# CHILTON'S IMPORT CAR MANUAL 1983-1990




**CHILTON BOOK COMPANY**

*ONE OF THE **ABC PUBLISHING COMPANIES,***
*A PART OF **CAPITAL CITIES/ABC, INC.***

Manufactured in USA



Chilton Way Radnor, Pa. 19089
ISBN 0-8019-7900-5
ISSN 0069-3634
Library of Congress Card Catalog No.76-648878

1 2 3 4 5 6 7 8 9 0    8 7 6 5 4 3 2 1 0 9

# ACKNOWLEDGEMENTS

AB Volvo, Göteborg, Sweden
American Honda Motor Company, Moorestown, New Jersey
American Isuzu Motors, Inc., Whittier, California
BMW of North America, Inc., Montvale, New Jersey
Branick Industries, Fargo, North Dakota
Chicago Rawhide Mfg. Company (Fuel/Water Separators), Elgin, Illinois
Chrysler Motors Corporation, Detroit, Michigan
Hyundai Motor America, Garden Grove, California
Mazda Motors of America, Inc., Compton, California
Mercedes-Benz of North America, Inc., Montvale, New Jersey
Mitsubishi Motor Sales, Inc. Fountain Valley, California
Nissan Motor Corporation of USA, Carson, California
Porsche Cars North America, Reno, Nevada
Racor Industries (Fuel/Water Separators), Modesto, California
Renault, Inc., Detroit, Michigan
Robert Bosch Corporation, Long Island City, New York
SAAB-Scania, New Haven, Connecticut
Subaru of America, Inc., Cherry Hill, New Jersey
Tokico America, Inc., Torrance, California
Toyo Kogyo, Ltd., Hiroshima, Japan
Toyota Motor Sales, USA, Inc., Torrance, California
Volkswagen of America, Inc., Troy, Michigan
Volvo, Inc., Rockleigh, New Jersey

# CONTENTS

# HOW TO USE THIS MANUAL

This manual is arranged in two sections:

## Car Section

Car sections are grouped by manufacturer and arranged in alphabetical order. The text and illustrations that comprise the service procedures in each Car Section are arranged in the following order of systems and components: Tune-Up, Engine Electrical, Engine Mechanical, Engine Lubrication, Engine Cooling, Emission Controls, Fuel System, Manual Transmission, Clutch, Automatic Transmission, Transaxle, Transfer Case, Drive Axle, Rear Suspension, Front Suspension, Steering, Brakes, and Chassis Electrical.

Specification charts are always located at the front of each section. All illustrations are located as close as possible to the pertinent text. Procedures are for all models in the particular section unless specifically noted otherwise.

## Unit Repair Section

The Unit Repair Section contains troubleshooting and overhaul procedures for the major components and systems of your car. This portion of the book is intended to be used in conjunction with the Car Sections.

Every major Unit Repair Section contains an Identification or Application chart to correlate the information contained in that section. The sections are usually arranged by brands, manufacturers or types of components rather than models of cars. All overhaul procedures in the Unit Repair Section begin with the component removed from the car. The reason for this division of material is an economic one. The steps involved in overhauling an engine are virtually the same for all engines. However, the operation of removing the engine from the car varies greatly from model to model. By combining where possible, and separating where necessary, we are able to publish the maximum amount of information.

## Locating Information

The Table of Contents, at the front of the book, lists the beginning of each Car and Unit Repair Section in the manual. The Index, also at the front of the book, is a comprehensive listing of all major mechanical sections and systems for every section in the book. The Index contains listings for Car Sections as well as for corresponding Unit Repair Sections.

To find where a particular Car Section is located in the book, you need only look in the Table of Contents. Once you have found the proper section, you may wish to find where specific procedures are located in that section. Turn to the Index at the front of the section. At the upper left-hand side is a listing of the main topics within the section and the page number they will be found on. Following the main topics is an alphabetical listing of all the procedures within the section and their page numbers.

---

### Safety Notice

Proper service and repair procedures are vital to the safe, reliable operation of all motor vehicles, as well as the personal safety of those performing repairs. This manual outlines procedures for servicing and repairing vehicles using safe effective methods. The procedures contain many NOTES, CAUTIONS and WARNINGS which should be followed along with standard safety procedures to eliminate the possibility of personal injury or improper service which could damage the vehicle or compromise its safety.

It is important to note that repair procedures and techniques, tools and parts for servicing motor vehicles, as well as the skill and experience of the individual performing the work vary widely. It is not possible to anticipate all of the conceivable ways or conditions under which vehicles may be serviced, or to provide cautions as to all of the possible hazards that may result. Standard and accepted safety precautions and equipment should be used when handling toxic or flammable fluids, and safety goggles or other protection should be used during cutting, grinding, chiseling, prying, or any other process that can cause material removal or projectiles.

Some procedures require the use of tools specially designed for a specific purpose. Before substituting another tool or procedure, you must be completely satisfied that neither your personal safety, nor the performance of the vehicle will be endangered.

### Part Numbers

Part numbers listed in this book are not recommendations by Chilton for any product by brand name. They are references that can be used with interchange manuals and aftermarket supplier catalogs to locate each brand supplier's discrete part number.

---

Although information in this manual is based on industry sources and is as complete as possible at the time of publication, the possibility exists that some car manufacturers made later changes which could not be included here. Information on very late models may not be available in some circumstances. While striving for total accuracy, Chilton Book Company cannot assume responsibility for any errors, changes, or omissions that may occur in the compilation of this data.

# Acura/Sterling

1

## Integra, Legend/825—All Models

# SERIAL NUMBER IDENTIFICATION

## Vehicle Identification Plate

Acura/Sterling vehicle identification numbers are mounted on the left top edge of the instrument panel and are visible from the outside. A vehicle identification number is also stamped on the clutch casing for the integra.

## Engine Number

The engine serial number is stamped into the right rear side of the engine (Integra) and front left side of the engine (Legend/825S/827). The first 5 digits indicate engine model identification. The remaining numbers refer to production sequence.

## Vehicle Identification Label

A vehicle/engine identification label is located under the hood, on the center of the cowl and on the driver's side door pillar.

## Transaxle Number

The transaxle serial number is stamped on the top of the transaxle/clutch case.

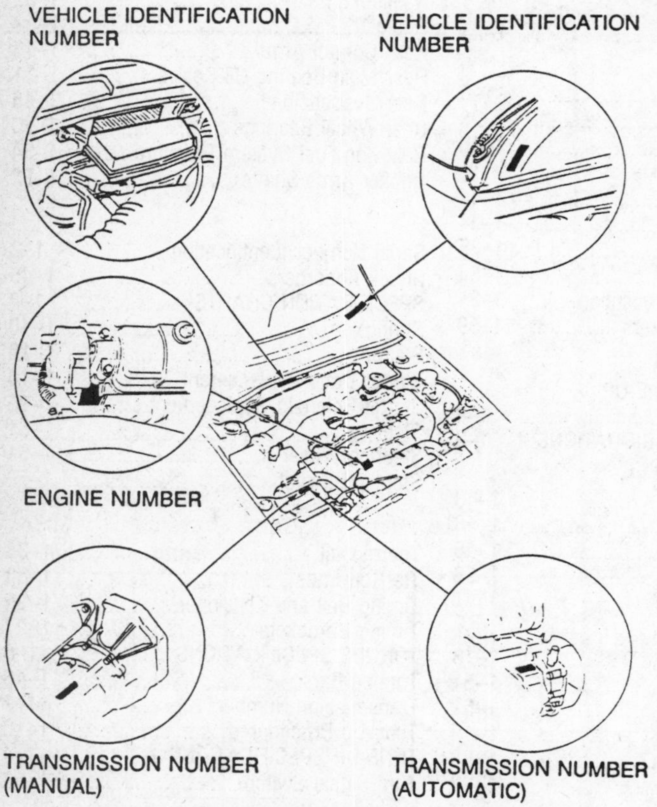


**Location of the of the identification numbers – Integra**

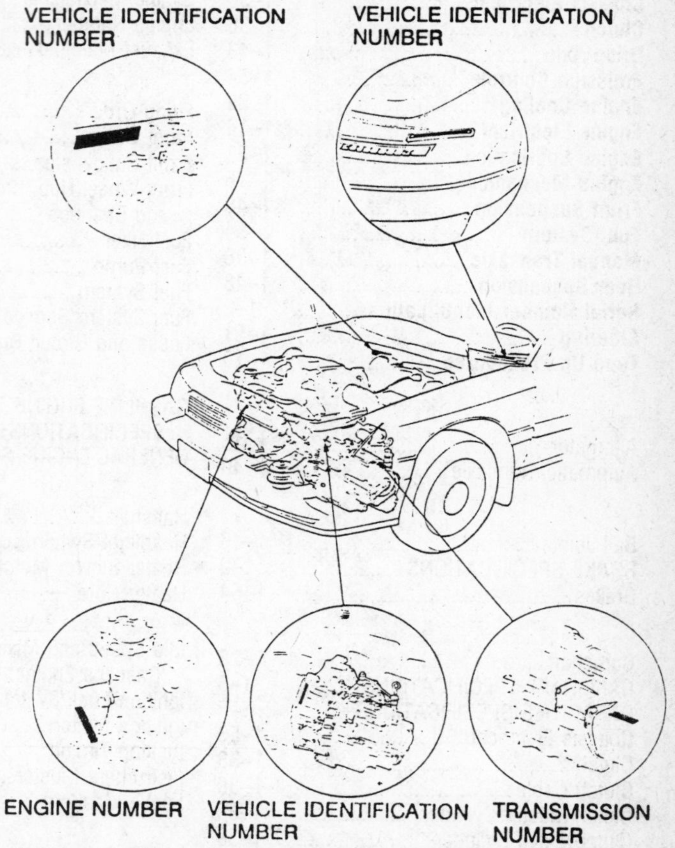


**Location of the of the identification numbers – Legend and 825S**

## ENGINE IDENTIFICATION

| Year | Model | Engine Displacement cu. in. (cc/liter) | Engine Series Identification | No. of Cylinders | Engine Type |
|---|---|---|---|---|---|
| 1986 | Integra | 97 (1590/1.6) | D16A1 | 4 | DOHC 16V |
| | Legend | 152 (2494/2.5) | C25A1 | 6 | OHC V6 |
| 1987 | Integra | 97 (1590/1.6) | D16A1 | 4 | DOHC 16V |
| | Legend | 152 (2494/2.5) | C25A1 | 6 | OHC V6 |

## ENGINE IDENTIFICATION

| Year | Model | Engine Displacement cu. in. (cc/liter) | Engine Series Identification | No. of Cylinders | Engine Type |
|---|---|---|---|---|---|
| 1987 | Legend Coupe | 163 (2675/2.7) | C27A1 | 6 | OHC V6 |
| | 825 | 152 (2494/2.5) | C25A1 | 6 | OHC V6 |
| 1988 | Integra | 97 (1590/1.6) | D16A1 | 4 | DOHC 16V |
| | Legend | 163 (2675/2.7) | C27A1 | 6 | OHC V6 |
| | Legend Coupe | 163 (2675/2.7) | C27A1 | 6 | OHC V6 |
| | 825 | 152 (2494/2.5) | C25A1 | 6 | OHC V6 |
| 1989-90 | Integra | 97 (1590/1.6) | D16A1 | 4 | DOHC 16V |
| | Legend | 163 (2675/2.7) | C27A1 | 6 | OHC V6 |
| | Legend Coupe | 163 (2675/2.7) | C27A1 | 6 | OHC V6 |
| | 825 | 163 (2675/2.5) | C27A1 | 6 | OHC V6 |

DOHC 16V Double Overhead Camshaft, 16 valve head
OHC Overhead Camshaft

## GENERAL ENGINE SPECIFICATIONS

| Year | Model | Engine Displacement cu. in. (cc) | Fuel System Type | Net Horsepower @ rpm | Net Torque @ rpm (ft. lbs.) | Bore × Stroke (in.) | Com-pression Ratio | Oil Pressure @ 3000 rpm |
|---|---|---|---|---|---|---|---|---|
| 1986 | Integra | 97 (1590) | PGM-FI | 113 @ 6250 | 99 @ 5500 | 2.95 × 3.54 | 9.3:1 | 60-78 |
| | Legend | 152 (2494) | PGM-FI | 151 @ 5800 | 154 @ 4500 | 3.31 × 2.95 | 9.0:1 | 71-82 |
| 1987 | Integra | 97 (1590) | PGM-FI | 113 @ 6250 | 99 @ 5500 | 2.95 × 3.54 | 9.3:1 | 60-78 |
| | Legend | 152 (2494) | PGM-FI | 151 @ 5800 | 154 @ 4500 | 3.31 × 2.95 | 9.0:1 | 71-82 |
| | Legend Coupe | 163 (2675) | PGM-FI | 161 @ 5900 | 162 @ 4500 | 3.43 × 2.95 | 9.0:1 | 71-82 |
| | 825 | 152 (2494) | PGM-FI | 151 @ 5800 | 154 @ 4500 | 3.31 × 2.95 | 9.0:1 | 71-82 |
| 1988 | Integra | 97 (1590) | PGM-FI | 113 @ 6250 | 99 @ 5500 | 2.95 × 3.54 | 9.5:1 | 60-78 |
| | Legend | 163 (2675) | PGM-FI | 161 @ 5900 | 162 @ 4500 | 3.43 × 2.95 | 9.0:1 | 71-82 |
| | Legend Coupe | 163 (2675) | PGM-FI | 161 @ 5900 | 162 @ 4500 | 3.43 × 2.95 | 9.0:1 | 71-82 |
| | 825 | 152 (2494) | PGM-FI | 151 @ 5800 | 154 @ 4500 | 3.31 × 2.95 | 9.0:1 | 71-82 |
| 1989-90 | Integra | 97 (1590) | PGM-FI | 118 @ 6500 | 103 @ 5500 | 2.95 × 3.54 | 9.5:1 | 60-78 |
| | Legend | 163 (2675) | PGM-FI | 161 @ 5900 | 162 @ 4500 | 3.43 × 2.95 | 9.0:1 | 71-82 |
| | Legend Coupe | 163 (2675) | PGM-FI | 161 @ 5900 | 162 @ 4500 | 3.43 × 2.95 | 9.0:1 | 71-82 |
| | 825 | 163 (2675) | PGM-FI | 161 @ 5900 | 162 @ 4500 | 3.43 × 2.95 | 9.0:1 | 71-82 |

PGM-FI—Electronic Fuel Injection

## TUNE-UP SPECIFICATIONS

| Year | Model | Engine Displacement cu. in. (cc) | Spark Plugs Type | Spark Plugs Gap (in.) | Ignition Timing (deg.) MT | Ignition Timing (deg.) AT | Compression Pressure (psi) | Fuel Pump (psi) | Idle Speed (rpm) MT | Idle Speed (rpm) AT | Valve Clearance In. | Valve Clearance Ex. |
|---|---|---|---|---|---|---|---|---|---|---|---|---|
| 1986 | Integra | 97 (1590) | ① | 0.039–0.043 | 0 ③ | 0 ③ | 164–192 | 36 | 750–850 | 750–850 | .0051–.0067 | .0059–.0075 |
| | Legend | 152 (2494) | ② | 0.039–0.043 | 3B ④ | 3B ④ | 135–178 | 36 | 670–770 | 670–770 | Hyd. | Hyd. |
| 1987 | Integra | 97 (1590) | ① | 0.039–0.043 | 0 ③ | 0 ③ | 164–192 | 36 | 750–850 | 750–850 | .0051–.0067 | .0059–.0075 |
| | Legend | 152 (2494) | ② | 0.039–0.043 | 3B ④ | 3B ④ | 135–178 | 36 | 670–770 | 670–770 | Hyd. | Hyd. |
| | Legend Coupe | 163 (2675) | ② | 0.039–0.043 | 15B ⑤ | 15B ⑤ | 142–171 | 36 | 630–730 | 630–730 | Hyd. | Hyd. |
| | 825 | 152 (2494) | ② | 0.039–0.043 | 3B ④ | 3B ④ | 135–178 | 36 | 670–770 | 670–770 | Hyd. | Hyd. |
| 1988 | Integra | 97 (1590) | ① | 0.039–0.043 | 12B ⑤ | 12B ⑤ | 135–192 | 36 | 700–800 | 650–750 | .0051–.0067 | .0059–.0075 |
| | Legend | 163 (2675) | ② | 0.039–0.043 | 15B ⑤ | 15B ⑤ | 142–171 | 36–41 | 630–730 | 630–730 | Hyd. | Hyd. |
| | Legend Coupe | 163 (2675) | ② | 0.039–0.043 | 15B ⑤ | 15B ⑤ | 142–171 | 36 41 | 630–730 | 630–730 | Hyd. | Hyd. |
| | 825 | 152 (2494) | ② | 0.039–0.043 | 3B ④ | 3B ④ | 135–178 | 36 41 | 670–770 | 670–770 | Hyd. | Hyd. |
| 1989 | Integra | 97 (1590) | ① | 0.039–0.043 | 12B ⑤ | 12B ⑤ | 135–192 | 36 | 700–800 | 650–750 | .0051–.0067 | .0059–.0075 |
| | Legend | 163 (2675) | ② | 0.039–0.043 | 15B ⑤ | 15B ⑤ | 142–171 | 36–41 | 630–730 | 630–730 | Hyd. | Hyd. |
| | Legend Coupe | 163 (2675) | ② | 0.039–0.043 | 15B ⑤ | 15B ⑤ | 142–171 | 36 41 | 630–730 | 630–730 | Hyd. | Hyd. |
| | 825 | 163 (2675) | ② | 0.039–0.043 | 15B ⑤ | 15B ⑤ | 142–171 | 36–41 | 630–730 | 630–730 | Hyd. | Hyd. |
| 1990 | SEE UNDERHOOD SPECIFICATIONS STICKER | | | | | | | | | | | |

**NOTE:** The Underhood Specifications sticker often reflects tune-up specification changes made in production. Sticker figures must be used if they disagree with those in this chart.

MT Manual transmission
AT Automatic transmission
NA Not adjustable
A After Top Dead Center
B Before Top Dead Center
Hyd. Hydraulic valve lash adjusters

① BCPR6EY-11
BCPR6EY-N11
Q20PR-U11

② BCPR6E-11
BCPR6EY-N11
Q20PR-U11

③ Vacuum advance hoses disconnected. White mark on crankshaft pulley

④ Vacuum advance hoses disconnected. Yellow mark on crankshaft pulley

⑤ Red mark on crankshaft pulley

## FIRING ORDERS

**NOTE: To avoid confusion, always replace spark plug wires one at a time.**

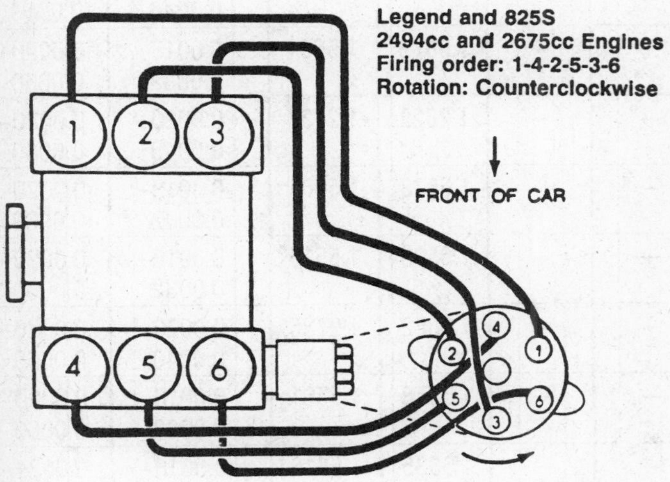


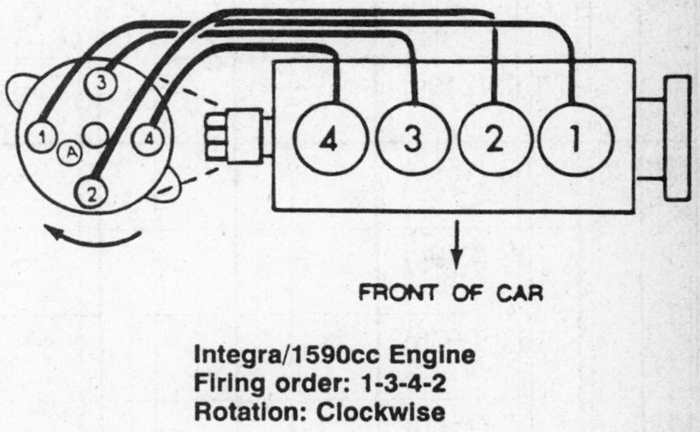


## CAPACITIES

| Year | Model | Engine Displacement cu. in. (cc) | Engine Crankcase (qts.) with Filter | Engine Crankcase (qts.) without Filter | Transmission (pts.) 4-Spd | Transmission (pts.) 5-Spd | Transmission (pts.) Auto. | Drive Axle (pts.) | Fuel Tank (gal.) | Cooling System (qts.) |
|---|---|---|---|---|---|---|---|---|---|---|
| 1986 | Integra | 97 (1590) | 4.5 | 4.0 | — | 4.8 | 5.0① | — | 13.2 | 6.0 |
| | Legend | 152 (2494) | 4.8 | 4.2 | — | 4.6 | 6.8① | — | 18.0 | 9.2 |
| 1987 | Integra | 97 (1590) | 4.5 | 4.0 | — | 4.8 | 5.0① | — | 13.2 | 6.0 |
| | Legend | 152 (2494) | 4.8 | 4.2 | — | 4.6 | 6.8① | — | 18.0 | 9.2 |
| | Legend Coupe | 163 (2675) | 4.8 | 4.2 | — | 4.6 | 6.8① | — | 18.0 | 9.2 |
| | 825 | 152 (2494) | 4.8 | 4.2 | — | 4.6 | 6.8① | — | 17.0 | 9.8 |
| 1988 | Integra | 97 (1590) | 4.5 | 4.0 | — | 4.8 | 5.0① | — | 13.2 | 6.0 |
| | Legend | 163 (2675) | 4.8 | 4.2 | — | 4.6 | 6.8① | — | 18.0 | 9.2 |
| | Legend Coupe | 163 (2675) | 4.8 | 4.2 | — | 4.6 | 6.8① | — | 18.0 | 9.2 |
| | 825 | 152 (2494) | 4.8 | 4.2 | — | 4.6 | 6.8① | — | 17.0 | 9.8 |
| 1989-90 | Integra | 97 (1590) | 4.5 | 4.0 | — | 4.8 | 5.0① | — | 13.2 | 6.0 |
| | Legend | 163 (2675) | 4.8 | 4.2 | — | 4.6 | 6.8① | — | 18.0 | 9.2 |
| | Legend Coupe | 163 (2675) | 4.8 | 4.2 | — | 4.6 | 6.8① | — | 18.0 | 9.2 |
| | 825 | 163 (2675) | 4.8 | 4.2 | — | 4.6 | 6.8① | — | 17.0 | 9.8 |

① Oil change capacity

## CAMSHAFT SPECIFICATIONS

All measurements given in inches.

| Year | Engine Displacement cu. in. (cc) | Journal Diameter 1 | 2 | 3 | 4 | 5 | Lobe Lift In. | Ex. | Bearing Clearance | Camshaft End Play |
|---|---|---|---|---|---|---|---|---|---|---|
| 1986 | 97 (1590) | — | — | — | — | — | 1.2822 | 1.2733 | 0.0020–0.0040 | 0.0020–0.0060 |
| | 152 (2494) | — | — | — | — | — | 1.5578 | 1.5561 | 0.0018–0.0032 | 0.0020–0.0060 |
| 1987 | 97 (1590) | — | — | — | — | — | 1.2822 | 1.2733 | 0.0020–0.0040 | 0.0020–0.0060 |
| | 152 (2494) | — | — | — | — | — | 1.5578 | 1.5561 | 0.0018–0.0032 | 0.0020–0.0060 |
| | 163 (2675) | — | — | — | — | — | 1.5535 | 1.5515 | 0.0018–0.0032 | 0.0020–0.0060 |
| 1988 | 97 (1590) | — | — | — | — | — | 1.2822 | 1.2735 | 0.0020–0.0040 | 0.0020–0.0060 |
| | 152 (2494) | — | — | — | — | — | 1.5578 | 1.5561 | 0.0018–0.0032 | 0.0020–0.0060 |
| | 163 (2675) | — | — | — | — | — | 1.5535 | 1.5515 | 0.0018–0.0032 | 0.0020–0.0060 |
| 1989-90 | 97 (1590) | — | — | — | — | — | 1.2822 | 1.2735 | 0.0020–0.0040 | 0.0020–0.0060 |
| | 163 (2675) | — | — | — | — | — | 1.5535 | 1.5515 | 0.0018–0.0032 | 0.0020–0.0060 |

## CRANKSHAFT AND CONNECTING ROD SPECIFICATIONS

All measurements are given in inches.

| Year | Engine Displacement cu. in. (cc) | Crankshaft Main Brg. Journal Dia. | Main Brg. Oil Clearance | Shaft End-play | Thrust on No. | Connecting Rod Journal Diameter | Oil Clearance | Side Clearance |
|---|---|---|---|---|---|---|---|---|
| 1986 | 97 (1590) | 2.1644–2.1654 | 0.0009–0.0017 ① | 0.0040–0.0140 | 3 | 1.7707–1.7717 | 0.0008–0.0015 | 0.0060–0.0120 |
| | 152 (2494) | 2.5187–2.5197 | 0.0009–0.0019 | 0.0040–0.0140 | 3 | 2.0463–2.0472 | 0.0010–0.0020 | 0.0060–0.0120 |
| 1987 | 97 (1590) | 2.1644–2.1654 | 0.0009–0.0017 ① | 0.0040–0.0140 | 3 | 1.7707–1.7717 | 0.0008–0.0015 | 0.0060–0.0120 |
| | 152 (2494) | 2.5187–2.5197 | 0.0009–0.0019 | 0.0040–0.0140 | 3 | 2.0463–2.0472 | 0.0010–0.0020 | 0.0060–0.0120 |
| | 163 (2675) | 2.5187–2.5197 | 0.0009–0.0019 | 0.0040–0.0140 | 3 | 2.0463–2.0472 | 0.0010–0.0020 | 0.0060–0.0120 |
| 1988 | 97 (1590) | 2.1644–2.1654 | 0.0009–0.0017 ① | 0.0040–0.0140 | 3 | 1.7707–1.7717 | 0.0008–0.0015 | 0.0060–0.0120 |
| | 152 (2494) | 2.5187–2.5197 | 0.0009–0.0019 | 0.0040–0.0140 | 3 | 2.0463–2.0472 | 0.0010–0.0020 | 0.0060–0.0120 |
| | 163 (2675) | 2.5187–2.5197 | 0.0009–0.0019 | 0.0040–0.0140 | 3 | 2.0463–2.0472 | 0.0010–0.0020 | 0.0060–0.0120 |

## CRANKSHAFT AND CONNECTING ROD SPECIFICATIONS

All measurements are given in inches.

| Year | Engine Displacement cu. in. (cc) | Crankshaft Main Brg. Journal Dia. | Crankshaft Main Brg. Oil Clearance | Crankshaft Shaft End-play | Crankshaft Thrust on No. | Connecting Rod Journal Diameter | Connecting Rod Oil Clearance | Connecting Rod Side Clearance |
|---|---|---|---|---|---|---|---|---|
| 1989-90 | 97 (1590) | 2.1644–2.1654 | 0.0009–0.0017 ① | 0.0040–0.0140 | 3 | 1.7707–1.7717 | 0.0008–0.0015 | 0.0060–0.0120 |
| | 163 (2675) | 2.5187–2.5197 | 0.0009–0.0019 | 0.0040–0.0140 | 3 | 2.0463–2.0472 | 0.0010–0.0020 | 0.0060–0.0120 |

① No. 1 oil clearance—0.0012-0.0190

## VALVE SPECIFICATIONS

| Year | Engine Displacement cu. in. (cc) | Seat Angle (deg.) | Face Angle (deg.) | Spring Test Pressure (lbs.) | Spring Installed Height (in.) | Stem-to-Guide Clearance (in.) Intake | Stem-to-Guide Clearance (in.) Exhaust | Stem Diameter (in.) Intake | Stem Diameter (in.) Exhaust |
|---|---|---|---|---|---|---|---|---|---|
| 1986 | 97 (1590) | 45 | 45 | — | — | 0.0010–0.0020 | 0.0020–0.0030 | 0.2591–0.2594 | 0.2579–0.2583 |
| | 152 (2494) | 45 | 45 | — | — | 0.0010–0.0020 | 0.0020–0.0030 | 0.2591–0.2594 | 0.2579–0.2583 |
| 1987 | 97 (1590) | 45 | 45 | — | — | 0.0010–0.0020 | 0.0020–0.0030 | 0.2591–0.2594 | 0.2579–0.2583 |
| | 152 (2494) | 45 | 45 | — | — | 0.0010–0.0020 | 0.0020–0.0030 | 0.2591–0.2594 | 0.2579–0.2583 |
| | 163 (2675) | 45 | 45 | — | — | 0.0010–0.0020 | 0.0020–0.0030 | 0.2591–0.2594 | 0.2579–0.2583 |
| 1988 | 97 (1590) | 45 | 45 | — | — | 0.0010–0.0020 | 0.0020–0.0030 | 0.2591–0.2594 | 0.2579–0.2583 |
| | 152 (2494) | 45 | 45 | — | — | 0.0010–0.0020 | 0.0020–0.0030 | 0.2591–0.2594 | 0.2579–0.2583 |
| | 163 (2675) | 45 | 45 | — | — | 0.0010–0.0020 | 0.0020–0.0030 | 0.2591–0.2594 | 0.2579–0.2583 |
| 1989-90 | 97 (1590) | 45 | 45 | — | — | 0.0010–0.0020 | 0.0020–0.0030 | 0.2591–0.2594 | 0.2579–0.2583 |
| | 163 (2675) | 45 | 45 | — | — | 0.0010–0.0020 | 0.0020–0.0030 | 0.2591–0.2594 | 0.2579–0.2583 |

## PISTON AND RING SPECIFICATIONS

All measurments are given in inches.

| Year | Engine Displacement cu. in. (cc) | Piston Clearance | Ring Gap Top Compression | Ring Gap Bottom Compression | Ring Gap Oil Control | Ring Side Clearance Top Compression | Ring Side Clearance Bottom Compression | Ring Side Clearance Oil Control |
|---|---|---|---|---|---|---|---|---|
| 1986 | 97 (1590) | 0.0004–0.0024 | 0.0060–0.0140 | 0.0060–0.0140 | 0.0080–0.0280 | 0.0012–0.0024 | 0.0012–0.0022 | — |
| | 152 (2494) | 0.0002–0.0013 | 0.0080–0.0140 | 0.0080–0.0140 | 0.0080–0.0280 | 0.0008–0.0018 | 0.0008–0.0018 | — |

## PISTON AND RING SPECIFICATIONS

All measurments are given in inches.

| Year | Engine Displacement cu. in. (cc) | Piston Clearance | Ring Gap Top Compression | Ring Gap Bottom Compression | Ring Gap Oil Control | Ring Side Clearance Top Compression | Ring Side Clearance Bottom Compression | Ring Side Clearance Oil Control |
|---|---|---|---|---|---|---|---|---|
| 1987 | 97 (1590) | 0.0004–0.0024 | 0.0060–0.0140 | 0.0060–0.0140 | 0.0080–0.0280 | 0.0012–0.0024 | 0.0012–0.0022 | — |
| | 152 (2494) | 0.0002–0.0013 | 0.0080–0.0140 | 0.0080–0.0140 | 0.0080–0.0280 | 0.0008–0.0018 | 0.0008–0.0018 | — |
| | 163 (2675) | 0.0006–0.0015 | 0.0080–0.0140 | 0.0140–0.0190 | 0.0080–0.0280 | 0.0006–0.0018 | 0.0006–0.0018 | — |
| 1988 | 97 (1590) | 0.0004–0.0024 | 0.0060–0.0140 | 0.0120–0.0180 | 0.0080–0.0280 | 0.0012–0.0022 | 0.0012–0.0022 | — |
| | 152 (2494) | 0.0002–0.0013 | 0.0080–0.0140 | 0.0080–0.0140 | 0.0080–0.0280 | 0.0008–0.0018 | 0.0008–0.0018 | — |
| | 163 (2675) | 0.0006–0.0015 | 0.0080–0.0140 | 0.0140–0.0190 | 0.0080–0.0280 | 0.0006–0.0018 | 0.0006–0.0018 | — |
| 1989-90 | 97 (1590) | 0.0004–0.0024 | 0.0060–0.0140 | 0.0120–0.0180 | 0.0080–0.0280 | 0.0012–0.0022 | 0.0012–0.0022 | — |
| | 163 (2675) | 0.0006–0.0015 | 0.0080–0.0140 | 0.0140–0.0190 | 0.0080–0.0280 | 0.0006–0.0018 | 0.0006–0.0018 | — |

## TORQUE SPECIFICATIONS

All readings in ft. lbs.

| Year | Engine Displacement cu. in. (cc) | Cylinder Head Bolts | Main Bearing Bolts | Rod Bearing Bolts | Crankshaft Pulley Bolts | Flywheel Bolts | Manifold Intake | Manifold Exhaust | Spark Plugs |
|---|---|---|---|---|---|---|---|---|---|
| 1986 | 97 (1590) | ① | 40 | 23 | 83 | ② | 16 | 23 | 13 |
| | 152 (2494) | ③ | ④ | 32 | 83 | ⑤ | 16 | ⑥ | 13 |
| 1987 | 97 (1590) | ① | 40 | 23 | 83 | ② | 16 | 23 | 13 |
| | 152 (2494) | ③ | ④ | 32 | 83 | ⑤ | 16 | ⑥ | 13 |
| | 163 (2675) | ③ | ④ | 33 | 83 | ⑤ | 16 | ⑥ | 16 |
| 1988 | 97 (1590) | ① | 46 | 23 | 83 | ② | 16 | 23 | 13 |
| | 152 (2494) | ③ | ④ | 32 | 83 | ⑤ | 16 | ⑥ | 13 |
| | 163 (2675) | ③ | ④ | 33 | 83 | ⑤ | 16 | ⑥ | 16 |
| 1989-90 | 97 (1590) | ① | 46 | 23 | 83 | ② | 16 | 23 | 13 |
| | 163 (2675) | ③ | ④ | 33 | 83 | ⑤ | 16 | ⑥ | 16 |

① 1st step – 22 ft. lbs.
2nd step – 48 ft. lbs.

② MT – 87 ft. lbs.
AT – 54 ft. lbs.

③ 1st step – 29 ft. lbs.
2nd step – 56 ft. lbs.

④ Cap bolt (9mm) – 29 ft. lbs.
Cap bridge bolt (11mm) – 49 ft. lbs.
Side bolt (10mm) – 36 ft. lbs.

⑤ MT – 76 ft. lbs.
AT – 54 ft. lbs.

⑥ 8mm nuts – 22 ft. lbs.
10mm nuts – 40 ft. lbs.

## BRAKE SPECIFICATIONS

All measurements in inches unless noted

| Year | Model | Lug Nut Torque (ft. lbs.) | Master Cylinder Bore | Brake Disc Minimum Thickness | Brake Disc Maximum Runout | Standard Brake Drum Diameter | Minimum Lining Thickness Front | Minimum Lining Thickness Rear |
|---|---|---|---|---|---|---|---|---|
| 1986 | Integra | 80 | — | ① | ② | — | 0.12 | 0.06 |
| | Legend | 80 | — | ③ | ④ | — | 0.12 | 0.06 |
| 1987 | Integra | 80 | — | ① | ② | — | 0.12 | 0.06 |
| | Legend | 80 | — | ③ | ④ | — | 0.12 | 0.06 |
| | Legend Coupe | 80 | — | ③ | ④ | — | 0.06 | 0.06 |
| | 825 | 80 | — | ③ | ④ | — | 0.12 | 0.06 |
| 1988 | Integra | 80 | — | ① | ② | — | 0.12 | 0.06 |
| | Legend | 80 | — | ③ | ④ | — | 0.06 | 0.06 |
| | Legend Coupe | 80 | — | ③ | ④ | — | 0.06 | 0.06 |
| | 825 | 80 | — | ③ | ④ | — | 0.06 | 0.06 |
| 1989-90 | Integra | 80 | — | ① | ② | — | 0.12 | 0.06 |
| | Legend | 80 | — | ③ | ④ | — | 0.06 | 0.06 |
| | Legend Coupe | 80 | — | ③ | ④ | — | 0.06 | 0.06 |
| | 825 | 80 | — | ③ | ④ | — | 0.06 | 0.06 |

① Front—0.67
Rear—0.31

② Front—0.004
Rear—0.006

③ Front—0.75
Rear—0.31

④ Front—0.004
Rear—0.004

## WHEEL ALIGNMENT

| Year | Model | | Caster Range (deg.) | Caster Preferred Setting (deg.) | Camber Range (deg.) | Camber Preferred Setting (deg.) | Toe-in (in.) | Steering Axis Inclination (deg.) |
|---|---|---|---|---|---|---|---|---|
| 1986 | Integra | Front | 1³⁄₁₆P-3³⁄₁₆P | 2³⁄₁₆P | 1½N-½P | ½N | ¹⁄₃₂N | NA |
| | | Rear | — | — | 1N-½N | ¾N | ¹⁄₁₆P | — |
| | Legend | Front | ¹¹⁄₁₆P-2¹⁄₁₆P | 1¹¹⁄₁₆P | 1N-1P | 0 | 0 | NA |
| | | Rear | — | — | 1N-1P | 0 | 0 | — |
| 1987 | Integra | Front | 1³⁄₁₆P-3³⁄₁₆P | 2³⁄₁₆P | 1½N-½P | ½N | ¹⁄₃₂N | NA |
| | | Rear | — | — | 1N-½N | ¾N | ¹⁄₁₆P | — |
| | Legend | Front | ¹¹⁄₁₆P-2¹⁄₁₆P | 1¹¹⁄₁₆P | 1N-1P | 0 | 0 | NA |
| | | Rear | — | — | 1N-1P | 0 | 0 | — |
| | Legend Coupe | Front | ¹¹⁄₁₆P-2¹⁄₁₆P | 1¹¹⁄₁₆P | 1N-1P | 0 | 0 | NA |
| | | Rear | — | — | 1N-1P | 0 | 0 | — |
| | 825 | Front | ¹¹⁄₁₆P-2¹⁄₁₆P | 1¹¹⁄₁₆P | 1N-1P | 0 | 0 | NA |
| | | Rear | — | — | 1N-1P | 0 | 0 | — |

## WHEEL ALIGNMENT

| Year | Model | | Caster Range (deg.) | Caster Preferred Setting (deg.) | Camber Range (deg.) | Camber Preferred Setting (deg.) | Toe-in (in.) | Steering Axis Inclination (deg.) |
|---|---|---|---|---|---|---|---|---|
| 1988 | Integra | Front | 1 3/16P-3 3/16P | 2 3/16P | 1½N-½P | ½N | 1/32N | NA |
| | | Rear | — | — | 1N-½N | ¾N | 1/16P | — |
| | Legend | Front | 11/16P-2 1/16P | 1 11/16P | 1N-1P | 0 | 0 | NA |
| | | Rear | — | — | 1N-1P | 0 | 0 | — |
| | Legend Coupe | Front | 11/16P-2 1/16P | 1 11/16P | 1N-1P | 0 | 0 | NA |
| | | Rear | — | — | 1N-1P | 0 | 0 | — |
| | 825 | Front | 11/16P-2 1/16P | 1 11/16P | 1N-1P | 0 | 0 | NA |
| | | Rear | — | — | 1N-1P | 0 | 0 | — |
| 1989-90 | Integra | Front | 1 3/16P-3 3/16P | 2 3/16P | 1½N-½P | ½N | 1/32N | NA |
| | | Rear | — | — | 1N-½N | ¾N | 1/16P | — |
| | Legend | Front | 11/16P-2 1/16P | 1 11/16P | 1N-1P | 0 | 0 | NA |
| | | Rear | — | — | 1N-1P | 0 | 0 | — |
| | Legend Coupe | Front | 11/16P-2 1/16P | 1 11/16P | 1N-1P | 0 | 0 | NA |
| | | Rear | — | — | 1N-1P | 0 | 0 | — |
| | 825 | Front | 11/16P-2 1/16P | 1 11/16P | 1N-1P | 0 | 0 | NA |
| | | Rear | — | — | 1N-1P | 0 | 0 | — |

NA—Not Available
N—Negative
P—Positive

# TUNE-UP PROCEDURES

## Ignition Timing

The timing marks are located on the crankshaft pulley, with a pointer on the timing belt cover; the 1590cc engine marks are visible from the driver's side of the engine compartment and the 2494cc and 2675cc timing marks are visible from the passengers side of the engine compartment.

In all cases, the timing is checked with the engine warmed to operating temperature (allow the cooling fan to turn **ON**), with the engine idling in **N**.

### ADJUSTMENT

#### *Integra*

**1986–87**

1. With the engine stopped, connect a tachometer according to the manufacturer's instructions.

**NOTE: On some models, pull back the rubber ignition coil cover to reveal the terminals.**

2. Connect a timing light to the engine according to the manufacturer's instructions.

3. Make sure all wires are clear of the cooling fan and hot exhaust manifolds. Start the engine. Point the timing light at the timing mark pointer and the crankshaft pulley.

4. Disconnect and plug the No. 2 and No. 5 vacuum hoses from the vacuum advance diaphragm. The pointer should be on the "white mark" (−2–2 degrees) on the crankshaft pulley.

5. If necessary, adjust the timing by loosening the distributor adjusting bolts and slowly rotate the distributor in the required direction while observing the timing marks.

**CAUTION**

***Do not grasp the top of the distributor cap while the engine is running as you might get a nasty shock. Instead, grab the distributor housing to rotate.***

After making the necessary adjustment, tighten the hold-down bolts, taking care not to disturb the adjustment and reinstall the cap on the upper adjusting bolt.

6. Unplug the No. 2 vacuum hose and check for 20 in. Hg (500mm Hg) of vacuum. If the vacuum is not to specification, check the hose and it's port on the throttle body.

7. Connect the No. 2 vacuum hose to the advance diaphragm. The timing should advance 4–8 degrees, half way between the **WHITE** and **RED** marks. If the timing does not advance, check the advance diaphragm.

8. Disconnect the No. 5 vacuum hose and check for vacuum. If the hose has no vacuum, check the ignition control solenoid valve. Rapidly open and release the throttle. The vacuum should momentarily go to 0. If the vacuum does not drop to 0, check the ignition control solenoid valve.

9. Connect the No. 5 vacuum hose to the advance diaphragm. The timing should advance to 10–14 degrees (on the **RED** mark). If the timing does not advance check the advance diaphragm.

**1988–90**

1. Connect a tachometer according to the manufacturer's instructions.

**NOTE: On some models, pull back the rubber ignition coil cover to reveal the terminals.**

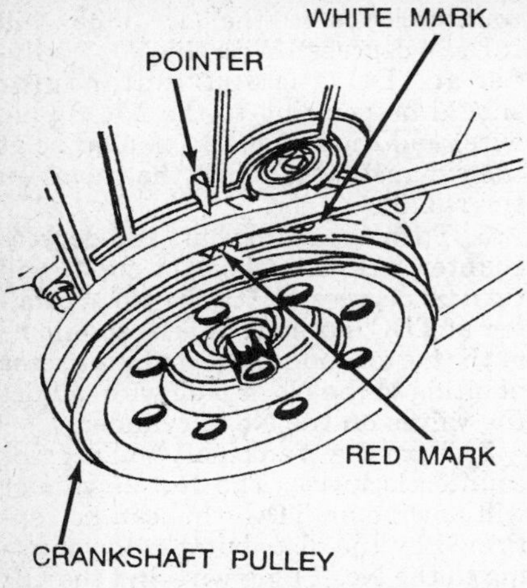


**Ignition timing marks – 1590cc engine**

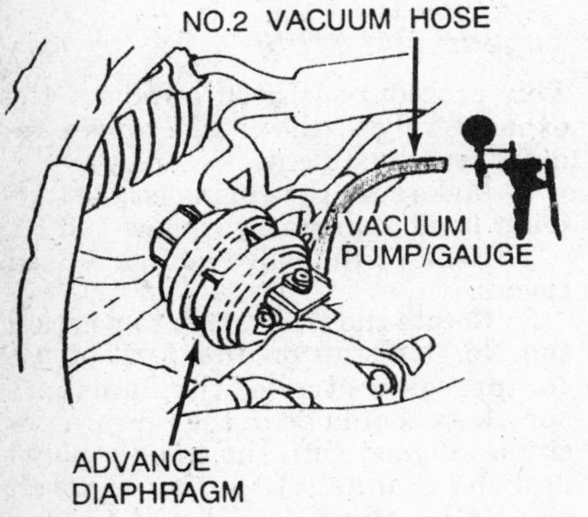


**Number 2 vacuum hose location**

2. Remove the main fuse box lid and connect the **Br/Bl** and **Br** terminals with a jumper wire.

3. Make sure all wires are clear of the cooling fan and hot exhaust manifolds. Start the engine. Point the timing light at the timing mark pointer and the crankshaft pulley.

4. The pointer should be on the **RED** mark (10–14 degrees BTDC) on the crankshaft pulley at 700–800 rpm (manual transaxle) or 650–750 rpm (automatic transaxle).

5. If necessary, adjust the timing by loosening the distributor adjusting bolts and slowly rotate the distributor in the required direction while observing the timing marks.

**CAUTION**

***Do not grasp the top of the distributor cap while the engine is running as you might get a nasty shock. Instead, grab the distributor housing to rotate.***

After making the necessary adjustment, tighten the hold-down bolts, taking care not to disturb the adjustment and reinstall the cap on the upper adjusting bolt.

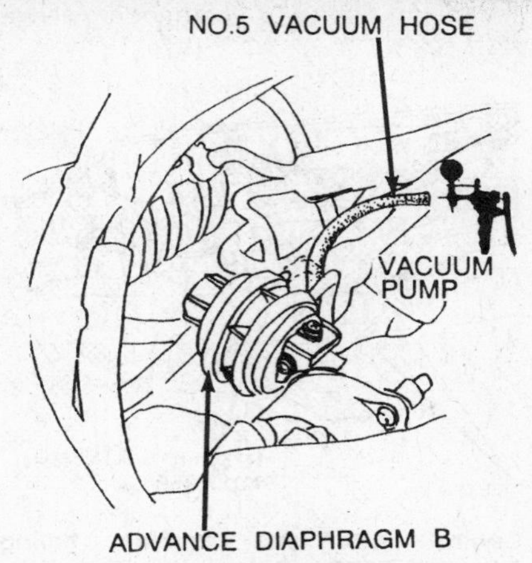


**Number 5 vacuum hose location**

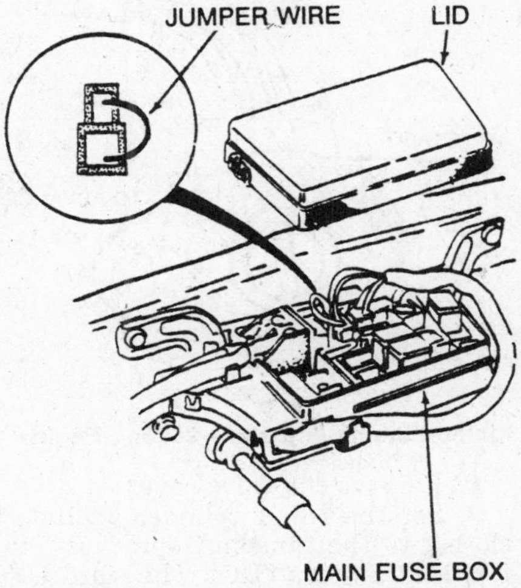


**Installing the jumper wire in the main fuse box for ignition timing – 1988–89 Integra**

6. Remove the jumper wire and put the lid on the main fuse box.

### Legend and 825S

#### 2494CC ENGINE

1. Disconnect the vacuum hoses from the vacuum advance diaphragm and, while the engine idles, check each hose for vacuum. The No. 4 and No. 11 hoses should both have vacuum. If the No. 11 hose has no vacuum, check the solenoid valve **A**. If the No. 4 hose has no vacuum, check the solenoid valve **B** vacuum hoses disconnected, plug the end of the hoses.

2. Stop the engine and connect a tachometer according to the manufacturer's instructions.

**NOTE: On some models, pull back the rubber ignition coil cover to reveal the terminals.**

3. Make sure all wires are clear of the cooling fan and hot exhaust manifolds. Start the engine. Point the timing light at the timing mark pointer and the crankshaft pulley.

4. Adjust the initial timing, if necessary to the following specification. The pointer should be on the **YELLOW** mark on the crankshaft pulley (3 degrees BTDC) at 670–770 rpm.

5. If necessary, adjust the timing by loosening the distributor adjusting bolt and slowly rotate the distributor in the required direction while observing the timing marks.

**CAUTION**

***Do not grasp the top of the distributor cap while the engine is running as you might get a nasty shock. Instead, grab the distributor housing to rotate.***

After making the necessary adjustment, tighten the hold-down bolts, taking care not to disturb the adjustment and reinstall the cap on the upper adjusting bolt.

6. Connect the No. 4 and No. 11 vacuum hoses to the vacuum advance and inspect the ignition timing at idle. The ignition timing 21–25 degrees (manual transaxle) **RED** mark at idle or 16–20 degrees (automatic transaxle) **RED** mark at idle. If the advance is not to specification, check the advance diaphragm and the distributor advance mechanism.

#### 2675CC ENGINE

1. Start the engine and warm to normal operating temperatures (the cooling fan should turn **ON**).

2. Stop the engine and connect a tachometer according to the manufacturer's instructions.

**NOTE: On some models, pull back the rubber ignition coil cover to reveal the terminals.**

3. Make sure all wires are clear of the cooling fan and hot exhaust manifolds. Start the engine. Point the timing light at the timing mark pointer and the crankshaft pulley.

4. Adjust the timing, if necessary to the following specification. The pointer should be on the **RED** mark on the crankshaft pulley (13–17 degrees BTDC) at 630 – 730 rpm.

5. If necessary, adjust the timing by turning the adjusting screw on the ignition timing adjuster in the control box as follows:

a. Remove the control box upper and lower cover.

b. Drill off the rivets, with a $^{3}/_{16}$ in. drill bit and separate the stay cover from the adjuster.

c. To adjust the timing, turn the adjusting screw (on the adjuster); clockwise to advance or counterclockwise to retard.

d. After adjusting, install the stay cover to the ignition timing adjuster

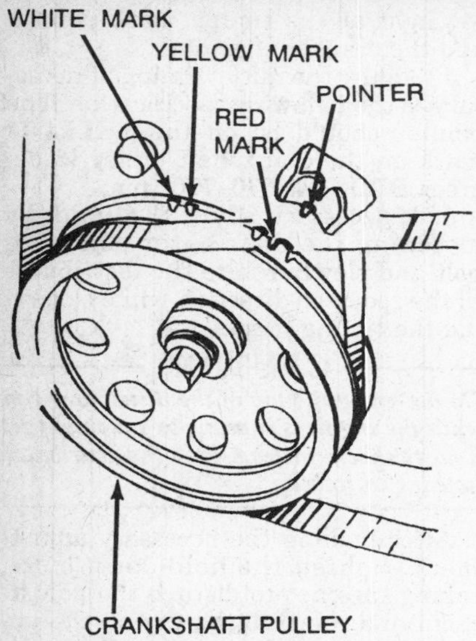


**Ignition timing marks—2494cc engine**

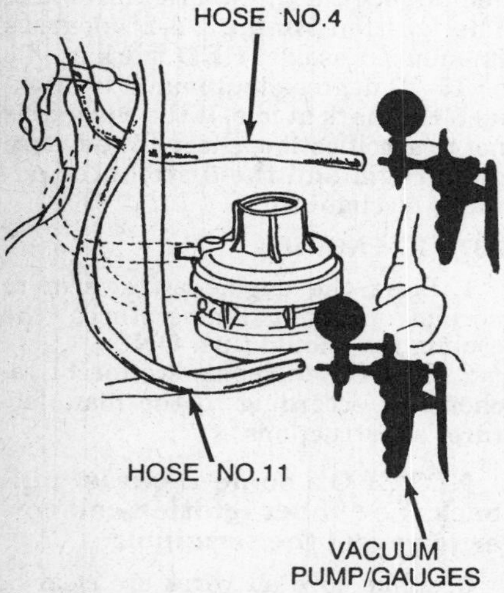


**Vacuum hose locations**

with new rivets and the adjuster to the control box.

## Valve Lash

The Acura Legend and the Sterling 825S engines use hydraulic lash adjusters on the intake valves and do not require periodic adjustment; ONLY the exhaust valves need adjustment.

### ADJUSTMENT

#### *Integra*

**NOTE: While all valve adjustments must be as accurate as possible, it is better to have the valve adjustment slightly loose than tight, as burned valves may result from overly tight adjustments.**

1. Make sure the engine is cold (cylinder head temperature below 100°F).

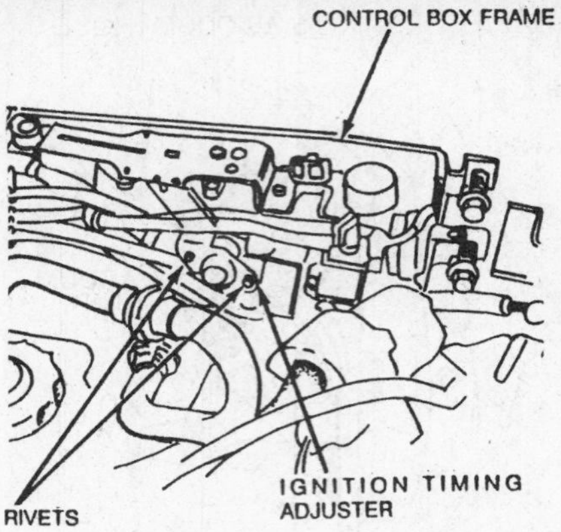


**Control box and ignition timing adjuster—2675cc Engine**

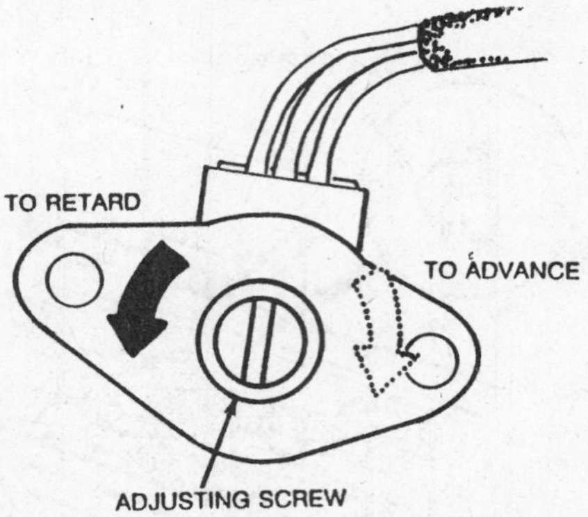


**Ignition timing adjuster—2675cc Engine**

2. Remove the valve cover.
3. Set the No. 1 cylinder (cylinder closest to the camshaft sprockets) to top dead center (TDC). The word **UP** should appear at the top and the **TDC** grooves on the pulley should align with the cylinder head surface. Double check this by checking the position of the distributor rotor. Using chalk or a pencil, mark the No. 1 spark plug wire's position at the distributor cap on the distributor body. Then, remove the cap and make sure the rotor points toward the mark.
4. With the No. 1 cylinder at TDC, adjust the valves of the No. 1 cylinder by performing the following procedures:
   a. Using a flat feeler gauge, 0.0051–0.0067 in. (intake) or 0.0059–0.0075 in., place it between the rocker arm and the valve stem; there should be a slight drag on the feeler gauge.
   b. If there is no drag or if the gauge cannot be inserted, loosen the valve adjusting the screw locknut.
   c. Turn the adjusting screw with a screwdriver to obtain the proper clearance.
   d. Hold the adjusting screw and torque the locknut(s) to 18 ft. lbs.
   e. Recheck the clearance.
5. Turn the crankshaft 180 degrees counterclockwise (the cam pulley will turn 90 degrees). With the No. 3 cylinder at TDC (the distributor rotor should be pointing to the No. 3 plug wire) and the **UP** marks should be at the exhaust side, adjust the valves on the No. 3 cylinder.
6. Turn the crankshaft 180 degrees counterclockwise (the cam pulley will turn 90 degrees). With the No. 4 cylinder at TDC (both **UP** marks should be at the bottom and the distributor rotor pointing to the No. 4 plug wire) adjust the valves on the No. 4 cylinder.
7. Turn the crankshaft 180 degrees counterclockwise. The No. 2 cylinder will now be on TDC (this can be confirmed by the distributor rotor pointing to the No. 2 plug wire and the **UP** marks should be at the intake side). The valves on the No. 2 cylinder may now be adjusted.

#### *Legend and 825S*

This procedure is used to adjust the exhaust valves; the intake valves require no adjustment.

1. Make sure the engine is cold (cylinder head temperature below 100°F).
2. Remove the valve and side head covers.
3. Rotate the crankshaft to position the No. 1 piston on the TDC of it's compression stroke; the camshaft sprockets should be in the upward position (aligned with the timing mark) and the crankshaft pulley V-notch should be aligned with the timing pointer on the timing cover.

**NOTE: Double check this by checking the position of the distributor rotor. Using chalk or a pencil, mark the No. 1 spark plug wire's position at the distributor cap on the distributor body. Then, remove the cap and make sure the rotor points toward the mark.**

4. To adjust the exhaust valves, perform the following procedures:
   a. Loosen the exhaust valve locknuts on all of the cylinders.
   b. Tighten the adjusting screw of the No. 1 cylinder, until it contacts the valve and tighten it 1½ turns. Tighten the locknut firmly.
   c. Perform the same procedure for the exhaust valves No. 2 and 4.
   d. Rotate the crankshaft 180 degrees and align the crankshaft pulley's V-notch with the timing pointer on the timing cover; the No. 5 piston is at TDC of it's compression stroke.
   e. Tighten the adjusting screw of the No. 5 cylinder, until it contacts the valve and tighten it 1½ turns. Tighten the locknut firmly.
   f. Perform the same procedure for the exhaust valves No. 3 and 6.

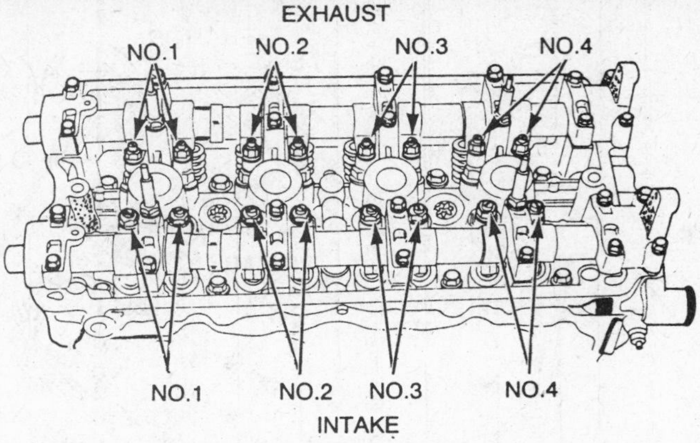


**Valve locations – 1590cc engine**

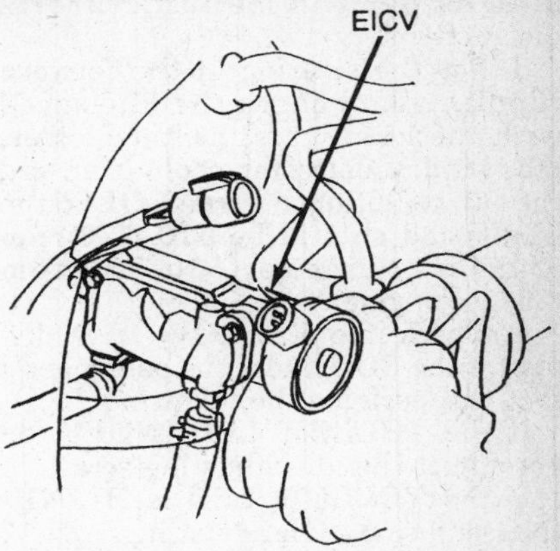


**EICV connector – 1590cc engine**

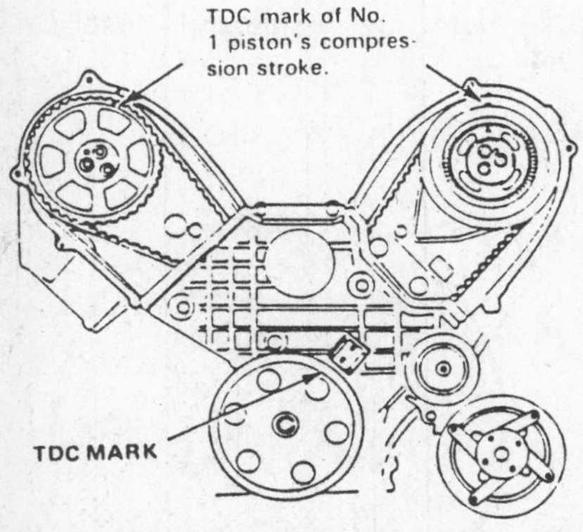


**Positioning the camshaft sprockets and crankshaft pulley on the TDC of the No. 1 piston's compression stroke – 2494cc and 2675cc engines**

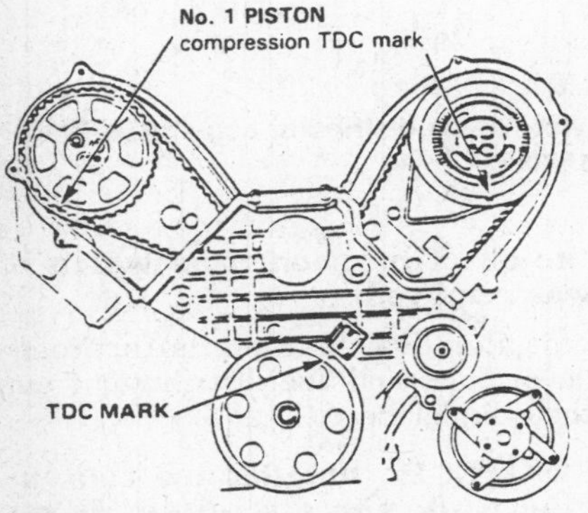


**Positioning the camshaft sprockets and crankshaft pulley on the TDC of the No. 5 piston's compression stroke – 2494cc and 2675cc engines**

5. After adjustment, use new gaskets and install the valve and side head covers.

## Idle Speed & Mixture

### ADJUSTMENT

**NOTE: The idle mixture is electronically controlled by the fuel injection system and is not adjustable.**

#### *Integra*

1. Start the engine and allow it to warm to normal operating temperatures; the cooling fan should turn **ON**.
2. Connect a tachometer to the engine as per the manufacturer's instructions.
3. With the engine idling, disconnect the connector at the **EICV** (1986–87) or the **EACV** (1988–90).
4. Check the idle speed with the headlights, heater blower, rear window defroster, cooling fan and the air conditioner turned **OFF**. Idle speed should be set to 500–600 rpm. If necessary, adjust the idle speed, by turning the idle adjusting screw on the top of the throttle body.
5. After the adjustment, turn the ignition switch **OFF** and reconnect the connector at the **EICV** or **EACV**.
6. Remove the **HAZARD** fuse at the battery terminal for at least 10 seconds to reset the ECU memory.
7. Start the engine and allow it to warm to normal operating temperatures; the cooling fan should turn **ON**.
8. Check the idle speed with the headlights, heater blower, rear window defroster, cooling fan and the air conditioner turned **OFF**. Idle speed should be 750–850 rpm (1986–87) or 650–750 rpm (1988–89)
9. Check the idle speed under the following conditions:

   With headlights and rear window defogger turned **ON**.

   With the air conditioner compressor turned **ON**.

   If equipped with an automatic transaxle, shift the transaxle into gear (except **P** or **N**), the idle should remain stable at:

   1986–87 manual transaxle – 750–850 rpm.

   1988–90 manual transaxle – 700–800 rpm.

**View of the EACV connector – 1590 engine**

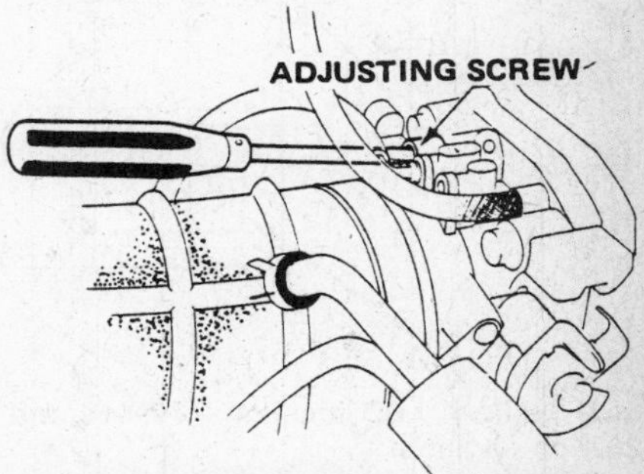


**Idle speed adjusting screw – 1590cc engine**

   1988–90 automatic transaxle – 650–750 rpm.

10. With the engine idling for 1 minute, with the fan switch turned on HI and the air conditioner turned **ON**, check the idle speed; it should be:

    1988–90 manual transaxle – 700–800 rpm.

    1988–90 automatic transaxle – 680–780 rpm.

#### *Legend and 825S*

1. Start the engine and allow it to warm to normal operating temperatures; the cooling fan should turn **ON**.
2. Connect a tachometer to the en-

gine as per the manufacturer's instructions.

3. Set the steering in the forward condition and check the idle speed with the headlights, heater blower, rear window defroster, cooling fan and the air conditioner turned **OFF**; the idle speed should be 670–770 rpm (2494cc engine) or 630–730 rpm (2675cc engine).

4. Check the **YELLOW** LED display at the ECU under the passenger's seat and perform the following:

If the **YELLOW** LED is **OFF**, do not adjust the idle adjusting screw.

If the **YELLOW** LED is **BLINKING**, adjust the idle adjusting screw ¼ turn clockwise.

If the **YELLOW** LED is **ON**, adjust the idle adjusting screw ¼ turn counter-clockwise.

**NOTE: The yellow LED may be lit at early stages, for example, when the mileage is within 310 miles (500 km). However, no adjustments should be made.**

Check that the **YELLOW** LED turns **OFF** after approximately 30 seconds. If it does not turn **OFF**, rotate the idle adjusting screw by ¼ turn in

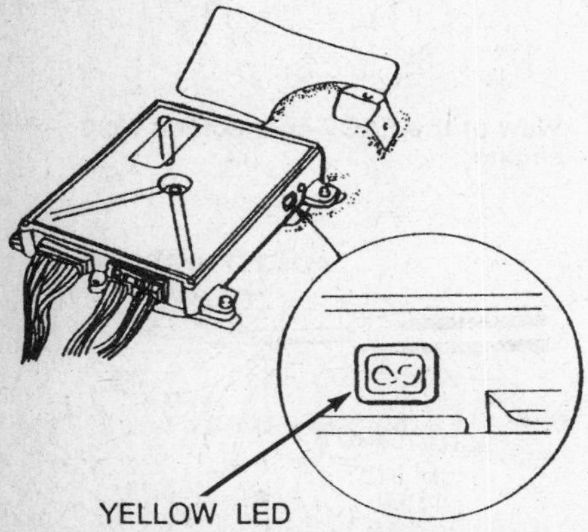

ECU "yellow" LED location—2494cc and 2675cc engines

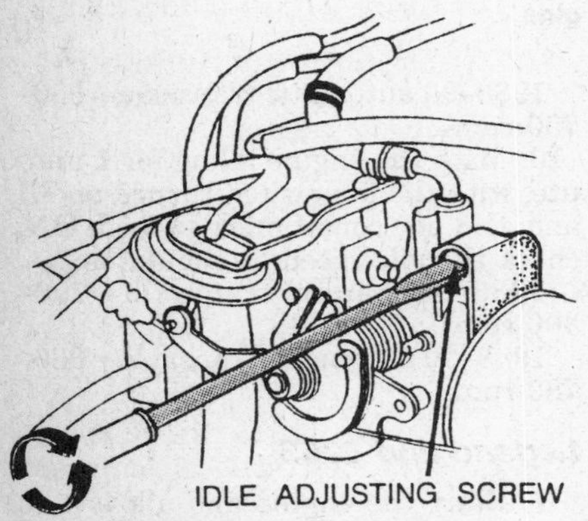

Adjusting of the idle adjusting screw—2494cc engine

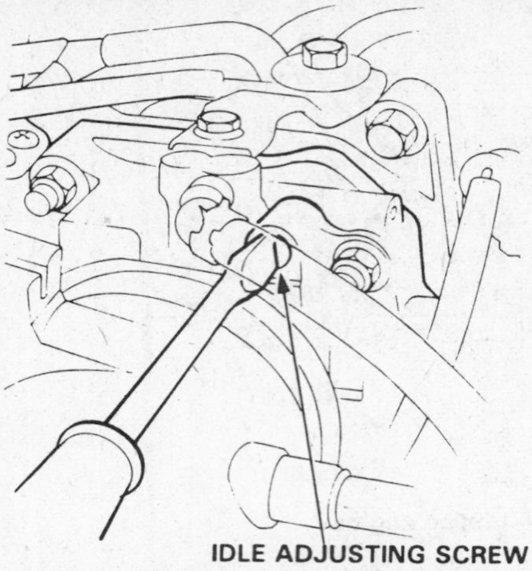

Adjusting of the idle adjusting screw—2675cc engine

the same direction and repeat this operation until the **YELLOW** LED turns **OFF**.

5. Check the idle speed under the following conditions:

With headlights and rear window defogger turned **ON**

With the steering wheel turning

With the air conditioner compressor turned **ON**

If equipped with an automatic transaxle, shift the transaxle into gear (except **P** or **N**), the idle should remain stable at 670–770 rpm (2494cc engine) or 630–730 rpm (2675cc engine).

# ENGINE ELECTRICAL

## Distributor

### REMOVAL & INSTALLATION

1. Disconnect the high tension and primary lead wires and the radio condenser wire from the distributor.

2. Label and disconnect the vacuum hoses (if equipped) or the electrical connectors (if equipped) from the distributor.

3. Remove the distributor cap hold-down screws and the distributor cap; move it aside.

4. Using chalk or paint, carefully mark the position of the distributor rotor in relation to the distributor housing, the distributor housing to the engine block.

**NOTE: This aligning procedure is very important because the distributor must be reinstalled in**

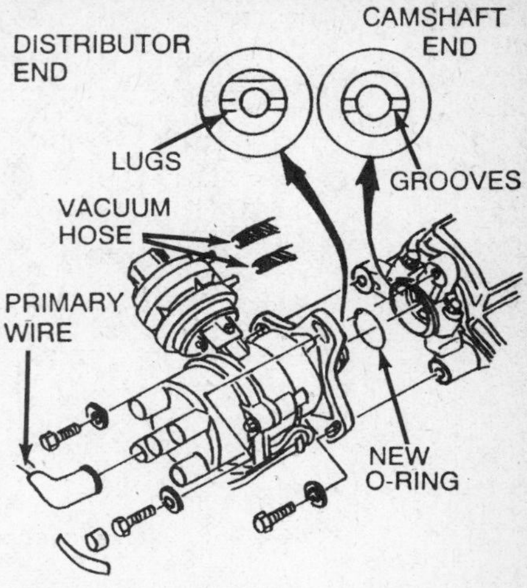

Distributor lug positioning—1590cc engine

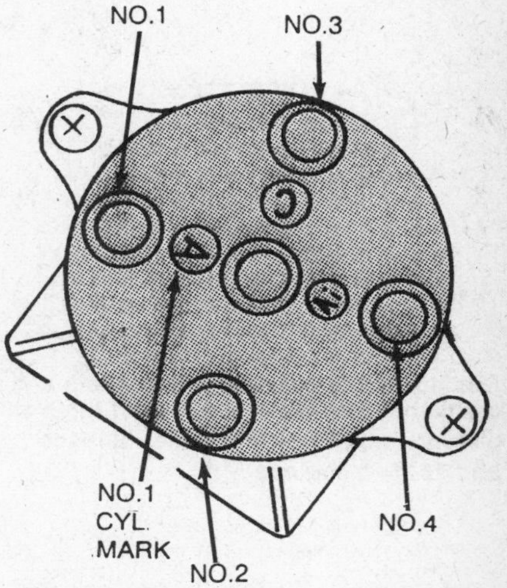

View of the distributor cap—1986–87 1590cc

**the exact location from which it was removed.**

5. Remove the distributor hold-down bolts and the distributor from the cylinder head.

**NOTE: Do not disturb the engine while the distributor is removed, for the timing will be altered.**

6. To install, lubricate the O-ring (integra) with engine oil, align the tip of the rotor with the mark on the distributor housing.

7. With the rotor and housing aligned, insert the distributor into the engine and align the mark on the housing with the mark on the block, cylinder head or extension housing.

**NOTE: The distributor is equipped with a coupling that connects them to the camshaft.**

**The lugs at the end of the coupling and it's mating grooves in the end of the camshaft are offset to prevent installing the distributor 180 degrees out of time.**

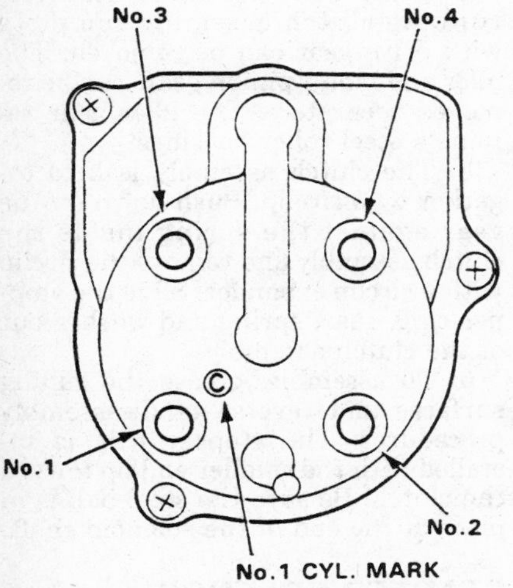


**View of the distributor cap – 1590cc (1988–90)**

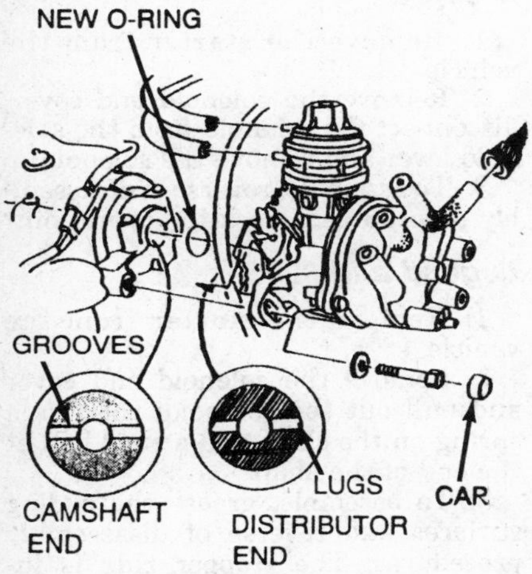


**Distributor lug positioning – 2494cc and 2675cc engines**

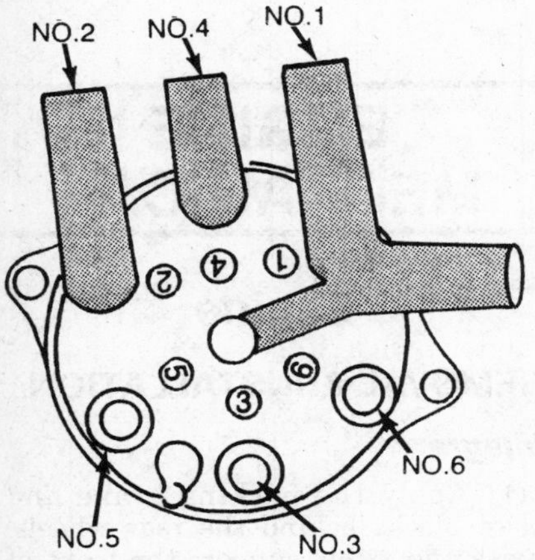


**Distributor cap wire locations – 2494cc and 2675cc engines**

8. When the distributor is fully seated in the engine, install and tighten the distributor retaining bolts.
9. Align and install the distributor cap, then install the hold-down screws.
10. Connect the vacuum hoses (if equipped) or the electrical connectors (if equipped). Install the high tension and primary wires and the radio condenser wire onto the coil.
11. Start the engine and check the ignition timing.

# Alternator

## PRECAUTIONS

- Observe the proper polarity of the battery connections by making sure the positive (+) and negative (−) terminal connections are not reversed. Mis-connection will allow current to flow in the reverse direction, resulting in damaged diodes and an overheated wire harness.
- Never ground or short out an alternator or regulator terminals.
- Never operate the alternator with it's or the battery's leads disconnected.
- Always remove the battery or disconnect the output lead while charging it.
- Always disconnect the ground cable when replacing any electrical components.
- Never subject the alternator to excessive heat or dampness if the engine is being steam cleaned.
- Never use arc welding equipment with the alternator connected.

## BELT TENSION ADJUSTMENT

The initial inspection and adjustment to the alternator drive belt should be performed after the first 3000 miles or if the alternator has been moved for any reason; afterward, inspect the belt tension every 30,000 miles. Before adjusting, inspect the belt for cracks or wear; be sure it's surfaces are free of grease and oil.

1. Push down on the belt halfway between pulleys with a force of about 22 lbs. The belt should deflect:

0.25–0.38 in. (7–10mm) – 1590cc engine

1986–88 – 0.71–0.87 in. (18–22mm) – 2494cc and 2675cc engines

1989–90 – 0.67–0.77 in. (17.0–19.5mm) – 2494cc and 2675cc engines.

2. If the belt tension requires adjustment, loosen the adjusting link bolt and move the alternator with a pry bar positioned against the front of the alternator housing.

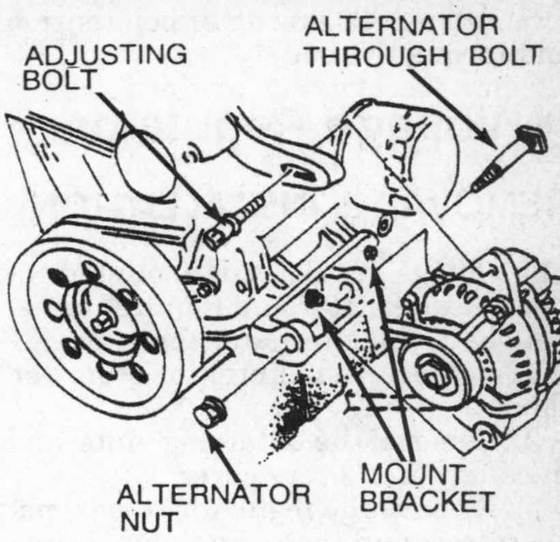


**Alternator mounting – 1590cc engine**

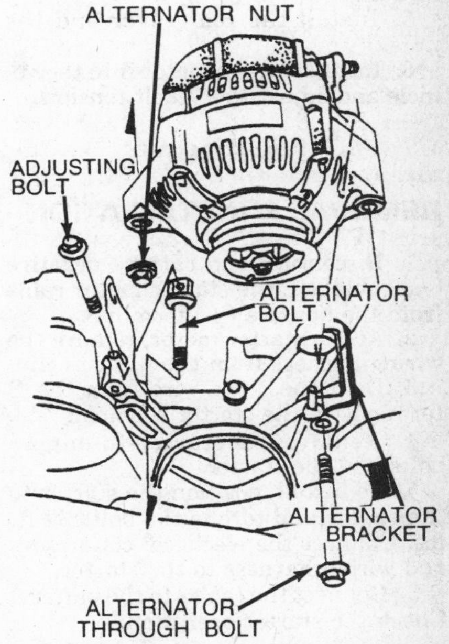


**Alternator mounting – 2494cc and 2675cc engines**

**NOTE: Do not apply pressure to any other part of the alternator.**

3. After obtaining the proper tension, tighten the adjusting link bolt.

**NOTE: Do not over-tighten the belt. Damage to the alternator bearings could result.**

## REMOVAL & INSTALLATION

1. Disconnect the negative (−) battery terminal.
2. Label and disconnect the wires from the plugs on the rear of the alternator.
3. Remove the alternator harness cover (if equipped), the alternator bolts, the V-belt and the alternator.
4. To install, position the alternator into the brackets, connect the V-belt and loosely install the bolts.

5. Adjust the alternator belt tension and torque the bolts.

## Voltage Regulator

### REMOVAL & INSTALLATION

The voltage regulator is mounted inside the alternator and requires disassembly of the alternator for removal.

1. Remove the alternator from the vehicle.
2. Remove the retaining nuts and the alternator's rear cover.
3. Remove the regulator-to-alternator screws and the regulator.
4. To install, position the regulator into the alternator and secure with screws.
5. Install the rear cover and the nuts.
6. Install the alternator into the vehicle and adjust the V-belt tension.

## Starter

### REMOVAL & INSTALLATION

1. Disconnect the battery negative (−) cable and the starter motor cable from the positive (+) terminal.
2. At the starter motor, remove the wiring harness from the harness clip.
3. Disconnect the wire from the **S** terminal on the starter solenoid.
4. Remove the starter-to-engine bolts and the starter.
5. To install, position the starter to the engine and torque the bolts 32 ft. lbs. Connect the electrical connectors and wiring harness to the starter.
6. Connect the cables to the battery. Check the starter operation.

### STARTER DRIVE REPLACEMENT

#### *Integra*

1. Remove the starter from the vehicle.
2. Remove the solenoid end cover, disconnect the solenoid from the solenoid lever and remove the solenoid.
3. Remove the end frame-to-motor bolts and the end frame.
4. The overrunning clutch assembly can be removed and the armature.
5. Separate the end cover, the field winding and the gear housing.
6. To assemble, grease the sliding surfaces and reverse of disassembly procedures. Check the operation.

#### *Legend and 825S*

1. Remove the starter from the vehicle.
2. Remove the solenoid end cover and pull out the solenoid; there is a spring on the shaft and a steel ball at the end of the shaft.
3. Remove the end frame-to-motor bolts and solenoid housing.
4. Remove the end frame. The overrunning clutch assembly complete with drive gear can be removed. The idler and motor pinion gears can be removed separately. The idler gear retains 5 steel roller bearings.
5. The clutch assembly is held together by a circlip. Push down on the gear against the spring inside the clutch assembly and remove the circlip with a circlip expander. Slide the stopper ring, gear, spring and washer out of the clutch assembly.
6. To assemble, grease the sliding surfaces and reverse of disassembly procedures. The stopper ring is installed with the smaller end lip toward the clutch. Be sure the steel ball is in place at the end of the solenoid shaft.

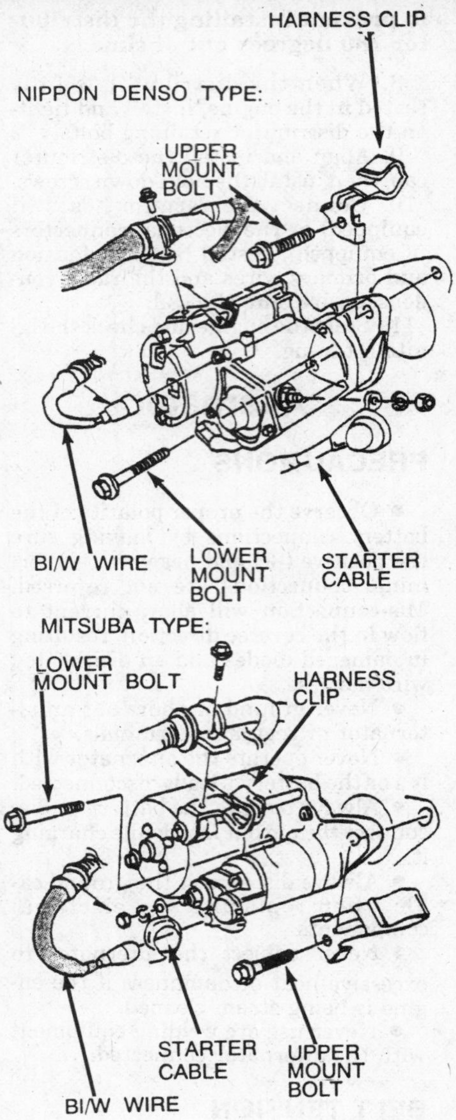


**Starter mounting—Integra**

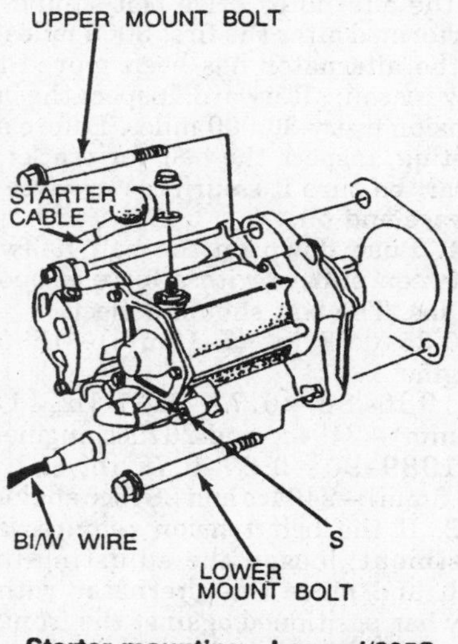


**Starter mounting—Legend/825S**

### STARTER SOLENOID REPLACEMENT

#### *Intergra*

1. Remove the starter from the vehicle.
2. Remove the solenoid end cover, disconnect the solenoid from the solenoid lever and remove the solenoid.
3. To assemble, reverse of disassembly procedures. Check the operation.

#### *Legend and 825S*

1. Remove the starter from the vehicle.
2. Remove the solenoid end cover and pull out the solenoid; there is a spring on the shaft and a steel ball at the end of the shaft.
3. To assemble, grease the sliding surfaces and reverse of disassembly procedures. The stopper ring is installed with the smaller end lip toward the clutch. Install the steel ball at the end of the solenoid shaft.

# ENGINE MECHANICAL

## Engine

### REMOVAL & INSTALLATION

#### *Integra*

1. Apply the parking brake and place blocks behind the rear wheels. Raise and safely support the front of the vehicle. Remove the engine and wheelwell splash shields.

2. Disconnect the battery cables from the battery; negative cable first. Remove the battery and the battery tray from the engine compartment (if necessary).

3. Using a scratch awl, scribe a line where the hood brackets meet the inside of the hood; this will help realign the hood during the installation. Disconnect and remove the washer fluid tube(s). Remove the hood-to-hinge bolts and the hood.

4. Drain the oil from the engine, the coolant from the radiator and the fluid from the transaxle.

**NOTE: Removal of the filler plug or radiator cap will speed the draining process.**

5. Remove the following items:

a. The air flow tube and the air intake duct.

b. The throttle control cable and/or clutch cable.

c. The coil wire and ignition primary leads.

d. The cruise control cable.

6. Relieve the fuel pressure by slowly loosening the service bolt on the top of the fuel filter about a turn.

**NOTE: Place a rag under the filter during this procedure to prevent fuel from spilling onto the engine.**

7. Disconnect the fuel hose from the fuel filter. Remove the special nut and the fuel hose.

8. Label and disconnect the following items:

a. The engine compartment subharness connector.

b. The engine secondary cable.

c. The brake booster vacuum hose.

9. Disconnect the control box connector(s). Remove the control box(s) from the bracket(s) and allow it hang next to the engine.

10. Loosen the throttle cable locknut and adjusting nut, then, slip the cable end out of the throttle bracket and remove it.

11. Remove the power steering pump-to-bracket bolts and V-belt, then, without disconnecting the hose, move the pump aside.

12. If equipped with an automatic transaxle, perform the following procedures:

a. Remove the center console.

b. Move the shift lever to the **R** position and remove the lock pin from the end of the shift cable.

13. If equipped with a manual transaxle, slide the retainer into place after driving in the spring pin.

14. Remove the radiator and heater hoses from the engine.

**NOTE: Label the heater hoses so they will be reinstalled in their original locations.**

15. Disconnect the oil cooler hoses from the transaxle (automatic transaxle), allow the fluid to drain from the hoses and prop the hoses up, near the radiator.

16. Remove the speedometer cable clip and pull the cable from the holder.

**NOTE: Do not remove the holder from the transaxle as it may cause the speedometer gear to fall into the transaxle.**

17. If equipped with air conditioning, perform the following procedures:

a. Loosen the drive belt adjusting bolts and remove the belt.

b. Remove the compressor-to-bracket bolts and wire it aside onto the front beam.

**NOTE: DO NOT disconnect the air conditioning freon lines. The compressor can be moved without discharging the system.**

c. Remove the lower compressor mounting bracket.

18. Disconnect the alternator wiring harness connectors. Remove the drive belt, the alternator mounting bolts and the alternator.

19. Squirt penetrating oil on the nuts holding the exhaust header pipe in place. Loosen and remove the nuts and pipe.

20. Remove the halfshaft as follows:

a. Place a floor jack under the lower control arm, then remove the ball joint cotter pin and nut.

**NOTE: Be certain the lower control arm is positioned securely on top of the floor jack so it doesn't suddenly jump or spring off when the ball joint remover is used.**

b. Using a ball joint puller, separate the ball joint from the front hub.

c. Slowly, lower the floor jack to lower the control arm.

d. Using a small pry bar, pry out the inboard CV-joint approximately 13mm on order to release the spring clip from the groove in the differential. Pull the steering knuckle assembly outward. Pull the halfshaft from the transaxle case.

21. Attach a lifting sling to the engine block and raise the hoist to remove the slack from the chain.

22. Remove the rear transaxle mount and the bolts from the front transaxle mount and the engine side mount.

23. Check that the engine and transaxle are free from any hoses or electrical connectors.

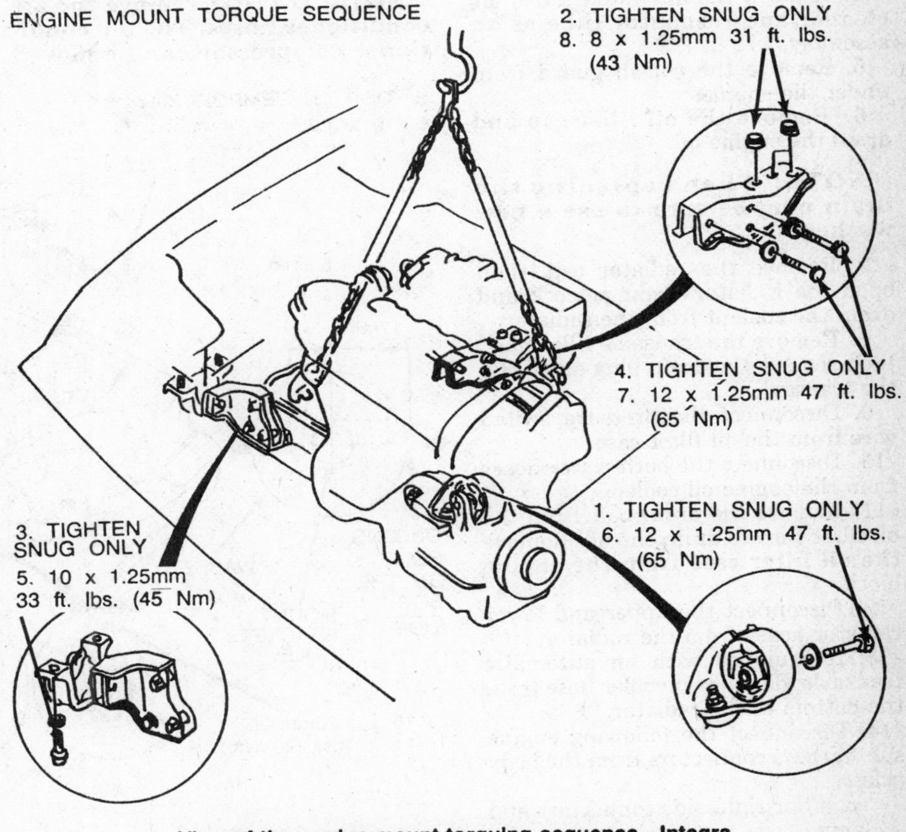


View of the engine mount torquing sequence—Integra

24. Slowly raise the engine up and out of the vehicle.
25. To install, reverse the removal procedures. Pay special attention to the following:
a. Torque the engine mounting bolts in the proper sequence or engine noise may develop.
b. Be sure the spring clip on the end of each halfshaft clicks into the differential.

**NOTE: Always use new spring clips on installation.**

c. Bleed the air from the cooling system.
d. Adjust the belt(s) tension and the throttle cable tension.
e. Check the clutch pedal freeplay.

### *Legend and 825S*

1. Apply the parking brake and place blocks behind the rear wheels. Raise and safely support the front of the vehicle.
2. Disconnect both battery cables from the battery. Remove the battery and the battery tray from the engine compartment.
3. Position the hood in the vertical position by removing the open stay mounting bolt on the hood side and fitting it to the mounting hole near the hinge.
4. Remove the air intake tube, air cleaner and resonator tube as an assembly.
5. Remove the splash guard from under the engine.
6. Remove the oil filler cap and drain the engine oil.

**NOTE: When replacing the drain plug be sure to use a new washer.**

7. Remove the radiator cap, then open the radiator drain petcock and drain the coolant from the radiator.
8. Remove the transaxle filler plug, then remove the drain plug and drain the transaxle.
9. Disconnect the pressure switch wire from the oil filter case.
10. Disconnect the both water hoses from the engine oil cooler.
11. Remove the drain bolt from the oil filter case to drain the oil. Remove the oil filter case from the engine block.
12. Disconnect the upper and lower radiator hoses from the radiator.
13. If equipped with an automatic transaxle, disconnect cooler hose from the bottom of the radiator.
14. Disconnect the following engine sub-harness connectors from the body side:
a. Four right side connectors and clamp
b. Both left side main fuse connectors
c. Coil wire, primary lead connectors and the condenser connector.
d. Both ground cables from the cylinder head and the transaxle.
15. Disconnect the connector from the power steering pump and both hoses. Disconnect the hose from the cruise control actuator and the hose from the power brake booster.
16. Using the following procedures relieve the fuel system pressure. Place a shop rag over the fuel filter to absorb any gasoline which may be sprayed on the engine while relieving the pressure. Slowly loosen the service bolt approximately one full turn. This will relieve any pressure in the system. Using a new sealing washer, tighten the service bolt.
17. Disconnect the fuel return hose from the pressure regulator. Remove the banjo nut and the fuel hose.
18. Disconnect the throttle cable from the throttle body and the rubber tube from the control box from the connection stay.
19. Remove the speed sensor from the transaxle.
20. Remove the air conditioning compressor as follows:
a. Remove the compressor clutch lead wire.
b. Loosen the belt adjusting bolt.

**NOTE: DO NOT remove the air conditioner hoses. The air conditioner compressor can be moved without discharging the air conditioner system.**

c. Remove the compressor mounting bolts, then lift the compressor out of the bracket with the hoses attached and hang it to the front bulkhead with a piece of wire.
21. Remove the exhaust pipe from the front and rear manifolds.
22. If equipped with an automatic transaxle, disconnect the control wire from the selector side of the transaxle.
23. If equipped with a manual transaxle, remove the gear change rod, the gear change extension and the clutch slave cylinder.
24. Remove the halfshaft as follows:
a. Remove the jackstands and lower the vehicle. Loosen the 32mm spindle nuts with a socket. Raise and safely support the vehicle.
b. Remove the front wheel and the spindle nut.
c. Remove the damper fork and the damper pinch bolts. Remove the damper fork.
d. Remove the ball joint bolt and separate the ball joint from lower control arm control.
e. Disconnect the tie rods from the steering knuckles.
f. Remove the sway bar bolts (Accord only).
g. Pull the front hub outward and off the halfshaft.
h. Using a small pry bar, pry out the inboard CV-joint approximately 13mm in order to release the spring

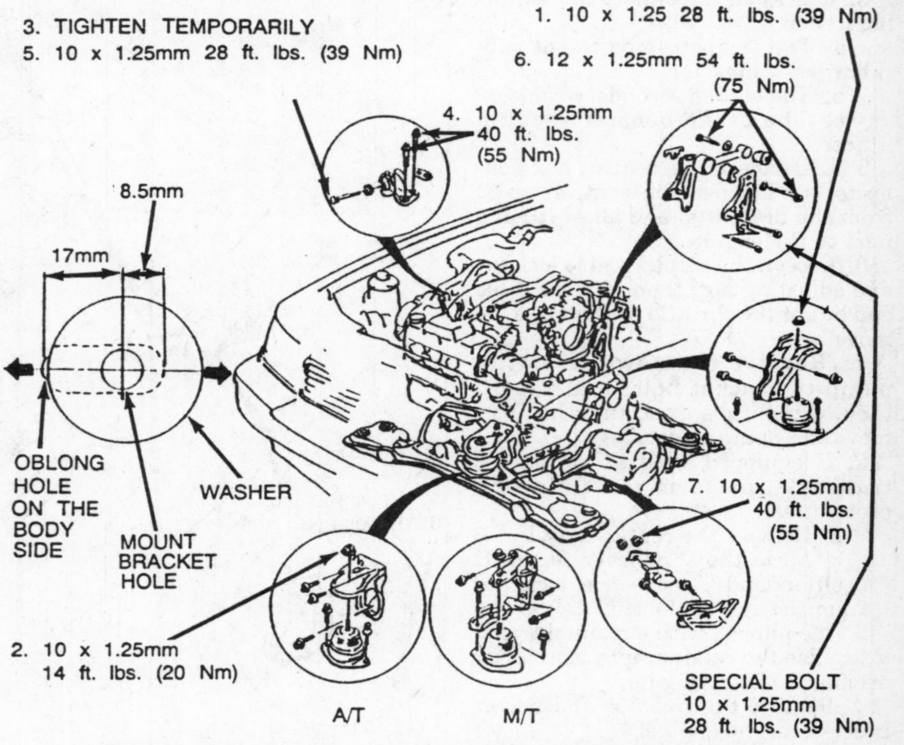

View of the engine mount torquing sequence—Legend and 825S

clip from the differential, then pull the halfshaft from the transaxle case.

**NOTE: When installing the halfshaft, insert the shaft until the spring clip clicks into the groove. Always use a new spring clip when installing the halfshaft.**

25. Attach a chain hoist to the engine and raise it enough to remove the slack.
26. Remove the engine side mount bracket bolts.
27. Remove the front engine mount nut, then remove the rear engine mount nut.
28. Loosen and remove the alternator belt. Disconnect the alternator wire harness and remove the alternator.
29. Remove the bolt from the rear torque rod at the engine, then loosen the bolt in the frame mount and swing the rod up and out of the way.
30. Tilt the engine about 30 degrees and raise the engine carefully from the vehicle checking that all wires and hoses have been removed from the engine/transaxle. Raise the engine all the way up and remove it from the vehicle.
31. Install the engine in the reverse order of removal, making the following checks:
    a. Torque the engine mounting bolts in the proper sequence to avoid excessive noise and vibration.
    b. Refill and bleed the air from the cooling system.
    c. Adjust the clutch pedal freeplay.
    d. Adjust the throttle cable tension and the alternator belt tension.
    e. Make sure the transaxle shifts properly.

## Cylinder Head

### REMOVAL & INSTALLATION

#### *Integra*

**CAUTION**

***Cylinder head temperature must be below 100°F.***

Before removing the cylinder head check the following:

Inspect the timing belt.

Turn the flywheel so the No. 1 cylinder is at TDC.

Mark all emission hoses before disconnecting them.

1. Disconnect the negative battery cable.
2. Drain the cooling system.
3. Remove the air cleaner:
    a. Remove the air cleaner cover and filter.
    b. Disconnect the hot/cold air intake ducts and remove the air chamber hose.
    c. Remove the air cleaner.
4. Relieve the fuel pressure using the following procedure:
    a. Slowly loosen the service bolt on the top of the fuel filter about one turn.

**NOTE: Place a rag under the filter during this procedure to prevent fuel from spilling onto the engine.**

    b. Disconnect the fuel return hose from the pressure regulator. Remove the special nut and the fuel hose.
5. Remove the brake booster vacuum tube from the intake manifold.
6. Remove the engine ground wire from the valve cover. Disconnect the throttle cable from the throttle body.
7. Disconnect the spark plug wires from the spark plugs and remove the distributor assembly.
8. Disconnect the hoses from the charcoal canister and from the No. 1 control box at the tubing manifold.
9. If equipped with air conditioning, disconnect the idle control solenoid hoses.
10. Disconnect the upper radiator heater and bypass hoses.
11. Disconnect the engine sub harness connectors and the following couplers from the cylinder head and the intake manifold:
    The 4 injector couplers
    The TA sensor connector
    The ground connector
    The TW sensor connector
    The throttle sensor connector
    The crankshaft angle sensor coupler
    The EAVC connector (if equipped)
    The CYL sensor connector (if equipped)
12. Remove the thermostat housing-to-intake manifold hose.
13. Disconnect the oxygen sensor coupler.
14. Remove the exhaust manifold bracket, the manifold bolts and the manifold.
15. Remove the bolts from the intake manifold and bracket.
16. Disconnect the breather chamber-to-intake manifold hose.
17. Remove the valve and upper timing belt covers.
18. Loosen the timing belt tensioner adjustment bolt and remove the belt.
19. Remove the lower timing belt cover bolts, the camshaft holder bolts, the camshaft holders, the camshafts and the rocker arms.
20. Remove the cylinder head bolts in the reverse order given in the head bolt torque sequence.

**NOTE: Unscrew the bolts ⅓ of a turn each time and repeat the sequence to prevent cylinder head warpage.**

21. Carefully, remove the intake mainfold from the cylinder head and the cylinder head from the engine.
22. Clean the gasket mounting surfaces.
23. To install, use new gaskets and

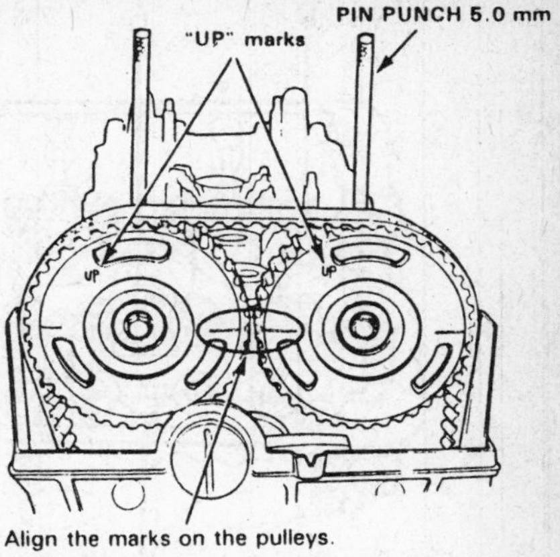

**Alignment of the camshaft marks—Integra**

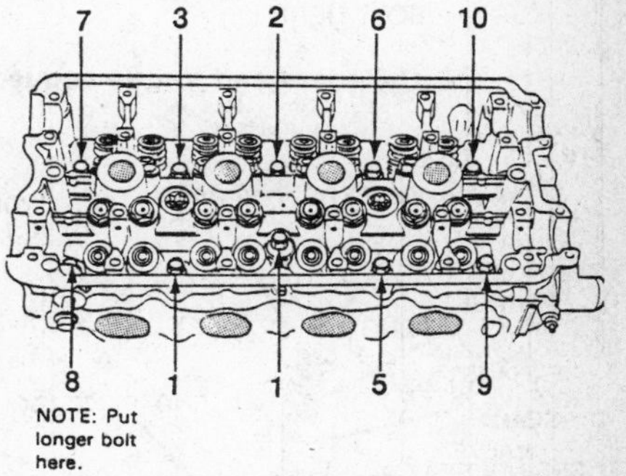

**Cylinder head torque sequence—1590cc engine 1986–87**

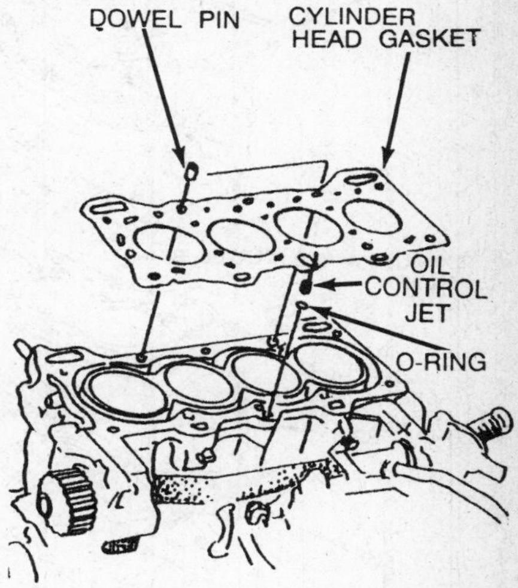

**Dowel pin and oil jet control locations—1590cc engine**

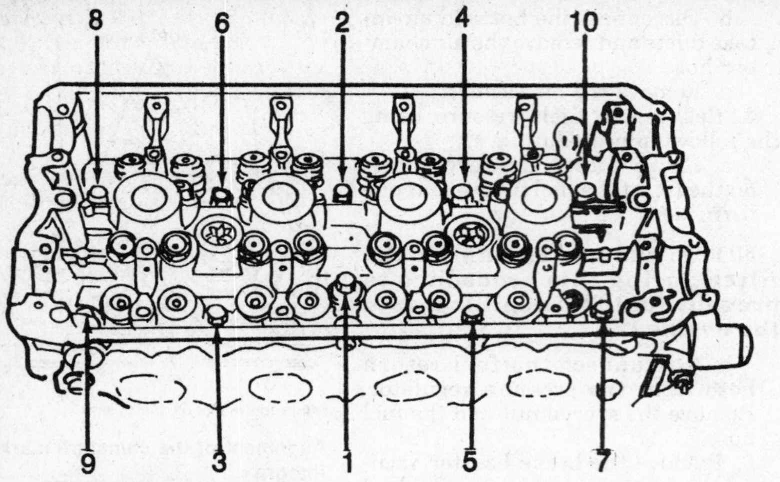


Cylinder head torque sequence – 1590cc engine 1988–89

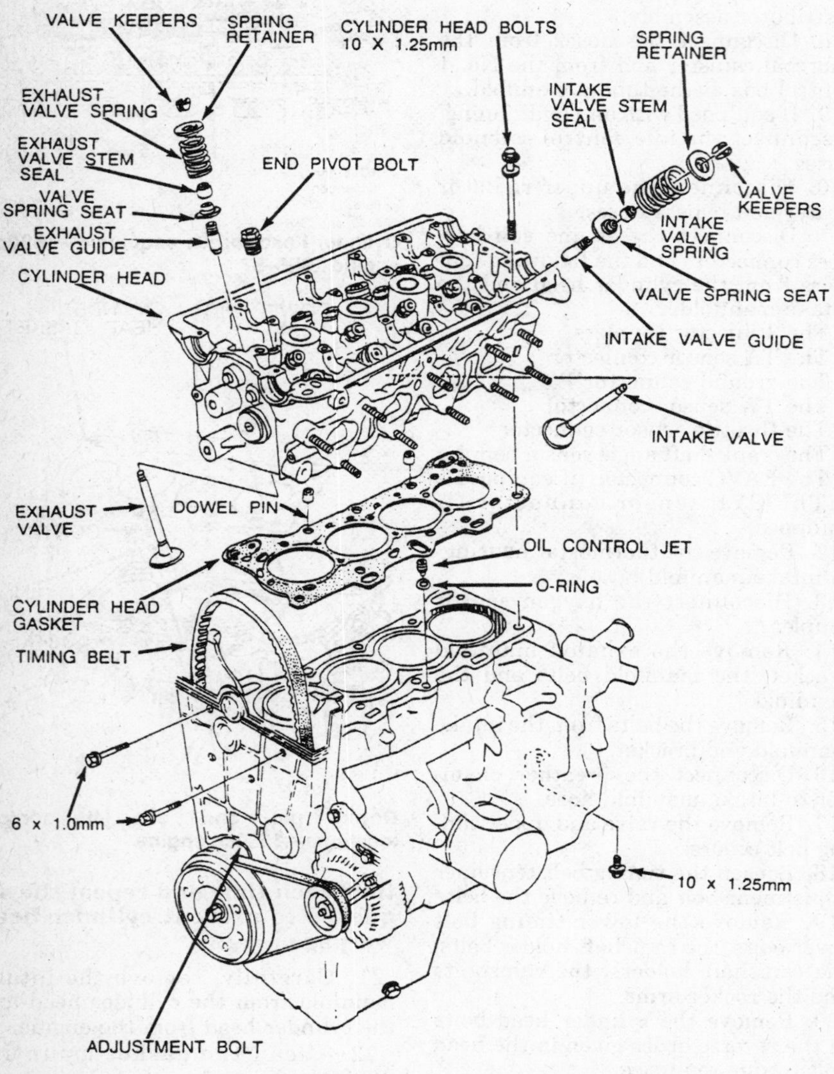


Cylinder head and related components – 1590cc engine

reverse the removal procedures, being sure to pay attention to the following points:

a. Be sure the No. 1 cylinder is at TDC and the camshaft pulleys **UP** mark is on the top before positioning the head in place.

b. The cylinder head dowel pins and oil control jet must be aligned.

c. Torque the cylinder head bolts in 2 progressive steps as shown in the torque sequence diagram. First to 22 ft. lbs. (30 Nm) in sequence, then to 48 ft. lbs. (67 Nm) in the same sequence.

d. Use the longer bolt in the No. 8 (1986–87) or No. 9 (1988–90) position.

e. After installation, check to see that all hoses and wires are installed correctly.

f. Adjust the valve clearance.

### Legend and 825S

**CAUTION**

***The cylinder head temperature must be below 100°F.***

Before removing the cylinder head check the following:

Inspect the timing belt.

Turn the flywheel so the No. 1 cylinder is at TDC.

Mark all emission hoses before disconnecting them.

1. Disconnect the battery ground cable.
2. Drain the cooling system.
3. Remove the vacuum hose from the brake booster.
4. Remove the secondary ground cable from the cylinder head and the transaxle housing.
5. Disconnect the radio noise condenser connector, ignition coil wire and the ignition primary connector.
6. Remove the air cleaner cover.
7. Relieve the fuel pressure using the following procedure:

a. Slowly loosen the service bolt on the top of the fuel filter about a turn.

**NOTE: Place a rag under the filter during this procedure to prevent fuel from spilling onto the engine.**

b. Disconnect the fuel return hose from the pressure regulator. Remove the special nut and the fuel hose.

8. Disconnect the throttle cable from the throttle valve.
9. Disconnect the charcoal canister hose from the throttle valve.
10. Disconnect the engine sub harness connectors and the following couplers from the cylinder head and the intake manifold:

The 6 injector couplers

The TA sensor connector
The temperature unit connector
The ground connector from the fuel pipe
The TW sensor connector
The throttle sensor connector
The crankshaft angle sensor EGR valve connector
The 4 wire harness clamps

11. Disconnect the oxygen sensor coupler.
12. Disconnect the cooling system hoses from the cylinder head.
13. Disconnect the spark plug wires from the spark plugs and remove the distributor assembly.
14. Remove the intake manifold cover from the intake manifold.
15. Remove the wire harness cover.
16. Remove the alternator pulley cover.
17. Remove the alternator and belt.
18. Remove the power steering pump and disconnect the pump hoses. Also, remove the hose clamp bolt on the body.
19. Disconnect the idle boost solenoid hoses.
20. Remove the cruise control actuator.
21. Remove the exhaust header pipe and pull it clear of the exhaust manifold.
22. Remove the air cleaner base mount bolts and disconnect the hose from the intake manifold to the breather chamber.
23. Remove the air cleaner base from the intake manifold.
24. Remove the EGR tube nuts from the cylinder hear.
25. Remove the exhaust manifold cover nuts.
26. Remove the air suction tube nuts from the exhaust manifold and air suction valve.
27. Remove the intake manifold assembly from the cylinder head.
28. Remove the water passage assembly from the front and rear of the cylinder head.
29. Remove the timing belt upper covers.
30. Loosen the tensioner adjustment bolt and remove the timing belt.

**NOTE: Advance the crankshaft by about 15 degrees before removing the timing belt to prevent interference between the piston and the valve.**

31. Remove the front and rear camshaft pulleys using the following procedure:
    a. Before removing the rear pulley, adjust the cam position so no valve is fully open.
    b. Remove the pulley mounting bolts with a universal holder and a double-end wrench. For the rear pulley, first remove the top two bolts and then the remaining bolt.
32. Remove the upper cover back plates.
33. Remove the valve covers and the head side covers.
34. Remove the bearing cap oil pipes, the bearing caps and the camshaft.
35. Remove the intake and exhaust inside rocker arms and pushrods.

**NOTE: Label all valve train components to ensure reinstallation in their proper locations.**

36. Remove the cylinder head bolts and remove the head.

**NOTE: Unscrew the cylinder head bolts $\frac{1}{3}$ of a turn in the reverse order of the torque sequence each turn until loose to prevent warpage to the cylinder head.**

37. Clean the gasket mounting surfaces.
38. To install, reverse of the removal procedure, taking note of the following items:
    a. Make sure the **UP** mark on the timing belt pulley is at the top.
    b. Turn the crankshaft so the No. 1 piston is at TDC.

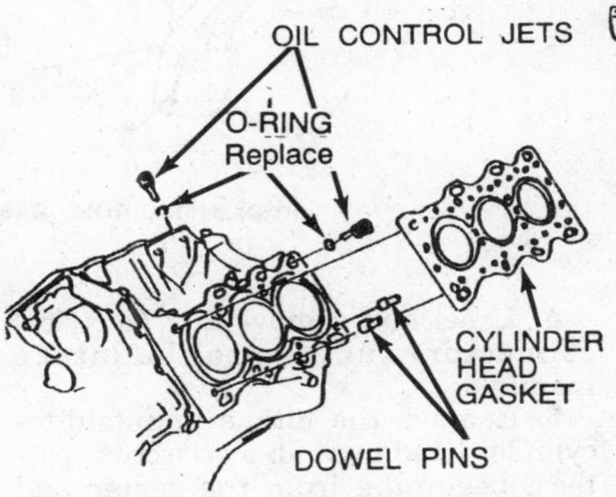


**Dowel pin and oil jet control locations – 2494cc and 2675cc engines**

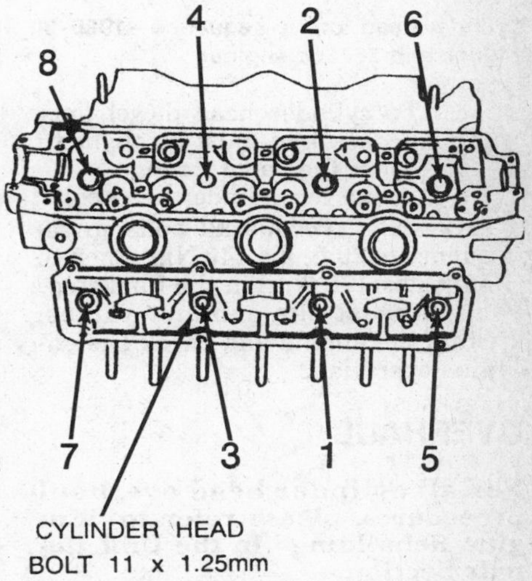


**Cylinder head torque sequence – 1986–88 2494cc and 2675cc engines**

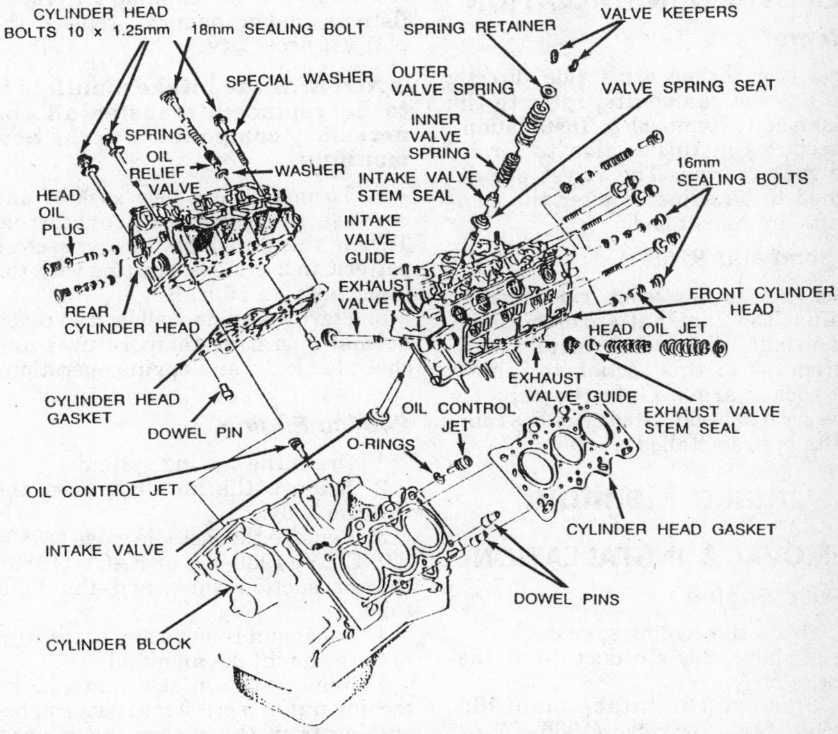


**Cylinder head and related components – 2494cc and 2675cc engines**

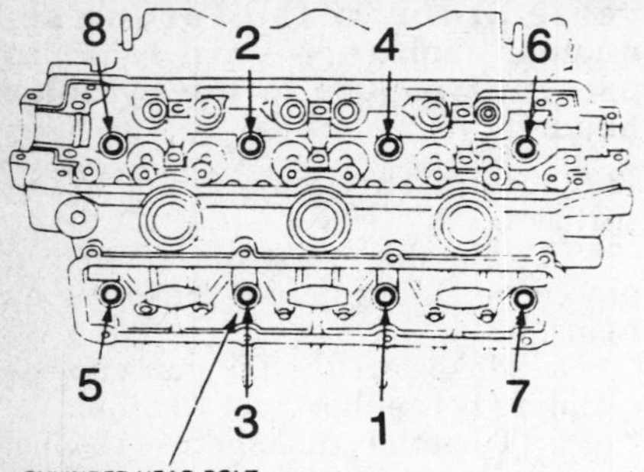


**Cylinder head torque sequence – 1989–90 2494cc and 2675cc engines**

c. The cylinder head dowel pins and oil control jet must be aligned.
d. Adjust the valve timing.
e. Torque the cylinder head bolts in 2 steps. Torque all bolts in sequence to 29 ft. lbs. (40 Nm), then to 56 ft. lbs. (78 Nm) in the final step.
f. Adjust the exhaust valves. Start the engine and check the engine operation.

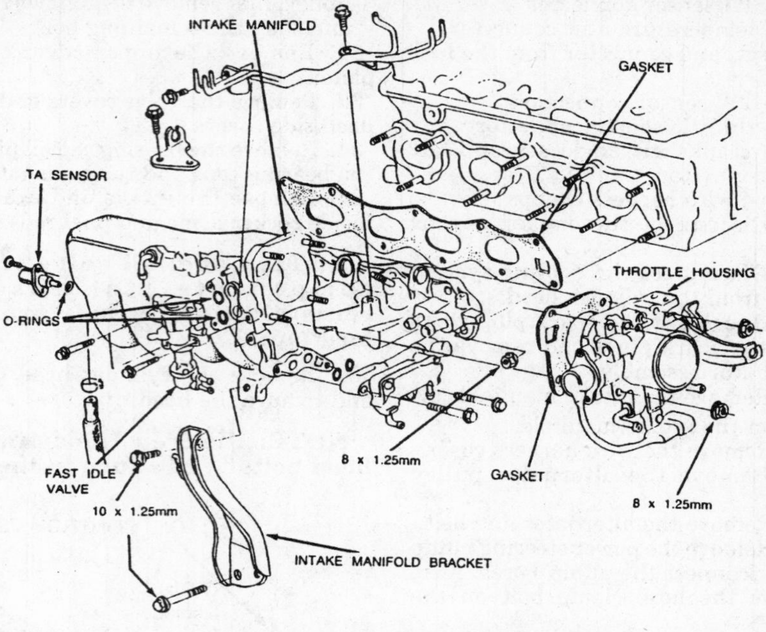


**Intake manifold assembly – 1590cc engine**

## OVERHAUL

**For all cylinder head overhaul procedures, please refer to "Engine Rebuilding" in the Unit Repair Section.**

## Rocker Arms/Shafts

### REMOVAL & INSTALLATION

#### *Integra*

Since the rocker arms ride directly against the camshafts, refer to the "Camshaft, Removal & Installation" procedures in this section to service the rocker arms. The valves are designed to be adjusted after the camshafts are reinstalled.

#### *Legend and 825S*

Since the rocker arms ride directly against the camshafts, refer to the "Camshaft, Removal & Installation" procedures in this section to service the rocker arms. Only the exhaust valves are to be adjusted after the camshafts are reinstalled.

## Intake Manifold

### REMOVAL & INSTALLATION

#### *1590cc Engine*

1. Drain the cooling system.
2. Remove the air duct from the throttle body.
3. Remove the intake manifold bracket, fast idle valve (1986–87) or the EVAC (1988–90).
4. Label and remove any electrical connectors running to the intake manifold.
5. Remove the intake manifold-to-cylinder head nuts, in a crisscross pattern, beginning from the center and moving out to both ends. Remove the manifold and the gasket.
6. Clean the gasket mounting surfaces. Inspect the manifold for cracks, flatness and/or damage; replace the parts, if necessary.

**NOTE: If the intake manifold is to be replaced, transfer all the necessary components to the new manifold.**

7. To install, use new gaskets and reverse the removal procedures. Torque the nuts/bolts in a crisscross pattern, in 2–3 steps, starting with the inner nuts, to 16 ft. lbs.
8. Start the engine, allow it to reach normal operating temperatures and check for leaks and engine operation.

#### *2494cc Engine*

1. Drain the cooling system.
2. Remove the air duct from the throttle body.
3. Remove the fast idle valve (1986–87), EICV (1986–87) or EACV (1988), the air suction valve and the EGR tube.
4. Label and remove any wires running to the intake manifold.
5. Remove the intake manifold attaching nut in a crisscross pattern, beginning from the center and moving out to both ends and the manifold.
6. Clean the gasket mounting surfaces. Inspect the manifold for cracks, flatness and/or damage; replace the parts, if necessary.

**NOTE: If the intake manifold is to be replaced, transfer all the necessary components to the new manifold.**

7. To install, use new gaskets and reverse the removal procedures. Torque the nuts/bolts in a crisscross pattern, in 2–3 steps, starting with the inner nuts, to 16 ft. lbs.
8. Start the engine, allow it to reach normal operating temperatures and check for leaks and engine operation.

#### *2675cc Engine*

1. Drain the cooling system.
2. Remove the air duct from the throttle body.
3. Remove the fast idle valve (1987), EICV (1986–87) or the EVAC (1988–90), the air suction valve and the EGR tube.
4. Label and remove any wires running to the intake manifold.
5. Remove the intake manifold attaching nut in a crisscross pattern, beginning from the center and moving out to both ends and the manifold.
6. Clean the gasket mounting surfaces. Inspect the manifold for cracks, flatness and/or damage; replace the parts, if necessary.

**NOTE. If the intake manifold is to be replaced, transfer all the necessary components to the new manifold.**

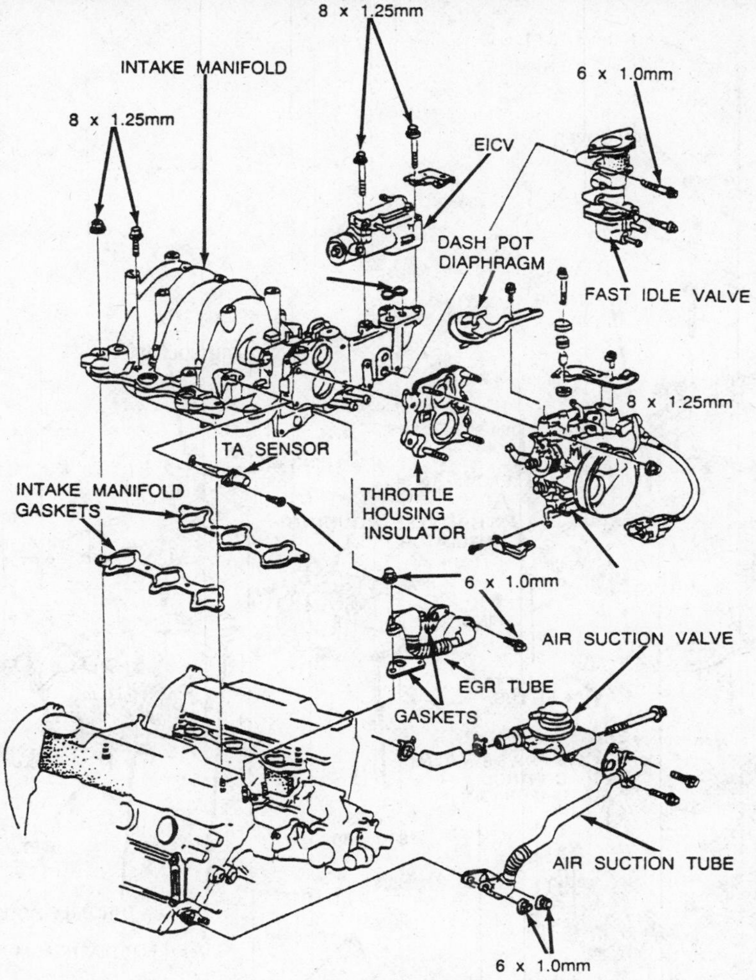


**Intake manifold assembly—2494cc engine**

7. To install, use new gaskets and reverse the removal procedures. Torque the nuts/bolts in a crisscross patter in 2–3 steps, starting with the inner nuts, to 16 ft. lbs.
8. Start the engine, allow it to reach normal operating temperatures and check for leaks and engine operation.

## Exhaust Manifold

### REMOVAL & INSTALLATION

**CAUTION**

***Do not perform this operation on a warm or hot engine.***

#### *1590cc Engine*

1. Remove the exhaust manifold shroud.
2. Remove the exhaust pipe-to-exhaust manifold nuts.
3. Remove the oxygen sensor (if equipped).
4. Remove the exhaust manifold bracket bolt.
5. Remove the exhaust manifold-to-cylinder head nuts in a crisscross pattern starting from the center and the manifold.
6. Clean the gasket mounting surfaces. Inspect the manifold for cracks, flatness and/or damage; replace the parts, if necessary.
7. To install, use new gaskets and reverse the removal procedures. Torque the manifold nuts in a crisscross pattern starting from the center, to 23 ft. lbs. and the exhaust pipe-to-manifold nuts to 40 ft. lbs.
8. Start the engine and check for leaks.

#### *2494cc and 2675cc Engines*

1. Remove the exhaust manifold shrouds.
2. Remove the exhaust pipe-to-exhaust manifold nuts.
3. Remove the oxygen sensors.
4. Remove the air suction tube.
5. Remove the exhaust pipe-to-exhaust manifold nuts.
6. Clean the gasket mounting surfaces. Inspect the manifold for cracks, flatness and/or damage; replace the parts, if necessary.
7. Remove the exhaust attaching nuts in a crisscross pattern starting from the center and the manifold.
8. To install, use new gaskets and reverse the removal procedures. Torque the manifold nuts/bolts in a crisscross pattern starting from the center, to 16 ft. lbs.

## Front Cover

### REMOVAL & INSTALLATION

#### *1590cc Engine*

1. Rotate the crankshaft to align the crankshaft pulley or flywheel pointer, at top dead center; the camshaft sprockets **UP** mark should be facing upward with the alignment marks aligned with the top of the cylinder head.
2. Remove the timing belt upper cover-to-engine bolts and the cover.
3. Loosen the alternator and remove the drive belt(s).
4. Remove the crankshaft pulley-to-crankshaft pulley bolt and the crankshaft pulley.
5. Remove the lower timing belt cover-to-engine bolts and the cover.
6. To install, reverse the removal procedures. Make sure the timing belt and the front oil seal are properly installed on the crankshaft and before replacing the cover. Torque the crankshaft pulley bolt to 83 ft. lbs. (1986–88) or 119 ft. lbs. (1989–90).

#### *2494cc and 2675cc Engines*

1. Rotate the crankshaft to align the crankshaft pulley or flywheel pointer, at Top Dead Center (TDC); the camshaft sprocket notches should align with the marks on the rear timing belt cover.
2. Remove the power steering pump (if equipped), the air conditioning (if equipped) and the alternator drive belts.
3. Remove the upper timing belt covers-to-engine bolts and the covers.
4. Remove the crankshaft pulley-to-crankshaft pulley bolt and the crankshaft pulley.
5. Remove the lower timing belt cover-to-engine bolts and the cover.
6. To install, reverse the removal procedures. Make sure the timing belt and the front oil seal are properly installed on the crankshaft and before replacing the cover. Torque the crankshaft pulley bolt to 83 ft. lbs. (1986–88) or 123 ft. lbs. (1989–90).

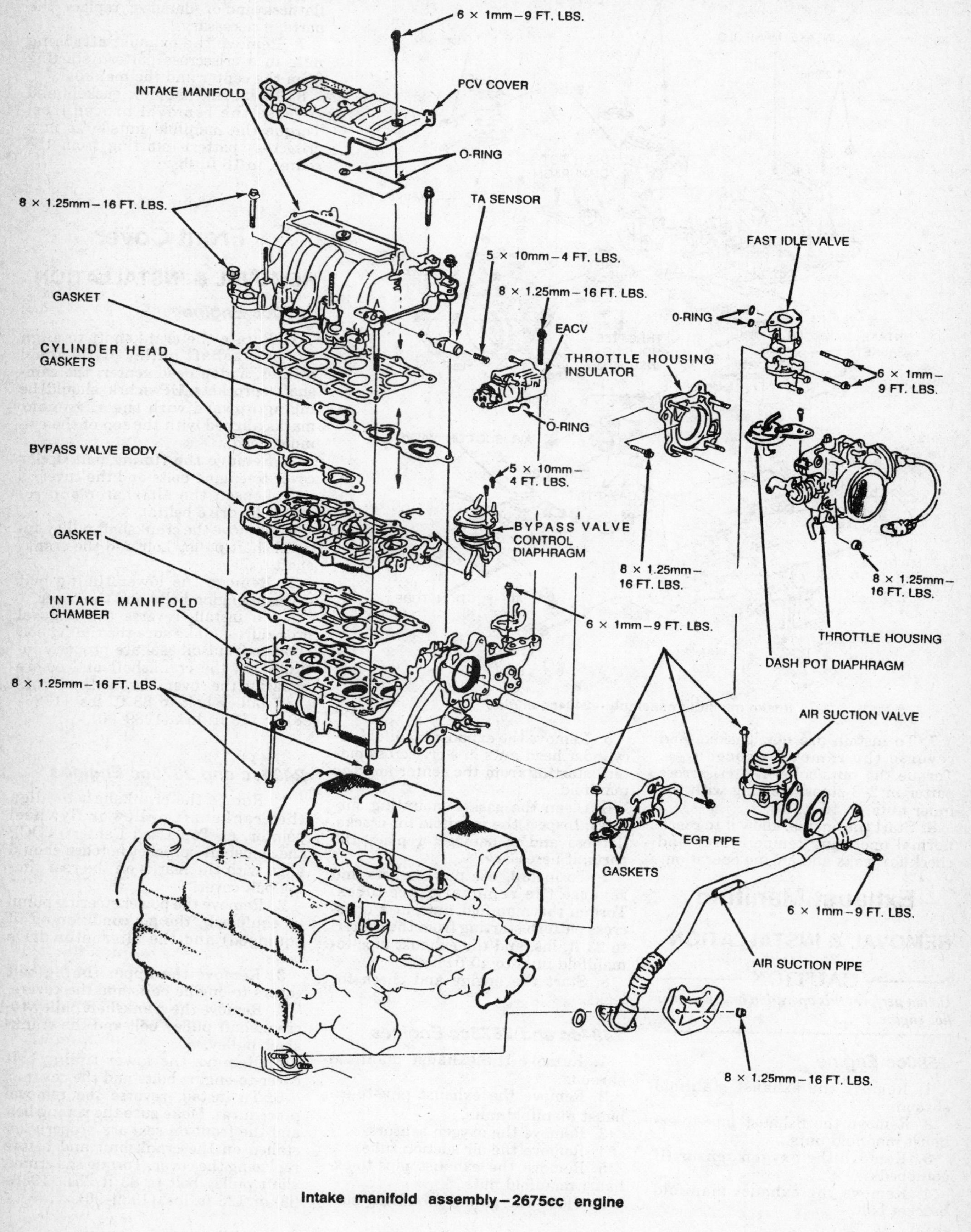


**Intake manifold assembly – 2675cc engine**

## OIL SEAL REPLACEMENT

### *1590cc Engine*

1. Remove the timng belt.
2. Slide the crankshaft sprocket and belt guides from the crankshaft.
3. Using a small prybar, pry the oil seal from the oil pump housing; be careful not to damage the seal's mounting surface.
4. Using a new oil seal, lubricate the seal lips with engine oil. Using a seal drive tool or equivalent, drive the new seal into the oil pump housing until it seats.
5. To complete the installation, reverse the removal procedures. Adjust the timing belt tension. Torque the crankshaft pulley bolt to 83 ft. lbs. (1986–88) or 119 ft. lbs. (1989–90).

### *2494cc and 2675cc Engines*

1. Remove the timing belt.
2. Slide the crankshaft sprocket and belt guides from the crankshaft.
3. Using a small prybar, pry the oil seal from the oil pump housing; be careful not to damage the seal's mounting surface.
4. Using a new oil seal, lubricate the seal lips with engine oil. Using a seal drive tool or equivalent, drive the new seal into the oil pump housing until it seats.
5. To complete the installation, reverse the removal procedures. Adjust the timing belt tension. Torque the crankshaft pulley bolt to 83 ft. lbs. (1986–88) or 123 ft. lbs. (1989–90).

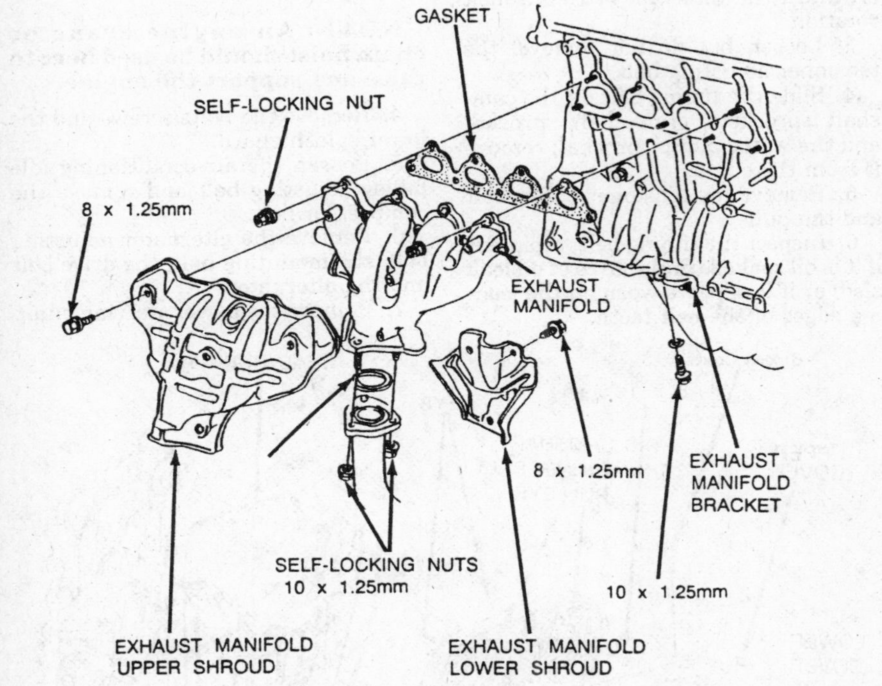


**Exhaust manifold assembly – 1590cc engine**

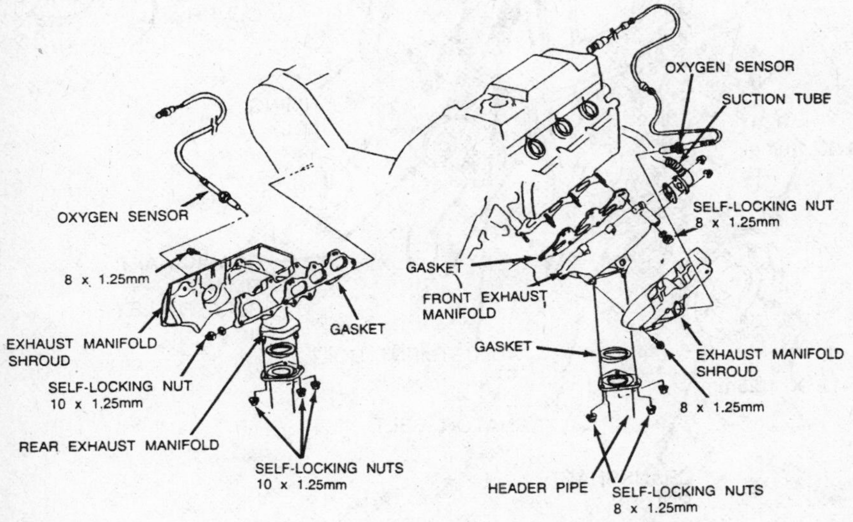


**Exhaust manifold assembly – 2494cc and 2675cc engines**

# Timing Belt And Tensioner

## ADJUSTMENT

### *1590cc Engine*

**NOTE: Always adjust the timing belt tension with the engine cold. The tensioner is spring-loaded to apply the proper tension to the belt automatically after making the following adjustments.**

1. Turn the crankshaft pulley until the No. 1 piston is at TDC of the compression stroke. This can be determined by observing the valves (all closed) or by feeling for pressure in the spark plug hole (with your thumb or a compression gauge) as the engine is turned.
2. Loosen the adjusting bolt on the tensioner pulley.
3. Rotate the crankshaft counterclockwise 3–teeth on the camshaft pulley to create tension on the timing belt.
4. Torque the adjusting bolt on the tensioner pulley to 33 ft. lbs. (45 Nm).
5. If the crankshaft pulley broke loose while turning the crank, torque it to 83 ft. lbs. (1986–88) or 119 ft. lbs. (1989–90).

**NOTE: Place the transaxle in gear and set the parking brake before torquing the crankshaft pulley bolt.**

### *Legend and 825S*

**NOTE: Always adjust the timing belt tension with the engine cold. The tensioner is spring-loaded to apply the proper tension to the belt automatically after making the following adjustments.**

1. Turn the crankshaft pulley until No. 1 is at TDC of the compression stroke. This can be determined by observing the valves (all closed) or by feeling for pressure in the spark plug hole (with your thumb or a compression gauge) as the engine is turned.
2. Rotate the crankshaft clockwise (as viewed from the pulley side of the

engine) 9–teeth on the camshaft pulley, (The blue mark on the camshaft pulley should match the pointer on the lower cover).

3. Loosen the adjusting bolt to create tension on the timing belt.

4. Torque the adjusting bolt to 31 ft. lbs. (43 Nm).

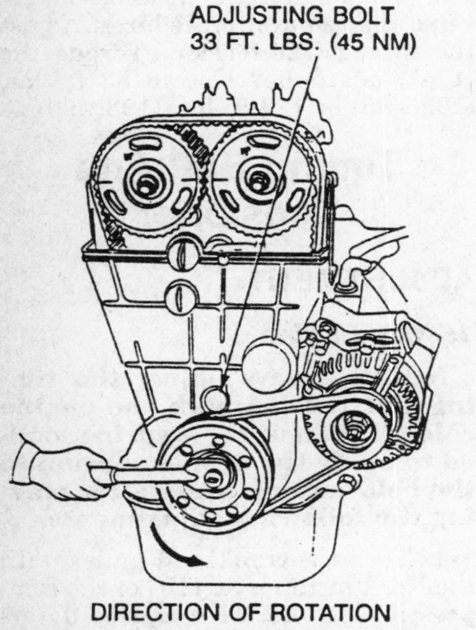


**Timing belt adjustment–1590cc engine**

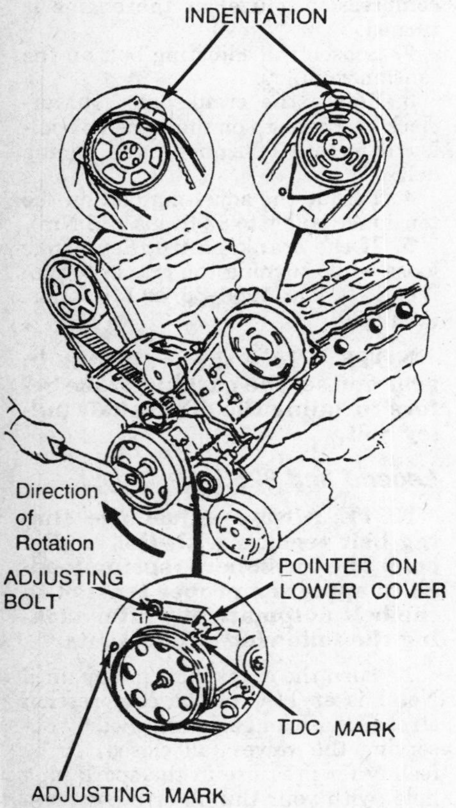


**Timing belt adjustment–2494cc and 2675cc engines**

## REMOVAL & INSTALLATION

### *1590cc Engine*

1. Rotate the crankshaft pulley until No. 1 is at TDC of the compression stroke. This can be determined by observing the valves (all closed) or by feeling for pressure in the spark plug hole (with your thumb or a compression gauge) as the engine is turned.

2. Remove the alternator belt, the power steering belt (if equipped) and the air conditioning belt (if equipped), crankshaft pulley and timing gear cover. Mark the direction of timing belt rotation.

3. Loosen but do not remove, the tensioner adjusting bolt.

4. Slide the timing belt off the camshaft sprockets, crankshaft sprocket and the water pump sprocket; remove it from the engine.

5. Remove the tensioner pulley bolt and the pulley.

6. Inspect the timing belt; replace it if it is oil soaked (find source of oil leak also) or if it appears worn on the leading edges of the belt teeth.

7. To install, reverse the removal procedures. Be sure to position the crankshaft and camshaft timing sprockets in the TDC position.

8. Adjust the timing belt tension.

### *2494cc and 2675cc Engines*

1. Remove the pulley cover and the harness cover from above the timing belt upper cover.

2. Remove the engine sub-harness clamp.

3. Remove the engine support bolts, loosen the side mount rubber and raise the side mount bracket.

**NOTE: An engine crane or chain hoist should be used here to raise and support the engine.**

4. Remove the bolts/screws and the lower splash guard.

5. Loosen the air conditioning idle pulley adjusting bolt and remove the compressor belt.

6. Remove the alternator adjusting bolt, the mounting bolt, the drive belt and the alternator.

7. Remove the power steering pump

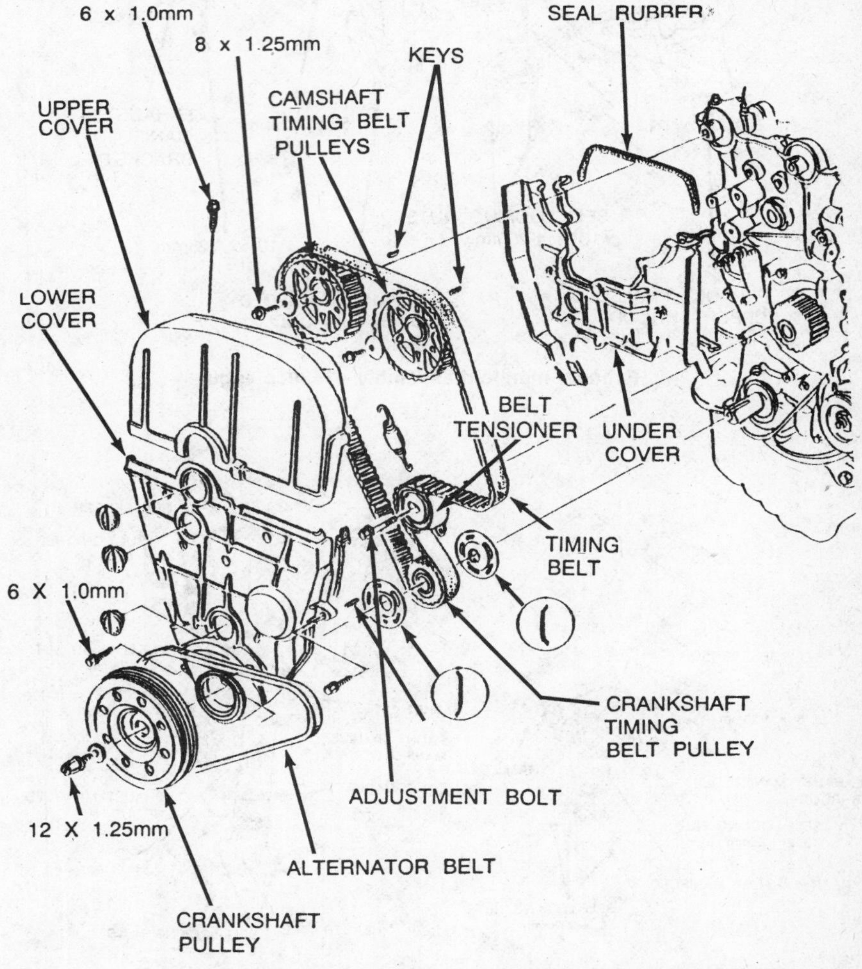


**Timing belt and sprocket assembly–1590cc engine**

bolt, the mounting bolt, the drive belt and the power steering pump.

**NOTE: During installation be sure to adjust all the belt tensions.**

8. Remove the front and rear upper covers.
9. Remove the special bolt and the crankshaft pulley.
10. Remove the lower cover.
11. Loosen the adjusting bolt and remove the timing belt.
12. Remove the adjustment pulley bolt and the pulley. Inspect the timing belt. Replace it if it is oil soaked (find source of oil leak also), or if it appears worn on the leading edges of the belt teeth.
13. To install, reverse the removal procedure. Be sure to install the belt with the arrow facing in the same direction it was facing during removal.
14. Remove all the spark plugs from the engine.
15. Advance the crankshaft by about 15 degrees from the No. 1 cylinder compression TDC. After adjusting the front and rear camshaft pulleys to the No. 1 cylinder compression TDC, return the crankshaft pulley by about 15 degrees again to adjust the TDC position.

**NOTE: Fabricate a universal holder to rotate the camshaft driving pulley.**

16. To fix the adjusting bolt with the timing belt tensioner at the belt loosening position, perform the following procedures:
    a. Push the tensioner bracket with a flat blade screwdriver to loosen the belt tension.
    b. DO NOT push on the timing belt.
17. To install the timing belt, perform the following procedures:
    a. Install the timing belt in the following sequence; crankshaft pulley, front crankshaft pulley, water pump pulley, tensioner and rear camshaft pulley.
    b. For ease of installation, advance the rear camshaft pulley by about a ½ tooth from the TDC position.
18. Loosen the adjusting bolt and retorque it after tensioning the belt.
19. Rotate the crankshaft 5–6 turns clockwise, so the belt may fit in position on the pulleys. Adjust the timing belt tension.

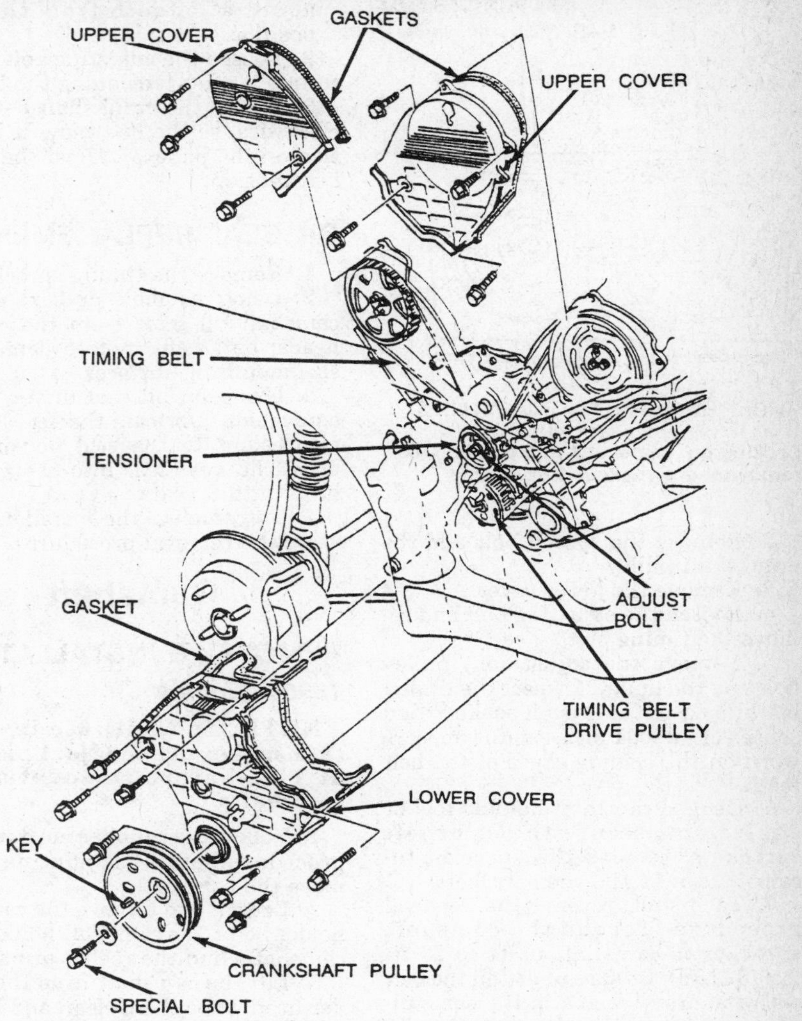


**Timing belt and sprocket assembly—2494cc and 2675cc engines**

## Timing Sprockets

### REMOVAL & INSTALLATION

#### *1590cc Engine*

1. Remove the timing belt; the No. 1 cylinder should be on the TDC of it's compression stroke.
2. Align the holes in the No. 1 camshaft bearing holders with the holes in the camshafts. Using 5.0mm pin punches, drive the into the holes to secure the camshafts.
3. Remove the camshaft sprocket-to-camshaft bolts, the washers and the sprockets; remove the sprocket with a pulley remover or a brass hammer.

**NOTE: Be careful not to loose the Woodruff key.**

4. Using a dial indicator, loosen the camshaft adjusting screws and check the camshaft endplay; it should be 0.002–0.006 in. (0.05–0.15mm).

**NOTE: Inspect the timing belt. Replace it if it is oil soaked (find source of oil leak also) or if it appears worn on the leading edges of the belt teeth.**

5. To install, reverse the removal procedure. Torque the camshaft sprocket-to-camshaft bolts to 27 ft. lbs. (38 Nm). Push the camshaft inward and torque the camshaft holder adjusting bolts to 9 ft. lbs. Be sure to position the crankshaft and camshaft timing sprockets in the top dead center position.

**NOTE: When installing the timing belt, do not allow oil to come in contact with the belt. Oil will cause the rubber to swell. Be careful not to bend or twist the belt unnecessarily, since it is made of fiberglass. Nor should you use tools having sharp edges when installing or removing the belt. Be sure to install the belt with the arrow facing in the same direction it was facing during removal.**

6. After installing the timing belt, adjust the belt tension.

#### *2494cc and 2675cc Engines*

1. Remove the timing belt.

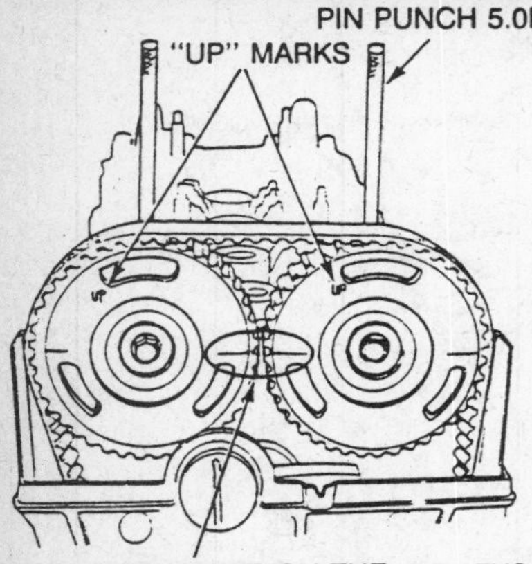


**Locking the camshafts into position to remove the sprockets–1.6L engine**

2. Remove the special bolt and the crankshaft pulley.
3. Remove the lower cover.
4. Loosen the adjusting bolt and remove the timing belt.
5. Remove the adjustment pulley bolt and the pulley. Inspect the timing belt. Replace it if it is oil soaked (find source of oil leak also) or if it appears worn on the leading edges of the belt teeth.
6. Using a camshaft holding tool or equivalent, secure the camshaft sprockets, remove the sprocket-to-camshaft bolts and the sprockets.
7. To install, reverse the removal procedure. Torque the camshaft sprocket-to-camshaft bolts to 23 ft. lbs. (32 Nm). Be sure to install the belt with the arrow facing in the same direction it was facing during removal.
8. Remove all the spark plugs from the engine.
9. Advance the crankshaft by about 15 degrees from the No. 1 cylinder compression TDC. After adjusting the front and rear camshaft pulleys to the No. 1 cylinder compression TDC, return the crankshaft pulley by about 15 degrees again to adjust the TDC position.
10. To fix the adjusting bolt with the timing belt tensioner at the belt loosening position, perform the following procedures:
   a. Push the tensioner bracket with a flat blade screwdriver to loosen the belt tension.
   b. DO NOT push on the timing belt.
11. To install the timing belt, perform the following procedures:
   a. Install the timing belt in the following sequence; crankshaft pulley, front crankshaft pulley, water pump pulley, tensioner and rear camshaft pulley.
   b. For ease of installation, advance the rear camshaft pulley by about a ½ tooth from the TDC position.
12. Loosen the adjusting bolt and retorque it after tensioning the belt.
13. Rotate the crankshaft 5–6 turns clockwise, so the belt may fit in position on the pulleys. Adjust the timing belt tension.

## OIL SEAL REPLACEMENT

1. Remove the timing sprockets.
2. Using a small prybar, pry the camshaft oil seals from the cylinder heads; be careful not to damage the seal mounting surfaces.
3. Using an oil seal driver tool or equivalent, lubricate the seal lips, apply sealant to the seal housing and drive the new seal into the cylinder head until it seats.
4. To complete the installation, reverse the removal procedures.

# Camshaft

## REMOVAL & INSTALLATION

### *1590cc Engine*

**NOTE: To facilitate installation, make sure the No. 1 piston is at TDC before removal of the camshafts.**

1. Follow the cylinder head removal procedure before attempting to remove the camshaft.
2. Loosen and remove the camshaft holder bolts, the camshaft holders, the camshafts and the rocker arms.
3. Lift the camshaft from the cylinder head, wipe them clean and inspect the lift ramps. Replace the camshaft(s) if the lobes are pitted, scored or excessively worn.

**To Install:**

4. Check the following before installing the camshafts:
   a. Be certain the keyways on the camshafts are facing **UP** (No. 1 cylinder at TDC).
   b. The valve locknuts should be loosened and the adjusting screws backed off before installation.
   c. Replace the rocker arms in there original positions.
5. Place the rocker arms on the pivot bolts and the valve stems.
6. Install the camshafts and the camshaft seals with the open side (spring) facing in and observe the following;
   a. The marks I or **E** are stamped on the camshaft holders.
   b. Do not apply oil to the holder mating surface of the camshaft seals.
7. Apply liquid gasket to the head mating surfaces of the No. 1 and No. 6 camshaft holders then install them along with the No. 2, 3, 4 and 5.
8. Temporarily tighten the camshaft holders while making sure the rocker arms are positioned on the valve stems.
9. Using an oil seal driver, special tool No. 07947–SB00100 or equivalent, press new oil seals into the No. 1 camshaft holders.
10. Tighten each bolt 2 turns at a time (in sequence) while checking that the rockers do not bind on the valves.
11. Install the camshaft pulley keys onto the grooves in the camshafts.
12. Push the camshaft pulleys onto the camshafts, then tight the retaining bolts to 27 ft. lbs. (38 Nm).
13. Adjust the valve timing, then check that all tubes, hoses and connectors have been installed correctly.

### *2494cc and 2675cc Engines*

**NOTE: To facilitate installation, make sure the No. 1 piston is at TDC before removal of the camshafts.**

1. Follow the Cylinder Head removal procedure before attempting to remove the camshaft.
2. Loosen and remove the camshaft bearing cap bolts, then remove the camshaft bearing caps, the camshafts and the rocker arms.
3. Lift the camshaft from the cylinder head, wipe them clean and inspect the lift ramps. Replace the camshaft(s) if the lobes are pitted, scored or excessively worn.

**To Install:**

4. Pour engine oil into the cylinder head hydraulic tappet mounting hole, up to the level of the oil path.
5. Install the hydraulic tappets into the cylinder head while observing the following;
   a. Do not rotate the hydraulic tappet while inserting it.
   b. Carefully follow the special start-up procedure given below after the head is reassembled to allow the lifters to fill with oil.
6. Pour engine oil into the oil fillers on the cylinder head.
7. Install the push rod and rocker arms while observing the following;
   a. Install each part in it's original position.
   b. Loosen the rocker arm adjusting screws and locknuts before installation.
8. Install the camshafts and the camshaft oil seals as follows;

**NOTE: The front camshaft has a groove in front driving the distributor.**

   a. Make sure the camshaft is mounted parallel with the rocker arm slipper surface.
   b. Advance the camshaft by 15

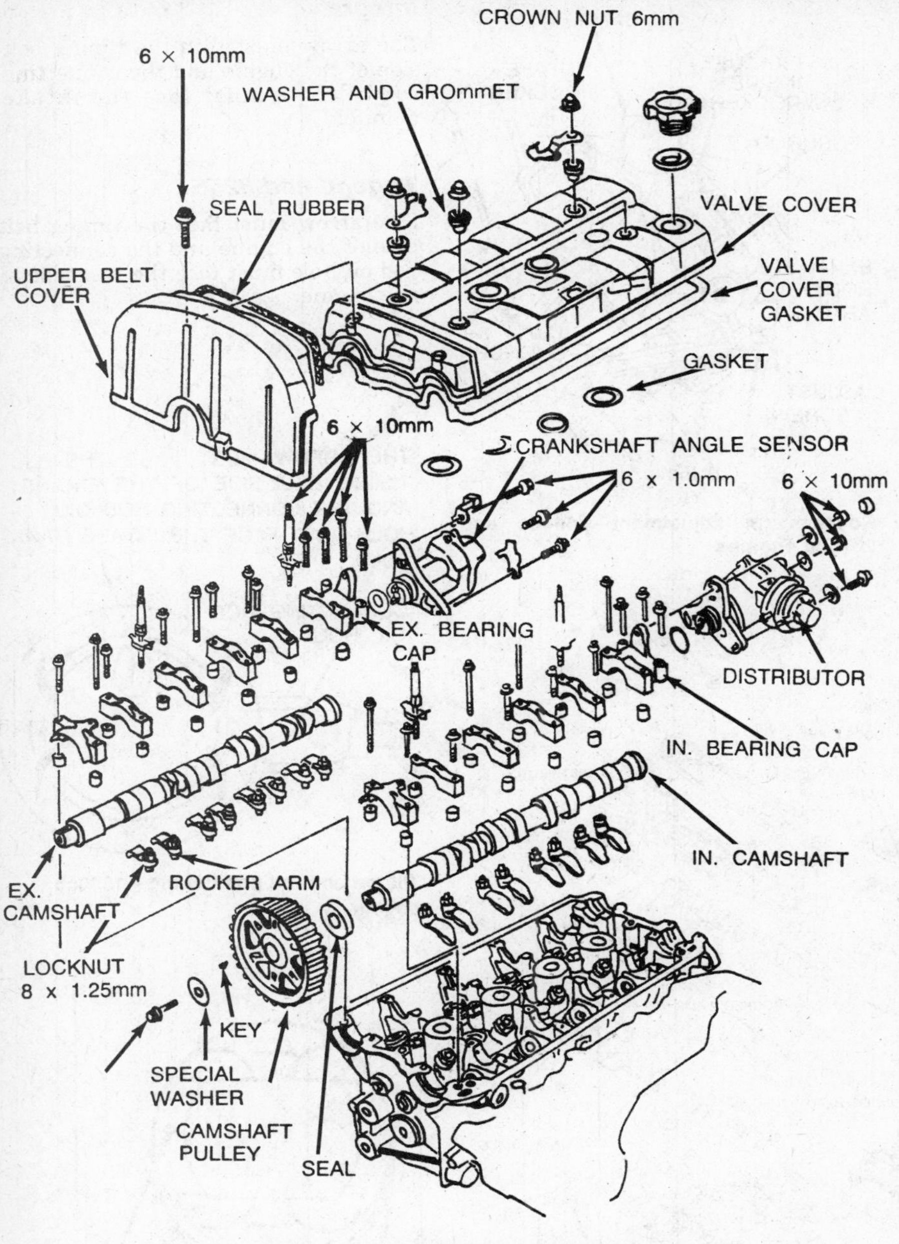


Camshaft installation – 1590cc engine

degrees from the No. 1 cylinder TDC of the compression stroke to prevent interference between the piston and the valve.

c. Place the rear camshaft on the cylinder head at the position where the cam is not pushing the valve.

d. Preset the oil seal, with it's spring side facing inward.

e. Install the rear camshaft sealing rubber.

f. Do not apply oil to the cam holder side of the oil seal.

9. Apply liquid gasket sealer to the camshaft oil seal mounting surface and on the head contact surface. Temporarily tighten the bearing caps as shown in the illustration.

10. Carefully fit the camshaft oil seal until it contacts the bearing cap.

11. Torque the bearing caps diagonally from the center of the head while observing the following;

a. Torque the 6mm bolts last.

b. Make sure the oil seal is properly positioned.

c. Torque the 8mm bolts to 20 ft. lbs. (28 Nm).

d. Torque the 6mm bolts to 9 ft. lbs. (12 Nm).

12. Install the upper timing belt cover plate.

13. Install the camshaft pulley.

14. Install the timing belt.

15. Adjust the timing belt tension and the valve timing.

16. Adjust the exhaust rocker arm screws as follows;

a. Adjust the front and rear camshafts at No. 1 TDC of the compression stroke. The No. 1, No. 2 and No. 4 cylinders now have the exhaust valves closed.

b. Tighten the adjusting screw from the No. 1 cylinder. (When you feel the screw contact the valve, tighten the screw 1½ turns). Tighten the locknut firmly.

c. Set the adjusting screws for No. 2 and No. 4 cylinders in the same way as Step b (above).

d. Rotate the crankshaft pulley 1 turn clockwise (as viewed from the pulleys side) to adjust the TDC of the No. 5 piston's compression stroke. The No. 3, No. 5 and No. 6 cylinders now have the exhaust valves closed.

e. Set the adjusting screws for No. 3 and No. 5 and No. 6 cylinders by tighten the adjusting screws when you feel the screw contact the valve, tighten the screw 1½ turns). Tighten the locknut firmly.

17. Install the valve covers and the head side covers. Replace the O-rings for the head side covers.

18. Follow the special start-up procedure given below.

### SPECIAL START-UP PROCEDURE

1. After the heads are reassembled, make sure the engine sits for at least 5 minutes to allow the hydraulic tappets to reach the proper oil level.

2. Remove the spark plugs. Have someone crank the engine; feel for compression from each cylinder at the spark plug holes. It may be necessary to crank the engine through several cycles to confirm compression.

If any cylinder does not have compression, it may be necessary to disassemble that head and check the suspected tappet.

If all cylinders have compression, reinstall the plugs and start the engine.

## Pistons and Connecting Rods

### POSITIONING

**For all piston and connecting rod overhaul procedures, please refer to "Engine Rebuilding" in the Unit Repair section.**

For correct piston and rod positioning refer to the illustrations.

901970

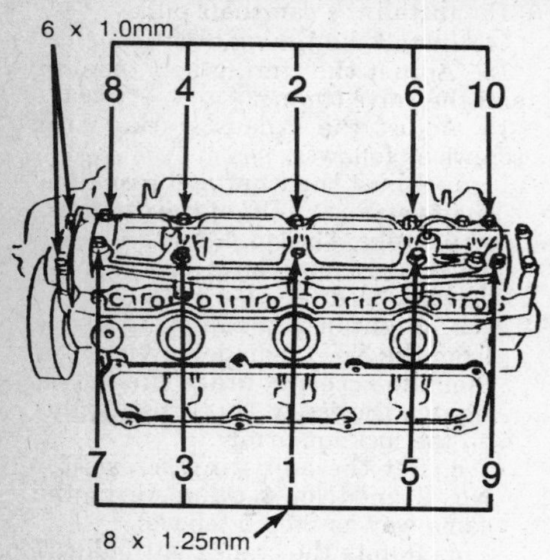


**Camshaft tightening sequence – 2494cc and 2675cc engines**

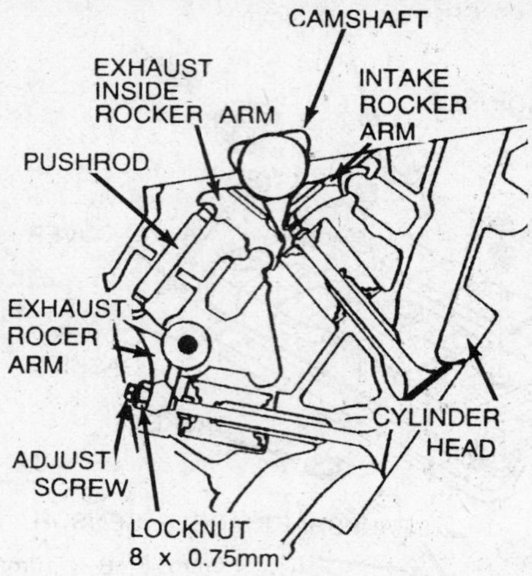


**Rocker arm adjustment – 2494cc and 2675cc engines**

### *Integra*

The arrow must face the timing belt side of the engine and the connecting rod oil hole must face the intake manifold.

### *Legend and 825S*

The arrow must face the timing belt side of the engine and the connecting rod oil hole must face the rear side of the engine.

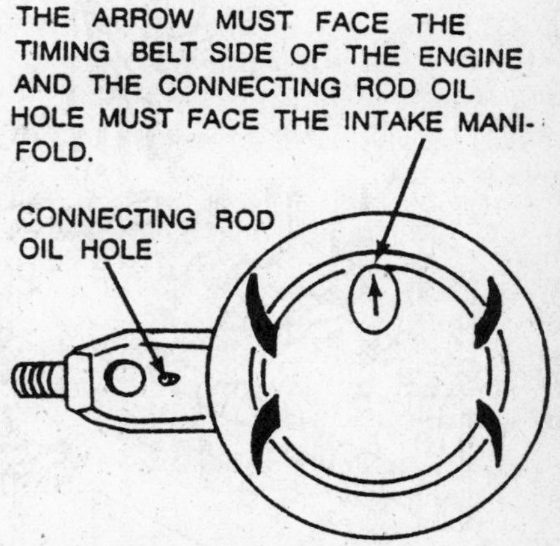


**Piston and rod positioning – 1590cc engine**

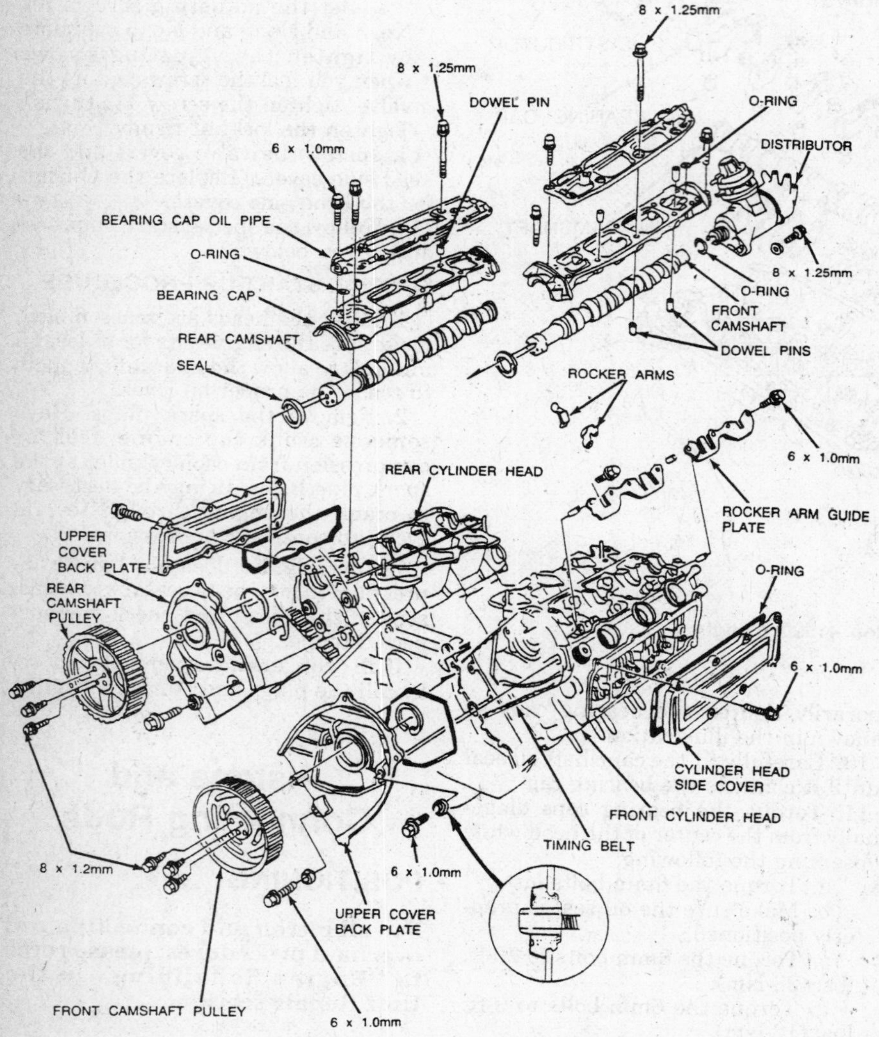


**Camshaft installation – 2494cc and 2675cc engines**

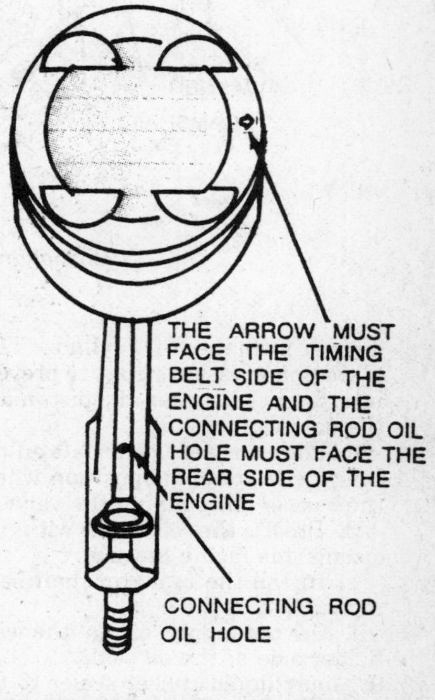


**Piston and rod positioning – 2494cc and 2675cc engines**

# ENGINE LUBRICATION

## Oil Pan

### REMOVAL & INSTALLATION

1. Drain the engine oil.
2. Raise and safely support the front of the vehicle. Remove the lower splash pan (if equipped).
3. Attach a chain to the bracket on the transaxle case and raise just enough to take the load off the center mount.

**NOTE: Do not remove the left engine mount.**

4. Remove the center beam and engine lower mount.
5. Loosen the oil bolts and remove the oil pan flywheel dust shield.

**NOTE: Loosen the bolts in a criss cross pattern beginning with the outside bolt. To remove the oil pan, lightly tap the corners of the oil pan with a mallet.**

6. Clean the gasket mounting surfaces.
7. To install, reverse the removal procedure. Apply sealant to the entire mounting surface of the cylinder block, except the crankshaft oil seal, before fitting the oil pan. Torque the bolts in a circular sequence, beginning in the center and working out toward the ends to 10 ft. lbs. (14 Nm).
8. Refill the crankcase.

## Rear Main Bearing Oil Seal

### REMOVAL & INSTALLATION

1. Remove the oil pan and the transaxle from the vehicle.
2. If equipped with a manual transaxle, perform the following procedures:
   a. Matchmark the pressure plate-to-flywheel.
   b. Insert the clutch alignment tool or equivalent, into the pilot bearing.
   c. Remove the pressure plate-to-flywheel bolts (gradually), the pressure and the clutch plate.
   d. Remove the flywheel-to-crankshaft bolts and the flywheel.
3. If equipped with an automatic transaxle, remove the flex plate-to-flywheel bolts and the flex plate.
4. Remove the rear oil seal housing-to-engine bolts and the gasket.
5. Using a pry bar, pry the oil seal from the housing.
6. Clean the gasket mounting surfaces. Check the flywheel or flex plate for cranks and/or damage; replace it, if necessary.
7. Using an oil seal installation tool or equivalent, drive the new oil seal into the rear oil seal housing until it seats.
8. Using sealant, apply a coat on the gasket mounting surface. Using oil, lubricate the oil seal lips.
9. To install, reverse the removal procedures. Torque the oil seal housing-to-engine bolts to 9 ft. lbs. (12 Nm); be careful not to damage the oil seal lip.
10. To complete the installation, reverse the removal procedures. Torque the flywheel-to-crankshaft bolts to 54 ft. lbs. (75 Nm) for automatic transaxles or 76 ft. lbs. (105 Nm) for manual transaxles. Refill the crankcase, start the engine and check for leaks.

## Oil Pump

### REMOVAL & INSTALLATION

#### *Integra*

1. Remove the oil pan.
2. Turn the crankshaft pulley and align the **T** mark on the crankshaft pulley with the timing mark on the cover.
3. Remove the cylinder head cover and the timing belt upper cover.
4. Remove the alternator drive belt.
5. Remove the crankshaft pulley and the timing belt lower cover.
6. Release the belt tensioner, remove the timing belt and the driven pulley.
7. Remove the oil screen.
8. Remove the oil pump-to-engine bolts and the oil pump assembly.
9. Remove the oil pump cover-to-oil pump screws and the cover.
10. Using a feeler gauge, check the inner rotor-to-outer rotor clearance; it should be 0.006 in. (0.14mm).
11. Using a straight edge and a feeler gauge, check the rotor-to-cover clearance; it should be 0.001–0.003 in. (0.03–0.08mm).
12. Using a feeler gauge, check the outer rotor-to-housing clearance; it should be 0.004–0.007 in. (0.1–0.18mm).
13. Inspect the rotors and pump housing for scoring and/or damage; replace the parts (if necessary).
14. Using a pry bar, pry the oil from the pump housing.
15. Using the oil seal installer tool or equivalent, drive the new oil seal into the housing until it seats and lubricate the lip with oil.

**To Install:**

16. Check that the oil pump turns freely.
17. Apply a light coat of oil to the seal lip.
18. Install the two dowel pins and a new O-ring on the cylinder block.
19. Apply sealant to the cylinder block mating surface of the oil pump and observe the following:
   a. Check the mating surfaces are clean and dry before applying the liquid gasket.
   b. Apply sealant evenly in a narrow bead centered on the mounting surface.
   c. To prevent oil leakage, apply sealant to the inner threads of the bolt holes.
   d. Do not allow the sealant to dry before assembly.
   e. Wait at least 30 minutes after assembly before filling the engine with oil.
20. Install the oil pump to the cylinder block.
21. Install the oil screen.
22. To complete the installation, use new gaskets and reverse of the removal procedures. Torque the oil pump-to-engine bolts to 9 ft. lbs. (12 Nm), the pickup tube-to-engine bolts to 9 ft. lbs. (12 Nm) and the pickup tube-to-oil pump housing bolts to 17 ft. lbs. (24 Nm). Refill the crankcase. Start the engine and check for leaks.

#### *Legend and 825S*

1. Remove the the oil pan.
2. Rotate the crankshaft pulley and

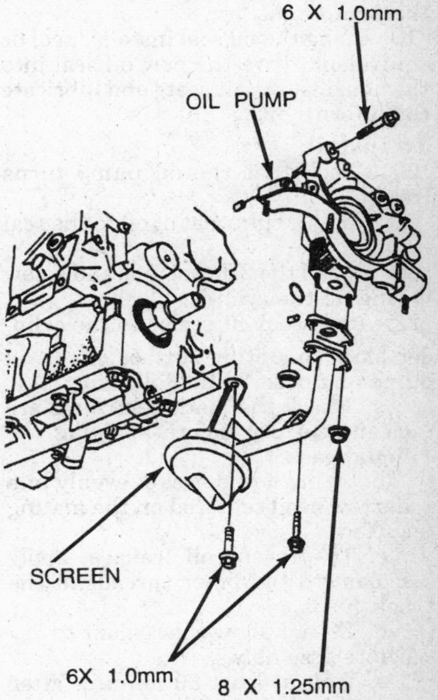


**Oil pump mounting – 1590cc engine**

align the timing mark on the crankshaft pulley with the timing mark on the cover, with the No. 1 cylinder at TDC of it's compression stroke.

3. Remove the timing belt upper cover.

4. Remove the alternator drive belt, power steering drive belt and the air compressor drive belt.

5. Remove the splash guard.

6. Remove the crankshaft pulley and the timing belt lower cover.

7. Release the belt tensioner, remove the timing belt and the driven pulley.

8. Remove the oil filter assembly.

9. Remove the oil screen and the low level switch (LS).

10. Remove the baffle plate.

11. Remove the oil pass pipe and joint.

12. Remove the mounting bolts and the oil pump assembly.

13. Remove the oil pump cover-to-oil pump screws and the cover.

14. Using a feeler gauge, check the inner rotor-to-outer rotor clearance; it should be 0.002–0.007 in. (0.04–0.018mm).

15. Using a straight edge and a feeler gauge, check the rotor-to-cover clearance; it should be 0.001–0.003 in. (0.02–0.07mm).

16. Using a feeler gauge, check the outer rotor-to-housing clearance; it should be 0.004–0.007 in. (0.1–0.18mm).

17. Inspect the rotors and pump housing for scoring and/or damage; replace the parts (if necessary).

18. Using a pry bar, pry the oil from the pump housing.

19. Using the oil seal installer tool or equivalent, drive the new oil seal into the housing until it seats and lubricate the lip with oil.

**To Install:**

20. Check that the oil pump turns freely.

21. Apply a light coat of oil to the seal lip.

22. Install the 2 dowel pins and a new O-ring on the cylinder block.

23. Apply sealant sealer to the cylinder block mounting surface of the oil pump and observe the following:

a. Check the mating surfaces are clean and dry before applying the liquid gasket.

b. Apply liquid gasket evenly in a narrow bead centered on the mating surface.

c. To prevent oil leakage, apply sealant to the inner threads of the bolt holes.

d. Do not allow the sealant to dry before assembly.

e. Wait at least 30 minutes after assembly before filling the engine with oil.

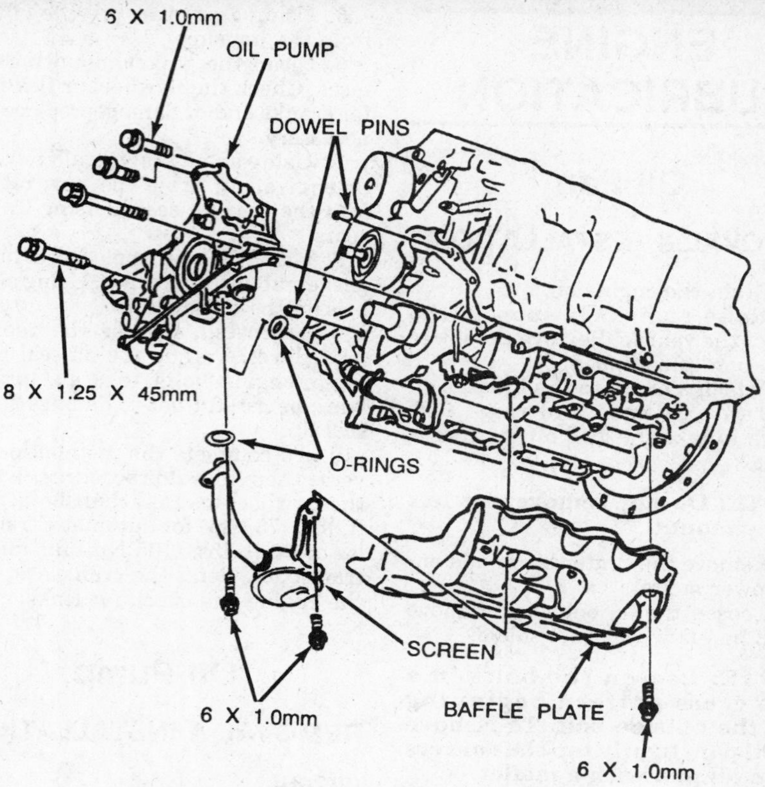


Oil pump mounting—2494cc and 2675cc engines

24. Install the oil pump to the cylinder block; apply sealant to the threads of the 8mm bolt. Torque the oil pump-to-cylinder head bolts to 9 ft. lbs. (12 Nm), the pickup tube-to-engine bolts to 9 ft. lbs. (12 Nm) and the pickup tube-to-oil pump bolts to 9 ft. lbs. (12 Nm).

25. To complete the installation, reverse the removal procedures. Refill the crankcase. Start the engine and check for leaks.

# ENGINE COOLING

## Radiator

### REMOVAL & INSTALLATION

**NOTE: When removing the radiator, take care not to damage the core and fins.**

1. Drain the cooling system.

2. Disconnect the thermo-switch wire and the fan motor wire. Remove the fan shroud (if equipped).

3. Disconnect the upper coolant hose at the upper radiator tank and the lower hose at the water pump connecting pipe. If equipped with an automatic transaxle, disconnect and plug the cooling lines at the bottom of the radiator.

4. Remove the hoses to the coolant reservoir.

5. Remove the radiator bolts and the radiator with the fan attached. The fan can be easily unbolted from the back of the radiator.

6. To install, reverse the removal procedure. Bleed the cooling system.

## Water Pump

### REMOVAL & INSTALLATION

1. Remove the timing belt from the water pump drive sprocket.

2. Drain the cooling system to a level below the water pump.

3. Remove the water pump-to-engine bolts and remove together with the drive sprocket.

4. To install, use a new O-ring and reverse the removal procedures. Bleed the cooling system.

5. Refill the cooling system. Start the engine, allow it to reach normal operating temperatures and check for leaks. Check and/or adjust the engine timing.

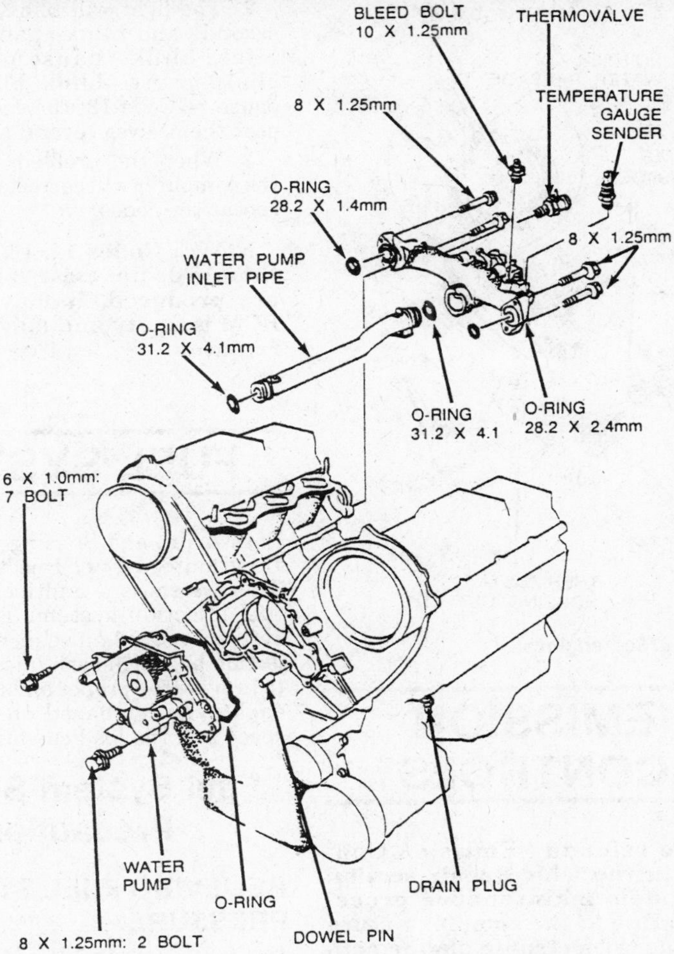


**Water pump mounting—2494cc and 2675cc engines**

## Thermostat

### REMOVAL & INSTALLATION

The thermostat is located under the thermostat housing.

1. Drain the cooling system to a level below the thermostat housing.
2. Remove the thermostat housing bolts, the housing and the thermostat.
3. Clean the gasket mounting surfaces.
4. To install, use new gaskets and reverse the removal procedures; install the thermostat's spring end toward the engine. Torque both cover bolts to 9 ft. lbs. (12 Nm). Refill and bleed the cooling system.

### COOLING SYSTEM BLEEDING

1. Move the temperature selector to the **MAX HEAT**.
2. Fill the coolant reservoir to the **MAX** mark.
3. Loosen the air bleed bolt in the water outlet and refill the radiator to the bottom of the filler neck with antifreeze/coolant. Tighten the bleed bolt as soon as the coolant starts to run out in a steady stream without any air bubbles in it.
4. With the radiator cap off, start the engine and allow it to warm up (the cooling fan should go on at least twice). Then, (if necessary) add more antifreeze/coolant to bring the level back up to the bottom of the filler neck.
5. Put the radiator cap on, restart the engine and check for any leaks.

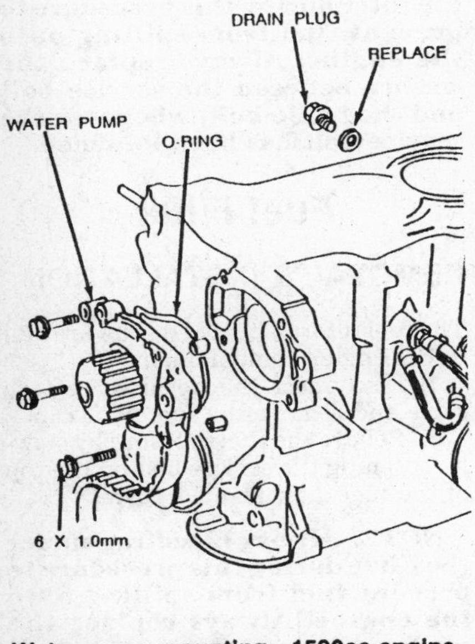


**Water pump mounting—1590cc engine**

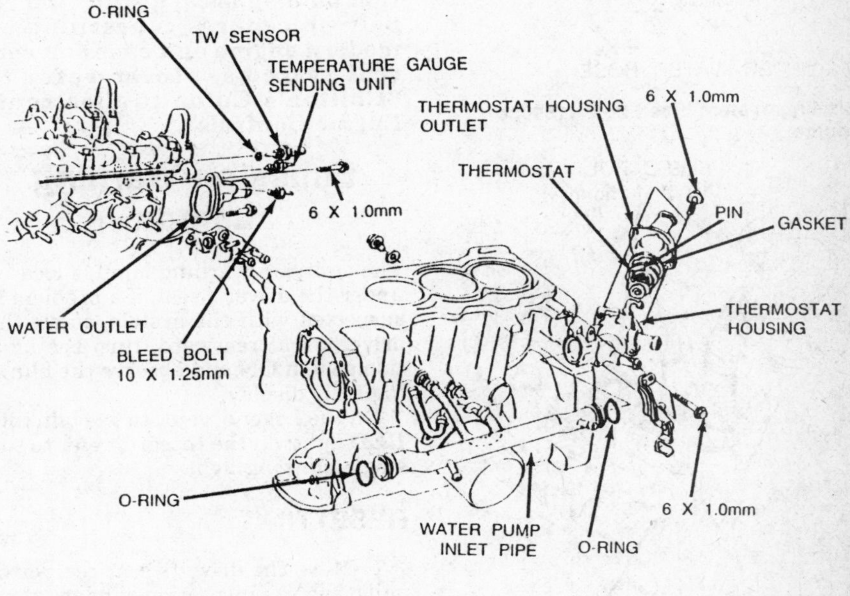


**Thermostat location—1590cc engine**

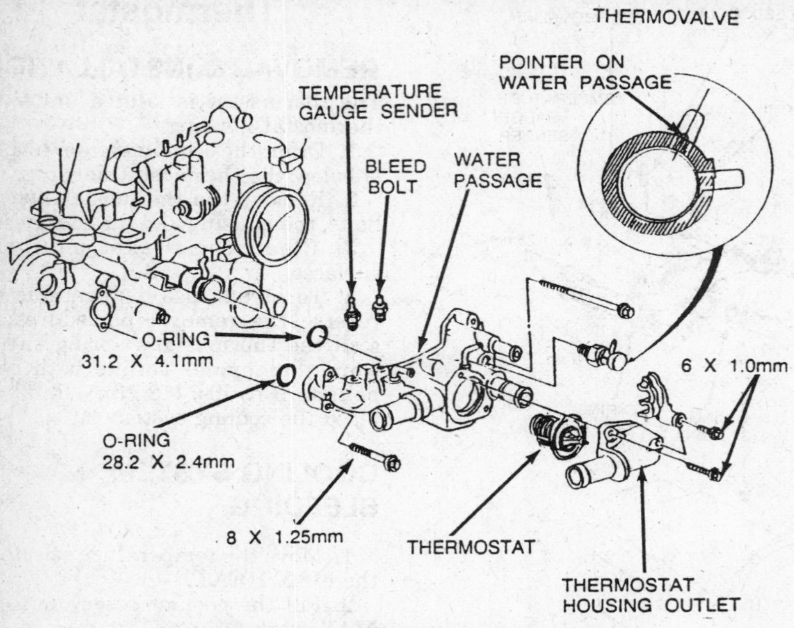


**Thermostat location – 2494cc and 2675cc engines**

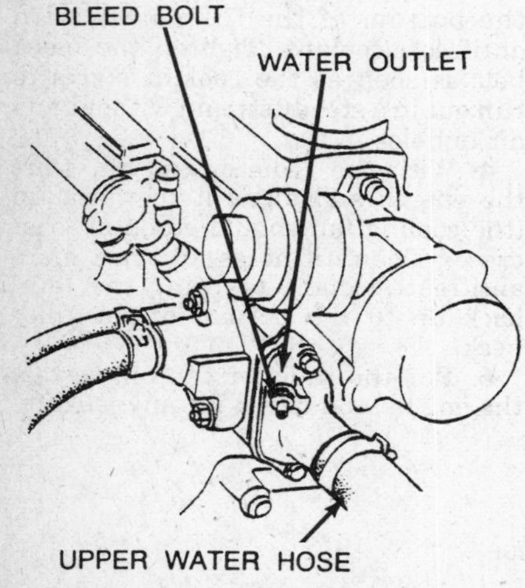


**Cooling system bleed bolt – 1590cc engine**

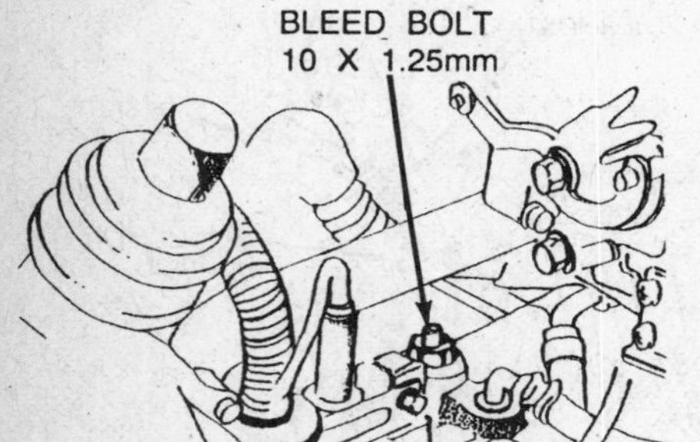

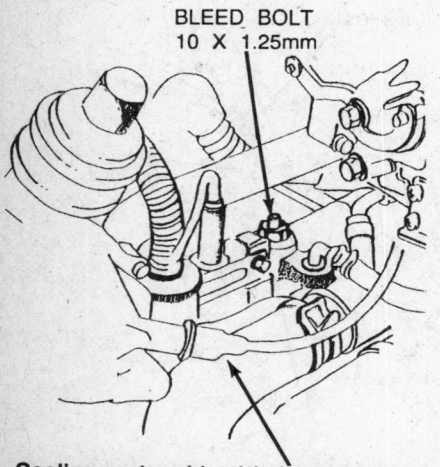

**Cooling system bleed bolt – 2494cc and 2675cc engines**

# EMISSION CONTROLS

**Please refer to "Emission Control" in the Unit Repair section for system maintenance procedures. Due to the complex nature of modern electronic engine control system, comprehensive diagnosis and testing procedures fall outside the confines of this repair manual. For complete information on diagnosis, testing and repair procedures concerning all modern engine and emission control systems, please refer to "Chilton's Guide to Electronic Engine Controls".**

## Emission Warning Lamps

The emission warning lamp is located under the driver's seal, if a problem is suspected with the system, move the driver's seat rearward, turn the ignition switch **ON** and observe the blinking LED display.

On the Legend, refer to the blinking **RED** light; on the Integra, refer to the single blinking light.

### RESETTING

1. Move the driver's seat rearward, pull down the inspection window, turn the ignition switch **ON** and observe the blinking light.

2. The light will blink, pause for 2 seconds and blink again. Example: blink, blink – pause = Code 2 or blink – pause – blink, blink, blink – pause = Code 13; the code(s) will repeat themselves several times.

3. When the problem is corrected, the computer will correct itself and not repeat the codes.

**NOTE: Codes 11, 16 and higher than 18 do not exist; if these codes are produced, it may mean the ECM is faulty and may need to be replaced.**

# FUEL SYSTEM

Both Acura and Sterling use Honda's Programmed Fuel Injection system. This system is a multiport electronic fuel injection system. The PGM-FI system is based on sequential port injection by which each injector is timed to provide the proper amount of fuel to each cylinder based on the engine speed and the load condition.

## Fuel System Service Precaution

### RELIEVING FUEL SYSTEM PRESSURE

1. Disconnect the negative battery cable and remove the fuel filler cap.
2. Relieve the fuel pressure by slowly loosening the service bolt on the top of the fuel filter about one turn.

**NOTE: Always place rag under the filter during this procedure to prevent fuel from spilling onto the engine. Always replace the washer between the service bolt and the banjo bolt, whenever the service bolt has been loosened.**

## Fuel Filter

### REMOVAL & INSTALLATION

The fuel filter is located on the firewall in the engine compartment.

1. Disconnect the negative battery cable and remove the fuel filler cap.
2. Relieve the fuel pressure by slowly loosening the service bolt on the top of the fuel filter about a turn.

**NOTE: Always place rag under the filter during this procedure to prevent fuel from spilling onto the engine. Always replace the washer between the service bolt**

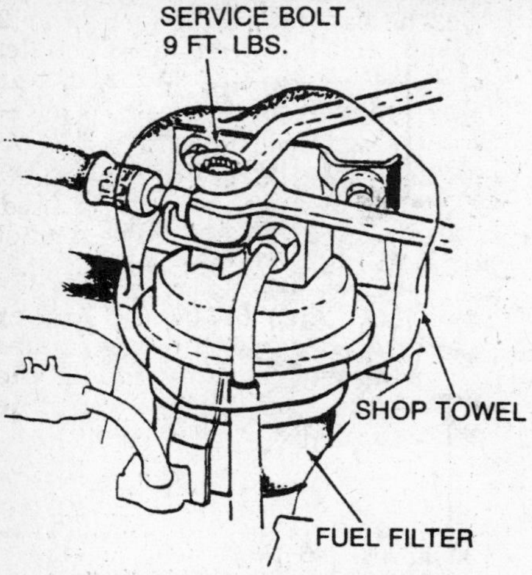


**Relieving the fuel system pressure**

**and the banjo bolt, whenever the service bolt has been loosened.**

3. Remove the fittings from the fuel filter.
4. Remove the fuel filter clamp and the fuel filter.
5. To assemble, use a new filter, washers and reverse the removal procedures.

## Electric Fuel Pump

### PRESSURE TESTING

1. Disconnect the negative battery cable and remove the fuel filler cap.
2. Relieve the fuel pressure by slowly loosening the service bolt on the top of the fuel filter about a turn.

**NOTE: Always place rag under the filter during this procedure to prevent fuel from spilling onto the engine. Always replace the washer between the service bolt and the banjo bolt, whenever the service bolt has been loosened.**

3. Using a fuel pressure gauge, attach it to the top of the fuel filter.
4. Start the engine and measure the fuel pressure with the engine idling and vacuum hose (from the pressure regulator) disconnected; the fuel pressure should be 35–41 psi. (240–279 kPa).
5. If the fuel pressure is not within specifications, check the fuel pump.
6. If the pressure is higher than specifications, check for a pinched or clogged fuel return hose or faulty pressure regulator.
7. If the pressure is lower than specifications, check a clogged filter, defective pressure regulator or leakage in the fuel line.
8. After inspection, remove the pressure gauge.

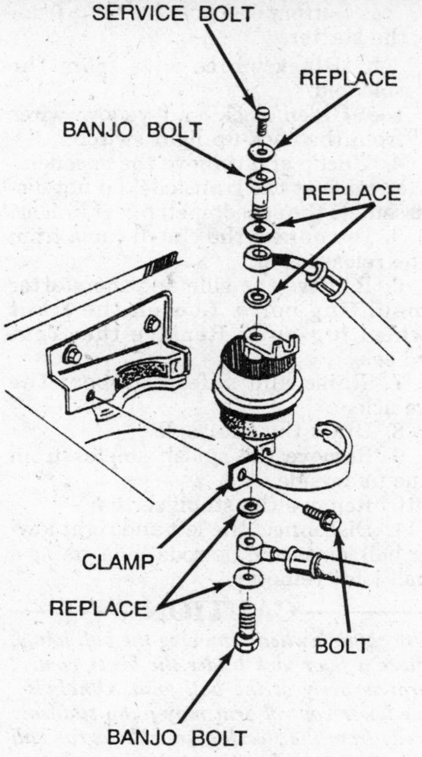


**Fuel filter assembly – Integra**

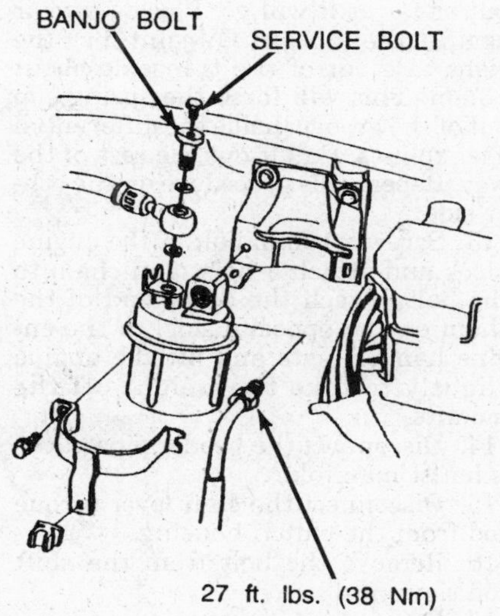


**Fuel filter assembly – Legend and 825S**

9. To assemble, use a new filter, washers and reverse the removal procedures.

### REMOVAL & INSTALLATION

#### *Integra*

1. Disconnect the negative battery cable.
2. Relieve the fuel pressure by slowly loosening the service bolt on the top of the fuel filter about 1 turn.

**NOTE: Place a rag under the filter during this procedure to prevent fuel from spilling onto the engine. Always replace the washer between the service bolt and the banjo bolt, whenever the service bolt has been loosened.**

3. Raise and safely support the vehicle.
4. Remove the left rear wheel.
5. Remove the fuel pump cover bolts and the cover.
6. Remove the fuel pump mount bolts and the fuel pump with it's mount.

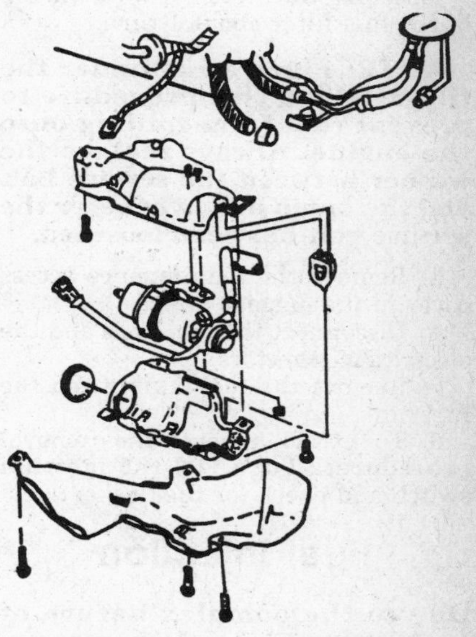

**Fuel pump mounting – Integra**

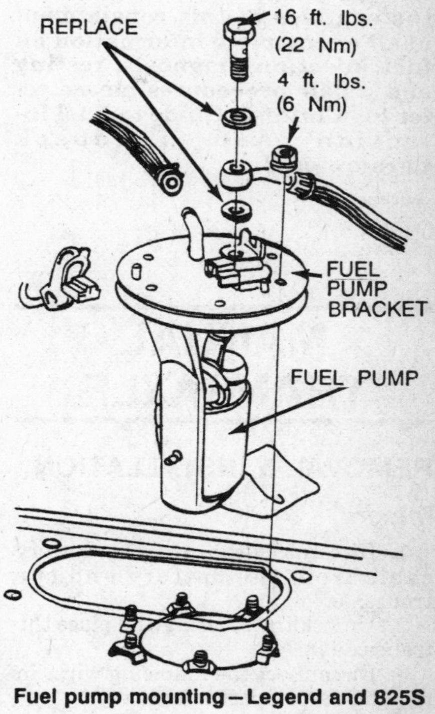


**Fuel pump mounting – Legend and 825S**

7. Disconnect the fuel lines and the electrical connectors.
8. Remove the clamp and remove the fuel pump from the mounting bracket.
9. Remove the fuel line and silencer from the pump.
10. To install, reverse the removal procedures. Turn **ON** the ignition switch and check for fuel leaks.

### *Legend and 825S*

1. Disconnect the negative battery cable.
2. Relieve the fuel pressure by slowly loosening the service bolt on the top of the fuel filter about 1 turn.

**NOTE: Place a rag under the filter during this procedure to prevent fuel from spilling onto the engine. Always replace the washer between the service bolt and the banjo bolt, whenever the service bolt has been loosened.**

3. Remove the maintenance access cover in the luggage area.
4. Disconnect the fuel lines and the electrical connectors.
5. Remove the fuel pump from the fuel tank.
6. To install, reverse the removal procedures. Turn **ON** the ignition switch and check for fuel leaks.

## Fuel Injection

**Due to the complex nature of modern fuel injection systems, comprehensive diagnosis and testing procedures fall outside the confines of this repair manual. For complete information on fuel injection diagnosis, testing and repair procedures please refer to "Chilton's Guide to Fuel Injection And Feedback Carburetors".**

# MANUAL TRANSAXLE

## REMOVAL & INSTALLATION

### *Integra*

1. Disconnect the negative battery cable from the battery and the transaxle.
2. Unlock the steering and place the transaxle in **N**.
3. Disconnect the following wires in the engine compartment:
   a. Battery (+) positive cable from the starter.
   b. Black/white wire from the solenoid.
   c. Green/black and yellow wires from the back-up light switch.
4. Unclip and remove the speedometer cable at the transaxle; do not disassemble the speedometer gear holder.
5. Disconnect the clutch cable from the release arm.
6. Remove the side and top starter mounting bolts. Loosen the front wheel lug nuts. Remove the front wheels.
7. Raise and safely support the vehicle.
8. Drain the transaxle.
9. Remove the splash shields from the underside.
10. Remove the stabilizer bar.
11. Disconnect the left and right lower ball joints and tie rods ends, using a ball joint remover.

**CAUTION**

***Use caution when removing the ball joints. Place a floor jack under the lower control arm securely at the ball joint. Otherwise, the lower control arm may jump suddenly away from the steering knuckle as the ball joint is removed.***

12. Turn the right steering knuckle out as far as it will go. Place a prybar against the inboard CV-joint, pry the right axle out of the transaxle about 13mm. This will force the spring clip out of the groove inside the differential gear splines. Pull it out the rest of the way. Repeat this procedure on the other side.
13. Screw a 10mm bolt at the engine block and attach a hoist and chain to the bolt; attach the other end of the chain on the opposite side, to the engine hanger plate and lift the engine slightly to take the weight off the mounts.
14. Disconnect the header pipe at the exhaust manifold.
15. Disconnect the shift lever torque rod from the clutch housing.
16. Remove the bolt from the shift rod clevis.
17. Raise the transmission jack securely against the transaxle to take up the weight.
18. Remove the bolts from the front transaxle mount at the front engine stiffener.
19. Remove the intake manifold bracket and the rear engine mount bracket.
20. Remove the transaxle housing bolts from the engine torque bracket.
21. Remove the remaining starter mounting bolts and take out the starter.
22. Remove the remaining transaxle mounting bolts.

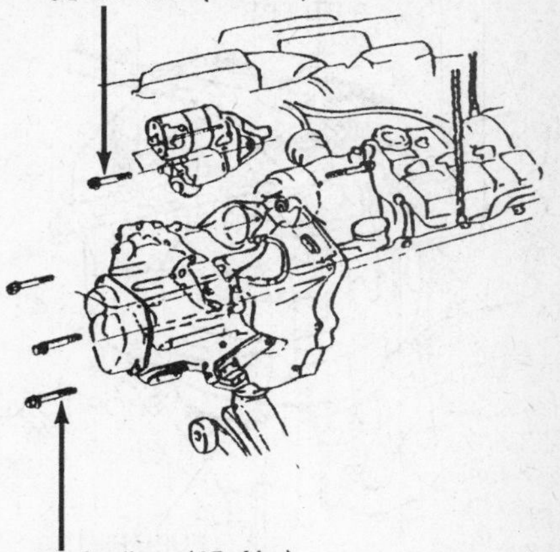


**Transaxle removal – Integra**

23. Pull the transaxle away from the engine until it clears the 14mm dowel pins, then lower on the transmission jack.
24. Separate the mainshaft from the clutch pressure plate and remove the transaxle by lowering the jack.

**To Install:**

25. Install the transaxle on a transmission jack. Clean and lubricate the clutch release bearing surfaces.
26. Make sure both 14mm dowel pins are installed in the clutch housing.
27. Raise the transaxle high enough to align the dowel pins with the matching holes in the block.
28. Roll the transaxle toward the engine and fit the mainshaft into the clutch disc splines. If the driver's side suspension was left in place, install new spring clips on both axles and carefully insert the left axle into the differential when installing the transaxle.

**NOTE: Install new 26mm spring clips on both axles. Make sure the axles fully bottom out. Slide the axle in until the spring clip engages the differential.**

29. Push and wiggle the transaxle until it fits flush with the flange.
30. Bolt the transaxle to the engine with the mounting bolts from the engine side. Torque the bolts to 50 ft. lbs. (68 Nm).
31. Install the rear mount bracket on the transaxle housing. Torque the mounting bolts to 47 ft. lbs. (65 Nm).
32. Install the engine torque bracket on the transaxle housing. Torque the mounting bolts to 33 ft. lbs. (45 Nm).
33. Loosely install the bolts for the front of the transaxle mount, then torque them in the sequence shown in the illustration.

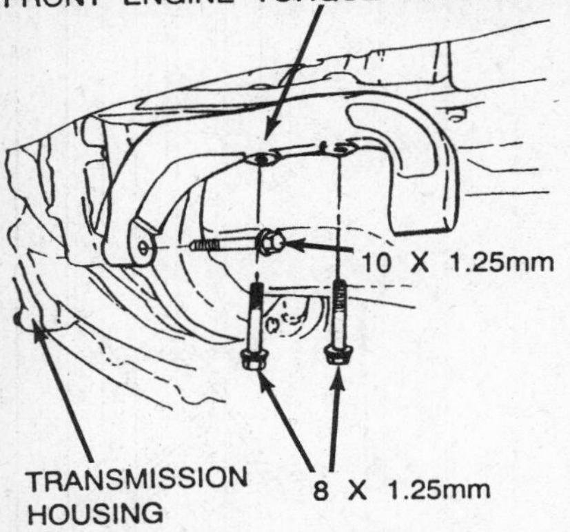


**Front transaxle mount tightening sequence**

34. Install the starter mounting bolts and torque them to 33 ft. lbs. (45 Nm).
35. Install the intermediate shaft, the right and left halfshaft.
36. Turn the right steering knuckle/axle assembly outward far enough to insert the free end of the axle into the transaxle. Repeat this procedure on the other side.

**NOTE: Make sure the axles fully bottom out. Slide the axle in until the spring clip engages the differential.**

37. Reconnect the shift rod and the shift lever torque rod.
38. Reconnect the lower arm to the ball joints and torque them to 33 ft. lbs. (45 Nm).
39. Reconnect the tie rod end ball joints and torque them to 33 ft. lbs. (45 Nm).
40. Install the engine and wheelwell splash shields.
41. Reconnect the exhaust header pipe.
42. Install the front wheels, lower the vehicle to the ground and tighten the lug nuts to 80 ft. lbs. (110 Nm).
43. Remove the chain hoist from the 10mm bolt on the cylinder head and the engine hanger plate.
44. Install the speedometer cable.
45. Install the transaxle housing bolts and torque them to 33 ft. lbs. (45 Nm).
46. Connect the clutch cable to the release arm, then attach the cable housing end to the transaxle bracket.
47. Connect the engine compartment wiring:
  a. Battery (+) positive cable from the starter.
  b. Black/white wire from the solenoid.
  c. Green/black and yellow wires from the back-up light switch.
48. With the ignition key turned **OFF**, connect the ground cable to the battery and the transaxle.
49. Refill the transaxle with SAE 30, 10W-30, 10W-40 or 20W-40 and adjust the clutch free-play.
50. Check the transaxle for smooth operation.

### *Legend and 825S*

1. Disconnect the both battery cables from the battery.
2. Disconnect the starter and ground cables.
3. Disconnect the back-up light wires from the engine harness.
4. Loosen the 6mm bolt attaching the harness holder at the side of the transaxle hanger and the release harness from the transaxle.
5. Loosen the 6mm bolts at the side of the battery base and the intake hose band.
6. Remove the air cleaner case assembly along with the intake hose.
7. Remove the 8mm bolts and the clutch slave cylinder with the clutch hose and the push rod.

**NOTE: Do not operate the clutch pedal once the slave cylinder has been removed.**

8. Remove the 8mm bolts and clutch damper assembly from the transaxle hanger bracket.
9. Remove the power steering speed sensor with the sensor hose intact.
10. Drain the oil from the transaxle.
11. Remove the halfshaft from the vehicle.
12. Remove the bolts securing the intermediate shaft and remove the shaft.
13. Remove the shift rod and the shift extension.
14. Remove the bolts attaching the torque rod bracket to the clutch case.

**NOTE: Replace the torque rod bolts whenever loosened or removed.**

15. Place a transmission jack securely beneath the transaxle.
16. Remove the sub frame center beam.
17. Attach a engine support chain with two 10mm bolts to the engine block, 1 on each bank.
18. Lift the engine slightly to take the weight off the mounts.
19. Remove the center stop bracket from the transaxle.
20. Remove the clutch cover.
21. Remove both rear engine mounting bolts from the transaxle.
22. Remove both front engine mounting bolts from the transaxle housing.
23. Remove the starter mounting bolts and the starter assembly.
24. Remove the remaining transaxle mounting bolts.
25. Pull the transaxle away from the engine until it clears the 14mm dowel pins and lower on the transmission jack.

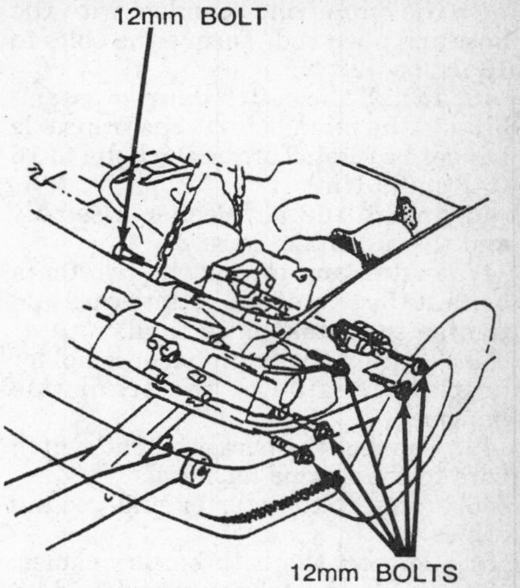


**Removing the transaxle – Legend and 825S**

**To Install:**

26. Install the transaxle on a transmission jack; clean and lubricate the clutch release bearing surfaces.
27. Make sure both 14mm dowel pins are installed in the clutch housing.
28. Raise the transaxle high enough to align the dowel pins with the matching holes in the block.
29. Roll the transaxle toward the engine and fit the mainshaft into the clutch disc splines.
30. Install the transaxle mounting bolts and torque to 55 ft. lbs. (75 Nm).
31. Install the starter and torque the mounting bolts.
32. Install the front engine mounting bolts and torque to 29 ft. lbs. (40 Nm).
33. Install the rear engine mounting bolts and torque to 29 ft. lbs. (40 Nm).
34. Install the center stopper bracket bolts and torque to 29 ft. lbs. (40 Nm).
35. Install the clutch cover.
36. Install the center beam.
37. Remove the transmission jack.
38. Install and torque the new torque rod bracket bolts to 29 ft. lbs. (40 Nm).

**NOTE: Replace the torque rod bolts whenever loosened or removed.**

39. Remove the engine support chain by removing the two 10mm bolts.
40. Install the shift rod and shift extension.
41. Install the intermediate shaft with the 8mm bolts. Torque the bolts to 29 ft. lbs. (40 Nm).
42. Install the right and left halfshaft.
43. Install the speed sensor.
44. Install the clutch slave cylinder

with the 8mm bolts complete with the hose and push rod. Torque the bolts to 16 ft. lbs. (22 Nm).

45. Install the clutch damper assembly and the 8mm bolts to the transaxle hanger bracket. Torque the bolts to 16 ft. lbs. (22 Nm).

46. Install the air cleaner assembly and the air intake hose.

47. Install and torque the two 6mm bolts at the side of the battery case and tighten the intake hose band.

48. Tighten the 6mm harness holder bolt at the side of the transaxle hanger.

49. Connect the back-up light switch wire to the engine harness.

50. Connect the starter and ground cables.

51. Connect the both battery cables.

52. Refill the transaxle with SAE 10W–30 or 10W–40 and adjust the free-play.

53. Check the transaxle for smooth operation.

## SHIFT LINKAGE ADJUSTMENT

The Acura and Sterling shift linkage is non-adjustable. However, if the linkage is binding or if there is excessive play, check the linkage bushings and pivot points. Lubricate with light oil or replace worn bushings (as necessary).

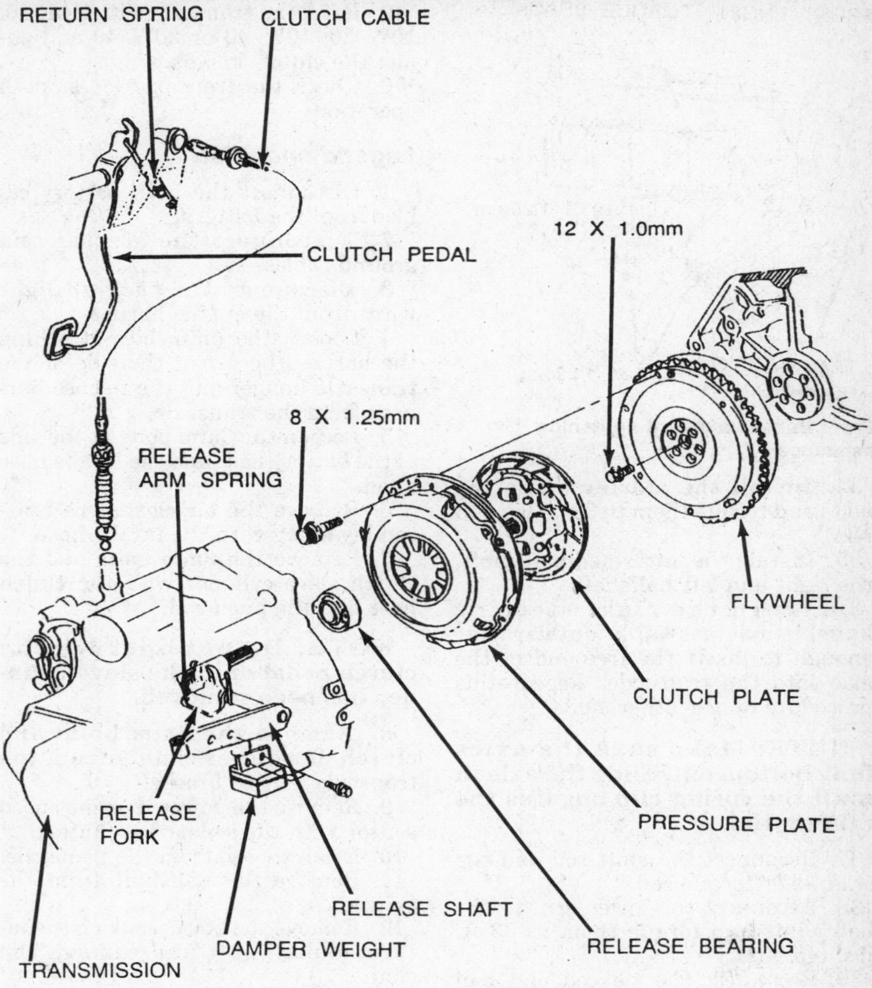


**Clutch assembly – Integra**

# CLUTCH

All models use a single dry disc with a diaphragm spring type pressure plate. On the Integra model the clutch is cable operated. However, on the Legend and 825S models, a hydraulic master and slave cylinder system is used.

## REMOVAL & INSTALLATION

1. Remove the transaxle.

2. Matchmark the flywheel and pressure plate for easy reassembly. Install the clutch alignment tool No. 07974-6890101 or equivalent, remove the pressure plate-to-clutch disc bolts, the pressure plate and the clutch disc.

**NOTE: Loosen the retaining bolts 2 turns at a time in a circular pattern. Removing a bolt while the rest are tight may warp the diaphragm spring.**

3. Remove the flywheel-to-crankshaft bolts and the flywheel. Inspect it for scoring and wear and reface or replace (as necessary).

4. To install the clutch, reverse the removal procedure and pay attention to the following points:

a. Make sure the flywheel and the end of the crankshaft are clean before assembly. Torque the flywheel-to-crankshaft bolts to 87 ft. lbs. (120 Nm) for Integra or 76 ft. lbs. (105 Nm) for Legend and 825S.

b. When installing the pressure plate, align the mark on the outer edge of the flywheel with the alignment mark on the pressure plate. Failure to align these marks will result in imbalance.

c. When torquing the pressure plate bolts, use a pilot shaft to center the friction disc. The pilot shaft can be bought at any large auto supply store or fabricated from a wooden dowel. After centering the disc, tighten the bolts 2 turns at a time, in a criss-cross pattern to avoid warping the diaphragm springs; torque to 19 ft. lbs. (26 Nm).

d. When installing the transaxle, make sure the mainshaft is properly aligned with the disc spline and the aligning pins are in place, before torquing the case bolts.

## PEDAL HEIGHT/FREE-PLAY ADJUSTMENT

### *Integra*

1. Adjust the clutch free-play at the release lever by turning the adjusting nut (at the transaxle).

**NOTE: The pedal height should be 5.67 in. (144mm) for 1986–87 or 5.87 in. (149mm) for 1988–90.**

2. Make sure there is $^5/_{32}$–$^{13}/_{64}$ in. (4.0–5.0mm) of free-play at the tip of the release arm after the adjustment.

3. If equipped with cruise control, turn the adjuster (above the clutch pedal) until the clutch pedal stroke is:

1986–87 – 5.31–5.51 in. (135–140mm)

1988–90 – 5.51–5.71 in. (140–145mm)

4. Tighten the locknut securely.

### *Legend and 825S*

Total clutch free-play is 0.35–0.59 in. (9–15mm).

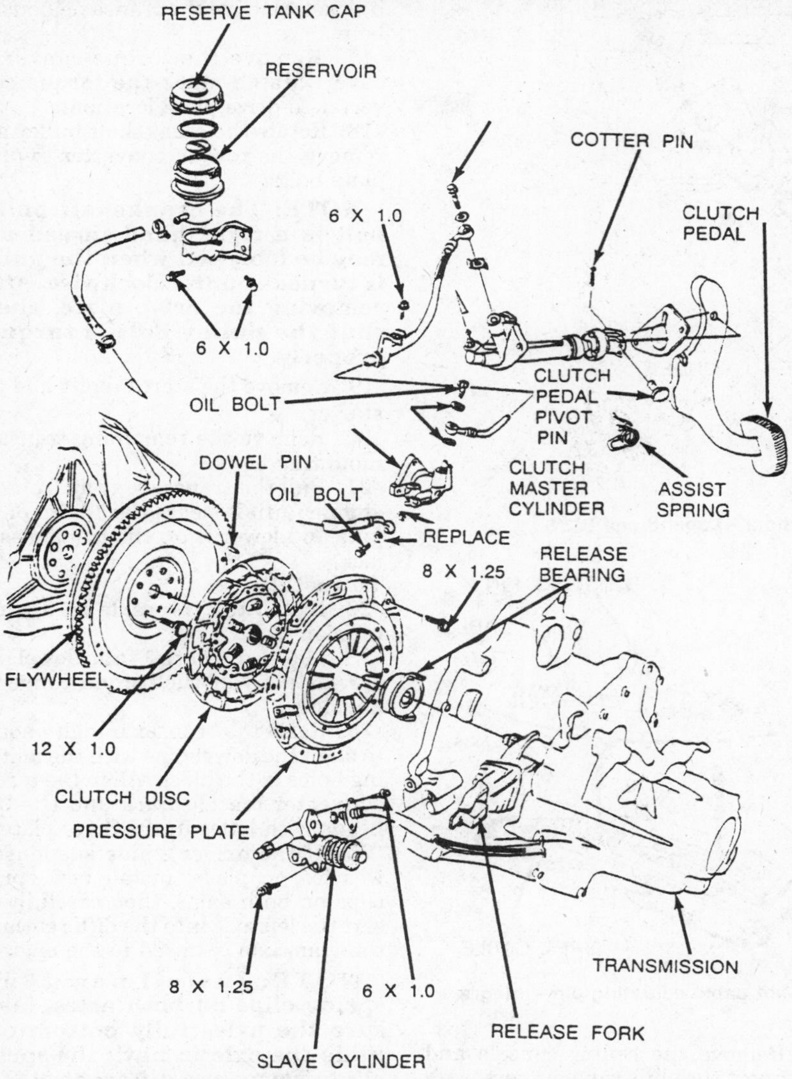


**Exploded view of the clutch assembly—Legend and 825S**

1. Loosen the locknut on the clutch pedal switch.
2. Loosen the lock nut on the clutch master cylinder push rod. Turn the push rod in or out to obtain the correct stroke and height at the clutch pedal.

Stroke at pedal—5.7–5.9 in. (145–150mm)

Clutch pedal height—7.0 in. (179mm) (to floor)

3. Tighten the lock nut on the clutch master cylinder push rod.
4. Screw the clutch pedal switch until it contacts the pedal.
5. Turn the switch another ¼–½ turn. Tighten the lock nut.

## Clutch Cable

### REMOVAL & INSTALLATION

#### *Integra*

1. Loosen the clutch cable adjusting nut (at the transaxle) near the release shaft arm.
2. Remove the cable from the release shaft arm by sliding the cable end retainer through the elongated hole in the release shaft arm.
3. From inside the vehicle, disconnect the cable from the clutch pedal and remove the clutch cable holder from the firewall. release the cable from the top of the clutch cable assembly.
4. Pull the cable out of the firewall and from the vehicle.
5. To install reverse the removal procedure and adjust the clutch free-play.

## Clutch Master Cylinder

### REMOVAL & INSTALLATION

#### *Legend and 825S*

The clutch master cylinder is located on the firewall in the engine compartment next to the brake master cylinder.

1. From the top of the clutch pedal, remove the cotter pin and pivot pin from the clutch pedal-to-pushrod junction.
2. Disconnect the hydraulic line (banjo bolt) from the clutch master cylinder.
3. Remove the master cylinder-to-firewall nuts and the master cylinder.
4. Disconnect the reservoir hose from the master cylinder by removing the clip.
5. To install, reverse the removal procedures. Torque the master cylinder-to-firewall nuts to 16 ft. lbs. (22 Nm). Refill the clutch master cylinder reservoir and bleed the system after installation.

## Clutch Slave Cylinder

### REMOVAL & INSTALLATION

#### *Legend and 825S*

1. Disconnect and plug the hydraulic line at the slave cylinder.
2. Remove the slave cylinder-to-clutch housing bolts and the slave cylinder.
3. To install, reverse the removal procedures. Torque the slave cylinder-to-clutch housing bolts to 16 ft. lbs. (22 Nm). Refill the clutch master cylinder reservoir and bleed the hydraulic system.

### BLEEDING THE HYDRAULIC CLUTCH SYSTEM

#### *Legend and 825S*

The hydraulic system must be bled whenever the system has been leaking or has been dismantled. The bleed screw is located on the slave cylinder.

1. Remove the bleed screw dust cap.
2. Attach a clear hose to the bleed screw. Immerse the other end of the hose in a clear jar ½ filled with brake fluid.
3. Refill the clutch master cylinder with fresh brake fluid.
4. Open the bleed screw slightly and have an assistant slowly depress the clutch pedal. Close the bleed screw when the pedal reaches the end of it's travel. Allow the clutch pedal to return slowly.
5. Repeat Steps 3–4 until all air bubbles are expelled from the system.
6. Discard the brake fluid in the jar. Replace the dust cap. Refill the master cylinder.

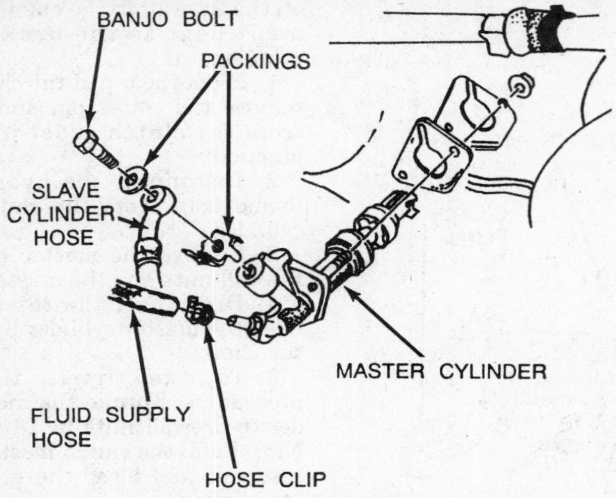


Exploded view of the clutch master cylinder—Legend and 825S

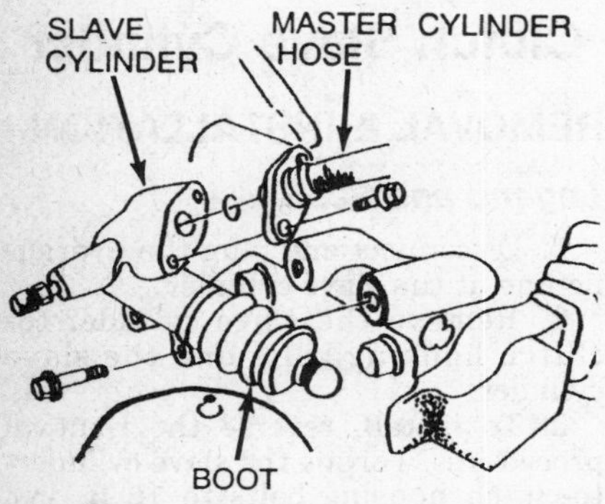


Exploded view of the slave cylinder—Legend and 25S

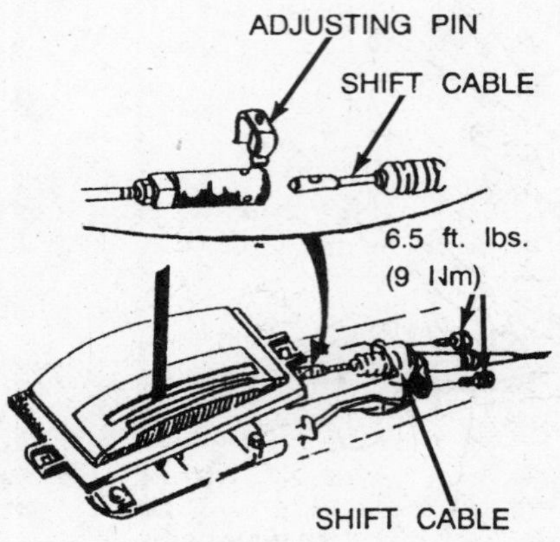


Shift cable adjusting pin—Integra

# AUTOMATIC TRANSAXLE

## REMOVAL & INSTALLATION

### *Integra*

1. Disconnect the negative battery cable and the ground cable from the transaxle. Raise and safely support the front of the vehicle.
2. Unlock the steering and place the transaxle in **N**.
3. Disconnect the following wires in the engine compartment:
   a. Battery (+) positive cable from the starter.
   b. Black/white wire from the solenoid.
4. Drain the transaxle.
5. Disconnect the speedometer cable.
6. Disconnect and plug the transaxle cooler hoses; wire them up next to the radiator so the ATF won't drain out.
7. Remove the center console and disconnect the shift cable by removing the adjusting pin.
8. Unscrew the cable guide bolt and pull out the throttle cable.
9. Remove the right and left halfshaft and intermediate shaft.
10. Screw a 10mm bolt at the cylinder head and attach a hoist and chain to the bolt; attach the other end of the chain to the engine hanger plate and lift the engine slightly to take the weight off the mounts.
11. Remove transaxle stop bracket (if equipped), the under cover and the engine splash shields.
12. Disconnect the header pipe from the exhaust manifold.
13. Using a transmission jack, place it under the transaxle and raise the it enough to take the weight off the mounts.
14. At the front of the engine bracket, remove the bolts from the front transaxle mount.
15. Remove the rear transaxle mount bracket bolts and the mount.
16. From the front transaxle mount bracket, remove the transaxle housing bolts.
17. Remove the torque converter cover. Match-mark the torque converter-to-drive plate location.
18. Rotate the crankshaft pulley and remove the torque converter-to-drive plate bolts.

**NOTE: The crankshaft pulley bolt is a right hand thread and may be loosened when the pulley is turned counterclockwise. After removing the drive plate, check that the pulley bolt is torqued properly.**

19. Remove the starter bolts and the starter.
20. Remove the remaining transaxle mounting bolts.
21. Pull the transaxle away from the engine until it clears the 14mm dowel pins and lower it on the transmission jack.

**To Install:**

22. Install the transaxle on a transmission jack.
23. Make sure both 14mm dowel pins are installed in the torque converter housing.
24. Raise the transaxle high enough to align the dowel pins with the matching holes in the block. Align the torque converter match-mark and the bolt heads with holes in the drive plate.
25. If the driver's side suspension was left in place, install new spring clips on both axles, then carefully insert the left axle into the differential as the transaxle is raised to the engine.

**NOTE: Install new 26mm spring clips on both axles. Make sure the axles fully bottom out. Slide the axle in until the spring clip engages the differential.**

26. Push and wiggle the transaxle until it fits flush with the flange.
27. Torque the transaxle-to-engine bolts (from the engine side) to 42 ft. lbs. (58 Nm).
28. Attach the torque converter to the drive plate with 12mm bolts and torque to 9 ft. lbs. (12 Nm). Rotate the crank as necessary to torque the bolts to ½ torque, then final torque in a criss-cross pattern. Check for free rotation after torquing the last bolt.
29. Install the shift cable.
30. Remove the transmission jack.
31. Install the torque converter cover plate.
32. Install the rear mount bracket on the transaxle housing. Torque the bolts to 48 ft. lbs. (65 Nm).
33. Install the front transaxle mount bracket. Torque the bolts to 33 ft. lbs. (45 Nm).
34. Loosely install the bolts for the front of the transaxle mount, then torque them in the sequence shown in the illustration to 18 ft. lbs. (24 Nm).

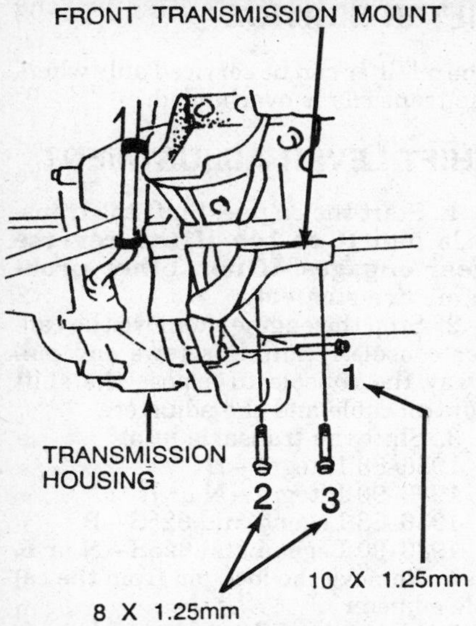


**Front transaxle mount tightening sequence**

35. Install the transaxle stop bracket (if equipped) and torque the bolts to 33 ft. lbs. (45 Nm). Install the starter mounting bolts and torque them to 33 ft. lbs. (45 Nm).
36. Install the intermediate shaft, the right and left halfshaft.
37. Turn the right steering knuckle/axle assembly outward far enough to insert the free end of the axle into the transaxle. Repeat this procedure on the other side.

**NOTE: Make sure the axles fully bottom out. Slide the axle in until the spring clip engages the differential.**

38. Reconnect the lower arm to the ball joints and torque them to 33 ft. lbs. (45 Nm).
39. Reconnect the tie rod end ball joints and torque them to 33 ft. lbs. (45 Nm).
40. Install the engine splash shields.
41. Reconnect the exhaust header pipe.
42. Install the front wheels, lower the vehicle to the ground and torque the lug nuts 80 ft. lbs. (110 Nm).
43. Remove the chain hoist from the 10mm bolt on the cylinder head and the engine hanger plate.
44. Install the speedometer cable.
45. Install the 3 top transaxle mounting bolts and torque them to 48 ft. lbs. (65 Nm).
46. Connect the cooler hoses and torque the banjo bolts to 21 ft. lbs. (29 Nm).
47. Attach the shift control cable to the shaft lever with the pin and clip, if removed. Check the adjustment.
48. Reinstall the center console.
49. Connect the engine compartment wiring:

a. Battery (+) positive cable to the starter.
b. Black/white wire from the solenoid.
c. Transaxle ground cable.

50. With the ignition key turned **OFF**, connect the ground cable to the battery and the transaxle.
51. Unscrew the dipstick from the top of the transaxle housing and add 2.5 qts. of Dexron® ATF through the hole. Reinstall the dipstick.

**NOTE: If the torque converter was replaced, the transaxle fill quantity is 5.7 qts.**

52. Start the engine, set the parking brake and shift the transaxle through all gears 3 times. Check for proper control cable adjustment.
53. Allow the engine to reach operating temperature with the transaxle in **N** or **P**, then turn it off and check the fluid level.
54. Install and adjust the throttle control cable. Road test.

### *Legend and 825S*

1. Disconnect the (−) negative and (+) positive battery cables from the battery.
2. Disconnect the starter motor and ground cables.
3. Drain the transmission fluid from the transaxle.
4. Remove the both 6mm bolts located at the side of the battery base and the intake hose band at the throttle body.
5. Remove the air cleaner assembly along with the intake hose.
6. Remove the speedometer gearbox complete with the power steering speed sensor hose.
7. Disconnect the throttle control cable from the transaxle housing.
8. Disconnect and plug the transaxle cooler hoses at the joint pipes; turn the ends up to prevent the transmission fluid from flowing out.
9. Near the oil cooler pipe bracket, disconnect the lockup control solenoid valve wire connector and the automatic speed pulser wire connector (1988–90).
10. Remove the center console, pry off the adjuster pin and disconnect the control cable.
11. Remove the control cable guide bolts and pull out the cable assembly; be careful not to bent the cable when removing it.
12. Remove the right/left halfshafts and the intermediate shaft.
13. Remove the torque converter case mounting bolts from the torque rod bracket.
14. Attach a chain hoist with two bolts and raise the engine slightly to unload the mounts.

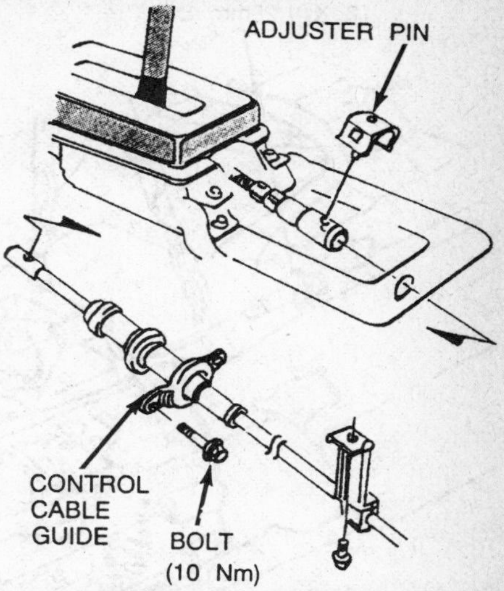


**Removing the control cable—Legend and 825S**

15. Remove the front engine mount bolts from the transaxle housing.
16. While holding the locknut, turn off the radius rod.
17. Remove the center beam.
18. Remove the center stopper bracket from the transaxle.
19. Remove the torque converter cover.
20. Place a transmission jack under the transaxle and raise the transaxle just enough to take the weight off the mounts.
21. Remove the both rear engine mount bolts from the transaxle.
22. Match-mark the torque converter-to-drive plate. Remove the plug and the drive plate bolts one at a time while rotating the crankshaft pulley.
23. Remove the starter-to-engine bolts and the starter.
24. Remove the remaining transaxle housing-to-engine bolts.
25. Pull the transaxle away from the engine and lower it from the vehicle.

**To Install:**

26. Install the transaxle on a transmission jack and raise to engine level.
27. Secure the transaxle to the engine with the mounting bolts.
28. Install the starter motor.
29. Align the match-marks and attach the torque converter-to-drive plate bolts; torque the bolts to 9 ft. lbs. (12 Nm). Rotate the crank as necessary to torque the bolts to ½ torque, the to the final torque, in a criss-cross pattern. Check for free rotation after torquing the last bolt.
30. Install the transaxle to the front engine mount bracket bolts and torque to 29 ft. lbs. (39 Nm).
31. Install the torque converter cover.
32. Install the center stopper bracket to the transaxle.

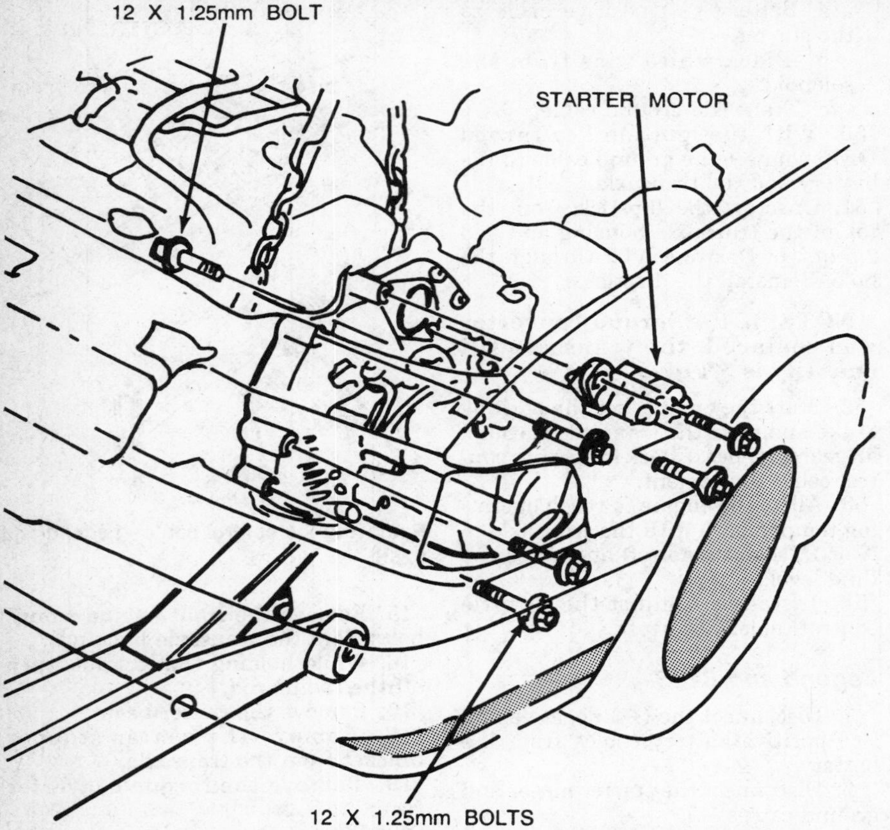


**Removing the automatic transaxle – Legend and 825S**

33. Install the center beam.
34. Connect the radius rod.
35. Remove the chain hoist from the engine.
36. Install the torque rod bracket and torque the bolts to 29 ft. lbs. (40 Nm).

**NOTE: Always replace the torque rod bolts with new ones whenever they have been loosened or removed.**

37. Remove the transmission jack.
38. Connect the intermediate shaft, then install the right and left halfshafts.
39. Route the control cables to the center console through the cable guide and secure with the bolt; be careful not to bent the cables.
40. Connect the control cable with the adjuster pin and reinstall the center console.
41. Connect the lockup control solenoid valve wire connectors.
42. Connect the cooler hoses to the joint pipes.
43. Connect the control cable on the throttle body side.
44. Install the speedometer gearbox.
45. Install the air cleaner assembly and the air intake hose.
46. Install the battery base bolts and tighten the intake hose band on the throttle body.
47. Refill the transaxle with ATF.
48. Connect the starter and ground cables.
49. Connect the battery cables.
50. Start the engine, set the parking brake, then shift the transaxle through all gears 3 times. Check for proper control cable adjustment.
51. Allow the engine reach operating temperature with the transaxle in **N** or **P**, then turn it **OFF** and check the fluid level. Road test the vehicle.

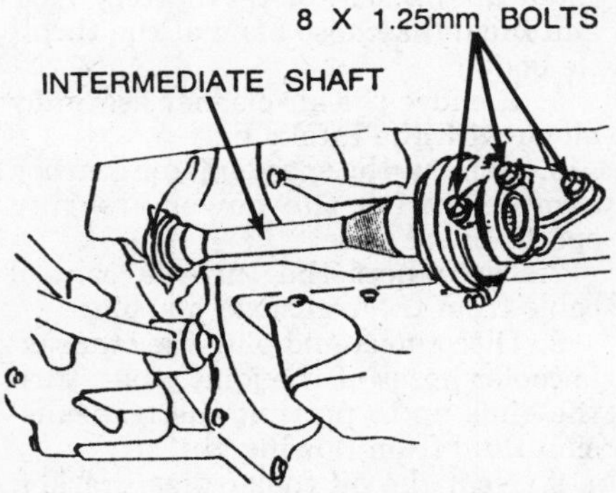


**Installing the intermediate shaft – Legend and 825S**

## FILTER SERVICE

The oil filter can be serviced only when the transaxle is overhauled.

## SHIFT LEVER ADJUSTMENT

1. Start the engine. Shift the transaxle into **R to see if the reverse gear engages. If not, other problems are suspect.**
2. Stop the engine. Remove the center console retaining screws and pull away the console to expose the shift control cable and the adjuster.
3. Shift the transaxle into:
1986–88 Integra – **D**
1989–90 Integra – **N** or **R**
1986–88 Legend and 825S – **R**
1989–90 Legend and 825S – **N** or **R**
4. Remove the lock pin from the cable adjuster.
5. Make sure the adjuster hole is aligned with the shift cable hole.

**NOTE: There are 2 holes in the end of the shift cable. They are positioned 90 degrees apart to allow cable adjustments in ¼ turn increments.**

6. If they are not perfectly aligned, loosen the locknut on the shift cable and adjust (as required).
7. Tighten the locknut and install the lock pin on the adjuster.

**NOTE: If the lock pin binds upon installation, the cable is still out of adjustment and must be readjusted.**

8. Install the center console. Start the engine and check the shift lever in all gears.

## THROTTLE CABLE ADJUSTMENT

1. Perform the following checks:
a. Make sure the throttle cable free-play is correct; it should be 0.39–0.47 in. (10–12mm).
b. The engine is operating at normal operating temperatures; the cooling fan turns **ON**.
c. The idle speed is correct.

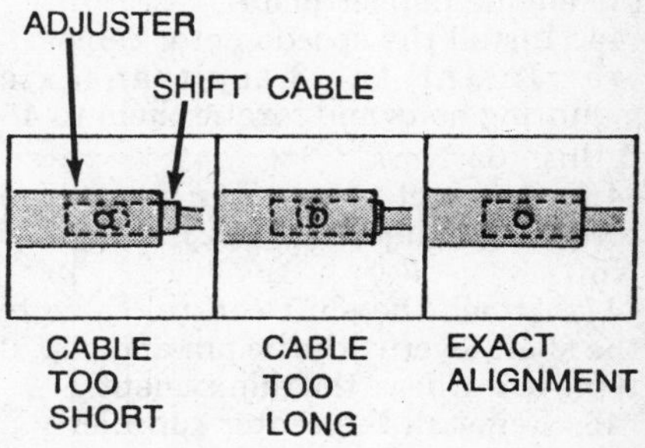


**Shift cable adjustment**

2. While working the throttle cable with your hand, remove the cable free-play.

3. Apply light thumb pressure to the throttle control lever and work the accelerator or throttle linkage; the lever should move as the engine speed increases above idle, (if not) adjust the cable.

4. Loosen the control cable nuts at the transaxle, synchronize the control lever to the throttle and tighten the locknuts.

**NOTE: To tailor the shift/lock-up characteristics to the driving expectations, adjust the control cable up to 3mm shorter than the synchronized point.**

# DRIVE AXLE

## Halfshaft

### REMOVAL & INSTALLATION

The front halfshaft assembly consists of a sub-axle shaft and a halfshaft with 2 universal joints.

A constant velocity ball joint is used for both universal joints, which are factory packed with special grease and enclosed in sealed rubber boots. The outer joint cannot be disassembled except for removal of the boot.

#### *Integra*

1. Loosen, but do not remove, the front wheel spindle nut with a 32mm socket.
2. Raise and safely support the front of the vehicle.
3. Drain the transaxle.
4. Remove the wheel lug nuts and the wheel.
5. Remove the spindle nut.
6. Using a floor jack to support the lower control arm, remove the lower arm ball joint cotter pin and nut.

**CAUTION**

***Make sure a floor jack is positioned securely under the lower control arm, at the ball joint. Otherwise, the lower control arm may jump suddenly away from the steering knuckle as the ball joint is removed.***

7. Separate the ball joint from the front hub with a ball joint puller.
8. Slowly lower the floor jack to lower the control arm.
9. Using a small pry bar with a 3.5 × 7mm tip, pry out the inboard CV-joint approximately ½ in. (12mm) in order to force the spring clip out of the groove in the differential side gears.

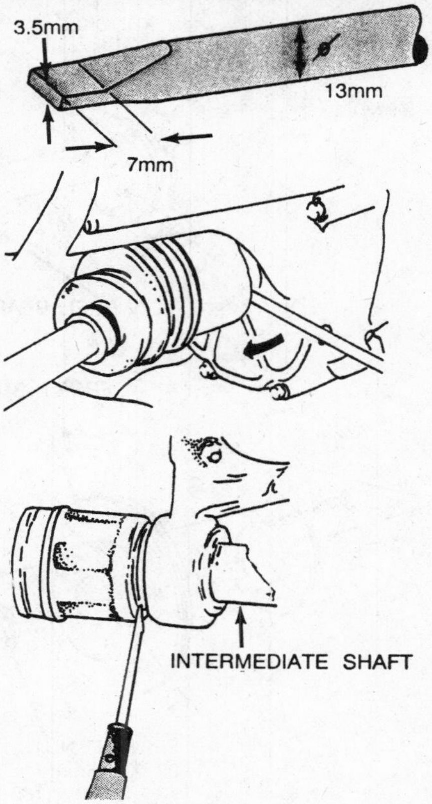

**Halfshaft removal—Integra**

**NOTE: Be careful not to damage the oil seal. Do not pull on the inboard CV-joint, it may come apart.**

10. Pull the halfshaft out of the differential or the intermediate shaft.
11. To install, reverse the removal procedure. If either the inboard or outboard joint boot bands have been removed for inspection or disassembly of the joint (only the inboard joint can be disassembled), be sure to repack the joint with a sufficient amount of bearing grease.

**NOTE: Make sure the CV-joint sub-axle bottoms so the spring clip may hold the halfshaft securely in the differential-intermediate shaft groove. Always replace the spring clip with a new one!**

#### *Legend and 825S*

1. Loosen the front wheel lug nuts.
2. Raise and safely support the front of the vehicle.
3. Drain the transaxle.

**NOTE: It is not necessary to drain the transaxle when the right (1986–87) or left (1988–90) halfshaft is removed.**

4. Remove the wheel lug nuts and then the wheel.
5. Raise the locking tab on the spindle nut and remove it with a 36mm socket wrench.
6. Remove the damper fork bolt, the damper pinch bolt and the damper fork.
7. Remove the knuckle-to-lower arm castle nut and separate the lower arm from the knuckle, using a bearing puller tool or equivalent.
8. Pull the knuckle outward and remove the halfshaft outboard joint from the knuckle, using a plastic tipped hammer.
9. Using a small pry bar with a 3.5 × 7mm tip, pry out the inboard CV-joint approximately ½ in. (12mm) in order to force the spring clip out of the groove in the differential side gears.

**NOTE: Be careful not to damage the oil seal. Do not pull on the inboard CV-joint, it may come apart.**

10. Pull the halfshaft out of the differential or the intermediate shaft.
11. To install, reverse the removal procedure. If either the inboard or outboard joint boot bands have been removed for inspection or disassembly of the joint (only the inboard joint can be disassembled), be sure to repack the joint with a sufficient amount of bearing grease.

**NOTE: Make sure the CV-joint sub-axle bottoms so the spring clip may hold the halfshaft securely in the differential-intermediate shaft groove. Always replace the spring clip with a new one!**

## Intermediate Shaft

### REMOVAL & INSTALLATION

1. Drain the oil from the transaxle.
2. Remove the 10mm bolts (Integra), the 8mm and 10mm bolt (Legend and 825S).
3. Lower the bearing support close to the steering gearbox and remove the intermediate shaft from the differential.

**NOTE: To avoid damage to the differential oil seal, hold the intermediate shaft horizontal until it clears the differential.**

4. To install, reverse the removal procedure.

### CV-JOINT OVERHAUL

**For all overhaul procedures, please refer to "CV-Joint Overhaul" in the Unit Repair Section.**

## Front Wheel Hub, Knuckle and Bearings

### REMOVAL & INSTALLATION

**NOTE: The following procedures for hub and wheel bearing removal and installation necessitate the use of many special tools and a hydraulic press. Do not attempt this procedure without these special tools.**

#### *Integra*

1. Pry the lock tab away from the spindle and loosen the nut. Slightly loosen the lug nuts.
2. Raise and safely support the front of the vehicle. Remove the front wheel and spindle nut.
3. Remove the brake caliper bolts and the caliper from the knuckle. Do not allow the caliper to hang by the brake hose, support it with a length of wire.
4. Remove the disc brake rotor retaining screws (if equipped). Screw two 8 × 1.25 × 12mm bolts into the disc brake removal holes and turn the bolts to press the rotor from the hub.

**NOTE: Only turn each bolt 2 turns at a time to prevent cocking the disc excessively.**

5. Remove the tie rod from the knuckle using a tie rod end removal tool. Use care not to damage the ball joint seals.
6. Use a floor jack to support the lower control arm, then, remove the cotter pin from the lower arm ball joint and the castle nut.

**CAUTION**

***Be sure to place the jack securely beneath the lower control arm at the ball joint. Otherwise, the tension from the torsion bar may cause the arm to suddenly jump away from the steering knuckle as the ball joint is removed.***

7. Remove the lower arm from the knuckle using the ball joint remover.
8. Loosen the pinch bolt which retains the shock in the knuckle. Tap the top of the knuckle with a hammer and slide it off the shock.
9. Remove the knuckle and hub, if still attached, by sliding the assembly off of the halfshaft.
10. Remove the hub from the knuckle using special tools and a hydraulic press.

**Bearing Removal:**

11. Remove the splash guard and the snapring.
12. Press the bearing outer race out of the knuckle using special tools and a hydraulic press.

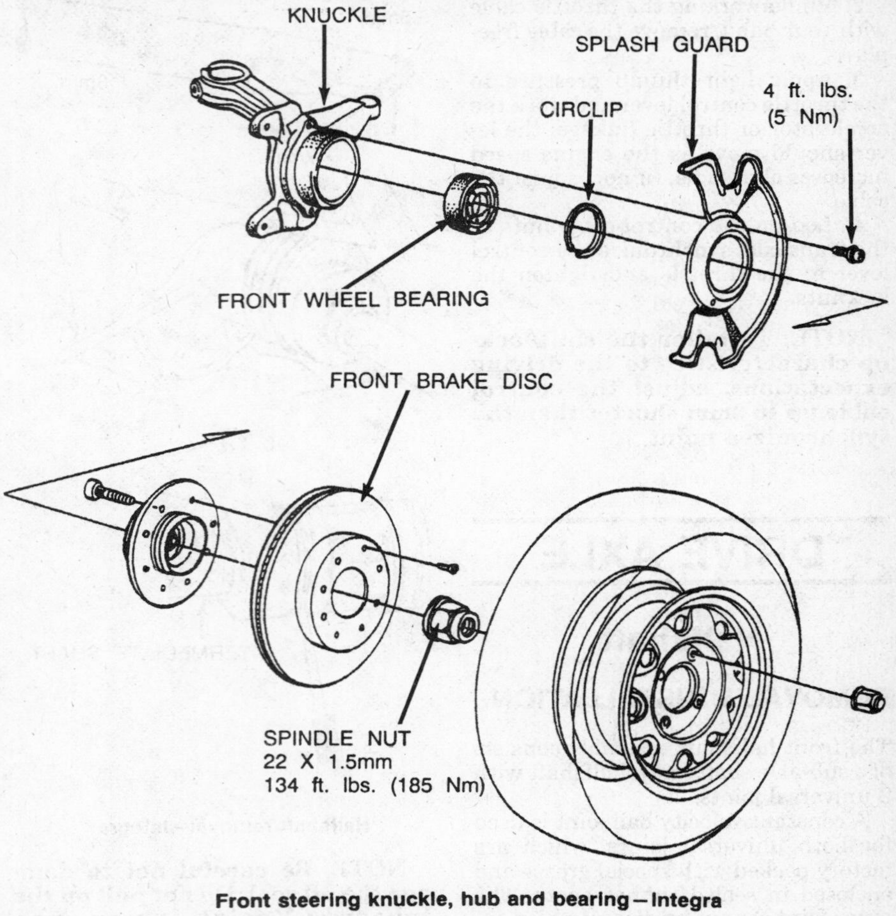


**Front steering knuckle, hub and bearing – Integra**

13. Remove the outboard bearing inner race from the hub using special tools and a bearing puller.

**NOTE: Whenever the wheel bearings are removed, always replace them with a new set of bearings and an outer dust seal.**

14. Clean all old grease from the halfshaft and spindles on the vehicle.
15. Remove the old grease from the hub and knuckle and thoroughly dry and wipe clean all components.
16. To install the bearings, press the bearing outer race into the knuckle using the special tools as used above, plus the installation base tool or equivalent.
17. Install the snapring and the splash guard.
18. Place the hub in the special tool fixture, set the knuckle in position on the press and apply downward pressure.
19. The remaining step are the reverse of the removal procedure. Use a new spindle nut and stake after torquing.

#### *Legend and 825S*

1. Pry the lock tab away from the spindle and loosen the 36mm nut. Slightly loosen the lug nuts.
2. Raise and safely support the front of the vehicle. Remove the front wheel and spindle nut.
3. Remove the bolts retaining the brake caliper and the caliper from the knuckle. Do not allow the caliper to hang by the brake hose, support it with a length of wire.
4. Remove the disc brake rotor retaining screws (if equipped). Screw the two 8 x 1.25 × 12mm bolts into the disc brake removal holes and turn the bolts to press the rotor from the hub.

**NOTE: Only turn each bolt 2 turns at a time to prevent cocking the disc excessively.**

5. Remove the tie rod from the knuckle using a tie rod end removal tool. Use care not to damage the ball joint seals.
6. Remove the cotter pin from the lower arm ball joint and the castle nut.
7. Remove the lower control arm from the knuckle using the ball joint remover.
8. Remove the cotter pin from the upper arm ball joint and the castle nut.
9. Remove the upper arm from the knuckle using the ball joint remover.

10. Remove the knuckle and hub by sliding the assembly off of the halfshaft.
11. Remove the back splash guard screws from the knuckle.
12. Remove the hub from the knuckle using special tools and a hydraulic press.

**Bearing Removal:**

13. Remove the splash guard, dust seal, snapring and outer bearing race.
14. Turn the knuckle over, remove the inboard dust seal, bearing and inner race and bearing.
15. Press the bearing outer race out of the knuckle using special tools and a hydraulic press.
16. Remove the outboard bearing inner race from the hub using special tools and a bearing puller.
17. Remove the outboard dust seal from the hub.

**NOTE: Whenever the wheel bearings are removed, always replace with a new set of bearings and outer dust seal.**

18. Clean all old grease from the halfshaft spindles on the vehicle.
19. Remove all old grease from the hub and knuckle and thoroughly dry and wipe clean all components.
20. To install the bearings, press the bearing outer race into the knuckle using the special tools used as above, plus the installing base tool.
21. Install the outboard ball bearing and inner race in the knuckle.
22. Install the snapring. Pack grease in the groove around the sealing lip of the outboard grease dust seal.
23. Drive the outboard grease seal into the knuckle, using a seal driver and hammer, until it is flush with the knuckle surface.
24. Install the splash guard, turn the knuckle upside down and install the inboard ball bearing and it's inner race.
25. Place the hub in the special tool fixture, set the knuckle in position on the press and apply downward pressure.
26. Pack grease in the groove around the sealing lip of the inboard dust seal.
27. Drive the dust seal into the knuckle using a seal driver.
28. To complete the installation, reverse the removal procedures. Use a new spindle nut and stake it after torquing.

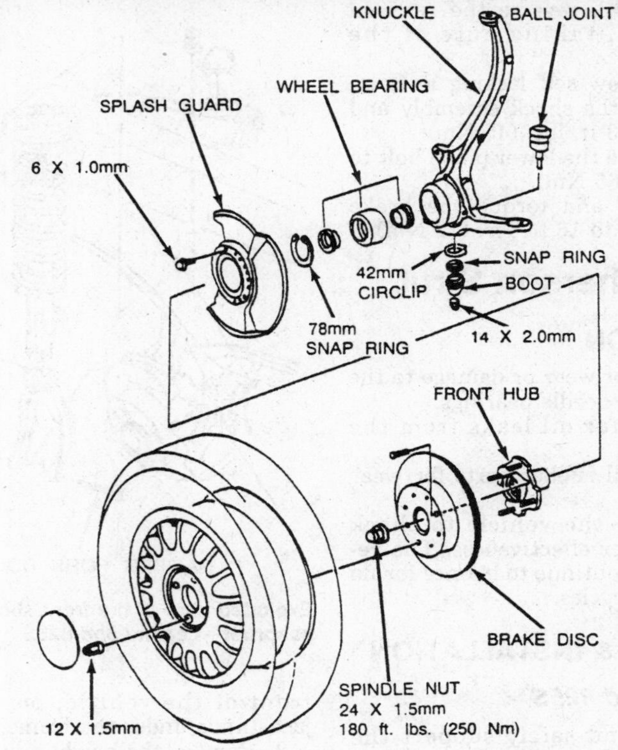


**Exploded view of the front steering knuckle, hub and bearing – Legend and 825S**

# FRONT SUSPENSION

The Integra suspension consists of 2 independent torsion bars and front shock absorbers similar to a front strut assembly but without a spring. Both lower forged radius arms are connected with a stabilizer bar.

The Legend and 825S models use a double wishbone system. The lower wishbone consists of a forged transverse link with a locating stabilizer bar. The lower end of the strut assembly has a fork shape to allow the halfshaft to pass through it. The upper arm is located in the wheel well and is twist mounted, angled forward from it's inner mount, to clear the strut assembly.

## Shock Absorbers

### REMOVAL & INSTALLATION

#### *Integra*

1. Raise and safely support the front of the vehicle. Remove the front wheels.
2. Remove the brake hose clamp bolt.
3. Place a floor jack beneath the lower control arm to support it.
4. Remove the lower shock-to-steering knuckle bolt and slowly lower the jack.

**CAUTION**

***Be sure the jack is positioned securely beneath the lower control arm at the ball joint.*** *Otherwise, the tension from the torsion bar may cause the lower control arm to suddenly jump away from the shock absorber as the pinch bolt is removed.*

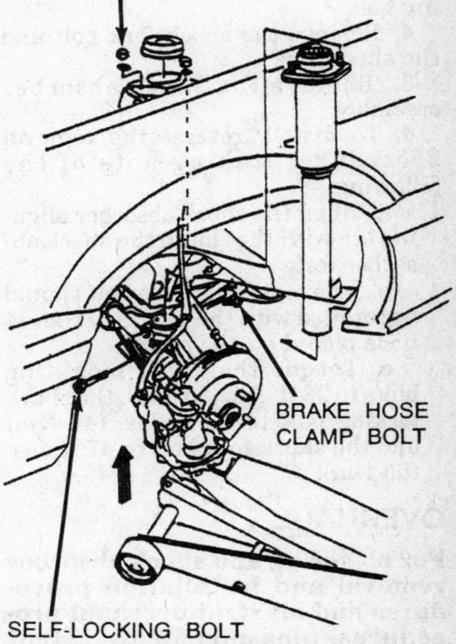


**Front shock absorber – Integra**

5. Compress the shock absorber by hand, remove the upper lock nuts and the shock from the vehicle.

6. To install, reverse the removal procedures, taking note of the following:

a. Use new self locking nuts on the top of the shock assembly and torque to 33 ft. lbs. (45 Nm).

b. Torque the lower pinch bolt to 47 ft. lbs. (65 Nm).

c. Install and torque the brake hose clamp to 16 ft. lbs. (22 Nm).

## MacPherson Strut

### INSPECTION

1. Check for wear or damage to the bushings and needle bearings.
2. Check for oil leaks from the struts.
3. Check all rubber parts for wear or damage.
4. Bounce the vehicle to check shock absorber effectiveness. The vehicle should continue to bounce for no more than 2 cycles.

### REMOVAL & INSTALLATION

#### *Legend and 825S*

1. Raise and safely support the front of the vehicle. Remove the front wheels.
2. Remove the brake hose clamps from the shock absorber.
3 Remove the shock absorber locking bolt.
4. Remove the shock fork bolt and the shock fork.
5. Remove the shock absorber assembly.
6. To install, reverse the removal procedures, taking note of the following:

a. Align the shock absorber aligning tab with the slot in the shock absorber fork.

b. The mounting base bolt should be torqued with the weight of the vehicle placed on the shock.

c. Torque the upper mounting bolts to 28 ft. lbs. (39 Nm), the shock locking bolt to 32 ft. lbs. (44 Nm) and the shock fork bolt to 47 ft. lbs. (65 Nm).

### OVERHAUL

**For all spring and shock absorber removal and installation procedures and all strut overhaul procedures, please refer to "Strut Overhaul" in the Unit Repair section.**

## Torsion Bar

### REMOVAL & INSTALLATION

#### *Integra*

1. Raise and safely support the front of the vehicle; position the jackstands under the frame.
2. Remove the height adjusting nut and the torque tube holder.
3. Remove the 30mm circlip.
4. Remove the torsion bar cap and the torsion bar clip by tapping the bar out of the torque tube.

**NOTE: The torsion bar will slide easier by moving the lower arm up and down.**

5. Tap the torsion bar backward, from the torque tube and remove the torque tube.
6. Inspect the torsion bar for cracks and/or damage; replace it, if necessary.
7. Install a new seal onto the torque tube. Coat the torque tube seal and tube with grease, install them on the rear beam.
8. Grease the ends of the torsion bar and insert into the torque tube from the rear.
9. Align the projection on the torque tube splines with the cutout in the torsion bar splines and insert the torsion bar approximately 0.394 in. (10mm).

**NOTE: The torsion bar will slide easier if the lower arm is moved up and down.**

10. Install the torsion bar clip, cap, the 30mm circlip and the torque tube cap.

**NOTE: Push the torsion bar forward so there is no clearance between the torque tube and the 30mm circlip.**

11. Coat the cap bushing with grease and install it on the torque tube. Install the torque tube holder.
12. Temporarily tighten the height adjusting nut.
13. Remove the jackstands and lower the vehicle to the ground. Adjust the torsion bar spring height.

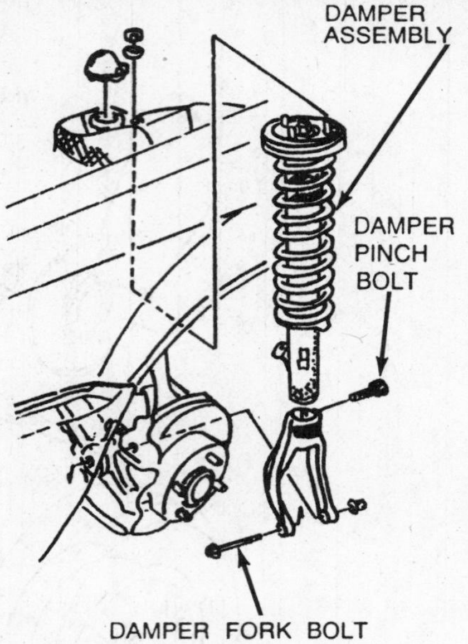


**Exploded view of the front shock absorber—Legend and 825S**

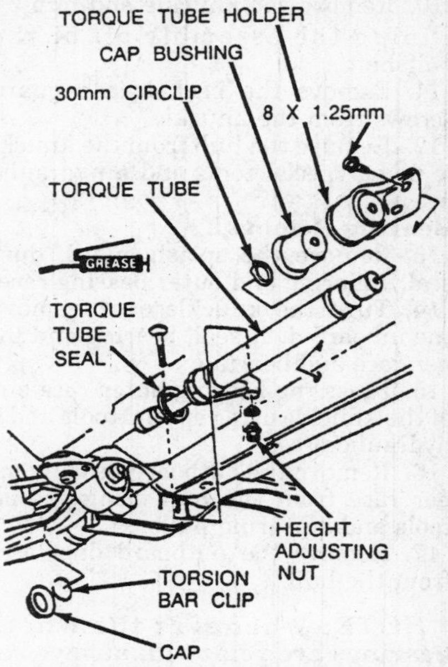


**Torsion bar assembly—Integra**

### ADJUSTMENT

1. Measure the torsion bar spring height between the ground and the highest point of the wheel arch. The measurement should be 25.7 in. (653mm).
2. If the spring height does not meet the specification above, make the following adjustment.

a. Raise and support the vehicle with the front wheels off the ground.

b. Adjust the spring height by turning the height adjusting nut. Tightening the nut raises the height and loosening the nut lowers the height.

**NOTE: The height varies 0.20 in. (5mm)/revolution of the adjusting nut.**

c. Lower the front wheels to the ground, then bounce the vehicle up and down several times and recheck the spring height to make sure it is within specifications.

## Ball Joints

### INSPECTION

Check ball joint play as follows:

a. Raise and safely support the front of the vehicle.

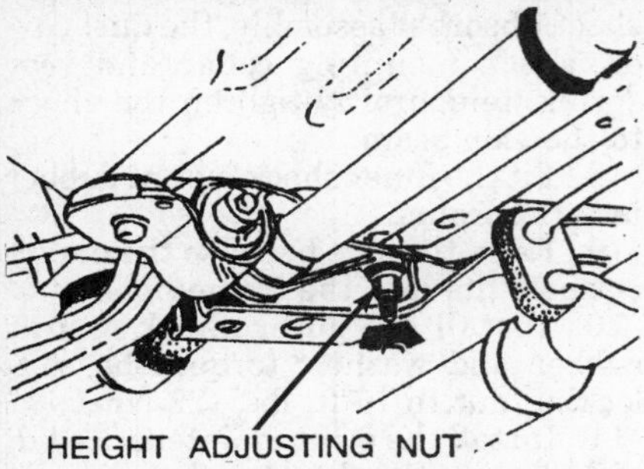

**Torsion bar adjustment — Integra**

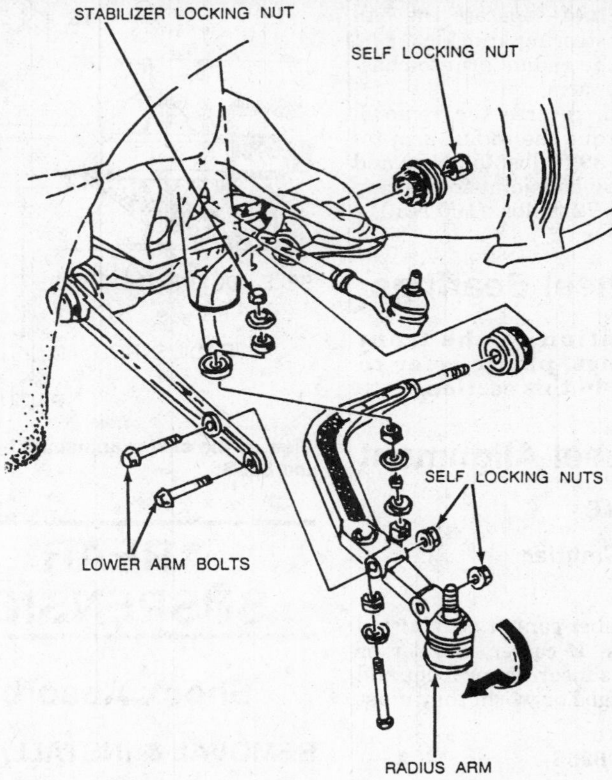

**Radius arm assembly — Integra**

b. Clamp a dial indicator onto the lower control arm and place the indicator tip on the knuckle, near the ball joint.

c. Place a pry bar between the lower control arm and the knuckle. Replace the lower control arm if the play exceeds 0.5mm.

### REMOVAL & INSTALLATION

#### *Integra*

The integra is equipped with only a lower ball joint. If the lower ball joint play exceeds 0.05mm, replace the lower ball joint and radius as an assembly.

#### *Legend and 825S*

**NOTE: This procedure is performed after the removal of the steering knuckle and requires the use of the following special tools or their equivalent: a Acura part No. 07GAF–SD40330 ball joint removal base, 07GAF–SD40320 ball joint installation base and 07GAG–SD40700 clip guide tool.**

1. Remove the steering knuckle from the vehicle.
2. Position the ball joint removal tool base or equivalent, on the ball joint, position the assembly in a shop press and press the ball joint from the steering knuckle.
3. Position the new ball joint into the hole of the steering knuckle.
4. Install the ball joint installer tool or equivalent, with the small end facing outward.
5. Position the ball joint installation base tool or equivalent, on the ball joint, position the assembly in a shop press and press the ball joint into the steering knuckle.
6. Seat the snapring in the groove of the ball joint.
7. Install the boot and snapring using the clip guide tool.

## Radius Arm

### REMOVAL & INSTALLATION

#### *Integra*

1. Raise and safely support the front of the vehicle. Remove the front wheels.
2. Place a floor jack beneath the lower control arm and remove the ball joint cotter pin/nut.

**CAUTION**

***Be sure to place the jack securely beneath the lower control arm at the ball joint. Otherwise, the tension from the torsion bar may cause the arm to suddenly jump away from the steering knuckle as the ball joint is removed.***

3. Using a ball joint remover tool or equivalent, remove the ball joint from the steering knuckle.
4. Remove the radius arm locking nuts and the stabilizer locking nut and separate the radius arm from the stabilizer bar.
5. Remove the lower arm bolts and the radius arm by pulling it down and forward.
6. To install, reverse the removal procedures. Tighten all the rubber bushings and damper parts only after the vehicle is placed back on the ground.

## Upper Control Arm

#### *Legend and 825S*

1. Raise and safely support the front of the vehicle on jackstands located under the frame. Remove the front wheel.
2. Remove the cotter pin and the upper control arm-to-steering knuckle nut.
3. Using a ball joint removal tool or equivalent, separate the upper control arm from the steering knuckle.
4. Remove the upper control arm-to-chassis nuts, washers and the upper control arm from the vehicle.
5. To install, reverse the removal procedures. Torque the upper control arm-to-chassis nuts to 47 ft. lbs. (65 Nm) and the upper control arm ball joint-to-steering knuckle nut to 32 ft. lbs. (42 Nm).

## Lower Control Arm

### REMOVAL & INSTALLATION

#### *Legend and 825S*

1. Raise and safely support the front of the vehicle. Remove the front wheels.
2. Disconnect the lower arm ball joint; be careful not to damage the seal.
3. Remove the stabilizer bar brackets, starting with the center brackets.
4. Remove the lower arm ball joint-to-steering knuckle nut. Using a ball

joint removal tool, separate the ball joint from the steering knuckle.

5. Remove the radius arm-to-chassis bolt and the arm.

6. To install, reverse the removal procedure. Torque the radius arm-to-chassis bolt to 39 ft. lbs. (55 Nm) and the radius arm ball joint-to-steering knuckle nut to 72 ft. lbs. (100 Nm).

## Front Wheel Bearings

**For information on the front wheel bearings, please refer to "Drive Axle" in this section.**

## Front Wheel Alignment

### ADJUSTMENT

#### Caster and Camber

**INTEGRA**

Caster and camber cannot be adjusted on the Integra. If caster, camber or kingpin angle is incorrect or front end parts are damaged or worn, they must be replaced.

**LEGEND AND 825S**

**NOTE: Wheel alignment adjustments must be performed in the following order: camber, caster and toe-in.**

The camber adjustment can be made by loosening the upper control arm nuts and sliding the ball joint until the camber meets specifications. The caster adjustment can be made by loosening the 16mm nuts on the front beam radius rods and turning the locknut to make the adjustment. Turning the nut clockwise decreases the caster; turning it counterclockwise increases the caster. After adjusting to specifications, hold the nylon locknut and lightly tighten the adjuster. Torque the 16mm nut to 58 ft. lbs. (80 Nm) and the locknut to 32 ft. lbs. (44 Nm) while holding the 16mm nut.

#### Toe-Out

Toe is the difference of the distance between the forward extremes of the front tires and the distance between the rearward extremes of the front tires. The fronts of the tires are further apart than the rear to counteract the pulling together effect of front wheel drive.

Toe-out can be adjusted by loosening the locknuts at each end of the tie rods. To increase toe-out, turn the right tie rod in the direction of forward wheel rotation and turn the left tie rod in the opposite direction. Turn both tie rods an equal amount until toe-out meets specification.

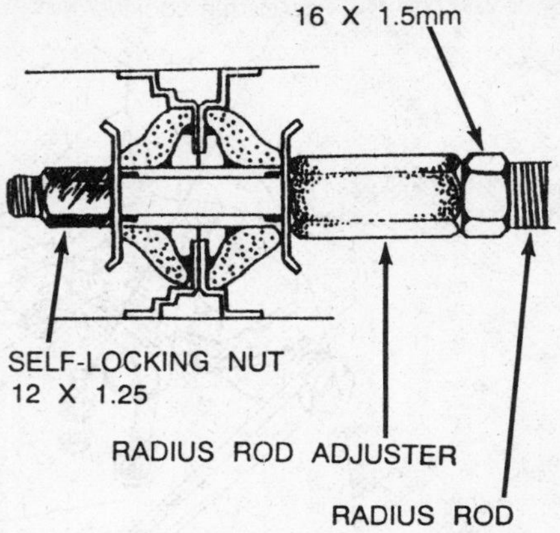


**View of the caster adjustment—Legend and 825S**

# REAR SUSPENSION

## Shock Absorber

### REMOVAL & INSTALLATION

#### 1986–88 Legend Sedan and 825S

1. Raise and safely support the rear of the vehicle.
2. Remove the rear wheels.
3. Place a jack under the lower arm and raise slightly.
4. Remove the 8mm nuts from the top of the assembly.
5. Lower the jack.
6. Remove the lower shock pinch bolt.
7. Remove the shock absorber from the hub assembly.
8. To install, reverse the removal procedures, torque the upper 8mm bolts to 16 ft. lbs. (22 Nm) and the lower pinch bolt to 47 ft. lbs. (65 Nm).

## MacPherson Strut

### REMOVAL & INSTALLATION

#### Integra

1. Raise and safely support the rear of the vehicle.
2. Remove the rear wheels.
3. Place a jack under the rear axle beam.
4. Remove the shock maintenance lid and the self locking nut.
5. Lower the jack gradually. Remove the self-locking bolt, rear spring and spring seat.

**To Install:**

6. Fit the upper spring seat into the frame.
7. Install the shock protector on the shock absorber assembly, the dust cover, shock mounting collar and rear spring; temporarily tighten the shock to the axle beam.
8. Fit the inner shock mount rubber into the frame.
9. Raise the axle beam so the damper shaft fits into the frame hole.
10. Install the outer shock mount rubber and washer; torque the self-locking nut to 16 ft. lbs. (22 Nm).
11. Install the strut maintenance lid.
12. Torque the shock on the rear axle beam with the weight of the vehicle placed on the ground. Torque the the strut-to-rear axle beam bolt to 40 ft. lbs. (55 Nm).

#### Legend Coupe and 1989–90 Legend sedan and 825S

1. Remove the carpet from the trunk.
2. Remove the upper strut mounting nuts.
3. Remove the parking brake cable-to-trailing arm clamp.
4. Remove the stabilizer linkage from the trailing arm.
5. Remove the upper arm mounting bolts.
6. Remove the lower strut mounting bolt.
7. Lower the rear suspension and remove the strut assembly.

**To Install:**

8. Lower the rear suspension and position the strut assembly in it's original position.
9. Loosely install the lower strut mounting bolt.
10. Install and torque the strut upper mounting nuts to 16 ft. lbs. (22 Nm) for 1986–88 or 28 ft. lbs. (39 Nm) for 1989–90.
11. Using a floor jack, raise the rear suspension until the weight of the vehicle is on the strut assembly.
12. Torque the strut-to-axle bolt to 47 ft. lbs. (65 Nm).
13. Install the parking brake clamp and the stabilizer linkage on the trailing arm.

### OVERHAUL

**For all spring and shock absorber removal and installation procedures, and all strut overhaul procedures, please refer to "Strut Overhaul" in the Unit Repair section.**

## Springs

### REMOVAL & INSTALLATION

#### 1986–88 Legend Sedan and 825S

1. Raise and safely support the rear of the vehicle.

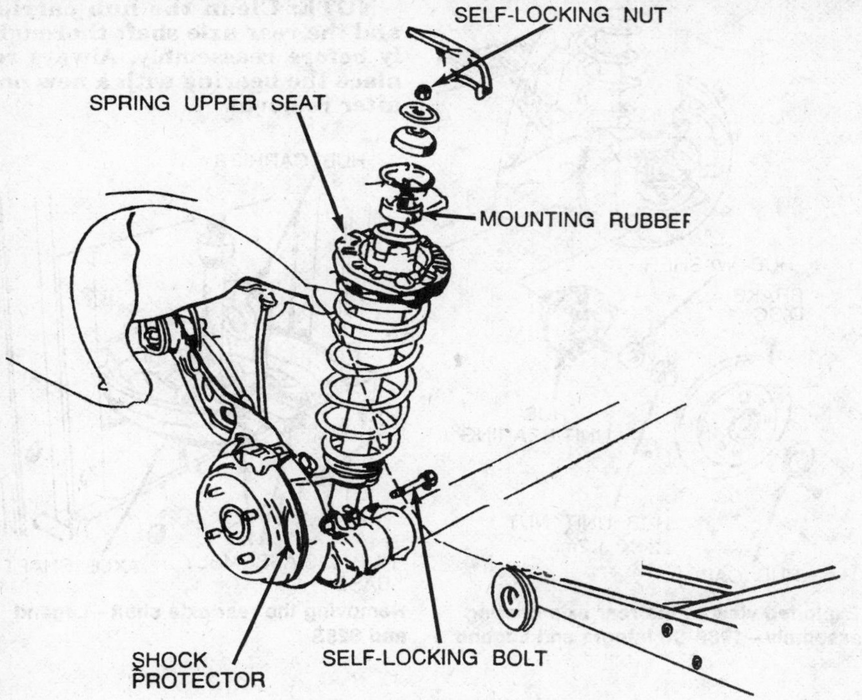


**Rear strut assembly-Integra**

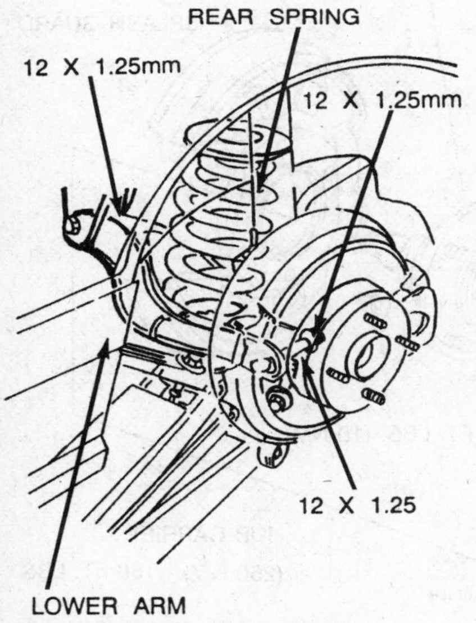


**View of the rear spring assembly—1986–88 Legend and 825S Sedan**

2. Place a floor jack under the lower arm.
3. Pull out the hub carrier lower bolt.
4. Loosen the lower arm outside bolt.
5. Pull out the lower arm inside bolt.
6. Lower the jack gradually and remove the rear spring.
7. To install, reverse the removal procedures. Install the rear spring with the lower end of the spring outside. Torque the lower arm-to-hub carrier nut/bolt to 54 ft. lbs. (75 Nm) (with the weight of the vehicle on the ground).

## Rear Control Arms

### REMOVAL & INSTALLATION

#### *Lower Control Arm*

The 1989–90 Legend and 825S models are equipped with 2 lower control arms, **A** and **B**.

1. Raise and safely support the rear of the vehicle with jackstands under the frame.
2. Remove the lower control arms-to-steering knuckle nut/bolt.
3. Remove the lower control arms-to-chassis nuts/bolts and the control arms from the vehicle.
4. To install, reverse the removal procedures. Torque the lower control arm **A**-to-chassis nut/bolt to 54 ft. lbs. (75 Nm), the lower control arm **B**-to-chassis nut/bolt to 16 ft. lbs. (22 Nm) and the lower control arms-to-steering knuckle nut/bolts to 47 ft. lbs. (65 Nm).

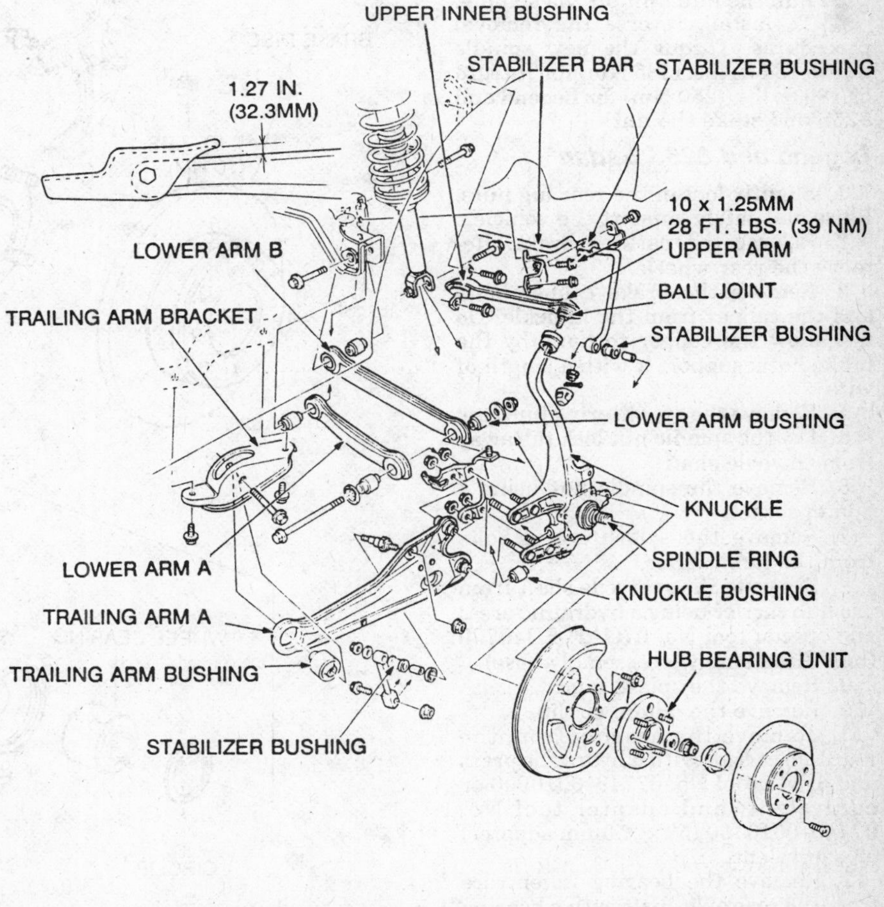


**Exploded view of the rear suspension system—Legend and 825S**

### *Trailing Arm*

The 1989–90 models, Legend and 825S, are equipped with trailing arms.

1. Raise and safely support the rear of the vehicle with jackstands under the frame.
2. Remove the trailing arm-to-steering knuckle nuts.
3. Remove the trailing arm-to-bracket nut/bolt and the trailing arm.
4. To install, reverse the removal procedures. Torque the trailing arm-to-steering knuckle nuts to 40 ft. lbs. (55 Nm) and the trailing arm-to-bracket nut/bolt to 47 ft. lbs. (65 Nm).

## Rear Wheel Hub Bearings

### REMOVAL & INSTALLATION

### *Integra and Legend Coupe*

1. Slightly loosen the rear lug nuts. Raise and safely support the vehicle.
2. Release the parking brake. Remove the rear wheels and the brake calipers.
3. Remove the brake disc.
4. Remove the rear bearing hub cap and nut.
5. Pull the hub unit off the spindle.
6. To install, reverse the removal procedures. Torque the new spindle nut to 134 ft. lbs. (185 Nm) for Integra or 180 ft. lbs. (250 Nm) for Legend and 825S and stake the nut.

### *Legend and 825S Sedan*

1. Slightly loosen the rear lug nuts. Raise and safely support the vehicle.
2. Release the parking brake. Remove the rear wheels.
3. Remove the brake caliper bolts and the caliper from the knuckle. Do not allow the caliper to hang by the brake hose; support it with a length of wire.
4. Remove the rear bearing hub cap.
5. Pry the spindle nut lock tab away from the axle shaft.
6. Remove the spindle nut using a 36mm socket.
7. Remove the splash guard bolts from the hub carrier.
8. Separate the rear axle shaft from the hub carrier using a hydraulic press and special tool No. 07GAF–SD40700 (hub disassembly/ reassembly base).
9. Remove the splash guard.
10. Remove the 68mm circlip.
11. Remove the bearing from the rear hub carrier with a hydraulic press and driver tool No. 07749–0010000 or equivalent, and adapter tool No. 07746–0010400 (52 × 55mm adapter) or equivalent.
12. Remove the bearing inner race from the rear axle shaft with a bearing remover or equivalent.

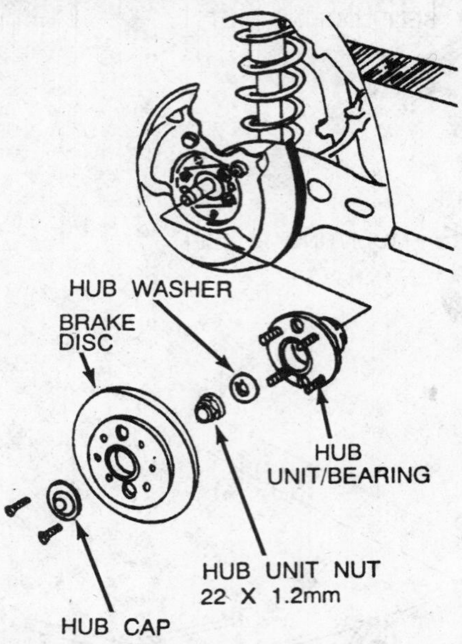


**Exploded view of the rear axle bearing assembly – 1989–90 Integra and Legend**

**NOTE: Clean the hub carrier and the rear axle shaft thoroughly before reassembly. Always replace the bearing with a new one after removal.**

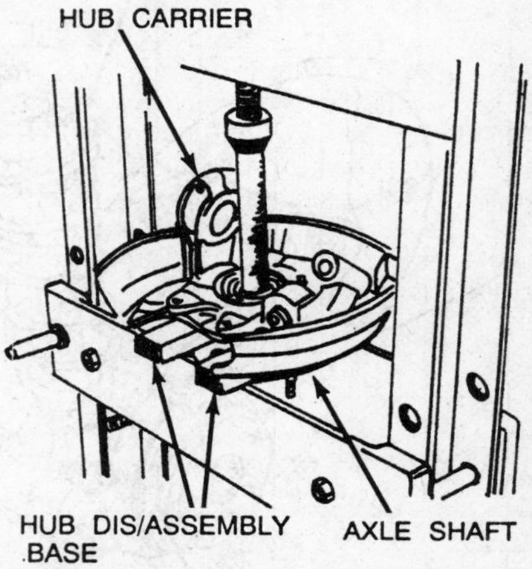


**Removing the rear axle shaft – Legend and 825S**

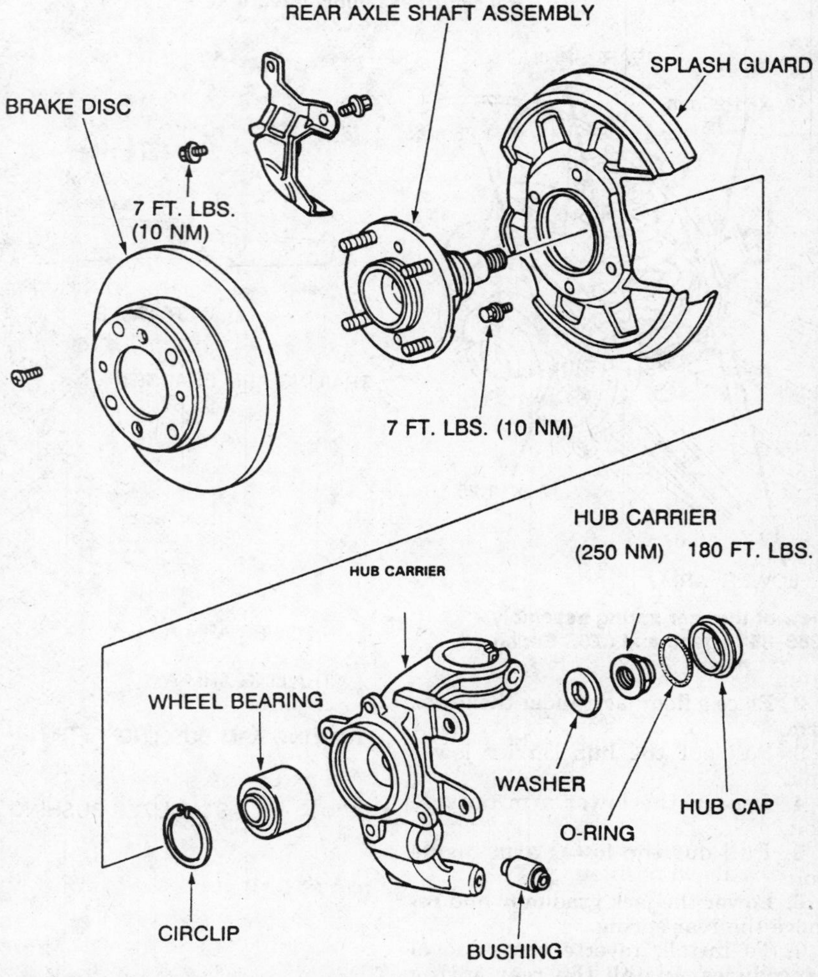


**Exploded view of the rear axle bearing assembly – 1986–88 Legend and 825S**

13. Press the bearing into the hub carrier using a hydraulic press and the following driver tools; 07749-0010000 or equivalent, tool No. 07746-0010500 (62 x 68mm adapter) or equivalent, and the hub disassembly/assembly base tool No. 07965-6920001 or equivalent.
14. Install the 68mm circlip into the groove in the hub carrier.
15. Install the splash guard.
16. Press the rear axle shaft into the hub carrier using a hydraulic press and the bearing support attachment tool No. 07GAF-SD40400 or equivalent.

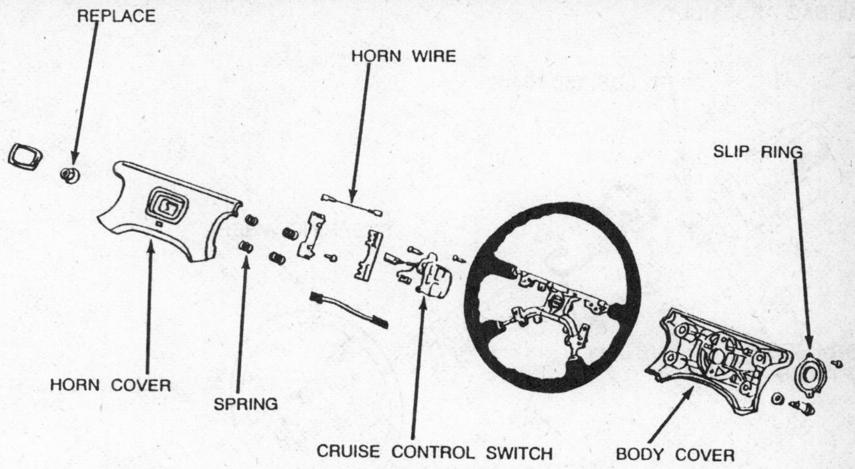


**Steering wheel—typical**

# STEERING

**CAUTION**

***The Legend (1988–90) and the Legend Coupe LS are equipped with a Supplemental Restraint System (SRS). Improper maintenance, including incorrect removal and installation of related components, can lead to personal injury caused by unintentional activation of the Airbag. Related components on these models should be serviced only by authorized service technicians.***

## Steering Wheel

### REMOVAL & INSTALLATION

#### *Without Airbag*

1. Place the steering wheel in the straight ahead position.
2. Disconnect the negative battery cable. Lift off the steering wheel pad.
3. Remove the steering wheel retaining nut and the horn pad.
4. If equipped with cruise control, remove the cruise control set/resume switch.
5. Gently hit the backside of each of the steering wheel spokes with equal force from the palms of your hands.

**NOTE: Avoid hitting the wheel or the shaft with excessive force. Damage to the shaft could result.**

6. To install, reverse of the removal procedure. Torque the steering wheel nut to 36 ft. lbs. (50 Nm).

#### *With Airbag*

1. Position the steering wheel in the straight ahead position.
2. Disconnect the (−) negative and (+) battery cables.
3. Remove the maintenance lid **A** below the airbag and the short connector.
4. Disconnect the short connector-to-airbag side of the connector.
5. Remove the maintainence lid **B** and the cruise control set/resume switch.
6. Using a Trox® T30 bit, remove the torx bolts and the airbag assembly.

**NOTE: Be sure to store the airbag in a safe place with the pad side facing upwards.**

7. Remove the steering wheel retaining nut. Gently hit the backside of each of the steering wheel spokes with equal force from the palms of your hands.

**NOTE: Avoid hitting the wheel or the shaft with excessive force. Damage to the shaft could result.**

8. To install, reverse of the removal procedure. Torque the steering wheel nut to 36 ft. lbs. (50 Nm).
9. Using new Torx® screws, torque the airbag to 7 ft. lbs. (10 Nm).
10. After installation, turn the ignition switch **ON** to the **II** position; the instrument panel SRS light should turn **ON** for about 8 seconds and turn **OFF**.
11. Make sure the horn buttons operate and the cruise control set/resume switch is in operation.

## Combination Switch

### REMOVAL & INSTALLATION

1. Remove the steering wheel.
2. Disconnect the column wiring harness and coupler.

**NOTE: Be careful not to damage the steering column or shaft.**

3. Remove the lower instrument panel cover and disconnect the wiper control unit connector. Remove the upper and lower column covers.
4. If equipped with an airbag, perform the following procedures:
   a. Disconnect the cable reel-to-SRS main harness electrical connector and the connector holder.
   b. Remove the cable reel and canceling sleeve.
5. Lift the combination switch from the steering column.

**To Install:**

6. Position the combination switch onto the steering column.
7. If equipped with an airbag, align the cancel sleeve grooves with the cable reel projections.
8. Install the upper and lower steering column covers. If equipped with an airbag, connect the wiper control unit harness connector and install the lower instrument panel.
9. If equipped with an airbag, perform the following procedures:
   a. Center the cable real by rotating it counterclockwise (approximately 2 turns) until the yellow gear tooth aligns with the mark on the cover.
   b. The arrow on the cable reel label must point straight upward.
10. To complete the installation, reverse the removal procedures.
11. After installation, turn the ignition switch **ON** to the **II** position; the instrument panel SRS light should turn **ON** for about 8 seconds and turn **OFF**.
12. Make sure the horn buttons operate and the cruise control set/resume switch is in operation.

## Ignition Lock/Switch

### REMOVAL & INSTALLATION

#### *Lock Assembly*

1. Remove the steering column housing upper and lower cover.

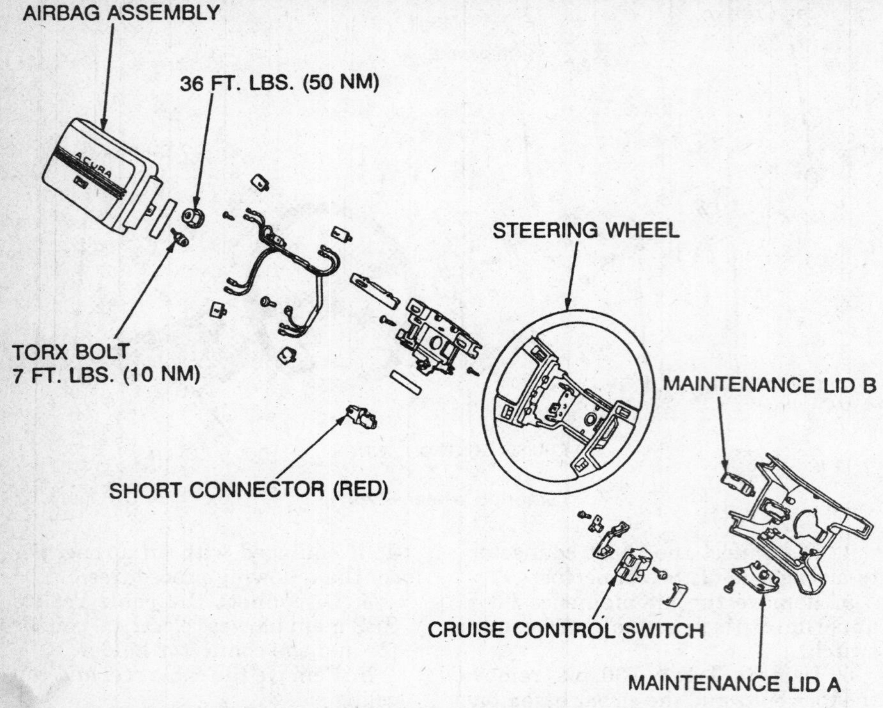

Exploded view of the steering wheel assembly with an air bag

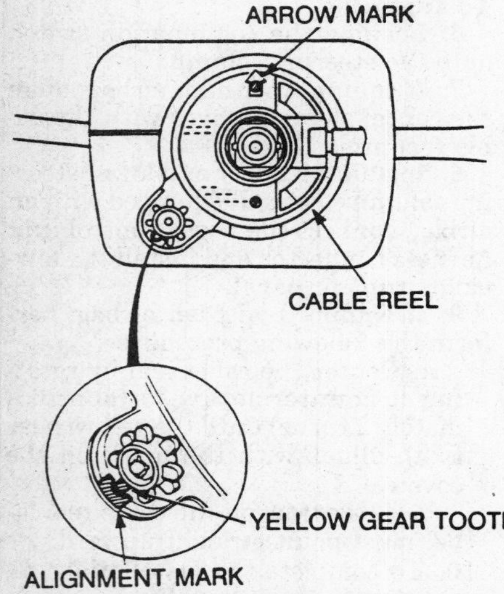

View of the cable reel alignment points—airbag system

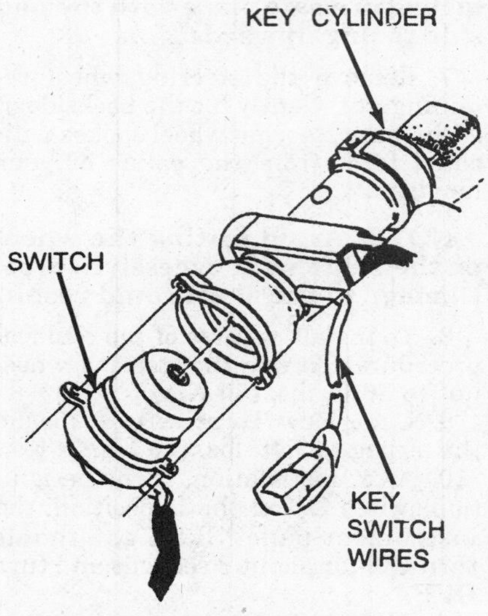

Ignition switch replacement

2. Disconnect the ignition switch wiring at the couplers.

3. The ignition switch assembly is held onto the column by shear bolts. Using a drill, remove the shear bolts, separate the ignition switch and remove it.

4. To install, reverse the removal procedure. Replace the shear bolts with new ones.

### *Switch Assembly*

1. Remove the steering column lower cover.

2. Disconnect the electrical connector at the switch.

3. Insert the key and turn it to the **I** position.

4. Remove the switch retaining screws and the switch (base) from the rest of the switch.

## Power Steering Gear

### REMOVAL & INSTALLATION

#### *Integra*

1. Remove the steering joint cover, the steering shaft connector bolts and pull the connector up off the pinion shaft.

2. Raise and safely support the front of the vehicle.

3. Remove the front wheels.

4. Remove the cotter pins and unscrew the tie rod end ball joint nuts halfway.

5. Break the tie rod ball joint nuts loose using a tie rod end removal tool or equivalent.

6. Remove the nuts and lift the tie rod ends out of the steering knuckles.

7. If equipped with a manual transaxle, perform the following procedures:

a. Remove the shift extension from the transaxle case.

b. Slide the pin retainer out of the way, drive out the spring pin with a punch and disconnect the shift control rod.

8. If equipped with an automatic transaxle, remove the shift cable guide from the floor and pull the shift cable down by hand.

9. Drain the power steering fluid.

10. Remove the front exhaust pipe. Clean the gasket areas thoroughly.

11. Disconnect the 3 fluid lines from the valve body.

12. Remove the gearbox mounting bolts.

13. Drop the gearbox far enough so the end of the pinion shaft comes out of it's hole in the frame channel and

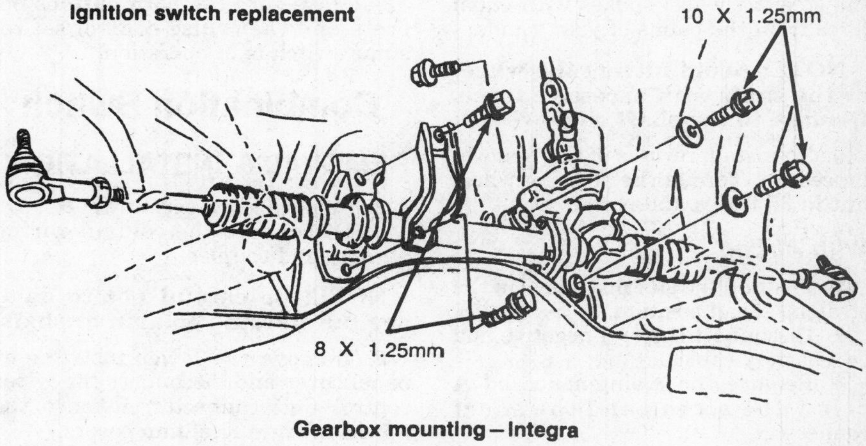

Gearbox mounting—Integra

rotate it forward until the shaft is pointing to the rear. Slide the gearbox to the right until the tie rod clears the rear beam, lower it from the vehicle to the left.

14. To install, reverse the removal procedures. Torque the power steering gear-to-chassis bolts to 32 ft. lbs. (44 Nm), the power steering gear clamp-to-chassis bolts to 29 ft. lbs. (40 Nm), the exhaust pipe-to-exhaust manifold nuts to 40 ft. lbs. (55 Nm), the tie rod ends-to-steering knuckle nuts to 29 ft. lbs. (40 Nm) and the shift extension-to-transaxle bolt to 7 ft. lbs. (10 Nm). Refill the reservoir with new power steering fluid. Start the engine and allow it run at fast idle, turn the steering wheel from lock-to-lock several times to bleed the air out. Check the fluid again and add if necessary. Check the system for leaks.

### Legend and 825S

1. Remove the steering joint cover and disconnect the steering shaft from the gearbox.
2. Drain the power steering fluid.
3. Remove the gearbox shield.
4. Using cleaning solvent and a brush, clean the control unit, it's lines and the end of the gearbox. Blow dry with compressed air (if possible).
5. Raise and safely support the front of the vehicle.
6. Remove the front wheels.
7. Remove the cotter pins and unscrew the tie rod end ball joint nuts halfway.
8. Break the tie rod ball joint nuts loose using a tie rod end removal tool or equivalent.
9. Remove the nuts and lift the tie rod ends from the steering knuckles.
10. If equipped with a manual transaxle, perform the following procedures:
    a. Remove the shift extension from the transaxle case.
    b. Disconnect the gearshift rod from the transaxle case by removing the 8mm spring pin.
11. If equipped with an automatic transaxle, remove the shift control cable from the clamp.
12. Remove the center beam bolts and the center beam.

**NOTE: Replace the self-locking nuts retaining the center beam (if worn).**

13. Disconnect the exhaust header pipe from the manifold. Replace the exhaust gasket and the self-locking nuts when reinstalling the pipe.
14. Remove the header pipe joint nuts and the header pipe.
15. Disconnect the 4 lines from the control unit.
16. Slide the tie rod all the way to the right side.
17. Slide the gear box right so the left tie rod clears the bottom of the rear beam and remove the gearbox.
18. To install, reverse the removal procedures. Torque the power steering gear-to-chassis bolts to 28 ft. lbs. (39 Nm), the exhaust pipe-to-exhaust manifold nuts to 40 ft. lbs. (55 Nm), the exhaust pipe-to-muffler nuts to 25 ft. lbs., the center beam-to-chassis bolts to 37 ft. lbs. (51 Nm), the shift extension-to-transaxle bolt to 7 ft. lbs. (10 Nm) and the tie rod end-to-steering knuckle nut to 32 ft. lbs. (44 Nm). Refill the reservoir with new power steering fluid. Start the engine and allow it to run at fast idle, turn the steering wheel from lock-to-lock several times to bled the air out. Check the fluid again and add (if necessary). Check the system for leaks.

## ADJUSTMENT

### Integra

1. Loosen the locknut on the rack guide screw with tool No. 07916–SA50001 or equivalent.
2. Tighten the guide screw until it compresses the spring against the guide; loosen it, torque it to about 3 ft. lbs. (4 Nm) and back it off about 25 degrees.
3. Torque the locknut to about 18 ft. lbs. (25 Nm) while preventing the guide screw from moving.

### Legend and 825S

1. Loosen the locknut on the rack guide screw with tool No. 07916–SA50001 or equivalent.
2. Tighten the guide screw until it compresses the spring against the guide; loosen it, torque it to about 2 ft. lbs. (3 Nm) and back it off about 20 degrees.
3. Torque the locknut to about 18 ft. lbs. (25 Nm) while preventing the guide screw from moving.

# Power Steering Pump

## REMOVAL & INSTALLATION

### Integra

1. Disconnect and plug the hoses from the reservoir.
2. Remove the 10mm flange bolts, the belt from the pulley and the pump assembly.
3. To install, reverse the removal procedures. Torque the power steering pump-to-engine bolts to 29 ft. lbs. (40 Nm). Be sure to observe the following:
    a. Connect the hoses tightly.
    b. Adjust the belt tension.
    c. Check the fluid level and add (if necessary).
    d. Bleed the air from the system.

### Legend and 825S

1. Remove the belt cover.
2. Drain the fluid from the system.
3. Disconnect and plug the inlet/outlet hoses from the pump.
4. Remove the belt by loosening the pump pivot bolt and adjusting nut.
5. Remove the pump assembly nut/bolt and the assembly.
6. To install, reverse the removal procedures. Torque the power steering pump-to-bracket bolt to 28 ft. lbs. (39 Nm) and the power steering pump-to-bracket nut to 16 ft. lbs. (22 Nm). Be sure to observe the following:
    a. Refill the reservoir with new fluid to the "Upper Level" on the reservoir.
    b. Connect the hoses tightly.
    c. Adjust the belt tension.
    d. Bleed the air from the system.
    e. Check the fluid level and add (if necessary).

## BELT ADJUSTMENT

1. Loosen the adjuster arm bolt.
2. Move the pump toward or away from the engine, until the belt can be depressed approximately $^3/_4$–$^{15}/_{16}$ in. (19–24mm) at the midpoint between both pulleys under moderate thumb pressure. If the tension adjustment is being made on a new belt, the deflection should only be about 11mm, to allow for the initial stretching of the belt.
3. Torque the bolt to 29 ft. lbs. (40 Nm) for Intrgra or 33 ft. lbs. (45 Nm) for Legend and 825S and recheck the adjustment.

## SYSTEM BLEEDING

1. Raise and safely support the front of the vehicle.
2. Refill the power steering pump reservoir to the full level.
3. Start the engine and turn the steering wheel from lock-to-lock (several times).
4. After the air bubbles have been eliminated from the system, refill the reservoir and lower the vehicle.

# Tie Rod Ends

## REMOVAL & INSTALLATION

### Integra

1. Raise and safely support the front of the vehicle. Remove the front wheel.
2. Loosen the tie rod end-to-power steering gear jam nut.

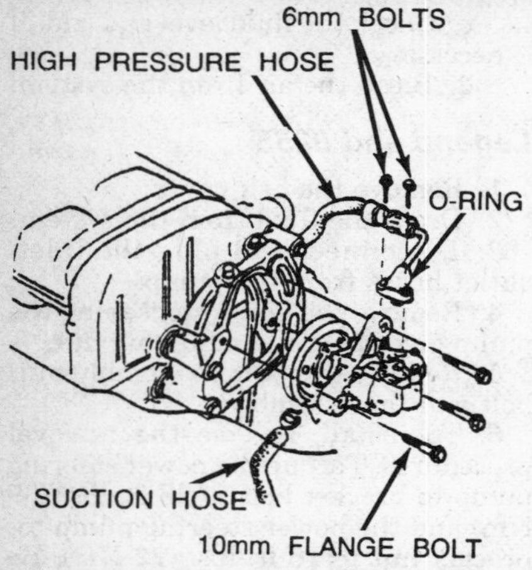

**Power steering pump mounting—Integra**

3. Remove the tie rod end-to-steering knuckle cotter pin and nut.
4. Using a tie rod removal tool or equivalent, separate the tie rod end from the steering knuckle.
5. While supporting the power steering rod, remove the tie rod end; be sure to count revolutions required to remove the tie rod end.
6. To install the new tie rod end, turn it the same amount of revolutions necessary to remove it and tighten the jam nut to 42 ft. lbs. (58 Nm) and the tie rod end-to-steering knuckle nut to 29 ft. lbs. (40 Nm).

### *Legend and 825S*

1. Raise and safely support the front of the vehicle. Remove the front wheels.
2. Remove the cotter pin and the nut from the tie rod end. Use a ball joint remover tool or equivalent, separate the tie rod from the steering knuckle.
3. Disconnect the air tube at the dust seal joint. Remove the tie rod dust seal bellows clamps and move the rubber bellows on the tie rod rack joints.
4. Straighten the tie rod lockwasher tabs at the tie rod-to-rack joint and remove the tie rod by turning it with a wrench.
5. To install, reverse the removal procedure. Always use a new tie rod lockwasher during reassembly. Torque the tie rod end-to-power steering gear to 40 ft. lbs. (55 Nm) and the tie rod end-to-steering knuckle nut to 32 ft. lbs. (44 Nm). Fit the locating lugs into the slots on the rack and bend the outer edge of the washer over the flat part of the rod, after the tie rod nut has been properly tightened.

# BRAKES

**For all brake system repair and service procedures not detailed below, please refer to "Brakes" in the Unit Repair section.**

## Master Cylinder

### REMOVAL & INSTALLATION

**CAUTION**

***Before removing the master cylinder, cover the body surfaces with fender covers and rags to prevent damage to painted surfaces by brake fluid.***

1. Disconnect and plug the brake lines at the master cylinder.
2. Remove the master cylinder-to-power booster bolts and the master cylinder from the vehicle.
3. To install, reverse the removal procedure. Torque the master cylinder-to-power booster bolts to 11 ft. lbs. (15 Nm). Bleed the brake system.

## Proportioning Valve

### REMOVAL & INSTALLATION

1. Disconnect and plug the hydraulic lines from the dual proportioning valve.
2. Remove the proportioning valve-to-bracket bolts and the valve from the vehicle.
3. To install, reverse the removal procedures. Bleed the brake system.

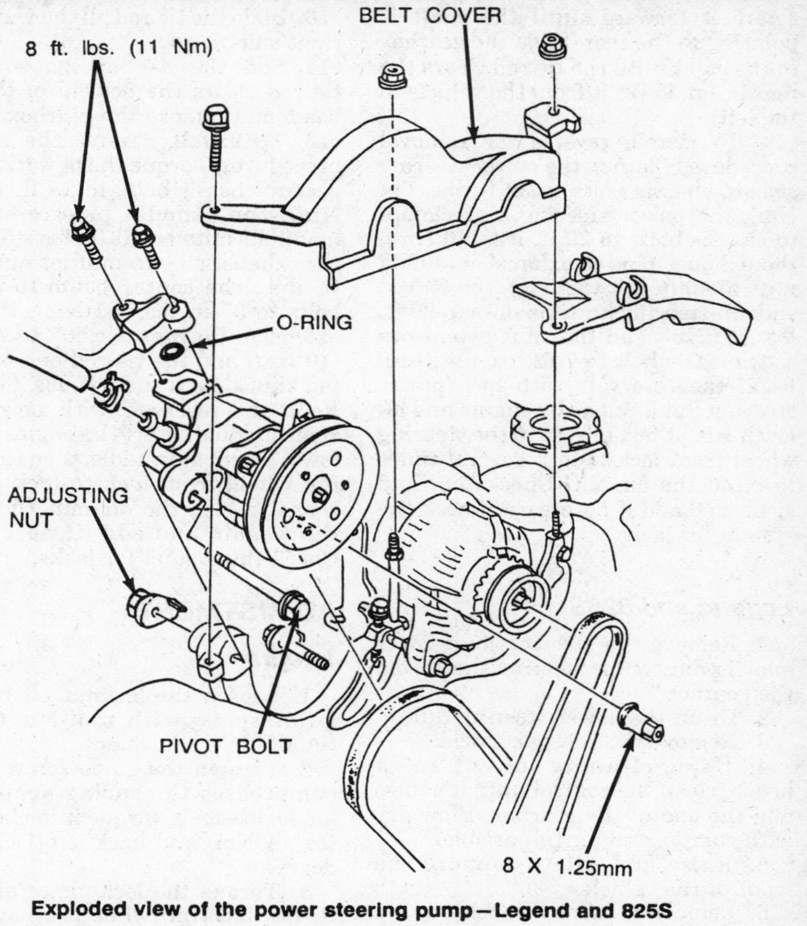

**Exploded view of the power steering pump—Legend and 825S**

## Vacuum Power Brake Booster

### INSPECTION

A preliminary check of the vacuum booster can be made as follows:

a. Depress the brake pedal several times using normal pressure; make sure the pedal height does not vary.
b. Hold the pedal in the depressed position and start the engine. The pedal should drop slightly.
c. Hold the pedal in the above position and stop the engine. The pedal should stay in the depressed position for approximately 30 seconds.
d. If the pedal does not drop when the engine is started or rises after the engine is stopped, the booster is not functioning properly.

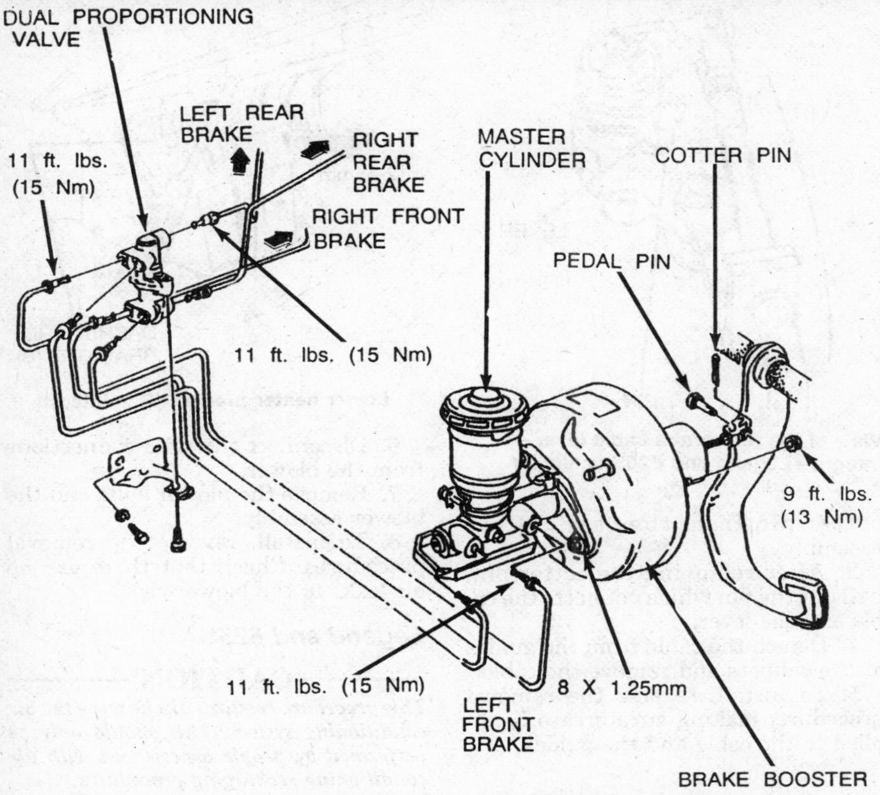


Master cylinder and booster assembly—typical

### REMOVAL & INSTALLATION

1. Disconnect the vacuum hose from the booster.
2. Disconnect and plug the brake lines at the master cylinder.
3. Remove the brake pedal-to-booster link pin and the booster nuts; the pushrod and nuts are located inside the vehicle under the instrument panel.
4. Remove the booster with the master cylinder attached.
5. To install, reverse the removal procedure. Torque the power brake booster-to-firewall nuts to 9 ft. lbs. (13 Nm) and the master cylinder-to-power brake booster nuts to 11 ft. lbs. (15 Nm). Check the vacuum booster pushrod-to-master cylinder piston clearance as outlined in the master cylinder removal procedure. Bleed the brake system before operating the vehicle.

## Anti-Lock Brake Booster (Modulator)

### REMOVAL & INSTALLATION

#### *Legend and 825S*

1. To relieve the accumulator line pressure, perform the following procedures:

a. Drain the fluid from the master cylinder and the modulator reservoir.

b. Remove the red cap from the bleeder screw on top of the power unit.

c. Using an anti-lock brake T-wrench or equivalent, turn the screw slowly 90 degrees (to collect the high pressure fluid from the reservoir) and 1 complete turn to drain the fluid.

d. Retighten the bleeder screw.

2. Disconnect and plug the lines from the hydraulic modulator.
3. Remove the mounting bolts and the modulator from the vehicle.
4. To install, reverse the removal procedures. Bleed the brake system.

## Disc Brake Pads

### REMOVAL & INSTALLATION

#### *Front*

1. Raise and safely support the front of the vehicle. Remove the front wheels.
2. Using a prybar (between the brake pad and the caliper), pry the brake caliper away from the vehicle until the piston is fully seated in the caliper.
3. Remove the lower caliper-to-cali-

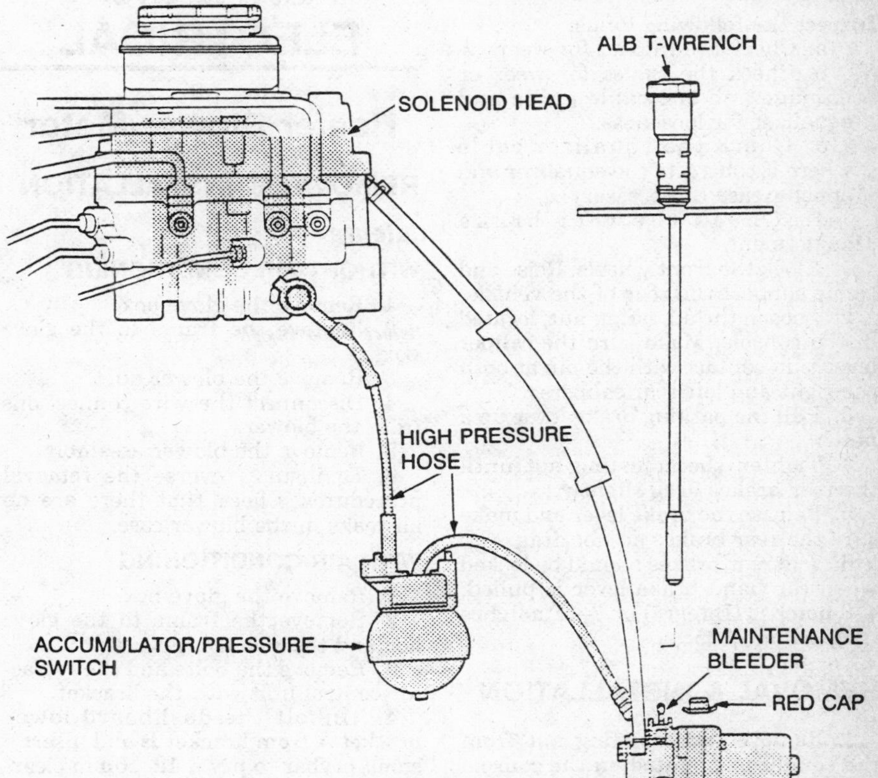


Bleeding the pressure from the anti-lock brake system

per support bolt and swing the caliper upward and away from the disc.

4. Remove the brake pad shim, the brake pad retainers and the pad.

5. Install new brake pads (coated with Molykote® M77, between the pads and shims), the shims and retainers.

6. Lower the calipers of the brake pad assemblies and torque the caliper bolt to 24 ft. lbs. (33 Nm).

### Rear

1. Raise and safely support the rear of the vehicle. Remove the rear wheels.

2. Using a prybar (between the brake pad and the caliper), pry the brake caliper away from the vehicle until the piston is fully seated in the caliper.

3. Remove the caliper-to-caliper support bolts and the caliper from the disc.

4. Remove the brake pads and shims.

5. To install, use new brake pads and reverse the removal procedures. Torque the caliper-to-caliper support bolts to 28 ft. lbs. (39 Nm).

## Parking Brake Cable

### ADJUSTMENT

Inspect the following items:

a. Check the ratchet for wear.

b. Check the cables for wear or damage and the cable guide and equalizer for looseness.

c. Check the equalizer cable where it contracts the equalizer and apply grease (if necessary).

d. Check the rear brake adjustment.

1. Block the front wheels. Raise and safely support the rear of the vehicle.

2. Loosen the adjusting nut, located in the console. Make sure the caliper lever is in contact with the pin at both the right and left rear calipers.

3. Pull the parking brake lever up a notch.

4. Tighten the adjusting nut until the rear brakes drag slightly.

5. Release the brake lever and make sure the rear brakes do not drag.

6. The rear brakes should be locked when the hand brake lever is pulled; 4–8 notches (Integra) or 7–11 notches (Legend and 825S).

### REMOVAL & INSTALLATION

1. Remove the adjusting nut from the equalizer mounted on the console and separate the cable from the equalizer.

2. Set the parking brake lever to a fully released position and remove the

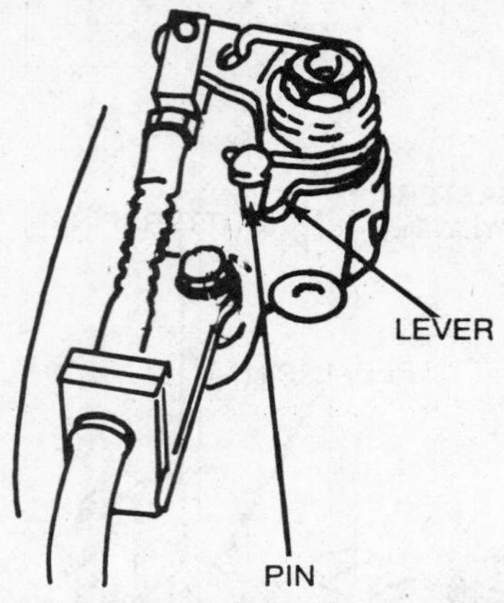

**View of the rear brake cable lever—Integra—Legend and 825S is similar**

cotter pin from the rear caliper assembly.

3. After removing the cotter pin, pull out the pin which connects the cable and the lever.

4. Detach the cable from the guides at the calipers and remove the cable.

5. To install, reverse the removal procedure, making sure grease is applied to the cable and the guides.

# CHASSIS ELECTRICAL

## Heater Blower Motor

### REMOVAL & INSTALLATION

#### Integra

**WITHOUT AIR CONDITIONING**

1. Remove the glove box.

2. Remove the frame to the glove box.

3. Remove the blower duct.

4. Disconnect the wire connections from the blower.

5. Remove the blower assembly.

6. To install, reverse the removal procedures. Check that there are no air leaks in the blower case.

**WITH AIR CONDITIONING**

1. Remove the glove box.

2. Remove the frame to the glove box and the side frame.

3. Remove the bolts and the retractor control unit with the bracket.

4. Unbolt the dashboard lower bracket **A** from bracket **B** and insert a small prybar to pry a 12–15mm clearance, to ease in the removal of the evaporator.

5. Loosen the sealing band toward the right side.

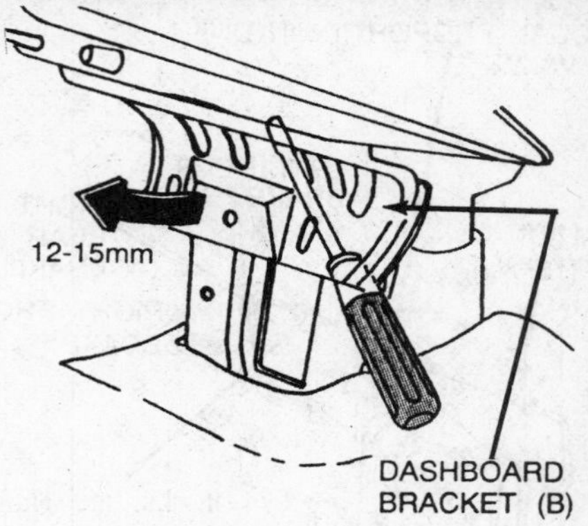

**Lower heater bracket "B"—Integra**

6. Disconnect the wire connections from the blower.

7. Remove the blower bolts and the blower assembly.

8. To install, reverse the removal procedures. Check that there are no air leaks in the blower case.

#### Legend and 825S

**CAUTION**

***This procedure requires discharging the air conditioning system. This should only be performed by people experienced with air conditioning recharging procedures.***

1. Disconnect the negative battery cable.

2. Remove the glove box lower cover screws and the cover.

3. Remove the glove box screws and the glove box.

4. Remove the glove box frame screws, the glove box frame, the clips and the heater duct.

5. Discharge the refrigerant from the air conditioning system.

6. Remove the evaporator.

7. Disconnect the wire connectors from the blower.

8. Remove the blower assembly bolts and the assembly.

9. To install, reverse the removal procedures. Check that there are no air leaks in the blower case. Recharge the air conditioning system.

## Heater Core

### REMOVAL & INSTALLATION

#### Integra

1. Drain the cooling system.

2. Disconnect the heater hoses at the firewall.

**NOTE: Coolant will run out of the heater hoses when disconnected, place a drain pan under them to catch the coolant.**

3. Disconnect the heater valve cable from the heater valve.

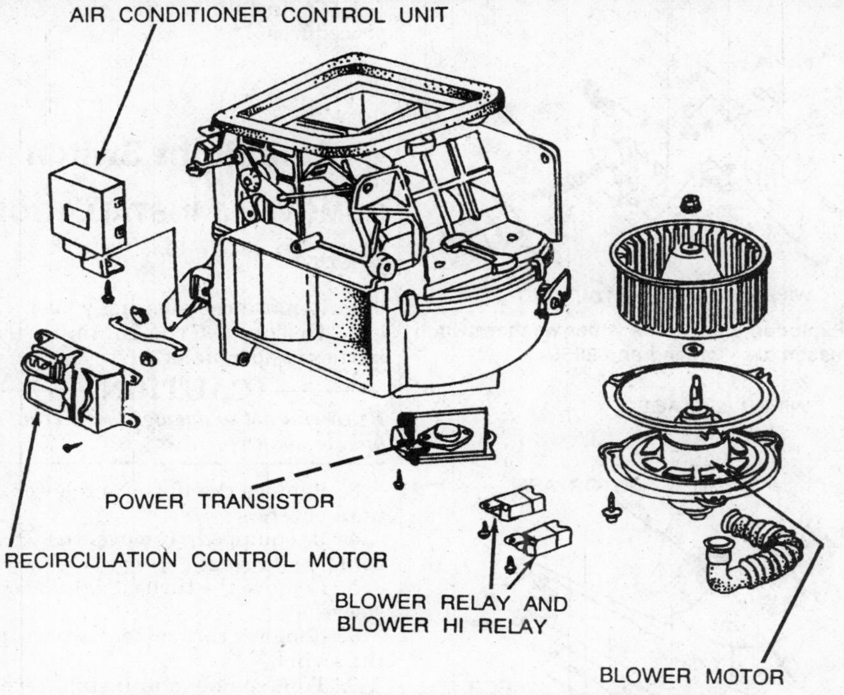


**Exploded view of the blower motor assembly—Legend and 825S**

4. Remove the heater assembly lower mounting nut.
5. Remove the console.
6. Disconnect the air mix cable from the heater.
7. Remove the dashboard assembly.
8. Disconnect the wire harness at the connector.
9. Remove the heater bolts and pull the heater assembly away from the body.
10. Remove the self tapping screws and the retaining plate.
11. Pull the heater core from the heater housing.
12. To install, reverse the removal procedures and observe the following:
    a. Apply sealant to the grommets.
    b. Do not interchange the inlet and outlet hoses.
    c. Bleed the cooling system.
    d. Connect all cable and adjust them properly.

### *Legend and 825S*

1. Drain the cooling system.
2. Disconnect the heater hoses at the firewall.

**NOTE: Coolant will run out of the heater hoses when disconnected, place a drain pan under them to catch the coolant.**

3. Remove the dashboard.
4. Disconnect the wire harness and the vacuum hoses.
5. Remove the heater mounting bolts and pull the heater assembly away from the body.

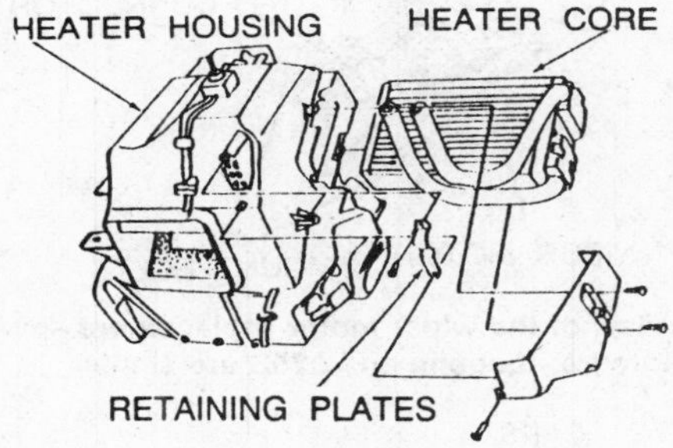


**Heater core replacement—Integra**

6. Remove the self tapping screws and the retaining plate.
7. Pull the heater core from the heater housing.
8. To install, reverse the removal procedures and observe the following:
    a. Apply sealant to the grommets.
    b. Do not interchange the inlet and outlet hoses.
    c. Bleed the cooling system.
    d. Connect all cables and adjust them properly.

## Radio

### REMOVAL & INSTALLATION

#### *Integra*

1. Disconnect the negative battery cable at the battery.
2. Remove the ashtray, the screws and the ashtray holder assembly.
3. Remove the screws from the rear radio bracket.
4. Disconnect the wiring harness and the antenna lead from the radio.
5. Slide out and remove the radio.
6. To install, reverse the removal procedures.

#### *Legend and 825S*

1. Disconnect the negative battery cable at the battery.
2. Remove the front console and the radio trim panel.
3. Remove the screws from the front of the radio panel.
4. Disconnect the wire harness and the antenna lead from the radio.
5. Slide out and remove the radio.
6. To install, reverse the removal procedures.

## Windshield Wiper Switch

### REMOVAL & INSTALLATION

#### *Integra*

1. Remove the steering wheel.
2. Disconnect the column wiring harness and coupler.

**CAUTION**

***Be careful not to damage the steering column or shaft.***

3. Remove the upper and lower column covers.
4. If equipped, remove the cruise control slip ring.
5. Remove the turn signal canceling sleeve.
6. Remove the switch retaining screws and the switch.
7. To assemble and install, reverse the removal procedures.

#### *Legend and 825S*

1. Remove the negative (−) cable from the battery.
2. Remove the dashboard lower panel and disconnect the 6-pin and 8-pin connectors from the wiper control unit on the lower panel.
3. Disconnect the 10-pin connector from the wiper/washer switch.
4. Remove the steering wheel, the steering column lower cover and disconnect the 6-pin connector from the winter position switch.
5. Remove the upper cover from the steering column.
6. Remove the screws and slide the wiper/washer switch out of the housing.
7. To install, reverse the removal procedures.

## Windshield Wiper Motor

### REMOVAL & INSTALLATION

1. Remove the negative (−) cable from the battery.
2. Remove the wiper arm nuts and the wiper arms.
3. Remove the front air scoop and hood seal located over the wiper linkage at the bottom of the windshield.
4. Disconnect the linkage from the wiper motor.
5. Remove the wiper motor water seal cover clamp and the cover.
6. Disconnect the wiper motor electrical connector, remove the motor mounting bolts and remove the motor.
7. To install, reverse the removal procedures. Coat the linkage joints with grease and make sure the linkage moves smoothly.

## Instrument Cluster

### REMOVAL & INSTALLATION

#### Integra

1. Remove the right and left switches from the instrument panel then disconnect the wire connecters from the switches.
2. Remove the upper instrument panel caps, the screws and the panel.
3. Remove the screws under the holes made by removing the switches.
4. Remove the rubber seal, loosen the column cover screws and the instrument panel.
5. Remove the gauge assembly screws and lift out the gauge assembly to disconnect the wire connectors.
6. Disconnect the speedometer cable and remove the gauge assembly.
7. To install, reverse the removal procedures.

#### Legend and 825S

**CAUTION**

***The Legend and 825S and Legend Coupe LS are equipped with a Supplemental Restraint System (SRS). Improper maintenance, including incorrect removal and installation of related components, can lead to personal injury caused by unintentional activation of the airbag. Related components on these models should be serviced only by authorized service technicians.***

1. Remove the screws and the instrument panel by disconnecting the wire harness.

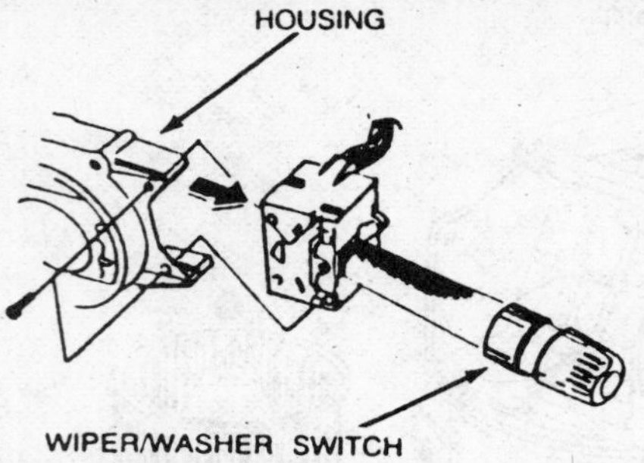


**Exploded view of the wiper/washer switch assembly—Legend and 825S**

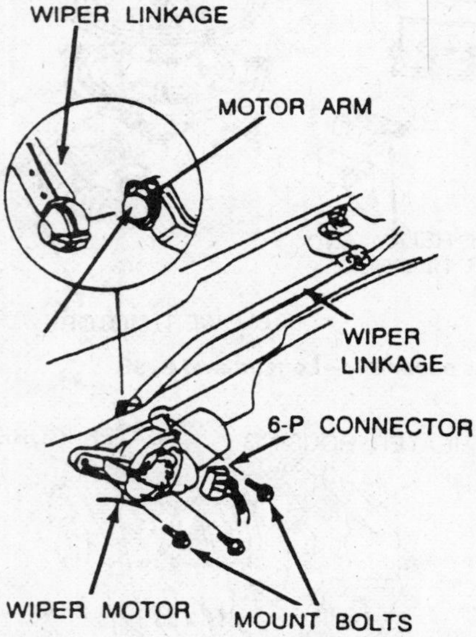


**View of the wiper motor replacement—Integra—Legend and 825S are similar**

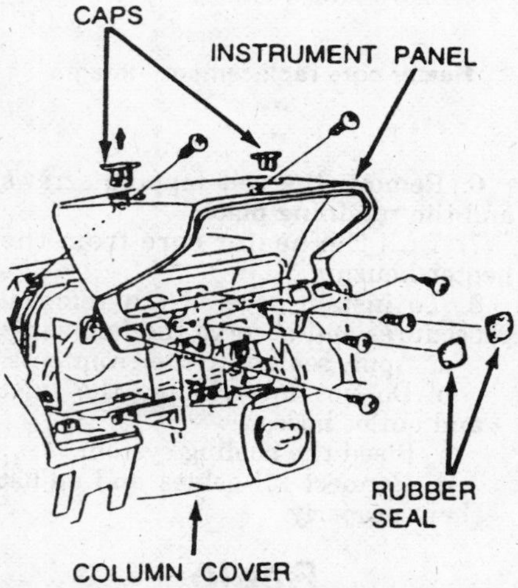


**Instrument cluster replacement—Integra**

2. Remove the gauge assembly screws and lift out the gauge assembly to disconnect the wire connectors.
3. Disconnect the speedometer cable and remove the gauge assembly.
4. To install, reverse the removal procedures.

## Headlight Switch

### REMOVAL & INSTALLATION

#### Integra

1. Remove the steering wheel.
2. Disconnect the column wiring harness and coupler.

**CAUTION**

***Be careful not to damage the steering column or shaft.***

3. Remove the upper and lower column covers.
4. If equipped, remove the cruise control slip ring.
5. Remove the turn signal canceling sleeve.
6. Remove the switch screws and the switch.
7. To assemble and install, reverse the above procedures.

#### Legend and 825S

1. Remove the negative (−) cable from the battery.
2. Remove the dashboard lower panel and disconnect the 14-pin connector from the lighting switch.
3. Remove the steering wheel, the steering column lower cover and disconnect the 3-pin connector from the slip ring.

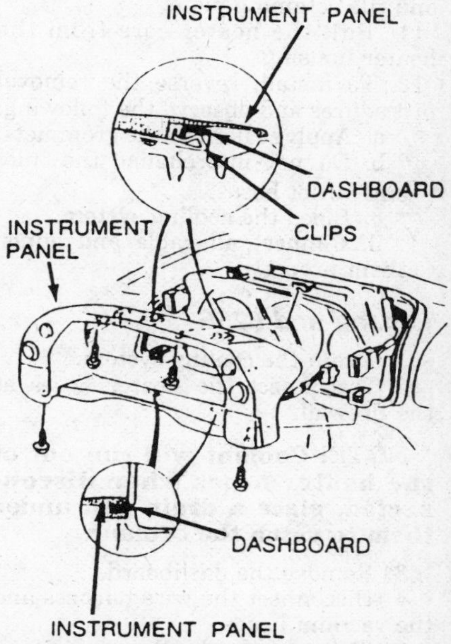


**Exploded view of the instrument panel—Legend and 825S**

4. Remove the upper cover from the steering column.

5. Remove the screws and slide the lighting switch out of the housing.

6. To install, reverse the removal procedures.

## Stoplight Switch

### REMOVAL & INSTALLATION

1. Loosen the brake light switch locknut and back off the brake light switch until it does not touch the brake pedal.

2. Loosen the pushrod locknut and screw the pushrod in or out until the pedal height (from the floor) is 7.05 in. (179mm) for Integra or 6.69 in. (171mm) for Legend and 825S and tighten the locknut.

3. Screw in the brake light switch until the plunger is fully depressed (threaded end touching the pad on the pedal arm).

4. Back off the switch ½ turn and tighten the locknut.

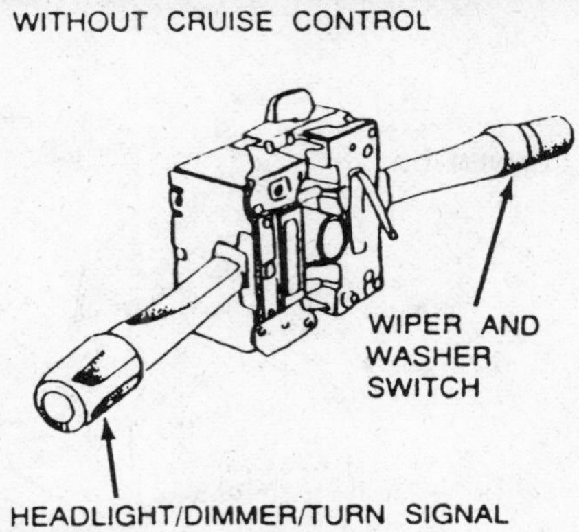


**Headlight switch replacement – Integra**

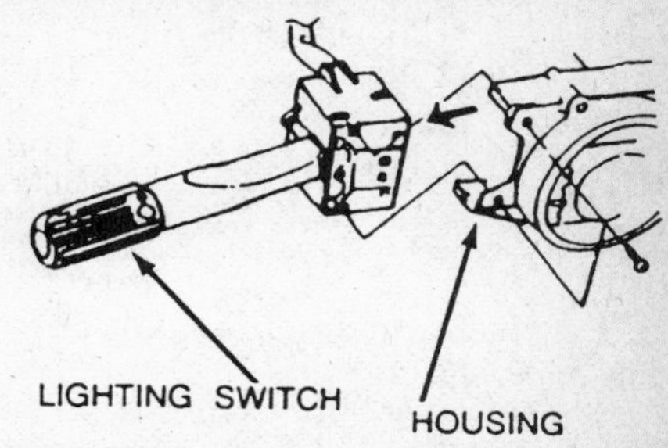


**Exploded view of the headlight switch – Legend and 825S**

## Fuses and Circuit Breakers

### LOCATION

#### *Integra*

The Integra fuse/relay box is located in the interior on the drivers side below the dashboard. There is also a main fuse box located in the engine compartment containing 2 – 45 amp and a 65 amp fuse. In addition to these, there is a 10 amp hazard fuse located at the positive battery terminal.

#### *Legend and 825S*

The Legend and 825S fuse box is located in the interior on the drivers side below the dashboard. There is also a relay box located in the left side of the engine compartment.

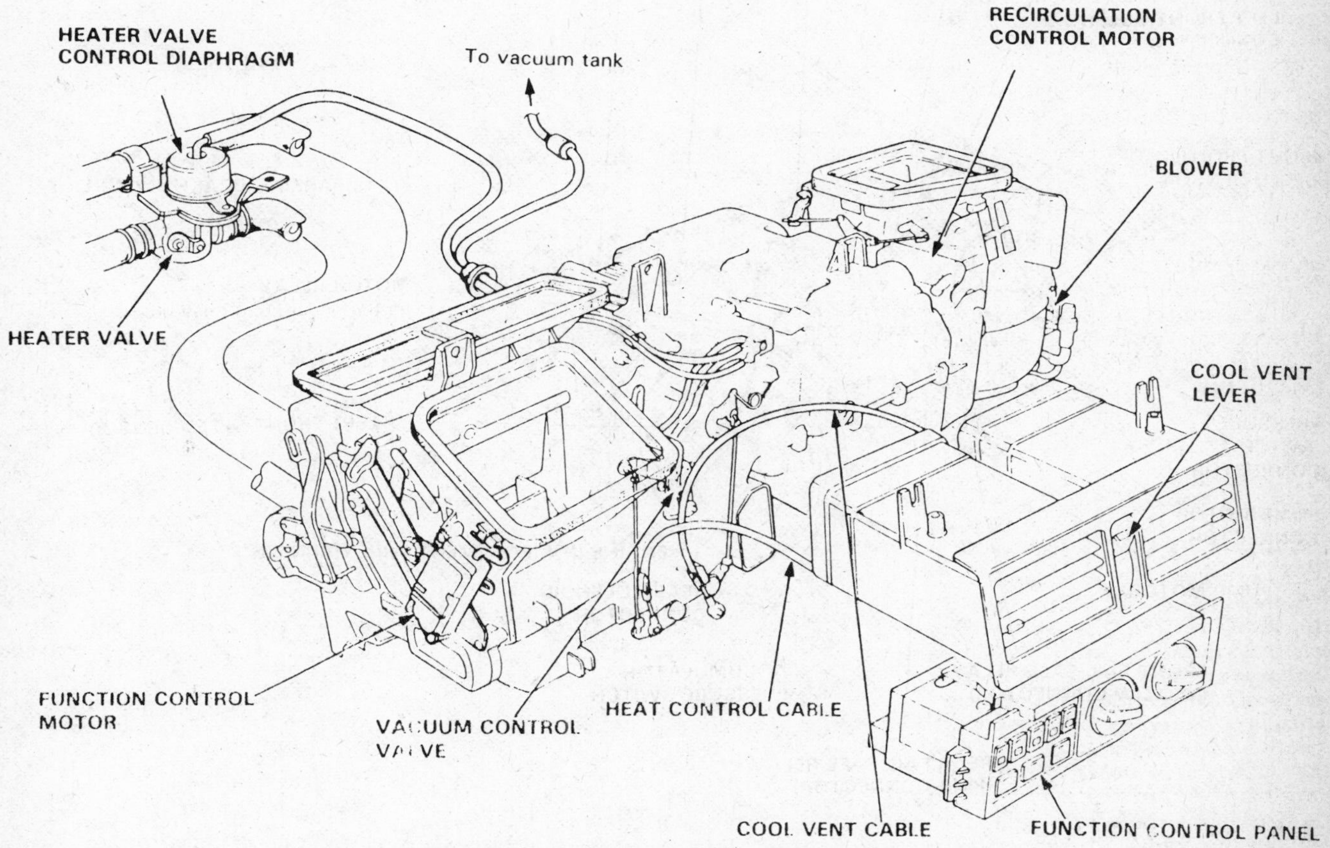


**View of the air and heating system components**

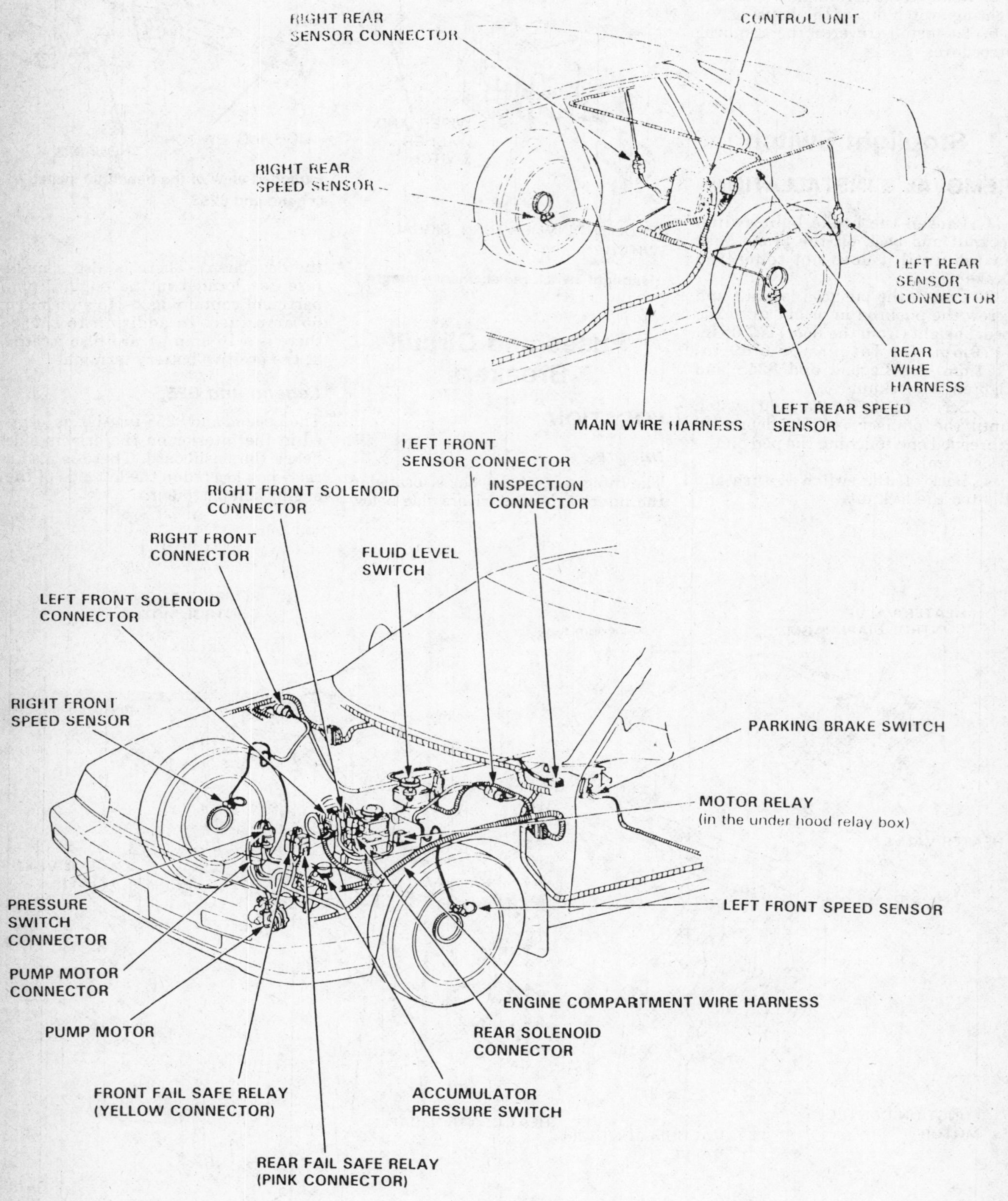
RIGHT REAR
SENSOR CONNECTOR
CONTROL UNIT
RIGHT REAR
SPEED SENSOR
LEFT REAR
SENSOR
CONNECTOR
REAR
WIRE
HARNESS
MAIN WIRE HARNESS
LEFT REAR SPEED
SENSOR
LEFT FRONT
SENSOR CONNECTOR
RIGHT FRONT SOLENOID
CONNECTOR
INSPECTION
CONNECTOR
RIGHT FRONT
CONNECTOR
FLUID LEVEL
SWITCH
LEFT FRONT SOLENOID
CONNECTOR
RIGHT FRONT
SPEED SENSOR
PARKING BRAKE SWITCH
MOTOR RELAY
(in the under hood relay box)
LEFT FRONT SPEED SENSOR
PRESSURE
SWITCH
CONNECTOR
PUMP MOTOR
CONNECTOR
ENGINE COMPARTMENT WIRE HARNESS
PUMP MOTOR
REAR SOLENOID
CONNECTOR
FRONT FAIL SAFE RELAY
(YELLOW CONNECTOR)
ACCUMULATOR
PRESSURE SWITCH
REAR FAIL SAFE RELAY
(PINK CONNECTOR)

Location of the anti-lock brake system components

# Audi 2

## 80, 90, 100, 200, 4000, 5000, Coupe, Quattro

# SERIAL NUMBER IDENTIFICATION

## Vehicle Identification Plate

### *1983–87 4000S and Coupe Models*

The vehicle identification number (VIN) is located on the left (driver's side) windshield pillar and in the engine compartment on the firewall.

### 1983–88 5000S Models and 1988–90 Models

The vehicle identification number (VIN) is located on a plate on top of the instrument panel. The (VIN) number is visible from outside through the left side of the windshield. The (VIN) number is also stamped into the upper right corner of the firewall. The vehicle identification plate is mounted on the right front wheel housing.

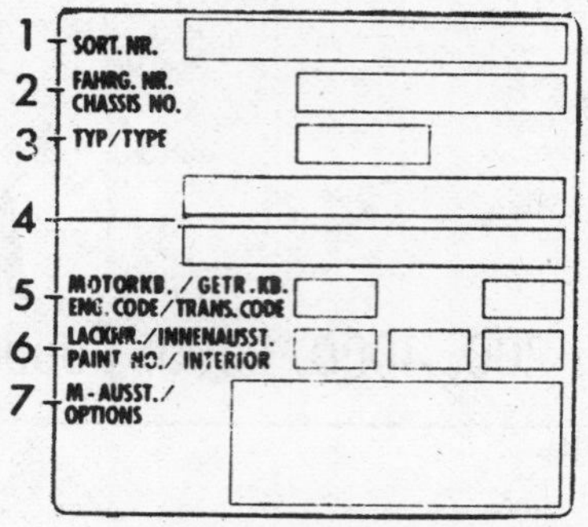


1. Production control no.
2. Vehicle identification no.
3. Type code number
4. Type designation
5. Engine and transmission code letter
6. Paint no./Interior
7. Optional equipment no.'s.

**Vehicle identification label showing the serial number location**

## Engine Number

### *4 Cylinder Engines*

The engine serial number is stamped into the left rear side of the engine block, below the cylinder head, next to the distributor.

### *5 Cylinder Engines*

The engine serial number is stamped into the left rear side of the engine block. In addition to the serial number, an engine code number is stamped into the starter end of the engine block, below the cylinder head mounting surface. This number indicates the exact, original cylinder bore of the engine, when manufactured.

## Vehicle Identification Label

On all models, a vehicle identification label is located on the inside of the luggage compartment lid.

## ENGINE IDENTIFICATION

| Year | Model | Engine Displacement cu. in. (cc/liter) | Engine Series Identification | No. of Cylinders | Engine Type |
|---|---|---|---|---|---|
| 1983 | 4000 | 105 (1715/1.7) | WT | 4 | OHC |
| | 4000 Coupe | 131 (2144/2.1) | WE | 5 | OHC |
| | 4000 Diesel | 97 (1588/1.6) | CR, CY | 4 | OHC |
| | 5000 Turbo | 131 (2144/2.1) | WK | 5 | OHC |
| | 5000 | 131 (2144/2.1) | WD | 5 | OHC |
| | 5000 Diesel | 121 (1986/2.0) | DE | 5 | OHC |
| | Quattro Turbo | 131 (2144/2.1) | WX | 5 | OHC |
| 1984 | 4000 | 109 (1780/1.8) | JN | 4 | OHC |
| | 4000 Quattro | 136 (2226/2.2) | KX | 5 | OHC |
| | 4000 Coupe | 131 (2144/2.1) | WE | 5 | OHC |
| | Coupe GT | 131 (2144/2.1) | KX | 5 | OHC |
| | Quattro Coupe | 131 (2144/2.1) | WU | 5 | OHC |
| | 5000 Turbo | 131 (2144/2.1) | KH | 5 | OHC |
| | 5000 | 131 (2144/2.1) | WU | 5 | OHC |
| | Quattro | 131 (2144/2.1) | WX | 5 | OHC |
| | Coupe | 131 (2144/2.1) | KM | 5 | OHC |
| 1985 | 4000 Coupe | 136 (2226/2.2) | KX | 5 | OHC |
| | 4000 S | 109 (1780/1.8) | MG | 4 | OHC |
| | 4000 S | 136 (2226/2.2) | KX | 5 | OHC |
| | Quattro | 136 (2226/2.2) | KZ | 5 | OHC |
| | Quattro Turbo | 131 (2144/2.1) | WX | 5 | OHC |

## ENGINE IDENTIFICATION

| Year | Model | Engine Displacement cu. in. (cc/liter) | Engine Series Identification | No. of Cylinders | Engine Type |
|---|---|---|---|---|---|
| **1985** | 5000 Turbo | 131 (2144/2.1) | KH | 5 | OHC |
| | 5000 S Wagon | 136 (2226/2.2) | KX, KZ | 5 | OHC |
| | 5000 S | 136 (2226/2.2) | KZ | 5 | OHC |
| | 5000 S Turbo | 131 (2144/2.1) | MC | 5 | OHC |
| | Coupe GT | 136 (2226/2.2) | KX | 5 | OHC |
| **1986** | 4000 Coupe | 136 (2226/2.2) | KX | 5 | OHC |
| | 4000 S | 109 (1780/1.8) | MG | 4 | OHC |
| | 4000 CS Quattro | 136 (2226/2.2) | JT | 5 | OHC |
| | 5000 Turbo | 136 (2226/2.2) | MC | 5 | OHC |
| | 5000 CS Turbo | 136 (2226/2.2) | MC | 5 | OHC |
| | 5000 CS Quattro Turbo | 136 (2226/2.2) | MC | 5 | OHC |
| | 5000 CS Quattro Wagon | 136 (2226/2.2) | MC | 5 | OHC |
| | 5000 S | 136 (2226/2.2) | MC | 5 | OHC |
| | 5000 S Wagon | 136 (2226/2.2) | MC | 5 | OHC |
| | Coupe GT | 136 (2226/2.2) | KX | 5 | OHC |
| **1987** | 4000 Coupe | 136 (2226/2.2) | KX | 5 | OHC |
| | 4000 S | 109 (1780/1.8) | MG | 4 | OHC |
| | 4000 CS Quattro | 136 (2226/2.2) | JT | 5 | OHC |
| | 5000 CS Turbo | 136 (2226/2.2) | MC | 5 | OHC |
| | 5000 CS Quattro Turbo | 136 (2226/2.2) | MC | 5 | OHC |
| | 5000 CS Quattro Wagon | 136 (2226/2.2) | MC | 5 | OHC |
| | 5000 S | 136 (2226/2.2) | MC | 5 | OHC |
| | 5000 S Wagon | 136 (2226/2.2) | MC | 5 | OHC |
| | Coupe GT | 136 (2226/2.2) | KX | 5 | OHC |
| **1988** | 80 | 121 (1983/2.0) | 3A | 4 | OHC |
| | 80 Quattro | 141 (2309/2.3) | NG | 5 | OHC |
| | 90 ① | 121 (1983/2.0) | 3A | 4 | OHC |
| | 90 | 141 (2309/2.3) | NG | 5 | OHC |
| | 90 Quattro | 141 (2309/2.3) | NG | 5 | OHC |
| | 5000 CS Turbo | 136 (2226/2.2) | MC | 5 | OHC |
| | 5000 CS Quattro Turbo | 136 (2226/2.2) | MC | 5 | OHC |
| | 5000 CS Quattro Wagon | 136 (2226/2.2) | MC | 5 | OHC |
| | 5000 S | 141 (2309/2.3) | NF | 5 | OHC |
| | 5000 S Wagon | 141 (2309/2.3) | NF | 5 | OHC |
| | 5000 S Quattro | 141 (2309/2.3) | NF | 5 | OHC |
| **1989-90** | 80 | 121 (1983/2.0) | 3A | 4 | OHC |
| | 80 Quattro | 141 (2309/2.3) | NG | 5 | OHC |
| | 90 | 121 (1983/2.0) | 3A | 4 | OHC |
| | 90 | 141 (2309/2.3) | NG | 5 | OHC |
| | 90 Quattro | 141 (2309/2.3) | NG | 5 | OHC |
| | 100 | 141 (2309/2.3) | NF | 5 | OHC |
| | 100 Quattro | 141 (2309/2.3) | NF | 5 | OHC |
| | 200 | 136 (2226/2.2) | MC | 5 | OHC |
| | 200 Quattro | 136 (2226/2.2) | MC | 5 | OHC |

① With automatic transmission

## GENERAL ENGINE SPECIFICATIONS

| Year | Model | Engine Displacement cu. in. (cc) | Fuel System Type | Net Horsepower @ rpm | Net Torque @ rpm (ft. lbs.) | Bore × Stroke (in.) | Compression Ratio | Oil Pressure @ rpm |
|---|---|---|---|---|---|---|---|---|
| 1983 | 4000 | 105 (1715) | CIS | 74 @ 5000 | 86.9 @ 3000 | 3.13 × 3.40 | 8.2:1 | 29 @ 2000 |
| | 4000 Coupe | 131 (2144) | CIS | 100 @ 5100 | 112.3 @ 3000 | 3.12 × 3.40 | 8.0:1 | 29 @ 2000 |
| | 4000 Diesel | 97 (1588) | DFI | 52 @ 4800 | 71.5 @ 2000 | 3.01 × 3.40 | 23.0:1 | 29 @ 2000 |
| | 5000 | 131 (2144) | CIS | 100 @ 5100 | 122.3 @ 4000 | 3.13 × 3.40 | 8.2:1 | 29 @ 2000 |
| | 5000 Turbo | 131 (2144) | CIS | 130 @ 5400 | 142 @ 3000 | 3.12 × 3.40 | 7.0:1 | 29 @ 2000 |
| | 5000 Diesel | 121 (1986) | DFI | 67 @ 4800 | 86.4 @ 3000 | 3.09 × 3.40 | 23.0:1 | 28 @ 2000 |
| | Quattro Turbo | 131 (2144) | CIS | 130 @ 5400 | 142 @ 3000 | 3.12 × 3.40 | 7.0:1 | 29 @ 2000 |
| 1984 | 4000 | 109 (1780) | CIS-E | 88 @ 5500 | 101 @ 3000 | 3.19 × 3.40 | 8.5:1 | 29 @ 2000 |
| | 4000 Quattro | 136 (2226) | CIS-E | 115 @ 5500 | 126 @ 3000 | 3.19 × 3.40 | 8.5:1 | 29 @ 2000 |
| | 4000 Coupe | 131 (2144) | CIS | 100 @ 5100 | 112.3 @ 3000 | 3.12 × 3.40 | 8.0:1 | 29 @ 2000 |
| | Coupe GT | 131 (2144) | CIS-E | 100 @ 5100 | 112.3 @ 3000 | 3.12 × 3.40 | 8.2:1 | 29 @ 2000 |
| | Quattro Coupe | 131 (2144) | CIS-E | 160 @ 5500 | 170 @ 3000 | 3.12 × 3.40 | 8.2:1 | 29 @ 2000 |
| | 5000 | 131 (2144) | CIS | 100 @ 5500 | 112 @ 3000 | 3.13 × 3.40 | 8.2:1 | 29 @ 2000 |
| | 5000 Turbo | 131 (2144) | CIS-E | 140 @ 5500 | 149 @ 2500 | 3.13 × 3.40 | 8.3:1 | 29 @ 2000 |
| | Quattro | 131 (2144) | CIS | 160 @ 5500 | 170 @ 3000 | 3.12 × 3.40 | 7.0:1 | 29 @ 2000 |
| | Coupe | 131 (2144) | CIS | 100 @ 5100 | 112.3 @ 3000 | 3.12 × 3.40 | 8.2:1 | 29 @ 2000 |
| 1985 | 4000 S | 109 (1780) | CIS-E | 88 @ 5500 | 101 @ 3000 | 3.19 × 3.40 | 8.5:1 | 29 @ 2000 |
| | 4000 S | 136 (2226) | CIS-E | 110 @ 5500 | 122 @ 2500 | 3.19 × 3.40 | 8.5:1 | 29 @ 2000 |
| | 4000 Coupe | 136 (2226) | CIS-E | 110 @ 5500 | 122 @ 2500 | 3.19 × 3.40 | 8.5:1 | 29 @ 2000 |
| | Quattro | 136 (2226) | CIS | 115 @ 5500 | 126 @ 3000 | 3.19 × 3.40 | 8.5:1 | 29 @ 2000 |
| | Quattro Turbo | 131 (2144) | CIS | 160 @ 5500 | 170 @ 3000 | 3.12 × 3.40 | 7.0:1 | 29 @ 2000 |
| | 5000 S | 136 (2226) | CIS-E | 110 @ 5500 | 122 @ 2500 | 3.19 × 3.40 | 8.5:1 | 29 @ 2000 |
| | 5000 S Turbo | 131 (2144) | CIS-E | 140 @ 5500 | 149 @ 2500 | 3.19 × 3.40 | 8.3:1 | 29 @ 2000 |
| | 5000 S Wagon | 136 (2226) | CIS-E | 110 @ 5500 | 122 @ 2500 | 3.19 × 3.40 | 8.5:1 | 29 @ 2000 |
| | 5000 Turbo | 131 (2144) | CIS-E | 140 @ 5500 | 149 @ 2500 | 3.13 × 3.40 | 8.3:1 | 29 @ 2000 |
| | Coupe GT | 136 (2226) | CIS-E | 110 @ 5500 | 110.6 @ 2500 | 3.19 × 3.40 | 8.5:1 | 29 @ 2000 |
| 1986 | 4000 S | 109 (1780) | CIS-E | 88 @ 5500 | 101 @ 3000 | 3.19 × 3.40 | 8.5:1 | 29 @ 2000 |
| | 4000 Coupe | 136 (2226) | CIS-E | 110 @ 5500 | 122 @ 2500 | 3.19 × 3.40 | 8.5:1 | 29 @ 2000 |
| | 4000 CS Quattro | 136 (2226) | CIS-E | 115 @ 5500 | 126 @ 3000 | 3.19 × 3.40 | 8.5:1 | 29 @ 2000 |
| | 5000 S | 136 (2226) | CIS-E | 110 @ 5500 | 122 @ 2500 | 3.19 × 3.40 | 8.5:1 | 29 @ 2000 |
| | 5000 S Wagon | 136 (2226) | CIS-E | 110 @ 5500 | 122 @ 2500 | 3.19 × 3.40 | 8.5:1 | 29 @ 2000 |
| | 5000 CS Turbo | 136 (2226) | CIS-E | 158 @ 5500 | 166 @ 3000 | 3.19 × 3.40 | 7.8:1 | 29 @ 2000 |
| | 5000 Turbo | 136 (2226) | CIS-E | 160 @ 5500 | 166 @ 3000 | 3.19 × 3.40 | 7.8:1 | 29 @ 2000 |
| | 5000 Quattro Turbo | 136 (2226) | CIS-E | 158 @ 5500 | 166 @ 3000 | 3.19 × 3.40 | 7.8:1 | 29 @ 2000 |
| | 5000 CS Quattro Wagon | 136 (2226) | CIS-E | 158 @ 5500 | 166 @ 3000 | 3.19 × 3.40 | 7.8:1 | 29 @ 2000 |
| | Coupe GT | 136 (2226) | CIS-E | 110 @ 5500 | 122 @ 2500 | 3.19 × 3.40 | 8.5:1 | 29 @ 2000 |
| 1987 | 4000 S | 109 (1780) | CIS-E | 88 @ 5500 | 101 @ 3000 | 3.19 × 3.40 | 8.5:1 | 29 @ 2000 |
| | 4000 Coupe | 136 (2226) | CIS-E | 110 @ 5500 | 122 @ 2500 | 3.19 × 3.40 | 8.5:1 | 29 @ 2000 |
| | 4000 CS Quattro | 136 (2226) | CIS-E | 115 @ 5500 | 126 @ 3000 | 3.19 × 3.40 | 8.5:1 | 29 @ 2000 |
| | 5000 S | 136 (2226) | CIS-E | 110 @ 5500 | 122 @ 2500 | 3.19 × 3.40 | 8.5:1 | 29 @ 2000 |
| | 5000 S Wagon | 136 (2226) | CIS-E | 110 @ 5500 | 122 @ 2500 | 3.19 × 3.40 | 8.5:1 | 29 @ 2000 |
| | 5000 CS Turbo | 136 (2226) | CIS-E | 158 @ 5500 | 166 @ 3000 | 3.19 × 3.40 | 7.8:1 | 29 @ 2000 |
| | 5000 Turbo | 136 (2226) | CIS-E | 160 @ 5500 | 166 @ 3000 | 3.19 × 3.40 | 7.8:1 | 29 @ 2000 |

## GENERAL ENGINE SPECIFICATIONS

| Year | Model | Engine Displacement cu. in. (cc) | Fuel System Type | Net Horsepower @ rpm | Net Torque @ rpm (ft. lbs.) | Bore × Stroke (in.) | Compression Ratio | Oil Pressure @ rpm |
|---|---|---|---|---|---|---|---|---|
| 1987 | 5000 Quattro Turbo | 136 (2226) | CIS-E | 158 @ 5500 | 166 @ 3000 | 3.19 × 3.40 | 7.8:1 | 29 @ 2000 |
| | 5000 CS Quattro Wagon | 136 (2226) | CIS-E | 158 @ 5500 | 166 @ 3000 | 3.19 × 3.40 | 7.8:1 | 29 @ 2000 |
| | Coupe GT | 136 (2226) | CIS-E | 110 @ 5500 | 122 @ 2500 | 3.19 × 3.40 | 8.5:1 | 29 @ 2000 |
| 1988 | 80 | 121 (1983) | CIS-M | 108 @ 5300 | 121 @ 3250 | 3.65 × 3.40 | 10.4:1 | 29 @ 2000 |
| | 80 Quattro | 141 (2309) | CIS-E | 130 @ 5700 | 140 @ 4500 | 3.25 × 3.40 | 10.0:1 | 29 @ 2000 |
| | 90 ① | 121 (1983) | CIS-M | 108 @ 5300 | 121 @ 3250 | 3.65 × 3.40 | 10.4:1 | 29 @ 2000 |
| | 90 | 141 (2309) | CIS-E | 130 @ 5700 | 140 @ 4500 | 3.25 × 3.40 | 10.0:1 | 29 @ 2000 |
| | 90 Quattro | 141 (2309) | CIS-E | 130 @ 5700 | 140 @ 4500 | 3.25 × 3.40 | 10.0:1 | 29 @ 2000 |
| | 5000 CS Turbo | 136 (2226) | CIS-E | 158 @ 5500 | 166 @ 3000 | 3.19 × 3.40 | 7.8:1 | 29 @ 2000 |
| | 5000 CS Quattro Turbo | 136 (2226) | CIS-E | 158 @ 5500 | 166 @ 3000 | 3.19 × 3.40 | 7.8:1 | 29 @ 2000 |
| | 5000 CS Quattro Wagon | 136 (2226) | CIS-E | 158 @ 5500 | 166 @ 3000 | 3.19 × 3.40 | 7.8:1 | 29 @ 2000 |
| | 5000 S | 141 (2309) | KE-III | 130 @ 5600 | 140 @ 4000 | 3.25 × 3.40 | 10.0:1 | 29 @ 2000 |
| | 5000 S Wagon | 141 (2309) | KE-III | 130 @ 5600 | 140 @ 4000 | 3.25 × 3.40 | 10.0:1 | 29 @ 2000 |
| | 5000 S Quattro | 141 (2309) | KE-III | 130 @ 5600 | 140 @ 4000 | 3.25 × 3.40 | 10.0:1 | 29 @ 2000 |
| 1989-90 | 80 | 121 (1983) | CIS | 108 @ 5300 | 121 @ 3200 | 3.25 × 3.65 | 10.5:1 | 29 @ 2000 |
| | 80 Quattro | 141 (2309) | CIS-EIII | 130 @ 5700 | 140 @ 4500 | 3.25 × 3.40 | 10.0:1 | 29 @ 2000 |
| | 90 ① | 121 (1983) | CIS | 108 @ 5300 | 121 @ 3200 | 3.25 × 3.65 | 10.5:1 | 29 @ 2000 |
| | 90 | 141 (2309) | CIS-EIII | 130 @ 5700 | 140 @ 4500 | 3.25 × 3.40 | 10.0:1 | 29 @ 2000 |
| | 90 Quattro | 141 (2309) | CIS-EIII | 130 @ 5700 | 140 @ 4500 | 3.25 × 3.40 | 10.0:1 | 29 @ 2000 |
| | 100 | 141 (2309) | CIS-EIII | 130 @ 5700 | 140 @ 4500 | 3.25 × 3.40 | 10.0:1 | 29 @ 2000 |
| | 100 Quattro | 141 (2309) | CIS-EIII | 130 @ 5700 | 140 @ 4500 | 3.25 × 3.40 | 10.0:1 | 29 @ 2000 |
| | 200 | 136 (2226) | CIS | 162 @ 5500 | 177 @ 3000 | 3.19 × 3.40 | 7.8:1 | 29 @ 2000 |
| | 200 Quattro | 136 (2226) | CIS | 162 @ 5500 | 177 @ 3000 | 3.19 × 3.40 | 7.8:1 | 29 @ 2000 |

① With automatic transmission
KE-III—KE-III Jetronic injection

## GASOLINE ENGINE TUNE-UP SPECIFICATIONS

| Year | Model | Engine Displacement cu. in. (cc) | Spark Plugs Type | Spark Plugs Gap (in.) | Ignition Timing (deg.) MT | Ignition Timing (deg.) AT | Compression Pressure (psi) | Fuel Pump (psi) | Idle Speed (rpm) MT | Idle Speed (rpm) AT | Valve Clearance In. | Valve Clearance Ex. |
|---|---|---|---|---|---|---|---|---|---|---|---|---|
| 1983 | 4000 | 105 (1715) | N8Y | .028 | 3A | 3A | NA | 64–74 | 850–1000 | 850–1000 | .008–.012 | .016–.020 |
| | 4000 Coupe | 131 (2144) | N8Y | .028 | 6B | 3A | NA | 64–74 | 725–925 | 850–1000 | .008–.012 | .016–.020 |
| | 5000 | 131 (2144) | N8Y | .028 | 6B | 3A | NA | 64–74 | 850–1000 | 850–1000 | .008–.012 | .016–.020 |
| | 5000 Turbo | 131 (2144) | N8Y | .028 | 21B | 21B | NA | 72–82 | 790–910 | 790–910 | .008–.012 | .016–.020 |
| | Quattro Turbo | 131 (2144) | N8Y | .028 | ① | ① | NA | 68–78 | 790–910 | 790–910 | .008–.012 | .016–.020 |
| 1984 | 4000 | 109 (1780) | N8Y | .032 | 6B | 6B | NA | 75–85 | 850–1000 | 850–1000 | Hyd. | Hyd. |
| | 4000 Coupe | 131 (2144) | N8GY | .032 | 8B | 8B | NA | 75–81 | 750–850 | 750–850 | Hyd. | Hyd. |

## GASOLINE ENGINE TUNE-UP SPECIFICATIONS

| Year | Model | Engine Displacement cu. in. (cc) | Spark Plugs Type | Spark Plugs Gap (in.) | Ignition Timing (deg.) MT | Ignition Timing (deg.) AT | Compression Pressure (psi) | Fuel Pump (psi) | Idle Speed (rpm) MT | Idle Speed (rpm) AT | Valve Clearance In. | Valve Clearance Ex. |
|---|---|---|---|---|---|---|---|---|---|---|---|---|
| 1984 | Quattro 4000 | 136 (2226) | N8GY | .028 | 8B | 8B | NA | 75–81 | 750–850 | 750–850 | Hyd. | Hyd. |
| | Coupe GT | 131 (2144) | N8BY | .032 | 8B | 8B | NA | 68–78 | 750–850 | 750–850 | Hyd. | Hyd. |
| | Quattro Coupe | 131 (2144) | N8GY | .032 | 8B | 8B | NA | 75–81 | 750–850 | 750–850 | Hyd. | Hyd. |
| | 5000 | 131 (2144) | N8Y | .028 | 6B | 6B | NA | 68–78 | 730–870 | 730–870 | Hyd. | Hyd. |
| | 5000 Turbo | 131 (2144) | N8BY | .028 | 6B | 6B | NA | 61–67 | 750–850 | 750–850 | Hyd. | Hyd. |
| | Quattro | 131 (2144) | N6GY | .028 | 6B | 6B | NA | 75–85 | 750–805 | 750–850 | Hyd. | Hyd. |
| | Coupe | 131 (2144) | N8GY | .032 | 6B | 6B | NA | 75–85 | 750–850 | 750–850 | Hyd. | Hyd. |
| 1985 | 4000 S | 109 (1780) | N8GY | .031 | 6B | 6B | NA | 75–82 | 800–1000 | 800–1000 | Hyd. | Hyd. |
| | 4000 S | 136 (2226) | N8GY | .032 | 8B | 8B | NA | 75–85 | 750–850 | 750–850 | Hyd. | Hyd. |
| | 4000 Coupe | 136 (2226) | N8GY | .032 | 8B | 8B | NA | 75–81 | 750–850 | 750–850 | Hyd. | Hyd. |
| | Quattro | 136 (2226) | N6GY | .028 | 6B | 6B | NA | 75–85 | 750–850 | 750–850 | Hyd. | Hyd. |
| | Quattro Turbo | 131 (2144) | N8GY | .028 | 8B | 8B | NA | 75–85 | 750–850 | 750–850 | Hyd. | Hyd. |
| | 5000 S | 136 (2226) | N8GY | .028 | 6B | 6B | NA | 73–84 | 750–850 | 750–850 | Hyd. | Hyd. |
| | 5000 Turbo | 131 (2144) | N8GY | .028 | 0 | 0 | NA | 84–91 | 750–850 | 750–850 | Hyd. | Hyd. |
| | 5000 S Wagon | 136 (2226) | N8GY | .028 | 6B | 6B | NA | 73–84 | 750–850 | 750–850 | Hyd. | Hyd. |
| | 5000 S Turbo | 131 (2226) | N8GY | .028 | 0 | 0 | NA | 84–91 | 750–850 | 750–850 | Hyd. | Hyd. |
| | Coupe GT | 136 (2226) | N8GY | .032 | 8B | 8B | NA | 75–81 | 750–850 | 750–850 | Hyd. | Hyd. |
| 1986 | 4000 S | 109 (1780) | N8GY | .031 | 6B | 6B | NA | 75–82 | 800–1000 | 800–1000 | Hyd. | Hyd. |
| | 4000 Coupe | 136 (2226) | N8GY | .032 | 8B | 8B | NA | 75–81 | 750–850 | 750–850 | Hyd. | Hyd. |
| | 4000 CS Quattro | 136 (2226) | N8GY | .032 | 8B | 8B | NA | 75–81 | 750–850 | 750–850 | Hyd. | Hyd. |
| | 5000 S | 136 (2226) | N8GY | .028 | 6B | 6B | NA | 75–85 | 750–850 | 750–850 | Hyd. | Hyd. |
| | 5000 Wagon | 136 (2226) | N8GY | .028 | 6B | 6B | NA | 75–85 | 750–850 | 750–850 | Hyd. | Hyd. |
| | 5000 S Wagon | 136 (2226) | N8GY | .028 | 6B | 6B | NA | 75–85 | 750–850 | 750–850 | Hyd. | Hyd. |
| | 5000 CS Turbo | 136 (2226) | N8GY | .028 | 0 | 0 | NA | 84–91 | 750–850 | 750–850 | Hyd. | Hyd. |

## GASOLINE ENGINE TUNE-UP SPECIFICATIONS

| Year | Model | Engine Displacement cu. in. (cc) | Spark Plugs Type | Spark Plugs Gap (in.) | Ignition Timing (deg.) MT | Ignition Timing (deg.) AT | Com-pression Pressure (psi) | Fuel Pump (psi) | Idle Speed (rpm) MT | Idle Speed (rpm) AT | Valve Clearance In. | Valve Clearance Ex. |
|---|---|---|---|---|---|---|---|---|---|---|---|---|
| 1986 | 5000 Turbo | 136 (2226) | N8GY | .028 | 0 | 0 | NA | 84–91 | 750–850 | 750–850 | Hyd. | Hyd. |
| | 5000 Quattro Turbo | 136 (2226) | N8GY | .028 | 0 | 0 | NA | 84–91 | 750–850 | 750–850 | Hyd. | Hyd. |
| | 5000 CS Quattro Wagon | 136 (2226) | N8GY | .028 | 6B | 6B | NA | 75–85 | 750–850 | 750–850 | Hyd. | Hyd. |
| | Coupe GT | 136 (2226) | N8GY | .032 | 8B | 8B | NA | 75–85 | 750–850 | 750–850 | Hyd. | Hyd. |
| 1987 | 4000 S | 109 (1780) | N8GY | .031 | 6B | 6B | NA | 75–82 | 800–1000 | 800–1000 | Hyd. | Hyd. |
| | 4000 Coupe | 136 (1780) | N8GY | .032 | 8B | 8B | NA | 75–81 | 750–850 | 750–850 | Hyd. | Hyd. |
| | 4000 CS Quattro | 136 (2226) | N8GY | .032 | 8B | 8B | NA | 75–81 | 750–850 | 750–850 | Hyd. | Hyd. |
| | 5000 S | 136 (2226) | N8GY | .028 | 6B | 6B | NA | 75–85 | 750–850 | 750–850 | Hyd. | Hyd. |
| | 5000 S Wagon | 136 (2226) | N8GY | .028 | 6B | 6B | NA | 75–85 | 750–850 | 750–850 | Hyd. | Hyd. |
| | 5000 CS Turbo | 136 (2226) | N8GY | .028 | 0 | 0 | NA | 84–91 | 750–850 | 750–850 | Hyd. | Hyd. |
| | 5000 Turbo | 136 (2226) | N8GY | .028 | 0 | 0 | NA | 84–91 | 750–850 | 750–850 | Hyd. | Hyd. |
| | 5000 Quattro Turbo | 136 (2226) | N8GY | .028 | 0 | 0 | NA | 84–91 | 750–850 | 750–850 | Hyd. | Hyd. |
| | 5000 CS Quattro Wagon | 136 (2226) | N8GY | .028 | 6B | 6B | NA | 75–85 | 750–850 | 750–850 | Hyd. | Hyd. |
| | Coupe GT | 136 (2226) | N8GY | .032 | 8B | 8B | NA | 75–85 | 750–850 | 750–850 | Hyd. | Hyd. |
| 1988 | 80 | 121 (1983) | NA | .031 | 6B | 6B | NA | 88–94 | 780–900 | 780–900 | Hyd. | Hyd. |
| | 80 Quattro | 141 (2309) | N9BYC | .031 | 15B | 15B | NA | 88–94 | 720–860 | 720–860 | Hyd. | Hyd. |
| | 90 ① | 121 (1983) | NA | .031 | 6B | 6B | NA | 88–94 | 780–900 | 780–900 | Hyd. | Hyd. |
| | 90 | 141 (2309) | N9BYC | .031 | 15B | 15B | NA | 88–94 | 720–860 | 720–860 | Hyd. | Hyd. |
| | 90 Quattro | 141 (2309) | N9BYC | .031 | 15B | 15B | NA | 88–94 | 720–860 | 720–860 | Hyd. | Hyd. |
| | 100 | 141 (2309) | N8GY | .031 | 15B | 15B | NA | 88–94 | 670–770 | 670–770 | Hyd. | Hyd. |
| | 100 Quattro | 141 (2309) | N8GY | .031 | 15B | 15B | NA | 88–94 | 670–770 | 670–770 | Hyd. | Hyd. |
| | 200 | 136 (2226) | N8GY | .028 | 0 | 0 | NA | 84–95 | 750–850 | 750–850 | Hyd. | Hyd. |
| | 200 Quattro | 136 (2226) | N8GY | .028 | 0 | 0 | NA | 84–95 | 750–850 | 750–850 | Hyd. | Hyd. |
| | 5000 CS Turbo | 136 (2226) | N8GY | .028 | 0 | 0 | NA | 84–95 | 750–850 | 750–850 | Hyd. | Hyd. |

## GASOLINE ENGINE TUNE-UP SPECIFICATIONS

| Year | Model | Engine Displacement cu. in. (cc) | Spark Plugs Type | Spark Plugs Gap (in.) | Ignition Timing (deg.) MT | Ignition Timing (deg.) AT | Compression Pressure (psi) | Fuel Pump (psi) | Idle Speed (rpm) MT | Idle Speed (rpm) AT | Valve Clearance In. | Valve Clearance Ex. |
|---|---|---|---|---|---|---|---|---|---|---|---|---|
| 1988 | 5000 CS Quattro Turbo | 136 (2226) | N8GY | .028 | 0 | 0 | NA | 84–95 | 750–850 | 750–850 | Hyd. | Hyd. |
| | 5000 CS Quattro Wagon | 136 (2226) | N8GY | .028 | 0 | 0 | NA | 84–95 | 750–850 | 750–850 | Hyd. | Hyd. |
| | 5000 S | 141 (2309) | N8GY | .031 | 15B | 15B | NA | 88–94 | 670–770 | 670–770 | Hyd. | Hyd. |
| | 5000 S Wagon | 141 (2309) | N8GY | .031 | 15B | 15B | NA | 88–94 | 670–770 | 670–770 | Hyd. | Hyd. |
| | 5000 S Quattro | 141 (2309) | N8GY | .031 | 15B | 15B | NA | 88–94 | 670–770 | 670–770 | Hyd. | Hyd. |
| 1989 | 80 | 121 (1983) | NA | .031 | 6B | 6B | NA | 88–94 | 780–900 | 780–900 | Hyd. | Hyd. |
| | 80 Quattro | 141 (2309) | N9BYC | .031 | 15B | 15B | NA | 88–94 | 720–860 | 720–860 | Hyd. | Hyd. |
| | 90 ① | 121 (1983) | NA | .031 | 6B | 6B | NA | 88–94 | 780–900 | 780–900 | Hyd. | Hyd. |
| | 90 | 141 (2309) | N9BYC | .031 | 15B | 15B | NA | 88–94 | 720–860 | 720–860 | Hyd. | Hyd. |
| | 90 Quattro | 141 (2309) | N9BYC | .031 | 15B | 15B | NA | 88–94 | 720–860 | 720–860 | Hyd. | Hyd. |
| | 100 | 141 (2309) | N8GY | .031 | 15B | 15B | 160–172 | 88–94 | 670–770 | 670–770 | Hyd. | Hyd. |
| | 100 Quattro | 141 (2309) | N8GY | .031 | 15B | 15B | 160–172 | 88–94 | 670–770 | 670–770 | Hyd. | Hyd. |
| | 200 | 136 (2226) | N8GY | .028 | 2 | 2 | 123–144 | 84–95 | 750–850 | 670–770 | Hyd. | Hyd. |
| | 200 Quattro | 136 (2226) | N8GY | .028 | 2 | 2 | 123–144 | 84–95 | 750–850 | 670–770 | Hyd. | Hyd. |
| 1990 | All | SEE UNDERHOOD SPECIFICATION STICKER | | | | | | | | | | |

B Before top dead center
A After top dead center
Hyd. Hydraulic lash adjusters—no adjustment is necessary.
NA Not available

① With automatic transmission
② Top dead center (not adjustable)

## FIRING ORDER

**NOTE: To avoid confusion, always replace spark plug wires one at a time.**

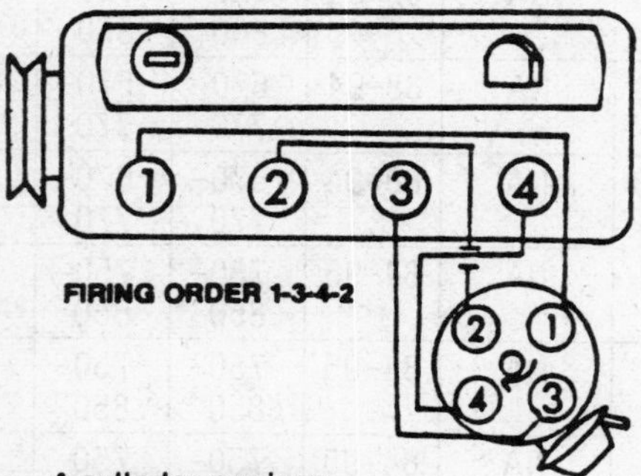


**4 cylinder engines**
**Firing order: 1–3–4–2**
**Distributor rotation: Clockwise**

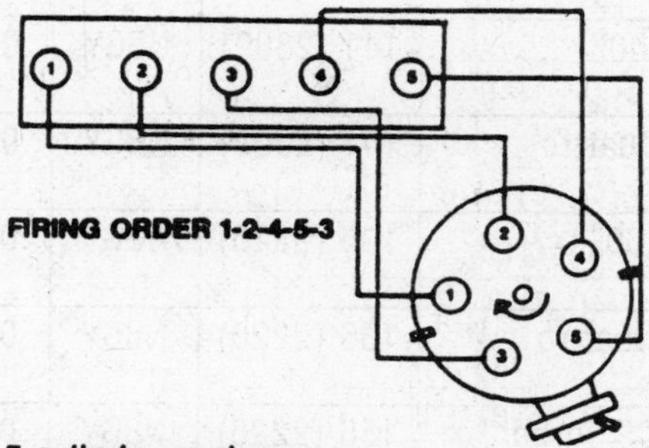


**5 cylinder engines**
**Firing order: 1–2–4–5–3**
**Distributor rotation: Clockwise**

## DIESEL ENGINE TUNE-UP SPECIFICATIONS

| Year | Engine Displacement cu. in. (cc) | Valve Clearance Intake (in.) | Valve Clearance Exhaust (in.) | Intake Valve Opens (deg.) | Injection Pump Setting (deg.) | Injection Nozzle Pressure (psi) New | Injection Nozzle Pressure (psi) Used | Idle Speed (rpm) | Cranking Compression Pressure (psi) |
|---|---|---|---|---|---|---|---|---|---|
| 1983 | 97 (1588) | .008–.012 | .016–.020 | NA | ① | 2306 | 2139 | 900-1000 | 493 |
| | 121 (1986) | .008–.012 | .016–.020 | NA | ② | 2306 | 2139 | 720-780 | 493 |

① The injection timing is .036 in. plunger stroke at top dead center. With the cold start knob pushed in, turn the injection pump body to adjust

② The injection timing is .037 in. plunger stroke at top dead center. With the cold start knob pushed in, turn the injection pump body to adjust

## CAPACITIES

| Year | Model | Engine Displacement cu. in. (cc) | Engine Crankcase with Filter | Engine Crankcase without Filter | Transmission (pts.) 4-Spd | Transmission (pts.) 5-Spd | Transmission (pts.) Auto. | Drive Axle (pts.) | Fuel Tank (gal.) | Cooling System (qts.) |
|---|---|---|---|---|---|---|---|---|---|---|
| 1983 | 4000 | 105 (1715) | 3.5 | 3.0 | 3.4 | 3.4 | 6.4 | 2.2 | 15.9 | 7.4 |
| | 4000 Diesel | 97 (1588) | 3.7 | 3.2 | — | 3.4 | 6.4 | 2.2 | 15.9 | 6.6 |
| | 4000 Coupe | 131 (2144) | 4.0 | 3.5 | — | 3.4 | 6.4 | 2.2 | 15.9 | 8.5 |
| | 5000 | 131 (2144) | 4.9 | 4.5 | 3.4 | 5.5 | 6.4 | 2.5 | 19.8 | 8.5 |
| | 5000 Diesel | 121 (1986) | 4.8 | 4.3 | — | 5.5 | 6.4 | 2.5 | 19.8 | 9.9 |
| | 5000 Turbo | 131 (2144) | 4.5 | 4.5 | — | — | 6.4 | 2.5 | 19.8 | 9.9 |
| | Quattro Turbo | 131 (2144) | 4.5 | 4.3 | — | — | 6.4 | 2.5 | 23.8 | 9.8 |
| 1984 | 4000 | 109 (1780) | 4.7 | 4.3 | 3.4 | 3.4 | 6.4 | 2.2 | 15.9 | 9.8 |
| | 4000 Coupe | 131 (2144) | 4.0 | 3.5 | — | 3.4 | 6.4 | 2.2 | 15.9 | 8.5 |
| | 4000 Quattro | 136 (2226) | 4.0 | 3.5 | — | 5.5 | — | 2.5 | 18.5 | 8.5 |
| | Quattro Coupe | 131 (2144) | 4.5 | 4.3 | — | 7.0 | 6.4 | 3.0 | 23.8 | 9.8 |
| | Coupe GT | 131 (2144) | 5.3 | 5.0 | — | 5.0 | 6.4 | 3.0 | 15.8 | 7.4 |
| | 5000 | 131 (2144) | 5.3 | 5.0 | — | 5.4 | 6.4 | 3.0 | 21.1 | 8.5 |
| | 5000 Turbo | 131 (2144) | 5.3 | 5.0 | — | 5.4 | 6.4 | 3.0 | 21.1 | 8.5 |
| | Quattro | 131 (2144) | 3.7 | 3.5 | — | 7.0 | 6.4 | 2.5 | 18.5 | 8.5 |
| | Coupe | 131 (2144) | 4.0 | 3.5 | — | 3.4 | 6.4 | 2.2 | 15.9 | 8.5 |
| 1985 | 4000 S | 109 (1780) | 3.7 | 3.5 | — | 4.2 | 6.4 | 2.2 | 15.8 | 6.9 |
| | 4000 S | 136 (2226) | 4.0 | 3.7 | — | 7.0 | 6.4 | 2.5 | 18.5 | 8.5 |
| | 4000 Coupe | 136 (2226) | 4.0 | 3.5 | — | 5.5 | 6.4 | 2.2 | 15.9 | 7.4 |
| | Quattro | 136 (2226) | 4.5 | 4.0 | — | 7.0 | 6.4 | 2.5 | 23.8 | 9.8 |
| | Quattro Turbo | 131 (2144) | 4.5 | 4.0 | — | 7.0 | 6.4 | 2.5 | 23.8 | 9.8 |
| | 5000 S | 136 (2226) | 5.3 | 5.0 | — | 5.4 | 6.4 | 3.0 | 21.0 | 8.5 |
| | 5000 Turbo | 131 (2144) | 5.0 | 4.5 | — | 5.5 | 6.4 | 3.0 | 21.1 | 8.6 |
| | 5000 S Wagon | 136 (2226) | 5.3 | 5.0 | — | 5.4 | 6.4 | 3.0 | 21.0 | 8.5 |
| | 5000 S Turbo | 131 (2144) | 5.3 | 5.0 | — | 5.4 | 6.4 | 3.0 | 21.0 | 8.5 |
| | Coupe GT | 136 (2226) | 4.0 | 3.7 | — | 5.0 | 6.4 | 3.0 | 15.8 | 7.4 |
| 1986 | 4000 S | 109 (1780) | 3.5 | 3.0 | — | 5.5 | 6.4 | 2.2 | 15.9 | 7.4 |
| | 4000 Coupe | 136 (2226) | 4.0 | 3.5 | — | 5.5 | 6.4 | 2.2 | 15.9 | 7.4 |
| | 4000 CS Quattro | 136 (2226) | 4.0 | 3.5 | — | 5.5 | 6.4 | 2.2 | 15.9 | 8.6 |
| | 5000 S | 136 (2226) | 5.3 | 5.0 | — | 5.4 | 6.4 | 3.0 | 21.0 | 8.5 |
| | 5000 Turbo | 136 (2226) | 5.0 | 4.5 | — | 5.5 | 6.4 | 3.0 | 21.0 | 8.6 |

## CAPACITIES

| Year | Model | Engine Displacement cu. in. (cc) | Engine Crankcase with Filter | Engine Crankcase without Filter | Transmission (pts.) 4-Spd | Transmission (pts.) 5-Spd | Transmission (pts.) Auto. | Drive Axle (pts.) | Fuel Tank (gal.) | Cooling System (qts.) |
|---|---|---|---|---|---|---|---|---|---|---|
| 1986 | 5000 CS Turbo | 136 (2226) | 5.3 | 5.0 | — | 5.4 | 6.4 | 3.0 | 21.0 | 8.5 |
| | 5000 S Wagon | 136 (2226) | 5.3 | 5.0 | — | 5.4 | 6.4 | 3.0 | 21.0 | 8.5 |
| | 5000 CS Quattro Turbo | 136 (2226) | 5.3 | 5.0 | — | 5.4 | 6.4 | 3.0 | 21.0 | 8.5 |
| | 5000 CS Quattro Wagon | 136 (2226) | 5.3 | 5.0 | — | 5.4 | 6.4 | 3.0 | 21.0 | 8.5 |
| | Coupe GT | 136 (2226) | 4.0 | 3.7 | — | 5.0 | 6.4 | 3.0 | 15.8 | 7.4 |
| 1987 | 4000 S | 109 (1780) | 3.5 | 3.0 | — | 5.5 | 6.4 | 2.2 | 15.9 | 7.4 |
| | 4000 Coupe | 136 (2226) | 4.0 | 3.5 | — | 5.5 | 6.4 | 2.2 | 15.9 | 7.4 |
| | 4000 CS Quattro | 136 (2226) | 4.0 | 3.5 | — | 5.5 | 6.4 | 2.2 | 15.9 | 8.6 |
| | 5000 S | 136 (2226) | 5.3 | 5.0 | — | 5.4 | 6.4 | 3.0 | 21.0 | 8.5 |
| | 5000 Turbo | 136 (2226) | 5.0 | 4.5 | — | 5.5 | 6.4 | 3.0 | 21.0 | 8.6 |
| | 5000 CS Turbo | 136 (2226) | 5.3 | 5.0 | — | 5.4 | 6.4 | 3.0 | 21.0 | 8.5 |
| | 5000 S Wagon | 136 (2226) | 5.3 | 5.0 | — | 5.4 | 6.4 | 3.0 | 21.0 | 8.5 |
| | 5000 CS Quattro Turbo | 136 (2226) | 5.3 | 5.0 | — | 5.4 | 6.4 | 3.0 | 21.0 | 8.5 |
| | 5000 CS Quattro Wagon | 136 (2226) | 5.3 | 5.0 | — | 5.4 | 6.4 | 3.0 | 21.0 | 8.5 |
| | Coupe GT | 136 (2226) | 4.0 | 3.7 | — | 5.0 | 6.4 | 3.0 | 15.8 | 7.4 |
| 1988 | 80 | 121 (1983) | 3.2 | 3.0 | — | 5.5 | 6.4 | 2.2 | 18.0 | 7.4 |
| | 80 Quattro | 141 (2309) | 3.7 | 3.5 | — | 5.5 | 6.4 | 2.2 | 18.5 | 8.5 |
| | 90 ① | 121 (1983) | 3.2 | 3.0 | — | — | 6.4 | 2.2 | 18.0 | 7.4 |
| | 90 | 141 (2309) | 3.7 | 3.5 | — | 5.5 | 6.4 | 2.2 | 18.0 | 8.5 |
| | 90 Quattro | 141 (2309) | 3.7 | 3.5 | — | 5.5 | 6.4 | 2.2 | 18.5 | 7.4 |
| | 100 | 141 (2309) | 5.0 | 4.5 | — | 5.5 | 6.4 | 3.0 | 21.1 | 8.5 |
| | 100 Quattro | 141 (2309) | 5.0 | 4.5 | — | 5.5 | 6.4 | 3.0 | 20.6 | 8.5 |
| | 200 | 136 (2226) | 5.0 | 4.5 | — | 5.5 | 6.4 | 3.0 | 20.6 | 8.5 |
| | 200 Quattro | 136 (2226) | 5.0 | 4.5 | — | 5.5 | 6.4 | 3.0 | 20.6 | 8.5 |
| | 5000 CS Turbo | 136 (2226) | 5.3 | 4.5 | — | 5.5 | 6.4 | 3.0 | 21.1 | 8.5 |
| | 5000 CS Quattro Turbo | 136 (2226) | 5.3 | 4.5 | — | 5.5 | 6.4 | 3.0 | 21.1 | 8.5 |
| | 5000 CS Quattro Wagon | 136 (2226) | 5.3 | 4.5 | — | 5.5 | 6.4 | 3.0 | 21.1 | 8.5 |
| | 5000 S | 141 (2309) | 5.3 | 4.5 | — | 5.5 | 6.4 | 3.0 | 21.1 | 8.5 |
| | 5000 S Wagon | 141 (2309) | 5.3 | 4.5 | — | 5.5 | 6.4 | 3.0 | 21.1 | 8.5 |
| | 5000 S Quattro | 141 (2309) | 5.3 | 4.5 | — | 5.5 | 6.4 | 3.0 | 21.1 | 8.5 |
| 1989-90 | 80 | 121 (1983) | 3.2 | — | — | 2.5 | 6.4 | — | 18 | 7.4 |
| | 80 Quattro | 141 (2309) | 3.7 | — | — | 6.0 | — | — | 18.5 | 8.5 |
| | 90 ① | 121 (1983) | 3.2 | — | — | — | 6.4 | — | 18 | 7.4 |
| | 90 | 141 (2309) | 3.7 | — | — | 5.0 | — | — | 18 | 8.5 |
| | 90 Quattro | 141 (2309) | 3.7 | — | — | 6.0 | — | — | 18.5 | 8.5 |
| | 100 | 141 (2309) | 5.0 | — | — | 5.0 | 7.0 | — | 21.1 | 8.5 |
| | 100 Quattro | 141 (2309) | 5.0 | — | — | 6.0 | — | — | 21.1 | 8.5 |
| | 200 | 136 (2226) | 5.0 | — | — | 5.0 | 7.0 | — | 20.6 | 8.5 |
| | 200 Quattro | 136 (2226) | 5.0 | — | — | 6.0 | — | — | 21.1 | 8.5 |

① With automatic transmission

## CRANKSHAFT AND CONNECTING ROD SPECIFICATIONS

All measurements are given in inches.

| Year | Engine Displacement cu. in. (cc) | Crankshaft Main Brg. Journal Dia. | Crankshaft Main Brg. Oil Clearance | Crankshaft Shaft End-play | Crankshaft Thrust on No. | Connecting Rod Journal Diameter | Connecting Rod Oil Clearance | Connecting Rod Side Clearance |
|---|---|---|---|---|---|---|---|---|
| **1983** | 97 (1588) | 2.1248 | 0.0010–0.0030 | 0.003–0.007 | 3 | 1.8807 | 0.0011–0.0034 | 0.014 |
| | 105 (1715) | 2.1247 | 0.0010–0.0030 | 0.003–0.007 | 3 | 1.8098 | 0.0011–0.0034 | 0.015 |
| | 121 (1986) | 2.3187 | 0.0006–0.0030 | 0.003–0.007 | 4 | 1.9107 | 0.005–0.0024 | 0.015 |
| | 131 (2144) | 2.2822 | 0.0006–0.0030 | 0.003–0.007 | 4 | 1.8098 | 0.006–0.0020 | 0.016 |
| **1984** | 109 (1780) | 2.1260 | 0.0010–0.0030 | 0.003–0.007 | 3 | 1.811 | 0.001–0.003 | 0.015 |
| | 131 (2144) | 2.2822 | 0.0006–0.0030 | 0.003–0.007 | 4 | 1.8098 | 0.0006–0.0020 | 0.016 |
| | 136 (2226) | 2.2818 | 0.0006–0.0030 | 0.003–0.007 | 4 | 1.8803 | 0.0006–0.0020 | 0.016 |
| **1985** | 109 (1780) | 2.1260 | 0.0010–0.0030 | 0.003–0.007 | 3 | 1.811 | 0.001–0.003 | 0.015 |
| | 131 (2144) | 2.2822 | 0.0006–0.0030 | 0.003–0.007 | 4 | 1.8098 | 0.0006–0.0020 | 0.016 |
| | 136 (2226) | 2.2818 | 0.0006–0.0030 | 0.003–0.007 | 4 | 1.8803 | 0.0006–0.0020 | 0.016 |
| **1986** | 109 (1780) | 2.1260 | 0.0010–0.0030 | 0.003–0.007 | 3 | 1.811 | 0.001–0.003 | 0.015 |
| | 136 (2226) | 2.2818 | 0.0006–0.0030 | 0.003–0.007 | 4 | 1.8803 | 0.0006–0.0020 | 0.016 |
| **1987** | 109 (1780) | 2.1260 | 0.0010–0.0030 | 0.003–0.007 | 3 | 1.811 | 0.001–0.003 | 0.015 |
| | 136 (2226) | 2.2818 | 0.0006–0.0030 | 0.003–0.007 | 4 | 1.8803 | 0.0006–0.0020 | 0.016 |
| **1988** | 121 (1983) | 2.1268–2.1276 | NA | NA | 3 | 1.8827–1.8835 | NA | NA |
| | 136 (2226) | 2.2818–2.2825 | 0.0006–0.0030 | 0.003–0.009 | 4 | 1.8487–1.8495 | 0.0004–0.0020 | 0.016 |
| | 141 (2309) | 2.2818–2.2825 | 0.0010–0.0020 | 0.003–0.009 | 4 | 1.8802–1.8810 | 0.0004–0.0020 | 0.016 |
| **1989–90** | 121 (1983) | 2.1268–2.1276 | NA | NA | 3 | 1.8827–1.8835 | NA | NA |
| | 136 (2226) | 2.2818–2.2825 | 0.0006–0.0030 | 0.003–0.009 | 4 | 1.8487–1.8495 | 0.0004–0.0020 | 0.016 |
| | 141 (2309) | 2.2818–2.2825 | 0.0010–0.0020 | 0.003–0.009 | 4 | 1.8802–1.8810 | 0.0004–0.0020 | 0.016 |

NA Not available

## PISTON AND RING SPECIFICATIONS

All measurements are given in inches.

| Year | Engine Displacement cu. in. (cc) | Piston Clearance | Ring Gap | | | Ring Side Clearance | | |
|---|---|---|---|---|---|---|---|---|
| | | | Top Compression | Bottom Compression | Oil Control | Top Compression | Bottom Compression | Oil Control |
| 1983 | 97 (1588) | 0.0011 | 0.012–0.020 | 0.012–0.020 | 0.010–0.016 | 0.002–0.004 | 0.002–0.003 | 0.001–0.002 |
| | 105 (1715) | 0.0011 | 0.012–0.018 | 0.012–0.018 | 0.012–0.018 | 0.0008–0.002 | 0.0008–0.002 | 0.0008–0.002 |
| | 121 (1986) | 0.0011 | 0.012–0.020 | 0.012–0.020 | 0.010–0.016 | 0.002–0.0035 | 0.002–0.003 | 0.001–0.002 |
| | 131 (2144) | 0.0011 | 0.010–0.020 | 0.010–0.020 | 0.010–0.020 | 0.0008–0.003 | 0.0008–0.003 | 0.0008–0.003 |
| 1984 | 109 (1780) | 0.0011 | 0.012–0.018 | 0.012–0.018 | 0.012–0.018 | 0.0008–0.012 | 0.0008–0.002 | 0.0008–0.002 |
| | 131 (2144) | 0.0011 | 0.010–0.020 | 0.010–0.020 | 0.010–0.020 | 0.0008–0.003 | 0.0008–0.003 | 0.0008–0.003 |
| | 136 (2226) | 0.0011 | 0.010–0.020 | 0.010–0.020 | 0.010–0.020 | 0.0008–0.003 | 0.0008–0.002 | 0.0008–0.002 |
| 1985 | 109 (1780) | 0.0011 | 0.012–0.018 | 0.012–0.018 | 0.012–0.018 | 0.0008–0.012 | 0.0008–0.002 | 0.0008–0.002 |
| | 131 (2144) | 0.0011 | 0.010–0.020 | 0.010–0.020 | 0.010–0.020 | 0.0008–0.003 | 0.0008–0.003 | 0.0008–0.003 |
| | 136 (2226) | 0.0011 | 0.010–0.020 | 0.010–0.020 | 0.010–0.020 | 0.0008–0.003 | 0.0008–0.002 | 0.0008–0.002 |
| 1986 | 109 (1780) | 0.0011 | 0.012–0.018 | 0.012–0.018 | 0.012–0.018 | 0.0008–0.002 | 0.0008–0.002 | 0.0008–0.002 |
| | 136 (2226) | 0.0011 | 0.010–0.020 | 0.010–0.020 | 0.010–0.020 | 0.0008–0.003 | 0.0008–0.003 | 0.0008–0.003 |
| 1987 | 109 (1780) | 0.0011 | 0.012–0.018 | 0.012–0.018 | 0.012–0.018 | 0.0008–0.002 | 0.0008–0.002 | 0.0008–0.002 |
| | 136 (2226) | 0.0011 | 0.010–0.020 | 0.010–0.020 | 0.010–0.020 | 0.0008–0.003 | 0.0008–0.003 | 0.0008–0.003 |
| 1988 | 121 (1983) | 0.0011 | 0.012–0.018 | 0.012–0.018 | 0.010–0.018 | 0.001–0.002 | 0.001–0.002 | 0.001–0.002 |
| | 136 (2226) | 0.0011 | 0.008–0.020 | 0.008–0.020 | 0.010–0.020 | 0.001–0.003 | 0.001–0.003 | 0.001–0.002 |
| | 141 (2309) | 0.0011 | 0.008–0.016 | 0.008–0.016 | 0.010–0.020 | 0.001–0.003 | 0.001–0.003 | 0.001–0.002 |
| 1989–90 | 121 (1983) | 0.0011 | 0.012–0.018 | 0.012–0.018 | 0.010–0.018 | 0.001–0.002 | 0.001–0.002 | 0.001–0.002 |
| | 136 (2226) | 0.0011 | 0.008–0.020 | 0.008–0.020 | 0.010–0.020 | 0.001–0.003 | 0.001–0.003 | 0.001–0.002 |
| | 141 (2309) | 0.0011 | 0.008–0.016 | 0.008–0.016 | 0.010–0.020 | 0.001–0.003 | 0.001–0.003 | 0.001–0.002 |

## VALVE SPECIFICATIONS

| Year | Engine Displacement cu. in. (cc) | Seat Angle (deg.) | Face Angle (deg.) | Spring Test Pressure (lbs.) | Spring Installed Height (in.) | Stem-to-Guide Clearance (in.) | | Stem Diameter (in.) | |
|---|---|---|---|---|---|---|---|---|---|
| | | | | | | Intake | Exhaust | Intake | Exhaust |
| 1983 | 97 (1588) | 45 | 45 | — | — | 0.039 | 0.051 | 0.3140 | 0.3130 |
| | 121 (1986) | 45 | 45 | — | — | 0.051 | 0.051 | 0.3140 | 0.3130 |

## VALVE SPECIFICATIONS

| Year | Engine Displacement cu. in. (cc) | Seat Angle (deg.) | Face Angle (deg.) | Spring Test Pressure (lbs.) | Spring Installed Height (in.) | Stem-to-Guide Clearance (in.) | | Stem Diameter (in.) | |
|---|---|---|---|---|---|---|---|---|---|
| | | | | | | Intake | Exhaust | Intake | Exhaust |
| 1983 | 105 (1715) | 45 | 45 | — | — | 0.039 | 0.051 | 0.3140 | 0.3130 |
| | 131 (2144) | 45 | 45 | — | — | 0.039 | 0.051 | 0.3140 | 0.3130 |
| 1984 | 109 (1780) | 45 | 45 | — | — | 0.039 | 0.051 | 0.3140 | 0.3130 |
| | 131 (2144) | 45 | 45 | — | — | 0.039 | 0.051 | 0.3140 | 0.3130 |
| | 136 (2226) | 45 | 45 | — | — | 0.039 | 0.051 | 0.3140 | 0.3130 |
| 1985 | 109 (1780) | 45 | 45 | — | — | 0.039 | 0.051 | 0.3140 | 0.3130 |
| | 131 (2144) | 45 | 45 | — | — | 0.039 | 0.051 | 0.3140 | 0.3130 |
| | 136 (2226) | 45 | 45 | — | — | 0.039 | 0.051 | 0.3140 | 0.3130 |
| 1986 | 109 (1780) | 45 | 45 | — | — | 0.039 | 0.051 | 0.3140 | 0.3130 |
| | 136 (2226) | 45 | 45 | — | — | 0.039 | 0.051 | 0.3140 | 0.3130 |
| 1987 | 109 (1780) | 45 | 45 | — | — | 0.039 | 0.051 | 0.3140 | 0.3130 |
| | 136 (2226) | 45 | 45 | — | — | 0.039 | 0.051 | 0.3140 | 0.3130 |
| 1988 | 121 (1983) | 45 | 45 | — | — | 0.039 | 0.051 | 0.3140 | 0.3130 |
| | 136 (2226) | 45 | 45 | — | — | 0.039 | 0.051 | 0.3140 | 0.3130 |
| | 141 (2309) | 45 | 45 | — | — | 0.039 | 0.051 | 0.3140 | 0.3130 |
| 1989-90 | 121 (1983) | 45 | 45 | — | — | 0.039 | 0.051 | 0.3140 | 0.3130 |
| | 136 (2226) | 45 | 45 | — | — | 0.039 | 0.051 | 0.3140 | 0.3130 |
| | 141 (2309) | 45 | 45 | — | — | 0.039 | 0.051 | 0.3140 | 0.3130 |

## TORQUE SPECIFICATIONS

All readings in ft. lbs.

| Year | Engine Displacement cu. in. (cc) | Cylinder Head Bolts | Main Bearing Bolts | Rod Bearing Bolts | Crankshaft Pulley Bolts | Flywheel Bolts | Manifold | | Spark Plugs |
|---|---|---|---|---|---|---|---|---|---|
| | | | | | | | Intake | Exhaust | |
| 1983 | 97 (1588) | ① | 47 | 33 | 58 ④ | 54 ⑤ | 18 | 18 | 14 |
| | 121 (1986) | ② | 47 | 33 | 253 | 54 ⑤ | 18 | 18 | — |
| | 105 (1715) | ① | 47 | 33 | 58 | 54 ⑤ | 16 | 16 | 14 |
| | 131 (2144) | ① | 47 | 36 ③ | 250 | 54 | 18 | 18 | 14 |
| 1984 | 109 (1780) | ① | 47 | 22 ⑥ | 145 | 54 ⑤ | 22 | 22 | 14 |
| | 131 (2144) | ① | 47 | 36 ③ | 250 | 54 ⑤ | 18 | 18 | 14 |
| | 136 (2226) | ① | 47 | 22 ⑥ | 253 | 54 ⑤ | 22 | 26 | 14 |
| 1985 | 109 (1780) | ① | 47 | 22 ⑥ | 145 | 54 ⑤ | 22 | 22 | 14 |
| | 131 (2144) | ① | 47 | 36 ③ | 250 | 54 ⑤ | 18 | 18 | 14 |
| | 136 (2226) | ① | 47 | 22 ⑥ | 253 | 54 ⑤ | 22 | 26 | 14 |
| 1986 | 109 (1780) | ① | 47 | 22 ⑥ | 145 | 54 ⑤ | 22 | 22 | 14 |
| | 136 (2226) | ① | 47 | 22 ⑥ | 253 | 54 ⑤ | 22 | 26 | 14 |
| 1987 | 109 (1780) | ① | 47 | 22 ⑥ | 145 | 54 ⑤ | 22 | 22 | 14 |
| | 136 (2226) | ① | 47 | 22 ⑥ | 253 | 54 ⑤ | 22 | 26 | 14 |
| 1988 | 121 (1983) | ① | 48 | 22 ⑥ | ⑦ | 74 | 15 | 18 | 14 |
| | 136 (2226) | ① | 48 | 22 ⑥ | 258 | 74 | 22 | 26 | 14 |
| | 141 (2309) | ① | 48 | 22 ⑥ | 258 | 74 | 22 | 26 | 14 |

## TORQUE SPECIFICATIONS

All readings in ft. lbs.

| Year | Engine Displacement cu. in. (cc) | Cylinder Head Bolts | Main Bearing Bolts | Rod Bearing Bolts | Crankshaft Pulley Bolts | Flywheel Bolts | Manifold Intake | Manifold Exhaust | Spark Plugs |
|---|---|---|---|---|---|---|---|---|---|
| 1989-90 | 121 (1983) | ① | 48 | 22 ⑥ | ⑦ | 74 | 15 | 18 | 14 |
| | 136 (2226) | ① | 48 | 22 ⑥ | 258 | 74 | 22 | 26 | 14 |
| | 141 (2309) | ① | 48 | 22 ⑥ | 258 | 74 | 22 | 26 | 14 |

**NOTE:** Always use new rod bearing bolts.

① In sequence 29 ft. lbs., 43 ft. lbs. and then tighten it a half turn more (180 degrees).

② In sequence 29 ft. lbs., 43 ft. lbs., and then tighten it a half turn more (180 degrees). Warm the engine and tighten the head bolts an additional quarter turn more (90 degrees).

③ Turbo and Quattro models 47 ft. lbs. Nut with notches—22 ft. lbs. plus a quarter turn.

④ Replacement bolt and washer 108 ft. lbs.

⑤ Models with a built in lug—145 ft. lbs.

⑥ Plus a quarter turn (90 degrees).

⑦ In sequence 66 ft. lbs., then a half turn more (180 degrees).

## BRAKE SPECIFICATIONS

All measurements in inches unless noted

| Year | Model | Lug Nut Torque (ft. lbs.) | Master Cylinder Bore | Brake Disc Minimum Thickness | Brake Disc Maximum Runout | Standard Brake Drum Diameter | Minimum Lining Thickness Front | Minimum Lining Thickness Rear |
|---|---|---|---|---|---|---|---|---|
| 1983 | 4000 | 65 | 0.825 | 0.413 ① | 0.002 | 7.910 | 0.078 | 0.098 |
| | 4000 Coupe | 65 | 0.825 | 0.413 ① | 0.002 | 7.910 | 0.078 | 0.098 |
| | 4000 Diesel | 65 | 0.825 | 0.413 ① | 0.002 | 7.910 | 0.078 | 0.098 |
| | 5000 | 80 | 0.875 | 0.807 | 0.004 | 9.094 | 0.078 | 0.098 |
| | 5000 Diesel | 80 | 0.875 | 0.807 | 0.004 | 9.094 | 0.078 | 0.098 |
| | 5000 Turbo | 80 | 0.875 | 0.807 ④ | 0.002 | 9.980 | 0.051 | 0.472 ② |
| | Quattro Turbo | 80 | 0.875 | 0.807 ④ | 0.002 | 9.980 | 0.051 | 0.472 ② |
| 1984 | 4000 | 65 | 0.825 | 0.413 ① | 0.002 | 7.910 | 0.078 | 0.098 |
| | 4000 Coupe | 65 | 0.825 | 0.413 ① | 0.002 | 7.910 | 0.078 | 0.098 |
| | 4000 Quattro | 80 | 0.810 | 0.472 ④ | 0.002 | 9.981 | 0.276 ② | 0.276 ② |
| | Coupe GT | 80 | 0.810 | 0.472 | 0.002 | 7.894 | 0.078 | 0.098 |
| | Quattro Coupe | 80 | 0.875 | 0.807 ④ | 0.002 | 9.980 | 0.051 | 0.472 ② |
| | 5000 | 80 | 0.875 | 0.807 | 0.004 | 9.094 | 0.078 | 0.098 |
| | 5000 Turbo | 80 | 0.875 | 0.807 ④ | 0.002 | 9.980 | 0.051 | 0.472 ② |
| | Quattro | 80 | 0.875 | 0.807 ④ | 0.002 | 9.980 | 0.051 | 0.472 ② |
| | Coupe | 80 | 0.810 | 0.472 | 0.002 | 7.913 | 0.276 ② | 0.098 |
| 1985 | 4000 S | 80 | 0.810 | 0.472 | 0.002 | 7.913 | 0.276 ② | 0.098 |
| | 4000 Coupe | 80 | 0.810 | 0.472 | 0.002 | 7.913 | 0.276 ② | 0.098 |
| | Quattro | 80 | 0.875 | 0.807 ④ | 0.002 | 9.980 | 0.051 | 0.472 ② |
| | Quattro Turbo | 80 | 0.875 | 0.807 ④ | 0.002 | 9.980 | 0.051 | 0.472 ② |
| | 5000 S | 80 | 0.810 | 0.787 | 0.002 | 9.094 | ③ | 0.098 |
| | 5000 S Turbo | 80 | 0.810 | 0.787 ④ | 0.002 | 9.981 | ③ | 0.281 |
| | 5000 S Wagon | 80 | 0.810 | 0.787 | 0.002 | 9.094 | ③ | 0.098 |
| | 5000 Turbo | 80 | 0.875 | 0.807 ④ | 0.002 | 9.980 | 0.051 | 0.472 ② |
| | Coupe GT | 80 | 0.810 | 0.472 | 0.002 | 7.894 | 0.078 | 0.098 |

## BRAKE SPECIFICATIONS

All measurements in inches unless noted

| Year | Model | Lug Nut Torque (ft. lbs.) | Master Cylinder Bore | Brake Disc Minimum Thickness | Brake Disc Maximum Runout | Standard Brake Drum Diameter | Minimum Lining Thickness Front | Minimum Lining Thickness Rear |
|---|---|---|---|---|---|---|---|---|
| 1986 | 4000 S | 80 | 0.810 | 0.472 | 0.002 | 7.913 | 0.276 ② | 0.098 |
| | 4000 Coupe | 80 | 0.810 | 0.472 | 0.002 | 7.913 | 0.276 ② | 0.098 |
| | 4000 CS Quattro | 80 | 0.810 | 0.728 | 0.003 | — | ③ | ③ |
| | 5000 S | 80 | 0.810 | 0.787 | 0.002 | 9.980 | 0.051 | 0.472 ② |
| | 5000 S Wagon | 80 | 0.810 | 0.787 ④ | 0.002 | 9.980 | 0.051 | 0.472 ② |
| | 5000 CS Turbo | 80 | 0.810 | 0.807 ④ | 0.002 | — | ③ | ③ |
| | 5000 Turbo | 80 | 0.875 | 0.807 ④ | 0.002 | 9.980 | 0.051 | 0.472 ② |
| | 5000 Quattro Turbo | 80 | 0.810 | 0.807 ④ | 0.002 | — | ③ | ③ |
| | 5000 CS Quattro Wagon | 80 | 0.810 | 0.807 ④ | 0.002 | — | ③ | ③ |
| | Coupe GT | 80 | 0.810 | 0.472 | 0.002 | 7.894 | 0.078 | 0.098 |
| 1987 | 4000 S | 80 | 0.810 | 0.472 | 0.002 | 7.913 | 0.276 ② | 0.098 |
| | 4000 Coupe | 80 | 0.810 | 0.472 | 0.002 | 7.913 | 0.276 ② | 0.098 |
| | 4000 CS Quattro | 80 | 0.810 | 0.728 | 0.003 | — | ③ | ③ |
| | 5000 S | 80 | 0.810 | 0.787 | 0.002 | 9.980 | 0.051 | 0.472 ② |
| | 5000 S Wagon | 80 | 0.810 | 0.787 | 0.002 | 9.980 | 0.051 | 0.472 ② |
| | 5000 CS Turbo | 80 | 0.810 | 0.807 ④ | 0.002 | — | ③ | ③ |
| | 5000 Turbo | 80 | 0.875 | 0.807 ④ | 0.002 | 9.980 | 0.051 | 0.472 ② |
| | 5000 Quattro Turbo | 80 | 0.810 | 0.807 ④ | 0.002 | — | ③ | ③ |
| | 5000 CS Quattro Wagon | 80 | 0.810 | 0.807 ④ | 0.002 | — | ③ | ③ |
| | Coupe GT | 80 | 0.810 | 0.472 | 0.002 | 7.894 | 0.078 | 0.098 |
| 1988 | 80 | 81 | 0.874 | 0.787 ⑤ | 0.002 | — | 0.078 | 0.078 ⑥ |
| | 80 Quattro | 81 | 0.874 | 0.787 ⑤ | 0.002 | — | 0.078 | 0.078 ⑥ |
| | 90 | 81 | 0.874 | 0.787 ⑤ | 0.002 | — | 0.078 | 0.078 ⑥ |
| | 90 Quattro | 81 | 0.874 | 0.787 ⑤ | 0.002 | — | 0.078 | 0.078 ⑥ |
| | 5000 CS Turbo | 81 | 0.875 | 0.787 ⑤ | 0.002 | — | ③ | 0.472 ② |
| | 5000 CS Quattro Turbo | 81 | 0.875 | 0.787 ⑤ | 0.002 | — | ③ | 0.472 ② |
| | 5000 CS Quattro Wagon | 81 | 0.875 | 0.787 ⑤ | 0.002 | — | ③ | 0.472 ② |
| | 5000 S | 81 | 0.810 | 0.787 ⑤ | 0.002 | — | ③ | 0.098 |
| | 5000 S Wagon | 81 | 0.810 | 0.787 ⑤ | 0.002 | — | ③ | 0.098 |
| | 5000 S Quattro | 81 | 0.810 | 0.787 ⑤ | 0.002 | — | ③ | 0.098 |
| 1989-90 | 80 | 81 | 0.874 | 0.787 ⑤ | 0.002 | — | 0.078 | 0.078 |
| | 80 Quattro | 81 | 0.874 | 0.787 ⑤ | 0.002 | — | 0.078 | 0.078 |
| | 90 ① | 81 | 0.874 | 0.787 ⑤ | 0.002 | — | 0.078 | 0.078 |
| | 90 | 81 | 0.874 | 0.787 ⑤ | 0.002 | — | 0.078 | 0.078 |
| | 90 Quattro | 81 | 0.874 | 0.787 ⑤ | 0.002 | — | 0.078 | 0.078 |
| | 100 | 81 | 0.874 | 0.787 ⑤ | 0.002 | — | ③ | 0.472 ② |
| | 100 Quattro | 81 | 0.874 | 0.787 ⑤ | 0.002 | — | ③ | 0.472 ② |
| | 200 | 81 | 0.874 | 0.905 ⑤ | 0.002 | — | ③ | 0.472 ② |
| | 200 Quattro | 81 | 0.874 | 0.905 ⑤ | 0.002 | — | ③ | 0.472 ② |

**NOTE:** Minimum lining thickness is as recommended by the manufacturer. Due to variations in state inspection regulations, the minimum allowable thickness may be different than recommended by the manufacturer.

① With ventilated discs—0.768 after refinishing—0.728 discard thickness
② Included backing plate
③ Replace the pads when the indicator on the dash turns on
④ All models with rear disc brakes—Minimum Thickness 0.335
⑤ All models with rear disc brakes minimum thickness 0.315
⑥ 0.275 in. including backing plate

## WHEEL ALIGNMENT

| Year | Model | Caster Range (deg.) | Caster Preferred Setting (deg.) | Camber Range (deg.) | Camber Preferred Setting (deg.) | Toe-in (in.) | Steering Axis Inclination (deg.) |
|---|---|---|---|---|---|---|---|
| 1983 | 4000 | 0–1P | 1/2P | 1 5/32N–5/32N | 21/32N | 5/64 | N/A |
| | 4000 Coupe | 0–1P | 1/2P | 1 5/32N–5/32N | 21/32N | 5/64 | N/A |
| | 4000 Diesel | 0–1P | 1/2P | 1 5/32N–5/32N | 21/32N | 5/64 | N/A |
| | 5000 | 1/2P–1 13/16P | 1 5/32P | 1N–0 | 1/2N | 0 | N/A |
| | 5000 Diesel | 1/2P–1 13/16P | 1 5/32P | 1N–0 | 1/2N | 0 | N/A |
| | 5000 Turbo | 1/2P–1 13/16P | 1 5/32P | 1N–0 | 1/2N | 0 | N/A |
| | Quattro Turbo | 27/32P–2 5/32P | 1 1/2P | 1 11/32N–11/32N | 27/32N | 0 | N/A |
| 1984 | 4000 | 0–1P | 1/2P | 1 5/32N–5/32N | 21/32N | 5/64 | N/A |
| | 4000 Coupe | 0–1P | 1/2P | 1 5/32N–5/32N | 21/32N | 5/64 | N/A |
| | 4000 Quattro | 15/16P–1 15/16P | 1 7/16P | 1 1/4N–1/4N | 3/4N | 5/64 | N/A |
| | Coupe GT | 0–1P | 1/2P | 1 5/32N–5/32N | 21/32N | 5/64 | N/A |
| | Quattro Coupe | 27/32P–2 5/32P | 1 1/2P | 1 11/32N–11/32N | 27/32N | 0 | N/A |
| | 5000 | 1/2P–1 13/16P | 1 5/32P | 1N–0 | 1/2N | 0 | N/A |
| | 5000 Turbo | 1/2P–1 13/16P | 1 5/32P | 1N–0 | 1/2N | 0 | N/A |
| | Quattro | 5/6P–2 1/6P | 1 1/2P | 1 1/3N–1/3N | 5/6N | 1/12 | N/A |
| | Coupe | 0–1P | 1/2P | 1 1/6N–1/6N | 2/3N | 1/3 | N/A |
| 1985 | 4000 S | 5/16P–1 5/16P | 1 7/16P | 1/6N–1 1/6N | 2/3N | 1/12 | N/A |
| | 4000 Coupe | 15/16P–1 5/16P | 1 7/16P | 1/6N–1 1/6N | 2/3N | 1/12 | N/A |
| | Quattro | 5/6P–2 1/6P | 1 1/2P | 1 1/3N–1/3N | 5/6N | 1/12 | N/A |
| | Quattro Turbo | 27/32P–2 5/32P | 1 1/2P | 1 11/32N–11/32N | 27/32N | 0 | N/A |
| | 5000 S | 11/32P–1 21/32P | 1P | 1N–0 ① ② | 1/2N | 0 ③ ④ | N/A |
| | 5000 S Turbo | 11/32P–1 21/32P | 1P | 1N–0 ① ② | 1/2N | 0 ③ ④ | N/A |
| | 5000 S Wagon | 11/32P–1 21/32P | 1P | 1N–0 ① ② | 1/2N | 0 ③ ④ | N/A |
| | 5000 Turbo | 11/32P–1 21/32P | 1P | 1N–0 ① ② | 1/2N | 0 ③ ④ | N/A |
| | Coupe GT | 0P–1P | 1/2P | 1 5/32N–5/32N | 21/32N | 5/64 | N/A |

## WHEEL ALIGNMENT

| Year | Model | Caster Range (deg.) | Caster Preferred Setting (deg.) | Camber Range (deg.) | Camber Preferred Setting (deg.) | Toe-in (in.) | Steering Axis Inclination (deg.) |
|---|---|---|---|---|---|---|---|
| 1986 | 4000 S | 15/16P–1 5/16P | 1 7/16P | 1/6N–1 1/6N | 2/3N | 1/12 | NA |
| | 4000 Coupe | 15/16P–1 5/16P | 1 7/16P | 1/6N–1 1/6N | 2/3N | 1/12 | NA |
| | 4000 CS Quattro | 15/16P–1 5/16P | 1 7/16P | 1/6N–1 1/6N | 2/3N | 1/12 | NA |
| | 5000 S | 11/32P–1 21/32P | 1P | 1N–0 ① ② | 1/2N | 0 ③ ④ | NA |
| | 5000 S Wagon | 11/32P–1 21/32P | 1P | 1N–0 ① ② | 1/2N | 0 ③ ④ | NA |
| | 5000 CS Turbo | 11/32P–1 21/32P | 1P | 1N–0 ① ② | 1/2N | 0 ③ ④ | NA |
| | 5000 Turbo | 11/32P–1 21/32P | 1P | 1N–0 ① ② | 1/2N | 0 ③ ④ | NA |
| | 5000 Quattro Turbo | 11/32P–1 21/32P | 1P | 1N–0 ① ② | 1/2N | 0 ③ ④ | NA |
| | 5000 CS Quattro Wagon | 11/32P–1 21/32P | 1P | 1N–0 ① ② | 1/2N | 0 ③ ④ | NA |
| | Coupe GT | 0P–1P | 1/2P | 1 5/32N–5/32N | 21/32N | 5/64 | NA |
| 1987 | 4000 S | 15/16P–1 5/16P | 1 7/16P | 1/6N–1 1/6N | 2/3N | 1/12 | NA |
| | 4000 Coupe | 15/16P–1 5/16P | 1 7/16P | 1/6N–1 1/6N | 2/3N | 1/12 | NA |
| | 4000 CS Quattro | 15/16P–1 5/16P | 1 7/16P | 1/6N–1 1/6N | 2/3N | 1/12 | NA |
| | 5000 S | 11/32P–1 21/32P | 1P | 1N–0 ① ② | 1/2N | 0 ③ ④ | NA |
| | 5000 S Wagon | 11/32P–1 21/32P | 1P | 1N–0 ① ② | 1/2N | 0 ③ ④ | NA |
| | 5000 CS Turbo | 11/32P–1 21/32P | 1P | 1N–0 ① ② | 1/2N | 0 ③ ④ | NA |
| | 5000 Turbo | 11/32P–1 21/32P | 1P | 1N–0 ① ② | 1/2N | 0 ③ ④ | NA |
| | 5000 Quattro Turbo | 11/32P–1 21/32P | 1P | 1N–0 ① ② | 1/2N | 0 ③ ④ | NA |
| | 5000 CS Quattro Wagon | 11/32P–1 21/32P | 1P | 1N–0 ① ② | 1/2N | 0 ③ ④ | NA |
| | Coupe GT | 0P–1P | 1/2P | 1 5/32N–5/32N | 21/32N | 5/64 | NA |
| 1988 | 80 | 3/4P–1 3/4P | 1 1/4P | 1 1/4N–1/4N | 3/4N | 5/64 | NA |
| | 80 Quattro | 3/4P–1 3/4P | 1 1/4P | 1 13/32N–13/32N | 27/32N | 5/64 | NA |
| | 90 | 3/4P–1 3/4P | 1 1/4P | 1 1/4N–1/4N | 3/4N | 5/64 | NA |
| | 90 Quattro | 3/4P–1 3/4P | 1 1/4P | 1 13/32N–13/32N | 27/32N | 5/64 | NA |
| | 5000 CS Turbo | 5/32N–1 1/2P | 27/32P | 1N–0 | 1/2N | 0 | NA |
| | 5000 CS Quattro Turbo | 11/32P–1 21/32P | 1P | 1N–0 | 1/2N | 1/64 | NA |
| | 5000 CS Quattro Wagon | 11/32P–1 21/32P | 1P | 1N–0 | 1/2N | 1/64 | NA |
| | 5000 S | 5/32N–1 1/2P | 27/32P | 1N–0 | 1/2N | 0 | NA |
| | 5000 S Wagon | 5/32N–1 1/2P | 27/32P | 1N–0 | 1/2N | 0 | NA |
| | 5000 S Quattro | 11/32P–1 21/32P | 1P | 1N–0 | 1/2N | 1/64 | NA |
| 1989–90 | 80 | 3/4P–1 3/4P | 1 1/4P | 1 1/4N–1/4N | 3/4N | 5/64 | NA |
| | 80 Quattro | 3/4P–1 3/4P | 1 1/4P | 1 13/32N–13/32N | 27/32N | 5/64 | NA |
| | 90 | 3/4P–1 3/4P | 1 1/4P | 1 1/4N–1/4N | 3/4N | 5/64 | NA |
| | 90 Quattro | 3/4P–1 3/4P | 1 1/4P | 1 13/32N–13/32N | 27/32N | 5/64 | NA |
| | 100 | 5/32N–1 1/2P | 27/32P | 1N–0 | 1/2N | 1/16N | NA |
| | 100 Quattro | 5/32N–1 1/2P | 27/32P | 1N–0 | 1/2N | 1/16N | NA |
| | 200 | 5/32N–1 1/2P | 27/32P | 1N–0 | 1/2N | 1/16N | NA |
| | 200 Quattro | 5/32N–1 1/2P | 27/32P | 1N–0 | 1/2N | 1/16N | NA |

N Negative
P Positive
NA No application
① Rear axle—5/6N–1/6N
② Maximum difference between left and right—Rear Axle—1/2N
③ Up to chassis No. EN096669—Rear Axle—1/30P–5/18P
④ from chassis No. EN096670—Rear Axle—1/30P–1/4P

# TUNE-UP PROCEDURES

Each tune-up adjustment will complement the effects of the other adjustments. Therefore, all adjustments should be completed to obtain maximum results.

Often, there may be a mid-Year change in the tune-up specifications or procedures. If the figures or specifications on the tune-up specifications sticker in the engine compartment, disagree with the "Tune-up Specifications" chart in this manual, the figures and/or procedures on the sticker must be followed.

## Ignition Timing

**NOTE: Ignition timing is not adjustable on 5 cylinder turbocharged engines.**

### STATIC ADJUSTMENT

1. Rotate the engine until the basic ignition timing mark is aligned with the ignition timing pointer on the bell housing and the distributor rotor points towards the No. 1 cylinder notch on the rim of the distributor housing.
2. The timing mark on the bell housing must be aligned with the mark on the flywheel.
3. This will place No. 1 cylinder at TDC (0 degree mark) on the compression stroke.
4. Connect a 12 volt test light between the ignition coil terminal No. 1 at the distributor and to ground. The lamp should go on.
5. Rotate the distributor clockwise slowly until the lamp goes out.
6. Rotate the distributor counterclockwise slowly, until the lamp goes on.
7. Tighten the distributor hold-down clamp.
8. The ignition timing is now set enough to start the engine.
9. Start and run the engine until it reaches normal operating temperature. The radiator fan must cycle at least once.
10. Check and adjust the ignition timing with test equipment or a timing light.

### DYNAMIC ADJUSTMENT

#### *1983–86 Engines*

Some tachometers, dwellmeters and oscilloscopes will not work with these ignition systems. Some test equipment may be damaged. Consult the manufacturer of the test equipment if there is any doubt.

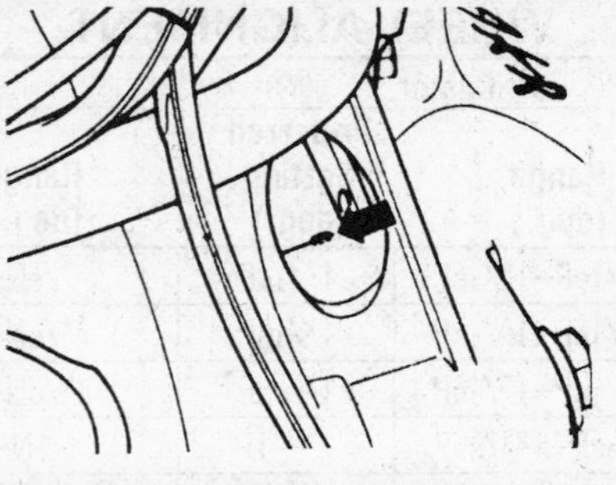

4 cylinder engine timing mark on bell housing aligned with mark on flywheel

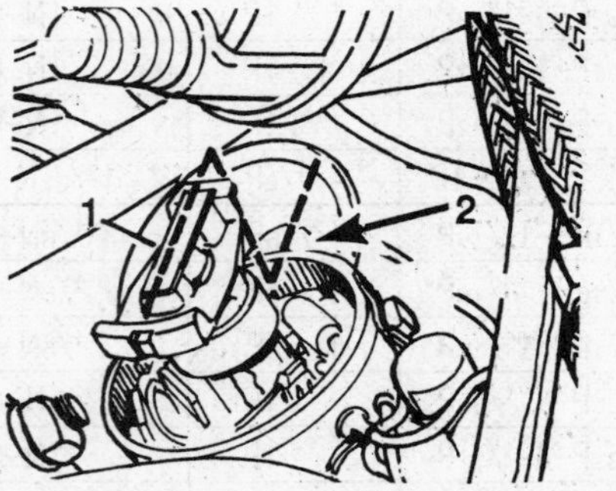


The distributor rotor (1) aligned with the No. 1 cylinder mark (2) on the rim of the distributor body. The dust cap is removed

On 1983–85 models, the idle stabilizer must be bypassed to check and/or adjust the ignition timing. To bypass the idle stabilizer, with the ignition off, disconnect the 2 electrical leads and plug them together. Check the ignition timing with the engine at the rpm specified on the sticker.

The idle stabilizer is located on top of the ignition control unit. It controls the idle speed by either advancing or retarding the ignition timing. This is done in accordance with the engine load. If the idle speed is erratic, or if the engine fails to start, bypass the idle stabilizer. If the idle improves, the idle stabilizer should be replaced.

**NOTE: 1986 models have an impedance transformer installed on top of the ignition control unit in place of an idle stabilizer. Do not disconnect the transformer when checking and/or adjusting the ignition timing.**

All 1983–86 engines require the distributor vacuum hoses to remain connected when checking or adjusting the timing.

To adjust the timing on 1983–85 engines:

1. Loosen the distributor clamp until it is just possible to turn the distributor by hand. Connect a timing light to the No.1 cylinder.

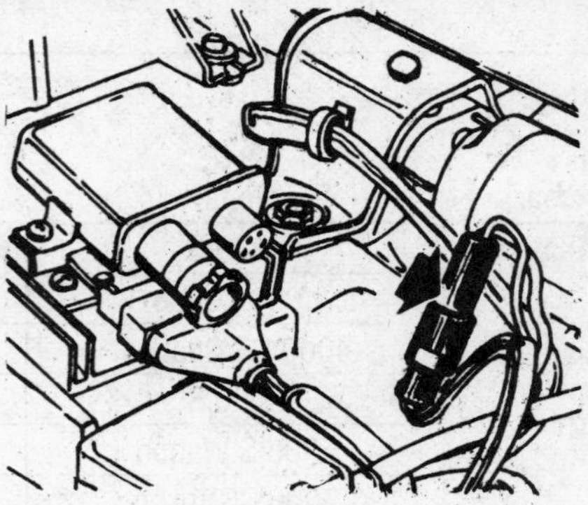

Bypass the idle stabilizer unit by connecting thye two plugs together (arrow)

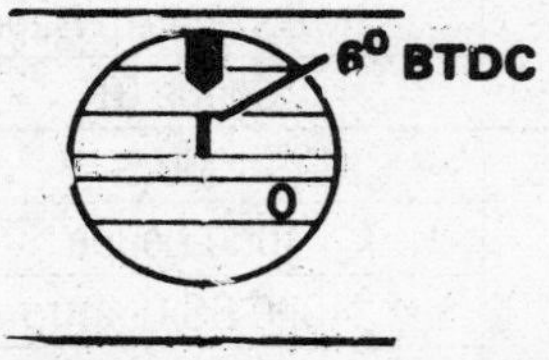


Timing mark alignment—4 cylinder engine

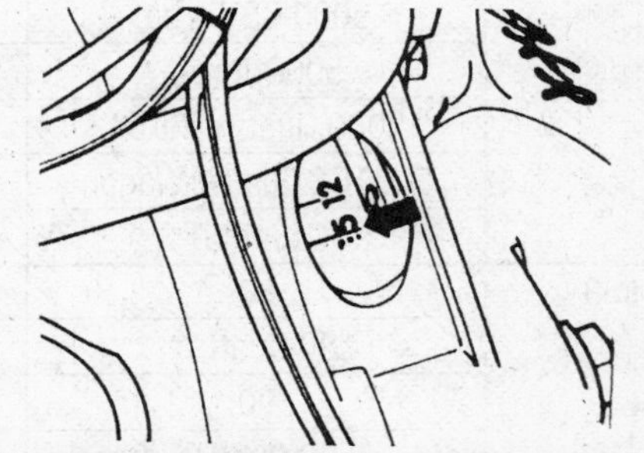

5 cylinder engine timing mark on bell housing aligned with mark on flywheel

2. Start and run the engine until it reaches normal operating temperature. The radiator fan must cycle at least 1 time.
3. With the engine at idle, aim the timing light in the timing window on the flywheel housing.

**NOTE: The ignition timing and idle speed should not be adjusted or checked with the radiator fan operating.**

4. Rotate the distributor until the notch on the flywheel aligns with the pointer on the bell housing.
5. Tighten the distributor hold down clamp and recheck the ignition timing.
6. Check the idle speed and adjust as required.

#### *1987–90 4 Cylinder Engine*

**NOTE: 1987–90 engine electronic control unit will retard or advance the timing for each cylinder as required by the cylinder's efficiency.**

1. Start and warm engine until oil temperature reaches at least 176°F (80°C).

2. Make certain fault code memory is clear, if equipped. All emission related component must be operating properly and throttle must be in the idle position.

**NOTE: Ignition timing, idle speed and CO (fuel/air mixture) must be checked and adjusted together for proper performance and economy.**

3. Shut engine **OFF**.

4. Connect tool VW 1367, equivalent or timing light, to battery, coil, plug wire and place TDC sensor in tranaxle housing recess. The ignition timing is display on the VW 1367 engine tester.

5. Start engine, make certain all electrical consumers are **OFF**, including air condition and radiator cooling fan.

6. Timing should be 4–8 degrees before TDC.

7. If adjustment is necessary, remove tamper proof seal covering distributor clamp bolt. Loosen clamp and turn distributor as needed.

8. Tighten distributor clamp to 18 ft. lbs. and install new seal.r

### *1987–88 5 Cylinder Engine*

**NOTE: 1987–90 engine electronic control unit will retard or advance the timing for each cylinder as required by the cylinder's efficiency.**

1. Start and warm engine until oil temperature reaches at least 176°F (80°C).

2. Make certain throttle is in the idle position.

3. Shut engine **OFF**.

4. Connect tool VW 1367, or equivalent, to battery, coil, plug wire and place TDC sensor in tranaxle housing recess. The ignition timing is display on the VW 1367 engine tester.

5. Insert a fuse in the fuel pump relay with fuse. Fuse must stay connected while checking or adjusting the timing. The electronic control unit will not provide a constant timing valve until 4 seconds after bridging the terminals.

6. Start engine, make certain no faults are stored in memory and air condition and all electrical loads are **OFF**.

7. Loosen the distributor and adjust timing to 13–17 degrees before TDC, if necessary.

8. Tighten distributor retaining bolt and remove fuse from fuel pump relay.

9. Raise engine to 2500 rpm.

10. Run engine at idle and check that

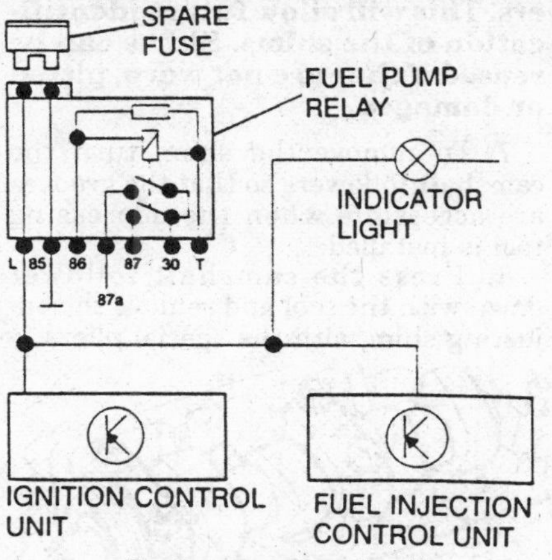


**Fuel pump relay circuit**

timing varies between 7–20 degrees before TDC.

11. Check that idle speed is 670–770 rpm, if not CO content will need to be adjusted.

### *1989–90 5 Cylinder Engine*

**NOTE: 1987–90 engine electronic control unit will retard or advance the timing for each cylinder as required by the cylinder's efficiency.**
**The ignition timing is controlled by the CIS-E III computer control system and requires the use of the special diagnostic connector located on the driveside footwell.**

1. Start and warm engine until oil temperature reaches at least 176°F (80°C).

2. Make certain throttle is in the idle position.

3. Shut engine **OFF**.

4. Connect tool VW 1367, or equivalent, to battery, coil, plug wire and place TDC sensor in tranaxle housing recess.

5. The ignition timing is display on the VW 1367 engine tester.

6. Start engine, make certain all electrical consumers are **OFF**, including air condition and radiator cooling fan.

7. Connect a jumper between the 2 lower terminal of the diagnostic test connecter. This jumper must stay connected while checking or adjusting the timing. The electronic control unit will not provide a constant timing valve until 4 seconds after bridging the terminals.

8. Loosen the distributor and adjust timing to 13–17 degrees before TDC, if necessary.

9. Tighten distributor retaining bolt and remove fuse from fuel pump relay.

10. Raise engine to 2500 rpm.

11. Run engine at idle and check that timing varies between 7–20 degrees before TDC.

12. Check that idle speed is 670–770

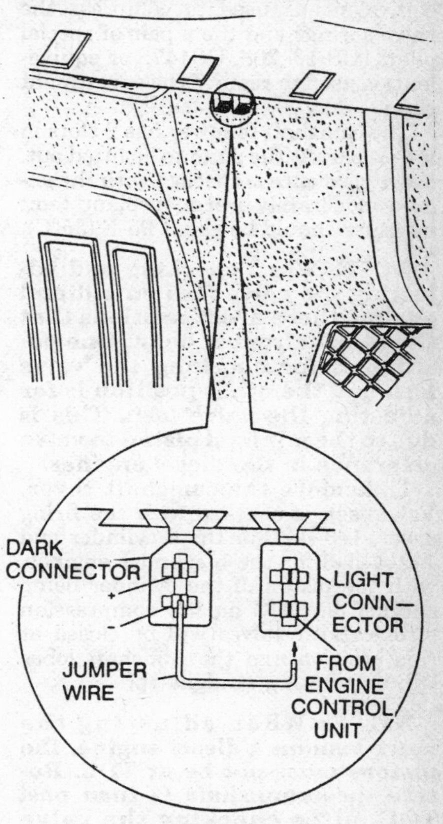


**Test connector**

rpm, if not CO content will need to be adjusted.

## Valve Lash

### ADJUSTMENT

#### *1983 4 and 5 Cylinder Engines*

**NOTE: Audi recommends checking the valve lash after the first 1000 miles and every 15,000 miles thereafter. All 1984–90 engines are equipped with hydraulic valve lash adjusters that eliminate the need for routine valve lash adjustments. Intermittent valve noise is normal when the engine is cold. If valve noise persists, check the camshaft lobes, shims and/or camshaft followers for wear. Replace if necessary.**

On all 1983 engines, the camshaft rides on a valve shim. The shim is seated inside a camshaft follower, that is installed over the valve spring and valve. Adjustments are made by installing a different size shim into the camshaft follower. Changes in the shim thickness will result in changes in the valve lash.

2 special tools must be used to remove and install the adjustment shims. A pry bar (VW 546, 2078 or

equivalent) is used to compress the valve springs and the a pair of special pliers (US 10–208, US4476 or equivalent) is used to remove the adjustment shim.

The camshaft follower has 2 slots in it that permit the shim to be lifted out. Valve clearance is checked with the engine moderately warm (coolant temperature should be about 95°F (35°C).

**NOTE: When checking and adjusting the valve lash on a diesel engine, there are 2 positions that the camshaft must be in. One position is for checking the valve lash and the other position is for adjusting the valve lash. This is due to the minimal piston to valve clearance in the diesel engines.**

1. Remove the camshaft cover. Valve lash is checked with the firing order, 1–3–4–2 for the 4 cylinder and 1–2–4–5–3 for the 5 cylinder engines, with the piston of the cylinder being checked at TDC on it's compression stroke. Both valves will be closed at this position and the camshaft lobes will be pointing straight up.

**NOTE: When adjusting the valve lash on a diesel engine, the pistons must not be at TDC. Rotate the crankshaft ¼ turn past TDC, after checking the valve lash, so that the valves do not contact the pistons when depressing the follower and removing the shim.**

2. Rotate the crankshaft by the crankshaft pulley bolt to position the camshaft for checking.

**NOTE: Do not rotate the engine using the camshaft sprocket bolt. This will stretch and/or break the timing belt. Always rotate the crankshaft clockwise.**

3. With the No. 1 piston at TDC of the compression stroke, determine the clearance using a feeler gauge. Adjust as necessary by replace the shim.
4. Continue checking the other cylinders in the firing order, turning the crankshaft to bring each piston to the top of it's compression stroke (¼ turn past on diesels).
5. If the clearance is within tolerance levels (± 0.002 in.), it is not necessary to readjust.
6. If adjustment is necessary, the shims will have to be removed and replaced with ones giving the correct clearance. Shims are available in 0.002 in. increments from 0.120 in.– 0.170 in.

**NOTE: The thickness of each adjusting shim is etched on 1 side. When installing, the size marks should face the camshaft followers. This will allow future identification of the shims. Shims can be reused if they are not worn, pitted or damaged.**

7. To remove the shim, turn the camshaft followers so that the grooves are accessible when the depressing tool is installed.
8. Press the camshaft follower down with the tool and remove the adjusting shim with the special pliers.

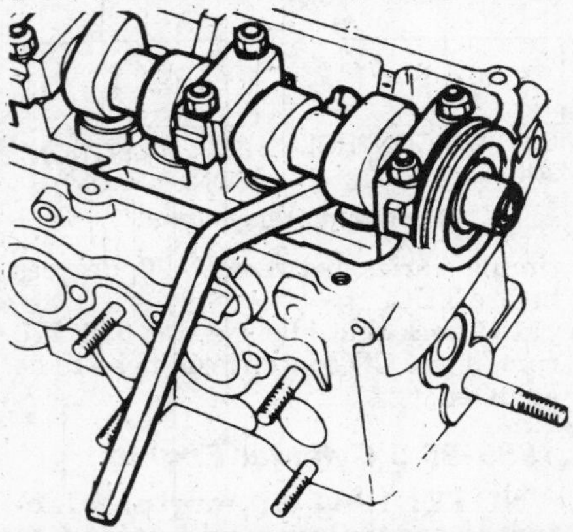

**Remove the adjusting discs with a special pry bar and pliers—don't press on the disc itself, but on the lip of the disc holder. Note the position of the camshaft lobes on no. 1 cylinder. This is the correct position for measuring valve clearance**

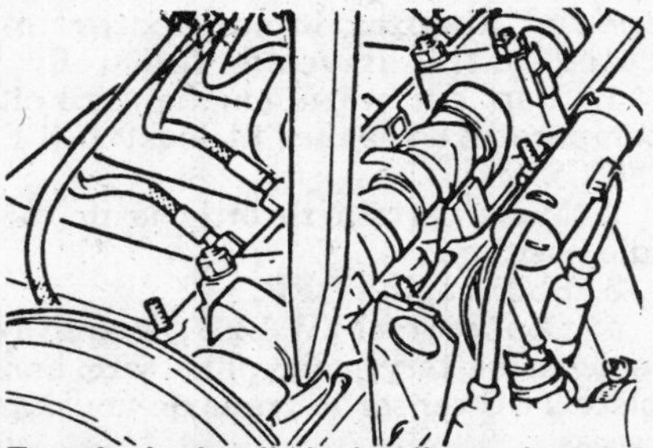

**Test the hydraulic lash adjuster by pushing down against the lifter with a suitable wooden dowel—if the lifter can be pushed down, replacement is indicated**

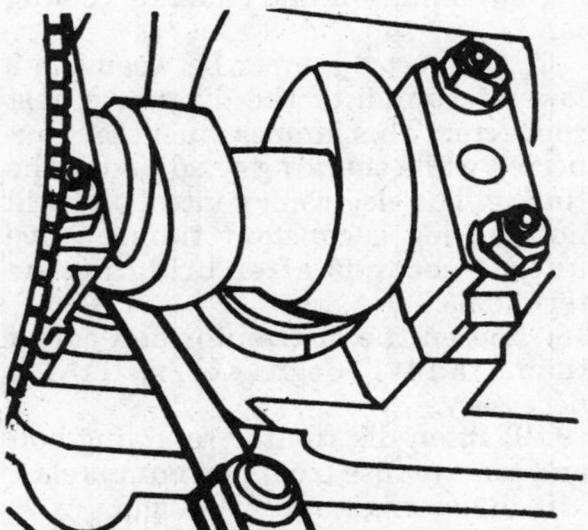

**Check the valve lash with a feeler gauge between the camshaft lobe and adjustment shim**

9. Replace the adjustment shim with a shim that will bring the clearance within the 0.002 in. tolerance level. If the clearance is too large, remove the existing shim and insert a thicker shim to bring the clearance up to specification. If the clearance is too small, insert a thinner shim.
10. Recheck all valve clearances after adjustment.
11. Install the camshaft cover with a new gasket.
12. Reconnect any vacuum hoses and cables that were removed.
13. Run the engine, check for leaks and listen for any excessive valve train noise.

# Idle Speed and Mixture Gasoline Engines

## IDLE SPEED ADJUSTMENT

**NOTE: The idle speed must be adjusted in conjunction with the CO percentage. It is suggested that the adjustment not be attempted unless the all of the necessary equipment is available.**

### *1983–88 Except 5 Cylinder Turbocharged and California Engines*

**NOTE: The ignition timing must be set to specifications before adjusting the idle speed.**

On 1983 4 cylinder 1.7L engines and 1984–88 4 cylinder 1.8L engines, check the idle speed with all vacuum hoses attached. If an adjustment is necessary, the oxygen sensor should remain connected and the crankcase vent hose to the valve cover should be disconnected and left open. The evaporative canister cap should also be removed.

On 1983 5 cylinder 2.1L engines: check the idle speed with the oxygen sensor and all vacuum hoses connected. If adjustment is necessary, disconnect and plug the crankcase vent hose at the camshaft cover. Remove the cap from the evaporative canister. On 5 cylinder, non turbocharged engines, disconnect the purge line. The idle speed stabilizer must also be bypassed, if equipped.

On 1984–87 5 cylinder 2.1L and 2.2L engines, check the idle speed with all vacuum hoses connected. If adjustment is necessary, the oxygen sensor should be connected, the crankcase vent hose to the valve cover should be disconnected and plugged and the evaporative canister cap should be removed.

**To adjust the idle speed:**

1. Connect a dwell/tachometer to the engine.

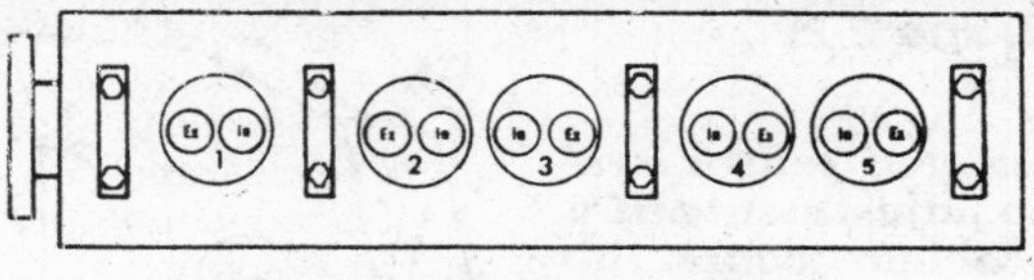

Valve location—5 cyl engine

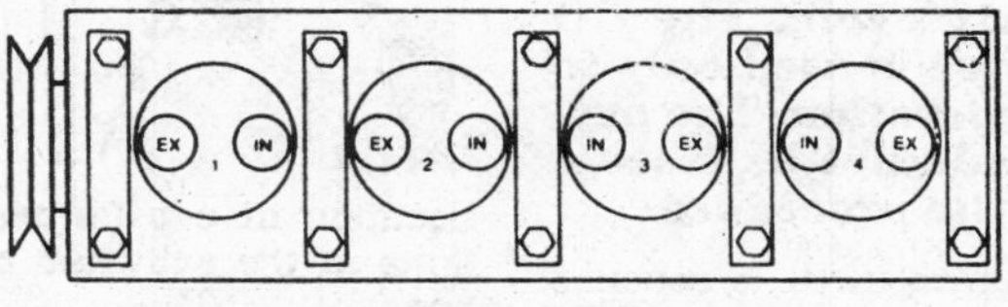

Valve location – 4 cylinder engines

2. Run the engine until the oil temperature is above 176°F (80°C). The radiator fan must cycle at least 1 time.
3. Turn the headlights on high beam.

**NOTE: Do not turn the A/C on and do not have a fuel pressure gauge connected in the fuel line while checking and adjusting the idle speed. If the fuel lines were disconnected, start the engine and run it at 3000 rpm briefly. Let the engine settle at idle for 2 minutes before proceding.**

4. Disconnect the PCV valve hose, if equipped.
5. Locate the idle speed adjusting screw in the throttle valve housing on the back of the intake manifold and adjust the idle to specifications.

**NOTE: Make sure that the radiator fan is not cycling when adjusting the idle speed. It may take several attempts to get the idle speed and CO percentage both within the correct range. Adjusting one will lead to a change in the other.**

6. Adjust the CO percentage after the idle speed adjustment.

### *1985–88 5 Cylinder Turbocharged and California Engines*

**NOTE: The ignition timing must be set before adjusting the idle speed.**

1. Connect a dwell/tachometer, according to the manufacturer's instructions.
2. Turn off all electrical accessories.
3. Run the engine until the oil temperature is above 175°F (80°C). The radiator fan must come on at least once.
4. Turn the ignition **OFF**.
5. Disconnect the PCV valve.
6. Disconnect the the oxygen sensor wire at the rear of the intake manifold.

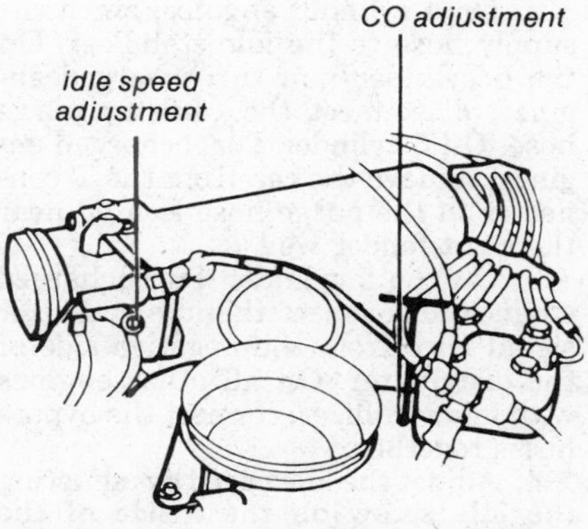


Idle speed and mixture adjustment screws – 4 cylinder gasoline engines

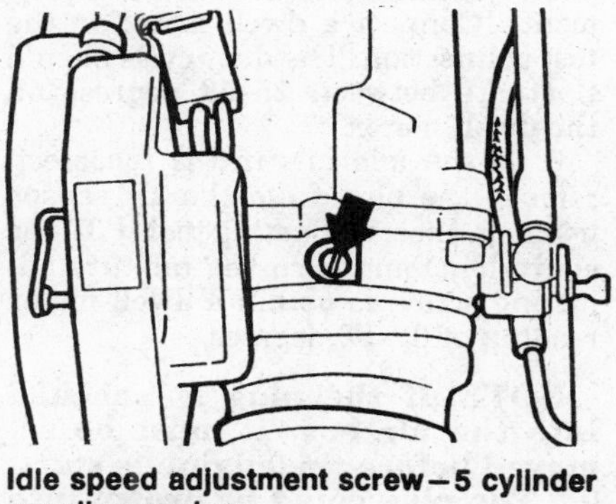

Idle speed adjustment screw – 5 cylinder gasoline engines

7. Unplug both wire leads at the idle stabilizer and connect them together.
8. Start the engine.
9. Locate the idle adjusting screw in the throttle valve housing on the intake manifold and adjust the idle to specifications.

**NOTE: The radiator fan must not cycle while adjusting the idle.**

10. Turn **OFF** the engine and reconnect the PCV valve, oxygen sensor wire and idle stabilizer.
11. Recheck the idle speed. If it has changed, the idle stabilizer will probably require replacement.
12. Adjust the CO percentage.

### *1989–90 5 Cylinder Engines*

Idle for these vehicles is not adjustable independently and must be set with CO (air/fuel mixture).

## IDLE MIXTURE ADJUSTMENT

**NOTE: An exhaust gas analyzer or CO percentage meter is required for this procedure.**

### *1983 Engines without Oxygen Sensor or Idle Stabilizer*

1. Run the engine until it reaches normal operating temperature.
2. Turn the high beams and A/C on. Set the ignition timing to specifications.
3. Adjust the idle speed to specifications.
4. Remove the charcoal filter hose from the air filter box.
5. Remove the plug from the CO percentage adjusting hole in the fuel distributor housing and insert tool VW–P377 or equivalent. Turn adjustment screw clockwise to raise the CO percentage or counterclockwise to decrease the CO percentage. Do not push down on the adjustment tool or accelerate the engine with the tool in place.
6. Remove the tool and accelerate the engine briefly before reading the CO percentage.

**NOTE: For 1983 models, a CO meter is not used to adjust the idle mixture. Audi specifies using the Siemens 451 or equivalent device when making adjustments and only using the CO meter to verify the settings. The purge hose or cap on the evaporative control system must also be removed to adjust CO.**

### *1983 Engines with Oxygen Sensor and Idle Stabilizer*

1. Connect Siemens 451 or equivalent, according to manufacturer's instructions.
2. Start the engine and allow it to reach operating temperature. Turn the ignition key **OFF**.
3. Remove the multipoint connectors from the idle stabilizer and connect them together.
4. Remove and plug the crankcase breather hose at the camshaft cover.
5. Connect the test hose probe to the CO test pipe next to the intake manifold. Some models have a blue rubber cap on the test pipe.
6. Disconnect the oxygen sensor wire and start the engine.
7. Insert adjusting tool VW–P377 and adjust CO percentage to specifica-

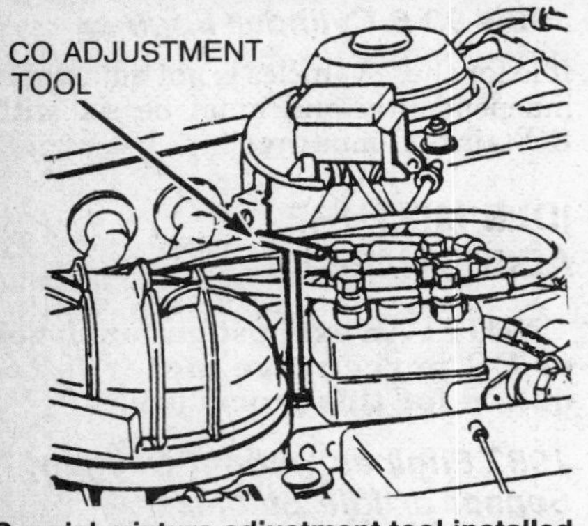


**Special mixture adjustment tool installed on typical CIS air flow sensor. Do not race the engine with the tool in place**

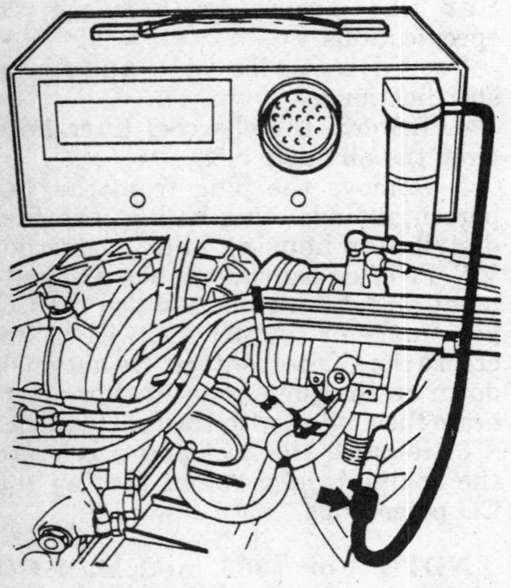

**Attach the CO tester to the tap tube as shown**

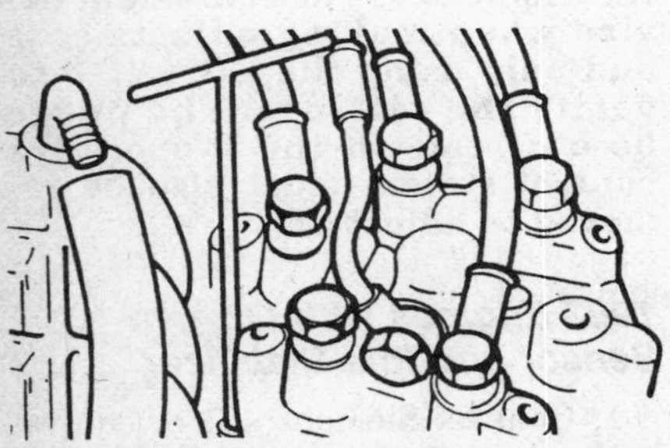

**Using the special tool to adjust the mixture**

tions. Check the underhood EPA sticker for the correct settings.

8. Remove the tool after each adjustments and accelerate the engine briefly before reading CO percentage.

9. Reconnect the oxygen sensor wire. Check CO percentage again.

10. Remove PCV hose and check idle speed.

11. Turn the engine off and reconnect the idle stabilizer. Start the engine and check the ignition timing.

12. Switch on all accessories. The timing should advance if the idle stabilizer is working properly.

### *1984 1.8L, 2.1L and 2.2L Engines*

**NOTE: The oxygen sensor system requires no adjustments. If a performance problem occurs, the system can be checked. A dwell meter is used to display the fuel injection's duty cycle. The CO percentage meter is used only to verify proper operation. The oxygen sensor should not be disconnected during the procedure.**

1. Run the engine until it reaches normal operating temperature. Disconnect but do not plug the crankcase ventilation hose at the camshaft cover.

2. On 4 cylinder engines, pinch the supply hose to the idle stabilizer. On the 5 cylinder non turbocharged engines, disconnect the canister purge hose. On 5 cylinder Turbocharged engines, remove the cap from the T-connector in the purge hose located near the right fender well.

3. On the 5 cylinder Turbocharged engines, disconnect the idle stabilizer signal wire from the negative side of the distributor. On all other engines with idle stabilizer, connect the bypass hoses together.

4. Adjust the idle speed by adjusting the idle screw on the inside of the throttle valve housing.

5. Connect a CO meter to the test point with adapter (US-4492 or equivalent). Connect a dwell meter to the test connection. The duty cycle should fluctuate between 25–59 degrees on the dwell meter.

6. If the idle mixture is incorrect, remove the plug from the air sensor housing. Insert adjusting tool (P377 or equivalent) and turn the mixture adjusting screw to obtain a dwell meter reading of 37–53 degrees.

**NOTE: If the plug is knocked into the air box, it must be removed before the engine is started. The plug could be drawn into the engine and cause severe damage to the internal components.**

7. Check the CO percentage. It should fluctuate between 0.3–1.2% with the oxygen sensor connected and 0.3–3.0% with the oxygen sensor disconnected. Recheck and adjust the idle speed as necessary.

8. Once the adjustments are completed, remove all test equipment and reconnect all vacuum lines and wires.

### *1985–90 4 Cylinder Engines*

**NOTE: On all models, the idle speed, mixture adjustment and ignition timing must be checked together. Exhaust gas mixture must be checked and adjusted by measuring milliamps (mA), using a**

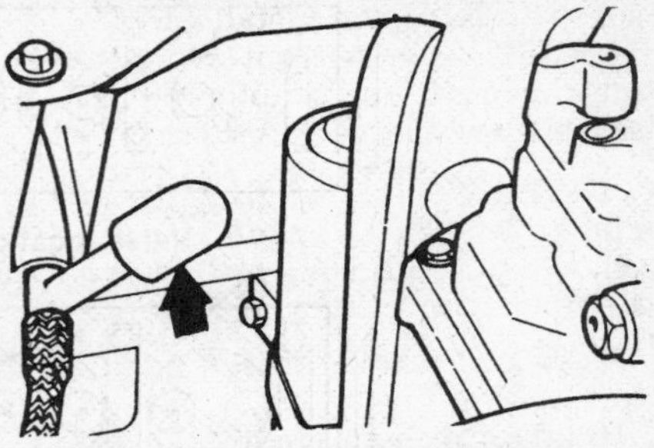

**Location of cap (arrow) and T-connections at the activated charcoal canister hose**

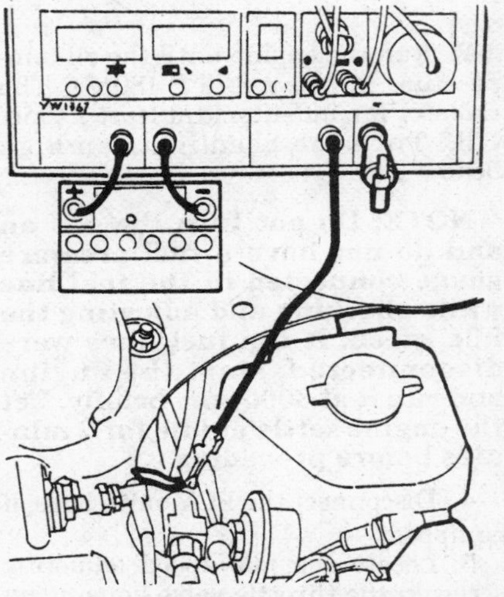

**Connect a tester to the oxygen sensor to the test connector as shown**

**special meter. The oxygen sensor must remain connected. Refer to the underhood vacuum diagram for all hose locations.**

1. Start and run the engine until it reaches normal operating temperature. The radiator fan must cycle at least 1 time.

2. Switch **OFF** all accessories.

**NOTE: The radiator fan must not be running during testing and/or adjusting.**

3. Pinch the hose to the idle speed boost valve.

4. Remove the crankcase breather hose from the valve cover and allow it to vent into the atmosphere.

5. Remove the cap from the T-piece at the canister.

6. Connect SIEMENS 451 tester or equivalent, according to the manufacturer's instructions.

7. Remove the cap from the CO test receptacle and insert the CO probe. The hose must fit tightly so that there is no exhaust leak.

8. To measure milliamps (mA), connect a digital multimeter to the differential pressure regulator. Remove the connector from the differential pres-

sure regulator and install adaptor VW 1515 A/1 or equivalent. Connect the multimeter to the adaptor and set the selector switch to DCA 20 mA scale.

**NOTE: If the engine does not run after the adaptor is connected, the connections are improper. Reverse the plug and repeat.**

9. Check the idle speed and adjust to specifications.
10. With the idle speed set, check the ignition timing and adjust to specifications.
11. Read the milliamp and CO values on the tester. The multimeter should read between 4–16 mA (reading fluctuates) and the CO value should be 0.3–1.2%.
12. If the current reading is less than 4 mA or more than 16 mA, remove the CO adjustment plug as follows:
   a. Stop the engine and remove the boot from the mixture control unit.
   b. Centerpunch the aluminum plug in the CO adjusting hole without knocking the plug in.
   c. Drill a hole $^3/_{32}$ in. (2.5mm) in diameter at the center of the plug $^9/_{64}$–$^5/_{32}$ in. (3.5–4mm) deep.
   d. Carefully clean up any metal shavings and insert a ⅛ in. sheet metal screw into the drilled hole. Remove the screw and plug, using a suitable tool.

**NOTE: If the plug is knocked into the mixture control unit, remove the air box cover and remove the plug. Do not run the engine unless the plug is retrieved.**

13. Start the engine and allow it to idle.
14. Adjust the current reading on the multimeter by turning the CO adjusting screw with tool P377 or equivalent, to obtain 8–12 mA on 1984–88 or 0–5 mA on 1988–90 vehicles (reading fluctuates).
15. Turn the adjusting screw clockwise to lower the current reading (CO higher) and counterclockwise to raise the current reading (CO lower).

**NOTE: Do not push adjustment downwards on the tool when making CO adjustments. Do not accelerate the engine with the tool in place. Remove the tool after each adjustment and accelerate the engine briefly before reading multimeter.**

16. After the CO adjustment is complete, recheck the idle speed and adjust if necessary. Reconnect the crankcase breather hose. If after reconnecting the breather hose, the current reading drops below specifications, the reading is being disturbed by "blow-by" from the crankcase. An oil change may be necessary.
17. Turn the ignition **OFF** and install a new mixture plug, flush with the mixture control unit.
18. Remove all test equipment, install the CO probe cap and remove the device used to pinch the idle speed boost valve hose.

### *1985–88 5 Cylinder Engines*

**NOTE: On all models, the idle speed, mixture adjustment and ignition timing must be checked together. Exhaust gas mixture must be checked and adjusted by measuring milliamps (mA), using a special meter. The oxygen sensor must remain connected. Refer to the underhood vacuum diagram for all hose locations.**

#### NON TURBOCHARGED ENGINES

**NOTE: Idle speed, ignition timing and oxygen sensor duty cycle (mixture) must be checked and adjusted together.**

1. Check that there are no leaks in the exhaust system and connect Siemens 451 tester or equivalent, according to the manufacturer's instructions. Make sure the TDC sending unit is installed snugly into the transaxle housing.
2. Remove the cap from the CO probe receptacle and install the CO test probe. Make sure the hose fits snugly so there is no exhaust leak.
3. Disconnect the crankcase breather hose at the cylinder head cover and plug the hose.
4. Disconnect both plugs at the idle stabilizer and plug the connectors together to bypass the unit. Make sure the connectors are tight.
5. Turn off all accessories. If any fuel lines were disconnected or replaced, start the engine and run it to 3000 rpm several times. Let idle for at least 2 minutes before continuing.
6. Start and run the engine until it reaches normal operating temperature. The radiator fan must cycle at least 1 time.

**NOTE: The radiator fan must not be running during any test and/or adjustment.**

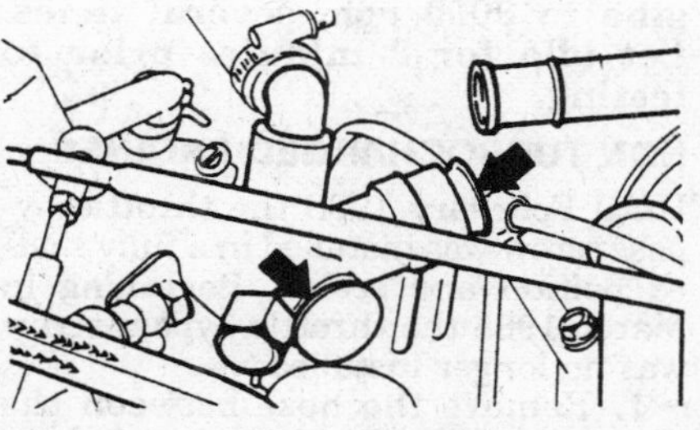

**Plug the crankcase breather hose as shown**

7. Check and adjust the idle speed.
8. Check and adjust the ignition timing. Turn the engine off.
9. Connect the dwell lead on the tester to the oxygen sensor blue/white test connection. Remove the cap from the charcoal canister purge line.
10. Remove the test lead from No. 1 ignition wire and TDC sending unit. Make sure the tester is on the 4 cylinder scale and press % button. Start the engine and check the oxygen sensor duty cycle (dwell) and CO percentage with the engine at idle.
11. The OXS duty cycle should be 25–65% (reading should fluctuate) and the CO should be between 0.3–1.2%. If the CO is more than 1.2%, but the duty cycle is correct, check for leaks in the intake or exhaust system, malfunctioning fuel distributor, or a faulty fuel injector spray pattern.
12. If the OXS duty cycle is less than 25% or more than 65%, remove the tamper-proof plug as follows:
   a. Stop the engine and remove the boot from the mixture control unit.
   b. Centerpunch the aluminum plug in the CO adjusting hole without knocking the plug in.
   c. Drill a hole $^3/_{32}$ in. (2.5mm) in diameter at the center of the plug $^9/_{64}$–$^5/_{32}$ in. (3.5–4mm) deep.
   d. Carefully clean up any metal shavings and insert a ⅛ in. sheet metal screw into the drilled hole. Remove the screw and plug, using a suitable tool.

**NOTE: If the plug is knocked into the mixture control unit, remove the air box cover and remove the plug. Do not run the engine unless the plug is retrieved.**

13. Using adjusting tool P377 or equivalent, adjust the OXS duty cycle (mixture) by turning the adjusting screw clockwise to lower the meter reading, or counterclockwise to increase the reading. Adjust to 44–56% (reading should fluctuate). The radiator fan must not cycle while checking or adjusting.

**NOTE: Do not push adjustment tool down while adjusting CO level. Never accelerate the engine with the tool in place and remove the tool and accelerate the engine briefly after each adjustment.**

14. Readjust the idle speed, if necessary.
15. Turn the engine off and remove the test equipment. Be sure to replace the CO probe cap to prevent exhaust leaks.
16. Reconnect the crankcase breath-

er hose and idle stabilizer. Install the cap to the charcoal canister purge line and replace the tamper-proof adjustment plug.

**TURBOCHARGED ENGINES**

**NOTE: The idle speed, ignition timing and oxygen sensor duty cycle (mixture) must be checked and adjusted together with the engine at normal operating temperature. The throttle valve must be in the idle position and all electrical accessories off. If the injector lines have been disconnected or replaced, start and run the engine to 3000 rpm several times. Let idle for 2 minutes prior to testing.**

1. Connect Siemens 451, VW 1367, or equivalent tester according to manufacturer's instructions. Make sure the TDC sensor is firmly seated into the transaxle housing.
2. Disconnect the green wire from terminal No. 1 of the ignition coil.
3. Remove the cap from the CO test tube and connect the hose from the CO tester. Make sure the hose connection is tight to eliminate any exhaust leak.
4. Disconnect and plug the crankcase ventilation hoses at the valve cover.
5. Remove the cap from the T-connection at the charcoal canister hose.
6. Start and run the engine until it reaches normal operating temperature. The cooling fan must cycle at least 1 time. Adjust the idle speed to specifications.

**NOTE: The cooling fan must not cycle while testing or adjusting.**

7. Turn the engine off and disconnect the test cable from terminal No. 1 of the ignition coil. Connect the cable to the blue/white wire of the oxygen sensor. Disconnect the test connections from No. 1 cylinder ignition cable and TDC sensor. Push the "Dwell Angle %" button on the tester.
8. Start the engine and allow it to idle. Raise the engine speed above 2000 rpm for 5 seconds and check the oxygen sensor duty cycle. The duty cycle should read 25–65% (reading should fluctuate) and the CO value should be 0.3–1.2% with the oxygen sensor connected.
9. If the CO value exceeds 1.2% with the duty cycle within 25–65%, check for a fault in the ignition system, leaks in the exhaust system or a problem with the fuel distributor. If the duty cycle is less than 25% or exceeds 65%, a CO adjustment is necessary.
10. Turn the engine off and remove the CO adjustment plug from the mixture control unit as follows:
   a. Stop the engine and remove the boot from the mixture control unit.
   b. Centerpunch the aluminum plug in the CO adjusting hole without knocking the plug in.
   c. Drill a hole $^3/_{32}$ in. (2.5mm) in diameter at the center of the plug $^9/_{64}$–$^5/_{32}$ in. (3.5–4mm) deep.
   d. Carefully clean up any metal shavings and insert a ⅛ in. sheet metal screw into the drilled hole. Remove the screw and plug, using a suitable tool.

**NOTE: If the plug is knocked into the mixture control unit, remove the air box cover and remove the plug. Do not run the engine unless the plug is retrieved.**

11. Using CO adjustment tool P377 or equivalent, turn the adjustment screw clockwise to lower the OXS duty cycle, or counterclockwise to raise it to obtain a reading of 42–58% (reading should fluctuate). Do not lift or press down on the adjustment tool when making adjustments. Remove the tool and briefly accelerate the engine after each adjustment. Never accelerate the engine with the tool in place.
12. Once the correct duty cycle reading is obtained, reset the idle speed if necessary.
13. Turn the engine off and disconnect the CO tester. Install the cap on the CO test tube, making sure it is tight to prevent exhaust leaks. Disconnect all test equipment and restore all disconnected hoses. Install the cap on the charcoal canister T-connection and drive in a new tamper-proof mixture plug.

### *1989–90 5 Cylinder Engines*

**NOTE: The idle speed, ignition timing and oxygen sensor duty cycle (mixture) must be checked and adjusted together with the engine at normal operating temperature. The throttle valve must be in the idle position and all electrical accessories off. If the injector lines have been disconnected or replaced, start and run the engine to 3000 rpm several times. Let idle for 2 minutes prior to testing.**

**NON TURBOCHARGED ENGINES**

Until February 1988 the throttle bypass screw was installed in a fully seated poition and sealed. Beginning in March 1988 the throttle bypass screw was no longer installed.

1. Remove the hose between the charcoal canister and intake air boot and vent to atmosphere. The elbow contains a calibrated bore, which must remain in thse intake air boot.
2. Remove the hose from the charcoal canister frequency valve and vent to atmosphere.
3. Remove the crankcase vent hose.
4. Plug the metal tube with cap from CO tap tube.
5. Disconnect the differential pressure regulator harness connector.
6. Connect test adapter VW 1315 A/1, or equivalent, between the differential pressure regulator and harness connector.
7. Set multimeter to 200 mA range and connect to the VW 1315 adapter.
8. Remove the cap from the CO tap tube.
9. Connect a SUN 105, or equivalent tester to CO tap. Hose must fit securely over the CO tap tube, so there is no exhaust leakage.
10. Start engine, briefly raise engine to 4000 rpm and snap throttle shut.
11. Meter should read negative 50–60 mA for a short time. If meter reads positive 50–60 mA reverse the test leads.
12. If no value is indicated check the idle switch for proper operation.
13. Measurement of the CO on SUN 105 should read 0.3–1.2 %.
14. If reading is incorrect, turn engine **OFF**.
15. Remove the intake air boot from the mixture control unit.
16. Center punch mixture adjustment screw plug. Drill a $^3/_{32}$ in. (2.5mm) hole in center of plug to a depth of $^9/_{64}$–$^5/_{32}$ in. (3.5–4.0mm). Clean up any shavings.

**NOTE: Applying grease to drill bit will help catch shavings.**

17. Screw a ⅛ in. (3mm) screw into plug and remove screw and plug with pliers.
18. Start engine and allow to idle.
19. Adjust CO by turning mixture tool P377, or equivalent, to obtain a valve of 0 ± 1 mA.

**NOTE: For service performed over 3280 ft. of elevation disconnect, the oxygen sensor (Green) wire prior to making adjustment and record mA measure. Reconnect oxygen sensor and adjust mA within ±1 mA of reading recorded with oxygen sensor disconnected.**

**TURBOCHARGED ENGINES**

1. Connect test adapter VW 1315 A/1, or equivalent, between the differential pressure regulator and harness connector.
2. Connect the VW 1367, or equivalent engine tester, making certain the TDC pickup is inserted into the transaxle housing as far as possible.

3. Set multimeter to 200 mA range and connect to the VW 1315 adapter.
4. Remove the cap from the CO tap tube.
5. Connect a SUN 105, or equivalent tester to CO tap. Hose must fit securely over the CO tap tube, so there is no exhaust leakage.
6. Disconnect and seal the crankcase breather hose to cylinder head cover.
7. Remove the T-connector at the charcoal canister hose.
8. Start engine and allow to idle.
9. Adjust idle adjustment screw to obtain a multimeter reading of 410–450 mA. Idle on VW 1367 should display 750–850 rpm – manual transaxle or 670–770 – automatic transaxle.
10. If idle is not within specification the idle stabilizer valve, temperature sensor or idle control unit may be defective.
11. Disconnect VW 1367 test lead from coil terminal and connect to oxygen sensor test (Blue/White) wire. Remove the TDC sensor.
12. Depress the "dwell-angle" button on the VW 1367 tester.
13. Start the engine and observe the oxygen sensor duty cycle. If duty cycle is 25%–65% and CO is greater than 1.2% there is a fuel, exhaust or ignition problem. If duty cycle is not 25%–65%, continue with adjust.
14. Turn ignition **OFF**.
15. Remove the intake air boot from the mixture control unit.
16. Center punch mixture adjustment screw plug. Drill a $^3/_{32}$ in. (2.5mm) hole in center of plug to a depth of $^9/_{64}$–$^5/_{32}$ in. (3.5–4.0mm). Clean up any shavings.

**NOTE: Applying grease to drill bit will help catch shavings.**

17. Screw a ⅛ in. (3mm) screw into plug and remove screw and plug with pliers.
18. Reinstall the intake air boot and start engine and allow to idle.
19. Adjust CO by turning mixture tool P377, or equivalent, to obtain a duty cycle fluctuation of 42%–58%.
20. Recheck idle speed after adjusting duty cycle.
21. Turn ignition **OFF**.
22. Disconnect test equipment and install cap on CO tap tube.
23. Reconnect the crankcase vent hoses and T-connector on charcoal canister hose.

**NOTE: The oxygen sensor duty cycle can drop below specification with the crankcase hose attached due to oil dilution. An oil change is a short term solution to this problem.**

## Idle Speed Diesel Engine

### ADJUSTMENTS

The idle speed of the engine can be adjusted by turning a control knob, located on the dash, either right or left. Turning the knob to the right increases the engine speed, while turning the knob to the left, decreases the engine speed.

#### *Initial Idle and Maximum No-Load Speed Adjustment*

1. Install diesel tachometer VW 1367 or equivalent.
2. Start the engine and warm up to normal operating temperature. Turn the control knob to the left until it touches the stop.
3. Using the adjuster screw on the injection pump, adjust the idle speed to 720–880 rpm on the non turbocharged diesel engine and 700–800 rpm on turbodiesel. Use a locking substance or a dab of paint to lock the idle adjuster screw into place on the pump.

**CAUTION**

***Use extreme care when adjusting the maximum no-load engine speed. Over-revving the engine could result in engine damage and personal injury.***

4. Increase the engine speed on the non turbocharged diesel engine to 5350–5450 rpm and set with the maximum speed adjuster screw, located on the injection pump. Lock the screw with a locking substance or a dab of paint. The 5000 Turbodiesel maximum no-load rpm is 5050–5150 rpm. Do not hold the engine at maximum rpm for more than 2 or 3 seconds.

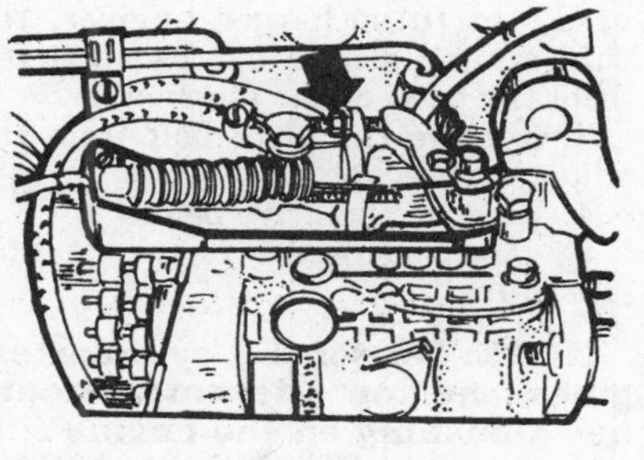

**Idle speed adjustment scew – diesel**

# ENGINE ELECTRICAL

**NOTE: Never disconnect any electrical connector with the ignition key ON, unless specified in repair procedure, or damage to electronic components may result.**

## Distributor

### REMOVAL

1. Disconnect the wiring harness connector from the distributor cap.
2. Unclip and remove the distributor cap and static shield with the spark plug wires still attached.
3. Disconnect and tag the vacuum lines at the distributor, if equipped.
4. Note the position of the rotor in relation to the distributor housing. Scribe a mark on the distributor and engine block for installation. Matchmark the tip of the rotor to the engine. Note the approximate position of the vacuum advance unit in relation to the engine.
5. Remove the distributor hold-down bolt and clamp.
6. Lift the distributor assembly from the engine. Note the position of the rotor as the distributor is removed.

### INSTALLATION

#### *Engine Timing Not Disturbed*

1. With the rotor pointing in the same direction as when removed, insert the distributor into the engine.
2. Once the distributor is seated into the engine, line up the marks on the distributor and engine with the metal tip of the rotor.
3. Make sure the vacuum advance unit, if equipped, is pointed in the same direction as it was pointed originally. If the marks on the distributor and the engine are lined up properly, this will be done automatically.
4. Install the distributor hold-down clamp and bolt.
5. Install the distributor cap and static shield.
6. Install the vacuum lines, if equipped.
7. Install the distributor wiring harness connector.
8. Start the engine. Adjust the ignition timing.

#### *Engine Timing Disturbed*

**NOTE: If the engine has been turned or disturbed in any manner (i.e. disassembled and rebuilt) while the distributor was removed, or if the marks were not drawn, it will be necessary to initially time the engine. Follow the procedure given below.**

1. It is necessary to place the No. 1 cylinder in the firing position (TDC) to correctly install the distributor. To locate this position, the ignition timing

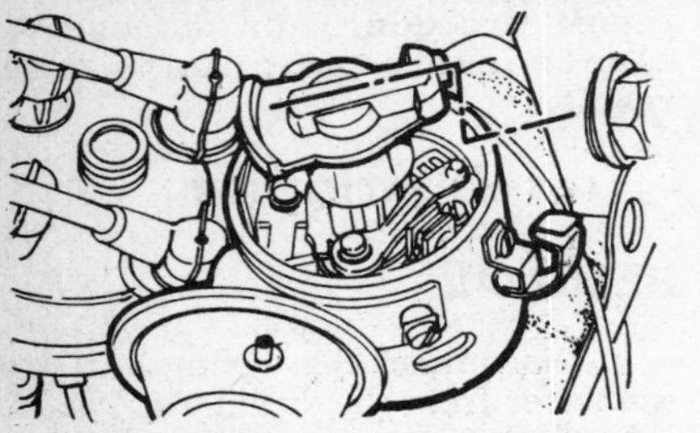

Rotor/distributor alignment for the No. 1 cylinder

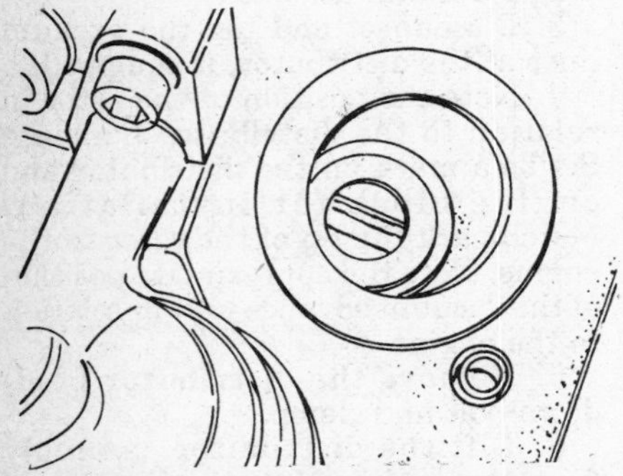

Oil pump driveshaft must be parallel to the crankshaft on 4 cylinder engines

marks on the flywheel and the clutch housing are used.

2. Remove the spark plug from the No. 1 cylinder. Turn the crankshaft until the piston in the No. 1 cylinder is moving up on the compression stroke. This can be determined by placing a finger over the spark plug hole and feeling the air being forced out of the cylinder. Stop turning the engine when the timing mark on the flywheel is aligned with the lug on the flywheel housing.

3. Remove the timing belt cover.

4. Align the mark on the camshaft sprocket with the upper edge of the drive belt cover or with the upper edge of the valve cover gasket mounting surfaces.

5. On 4 cylinder engines, align the oil pump drive pinion lug so that it aligns with the threaded hole.

6. Oil the distributor housing lightly where it bears on the cylinder block.

7. Install the distributor so that the rotor tip, points to the mark on the distributor housing for the No. 1 cylinder.

8. On 4 cylinder engines, when the distributor shaft has reached bottom, move the rotor back and forth slightly until the drive lug on the oil pump shaft enters the slots cut into the end of the distributor shaft and the distributor assembly slides down into place.

9. Clean the distributor cap and check for signs of cracking or carbon tracks. Install the cap and continue the installation procedure.

# Alternator

## PRECAUTIONS

When performing any service to the charging system, the following precautions must be observed:

- Leads or cables to any part of the charging circuit should be disconnected only after the engine has been switched **OFF** and has stopped running.
- When working on the electrical system, always disconnect the lead from the negative battery terminal.
- When performing tests with the engine running, the battery must always be connected.
- Temporary connections should never be made to the alternator. Always make firm connections.
- The alternator warning light on the instrument panel should go out when the engine reaches idle speed, or shortly after.

## REMOVAL & INSTALLATION

**NOTE: On models with 4 cylinder engines, the procedure can be done from the top of the vehicle. On 5 cylinder models, it is easier to remove and install the alternator from below the vehicle. On 5 cylinder diesel engine models, the undercover will have to be removed to gain access to the alternator.**

### *All Engines*

1. Disconnect the negative battery cable.

2. Disconnect and tag the alternator wiring. Various arrangements of plug-in or bolt-on connections are used. On turbocharged engines, the cold air housing must be removed from the back of the alternator.

3. Remove the pivot bolt from the adjusting bracket.

4. Remove the drive belt.

5. Unbolt and remove the alternator.

**NOTE: On some 4 cylinder engines, the top alternator mount has a bushing on the engine side of the mount. Check the condition of the bushing and replace if necessary, before installing the alternator.**

6. To install, hold the alternator in position and install the pivot bolts.

7. Install the drive belt and adjusting bolt.

8. Adjust the belt tension.

9. Connect the electrical connections, making sure that they are installed in their original locations.

10. Connect the negative battery cable.

## BELT TENSION ADJUSTMENT

The drive belts are correctly tensioned when the longest span of belt between pulleys can be depressed ⅛–½ in. using moderate thumb pressure. To adjust, loosen the slotted adjusting bracket bolt on the alternator. If the alternator hinge bolts are very tight, it may be necessary to loosen them slightly to move the alternator. Move the alternator in or out to obtain the correct tension. Tighten the adjusting bolt when finished.

V-belts under 39 in. in length should deflect about ⅛ in. Belts over 40 in. long should deflect about ½ in.

# Starter

## REMOVAL & INSTALLATION

### *All Engines*

**NOTE: A starter relay is used on vehicles with an alarm system. This relay supplies power to the starter. The alarm control unit will switch open the relay's ground, if any attempt to bypass the ignition circuit is detected. This prevents the starter from operating.**

1. Disconnect the negative battery cable.

2. Raise and safely support the vehicle safely.

3. Disconnect and tag the starter wiring.

4. On 4 cylinder engines, remove the starter support bracket bolts. Remove the starter mounting bolts from the rear of the starter.

5. On 5 cylinder engines, 1 bolt goes through the transaxle with a nut on the end of the bolt.

6. Remove the starter from the engine.

7. Installation is the reverse of the removal procedure.

# Starter Drive

## REMOVAL

**NOTE: In order to complete this procedure, a pair of circlip pliers and special tool US 1078, a gear puller, are needed.**

1. Remove the starter from the vehicle.

2. Remove the solenoid from the starter motor.

3. Remove the 2 long housing screws and remove the end plate.

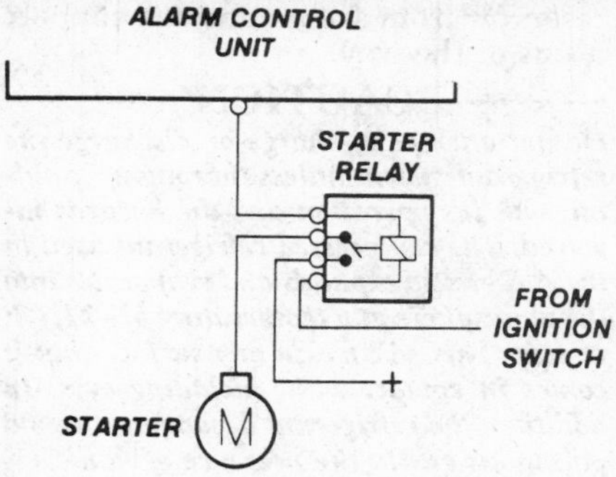


Starter relay circuit

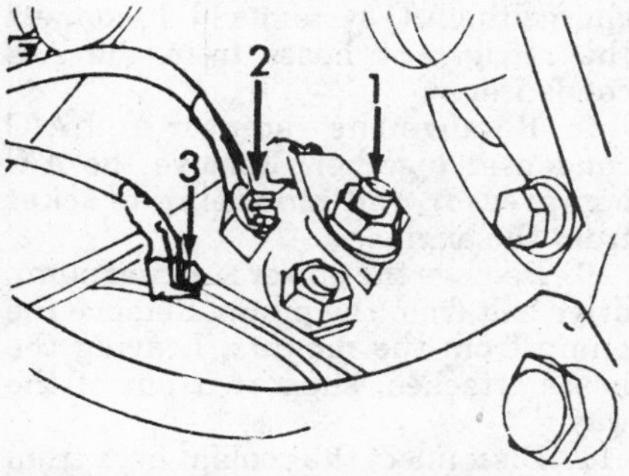


Starter motor electrical connections: (1) solenoid, (2) coil, (3) positive battery cable

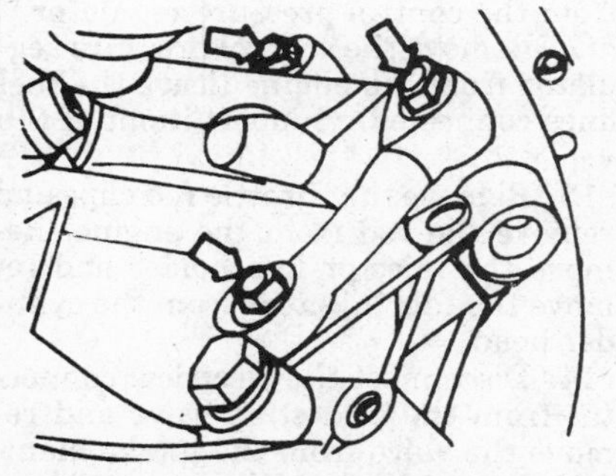

Starter motor mounting bolts—all models similar

4. Lift the brushes to free them from the commutator and remove the brush holder.
5. Lightly tap the field coil housing, until free from the housing and remove from the starter drive housing.
6. Remove the nut and bolt that serves as a pin for the shift lever. Be careful to retain all the associated washers.
7. Remove the shift lever.
8. Slide the armature/starter drive assembly out of the starter drive housing.
9. Using tool No. VW421, press the stop ring down and remove the circlip from the end of the armature shaft.
10. Remove the stop ring, using the gear puller tool No. 1078.
11. Slide the starter drive off of the armature shaft.

#### INSTALLATION

1. Lubricate the drive pinion lightly with multi-purpose grease and slide the starter drive onto the armature shaft.
2. Install the stop ring and press it over the circlip groove.

**NOTE: When installing the stop ring, the groove must always be on the side closest to the front of the starter (the side nearest to the starter drive).**

3. Install the circlip. Using the gear puller tool No. 1078, pull the stop ring up into place against the circlip.
4. Lightly grease the shaft.
5. Install the armature/starter drive assembly into the starter drive housing.
6. Install the shift lever.
7. Ease the field coil housing over the armature assembly and fit it into the starter drive housing.
8. Install the brush holder and the end plate.
9. Install the solenoid.
10. Install the starter.

#### SOLENOID REPLACEMENT

1. Remove the starter.
2. Remove the 3 solenoid switch retaining screws from the back of the starter drive housing.
3. Withdraw the solenoid, being careful to unhook it from the shift lever.
4. Installation is in the reverse of the removal procedure. In order to facilitate proper engagement of the shift lever upon installation, the drive pinion should be pulled out as far as possible.

## Diesel Glow Plug

#### REMOVAL & INSTALLATION

1. Disconnect the negative battery cable. Disconnect the electrical connector from the glow plug.
2. Remove the glow plug from the cylinder head.
3. Clean and inspect the glow plug for correct operation.
4. To install, reverse the removal procedures.

#### TESTING

1. Remove the electrical wire and bus-bar from the glow plugs.
2. Using a test light, connect the spring clip to the (+) positive battery terminal. Touch the probe to each glow plug.
3. If the light turns **ON**, the glow plug is functioning properly. If the light does not turn on, the glow plug is defective and must be replaced.

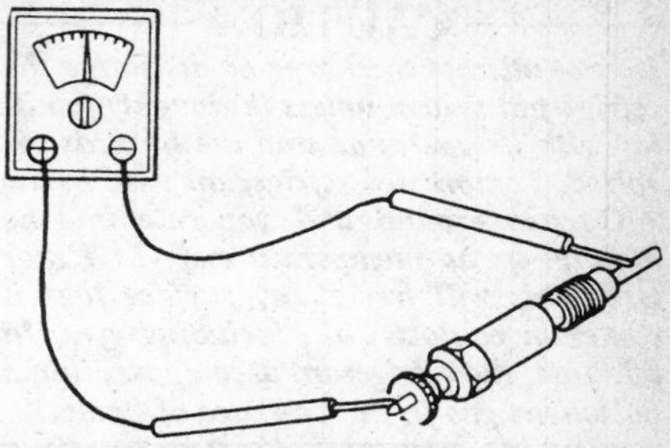

Testing glow plug continuity with an ohmmeter—typical

4. When installing the glow plug, torque the plug to 29 ft. lbs. (40 Nm).

# GASOLINE ENGINE MECHANICAL

## Engine

#### REMOVAL & INSTALLATION

***All Models with 4 Cylinder Gasoline Engine***

**NOTE: Removal of the hood will make engine removal and installation easier. Be sure to mark the location of each hood hinge, so the hood can be reinstalled in the same position.**

1. Disconnect the negative battery cable.
2. Remove the 2 grille retaining clips on the top of the grille. Remove the screw on the bottom and remove the grille.
3. Loosen the right and left sides of the A/C condenser. Tie the condenser away from the radiator.
4. Remove the rubber air duct from the throttle valve housing.
5. Remove the hose from the air duct to the auxiliary air regulator.
6. Disconnect the fuel lines from the cold start valve and fuel injectors. Cap the end of the fuel lines. Remove the injectors from the cylinder head.
7. Remove the fuel distributor, air flow sensor, fuel injectors and the air cleaner from the vehicle, as an assembly.
8. Remove the front engine mount to chassis bolts and remove the mount.
9. Loosen the nuts on the outer half of the crankshaft pulley and remove the V-belt.

**CAUTION**

***Do not attempt to charge or discharge the refrigerant system unless thoroughly familiar with its operation and the hazards involved. Compressed refrigerant used in the A/C system expands and evaporates into the atmosphere at a temperature of –21.7°F or less. This will freeze any surface that it comes in contact with, including eyes. In addition, the refrigerant decomposes into a poisonous gas in the presence of flame.***

10. Discharge the A/C system, following the caution for discharging refrigerant.
11. Remove all A/C lines from the compressor and plug the open connections.
12. Remove the crankcase ventilation hose from the valve cover.
13. Support the A/C hoses away from the engine.
14. Remove the A/C compressor mounting bolts and remove the compressor.
15. Open the heater control valve all the way.
16. Remove the cap on the expansion tank and drain the cooling system.
17. Remove the upper and lower radiator hoses from the radiator.
18. Disconnect and tag the radiator fan wiring and thermo switch at the radiator. Remove the radiator with the fan and shroud as an assembly.
19. Remove the power steering pump, if equipped, with hoses attached, move out of the way and secure to body.
20. On manual transaxle models, disconnect the clutch cable at the release lever.
21. Disconnect and tag the engine wiring.
22. Remove the control pressure regulator (above the oil filter) from the engine leaving all the fuel lines connected. Support it out of the way.
23. Remove the air hose from the back of the alternator, if equipped.
24. Disconnect the blue wire from the alternator at the plug located between the battery and the rear of the engine, if equipped.
25. Remove the charcoal filter hose at the intake air duct.
26. Remove the heater hoses from the engine.
27. Remove the throttle cable from the engine.
28. Disconnect and tag all vacuum hoses at the engine.
29. Remove the hose from the auxiliary regulator to the air inlet duct.
30. Remove the 3 upper engine to transaxle mounting bolts.
31. Remove the right and left engine mount nuts.
32. Raise and support the vehicle safely. Disconnect the exhaust pipe from the exhaust manifold.
33. Remove the flywheel cover plate. On automatic transaxle models, remove the torque converter to flywheel mounting bolts.

**NOTE: Matchmark the converter to flywheel for installation.**

34. Remove the front engine mounting bolts and remove the mount.
35. Disconnect and tag the starter wiring and remove the starter.
36. Remove the 2 lower engine to transaxle mounting bolts.
37. Loosen the right and left engine mount nuts on the sub-frame.
38. Remove the bolt from the front exhaust pipe support.
39. Support the transaxle.
40. Lift the engine until the weight is taken off of the engine mounts and carefully separate the engine and transaxle.
41. Remove the engine from the vehicle.
42. To install, reverse the removal procedures. Tighten the engine-to-transaxle bolts to 40 ft. lbs., starter bolts to 14 ft. lbs. Tighten the cold start valve, pressure control regulator and radiator mounting bolts to 7 ft. lbs. Use a new gasket on the cold start valve when installing.

**NOTE: Tighten the engine and subframe mounting bolts while the engine is running at idle. Tighten the front engine mount bolts to 18 ft. lbs. and the right and left engine mount bolts to 25 ft. lbs.**

### Models with 5 Cylinder Turbocharged Engine

**NOTE: Tag all hoses and wiring during removal to use as reference during reassembly.**

1. Remove the rear seat bottom and disconnect the negative battery cable.
2. Open the heater control valve all the way and drain the cooling system.
3. Remove the fuel injector cooling fan blower motor and intake hose from the engine.
4. Remove the upper radiator cover, grille, bumper strip. Disconnect the wiring harness in bumper for turnsignals and headlights and remove the bumper.
5. Disconnect the electrical connector from the coolant fan. Remove the upper radiator hose from the engine. Remove the radiator to expansion tank hose from the tank and the bleeder hose from the auxiliary radiator.
6. Disconnect the wire from the thermo switch. Remove the radiator mounting bolts, right-side radiator cover and bottom radiator cover.
7. Remove the windshield washer reservoir from the mount and support it out of the way.

**CAUTION**

***Do not attempt to charge or discharge the refrigerant system unless thoroughly familiar with it's operation and the hazards involved. The compressed refrigerant used in the A/C system expands and evaporates into the atmosphere at a temperature of –21.7°F or less. This will freeze any surface that it comes in contact with, including eyes. In addition, the refrigerant decomposes into a poisonous gas in the presence of flame.***

8. Following all precautions, discharge the A/C system and disconnect the refrigerant hoses from the A/C condenser.
9. Remove the radiator and A/C condenser together. Remove the A/C compressor and mounting bracket from the engine.
10. Remove the power steering pump drive belt from the pump. Remove the pump from the mounts. Leaving the hoses attached, support it out of the way.
11. Disconnect the coolant hose from the thermostat housing, wires from the oil pressure switch and temperature sender. Disconnect the wire plugs from the control pressure regulator.
12. Remove the control pressure regulator from the engine (leave the fuel lines connected). Support it out of the way.
13. Remove the throttle rod clips and remove the rod from the engine. Remove the injector line holder and remove the fuel injectors from the cylinder head.
14. Disconnect the electrical connector from the cold start valve and remove the valve from the intake manifold. Leave the fuel line connected.
15. At the throttle body, disconnect the electrical connectors from the throttle valve switches and intake air temperature switch.
16. Disconnect the air intake hose. Disconnect the wire from the auxiliary air regulator, pull off the vacuum hoses and disconnect the breaker hose from the engine.
17. At the two-way valve, remove and tag the vacuum hoses. Remove the thermo-pneumatic valve (leave the vacuum lines connected) and the rpm sensor.
18. Disconnect the speedometer cable from the transaxle.
19. Remove the distributor from the engine.
20. Disconnect and tag the thermo-time switch and overheating warning lamp connectors. Disconnect the heater hoses from the engine.
21. At the left engine mount, disconnect the brake booster from the firewall (with the reservoir) and leave

the lines connected. On Quattro models, disconnect the differential lock control lights connector. Disconnect the backup light switch wires.

22. Disconnect the tie rods from the steering rack. Disconnect the steering linkage.

23. On manual transaxle models, remove the clutch slave cylinder from the bell housing (leave the line attached), the bracket and pin (under the transaxle bracket).

24. Disconnect the left engine mount ground strap. Disconnect the vacuum hose from the auxiliary air valve.

25. Remove the air duct from the intercooler and remove the intercooler.

26. Disconnect and tag the electrical connectors from the alternator. Remove the oil cooler (leave the lines attached). Disconnect and tag the starter wiring.

27. Disconnect the exhaust pipe at the turbocharger. Remove the transaxle cover plates and the right side transaxle mount. Disconnect the axleshafts from the transaxle. On Quattro models, disconnect the driveshaft from the rear of the transaxle.

28. On Quattro models at the transaxle, disconnect the differential lock, remove the front and rear circlips and push back the boot. Disconnect the cable.

29. Remove the left-side transaxle mounting bolt and mounts from both sides.

30. At both front wheels, remove the ball joint pinch bolts. At the subframe, remove the mounting bolts and subframe. Separate the ball joints from the steering knuckle.

31. Install an engine lifting device on the engine. Raise the engine slightly and remove the left and right engine mounts. Lower the engine/transaxle assembly from the vehicle.

32. Raise the front of the vehicle and slide the engine/transaxle assembly from under the vehicle.

33. Separate the engine from the transaxle.

34. Installation is the reverse of the removal procedures

### Models with 5 Cylinder Non Turbocharged Engine

**NOTE: Tag all hoses and wiring during removal to use as reference during reassembly.**

1. Disconnect the negative battery cable.

2. Drain the cooling system.

3. Disconnect the radiator and heater hoses from the engine.

4. Remove the control pressure regulator from the engine, without disconnecting the fuel lines.

5. Remove the cold start valve from the intake manifold, without disconnecting the fuel lines.

6. Pull out the fuel injectors from the cylinder head and support the injectors and fuel lines out of the way.

**NOTE: Protect the fuel injectors and the cold start valve with caps.**

7. Loosen the air duct and vacuum hoses from the throttle valve assembly.

8. Remove the air box cover and filter.

9. At the top of the grille, pull the hood latch cable guide off of its bracket.

10. If equipped with A/C, proceed with the following procedures:

a. Remove the 2 clips from the top of the grille and the screw from the bottom. Remove the grille.

b. Remove the condenser mounting bolts.

c. Remove the air duct to auxiliary air regulator hose and remove the air duct from the throttle valve housing.

d. Remove the fuel distributor, air flow sensor, fuel injectors and air box, as a unit.

**NOTE: When removing the fuel injectors, leave all of the lines connected and cover the fuel injectors with caps.**

e. Remove the accessorie(s) drive belts.

**CAUTION**

***Do not attempt to charge or discharge the refrigerant system unless thoroughly familiar with its operation and the hazards involved. The compressed refrigerant used in the air conditioning system, expands and evaporates into the atmosphere at a temperature of –21.7°F or less. This will freeze any surface that it comes in contact with, including eyes. In addition, the refrigerant decomposes into a poisonous gas in the presence of flame.***

f. Discharge the refrigerant from the A/C system. Remove and plug the A/C hoses, move them away from the engine.

g. Remove the upper/lower compressor mounting bolts and remove the compressor from the engine.

11. Remove the power steering pump from the engine, leaving the hose connected.

12. Remove the vacuum amplifier.

13. Remove the EGR control valve.

14. Remove the windshield washer reservoir from its holder.

15. Remove the distributor cap and ignition wires. Remove the distributor vacuum hose(s).

**NOTE: Tape the distributor dust cap on to prevent it from falling off.**

16. Disconnect the throttle linkage from the engine.

17. If equipped with an automatic transaxle, remove the throttle pushrod.

18. Disconnect the oil pressure and water temperature sensor wiring.

19. Remove the exhaust pipe to manifold nuts. On turbocharged models, remove the exhaust pipe to wastegate nuts.

20. Remove the exhaust pipe support bracket from the transaxle.

21. Remove the front engine mount bolts and remove the mount. Disconnect the ground strap on left engine mount, if equipped.

22. Tag and disconnect all wires from the starter and remove the starter.

23. Tag and disconnect all wires leading from the alternator and remove the alternator.

24. On cars equipped with an automatic transaxle, through the starter mounting hole, remove the torque converter mounting bolts.

25. Remove the lower engine to transaxle mounting bolts.

26. Support the transaxle and lower the vehicle.

27. Remove the upper engine to transaxle mounting bolts.

28. Remove the left engine support bracket.

29. Loosen the right engine bracket from the right engine mount.

30. Lift the engine until the crankshaft V-belt pulley is behind the grille opening.

31. Carefully detach the engine from the transaxle.

32. Remove the engine assembly by turning it to the right while lifting it out.

33. To install, reverse the removal procedures. Torque the engine-to-transaxle mounting bolts to 43 ft. lbs., the torque converter-to-drive plate bolts to 14 ft. lbs., the starter bolts to 14 ft. lbs., the A/C mounting bolts to 29 ft. lbs. and the power steering pump and the control pressure regulator mounting bolts to 14 ft. lbs.

**NOTE: Tighten the engine and subframe mounting bolts, while the engine is running at idle, to 32 ft. lbs.**

### Quattro, Quattro Turbo and Quattro Coupe

1. Disconnect the negative battery cable. Open the heater control valve, remove the cap from the expansion valve and drain the coolant by removing the lower radiator hose.

2. Remove the intake hose from the

injector cooling blower motor. Remove the upper radiator cover screws and cover. Remove the upper radiator hose.

3. Disconnect the coolant fan electrical connector. Remove the coolant hose between the radiator and the expansion tank. Remove the bleeder hose to the auxiliary radiator. Disconnect the thermo switch electrical connector.

4. Remove the radiator mountings and the right and bottom radiator covers. Remove the windshield washer reservoir.

5. Disconnect the A/C lines at the condenser. Remove the radiator and the condenser as an assembly. Remove the upper compressor mounting bracket attaching bolts and the compressor to bracket attaching bolts. Remove the compressor and bracket.

6. Remove the power steering pump and its drive belt. position the pump out of the way without disconnecting the hoses. Disconnect the coolant hose at the thermostat housing.

7. Disconnect the electrical connectors at the oil pressure switch, temperature sender and control pressure regulator. Remove the injector cooling air distributor hose and motor.

8. Remove the control pressure regulator. leaving all the fuel lines attached. Remove the throttle cable and remove the holder foe the injector lines and pull out the injectors.

9. Disconnect the electrical connector at the cold start valve. Remove the cold start valve and leave the fuel lines connected.

10. Disconnect the electrical connectors of the 2 throttle valve switches and intake temperature switch. Disconnect the air intake hose and position the wiring out of the way.

11. Disconnect the electrical connector of the auxiliary air regulator, the vacuum hoses, engine breather hose and the electrical connector of the injector cooling fan and position the wiring out of the way. Disconnect the vacuum hoses of the 2 way valve.

12. Remove the thermo pneumatic valve , leaving the vacuum hoses connected. Remove the rpm sensor. Disconnect the speedometer cable at the transaxle.

13. Remove the distributor and the number 4 ignition wire from the distributor. Disconnect the electrical connector for the Hall sender at the distributor. Disconnect the connectors for the thermo time switch and the overheating warning lamp.

14. Disconnect the heater hoses from the engine. Disconnect the hydraulic brake booster with the reservoir from the motor mount, leaving the lines connected. Disconnect the electrical connector for the differential lock control lights and the back-up light switch.

15. Disconnect the tie rod bracket on the steering rack. Disconnect the shift linkage. Remove the clutch slave cylinder, leaving the hydraulic line connected. Remove the bracket and pin from the transaxle. Do not operate the clutch pedal after removing the slave cylinder.

16. Disconnect the ground strap from the left engine mount and the vacuum hose from the auxiliary air valve. Remove the oil cooler air duct. Remove the intercooler.

17. Disconnect the alternator electrical connectors. Remove the oil cooler, leaving the lines connected. Disconnect the starter electrical connectors. Disconnect the exhaust pipe at the flange.

18. Remove the transaxle cover plates and the right side transaxle mount. Disconnect the axle shafts at the transaxle. Disconnect the differential lock cable by removing the the front and rear circlip, pushing the back the boot and disconnect the cable from the mounting.

19. Remove the transaxle mounting bolts and remove the transaxle mounts. Remove the attaching bolts for the ball joints. Disconnect the rear subframe mounts. Remove the subframe mounting bolts, remove the subframe and press the ball joint out of the strut.

20. Attach a suitable engine lift to the proper engine locations and slightly lift the engine. Remove the engine side mounts and lower the engine and transaxle assembly.

21. Raise and support the vehicle safely. Remove the the engine and transaxle assembly from underneath the vehicle. Once the assembly is secure in a suitable engine stand, remove the transaxle from the engine.

22. The installation is the reverse order of the removal procedure.

## Cylinder Head

**NOTE: Before removing or installing the cylinder head, align the engine timing marks at TDC. Rotate the crankshaft mark away about ¼ turn (BTDC). This will prevent the valves from hitting the piston heads. Be sure to turn the crankshaft to the proper position after cylinder head installation.**

### REMOVAL & INSTALLATION

**NOTE: Cylinder head removal should not be attempted unless the engine is cold.**

1. Disconnect the negative battery cable.

2. Drain the cooling system.

3. Disconnect the air duct from the throttle valve assembly on all models except the Turbo and Quattro. On the Turbo and Quattro, remove the hose which runs between the air duct and the turbocharger.

4. Disconnect the throttle cable from the throttle valve assembly.

5. Remove the air duct for the injector cooling fan on the Turbo and Quattro.

6. Clean and remove the fuel injectors and all other fuel lines.

**NOTE: Protect the fuel injectors and the cold start valve with caps.**

7. Tag and disconnect all vacuum and PCV lines.

8. Remove the hose which runs from the intake manifold to the turbocharger on the Turbo and Quattro.

9. Tag and disconnect all electrical lines leading to the cylinder head.

10. Remove the intake manifold.

11. Disconnect all radiator and heater hoses where they are attached to the cylinder head. Position them out of the way.

12. Tag and remove all spark plug wires.

13. Remove the distributor. To aid installation, scribe a mark on the body of the distributor and the cylinder head.

14. Separate the exhaust manifold from the exhaust pipe.

**NOTE: Exhaust pipe detachment differs slightly on the Turbo and Quattro. First the exhaust pipe must be unbolted from the turbocharger. Second, it must be unbolted from the wastegate at the rear of the engine.**

15. Disconnect the EGR valve and oxygen sensor from the exhaust manifold.

16. Remove the heat deflector shield.

17. Remove the oil lines (2) from the turbocharger.

18. Remove the exhaust manifold.

**NOTE: When removing the exhaust manifold on the Turbo and Quattro, the manifold, turbocharger and wastegate should all be removed as 1 unit.**

19. Remove the air hose cover from the back of the alternator.

20. Tag and disconnect all wires coming from the back of the alternator and remove the alternator from the engine.

21. Disconnect and plug the hoses coming from the power steering pump.

22. Remove the power steering pump and the V-belt.

23. Remove the timing belt cover and belt.
24. Remove the valve cover.
25. Loosen the cylinder head bolts in the reverse order of the tightening sequence.
26. Remove the bolts and lift the cylinder head off of the engine.
27. Clean the cylinder head and engine block mating surfaces thoroughly and install the new gasket without any sealing compound. Make sure the words **TOP** or **OBEN** are facing **UP**, when the gasket is installed.
28. Place the cylinder head on the engine block and install bolts No. 8 and 10 first. These holes are smaller and will properly locate the gasket and the head on the engine block.
29. Install the remaining bolts. Tighten them in 3 stages as follows: Step 1–29 ft. lbs., Step 2–43 ft. lbs. and Step 3–Tighten ½ turn more (180 degrees).

**NOTE: Do not re-torque the cylinder head bolts at the 1000 mile maintenance nor at the 1000 mile interval following repairs.**

30. Installation of all other components is in the reverse order of removal.

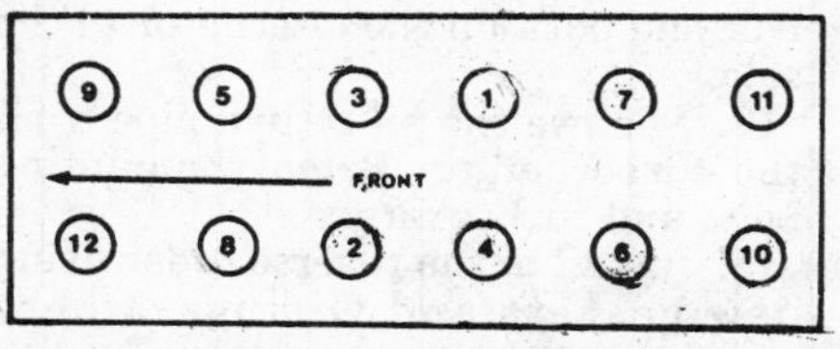

**Torque sequence for all 5 cylinder engines**

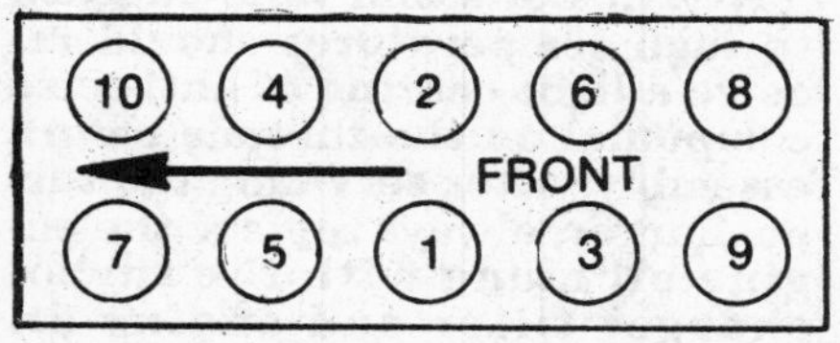

**Torque sequence for all 4 cylinder engines**

## OVERHAUL

**NOTE: For all cylinder head overhaul procedures, please refer to "Engine Rebuilding" in the Unit Repair Section.**

# Intake Manifold

## REMOVAL & INSTALLATION

### *4 Cylinder Engines*

1. Disconnect the negative battery cable. Relieve the fuel pressure in the system.
2. Disconnect the throttle cable at the throttle valve housing.
3. Disconnect the wiring for the cold start valve and thermo time switch.
4. Disconnect the ground wire from the intake manifold.
5. Remove the fuel line from the cold start valve. Cap the valve and line.
6. Remove the air boot from the throttle valve housing and sensor plate housing.
7. Disconnect and tag the vacuum hoses at the manifold.
8. Remove the fuel injectors from the cylinder head, without disconnecting the fuel lines from the injectors.
9. Remove the control pressure regulator line and move the regulator out of the way.
10. Remove the 2 straps that connect the intake and exhaust manifolds.
11. Disconnect the CO percentage check tube from the intake manifold.
12. Remove the intake manifold mounting nuts and remove the manifold from the engine.

**NOTE: Before loosening the intake manifold mounting nuts, soak the nuts and studs with spray lubricant. The stud are very difficult to replace with the cylinder head installed on the engine and this will aid in removal, without breaking the studs off in the cylinder head.**

13. Clean the gasket mating surfaces of the engine and intake manifold.
14. Before installation, hold the intake manifold gasket up to the engine and check for proper fit. Trim, if necessary.
15. Install the intake manifold on the cylinder head. Tighten the 6mm nuts to 7 ft. lbs. and the 8mm nuts to 18 ft. lbs.
16. The remainder of the installation is the reverse of the removal procedure.
17. Lubricate the fuel injector O-rings with a drop of engine oil, before installation in the cylinder head.
18. When finished, run the engine and check for leaks.

### *5 Cylinder Engines*

1. Disconnect the negative battery cable.
2. Relieve the fuel system pressure.
3. On non turbocharged engines, disconnect the air duct from the throttle valve assembly. On turbocharged engines, remove the hose between the air duct and turbocharger.
4. Disconnect the throttle cable/rod from the throttle valve assembly.
5. On turbocharged engines, remove the air duct for the injector cooling fan.
6. Remove the fuel injectors from the cylinder head, with the fuel lines attached.
7. Disconnect the cold start valve wiring and remove the fuel line from the valve.

**NOTE: Protect the fuel injectors and cold start valve with caps.**

8. Tag and disconnect all vacuum and PCV lines.
9. Tag and disconnect all electrical lines leading to the cylinder head.
10. On turbocharged engines, remove the hose which runs from the intake manifold to the turbocharger (intercooler on the Quattro).
11. Remove the auxiliary air regulator. Remove the air box cover and filter element.
12. Remove the intake manifold mounting nuts and remove the manifold from the engine.
13. Clean the gasket mating surfaces on the manifold and engine.
14. Using a new gasket, install the manifold on the cylinder head and tighten the nuts to 15 ft. lbs.
15. The remainder of the installation is the reverse of the removal procedure.
16. Always use new gaskets and O-rings where necessary.
17. Check the engine oil level and correct, if necessary.
18. When finished, run the engine and check for leaks.

# Exhaust Manifold

## REMOVAL & INSTALLATION

### *All Non-Turbocharged Engines*

**NOTE: Although not necessary, more working clearance will be found by removing the intake manifold before removing the exhaust manifold. Before starting, soak the manifold studs with lubricant to aid in the removal, without breaking the studs off in the cylinder head.**

1. Raise and support the vehicle safely. Disconnect the exhaust pipe from the exhaust manifold.
2. Disconnect the EGR valve and oxygen sensor, from the manifold.
3. Remove the heat deflector shield on 4 cylinder engines.
4. Disconnect the CO probe receptacle tube.
5. Remove the exhaust manifold mounting nuts and remove the manifold from the engine.
6. Clean the gasket mating surfaces of the manifold and engine.
7. Using a new gasket, install the manifold on the engine and tighten the nuts to 22 ft. lbs.

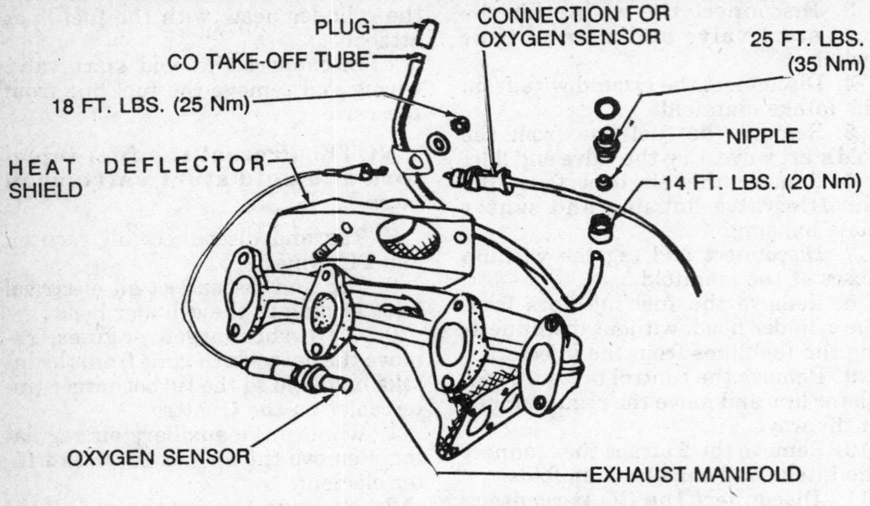


**4 cylinder gasoline engine exhaust manifold mounting**

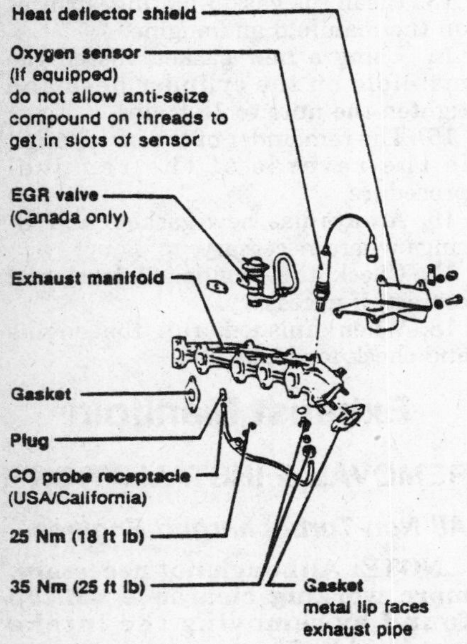


**5 cylinder gasoline engine exhaust manifold mounting**

**NOTE: Always replace the old mounting nuts with new brass nuts. Check the condition of the studs before installation. The oxygen sensor, EGR tube, bolts and nuts exposed to high temperatures should receive a light coating of anti-seize compound on the threads before assembly.**

8. Connect the exhaust pipe to the manifold, using a new gasket and tighten nuts to 26 ft. lbs.
9. Install and tighten the CO measuring tube to 22 ft. lbs.
10. The remainder of the installation is the reverse of the removal procedure.
11. When finished, run the engine and check for leaks.

### *Turbocharged Engines*

1. Remove the hose which runs between the air duct and the turbocharger.
2. If the intake manifold has not been removed, disconnect the hose which runs from the intake manifold to the turbocharger or intercooler.
3. Disconnect the exhaust pipe from the turbocharger.
4. Disconnect the exhaust pipe from the wastegate on the rear of the manifold.
5. Disconnect the EGR valve and the oxygen sensor, if necessary, from the manifold on gasoline engine models.
6. Remove the oil lines (2) from the turbocharger.
7. Remove the line from the bottom of the turbocharger to the intercooler, if equipped.

**NOTE: The manifold, turbocharger and wastegate are removed as 1 unit.**

8. Remove the manifold assembly.
9. Installation is the reverse of the removal procedure. Always use new gaskets and O-rings where necessary.

**NOTE: The oxygen sensor, EGR tube, bolts and nuts exposed to high temperatures should receive a light coating of anti-seize compound on the threads before assembly.**

10. Install and tighten the wastegate nuts to 22 ft. lbs.
11. Tighten the exhaust manifold mounting nuts to 26 ft. lbs.
12. Tighten the exhaust pipe nuts to 26 ft. lbs.
13. Start engine allow to reach normal operating temperature.
14. Check for leaks, and proper engine operation.

# Turbocharger

## REMOVAL & INSTALLATION

### *5 Cylinder Engines*

1. Disconnect the negative battery cable.
2. Spray all mounting bolts with a rust solvent.
3. Relieve the fuel system pressure.
4. Remove the vacuum tube between the intake air boot and turbocharger.
5. Remove the intake boot and crankcase ventilation hose. Remove the hose assembly between the intake manifold and throttle housing.
6. Remove the air box cover and remove the filter element.
7. Remove the right side engine mount heat shield.
8. Remove the oil supply pipe from the turbocharger. Remove the exhaust pipe from the corrugated pipe. Loosen the exhaust pipe at the transaxle mount and catalytic converter.
9. Remove the retaining clamp from the starter housing and sensor air hose.
10. Remove the exhaust pipe from the turbocharger.
11. Remove the alternator support bolt and position the alternator to the side.
12. Remove the oil return pipe from the turbocharger. Remove mounting bolts and turbocharger.
13. Install in the reverse order using new gaskets and O-rings, where necessary.

**NOTE: Bolts and nuts exposed to high temperatures should receive a light coating of anti-seize compound on the threads before assembly. After servicing the turbocharger, always replace the engine oil along with the turbocharger filter and engine oil filter.**

## TROUBLESHOOTING

**NOTE: For more information on turbocharging, please refer to "Turbocharging" in the Unit Repair Section.**

# Turbocharger Wastegate

## REMOVAL & INSTALLATION

**NOTE: Although not necessary, more working clearance will be found by removing the intake manifold before removing the wastgate. Before starting, soak the studs with lubricant to aid in**

**the removal, without breaking the studs off in the cylinder head.**

1. Intake manifold removal will provide more clearance for wastegate removal and installation.
2. Remove the wastegate to exhaust pipe connecting tube. There are 3 bolts on the top and on the bottom.
3. Remove the mounting bolt for the tube leading from the wastegate to the exhaust manifold.
4. Remove the vacuum line from the end of the wastegate.
5. Remove the 4 mounting bolts and remove the wastegate from the exhaust manifold.
6. Installation is in the reverse order of removal.

**NOTE: Bolts and nuts exposed to high temperatures should receive a light coating of anti-seize compound on the threads before assembly.**

## Timing Belt Cover

### REMOVAL & INSTALLATION

#### *4 Cylinder Engines*

**UPPER COVER**

1. Loosen the alternator adjusting bolts, pivot the alternator over and slip the drive belt off.
2. Loosen the A/C compressor mounting bolts and remove the drive belt.
3. Remove the valve cover nuts and remove the valve cover and retaining straps.
4. Remove the upper timing belt cover nuts. Note the position of the washers and spacers while removing the cover.
5. Installation is the reverse of the removal procedure.
6. Adjust the drive belt tension when finished.

**LOWER COVER**

1. Remove the upper timing belt cover.
2. Using the large bolt on the crankshaft sprocket, rotate the engine until the No. 1 cylinder is at TDC of the compression stroke. At this point, both valves for No. 1 cylinder will be closed and the **0** mark on the flywheel will be aligned with the pointer on the bell housing.
3. Remove the crankshaft pulley retaining bolts and loosen the crankshaft sprocket bolt, if the sprocket or rear cover is to be serviced.

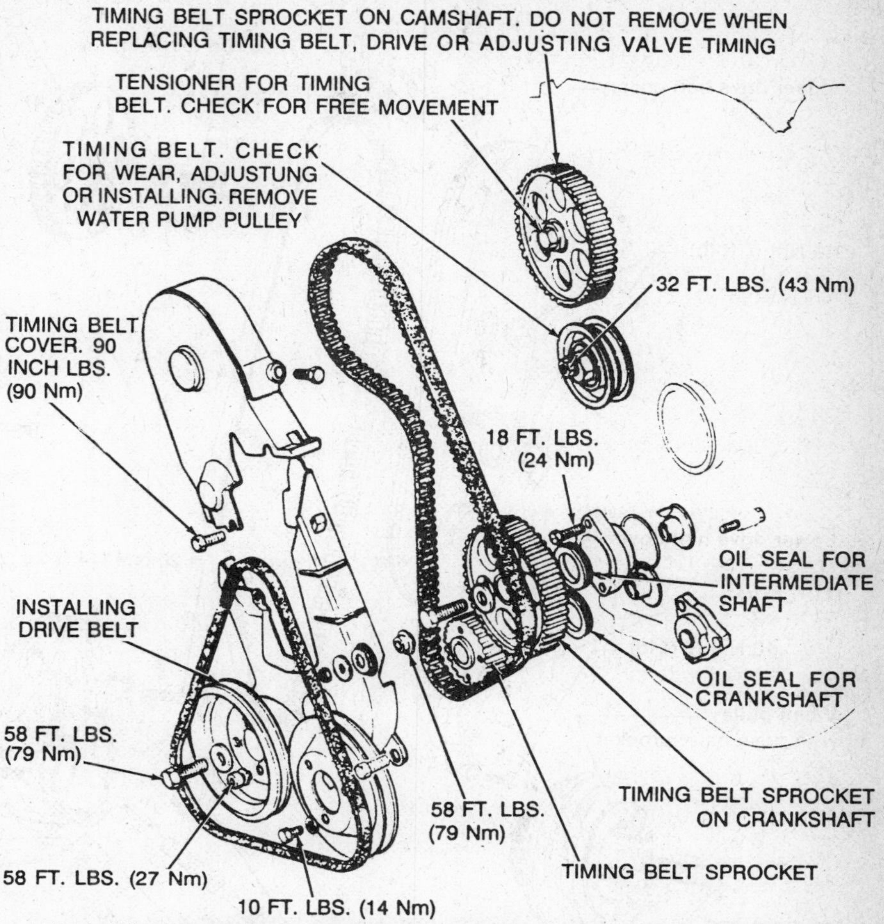


**4 cylinder gasoline engine timing belt, sprockets and covers—exploded view**

**NOTE: To remove the crankshaft sprocket bolt, on manual transaxle models, place the vehicle n 5th gear and have an assistant apply the brake. The will stop the engine from rotating while loosening the bolt. On automatic transaxle models, remove the starter and hold the flywheel from turning, using a flywheel holding tool VW 10-201 or equivalent.**

4. Remove the crankshaft pulley.
5. Remove the water pump pulley retaining bolts and remove the pulley.
6. Remove the lower cover retaining nuts and remove the cover. Take care not to lose any of the washers or spacers.
7. Installation is the reverse of the removal procedure.
8. Tighten the crankshaft sprocket bolt to 66 ft. lbs. plus ½ additional turn.

#### *5 Cylinder Engines*

**UPPER COVER**

1. Loosen the alternator adjusting bolts and remove the drive belt.
2. Loosen the power steering pump adjusting bolts and remove the drive belt.
3. Remove the retaining nuts and remove the timing belt cover. Take care not to lose any of the washers or spacers.
4. Installation is the reverse of the removal procedure.
5. Adjust the drive belt tension when finished.

**LOWER COVER**

1. Remove the upper timing belt cover.
2. Loosen the A/C compressor mounting bolts and remove the drive belt.
3. Remove the crankshaft balancer center bolt.

**NOTE: To remove the crankshaft balancer bolt, on manual transaxle models, place the vehicle in 5th gear and have an assistant apply the brake. The will stop the engine from rotating while loosening the bolt. On automatic transaxle models, remove the starter and hold the flywheel from turning, using a flywheel holding tool VW 10-201 or equivalent. This bolt is extremely tight.**

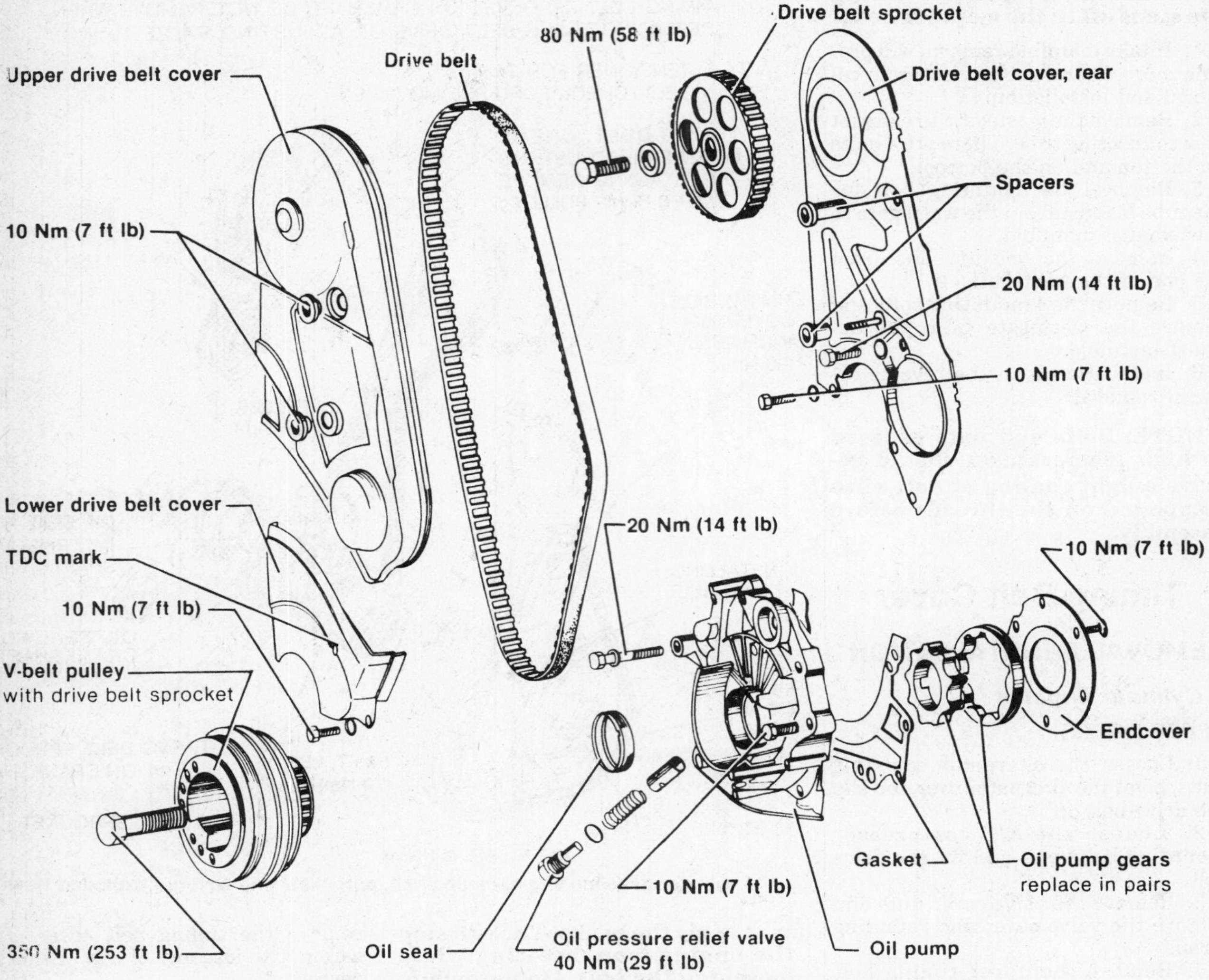


**5 cylinder gasoline engine timing belt, sprockets and cover—exploded view**

4. Remove the lower timing belt cover bolts and remove the cover.
5. Installation is the reverse of the removal procedure.
6. Use the same procedure to install the crankshaft center bolt as when removing the bolt. Apply a locking compound on the bolt threads and tighten the bolt to 258 ft. lbs. in several steps.
7. Adjust the drive belt tension when finished.

## Timing Belt

### REMOVAL & INSTALLATION

#### *4 Cylinder Engines*

1. Using the large bolt on the crankshaft sprocket, rotate the engine until the No. 1 cylinder is at TDC of the compression stroke. At this point, both valves will be closed and the **0** mark on the flywheel will be aligned with the pointer on the bell housing. If the belt hasn't jumped teeth the timing mark on the rear face of the camshaft sprocket should be aligned with the upper left edge of the valve cover.
2. Remove the upper and lower timing belt covers.
3. While holding the large hex nut on the tensioner pulley, loosen the smaller pulley locknut.
4. Turn the tensioner counterclockwise to relieve the tension on the timing belt.
5. Carefully slide the timing belt off of the sprockets and remove the belt.
6. If the engine had moved or jumped timing, use the large bolt on the crankshaft sprocket, rotate the engine until the No. 1 cylinder is at TDC of the compression stroke. At this point, both valves will be closed and the **0** mark on the flywheel will be aligned with the pointer on the bell housing and rotate the camshaft until the timing mark on the rear face of the camshaft sprocket is aligned with the upper left edge of the valve cover.
7. Install the crankshaft pulley and check that the notch on the pulley is aligned with the mark on the intermediate shaft sprocket. If not, rotate the intermediate shaft until they align.

**NOTE: If the timing marks are not correctly aligned with the No. 1 piston at TDC of the compression stroke and the belt is installed, valve timing will be incorrect. Poor performance and possible engine damage can result from the improper valve timing.**

8. Remove the crankshaft pulley. Note the pulley location on the crankshaft sprocket so that it can be replaced in the same position. Hold the large nut on the tensioner pulley and loosen the smaller locknut. Turn the tensioner counterclockwise to loosen and install the timing belt.

9. Slide the timing belt onto the sprockets and adjust the belt tension. The timing belt tension is correct when the belt can be twisted 90 degrees between the thumb and fore finger.
10. The remainder of the installation is the reverse of the removal procedure.

### *5 Cylinder Engines*

1. Using the large bolt on the crankshaft sprocket, rotate the engine until the No. 1 cylinder is at TDC of the compression stroke. Align the TDC mark **0** with the cast mark on the bell housing. If the belt hasn't jumped teeth the timing mark on the rear face of the camshaft sprocket should be aligned with the upper left edge of the valve cover.
2. Remove the alternator and A/C compressor drive belts.
3. Remove the upper and lower timing belt covers.
4. Loosen the water pump bolts only enough to turn the pump clockwise.

**NOTE: By loosening the water pump bolts, the coolant may drain from the engine at the water pump. If necessary, drain the cooling system, remove the water pump and reinstall it with a new O-ring.**

5. Slide the timing belt off the sprockets.
6. If necessary, turn the camshaft until the notch on the back of the sprocket is in line with the left side edge of the cylinder head gasket surface.
7. If necessary, align the TDC **0** mark with the with the lug cast on the bell housing.
8. Install the timing belt and turn the water pump counterclockwise to tighten the belt. Tighten the water pump bolts to 15 ft. lbs.

**NOTE: The timing belt is correctly tensioned when it can be twisted 90 degrees with the thumb and index finger along with the straight run between the camshaft sprocket and water pump. Belt must not be jammed between the oil pump and sprocket when installing the vibration damper.**

9. Install the timing belt covers and tighten the bolts to 7 ft. lbs.
10. Install the alternator and A/C compressor belts. These belts are correctly tensioned when they can be depressed ⅜ in. along their longest straight run.

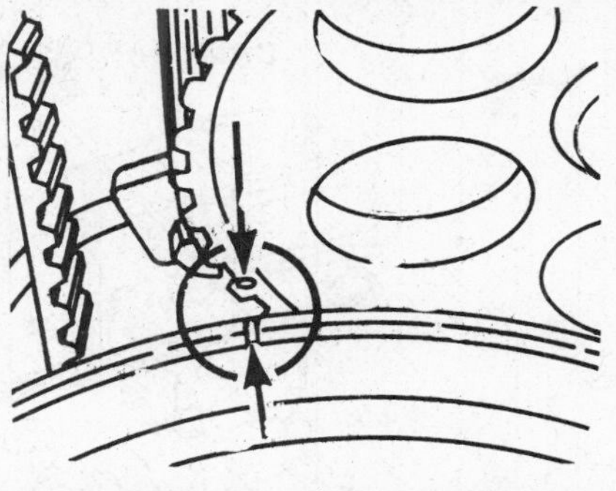

**Crankshaft pulley and intermediate shaft sprocket alignment – 4 cylinder engines**

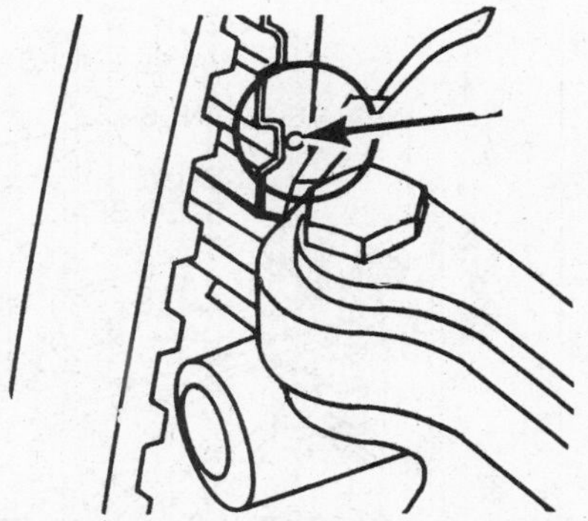

**Camshaft sprocket alignment – 4 and 5 cylinder gasoline engines**

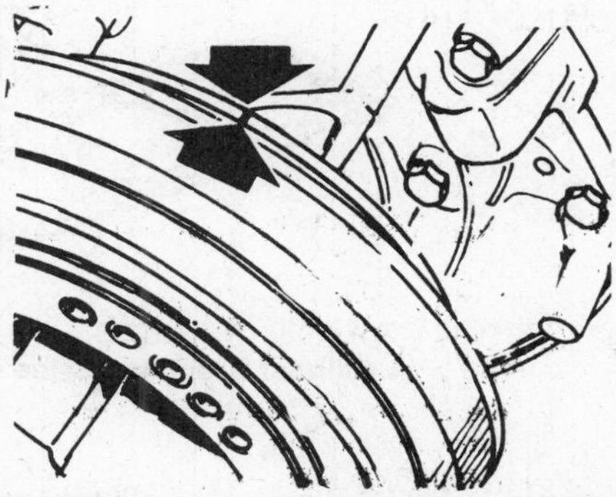

**Crankshaft pulley alignment marks – 5 cylinder engines**

## TENSION ADJUSTMENT

### *4 Cylinder Engines*

1. Holding the large bolt on the tensioner pulley, loosen the small nut and turn the tensioner clockwise to tighten and counterclockwise to loosen.
2. The belt is correctly tensioned when it can be twisted 90 degrees with the thumb and forefinger, midway between the camshaft and the intermediate shaft drive sprockets.

### *5 Cylinder Engines*

1. Loosen the water pump adjusting bolts and rotate the pump clockwise to tighten and counterclockwise to loosen.

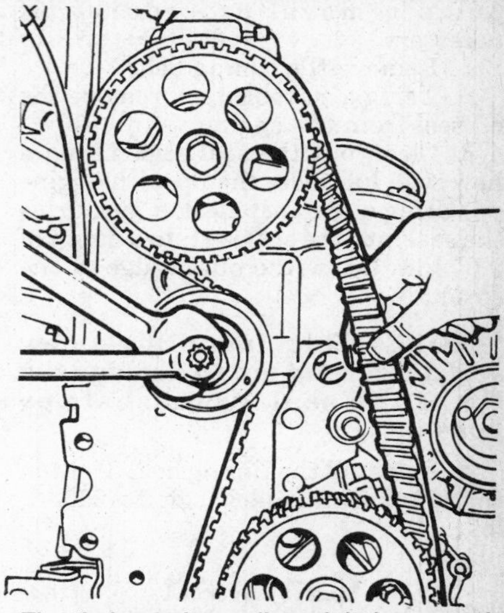

**The timing belt on all models is correctly tensioned when it can be twisted 90° with thumb and forefinger**

2. The belt is correctly tensioned when it can be twisted 90 degrees with the thumb and forefinger, midway between the camshaft drive sprocket and the water pump.

# Timing Sprockets

## REMOVAL & INSTALLATION

### *All Models*

All Gasoline engine timing belt sprockets are located by keys on their respective shafts. Each sprocket is retained by a bolt. To remove any or all of the sprockets, first remove the timing belt cover(s) and timing belt.

1. Remove the center retaining bolt for the sprocket.
2. Pull the sprocket off of the shaft.
3. If the sprocket is sticking on the shaft, use a gear puller. Do not hammer on the sprocket or damage may occur.

**NOTE: On 4 cylinder diesel engine camshafts, loosen the center bolt 1 turn and tap the rear of the sprocket with a rubber mallet. When the sprocket loosens, remove the bolt and sprocket.**

4. Remove the sprocket, being careful not to lose the key.
5. Installation is in the reverse order of removal.

**NOTE: Always check valve timing after removing the drive sprockets.**

## OIL SEAL REPLACEMENT

On 5 cylinder engines, the oil seal is a part of the oil pump. Refer to the pump removal procedures, if necessary.

1. Remove the timing belt.
2. Using a suitable tool, remove the oil seal from the engine.
3. Clean out the seal seat. Using a new seal, lubricate the lip with engine oil. Using a seal installation tool, drive the seal into the seal seat, to a depth of 0.079 in. below the outer edge of the cover.

**NOTE: When installing a new seal, be careful not to damage the lip of the seal, crankshaft or housing.**

4. Reinstall the timing belt. Tighten the crankshaft pulley bolt to 253 ft. lbs.

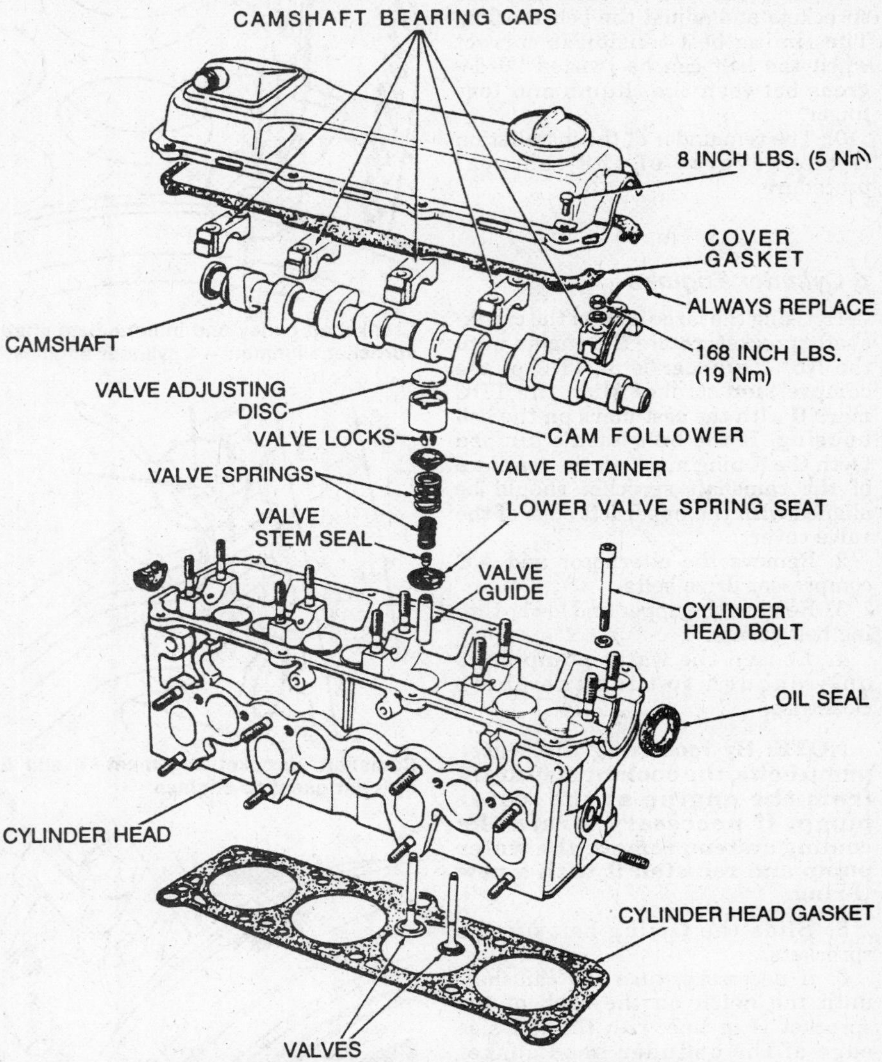


**4 cylinder gasoline engine cylinderhead – exploded view**

## Camshaft

### REMOVAL & INSTALLATION

#### *4 Cylinder Engines*

#### 80 AND 90 MODELS

1. Remove the upper drive belt, vacuum lines to valve cover and valve cover.
2. Using the large bolt on the crankshaft sprocket, rotate the engine until the No. 1 cylinder is at TDC of the compression stroke. At this point, both valves will be closed and the **0** mark on the flywheel will be aligned with the pointer on the bell housing. If the belt hasn't jumped teeth the timing mark on the rear face of the camshaft sprocket should be aligned with the upper left edge of the valve cover.
3. Remove the timing belt from the camshaft sprocket.
4. Remove the camshaft timing belt sprocket, take care not to lose woodruff key.
5. First remove bearing caps 1 and 3. Bearing cap 1 is located at the sprocket. Next remove bearing caps 2 and 5, alternately and diagonally. Bearing cap 5 is opposite end as cam sprocket. There is no bearing cap No. 4.
6. Remove the camshaft from the cylinder head.
7. Lubricate the camshaft journals, lobes and contact faces of the caps with assembly lube or gear oil before reinstallation.
8. Replace the camshaft oil seal in the cylinder head.

**NOTE: The bearing caps are offset, before installing the camshaft, set the bearing caps into position the check that they are facing in the correct direction. The numbers on the bearing caps are not always on the same side.**

9. Install the bearing caps in the proper order, observing the off-center position.
10. Install bearing caps 2 and 5 and tighten to 15 ft. lbs.
11. Install bearing caps 1 and 3 and tighten to 15 ft. lbs.
12. Mount camshaft sprocket and tighten to 59 ft. lbs.
13. Installation of the remaining components is in the reverse order of removal. When installing the crankshaft timing belt sprocket, be sure that the lug on the sprocket is properly installed into the slot.
14. Coat new camshaft seal with oil and press into cylinder head until flush, using tool VW 10-203, or equivalent.

**NOTE: Always recheck the valve timing and valve clearance after the camshaft has been removed.**

#### EXCEPT 80 AND 90 MODELS

1. Remove the timing belt from the camshaft sprocket.
2. Remove the PCV line from the valve cover.
3. Remove the valve cover.
4. Remove the camshaft timing belt sprocket.
5. First remove bearing caps 1, 3 and 4. Loosen bearing cap 2 afterwards.
6. Remove the camshaft from the cylinder head.
7. Lubricate the camshaft journals, lobes and contact faces of the caps with assembly lube or gear oil before reinstallation.
8. Replace the camshaft oil seal in the cylinder head.
9. Install the bearing caps in the proper order, observing the off-center position.

10. Lightly tighten bearing cap number 2 before installing bearing caps 4, 1 and 3. Tighten all the nuts to 14 ft. lbs.

**NOTE: Tighten the bearing caps diagonally. Observe off center bearing position. The numbers on the bearing caps are not always on the same side.**

11. Replace the camshaft seal under the No. 1 bearing cap.
12. Installation of the remaining components is in the reverse order of removal. When installing the crankshaft timing belt sprocket on 4 cylinder engines, be sure that the lug on the sprocket is properly installed into the slot on the crankshaft.

**NOTE: Always recheck the valve timing and valve clearance after the camshaft has been removed.**

### *5 Cylinder Engines*

#### EXCEPT 80 AND 90 MODELS

1. Remove the upper drive belt cover, valve cover and upper part of intake manifold, if necessary.
2. Using the large bolt on the crankshaft sprocket, rotate the engine until the No. 1 cylinder is at TDC of the compression stroke. Align the TDC mark **0** with the cast mark on the bell housing. If the belt hasn't jumped teeth the timing mark on the rear face of the camshaft sprocket should be aligned with the upper left edge of the valve cover.
3. Remove the timing belt from the camshaft sprocket. Remove the camshaft sprocket.
4. Diagonally loosen bearing caps 2 and 4 and remove the bearing caps.
5. Diagonally loosen bearing caps 1 and 3 and remove the bearing caps.
6. Lift the camshaft out of the cylinder head.
7. When installing, lightly oil the camshaft and bearing journals, with clean engine oil.
8. Position the caps on the same journals from which they were removed.
9. Tighten the nuts of caps 2 and 4 until snug.
10. Tighten all nuts to 15 ft. lbs.
11. Install the camshaft sprocket and timing belt. Install the valve cover. The camshaft sprocket bolt is tightened to 58 ft. lbs.

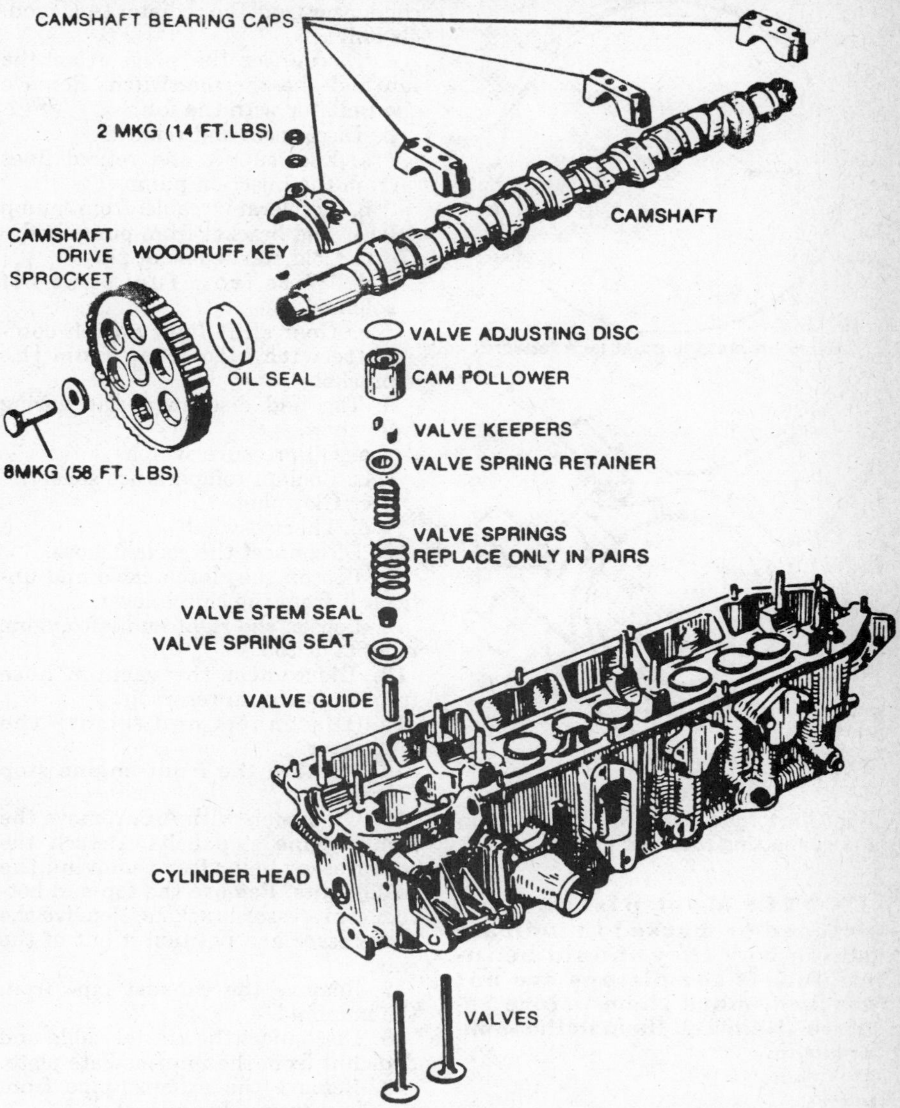


**5 cylinder gasoline engine cylinder head—exploded view**

#### 80 AND 90 MODELS

1. Remove the upper drive belt cover, valve cover and upper part of intake manifold, if necessary.
2. Using the large bolt on the crankshaft sprocket, rotate the engine until the No. 1 cylinder is at TDC of the compression stroke. Align the TDC mark **0** with the cast mark on the bell housing. If the belt hasn't jumped teeth the timing mark on the rear face of the camshaft sprocket should be aligned with the upper left edge of the valve cover.
3. Remove the timing belt from the camshaft sprocket. Remove the camshaft sprocket.
4. Remove bearing caps 1 and 3.
5. Diagonally loosen bearing caps 2 and 4 and remove the bearing caps.
6. Lift the camshaft out of the cylinder head.
7. When installing, lightly oil the camshaft and bearing journals, with clean engine oil.
8. Position the caps on the same journals from which they were removed.
9. Install bearing caps 2 and 4. Tighten alternately and diagonally to 15 ft. lbs.
10. Install bearing caps 1 and 3. Tighten bearing caps 1 and 3 to 15 ft. lbs.
11. Install the camshaft sprocket and timing belt. Install the valve cover. The camshaft sprocket bolt is tightened to 59 ft. lbs.

## Piston and Connecting Rod

### POSITIONING

**For all piston and connecting rod overhaul procedures, please refer to "Engine Rebuilding" in the Unit Repair section.**

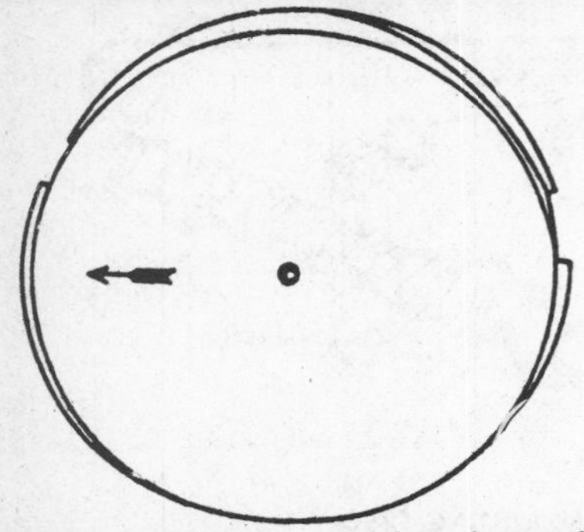

Arrow on pistons must face forward

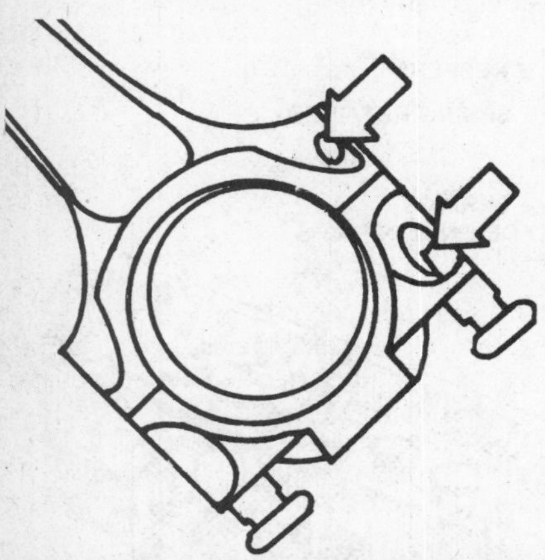

Align the forged marks when assembling the connecting rods and caps

**NOTE: Most pistons are notched or marked to indicate which way they should be installed. If the pistons are not marked, mark them before removal. Reinstall them in the same position.**

# DIESEL ENGINE MECHANICAL

## Engine

### REMOVAL & INSTALLATION

#### *4000 Models*

1. Disconnect the negative battery cable.
2. Remove the engine and transaxle cover plates.
3. Open the heater control valve fully and open the cap on the expansion tank.
4. Drain the coolant.
5. Detach the radiator cowl from the radiator and remove complete with both fans (A/C models only).
6. Remove the grille and detach the condenser from the radiator (A/C models only).
7. Disconnect the plugs from the fan and the thermo-switch. Remove the radiator with the fan.
8. Disconnect and remove:
   a. Fuel supply and return lines from the injection pump
   b. Accelerator cable from pump lever and bracket from pump body
   c. Cold start cable at pin
   d. Wire from fuel shut-off solenoid
   e. Gear shift light switch complete with all wiring from the bracket
9. Tag and disconnect the wiring from the:
   a. Oil pressure switch
   b. Coolant temperature sensors
   c. Glowplugs
   d. Thermoswitch
10. Disconnect the coolant hose.
11. Loosen the clutch cable and unhook it from the clutch lever.
12. Loosen the right and left engine mounts at top.
13. Disconnect the vacuum hose from the vacuum reservoir.
14. Disconnect and remove the alternator.
15. Remove the front engine stop bolts.
16. On models with A/C, remove the front engine stop bolts. Detach the compressor belt after removing the pulley nuts. Remove the top and bottom compressor brackets. Remove the compressor and position it out of the way.
17. Remove the exhaust pipe from the manifold.
18. Disconnect the starter cable and detach it from the intermediate plate.
19. Remove the exhaust pipe from the front transaxle support.
20. Remove the starter.
21. Remove the bottom 2 transaxles-to-engine bolts. Remove the flywheel cover plate.
22. Support the transaxle with a jack or install transaxle support bar VW 785/1B.
23. Attach a lifting apparatus to the engine and raise the engine/transaxle until the transaxle housing touches the steering rack.
24. Raise the transaxle jack or adjust the support bar. Remove the upper 3 transaxle-to-engine bolts.
25. Pry the engine/transaxle apart and lift the engine out of the engine compartment.
26. Installation is in the reverse order of removal. Please note the following:
   a. Place the intermediate plate on the dowel sleeves and stick it to engine block with grease.
   b. Place the starter on the engine carrier before installing the engine.

**CAUTION**

***Do not interchange fuel supply and return pipe union screws. For identification, the fuel return pipe union screw is marked OUT on the screw head.***

   c. Connect the starter cable so it cannot touch the engine.
   d. Install the engine mounts free of tension.
27. Tightening torques for installation are as follows:
   a. Cover plate-to-transaxle/engine—7 ft. lbs.
   b. Exhaust pipe-to-transaxle—18 ft. lbs.
   c. Front engine stop-to-engine block—18 ft. lbs.
   d. Stop housing-to-front cross member—18 ft. lbs.
   e. Engine mounts—25 ft. lbs.
   f. Engine-to-transaxle (12 M)—40 ft. lbs.
   g. Starter bolts—14 ft. lbs.

#### *5000 Models*

1. Disconnect the negative battery cable.
2. Remove the air cleaner.
3. Remove the cover plates underneath the engine and the transaxle.
4. Remove the front grille.
5. Remove the windshield washer reservoir from its holder.
6. Remove the hydraulic fluid reservoir from its holder.
7. Pull the hood latch cable guide out of its bracket.
8. Remove the cap on the expansion tank and drain the radiator.
9. Remove all radiator and heater hoses.
10. Remove the V-belt for the power steering pump and remove the power steering pump with the hoses connected.
11. On models equipped with A/C, loosen the condenser mounting bolts and tilt it away from the radiator.
12. Remove the auxiliary radiator.
13. Remove the fuel filter and plug the fuel lines.
14. Detach the accelerator cable.
15. Tag and disconnect all electrical wiring coming from the cylinder head.
16. Loosen the fuel return pipe on the injection pump.
17. Disconnect the idle speed control cable from the injection pump lever.
18. Remove the cover plate for the right engine mount.
19. Remove the front engine mount bolts and remove the mount from the crossmember.
20. Tag and disconnect all wiring from the alternator and remove the alternator and its bracket.
21. Remove the exhaust pipes from the manifold.

22. Remove the exhaust pipe support bracket from the transaxle.
23. Tag and disconnect all wiring from the starter and remove the starter.
24. On cars equipped with air conditioning, remove the compressor mounting bolts along with the mount. Leave the hoses connected and tie the compressor out of the way with wire.
25. Remove the lower engine/transaxle bolts.
26. Remove the flywheel cover plate from the transaxle.
27. Support the transaxle.
28. Remove the left engine bracket.
29. Lift the engine/transaxle up until the transaxle housing touches the steering housing.
30. Remove the upper engine/transaxle bolts.
31. Carefully pry the engine/transaxle apart.
32. Turn the engine to the right and lift up at the same time.
33. Turn the engine 90 degrees and lift it out.
34. Proceed in the reverse order for installation and note the following:
  a. Tighten the engine/transaxle bolts to 43 ft. lbs.
  b. Tighten all engine mount bolts to 33 ft. lbs.
  c. Tighten the exhaust pipe-to-manifold bolts to 22 ft. lbs.

## Cylinder Head

### REMOVAL & INSTALLATION

**NOTE: Cylinder head removal should not be attempted unless the engine is cold.**

1. Disconnect the negative battery cable.
2. Drain the cooling system.
3. Remove the air cleaner.
4. Clean and disconnect the fuel (injector) lines.
5. Tag and disconnect all electrical wires and leads.
6. Disconnect and plug all lines coming from the brake booster vacuum pump and remove the pump.
7. Disconnect the air supply tubes (turbocharged diesels only) and unbolt and remove the intake manifold.
8. Disconnect and plug all lines coming from the power steering pump and remove the pump and V-belt.
9. Disconnect and remove the oil supply and return lines from the turbocharger, if equipped.
10. Remove the exhaust manifold heat shields, if equipped.
11. Separate the exhaust pipe from the exhaust manifold or turbocharger and remove the manifold.

**NOTE: On Turbodiesels, the exhaust manifold is removed with the turbocharger and wastegate attached.**

12. Disconnect all radiator and heater hoses where attached to the cylinder head and position them out of the way.
13. Remove the timing belt cover and remove the timing belt.
14. Remove the injection pump belt cover and remove the belt.
15. Remove the PCV hose.
16. Remove the cylinder head cover.
17. Loosen the cylinder head bolts in the reverse order of the tightening sequence.
18. Remove the bolts and lift the cylinder head straight off.

**CAUTION**

***If the cylinder head sticks on the engine, loosen it by compression or tap it upward with a soft rubber mallet. Do not force anything between the head and the engine block to pry it upward. This may result in serious damage.***

19. Clean the cylinder head and engine block mating surfaces thoroughly and install the new gasket without any sealing compound. Make sure the words **TOP** or **OBEN** are facing up when the gasket is installed.

**NOTE: Depending upon piston height above the top surface of the engine block, there are 3 gaskets of different thicknesses which can be used. Be sure that the new gasket has the same number of notches and the same identifying number as the one being replaced.**

20. Place the cylinder head on the engine block and install bolts No. 8 and 10 first. These holes are smaller and will properly locate the gasket and the head on the engine block.
21. Install the remaining bolts. Tighten them in 3 stages as follows: Step 1: 29 ft. lbs.; Step 2: 43 ft. lbs.; Step 3: Tighten ½ turn more (180 degrees).
22. Installation of all other components is in the reverse order of removal. See the appropriate section for injection timing.
23. After reassembly, start the engine and let it run until it reaches normal operating temperature (when the radiator fan switches on). Stop the engine, remove the cylinder head cover and tighten the head bolts an additional ¼ turn (90 degrees), following the tightening sequence.

**NOTE: On all diesel engines using M12, 12 point cylinder head bolts, never reinstall old bolts. Always replace cylinder head bolts.**

24. After about 1000 miles, remove the cylinder head cover and retighten the cylinder head bolts, turning the bolts in sequence ¼ turn (90 degrees) WITHOUT loosening them first. This is done 1 bolt at a time, in the proper sequence, without interruption.

## Intake Manifold

### REMOVAL & INSTALLATION

1. Disconnect the negative battery cable.
2. Drain the cooling system.
3. Disconnect the hose that runs between the air duct and the turbocharger (turbocharged diesel only).
4. Remove the air cleaner.
5. Disconnect the plug all lines coming from the brake booster vacuum pump and remove the pump.
6. Disconnect the PCV line.
7. Disconnect and remove the blow-off valve and disconnect the hose which runs from the intake manifold to the turbocharger (turbocharged diesel only).
8. Remove the manifold.
9. Installation is in the reverse order of removal.

## Exhaust Manifold

### REMOVAL & INSTALLATION

#### *Except Turbodiesel*

Although it is not imperative to remove the intake manifold in order to remove the exhaust manifold, intake manifold removal will make everything more accessible.

1. Unbolt and separate the exhaust pipe from the exhaust manifold.
2. Disconnect the EGR valve from the manifold.
3. Remove the heat deflector shield on the 4 cylinder engines.
4. Remove the exhaust manifold from the engine.
5. Installation is the reverse of the removal procedure.

#### *Turbodiesel*

1. Remove the hose from the air duct to the turbocharger.
2. If the intake manifold has not been removed, disconnect the hose which runs from the intake manifold to the turbocharger or intercooler.
3. Unbolt the exhaust pipe from the turbocharger.
4. Unbolt the exhaust pipe from the wastegate on the rear of the manifold.
5. Disconnect the EGR valve.
6. Remove the lines from the turbocharger.
7. Remove the line from the bottom of the turbocharger to the intercooler.

**NOTE: The manifold, turbocharger and wastegate are removed as an assembly.**

8. Remove the manifold assembly.
9. Installation is the reverse of the removal procedure.

## Turbocharger

### REMOVAL & INSTALLATION

#### *4 Cylinder Turbodiesel*

1. Disconnect the negative battery cable. Remove the engine/transaxle cover plate.
2. Removal of the intake manifold is not absolutely necessary, but will greatly aid in the accessibility of all related nuts and bolts.
3. Loosen the hose clamps and remove the hose which leads to the intake manifold or intercooler.
4. Loosen the hose clamps and remove the hose which leads to the air cleaner. Loosen the left and right stabilizer bar clamps and push the stabilizer bar down.
5. Unbolt the oil supply (upper) and return (lower) lines and position them out of the way. Remove the turbocharger heat shield.
6. Remove the exhaust pipe mounting nuts and pull the exhaust pipe away from the turbocharger.
7. Remove the turbocharger mounting nuts and pull the turbocharger off of the exhaust manifold.
8. Installation is in the reverse order of removal. Note the following:
   a. Use new gaskets.
   b. Tighten the turbocharger-to-exhaust manifold bolts to 33 ft. lbs. Coat bolt threads with high temperature grease before installation.
   c. Tighten the turbocharger-to-exhaust pipe bolts to 18–29 ft. lbs.

#### *5 Cylinder Turbodiesel*

1. Disconnect the negative battery cable. If the battery interferes with space requirements, remove it.
2. Spray all mounting bolts with a rust solvent.
3. Remove the front grille.
4. Remove the vacuum tube between the intake air boot and turbocharger.
5. Remove the intake boot and crankcase ventilation hose. Remove the hose assembly between the intake manifold and throttle housing.
6. Remove the air filter housing cover.
7. Remove the right side engine mount heat shield and engine cover plate.
8. Remove the oil supply pipe from the turbocharger. Remove the exhaust pipe from the corrugated pipe and loosen the exhaust pipe at the transaxle mount and catalytic converter.
9. Remove the retaining clamp from the starter housing and sensor air hose.
10. Remove the exhaust pipe from the turbocharger and remove the exhaust bracket from the transaxle.
11. Remove the alternator support bolt and position the alternator to the side.
12. Remove the oil return pipe from the turbocharger. Remove mounting bolts and turbocharger.
13. Installation is the reverse of the removal procedure.

**NOTE: Always change the oil and oil filter(s) after turbocharger service.**

## Turbocharger Wastegate

### REMOVAL & INSTALLATION

The wastegate on the 4 cylinder engine is a press-fit and cannot be removed. The wastegate on the 5 cylinder engine is removed by disconnecting the air hose and unbolting it from the turbocharger unit.

### TROUBLESHOOTING

**For more information on Turbocharging, please refer to "Turbocharging" in the Unit Repair Section.**

## Front Cover

### REMOVAL & INSTALLATION

There are 2 drive belts on 5 cylinder diesel engines. 1 belt at the front on the engine and 1 at the rear. The front cover is removed in the same manner as the gasoline engine, with 2 exceptions. The cover has an upper and lower half. To remove the upper half, follow the procedure for the gasoline engine. To remove the lower half, use the following procedure.

1. Remove the upper cover.
2. Unscrew the crankshaft pulley retaining bolts and remove the pulley.
3. Unscrew the retaining nuts and remove the lower cover.
4. Installation is in the reverse order of removal.

To remove the rear belt cover on 5 cylinder diesels, use the following procedure.

5. Remove the outside half of the vacuum pump pulley and remove the V-belt.
6. Unscrew the retaining bolts and remove the rear timing belt cover. Take care not to lose any of the washers or spacers.
7. Installation is in the reverse order of removal.

## Timing Belt

### REMOVAL & INSTALLATION

#### *4 Cylinder Engine*

**NOTE: This procedure will require a number of special tools and a certain expertise with diesel engines.**

1. Remove the timing belt cover. Remove the cylinder head cover.
2. Turn the engine so that No. 1 cylinder is at TDC and fix the camshaft in position with tool 2065A. Align the tool as follows:
   a. Turn the camshaft until 1 end of the tool touches the cylinder head.
   b. Measure the gap at the other end of the tool with a feeler gauge.
   c. Take half of the measurement and insert a feeler gauge of this thickness between the tool and the cylinder head; turn the camshaft so that the tool rests on the feeler gauge.
   d. Insert a second feeler gauge of the same thickness between the other end of the tool with the cylinder head.
3. Lock the injection pump sprocket in position with pin 2064.
4. Check that the marks on the sprocket, bracket and pump body are in alignment (engine at TDC).
5. Loosen the timing belt tensioner. Remove the V-belt from the crankshaft.
6. Remove the timing belt.
7. Check that the TDC mark on the flywheel is aligned with the reference marks.
8. Loosen the camshaft sprocket bolt ½ turn and loosen the gear from the camshaft end by tapping it with a rubber mallet.
9. Install the timing belt and remove pin 2064 from the injection pump sprocket.
10. Tension the belt by turning the tensioner to the right. Check the belt tension as detailed later in the section.
11. Tighten the camshaft sprocket bolt to 33 ft. lbs.
12. Remove the tool from the camshaft.
13. Turn the crankshaft 2 turns in the direction of engine rotation (clockwise) and strike the belt once with a rubber mallet between the camshaft sprocket and the injection pump sprocket.
14. Check the belt tension again. Check the injection pump timing.

### *5 Cylinder Engine*

**NOTE: This procedure will require the use of a number of special tools.**

1. Remove all V-belts on the front of the engine.
2. Remove the outside half of the vacuum pump pulley and remove the V-belt.
3. Remove the front timing belt covers.
4. Remove the rear timing belt cover.
5. Remove the cylinder head cover.
6. Using the large bolt on the crankshaft sprocket, rotate the engine until the No. 1 cylinder is at TDC of the compression stroke. At this point, both of the valves will be closed and the mark on the flywheel will be aligned with the pointer on the clutch housing.
7. Align the marks on the injection pump sprocket mounting plate.

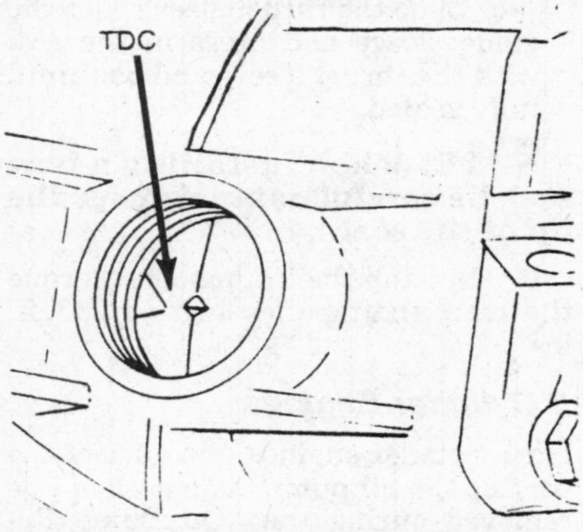


**Timing mark aligned on bell housing with mark on flywheel**

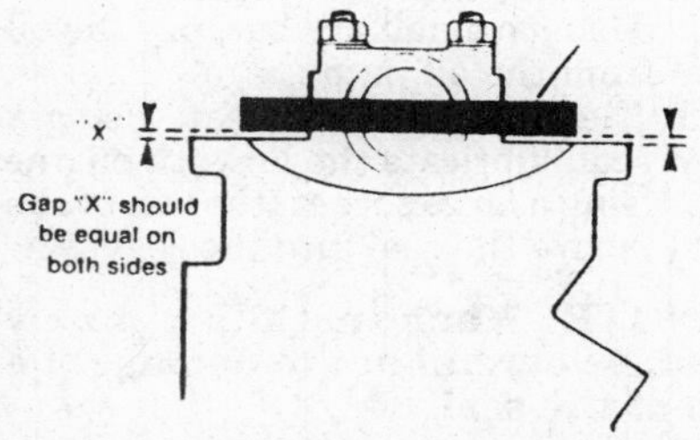


**Install the camshaft locking tool in the rear of the camshaft as shown**

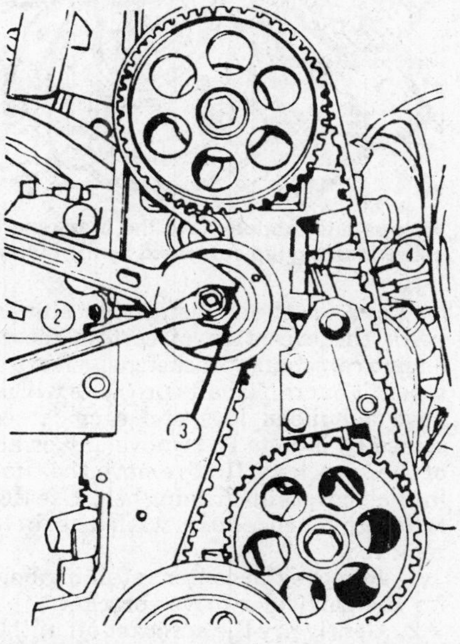

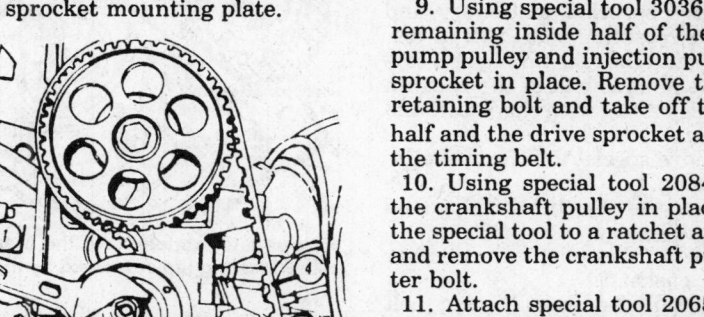

**4 cylinder diesel engine timing belt tensioning**

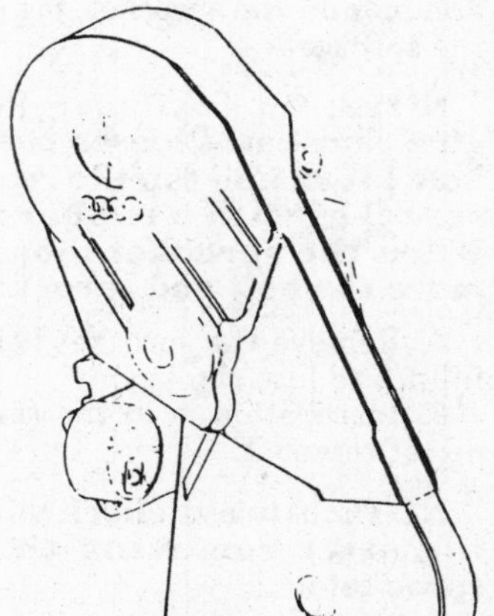
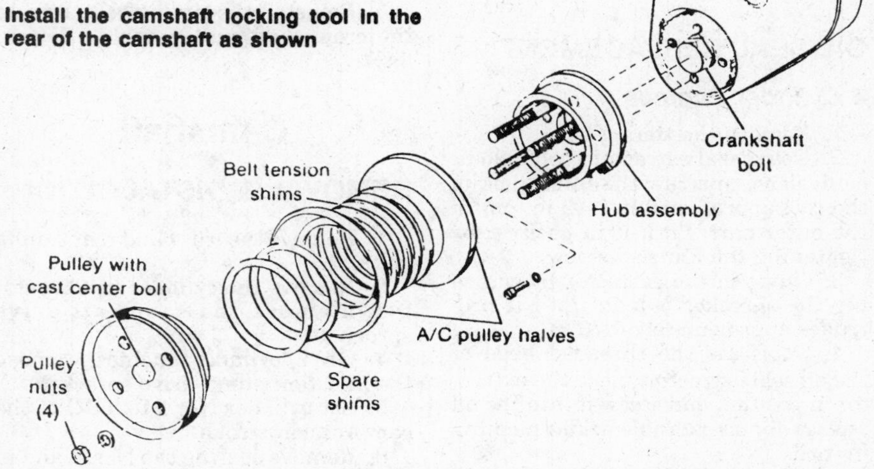


**4 cylinder diesel engine crankshaft sprocket and pulley—exploded view**

8. Using special tool 2064 (a pin), lock the injection pump sprocket in place so that it will not be allowed to move and alter the valve timing.
9. Using special tool 3036, hold the remaining inside half of the vacuum pump pulley and injection pump drive sprocket in place. Remove the center retaining bolt and take off the pulley half and the drive sprocket along with the timing belt.
10. Using special tool 2084 to hold the crankshaft pulley in place, attach the special tool to a ratchet and loosen and remove the crankshaft pulley center bolt.
11. Attach special tool 2065A to the rear of the camshaft so that it will not be allowed to move and alter the valve timing.
12. Loosen the adjusting bolts on the water pump and rotate the water pump housing by hand counter-clockwise to relieve the tension on the timing belt.
13. Unbolt and remove the crankshaft pulley and slide the timing belt off the sprockets. Discard the timing belt.

**To Install:**

14. Verify that the No. 1 cylinder is still at TDC and the mark on the flywheel is aligned with the pointer on the clutch housing.
15. Loosen the camshaft sprocket bolt approximately 1 turn and lightly tap the gear loose from the camshaft with a rubber mallet.
16. Install the new timing belt.
17. Rotate the water pump housing clockwise by hand to place tension on the timing belt. Tighten the water pump retaining bolts.
18. With special tool VW210, check the timing belt tension. The reading on the tool scale should be between 12 and 13.
19. Repeat Steps 4 and 5 until the specified timing belt tension in obtained. Torque the water pump retaining bolts to 14 ft. lbs.
20. Torque the camshaft sprocket bolt to 33 ft. lbs. and remove special tool 2065a.
21. Install the injection pump drive sprocket with the timing belt.
22. Verify that the No. 1 cylinder is still at TDC.
23. Tighten the injection pump sprocket retaining bolt enough so that the sprocket may be turned by hand.
24. With special tool VW210, check the timing belt tension. The reading on the tool scale should be between 12 and 13.
25. If the timing belt tension is not as specified, loosen the injection pump mounting bracket bolts and move the injection pump as required (away from the engine to tighten).

26. Repeat Steps 11 and 12 until the specified timing belt tension is obtained. Torque the mounting bracket bolts to 18 ft. lbs. Hold the injection pump drive sprocket stationary and torque the retaining bolt to 72 ft. lbs.
27. Reinstall the rear timing belt cover and the outside half of the vacuum pump pulley along with the V-belt and the tension.
28. Remove special tool from the injection pump.
29. Check the injection timing and adjust if necessary.
30. Reinstall the cylinder head cover with new gaskets.
31. Reinstall the front timing belt covers.
32. Reinstall the front V-belts and adjust the tension.

## TENSION ADJUSTMENT

### *Front Belt*

1. Remove the front timing belt covers to gain access to the front timing belt.
2. With special tool VW210, check the timing belt tension. The reading on the tool scale should be between 12 and 13.
3. If the timing belt tension is not as specified, loosen the water pump retaining bolts and rotate the water pump housing clockwise by hand to place tension on the timing belt (counter clockwise to relieve the tension). Tighten the water pump retaining bolts.
4. Repeat Steps 3 and 4 until the specified timing belt tension in obtained. Torque the water pump retaining bolts to 14 ft. lbs.
5. Reinstall the front timing belt covers.

### *Rear Belt*

1. Remove the rear timing belt cover to gain access to the rear timing belt.
2. With special tool VW210, check the timing belt tension. The reading on the tool scale should be between 12 and 13.
3. If the timing belt tension is not as specified, loosen the injection pump mounting bracket bolts and move the injection pump as required (away from the engine to tighten).
4. Repeat Steps 2 and 3 until the specified timing belt tension is obtained. Torque the mounting bracket bolts to 18 ft. lbs.
5. Reinstall the rear timing belt cover.

# Timing Sprockets

## REMOVAL & INSTALLATION

All of the drive sprockets are located by keys on their respective shafts (with the exception of certain diesel engine camshaft sprockets which are a taper fit or crankshaft sprockets which have a built-in lug) and each is retained by a bolt. To remove any or all of the sprockets, first remove the timing belt covers and timing belt. Use the following procedure with the belt removed.

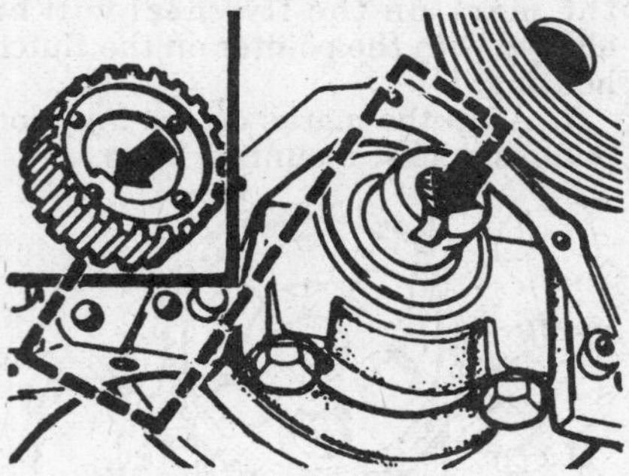

**Various late models have the crankshaft pulley locating lug contained by the pulley**

1. Remove the center retaining bolt for the particular drive sprocket.
2. Gently pry the sprocket off of the shaft.
3. If the sprocket is stubborn in coming off, use a gear puller. Don't hammer on the sprocket; it may crack the sprocket.

**NOTE: On 4 cylinder diesel engine camshafts, loosen the center bolt 1 turn and tap the rear of the sprocket with a rubber mallet. When the sprocket loosens, remove the bolt and sprocket.**

4. Remove the sprocket being careful not to lose the key.
5. Installation is in the reverse order of removal.

**NOTE: Always check valve timing after removing the drive sprockets.**

## OIL SEAL REPLACEMENT

### *4 Cylinder Engines*

1. Remove the timing belt.
2. Using seal extractor tool 2085 or equivalent, unscrew the inner part of the tool approximately 0.12 in. out of the outer part. Lock it in position by tightening the knurled screw.
3. Guide in the extractor by screwing the sprocket bolt in until it protrudes approximately 0.79 in.
4. Lubricate the threaded head of the oil seal extractor. place the extractor in position and screw it into the oil seal as far as possible while pushing inward.
5. Loosen the knurled screw and turn the inner part of the tool against the crankshaft until the seal is pulled out.
6. Clamp the extractor in a suitable vise and remove the oil seal with a suitable pair of pliers.
7. Using tool 10-203 or equivalent, press the tool in a depth of $^{3}/_{32}$ in. Install the new seal flush with the front cover.
8. The following seal removal & installation procedure is for the 4000 turbocharged diesel engine:
   a. Insert the bolt of tool 3083 or equivalent into the crankcase to guide the seal extractor tool 2085 or equivalent and remove the old seal.
   b. Slide the sleeve of tool 3083 or equivalent onto the crankcase journal. Dip the new seal in clean engine oil and slide it over the sleeve.
   c. Slide the thrust sleeve over the guide sleeve and press in the seal with the thrust sleeve and bolt until fully seated.

**NOTE: When installing a new seal, be careful not to damage the lip of the seal.**

9. Reinstall the timing belt. Torque the crankshaft pulley bolt to 253 ft. lbs.

### *5 Cylinder Engines*

On 5 cylinder engines, the oil seal is a part of the oil pump. The seal can be removed during the "Oil Pump Removal & Installation" procedures or it can be replaced as follows:

1. Remove the timing belt.
2. Using a small pry bar, pry the oil seal from the oil pump.
3. Clean out the seal seat. Using a new seal, lubricate the lip with engine oil. Using a large socket (the dia. of the seal), drive the seal into the seal seat.

**NOTE: When installing a new seal, be careful not to damage the lip of the seal.**

4. Reinstall the timing belt. Torque the crankshaft pulley bolt to 253 ft. lbs.

# Camshaft

## REMOVAL & INSTALLATION

1. Remove the front and rear timing belts.
2. Remove the cylinder head cover.
3. Remove the camshaft drive sprocket.
4. On 5 cylinder engines, remove the injection pump drive sprocket.
5. Set cylinder No. 1 to TDC of the compression stroke.
6. Remove bearing cap Nos. 1 and 4.
7. Diagonally loosen bearing cap Nos. 2 and 3 and remove.

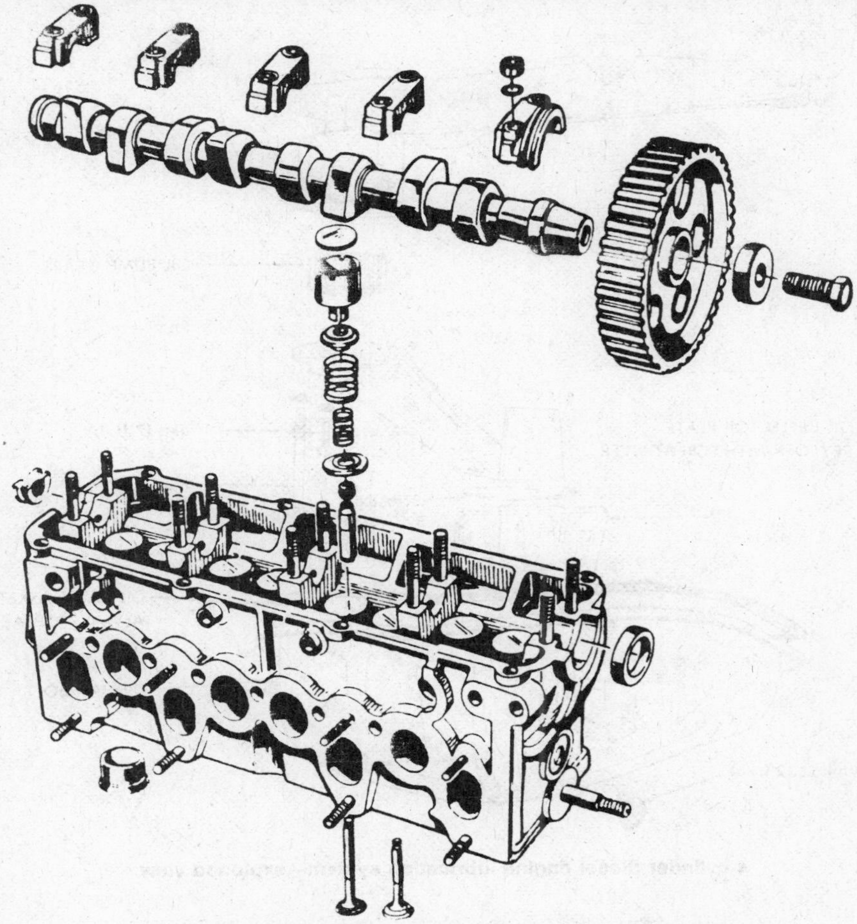

4 cylinder diesel cylinder head—exploded view

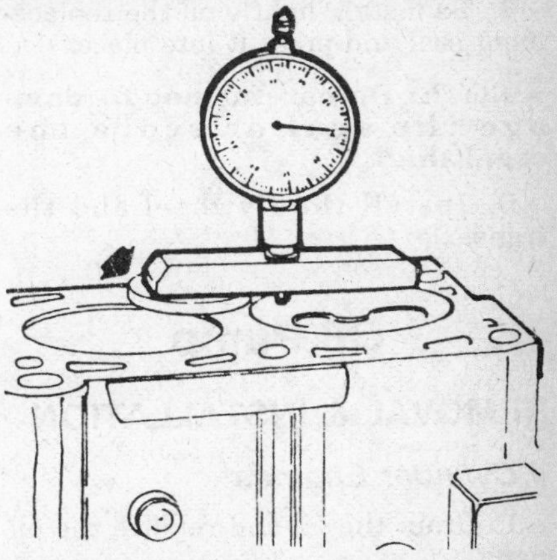

Piston projection measurement—diesel engines

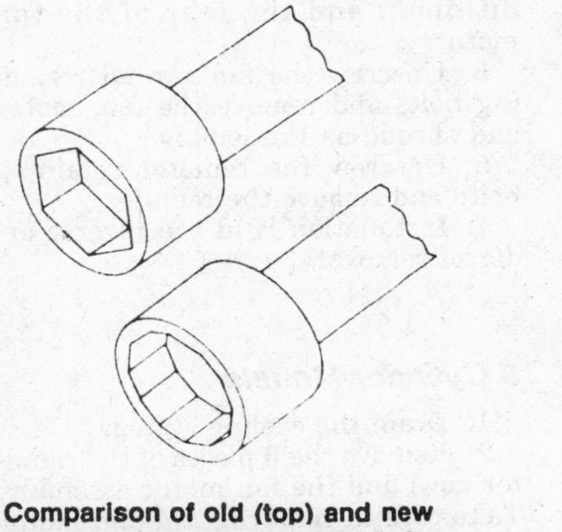

Comparison of old (top) and new (bottom) style cylinder head bolts

8. Remove the camshaft from the cylinder head.
9. Lubricate the camshaft journals, lobes, bearing shells and the contact faces of the caps with assembly lube or gear oil before reinstallation.
10. Replace both camshaft oil seals.

**NOTE: The cam lobes for the No. 1 cylinder must face upward.**

11. Install bearing caps Nos. 2 and 3 tightening alternately and diagonally.
12. Install bearing caps Nos. 1 and 4.
13. Replace the seal in the No. 1 bearing cap.
14. Installation of the remaining components is in the reverse order of removal.

**NOTE: Always recheck the valve clearance and valve timing, after the camshaft has been removed.**

## Pistons and Connecting Rods

### POSITIONING

**NOTE: Most pistons are notched or marked to indicate which way they should be installed. If the pistons are not marked, mark them before removal. Reinstall the pistons in the same position.**

# ENGINE LUBRICATION

## Oil Pan

### REMOVAL & INSTALLATION

#### *All Engines*

1. Raise and support the vehicle safely.
2. Drain the oil from the crankcase. Remove the cover plate from under the engine, if equipped.
3. Remove the 4 bolts from the subframe and lower the subframe. Remove the oil pan bolts while supporting the pan.
4. Lower the pan from the engine. Discard the gasket.
5. Coat both sides of a new gasket with sealer and install the gasket and oil pan.
6. Tighten the pan bolts to 7 ft. lbs. on 4 cylinder engines and 15 ft. lbs. on 5 cylinder engines.

## Rear Main Bearing Oil Seal

### REPLACEMENT

#### *All Engines*

The rear main oil seal is located at the rear of the engine block. It can be found in a housing behind the flywheel. To replace the seal it is necessary to remove the transaxle.

1. Remove the transaxle.
2. Remove the flywheel.
3. Using special tool VW2086 or a suitable tool, pry the old seal out of its housing.

4. To install, lightly oil the replacement seal and press it into place.

**NOTE: Be careful not to damage the seal or score the crankshaft.**

5. Install the flywheel and the transaxle.

## Oil Pump

### REMOVAL & INSTALLATION

#### *4 Cylinder Engines*

1. Drain the oil and remove the oil pan.
2. Remove the oil pump mounting bolts and pull the pump down and out of the engine.
3. Unscrew the 2 bolts and separate the pump halves.
4. Clean the lower half in solvent.
5. To remove the oil strainer for cleaning, bend out the metal rim of the oil strainer cover plate and remove it.
6. Examine the gears and the driveshaft for any wear or damage. Replace them if necessary.
7. Reassemble the pump halves.
8. Prime the pump with oil and install in the reverse order of removal.

#### *5 Cylinder Engines*

1. Loosen and remove the crankshaft pulley bolt.
2. Remove the timing belt covers.
3. Loosen the water pump bolts and turn the pump body clockwise.
4. Remove the timing belt and V-belt pulley with the timing belt sprocket.
5. Remove the dipstick and drain the engine oil.
6. Remove the front bolts on the sub frame and remove the oil pan.
7. Remove the oil suction pipe from the base of the oil pump and bracket to the engine block.
8. Remove the oil pump bolts and remove the oil pump from the front of the engine.
9. Installation is the reverse of the removal procedure.

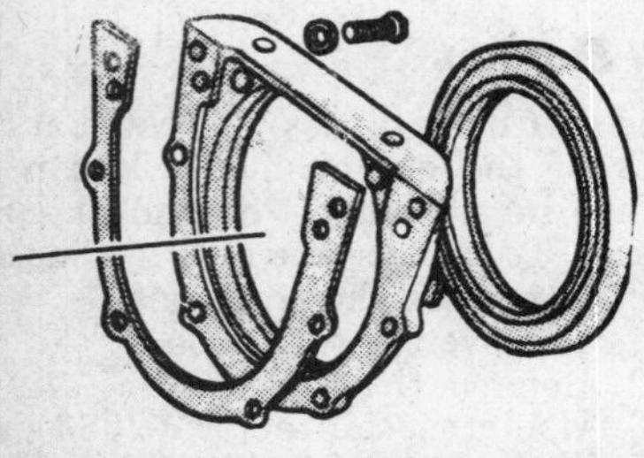

**Rear main oil seal (circular)—4000 and 5000**

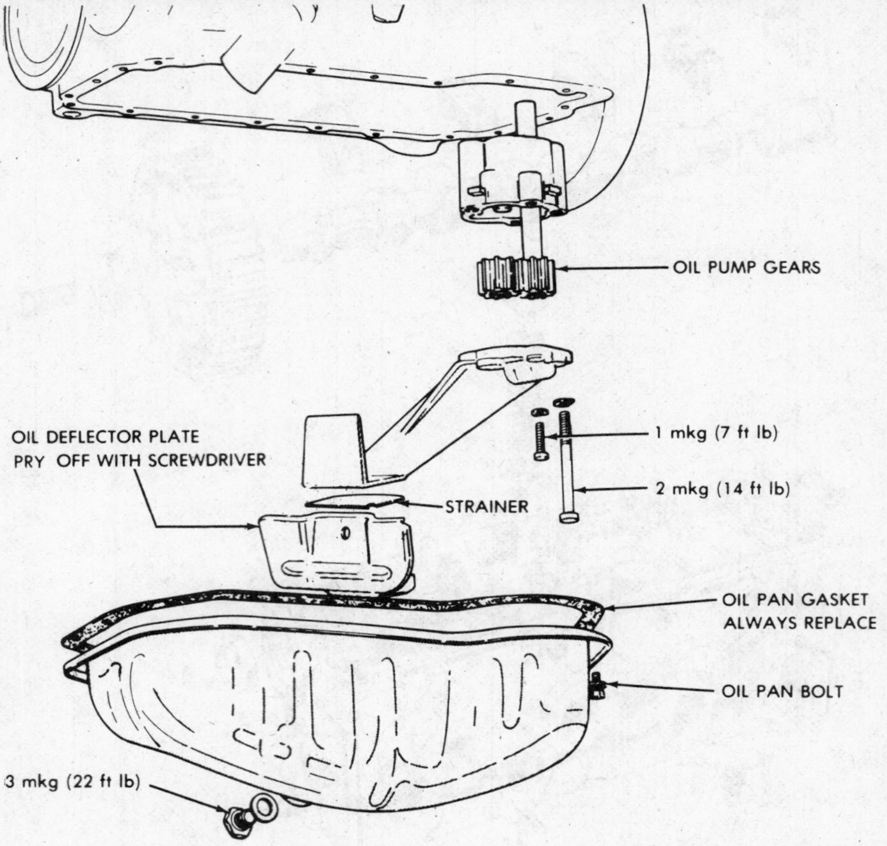


**4 cylinder diesel engine lubrication system—exploded view**

# ENGINE COOLING

**NOTE: When replacing or adding coolant, use only a phosphate-free coolant/antifreeze.**

## Radiator

### REMOVAL & INSTALLATION

#### *4 Cylinder Models*

**NOTE: The 80 and 90 series vehicles use a dual fan electric/belt driven assembly. Replacement is similar to the other 4 cylinder engines.**

1. Drain the cooling system.
2. If equipped with A/C, remove the grille and detach the condenser from the radiator.
3. Remove the upper and lower radiator hoses, the expansion tank supply hose and the expansion tank vent hose. Being careful not to crimp them, tie all hoses back out of the way.
4. Disconnect the wiring at the temperature switch (2 switches if air conditioned) and the rear of the fan motor.
5. Unscrew the fan shroud retaining bolts and remove the fan, motor and shroud as 1 assembly.
6. Unscrew the radiator retaining bolts and remove the radiator.
7. Installation is in the reverse order of removal.

#### *5 Cylinder Models*

1. Drain the cooling system.
2. Remove the 3 pieces of the radiator cowl and the fan motor assembly. Take care in removing the fan motor connectors to avoid bending them.
3. Remove the upper and lower radiator hoses and the coolant tank supply hose.
4. Disconnect the coolant temperature switch located on the lower right side of the radiator.
5. Remove the radiator mounting bolts and lift out the radiator.
6. Installation is the reverse of removal. Torque radiator mounting bolts to 14 ft. lbs. and cowl bolts to 7 ft. lbs.

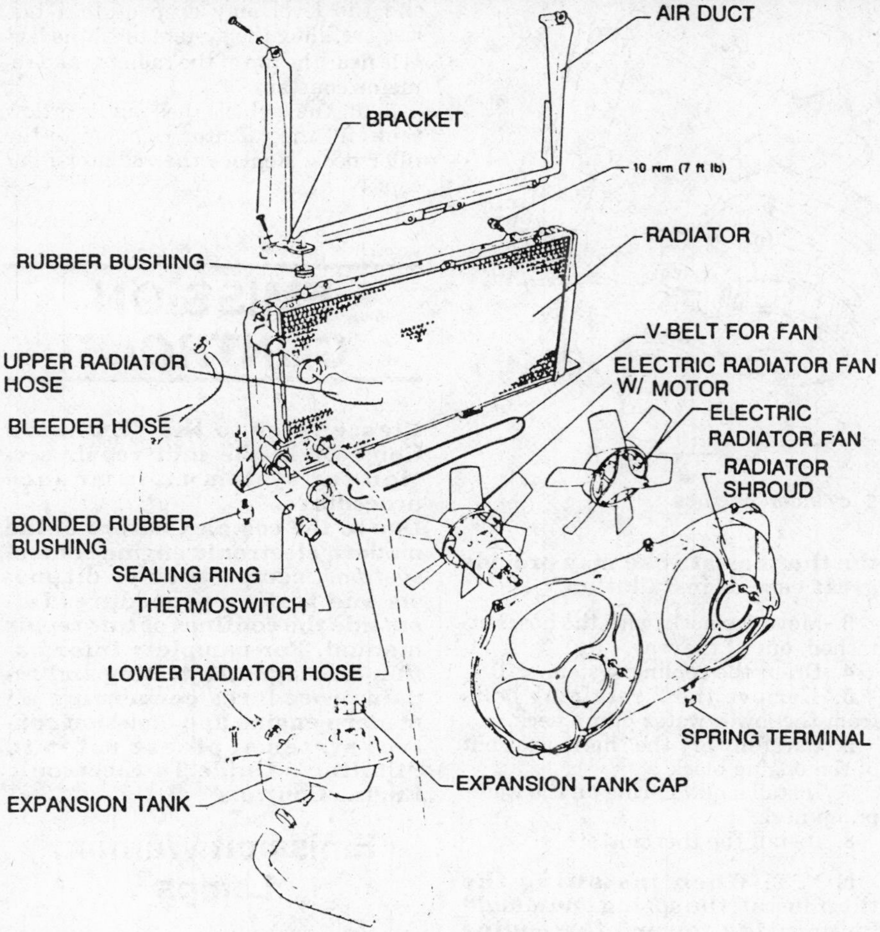


4 cylinder dual fan—80 model shown

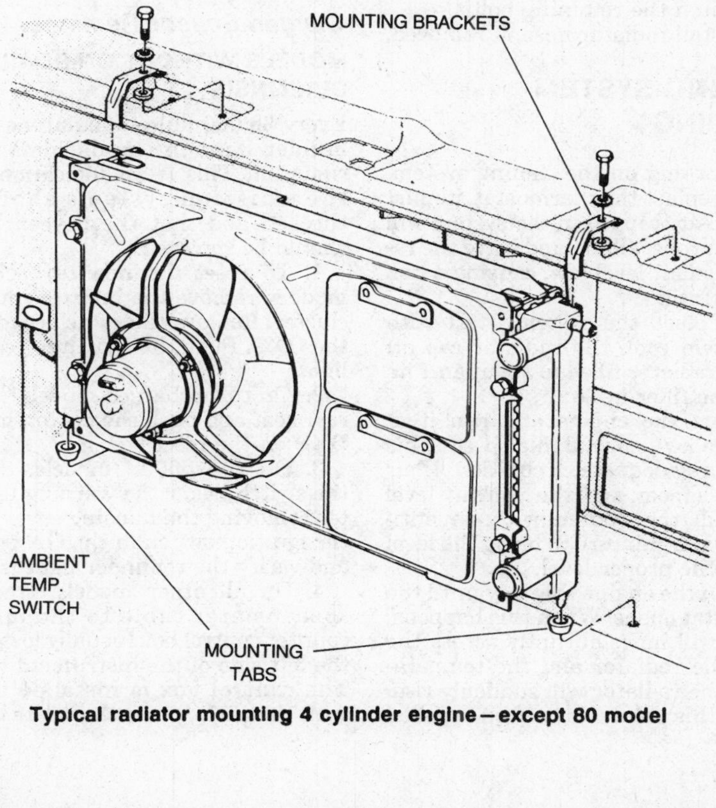


Typical radiator mounting 4 cylinder engine—except 80 model

## Water Pump

### REMOVAL & INSTALLATION

#### *All 4 Cylinder Engines and 5 Cylinder Gasoline Engines*

1. Drain the cooling system.
2. Remove the V-belts, timing belt covers. On 5 cylinder engines, remove the timing belt from the water pump.
3. On 4 cylinder engines, remove the water pump pulley retaining bolts and remove the pulley. Remove the pump retaining bolts (take note of various lengths and locations). Turn the pump slightly and lift from engine block.
4. Always replace the old gasket or O-ring.
5. Installation is the reverse of the removal procedure.
6. Reinstall the timing belt on 5 cylinder engine and properly tension the belt with the water pump.

#### *5 Cylinder Diesel Engine*

1. Drain the coolant from the cooling system.
2. If equipped with power steering, loosen the pump adjustment and remove the V-belt. Remove the power steering pump (with the hoses) and lay it aside.
3. Remove both of the drive belt covers.
4. Turn the crankshaft, so that the No. 1 cylinder is at the TDC of the compression stroke; the mark on the flywheel aligns with the mark on the clutch housing and the mark on the injection pump aligns with the mark on the mounting plate.
5. Using tool No. 2064, secure the injection pump sprocket. Using tool No. 3036, secure the vacuum pump belt pulley and the injection pump drive sprocket.
6. Remove the injection pump drive sprocket retaining bolt and the belt pulley, the injection pump drive sprocket and the drive belt.
7. Remove the cylinder head cover. Using tool No. 2065A, secure camshaft.
8. Loosen the camshaft sprocket retaining bolt (1 turn). Insert a drift, through the hole in the camshaft cover and drive the camshaft sprocket off its seat.
9. Slide the timing belt from the water pump sprocket.

**NOTE: When removing the timing belt, be careful not to move the timing mark positions.**

10. Remove the water pump-to-engine bolts and the pump from the engine.
11. To install, use a new gasket, seal-

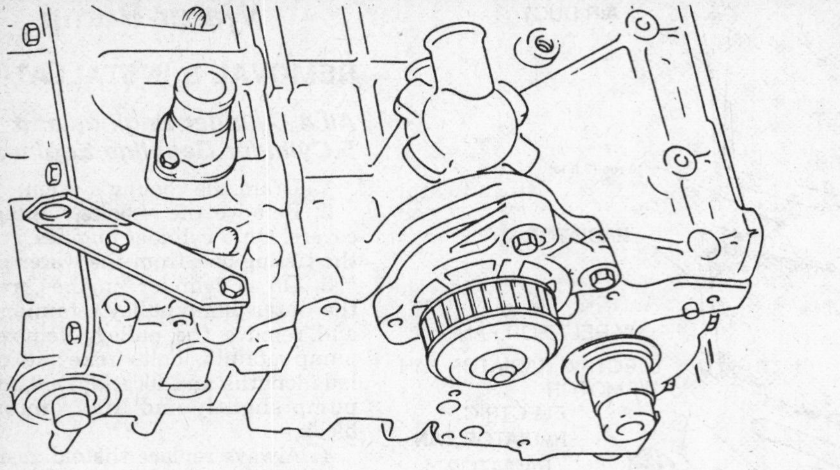

Water pump mounting—5 cylinder engines

ant and reverse the removal procedures. Torque the water pump bolts to 14 ft. lbs., the camshaft sprocket bolt to 33 ft. lbs. and the injection pump drive sprocket bolt to 72 ft. lbs. Adjust the drive belts and refill the cooling system.

## Thermostat

### REMOVAL & INSTALLATION

#### *4 Cylinder Engines*

The thermostat is located in the lower radiator hose neck on the bottom of the water pump housing.

1. Drain the cooling system.
2. Remove the 2 retaining bolts from the lower water pump neck.

**NOTE: It is not necessary to disconnect the lower radiator hose. But removing the hose for the thermostat yoke may provide great ease of installation.**

3. Move the neck, with the hoses attached, out of the way.
4. Carefully pry the thermostat out of the water pump housing.
5. Install with new gasket or O-ring.
6. Install the radiator hose, if removed.

#### *5 Cylinder Engines*

The thermostat is located in the lower radiator hose neck, on the left side of the engine block, behind the water pump housing.

1. Drain the cooling system.
2. Remove the 2 retaining bolts from the lower water pump neck.

**NOTE: It is not necessary to disconnect the lower radiator hose. But removing the hose for the thermostat yoke may provide great ease of installation.**

3. Move the neck, with the hoses attached, out of the way.
4. Drain the cooling system.
5. Remove the 2 retaining bolts from the lower water pump neck.
6. Carefully pry the thermostat out of the engine block.
7. Install a new O-ring on the water pump neck.
8. Install the thermostat.

**NOTE: When installing the thermostat, the spring end should be pointing toward the engine block.**

9. Reposition the water pump neck and tighten the retaining bolts.
10. Install radiator hose, if removed.

### COOLING SYSTEM BLEEDING

After working on the cooling system, even to replace the thermostat, it must be bled. Air trapped in the system will prevent proper filling and leave the radiator coolant level low, causing a risk of overheating.

1. To bleed the system, start with the system cool, the radiator cap off and the radiator filled to about an 1 in. below the filler neck.
2. Start the engine and run it at slightly above normal idle speed. This will insure adequate circulation. If air bubbles appear and the coolant level drops, fill the system with an antifreeze/water mixture to bring the level back to the proper level.
3. Run the engine this way until the thermostat opens. When this happens, coolant will move abruptly across the top of the radiator and the temperature of the radiator will suddenly rise.
4. At this point, air is often expelled and the level may drop quite a bit. Keep refilling the system until the level is near the top of the radiator and remains constant.
5. If the vehicle has an overflow tank, fill the radiator right up to the filler neck. Replace the radiator filler cap.

# EMISSION CONTROLS

**Please refer to the "Emission Control" in the unit repair section for system maintenance procedures.**
**Due to the complex nature of the modern electronic engine control systems, comprehensive diagnosis and testing procedures fall outside the confines of this repair manual. For complete information on diagnosis, testing and repair procedures concerning all modern engine and emission control systems, please refer to "Chilton's Guide To Electronic Engine Controls".**

## Emission Warning Lamps

### MAINTENANCE REMINDER LIGHT RESET

#### *Oxygen Sensor Reminder*

##### MODELS WITHOUT ON-BOARD DIAGONSIS

Every 30,000 miles a maintenance reminder light in the dashboard will come on. This is an indications that the emission systems should be checked and that the oxygen sensor should be replaced.

1. To reset the non turbocharged models, remove the instrument panel cluster. Remove the switch cover near the **OXS**. Push the switch to reset the light.
2. On turbocharged models, lift the rear seat and push the button marked **OXS** on the reset box.
3. On the 5000S models, depress the switch below the warning light after removing the housing cover. Place the ignition switch in the **ON** position and verify the reminder light is out.
4. On all other models, trace the speedometer cable to the mileage counter control box (usually located on the left side of the instrument panel). The control box is installed in-line with the cable, press the white button

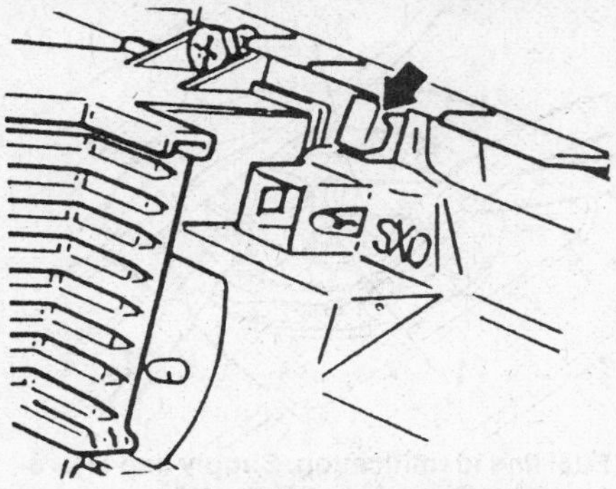

Maintenance reminder light reset button location 5000 non-turbo models

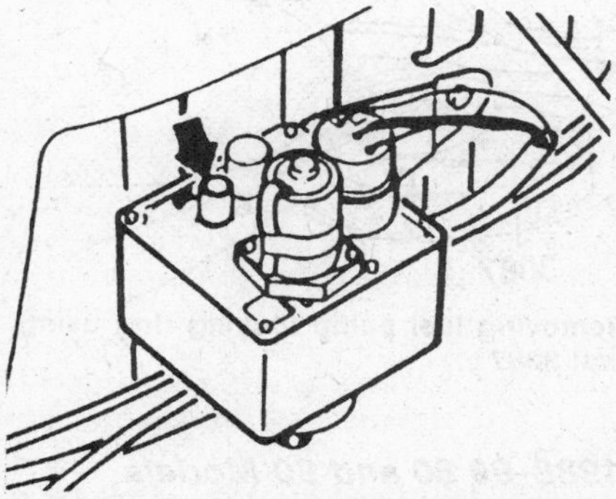

Maintenance reminder light reset button location 5000 turbo models

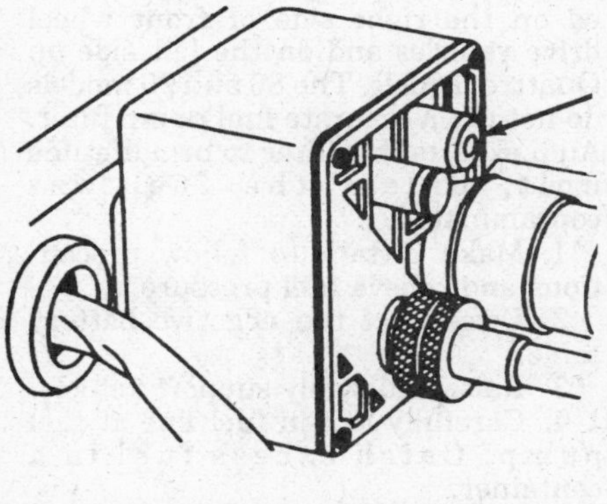

Maintenance reminder light reset button location all other models

on the control box and check to see that the reminder light has gone out.

#### 1985–88 MODELS WITH ON-BOARD DIAGNOSIS

The indicator light comes on whenever a fault develops which could cause the vehicle to fail an exhaust emission test. The light will remain on while driving as long as the fault exists. The light will go out after the fault has been repaired or no longer exists. Once the fault has been corrected, the permanent memory can be cleared the with the following procedures:

1. With the ignition **OFF**, Insert a fuse in the top of the fuel pump relay.
2. Turn ignition **ON**.
3. Wait at least 4 seconds, then remove the fuse.
4. Repeat Step 3, three times until indicator flashes code 4443.
5. Reinsert fuse in top of fuel pump relay for 4 seconds.
6. Repeat Step 5, until indicator flashes code 0000.
7. Reinsert fuse in top of fuel pump relay.
8. Wait at least 10 seconds, then remove fuse.
9. Memory is clear.

### *1989–90 80, 90, 100 and 200 Models*

Diagnosis connectors have been added to the drivers side footwell. It is not possible to activate fault memory by means of the fuel pump relay, as in older models. If the indicator light comes on when a fault develops, the light will remain on while driving as long as the fault exists. The light will go out after the fault has been repaired or no longer exists.

# GASOLINE FUEL SYSTEM

## Fuel System Service Precaution

When working with the fuel system certain precautions should be taken; always work in a well ventilated area, keep a dry chemical (Class B) fire extinguisher near the work area. Always disconnect the negative battery cable and do not make any repairs to the fuel system until all the necessary steps for repair have been reviewed.

### RELIEVING FUEL SYSTEM PRESSURE

Modern fuel injection systems operate under high pressure, this makes it necessary to first relieve the system of pressure before servicing. The pressurized fuel when released may ignite or cause personal injury.

1. If possibly, disconnect the power to the fuel pump, by remove fuss or relay, with the engine running. When the engine stalls, fuel pressure should be greatly reduced.
2. Remove the negative battery cable or the fuel pump relay, to prevent the fuel pump from activating.
3. Carefully loosen the fuel line on the control pressure regulator or component to be serviced.
4. Wrap a clean rag around the connection while loosening to catch any fuel.
5. After service is complete, discard the fuel soaked rag in the proper manner and reconnect negative battery cable, relay or fuses.

## Fuel Filter

### REMOVAL & INSTALLATION

#### *4 Cylinder Models except 80 and 90 vehicles*

**NOTE: The 1983–84 4000 has 2 fuel filters, 1 for the fuel pump and 1 for the fuel distributor. Both should be replaced every 15,000 miles. The fuel pump filter is underneath the vehicle, below the fuel tank.**

#### PUMP FILTER

1. Loosen the fuel line clamps on each end of the filter and disconnect the filter from the lines.
2. Install a new filter. Make sure

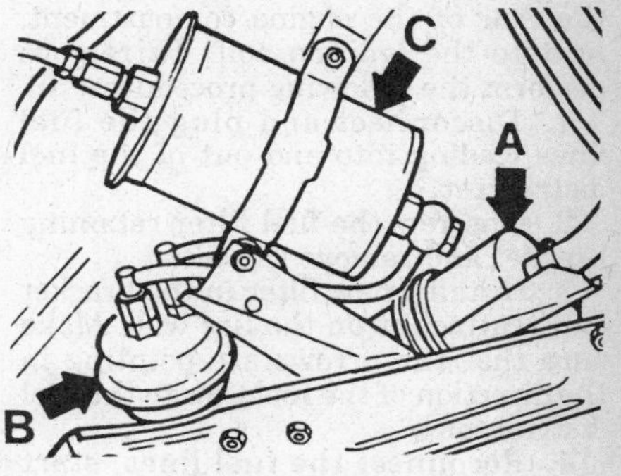


A—Fuel pump
B—Accumulator
C—Fuel filter

View of the fuel filter located at the right-rear undercarriage—1985 and later 4000S Coupe

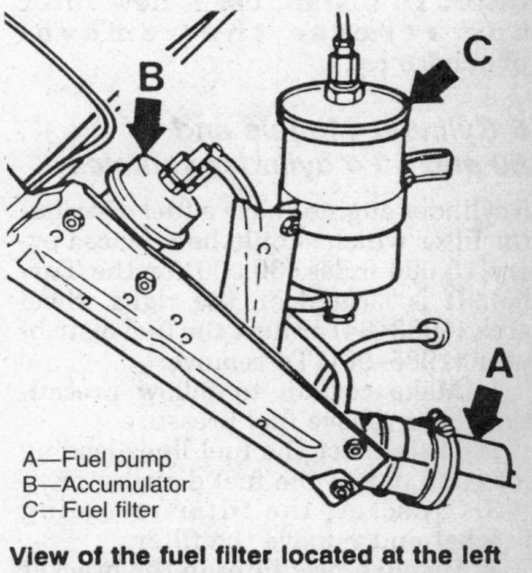


View of the fuel filter located at the left rear undercarriage – 80 and 90 and Quattro models

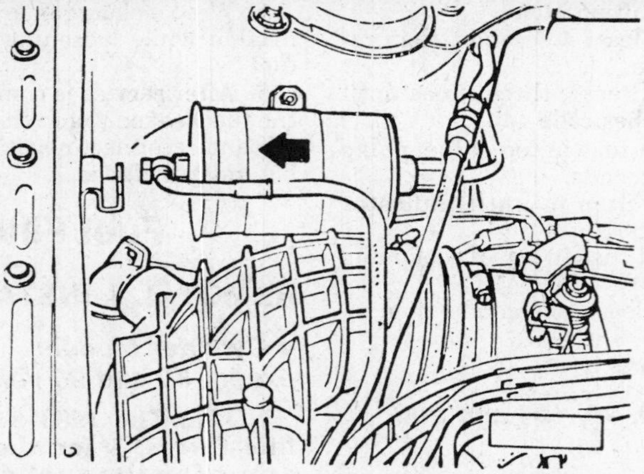

Typical fuel filter location—100, 200 and 5000 models

that the arrow points in the direction of fuel flow to the fuel pump.

3. Tighten the fuel line clamps and secure the new filter. Start the engine and check for leaks.

#### FUEL DISTRIBUTOR FILTER

The fuel distributor filter is located at the rear of the engine compartment, next to the ignition coil. To remove perform the following procedures:

1. Disconnect and plug the fuel lines leading into and out of the fuel distributor.
2. Unscrew the fuel filter retaining bracket and remove the filter.
3. Install a new filter in the bracket and reattach it on the fire wall. Make sure that the arrows are pointing in the direction of the fuel flow to the fuel distributor.
4. Reconnect the fuel lines, start the engine and check for leaks.

**NOTE: All 1985–87 4000 models have a fuel pump filter located in the line between the fuel tank and the fuel pump. To remove: disconnect the fuel lines and remove the filter. To install, use a new filter and reverse the removal procedures.**

#### *5 Cylinder Models and 80 and 90 4 cylinder vehicles*

5 cylinder engines have a fuel distributor filter which should be replaced every 15,000 miles (30,000 for the Turbo). It is located on the right wheel arch (1983–84) or next the fuel distributor (1985–90). To remove:

1. Make certain to follow precautions and relieve fuel pressure.
2. Disconnect the fuel lines leading into and out of the fuel distributor.
3. Unscrew the filter retaining bracket and remove the filter.
4. Install a new filter in the bracket and reattach bracket to vehicle. Make sure that the arrows are pointing in the direction of the fuel flow to the distributor.
5. Reconnect the fuel lines, start the engine and check for leaks.

## Electric Fuel Pump

### REMOVAL & INSTALLATION

#### *1983–87 4000 Models*

The fuel pump is located at the right rear of the undercarriage. On the 1985–87 4000 Quattro, the fuel pump is located at the left rear of the undercarriage.

1. Disconnect the battery ground.
2. Clean all fuel and electrical connections.
3. Disconnect the pump wiring.
4. Disconnect the fuel lines.
5. Unbolt and dismount the pump.
6. Installation is the reverse of removal. Torque the mounting bolts to 14 ft. lbs.

#### *1985–90 All Models Except 80 and 90 Models*

The fuel pump is located in the fuel tank.

1. Remove the floor cover from the luggage compartment.
2. Disconnect the negative battery cable and the electrical connector from the fuel gauge sender.
3. Mark and remove the hoses from the fuel gauge sender.
4. Using tool No. 3087, loosen the fuel gauge sender-to-fuel tank retaining ring. Pull out the fuel gauge fuel pump assembly.
5. From inside the assembly housing, pull off the fuel hoses, detach the electrical connections and remove the gravity vent valve.
6. To install, reverse the removal procedures. Start the engine and check for leaks.

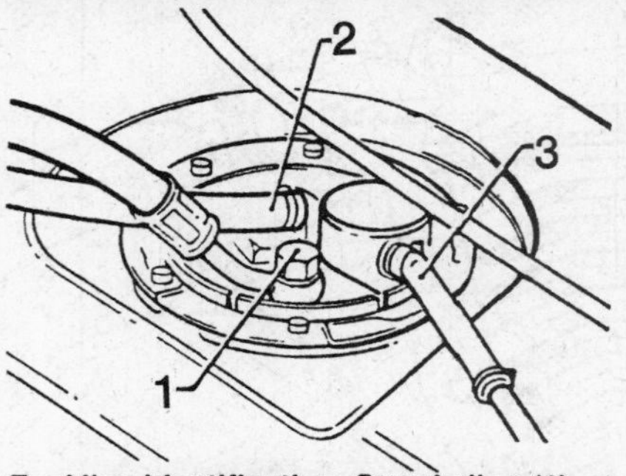


Fuel line identification. Supply line (1), return line (2) and vent hose (3)

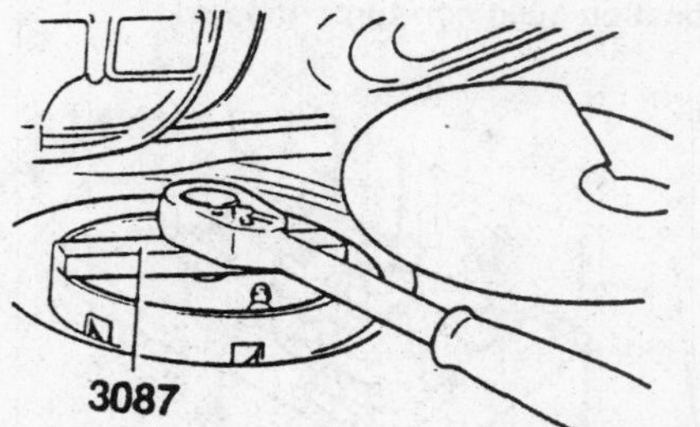


Removing fuel pump locking ring using tool 3087

#### *1988–90 80 and 90 Models*

The fuel pump is located under the vehicle on a bracket in front of the fuel tank. The fuel pump assembly is located on the right side of front wheel drive vehicles and on the left side on Quattro models. The 80 and 90 models do not use a separate fuel pump filter. Audi expects this filter to be a lifetime unit, unless the fuel was contaminated.

1. Make certain to follow precautions and relieve fuel pressure.
2. Disconnect the negative battery cable.
3. Raise and safely support vehicle.
4. Carefully loosen fuel line at fuel pump. Catch excess fuel in a container.
5. Remove fuel pump electrical connectors and remove the fuel pump.
6. Install fuel pump. Connect the fuel lines.
7. Connect the fuel pump electrical connectors.
8. Lower vehicle and connect the negative battery cable.
9. Replace and relays or fuses, that had been removed. Start engine and inspect for fuel leakage.

### PRESSURE TESTING

**CAUTION**

***When performing this test, do not smoke or have any open flame around.***

**NOTE: The fuel tank is pressurized. Do not open the fuel tank**

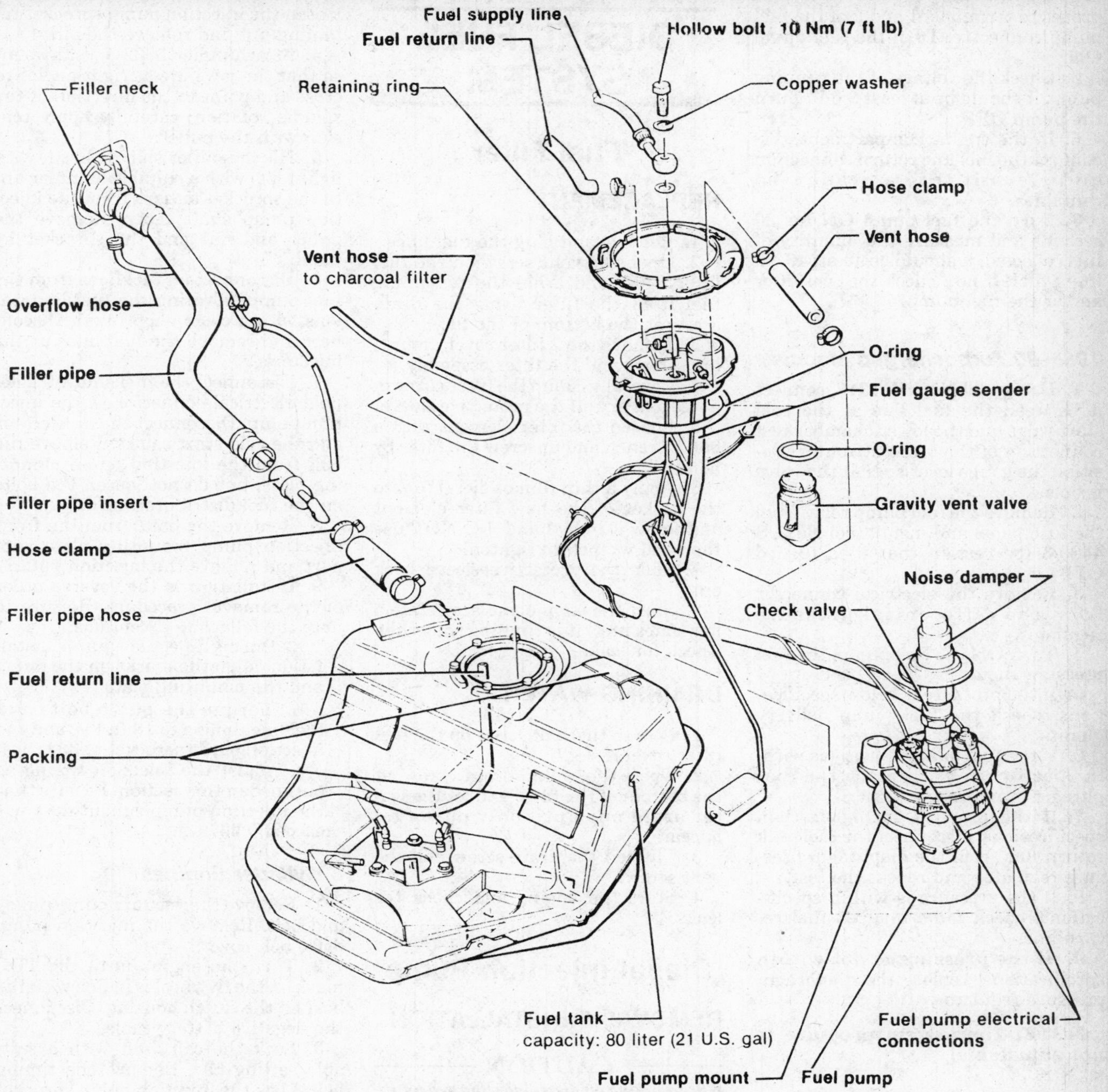


In-tank electric fuel pump and components

**cap until after the fuel pump delivery rate has been tested.**

### *1983 All Models*

1. Using tool No. US 4480/3, connect it in place of the fuel pump relay with the switch **OFF**.
2. At the input side of the fuel filter, disconnect the fuel line and place it into a graduated flask.
3. Turn the fuel pump **ON** for 30 second; the pump should deliver about 60 cu. in. of fuel.
4. If not within specifications, check the fuel pump filter. If the fuel pump filter is operating properly, replace the fuel pump.
5. Install the input hose onto the filter. Remove the output hose from the filter and place filter output into the flask.
6. Turn the fuel pump **ON** for 30 seconds; the amount of fuel collected should be the same, if not replace the fuel filter.
7. Replace the output line onto the fuel filter.

### *1985–90 Non Turbocharged Models*

1. Using tool No. US 4480/3, connect it in place of the fuel pump relay with the switch **OFF**.
2. Remove the fuel pump cover from the floor of the trunk, on 80 and 90 models raise and safely support vehicle to access the pump.
3. At the fuel pump connecting plug, pull back the rubber cover, leave the plug connected to the pump.
4. Using a voltmeter, connect the

probes to terminals 1 and 2 of the fuel pump connector. Turn the fuel pump **ON**.

5. Check the voltage of the running pump, it should be at least 9.0 V. Turn the pump **OFF**.

6. In the engine compartment, disconnect the fuel line return connection and place it into a graduated container.

7. Turn the fuel pump **ON** for 30 seconds and measure the quantity of fuel collected, it should be about 46 cu. in. of fuel. If not, check the fuel filter and/or the fuel pump.

#### *1985–90 Turbocharged Models*

1. Using tool No. VW 1318, connect it between the fuel line at the cold start valve and the lower chamber test connection of the fuel distributor. Position the gauge lever so that the valve is open.

2. Remove the fuel pump relay from the fuse panel and install tool No. US 4480/3 (be certain that it is turned **OFF**).

3. Remove the electrical connector from the differential pressure regulator.

4. Turn **ON** the fuel pump, the fuel pressure should be 75–82 psi.

5. If the pressure is below specifications, check the fuel pump delivery quantity.

6. If the fuel pump delivery is within specifications, replace the diaphragm pressure regulator.

7. If the pressure is higher than specifications, disconnect the fuel tank return line from the diaphragm pressure regulator and repeat the test.

8. If the pressure is within specifications, check for a plugged fuel return line.

9. If the pressure is not within specifications, replace the diaphragm pressure regulator.

**NOTE: The system pressure is not adjustable.**

## Fuel Injection

**Due to the complex nature of the modern electronic engine control systems, comprehensive diagnosis and testing procedures fall outside the confines of this repair manual. For complete information on diagnosis, testing and repair procedures concerning all modern engine and emission control systems, please refer to "Chilton's Guide To Fuel Injection And Feedback Carburetors".**

# DIESEL FUEL SYSTEM

## Fuel Filter

### REPLACEMENT

1. Remove and plug the fuel lines.

2. Open the vent screw on the fuel filter cover and drain the remaining fuel from the filter using the drain screw at the bottom of the filter.

3. Remove the 2 filter cover mounting screws and the filter assembly.

4. Carefully clamp the filter cover in a vise and pry off the protective sleeve.

5. Loosen the filter element with a band wrench and unscrew the filter by hand.

6. Apply a thin film of diesel fuel to the gasket of the new filter element and screw it in by hand. DO NOT use the band wrench to tighten.

7. Slide the protective sleeve back on.

8. Start the engine and accelerate a few times until it is running smoothly. Check for leaks.

### DRAINING WATER

1. Loosen the vent screw on the fuel filter cover.

2. Open the water drain screw at the bottom of the filter and let the water drain out until only pure fuel appears.

3. Tighten the drain screw and the vent screw.

4. Start the engine and check for leaks.

## Diesel Injection Pump

### REMOVAL & INSTALLATION

**CAUTION**

***When working on diesel injection system everything must be kept extremely clean. Wipe pipe unions clean before loosening. DO NOT use cold water if degreasing a hot injection pump, the sudden contraction of the metal can cause the pump to seize.***

#### *4 Cylinder Engines*

1. Turn the engine until the TDC mark on the flywheel is in line with the boss on the bellhousing. Disconnect the negative battery cable.

2. Lock the camshaft with a suitable setting bar and remove the timing belt.

3. Lock the injection pump sprocket with pin 2064 or equivalent. Slightly loosen the injection pump sprocket retaining nut and remove the pin.

4. Attach puller 3032 or equivalent so that the jaws are at right angles to cross and point in the direction of the spindle rotation, carefully apply tension with the puller.

5. Hit the puller spindle head (with light taps) with a suitable hammer until the sprocket loosens from the injection pump shaft taper. Remove the puller and nut and the sprocket by hand.

6. Disconnect all fuel lines from the fuel pump, covering the fuel line unions with a clean shop towel. Disconnect and remove the fuel lines at the injectors.

7. Disconnect the fuel shut-off solenoid electrical connector at the injection pump. Disconnect the accelerator and the cold start cables. Remove the bolt from the injection pump mounting plate, but do not loosen the bolts on the fuel distributor head.

8. Remove the bolts from the front injection pump mounting plate support and remove the injection pump.

9. Installation is the reverse order of the removal procedure. Be sure to note the following exceptions:

   a. During injection pump installation, align the marks on the pump and the mounting plate.

   b. Torque the pump bolts and fuel line unions to 18 ft. lbs. and the injection pump sprocket to 33 ft. lbs.

   c. Adjust the injection timing as outlined in this section. Be sure that the injection pump runout does not exceed 0.0079 in.

#### *5 Cylinder Engines*

1. Remove the vacuum pump pulley and belt. Remove the injection pump drive belt cover.

2. Turn the engine until the TDC mark on the flywheel is in line with the boss on the clutch housing. Disconnect the negative battery cable.

3. Lock the camshaft with a suitable setting bar. Remove the timing belt. Lock the injection pump sprocket with pin 2064 or equivalent.

4. Secure the vacuum pump belt pulley and injection pump drive sprocket with tool 3036 or equivalent.

5. Loosen and remove the drive sprocket attaching bolt and remove the drive sprocket with the timing belt.

6. Attach puller 3032 or equivalent so that the jaws are at right angles to cross and point in the direction of the spindle rotation, carefully apply tension with the puller.

7. Hit the puller spindle head (with light taps) with a suitable hammer until the sprocket loosens from the injection pump shaft taper. Remove the

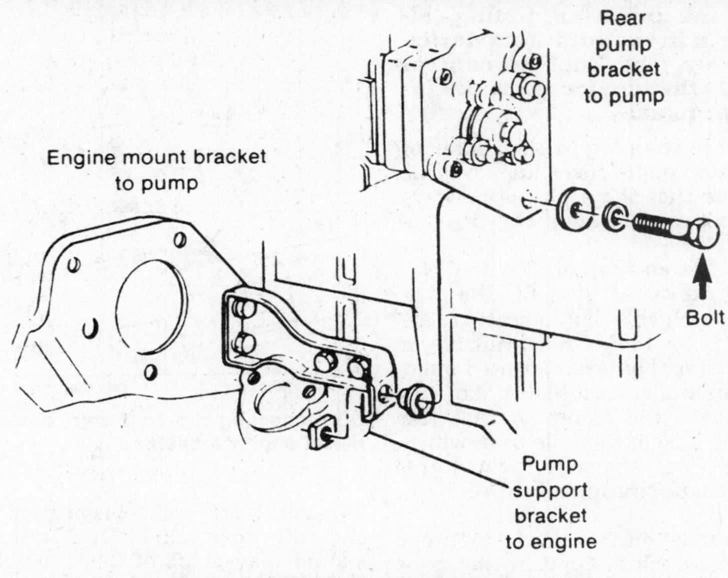


**4 cylinder diesel engine injection pump mounting**

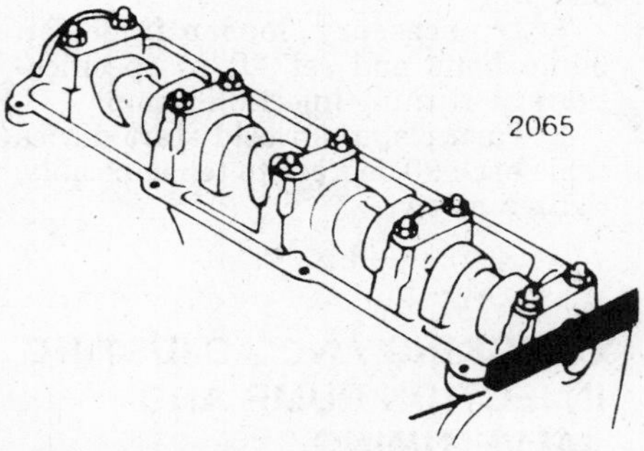


**Camshaft locking bar installed on camshaft**

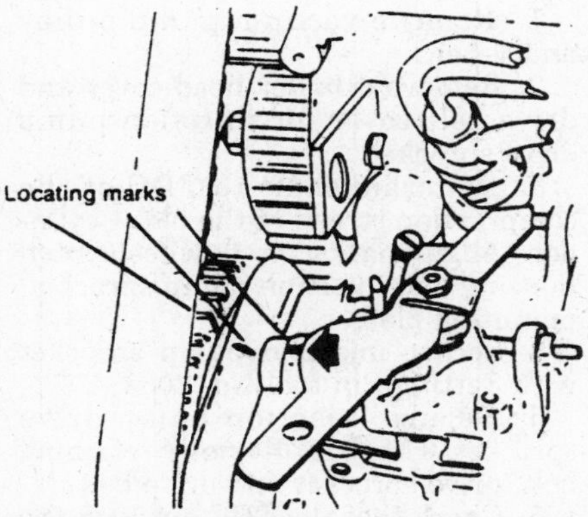


**4 cylinder diesel engine injection pump alignment marks**

puller and nut and the sprocket by hand.

8. Disconnect all fuel lines from the fuel pump, covering the fuel line unions with a clean shop towel. Disconnect and remove the fuel lines at the injectors.

9. Disconnect the fuel shut-off solenoid electrical connector at the injection pump, accelerator and the cold start cables.

10. Remove the coolant hoses from the cold start device. Remove the 4 bolts from the injection pump mounting plate and 1 bolt from the support bracket and remove the injection pump.

**NOTE: To remove the rear attaching bolt at the mounting plate, use a 6mm hex key socket with a 8.6 in. extension.**

11. Install the injection pump, aligning the marks on the pump and the mounting plate. Install the attaching bolts loosely. Align the rear support so that it contacts the cylinder block and injection pump free of tension and tighten it in this position.

12. During injection pump sprocket installation, be sure that the injection pump runout does not exceed 0.0079 in. Install the injection pump sprocket, turning it to align the marks on the gear and mounting plate.

**5 cylinder diesel engine installing fuel injection pump drive belt**

**5 cylinder diesel engine fuel injection pump and mounting bracket alignment marks**

13. Lock the pump with tool 2064 or equivalent and torque the attaching bolts to 33 ft. lbs. Install the timing belt with the injection pump drive sprocket on the camshaft.

14. Tighten the drive sprocket attaching bolt so that the drive sprocket can still be turned manually. Using tool VW210 or equivalent, check the timing belt tension.

15. If the scale of the tool does not read 12-13 adjust the drive belt tension by loosening the bolts and moving the plate pump. Be sure the TDC mark on the flywheel is aligned with the reference mark.

16. Secure the injection pump drive sprocket with the setting bar and torque the sprocket attaching bolt to 72 ft. lbs. Remove tool 2064 or equivalent.

17. Connect the coolant hoses to the cold start valve. Loosen the cold start device cable by loosening the screw on the slip collar. Do not loosen the cable clamping nut.

18. Hold the cold start lever to the left while turning the collar a ¼ turn to allow the cable clamp to slide to the left of the collar slot. Install the adapter 2066 or equivalent and a small dial indicator with a 0.0984 in. preload in place of the plug on the injection pump.

19. Remove the cover plate below the engine. Slowly turn the crankshaft counterclockwise until the dial indicator needle stops moving. Zero the dial indicator with approximately 0.03997 in. preload.

20. Turn the crankshaft clockwise until the TDC mark on the flywheel is aligned with the reference mark. The dial indictor should read, 0.0315–0.0354 in. On vehicles without a turbocharger and 0.0346–0.0386 in. on vehicles equipped with a turbocharger.

21. If it is necessary, loosen the injection pump bolts and set the lift by turning the injection pump. Set to 0.0327–0.343 in. On vehicles without a turbocharger and 0.0358–0.0374 in. on vehicles equipped with a turbocharger. Torque the injection pump attaching bolts to 18 ft. lbs.

22. Retention the cold start device cable by rotating the slip collar back a ¼ turn and tightening the slip collar screw. Connect the coolant hoses to the cold start device.

23. Reconnect all fuel lines, the shut-off solenoid and all other disconnect electrical connectors. Torque the fuel injection line unions to 18 ft. lbs. Re-install the timing belt cover. Start the engine and adjust the idle speeds as necessary.

## INJECTION TIMING

### *4 Cylinder Engines*

**NOTE: Before checking or adjusting the injection timing, always push in the cold start device completely. The knob to control the cold start device is on the instrument panel.**

1. Locate the plug in the center of the injection pump cover. Remove this plug. Note that the seal must always be replaced whenever the plug is removed.

2. VW has an adapter (VW tool No. 2066 or equivalent) that fits the plug opening to which a dial indicator is attached. If this tool is not available, a dial indicator that is substituted must have a range of at least (0–0.120 in. (0–3mm). Place the gauge so that the plunger will be in the hole from which the plug was removed. Preload the gauge to approximately 0.097 in. (2.5mm).

3. Turn the engine slowly counterclockwise, which is opposite the normal rotation, until the needle on the dial indicator stops moving. Zero the gauge.

**NOTE: Do not try to rotate the engine by turning the camshaft drive nut. This will only damage the drive belt.**

4. With the dial indicator on 0, turn the engine clockwise, which is the normal rotation, until the TDC mark on the flywheel is aligned with the boss on the belt housing. The gauge should read 0.032 in. on regular diesels and 0.035 in. on turbocharged diesels.

5. If the reading cannot be obtained, loosen the bolts on the mounting plate and injector support. Set the regular diesel lift of the pump to 0.032 in. by turning the pump; set the turbodiesel lift to 0.035 in. by turning the pump. Tighten the mounting bolts and recheck the injection timing.

6. Replace the seal on the center plug and install the plug.

### *5 Cylinder Engines*

1. Set crankshaft to TDC of the compression stroke of the No. 1 cylinder. Align marks on the flywheel/clutch housing and injection pump sprocket mounting plate.

2. Loosen cold start device cable by loosening screw (1) on clamp and turning clamp 90 degrees. Do not loosen screw (2).

3. Install adaptor and small dial indicator with 0.097 in. (2.5mm) preload in place of injection pump cover.

4. Turn the crankshaft counterclockwise slowly until the dial indicator stops moving.

5. Zero the dial indicator with about 0.04 in. (1mm) preload.

6. Turn crankshaft clockwise until

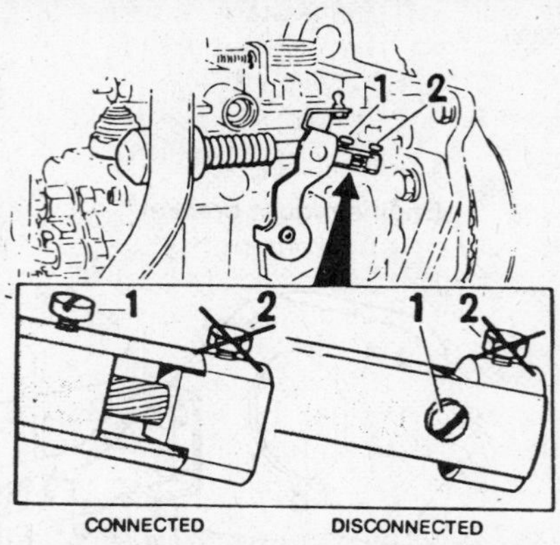


**Disconnecting the cold start device on diesel engine models**

TDC mark on flywheel is aligned with the reference mark. Dial indicator should read a lift of 0.031–0.035 in. (0.80–0.90mm) diesel or 0.035–0.038 in. (0.88–0.98mm) for turbocharged diesel.

7. If necessary, loosen injection pump bolts and set lift to specifications by turning injection pump.

8. Turn clamp on cold start device cable back 90 degrees to tension cable, tighten screw.

## CHECKING AND ADJUSTING INJECTION PUMP AND VALVE TIMING

### *All Engines*

1. Remove vacuum pump pulley and V-belt.

2. Remove cylinder head cover and drive belt cover for injection pump drive sprocket.

3. Set crankshaft to TDC of the compression stroke of the No. 1 cylinder. Align marks on flywheel/clutch housing and injection pump sprocket/mounting plate.

4. Secure injection pump sprocket with Setting Pin tool No. 2064.

5. Secure injection pump drive sprocket with bar. Remove retaining bolt, drive sprocket and drive belt.

6. Check that the TDC mark on the flywheel is still aligned with reference mark. Adjust if necessary.

7. Setting Bar tool No. 2065 A should fit in camshaft slot. If not, timing must be set as follows:

a. Turn crankshaft so that setting bar will fit.

b. Remove camshaft drive belt cover and loosen camshaft sprocket retaining bolt about 1 turn.

c. Loosen the camshaft sprocket by tapping with a drift inserted through hole in cover.

d. Turn crankshaft until TDC mark on flywheel and boss on clutch housing are aligned.

e. Tighten the camshaft sprocket bolt to 33 ft. lbs. and remove setting bar.

8. Install injection pump drive sprocket with drive belt. Tighten the drive sprocket retaining bolt until drive sprocket can just be turned by hand.

9. Check the drive belt tension. If necessary, adjust by loosening bolts and moving mounting plate with pump.

**NOTE: The belt is correctly tensioned when it can be twisted 90 degrees with the thumb and forefinger midway between the camshaft and intermediate shaft drive sprockets.**

10. Check that the TDC mark on flywheel is aligned. Adjust if necessary.

11. Secure injection pump drive sprocket with bar and tighten retaining bolt to 72 ft. lbs.

12. Remove the Setting Pin tool No. 2064 from injection pump.

13. Check injection timing. Adjust if necessary.

14. Install belt cover and cylinder head cover.

## Injection Nozzle

### REMOVAL & INSTALLATION

**NOTE: A loud knocking in 1 or more cylinders can be caused by a faulty injector. Locate by loosening pipe union on each cylinder in turn with engine at fast idle. If engine speed remains constant, that injector is faulty.**

**CAUTION**

*To avoid damage, keep injector parts clean when removing, installing, disassembling and assembling.*

1. Clean all injector pipe fittings.
2. Remove injector pipes.
3. Disconnect fuel return hoses.
4. Remove injectors, using tool No. US 2775 or equivalent.
5. Remove heat shields from injectors and discard.
6. Install new heat shields on injectors.
7. Install injectors and tighten to 51 ft. lbs.
8. Install injector pipes and tighten to 18 ft. lbs.
9. Reconnect fuel return hoses.
10. Start engine and accelerate a few times to clear air bubbles. Check for leaks.

# MANUAL TRANSAXLE

The transaxle is combined with the differential in a transaxle assembly.

### REMOVAL & INSTALLATION

**NOTE: If the flywheel has been removed from the crankshaft for any reason, tighten the mounting bolts to: Bolt without shoulder–72 ft. lbs.; bolt with shoulder–54 ft. lbs. Coat all threads with a locking compound.**

#### *1983–87 4000 Models Except Quattro and 1988–90 80 and 90 Models Except Quattro*

This procedure can be performed with the engine installed.

1. Disconnect the negative battery cable.
2. Unplug the 2 electrical connectors for the back-up lights. They can be found between the ignition coil and the fuel distributor filter.
3. Remove the upper engine/transaxle bolts.
4. Using special tool 3016 (or a pair of pliers), detach the speedometer cable from the transaxle.
5. Detach the clutch cable from the clutch lever.
6. Unbolt the exhaust pipe from the exhaust manifold.
7. Unscrew the 3 mounting bolts and remove the center engine mount.
8. Unbolt the front exhaust pipe from the support bracket and unbolt it from the catalytic converter or muffler.
9. Unscrew the 6 screws and remove the left halfshaft from the transaxle. Wire the halfshaft up and out of the way. Repeat the procedure for the right halfshaft.

**NOTE: When wiring the halfshaft, tighten the wire only enough so as to relieve any downward pressure on them.**

10. Remove the cover plate.
11. Tag and disconnect all wires leading to the starter and remove the starter.
12. Remove the bolt from the shift rod coupling.
13. Pry off the linkage coupling with a suitable small prybar.
14. Pull the shift rod coupling off of the shift rod. Place a transaxle jack under the transaxle, support it by lifting up slightly.
15. Loosen the left (chassis) bolt on the rear transaxle support. Remove the 2 bolts (some models have a single bolt) from the right (transaxle) side of the support and pivot the support out of the way.
16. Remove the rubber mounting block.
17. Unscrew 3 bolts and remove the front transaxle support.
18. Remove the lower engine/transaxle bolts.
19. Carefully pry the transaxle apart from the engine and remove it.
20. Installation is in the reverse order of removal. Note the following:

a. Make sure that all engine/transaxle mounts are correctly aligned and free of tension.

b. Check for proper adjustment of the gear shift lever.

c. Secure the bolt on the shift rod coupling with wire.

d. Tighten the engine/transaxle bolts to 40 ft. lbs.

e. Tighten the halfshaft-to-drive flange bolts to 33 ft. lbs.

f. Tighten the subframe-to-body bolts to 51 ft. lbs.

g. Tighten the front transaxle support-to-transaxle bolts to 18 ft. lbs.

h. Tighten the rubber mount-to-body bolts to 29 ft. lbs. on 1983 or 80 ft. lbs. except 1983.

i. Tighten the rubber mount-to-transaxle bolts to 40 ft. lbs.

j. Tighten the rubber mount-to-crossmember bolts to 18 ft. lbs.

#### *1984–87 4000 Quattro Models*

1. Disconnect the negative battery cable.
2. Disconnect the rpm sensor.
3. Remove the upper engine-to-transaxle bolts.
4. Using tool No. 3016, disconnect the speedometer cable from the transaxle.
5. Disconnect the tie rod coupling from the steering rack.

**CAUTION**

*When removing the tie rod coupling, remove the self-locking nuts (first) and the mounting bolts.*

6. Disconnect the transaxle switch electrical connector from the transaxle.
7. At the clutch slave cylinder, drive out the lock pin, remove the cylinder (leave the hydraulic line attached) and move it aside.
8. Disconnect the shift linkage from the transaxle.
9. Using an Engine Support tool No 10–222, place it on the vehicle and support the engine and remove the left-axle shaft from the transaxle.
10. At the rear of the transaxle, dis-

connect the driveshaft and the differential lock cable.
11. Remove the transaxle cover plate and turn the spindle of the engine support tool to raise the engine.
12. At the right transaxle mount, remove the axle shaft deflector and the transaxle mount.
13. Remove the front exhaust pipe. Disconnect the right axle shaft from the transaxle.
14. At the left side of the transaxle, remove the gine slightly.
15. Place a Transaxle Support Lift tool No. VWAG 1383 under the transaxle and secure it to the transaxle.
16. Remove the lower engine-to-transaxle bolts, push the transaxle back and lower it from the vehicle.

**CAUTION**

***When removing the transaxle, make sure that the axle shafts, driveshaft, tie rods and shift linkage do not interfere.***

**NOTE: If the pickup eye is still in place on the transaxle housing (near the starter), remove it with a hacksaw to provide easier access to the exhaust pipe.**

17. To install, reverse the removal procedures. Tightening bolts to the following torque:
    a. Torque the engine-to-transaxle bolts to 43 ft. lbs.
    b. Torque the transaxle mounting-to-transaxle bolts to 29 ft. lbs.
    c. Torque the transaxle mount-to-frame bolts to 32 ft. lbs.
    d. Torque the axle shafts-to-transaxle bolts to 33 ft. lbs.
    e. Torque the tie rod coupling-to-steering rack bolts to 29 ft. lbs.
    f. Torque the driveshaft-to-transaxle bolts to 39 ft. lbs.
18. Adjust the shift linkage.

### 1988–90 80 and 90 Quattro Models

1. Disconnect the negative battery cable.
2. Remove the 3 upper engine to transaxle bolts.

**NOTE: Tag all bolts during removal, so all bolts can be replaced in their correct locations, as they are not all the same size.**

3. Disconnect the ground strap from the transaxle.
4. Remove the wiring connectors fro the speedometer sender and the multifunction switch.
5. Disconnect the wiring for the oxygen sensor and oxygen sensor heating element.
6. Remove the engine protection plate.
7. Disconnect the exhaust pipe from the manifold.
8. Separate the exhaust pipe behind the catalyst and remove the pipe and catalyst.
9. Matchmark and remove the driveshaft.
10. Remove the rear crossmember.
11. Remove the shift rod securing bolt at the transaxle and let the shift rod hang.
12. Remove the transaxle cover plate.
13. Remove the right axle shaft shield.
14. Disconnect the left and right axle shafts, turn the steering to the right lock and tie both shafts up.
15. Remove the clutch slave cylinder.
16. Remove the tie rod coupling from the steering rack and turn wheel to the left.
17. Support the engine with tool 10–222A, or equivalent.
18. Support the transaxle with tool VW 1383, or equivalent.
19. Remove the transaxle strut at the left rear and front engine mount.
20. Remove the heat shield from the bonded rubber bushing.
21. Remove the bonded rubber bushing support bracket from the transaxle.
22. Remove the bonded rubber bushing.
23. Remove the bolt from the seatbelt tension in cable guide at the left rear of the transaxle. Position the cables and guide out of the way.
24. Lower the right rear subframe by loosening the mounting bolts.
25. Remove the remaining transaxle to engine bolts.
26. Remove the transaxle.
27. When install transaxle, make certain alignment bushings are in the cylinder block before reassembly.
28. Press clutch master cylinder in with a lever, until retaining bolt can be installed.

**NOTE: A replacement bolt for mounting the clutch slave cylinder is available from Audi, with a pointed tip for easier installation.**

29. Installation is the reverse order of the removal procedure.
30. Tighten subframe mounting bolts to 25 ft. lbs., plus an additional 90 degree turn.
31. Tighten transaxle retaining bolts as follows: Torque the 8mm bolts to 18 ft. lbs., the 10mm bolts to 33 ft. lbs. and the 12mm bolts to 48 ft. lbs.
32. Torque the driveshaft to flange bolts to 33 ft. lbs. and the driveshaft to transaxle and final drive bolts to 40 ft. lbs.
33. Torque the tie rod coupling to steering rack to 33 ft. lbs.

### 1983–88 5000

The manual transaxle may be removed with the engine in place.

1. Disconnect the battery ground.
2. Remove the air filter (diesel only).
3. Remove the windshield washer bottle.
4. Remove the upper engine-transaxle bolts.
5. Raise and support the vehicle.
6. Disconnect the speedometer cable from the transaxle.
7. Disconnect all wires and hoses connected to the transaxle.
8. Drive out the clutch slave cylinder lockpin and remove the slave cylinder. Leave the hydraulic line connected.
9. Support the engine, either from above with a hoist or from below with a jack.
10. Remove the heat shield.
11. Remove the lower engine/transaxle splash shield (diesel only).
12. Disconnect the exhaust pipe from the manifold.
13. Remove the right side guard plate.
14. Disconnect the driveshafts from the flanges and support them out of the way with wires. On the Quattro, disconnect the front/rear driveshaft at the rear output shaft on the transaxle and wire it out of the way.
15. Disconnect the back-up light switch.
16. Pry off the shift and adjusting rods.
17. Remove the lower engine-transaxle bolts.
18. Remove the starter.
19. Remove the sub-frame skid plate.
20. Install a jack under the transaxle and lift it slightly.
21. Remove both transaxle-to-subframe bolts.
22. Remove the right side transaxle bracket.
23. Slide the transaxle back off the locating dowels and remove it from the car.
24. When installing, place the driveshafts on top of the sub-frame; tighten the lower bolts first. Tighten the transaxle bracket, sub-frame and upper bolts. Driveshaft bolts are torqued to 32 ft. lbs.; transaxle bracket bolts to 29 ft. lbs.; sub-frame support bolts to 29 ft. lbs.; sub-frame to body bolts to 80 ft. lbs. and the transaxle to engine bolts to 40 ft. lbs. Install all other parts in reverse order of removal.

### 1989–90 100 Models

1. Disconnect the negative battery cable.
2. Remove the upper engine to transaxle bolts.

**NOTE: Tag all bolts during removal, so all bolts can be replaced in their correct locations, as they are not all the same size.**

3. Disconnect the ground strap from the transaxle, if equipped.
4. Remove the wiring connectors fro the speedometer sender and the multifunction switch.
5. Support the engine with tool 10–222A, or equivalent.
6. Disconnect the wiring for the oxygen sensor and oxygen sensor heating element.
7. Remove the splash shield, if equipped.
8. Disconnect the exhaust pipe from the manifold.
9. Separate the exhaust pipe behind the catalyst and remove the pipe and catalyst.
10. Remove the bolt for the shift rod a th the transaxle and separate.
11. Remove the heat shield from the right inner CV-joint.
12. Remove the axle shafts from the flanges and tie up out of the way.
13. Remove the heat shield for the bonded rubber bushing on the right side.
14. Support the transaxle with tool VW 1383, or equivalent.
15. Remove the strut at the rear of the transaxle.
16. Remove the clutch slave cylinder. Do not remove the hydraulic line from the slave cylinder.
17. Remove the lower transaxle to engine bolts.
18. Pry transaxle back and lower assembly.
19. Remove the transaxle.

**To install:**

20. When install transaxle, make certain alignment bushings are in the cylinder block before reassembly.
21. Press clutch master cylinder in with a lever, until retaining bolt can be installed.

**NOTE: A replacement bolt for mounting the clutch slave cylinder is available from Audi, with a pointed tip for easier installation.**

22. Installation is the reverse order of the removal procedure.
23. Tighten subframe mounting bolts to 25 ft. lbs., plus an additional 90 degree turn.
24. Tighten transaxle retaining bolts as follows: Torque the 8mm bolts to 18 ft. lbs., the 10mm bolts to 33 ft. lbs. and the 12mm bolts to 48 ft. lbs.
25. Torque the driveshaft to flange bolts to 33 ft. lbs. and the driveshaft to transaxle and final drive bolts to 40 ft. lbs.
26. Torque the tie rod coupling to steering rack to 33 ft. lbs.

### *1989–90 200 Models*

1. Disconnect the negative battery cable.
2. Remove the upper engine to transaxle bolts.
3. Remove the connector for the speedometer sender by pressing in the clips. Vehicles with turbocharger unscrew the cover plate (it cannot be removed yet).
4. Remove the clip from the clutch slave cylinder and drive out spring pin, if equipped. Remove the bolt securing the clutch slave cylinder to the transaxle and remove the cylinder. Leave the hydraulic line connected.
5. Support the engine, using tool 10–222A, or equivalent. Tie up coolant hoses and cables, as needed.
6. Remove the right side guard plate.
7. Disconnect the axle shafts from the flanges and rest both axle shafts on top of the subframe.
8. Tag and disconnect the wire from the back-up light switch, on quattro models tag and disconnect vacuum hoses at the servo.
9. Pry off the shift and adjusting rods.
10. Remove the lower engine transaxle bolts.
11. Remove the starter.
12. Remove the guard plate from the subframe.
13. Install tool US 618 and 618–1, or equivalent on transaxle jack and lift transaxle slightly.
14. Remove both rear subframe mounting bolts.
15. Remove both transaxle support bolts from the subframe.
16. Remove the bracket from the transaxle, push tension system cable and bracket off the retainer on transaxle. The retainer can only be removed with the transaxle out of the vehicle.
17. Remove the right side transaxle bracket.
18. Pull transaxle off dowel sleeves.
19. Lower transaxle and take out from below.
20. Before install transaxle, rest both axle shafts on top of the subframe.
21. Lubricate mainshaft splines.
22. Install transaxle onto dowels and install the lower bolts.
23. Install the tensioning system bracket and cable to the transaxle.
24. Tighten the transaxle bracket and subframe upper bolts to 29 ft. lbs.
25. Installation is the reverse order of the removal procedure.
26. Check alignment of transaxle and torque transaxle to engine bolts to 40 ft. lbs.
27. Torque subframe to body bolts to 80 ft. lbs.
28. Torque axle shaft to drive flange bolts to 58 ft. lbs.

### *1984–88 5000 Quattro, 5000 Quattro Turbo and 4000 Quattro Coupe*

1. Disconnect the negative battery cable and disconnect the rpm sensor.
2. Remove the upper engine to transaxle attaching bolts. Disconnect the speedometer.
3. Disconnect the tie rod coupling from the steering rack, first removing the self locking nuts below the tie rod coupling and second, the mounting bolts.
4. Drive out the clutch slave cylinder lock pin. Remove the clutch slave cylinder leaving the hydraulic lines attached. Disconnect the back-up light switch and shift linkage.
5. Attach tool 10–222 or equivalent and support the engine with a suitable engine hoist. Remove the deflector for the axle shaft and the right transaxle mount. Remove the right transaxle mount.
6. Disconnect the exhaust pipe at the flange and the right axle shaft at the transaxle. Remove the left transaxle mount and disconnect the left axle shaft at the transaxle.
7. Disconnect the driveshaft at the transaxle. Disconnect the differential lock cable and remove the transaxle cover plate.
8. Raise the engine slightly and place a suitable transaxle jack under the transaxle. Remove the lower engine to transaxle bolts.
9. Remove the transaxle from underneath the vehicle. On the Quattro Turbo models, remove the transaxle towards the rear of the vehicle, making sure the transaxle clears the axle shafts, driveshafts, tie rods and shift linkage.
10. Installation is the reverse order of the removal procedures. Torque the exhaust pipe flange attaching bolts to 18 ft. lbs. Torque the exhaust pipe to transaxle mount attaching bolts to 22 ft. lbs. Torque the tie rod coupling to the steering rack attaching bolts and the transaxle mount to transaxle attaching bolts to 29 ft. lbs.
11. Torque the transaxle mount to sub-frame attaching bolts and driveshaft attaching bolts to 32 ft. lbs. Torque the engine to transaxle mounting bolts to 43 ft. lbs. Torque the axle shaft to the transaxle mounting bolts to 58 ft. lbs.

## LINKAGE ADJUSTMENTS

### *4000, Coupe, 80 and 90 Models Except Quattro*

#### 4 SPEED

**NOTE: This procedure will require special tool VW 3014.**

1. Place the shift lever in the **N** position.
2. Working under the car, loosen the clamp nut on the shift rod. Check that the shift finger slides freely on the shift rod.
3. Inside the car, remove the shift knob and the boot. It is not necessary to remove the console.
4. Align the holes in the shifter base with the holes in the bearing plate directly below it and tighten the bolts.
5. Install the Special Tool VW 3014 with the locating pin toward the front.
6. Push the shift lever to the left side of the tool cutout and tighten the lower knurled knob to secure the tool.
7. Move the top slide of the tool to the left side stop and tighten the upper knurled knob.
8. Push the shift lever into the right cutout of the slide. Align the shift rod and the shift finger under the vehicle and tighten the clamp nut.
9. Remove the special tool.
10. Place the shift lever in the first gear position. Press the lever to the left side against the stop. Release the lever; it should spring back ¼–½ in. If not, move the lever housing slightly sideways to correct. Check that all gears can be engaged easily.

**5 SPEED**

1. Place the shift lever in the **N** position.
2. Working under the vehicle, loosen the clamp nut on the shift rod. Be certain that the shift finger slides freely on the shift rod.
3. Working inside the vehicle, remove the gearshift lever knob and the boot.
4. Loosen the shifter base plate bolts slightly. Align the holes in the plate with the holes in the bearing housing and tighten the bolts.
5. Using the Alignment tool No. 3057, slip it over the gearshift lever and make sure that the locating pin is in the front centering hole.
6. Position the shift lever to the right cut out of slide 5/R and tighten the lower knurled nut of the tool.
7. At the top of the tool, move the slide with the gearshift lever to the right stop. Tighten the upper knurled nut of the tool.
8. Position the gearshift lever into the left cut-out (¾) of the slide. Adjust the shift rod and the shift finger (with the transaxle in Neutral) and tighten the clamp nut.
9. Remove the tool and check the shifting of the gears for smoothness.

### *5000 Models*

1. Remove the gear shift boot.
2. Position the shift lever in neutral.

**View of the 1985 and later shift rod coupling used on the 4000 Sedan and Coupe GT**

**Loosen the clamp nut on the shift rod—4000**

3. The seam on the plastic stop bracket should line up with the center hole in the curved stop plate. If not, proceed below:

**NOTE: On the Quattro, adjust the adjusting rod (center-to-center) to 5.275 in. (134mm) and install the rod.**

4. Loosen the 4 bolts at the base of the shifter.
5. Align the holes in the shifter base with the holes in the bearing plate directly below it.
6. Tighten the bolts.
7. Loosen the clamp between the front and rear shift rods; the rear shift rod must move freely.
8. Make certain that the front shift rod is in the neutral position.
9. Using the shifter locating tool No. 3048, place it on the stop plate with the shift lever resting in the notch. Tighten the shift rod clamp.

**NOTE: On the 1984–88 models, a bearing pin is used. Adjust the**

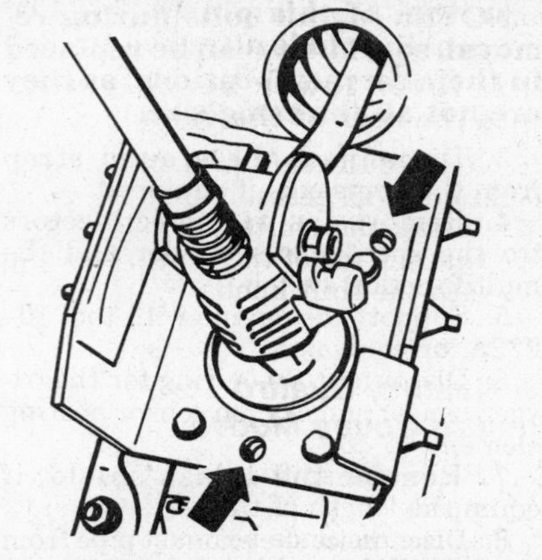

**Align the centering holes of the stop lever bearing (arrows), then tighten the bolts on 5000 models**

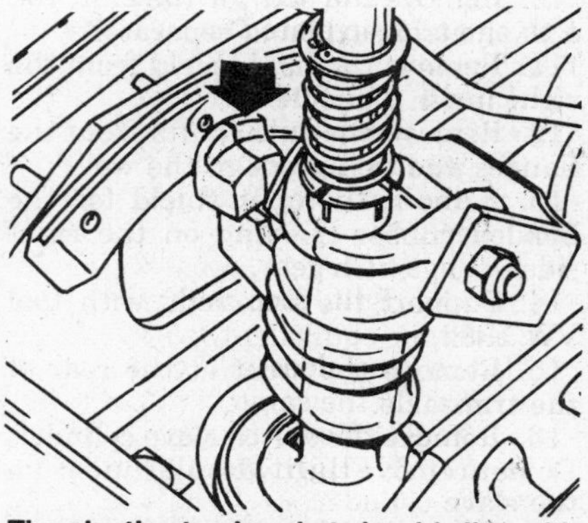

**The plastic stop bracket should align with the curved stop plate—5000**

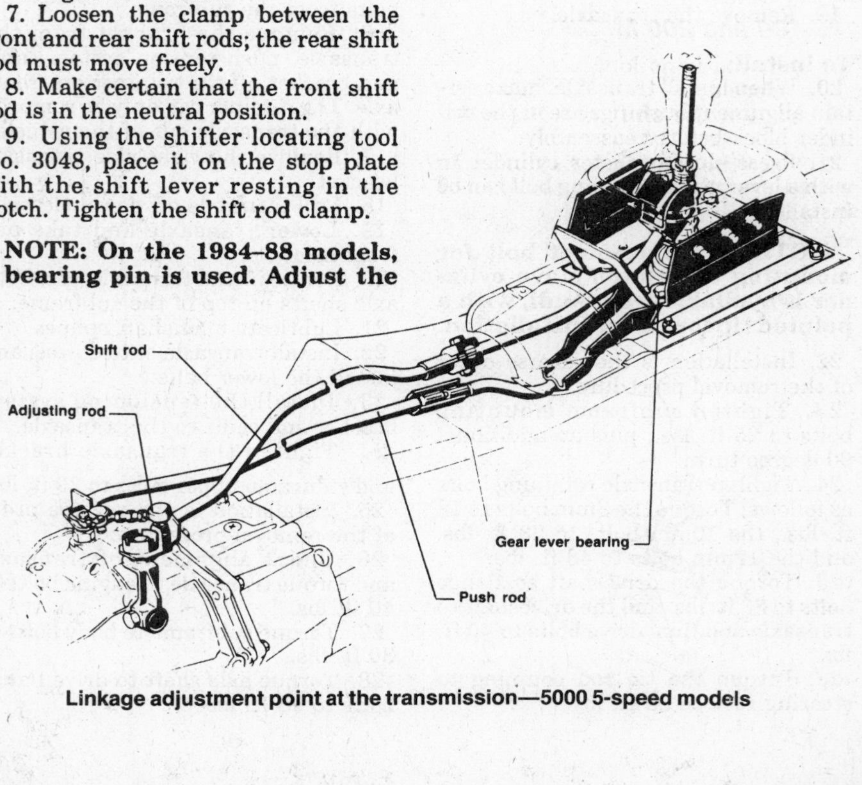


**Linkage adjustment point at the transmission—5000 5-speed models**

**projection of this pin to 11/16 in. The bearing pin is attached to the shift lever lower bearing and faces the rear of the vehicle.**

10. Release the shifter and check its operation in all gears.
11. Install the shifter boot, making sure that the top of the boot is in contact with the shift knob.

### *All Quattro, Quattro Turbo and Quattro Coupe Models*

1. Place the shift lever in neutral. Adjust the length of the adjusting rod so that the distance between the center point of the end holes is 5.275 in.
2. Loosen the clamp nut, making sure that the shift rod moves freely. Loosen the bolts slightly, align the centering holes of the gearshift lever housing and stop plate and tighten the bolts.
3. Install tool 3048 or equivalent, tighten the clamp nut and remove the tool. Engage first gear, press the shaft lever to the left, stop and release the shift lever.
4. Engage fifth gear, press the shaft lever to the right, stop and release te shift lever.
5. If the lever does not spring back approximately the same distance as in Steps 3 and 4, move the gear shift lever housing slightly in the slots sideward.
6. Make sure that all gears engage easily without jamming.

### *ALL 100 and 200 Models*

The shift rod is no longer splined on newer models.

1. Loosen the shift rod clamping bolt.
2. Place the gear shift in a vertical position so that the dimensions are equal on both sides and retighten shift rod clamp bolt.

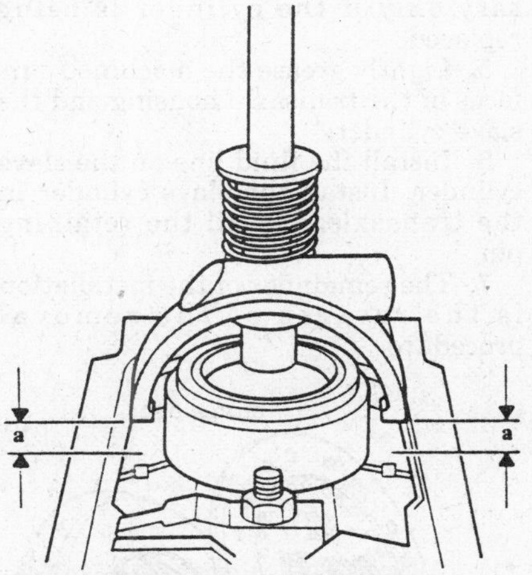


**Keep shifter centered for proper adjustment**

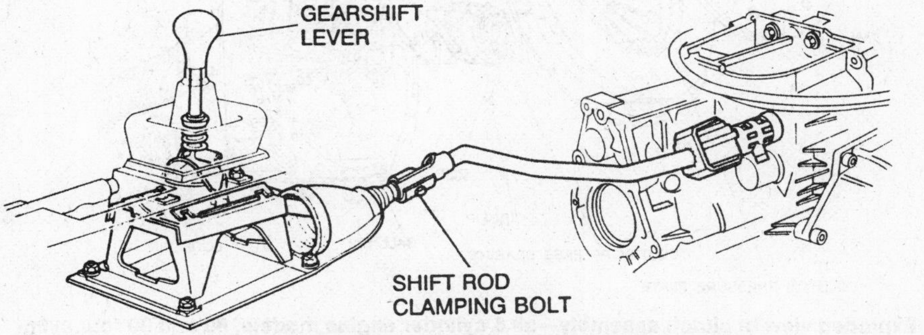


**Manual shift linkage—80, 90, 100 and 200 models**

# CLUTCH

## REMOVAL & INSTALLATION

### *All Models*

1. Remove the transaxle.
2. Mark the relationship of the pressure plate to the flywheel (only if it is to be reused).
3. Using tool No. 10–201, lock the flywheel. Unbolt the pressure plate from the flywheel, loosening the bolts alternately, a little at a time, to prevent warpage.
4. To install the clutch, place the driven plate on the pressure plate, making sure that the spring cage is facing the pressure plate.
5. Hold the clutch assembly against the flywheel, aligning the marks made in Step 2 and the dowel pins on the flywheel with the pressure plate. Insert a dummy shaft tool No. US 219 (1984–88 4000 Sedan and Coupe) or 10–213 (for all others) through the pressure plate and the driven plate into the crankshaft pilot bearing.
6. Install the pressure plate bolts finger tight. Tighten the bolts evenly, in rotation, to avoid distortion. Torque the bolts to 24 ft. lbs. (1983) or 18 ft. lbs. (1984–90). Remove the dummy shaft.
7. The clutch release bearing in the front of the transaxle should be checked before reassembly. It is retained by 2 springs.
8. Replace the transaxle. Torque the engine-to-transaxle bolts to 40 ft. lbs. and the axle shaft to 28 ft. lbs. (1983) or 58 ft. lbs. (1984–90).

## PEDAL FREE-PLAY ADJUSTMENT

### *4000 Models*

Free-play is the distance that the pedal travels from the released position to the point at which clutch spring pressure can first be felt. This can be measured by placing a yardstick alongside the clutch pedal. Free-play should be 5/8 in. (1983 Sedan) or 9/16 in. (1984–87 Sedan and Coupe), measured at the pedal.

1. Locate the clutch cable bracket by the oil filter.
2. Loosen the upper cable nut.
3. Turn both nuts clockwise to reduce pedal free-play or counterclockwise to increase it.
4. When adjustment is correct, tighten the upper nut to lock the cable in position.

## PEDAL HEIGHT ADJUSTMENT

### *All Models*

The clutch pedal should be at rest 3/8 in. above the brake pedal. To adjust the pedal height, remove the cotter pin holding the clutch master cylinder clevis to the pedal, loosen the locknut on the clevis shaft and turn the shaft to give the required pedal height. Tighten the locknut and install the clevis on the pedal.

# Clutch Cable

## REMOVAL & INSTALLATION

### *All 4 Cylinder Engines Models*

1. Loosen the adjustment nut on the end of the cable, at the transaxle.
2. Disengage the cable from the clutch arm on the transaxle.
3. Unhook the cable from the pedal. Remove the threaded eye from the end of the cable. Remove the adjustment nut(s).
4. Remove the C-clip which holds the outer cable at the adjustment point. Remove all the washers and bushings, first noting their locations.
5. Pull the cable out from the firewall toward the engine compartment side.

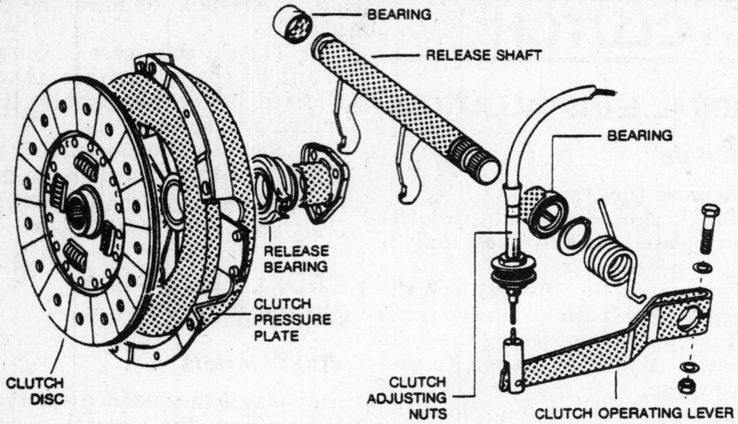


**Exploded view of the 4000 models clutch—except Quattro**

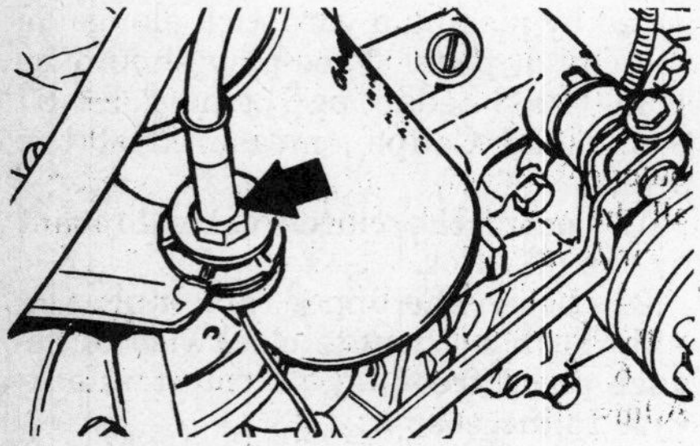

**Clutch cable adjustment nut**

6. Install and connect the new cable. Adjust the pedal free-play.

## Clutch Master Cylinder

### REMOVAL & INSTALLATION

**NOTE: The use of a pressure bleeder is necessary for this procedure. Before beginning, remove and plug the fluid line from the reservoir to the master cylinder. Empty the fluid in the line into a suitable container. Use care not spill any fluid on a painted surface.**

#### *All 5 Cylinder Engine Models*

1. Locate the master cylinder under the instrument panel, behind the clutch pedal.
2. Remove and plug the line leading to the slave cylinder from the end of the master cylinder.
3. Remove the circlip and the pin which attaches the clevis to the clutch pedal.
4. Remove the 2 master cylinder mounting bolts from the pedal mounting.
5. Remove and plug the reservoir line. Remove the master cylinder.
6. Installation is in the reverse order of removal. Tighten the master cylinder mounting bolts to 15 ft. lbs.
7. Bleed the clutch system when finished.

## Clutch Slave Cylinder

### REMOVAL & INSTALLATION

#### *5 Cylinder Engine Models*

1. Locate the slave cylinder on top of the transaxle housing.
2. Remove the retaining clip from the pin.
3. Drive out the slave cylinder lock pin, using a small punch.
4. Remove and plug the fluid line at the slave cylinder. This step is necessary only if the cylinder is being replaced.
5. Lightly grease the machined surfaces of the transaxle housing and the slave cylinder.
6. Install the fluid line on the slave cylinder. Install the slave cylinder in the transaxle. Install the retaining pin.
7. The remainder of the installation is the reverse of the removal procedure.
8. If the fluid line was removed, bleed the system.

### BLEEDING THE HYDRAULIC CLUTCH SYSTEM

Audi recommends that the clutch system be bled, using a pressure bleeder. The bleeder tank and fittings may be purchased at an auto supply store. Follow the instructions that come with the bleeder tank, for the proper bleeding procedure. The maximum line pressure must not exceed 36 psi.

# AUTOMATIC TRANSAXLE

### REMOVAL & INSTALLATION

#### *1983 087 and 089*

The procedures may vary slightly between 087 and 089 transaxles dependant upon the model vehicle that the transaxle is installed in. Adjust the following procedures as needed.

1. Disconnect the negative battery cable.
2. Remove the windshield washer bottle from the holder on the firewall.
3. Drain the cooling system. Raise and support the vehicle safely.
4. Disconnect and plug the hoses at the transaxle cooler.
5. Remove the upper end of the accelerator linkage rod.
6. Disconnect the speedometer cable at the transaxle.
7. Remove the upper engine to transaxle bolts.

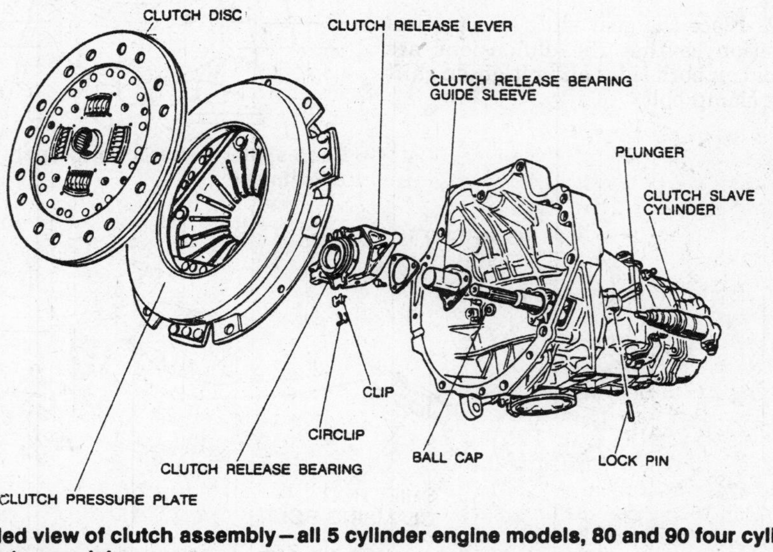


**Exploded view of clutch assembly—all 5 cylinder engine models, 80 and 90 four cylinder engine models**

8. Raise the engine enough to take the weight off of the engine mounts.
9. Remove the skid plate from the sub-frame.
10. Disconnect the exhaust pipe from the exhaust manifold and converter.
11. Remove the exhaust pipe from the hanger and remove it from the vehicle.
12. Remove the right halfshaft guard plate.
13. Disconnect the right and left halfshafts from the transaxle.
14. Remove the starter motor.
15. Disconnect the shifter cable and holder from the transaxle.
16. Remove the lower accelerator linkage rod.
17. Remove the accelerator cable from the transaxle support.
18. Remove the right side guard plate from the sub-frame.
19. Remove both transaxle mounts from the sub-frame.
20. Rotate the torque converter and remove each bolt as it appears in the starter opening.
21. Place a jack under the transaxle and raise it slightly.
22. Remove the lower engine to transaxle bolts.
23. Remove the rear sub-frame mounting bolts.
24. Swing both halfshafts rearward out of the way. Secure them with wire.

**NOTE: If the torque converter drive plate is removed from the crankshaft, tighten the mounting bolts to: Bolt without shoulder—73 ft. lbs.; bolt with shoulder—54 ft. lbs. Coat all threads with a locking compound.**

25. Separate the transaxle from the engine and carefully lower the transaxle onto the jack.
26. Installation is the reverse of the removal procedure.

**NOTE: Before installation, make sure that the torque converter is fully seated on the one-way clutch support. When the converter is properly seated, the distance between the converter cover nose and the end of the bell housing should be 0.393 in. (10mm).**

27. Install the lower engine to transaxle bolts first. The transaxle to sub-frame bolts are installed second.
28. Observe the following torques during installation: Converter bolts 22 ft. lbs.; transaxle to engine bolts 40 ft. lbs; starter bolts 40 ft. lbs.; sub-frame to body 80 ft. lbs. Proper bolt torque is important; use a suitable torque wrench to tighten all fasteners.
29. Adjust the throttle kickdown switch, as detailed below.

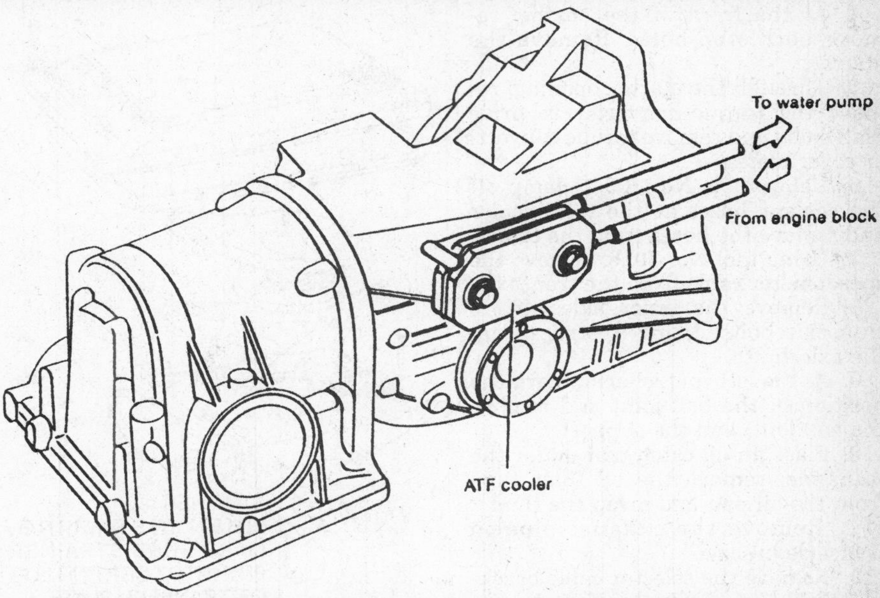


**Automatic transaxle models have the transaxle oil cooler mounted on the right side of the differential (1894) or on the rear of the transaxle (except 1984)**

### *Model 087*

**1984–90**

1. Disconnect the negative battery cable.
2. Raise and support the vehicle safely.
3. At the transaxles relay lever, remove the retaining clip and disconnect the pushrod socket.
4. Using tool No. 3016, disconnect the speedometer cable from the transaxle to engine bolts.
5. Using the Engine Support tools No. 10–222/1 and 10–222, install them to the engine and support it. Loosen the engine mounting bolts.
6. Disconnect the exhaust pipe from the exhaust manifold and from the converter. Remove the exhaust pipe from the vehicle.
7. Remove the right axleshaft guard plate and the axleshafts to transaxle bolts. Using wire, support the axleshafts.
8. Remove the starter. Through the starter hole, remove the torque converter to drive plate bolts.
9. Using tools No. 3094, clamp off the coolant hoses at the ATF cooler and remove the hoses from the cooler.
10. Place an oil pan under the transaxle. Remove the filler tube from the oil pan and drain the fluid.
11. At the accelerator pushrod, remove the circlip. Remove the accelerator cable support. Remove the accelerator cable from the transaxle operating lever.
12. Remove the selector cable bracket, circlip and cable from the transaxle shifting lever.
13. At the sub-frame, remove the front bolts. Using tool No. US 4470, support the transaxle and raise it slightly.
14. On the 4000 models, remove the center bolt from the transaxle mount; on all other models, remove the mounts from both sides of the transaxle and the lower transaxle to engine bolts.
15. Separate the transaxle from the engine and lower it from the vehicle. Be sure to secure the torque converter.

**NOTE: When installing the transaxle, should the torque converter slip off the one-way clutch support, the oil pump shaft could be pulled from the oil pump. This may cause severe damage when bolting the transaxle to the engine.**

16. To install, reverse the removal procedures. Torque the engine to transaxle bolts to 41 ft. lbs., the sub-frame bolts to 52 ft. lbs., the torque converter to drive plate bolts to 22 ft. lbs., the axleshaft to transaxle bolts 33 ft. lbs. and the transaxle mount center bolt to 30 ft. lbs. Refill the transaxle. Adjust the accelerator linkage and align the engine to transaxle mounts (if necessary).

### *Model 089*

**1984–90**

1. Disconnect the negative battery cable.
2. Remove the upper engine to transaxle bolts. Raise and support the vehicle safely.
3. Using the engine support tool No. 10–222A, secure it to the engine and the vehicle.

4. At the front of the engine, remove both stop bolts. Remove the starter.
5. Through the starter opening, remove the torque converter to drive plate bolts and remove torque converter cover plate.
6. Using tools No. 3094, clamp off the coolant hoses at the ATF cooler and remove the hoses from the cooler.
7. Using tool No. 3016, remove the speedometer cable from the transaxle.
8. Remove the inner axleshaft to transaxle bolts. Using a wire, tie up the axleshafts.
9. At the left control arm, mark the position of the ball joint and remove the ball joint and the support.
10. Place an oil catch pan under the transaxle, remove the oil filler tube from the oil pan and drain the fluid.
11. Remove the exhaust pipe to transaxle bracket.
12. Remove the selector cable bracket from the transaxle. At the transaxle shift lever, remove the selector cable circlip and the cable.
13. At the transaxle, remove the accelerator cable bracket and the cable from the operating lever.
14. From the transaxle mount, remove the center bolt. Using the engine support tool, lift the engine slightly.
15. Remove the throttle cable bracket bolts and the bracket.
16. Using tool No. 4470, support the transaxle and lift it slightly. Remove the lower transaxle to engine bolts.
17. Separate the engine from the transaxle and lower it from the vehicle. Be sure to secure the torque converter.

**NOTE: When installing the transaxle, should the torque converter slip off the one-way clutch support, the oil pump shaft could be pulled from the oil pump. This may cause severe damage when bolting the transaxle to the engine.**

18. To install, reverse the removal procedures. Tighten the engine to transaxle bolts to 41 ft. lbs., the sub frame bolts to 52 ft. lbs., the torque converter to drive plate bolts to 22 ft. lbs., the axleshaft to transaxle bolts to 33 ft. lbs., the ball joint to control arm bolts to 48 ft. lbs. and the transaxle mount center bolt to 30 ft. lbs. Refill the transaxle. Adjust the accelerator linkage and align the engine to transaxle mounts (if necessary).

## PAN REMOVAL AND FILTER SERVICE

The automatic transaxle fluid should be changed and the pan cleaned out every 20,000 miles. The interval should be shortened to 12,000 miles under severe use such as city driving or trailer towing.

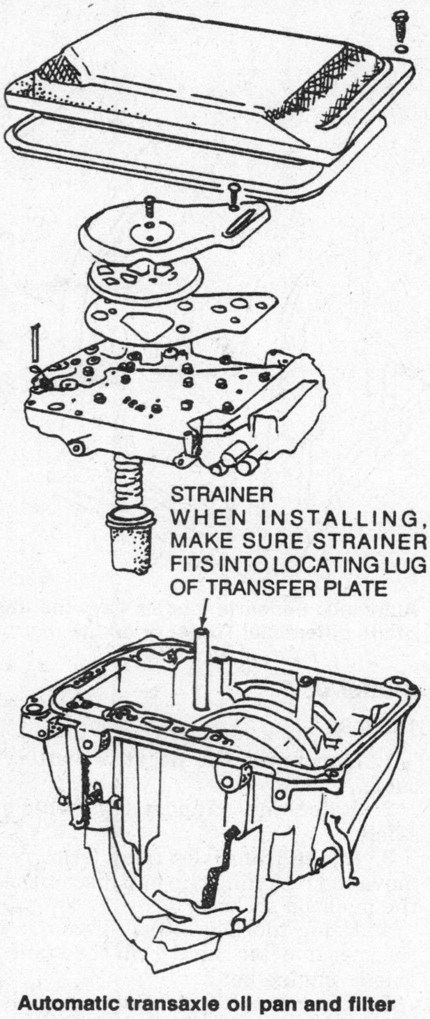
STRAINER
WHEN INSTALLING, MAKE SURE STRAINER FITS INTO LOCATING LUG OF TRANSFER PLATE

Automatic transaxle oil pan and filter

1. Start and run the engine in Neutral, for 1 or 2 minutes.
2. Make sure that the vehicle is parked on level ground. Stop the engine.
3. Place a pan of at least 4 quarts capacity under the transaxle.
4. To drain the fluid, remove the oil filler tube from the transaxle pan, after wiping the area clean.
5. Remove pan bolts and remove the pan. Clean out the pan.

**NOTE: After removing the pan, remove the oil filter, wash it clean in solvent, use a new gasket and reinstall it. Tighten the screws to 26 inch lbs.**

6. Install the pan and a new rubber gasket. Do not use any sealer on the gasket. Tighten the bolts to 7 ft. lbs. (1983) or 15 ft. lbs. (1984–89). Wait 10 minutes and retighten the bolts.
7. Clean off the filler tube, particularly the threads and install it in the pan.
8. Pour in fluid through the dipstick filler tube. The proper transaxle fluid is Dexron® II.
9. Start the engine and, with the wheels raised and the vehicle supported safely, shift through all the positions.
10. The level should reach the tip of the dipstick. Add fluid until the level reaches this point.
11. Take a short test drive. Fill the transaxle until the level is between the marks on the dipstick. Retighten the pan bolts.

**NOTE: If the transaxle is overfilled, the excess must be drained.**

## KICKDOWN SWITCH ADJUSTMENT

### *1984–88 Models*

1. Position the accelerator pedal in the fully released position.
2. Check the distance between the pedal lower edge and the pedal stop. Clearance should be 3.0 in.
3. If not, loosen the lockbolt which holds the cable at the pedal and place the pedal to give the 3 in. clearance. Tighten the lockbolt.
4. Press the pedal to the full throttle position but not into the kickdown detent. The kickdown take-up spring should not be compressed and the throttle valve should be wide open.
5. Press the accelerator lever to the stop (kickdown position); the operating lever must contact the stop and the pushrod's kickdown spring must be compressed to:

4000, 80, 90 model 087, 1984–87 – $^{13}/_{32}$ in.
4000, 80, 90 model 089, 1984–87 – $^{5}/_{16}$ in.
5000 model 087, 1984–88 – $^{5}/_{16}$ in.

6. Adjust the shift linkage, as detailed below.

### *087 Models*

#### 1989–90

The accelerator control is to be adjusted so that a closed throttle the operating lever on the transaxle is at the not throttle position. If adjustment is incorrect, shift speeds will be too high at part throttle and main pressure will be too high at idle.

1. Put selector in **P**.
2. Apply parking brake.
3. Adjust accelerator control in idle position with closed throttle.
4. Disconnect the locks on ball sockets and and disconnect the pull rod from the levers of the routing guide.
5. Disconnect the rods for cruise control.

6. Loosen locknut on the pull rod.
7. Position lever for pull rod approximately 0.040 in. (1mm) before stop.
8. Install pull rod, without tension. Ball socket must be twisted to be in line with ball and throttle lever must contact the stop.

**NOTE: Turbocharged vehicles have 2 pull rods.**

9. Loosen push rod length adjusting bolt B.
10. Push operating lever into the no throttle position, the throttle valve must contact the idle stop.
11. Tighten the push rod length adjusting bolt B.
12. Adjust the push rod length by shifting the adjusting plate. The push rod must install on the operating lever without tension.

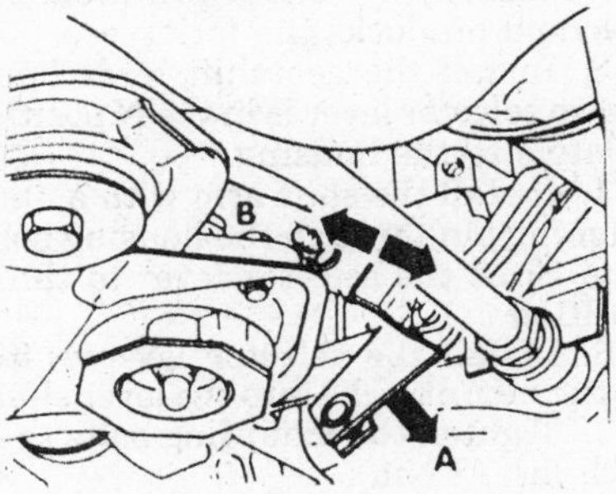


Adjusting transaxle pushrod

13. Remove the push rod from the operating lever.
14. Have an assistant depress the accelerator pedal to the stop.
15. Depress the operating lever to the kickdown stop.
16. Using pliers, pull the accelerator pedal cable back and fasten.
17. Check that the operating lever is in contact with the kickdown stop, readjust the pedal cable, if necessary.
18. Install the push rod onto operating lever and secure.
19. Check throttle lever operation.
20. Push accelerator cable through full throttle position to kickdown stop.
21. Transaxle lever must be in contact with stop.
22. Over center spring must be compressed approximately 0.320 in. (8mm).
23. Release accelerator pedal and install rod to cruise control. Rod must be tension free, adjust as necessary.

### *089 Models*

#### 1988–90

1. Remove covering for throttle control.
2. Loosen the 2 cable locking nuts.
3. Turn the throttle to the full throttle position and hold.

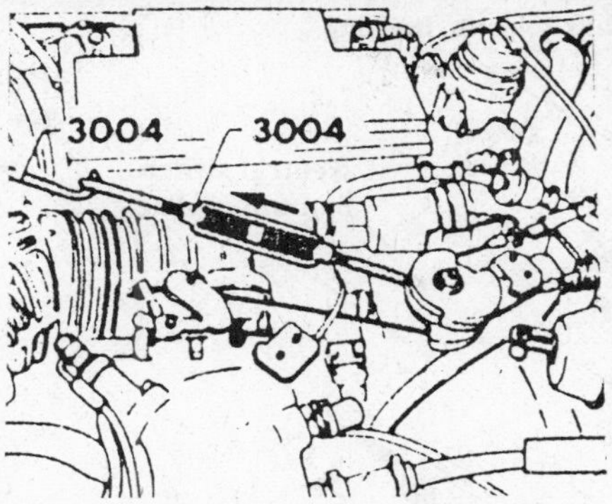


Adjusting throttle control

4. Using tool 3004, or a pair of appropriate sized turnbuckles, hold the throttle cable brackets at full open throttle. Attach an end on the lever lower cable bracket and an end on the end of the hood gas strut.
5. Insert a $^{11}/_{16}$ in. (17mm) spacer between the accelerator pedal and pedal stop.
6. An assistant is needed to push the pedal down to the stop.
7. Pull accelerator cable and install locking clip.
8. Pull cable to transaxle until pressure against spring from transaxle kickdowm position is felt.
9. Tight the nut on cable side against the bracket, next tighten the nut on pivot side against bracket.
10. Remove tool 3004 or turnbuckles.
11. Throttle lever must rest against the idel stop when the accelerator is released.
12. Press accelerator to full throttle position, not kickdown.
13. The pressure point for full throttle position of the accelerator pedal must be approximately ¾ in. (19mm) away from the pedal stop.
14. Press the accelerator to the pedal (kickdown) stop.
15. Transaxle operating lever must contact the kickdown stop.
16. The spring between the cable brackets must be stressed.
17. For vehicles with cruise control, adjust the coupling rod by moving the ball end 0.039–0.059 in. (1–1.5mm).
18. For vehicles with cruise control the A/C switch must only switch **ON** at kickdown and not a WOT, approximately $^{3}/_{16}$ in. (2mm) between the switch and cable bracket at wide-open throttle (not kickdown).

## NEUTRAL SAFETY SWITCH ADJUSTMENT

The neutral safety switch prevents the engine from being started with the transaxle in any position other than **PARK** or **NEUTRAL**. It also activates the back-up lights. The switch is at the base of the shift lever, inside the floorshift console. To replace or adjust the switch:

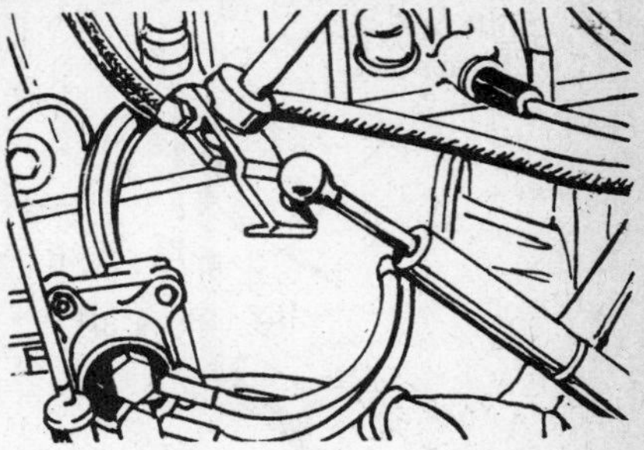

Kickdown detent linkage—typical of all models

1. Remove the 4 screws which hold the console to the floor.
2. Shift into **NEUTRAL**. Remove the 2 screws which hold the shift position indicator plate to the console. Remove the shift knob and the console.
3. Disconnect the switch electrical leads. These are: red/black—neutral safety; black—back-up lights; blue/red—back-up lights. The back-up light wires are at the front.
4. Remove the 2 switch retaining screws. Remove the switch.
5. Install the new switch so that the neutral safety switch contacts are together.
6. Install the electrical connectors. Hold the footbrake while making sure that the engine will start only in **NEUTRAL** and **PARK**. Make sure that the back-up lights operate only in **REVERSE**. If the switch does not operate properly, it may have to be moved on its slotted mounting bracket.
7. Replace the console cover when adjustment is complete.

## SHIFT LINKAGE ADJUSTMENT

The function of this adjustment is to make sure that the transaxle is fully engaged in each shift position. If this is not done, the transaxle may be only partially engaged in a certain range position. This would result in severe damage due to slippage.

### *All Vehicles without Shiftlock*

1. Remove the floor console. Place the selector lever in **PARK**.
2. Loosen the cable clamp nut at the transaxle end.
3. Press the selector lever on the transaxle into the **PARK** position to the stop.
4. Tighten the clamp nut to 6 ft. lbs. Install the console.

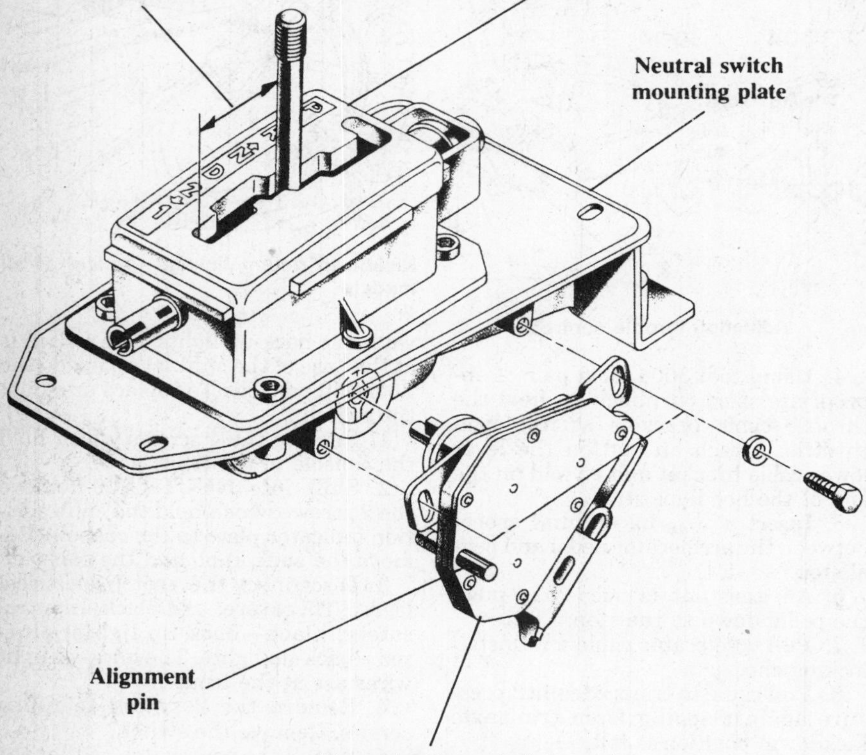


Automatic transaxle neutral safety switch—typical before 1988

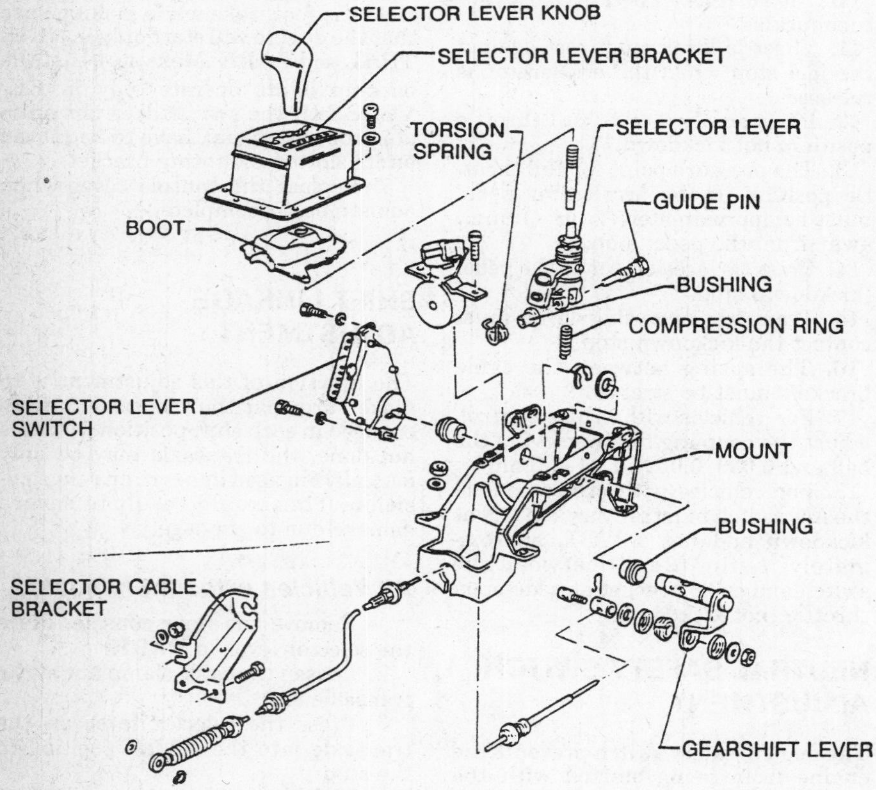


Shiftlock II—automatic shifter assembly

### *Vehicles With Shiftlock II*

**1988–1990**

The Shiftlock II system is dependent on fuse S12, brake light switch circuit, interior light relay control unit, driver's door switch circuit and vehicle speed.

With ignition switch **ON** the selector cannot be shifted out of **P** or **N** unless the brake pedal is depressed. At speeds under 3.7 mph, when shifted into **N** the shifter should lock in **N** after 1 second, unless the brake pedal is depressed. At speeds above 3.7 mph the shifter should not lock.

1. Adjust the solenoid switch, using a 1mm gauge between the selector lever and solenoid switch. With lever in **R** push the solenoid against the gauge and tighten to 7 ft. lbs. (0.1 Nm).
2. Center the lower bore of fork piece and supply voltage to switch. The solenoid pin locks the fork piece.
3. Install the gearshift lever housing so selector lever is in the **N** position relative to the housing.
4. Install the shift arm with a 4mm aligning pin through the housing bore.
5. Shift the selector lever to the **N** position.
6. Install the selector lever switch so the mount locks into the lever shaft.
7. Tighten the mounting bolts to 44 inch lbs. (5 Nm).
8. Remove aligning pin.
9. Check for correct operation.
10. If shifter does not function properly, it may be necessary to check the electronic control systems.

## BAND ADJUSTMENTS

### *All Models*

**SECOND GEAR BRAKE BAND**

1. Loosen the locknut.
2. Tighten the adjusting screw to 7 ft. lbs.
3. Loosen the adjusting screw and retighten it to 4 ft. lbs.
4. Loosen the screw exactly 2½ turns.
5. Hold the screw in this position and tighten the locknut.

# DRIVE AXLE

## Halfshaft

### REMOVAL & INSTALLATION

#### *4000, Coupe, 80 and 90 Models Except Quattro Turbo*

**NOTE: Never remove or install the axle nut with the wheel off the**

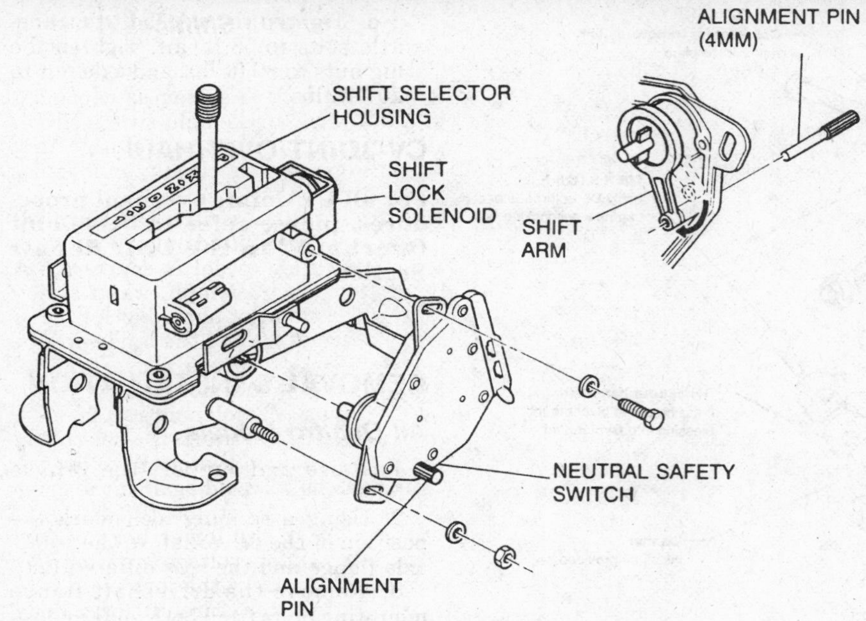

Adjusting neutral safety switch

**ground. The vehicle must be resting on the ground for these operations.**

1. Remove the halfshaft end nut (4000) or bolt (80 and 90).
2. Unbolt and remove the halfshaft to transaxle drive flange bolts.
3. Mark the position of the ball joint on the control arm, remove the 2 retaining nuts and remove the ball joint.
4. On 80 and 90 models, remove the ball joint to steering knuckle bolt and separate the knuckle from the ball joint. Remove the mounting bolts for the control arm/stablizer and push control arm downward, if necessary.

**NOTE: On 4000 models with manual transaxles, only remove the right side ball joint.Use puller 1389, or equivalent, to remove haftshaft, if necessary. Never use heat.**

5. Pull the pivot mounting outward and remove the halfshaft.
6. Installation is the reverse of the removal procedure.
7. When install the right halfshaft, take care not to damage the boot on the cover plate.
8. Tighten the ball joint to control arm/knuckle nuts/bolt to 47 ft. lbs. Tighten the halfshaft flange bolts to 33 ft. lbs.
9. Always use a new self-locking axle nut/bolt and tighten to 167 ft. lbs.
10. Check for proper alignment when finished.

### *4000, Coupe, 80 and 90 Quattro and Turbo Models*

1. With the vehicle on the ground, loosen the halfshaft end nut.

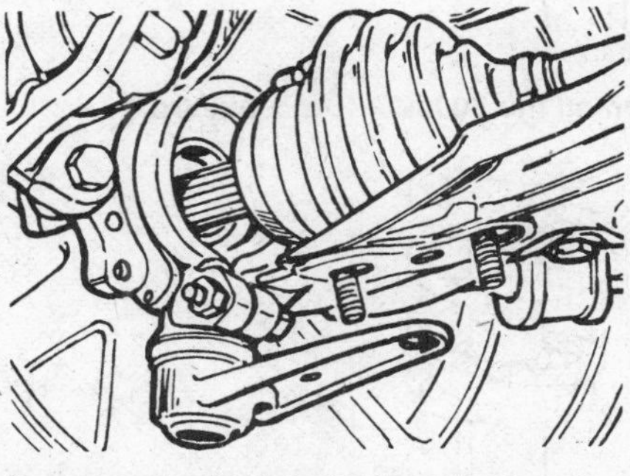
Remove the halfshafts by pivoting the control arm outward

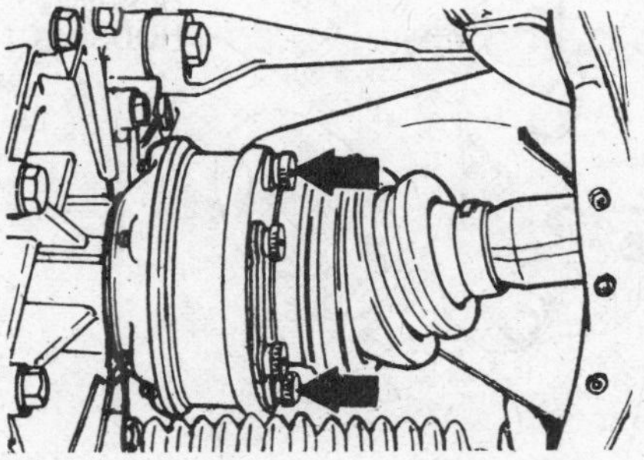
Remove the halfshaft retaining bolts at the transaxle

2. Raise and support the vehicle safely.
3. Remove the end nut and the wheel assembly. Remove the right backing plate.
4. Remove the halfshaft to transaxle flange bolts. Support the halfshaft with wire.
5. Using an Axle Shaft Press tool No. OTC 827-B or equivalent, attach it to the wheel hub and press the halfshaft from the hub.
6. Using the locking compound D-6, apply a ¼ in. bead around the front edge of the spline section of the halfshaft.

**NOTE: After applying the locking compound, allow it to dry for at least an hour.**

7. To install, reverse the removal procedure. Be sure to replace the inner CV-joint gasket. Tighten the halfshaft to transaxle flange bolts to 58 ft. lbs., the halfshaft to wheel hub nut to 203 ft. lbs. and the wheel bolts to 80 ft. lbs.

### *5000, 100 and 200 Models*

**NOTE: Never remove or install the axleshaft nut with the wheel off the ground. The vehicle must be resting on the ground for these operations. A puller is required for this job.**

1. Remove the axle nut.
2. Raise and support the vehicle safely. Remove the wheels.
3. On the right side, remove the halfshaft skid plate.
4. Disconnect the halfshaft from the transaxle. Using wire, support the halfshaft.
5. Using a 4-armed puller mounted on the wheel hub, press the halfshaft out of the hub.
6. Guide the inside end of the shaft up over the transaxle and out of the hub.
7. If equipped with an automatic transaxle, perform the following:
   a. Remove the stabilizer bar clamps.
   b. Remove the ball joint-to-hub bolt. Remove the ball joint from the hub.
   c. Press the halfshaft from the hub.
   d. Swing the suspension strut outward and press the halfshaft from the hub.
8. When installing, make certain that the splines are clean and free of grease. Apply a ¼ in. bead of RTV silicone sealant around the leading edge of the splines. Allow it to harden at least 1 hour. Torque the shaft-to-transaxle bolts to 32 ft. lbs. and the axle nut to 203 ft. lbs.

### *Quattro, Quattro Turbo and Quattro Coupe*

1. Remove the wheel cover and loosen the lug nuts. Remove the dust cover and the axle nut.
2. Raise and support the vehicle safely. Remove the lug nuts and wheel assembly. Remove the right backing plate.
3. Disconnect the axleshaft at the transaxle flange and position it out of the way.

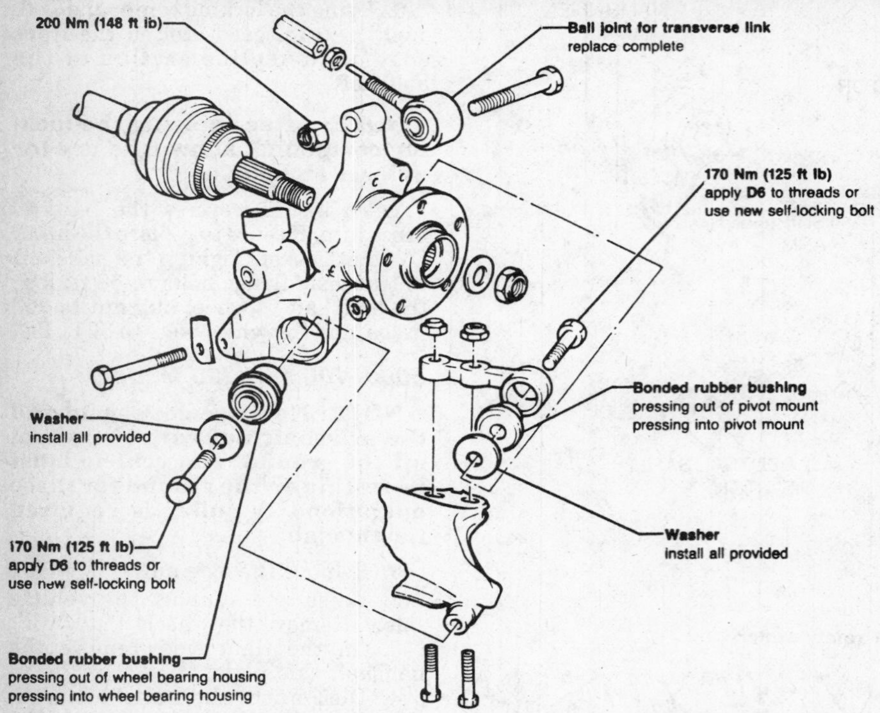


Exploded view of the rear suspension on the 5000CS Turbo Quattro

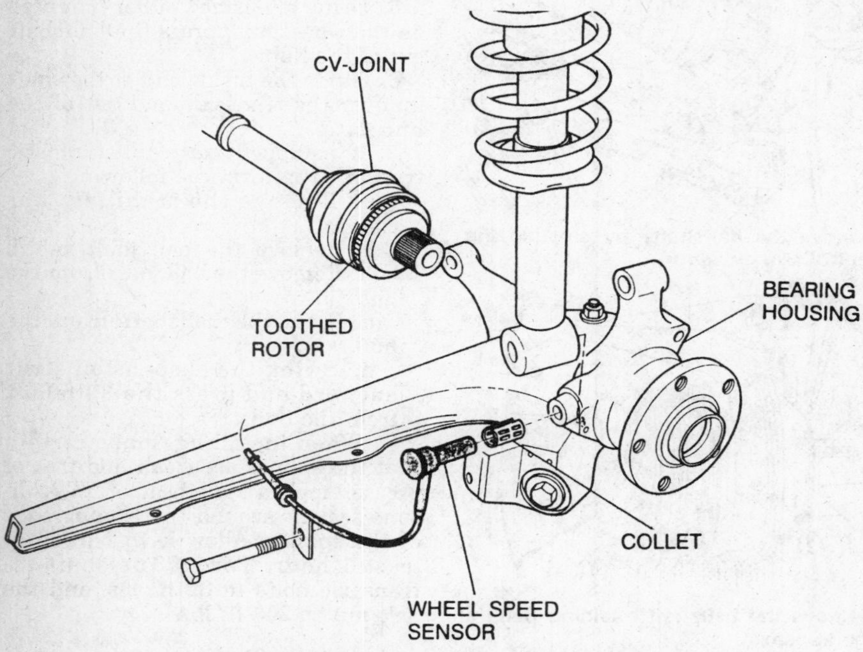


Rear axle speed sensor mounting – 200 shown

4. Using a suitable puller, press out the stub axle from the hub. Use only a mechanical or hydraulic puller to remove the stub axle. Never use hot air blower or a flame to heat the stub axle.
5. Installation is the reverse of the removal procedure, with the following exceptions:
   a. Replace the gasket on the inner CV-joint.
   b. Make sure that the splines on the stub axle and the wheel hub are free of oil, grease and old locking compound.
   c. Apply a bead of suitable locking compound approximately $^{13}/_{64}$ in. wide around the splines and install the stub axleshaft. Allow at least 1 hour for the locking compound to harden.
   d. Tighten the axleshaft to transaxle bolts to 58 ft. lbs. Tighten the lug nuts to 80 ft. lbs. and axle nut to 207 ft. lbs.

### CV-JOINT OVERHAUL

**For all CV Joints overhaul procedures, please refer to "CV-Joint Overhaul" in the Unit Repair Section.**

## Driveshaft

### REMOVAL & INSTALLATION

#### *All Quattro Models*

1. Raise and support the vehicle safely.
2. Using a scribing tool, mark the position of the driveshaft to the transaxle flange and the rear differential.
3. Remove the driveshaft flange mounting bolts from both ends and remove the driveshaft from the vehicle. Remove the center bearing bolts.
4. To install reverse the removal procedures.
5. Align scribe marks and install driveshaft.
6. Tighten the driveshaft to transaxle/differential flange bolts to 39 ft. lbs. (4000, 80, 90 Quattro) or 33 ft. lbs. (5000, 100, 200 Quattro) and the driveshaft center bearing to frame bolts to 14 ft. lbs.

## Rear Axle Shafts

### REMOVAL & INSTALLATION

#### *4000, 80 and 90 Quattro Models*

1. With the vehicle resting on the ground, loosen the axleshaft nut.
2. Raise and support the vehicle safely.
3. Remove the axleshaft nut, wheel bolts and wheel assembly.
4. Remove the ball joint nut. Using the Ball Joint Removal tool No. 1078 or equivalent, separate the ball joint from the strut.
5. Using a suitable tool, pry downward on the lower control arm to remove the ball joint from the control arm, if necessary loosen lower control arm mounting bolts.
6. Remove the tie rod to strut nut. Using a tie rod removal tool, separate the tie rod end from the strut.
7. Pull the brake hose and parking brake cable, with grommets, from the holding fixture.
8. Remove the inner axleshaft flange bolts. Separate the shaft from the flange and support it.
9. Using an Axle Shaft Pulling tool No. OTC 827-B or equivalent, attach

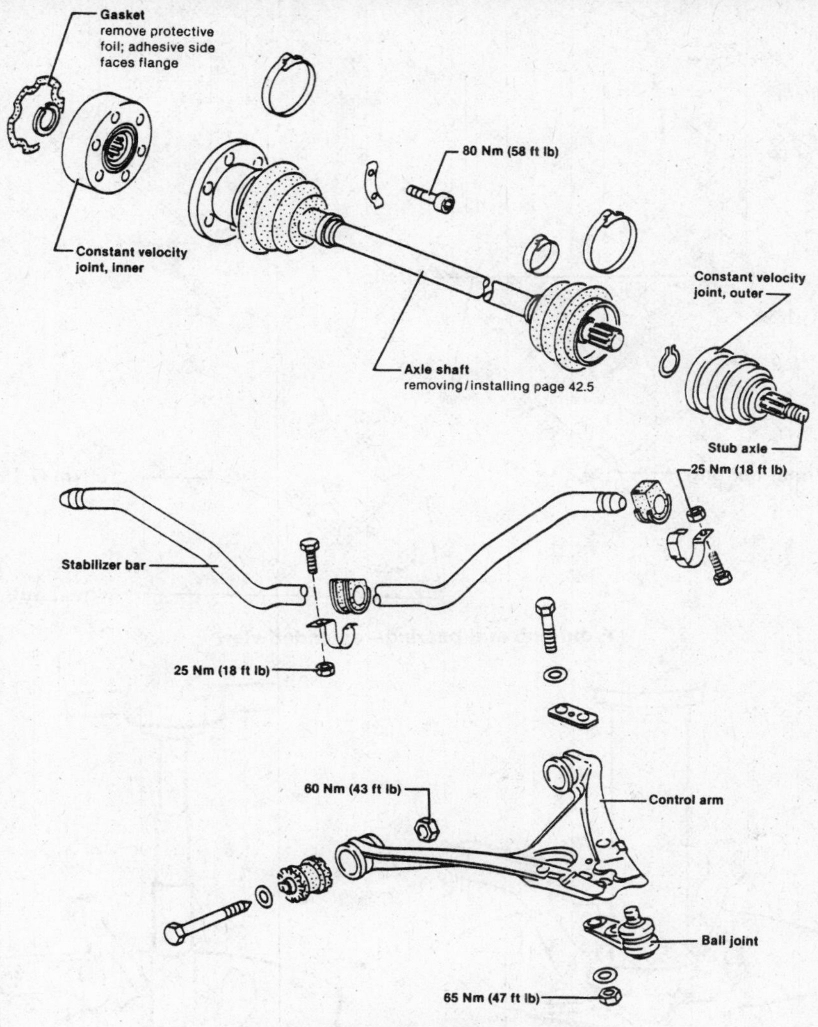


**Rear drive axle—Quattro models**

it to the wheel hub and press the axleshaft out of the hub.

10. Clean the axleshaft splines of any grease, dirt or locking compound. Using the locking compound D-6, apply a ¼ in. bead around the outer edge of the splines.

**NOTE: Allow the locking compound to dry for an hour before installation.**

11. To install, use a new inner flange gasket and reverse the removal procedures. Tighten the inner axleshaft flange bolts to 58 ft. lbs., the axleshaft to hub nut to 203 ft. lbs.(4000) or 238 ft. lbs. (80 and 90), the wheel bolts to 80 ft. lbs. and the ball joint nut to 47 ft. lbs.

### *5000 Quattro Models*

1. With the vehicle weight on the ground, loosen the axleshaft end nut.
2. Raise and support the vehicle safely.
3. Remove the axleshaft nut, wheel bolts and wheel assembly.
4. Remove the brake caliper to strut retaining bolts and remove the caliper, without disconnecting the line. Using wire, support the caliper.
5. Remove the brake rotor. Remove the inner axleshaft flange bolts and support the axleshaft.

**NOTE: When removing the right side axleshaft, remove the fuel tank cover plate first.**

6. Remove the transverse link to wheel bearing housing nut and remove the link.
7. Remove the trapezoidal arm to crossmember nut and bolt. Pry the arm downward.
8. Using an Axle Shaft Pulling tool No. OTC 827–B or equivalent, attach it to the wheel hub and remove the axleshaft from the hub.
9. Clean the axleshaft splines of any grease, dirt or locking compound. Using the locking compound D-6, apply a ¼ in. bead around the outer edge of the splines.

**NOTE: Allow the locking compound to dry for an hour before installation.**

10. To install, use a new inner flange gasket and reverse the removal procedures.
11. Tighten the axleshaft flange bolts to 58 ft. lbs., the axleshaft to hub nut to 266 ft. lbs., the wheel bolts to 80 ft. lbs., the brake caliper to wheel bearing housing bolt to 48 ft. lbs., the trapezoidal arm to crossmember nut to 63 ft. lbs. and the transverse link to wheel bearing housing nut to 148 ft. lbs.

### *100 and 200 Quattro Models*

1. With the vehicle weight on the ground, loosen the axleshaft end nut.
2. Raise and support the vehicle safely.
3. Remove the axleshaft nut, wheel bolts and wheel assembly.
4. Remove the brake caliper to strut retaining bolts and remove the caliper, without disconnecting the line. Using wire, support the caliper.
5. Remove the brake rotor. Remove the inner axleshaft flange bolts and support the axleshaft.
6. Remove the fuel tank cover plate, if necessary.
7. Remove the transverse link to wheel bearing housing nut and remove the link.
8. Remove the trapezoidal arm to crossmember nut and bolt. Pry the arm downward.
9. Remove the mounting bolt for suspension strut.
10. Before removing axle shaft, pull speed sensor out of the housing slightly.
11. Press down on wheel bearing housing and remove the axle shaft.
12. Clean the axleshaft splines of any grease, dirt or locking compound.

**To install:**

13. Use a new inner flange gasket and reverse the removal procedures.
14. Tighten the axleshaft flange bolts to 59 ft. lbs. (80 Nm).
15. Install caliper on housing.

**NOTE: Some bolts are self-locking type. Audi recommends always using new self-locking type bolts.**

16. Install new bolts and torque to 25 ft. lbs. (35 Nm).
17. Adjustment of parking brake assembly may be necessary.
18. Install the axleshaft bolt and washer assembly, tighten until just snug.
19. Make certain speed sensor sleeve

is in place and install speed sensor , by hand, until seated

20. Install wheels.

21. Lower vehicle and torque axleshaft bolts to 147 ft. lbs. (200 Nm) and then tighten axleshaft bolts an additional ¼ turn (90 degrees).

## Front Wheel Hub, Knuckle and Bearings

### REMOVAL & INSTALLATION

#### *All 4000, Coupe, 80 and 90 Models*

**NOTE: Audi 80 and 90 models use 2 types of front wheel bearing housing assemblies. A single piece unit that can not be separated from the strut and a bearing housing that is removable from the strut for service. The repair procedures are similar for both with the exception that the single piece unit housing, if defective, must be replaced as a strut assembly.**

1. Remove the halfshafts.
2. Remove the strut housing to body nuts and remove the strut/hub assembly from the vehicle.
3. Remove the brake disc and splash shield.
4. Using an arbor press with tools No. VW 408A, VW 295A, VW 402 and Base Plate tool No. VW 401, press the wheel hub from the strut housing.
5. Using a pair of snapring pliers, remove the snaprings from both sides of the wheel bearing.
6. Using an arbor press with tools No. VW 408A, VW 442, VW 401 and VW 402, press the wheel bearing from the strut housing.
7. Using the Wheel Puller tool No. VW 295A, pull the wheel bearing race from the wheel hub.
8. Place new grease inside the strut housing before installing the new bearing.
9. Using an arbor press and tools No. VW 412, VW 455 and VW 401, press the new wheel bearing and wheel hub into the strut housing. Be sure to replace the snaprings.
10. To install the strut/wheel hub assembly, reverse the removal procedures. Tighten the strut to body nuts to 44 ft. lbs.

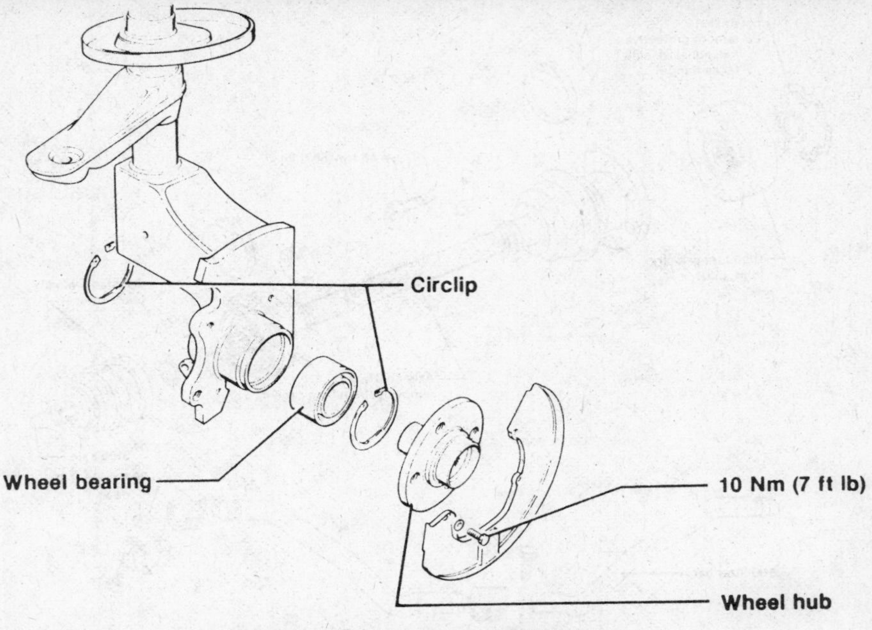

Front hub and bearing—exploded view

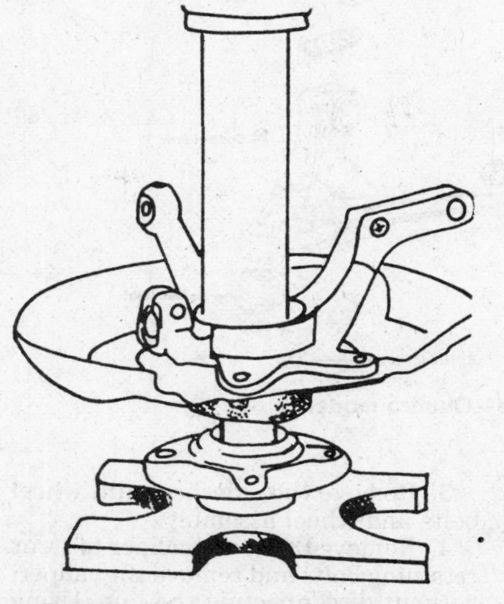
Pressing the hub from the spindle

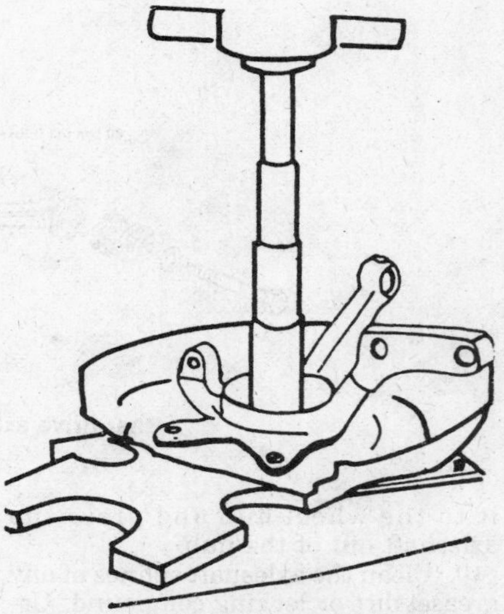
Pressing the bearing from the spindle

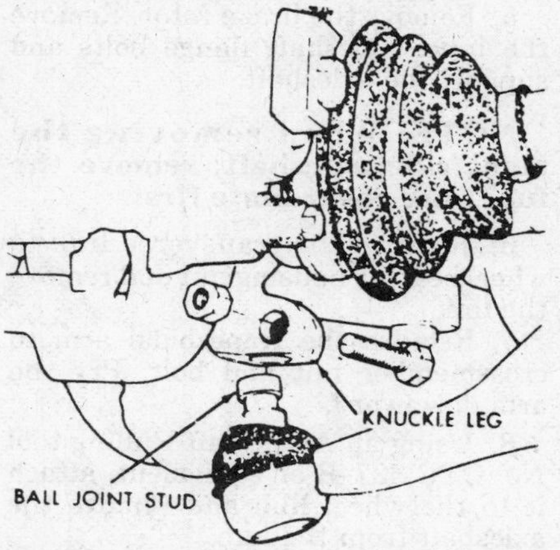

Separate the ball joint from the knuckle to remove the axleshaft

#### *All 5000 and 100 Models*

1. Remove the halfshafts.
2. Remove the strut to vehicle nuts and remove the strut from the vehicle.
3. Remove the disc brake rotor and splash shield.
4. Using an arbor press with tools No. VW 412, VW 420 and VW 295A, press the wheel hub from the strut housing.
5. Using a pair of snapring pliers, remove the snaprings from both sides of the wheel bearing.
6. Using an arbor press with tool No. 40–20, press the wheel bearing from strut housing.
7. Using the tools No. VW 295A and US 1078, press the bearing race from the wheel hub.
8. Install the outer snapring into the strut housing. Using an arbor press with tools No. VW 411, 40–20,A and VW 402, press the new wheel bearing into the strut housing until it seats against the snapring. Install the inner snapring.
9. Using an arbor press and tool No.

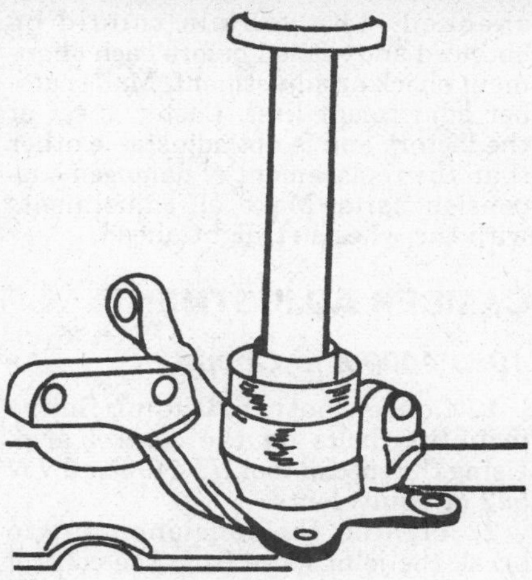

Pressing the new bearing into the spindle

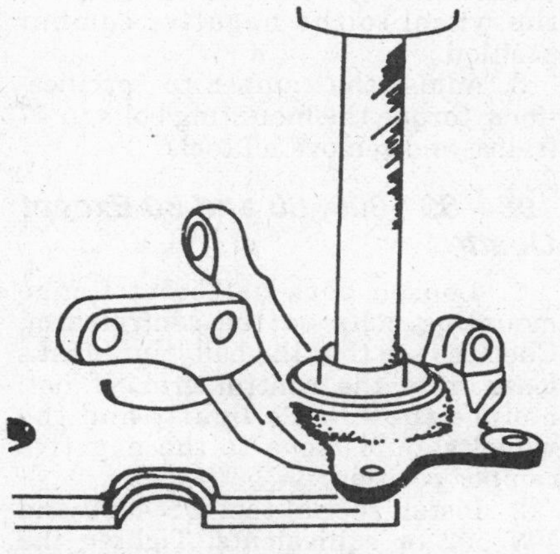

Pressing the inner bearing race from the spindle

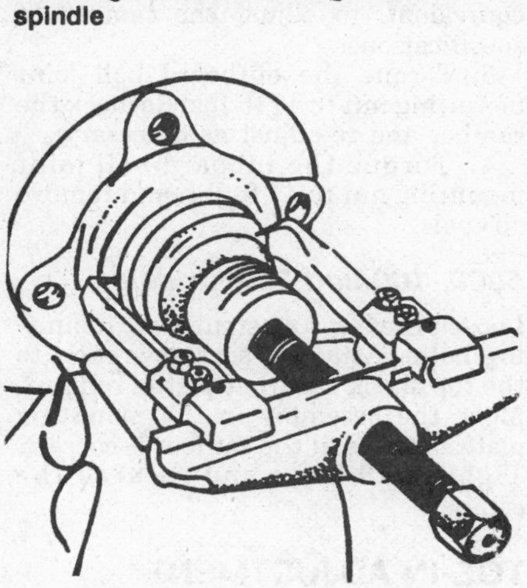

Removing the outer bearing race from the hub

40-21, press the wheel hub into the strut housing.

10. To install, reverse the removal procedures. Tighten the strut to body nuts to 43 ft. lbs. and reset the alignment when finished.

# FRONT SUSPENSION

All models use MacPherson struts. The strut unit, steering arm and steering knuckle are all combined in 1 strut assembly. There is no upper control arm.

**CAUTION**

***Exercise extreme caution when working with the front suspension. Coil springs and torsion bars are under great tension and can cause severe injury if their pressure is released suddenly.***

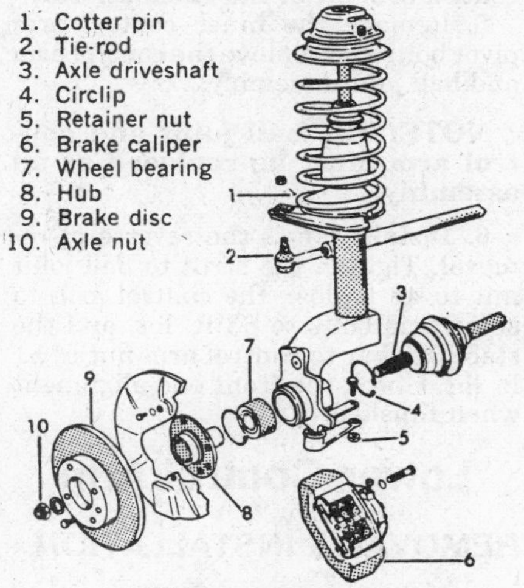


4000 front suspension

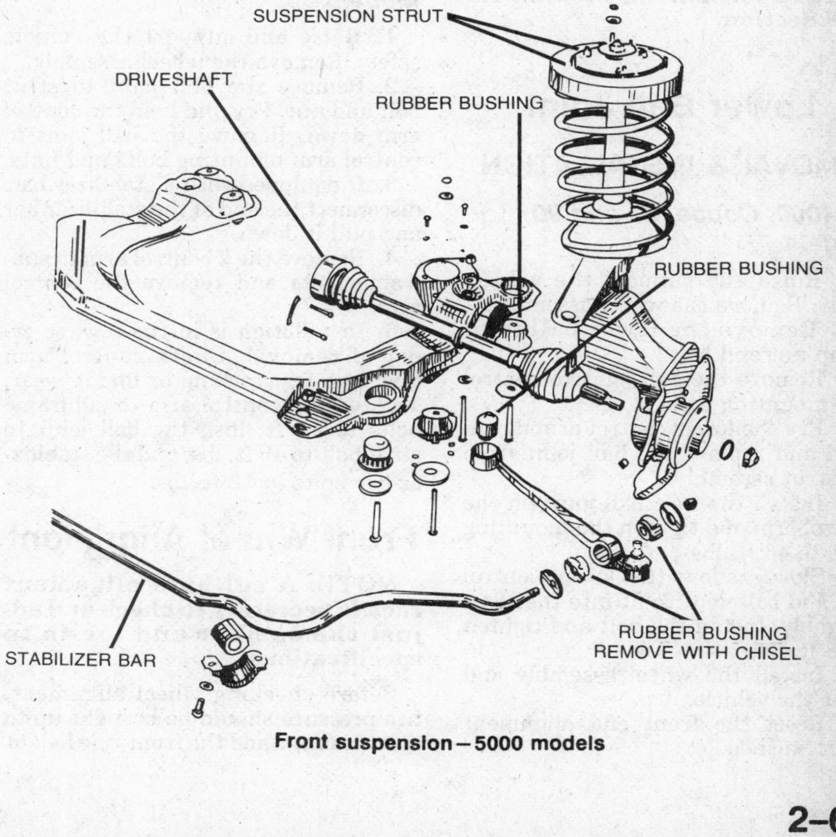


Front suspension – 5000 models

## MacPherson Strut

### REMOVAL & INSTALLATION

#### *All Models*

1. With the vehicle on the ground, remove the front axle nut and loosen the wheel bolts.
2. Raise and support the vehicle safely. Remove the wheel assembly.
3. Remove the brake caliper mounting bolts and disconnect the brake line bracket. Remove speed sensor if equipped.
4. Remove the brake caliper, with the line still attached and support it out of the way.
5. Remove disc brake rotor.
6. Remove the ball joint clamp bolt and nut.
7. Remove the tie rod end nut and separate the tie rod end from the strut.
8. If equipped with a stabilizer bar, remove the retaining bolt and remove the stabilizer bar end clamps. Pivot the stabilizer bar downward.
9. Remove the 2 center stabilizer bar clamps and unbolt it from the lower control arm.
10. Pry the lower control arm down and separate the ball joint from the strut, while alternately turning the steering wheel from right to left.
11. Using the tool No. OTC 827B or equivalent, press the halfshaft out of the hub.
12. On 4000, 80 and 90 models, support the strut assembly, hold the

shock absorber piston rod with an internal socket wrench and remove the retaining nut. Remove the strut assembly from the vehicle.

13. On 5000, 100 and 200 models, remove the upper strut cover, support the strut assembly and remove the 3 strut retaining nuts. Remove the strut assembly.

14. Installation is the reverse of the removal procedure. Note the following during installation:

a. When installing the stabilizer bar, the position is correct if the clamps are difficult to install in the rubber bushings. Attach the clamps loosely, take a short test drive to bring the bushings into the correct position and tighten to 18 ft. lbs.

b. Tighten the ball joint bolt to 36 ft. lbs. on 4000, 80, 90 models or 47 ft. lbs. on 5000 models or 48 ft. lbs. plus an additional ¼ turn (90 degrees) on 100 and 200 models.

c. Tighten the axleshaft end nut to 167 ft. lbs. on the 4000, 80 and 90, 203 ft. lbs. on Quattro and Quattro Turbos and 237 ft. lbs. on all other 5000, 100 and 200 models.

d. Make certain speed sensor and sleeve are completely seated, by hand.

### OVERHAUL

**For all spring and shock absorber removal and installation procedures and any other strut overhaul procedures, please refer to "Strut Overhaul" in the Unit Repair Section.**

## Lower Ball Joint

### REMOVAL & INSTALLATION

#### *All 4000, Coupe, 80 and 90 Models*

1. Raise and support the vehicle safely. Remove the wheel assembly.
2. Remove the lower ball joint clamp nut and bolt.
3. Remove the ball joint to control arm mounting bolts.
4. Pry the lower control arm downward and remove the ball joint from the strut assembly.
5. Install the new ball joint on the control arm and tighten the mounting bolts to 46 ft. lbs.
6. Slowly allow the lower control arm and ball joint to fit into the strut assembly. Install the bolt and tighten to 48 ft. lbs.
7. Install the wheel assembly and lower the vehicle.
8. Reset the front end alignment when finished.

## Lower Control Arm and Ball Joint

### REMOVAL & INSTALLATION

#### *All 5000 and 100 Models*

1. Raise and support the vehicle safely. Remove the wheel assembly. Remove the ball joint clamp nut.
2. Pry and hold the control arm and ball joint assembly down to remove it from the strut.
3. Remove the nut on the end of the stabilizer bar.
4. Loosen the control arm to subframe mounting bolts and pull the control arm off of the stabilizer bar.
5. Remove the inner control arm pivot bolts and remove the control arm and ball joint assembly.

**NOTE: The ball joint and control arm must be replaced as an assembly.**

6. Installation is the reverse of removal. Tighten the strut to ball joint nut to 48 ft. lbs., the control arm to sub-frame bolts to 63 ft. lbs. and the stabilizer bar to control arm nut to 81 ft. lbs. Check the front end alignment when finished.

## Lower Control Arm

### REMOVAL & INSTALLATION

#### *All 4000, Coupe, 80 and 90 Models*

1. Raise and support the vehicle safely. Remove the wheel assembly.
2. Remove the ball joint to strut bolt and nut. Pry and hold the control arm down. Remove the ball joint to control arm mounting bolts and nuts.
3. If equipped with a stabilizer bar, disconnect the end of the stabilizer bar and pull it down.
4. Remove the 2 control arm to subframe bolts and remove the control arm.
5. Installation is in the reverse order of removal. Check control arm bushings for cracking or undue wear. Tighten the control arm to subframe bolts to 43 ft. lbs.; the ball joint to strut bolt to 46 ft. lbs. and the stabilizer bar bolts to 18 ft. lbs.

## Front Wheel Alignment

**NOTE: A suitable alignment rack is necessary to check and adjust the camber and toe-in to specifications.**

Before checking wheel alignment, tire pressure should be brought up to specifications and the front ride height checked. The vehicle should be bounced and settled before each alignment check or adjustment. Make camber adjustment first. Caster is set at the factory and is not adjustable other than the replacement of damaged suspension parts. Make all adjustments with the wheels straight ahead.

### CAMBER ADJUSTMENT

#### *1983 4000 and Coupe*

1. Loosen both ball joint flange mounting bolts on the control arm. Using the special tool US 4490 and VW 582 or equivalents.
2. Tighten the tensioner nut to break the joint loose from the control arm. Loosen the tensioner nut until the wheel has negative camber. When the wheel nut is loosened, the weight of the vehicle on the wheels will move the wheel to the negative camber position.
3. Adjust the camber to specifications, torque the mounting bolts to 47 ft. lbs. and remove all tools.

#### *1984–89 4000, 80 and 90 Except Quattro*

1. Loosen both ball joint flange mounting bolts on the control arm. Check so see that the ball joint breaks loose from the control arm. If not, bounce the vehicle lightly and the wheel should move to the negative camber position.
2. Install special tool US 4490 and VW 552 or equivalents. Tighten the tensioning nut on tool VW 552 or equivalent, to adjust the camber to specifications.
3. Torque the outboard ball joint mounting nut to 47 ft. lbs. Recheck the camber and re-adjust as necessary.
4. Torque the inboard ball joint mounting nut to 47 ft. lbs. and remove all tools.

#### *5000, 100 and 200 Models*

Loosen the 3 spring strut plate mounting bolts. Attach a socket wrench to the top shock absorber piston rod nut. Move the assembly in the mounting plate slots, until the camber is correct. Tighten all bolts and recheck the camber.

### TOE-IN ADJUSTMENT

#### *All Models*

Toe-in can be determined by using a toe-in gauge. Measuring and comparing the distance between front and rear distance on wheels. If at all possible, optical measuring equipment and special tool 3075 should be used; it will give a much more accurate measurement.

1. Turn steering gear to the center position.
2. Remove lower pinion rack-cap bolt and attach centering tool 3075 with tool bracket into bolt hole and over mounting nut of the left tie rod, or use an equivalent centering tool. Insert a bolt in hole marked with "L" in centering tool 3075 to lock steering.
3. Measure and divide the total toe in half.
4. Loosen clamps and outer locknut on both rods.
5. Adjust each tie rod until specified setting for toe is reached.
6. Tighten clamps and locknuts, on tie rods.
7. Reposition steering wheel if necessary to obtain horizontal spokes.
8. Remove centering tool from rack assembly.
9. Install cap-bolt and torque to 14 ft. lbs. (20 Nm).

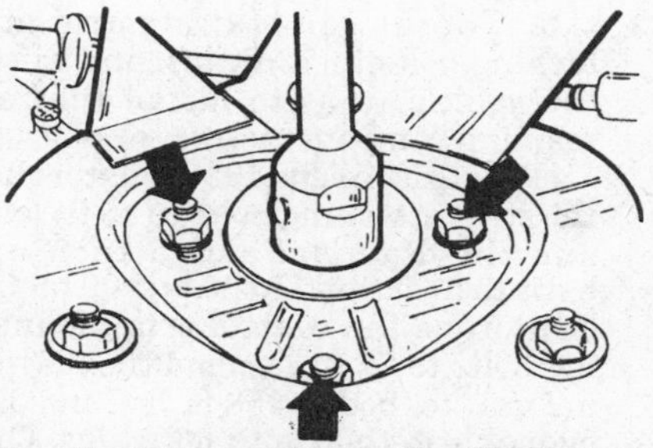
To adjust the camber on the 5000, move the strut assembly in the slots of the spring strut mounting plate

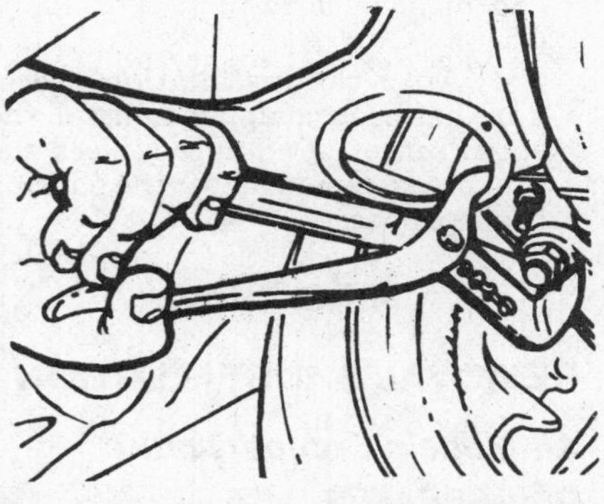
Adjusting the camber on the 4000 and Quattro without the special tool

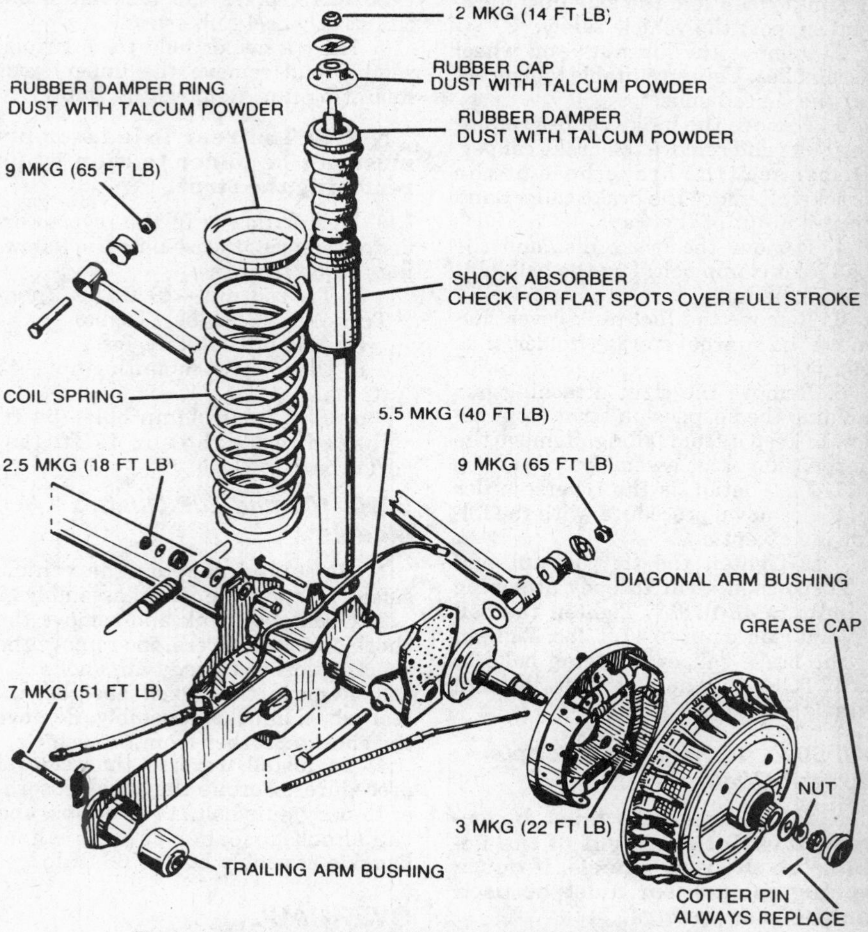

Rear suspension on the 5000 (exc. Quattro)—4000 similar

# REAR SUSPENSION

## Shock Absorbers

### REMOVAL & INSTALLATION

#### *1983 5000 Models*

If the vehicle is to be raised to remove the shock absorber, the spring tensioner tool 3004 or equivalent must be used to support the rear axle before removing any of the shock absorber nuts and or bolts. If the vehicle does not have to be raised, the spring tensioner tool 3004 or equivalent is not required.

1. Open the trunk and loosen the carpet trim. Remove the stem from the shock absorber upper mounting stud.
2. Remove the nut and bushing from the upper mount. Remove the shock absorber lower attaching bolt and remove the shock absorber.
3. Installation is the reverse of the removal procedure, with the following exception. Tighten the shock absorbers upper attaching nut to 14 ft. lbs. and the lower attaching bolt to 43 ft. lbs.

## MacPherson Struts

**For all spring and shock absorber removal and installation procedures and any other strut overhaul procedures, refer to "Strut Overhaul" in the Unit Repair section.**

### REMOVAL & INSTALLATION

#### *All 4000, 80 and 90 Models Except Quattro*

**NOTE: Always remove and install the suspension struts 1 at a time. Do not allow the rear axle to hang in place as this may cause damage to the brake lines.**

1. With the vehicle at ground level, open the trunk and remove the sheet metal trim from around the shock tower.
2. Remove the rubber cap.
3. Remove the strut mounting nut.
4. Raise and support the vehicle safely.
5. Remove the lower strut mounting bolt from the axle beam and remove the strut.
6. Installation is the reverse of removal. Torque the upper strut mounting bolt to 14 ft. lbs. and the lower strut mounting bolt to 43 ft. lbs.

#### *1983–85 Quattro, Quattro Turbo and Quattro Coupe Models*

1. Loosen the lug nuts, remove the

axle nut cover and the axle nut. Raise and support the vehicle safely.

2. Remove the lug nuts and wheel assemblies. Using a suitable tool, press off the tie rod ends.

3. Remove the brake caliper retaining bolts and remove the brake caliper. Disconnect the brake hose at the bracket. Remove the brake caliper and secure it out of the way.

4. Remove the brake disc and the ball joint clamp bolt. Pry the ball joint out of the hub.

5. Remove the fuel tank cover. Remove the sunroof storage holder, if so equipped.

6. Remove the strut attaching nut holding the suspension strut from below to keep it from falling. Remove the suspension strut assembly.

7. Installation is the reverse order of the removal procedure, with the following exceptions:

a. Tighten the tie rod nut and suspension strut to body attaching nuts to 43 ft. lbs. Tighten the ball joint clamp nut to 47 ft. lbs. Tighten the brake caliper retaining bolts to 47 ft.lbs., lug nuts to 80 ft. lbs. and axle nut to 203 ft. lbs.

#### *All 5000, 100 and 200 Models Except Quattro*

**NOTE: The struts must be removed with the weight of the vehicle on the rear wheels. If not, a spring compressor must be used on the rear springs.**

1. If the vehicle is not on its wheels, install the spring compressor and compress the spring. DO NOT attempt to remove the shock with the rear wheels raised without a compressor.

2. Remove the upper strut mounting nut.

3. Remove the lower strut mounting nut.

4. Remove the shock absorber.

5. Installation is the reverse of removal. Torque the lower mounts to 40 ft. lbs. (1983) or 66 ft. lbs. (1984–86) and the upper to 14 ft. lbs.

#### *4000, 80 and 90 Quattro Models*

1. Loosen the lug nuts and remove the axle nut cover.

2. Remove the axle nut and raise and support the vehicle safely. Remove the wheels.

3. Using a tie rod end puller, remove the tie rod end.

4. Remove the brake caliper mounting bolts. Disconnect the brake line from its bracket and position the caliper out of the way.

5. Remove the brake disc and the ball joint clamp bolt and pry the ball joint out of the hub.

6. Using a 4 arm puller tool No. OTC 8278, press the halfshaft from the strut/wheel hub assembly.

7. Have a helper hold the strut assembly and remove the upper strut mounting nut. Remove the strut.

**NOTE: The rear axle assembly must not be under tension while removing the strut.**

8. Installation is in the reverse order of removal. Please note the following torque figures:

a. Tie rod nut – 29 ft. lbs. (non-Turbo) or 43 ft. lbs. (Turbo).

b. Axle nut – 203 ft. lbs.

c. Upper strut mounting nut – 43 ft. lbs.

d. Ball joint clamp bolt – 54 ft. lbs. (non-Turbo) or 47 ft. lbs. (Turbo).

#### *5000, 100 and 200 Quattro Models*

1. Raise and support the vehicle safely. Remove the wheel assembly.

2. Open the trunk and remove the shock absorber covers, the remove the shock absorber-to-body nuts/bolts.

3. Remove the shock absorber-to-rear wheel knuckle assembly. Remove the shock absorber from the vehicle.

4. To install, reverse the removal procedures. Torque the shock absorber-to-body nuts/bolts to 15 ft. lbs. and the shock absorber-to-rear wheel knuckle assembly bolt to 66 ft. lbs.

### OVERHAUL

**For all spring and shock absorber removal and installation procedures and any other strut overhaul procedures, refer to "Strut Overhaul" in the Unit Repair section.**

## Rear Axle Assembly

### REMOVAL & INSTALLATION

#### *1983–90 All 4WD Models*

1. Raise and support the vehicle safely. Remove the wheel assembly. Detach the muffler hanger bands. Lower and support the muffler and tail pipe.

2. Remove the parking brake cable to equalizer nut. Pry the cable sleeve from the bracket. Remove both parking brake cables at the brackets and disconnect the brake hoses at the brake line brackets. Cap all hoses and lines. Models equipped with anti-lock brakes, disconnect the speed sensor.

3. Remove the nuts from the bolts attaching the trailing arms to the body. Do not remove the bolts at this time. On the right side, disconnect the spring from the brake pressure regulator.

4. Remove the bolts attaching the diagonal arms to the axle and remove the bolts attaching the strut to the axle. Slide out the trailing arm to the body attaching bolts and carefully remove the axle from the vehicle.

**NOTE: All bolts through rubber bushings should be tighten with the weight of the vehicle on its wheels. This is done to preset the bushings in a level non-stressed position, to avoid poor handling or tire wear.**

5. Installation is the reverse order of the removal procedure, with the following exceptions:

a. After positioning the axle in the vehicle, install both trailing arm bolts finger tight. Install the wheel and tire assemblies and lower the vehicle.

b. Torque the trailing arm attaching bolts to 72 ft. lbs. and raise the vehicle so as to install the remaining components.

c. Models except 1988–90, torque the strut attaching bolts to 43 ft. lbs. and the diagonal arm attaching bolts to 51 ft. lbs. On 80 and 90 models, torque the control arm mounting bolts to 72 ft. lbs. and the diagonal arm-to- body to 58 ft. lbs. and diagonal arm-to-axle to 66 ft. lbs. On 100 models, torque the control arm mounting bolts to 72 ft. lbs. and the diagonal arm-to- body to 66 ft. lbs. and diagonal arm-to-axle to 70 ft. lbs.

d. After the installation procedure has been completed, install the speed sensor, if equipped, bleed the brake system and adjust the parking brake as necessary.

## Axle Stub

### REMOVAL & INSTALLATION

#### *All Models Except Quattro*

##### DRUM BRAKES

1. Raise and support the vehicle safely. Remove the wheel assembly.

2. Disconnect the brake lines on both sides. Plug the lines.

3. Pry off the grease cap and remove the cotter pin, nut and washer. Remove the brake drum.

4. Remove the bearing inner race from the brake drum.

5. To remove the axle shaft, carefully (the spring can fly out) pry out the brake shoe retaining spring. Remove the brake shoes complete with pressure rod and spring, bottom bracket first. Disconnect the handbrake cable.

6. Remove the axle stub mounting

bolts and remove the axle and backing plate.

7. To replace the bearings and seal, pry the seal out of the brake drum and remove the inner race of the roller bearing.

8. Drive the roller bearing outer race from the brake drum, using a suitable mandrel. Remove the snapring and drive the outer roller bearing race from the drum. Clean the race seating surfaces in the drum.

9. Replace the snapring and drive in the outer race of the outer bearing.

10. Drive in the outer race of the inner roller bearing. Use a brass punch to seat the race evenly.

11. Lightly coat the inner race of the inner roller bearing with wheel bearing grease and push it into the outer race.

12. Drive a new shaft seal into position (the open side of the seal should face the roller bearing). Fill the space between the 2 roller bearings with approximately 10 oz. of wheel bearing grease.

13. Coat the inner race of the outer roller bearing with grease and install the inner race.

14. If removed, reinstall the stub axle and brake backing plate with the groove in the stub axle facing upward. Tighten the bolts to 14–15 ft. lbs. for 8 G-bolts or to 22 ft. lbs. for 10 K-bolts. Connect the brake lines, if removed.

15. Assemble the brake shoes, connect the handbrake cable and insert the brake shoes on the bottom bracket first. Connect the shoes at the wheel cylinder. Replace the retaining springs, with caution.

16. Install the brake drum, washer, nut, castellated nut and a new cotter pin.

17. Wheel bearing play should be 0.001–0.002 in. It can be measured with a dial indicator. Fill the end cap with approximately 10 oz. of wheel bearing grease and tap lightly into place.

18. Install the wheel assembly. Bleed the brake system and lower the vehicle.

**DISC BRAKES**

1. Raise and support the vehicle safely. Remove the wheel assembly.

2. Remove the caliper assembly, it may not be necessary to disconnect the hydraulic lines from the caliper or the parking brake cable. Suspend caliper with wire do not let caliber hang by brake hose.

3. Pry off the grease cap and remove the cotter pin, nut and washer.

4. Remove the outer bearing.

5. Remove the rotor.

6. Remove the bearing inner bearing and seal, using a soft drift or press.

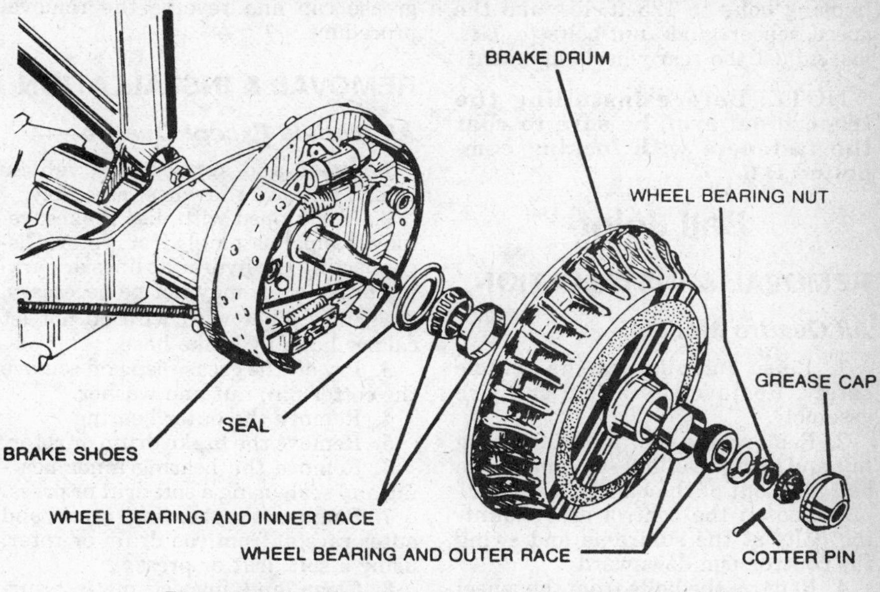


**Rear wheel bearing – typical of all models except Quattro**

7. Remove the bearing inner and outer race(s) from the rotor, using a soft drift or press.

8. If equipped with anti-lock brakes remove the speed sensor assembly.

9. Remove the splash shield and axle stud from the axle.

10. Install axle stub and torque bolts to 22 ft. lbs.

11. Clean and inspect mating surfaces for bearing races.

12. Install new races in the rotor, using soft drift or press.

13. Install new properly greased inner bearing and seal.

14. Install the rotor, outer bearing, washer, nut and adjust bearing play.

15. Install the cotter pin and dust cap.

16. Install the caliper assembly.

17. If hydraulic lines had be removed, install and bleed brakes.

18. If parking brake cable was removed, install and adjust as necessary.

19. Install the wheel assembly.

20. Lower vehicle and check brakes for proper operation.

# Rear Control Arms

## REMOVAL & INSTALLATION

### *1984–87 4000 Quattro and 1888–90 80 and 90 Quattro Models*

1. Raise and support the vehicle safely, under the frame and differential.

2. Using a scribing tool, mark the position of the ball joint carrier with the control arm.

3. Remove the ball joint carrier-to-control arm nuts and the lock plate. Separate the ball joint carrier from the control arm.

4. Remove the control arm-to-sub-frame bolts and the control arm from the vehicle.

5. To install, reverse the removal procedures. Audi recommends always using new replacement nuts. Torque the control arm-to-sub-frame bolts to 43 ft. lbs. Check the rear wheel alignment.

### *1986–88 5000 Quattro and 1989–90 100 and 200 Quattro Models*

On these vehicles, the control arm is know as the trapezoidal arm. It is connected to the wheel bearing housing and to 2 separate cross-members. It is recommended to use new self-locking nuts on all applications.

1. Raise and support the vehicle safely, under the frame and differential.

2. Remove the wheel. Along the trapezoidal arm, remove the speed sensor wiring bracket nuts/bolts and the guide.

3. Remove the wheel bearing housing-to-trapezoidal arm front and rear bolts.

4. Remove the trapezoidal arm-to-rear cross-member bolt.

5. At the brake pressure regulator, disconnect the spring.

6. Remove the trapezoidal arm-to-front cross-member nut and the trapezoidal arm from the vehicle.

7. To install, reverse the removal procedures. Torque the trapezoidal arm-to-front cross-member nut to 44 ft. lbs., the trapezoidal arm-to-rear cross-member bolt to 63 ft. lbs., the trapezoidal arm-to-wheel bearing

housing bolts to 125 ft. lbs. and the speed sensor guide nut/bolts to 7 ft. lbs. Adjust the rear wheel alignment.

**NOTE: Before installing the trapezoidal arm, be sure to coat the fasteners with locking compound D-6.**

## Ball Joint

### REMOVAL & INSTALLATION

#### All Quattro Models

1. Raise and support the vehicle safely. Remove the wheel and tire assembly.
2. Remove the ball joint attaching nut and using a suitable tool, press the ball joint out of the ball joint carrier.
3. Loosen the control arm mounting bolts at the subframe and swing the control arm downward.
4. Remove the bolts from the wheel bearing housing and insert (2) M8 × 40mm bolts approximately 1 in. into the wheel bearing housing.
5. Push the preassembled tool 40-204A or equivalent over the ball joint. Attach the ball joint mounting nut with a large washer onto the joint and tighten it as far as possible.
6. Pull out the ball joint by turning the installed bolts counterclockwise 1 at a time.
7. Using tool VW 415A or equivalent, drive the ball joint into the wheel bearing housing until seated. But before driving the ball joint into place, align the holes with the wheel bearing housing.
8. Torque the ball joint to 29 ft. lbs. Swivel the control arm into place and torque the ball joint nut to 54 ft. lbs. Tighten the control arm mountings with the vehicle wheels touching the ground.

## Rear Wheel Bearings

### ADJUSTMENT

#### All Models Except Quattro

1. Raise and support the vehicle safely.
2. Remove the grease cap.
3. Remove the cotter pin and the locking nut.
4. While turning the wheel (so that the wheel bearing does not jam), tighten the adjusting nut firmly.
5. Back the nut off slightly. Using a screwdriver, try to move the thrust washer with just finger pressure; when the thrust washer can be moved slightly, the correct adjustment has been met.
6. To install, place new grease in the grease cap and reverse the removal procedure.

### REMOVAL & INSTALLATION

#### All Models Except Quattro

1. Raise and support the vehicle safely. Remove the wheel assembly.
2. If equipped with disc brakes, remove caliper assembly from rotor. Disconnecting the hydraulic lines or parking brake cable may not be necessary. Suspend caliper with wire do not let caliber hang by brake hose.
3. Pry off the grease cap and remove the cotter pin, nut and washer.
4. Remove the outer bearing.
5. Remove the brake drum or rotor.
6. Remove the bearing inner bearing and seal, using a soft drift or press.
7. Remove the bearing inner and outer race(s) from the drum or rotor, using a soft drift or press.
8. Clean and inspect mating surfaces for bearing races.
9. Install new races, using soft drift or press.
10. Install new properly greased inner bearing.
11. Install seal.
12. Install drum or rotor, outer bearing, washer, nut and adjust bearing play.
13. Install cotter pin and dust cap.
14. If disc brakes, install caliper assembly.
15. If hydraulic lines had be removed, install and bleed brakes.
16. If parking brake cable had been remove, install and adjust as necessary.
17. Install the wheel assembly.
18. Lower vehicle and check brakes for proper operation.

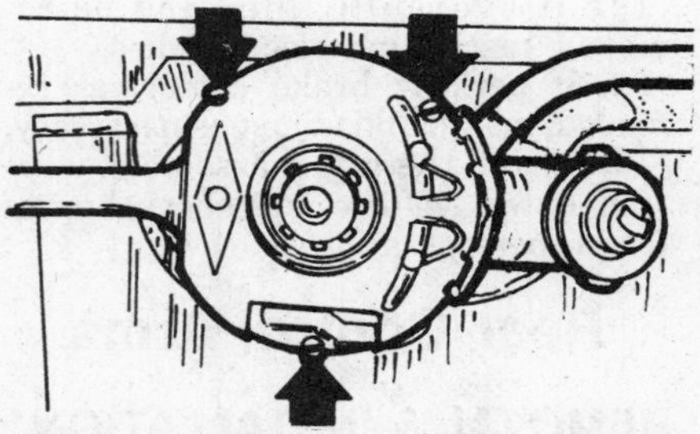

Steering column switch mounting screws—4000

## Rear Wheel Alignment

Only Quattro models are provided with rear wheel camber and toe adjustments.

**NOTE: It is advised to take the vehicle to a qualified alignment shop to have the alignment performed correctly.**

# STEERING

## Steering Wheel

### REMOVAL & INSTALLATION

**CAUTION**

***Vehicles equipped with airbags present a great danger to inexperienced personnel. Testing, assembly and repair work on the steering wheel/airbag assembly must only be conducted by trained service personnel. Repair, storage and transportation of airbag units are subject to laws for explosive materials. Never test an airbag circuit with a test light or voltmeter or unit may trigger. If removed from the vehicle the airbag trigger plate must always face upwards.***

#### All Models without Airbag

1. Center the steering wheel. Disconnect the negative battery cable.
2. Pull off the center horn pad and disconnect the wire. Mark the relationship of the steering wheel to the steering shaft.
3. Remove the steering wheel mounting nut and remove the steering wheel. A steering wheel puller should not be necessary.
4. To install, align the matchmarks and tighten the nut to 36 ft. lbs. (5000, 1983), 29–30 ft. lbs. all other models.

**NOTE: Never strike or pound on the steering wheel. The collapsible steering column may be damaged.**

#### All Models with Airbag

1. Center the steering wheel. Disconnect the negative battery cable.
2. Remove the side trim from center console, disconnect the power supply connector to the airbag.

**CAUTION**

***The power connector to the airbag must be disconnected, as the airbag can trigger with the vehicle battery disconnected, due to the use of the energy reserve circuit.***

3. Remove the screws for the upper steering column trim and remove the upper trim.
4. Separate the connector for the airbag spiral spring.
5. Remove the airbag torx® head retaining bolts.
6. Unhook the airbag unit, lift up safety clamp and remove the airbag wiring at the terminal.
7. Remove the steering wheel mounting nut and remove the steering wheel. A steering wheel puller may be necessary.
8. If removing sprial spring, wheel

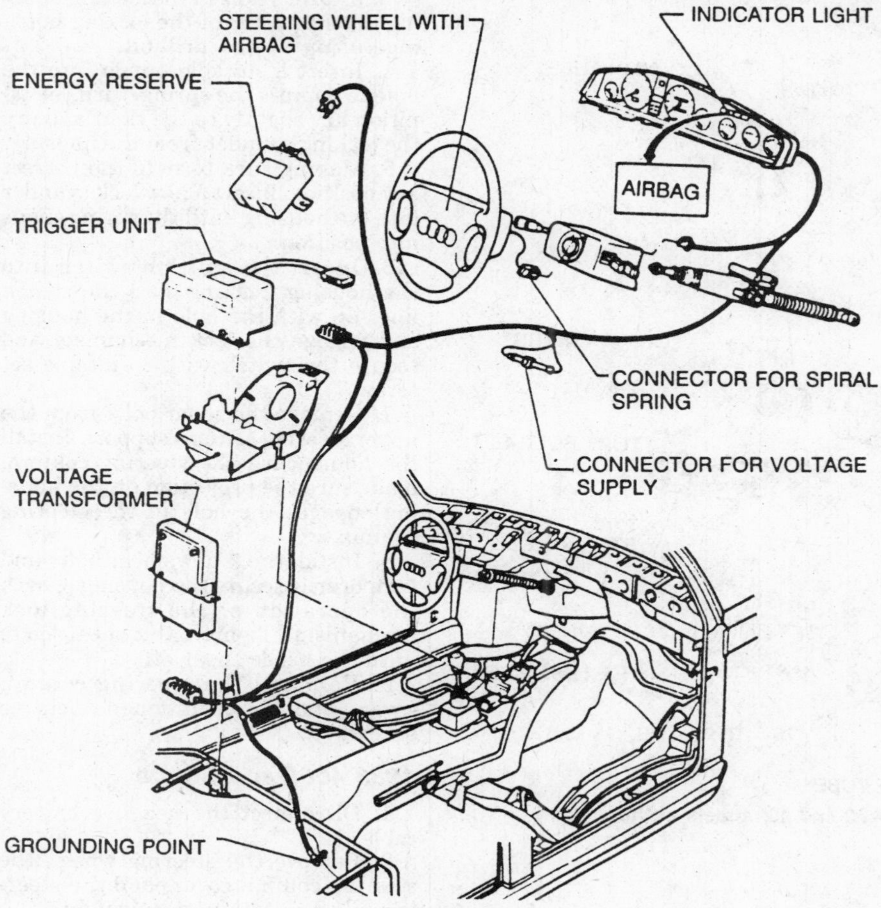


**Airbag system—200 shown**

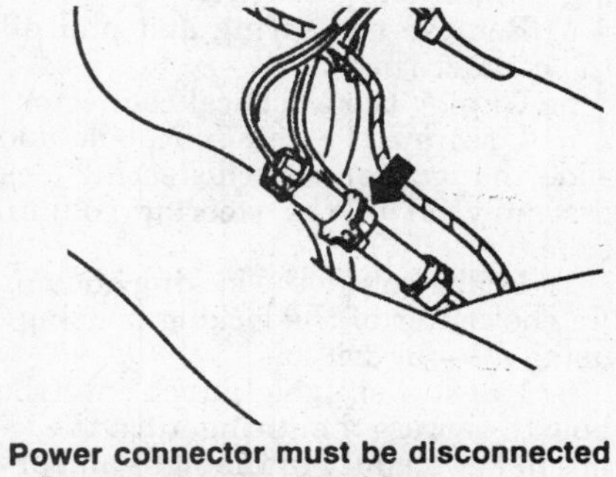

**Power connector must be disconnected—Steering wheel with airbag**

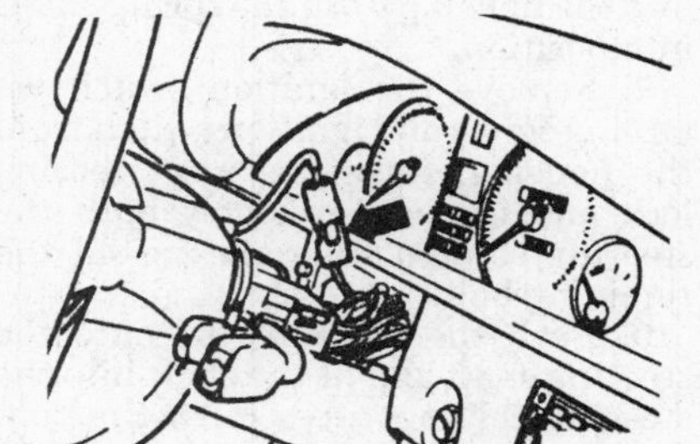

**Connector for airbag spiral spring**

must be straight ahead position. Do not twist spring after removing it.

9. To install, align the matchmarks and tighten the nut to 30 ft. lbs.

**NOTE: Never strike or pound on the steering wheel. The collapsible steering column may be damaged.**

10. Reinstall airbag, airbag connector and reinstall torx® head screws. Torque the Torx® head screws to 53 inch lbs.

11. Install steering column upper trim.

12. Connect airbag system power connector.

13. Install the side trim on center console.

14. Connect the negative battery cable.

## Combination Switch

### REMOVAL & INSTALLATION

#### *All 4000 and Coupe Models*

1. Disconnect the negative battery cable. Pull off the center horn pad. Re-

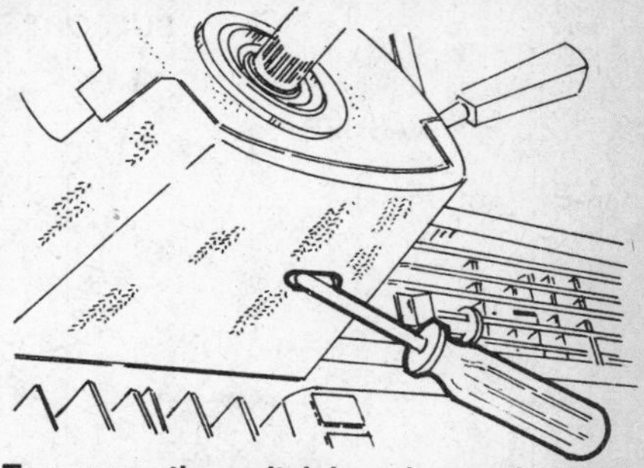

**To remove the switch housing on the 5000, insert a screwdriver and loosen the screw**

move the nut and washer securing the steering wheel and remove the steering wheel, spring and horn contacts.

2. Remove the steering column upper and lower covers. Remove the screws securing the combination switch to the steering lock housing.

3. Disconnect and tag the switch wiring. Remove the combination switch.

4. Installation is the reverse of removal procedure.

#### *5000, 80, 90, 100 and 200 Models*

1. Disconnect the negative battery cable. Remove the steering wheel. Take note of safety cautions regarding vehicles with airbags.

2. Remove the screws securing the combination switch housing through the access hole provided.

3. Pull the housing and switch assembly forward to clear the steering shaft and disconnect the wiring harness connectors. Insert a screwdriver into the slot at the bottom right of the switch housing. Loosen the screw and pull the housing off enough to unplug the electrical connectors.

4. The switches can be removed from the housing by removing the retaining screws.

5. Installation is the reverse of removal procedure.

## Ignition Lock/Switch

### REMOVAL & INSTALLATION

#### *1983 5000 Models*

1. Disconnect the negative battery cable. Lower the air conditioning ducts as required and remove the combination switch assembly.

2. Disconnect the wiring harness from the switch. Support the steering column and drill out the 2 shear bolts using a $^{5}/_{16}$ in. drill bit.

3. Remove the steering lock and switch assembly from the vehicle. Remove the screw from the bottom of the lock housing and remove the ignition

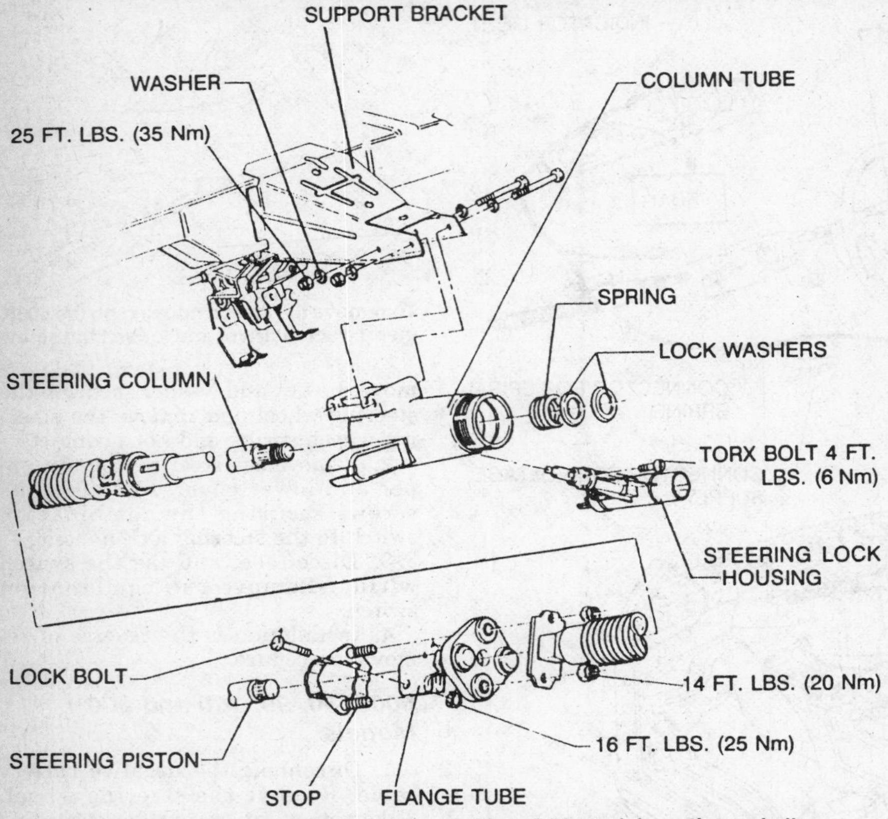


**Exploded view of steering column – 80 and 90 models – others similar**

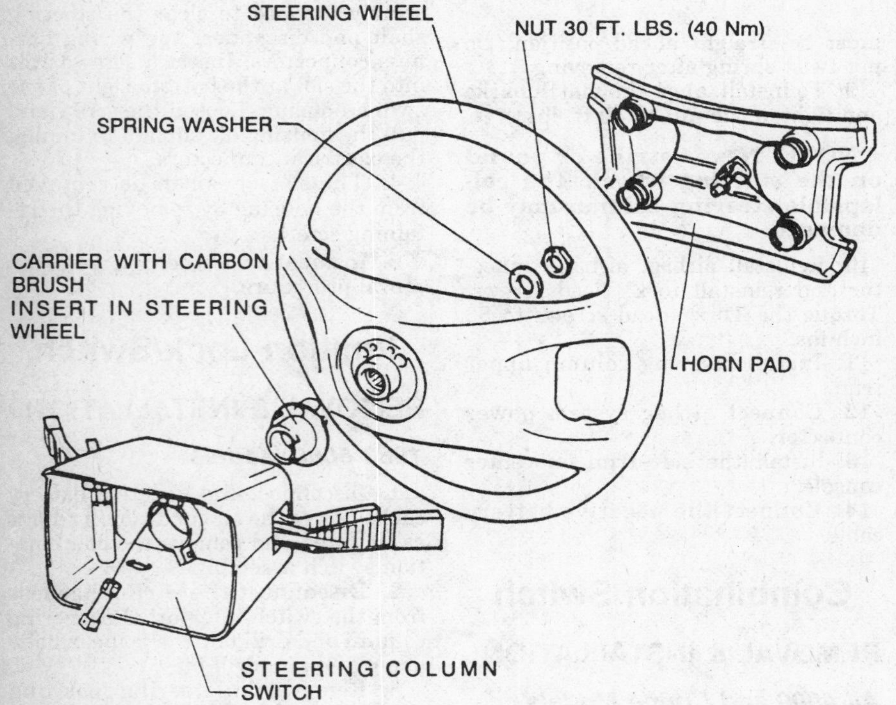


**Steering wheel and combination switch mounting – 80 and 90 models shown; 5000 and 100 similar**

switch. Drill a hole in the locking housing (in the center of the locking housing), using a ⅛ in. drill bit.

4. Insert a suitable punch into the hole to depress the spring, turn the ignition key slightly to the right and pry the locking cylinder from the housing.

5. Making sure to note the correct key position, insert a new lock cylinder into the housing until the spring snaps into position.

6. Insert the ignition switch into the housing, making sure the switch lines-up with the hole in the housing and engage the lock mechanism and secure the switch with a suitable set screw.

7. Remove the shear bolts from the upper steering column support. Install the housing on the steering column, make sure the projection on the housing engages the hole in the steering column.

8. Install the 2 new shear bolts and temporarily secure the housing. Check the operation of the steering lock mechanism. Tighten the shear bolts until the heads shear off.

9. Reinstall the steering column covers and air conditioner ducts as necessary.

### *1983 4000 and Coupe*

1. Disconnect the negative battery cable.

2. Remove the steering wheel, the steering column covers and the steering column combination switches.

3. Pry the lock washer off the steering column and discard it.

4. Remove the spring and pull off the contact ring.

5. Unplug the electrical connector.

6. Unscrew the retaining bolt and slide the ignition switch/steering lock assembly off of the steering column tube.

7. Drill a hole in the locking housing (in the center of the locking housing), using a ⅛ in. drill bit.

8. Insert a suitable punch into the hole to depress the spring, turn the ignition key slightly to the right and pry the locking cylinder from the housing. Making sure to note the correct key position, insert a new lock cylinder into the housing until the spring snaps into position.

9. Remove the ignition switch retaining screw and ignition switch from the housing. Push the new steering lock and ignition assembly onto the steering column tube and install the retaining bolt.

10. Push the support ring onto the steering shaft and fit the shaft into the steering column tube. Push the contact ring onto the steering shaft and install the spring and lock washer, be sure to fully compress the spring.

11. To finish this procedure, install the rest of the components in the reverse order of the removal procedure.

#### 1984–88 5000 Models and 1989–90 100 and 200 Models

1. Disconnect the negative battery cable. Remove the steering wheel. Take note of safety cautions regarding vehicles with airbags.
2. Remove the instrument cluster attaching bolts. Disconnect the speedometer cable at the transaxle.
3. Pull the instrument cluster forward and detach the speedometer cable at the speedometer. Disconnect the electrical connectors at the instrument cluster and remove the instrument cluster.
4. Remove the locking compound around the ignition switch and remove the switch. To remove the ignition lock cylinder go on with this procedure.
5. Support the steering column and drill out the 2 shear bolts using a 1/8 in. drill bit. Loosen the steering column bolts. Remove the left lower dash panel and the left air deflector.
6. Slide the steering column tube with the steering column downward and remove the steering lock from the steering column clamp. Drill a hole in the locking housing (in the center of the locking housing), using a 1/8 in. drill bit.
7. Push the retaining spring in with a suitable punch and remove the lock cylinder.
8. Installation is the reverse order of the removal procedure.

#### 1984–87 4000, Coupe Models 1988–90 80 and 90 Models

1. Disconnect the negative battery cable.
2. Remove the steering wheel, the steering column covers and the steering column combination switches.
3. Pry the lock washer off the steering column and discard it.
4. Remove the spring and pull off the contact ring.
5. Unplug the electrical connector.
6. Unscrew the retaining bolt and slide the ignition switch/steering lock assembly off of the steering column tube.
7. Installation is in the reverse order of removal. Use a new lock washer.

#### 1988–90 80 and 90 Models

1. Disconnect the negative battery cable.
2. Remove the steering wheel, the steering column covers and the steering column combination switches.
3. Remove instrument cluster retaining screws.
4. Tilt the instrument cluster backwards slightly and remove the electrical connectors.
5. Remove the instrument cluster.
6. Remove the locking compound from the ignition switch screws.
7. Remove the electrical connector from switch.
8. Remove screws and remove the switch.
9. Installation is in the reverse order of removal. Install the ignition switch in the **OFF** position.

## Manual Steering Gear

### REMOVAL & INSTALLATION

#### 1983 4000 and Coupe Models

1. Raise and support the front of the vehicle on jackstands.
2. At the steering gear, remove the tie rods from the steering drive pawl bracket by prying them off with a small pry bar.
3. At the steering gear-to-steering column lower flange tube, push back the dust cap. Loosen the steering column-to-steering gear clamp bolt and pry the clamp back. Remove the seal ring from the steering gear.
4. Using a brass drift, drive the steering column lower flange off the steering gear.
5. Remove the steering gear-to-body bolts, turn the wheels to the right lock and remove the steering gear through the opening in the right wheel well.
6. To install, reverse the removal procedures. Torque the flange tube bolt to 18 ft. lbs., the tie rod end ball joint nut to 22 ft. lbs. and the steering gear-to-body nuts to 25 ft. lbs.

### ADJUSTMENT

The tie rod is only adjustable on the left-side on 4 cylinder models and on both sides on 5 cylinder models.

1. At the steering gear cover, loosen the locknut. Tighten the adjusting screw until it touches the thrust washer. While holding the screw, tighten the locknut.
2. If the steering rattles, is too tight or does not center, readjust the adjusting screw.

**NOTE: When turning the steering wheel with the wheels off the ground, be careful not to turn it too hard against the stops for damage may result.**

## Power Steering Gear

### REMOVAL & INSTALLATION

#### 1983 4000 and Coupe Models

1. Raise and support the front of the vehicle on jackstands.
2. Disconnect the pressure hoses from the power steering gear and drain the fluid from the system.
3. At the power steering gear, pull the rubber cap back and disconnect the steering column clamp from the power steering gear pinion.
4. Remove the tie rods from the steering drive pawl at the power steering gear.
5. Remove the power steering gear-to-frame bolts and the steering gear from the vehicle.
6. To install, reverse the removal procedures. Bleed the hydraulic system.

#### 1984–87 4000, Coupe and 1988–89 80 and 90 Models

1. Raise and support the front of the vehicle on jackstands.
2. Remove the lower left instrument panel cover, the steering column-to-steering gear clamp bolt and the steering column-to-dash bolts. Remove the steering column from the vehicle.
3. Using a pair of visegrips, clamp off the fluid return line to the reservoir. Disconnect the fluid pressure line from the steering gear.
4. At the steering column boot, press in on the clips and remove the boot from the panel. From inside the vehicle, remove the fluid return line from the control valve body. On 1988–90 5 cylinder models, push off the dash panel boot and push the boot into the passenger compartment to access the pressure and return line.
5. At the left wheel housing, disconnect the steering gear from the frame.
6. At the steering rack, remove the tie rod coupling locknuts/bolts and the tie rods from the rack. Push the rack back into the steering housing.
7. Disconnect the steering assembly from the firewall. Turn the wheels to the right. Remove the assembly between the left wheel housing and the control arm.
8. To install, reverse the removal procedures. Bleed the hydraulic system.

#### 1984–88 5000 Models and 1989–90 100 and 200 Models

1. Raise and support the vehicle safely.
2. Pry off the lock plate and remove both tie rod mounting bolts from the steering rack, inside the engine compartment. Pry the tie rods out of the mounting pivot.
3. Remove the lower instrument panel trim.
4. Remove the pressure and return lines from the steering gear control valve body.

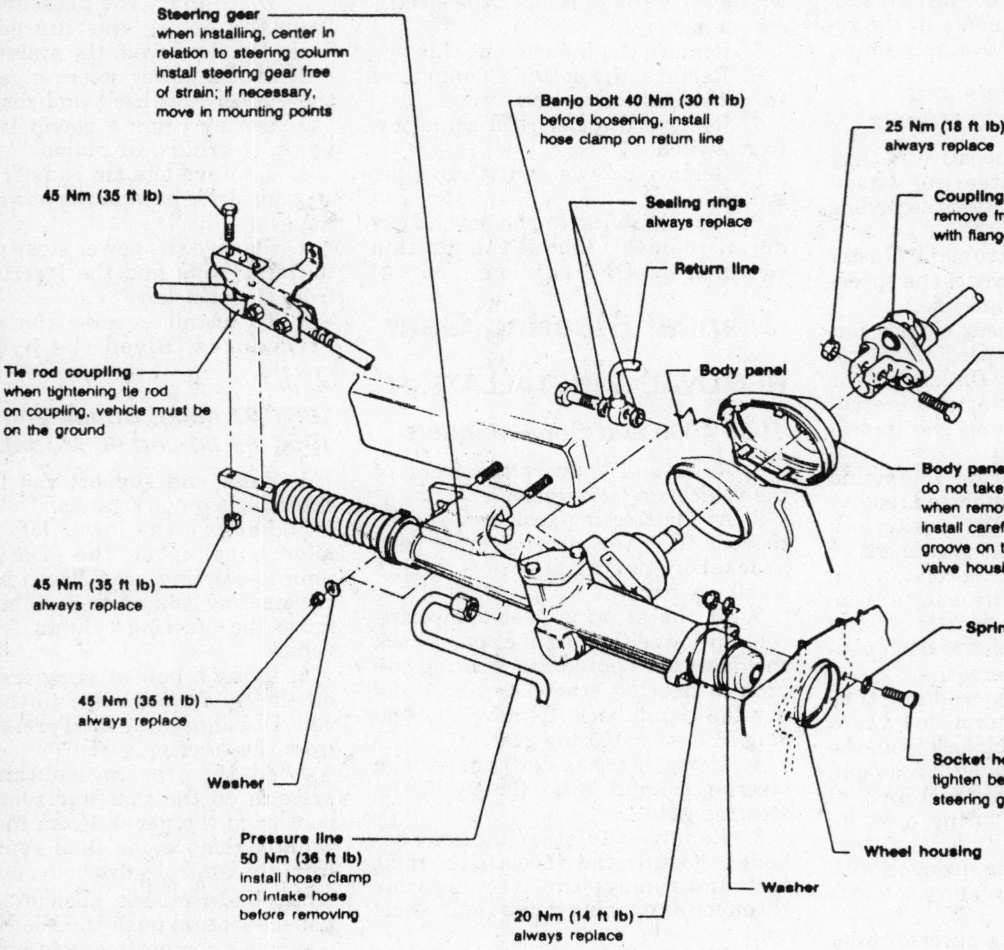


Power steering gear mounting – 80 and 90 models

5. Remove the shaft clamp bolt, pry off the clip and drive the shaft toward the inside of the vehicle with a brass drift.
6. Remove the steering gear mounting bolts at both ends. There is a single bolt at the right end.
7. Turn the wheels all the way to the right and remove the steering gear through the opening in the right wheel housing.
8. For installation, temporarily install the tie rod mounting pivot to the rack with both mounting bolts. Remove 1 bolt, install the tie rod and replace the bolt. Do the same on the other tie rod. Make sure to install the lock plate.
9. On all models except the 100 and 200, torque the tie rod to 39 ft. lbs., the mounting pivot bolt to 15 ft. lbs. and the steering gear-to-body mounting bolts to 15 ft. lbs. On 100 and 200 models, torque the tie rod to 44 ft. lbs., pivot bolt to 30 ft. lbs. and gear-to-body bolts to 15 ft. lbs.
10. Install hose lines with O-rings and torque to 30 ft. lbs.

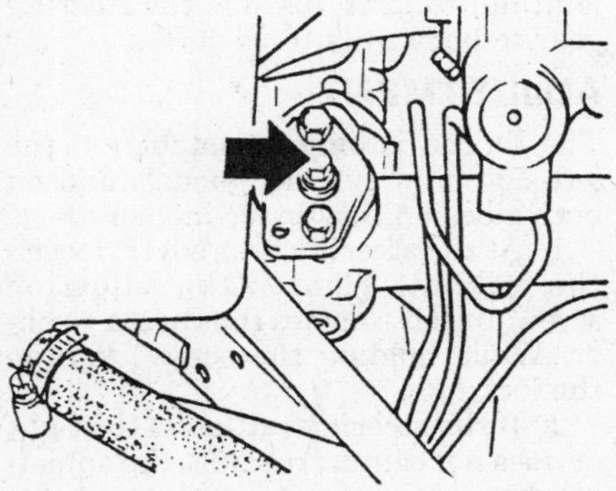

Steering gear adjustment bolt

11. Bleed the hydraulic system.

## ADJUSTMENT

1. Position the wheels in the straight-ahead position.
2. On top of the steering gear, loosen the locknut. Turn the adjusting nut until it bottoms against the thrust piece. While holding the adjusting screw, tighten the locknut.
3. If the steering rattles, is too tight or does not center, readjust the adjusting screw.

# Power Steering Pump

## REMOVAL & INSTALLATION

### *All Models*

1. Remove the hoses from the pump. Plug the openings.
2. Remove the belt adjusting bolt, push the pump to 1 side and remove the belt.
3. Support the pump, remove the mounting bolts and lift out the pump.
4. Installation is the reverse. Be sure to fill the pump suction chamber with hydraulic fluid before attaching lines or the pump may be damaged.

## BELT ADJUSTMENT

1. Loosen the pump mounting bolts.

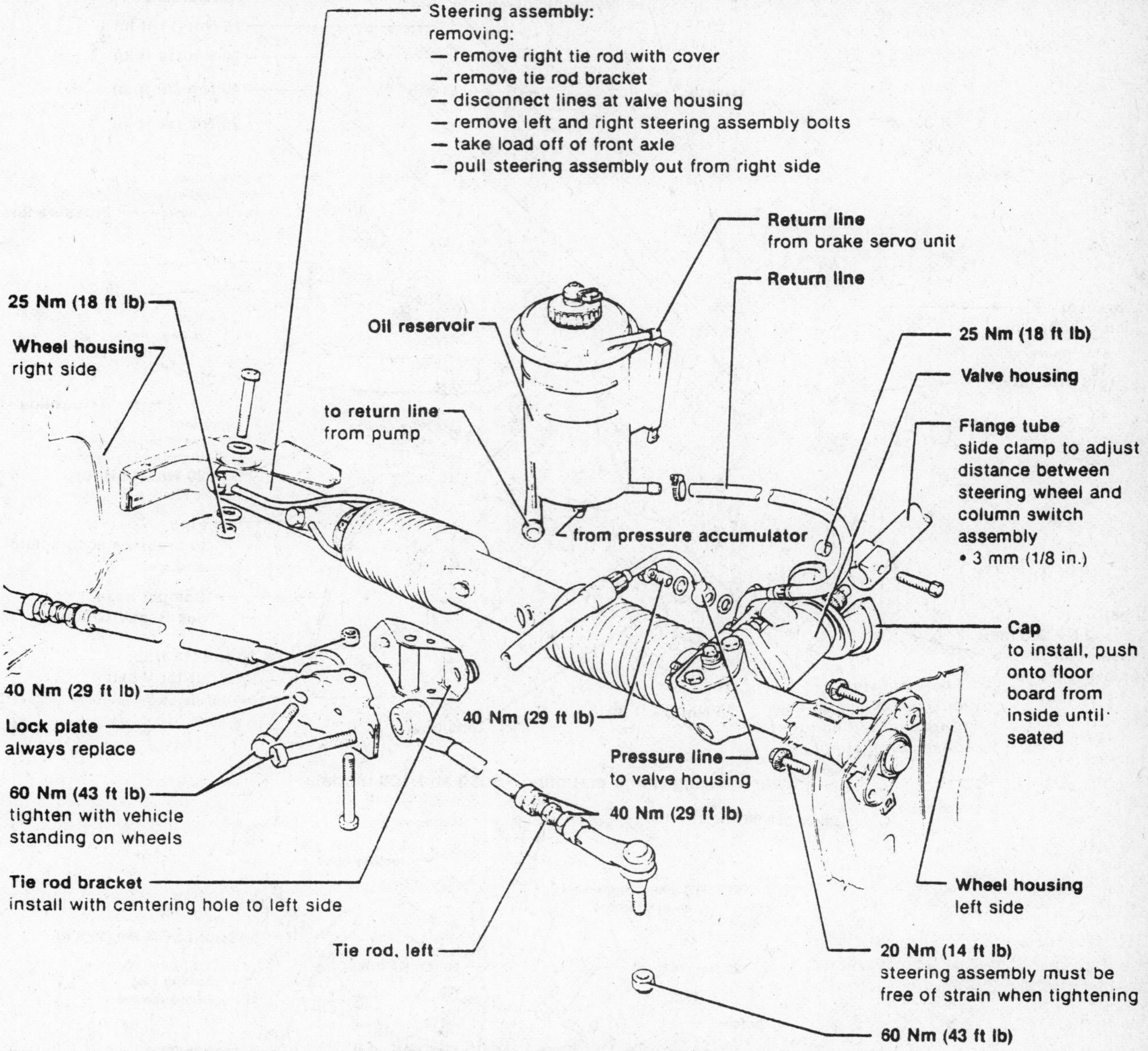


**Power steering gear mounting—5000 and 100 models**

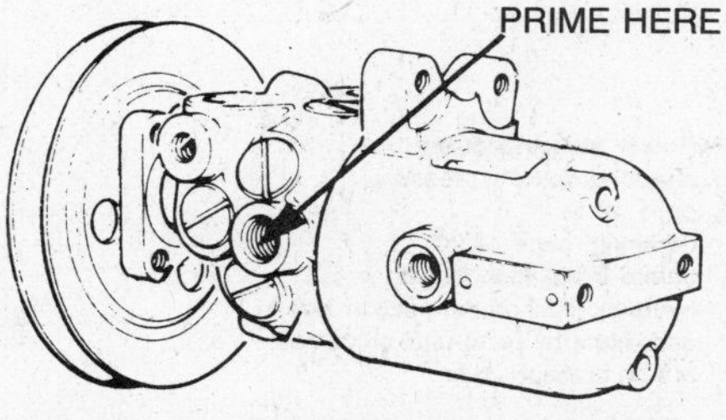


**Prime the power steering pump with hydraulic fluid before installing**

2. Turn the pump adjusting bolt until the center of the belt can be depressed ⅜ in. (10 mm).
3. After adjustment, tighten the mounting bolts.

## SYSTEM BLEEDING

1. Fill the reservoir to the **FULL** mark.
2. Raise and support the front of the vehicle on jackstands.
3. Turn the steering wheel (with the engine NOT running) from lock to lock (several times) to remove the air from the system.
4. Add fluid to the reservoir until the level is maintained at $1^3/_{16}$ in. (30mm) below the **FULL** mark.
5. Start the engine. As the fluid in the reservoir continues to drop, add fluid to maintain the $1^3/_{16}$ in. (30mm) level.

**NOTE: When turning the steering wheel, DO NOT use more force than necessary to turn it.**

6. Keep bleeding the system until no more air bubbles appear in the reservoir.
7. Turn **OFF** the engine and pump the brake pedal at least 20 times.
8. Replenish the fluid to the proper level.

# Tie Rod Ends

## REMOVAL & INSTALLATION

**NOTE: A puller or press is required for this job.**

1. Raise and support the vehicle safely. Remove the front wheels.
2. Disconnect the outer end of the steering tie rod from the steering knuckle by removing the cotter pin

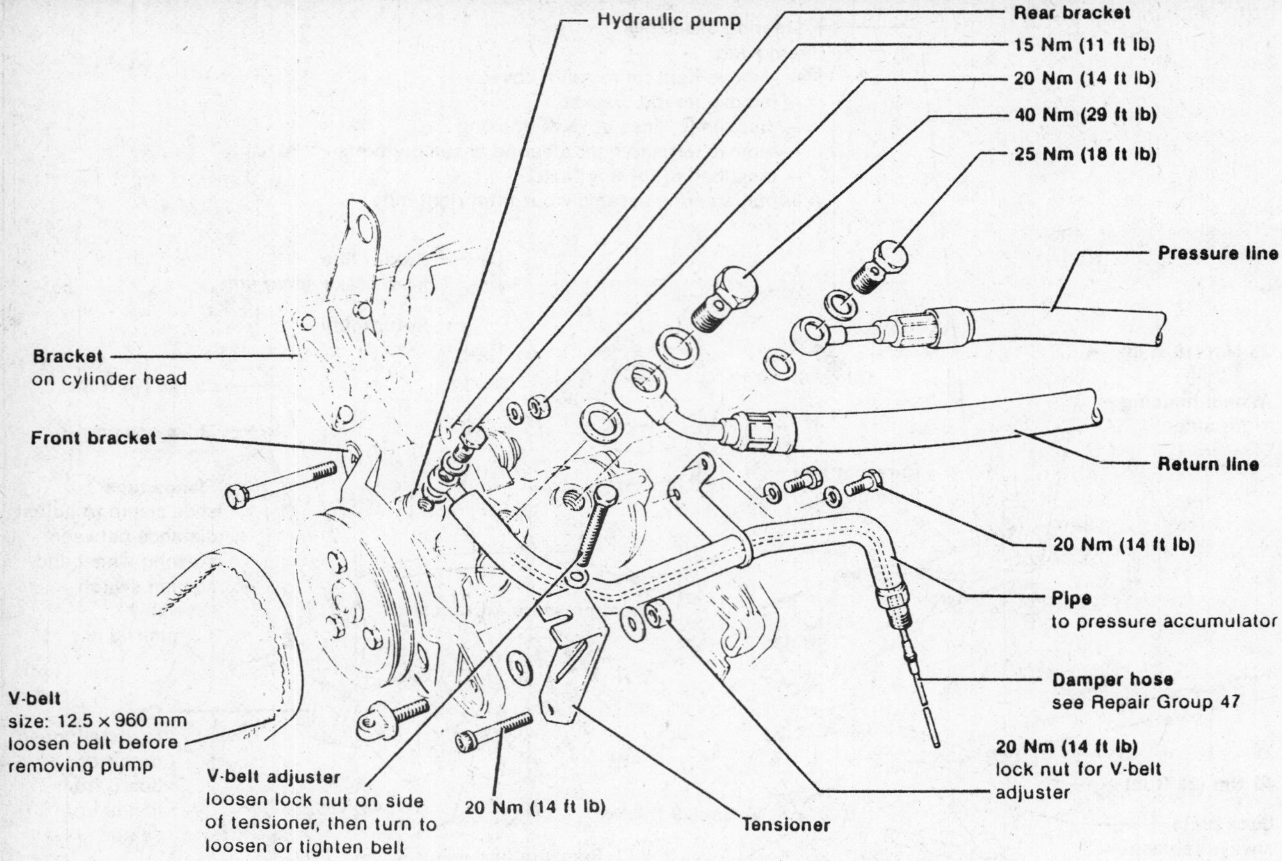


**Power steering pump mounting—5000 and 100 models**

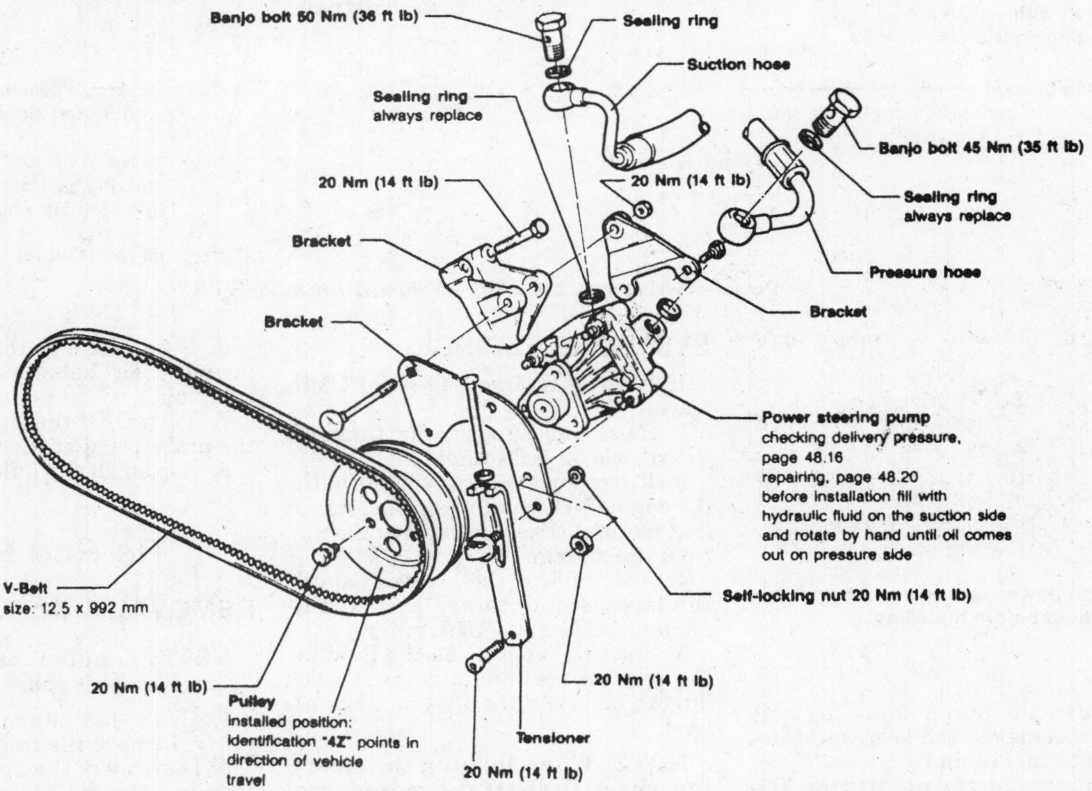


**Power steering pump mounting—80 and 90 models with 5 cylinder engine**

and nut and pressing out the tie rod end. A small puller or press is required to free the tie rod end.

3. Under the hood, pry off the lock plate and remove the mounting bolts from both tie rod inner ends. Pry the tie rod out of the mounting pivot.

4. Install the mounting pivot to the rack with both mounting bolts.

5. Remove 1 bolt, install the tie rod and replace the bolt. Do the same on the other tie rod.

6. Make sure to install the lock plate. The inner tie rod end bolts should be torqued to:

1983 4000 and Coupe – 40 ft. lbs.
1984–87 4000, Coupe – 32 ft. lbs.
1984–88 5000 – 44 ft. lbs.
1988–90 80 and 90 – 32 ft. lbs.
1989–90 100 and 200 – 44 ft. lbs.

7. If replacing the adjustable left tie rod, adjust it to the same length as the old one. Check the toe-in when the job is done.

8. Use new cotter pins when installing the outer tie rod end. Torque the nut to 22 ft. lbs. (4000, Coupe, 80 and 90) or 43 ft. lbs. (5000 and 100).

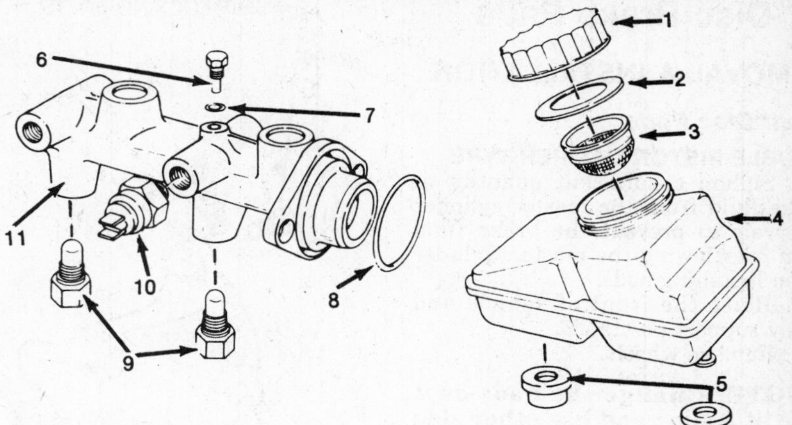

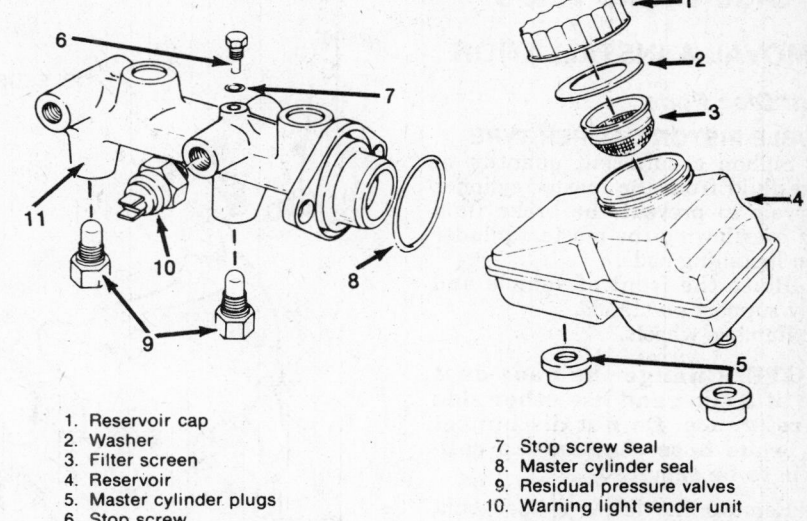

1. Reservoir cap
2. Washer
3. Filter screen
4. Reservoir
5. Master cylinder plugs
6. Stop screw
7. Stop screw seal
8. Master cylinder seal
9. Residual pressure valves
10. Warning light sender unit
11. Brake master cylinder housing

**4000 master cylinder—5000 similar**

# BRAKES

**For all brake system repair and service procedures not detailed below, please refer to "Brakes" in the Unit Repair Section.**

## Master Cylinder

### REMOVAL & INSTALLATION

#### *All Models*

1. Have an assistant hold the brake pedal down about 1½ in. Disconnect the brake lines nearest the firewall.

2. Hold a container under the fitting disconnected in Step 1 and have the assistant release the pedal. The contents of the reservoir will drain into the container. Discard the used fluid.

3. Disconnect the other brake line.

4. Disconnect the stoplight switch from the master cylinder.

5. Remove the master cylinder from the power brake unit. Be careful not to lose the sealing ring between the 2 units.

6. Installation is the reverse of removal.

7. Transfer the reservoir from the master cylinder to the new unit.

**NOTE: Bench bleeding master cylinder will speed the on vehicle bleeding procedure. Raise the front or rear of the vehicle, if necessary, to maintain bleeding locations at the highest point in the hydraulic system.**

8. Master cylinder bolt torque is 17 ft. lbs. Fill and bleed the system. There should be a pedal free-play of 0.2 in. Free-play can be adjusted with the linkage, inside.

## Proportioning Valve

### CHECKING

#### *All Models*

1. With the wheels on the ground, depress the brake pedal firmly.

2. Release the pedal suddenly and check that the lever on the proportioning valve moves.

3. If the lever does not move, the valve will probably require replacement.

**NOTE: It is normal for small quantities of brake fluid to escape through the vent hole.**

### REMOVAL & INSTALLATION

#### *All Models*

1. Remove and plug the 4 brake lines leading from the proportioning valve.

2. Disconnect the spring which is attached to the valve and the axle beam.

3. Remove the 2 mounting bolts and remove the valve.

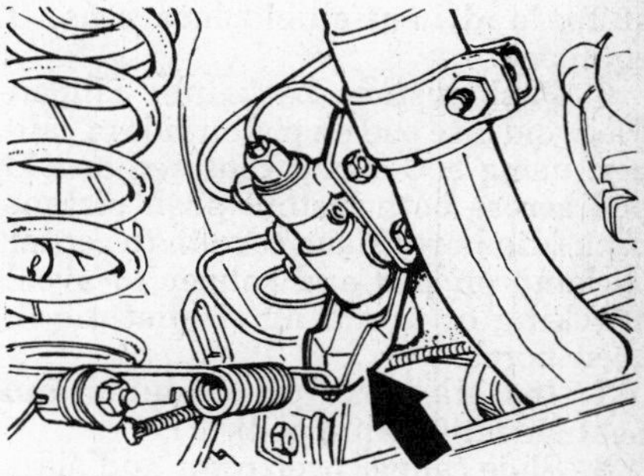

**5000 brake proportioning valve; when checking, the lever (arrow) should move**

**NOTE: Do not disassemble the valve.**

4. Installation is in the reverse order of removal.

5. Bleed the brake system when finished.

## Power Brake Booster

### REMOVAL & INSTALLATION

#### *All Models*

1. Remove the master cylinder. Do not disconnect the brake lines.

2. Disconnect the vacuum hose from the power brake booster.

3. From under the dash, disconnect the pushrod from the brake pedal, remove the power brake booster to firewall nuts and remove the booster from the vehicle.

4. To install, reverse the removal procedures.

# Disc Brake Pads

## REMOVAL & INSTALLATION

### *Front Disc Pads*

#### DOUBLE PISTON CALIPER TYPE

1. Siphon a sufficient quantity of brake fluid from the master cylinder reservoir to prevent the brake fluid from overflowing the master cylinder when installing pads.
2. Raise the front of vehicle and safely support on stands.
3. Remove wheels.

**NOTE: Change the pads on 1 axle at a time and use other side for reference. Do not disconnect the brake hoses, unless the caliper is to be serviced.**

4. Remove the lower caliper bolt, hold guide pin with open end wrench, while loosening. Disconnect the wear indicator, if equipped.
5. Swing brake caliper up and remove brake pads, taking note of spacer shims and heat-shield locations, if equipped.
6. Push pistons back into caliper. Place old disc pad on piston side of caliper, using a C-clamp centered on old pad across both piston, push pistons back into bore. Make certain to center C-clamp on pad and caliper to avoid cracking or jamming th pistons in their bores.
7. Install brake pads, shims and heat shield (if equipped).
8. Slide caliper over rotor and align pins.
9. Install guide pins and torque to 26 ft. lbs. (35 Nm).
10. Connect the wear indicator and install wheels.
11. Lower evehicle and fill master cylinder.
12. Pump the brake pedal slowly several time to force pads against the rotors.
13. Check master cylinder level again and add fluid if needed.

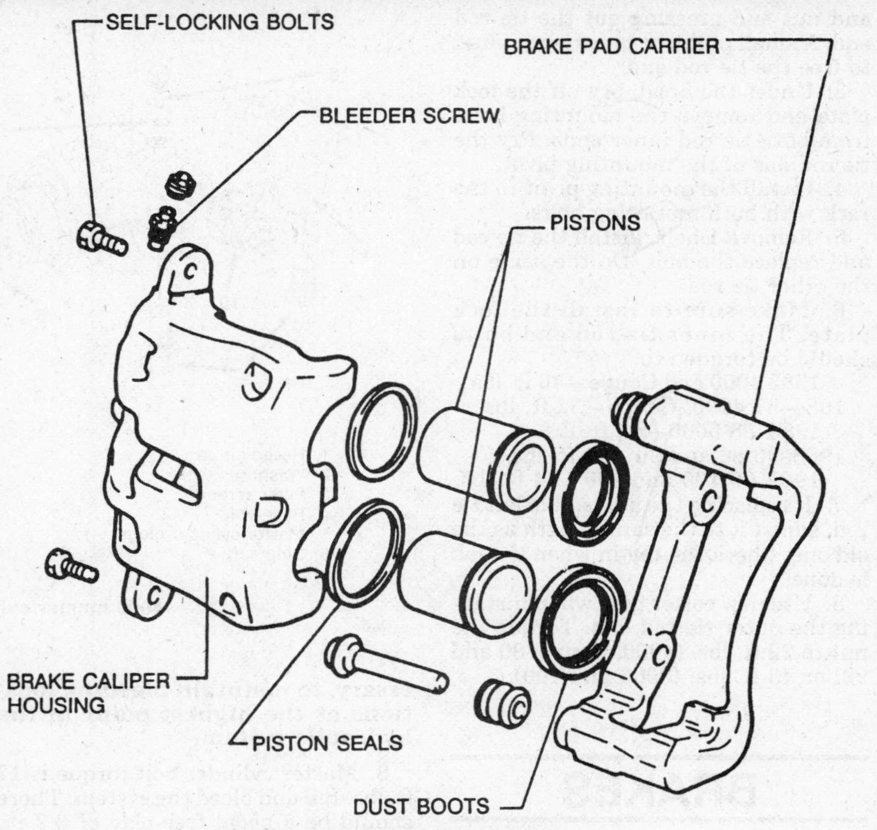

Double piston type caliper

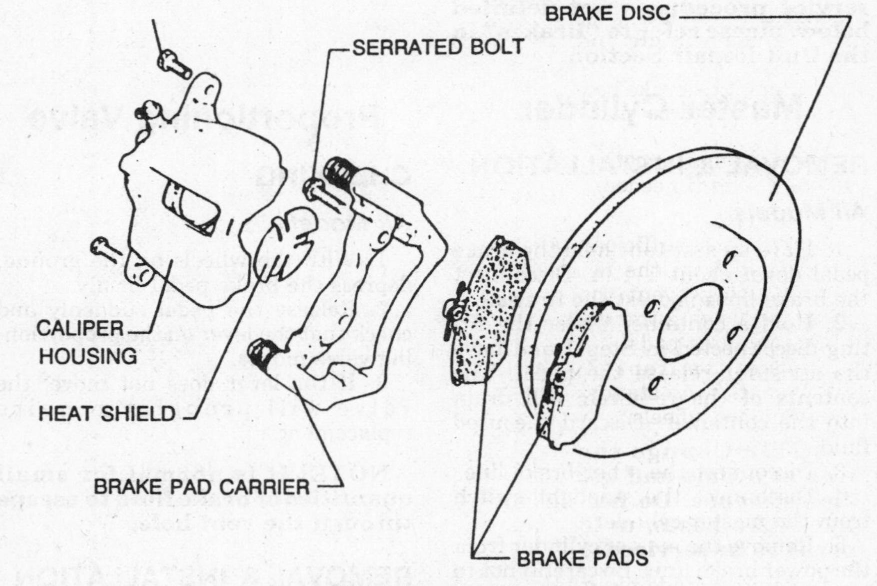

Girling type front brakes

#### GIRLING TYPE

1. Siphon a sufficient quantity of brake fluid from the master cylinder reservoir to prevent the brake fluid from overflowing the master cylinder when installing pads.
2. Raise the front of vehicle and safely support on stands.
3. Remove wheels.

**NOTE: Change the pads on 1 axle at a time and use other side for reference. Do not disconnect the brake hoses, unless the caliper is to be serviced.**

4. Remove the lower caliper bolt, hold guide pin with open end wrench, while loosening. Disconnect the wear indicator, if equipped.
5. Swing brake caliper up and remove brake pads, taking note of spacer shims and heat-shield locations, if equipped.
6. Push piston back into caliper, using a C-clamp in bore of piston. Make certain to center C-clamp on piston and caliper to avoid cracking or jamming the piston in the bore.
7. Install brake pads, shims and heat shield (if equipped).
8. Slide caliper over rotor and align pins.
9. Install guide pins and torque to 25 ft. lbs. (35 Nm).

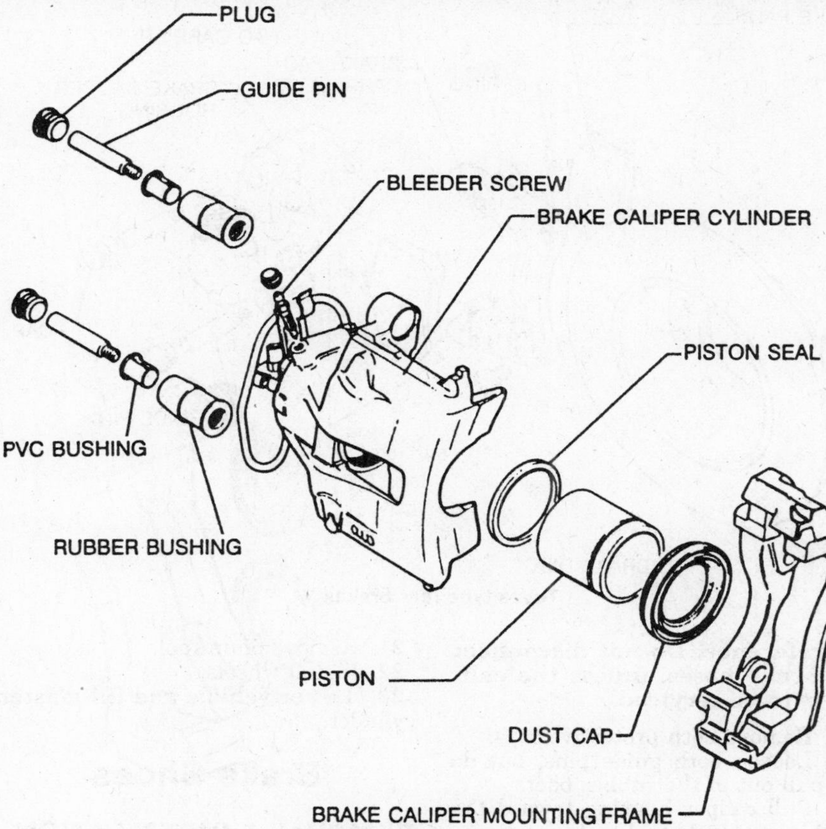

Teves type front brakes

10. Install wheels.
11. Lower vehicle and fill master cylinder.
12. Pump the brake pedal slowly several time to force pads against the rotors.
13. Check master cylinder level again and add fluid if needed.

**TEVES TYPE**

1. Siphon a sufficient quantity of brake fluid from the master cylinder reservoir to prevent the brake fluid from overflowing the master cylinder when installing pads.
2. Raise the front of vehicle and safely support on stands.
3. Remove wheels.

**NOTE: Change the pads on 1 axle at a time and use other side for reference. Do not disconnect the brake hoses, unless the caliper is to be serviced.**

4. Remove guide pin caps.
5. Remove guide pins.
6. Remove brake hose retaining clip or bracket.
7. Swing caliper up and secure in position, using a wire. Do not allow caliper to hang from brake hose.
8. Remove brake pads, taking note of spacer shims and heat-shield locations. Disconnect the wear indicator, if equipped.
9. Push piston back into caliper, using a C-clamp in bore of piston. Make certain to center C-clamp on piston and caliper to avoid cracking or jamming the piston in the bore.
10. Install brake pads, shims and heat shield (if equipped).
11. Slide caliper over rotor and align pins.
12. Install guide pins and torque to 18 ft. lbs. (25 Nm).
13. Install brake hose clip.
14. Install wheels.
15. Lower vehicle and fill master cylinder.
16. Pump the brake pedal slowly several time to force pads against the rotors.
17. Check master cylinder level again and add fluid if needed.

### *Rear Disc Pads*

**GIRLING TYPE**

1. Siphon a sufficient quantity of brake fluid from the master cylinder reservoir to prevent the brake fluid from overflowing the master cylinder when installing pads.
2. Raise the rear of vehicle and safely support on stands.
3. Remove wheels.

**NOTE: Change the pads on 1 axle at a time and use other side**

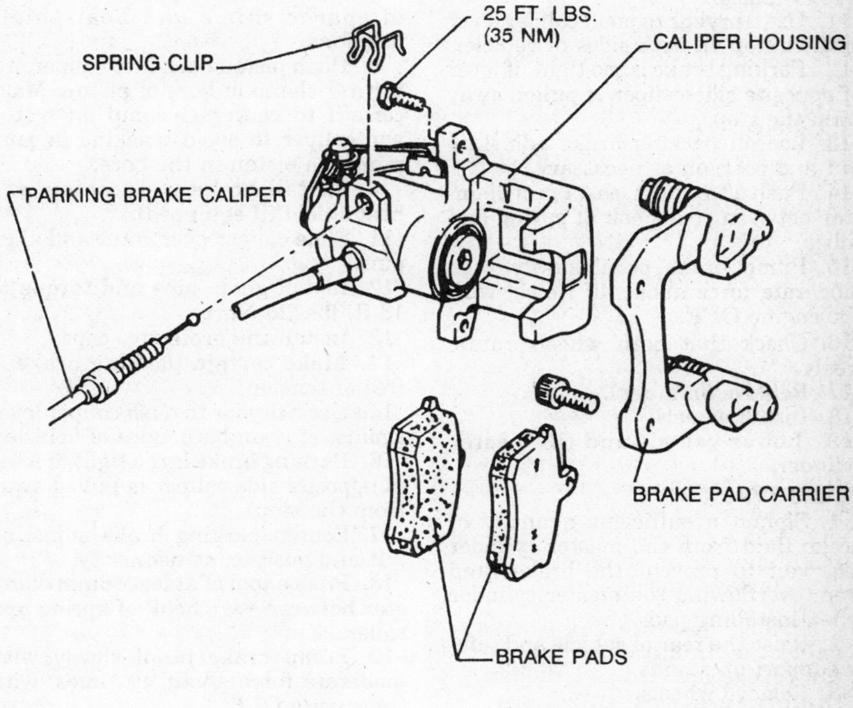

Girling type rear brakes

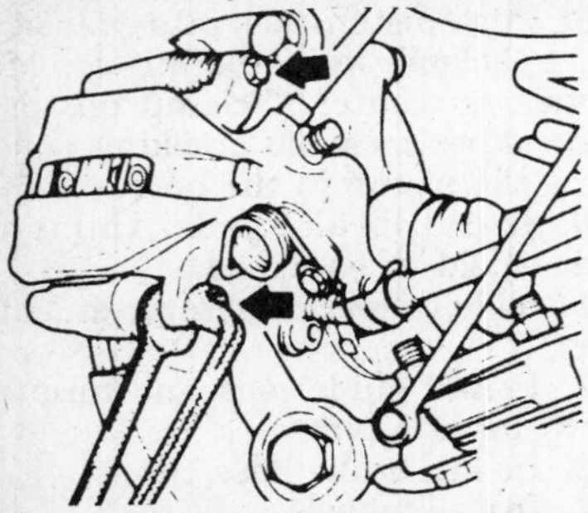

Holding guide pin with open-end wrench

**for reference. Do not disconnect the brake hoses, unless the caliper is to be serviced.**

4. Remove brake caliper housing, hold guide pin with open end wrench while loosening bolts. Disconnect the wear indicator, if equipped.
5. Remove brake pads, taking note of spacer shims and heat-shield locations.
6. Screw piston into housing by turning is clockwise with a socket head wrench while pushing in firmly.
7. Install brake pads, shims and heat shield (if equipped).
8. Install caliper on housing.

**NOTE: The bolts are self-locking type and Audi recommends always using new bolts.**

9. Install new bolts and torque to 25 ft. lbs. (35 Nm).
10. Make certain parking brake is free of tension.
11. Use a prybar to push caliper lever against stop on both sides of vehicle.
12. Parking brake is too tight, if lever of opposite side caliper is pulled away from the stop.
13. Loosen parking brake adjusting nut and position as necessary.
14. Push a tool of at least 6mm diameter between rear hook of spring and roller.
15. Pump brake pedal slowly with moderate force about 40 times, with the engine **OFF**.
16. Check that both wheels rotate freely.
17. Remove 6mm tool.
18. Install wheels.
19. Lower vehicle and fill master cylinder.

#### TEVES TYPE

1. Siphon a sufficient quantity of brake fluid from the master cylinder reservoir to prevent the brake fluid from overflowing the master cylinder when installing pads.
2. Raise the rear of vehicle and safely support on stands.
3. Remove wheels.

**NOTE: Change the pads on 1 axle at a time and use other side for reference. Do not disconnect the brake hoses, unless the caliper is to be serviced.**

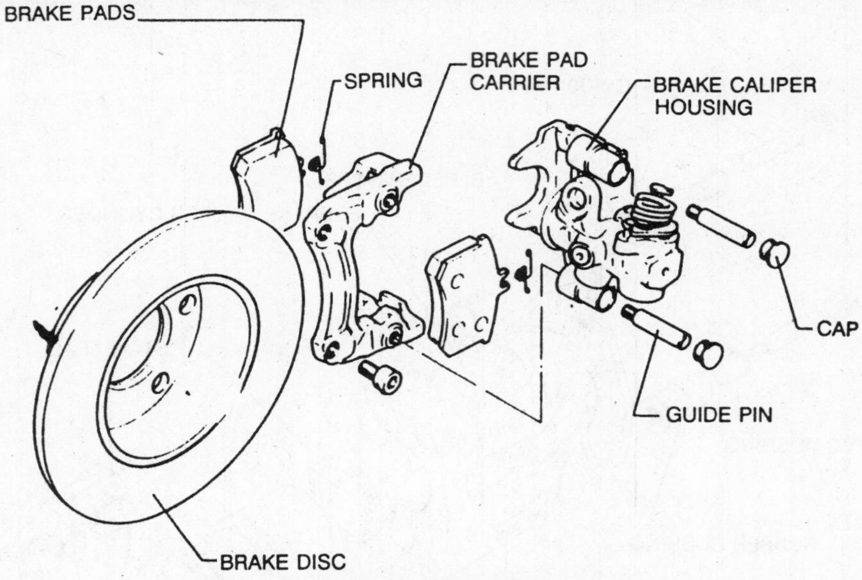


Teves type rear brakes

4. Remove both protective caps.
5. Loosen both guide pins, but do not pull out of the rubber boots.
6. Pull caliper housing toward the outside of vehicle by hand.
7. Swing the caliper housing to the rear and remove. Do not allow caliper to hang from brake hose. Disconnect the wear indicator, if equipped.
8. Remove brake pads, taking note of spacer shims and heat-shield locations.
9. Push piston back into caliper, using a C-clamp in bore of piston. Make certain to center C-clamp on piston and caliper to avoid cracking or jamming the piston in the bore.
10. Install brake pads, shims and heat shield (if equipped).
11. Slide caliper over rotor and align pins.
12. Install guide pins and torque to 18 ft. lbs.(25 Nm).
13. Install the protective caps.
14. Make certain parking brake is free of tension.
14. Use a prybar to push caliper lever against stop on both sides of vehicle.
16. Parking brake is too tight, if lever of opposite side caliper is pulled away from the stop.
17. Loosen parking brake adjusting nut and position as necessary.
18. Push a tool of at least 6mm diameter between rear hook of spring and roller.
19. Pump brake pedal slowly with moderate force about 40 times, with the engine **OFF**.
20. Check that both wheels rotate freely.
21. Remove 6mm tool.
22. Install wheels.
23. Lower vehicle and fill master cylinder.

## Brake Shoes

### REMOVAL & INSTALLATION

1. Raise the rear of the vehicle and support it with jackstands.
2. Remove the wheels an then remove the brake drum.

**NOTE: If the drum does not come off easily, the brakes will have to be backed off. First, push the lever on the proportioning valve toward the rear axle to relieve residual brake pressure. Next remove the plug on the backing plate and insert a small prytool in hole and pry up on adjusting wedge until stop.**

3. Turn and remove the washers to release the brake shoe retaining springs.
4. Remove the lower return springs.
5. Lift shoes off backing plate.
6. Disconnect the parking brake cable by pressing the spring toward the front of the vehicle and unhooking the cable from the brake lever.
7. Secure shoes in a vise. Unhook the upper return spring and adjusting wedge.
8. Unhook tensioning spring.
9. Lift out the brake shoes. Make sure to take note of how the adjuster mechanism fits into the brake shoe web.

**To Install:**

10. Check the wheel cylinder for fro-

zen pistons or leaks. If any are found, rebuild or replace the wheel cylinder.

11. Inspect old springs. If old springs are damaged or have been overheated, they should be replaced. Indications of overheated springs are paint discoloration and distortion.
12. Inspect the brake drum and recondition or replace if necessary.
13. Clean and lubricate all contact points on the backing plate.
14. Install tensioning spring and place shoe on push rod.
15. Insert adjusting wedge, with lug toward the backing plate.
16. Install the next shoe, with lever in push rod.
17. Connect the upper return spring.
18. Hook the parking brake cable onto the lever.
19. Install shoes onto the wheel cylinder pistons.
20. Connect the lower return spring and lift the shoes onto the lower support.
21. Connect the adjusting wedge spring.
22. Install the shoe retaining springs and retainers.
23. Install the brake drum and adjust the wheel bearing.
24. Install the wheels and lower vehicle.
25. Depress the brake pedal firmly several times to set the rear brake shoes.

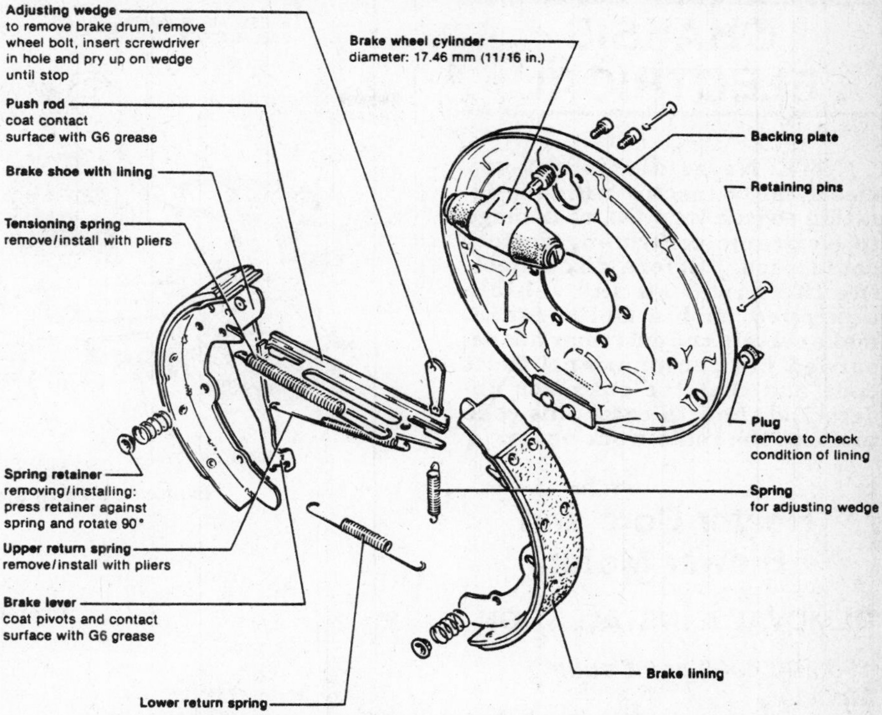

**Rear wheel cylinder mounting—all models with rear drum brakes**

## Wheel Cylinder

### REMOVAL & INSTALLATION

#### *All Models with Rear Drum Brakes*

1. Raise and support the vehicle safely.
2. Remove the wheel, brake drum and brake shoes.
3. Disconnect the brake line and plug the opening.
4. Remove the 2 mounting screws from the backing plate.
5. Remove the wheel cylinder.
6. To install, reverse the removal procedures. Bleed the brake system.

## Parking Brake Cable

### ADJUSTMENT

#### *Drum Brake Models*

**NOTE: Because of self-adjusting rear brakes, adjustment is only necessary after replacement of any of the brake components.**

1. Raise and support the vehicle safely.
2. Release the parking brake lever.
3. Depress the brake pedal once.
4. Pull the parking brake lever onto the second tooth.
5. Tighten the adjusting nut on the parking brake cable equalizer bar until the wheels can just be turned by hand.
6. Release the lever and check that both wheels rotate freely.
7. Turn the ignition switch **ON** and check that the brake warning light comes on, when the parking brake lever is pulled up to the first tooth and goes out when it is released.

#### *Disc Brake Models*

**NOTE: Because of the self-adjusting rear brakes, adjustment is only necessary after replacement of any of the brake components.**

1. Raise and support the vehicle safely.
2. Release the parking brake lever.
3. Check that the parking brake levers at the rear calipers stay on the stop. If not, loosen the adjusting nut.
4. Depress the brake pedal approximately 40 times and pull the parking brake lever to the 3rd tooth.

**NOTE: Always make sure basic adjustment on rear brakes is correct first. Refer to disc brake service.**

5. Tighten the adjusting nut on the parking brake equalizer bar until the rear wheels can just be turned by hand.
6. Release the brake and check that both wheels rotate freely and that the parking brake levers at the rear calipers stay on the stops.
7. Turn the ignition switch **ON** and check that the brake warning light comes **ON** when the parking brake is pulled to the first tooth and goes **OFF** when it is release.

### REMOVAL & INSTALLATION

#### *All Models*

1. Raise and support the rear of the car. Release the parking brake.
2. Remove the rear brake drums, models without disc brakes.
3. Disconnect the cable from the shoe assembly by pushing the spring forward and removing the cable from the adjusting arm on models without disc brakes.
4. Pull the parking brake cable out of its retaining clip on the caliper, on models with disc brakes.
5. Remove the cable compensating spring.
6. Back off the equalizer nut and guide the cable through the trailing arms and supports.
7. Installation is the reverse of removal.
8. Adjust if necessary.

**NOTE: When installing the parking brake cables on the Turbo and Quattro, the cable coupling should connect the 2 cables on the right side of the equalizer bar.**

# CHASSIS ELECTRICAL

**NOTE: Never disconnect any electrical connector with the ignition switch turn On, or damage to electronic controlling devices could occur. Before disconnecting the power on any vehicle equipped with a Delta radio, make certain the customer has recorded his personal anti-theft code and that the customer understands how to enter this code to make the radio work again.**

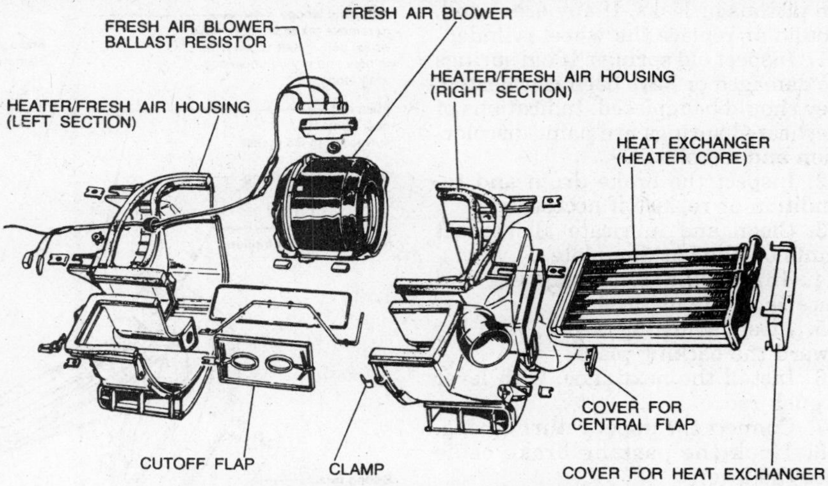

**Exploded view of the 4000 heater assembly**

## Heater Core and Blower Motor

### REMOVAL & INSTALLATION

#### *1983 All 4000 and Coupe Models*

1. Disconnect the negative battery cable.
2. Drain the engine coolant into a suitable clean container and save for re-use.
3. Trace the heater hoses coming from the firewall and disconnect them. One leads to the back of the cylinder head and the other leads to the heater valve located above and behind the oil filter.
4. Detach the cable for the heater valve.
5. Remove the center console.
6. Remove the left and right covers below the instrument panel.
7. Pull off the fresh air/heater control knobs.
8. Pull off the trim plate.
9. Remove the screws (2) for the controls.
10. Remove the center cover mounting screws (2 top and 2 bottom) and remove the cover.
11. Detach the right, left and center air ducts.
12. Remove the heater housing retaining spring.
13. Remove the cowl for the air plenum which is located under the hood and in front of the windshield.
14. Remove the heater housing mounting screws (4) and remove the heater housing. The mounting screws are under the hood where the air plenum was.
15. Remove the blower motor and the heater core from the assembly.
16. Installation is in the reverse order of removal. Be sure to replace all sealing material.

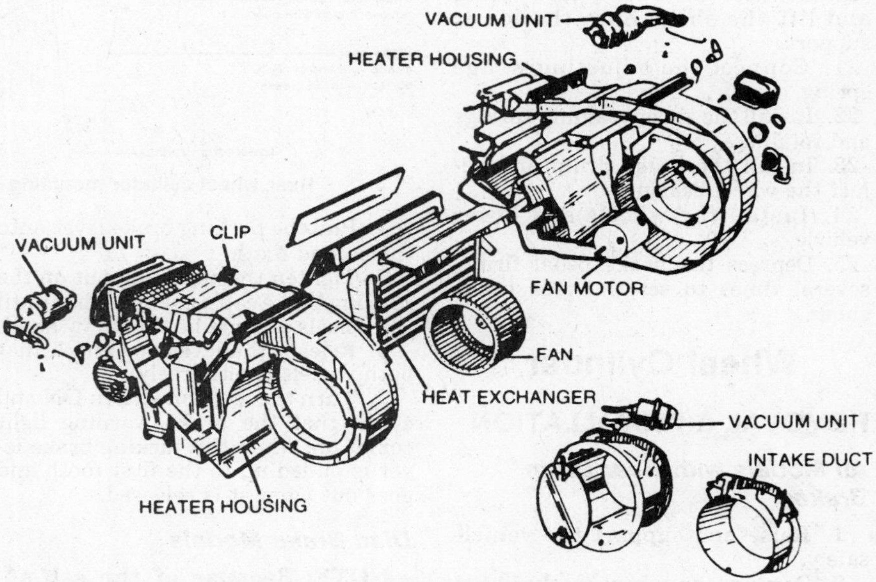

**Exploded view fo the 100, 200 and 5000 heater assembly**

#### *1983–88 5000 Models and 1989–90 100 and 200 Models*

**NOTE: Blower or core removal requires removal and disassembly of the entire unit.**

1. Disconnect the battery ground.
2. Drain the cooling system.

**CAUTION**

*If the vehicle is equipped with air conditioning, the A/C system must be discharged. Do Not attempt to discharge the freon unless familiar with air conditioning.*

3. Discharge the air conditioning system.
4. Disconnect the:
   a. Temperature sensor connector
   b. Evaporator/heater connector clamp
   c. Temperature control cable
   d. Fresh air door vacuum hose
5. Disconnect the main harness connector.
6. Loosen the case retaining strap.
7. Remove the coolant hoses at the heater core tubes.
8. Remove the yellow, green and red vacuum hoses from the heater case.
9. Remove the air duct hoses.
10. Remove the heater case mounting screws (2 in the passenger compartment, 1 in the engine compartment). On A/C equipped cars, remove the 4 evaporator housing mounting screws in the passenger compartment.
11. Support the heater/evaporator unit and pull it away from the firewall.
12. Remove the control cable grommet to facilitate case removal.
13. The case halves may be separated

by removing the clips at the top and bottom with a small pry bar.

14. Remove the blower motor and the heater core from the unit.

15. Installation is the reverse of removal. Replace all sealing material. Evacuate, charge and leak test the system.

**CAUTION**

***Freon will freeze any surface it contacts, including skin and eyeballs. It also turns into a poisonous gas in the presence of an open flame. Wear eye protection and suitable gloves when working on or around the air conditioning system.***

## Heater Blower Motor

### REMOVAL & INSTALLATION

#### *4000, Coupe, 80 and 90 Models*

1. Disconnect the negative battery cable.
2. Remove the air plenum from the cowl.
3. Remove the ballast resistor.
4. At the blower motor, disconnect the electrical connector.
5. Remove the blower mounting bolts and the blower from the heater assembly.
6. To install, reverse the removal procedures.

## Heater Core

### REMOVAL & INSTALLATION

#### *1984–89 4000, Coupe, 80 and 90 Models*

1. Disconnect the negative battery cable.
2. At the radiator, pull off the bottom hose and drain the coolant into a container for reuse.
3. Remove the heater hoses from the heat exchanger.
4. At the heater assembly control valve, disconnect the control wire.
5. Remove the console. Remove the left and the right heater covers from below the dashboard. On 80 and 90 Models, remove the instrument panel.
6. Discharge the air conditioning system and remove the refrigerant lines from the evaporator.
7. At the heater control unit, pull off the control knobs.
8. Remove the trim plate from the heater control unit.
9. At the heater control unit, remove the retaining screws and the center cover.
10. Remove the heater air ducts and the heater assembly retaining springs.
11. Remove the air plenum from the cowl and the heater assembly from the vehicle.
12. Separate the heater unit and remove the heater core.
13. Installation is the reverse order of the removal procedure.
14. Refill the cooling system and evacuate and recharge the air conditioning system if equipped.

## Radio

**NOTE: Before disconnecting the power on any vehcle equipped with a Delta radio, make certain the customer has recorded his personal anti-theft code and that the customer understands how to enter this code to make the radio work again.**

The 80, 90, 100 and 200 models use dual power antenna amplifiers and dual antenna. The front windshield antenna and amplifier for moderate strength FM signals and the rear amplifier and rear window defogger elements for AM and FM signals.

### REMOVAL & INSTALLATION

The radio is usually a dealer-installed or aftermarket unit; thus no specific removal and installation procedures can be given. The following information applies generally to all car radios.

Care should be taken during installation to avoid reversing the ground and power leads. Reversal of these leads will cause serious damage to the radio. The power lead usually has an in-line fuse.

If the speaker needs replacement, it should be replaced with the same impedance, measured in ohms. Mismatched impedance can cause rapid transistor failure as well as poor radio performance. This should also be taken into consideration when adding a second speaker.

The radio should never be operated without a speaker connected or with the speaker leads shorted. This will result in transistor failure.

## Windshield Wiper Switch

### REMOVAL & INSTALLATION

The windshield wiper switch is incorporated with the combination switch located on the steering column. On some models, if the wiper switch has to be replaced, the combination switch must be replaced.

#### *All 4000, Coupe, 80 and 90 Models*

1. Disconnect the negative battery cable. Pull off the horn pad and remove the steering wheel.
2. Remove the steering column cover. Remove the 3 screws on the turn signal switch.
3. Pull the turn signal switch and the wiper switch from the column.
4. Installation is the reverse order of the removal procedure.

#### *All 5000, 100 and 200 Models*

1. Disconnect the negative battery cable. Remove the steering wheel. Take note of safety cautions regarding vehicles with airbags.
2. Insert a suitable (Phillips head) tool into the slot at the bottom of the steering column cover and loosen the screw(s).
3. Pull the switch and the top of the cover assembly off of the steering column. Remove the 2 screws inside the cover to remove the wiper switch from the cover.
4. Installation is the reverse order of the removal procedure.

## Windshield Wiper Motor and Linkage

### REMOVAL & INSTALLATION

#### *All Models*

1. Disconnect the negative battery cable and disconnect the wiring harness connector at the motor. Pry off the wiper arms and remove the nuts from the studs in the cowl.
2. Remove the brace-to-body screws. While holding the crank, remove the nut securing the crank to the wiper motor and remove the crank.
3. Remove the bolts securing the wiper motor to the support and remove the motor.
4. Connect the new motor to the wiring harness, run the motor 2 revolutions and turn the wiper switch to the off position. The wiper motor should stop in the park position. Remove the linkage followed by the motor.
5. To install, reverse the removal procedures. Make sure that the crank is installed in the proper position.

## Instrument Cluster

### REMOVAL & INSTALLATION

#### *4000 and Coupe Models*

1. Disconnect the negative battery cable.
2. Remove the retaining screws for the instrument cluster cover. Remove the cover and the trim strip.
3. From the top of the instrument cluster, remove the 4 multipoint connectors.

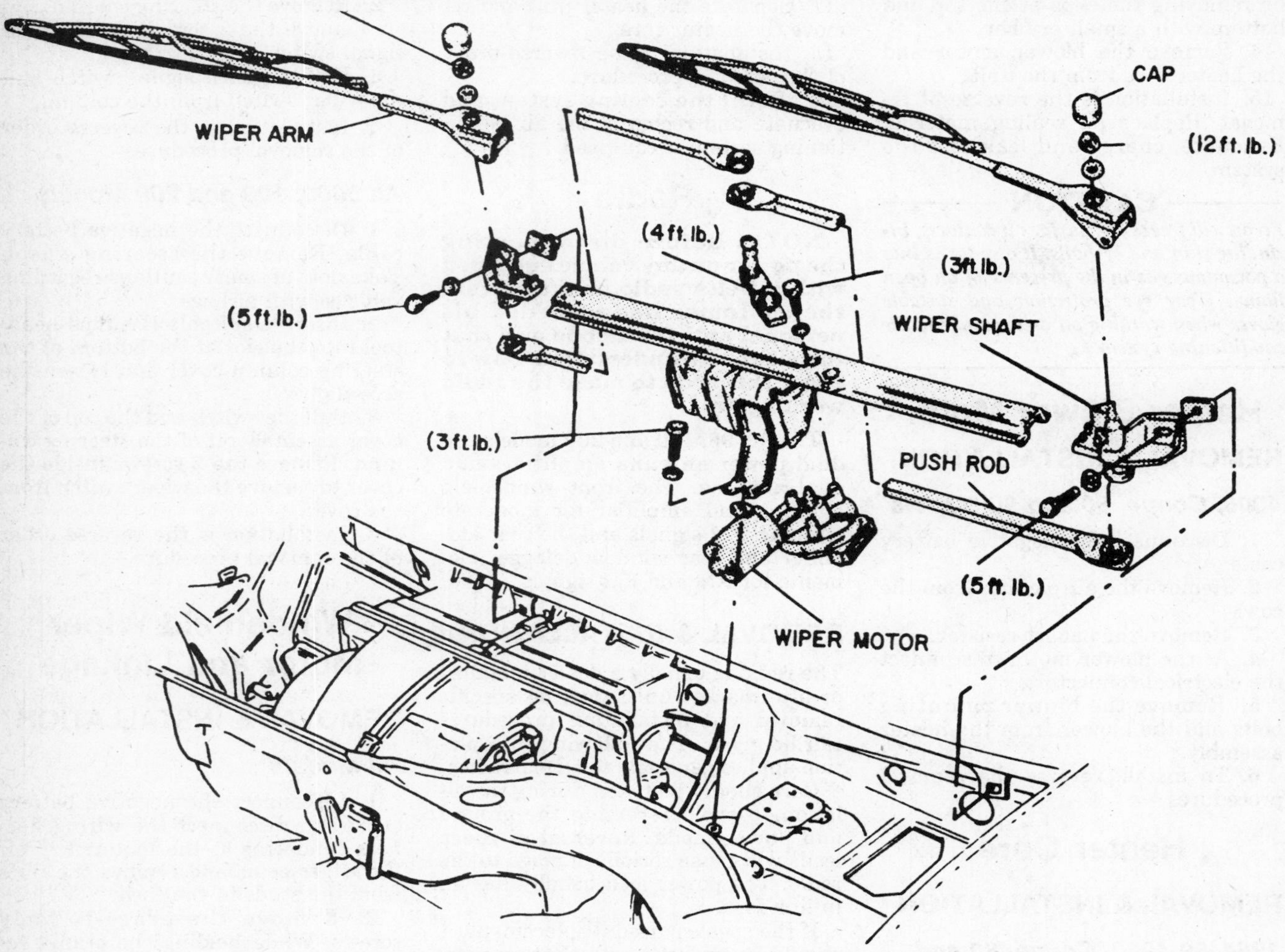


Windshield wiper assembly—5000 models—others similar

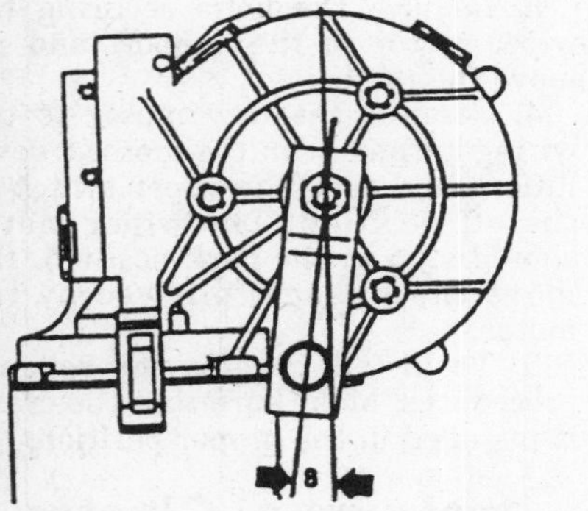


Wiper crank in the park position (at 8 degrees) for the 4000 models and the Coupe GT

4. Unscrew the speedometer cable.
5. Remove each switch panel from the side of the instrument cluster.
6. Remove the instrument cluster retaining screws and remove the cluster.
7. Installation is in the reverse order of removal.

### *1983 5000 Models*

1. Disconnect the negative battery cable.
2. Remove the instrument panel trim.
3. Remove the instrument cluster cover retaining screws and remove the cover.
4. Remove the upper portion of the cluster cover and remove the lower portion.
5. Loosen the instrument cluster retaining screws and slide it forward enough to remove the multipoint connectors and the speedometer cable.
6. Remove the cluster retaining screws and remove the cluster.
7. Installation is in the reverse order of removal.

### *1984–88 5000 Models*

1. Disconnect the negative battery cable. Pull of the the horn pad and remove the steering wheel.
2. Remove the instrument cluster attaching bolts. Disconnect the speedometer cable at the transaxle.
3. Pull out the instrument cluster and disconnect the speedometer cable at the speedometer head. Disconnect (and tag) all necessary electrical connectors and remove the instrument cluster.
4. Installation is the reverse order of the removal procedure.

### *1988–90 Models*

1. Disconnect the negative battery cable. Remove the steering wheel. Take note of safety cautions regarding vehicles with airbags.
2. Loosen the clamp on steering column switch.
3. Pull forward and remove electrical connector.
4. Remove steering column switches.
5. Tilt instrument cluster back and remove the connector retainers.
6. Remove the electrical connectors.
7. Remove the retaining screws for the instrument cluster and remove the instrument cluster.
8. Installation is in the reverse order of removal.

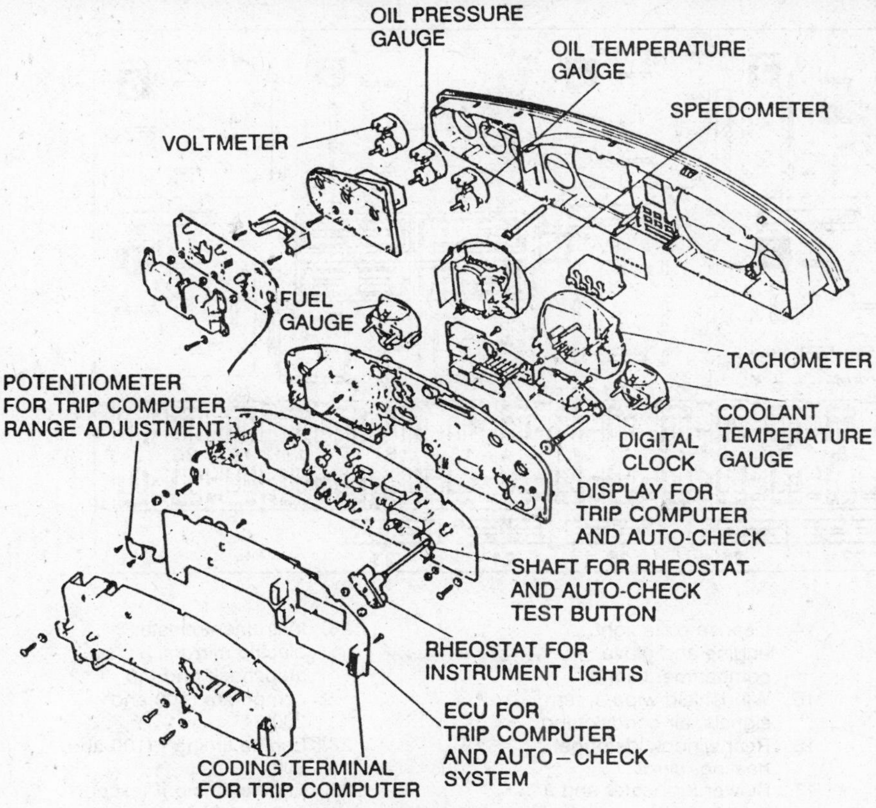


**Instrument cluster – typical**

## Headlight Switch

### REMOVAL & INSTALLATION

#### *Instrument Panel Mounted*

1. Remove the instrument cluster cover as previously outlined in this section.
2. Disconnect the wiring harness connector from the headlight switch.
3. Depress the clips on the headlight switch retainer and remove the switch from the instrument cluster.
4. Installation is the reverse order of the removal procedure.

**NOTE: On some of the later models the headlight switch could be incorporated with the combination switch. If this is the case remove the combination switch.**

#### *Steering Column Mounted*

1. Disconnect the negative battery cable.
2. Remove the steering wheel. Take note of safety cautions regarding vehicles with airbags. Remove the horn cover (pry it off by hand), remove the nut and washer securing the steering wheel and remove the steering wheel, spring and horn contact.
3. Remove the screws securing the combination switch housing through the access hole provided.
4. Pull the housing and switch assembly forward to clear the steering shaft and disconnect the wiring harness connectors. Insert a screwdriver into the slot at the bottom right of the switch housing. Loosen the screw and pull the housing off enough to unplug the electrical connectors.
5. The switches can be removed from the housing by removing the retaining screws.
6. Installation is the reverse of removal procedure.

## Stoplight Switch

### REMOVAL & INSTALLATION

#### *All Models*

1. Disconnect the negative battery cable.
2. Disconnect the stoplamp switch wire connector from the switch.
3. If the stoplight switch is located behind the brake pedal. Remove the hairpin retainer and outer nylon washer from the pedal pin. Slide the stoplamp switch off the brake pedal pin just far enough for the outer side plate of the switch to clear the pin. Remove the switch.
4. If the stoplight switch is located in the master cylinder, use a suitable wrench and remove the switch from the master cylinder.
5. Installation is the reverse order of the removal procedure. If the switch was located in the master cylinder, be sure to top off the master cylinder reservoir and bleed the brake circuit.

## Fuse Box

**NOTE: Audi recommends, disconnect the negative battery cable, before working on any part of the electrical system. Before disconnecting the power on any vehicle equipped with a Delta radio, make certain the customer has recorded his personal anti-theft code and that the customer understands how to enter this code to make the radio work again.**

### LOCATION

The fuse box for all 4000 and Coupe models can be found underneath the left side of the dashboard, behind the rear panel of the package tray or, under the left rear side of the engine compartment. The fuse box other models is located under the hood, at the rear of the engine compartment. The relays are also plugged into the fuse box. In the cover of each fuse box (and in the Owner's Manual) is a chart which tells which circuit the fuse protects and its correct amperage. The chart also tells which circuit the relays are connected to. Each model may also use in-line fuses for certain circuits; fuel pump, battery, air conditioning and power door locks (if equipped).

#### *Fuse Color Codes*

The number on the face of the fuse is the amperage rating.

1. Brown – 5-Amp
2. Red – 10-Amp
3. Blue – 15-Amp
4. Yellow – 25-Amp
5. Green – 30-Amp

#### *Auxilary Relay*

An auxilary relay panel, usually located under the leftside of the instrument panel may contain addition relays.

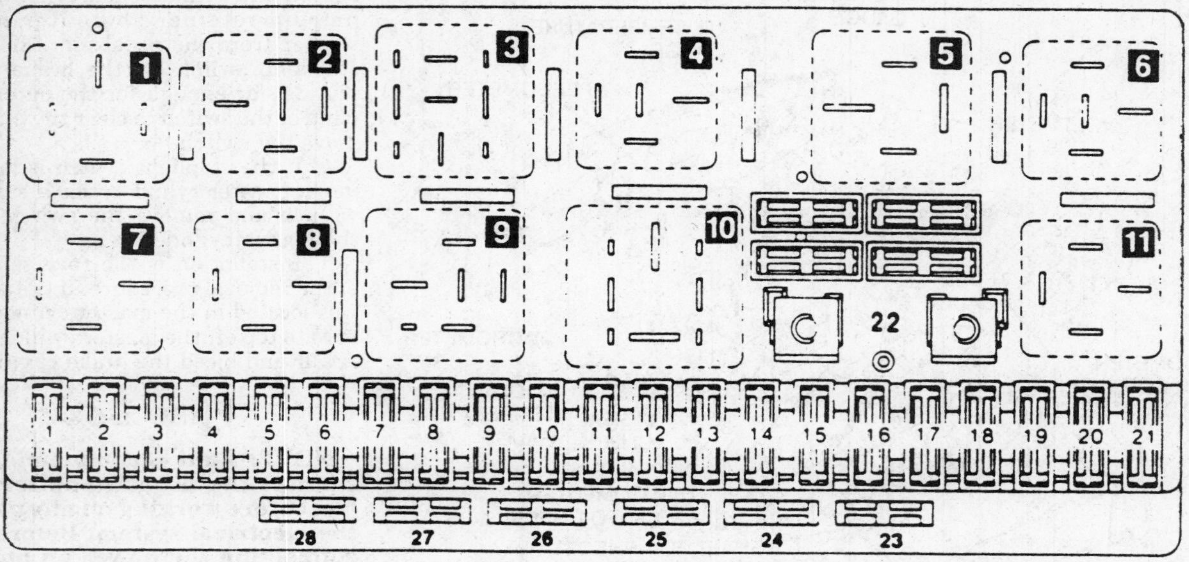


FUSE ASSIGNMENTS
1. Fog lights
2. Emergency flashers
3. Horn, brake lights
4. Clock,front cigarette lighter, interior lights, makeup mirror, radio, luggage compartment, trip computer, A/C controller
5. Radiator cooling fan
6. Side marker lights – Right
7. Side marker lights – Left
8. High beam – Right, High beam indicator light
9. High beam – Left
10. Low beam – Right
11. Low beam – Left
12. Combination instrument, backup lights, differential locks, autocheck system, cruise control, anti-lock brake, control unit cooling fan
13. Fuel pump
14. License plate light, engine and glove compartment lights
15. Windshield wipers, turn signals, air conditioning
16. Rear window defogger, heating mirror
17. Blower for heater and a/c system
18. Electric mirrors, windows or sunroof
19. Central locking system (and fuel injection – 100)
20. Radiator fan – Low speed, radiator fan delay
21. Rear cigarette lighter (except 100 and 200)
21. Diagnostic (100 and 200)
22. Not used
23. Passenger seat adjuster, memory switch controls – Driver's seat
24. Engine timing I (80 and (90)
25. Seat heating
26. Instrument cluster, electric mirrors, autocheck and trip computers (100 and 200)
27. Engine timing I (100 and 200)
28. Engine timing II (except 100 and 200)
28. Fuel injection control II (100 and 200)

RELAY ASSIGNMENTS
1. Fog Lights
2. Radiator cooling fan (stage 2)
3. Upshift system
4. Not used
5. Load reduction
6. Radiator (stage 2) or A/C blower
7. Horn
8. Auto transmission or Anti-theft
9. Intermittent wiper
10. Fuel pump relay
11. Radiator cooling (stage 1) or A/C

**Fuse and relay locations**

# BMW 3

## 318, 320, 325, 524, 525, 528, 533, 535, 633, 635, 733, 735, 750, L6, L7, M3, M5, M6—All Models

# SERIAL NUMBER IDENTIFICATION

## Vehicle Identification Plate

The manufacturer's plate is located in the engine compartment of the right side inner fender panel or support, or on the right side of the firewall.

## Engine Number

The engine number is located on the left rear side of the engine, above the starter motor.

## Vehicle Identification Number

The VIN is located on a plate on the upper left of the instrument panel, visible through the windshield.

## Chassis Number

The chassis number can be found in the engine compartment on the right inner fender support or facing forward on the right side of the heater bulkhead. A label is also attached to the upper steering column cover inside the vehicle. On 1987 models, it appears on the left/front door jamb and on all major components.

Engine serial number location

Under hood serial number location—typical

## ENGINE IDENTIFICATION

| Year | Model | Engine Displacement cu. in. (cc/liter) | Engine Series Identification | No. of Cylinders | Engine Type |
|---|---|---|---|---|---|
| 1983 | 320i | 108 (1766/1.8) | — | 4 | OHC |
| | 325e | 165 (2693/2.7) | M20B27 | 6 | OHC |
| | 528e | 165 (2693/2.7) | M20B27 | 6 | OHC |
| | 533i | 196 (3210/3.2) | M30B32 | 6 | OHC |
| | 633CSi | 196 (3210/3.2) | M30B32 | 6 | OHC |
| | 73i | 196 (3210/3.2) | M30B32 | 6 | OHC |
| 1984 | 318i | 108 (1766/1.8) | M10B18 | 4 | OHC |
| | 325e | 165(2693/2.7) | M20B27 | 6 | OHC |
| | 528e | 165(2693/2.7) | M20B27 | 6 | OHC |
| | 533i | 196 (3210/3.2) | M30B32 | 6 | OHC |
| | 633CSi | 196 (3210/3.2) | M30B32 | 6 | OHC |
| | 733i | 196 (3210/3.2) | M30B32 | 6 | OHC |
| 1985 | 318i | 108 (1766/1.8) | M10B18 | 4 | OHC |
| | 325e | 165 (2693/2.7) | M20B27 | 6 | OHC |
| | 528e | 165 (2693/2.7) | M20B27 | 6 | OHC |
| | 524td | 149 (2443/2.4) | M21D24 | 6 | OHC |
| | 533i | 196 (3210/3.2) | M30B32 | 6 | OHC |
| | 633CSi | 196 (3210/3.2) | M30B32 | 6 | OHC |
| | 733i | 196 (3210/3.2) | M30B32 | 6 | OHC |
| 1986 | 325e | 165 (2693/2.7) | M20B27 | 6 | OHC |
| | 528e | 165 (2693/2.7) | M20B27 | 6 | OHC |

## ENGINE IDENTIFICATION

| Year | Model | Engine Displacement cu. in. (cc/liter) | Engine Series Identification | No. of Cylinders | Engine Type |
|---|---|---|---|---|---|
| 1986 | 524td | 149 (2443/2.4) | M21D24 | 6 | OHC |
| | 535i | 209 (3428/3.4) | M30B34 | 6 | OHC |
| | 635CSi | 209 (3428/3.4) | M30B34 | 6 | OHC |
| | 735i | 209 (3428/3.4) | M30B34 | 6 | OHC |
| 1987 | 325 | 165 (2693/2.7) | M20B27 | 6 | OHC |
| | 325i | 152 (2494/2.5) | M20B25 | 6 | OHC |
| | 528e | 165 (2693/2.7) | M20B27 | 6 | OHC |
| | 325iS | 152 (2494/2.5) | M20B25 | 6 | OHC |
| | 535i | 209 (3428/3.4) | M30B34 | 6 | OHC |
| | 635CSi | 209 (3428/3.4) | M30B35MZ | 6 | OHC |
| | 735i | 209 (3428/3.4) | M30B35MZ | 6 | OHC |
| | M5 | 210.6 (3453/3.5) | S38Z | 6 | DOHC |
| | M6 | 210.6 (3453/3.5) | S38Z | 6 | DOHC |
| 1988 | 325 | 165 (2693/2.7) | M20B27 | 6 | OHC |
| | 528e | 165 (2693/2.7) | M20B27 | 6 | OHC |
| | 325i | 152 (2494/2.5) | M20B25 | 6 | OHC |
| | 325iS | 152 (2494/2.5) | M20B25 | 6 | OHC |
| | 325iX | 152 (2494/2.5) | M20B25 | 6 | OHC |
| | 535i | 209 (3428/3.4) | M30B34 | 6 | OHC |
| | 635CSi | 209 (3428/3.4) | M30B35MZ | 6 | OHC |
| | L6 | 209 (3428/3.4) | M30B35MZ | 6 | OHC |
| | 735i | 209 (3428/3.4) | M30B35MZ | 6 | OHC |
| | M3 | 140.4 (2302/2.3) | S14 | 4 | DOHC |
| | M5 | 210.6 (3453/3.5) | S38Z | 6 | DOHC |
| | M6 | 210.6 (3453/3.5) | S38Z | 6 | DOHC |
| | 750iL | 304.4 (4988/5.0) | M70 | 12 | DOHC |
| 1989-90 | 325 | 165 (2693/2.7) | M20B27 | 6 | OHC |
| | 325i | 152 (2494/2.5) | M20B25 | 6 | OHC |
| | 325iS | 152 (2494/2.5) | M20B25 | 6 | OHC |
| | 325iX | 152 (2494/2.5) | M20B25 | 6 | OHC |
| | 525 | 152 (2494/2.5) | M20B25 | 6 | OHC |
| | 535i | 209 (3428/3.4) | M30B34 | 6 | OHC |
| | 635CSi | 209 (3428/3.4) | M30B35MZ | 6 | OHC |
| | L6 | 209 (3428/3.4) | M30B35MZ | 6 | OHC |
| | 735i | 209 (3428/3.4) | M30B35MZ | 6 | OHC |
| | 735iL | 209 (3428/3.4) | M30B35MZ | 6 | OHC |
| | M3 | 140.4 (2302/2.3) | S14 | 4 | DOHC |
| | M5 | 210.6 (3453/3.5) | S38Z | 6 | DOHC |
| | M6 | 210.6 (3453/3.5) | S38Z | 6 | DOHC |
| | 750iL | 304.4 (4988/5.0) | M70 | 12 | DOHC |

## GENERAL ENGINE SPECIFICATIONS

| Year | Model | Engine Displacement cu. in. (cc) | Fuel System Type | Net Horsepower @ rpm | Net Torque @ rpm (ft. lbs.) | Bore × Stroke (in.) | Com-pression Ratio | Oil Pressure @ rpm |
|---|---|---|---|---|---|---|---|---|
| 1983 | 320i | 108 (1766) | EFI | 101 @ 5800 | 100 @ 4500 | 3.504 × 2.793 | 8.8:1 | 57 @ 4000 |
| | 325e | 165 (2693) | EFI | 121 @ 4250 | 170 @ 3250 | 3.307 × 3.189 | 9.0:1 | 71 @ 5000 |
| | 528e | 165 (2693) | EFI | 121 @ 4250 | 170 @ 3250 | 3.307 × 3.189 | 9.0:1 | 71 @ 5000 |
| | 533i | 196 (3210) | EFI | 181 @ 6000 | 195 @ 4000 | 3.504 × 3.386 | 8.8:1 | 64 @ 6000 |
| | 633CSi | 196 (3210) | EFI | 181 @ 6000 | 195 @ 4000 | 3.504 × 3.386 | 8.8:1 | 64 @ 6000 |
| | 733i | 196 (3210) | EFI | 181 @ 6000 | 195 @ 4000 | 3.504 × 3.386 | 8.8:1 | 64 @ 6000 |
| 1984 | 318i | 108 (1766) | EFI | 101 @ 5800 | 103 @ 4500 | 3.504 × 2.793 | 9.0:1 | 64 @ 4000 |
| | 325e | 165 (2693) | EFI | 121 @ 4250 | 170 @ 3250 | 3.307 × 3.189 | 9.0:1 | 71 @ 5000 |
| | 528e | 165 (2693) | EFI | 121 @ 4250 | 170 @ 3250 | 3.307 × 3.189 | 9.0:1 | 71 @ 5000 |
| | 533i | 196 (3210) | EFI | 181 @ 6000 | 195 @ 4000 | 3.504 × 3.386 | 8.8:1 | 64 @ 6000 |
| | 633CSi | 196 (3210) | EFI | 181 @ 6000 | 195 @ 4000 | 3.504 × 3.386 | 8.8:1 | 64 @ 6000 |
| | 733i | 196 (3210) | EFI | 181 @ 6000 | 195 @ 4000 | 3.504 × 3.386 | 8.8:1 | 64 @ 6000 |
| 1985 | 318i | 108 (1766) | EFI | 101 @ 5800 | 103 @ 4500 | 3.504 × 2.793 | 9.0:1 | 64 @ 4000 |
| | 325e | 165 (2693) | EFI | 121 @ 4250 | 170 @ 3250 | 3.307 × 3.189 | 9.0:1 | 71 @ 5000 |
| | 528e | 165 (2693) | EFI | 121 @ 4250 | 170 @ 3250 | 3.307 × 3.189 | 9.0:1 | 71 @ 5000 |
| | 524td | 149 (2443) | DFI | 114 @ 4800 | 155 @ 2400 | 3.15 × 3.19 | 22:1 | 71 @ 6000 |
| | 533i | 196 (3210) | EFI | 181 @ 6000 | 195 @ 4000 | 3.504 × 3.386 | 8.8:1 | 64 @ 6000 |
| | 633CSi | 196 (3210) | EFI | 181 @ 6000 | 195 @ 4000 | 3.504 × 3.386 | 8.8:1 | 64 @ 6000 |
| | 733i | 196 (3210) | EFI | 181 @ 6000 | 195 @ 4000 | 3.504 × 3.386 | 8.8:1 | 64 @ 6000 |
| | 535i | 209 (3428) | EFI | 182 @ 5400 | 213 @ 4000 | 3.62 × 3.38 | 8.0:1 | 71 @ 6000 |
| | 635CSi | 209 (3428) | EFI | 182 @ 5400 | 213 @ 4000 | 3.62 × 3.38 | 8.0:1 | 71 @ 6000 |
| | 735i | 209 (3428) | EFI | 182 @ 5400 | 213 @ 4000 | 3.62 × 3.38 | 8.0:1 | 71 @ 6000 |
| 1986 | 325e | 165 (2693) | EFI | 121 @ 4250 | 170 @ 3250 | 3.307 × 3.189 | 9.0:1 | 71 @ 5000 |
| | 528e | 165 (2693) | EFI | 121 @ 4250 | 170 @ 3250 | 3.307 × 3.189 | 9.0:1 | 71 @ 5000 |
| | 524td | 149 (2443) | DFI | 114 @ 4800 | 155 @ 2400 | 3.15 × 3.19 | 22:1 | 71 @ 6000 |
| | 535i | 209 (3428) | EFI | 182 @ 5400 | 213 @ 4000 | 3.62 × 3.38 | 8.0:1 | 71 @ 6000 |
| | 635CSi | 209 (3428) | EFI | 182 @ 5400 | 213 @ 4000 | 3.62 × 3.38 | 8.0:1 | 71 @ 6000 |
| | 735i | 209 (3428) | EFI | 182 @ 5400 | 213 @ 4000 | 3.62 × 3.38 | 8.0:1 | 71 @ 6000 |
| 1987 | 325 | 165 (2693) | EFI | 121 @ 4250 | 170 @ 3250 | 3.307 × 3.189 | 9.0:1 | 71 @ 5000 |
| | 528e | 165 (2693) | EFI | 121 @ 4250 | 170 @ 3250 | 3.307 × 3.189 | 9.0:1 | 71 @ 5000 |
| | 325i | 152 (2494) | EFI | 167 @ 5800 | 164 @ 4300 | 3.307 × 2.953 | 8.8:1 | 71 @ 5000 |
| | 325iS | 152 (2494) | EFI | 167 @ 5800 | 164 @ 4300 | 3.307 × 2.953 | 8.8:1 | 71 @ 5000 |
| | 535i | 209 (3428) | EFI | 182 @ 5400 | 213 @ 4000 | 3.62 × 3.38 | 8.0:1 | 71 @ 6000 |
| | 635CSi | 209 (3428) | EFI | 208 @ 5700 | 225 @ 4000 | 3.62 × 3.38 | 9.0:1 | 64 @ 6200 |
| | 735i | 209 (3428) | EFI | 208 @ 5700 | 225 @ 4000 | 3.62 × 3.38 | 9.0:1 | 64 @ 6200 |
| | M5 | 210.6 (3453) | EFI | 256 @ 6500 | 239 @ 4500 | 3.67 × 3.30 | 9.8:1 | 71 @ 6900 |
| | M6 | 210.6 (3453) | EFI | 256 @ 6500 | 239 @ 4500 | 3.67 × 3.30 | 9.8:1 | 71 @ 6900 |
| 1988 | 325 | 165 (2693) | EFI | 121 @ 4250 | 170 @ 3250 | 3.307 × 3.189 | 9.0:1 | 71 @ 5000 |
| | 528e | 165 (2693) | EFI | 121 @ 4250 | 170 @ 3250 | 3.307 × 3.189 | 9.0:1 | 71 @ 5000 |
| | 325i | 152 (2494) | EFI | 167 @ 5800 | 164 @ 4300 | 3.307 × 2.953 | 8.8:1 | 71 @ 6000 |
| | 325iS | 152 (2494) | EFI | 167 @ 5800 | 164 @ 4300 | 3.307 × 2.953 | 8.8:1 | 71 @ 6000 |

## GENERAL ENGINE SPECIFICATIONS

| Year | Model | Engine Displacement cu. in. (cc) | Fuel System Type | Net Horsepower @ rpm | Net Torque @ rpm (ft. lbs.) | Bore × Stroke (in.) | Com-pression Ratio | Oil Pressure @ rpm |
|---|---|---|---|---|---|---|---|---|
| 1988 | 325iX | 152 (2494) | EFI | 167 @ 5800 | 164 @ 4300 | 3.307 × 2.953 | 8.8:1 | 71 @ 6000 |
| | 535i | 209 (3428) | EFI | 182 @ 5400 | 213 @ 4000 | 3.62 × 3.38 | 8.0:1 | 71 @ 6100 |
| | 635CSi | 209 (3428) | EFI | 208 @ 5700 | 225 @ 4000 | 3.62 × 3.38 | 9.0:1 | 64 @ 6200 |
| | L6 | 209 (3428) | EFI | 208 @ 5700 | 225 @ 4000 | 3.62 × 3.38 | 9.0:1 | 64 @ 6200 |
| | 735i | 209 (3428) | EFI | 208 @ 5700 | 225 @ 4000 | 3.62 × 3.38 | 9.0:1 | 64 @ 6200 |
| | M3 | 104.4 (2302) | EFI | 194 @ 6750 | 166 @ 4750 | 3.67 × 3.30 | 10.5:1 | 71 @ 7250 |
| | M5 | 210.6 (3453) | EFI | 256 @ 6500 | 239 @ 4500 | 3.67 × 3.30 | 9.8:1 | 71 @ 6800 |
| | M6 | 210.6 (3453) | EFI | 256 @ 6500 | 239 @ 4500 | 3.67 × 3.30 | 9.8:1 | 71 @ 6800 |
| 1989-90 | 325 | 165 (2693) | EFI | 121 @ 4250 | 170 @ 3250 | 3.307 × 3.189 | 9.0:1 | 71 @ 5000 |
| | 325i | 152 (2494) | EFI | 167 @ 5800 | 164 @ 4300 | 3.307 × 2.953 | 8.8:1 | 71 @ 6000 |
| | 325iS | 152 (2494) | EFI | 167 @ 5800 | 164 @ 4300 | 3.307 × 2.953 | 8.8:1 | 71 @ 6000 |
| | 325iX | 152 (2494) | EFI | 167 @ 5800 | 164 @ 4300 | 3.307 × 2.953 | 8.8:1 | 71 @ 6000 |
| | 525i | 152 (2494) | EFI | 167 @ 5800 | 164 @ 4300 | 3.31 × 3.295 | 8.8:1 | 71 @ 6000 |
| | 535i | 209 (3428) | EFI | 182 @ 5400 | 213 @ 4000 | 3.62 × 3.38 | 8.0:1 | 71 @ 6100 |
| | 635CSi | 209 (3428) | EFI | 208 @ 5700 | 225 @ 4000 | 3.62 × 3.38 | 9.0:1 | 64 @ 6200 |
| | L6 | 209 (3428) | EFI | 208 @ 5700 | 225 @ 4000 | 3.62 × 3.38 | 9.0:1 | 64 @ 6200 |
| | 735i | 209 (3428) | EFI | 208 @ 5700 | 225 @ 4000 | 3.62 × 3.38 | 9.0:1 | 64 @ 6200 |
| | 735iL | 209 (3428) | EFI | 208 @ 5700 | 225 @ 4000 | 3.62 × 3.38 | 9.0:1 | 64 @ 6200 |
| | M3 | 104.4 (2302) | EFI | 194 @ 6750 | 166 @ 4750 | 3.67 × 3.30 | 10.5:1 | 71 @ 7250 |
| | M5 | 210.6 (3453) | EFI | 256 @ 6500 | 239 @ 4500 | 3.67 × 3.30 | 9.8:1 | 71 @ 6800 |
| | M6 | 210.6 (3453) | EFI | 256 @ 6500 | 239 @ 4500 | 3.67 × 3.30 | 9.8:1 | 71 @ 6800 |

EFI Electronic Fuel Injection
DFI Diesel Fuel Injection

## GASOLINE ENGINE TUNE-UP SPECIFICATIONS

| Year | Model | Engine Displacement cu. in. (cc) | Spark Plugs Type | Spark Plugs Gap (in.) | Ignition Timing (deg.) MT | Ignition Timing (deg.) AT | Com-pression Pressure (psi) | Fuel Pump (psi) | Idle Speed (rpm) MT | Idle Speed (rpm) AT | Valve Clearance In. | Valve Clearance Ex. |
|---|---|---|---|---|---|---|---|---|---|---|---|---|
| 1983 | 320i | 108 (1766) | WR9DS | 0.024 | 25B @ 2200 | 25B @ 2200 | 128 | 64-74 | 850 | 900 | 0.007 | 0.007 |
| | 325e | 165 (2693) | WR9LS | 0.024 | ① | ① | 149 | 33-38 | ① | ① | 0.010 | 0.010 |
| | 528e | 165 (2693) | WR9LS | 0.024 | ① | ① | 149 | 33-38 | ① | ① | 0.010 | 0.010 |
| | 533i | 196 (3210) | WR9LS | 0.024 | ① | ① | 149 | 35 | ① | ① | 0.012 | 0.012 |
| | 633CSi | 196 (3210) | WR9LS | 0.024 | ① | ① | 149 | 35 | ① | ① | 0.012 | 0.012 |
| | 733i | 196 (3210) | WR9LS | 0.024 | ① | ① | 149 | 35 | ① | ① | 0.012 | 0.012 |
| 1984 | 318i | 108 (1766) | WR9DS | 0.024 | ① | ① | 149 | 43 | 750 | 750 | 0.008 | 0.008 |
| | 325e | 165 (2693) | WR9LS | 0.024 | ① | ① | 149 | 33-38 | 700 | 700 | 0.010 | 0.010 |
| | 528e | 165 (2693) | WR9LS | 0.024 | ① | ① | 149 | 33-38 | 700 | 700 | 0.010 | 0.010 |
| | 533i | 196 (3210) | WR9LS | 0.024 | ① | ① | 149 | 35 | 700 | 700 | 0.012 | 0.012 |
| | 633CSi | 196 (3210) | WR9LS | 0.024 | ① | ① | 149 | 35 | 700 | 700 | 0.012 | 0.012 |
| | 733i | 196 (3210) | WR9LS | 0.024 | ① | ① | 149 | 35 | 700 | 700 | 0.012 | 0.012 |

## GASOLINE ENGINE TUNE-UP SPECIFICATIONS

| Year | Model | Engine Displacement cu. in. (cc) | Spark Plugs Type | Spark Plugs Gap (in.) | Ignition Timing (deg.) MT | Ignition Timing (deg.) AT | Com-pression Pressure (psi) | Fuel Pump (psi) | Idle Speed (rpm) MT | Idle Speed (rpm) AT | Valve Clearance In. | Valve Clearance Ex. |
|---|---|---|---|---|---|---|---|---|---|---|---|---|
| 1985 | 318i | 108 (1766) | WR9DS | 0.033 | ① | ① | 149 | 43 | 750 | 750 | 0.008 | 0.008 |
| | 325e | 165 (2693) | WR9LS | 0.029 | ① | ① | 149 | 33-38 | 700 | 700 | 0.010 | 0.010 |
| | 528e | 165 (2693) | WR9LS | 0.029 | ① | ① | 149 | 33-38 | 700 | 700 | 0.010 | 0.010 |
| | 533i | 196 (3210) | WR9LS | 0.024 | ① | ① | 149 | 35 | 700 | 700 | 0.012 | 0.012 |
| | 633CSi | 196 (3210) | WR9LS | 0.024 | ① | ① | 149 | 35 | 700 | 700 | 0.012 | 0.012 |
| | 535i | 209 (3428) | WR9LS | 0.029 | ① | ① | 149 | 43 | 800 | 800 | 0.012 | 0.012 |
| | 635CSi | 209 (3428) | WR9LS | 0.029 | ① | ① | 149 | 43 | 800 | 800 | 0.012 | 0.012 |
| | 733i | 196 (3210) | WR9LS | 0.024 | ① | ① | 149 | 35 | 700 | 700 | 0.012 | 0.012 |
| | 735i | 209 (3428) | WR9LS | 0.029 | ① | ① | 149 | 43 | 800 | 800 | 0.012 | 0.012 |
| 1986 | 325e | 165 (2693) | WR9LS | 0.029 | ① | ① | 149 | 33-38 | 700 | 700 | 0.010 | 0.010 |
| | 528e | 165 (2693) | WR9LS | 0.029 | ① | ① | 149 | 33-38 | 700 | 700 | 0.010 | 0.010 |
| | 535i | 209 (3428) | WR9LS | 0.029 | ① | ① | 149 | 43 | 800 | 800 | 0.012 | 0.012 |
| | 635CSi | 209 (3428) | WR9LS | 0.029 | ① | ① | 149 | 43 | 800 | 800 | 0.012 | 0.012 |
| | 535i | 209 (3428) | WR9LS | 0.029 | ① | ① | 149 | 43 | 800 | 800 | 0.012 | 0.012 |
| 1987 | 325 | 165 (2693) | WR9LS | 0.029 | ① | ① | 149 | 33-38 | 700 | 700 | 0.010 | 0.010 |
| | 528e | 165 (2693) | WR9LS | 0.029 | ① | ① | 149 | 33-38 | 700 | 700 | 0.010 | 0.010 |
| | 325i | 152 (2494) | W8LCR | 0.029 | ① | ① | 149 | 43 | 720 | 720 | 0.010 | 0.010 |
| | 325iS | 152 (2494) | W8LCR | 0.029 | ① | ① | 149 | 43 | 720 | 720 | 0.010 | 0.010 |
| | 535i | 209 (3428) | WR9LS | 0.029 | ① | ① | 149 | 43 | 800 | 800 | 0.012 | 0.012 |
| | 635CSi | 209 (3428) | WR9LS | 0.029 | ① | ① | 149 | 43 | 800 | 800 | 0.012 | 0.012 |
| | 735i | 209 (3428) | WR9LS | 0.029 | ① | ① | 149 | 43 | 800 | 800 | 0.012 | 0.012 |
| | M5 | 210.6 (3453) | X5DC | 0.029 | ① | ① | 149 | 43 | 800 | — | 0.013 | 0.013 |
| | M6 | 210.6 (3453) | X5DC | 0.029 | ① | ① | 149 | 43 | 800 | — | 0.013 | 0.013 |
| 1988 | 325 | 165 (2693) | WR9LS | 0.027 | ① | ① | 149 | 36 | 720 | 720 | 0.010 | 0.010 |
| | 528e | 165 (2693) | WR9LS | 0.027 | ① | ① | 149 | 36 | 720 | 720 | 0.010 | 0.010 |
| | 325i | 152 (2494) | WR9LS | 0.027 | ① | ① | 149 | 43 | 760 | 760 | 0.010 | 0.010 |
| | 325iS | 152 (2494) | WR9LS | 0.027 | ① | ① | 149 | 43 | 760 | 760 | 0.010 | 0.010 |
| | 325iX | 152 (2494) | WR9LS | 0.027 | ① | ① | 149 | 43 | 760 | 760 | 0.010 | 0.010 |
| | 535i | 209 (3428) | WR9LS | 0.027 | ① | ① | 149 | 43 | 800 | 800 | 0.012 | 0.012 |
| | 635CSi | 209 (3428) | WR9LS | 0.027 | ① | ① | 149 | 43 | 800 | 800 | 0.012 | 0.012 |
| | L6 | 209 (3428) | WR9LS | 0.027 | ① | ① | 149 | 43 | 800 | 800 | 0.012 | 0.012 |
| | M3 | 140.4 (2302) | WR9LS | 0.027 | ① | ① | 149 | 43 | — | — | 0.012 | 0.012 |
| | M5 | 210.6 (3453) | WR9LS | 0.027 | ① | ① | 149 | 43 | 850 | — | 0.013 | 0.013 |
| | M6 | 210.6 (3453) | WR9LS | 0.027 | ① | ① | 149 | 43 | 850 | — | 0.013 | 0.013 |
| | 735i | 209 (3428) | W8LCR | 0.027 | ① | ① | 149 | 43 | ① | ① | 0.012 | 0.012 |
| | 750i | 304 (4988) | F8LCR | 0.027 | ① | ① | 176 | 43 | 700 | 700 | NA | NA |
| 1989 | 325 | 165 (2693) | WR9LS | 0.027 | ① | ① | 149 | 36 | 720 | 720 | 0.010 | 0.010 |
| | 325i | 152 (2494) | WR9LS | 0.027 | ① | ① | 149 | 43 | 760 | 760 | 0.010 | 0.010 |
| | 325iS | 152 (2494) | WR9LS | 0.027 | ① | ① | 149 | 43 | 760 | 760 | 0.010 | 0.010 |
| | 325iX | 152 (2494) | WR9LS | 0.027 | ① | ① | 149 | 43 | 760 | 760 | 0.010 | 0.010 |

## GASOLINE ENGINE TUNE-UP SPECIFICATIONS

| Year | Model | Engine Displacement cu. in. (cc) | Spark Plugs Type | Spark Plugs Gap (in.) | Ignition Timing (deg.) MT | Ignition Timing (deg.) AT | Compression Pressure (psi) | Fuel Pump (psi) | Idle Speed (rpm) MT | Idle Speed (rpm) AT | Valve Clearance In. | Valve Clearance Ex. |
|---|---|---|---|---|---|---|---|---|---|---|---|---|
| 1989-90 | 525i | 152 (2494) | WR9LS | 0.027 | ① | ① | 149 | 43 | 760 | 760 | 0.010 | 0.010 |
| | 535i | 209 (3428) | WR9LS | 0.027 | ① | ① | 149 | 43 | 800 | 800 | 0.012 | 0.012 |
| | 635CSi | 209 (3428) | WR9LS | 0.027 | ① | ① | 149 | 43 | 800 | 800 | 0.012 | 0.012 |
| | L6 | 209 (3428) | WR9LS | 0.027 | ① | ① | 149 | 43 | 800 | 800 | 0.012 | 0.012 |
| | M3 | 140.4 (2302) | WR9LS | 0.027 | ① | ① | 149 | 43 | – | – | 0.012 | 0.012 |
| | M5 | 210.6 (3453) | WR9LS | 0.027 | ① | ① | 149 | 43 | 850 | – | 0.013 | 0.013 |
| | M6 | 210.6 (3453) | WR9LS | 0.027 | ① | ① | 149 | 43 | 850 | – | 0.013 | 0.013 |
| | 735i | 209 (3428) | W8LCR | 0.027 | ① | ① | 149 | 43 | ① | ① | 0.012 | 0.012 |
| | 735iL | 209 (3428) | W8LCR | 0.027 | ① | ① | 149 | 43 | ① | ① | 0.012 | 0.012 |
| | 750iL | 304 (4988) | F8LCR | 0.027 | ① | ① | 176 | 43 | 700 | 700 | NA | NA |
| 1990 | All SEE UNDERHOOD SPECIFICATIONS | | | | | | | | | | | |

**NOTE:** The underhood specifications sticker often reflects tune-up specification changes made in production. Sticker figures must be used if they disagree with those in this chart.

NA Not available

B Before Top Dead Center

① Motronic injection system—controlled by computer, please refer to the underhood sticker for specifications

## DIESEL ENGINE TUNE-UP SPECIFICATIONS

| Year | Engine Displacement cu. in. (cc) | Valve Clearance Intake (in.) | Valve Clearance Exhaust (in.) | Intake Valve Opens (deg.) | Injection Pump Setting (deg.) | Injection Nozzle Pressure (psi) New | Injection Nozzle Pressure (psi) Used | Idle Speed (rpm) | Cranking Compression Pressure (psi) |
|---|---|---|---|---|---|---|---|---|---|
| 1985 | 149 (2443) | 0.012 | 0.012 | NA | 3.5B | 2133–2470 | 1920 | 750 | 284 |
| 1986 | 149 (2443) | 0.012 | 0.012 | NA | 3.5B | 2133–2247 | 1920 | 750 | 284 |

B Before Top Dead Center

NA Not available

## FIRING ORDERS

**NOTE: To avoid confusion, always replace spark plug wires one at a time.**

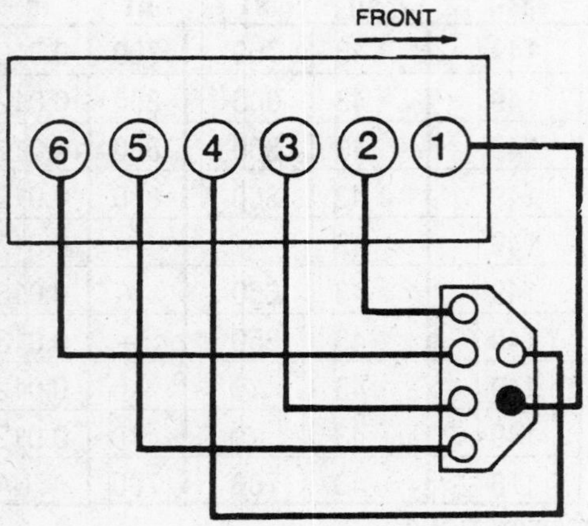


**325, 325e, 325i, 528e, 533i, 535i, M5, and 1982 and later 633CSi, 635CSi, M6, and 733i, 735i**
**Firing order: 1–5–3–6–2–4**

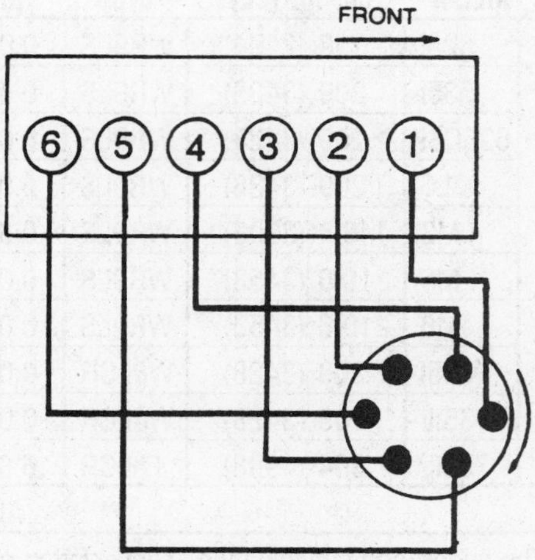


**528i, 1981 633CSi and 733i**
**Firing order: 1–5–3–6–2–4**

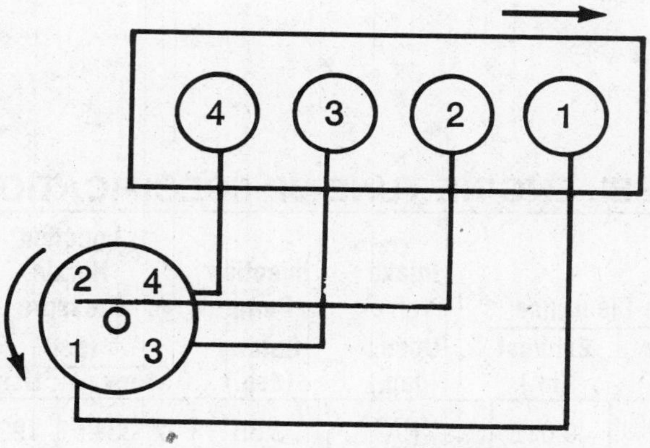


**320i, 318i firing order: 1-3-4-2**

## CAPACITIES

| Year | Model | Engine Displacement cu. in. (cc) | Engine Crankcase with Filter | Engine Crankcase without Filter | Transmission (pts.) 4-Spd | Transmission (pts.) 5-Spd | Transmission (pts.) Auto. | Drive Axle (pts.) | Fuel Tank (gal.) | Cooling System (qts.) |
|---|---|---|---|---|---|---|---|---|---|---|
| 1983 | 320i | 108 (1766) | 4.5① | 4.25② | 2.2 | — | 4.2 | 1.9 | 15.3 | 7.4 |
| | 528e | 165 (2693) | 4.5 | 4.2 | — | 3.4 | 4.2 | 3.8 | 16.6 | 12.7 |
| | 533i | 196 (3210) | 6.0 | 5.3 | — | 2.65 | 6.3 | 3.6 | 16.6 | 12.7 |
| | 633CSi | 196 (3210) | 6.0 | 5.25 | 2.4 | — | 4.2 | 3.2 | 16.5 | 12.7 |
| | 733i | 196 (3210) | 6.0 | 5.25 | — | 2.4 | 4.0 | 3.8 | 22.5 | 12.7 |

## CAPACITIES

| Year | Model | Engine Displacement cu. in. (cc) | Engine Crankcase with Filter | Engine Crankcase without Filter | Transmission (pts.) 4-Spd | Transmission (pts.) 5-Spd | Transmission (pts.) Auto. | Drive Axle (pts.) | Fuel Tank (gal.) | Cooling System (qts.) |
|---|---|---|---|---|---|---|---|---|---|---|
| 1984 | 318i | 108 (1766) | 4.5 | 4.2 | — | 2.4 | 6.3 | 1.9 | 14.5 | 7.4 |
| | 528e | 165 (2693) | 4.5 | 4.2 | — | 3.4 | 4.2 | 3.8 | 16.6 | 12.7 |
| | 533i | 196 (3210) | 6.0 | 5.3 | — | 2.65 | 6.3 | 3.6 | 16.6 | 12.7 |
| | 633CSi | 196 (3210) | 6.0 | 5.25 | 2.4 | — | 4.2 | 3.2 | 16.5 | 12.7 |
| | 733i | 196 (3210) | 6.0 | 5.25 | — | 2.4 | 4.0 | 3.8 | 22.5 | 12.7 |
| 1985 | 318i | 108 (1766) | 4.5 | 4.2 | — | 2.4 | 6.3 | 1.9 | 14.5 | 7.4 |
| | 325e | 165 (2693) | 4.5 | 4.2 | — | 2.4 | 6.3 | 3.4 | 14.5 | 7.4 |
| | 325es | 165 (2693) | 4.5 | 4.2 | — | 2.4 | 6.3 | 3.4 | 14.5 | 7.4 |
| | 528e | 165 (2693) | 4.5 | 4.2 | — | 3.4 | 4.2 | 3.8 | 16.6 | 12.7 |
| | 524td | 149 (2443) | 6.1 | 5.3 | — | 3.4 | 6.4 | 4.0 | 16.6 | 12.7 |
| | 535i | 209 (3428) | 6.1 | 5.3 | — | 3.4 | 6.4 | 4.0 | 16.6 | 12.7 |
| | 635CSi | 209 (3428) | 6.1 | 5.3 | — | 3.4 | 6.4 | 4.0 | 16.6 | 12.7 |
| | 735i | 209 (3428) | 6.1 | 5.3 | — | 3.4 | 6.4 | 4.0 | 22.5 | 12.7 |
| 1986 | 325e | 165 (2693) | 4.5 | 4.2 | — | 2.4 | 6.3 | 3.4 | 14.5 | 7.4 |
| | 325es | 165 (2693) | 4.5 | 4.2 | — | 2.4 | 6.3 | 3.4 | 14.5 | 7.4 |
| | 524td | 149 (2443) | 6.1 | 5.3 | — | 3.4 | 6.4 | 4.0 | 16.6 | 12.7 |
| | 528e | 165 (2693) | 4.5 | 4.2 | — | 3.4 | 4.2 | 3.8 | 16.6 | 12.7 |
| | 535i | 209 (3428) | 6.1 | 5.3 | — | 3.4 | 6.4 | 4.0 | 16.6 | 12.7 |
| | 635CSi | 209 (3428) | 6.1 | 5.3 | — | 3.4 | 6.4 | 4.0 | 16.6 | 12.7 |
| | 735i | 209 (3428) | 6.1 | 5.3 | — | 3.4 | 6.4 | 4.0 | 22.5 | 12.7 |
| 1987 | 325 | 165 (2693) | 4.5 | 4.2 | — | 2.6 | 6.4 | 3.6 | 15.3 | 12.7 |
| | 528e | 165 (2693) | 4.5 | 4.2 | — | 3.4 | 6.4 | 3.8 | 16.6 | 11.6 |
| | 535i | 209 (3428) | 6.1 | 5.3 | — | 3.4 | 6.4 | 4.0 | 16.6 | 12.7 |
| | 635CSi | 209 (3428) | 6.1 | 5.3 | — | 3.4 | 6.4 | 4.0 | 16.6 | 12.7 |
| | 735i | 209 (3428) | 6.1 | 5.3 | — | 3.4 | 6.4 | 3.6 | 21.4 | 12.7 |
| | M5 | 210.6 (3453) | 6.1 | 5.3 | — | 2.6 | 6.4 | 4.0 | 16.6 | 12.7 |
| | M6 | 210.6 (3453) | 6.1 | 5.3 | — | 2.6 | 6.4 | 4.0 | 16.6 | 12.7 |
| 1988 | 325 | 165 (2693) | 4.5 | 4.2 | — | 2.6 | 6.4 | 3.6 | 16.4 | 11.6 |
| | 325i | 152 (2494) | 5.0 | 4.75 | — | 2.6 | 6.4③ | 3.6④ | 16.4 | 11.0 |
| | 325iS | 152 (2494) | 5.0 | 4.75 | — | 2.6 | 6.4③ | 3.6④ | 16.4 | 11.0 |
| | 325iX | 152 (2494) | 5.0 | 4.75 | — | 2.6 | 6.4③ | 3.6④ | 16.4 | 11.0 |
| | 528e | 165 (2693) | 4.5 | 4.2 | — | 3.4 | 6.4 | 3.8 | 16.6 | 11.6 |
| | 535i | 209 (3428) | 6.1 | 5.3 | — | 2.6 | 6.4 | 4.0 | 16.6 | 11.6 |
| | 535iS | 209 (3428) | 6.1 | 5.3 | — | 2.6 | 6.4 | 4.0 | 16.6 | 12.7 |
| | 635CSi | 209 (3428) | 6.1 | 5.3 | — | 3.4 | 6.4 | 4.0 | 16.6 | 12.7 |
| | L6 | 209 (3428) | 6.1 | 5.3 | — | 3.4 | 6.4 | 4.0 | 16.6 | 12.7 |
| | 735i | 209 (3428) | 6.1 | 5.3 | — | 2.6 | 6.4 | 4.0 | 21.4 | 12.7 |
| | M3 | 104.4 (2302) | 5.0 | 4.75 | — | 2.6 | 6.4 | 3.6 | 16.4 | NA |
| | M5 | 210.6 (3453) | 6.1 | 5.3 | — | 2.6 | 6.4 | 4.0 | 16.6 | 12.7 |

## CAPACITIES

| Year | Model | Engine Displacement cu. in. (cc) | Engine Crankcase with Filter | Engine Crankcase without Filter | Transmission (pts.) 4-Spd | Transmission (pts.) 5-Spd | Transmission (pts.) Auto. | Drive Axle (pts.) | Fuel Tank (gal.) | Cooling System (qts.) |
|---|---|---|---|---|---|---|---|---|---|---|
| 1988 | M6 | 210.6 (3453) | 6.1 | 5.3 | — | 2.6 | 6.4 | 4.0 | 16.6 | 12.7 |
| | 750iL | 304 (4988) | 7.9 | 6.8 | — | 2.6 | 6.4 | 4.0 | 21.4 | 12.7 |
| 1989-90 | 325 | 165 (2693) | 4.5 | 4.2 | — | 2.6 | 6.4 | 3.6 | 16.4 | 11.6 |
| | 325i | 152 (2494) | 5.0 | 4.75 | — | 2.6 | 6.4③ | 3.6④ | 16.4 | 11.0 |
| | 325iS | 152 (2494) | 5.0 | 4.75 | — | 2.6 | 6.4③ | 3.6④ | 16.4 | 11.0 |
| | 325iX | 152 (2494) | 5.0 | 4.75 | — | 2.6 | 6.4③ | 3.6④ | 16.4 | 11.0 |
| | 525i | 152 (2494) | 5.0 | 4.75 | — | 2.6 | 6.4 | 3.6 | 16.4 | 11.0 |
| | 535i | 209 (3428) | 6.1 | 5.3 | — | 2.6 | 6.4 | 4.0 | 16.6 | 11.6 |
| | 535iS | 209 (3428) | 6.1 | 5.3 | — | 2.6 | 6.4 | 4.0 | 16.6 | 12.7 |
| | 635CSi | 209 (3428) | 6.1 | 5.3 | — | 3.4 | 6.4 | 4.0 | 16.6 | 12.7 |
| | L6 | 209 (3428) | 6.1 | 5.3 | — | 3.4 | 6.4 | 4.0 | 16.6 | 12.7 |
| | 735i | 209 (3428) | 6.1 | 5.3 | — | 2.6 | 6.4 | 4.0 | 21.4 | 12.7 |
| | 735iL | 209 (3428) | 6.1 | 5.3 | — | 2.6 | 6.4 | 4.0 | 21.4 | 12.7 |
| | M3 | 104.4 (2302) | 5.0 | 4.75 | — | 2.6 | 6.4 | 3.6 | 16.4 | NA |
| | M5 | 210.6 (3453) | 6.1 | 5.3 | — | 2.6 | 6.4 | 4.0 | 16.6 | 12.7 |
| | M6 | 210.6 (3453) | 6.1 | 5.3 | — | 2.6 | 6.4 | 4.0 | 16.6 | 12.7 |
| | 750iL | 304 (4988) | 7.9 | 6.8 | — | 2.6 | 6.4 | 4.0 | 21.4 | 12.7 |

NA Not available

① With chrome plated guide tube for dipstick—4.25

② With chrome plated guide tube for disptick—4.0

③ 325iX Transfer case—1.1

④ 325iX Front drive axle—1.5

## CRANKSHAFT AND CONNECTING ROD SPECIFICATIONS

All measurements are given in inches.

| Year | Engine Displacement cu. in. (cc) | Crankshaft Main Brg. Journal Dia. | Crankshaft Main Brg. Oil Clearance | Crankshaft Shaft End-play | Crankshaft Thrust on No. | Connecting Rod Journal Diameter | Connecting Rod Oil Clearance | Connecting Rod Side Clearance |
|---|---|---|---|---|---|---|---|---|
| 1983 | 108 (1766) | 2.3622 | 0.0012–0.0027 | 0.003–0.007 | 3 | 1.8898 | 0.0012–0.0028 | 0.0016 |
| | 165 (2693) | 2.3622 | 0.0012–0.0027 | 0.003–0.007 | 4 | 1.7717 | 0.0012–0.0028 | 0.0016 |
| | 196 (3210) | 2.3622 | 0.0012–0.0027 | 0.003–0.007 | 4 | 1.8898 | 0.0012–0.0028 | 0.0016 |
| 1984 | 108 (1766) | 2.1654 | 0.0012–0.0027 | 0.003–0.007 | 3 | 1.8898 | 0.0012–0.0028 | 0.0016 |
| | 165 (2693) | 2.3622 | 0.0012–0.0027 | 0.003–0.007 | 4 | 1.7717 | 0.0012–0.0028 | 0.0016 |
| | 196 (3210) | 2.3622 | 0.0012–0.0027 | 0.003–0.007 | 4 | 1.8898 | 0.0012–0.0028 | 0.0016 |
| 1985 | 108 (1766) | 2.1654 | 0.0012–0.0027 | 0.003–0.007 | 3 | 1.8898 | 0.0012–0.0028 | 0.0016 |
| | 149 (2443) | ② | 0.0008–0.0018 | 0.0031–0.0064 | 4 | 1.7707–1.7713 | 0.0008–0.0022 | — |

## CRANKSHAFT AND CONNECTING ROD SPECIFICATIONS

All measurements are given in inches.

| Year | Engine Displacement cu. in. (cc) | Crankshaft Main Brg. Journal Dia. | Crankshaft Main Brg. Oil Clearance | Crankshaft Shaft End-play | Crankshaft Thrust on No. | Connecting Rod Journal Diameter | Connecting Rod Oil Clearance | Connecting Rod Side Clearance |
|---|---|---|---|---|---|---|---|---|
| 1985 | 165 (2693) | 2.3622 | 0.0012–0.0027 | 0.003–0.007 | 4 | 1.7717 | 0.0012–0.0028 | 0.0016 |
| | 209 (3428) | 2.3622 | 0.0012–0.0027 | 0.003–0.007 | 4 | 1.8898 | 0.0012–0.0028 | 0.0016 |
| 1986 | 149 (2443) | ② | 0.0008–0.0018 | 0.0031–0.0064 | 4 | 1.7707–1.7713 | 0.0008–0.0022 | 0.0016 |
| | 165 (2693) | 2.3622 | 0.0012–0.0027 | 0.003–0.007 | 4 | 1.7717 | 0.0012–0.0028 | 0.0016 |
| | 209 (3428) | 2.3622 | 0.0012–0.0027 | 0.003–0.007 | 4 | 1.8898 | 0.0012–0.0028 | 0.0016 |
| 1987 | 152 (2494) | 2.3622 | 0.0012–0.0027 | 0.030–0.007 | 4 | 1.7717 | 0.0012–0.0028 | 0.0016 |
| | 165 (2693) | 2.3622 | 0.0012–0.0027 | 0.003–0.007 | 4 | 1.7717 | 0.0012–0.0028 | 0.0016 |
| | 209 (3428) | 2.3622 | 0.0012–0.0027 | 0.003–0.007 | 4 | 1.8898 | 0.0012–0.0028 | 0.0016 |
| | 210.6 (3453) | 2.3622 | 0.0012–0.0027 | 0.003–0.007 | 4 | 1.88877–1.88940 | 0.0012–0.0028 | 0.0016 |
| 1988 | 140.4 (2302) | 2.1653 | 0.0012–0.0028 | 0.0033–0.0068 | 3 | 1.88877–1.88940 | 0.0012–0.0028 | 0.0016 |
| | 152 (2494) | 2.3622 | 0.0012–0.0027 | 0.0033–0.0068 | 4 | 1.7717 | 0.0012–0.0028 | 0.0016 |
| | 165 (2693) | 2.3622 | 0.0012–0.0027 | 0.0033–0.0068 | 4 | 1.7717 | 0.0012–0.0028 | 0.0016 |
| | 209 (3428) | 2.3622 | 0.0012–0.0027 | 0.0033–0.0068 | 4 | 1.8898 | 0.0012–0.0028 | 0.0016 |
| | 210.6 (3453) | 2.3622 | 0.0012–0.0027 | 0.0033–0.0068 | 4 | 1.88877–1.88940 | 0.0012–0.0028 | 0.0016 |
| | 304 (4988) | 2.9521–2.9523 | 0.0010–0.0030 | 0.0033–0.0068 | — | 1.7707–1.7713 | 0.0006–0.0023 | 0.0016 |
| 1989-90 | 140.4 (2302) | 2.1653 | 0.0012–0.0028 | 0.0033–0.0068 | 3 | 1.88877–1.88940 | 0.0012–0.0028 | 0.0016 |
| | 152 (2494) | 2.3622 | 0.0012–0.0027 | 0.0033–0.0068 | 4 | 1.7717 | 0.0012–0.0028 | 0.0016 |
| | 165 (2693) | 2.3622 | 0.0012–0.0027 | 0.0033–0.0068 | 4 | 1.7717 | 0.0012–0.0028 | 0.0016 |
| | 209 (3428) | 2.3622 | 0.0012–0.0027 | 0.0033–0.0068 | 4 | 1.8898 | 0.0012–0.0028 | 0.0016 |
| | 210.6 (3453) | 2.3622 | 0.0012–0.0027 | 0.0033–0.0068 | 4 | 1.88877–1.88940 | 0.0012–0.0028 | 0.0016 |

## CRANKSHAFT AND CONNECTING ROD SPECIFICATIONS

All measurements are given in inches.

| Year | Engine Displacement cu. in. (cc) | Crankshaft Main Brg. Journal Dia. | Crankshaft Main Brg. Oil Clearance | Crankshaft Shaft End-play | Crankshaft Thrust on No. | Connecting Rod Journal Diameter | Connecting Rod Oil Clearance | Connecting Rod Side Clearance |
|---|---|---|---|---|---|---|---|---|
| 1989-90 | 304 (4988) | 2.9521–2.9523 | 0.0010–0.0030 | 0.0033–0.0068 | — | 1.7707–1.7713 | 0.0006–0.0023 | 0.0016 |

**NOTE:** BMW does not specify side clearance. The figure given expresses maximum permissible deviation from parallel of connecting rod bearing bores, with the shells 150mm or 5.905 in. apart

① 528i, 530i, 533i, 630CSi – 0.0009–0.0027
320i, 733i – 0.0009–0.0031
528e – 0.0013–0.0027

② Yellow – 2.3616–2.3618
Green – 2.3613–2.3615
White – 2.3611–2.3613

## VALVE SPECIFICATIONS

| Year | Engine Displacement cu. in. (cc) | Seat Angle (deg.) | Face Angle (deg.) | Spring Test Pressure (lbs.) | Spring Installed Height (in.) | Stem-to-Guide Clearance (in.) Intake | Stem-to-Guide Clearance (in.) Exhaust | Stem Diameter (in.) Intake | Stem Diameter (in.) Exhaust |
|---|---|---|---|---|---|---|---|---|---|
| 1983 | 108 (1766) | 45 | 45.5 | 64 @1.48 | 1.71① | 0.0010–0.0020 ② | 0.0010–0.0020 ② | 0.3149 | 0.3149 |
| | 165 (2693) | 45 | 45 | NA | NA | 0.031③ | 0.031③ | 0.3149 | 0.3149 |
| | 196 (3210) | 45 | 45.5 | 64 @ 1.48 | 1.71① | 0.031③ | 0.031③ | 0.3149 | 0.3149 |
| 1984 | 108 (1766) | 45 | 45.5 | 64 @ 1.48 | 1.71① | 0.031③ | 0.031③ | 0.3149 | 0.3149 |
| | 165 (2693) | 45 | 45 | NA | NA | 0.031③ | 0.031③ | 0.275 | 0.275 |
| | 196 (3210) | 45 | 45.5 | 64 @ 1.48 | 1.71① | 0.031③ | 0.031③ | 0.3149 | 0.3149 |
| 1985 | 108 (1766) | 45 | 45.5 | 64 @ 1.48 | 1.71① | 0.031③ | 0.031③ | 0.3149 | 0.3149 |
| | 149 (2443) | 45 | NA | NA | NA | 0.031③ | 0.031③ | 0.275 | 0.275 |
| | 165 (2693) | 45 | 45 | NA | NA | 0.031③ | 0.031③ | 0.275 | 0.275 |
| | 209 (3248) | 45 | 45.5 | 64 @ 1.48 | 1.71① | 0.031③ | 0.031③ | 0.3149 | 0.3149 |
| 1986 | 149 (2443) | 45 | NA | NA | NA | 0.031③ | 0.031③ | 0.275 | 0.275 |
| | 165 (2693) | 45 | 45 | NA | NA | 0.031③ | 0.031③ | 0.275 | 0.275 |
| | 209 (3248) | 45 | 45.5 | 64 @ 1.48 | 1.71① | 0.031③ | 0.031③ | 0.3149 | 0.3149 |
| 1987 | 152 (2494) | 45 | 45.5 | 64 @ 1.48 | 1.71① | 0.031③ | 0.031③ | 0.3149 | 0.3149 |
| | 165 (2693) | 45 | 45 | NA | NA | 0.031③ | 0.031③ | 0.275 | 0.275 |
| | 209 (3428) | 45 | 45.5 | 64 @ 1.48 | 1.71① | 0.031③ | 0.031③ | 0.3149 | 0.3149 |
| | 210.6 (3453) | 45 | NA | NA | NA | 0.025③ | 0.031③ | 0.276 | 0.276 |
| 1988 | 140.4 (2302) | 45 | NA | NA | NA | 0.025③ | 0.031③ | 0.276 | 0.276 |
| | 152 (2494) | 45 | NA | NA | NA | 0.031③ | 0.031③ | 0.275 | 0.275 |
| | 165 (2693) | 45 | NA | NA | NA | 0.031③ | 0.031③ | 0.275 | 0.275 |
| | 209 (3248) | 45 | NA | NA | NA | 0.031③ | 0.031③ | 0.315 | 0.315 |
| | 210.6 (3453) | 45 | NA | NA | NA | 0.025③ | 0.031③ | 0.276 | 0.276 |
| | 304 (4988) | 45 | NA | NA | NA | 0.020③ | 0.020③ | 0.275 | 0.275 |

## VALVE SPECIFICATIONS

| Year | Engine Displacement cu. in. (cc) | Seat Angle (deg.) | Face Angle (deg.) | Spring Test Pressure (lbs.) | Spring Installed Height (in.) | Stem-to-Guide Clearance (in.) | | Stem Diameter (in.) | |
|---|---|---|---|---|---|---|---|---|---|
| | | | | | | Intake | Exhaust | Intake | Exhaust |
| 1989-90 | 140.4 (2302) | 45 | NA | NA | NA | 0.025③ | 0.031③ | 0.276 | 0.276 |
| | 152 (2494) | 45 | NA | NA | NA | 0.031③ | 0.031③ | 0.275 | 0.275 |
| | 165 (2693) | 45 | NA | NA | NA | 0.031③ | 0.031③ | 0.275 | 0.275 |
| | 209 (3248) | 45 | NA | NA | NA | 0.031③ | 0.031③ | 0.315 | 0.315 |
| | 210.6 (3453) | 45 | NA | NA | NA | 0.025③ | 0.031③ | 0.276 | 0.276 |
| | 304 (4988) | 45 | NA | NA | NA | 0.020③ | 0.020③ | 0.275 | 0.275 |

① A dimension of 1.8110 applies to some springs, depending upon manufacturer. Figure given is free height

② Wear limit: .006 in.

③ Tilt clearance

## PISTON AND RING SPECIFICATIONS

All measurments are given in inches.

| Year | Engine Displacement cu. in. (cc) | Piston Clearance | Ring Gap Top Compression | Ring Gap Bottom Compression | Ring Gap Oil Control | Ring Side Clearance Top Compression | Ring Side Clearance Bottom Compression | Ring Side Clearance Oil Control |
|---|---|---|---|---|---|---|---|---|
| 1983 | 108 (1766) | 0.0018 | 0.0120–0.0180 | 0.0080–0.0160 | 0.0100–0.0200 | 0.002–0.004 | 0.002–0.003 | 0.001–0.002 |
| | 165 (2693) | 0.0004–0.0016 | 0.0120–0.0200 | 0.0120–0.0200 | 0.0100–0.0200 | 0.0016–0.0028 | 0.0012–0.0024 | 0.0008–0.0017 |
| | 196 (3210) | 0.0008–0.0020 | 0.0120–0.0280 | 0.0080–0.0160 | 0.0100–0.0200 | 0.0020–0.0032 | 0.0016–0.0028 | 0.0008–0.0028 |
| 1984 | 108 (1766) | 0.0008–0.0020 | 0.0120–0.0280 | 0.0080–0.0160 | 0.0100–0.0200 | 0.0024–0.0035 | 0.0012–0.0028 | 0.0008–0.0024 |
| | 165 (2693) | 0.0004–0.0016 | 0.0120–0.0200 | 0.0120–0.0200 | 0.0100–0.0200 | 0.0016–0.0028 | 0.0012–0.0024 | 0.0008–0.0017 |
| | 196 (3210) | 0.0008–0.0020 | 0.0120–0.0280 | 0.0080–0.0160 | 0.0100–0.0200 | 0.0020–0.0032 | 0.0016–0.0028 | 0.0008–0.0028 |
| 1985 | 108 (1766) | 0.0008–0.0020 | 0.0120–0.0280 | 0.0080–0.0160 | 0.0100–0.0200 | 0.0024–0.0035 | 0.0012–0.0028 | 0.0008–0.0024 |
| | 149 (2443) | 0.0010–0.0013 | 0.0008–0.0016 | 0.0080–0.0160 | 0.0100–0.0200 | 0.0024–0.0025 | 0.0020–0.0031 | 0.0012–0.0024 |
| | 165 (2693) | 0.0004–0.0016 | 0.0120–0.0200 | 0.0120–0.0200 | 0.0100–0.0200 | 0.0016–0.0028 | 0.0012–0.0024 | 0.0008–0.0017 |
| | 209 (3428) | 0.0008–0.0020 | 0.0120–0.0020 | 0.0080–0.0160 | 0.0100–0.0200 | 0.020–0.032 | 0.0016–0.0028 | 0.0008–0.0020 |
| 1986 | 149 (2443) | 0.0008–0.0020 | 0.0120–0.0200 | 0.0080–0.0160 | 0.0100–0.0200 | 0.020–0.032 | 0.0016–0.0028 | 0.0008–0.0020 |
| | 165 (2693) | 0.0004–0.0016 | 0.0120–0.0200 | 0.0120–0.0200 | 0.0100–0.0200 | 0.0016–0.0028 | 0.0012–0.0024 | 0.0008–0.0017 |
| | 209 (3428) | 0.0008–0.0020 | 0.0120–0.0020 | 0.0080–0.0160 | 0.0100–0.0200 | 0.020–0.032 | 0.0016–0.0028 | 0.0008–0.0020 |
| 1987 | 152 (2494) | 0.0004–0.0016 | 0.0120–0.0200 | 0.0120–0.0200 | 0.0100–0.0200 | 0.0016–0.0028 | 0.0012–0.0024 | 0.0008–0.0017 |

## PISTON AND RING SPECIFICATIONS

All measurments are given in inches.

| Year | Engine Displacement cu. in. (cc) | Piston Clearance | Ring Gap Top Compression | Ring Gap Bottom Compression | Ring Gap Oil Control | Ring Side Clearance Top Compression | Ring Side Clearance Bottom Compression | Ring Side Clearance Oil Control |
|---|---|---|---|---|---|---|---|---|
| 1987 | 165 (2693) | 0.0004–0.0016 | 0.0120–0.0200 | 0.0120–0.0200 | 0.0100–0.0200 | 0.0016–0.0028 | 0.0012–0.0024 | 0.0008–0.0017 |
| | 209 (3428) | 0.0008–0.0020 | 0.0120–0.0200 | 0.0080–0.0160 | 0.0100–0.0200 | 0.020–0.032 | 0.0016–0.0028 | 0.0008–0.0020 |
| | 210.6 (3453) | 0.0012–0.0024 | 0.0120–0.0220 | 0.0120–0.0220 | 0.0100–0.0200 | 0.0024–0.0035 | 0.0024–0.0035 | 0.0008–0.0020 |
| 1988 | 140 (2302) | 0.0012–0.0024 | 0.0120–0.0220 | 0.0120–0.0220 | 0.0100–0.0200 | 0.0024–0.0035 | 0.0024–0.0035 | 0.0008–0.0020 |
| | 152 (2494) | 0.0004–0.0016 | 0.0120–0.0200 | 0.0120–0.0200 | 0.0100–0.0200 | 0.0016–0.0028 | 0.0012–0.0024 | 0.0008–0.0017 |
| | 165 (2693) | 0.0004–0.0016 | 0.0120–0.0200 | 0.0120–0.0200 | 0.0100–0.0200 | 0.0016–0.0028 | 0.0012–0.0024 | 0.0008–0.0017 |
| | 209 (3428)③ | 0.0008–0.0020 | 0.0120–0.0200 | 0.0080–0.0160 | 0.0100–0.0200 | 0.020–0.032 | 0.0016–0.0028 | 0.0008–0.0020 |
| | 209 (3428)④ | 0.0008–0.0020 | 0.008–0.018 | 0.016–0.026 | 0.016–0.024 | 0.0016–0.0028 | 0.0012–0.0024 | 0.0008–0.0022 |
| | 210.6 (3453) | 0.0012–0.0024 | 0.0120–0.0220 | 0.0120–0.0220 | 0.0100–0.0200 | 0.0024–0.0035 | 0.0024–0.0035 | 0.0008–0.0020 |
| | 304 (4988) | 0.0004–0.0013 | 0.0080–0.0160 | 0.008–0.016 | 0.0100–0.0200 | 0.0016–0.0025 | 0.0012–0.0028 | 0.0008–0.0022 |
| 1989-90 | 140 (2302) | 0.0012–0.0024 | 0.0120–0.0220 | 0.0120–0.0220 | 0.0100–0.0200 | 0.0024–0.0035 | 0.0024–0.0035 | 0.0008–0.0020 |
| | 152 (2494) | 0.0004–0.0016 | 0.0120–0.0200 | 0.0120–0.0200 | 0.0100–0.0200 | 0.0016–0.0028 | 0.0012–0.0024 | 0.0008–0.0017 |
| | 165 (2693) | 0.0004–0.0016 | 0.0120–0.0200 | 0.0120–0.0200 | 0.0100–0.0200 | 0.0016–0.0028 | 0.0012–0.0024 | 0.0008–0.0017 |
| | 209 (3428)③ | 0.0008–0.0020 | 0.0120–0.0200 | 0.0080–0.0160 | 0.0100–0.0200 | 0.020–0.032 | 0.0016–0.0028 | 0.0008–0.0020 |
| | 209 (3428)④ | 0.0008–0.0020 | 0.008–0.018 | 0.016–0.026 | 0.016–0.024 | 0.0016–0.0028 | 0.0012–0.0024 | 0.0008–0.0022 |
| | 210.6 (3453) | 0.0012–0.0024 | 0.0120–0.0220 | 0.0120–0.0220 | 0.0100–0.0200 | 0.0024–0.0035 | 0.0024–0.0035 | 0.0008–0.0020 |
| | 304 (4988) | 0.0004–0.0013 | 0.0080–0.0160 | 0.008–0.016 | 0.0100–0.0200 | 0.0016–0.0025 | 0.0012–0.0028 | 0.0008–0.0022 |

① Mahle – 0.0008-0.0020
KS – 0.0012-0.0024

② Mahle – 0.0020-0.0032
KS – 0.0016-0.0028

③ B34 used in 535i

④ B35 used in 6 and 7 series cars

## BRAKE SPECIFICATIONS

All measurements in inches unless noted

| Year | Model | Lug Nut Torque (ft. lbs.) | Master Cylinder Bore | Brake Disc Minimum Thickness | Brake Disc Maximum Runout | Standard Brake Drum Diameter | Minimum Lining Thickness Front | Minimum Lining Thickness Rear |
|---|---|---|---|---|---|---|---|---|
| 1983 | 320i | 59–65 | .812 | .827 | 0.008 | 10.04 | — | — |
| | 533i | 65–79 | — | .787 | 0.008 | — | 0.079 | 0.079 |
| | 633CSi | 65–79 | — | .960F/.315R | 0.008 | — | 0.079 | 0.079 |
| | 733i | 65–79 | — | .906F/.315R | 0.008 | — | 0.079 | 0.079 |
| 1984 | 318i | 65–79 | — | .421 | 0.008 | 9.035 | 0.079 | 0.059 |
| | 533i | 65–79 | — | .787 | 0.008 | — | 0.079 | 0.079 |
| | 633CSi | 65–79 | — | .906F/.315R | 0.008 | — | 0.079 | 0.079 |
| | 733i | 65–79 | — | .906F/.315R | 0.008 | — | 0.079 | 0.079 |
| 1985 | 318i | 65–79 | — | .421 | 0.008 | 9.035 | 0.079 | 0.059 |
| | 325e | 65–79 | — | .421 | 0.008 | — | 0.079 | 0.079 |
| | 528e | 65–79 | — | .787F/.315R | 0.008 | — | 0.079 | 0.079 |
| | 524td | 65–79 | — | .787F/.315R | 0.008 | — | 0.079 | 0.079 |
| | 535i | 65–79 | — | .906F/.315R | 0.008 | — | 0.079 | 0.079 |
| | 635CSi | 65–79 | — | .906F/.315R | 0.008 | — | 0.079 | 0.079 |
| | 735i | 65–79 | — | .906F/.315R | 0.008 | — | 0.079 | 0.079 |
| 1986 | 325e | 65–79 | — | .421 | 0.008 | — | 0.079 | 0.079 |
| | 528e | 65–79 | — | .787F/.315R | 0.008 | — | 0.079 | 0.079 |
| | 524td | 65–79 | — | .787F/.315R | 0.008 | — | 0.079 | 0.079 |
| | 535i | 65–79 | — | .906F/.315R | 0.008 | — | 0.079 | 0.079 |
| | 635CSi | 65–79 | — | .906F/.315R | 0.008 | — | 0.079 | 0.079 |
| | 735i | 65–79 | — | .906F/.315R | 0.008 | — | 0.079 | 0.079 |
| 1987 | 325i | 65–79 | — | .421 | 0.008 | — | 0.079 | 0.079 |
| | 325iS | 65–79 | — | .421 | 0.008 | — | 0.079 | 0.079 |
| | 528e | 65–79 | — | .787F/.315R | 0.008 | — | 0.079 | 0.079 |
| | 535i | 65–79 | — | .906F/.315R | 0.008 | — | 0.079 | 0.079 |
| | 635CSi | 65–79 | — | .906F/.315R | 0.008 | — | 0.079 | 0.079 |
| | 735i | 65–79 | — | .906F/.315R | 0.008 | — | 0.079 | 0.079 |
| | M5 | 65–79 | — | 1.102F/.315R | 0.008 | — | 0.079 | 0.079 |
| | M6 | 65–79 | — | .906F/.315R | 0.008 | — | 0.079 | 0.079 |
| 1988 | 325 (All) | 65–79 | — | .787F/.315R | 0.008 | — | 0.079 | 0.079 |
| | 528e | 65–79 | — | .787F/.315R | 0.008 | — | 0.079 | 0.079 |
| | 535i | 65–79 | — | .787F/.315R | 0.008 | — | 0.079 | 0.079 |
| | 635CSi | 65–79 | — | .906F/.315R | 0.008 | — | 0.079 | 0.079 |
| | M3 | 65–79 | — | .905F/.394R | 0.008 | — | 0.079 | 0.079 |
| | M5 | 65–79 | — | 1.102F/.315R | 0.008 | — | 0.079 | 0.079 |
| | M6 | 65–79 | — | 1.024F/.315R | 0.008 | — | 0.079 | 0.079 |
| | 735i | 65–79 | — | .906F/.315R | 0.008 | — | 0.079 | 0.079 |
| | 750iL | 65–79 | — | NA F/.709R | 0.008 | — | 0.079 | 0.079 |

## BRAKE SPECIFICATIONS

All measurements in inches unless noted

| Year | Model | Lug Nut Torque (ft. lbs.) | Master Cylinder Bore | Brake Disc Minimum Thickness | Brake Disc Maximum Runout | Standard Brake Drum Diameter | Minimum Lining Thickness Front | Minimum Lining Thickness Rear |
|---|---|---|---|---|---|---|---|---|
| 1989-90 | 325 (All) | 65–79 | — | .787F/.315R | 0.008 | — | 0.079 | 0.079 |
| | 525i | 65–79 | — | .787F/.315R | 0.008 | — | 0.079 | 0.079 |
| | 535i | 65–79 | — | .787F/.315R | 0.008 | — | 0.079 | 0.079 |
| | 635CSi | 65–79 | — | .906F/.315R | 0.008 | — | 0.079 | 0.079 |
| | M3 | 65–79 | — | .905F/.394R | 0.008 | — | 0.079 | 0.079 |
| | M5 | 65–79 | — | 1.102F/.315R | 0.008 | — | 0.079 | 0.079 |
| | M6 | 65–79 | — | 1.024F/.315R | 0.008 | — | 0.079 | 0.079 |
| | 735i | 65–79 | — | .906F/.315R | 0.008 | — | 0.079 | 0.079 |
| | 735iL | 65–79 | — | .906F/.315R | 0.008 | — | 0.079 | 0.079 |
| | 750iL | 65–79 | — | NA F/.709R | 0.008 | — | 0.079 | 0.079 |

F Front
R Rear
① 1984 Models—.9213F

## TORQUE SPECIFICATIONS

All readings in ft. lbs.

| Year | Engine Displacement cu. in. (cc) | Cylinder Head Bolts | Main Bearing Bolts | Rod Bearing Bolts | Crankshaft Pulley Bolts | Flywheel Bolts | Manifold Intake | Manifold Exhaust | Spark Plugs |
|---|---|---|---|---|---|---|---|---|---|
| 1983 | 108 (1766) | ① | 42–46 | 38–41 | 101–108 | 72–83 | 15–20 | 22–24 | 15–21 |
| | 165 (2693) | ⑤ | 42–45⑫ | ⑨ | 283–311 | 71–81 | 22–24 | 22–24 | 15–21 |
| | 196 (3210) | ④ | 42–46 | 38–41 | 318–333 | 75–83⑦ | 16–17 | 22–24 | 15–21 |
| 1984 | 108 (1766) | ⑩ | 42–46 | 38–41 | 130–145 | 71–81 ⑦ | 22–24 | 22–24 | 15–21 |
| | 165 (2693) | ⑤ | 42–45⑫ | ⑨ | 283–311 | 71–81 | 22–24 | 22–24 | 15–21 |
| | 196 (3210) | ④ | 42–46 | 38–41 | 318–333 | 75–83⑦ | 16–17 | 22–24 | 15–21 |
| 1985 | 108 (1766) | ⑩ | 42–46 | 38–41 | 103–145 | 71–81⑦ | 22–24 | 22–24 | 15–21 |
| | 149 (2443) | ⑧ | 44–49⑫ | ⑨ | 283–311 | 71–81 | 14–17 | 14–17 | — |
| | 165 (2693) | ⑤ | 42–45⑫ | ⑨ | 283–311 | 71–81 | 22–24 | 22–24 | 15–21 |
| | 196 (3210) | ④ | 42–46 | 38–41 | 318–333 | 75–83⑦ | 16–17 | 22–24 | 15–21 |
| | 209 (3428) | ⑪ | 42–45⑫ | 38–41 | 311–325 | 71–81 | 22–24 | 22–24 | 15–21 |
| 1986 | 149 (2443) | ⑧ | 44–49⑫ | ⑨ | 283–311 | 71–81 | 14–17 | 14–17 | — |
| | 165 (2693) | ⑤ | 42–45⑫ | ⑨ | 283–311 | 71–81 | 22–24 | 22–24 | 15–21 |
| | 209 (3428) | ⑪ | 42–45⑫ | 38–41 | 311–325 | 71–81 | 22–24 | 22–24 | 15–21 |
| 1987 | 152 (2494) | ⑤ | 42–45⑫ | ⑨ | 283–311 | 71–81 | 22–24 | 22–24 | 15–21 |
| | 165 (2693) | ⑤ | 42–45⑫ | ⑨ | 283–311 | 71–81 | 22–24 | 22–24 | 15–21 |
| | 209 (3428) | ⑪ | 42–45⑫ | 38–41 | 311–325 | 71–81 | 22–24 | 22–24 | 15–21 |
| | 210.6 (3453) | ⑬ | 14.5–17.5⑫ | ⑭ | 311–325 | 71–81 | 14–17 | 6.5–7 | 15–21 |
| 1988 | 140.4 (2302) | ⑬ | 14.5–17.5⑫ | ⑭ | 311–325 | 75.5–76.5 | 6.5–7.0 | 6.5–7.0 | 15–21 |
| | 152 (2494) | ⑤ | 42–45 | ⑨ | 283–311 | 75.5–76.5 | 22–24 | 16–18⑱ | 15–21 |
| | 165 (2693) | ⑤ | 42–45 | ⑨ | 283–311 | 75.5–76.5 | 22–24 | 16–18⑱ | 15–21 |

## TORQUE SPECIFICATIONS

All readings in ft. lbs.

| Year | Engine Displacement cu. in. (cc) | Cylinder Head Bolts | Main Bearing Bolts | Rod Bearing Bolts | Crankshaft Pulley Bolts | Flywheel Bolts | Manifold Intake | Manifold Exhaust | Spark Plugs |
|---|---|---|---|---|---|---|---|---|---|
| 1988 | 209 (3428) | ⑪ | 42–45 | 38–41 | 311–325 | 75.5–76.5 | 22–24 | 16–18⑱ | 15–21 |
| | 210.6 (3453) | ⑬ | 14.5–17.5⑫ | ⑭ | 311–325 | 75.5–76.5 | 14–17⑰ | 6.5–7 | 15–21 |
| | 304 (4988) | ⑮ | ⑯ | ⑨ | 311–325 | 74 | 16–18 | 16–18 | 15–21 |
| 1989-90 | 140.4 (2302) | ⑬ | 14.5–17.5⑫ | ⑭ | 311–325 | 75.5–76.5 | 6.5–7.0 | 6.5–7.0 | 15–21 |
| | 152 (2494) | ⑤ | 42–45 | ⑨ | 283–311 | 75.5–76.5 | 22–24 | 16–18⑱ | 15–21 |
| | 165 (2693) | ⑤ | 42–45 | ⑨ | 283–311 | 75.5–76.5 | 22–24 | 16–18⑱ | 15–21 |
| | 209 (3428) | ⑪ | 42–45 | 38–41 | 311–325 | 75.5–76.5 | 22–24 | 16–18⑱ | 15–21 |
| | 210.6 (3453) | ⑬ | 14.5–17.5⑫ | ⑭ | 311–325 | 75.5–76.5 | 14–17⑰ | 6.5–7 | 15–21 |
| | 304 (4988) | ⑮ | ⑯ | ⑨ | 311–325 | 74 | 16–18 | 16–18 | 15–21 |

① 320i, 528i, 633CSi & 733i '79–'80
Step 1—25–32
Step 2—49–52
Step 3—56–59
Step 4—56–59 (after warm-up)
633CSi & 733i—'81–'82
Step 1—25–32
Step 2—49–51
Step 3—54–59
Step 4—20–30 degrees (after warm-up)

② Flat hex nut—174–188
Shoulder hex nut: 318–333

③ Step 1—22–25
Step 2—43–47

④ Step 1—25–29
Step 2—42–45
Wait 20 minutes
Step 3—56–59
Step4—20°–30°'

⑤ Step 1—29–33
Wait 20 minutes
Step 2—43–47
Warm engine fully
Step 3—20°–30°

⑥ Then turn additional 70°

⑦ First coat w/Loctite® 270 or equivalent

⑧ Step 1—50–60
Wait 15 minutes
Step 2—70–76
Run engine hot—25 minutes
Step 3—Turn 85°–95° angle torque
Crossbolts—28–34

⑨ Torque to 14.5 ft. lbs.
Turn 70° angle torque

⑩ Step 1—42–44
Wait 15 minutes
Step 2—30°–36° angle torque
Run engine warm—25 minutes
Step 3—20°–30° angle torque

⑪ Step 1—42–44
Wait 15 minutes
Step 2—30–36
Run engine warm—25 minutes
Step 3—30°–40° angle torque

⑫ Step 1—Torque to figure shown
Step 2—Turn 47°–53° angle torque

⑬ Step 1—35–37
Step 2—57–59
Wait 15 minutes
Step 3—71–73

⑭ Step 1—7
Step 2—21.5
Step 3—60°–62° angle torque

⑮ Step 1—22
Wait 15 minutes
Step 2—Turn 120° angle torque

⑯ Step 1—14.5
Step 2—Turn 70° angle torque

⑰ Applies to (larger) M8 bolts. Torque M6 (smaller) bolts to 6.5–7.0

⑱ Coat the threads of the upper row of bolts with a locking type sealer

## WHEEL ALIGNMENT

| Year | Model | | Caster Range (deg.) | Caster Preferred Setting (deg.) | Camber Range (deg.) | Camber Preferred Setting (deg.) | Toe-in (in.) | Steering Axis Inclination (deg.) |
|---|---|---|---|---|---|---|---|---|
| 1983 | 320i | Front | — | 8 5/16P | — | 0 | 1/16 | 10 5/16P |
| | | Rear | — | — | — | 2N | 1/32P | — |
| | 63CSi | Front | — | 8¼P | — | 5/16N | 5/64P | 12 3/16P |
| | | Rear | — | — | — | 2 5/16N | 5/64P | — |
| | 733i | Front | — | 8¼P | — | ⅓N | .078 | 12 3/16P |
| | | Rear | — | — | — | 2N | .08 | — |
| 1984 | 318i | Front | 8¼P-9¼P | 8¾P | 1 1/10N-1/10N | ⅔N | 0.079① | 13 2/3P |
| | | Rear | — | — | — | 1 13/16N | 0.079① | — |
| | 528e | Front | 7¾P-8¾P | 8¼P | ½N-1/10P | 1/13N | 3/32P | 12 3/16P |
| | | Rear | — | — | — | 2N | 3/32P | — |
| | 533i | Front | 7¾P-8¾P | 8¼P | ½N-1/10P | 1/13N | 3/32P | 12 3/16P |
| | | Rear | — | — | — | 2N | 3/32P | — |
| | 633CSi | Front | — | 8¼P | — | 5/16N | 5/64P | 12 3/16P |
| | | Rear | — | — | — | 2 5/16N | 5/64P | — |
| | 733i | Front | 9P-10P | 9½P | ½N-1/12P | 0 | ½ | 11 1/3P |
| | | Rear | — | — | — | 2N | 3/32P | — |
| 1985 | 318i | Front | 8¼P-9¼P | 8¾P | 1 1/10N-1/10N | ⅔N | 0.079① | 13 2/3P |
| | | Rear | — | — | — | 1 13/16N | 0.079① | — |
| | 325e | Front | 8¼P-9¼P | 8¾P | 1 1/10N-1/10N | ⅔N | 0.079① | 13 2/3P |
| | | Rear | — | — | — | 1 13/16N | 0.079① | — |
| | 528e | Front | 7¾P-8¾P | 8¼P | ½N-1/10P | ⅓N | 3/32P | 12 13/16P |
| | | Rear | — | — | — | 2N | 3/32P | — |
| | 533i | Front | 7¾P-8¾P | 8¼P | ½N-1/10P | ⅓N | 3/32P | 12 13/16P |
| | | Rear | — | — | — | 2N | 3/32P | — |
| | 635CSi | Front | 7¾P-8¾P | 8¼P | ½N-1/10P | ⅓N | 0.079① | 12 3/16P |
| | | Rear | — | — | — | 2 1/3N | 0.079① | — |
| | 735i | Front | 9P-10P | 9½P | ½N-½P | 0 | 0.020 ② | 11 1/3P |
| | | Rear | — | — | — | 2 1/3N | 0.079① | — |
| 1986 | 325e | Front | 8¼P-9½P | 8¾P | 1 1/10N-1/10N | ⅔N | 0.079① | 13 2/3P |
| | | Rear | — | — | — | 1 13/16N | 0.079① | — |
| | 528e | Front | 7¾P-8¾P | 8¼P | ½N-1/10P | 1/3N | 0.079① | 12 13/16P |
| | | Rear | — | — | — | 2 1/3N | 0.079① | — |
| | 535i | Front | 7¾P-8¾P | 8¼P | ½N-1/10P | 1/3N | 0.079① | 12 13/16P |
| | | Rear | — | — | — | 2 1/3N | 0.079① | — |
| | 635CSi | Front | 7¾P-8¾P | 8¼P | ½N-1/10P | ⅓N | 0.079① | 12 13/16P |
| | | Rear | — | — | — | 2 1/3N | 0.079① | — |
| | 735i | Front | 9P-10P | 9½P | ½N-½P | 0 | 0.020 ② | 11 1/3P |
| | | Rear | — | — | — | 2 1/3N | 0.079① | — |

## WHEEL ALIGNMENT

| Year | Model | | Caster Range (deg.) | Caster Preferred Setting (deg.) | Camber Range (deg.) | Camber Preferred Setting (deg.) | Toe-in (in.) | Steering Axis Inclin-ation (deg.) |
|---|---|---|---|---|---|---|---|---|
| 1987 | 325e | Front | 8¼P-9¼P | 8¾P | $1\frac{1}{10}$N-$\frac{1}{10}$N | ⅔N | 0.079① | 13⅔P |
| | | Rear | – | – | 1½N-2⅓N | 1⅚N | 0.079① | – |
| | 528e | Front | 7¾P-8¾P | 8¼P | ½N-$\frac{1}{10}$P | ⅓N | 0.079① | $12\frac{13}{16}$P |
| | | Rear | – | – | – | 2⅓N | 0.079① | – |
| | 535i | Front | 7¾P-8¾P | 8¼P | ½N-$\frac{1}{10}$P | ⅓N | 0.079① | $12\frac{13}{16}$P |
| | | Rear | – | – | – | 2⅓N | 0.079① | – |
| | 325 | Front | 8P-9P | 8½P | $1\frac{1}{10}$N-⅙P | ⅔N | 0.079 | $13\frac{5}{16}$P |
| | | Rear | – | – | 1⅓N-2⅓P | $1\frac{5}{16}$N | 0.079 | – |
| | 325③ | Front | 8¼P-8¾P | 8¾P | 1⅔N-⅔N | 1⅙N | 0.079 | 14⅓P |
| | | Rear | – | – | 1⅓N-2⅓P | $1\frac{5}{16}$N | 0.079 | – |
| | 325iX | Front | 1P-1⅓P | 1⅓ | 1½P-½N | 1N | 0.024 | 12⅔P |
| | | Rear | – | – | 1¾N-2¾N | 2¼N | 0.102 | – |
| | 635CSi | Front | 7½P-8½P | 8P | ⅚N-⅙P | ⅓N | 0.079 | 12P |
| | | Rear | – | – | 2⅚N-1⅚N | 2⅓N | 0.079⑤ | – |
| | M6 | Front | 7½P-8½P | 8¼P | ⅚N-⅙P | ⅓N | 0.079 | 12P |
| | | Rear | – | – | 2⅚N-1⅚N | 2⅓N | 0.079① | – |
| | 528e | Front | 7½P-8½P | 8P | ⅚N-⅙P | ⅓N | 0.079⑤ | 12P |
| | | Rear | – | – | 1⅚N–2⅚N | 2⅓N | 0.079⑤ | – |
| | 535i | Front | 7½P-8½P | 8P | ⅚N-⅙P | ⅓N | 0.079⑤ | 12P |
| | | Rear | – | – | 1⅚N–2⅚N | 2⅓N | 0.079⑤ | – |
| | M5 | Front | 7½P-8½P | 8P | ⅚N-⅙P | ⅓N | 0.098① | 12P |
| | | Rear | – | – | 1⅚N–2⅚N | 2⅓N | 0.098① | – |
| | 735i | Front | 7½P-8½P | 8P | ¾N-¼P | ¼N | 0.087⑥ | 12P |
| | | Rear | – | – | – | 2⅓N | 0.079① | – |
| 1988 | 325e | Front | 8P-9P | 8½P | $1\frac{1}{10}$N-$\frac{1}{10}$N | ⅔N | 0.079 | $13\frac{5}{16}$P |
| | | Rear | – | – | 1⅓N-2⅓N | $1\frac{5}{16}$N | 0.079 | – |
| | 325 | Front | 8P-9P | 8½P | $1\frac{1}{10}$N-⅙N | ⅔N | 0.079 | $13\frac{5}{16}$P |
| | | Rear | – | – | 1⅓N-2⅓P | $1\frac{5}{16}$N | 0.079 | – |
| | 325③ | Front | 8¼P-8¾P | 8¾P | 1⅔N-⅔N | 1⅙N | 0.079 | 14⅓P |
| | | Rear | – | – | 1⅓N-2⅓P | $1\frac{5}{16}$N | 0.079 | – |
| | 325iX | Front | 1P-1⅔P | 1⅓P | 1½N-½N | 1N | 0.024 | 12⅔P |
| | | Rear | – | – | 1¾N-2⅓P | $1\frac{5}{16}$N | 0.079 | – |
| | 325iX③ | Front | 1P-1⅔P | 1⅓P | $1\frac{15}{16}$N-$\frac{5}{16}$N | 1⅓N | 0.024 | 12⅔P |
| | | Rear | – | – | 1¾N-2⅓P | $1\frac{5}{16}$N | 0.079 | – |
| | 325 Convertible | Front | 8P-9P | 8½P | $1\frac{1}{10}$N-⅙N | ⅔N | 0.079 | $13\frac{5}{16}$P |
| | | Rear | – | – | 1⅓N-2⅓N | 1⅚N | 0.079 | – |
| | 528e | Front | 7¾P-8¾P | 8¼P | ½N-$\frac{1}{10}$P | ⅓N | 0.079① | $12\frac{13}{16}$P |
| | | Rear | – | – | – | 2⅓N | 0.079① | – |

## WHEEL ALIGNMENT

| Year | Model | | Caster Range (deg.) | Caster Preferred Setting (deg.) | Camber Range (deg.) | Camber Preferred Setting (deg.) | Toe-in (in.) | Steering Axis Inclination (deg.) |
|---|---|---|---|---|---|---|---|---|
| 1988 | 535i | Front | 7¾P-8¾P | 8¼P | ½N-⅒P | ⅓N | 0.079① | 12 13/16P |
| | | Rear | — | — | — | 2⅓N | 0.079① | — |
| | 635CSi | Front | 7½P-8½P | 8P | ⅚N-⅙P | ⅓N | 0.079⑤ | 12P |
| | | Rear | — | — | 2⅚N-1⅚N | 2⅓N | 0.079⑤ | — |
| | M6 | Front | 7¾P-8¾P | 8P | ⅚N-⅙P | ⅓N | 0.079⑤ | 12P |
| | | Rear | — | — | 2⅚N-1⅚N | 2⅓N | 0.079⑤ | — |
| | 528e | Front | 7½P-8½P | 8P | ⅚N-⅙P | ⅓N | 0.079⑤ | 12P |
| | | Rear | — | — | 1⅚N–2⅚N | 2⅓N | 0.079⑤ | — |
| | 535i | Front | 7½P-8½P | 8P | ⅚N-⅙P | ⅓N | 0.079⑤ | 12P |
| | | Rear | — | — | 1⅚N–2⅚N | 2⅓N | 0.079⑤ | — |
| | M5 | Front | 7½P-8½P | 8P | ⅚N-⅙P | ⅓N | 0.098 | 12P |
| | | Rear | — | — | 1⅚N–2⅚N | 2⅓N | 0.098 | — |
| | 735i | Front | 7½P-8½P | 8P | ¾N-¼P | ¼N | 0.087⑥ | 12P |
| | | Rear | — | — | 2⅚N-1⅚N | 2⅓N | 0.087 | — |
| | 750iL | Front | 7½P-8½P | 8P | ¾N-¼P | ¼N | 0.087⑥ | 12P |
| | | Rear | — | — | 2⅚N-1⅚N | 2⅓N | 0.087 | — |
| 1989-90 | 325e | Front | 8P-9P | 8½P | 1⅒N-⅒N | ⅔N | 0.079 | 13 5/16P |
| | | Rear | — | — | 1⅓N-2⅓N | 1 5/16N | 0.079 | — |
| | 325 | Front | 8P-9P | 8½P | 1⅒N-⅙N | ⅔N | 0.079 | 13 5/16P |
| | | Rear | — | — | 1⅓N-2⅓P | 1 5/16N | 0.079 | — |
| | 325③ | Front | 8¼P-8¾P | 8¾P | 1⅔N-⅔N | 1⅙N | 0.079 | 14⅓P |
| | | Rear | — | — | 1⅓N-2⅓P | 1 5/16N | 0.079 | — |
| | 325iX | Front | 1P-1⅔P | 1⅓P | 1½N-½N | 1N | 0.024 | 12⅔P |
| | | Rear | — | — | 1¾N-2⅓P | 1 5/16N | 0.079 | — |
| | 325iX③ | Front | 1P-1⅔P | 1⅓P | 1 15/16N-5/16N | 1⅓N | 0.024 | 12⅔P |
| | | Rear | — | — | 1¾N-2⅓P | 1 5/16N | 0.079 | — |
| | 325 Convertible | Front | 8P-9P | 8½P | 1⅒N-⅙N | ⅔N | 0.079 | 13 5/16P |
| | | Rear | — | — | 1⅓N-2⅓N | 1⅚N | 0.079 | — |
| | 525i | Front | 7½P-8½P | 8P | ¾N-¼P | ¼N | 0.087⑥ | 12P |
| | | Rear | — | — | — | 2⅓N | 0.079① | — |
| | 535i | Front | 7¾P-8¾P | 8¼P | ½N-⅒P | ⅓N | 0.079① | 12 13/16P |
| | | Rear | — | — | — | 2⅓N | 0.079① | — |
| | 635CSi | Front | 7½P-8½P | 8P | ⅚N-⅙P | ⅓N | 0.079⑤ | 12P |
| | | Rear | — | — | 2⅚N-1⅚N | 2⅓N | 0.079⑤ | — |
| | M6 | Front | 7¾P-8¾P | 8P | ⅚N-⅙P | ⅓N | 0.079⑤ | 12P |
| | | Rear | — | — | 2⅚N-1⅚N | 2⅓N | 0.079⑤ | — |
| | 528e | Front | 7½P-8½P | 8P | ⅚N-⅙P | ⅓N | 0.079⑤ | 12P |
| | | Rear | — | — | 1⅚N–2⅚N | 2⅓N | 0.079⑤ | — |

## WHEEL ALIGNMENT

| Year | Model | | Caster Range (deg.) | Caster Preferred Setting (deg.) | Camber Range (deg.) | Camber Preferred Setting (deg.) | Toe-in (in.) | Steering Axis Inclin-ation (deg.) |
|---|---|---|---|---|---|---|---|---|
| 1989-90 | 535i | Front | 7½P-8½P | 8P | 5/6N-1/6P | 1/3N | 0.079⑤ | 12P |
| | | Rear | — | — | 1 5/6N-2 5/6N | 2⅓N | 0.079⑤ | — |
| | M5 | Front | 7½P-8½P | 8P | 5/6N-1/6P | 1/3N | 0.098 | 12P |
| | | Rear | — | — | 1 5/6N-2 5/6N | 2⅓N | 0.098 | — |
| | 735iL | Front | 7½P-8½P | 8P | ¾N-¼P | ¼N | 0.087⑥ | 12P |
| | | Rear | — | — | 2 5/6N-1 5/6N | 2 1/3N | 0.087 | — |
| | 750iL | Front | 7½P-8½P | 8P | ¾N-¼P | ¼N | 0.087⑥ | 12P |
| | | Rear | — | — | 2 5/6N-1 5/6N | 2 1/3N | 0.087 | — |

All 300, 500 and 700 series models aligned with 150 lbs. in each front seat, 150 lbs. in rear seat and 46 lbs. in trunk. All 600 series models aligned with 150 lbs. in each front seat and 30 lbs. in trunk on left side

F Front
R Rear
N Negative
P Positive
① .083 with TRX tires
② .024 with TRX tires
③ With "M" suspension
④ .122 with 16 in. rims
⑤ .083 with TRX 390 rims
⑥ .094 with TRX 415 rims

# TUNE-UP PROCEDURES

## Electronic Ignition

### AIR GAP ADJUSTMENT

Breaker points and condensers are not used with the electronic ignition. The air gap between the rotating teeth and the stator teeth can be checked with a brass or plastic feeler gauge. This is not required on 1984–89 models. No adjustment is possible. If the gap is not 0.012–0.028 in., the unit should be replaced.

**CAUTION**

***All repair work to the electronic ignition system should be done with the engine stopped and the ignition switch OFF.***

Most models are equipped with a Motronic engine control system. This system uses various engine sensors including an oxygen sensor in the exhaust to monitor engine conditions. The monitored information is fed to a Motronic (computer) unit, which in turn controls the air/fuel mixture entering the engine.

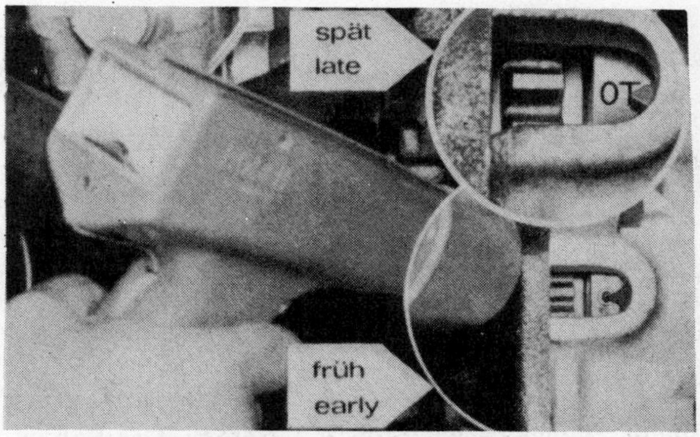

**Ignition timing marks at flywheel**

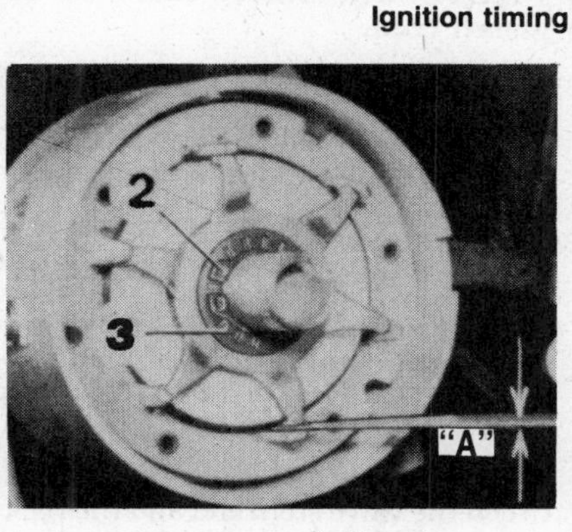

2. Circlip 3. Expander

**Measuring rotor to stator clearance (A)**

## Ignition Timing

### ADJUSTMENT

1. The engine should be at normal operating temperature. Adjust the idle speed (except on cars with Motronic injection. See below).
2. Remove and plug distributor vacuum lines. Connect a timing light to the No. 1 spark plug wire and start the engine. Align the marks on the flywheel with the bell housing indicator, by rotating the distributor body. Tighten the distributor body clamp.

## COMPUTER CONTROLLED IGNITION TIMING CHART

| Car/Model | Unit Number | RPM | Timing BTDC |
|---|---|---|---|
| 325e | 0261200021 | 650-750 | 4-12 |
| 325e | 0261100007 | 650-750 | 6-12 |
| 528e | 0261200007 | 650-750 | 4-12 |
| 528e | 0261200021 | 650-750 | 6-12 |
| | 0261200027 | | |
| 533i | 0261200008 | 650-750 | 6-14 |
| 535i | 0261200059 | 750-850 | 10-16 |
| M5 | 0261200079 | 800-900 | −3-3① |
| 633CSi | 0261200008 | 650-750 | 10-16 |
| 635CSi | 0261200059 | 750-850 | 10-16 |
| M6 | 0261200079 | 800-900 | −3-3① |
| 733i | 0261200008 | 600-700 | 6-14 |
| 735i | 0261200059 | 700-800 | 10-16 |

① That is − 3° after top dead center to 3° before top dead center

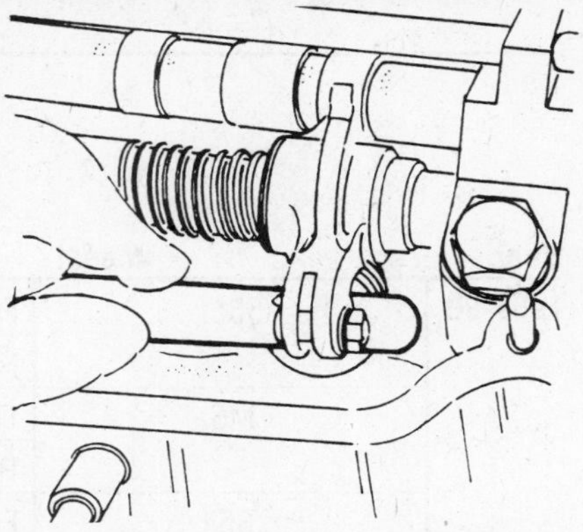

Checking valve clearance with a flat feeler gauge

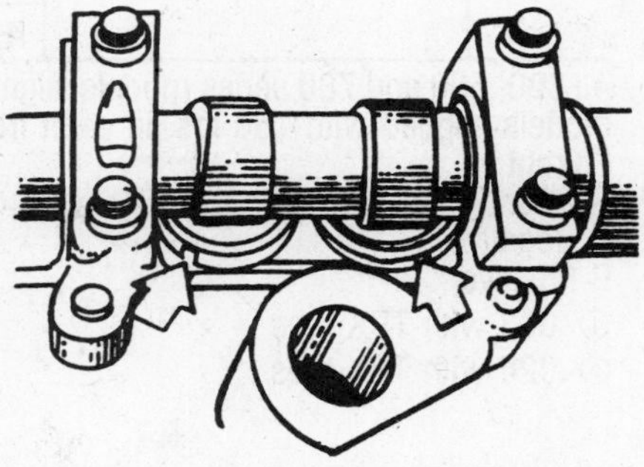

**On M5 and M6 DOHC engines, rotate the valve tappets so the grooves machined in the tops are facing as shown before attempting to measure valve clearance**

| Cylinder Firing-Piston at TDC | Exhaust Valve Closing, Intake Valve Opening On Opposite Cylinder |
|---|---|
| **6 CYLINDER** | |
| 1 | 6 |
| 5 | 2 |
| 3 | 4 |
| 6 | 1 |
| 2 | 5 |
| 4 | 3 |
| **4 CYLINDER** | |
| 1 | 4 |
| 3 | 2 |
| 4 | 1 |
| 2 | 3 |

**NOTE: The flywheel mark is either a pressed-in steel ball or a long tapered peg on the side of the starter ring gear.**

3. On cars with the Motronic control unit, the timing can be checked; however, timing cannot be adjusted. The only cure for improper timing is to replace the control unit. Also, timing must be within a specified range, as the computer changes the timing slightly to allow for various changes in operating condition. In other words, the timing does not have to be right on, but anywhere within the specified range.

4. The engine should be at normal operating temperature and the operation should be performed at normal room temperatures. The engine rpm should be within the specified range under the control of the computer.

5. Look up the control unit number on the unit itself. On 3, 5, and 6 Series cars, the unit is in the glove box; on the 7 Series, it is in the right side speaker cutout. Find the control unit number on the underside of unit and then reference that number on the Computer Controlled Ignition Timing Chart.

6. Connect a tachometer and a timing light to the engine (the latter to the No. 1 cylinder). Start the engine and check the rpm. If it is not correct, check the idle speed and reset it as necessary. Then, operate the timing light to see if timing is within the range specified on the chart. If it is significantly outside the range, the Motronic control unit must be replaced.

# Valve Lash

## ADJUSTMENT

### *Gasoline Engines*

#### EXCEPT M3, M5 AND M6

All BMW gasoline engines except the M series, dual overhead designs, are equipped with an overhead camshaft operating the intake and exhaust valves through rocker arm linkage.

**NOTE: The valves must be adjusted cold.**

1. Disconnect the negative battery cable. Remove the rocker cover.

2. Rotate the engine until the No. 1 cylinder is at TDC on the compression stroke.

**NOTE: Locate No. 1 cylinder firing position by the distributor rotor-to-cap position, or by observing the valve action in the opposite cylinder. Refer to following charts:**

3. Measure the valve clearance between the valve stem end and the rocker arm on the No. 1 cylinder (refer to the specifications for valve clearance).

4. Adjust the clearance by loosening the locknut on the rocker arm and turning the eccentric with a bent rod inserted through a hole provided on the surface of the eccentric.

5. When the proper clearance is obtained, tighten the locknut and recheck the valve clearance. Complete the adjustment on both valves.

6. Rotate the engine crankshaft to the next cylinder in the firing order, adjust the valves and repeat the procedures until all the valves are adjusted.

7. Replace the rocker cover, using a new gasket.

#### M3, M5 AND M6

**NOTE: To perform this procedure, a special tool is needed to depress the valves against spring pressure to gain access to the valve adjusting discs. Use BMW Tool 11 3 170 or equivalent. Also needed are: compressed air to lift valve adjusting discs that must be replaced out of the valve tappet; an assortment of adjusting discs of various thicknesses and a precise outside michrometer.**

1. Make sure the engine is overnight cold. Disconnect the negative battery cable. Remove the rocker cover.

Adjusting of engine valve clearance with bent rod after loosening the locknut (1)

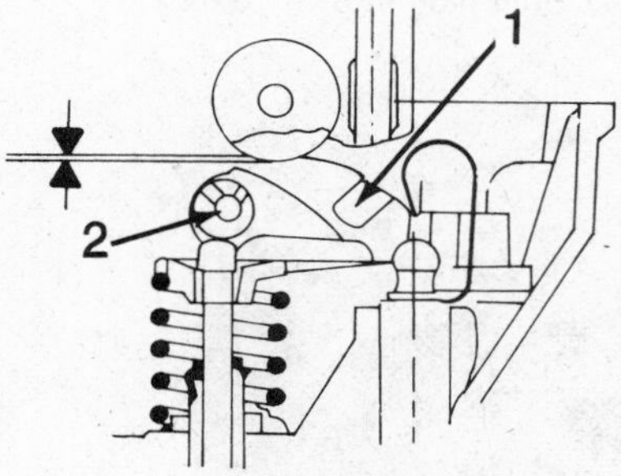


A back-up wrench should be used at (1) when adjusting valves. The locknut that holds the adjusting eccentric is at (2). "V" shows the valve clearance

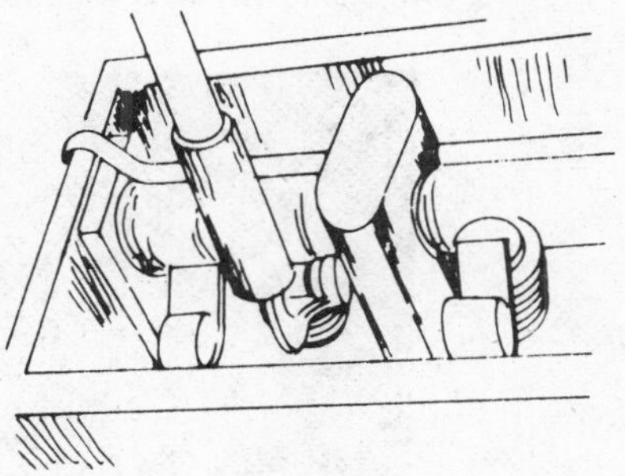

Tighten the adjusting nut with special tools 11 1 1809 and 00 2 050 or equivalent (525 td)

2. Turn the engine until the No. 1 cylinder intake valve cams (The intake cam is labeled **A** on the head) are both straight up.

3. Then, slide a flat feeler gauge in between each of the cams and the adjacent valve tappet. Check to see if the clearance is within the specified range. If it is, proceed with checking the remaining clearances as described starting in Step 8. If not, switch gauges and measure the actual clearance. When actual clearance is achieved, proceed with Steps 4–7.

4. Turn the tappets so the grooves machined into their edges are aligned as shown. Looking at the valves from the center of the engine, the right hand tappet's groove should be at about 5 o'clock and the left hand tappet's groove should be at about 7 o'clock. Use the end of the special tool required for the camshaft involved—in this case the **A** or intake camshaft (the exhaust camshaft end is labeled **E** on the engine and tool). Slide the proper end of the tool, going from the center of the engine outward, under the cam, with the heel of the tool pivoting on the inner side of the camshaft valley. Force the handle downward until the handle rests on the protrusion on the center of the cylinder head.

5. Use compressed air to pop the disc out of the tappet. Read the thickness dimension on the disc.

6. Determine the thickness required as follows:

a. If the valve clearance is too tight, try the next thinner disc.

b. If the valve clearance is too loose, try the next thicker disc.

7. Slip the thinner or thicker disc into the tappet with the letter facing downward. Rock the valve spring depressing tool out and remove it. Then, recheck the clearance. Change the disc again, if necessary, until the clearance falls within the specified range.

8. Turn the engine in firing order sequence (1–5–3–6–2–4 for the 6 cylinder engines or, for the M3, 1–3–4–2), turning the crankshaft forward ⅓ of a turn each time to get the intake cams to the upward position for each cylinder. Measure the clearance as in Step 3 and, if it is outside the specified range, follow Steps 4–7 to adjust either or both valves. Repeat this for all the intakes, and then turn the engine until No. 1 cylinder exhaust valves are upward.

9. Follow the same sequence for all the exhaust valves, going through the firing order, checking clearance as described in Step 3 and adjusting the valves as in Steps 4–7. Note that it is necessary, however, to use the opposite end of the special tool—the end marked **E** to depress the exhaust valves.

10. When all the clearances are in the specified range, replace the cam cover, start the engine, and check for leaks.

### *Diesel Engine*

1. Disconnect the negative battery cable. Remove the rocker cover.

2. Rotate the engine (using a socket on the crankshaft pulley nut) until the No. 1 cylinder is at TDC on the firing stroke. Line up the timing marks and also ensure that both No. 1 cylinder valves are loose; if they are not, turn the engine 360 degrees.

3. Use a 12mm backup wrench on the nut. Then, loosen the locknut. Slide a flat feeler gauge of the proper size (.012 in.) into the gap shown in the illustration. If it is necessary to change the clearance, rotate the eccentric, making sure the clearance is always taken up by turning the eccentric toward the operator or away from the centerline of the engine. Tighten the nut, and recheck the clearance, readjusting it if necessary. Repeat this step for the other valve on No. 1 cylinder.

4. Repeat the step above for each cylinder. Turn the engine ⅓ turn forward and adjust each cylinder in the firing order of 1–5–3–6–2–4.

5. Replace the valve rocker cover.

# Idle Speed and Mixture Gasoline Engines

## ADJUSTMENT

**NOTE: The idle speed and mixture can be adjusted ONLY with the aid of a CO meter. If this tool is not available, do not attempt any of the following procedures. The idle mixture can be adjusted ONLY with the aid of a CO meter on most models; on the 318i, it can be adjusted ONLY with a BMW digital mixture adjustment unit 12 6 400. Idle speed is not adjustable on any model with the Motronic control unit except the M5 and M6. If idle speed is incorrect, either the idle valve or the idle control unit must be replaced. See the fuel injection unit repair section.**

Note that several special tools are required to drill out the anti-tamper plug for the adjustment screw and to turn the adjustment screw. Get a new anti-tamper plug before beginning work.

### *318i*

1. The engine must be run until it is at operating temperature. Ignition

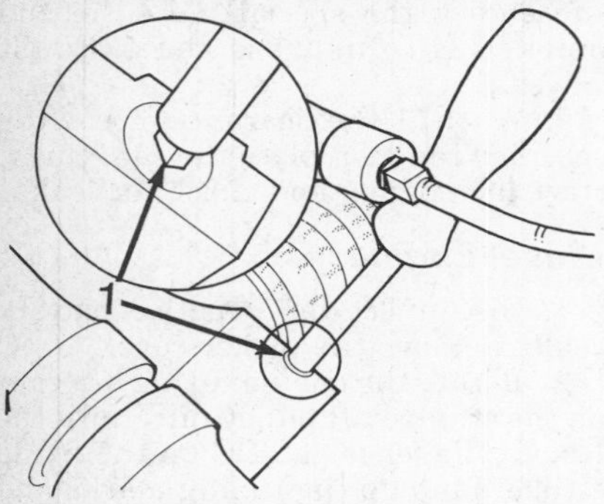


Drilling the anti-tamper plug on the 318i

Adjusting CO level with special tool. Hole plug shown—320i

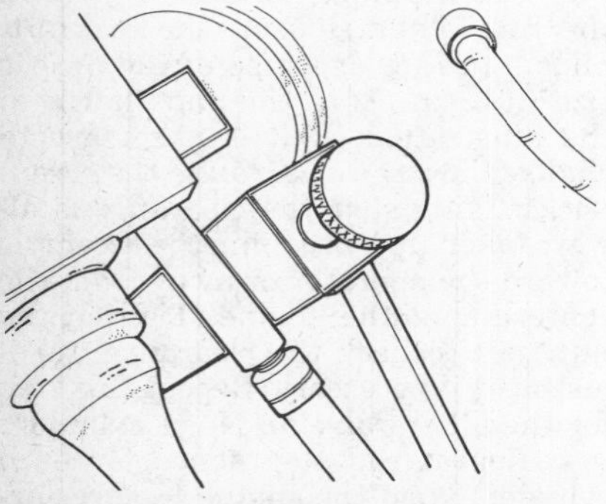

Special tool adjusting the CO on 318i

Remove plug (3) and use special tool 13-1-060 or equivalent to adjust the CO level with the screw in the bottom of the air intake sensor—530i, 528i, 528e, 630CSi, 633CSi and 733i

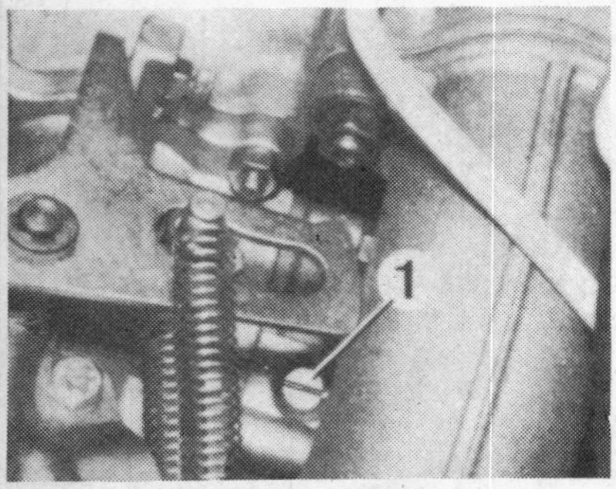


Idle speed screw location—320i

timing and valve clearances must be correct. Connect the BMW digital mixture measurement unit 12 6 400 or equivalent according to the instrument instructions. Disconnect the hose going to the active carbon filter on the throttle housing and do not plug the open connections.

2. Operate the engine to at least 3000 rpm for at least 30 seconds to ensure that the oxygen sensor is at operating temperature.

3. Disconnect the oxygen sensor wire, and fasten it where it cannot touch a ground. The nominal value to be looked for will now appear in the test unit's display. Make note of it and then reconnect the oxygen sensor into the test unit. The actual value will appear in the display. If the actual value is within plus or minus 0.3 volts of the nominal value, CO is within tolerance. If not, proceed as follows.

4. Drill a hole through the tamper plug with a special tool 13 1 092 or equivalent. Then screw special tool 13 1 094 or equivalent into the plug, and use the slide hammer on the tool to draw the plug out.

5. Use a special tool 13 1 060 to turn the adjusting screw to bring the actual valve to within 0.3 volt of the nominal value plug or minus. Turn off the engine, disconnect the test unit and reconnect the oxygen sensor wire to the oxygen sensor. Replace the anti-tamper plug with a new one.

### *320i*

1. Run the engine to normal operating temperature.

2. Adjust the engine idle speed with the screw located near the throttle valve linkage.

3. Detach the exhaust check valve and plug the hose.

4. To adjust the CO, remove the plug from the fuel distributor and with a special wrench, adjust the CO level to a maximum of 2.0% for the 49 state vehicles or 3.5% for California cars.

5. Reconnect the exhaust check valve hose and check the idle speed.

### *325, 325e, 325i and 325iS*

1. Disconnect the hose, leading from the throttle housing, that goes to the carbon canister. Do not plug the openings. Remove the bolts on either side of the exhaust manifold plug.

2. Remove the plug in the exhaust manifold, install the test nipple BMW part No. 13 0 100 or equivalent and connect the CO tester 13 0 070 or equivalent into the open nipple.

3. With the engine valve clearances correctly adjusted, ignition timing correct and the engine at operating temperature, measure the CO percentage at idle speed. CO nominal value is 0.2–1.2%.

4. If the CO level is within the specified range, disconnect the test unit, replace the plug in the exhaust manifold, and conclude the test. If not, adjust the CO as described below.

5. Turn off the engine and then unplug the oxygen sensor plug. Drill a hole in the anti-tamper plug in the throttle body with special tool No. 13 1 092 or equivalent. Then screw the special extractor tool No. 13 1 094 or equivalent into the hole drilled into

the plug and draw the plug out with the impact mass. Finally, use an adjustment tool 13 1 060 or 13 1 100 or equivalent to turn the adjustment, with the engine running, until the CO meets nominal values.

6. When the adjustment is complete, install a new anti-tamper plug, and reconnect the oxygen sensor plug and the carbon canister hose. Also, remove the nipple in the exhaust manifold and replace the plug. Reinstall the exhaust manifold bolts.

### *528e*

1. Pull the canister purge hose off the solenoid, leave it unplugged.

2. Connect the CO meter 13 0 070 or equivalent to the manifold via the nipple 13 0 100.

3. With the engine valve clearances correctly adjusted, ignition timing correct and the engine at operating temperature, measure the CO percentage at idle speed. CO nominal value is 0.2–1.2%.

4. If the CO level is within the specified range, disconnect the test unit, replace the plug in the exhaust manifold, and conclude the test. If not, adjust the CO as described below.

5. Turn off the engine and then unplug the oxygen sensor plug. Drill a hole in the anti-tamper plug in the throttle body with special tool No. 13 1 092 or equivalent. Then screw the special extractor tool No. 13 1 094 or equivalent into the hole drilled into the plug and draw the plug out with the impact mass. Finally, use an adjustment tool 13 1 060 or 13 1 100 or equivalent to turn the adjustment, with the engine running, until the CO meets nominal values.

6. When the adjustment is complete, install a new anti-tamper plug, and reconnect the oxygen sensor plug and the carbon canister hose. Also, remove the nipple in the exhaust manifold and replace the plug. Reconnect the hose to the solenoid.

### *525i, 533i, 535i, 633CSi, 635CSi, 733i, 735i and 735iL*

1. Make sure the idle speed is correct. The engine must be hot. Disconnect the evaporative emissions canister purge hose at the bottom of the solenoid mounted on the firewall. Leave the openings unplugged.

2. Unscrew the bolts on the exhaust manifold and install a nipple (part No. 13 0 100 or equivalent) and connect the CO test unit 13 0 070 or equivalent. CO should be 0.2–1.2%. If CO is not within limits, adjust it as described below.

3. Turn off the engine and unplug the oxygen sensor plug. Then, remove the air flow sensor by removing the air

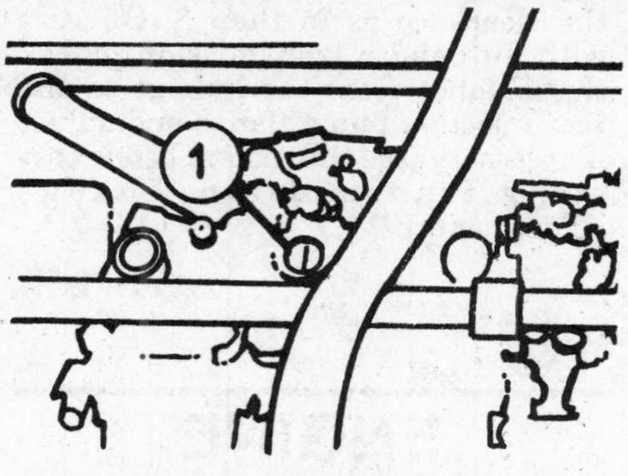


**On the M5 and M6 engines, adjust idle speed by turning this screw (1)**

cleaner and removing the 3 mounting bolts to separate the airflow sensor from it.

4. Use special tool 13 1 092 or equivalent to remove the anti-tamper plug. Use this tool to drill a hole in the plug and then use 13 1 094 or equivalent to pull it. The second tool should be screwed into the hole already drilled; use the slide hammer to pull the plug out.

5. Once the plug is removed, install the air flow sensor back onto the air cleaner and reinstall the air cleaner. With the engine idling hot and the oxygen sensor plug still disconnected, measure the CO and adjust it with Tool 13 1 060 or 13 1 100 or equivalent. The CO level must meet the nominal value of 0.2–1.2%.

6. Once the level is adjusted, stop the engine and reconnect the oxygen sensor plug. Then, remove the air flow sensor, put it on a bench, and install a new anti-tamper plug. Reinstall the airflow sensor and air cleaner. Reconnect the canister purge hose to the solenoid.

### *M3*

**NOTE: This test must be performed at essentially sea level altitude. In an area well above sea level, it will be necessary to use a BMW Service tester or equivalent device from another source and run the test with the system's altitude correction box connected.**

1. Make sure the engine is at operating temperature, and that the air cleaner is in reasonably clean condition. All basic engine tuning factors (spark plug condition and gap, valve adjustment, ignition timing, etc.) must be correct. Turn off all accessories.

2. A special electrical fitting (BMW special tool 13 4 010 or equivalent) is required to disable the Motronic control system's throttle valve switch. Pull off the electrical connector leading to the throttle valve switch. Then,

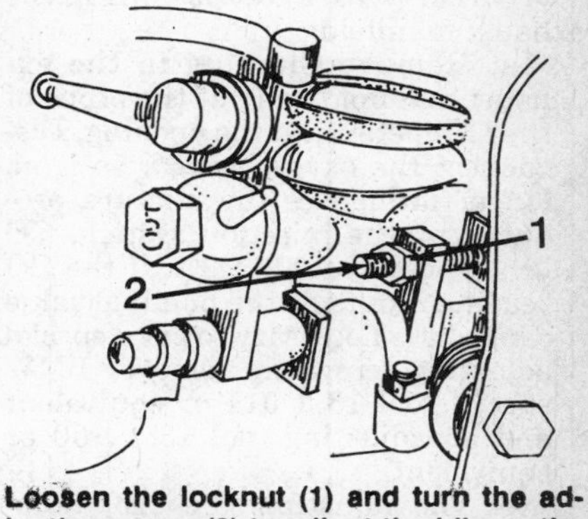


**Loosen the locknut (1) and turn the adjusting screw (2) to adjust the idle on the diesel engine**

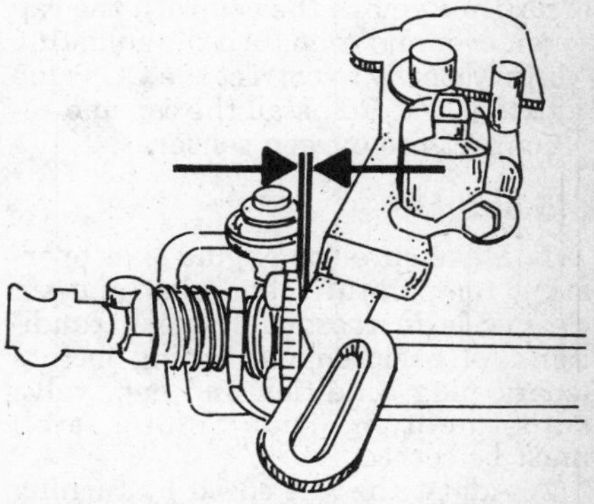

**Check the play "S" between the knurled screw and the throttle lever (524 td)**

plug the special tool into the open end of the connector.

3. Adjust the idle speed to specification by turning the screw located just above the "M" on the valve cover. Make sure to restore the throttle valve switch when the idle speed is correct.

4. Make sure the engine is in good basic tune, including proper spark plug gap and valve clearances. The engine must be at operating temperature.

- On cars with no test openings in the exhaust manifold:

a. With a CO meter in the tailpipe, disconnect the oxygen sensor so it no longer influences the mixture produced by the injection system. CO level should be zero. If there is a CO reading, it is necessary to get a special adjusting screw cap remover BMW special tool 13 1 011 or equivalent and an adjusting tool 13 1 100 or equivalent.

b. The adjusting screw cap is located on the top surface of the airflow sensor; the adjusting screw is accessible in the aperture underneath. Remove the cap with the cap remover and then turn the adjusting screw slowly to correct the CO value to 0. Reinstall the cap and reconnect the oxygen sensor.

- On cars with a test opening in the exhaust manifold:

a. Remove the plug in the exhaust manifold and put the probe of the CO meter into the opening. Disconnect the oxygen sensor so it no longer influences the mixture produced by the injection system. CO level should be 0.8–1.2%. If the CO reading is outside the nominal value range, it is necessary to get a special adjusting screw cap remover BMW special tool 13 1 011 or equivalent and an adjusting tool 13 1 100 or equivalent.

b. The adjusting screw cap is located on the top surface of the airflow sensor; the adjusting screw is accessible in the aperture underneath. Remove the cap with the cap remover and then turn the adjusting screw slowly to correct the CO value to .8–1.2%. Reinstall the cap and reconnect the oxygen sensor.

#### *M5 and M6*

1. Make sure the engine is at operating temperature, and that the air cleaner is in reasonably clean condition. All basic engine tuning factors (spark plug condition and gap, valve adjustment, ignition timing, etc.) must be correct.
2. Adjust the idle speed by turning the screw shown in the illustration.
3. To adjust CO, first remove the cap located at the center of the top surface of the airflow sensor. Use a special tool 13 1 100 to turn the airflow control screw in the airflow sensor, accessible after the anti-tamper cap is removed. CO must be 0.4–1.2%.
4. Install a new cap when CO meets specification.

## Idle Speed Diesel Engine

### ADJUSTMENT

1. Valve clearance must be correct. Run the engine until it reaches operating temperature. Make sure all electrical accessories are shut off. Check to make sure the throttle lever is resting on the idle adjusting screw. Shut the engine off.
2. Check the play between the throttle lever and the knurled screw. It should be 0.020–0.012 in. Hold the hexagonal nut associated with the screw with the knurled head, and then turn that screw until the play is correct.
3. Loosen the locknut (1) and turn the adjusting screw (2) to give the correct idle speed. Tighten the locknut.
4. Repeat the clearance check of Step 2. If not to specification, readjust the clearance as in Step 3. On cars with automatic transmission, check the distance from the linkage to the rear injection pump flange and adjust if necessary (see the section below covering transmission linkage adjustments).

# ENGINE ELECTRICAL

## Distributor

### REMOVAL & INSTALLATION

#### *4 Cylinder Engines Except M3*

1. Disconnect the negative battery cable. On all engines so equipped, remove the weather-proof rubber cap protecting the distributor cap and wires from moisture. Prior to removal, using paint, chalk or a sharp instrument, scribe alignment marks showing the relative position of the distributor body to its mount on the rear of the cylinder head.
2. Following the firing order illustration at the beginning of this section, mark each spark plug wire with a dab of paint or chalk noting its respective cylinder. It will be easier and faster to install the distributor and get the firing order right if the plug wires are left in the cap.
3. Pull up and disconnect the secondary wire (high tension cable leading from the coil to the center of the distributor cap), and remove the spark plug loom retaining nut(s) from the cylinder head cover. Disconnect the vacuum line(s) from the vacuum advance unit.
4. Disconnect the primary wire (low tension wire running from one of the coil terminals to the side of the distributor) at the distributor. On electronic ignition distributors, disconnect the plug.
5. Unsnap the distributor retaining clasps and lift off the cap and wire assembly. On all engines equipped with a dust cap under the rotor, remove the rotor, remove the dust cap and reinstall the rotor.
6. Now, with the aid of a remote starter switch or a friend, "bump" the starter a few times until the No. 1 piston is at TDC of its compression stroke. At this time, the notch scribed on the metal tip of the distributor rotor must be aligned with a corresponding notch scribed on the distributor case. Before removing the distributor,

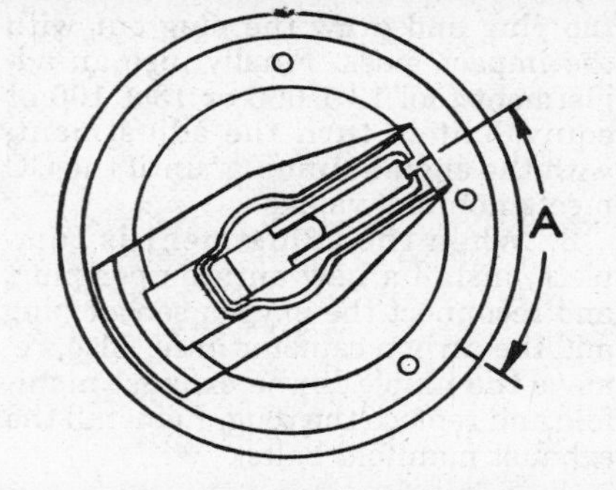


Distance (A) rotor moves from the housing mark during the removal of the electronic distributor

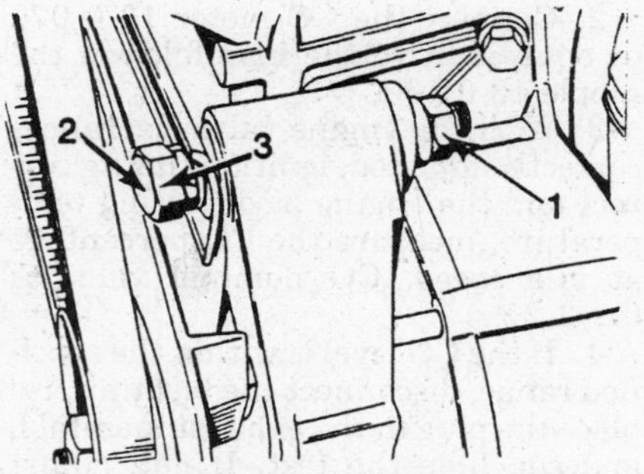


Loosen the locknut (1) at the rear of the alternator, and then turn the bolt (3) and tighten to 4.0–4.3 ft. lb. Hold the bolt in position while tightening the nut—318i

make sure that these 2 marks coincide as per the illustration.

7. Loosen the clamp bolt at the base of the distributor (where it slides into its mount) and lift the distributor up and out. Notice that the rotor turns clockwise as the distributor is removed. This is because the distributor is gear driven and must be compensated for during installation.
8. To install the distributor, position it in the block. Remember to rotate the rotor approximately 1.4 in. counterclockwise (see illustration) from the notch scribed in the distributor body. This will ensure that when the distributor is fully seated in its mount, the marks will coincide. Adjust the ignition timing as described earlier. Tighten the clamp bolt to 8.0 ft. lbs.
9. Reinstall the cap and wires.

#### *M3 Engine and 6 Cylinder Engines*

**NOTE: Most 6 cylinders and the 4 cylinder engine used on the M3 use a distributor which is contained within the engine. Other than distributor cap and rotor removal and installation, no service is possible.**

## INSTALLATION

### *TIMING DISTURBED*

Sometimes, the engine is accidentally turned over while the distributor is removed; in this case, it will be necessary to find TDC position for No. 1 cylinder before installing the distributor. Check the exact position of the crankshaft via the timing marks on the flywheel or front pulley, and obtain exact alignment as indicated by them. Then, proceed to install the distributor.

# Alternator

## PRECAUTIONS

Several precautions must be observed with alternator equipped vehicles to avoid damaging the unit. They are as follows:

- If the battery is removed for any reason, make sure that it is reconnected with the correct polarity. Reversing the battery connections may result in damage to the one-way rectifiers.
- When utilizing a booster battery as a starting aid, always connect it as follows: positive to positive, and negative (booster battery) to a good ground on the engine the car being started.
- Never use a fast charger as a booster to start cars with alternating-current (AC) circuits.
- When servicing the battery with a fast charger, always disconnect the battery cables.
- Never attempt to polarize an alternator.
- Avoid long soldering times when replacing diodes or transistors. Prolonged heat is damaging to alternators.
- Do not use test lamps of more than 12 volts for checking diode continuity.
- Do not short across or ground any of the terminals on the alternator.
- The polarity of the battery, alternator, and regulator must be matched and considered before making any electrical connections within the system.
- Never operate the alternator on an open circuit. Make sure that all connections within the circuit are clean and tight.
- Turn off the ignition switch and then disconnect the battery terminals when performing any service on the electrical system or charging the battery.
- Disconnect the battery ground cable if arc welding is to be done on any part of the car.

## BELT TENSION ADJUSTMENT

The fan belt tension is adjusted by moving the alternator on the slack adjuster bracket. The belt tension is adjusted to a deflection of approximately ½ in. under moderate thumb pressure in the middle of its longest span. On many late model engines, the position of the top of the alternator is adjusted via a bolt that is geared to the bracket. This bolt is turned to position the alternator and determine tension, and then is locked in position with a lockbolt.

## REMOVAL & INSTALLATION

1. Disconnect the battery ground cable.

2. Disconnect the wires from the rear of the alternator, marking them for later installation. Note that there is a ground wire on some models. On the 735i and 735iL, remove the cap and then disconnect the positive terminal at the junction box on the fender well. On the 325, M3, 633CSi, 635CSi, 733i and 735i and 735iL, it may be easier to remove the alternator mounting bolts, turn it, and then remove the wires.

- On the M5 and M6:

  a. Unscrew the nut and loosen the hose clamp. Pull of the plug. Then, lift out the air cleaner and airflow sensor.

  b. Make sure the engine is cool. Place a pan underneath and then disconnect the lower radiator hose.

- On the 1988–89 325, and the M3 and 528e, remove the airflow sensor.
- On the 735i and 735iL, make sure the engine is cool. Place a pan underneath and then disconnect the lower radiator hose.

3. Loosen the adjusting and pivot bolts, and remove the belt on those models with a standard mounting system. If the alternator has the tensioning bolt described in Step 4, loosen the lockbolt, turn the tensioning bolt so as to eliminate belt tension and then remove the belt. Remove the bolts and remove the alternator. On the 633CSi, 635CSi, 733i, 735i and 735iL, it may be necessary to loosen the fan cowl to get at the mounting bolts. On the 535i and 525i, it may be necessary to disconnect a power steering line that runs near the alternator.

**To install:**

4. Install the alternator in position and install the retaining bolts.

5. Adjust the belt tension to approximately ⅜ in., measured between the balancer and the alternator pulley.

6. On all 1984–90 models, a unique tensioning system is used. See the illustration for the 318i – the other models are similar. The tensioning bolt on the front of the alternator must be turned so as to tension the belt, using a torque wrench, until the torque is approximately 5 ft. lbs. Then, hold the adjustment with one wrench while tightening the locknut at the rear of the unit. Make sure that, if the unit has a ground wire on the alternator, it has been reconnected. On the M5 and M6, 735i and 735iL, make sure to reconnect the radiator hose, refill and bleed the cooling system. On the M5, M6, and 528e securely reinstall the air cleaner and airflow sensor. On the 528e, if the power steering line had to be disconnected, reconnect it securely, refill, and bleed the system.

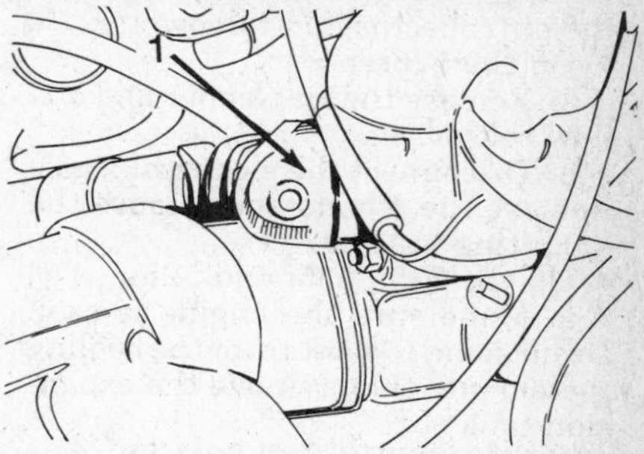

**In 318i starter removal, remove the nut and detach the bracket (1)**

# Starter

## REMOVAL & INSTALLATION

1. Disconnect the battery ground cable.

2. On fuel injected 6 cylinder models with 6 identical intake tubes, it may be necessary to remove No. 6 intake tube for clearance. On injected 4 cylinder models, remove the intake cowl from the mixture control unit. On the 318i, remove the wire holding bracket.

- On the 325 up to 1987:

  a. Disconnect the positive terminal at the junction box on the fender well. Then, remove the air cleaner with the flow sensor.

  b. Unscrew the air collector bracket that's in the way.

  c. Unscrew the nut that fastens a wiring bracket near the starter.

  d. Make sure the engine is cool and then drain the coolant into a clean container. Disconnect the heater hose that runs near the starter. Remove the coolant pipe if doing so is necessary for clearance.

- On the 1988–90 325 and the M3:

  a. Remove the air cleaner and airflow sensor. Then, remove the mounting bolts for the bracket for the air collector and remove it.

- On the 528e:

a. Remove the air cleaner and airflow sensor.

b. Disconnect the electrical leads. Remove the 3 bolts and remove the mounting bracket.

- On the 533i, 535i and 525i:

a. Make sure the engine is cool. Drain some coolant from the cooling system and then remove the expansion tank.

- On the 633CSi and 635CSi:

a. Make sure the engine is cool and drain some coolant out. Disconnect the heater hose that is near the starter.

b. Operate the brake pedal hard 20 times. Disconnect the power steering line that would otherwise prevent access to the starter.

c. Cut off the straps and remove the solenoid switch insulating cover, located right near the solenoid.

- On the M5 and M6:

a. Remove the exhaust manifold.

b. Cut off the straps and remove the solenoid switch insulating cover, located right near the solenoid.

3. Remove the starter solenoid wire leads, marking them for later installation, unless they have already been removed. On 4 cylinder models, disconnect the mounting bracket at the block. On the 1988–90 325 and the M3, drain coolant out of the engine and then disconnect the heater hose located near the starter; also unscrew and remove the coolant pipe if necessary for clearance.

**NOTE: Remove the accelerator cable holder on automatic transmission equipped vehicles.**

4. Unbolt and remove the starter. On the 325 up to 1987, the lower nut can be removed more easily from underneath. On late model 533, 525i, 535i, 733i, 735i and 735iL, M5 and M6, it may be necessary to use a box wrench with an angled handle to unscrew the main starter mounting bolts. On the 528e, 633CSi and 635CSi, the final mounting bolt must be removed from underneath. On the 1988–90 325 and the M3. the starter must be pulled out from above.

**To install:**

5. Install the starter and install the retaining bolts. Install all removed components on all models.

6. Make sure to reconnect all hoses and refill and bleed the cooling system or power steering system.

7. Where the solenoid switch cover has been unstrapped, reinstall it with new straps to locate it properly for electrical safety.

## STARTER DRIVE REPLACEMENT

The starter must be disassembled to replace the starter drive. A circlip retains the drive gear on the armature shaft and must be removed before the drive gear can be replaced.

1. Remove the field coil wires from the solenoid and remove the solenoid mounting bolts.
2. Disengage the solenoid plunger from the starter drive and remove the solenoid from the starter motor.
3. Remove the small dust cap from the end of the motor.
4. Remove the C-clip, shims and gasket from the end of the starter motor shaft.
5. Remove the 2 long pole housing screws from the housing. Lift off the pole housing cap, the brushes and the brush plate.
6. Remove the intermediate bearing screws and remove the pole housing.
7. Remove the rubber seal and washer from the engaging lever housing.
8. Remove the engaging lever screw and pull the armature out of the drive bearing.
9. Push back the thrust washer or thrust bearing race on the drive pinion end of the motor shaft in order to remove the C-clip retainer.
10. Remove the starter drive pinion and bracket.

**To install:**

11. Install the starter pinion and bracket. Secure them on the shaft with the thrust washer and C-clip. Lubricate the coarse threads, engaging ring and bearing with high temperature silicone grease.
12. Install the armature and shaft into the drive bearing, making sure that the tabs of the engaging lever are installed over the engaging ring. Lubricate the engaging lever with silicone grease.
13. Install the washer and rubber seal into the engaging lever housing, making sure the tabs on the seal and washer point toward the armature.
14. Position the pole housing so that the groove faces toward the rubber pad and install the pole housing into the drive bearing. Secure the screws with Loctite® No. 270.
15. Check the commutator bearing for looseness and then guide the field coil wires into the rubber seal.
16. Install the pole housing screws through the pole housing cap and locating slots in the brush plate. Install the brushes and pole housing cap on the starter.
17. Check armature axial play to 0.004–0.006 in. (0.1–0.15mm) (0.004–0.008 in. on 1984–90 models) and correct any excessive play with additional shims.
18. Install end gasket, shims and C-clip on the end of the motor shaft. Install the dust cover on the end of the starter motor (over the shaft, end gasket and shims).
19. Install the solenoid on the starter and attach the field coil wires to the solenoid.

# Diesel Glow Plugs

## REMOVAL & INSTALLATION

1. Disconnect the negative battery cable. Unscrew the electrical connection. Unscrew the glow plug with a suitable deep well socket or BMW special socket 12 2 100.
2. Coat the threads on the replacement plug with a copper paste such as CRC or equivalent. Install the plug and torque it to 14–22 ft. lbs. Install leads only after the plug is fully torqued to prevent twisting the wires.

## TESTING

1. Remove the cover from the heating time control unit for the glow plugs. Unplug both plugs. The engine compartment must be about 68°F.
2. Apply the test leads of an ohmmeter between the battery ground (–) and each of the lead tips G1–G6 on the No. 2 plug. Resistance must be 0.4–.6 ohms. If outside limits, replace the associated glow plug.
3. It is also possible to test amperage draw. Connect the test leads of an ammeter between the battery (+) terminal and each of the connectors G1–G6 on plug No. 2. Connect each for 5 seconds and then read the amperage. It should be 13–15 amps.

**Measure the electrical resistance at plug (2). Plug (1) must also be unplugged before making electrical tests, however**

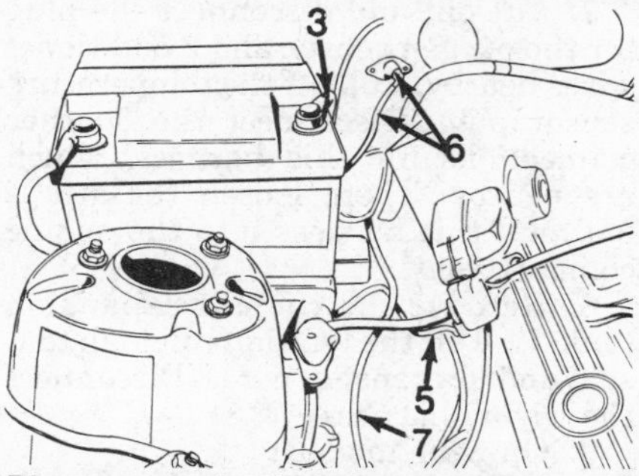


Disconnect wire (3) and ground (5), pull off plugs on temperature sensor (6), and on oxygen sensor (7)—318i

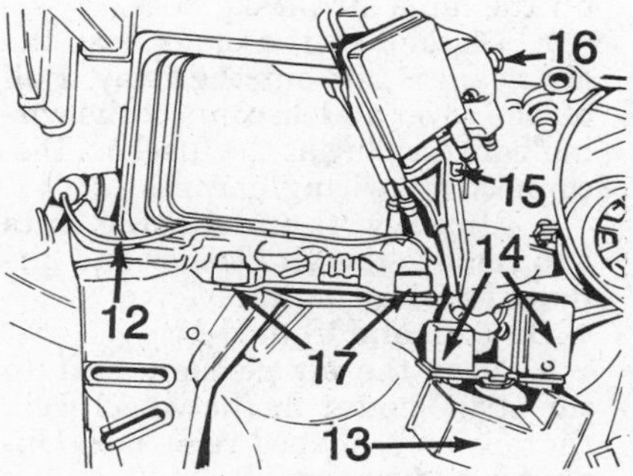


Disconnect wire (12), lift off cap (13) and remove relay (14), disconnect plug (15), open hose strap (16). Loosen nuts (17) and remove the air cleaner—318i

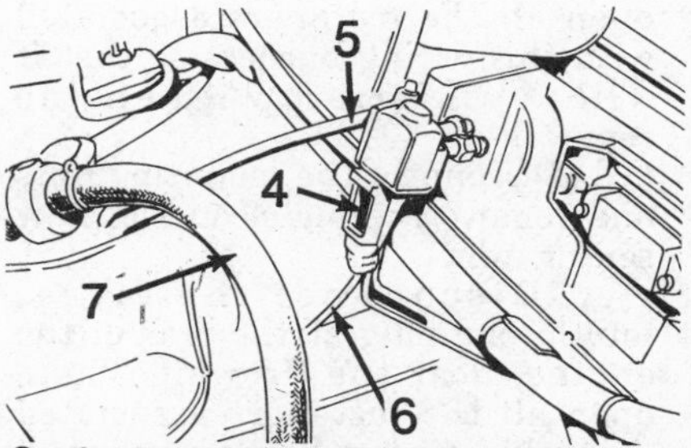


On the 318i, pull off the plug (4) and vacuum hoses (5 and 6). Detach vacuum hose (7). When installing, make sure (5) goes to the distributor, and (6) to the intake manifold.

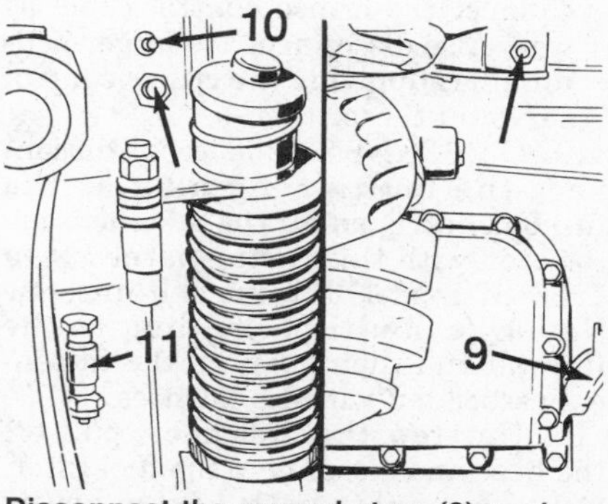


Disconnect the ground strap (9), and engine shock absorber (11) on the 318i. During installation, note that the pin (10) must fit into a bore in the axle carrier.

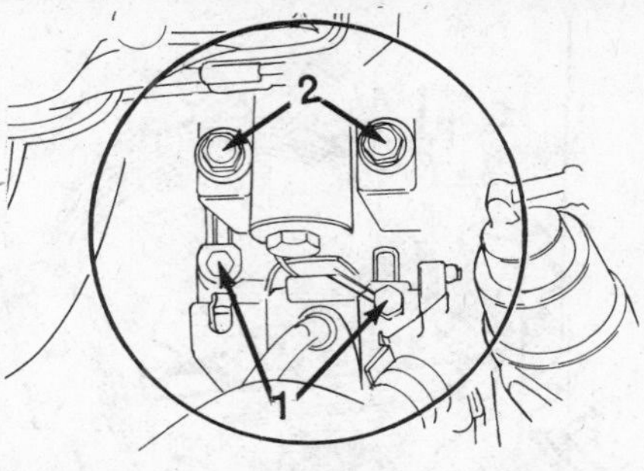


Remove bolts (1 and 2), then remove the bolt at the base of the A/C compressor—1984–87 318i

# ENGINE MECHANICAL

## Engine

### REMOVAL & INSTALLATION

#### *1984–85 318i*

1. Disconnect the negative battery cable. Remove the transmission from the vehicle.
2. Scribe hood hinge locations on the hood, and then remove it.
3. Detach the 2 mounting bolts and remove the power steering pump with hoses attached. Suspend the pump securely so that hoses will not be damaged.
4. Looking at the top of the air conditioning compressor, loosen the 2 outer bolts (bolts screwing into the compressor) and remove the 2 bolts fastening the mounting bracket to the engine. Then, support the unit and remove the hinge nut and bolt form the bottom of the unit. Finally, pull the unit away from the engine and support it to avoid putting strain on refrigerant hoses.

**NOTE: Do not disconnect any air conditioning hoses!**

5. Remove the radiator cap and drain coolant. Detach radiator hoses. Then, on air conditioned cars, disconnect the wires at the temperature switches. Unscrew and remove the cover located at the left side of the radiator (driver's side). Unscrew and disconnect transmission oil cooler lines at the radiator (automatic only), and plug openings. Finally, remove the mounting bolt located at the top, lift the radiator upward until it clears the rubber mounts on the bottom, and remove it.
6. Disconnect both battery leads and the battery-to-alternator wire. Disconnect the engine ground strap.
7. Open clips that hold the wiring harness running along the fender just behind the battery. Disconnect plugs from the temperature sensor and oxygen sensor.
8. Remove the glovebox liner. Unplug plugs at the idle control and L-Jetronic units. Unplug the connector that also comes out of this harness. Then, pull the harness through into the engine compartment.
9. Disconnect all 3 coil wires and wire to the electronic ignition unit. Take the wires out of the clips mounted nearby.
10. At the air cleaner, disconnect the wire mounted on the side of the air cleaner housing, and disconnect the plug. Lift off the L-shaped cap of the relay mounted nearby, and then remove the relay. Loosen the strap and disconnect the inlet hose. Loosen the 2 mounting nuts and remove the air cleaner.
11. Go to the relay box mounted in between the cowl and suspension strut on the driver's side. Remove the top of the box and lift out and disconnect the plug on the outboard side. Remove the rubber guard from the TCI control unit nearby and pull off the plug connected to that. Open both associated wire straps.
12. Going to the rear of the intake manifold, unscrew the clamp and pull off the large vacuum hose. Label and then disconnect the small vacuum hoses running to the distributor and intake manifold.
13. Disconnect the throttle cable. Remove the hose clamp and hose nearby.
14. Detach fuel hoses at the injection system, and with them the associated hose holder. Collect fuel in a metal pan.
15. Attach a suitable hoist to hooks at front and rear of the engine and support the engine securely.
16. Detach both engine mounts and the vibration damper. Lift out the engine, taking care not to permit the engine to shift and hit anything on the way out.

**To install:**

17. Install the engine in reverse order, keeping these points in mind:
    a. The locating mandrel on the front of the engine must be guided into the front suspension carrier.
    b. Adjust the throttle cable for smooth operation.
    c. Adjust the fan, air conditioning compressor, and power steering pump drive belts.

#### *320i*

1. Remove the transmission as detailed later.
2. Scribe lines, around the hood

hinges and then remove the hood.

3. Disconnect the upper and lower radiator hoses and then remove the radiator.

4. Unscrew and remove the air filter housing.

5. On models equipped with air conditioning, detach the compressor and position it out of the way with wires. Do not disconnect the refrigerant lines.

6. Disconnect the battery cables (negative cable first) and remove the battery.

7. Disconnect all fuel lines at the fuel distributor. Pull the hose off the charcoal canister. Disconnect the ground wire from the front axle carrier.

8. Unscrew the retaining nut and lift the accelerator cable from the holders toward the side. Push the nipple out toward the rear and then disconnect the cable.

9. Tag and disconnect all remaining wires and hoses which may interfere with engine removal.

10. Lift out the relay socket and then pull out the 2 relays to the side of the housing. Disconnect the plug underneath and then lift out the wire harness from its holder on the wheel arch.

11. Open the glove box and disconnect the plug on the left-hand side. Pull the harness out through the hole in the firewall (into the engine compartment). Pull the harness out of its holders.

12. Attach an engine hoist or the like to the front and rear of the engine.

13. Unbolt the left engine mount and the upper engine damper.

14. Unbolt the right engine mount and lift out the engine.

**To install:**

15. Install the engine into the engine compartment and install the motor mount nuts.

16. Slide the electrical harness in through the firewall and connect it to the control unit.

17. Connect all the wires and hoses to the engine components, making sure to properly route the wiring.

18. Install the accelerator cable and its retaining nut. When installing the accelerator cable, push the cable through the eye on the lever, attach it and then press the nipple into the eye. Attach the cable to the holder.

19. Connect the fuel lines and the vacuum lines. Install the radiator and connect the hoses.

20. On models equipped with air conditioning install the compressor and connect the wiring to it.

21. Install the air filter housing. With the aid of an assistant, install the hood, aligning the scribe marks made on the hood.

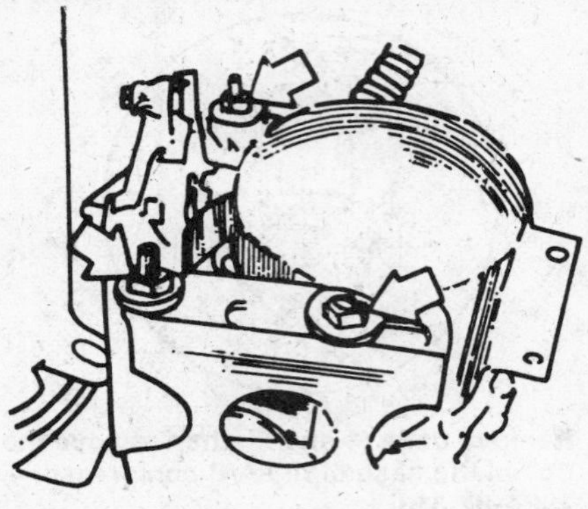

**Remove the three arrowed bolts and remove the compressor – 1988–89 318i and M3**

### *1983–87 325, 325e, 325i and 325iS*

1. Disconnect the battery ground cable. Remove the transmission as described in the appropriate section.

2. Without disconnecting hoses, loosen and remove the 3 power steering pump bolts and remove the pump and belts and support the pump out of the way.

3. Remove the drain plug and remove the coolant from the radiator. Then, remove the radiator (see the appropriate procedure).

4. Without disconnecting hoses, remove the 3 mounting bolts and remove the air conditioner compressor and drive belt and support the compressor out of the way.

5. Remove the through-bolts to disconnect the engine hood supports and then open the hood and support it securely.

**CAUTION**

***The hood must be propped in a secure manner! If it falls during work serious injury could result.***

6. Remove the trim panel inside the glovebox.

- On 325e models:

a. Disconnect the plugs going to the engine control computer; 2 are located in the wiring, and one directly on the unit.

b. Unscrew the idle control unit near the main control computer and pull off its plugs. On automatic transmission-equipped cars, disconnect the plug leading to the vehicle wiring harness.

- On 325i and 325iS models:

a. Pull the main, multiprong plug off the control unit. Also unplug one plug in a wire coming into the unit, located below the unit and to the left.

b. If the car has an automatic transmission, disconnect the plug for the main wiring harness.

7. Lift out and disconnect the plug for the oxygen sensor and 2 additional wires nearby. Pull off the temperature sensor plug. Disconnect the 3 other connections for this harness, which are nearby. Then, loosen the straps and pull this harness into the engine compartment.

8. Remove the coolant expansion tank. Pull off the ignition coil high tension and low tension wires. Disconnect the wiring harness.

9. On 325e models:

a. Disconnect the accelerator cable and cruise control cable. Pull off the vacuum hoses going to the throttle body. Loosen the clamp and pull off the large air intake hose.

b. Disconnect the plugs near the air cleaner. Lift out the relay. Pull off the cover and disconnect the wiring harness plug at the fusebox. Disconnect the wiring harness.

c. Unscrew the mounting nuts and remove the air cleaner and airflow sensor as a unit.

- On 325i and iS models:

a. Near the air cleaner, next to the strut mount in the wheel well, there is an L-shaped relay box. Unplug it and remove it.

b. Loosen the clamp on the air intake hose.

c. Disconnect the multiprong connector from the airflow sensor (integral with the air cleaner). Then, open all the fasteners associated with this wiring harness so that it will not interfere with engine removal.

d. Disconnect the mounting nuts and remove the air cleaner/airflow sensor unit.

e. Disconnect the large, multiprong plug at the rear of the engine, near the firewall. Then, open all the fasteners associated with this wiring harness as well. Also, disconnect the 2 vacuum hoses nearby.

f. Disconnect the accelerator cable. If the car has cruise control, disconnect the cruise control cable as well. Also disconnect the large vacuum line supplying the cruise control servo on these cars.

10. On 1983–85 325e cars, disconnect the multiprong plug at the fusebox and open all the fasteners associated with this wiring harness. On 1986–87 models lift out and unscrew the large, multi-prong plug at the firewall and then open up the fasteners associated with its harness.

11. Unscrew the fuel lines, pull off the hose and disconnect the fuel filter.

12. Disconnect both heater hoses. Disconnect the engine ground strap. Unbolt the engine mounts.

13. Lift out the engine with a suit-

able hoist, using hooks at front and rear.

**To install:**

14. To install, reverse the procedures used for removal and lower the engine into the engine compartment. When the engine is positioned, the guide pin must fit in the bore of the axle carrier.

Torque the mounting bolts on the front axle carrier (small bolt) to 18–20 ft. lb.; the larger bolt to 31–35 ft. lb. Torque the mount-to-bracket bolts to 31–35 ft. lbs.

Torque the engine-to-bracket mounts to (small bolt) 16–17 ft. lb., (large bolt) 31–35 ft. lb.

15. Connect the fuel lines, use new hose clamps to connect the fuel lines to the fuel filter. Connect all of the multiprong plugs and all vacuum hoses.

16. Connect the accelerator cable and cruise control cable to the throttle body and adjust the accelerator cable and cruise control cable.

17. Install the coolant recovery tank, use a new hose clamp on the coolant expansion tank.

18. Install the air cleaner and reconnect all electrical plugs. Connect and install the "L" shaped relay box on the wheel well.

19. Reconnect the wiring to the main control unit and install the idle control unit.

20. Install the air conditioning compressor and power steering pump, properly route the accessory drive belt. Adjust the belt tension.

21. Install the radiator and connect the hoses.

22. Install the transmission.

23. Install the hood support and lower the hood.

24. Make sure all fluid levels are correct before starting the engine. Bleed air from the cooling system.

### 1988–90 325, 325e, 325i and 325iS

1. Disconnect the battery ground cable. Remove the transmission as described in the appropriate section.

2. Without disconnecting hoses, loosen and remove the 3 power steering pump bolts and remove the pump and belts and support the pump out of the way.

3. Remove the drain plug and remove the coolant from the radiator. Then, remove the radiator (see the appropriate procedure). Unbolt and remove the fan from the engine. Store it in an upright position.

4. Without disconnecting hoses, remove the 4 mounting bolts (they run through the compressor body) and remove the air conditioner compressor and drive belt and support the compressor out of the way.

5. Remove the through-bolts to disconnect the engine hood supports and then open the hood and support it securely.

**CAUTION**

***The hood must be propped in a secure manner! If it falls during work serious injury could result.***

6. Disconnect the accelerator cable. If the car has cruise control, disconnect the cruise control cable. If the car has an automatic transmission, disconnect the throttle cable leading to the transmission.

7. Pull the large, multiprong plug off the airflow sensor (an integral part of the air cleaner). Loosen the clamp and disconnect the air intake hose at the airflow sensor. Remove the 2 mounting nuts and remove the air cleaner/airflow sensor unit.

8. Disconnect the coolant expansion tank hose. Disconnect the large, multiprong connector near ther air intake hose.

9. The diagnosis plug is a large, screw-on connector located near the thermostat and associated hoses. Unscrew and disconnect this connector.

10. Disconnect the 2 large coolant hoses connecting to the thermostat.

11. Make sure the engine is cold. Place a metal container under the connection to collect fuel; then, disconnect the fuel line at the connection right near the thermostat housing by unscrewing it. Unfasten the fuel line clip about a foot away from this connection.

12. Disconnect the 2 electrical plugs near the diagnosis plug connector. Disconnect the bracket for the dipstick guide tube.

13. Remove the 2 bolts which attach 2 water pipes going to the engine to mounting brackets.

14. Disconnect the 2 heater hoses at the heater core (near the firewall). Remove the coolant hose running to the top of the block.

15. Place a metal container under the connection to collect fuel; then, disconnect the remaining fuel hose supplying the engine injectors. Disconnect the 3 electrical connectors nearby.

16. Remove the bolt from the mounting brace connecting with the cylinder head.

17. Mark and then disconnect the 2 electrical leads from the starter. Unbolt the starter and lift it out from above.

18. Place a metal container under the connection to collect fuel; then, disconnect the fuel pipe that runs right near the starter.

19. Label electrical connectors on the alternator. Then, pull off the rubber caps for the 2 connectors which are attached with nuts and remove the nuts and any washers. Disconnect the plug-on connector.

20. Disconnect the electrical leads for the coil. Loosen the clips attaching the leads under the distributor and pull the harness away to the left. Disconnect the oil pressure sending unit.

21. Place a drain pan underneath the 2 connections and then disconnect the oil cooler pipes at the crankcase by unscrewing the flare nut fittings.

22. Take the cover off the relay box. Then, lift out the relays and their mounting sockets. Place the relays and associated wiring on top of the engine so they will come out with it.

23. Loosen its mounting clamp and then remove the carbon canister. There is a plate nearby to which a number of electrical leads are connected. Remove the mounting screws and move the plate aside so that it will clear the dipstick guide tube when the engine is removed.

24. Remove the 2 bolts that fasten the wiring harness to the firewall. Then, disconnect the engine ground strap.

25. Remove both engine mount through-bolts. Lift out the engine with a suitable hoist, using hooks at front and rear.

**To install:**

26. To install, reverse the procedures used for removal and lower the engine into the engine compartment. When the engine is positioned, the guide pin must fit in the bore of the axle carrier. Torque the mounting bolts on the front axle carrier (small bolt) to 18–20 ft. lb.; the larger bolt to 31–35 ft. lb. The mount-to-bracket bolts are torqued to 31–35 ft. lb. Engine-to-bracket mounts are torqued to (small bolt) 16–17 ft. lb., (large bolt) 31–35 ft. lb.

27. Connect the fuel lines, use new hose clamps to connect the fuel lines to the fuel filter. Connect all of the multiprong plugs and all vacuum hoses.

28. Connect the accelerator cable and cruise control cable to the throttle body and adjust the accelerator cable and cruise control cable.

29. Install the coolant recovery tank, use a new hose clamp on the coolant expansion tank.

30. Install the air cleaner and reconnect all electrical plugs. Connect and install the relays in the relay box.

31. Reconnect the wiring to the main control unit and install the idle control unit.

32. Install the air conditioning compressor and power steering pump, properly route the accessory drive belt. Adjust the belt tension.

33. Install the radiator and connect the hoses.
34. Install the transmission.
35. Install the hood support and lower the hood.
36. Make sure all fluid levels are correct before starting the engine. Bleed air from the cooling system.

### M3

1. Disconnect the battery ground cable. Remove the transmission as described elsewhere.
2. Remove the splash guard from underneath the engine. Put a drain pan underneath and then drain coolant from both the radiator and block.
3. Loosen the hose clamps at either end of the air intake hose leading to the air intake sensor. Pull off the hose. Then, pull both electrical connectors off the air cleaner/airflow sensor unit. Remove both mounting nuts and remove the unit.
4. Disconnect the accelerator and cruise control cables. Unscrew the nuts mounting the cable housing mounting bracket and set the housings and bracket aside.
5. Loosen the clamp and disconnect the brake booster vacuum hose.
6. Loosen the clamp and disconnect the other end of the booster vacuum hose at the manifold. Remove the nut from the intake manifold brace.
7. Loosen the hose clamp and disconnect the air intake hose at the manifold. Then, remove all 6 nuts attaching the manifold assembly to the outer ends of the intake throttle necks and remove the assembly.
8. Put a drain pan underneath and then loosen the hose clamps and disconnect the coolant expansion tank hoses. Disconnect the engine ground strap.
9. Disconnect the ignition coil high tension lead. Then, label and then disconnect the 2 plugs on the front of the block, nearby. Remove the nut fastening another lead farther forward of the 2 plugs and move the lead aside so it will not interfere with engine removal.
10. Label and then disconnect the 2 plugs from the rear of the alternator. Label the 2 additional leads and then remove the nuts and disconnect those leads. It's best to reinstall nuts once the leads are removed to keep them from being mixed up.
11. Remove the cover for the electrical connectors from the starter. Label the leads and then remove the attaching nuts and disconnect them. Reinstall the nuts.
12. There is a wire running to a connector on the oil pan to warn of low oil level. Pull off the connector, unscrew the carrier for the lead, and then pull the lead out from above. Pull off the 2 connectors near where the lead for the low oil warning system ran and unclip the wires from the carrier.
13. Find the vacuum hose leading to the fuel pressure regulator. Pull it off. Label and then disconnect the 2 plugs nearby. Unscrew the mounting screw for another electrical lead connecting with the top of the block and remove the lead and its carrier.
14. There is a vacuum hose connecting with one of the throttle necks. Disconnect it and pull it out of the intake manifold bracket. Pull off the electrical connector nearby. Pull out the rubber retainer, and then pull the idle speed control out and put it aside. The engine wiring harness is located nearby. Take it out of its carriers.
15. All the fuel injectors are plugged into a common plate. Carefully and evenly pull the plate off the injectors, pull it out past the pressure regulator, and lay it aside.
16. Loosen the clamp and then disconnect the PCV hose. Label and then disconnect the 2 fuel lines connecting with the injector circuit (it's important to label them so that they can be installed correctly!). Put a drain pan underneath and then disconnect the heater hose from the cylinder head.
17. Loosen the clamp near the throttle necks and then pull the engine wiring harness out and put it aside. Put a drain pan underneath and then disconnect the heater hose that connects to the block.
18. Loosen the mounting clamp for the carbon canister, slide it out of the clamp, and place it aside with the hoses still connected.
19. Note the routing of the 2 oil cooler lines where they connect at the base of the oil filter. Label them if necessary. Put a drain pan underneath and then unscrew the flared connectors for the 2 lines.
20. Unbolt and remove the fan. Store it in an upright position. See the appropriate procedure later in this section and remove the radiator.
21. Support the power steering pump. Remove the adjusting bolt and disconnect and remove the belt. Then, remove the 2 sets of nuts and bolts on which the unit hinges. Pull the unit aside and hang it so there will not be strain on the hoses.
22. Remove the adjusting bolt for the air conditioning compressor and disconnect and remove the belt. Then, remove the nut at one end of the hinge bolt and pull the bolt out, suspending the compressor to reduce the load on the bolt and to keep it from falling. Move the compressor aside and hang it so there will not be strain on the hoses.
23. Remove the through-bolts to disconnect the engine hood supports and then open the hood and support it securely.

**CAUTION**

***The hood must be propped in a secure manner! If it falls during work serious injury could result.***

24. Suspend the engine with a lifting crane via the hooks at the front and rear of the cylinder head. Then, remove the nuts for the engine mounting bolts. The mounts are on the axle carrier and the nut is at the top on the left and on the bottom on the right. Then, carefully lift the engine out of the compartment, avoiding contact between it and the components remaining in the car.

**To install:**

25. Keep these points in mind during installation:
    a. Torque the engine mounting bolts to 32.5 ft. lbs.
    b. Adjust the belt tension for the air conditioning compressor and power steering pump drive belts to give ½–¾ in. deflection.
    c. Torque the oil cooler line flare nuts to 25 ft. lbs.
    d. When reconnecting the intake manifold to the throttle necks, inspect and, if necessary, replace the O-rings. Torque the mounting nuts to 6.5 ft. lbs.
26. To install, reverse the procedures used for removal and lower the engine into the engine compartment. When the engine is positioned, the guide pin must fit in the bore of the axle carrier. Torque the mounting bolts on the front axle carrier (small bolt) to 18–20 ft. lb.; the larger bolt to 31–35 ft. lb. The mount-to-bracket bolts are torqued to 31–35 ft. lb.
27. Install the intake manifold assembly and connect the fuel lines, use new hose clamps to connect the fuel lines to the fuel filter. Connect all of the multiprong plugs and all vacuum hoses.
28. Connect the accelerator cable and cruise control cable to the throttle body and adjust the accelerator cable and cruise control cable.
29. Install the coolant recovery tank, use a new hose clamp on the coolant expansion tank.
30. Install the air cleaner and reconnect all electrical plugs. Connect and install the relays in the relay box.
31. Reconnect the wiring to the main control unit and install the idle control unit.
32. Install the air conditioning compressor and power steering pump, properly route the accessory drive belt. Adjust the belt tension.
33. Install the radiator and connect the hoses.
34. Install the transmission.

35. Install the hood support and lower the hood.
36. Make sure all fluid levels are correct before starting the engine. Bleed air from the cooling system.

### 524td

1. Disconnect the negative battery cable. Remove the transmission as detailed later in this section.
2. Remove the adjusting and hinge bolts for the power steering pump support the pump out of the way securely without placing any strain on the hoses.
3. Remove the adjusting and hinge bolts for the air conditioning compressor; support the compressor out of the way without placing any strain on the hoses (do not attempt to disconnect them!)
4. Remove the drain plug from a block, and drain the coolant. Then, remove the radiator as described later in this section. Remove the circlip and disconnect the power lead, nearby.
5. Remove the ground wires from the hood. Disconnect the gas pressure hood props and then securely prop up the engine hood so it is wide open.
6. Disconnect the negative and positive battery leads.
7. Disconnect the primary electrical connection. Lift off the cover and pull off plugs. Disconnect the wire. Remove the preheating time control.
8. Remove the coolant overflow tank by disconnecting wiring and the coolant hose, removing the 2 mounting nuts, and then pulling it off the mounting studs.
9. Remove the cover and cap. Disconnect the plug. Then, pull off all 3 relays.
10. Remove the wiring harness fasteners at the body.
11. Disconnect the accelerator and cruise control cables.
12. Disconnect the fuel hoses running between the injection pump and the filter system (supply and return).
13. Disconnect the 5 vacuum hoses connecting to the rear of the engine block.
14. Disconnect the plug near the rear of the cylinder head and disconnect the ground wire nearby.
15. Disconnect the water hoses for the heater.
16. Disconnect the hoses going into the air cleaner. The large air intake hose is twisted to release it prior to removing it. Unscrew the wingnuts, release the clamps, and remove the air cleaner.
17. Place a bucket underneath the oil cooler and then disconnect both oil lines. Disconnect the manifold pressure line going to the turbo wastegate.
18. Disconnect the multi-prong plug on the control unit in the glovebox. Disconnect the engine wiring harness and pull it into the engine compartment.
19. Disconnect the wiring running near one of the engine mounts. Disconnect the engine ground strap.
20. Attach a lifting sling to the engine lifting hoods. Apply tension enough to support the engine. Pull the center-bolts out of both engine mounts and remove the engine.

**To install:**

21. To install, guide the engine into the engine compartment, carefully. The engine mounting system has a guidepin that must be fitted into a corresponding bore in the front axle to locate the engine properly for installing of the mount through-bolts.
22. Connect the electrical leads to the control unit and the ground strap to the body.
23. Connect the oil cooler lines and connect the pressure line to the turbocharger. Install the air cleaner and connect all hoses to the air cleaner assembly.
24. Reconnect the water hoses to the heater. Connect the vacuum lines to the rear of the engine block. Connect the fuel lines between the injection pump and the filler system.
25. Connect the accelerator and cruise control cables. Connect all the plugs and wiring at the relay box and the timed heater unit.
26. Install the radiator and all hoses. Reattach the air conditioning compressor and the power steering pump.
27. Install the transmission. Install the hood support struts.
28. Top off all of the fluids. Connect the battery cables. Run the engine and check for proper timing and idle.

### 528e

1. Disconnect the negative battery cable. Remove the transmission as detailed later. Disconnect the exhaust pipe from the exhaust manifold.
2. Remove the splash guard.
3. With the hoses still attached, remove the power steering pump and position it out of the way.
4. Unscrew the drain plug on the engine block, remove the upper and lower radiator hoses and drain the cooling system. After draining, remove the radiator.
5. With the refrigerant hoses still connected, remove the air conditioning compressor and position it out of the way.
6. Disconnect the gas pressure springs, scribe around the hinges and then remove the hood.
7. Disconnect the battery cables (negative first) and remove the battery.
8. Disconnect the accelerator and cruise control cables. Disconnect all hoses from the throttle housing (make sure to tag them all). Disconnect the air duct.
9. Remove the air filter housing along with the air flow sensor.
10. Tag and disconnect all remaining lines, hoses and wires which may interfere with engine removal.
11. Tag and disconnect all plugs and wires attached to the control unit in the glove box. Unscrew the straps on the firewall and pull the wire harness through to the engine compartment.
12. Disconnect the engine ground strap and then loosen both engine mounts.
13. Attach an engine lifting hoist to the front and rear of the engine, remove the engine mount bolts and then lift out the engine.

**To install:**

14. To install, reverse the procedures used for removal and lower the engine into the engine compartment. When the engine is positioned, the guide pin must fit in the bore of the axle carrier. Torque the mounting bolts on the front axle carrier (small bolt) to 18–20 ft. lb.; the larger bolt to 31–35 ft. lb. The mount-to-bracket bolts are torqued to 31–35 ft. lb.
15. Connect all of the electrical wiring and all vacuum hoses.
16. Connect the accelerator cable and cruise control cable to the throttle body and adjust the accelerator cable and cruise control cable.
17. Install the air cleaner and reconnect all electrical plugs.
18. Reconnect the wiring to the main control unit.
19. Install the air conditioning compressor and power steering pump, properly route the accessory drive belt. Adjust the belt tension.
20. Install the radiator and connect the hoses.
21. Install the transmission.
22. Install the hood support and lower the hood.
23. Make sure all fluid levels are correct before starting the engine. Bleed the air from the cooling system.

### 525i, 533i, 535i, 633CSi and 635CSi

1. Disconnect both battery connections (negative first). There is a lead coming from the engine to the positive battery terminal. Disconnect it at the battery. On the 600 Series cars, disconnect the ground strap.
2. Unscrew the ground strap for the hood. Support the hood securely and then disconnect the gas props. Then, raise the hood until it is vertical and securely fasten it in place.
3. Remove the transmission as de-

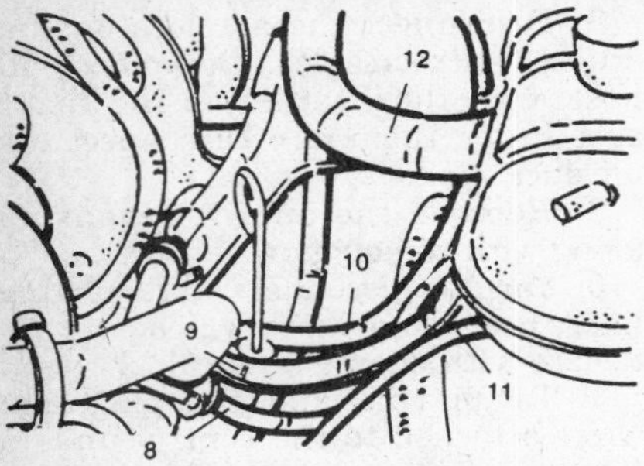


On the 630CSi and 633CSi, also disconnect the hoses shown, which are routed and coded as follows: 8–white from the booster blowoff valve to the white capped valve; 9–black from the booster blowoff valve to the blue capped valve; 10–blue from the booster blowoff valve to the blue capped valve; 11–red from the pressure converter to the EGR valve. Also detach the overflow tank hose (12)

scribed later in this section. With the engine cool, place a clean container underneath the coolant drain plug in the side of the block. Remove the plug and drain all coolant from the block. Remove the fan and radiator.

4. Support the power steering pump. Remove the 3 mounting bolts and then hang the pump out of the way in a position that will not put stress on the hoses.

5. Support the air conditioning compressor. Remove the 3 mounting bolts and then hang the compressor out of the way in a position that will not put stress on the hoses.

- On the 533i and 633i:

a. Pull off the plug at the airflow sensor and remove associated wiring. Remove the hoses and pipes connected to the air cleaner and airflow sensor. If it looks like it will be confusing to reconnect all hoses to the proper connections, label them. Then, remove the nuts and remove the airflow sensor and air cleaner as an assembly.

b. Pull off the plugs on the idle control and Digital Motor Electronics (DME) control in the glove box. Pull the wires through into the engine compartment. Disconnect the ground wire associated with the DME. Disconnect the oxygen sensor. Disconnect the DME wiring harness on the firewall.

c. Disconnect both (+) and (–) low tension and the high tension wire from the coil. Disconnect the wires from the solenoid nearby. Pull the wiring harness out of the holders. On the 633i, also disconnect the harness at the fuse box.

- On the 525i, 535i and 635i:

a. Pull the wire leading to the oxygen sensor out of the clips under the floor. Disconnect the sensor at the exhaust pipe.

b. Pull off the plug at the airflow sensor and remove associated wiring. Remove the hoses and pipes connected to the air cleaner and airflow sensor. If it looks like it will be confusing to reconnect all hoses to the proper connections, label them. Then, remove the nuts and remove the airflow sensor and air cleaner as an assembly.

c. Pull the large, multiprong plug off the DME box in the glove compartment. Disconnect the smaller plug that's connected to the same harness and plugged in nearby. Then, run the entire harness back into the engine compartment.

d. Disconnect the engine ground wire located at the rear of the block. Unclip the harness for the DME from the firewall.

e. Disconnect both (+) and (–) low tension and the high tension wire from the coil. Disconnect the wires from the solenoid nearby. Pull the wiring harness out of the holders.

6. Pull off the fuse box cover and the cap nearby. Remove the 3 relays (they have metal covers) on one side of the fusebox. Then, disconnect the wiring harness that leads into the fusebox. On the 635i, unclamp the harness where it is clamped to the fender well and remove the diagnosis socket (located right near the fusebox).

7. Disconnect the accelerator and cruise control cables.

8. Unclamp and remove the coolant hose that leads to the expansion tank. Disconnect the fuel return line nearby, collecting any fuel in a metal container for safe disposal. Unclip the wiring harness clips on the 2 wires that run through this area of the engine compartment.

9. Disconnect the fuel supply line, collecting any fuel in a metal container for safe disposal. Disconnect the 2 heater hoses at connections nearby.

10. Pull the main vacuum supply hose off at the intake manifold.

11. Disconnect the remaining main coolant hose and plug it.

12. Install a lifting sling to the 2 hooks on top of the engine. Unbolt the left side engine mount. Remove the main engine ground strap. Unbolt the right side engine mount. Carefully pull the engine out of the compartment.

**To install:**

13. To install, reverse the procedures used for removal and lower the engine into the engine compartment. When the engine is positioned, the guide pin must fit in the bore of the axle carrier. Torque the mounting bolts on the front axle carrier (small bolt) to 18–20 ft. lb.; the larger bolt to 31–35 ft. lb. The mount-to-bracket bolts are torqued to 31–35 ft. lb.

14. Install the intake manifold assembly and connect the fuel lines, use new hose clamps to connect the fuel lines to the fuel filter. Connect all of the multiprong plugs and all vacuum hoses.

15. Connect the accelerator cable and cruise control cable to the throttle body and adjust the accelerator cable and cruise control cable.

16. Install the coolant recovery tank, use a new hose clamp on the coolant expansion tank.

17. Install the air cleaner and reconnect all electrical plugs. Connect and install the relays in the relay box.

18. Reconnect the wiring to the main control unit and install the idle control unit.

19. Install the air conditioning compressor and power steering pump, properly route the accessory drive belt. Adjust the belt tension.

20. Install the radiator and connect the hoses.

21. Install the transmission.

22. Install the hood support and lower the hood.

23. Make sure all fluid levels are correct before starting the engine. Bleed air from the cooling system.

### M5 and M6

1. Disconnect the battery negative cable. Then, disconnect the positive cable. Scribe matchmarks and then remove the hood.

2. Remove the fan. Remove the drain plugs in the block and radiator. Disconnect the hoses and remove the radiator.

3. Support the power steering pump. Remove the 3 mounting bolts and then hang the pump out of the way in a position that will not put stress on the hoses.

4. Support the air conditioning compressor. Remove the 3 mounting bolts and then hang the compressor out of the way in a position that will not put stress on the hoses.

5. Remove the transmission as described later in this section.

6. Remove the attaching bolt and, with an appropriate puller, remove the vibration damper from the front of the engine.

7. Remove the 2 bolts at either end and remove the cross brace that runs under the engine. Remove the heat shield nearby.

8. Disconnect the electrical connector going to the airflow sensor. Pull the electrical leads out of the wiring holders. Loosen the hose clamp for the air intake hose. Remove the mounting nut for the air cleaner. Then, remove the air cleaner and airflow sensor as an assembly.

9. Disconnect the large vacuum

hose at the bottom of the intake manifold.

10. Disconnect the PCV hoses where they connect to the top of the manifold. Disconnect the throttle cable that runs across the top of the manifold, and the hose running near the front. Remove the bolts fastening the manifold to the outer ends of the intake tubes and remove it.

11. Working inside the glove compartment, disconnect the plug that connects to the DME control. Then, guide the leads through and into the engine compartment. Disconnect the high tension lead and the 2 low tension leads at the coil. Then, unfasten the wiring harness holders for the harness running to the coil where the harness runs along the fender well.

12. Disconnect the fuel hose connection at the rear of the fuel manifold on top of the engine, and collect fuel in a metal container for safe disposal. Disconnect the vacuum hose that runs along the firewall nearby.

13. Disconnect the plugs for the reference mark and speed sensors. Disconnect the hoses on the coolant expansion tank.

14. Working on the fuse box, pull off the large electrical connector. Pull off the diagnosis socket. Disconnect the remaining leads.

15. Disconnect the heater hoses near the firewall. Using a backup wrench, disconnect the 2 lines at the oil cooler. Disconnect the low pressure fuel line at the pressure regulator.

16. Disconnect the starter leads. Cut the straps and remove the solenoid heat shield.

17. Attach a lifting sling to the engine and support the assembly with a crane. Disconnect the ground lead. Then, disconnect the left side engine mount, removing the nut from underneath and then unscrewing the bolt out the top. Do the same for the right mount (the nut is underneath). Carefully lift the engine out of the compartment, tilting the front of the engine upward for clearance.

**To install:**

18. Keep these points in mind during installation:

a. Torque the engine mounting bolts to 32.5 ft. lbs.

b. Adjust the belt tension for the air conditioning compressor and power steering pump drive belts to give ½–¾ in. deflection.

c. Torque the oil cooler line flare nuts to 25 ft. lbs.

d. When reconnecting the intake manifold to the throttle necks, inspect and, if necessary, replace the O-rings. Torque the mounting nuts to 6.5 ft. lbs.

19. To install, reverse the procedures used for removal and lower the engine into the engine compartment. When the engine is positioned, the guide pin must fit in the bore of the axle carrier. Torque the mounting bolts on the front axle carrier (small bolt) to 18–20 ft. lb.; the larger bolt to 31–35 ft. lb. The mount-to-bracket bolts are torqued to 31–35 ft. lb.

20. Install the intake manifold assembly and connect the fuel lines, use new hose clamps to connect the fuel lines to the fuel filter. Connect all of the multiprong plugs and all vacuum hoses.

21. Connect the accelerator cable and cruise control cable to the throttle body and adjust the accelerator cable and cruise control cable.

22. Install the coolant recovery tank, use a new hose clamp on the coolant expansion tank.

23. Install the air cleaner and reconnect all electrical plugs. Connect and install the relays in the relay box.

24. Reconnect the wiring to the main control unit and install the idle control unit.

25. Install the air conditioning compressor and power steering pump, properly route the accessory drive belt. Adjust the belt tension.

26. Install the radiator and connect the hoses.

27. Install the transmission.

28. Install the hood support and lower the hood.

29. Make sure all fluid levels are correct before starting the engine. Bleed air from the cooling system.

### *733i and 735i*

#### 1983–86 (M30 B34 Engine)

1. Scribe marks for the location of hood hinges on the hood and remove the hood.

2. Disconnect battery positive and negative cables. Unscrew the ground strap at the body. Disconnect the wire that's attached to the positive battery connector at the connector. Remove the battery.

3. Remove the transmission as described later in this section.

4. Drain the coolant, and then remove the fan and radiator (refer to the cooling system section later in this section).

5. Remove the power steering pump adjusting bolt and hinge nut and bolt. Leave the hoses connected. Suspend the pump while removing the bolts and then wire it in a position that will keep tension off the hoses.

6. In a similar way, loosen and remove the adjusting bolt and the 2 hinge nuts and bolts for the air conditioning compressor. Leave the hoses connected. Suspend the compressor as it is being detached and then wire it in such a position that the hoses will not be stressed.

7. Disconnect the plug (2) and lift out the wiring. Pull off hoses (3 and 4). Loosen the hose clamp (5). Unscrew the air cleaner and airflow sensor.

8. Working under the dash, unscrew the right radio speaker cover. Disconnect the retaining strap for the glovebox. Then, pull off the plug for the idle control unit (located right under the glove-box), and the DME unit plug and 2 other plugs nearby on the right kick panel.

9. Front the front of the cowl in the engine compartment, lift out the master relay and unscrew the socket. Take off its rubber ring and lift out the oxygen sensor plug. Disconnect the wire. Unstrap the wiring harness. Then, disconnect the heater hose.

10. Remove the cover and protective cap from the fusebox. Pull off the connector and the 2 relays nearby. Pull off the wire and hose just below the fusebox. Then, disconnect the wiring harness. Unscrew the fuel line nearby.

11. Working near the air cleaner, remove the windshield washer fluid tank, disconnect the electrical plug at the airflow sensor, and then remove the air cleaner with the airflow sensor attached.

12. Working just in front of the right door, disconnect the additional multiprong connector for the DME control unit. Disconnect the small plug nearby.

13. Working just below the windshield on the right side of the car, lift out the master relay and unscrew the socket nearby. Disconnect the wire at the strut tower. Loosen the firewall clamps and pull the wiring harness off on this side. Disconnect the other heater hose nearby.

14. Working at the relay box near the coolant reservoir, lift off the cap and disconnect the multiprong wiring connector. Lift the 2 relays from the box. Take the wiring harness out of the clamps.

15. Unscrew the fuel line at the pressure regulator. Disconnect the dipstick tube bracket. Loosen the clamp and unscrew the wiring harness for the oxygen sensor on the floor panel.

16. Disconnect the coil primary and secondary wires and the plug right nearby. Disconnect the air conditioning compressor wires and lift the wires out the holders.

17. Disconnect the throttle and cruise control cables. Pull off the fuel hose nearby. Disconnect the water hoses at the front of the engine.

18. Look around the engine compartment and disconnect any remaining vacuum hoses or wires.

19. Attach lifting hooks to the 2 lift points on the engine – it may be neces-

sary to disconnect a water hose to gain access to one of them. Support the engine with a crane.

20. Unscrew the attaching bolt for the left side engine mount near the steering box. Do the same for the right side mount and ground strap. Unbolt the engine vibration damper. Carefully lift the engine out of the car.

**To install:**

21. To install, reverse the procedures used for removal and lower the engine into the engine compartment. When the engine is positioned, the guide pin must fit in the bore of the axle carrier. Torque the mounting bolts on the front axle carrier (small bolt) to 18–20 ft. lb.; the larger bolt to 31–35 ft. lb. The mount-to-bracket bolts are torqued to 31–35 ft. lb.

22. Connect the fuel lines, use new hose clamps to connect the fuel lines to the fuel filter. Connect all of the multiprong plugs and all vacuum hoses.

23. Connect the accelerator cable and cruise control cable to the throttle body and adjust the accelerator cable and cruise control cable.

24. Install the washer fluid tank, use a new hose clamp on the coolant expansion tank.

25. Install the air cleaner and reconnect all electrical plugs. Connect and install the relays in the relay box.

26. Reconnect the wiring to the main control unit and install the idle control unit.

27. Install the air conditioning compressor and power steering pump, properly route the accessory drive belt. Adjust the belt tension.

28. Install the radiator and connect the hoses.

29. Install the transmission.

30. Install the hood support and lower the hood.

31. Make sure all fluid levels are correct before starting the engine. Bleed air from the cooling system.

### *735i and 735iL*

#### 1987–90 (M30 B35 Engine)

1. Disconnect the negative battery cable and then the positive. Remove the transmission as described later in this section. Scribe hinge locations and remove the hood, or remove support struts and prop it securely all the way up.

2. Remove the splash guard from underneath the engine. Then, with the engine cool, remove the drain plugs in the radiator and block and drain the engine coolant.

3. Loosen the power steering pump bolts from underneath. Turn the adjusting pinion so as to loosen the belt and remove the belt. Then, remove the mounting bolts and remove the power steering pump without disconnecting the hoses. Support the pump out of the way so as to avoid stressing the hoses.

4. Do the same with the air conditioner compressor (this unit does not have the belt adjusting pinion—it is necessary only to loosen all the bolts and push the compressor toward the engine to remove the belt.

5. Loosen the air intake hose clamp and disconnect the hose. Remove the mounting nut and then remove the air cleaner.

6. The unit on the opposite side of the intake hose from the air cleaner contains the idle speed control valve, which must be removed next. Loosen the hose clamps and pull off the hoses. Disconnect the electrical connector. Remove the mounting nut and then pull the idle speed control out of the air intake hose.

7. Pull off the 3 retainers for the airflow sensor, and then pull the unit off its mountings, disconnecting the vacuum hose from the PCV system at the same time.

8. Working on the coolant expansion tank, disconnect the electrical connector. Remove the nuts on both sides. Loosen their clamps and then disconnect all 3 hoses and remove the tank.

9. Disconnect the heater hoses at both the control valve and at the heater core.

10. Disconnect the throttle and cruise control cables at the throttle lever. Unbolt the cable housing retainer and remove the housing and cables.

11. Pull off the 4 low amperage starter connectors and disconnect the high amperage connector coming from the battery.

12. Loosen its clamp and then disconnect the coolant hose the runs to the alternator.

13. Disconnect the connecting plug for the oxygen sensor, as well as the 2 other plugs nearby.

14. Loosen the clamps and then disconnect the fuel supply and return pipes, draining fuel into a metal container for safe disposal.

15. Disconnect the fuel pipe at the injector supply manifold. Disconnect the plug nearby. Disconnect the electrical connector at the throttle body. Lift off the protective caps and then remove the attaching nuts for the protective cover for the wiring harness for the injectors and remove it.

16. Disconnect the ground strap at the block. Remove the engine mount nut from the top on both sides.

17. Attach a lifting sling to the engine and support the assembly with a crane. Disconnect the ground lead. Carefully lift the engine out of the compartment, tilting the front of the engine upward for clearance.

**To install:**

18. Keep these points in mind during installation:

a. Torque the engine mounting bolts to 32.5 ft. lbs.

b. Adjust the belt tension for the air conditioning compressor and power steering pump drive belts to give ½–¾ in. deflection.

c. Torque the oil cooler line flare nuts to 25 ft. lbs.

d. When reconnecting the intake manifold to the throttle necks, inspect and, if necessary, replace the O-rings. Torque the mounting nuts to 6.5 ft. lbs.

19. To install, reverse the procedures used for removal and lower the engine into the engine compartment. When the engine is positioned, the guide pin must fit in the bore of the axle carrier. Torque the mounting bolts on the front axle carrier (small bolt) to 18–20 ft. lb.; the larger bolt to 31–35 ft. lb. The mount-to-bracket bolts are torqued to 31–35 ft. lb.

20. Connect the fuel lines, use new hose clamps to connect the fuel lines to the fuel filter. Connect all of the multiprong plugs and all vacuum hoses.

21. Connect the accelerator cable and cruise control cable to the throttle body and adjust the accelerator cable and cruise control cable.

22. Install the coolant recovery tank, use a new hose clamp on the coolant expansion tank.

23. Install the air cleaner and reconnect all electrical plugs. Connect and install the relays in the relay box.

24. Reconnect the wiring to the main control unit and install the idle control unit.

25. Install the air conditioning compressor and power steering pump, properly route the accessory drive belt. Adjust the belt tension.

26. Install the radiator and connect the hoses.

27. Install the transmission.

28. Install the hood support and lower the hood.

29. Make sure all fluid levels are correct before starting the engine. Bleed air from the cooling system.

## Cylinder Head

### REMOVAL & INSTALLATION

#### *318i*

**NOTE: In order to perform this procedure, it is necessary to have a special tool (angle gauge) that will accurately measure the angle at which the cylinder head bolts are torqued.**

1. Disconnect exhaust pipes at the

**Alignment of dowel pin hole and camshaft flange notch with the cast projection of the cylinder head—four cylinder engine**

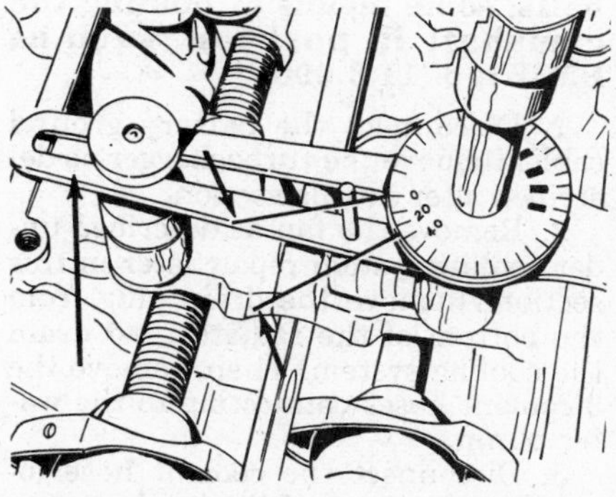

**On the final torquing step for 318i cylinder head bolts, tighten head bolts the specified angle, as shown**

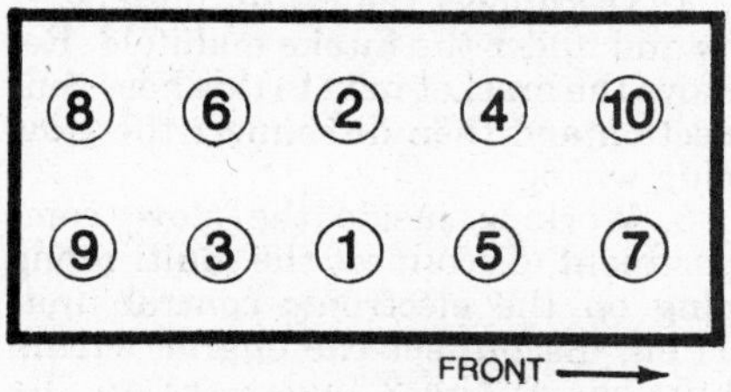


**4-cylinder head torque sequence**

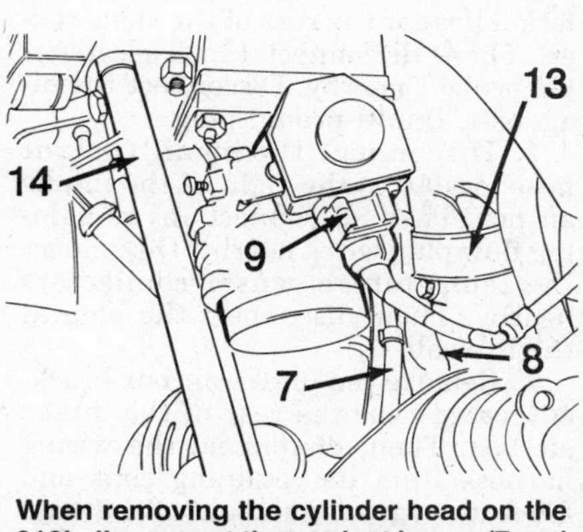


**When removing the cylinder head on the 318i, disconnect the coolant hoses (7 and 8), disconnect the plug (9) and vacuum hose (13), and unscrew the support (14)**

exhaust manifold and remove the pipe clamp on the transmission.

2. Disconnect the battery ground cable. Remove the drain plug and drain coolant.

3. Disconnect the wire and plug on the air cleaner. Loosen the clamp and disconnect the air intake hose. Then unscrew the nuts and remove the air cleaner.

4. Disconnect the throttle cable. Remove the dipstick tube locating bracket.

5. Disconnect the throttle position electronic plug. Disconnect the coolant and vacuum hoses nearby. Unscrew the support for the throttle body nearby.

6. Detach the fuel supply and return hoses and the hose mounting clamp.

7. Disconnect the intake manifold, distributor, and power brake unit vacuum hoses.

8. Disconnect the diagnosis plug, alternator wiring, and other plugs (2) nearby. Disconnect the coolant hoses at the cylinder head.

9. Disconnect any electrical plugs on the starter and injection system. This includes pulling off each injection plug and opening up the wiring straps.

10. Remove the distributor cap, disconnect distributor wiring plugs, wiring harness, and all plug wires.

11. Disconnect the coolant hoses going into the firewall.

12. Remove the cylinder head cover. Remove the bracket near the upper timing case over. Then, remove bolts and remove the upper timing case cover.

13. Rotate the engine until the TDC mark on the front pulley is aligned with the mark on the front cover and the distributor rotor is aligned with the mark on the side of the distributor (No. 1 cylinder is at TDC). Then, remove the distributor.

14. Remove the timing chain tensioner piston as described below.

15. Remove the retaining bolts and pull off the upper timing chain sprocket. **Do not rotate crankshaft while the sprocket is off!**

16. Loosen the cylinder head bolts in reverse order of the torquing sequence and remove. Lift off the cylinder head.

**To install:**

17. Install the cylinder head in position, noting these points:

a. Use a new head gasket.

b. Lightly oil all head bolts, keeping oil out of the threaded holes in the block.

c. Torque in the sequence shown in 4 stages:

25–29 ft. lb.

42–45 ft. lb.

Wait 20 minutes—adjust the valves during this time

56–59 ft. lb.

Run the engine until it is warm

Torque bolts to 25 degrees (on the angle gauge)

d. When installing the timing chain sprocket, first make sure the notch in the camshaft flange is aligned with the cast tab on the cylinder head. The dowel pin will then align with the bore in the sprocket at the 6 o'clock position.

e. When installing the upper timing cover, pack sealer into the crevices between block and the top of lower cover. Install all bolts finger tight. Tighten outer bolts first, from top to bottom on left, and top to bottom on right. Finally, torque the 2 front bolts.

Sprocket-to-camshaft torque—5 ft. lb.

Chain tensioner plug—22–29 ft. lbs.

Timing case cover—7–8 ft. lb.

### *320i*

1. Remove the air cleaner and disconnect the breather tube. Remove the intake manifold.

2. Disconnect the battery ground cable and drain the cooling system.

3. Remove the choke cable, if so equipped.

4. Disconnect the throttle linkage. Pull the torsion shaft towards the firewall until the ball is free of the torsion shaft.

5. Remove and tag the vacuum hoses.

6. Disconnect the coolant hoses from the cylinder head.

7. Disconnect the electrical wiring and connectors from the cylinder head and engine components.

8. Remove the cylinder head cover and the front upper timing case cover.

9. Rotate the engine until the distributor rotor points to the notch on the distributor body edge and the tim-

Timing chain tensioner plug removal or installation—typical

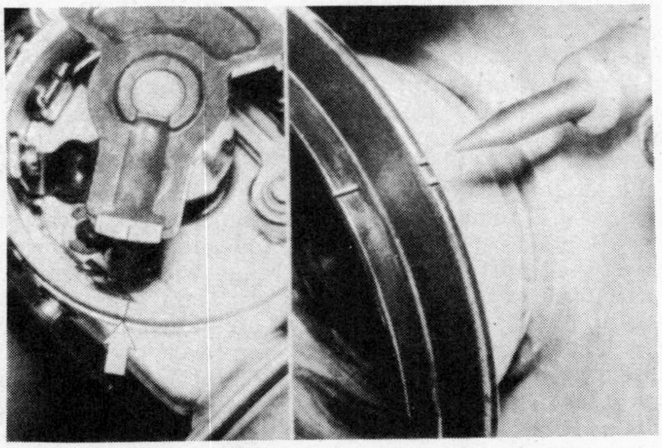

Alignment of distributor rotor and belt pulley notch—typical

ing indicator points to the first notch on the belt pulley. No. 1 piston should now be at TDC on its firing stroke.

10. Remove the timing chain tensioner piston by removing the plug in the side of the block.

**CAUTION**

***The plug is under heavy spring tension.***

11. Open the lockplates, remove the retaining bolts and remove the timing chain sprocket from the camshaft.

**NOTE: The dowel pin hole in the camshaft flange should be in the 6 o'clock position while the notch at the top of the cam flange should be aligned with the cast projection on the cylinder head and in the 12 o'clock position for proper installation.**

12. Remove the exhaust pipe from the exhaust manifold and remove the dipstick holder.

13. Unscrew the cylinder head bolts in the reverse of the tightening sequence and remove the cylinder head.

**To install:**

14. Install the cylinder head in position, noting the following points:

a. Tighten the cylinder head bolts in 3 stages, following the illustrated sequence. Adjust the valves, start the engine and bring to normal operating temperature. Stop the engine and allow it to cool to approximately 95°F (35°C). Retorque the cylinder head bolts to specifications and readjust the valves.

**NOTE: The cylinder head bolts should be retorqued after 600 miles (1000 km) of driving.**

b. Check the projection of the cylinder head dowel sleeves in the cylinder block mating surface. Maximum height is 0.20 in.

c. Match the cylinder head gasket to the cylinder block and head to verify coolant flow passages are correct.

d. Adjust timing and idle speed.

e. Bleed the cooling system. Set the heater valve to the warm position and fill the cooling system.

f. Run the engine to normal temperature and when the thermostat has opened, release the pressure cap to the first position. Squeeze the upper and lower radiator hoses in a pumping effect, to allow trapped air to escape through the radiator.

g. Recheck the coolant level and close the pressure cap to its second catch position.

### *524td*

**NOTE: To perform this procedure, a number of special tools will be needed. These include a dial indicator with a bridge that will allow the gauge to measure piston protrusion while the edges of the bridge rest on the block deck on either side of the piston; and an angle gauge for measuring turning angle of cylinder head bolts; some means of holding the camshaft in position, such as BMW tool 11 3 090.**

1. Disconnect the battery ground cable. Remove the turbocharger as described later in this section.

2. Remove the fan as described under cooling system repair later in this section. Remove the drain plug from the bottom of the radiator and drain the cooling system. Then, remove the 3 coolant hoses connecting to the water pump.

3. Disconnect the coolant hose located at the front of the intake manifold. Disconnect the electrical plug near this hose connection. Disconnect the injector leakoff line that also connects near these connections.

4. Disconnect the heater hose nearby and under the intake manifold. Remove the bracket next to this hose connection and then disconnect the glow plug wiring.

5. Working inside the glove compartment, disconnect the multi-prong plug on the electronic control unit. Then, disconnect the engine wiring harness at the 2 fasteners on the firewall and pull the harness into the engine compartment.

6. Disconnect the crankcase ventilation hose at the rear of the valve cover. Then, disconnect the 3 electrical plugs right nearby. Disconnect the diagnostic (multi-prong) plug.

7. Disconnect the small coolant hose located to the right of the intake air box. Then, disconnect any remaining flow plug wires nearby. Disconnect the temperature sensor connectors nearby. Then, disconnect the plug at the firewall.

8. Remove the intake air box bracket located near the rear of the intake air box. Then, disconnect the wiring harness from its retaining clips and move it downward and out of the way.

9. Disconnect the transmission dipstick tube bracket at the intake manifold. Disconnect the air hose at the

Check the height above the block deck of each piston at the locations "A" and "B" shown

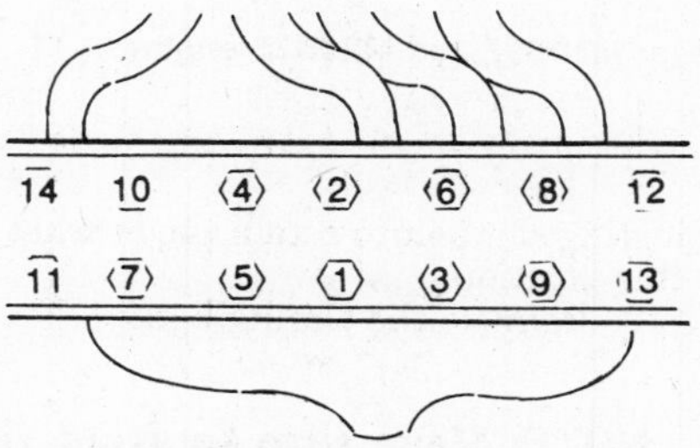


Cylinder head tightening or loosening (14–1) sequence for the 524 td

manifold, nearby. Disconnect the wire at the intake pressure relief valve, nearby.

10. Remove the crankcase ventilation system oil trap from the valve cover by first disconnecting the hose and then unbolting it and removing it with its gasket.

11. Use a crowfoot wrench to unscrew and remove the injection lines at the pump and injectors. Plug all openings with clean, protective caps.

12. Remove the cam cover. Then, turn the engine until No. 1 cylinder is at TDC (No. 6 cylinder's valves overlap). Either lock the crank in position with a pin such as BMW special tool 11 2 300 or equivalent, or make sure the crankshaft is completely undisturbed until the engine is reassembled.

13. Remove the coolant hose which runs across the front of the timing belt cover and remove the timing belt cover. Then, loosen the camshaft sprocket retaining bolt. Loosen the bolt and nut which position the timing belt tensioner and then remove the timing belt.

14. Remove the cylinder head bolts in the order of 14–1, going in rotation in several stages. Lift the head off the engine.

15. Clean the block deck and cylinder head lower surfaces with a solvent and wooden scraper (to avoid scoring either surface).

16. Set up and zero a dial indicator it will be possible to measure the protrusion of the pistons above the block deck. Measure the protrusion of each piston along the center-line of the block on the flat surface at both the front and rear of the piston. Rock the engine back and forth for each cylinder until absolute maximum protrusion is obtained. Average the 2 readings for each piston and record the average. Return the crankshaft to No. 6 cylinder overlap position. Note the highest protrusion. Compare it to these figures and select a head gasket of the appropriate thickness from the protrusion figure:

1 hole 0.025–0.030
2 holes 0.031–0.035
3 holes 0.036–0.042

**NOTE: Gaskets have one, 2, or 3 holes along one edge to indicate the thickness classification.**

17. Clean all the cylinder head bolts with solvent and give them a very light coating of engine oil. Make sure the bolts are not heavily coated with oil and that the bolt holes do not contain any oil, as this will interfere with torquing and might even crack the cylinder block.

**To install:**

18. Turn the camshaft so that the valves on cylinder No. 6 are at the overlap position. Make sure the camshaft does not turn from this position, or the valves may be bent when the head is installed. Use a jig such as BMW tool 11 3 090 or equivalent. Install the bolts and then torque them in the numbered order shown in the illustration (1–14) to ⅓ the torque figure shown in the chart at the front of this section. Then, retorque them to ⅔ of that figure in the numbered order. Finally, retorque them, again in numbered order, to the full torque figure.

19. Install and adjust the timing belt. Adjust the valves and install the cam cover. Then, install the timing belt cover. Install the injection pump lines and torque the fittings to 14–18 ft. lbs. Bleed the fuel system. Reconnect all electrical lines, hoses, and other fittings so the engine is ready to run. Use a new gasket on the crankcase ventilation system oil trap. Refill the cooling system.

20. Start the engine and run it at about 1000 rpm until it is hot. Then, remove the cam cover and again in numerical order, final-torque the bolts by accurately turning them exactly another 90 degrees tighter. Use a tool designed for angle torquing such as BMW 11 2 110. Replace the cam cover.

### *1983–87 325, 325e, 325i, 325iS, 325iX and 528e*

1. Disconnect the battery ground cable. Make sure the engine is cool. Disconnect the exhaust pipes at the manifold and at the transmission clamp. Remove the drain plug at the bottom of the radiator and drain the coolant. Drain the engine oil.

2. Disconnect the accelerator and cruise control cables. If the car has an automatic transmission, disconnect the throttle cable that goes to the transmission.

3. Working at the front of the block, disconnect the upper radiator hose, the bypass water hose, and several smaller water hoses nearby. Remove the diagnosis plug located at the front corner of the manifold. Remove the bracket located just underneath. Disconnect the fuel line and drain the contents into a metal container for safe disposal.

- On the 325, 325i, 325iS and 325iX:

a. Working on the air cleaner/airflow sensor, disconnect the vacuum hoses, labeling them if necessary. Disconnect all electrical connectors and unclip and remove the wiring harness. There is a relay located in an L-shaped box near the strut tower. Disconnect and remove it. Unclamp and remove the air hose. Remove the mounting nuts and remove the assembly.

b. Disconnect the hose at the coolant overflow tank. Disconnect the idle speed positioner vacuum hose and then remove the positioner from the manifold.

c. If the car has 4 wheel drive, disconnect the vacuum hose from the servo mounted on the manifold.

d. Place a drain pan underneath and then disconnect the 2 water connections at the front of the intake manifold. Disconnect the electrical connector nearby.

- On the 325e and 528e:

a. Working near the air cleaner/air flow sensor unit, disconnect the vacuum hoses at the intake manifold and at the air intake hose. Disconnect the 2 electrical connectors and then remove the wiring harness. Pull off the large hose leading into the unit and loosen the clamp where the air intake hose connects at the intake manifold. Remove the mounting nuts and remove the air cleaner/airflow sensor.

b. Disconnect the water hoses at the throttle body. Disconnect the electrical connector underneath the throttle body. Disconnect the bracket under the intake manifold tube nearby.

4. On all models, disconnect the heater water hoses. Press down (in the arrowed direction) on the vent tube collar shown in the illustration and install the special tool or a similar device to retain the collar in the unlocked position. Disconnect the vent tube and

**Alignment of dowel pin (1) with the sprocket and upper bolt hole and cylinder head cast tab—six cylinder engines**

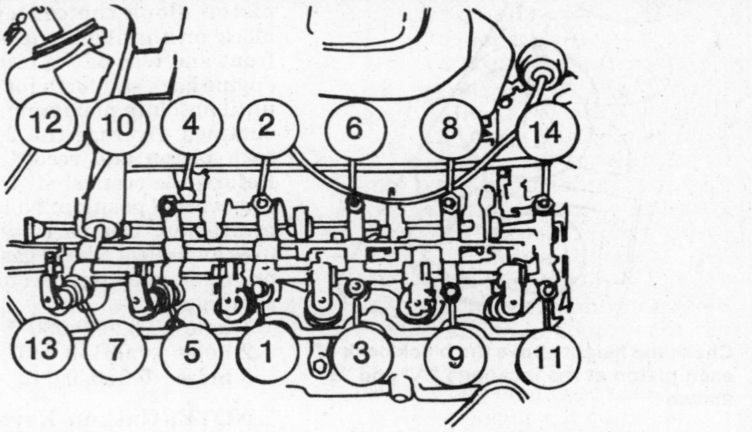


**Cylinder head torque sequence for the M20B27 and M20B25 engines**

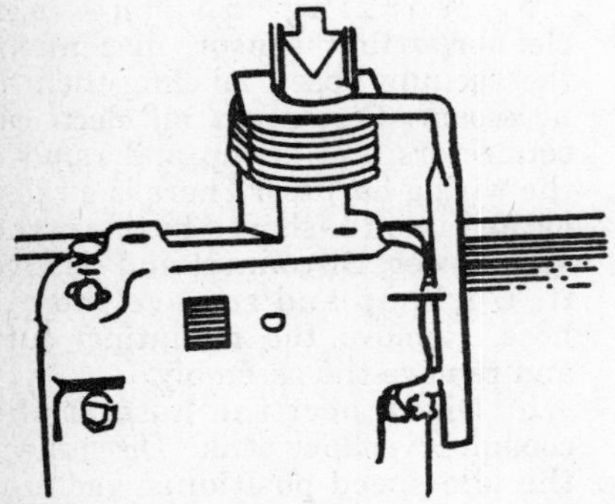

**On the 325e and 528e, you'll have to press the vent tube downward (in the direction of the arrow) and then lock the collar in that position with a tool such as 11 1 290. Then, disconnect the tube.**

inspect its O-ring seal, replacing it if necessary.

5. Unbolt the dipstick tube at the manifold. Remove the fuel hose bracket at the cylinder head. Make sure the engine is cold. Then, place a metal container under the connection and disconnect the fuel hose at the connection nearby.

6. Disconnect the high tension lead from the coil. Put a drain pan nearby and then disconnect and remove the coolant expansion tank.

- On the 325, 325i, iS and iX:

  a. If the car has 4 wheel drive, disconnect the intake manifold vacuum hose leading the the servo that engages 4 wheel drive.

  b. Disconnect the fuel injector electrical connectors at all 6 injectors, as well as the 2 additional electrical connectors to sensors on the head. Disconnect the oil pressure sending unit connector. Then, unfasten the carriers and remove this wiring harness toward the left side of the car.

- On 325e and 528e cars:

  a. There is a bracket with various vacuum and electrical fittings that runs from the cam cover over toward the intake manifold. Disconnect the electrical connector connected on this bracket and the plug to its left. Remove the nuts fastening the bracket to the cam cover and the gasketed flange on the opposite end and remove the bracket. Inspect the gasket and supply a new one for use in installation, if necessary. Unplug the fuel injectors.

  b. Disconnect the DME plugs nearby. Disconnect the 4 plugs located near the front 3 fuel injectors and any remaining injector connectors. Unplug the oil pressure sending unit connector. Then, unfasten the mounting clips and pull the wiring harness out toward the left.

7. Disconnect the coil high tension wire and disconnect the high tension wires at the plugs. Then, disconnect the tube in which the wires run at the cam cover. Disconnect the PCV hose. Then, remove the 8 retaining nuts and remove the cam cover.

8. Turn the crankshaft so that the TDC line is lined up with the indicator and the valves of No. 6 cylinder are in overlapping (slightly open) position.

9. Remove the distributor cap. Then, unscrew and remove the rotor. Unscrew and remove the adapter just underneath the rotor. Remove the cover underneath the adapter. Check its O-ring and replace it if necessary.

10. Remove the distributor mounting bolts and the protective cover.

11. These engines are equipped with a rubber drive and timing belt. Remove the belt covers as described later in this section. To loosen belt tension, loosen the tension roller bracket pivot bolt and adjusting slot bolt. Push the roller and bracket away from the belt to release the tension, hold the bracket in this position, and retighten the adjusting slot bolt to retain the bracket it this position.

12. Remove the timing belt.

**NOTE: Make sure to avoid rotating both the engine and camshaft from this point onward.**

13. Remove the cylinder head mounting bolts in exact reverse order of the tightening sequence shown. Then, remove the cylinder head.

**To install:**

14. Install the head with a new gasket. Check that all passages line up with the gasket holes. Clean the threads on the head bolts and coat with a *very light* coating of oil. Keep oil out of the bolt cavities in the head, or the head could be cracked or proper torquing affected.

15. Install the bolts and torque in stages, with waiting periods, and to the figures as described in specifications. Torque them in the numbered order, as shown in the applicable illustration. Then, adjust the valves.

16. Clean both cylinder head and block sealing surfaces thoroughly with a hardwood scraper. Inspect the surfaces for flatness. Note that the M20B25 engine gasket is coded 2.5 and the M20B27 engine gasket is coded 2.7. Complete the installation by reversing all removal procedures. Make sure to refill the engine oil pan and cooling system with proper fluids and to bleed the cooling system. Replace the gaskets for the exhaust system connections, if necessary. Coat the studs with CRC® copper paste or equivalent. Note that the plugs for the DME reference mark and speed signals should be connected so that the gray plug goes to the socket with a ring underneath.

**NOTE: Align the timing marks when installing the timing belt. The crankshaft sprocket mark must point at the notch in the flange of the front engine cover. The camshaft sprocket arrow must point at the alignment mark on the cylinder head. Also, the No. 1 piston must be at TDC of the compression stroke. BMW recommends that the timing belt be replaced every time the cylinder head is removed and the belt is disturbed as a consequence. Tension the belt.**

17. Start the engine and run it until it is hot. Stop the engine and again remove the cam cover. Using an angle gauge, tighten the head bolts 25 degrees farther in numbered order. Reinstall the cam cover.

### *1988–90 325, 325e, 325i, 325iS, 325iX and 528e*

1. Disconnect the battery ground cable. Disconnect the oxygen sensor plug.
2. Remove the bolts attaching the 2 exhaust pipes to the manifold. Then, unfasten the bracket which supports the pipes at the transmission and lower them slightly. Support them from the chassis with wire or another suitable means.
3. Put drain pans underneath and then remove the drain plugs from the radiator and block to drain coolant.
4. Disconnect the accelerator cable. On cars with cruise control, disconnect the cruise control cable; on cars with automatic transmissions, disconnect the transmission throttle cable.
5. Disconnect the large electrical plug from the airflow sensor unit. Loosen the clamp on the air intake hose. Remove the mounting nuts for the airflow sensor/air cleaner unit and lift it for access. Disconnect the remaining hose and electrical plug and then remove the unit.
6. The diagnosis plug is located on the front of the engine, near the thermostat housing. It is a large, multiprong plug. Disconnect it. Then, disconnect the 5 coolant hoses, 2 of small diameter, and 3 of large diameter, from the thermostat housing and cylinder head.
7. Make sure the engine is cool. With a metal container to collect fuel, carefully and slowly loosen the clamp on the fuel hose where it connects right near the diagnosis plug. When fuel pressure has been relieved, disconnect the hose and collect any remaining fuel in the cup.
8. There is a brace connected to the head at the front. Remove the bolt fastening this brace to the head. Disconnect the 2 electrical connectors nearby. Disconnect the fuel line nearby, draining the fuel into a metal container.
9. Place a drain pan underneath and then disconnect the 2 water connections at the front of the intake manifold. Disconnect the electrical connector nearby.
10. Disconnect the 2 heater hoses at the firewall and drain any coolant into a pan.
11. Press down (in the arrowed direction) on the PCV vent tube collar and install the special tool or a similar device to retain the collar in the unlocked position. Disconnect the vent tube and inspect its O-ring seal, replacing it if necessary.
12. Disconnect the electrical leads going to the coil. Unbolt and remove the fan and then store it in an upright position. Unbolt the coolant pipe located near the fan and remove it.
13. Then, remove the 8 retaining nuts and remove the cam cover. Turn the crankshaft so that the TDC line is lined up with the indicator and the valves of No. 6 cylinder are in overlapping (slightly open) position.
14. Remove the distributor cap. Then, unscrew and remove the rotor. Unscrew and remove the adapter just underneath the rotor. Remove the cover underneath the adapter. Check its O-ring and replace it if necessary.
15. Remove the mounting nut and the protective cover. Then, disconnect the wiring clip underneath the distributor and move the leads away, so they are in front of the pulley.
16. These engines are equipped with a rubber drive and timing belt. Remove the belt covers as described later in this section. To loosen belt tension, loosen the tension roller bracket pivot bolt and adjusting slot bolt. Push the roller and bracket away from the belt to release the tension, hold the bracket in this position, and retighten the adjusting slot bolt to retain the bracket it this position.
17. Remove the timing belt.

**NOTE: Make sure to avoid rotating both the engine and camshaft from this point onward.**

18. Remove the cylinder head mounting bolts in exact reverse order of the tightening sequence shown above. Then, remove the cylinder head.

**To install:**

19. Install the head with a new gasket. Check that all passages line up with the gasket holes. Clean the threads on the head bolts and coat with a *very light* coating of oil. Keep oil out of the bolt cavities in the head, or the head could be cracked or proper torquing affected.
20. Install the bolts and torque in stages, with waiting periods, and to the figures as described in specifications. Torque them in the numbered order, as shown in the applicable illustration. Then, adjust the valves.
21. Clean both cylinder head and block sealing surfaces thoroughly with a hardwood scraper. Inspect the surfaces for flatness as described in the Engine Rebuilding section. Note that the M20B25 engine gasket is coded 2.5 and the M20B27 engine gasket is coded 2.7. Make sure all openings match precisely. Complete the installation by reversing all removal procedures. Make sure to refill the engine oil pan and cooling system with proper fluids and to bleed the cooling system.
22. Replace the gaskets for the exhaust system connections, if necessary. Coat the studs with CRC® copper paste or equivalent. Note that the plugs for the DME reference mark and speed signals should be connected so that the gray plug goes to the socket with a ring underneath.

**NOTE: Align the timing marks when installing the timing belt. The crankshaft sprocket mark must point at the notch in the flange of the front engine cover. The camshaft sprocket arrow must point at the alignment mark on the cylinder head. Also, the No. 1 piston must be at TDC of the compression stroke. BMW recommends that the timing belt be replaced every time the cylinder head is removed and the belt is disturbed as a consequence. Tension the belt.**

23. Start the engine and run it until it is hot. Stop the engine and again remove the cam cover.
24. Using an angle gauge, tighten the head bolts 25 degrees farther in numbered order. Reinstall the cam cover.

### *M3*

**NOTE: This is an extremely difficult operation involving the use of a number of special tools. It is necessary to remove both of the camshafts to complete it. Refer to the camshaft removal and installation procedure below for information on those special tools required for that part of the job. It is also necessary to have a set of metric hex wrenches.**

1. Disconnect the negative battery cable. Remove the splash guard from underneath the engine. Put drain pans underneath and then remove the drain plugs from both the radiator and block to drain all coolant.
2. Loosen the hose clamps for the

air intake hose located next to the radiator and then remove the hose. Disconnect the 2 electrical connectors for the airflow sensor. Then, remove the 2 attaching nuts and remove the air cleaner/ airflow sensor unit.

3. Disconnect the accelerator and cruise control cables. Unbolt the cable mounting bracket and move the cables and bracket aside.

4. Remove the attaching nut, pull off the clamp, and then detach the vacuum hose from the brake booster.

5. Loosen the hose clamp and remove the air intake hose from the intake manifold. Remove the nut from the manifold brace, nearby.

6. Loosen the clamp and disconnect the other end of the booster vacuum hose at the manifold. Remove the nut from the intake manifold brace.

7. Loosen the hose clamp and disconnect the air intake hose at the manifold. Then, remove all 6 nuts attaching the manifold assembly to the outer ends of the intake throttle necks and remove the assembly.

8. Put a drain pan underneath and then loosen the hose clamps and disconnect the coolant expansion tank hoses. Disconnect the engine ground strap.

9. Disconnect the ignition coil high tension lead. Label and then disconnect the 2 plugs on the front of the block, nearby. Remove the nut fastening another lead farther forward of the 2 plugs and move the lead aside so it will not interfere with engine removal.

10. Find the vacuum hose leading to the fuel pressure regulator. Pull it off. Label and then disconnect the 2 plugs nearby. Unscrew the mounting screw for another electrical lead connecting with the top of the block nearby and remove the lead and its carrier.

11. There is a vacuum hose connecting with one of the throttle necks. Disconnect it and pull it out of the intake manifold bracket. Pull off the electrical connector nearby. Pull out the rubber retainer, and then pull the idle speed control out and put it aside. The engine wiring harness is located nearby. Take it out of its carriers.

12. All the fuel injectors are plugged into a common plate. Carefully and evenly pull the plate off the injectors, pull it out past the pressure regulator, and lay it aside.

13. Loosen the clamp and then disconnect the PCV hose. Label and then disconnect the 2 fuel lines connecting with the injector circuit (it's important to label them so that they can be installed correctly!). Put a drain pan underneath and then disconnect the heater hose from the cylinder head.

14. Loosen the clamp near the throttle necks and then pull the engine wiring harness out and put it aside. Put a drain pan underneath and then disconnect the heater hose that connects to the block.

15. Remove the bolts from the flanges connecting the exhaust pipes to the exhaust manifold. Provide new gaskets and self-locking nuts. Disconnect the oxygen sensor plug.

16. Put a drain pan underneath and then disconnect the 2 radiator hoses from the pipe at the front of the block.

17. See the procedures below for removal of the front timing cover and timing chain. It is not necessary to remove the timing chain completely, but it is necessary to remove the cam cover, front covers (for the camshaft drive sprockets), and the upper guide rail for the timing chain, and then turn the engine to TDC firing position for No. 1. Then, the procedure will be to remove the timing chain tensioner. Note the relationship between the chain and both the crankshaft and camshaft sprockets, and then remove both camshaft drive sprockets. Leave the chain in a position that will not interfere with removal of the head and which will minimize disturbing its routing through the areas on the front of the block.

18. Remove the camshafts as described below.

19. Prepare a clean work area and a way to store the cam followers in order – preferably some sort of rack. Remove the cam followers one at a time, keeping them in exact order for installation in the same positions.

20. Pull off the spark plug connectors. Remove the 2 nuts from the cam cover, located just to one side of the row of spark plugs. Then remove the ignition lead tube. Then, remove the 8 remaining nuts and remove the cam cover. Provide new gaskets.

21. Remove the bolts (some are accessible from below) that retain the timing case to the head at the front (the timing case houses the lifters and the camshaft lower bearing saddles.) Note that one bolt, on the right (passenger's) side of the car, is longer and retains the shaft for the upper timing chain tensioning rail.

22. Remove the coolant pipe that runs along the left/rear of the block. Remove one bolt at the left/front of the block that is located outside the cam cover. Then, go along in the area under the cam cover and remove all the remaining (42) bolts for the timing case (arrows in the illustration point them out). Remove the timing case.

23. Remove the 2 hex bolts fastening the head to the block at the front. These are located outside the cam cover and just behind the water pump drive belt. Then, remove the head bolts located under the cam cover in reverse order of the 4 cylinder engine cylinder head torque sequence (10–1).

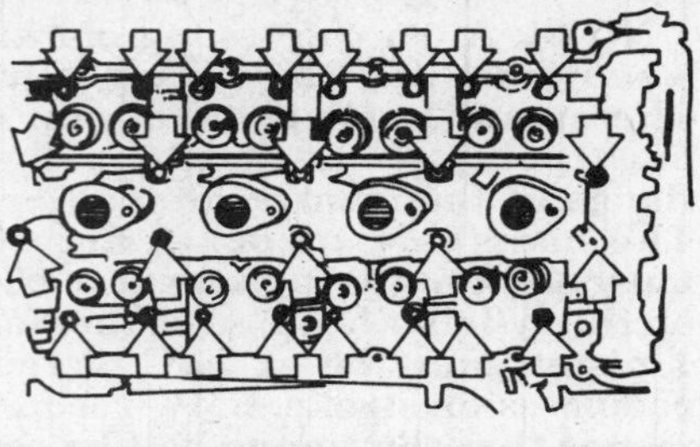

**Removing the timing case for the M3. Remove all arrowed bolts**

**To install:**

24. Make checks of the lower cylinder head and block deck surface to make sure they are true. Clean both cylinder head and block sealing surfaces thoroughly with a hardwood scraper. Lubricate the head bolts with a light coating of engine oil. Make sure there is no oil or dirt in the boltholes in the block. Install a new head gasket, making sure that all bolt, oil, and coolant holes line up. Install the bolts as follows:

a. Torque them, in the order shown in the illustration for 4 cylinder engines (1–10) to 35–37 ft. lbs.

b. Then, torque them, in order, to 57–59 ft. lbs.

c. Wait 15 minutes.

d. Torque them, in order, to 71–73 ft. lbs.

e. Remember to reinstall the bolts that go outside the cylinder head cover and fasten the front of the head to the block at front and rear.

25. BMW recommends checking the fit of each tappet in the timing case. If the engine is not a high mileage one, has had no lubrication problems, and has exhibited no particular tappet noise, it may be reasonable to skip this step. On the other hand, if the engine exhibits abuse, has been run a great many miles, or has had tappet noise, it is easy to replace worn tappets at this time, and it would be wise to check them. The procedure is as follows:

a. Measure a tappet's outside diameter with a michrometer. Then, zero an inside michrometer at this exact dimension.

b. Then, use the inside michrometer to measure the tappet bore that corresponds to this particular tappet. If the resulting measurement is 0.0001–0.0026 in. the tappet may be reused. If it is worn past this dimension, replace it with a new one. If the tappet is being replaced, repeat steps a and b to make sure it will now meet specifications. If the bore were to be worn so much that even a new tappet would not restore clearance to specification, it would be necessary to replace the timing case.

c. Repeat for all the remaining tappets. Make sure to measure each tappet and its *corresponding bore* only!

26. The remaining steps of installation are the reverse of the removal procedure. Note the following specifics, during work:

a. Before remounting the timing case, replace the O-ring in the oil passage located at the left/front of the block. Also, check the O-rings in the tops of the spark plug bores and replace these as necessary.

b. Install the timing case and torque the bolts in several stages. The smaller (M7) bolts are torqued to 10–12 ft. lbs.; the larger (M8) bolts are torqued to 14.5–15.5 ft. lbs. Install each tappet back into the same bore.

c. When bolting the exhaust pipes to the flange at the manifold, use new gaskets and self-locking nuts and torque the nuts to 36 ft. lbs.

d. When reinstalling the intake manifold, check and, if necessary, replace the O-rings where the manifold tubes connect to the throttle necks. Torque the nuts to 6.5 ft. lbs.

d. Make sure to refill the radiator and bleed the cooling system.

### *525i, 533i, 535i, 633CSi, 635CSi, 733i and 1983–86 735i (M30 B32 and M30 B34 engines)*

1. Unbolt the exhaust pipes at the exhaust manifold. Unclamp the exhaust pipe at the transmission.

2. Disconnect the battery negative and positive cables and drain the coolant by removing the plugs from the radiator and block.

3. Disconnect the throttle, accelerator, and cruise control cables at the throttle body.

4. These engines are all virtually identical, but wiring harnesses vary from model to model. Systematically disconnect all wiring that goes to the cylinder head or would obstruct its removal. This includes: wiring to the airflow sensor; ignition wiring and, where used, the ignition wiring tube; wires to the fuel injectors; on some models it may be necessary to disconnect the alternator wiring; on many, it will be necessary to disconnect the main harness to the fuse box. On 535, 635, and 735 Series cars, it is necessary to disconnect the starter wiring.

5. Disconnect fuel lines, vacuum lines, and heater and coolant hoses that are in the way. Disconnect DME plugs on those models so equipped. Note that the gray plug connects to the plug with a ring underneath, for proper installation.

6. Remove the air cleaner and the windshield washer tank.

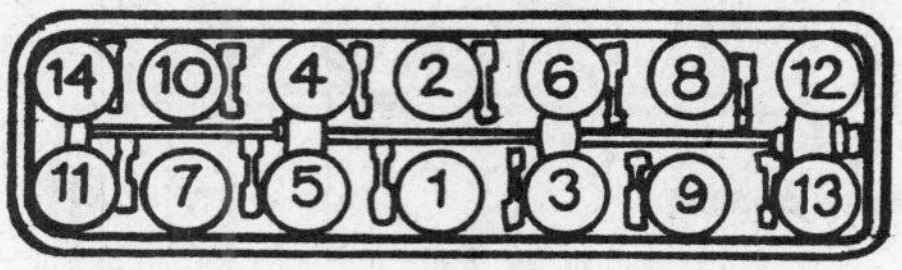


**Cylinder head torque sequence for the M30B34 engine until 12/86 and the S38Z engine used in the M5 and M6**

7. Remove the rocker cover. On 535, 635, and 735 Series cars, disconnect the injector electrical connections, cold start valve, and idle positioner. Disconnect the ground lead on all engines. Then, complete disconnecting the engine wiring harness by disconnecting the oil pressure sending unit and set the harness aside.

8. See the procedures below for removal of the front cover and timing chain and tensioner. Remove the upper timing case cover, tensioner piston, and then open the lockplates and remove the timing chain upper sprocket. Make sure to suspend the sprocket so the timing chain position isn't lost.

9. Loosen the cylinder head bolts following strictly the illustration in reverse order – 14–1. Then, install 4 special pins BMW part No. 11 1 063 or equivalent. This is necessary to keep the rocker arm shafts from moving. Then, lift off the head.

**To install:**

10. Make checks of the lower cylinder head and block deck surface to make sure they are true. Install a new head gasket, making sure that all bolt, oil, and coolant holes line up. Use a gasket marked M 30 B 34 for the larger engine used in 735i. Use a 0.3mm thicker gasket if the head has been machined.

11. Apply a very light coating of oil to the head bolts. Don't let oil get into the boltholes or apply excessive amounts of oil, or torque could be incorrect and the block could crack. Use the newer type of bolt without a collar. Install the bolts, finger tight.

12. Torque bolts 1–6 in the order shown in the illustration to 42–44 ft. lbs. Remove the 4 pins holding the rocker shafts in place. Now, complete the first stage of torquing by torquing bolts 7–14 in the order shown, to the specifications shown in the Specifications chart for the first stage of torquing. Follow the remaining torquing procedures as described in the Specifications chart. Wait between steps as mentioned. Adjust the valves. Then, reassemble the engine as described below and run it until hot. Then, again remove the valve cover, and either immediately or at any time later (engine temperature isn't critical), turn the head bolts, in order, the number of degrees specified in the specifications chart, using special tool BMW 11 2 110 or equivalent.

13. Reinstall the timing sprocket to the camshaft. Make sure the cam is in proper time, that new lockplates are used, and that nuts are properly torqued. See the procedure for timing chain removal and installation below.

14. When reinstalling the timing cover, make sure to apply a liquid sealer to the joints between upper and lower timing covers. The remainder of installation is the reverse of removal. Note these points.

a. Adjust throttle, speed control, and accelerator cables. Inspect and if necessary replace the exhaust manifold gasket.

b. When reinstalling the cylinder block coolant plug, coat it with sealer. Make sure to refill the cooling system and bleed it (see the Cooling System procedure below).

### *525i, 535i, 635CSi and 1987–90 735i and 735iL (M30 B35 engine)*

1. Unbolt the exhaust pipe connections at the manifold and at the transmission pipe clamp. Disconnect the negative battery cable.

2. Remove the splash shield from under the engine. With the engine cool, remove the drain plugs from the bottom of the radiator and block. Drain the engine oil.

3. Remove the fan. Lift out the expansion rivets on either side and remove the fan shroud.

4. Loosen the hose clamp and disconnect the air inlet hose. Remove the mounting nut and remove the air cleaner.

5. The unit on the opposite side of the intake hose from the air cleaner contains the idle speed control valve, which must be removed next. Loosen the hose clamps and pull off the hoses. Disconnect the electrical connector. Remove the mounting nut and then pull the idle speed control out of the air intake hose.

6. Pull off the 3 retainers for the airflow sensor, and then pull the unit off its mountings, disconnecting the vacuum hose from the PCV system at the same time.

7. Working on the coolant expansion tank, disconnect the electrical connector. Remove the nuts on both sides. Loosen their clamps and then disconnect all 3 hoses and remove the tank.

8. Disconnect the heater hoses at both the control valve and at the heater core.

9. Disconnect the throttle and cruise control cables at the throttle lever. Unbolt the cable housing retainer and remove the housing and cables.

10. Disconnect the 4 plugs near the thermostat housing. Loosen the hose clamps and pull off the 2 coolant hoses.
11. Disconnect the plug in the line leading to the oxygen sensor. Disconnect the other 2 plugs nearby.
12. Disconnect the fuel supply and return lines, collecting fuel in a metal container for safe disposal.
13. Disconnect the fuel pipe running along the cylinder head, near the manifold. Pull off the electrical connector at the throttle body. Remove the caps, then remove the attaching bolts and remove the wiring harness carrier and harness for the fuel injectors.
14. Disconnect the coil high tension lead. Disconnect the high tension wires at the plugs. Then, remove the mounting nuts and remove the carrier for the high tension wires from the head.
15. Remove the attaching nuts for the cam cover and remove it.
16. Turn the engine until the timing marks are at TDC and the No. 6 valves are at overlap (both slightly open) position.
17. Remove the upper timing case cover as described below. Remove the timing chain tensioner piston as also described below.
18. Remove the 4 upper timing chain sprocket bolts and pull the sprocket off, *holding it upward and then supporting it securely so the relationship between the chain and sprockets top and bottom will not be lost* .
19. Disconnect the upper radiator hose at the thermostat housing. Remove the 3 bolts and remove the support for the intake manifold.
20. Remove the cylinder head bolts in the opposite of numbered order. Then, install 4 special pins BMW part No. 11 1 063 or equivalent. This is necessary to keep the rocker arm shafts from moving. Then, lift off the head.
21. Make checks of the lower cylinder head and block deck surface to make sure they are true. Install a new head gasket, making sure that all bolt, oil, and coolant holes line up. Use a gasket marked M30 B35. Use a 0.3mm thicker gasket if the head has been machined.

**To install:**

22. Apply a very light coating of oil to the head bolts. Don't let oil get into the boltholes or apply excessive amounts of oil, or torque could be incorrect and the block could crack. Use the newer type of bolt without a collar. Install the bolts, finger tight.
23. Torque bolts 1–6 in the order shown in the illustration to 42–44 ft. lbs. Remove the 4 pins holding the rocker shafts in place. Now, complete the first stage of torquing by torquing bolts 7–14 in the order shown, to the same specification. Adjust the valves after a 15 minute wait. Tighten the bolts, in the order shown, with a torque angle gauge 30–36 degrees, using special tool BMW 11 2 110 or equivalent. Then, reassemble the engine as described below and run it until hot (25 minutes). Then, again remove the valve cover, and either immediately or at any time later (engine temperature isn't critical), turn the head bolts, in order, 30–40 degrees.

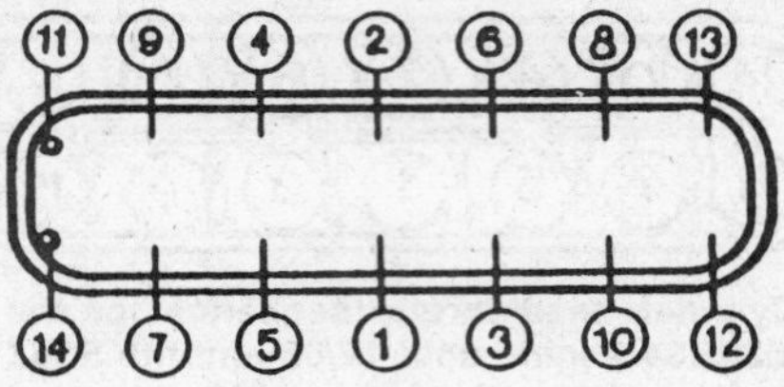


**Torque head bolts in the order shown—M30 B35 engine from 12/'86 on**

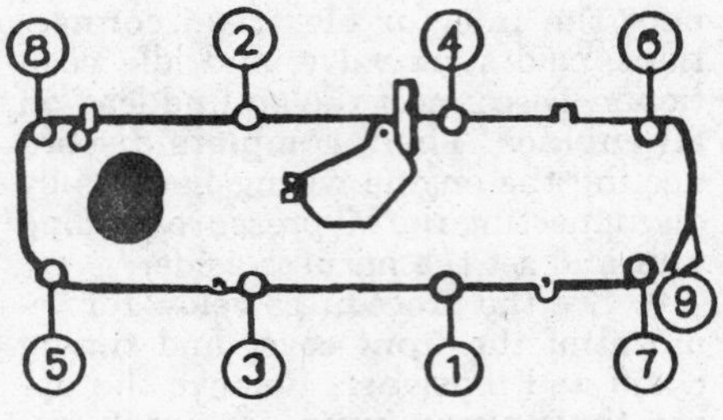


**Torque the cam cover bolts on the M30 B34 and B35 engines in the order shown**

24. Reinstall the timing sprocket to the camshaft. Make sure the cam is in proper time, that new lockplates are used, and that nuts are properly torqued. See the procedure for timing chain removal and installation below.
25. When reinstalling the timing cover, make sure to apply a liquid sealer to the joints between upper and lower timing covers. The remainder of installation is the reverse of removal. Note these points:
a. Adjust throttle, speed control, and accelerator cables. Inspect and if necessary replace the exhaust manifold gasket.
b. When reinstalling the cylinder block coolant plug, coat it with sealer. Make sure to refill the cooling system and bleed it (see the Cooling System procedure below). Make sure to refill the oil pan with the correct amount of specified oil.
c. Make sure to install the timing chain so that the down pin on the camshaft sprocket is at the lower left (8 o'Clock) when its tapped bores are at right angles to the engine. Torque the sprocket bolts to 6.5–7.5 ft. lbs.
d. Check the cam cover gasket, replacing as necessary. Retighten cam cover bolts in the order shown. Torque the bolts to 6.5–7.5 ft. lbs.
e. When reinstalling the fan shroud, make sure all guides are located properly.
f. Coat the tapered portion of the exhaust pipe connection flange with CRC® Copper Paste or equivalent. Torque the attaching nuts to 4.5 ft. lbs., and then loosen one and a half turns.

### *M5 and M6*

**NOTE: This is an extremely difficult operation involving the use of a number of special tools. It is necessary to remove both of the camshafts to complete it. Refer to the camshaft removal and installation procedure below for information on those special tools.**

1. Disconnect the negative battery cable. Scribe matchmarks where the hood hinges attach to the hood. Then, disconnect the support struts, unbolt the hood at the hinges and remove it.
2. Disconnect the electrical connector at the airflow sensor. Loosen the hose clamp at the air intake hose going to the air cleaner, remove the air cleaner attaching nut, and remove the air cleaner and airflow sensor.
3. Disconnect the large vacuum hose that connects to the bottom of the intake manifold. Disconnect the PCV hoses where they connect to the top of the manifold. Disconnect the throttle cable that runs across the top of the manifold, and the hose running near the front. Remove the bolts fastening the manifold to the outer ends of the intake tubes and remove it.
4. With the engine cool, drain the coolant from the block. Disconnect the exhaust pipe at the manifold.
5. Working underneath, remove the heat shields. Remove the cross brace and stabilizer bar where they connect to the engine carrier. Remove the exhaust manifold as described below.
6. Disconnect the upper radiator hose. Pull the 3 plugs off the water manifold that connects with the upper radiator hose. Pull off the plug coming from the same harness and connecting to the top of the engine. Then, unclip this harness and pull it out of the way.
7. Loosen the retaining straps and disconnect the electrical connector that runs directly across the front of the block. Disconnect the fuel pipe on the driver's side of the block, collecting fuel in a metal container for safe disposal.
8. Pull the electrical connector off the throttle bypass valve. Disconnect the water hose and remove the bypass valve. Disconnect the large hose just to the right of the throttle bypass valve.

Remove the wiring harness clips just to the right.

9. Going to the rear of the engine, disconnect the fuel return line and collect fuel in a metal container for safe disposal. Disconnect both heater hoses. Remove the conduit for the injector wiring harness from the head. Remove the 2 bolts in the front of the head which run down into the timing cover.

10. See the procedures below for removal of the front timing cover and timing chain. It is not necessary to remove the timing chain completely, but it will be necessary to remove the cam cover, front covers (for the camshaft drive sprockets), and the upper guide rail for the timing chain, and then turn the engine to TDC firing position for No. 1. Then, it will be necessary to remove the timing chain tensioner. Note the relationship between the chain and both the crankshaft and camshaft sprockets, and then remove both camshaft drive sprockets. Leave the chain in a position that will not interfere with removal of the head and which will minimize disturbing its routing through the areas on the front of the block.

11. Remove the camshafts as described below.

12. Prepare a clean work area and a way to store the cam followers in order—preferably some sort of rack. Remove the cam followers one at a time, keeping them in exact order for installation in the same positions.

13. Remove the coolant pipe that runs across the front of the block. Remove the bolts (some are accessible from below) that retain the timing case to the head at the front (the timing case houses the lifters and the camshaft lower bearing saddles.) Then, go along in the area under the cam cover and remove all the remaining bolts for the timing case. Remove the timing case.

14. Loosen the head bolts in reverse of the tightening order shown. Remove the cylinder head.

**To install:**

15. Make checks of the lower cylinder head and block deck surface to make sure they are true. Lubricate the head bolts with a light coating of engine oil. Make sure there is no oil or dirt in the boltholes in the block. Install a new head gasket, making sure that all bolt, oil, and coolant holes line up. Use a gasket type M6 marked 3.5M 88.3.

16. Replace the O-ring in the head at the right/rear where the coolant pipe comes up from the block. Coat the pipe with a Silastic sealer.

17. Install the head onto the block. Install the head bolts and tighten in numbered order according to Specifications.

Removing the rocker arm shaft with special tool—four cylinder engine

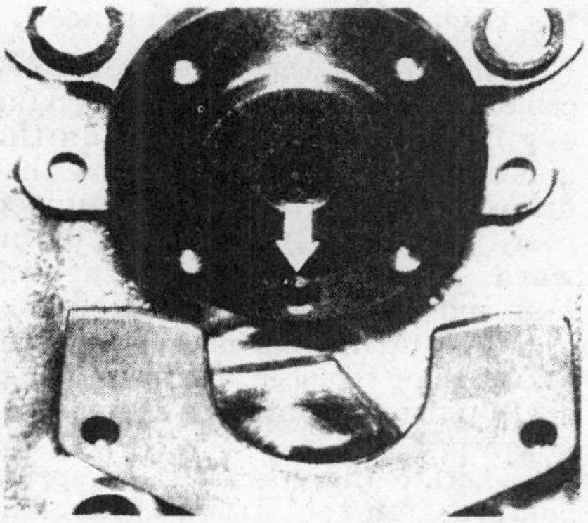

Removal of camshaft and rocker arm retainer plate from the cylinder head, showing the dowel pin hole on four cylinder engine

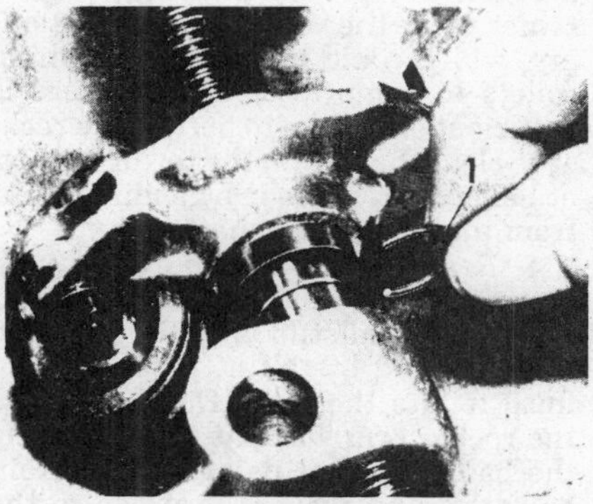

Circlip location on the rocker arm shaft

18. When installing the timing case, replace the O-rings in the 2 small oil passages in the ends of the head. Inspect the 6 O-rings in the center of the block and replace them if necessary. Coat all sealing surfaces with silastic sealer. Tighten the bolts evenly, torquing the smaller (M7) bolts to 10–12 ft. lbs. and the larger (M8) bolts to 14.5–15.5 ft. lbs. Install all lifters back into the same bores.

19. Install the camshafts as described below.

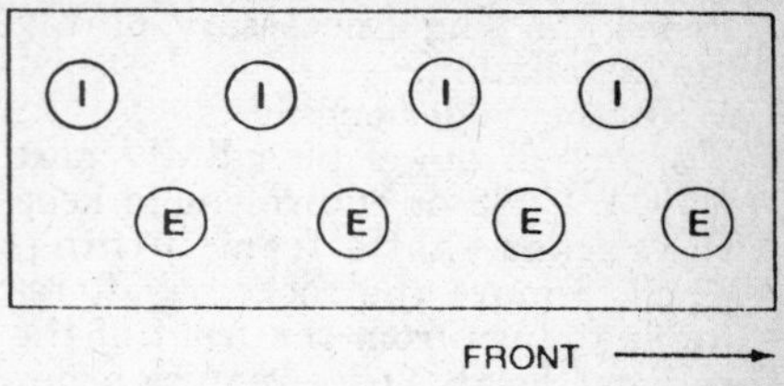


4-cylinder valve location

20. As described under the camshaft and timing chain removal and installation procedures below, reroute the timing chain as necessary and remount the drive sprockets for the camshaft. Install the tensioning rail that goes at the top of the timing chain.

21. Install the front cover according to the procedure below.

22. Continue to reverse the removal procedure. Note these points while working:

a. When reinstalling the intake manifold, inspect the O-rings and replace as necessary.

b. Refill the cooling system with an appropriate anti-freeze/water mix for the climate and bleed the cooling system.

### OVERHAUL

**NOTE: For all cylinder head overhaul procedures, please refer to "Engine Rebuilding" in the Unit Repair Section.**

## Rocker Arms/Shafts

### REMOVAL & INSTALLATION

#### *All Models Except 325, 325e, 325i, 325iS, 325iX and 524td, and 528e*

1. Disconnect the negative battery cable. Remove the cylinder head.

2. Remove the camshaft.

3. On 6 cylinder engines, remove the retaining bolts and remove the end cover from the rear of the cylinder head. Slide the thrust rings and rocker arms rearward and remove the circlips from the rocker arm shafts.

4. On 4 cylinder engines:

a. Remove the distributor flange from the rear of the cylinder head.

b. Using a long punch, drive the rocker arm shaft from the rear to the front of the cylinder head.

**NOTE: Be sure all circlips are off the shaft before attempting to drive the shaft from the cylinder head.**

c. The intake rocker shaft is not plugged at the rear, while the exhaust rocker shaft must be plugged.

Renew the plug if necessary, during the installation.

5. On 6 cylinder engines:

a. Install dowel pins BMW part No. 11 1 063 or equivalent to keep the rocker shafts from turning. Then, remove the rocker shaft retaining plugs from the front of the cylinder head. These require a hex head wrench. Then, push back the rocker arms against spring pressure and remove the circlips retaining the shafts. Remove the dowel pins. If the rocker shafts have welded plugs, the shafts will have to be pressed out of the head with a tool such as 11 3 050 or equivalent.

**CAUTION**

***There is considerable force on the springs positioning the rockers. They may pop out! Be cautious and wear safety glasses.***

b. Install a threaded slide hammer into the ends of the rear rocker shafts and remove.

**To install:**

6. The rocker arms, springs, washers, thrust rings and shafts should be examined and worn parts replaced. Special attention should be given to the rocker arm cam followers. If these are loose, replace the arm assembly. The valves can be removed, repaired or replaced, as necessary, while the shafts and rocker arms are out of the cylinder head.

7. Install the rocker arms in position, noting the following procedures:

a. Design changes of the rocker arms and shafts have occurred with the installation of a bushing in the rocker arm and the use of 2 horizontal oil flow holes drilled into the rocker shaft for improved oil supply. Do not mix the previously designed parts with the later design.

b. When installing the rocker arms and components to the rocker shafts, install locating pins in the cylinder head bolt bores to properly align the rocker arm shafts. Note that on 6 cylinder engines, the longer rocker shafts go on the chain end of the engine; the openings face the bores for the cylinder head bolts; and the plug threads face outward. The order of installation is: spring, washer, rocker arm, thrust washer, circlip. Note also that newer, short springs may be used with the older design.

c. Install sealer on the rocker arm shaft retaining plugs and rear cover.

d. On the 4 cylinder engines, position the rocker shafts so that the camshaft retaining plate ends can be engaged in the slots of shafts during camshaft installation.

e. Adjust the valve clearance.

### *524td*

**NOTE: To replace the rocker arms on the 524td, it is necessary to use a special tool which allows the valve involved to be opened and works against the camshaft. Use BMW Tool 11 3 120 or the equivalent. It is also necessary to have a special tool designed to remove the rocker pivots from the head. Because these are retained by an adhesive, it will be necessary to get an adhesive designed to retain the rocker pivots on this engine. It is also necessary, of course, to have the special tools required to adjust the valves after the rockers have been replaced.**

1. Disconnect the negative battery cable. Remove the cam cover. Turn the engine over with a wrench on the crankshaft pulley so the cams that drive the vacuum pump (mounted over the camshaft) are pointed downward. Then, remove the attaching nuts and remove the vacuum pump.

2. Pull off the spring clip for each rocker being replaced. Turn the crankshaft so the cams involved are pointing downward.

3. Locate the special valve spring compression tool around the camshaft. Make sure that if the valve will not depress easily, the crankshaft is turned. If the piston is right near top center, the valve may hit it. Also, make sure not to depress the valve spring retainer while the valve remains stationary, which could permit the retaining collets to come loose. When there is sufficient clearance to permit the rocker to clear the ball on the top of the pivot ballstud, remove it by sliding it out from under the camshaft.

4. Remove the ballstud by clamping the special tool on it and pulling it out. Coat a new ballstud with the required adhesive and install it, pressing it in until it hits the stop. Do not replace the rocker arm without also replacing the ballstud. If re-using parts, retain ballstuds and rockers in order so the same parts will be used together.

**To install:**

5. Install the rocker in reverse order. Press the spring clip into the groove in the top of the ballstud from the outboard side so the end of the clip will retain the rocker. Adjust the valves as described earlier in this section.

6. Install the vacuum pump with the cams that are under it turned downward. Make sure that the vacuum pump pipe is at the rear and that its drive cam will line up with the follower on the pump plunger. Make sure to install the seal on the pipe. Replace the cam cover in reverse or removal.

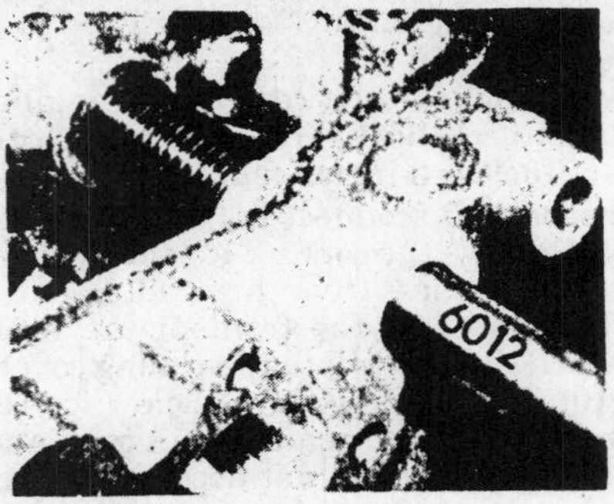


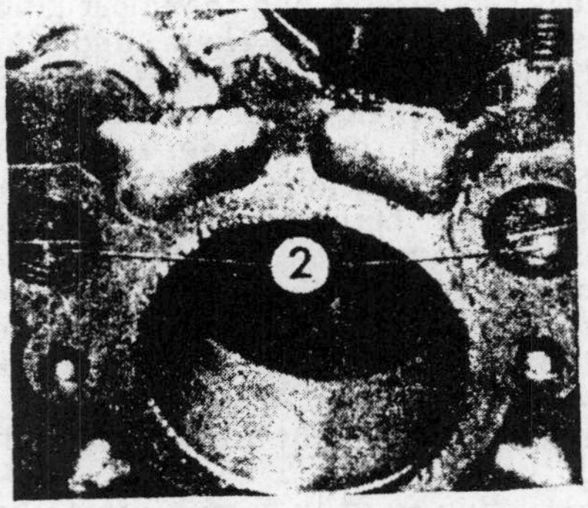


Rocker arm shaft locking bolt (2) location—six cylinder engine

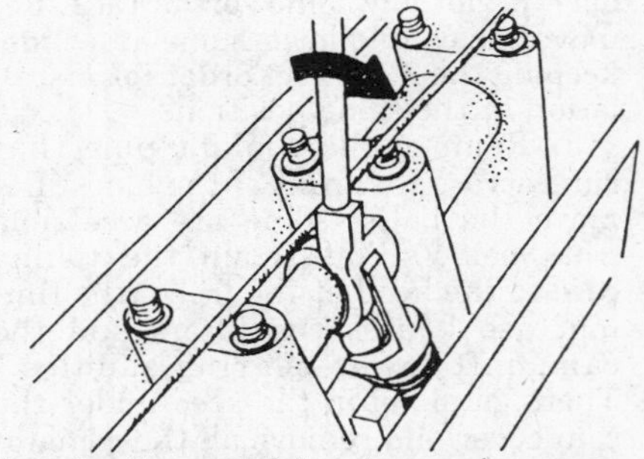

Locate the special valve spring compressing tool around the camshaft, as shown, to force the valve downward. This will give clearance to permit removal of the rocker arm

1. Set screw
2. Eccentric
3. Washer
4. Locking nut

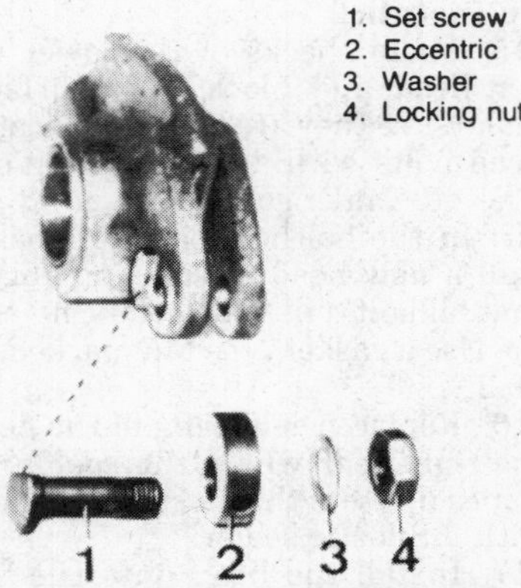


Rocker arm valve adjusting mechanism

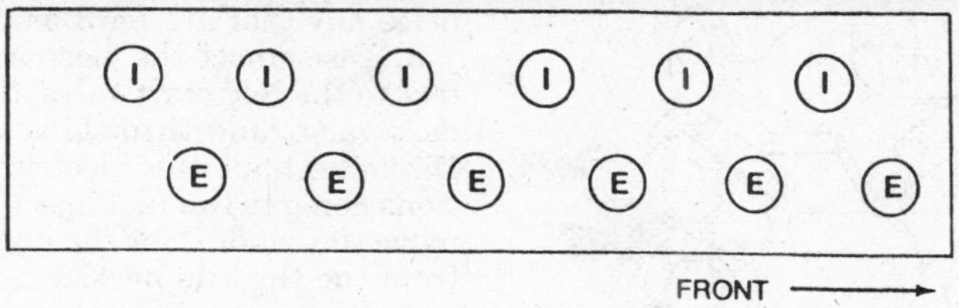


6-cylinder valve location

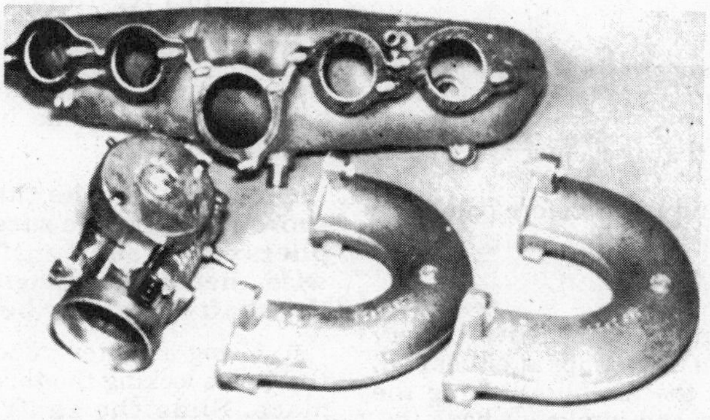

Induction system with induction tubes secured with nuts and washers

3. Spring
4. Washer
5. Rocker arm
6. Thrust ring

**Installed position of rocker arm components**

### *325, 325e, 325i, 325iS, 325iX and 528e*

The cylinder head must be removed before the rocker arm shafts can be removed.

1. Disconnect the negative battery cable. Remove the cylinder head.
2. Mount the head on BMW stand 11 1 060 and 00 1 490 or equivalent. Secure the head to the stand with one head bolt.
3. Remove the camshaft sprocket bolt and remove the camshaft distributor adapter and sprocket. Reinstall the adapter on the camshaft.
4. Adjust the valve clearance to the maximum allowable on all valves.
5. Remove the front and rear rocker shaft plugs and lift out the thrust plate.
6. Remove the spring-clips from the rocker arms by lifting them off.
7. Remove the exhaust side rocker arm shaft:
   a. Set the No. 6 cylinder rocker arms at the valve overlap position (rocker arms parallel), by rotating the camshaft through the firing order.
   b. Push in on the front cylinder rocker arm and then turn the camshaft in the direction of the intake rocker shaft, using a ½ in. drive breaker bar and a deep well socket to fit over the camshaft adapter. Slide each rocker arm to one side as it develops sufficient clearance away from its actuating cam and the valve it actuates. Rotate the camshaft until all of the rocker arms are relaxed.
   c. Remove the rocker arm shaft.
8. Remove the intake side rocker arm shaft:
   a. Turn the camshaft in the direction of the exhaust rocker arm.
   b. Use a deep well socket and ½ in. drive breaker bar on the camshaft adapter to turn the camshaft. Slide each rocker arm to one side as it develops sufficient clearance away from its actuating cam and the valve it actuates. Rotate the camshaft until all of the rocker arms are relaxed.
   c. Remove the rocker arm shaft.
9. Install the rocker arm shafts by reversing the removal procedure. Bear the following points in mind:
   a. The large oil bores in the rocker shafts must be installed downward (toward the valve guides) and the small oil bores and grooves for the guide plate face inward toward the center of the head.
   b. The straight sections of the spring clamps must fit into the grooves in the rocker arm shafts.
   c. The guide plate must fit into the grooves in the rocker arm shafts.
   d. Adjust the valve clearance.

# Intake Manifold

## REMOVAL & INSTALLATION

### *318i and 320i*

1. Disconnect the negative battery cable. Remove the air cleaner and drain the cooling system.
2. Disconnect the accelerator cable and remove the vacuum hoses from the air collector. Tag the hoses.
3. Remove the injection line holder from No. 4 intake tube.
4. Remove the No. 3 intake tube and disconnect the vacuum and coolant lines from the throttle housing.
5. Disconnect the hoses at the EGR valve and remove the wire plugs at the temperature timing switch.
6. Remove the cold start valve from the air collector.
7. Disconnect the vacuum hose and electrical connections at the timing valve.
8. Disconnect the remaining intake tubes at the collector. Disconnect the collector brackets at the engine and remove the collector.
9. Remove the air intake tubes from the manifold and remove the injector valves.
10. Remove the intake manifold.

**To install:**

11. To install the manifold, use new gaskets and install the manifold to the engine.
12. Install the air intake tubes and the injector valves. Install the collector and bracket.
13. Connect the vacuum line and electrical connections to the timing valve. Install the cold start valve.
14. Connect the line at the EGR valve and the electrical connections at the temperature timing switch.
15. Connect all vacuum, cooling and fuel lines at the throttle housing. Install the accelerator cable and vacuum hoses to the air collector.
16. Install the air cleaner and fill the cooling system. Check all hose connections and fluid levels before operating the engine.

### All 6 Cylinder Models Except 524td, M5 and M6

**NOTE: Slight variations may exist among models due to model changes and updating but basic removal and installation remains the same.**

1. Disconnect the battery ground cable and drain the cooling system.
2. Disconnect the wire harness at the air flow sensor. Remove the air cleaner and sensor as an assembly. Disconnect the air intake hose running from the air cleaner to the manifold.
3. Remove and tag the vacuum hoses and electrical plugs. Disconnect the accelerator linkage (and cruise control linkage, if so-equipped) from the throttle housing.
4. Disconnect the coolant hoses from the throttle housing.
5. Working from the rear of the collector housing, disconnect the vacuum lines, and starting valve connector, fuel line and air line. Tag the hoses and lines for ease of assembly.
6. Remove the EGR valve and line.
7. Remove all intake pipes.
8. Remove the air collector housing from the engine. On later models with a single intake manifold casting, remove the nuts and remove the throttle valve body.
9. Disconnect the plugs at the injector valves and remove the valves.
10. Disconnect the wire plugs at the coolant temperature sensor, the temperature time switch and the temperature switch.
11. Pull the wire loom upward through the opening in the intake manifold neck.
12. Remove the coolant hoses from the intake neck.
13. Remove the retaining bolts or nuts and remove either front, rear or both intake manifold necks. On later models, remove the entire assembly.

**NOTE: Mark the heater hoses for proper reinstallation.**

**To install:**

14. To install the manifold, use new gaskets and install the manifold to the engine.
15. Install the air intake tubes and the injector valves. Install the collector and bracket.
16. Connect the vacuum line and electrical connections to the timing valve. Install the cold start valve.
17. Connect the line at the EGR valve and the electrical connections at the temperature timing switch.
18. Connect all vacuum, cooling and fuel lines at the throttle housing. Install the accelerator cable and vacuum hoses to the air collector.

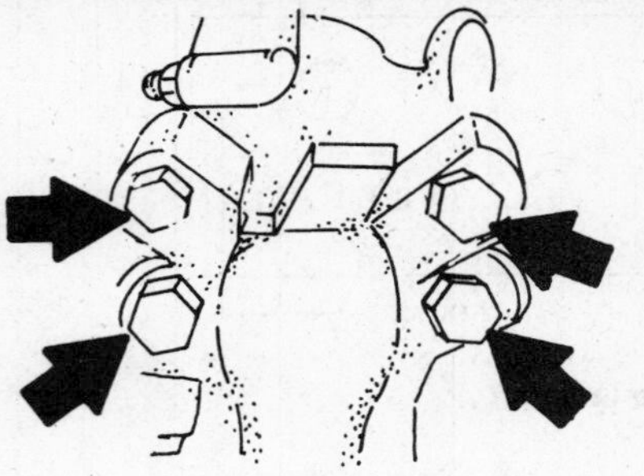

Remove the four arrowed bolts to remove the turbocharger (524 td)

19. Install the air cleaner and fill the cooling system. Check all hose connections and fluid levels before operating the engine.

### 524td

1. Disconnect the negative battery cable. Loosen the clamps at either end, and remove the air hose linking the turbocharger and intake air box.
2. Using a crowfoot type wrench, disconnect the injection lines at both the pump and injectors, remove the lines as an assembly, and plug all openings.
3. Remove any remaining hoses or wires interfering with manifold removal. Then, remove the retaining nuts and remove the manifold.
4. Clean both gasket surfaces, install a new gasket, and put the manifold into position. Install the retaining nuts. Torque the nuts to the figure shown in the torque chart at the beginning of this section.
5. Reinstall the injection lines, torquing the connections to 14–18 ft. lbs. Bleed the injection system. Reconnect all hoses and wires that had to be disconnected. Reconnect the hose linking the turbocharger and manifold. Make sure connections are properly positioned and that the clamps are tight.

### M5 and M6

The M5 and M6 employ a manifold chamber in combination with 6 throttle necks (one for each cylinder), each of which contains its own throttle. The throttle necks are divided into 3 assemblies each containing the necks for 2 adjacent cylinders.

1. Disconnect the negative battery cable. Remove the nuts at the outer ends of the throttle necks (these attach the manifold to the outer ends of the necks). Loosen the hose clamps for the crankcase ventilation hoses and for the air intake hose. Disconnect the accelerator cable.
2. Pull the intake manifold off the throttle necks. Check O-rings and replace any that are hard or cracked.
3. Disconnect the electrical connectors to the cold start valve, throttle bypass valve, and throttle valve switch. Disconnect all the electrical connections going to the fuel injectors and remove the conduit for the injector wires from the throttle necks.
4. Disconnect the vacuum hoses for the fuel pressure regulator and the heater temperature sensor. Disconnect the fuel return pipe, and collect the fuel in a metal container for safe disposal.
5. Remove the attaching nuts and bolts, and remove the injection pipe and injectors.

**NOTE: Clean the throttle shaft thoroughly and be sure not to use pliers on the shaft surface. Otherwise, needle bearings on which the shaft rides may be damaged.**

6. Using a center punch, drive out the 4 pins locking the throttle shaft in place. Slide the shaft out of the bearings.
7. Unscrew its mounting nuts and remove the throttle bypass valve. Disconnect the air hoses from this valve.
8. Remove the nuts attaching the throttle valve necks to the head and remove them.
9. Remove the connecting pipes that run between the valve neck units. Replace O-rings if necessary. Replace all gaskets and make sure gasket surfaces on the head and inner ends of valve necks are clean.
10. Install in reverse order, providing new pins for the throttle shaft and coating its bearing surfaces with Molykote Longterm® before assembly.
11. Replace the sleeves in the intake manifold, if necessary. Replace the crankcase ventilation hose connecting the intake manifold and crankcase.

### M3

**NOTE: A Torx® nut driver is needed to perform this operation.**

1. Disconnect the negative battery cable. Remove the capnuts (2 each) at the outer ends of the 4 throttle necks. Then remove the mounting nuts underneath.
2. Make sure the engine has cooled off. Loosen the hose clamps for the air intake lines and for the fuel lines where they connect with the injection pipe. Collect fuel in a metal container.
3. Disconnect the throttle cable.
4. Pull off the intake manifold. Cut off the crankcase ventilation hose running to it from the crankcase. Then, remove the manifold and place it aside. Supply a new crankcase ventilation hose.
5. Pull off the throttle valve switch

plug. Carefully pull the injector plug plate evenly off all 4 injectors.

6. Pull the fuel pressure regulator vacuum hose off the pressure regulator.

7. Remove the 2 mounting bolts for the injector pipe. Then, carefully lift off the pipe and injectors.

8. Unscrew the nut attaching the ball joint at the end of the throttle actuating rod to the throttle linkage. Supply a new self-locking nut.

9. Remove the Torx® nuts attaching the throttle necks to the cylinder head. Then, remove the 4 throttle necks as an assembly.

10. Separate the throttle neck assemblies by pulling them apart at the connecting pipe.

11. Inspect the O-rings in the connecting pipe and at the outer ends of the throttle necks. Replace as necessary.

12. Reverse the removal procedure to install. Use the new throttle linkage self-locking nut and the new crankcase ventilation hose.

13. Torque the nuts attaching the throttle necks to the head and the intake manifold to the throttle necks to 6.5–7.0 ft. lbs. Adjust the throttle cable.

## Exhaust Manifold

### REMOVAL & INSTALLATION

#### *All Except 524td, M3, M5 and M6*

The exhaust manifolds are referred to as exhaust gas recirculation reactors.

The removal and installation procedures are basically the same for all models. The 4 cylinder manifold (used on the 320i model), is a one piece, one outlet unit, while the 6 cylinder manifold assembly consists of a 2 piece, double outlet to the exhaust pipe. One piece can be replaced independently of the other.

1. Disconnect the negative battery cable. Remove the air volume control and if necessary, air cleaner.

2. Disconnect the exhaust pipe at the reactor outlet(s).

3. Remove the guard plate from the reactor(s).

4. Disconnect the air injection pipe fitting, the EGR counterpressure line, EGR pressure line and any supports.

**NOTE: An exhaust filter is used between the reactor and the EGR valve and must be disconnected. Replace the filter if found to be defective.**

5. Remove the retaining bolts or nuts at the reactor and remove it from the cylinder head.

6. Install the manifold, using new gaskets. Install the air injection fittings.

7. Connect the exhaust pipe at the reactor. Install the air cleaner.

#### *524td*

1. Disconnect the negative battery cable. Remove the turbocharger, oil lines, and piping as described below.

2. Remove the nuts and disconnect the exhaust pipe at the manifold.

3. Remove the manifold bolts and remove the manifold. Clean both gasket surfaces.

4. Install the gasket, manifold, and attaching nuts. Torque the nuts to the figure shown in the torque chart at the beginning of this section.

5. Install the turbocharger and associated piping as described below.

#### *M5 and M6*

1. Disconnect the negative battery cable. With the engine cool, remove the drain plug from the block. Remove the 3 electrical connectors from the front of the coolant manifold that runs along the left side of the engine. Disconnect the radiator hose from the front of this pipe. Then, remove all the mounting bolts for this pipe and remove it. Inspect the O-rings (one for each cylinder, located in the block), and replace any that are worn or damaged.

2. Disconnect the exhaust pipe at the manifold. Remove the heat shields from underneath the engine.

3. Remove the cross brace that runs under the engine by removing the 2 bolts from either end and then removing it.

4. Disconnect the stabilizer bar near both ends where it is bushed to the engine carrier.

5. Attach a lifting sling to the engine. Remove the nut from the right side engine mount and lift the engine slightly for clearance.

6. Remove the mounting bolts and remove the manifold.

7. Clean all gasket material from the surfaces of the manifold and head and replace the gaskets.

8. To install, position the manifold, torquing the manifold bolts to 36–40 ft. lbs. and the coolant pipe mounting bolts to 7.5–8.5 ft. lbs. Make sure to refill the cooling system with fresh anti-freeze/water mix and bleed it.

#### *M3*

1. Disconnect the negative battery cable. With the engine cool, remove the drain plug from the block. Remove the 3 electrical connectors from the front of the coolant manifold that runs along the left side of the engine. Disconnect the radiator hose from the front of this pipe. Then, remove all the mounting bolts for this pipe and remove it. Inspect the O-rings (one for each cylinder, located in the block), and replace any that are worn or damaged.

Position of crankshaft woodruff key (1)

2. Disconnect the exhaust pipe at the manifold flange. Remove the heat shields from underneath the engine.

3. Remove the mounting nuts at the cylinder head and remove the manifold.

4. Clean all gasket material from the surfaces of the manifold and head and replace the gaskets.

5. To install, position the manifold on the head, torquing the manifold bolts to 6.5–7.0 ft. lbs. and the coolant pipe mounting bolts to 7.5–8.5 ft. lbs. Torque the bolts at the flange attaching manifold and exhaust pipe first to 22–25 ft. lbs. and then to 36–40 ft. lbs. Make sure to refill the cooling system with fresh anti-freeze/water mix and bleed it.

## Turbocharger

### REMOVAL & INSTALLATION

#### *524td*

1. Disconnect the negative battery cable. Disconnect the connecting hoses and remove the air cleaner. Disconnect the turbo inlet and outlet air hoses.

2. Remove the EGR pipe and EGR valve.

3. Unbolt the banjo connector for the oil pressure line going to the turbocharger at the side of the block. Remove the clamps and disconnect the oil drain line from the turbo at the block. Disconnect the exhaust pipe at the turbo exhaust outlet.

4. Remove the 4 bolts attaching the turbocharger to the exhaust manifold, and remove it.

5. Installation is the reverse of removal. Replace gaskets on the EGR valve and seals on the high pressure oil line. Coat EGR valve studs with a copper paste and replace the self-locking nuts.

## Timing Chain Cover

### REMOVAL & INSTALLATION

#### *318i and 320i*

There are 2 timing chain covers, one upper and one lower, which must be removed to service the timing chain and sprocket assemblies.

1. Remove the cylinder head cover. Disconnect the negative battery cable. Disconnect the air injection line at the front of the thermal reactor (if so equipped). On the 318i, disconnect the bracket located on the driver's side of the upper cover.
2. Remove 8 bolts which retain the upper timing gear cover to the cylinder head and lower timing gear cover. remove the upper cover, taking note of the placement of the alternator ground wire.
3. Drain the cooling system and remove the radiator, preheater intake air assembly (carburetor equipped cars only) and radiator hoses.
4. Bend back the lockplates for the fan retaining bolts. Remove the bolts and lift off the fan.
5. Loosen the alternator retaining bolts. Push the alternator toward the engine and remove the fan pulley and the alternator drive (fan) belt. On the 318i, remove the alternator and tensioning bar. remove the 4 mounting bolts from the air pump bracket (where it attaches to the block), and remove the pump and bracket; then remove the bolt attaching the tensioning bar to the block and remove the tensioning bar.
6. Disconnect the coolant hoses from the water pump. Remove the 6 retaining bolts and copper sealing washers and lift off the water pump.
7. Unscrew the plug and remove the spring from the cam chain tensioner assembly, taking care to cushion the sudden release of spring tension. Remove the plunger (piston).
8. On the 320i, disconnect the multiple plug and cable lead from the alternator. Remove the alternator with its bearing block and clamping strap.
9. Remove the flywheel inspection plate and block the ring gear from turning with a small prybar.
10. Unscrew the crankshaft pulley nut and pull off the belt pulley.
11. Remove the bolts which retain the lower cover to the cylinder black and oil pan. On the 318i, remove the bolts retaining the brace plate and remove it. Also on the 318i, loosen the oil pan lower retaining bolts not directly involved with the lower cover. With a sharp knife, carefully separate the lower edge of the timing cover from the upper edge of the oil pan gasket at the front.
12. Remove the lower timing cover. At this time, it is advisable to replace the timing cover seal (sealing ring) with a new one. The sealing ring is a press fit into the cover.
13. Clean the mating surfaces of the timing covers, oil pan, cylinder head, and cylinder block. Replace all gaskets (except the oil pan gasket), and seal them at the corners with sealing compound such as Permatex® No. 2. If the oil pan gasket has been damaged, remove the oil pan and replace the gasket.

**To install:**

14. Reverse the above procedure to install, taking care to tighten the upper timing gear cover retaining bolts in the following sequence (as per the illustration): handtighten 1 and 2, then torque 3–8 in numerical order, and finally 1 and 2 to 6.5–7.9 ft. lbs.
15. Note that on the 318i, the mounting web for the tensioning piston must be in the oil pocket. On the 318i, also make sure to pack the bores between the lower cover (at the top) and block with sealer.

#### *6 Cylinder Models Except 325, 325e, 325i, 325iS, 325iX, 524td, 528e, M5 and M6*

**NOTE: On 533, 535, 600CS Series, and 700 Series engines, this procedure requires the use of a special gauge, to be made to a certain dimension, as in Step 16.**

1. Disconnect the negative battery cable. Remove the cylinder head cover. Remove the distributor as described earlier in this chapter. On all 3.3Lmodels, detach the distributor guard and the air line going to the thermal reactor. On models with DME, follow this procedure to remove the distributor:
   a. Remove the distributor cap, which screws onto the cover directly in front of the camshaft.
   b. Then, if the rotor is of the slide-on type, simply pull the rotor off and then remove the cover underneath it.
   c. If the rotor is of the screw-on type, unscrew it from the distributor shaft, then unscrew the adapter underneath and, finally remove the cover underneath the adapter.
2. Drain the coolant to below the level of the thermostat and remove the thermostat housing cover.
3. Remove the 8 bolts (nine on M30B35MZ) and remove the upper timing case cover with the worm drive which drives the distributor (pre DME cars only).
4. Remove the piston which tensions the timing chain, working carefully because of very high spring pressure.
5. Remove the cooling fan and all drive belts. On late model 600 Series cars, the alternator must be swung aside by loosing the front bolt and removing the 2 side bolts. On all cars with the M30B35MZ engine, remove its attaching bolts and then remove the drive pulley from the water pump. The power steering pump must be removed, leaving the pump hoses connected and supporting the pump out of the way but so that the hoses are not stressed.
6. Remove the flywheel housing cover and lock the flywheel in position with an appropriate special tool.
7. Unscrew the nut from the center of the pulley and pull the pulley/vibration damper off the crankshaft.
8. Detach the TDC position transmitter on 600CS Series, 700 Series, and certain 528i models.
9. Loosen all the oil pan bolts, and then unscrew all the bolts from the lower timing case cover, *noting their lengths for reinstallation in the same positions. Carefully* use a knife to separate the gasket at the base of the lower timing cover. Then, remove the cover.

**To install:**

10. To install the lower cover, first coat the surfaces of the oil pan and block with sealer. Put it into position on the block, making sure the tensioning piston holding web (cast into the block) is in the oil pocket. Install all bolts; then tighten the lower front cover bolts evenly; finally, tighten the oil pan bolts evenly.
11. Inspect the hub of the vibration damper. If the hub is scored, install the radial seal so the sealing lip is in front of or to the rear of the scored area. Pack the seal with grease and install it with a sealer installer.
12. Install the pulley/damper and torque the bolt to specifications. When installing, make sure the key and keyway are properly aligned.
13. Remove the flywheel locking tool and reinstall the cover. Reinstall and tension all belts.
14. Before installing the upper cover, use sealer to seal the joint between the back of the lower timing cover and block at the top. On some models, there are sealer wells which are to be filled with sealer. If these are present, fill them carefully. Check the cork seal at the distributor drive coupling, and replace it if necessary.
15. On all but M30B35MZ engines: See the illustration for 4 cylinder engines above, and tighten bolts 1 and 2 (the lower bolts) slightly. Then, tighten bolts 3–8. Finally, fully tighten the

lower bolts. On M30B35MZ engines, note that the top bolt on the driver's side and the bottom bolt on the passenger's side are longer. On these engines, tighten the 2 bolts that run down into the lower timing cover first; then tighten the remaining 6 bolts (3 on each side).

16. On the M30B35MZ engine, simply install the TDC transmitter and its mounting bracket. On remaining engines, install the TDC position transmitter loosely, if so equipped. With the engine at exactly 0 degrees Top Center, as shown by the marker on the front cover, adjust the position of the transmitter with a gauge which should be made to conform to the dimensions shown in the illustration: i.e. it must fit the curve on the outside of the balancer, and incorporate a notch (for the pin on the balancer) and a ridge against which the transmitter must rest. The straight line distance between the center of the notch and bottom of the ridge must be exactly 37.5mm. Then, tighten the transmitter mounting screw.

17. Just before installing the upper timing case cover, check the condition of that area of the head gasket. It will usually be in good condition. If it should show damage, it must be replaced.

18. If the car has the DME type distributor, inspect the sealing O-rings and replace as necessary. If it uses the DME distributor with the screw-off type rotor, make sure the bolt at the center of the rotor has its seal in place and that it is installed with a sealer designed to prevent the bolt from backing out.

19. Complete the installation, making sure to bleed the cooling system.

### 524td

1. Disconnect the negative battery cable. Disconnect the hoses and remove the air cleaner. Remove the belt driving the alternator and fan. Remove the attaching nuts and remove the fan, keeping it in the vertical position.

2. Remove the air hose running along the top edge of the cover. remove the attaching bolts and remove the cover.

3. If removing the cover to replace the timing belt, proceed further to remove the vibration damper:

a. Remove the remaining accessory drive belts.

b. Remove the belts and remove the fan drive pulley.

c. Remove the center bolt, and pull the pulley and vibration damper off the hub.

4. Install the damper and pulley in position, torquing the center bolt for the vibration damper to the specifications shown in the torque specifications chart. Adjust belt tension. Install the cover and all drive belts.

### M3

1. Disconnect the negative battery cable. Drain the cooling system through the bottom of the radiator. Remove the radiator and fan as described later in this section.

2. Disconnect all electrical plugs, remove the attaching nuts, and remove the air cleaner and airflow sensor.'

3. Note and if necessary mark the wiring connections. Then, disconnect all alternator wiring. Unbolt the alternator and remove it and the drive belt.

4. Unbolt the power steering pump. Remove the belt and then move the pump aside, supporting it out of the way but in a position where the hoses will not be stressed.

5. Remove the 3 bolts from the bottom of the bell housing and the 2 bolts below it which fasten the reinforcement plate in place.

6. Remove the drain plug and drain the oil from the lower oil pan. Then, remove the lower oil pan bolts and remove the lower pan.

7. Remove the 3 bolts fastening the bottom of the front cover to the front of the oil pan. Loosen all the remaining oil pan bolts so the pan may be shifted downward just slightly to separate the gasket surfaces.

8. Remove the water pump as described below. Remove the center bolt and use a puller to remove the crankshaft pulley.

9. Remove the piston for the timing chain tensioner as described below under Timing Chain and Sprockets Removal & Installation.

10. Remove the 2 bolts attaching the top of the front cover to the cylinder head. Then, remove all the bolts fastening the cover to the block.

11. Run a knife carefully between the upper surface of the oil pan gasket and the lower surface of the front cover to separate them without tearing the gasket. If the gasket is damaged, remove the oil pan and replace it, as described later in this section.

**To install:**

12. Before reinstalling the cover, use a file to break or file off flashing at the top/rear of the casting on either side so the corner is smooth. Replace all gaskets, coating them with silicone sealer. Where gasket ends extend too far, trim them off. Apply sealer to the area where the oil pan gasket passes the front of the block.

13. Slide the cover straight on to avoid damaging the seal. Install all bolts in their proper positions. Coat the 3 bolts fastening the front cover to the upper oil pan with a sealer such as Loctite® 270® or equivalent.

14. Tighten the bolts at the top, fastening the lower cover to the upper cover first. Then, tighten the remaining front cover bolts and, finally, the oil pan bolts (to 7 ft. lbs.). If the car has the DME type distributor, inspect the sealing O-rings and replace as necessary. If it uses the DME distributor with the screw-off type rotor, make sure the bolt at the center of the rotor has its seal in place and that it is installed with a sealer designed to prevent the bolt from backing out.

15. Reverse the remaining portions of the removal procedures, making sure to fill and bleed the cooling system and to refill the oil pan with the correct oil.

16. Torque the oil drain plug to 24 ft. lbs. and both upper and lower oil pan bolts to 7 ft. lbs.

### M5 and M6

1. Disconnect the battery ground cable. Pull out the plug and remove the wiring leading to the airflow sensor. Loosen the hose clamp and disconnect the air intake hose. Remove the mounting nut and remove the air cleaner and airflow sensor as an assembly.

2. Remove the radiator and fan. See appropriate procedures below. Remove the flywheel housing cover and install a lock to lock the position of the flywheel. Remove the mounting nut for the vibration damper with a deepwell socket. Pull the damper off with a puller.

3. Remove the pipe that runs across in front of the front cover. Remove the mounting bolts and remove the water pump pulley.

4. Loosen the top/front mounting bolt for the alternator. Remove the lower/front bolt. Loosen the 2 side bolts. Swing the alternator aside.

5. Remove the power steering pump mounting bolts. Make sure to retain the spacer that goes between the pump and oil pan. Swing the pump aside and support it so the hoses will not be under stress.

6. Remove the flywheel housing cover and lock the flywheel in position with an appropriate special tool.

7. Unscrew the nut from the center of the pulley and pull the pulley/vibration damper off the crankshaft.

8. Remove the bolts at the top, fastening the lower front cover to the upper front cover. Remove the bolts at the bottom, fastening the lower cover to the oil pan. Loosen the remaining oil pan mounting bolts.

9. Run a knife carefully between the upper surface of the oil pan gasket and

the lower surface of the front cover to separate them without tearing the gasket.

10. Loosen and then remove the remaining front cover mounting bolts, noting the locations of the TDC sending unit on the upper/right side of the engine and the suspension position sending unit on the upper left. Also, keep track of the bolts that mount these accessories, as their lengths are slightly different. If necessary, lay the bolts out in a clean area in a pattern similar to that in which they are positioned on the engine. Remove the timing cover, pulling it off squarely.

**To install:**

11. Before reinstalling the cover, use a file to break or file off flashing at the top/rear of the casting on either side so the corner is smooth. Replace all gaskets, coating them with silicone sealer. Where gasket ends extend too far, trim them off. Apply sealer to the area where the oil pan gasket passes the front of the block.

12. Slide the cover straight on to avoid damaging the seal. Install all bolts in their proper positions. Tighten the bolts at the top, fastening the lower cover to the upper cover first. Then, tighten the remaining front cover bolts and, finally, the oil pan bolts. If the car has the DME type distributor, inspect the sealing O-rings and replace as necessary. If it uses the DME distributor with the screw-off type rotor, make sure the bolt at the center of the rotor has its seal in place and that it is installed with a sealer designed to prevent the bolt from backing out.

13. Complete the installation procedure, making sure to refill and bleed the cooling system.

## Timing Chain Cover Oil Seal

### REMOVAL & INSTALLATION

#### *All Models Except 325, 325e, 325i, 325iS, 325iX, 524td and 528e*

1. Disconnect the negative battery cable. Position the No. 1 piston at TDC on the beginning of its compression stroke.
2. Remove the flywheel guard and lock the flywheel with a locking tool.
3. Remove the drive belts and the fan.
4. Remove the retaining nut and remove the vibration damper from the crankshaft.

**NOTE: The Woodruff key should be at the 12 o'clock position on the crankshaft.**

5. Remove the seal from the timing housing cover with a small pry bar.
6. Using a special seal installer or equivalent, lubricate and install the seal in the cover. This tool is used to press the seal into the bore with even pressure around the entire perimeter.

**NOTE: If the balancer hub has serious scoring on the sealing surface, position the seal in the cover so that the sealing lip is in front of or behind the scored groove.**

7. Lubricate the balancer hub and install it on the crankshaft, being careful not to damage the seal.
8. Complete the assembly, using the reverse of the removal procedure. Be sure to remove the flywheel locking tool before attempting to start the engine.

#### *325, 325e, 325I, 325IS, 325IX and 528e*

The 325 and 528e have 2 oil seals on the front engine cover. One is on the crankshaft and the other is on the intermediate shaft.

1. Disconnect the negative battery cable. Remove the front engine cover.
2. Press the 2 radial oil seals out of the front engine cover.
3. Install the oil seals flush with the front engine cover using BMW tools 24 1 050, 33 1 180 and 005 5 500 or equivalents.
4. Install the front engine cover.

#### *524td*

**NOTE: A number of special tools are necessary to complete this operation. They include: A wrench designed to hold the vibration damper hub BMW 11 2 150 or equivalent; a puller for the vibration damper hub; a pin to hold the vibration damper hub 11 2 040; a puller to remove the timing belt sprocket from the crankshaft such as BMW 00 7 501 and 11 2 131; seal installer 24 1 040 and 24 1 050; and special tools designed to protect the seals when the front engine cover is installed – 11 2 211 and 11 2 212. Equivalents may be available from other sources.**

1. Disconnect the negative battery cable. Remove the timing belt cover and vibration damper as described above.
2. Remove the radiator. Install the special wrench on the vibration damper hub. Then, unscrew the bolt at the center until it is about 3 turns out. Attach a puller such as 00 7 501 with bolts 11 2 132. The 2 outer bolts screw into holes in the outer rim of the damper hub. Then, turn the center bolt of the puller so it forces the hub off by pressing against the center bolt.
3. Remove the timing belt as described below. Then, use the special tool or another suitable means to hold the intermediate shaft stationary while removing the bolt at the center. Then, remove the intermediate shaft washer and sprocket.
4. Screw the bolt into the center of the crankshaft until it is about 3 turns out. Screw the outer bolts for the puller into the outer edge of the crankshaft sprocket until they are secure. Then, screw in the center bolt of the puller to force the crankshaft sprocket off.
5. Remove the arrowed bolts, and oil pan bolts labeled 4, 5, and 6. Loosen the other pan bolts. Then carefully use a sharp knife to separate the oil pan gasket from the front cover. Remove the cover.
6. From the rear of the cover, press the oil seals outward. Then use tools such as 24 1 040 and 24 1 050 to press in new seals. Replacement seals must be pressed in until 0.039–0.079 in. indented. Apply clean engine oil to the sealing lips.

**To install:**

7. Install tools such as 11 2 211 (crankshaft) and 11 2 212 (intermediate shaft) to the ends of these shafts to protect the seals. Then, install the front cover.
8. Install the seal in position. Keep the following points in mind:
   a. Install the crankshaft sprocket with the Woodruff key in the proper position and the step forward.
   b. When installing the intermediate shaft sprocket, make sure the centering pin slides into its bore.

## Timing Chain and Tensioner

### REMOVAL & INSTALLATION

#### *All Models Except 325, 325e, 325i, 325iS, 325iX, 524td, 528e, M3, M5 and M6*

1. Disconnect the negative battery cable. Rotate the crankshaft to set the No. 1 piston at TDC, at the beginning of its compression stroke.
2. Remove the distributor (6 cylinder engines only).
3. Remove the cylinder head cover, air injection pipe and guard plate.
4. Drain the cooling system and remove the thermostat housing.
5. Remove the upper timing housing cover.
6. Remove the timing chain tensioner piston by unscrewing the cap *cautiously*.

Location of upper (4) and lower (3) guide rail retainers

Installation of the timing cover housing showing special sealing locations

**NOTE: The piston is under heavy spring tension.**

7. Remove the drive belts and fan.
8. Remove the flywheel guard and lock the flywheel with a locking tool.
9. Remove the vibration damper assembly.

**NOTE: The crankshaft Woodruff key should be in the 12 o'clock position.**

10. Remove upper and lower timing covers as described above.
11. Turn the crankshaft so that the No. 1 cylinder is at firing position. On the 318i, this will put the top sprocket locating pin at 6 o'clock. Open the camshaft lockplates if so equipped, remove the bolts and remove the camshaft sprocket.

• On 4 cylinder engines (except 318i):

a. Remove the bottom circlip holding the chain guide rail to the block. Loosen the upper pivot pin until the guide rail rests against the forward part of the cylinder head gasket.

b. Remove the timing chain from the sprockets and remove the guide rail by pulling downward and swinging the rail to the right.

c. Remove the chain from the guide rail and remove it from the engine.

• On the 318i engine, take the timing chain off top and bottom sprockets and remove carefully from the guide rail.

12. On 6 cylinder engines remove the chain from the lower sprocket, swing the chain to the right front and out of the guide rail and remove the chain from the engine.

**To install:**

13. Install the chain in position, but note the following:
14. Be sure that No. 1 piston remains at the top of its firing stroke and the key on the crankshaft is in the 12 o'clock position.
15. On 4 cylinder engines:

a. Position the camshaft flange so that the dowel pin bore is located at the 6 o'clock position and the notch in the top of the flange aligns with the cast tab on the cylinder head.

b. On all models but the 318i, position the chain in the chain guide rail and move the rail upward and to the left, engaging the lower locating pivot pin and threading the upper pivot pin into the block. Install the circlip on the lower guide pin. On the 318i, simply locate the chain carefully in the guide rail.

c. Engage the chain on the crankshaft sprocket and fit the camshaft sprocket into the chain.

d. Align the gear dowel pin to the camshaft flange and bolt the sprocket into place. Use new lockplates (where so equipped), and secure the bolt heads.

16. On 6 cylinder engines:

a. Position the camshaft flange so that the dowel pin bore is between the 7 and 8 o'clock position and the upper flange bolt hole is aligned with the cast tab on the cylinder head.

b. Position the chain on the guide rail and swing the chain inward and to the left.

c. Engage the chain on the crankshaft gear and install the camshaft sprocket into the chain.

d. Align the gear dowel pin to the camshaft flange and bolt and sprocket into place. Torque the sprocket bolts to 5 ft. lbs. (6.5–7.5 on the M30B35 engine).

17. Install the chain tensioner piston, spring and cap plug, but do not tighten.
18. To bleed the chain tensioner, fill the oil pocket, located on the upper timing housing cover, with engine oil and move the tensioner back and forth with a screwdriver until oil is expelled at the cap plug. Tighten the cap plug securely.
19. Complete the assembly in the reverse order of removal. Check the ignition timing and the idle speed. Be sure the flywheel holder is removed before any attempt is made to start the engine.

### *M3*

1. Disconnect the negative battery cable. Remove the timing case cover as described above.
2. Refer to the camshaft removal procedure below. Follow the procedure to the point where the 2 camshaft drive sprockets are unbolted and remove them. It is not necessary to remove the cover from the rear of the head.
3. Make sure to catch the washer and lockwashers which will be released at the front as the rest of this step is performed. Now, remove the 2 mounting bolts for the guide rail, which is located on the left (driver's) side of the engine. These are accessible from the rear.
4. Pull the guide rail forward and then turn it clockwise on its axis, look-

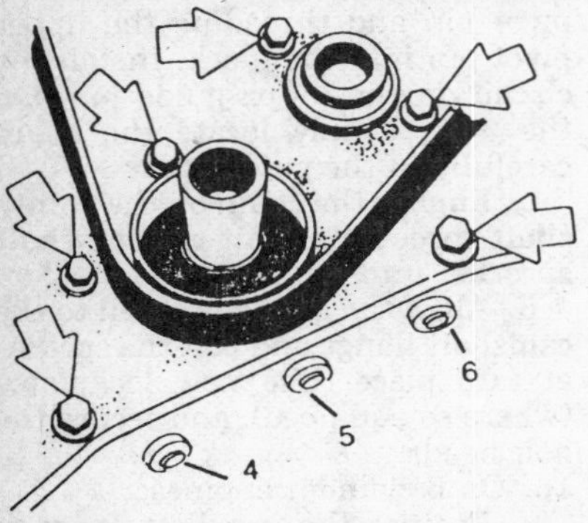

Remove the three oil pan bolts (4, 5, 6) to remove the front cover (524 td). Remove the other arrowed bolts, also

ing at it from above, to free it from the chain.

5. Note the relationships between timing chain and sprocket marks. Remove the chain by separating it from the sprockets at top and bottom.

**To install:**

6. Engage the timing chain with the crankshaft sprocket so marks line up. Route the chain up through where the guide rail will go. Install the guide rail in reverse of the removal procedure.

7. Then engage the chain with the driver's side (E) sprocket with the marks lined up. Bolt this sprocket and the lockplate onto the front end of the intake camshaft. Use the adapter to keep the sprocket from turning, and torque the bolts to 6–7 ft. lbs. Turn this camshaft in the direction opposite to normal rotation to tension the timing chain on that side.

8. Now, engage the timing marks with the mark on the passenger's side ("A") sprocket and then install the sprocket and lockplate onto the front end of the exhaust camshaft. Again, use the adapter to keep the sprocket from turning, and torque the bolts to 6–7 ft. lbs. Make sure the timing chain has stayed in time.

9. Slide the chain tensioner piston into its cylinder. Install a new seal. Now install the spring with the conical end out. Install the cap which retains the spring and torque it to 29 ft. lbs.

10. Turn the engine one revolution in the normal direction of rotation. Recheck the timing. With the crankshaft at TDC, one groove on each camshaft faces inward and another on each faces the cast boss on the nearby bearing cap.

11. Perform the remaining procedures for camshaft installation, including installing and centering the top chain guide rail and centering it.

12. Install the timing case cover as described above.

*M5 and M6*

1. Disconnect the negative battery cable. Remove the fan shroud and the fan. Remove the cylinder head cover. Remove the timing cover as described above.

2. Refer to the camshaft removal procedure below. Follow the procedure to the point where the 2 camshaft drive sprockets are unbolted and remove them. It is not necessary to perform Step 4 to remove the cover from the rear of the head.

3. Refer to the procedure below and remove the water pump.

4. Remove the 2 mounting bolts for the guide rail, which is located on the left (driver's) side of the engine. These are accessible from the rear. Turn the guide rail counterclockwise on its axis, looking at it from above to clear the chain and block and remove it. Be careful to retain all washers.

5. Note the relationships between timing chain and sprocket marks. Remove the timing chain.

**To install:**

6. Install the timing chain with the marks on all 3 sprockets aligned with marked links on the chain. Make sure the chain runs on the inside of the guide sprocket on the left side of the engine and along the groove in the lower tensioning rail. Install the chain onto the camshaft drive sprockets and then install the sprockets onto the camshafts (note that the exhaust side sprocket is marked **A** and the intake sprocket is marked **E**. Then, install the guide rail with all washers and lockwashers by rotating it into position in reverse of the removal procedure.

7. Tighten the camshaft drive sprockets, install the chain tensioner, and install the upper guide rail as described in the camshaft removal and installation procedure. Reverse the remaining removal steps to complete the procedure. Make sure to refill the cooling system with an appropriate antifreeze/water mix and to bleed the cooling system.

## Timing Belt and Front Engine Cover

### REMOVAL & INSTALLATION

*325, 325e, 325i, 325iS, 325iX and 528e*

The 325 and 528e are equipped with a rubber drive and timing belt and the distributor guard plate is actually the upper timing belt cover.

1. Disconnect the negative battery cable. Remove the distributor cap and rotor. Remove the inner distributor cover and seal.

2. Remove the 2 distributor guard plate attaching bolts and one nut. Remove the rubber guard and take out the guard plate (upper timing belt cover).

3. Rotate the crankshaft to set No. 1 piston at TDC of its compression stroke.

**NOTE: At TDC of No. 1 piston compression stroke, the camshaft sprocket arrow should align directly with the mark on the cylinder head.**

4. Remove the radiator.

5. Remove the lower splash guard and take off the alternator, power steering and air conditioning belts.

6. Remove the crankshaft pulley and vibration damper.

7. Hold the crankshaft hub from rotating with special BMW tool 11 2 150 or equivalent. Remove the crankshaft hub bolt.

8. Install the hub bolt into the crankshaft about 3 turns and use BMW tools 00 7 501 and 11 2 132 or a gear puller, to remove the crankshaft hub.

9. Remove the bolt from the engine end of the alternator bracket. Loosen the alternator adjusting bolt and swing the bracket out of the way.

10. Lift out the TDC transmitter and set it out of the way.

11. Remove the remaining bolt and lift off the lower timing belt cover.

12. Loosen the 2 tensioner pulley bolts and release the tension on the belt by pushing on the tensioner pulley bracket.

13. Mark the running direction of the timing belt and remove the belt.

14. Remove the 3 bolts across the front of the oil pan and loosen the remaining oil pan bolts. Try not to damage the oil pan gasket. Remove the 6 front engine cover bolts and remove the front engine cover.

**To install:**

15. Install the cover, noting the following:

   a. To tighten the timing belt, turn the engine in the direction of normal engine operation, with a ½ in. drive rachet wrench on the crankshaft bolt. When the timing belt is tight, then torque the 2 tensioner bolts.

   b. Align the hub centering pin through the hole in the vibration damper for proper installation.

   c. Align the timing marks when installing the timing belt. The crankshaft sprocket mark must point at the notch in the flange of the front engine cover. The camshaft sprocket arrow must point at the alignment mark on the cylinder head. Also, the No. 1 piston must be at TDC of the compression stroke.

   d. If the oil pan gasket is dam-

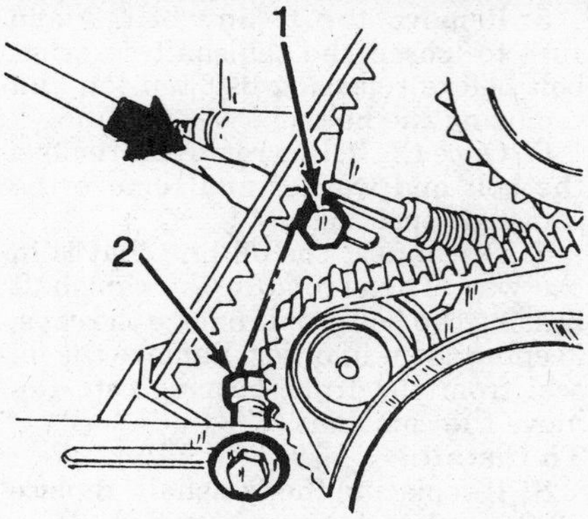


1. Tensioner adjusting slot bolt
2. Tensioner bracket pivot bolt

**Releasing the tension on timing belt—528e**

1. Front oil pan bolts

**Bolt location for front engine cover—528e**

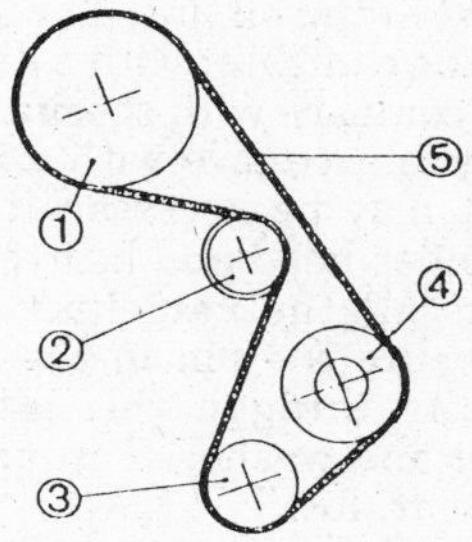


1. Camshaft sprocket
2. Tensioner roller
3. Crankshaft sprocket
4. Intermediate shaft sprocket
5. Tining drive belt

**Location of timing belt sprockets and belt tensioner—528e**

aged, it must be replaced.

e. Check and replace front cover oil seals if needed.

f. Use BMW tools 11 2 211 (crankshaft seal aligner) and 11 2 212 (intermediate shaft seal aligner) or equivalent to install the front engine cover without damaging the oil seals.

g. Check the engine oil level.

h. Install engine coolant and bleed the cooling system. Bring the engine up to operating temperature and loosen the bleed screw on top of

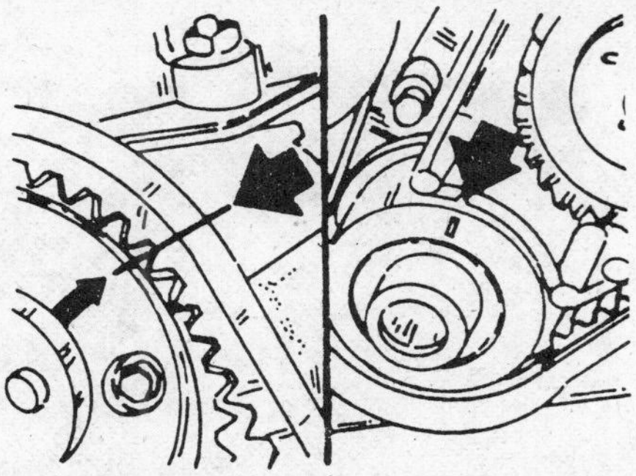

**Crankshaft sprocket timing marks aligned for installation of the timing belt—528e**

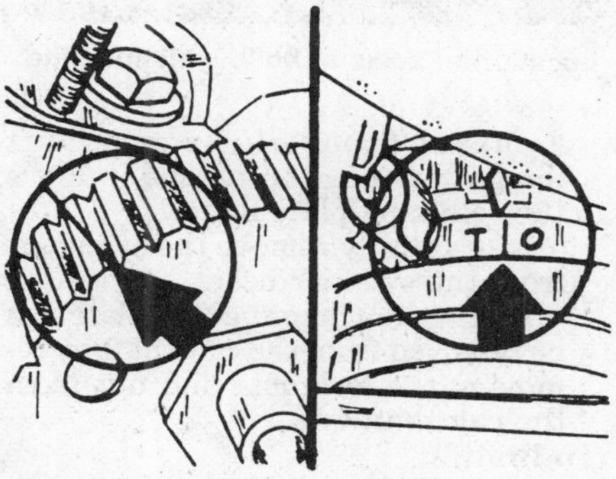


**Aligning the marks for timing belt installation—528e**

the thermostat housing. Continue to bleed until escaping coolant is free of bubbles. Add coolant to the expansion tank if needed.

### *524td*

**NOTE: To perform this procedure, it is necessary to have a means to hold the camshaft stationary such as BMW special tool 11 3 090 and a pin to hold the injection pump gear stationary such as BMW 13 5 340. The engine must be cold.**

1. Disconnect the negative battery cable. Turn the engine to No. 1 cylinder at TDC, valves of No. 6 overlapping. Remove the timing belt cover and front pulley as described above. Loosen the camshaft pulley bolt, and the bolt and nut mounting the tensioner.

2. Mark the direction the belt rotates and remove it.

3. Position the camshaft at TDC,No. 6 cylinder valves overlapping and lock it there. Lock the injection pump in position with the pin 13 5 340.

**To install:**

4. Install the new belt with the timing marks on the sprockets and belt lined up. Turn the camshaft sprocket so as to begin tensioning the belt and seat it in the grooves. When the belt is in its normal, installed position, re-

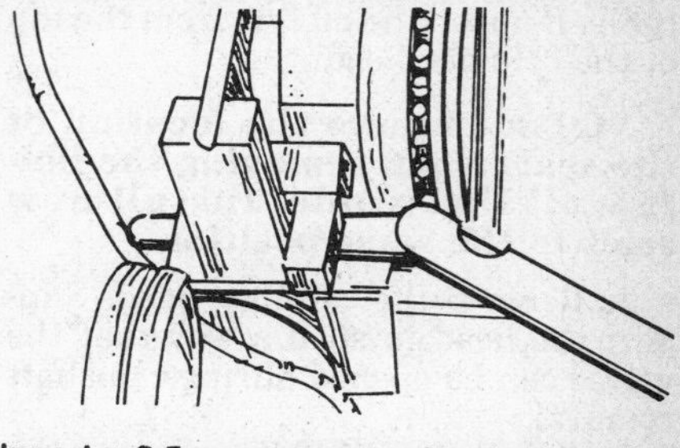

**Insert a 2.5mm gauge under the exhaust side of the jig holding the camshaft for new drive belts (524 td)**

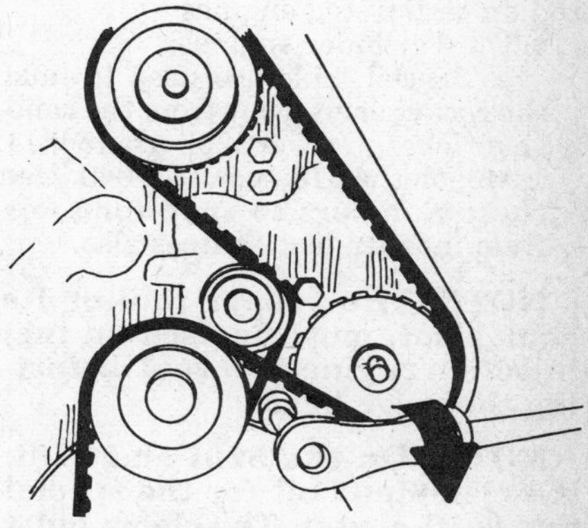

**Adjusting the belt tension. Turn the torque wrench in the direction shown to apply the proper tension (see text)**

move the pin holding the injection pump sprocket.

5. Insert a 2.5mm thick feeler gauge under the exhaust side of the jig holding the camshaft if the belt is new or had been used less than 10,000 miles.

6. Torque the nut which rotates the tensioner (2) in the direction shown in the illustration. For belts with 10,000 miles or less on them, torque to 30.5–32.5 ft. lbs. For belts with more mileage, torque to 22–25 ft. lbs.

7. Tighten the locknut for the tensioner (3) and then tighten (1), the camshaft sprocket bolt, and (2). Remove the camshaft-holding jig.

8. Rotate the engine in the forward direction one full turn and then recheck that timing marks are all lined up.

9. Adjust the static timing of the injection pump as described below. Reinstall the timing belt cover and front pulley in the reverse of removal. Refer to the appropriate procedure above.

# Camshaft

## REMOVAL & INSTALLATION

### *All Models Except 325, 325e, 325i, 325iS, 325iX, 524td, 528e, M3, M5 and M6*

1. Disconnect the negative battery

cable. Remove the oil line from the top of the cylinder head.

**NOTE: Observe the location of the seals when removing the hollow oil line studs. Install new seals in the same position.**

2. Remove the cylinder head. Support the head in such a way that the valves can be opened during camshaft removal.
3. Adjust the valve clearance to the maximum clearance on all rocker arms.
4. Remove the fuel pump and pushrod on carbureted engines.

• On 4 cylinder engines:

a. Special tools are used to hold the rocker arms away from the camshaft lobes. On the 320i, use tool 11 1 040; on the 318i, use 11 0 040. Use these numbers to shop for tools from independent sources also.

**NOTE: The proper tool or its equivalent, must be used on fuel injection engines to avoid distorting the valve heads.**

**NOTE: On the 320i and 318i, the clamping bolt for the special tool is off-center. The clamp must be mounted so the shorter end faces the exhaust side of the engine, or the valve heads may contact each other. On the 318i, install 2 dowel pins in the head.**

• On 6 cylinder engines:

a. A special tool set (11 1 060 and 00 1 490) or its equivalent, is used to hold the rocker arms away from the camshaft lobes. When installing the tool, move the intake rocker arms of No. 2 and 4 cylinders forward approximately 1/4 in. and tighten the intake side nuts to avoid contact between the valve heads. On the 6, turn the camshaft 15 degrees clockwise to install the tool. On these engines, to avoid contact between the valve heads, first tighten the tool mounting nuts on the exhaust side to the stop and then tighten the intake side nuts slightly. Reverse this exactly during removal.

5. Remove the camshaft.

• On 4 cylinder engines:

a. Turn the camshaft until the flange is aligned with the cylinder head boss. Remove the guide plate retaining bolts and move the plate downward and out of the slots on the rocker arm shafts.

b. Carefully remove the camshaft from the cylinder head.

c. Remove the 2 plugs behind the guide plate (at top), coat with Loctite® No. 270® or equivalent, and replace them.

• On 6 cylinder engines:

a. Rotate the camshaft so that the 2 cutout areas of the camshaft flange are horizontal and remove the retaining plate bolts.

b. Carefully remove the camshaft from the cylinder head.

c. The flange and guide plate can be removed from the camshaft by removing the lockplate and nut from the camshaft end.

Location of seals at hollow oil line stud

**To install:**

6. Install the camshaft and associated components in the reverse order of removal, but observe the following:

a. After installing the camshaft guide plate, the camshaft should turn easily. Measure and correct the camshaft end play.

b. The camshaft flange must be properly aligned with the cylinder head before the sprocket is installed. Refer to the disassembly procedure.

c. Install the oil tube hollow stud washer seals properly, one above and one below the oil pipe. On 6 cyl. engines, the arrow on the oil line must face forward.

d. Install the cylinder head. Adjust the valves.

### *524td*

**NOTE: To complete this procedure, it is necessary to have several special tools to install a new oil seal. Use BMW tools 11 2 212, 11 3 080, and 00 5 500.**

1. Disconnect the negative battery cable. Remove the cam cover and vacuum pump as described below.
2. Remove the exhaust side rocker arm of cylinder No. 2 and the intake rocker arm of cylinder No. 3. See the Rocker Arm Removal & Installation procedure above. It is not necessary to disturb the rocker pedestals; keep the rockers in order of reinstallation in the same positions.
3. Turn the crankshaft until it is at TDC with No. 6 cylinder's valves in overlap position.
4. Remove the front cover.
5. Remove the timing belt. Make sure to loosen the camshaft sprocket bolt before releasing belt tension and removing the belt.
6. Once the belt is removed, remove the bolt and washer and remove the camshaft sprocket.
7. Disconnect the oil line that is in the way. Then, remove the camshaft bearing cap bolts and remove the caps, keeping them in order. Remove the oil seal from the front bearing cap. Remove the camshaft.

**To install:**

8. If replacing the camshaft, replace all the rocker arms as described above. Also, transfer the steels ring that drives the vacuum pump to the new camshaft.
9. Oil all bearing surfaces with clean engine oil and install the camshaft. Install the caps and bolts, and torque M6 bolts to 6–7 ft. lbs. M8 bolts should be torqued to 15–17 ft. lbs. The front bearing cap lower surface must be coated with a brush-on universal sealing compound – 3 Bond Silicone 1207 or equivalent.
10. Install a seal installer 11 2 212 or equivalent onto the end of the camshaft. Lubricate the lip of the seal with clean engine oil. Then, press the seal into the bore of the bearing, using a suitable seal installer part no. 11 3 080 and 00 5 500 or equivalent. The seal must be pressed in until it hits the stop.
11. Install the oil line. Check the end play of the camshaft with a dial indicator and compare with specifications. If end play is excessive with a new camshaft, it may be necessary to replace the cylinder head and bearing caps.
12. Install the camshaft sprocket making sure the pin in the camshaft flange fits through the bore in the sprocket and washer. Torque the bolt to 47–51 ft. lbs.
13. Install the timing belt and tension it as described above. Reverse the remaining removal procedures.

### *325, 325e, 325i, 325iS, 325iX and 528e*

The cylinder head and the rocker arm shafts must be removed before the camshaft can be removed.

1. Disconnect the negative battery cable. Remove the cylinder head.
2. Mount the head on a stand. Secure the head to the stand with one head bolt.
3. Remove the camshaft sprocket bolt and remove the camshaft distributor adapter and sprocket. Reinstall the distributor adapter on the camshaft.
4. Adjust the valve clearance to the maximum allowable on all valves.
5. Remove the front and rear rocker

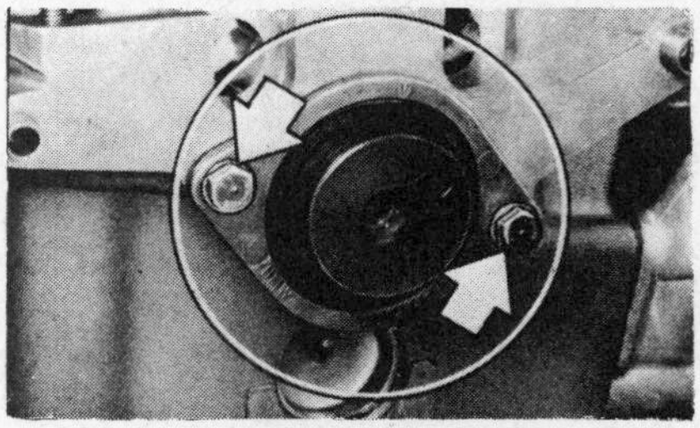

**Removing camshaft thrust bearing cover—528e**

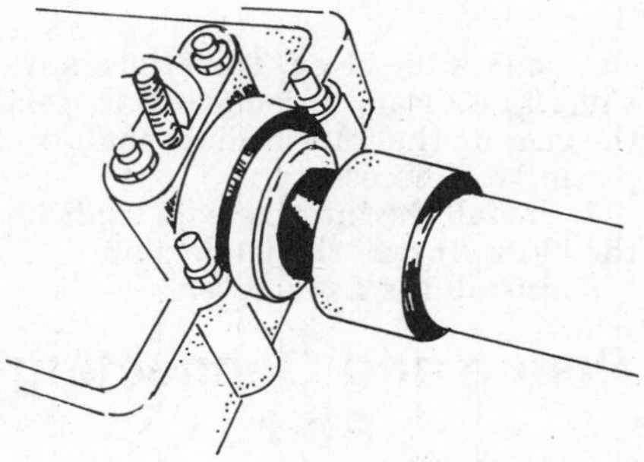

**Installing the front camshaft oil seal – 524 td**

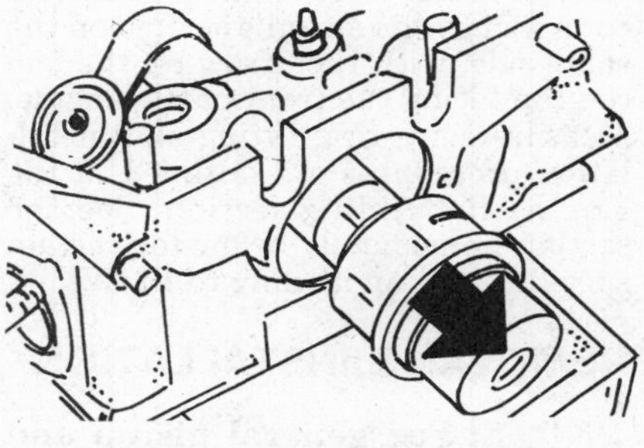

**Pulling out the camshaft—528e**

shaft plugs and lift out the thrust plate.

6. Remove the clips from the rocker arms by lifting them off.

7. Remove the exhaust side rocker arm shaft:

a. Set the No. 6 cylinder rocker arm to the valve overlap position (both rocker arms parallel).

b. Push in on the rocker arm on the front cylinder and turn the camshaft in the direction of the intake rocker shaft, using a ½ in. breaker bar and a deep well socket to fit over the camshaft adapter. Rotate the camshaft until all of the rocker arms are relaxed.

c. Remove the rocker arm shaft.

8. Remove the intake side rocker arm shaft:

a. Turn the camshaft in the direction of the exhaust valves.

b. Use a deep well socket and ½ in. drive breaker bar on the camshaft adapter to turn the camshaft until all of the rocker arms are relaxed.

c. Pull out the rocker arm shaft.

9. Remove the camshaft thrust bearing cover. Check the radial oil seal and round cord seal and replace them if needed.

10. Pull out the camshaft.

**To install:**

11. Install the camshaft, noting the following:

a. Use BMW tool 11 2 212 or equivalent over the end of the camshaft during installation of the thrust bearing cover; this will protect the oil seals and guide the cover on.

b. The rocker arm thrust plate must be fit into the grooves in the rocker shafts.

c. The straight side of the springclip must be installed in the groove of the rocker arm shafts.

d. The large oil bores in the rocker shafts must be installed down to the valve guides and the small oil bores must face inward toward the center of the head.

e. Adjust the valve clearance.

### *M3, M5 and M6*

**NOTE: To perform this operation it is necessary to have an expensive jig, special tool No. 11 3 010 or equivalent. This is necessary to permit safe removal of the camshaft bearing caps and then safe release of the tension the valve springs put on the camshafts. The job also requires an adapter to keep the camshaft sprockets from turning while loosening and tightening their mounting bolts.**

1. Disconnect the negative battery cable. Remove the cylinder head cover. Remove the fan cowl and the fan.

2. Remove the mounting bolts and remove the distributor cap. Remove the mounting screws and remove the rotor. Unscrew the distributor adapter and the protective cover underneath. Inspect the O-ring that runs around the protective cover and replace it, if necessary.

3. Remove the 2 bolts and remove the protective cover from in front of the right side (intake) camshaft. Remove the bolts and remove the distributor housing from in front of the left (exhaust) side cam. Inspect the O-rings, and replace them if necessary.

4. Remove the 6 mounting bolts from the cover at the rear end of the cylinder head and remove it. Replace the gasket. Note that on the M3, 2 of these bolts are longer. These fit into the 2 holes that are sleeved.

5. Remove the 2 nuts, located at the front of the head, which mount the upper timing chain guide rail. Then, remove the upper guide rail.

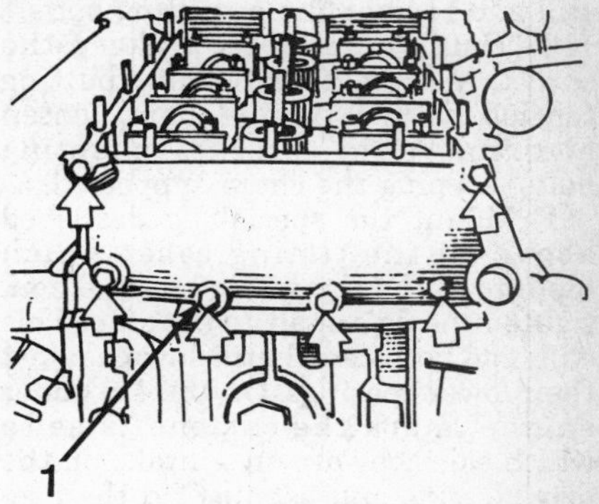


**On the rear cover of the M3, install the longer bolts into the two holes marked "1"**

6. Turn the crankshaft to set the engine at No. 1 cylinder TDC. On the 6 cylinder engine, valves for No. 6 will be at overlap position – both valves just slightly open with timing marks, of course, at TDC. On the 4 cylinder engine, valves for No. 4 cylinder will be at overlap position – both valves just slightly open with timing marks, of course, at TDC.

7. Remove the cap for the timing chain tensioner, located on the right side of the front timing cover. Then, slide off the damper housing. Remove the seal, discard it, and supply a new one for reassembly.

**CAUTION**

***The next item to be removed is a plug which keeps the tensioner piston inside its hydraulic cylinder against considerable spring pressure. Use a socket wrench and keep pressure against the outer end of the plug, pushing inward, so that spring pressure can be released very gradually once the plug's threads are free of the block.***

8. Remove the plug as described in the caution, and then release spring tension. Remove the spring and then the piston. Check the length of the spring. It must be 6.240–6.280 in. in length; otherwise, replace it to maintain stable timing chain tension.

**NOTE: The timing chain should remain engaged with the crankshaft sprocket while removing the camshafts. Otherwise, it will be necessary to do additional work to restore proper timing. Devise a way to keep the timing chain under slight tension by supporting it at the top while removing the camshaft sprockets in the next step.**

9. Pry open the lockplates for the camshaft sprocket mounting bolts. Install an adapter to hold the sprockets

still and remove the mounting bolts.

10. Using an adapter to keep the sprockets from turning and putting tension on the timing chain, loosen and remove the sprocket mounting bolts, keeping the chain supported.

11. Mount the special jig described above on the timing case (which mounts to the top of the head). Then, tighten the jig's shaft to the stop. This will hold both camshafts down against their lower bearings. On the 4 cylinder engine, mark the camshafts as to which side they are on—intake on the driver's side and exhaust on the passenger's side. Also, mark the camshafts as to which end faces forward.

12. Remove the mounting bolts and remove the camshaft bearing caps. It is possible to save time by keeping the caps in order, although they are marked for installation in the same positions.

13. Once all bearing caps are removed, slowly crank backwards on the jig shaft to gradually release the tension on the camshafts. Once all tension is released, remove the camshafts.

14. Carefully remove the camshafts in such a way as to avoid nicking any bearing surfaces or cams.

**To install:**

15. Oil all bearing and cam surfaces with clean engine oil. Carefully install the camshafts (marked E for intake and A for exhaust) so as to avoid nicking any wear surfaces. The camshafts should be turned so that the groove between the front cam and sprocket mounting flange faces straight up. Install the special jig and tighten down on the shaft to seat the camshafts.

16. Install all bearing caps in order (or as marked). Torque the attaching bolts to 15–17 ft. lbs. Then, release the tension provided by the jig by turning the bolt and remove the jig.

17. Install the intake sprocket (marked E), install the lockplate, and install the mounting bolts. Use the adapter to keep the sprocket from turning, and torque the bolts to 6–7 ft. lbs. Do the same for the exhaust side sprocket. Make sure the timing chain stays in time.

18. Now, slide the timing chain tensioner piston into the opening in the cylinder in the block. Install the spring with the conically wound end facing the plug (or outward). Install the plug into the end of the sprocket and then install it over the spring and use the socket wrench to depress the spring until the plug's threads engage with those in the block. Start the threads in carefully and then torque the plug to 27–31 ft. lbs. Install a new seal, connector, damper housing, and the outside cap with a new cap seal. Torque the outside cap to 16–20 ft. lbs. on the engine used in the M5 and M6 and 29 ft. lbs. on the M3 engine.

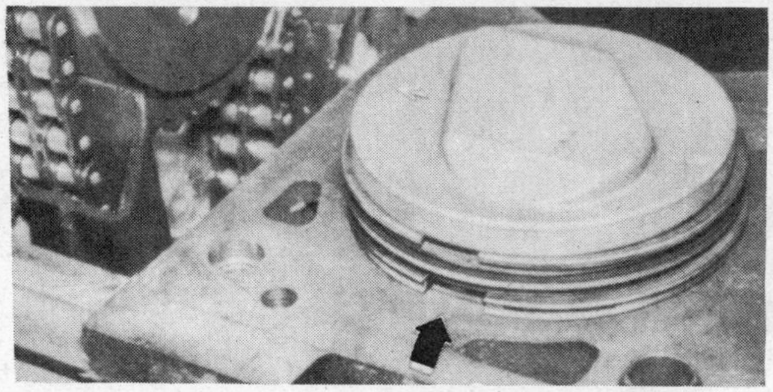

Location of piston in the cylinder bore with ring gaps located 180° apart

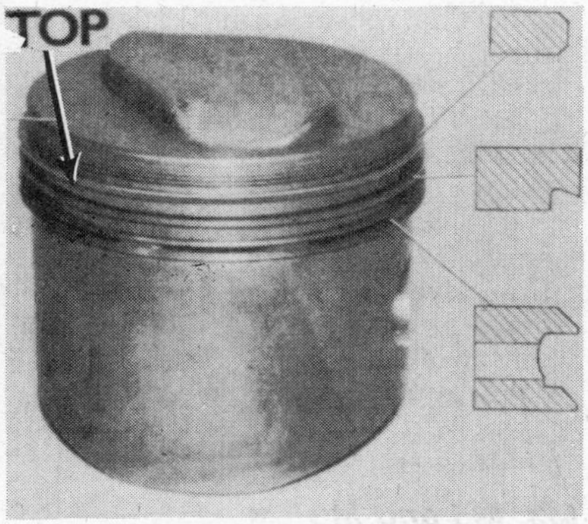


Proper piston ring installation—typical

19. Crank the engine forward just one turn in normal direction of rotation. Now, one camshaft groove on each side should face toward the center of the head and one on each side should face the case boss on the front bearing cap. Lock the sprocket mounting bolts with the tabs on the lockplates.

20. Reverse the remaining removal procedures to complete the installation. Before final tightening of the mounting nuts for the guide rail for the top of the timing chain, go back and forth, measuring the clearance between the sprockets and the center of the guide rail to center it. Then, tighten the mounting nuts.

## Intermediate Shaft

### REMOVAL & INSTALLATION

#### *325, 325e, 325i, 325iS, 325iX, 524td and 528e*

1. Disconnect the negative battery cable. Remove the front cover as detailed previously.

2. Remove the intermediate shaft sprocket.

3. Loosen and remove the 2 retaining screws and then remove the intermediate shaft guide plate.

4. Carefully slide the intermediate shaft out of the block. Turn the crankshaft if necessary to remove it. Inspect the gear on the intermediate shaft, replacing it if necessary.

5. Install the intermediate shaft ito the block. Install the guide plate.

6. Install the front cover.

## Piston and Connecting Rod

### POSITIONING

Reference numbers on the pistons and connecting rods must be located on the same side, with the arrow on the piston top facing the front of the engine. Measurement, ring fitting and installation procedures are outlined in the Engine Rebuilding section. See the section immediately below for certain specifics that apply only to BMWs.

### REMOVAL & INSTALLATION

**NOTE: For general piston and connecting rod overhaul procedures, please refer to "Engine Rebuilding" in the Unit Repair Section. The points below apply only to the particulars of BMW engine rebuilding. Keep them in mind when rebuilding these engines.**

- The pistons and connecting rods may be removed from the engine after the cylinder head, oil pan and oil pump are removed. It may be necessary to first remove a ridge worn into the cylinder above the top ring. See the engine rebuilding section. The connecting rods and caps are marked for each cylinder with No. 1 cylinder at the sprocket end of the engine. Codes pairing the connecting rods with the matching cap are located on the exhaust side of the engine. However, it is a good idea to mark the exact relationship between each rod and the crankshaft to ensure replacement in the exact same position, in case the bearings can be re-used.
- On the 524td engine, oil nozzles which are critically aimed must be protected from damage by studs (11 2

050) which screw into the connecting rod cap bolt holes before the rod and piston are shoved upward and out the top of the block. Make sure each crankpin is precisely at BDC prior to removal.

- To disassemble rods and pistons, remove the circlip and press out the piston pin. Note that pistons and piston pins come as a matched set. Do not mix them up.

b. A piston pin must always slide through the connecting rod under light pressure.

- If replacing pistons, make sure all are of the same make and weight class (marked "+" or "–" on the crown).
- Piston installed clearance must meet specifications. On the 318i, check installed clearance at a point measured up from the lower skirt edge, depending on the piston manufacturer: Mahle – 0.551 in.; KS – 1.215 in.; Alcan – 0.610 in.
- On the M20B27 engine used in 325e and 528e models, check piston diameter according to total height and manufacturer. On pistons 2.705 in. high manufactured by Mahle, check the diameter at a point 0.315 in. above the low point on the skirt; on those of this height manufactured by KS, check diameter 0.551 in. above the low point of the skirt. If the total height is 3.059 in., check the diameter of both Mahle and KS pistons 0.905 in. above the low point of the skirt. On the M20B25 engine used in 325i, check the diameter 0.354 in. above the low point of the skirt.
- On the 3.3L engine, measure Mahle pistons 1.024 in. up from the lower skirt edge, and KS pistons 1.340 in. up from the skirt edge. On the 3.5 liter engine, measure 0.551 in. up from the skirt edge.
- On the 3.5L, M30 B34 engine, measure the Mahle pistons at a point 0.551 in. up from the bottom of the skirt.
- On the 3.5L, M30 B35 engine, measure Alcan piston diameter at a point 0.531 in. from the lowest point of the skirt; measure Mahle pistons at a point 0.866 in. from the lowest point of the skirt.
- On the 524td engine, the dimensions are: Alcan 0.591; KS 0.709; Mahle/Konig 0.472. Measure 0.551 in. up from the skirt edge.
- On the engines used in the M3, M5, and M6, measure the piston at a point 0.236 in. below the deepest part of the skirt.
- Lubricate the piston and rings with engine oil prior to installation. Offset ring gaps 120 degrees apart. Install circlips facing *downward*.
- The side of rings marked "TOP" must face upward. 2.5L, 2.7L, 3.3L and 3.5L engines and the M3 engine use a plain compression ring at top, tapered or beveled second compression ring, and an oil control ring at the bottom. The 524td uses a keystone ring at the top, a taper face lower compression ring, and a beveled oil control ring with a rubber-lined expander at the bottom.

# ENGINE LUBRICATION

## Oil Pan

### REMOVAL & INSTALLATION

#### 320i

1. Raise and support the vehicle. Drain the engine oil.
2. Loosen the steering gear bolts and pull the steering box off the front axle carrier.
3. Remove the oil pan bolts and separate the pan from the engine block.
4. Swing the oil pan downward while rotating the crankshaft to allow the pan to clear the crankpin and remove the pan toward the front.
5. Install the oil pan, using new gaskets. Install the steering gear box.
6. Fill the engine to the correct level with oil.

#### 318i

1. Remove the dipstick. Remove the lower pan by draining oil, removing pan bolts, and removing the lower pan.
2. Remove the oil pump.
3. Unscrew the ground strap, located at the right rear of the upper pan.
4. Remove the bottom 3 flywheel housing bolts, and 2 reinforcement plate bolts, and remove the reinforcement plate.
5. Remove upper pan bolts, and remove the upper pan.
6. Clean all 4 sealing surfaces. Replace both gaskets. Coat the mating surfaces on the timing case and end covers with sealer. Install the oil pump.
7. Install the oil pan, torquing pan bolts to 7–8 ft. lb.
8. Install the bottom flywheel bolts. Fill the engine to the correct level with oil.

#### 524td

1. Drain the oil out of the oil pan. Disconnect the electrical connector for the wire running to the base of the oil pan.
2. Disconnect the turbocharger drain hose running into the side of the oil pan.
3. Remove the flywheel/torque converter cover by removing the 4 bolts from underneath the the 3 from the clutch or converter housing.
4. Remove the oil pan bolts and lower it until it is possible to gain access to the oil pump mounting bolts. Remove those bolts (one on one side of the crankshaft and 2 on the other side) then lower the pan with the pump inside it.
5. Clean all the sealing surfaces. Coat the joints between the block and timing case cover and end cover with a sealing compound. Use a new pan gasket.
6. Guide the oil pump driveshaft into the upper bearing in one side of the block. Guide the pan with the pump inside it upward until it is possible to bolt the oil pump into position. Then, bolt the pan into position. Complete the procedure in reverse order.

#### 533i and 1983–84 633CSi, 525i, 535i, 635CSi, M5 and M6

1. Disconnect the engine ground lead. Disconnect the electrical connector and separate the leads from the air cleaner/air flow sensor. Loosen the hose clamp and disconnect the air intake hose. Remove the mounting nut and remove the air cleaner and the airflow sensor as a unit. Remove the fan shroud.
2. Drain the engine oil.
3. Loosen the belt tension and remove the alternator drive belt. Loosen the upper/front mounting bolt for the alternator and the 2 bolts on the side of the block that mount it at the rear. Remove the lower/front mounting bolt. Then, swing the alternator to the side.
4. Loosen the power steering pump mounts and remove the drive belt. Then, remove the mounting bolts and remove the pump and pump mounting bracket. Make sure to retain spacers. If the car has air conditioning, remove the nuts and bolts that fasten the compressor to the hinge type mounting bracket. Make sure the compressor is suspended so there is no tension on the hoses. Unbolt the hinge type mounting bracket and remove it.
5. Remove the brace plate located under the oil pan. Remove those oil pan bolts that can be reached.
6. Remove the engine ground strap. Remove the engine mount through bolts. Attach a lifting sling to the hooks on top of the engine. Lift the engine slightly for clearance.
7. Shift the power steering pump out of the way and support it so no tension will be placed on the hoses.
8. Remove the remaining oil pan

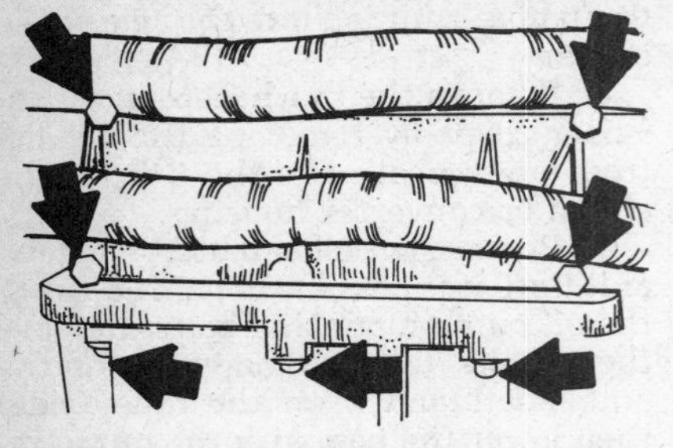

Removing the bolts (arrowed) to remove the flywheel or torque converter cover

Rear main bearing oil seal and end cover housing showing special sealing locations

When removing the upper oil pan on the 318i, remove the arrowed bolts from the bell housing and reinforcing plate, and remove the plate

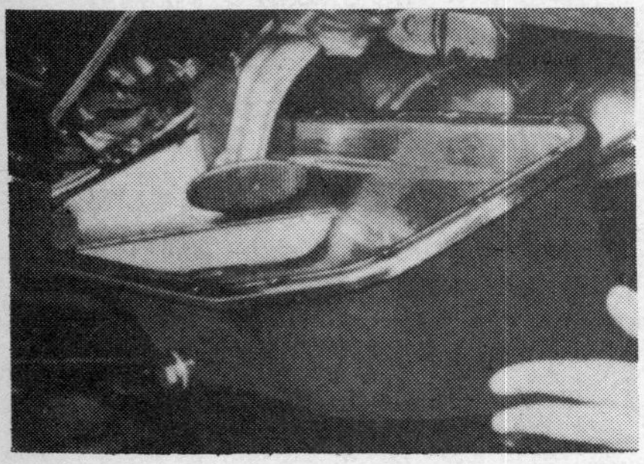

Removal of engine oil pan—typical

mounting bolts. Turn the crankshaft so the rods for cylinders 5 and 6 are as high as possible. Then, remove the pan.

9. Clean all sealing surfaces and supply a new gasket. Apply a liquid sealer to the joints between the block and the timing cover on the front and the rear main seal cover at the rear.

10. Install the oil pan in reverse order. Torque the pan bolts to 6.5–7.5 ft. lbs. Make sure to refill the pan with the required amount of the correct oil. Mount all accessories securely and adjust the drive belts.

### 1983–86 733i and 735i (M30 B34 Engine)

1. Disconnect the negative battery cable. Remove the alternator drive belt, remove the alternator mounting bolts and move it aside.

2. Loosen the adjusting and mounting bolts and remove the power steering pump belt. Remove the power steering pump hinge bolt and nut. Remove the 2 bolts shown, keeping any shims that may have been used in assembly together with the bolt they were on.

3. Drain coolant out of the block. Drain the oil pan. Remove the plug from the block and drain the engine of coolant.

4. Remove the 2 attachments fastening the stabilizer bar to the body.

5. Remove the 2 bolts and nuts shown and move this bracket away from the engine.

6. Remove the bolts and remove the clutch housing cover. Remove all the oil pan bolts that can be reached.

7. Disconnect the oil level sending unit wire. Then, unfasten both engine mounts by removing the nuts from the ends of the bolts.

8. Disconnect the radiator hoses that's near one of the lifting hooks, and securely connect a lifting sling to the engine. Raise the engine.

9. Swing out and tie down the power steering bracket. Then, unscrew the remaining oil pan bolts.

10. Pull the oil pan down. Turn the crankshaft so the rods for cylinders 5 and 6 are in the highest position, pull the stabilizer bar away, and then remove the pan.

11. Install in reverse order, paying attention to these points:

a. Clean all gasket surfaces thoroughly. Use a new gasket and coat all mating surfaces on the timing cover and clutch housing cover with a liquid sealer.

b. Torque the stabilizer bar attachment bolts to 16 ft. lbs.

c. Make sure spacers are used on the power steering pump brace (removed in Step 2) so there will not be any torque on the bracket due to misalignment.

### 1987–90 735i, 735iL (M30 B35 Engine)

1. Disconnect the negative battery cable. Loosen the hose clamp for the air intake hose. Remove the mounting nut for the air cleaner, and remove the air cleaner. Remove the fan and shroud.

2. Disconnect the electrical plug and overflow hose from the coolant expansion tank. Be careful not to kink the hose. Remove the mounting nuts and remove the tank.

3. Remove the splash guard for the power steering pump. Loosen the locknut for the pump adjustment and remove the through bolt that mounts the pump lower bracket (which contains the adjustment mechanism) to the block. Swing the bracket aside. Unscrew the bolt attaching the power steering pump lines to the block and shift them aside too.

4. Disconnect the electrical plug for the suspension leveling switch on the left side engine mounting bracket. Remove the oil pan drain plug and drain the oil.

5. Remove the bracket for the exhaust pipes located near the oil pan.

6. Disconnect the ground strap from the engine. Remove the nuts and washers attaching the engine to the mounts on both sides.

7. Attach an engine lifting sling to the hooks at either end of the cylinder head. Lift the engine as necessary for clearance.

8. Remove all oil pan mounting bolts and remove the pan. Clean both sealing surfaces and supply a new gasket. Coat the 4 joints (between the block and timing case cover at the front and the block and rear main seal housing cover at the rear) with a sealer such as 3 Bond Silicone Sealer®. Install the oil pan bolts and torque them to 6.5–7.5 ft. lbs.

9. Reverse the remaining proce-

dures to install the oil pan. Torque the engine mount nuts to 31–34 ft. lbs. Refill the oil pan with the required amount and type of oil.

### *325, 325e, 325i, 325iS, 325iX and 528e*

1. Disconnect the negative battery cable. Raise the vehicle and support it. Drain the engine oil.
2. Remove the front lower splash guard. This may not be necessary for access on 1988–90 models.
3. Disconnect the electrical terminal from the oil sending unit.
4. On 1987 and earlier models, skip to Step 5. On 1988–90 models, remove the power steering gear from the front axle carrier as described later in this section.
5. Remove the flywheel cover.
6. Remove the oil pan bolts and lower the oil pan. Remove the oil pump bolts and take out the oil pump and oil pan.
7. Install the oil pan, paying attention to the following points:
   a. Clean the gasket surfaces and use a new gasket on the oil pan.
   b. Coat the joints on the ends of the front engine cover with a universal sealing compound.
   c. Install the sending unit wire and the engine oil. If the power steering gear was removed, make sure to refill and bleed this system.

### *M3*

1. Remove the dipstick. Remove the splash guard from underneath the engine.
2. Remove the drain plug and drain the oil. Unscrew all the bolts for the lower oil pan and remove it.
3. Remove the oil pump as described below.
4. Remove the lower flywheel housing cover by removing the 3 bolts at the bottom of the flywheel housing and the 2 bolts in the cover just ahead of the flywheel housing.
5. Disconnect the oil pressure sending unit plug. Unbolt the oil pan bracket. Disconnect the ground lead. Loosen its clamp and disconnect the crankcase ventilation hose.
6. Remove the oil pan bolts and remove the upper oil pan. Clean all sealing surfaces. Supply a new gasket and the coat the joints where the timing case cover and block meet with a brush-on sealant. Install the pan and torque the bolts evenly to 7 ft. lbs.
7. Reverse the remaining removal procedures to install, cleaning all sealing surfaces and using a new gasket on the lower pan, also. Torque the lower pan bolts, also, to 7 ft. lbs.
8. Install the oil pan drain plug, torquing to 24 ft. lbs. Refill the oil pan with the required amount of approved oil. Start the engine and check for leaks.

# Rear Main Bearing Oil Seal

## REMOVAL & INSTALLATION

The rear main bearing oil seal can be replaced after the transmission, and clutch/flywheel or the converter/flywheel has been removed from the engine.

Removal and installation, after the seal is exposed, is as follows.

1. Drain the engine oil and loosen the oil pan bolts. Carefully use a knife to separate the oil pan gasket from the lower surface of the end cover housing.
2. Remove the 2 rear oil pan bolts.
3. Remove the bolts around the outside of the cover housing and remove the end cover housing from the engine block. Remove the gasket from the block surface.
4. Remove the seal from the housing. Coat the sealing lips of the new seal with oil. Install a new seal into the end cover housing with a special seal installer BMW Tool No. 11 1 260 backed up by a mandrel, Tool No. 00 5 500 or equivalent. On 1984–89 3.3 and 3.5L engines, and 1988–89 2.5 and 2.7L engines, press the seal in until it is about 0.039–0.079 in. deeper than the standard seal, which was installed flush.
5. While the cover is off, check the plug in the rear end of the main oil gallery. If the plug shows signs of leakage, replace it with another, coating it with Loctite® 270® or equivalent to keep it in place.

**NOTE: Fill the cavity between the sealing lips of the seal with grease before installing. On 1984–86 engines, lubricate the seal with oil.**

6. On all 1983–90 engines, coat the mating surface between the oil pan and end cover with sealer. Using a new gasket, install the end cover on the engine block and bolt it into place.
7. Complete the installation. If the oil pan gasket has been damaged, replace it. Install the transmission.

# Oil Pump

## REMOVAL & INSTALLATION

### *All Models Except 325, 325e, 325i, 325iS, 325iX, M3, 524td and 528e*

1. Remove the oil pan. On the 318i and M3, only the lower section of the pan need be removed.
2. Remove the bolts retaining the sprocket to the oil pump shaft and remove the sprocket.
3. On 4 cylinder engines:
   a. Remove the oil pump retaining bolts and lower the oil pump from the engine block.
   b. Check the installed location of the O-ring seal, between the housing and the pressure safety line and make sure it is installed so it will seal properly.
   c. Torque the sprocket retaining nut to 18–22 ft. lbs.
   d. Be sure that the oil bore in the shim(s) is correctly positioned during the oil pump installation. If there is a lot of play in the drive chain, add one or more shims. The drive chain should give slightly under light thumb pressure.
4. On 6 cylinder engines:
   a. Remove the oil pump retaining bolts and lower the oil pump from the engine block. On 6 cyl. engines other than the M30B35, there are 3 bolts at the front and 2 bolts attaching the rear of the oil pickup to the lower end of a support bracket. It is necessary to remove all 5 bolts. On the M30B35, there are only 3 bolts.
   b. Do not loosen the chain adjusting shims from the 2 mounting locations.
   c. Add or subtract shims between the oil pump body and the engine block to obtain a slight movement of the chain under light thumb pressure.
5. Install the oil pump in position.

**CAUTION**

***When used, the 2 shim thicknesses must be the same. Tighten the pump holder at the pick-up end after shimming is completed to avoid stress on the pump.***

6. On 6 cylinder engines, other than the M30B35, after the main pump mounting bolts are torqued, loosen the bolts at the bracket on the rear of the pick-up, allowing the pick-up to assume its most natural position. This will relieve tension on the bracket. Tighten the bolts. On the M30B35, torque the oil pump mounting bolts to 16 ft. lbs. and the sprocket bolts to 19 ft. lbs.

### *325, 325e, 325i, 325iS, 325iX, M3 and 528e*

1. Raise the vehicle and support it. Drain the engine oil.
2. Remove the front lower splash guard.
3. Disconnect the electrical terminal from the oil sending unit.
4. Remove the flywheel cover.

5. Remove the 3 oil pan bolts—one on one side and 2 on the other and lower the oil pan. Remove the oil pump bolts and take out the oil pump and oil pan.

6. Installation is the reverse of removal. Installation notes:

a. Clean the gasket surfaces and use a new gasket on the oil pan.

b. Positioning the pump for installation of its mounting bolts, guide the pump driveshaft into the hole in the center of the drive gear.

c. Coat the joints on the ends of the front engine cover with a universal sealing compound.

d. Install the sending unit wire and the engine oil.

### 524td

On the diesel, the pump comes down as the oil pan is removed.

# ENGINE COOLING

## Radiator

### REMOVAL & INSTALLATION

Remove the radiator as follows:

1. Disconnect the negative battery cable. Drain the cooling system. On 3.3L and 3.5L engines and on the M3, this requires removing the plug from the bottom radiator tank.

2. If the car has a coolant expansion tank, remove the cap, disconnect the hose at the radiator, and drain the coolant into a clean container. If the car has a splash guard, remove it.

3. Disconnect and remove the coolant hoses.

4. Disconnect the automatic transmission oil cooler lines and plug their openings as well as the openings in the cooler.

5. Disconnect any of the temperature switch wire connectors (used in many applications—especially if the car has air conditioning).

6. Remove the shroud from the radiator. On some models, this is done by simply pressing plugs toward the rear of the car. On others, there are metal slips that must be pulled upward and off to free the shroud from the radiator. The shroud will remain in the vehicle, resting on the fan on most models. On the 735i and 735iL, remove the fan and shroud together (make sure to store the fan in a vertical position!). The fan must be held stationary with some sort of flat blade cut to fit over the hub and drilled to fit over 2 of the studs on the front of the pulley (or it is possible to use BMW special tool 11 5 020). Then, unscrew the retaining nut at the center of the fluid drive hub turning it *clockwise* to remove it because it has left hand threads.

- On the 318i, remove the cover from the left side of the radiator.
- On late model cars with the M30 B35 engine, remove the fan and shroud; then, spread the retaining clip and pull the oil cooler out to the right. Remove the radiator retaining bolts (or single bolt on some models) and lift the radiator from the vehicle.
- Note that on the 1983–88 3.3L and 3.5L engines, there are 2 bolts at the top/rear of the radiator and 2 bolts at the bottom rear.

7. The radiator is installed in the reverse order of removal. Fill and bleed the cooling system.

- Note that, on the M3, there are rubber washers that go on either side of the mounting brackets at the top and that the bottom of the unit is suspended by rubber bushings into which prongs located on the bottom tank will fit. Make sure all parts fit right when the unit is installed. On all models, check that rubber mounts are located so as to effectively isolate the radiator from the chassis, as this will help ensure reliable radiator performance and long life. Note that if the car uses plastic upper and lower radiator tanks and has a radiator drain plug, be careful not to overtorque the plug—use only 1.2–2 ft. lbs. Torque engine oil cooler pipes to 18–21 ft. lbs. and transmission cooler pipes to 13–15 ft. lbs. Torque the thermostatic fan hub on the 735i and 735iL to 29–36 ft. lbs.

## Water Pump

### REMOVAL & INSTALLATION

#### All Models Except 325, 325e, 325i, 325iS, 325iX, M3, 524td and 528e

1. Disconnect the negative battery cable. Drain the cooling system and remove the radiator.

2. Remove the fan blades. Loosen the drive belts and remove as necessary. On the 318i, M3, and 1983–85 733i, and the 735i and 735iL, this requires holding the fan pulley via the locating posts (fabricate some sort of flat blade cut to fit over the hub and drilled to fit over 2 of the studs on the front of the pulley, or use BMW special tool 11 5 020. Then turn the coupling nut clockwise (left hand threads) to remove the fan and clutch. Store in a vertical position.

3. On the M3, next loosen the alternator bolts to release belt tension.

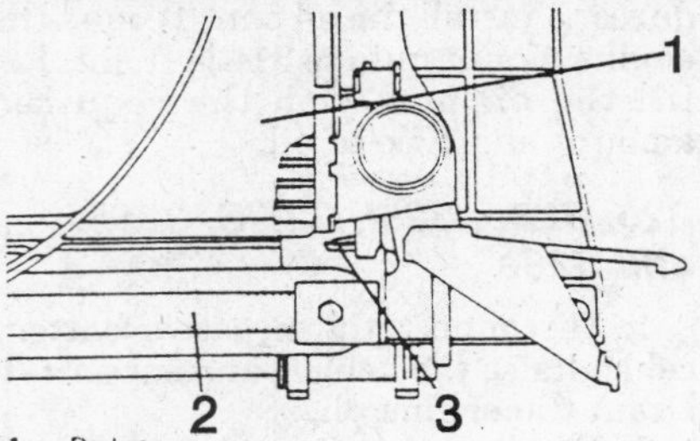


**Late model 5,6,and 7 Series cars with the M30 B35 engine have an oil cooler that must be removed before removing the radiator (1). To remove the oil cooler (2), remove the clip (3) and then pull the cooler out to the right.**

Then, on all models, unbolt and remove the belt pulley from the pump flange and disconnect the coolant hoses.

4. On 1983–85 3.3L and all 3.5L engines, remove the lifting hook that's in the way before removing the 2 bolts. In addition, on the M5, M6 models, remove the air cleaner and airflow sensor as an assembly before removing the pump. Remove the retaining bolts and remove the water pump from the engine.

5. The installation is in the reverse of the removal procedure. Use a new gasket and bleed the cooling system.

#### 325, 325e, 325i, 325iS, 325iX, M3, and 528e

1. Disconnect the negative battery cable. Drain the cooling system.

2. Remove the distributor cap and rotor. Remove the inner distributor cap and rubber sealing ring.

3. The fan must be held stationary with some sort of flat blade cut to fit over the hub and drilled to fit over 2 of the studs on the front of the pulley (or use BMW special tool 11 5 030). Remove the fan coupling nut (left hand thread—turn clockwise to remove).

4. Remove the belt and pulley.

5. Remove the rubber guard and distributor and or upper timing belt cover.

6. Compress the timing tensioner spring and clamp pin with BMW special tool 11 5 010 or equivalent.

**NOTE: Observe the installed position of the tensioner spring pin on the water pump housing for reinstallation purposes.**

7. Remove the water hoses, remove the 3 water pump bolts and remove the pump.

8. Clean the gasket surfaces and use a new gasket.

Measuring belt deflection

Bleeding of the cooling system with bleeder screw

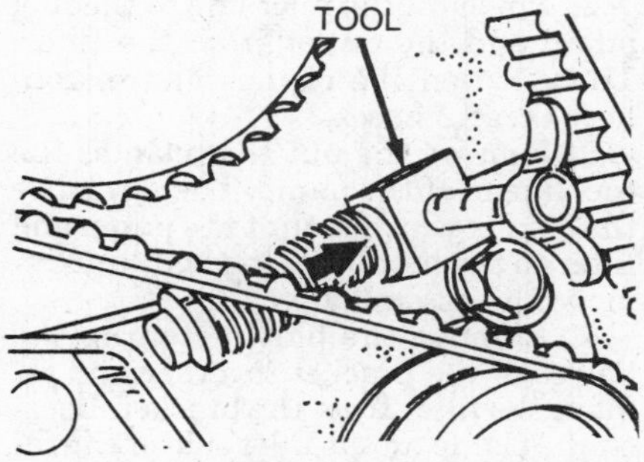


Compress tensioner spring with special tool during water pump removal—528e

Removing water pump retaining bolts—528e

9. Install the water pump in position. Note the position of the tensioner spring pin.

10. Add coolant and bleed the cooling system.

### *524td*

1. Remove the fan cowl. Hold the fan pulley with the blade of a screwdriver and remove the nut which fastens the fan in place, turning it clockwise because of the use of left hand threads. Drain the cooling system.

2. Remove the front cover as described earlier in this section. Unclamp and detach the water pump outlet hose at the pump.

3. Remove the water pump mounting bolts. Remove the pump, pushing the timing belt to one side for clearance.

4. Clean both surfaces of gasket material, and install a new gasket coated with sealer.

5. Install the water pump in reverse order. Refill the cooling system and bleed it.

# Thermostat

## REMOVAL & INSTALLATION

The thermostat is located near the water pump, either on the cylinder head or intake manifold on some models and is located between 2 coolant hose sections on other models. On the diesel, it is located right above the water pump. Remove the fan to gain access to it. See the water pump removal procedure for special procedures required to remove the fan.

The removal and installation of the thermostat is accomplished in the conventional manner. Always drain some coolant out and save it in a clean container before removing the thermostat. On the M5, M6 engine, the forward (removable) portion of the housing has a hose connected to it. The hose need not be disconnected to remove the housing. Note that on the 1983–87 3.3L and all 3.5L engines and the diesel, there is not only a thermostat housing gasket, but an inner rubber seal to keep the closed thermostat from leaking. On the engine used in the M5, M6, there is a large O-ring seal for the main portion of the housing and a small, O-ring located above it in a small passage. The M20B27 and M20B25 engines also use the large O-ring which must be replaced with the thermostat. Replace both these seals on all models.

Note that thermostats for 3.5L engines built in 1986–90 carry an "A" designation. The thermostat for M20B27 and M20B25 engines in 1986–90 models is smaller in diameter. On all models except M3, the thermostat is installed with the thermostatic sensing unit facing inward and the cross-band facing outward. Refill and bleed the cooling system.

On the M3, the thermostat is installed in a coolant lines with a thir connection that goes to the block. To replace it, first drain coolant and then note the routing of hoses. Loosen all 3 hose clamps and then replace the unit. Refill and bleed the system.

## COOLING SYSTEM BLEEDING

### *With Bleeder Screw on Thermostat Housing*

Set the heat valve in the **WARM** position, start the engine and bring it to normal operating temperature. Run the engine at fast idle and open the venting screw on the thermostat housing until the coolant comes out free of air bubbles. Close the bleeder screw and refill the cooling system.

### *Without Bleeder Screw*

Fill the cooling system, place the heater valve in the WARM position, close the pressure cap to the second (fully closed) position. Start the engine and bring to normal operating temperature. Carefully release the pressure cap to the first position and squeeze the upper and lower radiator hoses in a pumping action to allow trapped air to escape through the radiator. Recheck the coolant level and close the pressure cap to its second position.

# EMISSION CONTROLS

**Please refer to "Emission Control" in the Unit Repair section**

**for system maintenance procedures. Due to the complex nature of modern electronic engine control systems, comprehensive diagnosis and testing procedures fall outside the confines of this repair manual. For complete information on diagnosis, testing, and repair procedures concerning all modern engine and emission control systems, please refer to Chilton's Guide to Electronic Engine Controls".**

## Emission Warning Lamps

### EGR WARNING LIGHT RESETTING

A warning light marked EGR is triggered at 25,000 miles, to alert the driver to service the exhaust gas recirculation system filter.

A triggering device, located under the dash and driven by the speedometer cable, can be reset to open the electrical contacts and extinguish the EGR warning light.

**NOTE: Two different sized buttons are mounted side by side on the triggering device. The small button is for the reactor light and the large button is for the EGR light. Press the button to reset.**

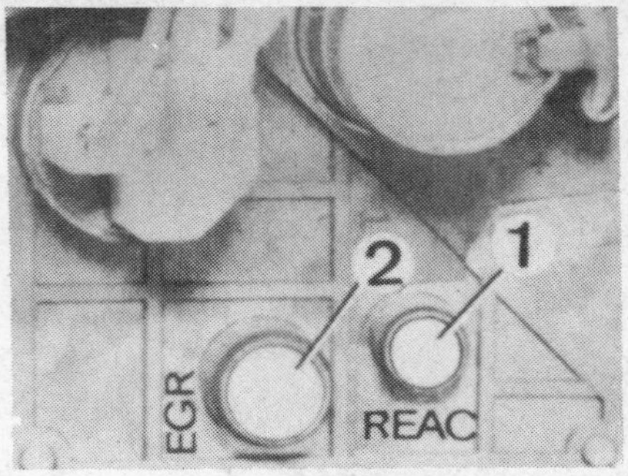


Triggering device with REACTOR (1) and the EGR (2) resetting buttons shown

# GASOLINE FUEL SYSTEM

## Fuel System Service Precaution

**CAUTION**

*Gasoline is extremely volatile and can easily be ignited. Work on fuel system parts only when the engine is cold. Keep all other sources of ignition away. Carefully observe all precautions given in the procedures as to clamping fuel lines, collecting fuel in a metal container, and disposing of it in a safe manner. Always relieve fuel system pressure before unclamping lines, as fuel injection systems maintain very high pressure, even when the engine is off.*

### RELIEVING FUEL SYSTEM PRESSURE

To relieve the pressure in the system, first find the fuel pump relay plug, located on the cowl. Unplug the relay, leaving it in a safe position where the connections cannot ground. If necessary, tape the plug in place or tape over the connector prongs with electrical tape. Then, start the engine and operate it until it stalls. Crank the engine for 10 seconds after it stalls to remove any residual pressure.

## Fuel Filter

### LOCATION

#### *320i, 318i, 325, 325e, 325i, 325iS, 325iX, M3, 528e, 733i, 735i and 735iL*

The inline filter is located directly above the final drive assembly and attached to the underside of the floor pan.

#### *533i, 525i, 535i, 633CSi, 635CSi, M5 and M6*

The inline filter is located behind the passenger side wheel, near the frame, above the final driveshaft. On 1986–88 models, it is mounted on a bracket onto which the fuel pump is also mounted.

### REMOVAL & INSTALLATION

#### *All Models Except 633CSi, M5 and M6*

The inline fuel filters on these BMW models are easily removed. On filters that are located near the fuel tank, it is necessary to clamp the fuel lines closed before disconnecting them, or fuel will run out continuously.

1. Disconnect the negative battery cable. Relieve fuel system pressure, as described above. Clamp the lines closed if the filter is mounted low, near the fuel tank. Then, loosen the clamps and disconnect the inlet and outlet hoses. Remove the hose clamps or slide them back, well off the connections to make it easier to pull off the hoses, if necessary.
2. The filters will usually be attached to a frame, floor pan or wheel well by a bracket. Loosen the bracket and remove the filter. On the 735 models with the M30 B35 engine, remove the phillips head screw clamping the filter inside the mounting band. Note the direction of flow and then remove the filter.
3. Observe the instructions on the inlet and outlet during installation.

#### *633CSi, M5 and M6*

1. Relieve fuel system pressure. Disconnect the battery cables. Working under the fuel tank, pull back the protective caps and then unscrew the attaching nuts and pull off the electrical connections for the fuel pump.
2. Pinch off the inlet line to the fuel pump and the outlet from the filter. Then, loosen the clamps and disconnect these 2 hoses.
3. Remove the nut that clamps the fuel line near the pump. Then, remove the 3 bolts which mount the pump and filter to the bottom of the body and remove the assembly.
4. Remove the bolt fastening the halves of the bracket together and remove the filter from the bracket. Loosen the clamp on the inlet side of the filter and disconnect the inlet line, noting the direction of flow (arrow). Remove the rubber bushing in which the filter is mounted, and mount it on the new filter.
5. Install the filter in exact reverse order, making sure all clamps are securely tightened. Operate the engine and check for leaks.

## Electric Fuel Pump

### PRESSURE CHECKING

#### *318i and 320i*

1. Relieve fuel system pressure, as described above. Connect a pressure gauge in the line leading from the fuel distributor on top of the injector pump to the warm-up regulator. Plug the open end of the line leading to the warm-up regulator, and make sure the gauge will read the pressure coming from the distributor.
2. Disconnect the wire plug on the mixture control unit, and turn on the ignition. The pressure should read 64–74 psi, or the fuel pump will have to be replaced.

#### *1982–86 325e, 528e, 533i and 633CSi*

Relieve fuel system pressure, as described above. Connect a pressure gauge in the line leading to the cold start valve from the injector feed circuit. With the engine idling, the pres-

Electric fuel pump assembly—typical

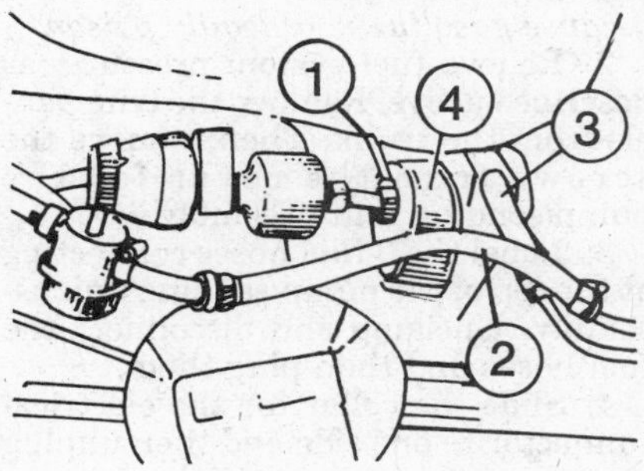


1. Suction line
2. Pressure line
3. Return line
4. Damper

**Note the arrangement of the fuel pump, lines, and damper on the 1987–89 325 series cars**

sure must be 33–38 psi, or the fuel pump (or filter) is defective.

### *1987–90 325, 325e, 325i, 325iS and 325iX*

1. Relieve fuel system pressure, as described above. Tee a pressure gauge into the fuel feed line in front of the pressure regulator.
2. Disconnect the fuel pump relay. Connect a remote starter switch between terminals KL30 and KL87 of the relay. Close the switch and check the pressure. It should be 43 psi. If not, the filter is severely clogged or the fuel pump is defective.

### *M3*

1. Relieve fuel system pressure, as described above. Tee a pressure gauge into the fuel return line at the pressure regulator. Then, clamp off the return line so pressure builds up to the maximum level the pump can produce.
2. Remove the trim from the cowl on the right (passenger's side). Then, unplug the fuel pump relay. Connect a remote starter switch between terminals 30 and 87 (left side and top holding the male side of the connector). Energize the switch and check the pressure. It must be 43 psi. Check the filter for excessive clogging. If it is okay, the pump is defective.

### *533i, 525i, 535i, 633CSi, 635CSi, 733i, 735i, 735iL, M5 and M6*

1. Relieve fuel system pressure, as described above. Tee a pressure gauge into the fuel feed line in front of the pressure regulator (on M5, M6, tee in between the cold start valve and the fuel rail). Plug the fuel return hose.
2. Pull off the pump relay. Jumper terminals 87 and 30. Measure the delivery pressure. It should be 43 psi on these models except the 1987–1990 735i, 735iL and 750iL. On these models, it should be 48 psi.

## REMOVAL & INSTALLATION

### *All 5 Series Except M5*

The fuel pump is an electrical unit, delivering fuel through a pressure regulator, to a fuel distributor or a ring-line for the injection valves. The fuel pump is mounted under the vehicle, near the fuel tank, or in the engine compartment.

1. Relieve fuel system pressure, as described above. Disconnect the negative battery connector. Push back any protective caps and disconnect the electrical connector(s).
2. If the fuel lines are flexible, pinch them closed with an appropriate tool. Disconnect the fuel lines and plug the ends.
3. Remove the retaining bolts and remove the pump and expansion tank as an assembly. On the 318i, the pump and mounting bracket come off together. On the 1983–85 733i and 1986 735i, remove the clamp bolt, bend the clamp open, and remove the pump.
4. The pump can be separated from the expansion tank after removal. On the 318i, separate the pump from the mounting bracket and slide the rubber mounting ring from the pump.
5. Install the pump in the correct position, be sure to use similar types of hose clamps, if any need replacing. The wrong type clamp can damage the pressure lines.
6. Run the engine and check the fuel lines for leakage. Check the fuel system pressure.

### *1987–90 325, 325e, 325i, 325iS, 325iX and M3*

1. Relieve fuel system pressure. Disconnect the negative battery connector. Going to the pump, which is under the car and near the fuel tank, push back any protective caps, note the routing and disconnect the electrical connector(s).
2. Securely clamp the suction hose (coming from the tank) and plug the discharge hose so no fuel can escape.
3. Open the hose clamp connecting the suction hose to the pump and disconnect it.
4. Remove the 3 attaching nuts which mount the pump and bracket to the floor pan and remove both as an assembly.
5. Remove the bolt passing through the 2 parts of the bracket and also mounting the hose attaching strap to the bracket. Then, pull the pump out of the bracket.
6. Loosen the hose clamp for the discharge hose and disconnect it at the pump. Pull the rubber ring off the pump.
7. Note the code number on the pump and make sure to replace it with one of the same number. Inspect all the rubber mounts on the pump mounting bracket and replace any that are cracked or crushed.
8. Install the pump in reverse order. Make sure to unclamp the hoses and then run the engine and check for leaks. Check the fuel system pressure.

### *633CSi, M5 and M6*

1. Disconnect the negative battery cable. Relieve fuel system pressure, as described above. Clamp the lines closed if the filter is mounted low, near the fuel tank. Then, loosen the clamps and disconnect the inlet and outlet hoses. Remove the hose clamps or slide them back, well off the connections to make it easier to pull off the hoses, if necessary.
2. The filters will usually be attached to a frame, floor pan or wheel well by a bracket. Loosen the bracket and remove the filter. On the 735 models with the M30 B35 engine, remove the phillips head screw clamping the filter inside the mounting band. Note the direction of flow and then remove the filter.

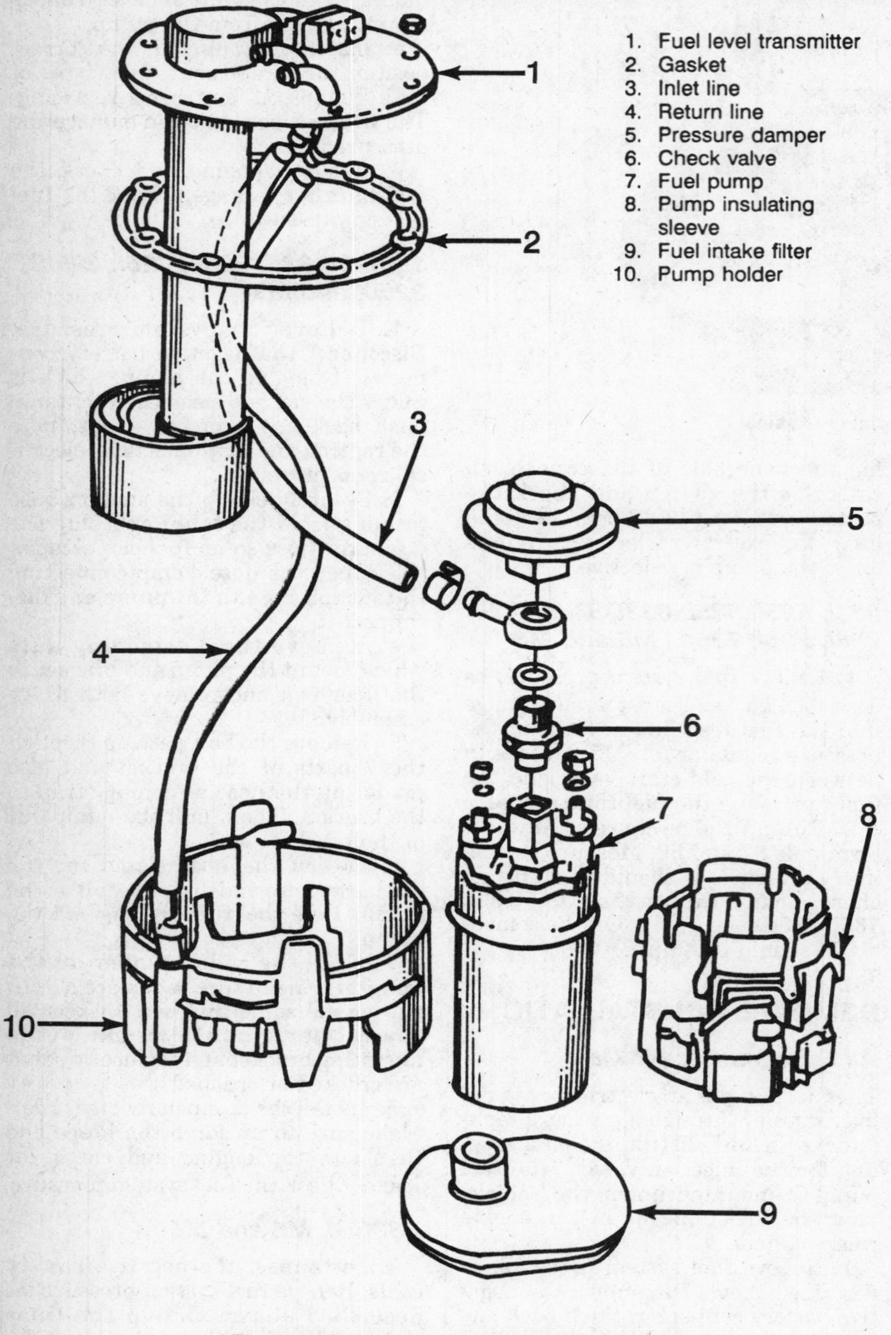


**The in-tank fuel pump used in 1987–89 735i**

3. Observe the instructions on the inlet and outlet during installation.

4. Remove the bolt fastening the halves of the bracket together and remove the filter from the bracket. Loosen the clamp on the outlet side of the fuel pump and disconnect the line. Then, slide off the rubber bushing in which the pump is mounted.

5. Check the code number on the side of the pump and make sure the replacement unit carries the same code.

6. Install the pump in exact reverse order, making sure all clamps are securely tightened. Operate the engine and check for leaks.

### *1987–90 735i and 735iL*

The pump on this car is mounted in the top of the tank along with the fuel level sending unit.

1. If the fuel pump is working well enough to drive the car, run it until the fuel level is as low as possible. If the car cannot be run, devise a safe way to draw fuel out of the tank until the level is low. The best means is some sort of pump and container system designed for this purpose, as siphoning is no longer considered safe *because gasoline is a deadly poison*.

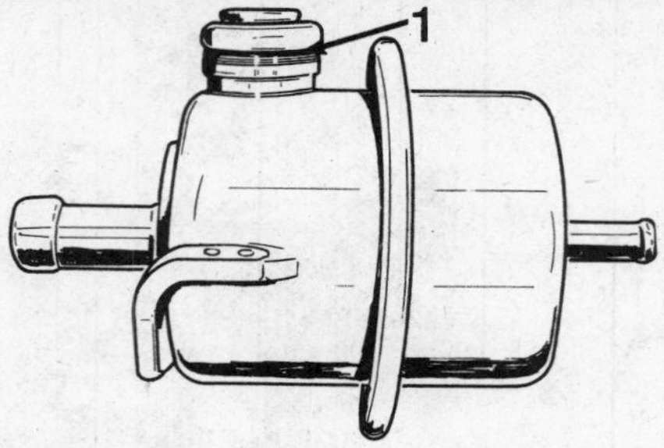


**On the 318i fuel pressure regulator, check the seal (1) and replace it if necessary**

2. Relieve fuel system pressure, as described above. Remove the trim panels from the trunk. Then, remove the screws from the cover for the pump/sending unit assembly.

3. Label the 3 fuel hoses connecting at the top of the pump/sending unit assembly. Unclamp and disconnect the fuel hoses and then plug them.

4. Slide the collar for the electrical connector to one side and then unplug the connector.

5. Remove the 8 attaching screws and remove the pump/sending unit assembly. Replace the gasket.

6. Press the 2 retaining locks for the pump unit inward and slide the pump out of the pump/sending unit assembly.

7. Note the routing of the fuel and electrical lines to the pump from the top of the pump/sending unit assembly. Loosen the 2 hose clamp screws and the screws attaching the electrical connectors to the pump. Disconnect the hose and connector.

8. Unscrew the pressure regulator from the top of the check valve. Then, unscrew the check valve from the top of the pump.

9. Pull the insulating sleeve off the pump. Then, loosen the retaining screw and slide the filter off the pump.

10. Install the pump in reverse order. Be careful to ensure that the 2 retaining locks fasten the pump in place in a secure manner. Operate the engine and check for leaks.

## Fuel Pressure Regulator

### REMOVAL & INSTALLATION

### *1983 733i*

1.Disconnect the negative battery cable. Relieve fuel system pressure, as described above. Clamp the lines closed if the filter is mounted low, near

the fuel tank. Then, loosen the clamps and disconnect the inlet and outlet hoses. Remove the hose clamps or slide them back, well off the connections to make it easier to pull off the hoses, if necessary.
2.The filters will usually be attached to a frame, floor pan or wheel well by a bracket. Loosen the bracket and remove the filter. Remove the phillips head screw clamping the filter inside the mounting band. Note the direction of flow and then remove the filter.
3.Observe the instructions on the inlet and outlet during installation.
4.Remove the bolt fastening the halves of the bracket together and remove the filter from the bracket. Loosen the clamp on the outlet side of the fuel pump and disconnect the line. Then, slide off the rubber bushing in which the pump is mounted.
5.Check the code number on the side of the pump and make sure the replacement unit carries the same code.
6.Install the pump in exact reverse order, making sure all clamps are securely tightened. Operate the engine and check for leaks.

#### *318i, 325, 325e, 325i, 325iS, 325iX, 528e, 1983–84 533i, All 525i, 535i, 1983–84 633CSi, All 635CSi, 1984 733i, 735i, 735iL, M5 and M6*

1. Remove the vacuum hose from the unit.
2. Loosen the clamp and pull off the fuel hose.
3. Remove the 2 bolts and pull the unit from the injection tube (318i, 325, M3, all models with M30 B35 engine), or from the body (other models).
4. Inspect the seal that seals the connection with the injection tube and replace it, if necessary.
5. Install the regulator in position, using new seals during installation.
6. Check the system for leaks.

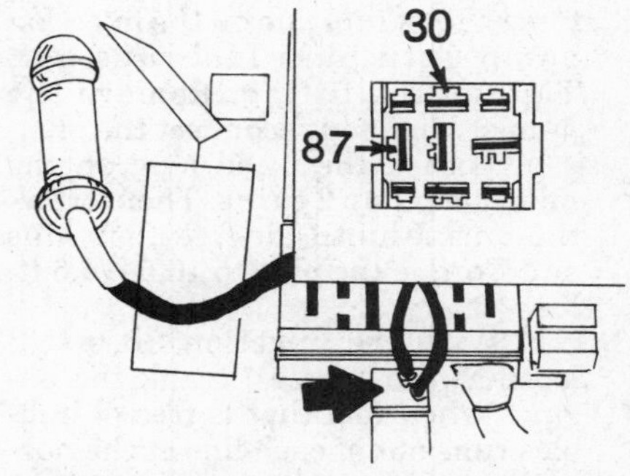


**Jumper terminals 30 and 87 to run the fuel transfer pump and prime the fuel system**

## Fuel Injection

**NOTE: Due to the complex nature of modern fuel injection systems, comprehensive diagnosis and testing procedures fall outside the confines of this repair manual. For complete information on fuel injection diagnosis, testing and repair procedures please refer to Chilton's Guide To Fuel Injection And Feedback Carburetors.**

# DIESEL FUEL SYSTEM

## Fuel Filter

### REPLACEMENT

1. Loosen the bleeder screw located on top of the filter mounting fitting with a regular screwdriver. Place a container under the filter and loosen the drain cock to drain a small amount of fuel (this will keep fuel from spilling when the filter is removed).
2. Disconnect the plug on the water level sensor. Unscrew the filter with a standard oil filter strap wrench.
3. Remove the water level sensor from the old filter and move it over to the new one.
4. Thoroughly coat the seal on top of the new filter with clean fuel. Start the filter onto the threads, turn it until the gasket touches, and then turn it just one half turn more by hand.
5. Disconnect the plug for the fuel transfer pump. Open the bleeder screw. Jumper terminals 30 and 87. When fuel that is bubble-free runs out of the bleed screw, tighten it. Remove the jumper and reconnect the plug.
6. Start the engine and operate it to check for leaks. Tighten the filter just a bit further, if necessary.

### DRAINING WATER FROM THE SYSTEM

1. Hold a half pint container under the bleeder screw and open the drain cock.2. Disconnect the plug for the fuel transfer pump. Open the bleeder screw. Jumper terminals 30 and 87.
3. Press the drain adapter in to open it. Drain until pure fuel runs out.
4. Remove the jumper and replace the plug.

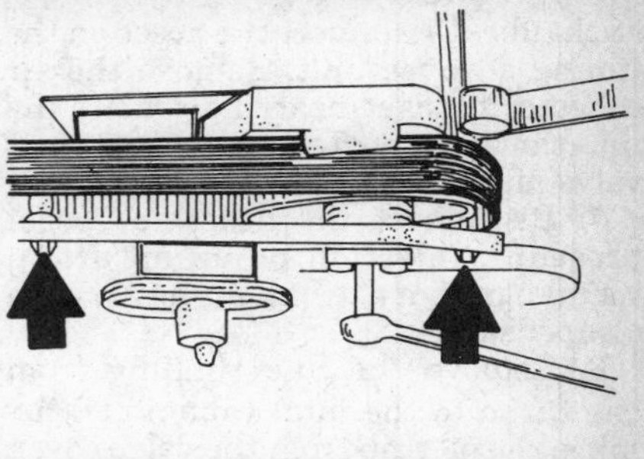

**Install bolts at the arrowed point to hold the injection pump installation**

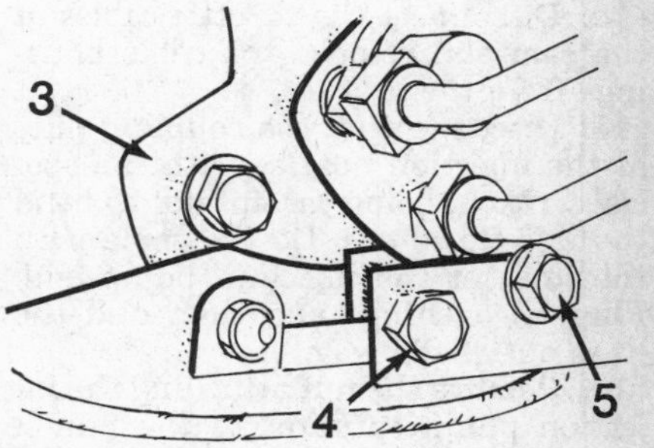


**Loosen the bolts shown (3–5) before starting injection pump installation**

## Diesel Injection Pump

### REMOVAL & INSTALLATION

**NOTE: This is a complex operation requiring several special tools. Use 13 5 020 or equivalent to remove injection lines. Use 13 5 010 and 13 5 061 or equivalent to press the injection pump off its sprocket. Also required are 2 M6 × 20mm bolts and plastic caps to seal openings.**

1. Remove the drain plugs from both the block and the radiator to completely drain coolant. Remove the fan cowl and fan as described earlier in this section.
2. Remove the oil filler cap to watch the valves. Turn the crankshaft with a socket wrench so tha No. 1 cylinder is at TDC firing position (No. 6 valves overlapping).
3. Disconnect and remove the upper and lower radiator hoses. Remove the alternator drive belt. Remove the timing belt cover, as described earlier in this section.
4. Using a backup wrench, use the special injection line wrench to disconnect the inlet line at the injection pump. Plug the opening.
5. Disconnect the fuel return line at the connector below the pump. Remove the wiring harness clamp nearby.
6. Remove the clamp for the oil dip-

stick tube. Disconnect the hoses on the timing advance unit. Remove the air collector bracket near the rear of the injection pump. Remove the pop off valve air connection.

7. Disconnect the hoses for boost pressure, injection pump oil drain, vacuum, and the altitude compensator.

8. Remove the line running from the turbo to the intake manifold. Remove the oil trap from the valve cover. Then pull off the 3 plugs nearby.

9. Disconnect the fuel shutoff and idle switch connectors.

10. Disconnect the throttle cables at the cam and remove the cable housings from the bracket.

11. Disconnect all the coupling nuts at the injection nozzles with the special wrench, being careful not to bend the injection lines. Do the same with the lines at the injection pump end. Plug all openings and then pull the lines out of the way.

12. Remove the nut attaching the injection pump sprocket to the pump. Then, bolt the special tools for pressing the pump off the sprocket to the sprocket. Turn the crankshaft as necessary to line the boltholes up so the bolts fastening the tool to the block on either side can be installed and then install them.

13. Remove the 2 nuts situated directly behind the front cover. Then, remove the 3 bolts that fasten the pump at the rear.

14. Turn the large bolt at the center of the special tool and press the pump out of the sprocket.

15. Pull off the EGR pressure converter hoses at the converter. Remove the wiring harness for the pump out of the clips. Remove the pump. Be careful not to disturb the pump shaft. The key must remain at the top (don't lose it).

**To install:**

16. Install the pump so the key fits through the slot in the sprocket. Then, install and tighten the 2 nuts situated directly behind the front cover. Make sure the pump rests tightly against its mounting on the front cover.

17. Remove the special tool used to press the pump out of the sprocket. Then, install the sprocket bolt and torque it to 33–35 ft. lbs.

18. Adjust the static timing as described below.

19. Perform the remaining procedures in reverse order. Install the injection lines. Bleed the fuel system as described above.

## Diesel Injection Timing

### ADJUSTMENT

**NOTE: To perform this procedure, a special dial indicator gauge and a timing pin, BMW tools 13 5 330 and 11 2 300 or equivalent are needed.**

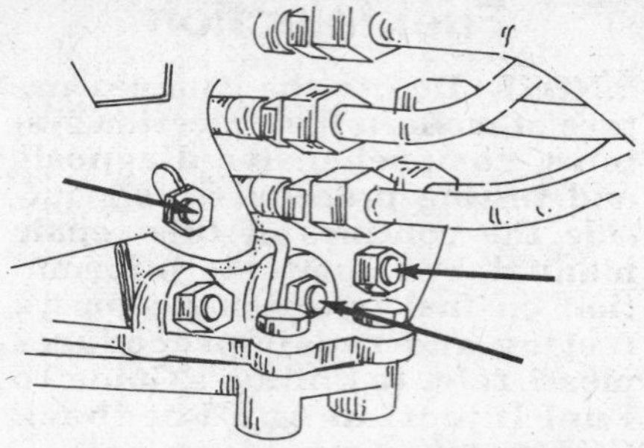

**Loosen the three arrowed bolts to turn the injection pump for timing it. These are at the rear of the pump**

1. Make sure the coolant temperature is above 68xF so the throttle lever will rest against the idle stop—not in the cold fast idle position.

2. Unfasten the coolant overflow tank and move it out of the way. Disconnect and plug the overflow hose.

3. Remove the plug in the injection pump head (between 2 of the lines going to the injectors). Install 13 5 330 or equivalent and hand tighten it. Remove the fan as described in the cooling system section. Turn the crankshaft, watching the dial gauge, in the forward direction until the gauge reaches its maximum value. Then, zero the gauge. Continue turning the engine toward TDC as while pressing the timing pin into the timing hole in the flywheel housing. The pin will lock into a hole in the flywheel, keeping the engine at TDC. Check that No. 6 valves are overlapping by removing the oil filler cap. Repeat the procedure, to set the engine at TDC firing position for No. 1, if the valves of No. 6 are not overlapping. Make sure to zero the gauge in the same way.

4. The reading should be 0.0256–0.0264 in. If it is within these limits, remove the gauges and replace the plug with a new gasket, restoring other parts disturbed to their normal condition. If the reading is incorrect, follow the rest of the steps.

5. Remove the bracket for the air collector that is near the injection pump. Remove the wiring harness from its clamps.

6. Remove the bolts 3, 4 and 5 at the rear of the pump (see the illustration).

7. Loosen the hose clamp that's in the way at the front of the pump. Loosen the 2 nuts behind the front cover just enough to permit turning the pump. To increase the reading or advance the timing, turn the pump toward the engine. When the figure is within tolerance, tighten the 2 nuts on the front cover and then tighten 3–5 in numerical order at the rear. Reverse the remaining procedures.

## Injection Nozzle

### REMOVAL & INSTALLATION

**NOTE: To remove these injection nozzles, a special tool BMW 13 5 020 or equivalent will be required. Also needed are caps to prevent the entry of dirt.**

1. Remove the oil trap located on the valve cover. Loosen the mounting clamps for the injection lines.

2. Disconnect the plugs associated with the injection system. There are a diagnostic plug and 2 others nearby.

3. Pull off the leakoff hoses for the injectors with a pair of pliers. Then, unscrew the coupling nuts on the injectors with the special tool 13 5 020 or equivalent.

4. Use the same tool to unscrew the coupling nuts on the injection pump. Make sure not to hit the lines with the tool handle and bend them.

5. Unscrew the injectors using the special tool. For No. 1 injector with the wire, run the plug through the tool to protect it. Make sure it is as close as possible to the middle.

**To install:**

6. Install in reverse order. Coat the threads of each injector with CRC and torque each injector to 25–33 ft. lbs.

7. When tightening injection lines to the pump, tighten No.4 cylinder's line first. All injection line fittings (both ends) are torqued to 10–18 ft. lbs. Leave the injector ends loose for bleeding.

8. Bleed the fuel system as follows:

a. Disconnect the electrical plug for the fuel transfer pump relay. Jumper the terminals numbered 30 and 87 to operate the fuel transfer pump. Then, loosen the banjo fitting for the inlet fuel line on the injection pump until pure fuel runs out. Tighten the fitting. Remove the jumper wire and reconnect the plug.

b. Loosen the bleed plug on the injection pump 2 turns. Then, crank the engine until air-free fuel runs out. Torque the plug to 10.5–14.5 ft. lbs.

c. With the injection lines still loose at the nozzles, crank the engine. When fuel that is free of bubbles runs out of each line at the nozzle, stop cranking the engine. Torque the nozzles with the special tool to 10–18 ft. lbs.

# MANUAL TRANSMISSION

## REMOVAL & INSTALLATION

### *320i and 318i*

1. Disconnect the negative battery cable. Drain the transmission. On 320i only, unscrew all transmission mounting bolts (4) accessible from above. Swing up the bracket mounted to the top/left bolt.

2. Disconnect the exhaust system support at the rear of the transmission.

3. Detach the exhaust pipe at the manifold.

4. Detach the driveshaft at the transmission by pulling out bolts from the rear of the coupling (the coupling remains attached to the driveshaft).

5. Remove the heat shield. Remove the bolts for the center bearing bracket, and pull the bracket downward. Bend the driveshaft downward and pull it out of the bearing journal.

6. Remove the bolt and disconnect the speedometer drive cable. Disconnect the back-up light switch wire, and pull the wire out of the clips on the transmission.

7. Remove the 2 Allen bolts at the top and pull the console off the transmission.

8. Disconnect the gearshift selector rod by pulling off the circlip, removing the washer and pulling the rod off the pin.

9. Detach the clutch slave cylinder line bracket at the front of the transmission, remove the mounting bolts from the slave cylinder mounting, and remove the slave cylinder.

10. Remove the flywheel housing cover.

11. Support the transmission securely at the center with a floor jack and wooden block.

12. Detach the crossmember by removing the nuts attaching it to the body at either end. On 318i, remove all front mounting bolts. Remove the 3 remaining front mounting bolts on the 320i, and pull the transmission out toward the rear.

**To install:**

13. Install the transmission in position under the vehicle. Align the input shaft and install the transmission. Bear the following points in mind:

a. Front mounting bolts are torqued to 18–19 ft. lbs. on the M8 transmissions; 34–37 on the M10 transmissions. Torque the crossmember rubber mounts to 31–35 ft. lbs.

b. On the 318i, the console has self-locking bolts which must be replaced for reassembly.

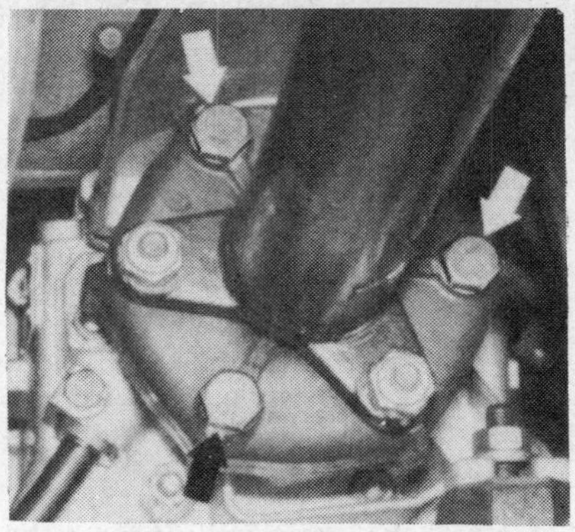

**Disconnecting driveshaft at transmission**

c. When reinstalling the clutch slave cylinder, make sure the bleeder screw faces downward.

d. When installing the driveshaft center support bearing, preload it forward 0.078 in. on 320i, 0.079–0.157 in. on 318i.

e. Replace the locknuts on the driveshaft coupling and tighten the nuts only – not the bolts to 31–35 ft. lbs.

f. Inspect the gasket at the joint between the exhaust manifold and pipe and replace it if necessary.

g. When reattaching exhaust system support at the rear, leave the attaching nut/bolt slightly loose; loosen the 2 nuts/bolts attaching the support via slots to the transmission; push the support toward the exhaust pipe until all tension is removed and then secure nuts and bolts.

### *6 Cylinder Models Except All 3 Series, 525i, 1983–84 533i, 535i, M5, 1983–84 633CSi, 635CSi, M6 and 1983–84 733i, 735i and 735iL*

1. Disconnect the negative battery cable. Remove the complete exhaust system. Drain the transmission.

2. Remove the circlip and washer at the selector rod and disengage the rod at the transmission.

3. Unzip the leather boot surrounding the gearshift lever. With a pointed object such as an ice pick, release the circlip at the bottom of the gearshift lever and then pull the lever upward and out of the transmission. Lubricate the nylon bushings at the bottom of the lever mechanism with a permanent lubricant for reassembly.

4. Remove the 3 bolts from the coupling at the front of the driveshaft out through the rear of the coupling, leaving the nuts/bolts attaching the driveshaft to the coupling in place.

5. Remove the heat shield. Remove the mounting bolts and remove the center bearing support bracket. Bend the driveshaft downward at the front and slide the spline out of the center bearing.

6. Support the transmission securely between the front axle carrier and oil pan with a floorjack and wooden block.

7. Remove the attaching bolt and pull out the speedometer cable. Disconnect the back-up light wiring electrical connectors and pull the wire out of the clips on the transmission.

8. Loosen the connection to the rubber bushing at the transmission, remove the mounting nuts at either end, and remove the crossmember. On the 633CSi, lower the transmission to the front axle carrier.

9. On the 633CSi, disconnect the mount for the clutch hydraulic line at the front of the transmission. Then, on all models, unscrew the mounting nuts and detach the clutch slave cylinder (with the line connected).

10. Remove the mounting nuts at the clutch housing and separate the transmission and clutch housing.

11. Pull the gearbox to the rear and out of the car.

**To install:**

12. Install the transmission in position and align the input shaft, keeping the following points in mind:

a. Use a slave cylinder to move the clutch throw-out arm to the correct position. Align the throw-out bearing. Grease the guide sleeve and groove in the throw-out bearing with a permanent lubricant.

b. Put the transmission into gear before installing.

c. Make sure, when installing the clutch slave cylinder, that the hose connection faces downward.

d. Preload the center bearing 0.08 in. toward the front.

e. When tightening the coupling, hold the bolt heads and torque only the nuts only to 75 ft. lbs. Use new nuts. Torque the transmission- to-engine bolts to 16–17 ft. lbs. (M8 transmission) or 31–35 ft. lbs. (M10 transmission); torque the bolt for the rubber bushing on the crossmember to 18 ft. lbs.

### *325, 325e, 325i, 325iS, 325iX, and M3*

1. Disconnect the negative battery cable. Raise the car and support it securely. Remove the exhaust system. Remove the cross brace and heat shield. On the 325iX, remove the transfer case as described later in this section.

2. Hold the nuts on the front with one wrench, and remove bolts from

the rear with another to disconnect the flexible coupling at the front of the driveshaft. Some models have a vibration damper at this point in the drivetrain. This damper is mounted on the transmission output flange with bolts that are pressed into the damper. On these models, unscrew and remove the nuts located behind the damper.

3. Loosen the threaded sleeve on the driveshaft. Get a special tool such as BMW 261040 to hold the splined portion of the shaft while turning the sleeve.

4. Remove its mounting bolts and remove the center driveshaft mount. Then, bend the driveshaft down at the center and pull it off the transmission output flange. Keep the sections of the driveshaft from pulling apart and suspend it from the car with wire.

5. Remove the retainer and washer, and pull out the shift selector rod.

6. Use a hex-head wrench to remove the 2 self-locking bolts that retain the shift rod bracket at the rear of the transmission and then remove the bracket. If the car has a shift arm, use a screwdriver to pry the spring clip up off the boss on the transmission case and swing it upward. Then, pull out the shift shaft pin.

7. Unscrew and remove the clutch slave cylinder and support it so the hydraulic line can remain connected.

8. The transmission incorporates sending units for flywheel rotating speed and position. Remove the heat shield that protects these from exhaust heat and then remove the retaining bolt for each sending unit. Note that the speed sending unit, which has *no* identifying ring goes in the bore on the right, and that the reference mark sending unit, which has a marking ring, goes in the bore on the left. If the sending units are installed in reverse positions, the engine will not run at all. Pull these units out of the flywheel housing.

9. Disconnect the wiring connector going to the backup light switch and pull the wires out of the harness.

10. *Support the transmission from underneath in a secure manner.* Remove mounting bolts and remove the crossmember holding the rear of the transmission to the body. Then, lower the transmission onto the front axle carrier.

11. Using a Torx® socket, remove the Torx® bolts holding the transmission flywheel housing to the engine at the front. Make sure to retain the washers with the bolts. Pull the transmission rearward to slide the input shaft out of the clutch disc and then lower the transmission and remove it from the car.

**To install:**

12. Install the transmission in position under the vehicle. Align the input shaft and install the transmission, keeping the following points in mind:

a. Coat the input shaft splines and flywheel housing guide pins with a light coating of a grease such as Microlube GL 261®.

b. Make sure the front mounting bolts are installed with their washers. Torque them to 46–58 ft. lbs.

c. Before reinstalling the 2 sending units for flywheel position and speed, make sure their faces are free of either grease or dirt and then coat them with a light coating of Molykote Longterm 2®. Inspect the O-rings and replace them if they are cut, cracked, crushed, or stretched.

d. When installing the shift rod bracket at the rear of the transmission, use new self-locking bolts and make sure the bracket is level before tightening them. Torque the shift rod bracket bolts to 16.5 ft. lbs. except on the M3, which uses an aluminum bracket. On the M3, torque these bolts to 8 ft. lbs.

e. Install the clutch slave cylinder with the bleed screw downward.

f. When installing the driveshaft center bearing, preload it forward 0.157–0.236 in. Check the driveshaft alignment with an appropriate tool such as BMW 26 1 030. Replace the nuts and then torque the center mount bolts to 16–17 ft. lb.

g. Torque the flexible coupling bolts to 83–94 ft. lb.

### *1983–84 533i, 633CSi, and 733i, All 525i, 535i, 635CSi, M5 and M6*

1. Disconnect the negative battery cable. Raise the car and support it securely. Disconnect and lower the exhaust system to provide clearance for transmission removal. Remove the heat shield brace and transmission heat shield.

2. Support the driveshaft and then unscrew the driveshaft coupling at the rear of the transmission. Use a wrench on both the nut and the bolt.

3. Working at the front of the driveshaft center bearing, unscrew the screw-on type ring type connector which attaches the driveshaft to the center bearing. Then, unbolt the center bearing mount. Bend the driveshaft down and pull it off the centering pin. If the car has a vibration damper, turn it and pull it back over the output flange before pulling the driveshaft off the guide pin. Suspend it from the car.

4. Pull off the wires for the backup light switch. Unscrew the passenger compartment console to disconnect it from the top of the transmission by removing the 2 self-locking bolts. Discard these and purchase replacements.

5. Pull out the locking clip, and disconnect the shift rod at the rear of the transmission. Take care to keep all the washers.

6. If the transmission is linked to the shift lever with an arm, use a screwdriver to lift the spring out of the holder on the bracket and then raise the arm. Pull out the shift shaft bolt.

7. If the car has a flywheel housing cover (semi-circular in shape), remove the mounting bolts and remove the cover.

8. If the car has DME, the speed sensor and reference mark sensor on the flywheel housing must be disconnected. Note their locations. The speed sensor goes in the upper bore, marked D. The reference mark sensor, which has a ring, goes in the lower bore, marked B. Check the O-rings for the sensors and install new ones if they are damaged.

9. Support the transmission securely. Then, unbolt and remove the rear transmission crossmember.

10. Remove the upper and lower attaching nuts and remove the clutch slave cylinder, supporting it so the hydraulic line need not be disconnected. Disconnect the reverse gear backup light switch nearby, and pull the wires out of the holders.

11. Unscrew the bolts fastening the transmission to the bell housing, using an angled box wrench. On late model cars there are some Torx® bolts; use a special Torx® wrench for these. Pull the transmission rearward until the input shaft has disengaged from the clutch disc and then lower and remove it.

**To install:**

12. To install the transmission, first put it in gear. Insert the guide sleeve of the input shaft into the clutch pilot bearing carefully. Turn the output shaft to rotate the front of the input shaft until the splines line up and it engages the clutch disc.

Perform the remaining portions of the procedure in reverse of removal, observing the following points:

a. Make sure the arrows on the rear crossmember point forward.

b. Preload the center bearing mount forward of its most natural position 0.079–0.157 in. On 7 Series cars with the M30 B35 engine only, and 6 Series cars with the 265/6 transmission (no integral clutch housing), preload the bearing 0.157–0.236 in.

c. In tightening the driveshaft screw on ring, use special Tool No. 26 1 040 or equivalent.

d. When reconnecting the nuts and bolt at the transmission coupling, replace the nuts with new ones and turn only the nut, holding the bolts stationary.

e. Make sure DME sensor faces are clean. Coat the sensor outside diameters with Molykote Longterm 2® or equivalent.

f. If the car has a shift arm (Step 6), lubricate the bolt with a light layer of Molykote Longterm 2® or equivalent.

g. Observe these torque figures in ft. lbs:

Transmission to bell housing—52–58 ft. lbs.

Rear/Top transmission Torx® bolts—46–58 ft. lbs.

Center mount to body—16–17 ft. lbs.

Front joint-to-transmission—83–94 ft. lbs.

### *735i and 735iL*

1. Disconnect the negative battery cable. Remove the exhaust system. Remove the attaching bolts and remove the heat shield mounted just to the rear of the transmission on the floorpan.
2. Support the transmission securely from underneath. Then, remove the crossmember that supports it at the rear from the body by removing the mounting bolts on both sides.
3. Using wrenches on both the bolt heads and on the nuts, remove the bolts passing through the vibration damper and front universal joint at the front of the driveshaft.
4. Remove its mounting bolts and remove the center driveshaft mount. Then, bend the driveshaft down at the center and pull it off the transmission output flange. Keep the sections of the driveshaft from pulling apart and suspend it from the car with wire.
5. Pull out the circlip, slide off the washer, and then pull the shift selector rod off the transmission shift shaft. Disconnect the backup light switch, nearby.
6. Lower the transmission slightly for access. Then, use a screwdriver to lift the spring out of the holder on the bracket and then raise the arm. Pull out the shift shaft bolt.
7. Remove the upper and lower attaching nuts and remove the clutch slave cylinder, supporting it so the hydraulic line need not be disconnected.
8. Unscrew the bolts fastening the transmission to the bell housing. Since these are Torx® bolts; use a special Torx® wrench. Make sure to retain the washer with each bolt to ensure that they can be readily removed later, if necessary. Pull the transmission rearward until the input shaft has disengaged from the clutch disc and then lower and remove the transmission.

**To install:**

9. Install the transmission in position under the vehicle. Align the input shaft and install the transmission. Follow these procedures:

a. Preload the center bearing mount forward of its most natural position 0.157–0.236 in.

b. When reconnecting the nuts and bolt at the transmission coupling, replace the nuts with new ones and turn only the nut, holding the bolts stationary.

c. When reconnecting the shift arm (Step 6), lubricate the bolt with a light layer of Molykote Longterm 2® or equivalent and check the O-ring for crushing, cracks or cuts, replacing it if it is damaged.

d. When installing the clutch slave cylinder, make sure the bleeder screw faces downward.

e. Observe these torque figures:

Center mount to body—16–17 ft. lbs.

Front joint-to-transmission—58.5 ft. lbs.

# CLUTCH

## REMOVAL & INSTALLATION

1. Disconnect the negative battery cable. On cars with DME, remove the heat shield and then the 2 attaching bolts; disconnect the speed and reference mark sensors at the flywheel housing. Mark the plugs for reinstallation.
2. Remove the transmission and clutch housing as described earlier in this chapter.
3. On late model 6 cylinder cars, a Torx® socket is required. If the car has a 265/6 transmission (without an integral clutch housing), remove the clutch housing.
4. Prevent the flywheel from turning, using a locking tool.
5. Loosen the mounting bolts one after another gradually (1–1½ turns at a time) to relieve tension from the clutch.
6. Remove the mounting bolts, clutch, and drive plate. Coat the splines of the transmission input shaft with Molykote® Longterm 2, Microlube® GL 2611, or equivalent. Make sure the clutch pilot bearing, located in the center of the crankshaft, turns easily.
7. Check the clutch driven disc for excess wear or cracks. Check the integral torsional damping springs (used with lighter flywheels only) for tight fit (so they cannot rattle or become dislocated). Inspect the rivets to make sure they are all tight. Check the flywheel to make sure it is not scored, cracked, or burned, even at a small spot. Use a straight edge to make sure the contact surface is true. Replace any defective parts.

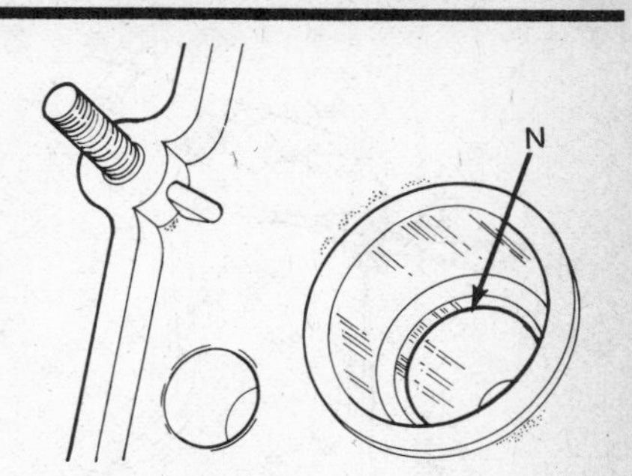


**Pack the groove ("N") with Molykote® Longterm 2 or equivalent before installing the transmission used on the 733i/735i, and 633CSi/35CSi/M6**

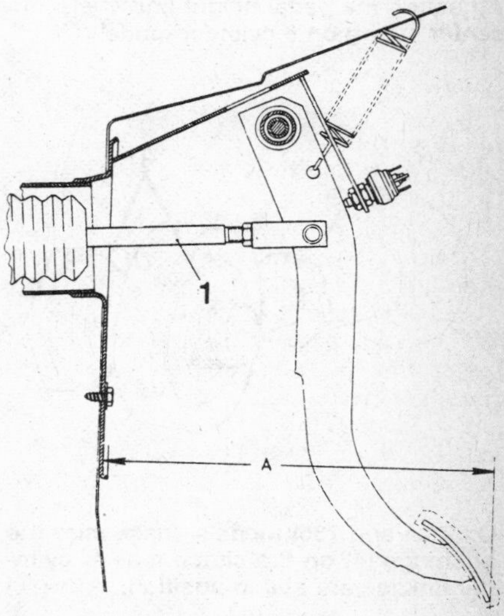


**Adjusting the pedal height on the 320i**

| Models | Dimension "A" (in.) | Dimension "B" (in.) |
|---|---|---|
| 733i, | 1.358 | 10.472–10.787 |
| 735i, | — | 10.433–10.827 |
| 633CSi, 635CSi, M6 | 1.358 | 10.669–11.102 |
| 528e, 524td, 533i, 535i | 1.358 | 9.843–10.276 |

**To install:**

8. To install, fit the new clutch plate and disc in place and install the mounting bolts.
9. When installing the clutch retaining bolts turn them in gradually to evenly tighten the clutch disc and to prevent warpage.

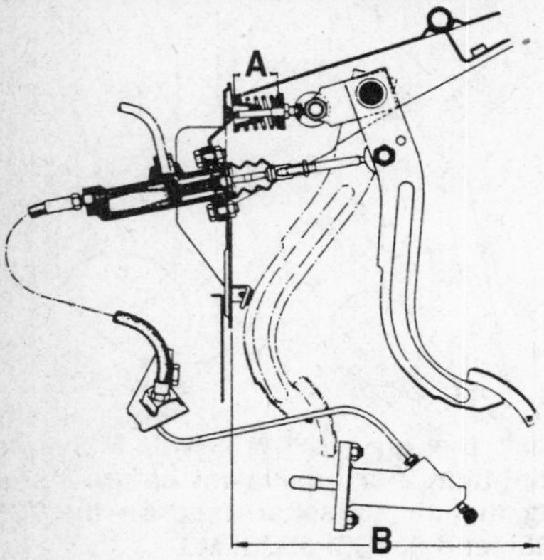


Adjusting the pedal height and over-center spring on 6 cylinder model

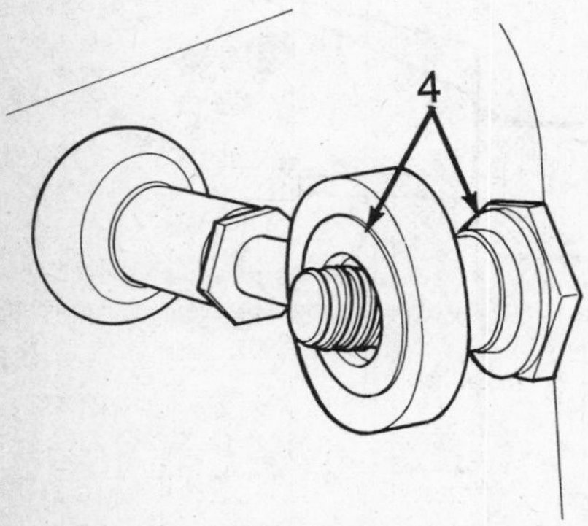


On 733i and 735i models, make sure the bushings (4) on the clutch master cylinder linkage are still in position.

10. Install the transmission and the clutch housing.
11. On vehicles equipped, install the speed and reference mark sensors. Install the heat shield.
12. Note that on late model 6 cylinder engines, the clutch pressure plate must fit over dowel pins. Torque the clutch mounting bolts to 16–17 ft. lbs., 17–19 ft. lbs. 1983–88 3.3L and 3.5L engines.

### PEDAL HEIGHT AND OVER-CENTER SPRING ADJUSTMENTS

#### *All 6 Cylinder Models Except 325, 325e, 325i, 325is and 325iX*

Measure the length of the over-center spring (Dimension "A") and, if necessary, loosen the locknut and rotate the shafts as necessary to get the proper clearance. Measure the distance (Dimension "B") from the firewall to the tip of the clutch pedal and move the pedal in or out, if necessary, by loosening the locknut and rotating the shaft. Specifications for the various models are shown below:

#### *All 4 Cylinder Models and 325, 325e, 325i, 325iS and 325iX*

Measure the distance between the bottom edge of the clutch pedal and the firewall. It should be 9.920–10.197 in. except on 325 models built in years up to 1986. On 325 up to 1986–9.961–10.394 (1987–90 325 models and M3 do not require clutch pedal adjustment. If out of specification, loosen the locknut and rotate the piston rod to correct it.

## Clutch Master Cylinder

### REMOVAL & INSTALLATION

1. Remove the necessary trim panel or carpet.
2. On the 320i, disconnect the accelerator cable and pull it forward out of the engine firewall.
3. Disconnect the pushrod at the clutch pedal.
4. Remove the cap on the reservoir tank. On some models, there is a clutch master cylinder reservoir, while on others there is a common reservoir shared with the brake master cylinder. Remove the float container (if equipped). Remove the screen (if equipped) and remove enough brake fluid from the tank until the level drops below the refill line or the connection for the filler pipe, if there is one.
5. Disconnect the coolant expansion tank without removing the hoses on models 733i, 735i and 735iL (latest models with the M30 B35 engine do not require this).
6. Remove the lower/left instrument panel trim. Then, remove the retaining nut from the end of the master cylinder actuating rod where the bolt passes through the pedal mechanism.
7. Disconnect the line to the slave cylinder and the fluid fill line going to the top of the master cylinder. Remove the retaining bolts and remove the master cylinder from the firewall.
8. Install the clutch master cylinder in position. On all models the piston rod bolt should be coated with Molykote® Longterm 2 or equivalent. Make sure all bushings remain in position. Bleed the system and adjust the pedal travel with the pushrod to 6 in.

## Clutch Slave Cylinder

### REMOVAL & INSTALLATION

1. Remove enough brake fluid from the reservoir until the level drops below the refill line connection.
2. Remove the circlip or retaining bolts depending on the model and pull the unit down.
3. Disconnect the line and remove the slave cylinder.
4. Install the slave cylinder on the transmission. On the 325 Series and M3, if the engine uses the 2-section flywheel, make sure a larger cylinder with a diameter of 0.874 in. is used instead of the usual cylinder (diameter 0.809 in.). Make sure to install the cylinder with the bleed screw facing downward. When installing the front pushrod, coat it with Molykote® Longterm 2 or equivalent anti-seize compound. Bleed the system.

### BLEEDING THE HYDRAULIC CLUTCH SYSTEM

1. Fill the reservoir.
2. Connect a bleeder hose from the bleeder screw to a container filled with brake fluid so that air cannot be drawn in during bleeding procedures.
3. Pump the clutch pedal about 10 times and then hold it down.
4. Open the bleeder screw and watch the stream of escaping fluid. When no more bubbles escape, close the bleeder screw and tighten it.
5. Release the clutch pedal and repeat the above procedure until no more bubbles can be seen when the screw is opened.
6. If this procedure fails to produce a bubble-free stream:
   a. Pull the slave cylinder off the transmission without disconnecting the fluid line.

**NOTE: Do not depress the clutch pedal while the slave cylinder is dismounted.**

   b. Depress the pushrod in the cylinder until it hits the internal stop. Then, reinstall the cylinder.

# AUTOMATIC TRANSMISSION

### REMOVAL & INSTALLATION

#### *3 Speed*

1. Disconnect the negative battery cable. Disconnect the accelerator cable.
2. On the 4 cylinder engine remove all of the transmission mounting bolts which are accessible from above.
3. Detach the oil filler neck and drain the oil.
4. On 4 cylinder engines remove the exhaust pipe support bracket and separate the pipe from the exhaust manifold. On the 318i and 325, remove the

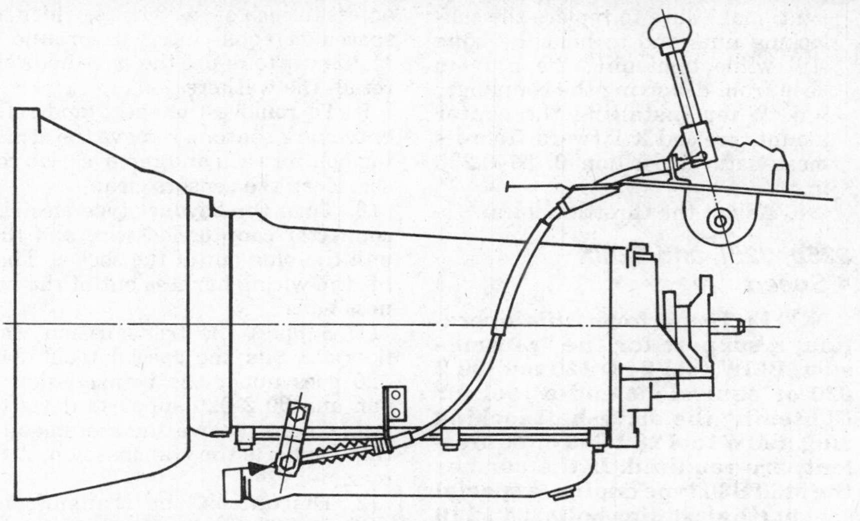

Adjusting the automatic transmission selector lever—733i and 735i

Remove the 4 torque convertor retaining bolts

exhaust system and detach the heat shield.

5. On all 6 cylinder engines except model 733i, remove the entire exhaust system.

6. Detach the oil cooler lines from the transmission and drain fluid.

7. Disconnect the propeller shaft at the transmission, On model 733i, use special clamping tool. On the 318i and 325, disconnect the selector rod.

8. Disconnect the speedometer cable.

9. Remove the heat guard and center bearing and bend down and pull off the propeller shaft.

10. Remove the torque converter cover and remove the 4 bolts that attach the torque converter to the drive plate. Turn the engine for this procedure, using the vibration damper.

**NOTE: On 6 cylinder models, the speed transmitter and reference transmitter must be unbolted and removed from the flywheel housing. For installation, the speed transmitter faces the gear ring. The reference transmitter has a plug with a grey ring and faces the flywheel. The engine will not start if the plugs are mixed up. Coat both with anti-seize compound before installing. Make sure their tips are clean.**

11. Support the transmission and disconnect the crossmember at the body.

12. Remove the remaining transmission mounting bolts.

13. Separate the transmission from the engine and take off the torque converter at the same time. On 733i, 735i and 735iL models, this is done by removing the protective grill on the side of the converter housing and gently prying it toward the transmission as the transmission is pulled rearward. On the 318i, lower the transmission onto the front axle carrier. Remove the grill from the torque converter housing and gently pry the torque converter backwards as the transmission is pulled off.

**To install:**

14. Install the transmission in position under the vehicle. Push the torque converter back against the stop on the main transmission and rotate it to align bolt holes with the drive plate holes before installing.

15. On 733i, 735i and 735iL models, drive connections on the front of the converter must be indented inside the converter housing at least 0.354 in.

16. Use new nuts on the driveshaft flexible coupling. Torque drive plate bolts to 16–17 ft. lb.

17. Install the exhaust suspension without twisting. When installing the propeller shaft preload the center bearing by 0.08 in. in the forward direction.

18. Make sure the torque converter

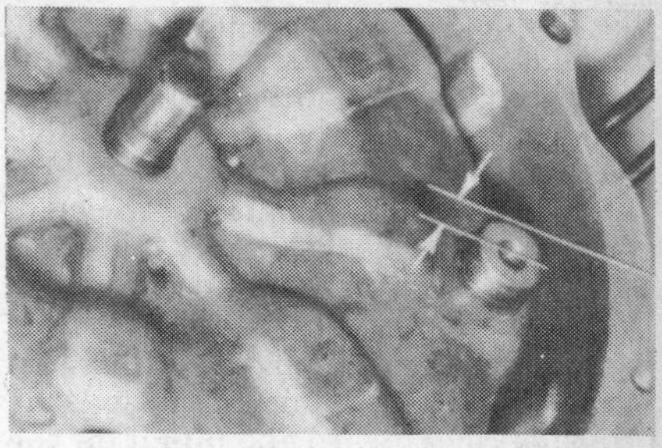

The torque converter is installed correctly if the drive shell mounting parts are located underneath the converter housing

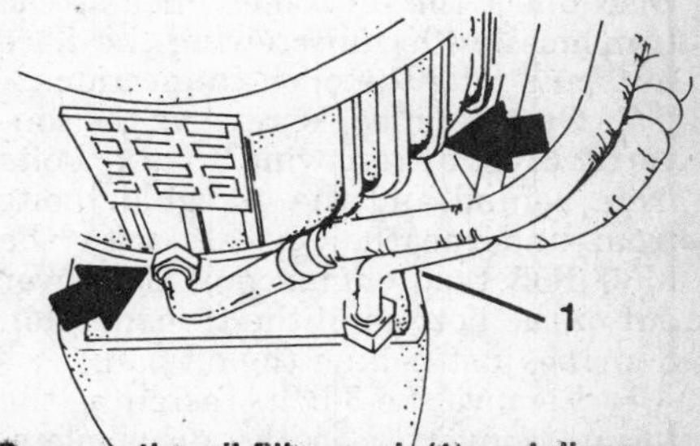


Remove the oil filler neck (1) and disconnect the arrowed hoses to drain fluid from the 4HP–22 transmission

is positioned correctly before installing. Replenish drained fluid with new fluid, only.

### *4 Speed Except 325e, 325i, and 325iX*

**NOTE: To perform this operation, a support for the transmission, BMW tool 24 0 120 and 00 2 020 or equivalent and a tool for tightening the driveshaft locking ring, BMW tool 26 1 040 or equivalent are required. If the car has the M30 B35 type engine, a special socket (that retains bolts) 24 1 110 or equivalent will be needed.**

1. Disconnect the battery ground cable. On both gas and diesel engines, loosen the throttle cable adjusting nuts, release the cable tension, and disconnect the cable at the throttle lever. Then, remove (and retain) the nuts, and pull the cable housing out of the bracket.

2. Disconnect the exhaust system at the manifold and hangers, and lower it out of the way. Remove the hanger that runs across under the driveshaft. Remove the exhaust heat shield from under the center of the car.

3. Support the transmission via a floorjack and the special tools. 24 0 120 goes under the transmission oil pan and 00 2 020 supports it via the jack. Then, remove the crossmember that supports the transmission at the rear.

4. Remove the driveshaft coupling through bolts and nuts or the CV-joint through bolts and nuts. Either type is located right at the rear of the transmission. Discard used self-locking coupling nuts. Keep the CV-joint clean, and replace its gasket.

5. Unscrew the transmission locking ring at the center mount (if equipped). Then, remove the bolts and remove the center mount. Bend the propshaft downward and pull it off the centering pin. Suspend it with wire from the underside of the car.

6. Drain the transmission oil and discard it. Remove the oil filler neck. Disconnect the oil cooler lines at the transmission by unscrewing the flare nuts and plug the open connections.

7. On most models, remove the converter cover by removing 3 Torx® bolts from behind and the 4 regular bolts from underneath. On cars with the M30 B35 type engine pull the cover out of the bottom of the transmission housing, just behind the oil pan.

8. Remove the 3 bolts fastening the torque converter to the drive plate, turning the flywheel as necessary to gain access from below. Use a special socket (that retains the bolts) 24 1 110 or equivalent on cars with the M30 B35 type engine.

9. On cars so-equipped, remove the guard for the speed and reference mark sensors. Remove the attaching bolt for each and remove each sensor (the diesel only has a reference mark sensor). Keep the sensors clean.

10. Disconnect the shift cable by loosening the locknut fastening it to the shift lever and disconnecting the cable at the cable housing bracket.

11. If the transmission has an electrical connection, turn the bayonet fastener to the left to release the connection, disconnect it, and pull the wire out of the ties.

12. Lower the transmission as far as possible. Then, remove all the Torx® or standard type bolts attaching the transmission to the engine.

13. Remove the small grill from the bottom of the transmission. Then press the converter off with a large screwdriver passing through this opening while sliding the transmission out.

**To install:**

14. Install the transmission under the vehicle and raise it into position. Observe the following points:

a. Make sure the converter is fully installed onto the transmission—so the ring on the front is inside the edge of the case.

b. When reinstalling the driveshaft, tighten the lockring with a special tool such as 26 1 040.

c. If the driveshaft has a simple coupling (524td), rather than a CV-joint, make sure to replace the self-locking nuts and to hold the bolts still while tightening the nuts to keep from distorting the coupling.

d. When installing the center mount, preload it forward from its most natural position 0.157–0.236 in.

e. Adjust the throttle cables.

### *325e, 325i, and 325iX 4 Speed*

**NOTE: To perform this operation, a support for the transmission, BMW tool 24 0 120 and 00 2 020 or equivalent and a tool for tightening the driveshaft locking ring, BMW tool 26 1 040 or equivalent, are required. If the car has the M30 B35 type engine, a special socket (that retains bolts) 24 1 110 or equivalent will also be needed.**

1. Disconnect the battery ground cable. Loosen the throttle cable adjusting nuts, release the cable tension, and disconnect the cable at the throttle lever. Then, remove (and retain) the nuts, and pull the cable housing out of the bracket.

2. Disconnect the exhaust system at the manifold and hangers, and lower it out of the way. Remove the hanger that runs across under the driveshaft. Remove the exhaust heat shield from under the center of the car.

3. On the 325iX with 4 wheel drive, remove the transfer case from the rear of the transmission as described below.

4. Drain the transmission oil and discard it. Remove the oil filler neck. Disconnect the oil cooler lines at the transmission by unscrewing the flare nuts and plug the open connections.

5. Support the transmission via a floorjack and the special tools. 24 0 120 goes under the transmission oil pan and 00 2 020 supports it via the jack. Separate the torque converter housing from the transmission by removing 3 Torx® bolts with a Torx® screwdriver from behind and the 4 regular bolts from underneath. Retain the washers used with the Torx® bolts.

6. On the 325iX, disconnect the front driveshaft as described below under the procedure for removing the transfer case.

7. Remove bolts attaching the torque converter housing to the engine, making sure to retain the spacer used behind one of the bolts. Then, loosen the 2 mounting bolts for the oil level switch just enough so that the plate can be removed while pushing the switch mounting bracket to one side.

8. Remove the 3 bolts attaching the torque converter to the drive plate. Turn the flywheel as necessary to gain access to each of the 3 bolts, which are spaced at equal intervals around it. Make sure to re-use the same bolts and retain the washers.

9. To remove the speed and reference mark sensors, remove the attaching bolt for each and remove each sensor. Keep the sensors clean.

10. Turn the bayonet type electrical connector counterclockwise and then pull the plug out of the socket. Then, lift the wiring harness out of the harness bails.

11. Support the transmission via a floorjack and the special tools. 24 0 120 goes under the transmission oil pan and 00 2 020 supports it via the jack. Then, remove the crossmember that supports the transmission at the rear.

12. Disconnect the transmission shift rod. Then, remove the nuts and then the through bolts from the damper-type U-joint at the front of the transmission.

13. Unscrew the transmission locking ring at the center mount (if equipped), using the special tool designed for this purpose 26 1 040 or equivalent). Then, remove the bolts and remove the center mount. Bend the propshaft downward and pull it off the centering pin. Suspend it with wire from the underside of the car.

14. Lower the transmission as far as possible. Then, remove all the Torx® or standard type bolts attaching the transmission to the engine.

15. Remove the small grill from the bottom of the transmission. Then press the converter off with a large screwdriver passing through this opening while sliding the transmission out.

**To install:**

16. Install the transmission in position under the vehicle and raise it into position. Observe the following points:

a. Make sure the converter is fully installed onto the transmission—so the ring on the front is inside the edge of the case.

b. When reinstalling the driveshaft, tighten the lockring with a special tool such as 26 1 040.

c. Make sure to replace the self-locking nuts on the driveshaft flexible joint and to hold the bolts still while tightening the nuts to keep from distorting it.

d. When installing the center mount, preload it forward from its most natural position 0.157–0.236 in.

e. When reconnecting the bayonet type electrical connector, make sure that the alignment marks are aligned after the plug it twisted into its final position.

f. When reinstalling the speed and reference mark sensors, inspect

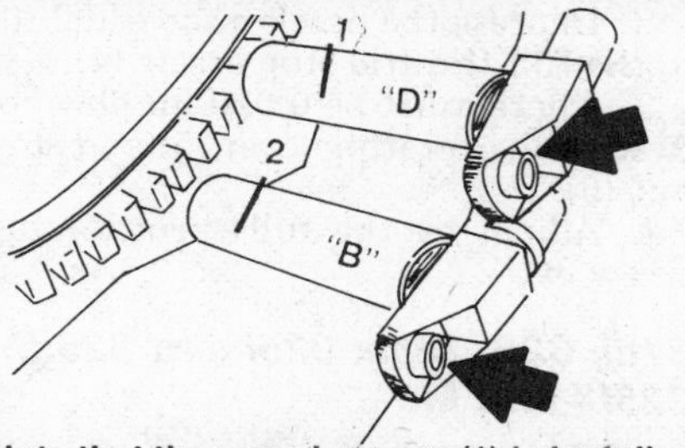


Note that the speed sensor (1) is installed into bore "D" and that the reference mark sensor (2) goes into bore "B"

the O rings used on the sensors and install new ones, if necessary. Make sure to install the speed sensor into the bore marked "D" and the reference mark sensor, which is marked with a ring, into the bore marked "B".

g. Torque the crossmember mounting bolts to 16–17 ft. lbs.

h. If O-rings are used with the transmission oil cooler connections, replace them.

i. Adjust the throttle cables.

## PAN REMOVAL

1. Raise and support the car securely.
2. Remove the drain plug and drain the transmission fluid from the pan.
3. With an open-end wrench, disconnect the oil filler tube where it connects to the bottom of the pan.
4. Remove the attaching bolts and brackets and separate the pan from the transmission. Clean all gasket surfaces.
5. Note the locations of the 2 magnets in the sump. Clean the sump of sediment with clean rags. Replace the magnets. Position a new gasket around the outer edge of the pan.

**To install:**

6. Position the pan on the transmission and install the bolts and brackets. Note that the short legs of the brackets locate inward and under the pan, while the longer, outer legs rest against the transmission housing itself.
7. Tighten the bolts evenly. Torque them to 6–6.5 ft. lbs. Reconnect the filler tube and install the drain plug. Refill the pan with the amount of fluid shown in specifications.
8. Start the engine and run it with the transmission in gear (put the selector in each position for at least a few seconds) for 10 minutes or so to get the transmission fluid hot. Then, with the engine still running, check and correct the fluid level according to the reading on the dipstick.

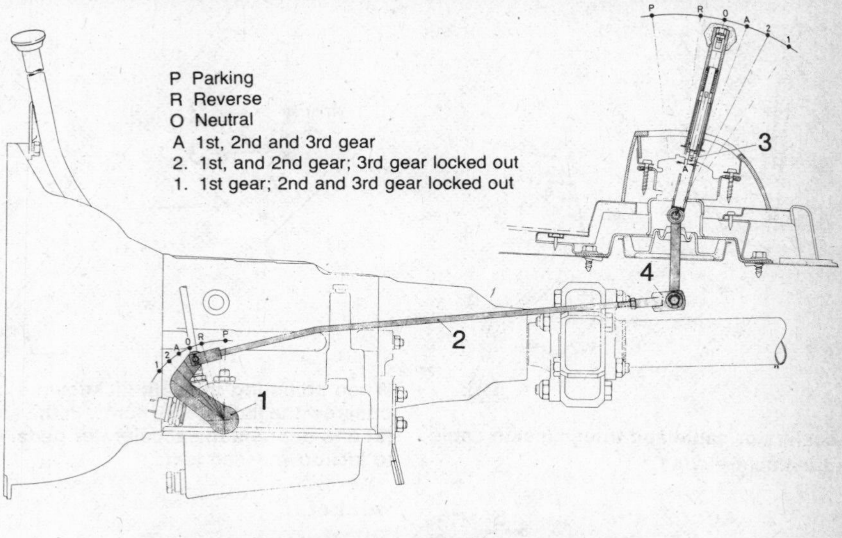


Selector lever adjustment—typical all models

## FILTER SERVICE

**NOTE: It is not possible to perform this procedure without special Torx® tools BMW 00 2 100 and 00 2 050.**

1. Remove the oil pan as described immediately above.
2. Remove all the Torx® head screws from both the center and the outer edges of the screen.
3. Clean the screen in a safe solvent. If the screen has a burnt residue that cannot be cleaned replace the screen.
4. Install the screen and oil pan. Fill the transmission to the correct level with the correct fluid.

## SELECTOR LEVER ADJUSTMENT

### *All Models Except 1983–84 633CSi, 635CSi and 733i, 735i, 735iL, M5 and M6*

1. Detach the selector rod (1) at the selector lever lower section (2).
2. Move the selector lever (3) on the transmission to position O or N.
3. Press the selector lever (4) against the stop (5) on the shift gate.
4. Adjust the length of the selector rod (1) until the pin (6) aligns with the bore in the selector lever lower section (2). Shorten the selector rod length by:

320i – 1 turn
318i, 325e, 325i, 325iX, 524td, 535, 633CSi and 733i – 1–2 turns
530i – 2–2½ turns

**NOTE: If equipped with air conditioning on the 4 cylinder models, plates (7) must be installed between the bearing bracket and float plate and selector rod (1) must be attached in bore (K) of selector lever (3).**

### *1983–84 633CSi, 635CSi, 735i, 735iL, M5 and M6*

1. Move the selector lever to "P" position. Loosen the nut.
2. Push the transmission leverto the forward or park position. Then push the cable rod in the opposite direction; tighten the nut to 7.0–8.5 ft. lbs.

## ACCELERATOR CABLE ADJUSTMENT

### *1983–84 533i, 525i, 535i, 633CSi, 733i and All 635CSi, 735i, 735iL, M5 and M6*

1. On the injection system throttle body, loosen the 2 locknuts at the end of the throttle cable and adjust the cable until there is a play of 0.010–0.030 in.
2. Loosen the locknut and lower the kickdown stop under the accelerator pedal. Have someone depress the accelerator pedal until he can feel the transmission detent. Then, back the kickdown stop back out until it just touches the pedal.
3. Check that the distance from the seal at the throttle body end of the cable housing is at least 1.732 in. from the rear end of the threaded sleeve. If this dimension checks out, tighten all the locknuts.

### *320i*

1. Adjust the accelerator cable at nuts (1) until the accelerator cable eye (2) has a play of 0.008–0.012 in.

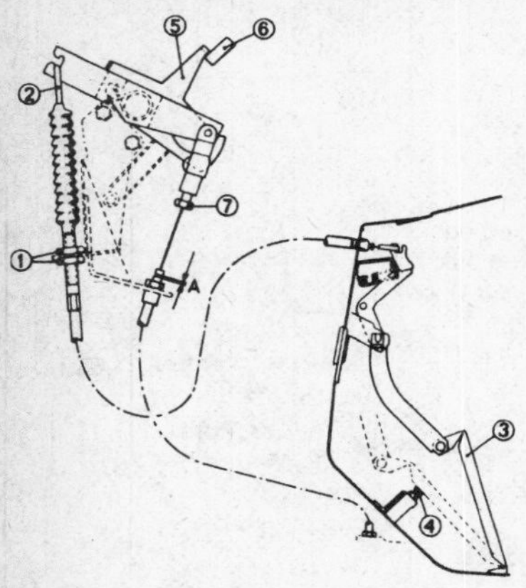

Accelerator cable and transmission cable adjustment—320i

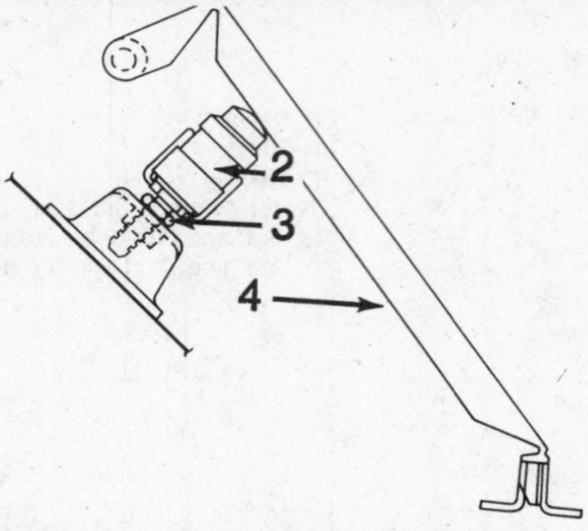

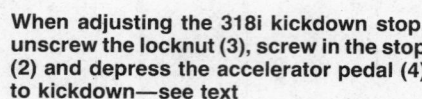

When adjusting the 318i kickdown stop, unscrew the locknut (3), screw in the stop (2) and depress the accelerator pedal (4) to kickdown—see text

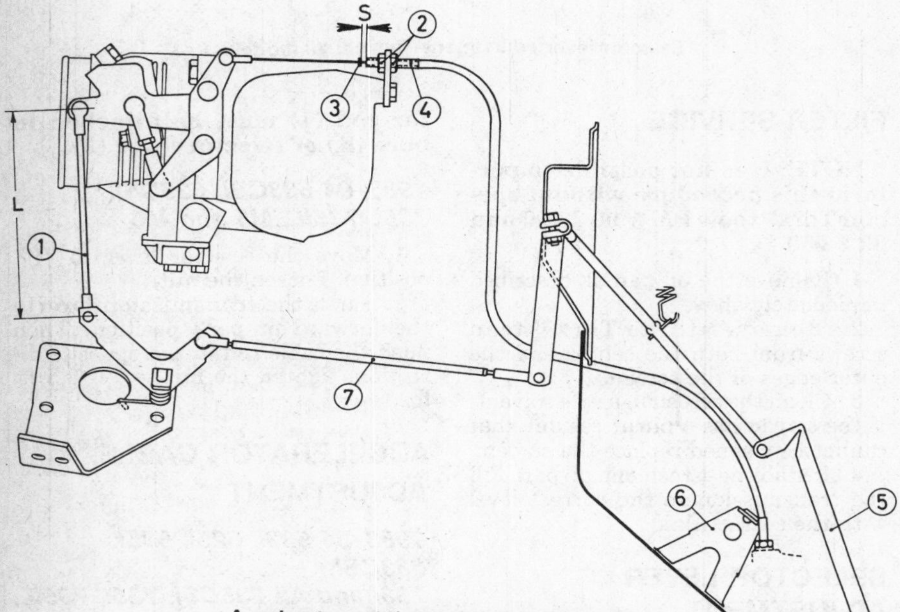

Accelerator cable adjustment—630i, 733i

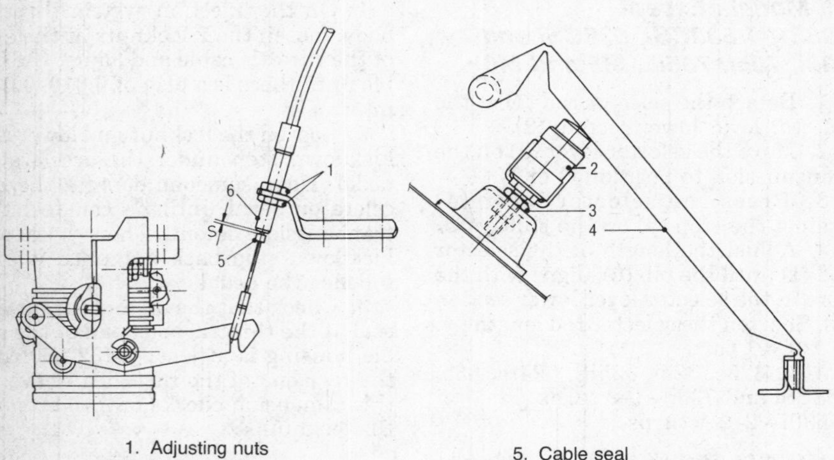

1. Adjusting nuts
2. Kickdown stop
3. Locknut
4. Accelerator pedal
5. Cable seal
6. End of cable sleeve
7. Distance between 5 and 6

Automatic transmission accelerator cable adjustment—528e

2. Depress the accelerator pedal (3) to the full throttle stop screw (4).

3. There must be 0.020 in. play between the operating lever (5) and stop nut (6).

4. Adjust by the full throttle stop screw (4).

### *318i, 325, 325e, 325i and 325iS, 325iX and M3*

1. Adjust the cable for zero tension with the throttle closed and accelerator pedal released.

2. Loosen the locknut on the throttle stop bolt. Now adjust the bolt inward just until it suspends the accelerator pedal at the point where the throttle just reaches wide open position. On automatic transmission equipped cars, make sure the throttle is in full detent position. Now, turn the stop screw 1½ turns lower to get a clearance of 0.020 in. between the accelerator pedal and stop bolt at full throttle. Tighten the locknut.

### *528e*

1. Adjust the freeplay (s) of the cable in N position to 0.010–0.030 in. (0.25–0.75mm). Use cable adjuster nuts (1) to adjust the freeplay.

2. In the passenger compartment, loosen the kickdown switch. Screw in the kickdown stop (2) all the way in the direction of the floor pan.

3. Press down on the accelerator pedal (4) to the transmission pressure point. Unscrew the kickdown stop (2) until it contacts the accelerator pedal.

4. Press the accelerator to the kickdown (wide open throttle position.

5. In kickdown position, the distance (s) must be 1.732 in. (44.0mm). The distance (s) equals the distance from the cable seal (5) to the end of the cable sleeve (6).

## TRANSMISSION CABLE ADJUSTMENT

### *320i*

**NOTE: The accelerator cable must be correctly adjusted.**

1. With the transmission in the **N** position, adjust play to 0.010–0.030 in. with the screw.

2. Depress the accelerator pedal to kickdown stop; play must now be 1.712–2.027 in. Make corrections with screw (4).

### *318i, 325, 325e, 325i, 325iS and M3*

1. Adjust the play in the cable "S" to 0.010–0.030 in. Make sure both cable locknuts are loose.

2. Back off the accelerator pedal

kickdown stop and then depress the accelerator pedal until the transmission just reaches the detent and some resistance is felt.

3. Run the kickdown stop out until it just touches the bottom of the pedal.

4. Depress the accelerator through the detent and hold while measuring distance "S" from the lead seal to the end of the sleeve. It must be at least 1.732 in. Adjust further, if necessary.

5. Tighten all locknuts.

### 524td

1. The engine must be at normal operating temperature so the operating lever on the injection pump rests on the idle stop. Adjust the play between the throttle cable stop and the end of the threads on the cable jacket to 0.010–0.030.

2. Then, loosen the nut that locks the accelerator pedal kickdown stop. Press the pedal down until it reaches the transmission detent. Screw the kickdown stop back out until it just touches the lower side of the accelerator pedal.

3. Press the accelerator pedal down until it has kicked down (extreme position). Make sure the distance measured above is at least 1.732 in. Readjust to obtain this figure, if necessary.

# TRANSFER CASE

## REMOVAL & INSTALLATION

### With Manual Transmission

**NOTE: To perform this procedure, a special, large wrench that locks onto flats on alternate sides of a section of the rear driveshaft is required. Use BMW special tool No. 26 1 060 or an equivalent that is available in the aftermarket.**

1. Disconnect the negative battery cable. Raise the car and support it securely at the 4 corners so it is possible to work underneath it safely. Remove the exhaust system. Unbolt and remove the exhaust system heat shields located behind and below the transfer case.

2. Unscrew the rear section of the driveshaft at the sliding joint located behind the output flange of the transfer case.

3. Hold the through-bolts stationary and remove the self-locking nuts from in front of the flexible coupling at the transfer case output flange. Discard all the self-locking nuts and replace them.

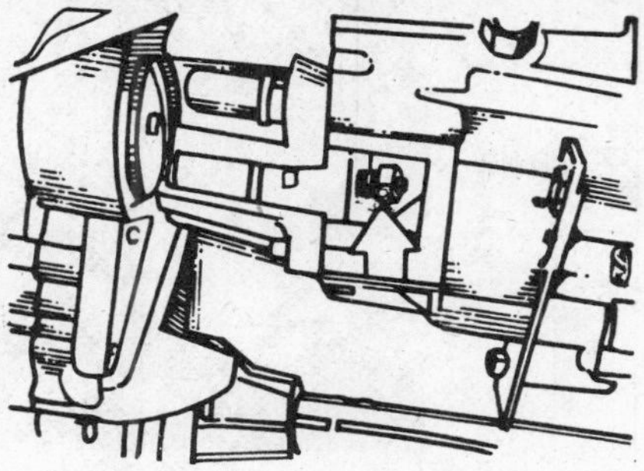

**The arrow shows the location of the flexible coupling linking the transmission output flange with the input flange of the transfer case.**

**CAUTION**

***During the next step, be careful not to let the driveshaft rest on the metal fuel line that crosses underneath it, or the line could be damaged!***

4. Slide the sections of the driveshaft together at the sliding joint and then pull the front of the driveshaft off the centering pin at the transmission output shaft.

5. Remove the nuts and through bolts from the flexible coupling linking the transmission output flange with the short driveshaft linking the transmission and the transfer case.

6. Support the transmission from underneath in a secure manner (supported squarely with a floorjack). Then, mark each of the 4 bolts fastening the crossmember that supports the transmission at the rear to the body (bolts are of different lengths). Remove the crossmember.

7. Lower the transmission/transfer case unit just enough to gain access to the bolts linking the 2 boxes together. Remove the 2 lower and 2 upper bolts. It is possible to gain access to the upper bolts using a socket wrench with a U-joint and extension.

8. There is a protective cap on the forward driveshaft where it links up with the transfer case. The cap is made of a brittle material, so it *must be handled carefully*. Gently slide the cap forward until is free of the transfer case.

9. Now, slide the transfer case to the rear so it can be separated from both the transmission and the forward driveshaft. When it is free, remove it.

**To install:**

10. Install the transfer case under the vehicle and raise it into position, bearing the following points in mind:

a. Inspect the dowel holes locating the transfer case with the transmission and the guide hole for the output shaft where it slides into the transfer case to make sure these parts will be properly located. Lubricate the guide pin and the splines of the front driveshaft section with grease.

b. When fitting the transfer case onto the transmission, check to make sure the output flange of the transmission is properly aligned with the flexible coupling. Put the through-bolts through the flexible coupling and then install and torque the nuts to 65 ft. lbs. while holding the bolts stationary, rather than turning them.

c. When reconnecting the transfer case to the gearbox, torque the bolts to 30 ft. lbs.

d. Before fitting the driveshaft back onto the rear of the transmission, retain the seal in the protective cap by applying grease to it.

e. Torque the transmission crossmember bolts to 17 ft. lbs.

f. Check the fluid level and fill with the recommended lubricant.

### With Automatic Transmission

**NOTE: To perform this procedure, a special, large wrench that locks onto flats on alternate sides of a section of the rear driveshaft is required. Use BMW special tool No. 26 1 060 or an equivalent that is available in the aftermarket.**

1. Disconnect the negative battery cable. Raise the car and support it securely at the 4 corners so it will be possible to work underneath it safely. Remove the exhaust system. Unbolt and remove the exhaust system heat shields located behind and below the transfer case.

2. Unscrew the rear section of the driveshaft at the sliding joint located behind the output flange of the transfer case.

3. Hold the through-bolts stationary and remove the self-locking nuts from in front of the flexible coupling at the transfer case output flange. Discard all the self-locking nuts and replace them.

**CAUTION**

***During the next step, be careful not to let the driveshaft rest on the metal fuel line that crosses underneath it, or the line could be damaged.***

4. Slide the sections of the driveshaft together at the sliding joint and then pull the front of the driveshaft off the centering pin at the transmission output shaft.

5. Remove the nuts and through bolts from the flexible coupling linking the transmission output flange with the short driveshaft linking the transmission and the transfer case.

6. Note the locations of all the washers and then loosen the retaining nut and disconnect the range selector

lever cable at the transmission by pulling out the pin. Be careful not to bend the cable in doing this. Then, loosen the nuts that position the cable housing onto the transmission and slide the cable housing backward so it can be separated from the bracket on the transmission housing.

7. There is a protective cap on the forward driveshaft where it links up with the transfer case. The cap is made of a brittle material, so it *must be handled carefully*. Gently slide the cap forward until is free of the transfer case.

8. Remove the drain plug in the bottom of the pan and drain the transmission fluid.

9. Support the transmission from underneath in a secure manner (supported squarely with a floorjack). Then, mark each of the 4 bolts fastening the crossmember that supports the transmission at the rear to the body (bolts are of different lengths). Remove the crossmember.

10. Remove the nine nuts fastening the transfer case to the transmission housing. Note the location of the wiring holder so it will be possible to reinstall it on the same bolt.

11. Slide the transfer case to the rear and off the transmission.

**To install:**

12. Install the transfer case under the vehicle and raise it into position, bearing the following points in mind:

a. Inspect the sealing surfaces as well as the dowel holes in the transfer case to make sure they will seal and locate properly. Clean the sealing surfaces and replace the gasket.

b. When sliding the transfer case back onto the transmission, turn the front driveshaft section slightly to help make the splines mesh.

c. When reconnecting the shift cable, inspect the rubber mounts and replace any that are cut, crushed, or cracked. Adjust the shift cable.

d. Before fitting the driveshaft back onto the rear of the transmission, retain the seal in the protective cap by applying grease to it.

e. When fitting the transfer case onto the transmission, check to make sure the output flange of the transmission is properly aligned with the flexible coupling. Put the through-bolts through the flexible coupling and then install and torque the nuts to 65 ft. lbs. while holding the bolts stationary, rather than turning them.

f. Torque the bolts holding the transfer case to the transmission to 65 ft. lbs.

g. Torque the transmission crossmember bolts to 17 ft. lbs.

h. Check the fluid level and fill with the recommended lubricant.

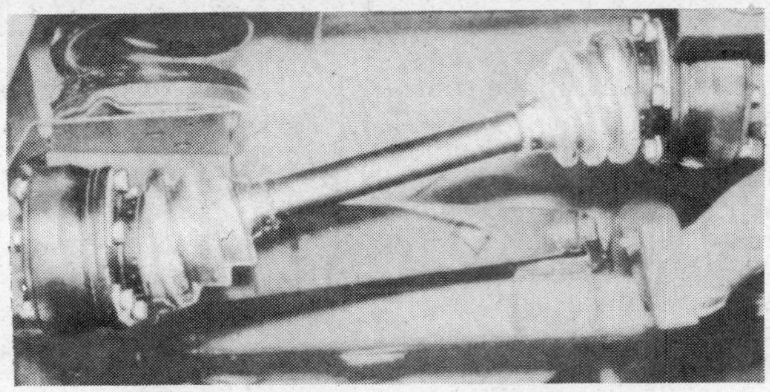

Constant velocity type output shaft

# DRIVE AXLE

## Halfshaft

### REMOVAL & INSTALLATION

#### *Except 4WD Front Axle—325iX*

1. Detach the output shaft at the final drive and drive flange.

2. On the 733i, support the control arm as the spring strut and shock absorber are detached.

3. The spring strut serves as a retaining strap and the trailing arm must be supported if the spring strut is detached.

4. Replace the bellows as follows:

a. Take off the sealing cover.

b. Remove the circlip.

c. Unscrew the clamp on the dust cover. Take off the dust cover.

d. Press off the inner cover.

e. Press the output shaft out of the constant velocity joint. Make sure in doing this that the bearing inner race is supported.

f. Place the dust cover and inside cover on the output shaft.

g. Coat the splined threads with Loctite® 270 or equivalent. Keep the compound out of ball races.

h. Press the joint and cap on and install the circlip.

i. Pack the joint and bellows with CV-joint grease. Clean the sealing surfaces to remove grease. Then, coat the larger diameter end of the bellows with an adhesive and secure with new clamps. Seal the cover with Curil or equivalent and install it.

#### *4WD Front Axle—325iX*

**NOTE: A number of special tools are required to perform this operation. Use the BMW factory numbers given to shop for these from factory sources, or to cross-reference similar tools that may be available in the aftermarket. Use 33 4 050 and 00 5 500 to drive in a new lockplate for the brake disc. The tie rod must be pressed off with 342 2 070. Control arms are pressed off with 31 2 160. Use 33 2 112 and 33 2 113 to press the output shafts out of the brake discs and 33 2 112, 33 2 124 and 33 4 042 to press them back in. On the left side, the output shaft is pulled out of the drive axle with 31 5 011 and 30 31 581. On the right side, 31 5 011 and 31 5 012 are used to pull the output shaft out of the axle.**

1. Raise the car and support it securely. Remove the front wheels. Remove the drain plug and drain the lube oil from the front axle.

2. Lift out the lockplate in the center of the brake disc with a screwdriver. Then, unscrew the collar nut.

3. Remove the attaching nut from each tie rod and then press the rod off the steering knuckle with 33 2 070.

4. Remove the retaining nut and then press the control arm off the steering knuckle on either side.

5. Mount 33 2 112 and 33 2 113 to the brake disc with 2 wheel bolts. Press the output shaft out of the center of the steering knuckle on that side. Repeat on the other side.

6. To remove the drive axle from the differential on the left side: Install special tool 31 5 011 by bolting it together around the axle so that the ring on its inner diameter fits into the groove on the shaft. Install 30 31 581 onto the shaft so it will rest against the housing ang the bolt heads of 31 5 011 will rest against it. Screw the 2 bolts in alternately in small increments to get even pressure on the shaft, pulling it out of the differential.

7. To remove the drive axle on the right side: Install 31 5 012 on the diameter of the shaft directly against the housing. Install 31 5 011 by bolting it together around the axle so that the ring on its inner diameter fits into the groove on the shaft. Screw the 2 bolts in alternately in small increments to get even pressure on the shaft, pulling it out of the differential.

**To install:**

8. Install the halfshafts, bearing the

following points in mind:

a. Install the shafts into the housing until the circlip inside engages in the groove of the shaft. It may be necessary to install the removal tool and tap against it with a plastic-headed hammer to drive the shaft far enough into the housing.

b. Before installing the shafts into the steering knuckle, coat the spline with light oil.

c. When installing the control arms onto the steering knuckle, torque the nut to 61.5 ft. lbs. and use a new cotter pin. When installing the tie rod onto the steering knuckle, torque to 61.5 ft. lbs. and use a new self-locking nut.

d. Drive a new lockplate into the brake disc with 33 4 050 and 00 5 500. Torque the nut to 181 ft. lbs.

e. Replace the drain plug and refill the final drive unit with the required lubricant.

### CV-JOINT OVERHAUL

**NOTE: For all CV-Joint overhaul procedures, please refer to "CV-Joint Overhaul" in the unit repair section.**

## Driveshaft and U-Joints

### REMOVAL & INSTALLATION

#### *320i, 635Csi, 1984–86 733i and 735i*

1. On the 5 and 6 series cars, remove the entire exhaust system. On the 1984–86 733i and 735i remove just the muffler.
2. On the 320i, detach the outer pipe at the manifold and support it at the transmission.
3. Remove the heat shield near the fuel tank, if so equipped. On 1984–86 733i, 735i, this requires loosening the automatic transmission rear crossmember bolts slightly on the right side for clearance. On 6 and 7 Series models now also use BMW Special Tool 26 1 040 or equivalent to loosen the threaded sleeve attaching the rear of the driveshaft to the front of the center bearing.
4. Disconnect the propeller shaft at the transmission by removing the nuts and bolts from the flexible coupling. If the car has a vibration damper where the shaft connects to the transmission, turn the damper 60 degrees counterclockwise and remove it with the rubber coupling.

**NOTE: On 733i, install a special clamping tool (BMW-261011) or equivalent around the coupling and remove the bolts.**

5. Loosen the center bearing bolts and remove them.
6. On 733i, with manual transmission, loosen the crossmember and push the left end forward.
7. Disconnect the propeller shaft at the final drive. Bend the propeller shaft down and pull out.

**To install:**

8. Installation is the reverse of removal.
9. The propeller shaft is balanced as an assembly and must only be renewed as a complete assembly.
10. Align the driveshaft with a gauge (BMW–21–1–000) (use 26 1 000 on 1984–86 733i, 735i) or equivalent by moving the center bearing sideways or by placing washers underneath the center bearing (this is not required on 6 Series cars).
11. On the 733i, remove the special coupling tool only after the nuts have been tightened to prevent stress on the coupling.
12. Preload the center bearing by 0.078 in. in the forward direction. (.157–.236 in. on 6 Series cars).
13. Wherever self-locking nuts are used, replace them. Hold the nut or bolt in place where is runs through a U-joint, and torque at the opposite end—where the driveshaft flange is located. Check the center bearing for lubrication and if it's dry, lubricate with Molykote® Longterm 2 or equivalent.

#### *325iX (4WD)*

**CAUTION**

***Never drive the car using front wheel drive when the rear propeller shaft is removed, or the lockup system in the transfer case may be damaged.***

1. Remove the exhaust system. Remove both exhaust system heat shields.
2. Loosen the threaded sleeve near the front of the driveshaft with 26 2 060 oor 26 1 040 or the equivalent. Turn the sleeve several turns outward, but do not disconnect it entirely.
3. Disconnect the driveshaft at the output flange of the transfer case by removing the nuts and through bolts.
4. Disconnect the driveshaft at the final drive by removing the nuts and through bolts.

**CAUTION**

***Make sure the drive axle does not rest on the fuel line that runs across under it.***

5. Slide the sections of the driveshaft together and then slide it out of the centering pin on the output flange of the transfer case. Remove it from the car.

**To install:**

6. Install the driveshaft in reverse order, bearing these points in mind:

a. Wherever self-locking nuts are used, replace them.

b. Hold the nut or bolt in place where is runs through a U-joint, and torque at the opposite end—where the driveshaft flange is located.

c. Check the center bearing for lubrication and if it's dry, lubricate with Molykote® Longterm 2 or equivalent.

#### *1987–90 735i and 735iL*

**NOTE: If the car has a front universal joint, use special tools 24 0 120 and 00 2 020 to support the transmission during this operation.**

1. Remove the exhaust system. Remove the heat shield from the floorpan. Remove the nuts and bolts fastening the propeller shaft to the transmission at the flexible coupling. Replace the self-locking nuts.
2. If the car has a front U-joint, support the transmission from underneath with tools 24 0 120 or the equivalent. When the transmission is securely supported, remove the 6 bolts and remove the rear transmission mounting crossmember.
3. Remove the self-locking nuts and then the bolts fastening the driveshaft to the final drive. Replace the self-locking nuts. Remove the propeller shaft, taking care to keep it protected from dirt.
4. Remove the bolts from the crossbrace underneath and remove the center propshaft mount. Then, bend the shaft at the middle and remove it from the car by pulling it off the centering pin on the forward end.

**To install:**

5. Install in reverse order, keeing the following points in mind:

a. Repack the CV joing with approved grease and replace the gasket, if necessary.

b. Check the center bearing for lubrication and if it's dry, lubricate with Molykote® Longterm 2 or equivalent.

c. If the vibration damper at the forward end of the driveshaft must be replaced, turn it 60 degrees to remove it.

d. When remounting the center mount, preload it forward from its most natural position 0.157–0.236 in.

e. Torque U-joint bolts to 52 ft. lbs. and CV-joint bolts to 51 ft. lbs.

#### *528e, 525i, 535i and 633CSi with CV-Joint*

**NOTE: To perform this procedure, procure a set of tools designed to support the transmission via the pan BMW tools 24 0 120 and 00 2 020 or equivalent.**

1. Support the transmission from underneath with the special tools and a floorjack. Remove the nuts and washers from the transmission mounts on top of the rear transmission mounting crossmember. Loosen but do not remove the nuts located underneath which fasten the crossmember to the body. Then, slide this crossmember as far to the rear as it will go.
2. Unscrew the fastening nuts on the forward end of the CV-joint and then discard them.
3. Using a prybar to keep the driveshaft from turning, remove the self locking nuts and bolts fastening the rear of the driveshaft to the final drive.
4. Remove the bolts fastening the center mount to the body. Bend the propshaft down and pull the CV-joint off the transmission flange. Cover the joint to keep it clean.

**To install:**

5. Replace the gasket that fits between the joint bolts. Install in reverse order, keeping these points in mind:
   a. Replace the self-locking nuts used at either end of the shaft.
   b. Preload the center mount forward by forcing the bracket 0.157–0.197 in. forward from the neutral position on 5 Series cars and 0.157–0.236 in. forward on 6 Series cars.

### *318i, 325, 325e, 325i, 325iS and M3*

1. Remove the mufflers. Unscrew and remove the exhaust system heat shield near the fuel tank.
2. Unbolt and remove the cross brace that runs under the driveshaft.
3. Support the transmission. The automatic transmission must be supported by the case and not the pan. BMW makes a jig and support (No. 24 0 120 and 00 2 020) for this. Loosen all transmission support bolts and remove. Remove the transmission rear support crossmember.
4. Lower the manual transmission for clearance. Remove the driveshaft bolts from the front coupling.

**CAUTION**

***Make sure the drive axle does not rest on the fuel line that runs across under it.***

5. Unscrew and remove bolts at the coupling near the final drive.
6. Loosen the threaded sleeve on the driveshaft with a tool such as BMW 26 1 040. Unbolt and remove the center mount.
7. Bend the driveshaft downward and remove it, being careful not to allow it to rest on the connecting line on the fuel tank.

**To install:**

8. Upon installation:
   a. Mount the holder for the oxygen sensor plug.
   b. Make sure the heat shield clears the fuel tank.
   c. Wherever self-locking nuts are used, replace them. On the transmission-end flange, tighten the nuts/bolts only on the flange side, holding the other end stationary.
   d. Preload the center mount to 0.079–0.157 in. in the forward direction on the 318i and 0.157–0.236 in. on other models before tightening the bolts. Torque the mounting bolts to 16 ft. lbs.
   e. Lubricate the center bearing with Molykote® Longterm 2 or equivalent if it is dry.
   f. Make sure to reinstall the bracket for the oxygen sensor plug.
   g. Make sure that there is sufficient clearance between the rear heat shield and fuel tank.

## Front Driveshaft and U-Joints

### REMOVAL & INSTALLATION

### *325iX (4WD)*

**CAUTION**

***Never drive the car with either driveshaft disconnected. This could damage the lock-up mechanism in the transfer case.***

1. Remove the nuts at the front drive axle input flange. Discard the nuts and replace them with new self-locking nuts. Remove the 6 through-bolts.
2. Gently push the driveshaft to the rear. Then, remove the coupling and centering disc from the front drive axle.
3. Pull the driveshaft and protective cap out of the front of the transfer case and remove it.

**To install:**

4. To install, reverse the removal procedure, bearing the following points in mind:
   a. Inspect the cap and seal for the area of the transfer case where the driveshaft engages. Replace parts, if necessary. After engaging the shaft with the transfer case, slide the protective cap back over the front of the transfer case.
   b. Inspect the seal on the output flange for the front drive axle and replace it if necessary.
   c. When reinstalling the coupling at the rear of the front drive axle, make sure the 3 arrows line up with the 3 flange arms.
   d. When installing the bolts and nuts for the front driveshaft coupling, install the bolts and then hold them stationary with a wrench while installing new self locking nuts.

Remove circlip (2) and dust guard (3)

Drive center bearing onto grooved ball bearing

## Center Bearing

### REMOVAL & INSTALLATION

### *All 5, 6, and 7 Series Cars Except 528e, 525i, 535i, 633CSi, M5 and M6 Without Splines*

1. Bend down the driveshaft and pull it out of the centering pin on the transmission.
2. Loosen the threaded bushing. On 1983–1986 733i, 735i and 735iL also remove the felt ring.
3. Mark the driveshaft position on slide with a punch mark and pull the front half of the propeller shaft out of the slide.
4. Remove the circlip and dust guard.
5. Using a standard puller remove the center bearing without the dust guard.
6. Use a puller and remove the grooved ball bearing in the center bearing. On 733i, 735i and 735iL, press the grooved ball bearing into the center mount.
7. Installation is the reverse of removal. Lubricate the splines with Molykote® Longterm 2 or equivalent. Drive the center bearing onto the grooved ball bearing with tool (BMW–24–1–050) or equivalent. On 733i, 735i and 735iL, check the in-

stalled position of the dust guard—it must be flush with the center mount.

### *1987–90 M5 and M6 528e, 525i, 535i and 633CSi Without Splines*

**NOTE: This type of propshaft has the 2 sections bolted together just behind the center bearing. Use a press and a puller to complete this operation.**

1. Remove the propeller shaft as described above. Matchmark the relationship between the forward and rear sections of the shaft at the center bearing.
2. Remove the bolt that fastens the forward U-joint section to the center mount.
3. Using a standard puller remove the center mount and bearing without the dust guard.
4. Press the old bearing out of the mount and press a new one in. Then, use a mandrel 24 1 040 or equivalent to drive the bearing center race onto the driveshaft.
5. Assemble the driveshaft in reverse order, lining up its halves with the matchmarks. Install the bolt fastening the shaft sections together with a locking type of sealer, torquing to 72 ft. lbs.

### *320i*

1. With the propeller shaft removed, mark the shaft's location to the coupling.
2. Remove the circlip and pull out the propeller shaft.
3. Using a standard puller remove the center bearing without its dust cover.
4. Drive the grooved ball bearing out of the center bearing.
5. Installation is the reverse of removal.

### *318i, 325, 325e, 325i, 325iS, 325iX and M3*

1. Remove the driveshaft as described above. Since the shaft is a balanced assembly, matchmark both halves so it can be reassembled in the same position.
2. Unscrew the threaded sleeve (1), and remove the front propshaft section. Remove the washer (2) and rubber ring (3). A BMW special tool is shown, but it is possible to loosen the sleeve with an ordinary wrench, provided a way is carefully devised to hold the propshaft against the torque required to loosen the sleeve without damaging it.
3. Lift out the circlip and remove the dustguard behind it.
4. Pull out the center mount and ball bearing with a puller.

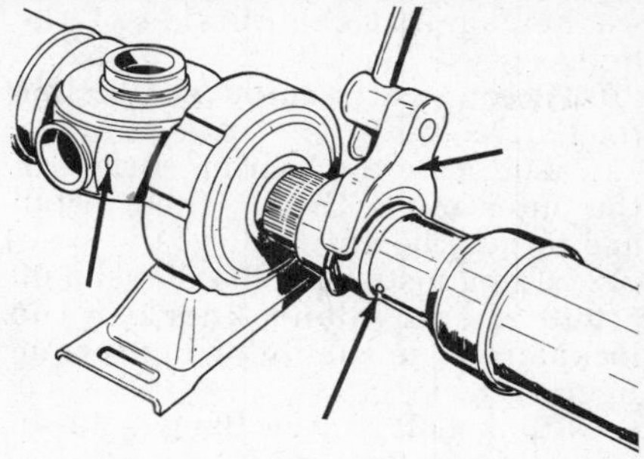

In replacing the center mount on the driveshaft on the 318i, unscrew the threaded sleeve as shown. Matchmark the assembly prior to taking it apart as shown by the arrows.

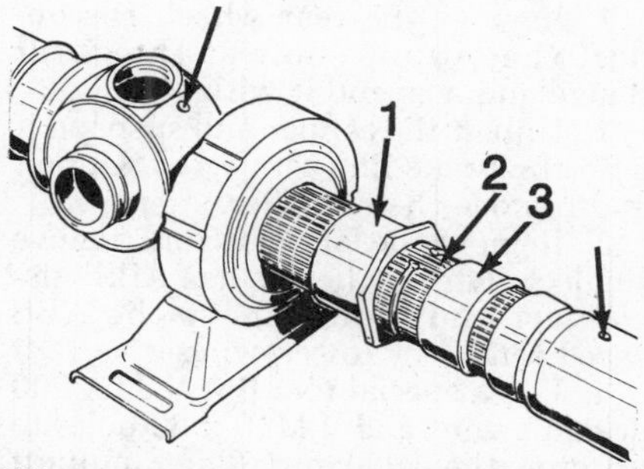


When assembling the driveshaft on the 318i, push on the threaded sleeve (1), washer (2), and rubber ring (3)

Wheel bearing with rear axle shaft removed—6 cylinder models

5. Lay the center mount on a flat plate and press the new ball bearing in with even pressure all around the outer race.
6. Install the dust guard and then drive the center mount onto the splined portion of the shaft. Make sure the dust guard is installed flush with the center mount and that the center mount will operate with adequate clearance.
7. Assemble the shaft with matchmarks aligned. Push on the threaded sleeve, washer, and rubber ring (do not tighten the threaded sleeve yet).
8. Install the driveshaft as described above. Then, tighten the threaded sleeve.

Driving out rear axle shaft—4 cylinder models

## Centering Ring

### REMOVAL & INSTALLATION

1. Fill the center with grease and using a 14mm (0.551 in.) dia. mandrel, drive out the ring.
2. Installation is the reverse of removal.

**NOTE: The shaft ring faces out.**

## Rear Axle Shaft, Wheel Bearings and Seals

### REMOVAL & INSTALLATION

### *6 Cylinder Models Except 325, 325e, 325i, 325iS, 325iX, 1983–84 733i, 735i and 735iL*

1. Remove the wheel.
2. Loosen the brake caliper and leave the brake line connected.
3. Remove the brake disc.
4. Remove the driving flange as follows:
   a. Disconnect the output shaft.
   b. Remove the lockplate.
   c. Loosen the collared nut and pull off the drive flange.
5. Tighten the collared nut and drive off the rear axle shaft.
6. Drive off the wheel bearings and seals toward the outside.
7. Installation is the reverse of removal.

### *320i*

1. Remove the wheel.
2. Remove the cotter pin from the castellated nut.
3. Apply the handbrake.
4. Loosen the castellated nut.
5. Release the handbrake.

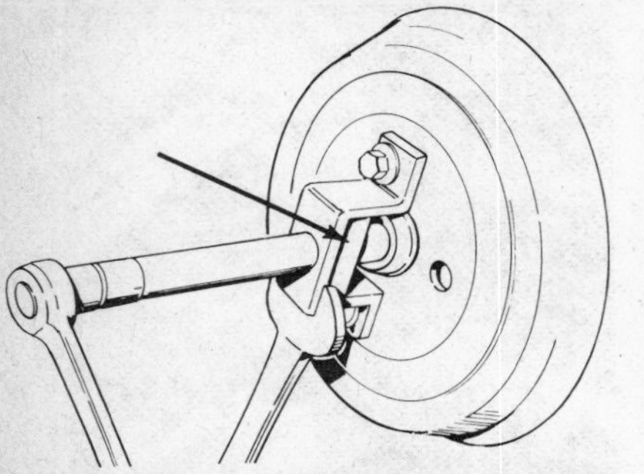

Removing the output shaft on the 318i. Use two wheel bolts to fasten the bridge (33 2 112), and then press the shaft out as shown.

6. Remove the brake drum.
7. Pull off the drive flange with a puller.
8. Disconnect the output shaft and tie it up.
9. Drive out the halfshaft with a plastic hammer using the castellated nut to protect the end of the shaft.
10. Drive out the bearing and sealing ring.
11. Take out the spacer sleeve and shim.
12. Installation is the reverse of removal.

### *318i, 325, 325e, 325i, 325iS, 325iX and M3*

1. Lift out the lockplate and remove the retaining nut from the output flange. Remove the flange.
2. Disconnect the output shaft from the final drive and suspend it.
3. Press out the output shaft with a special tool set 33 2 110 or equivalent. Bolt the bridge to the brake drum (or disc) with 2 wheel bolts and hold it with an open-end wrench. Force the output shaft toward the center of the car via the spindle by turning the threaded portion of the tool.
4. Drive out the rear axle shaft with tool 33 4 010 or equivalent.
5. Lift out the circlip. Then, pull out the wheel bearings with special tool 33 4 040 or equivalent. On models with disc brakes and larger bearings, use 33 4 031.
6. Pull out the seal with a tool such as 33 4 045.
7. If the inner bearing shell is damaged, pull it off with a puller and thrust pad.

**To install:**

8. To install, pull in the wheel bearing assembly, pull in the seal, insert the circlip and then pull in the rear axle shaft, all in reverse of steps above. Use 33 4 040 except on 325e; on that model, use 33 4 049. Install the axle shaft seal with a tool such as 33 4 045.
9. To install the output shaft, screw the threaded spindle into the shaft all the way, and then use the nut and washer against the outside of the bridge.
10. Reconnect the output shaft to the final drive.
11. Lubricate the bearing surface of the outer nut with oil. Then install and torque the nut.
12. Using installers 33 4 050 and 00 5 000 or equivalent, knock in the lockplate. Use the following torque figures:

Output shaft to drive flange – 42–46 ft. lbs.

Drive flange hub to output shaft – 140–152 ft. lbs.

### *1983 528e, 525i, 535i and 633CSi and 1983–84 733i, M5, M6, 735i and 735iL*

1. Remove the rear wheel. Disconnect the output shaft at the outer flange and suspend it with wire.
2. Unbolt the caliper and suspend it with the brake line connected. Unbolt and remove the rear disc.
3. Remove the large nut and remove the lockplate. If the car has ABS, disconnect and then remove the ABS speed sensor by unscrewing it.
4. Use a special tool BMW 33 4 000 or equivalent and 2 M10 x 30 bolts to unscrew the collar nut. Then, pull off the drive flange with tools 00 7 501 and 00 7 502.
5. Screw on the collar nut until it is just flush with the end of the shaft and use a soft (nylon) hammer to knock out the shaft.
6. Remove the circlip. Then, use special tools 33 4 031, 33 4 032 and 33 4 038 or equivalent to pull off the wheel bearings.
7. Pull the inner bearing race off the axle shaft with special tool 00 7 500 or equivalent.
8. Pull the new bearing assembly in with special tools 33 4 036, 33 4 032, and 33 4 038 or equivalent.
9. Install special tool 33 4 037 or equivalent. Then, reinstall the circlip.
10. Pull the rear axle shaft through with special tools 23 1 300, 33 4 080 and 33 4 020 or equivalent.
11. Use special tool 33 4 000 or equivalent to tighten the collar nut.
12. Fit special tool 33 4 060 or equivalent into the lockplate and top it in with a slide hammer 00 5 000 or equivalent.
13. Reconnect the output shaft. Remount the brake disc and caliper.

## Front Wheel Drive Hub, Knuckle and Bearings

### REMOVAL & INSTALLATION

**NOTE: A number of special tools are required to perform this operation. Read through the procedure and procure these before attempting to start work. Factory part numbers for tools are given, but it is possible to shop for equivalent tools, using these part numbers, in the aftermarket.**

1. Raise the car and support it securely. Remove the output halfshaft as described above. Then, remount the control arm with nuts just finger tight, to keep the spring strut in position.
2. Remove the upper and lower attaching bolts and remove the brake caliper, suspending it nearby with wire so that there is no tension on the brake hose.
3. Remove the Allen bolt and remove the brake disc.
4. Bolt special tool 31 2 090 or equivalent to the knuckle with its 3 bolts. Then, mount 33 1 307 hooked around the tie rod arm and press the drive flange off. If it is scored, pull the bearing's inner race out of the drive flange with 33 1 307 and 00 7 500 or equivalent.
5. Compress the snapring with snap ring pliers and remove it.
6. Remove 31 2 090 or the equivalent and replace 33 1 307 or its equivalent with a tool such as 31 2 070. Again install and use the combination, this time to press out the bearing.
7. Screw out the spindle of 31 2 090 and install 33 4 032 or equivalent so it is flush with the surface of 31 2 090. Use 33 4 034 and 33 4 038 to pull in the new bearing. Then, remove 31 2 090.
8. Install the circlip again, with snap-ring pliers, *making sure the open end faces downward.*
9. Pull the drive flange into place with 33 4 032 or equivalent, 33 4 038 or equivalent, 33 4 045 or equivalent, and 33 4 048 or equivalent.
10. Install the brake disc and caliper and the wheel in reverse order.

# FRONT SUSPENSION

## MacPherson Strut Assembly

**For removal of spring from struts and all strut overhaul procedures, please refer to "Strut Overhaul" in the Unit Repair section.**

Lock wire location at strut assembly

**CAUTION**

*MacPherson strut springs are under tremendous pressure and any attempt to remove them without proper tools could result in serious personal injury.*

## REMOVAL & INSTALLATION

### 318i, 325, 325e, 325i 325iS and M3

1. Remove the front wheel. Disconnect the brake pad wear indicator plug and ground wire. Pull the wires out of the holder on the strut.
2. Unbolt the caliper and pull it away from the strut, suspending it with a piece of wore from the body. Do not disconnect the brake line.
3. Remove the attaching nut and then detach the push rod on the stabilizer bar at the strut.
4. Unscrew the attaching nut and press off the guide joint. Use special tool 31 1 110 or equivalent except for M3; on M3, use 31 2 160 or equivalent.
5. Unscrew the nut and press off the tie rod joint.
6. Press the bottom of the strut outward and push it over the guide joint pin. Use 32 2 070 or equivalent for all but M3; for M3, use 31 2 160 or equivalent. Support the bottom of the strut.
7. Unscrew the nuts at the top of the strut (from inside the engine compartment) and then remove the strut.

**To install:**

8. Install in reverse order, keeping the following points in mind:
   a. Replace the self-locking nuts that fasten the top of the strut.
   b. Tie rod and guide joints must have both pins and both bores clean for reassembly. Replace both self-locking nuts.
   c. Torque the control arm to spring strut attaching nut to 43–51 ft. lb. Torque the spring strut to wheel well nuts to 16–17 ft. lb.

### 325iX

**NOTE: A number of special tools are required to perform this operation. Read through the procedure before attempting to start work. Factory part numbers for tools are given, but it is possible to shop for equivalent tools, using these part numbers, in the aftermarket.**

1. Raise the vehicle and support it securely by the chassis. Remove the front wheel. Unplug the ABS pulse transmitter.
2. Lift out the lockplate at the center of the brake disc with a screwdriver. Unscrew the collar nut.
3. Disconnect the brake pad wear indicator plug and the ground wire. Pull the wires and brake hose out of the clip on the spring strut. Then, disconnect the small rod at the strut.
4. Remove the brake caliper mounting bolts and support the assembly nearby with a piece of wire, keeping stress off the brake hose.
5. Remove the attaching nut from the tie rod end. Then press the stud off the knuckle with a tool such as 32 2 070.
6. Remove the attaching nut for the control arm and then press the stud off the knuckle with a tool such as 31 2 160.
7. Mount a tool such as 33 2 112 and 33 2 113 to the brake disc with 2 of the wheel bolts. Then, press the output shaft out of the center of the knuckle.
8. Support the spring strut from underneath. Remove the cap from the center of the wheel house. Remove the 3 bolts from the upper mount near the wheel housing. Remove the strut.

**To install:**

9. Install the strut, keeping these points in mind:
   a. Torque the nuts attaching the strut to the wheel house to 16 ft. lbs.
   b. Lubricate the splines of the output shaft with oil before pressing it back into the center of the knuckle. Use tools 33 2 112, 332 114, and 33 4 038 or equivalent.
   c. Keep grease off the studs for the control arm and tie rod end. Replace the cotter pin on the control arm and the self-locking nut on the tie rod end. Torque the control arm stud nut to 61.5 ft. lbs. Torque the tie rod nut to 61.5 ft. lbs. and then tighten it further to install the cotter pin, if necessary.
   d. Replace the lockplate in the center of the disc with tools such as 005 500 and 33 4 050.
   e. Torque the bolts attaching the caliper to the steering knuckle to 63–79 ft. lbs.

### 320i

1. Raise the vehicle and support safely. Remove the wheel.
2. Detach the bracket at the strut assembly.
3. Disconnect and suspend the bake caliper with a wire from the vehicle body. Do not disconnect the brake line.
4. Remove the cotter pin and castle nut. Press the tie rod off the steering knuckle.
5. Remove the 3 retaining nuts and detach the strut assembly at the wheel house.
6. Installation is the reverse of removal.

### 524td, 528e, 1983–84 533i, 525i, 535i, 1983–84 633CSi, 635CSi, M5, M6 and 1987–90 735i and 735iL

1. Raise the vehicle and support it securely. Remove the front wheel.
2. Disconnect the brake caliper and suspend it with a piece of wire so there is no tension on the brake hose (do not disconnect the hose).
3. If removing the left side strut, lift the electrical plug out of the clip on the strut, disconnect the ground wire, and disconnect the plug.
4. On cars with ABS, disconnect the ABS pulse transmitter at the strut.
5. Disconnect the stabilizer push rod at the bracket on the side of the strut; To do this, use a wrench to hold the rod end on the flats just outside the bracket and unscrew the nut from the inside of the bracket.
6. Remove the bolts from the underside of the tie rod arm that attach the bottom of the strut to the arm. Then, move the strut outward.
7. On the 735i and 735iL, remove the cap. Support the bottom of the strut and then remove the 3 nuts attaching the strut to the top of the fender well.
8. Installation is the reverse of removal. Use new self-locking nuts on the studs that pass through the fender well. Align the bottom of the strut with the tie rod arm so the tab on the arm fits into the notch on the bottom of the strut.

### 1983–84 733i and 1985–86 735i

1. Raise the vehicle and support it safely by the body. Remove the front wheel. Detach the brake line bracket and clamp from the strut.
2. Pull off the rubber cover, and then use an Allen type wrench to unbolt the anti-lock sensor at the rear of the caliper. Remove it.
3. Pull the anti-lock sensor electrical connector out of the holder and unplug it. Disconnect the ground wire.

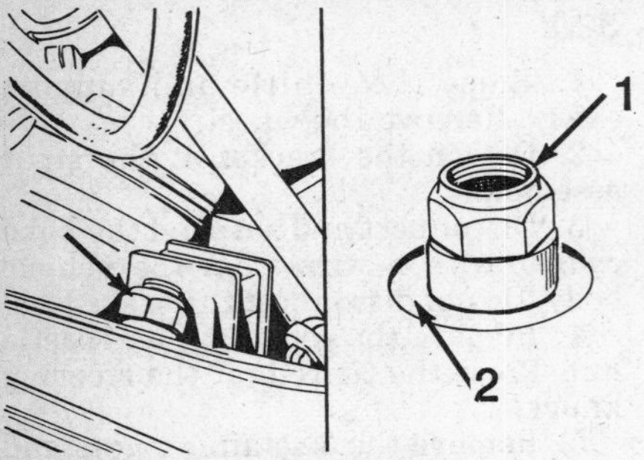


In replacing the nut located in the center of the control arm, use a replacement nut (1) and washer (2) of the type shown

4. Detach the caliper and suspend it from the body without disconnecting the brake line.
5. Support the strut in a secure manner at the bottom. Remove the self-locking nut and through bolt connecting the lower end of the vibration strut where it connects to the control arm.
6. Then, remove the 3 self-locking nuts from the top of the strut housing in the engine compartment, and remove the strut.

**To install:**

7. Install the strut in reverse order, noting the following points:
   a. Use new self-locking nuts on the top of the strut housing and at the connection to the control arm.
   b. When reconnecting the lower strut to the track arm, clean the bolt threads and bolt holes and install the bolts with a special bolt tightener HWB No. 81 22 9 400 086 or equivalent.

### OVERHAUL

**NOTE: For all spring and shock absorber removal and installation procedures, and all strut overhaul procedures, please refer to "Strut Overhaul" in the unit repair section.**

## Control Arm

### REMOVAL & INSTALLATION

#### *528e and 533i*

1. Raise the vehicle and support safely. Remove the wheel.
2. Disconnect the stabilizer at the control arm.
3. Remove the tension strut nut on the control arm.
4. Disconnect the control arm at the front axle support and remove it from the tension strut.
5. Remove the lock wire, remove the bolts and take the control arm off the spring strut.

Vibration strut attaching bolt—733i

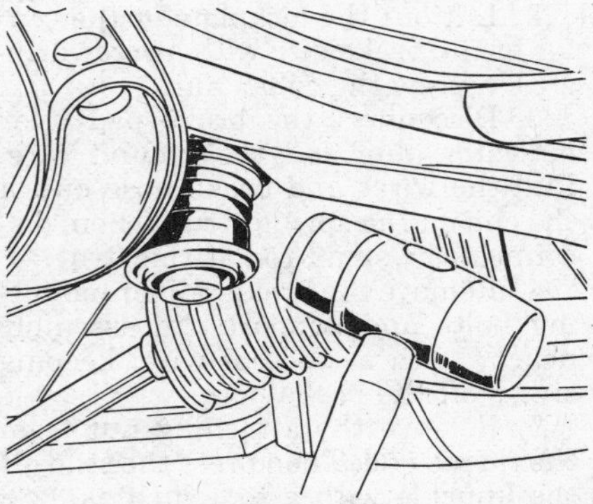

On the 318i, knock the pin loose with a soft hammer, as shown

6. Remove the cotter pin and nut.
7. Using special tool BMW 00-7-500 or equivalent, pull the guide joint from the tie rod arm.
8. Install the control arm to the front axle and reverse the removal procedure.

#### *524td, 1984 533i, 525i, 535i, 1983–84 633CSi, 635i, M5, M6 and 1987–90 735i and 735iL*

1. Raise and support the vehicle securely. Remove the wheel.
2. Remove the 3 bolts that fasten the bottom of the strut to the steering knuckle.
3. Remove the cotter pin and castellated nut. Use a ball joint remover (BMW 31 1 110 or equivalent) to press the ball joint end of the control arm off the steering knuckle.
4. Remove the self locking nut. Then, remove the through bolt and the 2 washers, slide the inner end of the strut and bushing out of the front suspension crossmember.

**To install:**

5. Install in reverse order, noting the following points:
   a. Make sure both washers are replaced to cushion the bushing where it contacts the suspension crossmember.
   b. Replace the bushing if it is worn or cracked.
   c. Use a new self-locking nut on the bolt fastening the inner end of the strut.
   d. Align the bottom of the strut with the steering knuckle so the tab on the arm fits into the notch on the bottom of the strut. Install the bolts with a locking type sealer.
   e. When installing the arm ball joint onto the steering knuckle, tighten the nut until a castellation lines up with the cotter pin hole and then use a new cotter pin in the nut.
   f. Final tighten the through bolt for the inner end of the arm after the car is on the ground at normal ride height.

#### *320i*

1. Disconnect the stabilizer at the control arm.
2. Disconnect the control arm at the front axle support.
3. Remove the cotter pin and castellated nut.
4. Press the control arm off the steering knuckle with special tool BMW 31-1-100 or equivalent.
5. Installation is the reverse of removal.

#### *318i, 325, 325e, 325I 325IS and M3*

1. Remove the front wheel. Disconnect the rear control arm bracket where it connects to the body by removing the 2 bolts.
2. Remove the nut and disconnect the thrust rod on the front stabilizer bar where it connects to the center of the control arm.
3. Unscrew the nut which attaches the front of the stabilizer bar to the crossmember and remove the nut from above the crossmember. Then, use a plastic hammer to knock this support pin out of the crossmember.
4. Unscrew the nut and press off the guide joint where the control arm attaches to the lower end of the strut. To do this, use a special tool such as 31 1 110 (31 2 160 for the M3) or equivalent.

**To install:**

5. Reverse the procedure to install. Keep these points in mind:
   a. Replace the self-locking nut that fastens the guide joint to the control arm.
   b. Make sure the support pin and the bore in the crossmember are clean before inserting the pin through the crossmember. Replace the original nut with a replacement nut and washer equivalent to those shown in the illustration.
   c. Torque the control arm-to-spring strut nut to 43–51 ft. lb. Torque the control arm support to crossmember nut to 29–34 ft. lb. Torque the push rod on the stabilizer bar to 29–34 ft. lb.

### 325iX

1. Remove the front wheel. Disconnect the rear control arm bracket where it connects to the body by removing the 2 bolts.
2. Remove the nut from the top of the stud that attaches to one corner of the control arm and runs through the crossmember.
3. Remove the cotter pin and then remove the nut from the balljoint stud where it passes through the steering knuckle. Then, press the balljoint stud out of the knuckle with a tool such as 31 2 160. Make sure to keep the stud and bore free of grease.
4. Reverse the procedure to install. Keep these points in mind:
   a. Make sure the support pin and the bore in the crossmember are clean before inserting the pin through the crossmember. Replace the original nut with a replacement nut and washer equivalent to those shown in the illustration.
   b. Torque the control arm-to-spring strut nut to 61.5 ft. lb. Turn the nut farther, as necessary to align the castellations with the cotter pin hole and install a new cotter pin. Torque the control arm support to crossmember nut to 30 ft. lb.

### 733i and 1985–86 735i

1. Raise the vehicle and support safely. Remove the wheel.
2. Disconnect the vibration strut from the control arm.
3. Disconnect the control arm from the axle carrier.
4. Disconnect the tie rod arm from the front strut.
5. Remove the cotter pin and castellated nut. Press off the control arm with special tool BMW 31-1-110 or equivalent.
6. Installation is the reverse of removal. Use new self-locking nuts on the connections at the vibration strut and axle carrier. When reconnecting the arm to the tie rod arm, use a bolt tightener HBW No. 81 22 9 400 086 and make sure the threads and bolt holes are clean.

## Front Wheel Bearings

### ADJUSTMENT

**NOTE: The wheel bearings for 318i and 325, 5 and 6 Series, and 7 Series for 1987–90 cannot be adjusted.**

### 320i, 533i, 633CSi, 733i, 735i and 735iL

1. Raise the vehicle, support it and remove the front wheel.
2. Remove the end cap, and then straighten the cotter pin and remove it. Loosen the castellated nut.
3. While continuously spinning the brake disc, torque the castellated nut down to 22–24 ft. lbs. Keep turning the disc thru-out this and make sure it turns at least 2 turns after the nut is torqued and held.
4. Loosen the nut until there is end play and the hub rotates with the nut.
5. Torque the nut to no more than 2 ft. lbs. Finally, loosen slowly just until castellations and the nearest cotter pin hole line up and insert a new cotter pin.
6. Make sure the slotted washer is free to turn without noticeable resistance; otherwise, there is no end play and the bearings will wear excessively.

### 528i

1. Remove the wheel. Remove the locking cap from the hub by gripping it carefully on both sides with a pair of pliers.
2. Remove the cotter pin from the castellated nut, and loosen the nut.
3. Spin the disc constantly while torquing the nut to 7 ft. lbs. Continue spinning the disc a couple of turns after the nut is torqued and held.
4. Loosen the castellated nut ¼–⅓ turn-until the slotted washer can be turned readily.
5. Fasten a dial indicator to the front suspension and rest the pin against the wheel hub. Preload the meter about 0.039 in. to remove any play.
6. Adjust the position of the castellated nut while reading the play on the indicator. Make the play as small as possible while backing off the castellated nut just until a new cotter pin can be inserted. The permissible range is 0.0008–0.004 in.
7. Install the new cotter pin, locking cap, and the wheel.

### REMOVAL & INSTALLATION (PACKING)

**NOTE: Wheel bearings on 318i, 325, 5 and 6 Series, and 7 Series for 1987–90 are permanently sealed bearings and do not require periodic disassembly and packing.**

1. Remove the wheel. Unbolt and remove the caliper. Hang it from the body. Do not disconnect or stress the hose. On models with a separate disc, remove the locking cap by gripping carefully on both sides with a pair of pliers, remove the cotter pin from the castellated nut, and remove the nut and, where equipped, the slotted washer. Then, remove the entire hub and bearing.
2. Remove the shaft sealing ring and take out the roller bearing.
3. On most models, the outer bearing race may be forced out through the recesses in the wheel hub. A BMW puller 00 8 550 or the equivalent may also be used. On the 733i, the recesses are not provided and a puller is necessary.

**To install:**

4. Clean all bearings and races and the interior of the hub with alcohol, and allow to air dry.

**NOTE: Do not dry with compressed air as this can damage the bearings by rolling them over one another unlubricated or force one loose from the cage causing injury. Replace all bearings and races if there is any sign of scoring or galling.**

5. Press in the outer races with a suitable sleeve. Pack a new shaft seal with graphite grease and refill the hub with fresh grease.
6. Assemble in this order: outer race; inner race; outer race; inner race; shaft seal.
7. If necessary, adjust the wheel bearing play as described above.

### 318i, 325, 325e, 325i, 325iS and M3

**NOTE: The bearings on the 318i and 325 are only removed if they are worn. They cannot be removed without destroying them (due to side thrust created by the bearing puller). They are not periodically disassembled, repacked and adjusted.**

1. Remove the front wheel and support the car. Remove the attaching bolts and remove and suspend the brake caliper, hanging it from the body so as to avoid putting stress on the brake line.
2. Remove the setscrew with an Allen wrench. Pull off the brake disc and pry off the dust cover with a small prybar.
3. Using a chisel, knock the tab on the collar nut away from the shaft. Unscrew and discard the nut.
4. Pull off the bearing with a puller set such as 31 2 101/102/104 and discard it. On the M3, use a puller set such as 31 2 102/105/106. On the M3, install the main bracket of the puller with 3 wheel bolts.
5. If the inside bearing inner race remains on the stub axle, unbolt and remove the dust guard. Bend back the inner dust guard and pull the inner race off with a special tool capable of getting under the race (BMW 00 7 500

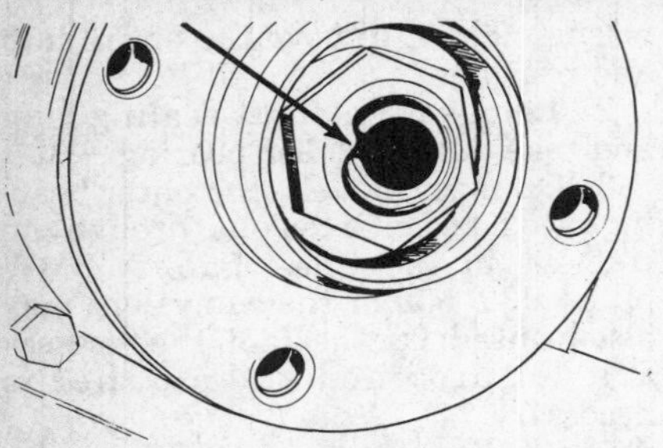

On 318i, unlock the collar nut as shown with a chisel, by applying force in the direction shown by the arrow

and 33 1 309 or equivalent). Reinstall the dust guard.

6. If the dust guard has been removed, install a new one. Install a special tool (BMW 31 2 120 or equivalent; on M3, use 31 2 110 or equivalent) over the stub axle and screw it in for the entire length of the guide sleeve's threads. Press the bearing on.

7. Reverse the remaining removal procedures to install the disc and caliper. Torque the wheel hub collar nut to 188 ft. lb. Lock the collar nut by bending over the tab.

#### *1983–86 733i and 735i*

1. Remove the front wheel. Detach the brake line clamp and bracket on the strut. On cars with ABS, remove the rubber boot and unbolt and remove the anti-lock sensor.

2. Detach the caliper without disconnecting the brake line and suspend it.

3. Use a tool such as 21 2 000 to remove the end cap. Remove the cotter pin and unscrew the castellated nut. Then, remove the stepped washer, brake disc, and wheel hub.

4. Use an Allen type wrench to unscrew the bolt and separate the disc from the wheel hub.

5. Lift out the shaft seal. Remove the tapered roller bearings. Knock out the outer races if they show scoring with a punch by tapping all around.

**To install:**

6. Press in new outer races with special tools such as 31 2 061 for the inside bearings and 31 2 062 for the outside bearings. Pack the 2 inner races with wheel bearing grease. The order of installation is: outer race, inner race, outer race, inner race, shaft seal. To install the seal, lubricate the sealing lip of the shaft seal with grease and install the seal with a tool such as 31 2 040. Repack all bearings thoroughly with wheel bearing grease before installation.

7. Install the bearing and adjust the wheel bearings as described above.

#### *524td, 528e, 525i, 535i, 1983–84 633CSi, 635CSi, M5 and M6*

1. Raise the vehicle and support it securely. Unbolt and remove the caliper, suspending it so the broke line will not be stressed. Remove th Allen bolt and remove the brake disc.

2. Remove the grease cap. Use a flat punch and hammer to push the punched-in area of the retaining nut away from the groove in the axle. If necessary, chisel the nut off. Then, use a socket 31 2 080 or equivalent to unscrew the bearing retaining nut.

3. Install a puller 31 2 100 or equivalent. Screw the tool's bolt inward to pull the bearing housing out of the axle.

**To install:**

4. Install a new bearing assembly cover on the stub axle. Use special tool set 31 2 110 to pull the new bearing assembly into the axle.

5. Install a washer and a new retaining nut. Torque the nut to 210 ft. lbs. Use a center punch and hammer to punch the inner edge of the nut into the indentation on the axle shaft. Install a new grease cap coated with a sealer such as HWB 88 228 407 420.

#### *1987–90 735i and 735iL*

1. Remove the front wheel and support the car. Remove the attaching bolts and remove and suspend the brake caliper, hanging it from the body so as to avoid putting stress on the brake line.

2. Remove the setscrew with an Allen wrench. Pull off the brake disc and pry off the dust cover with a small prybar.

3. Using a chisel, knock the tab on the collar nut away from the shaft. Unscrew and discard the nut.

4. Install a puller collar such as 31 2 105 to the bearing housing with 3 bolts. Install a puller such as 31 2 102 and 312 2 106 and pull off the bearing and discard it.

5. If the inside bearing inner race remains on the stub axle, unscrew and remove the dust guard, using a socket extension. Bend back the inner dust guard and pull the inner race off with a special tool capable of getting under the race (BMW 31 2 100 and 31 2 102 or equivalent). Reinstall the dust guard and install a new dust cover.

6. Then install a special tool (BMW 31 2 110 or equivalent) over the stub axle and screw it in for the entire length of the guide sleeve's threads. Slide the bearing on and follow it with 31 2 100 or equivalent, and use this tool to press the bearing on.

7. Reverse the remaining removal procedures to install the disc and caliper. Torque the wheel hub collar nut to 210 ft. lb. Lock the collar nut by bending over the tab.

8. Install a new grease cap coated with a sealer such as HWB 88 228 407 420.

## Front Wheel Alignment

### Adjustment

#### *Caster and Camber*

Caster and camber are not adjustable, except for replacement of bent or worn parts.

Camber that is out of specification because of excessive tolerances can be corrected by installing eccentric mounts. This cannot be done to correct misalignment caused by a collision, however.

#### *Toe-in Adjuatment*

Toe-in is adjusted by changing the length of the tie rod and tie rod end assembly. Center the steering by aligning marks on the steering shaft and the steering housing. Then, loosen the clamp bolt on either end of each tie rod and turn the tie rod, using a wrench on the flats. When adjusting the tie rod ends, adjust each by equal amount (by turning in the opposite direction) to increase or decrease the toe-in measurement.

# REAR SUSPENSION

## MacPherson Strut Assembly

**For all spring and shock absorber removal and installation procedures and any other strut overhaul procedures, please refer to "Strut Overhaul" in the Unit Repair section.**

**CAUTION**

***MacPherson strut springs are under tremendous pressure and any attempt to remove them without proper tools could result in serious personal injury.***

### REMOVAL & INSTALLATION

1. On 1987–90 735i and 735iL, remove the rear seat and back rest. On 1983–86 733i and 735i, remove the trim from over the wheel well in the trunk.

2. Jack up the car and support the control arms.

**CAUTION**

***The coil spring, shock absorber assembly acts as a strap so the control arm should always be supported.***

3. On 1987–90 735i and 735iL if the car has automatic ride control (for other models skip to Step 4):
   a. Pull off and bridge (electrically) the low pressure switch electrical connection and turn on the ignition.
   b. Disconnect the control rod nut, holding the collar with an 8mm wrench against torque. Don't disconnect the rod at the ball joint.
   c. Operate the lever on the control switch in the "discharge" direction for about 20 seconds to discharge fluid from the lines.
   d. Disconnect the hydraulic line on the shock absorber.
4. Remove the lower shock retaining bolt.
5. Remove trim if necessary and disconnect the upper strut retaining nuts at the wheel arch and remove the assembly.

**To install:**

6. Install in reverse order, using new gaskets between the unit and the wheel arch, and new self-locking nuts on top of the strut. Torque the shock-to-body nuts to 16–17 ft. lbs.; spring retainer-to-wheel house nuts (6 cyl.) to 16–17 ft. lbs.; lower bolt to 52–63 ft. lbs. (4 cyl.), 90–103 ft. lbs. (6 cyl.). On the 733i, 735i and 735iL, replace the gasket that goes between the top of the strut and the lower surface of the wheel well. Final torquing of the lower strut bolt should be done with the car in the normal riding position.

# Shock Absorber

**CAUTION**

***Strut springs are under tremendous pressure and any attempt to remove them without proper tools could result in serious personal injury.***

## REMOVAL & INSTALLATION

### *318i and 325*

1. Jack up the car and support the control arms.

**CAUTION**

***On the 318i and 325, the spring and shock absorber are separate. The control arm must be securely supported throughout this procedure.***

2. Remove the lower shock retaining bolt.
3. Remove trim if necessary and disconnect the upper strut retaining nuts at the wheel arch and remove the assembly.

**NOTE: On the 318i and 325, this is located behind the trim panel in the trunk. The shock absorber, because it is separate from the spring, may now be replaced.**

**To install:**

4. Install in reverse order, using new gaskets between the unit and the wheel arch, and new self-locking nuts on top of the strut.
5. Torque the shock-to-body nuts to 16–17 ft. lb.; spring retainer-to-wheel house nuts (6 cyl.) to 16–17 ft. lb.; lower bolt to 52–63 ft. lb. (4 cyl.), 90–103 ft. lb. (6 cyl.).
6. Final torquing of the lower strut bolt should be done with the car in the normal riding position.

## OVERHAUL

**NOTE: For all spring and shock absorber removal and installation procedures, and all strut overhaul procedures, please refer to "Strut Overhaul" in the unit repair section.**

# Rear Spring

## REMOVAL & INSTALLATION

### *318i, 325, 325e, 325i, 325iS, 325iX, and M3*

1. Disconnect the rear portion of the exhaust system and hang it from the body.
2. Disconnect the final drive rubber mount, push it down, and hold it down with a wedge.
3. Remove the bolt that connects the rear stabilizer bar to the strut on the side being worked on. Be careful not to damage the brake line.

**NOTE: Support the lower control arm securely with a jack or other device that will permit it to be lowered gradually, while maintaining secure support.**

4. Then, to prevent damage to the output shaft joints, lower the control arm only enough to slip the coil spring off the retainer.
5. Make sure, in replacing the spring, that the same part number, color code, and proper rubber ring are used. Reverse all removal procedures to install, making sure that the spring is in proper position, keeping the control arm securely supported until the shock bolt is replaced, and tightening stabilizer bar and lower shock mount bolts with the control arm in the normal ride position. Torque the stabilizer bolt to 22–24 ft. lbs., and the shock bolt to 52–63 ft. lbs.

# Stabilizer Bar

## REMOVAL & INSTALLATION

1. Disconnect the stabilizer from the trailing arm on either side by removing the connecting bolt from the lower end of the link.
2. Disconnect the stabilizer on the crossmember.
3. Check the rubber bushings for wear and replace as necessary.

# Rear Control Arm

## REMOVAL & INSTALLATION

### *524td, 528e, 525i, 535i and M5*

1. Apply the parking brake and then remove the rear wheel. Disconnect the driveshaft at the outer flange by removing the bolts.
2. Remove the parking brake lever.
3. Plug the front hose to prevent loss of brake fluid in the reservoir.
4. Support the body.
5. Disconnect the brake line at the brake hose.
6. Disconnect the stabilizer and coil spring at the control arm.
7. Disconnect the control arm at the axle carrier.
8. Installation is the reverse of removal. Bleed the system.

### *733i, 735i and 735iL*

1. Remove the rear wheel.
2. Apply the parking brake to hold the driveshaft stationary. Disconnect the output shaft at the drive flange. Hang the shaft from the body by a piece of wire.
3. Disconnect the parking brake cable at the lever as described later in this section.
4. Remove the float housing from the brake fluid reservoir and then remove as much fluid as possible from the reservoir, using a syringe used only for brake fluid (or a new one).
5. Pull the brake cable housing out of the mounting bracket near the control arm. Disconnect the brake line.
6. On 735i and 735iL models with ABS: *Carefully, to avoid damaging the rubber grommet in which it is mounted,* pull the wiring for the pulse transmitter out of its mount so it will be possible to unplug it. Then, do so.
7. Support the trailing arm from underneath in a secure manner.
8. Remove the nuts and then remove the 2 through bolts to disconnect the control arm from the rear axle carrier.
9. If the car has a stabilizer bar, remove the bolts and remove the attaching bracket for the stabilizer bar.

1. Spacer ring 2. Washer 3. Wishbone

**Detaching the lower arm at front axle beam**

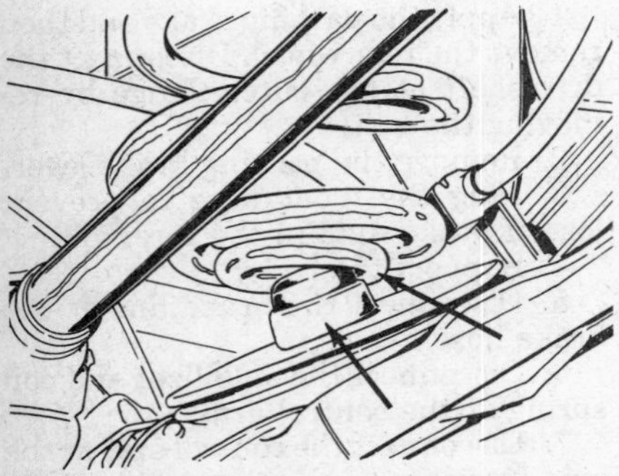

**On the 318i, lower the trailing arm just enough to get the spring off the locating tang**

10. Disconnect the shock absorber and remove the control arm.
11. Installation is the reverse of removal. When reattaching the control arm, insert the bolt on the inner bracket first. Final tighten all mounting bolts with the car resting on its wheels. Torque the bolts attaching the control arm to the axle carrier to 49–54 ft. lbs. Refill and bleed the brake system.

## Trailing Arm

### REMOVAL & INSTALLATION

#### *528e, 533i, 633CSi*

1. Raise the vehicle and remove the rear wheel. Apply the parking brake and disconnect the output shaft at the rear axle shaft. Then, disconnect the parking brake cable at the handbrake. Remove the parking brake lever.
2. Remove the rear wheel.
3. Using vise grips, clamp the front hose to prevent loss of fluid.
4. Support the body.
5. Pull the parking brake cable out of the pipe.
6. Disconnect the stabilizer and spring strut at the trailing arm.
7. Disconnect the brake line at the brake hose.
8. Disconnect the driveshaft at the outboard flange.
9. Disconnect the brake pad wear indicator wire at the right trailing arm and take the wire out of the clamps.
10. Disconnect the trailing arm at the rear axle support.
11. Installation is the reverse of removal. Refill and bleed the brake system.

#### *318i, 320i, 325, 325e, 325i, 325iS, 325iX and M3*

1. Raise the vehicle and remove the rear wheel. Apply the parking brake and disconnect the output shaft at the rear axle shaft. Then, on the 320i, disconnect the parking brake cable at the handbrake. On the 318i and 325, remove the parking brake lever.
2. Remove the brake fluid from the master cylinder reservoir on the 318i and 325. To do this, it will be necessary to remove the strainer at the top of the reservoir and use a new syringe or one used only with brake fluid. Disconnect the brake line connection on the rear control arm on both types of car. Plug the openings.
3. Support the control arm securely. Disconnect the shock absorber at the control arm. On 318i and 325, lower the control arm slowly and remove the spring. On the 320i, the control arm need not be lowered slowly because the spring is integral with the strut.
4. Remove the nuts and then slide the bolts out of the mounts where the control arm is mounted to the axle carrier.

**To install:**

5. Install in reverse order. Install the bolt that goes into the inner bracket first.
6. Torque the bolts holding the trailing arm to the axle carrier to 48–54 ft. lb.
7. On the 318i and 325, make sure the spring is positioned properly top and bottom. Torque the strut bolt to 52–63 ft. lb.
8. Reinstall the handbrake or reconnect the cable and adjust. Then apply the brake and reconnect the output shaft.
9. Reconnect the brake line, replenish with the proper brake fluid, and bleed the system.

## Rear Wheel Bearings

### ADJUSTMENT AND REMOVAL & INSTALLATION

**NOTE: For these procedures, refer to "Rear Axle Shaft, Wheel Bearings, and Seals" in the Drive Axle section.**

# STEERING

## Steering Wheel

### REMOVAL & INSTALLATION

**NOTE: Remove and install steering wheel in straight ahead position. Mark the relationship between the wheel and spindle.**

1. Disconnect the negative battery cable. Remove steering wheel pad or BMW emblem. Mark the relationship between the steering wheel and shaft for installation in the same position. On 1986–90 models, unlock the steering wheel lock with the key. Otherwise, the wheel cannot be removed.
2. Unscrew retaining nut and remove the wheel.

**CAUTION**

***Be careful not to damage the direction signal cancelling cam, which is right under the steering wheel, in performing this operation. On models equipped with air bags, it is important to avoid banging on the wheel in any way.***

3. Installation is the reverse of removal. Lubricate the direction signal cancelling cam. Replace the self-locking nut on all models, and torque it to 58 ft. lbs.

## Turn Signal, Dimmer Switch and Wiper Switch

### REMOVAL & INSTALLATION

#### *318i, 320i, 533i and 633CSi*

1. Turn the steering wheel to the straight ahead position. Remove the steering wheel and the lower steering column cover.
2. Disconnect the negative cable from the battery. Disconnect the direction signal switch multiple connector from under the dash by squeezing in the locks on either side and pulling it off.
3. Remove the cable straps from the column.
4. Loosen the mounting screws and remove the switch and harness.

**To install:**

5. Install in reverse order, noting the following points:
   a. Make sure to mount the ground wire.
   b. Make sure the switch is in the middle position and that the follower faces the center of the cancelling

cam on the steering column shaft. Then, before finally tightening the switch mounting screws, adjust the switch on slotted mounting holes so the gap between the cam and follower is 0.118 in.

### 325, 325e, 325i, 325iS, 325iX and M3

1. Turn the steering wheel to the straight ahead position. Remove the steering wheel and the lower steering column cover. Remove the 5 retaining screws and remove the lower/left instrument panel cover.

2. Disconnect the negative cable from the battery. If the turn signal switch is to be replaced, remove the screw at top/left and the ground wire attaching screw at the bottom left. If the wiper switch is to be replaced, remove the 2 similar screws on the right side.

3. To disconnect the turn signal/dimmer switch wiring:

a. Lift the plug and flasher relay out of the clip on the left side of the steering column and unplug the relay. Unplug the horn lead just above.

b. Cut the straps retaining the wiring and then disconnect the plug the turn signal/dimmer switch wiring goes to just below.

4. To disconnect the wiper switch wiring, cut the 2 wire straps and disconnect the plug the wiper switch wiring connects with the the lower /left column.

5. Installation is performed in the reverse of removal. Make sure to inspect the ground wires carefully for any breaks in insulation or other problems (if the switch is being re-used) and ensure that they are properly connected.

### 524td, 525i, 528e, 535i, 635CSi, M5 and M6

1. Disconnect the battery ground cable. Remove the steering wheel as described above.

2. Remove the instrument panel trim which is near the bottom of the steering wheel on the left side.

3. Remove the 2 screws from underneath and remove the steering column lower cover.

4. Disconnect the electrical connectors near the bottom of the column and at the area just under the front of the dash.

5. Unscrew the 2 screws fastening the switch and one ground wire to the column just to the left of the steering shaft. Pull off the plug connecting the switch to the relay on the right side of the column. Remove the switch.

6. Installation is the reverse of removal.

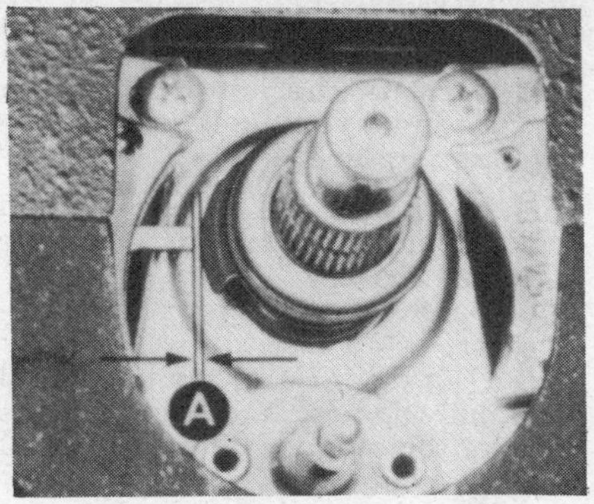


Turn signal switch adjustment

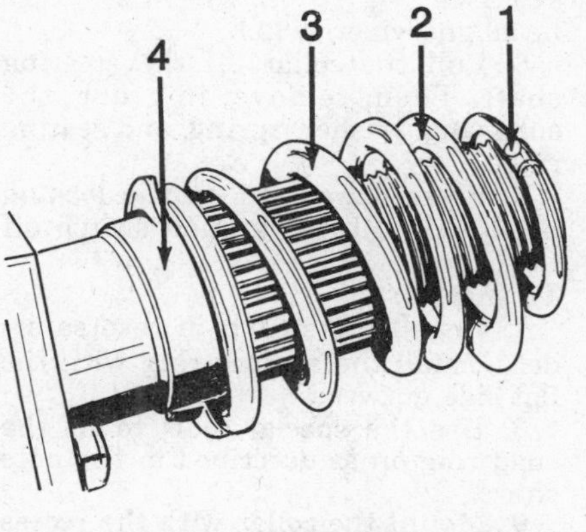


When removing the 318i steering lock, remove the snap ring (1), washer (2), spring (3), and seating ring (4)

### 1983–85 733i and 1985–86 735i

1. Disconnect the negative battery cable. Remove the steering wheel as described above.

2. Remove the lower steering column cover.

3. Remove the 2 Phillips type screws located to the left of the steering shaft (the lower screw mounts a ground wire).

4. Disconnect the electrical connector for the switch and the flasher relay, located along the front of the column. Pull the flasher relay out of the holder.

5. Follow the wiring to the area under the dash. Open ties and unplug the electrical connector. Remove the switch.

6. Install in reverse order, making sure to retie electrical wiring going under the dash and to reconnect the ground wire to the lower switch mounting screw.

### 1987–90 735i and 735iL

1. Disconnect the battery ground. Remove the steering wheel as described above.

2. Remove the instrument panel trim below and to the left of the steering wheel.

3. Remove the lower steering column cover.

4. Compress its retaining hook and then pull off the flasher relay socket facing downward.

5. On cars with airbags, drive out the pin and pry out the expansion rivet. Then, on all cars, remove the upper steering column cover.

6. Pull off the connector plug. This is located between the column and the dash in front of and just above where the steering wheel is normally located.

7. Compress the retaining hooks and remove the switch (located to the left of the steering shaft). Disconnect all electrical plugs and remove the switch.

8. Install in reverse order.

## Ignition Switch

## REMOVAL & INSTALLATION

### Except Below

1. Disconnect negative battery terminal.

2. Remove lower steering column casing.

3. On 320i, 633CSi, 733i and 528e models, shear off the 4 tamper-proof screws with a chisel or other tool.

4. Unscrew the set screw and remove the switch.

5. Disconnect the central fuse/relay plate plug.

6. Installation is the reverse of removal.

**NOTE: Turn ignition key all the way back and set the switch at the 0 position before installing. Marks on the switch must be opposite each other.**

### 318i, 325, 325e, 325i, 325iS, 325iX and M3

1. Disconnect the battery ground cable. Remove the steering wheel.

2. Remove the 4 screws, and remove the lower steering column cover.

3. Disconnect the turn signal/wiper switch by removing the 4 screws and disconnecting the wires.

4. Remove the collar from the steering column shaft. Then, remove the snap ring (1), washer (2), spring (3) and seating ring (4).

**CAUTION**

***In the next step, pry carefully. Don't use too much force, because a screwdriver can slip and cause injury!***

5. Pry off the steering spindle bearings with 2 screwdrivers. Pry by the *inner race only*

6. Disconnect the main electrical

plug at the bottom of the steering column.

7. Use a chisel to remove the tamperproof screw. Pull the lock assembly with the upper section of the casting off the outer column.

8. With a suitable tool, press downward on the lock and then slide the switch off, noting the switch position and that of the lock assembly.

**To install:**

9. To install, reverse the above procedure, noting these points:

a. When installing the switch, make sure its position is the same in relationship with the lock, so the actions of the 2 will be synchronized.

b. Use a Torx® screwdriver for the tamperproof screw.

c. Drive the steering spindle bearings back on by the inner races only.

d. When installing the seating ring that goes on the shaft, make sure the spring seat faces outward. Use a piece of pipe slightly larger than the shaft and tap it with a hammer to install the snap ring. Then, make sure the collar that goes on next locks the snap ring in place.

### *1985–86 524td, 525i, 528e, 535i and 635i*

1. Disconnect the battery ground cable. Remove the steering wheel as described above.

2. Remove the instrument panel lower trim and the steering column lower cover.

3. Unplug the flasher relay and then pull the relay and holder off the front of the column. Then, remove the 4 Phillips screws retaining the headlight dimmer and wiper combination switch.

4. Use a hammer and chisel to shear off the 5 screws mounting the switch.

5. Remove the setscrew. Then, press downward on the steering column and pull the steering lock out.

**To install:**

6. Install in reverse order, using new shear-off type screws to mount the switch.

7. Make sure to install the switch so it is properly positioned in relation to the steering lock.

8. Apply paint to the setscrew to lock it in position after it has been installed and tightened.

### *524td, 528e, 1987–90 525i, 535i, M5, 635Csi and M6*

**NOTE: To perform this operation, use special tools 32 3 052 and 32 3 050 or equivalent. These are a sleeve, tapered at the outer end, which permits mounting a snapring over the threaded end of the steering shaft without damaging those threads. There is also a pipe which fits over the sleeve and permits the snapring to be forced down the sleeve while being kept square.**

1. Disconnect the battery ground cable. Remove the steering wheel as described above.

2. Remove the steering column lower cover.

3. Unplug the flasher relay and then pull the relay and holder off the front of the column. Pull the plug off the horn contact.

4. Note the location of the 2 ground wires. Then, remove the 4 Phillips screws and remove the headlight/wiper switch.

5. Pull the collar off the steering shaft. Then, remove, in order, the snap ring, washer, spring, and seating ring.

6. Press downward on the locking hook and pull the ignition switch off the column.

**To install:**

7. Install the switch in reverse order. Install the seating ring with the flat side outward.

8. Use the special tools to fit the snap ring on as described in the note above.

9. Mount the collar with the recess downward. Make sure to reconnect the ground wires to the bottom/left Phillips screw.

### *1983–84 733i*

1. Disconnect the negative battery cable. Remove the outer steering column cover.

2. Lift the flasher relay out of its holding clamp. Unscrew the attaching screw and pull out the switch.

3. Open the wire strap and pull off the plug.

4. Install in reverse order noting these points:

a. With the ignition key in the new switch, turn the key slowly back and forth while sliding in the switch until it engages. Apply a new coating of locking sealer.

b. Connect the black wire from the ignition switch to the black wire coming from the power saving relay. Use new straps to tie the wiring harness back in place.

### *1985–86 735i*

1. Disconnect the battery ground cable. Remove the steering wheel as described above.

2. Remove the steering column lower cover.

3. Then, remove the 4 Phillips screws retaining the headlight dimmer and wiper switches.

4. Use a hammer and chisel to shear off the 4 screws mounting the switch to the switch plate.

5. Remove the setscrew. Then, pull the ignition switch out.

**To install:**

6. To synchronize the positions of the ignition lock and switch, use the key to turn the ignition lock as far back from the on position as it will go, and set the ignition switch to the **O** position.

7. Complete the installation in reverse order, using new shear-off type screws to mount the switch.

8. Make sure to install the switch so it is properly positioned in relation to the steering lock.

9. Apply clear lacquer to the setscrew to lock it in position after it has been installed and tightened.

### *1987–90 735i and 735iL*

1. Disconnect the battery ground cable. Remove the steering wheel as described above. Remove the instrument panel trim located just below the steering column.

2. Remove the steering column cover casing by removing the 2 screws from underneath and the 2 from the front of the column.

3. Remove the bolt and nut fastening the lower end of the steering spindle (the bolt passes through a groove in the spindle). Mark alignment of the steering shaft splines with a spot of paint on each side.

4. Remove the bolts and nuts at the forked lower end of the steering column. Replace the nuts, which are self-locking.

5. Remove the 2 bolts fastening the upper column to the dash. Remove the column by pressing it downward.

6. Pull off the ignition switch connector. Then, compress the locking hooks and pull off the combination switch.

7. Turn the ignition switch to **R** position. Use a center punch to press the retainer into the locking bore in the case and then pull the ignition switch out of the case.

**To install:**

8. Install in reverse order, noting the following points:

a. Make sure to remount the spacer sleeve that goes in the column mounting bracket.

b. After realigning the splines of the steering shaft and lower column, tighten the adjusting nut so the sliding force of the column is about 10 lbs.

c. Make sure the bolt which fastens the steering spindle in place passes through the groove in the spindle.

d. Check the position of the concave collar located just under the

Tie rod arm-to-shock absorber retaining bolts—733i

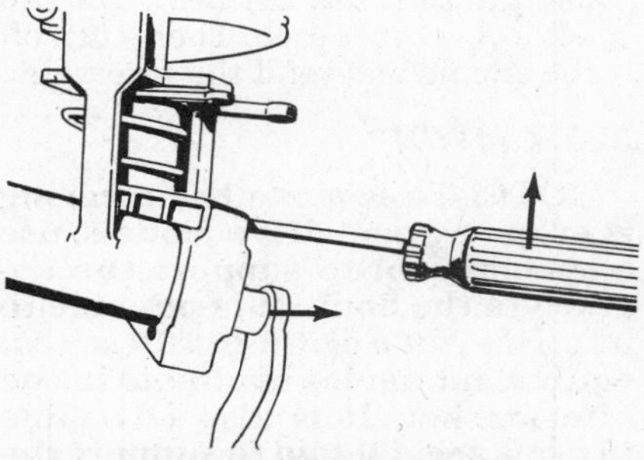

On the 318i, press down the locking hook with a screwdriver, as shown, and remove the ignition switch

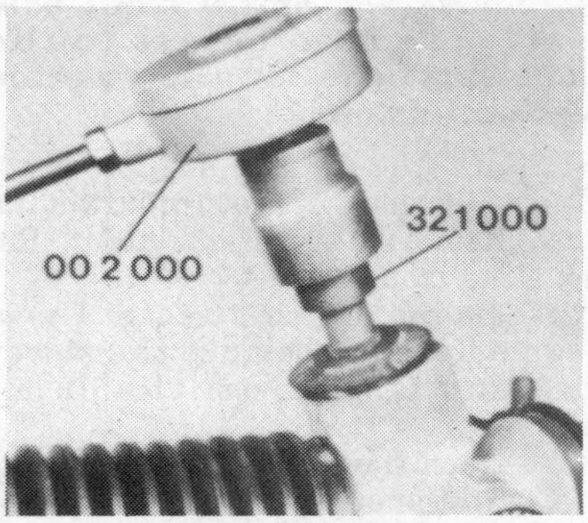


Pressure pad adjustment—320i

steering wheel. It must fit over the snapring.

e. Double check to make sure to replace all self-locking nuts.

## Manual Steering Gear

### REMOVAL & INSTALLATION

#### *320i*

1. Loosen the front wheels.
2. Remove the cotter pin and castle nut.
3. Press the tie rods off of the steering knuckles.
4. Detach the steering at the front axle support.

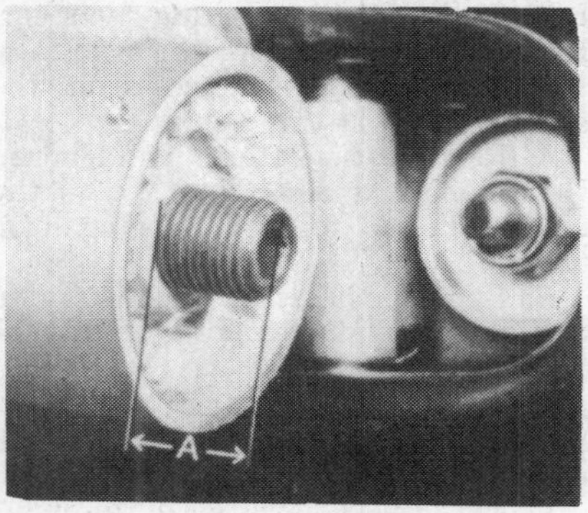


Steering adjustment 320i

Turning torque adjustment—320i

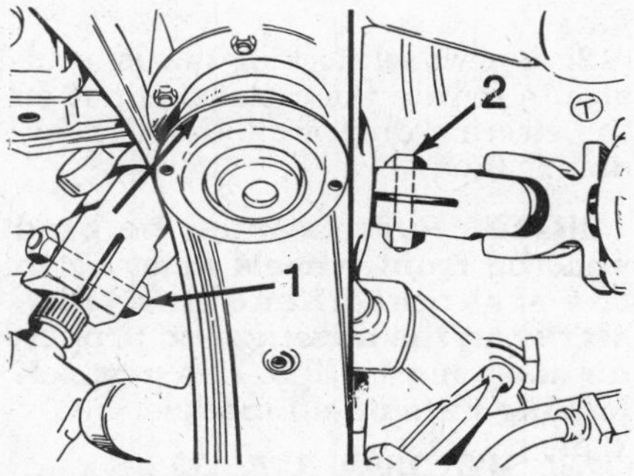


On the 318i, remove the pinch bolt (1), and through bolt (2)

5. Pull the steering gear off of the steering spindle.
6. Installation is the reverse of removal.

**NOTE: Turn the steering wheel until the wheels point straight ahead. The mark on the dust seal must be between the marks on the gear box.**

### ADJUSTMENT

#### *320i*

1. Remove the steering gear from the car.
2. Clamp the special tool 32–1–100,

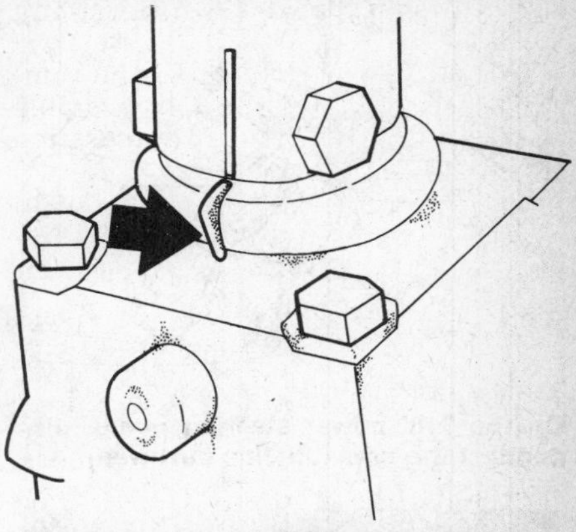

On late model 733i and 735is, line up the marks on the steering shaft and gearbox to put the steering wheel in the straight ahead position.

or equivalent, in a vise and place the steering gear assembly into the tool.

3. Unscrew the nut on the steering damper and slide it back.
4. Remove the cap and unscrew the socket head cap about ½ in..
5. Pressure pad adjustment:
   a. Remove the cotter pin. Tighten the set screw with special 32–1–100, or equivalent, and a torque wrench, to 4 ft. lbs. Loosen the set screw by one full castle slot to align the cotter pin bore.
   b. Use special tools 32–1–00 and 00–2–000 or equivalent to move rack to the left and right over the entire stroke and check for sticking and hooking. If this is the case, loosen the set screw by one more castle slot and insert the cotter pin.
   c. Repeat test. If there is still sticking or hooking, replace rack, drive pinion or the entire steering gear. Never loosen the screw by 2 castle slots regardless of circumstances.
6. Turning torque adjustment:
   a. Move rack to the center position. Place special tools 00–2–000 and 32–1–000 or equivalent on the drive pinion, check the turning torque. If it is not between 7.8 and 11.2 ft. lbs., adjust the set screw.
   b. Turn to the right to increase friction, and turn to the left to decrease friction.
   c. Install cap.

## Power Steering Gear

### REMOVAL & INSTALLATION

#### *5, 6 and 7 Series*

1. Turn the steering to left lock.
2. On 1985–90 models, which share the hydraulic system with the power brakes, discharge pressure from the

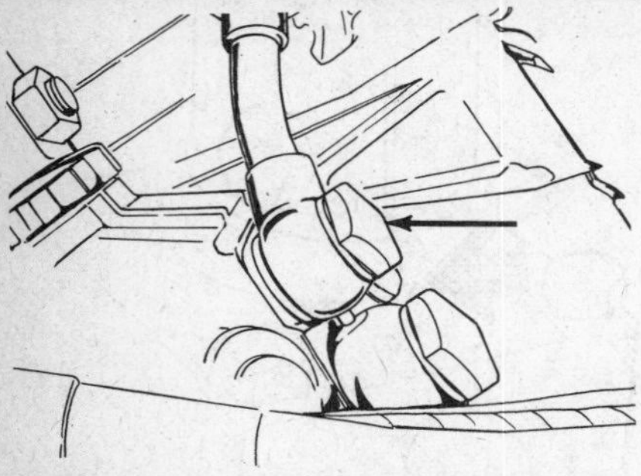

On the 318i power steering pump, disconnect the pressure line (arrowed)

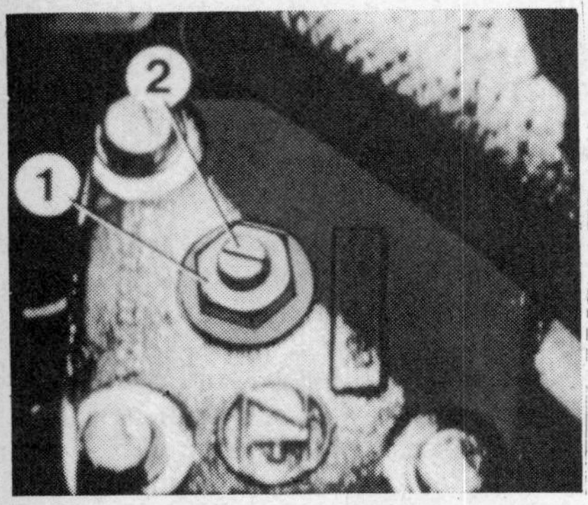


1. Locknut 2. Adjusting nut

Power steering adjustment

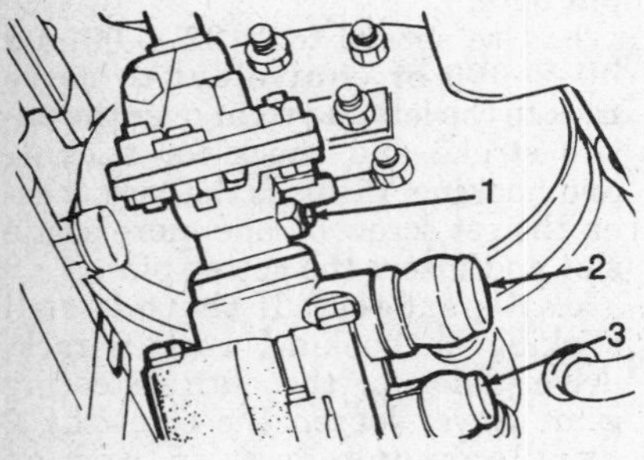


1. Screw
2. Hose
3. Hose

Coupling flange and steering box

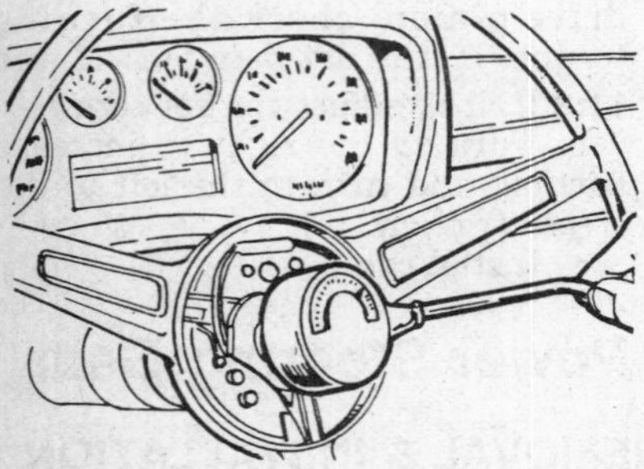

Friction gauge installation

system by operating the brake pedal hard about 20 times. Then, drain brake fluid out of the reservoir. Remove the 2 mounting nuts/bolts and remove the pipe connecting the steering unit and the rest of the system.

3. On all other systems, drain the steering fluid at this point.

4. Remove the cotter pin and loosen the castellated nut. Then, press the center tie rod off the steering drop arm.

5. Remove the screw or nut(s) and bolt(s) and slide the U-joint off the steering box or slide the flange coupling the steering column and steering gear upward. Replace all self-locking nuts.

6. Disconnect the hoses at the steering gear and plug the openings.

7. Detach and remove the steering gear mounting bolts at the front axle carrier, working below it. Be careful to retain all washers—they are used on both side of the front axle carrier members.

**To install:**

8. Installation is the reverse of removal. Use new seals on the hydraulic lines.

9. The U-joint bolts must pass through the locking grooves on the steering shaft and steering unit shaft.

10. When reinstalling the gearbox on 6 and 7 Series cars, line up marks on the steering shaft and gearbox so the steering wheel will be in the straight ahead position.

11. Use a new cotter pin on the castellated nut. Replace all self-locking nuts.

12. A new, self locking nut is available to replace the castellated nut on the steering drop arm. Use new hydraulic fluid.

**NOTE: System must be bled and the front wheels must be in the straight ahead position. Marks on the housing and propeller shaft must align. Use new self locking nuts on all models.**

### *318i, 325, 325e, 325i, 325iS and M3*

1. Support the car securely and remove front wheels. Remove the pinch bolt (1) and loosen bolt (2). Press the spindle off the steering gear.

2. Use a syringe to empty the power steering fluid reservoir. Loosen the clamp and pull off the hydraulic fluid return line from the power steering unit. Discard drained fluid.

3. Detach the pressure line (arrowed). Seal off openings.

4. Unscrew left and right side nuts, and press off the tie rods where they connect to the spring struts. For most of these models, use a tool such as 32 0 070; however, for the M3, use 32 1 160 or equivalent.

5. Remove the bolts attaching the steering unit to the front axle carrier and remove it.

**To install:**

6. Install in reverse order, keeping the following points in mind:

a. The steering unit bolts to the rear holes of the axle carrier. Use new self-locking nuts and torque them to 29–34 ft. lb.

b. When reconnecting tie rods to the spring struts, make sure tie rod pins and strut bores are clean. Replace self-locking nuts, coat threads with Loctite® 270 or equivalent, and torque to 40–48 ft. lb.

c. Replace the seals on the power steering pump connection, and torque the bolt to 29–32 ft. lb.

d. Refill the fluid reservoir with specified fluid. Idle the engine and turn the steering wheel back and forth until it has reached right and left lock 2 times each. Then, turn off the engine and refill the reservoir.

### *325iX (4WD)*

**NOTE: To remove the steering gear on 4 wheel drive models, use a special tool to support the engine via the body. It is possible to use BMW Tool 00 0 200 or an equivalent device available in the aftermarket. It is also advisable to use a special tool to support the front axle carrier without damaging it. Another tool such 00 0 200 would do this job. It is necessary to remove the entire front axle carrier to gain access to the mounting bolts for the steering gear on this model.**

1. Raise the car and support it securely a few feet off the ground via the body. Remove the splash guard. Remove the front wheels.

2. Remove the air cleaner. Use a clean syringe to remove the power steering fluid from the pump reservoir.

3. Attach the support tool and connect it to the engine hooks to be sure the engine is securely supported.

4. Remove the through bolts from the right and left engine mounts.

5. Disconnect both the hydraulic lines running from the power steering pump to the steering gear, and then plug the openings.

6. Loosen both the retaining bolts and then disconnect the steering column spindle off the steering gear.

7. Remove the retaining nuts on both sides and then use a tool such as 32 2 070 to press the tie rod ends off the steering knuckles. Be careful to keep grease out of the bores and off the tie rod ballstuds.

8. Remove the cotter pins, remove the retaining nuts on both sides and then use a tool such as 31 2 160 to press the control arm balljoint studs out of the steering knuckles. Be care-

Power steering reservoir—typical

ful to keep grease out of the bores and off the control arm ballstuds.

9. Remove the 2 bolts on either side attaching the control arm brackets to the body.

10. Remove the 2 bolts and remove the stabilizer bar mounting brackets from the front axle carrier on both sides.

11. Support the front axle carrier with a floorjack, assisted by the special tool mentioned in the note above or by another safe means that will not put stress on the axle carrier. Then, remove the (2) mounting bolts on either side and remove the axle carrier. Remove the 3 mounting bolts and remove the steering gear from the axle carrier.

**To install:**

12. Install in reverse order, noting these points:

a. Clean the bores into which the axle carrier bolts are mounted. Use some sort of locking sealer and torque the bolts to 30 ft. lbs.

b. Torque the mounting bolts holding the steering gear to front axle carrier to 30 ft. lbs.

c. Install new cotter pins on the retaining nuts for the control arm ballstuds. Torque to 61.5 ft. lbs.

d. Replace the self-locking nuts on the tie rod end ballstuds and connecting the steering column spindle to the steering box. Torque tie rod ballstud nuts to 24–29 ft. lbs.

e. Replace the gaskets on power steering hydraulic lines. Refill the fluid reservoir with specified fluid. Idle the engine and turn the steering wheel back and forth until it has reached right and left lock 2 times each. Then, turn off the engine and refill the reservoir.

### ADJUSTMENT

1. Remove the steering wheel center.

2. With the front wheels in the straight ahead position, remove the cotter pin and loosen the castle nut.

3. Press the center tie rod off the steering drop arm.

Power steering belt adjustment

4. Turn the steering wheel to the left about one turn. Install a friction gauge and turn the wheel to the right, past the point of pressure and the gauge should read 0.72–0.87 ft. lbs.

5. To adjust, turn the steering wheel about one turn to the left. Loosen the counter nut and turn the adjusting screw until the specified friction is reached when passing over the point of pressure.

## Power Steering Pump

### REMOVAL & INSTALLATION

#### *All Models Except 733i, 735i and 735iL*

**NOTE: On 5, 6 and 7 Series models built in 1986–89, the power steering pump operates the power brakes. On these cars, depress the brake pedal repeatedly until all boost pressure has been discharged.**

1. Detach the steering pump hoses. Seal off all openings. Loosen the locknut and turn the adjusting bolt to release belt tension, and remove the belt.

2. On 6 Series models, remove the splash guard. Remove bolts from the brackets holding the front and rear of the pump.

3. Installation is the reverse of removal. Torque pump mounting bolts to 16–17 ft. lbs. On 3 series cars with a toothed drive belt adjusting nut, torque the adjusting nut to 5.8–6.1 ft. lbs. to get the correct belt tension.

**NOTE: Bleed the system and torque the hose connections to 35 ft. lbs. (29–32 ft. lb – 318i and 325).**

#### *733i, 735i and 735iL*

**NOTE: When the pump is damaged, the pressure control regulator must also be replaced.**

1. Discharge the hydraulic accumulator, by depressing the brake pedal with the force required for full stop breaking (about 20 times).

2. Use a syringe to draw the fluid out of the pump reservoir and discard it. Detach all hoses at the pump and plug the openings.

3. Loosen the 2 locknuts and turn the adjusting pinion nut to release the belt tension. Remove the drive belt.

4. Remove bolts from the brackets holding the pump in place at both top and bottom.

**To install:**

5. Install in reverse order. Reconnect the hoses to the pump in such a way that they will not rub against body parts.

6. Note that on all models, the belt tension is released or tightened by unscrewing the splash guard, loosening the locknut and bolts at top and bottom of the pump, and then turning the geared locking element.

7. In adjusting the belt, torque this locking element in the tightening direction to 5.9–6.1 ft. lbs. and then tighten the locknut. Use new seals on the hydraulic lines.

**NOTE: Run the engine 10 minutes and turn the steering wheel several times from stop to stop. Operate the brake booster quickly, to obtain hard resistance, about 10 times to discard the oil leaving the return hose.**

8. Stop the engine, drain the oil from the tank and connect the booster return hose on the tank.

### BELT ADJUSTMENT

Tighten the belt so that when pressure is applied to the belt, the distance between both belt pulleys is 5–10mm.

On 733i, 735i and 735iL models and 3 Series models, torque the geared locking element in the tightening direction to 5.9–6.1 ft. lbs. and then tighten the locknut.

### SYSTEM BLEEDING

1. Fill the reservoir to the edge with the proper fluid.

2. Start the engine and all oil until the oil level remains constant.

3. Turn the steering wheel from lock to lock quickly until air bubbles are no longer present in the reservoir.

4. On models incorporating a combination power steering and power brake system, operate the brake pedal to discharge the hydraulic accumulator until the oil level stops rising or noticeable resistance on the brake pedal is felt.

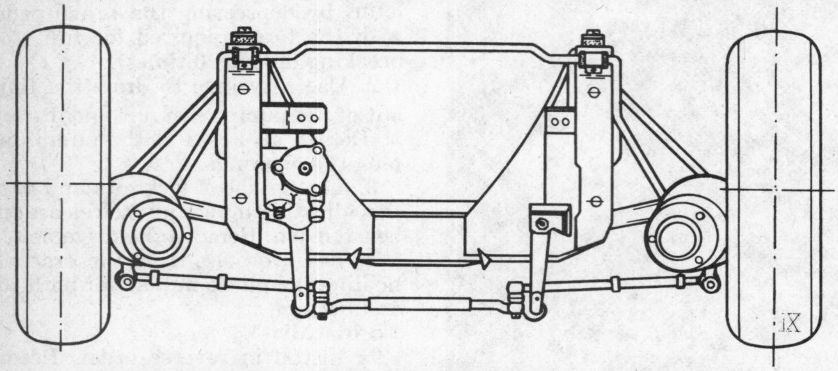


Recirculating-ball type steering linkage—all except 318i and 320i

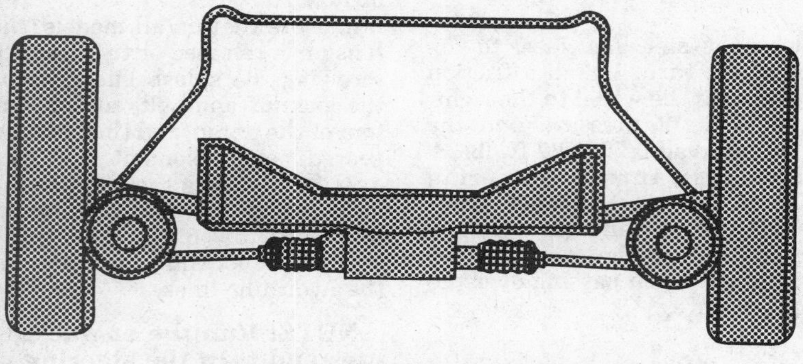

Rack and pinion steering linkage—318i and 320i

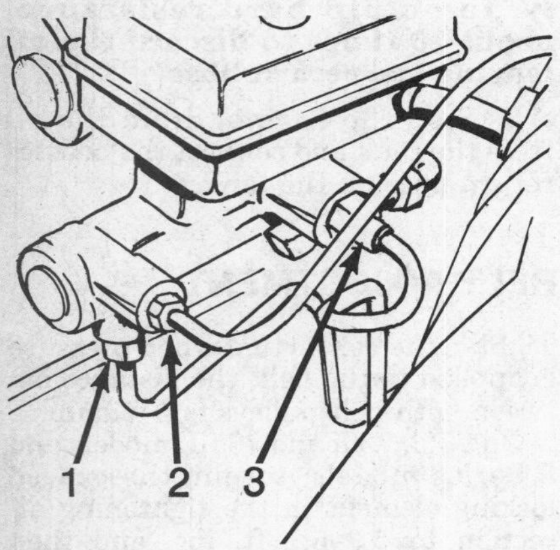


1. Right front
2. Left front
3. Rear wheels

Master cylinder—320i

## Tie Rod Ends

### REMOVAL & INSTALLATION

#### *All Models*

1. Raise and support the vehicle. Loosen the clamping bolt that retains the toe-in adjustment by keeping the tie rod end from turning in relation to the tie rod.

2. Remove the cotter pin and castellated or self-locking nut from the bottom of the tie rod end. Then, press the tie rod end out of the steering knuckle with a tool such as 32 2 050 (on the M3, use 32 1 160 or equivalent). Then, unscrew the tie rod end from the tie rod and remove it, counting the number of turns required.

3. Install in reverse order, using a new cotter pin or castellated nut. Recheck the front alignment and reset the toe-in if necessary. Torque the castellated or self-locking nut to 26.5 ft. lbs. and the clamping screw to 10 ft. lbs. Final torque the clamping bolt with the car resting on its wheels.

# BRAKE SYSTEM

**For all brake system repair and service procedures not detailed below, please refer to "Brakes" in the Unit Repair section.**

## Master Cylinder

### REMOVAL & INSTALLATION

#### *533i and 633i*

1. Disconnect the negative battery cable. Remove the air cleaner if necessary for access.
2. Drain and disconnect the brake fluid reservoir from the master cylinder. The brake fluid reservoir will be mounted in one of 2 ways: (1) assembled directly on top of the master cylinder; it is removed by tilting the reservoir to one side and lifting it off of the master cylinder, or (2) the reservoir is mounted in the engine compartment where it is attached to the inner fender sheet metal by means of attaching bolts; carefully disconnect hoses leading to the master cylinder and allow the reservoir to drain.
3. Disconnect all brake lines from the master cylinder.
4. Remove the master cylinder-to-power booster attaching nuts, and remove the master cylinder. On 7 Series cars, check that the new master cylinder is of the same diameter as the old one.

**NOTE: Observe the correct seating of the master cylinder- to-power booster seals.**

**To install:**

5. Bench-bleed the master cylinder.

**NOTE: Check for proper seating of the master cylinder- to-power booster O-ring. Check clearance between the master cylinder piston and push rod with Plastigage® or equivalent, and, if necessary, adjust to 0.002 in. by placing shims behind the head of the push rod.**

6. Position the master cylinder onto the studs protruding from the power booster; install and tighten the attaching nuts.
7. Connect all brake lines.
8. Install the brake fluid reservoir and fill with brake fluid.

**NOTE: An alternate method to bench bleeding the master cylinder is to bleed the master cylinder in the vehicle by opening (only slightly) the brake line fitting at the master cylinder, and allowing the fluid to flow from the master cylinder into a container, however, this method should be considered as an ALTERNATE METHOD ONLY as it is more difficult to control the fluid leaving the master cylinder during bleeding, thereby increasing the chance of accidentally splashing brake fluid onto the painted surface of the vehicle.**

9. Bleed the brake system.

#### *318i, 320i, 325, 325e, 325I and 325iS, 325iX, M3*

1. Disconnect the negative battery

cable. Remove the fuel mixture control unit on the 320i. Disconnect the fluid level indicator plug.

2. Disconnect the clutch master cylinder hose at the fluid reservoir.

3. Drain and then disconnect the brake fluid reservoir from the master cylinder

4. Disconnect the brake lines from the master cylinder.

5. On the 320i, working from the underside of the left-side inner fender panel (wheel opening area) remove the 2 master cylinder support bracket attaching nuts.

6. Remove the master cylinder-to-power booster attaching nuts, and remove the master cylinder. Inspect the rubber vacuum seal in the end of the unit and replace, if necessary.

7. Install in reverse order of removal.

**NOTE: Bench bleed the master cylinder prior to installation. Refer to the aforementioned note concerning an ALTERNATE bleeding procedure.**

8. Bleed the brake system.

### 524td, 525i, 528e, 535i, 635CSi, M5 and M6

#### WITH VACUUM POWER BRAKES

1. Disconnect the negative battery cable. Using a syringe that is new or has been used only for brake fluids, draw off all brake fluid from the brake fluid reservoir. Disconnect the fluid line going to the clutch master cylinder and plug it.

2. Disconnect the 2 brake lines connected to the side of the master cylinder.

3. Remove the 2 mounting bolts and remove the master cylinder from the power booster.

4. Inspect the rubber O-ring located in the groove of the rear of the master cylinder. Replace it if it is damaged.

5. Install in reverse order. Bleed the system.

#### WITH HYDRAULIC POWER BRAKES

1. Disconnect the negative battery cable. Operate the brake pedal with maximum force about 20 times to remove all residual hydraulic pressure. Using a syringe that is new or has been used only for brake fluids, draw off all brake fluid from the brake fluid reservoir.

2. Disconnect the hydraulic hoses and remove the fluid storage tank from the top of the master cylinder.

3. Remove the 2 bolts fastening the master cylinder to the booster and remove it.

4. Install the master cylinder in reverse order. Bleed the system.

### 733i, 735i and 735iL

1. Disconnect the negative battery cable. Drain and disconnect the fluid reservoir on 733i models built through 1982 and on 1986–90 models.

2. Disconnect the 2 brake lines from the outboard side of the master cylinder.

3. Remove the master cylinder-to-hydraulic booster attaching bolts, and remove the master cylinder.

4. Install in the reverse order of removal.

**NOTE: Bench bleed the master cylinder prior to installation. Refer to the aforementioned note concerning an ALTERNATE bleeding procedure.**

# Proportioning Valve

## REMOVAL & INSTALLATION

### 318i, 325, 325e, 325i, 325iS, 325iX and M3

1. Disconnect the negative battery cable. Draw off hydraulic fluid from the master cylinder with a syringe or hose used only with clean brake fluid.

2. Disconnect the brake lines at the top and bottom of the proportioning valve.

3. Remove the clamp from the valve and disconnect the pressure connection at the union.

4. Check day/year codes, reduction factor, and switch-over pressure to make sure the new valve is identical.

5. Install in reverse order. Bleed the system.

### 320i

1. Disconnect the negative battery cable. Draw off brake fluid from the master cylinder with a syringe or hose used only with clean brake fluid.

2. Disconnect the 4 brake lines at the proportioning valve.

3. Unscrew the 2 mounting bolts from the inner front/left wheel well. Replace this part with one bearing the code "25" and having a piston diameter of 0.709 in.

4. Install in reverse order. Bleed the system.

# Vacuum Operated Power Brake Booster

## REMOVAL & INSTALLATION

### 318i, 325, 325e, 325i, 325iS, 325iX and M3

1. Disconnect the negative battery cable. Draw off brake fluid in the reservoir and discard.

2. Remove the reservoir and disconnect the clutch hydraulic hose.

3. Disconnect all brake lines from the master cylinder.

4. Remove the instrument panel trim from the bottom/left inside the passenger compartment.

5. Remove the return spring from the brake pedal. Press off the clip and remove the pin which connects the booster rod to the brake pedal.

6. Remove the 4 nuts and pull the booster and master cylinder off in the engine compartment.

7. If the filter in the brake booster is clogged, it will have to be cleaned. To do this, remove the dust boot, retainer, damper, and filter, and clean the damper and filter. Make sure when reinstalling that the slots in the damper and filter are offset 180 degrees.

8. Install in reverse order. Adjust the stoplight switch for a clearance of 0.197–0.236 in.

9. Inspect the rubber seal between the master cylinder and booster and replace it if necessary.

### 320i

1. Disconnect the negative battery cable. Remove the master cylinder.

2. Disconnect the vacuum line at the power booster.

3. Remove the brake pedal apply-rod to power booster push rod pin.

4. Remove the power booster attaching nuts, and remove the power booster.

5. Install in the reverse order of removal.

**NOTE: If the original power booster unit is to be reused, remove the dust boost and clean the silencer and filter. Position the slots in the silencer 180 degrees away from the slots in the filter.**

6. Adjust the extended visible length of the brake light switch head to 0.20–0.24 in..

### 1984–85 528e, 533i and 633CSi

1. Disconnect the negative battery cable. Remove the coolant reservoir.

2. Remove the master cylinder.

3. Disconnect the vacuum hose at the power booster.

4. Disconnect the power booster apply rod at the brake pedal.

5. Remove the power booster attaching bolts.

6. Remove the power booster.

**To install:**

7. Install in the reverse order of removal.

**NOTE: If the original power booster unit is to be reused, remove the dust boot and clean the silencer and filter. Position the**

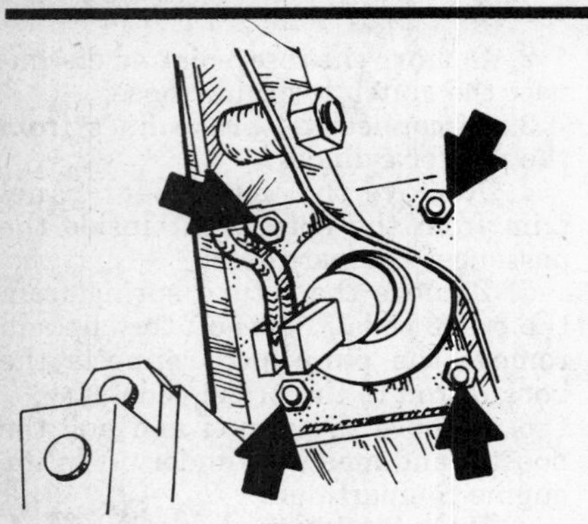

Remove the four arrowed bolts to remove the hydraulic brake booster (5-series cars

**slots in the silencer 180 degrees away from the slots in the filter.**

8. Adjust the brake pedal distance to 0.055–9.450 in. Adjust the stop light switch distance as described below:

a. Disconnect the electrical connector and loosen the locknut.

b. Measure the distance between the button on the end of the switch and the brake pedal. It must be 0.197–0.236 in. If necessary, turn the stoplight switch to adjust the distance.

c. Tighten the locknut and reconnect the electrical connector.

### *524td, 528e, 1986–90 525i, 535i, 635CSi, M5 and M6*

1. Disconnect the negative battery cable. Remove all brake fluid from the master cylinder with a syringe or hose used only with clean brake fluid.
2. Disconnect the electrical plugs from the cap on the fluid reservoir. Disconnect the hose going to the hydraulic clutch.
3. Disconnect the 2 brake lines on the outboard side of the master cylinder.
4. Remove the instrument panel trim located in the bottom/left area of the panel.
5. Disconnect and remove the pedal return spring. Then, remove the retaining clip and pull out the clevis pin connecting the pedal linkage to the booster.
6. Remove the 4 nuts and washers from the firewall, under the brake pedal. Then, remove the booster and master cylinder from the engine compartment.
7. Remove the 2 mounting bolts and disconnect the master cylinder from the booster.

**NOTE: If the original power booster unit is to be reused, remove the dust boot and clean the silencer and filter. Position the slots in the silencer 180 degrees away from the slots in the filter.**

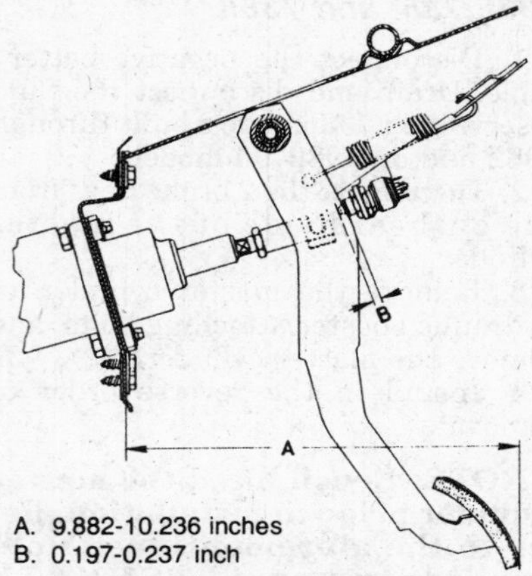


A. 9.882-10.236 inches
B. 0.197-0.237 inch

Brake pedal adjustment—733i

8. Check the O-ring located in the end of the master cylinder and replace it if it is worn or cracked.

**To install:**

9. Install the booster in reverse order, adjusting the stoplight switch as described in the next step and bleeding the system.
10. To adjust the stoplight switch:

a. Disconnect the electrical connector and loosen the locknut.

b. Measure the distance between the button on the end of the switch and the brake pedal. It must be 0.197–0.236 in. If necessary, turn the stoplight switch to adjust the distance.

c. Tighten the locknut and reconnect the electrical connector.

## Hydraulically Operated Power Brake Booster

### REMOVAL & INSTALLATION

#### *733i, 735i and 735iL*

1. Disconnect the negative battery cable. Release the pressure in the hydraulic accumulator by operating the brake pedal (with the engine not running) 20 times with a force equivalent to that necessary to bring the vehicle to a complete stop. Use a syringe to draw off the brake fluid in the master cylinder reservoir.
2. Remove the lower left instrument panel trim.
3. Disconnect the power booster aply-rod at the brake pedal. This is done by pulling off the bayonet clip and then pulling the pin out of the piston rod.
4. Remove the master cylinder as describe above.
5. Disconnect the fluid lines at the brake booster.
6. Remove the 4 power booster to pedal base assembly attaching bolts, and remove the power booster.

**To install:**

7. Install in the reverse order of removal. The hydraulic return line connection must be tightened with 34 3 153 or equivalent and the pressure line with 34 3 152 or equivalent. The adjustments of Steps 8 and 9 are not required on those cars.
8. Adjust the distance between the brake pedal and the fire wall to 9.882–10.236 in.
9. Adjust the extended visible length of the brake light switch head (plunger) to 0.197–0.237 in.

## Hydraulically Operated Power Brake Booster and Master Cylinder

### REMOVAL & INSTALLATION

#### *524td, 528e, 525i, 535i, 635CSi, M5 and M6*

**NOTE: Special wrenches must be used to tighten hydraulic lines for the hydraulic booster. Use BMW tools 34 3 153 and 34 3 152 or equivalent.**

1. Disconnect the negative battery cable. With the engine off, discharge all pressure from the system by applying the brake pedal 20 times full force. Using a syringe or similar tool used only with brake fluids, draw excess brake fluid out of the reservoir.
2. Remove the lower/left instrument panel trim. The, lift out the spring clip and remove the clevis pin fastening the piston rod to the brake pedal.
3. Disconnect the electrical connector and then pull of the reservoir.
4. Disconnect the brake hydraulic lines at the master cylinder. Disconnect the hydraulic hoses at the brake booster.
5. Remove the bolts from the driver's side of the pedal base assembly and remove the booster and master cylinder. To separate the master cylinder and booster to replace the booster, remove the 2 bolts.
6. Measure the distance from the end of the threads on the piston rod to the outer end of the forked fitting for the clevis pin. Then, transfer the fitting over to the new booster, screwing it on until the dimension is the same.

**To install:**

7. Install in reverse order, keeping the following points in mind:

a. When reattaching the hydraulic fittings to the booster, make sure everything is clean and use the special tools to tighten the fittings.

b. Check the rubber seals for the master cylinder reservoir and replace them is necessary.

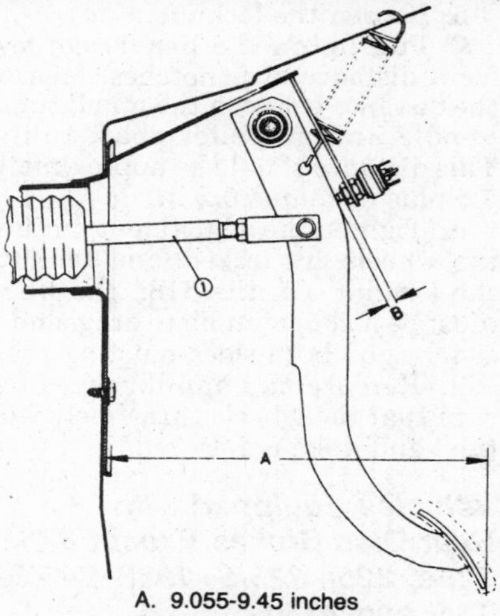


A. 9.055-9.45 inches
B. 50 mm (1.97 inches)

**Brake Pedal Adjustment 528i, 528e, 630CSi, and 633CSi**

c. Bleed the brakes. Test operation and boost of the system before driving the vehicle.

## Disc Brake Pads

### REMOVAL & INSTALLATION

#### *Front Disc Brakes*

##### ALL MODELS EXCEPT 528e

1. Raise the front of the vehicle and safely support it. Remove the wheel.
2. Siphon a sufficient quantity of hydraulic fluid from the master cylinder reservoir to prevent the fluid from overflowing the master cylinder when removing the brake pads. This is necessary as the pistons must be forced back into the cylinder bore to provide sufficient clearance to remove the pads.
3. If so equipped, disconnect the electrical connector from the brake pad wear indicator and then pull the wires out of the clamp.
4. Remove the pad retaining pins and any retaining clips holding them.
5. Remove the anti-rattle and spreader springs. note the correct positioning of the springs prior to removal. Replace if necessary.
6. Force the old pads away from the brake disc (rotor) for easy withdrawal and then lift the pads out of the caliper.

**To install:**

7. Check the brake disc (rotor) for scoring or signs of excess wear..
8. Examine the dust boot for cracks or damage and push the pistons back into the cylinder bores. If the pistons are frozen or if the caliper is leaking hydraulic fluid, it will require overhaul or replacement.
9. Slip the new pads into the caliper and then install one pad retaining pin and clip. Position the anti-rattle springs and/or spreader springs and then install the other pad retaining pin and clip.
10. Refill the master cylinder with the correct brake fluid.
11. Replace the wheel and lower the vehicle. Pump the brake pedal several times to bring the brakes into correct adjustment. Road test the vehicle.

**NOTE: If a firm pedal cannot be obtained, the system will require bleeding.**

##### 528e

1. Raise and safely support the front of the vehicle.. Remove the wheel.
2. Siphon a sufficient quantity of hydraulic fluid from the master cylinder reservoir to prevent the fluid from overflowing the master cylinder while removing the pads. This is necessary as the pistons must be forced into the cylinder bore to provide sufficient clearance to remove the pads.
3. Grasp the caliper from behind and pull it outward. This will push the piston back into the cylinder bore.
4. Disconnect the brake pad lining wear indicator.
5. Remove the plastic caps and then unscrew and remove the 2 socket head guide pins. Press out the pad clamp and then lift off the caliper and position it out of the way.
6. Remove the brake pads.

**To install:**

7. Check the brake disc (rotor) for scoring or signs of excess wear.
8. Examine the dust boot for cracks or damage and push the piston back into the cylinder bore. If the piston if frozen of if the caliper is leaking hydraulic fluid, it will require overhaul or replacement.
9. Slip the new pads into the mounting bracket and then install the caliper in the reverse order of removal.
10. Refill the master cylinder with the proper brake fluid.
11. Replace the wheel and lower the vehicle. Pump the brake pedal several times to bring the brakes into correct adjustment. Road test the vehicle.

**NOTE: If a firm pedal cannot be obtained, the system will require bleeding.**

#### *Rear Disc Brakes*

##### ALL EQUIPPED MODELS EXCEPT 528e, 6 AND 7 SERIES

**NOTE: The position of the caliper piston must be checked with a special BMW gauge (or equivalent) 34 1 000 series (specific by the model) and, if necessary, aligned with a special tool such as 34 1 060 or equivalent.**

1. Support the rear of the vehicle in a raised position, and remove the rear wheels.
2. Drive out the retaining pins.
3. Remove the cross springs (anti-rattle clips).
4. Using a BMW special hook, tool 34-1-010 or an equivalent tool, pull the pads out and away from the caliper.
5. Using a BMW special tool 34-10050, press the piston into the caliper to the fully retracted position. Drain fluid from the master cylinder first as doing this will displace fluid and raise the level there.
6. Check the 20 degree position of the caliper piston with a BMW special gauge 34-1-000 or an equivalent gauge. The 20 degree step must face the inlet or the brake disc.
7. Install the new brake pads, making sure to reinstall the anti-rattle clips. Install the rear wheel.

##### 6 AND 7 SERIES

**NOTE: The position of the caliper piston must be checked with a special BMW gauge (or equivalent) 34 1 000 series (specific by model) and, if necessary, aligned with a special tool such as 34 1 060 or equivalent.**

1. Remove the rear wheel. Disconnect the right rear plug for the pad wear indicator. Take the wires out of the clamp.
2. Drive out the retaining pins and remove the cross spring.
3. Pull the pads straight out with a tool which will grab them via the backing plate holes. If the pads are to be reused, make sure not to mix them up, they must be reinstalled in the same place.

**To install:**

4. When using new pads, note both the color code and make. Replace all 4 pads on rear axle together if any pads are excessively worn.
5. Install a new wear sensor on the right side of the left brake pad (thicker side toward disc).
6. Use a brush and alcohol to clean the guide surface of the housing opening.
7. Force the pistons back into the caliper with an appropriate special tool (for example BMW 34 1 050). Forcing the pistons back will displace the fluid in the caliper and raise the level in the master cylinder. Drain some fluid out of the master cylinder reservoir before proceeding.
8. The step on the piston must face the side of the caliper where the disc enters the caliper when the vehicle is

moving forward. If necessary, correct the angle of the piston with a special tool such as BMW 34 1 060. Measure the angle with BMW gauge 34 1 100 or equivalent.

9. Reinstall pads in reverse order. Check the cross spring and retaining pins and replace if necessary. Pump the brake pedal until all motion has been taken out of the pads and they rest at the calipers. Keep the master cylinder fluid reservoir full while doing this.

**528e**

1. Raise and safely support the rear of the vehicle.. Remove the wheel.
2. Siphon a sufficient quantity of hydraulic fluid from the master cylinder reservoir to prevent the fluid from overflowing the master cylinder while removing the pads. This is necessary as the pistons must be forced into the cylinder bore to provide sufficient clearance to remove the pads.
3. Grasp the caliper from behind and pull it outward. This will push the piston back into the cylinder bore.
4. Disconnect the brake pad lining wear indicator.
5. Remove the plastic caps and then unscrew and remove the 2 socket head guide pins. Press out the pad clamp and then lift off the caliper and position it out of the way.
6. Remove the brake pads.

**To install:**

7. Check the brake disc (rotor) for scoring or signs of excess wear.
8. Examine the dust boot for cracks or damage and push the piston back into the cylinder bore. If the piston if frozen of if the caliper is leaking hydraulic fluid, it will require overhaul or replacement.
9. Slip the new pads into the mounting bracket and then install the caliper in the reverse order of removal.
10. Refill the master cylinder with the proper brake fluid.
11. Replace the wheel and lower the vehicle. Pump the brake pedal several times to bring the brakes into correct adjustment. Road test the vehicle.

**NOTE: If a firm pedal cannot be obtained, the system will require bleeding.**

## Brake Shoes

### REMOVAL & INSTALLATION

#### *Rear Drum Brakes*

**318i AND 320i**

1. Raise and safely support the rear of the vehicle and remove the Allen screw from the brake drum. Remove the brake drum.
2. Turn the retainers 90 degrees and remove the retaining springs at the center of both shoes.
3. Disconnect the return springs at the bottom with a return spring tool, noting their exact locations. Disconnect the bottoms of the shoes from the retainers.
4. Pull the tops of the shoes out of the brake cylinder piston rods, and pull slightly away from their mountings for clearance. Then, disconnect the parking brake cable from the actuating hook, and remove the shoes.
5. Measure the brake linings-minimum thickness is .118 in. Also check the return spring for signs of heat damage and replace, if necessary.
6. Install in reverse order, making sure to connect the long end of the return spring between the parking brake lever and brake shoe.

## Rear Wheel Cylinder

### REMOVAL & INSTALLATION

1. Remove the rear brake drum.
2. Loosen the wheel cylinder bleeder screw. DO NOT remove the bleeder screw.
3. Disconnect the brake line from the wheel cylinder.
4. Turn the brake shoe adjusting cams as far to the outside as possible.
5. Remove the wheel cylinder attaching bolts, and remove the wheel cylinder.
6. Install in the reverse order of removal.

## Parking Brake Cable

### ADJUSTMENT

#### *Vehicles Equipped with Rear Drum Brakes*

1. Support the rear of the vehicle in the raised position.
2. Fully release the handbrake.
3. On vehicles with adjustable brakes, while rotating the tire and wheel assembly, turn the left hand eccentric adjustment nut counterclockwise and the right-hand eccentric adjustment nut clockwise until the brake shoes are tight against the drum and the wheel will no longer rotate. On vehicles with self-adjusting brakes, simply operate the pedal hard several times to ensure automatic adjusters have taken up the slack.
4. Loosen the eccentric nuts by 1/8 of a turn, so that the wheel is just able to turn, on vehicles with adjustable brakes.
5. Push up the rubber sleeve on the handbrake lever until the locknut is visible.
6. Loosen the locknut.
7. Pull up on the handbrake lever for a distance of 5 notches. Measure the distance between the middle of the handle and propeller shaft tunnel. This distance should be approximately 4.5 plus or minus 0.2 in.
8. Tighten the adjustment nut until the wheels are locked, and retighten the locknut. On the 318i, the wheels must be just beginning to drag, and resistance on both sides must be equal.
9. Release the handbrake. Make sure that the wheels turn freely when the handbrake is released.

#### *Vehicles Equipped with Rear Disc Brakes Except 325, 325e, 325i, 325iS, 1983–84 733i, 735i and 735iL*

The procedure for adjusting the handbrake on vehicles equipped with rear disc brakes is similar to the procedure for adjusting the handbrake on vehicles equipped with rear drum brakes with one exception.

The mechanism for adjusting the brake shoes is a star wheel type adjuster. Insert a screwdriver through the 0.6 in. hole, and turn the adjusting star wheel until the brake disc can no longer be moved. Proceed as though adjusting the handbrake on vehicles equipped with rear drum brakes.

#### *325, 325e, 325i and 325iS, 325iX, M3*

1. Remove one bolt on each rear wheel with the vehicle securely supported. Make sure the handbrake is off and cable properly adjusted.
2. Turn the wheels until the bolt hole is about 30 degrees behind the 12 o'clock position. Then it is possible to reach the star wheel adjuster with a long screwdriver.
3. Turn the left side adjusting nut up, or the right side nut down, to tighten the adjustment until the shoes prevent the disc from being turned by hand. Now loosen the adjustment 3–4 threads. Make sure the disc turns easily.

#### *1983–84 733i, 735i and 735iL*

1. The parking brake should be adjusted when the lever can be pulled up more than 8 notches. First, remove the cover pate on the console (the handbrake lever protrudes through this plate). Then, loosen the locknuts and loosen the adjusting nuts (2) for the cables until they are nearly at the ends of the threads.
2. Support the car securely off the rear wheels. Remove one wheel bolt from each rear wheel. Then, rotate one wheel until the hole left by removing the bolt is about 45 degrees counter-

To disconnect the rear brake cable on the 735i, pull the spreader lock assembly (A) out of the housing and remove the pin at the lower end. Disconnect the cable at (B); pull the inner portion of the spreader lock (C) out of the housing.

clockwise from the 6 o'clock position. This will line the hole in the wheel with the star wheel which adjusts the rear brake shoes (used for parking only). If it is difficult to turn the star wheel it will help to remove the rear wheel and, if necessary, the brake disc.

3. Turn the adjusting star wheel with a screwdriver until the rear wheel or brake disc can no longer be turned. Then, back it off 4 to 6 threads.

4. In the passenger compartment, pull the handbrake up 4 notches. Then, turn the cable adjusting nuts in the tightening direction until the rear wheels can just barely be turned. Make sure the adjustment is uniform. Lock the adjusting nuts in position.

5. Release the handbrake and make sure the wheels can now be turned easily, repeating Step 4 to correct a failure to release if necessary.

## REMOVAL & INSTALLATION

### *318i and 320i*

1. Remove the brake drum as described above. Pull off the rubber boot at the handbrake lever, loosen and remove the locknuts on the appropriate side, and disconnect the cable at the handbrake lever.

2. Remove the brake shoes as described in Unit Repair.

3. Then, on 320i, pull the cable out of the holder toward the rear of the car. On 318i, disconnect the cable on the rear suspension arm, compress the locking clamp, and disconnect the cable on the backing plate and pull it out.

**To install:**

4. Install the cable in position, making sure the cable holders are both located properly—one in the protective tube, and the other in the backing plate.

5. On the 318i, make sure the clamp which locates the tube is properly connected.

6. Adjust the brakes as described at the front of this chapter.

### *325, 325e, 325i, 325iS and 325iX*

1. Remove the rubber boot at the base of the handbrake by pulling up the clamp at the front and lifting it out at the rear.

2. Lift out the ashtray at the rear of the console. Remove the bolt located under the ashtray. Then, pull the console to the rear to disconnect it and remove it.

3. Unscrew and remove the parking brake cable nuts.

4. Remove the parking brake shoes. Locate the cable spread outboard of the brake disc. Pull the outer portion of the spreader to the rear and remove it. Then, press out the pin and pull the unit off.

5. Disconnect the brake cable at the trailing arm. Then, pull the cable out of the protective tube. Disconnect the cable support at the rear disc and then pull the assembly out.

**To install:**

6. Install in reverse order. The sliding surfaces of the cable spreader should be coated with Molykote® G paste or equivalent.

7. Make sure the cable holder rests on the protective tube.

8. To adjust the cable, pull the brake up just 5 notches, and then tighten the nuts until the right and left rear wheels just begin to drag uniformly. Release the brake and make sure the wheels turn freely.

### *1983–84 733i and 1983–86 735i*

1. Lift out the cover plate that surrounds the handbrake lever. Remove the locknuts and adjusting nuts from the front ends of the brake cables.

2. Remove the rear brake discs.

3. Disconnect the spreader locks from the backing plates: first, rock the lower end of the spreader lock outward, and then pull out the pin. Press the cable connection out of the spreader lock. Pull the spreader lock out of the housing. Pull the cable through the backing plate.

4. Detach the parking brake cable at the trailing arm and remove it.

5. To install, reverse the removal procedures, giving the sliding surfaces and pin of the spreader lock a light coating of an lubricant such as Molykote® G paste. Adjust the handbrake as described above.

### *1987–90 735i and 735iL*

1. Remove the rear brake discs. Refer to the Brake Unit Repair Section.

2. Using brake spring pliers, disconnect the upper return spring for the parking brake shoes. Then, using a special tool 34 4 000 or the equivalent, turn the retaining springs for the parking brake shoes 90 degrees to unlock them and then disconnect them.

**CAUTION**

***In performing the next step, watch the pin for the expander lock and keep it if it falls out.***

3. Separate the parking brake shoes at the top and then remove them from below.

4. Disconnect the spreader locks from the backing plates: first, rock the lower end of the spreader lock outward, and then pull out the pin. Press the cable connection out of the spreader lock. Pull the spreader lock out of the housing. Pull the cable through the backing plate.

5. Disconnect the parking brake cable at the trailing arm.

6. Working inside the car, remove the console cover as follows:

a. Lift out the air grille and remove the 2 nuts underneath.

b. Remove the cap and unscrew the mounting bolt that's located at the forward end of the console on the right side. Lift out the cover that the bolt retains.

c. Remove the bolt on the left side of the forward end of the console. If the car has power windows, disconnect the plugs. Then, lift the console and remove air ducts.

d. Turn the retainer 90 degrees and peel the rubber cover downward. Now, unscrew the adjusting nuts on the parking brake cables and pull them out.

7. Install the cable in position. Adjust the parking brake as described above.

### 5 and 6 Series

1. Remove the parking brake shoes as described in the Unit Repair section.
2. Disconnect the negative battery cable, loosen the mounting screw and pull off the footwell nozzle.
3. Unscrew mounting bolts, and pull the tray at the front of the footwell out far enough to disconnect the wires. Then, remove the tray.
4. Remove the rubber boot from the handbrake lever. Unscrew the locknuts and remove them and pull the cable out of the brake lever.
5. Working under the car, detach the brake cable at the suspension arm. Remove the 2 mounting nuts at the brake backing plate, and then pull the cable out of the protective tube.
6. Install the cable in the reverse order of removal.

# CHASSIS ELECTRICAL

## Heater Assembly and Blower

### REMOVAL & INSTALLATION

#### 320i

1. Disconnect the battery ground.
2. Move the selector lever to the **WARM** position.
3. Drain the cooling system.
4. Loosen the hose clamp, and remove the heater core return hose.
5. Disconnect the heater hose between the hot water control valve and the engine.
6. Remove the package tray.
7. Remove outer tube casing.
8. Remove the lower center trim panel.
9. Remove the left side outer trim panel.
10. Remove the upper section of the steering tube casing.
11. Remove the heater control knobs.
12. Remove the heater control trim panel.
13. Remove the right side trim panel.
14. Disconnect the heater electrical lead.
15. Remove the heater housing retaining nuts.
16. Disconnect the left side distribution duct, and move the steering tube outer casing retaining bracket out of the way.
17. Remove the glove box lower trim panel.
18. Disconnect the left side distribution duct, and lift out the heater housing.
19. Remove the housing rivets.
20. Remove the housing clamps, and separate the housing halves.
21. Disconnect the bowden cable from the hot water control valve.
22. Remove the hot water control valve and hose from the water valve bracket on the heater housing.
23. Remove the rubber sleeves from the heater core inlet and outlet tubes.
24. Disconnect the electrical leads at the blower motor.
25. Disconnect the electrical leads at the blower resistor in the heater housing.
26. Open the blower motor support clamps, and remove the blower motor and fan as an assembly.
27. Install in the reverse order of removal.
28. Check operation of the heater controls. Adjust if necessary.

#### 528e and 533i

1. Remove the center tray. Remove the instrument panel trim to bottom right of tray.
2. Remove the glove box and remove heater controls at water valve and at air doors. Remove center console if equipped.
3. Disconnect the battery ground.
4. Push the selector lever to the **WARM** position.
5. Drain the coolant and remove the air conditioning evaporator:
   a. Drain the refrigerant slowly out of the low side Schrader® valve. If not trained and experienced in refrigeration work, leave this to a specialist.
   b. Take off the no-drip tape type insulation and disconnect both refrigerant lines from the evaporator.

**NOTE: Plug the refrigerant lines immediately to prevent moisture and contaminants from entering the system.**

   c. Pull the temperature sensor out of the evaporator housing.
   d. Disconnect the evaporator/heater control electrical connector.
   e. Remove the right and left screw from the housing (from area where the housing meets the passenger compartment carpeting).
   f. Remove the floor pan to evaporator housing bracket. Lift the housing slightly and pull it from under the dash.

**CAUTION**

***Do not bend the temperature sensor or it will have to be replaced.***

   g. Disconnect the blower wires and the blower resistor wire. Lift the evaporator slightly and pull the adapter and evaporator from under the dash.

6. Disconnect the heater hoses from the heater core, and remove the rubber seal.
7. Remove the lower instrument panel center trim.
8. Disconnect the heater controls at the instrument panel.
9. Disconnect the control shafts at the joints.
10. Disconnect the multiple electrical connector at the heater.
11. Remove the instrument panel center cover.
12. Working from inside the engine compartment, remove the upper section of the fire shield.
13. Remove the heater assembly retaining nuts, and lift out the heater.
14. Open the heater housing clips, and separate the housing halves and remove the heater core.
15. Disconnect the electrical leads at the blower motor, and remove the motor.
16. Install in the reverse order of removal.

#### 1983–86 733i and 735i

1. Disconnect the negative battery cable. Drain the coolant from the system.
2. Discharge the refrigerant from the air conditioner or have this done by someone trained in this type of work if not familiar with it.
3. Remove the instrument trim panel.
4. Remove the cowl fresh air grille.
5. Remove the heater assembly cover attaching screws, and remove the cover.
6. Disconnect the heater hoses at the heater core.
7. Disconnect the vacuum lines at the heater.
8. Bend open the heater duct mounting clamp.
9. Disconnect the central electrical lead.
10. Pull the duct cover downward, and remove it.
11. Remove the center strut attaching bolts (4).
12. Remove the insulation from the refrigerant lines.

13. Disconnect the refrigerant lines from the evaporator.
14. Disconnect the evaporator drain tube.
15. Remove the heater assembly retaining bolts, remove the heater and the heater core.
16. Install in the reverse order of removal.

## Heater Assembly and Heater Core

### REMOVAL & INSTALLATION

#### *524td, 528e, 533i, 633CSi, 525i, 535i, 635CSi, M5 and M6*

1. Disconnect the battery ground. Remove the instrument panel trim at bottom left. Remove the package tray.
2. If not trained in air conditioning work, have the air conditioning system discharged professionally. Otherwise, discharge it carefully through the Schrader® valve, and then cap the valve off.
3. Remove the 2 bolts and remove the trim panel underneath the evaporator unit.
4. Remove the tape type insulation. Get caps for the refrigerant lines. *Using a backup wrench*, disconnect the low and high pressure lines and cap them.
5. Disconnect the electrical connector for the evaporator. Disconnect the temperature sensor plug, accessible from the outside of the evaporator housing.
6. Remove the 2 bolts and then remove the bracket that braces the housing at the firewall. Remove the mounting bolt from either side of the housing.
7. Unclip both fasteners and remove the housing.
8. Now, move into the engine compartment and remove the rubber insulator from the cowl.
9. Remove the mounting bolts for the cover which is located under the windshield.
10. Remove the mounting nuts for the heater housing located on either side of the blower.
11. Drain the cooling system and disconnect the 2 hoses at the core.
12. Working inside the car, remove the 3 electrical connectors for the heater housing. Pull off the 2 air ducts.
13. Remove the 2 mounting nuts and remove the heater unit.
14. Remove the 4 air duct connections from the housing. Push the retaining bar back and then split and remove the 2 blower shells.
15. Remove the 13 retaining clips from the housing halves and split the housing. Then, remove the core.

**To install:**

16. To install, reverse the removal procedure, noting the following points:
    a. Cement a new rubber seal on the core.
    b. Make sure that when reassembling the halves of the housing, all the distributor door flap shafts pass through the holes in the housing.
    c. Before reconnecting the refrigerant lines, coat the threads with clean refrigerant oil.
    d. Refill the cooling system with clean coolant and bleed it.
    e. Have the air conditioning system evacuated and recharged or do so if qualified.

## Heater Core

### REMOVAL & INSTALLATION

#### *1987–90 735i and 735iL*

1. Disconnect the negative battery cable. Drain coolant from the cooling system (engine cooled off). Remove the center console.
2. Remove the 2 bolts and remove the right core mounting bracket. Lift out the front blower motor.
3. Remove the core cover screws. Loosen the wire straps and clips and remove the cover.
4. Unscrew the 6 mounting bolts and lift out the 3 heater pipes. Replace the O-rings. Then, lift out the core from the right side.
5. Install in reverse order. Refill and bleed the cooling system.

#### *318i, 325, 325e, 325i, 325iS, 325iX and M3*

1. Disconnect the negative battery cable. Remove the package tray. Remove bolts and remove the left/lower dish trim panel.
2. Drain the coolant, loosen the bolt and remove the clamp bracing the 2 lines going to the heater core.
3. Remove the left side duct carrying air from the heater to the rear seat duct.
4. Unscrew the bolts and remove the lower heater discharge duct.
5. Unscrew the bolts fastening the water lines from the engine compartment to the lines coming down from the heater core. Remove and discard the O-ring seals.
6. Unscrew the bolts, separate the halves of the core housing, and pull the core out of the housing.
7. Installation is the reverse of removal. Replace the O-ring seals for the water lines.

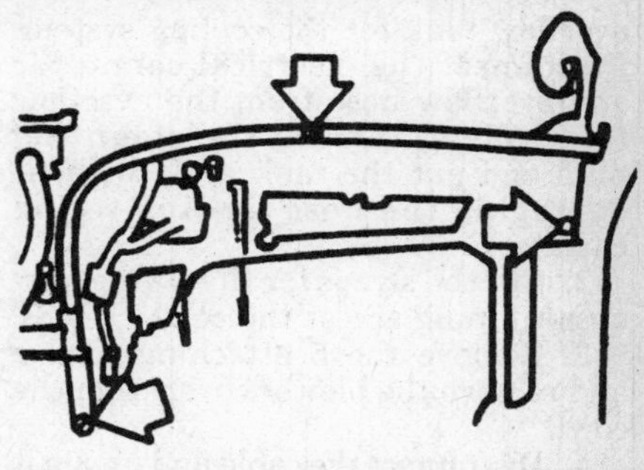

**Remove the two arrowed screws to remove the heater core on 1987-88 735i**

## Blower Motor

### REMOVAL & INSTALLATION

#### *318i, 325, 325e, 325i, 325iS, 325iX and M3*

1. Disconnect the negative battery cable. The blower is accessible by removing the cover at the top of the firewall in the engine compartment. To remove the cover, pull off the rubber strip, cut off the wire that runs diagonally across the cover, unscrew and remove the bolts, and pull the cover aside.
2. Open the retaining straps, swing them aside, and then remove the blower cover.
3. Pull off both connectors. Disengage the clamp that fastens the assembly in place by pulling the bottom in the direction of the operator. Now, lift out the motor/fan assembly, being careful not to damage the air damper underneath.

#### *524td, 528e, 533i, 525i, 535i, 633CSi, 635CSi, M5 and M6*

1. Disconnect the battery ground cable.
2. Remove the rubber insulator from the cowl. Remove the mounting bolts for the cover which is located under the windshield.
3. Push back the 3 retaining tabs and remove the 2 shells that cover the blower wheels.
4. Disconnect the electrical connector for the motor. Unclip the retaining strap for the motor and remove the motor and blower wheels.
5. Replace the motor and blower wheels as an assembly (prebalanced). The motor will fit into the housing only one way. Reverse all procedures to install, making sure the flat surface on the inlet cowls face the body.

#### *1987–90 735i and 735iL*

1. Disconnect the battery ground cable. Pull the rubber cover off the

overflow tank for the cooling system. Disconnect the electrical connector and overflow hose from the overflow tank. Then, remove the mounting nuts and put the tank aside without damaging the hose leading to the radiator.

2. Cut the straps for the wiring harness running across the cowl.

3. Remove the 5 attaching screws and remove the blower cover from the cowl.

4. Disconnect the cable and unclip it where it is clipped to the blower cover. Then, open the plastic retainer and take off the cover.

5. Disconnect the electrical connector. Lift off the metal retainer for the blower motor and remove the blower motor.

6. Install a new, prebalanced motor and blower assembly. Install in reverse order.

## Radio

### REMOVAL & INSTALLATION

#### *318i and 320i*

1. Disconnect the negative battery cable.

2. Unscrew the shift lever and lift off the boot.

3. Remove the phillips head screws which retain the console to the dash and transmission tunnel.

4. Remove the phillips head screws which retain the left and right-hand side panels of the console to the radio mounting bracket. Remove the side panels, exposing the radio mounting bracket. (The radio mounting bracket houses the speaker.)

5. Disconnect the antenna cable from the radio. Disconnect the radio ground cable (if so equipped) from the left-hand heater mounting bolt. Disconnect the power lead for the radio from the existing plug location inline to the hazard warning switch.

6. Lift the radio mounting bracket forward. The radio may now be disconnected from the speaker by removing the speaker multiple plug from the back of the radio.

7. Pry off the radio control knobs exposing the mounting nuts. Unscrew the mounting nuts and remove the radio from its bracket.

**To install:**

8. Install the radio in its mounting bracket and install the mounting nuts.

9. Install the radio control knobs. Connect the speaker plug to the radio and connect the power and ground leads to the radio.

10. Install the side console panels and install the console retaining screws.

11. Install the shift lever boot, if equipped. Connect the negative battery cable and check the operation of the radio.

#### *528e*

1. Disconnect the negative battery cable. Pull off the radio knobs and ornamental rings.

2. Push up on spring catches and remove them from the control shafts. Remove the radio mask.

3. Remove the bolts from supports on both sides of the radio.

4. Disconnect the automatic antenna lead, the antenna, the right and left speaker wires and the power supply.

5. Connect the power, speaker and antenna leads to the radio and install it in the dash.

6. Install the radio mask, ornamental rings, face plate and control knobs to the radio.

7. Connect the negative battery cable and check the radio for proper operation.

#### *All Models Equipped with Electronically Tuned Radio (ETR)*

Most models after 1984 are equipped with an electronically tuned stereo system, this system uses push buttons instead of knobs for radio control.

To remove the ETR radio receiver, first disconnect the negative battery cable then, remove the screws retaining the trim around the radio (and the A/C and heating control panel). Remove the screws retaining the radio. Slide it out of the dash and disconnect the wiring.

The radio is installed by simply connecting the wiring and sliding it back into place in the dash and securing it with the screws. Reinstall the trim around the radio and connect the battery cable. Check the radio operation.

## Windshield Wiper Switch

### REMOVAL & INSTALLATION

**NOTE: On many models, this switch is a combination unit which also controls the direction signals and headlight dimming. On 325, 325e, 325i, 325iS, 325iX and M3, this switch is mounted right next to the turn signal switch and its removal is covered specifically under the above procedure.**

#### *All Models Except 1987–90 735i and 735iL*

The wiper switch is located on the steering column and in most cases the steering wheel will have to be removed, along with the lower steering column trim panels, to gain access to the switch.

After the retaining screws and electrical connectors are removed, the switch can be lifted from the plate of the steering column.

**CAUTION**

***To avoid possible electrical short-circuits, the negative battery cable should be removed before the repairs are attempted.***

#### *1987–90 735i and 735iL*

1. Disconnect the negative battery cable. Remove the steering wheel as described earlier. Remove the lower/left instrument panel trim.

2. Remove the screws and remove the lower steering column cover.

3. Push the locking hook for the flasher back and remove the relay, socket facing downward.

4. Take off the upper steering column cover. If the car has airbags, drive out the pins and lift out the expansion rivet first.

5. Press the retaining hooks inward on both sides, pull the switch out, and then disconnect the electrical connector.

6. Installation is the reverse of removal.

## Windshield Wiper Motor

The electric wiper motor assembly is located under the engine hood, at the top of the cowl panel. A few models have covers over the wiper motor assembly, while others have the motors exposed. Link rods operate the left and right wiper pivot assemblies from a drive crank bolted to the wiper motor output shaft.

### REMOVAL & INSTALLATION

#### *320i, 524td, 528e, 528i, 533i, 525i, 535i, 633CSi, 635CSi, M5 and M6*

1. Disconnect the negative battery cable. Remove the cowl cover to expose the wiper motor (320i, 530i and all 5 and 6 Series cars after 1983).

2. Disconnect the wiper motor crank arm from the motor output shaft by removing the nut and pulling off the crank arm.

3. Remove the motor retaining screws and disconnect the electrical connector.

4. Remove the wiper motor from the vehicle.

5. Reverse the procedure to install the motor.

### 318i, 325, 325e, 325i 325iS, 325iX and M3

1. Disconnect the negative battery cable. Remove the heater motor, as described above. Remove the bracket bracing the windshield wiper motor, which is now visible.
2. Disconnect the electrical connector for the motor.
3. Lift out the grill located at the top of the cowl and disconnect the linkages to both wiper arms at the left side shaft mounts.
4. Disconnect both wiper arms from their shafts by lifting the cover, unscrewing the nut, and pulling the arm off. Then, remove the cover, nut and washer surrounding the shafts and holding the console in place. Now remove the entire console.
5. With the motor still mounted, remove the nut retaining the linkage to the motor shaft. Then, unbolt and remove the motor from the console.
6. Installation is the reverse of removal.

### 1983–84 733i and 1985–86 735i

1. Disconnect the negative battery cable. Remove the mounting screws and remove the grill from the cowl.
2. The wiper motor is located under a cover located in front of the windshield on the left side of the car. Unscrew the 2 mounting screws on the firewall and the 2 directly in front of the windshield. Pull the rubber seal out part way and move the cover slightly away from its normal position. Disconnect the hose from the cover and then tilt the cover forward.
3. Remove the wiper motor cover and unplug the electrical connector.
4. Remove both wiper arms. Unscrew the collar nuts and disconnect both wiper shaft mounts. Turn back the rubber pad and disconnect the linkage for the right wiper. Unscrew and remove the 2 mounting bolts and pull the spacer tube apart; remove the motor. Note the exact position of the motor crank.
5. Disconnect the linkage and pull the crank off the motor. The motor may be removed from the bracket after removing the 3 mounting bolts.

**To install:**

6. Install in reverse order, noting these points:
   a. Install the crank in the position shown to get proper parking of the wipers.
   b. When remounting the motor, make sure the bumpers that rest against the firewall are properly positioned.
   c. Situate the rubber pad so the motor has proper support.
   d. When reassembling the wiper

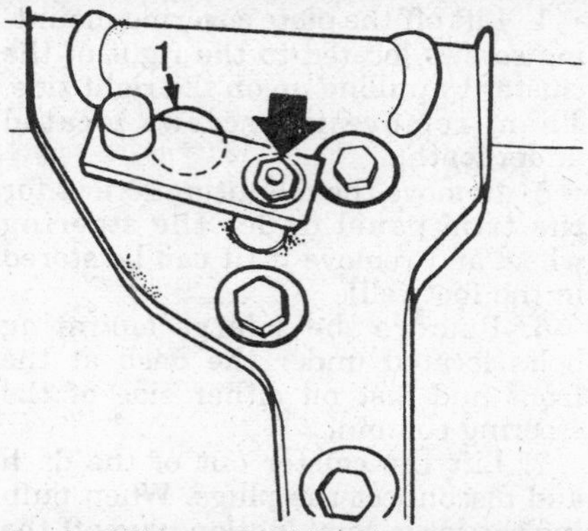


**On the 735i and 733i (1983 and later), install the motor crank in the position shown, with the bolt (1) half hidden by the upper edge of the crank.**

shaft mounts, install the diaphragm spring and then the ring and torque to only 9 ft. lbs.
   e. When reinstalling the outer cover, take care not to pinch any vacuum hoses.

### 1987–90 735i and 735iL

1. Disconnect the negative battery cable. Make sure the wipers are in the parked position. Remove the heater blower as described above. Take off the cover near the blower.
2. Disconnect the heater cable and lift out the linkage. Disconnect the temperature sensor.
3. Disconnect the clips, lift the cowl cover slightly and then remove the fresh air inlet cowls on either side. Then, remove the cover.
4. Unscrew bolts and remove the mounting bracket for the wiper housing. Remove the left wiper arm by pulling up the cover, loosening the pinch bolt, and removing it. Remove the right wiper by pulling up the cover, removing the through bolt and then pulling it off.
5. Lift out the clips and remove the cover for the linkage.
6. Unscrew and remove the nuts fastening the linkage to the cowl. Pull the linkage arms downward and out of the cowl.
7. Mark the relationship between the linkage lever and the motor. Remove the nut and disconnect the linkage at the motor shaft. Disconnect the electrical connector and remove the linkage.
8. Remove the 3 mounting bolts and remove the wiper motor. If installing a new motor, connect the motor and operate it until it reaches parked position; then install the linkage so that the shaft lever and linkage link are in a straight line.

**To install:**

9. Perform the remaining portions of the installation in reverse order, noting these points:
   a. Make sure the wiper arms are pressed all the way onto the linkage shafts so the contact pressure control will work.
   b. Make sure the inlet cowling is installed in proper relation to the blower housing and fresh air flap.

## Instrument Cluster

### REMOVAL & INSTALLATION

### 318i, 325, 325e, 325i 325iS, 325iX, and M3

1. Disconnect the negative battery cable. Remove the attaching screws and remove the lower instrument panel trim from under the steering column.
2. Remove the mounting nuts for the trim just under the instrument carrier, and remove it.
3. Unscrew the 4 screws underneath and 2 above the instrument carrier, and remove trim that surrounds the instrument carrier.
4. Remove the 2 screws at the top of the carrier, lift it out of the instrument panel, and then disconnect the plugs. To disconnect the combination plug, first pull the sliding clamp off the center.
5. Installation is the reverse of removal.

### 320i

1. Disconnect the negative battery cable.
2. Remove the steering wheel assembly.
3. Remove the bottom center instrument trim panel.
4. Disconnect the speedometer cable, loosen the knurled nut and pull the instrument assembly outward.
5. Remove the electrical plugs and wires.
6. Remove the instrument cluster from the dash.
7. Reverse the removal procedure to install.

### 528e

1. Remove the negative battery cable.
2. Remove the lower instrument trim panel.
3. Disconnect the speedometer cable.
4. Loosen the knurled nuts on the cluster back.
5. Loosen the steering column to dash screws.
6. Pull the instrument cluster outward and remove the electrical wires and connectors.

7. Remove the cluster from the dash panel.
8. Reverse the removal procedure to install the cluster.

### 533i, 535i and 633CSi

1. Disconnect the negative battery cable.
2. Remove the steering wheel assembly.
3. Remove the bottom center instrument trim panel.
4. Remove the cover from the "INQUIRY" unit.
5. Remove the 3 retaining screws and remove the "INQUIRY" printed circuit board.
6. Remove the light switch, leaving the wiring connected.
7. Remove the left air control knob and remove the bezel cover.
8. Remove the fog lamp switch and leave the wiring attached.
9. Remove the screws from the instrument cluster and loosen the steering column control base screws.
10. Disconnect the speedometer cable.
11. Push downward on the upper section casing and the steering column, so that the instrument cluster can be removed at an angle. Disconnect the electrical wiring and connectors.
12. Reverse the removal procedure to install the instrument cover.

### 524td, 528e, 1986–90 535i, 525i and M5

1. Disconnect the battery ground cable. Unscrew the 2 retaining screws in the hood above the instrument carrier.
2. Lift the carrier out far enough to unplug all the plugs and remove it. Before pulling off the combination plug, pull the sliding clip off the side of the plug.
3. Install in reverse order.

### 1983–84 633CSi, 1985–90 635CSi and M6

1. Disconnect the battery ground cable. Remove the steering wheel as described earlier.
2. Lift the glass cover off the check control, located to the left of the instrument cluster. Unscrew the 3 mounting screws, lift off the housing, and pull off the plugs while removing it.
3. Remove the fog light switch from the dash without disconnecting the wiring.
4. Lift off the plate covering mounting screws located to the right of the cluster by pulling up on the right side. Then, remove the screws located underneath.
5. Remove the mounting screws for the trim panel under the steering wheel and remove it (it can be stored in the footwell).
6. Remove the 2 large mounting bolts located under the dash at the front and just on either side of the steering column.
7. Lift the cluster out of the dash and disconnect the plugs. When pulling the large combination plug off the carrier, first push the clip off the plug.
8. Installation is the reverse of removal.

### 1983–84 733i and 1985–86 735i

1. Disconnect the negative battery cable. Remove the 3 bolts from the top of the instrument cluster.
2. Lift the instrument cluster out of the dash. Disconnect all electrical connectors. Note that the combination plugs have a slide clamp that must be removed before they can be pulled apart.
3. Install in reverse order.

### 1987–90 735i and 735iL

1. Remove the steering wheel as described earlier. Remove the 2 large screws located under the cluster hood.
2. Pry the cluster out slightly from the top and pull it forward and down until it touches the steering column.
3. Press the levers next to the electrical connector plugs upward and then pull the plugs off the cluster. Remove the cluster.
4. The cluster may be further disassembled by turning the toggle screws 90 degrees.
5. Install the cluster in reverse order. Make sure the levers that lock the electrical connector plugs are upward before trying to connect them.

## Headlight Switch

### REMOVAL & INSTALLATION

### 318i, 325, 325e, 325i 325iS, 325iX, and M3

1. Disconnect the battery ground cable. Remove the lower/left trim panel screws and remove the panel.
2. Unscrew the knob from the switch.
3. Pull off the connector plug from behind the dash panel. Pull out the switch from behind and remove it.
4. Install in reverse order.

### 524td, 528e, 525i, 535i, M5, 733i, 735i and 735iL

1. Disconnect the negative battery cable. The switch is pressed into the left side of the dash. Pry the switch out using a small screwdriver top and bottom.
2. Unplug the switch. Install in reverse order.

### 1983–84 633CSi, 635CSi, M6

1. Disconnect the battery ground. Remove the lower left instrument panel trim.
2. Unscrew and remove the light switch knob.
3. Remove the 4 bolts and remove the brace located under the instrument panel.
4. Pull off the switch plug. Then, pull the switch out of the dash from behind.
5. Install in reverse order.

## Stoplight Switch

### REMOVAL & INSTALLATION

### All Models

1. Disconnect the negative battery cable. Disconnect the electrical connector to the switch.
2. Loosen the locknut and then turn the switch outward to remove it.
3. Screw the new switch in. Adjust the gap between the pedal and actuator on the switch to 0.197–0.236 in. Tighten the locknut.

## Fuse and Circuit Breakers

### LOCATION

The fuse box is located under the engine hood on the left side, near the upper strut housing or near the battery, on the remaining models.

Various relays are also mounted on the fuse box for easy accessibility.

# Chrysler Corp. Imports

## Colt, Champ, Challenger, Conquest, Sapporo, Vista

# 4

# SERIAL NUMBER IDENTIFICATION

## Vehicle Identification Plate

The Vehicle Information Code and Chassis Number plate is attached to the bulkhead (firewall) in the engine compartment. The plate shows model code, engine model, transaxle model and body color code.

## Engine Number

The engine number is stamped at the right front side, on the top edge of the cylinder block and contains the engine model number and engine serial number.

## Vehicle Identification Label

The vehicle identification plate is mounted on the instrument panel, adjacent to the lower corner of the windshield on the driver's side and is visible through the windshield. A standardized 17 digit Vehicle Identification Number (VIN) is used.

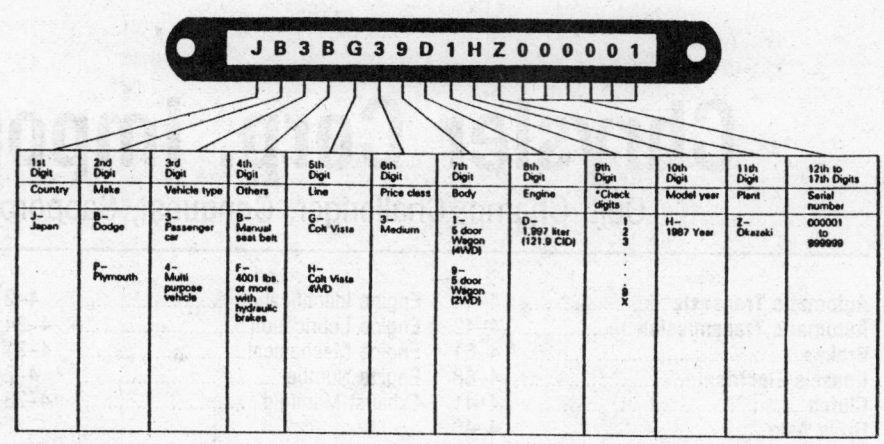

| 1st Digit | 2nd Digit | 3rd Digit | 4th Digit | 5th Digit | 6th Digit | 7th Digit | 8th Digit | 9th Digit | 10th Digit | 11th Digit | 12th to 17th Digits |
|---|---|---|---|---|---|---|---|---|---|---|---|
| Country | Make | Vehicle type | Others | Line | Price class | Body | Engine | *Check digits | Model year | Plant | Serial number |
| J– Japan | B– Dodge | 3– Passenger car | B– Manual seat belt | G– Colt Vista | 3– Medium | 1– 5 door Wagon (4WD) | D– 1,997 liter (121.9 CID) | 1<br>2<br>3<br>.<br>.<br>.<br>9<br>X | H– 1987 Year | Z– Okazaki | 000001 to 999999 |
| | P– Plymouth | 4– Multi purpose vehicle | F– 4001 lbs. or more with hydraulic brakes | H– Colt Vista 4WD | | 9– 5 door Wagon (2WD) | | | | | |

NOTE
* "Check digit" means a single number or letter X used to verify the accuracy of transcription of vehicle identification number.

Typical Vehicle Indentification Code plate

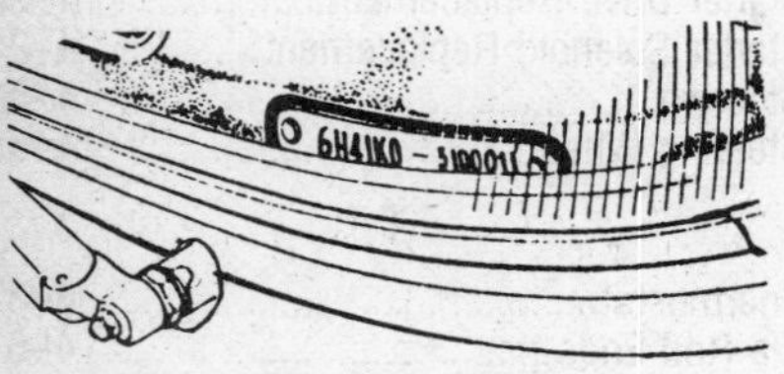


Serial number location

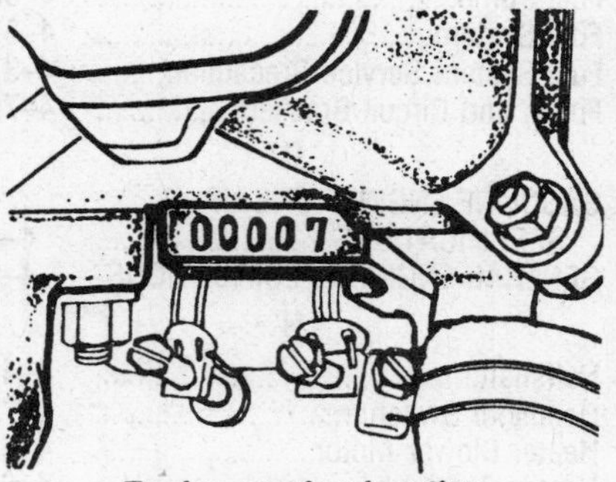


Engine number location

Engine model number

## ENGINE IDENTIFICATION

| Year | Model | Engine Displacement cu. in. (cc/liter) | Engine Series Identification | No. of Cylinders | Engine Type |
|---|---|---|---|---|---|
| 1983 | Champ | 86.0 (1410/1.4) | G12B, 4G12 | 4 | OHC |
| | Colt | 86.0 (1410/1.4) | G12B, 4G12 | 4 | OHC |
| | Champ | 97.5 (1597/1.6) | G32B, 4G32 | 4 | OHC |
| | Colt | 97.5 (1597/1.6) | G32B, 4G32 | 4 | OHC |
| | Challenger | 155.9 (2555/1.6) | G54B, 4G54 | 4 | OHC |
| | Sapporo | 155.9 (2555/1.6) | G54B, 4G54 | 4 | OHC |
| 1984 | Colt | 86.0 (1410/1.4) | G12B, 4G12 | 4 | OHC |
| | Colt | 97.5 (1597/1.6) | G32B, 4G32 | 4 | OHC |
| | Colt Vista | 121.9 (1997/2.0) | G63B | 4 | OHC |
| | Conquest | 155.9 (2555/2.6) | G54B, 4G54 | 4 | OHC |

## ENGINE IDENTIFICATION

| Year | Model | Engine Displacement cu. in. (cc/liter) | Engine Series Identification | No. of Cylinders | Engine Type |
|---|---|---|---|---|---|
| 1985 | Colt | 89.6 (1468/1.5) | G15B | 4 | OHC |
| | Colt | 97.5 (1597/1.6) | G32B, 4G32 | 4 | OHC |
| | Colt Vista | 121.9 (1997/2.0) | G63B | 4 | OHC |
| | Conquest | 155.9 (2555/2.6) | G54B, 4G54 | 4 | OHC |
| 1986 | Colt | 89.6 (1468/1.5) | G15B | 4 | OHC |
| | Colt | 97.5 (1597/1.6) | G32B, 4G32 | 4 | OHC |
| | Colt Vista | 121.9 (1997/2.0) | G63B | 4 | OHC |
| | Conquest | 155.9 (2555/2.6) | G54B, 4G54 | 4 | OHC |
| 1987 | Colt | 89.6 (1468/1.5) | G15B | 4 | OHC |
| | Colt | 97.5 (1597/1.6) | G32B, 4G32 | 4 | OHC |
| | Colt Vista | 121.9 (1997/2.0) | G63B | 4 | OHC |
| | Conquest | 155.9 (2555/2.6) | G54B, 4G54 | 4 | OHC |
| 1988 | Colt | 89.6 (1468/1.5) | G15B | 4 | OHC |
| | Colt | 97.5 (1597/1.6) | G32B | 4 | OHC |
| | Colt Vista | 121.9 (1997/2.0) | G63B | 4 | OHC |
| | Conquest | 155.9 (2555/2.6) | G54B | 4 | OHC |
| 1989-90 | Colt | 89.6 (1468/1.5) | 4G15,G15B | 4 | OHC |
| | Colt | 97.3 (1595/1.6) | 4G61 | 4 | OHC |
| | Colt Vista | 121.9 (1997/2.0) | G63B | 4 | OHC |
| | Conquest | 155.9 (2555/2.6) | G54B | 4 | OHC |

## GENERAL ENGINE SPECIFICATIONS

| Year | Model | Engine Displacement cu. in. (cc) | Fuel System Type | Net Horsepower @ rpm | Net Torque @ rpm (ft. lbs.) | Bore × Stroke (in.) | Com-pression Ratio | Oil Pressure @ rpm |
|---|---|---|---|---|---|---|---|---|
| 1983 | Colt | 86.0 (1410) | Carb | 70 @ 5200 | 78 @ 3000 | 2.91 × 3.23 | 8.8:1 | 50-64 |
| | Colt | 97.5 (1597) | Carb | 77 @ 5200 | 87 @ 3000 | 3.03 × 3.39 | 8.5:1 | 57-71 |
| | Challenger | 155.9 (2555) | Carb | 105 @ 5000 | 139 @ 2500 | 3.59 × 3.86 | 8.2:1 | 50-64 |
| | Sapporo | 155.9 (2555) | Carb | 105 @ 5000 | 139 @ 2500 | 3.59 × 3.86 | 8.2:1 | 50-64 |
| 1984 | Colt | 86.0 (1410) | Carb | 70 @ 5200 | 78 @ 3000 | 2.91 × 3.23 | 8.2:1 | 50-64 |
| | Colt | 9.75 (1597) | Carb | 77 @ 5200 | 87 @ 3000 | 3.03 × 3.39 | 8.5:1 | 57-71 |
| | Colt Vista | 97.5 (1597) | EFI/Turbo | 102 @ 5000 | 122 @ 3000 | 3.03 × 3.39 | 7.6:1 | 57-71 |
| | Conquest | 155.9 (2555) | EFI | 145 @ 5000 | 185 @ 2500 | 3.59 × 3.86 | 7.0:1 | 50-64 |
| 1985 | Colt | 89.6 (1468) | Carb | 77 @ 5300 | 84 @ 3000 | 2.97 × 3.23 | 9.4:1 | 50-64 |
| | Colt | 97.5 (1597) | EFI/Turbo | 102 @ 5500 | 122 @ 3000 | 3.03 × 3.39 | 7.6:1 | 57-71 |
| | Colt Vista | 121.9 (1997) | Carb | 88 @ 5000 | 108 @ 3500 | 3.35 × 3.45 | 8.5:1 | 57-71 |
| | Conquest | 155.9 (2555) | EFI | 145 @ 5000 | 185 @ 2500 | 3.59 × 3.86 | 7.0:1 | 50-64 |

## GENERAL ENGINE SPECIFICATIONS

| Year | Model | Engine Displacement cu. in. (cc) | Fuel System Type | Net Horsepower @ rpm | Net Torque @ rpm (ft. lbs.) | Bore × Stroke (in.) | Compression Ratio | Oil Pressure @ rpm |
|---|---|---|---|---|---|---|---|---|
| 1986 | Colt | 89.6 (1468) | Carb | 68 @ 5000 | 84 @ 3000 | 2.97 × 3.23 | 9.4:1 | 50-64 |
| | Colt | 97.5 (1597) | EFI/Turbo | 102 @ 5500 | 122 @ 3000 | 3.03 × 3.39 | 7.6:1 | 57-71 |
| | Colt Vista | 121.9 (1997) | Carb | 88 @ 5000 | 108 @ 3500 | 3.35 × 3.45 | 8.5:1 | 57-71 |
| | Conquest | 155.9 (2555) | EFI | 145 @ 5000 | 185 @ 2500 | 3.59 × 3.86 | 7.0:1 | 50-54 |
| | Conquest | 155.9 (2555) | EFI/Turbo | 170 @ 5000 | 220 @ 2500 | 3.59 × 3.86 | 7.0:1 | 50-54 |
| 1987 | Colt | 89.6 (1468) | Carb | 68 @ 5000 | 84 @ 3000 | 2.97 × 3.23 | 9.4:1 | 50-64 |
| | Colt | 97.5 (1597) | EFI/Turbo | 102 @ 5500 | 122 @ 3000 | 3.03 × 3.39 | 7.6:1 | 57-71 |
| | Colt Vista | 121.9 (1997) | Carb | 88 @ 5000 | 108 @ 3500 | 3.35 × 3.45 | 8.5:1 | 57-71 |
| | Conquest | 155.9 (2555) | EFI | 145 @ 5000 | 185 @ 2500 | 3.59 × 3.86 | 7.0:1 | 55-70 |
| | Conquest | 155.9 (2555) | EFI/Turbo | 170 @ 5000 | 220 @ 2500 | 3.59 × 3.86 | 7.0:1 | 55-70 |
| 1988 | Colt | 89.6 (1468) | Carb | 68 @ 5000 | 84 @ 3000 | 2.97 × 3.23 | 9.4:1 | 50-64 |
| | Colt | 97.5 (1597) | EFI/Turbo | 102 @ 5500 | 122 @ 3000 | 3.03 × 3.39 | 7.6:1 | 57-71 |
| | Colt Vista | 121.9 (1997) | EFI | 96 @ 5000 | 113 @ 3500 | 3.35 × 3.46 | 8.5:1 | 48-65 |
| | Conquest | 155.9 (2555) | EFI/Turbo | 188 @ 5000 | 234 @ 2500 | 3.59 × 3.86 | 7.0:1 | 55-70 |
| 1989-90 | Colt | 89.6 (1468) | EFI | 81 @ 5500 | 91 @ 3000 | 2.97 × 3.23 | 9.4:1 | 50-64 |
| | Colt | 97.3 (1595) | EFI/Turbo | 135 @ 6000 | 141 @ 3000 | 3.24 × 2.95 | 8.0:1 | 50-64 |
| | Colt Vista | 121.9 (1997) | EFI | 99 @ 5000 | 116 @ 4000 | 3.35 × 3.46 | 8.5:1 | 48-65 |
| | Conquest | 155.9 (2555) | EFI/Turbo | 188 @ 5000 | 234 @ 2500 | 3.59 × 3.86 | 7.0:1 | 55-70 |

## GASOLINE ENGINE TUNE-UP SPECIFICATIONS

| Year | Model | Engine Displacement cu. in. (cc) | Spark Plugs Type | Spark Plugs Gap (in.) | Ignition Timing (deg.) MT | Ignition Timing (deg.) AT | Compression Pressure (psi) | Fuel Pump (psi) | Idle Speed (rpm) MT | Idle Speed (rpm) AT | Valve Clearance In. | Valve Clearance Ex. |
|---|---|---|---|---|---|---|---|---|---|---|---|---|
| 1983 | Colt | 86.0 (1410) | BRP6ES-11 | 0.039–0.043 | 5B | — | NA | 3.7–5.1 | 650 | — | 0.006 | 0.010 |
| | Colt | 97.5 (1597) | BRP6ES-11 | 0.039–0.043 | 5B | 5B | NA | 3.7–5.1 | 650 | 700 | 0.006 | 0.010 |
| | Challenger | 155.9 (2555) | BPR6ES-11 | 0.039–0.043 | 7B | 7B | NA | 3.7–5.1 | 650 | 700 | 0.006 | 0.010 |
| | Sapporo | 155.9 (2555) | BPR6ES-11 | 0.039–0.043 | 7B | 7B | NA | 3.7–5.1 | 650 | 700 | 0.006 | 0.010 |
| 1984 | Colt | 86.0 (1410) | BPR6ES-11 | 0.039–0.043 | 5B | — | NA | 2.7–3.7 | 650 | 650 | 0.006 | 0.010 |
| | Colt | 97.5 (1597) | BPR6ES-11 | 0.039–0.043 | — | 5B | NA | 2.4–3.4 | 700 | 700 | 0.006 | 0.010 |
| | Colt Vista | 97.5 (1597) | BPR6ES-11 | 0.039–0.043 | 8B | — | NA | 35.6 | 650 | 700 | 0.006 | 0.010 |
| | Conquest | 155.9 (2555) | BPR6ES-11 | 0.039–0.043 | 10B | 10B | NA | 4.6–6.0 | 850 | 850 | 0.006 | 0.010 |

## GASOLINE ENGINE TUNE-UP SPECIFICATIONS

| Year | Model | Engine Displacement cu. in. (cc) | Spark Plugs Type | Spark Plugs Gap (in.) | Ignition Timing (deg.) MT | Ignition Timing (deg.) AT | Compression Pressure (psi) | Fuel Pump (psi) | Idle Speed (rpm) MT | Idle Speed (rpm) AT | Valve Clearance In. | Valve Clearance Ex. |
|---|---|---|---|---|---|---|---|---|---|---|---|---|
| 1985 | Colt | 89.6 (1468) | BPR6ES-11 | 0.039–0.040 | 8B | 8B | NA | NA | 700 | 750 | 0.006 | 0.010 ① |
| | Colt | 97.5 (1597) | BPR6ES-11 | 0.039–0.040 | 8B | 8B | NA | 35.6 | 700 | 700 | 0.006 | 0.010 |
| | Colt Vista | 121.9 (1997) | BPR6ES-11 | 0.039–0.040 | 5B | 5B | NA | 4.5–5.5 | 700 | 700 | 0.006 | 0.010 |
| | Conquest | 155.9 (2555) EFI | BPR6ES-11 | 0.039–0.040 | 10B | 10B | NA | 4.6–6.0 | 850 | 850 | 0.006 | 0.010 |
| | Conquest | 155.9 (2555) | BPR6ES-11 | 0.039–0.043 | 10B | 10B | NA | 35.6 6.0 | 850 | 850 | 0.006 | 0.010 |
| 1986 | Colt | 89.6 (1468) | BPR6ES-11 | 0.039–0.040 | 8B | 8B | NA | NA | 700 | 750 | 0.006 | 0.010 ① |
| | Colt | 97.5 (1597) | BPR6ES-11 | 0.039–0.040 | 8B | 8B | NA | 35.6 | 700 | 700 | 0.006 | 0.010 |
| | Colt Vista | 121.9 (1997) | BPR6ES-11 | 0.039–0.040 | 5B | 5B | NA | 4.5–5.5 | 700 | 700 | Hyd. ② | Hyd. ② |
| | Conquest | 155.9 (2555) | BPR6ES-11 | 0.039–0.040 | 10B | 10B | NA | 4.6–6.0 | 850 | 850 | 0.006 | 0.010 |
| | Conquest | 155.9 (2555) | BPR6ES-11 | 0.039–0.043 | 10B | 10B | NA | 35.6 6.0 | 850 | 850 | 0.006 | 0.010 |
| 1987 | Colt | 89.6 (1468) | BPR6ES-11 | 0.039–0.040 | 8B | 8B | NA | NA | 700 | 750 | 0.006 | 0.010 ① |
| | Colt | 97.5 (1597) | BPR6ES-11 | 0.039–0.040 | 8B | 8B | NA | 35.6 | 700 | 700 | 0.006 | 0.010 |
| | Colt Vista | 121.9 (1997) | BPR6ES-11 | 0.039–0.040 | 5B | 5B | NA | 4.5–5.5 | 700 | 700 | Hyd. ② | Hyd. ② |
| | Conquest | 155.9 (2555) | BPR6ES-11 | 0.039–0.040 | 10B | 10B | NA | 4.6–6.0 | 850 | 850 | 0.006 | 0.010 |
| | Conquest | 155.9 (2555) | BPR6ES-11 | 0.039–0.040 | 10B | 10B | NA | 35.6 5.5 | 850 | 850 | 0.006 | 0.010 |
| 1988 | Colt | 89.6 (1468) | BPR6ES-11 | 0.039–0.040 | 8B | 8B | NA | NA | 700 | 750 | 0.006 | 0.010 ① |
| | Colt | 97.5 (1597) | BPR6ES-11 | 0.039–0.040 | 8B | 8B | NA | 35.6 | 700 | 700 | 0.006 | 0.010 |
| | Colt Vista | 121.9 (1997) | BPR6ES-11 | 0.039–0.040 | 5B | 5B | NA | 4.5–5.5 | 700 | 700 | Hyd. ② | Hyd. ② |
| | Conquest | 155.9 (2555) | BPR6ES-11 | 0.039–0.040 | 10B | 10B | NA | 35.6 5.5 | 850 | 850 | Hyd. | Hyd. ② |
| 1989 | Colt | 89.6 (1468) | BPR6ES-11 | 0.039–0.043 | 5B | 5B | NA | 47.6 | 750 | 750 | 0.006 | 0.010 ① |
| | Colt | 97.3 (1595) | BPR6ES-11 | 0.028–0.031 | 5B | – | NA | 47.6 | 750 | – | Hyd. | Hyd. |

## GASOLINE ENGINE TUNE-UP SPECIFICATIONS

| Year | Model | Engine Displacement cu. in. (cc) | Spark Plugs Type | Spark Plugs Gap (in.) | Ignition Timing (deg.) MT | Ignition Timing (deg.) AT | Com-pression Pressure (psi) | Fuel Pump (psi) | Idle Speed (rpm) MT | Idle Speed (rpm) AT | Valve Clearance In. | Valve Clearance Ex. |
|---|---|---|---|---|---|---|---|---|---|---|---|---|
| 1989 | Colt Vista | 121.9 (1997) | W20EPR-11 | 0.039–0.043 | 5B | 5B | NA | 47.6– | 700 | 700 | Hyd. | Hyd. ② |
| | Conquest | 155.9 (2555) | BUR7EA-11 | 0.039–0.043 | 10B | 10B | NA | 33.6 | 850 | 850 | Hyd. | Hyd. ② |
| 1990 | SEE UNDERHOOD SPECIFICATIONS STICKER | | | | | | | | | | | |

**NOTE:** The underhood specifications sticker often reflects tune-up specification changes in production. Sticker figures must be used if they disagree with those in this chart

① Jet valve clearance – 0.006 in.

② Jet valve clearance – 0.010 in.

## FIRING ORDERS

**NOTE: To avoid confusion, always replace spark plug wires one at a time.**

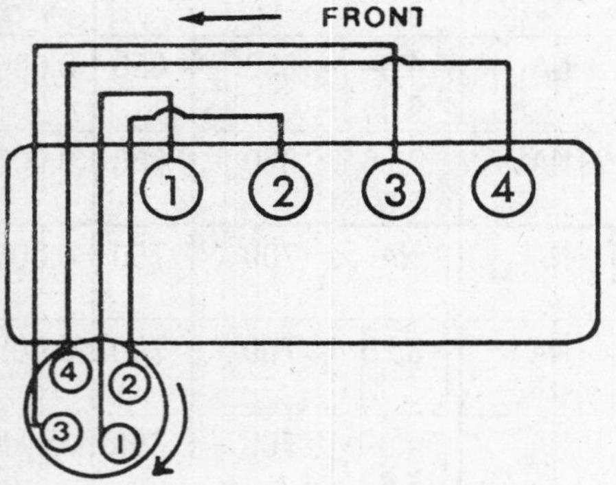


1410, 1468, 1597, 1997cc engines

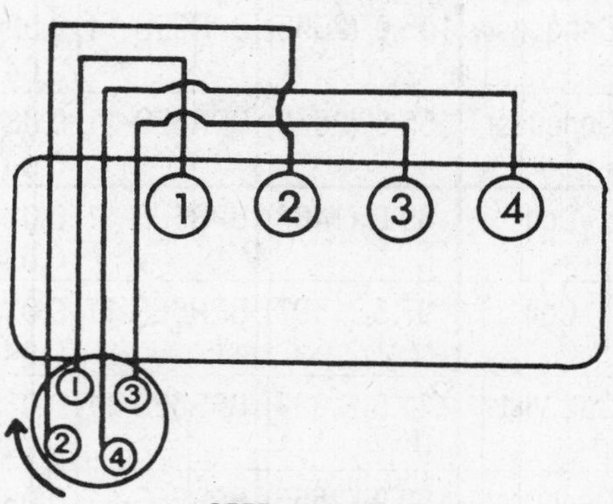


2555cc engines

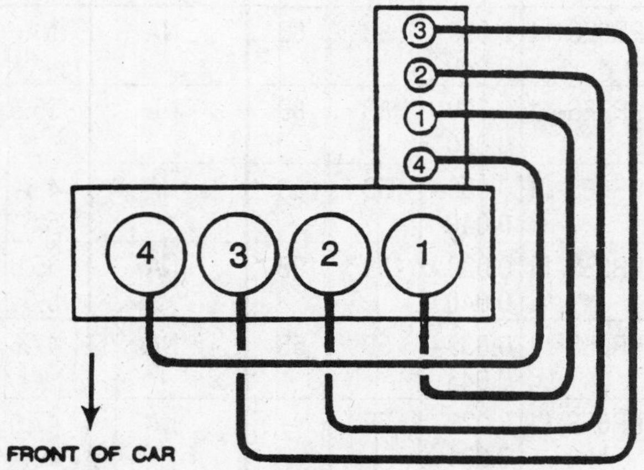


1595cc (1.6L) DOHC
Firing Order: 1–3–4–2

## CAPACITIES

| Year | Model | Engine Displacement cu. in. (cc) | Engine Crankcase with Filter | Engine Crankcase without Filter | Transmission (pts.) 4-Spd | Transmission (pts.) 5-Spd | Transmission (pts.) Auto. | Drive Axle (pts.) | Fuel Tank (gal.) | Cooling System (qts.) |
|---|---|---|---|---|---|---|---|---|---|---|
| 1983 | Colt | 86.0 (1410) | 4.0 | 3.5 | 4.4 | — | — | — | 10.6 | 4.7 |
| | Colt | 97.5 (1597) | 4.0 | 3.5 | 4.4 | — | 9.5 | — | 10.6 | 4.7 |
| | Champ | 86.0 (1410) | 4.0 | 3.5 | 4.4 | — | — | — | 10.6 | 4.7 |
| | Champ | 97.5 (1597) | 4.0 | 3.5 | 4.4 | — | 9.5 | — | 10.6 | 4.7 |
| | Challenger | 155.9 (2555) | 4.5 | 4.0 | — | 4.8 | 14.4 | 2.7 | 15.8 | 9.5 |
| | Sapparo | 155.9 (2555) | 4.5 | 4.0 | — | 4.8 | 14.4 | 2.7 | 15.8 | 9.5 |
| 1984 | Colt | 86.0 (1410) | 4.0 | 3.5 | 4.4 | — | 9.5 | — | 10.6① | 4.7 |
| | Colt | 97.5 (1597) | 4.0 | 3.5 | 4.4 | — | 9.5 | — | 10.6① | 4.7 |
| | Colt Vista | 121.9 (1997) | 4.5 | 4.0 | 4.4 | 4.9 | 9.5 | — | 13.2 | 7.4 |
| | Conquest | 155.9 (2555) | 4.5 | 4.0 | — | 4.8 | 12.3 | 2.7 | 19.8 | 9.7 |
| 1985 | Colt | 89.6 (1468) | 3.5 | 3.0 | 3.6 | 3.8 | 9.5 | — | 11.9 | 5.3 |
| | Colt | 97.5 (1597) | 4.0 | 3.5 | — | 3.8 | 9.5 | — | 11.9 | 5.3 |
| | Colt Vista | 121.9 (1997) | 4.0 | 3.5 | — | 4.9② | 9.5 | — | 13.2③ | 7.4 |
| | Conquest | 155.9(2555) | 4.5 | 4.0 | — | 4.8 | 14.4 | 2.7 | 19.8 | 9.5 |
| 1986 | Colt | 89.6 (1468) | 3.5 | 3.0 | 3.6 | 3.8 | 9.5 | — | 11.9 | 5.3 |
| | Colt | 97.5 (1597) | 4.0 | 3.5 | — | 3.8 | 9.5 | — | 11.9 | 5.3 |
| | Colt Vista | 121.9 (1997) | 4.0 | 3.5 | — | 4.9② | 9.5 | — | 13.2③ | 7.4 |
| | Conquest | 155.9(2555) | 4.5 | 4.0 | — | 4.8 | 14.4 | 2.7 | 19.8 | 9.5 |
| 1987 | Colt | 89.6 (1468) | 3.5 | 3.0 | 3.6 | 3.8 | 9.5 | — | 11.9 | 5.3 |
| | Colt | 97.5 (1597) | 4.0 | 3.5 | — | 3.8 | 9.5 | — | 11.9 | 5.3 |
| | Colt Vista | 121.9 (1997) | 4.0 | 3.5 | — | 4.9② | 9.5 | — | 13.2③ | 7.4 |
| | Conquest | 155.9(2555) | 4.5 | 4.0 | — | 4.8 | 14.4 | 2.7 | 19.8 | 9.5 |
| 1988 | Colt | 89.6 (1468) | 3.5 | 3.0 | 3.6 | 3.8 | 9.5 | — | 11.9 | 5.3 |
| | Colt | 97.5 (1597) | 4.0 | 3.5 | — | 3.8 | 9.5 | — | 11.9 | 5.3 |
| | Colt Vista | 121.9 (1997) | 4.0 | 3.5 | — | 4.9② | 9.5 | — | 13.2③ | 7.4 |
| | Conquest | 155.9(2555) | 4.5 | 4.0 | — | 4.8 | 14.4 | 2.7 | 19.8 | 9.5 |
| 1989-90 | Colt | 89.6 (1468) | 4.0 | 3.5 | ④ | ④ | 9.5 | — | 13.2 | 5.3 |
| | Colt | 97.3 (1595) | 4.0 | 3.5 | ④ | ④ | 9.5 | — | 13.2 | 5.3 |
| | Colt Vista | 121.9 (1997) | 4.0 | 3.5 | — | 4.9② | 9.5 | — | 13.2③ | 7.4 |
| | Conquest | 155.9(2555) | 4.5 | 4.0 | — | 4.8 | 14.4 | 2.7 | 19.8 | 9.5 |

① RS and LS—13.2

② 4WD—4.4 pts.
Transfer case—1.5 pts.

③ 4WD—14.5 gals.

④ KM200—3.6 pts.
KM201, 206—3.8 pts.
KM210—4.4 pts.

## CAMSHAFT SPECIFICATIONS

All measurements given in inches.

| Year | Engine Displacement cu. in. (cc) | Journal Diameter 1 | 2 | 3 | 4 | 5 | Lobe Height In. | Ex. | Bearing Clearance | Camshaft End Play |
|---|---|---|---|---|---|---|---|---|---|---|
| 1983 | 86.0 (1410) | 1.339 | 1.339 | 1.339 | 1.339 | 1.339 | 1.500 | 1.504 | .0020–.0035 | .004–.008 |
| | 97.5 (1597) | 1.339 | 1.339 | 1.339 | 1.339 | 1.339 | 1.433 | 1.433 | .0020–.0035 | .004–.008 |
| | 155.9 (2555) | 1.339 | 1.339 | 1.339 | 1.339 | 1.339 | 1.660 | 1.663 | .0020–.0045 | .004–.008 |
| 1984 | 86.0 (1410) | 1.339 | 1.339 | 1.339 | 1.339 | 1.339 | 1.500 | 1.504 | .0020–.0035 | .004–.008 |
| | 97.5 (1597) | 1.339 | 1.339 | 1.339 | 1.339 | 1.339 | 1.433 | 1.433 | .0020–.0035 | .004–.008 |
| | 97.5 (1597) Turbo | 1.339 | 1.339 | 1.339 | 1.339 | 1.339 | 1.660 | 1.663 | .0020–.0045 | .004–.008 |
| 1985 | 89.6 (1468) | 1.8110 | 1.8110 | 1.8110 | 1.8110 | 1.8110 | 1.500 | 1.504 | .0020–.0035 | .004–.008 |
| | 97.5 (1597) | 1.336 | 1.336 | 1.336 | 1.336 | 1.336 | 1.433 | 1.433 | .0020–.0035 | .004–.008 |
| | 121.9 (1997) | 1.340 | 1.340 | 1.340 | 1.340 | 1.340 | 1.656 | 1.656 | .0020–.0035 | .004–.008 |
| | 155.9 (2555) | 1.339 | 1.339 | 1.339 | 1.339 | 1.339 | 1.669 | 1.669 | .0020–.0045 | .004–.008 |
| 1986 | 89.6 (1468) | 1.8110 | 1.8110 | 1.8110 | 1.8110 | 1.8110 | 1.500 | 1.504 | .0015–.0031 | .002 .008 |
| | 97.5 (1597) | 1.336 | 1.336 | 1.336 | 1.336 | 1.336 | 1.431 | 1.431 | .0020–.0035 | .002–.006 |
| | 121.9 (1997) | 1.340 | 1.340 | 1.340 | 1.340 | 1.340 | 1.656 | 1.656 | .0020–.0035 | .004–.008 |
| | 155.9 (2555) | 1.339 | 1.339 | 1.339 | 1.339 | 1.339 | 1.669 | 1.669 | .0020–.0035 | .004–.008 |
| 1987 | 89.6 (1468) | 1.8110 | 1.8110 | 1.8110 | 1.8110 | 1.8110 | 1.500 | 1.541 | .0015–.0031 | .002 .008 |
| | 97.5 (1597) | 1.336 | 1.336 | 1.336 | 1.336 | 1.336 | 1.431 | 1.431 | .0020–.0035 | .002–.006 |
| | 121.9 (1997) | 1.340 | 1.340 | 1.340 | 1.340 | 1.340 | 1.656 | 1.656 | .0020–.0035 | .004–.008 |
| | 155.9 (2555) | 1.340 | 1.340 | 1.340 | 1.340 | 1.340 | 1.671 | 1.671 | .0020–.0035 | .004–.008 |
| 1988 | 89.6 (1468) | 1.8110 | 1.8110 | 1.8110 | 1.8110 | 1.8110 | 1.500 | 1.541 | .0015–.0031 | .002 .008 |
| | 97.5 (1597) | 1.336 | 1.336 | 1.336 | 1.336 | 1.336 | 1.431 | 1.431 | .0020–.0035 | .002–.006 |
| | 121.9 (1997) | 1.340 | 1.340 | 1.340 | 1.340 | 1.340 | 1.656 | 1.656 | .0020–.0035 | .004–.008 |
| | 155.9 (2555) | 1.340 | 1.340 | 1.340 | 1.340 | 1.340 | 1.671 | 1.671 | .0020–.0035 | .004–.008 |

## CAMSHAFT SPECIFICATIONS

All measurements given in inches.

| Year | Engine Displacement cu. in. (cc) | Journal Diameter | | | | | Lobe Height | | Bearing Clearance | Camshaft End Play |
|---|---|---|---|---|---|---|---|---|---|---|
| | | 1 | 2 | 3 | 4 | 5 | In. | Ex. | | |
| 1989-90 | 89.6 (1468) | 1.8110 | 1.8110 | 1.8110 | 1.8110 | 1.8110 | 1.532 | 1.535 | .0015–.0031 | .002 .008 |
| | 97.3 (1595) | 1.020 | 1.020 | 1.020 | 1.020 | 1.020 | 1.385 | 1.374 | .0020–.0035 | .004–.008 |
| | 121.9 (1997) | 1.340 | 1.340 | 1.340 | 1.340 | 1.340 | 1.657 | 1.657 | .0020–.0035 | .004–.008 |
| | 155.9 (2555) | 1.340 | 1.340 | 1.340 | 1.340 | 1.340 | 1.671 | 1.671 | .0020–.0035 | .004–.008 |

## CRANKSHAFT AND CONNECTING ROD SPECIFICATIONS

All measurements are given in inches.

| Year | Engine Displacement cu. in. (cc) | Crankshaft | | | | Connecting Rod | | |
|---|---|---|---|---|---|---|---|---|
| | | Main Brg. Journal Dia. | Main Brg. Oil Clearance | Shaft End-play | Thrust on No. | Journal Diameter | Oil Clearance | Side Clearance |
| 1983 | 86.0 (1410) | 1.8898 | .0008–.0028 | .002–.007 | 3 | 1.6535 | .0004–.0024 | .004–.010 |
| | 97.5 (1597) | 2.2441 | .0008–.0028 | .002–.007 | 3 | 1.7717 | .0004–.0028 | .004–.010 |
| | 155.9 (2555) | 2.5984 | .0008–.0028 | .002–.007 | 3 | 2.0866 | .0008–.0028 | .004–.010 |
| 1984 | 86.0 (1410) | 1.8898 | .0008–.0028 | .002–.007 | 3 | 1.6535 | .0004–.0024 | .004–.010 |
| | 97.5 (1597) | 2.2441 | .0008–.0028 | .002–.007 | 3 | 1.7717 | .0004–.0028 | .004–.010 |
| | 121.9 (1997) | 2.2441 | .0008–.0028 | .002–.007 | 3 | 1.7717 | .0008–.0020 | .004–.010 |
| | 155.9 (2555) | 2.5984 | .0008–.0028 | .002–.007 | 3 | 2.0866 | .0008–.0028 | .004–.010 |
| 1985 | 89.6 (1468) | 1.8898 | .0008–.0028 | .002–.007 | 3 | 1.6535 | .0004–.0024 | .004–.010 |
| | 97.5 (1997) | 2.2441 | .0008–.0028 | .002–.007 | 3 | 1.7717 | .0008–.0020 | .004–.010 |
| | 121.9 (1997) | 2.2441 | .0008–.0028 | .002–.007 | 3 | 1.7717 | .0008–.0020 | .004–.010 |
| | 155.9 (2555) | 2.5984 | .0008–.0028 | .002–.007 | 3 | 2.0866 | .0008–.0028 | .004–.010 |
| 1986 | 89.6 (1468) | 1.8898 | .0008–.0028 | .002–.007 | 3 | 1.6535 | .0004–.0024 | .004–.010 |
| | 97.5 (1597) | 2.2441 | .0008–.0028 | .002–.007 | 3 | 1.7717 | .0004–.0028 | .004–.010 |
| | 121.9 (1997) | 2.2441 | .0008–.0028 | .002–.007 | 3 | 1.7717 | .0008–.0020 | .004–.010 |

## CRANKSHAFT AND CONNECTING ROD SPECIFICATIONS

All measurements are given in inches.

| Year | Engine Displacement cu. in. (cc) | Crankshaft | | | | Connecting Rod | | |
|---|---|---|---|---|---|---|---|---|
| | | Main Brg. Journal Dia. | Main Brg. Oil Clearance | Shaft End-play | Thrust on No. | Journal Diameter | Oil Clearance | Side Clearance |
| 1986 | 155.9 (2555) | 2.5984 | .0008–.0028 | .002–.007 | 3 | 2.0866 | .0008–.0028 | .004–.010 |
| | 155.9 (2555) Turbo | 2.3622 | .0008–.0020– | .002–.007– | 3 | 2.0866 | .0008–.0024– | .004–.0010– |
| 1987 | 89.6 (1468) | 1.8898 | .0008–.0028 | .002–.007 | 3 | 1.6535 | .0004–.0024 | .004–.010 |
| | 97.5 (1597) | 2.2441 | .0008–.0028 | .002–.007 | 3 | 1.7717 | .0004–.0028 | .004–.010 |
| | 121.9 (1997) | 2.2441 | .0008–.0028 | .002–.007 | 3 | 1.7717 | .0008–.0020 | .004–.010 |
| | 155.9 (2555) | 2.5984 | .0008–.0028 | .002–.007 | 3 | 2.0866 | .0008–.0028 | .004–.010 |
| | 155.9 (2555) Turbo | 2.3622 | .0008–0.0020– | .002–0.007– | 3 | 2.0866 | .0008–.0024– | .004–.0010– |
| 1988 | 89.6 (1468) | 1.8898 | .0008–.0018 | .002–.007 | 3 | 1.6535 | .0006–.0017 | .004–.010 |
| | 97.5 (1597) | 2.2441 | .0008–.0019 | .002–.007 | 3 | 1.7717 | .0008–.0019 | .004–.010 |
| | 121.9 (1997) | 2.2441 | .0008–.0028 | .002–.007 | 3 | 1.7717 | .0006–.0020 | .004–.010 |
| | 155.9 (2555) Turbo | 2.3622 | .0008–.0020– | .002–.007– | 3 | 2.0866 | .0008–.0020– | .004–.010– |
| 1989-90 | 89.6 (1468) | 1.89 | .0008–.0018 | .002–.007 | 3 | 1.65 | .0006–.0017 | .004–.010 |
| | 97.3 (1595) Turbo | 2.24 | .0008–.0020 | .002–.007 | 3 | 1.77 | .0008–.0020 | .004–.010 |
| | 121.9 (1997) | 2.24 | .0008–.0020 | .002–.007 | 3 | 1.77 | .0006–.0020 | .004–.010 |
| | 155.9 (2555) Turbo | 2.36 | .0008–.0018– | .002–.007– | 3 | 2.09 | .0008–.0020– | .004–.010– |

## VALVE SPECIFICATIONS

| Year | Engine Displacement cu. in. (cc) | Seat Angle (deg.) | Face Angle (deg.) | Spring Test Pressure (lbs.) | Spring Installed Height (in.) | Stem-to-Guide Clearance (in.) | | Stem Diameter (in.) | |
|---|---|---|---|---|---|---|---|---|---|
| | | | | | | Intake | Exhaust | Intake | Exhaust |
| 1983 | 86.0 (1410) | 45 | 45 | 69 @ 1.417 | 1.417 | .0012–.0024 | .0020–.0035 | .3147–.3153 | .3147–.3153 |
| | 97.5 (1597) | 45 | 45 | 61 @ 1.470 | 1.470 | .0012–.0024 | .0020–.0035 | .3147–.3153 | .3147–.3153 |
| | 155.9 (2555) | 45 | 45 | 61 @ 1.590 | 1.590 | .0012–.0024 | .0020–.0035 | .3147–.3153 | .3147–.3153 |

## VALVE SPECIFICATIONS

| Year | Engine Displacement cu. in. (cc) | Seat Angle (deg.) | Face Angle (deg.) | Spring Test Pressure (lbs.) | Spring Installed Height (in.) | Stem-to-Guide Clearance (in.) Intake | Stem-to-Guide Clearance (in.) Exhaust | Stem Diameter (in.) Intake | Stem Diameter (in.) Exhaust |
|---|---|---|---|---|---|---|---|---|---|
| 1984 | 86.0 (1410) | 45 | 45 | 69 @ 1.417 | 1.417 | .0012–.0024 | .0020–.0035 | .3147–.3153 | .3147–.3153 |
| | 97.5 (1597) | 45 | 45 | 61 @ 1.470 | 1.470 | .0012–.0024 | .0020–.0035 | .3147–.3153 | .3147–.3153 |
| | 97.5 (1597) Turbo | 45 | 45 | 61 @ 1.470 | 1.470 | .0012–.0024 | .0020–.0035 | .3147–.3153 | .3147–.3153 |
| 1985 | 89.6 (1468) | 45 | 45 | 69 @ 1.417 | 1.417 | .0012–.0024 | .0020–.0035 | .3147–.3153 | .3147–.3153 |
| | 97.5 (1597) | 45 | 45 | 61 @ 1.470 | 1.470 | .0012–.0024 | .0020–.0035 | .3147–.3153 | .3147–.3153 |
| | 121.9 (1997) | 45 | 45 | 40 @ 1.591 | 1.591 | .0012–.0024 | .0020–.0035 | .3147–.3153 | .3147–.3153 |
| 1986 | 89.6 (1468) | 45 | 45 | 69 @ 1.417 | 1.417 | .0012–.0024 | .0020–.0035 | .3147–.3153 | .3147–.3153 |
| | 97.5 (1597) | 45 | 45 | 61 @ 1.470 | 1.470 | .0012–.0024 | .0020–.0035 | .3147–.3153 | .3147–.3153 |
| | 121.9 (1997) | 45 | 45 | 40 @ 1.591 | 1.591 | .0012–.0024 | .0020–.0035 | .3147–.3153 | .3147–.3153 |
| | 155.9 (2555) | 45 | 45 | 61 @ 1.590 | 1.590 | .0012–.0024 | .0020–.0035 | .3147–.3153 | .3147–.3153 |
| 1987 | 89.6 (1468) | 45 | 45 | 69 @ 1.417 | 1.417 | .0012–.0024 | .0020–.0035 | .3147–.3153 | .3147–.3153 |
| | 97.5 (1597) | 45 | 45 | 61 @ 1.470 | 1.470 | .0012–.0024 | .0020–.0035 | .3147–.3153 | .3147–.3153 |
| | 121.9 (1997) | 45 | 45 | 40 @ 1.591 | 1.591 | .0012–.0024 | .0020–.0035 | .3147–.3153 | .3147–.3153 |
| | 155.9 (2555) | 45 | 45 | 61 @ 1.590 | 1.590 | .0012–.0024 | .0020–.0035 | .3147–.3153 | .3147–.3153 |
| 1988 | 89.6 (1468) | 45 | 45 | 53 @ 1.469 | 1.469 | .0008–.0020 | .0020–.0035 | .260 | .260 |
| | 97.5 (1597) | 45 | 45 | 62 @ 1.469 | 1.469 | .0012–.0024 | .0020–.0035 | .320 | .320 |
| | 121.9 (1997) | 45 | 45 | 40 @ 1.591 | 1.591 | .0012–.0024 | .0020–.0035 | .310 | .310 |
| | 155.9 (2555) | 45 | 45 | 40.4 @ 1.591 | 1.591 | .0012–.0024 | .0020–.0035 | .315 | .315 |
| 1989-90 | 89.6 (1468) | 45 | 45 | 53 @ 1.469 | 1.469 | .0008–.0020 | .0020–.0035 | .260 | .260 |
| | 97.3 (1595) | 45 | 45 | 53 @ 1.469 | 1.469 | .0008–.0019 | .0020–.0033 | .258 | .257 |
| | 121.9 (1997) | 45 | 45 | 40.4 @ 1.591 | 1.591 | .0012–.0024 | .0020–.0035 | .310 | .310 |
| | 155.9 (2555) | 45 | 45 | 73 @ 1.591 | 1.591 | .0012–.0024 | .0020–.0035 | .315 | .315 |

## PISTON AND RING SPECIFICATIONS

All measurments are given in inches.

| Year | Engine Displacement cu. in. (cc) | Piston Clearance | Ring Gap Top Compression | Ring Gap Bottom Compression | Ring Gap Oil Control | Ring Side Clearance Top Compression | Ring Side Clearance Bottom Compression | Ring Side Clearance Oil Control |
|---|---|---|---|---|---|---|---|---|
| 1983 | 86.0 (1410) | .0008–.0016 | .0080–.0160 | .0080–.0160 | .0080–.0200 | .0012–.0028 | .0008–.0024 | Snug |
| | 97.5 (1597) | .0008–.0016 | .0080–.0160 | .0080–.0160 | .0080–.0200 | .0012–.0028 | .0008–.0024 | Snug |
| | 155.9 (2555) | .0008–.0016 | .0098–.0177 | .0098–.0177 | .0078–.0354 | .0008–.0024 | .0008–.0024 | Snug |
| 1984 | 86.0 (1410) | .0008–.0016 | .0080–.0160 | .0080–.0160 | .0080–.0200 | .0012–.0028 | .0008–.0024 | Snug |
| | 97.5 (1597) | .0008–.0016 | .0100–.0160 | .0080–.0140 | .0080–.0280 | .0012–.0028 | .0008–.0024 | Snug |
| 1985 | 89.6 (1468) | .0008–.0016 | .0080–.0160 | .0080–.0160 | .0080–.0200 | .0012–.0028 | .0008–.0024 | Snug |
| | 97.5 (1597) | .0008–.0016 | .0100–.0160 | .0080–.0140 | .0080–.0280 | .0012–.0028 | .0008–.0024 | Snug |
| | 121.9 (1997) | .0008–.0016 | .0100–.0180 | .0080–.0160 | .0080–.0028 | .0020–.0040 | .0010–.0020 | Snug |
| | 155.9 (2555) | .0008–.0016 | .0098–.0177 | .0098–.0177 | .0078–.0354 | .0024–.0039 | .0008–.0024 | Snug |
| 1986 | 89.6 (1468) | .0008–.0016 | .0080–.0160 | .0080–.0160 | .0080–.0200 | .0012–.0028 | .0008–.0024 | .0010–.0030 |
| | 97.5 (1597) | .0008–.0016 | .0100–.0160 | .0080–.0140 | .0080–.0280 | .0012–.0028 | .0008–.0024 | Snug |
| | 121.9 (1997) | .0008–.0016 | .0100–.0180 | .0080–.0160 | .0080–.0028 | .0020–.0040 | .0010–.0020 | Snug |
| | 155.9 (2555) | .0008–.0016 | .0098–.0177 | .0098–.0177 | .0078–.0354 | .0024–.0039 | .0008–.0024 | Snug |
| | 155.9 (2555) Turbo | .0008–.0016 | .0120–.0200 | .0100–.0160 | .0120–.0310 | .0020–.0040 | .0010–.0020 | Snug |
| 1987 | 89.6 (1468) | .0008–.0016 | .0080–.0160 | .0080–.0160 | .0080–.0200 | .0012–.0028 | .0008–.0024 | Snug |
| | 97.5 (1597) | .0008–.0016 | .0100–.0160 | .0080–.0140 | .0080–.0280 | .0012–.0028 | .0008–.0024 | Snug |
| | 121.9 (1997) | .0008–.0016 | .0100–.0180 | .0080–.0160 | .0080–.0028 | .0020–.0040 | .0010–.0020 | Snug |
| | 155.9 (2555) | .0008–.0016 | .0098–.0177 | .0098–.0177 | .0078–.0354 | .0024–.0039 | .0008–.0024 | Snug |
| | 155.9 (2555) Turbo | .0008–.0016 | .0120–.0200 | .0100–.0160 | .0120–.0310 | .0020–.0040 | .0010–.0020 | Snug |
| 1988 | 89.6 (1468) | .0008–.0016 | .0079–.0138 | .0079–.0138 | .0079–.0276 | .0012–.0028 | .0008–.0024 | Snug |
| | 97.5 (1597) | .0012–.0019 | .0098–.0157 | .0079–.0138 | .0080–.0280 | .0012–.0028 | .0008–.0024 | Snug |
| | 121.9 (1997) | .0004–.0012 | .0098–.0157 | .0079–.0138 | .0079–.0276 | .0012–.0028 | .0008–.0024 | Snug |

## PISTON AND RING SPECIFICATIONS

All measurments are given in inches.

| Year | Engine Displacement cu. in. (cc) | Piston Clearance | Ring Gap Top Compression | Ring Gap Bottom Compression | Ring Gap Oil Control | Ring Side Clearance Top Compression | Ring Side Clearance Bottom Compression | Ring Side Clearance Oil Control |
|---|---|---|---|---|---|---|---|---|
| 1988 | 155.9 (2555) Turbo | .0012–.0020 | .0118–.0177 | .0098–.0157 | .0118–.0315 | .0020–.0035 | .0008–.0024 | Snug |
| 1989-90 | 89.6 (1468) | .0008–.0016 | .0079–.0138 | .0079–.0138 | .0079–.0276 | .0012–.0028 | .0008–.0024 | Snug |
| | 97.3 (1595) Turbo | .0012–.0020 | .0098–.0157 | .0138–.0197 | .0079–.0276 | .0012–.0028 | .0012–.0028 | Snug |
| | 121.9 (1997) | .0004–.0012 | .0098–.0157 | .0079–.0138 | .0079–.0276 | .0012–.0028 | .0008–.0024 | Snug |
| | 155.9 (2555) Turbo | .0012–.0020 | .0118–.0177 | .0098–.0157 | .0118–.0315 | .0020–.0035 | .0008–.0024 | Snug |

## TORQUE SPECIFICATIONS

All readings in ft. lbs.

| Year | Engine Displacement cu. in. (cc) | Cylinder Head Bolts | Main Bearing Bolts | Rod Bearing Bolts | Crankshaft Pulley Bolts | Flywheel Bolts | Manifold Intake | Manifold Exhaust | Spark Plugs |
|---|---|---|---|---|---|---|---|---|---|
| 1983 | 86.0 (1410) | 50-54 | 37-39 | 23-25 | 37-43 | 94-101 | 11-14 | 11-14 | 15–22 |
| | 97.5 (1597) | 50-54 | 36-40 | 23-25 | 44-50 | 94-101 ① | 11-14 | 11-14 | 15–22 |
| | 155.9 (2555) | 65-72 | 55-61 | 33-34 | 80-90 | 94-101 ① | 11-14 | 11-14 | 15–22 |
| 1984 | 86.0 (1410) | 50-54 | 37-39 | 23-25 | 37-43 | 94-101 | 11-14 | 11-14 | 15–22 |
| | 97.5 (1597) | 50-54 | 36-40 | 23-25 | 44-50 | 94-101 ① | 11-14 | 11-14 | 15–22 |
| | 97.5 (1597) | 65-72 | 55-61 | 33-34 | 80-90 | 94-101 ① | 11-14 | 11-14 | 15–22 |
| 1985 | 89.6 (1468) | 50-54 | 37-39 | 23-25 | 37-43 | 94-101 | 11-14 | 11-14 | 15–22 |
| | 97.5 (1597) | 50-54 | 36-40 | 23-25 | 44-50 | 94-101 ① | 11-14 | 11-14 | 15–22 |
| | 121.9 (1997) | 65-72 | 37-39 | 33-35 | 80-94 | 94-101 | 11-14 | 11-14 | 15–22 |
| | 155.9 (2555) | 65-72 | 55-61 | 33-34 | 80-94 | 94-101 | 11-14 | 11-14 | 15–22 |
| 1986 | 89.6 (1468) | 50-54 | 37-39 | 23-25 | 51-72 | 94-101 | 11-14 | 11-14 | 15–22 |
| | 97.5 (1597) | 50-54 | 36-40 | 23-25 | 80-93 | 94-101 ① | 11-14 | 11-14 | 15–22 |
| | 121.9 (1997) | 65-72 | 37-39 | 37-38 | 80-94 | 94-101 ① | 11-14 | 11-14 | 15–22 |
| | 155.9 (2555) | 65-72 | 55-61 | 33-34 | 80-94 | 94-101 | 11-14 | 11-14 | 15–22 |
| 1987 | 89.6 (1468) | 50-54 | 37-39 | 23-25 | 51-72 | 94-101 | 11-14 | 11-14 | 15–22 |
| | 97.5 (1597) | 50-54 | 36-40 | 23-25 | 80-93 | 94-101 ① | 11-14 | 11-14 | 15–22 |
| | 121.9 (1997) | 65-72 | 37-39 | 37-38 | 80-94 | 94-101 ① | 11-14 | 11-14 | 15–22 |
| | 155.9 (2555) | 65-72 | 55-61 | 33-34 | 80-94 | 94-101 | 11-14 | 11-14 | 15–22 |
| 1988 | 89.6 (1468) | 50-54 | 37-39 | 23-25 | 51-72 | 94-101 | 11-14 | 11-14 | 15–22 |
| | 97.5 (1597) | 50-54 | 36-40 | 23-25 | 80-93 | 94-101 ① | 11-14 | 11-14 | 15–22 |
| | 121.9 (1997) | 65-72 | 37-39 | 37-38 | 80-94 | 94-101 ① | 11-14 | 11-14 | 15–22 |
| | 155.9 (2555) | 65-72 | 55-61 | 33-34 | 80-94 | 94-101 | 11-14 | 11-14 | 15–22 |
| 1989-90 | 89.6 (1468) | 51-54 | 36-40 | 23-25 | 51-72 | 94-101 | 11-14 | 11-14 | 15–22 |
| | 97.5 (1595) | 65-72 | 47-51 | 36-38 | 80-94 | 94-101 ① | 11-14 | 18-14 | 15–22 |
| | 121.9 (1997) | 65-72 | 37-39 | 37-38 | 80-94 | 94-101 ① | 11-14 | 11-14 | 15–22 |
| | 155.9 (2555) | 65-72 | 55-61 | 33-34 | 80-94 | 94-101 | 11-14 | 11-14 | 15–22 |

① With automatic transmission—84-90 ft.lbs.

## BRAKE SPECIFICATIONS

All measurements in inches unless noted

| Year | Model | Lug Nut Torque (ft. lbs.) | Master Cylinder Bore | Brake Disc Minimum Thickness | Brake Disc Maximum Runout | Standard Brake Drum Diameter | Minimum Lining Thickness Front | Minimum Lining Thickness Rear |
|---|---|---|---|---|---|---|---|---|
| 1983 | Colt | 51-58 | .8125 | .450 | .006 | 7.100 | .040 | .040 |
| | Challenger | 51-58 | .8750 | .430②③ | .006 | 9.000⑦ | .040 | .040 |
| | Sapporo | 51-58 | .8750 | .430②③ | .006 | 9.000⑦ | .040 | .040 |
| 1984 | Colt | 51-58 | .8150① | .450⑧ | .006 | 7.100 | .040 | .040 |
| | Colt Vista | 51-58 | .8750 | .650⑥ | .006 | 8.000⑤ | .040 | .040 |
| | Conquest | 51-58 | .8750 | .880④ | .006 | — | .040 | .040 |
| 1985 | Colt | 51-58 | .8125① | .450⑧ | .006 | 7.100 | .040 | .040 |
| | Colt | 51-58 | .8750 | .650⑥ | .006 | 8.000⑤ | .040 | .040 |
| | Conquest | 51-58 | .9400 | .880④ | .006 | — | .040 | .040 |
| 1986 | Colt | 51-58 | .8125① | .450⑧ | .006 | 7.100 | .040 | .040 |
| | Colt Vista | 51-58 | .8750 | .650⑥ | .006 | 8.000⑤ | .040 | .040 |
| | Conquest | 51-58 | .9400 | .880④ | .006 | — | .040. | .040 |
| 1987 | Colt | 51-58 | .8125① | .450⑧ | .006 | 7.100 | .040 | .040 |
| | Colt Vista | 51-58 | .8750 | .650⑥ | .006 | 8.000⑤ | .040 | .040 |
| | Conquest | 51-58 | .9400 | .880④ | .006 | — | .040 | .040 |
| 1988 | Colt | 51-58 | .8125① | .450⑧ | .006 | 7.100 | .040 | .040 |
| | Colt Vista | 51-58 | .8750 | .650⑥ | .006 | 8.000⑤ | .040 | .040 |
| | Conquest | 51-58 | .9400 | .880④ | .006 | — | .040 | .040 |
| 1989-90 | Colt | 51-58 | .8110① | .450⑧ | .006 | 7.100 | .040 | .040 |
| | Colt Vista | 51-58 | .8750 | .650⑥ | .006 | 8.000⑤ | .040 | .040 |
| | Conquest | 51-58 | .9400 | .880④ | .006 | — | .040 | .040 |

① Colt Turbo—0.8750
② With rear disc brakes—discard at 0.330
③ Front
④ Rear—0.650 in.
⑤ 4WD—9.000 in.
⑥ 4WD—0.880 in.
⑦ With rear drum brakes
⑧ 84-88 Turbo—0.645

## WHEEL ALIGNMENT

| Year | Model | Caster Range (deg.) | Caster Preferred Setting (deg.) | Camber Range (deg.) | Camber Preferred Setting (deg.) | Toe-in (in.) | Steering Axis Inclination (deg.) |
|---|---|---|---|---|---|---|---|
| 1983 | Colt | ½-1⅛ | 13/16 | 0-1 | ½ | 5/64-5/32 | 12 11/16 |
| | Challenger | 2 3/16-3 3/16 | 2 11/16 | 11/16-1 11/16 | 1 3/16 | 0-9/32 | 9½ |
| | Sapporo | 2 3/16-3 3/16 | 2 11/16 | 11/16-1 11/16 | 1 3/16 | 0-9/32 | 9½ |
| 1984 | Colt | ½-1⅛ | 13/16 | 0-1 | ½ ① | 5/64-5/32 | 12 11/16 |
| | Colt Vista | 5/16-1 5/16 | 13/16 ⑤ | 1/16N-15/16P | 7/16 ④ | ⅛ | NA |
| | Conquest | — | 5 5/16 | — | 0 | 5/64-13/64 | NA |
| 1985 | Colt | 3/16-1 3/16 | 11/16 | ½N-½P | 0 | 0 | NA |
| | Colt Vista | 5/16-1 5/16 | 13/16 ⑤ | 1/16N-15/16P | 7/16 ④ | ⅛ | NA |
| | Conquest | — | 5 5/16 | — | 0 ② | 5/64-13/64 | NA |

## WHEEL ALIGNMENT

| Year | Model | Caster Range (deg.) | Caster Preferred Setting (deg.) | Camber Range (deg.) | Camber Preferred Setting (deg.) | Toe-in (in.) | Steering Axis Inclination (deg.) |
|---|---|---|---|---|---|---|---|
| 1986 | Colt | $\frac{3}{16}$-$1\frac{3}{16}$ | $\frac{11}{16}$ | ½N-½P | 0 | 0 | NA |
| | Colt Vista | $\frac{5}{16}$-$1\frac{5}{16}$ | $\frac{13}{16}$ ⑤ | $\frac{1}{16}$N-$\frac{15}{16}$P | $\frac{7}{16}$ ④ | ⅛ | NA |
| | Conquest | — | $5\frac{13}{16}$ | — | -½N | 0 | NA |
| 1987 | Colt | $\frac{3}{16}$-$1\frac{3}{16}$ | $\frac{11}{16}$ | ½N-½P | 0 | 0 | NA |
| | Colt Vista | $\frac{5}{16}$-$1\frac{5}{16}$ | $\frac{13}{16}$ ⑤ | $\frac{1}{16}$N-$\frac{15}{16}$P | $\frac{7}{16}$ ④ | ⅛ | NA |
| | Conquest | — | $5\frac{13}{16}$ | — | -½N ③ | 0 | NA |
| 1988 | Colt | $\frac{3}{16}$-$1\frac{3}{16}$ | $\frac{11}{16}$ | ½N-½P | 0 | 0 | NA |
| | Colt Vista | $\frac{5}{16}$-$1\frac{5}{16}$ | $\frac{13}{16}$ ⑤ | $\frac{1}{16}$N-$\frac{15}{16}$P | $\frac{7}{16}$ ④ | ⅛ | NA |
| | Conquest | — | $5\frac{13}{16}$ | — | -½N ③ | 0 | NA |
| 1989-90 | Colt | $2\frac{1}{6}$-$2\frac{5}{6}$ | $2\frac{1}{3}$ | ½N-½P | 0 | 0 | NA |
| | Colt Vista | $\frac{5}{16}$-$1\frac{5}{16}$ | $\frac{13}{16}$ ⑤ | $\frac{1}{16}$N-$\frac{15}{16}$P | $\frac{7}{16}$ ④ | 0 | NA |
| | Conquest | — | $5\frac{13}{16}$ | — | -½N ③ | 0 | NA |

N Negative
P Positive
① Rear
⅝ degree camber
0 in. toe-in
② Rear
-$\frac{5}{16}$ degree camber
$\frac{5}{16}$ in. toe-in
③ Rear
0 degree camber
0 in. toe-in
④ Rear
⅝ degree camber
0 degrees toe-in
⑤ FWD Front
$\frac{13}{16}$ degree caster
$\frac{13}{16}$ degree camber
⑥ FWD Rear
0 degrees caster
0 degrees toe-in

# TUNE-UP PROCEDURES

## Ignition Timing

### ADJUSTMENT

#### *Except 1595cc DOHC Engine*

**CAUTION**

***When performing this or any other adjustment with the engine running, be very careful of the cooling fan blades.***

1. Attach the timing light according to the manufacturer's instructions.
2. Locate the timing tab line on the front of the engine and the notch on the crankshaft pulley. Mark them so they are easily recognizable with the timing light.
3. Start the engine and allow it to reach operating temperature.
4. Point the timing light at the crankshaft pulley marks. The marked line should align with the pulley notch.
5. If the marks do not align, loosen the distributor mounting nut and rotate the distributor slowly in either direction to align the timing marks.
6. Tighten the mounting nut when the ignition timing is correct. Stop the engine and remove the timing light.

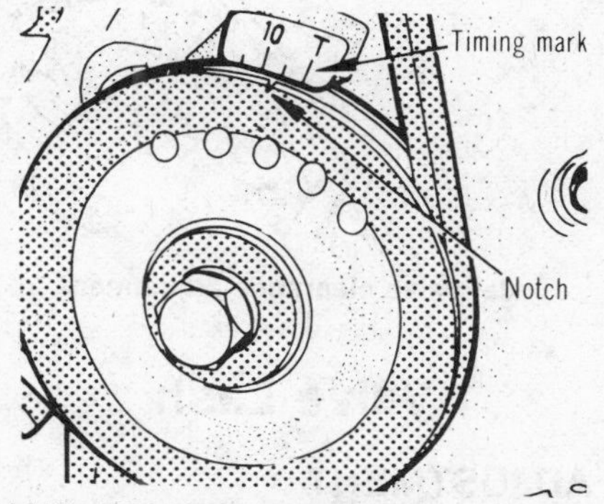


**1410, 1468, 1597 and 1997cc engine timing marks**

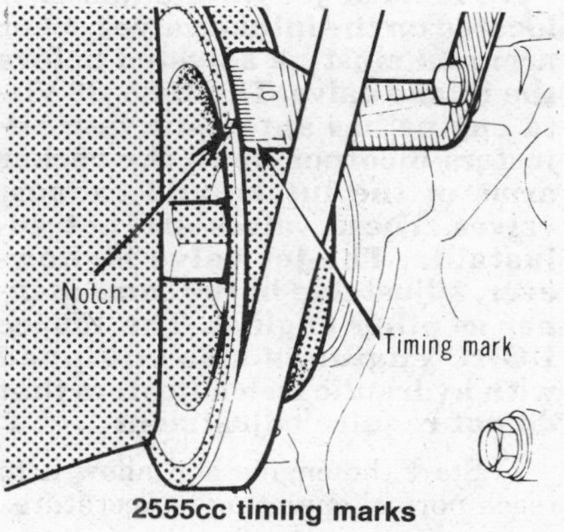


**2555cc timing marks**

#### *1595cc DOHC Engine*

1. Run the engine until the normal operating temperature is reached. Shut off the engine. Make sure all lights and electrical accessories are off. Make sure the electric cooling fan is not operating when timing. Disconnect the fan harness if necessary, but take care not to allow the engine to overheat.
2. Connect a timing light following the light manufacturer's instructions.
3. Insert a paper clip along the terminal surface of the terminal parallel to the fastener side of the ignition connecter harness in the engine compartment.
4. Connect a tachometer to the paper clip. Start the engine and check the curb idle speed. The idle speed should be 750 rpm, plus or minus 100 rpm.
5. Shut off the engine, connect a lead wire with alligator clips to the terminal for ignition-timing adjustment, and ground it to a good chassis grounding point.
6. Start the engine and point the timing light at the pulley and timing

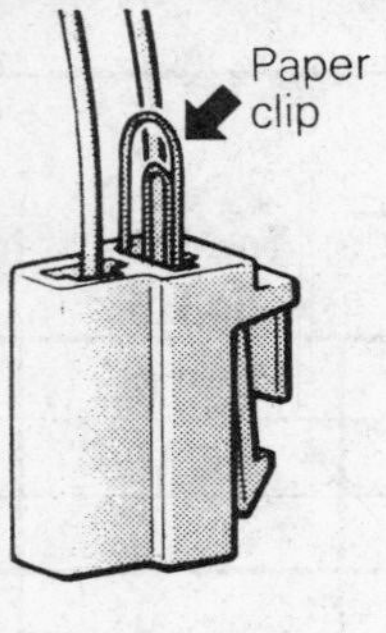


Paper clip installation

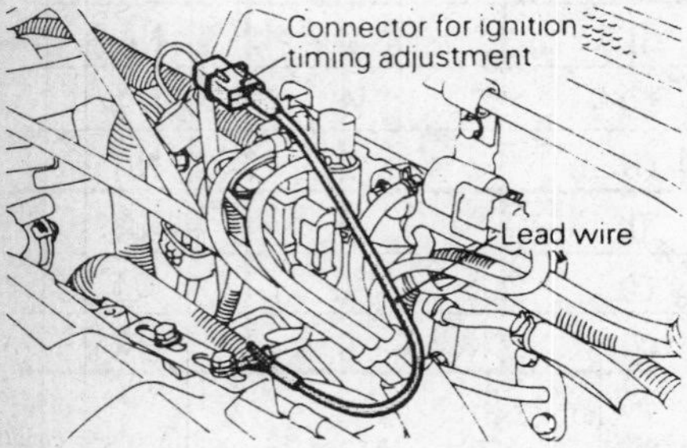


Lead wire connection

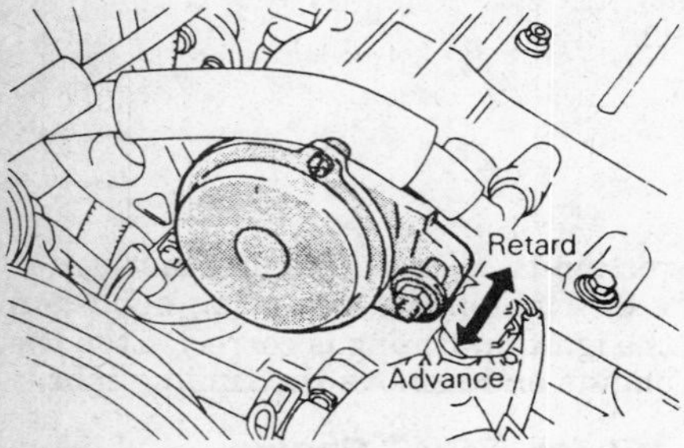


Timing adjustment with crank angle sensor

cover marks. The base timing is 5 degrees before top dead center.

7. If timing adjustment is necessary, loosen the crank angle sensor pivot bolt and turn the sensor. Turning the sensor to the right advances the timing, to the left retards it. Tighten the sensor pivot bolt when correct timing is reached. Do not allow the engine to overheat.

8. Stop the engine and disconnect the ground wire. Start the engine and check the curb idle speed. Check the ignition timing, it should now be about 8 degrees before top dead center.

9. Timing may vary depending upon the engine control module. If the timing is not about 8 degrees, check the base timing again. If the base timing is still 5 degrees, the ignition timing is functioning normally.

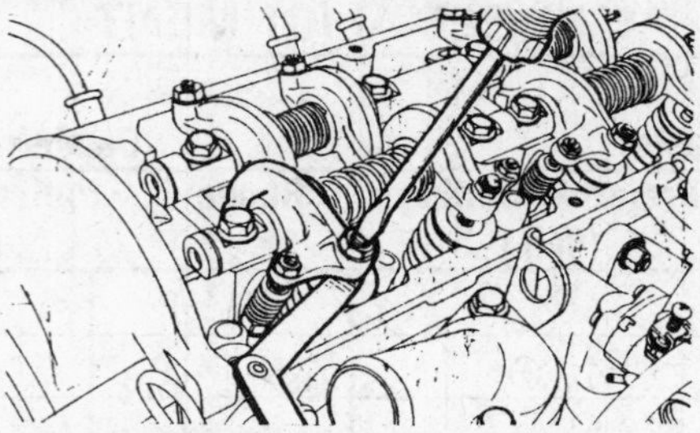

Adjusting valve clearance all engines

| Exhaust Valve Closing | Adjust |
|---|---|
| No. 1 cylinder | No. 4 cylinder valves |
| No. 2 cylinder | No. 3 cylinder valves |
| No. 3 cylinder | No. 2 cylinder valves |
| No. 4 cylinder | No. 1 cylinder valves |

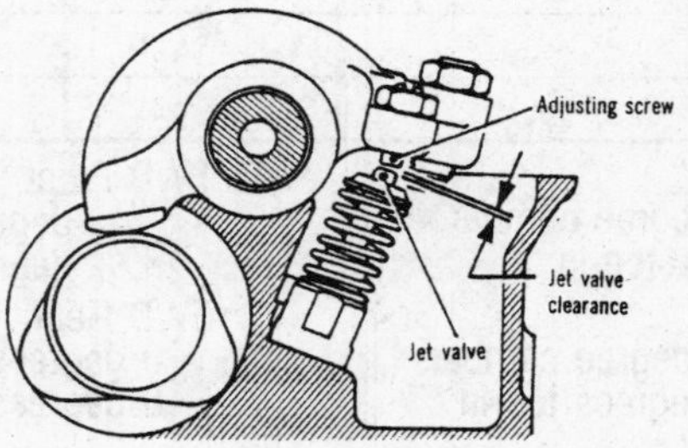


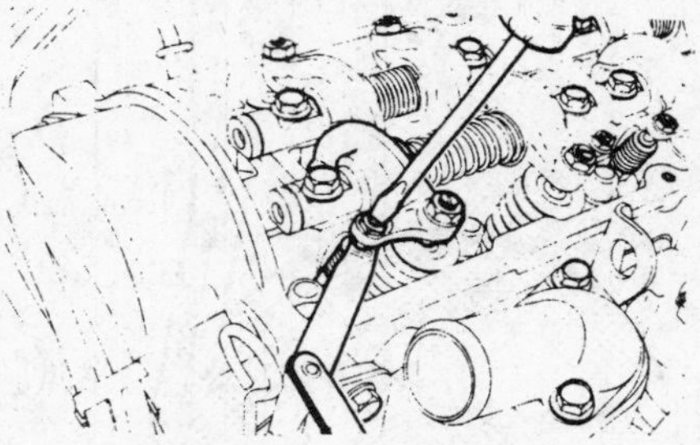

Jet valve clearance adjustment

## Valve Lash

### ADJUSTMENT

#### *Except 1595cc DOHC Engine*

**NOTE: The jet valve adjuster is located on the intake valve rocker arm and must be adjusted before the intake valve. The 1985–89 Vista engine has automatic lash adjusters incorporate in the rocker arms of the intake and exhaust valves. These valves are not adjustable. The jet valve is, however, adjustable in the same manner as other engines. The 1595cc DOHC engine is also equipped with hydraulic lash adjusters that do not require adjustment.**

1. Start the engine and allow it to reach normal operating temperature.

2. Shut off the engine and remove the air cleaner. Remove all spark plugs from the cylinder head.

3. Remove the rocker arm cover.

4. Turn the crankshaft clockwise until the notch on the pulley is lined up with the **T** mark on the lower pulley. This brings No. 1 and No. 4 pistons to top dead center.

5. To determine which cylinder piston is at top dead center on the compression stroke, move the rocker arms of both cylinders up and down by hand. If the intake and exhaust rocker arms of one cylinder are both movable, the piston in that cylinder is at top dead center on the compression stroke.

6. When No. 1 piston is at top dead center on the compression stroke the following valves can be adjusted: No. 1 intake, exhaust and jet valve – No. 2 intake and jet valve – No. 3 exhaust.

7. If the jet valve clearance is not as specified, loosen the rocker arm locknut of the intake valve and loosen the adjusting screw 2 or more turns.

8. Loosen the jet valve locknut and adjust the clearance using a feeler gauge while turning the adjusting screw.

9. While holding the adjusting screw with a screw driver to prevent it from turning, tighten the locknut.

10. To adjust the intake and exhaust valve clearances, loosen the rocker arm locknut and adjust the clearance using a feeler gauge while turning the adjusting screw.

11. While holding the adjusting screw with a screw driver to prevent it from turning, tighten the locknut.

12. Turn the crankshaft 1 full revolution to line up the notch on the crankshaft pulley with the **T** mark on the timing belt lower cover. This will bring No. 4 piston to TDC on the compression stroke. The valves to be adjusted are: No. 2 exhaust – No. 3 intake and jet valve and No. 4 intake, exhaust and jet valve.

## Idle Speed

### ADJUSTMENT

#### *Carbureted Engine*

Set the idle with all accessories off and the transmission in neutral.

1. Have the engine at normal operating temperature.

2. Operate the engine at 2000–3000 rpm for over 5 seconds, then allow to idle for 2 minutes.

3. Using a tachometer, set the idle to specifications, using the idle adjusting screw on the base of the carburetor.

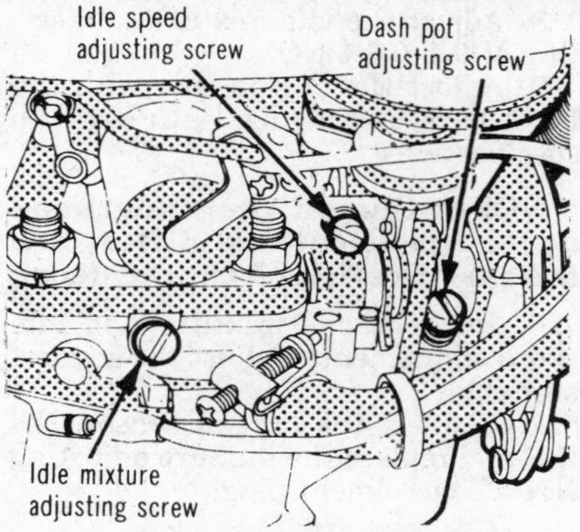


**Idle speed adjusting screw**

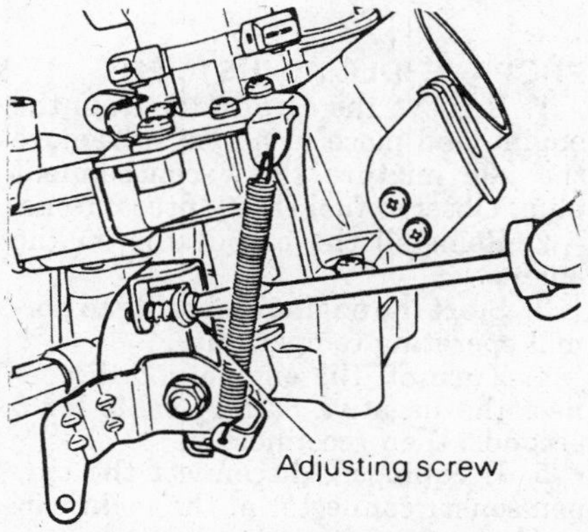


**Fuel injection unit idle speed adjusting screw**

### *Throttle Body Injection (ECI)*

**NOTE: This adjustment MUST be made any time the Idle Speed Control (ISC) servo, Throttle Position Sensor (TPS), mixing body or throttle body has been removed. A digital voltmeter is essential for this operation.**

1. Run the engine to normal operating temperature, then shut it off.
2. Disconnect the accelerator cable at the throttle lever on the mixing body.
3. Loosen the screws holds the TPS and turn it fully clockwise. Tighten the screws.
4. Turn the ignition switch to the **ON** position for at least 15 seconds, then turn if **OFF**. This will automatically set the ISC servo to the proper position.
5. Disconnect the ISC servo wiring connector.
6. Start the engine and check the idle speed with a tachometer. Idle speed should be 700 rpm. If not, adjust it with the adjusting screw.
7. Insert the digital voltmeter test probes in the TPS connector GW and B holes.
8. Turn the ignition switch to the **ON** position. DO NOT START THE ENGINE.
9. Read the voltage. If indicated voltage is not 0.45–0.51, loosen the PTS mounting screw and turn the sensor clockwise or counterclockwise until the indicated voltage is 0.48V. Tighten the screws and apply a threadlocking sealant.
10. Open the throttle valve fully and let it close. Recheck the indicated voltage. Adjust if necessary.
11. Remove the voltmeter and reconnect the wiring.
12. Start the engine. Recheck the idle speed. Adjust if necessary and stop the engine.
13. Turn the ignition switch to the **ON** position for at least 15 seconds, then turn it **OFF**.
14. Connect the cable, and adjust if necessary to remove any slack, using the adjusting nut at the throttle level.

### *Multipoint Injection (MPI)*

The curb idle speed is controlled electronically and should not require adjustment.

## Idle Mixture

### ADJUSTMENT

#### *Carbureted Engines*

#### CARBURETOR WITH ROLL PIN AND CONCEALMENT PLUG

**NOTE: A carbon monoxide (CO) meter is necessary when performing the carburetor mixture adjustment.**

1. Remove the carburetor from the engine. Observing all fuel handling precautions, drain the fuel from the carburetor bowl.
2. Place the carburetor upside down, in a vise and carefully tighten to hold carburetor securely.
3. With an appropriate pin punch, remove the roll pin from the carburetor base and the concealment plug from over the mixture adjustment screw.

**NOTE: Some carburetors may only have a roll pin installed over the mixture adjusting screw channel to prevent tampering.**

4. Reinstall the carburetor and start the engine. Bring to normal operating temperature.
5. When equipped, disconnect or clamp off the hose between the Pulse air feeder and the air cleaner.
6. Operate the engine between 2000– 3000 rpm for approximately 5 seconds and then allow to idle for approximately 2 minutes.

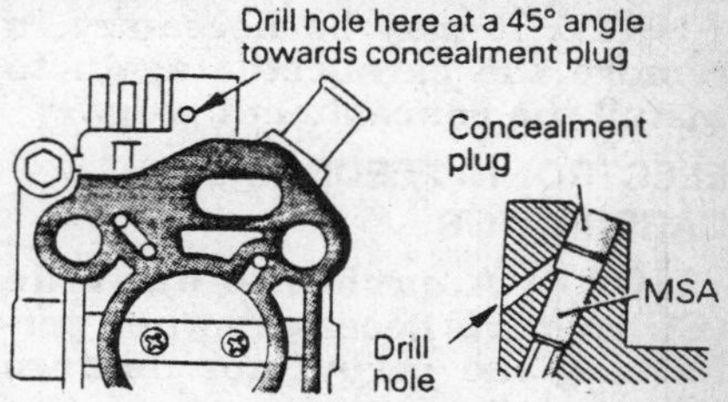


**Drilling of carburetor base to remove concealment plug, exposing the mixture adjustment screw**

7. Adjust the idle mixture to a setting of 0.5% on the (CO) meter, up to 1984 models and 0.1–0.3% for 1985–89.

**NOTE: Should the underhood decal specifications differ, use the specifications from the decal.**

8. Replace the roll pin and if equipped, the concealment plug. Reset the engine idle speed as required.

**NOTE: It may be necessary to remove the carburetor again to install the roll pin and plug.**

#### CARBURETOR WITH CONCEALMENT PLUG

**NOTE: A carbon monoxide (CO) meter is necessary when performing the carburetor mixture adjustment.**

1. Remove the carburetor from the engine. Observing all fuel handling precautions, drain the fuel from the carburetor bowl.
2. Place the carburetor upside down, in a vise and carefully tighten to hold carburetor securely.
3. With a $^1/_{64}$ in. pilot bit, drill a hole in the carburetor base casting to the edge of the concealment plug. Enlarge the drilled hole to ⅛ in.
4. With an appropriate pin punch, remove the concealment plug from over the mixture adjustment screw.
5. Reinstall the carburetor and start the engine. Bring to normal operating temperature.
6. When equipped, disconnect or clamp off the hose between the Pulse air feeder and the air cleaner.
7. Operate the engine between 2000–3000 rpm for approximately 5 seconds and then allow to idle for approximately 2 minutes.
8. Adjust the idle mixture to a setting of 0.5% on the CO meter, up to 1984 models and 0.1–0.3 for 1985–89.

**NOTE: Should the underhood decal specifications differ, use the specifications from the decal.**

9. Replace the concealment plug. Reset the engine idle speed as required.

**NOTE: It may be necessary to remove the carburetor again to install the concealment plug.**

### ELECTRONIC FEEDBACK CARBURETOR

**NOTE: A carbon monoxide (CO) meter is necessary when performing the carburetor mixture adjustment.**

1. Remove the carburetor from the engine. Observing all fuel handling precautions, drain the fuel from the carburetor bowl.
2. Place the carburetor upside down, in a vise and carefully tighten to hold carburetor securely.
3. With a 5/64 in. pilot bit, drill a hole in the carburetor base casting to the edge of the concealment plug. Enlarge the drilled hole to 1/8 in.
4. With an appropriate pin punch, remove the concealment plug from over the mixture adjustment screw.
5. Reinstall the carburetor and start the engine. Bring to normal operating temperature.
6. Disconnect the oxygen sensor. 1985–89 models, disconnect the battery cable for 3 seconds and then reconnect.
7. Operate the engine between 2000–3000 rpm for approximately 5 seconds and then allow to idle for approximately 2 minutes.
8. Adjust the idle mixture to a setting of 0.5% on the CO meter, up to 1984 models and 0.1–0.3% for 1985–89.

**NOTE: Should the underhood decal specifications differ, use the specifications from the decal.**

9. Connect the oxygen sensor and replace the mixture adjusting screw concealment plug.

**NOTE: It may be necessary to remove the carburetor again to install the concealment plug.**

10. Reset the engine idle speed as required.

### ELECTRONIC FEEDBACK CARBURETOR WITH IDLE SPEED CONTROL

**NOTE: A carbon monoxide (CO) meter is necessary when performing the carburetor mixture adjustment.**

1. Remove the carburetor from the engine. Observing all fuel handling precautions, drain the fuel from the carburetor bowl.
2. Place the carburetor upside down, in a vise and carefully tighten to hold carburetor securely.
3. With a 5/64 in. pilot bit, drill a hole in the carburetor base casting to the edge of the concealment plug. Enlarge the drilled hole to 1/8 in.
4. With an appropriate pin punch, remove the concealment plug from over the mixture adjustment screw.
5. Reinstall the carburetor and start the engine. Bring to normal operating temperature. Stop the engine and relax the accelerator cable.
6. Switch on the ignition switch, wait 18 seconds and then turn the switch off. Disconnect the oxygen sensor and ISC actuator.
7. Start the engine and operate between 2000 and 3000 rpm for approximately 5 seconds and then allow to idle for approximately 2 minutes.
8. Adjust the idle mixture to a setting of 0.1–0.3% CO.
9. Adjust the engine rpm with the ISC adjustment screw to specifications.

**NOTE: Should the underhood decal specifications differ, use the specifications from the decal.**

10. Recheck the mixture and idle speed adjustments. Adjust the accelerator cable.
11. Connect the oxygen sensor, the ISC and replace the mixture adjusting screw concealment plug.

**NOTE: It may be necessary to remove the carburetor again to install the concealment plug.**

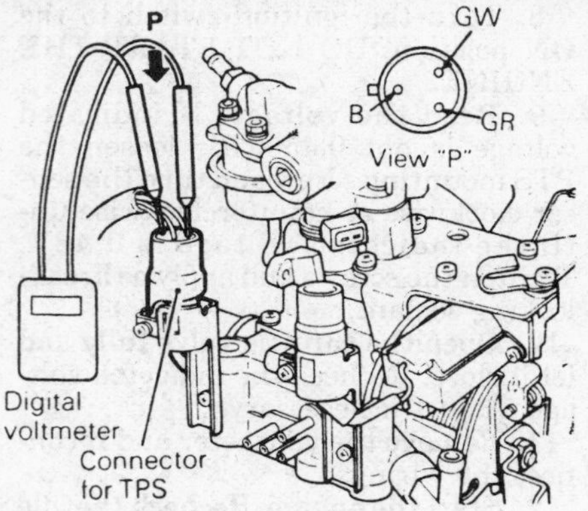

Digital voltmeter connections

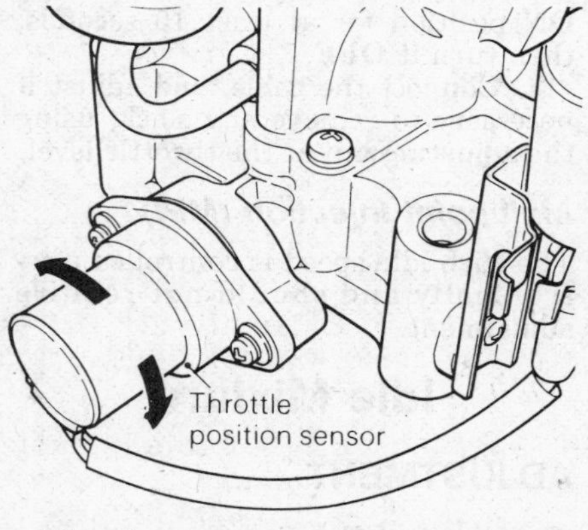

Throttle position sensor adjustment

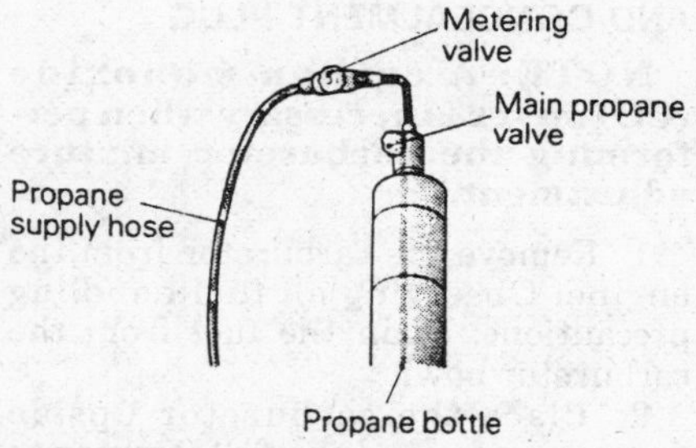

Components necessary to perform the Propane Idle Enrichment procedure

### PROPANE IDLE ADJUSTMENT

1. Remove the carburetor from the engine and place in a vise to remove the idle mixture screw concealment plug. Observe fuel safety precautions.
2. Reinstall the carburetor on the engine.
3. Start the engine and bring to normal operating temperature.
4. Turn off the engine and disconnect the negative battery cable for 5 seconds, then reconnect it.
5. If equipped, disconnect the oxygen sensor connector at the main wiring harness.
6. Start the engine and operate the engine at a speed of 2000–3000 rpm for 5 seconds. Lights, cooling fan and all accessories must be off.
7. Allow the engine to operate at curb idle for 2 minutes.
8. If necessary, adjust the ignition timing.
9. Disconnect the fresh air duct from the air cleaner and insert the propane supply hose into the air cleaner about 4–6 in.
10. Be sure both valves are closed on the propane bottle and it is in an upright and safe position.
11. Open the main propane valve and slowly open the metering valve until maximum engine speed is achieved. Excessive amounts of propane will cause engine speed to reduce. Fine tune the metering valve to obtain the highest engine rpm.
12. With the propane still flowing, adjust idle speed screw to obtain the specified enriched rpm. Fine tune the the metering valve again to obtain the highest engine rpm. If there is a change in the enriched rpm, readjust the idle speed screw to obtain the specified enriched rpm.
13. Turn off the propane main valve and allow the engine speed to stabilize.
14. Slowly adjust the idle mixture screw to obtain the specified curb idle speed.

15. Recheck the maximum enriched idle speed again by using the propane metering valve. If the enriched speed varies by more than 25 rpm than the specified enriched rpm, perform the adjustment again.

16. Turn off both propane valves and remove the bottle and hose.

17. Reconnect the oxygen sensor connector to the main wiring.

18. Reinstall the idle mixture screw concealment plug and connect the fresh air duct to the air cleaner.

# ENGINE ELECTRICAL

## Distributor

### REMOVAL & INSTALLATION

Before removing the distributor, position No. 1 cylinder at TDC on the compression stroke and align the timing marks before distributor removal.

1. Disconnect the negative battery cable from the battery.
2. Disconnect the spark plug wires from the distributor cap.
3. Disconnect the ignition coil high tension wire from the distributor cap.
4. Remove the vacuum line (lines) from the advance unit.
5. Remove the cap from the distributor.
6. Verify the rotor points to the No. 1 cylinder position and the timing marks on the crankshaft pulley and the timing tab are aligned at TDC.
7. Mark the distributor body to the exact place the rotor points. Matchmark both the distributor mounting flange and the cylinder head.
8. Loosen and remove the retaining nut from the mounting stud. Lift the distributor from the cylinder head. The rotor may turn slightly from the mark on the distributor body. Make note of how far. When the distributor is reinstalled, this is the point to position the rotor.
9. If the engine has not been disturbed, i.e. the crankshaft was not turned, then reinstall the distributor in the reverse order or removal. Carefully align the matchmarks. Always check the ignition timing whenever the distributor has been removed.
10. If the engine has been disturbed, i.e. rotated while the distributor was out, proceed as follows:

a. Turn the crankshaft so that the No. 1 piston is on the compres-

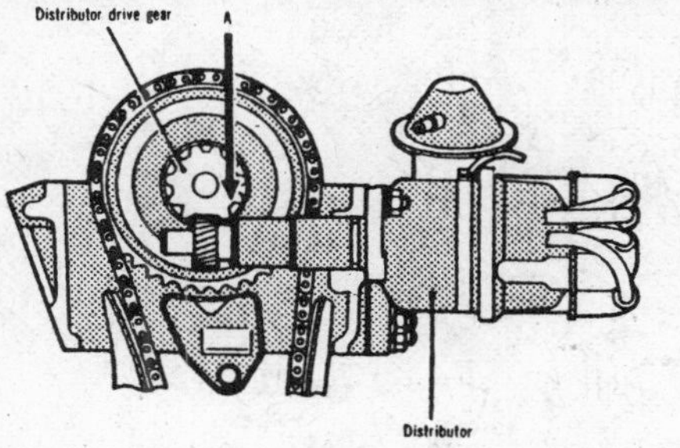


**Distributor installation—cylinder head mounted distributors**

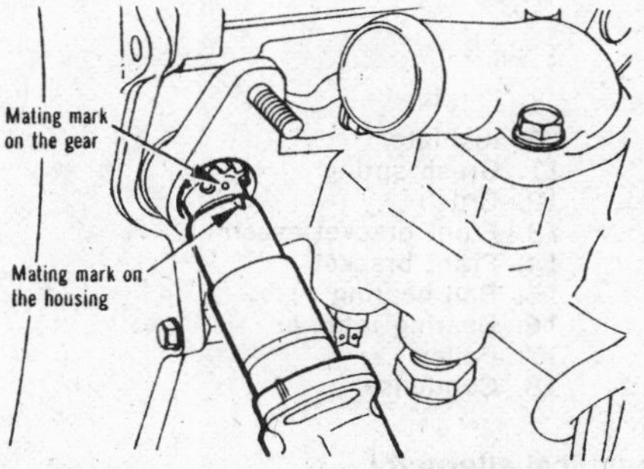


**Aligning mating marks for installation of cylinder head mounted distributors**

sion stroke and the timing marks are aligned.

b. Turn the distributor shaft so that the rotor points approximately 15 degrees before the rotor position that was marked on the distributor.

c. Insert the distributor, if resistance is met, slight wiggling of the rotor shaft will help seat the distributor.

d. When the distributor seats against the head, align the matchmarks and install the retaining nut. Do not tighten the retaining nut all the way, as the timing must be checked. Reinstall the rotor, cap, plug wires, coil lead, primary lead (or harness) and connect the vacuum hoses. Connect the negative battery cable. Start the engine, allow it to reach operating temperature and check the ignition timing.

## Alternator

### PRECAUTIONS

There are numerous precautions which must be strictly observed in order to avoid damaging the unit.

- Reversing the battery connections will result in damage to the diodes.
- Booster batteries should be connected from negative to negative and positive to positive.
- Never use a fast charger as a booster to start the car.
- When servicing the battery with a fast charger, always disconnect the car battery cables.

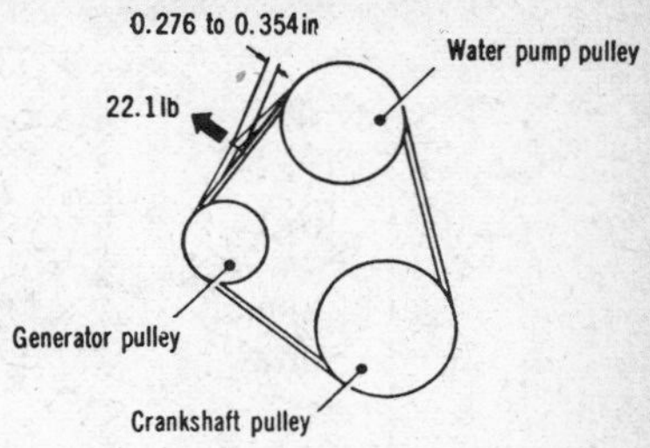


**Belt tension adjustment**

- Never attempt to polarize an alternator.
- Avoid long soldering times when replacing diodes or transistors. Prolonged heat is damaging to alternators.
- Do not use test lamps of more than 12 volts (V) for checking diode continuity.
- Do not short across or ground any of the terminals to the alternator.
- The polarity of the battery, alternator, and regulator must be matched and considered before making any electrical connections within the system.
- Never operate the alternator on an open circuit. Make sure that all connections within the circuit are clean and tight.
- Disconnect the battery terminals when performing any service on the electrical system. This will eliminate the possibility of accidental reversal of polarity.
- Disconnect the battery ground cable if arc welding is to be done on any part of the car.

### BELT REPLACEMENT AND TENSIONING

1. Check the drive belt(s) for cracking, fraying and any other deterioration. Replace if necessary.
2. To replace the belt, loosen the stationary mounting bolt and and pivot bolt. If the unit is equipped with an adjustment bolt, loosen it to provide the necessary slack for belt removal. Pivot the driven component in its bracket. Remove the old belt and slip the replacement belt over the pulleys.
3. Move the driven component over, or tighten the adjustment bolt, until the belt can be deflected ¼–⅜ in. at its midpoint.
4. Tighten the mounting and pivot bolts.

### REMOVAL & INSTALLATION

#### *Rear Wheel Drive*

1. Disconnect the negative battery cable.

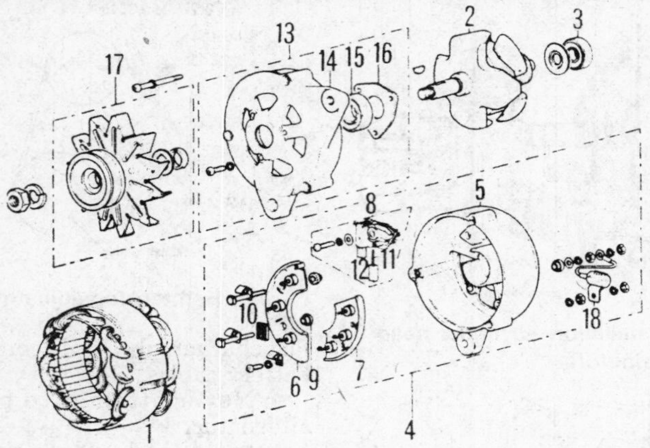


1. Stator
2. Rotor
3. Ball bearing
4. Rear bracket assembly
5. Rear bracket
6. Heat sink complete (+)
7. Heat sink complete (−)
8. Brush holder assembly
9. Insulator
10. Insulator
11. Brush spring
12. Brush
13. Front bracket assembly
14. Front bracket
15. Ball bearing
16. Bearing retainer
17. Pulley
18. Condenser

**Exploded view of the typical alternator**

2. Disconnect the wire connectors from the alternator.
3. On vehicles with air conditioning remove the discharge and suction hose connections and remove the compressor.
4. Remove the alternator.
5. Reverse the removal procedure to install. Adjust the belt to proper tension.

### *Front Wheel Drive*

1. Disconnect the negative battery cable.
2. Remove the condenser fan motor.
3. Remove the power steering pump from the bracket and hold it on the oil reservoir using wire.
4. Remove the power steering pump bracket.
5. Disconnect the wiring connectors from the alternator.
6. Remove the lock bolt and the support bolt.
7. Remove the alternator and the adjusting bolt.
8. Install in the reverse order of removal. Adjust the belt to the proper tension. Adjust the front leg to front leg to front case clearance as follows:
   a. Push the support bolt to the normal position without installing the nut.
   b. Push the alternator forward.
   c. Insert shims between the front leg and the front case and determine the number of shims necessary. The number of shims used should be just enough so that there is no fall under natural conditions.
   d. Insert the decided number of shims at the clearance point at rear side of the alternator.
   e. Tighten the support bolt and the brace bolt.

## Voltage Regulator

### REMOVAL & INSTALLATION

The voltage regulator is a solid state unit built into or mounted on the alternator. The regulator is non-adjustable and is serviced, when necessary, by replacement.

## Starter

### REMOVAL & INSTALLATION

1. Disconnect the battery ground cable and the starter motor wiring.
2. Remove the 2 starter attaching bolts and remove the starter motor.
3. Clean both surfaces of the starter motor flange and the rear plate.
4. Position the starter in the housing opening.
5. Install the attaching bolts. Tighten evenly to avoid binding.
6. Install the starter wiring and connect the battery cable.

### STARTER DRIVE REPLACEMENT

#### *Direct Drive Starter*

**NOTE: Starter is removed from car.**

1. Remove the wire connecting the starter solenoid to the starter.
2. Remove 2 screws holding the starter solenoid on the starter drive housing and remove the solenoid.
3. Remove the 2 long through bolts at the rear of the starter and separate the armature yoke from the armature.
4. Carefully remove the armature and the starter drive engagement lever from the front bracket, after making a mental note of the way they are positioned along with the attendant spring and spring retainer.
5. Loosen the 2 screws and remove the rear bracket.
6. Tap the stopper ring at the end of the drive gear engagement shaft in towards the driver gear to expose the snapring. Remove the snapring.
7. Pull the stopper, drive gear and overrunning clutch from the end of the shaft.

Inspect the pinion and spline teeth for wear and damage. If the engagement teeth are damaged, visually check the flywheel ring gear through the starter hole to insure that it is not damaged. It will be necessary to turn the engine over by hand to completely inspect the ring gear.

Check the brushes for wear. Their service limit length is 0.453 in. Replace if necessary.

Assembly is performed in the following manner.

8. Install the spring retainer and spring on the armature shaft.
9. Install the overrunning clutch assembly on the armature shaft.
10. Fit the stopper ring with its open side facing out on the shaft.
11. Install a new snapring and , using a gear puller, pull the stopper ring into place over the snapring.
12. Fit the small washer on the front end of the armature shaft.
13. Fit the engagement lever into the overrunning clutch and refit the armature into the front housing.
14. Fit the engagement lever spring and spring retainer into place and slide the armature yoke over the armature. Make sure the yoke is positioned with the spring retainer cut-out space in line with the spring retainer.

**NOTE: Make sure the brushes are seated on the commutator.**

15. Replace the rear bracket and 2 retainer screws.
16. Install the 2 though bolts in the end of the yoke.
17. Refit the starter solenoid, making sure the plunger is fit over the engagement lever. Install the screws and connect the wire running from the starter yoke to the starter solenoid.

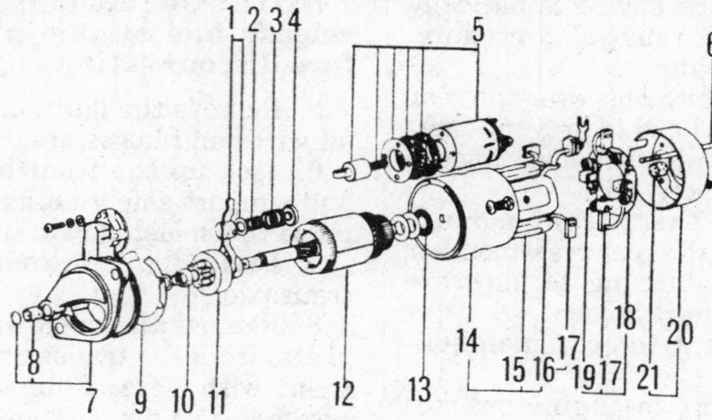


1. Lever assembly
2. Lever spring (A)
3. Lever spring (B)
4. Spring retainer
5. Electromagnetic switch
6. Through bolt
7. Front bracket
8. Front bracket bearing
9. Plate
10. Stop ring
11. Overrunning clutch
12. Armature
13. Insulating washer
14. Yoke assembly
15. Pole piece
16. Field coil
17. Brush
18. Brush holder
19. Brush spring
20. Rear bracket
21. Rear bracket bearing

Exploded view of the typical starter

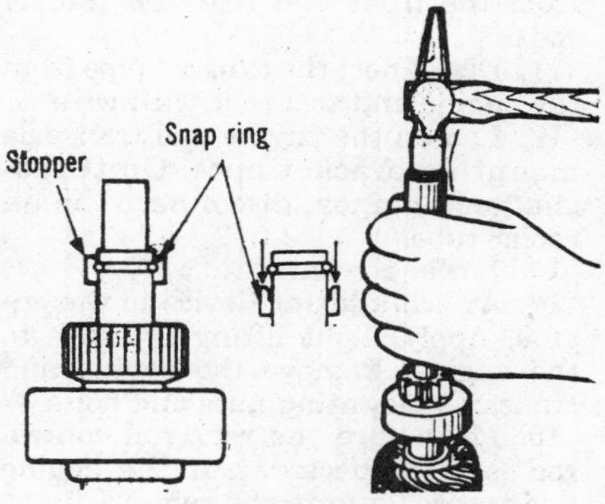


Removing the starter drive

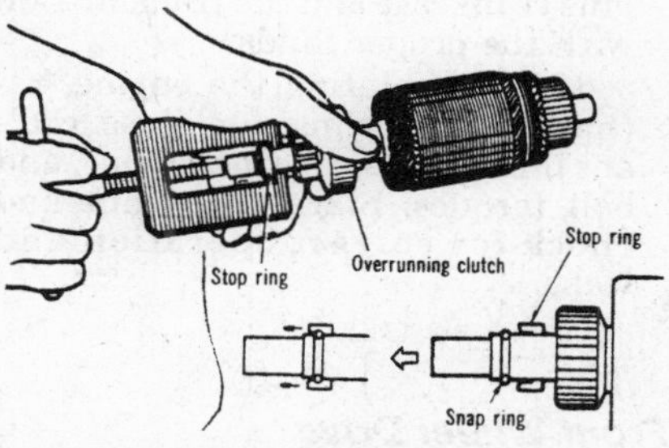


Installing the snap-ring stopper

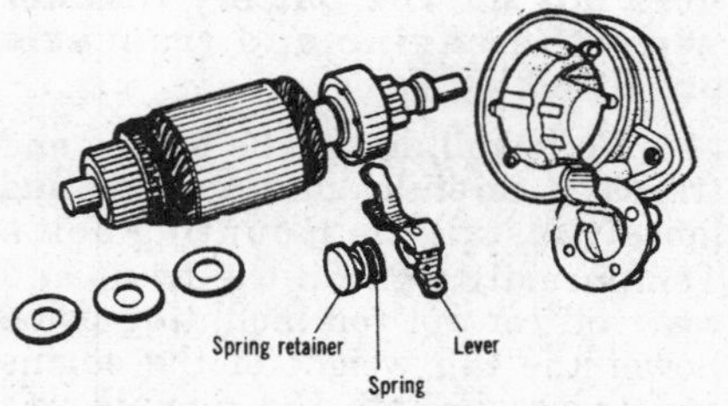


Removing the starter armature and lever

### *Reduction Drive Starter*

**NOTE: Starter removed from car.**

1. Remove the wire connecting the starter solenoid to the starter.
2. Remove the 2 screws holding the solenoid and, pulling out, unhook it from the engagement lever.
3. Remove the 2 through bolts in the end of the starter and remove the 2 bracket screws. Pull off the rear bracket.

**NOTE: Since the conical spring washer is contained in the rear bracket, be sure to take it out.**

4. Remove the yoke and brush holder assembly while pulling the brush upward.
5. Pull the armature assembly out of the mounting bracket.
6. On the side of the armature mounting bracket, there is a small dust shield held on by 2 screws, remove the shield. Remove the snapring and washer located under the shield.
7. Remove the remaining bolts in the mounting bracket and separate the reduction case.

**NOTE: Several washers will come out of the reduction case when separated. These adjust the armature end play; do not lose them.**

8. Remove the reduction gear, lever and lever spring from the front bracket.
9. Use a brass drift or a deep socket to knock the stopper ring on the end of the shaft in toward the pinion. Remove the snapring. Remove the stopper, pinion and pinion shaft assembly.
10. Remove the ball bearings at both ends of the armature.

**NOTE: The ball bearings are pressed into the front bracket and are not replaceable. Replace them together with the bracket.**

Inspect the pinion and spline teeth for wear or damage. If the pinion drive teeth are damaged, visually check the engine flywheel ring gear. Check the flywheel ring gear by looking through the starter motor mounting hole. It will be necessary to turn the engine over by hand to completely inspect the ring gear.

Check the starter brushes for wear. Their service limit length is 0.453 in. Replace if necessary.

Assembly is the reverse of disassembly procedure. Be sure to replace all the adjusting and thrust washers that was removed. When replacing the rear bracket, fit the conical spring pinion washer with its convex side facing out. Make sure that the brushes seat themselves on the commutator.

## STARTER SOLENOID REPLACEMENT

1. Disconnect the negative battery cable.
2. Remove the starter from the vehicle.
3. Disconnect the field coil wire from the **M** terminal of the solenoid.
4. Remove the mounting screws and remove the solenoid.
5. Installation is the reverse of the removal procedure.

# ENGINE MECHANICAL

## Engine

### REMOVAL & INSTALLATION

#### *Rear Wheel Drive*

The factory recommends removing the engine and transmission as a unit.

1. Disconnect and remove the battery and tray.
2. Drain the cooling system.
3. Disconnect the coil, throttle positioner solenoid, fuel cut-off solenoid, alternator, starter, transmission switch, backup light switch, and temperature and oil pressure gauge sending units.
4. On cars with air conditioning, the refrigerant must be released from the system. After the system has been drained, disconnect and cap lines at the compressor and condenser.

5. Remove all air cleaners hoses. Remove the wing nut (and snap clips) and the air cleaner to cover.
6. Remove the 2 retaining nuts and bracket and remove the air cleaner housing.
7. Disconnect the accelerator cable.
8. Remove and plug the radiator hose.
9. Remove the exhaust manifold nuts and drop the pipe down and out of the way.
10. Disconnect and cap the fuel lines at the pump. On cars with fuel injection, see Fuel Pump Removal for the procedure necessary to bleed the pressure from the system before disconnecting the lines.
11. Disconnect the vacuum hose from the canister purge valve located on the passenger side firewall. Remove the purge hose which runs from the valve to the intake manifold.
12. Scribe a line around the hood hinges and then remove the hood. Place it away from the work area to avoid it being scratched or dented.
13. Remove the grill, radiator cross panel and the radiator. Disconnect and plug the oil cooler lines on automatic transmission equipped cars. Disconnect and plug the engine oil cooler lines (at the engine) on turbo models. Remove and secure the power steering pump (with hoses connected) out of the way.
14. Jack up the front of the car and support it on jackstands. Remove the splash shield.
15. Drain the engine oil and the transmission fluid. Remove the driveshaft.
16. Disconnect the speedometer cable and back-up switch wire. Remove the neutral switch on automatic cars.
17. Disconnect the clutch cable from the clutch lever.
18. Remove the control rod and the cross shaft that are located under the transmission.
19. Untie and open the leather shift boot. Pull the rug back. Remove the 4 retaining bolts and remove the shift lever.
20. On automatic transmission: Disconnect the transmission control rod from the shift linkage.
21. Attach the lifting device to the 2 engine brackets provided by the factory, one near the water neck at the front and the other on the passenger's side at the rear.
22. Raise the engine a slight amount and remove the retaining nuts on the side mounts and the rear crossmember mount.
23. Lift the engine out of the compartment.
24. Check the condition of the engine mounts. There are 3: left front, right front and rear. Replace, if required.
25. Installing the engine is basically a reverse of the removal procedure, noting the following:

a. Drape heavy rags over the rear of the cylinder head to prevent damaging the firewall when lowering the engine into place.

b. Tighten the 2 front mounts first and then the rear crossmember mount. All tightening torques are listed in the chart below:

Front mount-to-crossmember–15–17 ft. lbs.

Front mount-to-engine bracket nut–15–17 ft. lbs.

Front engine block-to-bracket bolt–29–36 ft. lbs.

Rear mount-to-support bracket–7–8.5 ft. lbs.

Rear mount-to-frame bolt–15–17 ft. lbs.

Crossmember-to-body bolt–(manual) 9–11 ft. lbs., (automatic) 7–8.5 ft. lbs.

c. Refill the cooling system, engine crankcase and the transmission with the proper fluids.

d. Before stating the engine, recheck the following: fuel lines, coolant lines, electrical connections, and bolt torques. Start the engine and check for correct operation and leaks.

### *Front Wheel Drive*

#### EXCEPT 4WD VISTA AND 1595cc DOHC ENGINE

The factory recommends that the engine and transaxle be removed as a unit.

1. Disconnect and remove the battery and the tray.
2. Remove the air cleaner assembly. Disconnect the purge control valve. Remove the purge control valve mounting bracket. Remove the windshield washer reservoir, radiator tank and carbon canister.
3. Drain the coolant from the radiator. Remove the radiator assembly with the electric cooling fan attached. Be sure to disconnect the fan wiring harness and the transmission cooler lines (if equipped).
4. Disconnect the following cables, hoses and wires from the engine and transaxle: clutch, accelerator, seedometer, heater hose, fuel lines, PCV vacuum line, high-altitude compensator vacuum hose (Calif. models), bowl vent valve purge hose (U.S.A. models), inhibitor switch (auto trans), control cable (auto trans), starter, engine ground cable, alternator, water temperature gauge, ignition coil, temperature sensor, back-up light (man. trans.), oil pressure wires, and the ISC cable on fuel injected cars.

**NOTE: On fuel injected models, release fuel system pressure before disconnecting any fuel lines.**

5. Remove the ignition coil. Be sure all wires and hoses are disconnected.
6. Jack up the front of the vehicle and support safely on jackstands. Remove the splash shield (if equipped).
7. Drain the lubricant out of the transaxle.
8. Remove the right and left driveshafts from the transaxle and support them with wire. Plug the transaxle case holes so dirt cannot enter.

**NOTE: The driveshaft retainer ring should be replaced whenever the shaft is removed.**

9. Disconnect the assist rod and the control rod from the transaxle. If the car is equipped with a range selector, disconnect the selector cable.
10. Remove the mounting bolts/bolt from the front and rear roll control rods.
11. Disconnect the exhaust pipe from the engine and secure it with wire.
12. Loosen the engine and transaxle mounting bracket nuts. On turbocharged engines, disconnect the oil cooler tube.
13. Lower the car.
14. Attach a lifting device to the engine. Apply slight lifting pressure to the engine. Remove the engine and transaxle mounting nuts and bolts.
15. Make sure the rear roll control rod is disconnected. Lift the engine and transaxle from the car.

**NOTE: Make sure the transaxle does not hit the battery bracket when the engine and transaxle are lifted.**

16. To install, lower the engine and transaxle carefully into position and loosely install the mounting bolts. Temporarily tighten the front and rear roll control rod mounting bolts. Lower the full weight of the engine and transaxle onto the mounts and tighten the nuts and bolts. Loosen and retighten the roll control rods.
17. The rest of the engine installation is the reverse of the removal. Make sure all cables, hoses and wires are connected. Fill the radiator with coolant, the transaxle with lubricant. Adjust the clutch cable and accelerator cable. Adjust the transaxle control rod. Start the engine and check for leaks.

#### 4WD VISTA

1. Remove the battery, battery tray and bracket.
2. Disconnect the engine oil pressure switch and power steering pump connectors.
3. Disconnect the alternator harness.

4. Remove the air cleaner.
5. Remove the high tension cable from the distributor.
6. Disconnect the engine ground wire at the firewall.
7. Remove the windshield washer bottle.
8. Disconnect the brake booster vacuum hose.
9. Disconnect and tag all other vacuum lines connected to the engine.
10. Drain the coolant.
11. Remove the coolant reservoir tank.
12. Remove the radiator.
13. Disconnect the heater hoses at the engine.
14. Disconnect the accelerator cable from the carburetor.
15. Disconnect the speed control cable at the carburetor.
16. Disconnect the speedometer cable at the transaxle.
17. If the car is equipped with air conditioning, the system must be evacuated.
18. Disconnect the hose at the air conditioning compressor and cap all openings immediately.
19. Disconnect the hoses at the power steering pump.
20. Disconnect the fuel return hose, then the fuel inlet hose, at the carburetor.
21. Disconnect the shift control cables at the transaxle.
22. Raise and support the car on jackstands.
23. Remove the lower cover and skid plate.
24. Drain the transaxle and transfer case.
25. Disconnect the exhaust pipe from the manifold.
26. See the procedures under Driveshaft, later in this section, and remove the driveshaft.
27. Remove the clutch slave cylinder as described later in this section.
28. Disconnect the halfshafts at the transaxle as described later in this section.
29. Remove the transfer case extension stopper bracket.

**NOTE: The 2 top stopper bracket bolts are easier to get at from the engine compartment, using a T-type box wrench.**

30. Lower the vehicle to the ground.
31. Remove the nuts only, from the engine mount-to-body bracket.
32. Remove the range select control valves from the transaxle insulator bracket.
33. Remove the nut only, from the transaxle mounting insulator.
34. Remove the front roll insulator nut.
35. Remove the front roll insulator nut.
36. Remove the rear insulator-to-engine nut.
37. Remove the grille and valance panel.
38. Remove the A/C condenser.
39. Take up the weight of the engine with a lifting device attached to the lifting eyes.
40. Remove all the mounting bolts.
41. Double check that all wiring, hoses and cable from the engine, transaxle and transfer case have been disconnected.. Move the assembly forward slightly to a point at which it will clear the floorpan, and lift the whole assembly clear of the car.
42. Installation is the reverse of removal. Observe the following torques:
Transaxle stopper–58 ft. lbs.
Engine-to-body bracket bolts–47 ft. lbs.
Rear insulator–29 ft. lbs.
Transaxle mount nuts–58 ft. lbs.
Heat shield–7 ft. lbs.
Front roll bracket nuts–36 ft. lbs.

### 1595cc DOHC ENGINE

1. Remove the hood. Disconnect the negative battery cable, the positive battery cable and remove the battery.
2. Relieve the fuel system pressure. Drain the cooling system and the engine oil. Disconnect the exhaust pipe from the turbocharger after removing the heat shields.
3. Remove the radiator. Remove the transaxle.
4. Remove the air cleaner. Disconnect the accelerator cable, the vacuum hose from the brake booster, and all vacuum hoses (label the hoses for correct installation).
5. Disconnect the high pressure fuel line and the fuel return hose. Remove their respective mounting O-rings.
6. Disconnect the heater hoses, the oxygen sensor, the coolant temperature sensor and the connection for the engine coolant temperature gauge unit.
7. Disconnect the engine coolant switch for the air conditioner. Disconnect the fuel injector wiring connection, the ignition coil, the power transistor, vacuum lines and the ISC motor.
8. On California models, disconnect the EGR temperature sensor.
9. Disconnect the detonation sensor, the throttle position sensor, the crankshaft angle sensor and the control wiring harness connectors.
10. Disconnect the oil pressure switch for the power steering. Disconnect the alternator wiring. Remove the wiring harness mounting clamps. Disconnect the engine oil pressure switch.
11. Remove the air conditioning compressor, with lines attached, and safety wire the assembly out of the way.
12. Remove the power steering pump, with hoses attached, and safety wire it out of the way.
13. Connect a chain hoist to the engine with a suitable lifting bracket. Take up slack on the engine. Check to be sure all cables, hoses, harness connectors and vacuum hoses have been disconnected.
14. Remove the engine mounting bracket. Disconnect the front engine roll stopper and the rear roll stopper. Carefully raise and remove the engine assembly.
15. Service as required. Install the engine in the reverse order of removal. Make sure all cables, vacuum lines, hose and wire connectors are installed or attached. Fill the radiator with the proper coolant mix. Fill the engine with the proper oil. Adjust the clutch and accelerator cable. Start the engine and check for leaks.

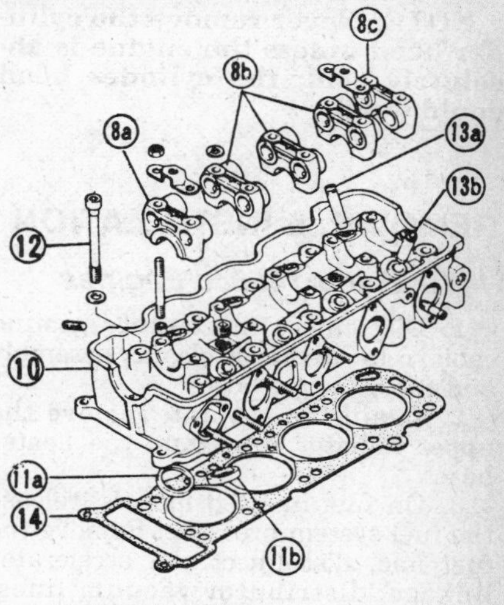


8a. Camshaft bearing cap
8b. No. 2, 3 and 4 caps
8c. Camshaft bearing cap (rear)
10. Cylinder head
11a. Intake valve seat ring
11b. Exhaust valve seat ring
12. Cylinder head bolt
13a. Exhaust valve guide
13b. Intake valve guide
14. Cylinder head gasket

**Exploded view of the cylinder head**

## Cylinder Head

The timing chain/belt and gear should be attached together in correct timing position and hung on wire except on 1410cc and 1468cc engines where only the timing belt needs to be removed. The head bolts on the 1410cc, 1468cc, 1597cc and 1997cc engines require a $^{5}/_{16}$ in. Allen socket for removal.

**NOTE: Never remove the cylinder head unless the engine is absolutely cold; the cylinder head could warp.**

## REMOVAL & INSTALLATION

### *1410cc and 1468cc Engines*

1. Disconnect the battery ground cable, remove the air cleaner assembly and the attached hoses.
2. Drain the coolant, remove the upper radiator hose, and the heater hoses.
3. On fuel injected models, release the fuel system pressure. Remove the fuel line, disconnect the accelerator linkage, distributor vacuum lines, purge valve, and water temperature gauge wire.
4. Remove the spark plug wires and the fuel pump. Remove the distributor, where necessary.
5. Disconnect the exhaust pipe from the exhaust manifold flange.
6. Remove the exhaust manifold assembly.
7. Remove the intake manifold and carburetor as a unit.
8. Turn the crankshaft to No. 1 piston at TDC on the compression stroke.

**NOTE: During the following procedure, do not turn the crankshaft after locating TDC.**

Remove the timing belt cover. Be sure that the knockout pin is at 12 o'clock and the cam sprocket mark and cylinder head pointer are aligned at 3 o'clock. Loosen the timing belt tensioner mounting. Move the tensioner toward the water pump and secure it in that position. Remove the rocker arm cover.

**NOTE: The cam pulley need not be removed.**

9. Loosen and remove the cylinder head bolts in 2 or 3 stages to avoid cylinder head warpage.
10. Remove the cylinder head from the engine block.
11. Clean the cylinder head and block mating surfaces and install a new cylinder head gasket.
12. Position the cylinder head on the engine block, engage the dowel pins front and rear and install the cylinder head bolts.
13. Tighten the head bolts in 3 stages and then torque to specifications.
14. Install the timing belt upper under cover on the 1597cc and 1997cc engines.
15. Locate the camshaft in original position. Pull the camshaft sprocket and belt or chain upward and install on the camshaft.

**NOTE: If the dowel pin and the dowel pin hole does not line up between the sprocket and the spacer or camshaft, move the camshaft by bumping either of the 2 projections provided at the rear of the No. 2 cylinder exhaust cam of the camshaft, with a light hammer or other tool, until the hole and pin align. Be certain the crankshaft does not turn.**

16. Install the camshaft sprocket bolt and the distributor gear and tighten. (The gear is used on 2555cc engines.)
17. Install the timing belt upper front cover and spark plug cable support.
18. Apply sealant to the intake manifold gasket on both sides. Position the gasket and install the intake manifold. Tighten nuts to specifications.

**NOTE: Be sure that no sealant enters the jet air passages when equipped.**

19. Install the exhaust manifold gaskets and the manifold assembly. Tighten the nuts to specifications.
20. Connect the exhaust pipe to the exhaust manifold and install the fuel pump. Install the purge valve.
21. Install the water temperature gauge wire, heater hoses and the upper radiator hose.
22. Connect the fuel lines, accelerator linkage, vacuum hoses and the spark plug wires.
23. Fill the cooling system and connect the battery ground cable. Install the distributor.
24. Temporarily adjust the valve clearance to the cold engine specifications.
25. Install the gasket on the rocker arm cover and temporarily install the cover on the engine.
26. Start the engine and bring it to normal operating temperature. Stop the engine and remove the rocker arm cover.
27. Adjust the valves to hot engine specifications.
28. Install the rocker arm cover and tighten securely.
29. Install the air cleaner, hoses, purge valve hose and any other removed unit.

### *1597cc and 1997cc Engines*

1. Disconnect the battery ground cable, remove the air cleaner assembly and the attached hoses.
2. Drain the coolant, remove the upper radiator hose, and the heater hoses.
3. On fuel injected models, release the fuel system pressure. Remove the fuel line, disconnect the accelerator linkage, distributor vacuum lines, purge valve, and water temperature gauge wire.
4. Remove the spark plug wires and the fuel pump. Remove the distributor, where necessary.
5. Disconnect the exhaust pipe from the exhaust manifold flange.
6. Remove the exhaust manifold assembly.
7. Remove the intake manifold and carburetor as a unit.
8. Turn the crankshaft to No. 1 piston at TDC on the compression stroke.

**NOTE: During the following procedure, do not turn the crankshaft after locating TDC.**

Align the timing mark on the upper under cover of the timing belt with that of the cam shaft sprocket. Matchmark the timing belt and the timing mark on the camshaft sprocket with a felt tip pen. Remove the sprocket and insert a 2 in. piece of timing belt or other material between the bottom of the camshaft sprocket and the sprocket holder on the timing belt lower front cover, to hold the sprocket and belt so that the valve timing will not be changed. Remove the timing belt upper under cover and rocker arm cover.

9. Loosen and remove the cylinder head bolts in 2 or 3 stages to avoid cylinder head warpage.
10. Remove the cylinder head from the engine block.
11. Clean the cylinder head and block mating surfaces and install a new cylinder head gasket.
12. Position the cylinder head on the engine block, engage the dowel pins front and rear and install the cylinder head bolts.
13. Tighten the head bolts in 3 stages and then torque to specifications.
14. Install the timing belt upper under cover on the 1597cc and 1997cc engines.
15. Locate the camshaft in original position. Pull the camshaft sprocket and belt or chain upward and install on the camshaft.

**NOTE: If the dowel pin and the dowel pin hole does not line up between the sprocket and the spacer or camshaft, move the camshaft by bumping either of the 2 projections provided at the rear of the No. 2 cylinder exhaust cam of the camshaft, with a light hammer or other tool, until the hole and pin align. Be certain the crankshaft does not turn.**

16. Install the camshaft sprocket bolt and the distributor gear and tighten. (The gear is used on 2555cc engines.)
17. Install the timing belt upper

front cover and spark plug cable support.

18. Apply sealant to the intake manifold gasket on both sides. Position the gasket and install the intake manifold. Tighten nuts to specifications.

**NOTE: Be sure that no sealant enters the jet air passages when equipped.**

19. Install the exhaust manifold gaskets and the manifold assembly. Tighten the nuts to specifications.
20. Connect the exhaust pipe to the exhaust manifold and install the fuel pump. Install the purge valve.
21. Install the water temperature gauge wire, heater hoses and the upper radiator hose.
22. Connect the fuel lines, accelerator linkage, vacuum hoses and the spark plug wires.
23. Fill the cooling system and connect the battery ground cable. Install the distributor.
24. Temporarily adjust the valve clearance to the cold engine specifications.
25. Install the gasket on the rocker arm cover and temporarily install the cover on the engine.
26. Start the engine and bring it to normal operating temperature. Stop the engine and remove the rocker arm cover.
27. Adjust the valves to hot engine specifications.
28. Install the rocker arm cover and tighten securely.
29. Install the air cleaner, hoses, purge valve hose and any other removed unit.

### 2555cc Engine

1. Disconnect the battery ground cable, remove the air cleaner assembly and the attached hoses.
2. Drain the coolant, remove the upper radiator hose, and the heater hoses.
3. On fuel injected models, release the fuel system pressure. Remove the fuel line, disconnect the accelerator linkage, distributor vacuum lines, purge valve, and water temperature gauge wire.
4. Remove the spark plug wires and the fuel pump. Remove the distributor, where necessary.
5. Disconnect the exhaust pipe from the exhaust manifold flange.
6. Remove the exhaust manifold assembly.
7. Remove the intake manifold and carburetor as a unit.
8. Turn the crankshaft to No. 1 piston at TDC on the compression stroke.

**NOTE: During the following procedure, do not turn the crankshaft after locating TDC.**

Remove the rocker arm cover. Position the camshaft sprocket dowel pin at the 12 o'clock position with the crankshaft pulley notch aligned with the timing mark **T** at the front of the timing chain case. Match the timing chain with the timing mark on the camshaft sprocket. Remove the camshaft sprocket bolt, distributor, gear and the sprocket from the camshaft.

9. Loosen and remove the cylinder head bolts in 2 or 3 stages to avoid cylinder head warpage.
10. Remove the cylinder head from the engine block.
11. Clean the cylinder head and block mating surfaces and install a new cylinder head gasket.
12. Position the cylinder head on the engine block, engage the dowel pins front and rear and install the cylinder head bolts.
13. Tighten the head bolts in 3 stages and then torque to specifications.
14. Install the timing belt upper under cover on the 1597cc and 1997cc engines.
15. Locate the camshaft in original position. Pull the camshaft sprocket and belt or chain upward and install on the camshaft.

**NOTE: If the dowel pin and the dowel pin hole does not line up between the sprocket and the spacer or camshaft, move the camshaft by bumping either of the 2 projections provided at the rear of the No. 2 cylinder exhaust cam of the camshaft, with a light hammer or other tool, until the hole and pin align. Be certain the crankshaft does not turn.**

16. Install the camshaft sprocket bolt and the distributor gear and tighten. (The gear is used on 2555cc engines.)
17. Install the timing belt upper front cover and spark plug cable support.
18. Apply sealant to the intake manifold gasket on both sides. Position the gasket and install the intake manifold. Tighten nuts to specifications.

**NOTE: Be sure that no sealant enters the jet air passages when equipped.**

19. Install the exhaust manifold gaskets and the manifold assembly. Tighten the nuts to specifications.
20. Connect the exhaust pipe to the exhaust manifold and install the fuel pump. Install the purge valve.
21. Install the water temperature gauge wire, heater hoses and the upper radiator hose.
22. Connect the fuel lines, accelerator linkage, vacuum hoses and the spark plug wires.

## COLD ENGINE SPECIFICATIONS

| | Inch | mm |
|---|---|---|
| Jet valve, if equipped | 0.003 | 0.07 |
| Intake valve | 0.003 | 0.07 |
| Exhaust valve | 0.007 | 0.17 |

## HOT ENGINE SPECIFICATIONS

| | Inch | mm |
|---|---|---|
| Jet valve, if equipped | 0.006 | 0.15 |
| Intake valve | 0.006 | 0.15 |
| Exhaust valve | 0.010 | 0.25 |

23. Fill the cooling system and connect the battery ground cable. Install the distributor.
24. Temporarily adjust the valve clearance to the cold engine specifications.
25. Install the gasket on the rocker arm cover and temporarily install the cover on the engine.
26. Start the engine and bring it to normal operating temperature. Stop the engine and remove the rocker arm cover.
27. Adjust the valves to hot engine specifications.
28. Install the rocker arm cover and tighten securely.
29. Install the air cleaner, hoses, purge valve hose and any other removed unit.

### 1595cc DOHC Engine

1. Drain the engine and radiator coolant.
2. Disconnect the negative battery cable.
3. Remove the radiator assembly.
4. Disconnect the accelerator cable. Disconnect the air flow sensor wiring connector.
5. Disconnect all of the breather and vacuum hoses to the air intake. Remove the air cleaner assembly.
6. Remove the PCV hose. Disconnect the water bypass hose, the heater hose and vacuum lines from the water inlet connector.
7. Disconnect the vacuum hose to the power brake booster.
8. Release the fuel system pressure, and disconnect the high pressure and fuel return lines. Remove the mounting O-rings.
9. Disconnect the oxygen sensor, engine coolant sensor, temperature gauge connection and the air conditioner coolant temperature switch.
10. Disconnect the fuel injector wiring harness, the ignition coil, power transistor, ISC motor and the EGR sensor connector.

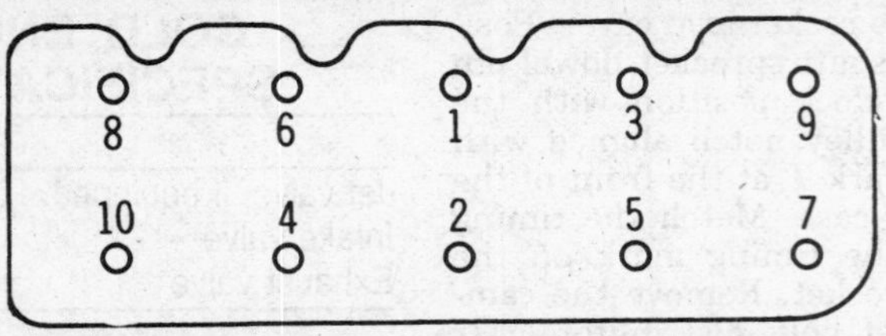


Head bolt torque sequence for the 1410, 1468, 1597 and 1997cc engines

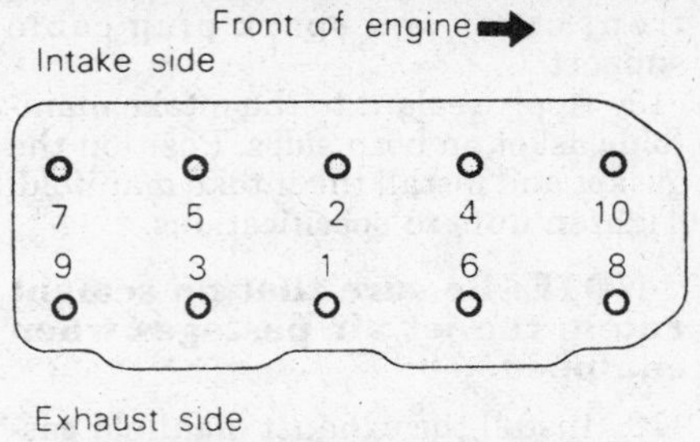


1595cc DOHC cylinder head bolt tightening sequence

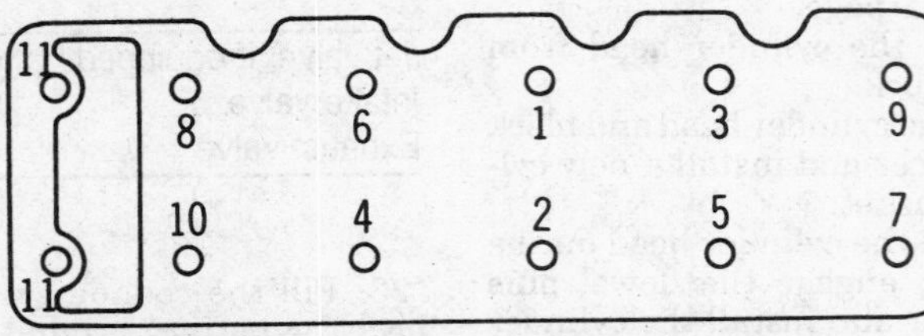


Cylinder head bolt tightening sequence— 2555cc

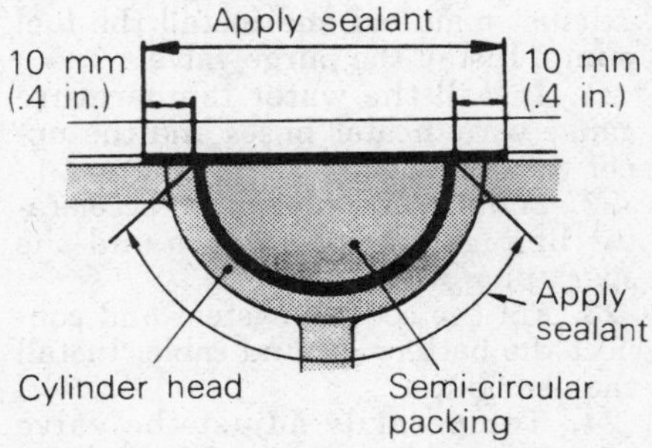


Half moon seal installation

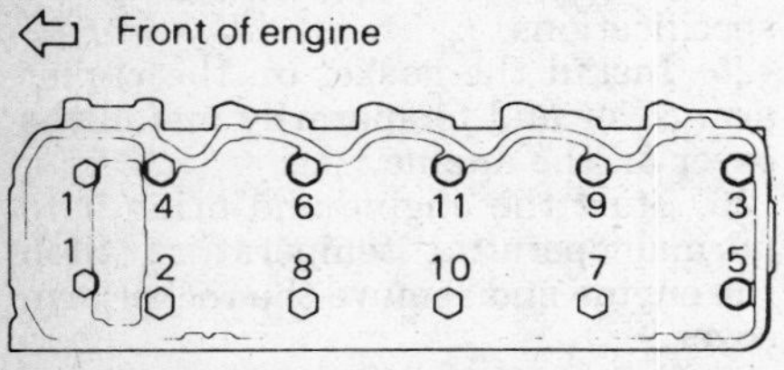


2555cc cylinder head bolt loosening sequence

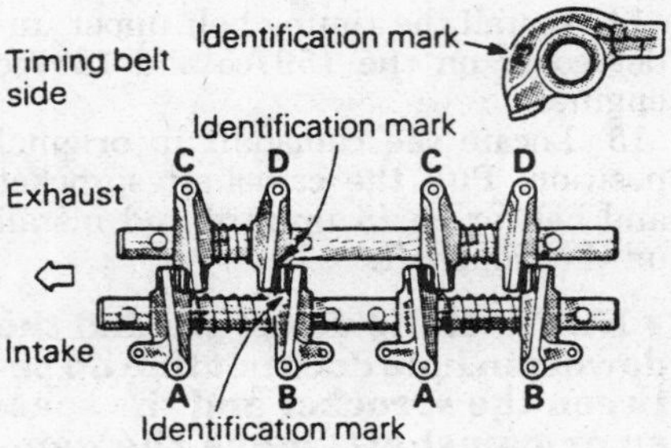


Correct assembly of rocker arm assembly, 1597cc, 1410cc and 1468cc engines

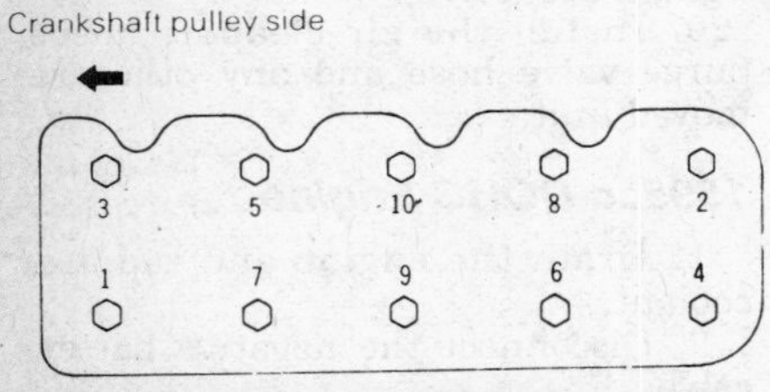


1410, 1468, 1597 and 1997cc cylinder head bolt loosening sequence

11. Disconnect the detonation sensor, throttle position sensor and crankshaft angle sensor wiring connectors.
12. Remove the center cover and the spark plug wires. Disconnect the control wire harness connector.
13. Remove the timing belt.
14. Remove the rocker cover and rear half moon seal.
15. Remove the heat shield, turbocharger water and oil lines.
16. Disconnect the exhaust pipe from the turbocharger.
17. Remove the turbocharger, exhaust manifold and intake manifold assemblies.
18. Remove the head mounting bolts. Start at the outer ends of the head and loosen, in a criss-cross manner, toward the center of the head. Make 2 or 3 passes to loosen the bolts, a little at a time, in sequence.
19. Remove the cylinder head. Clean all gasket mounting surfaces. Make sure that no gasket material gets into the cylinders, coolant passages or oil passages.
20. Position the cylinder head, with a new gasket, on the engine. Install and tighten the head mounting bolts. Tighten the head bolts from the center outwards, following the illustration provided. Tighten in 3 steps. Torque to 65–72 ft. lbs.
21. Install the components in the reverse order of removal.

## OVERHAUL

**For all cylinder head procedures, please refer to the "Engine Rebuilding" in the Unit Repair Section.**

# Rocker Arm/Shaft

To service the rocker arm or camshaft while the cylinder head is still mounted on the cylinder block and in the car:

1. Remove the breather hoses, purge hose and air cleaner. Disconnect the spark plug cables.
2. Turn the crankshaft until number 1 piston is on TDC.
3. Refer to the cylinder head removal. Remove the cam sprocket timing chain/belt and rocker arm cover.

## REMOVAL & INSTALLATION

### *Except 1595cc DOHC, 1997cc and 2555cc Engines*

If the cylinder head has been removed from the car or the preceding steps have been followed:

1. Matchmark the camshaft/rocker arm bearing caps to their cylinder head location. (Except 1410cc and 1468cc engine).
2. Loosen the bearing cap bolts, or the rocker shaft bolts (1410cc and 1468cc engine) from the cylinder head but do not remove them from the caps or shafts. Lift the rocker assembly from the cylinder head as a unit.
3. The rocker arm assembly can be disassembled by the removal of the mounting bolts (and dowel pins on some models) from the bearing caps and/or shafts.

**NOTE: Keep the rocker arms and springs in the same order as disassembly. The left and right springs have different tension ratings and free length. Observe the location of the rocker arms as they are removed. Exhaust and intake, right and left, are different. Do not get them mixed up.**

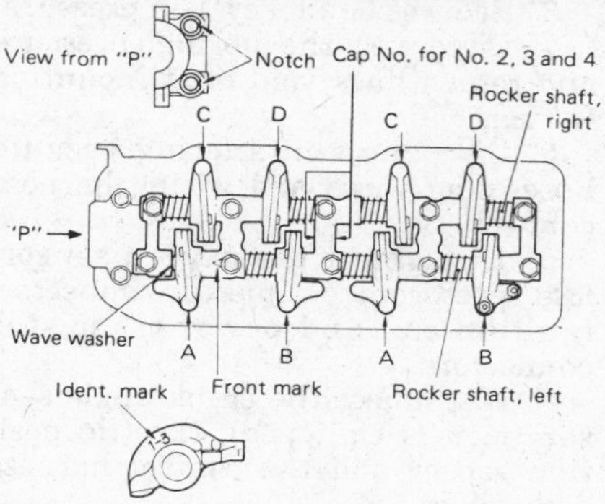


Rocker arm application

| | Ident. mark | In. | Ex. |
|---|---|---|---|
| No. 1 & 3 cyl. | 1–3 | A | C |
| No. 2 & 4 cyl. | 2–4 | B | D |

**1997cc engine rocker arm shaft assembly**

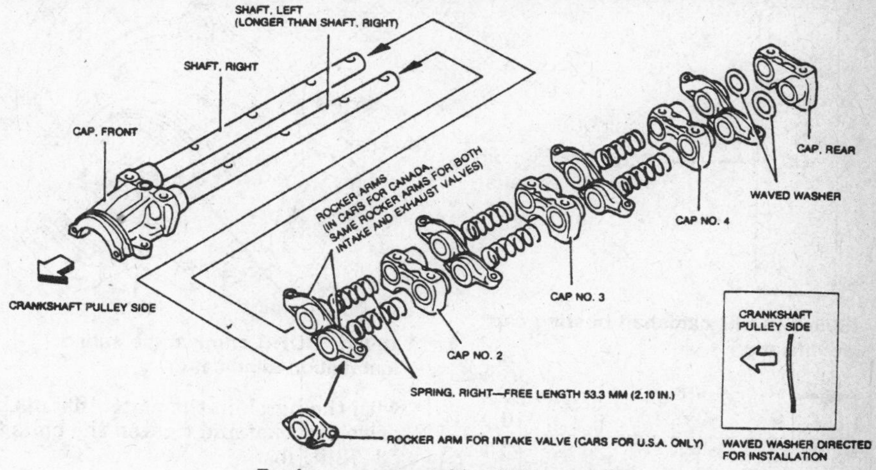


**Rocker arm assembly, 1597cc engine**

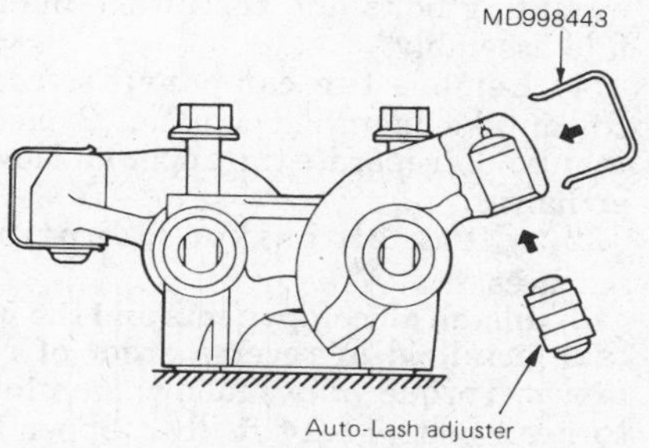


**Automatic lash adjuster installation**

### *1997cc and 2555cc Engines with Automatic Lash Adjusters*

**NOTE: A special tool, MD998443, is required for this procedure.**

1. Remove the rocker cover and gasket, and the timing belt cover.
2. Turn the crankshaft so that the No. 1 piston is a TDC compression. At this point, the timing mark on the camshaft sprocket and the timing mark on the head to the left of the sprocket will be aligned.
3. Remove the camshaft bearing cap bolts.
4. Install the automatic lash adjuster retainer tool MD998443, to keep the adjuster from falling out of the rocker arms.
5. Lift off the bearing caps and rocker arm assemblies.
6. The rocker arms may now be removed from the shaft.

**NOTE: Keep all parts in the order in which they were removed. None of the parts are interchangeable. The lash adjusters are filled with diesel fuel, which will spill out if they are inverted. If any diesel fuel is spilled, the adjusters must be bled. The bleeding procedure can be found following this procedure.**

| Model | Item | Torque ft. lbs. |
|---|---|---|
| Colt | • Oil Pipe | 11–14 |
| | • Turbocharger-To-Manifold | 38–52 |
| | • Oil Return Pipe | 6–7 |
| | • Oil Pipe Flare Nut | 21–25 |
| | • Oxygen Sensor | 30–35 |
| | • Converter-To-Support Bracket | 9–11 |
| Conquest | • Oil Pipe Fitting | 17–20 |
| | • Turbocharger Mounting Nuts | 37–50 |
| | • Oil Return Pipe | 6–7 |
| | • Oil Pipe-To - Fitting | 13–17 |

7. Check all parts for wear or damage. Replace any damaged or excessively worn parts.
8. Assemble all parts in reverse order of removal. Note the following:
   a. The rocker shafts are installed with the notches in the ends facing up.
   b. The left rocker shaft is longer than the right.
   c. The wave washers are installed on the left shaft.
   d. Coat all parts with clean engine oil prior to assembly.
   e. Insert the lash adjuster from under the rocker arm and install the special holding tool. If any of the diesel fuel is spilled, the adjuster must be bled.
   f. Tighten the bearing cap bolts, working from the center towards the ends to 15 ft. lbs.
   g. Check the operation of each lash adjuster by positioning the camshaft so that the rocker arm bears on the low, or round portion of the cam (pointed part of the can faces straight down). Insert a thin steel wire, or tool MD998442, in the hole in the top of the rocker arm, over the lash adjuster and depress the check ball at the top of the adjuster. While holding the check ball depressed, move the arm up and down. Looseness should be felt. Full plunger stroke should be .0866 in. (2.2mm). If not, remove, clean and bleed the lash adjuster.

### *1595cc DOHC Engine*

1. With the cylinder head removed from the vehicle. Remove the crank angle sensor.
2. Remove both camshaft drive sprockets.
3. Remove both rear (opposite end of the drive sprockets) camshaft bearing caps.
4. Remove both front bearing caps and front oil seals.
5. Remove the remaining camshaft bearing caps alternating from the rear of the head to the front.
6. Remove the camshafts.
7. Remove the rocker arms and the lash adjusters. Remove the valve body assembly from the rear of the cylinder head.
8. Clean and inspect all parts. Check the rollers on the end of the rocker arms. If the rollers are warn on do not rotate smoothly, replace as necessary.
9. Install the lash adjusters and rocker arms. Lubricate them prior to installation. Install the valve body. Lu-

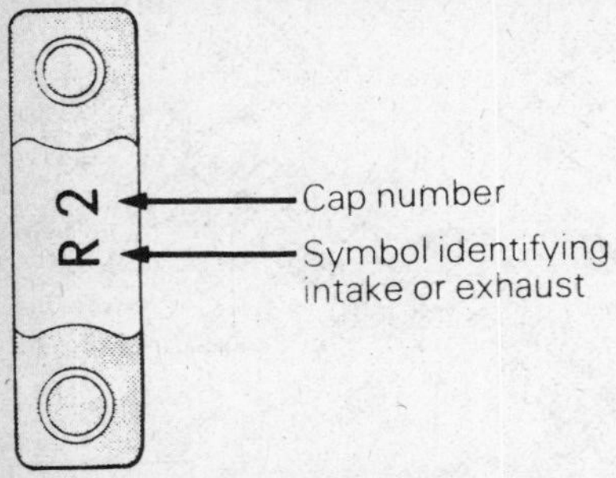


**1595cc DOHC camshaft bearing cap identification**

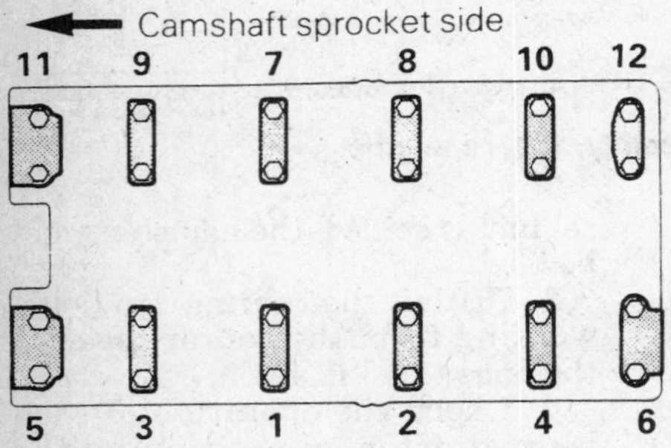


**1595cc DOHC camshaft bearing cap installation tightening sequence**

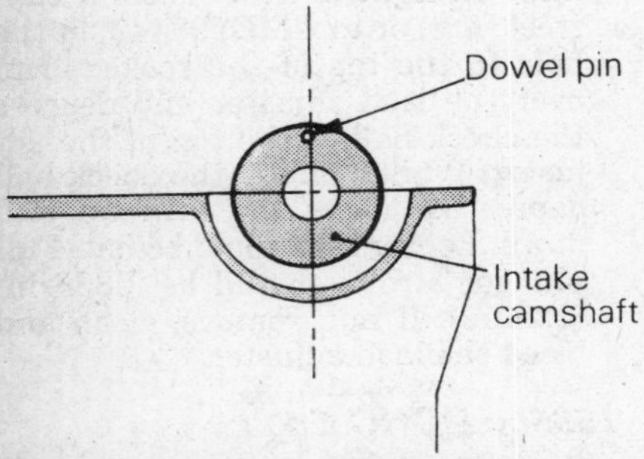


**1595cc DOHC intake camshaft dowel pin position**

bricate the camshafts. Place the camshafts in position. The intake side camshaft has a slit in the rear to drive the crank angle sensor. The bearing caps Nos. 2 to 5 are the same shape. When installing them, check the top markings to identify the intake or exhaust side. L or R is marked on the front caps, L for the intake side; R for the exhaust side.

10. Tighten the bearing caps, in 2 or 3 steps, to 14–15 ft. lbs. in the illustration order shown.

11. Make sure that the rocker arm is properly mounted on the lash adjuster and valve stem tip.

12. Install the front oil seals. Turn the intake camshaft until the front dowel pin is facing straight up at the twelve o'clock position. Install the crank angle sensor with the punch mark on the sensor housing aligned

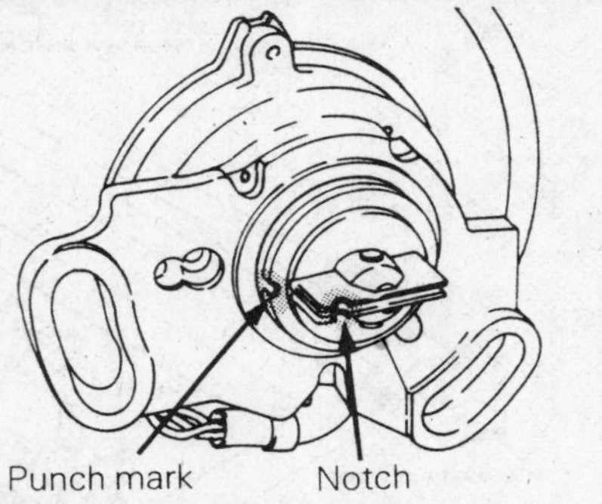


**1595cc DOHC crank angle sensor installation alignment**

with the notch in the plate. Install the drive sprocket and tighten the bolts to 58–72 ft. lbs.

## Intake Manifold

### REMOVAL & INSTALLATION

#### *Except Multipoint Fuel Injection*

1. Remove the air cleaner.
2. Disconnect the fuel line and EGR lines on models so equipped.
3. Disconnect the throttle positioner solenoid and fuel cut-off solenoid wires.
4. Disconnect the accelerator linkage and, if equipped with automatic transmission, the shift cables at the carburetor or injection pump.
5. If equipped, remove the injection mixer assembly.
6. On the 1597cc engine, remove the fuel pump and the thermostat housing. Disconnect the choke coolant hose at the manifold. Disconnect the power brake booster vacuum line.
7. Drain the coolant.
8. Remove the water hose from carburetor and cylinder head.
9. Remove the heater and water outlet hoses.
10. Disconnect the water temperature sending unit.
11. Remove the manifold.
12. Clean all mounting surfaces. Before reinstalling the manifold, coat both side with gasket sealer.

**NOTE: If the engine is equipped with the jet air system, take care not to get any sealer into the jet air intake passage.**

13. Installation is the reverse of removal.

#### *Multipoint Fuel Injection*

1. Drain the cooling system and disconnect the negative battery cable. Disconnect the air intake hose, accelerator cable and the throttle body stay.
2. Disconnect the water by-pass hose and the vacuum hose to the power brake booster.
3. Relieve the fuel system pressure.
4. Disconnect the fuel high pressure and return lines, and their mounting O-rings.
5. Disconnect interfering vacuum hose, plug wires and wiring harness connections.
6. Disconnect the oxygen sensor, idle speed control, injector connector, ignition coil and power transistor connectors.
7. Disconnect the crank angle sensor (models equipped), throttle position sensor and the control harness connectors.
8. Remove the fuel delivery pipe, fuel injector, and pressure regulator as an assembly. Remove the mounting grommets and O-rings.
9. Remove the intake manifold lower support stay shield and the end tension bracket.
10. Remove the intake manifold mounting bolts and the intake manifold assembly.
11. Remove the components from the intake manifold, and on 2 piece manifolds, separate the upper and lower halves.
12. Clean all gasket mounting surfaces.
13. Install all components and the intake manifold in reverse order of removal. Torque values follow: manifold to head bolts 11–14 ft. lbs.; upper to lower manifold 11–14 ft. lbs.; fuel deiivery manifold 7–9 ft. lbs.; throttle body 11–16 ft. lbs. on DOHC and 1997cc; 7–9 ft. lbs. on 1468cc.

## Exhaust Manifold

### REMOVAL & INSTALLATION

1. Remove the air cleaner assembly.
2. Remove the manifold heat stove and hose. Disconnect the EGR lines and reed valve, if equipped. On turbocharged models, remove the turbocharger.
3. Disconnect the exhaust pipe bracket from the engine block.
4. Remove the exhaust pipe flange bolts (1 bolt and nut may have to be removed from under the car).
5. Remove the manifold flange stud nuts and remove the manifold from the cylinder head.
6. Installation is the reverse of removal. Port liner gaskets may be used along with the exhaust manifold gaskets on some engine models.

## Turbocharger

### REMOVAL & INSTALLATION

**NOTE: Make sure that the engine and turbocharger are cold,**

**preferably overnight, before removing the unit. If replacing the turbocharger, change the engine oil and filter.**

1. Drain the cooling system and disconnect the negative battery cable. For clearance on some models, it will be necessary to remove the radiator. Remove the heat shield.
2. Disconnect the air intake hose and vacuum lines. Remove the oxygen sensor from the catalytic converter.
3. Remove the converter-to-turbocharger nuts.
4. Disconnect the hose from the oil return pipe and time chain case.
5. Remove the oil pipe from the turbocharger and oil filter housing.
6. Remove the air intake pipe connecting bolt.
7. Remove the turbocharger mounting nuts and lift the unit off the engine.
8. Installation is the reverse of removal. Torque all parts to the specification. Before the oil flare nut is installed at the top of the unit, pour clean engine oil into the turbocharger. Always use new gaskets.

## TROUBLESHOOTING

**For more information on turbocharging, please refer to "Turbocharging" in the Unit Repair Section.**

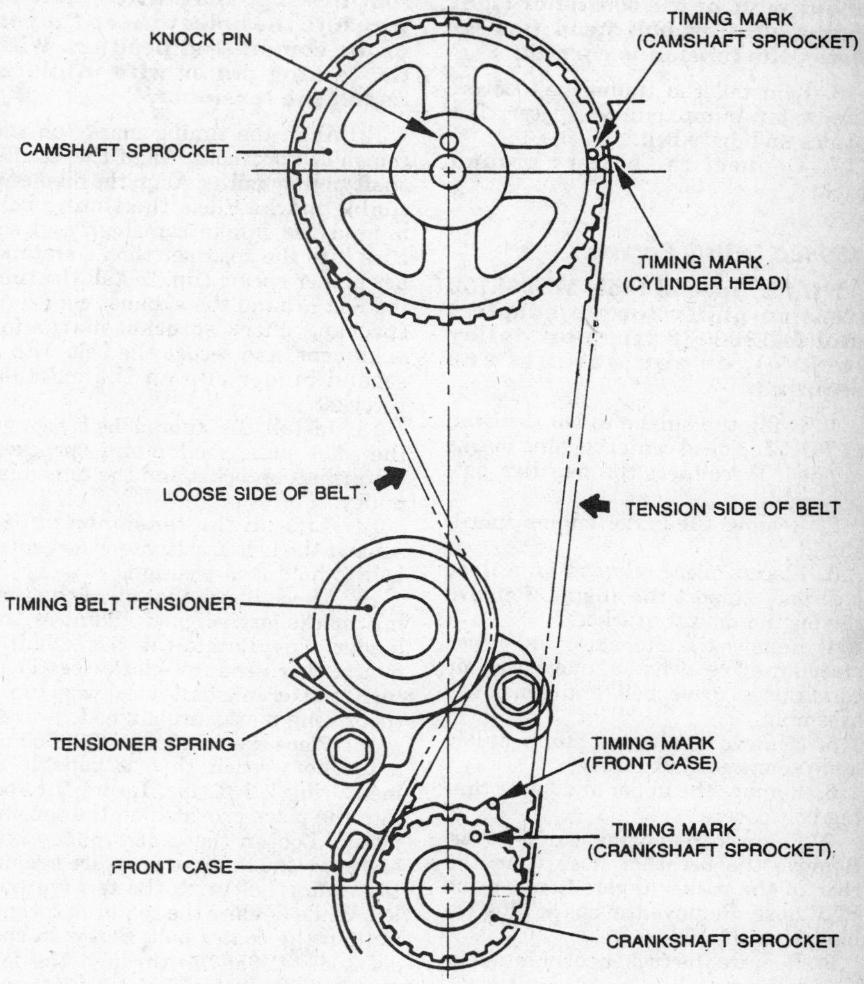


1410 and 1468cc engine timing belt installation

# Timing Gear Cover, Chain/Belt, Sprockets and Tensioner

**NOTE: The timing chain case is cast aluminum, so exercise caution when handling this part.**

The following outlines are the recommended removal and installation procedures for the timing chain or belt. Some modifications to the procedures may be necessary due to added accessories, sheet metal parts, or emission control units and connecting hoses.

## REMOVAL & INSTALLATION

### *1410cc and 1468cc Engine*

1. Turn the engine until the No. 1 piston is on TDC with the timing marks aligned.
2. Disconnect the ground (negative) battery cable.
3. Remove the fan drive belt, the fan blades, spacer and water pump pulley.
4. Remove the timing belt cover.
5. Loosen the timing belt tensioner mounting bolt and move the tensioner toward the water pump. Temporarily secure the tensioner.
6. Remove the crankshaft pulley and slide the belt off of the camshaft and crankshaft drive sprockets.
7. Inspect the drive sprockets for abnormal wear, cracks or damage and replace if necessary. Remove and inspect the tensioner. Check for smooth pulley rotation, excessive play or noise. Replace tensioner if necessary.
8. Reinstall the tensioner, if it was removed and temporarily secure it close to the water pump.
9. Make sure that the timing mark on the camshaft sprocket is aligned with the pointer on the cylinder head and that the crankshaft sprocket mark is aligned with the mark on the engine case.
10. Install the timing belt on the crankshaft sprocket.
11. Install the belt counterclockwise over the camshaft sprocket making sure there is no play on the tension side of the belt. Adjust the belt fore and aft so that it is centered on the sprockets.
12. Loosen the tensioner from it's temporary position so that the spring pressure will allow it to contact the timing belt.
13. Rotate the crankshaft 2 complete turns in the normal rotation direction to remove any belt slack. Turn the crankshaft until the timing marks are lined up. If the timing has slipped, remove the belt and repeat the procedure.
14. Tighten the tensioner mounting bolts, slotted side (right) first, then the spring side.
15. Once again rotate the engine 2 complete revolutions until the timing marks line up. Recheck the belt tension.

**NOTE: When the tension side of the timing belt and the tensioner are pushed in horizontally with a moderate force (about 11 lbs.) and the cogged side of the belt covers**

**about 1/4 in. of the tensioner right side mounting bolt head (across flats), the tension is correct.**

16. Reinstall the timing belt cover, the water pump pulley, spacer, fan blades and drive belt.
17. Connect the battery ground cable.

### *1595cc DOHC Engine*

**NOTE: Special tools MD998752 (tension pulley torque adapter) and MD998738 (tension pulley locker), or equivalents are required.**

1. Bring the engine to No. 1 piston at TDC (top dead center) timing marks aligned. Disconnect the negative battery cable.
2. Remove the under engine splash shield.
3. Place a piece of wood on a floor jack and support the engine. Remove the engine mount bracket.
4. Remove the alternator and power steering drive belts. Remove the air conditioner drive belt and tensioner assembly.
5. Remove the water pump pulley and the crankshaft pulley.
6. Remove the upper and lower timing belt covers.
7. Remove the engine center cover. Remove the breather hose from the rear of the rocker cover. Remove the PCV hose. Remove the spark plug cables from the plugs.
8. Remove the rocker cover and rear half-moon seal.
9. Confirm the the engine is still at No. 1 TDC. The timing marks on the camshaft sprocket and the upper surface of the cylinder head should coincide. The dowel pin on the front of the camshafts should be in the twelve o'clock position. Remove the automatic belt tensioner. Loosen the tensioner pulley center bolt.
10. If the timing belt is to reused, mark an arrow, on the belt, in the direction of rotation, for installation reference. Remove the timing belt.
11. Install the automatic tensioner, after reset.

**NOTE: To reset the tensioner: Keep the adjuster level and clamp it in a soft jawed vise. Clamp with the extended adjuster on one side, and the end mounting a plug on the other side. If the plug extends out of the adjuster body, place a suitable hole sized washer over the plug so that the vise jaw pushes on the washer, not the plug. Close the vise slowly, forcing the adjuster back into the body. When the hole in the adjuster boss aligns with the adjuster rod, insert a snug fitting pin or wire into the holes to keep the rod in the compressed position. With the locking pin or wire in place, install the tensioner.**

12. Align the timing marks on the camshaft sprockets. Align the crankshaft timing marks. Align the oil pump timing marks.Place the timing belt around the intake camshaft and secure it to the sprocket with a stationary binder spring clip. Install the timing belt around the exhaust camshaft sprocket, check sprocket marks for alignment, and secure the belt with a second binder clip on the exhaust sprocket.
13. Install the timing belt around the idler pulley, oil pump sprocket, crankshaft sprocket and the tensioner pulley.
14. Lift up the tensioner pulley against the belt and tighten the center bolt to hold it in position.
15. Check to see that all of the timing marks are aligned. Remove the binder clips. Rotate the crankshaft a quarter turn counter-clockwise. Then turn the crankshaft clockwise until the timing marks are aligned.
16. Place special tool MD998752 on a torque wrench that is capable of measuring 2.2 ft. lbs. Insert the tool into the place provided on the tension pulley. Loosen the center pulley bolt and apply 2.2 ft. lbs of pressure against the timing belt with the tension pulley. While holding the required torque, tighten the center bolt. Screw in special tool MD998738 through the left engine support bracket until it contacts the tensioner arm bracket. Turn the tool a little more to secure the tensioner and remove the locking wire place into the automatic adjuster when it was reset.
17. Remove the special tool. Rotate the crankshaft 2 complete turns clockwise and let alone for about fifteen minutes. Then measure the protrusion of the automatic adjuster. It should be .015–.018 in. If the proper amount of protrusion is not present, repeat the tensioning process.

### *1597cc Engine*

1. Drain the coolant and remove the radiator on rear wheel drive cars only. Disconnect the battery cable.
2. Remove the alternator and accessory belts. Remove the belt cover.
3. Rotate the crankshaft to bring No. 1 piston to TDC on the compression stroke. Align the notch on the crankshaft pulley with the **T** mark on the timing indicator scale and the timing mark on the upper under cover of the timing belt with the mark on the camshaft sprocket. Mark and remove the distributor.

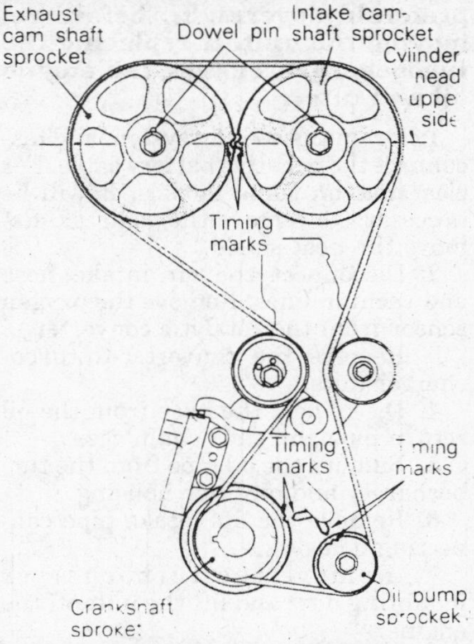


**1595cc DOHC timing mark alignment for timing belt installation**

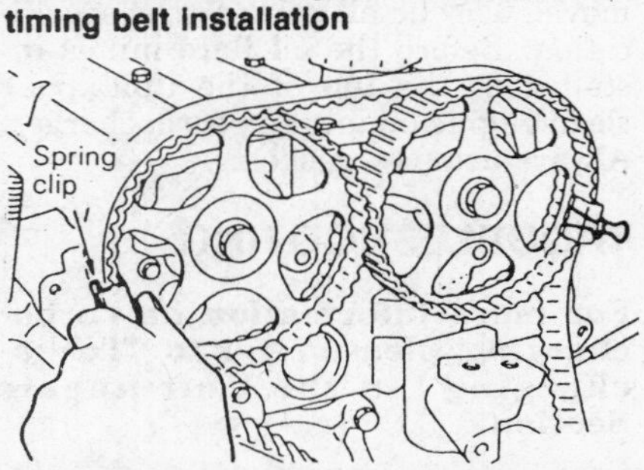


**Using binder clips to secure the timing belt**

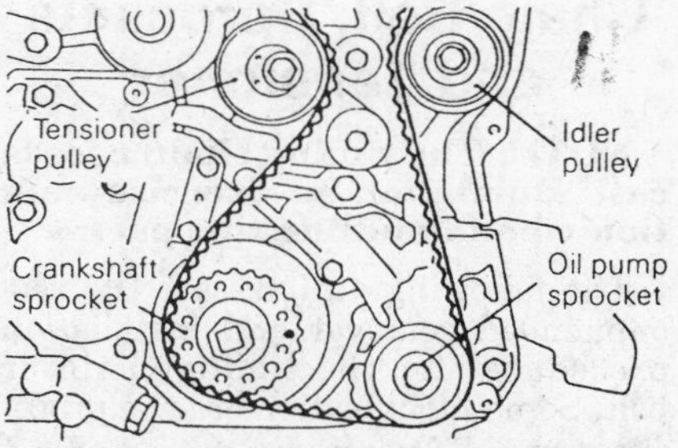


**Installing the timing belt around the idler pulley, oil pump sprocket, crankshaft sprocket and tensioner**

4. Remove the crankshaft pulley and bolt.
5. Remove the lower splash shield, if necessary for working room.
6. Remove the timing belt covers, upper front and lower front.
7. Remove the crankshaft sprocket bolt.
8. Loosen the tensioner mounting nut and bolt. Move the tensioner away from the belt and retighten the nut to keep the tensioner in the off position. Remove the belt.
9. Remove the camshaft sprocket, crankshaft sprocket, flange and tensioner.

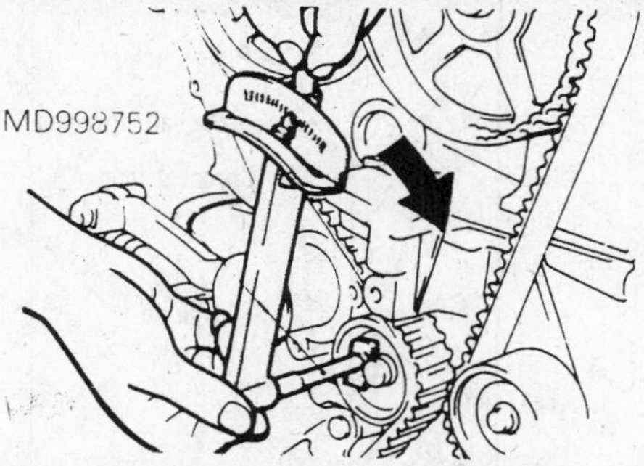


**Using special tool MD998752–1595cc DOHC**

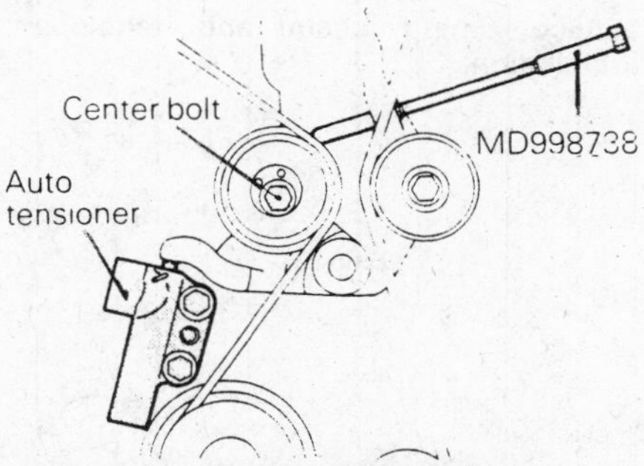


**Using special tool MD998738–1595cc DOHC**

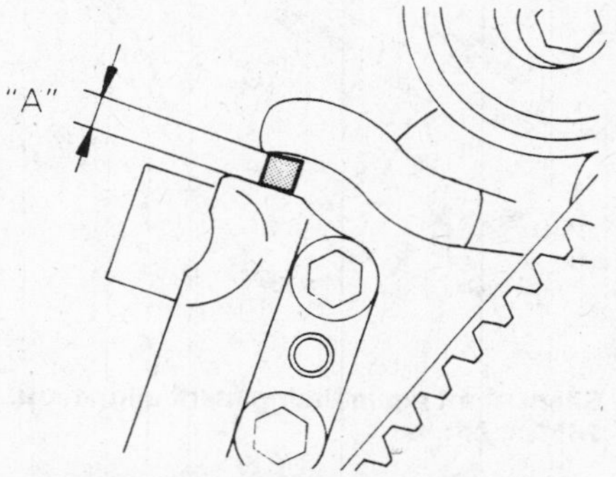


**1595cc DOHC automatic tensioner extension measurement**

10. The water pump or cylinder head may be removed at this point, depending upon the type of repairs needed.
11. Raise the front of the car and support it safely. Remove any interfering splash pans.
12. Drain the oil pan and remove the pan from the block.
13. Remove the oil pump sprocket and cover.
14. Remove the front cover and oil pump as a unit.
15. Install a new front seal in the cover. Install a new gasket on the front of the cylinder block and install the front cover.
16. Tighten the front cover bolts to 11–13 ft. lbs. Install the oil screen and oil pan. Tighten the bolts to 5 ft. lbs.
17. If the cylinder head and/or water pump had been removed, reinstall them, using new gaskets.

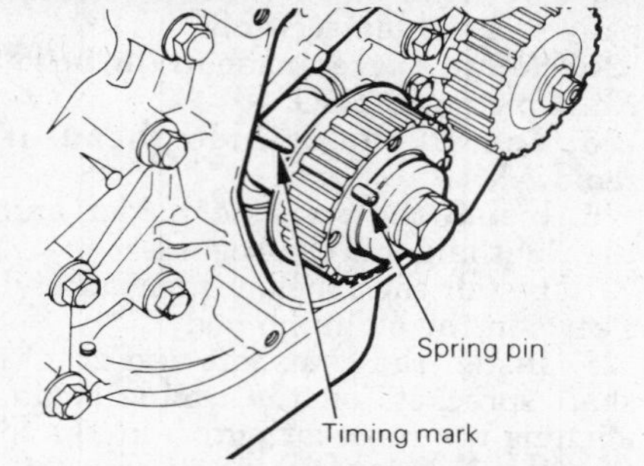


**1597cc crankshaft sprocket timing mark alignment**

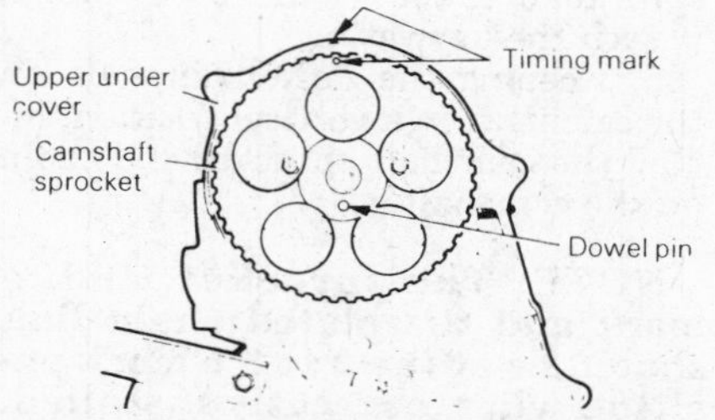


**1597cc camshaft sprocket installation alignment**

18. Install the upper and lower under covers.
19. Install the spacer, flange and crankshaft sprocket and tighten the bolt to 43.5–50 ft. lbs.
20. Align the timing mark on the crankshaft sprocket with the timing mark on the front case.
21. Align the camshaft sprocket timing mark with the upper under cover timing mark.
22. Install the tensioner spring and tensioner. Temporarily tighten the nut. Install the front end of the tensioner spring (bent at right angles) on the projection of the tensioner and the other end (straight) on the water pump body.
23. Loosen the nut and move the tensioner in the direction of the water pump. Lock it by tightening the nut.
24. Ensure that the sprocket timing marks are aligned, and install the timing belt. The belt should be installed on the crankshaft sprocket, the oil pump sprocket, and then the camshaft sprocket, in that order, while keeping the belt tight.
25. Loosen the tensioner mounting bolt and nut and allow the spring tension to move the tensioner against the belt.

**NOTE: Make sure the belt comes in complete mesh with the sprocket by lightly pushing the tensioner up by hand toward the mounting nut.**

26. Tighten the tensioner mounting nut and bolt.

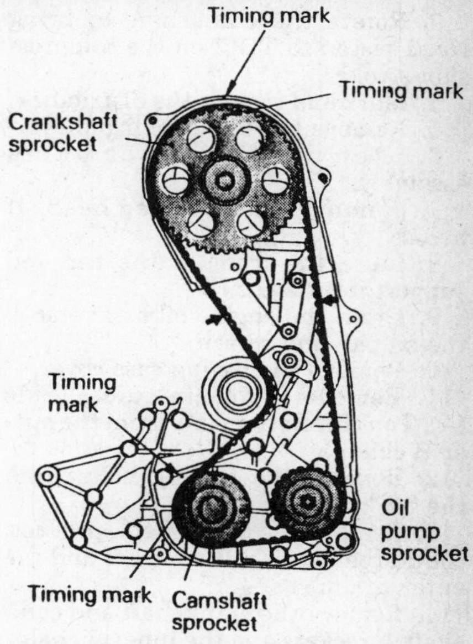


**Timing belt installation, 1597cc engine**

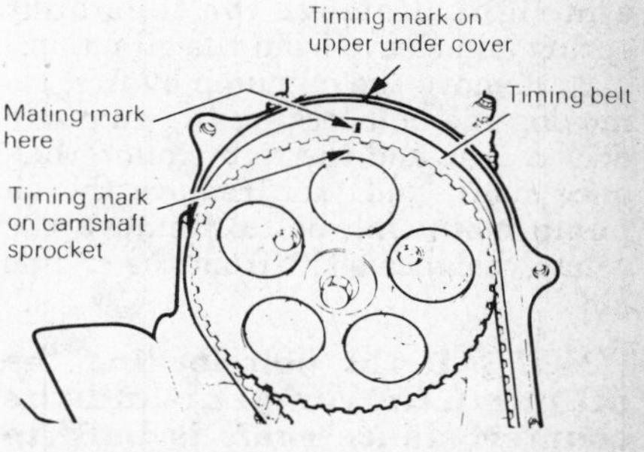


**Camshaft timing mark alignment on the 1597cc engine**

**NOTE: Be sure to tighten the nut before tightening the bolt. Too much tension could result from tightening the bolt first.**

27. Recheck all sprocket alignments.
28. Turn the crankshaft through a complete rotation in the normal direction. Do not turn in a reverse direction or shake or push the belt.
29. Loosen the tensioner bolt and nut. Retighten the nut and then the bolt.
30. Install the lower and upper front outer covers.
31. Install the crankshaft pulley and tighten the bolts to 7.5–8.5 ft. lbs.
32. Install the alternator and belt and adjust. Install the distributor.
33. Install the radiator, fill the cooling system and inspect for leaks.

### *2555cc Engines with Silent Shaft (Chain Equipped)*

1. Drain the coolant and remove the radiator. Disconnect the battery ground cable.
2. Remove the alternator and accessory belts.

3. Rotate the crankshaft to bring No. 1 piston to TDC, on the compression stroke.
4. Mark and remove the distributor.
5. Remove the crankshaft pulley.
6. Remove the water pump assembly.
7. Remove the cylinder head, if necessary.
8. Raise the front of the car and support it safely.
9. Drain the engine oil and remove the oil pan and screen.
10. Remove the timing case cover.
11. Remove the chain guides.(Side (A), Top (B), Bottom (C), from the outer B chain.)
12. Remove the locking bolts from the "B" chain sprockets.
13. Remove the crankshaft sprocket, counterbalance shaft sprocket and the outer chain.
14. Remove the crankshaft and camshaft sprockets and the inner A chain.
15. Remove the camshaft sprocket holder and the chain guides, both left and right. Remove the tensioner spring and sleeve from the oil pump.
16. Remove the oil pump by first removing the bolt locking the oil pump driven gear and the right counterbalance shaft, and then remove the oil pump mounting bolts. Remove the counterbalance shaft from the engine block.

**NOTE: If the bolt locking the oil pump driven gear and the counterbalance shaft is hard to loosen, remove the oil pump and the shaft as a unit.**

17. Remove the left counterbalance shaft thrust washer and take the shaft from the engine block.
18. Install the right counterbalance shaft into the engine block.
19. Install the oil pump assembly. Do not lose the Woodruff key from the end of the counterbalance shaft. Torque the oil pump mounting bolts to 6–7 ft. lbs.
20. Tighten the counterbalance shaft and the oil pump driven gear mounting bolt.

**NOTE: The counterbalance shaft and the oil pump can be installed as a unit, if necessary.**

21. Install the left counterbalance shaft into the engine block.
22. Install a new O-ring on the thrust plate and install the unit into the engine block, using a pair of bolts without heads, as alignment guides.

**NOTE: If the thrust plate is turned to align the bolt holes, the O-ring may be damaged.**

23. Remove the guide bolts and install the regular bolts into the thrust plate and tighten securely.
24. Rotate the crankshaft to bring No. 1 piston to TDC.
25. Install the cylinder head, if removed.
26. Install the sprocket holder and the right and left chain guides.
27. Install the tensioner spring and sleeve on the oil pump body.
28. Install the camshaft and crankshaft sprockets on the timing chain, aligning the sprocket punch marks to the plated chain links.
29. While holding the sprocket and chain as a unit, install the crankshaft sprocket over the crankshaft and align it with the keyway.
30. Keeping the dowel pin hole on the camshaft in a vertical position, install the camshaft sprocket and chain on the camshaft.

**NOTE: The sprocket timing mark and the plated chain link should be at the 2 to 3 o'clock position when correctly installed. The chain must be aligned in the right and left chain guides with the tensioner pushing against the chain. The tension for the inner chain is predetermined by spring tension.**

31. Install the crankshaft sprocket for the outer B chain.
32. Install the 2 counterbalance shaft sprockets and align the punched mating marks with the plated links of the chain.
33. Holding the 2 shaft sprockets and chain, install the outer chain in alignment with the mark on the crankshaft sprocket. Install the shaft sprockets on the counter balance shaft and the oil pump driver gear. Install the lock bolts and recheck the alignment of the punch marks and the plated links.
34. Temporarily install the chain guides, side (A), top (B), and bottom (C).
35. Tighten side (A) chain guide securely.
36. Tighten bottom (B) chain guide securely.
37. Adjust the position of the top (B) chain guide, after shaking the right and left sprockets to collect any chain slack, so that when the chain is moved toward the center, the clearance between the chain guide and the chain links will be approximately $^{9}/_{64}$ in. Tighten the Top (B) chain guide bolts.
38. Install the timing chain cover using a new gasket, being careful not to damage the front seal.
39. Install the oil screen and the oil pan, using a new gasket. Torque the bolts to 4.5–5.5 ft. lbs.
40. Install the crankshaft pulley, alternator and accessory belts, and the distributor.

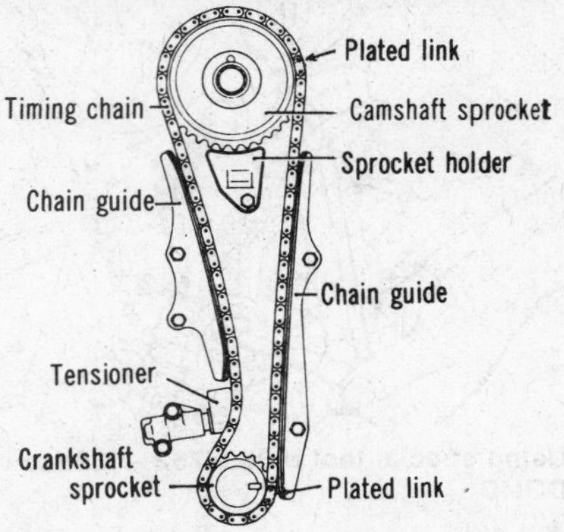


**2555cc timing chain and tensioner installation**

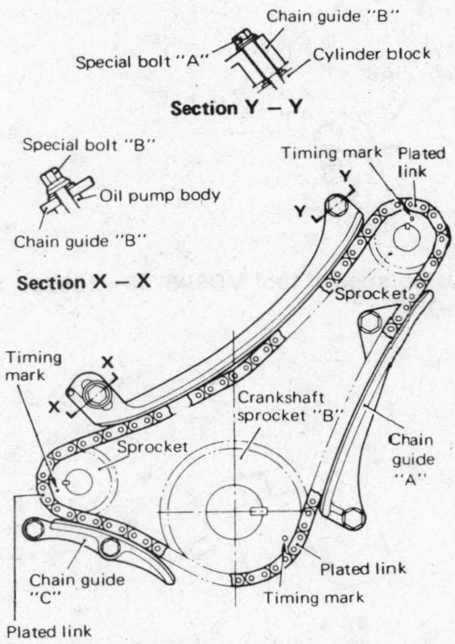


**Silent shaft chain timing mark alignment, 2555cc engine**

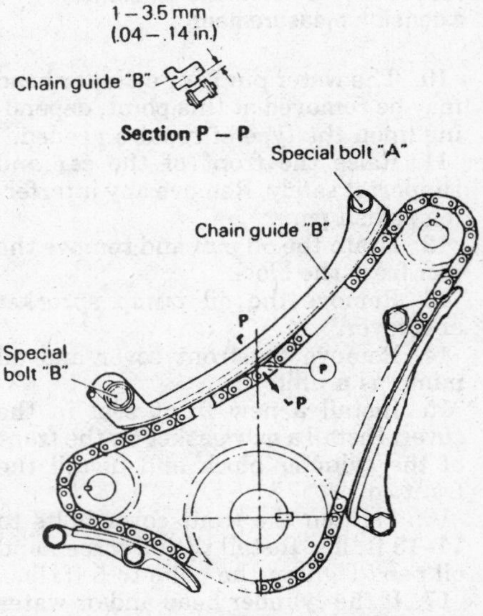


**Location of special bolts for chain guide "B", 2555cc engine**

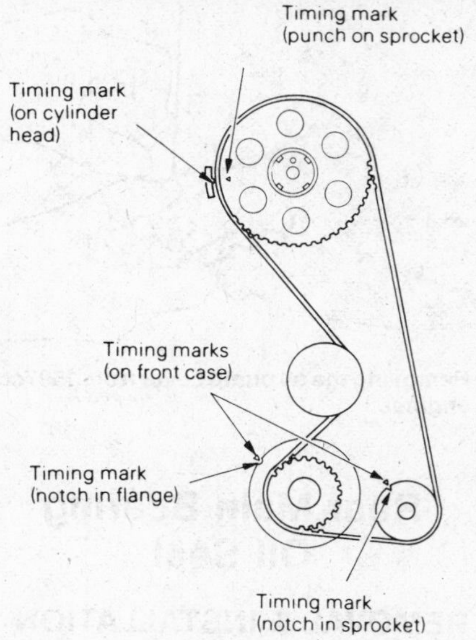


**1997cc timing mark alignment**

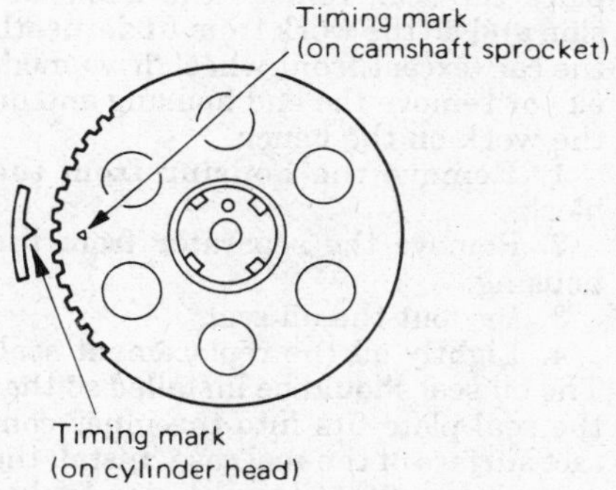


**Camshaft timing mark alignment for #1 TDC, on the 1997cc engine**

41. Install the oil pressure switch, if removed, and install the battery ground cable.

42. Install the fan blades, radiator, fill the system with coolant and start the engine.

### *1997cc Engine*

**NOTE: An 8mm diameter metal bar is needed for this procedure.**

1. Remove the water pump drive belt and pulley.
2. Remove the crank adapter and crankshaft pulley.
3. Remove the upper and lower timing belt covers.
4. Move the tensioner fully in the direction of the water pump and temporarily secure it there.
5. If the timing belt is to be reused, make a paint mark on the belt to indicate the direction of rotation. Slip the belt from the sprockets.

**NOTE: Place the belt in an area where it will not be contacted by oil or other petroleum distilled.**

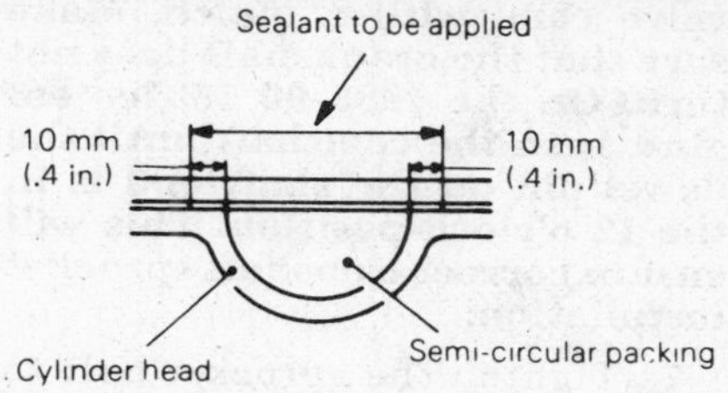


**Sealant application on the rocker cover rear seal projections used for turning the shaft in hard-to-turn installations**

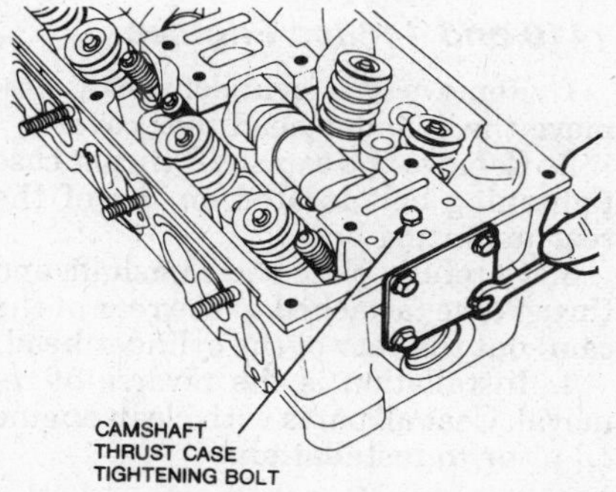


**Rear camshaft cover on 1410 and 1468cc engines**

6. Remove the camshaft sprocket bolt and pull the sprocket from the camshaft.
7. Remove the crankshaft sprocket bolt and pull the crankshaft sprocket and flange from the crankshaft.
8. Remove the plug on the left side of the block and insert an 8mm diameter metal bar in the opening to keep the silent shaft in position.
9. Remove the oil pump sprocket retaining nut and remove the oil pump sprocket.
10. Loosen the right silent shaft sprocket mounting bolt until it can be turned by hand.
11. Remove the belt tensioner and remove the timing belt.

**NOTE: Do not attempt to turn the silent shaft sprocket or loosen its bolt while the belt is off.**

12. Remove the silent shaft belt sprocket from the crankshaft.
13. Check the belt for wear, damage or glossing. Replace it if any cracks, damage, brittleness or excessive wear are found.
14. Check the tensioners for a smooth rate of movement.
15. Replace any tensioner that shows grease leakage through the seal.
16. Install the silent shaft belt sprocket on the crankshaft, with the flat face toward the engine.
17. Apply light engine oil on the outer face of the spacer and install the spacer on the right silent shaft. The side with the rounded shoulder faces the engine.
18. Install the sprocket on the right silent shaft and install the bolt fingertight.
19. Install the silent shaft belt and adjust the tension, by moving the tensioner into contact with the belt, tight enough to remove all slack. Tighten the tensioner bolt to 21 ft. lbs.
20. Tighten the silent shaft sprocket bolt to 28 ft. lbs.
21. Install the flange and crankshaft sprocket on the crankshaft. The flange conforms to the front of the silent shaft sprocket and the timing belt sprocket is installed with the flat face toward the engine.

**NOTE: The flange must be installed correctly or a broken belt will result.**

22. Install the washer and bolt in the crankshaft and torque it to 94 ft. lbs.
23. Install the camshaft sprocket and bolt and torque the bolt to 72 ft. lbs.
24. Install the timing belt tensioner, spacer and spring.
25. Align the timing mark on each sprocket with the corresponding mark on the front case.
26. Install the timing belt on the sprockets and move the tensioner against the belt with sufficient force to allow a deflection of 5–7mm along its longest straight run.
27. Tighten the tensioner bolt to 21 ft. lbs.
28. Install the upper and lower covers, the crankshaft pulley and the crank adapter. Tighten the bolts to 21 ft. lbs.
29. Remove the 8mm bar and install the plug.

## Camshaft

### REMOVAL & INSTALLATION

#### *Except 1410cc, 1468cc and 1595cc DOHC Engines*

1. Matchmark the rocker arm bearing caps to the cylinder head.
2. Remove the bearing cap bolts from the cylinder head, but do not remove them from the bearing caps and shafts. Lift the rocker arm assembly from the cylinder head.
3. Make sure the timing marks on the camshaft sprocket and head are properly aligned, so that No. 1 piston is at TDC of the compression stroke. If the camshaft sprocket is to be removed, do so before removing the camshaft from the head. If not, it will be difficult to remove the sprocket bolt. So, prior to removing the bearing caps or belt, remove the camshaft sprocket bolt and lift off the sprocket and belt. Discard the camshaft oil seal.
4. Remove the camshaft from the bearing saddles.

**NOTE: On some engines, a distributor drive gear and spacer are used on the front of the camshaft.**

5. The valves, valve springs, and valve guide seals can now be removed from the cylinder head.

6. Installation is the reverse of removal. Coat all parts with clean engine oil prior to installation. Use a seal driver MD998364 or equivalent, for engines except the 1985–90 1997cc and MD998307 or equivalent, for 1985–88 1997cc engines, install a new oil seal after the camshaft is in place.

**NOTE: If the dowel pin hole of the camshaft sprocket will not align with the dowel pin on the camshaft on the 1597cc engine, the shaft can be easily turned by striking the projections on the shaft, just behind No. 2 exhaust valve cam, with a punch. Make sure that the crankshaft does not turn. On the 1985–90 1997cc engine, turn the camshaft until the dowel pin on the shaft end is in the 12 o'clock position. This will ensure correct camshaft sprocket installation.**

7. Tighten the sprocket bolt to 50–60 ft. lbs. on the 1994cc, 1997cc and 2555cc engines; 44–55 ft. lbs. on the 1597cc. Tighten the rocker cover bolts to 5 ft. lbs.

### *1410 and 1468cc Engines*

1. Remove the cylinder head. Remove the cylinder head rear cover.
2. Remove the camshaft thrust case tightening bolt located on top of the rear mounting boss.
3. Carefully slide the camshaft and thrust case (attached to the rear of the cam) out the rear of the cylinder head.
4. Installation is the reverse of removal. Coat all parts with clean engine oil prior to installation.

### *1595cc DOHC Engine*

Refer to the proceeding Rocker Arm and Shaft section.

## Piston and Connecting Rod

### POSITIONING

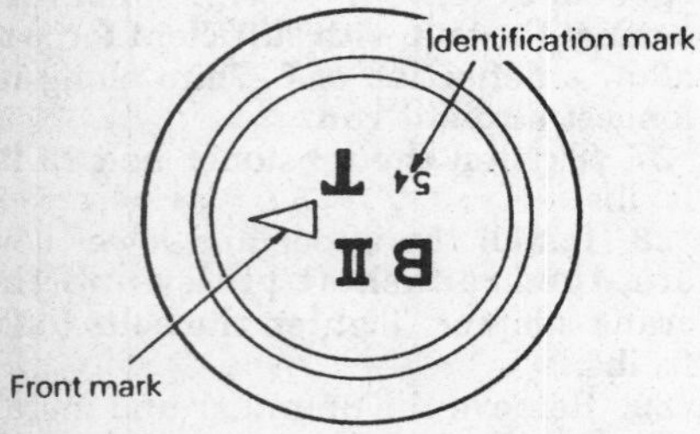


**Typical piston identification and direction indicator**

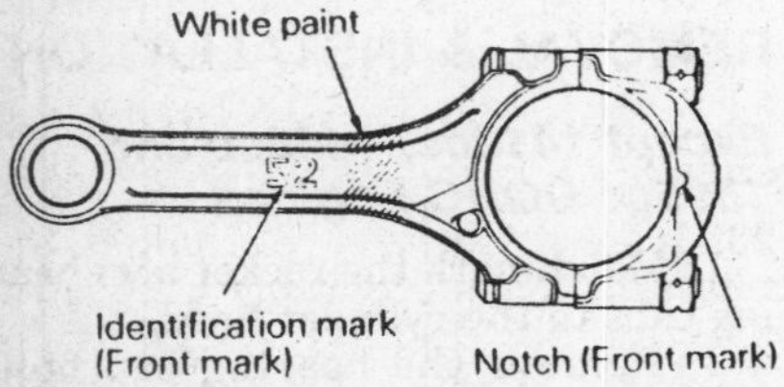


**Typical connecting rod identification and front indicator**

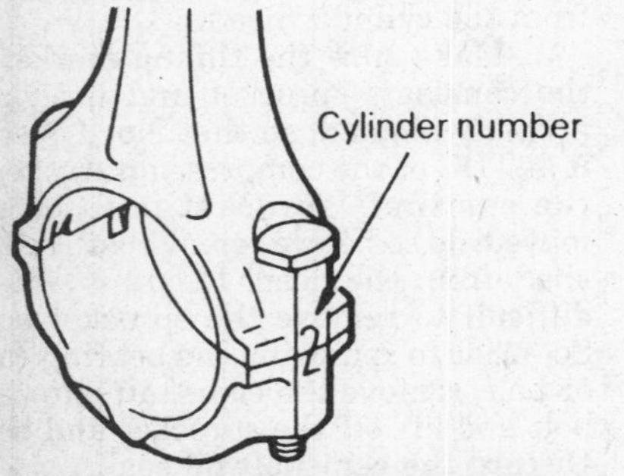


**Location of cylinder number on connecting rod**

**For all piston and connection rod overhaul procedures, please refer to "Engine Rebuilding" in the Unit Repair Section.**

# ENGINE LUBRICATION

## Oil Pan

### REMOVAL & INSTALLATION

The engine may have be raised off its mount for the pan to clear the suspension crossmember. However, on most front wheel drive models, there is usually enough clearance without raising the engine.

1. Remove the underbody splash shield.
2. Unbolt the left and right engine mounts (except front wheel drive).
3. Jack up the engine under the the bell housing (except front wheel drive).
4. Remove the oil pan.
5. Installation is the reverse of removal.

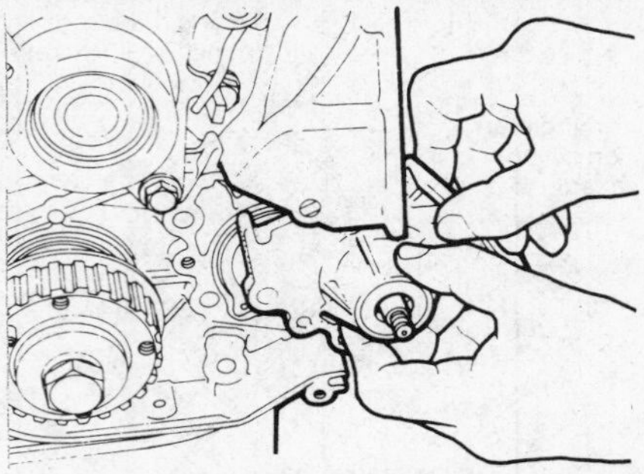

**Removing the oil pump cover from 1597cc engines**

## Rear Main Bearing Oil Seal

### REMOVAL & INSTALLATION

The rear main oil seal is located in a housing on the rear of the block. To replace the seal, remove the transmission and do the work from underneath the car (except front wheel drive models) or remove the end housing and do the work on the bench.

1. Remove the housing from the block.
2. Remove the separator from the housing.
3. Pry out the oil seal.
4. Lightly oil the replacement seal. The oil seal should be installed so that the seal plate fits into the inner contact surface of the seal case. Install the separator with the oil holes facing down.

## Oil Pump

### REMOVAL & INSTALLATION

### *1410cc and 1468cc Engines*

1. Remove the timing belt as previously described.
2. Remove the oil pan as previously described.
3. Remove the oil screen.
4. Unbolt and remove the front case assembly.
5. Remove the oil pump cover.
6. Remove the inner and outer gears from the front case.

**NOTE: The outer gear has no identifying marks to indicate direction of rotation. Clean the gear and mark it with an indelible marker.**

7. Remove the plug, relief valve spring and relief valve from the case.
8. Check the front case for damage or cracks. Replace the front seal. Replace the oil screen O-ring. Clean all parts thoroughly with a safe solvent.

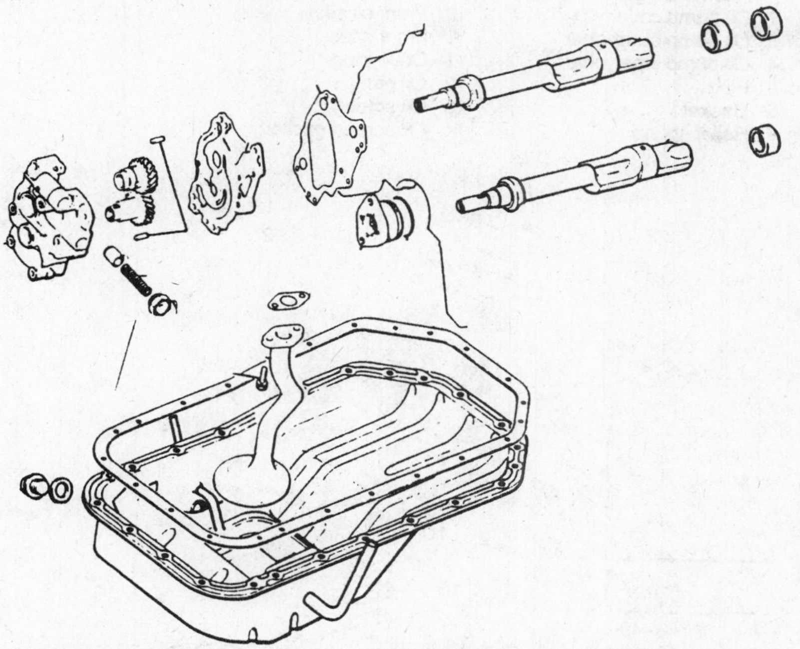

Exploded view of oil pump, oil pan and silent shafts, 2555cc engine

9. Check the pump gears for wear or damage. Clean the gears thoroughly and place them in position in the case to check the clearances. There is a crescent-shaped piece between the 2 gears. This piece is the reference point for 2 measurements. Use the following clearances for determining gear wear:

Outer gear face-to-case–0.0039–0.0079 in.

Outer gear teeth-to-crescent–0.0087–0.0134 in.

Outer gear end-play–0.0016–0.0039 in.

Inner gear teeth-to-crescent–0.0083–0.0126 in.

Inner gear end-play–0.0016–0.0039 in.

10. Check that the relief valve can slide freely in the case.

11. Check the relief valve spring for damage. The relief valve free length should be 1.850 in. Load/length should be 9.5 lb. at 1.575 in.

12. Thoroughly coat both oil pump gears with clean engine oil and install them in the correct direction of rotation.

13. Install the pump cover and torque the bolts to 7 ft. lbs.

14. Coat the relief valve and spring with clean engine oil, install them and tighten the plug to 30–36 ft. lbs.

15. Position a new front case gasket, coated with sealer, on the engine and install the front case. Torque the bolts to 10 ft. lbs. Note that the bolts have different shank lengths.

16. Coat the lips of a new seal with clean engine oil and slide it along the crankshaft until it touches the front case. Drive it into place with a seal driver.

17. Install the sprocket, timing belt and pulley.

18. Install the oil screen.

19. Thoroughly clean both the oil pan and engine mating surfaces. Apply a 4mm wide bead of RTV sealer in the groove of the oil pan mating surface. 4mm is usually the first cut mark on the nozzle that comes with the tube of sealer.

**NOTE: The sealer will set in approximately 15 minutes.**

20. Tighten the oil pan bolts to 5–6 ft. lbs.

### *1595cc DOHC and 1597cc Engines*

1. Remove the timing belt.
2. Drain the oil.
3. Remove the oil filter (DOHC). Remove the oil pan and screen.
4. Remove the oil filter bracket (DOHC). Unbolt and remove the front case assembly.

**NOTE: On 1597cc: if the front case assembly is difficult to remove from the block, there is a groove around the case into which a pry bar may be inserted, to aid in removal. Pry slowly and evenly. Don't hammer.**

5. On 1597cc: Remove the oil pressure relief plug, spring and plunger.
6. On 1597cc: Remove the nut and pull off the oil pump sprocket.
7. On 1597cc: Remove the oil pump cover.
8. On 1597cc: Remove the pump rotor.
9. Check the case for cracks and damage.
10. Check the oil screen for damage.
11. Replace the oil screen O-ring.
12. Thoroughly clean all parts in a safe solvent.
13. On 1597cc: Place the rotor back in the case to check clearances.

Side clearance–0.0024–0.0047in.

Tip clearance–0.0016–0.0047 in.

Body clearance–0.0039–0.0063 in.

Shaft-to-cover clearance–0.0008–0.0020 in.

14. On 1597cc: Check that the relief valve plunger slides smoothly in its bore.
15. On 1597cc: Check the relief valve spring. The free length should be 1.850 in.; the load length should be 9.5 lb. at 1.575 in.
16. On 1597cc: Install a new oil seal, coated with clean engine oil, into the oil pump cover. Drive it into place using a hammer and flat block.
17. On 1597cc: Install a new cover gasket in the groove in the case.
18. On 1597cc: Coat the rotor with clean engine oil and install it in the cover.
19. On 1597cc: Install the cover and tighten the bolts.
20. On 1597cc: Install the sprocket and tighten the nut to 28 ft. lbs.
21. On 1597cc: Coat the oil relief valve plunger with clean engine oil and install it, along with the spring and plug.
22. Install a new case gasket, coated with sealer, on the block and install the case. Torque the case bolts: On 1597cc: 13 ft. lbs. On 1595cc DOHC 20–25 ft. lbs.

**NOTE: There are 2 different lengths of case bolts.**

23. Install the screen. Tighten the bolts: On 1597cc: 18 ft. lbs. On 1595cc DOHC: 11–16 ft. lbs.
24. Install the oil pan as previously described.

### *1997cc and 2555cc Engines*

1. Remove the timing chain as previously described.
2. Remove the oil pump cover and gears.
3. Remove the relief valve plug, spring and plunger.
4. Thoroughly clean all parts in a safe solvent and check for wear and damage.
5. Clean all orifices and passages.
6. Place the gear back in the pump body and check clearances.

Gear teeth-to-body–0.0041–0.0059 in.

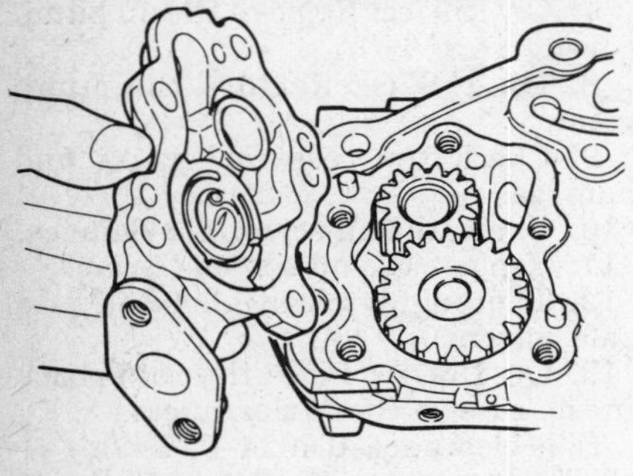

Oil pump cover removal from the 1997cc engine

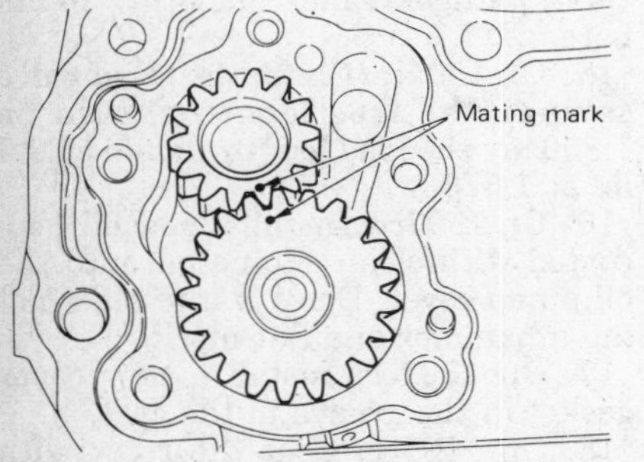


Oil pump gear mating marks on the 1997cc engine

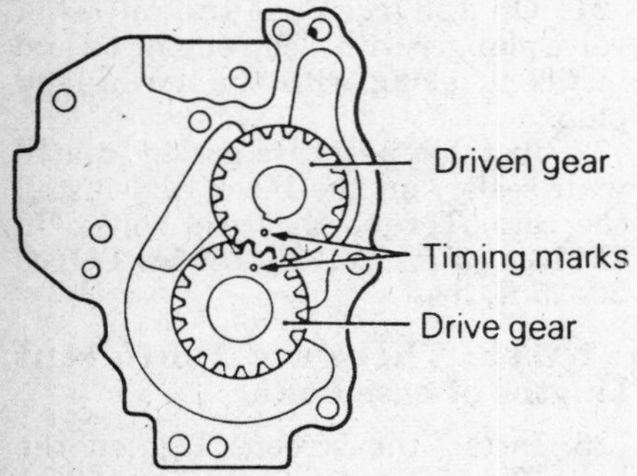


Installation of oil pump drive and driven gears and matching of timing marks, 2555cc engine

Driven gear end play–0.0024–0.0047 in.

Drive gear-to-bearing (front end)–0.0008–0.0018 in.

Drive gear-to-bearing (rear end)–0.0017–0.0026 in.

**NOTE: If gear replacement is necessary, the entire pump body must be replaced.**

7. Check the relief valve spring for wear or damage. Free length should be 1.850 in.; load length should be 9.5 lb at 1.575 in.

1. Front case gasket
2. Oil pump cover
3. Oil pump outer gear
4. Oil pump inner gear
5. Plug
6. Gasket
7. Relief spring
8. Relief plunger
9. Front oil seal
10. Front case
11. Drain plug
12. Oil pan
13. Oil screen
14. Oil screen gasket

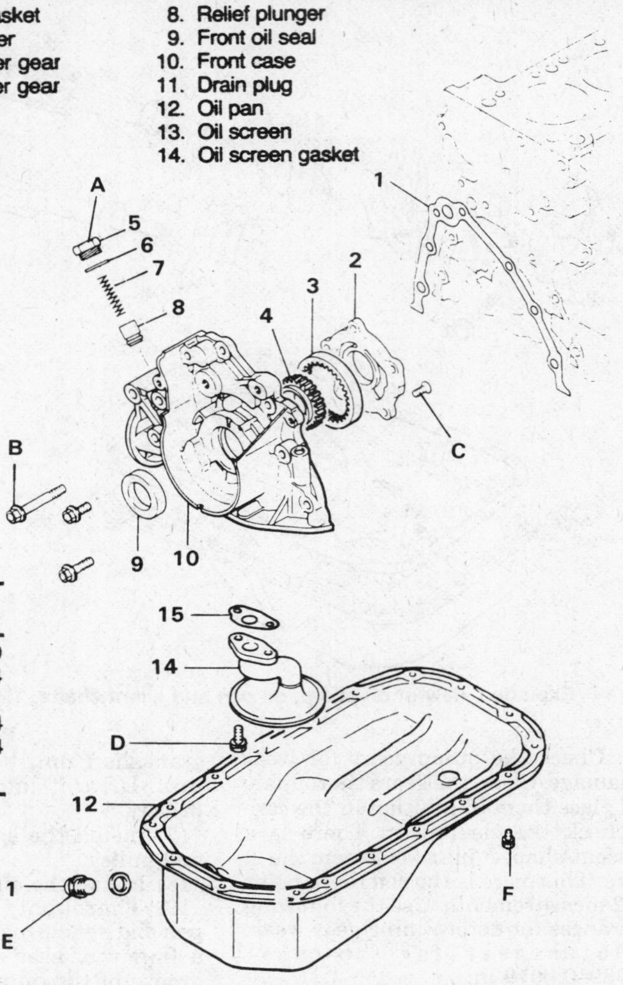


| | Nm |
|---|---|
| A | 40–49 |
| B | 12–14 |
| C | 8–9 |
| D | 18–24 |
| E | 35–44 |
| F | 6–7 |

1410 and 1468cc engine oil pump, front case and oil pan

8. Assembly is the reverse of disassembly. Make sure that the gears are installed with the mating marks aligned.

# ENGINE COOLING

## Radiator

### REMOVAL & INSTALLATION

1. Remove the splash panel from the bottom of the car. Drain the radiator by opening the petcock. Remove the shroud on models so equipped. On the Conquest, remove the battery.
2. Disconnect the radiator hoses at the engine. On automatic transmission cars, disconnect and plug the transmission lines to the bottom of the radiator.
3. Remove the 2 retaining bolts from either side of the radiator. Lift out the radiator. On front wheel drive models, disconnect the electric fan wiring harness. Do not remove the fan motor, blades or bracket – remove as a unit with the radiator.
4. Install the radiator in the reverse order of removal. Tighten the retaining bolts gradually in a crisscross pattern.

**CAUTION**

***Work around the electric cooling fan when the engine is cold or disconnect the negative battery cable. On some models, the fan will run to cool the engine even when the ignition is off.***

## Water Pump

### REMOVAL & INSTALLATION

#### *Rear Wheel Drive*

1. Drain the cooling system.
2. Remove the fan shroud and radi-

ator if necessary for working room.
3. Remove the alternator belt and accessory belts.
4. Remove the fan blades and/or automatic hub, if equipped.
5. Remove the water pump assembly from the timing chain case or the cylinder block.
6. Installation is the reverse of removal.
7. Fill the radiator with coolant and test for leaks.

### *Front Wheel Drive*

1. Drain the cooling system.
2. Remove the drive belt and water pump pulley.
3. Remove the timing belt covers and timing belt tensioner, as explained earlier.
4. Remove the water pump bolts and alternator bracket.
5. Remove the water pump.

**NOTE: The pump is not rebuildable. If there are signs of damage, or leakage from the seals or vent hole, the unit must be replaced.**

6. Discard the O-ring in the front end of the water pipe. Install a new O-ring coated with water.
7. Using a new gasket, mount the water pump and alternator bracket on the engine. Torque the bolts with a head mark **4** to 10 ft. lbs.; the bolts with a head mark **7** to 20 ft. lbs.
8. The remainder of assembly is the reverse of disassembly. Fill the system with coolant.

## Thermostat

### REMOVAL & INSTALLATION

#### *Rear Wheel Drive*

The thermostat is located in the intake manifold under the upper radiator hose.

1. Drain the coolant below the level of the thermostat.
2. Remove the 2 retaining bolts and lift the thermostat housing off the intake manifold with the hose still at position).
3. Raise the small cone-shaped cover on the throttle cable to expose the nipple.

**NOTE: It is not necessary to remove the upper radiator hose.**

4. Lift the thermostat out of the manifold.
5. Install the thermostat in the reverse order of removal. Use a new gasket and coat the mating surfaces with sealer.

#### *Front Wheel Drive*

1. Drain the cooling system to a point below the thermostat level.
2. Remove the air cleaner.
3. Disconnect the hose at the thermostat water pipe.
4. Remove the water pipe support bracket nut.

**NOTE: This nut is also an intake manifold nut. It is VERY difficult to get to. A deep offset 12mm box wrench is used to remove or replace it.**

5. Unbolt and remove the thermostat housing and pipe.
6. Lift out the thermostat. Discard the gasket.
7. Clean the mating surfaces of the housing and manifold thoroughly.
8. Install the thermostat with the spring facing downward and position a new gasket. The jiggle valve in the thermostat should be on the manifold side.
9. Install the housing and pipe assembly. Torque the housing bolts to 10 ft. lbs.; the intake manifold nut to 14 ft. lbs.
10. Refill the system with coolant.

# EMISSION CONTROLS

**Please refer to "Emission Control" in the Unit Repair section for system maintenance procedures. Due to the complex nature of modern electronic engine control systems, comprehensive diagnosis and testing procedures fall outside the confines of this repair manual. For complete information on diagnosis, testing and repair procedures concerning all modern engine and emission control systems, please refer to "Chilton's Guide to Electronic Engine Controls".**

### MAINTENANCE REMINDER LAMP

An EGR maintenance reminder lamp will illuminate at approximately 50,000 miles and after the EGR inspection/service has been accomplished, the lamp timer switch must be reset.

The reset button is located on the back of the instrument panel, on the left side of the speedometer cable junction or below it. It is only necessary to slide the switch from on side of the switch to the other, to reset the sensor.

# FUEL SYSTEM

## Fuel System Service Precaution

### RELIEVING FUEL SYSTEM PRESSURE

**NOTE: Be sure to reduce the internal pressure. If the hose is removed from the fuel main pipe without reducing the internal pressure, fuel will gush out.**

1. Start the engine and then disconnect the fuel gauge unit connector, which is located in the luggage compartment.
2. After the engine has been stopped, set the ignition to the **OFF** position.
3. Disconnect the battery cable from the negative terminal of the battery.

## Fuel Filter

### REPLACEMENT

The fuel filter should be replaced every 12,000 miles. On carburetor equipped models, the filter is usually located on the left-handed inner fender near the master cylinder. Loosen both hose clamps and remove the lines from the filter. Pull the filter from its bracket and discard it. Snap the replacement filter into the bracket. Install the lines on the filter and tighten the hose clamps. Start the engine and check for leaks.

**NOTE: On models with fuel injection, relieve fuel system pressure before removing filter.**

On multipoint fuel injected models, remove the air cleaner. Be sure the fuel system pressure has been relieved, hold the fuel filter connection nut firmly and remove the line eye bolt. Remove the filter.

**NOTE: Some pressure may still remain in the system, cover the filter connections with a rag to prevent splashing.**

## Mechanical Fuel Pump

A mechanical fuel pump is used and is attached to the engine. A cartridge type fuel filter is used and is located in the engine compartment.

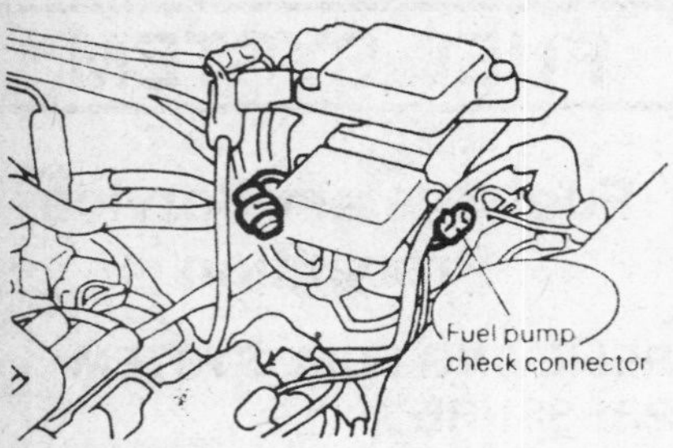


**Colt Turbo fuel pump test connectors**

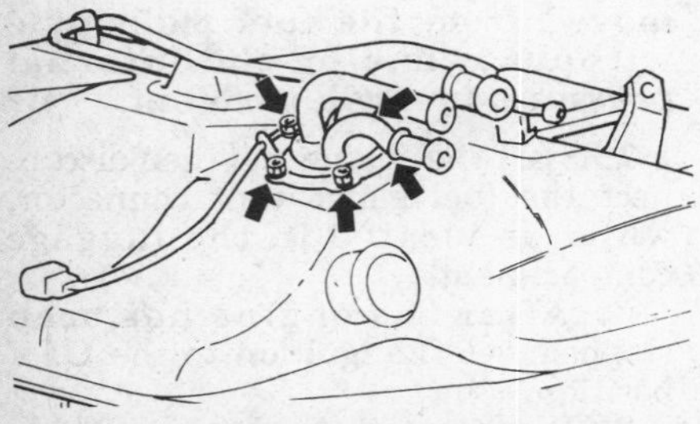

**Colt Turbo electric fuel pump location. The arrows indicate the mounting bolts**

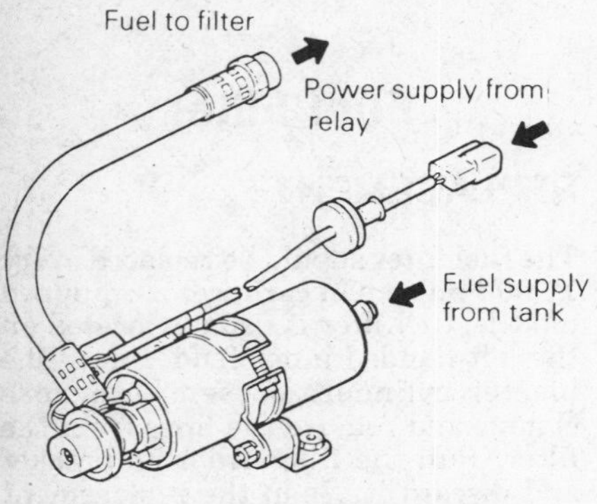


**Conquest electric fuel pump**

### TESTING

Disconnect the fuel line from the carburetor and attach a pressure tester to the end of the line. Crank the engine. The pressure should agree with the figure given in the "Tune-Up Specification" chart.

### REMOVAL & INSTALLATION

The pump is mounted on the front side of the engine and is driven by an eccentric on the camshaft.

1. Remove the fuel lines.
2. Unbolt the pump mounting bolts, remove the pump, insulator, and gasket.
3. Coat both sides of a new insulator and gasket with sealer and install the pump in the reverse order of removal.

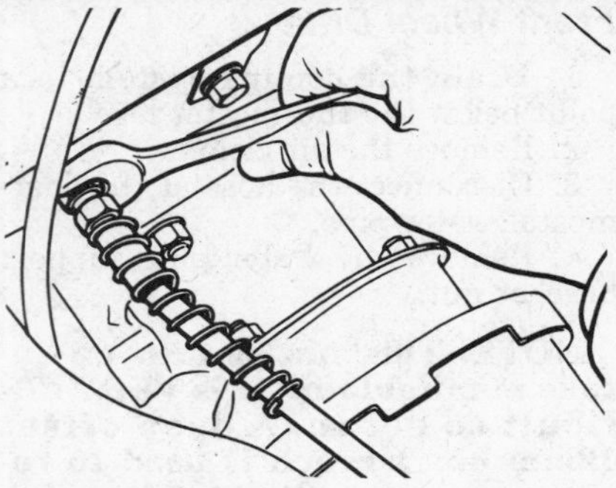

**Throttle linkage adjustment (typical)**

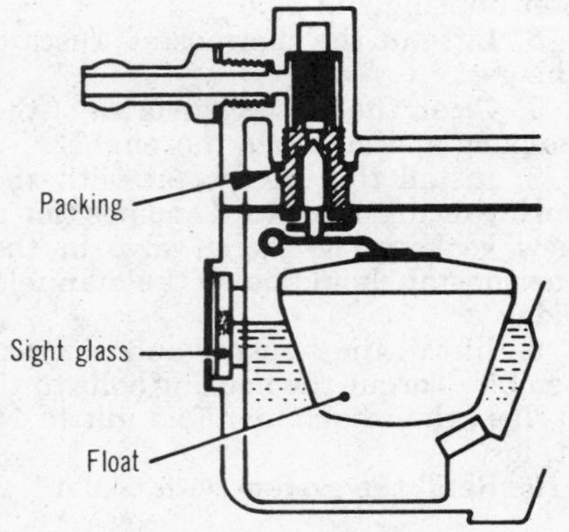


**Float level adjustment—1983**

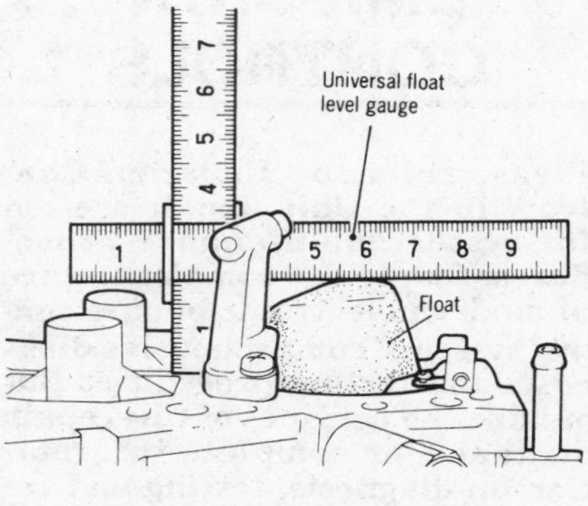


**Dry float level adjustment**

## Electric Fuel Pump

An electric fuel pump is used and is located either in or on the fuel tank or behind the left rear wheel, A high pressure fuel filter is used and is located in the engine compartment.

There is a connector for checking the fuel function in the engine compartment, under the battery. The fuel pump can be operated by connecting the terminals with jumper wires.

1. Connect jumper wires to terminals 1 and 2 of fuel pump check connector, and check to ensure that when operating, the sound of fuel pump can be heard.
2. When no operating sound can be heard, check for defective connector, wiring, etc.
3. If there is nothing wrong with connector and wiring, disconnect the fuel pump connector at the pump and energize the pump. If pump still fails to operate, replace it.

## Carburetor

### REMOVAL & INSTALLATION

1. Remove the solenoid valve wiring.
2. Disconnect the air cleaner breather hose, air duct and vacuum tube.
3. Remove the air cleaner.
4. Remove the air cleaner case.
5. Disconnect the accelerator and shift cables (automatic transmission) at the carburetor.
6. Disconnect the purge valve hose; remove the vacuum compensator, and fuel lines.
7. Drain the coolant.
8. Remove the water hose between the carburetor and the cylinder head.
9. Remove the carburetor.
10. Installation is the reverse of removal.

### THROTTLE LINKAGE ADJUSTMENT

Adjust the stopper bolt to a distance of 0.750–0.040 in. from inside of the bolt holding bracket, to the contact point of the pedal lever while holding the carburetor throttle plates closed. The yoke at the carburetor end of the accelerator rod is serrated to allow the yoke to be loosened and moved so that a minimal readjustment of the stopper adjusting bolt is needed to give the proper throttle release and opening.

### FLOAT LEVEL ADJUSTMENT

#### *1983*

A sight glass is fitted at the float chamber and the fuel level can be checked without disassembling the carburetor. Normal fuel level is within the level mark on the sight glass.

The fuel level adjustment is corrected by increasing or decreasing the number of needle valve packings. The float level may be off 0.160 in., above or below the level mark and the operation of the engine would not be affected.

#### *1984–90 (Dry Setting)*

1. Invert the float chamber cover assembly without a gasket.
2. Position a universal float level

gauge and measure the distance from the bottom of the float to the surface of the float chamber cover. The distance should by 0.787 in. (20mm), 0.0394 in. (1mm).

3. If the reading is not within this range, the shim under the needle seat must be changed. Shim kits are available which contain 3 shims; 0.0118 in. (0.3mm), 0.0157 in. (0.4mm) and 0.0196 in. (0.5mm).

## FAST IDLE ADJUSTMENT

1. Start the engine and open the throttle valve about 45 degrees. Manually close the choke valve and slowly return the throttle valve to the stop position.
2. With a tachometer, check that the fast idle speed is 2000 rpm or lower. (Not less than 1700 rpm). Adjust the speed as necessary with the fast idle speed screw.
3. Cold start the engine and check the automatic choke and fast idle operation.

## AUTOMATIC CHOKE ADJUSTMENT

### *1983–84*

The choke is adjusted by turning the screw located on the choke spring bracket. The latest model years could have a tamper resistant cover on the screw. If choke adjustment is absolutely necessary, then the cover could be removed to make the adjustment. A new cover should be installed on the screw after the adjustment is made.

### *1985–90*

1. Remove the air cleaner and choke mechanism cover.

**NOTE: Some models might have headless, tamperproof screws securing the choke mechanism cover. These have to be drilled out. In that case, it's easier to remove the carburetor.**

2. Remove the bracket bridging the choke spring gear and choke actuating cam.
3. Slip the choke strangler spring from the choke lever. Align the scribed black line on the choke gear with the mark below the teeth on the actuating cam and reassemble all parts.
4. Temporarily tighten the lower bracket screw.
5. Move the arm at the upper screw to align the center line scribed in the notch on the arm with the punch mark on the float chamber.
6. Tighten the screws.
7. Install the cover with new screws.

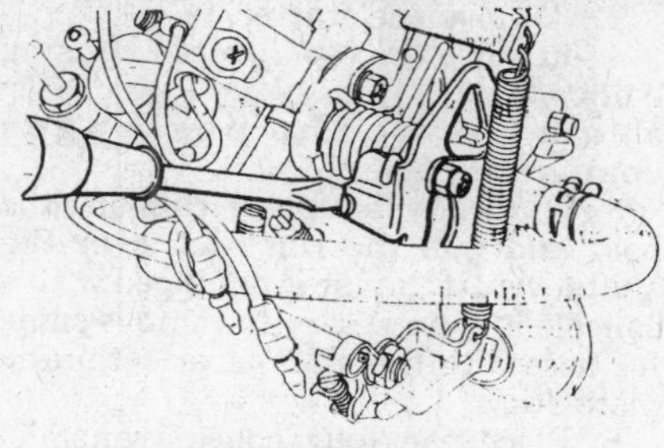

**Choke adjustment**

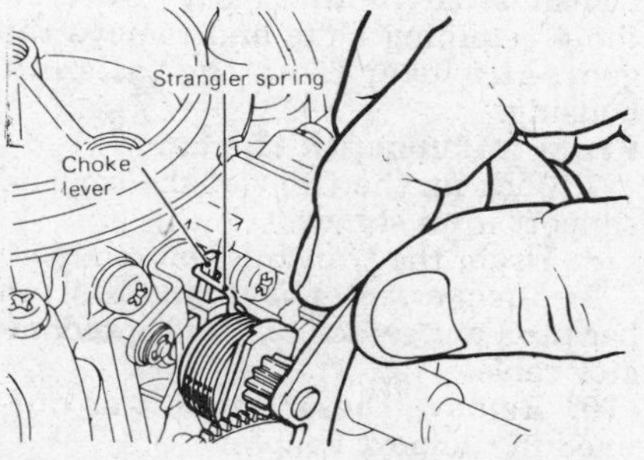


**Removing the choke bracket bridge on 1985–86 models with feedback carburetor**

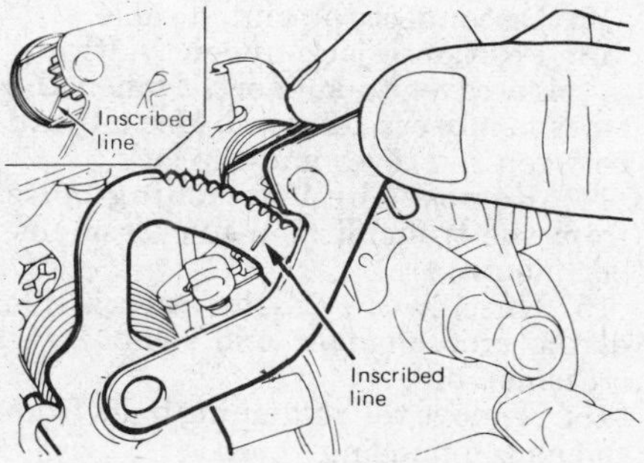


**Aligning the choke gear and cam mating marks**

## THROTTLE OPENER ADJUSTMENT (IDLE-UP)

### *1983–84*

This system is not available in California. The throttle opener increases engine rpm if it drops below a specified amount. The system can be adjusted.

1. Check and adjust curb idle if needed.
2. Turn off all accessories and disconnect the electric radiator fan and hook a tachometer to the engine.
3. If equipped with air conditioning, switch the system on.
4. Warm up the engine and set the transaxle in neutral.
5. Remove the pressure on throttle opener by lifting on the unit with a finger. Do not push up on the throttle opener lever or rod.
6. Adjust the throttle opener screw to obtain 800–900 rpm.

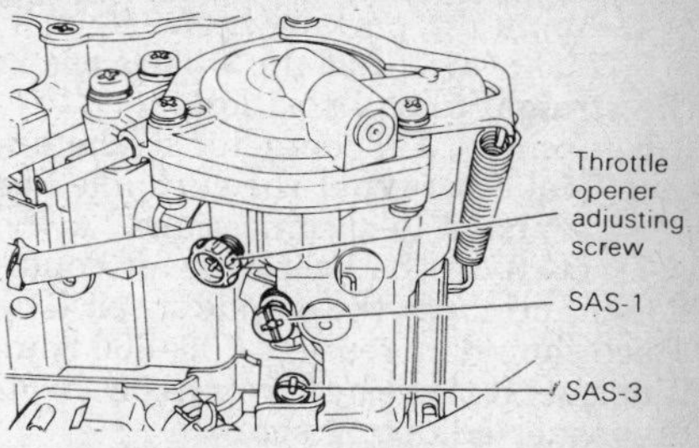


**Throttle opener adjustment location**

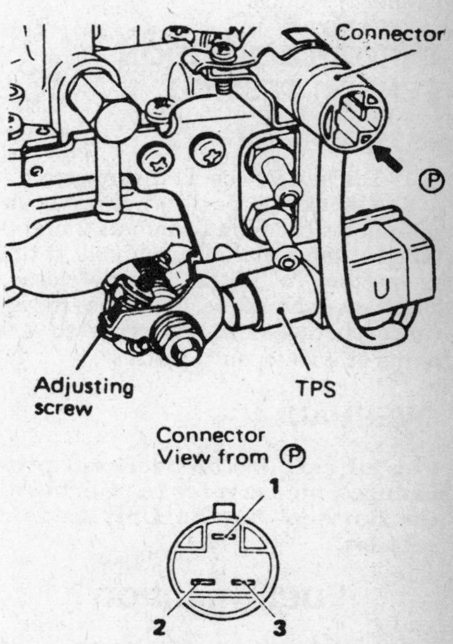


**Throttle position sensor testing**

**NOTE: Turn the A/C switch on and off several times to check the throttle opener operation (lever up/down).**

### *1985–90*

#### EXCEPT 4WD VISTA

1. Check the vacuum hoses and electrical connectors.
2. Disconnect the vacuum hose at the throttle opener nipple.
3. Connect a vacuum pump to the throttle opener nipple.
4. Connect a tachometer to the engine.
5. Run the engine to normal operating temperature at idle.
6. Apply 300mm Hg. (11.8 in. Hg.) vacuum with the pump. The idle speed should increase. If not, replace the throttle opener dashpot.

#### 4WD VISTA

1. Turn all lights and accessories off.
2. Place the transaxle in neutral.
3. Disconnect the electric fan connector.

4. Apply the parking brake.
5. Make sure that the wheels are in the straight ahead position.
6. Connect a tachometer to the engine. Make sure that the curb idle has been adjusted to specification.
7. Turn on the heater or air conditioner and check the engine speed. The speed should increase to 700–800 rpm. If not, set it there by turning the throttle opener adjusting screw.
8. Turn the A/C or heater off and on several times to verify that the throttle opener responds.

### THROTTLE POSITION SENSOR TESTING

#### *1985–90*

1. Disconnect the TPS connector.
2. Check the resistance with an ohmmeter between terminals 2 and 3 (the bottom, adjacent terminals in the connector). With the throttle closed, resistance should be 1.2 ohms. Resistance should slowly increase to 4.9 ohms at wide open throttle.

### OVERHAUL

**For all carburetor overhaul procedures, please refer to "Carburetor Service" in the Unit Repair section.**

## Fuel Injection

**Due to the complex nature of modern fuel injection systems, comprehensive diagnosis and testing procedures fall outside the confines of this repair manual. For complete information on fuel injection diagnosis, testing and repair procedures, please refer to "Chilton's Guide To Fuel Injection and Feedback Carburetors".**

# MANUAL TRANSMISSION

### REMOVAL & INSTALLATION

#### *Rear Wheel Drive Except Conquest*

NOTE: **The clutch housing and transmission are removed as a unit.**

1. Disconnect the battery cables, negative (ground) cable first.
2. Remove the battery cable from the starter and fasten it away from the transmission.
3. Remove the starter.
4. Remove the top 2 clutch housing bolts.

**From inside the passenger compartment:**

5. Untie the leather or rubber shift boot and pull the rug back over the shift lever. If the car is equipped with a console it is necessary to remove same for access to the shift lever retaining plate etc.
6. Place the four speed transmission in second gear and the five speed transmission in first gear. Unscrew the 4 retaining bolts and remove the gearshift lever from the tailshaft housing.

**From underneath the car:**

7. Jack up the front of the car and support it on stands.
8. Drain the transmission oil.
9. Disconnect the transmission backup light switch and the speedometer cable.
10. Remove the driveshaft as outlined in the next chapter.
11. Disconnect the exhaust pipe at the manifold and the engine side bracket. Drop the pipe down and out of the way.
12. Disconnect the clutch cable.
13. Position a jack under the transmission cover to support it when the crossmember is removed. Use a board between the cover and the jack.
14. Remove the 2 attaching bolts from the transmission-to-crossmember mount.
15. Unscrew the 2 bolts at each side of the crossmember and remove the crossmember.
16. Remove the remaining bolts from the clutch housing.
17. Pull the transmission rearward and lower it to the floor. When removing the transmission, pull it straight back so as not to damage the pilot bearing, clutch disc, or pressure plate.
18. Installation of the transmission is basically the reverse of the removal procedure, noting the following points:
    a. When installing the gearshift assembly, position the lever in First gear so that the nylon bushing is vertical. Make sure that no dirt enters the transmission housing during the installation of the shifter.
    b. Refill the transmission with gear oil.
    c. Adjust the clutch.

#### *Conquest*

1. Raise and support the front and rear of the car on jackstands.
2. Remove the driveshaft.
3. Drain the transmission.
4. Disconnect the speedometer cable and switch connector at the transmission.
5. Remove the clutch slave cylinder.
6. Remove the bell housing cover.
7. Remove the starter.
8. Remove the 2 upper transmission mounting bolts.
9. Support the transmission with a floor jack.
10. Remove the remaining transmission mounting bolts.
11. Remove the engine support bracket, insulator assembly and ground strap.
12. Place the shift lever in the **NEUTRAL** position. Remove the trim plate and unbolt the shifter assembly, removing it and the stopper plate underneath it.
13. Cover the rear of the cylinder head with a heavy cloth to prevent damage from contact with the firewall.
14. Slowly lower the jack, pull it rearward to disengage the transmission from the clutch.
15. Installation is the reverse of removal. Torque the transmission mounting bolts to 35 ft. lbs.; the starter bolts to 20 ft. lbs.

# MANUAL TRANSAXLE

### REMOVAL & INSTALLATION

#### *Colt and Champ*

1. Disconnect the battery ground (negative) cable.
2. Disconnect from the transaxle: the clutch cable, speedometer cable, back-up light harness, starter motor and the 4 upper bolts connecting the engine to the transaxle.
3. On cars with a turbocharger, remove the air cleaner case, the actuator mounting bolts, the pin coupling, the actuator and shaft and remove the actuator. Discard the collar used with the pin and replace it with a new collar. On cars with a five speed transaxle, disconnect the selector control valve.
4. Jack up the car and support on jackstands.
5. Remove the front wheels. Remove the splash shield. Drain the transaxle fluid.
6. Remove the shift rod and extension. It may be necessary to remove any heat shields that interfere.
7. On models equipped, remove the stabilizer bar from the lower arm and disconnect the lower arm from the body side.
8. Remove the right and left driveshafts from the transaxle case. See halfshaft removal in this section.
9. Disconnect the range selector ca-

ble (if equipped). Remove the engine rear cover.

10. Support the weight of the engine from above (chain hoist). Support the transaxle and remove the remaining lower mounting bolts.

11. Remove the transaxle mount insulator bolt.

12. Remove (slide back and away from the engine) and lower the transaxle.

13. To install reverse the removal procedure. Be sure to connect all controls and wiring. Use new retaining rings when installing the driveshafts.

### *2WD Vista*

1. Remove the battery and tray.
2. Remove the coolant reservoir.
3. Remove the air cleaner.
4. Disconnect the clutch cable, speedometer cable, and backup light wiring from the transaxle.
5. Remove the upper 5 engine-to-transaxle bolts.
6. Disconnect the select control lever and switch harness.
7. Remove the starter.
8. Disconnect and tag all wiring from the transaxle.
9. Jack up and support the front end.
10. Remove the wheels.
11. Drain the transaxle fluid.
12. Remove the extension and shift rod from the engine compartment.
13. Remove the stabilizer and strut bar from the lower control arm.
14. Remove the left and right axle shafts.
15. Support the transaxle with a floor jack, taking care to avoid damaging the pan.
16. Remove the bell housing cover.
17. Remove the remaining transaxle-to-engine bolts.
18. Remove the transaxle mounting bolt.
19. Lower the jack and slide the transaxle from under the car.
20. Installation is the reverse of removal. Torque the mount bolt to 30 ft. lbs.; the engine-to-transaxle bolts to 45 ft. lbs.

### *4WD Vista*

1. Disconnect the battery cables at the battery. Remove the coolant reserve tank.
2. Disconnect the speedometer cable, shift control cable and back-up light harness at the transaxle.
3. Remove the range select control valves and connectors.
4. Tag and disconnect all other wiring attached to the transaxle.
5. Remove the clutch slave cylinder.
6. Remove the vacuum reservoir tank.
7. Disconnect the starter wiring.
8. Remove the upper 5 engine-to-transaxle bolts.
9. Raise and support the car on jackstands.
10. Remove the front wheels, lower engine cover and skid plate.
11. Drain the transaxle and transfer case.
12. Remove the driveshaft.
13. Remove the transfer case extension housing.
14. Remove the left and right halfshafts.
15. Disconnect the right strut from the lower arm.
16. Remove the right fender liner.
17. Take up the weight of the transaxle with a floor jack.

**NOTE: Use a wide board on the floor jack pedestal to help spread the weight over a large area of the transaxle.**

18. Remove the bell housing cover bolts and remove the cover.
19. Remove the remaining engine-to-transaxle bolts.
20. Remove the transaxle mount insulator bolt.
21. Remove the transaxle mounting bracket attaching bolts.
22. Move the transaxle/transfer case assembly to the right. Tilt the right side of the transaxle down, until the transfer case is about level with the upper part of the steering rack tube, then turn it to the left and lower the assembly. Observe the following torques:

Transaxle mount insulator nut–55–58 ft. lbs.

Transaxle mounting bracket bolts–25–30 ft. lbs.

Engine-to-transaxle bolts–45 ft. lbs.

# CLUTCH

## REMOVAL & INSTALLATION

1. On the 4WD Vista, remove the slave cylinder. Remove the transmission or transaxle as outlined.
2. Insert a pilot shaft or an old input shaft into the center of the clutch disc, pressure plate, and the pilot bearing in the crankshaft.
3. With the pilot tool supporting the clutch disc, loosen the pressure plate bolts gradually and in a criss-cross pattern.
4. Remove the pressure plate and clutch disc.
5. Clean the transmission and clutch housing. Clean the flywheel surface with a non-oil based solvent.

**NOTE: Before assembly, slide the clutch disc up and down on the transmission input shaft to check for any binding. Remove any rough spots with crocus cloth and then lightly coat the shaft with Lubriplate.**

To remove the throwout bearing assembly:

6. Remove the return clip and take out the throwout bearing carrier and the bearing.
7. To replace the throwout arm use a $^{3}/_{16}$ in. punch, knock out the throwout shaft spring pin and remove the shaft, springs, and the center lever.
8. Do not immerse the throwout bearing in solvent; it is permanently lubricated. Blow and wipe it clean. Check the bearing for wear, deterioration, or burning. Replace the bearing if there is any question about its condition.
9. Check the shafts, lever, and springs for wear and defects. Replace them if necessary.
10. Examine the clutch disc for the following before reusing it: loose rivets, burned facing, oil or grease on the facing, less than 0.012 in. left between the rivet head and the top of the facing.
11. Check the pressure plate and replace it if any of the following conditions exist: scored or excessive wear, bent or distorted diaphragm, loose rivets.
12. Insert the control lever into the clutch housing. Install the 2 return springs and the throwout shaft.
13. Lock the shift lever to the shaft with the spring pin.
14. Fill the shaft oil seal with multipurpose grease.
15. Install the throwout bearing carrier and the bearing. Install the return clip.
16. Grease the carrier groove and inner surface.
17. Lightly grease the clutch disc splines.

**NOTE: The clutch is installed with the larger boss facing the transmission.**

18. Support the clutch disc and pressure plate with the pilot tool.
19. Turn the pressure plate so that its balance mark aligns with the notch in the flywheel.
20. Install the pressure plate-to-flywheel bolts hand-tight. Using a torque wrench and, working in a criss-cross pattern, tighten the bolts to 11–15 ft. lbs.
21. Install the transmission as outlined.
22. Adjust the clutch as described in the following section.

## CLUTCH ADJUSTMENTS Front Wheel Drive (in.)

| Model | Pedal Height |
|---|---|
| 1983–84 Colt | 7.10–7.30 |
| 1985–90 Colt, Vista | 6.20–6.40 |
| 1985–90 4WD Vista | 7.10–7.30 |
| **Model** | **Pedal Free-play** |
| 1983–84 Colt | 0.80–1.20 |
| 1985–90 Vista | 0.60–0.80 |
| 1985–90 4WD Vista | 0.04–0.12 |
| **Model** | **Cable Free-play** |
| 1983–84 Colt | 0.20–0.24 |
| 1985–90 Colt, Vista | 0.00–0.04 |
| **Model** | **Pedal-to-floorboard Clearance** |
| 1983–84 Colt | 1.40–1.60 |
| 1985–90 Colt | 3.10+ |
| 1985–90 2WD, 4WD Vista | 3.10+ |

## CLUTCH ADJUSTMENTS Rear Wheel Drive (in.)

| Model | Pedal Height |
|---|---|
| 1983 | 7.1 |
| 1985–90 | 7.4–7.6 |
| **Model** | **Pedal Stroke** |
| 1983–84 | 6.0 |
| **Model** | **Pedal Free-play** |
| 1985–90 | 0.04–0.10 |
| **Model** | **Pedal Pad Surface-to-floor** |
| 1985–90 | 1.4 |

### ADJUSTMENTS

#### *Pedal Height*

1. Measure the distance between the floor and the top of the clutch pedal.
2. Refer to the chart above for proper distance. Loosen the clutch switch locknut and move the switch in or out as necessary.

#### *Cable and Free–Play*

**EXCEPT HYDRAULIC CLUTCH MODELS**

1. Slightly pull the cable out from the firewall.
2. Turn the adjusting wheel on the cable until the play between the wheel and the cable is within the dimension listed in the accompanying chart.
3. Check the clutch free-play.
   a. Jack up the front of the car and support it on stands.
   b. Slide under and remove the rubber cover from the clutch housing.
   c. Using a 0.030 in. feeler gauge, check the clearance between the pressure plate diaphragm spring and the throwout bearing.
4. If the free travel is not correct, make further adjustments at the cable adjusting wheel.

**NOTE: Each turn of the adjusting wheel equals 0.060 in. of adjustment to the wheel and retainer clearance.**

5. Lower the car and check the clutch operation.

**HYDRAULIC CLUTCH EQUIPPED MODELS**

If free-play and pedal surface-to-floorboard adjustments are not within specification, there is air in the system. Follow the procedures listed below for bleeding the hydraulic system.

## Clutch Cable

### REMOVAL & INSTALLATION

1. Loosen the cable adjusting wheel inside the engine compartment.
2. Loosen the clutch pedal adjusting bolt locknut and loosen the adjusting bolt.
3. Remove the cable end from the clutch throwout lever.
4. Remove the cable end from the clutch pedal.
5. Installation is the reverse of removal.

**NOTE: Lubricate the cable with engine oil and after installation, install pads isolating the cable from the intake manifold and from the rear side of the engine mount insulator on coupe, sedan, and hatchbacks only.**

## Clutch Master Cylinder

### REMOVAL & INSTALLATION

1. Loosen the bleeder screw on the slave cylinder and drain the system.
2. Disconnect the pushrod from the clutch pedal.
3. Disconnect the clutch pedal from the pedal bracket.
4. Disconnect the fluid line from the master cylinder.
5. Unbolt and remove the master cylinder.
6. Installation is the reverse of removal. Bleed the system.

**NOTE: On the 4WD Vista, the lower master cylinder mounting nut is accessed from inside the car.**

## Clutch Slave Cylinder

### REMOVAL & INSTALLATION

1. Disconnect the clutch hose from the slave cylinder.
2. Unbolt and remove the cylinder from the clutch housing.
3. Installation is the reverse of removal. Bleed the system.

### BLEEDING THE SYSTEM

**NOTE: An assistant is needed for the bleeding operation.**

1. Raise and support the car on jackstands.
2. Loosen the bleeder screw at the slave cylinder.
3. Make sure that the master cylinder is full.
4. Attach a length of rubber hose to the bleeder screw nipple and place the other end in a glass jar half full of clean brake fluid.
5. Have the assistant push the clutch pedal down slowly to the floor. If air is in the system, bubbles will appear in the jar as the pedal is being depressed.
6. When the pedal is at the floor, tighten the bleeder screw.
7. Repeat Steps 5 and 6 until no bubbles are found. Check the master cylinder level frequently to make sure of fluid level.

# AUTOMATIC TRANSMISSION

### REMOVAL & INSTALLATION

#### *TorqueFlite A–904*

1. The transmission and converter must be removed as an assembly; otherwise, converter drive plate, pump bushing, or the oil seal may be damaged. The drive plate will not support a load; therefore, none of the weight of the transmission should be allowed to rest on the plate during removal.
2. Disconnect negative cable from the battery for safety.
3. Remove the cooler lines at transmission.
4. Remove starter motor and cooler line bracket.
5. Loosen pan to drain transmission.

6. Rotate engine clockwise with socket wrench on crankshaft pulley bolt to position the bolts attaching torque converter to drive plate, and remove them.
7. Mark parts for reassembly then disconnect driveshaft at rear universal joint. Carefully pull shaft assembly out of the extension housing.
8. Disconnect gearshift rod and torque shaft assembly from transmission.
9. Disconnect throttle rod from lever at the left-side of transmission. Remove linkage bell crank from transmission if so equipped.
10. Remove the oil filter tube and speedometer cable.
11. Support the rear of the engine with jack or similar device.
12. Raise transmission slightly with service jack to relieve load on the supports.
13. Remove bolts securing transmission mount to crossmember and crossmember to frame, then remove crossmember.
14. Remove all bellhousing bolts.
15. Carefully work transmission converter assembly rearward off engine block dowels and disengage converter hub from end of crankshaft. Attach a small C-clamp to edge of bellhousing to hold converter in place during transmission removal.
16. Lower transmission and remove assembly from under the vehicle.
17. To remove converter assembly, remove C-clamp from edge of bellhousing, then carefully slide assembly out of transmission.
18. Follow the removal procedure in reverse order to install TorqueFlite transmission.

### *JM600*

1. Drain the fluid.
2. Disconnect the battery ground.
3. Remove the dipstick and unbolt the filler tube.
4. Raise the front and rear of the car and support it on jackstands.
5. Remove the 2 topmost transmission-to-engine bolts.
6. Remove the starter.
7. Disconnect the oil cooler lines and cap them to avoid spillage.
8. Remove the bell housing cover.
9. Turn the crankshaft so that the torque converter bolts appear and remove them, turning the crankshaft for each bolt in turn.
10. Disconnect the speedometer cable at the transmission.
11. Disconnect the linkage and cross shaft.
12. Disconnect the ground strap.
13. Matchmark the flanges and remove the driveshaft.
14. Support the transmission with a transmission jack, and the engine with a floor jack.
15. Remove the rear engine support bracket.
16. Remove the remaining engine-to-transmission bolts.
17. Slowly lower the transmission while pulling it rearward to disengage it from the engine. Be careful to avoid dropping the torque converter.
18. Installation is the reverse of removal. Torque the torque converter-to-flywheel bolts to 42–46 ft. lbs.; the transmission-to-engine bolts to 32–40 ft. lbs. Adjust the linkage, fill the unit and roadtest the car.

## PAN AND FILTER SERVICE

### *TorqueFlite A-904*

1. Raise and support the vehicle.
2. Loosen the pan bolts from one end to the other allowing the fluid to drain out.
3. Unbolt the old filter from the pan.
4. Clean the pan and install a new filter. Tighten filter bolts to 35 inch lbs.
5. Install the pan and new gasket. Torque pan bolts to 6–9 ft. lbs.
6. Add 4 quarts of Dexron®II fluid, start the engine and move the lever through all positions, pausing momentarily in each. Add enough fluid to bring the level to the full mark on the dipstick.

### *JM600*

1. Jack up the front of the car and support it safely on stands.
2. Slide a drain pan under the transmission. Loosen the rear oil pan bolts first, to allow most of the fluid to drain off.
3. Remove the remaining bolts and drop the pan.
4. Discard the old gasket, clean the pan, and install the pan with a new gasket.
5. Tighten the pan bolts to 4–6 ft. lbs. in a criss-cross pattern. Lower car. The transmission case is aluminum, so don't exert too much force on the bolts.
6. Refill the transmission through the dipstick tube. Check the fluid level.

## KICKDOWN BAND ADJUSTMENT

### *TorqueFlite A-904*

The kickdown band adjusting screw is located on the left side of the transmission case.

1. Loosen the locknut and back off approximately 5 turns. Test the adjustment screw for free turning in the transmission case.

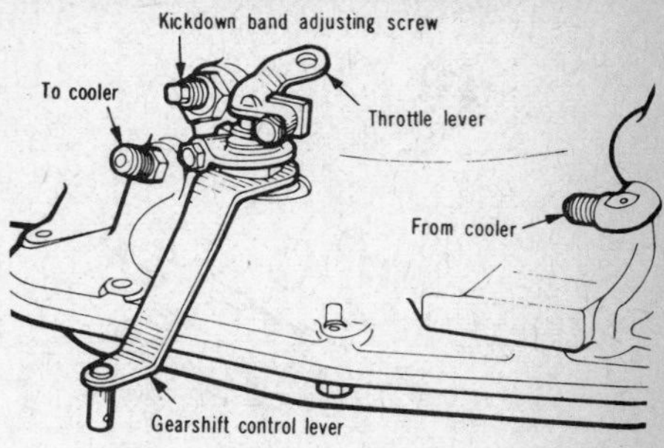


**TorqueFlite kickdown band adjustment points**

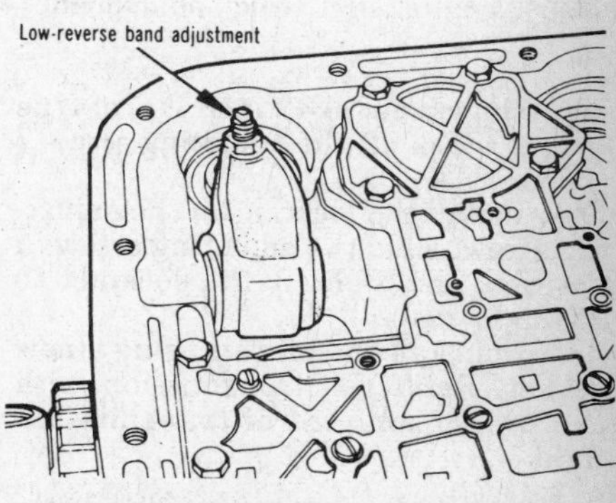


**TorqueFlite low/reverse band adjustment**

2. Tighten the adjusting screw to 69 inch lbs. (the torque specifications shown are true torque with no adapter on the wrench).
3. Back off the adjusting screw 3½ turns.
4. Hold the adjusting screw to prevent turning and secure the locknut to 30–40 ft. lbs.

## KICKDOWN SWITCH ADJUSTMENT

### *JM600*

The kickdown switch is located on the upper post of the accelerator pedal. With the pedal fully depressed, a click should be heard just before the pedal bottoms out. If not, loosen the locknut and extend the switch until the pedal lever contacts the switch and a click is heard at the proper time.

## LOW AND REVERSE BAND ADJUSTMENT

### *TorqueFlite A-904*

1. Raise and safely support the front of the car. Drain the transmission fluid and remove the oil pan.
2. The allen socket head adjusting screw is located at the servo end of the strut. Loosen and remove the locknut from the adjusting screw. Tighten the

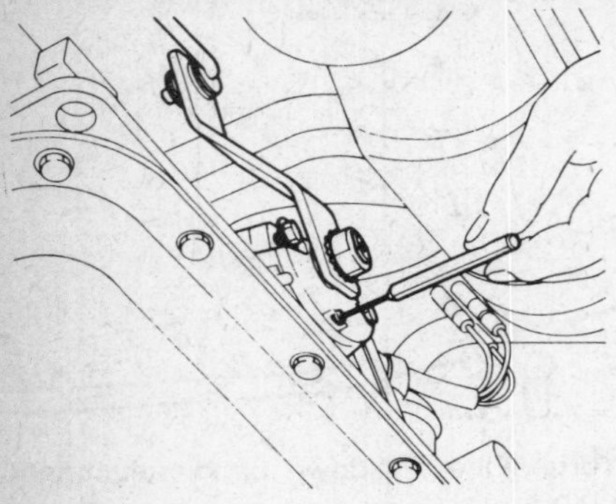

JM600 neutral start switch adjustment

adjusting screw to 43 inch lbs. of true torque. Back off the adjusting screw 7 turns.

3. Install the locknut on the adjusting screw. Hold the adjusting screw in position and tighten the locknut to 25–35 ft. lbs.

4. Reinstall the oil pan using a new gasket. Refill the transmission with the proper amount of transmission fluid.

## NEUTRAL SAFETY SWITCH ADJUSTMENT

### *TorqueFlite A-904*

1. The inhibitor (neutral) switch is located at the base of the shift control under the console cover.

2. Loosen the set screw that retains the shift lever handle to the shift lever. Remove the handle.

3. Remove the screws at the top and rear of the console, place the shift lever in **L** and remove the console. Put the lever in the **P** position.

4. Remove the top and side shift indicator panel mounting screws and pull the panel up. The inhibitor switch can now be disconnected and removed if necessary.

5. Adjust the switch by moving the selector lever to the **N** position. Loosen the mounting screws and adjust the inhibitor switch so that the pin on the forward end of the rod assembly will be in the position near the lobe of the detent plate and that this position will be at the front end of the range of the N connection of the switch. Temporarily tighten the switch mounting screws. After adjusting the selector lever clearance to 0.059 in., tighten the mounting screws.

6. To test the switch, disconnect the wiring connector and set the selector lever in each of its positions. With a continuity tester connected, current should be available in the park, neutral and reverse positions only. Replace the switch if necessary. Install the console and shift handle.

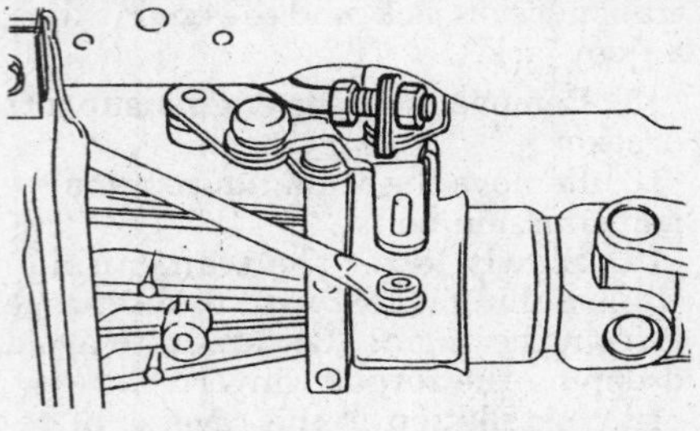

TorqueFlite throttle rod adjustment point

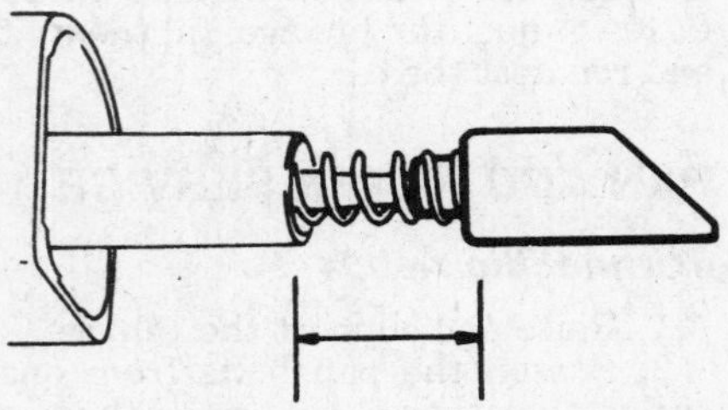

JM600 throttle rod adjustment point

### *JM600*

1. Place the selector lever in **NEUTRAL.**

2. Raise and support the car on jackstands.

3. Remove the lower screw on the neutral start switch.

4. Loosen the switch attaching bolts.

5. Insert a pin, 0.079 in. (2mm) in diameter, into the lower screw hole in the switch. Move the switch until the pin drops into a hole in the rotor behind the switch.

6. Hold the switch in that position and tighten the attaching bolts to 5 ft. lbs.

7. Using an ohmmeter, check the switch across the leads for continuity.

## THROTTLE ROD ADJUSTMENT

### *TorqueFlite A-904*

Warm the engine until it reaches the normal operating temperature. With the carburetor automatic choke off the fast idle cam, adjust the engine idle speed by using a tachometer. Then make the throttle rod adjustment.

1. Install each linkage. Loosen its bolts so that the rods B and C can slide properly.

2. Lightly push the rod A or the transmission throttle lever and the rod C toward the idle stopper and set the rods to idle position. In this case the carburetor automatic choke must be fully released. Tighten the bolt securely to connect the rods B and C.

3. Make sure that when the carburetor throttle valve is wide-open, the transmission throttle lever smoothly moves from idle to wide-open position (operating angle; 45–54 degrees) and that there is some room in the lever stroke.

**NOTE: Make sure that when the throttle linkage alone is returned slowly from the fully open throttle position, that the transmission throttle lever completely returns to the idle position by spring force.**

### *JM600*

1. Apply chassis lube to all sliding parts.

2. Place the selector in the **NEUTRAL** position.

3. Turn the adjusting cam until the distance between the adjusting cam and the selector lever end is 15–16mm.

## DOWNSHIFT SOLENOID INSPECTION

### *JM600*

1. Raise and support the car on jackstands.

2. Uncouple the connectors on the wiring at the solenoid.

**NOTE: Transmission fluid will drain from the hole after the solenoid is removed. Have a drain pan ready to catch it.**

3. Remove the solenoid and O-ring.

4. Connect a 12V source across the solenoid wire to verify that the plunger is operational. If not, replace it.

5. Apply a coating of clean transmission fluid to the O-ring and install the solenoid. Refill the transmission.

# AUTOMATIC TRANSAXLE

## REMOVAL & INSTALLATION

### *KM Series*

**NOTE: The transaxle and converter must be removed and installed as an assembly.**

1. Remove the battery and tray. On cars with a turbocharger, remove the air cleaner case.

2. Disconnect the throttle control cable at the carburetor and the manual control cable at the transaxle.

3. Disconnect from the transaxle: the inhibitor switch (neutral safety) connecter, fluid cooler hoses and the 4

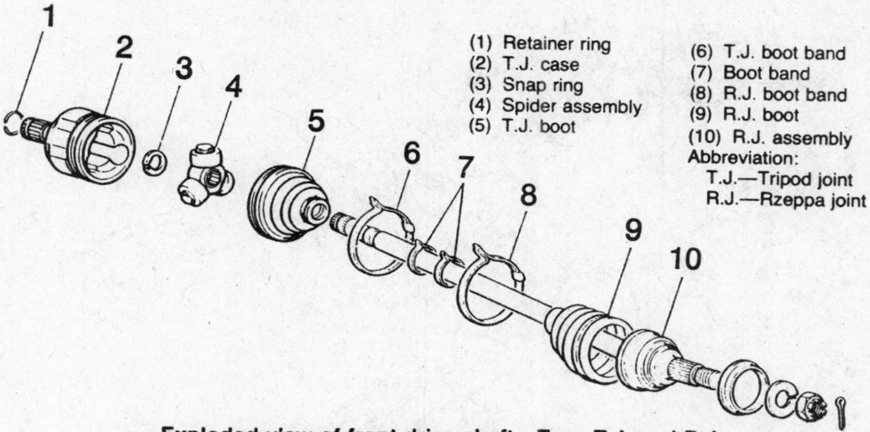


**Exploded view of front drive shaft—Type T.J. and R.J.**

upper bolts connecting the engine to the transaxle.

**NOTE: Cap oil cooler hoses to prevent fluid loss.**

4. Jack up the car and support on jackstands.
5. Remove the front wheels. Remove the engine splash shield.
6. Drain the transaxle fluid.
7. Disconnect the stabilizer bar at the lower arms, and disconnect the control arms from the body. Remove the right and left driveshafts from the transaxle case. See halfshaft removal in this section.
8. Disconnect the speedometer cable. Remove the starter motor.
9. Remove the lower cover from the converter housing. Remove the 3 bolts connecting the converter to the engine drive plate.

**NOTE: Never support the full weight of the transaxle on the engine drive plate.**

10. Turn and force the converter back and away from the engine drive plate.
11. Support the weight of the engine from above (chain hoist). Support the transaxle and remove the remaining mounting bolts.
12. Remove the transaxle mount insulator bolt.
13. Remove (slide away from the engine) and lower the transaxle and converter a an assembly.
14. To install reverse the removal procedure. Be sure to connect all controls, wiring and hoses. Use new retaining rings when installing the drive axles. Torque all indicated 7T bolts to 39 ft. lbs.; all indicated 10T bolts to 25 ft. lbs.

## PAN AND FILTER SERVICE

### *KM Series*

1. Jack up the front of the car and support it safely on jackstands. Remove splash shield.
2. Slide a drain pan under the differential drain plug. Loosen and remove the plug and drain the fluid. Move the drain pan under the transaxle oil pan, remove the plug and drain the fluid. The transmission fluid cannot all be drained by just draining the oil pan.
3. Remove the pan retaining bolts and remove the pan.
4. The filter may be serviced at this time.
5. Use a new oil pan gasket and reinstall the pan in the reverse order of removal.
6. Replace both drain plugs. Lower car. Refill the transmission with 4.2 qts. of Dexron®II fluid. Start the engine and allow to idle for at least 2 minutes. With the parking brake applied, move the selector to each position ending in neutral.
7. Add sufficient fluid to bring the level to the lower mark. Recheck the fluid level after the transmission is up to normal operating temperature.

## KICKDOWN BAND ADJUSTMENT

### *KM170, KM176*

**NOTE: No adjustment is possible on most other KM Series Transaxles.**

1. Wipe all dirt and other contamination from the kickdown servo cover and surrounding area. The cover is located to the right of the dipstick hole.
2. Remove the snapring and then the cover.
3. Loosen the locknut.
4. Holding the kickdown servo piston from turning, tighten the adjusting screw to 7.2 ft. lbs. (84 inch lbs.) and then back it off. Repeat the tightening and backing off 2 times in order to ensure seating of the band on the drum.
5. Tighten the adjusting screw to 3.6 ft. lbs. (42 inch lbs.) and back off 3.5 turns (counterclockwise) on KM170; 2–2 1/4 on KM176.
6. Holding the adjusting screw against rotation, tighten the locknut nut to 11–15 ft. lbs. on KM170; 18–23 ft. lbs on KM176.
7. Install a new seal ring (D-shaped) in the groove in the outside surface of the cover. Use care not to distort the seal ring.
8. Install the cover and then the snapring.

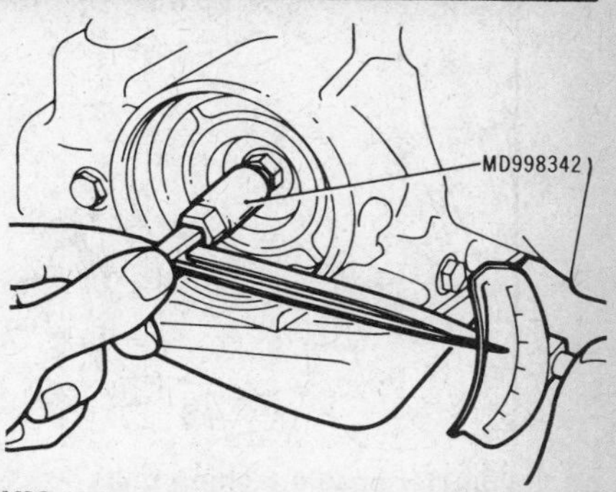


**KM 170, 176 kickdown band adjustment point**

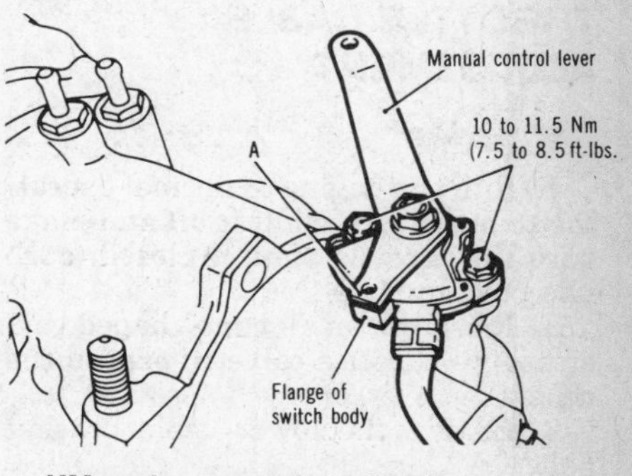


**KM series neutral start switch adjustment**

## NEUTRAL SAFETY SWITCH ADJUSTMENT

### *KM Series*

1. Place manual control lever in the **Neutral** position.
2. Loosen the 2 switch attaching bolts. Switch is located on side of transmission.
3. Turn the switch body until the flat end of the manual lever overlaps the square end of the switch body flange.
4. While keeping the switch body flange and manual lever aligned torque the 2 attaching bolts to 7.5–8.5 ft. lbs.

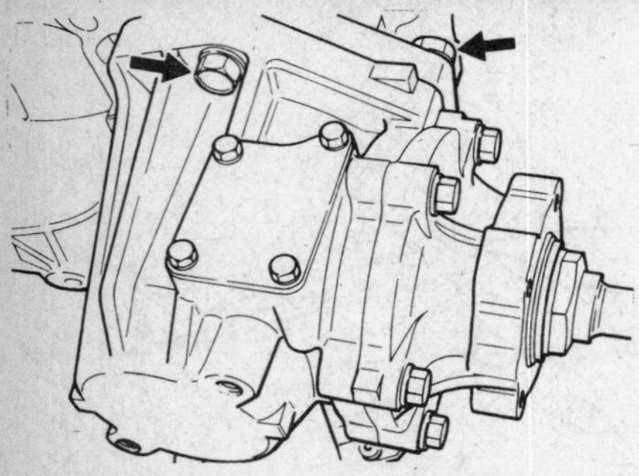

Transfer case attaching bolts

## THROTTLE CABLE ADJUSTMENT

### *KM Series*

1. Run the engine to normal operating temperature. Shut it off and make sure the throttle plate is closed (curb idle position).
2. Raise the small cone-shaped cover on the throttle cable to expose the nipple.
3. Loosen the lower cable bracket bolt.
4. Move the lower cable bracket until the distance between the nipple and the lower cover directly underneath it is 0.02–0.06 in.
5. Tighten the bracket bolt to 9–11 ft. lbs.

# TRANSFER CASE

## REMOVAL & INSTALLATION

### *4WD Vista*

1. Remove the transaxle as described above.
2. Unbolt the transfer case from the transaxle and using a small prybar, separate the two.
3. Installation is the reverse of removal. Torque the attaching bolts to 40–43 ft. lbs.

# DRIVE AXLE

## Halfshafts

## REMOVAL & INSTALLATION

### *Except 4WD Vista*

1. Remove the hub center cap and loosen the driveshaft (axle) nut. Loosen the wheel lug nuts.
2. Lift the car and support it on

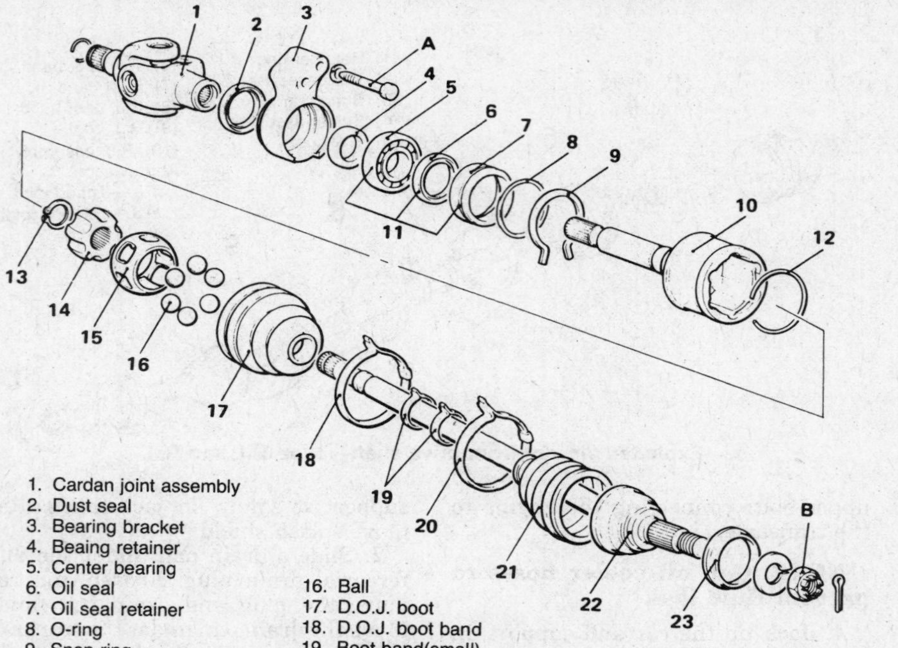


1. Cardan joint assembly
2. Dust seal
3. Bearing bracket
4. Beaing retainer
5. Center bearing
6. Oil seal
7. Oil seal retainer
8. O-ring
9. Snap ring
10. D.O.J. outer race
11. Center bearing assembly
12. Circlip
13. Snap ring
14. D.O.J. inner race
15. D.O.J. cage
16. Ball
17. D.O.J. boot
18. D.O.J. boot band
19. Boot band(small)
20. B.J. boot band
21. B.J. boot
22. B.J. Assembly
23. Dust cover

B.J.—Birfield joint
D.O.J.—Double offset joint

**4-wd Vista halfshaft**

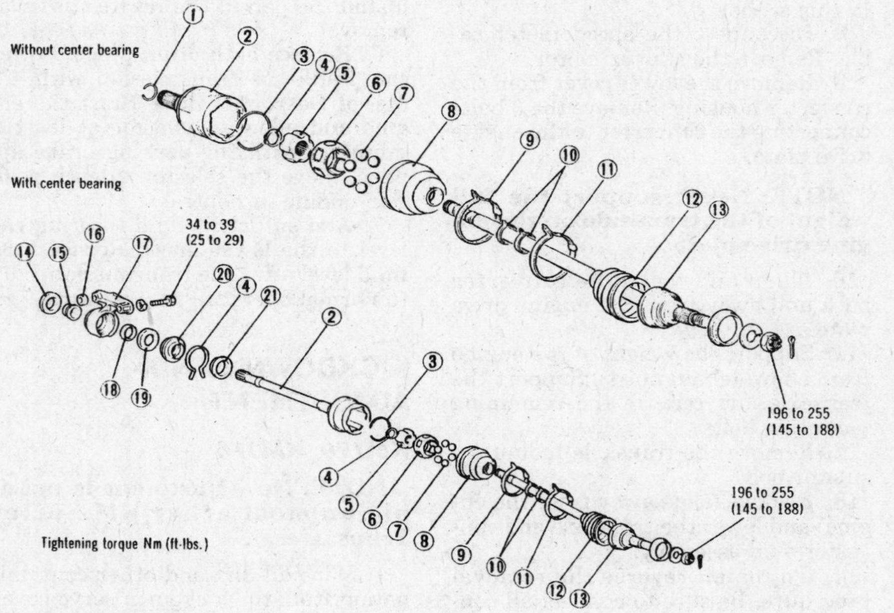


(1) Retainer ring
(2) D.O.J. outer race
(3) Circlip
(4) Snap ring
(5) D.O.J. inner race
(6) D.O.J. cage
(7) Ball
(8) D.O.J. boot
(9) D.O.J. boot band
(10) Boot band
(11) B.J. boot band
(12) B.J. boot
(13) B.J. assembly
(14) Dust cover
(15) Sleeve
(16) Spacer
(17) Center bearing bracket
(18) Bearing retainer
(19) Dust cover
(20) Center bearing assembly
(21) Dust cover

Abbreviation:
D.O.J.—Double offset joint
B.J. —Birfield joint

**Exploded view of front drive shaft—Type D.O.J. and B.J.**

jackstands. Remove the front wheels. Remove the engine splash shield.
3. Remove the lower ball joint and strut bar from the lower control arm.
4. Drain the transaxle fluid.

**NOTE: On models with turbocharger, remove the snapring which secures the center bearing.**

5. Insert a pry bar between the transaxle case (on the raised rib) and the driveshaft double off-set joint case (DOJ) or tripod joint (TJ). Do not insert the pry bar too deeply or the oil seal will be damaged. Move the bar to the right to withdraw the left driveshaft; to the left to remove the right driveshaft.

**NOTE: In the case of the TJ–RJ driveshaft be sure to hold the TJ case and pull out the shaft straight. Simply pulling the shaft out of position could cause damage to the TJ boot or the spider assembly slipping from the case.**

6. Plug the transaxle case with a clean rag to prevent dirt from entering the case.
7. Use a puller-driver mounted on the wheel studs to push the driveshaft from the front hub. Take care to prevent the spacer from falling out of place.

**NOTE: On models with a center bearing, after forcing out the driveshaft, remove it by lightly tapping the DOJ outer race with a plastic hammer.**

8. Assembly is the reverse of removal. Insert the driveshaft into the hub first, then install the transaxle end. Torque the shaft nut to 180 ft. lbs.

**NOTE: Always use a new retaining ring every time the driveshaft is removed.**

9. Installation of the old parts is the reverse of removal after they have been re-greased. To install the kit, use the grease supplied with the kit and apply an amount to the inner race and cage. Install the inner race and cock slightly.
10. Apply grease to the balls and install them in the cage. Place the inner race on the driveshaft and install the snap-ring. Apply grease to the outer race and install. Install the boots and bands.
11. Install the driveshaft using a new retainer ring.

### *4WD Vista*

#### LEFT SIDE

1. Remove the hub cap and halfshaft nut.
2. Raise and support the car on jackstands.
3. Remove the front wheels.
4. Drain the transaxle fluid.
5. Disconnect the lower ball joint from the knuckle.
6. Remove the strut and stabilizer bar from the lower arm.
7. Remove the center bearing ssnapring from the bearing bracket.
8. Lightly tap the double off-set joint outer race with a wood mallet and disconnect the halfshaft from the cardan joint.
9. Disconnect the halfshaft from the bearing bracket.
10. Using a 2-jawed puller secured to the hub lugs, press the halfshaft from the hub.
11. Unbolt and remove the bearing bracket.
12. Using a wood mallet, lightly tap the cardan joint yoke and remove it from the transaxle. Never pry the cardan joint from the transaxle. Prying will damage the cardan joint dust cover.
13. Install the cardan joint.
14. Apply a coating of chassis lube on the center bearing.
15. Attach a new O-ring to the oil seal retainer.
16. Install the bearing bracket. Torque the bolts to 40 ft. lbs.
17. Insert the center bearing in the bearing bracket, making sure it is fully seated, then secure it with the ssnapring.
18. Coat the halfshaft splines with chassis lube and slide it into the cardan joint.
19. Slide the halfshaft into the hub and install the nut. Torque the nut to 188 ft. lbs.

#### RIGHT SIDE

The right side shaft is serviced in the same manner as those on other front wheel drive models. See the procedures above.

## CV–JOINT OVERHAUL

**For all CV-Joint removal, installation and overhaul procedures, please refer to "CV-Joint Overhaul" in the Unit Repair section.**

# Driveshafts and U–Joints

## REMOVAL & INSTALLATION

### *All Except 4WD Vista*

1. Matchmark the rear flange yoke and the differential pinion flange.
2. On late models with a 2 piece driveshaft, remove the center support mounting bolts. Remove the bolts from the rear flange. Remove the driveshaft by pulling it from the rear of the transmission extension housing.

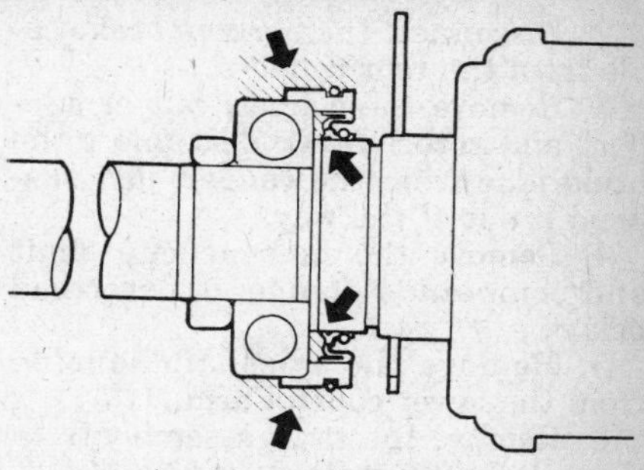
Lubricant application points

**NOTE: Place a container under the transmission extension housing to collect any oil leakage when the driveshaft is removed.**

3. To install the shaft, align the front sleeve yoke with the splines of the transmission output shaft and push the driveshaft into the extension housing.

**NOTE: Be careful not to damage the rear transmission seal lip upon installation.**

4. Align the matchmarks on the rear yokes, install the bolts, and tighten securely. Secure center support mounting bolts.
5. Inspect the oil level of the transmission.

### *4WD Vista*

1. Raise and support the car on jackstands.
2. Drain the transfer case.
3. Matchmark the differential companion flange and the driveshaft flange yoke.
4. Unbolt the driveshaft from the differential flange.
5. Remove the 2 center bearing attaching nuts.

**NOTE: Make sure the flat washer and the adjusting spacer are not interchanged. Keep them separate for assembly.**

6. Pull the driveshaft from the transfer case. Be careful to avoid damaging the transfer case oil seal.
7. Installation is the reverse of removal. Torque the center bearing nuts to 25–30 ft. lbs.; the driveshaft-to-differential flange nuts to 20–25 ft. lbs.

# Rear Axle Shaft and/or Bearing

## REMOVAL & INSTALLATION

### *Conquest*

1. Raise and support the car on jackstands.

2. Disconnect the parking brake cable from the rear calipers.
3. Remove the caliper, caliper support and rotor. Don't disconnect the brake line from the caliper, just suspend it out of the way.
4. Remove the intermediate shaft and companion flange as described below.
5. Remove the axleshaft housing from the lower control arm.
6. Remove the strut assembly from the axleshaft housing.
7. Loosen the companion flange mounting nut and tap the axleshaft out of the housing with a plastic mallet. Be careful to avoid scratching the oil seal.
8. Remove the spacer and dust covers from inside the housing.

**NOTE: Don't remove the bearings unless they are to be replaced, since they will be damaged during removal.**

9. Remove the outer bearing with a puller.
10. Using a brass drift, drive the inner bearing and seal from the housing.
11. Press the new outer bearing onto the shaft with the seal side facing the flange side of the shaft.
12. Pack the housing with lithium based wheel bearing grease.
13. Press the inner bearing onto the shaft with the seal side facing the companion flange side of the shaft.
14. Grease the seal bore in the housing and drive the new seal into position.
15. Install the dust covers.
16. Insert the axleshaft and spacer into the housing and attach the companion flange.
17. Place the housing in a vise and install and tighten the companion flange nut to 200–220 ft. lbs.
18. Install all other parts in reverse order of removal. Check axleshaft end-play with a dial indicator. End-play should be 0.031 in. If end-play exceeds the limit, either the bearing needs replacing or the shaft bearings are not assembled properly.

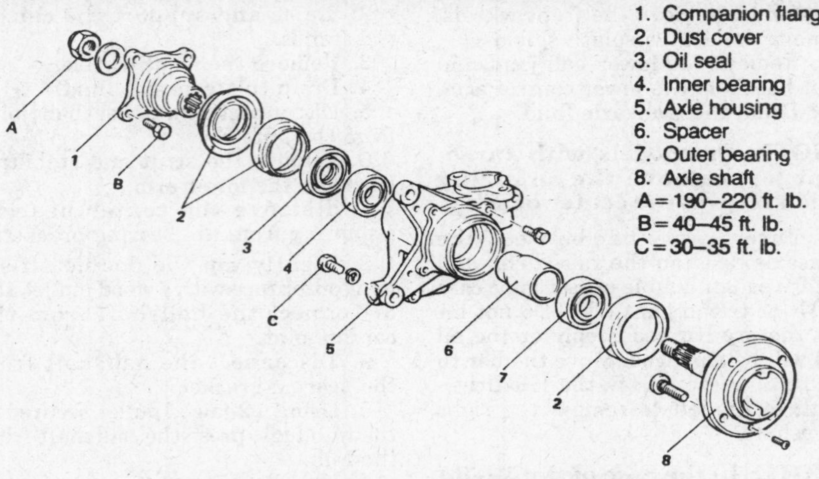


Conquest rear axle axleshaft and housing assembly

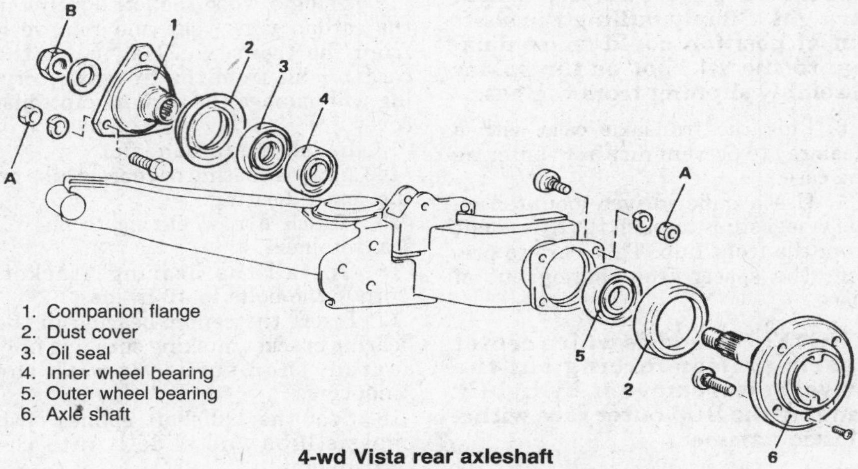


4-wd Vista rear axleshaft

### *4WD Vista*

1. Raise and support the rear of the car on jackstands placed under the frame.
2. Remove the rear wheels.
3. Remove the brake drums.
4. Remove the 3 bolts securing the axleshaft flange to the intermediate shaft flange.
5. Using special tool MB900767, remove the axleshaft flange nut.
6. Using a slidehammer connected to a 2-jawed adapter secured under 2 lug nuts, pull the axleshaft from the housing.
7. Remove the lower arm as described later in this section.
8. Using special tool MB990560, remove the dust cover and the outer wheel bearing and seal from the axleshaft at the same time. Discard the seal.
9. Using driver MB990938 and adapter MB990927, or equivalent, drive the inner bearing and seal from the housing. The new bearing should be thoroughly packed with chassis lube and driven into place with the same tools.
10. Install a new inner bearing seal with a seal driver.
11. Using a special tool MB990799, or similar driver, tape a new dust cover into place. Tap evenly around the tool to seat the cover.
12. Coat the lip of a new seal with chassis lube and pack the new outer bearing thoroughly with chassis lube.
13. Using MB990560 and a press, install the bearing and seal.
14. Mount the inner arm in a vise and, using a press, install the axleshaft.
15. Install the axleshaft and inner arm assembly.
16. Torque the axleshaft nut to 160 ft. lbs.
17. Connect the axleshaft and intermediate shaft flanges and torque the bolts to 43 ft. lbs.

## Intermediate Shaft

### REMOVAL & INSTALLATION

#### *Conquest*

1. Remove the 4 bolts and separate the intermediate shaft from the companion flange.
2. Using a slidehammer and adapter, remove the intermediate shaft from the differential. Be careful to avoid damaging the oil seal.
3. If the oil seal is to be replaced, pry it from the housing.
4. Installation is the reverse of removal. Coat the part of the intermediate shaft that passes through the seal, with chassis lube. The shaft can be driven into place using the

slidehammer. Before and after coupling the intermediate shaft and companion flange, check to make sure that the shaft does not slide from the differential housing.

### *4WD Vista*

1. Raise and support the rear on jackstands placed under the frame.
2. Disconnect the intermediate shaft and axleshaft flanges.
3. Using a small prybar, pry the intermediate shaft from the differential, being careful to avoid scratching the oil seal.
4. Installation is the reverse of removal. Torque the flange bolts to 43 ft. lbs.

## Front Wheel Hub, Knuckle and Bearing

### REMOVAL & INSTALLATION

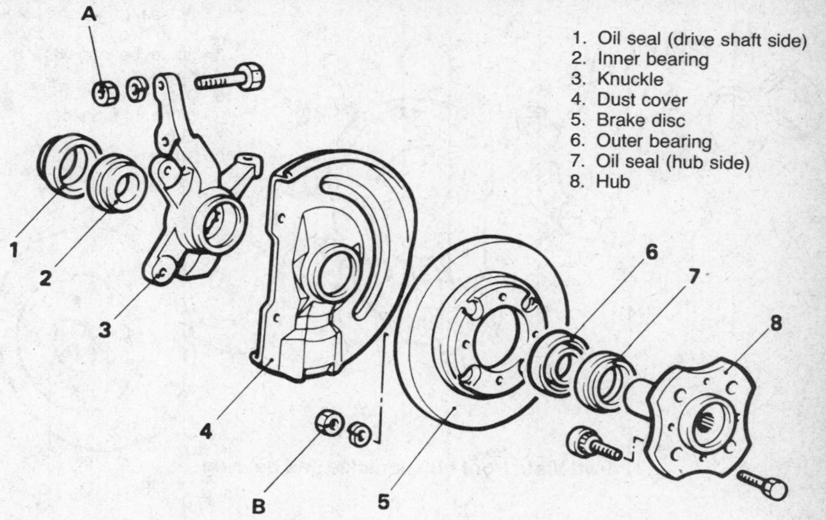


Front hub and knuckle used on 1984 Colt Turbo and 1985 and later Colt

### *1983–84 Non-Turbocharged*

**NOTE: A press and several special tools are needed for this procedure.**

1. Remove the axle shaft.

**NOTE: Keep the bearing spacers separate for installation.**

2. Remove the caliper, and suspend it out of the way, without disconnecting the brake line.
3. Disconnect the tie rod end from the knuckle.
4. Disconnect the strut from the knuckle and remove the hub and knuckle assembly.
5. Pry the hub and knuckle assembly apart. If separation is difficult, mount the knuckle in a vise and drive out the hub with a plastic mallet. Drive out the oil seals, bearings and races with a brass drift.
6. Inspect all parts for wear and damage; replace any suspect parts.
7. Install the outer races of the inner and outer bearings, using a brass drift or press. If a press is used, 4400 lb. installation pressure is necessary.
8. Apply lithium based wheel bearing grease to the inside of the knuckle, the oil seals and bearings. Thoroughly pack the bearings making sure that clean grease permeates all cavities.
9. If separated, assemble the hub and rotor. Torque the bolts to 36 ft. lbs.
10. Install the inner race of the outer bearing using a brass drift. Using a driver, install the outer oil seal.
11. Using special tool MB990776–A, hold the inner race of the outer bearing, while pressing the hub into the knuckle. 1100 lb. of press pressure is needed.
12. After installing the inner race of the inner bearing, install the inner oil seal.

**NOTE: At this point, the correct spacer between the front axle and hub must be determined. The spacers are vital for establishing front wheel bearing preload.**

13. Install spacer selection gauge MB9907959 on the hub and tighten the nut to 14–15 ft. lbs. Prevent the tool from turning while tightening the nut.
14. Rotate the hub and tool several turns to seat the bearings.
15. Install a dial indicator on the tool and load about 5mm of travel on the indicator, then zero the dial.
16. While holding the threaded stud of the tool with a wrench, back off the nut until travel no longer registers on the gauge. Note the total indicator reading.

**NOTE: Be sure that the tool does not turn during this procedure. Hold it in a vise if necessary. Be sure to back off the nut SLOWLY to give an accurate indicator reading.**

17. Repeat Step 16 and average the two readings. Use the averaged reading to calculate what spacers will be needed.
18. Install the spacer in the hub with the chamfered side toward the knuckle.
19. Installation of the hub and knuckle is the reverse of the removal. Observe the following torques:
   Axleshaft nut–88–130 ft. lbs.
   Knuckle-to-strut–55–65 ft. lbs.
   Ball joint-to-arm–70–88 ft. lbs.
   Lower arm-to-strut–70–88 ft. lbs.
   Knuckle-to-tie rod–11–25 ft. lbs.

### *1984 Turbocharged Colt and 1985–90 Colt and 2WD Vista*

**NOTE: The following procedure requires the use of several special tools.**

1. Remove the axleshaft nut.
2. Raise and support the car with jackstands positioned so that the wheels hang freely.
3. Remove the wheels.
4. Remove the caliper and suspend it out of the way without disconnecting the brake hose.
5. Disconnect the lower ball joint from the knuckle.
6. Disconnect the tie rod end from the knuckle.
7. Using a 2-jawed puller, press the axleshaft from the hub.
8. Unbolt the strut from the knuckle. Remove the hub and knuckle assembly from the car.
9. Install first the arm, then the body of special tool MB991056 (Colt) or MB991001 (Vista) on the knuckle and tighten the nut.
10. Using special tool MB990998 or MB990781, separate the hub from the knuckle.

**NOTE: Prying or hammering will damage the bearing. Use these special tools, or their equivalent to separate the hub and knuckle.**

11. Place the knuckle in a vise and separate the rotor from the hub.
12. Using special tools, C–293–PA, SP–3183 and MB990781, remove the

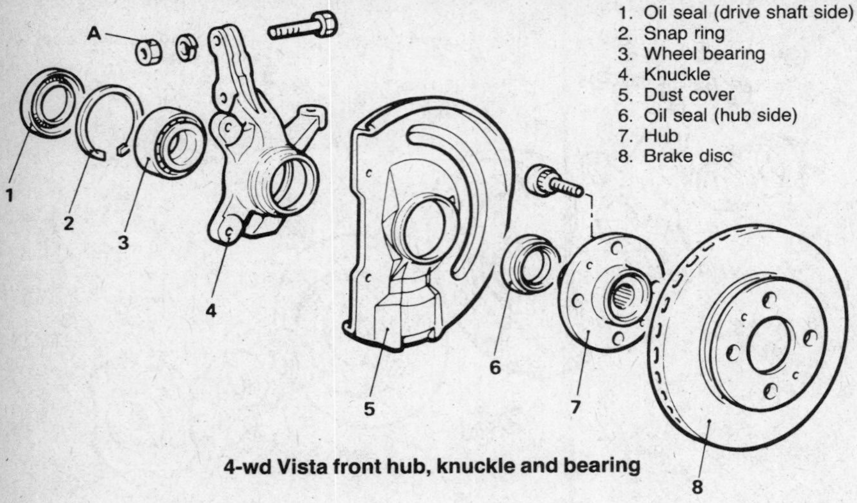


1. Oil seal (drive shaft side)
2. Snap ring
3. Wheel bearing
4. Knuckle
5. Dust cover
6. Oil seal (hub side)
7. Hub
8. Brake disc

4-wd Vista front hub, knuckle and bearing

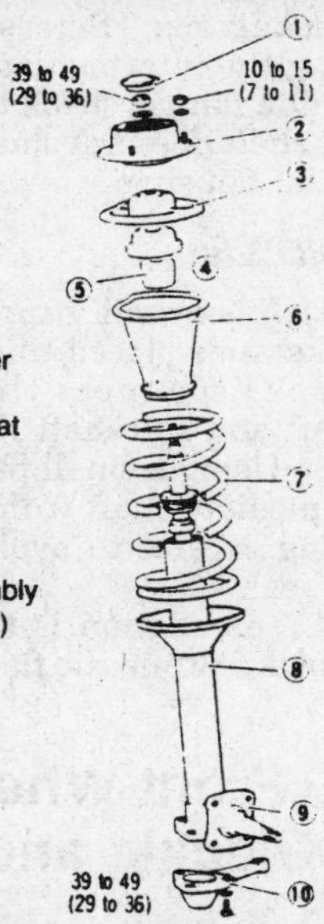

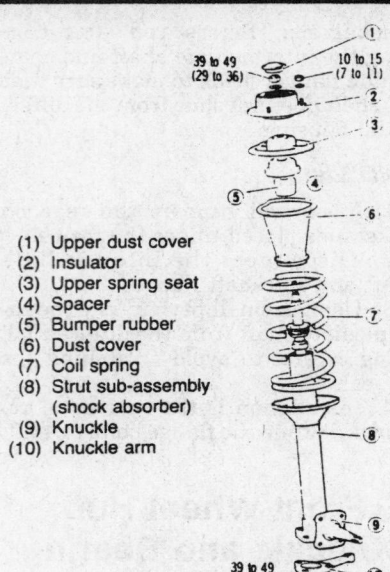

(1) Upper dust cover
(2) Insulator
(3) Upper spring seat
(4) Spacer
(5) Bumper rubber
(6) Dust cover
(7) Coil spring
(8) Strut sub-assembly (shock absorber)
(9) Knuckle
(10) Knuckle arm

Front strut on all rear wheel drive cars except Conquest

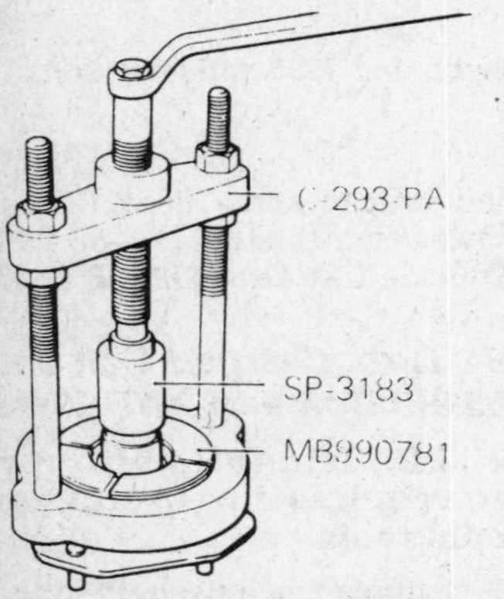


Removing the outer bearing inner race from the hub, using the special tools described

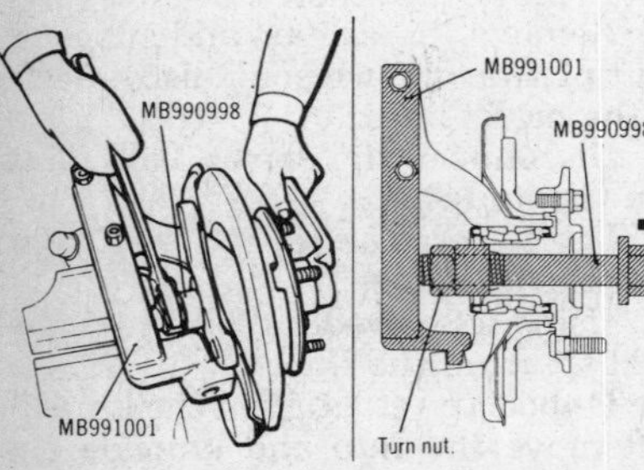


Using special tools to remove the hub from the knuckle

outer bearing inner race.

13. Drive the oil seal and inner bearing inner race from the knuckle with a brass drift.

14. Drive out both outer races in a similar fashion.

**NOTE: Always replace bearings and races as a set. Never replace just an inner or outer bearing. If either is in need of replacement, both sets must be replaced.**

15. Thoroughly clean and inspect all parts. Any suspect part should be replaced.

16. Pack the wheel bearings with lithium based wheel bearing grease. Coat the inside of the knuckle with similar grease and pack the cavities in the knuckle. Apply a thin coating of grease to the outer surface of the races before installation.

17. Using special tools C–3893 and MB990776, install the outer races.

18. Install the rotor on the hub and torque the bolts to 36–43 ft. lbs.

19. Drive the outer bearing inner race into position.

20. Coat the out rim and lip of the oil seal and drive the hub side oil seal into place, using a seal driver.

21. Place the inner bearing in the knuckle.

22. Mount the knuckle in a vise. Position the hub and knuckle together. Install tool MB99098 and tighten the tool to 147–192 ft. lbs. Rotate the hub to seat the bearing.

23. With the knuckle still in the vise measure the hub starting torque with an in. lb. torque wrench and tool MB990998. Starting torque should be 11.5 inch lbs., or less. If the starting torque is 0, measure the hub bearing axial play with a dial indicator. If axial play exceeds 0.0078 in., while the nut is tightened to 145–192 ft. lbs., the assembly has not been done correctly. Disassemble the knuckle and hub and start again.

24. Remove the special tool.

25. Place the outer bearing in the hub and drive the seal into place.

26. The remainder of installation is the reverse of removal.

### 4WD Vista

**NOTE: The following procedure requires the use of several special tools.**

1. Remove the hub cap and halfshaft nut.

2. Raise and support the car on jackstands.

3. Remove the front wheels.

4. Drain the transaxle fluid.

5. Disconnect the lower ball joint from the knuckle.

6. Remove the strut and stabilizer bar from the lower arm.

7. Remove the center bearing snapring from the bearing bracket.

8. Lightly tap the double off-set joint outer race with a wood mallet and disconnect the halfshaft from the cardan joint.

9. Disconnect the halfshaft from the bearing jacket.

10. Using a 2-jawed puller secured to the hub lugs, press the halfshaft from the hub.

11. Unbolt the strut from the hub. Remove the hub and knuckle assembly from the car.

12. Install first the arm, then the body of special tool MB991001 on the knuckle and tighten the nut.

13. Using special tool MB9900998, separate the hub from the knuckle and tighten the nut.

**NOTE: Prying or hammering will damage the bearing. Use these special tools, or their equivalent, to separate the hub and knuckle.**

14. Matchmark the hub and rotor. The rotor should slide from the hub. If not, insert M8x1.25 bolts in the holes between the lugs and tighten them alternately to press the hub from the rotor. NEVER HAMMER THE ROTOR TO REMOVE IT!

15. Using a 2-jawed puller, remove the outer bearing inner race.

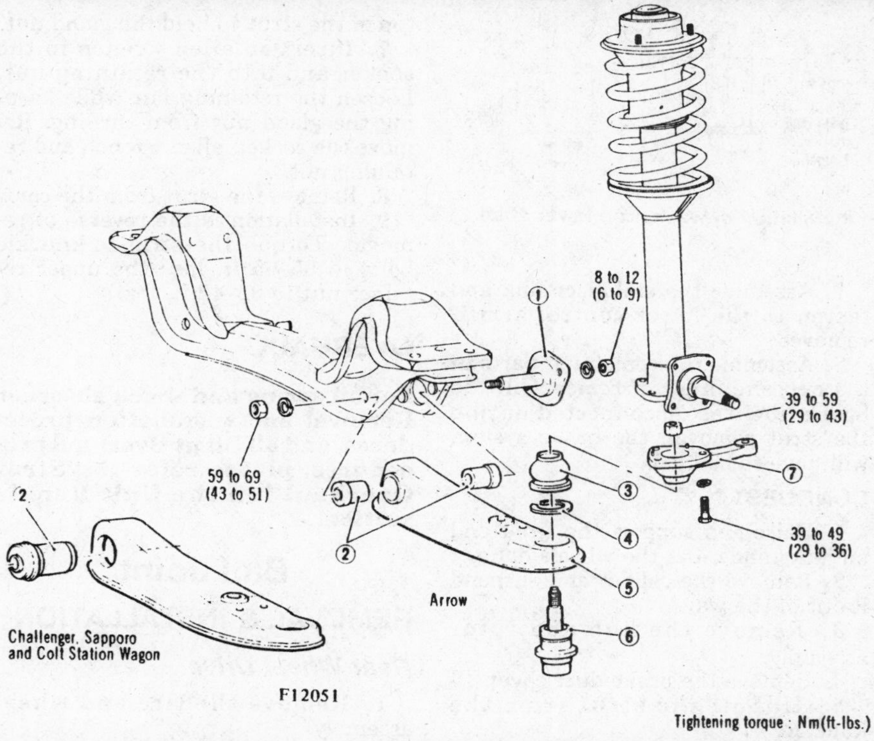


**Lower control arm and ball joint used on all rear wheel drive cars, except Conquest**

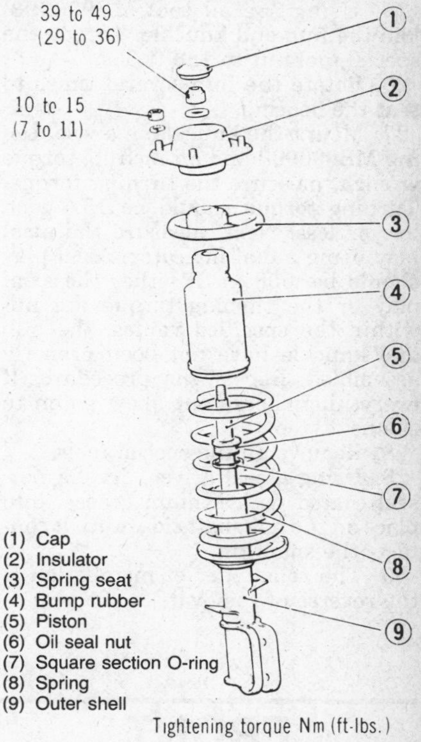


**1983–84 Colt FWD front strut assembly**

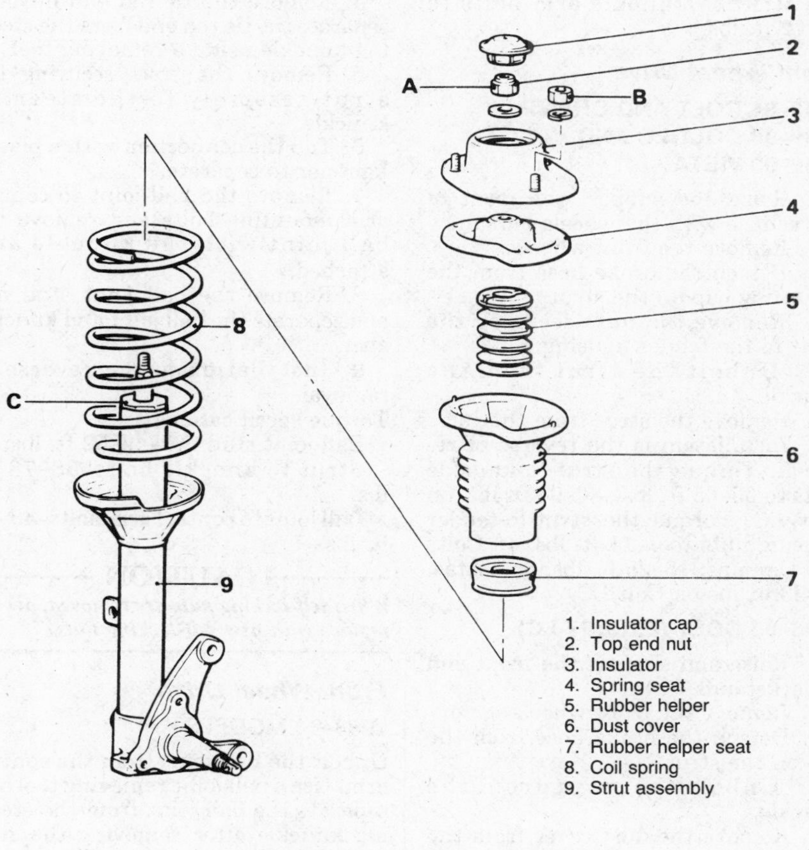


**Conquest front strut**

16. Remove and discard the outer oil seal.
17. Remove and discard the inner oil sea.
18. Remove the bearing snapring from the knuckle.
19. Using special tools C–4628 and MB991056 or MB991001, remove the bearing from the knuckle. Using a driver, drive the bearing from the knuckle.

**NOTE: Always replace bearings and races as a set. Never replace just an inner or outer bearing. If either is in need of replacement, both sets must be replaced.**

20. Thoroughly clean and inspect all parts. Any suspect part should be replace.
21. Pack the wheel bearings with lithium based wheel bearing grease. Coat the inside of the knuckle with similar grease and pack the cavities in the knuckle. Apply a thin coating of grease to the outer surface of the races before installation.
22. Using special tools C–4171 and MB990985, press the bearing into place in the knuckle. Install the snapring.
23. Coat the lips of a new hub-side seal with lithium grease. Using a seal driver, install the seal. Make sure it is flush.
24. Install the rotor on the hub.

25. Using special tool MB990998, join the hub and knuckle. Torque the special tool nut to 188 ft. lbs.

26. Rotate the hub several times to seat the bearing.

27. Mount the knuckle in a vise. Using MB990998 and an inch lb. torque wrench, measure the turning torque. Turning torque should be 15.6 inch lbs. or less. Next, measure the axial play using a dial indicator. Axial play should be .008 in. If either the axial play or the turning torque are not within the specified values, the hub and knuckle have not been properly assembled. Repeat the procedure. If everything checks out okay, go on to the next step.

28. Remove all the special tools.

29. Using a seal driver, drive a new seal coated with lithium grease, into place on the halfshaft side, until it contacts the snapring.

30. The remainder of installation is the reverse of removal.

# FRONT SUSPENSION

## MacPherson Strut

### REMOVAL & INSTALLATION

#### *Rear Wheel Drive*

**ALL EXCEPT CONQUEST**

1. Loosen the lug nuts, jack up the front of the car (after blocking the rear wheels) and support safely on jackstands.

2. Remove the brake caliper, hub and brake disc rotors. Disconnect the stabilizer link from the lower arm, remove the 3 steering knuckle-to-strut assembly bolts.

3. Carefully force the lower control arm down and separate the strut assembly and the steering knuckle. Unscrew the 3 retaining nuts at the top and remove the strut assembly.

**NOTE: On some models the lower splash shield may interfere with the strut removal.**

4. To install the strut, position the strut assembly in the fender. Install the upper retaining nuts hand tight.

5. Apply sealer on the mounting flange and fasten the strut assembly to the steering knuckle. Connect the brake hose if removed.

6. Tighten the upper retaining nuts to 7–11 ft. lbs. Torque the knuckle bolts to 30–36 ft. lbs.

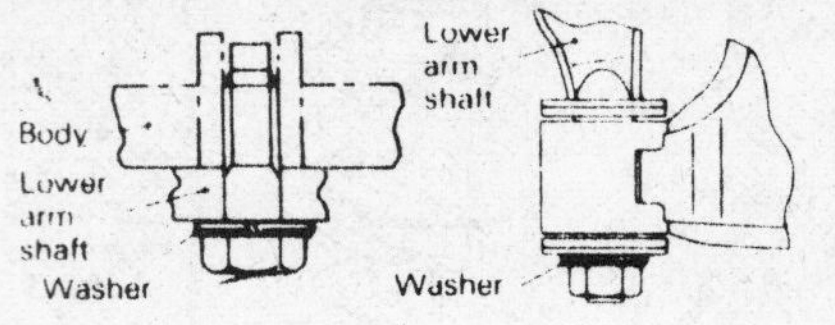


Installation of washer on lower shaft

7. Assemble the stabilizer link and fasten to the lower control arm if removed.

8. Assemble the remaining parts in the opposite order of removal. If the brake line was disconnected during the strut removal, the brake system will have to be bled.

**CONQUEST**

1. Raise and support the front end on jackstands. Let the wheels hang.

2. Remove the caliper and suspend it out of the way.

3. Remove the hub and rotor assembly.

4. Remove the brake dust cover.

5. Unbolt the strut from the knuckle.

6. Remove the strut to fender mounting nuts and remove the strut. Install in the reverse order. Torque the strut to fender nuts; 18–25 ft. lbs.; the strut to knuckle arm bolts to 58–72 ft. lbs.

#### *Front Wheel Drive*

**1983–84 COLT AND CHAMP, 1989–90 COLT LC AND 1985–90 VISTA**

1. Raise and support the front of the vehicle with the wheels hanging.

2. Remove the front wheels.

3. Detach the brake hose from the mounting clip on the strut.

4. Remove the nuts securing the strut to the fender housing.

5. Unbolt the strut from the knuckle.

6. Remove the strut from the car.

7. Installation is the reverse of removal. Torque the strut-to-knuckle bolts to 55–65 ft. lbs.; 80–94 ft. lbs. on Colt LC. Torque the strut-to-fender housing nuts to 7–11 ft. lbs. on Colts and Champs; 18–25 ft. lbs. on Vistas. 25–33 ft. lbs on Colt LC.

**1985–90 COLT (EXCEPT LC)**

1. Raise and support the front end on jackstands.

2. Remove the front wheels.

3. Detach the brake hose from the clip on the strut.

4. Unbolt the strut from the knuckle.

5. Remove the dust cover from the upper end of the strut.

6. Insert a ½ in. drive socket in the top of the strut to hold the gland nut.

7. Insert an allen wrench in the socket and into the retaining nut. Loosen the retaining nut while keeping the gland nut from turning. Remove the socket, allen wrench and retaining nut.

8. Remove the strut from the car.

9. Installation is the reverse of removal. Torque the strut-to-knuckle bolts to 55–65 ft. lbs.; the upper retainer nut to 33–43 ft. lbs.

### OVERHAUL

**For all spring and shock absorber Removal and Installation procedures, and all Strut Overhaul procedures, please refer to "Strut Overhaul" in the Unit Repair section.**

## Ball Joint

### REMOVAL & INSTALLATION

#### *Rear Wheel Drive*

1. Remove the tire and wheel assembly.

2. Remove the brake caliper and support from the mounting adapter.

3. Anchor assembly out of the way with wire to the strut spring.

4. Remove the tie rod end nut and separate the tie rod end from the steering knuckle using a removing tool.

5. Remove the bolts securing the strut assembly to the steering knuckle.

6. Tap the connection with a plastic hammer to separate.

7. Remove the ball joint to control arm mounting bolts and remove the ball joint with the knuckle arm attached.

8. Remove the ball joint stud nut and separate the ball joint and knuckle arm.

9. Installation is the reverse of removal.

Torque specifications are:

Ball joint stud nut–43–52 ft. lbs.

Strut to knuckle bolts–58–78 ft. lbs.

Ball joint to control arm bolts–43–51 ft. lbs.

**CAUTION**

***When self-locking nuts are removed, always replace with new self-locking nuts.***

#### *Front Wheel Drive*

**1983–84 MODELS**

Unbolt the ball joint from the control arm. Use a ball joint removing tool and separate the ball joint from the steering knuckle after removing the stud retaining nut. Install in the reverse order.

Torque specifications are:
Ball joint to control arm–69–87 ft. lbs.
Ball joint stud nut–40–51 ft. lbs.

#### 1985–90 COLT

The ball joint is not replaceable. The ball joint and lower control arm must be replaced as an assembly.

#### 1985–87 VISTA

**NOTE: On some models covered in the above year span, and on all late model Vistas, ball joint replacement requires Control Arm replacement. If the ball joint is replaceable the procedure requires a hydraulic press.**

1. Disconnect the lower arm.
2. Remove the ball joint dust cover.
3. Using snapring pliers, remove the snapring from the ball joint.
4. Using an adapter plate and driver, such as tool MB990800, press the ball joint from the arm.
5. Installation is the reverse of removal, inverting the tool in the press for installation. Coat the lip and interior of the dust cover with lithium based chassis lube.

## Lower Control Arm

### REMOVAL & INSTALLATION

#### *Rear Wheel Drive*

#### EXCEPT CONQUEST

1. Loosen the lug nuts and then raise the front end of the car.
2. Remove the caliper, hub and disc.
3. Disconnect the stabilizer link and strut bar from the lower control arm. Depending on year, remove idler arm support from the chassis and move steering linkage to gain clearance.
4. Remove the 3 steering knuckle-to-strut assembly bolts.
5. Carefully force the lower control arm down and separate the strut assembly and the steering knuckle.
6. Unscrew the 3 retaining nuts at the top and withdraw the strut assembly, if necessary.
7. Using a puller, disconnect the steering knuckle arm and the tie-rod ball joint.
8. Again using a puller, disconnect the knuckle arm and the lower arm ball joint.
9. Remove the control arm-to-crossmember bolts and remove the control arm.
10. Install the lower arm on the crossmember. Tighten the bolts to 58–69 ft. lbs. The chamfered end of the nut should be facing the round surface of the bracket.
11. Tighten the steering knuckle arm-to-control arm ball joint nut to 52–69 ft. lbs.
12. Install the strut assembly into the fender. Tighten the top mounting nuts to 18–25 ft. lbs.
13. Apply sealer to the lower end of the strut. Install and tighten the strut-to-steering knuckle arm bolts to 58–72 ft. lbs.
14. Assemble the stabilizer link and fasten it and strut bar to the lower control arm.
15. Install the backing plate, brake disc, hub, and caliper. Tighten strut bar to 18–25 ft. lbs.
16. Install the wheel and lower the car.
17. Jounce the car up and down a few times and then tighten the stabilizer bolt to 7–10 ft. lbs.

#### CONQUEST

**NOTE: This procedure requires the use of a special tool.**

1. Raise and support the front end on jackstands.
2. Remove the front wheels.
3. Remove the caliper and suspend it out of the way.
4. Remove the hub and rotor assembly.
5. Disconnect the stabilizer bar and strut bar from the lower arm.
6. Using a separator, remove the attaching nut and disconnect the tie rod from the knuckle arm.
7. Unbolt the strut from the knuckle arm.
8. Unbolt the lower control arm and knuckle arm assembly from the crossmember.
9. Using special tool MB990635, separate the knuckle arm from the lower control arm.
10. Installation is the reverse of removal. Apply sealant to the flange of the knuckle arm where it mates with the strut. Torque the lower control arm shaft bolt to 60–70 ft. lbs.; the ball joint-to-knuckle arm nut to 45–55 ft. lbs.

#### *Front Wheel Drive Models*

#### 1983–84 ALL MODELS

1. Loosen front wheel lugs, block rear wheels, jack up the front of the car and support on jackstands.
2. Remove the front wheels. Remove the lower splash shield.
3. Disconnect the lower ball joint by unfastening the nuts and bolts mounting it to the control arm. It is not necessary to remove the ball joint from the knuckle.
4. Remove the strut bar and the control arm inner mounting nut and bolt. Remove the control arm.
5. Assembly is the reverse of removal.

Torque Specifications are:
Inner mount bolt–69–87 ft. lbs.
Ball joint mount–69–87 ft. lbs.
Ball joint nut–40–51 ft. lbs.

#### 1985–90 COLT

1. Raise and support the front end. Remove the wheels. Remove the splash shield. On models equipped, remove the center crossmember.
2. Disconnect the stabilizer bar from the lower arm.
3. Using a ball joint separator, disconnect the ball joint from the knuckle.
4. Unbolt the lower arm from the body and remove it from the car.

**NOTE: The ball joint cannot be separated from the control arm, but must be replaced as an assembly.**

5. If the stabilizer bar is to be removed, disconnect the tie rod from the knuckle, and unbolt and remove the stabilizer.
6. Check all parts for wear and damage and replace any suspect part.
7. Using an inch lb. torque wrench, check the ball joint starting torque. Nominal starting effort should be 22–87 inch lbs. Replace it if otherwise.
8. Installation is the reverse of removal. Use a new dust cover, the lip and inside of which is coated with lithium based chassis lube. The dust cover should be hammered into place with a driver, such as tool MB990800. Install the stabilizer bar so that the serrations on the horizontal part protrude 6mm to the inside of the clamp and 23mm of threaded stud appear below the nut at the control arm. The washer on the lower arm shaft should be installed as shown in the accompanying illustration. The left side lower arm shaft has left-handed threads. The lower arm shaft nut must be torqued with the wheels hanging freely. Observe the following torques:

Knuckle-to-strut–54–65 ft. lbs. 1989–90; 80–94 ft. lbs. lbs.
Lower arm shaft-to-body–69–87 ft. lbs.
Stabilizer bar-to-body–12–20 ft. lbs.
Ball joint-to-knuckle–44–53 ft. lbs.
Lower arm-to-shaft–70–88 ft. lbs.
Rear Shaft bushing bracket-to-body–43–58 ft. lbs.

#### 1985–90 VISTA

1. Raise and support the front end.
2. Remove the wheels.
3. Disconnect the stabilizer bar and strut bar from the lower arm.
4. Remove the nut and disconnect the ball joint from the knuckle with a separator.
5. Unbolt the lower arm from the crossmember.

6. Check all parts for wear or damage and replace any suspect part.
7. Using an inch lbs. torque wrench, check the ball joint starting torque. Starting torque should be 20–86 inch lbs. If it is not within that range, replace the ball joint.
8. Installation is the reverse of removal. Tighten all fasteners with the wheels hanging freely. Observe the following torques:

Ball joint-to-knuckle–44–53 ft. lbs.

Arm-to-crossmember–2wd: 90–111 ft. lbs.; 4wd: 58–68 ft. lbs.

Stabilizer bar hanger brackets–7–9 ft. lbs.

When installing the stabilizer bar, the nut on the bar-to-crossmember bolts and the bar-to-lower arm bolts, are not torqued, but turned on until a certain length of thread is exposed above the nut:

2wd stabilizer bar-to-crossmember–0.31–0.39 in.

2wd stabilizer bar-to-lower control arm–0.31–0.39 in.

4wd stabilizer bar-to-crossmember–0.31–0.39 in.

4wd stabilizer bar-to-lower arm–0.51–0.59.

## Front Wheel Bearings

**NOTE: Please refer to the "Drive Axle" Section for FWD Models.**

### ADJUSTMENT

#### *Rear Wheel Drive*

1. Remove the wheel and dust cover. Remove the cotter pin and lock cap from the nut.
2. Torque the wheel bearing nut to 14.5 ft. lbs. (19.6 Nm) and then loosen the nut. Retorque the nut to 3.6 ft. lbs. (4.9 Nm) and install the lock cap and cotter pin.
3. Install the dust cover and the wheel.

### REMOVAL & INSTALLATION

1. Remove the caliper (pin type) or the caliper and support (sliding type).

**NOTE: On sliding type calipers, remove the caliper and support as a unit by unfastening the bolts holding it to the adapter. Support the caliper with wire, do not allow the weight to be supported by the brake hose.**

2. Pry off the dust cap. Tap out and discard the cotter pin. Remove the locknut.
3. Being careful not to drop the outer bearing, pull off the brake disc and wheel hub.

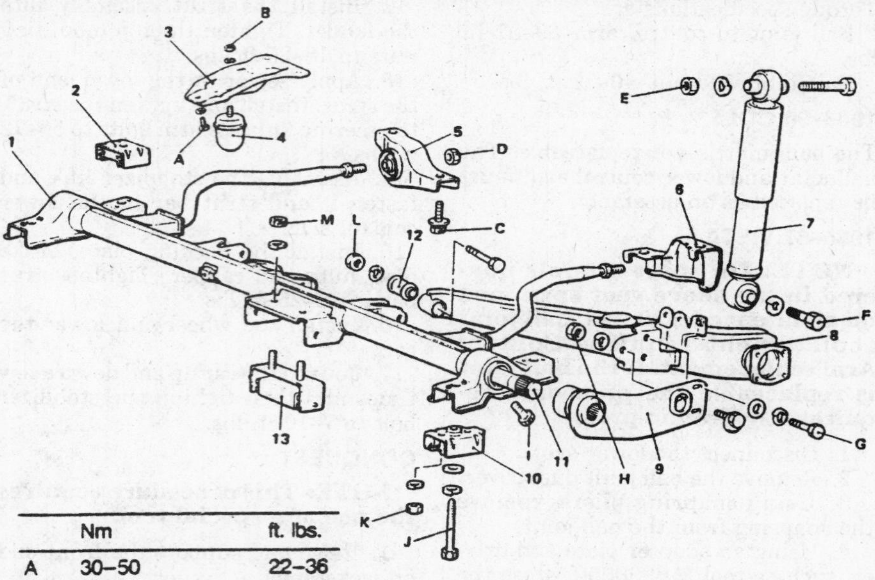

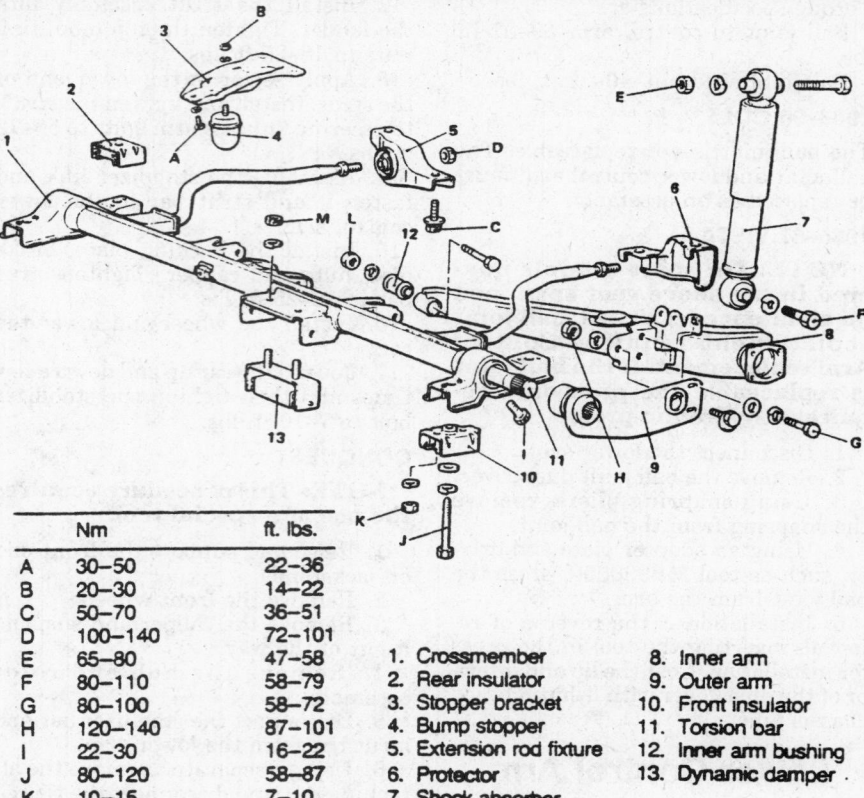

| | Nm | ft. lbs. |
|---|---|---|
| A | 30–50 | 22–36 |
| B | 20–30 | 14–22 |
| C | 50–70 | 36–51 |
| D | 100–140 | 72–101 |
| E | 65–80 | 47–58 |
| F | 80–110 | 58–79 |
| G | 80–100 | 58–72 |
| H | 120–140 | 87–101 |
| I | 22–30 | 16–22 |
| J | 80–120 | 58–87 |
| K | 10–15 | 7–10 |
| L | 70–90 | 51–65 |
| M | 19–28 | 14–20 |

1. Crossmember
2. Rear insulator
3. Stopper bracket
4. Bump stopper
5. Extension rod fixture
6. Protector
7. Shock absorber
8. Inner arm
9. Outer arm
10. Front insulator
11. Torsion bar
12. Inner arm bushing
13. Dynamic damper

4wd Vista rear suspension

4. Remove the grease inside the wheel hub.
5. Using a brass drift, carefully drive the outer bearing race out of the hub.
6. Remove the inner bearing seal and bearing.
7. Check the bearings for wear or damage and replace them if necessary.
8. Coat the inner surface of the hub with grease.
9. Grease the outer surface of the bearing race and drift it into place in the hub.
10. Pack the inner and outer wheel bearings with grease. (see repacking.)

**NOTE: If the brake disc has been removed and/or replaced; tighten the retaining bolts to 25–29 ft. lbs.**

11. Install the inner bearing in the hub. Being careful not to distort it, install the oil seal with its lip facing the bearing. Drive the seal on until its outer edge is even with the edge of the hub.
12. Install the hub/disc assembly on the spindle, being careful not to damage the oil seal.
13. Install the outer bearing, washer, and spindle nut. Adjust the wheel bearing.

## Front Wheel Alignment

### CASTER AND CAMBER

Caster is preset at the factory. It requires adjustment only if the suspension and steering linkage components are damaged, in which case, repair is accomplished by replacing the damaged part. A slight caster adjustment can be made by moving the nuts on the front anchors of the strut bars.

### TOE-IN

Toe-in is the difference in the distance between the front wheels, as measured at both the front and the rear of the front tires.

Toe-in is adjusted by turning the tie rod turnbuckles as necessary. The turnbuckles should always be tightened or loosened the same amount for both tie rods; the difference in length between the 2 tie rods should not exceed 0.2 in. On the Challenger and Sapporo, only the left tie rod is adjustable.

# REAR SUSPENSION

## Shock Absorbers

### REMOVAL & INSTALLATION

#### *1983–90 Except 4WD Vista*

1. Remove the hub cap or wheel cover. Loosen the lug nuts.
2. Raise the rear of the car. Support the car with jackstands.

**NOTE: The body sill is marked with 2 dimples to locate the support position. Never place a stand anywhere but between these marks or the body can be damaged.**

3. Remove the wheel. Remove the upper mounting bolt and nut.
4. While holding the bottom stud mount nut with one wrench, remove the locknut with another wrench.
5. Remove the shock absorber.
6. Check the shock for:
   a. Excessive oil leakage; some minor weeping is permissible.
   b. Bent center rod, damaged outer case, or other defects.
   c. Pump the shock absorber several times, if it offers even resistance on full strokes it may be considered serviceable.
7. Install the upper shock mounting nut and bolt. Hand tighten the nut.
8. Install the bottom eye of the shock over the spring stud. Tighten the lower nut to 12–15 ft. lbs. on rear wheel drive models; 47–58 ft. lbs. on front wheel drive models.
9. Finally, tighten the upper nut to 47–58 ft. lbs. on all models except station wagons, which are tightened to 12–15 ft. lbs.

#### *4WD Vista*

1. Raise and support the rear end on jackstands under the frame.
2. Remove the rear wheels.
3. Using a floor jack, raise the inner control arm slightly.
4. Unbolt the top, then the bottom of the shock absorber. Remove it from the car.
5. Installation is the reverse of removal. Torque the top nut to 55–58 ft. lbs.; the bottom bolt to 75–80 ft. lbs.

## MacPherson Strut

### REMOVAL & INSTALLATION

#### *Conquest*

1. Raise and support the rear end on jackstands.

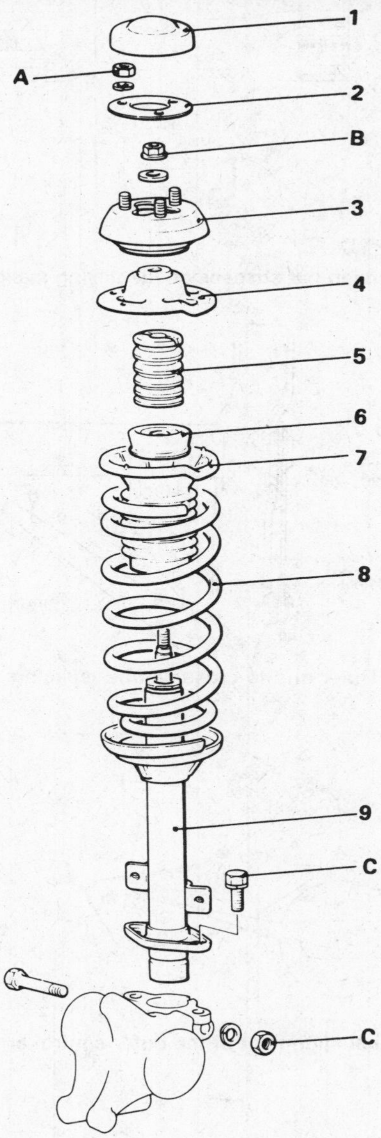


1. Strut house cap
2. Gasket
3. Strut insulator
4. Spring seat
5. Rubber helper
6. Rubber helper seat
7. Dust cover
8. Coil spring
9. Strut

**Conquest rear strut**

2. Remove the rear wheels.
3. Unclip the brake hose at the strut.
4. Unbolt the intermediate shaft from the companion flange.
5. Unbolt the strut assembly from the axleshaft housing. Remove the housing coupling bolts. Separate the strut from the housing by pushing the housing downward while prying open the coupling on the housing.
6. Remove the strut upper end attaching nuts, found under the side trim in the cargo area.
7. Lift out the strut.
8. Installation is the reverse of removal. Torque the upper end nuts to 20–25 ft. lbs.; the strut-to-housing bolts to 50 ft. lbs.; the coupling bolt to 50 ft. lbs.

#### *Colt LC*

1. Raise and support the rear of the vehicle from a frame point, allow the lower arms and suspension to hang. Remove the wheels.
2. Place a block of wood on a floor jack, and position the jack under the axle beam. Raise the axle slightly to relax the strut and to support the axle when the strut is removed. Position a jackstand that will support the axle should the jack fail.
3. Take care in jacking that no contact is made on the lateral rod.
4. On hatchback models, remove the trunk side trim.
5. Remove the upper dust cover cap.
6. Remove the upper mounting nuts. Remove the lower mounting bolt and nut.
7. Remove the strut.
8. Install in the reverse order. Torque the lower mounting bolt and nut to 58–72 ft. lbs.; The upper mounting nuts to 18–25 ft. lbs.

### OVERHAUL

**For all strut overhaul procedures, please refer to "Strut Overhaul" in the Unit Repair section.**

## Springs

### REMOVAL & INSTALLATION

#### *Leaf Springs*

##### REAR WHEEL DRIVE EXCEPT CONQUEST

1. Remove the hub cap or wheel cover. Loosen the lug nuts.
2. Raise the rear of the car. Install a stand at the exact point at which the 2 dimples locate the support point on the sill flange. Damage to the unit body can result from installing a stand at any other location.
3. Disconnect the lower mounting nut of the shock absorber.
4. Remove the 4 U-bolt fastening nuts from the spring seat.

**NOTE: It's not necessary to remove the shock absorber, leave the top connected.**

5. Place a floor jack under the rear axle and raise it just enough to remove the load from the springs. Remove the spring pad and seat.

6. Remove the 2 rear shackle attaching nuts and remove the rear shackle.
7. Remove the front pin retaining nut.
8. Remove the 2 pin retaining bolts and take off the pin.

**NOTE: It is a good safety practice to replace used suspension fasteners with new parts.**

9. Install the front spring eye bushings from both sides of the eye with the bushing flanges facing out.
10. Insert the spring pin assembly from the body side and fasten it with the bolts. Temporarily tighten the spring pin nut.
11. Install the rear eye bushings in the same manner as the front, insert the shackle pins from the outside of the car, and temporarily tighten the nut after installing the shackle plate.
12. Install the pads on both sides of the spring, aligning the pad center holes with the spring center bolt collar, and then install the spring seat with its center hole through the spring center collar.
13. Attach the assembled spring and spring seat to the axle housing with the axle housing spring center hole meeting with the spring center bolt and install the U-bolt nuts. Tighten the nuts to 33–36 ft. lbs.
14. Tighten the lower shock absorber nut to 12–15 ft. lbs. on all models.
15. Lower the car to the floor, jounce it a few times, and then tighten the spring pin and shackle pin nuts to 36–43 ft. lbs.

### *Coil Springs*

#### FRONT WHEEL DRIVE AND STATION WAGONS EXCEPT 4WD VISTA

1. Raise and support the car safely allowing the rear axle to hang unsupported.
2. Place a jack under the rear axle, and remove the bottom bolts or nuts of the shock absorbers.
3. Lower the rear axle and remove the left and right coil springs.
4. Installation is the reverse of removal.

**NOTE: When installing the spring, pay attention to the difference in shape between the upper and lower spring seats.**

## Torsion Bar and Control Arms

Instead of springs, the 4WD Vista uses transversely mounted torsion bars housed inside the rear crossmember, attached to which are inner and outer control arms. The conventional style shock absorbers are mounted on the inner arms.

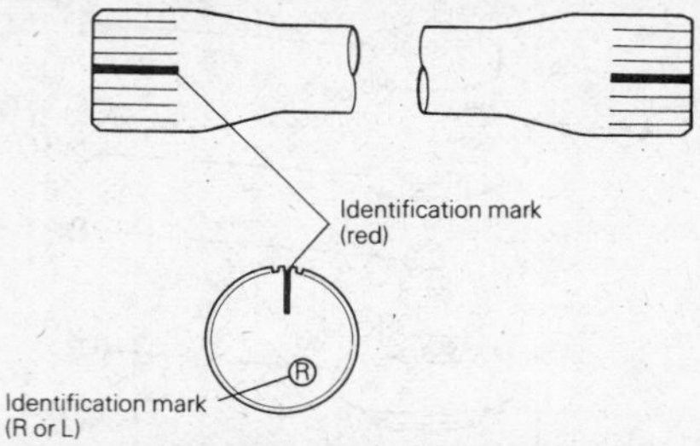


**Torsion bar suspension identifying marks**

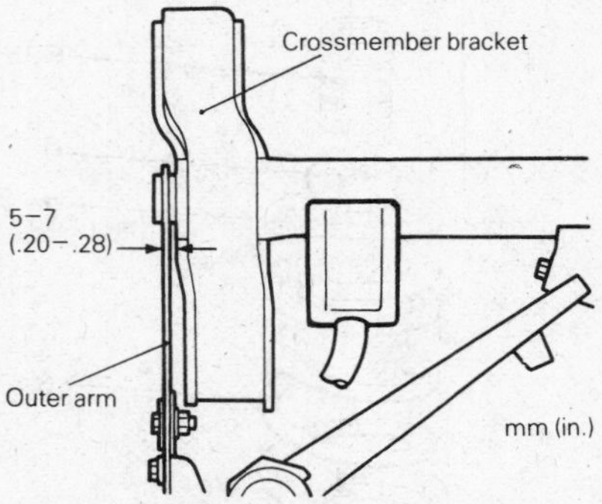


**Outer arm-to-crossmember spacing**

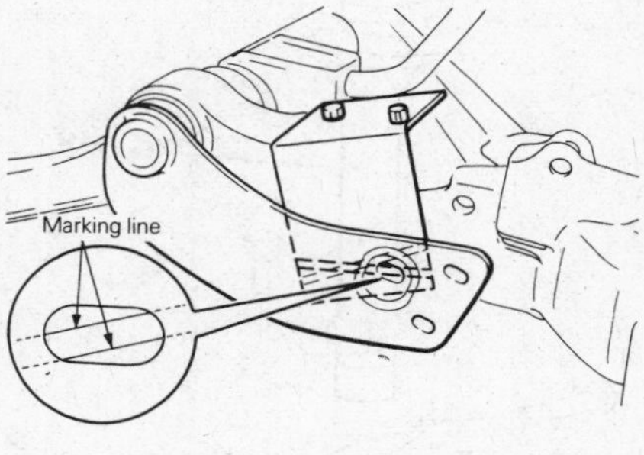


**Final alignment of the outer control arm**

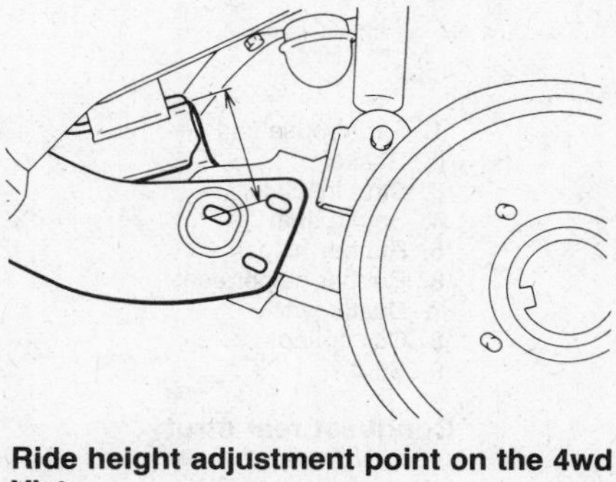

**Ride height adjustment point on the 4wd Vista**

### REMOVAL & INSTALLATION

#### *4WD Vista*

1. Raise and support the car with jackstands under the frame.
2. Remove the differential as described above.
3. Remove the intermediate shafts and axleshafts.
4. Remove the rear brake assemblies.
5. Disconnect the brake lines and parking brake cables from the inner arms.
6. Remove the main muffler.
7. Raise the inner arms slightly with a floor jack and disconnect the shock absorbers.
8. Matchmark, precisely, the upper ends of the outer arms, the torsion bar ends and the top of the crossmember bracket and remove the inner and outer arm attaching bolts.
9. Remove the extension rods fixtures' attaching bolts.
10. Remove the crossmember attaching bolts and remove the rear suspension assembly from the car.
11. Unbolt and remove the damper from the crossmember.
12. Remove the front and rear insulators from both ends of the crossmember.
13. Loosen, but do not remove, the lockbolts securing the outer arm bushings at both ends of the crossmember.
14. Pull the outer arm from the crossmember. Many times, the torsion bar will slide out of the crossmember with the outer arm.
15. Remove the torsion bar from either the crossmember or outer arm.
16. Inspect all parts for wear or damage. Inspect the crossmember for bending or deformation.
17. Inner arm bushings may be replaced at this time using a press. The thicker end of the bushings goes on the inner side.
18. Prior to installation note that the torsion bars are marked with an L or R on the outer end, and are not interchangeable.
19. If the original torsion bars are being installed, align the identification marks on the torsion bar end, crossmember and outer arm, install the torsion bar and arm and tighten the lockbolts. Skip Step 20. If new torsion bars are being installed, proceed to Step 20.
20. A special alignment jig must be fabricated. See the accompanying illustration for the dimension needed to make this jig. The jig is bolted to the rear insulator hole on the crossmember bracket as shown. Insert the torsion bar into the outer arm, aligning the red identification mark on the torsion bar end with the matchmark made on the outer arm top side. Install the torsion bar and arm so that the center of the flanged bolt hole on the arm is 32mm below the lower marking line on the jig. Then, pull the outer

arm off of the torsion bar, leaving the bar undisturbed in the crossmember. Reposition the arm on the torsion bar, 1 serration counterclockwise from its former position. This will make the previously measured dimension, 33mm above the lower line. In any event, when the outer arm and torsion bar are properly positioned, the marking lines on the jig will run diagonally across the center of the toe-in adjustment hole as shown. When the adjustment is complete, tighten the lockbolts. The clearance between the outer arm and the crossmember bracket, at the torsion bar, should be 5.0–7.0mm.

21. The remainder of installation is the reverse of removal. Observe the following torques:

Extension rod fixture bolts–45–50 ft. lbs.

Extension rod-to-fixture nut–95–100 ft. lbs.

Shock absorber lower bolt–75–80 ft. lbs.

Outer arm attaching bolts–65–70 ft. lbs.

Toe-in bolt–95–100 ft. lbs.

Lockbolts–20–22 ft. lbs.

Crossmember attaching bolts–80–85 ft. lbs.

Front insulator nuts–7–10 ft. lbs.

Inner arm-to-crossmember bolts–60–65 ft. lbs.

Damper-to-crossmember nuts–15–20 ft. lbs.

22. Lower the car to the ground and check the ride height. The ride height is checked on both sides and is determined by measuring the distance between the center line of the toe-in bolt hole on the outer arm, and the lower edge of the rebound bumper. The distance on each side should be 4.00–4.11 inches. If not, or if there is a significant difference between sides, the torsion bar(s) positioning is wrong.

## Lower Control Arm

### REMOVAL & INSTALLATION

#### *Rear Wheel Drive Except Conquest*

1. Support the vehicle body on safety stands. Use a jack under the rear axle to raise the rear axle assembly slightly.
2. Remove the wheel and the upper control arm rod.
3. Detach the parking brake rear cable from the lower arm.
4. Remove the lower arm from the rear axle housing and from the bracket attached to the body.
5. Temporarily install the lower arm (check for marking on left side arm) and torque the bolts to 94–108 ft. lbs. Torque the assist link bushing bolt to 47–58 ft. lbs.
6. With the special nut assembly placed securely against the rear axle housing bracket, install the upper control arm rod to the bracket. Torque the bolt to 94 ft. lbs. Always use new bolts.

#### *Conquest*

1. Raise and support the rear end on jackstands. Allow the wheels to hang freely.
2. Remove the rear wheels.
3. Disconnect the parking brake cable from the lower arm.
4. Disconnect the stabilizer bar.
5. Unbolt the lower control arm from the axleshaft housing.
6. Unbolt the lower control arm from the front support.
7. Unbolt the lower control arm from the crossmember and remove it.
8. Installation is the reverse of removal. Apply a thin coating of chassis lube to the cutout portion of the lower arm-to-axleshaft housing shaft. Do not allow the grease to touch the bushings. Insert the shaft with the mark on its head facing downward. When positioning the lower control arm on the crossmember, align the mark on the crossmember with the line on the plate. Torque follows;

Lower control arm-to-front support bolts–108 ft. lbs.

Arm-to-crossmember bolts–108 ft. lbs.

Arm to axleshaft housing bolts–60 ft. lbs.

Arm locking pin–15 ft. lbs.

9. Have the rear wheel alignment checked.

## Trailing Arm

### REMOVAL & INSTALLATION

#### *Front Wheel Drive Except 4WD Vista and Torsional Suspension*

1. Support the side frame on jack stands and remove the rear wheels. Remove the rear brake assembly.
2. Remove the muffler and jack the control arm just enough to raise it slightly.
3. Remove the shock absorber and lower the jack. Remove the coil spring and temporarily install the shock absorber to the control arm.
4. Disconnect the brake hoses at the rear suspension arms and remove the rear suspension from the body as an assembly.
5. Install the fixture-to-body bolts and torque to 36–51 ft. lbs.
6. Install the coil springs and loosely install the shock absorbers. Tighten the shock absorber bolts to specification after the vehicle is lowered to the floor.

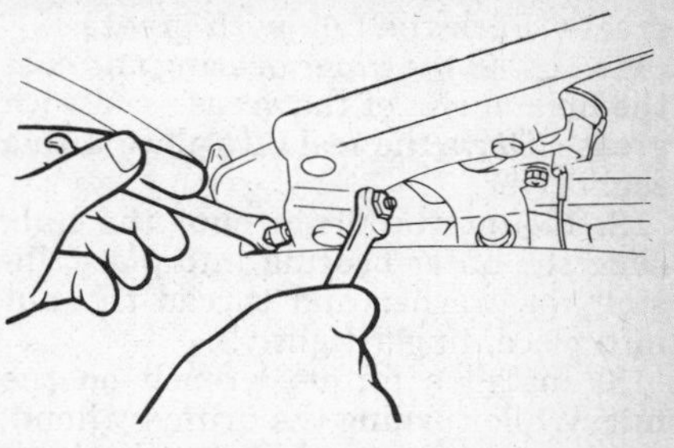

Lever adjustment—Colt Vista

7. Install the rear brake assembly.
8. Lower the vehicle and tighten the suspension arm end nuts on all except Colt Vista to 36–51 ft. lbs. (Colt Vista-94–108 ft. lbs. and the shock bolts to 47–58 ft. lbs. for all models.
9. Install the brake drums and wheels.
10. Bleed the brake system and adjust the rear brake shoe clearance.

## Rear Wheel Bearings

**NOTE: For all RWD models, please refer to the "Drive Axle" section.**

### REMOVAL & INSTALLATION

#### *Except 1985–90 Colt*

1. Loosen the lug nuts, raise the rear of the car and support it on jackstands. Remove the wheel.
2. Remove the grease cap, cotter pin, nut and washer.
3. Remove the brake drum. While pulling the drum, the outer bearing will fall out. Do not drop it.
4. Pry out the grease seal and discard it.
5. Remove the inner bearing.
6. Check the bearing races. If any scoring, heat checking or damage is noted, they should be replaced.

**NOTE: When bearing or races need replacement, replace them as a set.**

7. Inspect the bearings. If wear or looseness or heat checking is found replace them.
8. If the bearings and races are to be replaced, drive out the races with a brass drift.
9. Before installing new races, coat them with lithium based wheel bearing grease. The races are most easily installed using a driver made for that purpose. They can, however, be driven into place with a brass drift. Make sure that they are fully seated.
10. Thoroughly pack the bearings with lithium based wheel bearing

grease. Pack the hub with grease.

11. Install the inner bearing and coat the lip and rim of the grease seal with grease. Drive the seal into place with a seal driver.

12. Mount the drum onto the hub, slide the outer bearing into place, install the washer and thread the nut into place, finger-tightly.

13. Install a torque wrench on the nut. While turning the drum by hand, tighten the nut to 15 ft. lbs. Back off the nut until it is loose, then tighten it to 4 ft. lbs. If the torque wrench is not all that accurate below 10 ft. lbs., use an in. lb. torque wrench and tighten the nut to 48 inch lbs.

14. Install the lock cap and insert a new cotter pin. If the lock cap and hole don't align, and repositioning the cap can't accomplish alignment, back off the nut no more than 15 degrees. If that won't align the holes either, try the adjustment procedure over again.

### *1985–90 Colt*

1. Loosen the lug nuts. Raise the rear of the car and support it on jackstands.
2. Remove the wheel.
3. Remove the grease cap.
4. Remove the nut.
5. Pull the drum off. The outer bearing will fall out while the drum is coming off. Do not drop it. On models with disc brakes; Remove the caliper assembly. Remove the disc rotor. Remove the hub assembly.
6. Pry out the oil seal. Discard it.
7. Remove the inner bearing.
8. Check the bearing races. If any scoring, heat checking or damage is noted, they should be replaced.

**NOTE: When bearing or races need replacement, replace them as a set.**

9. Inspect the bearings. If wear or looseness or heat checking is found, replace them.
10. If the bearings and races are to be replaced, drive out the race with a brass drift.
11. Before installing new races, coat them with lithium based wheel bearing grease. The races are most easily installed using a driver made for that purpose. They can, however, be driven into place with a brass drift. Make sure that they are fully seated.
12. Thoroughly pack the bearings with lithium based wheel bearing grease. Pack the hub with grease.
13. Install the inner bearing and coat the lip and rim of the grease seal with grease. Drive the seal into place with a seal driver.
14. Models with drum brakes: Mount the drum on the axleshaft. Install the

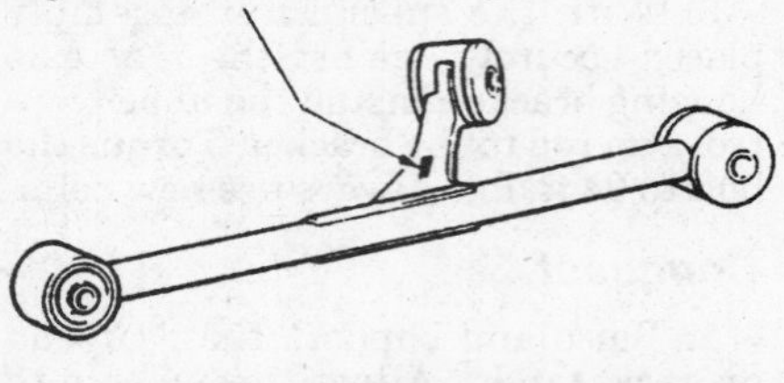


**Rear lower control arm identifying marks for all rear wheel drive cars except Conquest**

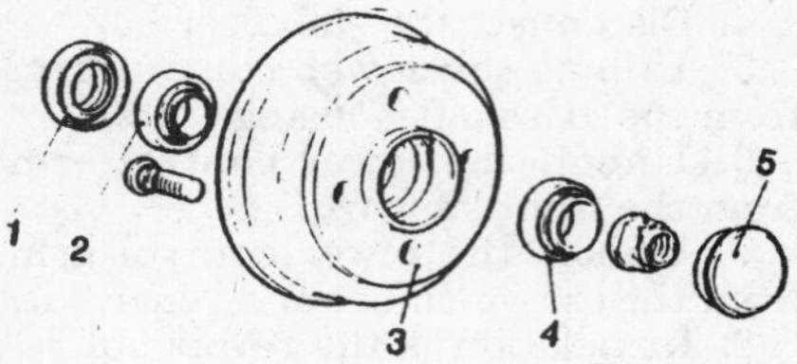


1. Oil seal
2. Inner bearing
3. Brake drum
4. Outer bearing
5. Hub cap

**Drum brake rear bearing assembly—1985–90 Colt**

outer bearing. Don't install the nut at this time.

15. Models with drum brakes: Using a pull scale attached to one of the lugs, measure the starting force necessary to get the drum to turn. Starting force should be 5 lbs. If the starting torque is greater than specific, replace the bearings.
16. Models with drum brakes: Install the nut on the axleshaft. Thread the nut on, by hand, to a point at which the back face of the nut is 2–3mm from the shoulder of the shaft (where the threads end).
17. Models with drum brakes: Using an inch lb. torque wrench, turn the nut counterclockwise 2 to 3 turns, noting the average force needed during the turning procedure. Turning torque for the nut should be about 48 in. lbs. If turning torque is not within 5 in. lbs., either way, replace the nut.
18. Models with drum brakes: Tighten the nut to 75–110 ft. lbs. On 1989–90 models; 108–145 ft. lbs.
19. Models with drum brakes: Using a stand mounted gauge, check the axial play of the wheel bearings. Play should be less than 0.0079 in. If play cannot be brought within that figure, the unit is assembled incorrectly.
20. Models with drum brakes: Pack the grease cap with wheel bearing grease and install it.
21. On disc brake models: Install the hub and bearing assembly. Tighten the nut to 108–145 ft. lbs. Install the rotor and caliper assembly.

# STEERING

## Steering Wheel

### REMOVAL & INSTALLATION

1. Pry off the steering wheel center foam pad.
2. Remove the steering wheel retaining nut.
3. Using a steering wheel puller, remove the wheel.
4. Be sure the front wheels are in a straight ahead position. Reverse the removal procedure. Tighten the nut to 30 ft. lbs.

## Turn Signal Switch

### REMOVAL & INSTALLATION

#### *Rear Wheel Drive*

1. Remove the steering wheel and have the tilt handle in the lowest position.
2. Remove the instrument cluster cover and column covers.
3. Remove the connectors from the column switch from the column tube.

**NOTE: Early models may have the turn signal and hazard switches mounted on a base plate. Removal of the attaching screws will allow these switches to be removed without removal of the remaining switches.**

4. Switch installation is the reverse of removal. Be sure that the switch is centered in the column or self-canceling will be affected.

#### *Front Wheel Drive*

1. Remove the steering wheel.
2. Remove the lap heater duct. On, depending on model, the lower knee protector assembly.
3. Remove the column covers.
4. On late models, remove the steering wheel. Remove the switch retaining screws, disconnect the wiring and remove the switch.
5. Installation is the reverse of removal.

## Ignition Lock and Switch

### REMOVAL & INSTALLATION

**NOTE: When replacing the ignition switch or key reminder switch only, remove the column cover, remove the screw holding the switch, and pull out the switch.**

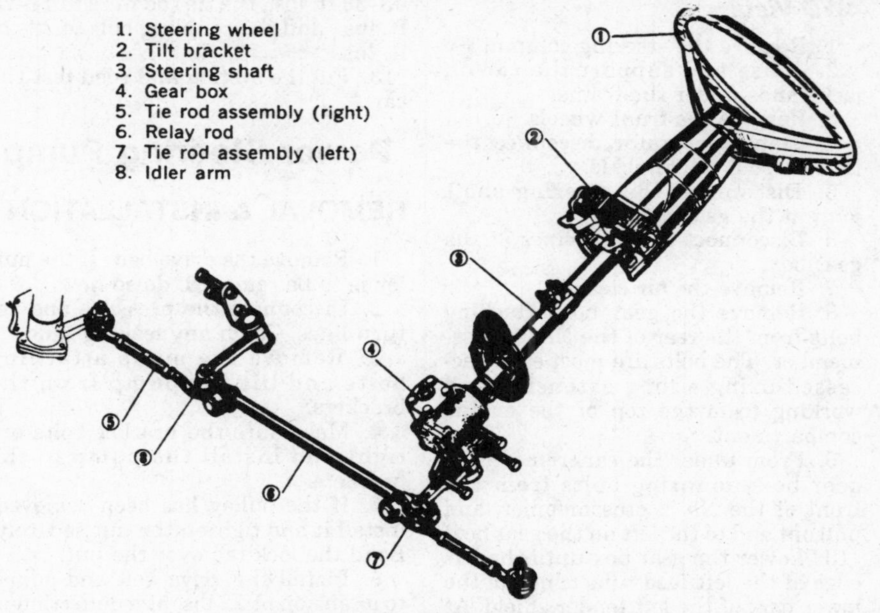


Rear wheel drive steering system

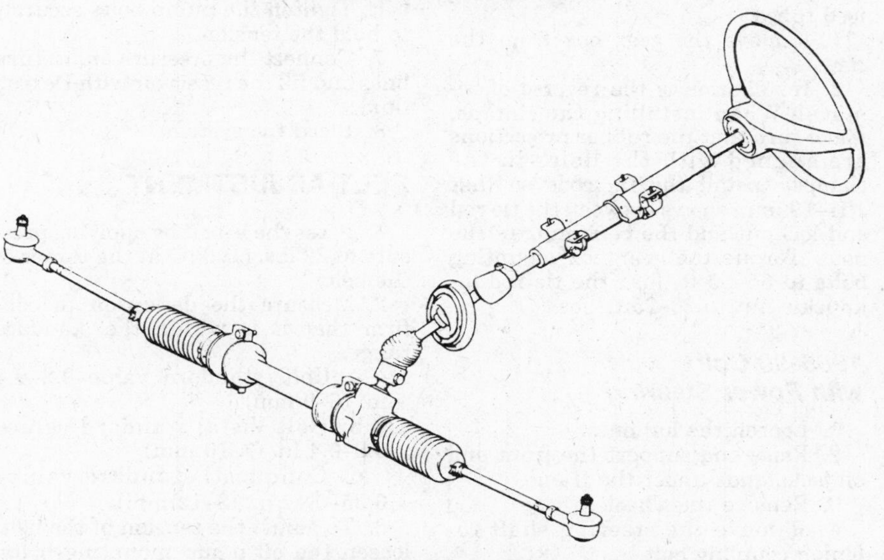

Typical rack and piston steering system

1. Remove the turn signal switch as described above.
2. Cut a notch in the lock bracket bolt head with a hacksaw.
3. Remove the bolt and lock.
4. Remove the column cover and unbolt and remove the ignition switch.
5. Install both lock and switch in reverse of removal.

**NOTE: When installing the lock, the bolt should be tightened until the head is crushed. When installing the switch, install the switch bolt loosely and insert and work the key a few times to make sure everything checks out before tightening the bolt.**

## Manual Steering Gear

### REMOVAL & INSTALLATION

#### *Rear Wheel Drive*

1. Remove the clamp bolt connecting the steering shaft with the steering gear housing mainshaft. Check for, or make, mating marks for the assembly.
2. Using appropriate pullers, disconnect the pitman arm and the relay rod at the linkage connection.
3. Remove the gearbox from the frame by removal of the attaching bolts.
4. Remove the pitman arm from the cross shaft. Check for mating marks.
5. Installation is the reverse of removal.

## Power Steering Gear

The power steering consists of a belt driven pump, a separate fluid reservoir, pressure and return lines, and a steering gear assembly with an integral control valve.

### REMOVAL & INSTALLATION

#### *Rear Wheel Drive*

1. Matchmark and disconnect the steering shaft from the gearbox main shaft.
2. Disconnect the tie rod end and pitman arm from the relay rod.
3. Remove the air cleaner and disconnect the pressure and return lines from the steering gear assembly.
4. Remove any interfering splash pans from underneath the vehicle.
5. If necessary, remove the kickdown linkage splash pan shield and bolts. Move the fuel line aside to avoid damage during removal.
6. Remove the frame bolts from the gearbox and lower the unit from the vehicle.
7. Installation is the reverse of removal. Make sure that all matchmarks align. After tightening the pitman arm nut make sure that the distance between the centerline of the lowest steering gear mounting bolt and the top of the pitman arm is 19.5mm. Observe the following torques:
   Pitman arm nut–94–109 ft. lbs.
   Steering gear mounting bolts–40–47 ft. lbs.
   Tie rod socket and relay rod–25–33 ft. lbs.
   High pressure hose–22–29 ft. lbs.
   Return hose–29–36 ft. lbs.

### ADJUSTMENT

**NOTE: The steering gear must be disconnected from the steering shaft.**

1. Measure the mainshaft preload with an inch lbs. torque wrench. The preload should be 3.5–6.9 inch lbs., with the cross-shaft adjusting bolt backed off.
2. Adjust the valve housing top cover to obtain the proper preload. When correct, lock the top cover with the locking nut.
3. Tighten the cross-shaft adjusting bolt until zero lash is present. Check the total starting torque to rotate the main shaft. The torque should be 5.2–8.7 inch lbs.
4. Adjust the cross-shaft until the required starting torque is obtained

and lock the adjusting bolt nut securely.

## Rack and Pinion Steering

### REMOVAL & INSTALLATION

#### *1983–84 Colt and Champ with Manual and Power Steering and 1985–90 Colt Manual Steering*

1. Loosen the lug nuts.
2. Raise and support the front end on jackstands under the frame.
3. Remove the wheels.
4. Remove the steering shaft-to-pinion coupling bolt.
5. Disconnect the tie rod ends with a separator. On cars with power steering, drain the fluid and disconnect the hoses at the gear unit.
6. Remove the clamps, or clamp and bolts securing the rack to the crossmember and remove the unit from the car.
7. Install the rubber mount for the gear box with the slit on the downside. The remainder of installation is the reverse of removal. Torque as follows:

Rack-to-crossmember–22–29 ft. lbs. on 1983–84 models, 45–60 ft. lbs. on 1985–90 models.

Coupling bolt–11–14 ft. lbs. on 1983–84 models, 22–25 ft. lbs. on 1985–89 models.

Tie-rod nuts–11–25 ft. lbs.

8. Fill the system and road test the car.

#### *2WD Vista*

1. Loosen the lug nuts.
2. Raise and support the front end on jackstands under the frame.
3. Remove the wheels.
4. Remove the steering shaft-to-pinion coupling bolt.
5. Disconnect the tie rod ends with a separator. On cars with power steering, disconnect the hoses at the gear unit.
6. Remove the crossmember support bracket from the crossmember on the right side of the car.
7. Unbolt the gearbox from the crossmember.

**NOTE: The gearbox is most easily removed using a ratchet and long extension, working from the engine compartment side.**

8. Pull the gearbox out the right side of the car. Pull it slowly to avoid damage.
9. Installation is the reverse of removal. Torque the rack clamp bolts to 43–58 ft. lbs., the tie rod nuts to 17–25 ft. lbs., and the coupling bolt to 22–25 ft. lbs. Fill the system and road test the car.

#### *4WD Vista*

1. Remove the steering column.
2. Raise and support the car on jackstands under the frame.
3. Remove the front wheels.
4. Using a separator, disconnect the tie rod from the knuckle.
5. Disconnect the steering shaft joint at the gear box.
6. Disconnect the fluid lines at the gear box.
7. Remove the air cleaner.
8. Remove the gear box attaching bolts from the rear of the No. 2 crossmember. The bolts are most easily accessed using a long extension and working from the top of the engine compartment.
9. From under the car, remove the gear box mounting bolts from the front of the No. 2 crossmember, and pull out and to the left on the gear box.
10. Lower the gear box until the left edge of the left feed tube contacts the lower part of the left fender shield. At this point, remove the left and right feed tubes.
11. Remove the gear box from the car.
12. Installation is the reverse of removal. When installing the clamps, make sure that the rubber projections are aligned with the holes in the clamps. Install the tie rods so that 191–193mm shows between the tie rod end locknut and the beginning of the boot. Torque the gear box mounting bolts to 55–60 ft. lbs.; the tie rod-to-knuckle nut to 20–25 ft. lbs.

#### *1985–90 Colt with Power Steering*

1. Loosen the lug nuts.
2. Raise and support the front end on jackstands under the frame.
3. Remove the wheels.
4. Remove the steering shaft-to-pinion coupling bolt.
5. Disconnect the tie rod ends with a separator.
6. Drain the fluid.
7. Disconnect the hoses from the gearbox.
8. Remove the band from the steering joint cover.
9. Unbolt and remove the stabilizer bar.
10. Remove the rear roll stopper-to-center member bolt and move the rear roll stopper forward.
11. Remove the rack unit mounting clamp bolts and take the unit out the left side of the car.
12. Installation is the reverse of removal. Make sure that the rubber isolators have their nubs aligned with the holes in the clamps. Apply rubber cement to the slits in the gear mounting grommet. Tighten the clamp bolt to 43–58 ft. lbs., the tie rod nuts to 11–25 ft. lbs., and the coupling bolt to 22–25 ft. lbs.
13. Fill the system and road test the car.

## Power Steering Pump

### REMOVAL & INSTALLATION

1. Remove the drive belt. If the pulley is to be removed, do so now.
2. Disconnect the pressure and return lines. Catch any leaking fluid.
3. Remove the pump attaching bolts and lift the pump from the brackets.
4. Make sure the bracket bolts are tight and install the pump to the brackets.
5. If the pulley has been removed, install it and tighten the nut securely. Bend the lock tab over the nut.
6. Install the drive belt and adjust to a tension of 22 lbs. at a deflection of 0.28–0.39 in. at the top center of the belt. Tighten the pump bolts securely to hold the tension.
7. Connect the pressure and return lines and fill the reservoir with Dexron fluid.
8. Bleed the system.

### BELT ADJUSTMENT

1. Press the V-belt by applying pressure of 22 lbs. (100 N) at the center of the belt.
2. Measure the deflection to confirm that it is within the standard range.
   a. Colt, standard value–0.2–0.4 in. (6–9 mm).
   b. Colt Vista, standard value–0.3–0.4 in. (7–10 mm).
   c. Conquest, standard value–0.35–0.47 in. (9–12 mm).
3. To adjust the tension of the belt, loosen the oil pump mounting bolts, move the oil pump, and then retighten the bolts.

### BLEEDING THE SYSTEM

1. The reservoir should be full of Dexron®II fluid.
2. Jack up the front wheels and support the vehicle safely.
3. Turn the steering wheel fully to the right and left until no air bubbles appear in the fluid. Maintain the reservoir level.
4. Lower the vehicle and with the engine idling, turn the wheels fully to the right and left. Stop the engine.
5. Install a tube from the bleeder screw on the steering gear box to the reservoir.
6. Start the engine, turn the steer-

ing wheel fully to the left and loosen the bleeder screw.

7. Repeat the procedure until no air bubbles pass through the tube.

8. Tighten the bleeder screw and remove the tube. Refill the reservoir as needed, and check that no further bubbles are present in the fluid. An abrupt rise in the fluid level after stopping the engine is a sign of incomplete bleeding. This will cause noise from the pump or control valve.

## Steering Linkage

**NOTE: The following applies to rear wheel drive cars. For front wheel drive component service, see the Rack and Pinion procedures above.**

### REMOVAL & INSTALLATION

#### *Tie Rods*

1. Using a puller, disconnect the tie rod ends from the steering knuckle.
2. Loosen the jam nut and remove the tie rod ends from the tie rod. The outer end is left-hand threaded and the inner is right-hand threaded.
3. Grease the tie rod threads and install the ends. Turn each end in an equal amount.
4. Install the tie rod assembly on the steering knuckle and relay rod. Tighten the castellated nuts to 29–36 ft. lbs. Use new cotter pins.
5. Adjust the toe-in.

#### *Relay Rod*

1. Disconnect the tie rod ends from the steering knuckles with a puller.
2. Again using the puller, disconnect the relay rod from the idler arm and the pitman arm.
3. Remove the relay arm.
4. Install the rod in the reverse order of removal. Tighten the tie rod end nuts to 29–36 ft. lbs. Tighten the relay rod-to-pitman arm nut and relay rod-to-idler arm nut to 29–43 ft. lbs. Always use new cotter pins.

#### *Idler Arm*

1. Disconnect the idler arm from the relay rod using a puller.
2. Remove the retaining bolts and remove the idler arm.
3. Mount the idler arm on the frame and tighten the bolts to 25–29 ft. lbs.
4. Attach the relay rod to the idler arm and tighten the stud nut to 29–43 ft. lbs. Use a new cotter pin.

# BRAKES

**For all brake system repair and service procedures not detailed below, please refer to "Brakes" in the Unit Repair section.**

## Master Cylinder

### REMOVAL & INSTALLATION

#### *Rear Wheel Drive*

**CAUTION**

***Be careful not to spill brake fluid on the painted surfaces of the car. The brake fluid will cause damage to the paint.***

1. Disconnect all hydraulic lines from the master cylinder. On models with remote reservoir, remove and plug the hoses from the master cylinder caps. If the master cylinder has a fluid level warning device, disconnect the wiring harness.
2. On non-power brake cars, remove the clevis pin that connects the master cylinder push rod to the brake pedal.
3. Loosen and remove the master cylinder mounting nuts, either from the firewall (manual brakes) or from the power brake booster. Remove the master cylinder.

**NOTE: Before installing the master cylinder, make sure that there is less than 0.03 in. clearance between the pushrod and master cylinder piston on all but the Conquest. On Conquest, the clearance should be 0.028–0.043 in.**

4. Mount the master cylinder to the firewall (manual brakes) or to the power brake booster.
5. Connect the push rod to the brake pedal (manual brakes).
6. Connect all brake lines and wiring harnesses and fill the master cylinder reservoirs with clean fluid.
7. Bleed the brake system.

#### *Front Wheel Drive*

1. Disconnect the fluid level sensor.
2. Disconnect the brake tubes from the master cylinder and cap them immediately.
3. On cars with a turbocharger, remove the reservoir from the reservoir holder.
4. Unbolt and remove the master cylinder from the booster.
5. Installation is the reverse of removal. Measure the master cylinder pushrod clearance; it should be 0.016–0.31 in. Torque the mounting bolts to 6–9 ft. lbs. (72–108 inch lbs.).

## Proportioning Valve/ Combination Valve

### REMOVAL & INSTALLATION

1. Disconnect the brake lines at the valve.

**NOTE: Use a flare wrench, if possible, to avoid damage to the flare nuts and brake lines.**

2. Remove the mounting bolts and the valve.
3. Install in the reverse order. Refill the master cylinder and bleed the brake system.

## Power Brake Booster

### REMOVAL & INSTALLATION

1. Remove the master cylinder.
2. Disconnect the vacuum line from the booster.
3. Remove the pin connecting the power brake operating rod and the brake lever.
4. Unbolt and remove the booster.
5. Replace the packing on both sides of the booster-to-firewall spacer with new packing.
6. If the check valve was removed, make sure the direction of installation marking on the valve is followed.
7. Installation is the reverse of removal. Torque the booster-to-firewall nuts to 6–9 ft. lbs. (54–108 inch lbs.). Torque the master cylinder-to-booster nuts to 6–9 ft. lbs.
8. Adjust the brake pedal and master cylinder pushrod as explained earlier.

## Front Disc Brake Pads

### REMOVAL & INSTALLATION

#### *1983 Challenger*

A sliding caliper disc brake is used.

1. Loosen the wheel lugs, block the rear wheels, raise the front of the car and support on jackstands. Remove the wheels.
2. Remove approximately half of the brake fluid from the master cylinder.
3. Remove the spring pin(s) and pull the stopper plug(s) from the upper end of the caliper.
4. Move the caliper back and forth to loosen, then remove the caliper from the support.

**NOTE: The hydraulic brake hose need not be removed from the caliper, but do not allow the caliper weight to hang from the hose. Secure the caliper with a piece of wire.**

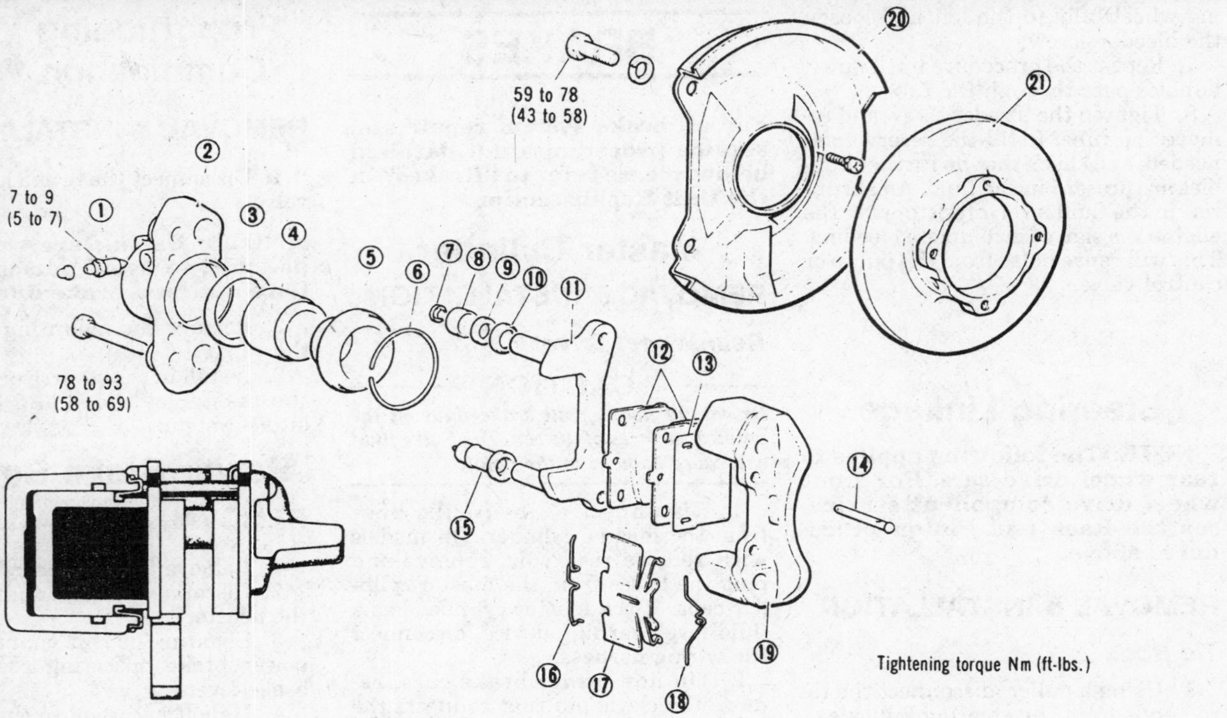


1. Bleeder screw
2. Caliper, inner
3. Piston seal
4. Piston
5. Dust seal
6. Retaining ring
7. Cap plug
8. Torque plate pin cap
9. Oil seal retainer
10. Wiper seal
11. Torque plate
12. Pad assembly
13. Anti-squeak shim
14. Pad retaining pin
15. Torque plate pin bushing
16. K-spring
17. Pad protector
18. M-pad
19. Caliper, outer
20. Dust cover
21. Brake disc

**Exploded view of the brake caliper used on 1983–84 Colt except turbo**

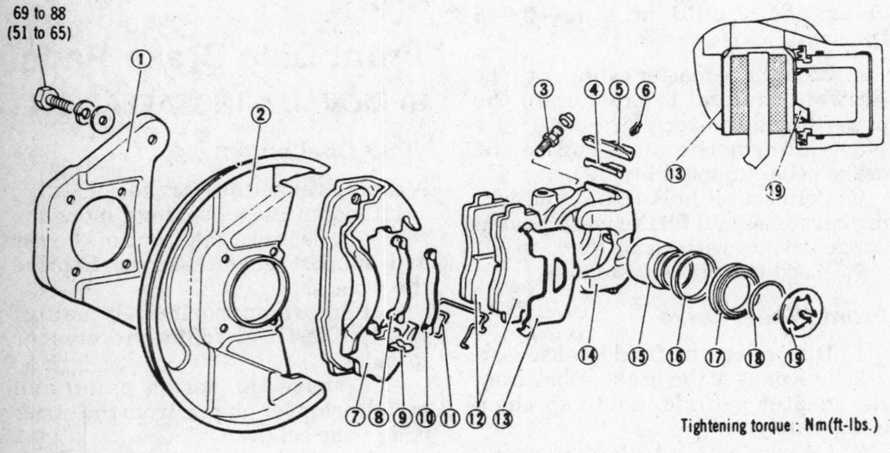


1. Disc brake adapter
2. Dust cover
3. Bleeder screw
4. Pad support plate
5. Stopper plug
6. Spigot pin
7. Caliper support
8. Pad clip (inner)
9. Pad clip B
10. Pad clip (outer)
11. Anti-rattle spring
12. Brake pad
13. Anti-squeak shim (outer)
14. Caliper body
15. Piston
16. Piston seal
17. Dust boot
18. Boot ring
19. Anti-squeak shim (inner)

**Exploded view of a typical sliding type caliper**

5. Take the time to examine the pad holder with its related clips and springs. All parts must be returned to the same place when reinstalling the old pads or replacing with new pads.

6. Remove the anti-squeak clips then remove the brake pads from the mounting bracket. Do not remove the caliper support springs (2 large wire hair pins).

7. Under each brake pad there is a pad support plate. These are not interchangeable and must be installed correctly.

8. Insert the new pads in the mounting bracket over the pad support plates and install the anti-squeak clips.

9. Seat the caliper piston fully into the caliper bore. Do this by opening the bleeder screw and push the piston in with a hammer handle, or C-clamp. If you meet too much resistance, the piston might be hanging up on a scored bore or have a gaulded piston wall, if so rebuild or replace the caliper.

10. Seat the caliper over the mounting bracket. Clean and apply No. 2 brake grease to the sliding surfaces,

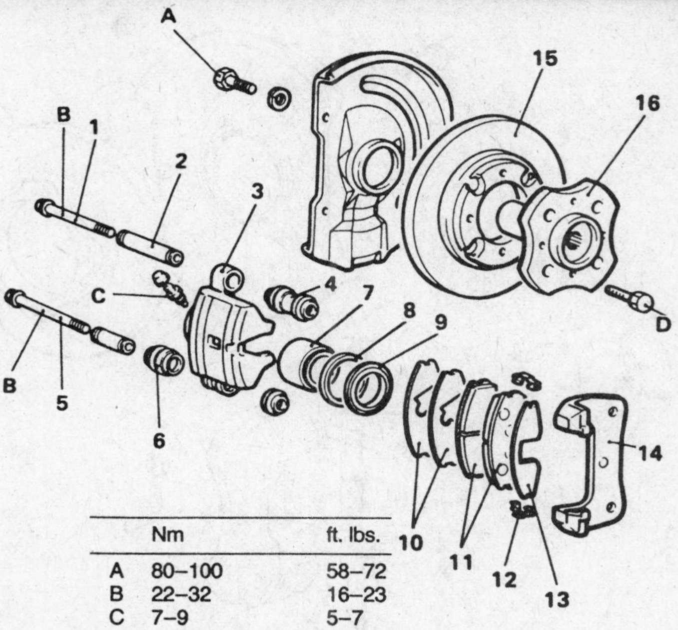

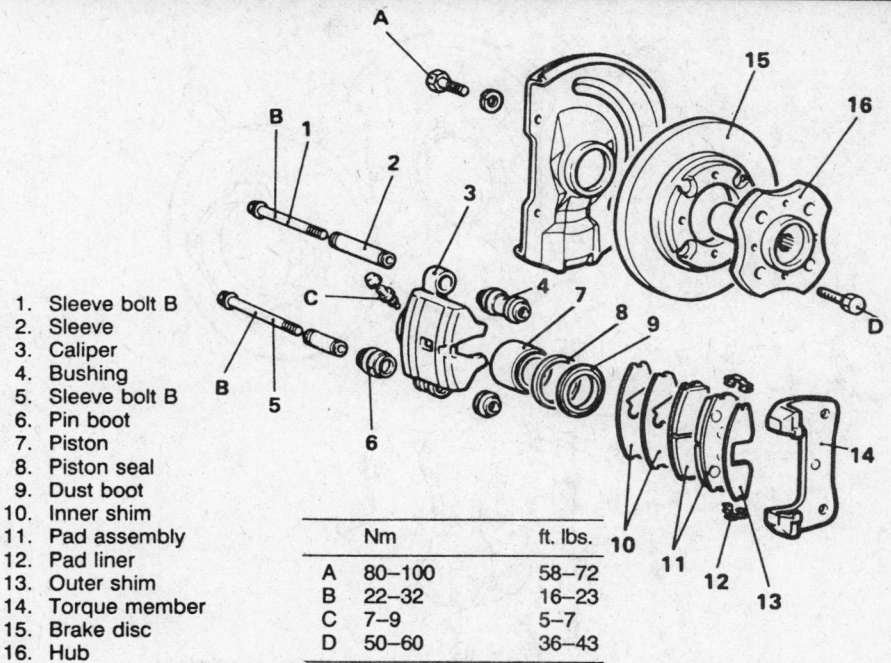

1. Sleeve bolt B
2. Sleeve
3. Caliper
4. Bushing
5. Sleeve bolt B
6. Pin boot
7. Piston
8. Piston seal
9. Dust boot
10. Inner shim
11. Pad assembly
12. Pad liner
13. Outer shim
14. Torque member
15. Brake disc
16. Hub

| | Nm | ft. lbs. |
|---|---|---|
| A | 80–100 | 58–72 |
| B | 22–32 | 16–23 |
| C | 7–9 | 5–7 |
| D | 50–60 | 36–43 |

**Exploded view of the brake caliper used on 1985–90 Colt except turbo**

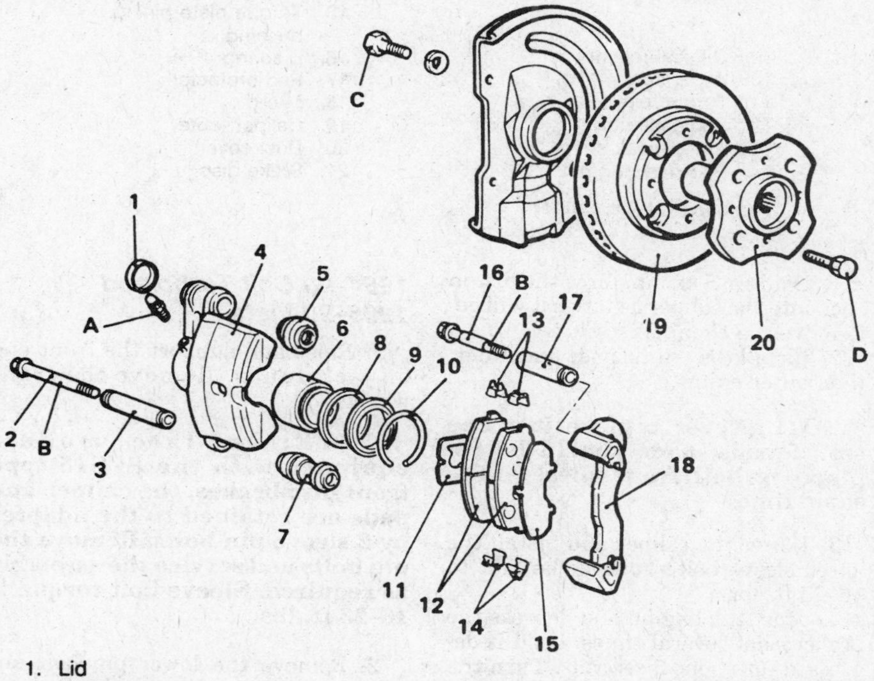


1. Lid
2. Lock pin
3. Sleeve
4. Caliper body
5. Guide pin boot
6. Piston
7. Lock pin boot
8. Piston seal
9. Piston boot
10. Boot ring
11. Inner shim
12. Pad assembly
13. Pad clip B
14. Pad clip C
15. Anti-squeak shim
16. Guide pin
17. Sleeve
18. Support mounting
19. Brake disc
20. Hub

| | Nm | ft. lbs. |
|---|---|---|
| A | 7–9 | 5–7 |
| B | 22–32 | 16–23 |
| C | 80–100 | 58–72 |
| D | 50–60 | 36–43 |

**Exploded view of the typical caliper used on the Vista and Turbo Colt**

plug plates and stopper plug. Install the caliper stopper plug and the spring pin.

11. Fill the master cylinder and bleed the brake system.
12. Install the tire and wheel, lower the car to the ground and road test. Pump the brakes several times. Do not move the car until a firm brake pedal is present.

### *1983–84 Front Wheel Drive without Turbochargers*

1. Raise and support the front end on jackstands.
2. Remove the front wheels.
3. Pry off the dust shield from the caliper.
4. Depress the center of the outboard spring clip and remove the clip by slipping the ends from the pins.
5. Remove the inboard spring clip with pliers.
6. Using pliers, pull the retaining pins from the caliper.
7. Lift the pads and anti-squeal shims from the caliper.
8. Clean all caliper parts, especially the torque plate shafts, with a solvent made for brake parts.

**NOTE: Replace all brake pads at the same time. Never replace the pads on 1 wheel only!**

9. If the dust protector or spring clips are weak, damaged or deformed, replace them.
10. Remove the cap from the master cylinder reservoir and, using a clean suction gun, remove about 1/4 in. of fluid.
11. Using a C-clamp, force the caliper piston back into the caliper as far as it will go.
12. Install the inboard pad and anti-squeal shim.
13. Install the outboard pad and anti-squeal shim.
14. Install the pins.
15. Install the 2 spring clips.
16. Install the dust shield.
17. Install the wheels and lower the car. Get in the car and depress the brake pedal a few times. The first couple of strokes on the pedal will feel overly long. However, the pads will set themselves and the stroke will return to normal. Pump the brakes several more times. Do not move the car until a firm brake pedal is present.

### *1985–90 Colt without Turbocharger*

1. Raise and support the front end on jackstands. Remove the wheels.

**NOTE: On late models equipped with the PFS15 type front disc brakes; the caliper and**

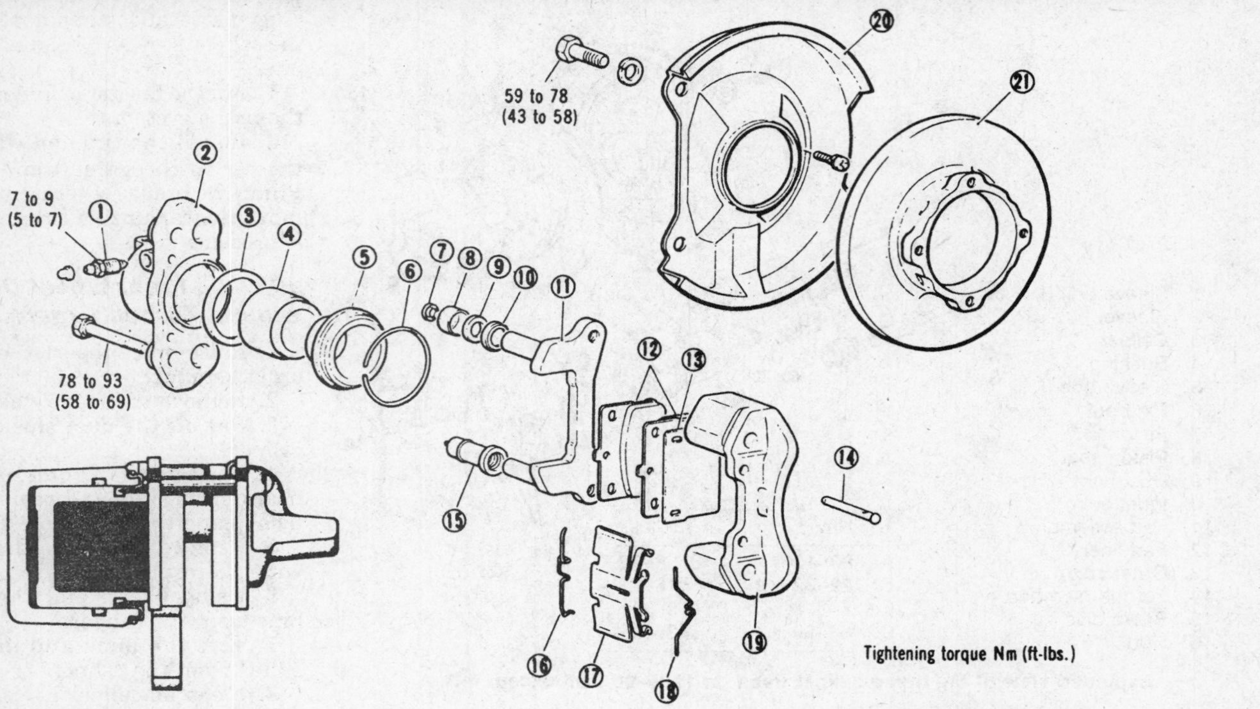

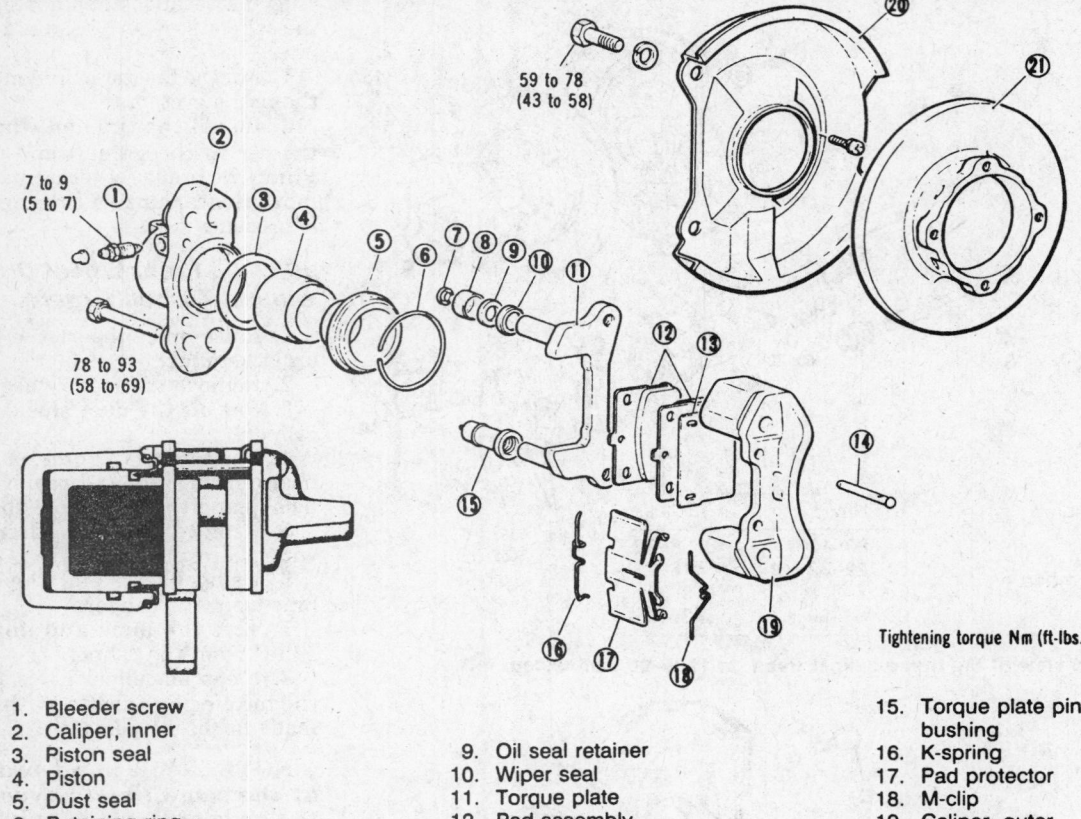

1. Bleeder screw
2. Caliper, inner
3. Piston seal
4. Piston
5. Dust seal
6. Retaining ring
7. Cap plug
8. Torque plate pin cap
9. Oil seal retainer
10. Wiper seal
11. Torque plate
12. Pad assembly
13. Anti-squeak shim
14. Pad retaining pin
15. Torque plate pin bushing
16. K-spring
17. Pad protector
18. M-clip
19. Caliper, outer
20. Dust cover
21. Brake disc

**Typical pin type caliper**

**pads are retained to the adapter by 2 sleeve pin bolts. Remove the pin bolts and service the assembly as required. Sleeve pin torque is 16–23 ft. lbs.**

2. Remove the lower sleeve bolt from the caliper and rotate the caliper upward.

**NOTE: There is a grease coating on the bolt. Make sure that it is not removed or contaminated.**

3. Support the caliper by suspending it with wire or string from a nearby suspension member.
4. Remove the inner, then outer shims from the caliper.
5. Lift out the brake pads.
6. Remove the pad liners.
7. Clean all parts in solvent made for brake parts.
8. Inspect the dust boot on the caliper piston. If it is torn or brittle, replace it. and consider rebuilding the caliper.
9. Inspect the shims and liners and replace them if damaged.
10. Remove the cap from the master cylinder reservoir and siphon off about ¼ in. of fluid.
11. Using a C-clamp, force the piston back into the caliper as far as it will go. Remove the clamp.
12. Install the liners, pads and inner, then outer shims.

**NOTE: Never replace just one set of pads, pads should be replaced on both front wheels at the same time.**

13. Lower the caliper and install the lower sleeve bolt. Torque the bolt to 16–23 ft. lbs.
14. Start the engine and depress the brake pedal several times. Hold it depressed for about 5 seconds. Turn the engine off.
15. Rotate the brake rotor a few times. Using a spring scale hooked to 1 of the lugs, measure the brake drag. Remove the pads and perform the spring scale test again. The difference between the drag test with and without the pads should not exceed 15 lbs. If the difference does exceed 15 lbs., the caliper will have to be rebuilt or replaced. Service if required. When servicing is complete, pump the brakes several times. Do not move the car until a firm brake pedal is present.

### *1984–90 Colt Turbo and 1985–90 Vista*

1. Raise and support the front end on jackstands. Remove the front wheels.

**NOTE: On late models equipped with the PFS15 type front disc brakes, the caliper and pads are retained to the adapter by 2 sleeve pin bolts. Remove the pin bolts and service the assembly as required. Sleeve bolt torque is 16–23 ft. lbs.**

2. Remove the lower pin bolt and rotate the caliper upwards. Support the caliper with wire or string from a nearby suspension member.
3. Remove the inner shim, the anti-squeal shim and the pads from the caliper support assembly.
4. Remove the clips from the pads.
5. Clean all parts in solvent made for brake parts.
6. Inspect the dust boot on the caliper piston. If it is torn or brittle, replace it, and consider rebuilding the caliper.
7. Inspect the shims and liners and

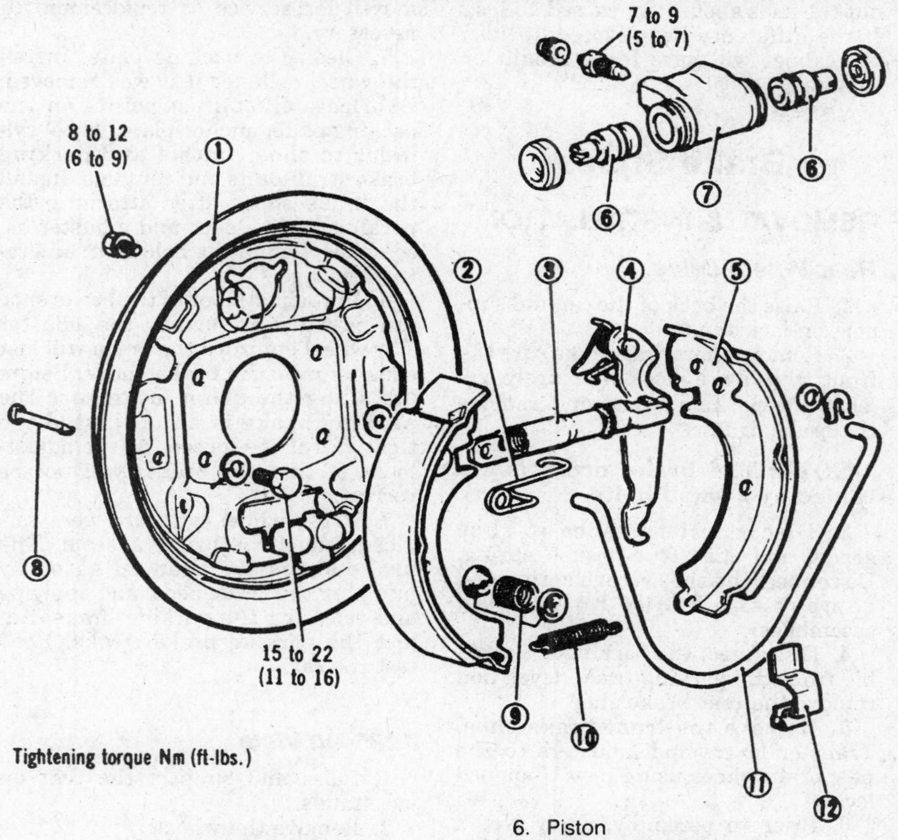


1. Backing plate
2. Spring
3. Adjuster
4. Parking lever
5. Shoe and lining assembly
6. Piston
7. Wheel cylinder body
8. Shoe hold spring pin
9. Shoe hold down spring
10. Shoe to shoe spring
11. Shoe return spring
12. Clip spring

**Typical rear drum brake system used on front wheel drive except Vista**

replace them if damaged.

8. Remove the cap from the master cylinder reservoir and siphon off about ¼ in. of fluid.

9. Using tool MB990520, force the piston back into the caliper as far as it will go. Remove the clamp.

10. Install the pads with clips attached and the proper shims, in position, on the support.

**NOTE: Never replace just one set of pads. Pads should be replaced on both front wheels at the same time.**

11. Lower the caliper and install the lower pin bolt. Torque the bolt to 16–23 ft. lbs.

12. Start the engine and depress the brake pedal. Hold it depressed for about 5 seconds. Turn the engine off.

13. Rotate the brake rotor a few times. Using a spring scale hooked to 1 of the lugs, measure the brake drag. Remove the pads and perform the spring scale test again. The difference between the drag test with and without the pads should not exceed 15 lbs. If the difference does exceed 15 lbs., the caliper will have to be rebuilt or replaced.

14. When servicing is complete, pump the brakes several times, do not operate the vehicle until a firm brake pedal is present. Bleed the brakes if necessary.

### *Conquest*

1. Raise and support the front end on jackstands.

2. Remove the front wheels.

3. Remove the caliper lower slide pin.

**NOTE: There is a grease coating on the bolt. Make sure that it is not removed or contaminated.**

4. Rotate the caliper upward and suspend it with string from a nearby suspension member.

5. Remove the brake pads and shims.

6. Remove the clips from the pads.

7. Clean all parts in solvent made for brake parts.

8. Inspect the dust boot on the caliper piston. If it is torn or brittle, replace it, and consider rebuilding the caliper.

9. Inspect the shims and liners and replace them if damaged.

10. Remove the cap from the master cylinder reservoir and siphon off about ¼ in. of fluid.

11. Using tool MB990520, force the piston back into the caliper as far as it will go. Remove the clamp.

12. Install the pads with clips attached and the proper shims, in position, on the support.

**NOTE: Never replace just one set of pads, pads should be replaced on both front wheels at the same time.**

13. Rotate the caliper back into position and install the lower slider pin. Torque the pin to 70 ft. lbs.

14. Start the engine and depress the brake pedal. Hold it depressed for about 5 seconds. Turn the engine off.

15. Rotate the brake rotor a few times. Using a spring scale hooked to 1 of the lugs, measure the brake drag. Remove the pads and perform the spring scale test again. The difference between the drag test with and without the pads should not exceed 15 lbs. If the difference does exceed 15 lbs., the caliper will have to be rebuilt or replaced.

16. When servicing is complete, pump the brakes several times, do not operate the vehicle until a firm brake pedal is present. Bleed the brakes if necessary.

# Rear Disc Brake Pads

## REMOVAL & INSTALLATION

### *Except Conquest*

1. Block the front wheels, jack up the rear of the car and support on jackstands. Remove the rear wheel and the caliper dust cover.

2. Disconnect the parking brake cable

3. Remove the spring pin and stopper plug.

4. Move the caliper back and forth to loosen, then remove the caliper from the support.

**NOTE: The brake hose need not be disconnected; however, do not suspend the weight of the caliper from the hose.**

5. Take time to examine the location of the various clips and springs. Remove the pads from the support. Do not mix up the inner and outer clips, they must be installed in the same location.
6. Seat the caliper piston by pushing in while turning clockwise (use a special tool). When fully seated, 1 of the grooves on the piston must be located vertically at 12 o'clock to accommodate a projection of the brake pad. Install new pads into the support and install the caliper.

### *Conquest*

1. Raise and support the rear end on jackstands.
2. Remove the wheels.
3. Disconnect the parking brake cable.
4. Remove the lower caliper lockpin, and (depending on year), the upper guide pin.

**NOTE: There is a grease coating on the bolt. Make sure that it is not removed or contaminated.**

5. Rotate the caliper upward (if upper guide pin removal is not required) and suspend it with string from a nearby suspension member.
6. Remove the brake pads and shims.
7. Remove the clips from the pads.
8. Clean all parts in solvent made for brake parts.
9. Inspect the dust boot on the caliper piston. If it is torn or brittle, replace it, and consider rebuilding the caliper.
10. Inspect the shims and liners and replace them if damaged.
11. Remove the cap from the master cylinder reservoir and siphon off about ¼ in. of fluid.
12. Using tool MB990652, align the grooves in the caliper and piston and force the piston back into the caliper as far as it will go. Remove the clamp.
13. Install the pads and shims after attaching the clips in reverse order of removal.

**NOTE: Never replace just one set of pads, pads should be replaced on both front wheels at the same time.**

14. Rotate the caliper back into position and install the lower slider pin. Torque the pin to 45 ft. lbs.
15. Start the engine and depress the brake pedal. Hold it depressed for about 5 seconds. Turn the engine off.
16. Rotate the brake rotor a few times. Using a spring scale hooked to 1 of the lugs, measure the brake drag. Remove the pads and perform the spring scale test again. The difference between the drag test with and without the pads should not exceed 15 lbs., If the difference does exceed 15 lbs., the caliper will have to be rebuilt or replaced.

## Brake Shoes

### REMOVAL & INSTALLATION

#### *Rear Wheel Drive*

1. Raise the back of the car and support on jackstands.
2. Remove the wheel. Make sure the front wheels are blocked securely, release the parking brake and remove the brake drum.

**NOTE: The brake drum is retained by 2 small bolts.**

3. Disconnect the shoe-to-shoe spring and the strut-to-shoe spring. Disconnect the shoe return spring and remove the brake hold-down assemblies.
4. Disconnect the parking brake cable from the parking brake lever and remove the rear brake shoe.
5. Remove the front brake shoe. Transfer levers and adjusters to the new brake shoes using new U-shaped locks.
6. Prior to assembly, apply No. 2 brake grease to the contact area of the strut and parking brake lever and strut and adjusting lever. After cleaning the backing plate apply grease to the brake shoe contact points.
7. Connect the parking brake and install the brake shoes with the adjusters and holddown assemblies. Install the return springs. The lining to drum clearance is automatically adjusted by applying the brakes several times after the drums have been installed. If the wheel cylinders have been rebuilt the brake system must be bled before correct adjustment is possible.

#### *1983–90 Front Wheel Drive except Vista*

1. Remove rear wheel and brake drum.
2. Remove the lower pressed metal spring clip, the shoe return spring (the large one piece spring between the 2 shoes), and the 2 shoe hold-down springs.
3. Remove the shoes and adjuster as an assembly. Disconnect the parking brake cable from the lever, remove the spring between the shoes and the lever from the rear (trailing) shoe. Disconnect the adjuster retaining spring and remove the adjuster, turn the star wheel in to the adjuster body after cleaning and lubricating the threads.
4. The wheel cylinder may be removed for service or replacement, if necessary.
5. Clean the backing plate. Install the wheel cylinder if it was removed. Lubricate all contact points on the backing plate, anchor plate, wheel cylinder to shoe contact and parking brake strut joints and contacts. Install the brake shoes after attaching the parking brake, lever and adjuster assemblies. Install the holddown and return springs.
6. Pre-adjustment of the brake shoe can be made by turning the adjuster star wheel out until the drum will just slide on over the brake shoes. Before installing the drum make sure the parking brake is not adjusted too tightly, if it is—loosen, or the adjustment of the rear brakes will not be correct.
7. If the wheel cylinders were serviced, bleed the brake system. The brake shoes are then adjusted by pumping the brake pedal and applying and releasing the parking brake, Adjust the parking brake stroke. Road test the car.

#### *1985–90 Vista*

1. Raise and support the rear on jackstands.
2. Remove the wheels.
3. Remove the brake drums.
4. Remove the shoe-to-strut spring.
5. Remove the shoe-to-shoe spring.
6. Remove the shoe hold-down spring.
7. Remove the shoe retainer clip.
8. Remove the leading shoe.
9. Remove the brake cable from the lever.
10. Remove the trailing shoe.
11. Remove the brake cable snapring and remove the cable.
12. Inspect all parts for wear or damage. Heat damage is a problem common to brake systems. Sign of heat damage are bluing and cracking. It's a good idea, when replacing brake shoes, to replace all the brake hardware, i.e., springs and clips.

**NOTE: Never replace shoes on one side only! Replace both sets of shoes at the same time.**

13. Assembly the parking brake and adjuster assemblies on the brake shoes. Install the brake shoes and holddowns. Connect the return springs. Apply a small amount of lithium based grease to the contact pads of the backing plate before installing the shoes. When installing the shoe-to-shoe spring and shoe-to-strut spring, set the adjuster lever all the way back against the shoe. When everything is assembled, pump the pedal several times and adjust the brakes.

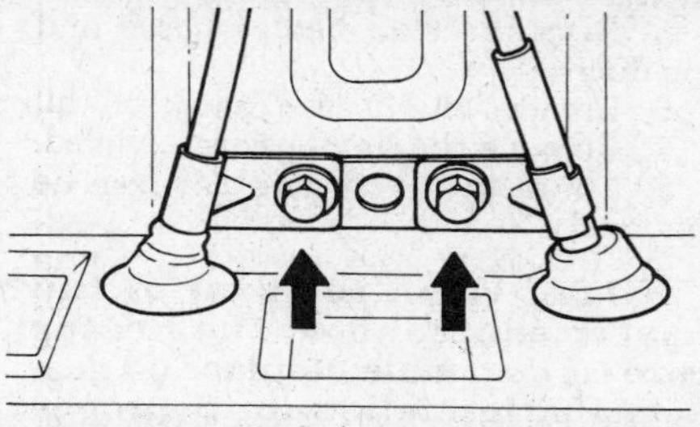

Location of cable clamp attaching bolts in passenger compartment—all except Vista

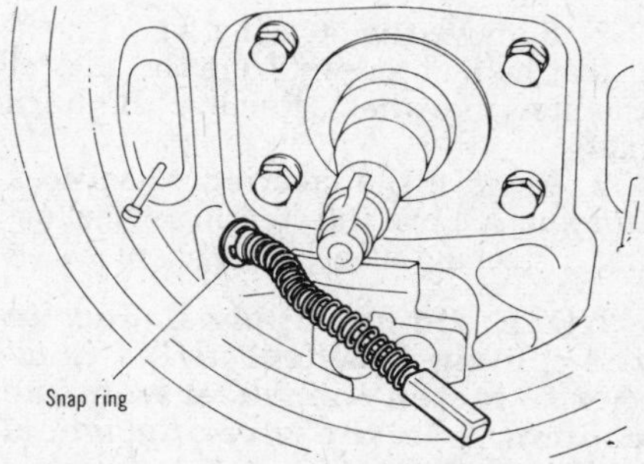


Cable snap ring on backing plate

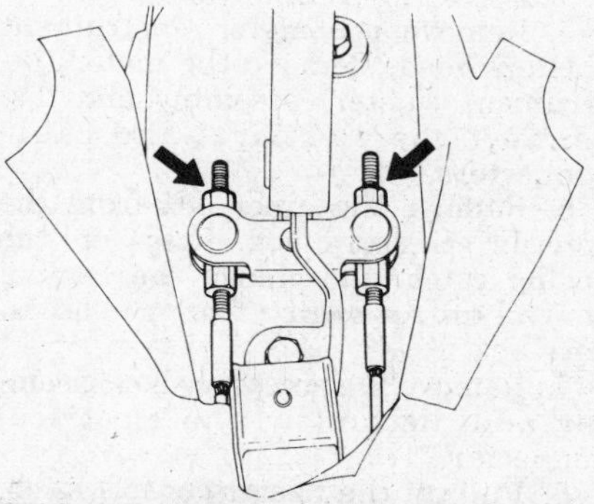

Cable adjusting nuts—front wheel drive models except Vista

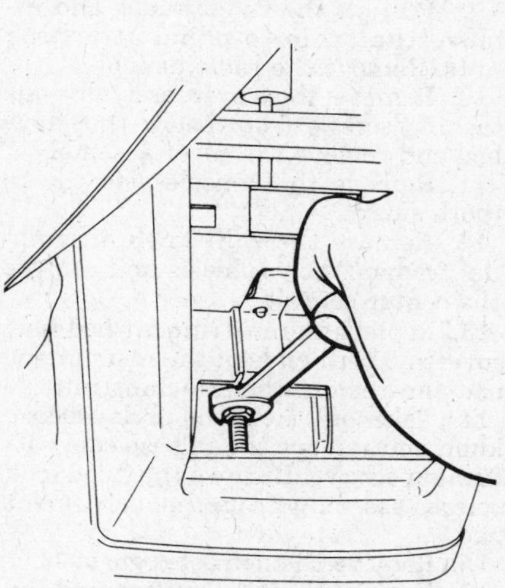

1985 and later Colt parking brake cable adjustment

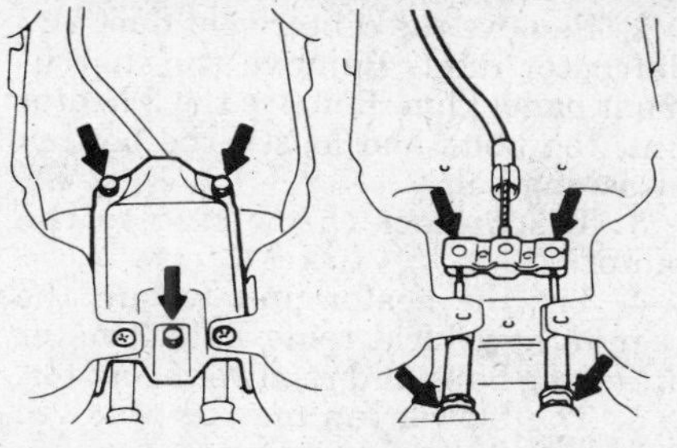

Parking brake equalizer cover bolts and cable coupler—Colt Vista

## Wheel Cylinders

### REMOVAL & INSTALLATION

**NOTE: Most wheel cylinders can be rebuilt while mounted in position on the brake backing plate. However, if the cylinder must be removed, disconnect the brake line and unbolt the cylinder after the brake shoes have be removed.**

1. Remove the brake shoes.
2. Place a bucket or some old newspapers under the brake backing plate to catch the brake fluid that will run out of the wheel cylinder. Disconnect the brake line and remove the cylinder mounting bolts. Remove the cylinder from the backing plate.
3. Install the cylinder in the reverse order. Bleed the brake system.

## Parking Brake Cable

### ADJUSTMENT

#### *1983–84*

Release the parking brake lever. Loosen the lock (rear) nuts on each side of the lever or on the frame bracket. Tighten the adjusting (front) nuts to increase tension, or loosen to reduce. Any adjustment must be made evenly on both sides. Be sure, after adjustment, that when the parking brake is released the rear wheels will turn freely with no brake shoe drag. Handbrake travel should be; 6 to 8 notches.

**NOTE: Lever stroke of less than 5 notches, will cause the adjuster to malfunction i.e., not adjust.**

#### *1985–90 Except Conquest*

1. Pull the parking brake lever up with a force of about 45 lbs. If that value cannot be determined, just pull it up as far as you can. The total number of clicks heard should be 5–7.
2. If the number of clicks was not within that range, release the lever and back off the cable adjuster locknut at the base of the lever and tighten the adjusting nut until there is no more slack in the cable.
3. Operate the lever and brake pedal several times, until no more clicks are heard from the automatic adjuster.
4. Turn the adjusting nut to give the proper number of clicks when the lever is raised full travel.
5. Raise and support the rear of the car on jackstands.
6. Release the brake lever and make sure that the rear wheels turn freely. If not, back off on the adjusting nut until they do.

#### *Conquest*

1. Pull up on the lever, counting the number of clicks. Total travel should yield 4–5 clicks.
2. If not, remove the center console and turn the adjusting nut on the lever rod to obtain the required travel.
3. Raise and support the rear of the car on jackstands.
4. With the parking brake released, make sure that the rear wheels turn freely.

### REMOVAL & INSTALLATION

#### *Rear Wheel Drive*

1. Block the front wheels, jack up the rear of the car and support with jackstands.
2. Release the parking brake. Pull off the clevis pins from both sides of the rear brake. Disconnect the cable from the extension lever.
3. On drum brake models (through 1980) loosen the parking brake lever mounting bolts and disconnect the front end of the rear cable from the equalizer. On 1981 and later models, remove brake drums, disconnect cable from lever, remove retaining clip and remove cable through brake backing plate. Remove the front cable after disconnecting the parking brake lever. On rear disc brake models, remove the rubber hanger from the center of the axle housing. Remove the parking brake lever and clevis pin linking the lever and cable. Remove the clips under the floor and remove the cable.
4. Install the cable. When installing, make sure that the cable clips do not interfere with a rotating part. Adjust the extension lever to stop first. Then adjust the left cable, then the right on the Challenger and Wagons.

#### *Front Wheel Drive Models*

1. Block front wheels, raise rear of car and support on jackstands.
2. Disconnect the brake cable at the parking brake lever (brakes released). Remove the cable clamps inside the driver's compartment (2 bolts). On

1985 Colt, remove the rear seat. Disconnect the clamps on the rear suspension arm.
3. Remove the rear brake drums and the brake shoes assemblies. Disconnect the parking brake cable from the lever on the trailing (rear) brake shoe. Remove the brake cables.
4. Install the cable and adjust.

# CHASSIS ELECTRICAL

## Heater Blower Motor

### REMOVAL & INSTALLATION

#### *1983 Colt Coupe, Sedan, and Rear Wheel Drive Hatchback*

1. Remove the instrument cluster (coupe and sedan). Remove the instrument cluster and the glove box (hatchback).
2. Remove the heater control bracket assembly.
3. Remove the motor assembly and disconnect the wire connection.
4. (Coupe and sedan) Remove the motor in a horizontal position while holding the control bracket down.
5. (Hatchback) Remove the motor through the glove box opening.
6. Installation is the reverse of removal.

#### *1983 Challenger and Sapporo*

1. Remove the lower instrument pad cover assembly from under the glove box.
2. Remove the passenger side console cover.
3. Remove the glove box-to-center support attaching screw.
4. Loosen the stops at either side of the glove box so that the glove box swings free.
5. Disconnect the glove box light.
6. Remove the glove compartment assembly from the instrument pad.
7. Remove the ducts, heater fan switch connector and control cables.
8. Remove 3 attaching bolts and lift out the blower assembly.
9. Remove the wiring bracket and the motor connector. Remove the vent tube and 3 motor attaching screws. Lift out the motor and remove the fan from the motor assembly.
10. Installation is the reverse of removal.

#### *1983–84 Front Wheel Drive*

1. Disconnect the battery ground cable. Remove the center console and parcel tray, if equipped.
2. Remove the center vent duct and defroster duct. Remove the instrument panel trim. Remove the 2 heater unit top bolts and loosen the bottom attaching bolt.
3. Disconnect the wiring to the motor.
4. Tilt the heater unit toward the rear of the vehicle, remove the 3 motor attaching bolts and remove the motor.
5. The blower fan may be removed from the shaft if necessary.
6. Installation is the reverse of the removal procedure.

#### *1985–90 Colt*

1. Remove the glove box and parcel tray.
2. Disconnect the changeover control wire and duct.
3. Remove the blower case.
4. Unbolt and remove the blower motor from the case.
5. The fan is removable from the motor shaft.
6. Installation is the reverse of removal.

#### *Vista*

1. Remove the upper and lower glove boxes.
2. Disconnect the wiring from the blower assembly.
3. Remove the blower motor mounting bolts and lift out the motor. If the entire blower case is to be removed, the instrument panel will have to be removed first.

#### *Conquest*

1. Remove the lower panel cover and the glove box.
2. Disconnect the air changeover cable from the blower.
3. Disconnect the duct from the blower.
4. Disconnect the blower wiring.
5. Unbolt and remove the blower motor.
6. Installation is the reverse of removal.

## Heater Core

**NOTE: The core is contained within the heater case. The core and case are removed as a unit.**

### REMOVAL & INSTALLATION

#### *1983 Station Wagon*

1. Drain the cooling system.
2. Remove the glove box, instrument cluster and console assembly.
3. Disconnect the heater control wires at the heater box.
4. Remove the heater control assembly.
5. Disconnect all heater hoses and air ducts.
6. Remove the heater assembly.
7. Remove the heater core.
8. Installation is the reverse of removal.

**NOTE: Upon removal of the heater control box, the heater core is removable. Replace all gaskets and insulation in its proper place.**

#### *1983 Challenger and Sapporo*

1. Disconnect the negative battery terminal.
2. Remove the steering wheel horn pad attaching screws, from the back of the steering wheel. Remove the horn pad.
3. Remove the steering wheel lock nut and remove the steering wheel using a steering wheel puller tool.

**NOTE: Do not apply impact to the column or wheel with a hammer to loosen the wheel from the column. Use the steering wheel puller tool.**

4. Loosen the tilt lock lever and lower the steering column fully.
5. Remove the meter (instrument cluster) hood. Remove the meter (instrument cluster) assembly and disconnect the electrical and cable connectors.
6. Remove the inner box from the console accessory box. Press on the spring catch, to remove the remote control mirror switch from the accessory box.
7. Remove the accessory box assembly and disconnect the electrical connector.
8. Pull off the heater control knob, pull out the control panel and take out the illumination harness.
9. Pull off the radio knobs and remove the radio to panel attaching nuts. Remove the radio panel.
10. Remove the cover assembly attaching screws from below the glove box and remove the cover assembly.
11. Remove the console side covers (both sides).
12. Remove the shift knob on manual transmission vehicles and remove the center console.
13. Remove the instrument pad bolt covers at both ends of the instrument pad and remove the attaching nuts.
14. Take off the hood lock release knob and remove the release cable attaching screws. Remove the hood lock release assembly from the instrument pad.
15. Remove the defroster garnish.
16. Remove the screws attaching the glove compartment to the center dash reinforcement.

17. Remove all remaining instrument pad attaching bolts.
18. Disconnect the clock, glove box, chime and dimmer control and remove the instrument pad.
19. Disconnect the defogger switch, radio, chime driver, defogger relay connectors and the antenna feeder end.
20. Remove the center reinforcement.
21. Set the heater temperature control to warm position and drain the coolant from the radiator.
22. From the engine compartment, remove the heater hoses from the heater assembly.
23. From under the dash, remove the heater ducts from the heater assembly. To remove the rear seat heater duct, move the outlet control link to the vent side, insert a finger into the outlet and remove the duct from inside heater.
24. Disconnect the power relay connector, remove 3 attaching bolts and remove the heater assembly. Remove the heater core.
25. The installation is the reverse of removal.
26. Connect the heater hoses in a fully seated position on the inlet and outlet fittings of the heater core assembly, so they will not leak.
27. Adjust the heater control cable by setting the control panel to cool and heater unit lever on cool and tighten the cable at that position.

**NOTE: In order to fill the engine cooling and heating system completely it may be necessary to open the water valve fully, run the engine to circulate the coolant and then stop the engine and add more coolant.**

#### *1983–84 Front Wheel Drive Colt and Champ Models*

1. Disconnect the battery ground cable.
2. Place the water valve lever in the hot position. Drain the coolant.
3. Remove the center console and parcel tray, if equipped.
4. Remove the center ventilation duct and the defroster duct. Disconnect the instrument trim panel and cluster hood.
5. Disconnect all control wires at the heater unit.
6. Disconnect the heater hose from the engine. Remove the clamps from the hoses. Disconnect the heater wiring harness.
7. Remove the 2 top mounting bolts and the 1 lower nut. Remove the heater assembly.
8. Installation is the reverse of removal. Be sure the grommets through which the heater hoses pass when entering the passenger compartment are secured when reinstalling.

#### *1985–90 Colt and Vista*

1. Disconnect the battery ground cable.
2. Set the heater control lever to warm.
3. Drain the cooling system.
4. Remove the instrument panel.
5. Remove the duct from between the heater unit and the blower case.
6. Disconnect the coolant hoses at the heater case.
7. Unbolt and remove the heater case.
8. Remove the hose and pipe clamps and remove the water valve.
9. Remove the core from the case.
10. Set the mixing damper to the closed position, and, with the damper in that position, install the rod so that the water valve is fully closed.
11. Place the damper lever in the vent position, and adjust the linkage so that the foot/def damper opens to the def side and the vent damper is level with the separator.
12. Install the hoses. They are marked for flow direction.
13. The remainder of assembly is the reverse of disassembly.

#### *Conquest*

1. Move the control lever to warm.
2. Drain the coolant at the radiator.
3. Disconnect the coolant hoses at the heater unit.
4. Remove the instrument panel and floor console.
5. Remove the center ventilation duct, defroster duct and lap heater duct.
6. Remove the center instrument panel brace.
7. Remove the heater control assembly.
8. Remove the 3 screws and lift out the heater case.
9. Check the core for leaks, clogging and bent fins. Replace or repair as necessary.
10. Installation is the reverse of removal. Replace any cracked hoses or damaged insulation. Refill the system and check for leaks.

## Radio

### REMOVAL & INSTALLATION

#### 1985–90 COLT

1. Remove the floor console.
2. Remove the radio and mounting bracket from the console.

**NOTE: The radio fuse is on the back of the radio. The left front speaker is accessed through the corner panel. To get to the right front speaker, remove the glove box and air duct. The rear speakers are easily accessed.**

#### VISTA

1. Remove the radio trim panel.
2. Remove the console side cover and disconnect the wiring connector and antenna cable.
3. Remove the mounting screws and slide the radio out of the panel.
4. The front speakers are accessed by removing the left or right trim panels. The rear speakers are accessed by removing the rear door trim panels.
5. Installation is the reverse of removal.

#### CONQUEST

1. Remove the front console box.
2. Remove the radio trim panel.
3. Remove the attaching screws and lift out the radio and mounting bracket.
4. To remove the front speaker, the instrument panel pad must first be removed.
5. The door speakers are accessed by removing the door trim panels.
6. The rear speakers are accessed by removing the rear trim panels.
7. Installation of all components is the reverse of removal.

## Windshield Wiper Switch

**NOTE: On all rear wheel drive cars, and Vista, the wiper switch is integral with the turn signal switch. For wiper switch service, follow the procedures listed under "Turn Signal Switch," earlier in this section.**

### REMOVAL & INSTALLATION

#### *1983–84*

1. Remove the instrument cluster.
2. Pull out on the wiper switch knob to remove it.
3. Remove the 2 attaching screws and pull the switch from the panel.
4. Installation is the reverse of removal.

#### *1985–90*

1. Remove the steering wheel.
2. Remove the steering column cover.
3. Pull out and remove the switch knob.
4. Remove the 2 mounting screws and pull the switch out.
5. Installation is the reverse of removal.

## Windshield Wiper Motor

### REMOVAL & INSTALLATION

#### *Except Vista, Conquest and 1985–90 Colt*

1. Remove the motor bracket and body retaining bolts. Remove the wiper arms and unbolt and remove the cowl panel.
2. Remove the wiper arm shaft nut on the driver's side of the car and pull the motor assembly out.
3. Remove the bushing and disconnect the motor crank arm and linkage.
4. Install the motor in the reverse order of removal.

#### *Vista and 1985–90 Colt*

1. Remove the wiper arms.
2. Remove the front cowl trim plate.
3. Remove the pivot shaft mounting nuts and push the pivot shaft toward the inside.
4. Disconnect the linkage from the motor and lift out the linkage.
5. Unbolt and remove the motor.
6. Installation is the reverse of removal.

**NOTE: When installing the arms, the at-rest position of the blade tips-to-windshield molding should be:**

Vista passenger's side–30mm, driver's side: 25mm.

Colt passenger's side–20mm, driver's side: 15mm.

#### *Conquest*

1. Remove the wiper arm and pivot shaft mounting nut, remove the arms and push the pivot shaft toward the inside.
2. Remove the cover from the wiper access hole on the right side of the front deck panel.
3. Loosen the wiper motor mounting bolts, pull the motor out slightly, disconnect the motor from the linkage, then remove the motor and linkage. If the motor's crank arm is to be removed, mark its position first.
4. Installation is the reverse of removal. Install the wiper arms so that the blade tip-to-windshield molding distance, at rest, is ½ in.

## Instrument Cluster

### REMOVAL & INSTALLATION

#### *Challenger and Sapporo*

1. Remove the battery ground cable.
2. Remove 3 screws from the top and 3 screws from the bottom of the cluster assembly.

**NOTE: 2 of the bottom screws are located behind the brake warning and fasten seat belt lens and the third bottom screw is located at the ash tray opening. A thin tipped screwdriver or a wire hook is required to remove the lenses to gain access to the screws.**

3. Move the instrument cluster away from the dash and disconnect the meter connections, heater fan connections, speedometer cable and any other connector or ground cables.
4. Remove the cluster assembly from the dash.
5. Installation is the reverse of removal.

#### *1983–84 Colt and Champ*

1. Remove the steering wheel.
2. Remove the heater control knobs.
3. Remove the cluster panel attaching screws.
4. Remove the light switch, wiper switch, clock and indicator connectors.
5. Remove the cluster panel.
6. Remove the combination meter attaching screws.
7. Pull the combination meter out slightly and disconnect the speedometer cable and electrical connectors. Lift out the combination meter.
8. Installation is the reverse of removal.

#### *1985–90 Colt*

1. Remove the steering wheel.
2. Remove the glove box.
3. Remove the instrument panel heater duct.
4. Remove the parcel tray.
5. Remove the steering column lower cover.
6. Disconnect the light switch and wiper switch connectors.
7. Remove the steering column upper cover.
8. Remove the instrument cluster hood screws and lift off the hood.
9. Remove the cluster mounting screws and pull the cluster slightly forward. Disconnect the speedometer cable and electrical connectors and lift out the cluster.
10. Installation is the reverse of removal.

#### *Vista*

1. Remove the steering wheel.
2. Remove the ashtray.
3. Pry off (carefully) the cluster hood cover.
4. Remove the cluster hood mounting screws.
5. Pull the hood slightly toward the front and release the connectors. Lift the hood off.
6. Remove the 4 cluster mounting screws, pull the cluster slightly toward the front and disconnect the speedometer cable and electrical connectors.
7. Lift out the cluster.
8. Installation is the reverse of removal.

#### *Conquest*

**CAUTION**

***The following procedure applies to both the conventional needle-type gauge cluster and to the liquid crystal display type. Because the LCD gauges are composed of very delicate components, they must not be subjected to severe shocks. Furthermore, the LCD gauges must not be disassembled.***

1. Remove the cluster hood attaching screws.
2. Pull outward on both bottom side edges of the hood, and, while holding it in that position, pull it upward and off.
3. Disconnect the wiring to the hood switches.
4. Remove the cluster case attaching screws.
5. Pull both sides of the lower part of the cluster case up and toward the rear of the vehicle.
6. Disconnect the speedometer cable from the back of the case.
7. Disconnect all wiring at the back of the case and lift the case out.
8. Installation is the reverse of removal.

## Headlight Switch

### REMOVAL & INSTALLATION

1. Disconnect the negative battery cable.
2. Disconnect the electrical connections from the switch.
3. Remove the knob and the ring nut.
4. Pull the switch back from behind the trim panel and out under the dash.
5. Installation is the reverse of the removal procedure.

## Fuse Box

### LOCATION

#### *Front Wheel Drive and Conquest*

The fuse block is located up under the instrument panel on the driver's side of the steering column.

#### *All Other Models*

The fuse block is located on the lower part of the driver's side front pillar post.

# Chevrolet Imports/GEO

**Chevrolet**—Nova, Spectrum, Sprint
**GEO**—Prizm, Metro

# 5

# SERIAL NUMBER IDENTIFICATION

## ENGINE IDENTIFICATION

| Year | Model | Engine Displacement cu. in. (cc/liter) | Engine Series Identification | No. of Cylinders | Engine Type |
|---|---|---|---|---|---|
| 1985 | Sprint | 61 (1000/1.0) | — | 3 | SOHC |
| | Spectrum | 90 (1471/1.5) | 4XC1-U | 4 | SOHC |
| | Nova | 97 (1600/1.6) | 4A-LC | 4 | SOHC |
| 1986 | Sprint | 61 (1000/1.0) | — | 3 | SOHC |
| | Spectrum | 90 (1471/1.5) | 4XC1-U | 4 | SOHC |
| | Nova | 97 (1600/1.6) | 4A-LC | 4 | SOHC |
| 1987 | Sprint | 61 (1000/1.0) | — | 3 | SOHC |
| | Spectrum | 90 (1471/1.5) | 4XC-U | 4 | SOHC |
| | Nova | 97 (1600/1.6) | 4A-LC | 4 | SOHC |
| 1988 | Sprint/Firefly | 61 (1000/1.0) | — | 3 | SOHC |
| | Spectrum | 90 (1471/1.5) | 4XC1-U | 4 | SOHC |
| | Spectrum | 90 (1471/1.5) | 4XC1-UT | 4 | SOHC |
| | Nova | 97 (1600/1.6) | 4A-LC | 4 | SOHC |
| | Nova | 97 (1600/1.6) | 4A-GEL | 4 | DOHC |
| 1989-90 | Metro | 61 (1000/1.0) | — | 3 | SOHC |
| | Spectrum | 90 (1471/1.0) | 4XC1-U | 4 | SOHC |
| | Prizm | 97 (1600/1.6) | 4A-FE | 4 | DOHC |

SOHC Single overhead cam engine
DOHC Dual overhead cam engine

## GENERAL ENGINE SPECIFICATIONS

| Year | Model | Engine Displacement cu. in. (cc) | Fuel System Type | Net Horsepower @ rpm | Net Torque @ rpm (ft. lbs.) | Bore × Stroke (in.) | Com-pression Ratio | Oil Pressure @ rpm |
|---|---|---|---|---|---|---|---|---|
| 1985 | Sprint | 61 (1000) | 2 bbl | 48 @ 5100 | 57 @ 3200 | 2.91 × 3.03 | 9.5:1 | 48 |
| | Spectrum | 90 (1471) | 2 bbl | 70 @ 4800 | 87 @ 3400 | 3.031 × 3.111 | 9.6:1 | 49 @ 5200 |
| | Nova | 97 1600) | 2 bbl | 70 @ 4800 | 85 @ 2800 | 3.19 × 3.03 | 9.0:1 | 34 @ 2000 |
| 1986 | Sprint | 61 (1000) | 2 bbl | 48 @ 5100 | 57 @ 3200 | 2.91 × 3.03 | 9.5:1 | 48 |
| | Spectrum | 90 (1471) | 2 bbl | 70 @ 5400 | 87 @ 3400 | 3.031 × 3.111 | 9.6:1 | 49 @ 5200 |
| | Nova | 97 (1600) | 2 bbl | 74 @ 4800 | 85 @ 2800 | 3.19 × 3.03 | 9.0:1 | 34 @ 2000 |
| 1987 | Sprint | 61 (1000) | 2 bbl | 48 @ 5100 | 77 @ 3200 | 2.91 × 3.03 | 9.5:1 | 48 |
| | Sprint | 61 (1000) | 2 bbl | 46 @ 4700 | 78 @ 3200 | 2.91 × 3.03 | 9.8:1 | 48 |
| | Sprint | 61 (1000) | EFI | 70 @ 5500 | 107 @ 3500 | 2.91 × 3.03 | 8.3:1 | 48 |
| | Spectrum | 90 (1471) | 2 bbl | 70 @ 5400 | 87 @ 3400 | 3.031 × 3.110 | 8.2:1 | 49 @ 5200 |
| | Spectrum | 90 (1471) | Turbo | 110 @ 5400 | 120 @ 3400 | 3.031 × 3.110 | 8.0:1 | 49 @ 5200 |
| | Nova | 97 (1600) | 2 bbl | 74 @ 5200 | 85 @ 2800 | 3.19 × 3.03 | 9:0:1 | 34 @ 2000 |

## GENERAL ENGINE SPECIFICATIONS

| Year | Model | Engine Displacement cu. in. (cc) | Fuel System Type | Net Horsepower @ rpm | Net Torque @ rpm (ft. lbs.) | Bore × Stroke (in.) | Com-pression Ratio | Oil Pressure @ rpm |
|---|---|---|---|---|---|---|---|---|
| 1988 | Sprint | 61 (1000) | 2 bbl | 48 @ 5100 | 77 @ 3200 | 2.91 × 3.03 | 9.5:1 | 48 |
| | Sprint | 61 (1000) | 2 bbl | 46 @ 4700 | 78 @ 3200 | 2.91 × 3.03 | 9.8:1 | 48 |
| | Sprint | 61 (1000) | EFI | 70 @ 5500 | 107 @ 3500 | 2.91 × 3.03 | 8.3:1 | 48 |
| | Spectrum | 90 (1471) | 2 bbl | 70 @ 5400 | 87 @ 3400 | 3.031 × 3.110 | 9.6:1 | 49 @ 5200 |
| | Spectrum | 90 (1471) | Turbo | 110 @ 5400 | 120 @ 3400 | 3.031 × 3.110 | 8.0:1 | 49 @ 5200 |
| | Nova | 97 (1600) | 2 bbl | 74 @ 5200 | 85 @ 2800 | 3.19 × 3.03 | 9.0:1 | 34 @ 2000 |
| | Nova | 97 (1600) | EFI | 110 @ 6600 | 98 @ 4800 | 3.19 × 3.03 | 9.4:1 | 56 @ 3000 |
| 1989-90 | Metro | 61 (1000) | EFI | 55 @ 5700 | 58 @ 3300 | 2.91 × 3.03 | 9.5:1 | 39 @ 4000 |
| | Metro | 61 (1000) | EFI | 49 @ 4700 | 58 @ 3300 | 2.91 × 3.03 | 9.5:1 | 39 @ 4000 |
| | Spectrum | 90 (1471) | 2 bbl | 70 @ 5400 | 87 @ 3400 | 3.031 × 3.110 | 9.6:1 | 49 @ 5200 |
| | Prizm | 97 (1600) | MFI | 102 @ 5800 | 101 @ 4800 | 3.19 × 3.03 | 9.5:1 | 56 @ 3000 |

① ER model
② LSI model

## GASOLINE ENGINE TUNE-UP SPECIFICATIONS

| Year | Model | Engine Displacement cu. in. (cc) | Spark Plugs Type | Spark Plugs Gap (in.) | Ignition Timing (deg.) MT | Ignition Timing (deg.) AT | Com-pression Pressure (psi) | Fuel Pump (psi) | Idle Speed (rpm) MT | Idle Speed (rpm) AT | Valve Clearance In. | Valve Clearance Ex. |
|---|---|---|---|---|---|---|---|---|---|---|---|---|
| 1985 | Sprint | 61 (1000) | R43CXLS | 0.039–0.043 | 10 | 6 | 199 | 3.5 | — | 850 | 0.006 | 0.008 |
| | Spectrum | 90 (1471) | BPR6ES-11 | 0.043 | 15 | 10 | 128-179 | 3.8–4.7 | 700 | 950 | 0.006 | 0.010 |
| | Nova | 97 (1600) | ⑥ | 0.043 | 0 | 0 | 160 | 2.5–3.5– | 650 | 800 | 0.008 | 0.012 |
| 1986 | Sprint | 61 (1000) | R43CXLS | 0.039–0.043 | 10 | 6 | 199 | 3.5 | 750 | 850 | 0.006 | 0.008 |
| | Spectrum | 90 (1471) | BPR6ES-11 | 0.040 | 15① | 10③ | 128-179 | 3.8–4.7 | 700 | 950 | 0.006 | 0.010 |
| | Nova | 97 (1600) | ⑥ | 0.043 | 0 | 0 | 160 | 2.5–3.5 | 650 | 750 | 0.008 | 0.012 |
| 1987 | Sprint | 61 (1000) | R43CXLS | 0.039–0.043 | 10 | 6 | 199 | 4.0 | 750⑪ | 850 | 0.006 | 0.008 |
| | Sprint | 61 (1000)⑨ | R43CXLS | 0.039–0.043 | 12 | — | 199 | 25–33 | 750 | — | 0.006 | 0.008 |
| | Spectrum | 90 (1471) | BPR6ES-11 | 0.040 | 15① | 10③ | 128-179 | 3.8–4.7 | 700 | 950 | 0.006 | 0.010 |
| | Spectrum | 90 (1471)⑨ | BPR6ES-11 | 0.040 | 15② | NA | 128-179 | 28.4⑤ | 950 | NA | 0.006 | 0.010 |
| | Nova | 97 (1600) | ⑥ | 0.043 | 0 | 0 | 160 | 2.5–3.5 | 650 | 800 | 0.008 | 0.012 |

## GASOLINE ENGINE TUNE-UP SPECIFICATIONS

| Year | Model | Engine Displacement cu. in. (cc) | Spark Plugs Type | Spark Plugs Gap (in.) | Ignition Timing (deg.) MT | Ignition Timing (deg.) AT | Compression Pressure (psi) | Fuel Pump (psi) | Idle Speed (rpm) MT | Idle Speed (rpm) AT | Valve Clearance In. | Valve Clearance Ex. |
|---|---|---|---|---|---|---|---|---|---|---|---|---|
| 1988 | Sprint | 61 (1000) | R43CXLS | 0.039–0.043 | 10 | 6 | 199 | 4.0 | 750⑪ | 850 | 0.006 | 0.008 |
| | Sprint | 61 (1000)⑨ | R43CXLS | 0.039–0.043 | 12 | – | 199 | 2.5–3.3 | 750 | – | 0.006 | 0.008 |
| | Spectrum | 90 (1471) | BPR6ES-11 | 0.040 0.043 | 15① | 10③ | 128-179 | 3.8–4.7 | 700 | 950 | 0.006 | 0.010 |
| | Spectrum | 90 (1471)⑨ | BPR6ES-11 | 0.040 | 15② | NA | 128-179 | 2.8④ | 950 | NA | 0.006 | 0.010 |
| | Nova | 97 (1600) | ⑥ | 0.043 | 0 | 0 | 128-178 | 3.5 | 650 | 750 | 0.008 | 0.012 |
| | Nova | 97 (1600)⑩ | BCPR5EP11 | 0.043 | | 10B④ | 142-179 | NA | 800 | 800 | ⑦ | ⑧ |
| 1989 | Metro | 61 (1000) | R43CXLS | 0.039–0.043 | ⑬ | ⑬ | 199 | 26 | 750 | 850 | Hyd. | Hyd. |
| | Spectrum | 90 (1471) | R42XLS | 0.040 | 15① | 10③ | 128-179 | 3.8–4.7 | 750 | 1000 | 0.006 | 0.010 |
| | Prizm | 97 (1600) | BCPRSEY | 0.031 | 10B | 10B | 142-191 | ⑫ | 700 | 700 | 0.006–0.010 | 0.008–0.012 |
| 1990 | SEE UNDERHOOD SPECIFICATIONS STICKER | | | | | | | | | | | |

**NOTE**—The underhood specifications sticker often reflects tune-up specification changes made in production. Sticker figures must be used if they disagree with those in this chart.

NA Not available

① @ 750 rpm

② @ 950 rpm

③ @ 1000 rpm

④ Use jumper wire to short circuit both terminals of the check engine connector located need the wiper motor. When the jumper wire is removed and the transaxle is in Neutral, the ignition timing should be more than 16 degrees BTDC (manual) or 12 degrees BTDC (automatic)

⑤ @ 900 rpm with pressure regulator connected

⑥ USA—BPR5EY11
Calif—BPR4EY11

⑦ Cold—0.006-0.010 in.
Hot—0.008-0.012 in.

⑧ Cold—0.008-0.012 in.
Hot—0.010-0.014 in.

⑨ Turbo engine

⑩ Twin Cam engine

⑪ ER Model—700 rpm

⑫ See "Pressure Testing" in text

⑬ See Underhood Sticker

## FIRING ORDERS

NOTE: To avoid confusion, always replace spark plug wires one at a time.

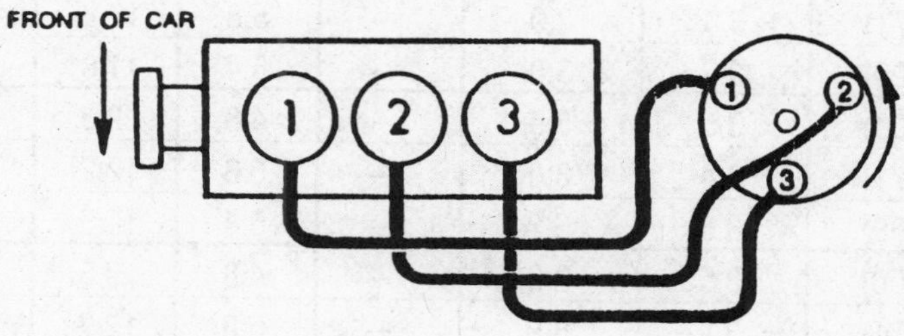


**GM Sprint and Metro 3–61 (1.0L)**
**Engine firing order:1–3–2**
**Distributor rotation: counterclockwise**

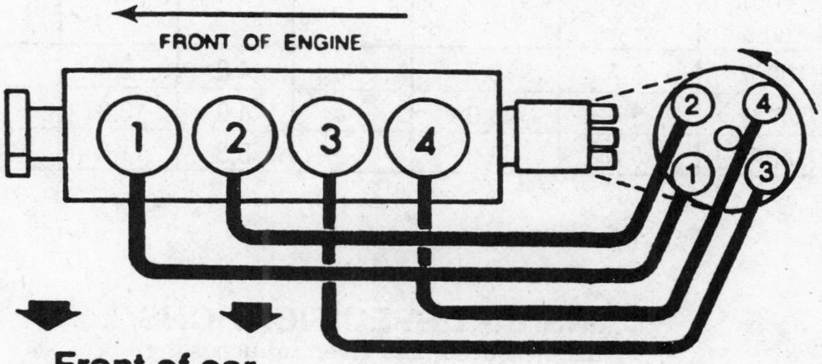


**GM (Isuzu) 4-90 (1.5L)**
**Engine firing order: 1-3-4-2**
**Distributor rotation: counterclockwise – Spectrum**

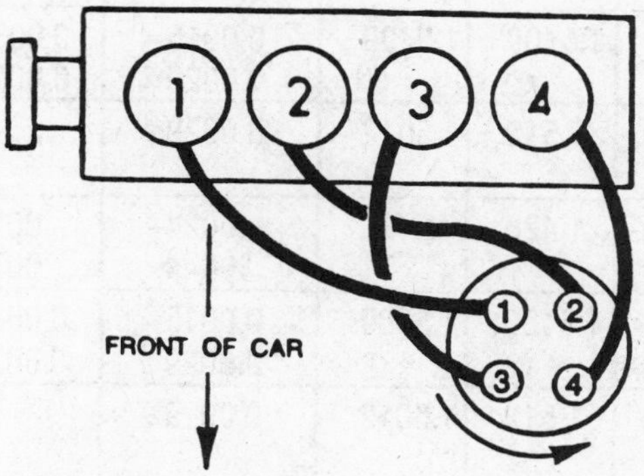


**1.6L 4A-LC 8-valve engine**
**Firing order: 1-3-4-2 – Nova**

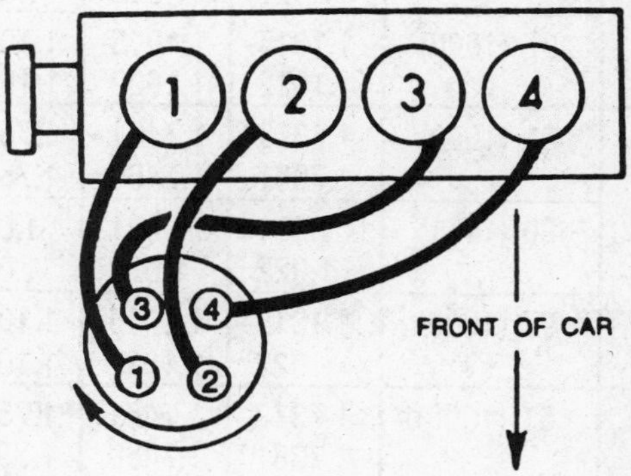


**1.6L 4A-GE and 4-AF 16-valve, twincam engine**
**Firing order: 1-3-4-2 – Nova and Prizm**

## CAPACITIES

| Year | Model | Engine Displacement cu. in. (cc) | Engine Crankcase with Filter | Engine Crankcase without Filter | Transmission (pts.) 4-Spd | Transmission (pts.) 5-Spd | Transmission (pts.) Auto. | Drive Axle (pts.) | Fuel Tank (gal.) | Cooling System (qts.) |
|---|---|---|---|---|---|---|---|---|---|---|
| 1985 | Sprint | 61 (1000) | 3.5 | 3.5 | — | 4.8 | — | — | 8.3 | 4.5 |
| | Spectrum | 90 (1471) | 3.4 | 3.0 | — | 5.8 | 12.2 | — | 11.0 | 6.8 |
| | Nova | 97 (1600) | 3.2 | 3.0 | — | 5.4 | 11.6 | — | 13.2 | 6.2 |
| 1986 | Sprint | 61 (1000) | 3.5 | 3.5 | — | 4.8 | 9.5 | — | 8.3 | 4.5 |
| | Spectrum | 90 (1471) | 3.4 | 3.0 | — | 5.8 | 12.2 | — | 11.0 | 6.8 |
| | Nova | 97 (1600) | 3.5 | 3.2 | — | 5.4 | 11.6 | — | 13.2 | 6.3 |
| 1987 | Sprint | 61 (1000) | 3.5 | 3.5 | — | 4.8 | 9.5 | — | 8.3 | 4.5 |
| | Spectrum | 90 (1471) | 3.4 | 3.0 | — | 5.8 | 12.2 | — | 11.0 | 7.5 |
| | Nova | 97 (1600) | 3.5 | 3.2 | — | 5.4 | 11.6 | — | 13.2 | 6.3 |
| 1988 | Sprint | 61 (1000) | 3.5 | 3.5 | — | 4.8 | 9.5 | — | 8.3 | 4.5 |
| | Spectrum | 90 (1471) | 3.4 | 3.0 | — | 5.8 | 12.2 | — | 11.0 | 6.8 |
| | Nova | 97 (1600) | 3.5 | 3.2 | — | 5.4 | 11.6 | — | 13.2 | 6.4 |
| | Nova | 97 (1600) Turbo | 3.9 | 3.6 | — | 5.4 | 16.6 | — | 13.2 | 6.3 |
| 1989-90 | Metro | 61 (1000) | 3.7 | 3.7 | — | 4.8 | 9.6 | — | 8.7 | 4.5 |
| | Spectrum | 90 (1471) | 3.4 | 3.0 | — | 4.0 | 13.8 | — | 11.0 | 6.8 |
| | Prizm | 97 (1600) | 3.4 | 3.2 | — | 5.8 | 11.6 | — | 13.0 | 6.3 |

## CAMSHAFT SPECIFICATIONS

All measurements given in inches.

| Year | Engine Displacement cu. in. (cc) | Journal Diameter 1 | Journal Diameter 2 | Journal Diameter 3 | Journal Diameter 4 | Journal Diameter 5 | Lobe Lift In. | Lobe Lift Ex. | Bearing Clearance | Camshaft End Play |
|---|---|---|---|---|---|---|---|---|---|---|
| 1985 | 61 (1000) | 1.7372–1.7381 | 1.7451–1.7460 | 1.7530–1.7539 | 1.7609–1.7618 | — | 1.512 | 1.5012 | 0.0029 | — |
| | 90 (1471) | 1.021–1.022 | 1.021–1.022 | 1.021–1.022 | 1.021–1.022 | 1.021–1.022 | 1.426 | 1.426 | .0024–.0044 | .0039–.0071 |
| | 97 (1600) | 1.1015–1.1022 | 1.1015–1.1022 | 1.1015–1.1022 | 1.1015–1.1022 | — | 1.5409 ① | 1.5409 ① | 0.0015–0.0029 | 0.0031–0.0071 |
| 1986 | 61 (1000) | 1.7372–1.7381 | 1.7451–1.7460 | 1.7530–1.7539 | 1.7609–1.7618 | — | 1.512 | 1.5012 | 0.0029 | — |
| | 90 (1471) | 1.021–1.022 | 1.021–1.022 | 1.021–1.022 | 1.021–1.022 | 1.021–1.022 | 1.426 | 1.426 | .0024–.0044 | .0039–.0071 |
| | 97 (1600) | 1.1015–1.1022 | 1.1015–1.1022 | 1.1015–1.1022 | 1.1015–1.1022 | — | 1.5409 ① | 1.5409 ① | 0.0015–0.0029 | 0.0031–0.0071 |
| 1987 | 61 (1000) | 1.7372–1.7381 | 1.7451–1.7460 | 1.7530–1.7539 | 1.7609–1.7618 | — | 1.512 | 1.5012 | 0.0029 | — |
| | 90 (1471) | 1.021–1.022 | 1.021–1.022 | 1.021–1.022 | 1.021–1.022 | 1.021–1.022 | 1.426 | 1.426 | .0024–.0044 | .0039–.0071 |
| | 97 (1600) | 1.1015–1.1022 | 1.1015–1.1022 | 1.1015–1.1022 | 1.1015–1.1022 | — | 1.5409 ① | 1.5409 ① | 0.0015–0.0029 | 0.0031–0.0071 |

## CAMSHAFT SPECIFICATIONS

All measurements given in inches.

| Year | Engine Displacement cu. in. (cc) | Journal Diameter 1 | 2 | 3 | 4 | 5 | Lobe Lift In. | Ex. | Bearing Clearance | Camshaft End Play |
|---|---|---|---|---|---|---|---|---|---|---|
| 1988 | 61 (1000) | 1.7372–1.7381 | 1.7451–1.7460 | 1.7530–1.7539 | 1.7609–1.7618 | — | 1.512 | 1.5012 | 0.0029 | — |
| | 90 (1471) | 1.021–1.022 | 1.021–1.022 | 1.021–1.022 | 1.021–1.022 | 1.021–1.022 | 1.426 | 1.426 | .0024–.0044 | .0039–.0071 |
| | 97 (1600) | 1.1015–1.1022 | 1.1015–1.1022 | 1.1015–1.1022 | 1.1015–1.1022 | — | 1.5409 ① | 1.5409– ① | 0.0015–0.0029 | 0.0031–0.0071 |
| | 97 (1600)② | 1.0610–1.0616 | 1.0610–1.0616 | 1.0610–1.0616 | 1.0610–1.0616 | 1.0610–1.0616 | 1.3998–1.4002 | 1.3998–1.4002 | 0.0014–0.0028 | 0.0031–0.0075 |
| 1989-90 | 61 (1000) | 1.0220–1.0228 | 1.1795–1.1803 | 1.1795–1.1803 | — | — | 1.5601–2.5664 | 1.5601–2.5664 | 0.008–.0024 | — |
| | 90 (1471) | 1.021–1.022 | 1.021–1.022 | 1.021–1.022 | 1.021–1.022 | 1.021–.022 | 1.426 | 1.426 | .00236–.00437 | .00394–.0071 |
| | 97 (1600) | 0.9822 | 0.9035 | 0.9035 | 0.9035 | — | 1.370 | 1.359 | .0014–.0028 | .0043 |

① Minimum lobe height
② Twin cam engine (4A-GEL)
③ Other than Metro model— 1.5911–1.5974

## CRANKSHAFT AND CONNECTING ROD SPECIFICATIONS

All measurements are given in inches.

| Year | Engine Displacement cu. in. (cc) | Crankshaft Main Brg. Journal Dia. | Main Brg. Oil Clearance | Shaft End-play | Thrust on No. | Connecting Rod Journal Diameter | Oil Clearance | Side Clearance |
|---|---|---|---|---|---|---|---|---|
| 1985 | 61 (1000) | ① | 0.0012 | 0.0083 | 3 | 1.6532 | 0.0015 | 0.0058 |
| | 90 (1471) | 1.8865–1.8873 | 0.0008–0.0020 | 0.0024–0.0095 | 2 | 1.5720–1.5726 | 0.0010–0.0023 | 0.0079–0.0138 |
| | 97 (1600) | 1.8892–1.8898 | 0.0005–0.0190 ② | 0.0008–0.0073 | 3 | 1.5742–1.5748 | 0.0008–0.0020 | 0.0059–0.0098 |
| 1986 | 61 (1000) | ① | 0.0012 | 0.0083 | 3 | 1.6532 | 0.0015 | 0.0058 |
| | 90 (1471) | 1.8865–1.8873 | 0.0008–0.0020 | 0.0024–0.0095 | 2 | 1.5720–1.5726 | 0.0010–0.0023 | 0.0079–0.0138 |
| | 97 (1600) | 1.8892–1.8898 | 0.0006–0.0019 ③ | 0.0008–0.0073 | 3 | 1.5742–1.5748 | 0.0008–0.0020 | 0.0059–0.0089 |
| 1987 | 61 (1000) | ① | 0.0012 | 0.0044–0.0122 | 3 | 1.6532 | 0.0012–0.0190 | 0.0039–0.078 |
| | 90 (1471) | 1.8865–1.8873 | 0.0008–0.0020 | 0.0024–0.0095 | 2 | 1.5720–1.5726 | 0.0010–0.00230 | 0.0079–0.0138 |
| | 97 (1600) | 1.8892–1.8898 1.8898 | 0.0006–0.0019 ③ | 0.0008–0.0073 | 3 | 1.5742–1.5748 | 0.0008–0.0020 | 0.0059–0.0089 |
| 1988 | 61 (1000) | ① | 0.0012 | 0.0044–0.0122 | 3 | 1.6532 | 0.0012–0.019 | 0.0039–0.078 |
| | 90 (1471) | 1.8865–1.8873 | 0.0008–0.0020 | 0.0024–0.0095 | 2 | 1.5720–1.5726 | 0.0010–0.0023 | 0.0079–0.0138 |

## CRANKSHAFT AND CONNECTING ROD SPECIFICATIONS

All measurements are given in inches.

| Year | Engine Displacement cu. in. (cc) | Crankshaft: Main Brg. Journal Dia. | Crankshaft: Main Brg. Oil Clearance | Crankshaft: Shaft End-play | Crankshaft: Thrust on No. | Connecting Rod: Journal Diameter | Connecting Rod: Oil Clearance | Connecting Rod: Side Clearance |
|---|---|---|---|---|---|---|---|---|
| 1989-90 | 61 (1000) | ① | 0.0012 | 0.0080–0.0073 | 3 | 1.6529–1.6535 | 0.0012–0.019 | 0.0039–0.078 |
| | 90 (1471) | 1.8865–1.8873 | 0.00079–0.00199 | 0.0024–0.0095 | 3 | 1.5526 | 0.0009–0.0229 | 0.0079–0.0138 |
| | 97 (1600) | 1.8865–1.8873 | 0.0006–0.0013 | 0.0008–0.0073 | 3 | 1.5420–1.5748 | 0.0008–0.0020 | 0.0059–0.0098 |

① Bearing cap stamped
No. 1 – 1.7710-1.7712
No. 2 – 1.7714-1.7716
No. 3 – 1.7712-17714
No. 4 – 1.7710-1.7712
② Maximum clearance – 0.0031
③ Maximum clearance – 0.0039

## VALVE SPECIFICATIONS

| Year | Engine Displacement cu. in. (cc) | Seat Angle (deg.) | Face Angle (deg.) | Spring Test Pressure (lbs.) | Spring Installed Height (in.) | Stem-to-Guide Clearance (in.) Intake | Stem-to-Guide Clearance (in.) Exhaust | Stem Diameter (in.) Intake | Stem Diameter (in.) Exhaust |
|---|---|---|---|---|---|---|---|---|---|
| 1985 | 61 (1000) | 45 | 45 | 60 | 1.63 | 0.0014 | 0.0020 | 0.2745 | 0.2740 |
| | 90 (1471) | 45 | 45 | 47 @ 1.57 | 1.57 | 0.0009–0.0022 | 0.0012–0.0025 | 0.2740–0.2750 | 0.2740–0.2744 |
| | 97 (1600) | 45 | 44.5 | 46.3 | 1.52 | 0.0010–0.0024 | 0.0012–0.0026 | 0.2744–0.2750 | 0.2742–0.2748 |
| 1986 | 61 (1000) | 45 | 45 | 60 | 1.63 | 0.0014 | 0.0020 | 0.2745 | 0.2740 |
| | 90 (1471) | 45 | 45 | 47 @ 1.57 | 1.57 | 0.0009–0.0022 | 0.0012–0.0025 | 0.2740–0.2750 | 0.2740–0.2744 |
| | 97 (1600) | 45 | 44.5 | 46.3 | 1.52 | 0.0010–0.0024 | 0.0012–0.0026 | 0.2744–0.2750 | 0.2742–0.2748 |
| 1987 | 61 (1000) | 45 | 45 | 60 | 1.63 | 0.0014 | 0.0020 | 0.2745 | 0.2740 |
| | 90 (1471) | 45 | 45 | 47 @ 1.57 | 1.57 | 0.0009–0.0022 | 0.0012–0.0025 | 0.2740–0.2750 | 0.2740–0.2744 |
| | 97 (1600) | 45 | 44.5 | 46.3 | 1.52 | 0.0010–0.0024 | 0.0012–0.0026 | 0.2744–0.2750 | 0.2742–0.2748 |
| 1988 | 61 (1000) | 45 | 45 | 60 | 1.63 | 0.0014 | 0.0020 | 0.2745 | 0.2740 |
| | 90 (1471) | 45 | 45 | 47 @ 1.57 | 1.57 | 0.0009–0.0022 | 0.0012–0.0025 | 0.2745–0.2750 | 0.2740–0.2744 |
| | 97 (1600)① | 45 | 44.5 | 32.2 | 1.366 | 0.0010–0.0024 | 0.0012–0.0026 | 0.2350–0.2356 | 0.2348–0.2354 |
| | 97 (1600) | 45 | 44.5 | 46.3 | 1.52 | 0.0010–0.0024 | 0.0012–0.0026 | 0.2744–0.2750 | 0.2742–0.2748 |

## VALVE SPECIFICATIONS

| Year | Engine Displacement cu. in. (cc) | Seat Angle (deg.) | Face Angle (deg.) | Spring Test Pressure (lbs.) | Spring Installed Height (in.) | Stem-to-Guide Clearance (in.) | | Stem Diameter (in.) | |
|---|---|---|---|---|---|---|---|---|---|
| | | | | | | Intake | Exhaust | Intake | Exhaust |
| 1989-90 | 61 (1000) | 45 | 45 | 44 @ 1.28 | — | 0.0008–0.0021 | 0.0014–0.0024 | 0.2148–0.2151 | 0.2146–0.2151 |
| | 90 (1471) | 45 | 45 | 47 @ 1.57 | 1.57 | 0.0009–0.0022 | 0.0118–0.00248 | 0.274–0.275 | 0.274–0.2744 |
| | 97 (1600) | 45 | 45.5 | 32.2 | 1.36 | 0.0031 | 0.0039 | 0.2350–0.2356 | 0.2348–0.2354 |

① Twin Cam Engine (4A-GEL)

## PISTON AND RING SPECIFICATIONS

All measurments are given in inches.

| Year | Engine Displacement cu. in. (cc) | Piston Clearance | Ring Gap | | | Ring Side Clearance | | |
|---|---|---|---|---|---|---|---|---|
| | | | Top Compression | Bottom Compression | Oil Control | Top Compression | Bottom Compression | Oil Control |
| 1985 | 61 (1000) | 0.0008–0.0015 | 0.0079–0.0129 | 0.0079–0.0129 | 0.0079–0.0275 | 0.0012–0.0027 | 0.0008–0.0023 | — |
| | 90 (1471) | 0.0011–0.0019 | 0.0098–0.0138 | — | 0.0039–0.0236 | 0.0010–0.0026 | — | — |
| | 97 (1600) | 0.0035–0.0043 | 0.0098–0.0185 | 0.0059–0.0165 | 0.0118–0.0402 | 0.0016–0.0031 | 0.0012–0.0028 | Snug |
| 1986 | 61 (1000) | 0.0008–0.0015 | 0.0079–0.0129 | 0.0079–0.0137 | 0.0079–0.0275 | 0.0012–0.0027 | 0.0008–0.0023 | — |
| | 90 (1471) | 0.0011–0.0019 | 0.0098–0.0138 | — | 0.0039–0.0236 | 0.0010–0.0026 | — | — |
| | 97 (1600) | 0.0035–0.0043 | 0.0098–0.0185 | 0.0059–0.0165 | 0.0118–0.0402 | 0.0016–0.0031 | 0.0012–0.0028 | Snug |
| 1987 | 61 (1000) | 0.0008–0.0015 | 0.0079–0.0129 | 0.0079–0.0137 | 0.0079–0.0275 | 0.0012–0.0027 | 0.0008–0.0023 | — |
| | 61 (1000)① | 0.0008–0.0015 | 0.0079–0.0119 | 0.0079–0.0119 | 0.0079–0.0237 | 0.0012–0.0030 | 0.0008–0.0023 | — |
| | 61 (1000) | 0.0008–0.0015 | 0.0079–0.0157 | ② | 0.0079–0.0275 | 0.0012–0.0027 | — | — |
| | 90 (1471) | 0.0011–0.0019 | 0.0098–0.0138 | ② | 0.0039–0.0236 | 0.0010–0.0026 | — | — |
| | 90 (1471)① | 0.0011–0.0019 | 0.0106–0.0153 | 0.0098–0.0145 | 0.0039–0.0236 | 0.0010–0.0026 | 0.0008–0.0024 | Snug |
| | 97 (1600) | 0.0035–0.0043 | 0.0098–0.0185 | 0.0059–0.0165 | 0.118–0.402 | 0.016–0.0031 | 0.0012–0.0028 | |
| 1988 | 61 (1000) | 0.0008–0.0015 | 0.0079–0.0129 | 0.0079–0.0137 | 0.0079–0.0275 | 0.0012–0.0027 | 0.0008–0.0023 | — |

## PISTON AND RING SPECIFICATIONS

All measurments are given in inches.

| Year | Engine Displacement cu. in. (cc) | Piston Clearance | Ring Gap Top Compression | Ring Gap Bottom Compression | Ring Gap Oil Control | Ring Side Clearance Top Compression | Ring Side Clearance Bottom Compression | Ring Side Clearance Oil Control |
|---|---|---|---|---|---|---|---|---|
| 1988 | 61 (1000)① | 0.0008–0.0015 | 0.0079–0.0119 | 0.0079–0.0119 | 0.0079–0.0237 | 0.0012–0.0030 | 0.0008–0.0023 | |
| | 61 (1000)④ | 0.0008–0.0015 | 0.0079–0.0157 | ② | 0.0079–0.0275 | 0.0012–0.0027 | – | – |
| | 90 (1471) | 0.0011–0.0019 | 0.0098–0.0138 | ② | 0.0039–0.0236 | 0.0010–0.0026 | – | – |
| | 90 (1471)① | 0.0011–0.0019 | 0.0106–0.0153 | 0.0098–0.0145 | 0.0039–0.0236 | 0.0010–0.0026 | 0.0008–0.0024 | – |
| | 97 (1600) | 0.0035–0.0043 | 0.0098–0.0185 | 0.0059–0.0165 | 0.118–0.402 | 0.016–0.0031 | 0.0012–0.0028 | Snug |
| | 97 (1600)③ | 0.0039–0.0047 | 0.0098–0.0138 | 0.0078–0.0118 | 0.0059–0.0031 | 0.0016–0.0031 | 0.0012–0.0028 | Snug |
| 1989-90 | 61 (1000) | 0.0008–0.0015 | 0.0079–0.0129 | 0.0079–0.0137 | 0.0079–0.0275 | 0.0012–0.0027 | 0.0008–0.0023 | – |
| | 90 (1471) | 0.0011–0.0019 | 0.250–0.350 | 0.250–0.350 | 0.10–0.60 | 0.0009–0.0026 | 0.00098–0.0026 | – |
| | 97 (1600) | 0.1124–0.0031 | 0.0098–0.0138 | 0.0059–0.0118 | 0.0039–0.0236 | 0.0016–0.0031 | 0.0012–0.0028 | – |

① Turbo engine
② ER model has only one compression ring
③ Twincam engine
④ ER model

## TORQUE SPECIFICATIONS

All readings in ft. lbs.

| Year | Engine Displacement cu. in. (cc) | Cylinder Head Bolts | Main Bearing Bolts | Rod Bearing Bolts | Crankshaft Pulley Bolts | Flywheel Bolts | Manifold Intake | Manifold Exhaust | Spark Plugs |
|---|---|---|---|---|---|---|---|---|---|
| 1985 | 61 (1000) | 48 | 38 | 25 | 50 | 44 | 17 | 17 | 20 |
| | 90 (1471) | ② | 65 | 25 | 108 | 22① | 17 | 17 | 18 |
| | 97 (1600) | 40-47 | 40-47 | 34-39 | 80-94 | 55-61 | 15-21 | 15-21 | 20 |
| 1986 | 61 (1000) | 48 | 38 | 25 | 50 | 44 | 17 | 17 | 20 |
| | 90 (1471) | ② | 65 | 25 | 108 | 22① | 17 | 17 | 18 |
| | 97 (1600) | 40-47 | 40-47 | 34-39 | 80-94 | 55-61 | 15-21 | 15-21 | 20 |
| 1987 | 61 (1000) | 48 | 38 | 25 | 50 | 44 | 17 | 17 | 20 |
| | 90 (1471) | ② | 65 | 25 | 108 | 22① | 17 | 17 | 18 |
| | 97 (1600) | 43 | 43 | 29 | 80-94 | 55-61 | 15-21 | 15-21 | 20 |
| 1988 | 61 (1000) | 48 | 38 | 25 | 50 | 44 | 17 | 17 | 20 |
| | 90 (1471) | ② | 65 | 25 | 108 | 22① | 17 | 17 | 18 |
| | 97 (1600) | 43 | 43 | 29 | 87 | 58 | 20 | 18 | 13 |
| | 97 (1600)③ | ④ | 44 | 36 | 101 | 58 | 20 | 18 | 13 |

## TORQUE SPECIFICATIONS

All readings in ft. lbs.

| Year | Engine Displacement cu. in. (cc) | Cylinder Head Bolts | Main Bearing Bolts | Rod Bearing Bolts | Crankshaft Pulley Bolts | Flywheel Bolts | Manifold Intake | Manifold Exhaust | Spark Plugs |
|---|---|---|---|---|---|---|---|---|---|
| 1989-90 | 61 (1000) | 54 | 40 | 26 | 8 | 45 | 17 | 17 | 18 |
| | 90 (1471) | ② | 65 | 25 | 108 | 22① | 17 | 17 | 18 |
| | 97 (1600) | 44 | 44 | 36 | 87 | 58⑤ | 14 | 18 | 20 |

① Tighten an additional 45 degrees after torquing
② 1st step—29 ft. lbs.; 2nd step—58 ft. lbs.
③ Twin cam engine (4A-GEL)
④ 1st—Torque in sequence to 22 ft. lbs.
2nd—Torque in sequence another ¼ turn
3rd—Torque in sequence another ¼ turn
⑤ Manual transmission—47 ft. lbs.

## BRAKE SPECIFICATIONS

All measurements in inches unless noted

| Year | Model | Lug Nut Torque (ft. lbs.) | Master Cylinder Bore | Brake Disc Minimum Thickness | Brake Disc Maximum Runout | Standard Brake Drum Diameter | Minimum Lining Thickness Front | Minimum Lining Thickness Rear |
|---|---|---|---|---|---|---|---|---|
| 1985 | Sprint | 29-50 | 0.825 | 0.315 | 0.0028 | 7.09 | 0.315 | 0.110① |
| | Spectrum | 65 | 0.810 | 0.378 | 0.0059 | 7.09 | 0.039 | 0.039 |
| | Nova | 76 | NA | 0.492 | 0.0059 | 7.87 | 0.039 | 0.039 |
| 1986 | Sprint | 29-50 | 0.825 | 0.315 | 0.0028 | 7.09 | 0.315① | 0.110① |
| | Spectrum | 65 | 0.810 | 0.378 | 0.0059 | 7.09 | 0.039 | 0.039 |
| | Nova | 76 | NA | 0.492 | 0.0059 | 7.87 | 0.039 | 0.039 |
| 1987 | Sprint | 29-50 | 0.825 | 0.315 | 0.0028 | 7.09 | 0.315① | 0.110① |
| | Spectrum | 65 | 0.810 | 0.378 | 0.0059 | 7.09 | 0.039 | 0.039 |
| | Nova | 76 | NA | 0.492 | 0.0059 | 7.87 | 0.039 | 0.039 |
| 1988 | Sprint | 29-50 | 0.825 | 0.315 | 0.0028 | 7.09 | 0.315① | 0.110① |
| | Spectrum | 65 | 0.810 | 0.378 | 0.0059 | 7.09 | 0.039 | 0.039 |
| | Nova | 76 | NA | 0.492 | 0.0059 | 7.87 | 0.039 | 0.039 |
| 1989-90 | Metro | 41 | 0.825 | 0.315 | 0.004 | 7.09 | 0.315 | 0.110① |
| | Spectrum | 65 | 0.810 | 0.378 | 0.0059 | 7.09 | 0.039 | 0.039 |
| | Prizm | 76 | NA | 0.669 | 0.0035 | 7.87 | 0.030 | 0.039 |

① Lining plus shoe rim

## WHEEL ALIGNMENT

| Year | Model | Caster Range (deg.) | Caster Preferred Setting (deg.) | Camber Range (deg.) | Camber Preferred Setting (deg.) | Toe-in (in.) | Steering Axis Inclination (deg.) |
|---|---|---|---|---|---|---|---|
| 1985 | Sprint | — | 3 3/16P | — | 1 | 1/16 | 12 3/16 |
| | Spectrum | 1¾P-2 2/4P | 2 ¼P | 7/16N-1 1/16P | 1 1/32P | 0 + 1/16 | ①② |
| | Nova | ¼-1¾P | 1P | 1¼N-¼P | ½N | 0 + 1/16 | 11¾-13¼ |

## WHEEL ALIGNMENT

| Year | Model | Caster Range (deg.) | Caster Preferred Setting (deg.) | Camber Range (deg.) | Camber Preferred Setting (deg.) | Toe-in (in.) | Steering Axis Inclination (deg.) |
|---|---|---|---|---|---|---|---|
| 1986 | Sprint | – | 3 3/16P | – | 1 | 1/16 | 12 3/16 |
| | Spectrum | 1¾P-2¾P | 2¼P | 7/16N-1 1/16P | 11/32P | 0 + 1/16 | ①② |
| | Nova | 1¾P-2¾P | 5/6P | ¾N-¼P | ¼P | 0 +0.078 | – |
| 1987 | Sprint | – | 3 3/16 | – | ¼ | 0 | 12 3/16 |
| | Spectrum | 1¾P-2¾P | 2¼P | 7/16N-1 1/16P | 11/32P | 0 + 1/16 | ①② |
| | Nova | 1/8-1½P | ⅞ | ¼N-¾P | ½N | 0.04-0.08 | – |
| 1988 | Sprint | – | 3 3/16 | – | ¼ | 0 | 12 3/16 |
| | Spectrum | 1¾P-2¾P | 2¼P | 7/16N-1 1/16P | 11/32P | 0 + 1/16 | ①② |
| | Nova | ⅛-1⅔P | 9/10P | ¾N-¼P | ¼N | 0-0.078 | – |
| | Nova Twin Cam | 1N-1½P | ¼P | ¾N-¼P | ¼N | 0-0.078 | – |
| 1989-90 | Metro | 1P-5P | 3P | 1N-1P | 0 | 0 | 25 11/16 |
| | Spectrum | 1¾-2¾P | 2¼P | 11/16N-1 5/16P | 5/16 | 0 | 16 |
| | Prizm | 11/16P-2 3/16P③ | 1 7/16P | 9/6N-1 5/16P | 3/16 | 3/64 | NA |
| | Prizm | 9/16P-2 2/8P④ | 1 5/16 | ½N-1P | ¼ | 3/64 | NA |

① Inside—37°40' full lock
② Outside—32°30' full lock
③ Manual transaxle
④ Automatic transaxle

# TUNE-UP PROCEDURES

## Ignition Timing

### ADJUSTMENT

#### *Nova and Prizm*

**EXCEPT TWINCAM**

1. Set the parking brake and place the transaxle in Neutral. Run the engine until normal operating temperatures are reached, then, turn OFF the engine.
2. Install a timing light to the No. 1 spark plug wire according to the manufacturer's instructions.

**NOTE: For inductive timing lights, the induction clip can simply be installed over the plug wire. For other lights, the pick-up wire must be connected between the spark plug boot and the spark plug. Connect a tachometer according to the manufacturer's instructions.**

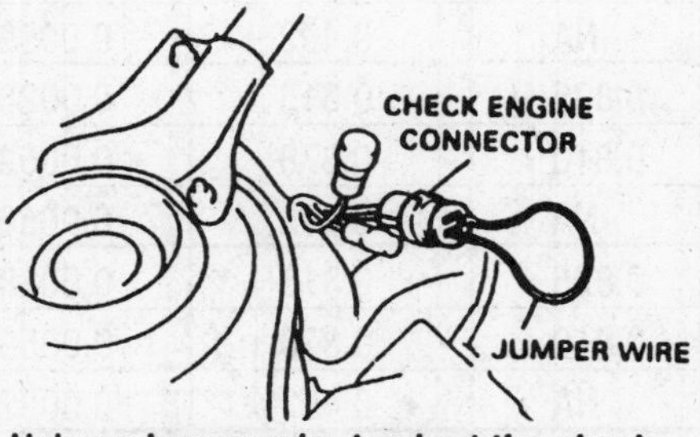

**Using a jumper wire to short the check engine connector-twincam engine—Nova and Prizm**

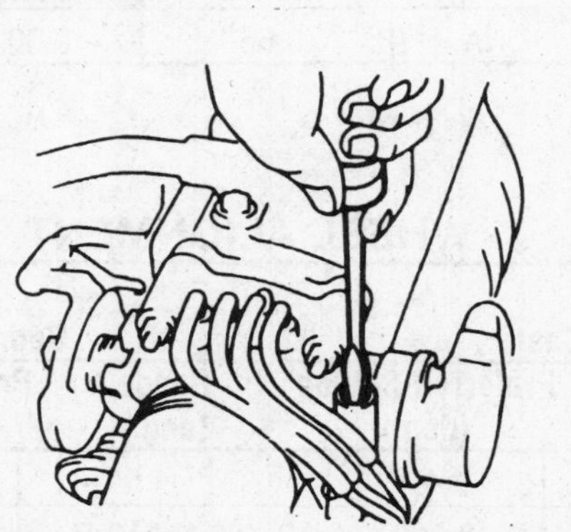
**Adjusting the idle speed screw-twincam engine—Nova and Prizm**

3. Disconnect and plug the distributor-to-intake manifold vacuum hoses.
4. Loosen the distributor flange hold-down bolt to finger tight.
5. Start the engine, then, check and/or adjust the engine rpm; it should be 750 or less.
6. Aim the timing light at the scale on the timing cover near the front pulley; the timing should be 0 degrees BTDC. If the timing is not correct, turn the distributor slightly to correct it. Once the reading is correct, tighten the hold-down bolt and recheck the timing.
7. Stop the engine, remove the timing light, then, unplug and reconnect the distributor vacuum hoses.

**TWINCAM**

1. Firmly apply the parking brake and place the transaxle in Neutral.
2. Run the engine until normal operating temperatures are reached, then, stop the engine.
3. Using a jumper wire, connect it to the check engine connector located near the wiper motor.
4. Using a timing light, connect it to the No. 1 spark plug wire. Loosen the distributor hold-down bolt until it is finger tight.

5. Start the engine, then, check and/or adjust the idle speed; it should be 800 rpm.

6. Aim the timing light at the timing cover plate near the crankshaft pulley; the notch on the crankshaft pulley should align the 10 degrees BTDC timing mark on the timing plate.

7. To adjust the engine timing, turn the distributor slightly to align the marks, then, tighten the hold-down bolt and recheck the timing.

8. When the adjustment is correct, remove the jumper wire from the check engine connector and recheck the timing marks. The timing should now be more than 16 degrees BTDC (manual) or more than 12 degrees BTDC (automatic).

### *Prizm*

1. Firmly apply the parking brake and place the transaxle in Neutral.

2. Connect a tachometer to the battery and the diagnostic connector. Do not ground the tachometer terminal.

3. Run the engine until normal operating temperatures are reached, then, stop the engine.

4. Remove the diagnostic connector cap and insert a jumper wire between terminals **E1** and **T**.

5. Using a timing light, connect it to the No. 1 spark plug wire. Loosen the distributor hold-down bolt until it is finger tight.

6. Start the engine, then, check and/or adjust the idle speed; it should be 700 rpm.

7. Aim the timing light at the timing cover plate near the crankshaft pulley; the notch on the crankshaft pulley should align with the specified timing mark on the timing plate. Use the timing specification noted on the undehood sticker.

8. To adjust the engine timing, turn the distributor slightly to align the marks, then, tighten the hold-down bolt and recheck the timing.

9. When the adjustment is correct, remove the jumper wire from diagnostic connector and install the cap.

10. Disconnect the ACV conncector.

11. Recheck the timing marks. The timing should now be 10 degrees BTDC.

12. Reconnect the ACV connector.

13. Disconnect the timing light.

### *Spectrum*

1. Set the parking brake and block the wheels.

2. Place the manual transmission in **Neutral** or the automatic transmission in**Park**.

3. Allow the engine to reach normal operating temperature. Make sure that the choke valve is open. Turn off all of the accessories.

4. If equipped with power steering, place the front wheels in a straight line.

5. Disconnect and plug the distributor vacuum line, the canister purge line, the EGR vacuum line and the ITC valve vacuum line at the intake manifold.

6. Connect a timing light to the No. 1 spark plug wire and a tachometer to the tachometer filter connector on the coil, tachometer filter is mounted near distributor hold down bolt.

**NOTE: Check the idle speed and adjust as needed.**

7. Loosen the distributor flange bolt.

8. Using the timing light, align the notch on the crankshaft pulley with the mark on the timing cover by turning the distributor.

**NOTE: Adjust the timing to 15 degrees BTDC at 750 rpm (MT) or 10 degrees BTDC at 1000 rpm (AT).**

9. After the timing marks have been aligned, tighten the distributor flange bolt, then reinstall all vacuum lines.

### *Sprint and Metro*

Before setting timing , make sure that the headlights, heater fan, engine cooling fan and any other electrical equipment is turned **OFF**. If any current drawing systems are operating, the idle up system will operate and cause the idle speed to be higher than normal.

1. Connect a tachometer to the negative terminal of the ignition coil. Connect a timing light to the No. 1 spark plug wire. Refer to the underhood sticker.

2. Start and run the engine until it reaches normal operating temperature.

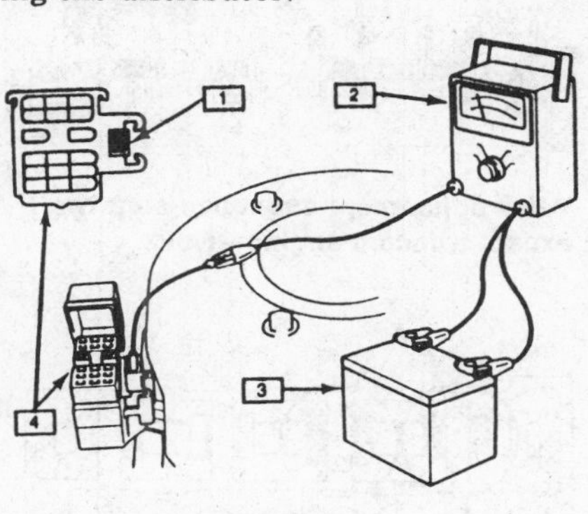


1. IG terminal
2. Tachometer
3. Battery
4. Diagnostic connector

**Tachometer connections – Prizm**

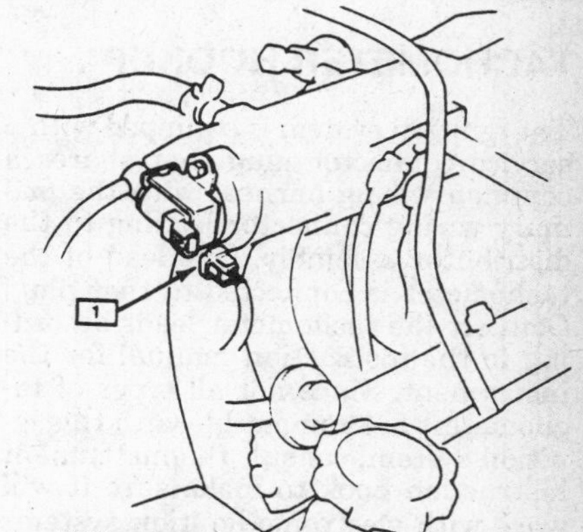


1. AVC connector

**Removing the AVC connector – Prizm**

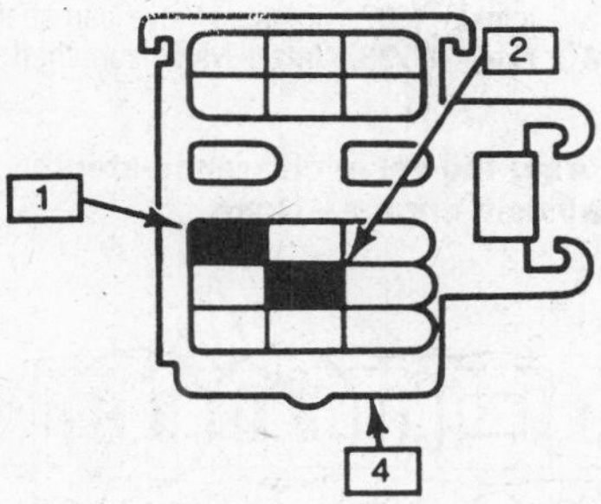

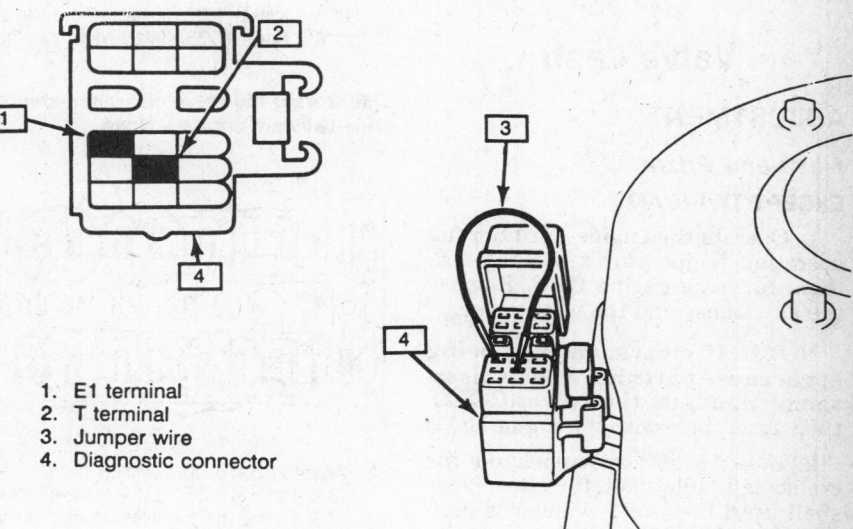

1. E1 terminal
2. T terminal
3. Jumper wire
4. Diagnostic connector

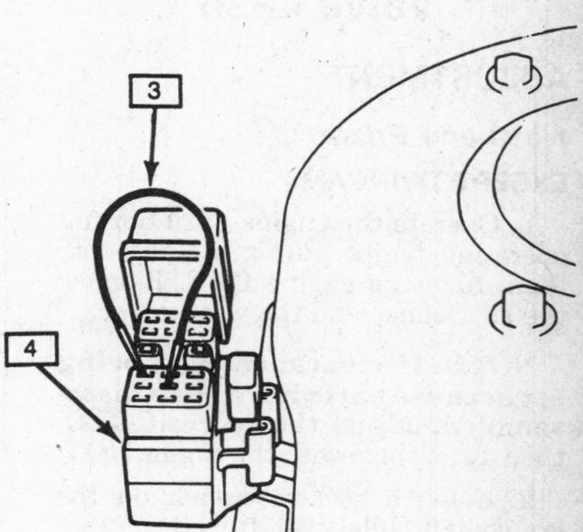


**Diagnostic connector with jumper wire – Prizm**

3. Check and/or adjust the idle speed. Correct speed should be 750 rpm for models with manual transaxles and 850 rpm on models with automatic transaxles.

**NOTE: To adjust the idle speed, turn the throttle adjustment screw on the carburetor.**

4. With the engine at the proper idle speed, aim the timing light at the crankshaft pulley and timing marks. The **V** timing mark on the pulley should be at the 10 degrees BTDC mark on the timing plate.

**NOTE: To adjust the ignition timing, loosen the distributor hold down bolt and rotate the distributor. When the V mark and the 10 degree mark are aligned, tighten the distributor hold down bolt and recheck the timing.**

5. With the timing adjusted, stop the engine and remove the testing equipment.

## TACHOMETER HOOKUP

The ignition system is equipped with a service connector plug that shares a common wiring harness with the primary wiring connector leading to the distributor assembly. One lead of the tachometer is connected to that plug. Connect the tachometer leads according to the instruction manual for the instrument. Since not all types of tachometers are compatible with this ignition system, consult the instrument instruction book to make sure it will work with electronic ignition systems and will not damage the system. Never ground the TACH terminal of the distributor assembly or damage to the ignition system will result.

# Valve Lash

## ADJUSTMENT

### *Nova and Prizm*

### EXCEPT TWINCAM

1. Operate the engine until normal operating temperatures are reached, then, turn the engine **OFF**. Remove the air cleaner and the valve cover.

**NOTE: If clearances are being set because parts have been disassembled, adjust the valves COLD, then, reset them with the engine HOT.**

2. Using a socket wrench on the crankshaft pulley bolt, turn the crankshaft until the No. 1 cylinder is positioned to the TDC of its compression stroke; the rocker arms of the No. 1 cylinder should be loose.

**NOTE: The notch on the crankshaft pulley should align with the 0 degrees mark on the timing plate.**

3. Using a 0.008 in. feeler gauge, adjust the intake valve clearance of cylinder No. 1 and 2. Using a 0.012 in. feeler gauge, adjust the exhaust valve clearance of cylinders No. 1 and 3.

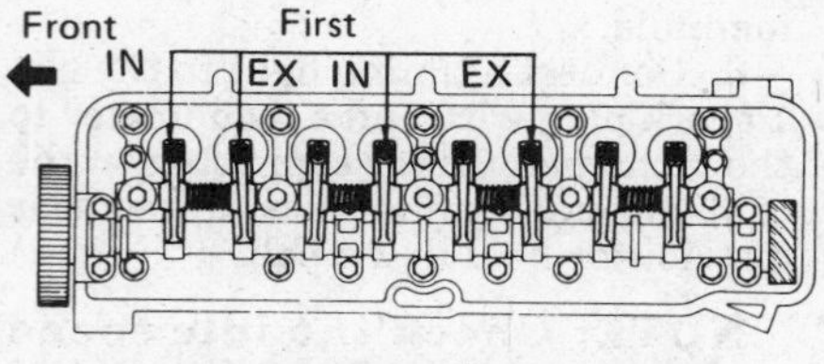


**Valve adjustment sequence-step one except twincam engine—Nova**

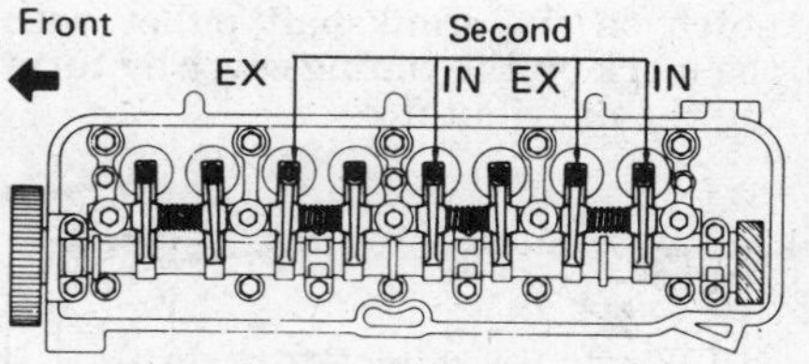


**Valve adjustment sequence-step two except twincam engine—Nova**

4. To adjust each valve, perform the following procedures:

a. Loosen the rocker arm adjusting nut; it may be necessary to back-off the adjusting screw.

b. Slide the feeler gauge between the rocker arm and valve tip. The surfaces will just touch, giving a very slight pull on the gauge.

c. Using a screwdriver (to turn the rocker arm screw) and a wrench (to hold the rocker arm lock nut), adjust the valve clearance, then, tighten the rocker arm lock nut.

d. Recheck the clearance and readjust (if necessary).

5. Rotate the crankshaft one complete revolution (360 degrees), then, realign the crankshaft pulley notch with the 0 degrees mark on the timing plate.

6. Using a 0.008 in. feeler gauge, adjust the intake valve clearance of cylinder No. 3 and 4. Using a 0.012 in. feeler gauge, adjust the exhaust valve clearance of cylinders No. 2 and 4.

7. To install, use a new gasket, sealant (if necessary) and reverse the removal procedures. Install the air cleaner. Adjust the engine timing and idle speed.

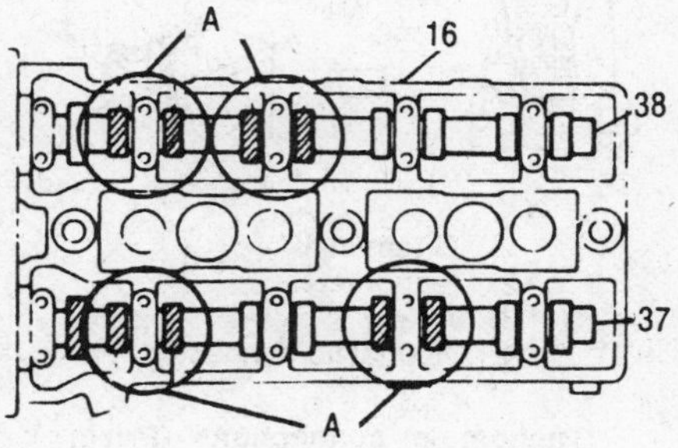


A. Adjust valves (1 & 2 intake) (1 & 3 exhaust)
16. Cylinder head
37. Exhaust valve camshaft
38. Intake valve camshaft

**Measuring the valve clearance-step one-twincam engine—Nova**

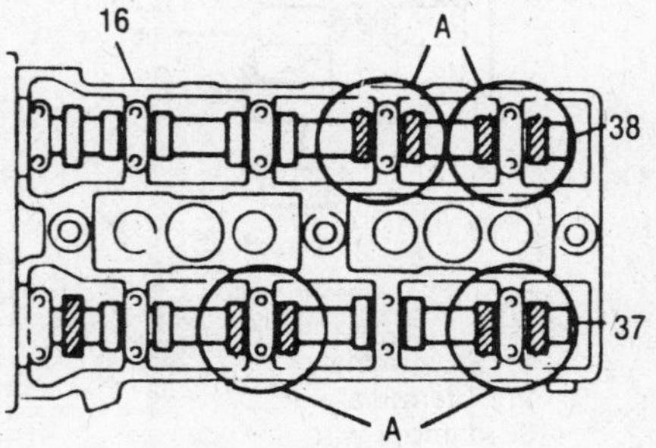


A. Adjust valves (3 & 4 intake) (2 & 4 exhaust)
16. Cylinder head
37. Exhaust valve camshaft
38. Intake valve camshaft

**Measuring the valve clearance-step two-twincam engine—Nova**

### TWINCAM

1. With the engine **COLD**, remove the valve covers.

2. To inspect the valve clearances, perform the following procedures:

a. Using a socket wrench on the crankshaft pulley, rotate the crankshaft until the No. 1 cylinder is positioned to the TDC of its compression stroke; the valve lifters of the No. 1 cylinder should be loose.

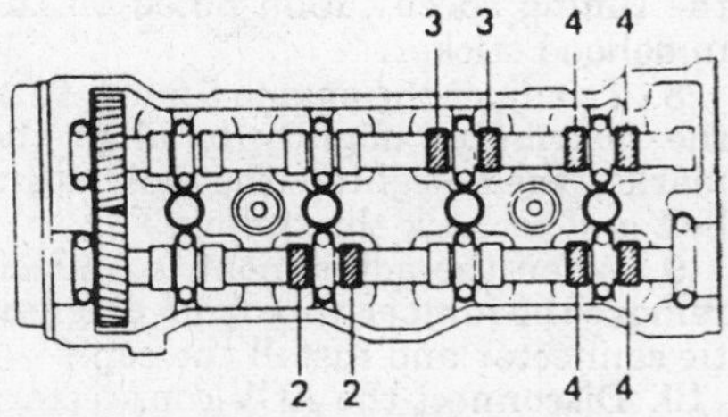


**Adjust these valves SECOND—Prizm**

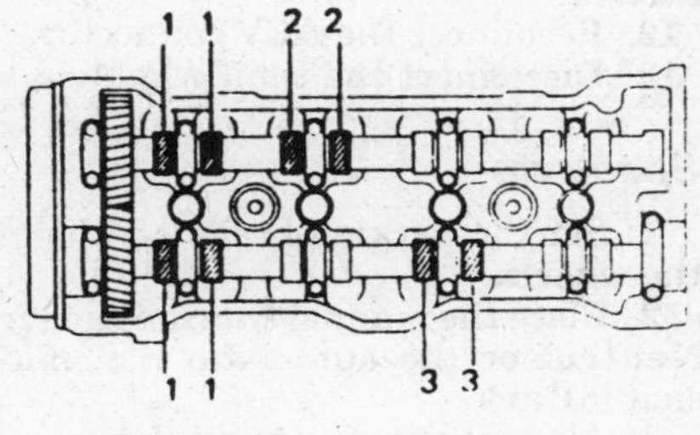


**Adjust these valves FIRST—Prizm**

| Measured Clearance (mm) | Installed Shim Thickness (mm) | | | | | | | | | | | | | | | | | | | | | | | | | | | | | | | | | | | | | | | | | | | | | | | | | | | | | | | |
|---|---|---|---|---|---|---|---|---|---|---|---|---|---|---|---|---|---|---|---|---|---|---|---|---|---|---|---|---|---|---|---|---|---|---|---|---|---|---|---|---|---|---|---|---|---|---|---|---|---|---|---|---|---|---|---|---|---|
| | 2.500 | 2.525 | 2.550 | 2.575 | 2.600 | 2.620 | 2.625 | 2.640 | 2.650 | 2.660 | 2.675 | 2.680 | 2.700 | 2.720 | 2.725 | 2.740 | 2.750 | 2.760 | 2.775 | 2.780 | 2.800 | 2.820 | 2.825 | 2.840 | 2.850 | 2.860 | 2.875 | 2.880 | 2.900 | 2.920 | 2.925 | 2.940 | 2.950 | 2.960 | 2.975 | 2.980 | 3.000 | 3.020 | 3.025 | 3.040 | 3.050 | 3.060 | 3.075 | 3.080 | 3.100 | 3.120 | 3.125 | 3.140 | 3.150 | 3.160 | 3.175 | 3.180 | 3.200 | 3.225 | 3.250 | 3.275 | 3.300 |
| 0.000 - 0.009 | | | | | | | | | | | 02 | 02 | 02 | 04 | 04 | 04 | 04 | 04 | 06 | 06 | 06 | 08 | 08 | 08 | 08 | 08 | 10 | 10 | 10 | 12 | 12 | 12 | 12 | 12 | 14 | 14 | 14 | 16 | 16 | 16 | 16 | 16 | 18 | 18 | 18 | 20 | 20 | 20 | 20 | 20 | 22 | 22 | 22 | 24 | 24 | 26 | 26 |
| 0.010 - 0.025 | | | | | | | | | | 02 | 02 | 02 | 02 | 04 | 04 | 04 | 04 | 06 | 06 | 06 | 06 | 08 | 08 | 08 | 08 | 10 | 10 | 10 | 10 | 12 | 12 | 12 | 12 | 14 | 14 | 14 | 14 | 16 | 16 | 16 | 16 | 18 | 18 | 18 | 18 | 20 | 20 | 20 | 20 | 22 | 22 | 22 | 22 | 24 | 24 | 26 | 26 |
| 0.026 - 0.029 | | | | | | | | | 02 | 02 | 02 | 02 | 04 | 04 | 04 | 04 | 06 | 06 | 06 | 06 | 08 | 08 | 08 | 08 | 10 | 10 | 10 | 10 | 12 | 12 | 12 | 12 | 14 | 14 | 14 | 14 | 16 | 16 | 16 | 16 | 18 | 18 | 18 | 18 | 20 | 20 | 20 | 20 | 22 | 22 | 22 | 22 | 24 | 24 | 26 | 26 | 28 |
| 0.030 - 0.040 | | | | | | | | 02 | 02 | 02 | 02 | 02 | 04 | 04 | 04 | 04 | 06 | 06 | 06 | 06 | 08 | 08 | 08 | 08 | 10 | 10 | 10 | 10 | 12 | 12 | 12 | 12 | 14 | 14 | 14 | 14 | 16 | 16 | 16 | 16 | 18 | 18 | 18 | 18 | 20 | 20 | 20 | 20 | 22 | 22 | 22 | 22 | 24 | 24 | 26 | 26 | 28 |
| 0.041 - 0.050 | | | | | | | | 02 | 02 | 02 | 02 | 02 | 04 | 04 | 04 | 06 | 06 | 06 | 06 | 06 | 08 | 08 | 08 | 10 | 10 | 10 | 10 | 10 | 12 | 12 | 12 | 14 | 14 | 14 | 14 | 14 | 16 | 16 | 16 | 18 | 18 | 18 | 18 | 18 | 20 | 20 | 20 | 22 | 22 | 22 | 22 | 22 | 24 | 24 | 26 | 26 | 28 |
| 0.051 - 0.070 | | | | | | 02 | 02 | 02 | 02 | 02 | 04 | 04 | 04 | 06 | 06 | 06 | 06 | 06 | 08 | 08 | 08 | 10 | 10 | 10 | 10 | 10 | 12 | 12 | 12 | 14 | 14 | 14 | 14 | 14 | 16 | 16 | 16 | 18 | 18 | 18 | 18 | 18 | 20 | 20 | 20 | 22 | 22 | 22 | 22 | 22 | 24 | 24 | 24 | 26 | 26 | 28 | 28 |
| 0.071 - 0.075 | | | | | 02 | 02 | 02 | 02 | 02 | 04 | 04 | 04 | 04 | 06 | 06 | 06 | 06 | 08 | 08 | 08 | 08 | 10 | 10 | 10 | 10 | 12 | 12 | 12 | 12 | 14 | 14 | 14 | 14 | 16 | 16 | 16 | 16 | 18 | 18 | 18 | 18 | 20 | 20 | 20 | 20 | 22 | 22 | 22 | 22 | 24 | 24 | 24 | 24 | 26 | 26 | 28 | 28 |
| 0.076 - 0.090 | | | | | 02 | 02 | 02 | 02 | 04 | 04 | 04 | 04 | 06 | 06 | 06 | 06 | 08 | 08 | 08 | 08 | 10 | 10 | 10 | 10 | 12 | 12 | 12 | 12 | 14 | 14 | 14 | 14 | 16 | 16 | 16 | 16 | 18 | 18 | 18 | 18 | 20 | 20 | 20 | 20 | 22 | 22 | 22 | 22 | 24 | 24 | 24 | 24 | 26 | 26 | 28 | 28 | 30 |
| 0.091 - 0.100 | | | | | 02 | 02 | 02 | 04 | 04 | 04 | 04 | 04 | 06 | 06 | 06 | 08 | 08 | 08 | 08 | 08 | 10 | 10 | 10 | 12 | 12 | 12 | 12 | 12 | 14 | 14 | 14 | 16 | 16 | 16 | 16 | 16 | 18 | 18 | 18 | 20 | 20 | 20 | 20 | 20 | 22 | 22 | 22 | 24 | 24 | 24 | 24 | 24 | 26 | 26 | 28 | 28 | 30 |
| 0.101 - 0.120 | | | | 02 | 02 | 04 | 04 | 04 | 04 | 04 | 06 | 06 | 06 | 08 | 08 | 08 | 08 | 08 | 10 | 10 | 10 | 12 | 12 | 12 | 12 | 12 | 14 | 14 | 14 | 16 | 16 | 16 | 16 | 16 | 18 | 18 | 18 | 20 | 20 | 20 | 20 | 20 | 22 | 22 | 22 | 24 | 24 | 24 | 24 | 24 | 26 | 26 | 26 | 28 | 28 | 30 | 30 |
| 0.121 - 0.125 | | | 02 | 02 | 02 | 04 | 04 | 04 | 04 | 06 | 06 | 06 | 06 | 08 | 08 | 08 | 08 | 10 | 10 | 10 | 10 | 12 | 12 | 12 | 12 | 14 | 14 | 14 | 14 | 16 | 16 | 16 | 16 | 18 | 18 | 18 | 18 | 20 | 20 | 20 | 20 | 22 | 22 | 22 | 22 | 24 | 24 | 24 | 24 | 26 | 26 | 26 | 26 | 28 | 28 | 30 | 30 |
| 0.126 - 0.140 | | | 02 | 02 | 04 | 04 | 04 | 04 | 06 | 06 | 06 | 06 | 08 | 08 | 08 | 08 | 10 | 10 | 10 | 10 | 12 | 12 | 12 | 12 | 14 | 14 | 14 | 14 | 16 | 16 | 16 | 16 | 18 | 18 | 18 | 18 | 20 | 20 | 20 | 20 | 22 | 22 | 22 | 22 | 24 | 24 | 24 | 24 | 26 | 26 | 26 | 26 | 28 | 28 | 30 | 30 | 32 |
| 0.141 - 0.149 | | | 02 | 02 | 04 | 04 | 04 | 06 | 06 | 06 | 06 | 06 | 08 | 08 | 08 | 10 | 10 | 10 | 10 | 10 | 12 | 12 | 12 | 14 | 14 | 14 | 14 | 14 | 16 | 16 | 16 | 18 | 18 | 18 | 18 | 18 | 20 | 20 | 20 | 22 | 22 | 22 | 22 | 22 | 24 | 24 | 24 | 26 | 26 | 26 | 26 | 26 | 28 | 28 | 30 | 30 | 32 |
| 0.150 - 0.250 | | | | | | | | | | | | | | | | | | | | | | | | | | | | | | | | | | | | | | | | | | | | | | | | | | | | | | | | | |
| 0.251 - 0.270 | 04 | 06 | 06 | 08 | 08 | 10 | 10 | 10 | 10 | 10 | 12 | 12 | 12 | 14 | 14 | 14 | 14 | 14 | 16 | 16 | 16 | 18 | 18 | 18 | 18 | 18 | 20 | 20 | 20 | 22 | 22 | 22 | 22 | 22 | 24 | 24 | 24 | 26 | 26 | 26 | 26 | 26 | 28 | 28 | 28 | 30 | 30 | 30 | 30 | 30 | 32 | 32 | 32 | 34 | 34 | | |
| 0.271 - 0.275 | 04 | 06 | 06 | 08 | 08 | 10 | 10 | 10 | 10 | 12 | 12 | 12 | 12 | 14 | 14 | 14 | 14 | 16 | 16 | 16 | 16 | 18 | 18 | 18 | 18 | 20 | 20 | 20 | 20 | 22 | 22 | 22 | 22 | 24 | 24 | 24 | 24 | 26 | 26 | 26 | 26 | 28 | 28 | 28 | 28 | 30 | 30 | 30 | 30 | 32 | 32 | 32 | 32 | 34 | 34 | | |
| 0.276 - 0.290 | 06 | 06 | 08 | 08 | 10 | 10 | 10 | 10 | 12 | 12 | 12 | 12 | 14 | 14 | 14 | 14 | 16 | 16 | 16 | 16 | 18 | 18 | 18 | 18 | 20 | 20 | 20 | 20 | 22 | 22 | 22 | 22 | 24 | 24 | 24 | 24 | 26 | 26 | 26 | 26 | 28 | 28 | 28 | 28 | 30 | 30 | 30 | 30 | 32 | 32 | 32 | 32 | 34 | 34 | | | |
| 0.291 - 0.300 | 06 | 06 | 08 | 08 | 10 | 10 | 10 | 12 | 12 | 12 | 12 | 12 | 14 | 14 | 14 | 16 | 16 | 16 | 16 | 16 | 18 | 18 | 18 | 20 | 20 | 20 | 20 | 20 | 22 | 22 | 22 | 24 | 24 | 24 | 24 | 24 | 26 | 26 | 26 | 28 | 28 | 28 | 28 | 28 | 30 | 30 | 30 | 32 | 32 | 32 | 32 | 32 | 34 | 34 | | | |
| 0.301 - 0.320 | 06 | 08 | 08 | 10 | 10 | 12 | 12 | 12 | 12 | 12 | 14 | 14 | 14 | 16 | 16 | 16 | 16 | 16 | 18 | 18 | 18 | 20 | 20 | 20 | 20 | 20 | 22 | 22 | 22 | 24 | 24 | 24 | 24 | 24 | 26 | 26 | 26 | 28 | 28 | 28 | 28 | 28 | 30 | 30 | 30 | 32 | 32 | 32 | 32 | 32 | 34 | 34 | 34 | | | | |
| 0.321 - 0.325 | 06 | 08 | 08 | 10 | 10 | 12 | 12 | 12 | 12 | 14 | 14 | 14 | 14 | 16 | 16 | 16 | 16 | 18 | 18 | 18 | 18 | 20 | 20 | 20 | 20 | 22 | 22 | 22 | 22 | 24 | 24 | 24 | 24 | 26 | 26 | 26 | 26 | 28 | 28 | 28 | 28 | 30 | 30 | 30 | 30 | 32 | 32 | 32 | 32 | 34 | 34 | 34 | 34 | | | | |
| 0.326 - 0.340 | 08 | 08 | 10 | 10 | 12 | 12 | 12 | 12 | 14 | 14 | 14 | 14 | 16 | 16 | 16 | 16 | 18 | 18 | 18 | 18 | 20 | 20 | 20 | 20 | 22 | 22 | 22 | 22 | 24 | 24 | 24 | 24 | 26 | 26 | 26 | 26 | 28 | 28 | 28 | 28 | 30 | 30 | 30 | 30 | 32 | 32 | 32 | 32 | 34 | 34 | 34 | 34 | | | | | |
| 0.341 - 0.350 | 08 | 08 | 10 | 10 | 12 | 12 | 12 | 14 | 14 | 14 | 14 | 14 | 16 | 16 | 16 | 18 | 18 | 18 | 18 | 18 | 20 | 20 | 20 | 22 | 22 | 22 | 22 | 22 | 24 | 24 | 24 | 26 | 26 | 26 | 26 | 26 | 28 | 28 | 28 | 30 | 30 | 30 | 30 | 30 | 32 | 32 | 32 | 34 | 34 | 34 | 34 | | | | | | |
| 0.351 - 0.370 | 08 | 10 | 10 | 12 | 12 | 14 | 14 | 14 | 14 | 14 | 16 | 16 | 16 | 18 | 18 | 18 | 18 | 18 | 20 | 20 | 20 | 22 | 22 | 22 | 22 | 22 | 24 | 24 | 24 | 26 | 26 | 26 | 26 | 26 | 28 | 28 | 28 | 30 | 30 | 30 | 30 | 30 | 32 | 32 | 32 | 34 | 34 | 34 | 34 | 34 | | | | | | | |
| 0.371 - 0.375 | 08 | 10 | 10 | 12 | 12 | 14 | 14 | 14 | 14 | 16 | 16 | 16 | 16 | 18 | 18 | 18 | 18 | 20 | 20 | 20 | 20 | 22 | 22 | 22 | 22 | 24 | 24 | 24 | 24 | 26 | 26 | 26 | 26 | 28 | 28 | 28 | 28 | 30 | 30 | 30 | 30 | 32 | 32 | 32 | 32 | 34 | 34 | 34 | 34 | | | | | | | | |
| 0.376 - 0.390 | 10 | 10 | 12 | 12 | 14 | 14 | 14 | 14 | 16 | 16 | 16 | 16 | 18 | 18 | 18 | 18 | 20 | 20 | 20 | 20 | 22 | 22 | 22 | 22 | 24 | 24 | 24 | 24 | 26 | 26 | 26 | 26 | 28 | 28 | 28 | 28 | 30 | 30 | 30 | 30 | 32 | 32 | 32 | 32 | 34 | 34 | 34 | 34 | | | | | | | | | |
| 0.391 - 0.400 | 10 | 10 | 12 | 12 | 14 | 14 | 14 | 16 | 16 | 16 | 16 | 16 | 18 | 18 | 18 | 20 | 20 | 20 | 20 | 20 | 22 | 22 | 22 | 24 | 24 | 24 | 24 | 24 | 26 | 26 | 26 | 28 | 28 | 28 | 28 | 28 | 30 | 30 | 30 | 32 | 32 | 32 | 32 | 32 | 34 | 34 | 34 | | | | | | | | | | |
| 0.401 - 0.420 | 10 | 12 | 12 | 14 | 14 | 16 | 16 | 16 | 16 | 16 | 18 | 18 | 18 | 20 | 20 | 20 | 20 | 20 | 22 | 22 | 22 | 24 | 24 | 24 | 24 | 24 | 26 | 26 | 26 | 28 | 28 | 28 | 28 | 28 | 30 | 30 | 30 | 32 | 32 | 32 | 32 | 32 | 34 | 34 | 34 | | | | | | | | | | | | |
| 0.421 - 0.425 | 10 | 12 | 12 | 14 | 14 | 16 | 16 | 16 | 16 | 18 | 18 | 18 | 18 | 20 | 20 | 20 | 20 | 22 | 22 | 22 | 22 | 24 | 24 | 24 | 24 | 26 | 26 | 26 | 26 | 28 | 28 | 28 | 28 | 30 | 30 | 30 | 30 | 32 | 32 | 32 | 32 | 34 | 34 | 34 | 34 | | | | | | | | | | | | |
| 0.426 - 0.440 | 12 | 12 | 14 | 14 | 16 | 16 | 16 | 16 | 18 | 18 | 18 | 18 | 20 | 20 | 20 | 20 | 22 | 22 | 22 | 22 | 24 | 24 | 24 | 24 | 26 | 26 | 26 | 26 | 28 | 28 | 28 | 28 | 30 | 30 | 30 | 30 | 32 | 32 | 32 | 32 | 34 | 34 | 34 | 34 | | | | | | | | | | | | | |
| 0.441 - 0.450 | 12 | 12 | 14 | 14 | 16 | 16 | 16 | 18 | 18 | 18 | 18 | 18 | 20 | 20 | 20 | 22 | 22 | 22 | 22 | 22 | 24 | 24 | 24 | 26 | 26 | 26 | 26 | 26 | 28 | 28 | 28 | 30 | 30 | 30 | 30 | 30 | 32 | 32 | 32 | 34 | 34 | 34 | 34 | 34 | | | | | | | | | | | | | |
| 0.451 - 0.470 | 12 | 14 | 14 | 16 | 16 | 18 | 18 | 18 | 18 | 18 | 20 | 20 | 20 | 22 | 22 | 22 | 22 | 22 | 24 | 24 | 24 | 26 | 26 | 26 | 26 | 26 | 28 | 28 | 28 | 30 | 30 | 30 | 30 | 30 | 32 | 32 | 32 | 34 | 34 | 34 | 34 | 34 | | | | | | | | | | | | | | | |
| 0.471 - 0.475 | 12 | 14 | 14 | 16 | 16 | 18 | 18 | 18 | 18 | 20 | 20 | 20 | 20 | 22 | 22 | 22 | 22 | 24 | 24 | 24 | 24 | 26 | 26 | 26 | 26 | 28 | 28 | 28 | 28 | 30 | 30 | 30 | 30 | 32 | 32 | 32 | 32 | 34 | 34 | 34 | 34 | | | | | | | | | | | | | | | | |
| 0.476 - 0.490 | 14 | 14 | 16 | 16 | 18 | 18 | 18 | 18 | 20 | 20 | 20 | 20 | 22 | 22 | 22 | 22 | 24 | 24 | 24 | 24 | 26 | 26 | 26 | 26 | 28 | 28 | 28 | 28 | 30 | 30 | 30 | 30 | 32 | 32 | 32 | 32 | 34 | 34 | 34 | 34 | | | | | | | | | | | | | | | | | |
| 0.491 - 0.500 | 14 | 14 | 16 | 16 | 18 | 18 | 18 | 20 | 20 | 20 | 20 | 20 | 22 | 22 | 22 | 24 | 24 | 24 | 24 | 24 | 26 | 26 | 26 | 28 | 28 | 28 | 28 | 28 | 30 | 30 | 30 | 32 | 32 | 32 | 32 | 32 | 34 | 34 | 34 | | | | | | | | | | | | | | | | | | |
| 0.501 - 0.520 | 14 | 16 | 16 | 18 | 18 | 20 | 20 | 20 | 20 | 20 | 22 | 22 | 22 | 24 | 24 | 24 | 24 | 24 | 26 | 26 | 26 | 28 | 28 | 28 | 28 | 28 | 30 | 30 | 30 | 32 | 32 | 32 | 32 | 32 | 34 | 34 | 34 | | | | | | | | | | | | | | | | | | | | |
| 0.521 - 0.525 | 14 | 16 | 16 | 18 | 18 | 20 | 20 | 20 | 20 | 22 | 22 | 22 | 22 | 24 | 24 | 24 | 24 | 26 | 26 | 26 | 26 | 28 | 28 | 28 | 28 | 30 | 30 | 30 | 30 | 32 | 32 | 32 | 32 | 34 | 34 | 34 | 34 | | | | | | | | | | | | | | | | | | | | |
| 0.526 - 0.540 | 16 | 16 | 18 | 18 | 20 | 20 | 20 | 20 | 22 | 22 | 22 | 22 | 24 | 24 | 24 | 24 | 26 | 26 | 26 | 26 | 28 | 28 | 28 | 28 | 30 | 30 | 30 | 30 | 32 | 32 | 32 | 32 | 34 | 34 | 34 | 34 | | | | | | | | | | | | | | | | | | | | | |
| 0.541 - 0.550 | 16 | 16 | 18 | 18 | 20 | 20 | 20 | 22 | 22 | 22 | 22 | 22 | 24 | 24 | 24 | 26 | 26 | 26 | 26 | 26 | 28 | 28 | 28 | 30 | 30 | 30 | 30 | 30 | 32 | 32 | 32 | 34 | 34 | 34 | 34 | 34 | | | | | | | | | | | | | | | | | | | | | |
| 0.551 - 0.570 | 16 | 18 | 18 | 20 | 20 | 22 | 22 | 22 | 22 | 22 | 24 | 24 | 24 | 26 | 26 | 26 | 26 | 26 | 28 | 28 | 28 | 30 | 30 | 30 | 30 | 30 | 32 | 32 | 32 | 34 | 34 | 34 | 34 | 34 | | | | | | | | | | | | | | | | | | | | | | | |
| 0.571 - 0.575 | 16 | 18 | 18 | 20 | 20 | 22 | 22 | 22 | 22 | 24 | 24 | 24 | 24 | 26 | 26 | 26 | 26 | 28 | 28 | 28 | 28 | 30 | 30 | 30 | 30 | 32 | 32 | 32 | 32 | 34 | 34 | 34 | 34 | | | | | | | | | | | | | | | | | | | | | | | | |
| 0.576 - 0.590 | 18 | 18 | 20 | 20 | 22 | 22 | 22 | 22 | 24 | 24 | 24 | 24 | 26 | 26 | 26 | 26 | 28 | 28 | 28 | 28 | 30 | 30 | 30 | 30 | 32 | 32 | 32 | 32 | 34 | 34 | 34 | 34 | | | | | | | | | | | | | | | | | | | | | | | | | |
| 0.591 - 0.600 | 18 | 18 | 20 | 20 | 22 | 22 | 22 | 24 | 24 | 24 | 24 | 24 | 26 | 26 | 26 | 28 | 28 | 28 | 28 | 28 | 30 | 30 | 30 | 32 | 32 | 32 | 32 | 32 | 34 | 34 | 34 | | | | | | | | | | | | | | | | | | | | | | | | | | |
| 0.601 - 0.620 | 18 | 20 | 20 | 22 | 22 | 24 | 24 | 24 | 24 | 24 | 26 | 26 | 26 | 28 | 28 | 28 | 28 | 28 | 30 | 30 | 30 | 32 | 32 | 32 | 32 | 32 | 34 | 34 | 34 | | | | | | | | | | | | | | | | | | | | | | | | | | | | |
| 0.621 - 0.625 | 18 | 20 | 20 | 22 | 22 | 24 | 24 | 24 | 24 | 26 | 26 | 26 | 26 | 28 | 28 | 28 | 28 | 30 | 30 | 30 | 30 | 32 | 32 | 32 | 32 | 34 | 34 | 34 | 34 | | | | | | | | | | | | | | | | | | | | | | | | | | | | |
| 0.626 - 0.640 | 20 | 20 | 22 | 22 | 24 | 24 | 24 | 24 | 26 | 26 | 26 | 26 | 28 | 28 | 28 | 28 | 30 | 30 | 30 | 30 | 32 | 32 | 32 | 32 | 34 | 34 | 34 | 34 | | | | | | | | | | | | | | | | | | | | | | | | | | | | | |
| 0.641 - 0.650 | 20 | 20 | 22 | 22 | 24 | 24 | 24 | 26 | 26 | 26 | 26 | 26 | 28 | 28 | 28 | 30 | 30 | 30 | 30 | 30 | 32 | 32 | 32 | 34 | 34 | 34 | 34 | 34 | | | | | | | | | | | | | | | | | | | | | | | | | | | | | |
| 0.651 - 0.670 | 20 | 22 | 22 | 24 | 24 | 26 | 26 | 26 | 26 | 26 | 28 | 28 | 28 | 30 | 30 | 30 | 30 | 30 | 32 | 32 | 32 | 34 | 34 | 34 | 34 | 34 | | | | | | | | | | | | | | | | | | | | | | | | | | | | | | | |
| 0.671 - 0.675 | 20 | 22 | 22 | 24 | 24 | 26 | 26 | 26 | 26 | 28 | 28 | 28 | 28 | 30 | 30 | 30 | 30 | 32 | 32 | 32 | 32 | 34 | 34 | 34 | 34 | | | | | | | | | | | | | | | | | | | | | | | | | | | | | | | | |
| 0.676 - 0.690 | 22 | 22 | 24 | 24 | 26 | 26 | 26 | 26 | 28 | 28 | 28 | 28 | 30 | 30 | 30 | 30 | 32 | 32 | 32 | 32 | 34 | 34 | 34 | 34 | | | | | | | | | | | | | | | | | | | | | | | | | | | | | | | | | |
| 0.691 - 0.700 | 22 | 22 | 24 | 24 | 26 | 26 | 26 | 28 | 28 | 28 | 28 | 28 | 30 | 30 | 30 | 32 | 32 | 32 | 32 | 32 | 34 | 34 | 34 | | | | | | | | | | | | | | | | | | | | | | | | | | | | | | | | | | |
| 0.701 - 0.720 | 22 | 24 | 24 | 26 | 26 | 28 | 28 | 28 | 28 | 28 | 30 | 30 | 30 | 32 | 32 | 32 | 32 | 32 | 34 | 34 | 34 | | | | | | | | | | | | | | | | | | | | | | | | | | | | | | | | | | | | |
| 0.721 - 0.725 | 22 | 24 | 24 | 26 | 26 | 28 | 28 | 28 | 28 | 30 | 30 | 30 | 30 | 32 | 32 | 32 | 32 | 34 | 34 | 34 | 34 | | | | | | | | | | | | | | | | | | | | | | | | | | | | | | | | | | | | |
| 0.726 - 0.740 | 24 | 24 | 26 | 26 | 28 | 28 | 28 | 28 | 30 | 30 | 30 | 30 | 32 | 32 | 32 | 32 | 34 | 34 | 34 | 34 | | | | | | | | | | | | | | | | | | | | | | | | | | | | | | | | | | | | | |
| 0.741 - 0.750 | 24 | 24 | 26 | 26 | 28 | 28 | 28 | 30 | 30 | 30 | 30 | 30 | 32 | 32 | 32 | 34 | 34 | 34 | 34 | | | | | | | | | | | | | | | | | | | | | | | | | | | | | | | | | | | | | | |
| 0.751 - 0.770 | 24 | 26 | 26 | 28 | 28 | 30 | 30 | 30 | 30 | 30 | 32 | 32 | 32 | 34 | 34 | 34 | 34 | 34 | | | | | | | | | | | | | | | | | | | | | | | | | | | | | | | | | | | | | | | |
| 0.771 - 0.775 | 24 | 26 | 26 | 28 | 28 | 30 | 30 | 30 | 30 | 32 | 32 | 32 | 32 | 34 | 34 | 34 | 34 | | | | | | | | | | | | | | | | | | | | | | | | | | | | | | | | | | | | | | | | |
| 0.776 - 0.790 | 26 | 26 | 28 | 28 | 30 | 30 | 30 | 30 | 32 | 32 | 32 | 32 | 34 | 34 | 34 | 34 | | | | | | | | | | | | | | | | | | | | | | | | | | | | | | | | | | | | | | | | | |
| 0.791 - 0.800 | 26 | 26 | 28 | 28 | 30 | 30 | 30 | 32 | 32 | 32 | 32 | 32 | 34 | 34 | 34 | | | | | | | | | | | | | | | | | | | | | | | | | | | | | | | | | | | | | | | | | | |
| 0.801 - 0.820 | 26 | 28 | 28 | 30 | 30 | 32 | 32 | 32 | 32 | 32 | 34 | 34 | 34 | | | | | | | | | | | | | | | | | | | | | | | | | | | | | | | | | | | | | | | | | | | | |
| 0.821 - 0.825 | 26 | 28 | 28 | 30 | 30 | 32 | 32 | 32 | 32 | 34 | 34 | 34 | 34 | | | | | | | | | | | | | | | | | | | | | | | | | | | | | | | | | | | | | | | | | | | | |
| 0.826 - 0.840 | 28 | 28 | 30 | 30 | 32 | 32 | 32 | 32 | 34 | 34 | 34 | 34 | | | | | | | | | | | | | | | | | | | | | | | | | | | | | | | | | | | | | | | | | | | | | |
| 0.841 - 0.850 | 28 | 28 | 30 | 30 | 32 | 32 | 32 | 34 | 34 | 34 | 34 | 34 | | | | | | | | | | | | | | | | | | | | | | | | | | | | | | | | | | | | | | | | | | | | | |
| 0.851 - 0.870 | 28 | 30 | 30 | 32 | 32 | 34 | 34 | 34 | 34 | 34 | | | | | | | | | | | | | | | | | | | | | | | | | | | | | | | | | | | | | | | | | | | | | | | |
| 0.871 - 0.875 | 28 | 30 | 30 | 32 | 32 | 34 | 34 | 34 | 34 | | | | | | | | | | | | | | | | | | | | | | | | | | | | | | | | | | | | | | | | | | | | | | | | |
| 0.876 - 0.890 | 30 | 30 | 32 | 32 | 34 | 34 | 34 | 34 | | | | | | | | | | | | | | | | | | | | | | | | | | | | | | | | | | | | | | | | | | | | | | | | | |
| 0.891 - 0.900 | 30 | 30 | 32 | 32 | 34 | 34 | 34 | | | | | | | | | | | | | | | | | | | | | | | | | | | | | | | | | | | | | | | | | | | | | | | | | | |
| 0.901 - 0.925 | 30 | 32 | 32 | 34 | 34 | | | | | | | | | | | | | | | | | | | | | | | | | | | | | | | | | | | | | | | | | | | | | | | | | | | | |
| 0.926 - 0.950 | 32 | 32 | 34 | 34 | | | | | | | | | | | | | | | | | | | | | | | | | | | | | | | | | | | | | | | | | | | | | | | | | | | | | |
| 0.951 - 0.975 | 32 | 34 | 34 | | | | | | | | | | | | | | | | | | | | | | | | | | | | | | | | | | | | | | | | | | | | | | | | | | | | | | |
| 0.976 - 1.000 | 34 | 34 | | | | | | | | | | | | | | | | | | | | | | | | | | | | | | | | | | | | | | | | | | | | | | | | | | | | | | | |
| 1.001 - 1.025 | 34 | | | | | | | | | | | | | | | | | | | | | | | | | | | | | | | | | | | | | | | | | | | | | | | | | | | | | | | | |

AVAILABLE SHIMS

| Shim No. | Thickness | Shim No. | Thickness |
|---|---|---|---|
| 02 | 2.500 (0.0984) | 20 | 2.950 (0.1161) |
| 04 | 2.550 (0.1004) | 22 | 3.000 (0.1181) |
| 06 | 2.600 (0.1024) | 24 | 3.050 (0.1201) |
| 08 | 2.650 (0.1043) | 26 | 3.100 (0.1220) |
| 10 | 2.700 (0.1063) | 28 | 3.150 (0.1240) |
| 12 | 2.750 (0.1083) | 30 | 3.200 (0.1260) |
| 14 | 2.800 (0.1102) | 32 | 3.250 (0.1280) |
| 16 | 2.850 (0.1122) | 34 | 3.300 (0.1299) |
| 18 | 2.900 (0.1142) | | |

**Intake valve clearance (cold):**
**0.15 – 0.25 mm (0.006 – 0.010 in.)**

**Example:** **A 2.800 mm shim is installed and the measured clearance is 0.450 mm. Replace the 2.800 mm shim with shim No. 24 (3.050 mm).**

Intake valve shim size chart-twincam engine – Nova and Prizm

| Measured Clearance (mm) | Installed Shim Thickness (mm) | | | | | | | | | | | | | | | | | | | | | | | | | | | |
|---|---|---|---|---|---|---|---|---|---|---|---|---|---|---|---|---|---|---|---|---|---|---|---|---|---|---|---|---|
| | 2.500 | 2.525 | 2.550 | 2.575 | 2.600 | 2.620 | 2.625 | 2.640 | 2.650 | 2.660 | 2.675 | 2.680 | 2.700 | 2.720 | 2.725 | 2.740 | 2.750 | 2.760 | 2.775 | 2.780 | 2.800 | 2.820 | 2.825 | 2.840 | 2.850 | 2.860 | 2.875 | 2.880 |
| 0.000 - 0.009 | | | | | | | | | | | | | | 02 | 02 | 02 | 02 | 02 | 04 | 04 | 04 | 06 | 06 | 06 | 06 | 06 | 08 | 08 |
| 0.010 - 0.025 | | | | | | | | | | | | | | 02 | 02 | 02 | 02 | 04 | 04 | 04 | 06 | 06 | 06 | 06 | 06 | 08 | 08 | 08 |
| 0.026 - 0.040 | | | | | | | | | | | | | 02 | 02 | 02 | 02 | 04 | 04 | 04 | 04 | 06 | 06 | 06 | 06 | 08 | 08 | 08 | 08 |
| 0.041 - 0.050 | | | | | | | | | | | | 02 | 02 | 02 | 02 | 04 | 04 | 04 | 04 | 06 | 06 | 06 | 06 | 08 | 08 | 08 | 08 | 10 |
| 0.051 - 0.070 | | | | | | | | | | | 02 | 02 | 02 | 04 | 04 | 04 | 04 | 04 | 06 | 06 | 06 | 08 | 08 | 08 | 08 | 08 | 10 | 10 |
| 0.071 - 0.090 | | | | | | | | | 02 | 02 | 02 | 02 | 04 | 04 | 04 | 04 | 06 | 06 | 06 | 06 | 08 | 08 | 08 | 08 | 10 | 10 | 10 | 10 |
| 0.091 - 0.100 | | | | | | | | 02 | 02 | 02 | 02 | 04 | 04 | 04 | 04 | 06 | 06 | 06 | 06 | 08 | 08 | 08 | 08 | 10 | 10 | 10 | 10 | 12 |
| 0.101 - 0.120 | | | | | | 02 | 02 | 02 | 02 | 02 | 04 | 04 | 04 | 06 | 06 | 06 | 06 | 06 | 08 | 08 | 08 | 10 | 10 | 10 | 10 | 10 | 12 | 12 |
| 0.121 - 0.140 | | | | | 02 | 02 | 02 | 02 | 04 | 04 | 04 | 04 | 06 | 06 | 06 | 06 | 08 | 08 | 08 | 08 | 10 | 10 | 10 | 10 | 12 | 12 | 12 | 12 |
| 0.141 - 0.150 | | | | | 02 | 02 | 02 | 04 | 04 | 04 | 04 | 06 | 06 | 06 | 06 | 08 | 08 | 08 | 08 | 10 | 10 | 10 | 10 | 12 | 12 | 12 | 12 | 14 |
| 0.151 - 0.170 | | | | 02 | 02 | 04 | 04 | 04 | 04 | 04 | 06 | 06 | 06 | 08 | 08 | 08 | 08 | 08 | 10 | 10 | 10 | 12 | 12 | 12 | 12 | 12 | 14 | 14 |
| 0.171 - 0.190 | | | 02 | 02 | 04 | 04 | 04 | 04 | 06 | 06 | 06 | 06 | 08 | 08 | 08 | 08 | 10 | 10 | 10 | 10 | 12 | 12 | 12 | 12 | 14 | 14 | 14 | 14 |
| 0.191 - 0.199 | | | 02 | 02 | 04 | 04 | 04 | 06 | 06 | 06 | 06 | 08 | 08 | 08 | 08 | 10 | 10 | 10 | 10 | 12 | 12 | 12 | 12 | 14 | 14 | 14 | 14 | 16 |
| 0.200 - 0.300 | | | | | | | | | | | | | | | | | | | | | | | | | | | | |
| 0.301 - 0.320 | 04 | 06 | 06 | 08 | 08 | 10 | 10 | 10 | 10 | 10 | 12 | 12 | 12 | 14 | 14 | 14 | 14 | 14 | 16 | 16 | 16 | 18 | 18 | 18 | 18 | 18 | 20 | 20 |
| 0.321 - 0.325 | 04 | 06 | 06 | 08 | 08 | 10 | 10 | 10 | 10 | 12 | 12 | 12 | 12 | 14 | 14 | 14 | 14 | 16 | 16 | 16 | 16 | 18 | 18 | 18 | 18 | 20 | 20 | 20 |
| 0.326 - 0.340 | 06 | 06 | 08 | 08 | 10 | 10 | 10 | 10 | 12 | 12 | 12 | 12 | 14 | 14 | 14 | 14 | 16 | 16 | 16 | 16 | 18 | 18 | 18 | 18 | 20 | 20 | 20 | 20 |
| 0.341 - 0.350 | 06 | 06 | 08 | 08 | 10 | 10 | 10 | 12 | 12 | 12 | 12 | 12 | 14 | 14 | 14 | 16 | 16 | 16 | 16 | 16 | 18 | 18 | 18 | 20 | 20 | 20 | 20 | 20 |
| 0.351 - 0.370 | 06 | 08 | 08 | 10 | 10 | 12 | 12 | 12 | 12 | 12 | 14 | 14 | 14 | 16 | 16 | 16 | 16 | 16 | 18 | 18 | 18 | 20 | 20 | 20 | 20 | 20 | 22 | 22 |
| 0.371 - 0.375 | 06 | 08 | 08 | 10 | 10 | 12 | 12 | 12 | 12 | 14 | 14 | 14 | 14 | 16 | 16 | 16 | 16 | 18 | 18 | 18 | 18 | 20 | 20 | 20 | 20 | 22 | 22 | 22 |
| 0.376 - 0.390 | 08 | 08 | 10 | 10 | 12 | 12 | 12 | 12 | 14 | 14 | 14 | 14 | 16 | 16 | 16 | 16 | 18 | 18 | 18 | 18 | 20 | 20 | 20 | 20 | 22 | 22 | 22 | 22 |
| 0.391 - 0.400 | 08 | 08 | 10 | 10 | 12 | 12 | 12 | 14 | 14 | 14 | 14 | 14 | 16 | 16 | 16 | 18 | 18 | 18 | 18 | 18 | 20 | 20 | 20 | 22 | 22 | 22 | 22 | 22 |
| 0.401 - 0.420 | 08 | 10 | 10 | 12 | 12 | 14 | 14 | 14 | 14 | 14 | 16 | 16 | 16 | 18 | 18 | 18 | 18 | 18 | 20 | 20 | 20 | 22 | 22 | 22 | 22 | 22 | 24 | 24 |
| 0.421 - 0.425 | 08 | 10 | 10 | 12 | 12 | 14 | 14 | 14 | 14 | 16 | 16 | 16 | 16 | 18 | 18 | 18 | 18 | 20 | 20 | 20 | 20 | 22 | 22 | 22 | 22 | 24 | 24 | 24 |
| 0.426 - 0.440 | 10 | 10 | 12 | 12 | 14 | 14 | 14 | 14 | 16 | 16 | 16 | 16 | 18 | 18 | 18 | 18 | 20 | 20 | 20 | 20 | 22 | 22 | 22 | 22 | 24 | 24 | 24 | 24 |
| 0.441 - 0.450 | 10 | 10 | 12 | 12 | 14 | 14 | 14 | 16 | 16 | 16 | 16 | 16 | 18 | 18 | 18 | 20 | 20 | 20 | 20 | 20 | 22 | 22 | 22 | 24 | 24 | 24 | 24 | 24 |
| 0.451 - 0.470 | 10 | 12 | 12 | 14 | 14 | 16 | 16 | 16 | 16 | 16 | 18 | 18 | 18 | 20 | 20 | 20 | 20 | 20 | 22 | 22 | 22 | 24 | 24 | 24 | 24 | 24 | 26 | 26 |
| 0.471 - 0.475 | 10 | 12 | 12 | 14 | 14 | 16 | 16 | 16 | 16 | 18 | 18 | 18 | 18 | 20 | 20 | 20 | 20 | 22 | 22 | 22 | 22 | 24 | 24 | 24 | 24 | 26 | 26 | 26 |
| 0.476 - 0.490 | 12 | 12 | 14 | 14 | 16 | 16 | 16 | 16 | 18 | 18 | 18 | 18 | 20 | 20 | 20 | 20 | 22 | 22 | 22 | 22 | 24 | 24 | 24 | 24 | 26 | 26 | 26 | 26 |
| 0.491 - 0.500 | 12 | 12 | 14 | 14 | 16 | 16 | 16 | 18 | 18 | 18 | 18 | 18 | 20 | 20 | 20 | 22 | 22 | 22 | 22 | 22 | 24 | 24 | 24 | 26 | 26 | 26 | 25 | 26 |
| 0.501 - 0.520 | 12 | 14 | 14 | 16 | 16 | 18 | 18 | 18 | 18 | 18 | 20 | 20 | 20 | 22 | 22 | 22 | 22 | 22 | 24 | 24 | 24 | 26 | 26 | 26 | 26 | 26 | 28 | 28 |
| 0.521 - 0.525 | 12 | 14 | 14 | 16 | 16 | 18 | 18 | 18 | 18 | 20 | 20 | 20 | 20 | 22 | 22 | 22 | 22 | 24 | 24 | 24 | 24 | 26 | 26 | 26 | 26 | 28 | 28 | 28 |
| 0.526 - 0.540 | 14 | 14 | 16 | 16 | 18 | 18 | 18 | 18 | 20 | 20 | 20 | 20 | 22 | 22 | 22 | 22 | 24 | 24 | 24 | 24 | 26 | 26 | 26 | 26 | 28 | 28 | 28 | 28 |
| 0.541 - 0.550 | 14 | 14 | 16 | 16 | 18 | 18 | 18 | 20 | 20 | 20 | 20 | 20 | 22 | 22 | 22 | 24 | 24 | 24 | 24 | 24 | 26 | 26 | 26 | 28 | 28 | 28 | 28 | 28 |
| 0.551 - 0.570 | 14 | 16 | 16 | 18 | 18 | 20 | 20 | 20 | 20 | 20 | 22 | 22 | 22 | 24 | 24 | 24 | 24 | 24 | 26 | 26 | 26 | 28 | 28 | 28 | 28 | 28 | 30 | 30 |
| 0.571 - 0.575 | 14 | 16 | 16 | 18 | 18 | 20 | 20 | 20 | 20 | 22 | 22 | 22 | 22 | 24 | 24 | 24 | 24 | 26 | 26 | 26 | 26 | 28 | 28 | 28 | 28 | 30 | 30 | 30 |
| 0.576 - 0.590 | 16 | 16 | 18 | 18 | 20 | 20 | 20 | 20 | 22 | 22 | 22 | 22 | 24 | 24 | 24 | 24 | 26 | 26 | 26 | 26 | 28 | 28 | 28 | 28 | 30 | 30 | 30 | 30 |
| 0.591 - 0.600 | 16 | 16 | 18 | 18 | 20 | 20 | 20 | 22 | 22 | 22 | 22 | 22 | 24 | 24 | 24 | 26 | 26 | 26 | 26 | 26 | 28 | 28 | 28 | 30 | 30 | 30 | 30 | 30 |
| 0.601 - 0.620 | 16 | 18 | 18 | 20 | 20 | 22 | 22 | 22 | 22 | 22 | 24 | 24 | 24 | 26 | 26 | 26 | 26 | 26 | 28 | 28 | 28 | 30 | 30 | 30 | 30 | 30 | 32 | 32 |
| 0.621 - 0.625 | 16 | 18 | 18 | 20 | 20 | 22 | 22 | 22 | 22 | 24 | 24 | 24 | 24 | 26 | 26 | 26 | 26 | 28 | 28 | 28 | 28 | 30 | 30 | 30 | 30 | 32 | 32 | 32 |
| 0.626 - 0.640 | 18 | 18 | 20 | 20 | 22 | 22 | 22 | 22 | 24 | 24 | 24 | 24 | 26 | 26 | 26 | 26 | 28 | 28 | 28 | 28 | 30 | 30 | 30 | 30 | 32 | 32 | 32 | 32 |
| 0.641 - 0.650 | 18 | 18 | 20 | 20 | 22 | 22 | 22 | 24 | 24 | 24 | 24 | 24 | 26 | 26 | 26 | 28 | 28 | 28 | 28 | 28 | 30 | 30 | 30 | 32 | 32 | 32 | 32 | 32 |
| 0.651 - 0.670 | 18 | 20 | 20 | 22 | 22 | 24 | 24 | 24 | 24 | 24 | 26 | 26 | 26 | 28 | 28 | 28 | 28 | 28 | 30 | 30 | 30 | 32 | 32 | 32 | 32 | 32 | 34 | 34 |
| 0.671 - 0.675 | 18 | 20 | 20 | 22 | 22 | 24 | 24 | 24 | 24 | 26 | 26 | 26 | 26 | 28 | 28 | 28 | 28 | 30 | 30 | 30 | 30 | 32 | 32 | 32 | 32 | 34 | 34 | 34 |
| 0.676 - 0.690 | 20 | 20 | 22 | 22 | 24 | 24 | 24 | 24 | 26 | 26 | 26 | 26 | 28 | 28 | 28 | 28 | 30 | 30 | 30 | 30 | 32 | 32 | 32 | 32 | 34 | 34 | 34 | 34 |
| 0.691 - 0.700 | 20 | 20 | 22 | 22 | 24 | 24 | 24 | 26 | 26 | 26 | 26 | 26 | 28 | 28 | 28 | 30 | 30 | 30 | 30 | 30 | 32 | 32 | 32 | 34 | 34 | 34 | 34 | 34 |
| 0.701 - 0.720 | 20 | 22 | 22 | 24 | 24 | 26 | 26 | 26 | 26 | 26 | 28 | 28 | 28 | 30 | 30 | 30 | 30 | 30 | 32 | 32 | 32 | 34 | 34 | 34 | 34 | 34 | | |
| 0.721 - 0.725 | 20 | 22 | 22 | 24 | 24 | 26 | 26 | 26 | 26 | 28 | 28 | 28 | 28 | 30 | 30 | 30 | 30 | 32 | 32 | 32 | 32 | 34 | 34 | 34 | 34 | | | |
| 0.726 - 0.740 | 22 | 22 | 24 | 24 | 26 | 26 | 26 | 26 | 28 | 28 | 28 | 28 | 30 | 30 | 30 | 30 | 32 | 32 | 32 | 32 | 34 | 34 | 34 | 34 | | | | |
| 0.741 - 0.750 | 22 | 22 | 24 | 24 | 26 | 26 | 26 | 28 | 28 | 28 | 28 | 28 | 30 | 30 | 30 | 32 | 32 | 32 | 32 | 32 | 34 | 34 | 34 | | | | | |
| 0.751 - 0.770 | 22 | 24 | 24 | 26 | 26 | 28 | 28 | 28 | 28 | 28 | 30 | 30 | 30 | 32 | 32 | 32 | 32 | 32 | 34 | 34 | 34 | | | | | | | |
| 0.771 - 0.775 | 22 | 24 | 24 | 26 | 26 | 28 | 28 | 28 | 28 | 30 | 30 | 30 | 30 | 32 | 32 | 32 | 32 | 34 | 34 | 34 | 34 | | | | | | | |
| 0.776 - 0.790 | 24 | 24 | 26 | 26 | 28 | 28 | 28 | 28 | 30 | 30 | 30 | 30 | 32 | 32 | 32 | 32 | 34 | 34 | 34 | 34 | | | | | | | | |
| 0.791 - 0.800 | 24 | 24 | 26 | 26 | 28 | 28 | 28 | 30 | 30 | 30 | 30 | 30 | 32 | 32 | 32 | 34 | 34 | 34 | 34 | 34 | | | | | | | | |
| 0.801 - 0.820 | 24 | 26 | 26 | 28 | 28 | 30 | 30 | 30 | 30 | 30 | 32 | 32 | 32 | 34 | 34 | 34 | 34 | 34 | | | | | | | | | | |
| 0.821 - 0.825 | 24 | 26 | 26 | 28 | 28 | 30 | 30 | 30 | 30 | 32 | 32 | 32 | 32 | 34 | 34 | 34 | 34 | | | | | | | | | | | |
| 0.826 - 0.840 | 26 | 26 | 28 | 28 | 30 | 30 | 30 | 30 | 32 | 32 | 32 | 32 | 34 | 34 | 34 | 34 | | | | | | | | | | | | |
| 0.841 - 0.850 | 26 | 26 | 28 | 28 | 30 | 30 | 30 | 32 | 32 | 32 | 32 | 32 | 34 | 34 | 34 | | | | | | | | | | | | | |
| 0.851 - 0.870 | 26 | 28 | 28 | 30 | 30 | 32 | 32 | 32 | 32 | 32 | 34 | 34 | 34 | | | | | | | | | | | | | | | |
| 0.871 - 0.875 | 26 | 28 | 28 | 30 | 30 | 32 | 32 | 32 | 32 | 34 | 34 | 34 | 34 | | | | | | | | | | | | | | | |
| 0.876 - 0.890 | 28 | 28 | 30 | 30 | 32 | 32 | 32 | 32 | 34 | 34 | 34 | 34 | | | | | | | | | | | | | | | | |
| 0.891 - 0.900 | 28 | 28 | 30 | 30 | 32 | 32 | 32 | 34 | 34 | 34 | 34 | 34 | | | | | | | | | | | | | | | | |
| 0.901 - 0.925 | 28 | 30 | 30 | 32 | 32 | 34 | 34 | 34 | 34 | | | | | | | | | | | | | | | | | | | |
| 0.926 - 0.950 | 30 | 30 | 32 | 32 | 34 | 34 | 34 | | | | | | | | | | | | | | | | | | | | | |
| 0.951 - 0.975 | 30 | 32 | 32 | 34 | 34 | | | | | | | | | | | | | | | | | | | | | | | |
| 0.976 - 1.000 | 32 | 32 | 34 | 34 | | | | | | | | | | | | | | | | | | | | | | | | |
| 1.001 - 1.025 | 32 | 34 | 34 | | | | | | | | | | | | | | | | | | | | | | | | | |
| 1.026 - 1.050 | 34 | 34 | | | | | | | | | | | | | | | | | | | | | | | | | | |
| 1.051 - 1.075 | 34 | | | | | | | | | | | | | | | | | | | | | | | | | | | |

| Measured Clearance (mm) | Installed Shim Thickness (mm) | | | | | | | | | | | | | | | | | | | | | | | | | | | | |
|---|---|---|---|---|---|---|---|---|---|---|---|---|---|---|---|---|---|---|---|---|---|---|---|---|---|---|---|---|---|
| | 2.900 | 2.920 | 2.925 | 2.940 | 2.950 | 2.960 | 2.975 | 2.980 | 3.000 | 3.020 | 3.025 | 3.040 | 3.050 | 3.060 | 3.075 | 3.080 | 3.100 | 3.120 | 3.125 | 3.140 | 3.150 | 3.160 | 3.175 | 3.180 | 3.200 | 3.225 | 3.250 | 3.275 | 3.300 |
| 0.000 - 0.009 | 08 | 10 | 10 | 10 | 10 | 10 | 12 | 12 | 12 | 14 | 14 | 14 | 14 | 14 | 16 | 16 | 16 | 18 | 18 | 18 | 18 | 18 | 20 | 20 | 20 | 22 | 22 | 24 | 24 |
| 0.010 - 0.025 | 10 | 10 | 10 | 10 | 10 | 12 | 12 | 12 | 14 | 14 | 14 | 14 | 14 | 16 | 16 | 16 | 18 | 18 | 18 | 18 | 18 | 20 | 20 | 20 | 22 | 22 | 22 | 24 | 26 |
| 0.026 - 0.040 | 10 | 10 | 10 | 10 | 12 | 12 | 12 | 12 | 14 | 14 | 14 | 14 | 16 | 16 | 16 | 16 | 18 | 18 | 18 | 18 | 20 | 20 | 20 | 20 | 22 | 22 | 24 | 24 | 26 |
| 0.041 - 0.050 | 10 | 10 | 10 | 12 | 12 | 12 | 12 | 14 | 14 | 14 | 14 | 16 | 16 | 16 | 16 | 18 | 18 | 18 | 18 | 20 | 20 | 20 | 20 | 22 | 22 | 22 | 24 | 24 | 26 |
| 0.051 - 0.070 | 10 | 12 | 12 | 12 | 12 | 12 | 14 | 14 | 14 | 16 | 16 | 16 | 16 | 16 | 18 | 18 | 18 | 20 | 20 | 20 | 20 | 20 | 22 | 22 | 22 | 24 | 24 | 26 | 26 |
| 0.071 - 0.090 | 12 | 12 | 12 | 12 | 14 | 14 | 14 | 14 | 16 | 16 | 16 | 16 | 18 | 18 | 18 | 18 | 20 | 20 | 20 | 20 | 22 | 22 | 22 | 22 | 24 | 24 | 26 | 26 | 28 |
| 0.091 - 0.100 | 12 | 12 | 12 | 14 | 14 | 14 | 14 | 16 | 16 | 16 | 16 | 18 | 18 | 18 | 18 | 20 | 20 | 20 | 20 | 22 | 22 | 22 | 22 | 24 | 24 | 24 | 26 | 26 | 28 |
| 0.101 - 0.120 | 12 | 14 | 14 | 14 | 14 | 14 | 16 | 16 | 16 | 18 | 18 | 18 | 18 | 18 | 20 | 20 | 20 | 22 | 22 | 22 | 22 | 22 | 24 | 24 | 24 | 26 | 26 | 28 | 28 |
| 0.121 - 0.140 | 14 | 14 | 14 | 14 | 16 | 16 | 16 | 16 | 18 | 18 | 18 | 18 | 20 | 20 | 20 | 20 | 22 | 22 | 22 | 22 | 24 | 24 | 24 | 24 | 26 | 26 | 28 | 28 | 30 |
| 0.141 - 0.150 | 14 | 14 | 14 | 16 | 16 | 16 | 16 | 18 | 18 | 18 | 18 | 20 | 20 | 20 | 20 | 22 | 22 | 22 | 22 | 24 | 24 | 24 | 24 | 26 | 26 | 26 | 28 | 28 | 30 |
| 0.151 - 0.170 | 14 | 16 | 16 | 16 | 16 | 16 | 18 | 18 | 18 | 20 | 20 | 20 | 20 | 20 | 22 | 22 | 22 | 24 | 24 | 24 | 24 | 24 | 26 | 26 | 26 | 28 | 28 | 30 | 30 |
| 0.171 - 0.190 | 16 | 16 | 16 | 16 | 18 | 18 | 18 | 18 | 20 | 20 | 20 | 20 | 22 | 22 | 22 | 22 | 24 | 24 | 24 | 24 | 26 | 26 | 26 | 26 | 28 | 28 | 30 | 30 | 32 |
| 0.191 - 0.199 | 16 | 16 | 16 | 18 | 18 | 18 | 18 | 20 | 20 | 20 | 20 | 22 | 22 | 22 | 22 | 24 | 24 | 24 | 24 | 26 | 26 | 26 | 26 | 28 | 28 | 28 | 30 | 30 | 32 |
| 0.200 - 0.300 | | | | | | | | | | | | | | | | | | | | | | | | | | | | | |
| 0.301 - 0.320 | 20 | 22 | 22 | 22 | 22 | 22 | 24 | 24 | 24 | 26 | 26 | 26 | 26 | 26 | 28 | 28 | 28 | 30 | 30 | 30 | 30 | 30 | 32 | 32 | 32 | 34 | 34 | | |
| 0.321 - 0.325 | 20 | 22 | 22 | 22 | 22 | 24 | 24 | 24 | 24 | 26 | 26 | 26 | 26 | 28 | 28 | 28 | 28 | 30 | 30 | 30 | 30 | 32 | 32 | 32 | 32 | 34 | 34 | | |
| 0.326 - 0.340 | 22 | 22 | 22 | 22 | 24 | 24 | 24 | 24 | 26 | 26 | 26 | 26 | 28 | 28 | 28 | 28 | 30 | 30 | 30 | 30 | 32 | 32 | 32 | 32 | 34 | 34 | | | |
| 0.341 - 0.350 | 22 | 22 | 22 | 24 | 24 | 24 | 24 | 24 | 26 | 26 | 26 | 28 | 28 | 28 | 28 | 28 | 30 | 30 | 30 | 32 | 32 | 32 | 32 | 32 | 34 | 34 | | | |
| 0.351 - 0.370 | 22 | 24 | 24 | 24 | 24 | 24 | 26 | 26 | 26 | 28 | 28 | 28 | 28 | 28 | 30 | 30 | 30 | 32 | 32 | 32 | 32 | 32 | 34 | 34 | 34 | | | | |
| 0.371 - 0.375 | 22 | 24 | 24 | 24 | 24 | 26 | 26 | 26 | 26 | 28 | 28 | 28 | 28 | 30 | 30 | 30 | 30 | 32 | 32 | 32 | 32 | 34 | 34 | 34 | 34 | | | | |
| 0.376 - 0.390 | 24 | 24 | 24 | 24 | 26 | 26 | 26 | 26 | 28 | 28 | 28 | 28 | 30 | 30 | 30 | 30 | 32 | 32 | 32 | 32 | 34 | 34 | 34 | 34 | | | | | |
| 0.391 - 0.400 | 24 | 24 | 24 | 26 | 26 | 26 | 26 | 26 | 28 | 28 | 28 | 30 | 30 | 30 | 30 | 30 | 32 | 32 | 32 | 34 | 34 | 34 | 34 | 34 | | | | | |
| 0.401 - 0.420 | 24 | 26 | 26 | 26 | 26 | 26 | 28 | 28 | 28 | 30 | 30 | 30 | 30 | 30 | 32 | 32 | 32 | 34 | 34 | 34 | 34 | 34 | | | | | | | |
| 0.421 - 0.425 | 24 | 26 | 26 | 26 | 26 | 28 | 28 | 28 | 28 | 30 | 30 | 30 | 30 | 32 | 32 | 32 | 32 | 34 | 34 | 34 | 34 | | | | | | | | |
| 0.426 - 0.440 | 26 | 26 | 26 | 26 | 28 | 28 | 28 | 28 | 30 | 30 | 30 | 30 | 32 | 32 | 32 | 32 | 34 | 34 | 34 | 34 | | | | | | | | | |
| 0.441 - 0.450 | 26 | 26 | 26 | 28 | 28 | 28 | 28 | 28 | 30 | 30 | 30 | 32 | 32 | 32 | 32 | 32 | 34 | 34 | 34 | | | | | | | | | | |
| 0.451 - 0.470 | 26 | 28 | 28 | 28 | 28 | 28 | 30 | 30 | 30 | 32 | 32 | 32 | 32 | 32 | 34 | 34 | 34 | | | | | | | | | | | | |
| 0.471 - 0.475 | 26 | 28 | 28 | 28 | 28 | 30 | 30 | 30 | 30 | 32 | 32 | 32 | 32 | 34 | 34 | 34 | 34 | | | | | | | | | | | | |
| 0.476 - 0.490 | 28 | 28 | 28 | 28 | 30 | 30 | 30 | 30 | 32 | 32 | 32 | 32 | 34 | 34 | 34 | 34 | | | | | | | | | | | | | |
| 0.491 - 0.500 | 28 | 28 | 28 | 30 | 30 | 30 | 30 | 30 | 32 | 32 | 32 | 34 | 34 | 34 | 34 | 34 | | | | | | | | | | | | | |
| 0.501 - 0.520 | 28 | 30 | 30 | 30 | 30 | 30 | 32 | 32 | 32 | 34 | 34 | 34 | 34 | 34 | | | | | | | | | | | | | | | |
| 0.521 - 0.525 | 28 | 30 | 30 | 30 | 30 | 32 | 32 | 32 | 32 | 34 | 34 | 34 | 34 | | | | | | | | | | | | | | | | |
| 0.526 - 0.540 | 30 | 30 | 30 | 30 | 32 | 32 | 32 | 32 | 34 | 34 | 34 | 34 | | | | | | | | | | | | | | | | | |
| 0.541 - 0.550 | 30 | 30 | 30 | 32 | 32 | 32 | 32 | 32 | 34 | 34 | 34 | | | | | | | | | | | | | | | | | | |
| 0.551 - 0.570 | 30 | 32 | 32 | 32 | 32 | 32 | 34 | 34 | 34 | | | | | | | | | | | | | | | | | | | | |
| 0.571 - 0.575 | 30 | 32 | 32 | 32 | 32 | 34 | 34 | 34 | 34 | | | | | | | | | | | | | | | | | | | | |
| 0.576 - 0.590 | 32 | 32 | 32 | 32 | 34 | 34 | 34 | 34 | | | | | | | | | | | | | | | | | | | | | |
| 0.591 - 0.600 | 32 | 32 | 32 | 34 | 34 | 34 | 34 | 34 | | | | | | | | | | | | | | | | | | | | | |
| 0.601 - 0.620 | 32 | 34 | 34 | 34 | 34 | 34 | | | | | | | | | | | | | | | | | | | | | | | |
| 0.621 - 0.625 | 32 | 34 | 34 | 34 | 34 | | | | | | | | | | | | | | | | | | | | | | | | |
| 0.626 - 0.640 | 34 | 34 | 34 | 34 | | | | | | | | | | | | | | | | | | | | | | | | | |
| 0.641 - 0.650 | 34 | 34 | 34 | | | | | | | | | | | | | | | | | | | | | | | | | | |
| 0.651 - 0.670 | 34 | | | | | | | | | | | | | | | | | | | | | | | | | | | | |
| 0.671 - 0.675 | 34 | | | | | | | | | | | | | | | | | | | | | | | | | | | | |
| 0.676 - 0.690 | | | | | | | | | | | | | | | | | | | | | | | | | | | | | |
| 0.691 - 0.700 | | | | | | | | | | | | | | | | | | | | | | | | | | | | | |
| 0.701 - 0.720 | | | | | | | | | | | | | | | | | | | | | | | | | | | | | |
| 0.721 - 0.725 | | | | | | | | | | | | | | | | | | | | | | | | | | | | | |
| 0.726 - 0.740 | | | | | | | | | | | | | | | | | | | | | | | | | | | | | |
| 0.741 - 0.750 | | | | | | | | | | | | | | | | | | | | | | | | | | | | | |
| 0.751 - 0.770 | | | | | | | | | | | | | | | | | | | | | | | | | | | | | |
| 0.771 - 0.775 | | | | | | | | | | | | | | | | | | | | | | | | | | | | | |
| 0.776 - 0.790 | | | | | | | | | | | | | | | | | | | | | | | | | | | | | |
| 0.791 - 0.800 | | | | | | | | | | | | | | | | | | | | | | | | | | | | | |
| 0.801 - 0.820 | | | | | | | | | | | | | | | | | | | | | | | | | | | | | |
| 0.821 - 0.825 | | | | | | | | | | | | | | | | | | | | | | | | | | | | | |
| 0.826 - 0.840 | | | | | | | | | | | | | | | | | | | | | | | | | | | | | |
| 0.841 - 0.850 | | | | | | | | | | | | | | | | | | | | | | | | | | | | | |
| 0.851 - 0.870 | | | | | | | | | | | | | | | | | | | | | | | | | | | | | |
| 0.871 - 0.875 | | | | | | | | | | | | | | | | | | | | | | | | | | | | | |
| 0.876 - 0.890 | | | | | | | | | | | | | | | | | | | | | | | | | | | | | |
| 0.891 - 0.900 | | | | | | | | | | | | | | | | | | | | | | | | | | | | | |
| 0.901 - 0.925 | | | | | | | | | | | | | | | | | | | | | | | | | | | | | |
| 0.926 - 0.950 | | | | | | | | | | | | | | | | | | | | | | | | | | | | | |
| 0.951 - 0.975 | | | | | | | | | | | | | | | | | | | | | | | | | | | | | |
| 0.976 - 1.000 | | | | | | | | | | | | | | | | | | | | | | | | | | | | | |
| 1.001 - 1.025 | | | | | | | | | | | | | | | | | | | | | | | | | | | | | |
| 1.026 - 1.050 | | | | | | | | | | | | | | | | | | | | | | | | | | | | | |
| 1.051 - 1.075 | | | | | | | | | | | | | | | | | | | | | | | | | | | | | |

AVAILABLE SHIMS mm (in.)

| Shim No. | Thickness | Shim No. | Thickness |
|---|---|---|---|
| 02 | 2.500 (0.0984) | 20 | 2.950 (0.1161) |
| 04 | 2.550 (0.1004) | 22 | 3.000 (0.1181) |
| 06 | 2.600 (0.1024) | 24 | 3.050 (0.1201) |
| 08 | 2.650 (0.1043) | 26 | 3.100 (0.1220) |
| 10 | 2.700 (0.1063) | 28 | 3.150 (0.1240) |
| 12 | 2.750 (0.1083) | 30 | 3.200 (0.1260) |
| 14 | 2.800 (0.1102) | 32 | 3.250 (0.1280) |
| 16 | 2.850 (0.1122) | 34 | 3.300 (0.1299) |
| 18 | 2.900 (0.1142) | | |

**Exhaust valve clearance (cold):**
**0.20 – 0.30 mm (0.008 – 0.012 in.)**

**Example:** **A 2.800 mm shim is installed and the measured clearance is 0.450 mm. Replace the 2.800 mm shim with shim No. 22 (3.000 mm).**

**Exhaust valve shim size chart-twincam engine—Nova and Prizm**

**NOTE: The crankshaft pulley notch will align with the 0 degrees mark on the timing plate.**

b. Using a feeler gauge, measure and record (valves not within specifications) the intake valve-to-lifter clearances of cylinders No. 1 and 2; the exhaust valve-to-lifter clearances of cylinders No. 1 and 3.

c. Rotate the crankshaft one complete revolution (360 degrees) and realign the crankshaft pulley notch with the 0 degrees mark on the timing plate; the valve lifters of the No. 4 cylinder should be loose.

d. Using a feeler gauge, measure and record (valves not within specifications) the intake valve-to-lifter clearances of cylinders No. 3 and 4; the exhaust valve-to-lifter clearances of cylinders No. 2 & 4.

3. Rotate the crankshaft pulley until the cam lobe (valve being worked on) is positioned in the upward direction.

4. Using the valve clearance adjustment tool set No. J-37141 or equivalent, press the valve lifter downward, then, secure it in downward position (using another tool) and remove the first tool.

5. Using a small screwdriver or a magnetic finger, remove the adjusting shim.

6. To select the correct valve shim(s), perform the following procedures:

a. Using a micrometer, measure the thickness of the old shim.

b. Using the valve clearance measurement (already acquired), subtract 0.008 in. (intake valve) or 0.010 in. (exhaust valve) from it; the new calculation is the difference between the old shim and the new shim.

c. Using the difference (just calculated), add it to the old shim thickness, then, select (from the chart) a new shim with the thickness closest to the new calculation.

7. Install the new shim and remove the hold-down tool.

8. After all valves have met specifications, use new gaskets, sealant (if necessary) and reverse the removal procedures. Adjust the engine timing and idle speed.

### *Spectrum*

1. Remove the cylinder head cover.

2. Rotate the engine until the notched line on the crankshaft pulley aligns with the 0 degree mark on the timing gear case. The position of the No. 1 piston should be at TDC of the compression stroke.

3. Set the intake valve to 0.006 in. (Cold) for No. 1 and 2 cylinders; exhaust valves to 0.010 in. (Cold) for No. 1 and 3 cylinders.

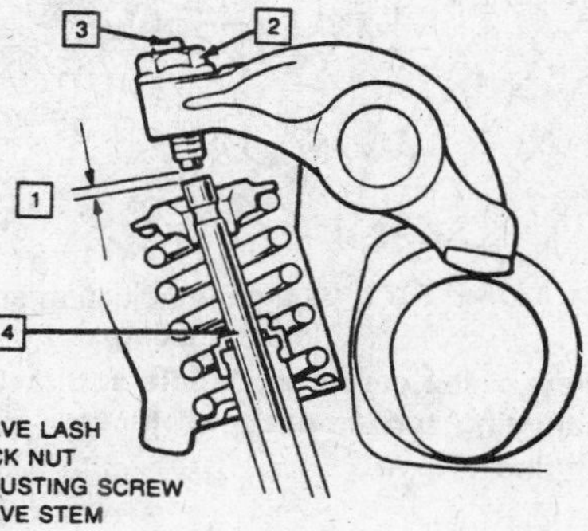


1. VALVE LASH
2. LOCK NUT
3. ADJUSTING SCREW
4. VALVE STEM

**Valve lash adjusting screw location—Sprint and Metro**

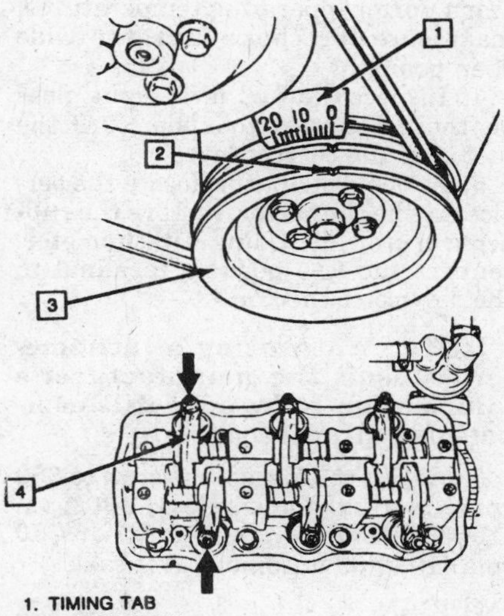


1. TIMING TAB
2. TIMING NOTCH
3. CRANKSHAFT PULLEY
4. NO. 1 CYLINDER

**Timing mark alignment for adjusting valve lash for No. 1 cylinder—Sprint and Metro**

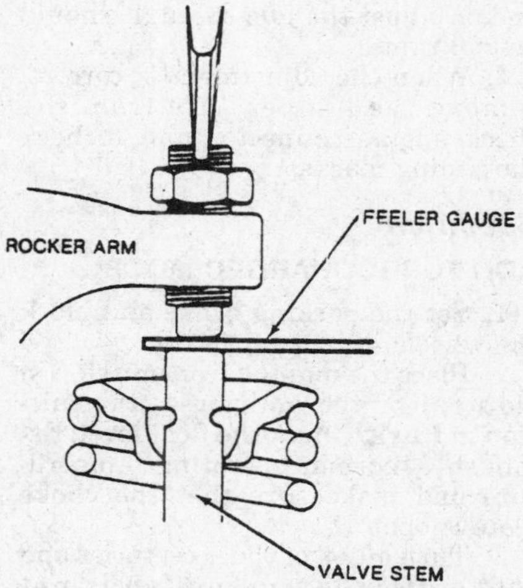


**Valve lash adjustment—Spectrum**

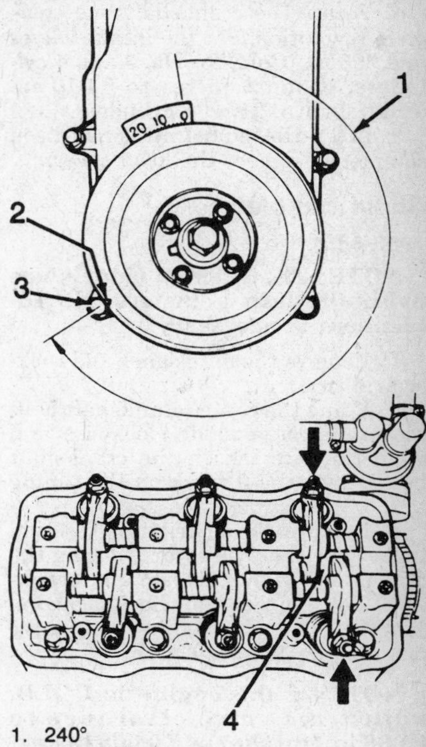


1. 240°
2. Timing notch
3. Left mounting bolt
4. No. 3 cylinder

**Timing mark alignment for adjusting valve lash on No. 3 cylinder—Sprint and Metro**

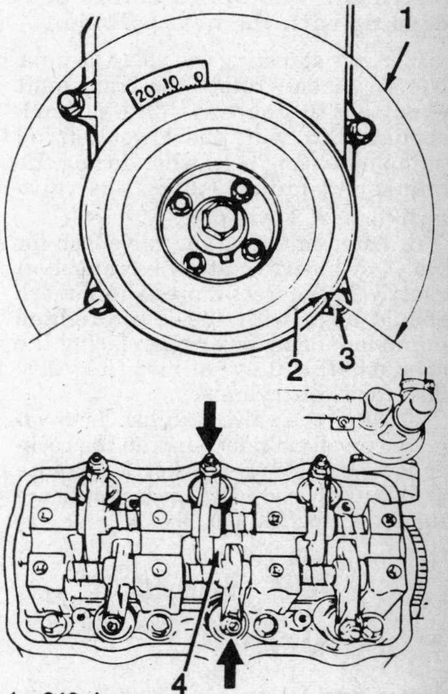


1. 240 degrees
2. Timing notch
3. Right mounting bolt
4. No. 2 cylinder

**Timing mark alignment for adjusting valve lash on No. 2 cylinder—Sprint and Metro**

4. Rotate the crankshaft one complete revolution. Set the intake valves to 0.006 in. (Cold) for No. 3 and 4 cylinders; exhaust valves to 0.010 in. (Cold) for No. 2 and 4 cylinders.

5. After the adjustment has been completed, replace the head cover.

### *Sprint and Metro*

#### 1985-88

**NOTE: The 1989-90 models use hydraulic lash adjusters. No adjustment is necessary.**

1. Remove the air cleaner and rocker arm cover.
2. Using the center crankshaft bolt, rotate the crankshaft clockwise and align the **V** mark on the crankshaft pulley with the **0** mark on the timing tab.
3. Remove the distributor cap and make sure that the rotor is facing the fuel pump. If not, rotate the crankshaft 360 degrees and check it again.
4. Check and/or adjust the valve lash for the No. 1 cylinder.

**NOTE: If the engine is COLD, adjust the valve clearance to 0.006 in. (intake) and 0.008 in. (exhaust). With a WARM engine, adjust the valve clearance to 0.010 in. (intake) and 0.012 in. (exhaust). After each adjustment, tighten the lock nut on the adjusting screw to 11–13 ft. lbs. and recheck the valve lash, before proceeding with the next cylinder.**

5. After adjusting the valve lash for No. 1 cylinder, rotate the crankshaft exactly 240 degrees. The **V** mark should align with the lower left oil pump mounting bolt, when facing the crankshaft pulley. Adjust the valve lash for No. 3 cylinder.
6. After adjusting the valve lash for No. 3 cylinder, rotate the crankshaft exactly 240 degrees more. The **V** mark should align with the lower rightoil pump mounting bolt, when facing the crankshaft pulley. Adjust the valve lash for No. 2 cylinder.
7. After the valve lash has been adjusted on all cylinders, install the rocker cover using a new gasket. Make sure that the valve adjustment locknuts are tightened to 11–13 ft. lbs.

# Idle Speed

## ADJUSTMENT

### *Nova and Prizm*

#### EXCEPT TWINCAM

1. Turn off all of the accessories, firmly set the parking brake and position the transaxle in neutral.

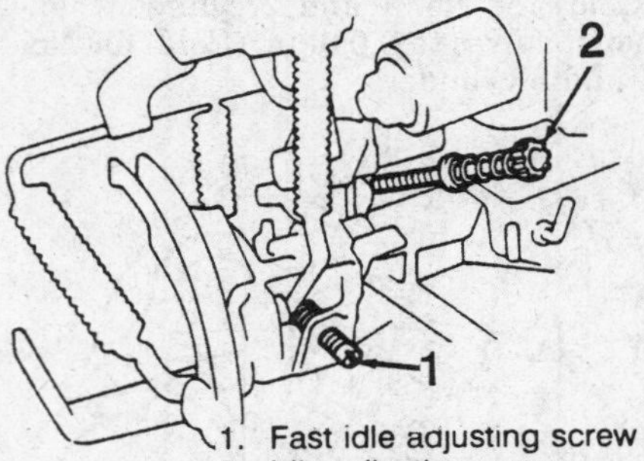


1. Fast idle adjusting screw
2. Idle adjusting screw

**View of the carburetor's idle and fast idle adjusting screws-except twincam engine—Nova**

2. Check and/or adjust the ignition timing.
3. Start the engine and allow it to reach normal operating temperatures; make sure the choke is in the wide open position.
4. Inspect the fuel level sight glass on the carburetor to make sure the fuel is at the correct level.
5. At the distributor, locate the service engine connector, remove the rubber cap from it. Using a tachometer, connect the (+) positive terminal to the service connector.

**NOTE: When using a tachometer, consult the manufacturer's information to be sure it is compatible with the system.**

6. Adjust the idle speed screw to 650 rpm (manual transaxles), 800 rpm (1985 automatic transaxles) or 750 rpm (1986-89 automatic transaxles).

#### TWINCAM

1. Make sure the ignition timing is correct.
2. Using a jumper wire, connect it to the check engine connector located near the wiper motor.
3. Start the engine, then, check and/or adjust the idle speed; it should be 800 rpm.
4. When the adjustment is correct, remove the jumper wire from the check engine connector and recheck the timing marks.

### *Spectrum*

#### NON-TURBOCHARGED MODEL

1. Set the parking brake and block the wheels.
2. Place the manual transmission in **Neutral** or the automatic transmission in **Park**. Check the float level. Establish a normal operating temperature and make sure that the choke plate is open.
3. Turn off all of the accessories and wait until the cooling fan is not operating.
4. If equipped with power steering, place the wheels in the straight forward position. Remove the air filter.
5. Disconnect and plug the distributor vacuum line, canister purge line, EGR vacuum line and ITC valve vacuum line.
6. Connect a tachometer to the coil tachometer connector and a timing light to the No. 1 spark plug wire. Check the timing and idle speed.
7. If the idle speed needs adjusting, turn the idle speed adjusting screw.
8. If equipped with A/C, adjust the system to **Max/Cold** and place the blower on **High** position. Set the fast idle speed by turning the adjust bolt of the Fast Idle Control Diaphragm to 850 rpm (MT) or 980 rpm (AT).
9. When adjustment is completed, turn the engine off, remove the test equipment, install the air filter and vacuum lines.

#### TURBOCHARGED MODEL

1. Set the parking brake.
2. Block the front wheels.
3. Place the select lever in **Neutral**.
4. Make the idling speed adjustment with the engine at normal operating temperature, with A/C Off and front wheels facing straight ahead.

**NOTE: All electrical equipment (lights, rear defogger, heater, etc.) should be turned off.**

5. Make sure Check Engine light is not on.

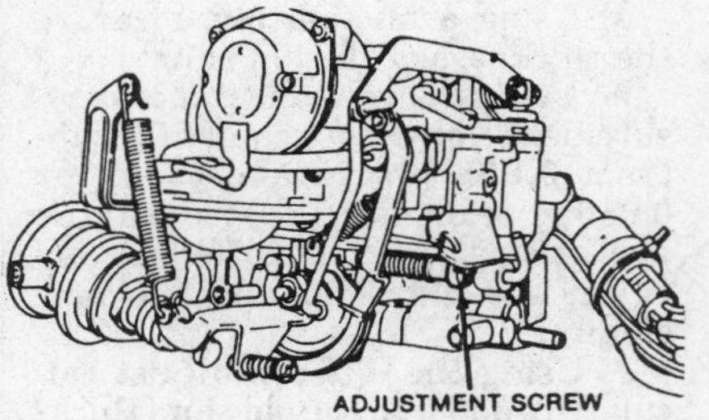


**Adjusting the idle speed screw—Spectrum**

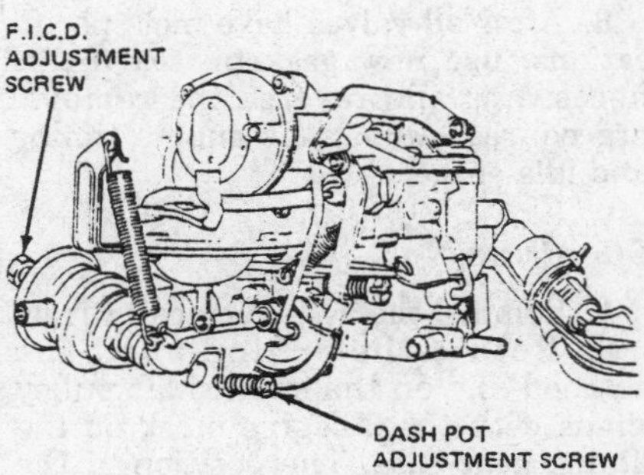


**Adjustment fast idle control device—Spectrum**

6. Ground Test terminal (ALDL connector).
7. Race over 2000 rpm to reset the position of idle air control valve.
8. Set idle adjust screw to 950 rpm.
9. Remove Test terminal, ground and clear ECM trouble code.

### *Sprint and Metro*

#### Carbureted Models

Check and/or adjust the accelerator cable free-play, ignition timing, valve lash and the emission control wiring and hoses. Make sure that the headlights, heater fan, engine cooling fan and any other electrical equipment is turned **OFF**. If any current drawing system is operating, the idle up system will operate and cause the idle speed to be higher than normal.

1. Connect a tachometer to the primary negative terminal of the ignition coil and refer to the underhood sticker.
2. Place the transaxle in Neutral, set the parking brake and block the wheels.
3. Start and run the engine until it reaches normal operating temperature.
4. Check and/or adjust the idle speed, it should be 700–800 rpm with manual transaxles, 800–900 rpm with automatic transaxles.

**NOTE: To adjust the idle speed, turn the throttle adjustment screw on the carburetor.**

5. With the engine at the proper idle speed, check and/or adjust the idle up speed.
6. Stop the engine and remove the tachometer.

#### FUEL INJECTED MODELS

The idle speed is controlled by the (ECM) Electronic Control Module and is not adjustable.

## Idle Mixture

### ADJUSTMENT

#### *Nova and Prizm*

**NOTE: The idle mixture for the twincam engine is not adjustable.**

**NOTE: Idle mixture does not require adjustment as a matter of routine maintenance. Only if the engine will not idle properly and all vacuum leaks, tune-up and mechanical problems have been eliminated as possible causes of the rough idle or stalling should the mixture adjustment be performed. Performing this procedure requires drills of 0.256 and 0.295 in. diameter. Be sure to have a source of compressed air to remove metal drillings.**

1. Remove the carburetor.
2. To remove the mixture adjusting plug, perform the following procedures:
   a. Plug all the carburetor vacuum ports so drillings will not be able to enter them.
   b. Using a center punch, mark the center of the mixture adjusting plug. Using a 0.256 in. drill, carefully drill a hole in the center of the plug.

**NOTE: Stop drilling as soon as the plug has been drilled through; there is only about 0.04 in. (1mm) clearance between the plug and the top of the mixture screw.**

   c. Using a small screwdriver, reach through the drilled hole and gently turn the mixture adjusting screw inward, until it just touches bottom.

**NOTE: If the screw is turned too tight, the tapered tip will become grooved, necessitating replacement.**

   d. Using a 0.295 in. drill, drill to force the plug from its seat.
3. Using compressed air, remove any metal filings. Remove the mixture screw by screwing it out all the way. Inspect the tip for grooving and the top for damage to the screwdriver groove and replace the screw (if necessary).
4. Install the mixture adjusting screw, by turning it in slowly and gently until it touches bottom, then, back it out (counting the number of turns) 3¼ turns.
5. Reinstall the carburetor, then, reconnect the vacuum hoses (refer to the Vacuum Hose Information label) and air cleaner.
6. Start the engine and allow it to reach normal operating temperatures.
7. Adjust the idle speed.

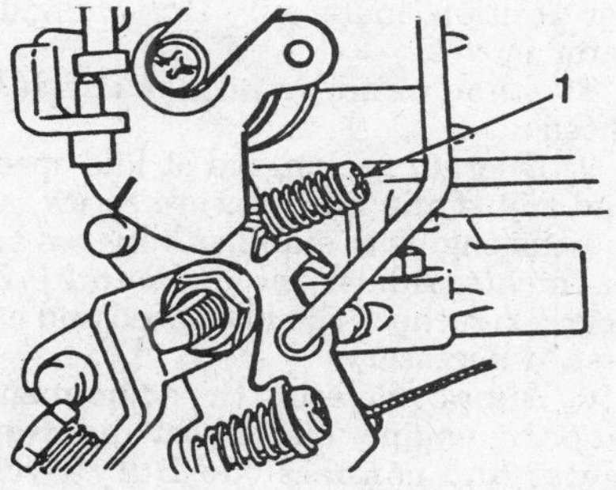


**Idle speed adjustment screw-carbureted engines – Sprint and Metro**

8. Adjust the idle mixture screw until the highest rpm is reached, then, readjust the idle speed screw to 700 rpm. Keep adjusting both screws until the maximum speed will not rise any higher, no matter how much the idle mixture screw is adjusted.
9. Adjust the idle mixture screw until the engine speed is 650 rpm.
10. Adjust the idle speed screw to 650 rpm (manual transaxles), 800 rpm (1985 automatic transaxles) or 750 rpm (1986-89 automatic transaxles).
11. Remove the air cleaner and EGR mounting bracket. Using a hammer and drift, tap a new idle mixture adjusting plug in place with the tapered end inward. Reinstall the air cleaner and EGR vacuum modulator bracket.

### *Spectrum*

**NOTE: The idle mixture screw is adjusted and sealed at the factory and no service adjustment is required. However, if the necessity of adjustment aries for some reason, adjusting by removing plug is possible but it must be plugged again after adjustment is completed.**

1. Remove the carburetor from the engine.
2. Using a center punch, make a punch mark on the idle mixture sealing plug. Drill a hole through the plug, insert a threaded screw and pull the plug from the throttle body.The width of the plug is about 0.39 in. (10 mm).

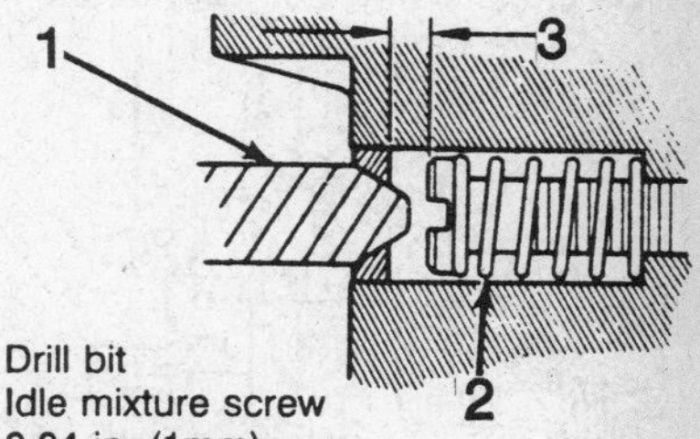


1. Drill bit
2. Idle mixture screw
3. 0.04 in. (1mm)

**Drilling the mixture adjusting screw plug from the carburetor base-except twincam engine – Nova**

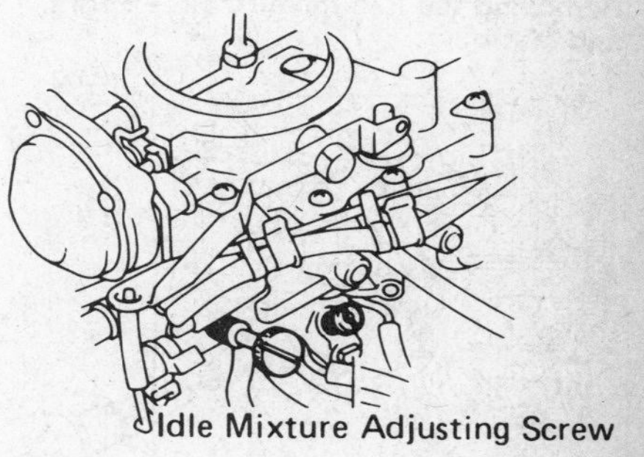


**Idle mixture adjustment – Nova**

**NOTE: If the idle mixture screw is damaged from the drilling process, replace the screw.**

3. Lightly seat the idle mixture screw, then back out 3 turns (MT) or 2 turns (AT). DO NOT overtighten the idle mixture screw.
4. Reinstall the carburetor and the air cleaner.
5. Adjust the idle speed.
6. Using a dwell meter, connect the positive lead to the duty monitor and the negative lead to ground. Place the meter dial on the 4 cylinder scale. Turn the idle mixture screw until the dwell meter reads 45 degrees (4 cylinder scale).
7. Turn A/C on **Max/Cold** and blower on **High** then adjust the bolt on the FICD and set the fast idle to 850 rpm (MT) or 980 (AT), if so equipped then stop the engine and remove the test equipment.
8. Drive a new idle mixture plug into the throttle body, flush with the throttle body apply Locktite No.262 or its equivalent to the plug.
9. Recheck all adjustments and road test.

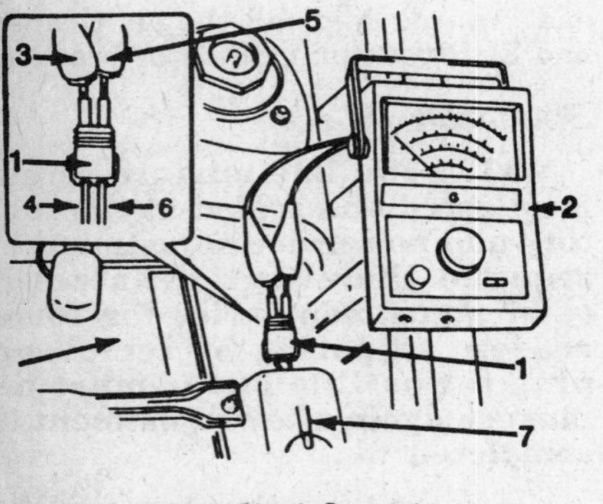


1. Duty Check Connector
2. Dwell Meter
3. Positive (+) Terminal
4. "Blue/Red" Wire
5. Negative (−) Terminal
6. "Black/Green Wire
7. Water Reservoir Tank
8. Battery

**Connecting a dwell meter to the duty cycle check connector – Sprint and Metro**

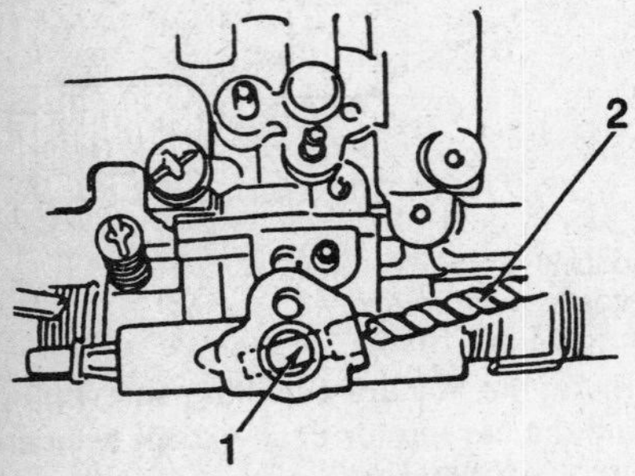


1. Mixture adjust screw pin
2. Drill

**Removing the idle mixture pin – Sprint and Metro**

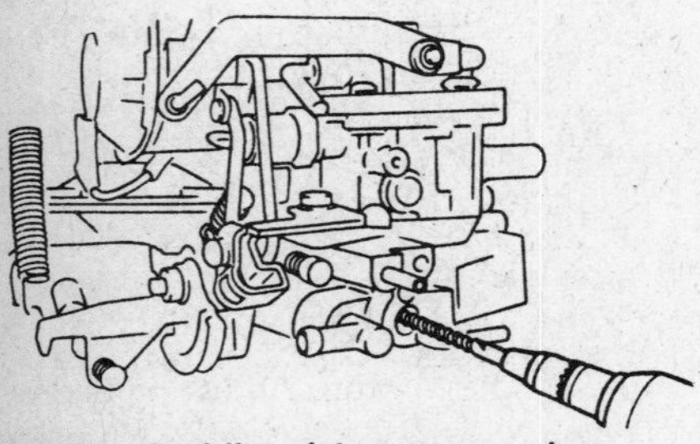

**Drilling the idle mixture screw plug – Spectrum**

### *Sprint and Metro*

#### CARBURETED MODELS

The carburetor is adjusted at the factory and no further adjustment should be necessary. However, if the engine performance is poor, the emission test fails, or the carburetor has been replaced or overhauled, an idle mixture adjustment is necessary. Before adjusting the idle mixture, check the timing/idle speed and the valve lash. Make sure that all electrical accessories are turned **OFF**.

1. Remove the carburetor from the intake manifold.
2. Using an $^{11}/_{64}$ in. bit, drill through the idle mixture screw housing, in line with the retaining pin. Use a punch to drive the pin from the housing.
3. Install the carburetor to the intake manifold by reversing the removal procedures.
4. Place the transaxle in Neutral, set the parking brake and block the wheels.
5. Start the engine and bring it to normal operating temperatures.
6. Disconnect the Duty Cycle Check connector, located near the water reservoir tank. Connect the positive terminal of a dwell meter to the blue/red wire and the negative terminal to the black/green wire.
7. Set the dwell meter to the 6 cylinder position, make sure that the indicator moves.
8. Check and/or adjust the idle speed.
9. Operate the engine at idle speed and adjust the idle mixture screw, allow the engine to stabilize between adjustments. Adjust the dwell to 21–27 degrees; recheck the idle speed and adjust, if necessary.
10. After completing the adjustment, stop the engine, disconnect the dwell meter and connect the Duty Cycle Check connector to the coupler.
11. Install a new idle mixture adjust screw pin in the throttle housing, drive it in place.

#### FUEL INJECTED MODELS

The idle mixture is controlled by the Electronic Control Module (ECM). No adjustments are possible.

# ENGINE ELECTRICAL

## Distributor

### REMOVAL & INSTALLATION

### *Nova and Prizm*

#### EXCEPT TWINCAM

The distributor uses vacuum and centrifugal advances for spark timing control. The voltage introduced into the pickup coil turns the ignition module **On** and **Off.** The ignition module turns the ignition coil **On** and **Off** creating high voltage for the spark plugs.

1. Disconnect the negative terminal from the battery.
2. Remove the No. 1 spark plug. Place your finger in the spark plug hole and rotate the crankshaft (clockwise) until you feel air being forced from the cylinder; this is the TDC of the No. 1 cylinder compression stroke. Align the crankshaft pulley notch with the 0 degrees mark on the timing plate.
3. Disconnect the distributor wire from the connector.

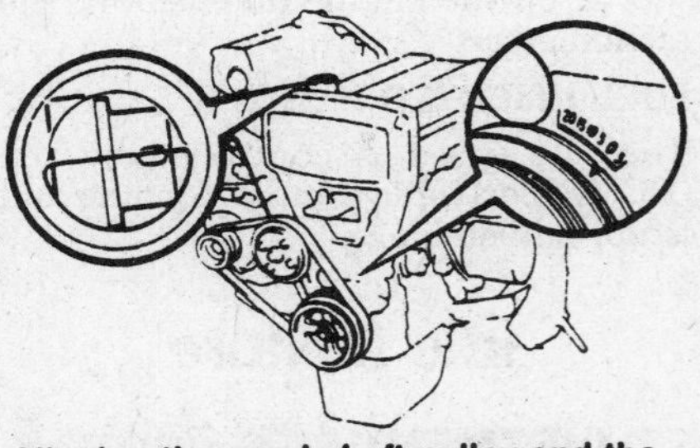

**Aligning the crankshaft pulley and the camshaft cavity-twincam engine – Nova and Prizm**

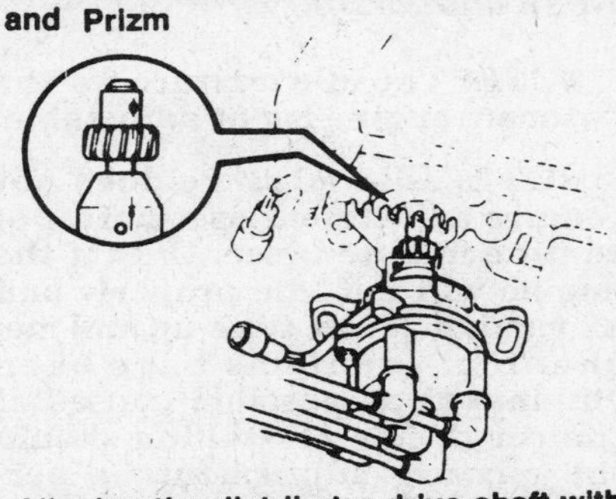

**Aligning the distributor drive shaft with the housing-twincam engine – Nova and Prizm**

4. Disconnect the hoses and the vacuum advance unit.
5. Disconnect the distributor cap and move it aside.
6. Using a piece of chalk, make alignment marks of the distributor housing-to-engine block and the rotor-to-distributor housing.
7. Remove the distributor hold-down bolt(s) and the distributor from the engine; the rotor must be rotated slightly to remove the distributor.
8. To install, use a new O-ring on the distributor housing, lubricate the drive gear teeth with engine oil, align the protrusion at the bottom of the distributor housing with the pin on the side of the distributor drive gear, mesh the gears and reverse the removal procedures. Check and/or adjust the ignition timing.

### TWINCAM

The distributor uses an electronic spark advance ESA system. The voltage introduced into the pick-up coils is monitored by the electronic control module ECM. The program within the ECM decides when to, using the collected data from the various sensors, turns the igniter module On and **OFF** at precisely the right moment.

1. Disconnect the negative terminal from the battery. Disconnect the spark plug wires from the spark plugs and the ignition coil.
2. Disconnect the distributor wire from the connector.
3. To position the No. 1 cylinder on the TDC of its compression stroke, perform the following procedures:
   a. Using a socket wrench on the crankshaft pulley bolt, rotate the crankshaft pulley until the notch is aligned with the 0 degree mark on the timing plate.

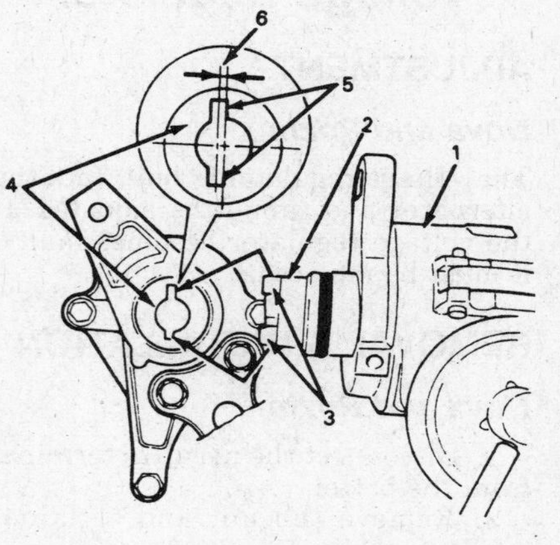


1. Distributor 4. Camshaft
2. Coupling 5. Slot
3. Dog 6. Offset

**Offset slot in distributor must align with offset slot in camshaft—Sprint and Metro**

   b. Remove the oil filler cap and look for the cavity in the camshaft; if it is not visible, rotate the crankshaft pulley one complete revolution.
4. Remove the distributor-to-engine hold-down bolts and the distributor from the engine.
5. Remove the distributor from the engine and the O-ring from the distributor; discard the O-ring.
6. To install the distributor, use a new O-ring and perform the following procedures:
   a. Turn the distributor to align the drive shaft drilled mark with housing cavity.
   b. Align the center of the distributor flange with the center of the cylinder head bolt hole, then, install the distributor.
   c. Install the hold-down bolt and torque it to 14 ft. lbs.
7. To complete the installation, reverse the removal procedures. Check and/or adjust the ignition timing.

**NOTE: When performing the ignition timing procedures, never allow the ignition coil terminal to touch ground for it could result in damage to the ignition coil and/or igniter.**

## *Spectrum*

### UNDISTURBED ENGINE

1. Disconnect the negative battery terminal from the battery.
2. Remove the distributor cap.
3. Mark and remove all electrical leads and vacuum lines connected to the distributor assembly.
4. Mark the relationship of the rotor to the distributor housing and the distributor housing to the engine.
5. Remove the hold-down bolt, clamp and distributor.
6. To install, reverse the removal procedures and check the timing.

### DISTURBED ENGINE

If the engine was cranked while the distributor was removed, you will have to place the engine on TDC of the compression stroke to obtain the proper ignition timing.

1. Remove the No. 1 spark plug.
2. Place your thumb over the spark plug hole. Crank the engine slowly until compression is felt. It will be easier if you have someone rotate the engine by hand, using a wrench on the crankshaft pulley.
3. Align the timing mark on the crankshaft pulley with the 0 degrees mark on the timing scale attached to the front of the engine. This places the engine at TDC of the compression stroke.
4. Turn the distributor shaft until the rotor points to the No. 1 spark plug tower on the cap.
5. Install the distributor into the engine. Be sure to align the distributor-to-engine block mark made earlier.
6. To complete the installation, reverse the removal procedures and check the timing.

## *Sprint and Metro*

1. Disconnect the negative battery cable.
2. Disconnect the wiring harness at the distributor and the vacuum line at the distributor vacuum unit.
3. Remove the distributor cap.

**NOTE: Mark the distributor body in reference to where the rotor is pointing. Mark the distributor hold down bracket and cylinder head for a reinstallation location point.**

4. Remove the hold down bolt and the distributor from the cylinder head. DO NOT rotate the engine after the distributor has been removed.
5. To install, aligning all of the reference marks and install the distributor into the off-set slot in the camshaft.
6. With the distributor installed, the hold down bolt hand tight and the cap on, run the engine and check the ignition timing.

# Alternator

**NOTE: For further information on the charging system, please refer to "Charging and Starting" in the Unit Repair section.**

### PRECAUTIONS

Several precautions must be observed with alternator equipped vehicles to avoid damage to the unit.

- If the battery is removed for any reason, make sure it is reconnected with the correct polarity. Reversing the battery connections may result in damage to the one-way rectifiers.
- When utilizing a booster battery as a starting aid, always connect the positive-to-positive terminals and the negative terminal from the booster battery to a good engine ground on the vehicle being started.
- Never use a fast charger as a booster to start vehicles with alternating-current (AC) circuits.
- Disconnect the battery cables when charging the battery with a fast charger.
- Never attempt to polarize an alternator.
- Avoid long soldering times when making alternator repairs. Prolonged head will damage the alternator.

- Do not use test lamps of more than 12V when checking diode continuity.
- Do not short across or ground any of the alternator terminals.
- The polarity of the battery, alternator and regulator must be matched and considered before making any electrical connections within the system.
- Never separate the alternator on an open circuit. Make sure all connections within the circuit are clean and tight.
- Disconnect the battery ground terminal when performing any service on electrical components.
- Disconnect the battery if arc welding is to be done on the vehicle.

## BELT TENSION ADJUSTMENT

### *Nova and Prizm*

The belt tension on most components is adjusted by moving the component (alternator) within the range of the slotted bracket. Check the belt tension every 12 months or 10,000 miles. Push in on the drive belt about midway between the crankshaft pulley and the driven component. If the belt deflects more than 9/16 in. or less than 3/8 in., adjustment is required.

1. Loosen the adjustment nut and bolt in the slotted bracket. Slightly loosen the pivot bolt.
2. Pull (don't pry) the component outward to increase tension. Push inward to reduce tension. Tighten the adjusting nut/bolt and the pivot bolt.
3. Recheck the drive belt tension and readjust (if necessary).

### *Spectrum*

**NOTE: The following procedures require the use of GM belt tension gauge No. BT-33-95-ACBN (regular V-belts) or BT-33-97M (poly V-belts).**

1. If the belt is cold, operate the engine (at idle speed) for 15 minutes; the belt will seat itself in the pulleys allowing the belt fibers to relax or stretch. If the belt is hot, allow it to cool, until it is warm to the touch.

**NOTE: A used belt is one that has been rotated at least one complete revolution on the pulleys. This begins the belt seating process and it must never be tensioned to the new belt specifications.**

2. Loosen the component-to-mounting bracket bolts.
3. Using a GM belt tension gauge No. BT-33-95-ACBN (standard V-belts) or BT-33-97M (poly V-belts), place the tension gauge at the center of the belt between the longest span.
4. Applying belt tension pressure on the component, adjust the drive belt tension to the correct specifications. The belt tension should deflect about 1/4 in. over a 7-10 in. span or 1/2 in. over a 13-16 in. span.
5. While holding the correct tension on the component, tighten the component-to-mounting bracket bolt.
6. When the belt tension is correct (70-110 inch lbs.), remove the tension gauge.

## REMOVAL & INSTALLATION

### *Nova and Prizm*

1. Disconnect the negative terminal from the battery.
2. Label and disconnect each alternator wiring connector.
3. Loosen the alternator adjusting lockbolt (located in the slotted bar at the bottom of the unit) and the hinge nut/bolt, located at the top of the unit. Turn the adjusting bolt to shift the alternator toward the block; remove the drive belt.
4. Remove the adjusting bolt, the hinge nut/bolt and the alternator.
5. To install, reverse the removal procedures.

**NOTE: The drive belt serrations which run along its length. Make sure serrations align with indentations on the pulleys; all serrations must ride inside the pulley surface.**

### *Spectrum*

1. Disconnect the negative battery terminal from the battery.

**CAUTION**

***Failure to disconnect the negative cable may result in injury from the positive battery lead at the alternator and may short the alternator and regulator during the removal process.***

2. Disconnect and label the two terminal plug and the battery leads from the rear of the alternator.
3. Loosen the mounting bolts. Push the alternator inwards and slip the drive belt off the pulley.
4. Remove the mounting bolts and remove the alternator.
5. To install, place the alternator in its brackets and install the mounting bolts. Do not tighten them yet.
6. Slip the belt back over the pulley. Pull outwards on the unit and adjust the belt tension. Tighten the mounting and adjusting bolts.
7. Install the electrical leads and the negative battery cable.

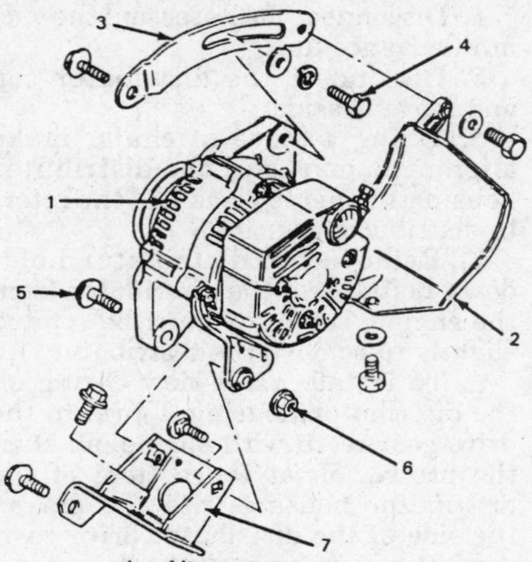


1. Alternator
2. Alternator cover
3. Alternator adjusting arm
4. Arm bolt
5. Alternator bolt
6. Alternator nut
7. Alternator bracket

**Alternator mounting-all engines—Sprint and Metro**

### *Sprint and Metro*

1. Disconnect the negative battery cable.
2. Disconnect the wiring connectors from the back of the alternator.
3. Remove the adjusting arm mounting bolt, the lower pivot bolt and the drive belt.
4. Remove the alternator.
5. To install, reverse the removal procedures. Adjust the drive belt to have 1/4-3/8 in. play on the longest run of the drive belt.

# Voltage Regulator

## ADJUSTMENT

### *Nova and Prizm*

The voltage regulator is built into the alternator and cannot be adjusted. If the voltage regulator becomes faulty, it must be replaced.

## REMOVAL & INSTALLATION

### *Nova and Prizm*

1. Disconnect the negative terminal from the battery.
2. Remove the nut and terminal insulator.
3. Remove the 3 nuts and the end cover.
4. Remove the 5 screws, brush holder and IC regulator.
5. To install, reverse the removal procedures.

### Spectrum, Sprint and Metro

A solid state regulator is mounted within the alternator. All regulator components are enclosed in a solid mold. The regulator is non-adjustable and requires no maintenance.

## Starter

**NOTE: For further information on the starting system, please refer to "Charging and Starting" in the Unit Repair section.**

### REMOVAL & INSTALLATION

#### Nova and Prizm

1. Disconnect the negative terminal from the battery.
2. Disconnect the electrical connectors from the starter terminals.
3. Remove the transaxle cable and bracket from the transaxle.
4. Remove the starter-to-engine bolts and the starter from the vehicle.
5. To install, reverse the removal procedures. Torque the starter-to-engine bolts to 29 ft. lbs.

#### Spectrum

1. Disconnect the negative battery terminal from the battery.
2. Disconnect the ignition switch lead wire and the battery cable from the starter motor terminal.
3. Remove the 2 mounting bolts from the starter and remove the starter.
4. To install, reverse the removal procedures.

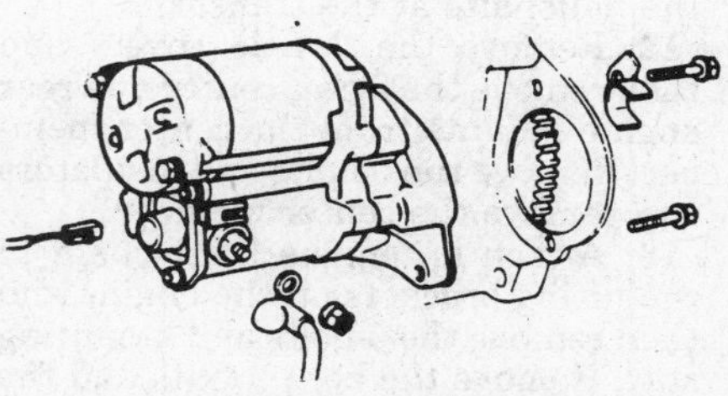

Starter removal – Nova and Prizm

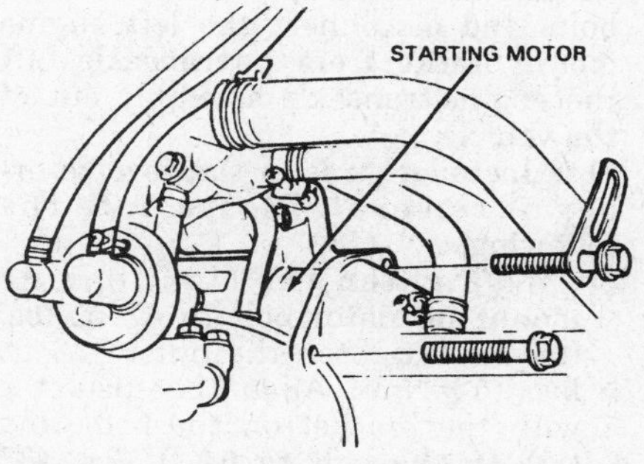


Starter motor mounting – Sprint and Metro

#### Sprint and Metro

1. Disconnect the negative battery cable.
2. Disconnect the ignition switch wire and the battery cable from the starter.
3. Remove the 2 engine-to-starter mounting bolts and remove the starter.
4. To install, reverse the removal procedures.

# ENGINE MECHANICAL

## Engine

### REMOVAL & INSTALLATION

#### Nova

##### EXCEPT TWINCAM

1. Disconnect the negative terminal from the battery. Drain the cooling system into a clean container; be sure to open block drain cocks.
2. Drain the engine crankcase and transaxle fluid.
3. Using a scratch awl, scribe the hood hinge-to-hood outline, then, using an assistant remove the hood.
4. Remove the air cleaner assembly and associated ducting.
5. From the radiator, remove the upper coolant hose and the overflow hose. Disconnect the coolant hose from the coolant pipe at the rear of the cylinder head and the coolant hose from the thermostat housing.
6. Disconnect the fuel hoses from the fuel pump.
7. Remove the drive belt from the alternator, the power steering pump (if equipped) and the A/C compressor (if equipped). If equipped with power steering, remove the power steering pump-to-engine bolts and move the pump aside, DO NOT disconnect the pressure hoses. If equipped with air conditioning, remove the compressor-to-engine bolts and move it aside; DO NOT disconnect the pressure hoses.
8. Label and disconnect the electrical connectors that will interfere with the engine removal.
9. Label and disconnect the vacuum hoses running between the engine and firewall or fender well mounted accessories.
10. Label and disconnect the electrical connectors from the transaxle.
11. Disconnect the speedometer cable from the transaxle.
12. Raise and support the vehicle on jackstands.
13. Disconnect the exhaust pipe-to-exhaust manifold bolts and separate the exhaust pipe from the manifold.
14. On Federal models, disconnect the air hose from the catalytic converter.
15. If equipped with an automatic transaxle, disconnect and plug the oil cooler tubes from the radiator.
16. Remove the under covers from both sides of the vehicle.
17. Disconnect the cable and the bracket from the transaxle.
18. Disconnect the steering knuckles from the lower control arms.
19. Disconnect the halfshafts from the transaxle.
20. Remove the flywheel cover. If equipped with an automatic transaxle, mark the torque converter-to-flexplate, then, remove the torque converter-to-flexplate bolts and move the torque converter back into the transaxle.
21. Disconnect the front and rear engine mounts from the center member.
22. Lower the vehicle.
23. Remove the radiator-to-chassis bolts and the radiator (with the fans) from the vehicle.
24. Using a overhead lift, attach it to and support the engine.
25. Remove the through bolt from right-side engine mount, then, the left-side transaxle mount bolt and the mount.
26. Remove the engine/transaxle assembly from the vehicle. Remove the transaxle-to-engine bolts and separate the transaxle from the engine, then, secure the engine to a work stand.
27. To install, reverse the removal procedures.

If equipped with an automatic transaxle, torque the torque converter-to-flexplate bolts to 58 ft. lbs.

Torque the halfshaft-to-transaxle bolts to 27 ft. lbs.

Torque the engine-to-crossmember mount bolts to 29 ft. lbs.

Torque the exhaust pipe-to-exhaust manifold to 46 ft. lbs.

Torque the power steering pump-to-bracket bolt to 29 ft. lbs.

Torque the power steering adjusting bolt to 32 ft. lbs.

Refill the cooling system, the transaxle and the engine with clean fluid.

Start the engine, allow it to reach normal operating temperatures and check for leaks.

##### TWINCAM

1. Disconnect the negative terminal from the battery.
2. Drain the cooling system into a clean container; be sure to open block drain cocks.
3. Drain the engine crankcase and transaxle fluid.

4. Using a scratch awl, scribe the hood hinge-to-hood outline, then, using an assistant remove the hood.
5. Remove the air cleaner assembly, the coolant tank reservoir and the PVC hose.
6. Disconnect the heater hoses from the water inlet housing and the fuel hose from the fuel filter.
7. If equipped with a manual transaxle, remove the clutch slave cylinder-to-transaxle bolts and the slave cylinder, then, move the cylinder aside.
8. Disconnect the vacuum hose from the charcoal canister.
9. Disconnect the speedometer cable from the transaxle and the accelerator cable from the throttle body.
10. If equipped with cruise control, perform the following procedures:
   a. Remove the cables from the throttle body.
   b. Disconnect the vacuum hose from the actuator.
   c. Remove the actuator cover bolts and the cover.
   d. Disconnect the actuator connector, then, remove the actuator.
11. Remove the ignition coil.
12. To remove the main wiring harness, perform the following procedures:
   a. Remove the right-side of the cowl panel and disconnect the No. 4 junction block connectors.
   b. Remove the ECM cover and disconnect the ECM connectors, then, pull the main wiring harness into the engine compartment.
13. Disconnect the No. 2 junction block connectors and the ground strap terminals.
14. Disconnect the windshield washer change valve connector, the battery cable from the starter, the cruise control vacuum pump and switch connectors.
15. Disconnect the vacuum hose from the power brake booster.
16. If equipped with air conditioning, perform the following procedures:
   a. Remove the vane pump pulley nut.
   b. Loosen the idler pulley adjusting and pulley nuts.
   c. Remove the compressor-to-bracket bolts, then, move the compressor aside and secure it.
   d. Disconnect the oil pressure connector.
   e. Remove the compressor bracket bolts, the vane pump bolts, then, move the vane pump and bracket aside and suspend it.
17. Raise and support the front of the vehicle on jackstands.
18. Remove the splash shields.
19. If equipped with an automatic transaxle, disconnect and plug the oil cooler from the radiator.
20. Remove the exhaust pipe-to-exhaust manifold bolts and separate the pipe from the manifold. Disconnect the oxygen sensor connector.
21. Remove the flywheel housing cover.
22. Remove the front and rear engine mounts from the center member, then, the center member.
23. Disconnect the right-side control arm from the steering knuckle and halfshafts from the transaxle.
24. Lower the vehicle.
25. Using a vertical hoist, secure the engine to it and support the engine; secure the engine wiring and hoses to the lift chain.
26. Remove the right-side engine mount, then, the left-side engine mount from the transaxle bracket.

**NOTE: When lifting the engine be careful not to damage the throttle position sensor or the power steering gear housing.**

27. Lift the engine/transaxle assembly from the vehicle.
28. To separate the transaxle from the engine, perform the following procedures:
   a. Remove the radiator fan temperature switch connector and the start injector time switch connector.
   b. Disconnect the vacuum hoses from the BVSV's.
   c. Remove the No. 1 and 2 hoses from the water bypass pipes.
   d. Disconnect the electrical connector from the back-up switch, the water temperature sensor and the water temperature switch.
   e. If equipped with an automatic transaxle, disconnect the neutral start switch connector and the transaxle solenoid connector, then, remove the torque converter-to-flexplate bolts; be sure to push the torque converter back into the transaxle.
   f. Remove the starter, the transaxle-to-engine bolts and the transaxle.
29. To install, reverse the removal procedures.

Torque the torque converter-to-flexplate bolts to 20 ft. lbs.

Torquethe starter-to-engine bolts to 29 ft. lbs.

Torquethe halfshaft-to-transaxle nuts to 27 ft. lbs.

Torquethe right-side control arm-to-steering knuckle nuts/bolts to 47 ft. lbs.

Torquethe cross member-to-chassis bolts to 29 ft. lbs.

Torquethe engine mounts-to-cross member bolts to 35 ft. lbs.

Torquethe exhaust pipe to-exhaust manifold nuts to 46 ft. lbs.

Refill the cooling system, the engine crankcase and transaxle.

Start the engine, allow it to reach normal operating temperatures and check for leaks.

### Prizm

1. Remove the battery. Scribe matchmarks around the hood hinges and then remove the hood. Remove the engine undercovers.
2. Drain the engine coolant and oil. Drain the gear oil from the transaxle.
3. Remove the air cleaner along with its hose.
4. Remove the coolant reservoir tank. Remove the radiator and cooling fan.
5. Disconnect the accelerator and throttle cables at the carburetor on models with automatic transmissions.
6. Disconnect the No. 2 junction block, the graound strap connector and the ground strap. Disconnect the vacuum hoses at the brake booster, power steering pump, A/C compressor and EBCV.
7. Disconnect the fuel lines at the fuel pump. Disconnect the heater hoses at the water inlet housing.
8. Disconnect the power steering pump and lay it aside with the hydraulic lines still attached. Do the same with the A/C compressor.
9. Disconnect the speedometer cable. On models with a manual transmission, remove the clutch release cylinder and position it out of the way with the hydraulic lines still attached.
10. Disconnect the shift control cables and then raise the front of the vehicle. Support it with safety stands.
11. Remove the 2 nuts from the flange and then disconnect the exhaust pipe at the manifold. Disconnect the halfshafts at the transaxle.
12. Remove the 2 hole covers and then remove the front, center and rear engine mounts from the center member. Remove the 5 bolts and insulators and remove the center member.
13. Attach an engine hoist chain to the lifting brackets on the engine and then remove the 3 bolts and mounting stay. Remove the bolt, 2 nuts and the thru-bolt and pull out the right side engine mount. Remove the 2 bolts and the left mounting stay. Remove the 3 bolts and disconnect the left engine mount bracket from the transaxle. Lift the engine/transaxle assembly out of the vehicle.
14. Installation is in the reverse order of removal. Please note the following:
   a. Tighten the right engine mount insulator bolt to 47 ft. lbs. (64 Nm); tighten the nut to 38 ft. lbs. (52 Nm). Align the insulator with the bracket on the body and tighten the bolt to 64 ft. lbs. (87 Nm).

b. Align the left engine mount insulator bracket with the transaxle bracket and tighten the bolt to 35 ft. lbs. (48 Nm).

c. Install the right mounting stay and tighten the 3 bolts to 31 ft. lbs. (42 Nm). Install the left stay and tighten the 2 bolts to 15 ft. lbs. (21 Nm).

d. Install the engine center member and tighten the 5 bolts to 45 ft. lbs. (61 Nm).

e. Install the front and rear engine mounts and bolts. Align the bolts holes in the brackets with the center member and tighten the front mount bolts to 35 ft. lbs. (48 Nm); tighten the center and rear mounts to 38 ft. lbs. (52 Nm). Install the 2 hole covers and tighten the rear mounting bolt to 58 ft. lbs. (78 Nm).

### *Spectrum*

1. Remove the hood and disconnect the negative battery cable.
2. Drain the cooling system.
3. Remove the air cleaner and the throttle cable at the carburetor.
4. Disconnect the heater hoses at the intake manifold, the coolant hose at the thermostat housing and the thermostat housing at the cylinder head.
5. On turbochraged models, remove the throttle cable, fuel lines, connectors at carburetor also remove turbocharger vacuum, oil and water lines.
6. Remove the distributor from the cylinder head.
7. Disconnect the $O_2$ sensor electrical connector.
8. Support the engine using a vertical lift and remove the right motor mount.
9. Disconnect the necessary electrical connectors and vacuum hoses.
10. Disconnect the flex hose at the exhaust manifold and the lower radiator hose at the block.
11. Remove the upper A/C compressor bolt and remove the belt.
12. Disconnect the power steering bracket at the block and remove the belt.
13. Disconnect the fuel lines from the fuel pump and the electrical connectors from under the carburetor.
14. Remove the upper starter bolt and raise the vehicle.
15. Drain the oil from the crankcase and remove the oil filter.
16. Disconnect the oil temperature switch connector.
17. Disconnect the exhaust pipe bracket at the block and the exhaust pipe at the manifold.
18. Remove the A/C compressor and move to one side. Do not disconnect the A/C refrigerant lines. Remove the alternator wires.
19. Remove the flywheel cover and the converter bolts, then install the Flywheel Holding tool No. J-35271 or equivalent.
20. Disconnect the starter wires and remove the starter.
21. Remove the front right wheel and inner splash shield.
22. Lower the engine by lowering the crossmember enough to gain access to the crankshaft pulley bolts, then remove the pulley.
23. Raise the engine and crossmember. Remove the engine support.
24. Lower the vehicle and support the transmission.

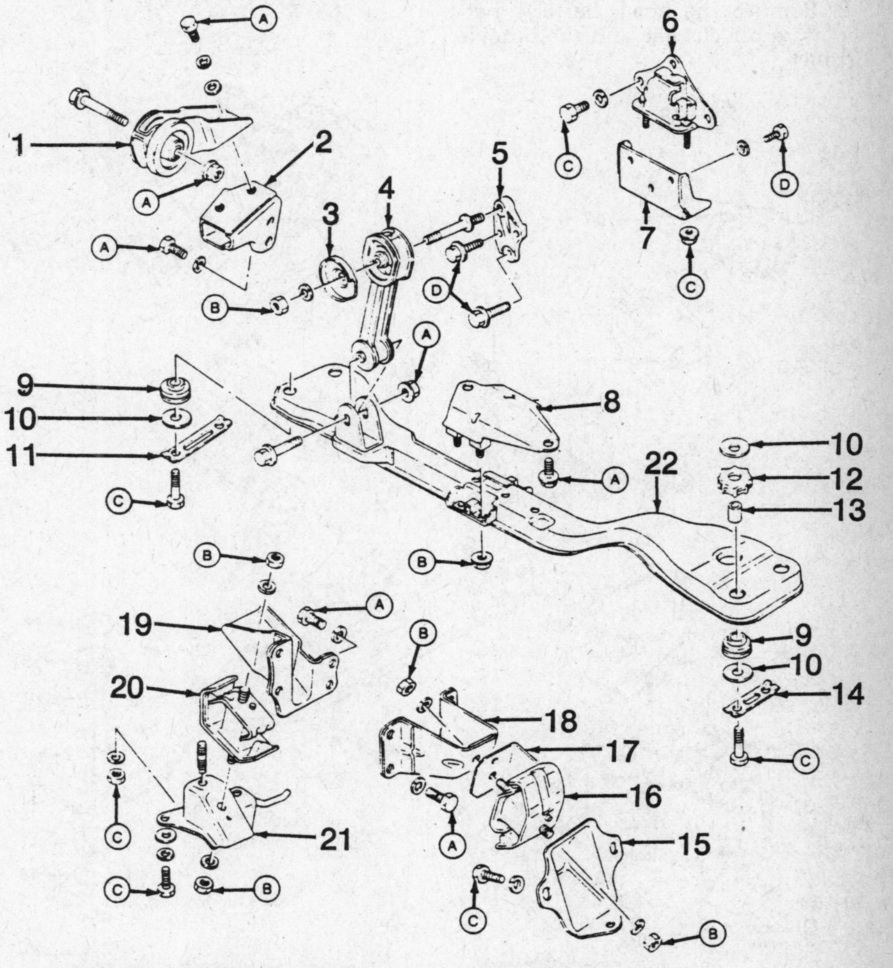

1. SIDE MOUNTING BUSHING
2. SIDE MOUNTING BRACKET
3. STOPPER PLATE
4. TORQUE ROD
5. TORQUE ROD BRACKET
6. TRANSMISSION L MOUNTING
7. BRACKET
8. TRANSMISSION MOUNTING
9. LOWER CUSHION
10. WASHER
11. REAR LOCK WASHER
12. UPPER CUSHION
13. SPACER
14. FRONT LOCK WASHER
15. FRONT MOUNTING BODY BRACKET
16. FRONT MOUNTING
17. INSULATOR
18. FRONT MOUNTING BRACKET
19. REAR MOUNTING BRACKET
20. REAR MOUNTING
21. REAR BODY BRACKET
22. TRANSMISSION MOUNTING MEMBER

BOLT AND NUT TIGHTENING TORQUE:

(A): 4.0 — 6.0 Kg-m
40 — 60N·m
29.0 — 43.0 LB-FT

(B): 4.0 — 5.0 Kg-m
40 — 50 N·m
29.0 — 36.0 LB-FT

(C): 5.0 — 6.0 Kg-m
50 — 60 N·m
36.5 — 43.0 LB-FT

(D): 1.8 — 2.8 Kg-m
18 — 28 N·m
13.5 — 20.0 LB-FT

**Engine mounting-automatic transaxle – Sprint and Metro**

25. Remove the transmission to engine bolts. Remove the engine.

26. To install, reverse the removal procedures, adjust the drive belts and refill the fluids.

### *Sprint and Metro*

1. Remove the battery cables.
2. Remove the hood, battery, battery tray, air cleaner and the outside air duct.
3. Drain the cooling system, engine oil and the transaxle.
4. Disconnect and tag the radiator, heater and vacuum hoses from the engine.
5. Disconnect the cooling fan wiring.

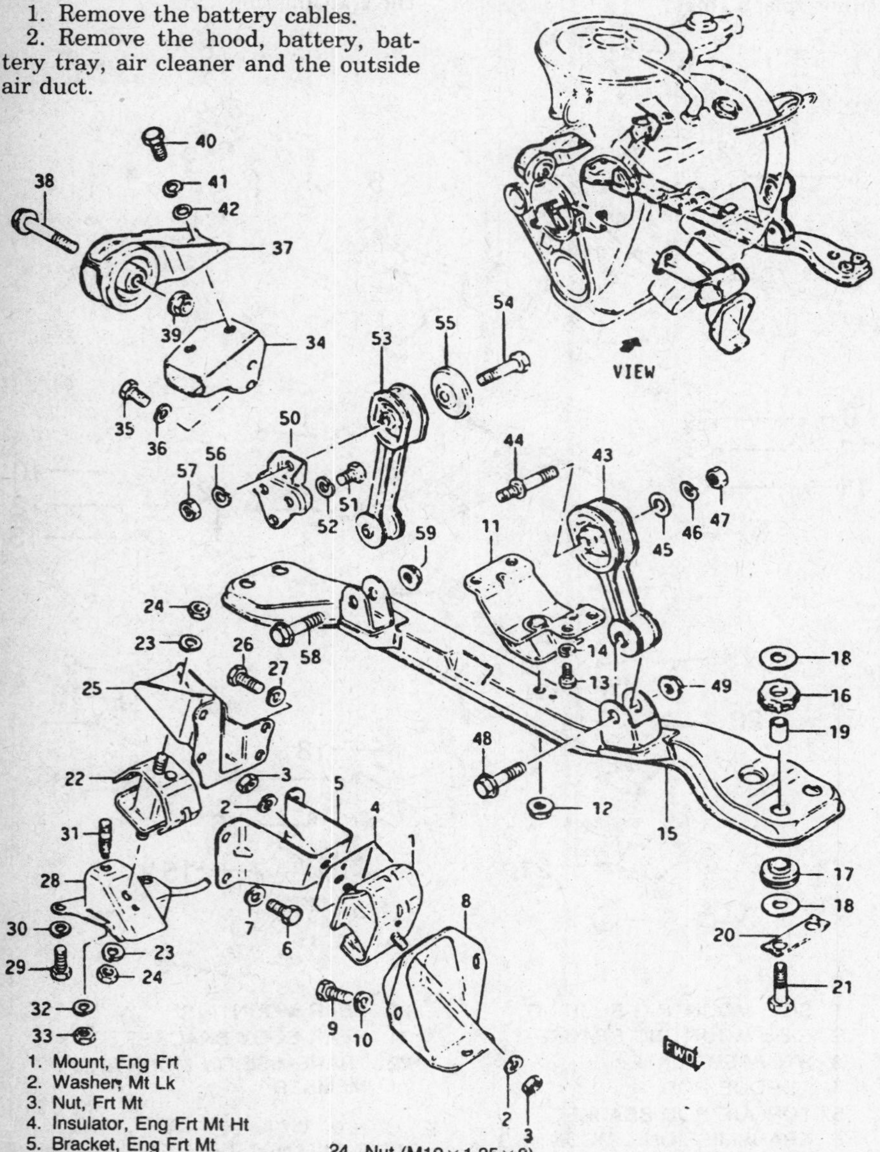


1. Mount, Eng Frt
2. Washer, Mt Lk
3. Nut, Frt Mt
4. Insulator, Eng Frt Mt Ht
5. Bracket, Eng Frt Mt
6. Bolt, Brkt
7. Washer, Brkt Mt
8. Bracket, Frt Mt Body
9. Bolt, Brkt
10. Washer, Brkt Lk
11. Mount, Trans
12. Nut, Trans Mt
13. Bolt (M8 × 1.25 × 20)
14. Washer
15. Member, Trans Mt
16. Cushion, Mt Mbr Upr
17. Cushion, Mt Mbr Lwr
18. Washer, Mt Mbr
19. Spacer, Mbr
21. Bolt, Mbr
22. Mount, Eng Rr
23. Washer, Mt
24. Nut (M10 × 1.25 × 8)
25. Bracket, Eng Rr Mt
26. Bolt, Brkt
27. Washer, Brkt Lk
28. Bracket, Rr Mt Body
29. Bolt, Brkt
30. Washer, Brkt Lk
31. Stud, Brkt
32. Washer, Brkt Lk
33. Nut, Brkt
34. Bracket, Eng Si Mt
35. Bolt, Si Brkt
36. Washer, Brkt Lk
37. Bushing, Eng Si Mt
38. Bolt, Mt Bush
39. Nut, Mt Bush
41. Washer, Lk
42. Washer, Bush
43. Rod, Eng Frt Torq
44. Stud, Frt Rod
45. Washer, Frt Rod
46. Washer, Rod Lk
47. Nut, Frt Rod
48. Bolt, Frt Rod
49. Nut, Frt Rod
50. Bracket, Rr Torq Rod
51. Bolt, Rod Brkt
52. Washer, Brkt Lk
53. Rod, Eng Rr Torq
54. Bolt, Rr Rod
55. Plate, Rr Torq Stopper
56. Washer, Rr Rod Lk
57. Nut, Rr Rod
58. Bolt, Rr Rod
59. Nut, Rr Rod

**Engine mounting-manual transaxle – Sprint and Metro**

6. Remove the cooling fan, shroud and radiator as an assembly.
7. Remove the fuel hoses from the fuel pump.
8. Remove the brake booster hose from the intake manifold, accelerator cable from the carburetor and speed control cable from the transaxle.
9. Remove the clutch cable and bracket from the transaxle.
10. Disconnect and tag the necessary wiring from the engine and transaxle.
11. Remove the A/C compressor adjusting bolt and drive belt splash shield.
12. Raise and support the vehicle safely.
13. Disconnect the exhaust pipe from the exhaust manifold.
14. Remove the A/C pivot bolt, the drive belt and the mounting bracket.
15. Disconnect the gearshift control shaft and extension rod at the transaxle.
16. Disconnect the ball joints.
17. Remove the axle shafts from the transaxle.
18. Remove the engine torque rods and the transaxle mount nut.
19. Lower the vehicle.
20. Remove the engine side mount and the mount nuts.
21. Connect a vertical hoist to the engine, then lift the engine and transaxle assembly from the vehicle.
22. To install, reverse the removal procedures. Refill the engine, the transaxle and the cooling system.

# Cylinder Head

## REMOVAL & INSTALLATION

### *Nova*

#### EXCEPT TWINCAM

1. Disconnect the negative terminal from the battery.
2. Drain the engine coolant into a clean container, opening both the radiator and cylinder block drain cocks.
3. Remove the air cleaner. Label and disconnect all vacuum hoses.
4. Raise and support the vehicle on jackstands. Drain the engine oil. Remove the exhaust pipe-to-exhaust manifold nuts and separate the exhaust pipe from the manifold. Remove the exhaust pipe bracket from the engine. Remove the hose from the catalytic converter pipe.
5. If equipped with power steering, loosen the power steering pump pivot bolt. Lower the vehicle.
6. Disconnect the accelerator and throttle cables from the carburetor and cable bracket.
7. Disconnect electrical harness from the cowl, the oxygen sensor and the distributor.

8. Disconnect the fuel hoses from the fuel pump.

9. Disconnect the upper radiator hose from the water outlet, then, remove the water outlet from the cylinder head. Remove the heater hose.

10. If equipped with power steering, remove the adjusting bracket from the engine.

11. Remove the PCV valve and the wiring harness that passes over the valve cover.

12. Label and disconnect the spark plug wires, the electrical connector and the vacuum hoses from the distributor.

13. Remove the upper timing belt cover-to-cylinder head bolts and the cover.

14. Remove the cylinder head cover-to-cylinder head bolts, the cover and the gasket.

15. Remove the alternator drive belt. Remove the water pump pulley-to-water pump bolts and the pulley.

16. Using socket wrench on the crankshaft pulley bolt, rotate the crankshaft to position the No. 1 cylinder on the TDC of its compression stroke; the crankshaft pulley notch is aligned with the 0 degrees mark on the timing plate and the No. 1 cylinder rocker arms are loose.

17. Remove the distributor-to-cylinder head hold-down bolts and the distributor.

18. Matchmark the timing belt and sprocket for reassembly in the same position; mark an arrow on the timing belt for rotation direction.

19. Loosen the idler pulley bolt. Move it so as to release the timing belt tension and snug the idler pulley bolt. Remove the timing belt; avoid twisting or bending it.

20. Loosen the head bolts (in sequence), in three stages, then, remove them. Lift the head directly off the block. If it is necessary to pry the head off the block, use a bar between the head and the projection provided on top of the block.

**NOTE: Do not pry except at the projection provided. Be careful not to damage the block or cylinder head sealing surface.**

21. Using a putty knife, clean the gasket mounting surfaces. Using a power wire brush, clean the cylinder head chambers.

22. To install, use new gaskets, sealant (if necessary) and reverse the removal procedures.

**NOTE: When installing the cylinder head gasket, position the side with the sealer facing upwards.**

23. Torque the cylinder head-to-engine bolts (in sequence), using three passes, to 43 ft. lbs., the camshaft sprocket-to-camshaft bolt to 34 ft. lbs. and the timing belt idler bolt to 27 ft. lbs.

24. Rotate the crankshaft through two complete revolutions and check the timing belt tension; the tension should be 0.024–0.28 in.

25. Adjust the valves with the engine **Cold**. Operate the engine until normal operating temperatures are reached and check for leaks. Readjust the valves with the engine **Hot**. Set the ignition timing.

### TWINCAM

1. Disconnect the negative terminal from the battery.

2. Drain the engine coolant. Remove the air cleaner assembly.

3. Disconnect the throttle cable and the cruise control cable (if equipped) from the throttle linkage. Remove the ignition coil.

4. From the rear of the cylinder head, remove the heater hose. Remove the vacuum hoses from the throttle body. Remove the water outlet hose from cylinder head and the radiator.

5. If equipped with cruise control, remove the actuator and the bracket assembly.

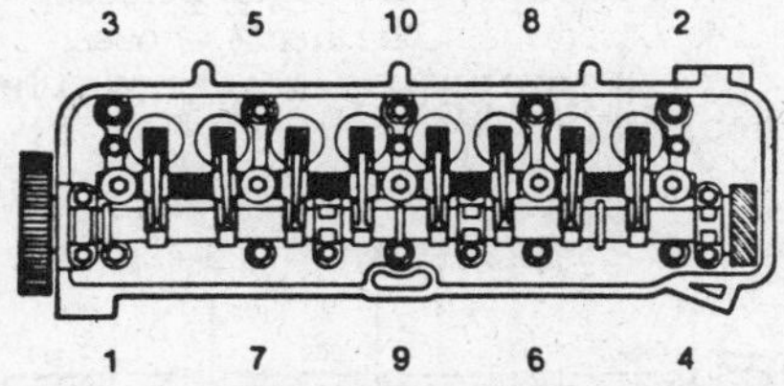


Cylinder head bolt loosening sequence-except twincam engine—Nova

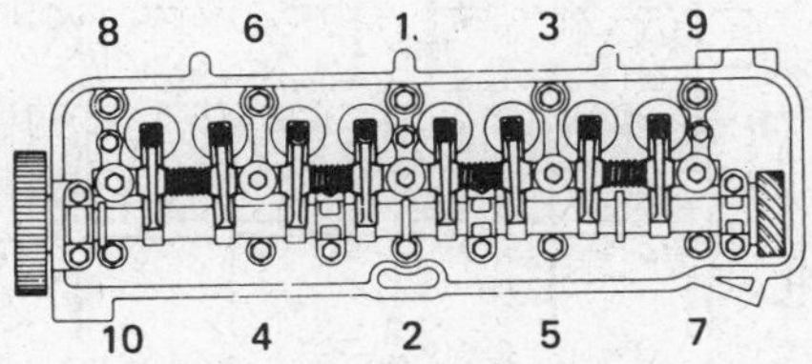


Cylinder head bolt torquing sequence except twincam engine—Nova

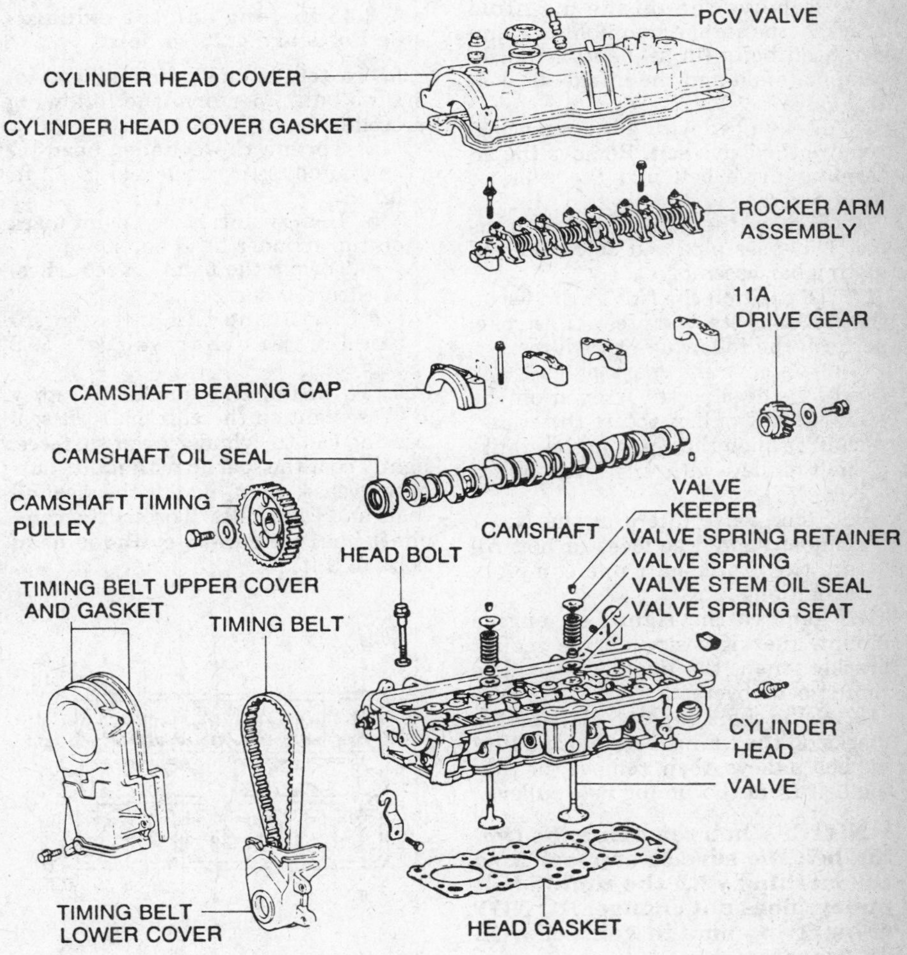


Exploded view of the cylinder head assembly-except twincam engine—Nova

6. Remove the hoses from the PCV valve and the power brake booster.
7. Remove the pressure regulator, the EGR valve (with lines) and the cold start injector hose.

**CAUTION**

***Before disconnecting any component in the fuel system, be sure to reduce the fuel pressure.***

8. Disconnect and remove the No. 1 fuel line.
9. From the auxiliary air valve, remove the No. 1 and No. 2 water by-pass hoses.
10. Remove the vacuum pipe and the cylinder head rear cover.
11. Label and disconnect the electrical harness connectors. Remove the distributor-to-cylinder hold-down bolt and the distributor.
12. Remove the exhaust manifold-to-cylinder head bolts and separate the exhaust manifold from the cylinder head.
13. Remove the fuel delivery pipe-to-engine bolts and the delivery pipe with the injectors; DO NOT drop the fuel injectors.
14. Remove the intake manifold bracket, the intake manifold-to-cylinder head bolts (in sequence), the intake manifold and the intake air control valve.
15. If equipped with power steering, remove the drive belt. Remove the alternator drive belt and the cylinder head covers.
16. Remove the water outlet with the No. 1 by-pass pipe and drive belt adjusting bar assembly.
17. To position the No. 1 cylinder on the TDC of its compression stroke, perform the following procedures:
    a. Remove the spark plugs.
    b. Using a socket wrench on the crankshaft pulley, rotate the crankshaft to align the notch in the crankshaft pulley with the idler pulley bolt.
    c. The valve lifters of the No. 1 cylinder should be loose; if not, rotate the crankshaft one complete revolution.
18. Remove the right-side engine mount, the right-side engine mount bracket, then, the upper and middle timing belt covers.
19. Using chalk or paint, place match marks on the timing belt and the timing belt pulleys, then, remove the timing belt from the timing belt pulleys.

**NOTE: When removing the timing belt, be sure to support it so the meshing with the timing belt pulleys does not change. DO NOT allow it to come in contact with oil or water.**

20. While securing the camshafts, remove each camshaft pulley-to-camshaft bolt, washer and pulley. Remove the inner timing belt cover.
21. Remove the camshaft bearing cap-to-cylinder head bolts, the caps (keep them in order) and the camshafts (keep them in order).
22. Using the cylinder head bolt removal sequence, remove the cylinder head bolts and lift the cylinder head from the engine.
23. Using a putty knife, clean the gasket mounting surfaces. Using a power wire brush, clean the carbon from the cylinder head cavities. Inspect the cylinder head for damage and/or warpage.

**NOTE: When cleaning the cylinder head, be careful, for the cylinder head is made of aluminum which is a soft material.**

**To install:**

24. To install the cylinder head, use a new gasket (make sure it is installed in the correct direction), lubricate the bolt threads in engine oil and reverse the removal procedures.

**NOTE: The intake-side bolts are 3.45 in. long and the exhaust-side bolts are 4.25 in. long.**

25. To torque the cylinder head-to-engine bolts, perform the following procedures:
    a. Torque the cylinder head-to-engine bolts (in sequence) to 22 ft. lbs.
    b. Using paint, place a paint mark on the cylinder head bolts.
    c. Torque the bolts (in sequence) ¼ turn (90 degrees).
    d. Retorque the bolts (in sequence) another ¼ turn (90 degrees).
26. To install the camshafts, apply RTV sealant to the camshaft oil seal bearing cap-to-cylinder head surfaces, lightly coat the seal lip with multi-purpose grease, then, install the new oil seals and camshafts. Torque the camshaft bearing cap-to-cylinder head bolts to 9 ft. lbs.
27. Install the camshaft pulleys-to-camshaft bolts to 34 ft. lbs. Align the timing belt marks with the camshaft pulley marks and install the timing belt onto the camshaft pulleys.
28. Using a wrench on the timing belt pulley, rotate the crankshaft two complete revolutions and check the timing belt alignment points.
29. To complete the installation, use new O-rings, new gaskets, sealant (if necessary) and reverse the removal procedures. Torque the intake manifold-to-cylinder head bolts to 20 ft. lbs., the exhaust manifold-to-cylinder head bolts to 18 ft. lbs. Refill the cooling system. Start the engine, allow it to reach normal operating temperatures and check for leaks. Check and/or adjust the ignition timing.

### Prizm

1. Disconnect the negative battery cable.
2. Drain the coolant.
3. Raise and support the vehicle safely.
4. Remove the right lower stone shield.
5. Remove the 2 mount nut and stud protectors.
6. Remove the 2 rear transaxle mount to main crossmember mount nuts.
7. Remove the two center mount to center crossmember nuts.
8. Lower the vehicle.
9. Remove the air cleaner assembly, disconnect the throttle cable and the cruise control actuator cable.
10. Disconnect the transaxle kick-down cable.
11. Disconnect all necessary electrical connections and vacuum lines.
12. Disconnect the fuel inlet line.
13. Disconnect the cold start injector pipe.
14. Remove the fuel rail.
15. Disconnect the coolant hoses.
16. Disconnect the heater hoses.
17. Remove the water outlet housing.

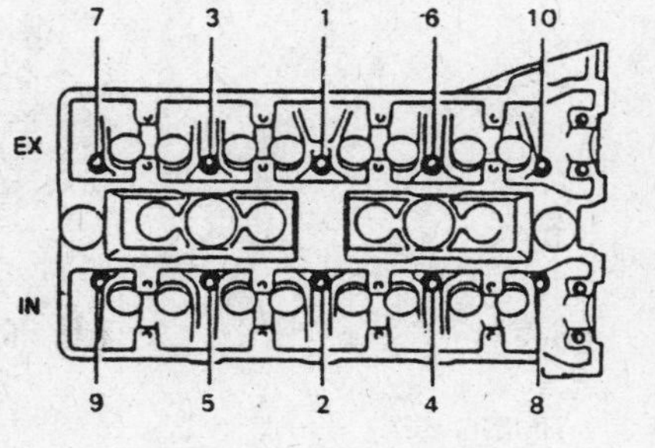

**Cylinder head bolt torquing sequence twincam engine—Nova**

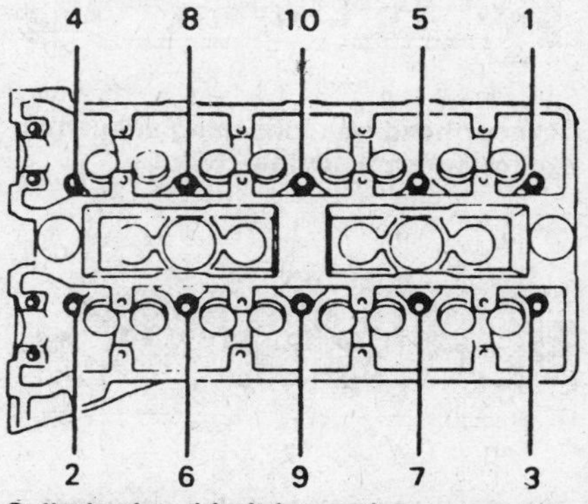

**Cylinder head bolt loosening sequence twincam engine—Nova**

18. Remove the water inlet housing.
19. Disconnect the spark plug wires.
20. Disconnect the PCV valve.
21. Remove the cylinder head cover.
22. Loosen the air conditioning compressor, power steering pump, and generator brackets as applicable.
23. Remove the accessory drive belts.
24. Remove the air conditioning idler pulley.
25. Disconnect the electrical connections at cruise control actuator.
26. Remove the cruise control actuator and bracket.
27. Remove windshield washer reservoir.
28. Support the engine with a J 28467-A support fixture or its equivalent.
29. Remove the right engine mount through bolt.
30. Raise the engine.
31. Remove the water pump pulley.
32. Lower the engine.
33. Disconnect the engine wiring harness from upper timing belt cover.
34. Raise and suitably support the vehicle.
35. Remove the cylinder head-to-cylinder block bracket.
36. Remove the exhaust manifold support bracket.
37. Disconnectemove the exhaust pipe from exhaust manifold.
38. Remove the upper timing belt cover.
39. Remove the center timing belt cover.
40. Remove the right engine mount bracket.
41. Remove the distributor.
42. Set the number 1 cylinder at TDC on its compression stroke. Turn the crankshaft pulley and align its

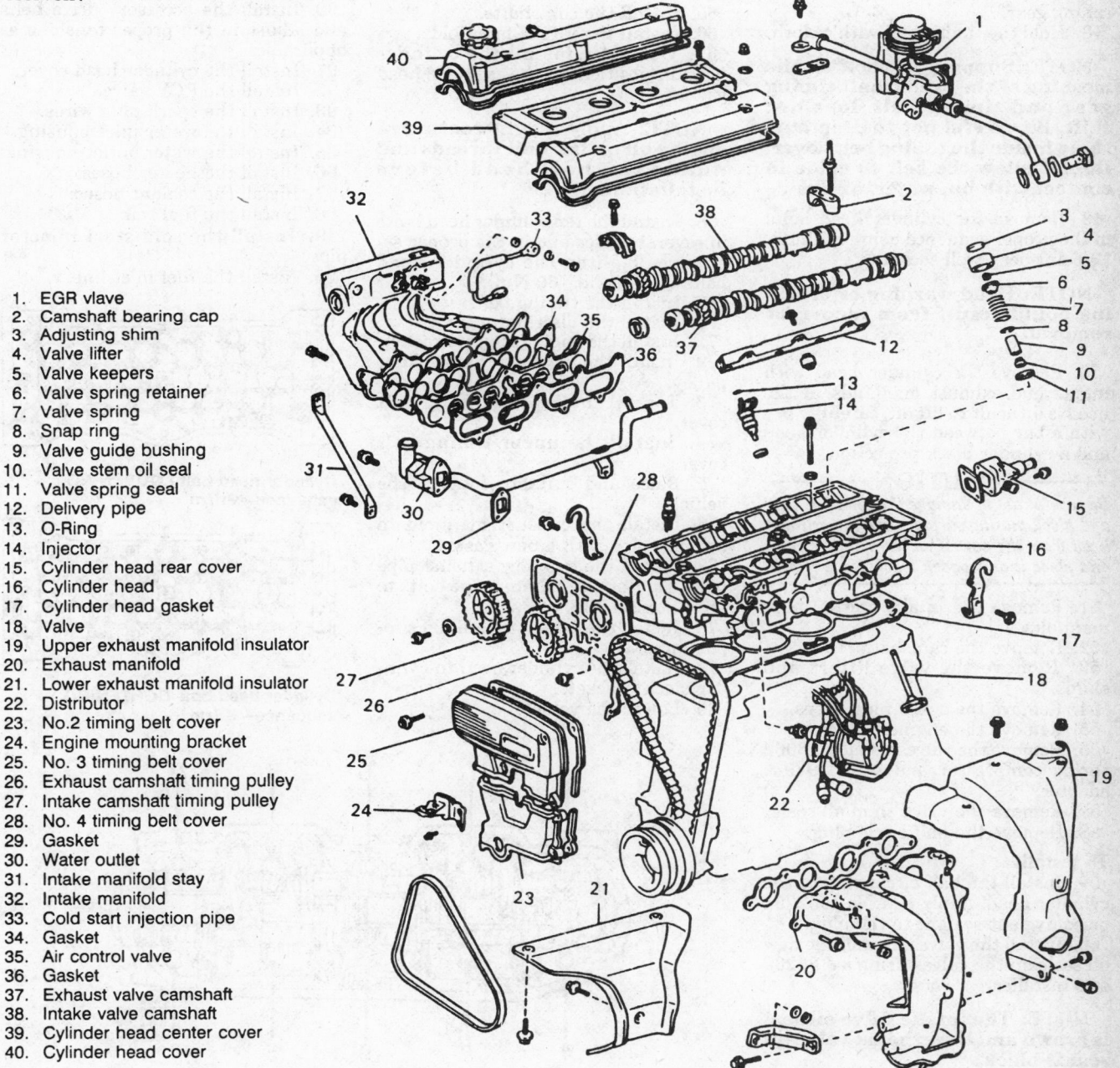

1. EGR vlave
2. Camshaft bearing cap
3. Adjusting shim
4. Valve lifter
5. Valve keepers
6. Valve spring retainer
7. Valve spring
8. Snap ring
9. Valve guide bushing
10. Valve stem oil seal
11. Valve spring seal
12. Delivery pipe
13. O-Ring
14. Injector
15. Cylinder head rear cover
16. Cylinder head
17. Cylinder head gasket
18. Valve
19. Upper exhaust manifold insulator
20. Exhaust manifold
21. Lower exhaust manifold insulator
22. Distributor
23. No.2 timing belt cover
24. Engine mounting bracket
25. No. 3 timing belt cover
26. Exhaust camshaft timing pulley
27. Intake camshaft timing pulley
28. No. 4 timing belt cover
29. Gasket
30. Water outlet
31. Intake manifold stay
32. Intake manifold
33. Cold start injection pipe
34. Gasket
35. Air control valve
36. Gasket
37. Exhaust valve camshaft
38. Intake valve camshaft
39. Cylinder head center cover
40. Cylinder head cover

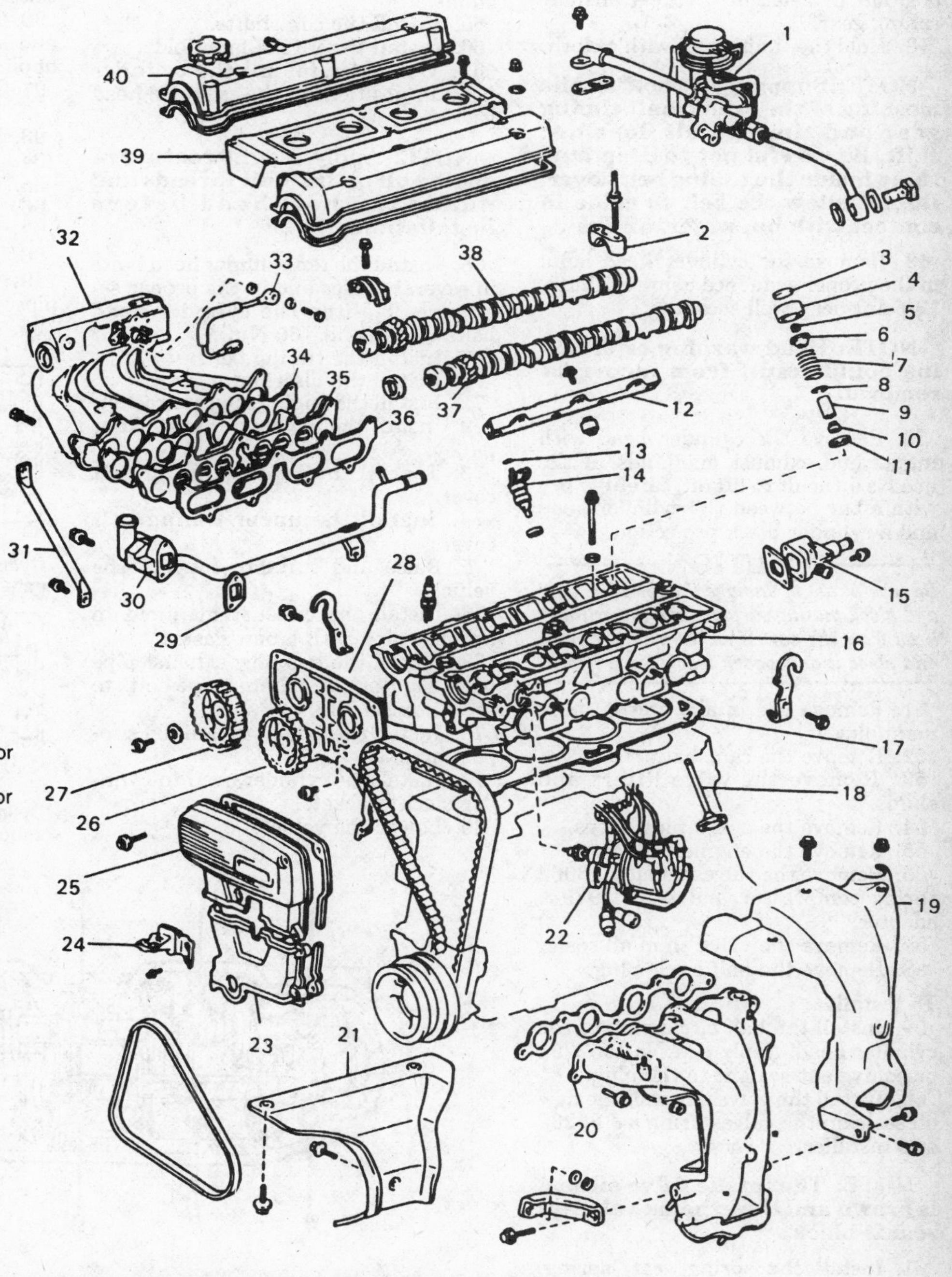

**Exploded view of the cylinder head assembly-twincam engine—Nova**

groove with the 0 mark of the timing belt cover.
43. Check that the camshaft gear hole is aligned with the exhaust camshaft cap mark.
44. Remove the plug from the lower timing belt cover.
45. Place alignment marks on the camshaft timing gear and belt.
46. Loosen the idler pulley mount bolt and push the idler pulley toward the left as far as it will go, then tighten it temporarily.
47. Remove the timing belt from the camshaft timing gear after marking its position in relation to the camshaft timing gear.
48. Hold the timing belt with a cloth.

**NOTE: Support the belt so the meshing of the crankshaft timing gear and timing belt does not shift. Be careful not to drop anything inside the timing belt cover. Do not allow the belt to come in contact with oil, water, or dust.**

49. Remove the cylinder head bolts in the proper sequence using a 10mm, 12 point deep well socket.

**NOTE: Head warping or cracking could result from incorrect removal.**

50. Remove the cylinder head with intake and exhaust manifolds. If the head is difficult to lift off, carefully pry with a bar between the cylinder head and a cylinder block projection.

**CAUTION**

***Be careful not to damage the cylinder head and block mating surface. Lift the cylinder head from the dowels on the cylinder block and place it on wooden blocks on a bench.***

51. Remove the intake and exhaust manifolds.
52. Remove the camshafts.
53. Remove the valve lifters and shims.
54. Remove the spark plug tubes.
55. Remove the engine hangers.
56. Remove the valves using a J 8062 spring compressor and a J 37979-A adapter.
57. Remove the valve stem oil seals.
58. Remove the half circle plug.

**To install**

59. Install the half circle plug to the cylinder head. Apply GM No.1052751 or equivalent sealant to the plug.
60. Install the valves. Install the new oil seals on the valves using a J 38232 seal installer.

**NOTE: The intake valve oil seal is brown and the exhaust valve oil seal is black.**

61. Install the spring seat, spring, and spring retainer on the cylinder head. Using a J 8062 spring compressor and a J 37979-A adapter, compress the valve springs and place the 2 keepers around valve stem. Remove the J 8062 spring compressor and the J 37979-A adapter.
62. Apply GM No.1052751 sealant to the spark plug tube hole of the cylinder head, and using a press, install a new spark plug tube to a protrusion height of 1.835–1.866 in. (46.6–47.4mm).
63. Install the engine hangers to the cylinder head.
64. Install the valve lifters and shims.
65. Install the camshafts.
66. Install the intake manifold.
67. Carefully install the cylinder head in position on the cylinder head gasket.

**NOTE: Apply a light coating of engine oil on the bolt threads and under the bolt head before installation.**

68. Install the ten cylinder head bolts in several passes and in the proper sequence. Tighten the cylinder head bolts to 44 ft. lb. (60 Nm).
69. Install the timing belt.
70. Install the distributor.
71. Install the engine mount bracket.
72. Install the air conditioning idler pulley.
73. Install the center timing belt cover.
74. Install the upper timing belt cover.
75. Raise and suitably support the vehicle.
76. Install the exhaust manifold to exhaust pipe with a new gasket.
77. Install the two new exhaust pipe bolts.Tighten the exhaust pipe bolts to 18 ft. lb. (25 Nm).
78. Install the exhaust manifold support bracket.
79. Install the cylinder head-to-cylinder block bracket.
80. Lower the vehicle.
81. Connect the engine harness to upper timing belt cover.
82. Raise the engine.
83. Install the water pump pulley.
84. Lower engine.
85. Install the right engine mount through bolt.Tighten to 64 ft. lbs. (87 Nm).
86. Remove the J 28467-A support fixture.
87. Install the windshield washer reservoir.
88. Install the cruise control actuator and bracket.
89. Connect the electrical connections at the cruise control actuator.
90. Install the accessory drive belts and adjust to the proper tensions as applicable.
91. Install the cylinder head cover.
92. Install the PCV valve.
93. Install the spark plug wires.
94. Install the water inlet housing.
95. Install the water outlet housing.
96. Install the heater hoses.
97. Install the coolant hoses.
98. Install the fuel rail.
99. Install the cold-start injector pipe.
100. Install the fuel inlet line.

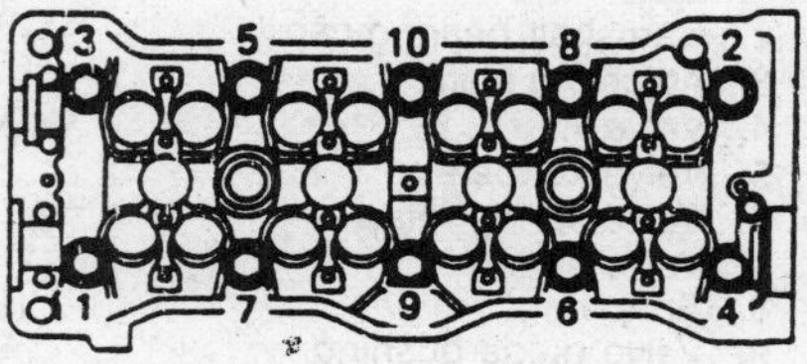


**Cylinder head bolt LOOSENING sequence–Prizm**

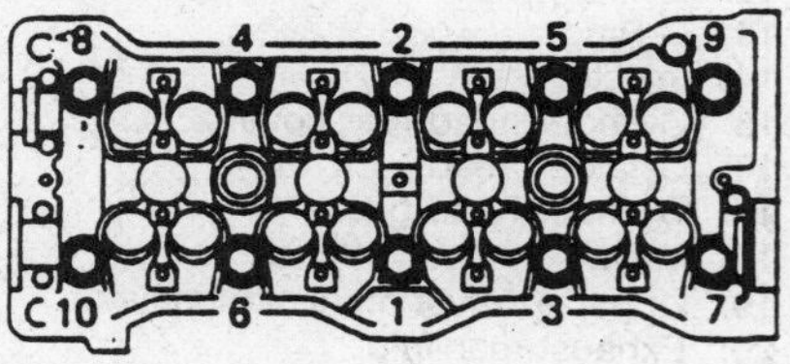


**Cylinder head bolt TIGHTENING sequence–Prizm**

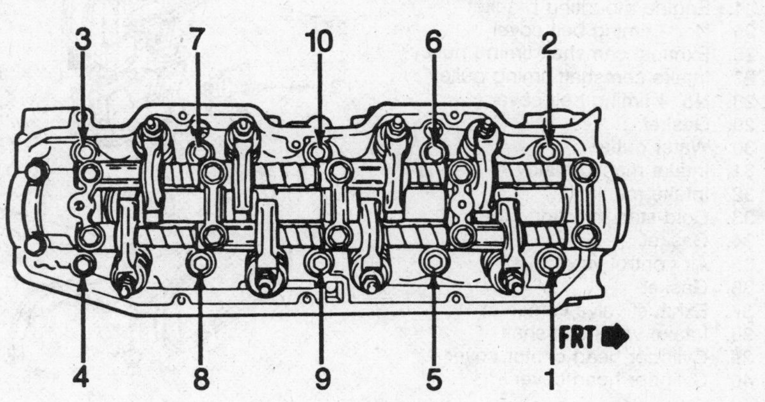


**Cylinder head bolt removal sequence–Spectrum**

101. Connect all necessary electrical connections and vacuum lines.
102. Install the transaxle kick-down cable.
103. Connect the cruise control actuator cable.
104. Connect the throttle cable.
105. Install the air cleaner assembly.
106. Raise and suitably support the vehicle.
107. Install the 2 rear mount-to-main crossmember nuts.
108. Install the 2 center transaxle mount-to-center crossmember nuts.
109. Tighten the rear transaxle mount-to-main crossmember nuts to (45 ft. lbs. (61 Nm).
110. Tighten the center transaxle mount-to-center crossmember nuts to (45 ft. lbs. (61 Nm).
111. Install both mount nut and stud protectors.
112. Install the right lower stone shield.
113. Lower vehicle.
114. Refill coolant.
115. Install the battery negative (-) cable.

### Spectrum

1. Disconnect the negative battery terminal from the battery.
2. Drain the cooling system.
3. Remove the air cleaner.
4. Disconnect the flex hose and oxygen sensor at the exhaust manifold.
5. Disconnect the exhaust pipe bracket at the block and the exhaust pipe at the manifold. On turbocharged model disconnect exhaust pipe at wastegate manifold and disconnect vacumm line for turbocharger control.
6. Disconnect the spark plug wires.
7. Remove the thermostat housing, the distributor, the vacuum advance hoses and the ground cable at the cylinder head.
8. Disconnect the fuel hoses at the fuel pump on non-turbocharged model.
9. From the carburetor, if so equipped, remove the necessary hoses and the throttle cable.
10. Remove engine harness asembly from fuel injectors and fuel line from fuel injector pipe on turbocharged model.
11. Disconnect the vacuum switching valve electrical connector and the heater hoses.
12. Remove the alternator, P/S and A/C adjusting bolts, brackets and drive belts.
13. Support the engine using a vertical hoist. Remove the right hand motor mount and the bracket at the front cover.
14. Rotate the engine to align the timing marks, then remove the timing gear cover.

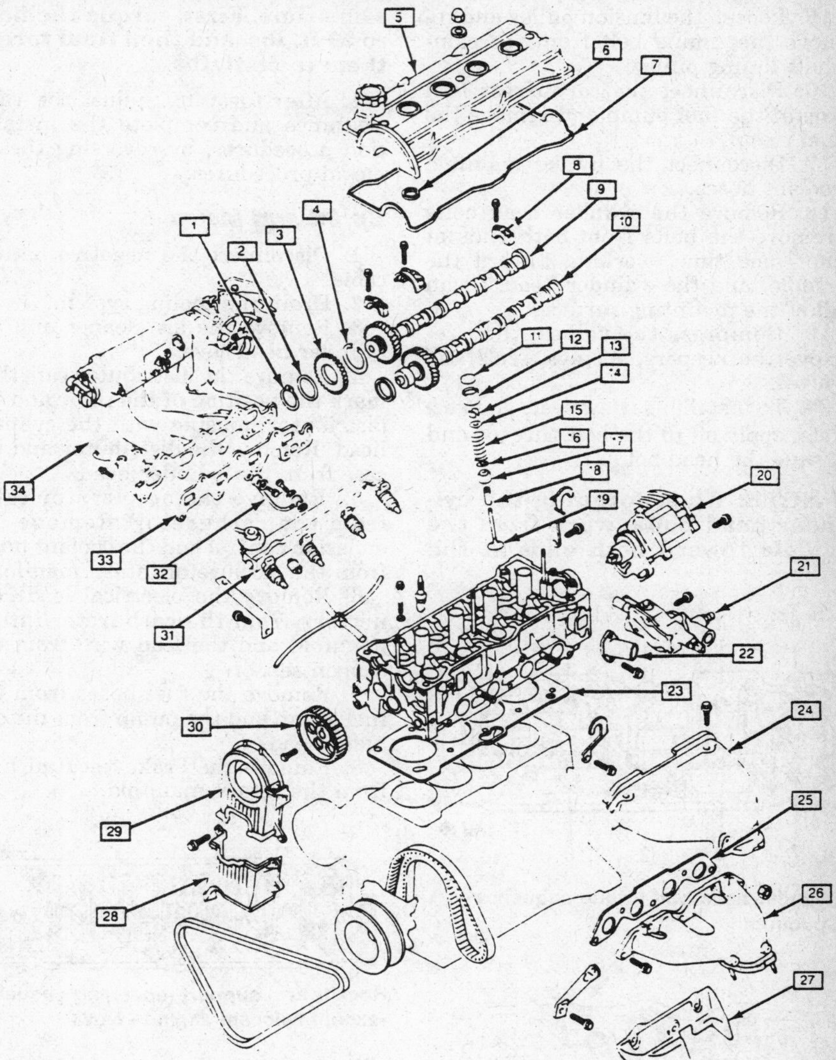

1. Camshaft snap ring
2. Wave washer
3. Camshaft sub gear
4. Camshaft gear spring
5. Cylinder head cover
6. Spark plug tube gasket
7. Cylinder head cover gasket
8. Camshaft bearing cap
9. Camshaft (intake)
10. Camshaft (exhaust)
11. Adjusting shim
12. Valve lifter
13. Valve keepers
14. Valve spring retainer
15. Valve spring
16. Valve spring seat
17. Valve stem oil seal
18. Valve guide bushing
19. Valve
20. Distributor
21. Water inlet housing
22. Water outlet housing
23. Head gasket
24. Exhaust manifold upper insulator
25. Exhaust manifold gasket
26. Exhaust manifold
27. Exhaust manifold lower insulator
28. Center timimg belt cover
29. Upper timing belt cover
30. Camshaft timimn gear
31. Fuel rail
32. Cold start injector pipe
33. Intake manifold gasket
34. Intake manifold

**Exploded view of the cylinder head assembly—Prizm**

15. Loosen the tension pulley and remove the timing belt from the camshaft timing pulley.
16. Disconnect the carburetor fuel line at the fuel pump and remove the fuel pump.
17. Disconnect the intake manifold coolant hoses.
18. Remove the cylinder head bolts (remove the bolts from both ends at the same time, working toward the middle) and the cylinder head. Clean all of the mounting surfaces.
19. Compress the valves; then remove the keepers, springs, seals and valves.
20. To install, use new seals and gaskets, apply oil to the bolt threads and torque the head bolts.

**NOTE: When torquing the cylinder head bolts, work from the middle toward both ends at the same time. First, torque the bolts to 29 ft. lbs. and then final torque them to 58 ft. lbs.**

21. After torquing, adjust the valve clearance and complete the installation procedures, by reversing the removal procedures.

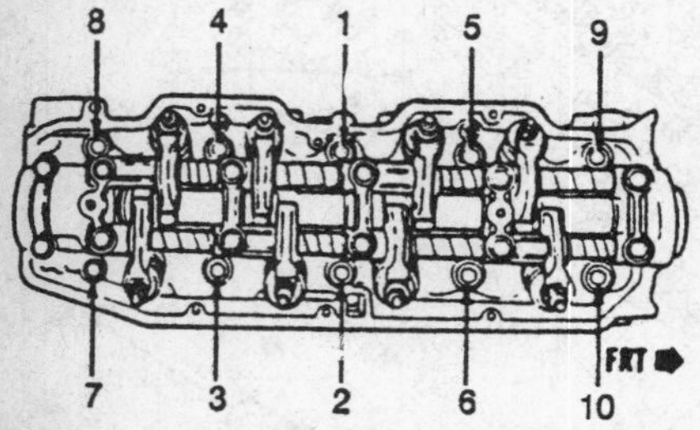


Cylinder head bolt torque sequence—Spectrum

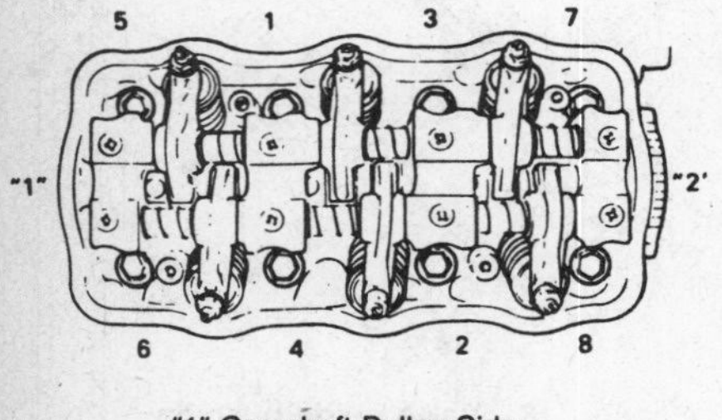


Cylinder head mounting bolt torque sequence—Sprint and Metro

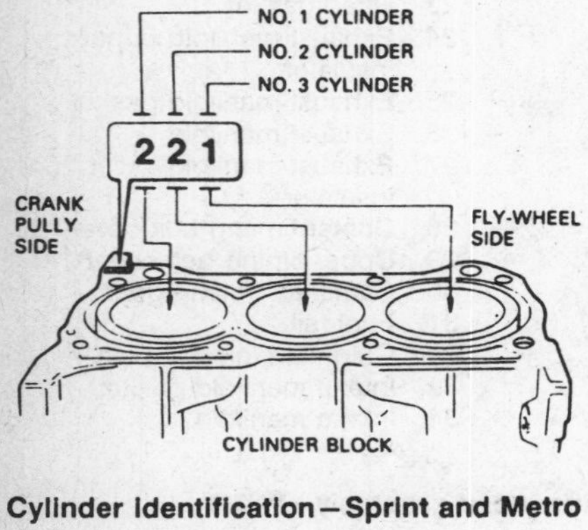


Cylinder identification—Sprint and Metro

### *Sprint and Metro*

1. Disconnect the negative battery cable.
2. Drain the cooling system.
3. Remove the air cleaner and the cylinder head cover.
4. Remove the distributor cap, then mark the position of the rotor and the distributor housing with the cylinder head. Remove the distributor and the case from the cylinder head.
5. Remove the accelerator cable from the carburetor. Remove the emission control and the coolant hoses from the carburetor/intake manifold.
6. Remove the electrical lead connectors from the carburetor/intake manifold and the lead wire from the oxygen sensor.
7. Remove the fuel hoses from the fuel pump and the pump from the cylinder head.
8. Remove the brake vacuum hose from the intake manifold.

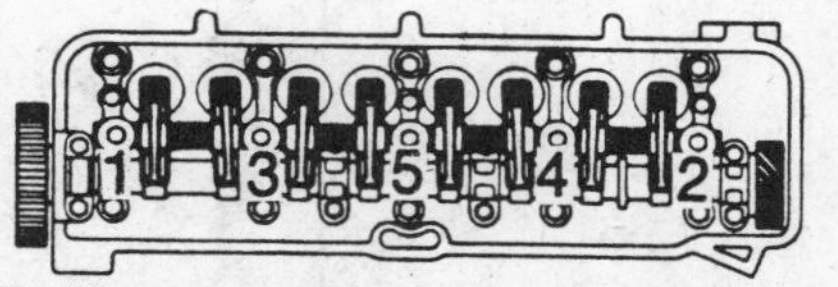


Rocker arm support loosening sequence -except twincam engine—Nova

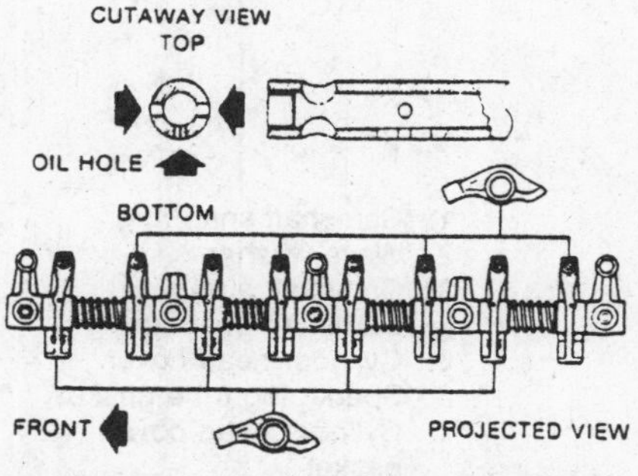


View of the rocker arm shaft assembly except twincam engine—Nova

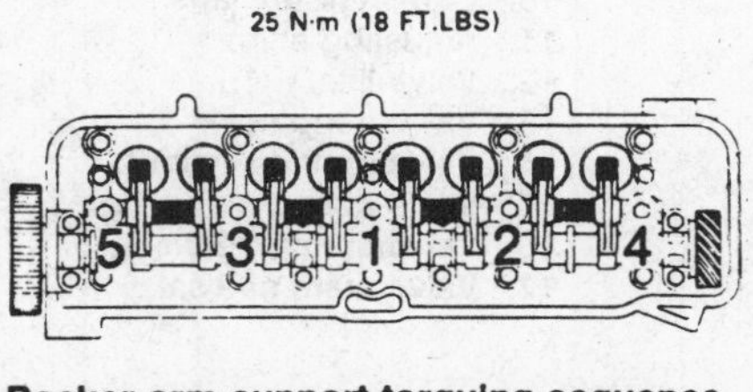


Rocker arm support torquing sequence - except twincam engine—Nova

9. Remove the crankshaft pulley, the outside cover, the timing belt and the tensioner from the front of the engine.
10. Remove the exhaust and the 2nd air pipes from the exhaust manifold.
11. Remove the exhaust/intake manifolds and the engine side mount from the cylinder head.
12. Loosen the rocker arm valve adjusters, turn back the adjusting screws so that the rocker arms move freely. Remove the rocker arm shaft retaining screws and pull out the shafts. Remove the rocker arms and springs from the cylinder head.

**NOTE: Make a note of the differences between the rocker arm shafts. The intake shaft's stepped end is 0.55 in., which faces the camshaft pulley; the exhaust shaft's stepped end is 0.59 in., which faces the distributor.**

13. Remove the mounting bolts and the cylinder head from the engine.
14. To install, use new gaskets and reverse the removal procedures. Torque the cylinder head bolts to 46–50.5 ft. lbs. and the rocker arm shaft screws to 7–9 ft. lbs. Adjust the valve clearances. Refill the cooling system. Check and/or adjust the ignition timing.

## OVERHAUL

**For all cylinder head overhaul procedures, please refer to the "Engine Rebuilding" in the Unit Repair section.**

# Rocker Arm/Shaft Assembly

## REMOVAL & INSTALLATION

### *Nova and Prizm*

#### EXCEPT TWINCAM

1. Remove the air cleaner and valve cover.
2. Remove the five rocker shaft assembly retaining bolts in several stages—note that they MUST be loosened in the correct sequence: Front bolt first, rear bolt second, forward—center bolt third, rearward-center bolt fourth and the center bolt fifth.
3. Remove the rocker arm/shaft assembly.
4. Inspect for wear by attempting to rock the rocker levers on the shaft. If negligible motion is felt, wear is acceptable. If there is noticeable wear, note the order of assembly and the fact that there are two types of rockers. Remove the bolts and slide the rockers, springs and pedestals from the shaft.

5. Using an internal dial indicator, measure the inside diameter of each rocker lever; using a micrometer, measure the shaft diameter at the rocker wear areas. Subtract the shaft shaft diameter from the rocker arm inside diameter; the difference must not exceed 0.0024 in. If necessary, replace the rockers and/or the shaft to correct the clearance problems.

6. Assemble the pedestals, rockers, springs and bolts in reverse order of disassembly. Using clean engine oil, lubricate wear surfaces thoroughly. Install the rocker arm shaft with the oil holes facing downward.

7. Loosen the valve adjusting screw lock nuts. Install the rocker arm assembly onto the cylinder head and start the bolts, tightening them finger tight. Torque the rocker arm assembly-to-cylinder head bolts (in sequence) using 3 passes to 18 ft. lbs.: center bolt – first, center/rearward bolt – second, center/forward bolt – third, rear bolt – fourth and front bolt – last. Perform the valve adjustment.

8. To complete the installation, use new gasket(s), sealant (if necessary) and reverse the removal procedures.

### Spectrum

1. Disconnect the negative battery terminal from the battery. Remove the PCV hoses.

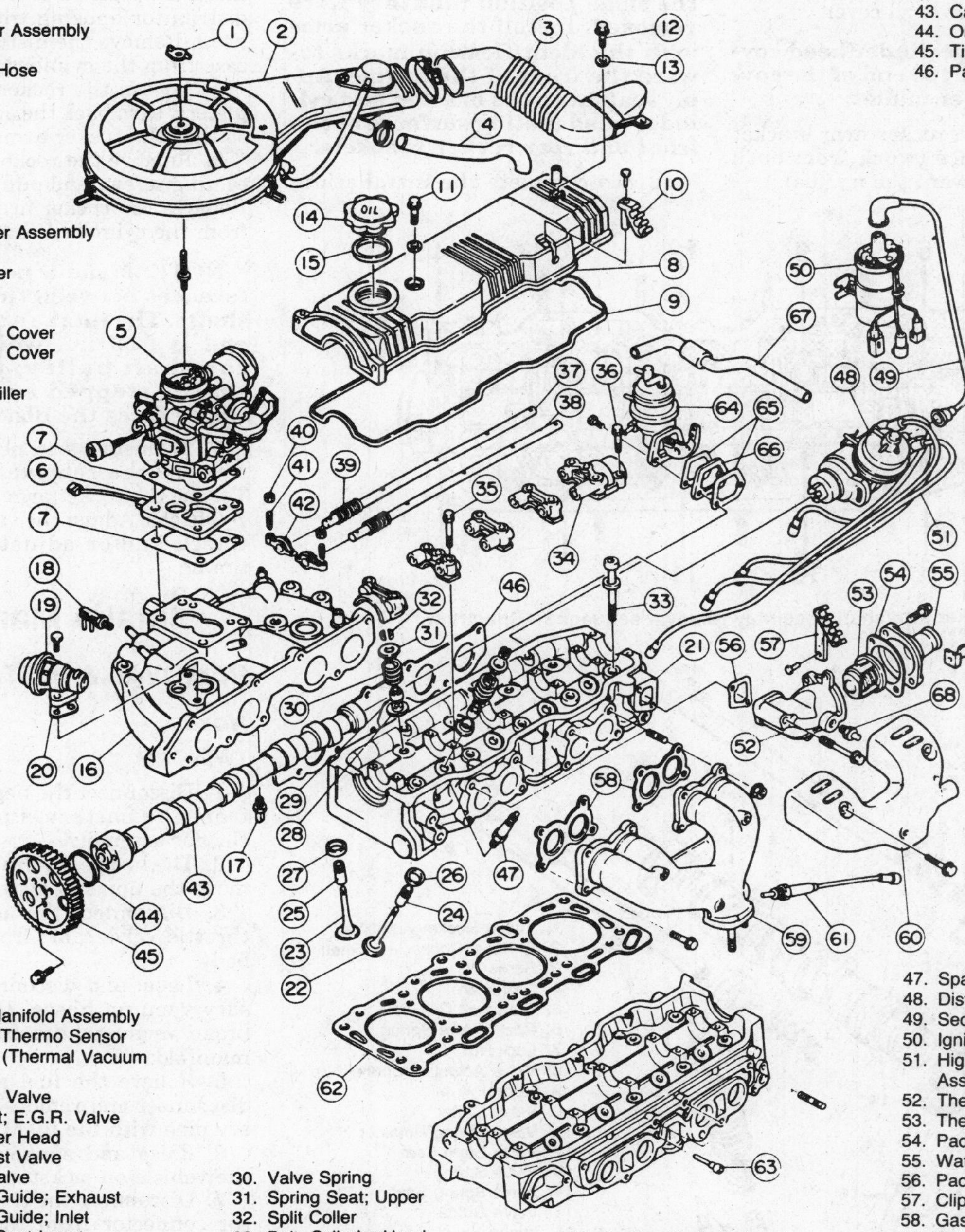

1. Wing Nut
2. Air Cleaner Assembly
3. Air Duct
4. TCA Flex Hose
5. Carburetor
6. EFE Heater Assembly
7. Packing
8. Head Cover
9. Packing
10. Clip
11. Bolt; Head Cover
12. Bolt; Head Cover
13. Packing
14. Cap; Oil Filler
15. Packing
16. Inlet Manifold Assembly
17. Water Thermo Sensor
18. T.V.V. (Thermal Vacuum Valve)
19. E.G.R. Valve
20. Gasket; E.G.R. Valve
21. Cylinder Head
22. Exhaust Valve
23. Inlet Valve
24. Valve Guide; Exhaust
25. Valve Guide; Inlet
26. Valve Seat Insert; Exhaust
27. Valve Seat Insert; Inlet
28. Spring Seat; Lower
29. Oil Controller
30. Valve Spring
31. Spring Seat; Upper
32. Split Coller
33. Bolt; Cylinder Head
34. Rocker Bracket
35. Bolt
36. Bolt
37. Rocker Shaft; Inlet
38. Rocker Shaft; Exhaust
39. Rocker Spring
40. Nut
41. Adjusting Screw
42. Rocker Arm
43. Camshaft
44. Oil Seal; Camshaft
45. Timing Pulley; Camshaft
46. Packing
47. Spark Plug
48. Distributor Assembly
49. Secondary Coad
50. Ignition Coil Assembly
51. Hightension Cable Assembly
52. Thermostat Housing
53. Thermostat
54. Packing
55. Water Outlet Pipe
56. Packing
57. Clip
58. Gasket
59. Exhaust Manifold
60. Hot Air Cover
61. $O_2$ Sensor
62. Gasket; Cylinder Head
63. Nozzle; Sonic Jet

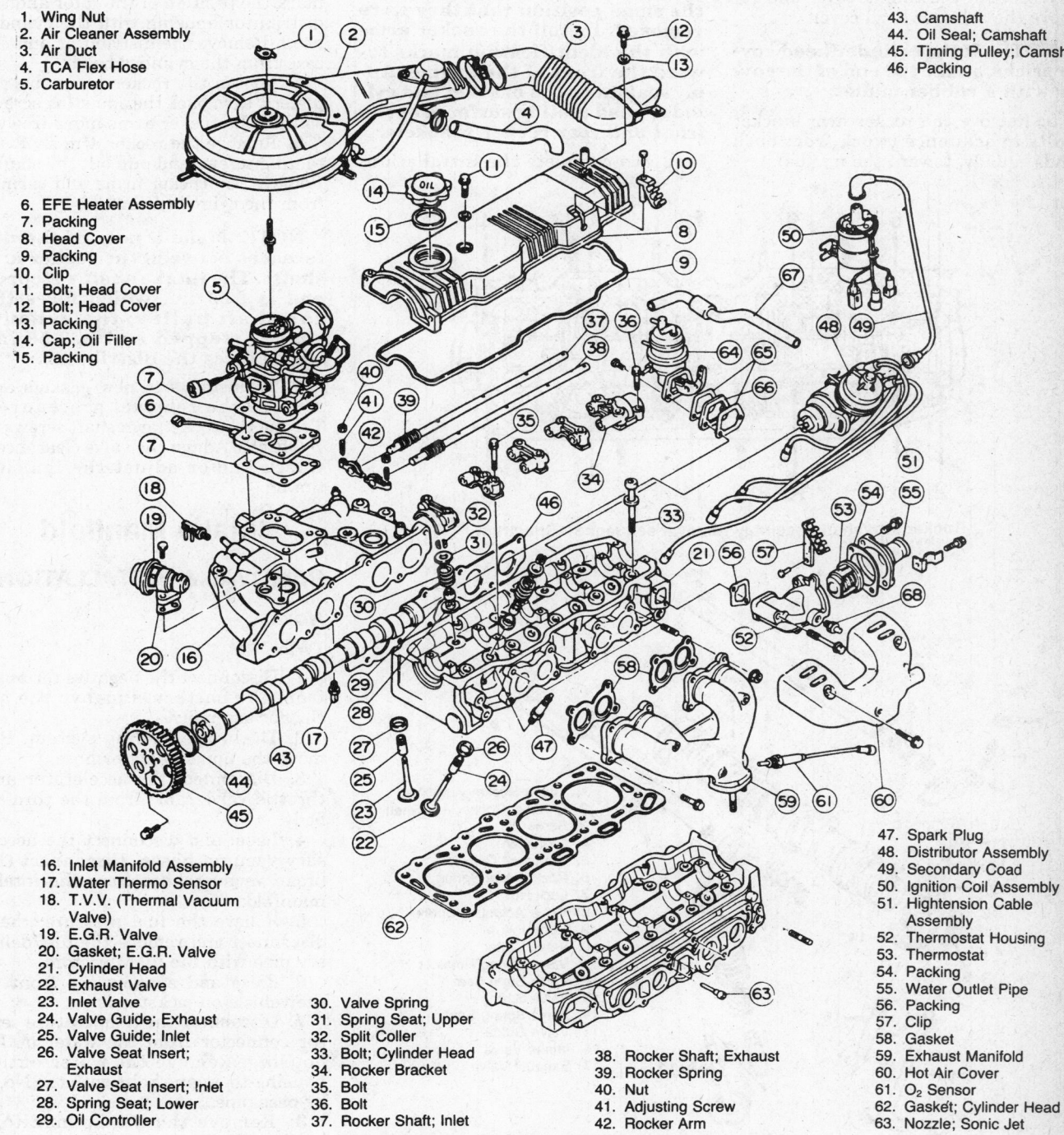

**Exploded view of the top of the engine – Spectrum**

2. Remove the spark plug wires from the mounting clip.
3. Remove the ground wire from the right rear side of the head cover.
4. Support the engine and remove the right side engine mounting rubber, bolts and plate.
5. Remove the mounting bracket on the timing cover.
6. Remove the four bolts holding the timing cover and the two bolts holding the cylinder head cover.
7. Loosen the timing cover and remove the cylinder head cover.

**NOTE: If the cylinder head cover sticks, strike the end of the cover with a rubber mallet.**

8. Remove the rocker arm bracket bolts in sequence (work from both ends equally, toward the middle).
9. Remove the rocker arm shafts and then the rocker arms from the shafts.
10. Using a putty knife, clean the sealing surfaces of the cover and the cylinder head.
11. To install, apply sealer to the sealing surfaces and reverse the removal procedures.

**NOTE: The rocker arm shafts are different from each other, make sure they are installed in the same position that they were removed. Install the rocker arms with the identification marks toward the front of the engine. Apply sealant to the bracket and cylinder head mating surfaces of the front and rear rocker brackets.**

12. To complete the installation, mount the rocker assemblies securely to the dowel pins on the cylinder head. Torque the rocker arm bolts to 16 ft. lbs. Start the engine and check for leaks.

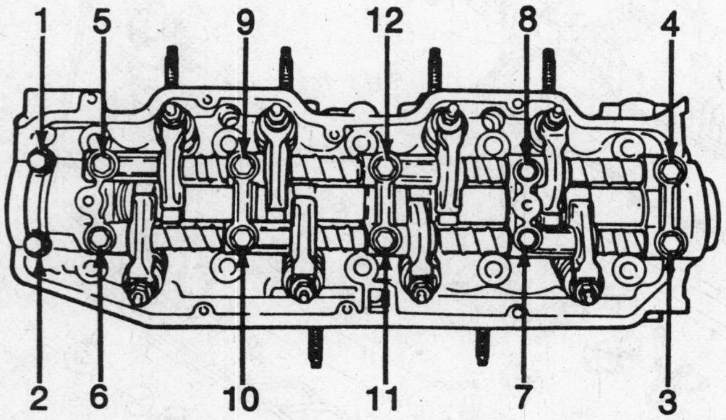

Rocker arm/shaft assembly removal sequence—Spectrum

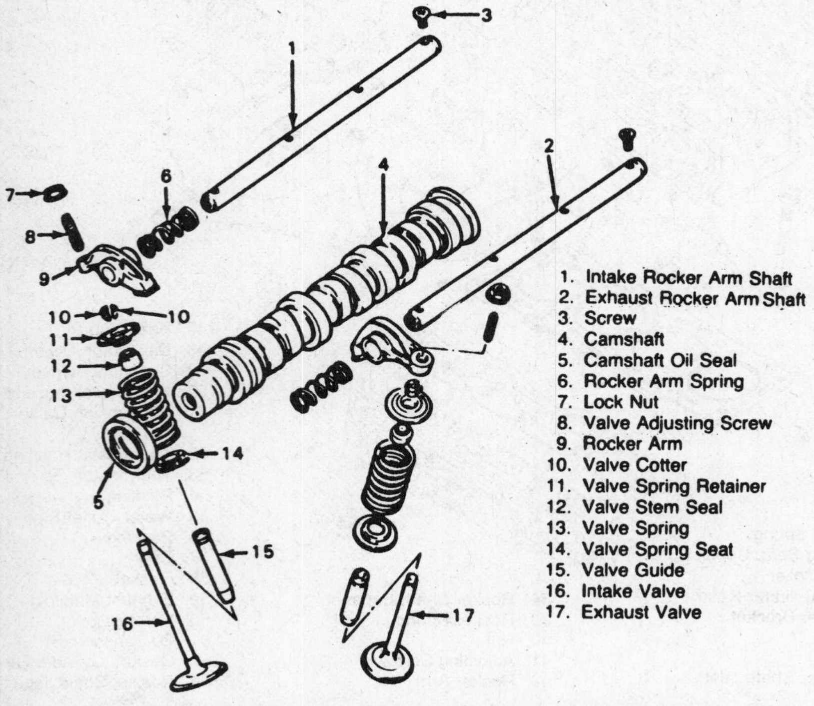

Exploded view of the rocker arm assembly—Sprint and Metro

### *Sprint and Metro*

1. Disconnect the negative battery cable.
2. Remove the air cleaner and the cylinder head cover.
3. Remove the distributor cap, then mark the position of the rotor and the distributor housing with the cylinder head. Remove the distributor and the case from the cylinder head.
4. Loosen the rocker arm valve adjusters, turn back the adjusting screws so that the rocker arms move freely.
5. Remove the rocker arm shaft retaining screws and pull out the shafts. Remove the rocker arms and springs from the cylinder head.

**NOTE: Make a note of the differences between the rocker arm shafts. The intake shaft's stepped end is 0.55 in., which faces the camshaft pulley; the exhaust shaft's stepped end is 0.59 in., which faces the distributor.**

6. To install, use new gaskets and reverse the removal procedures. Torque the rocker arm shaft screws to 7–9 ft. lbs. Adjust the valve clearances. Check and/or adjust the ignition timing.

# Intake Manifold

## REMOVAL & INSTALLATION

### *Nova*

#### TWINCAM

1. Disconnect the negative terminal from the battery. Remove the air cleaner assembly.
2. Drain the cooling system. Remove the upper radiator hose.
3. Disconnect the accelerator and throttle valve cable from the throttle body.
4. Label and disconnect the necessary vacuum hoses. Disconnect the brake vacuum hose from the intake manifold.
5. Relieve the fuel pressure, then, disconnect and remove the fuel delivery pipe with the fuel injectors.
6. Raise and support the front of the vehicle on jackstands.
7. Disconnect the temperature sensor connector from the water outlet housing. Remove the water outlet housing-to-engine bolts with the No. 1 by-pass pipe.
8. Remove the intake manifold bracket, the intake manifold-to-engine bolts, the intake manifold (with the air

control valve) and gaskets from the cylinder head.

9. Using a putty knife, clean the gasket mounting surfaces. Inspect the intake manifold and air control valve for damage and/or warpage; maximum warpage for both is 0.002 in., if the warpage is greater, replace the intake manifold or air control valve.

10. To install, use new gaskets and reverse the removal procedures. Torque the intake manifold-to-cylinder head bolts to 20 ft. lbs., the intake manifold bracket-to-engine bolts to 20 ft. lbs. and the fuel delivery pipe-to-engine bolts to 13 ft. lbs. Start the engine and check for leaks.

### *Prizm*

1. Disconnect the battery negative (-) cable.
2. Drain coolant.
3. Remove the air cleaner assembly.
4. Disconnec the throttle cable and accelerator cable from bracket (automatic transaxle).
5. Disconnect all necessary vacuum hoses.
6. Disconnect the following connectors:
   Throttle position sensor
   Cold start injector
   Injector connectors
   Air control valve and vacuum sensor
7. Disconnect the cold start injector pipe.
8. Disconnect the water hose from air valve.
9. Raise and suitably support the vehicle.
10. Remove the intake manifold bracket.
11. Lower vehicle.
12. Remove the 7 bolts, 2 nuts, ground cable, intake manifold, and gasket.
13. Measure the intake manifold with a straight edge and a feeler gage at the cylinder head mating surface. If warpage exceeds 0.008 in. (0.2 mm), replace the intake manifold.

**To install:**

14. Install the new gasket, intake manifold, 7 bolts, 2 nuts, and ground cable connector.
15. Raise and suitably support the vehicle.
16. Install the intake manifold bracket.
17. Lower vehicle.
18. Tighten the intake manifold bolts to 14 ft. lbs. (19 Nm).
19. Connect the water hose to the air valve.
20. Connect the cold-start injector pipe.
21. Connect the following connectors:
   Throttle position sensor
   Cold start injector
   Air control Valve
   Vacuum sensor
22. Connect all the vacuum hoses.
23. Connect the throttle and accelerator cables to bracket (automatic transaxle).
24. Refill coolant.
25. Install the air cleaner assembly.
26. Connect the battery negative (-) cable.

### *Spectrum*

#### NON-TURBOCHARGED MODEL

1. Disconnect the negative battery terminal from the battery. Drain the cooling system.
2. Remove the bolt securing the alternator adjusting plate to the engine.
3. Disconnect and label all of the hoses attached to the air cleaner and remove the air cleaner.
4. Disconnect the air inlet temperature switch wiring connector.
5. Disconnect and label the hoses, electrical connectors, and control cable attached to the carburetor.
6. If equipped with A/C, disconnect the FIDC vacuum hose, the pressure tank control valve hose, the distributor/3-way connector hose and the VSV wiring connector.
7. Remove the carburetor attaching bolts (located beneath the intake manifold), then remove the carburetor and the EFE heater.
8. At the intake manifold, remove the PCV hose, the water bypass hose, the heater hoses, the EGR valve/canister hose, the distributor vacuum advance hose and the ground wires.
9. Disconnect the thermometer unit switch wiring connector.
10. Remove the intake manifold attaching nuts/bolts and the intake manifold.
11. Clean the sealing surfaces of the intake manifold and cylinder head.
12. To install, use new gaskets and reverse the removal procedures. Torque the intake manifold to 17 ft. lbs.; then adjust the engine control cable and the alternator belt tension. Refill the engine with coolant and check for leaks.

#### TURBOCHARGED MODEL

1. Disconnect the negative battery terminal from the battery.
2. Remove pressure regulator and oil seperator.
3. Disconnect vacuum line from VSV and remove vacuum switching valve from bracket.
4. Remove oil seperator/VSV bracket and hanger as an assembly.
5. Remove throttle valve assembly and engine harness assembly (mark or tag harness connections if necessary).
6. Remove Idle Air Control Valve, Relief Valve and MAP sensor.
7. Disconnect vacuum line from Back Pressure transducer and unclip transducer from hold down bracket.
8. Remove EGR valve and adaptor plate.
9. Remove Fuel injectors and fuel pipe connected to rail as one unit and postion out of way then remove Intake Manifold with common chamber
10. To install, use new gaskets and reverse the removal procedures. Torque the intake manifold to 17 ft. lbs. Start and run engine check for leaks.

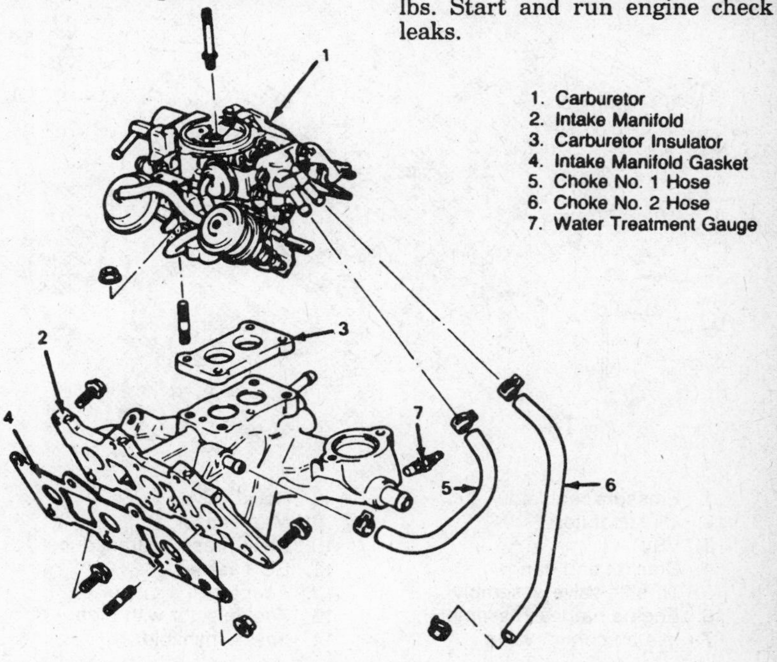


Carburetor and intake manifold mounting – Sprint and Metro

### *Sprint and Metro*

#### NON TURBOCHARGED ENGINES

1. Disconnect the negative battery cable.
2. Drain the cooling system.
3. Disconnect the air cleaner element, the EGR modulator, the warm air, the cool air, the 2nd air and the vacuum hoses from the air cleaner case.
4. Remove the air cleaner case, the electrical lead wires and the accelerator cable from the carburetor.
5. Disconnect the emission control and the fuel hoses from the carburetor.
6. Remove the water hoses from the choke housing.
7. Remove the electrical lead wires, the emission control, the coolant and the brake vacuum hoses from the intake manifold.
8. Remove the intake manifold from the cylinder head.
9. Clean the mating gasket surfaces.
10. To install, use new gaskets and reverse the removal procedures. Torque the intake manifold-to-cylinder head bolts to 14–20 ft. lbs. Refill the cooling system.

#### TURBOCHARGED ENGINES

1. Disconnect the negative battery cable.
2. Drain the cooling system when the engine is cool.

**CAUTION**

***The fuel delivery pipe is under high pressure even after the engine is stopped, direct removal of the fuel line may result in dangerous fuel spray. Make sure to release the fuel pressure according to the procedure outlined under Fuel System in this section.***

3. Remove the surge tank together with the throttle body.
4. Disconnect the fuel injector couplers.
5. Disconnect the fuel hoses from the delivery pipe.
6. Remove the delivery pipe together with the injectors.
7. Disconnect the water temperature gauge wire (Yellow/White).
8. Disconnect the starter injector time switch coupler (Brown).
9. Disconnect the water temperature sensor coupler (Green).
10. Disconnect the radiator fan switch coupler.
11. Disconnect the water hoses and the EGR vacuum hoses.
12. Remove the intake manifold.
13. Installation is the reverse of removal, with the following precautions:
    a. Use a new intake manifold gasket.
    b. If an injector was removed from the delivery pipe a new O-ring should be used.
    c. Torque the intake manifold retaining bolts to 17 ft. lbs.
    d. After the ignition is turned on check for fuel leaks.

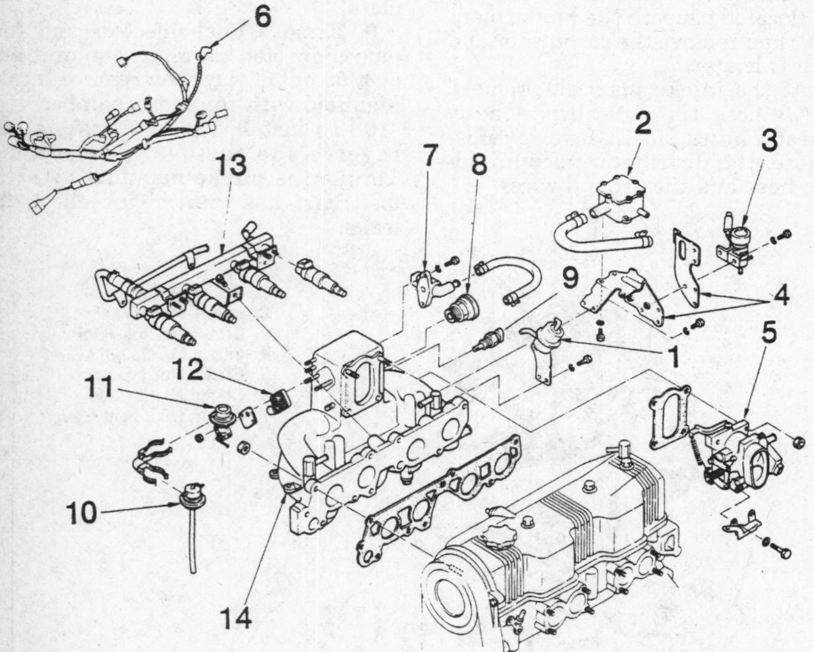


1. Pressure regulator
2. Oil separator
3. VSV
4. Bracket and hanger
5. Throttle valve assembly
6. Engine harness assembly
7. Idle air control valve
8. Relief valve
9. Map sensor
10. Back pressure transducer
11. EGR valve
12. Adaptor
13. Fuel injector with pipe
14. Intake manifold

**Intake manifold turbocharged model—Spectrum**

## Exhaust Manifold

### REMOVAL & INSTALLATION

#### *Nova and Prizm*

##### TWINCAM

1. Disconnect the negative terminal from the battery.
2. Remove the exhaust manifold heat shield.
3. Raise and support the front of the vehicle on jackstands.
4. Remove the exhaust pipe-to-exhaust manifold nuts and separate the pipe from the manifold. Remove the exhaust manifold bracket from the exhaust manifold, the exhaust manifold-to-engine bolts, the exhaust manifold and gasket (discard the gasket) from the cylinder head.
5. Using a putty knife, clean the gasket mounting surfaces. Inspect the exhaust manifold for damage and/or warpage; maximum warpage is 0.012 in., if the warpage is greater, replace the exhaust manifold.
6. To install, use a new gasket and reverse the removal procedures. Torque the exhaust manifold-to-cylinder head bolts to 18 ft. lbs. Start the engine and check for leaks.

#### *Spectrum*

**NOTE: On turbocharged model refer to section on Turbocharger Removal & Installation.**

1. Disconnect the negative battery terminal from the battery and the $O_2$ sensor wiring connector.
2. Disconnect the Thermostatic Air Cleaner (TAC) flex hose.
3. Remove the hot air cover and raise the vehicle.
4. Disconnect the exhaust pipe from the exhaust manifold and lower the vehicle.
5. Remove the nuts and bolts securing the exhaust manifold to the cylinder head. Clean the gasket mounting surfaces.
6. To install, use new gaskets and reverse the removal procedures. Torque the exhaust manifold to 17 ft. lbs. or 21 ft. lbs. turbocharged model then start the engine and check for leak

### Sprint and Metro

#### NON TURBOCHARGED ENGINES

1. Disconnect the negative battery cable.
2. Raise and support the vehicle on jackstands.
3. Remove the exhaust pipe at the exhaust manifold.
4. Remove the lower heat shield bolt and the 2nd air pipe at the exhaust manifold.
5. If equipped, remove the A/C drive belt and the lower adjusting bracket.
6. Lower the vehicle.
7. Remove the spark plug and the oxygen sensor wires.
8. Remove the hot air shroud from the exhaust manifold.
9. Remove the 2nd air valve hoses, the valve and the pipe from the exhaust manifold.
10. Remove the mounting bolts and the exhaust manifold.
11. Clean the gasket mating surfaces.
12. To install, use a new gasket and reverse the removal procedures. Torque the exhaust manifold fasteners to 14–20 ft. lbs. and the exhaust pipe to 30–43 ft. lbs.

#### TURBOCHARGED ENGINES

1. Remove the turbocharger assembly. Refer to the Turbocharger removal and installation procedure which follows.
2. Remove the exhaust manifold.
3. Installation is the reverse of removal. Install a new gasket.

## Turbocharger

### REMOVAL & INSTALLATION

#### Spectrum

1. Disconnect the negative battery terminal from the battery.
2. Remove lower and upper heat protector shield covering turbocharger assembly.
3. Remove manifold heat protecter and unplug oxygen sensor.
4. Disconnect vacuum pipe from wastegate and positon out of the way.
5. Disconnect water lines.
6. Disconnect oil lines return and delivery.
7. Disconnect exhaust pipe from wastegate manifold.

**NOTE: Exhaust manifold studs should be soaked with CRC or equivalent to prevent studs from breaking before removal.**

8. Remove turbocharger and wastegate as an assembly.
9. To install, use new a gasket on exhaust manifold to turbocharger housing and reverse the removal procedures. Refill all fluid levels, run engine check for leaks.

#### Sprint and Metro

1. Disconnect the battery ground cable.
2. Drain the cooling system when the engine is cool.
3. Remove the hood.
4. Remove the front grille by removing the four screws and pulling it forward.
5. Remove the intercooler.
6. Remove the radiator hoses.
7. Disconnect the radiator fan motor coupler.
8. Disconnect the front upper member.
9. Remove the A/C condensor, if so equipped.
10. Remove the radiator.
11. Disconnect the front bumper from the damper flange. Place a stand under the front bumper to prevent it from dropping, and remove the couplers clamps and bolts and pull the bumper towards yourself.
12. Disconnect the exhaust pipe bolts.
13. Remove the A/C compressor, if so equipped.
14. Remove the turbocharger cover.
15. Unclamp the oxygen sensor wire.
16. Remove the turbocharger side cover.
17. Lower the exhaust pipe support bracket bolt.
18. Remove the upper exhaust pipe together with the lower exhaust pipe.
19. Disconnect the air outlet pipe.
20. Disconnect the air inlet hose clamp bolt on the cylinder head.
21. Disconnect the air inlet pipe.
22. Disconnect the air inlet pipe from the cylinder block.
23. Disconnect the oil drain hose.
24. Disconnect the water pipe cylinder head clamp bolt.
25. Disconnect the water hoses.

**NOTE: Never adjust or disassemble turbocharger assembly.**

26. Installation is the reverse of removal. Always use new gaskets during installation. Recharge A/C system.

**CAUTION**

***Use care when discharging and/or charging the A/C system. Please refer to "Air Conditioning" in the Unit Repair section***

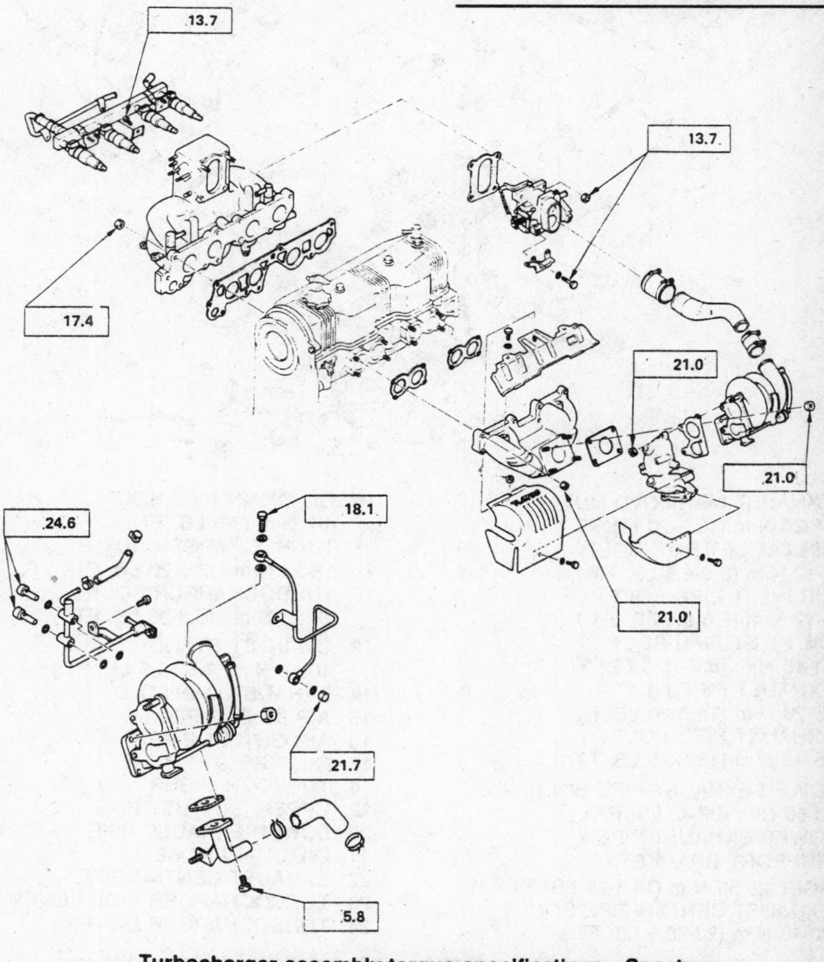


**Turbocharger assembly torque specifications—Spectrum**

## TROUBLESHOOTING

**For more information on turbocharging, please refer to Turbocharging in the Unit Repair section.**

# Combination Manifold

## REMOVAL & INSTALLATION

### *Nova and Prizm*

#### EXCEPT TWINCAM

1. Disconnect the negative terminal from the battery.
2. Remove the air cleaner assembly. Label and disconnect the vacuum hoses.
3. Disconnect the throttle valve and the accelerator cables from the carburetor. Label and disconnect the electrical connectors from the carburetor.
4. Disconnect the fuel line from the fuel pump and drain the excess fuel into a metal container.
5. Disconnect or remove any emission control hardware that may be the way. Remove the carburetor-to-combination manifold nuts and the carburetor from the combination manifold; discard the gasket.

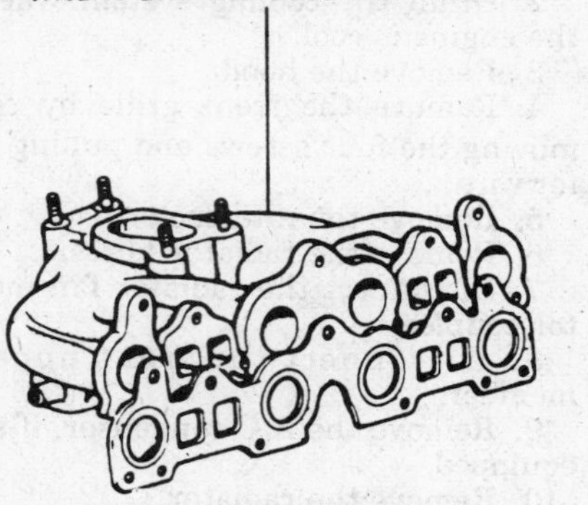


**Combination manifold and gasket—Nova and Prizm**

6. Remove the Early Fuel Evaporation (EFE) gasket. Remove the vacuum line, the dashpot bracket and the carburetor heat shield.
7. Raise and support the front of the vehicle. Remove the exhaust pipe-to-combination manifold bolts, the exhaust bracket from the engine and the air hose from the catalytic converter pipe.
8. Lower the vehicle.
9. Disconnect the brake vacuum hose from the combination manifold. Remove the accelerator and throttle cable brackets.
10. Working from the center outward, remove the combination manifold-to-cylinder head nuts in several stages so tension is gradually released.
11. Remove the combination manifold from the cylinder head.
12. Using a putty knife, clean the gasket mounting surfaces. Inspect the manifold for damage and/or warpage.
13. To install, use new gaskets and reverse the removal procedures. Torque the combination manifold-to-cylinder head bolts to 18 ft. lbs. Start the engine and check for leaks.

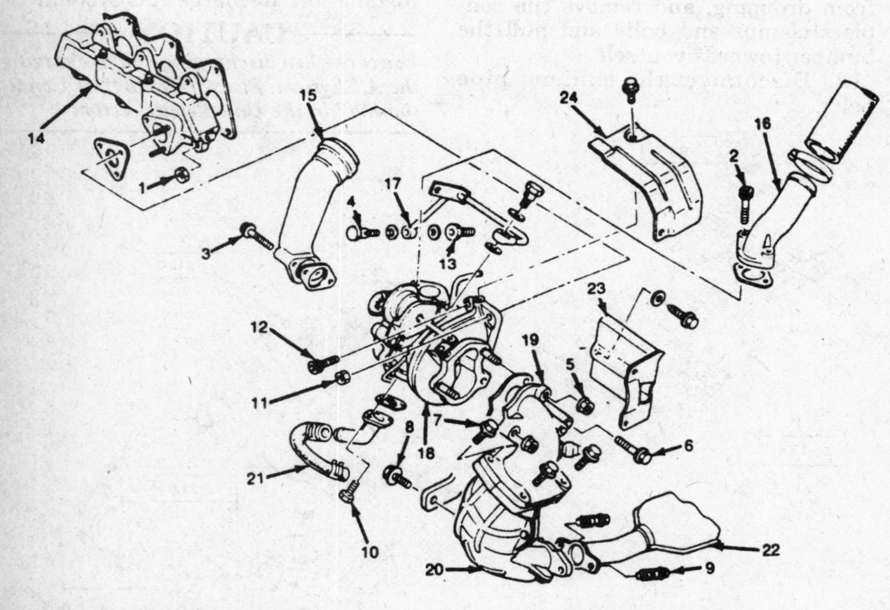


1. EXHAUST MANIFOLD NUT 18-28 N·m (13.5-20 LB. FT.)
2. AIR OUTLET PIPE BOLT 8-12 N·m (6.0-8.5 LB. FT.)
3. AIR INLET PIPE BOLT 8-12 N·m (6.0-8.5 LB. FT.)
4. OIL INLET PIPE BOLT 11-15 N·m (8.0-10.5 LB. FT.)
5. EXHAUST PIPE NUT 18-28 N·m (13.5-20 LB. FT.)
6. EXHAUST PIPE BOLT 25-35 N·m (18.5-25 LB. FT.)
7. LOWER EXHAUST PIPE BOLT 40-60 N·m (29-43 LB. FT.)
8. LOWER EXHAUST PIPE SUPPORT BRACKET BOLT 25-35 N·m (18.5-25 LB. FT.)
9. EXHAUST CENTER PIPE BOLT 30-40 N·m (22-28.5 LB. FT.)
10. OIL DRAIN PIPE BOLT 4-7 N·m (3-5 LB. FT.)
11. TURBOCHARGER NUT 18-28 N·m (13.5-20 LB. FT.)
12. TURBOCHARGER BOLT 18-28 N·m (13.5-20 LB. FT.)
13. OIL INLET STAND 10-15 N·m (7.5-10.5 LB. FT.)
14. EXHAUST MANIFOLD
15. AIR INLET PIPE
16. AIR OUTLET PIPE
17. OIL PIPE
18. TURBOCHARGER
19. UPPER EXHAUST PIPE
20. LOWER EXHAUST PIPE
21. OIL DRAIN HOSE
22. EXHAUST CENTER PIPE
23. TURBOCHARGER SIDE COVER
24. TURBOCHARGER COVER

**Turbocharger and component mounting-exploded view—Sprint and Metro**

# Timing Belt Front Covers

## REMOVAL & INSTALLATION

### *Nova*

#### EXCEPT TWINCAM

This engine uses a 3 piece timing belt cover assembly; any individual cover can be removed by performing one of the following procedures.

**Upper**

1. Disconnect the negative terminal from the battery.
2. Loosen the water pump pulley bolts and remove the alternator/water pump drive belt. If equipped with pow-

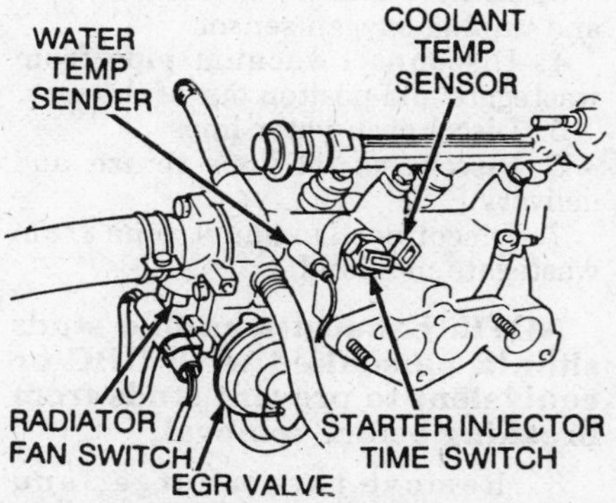


**Temperature sensor locations on intake manifold-turbocharged engine—Sprint and Metro**

er steering, remove the power steering pump drive belt.

3. Remove the water pump pulley bolts and pulley. Drain the cooling system.

4. Disconnect the upper radiator hose from the water pump outlet. Label and disconnect all vacuum hoses that may be in the way.

5. Remove the upper timing belt front cover-to-engine bolts.

**NOTE: To remove the lower timing belt cover-to-engine bolts, it may be necessary to raise and support the vehicle, then, remove them from underneath.**

6. Remove the upper timing belt front cover and gasket.

7. Using a putty knife, clean the gasket mounting surfaces.

8. To install, use a new gasket, sealant (if necessary) and reverse the removal procedures. Adjust the drive belts. Refill the cooling system. Start the engine, allow it to reach normal operating temperatures and check for leaks.

#### Middle

1. Remove the upper timing belt front cover.

2. If equipped with air conditioning, loosen the idler pulley mounting bolt. Loosen the adjusting nut, then, remove the A/C drive belt, the idler pulley (with adjusting bolt).

3. Remove the alternator bolts and move it aside.

4. Remove the middle timing belt front cover-to-engine bolts, the cover and gasket.

5. Using a putty knife, clean the gasket mounting surfaces.

6. To install, use a new gasket, sealant (if necessary) and reverse the removal procedures. Adjust the drive bolts. Refill the cooling system. Start the engine, allow it to reach normal operating temperatures and check for leaks.

#### Lower

1. Disconnect the negative terminal from the battery.

2. Loosen the alternator adjusting bolts and remove the drive belt.

3. If equipped with air conditioning, remove the drive belt.

4. Raise and support the front of the vehicle on jackstands.

5. Remove the right-side under cover, the flywheel cover, the crankshaft pulley-to-crankshaft bolt and the crankshaft pulley.

6. Remove the lower timing belt front cover-to-engine bolts, the cover and gasket.

7. Using a putty knife, clean the gasket mounting surfaces.

8. To install, use a new gasket, sealant (if necessary) and reverse the removal procedures. Torque the crankshaft pulley-to-crankshaft bolt to 80–94 ft. lbs. Adjust the drive belt(s).

#### TWINCAM

This engine uses a three-piece timing belt front cover assembly of an interlocking design. To removal any portion of the cover, disassembly must start from the top and work to the bottom.

1. Disconnect the negative terminal from the battery.

2. Raise and support the front of the vehicle, then, remove the right-side wheel assembly.

3. Remove the under carriage splash shield and drain the cooling system.

4. Disconnect the accelerator cable, the cruise control cable (if equipped), the cruise control actuator (if equipped) and the ignition coil.

5. Remove the water outlet housing-to-engine bolts and the housing.

6. Remove the drive belt from the power steering pimp (if equipped) and the alternator. Disconnect the spark plug wires from the spark plugs and the spark plugs from the engine.

7. To position the No. 1 cylinder on the TDC of its compression stroke, perform the following procedures:

   a. Using a socket wrench on the crankshaft pulley bolt, rotate the crankshaft to align the notch on the crankshaft pulley with the idler pulley bolt.

   b. Remove the oil filler cap and look for the hole in the camshaft; if it cannot be seen, rotate the crankshaft one complete revolution and check for it again.

8. Remove the right-side engine mount, the water pump pulley bolts and the pulley.

9. To remove the crankshaft pulley, perform the following procedures:

   a. Using the crankshaft pulley holding tool No. J-8614-01 or equivalent, secure and hold the pulley while removing the crankshaft pulley-to-crankshaft bolt.

   b. Using the crankshaft pulley puller tool No. J-1859-01 or equivalent, press the crankshaft pulley from the crankshaft.

10. Remove the timing belt front covers-to-engine bolts, the covers and the gaskets.

11. Using a putty knife, clean the gasket mounting surfaces.

12. To install, use new gaskets, sealant (if necessary) and reverse the removal procedures.

13. Using the crankshaft pulley holding tool No. J-8614-01 or equivalent, secure and hold the pulley while installing the crankshaft pulley-to-crankshaft bolt.

14. To complete the installation, reverse the removal procedures. Adjust the drive belts. Refill the cooling system. Start the engine, allow it to reach normal operating temperatures and check for leaks.

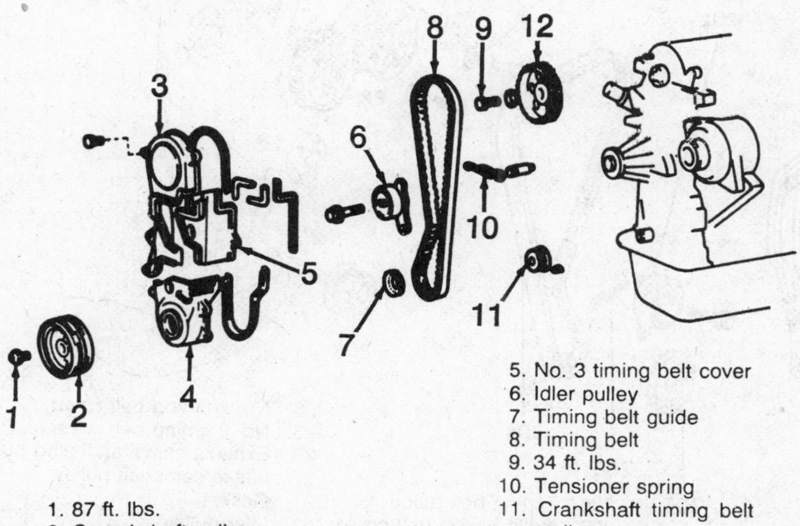


1. 87 ft. lbs.
2. Crannkshaft pulley
3. No. 1 timing belt cover
4. NO. 2 timing belt cover
5. No. 3 timing belt cover
6. Idler pulley
7. Timing belt guide
8. Timing belt
9. 34 ft. lbs.
10. Tensioner spring
11. Crankshaft timing belt pulley
12. Camshaft timing belt pulley

**Exploded view of the timing belt assembly-except twincam engine—Nova**

### *Prizm*

For front cover removal procedures on the Prizm, please refer to the Timing Belt and Tensioner procedure.

### *Spectrum*

1. Disconnect negative battery cable.

2. Support the engine.

3. Remove the front mount bracket attached to the front cover.
4. Remove front cover.
5. To install, reverse the removal procedures.

## Timing Belt and Tensioner

### ADJUSTMENT

#### Nova and Prizm

1. Remove the front cover assembly.
2. Using finger pressure on the longest span between pulleys (except twincam) or between the camshaft pulleys (twincam), measure the timing belt deflection; 4.4 lbs. at 0.24–0.28 in. (except twincam) or 0.16 in. (twincam).
3. If adjustment is not correct, loosen the idler pulley bolt and correct the belt tension.
4. To install, the front covers, reverse the removal procedures.

#### Spectrum

1. Remove the front cover.
2. Loosen the timing belt tension pulley bolt.

**NOTE: If the belt has been removed or replaced with a new one, perform the following procedures to stretch the belt.**

3. Using an Allen wrench, insert it into the hexagonal hole of the tension pulley. Hold the pulley stationary and temporarily tighten the tension pulley-to-engine bolt.
4. Rotate the crankshaft two complete revolutions and align the crankshaft timing pulley groove with the mark on the oil pump.
5. Loosen the tension pulley-to-engine bolt.
6. Using the Allen wrench and a timing belt tension gauge, apply 38 ft. lbs. of tension to the timing belt, hold the pulley stationary and torque the tension pulley-to-engine bolt to 37 ft. lbs.
7. To complete the adjustment, install the front cover.

### REMOVAL & INSTALLATION

#### Nova

1. Remove the front covers.
2. Remove the No. 1 spark plug. Using a socket wrench on the crankshaft pulley bolt, rotate the engine (clockwise) to position the No. 1 cylinder on the TDC of its compression stroke.

**NOTE: The TDC of the No. 1 cylinder is located when air is expelled from the cylinder.**

3. If reusing the timing belt, mark an arrow showing direction of rotation and matchmark the belt to both pulleys.
4. Loosen the idler pulley mounting bolt and push the idler pulley relieve the belt tension, then, retighten the mounting bolt.
5. Remove the timing belt.

**NOTE: Be careful not to bend, twist or turn the belt inside out. Keep grease or water from contacting it. Inspect the belt for cracks, missing teeth or general wear, replace it (if necessary).**

6. Install the timing belt by realigning the matchmarks, the belts directional arrow facing clockwise and adjust the timing belt tension. Rotate the crankshaft 2 complete revolutions and recheck the alignment.
7. To complete the installation, reverse the removal procedures. Torque the idler pulley mounting bolt to 27 ft. lbs. Adjust the timing belt tension. Check and/or adjust the timing.

#### Prizm

1. Raise the front of the vehicle and support it with safety stands. Remove the right wheel and undercover. Remove the air cleaner.
2. Remove the 2 mount nut and stud protectors.
3. Remove the 2 rear transaxle mount to main crossmember nuts.

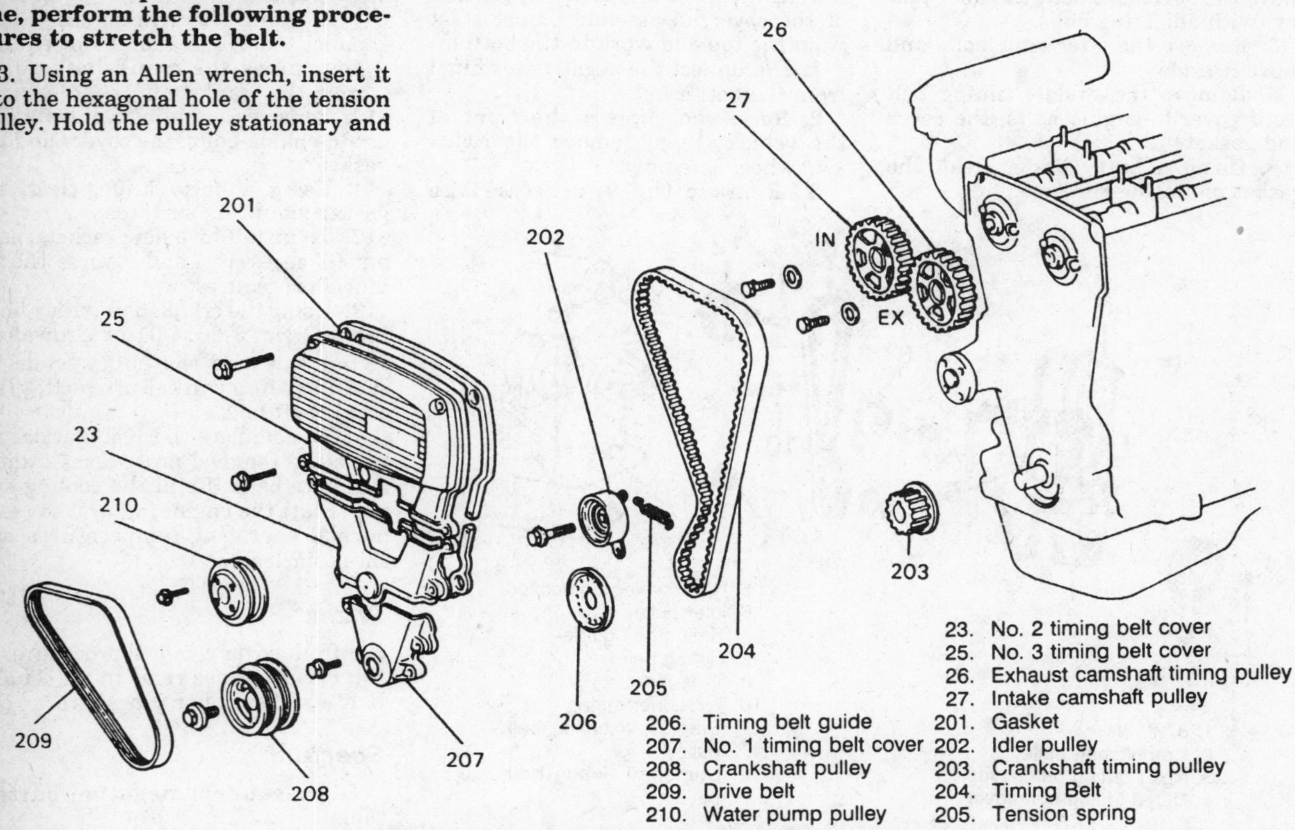


23. No. 2 timing belt cover
25. No. 3 timing belt cover
26. Exhaust camshaft timing pulley
27. Intake camshaft pulley
201. Gasket
202. Idler pulley
203. Crankshaft timing pulley
204. Timing Belt
205. Tension spring
206. Timing belt guide
207. No. 1 timing belt cover
208. Crankshaft pulley
209. Drive belt
210. Water pump pulley

**Exploded view of the timing belt assembly-twincam engine—Nova**

4. Remove the 2 center transaxle mount to center crossmember nuts.

5. lower the vehicle.

6. Remove the drive belts. Remove the power steering pump and the A/C compressor (and their brackets!) and position them out of the way. Leave the hydraulic and refrigerant lines connected.

7. Remove the spark plugs and the cylinder head cover. Be sure to scrape off any left-over gasket material. Rotate the crankshaft pulley so that the **0** mark is in alignment with the groove in the No. 1 front cover. Check that the lifters on the No. 1 cylinder are loose; if not, turn the crankshaft 1 complete revolution (360 degrees).

8. Position a floor jack under the engine and remove the right side engine mounting insulator.

9. Remove the water pump and crankshaft pulleys. The crankshaft pulley will require a two-armed puller.

10. Loosen the 9 bolts and remove the Nos. 1, 2 and 3 front covers. Remove the timing belt guide.

11. Loosen the bolt on the idler pulley, push it to the left as far as it will go and then retighten it. If reusing the timing belt, draw an arrow on it in the direction of engine revolution (clockwise) and then matchmark the belt to the pulleys as indicated.

12. Remove the timing belt. Remove the idler pulley bolt, the pulley and the tension spring.

13. Remove the crankshaft timing pulley.

14. Lock the camshaft and remove the camshaft timing pulleys.

**To install:**

15. Install the camshaft timing pulley so it aligns with the knockpin on the exhaust camshaft. Tighten the pulley to 34 ft. lbs. (47 Nm). Align the mark on the No. 1 camshaft bearing cap with the center of the small hole in the pulley.

16. Install the crankshaft timing pulley so that the marks on the pulley and the oil pump body are in alignment.

17. Install the idler pulley and its tension spring, move it to the left as far as it will go and tighten it temporarily.

18. Align the matchmarks made during removal and then install the timing belt on the camshaft pulley. Loosen the idler pulley set bolt. Make sure the timing belt meshing at the crankshaft pulley does not shift.

19. Rotate the crankshaft clockwise 2 revolutions from TDC to TDC. Make sure that each pulley aligns with the marks made previously. If the marks are not in alignment, the valve timing is wrong. Shift the timing belt meshing slightly and then repeat Steps 14–15.

20. Tighten the set bolt on the timing belt idler pulley to 27 ft. lbs. (37 Nm). Measure the timing belt deflection at the top span between the 2 camshaft pulleys. It should deflect no more than 0.16 in. at 4.4 lbs. of pressure. If deflection is greater, readjust by using the idler pulley.

21.Raise the engine and install the water pump pulley.

22. Lower the engine.

23. Install the right engine mount through bolt and tighten to 64 ft. lbs.

24. Remove the engine support.

25. The remainder of the installation is the reverse of removal.Tighten the center transaxle mount to center crossmember nuts to 45 ft. lbs. and the rear transaxle mount to main crossmember nuts to 45 ft. lbs.

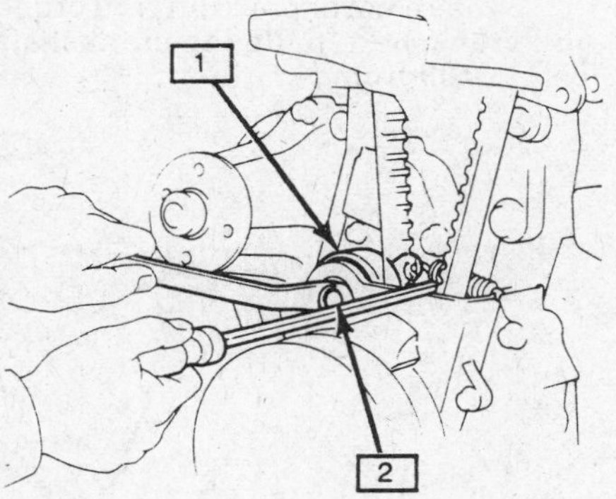


1. Idler pulley
2. Idler pulley mount bolt

**Moving the idler pulley to the left—Prizm**

### *Spectrum*

1. Remove the engine and mount the engine to an engine stand.

2. Remove the accessory drive belts.

3. Remove the engine mounting bracket from the timing cover.

4. Rotate the crankshaft until the notch on the crankshaft pulley aligns with the 0 degree mark on the timing cover and the No. 4 cylinder is on TDC of the compression stroke.

5. Remove the starter and install the flywheel holding tool No. J–35271 or equivalent.

6. Remove the crankshaft bolt, boss and pulley.

7. Remove the timing cover bolts and the timing cover.

8. Loosen the tension pulley bolt.

9. Insert an Allen wrench into the tension pulley hexagonal hole and

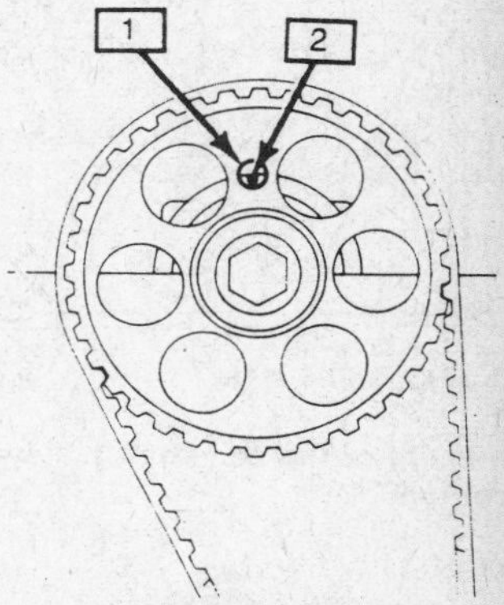


1. Camshaft gear hole
2. Exhaust camshaft cap mark

**Aligning the canshaft gear hole and the exhaust camshaft cap mark—Prizm**

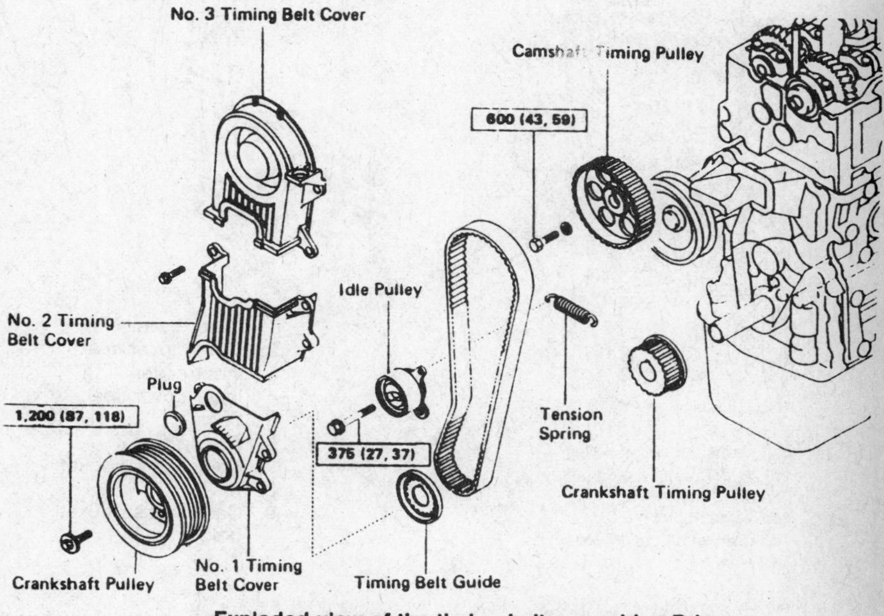


**Exploded view of the timing belt assembly—Prizm**

loosen the timing belt by turning the tension pulley clockwise.

10. Remove the timing belt.
11. Remove the head cover.

**NOTE: Inspect the timing belt for signs of cracking, abnormal wear and hardening. Never expose the belt to oil, sunlight or heat. Avoid excessive bending, twisting or stretching.**

**To install:**

12. Position the Woodruff key on the crankshaft followed by the crankshaft timing gear. Align the groove on the timing gear with the mark on the oil pump.
13. Align the camshaft timing gear mark with the upper surface of the cylinder head and the dowel pin in its uppermost position.
14. Place the timing belt arrow in the direction of the engine rotation and install the timing belt. Tighten the tension pulley bolt.
15. Turn the crankshaft two complete revolutions and realign the crankshaft timing gear groove with the mark on the oil pump.
16. Loosen the tension pulley bolt and apply tension to the belt with an Allen wrench. Torque the pulley bolt to 37 ft. lbs. while holding the pulley stationary.
17. Adjust the valve clearances.
18. To complete the installation, reverse the removal procedures. Torque the crankshaft pulley-to-crankshaft bolt to 109 ft. lbs.

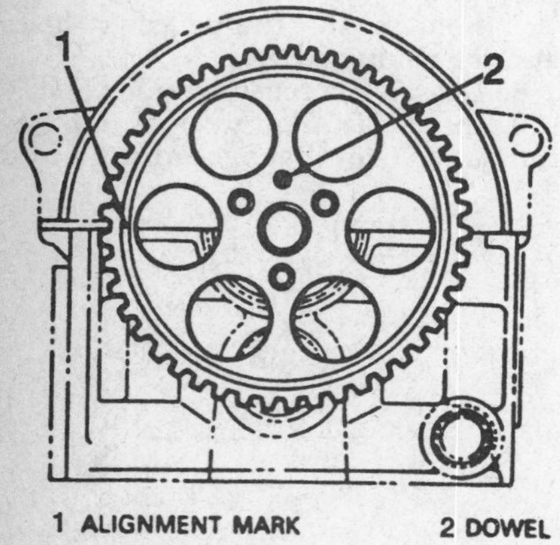


**Alignment of the camshaft pulley—Spectrum**

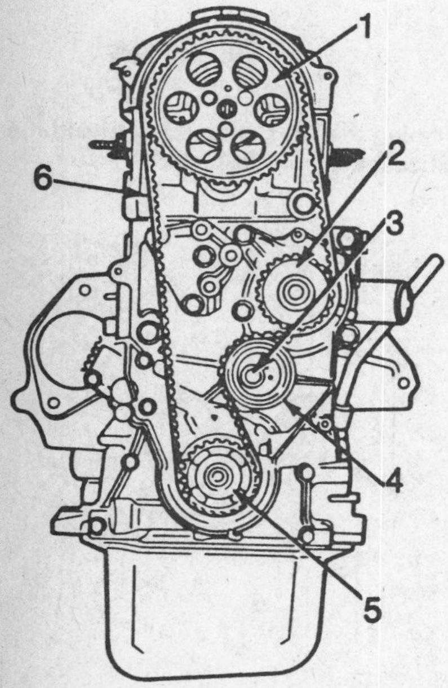


1. Camshaft timing pulley
2. Water pump timing pulley
3. Bolt
4. Tension pulley
5. Crankshaft timing pulley
6. Timing belt

**Timing belt assembly—Spectrum**

# Timing Cover, Belt and Tensioner

## REMOVAL & INSTALLATION

### *Sprint and Metro*

1. Disconnect the negative battery cable.
2. Loosen the water pump pulley bolts and the alternator adjusting bolt.
3. If equipped, remove the A/C compressor adjusting bolt.
4. Raise and support the vehicle on jackstands.
5. Remove the drive belt splash shield, the right fender plug and the drive belts.
6. Remove the crankshaft and the water pump pulleys.
7. Remove the bolts from the bottom of the belt cover.
8. Lower the vehicle.

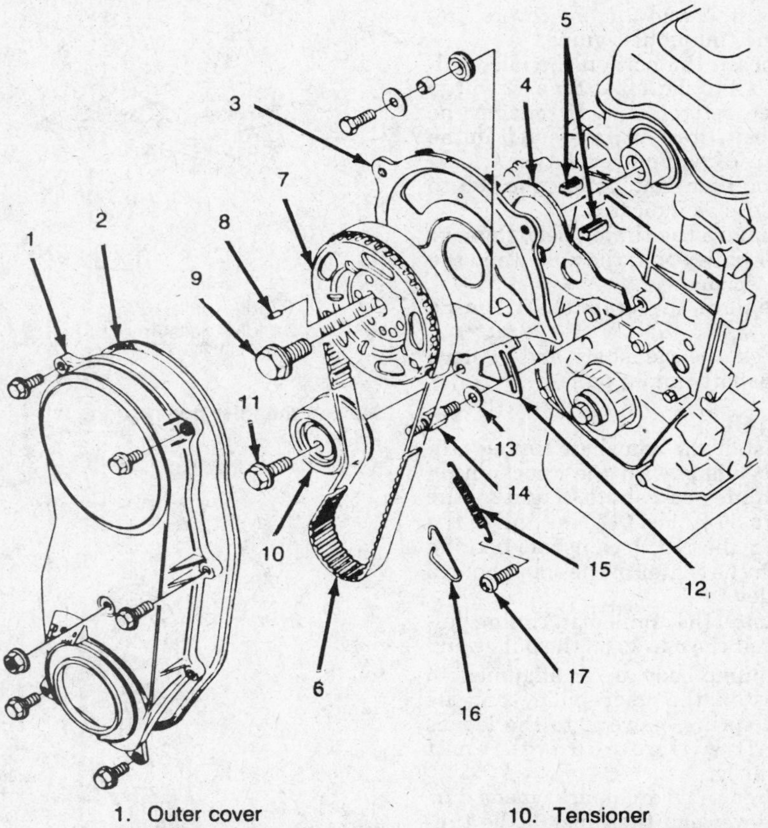


1. Outer cover
2. Outer cover seal
3. Inner cover
4. Inner cover seal
5. Seal
6. Timing belt
7. Camshaft sprocket
8. Pin
9. Camshaft sprocket bolt
10. Tensioner
11. Tensioner bolt
12. Tensioner plate
13. Washer
14. Tensioner stud
15. Tensioner spring
16. Spring damper
17. Spring screw

**Timing belt, tensioner and sprockets-exploded view—Sprint and Metro**

9. Remove the bolts from the top of the belt cover and the cover.
10. Remove the cylinder head cover and loosen the rocker arm adjusting bolts.
11. Remove the distributor cap.
12. Loosen the tensioner pulley and adjusting stud bolt.
13. Remove the timing belt, the tensioner, the tensioner plate and spring.

**To install:**

14. Install the tensioner assembly but DO NOT tighten the bolts.
15. Turn the camshaft pulley clockwise and align the mark on the pulley with theVmark on the inside cover.
16. Using a 17mm wrench, turn the crankshaft clockwise and align the punch mark on the crankshaft pulley with the arrow mark on the oil pump.
17. With the timing marks aligned, install the timing belt so that there is no belt slack on the right side (facing the engine) of the engine, apply belt tension with the tensioner pulley.
18. Turn the crankshaft 1 rotation clockwise to remove the belt slack. Torque the tensioner stud, first, and then the tensioner bolt to 17–21 ft. lbs.
19. To complete the installation, use new gaskets and reverse the removal procedures. Torque the crankshaft pulley to 7–9 ft. lbs. Adjust the valve clearances.

## Timing Sprockets

### REMOVAL & INSTALLATION

#### *Nova*

#### EXCEPT TWINCAM

1. Remove the timing belt.
2. To remove the crankshaft timing belt pulley, simply pull it and the key from the crankshaft.
3. To remove the camshaft pulley, perform the following procedures:
   a. Remove the valve cover.
   b. Using an open end wrench, place it on the camshaft flats to secure it.
   c. Using a socket wrench on the camshaft pulley bolt, remove the camshaft pulley bolt and the camshaft pulley.
4. To install the timing belt pulleys, reverse the removal procedures. Torque the camshaft pulley-to-camshaft bolt to 34 ft. lbs.
5. After installing the crankshaft pulley bolt, rotate the crankshaft two complete revolutions and recheck the alignment. Check and/or adjust the timing belt tension. Torque the idler pulley mounting bolt to 27 ft. lbs.
6. To complete the installation, reverse the removal procedures.

#### TWINCAM

1. Remove the timing belt.

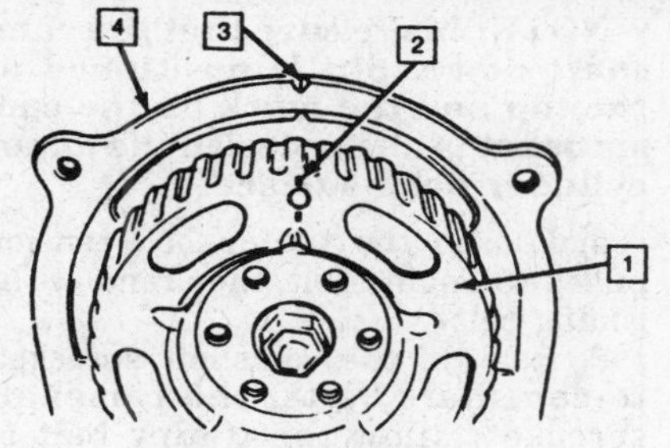

1. CAMSHAFT PULLEY
2. TIMING MARK
3. "V" MARK
4. BELT INSIDE COVER

**Camshaft sprocket and inner belt cover timing mark alignment—Sprint and Metro**

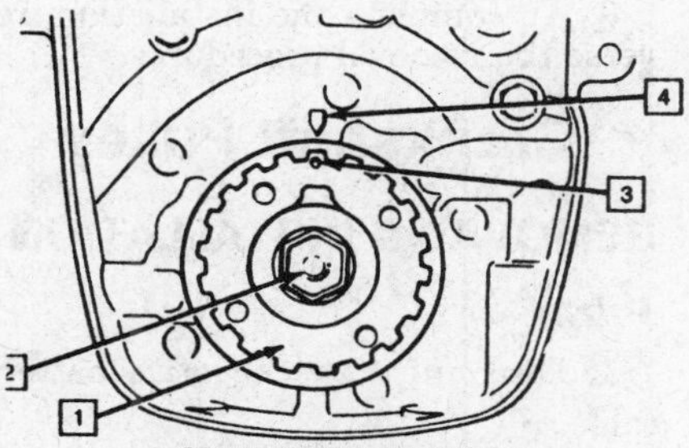

1. CRANK TIMING BELT PULLEY
2. PULLEY BOLT (17 mm)
3. PUNCH MARK
4. ARROW MARK

**Crankshaft sprocket and oil pump timing mark alignment—Sprint and Metro**

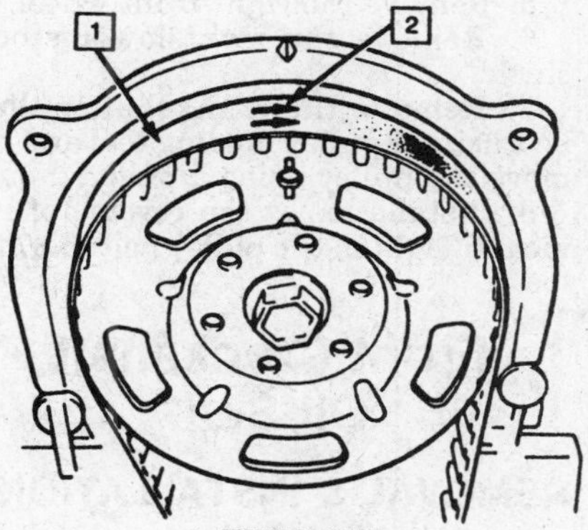

1. TIMING BELT
2. ARROW MARK

**Arrow marks on timing belt show direction of rotation—Sprint and Metro**

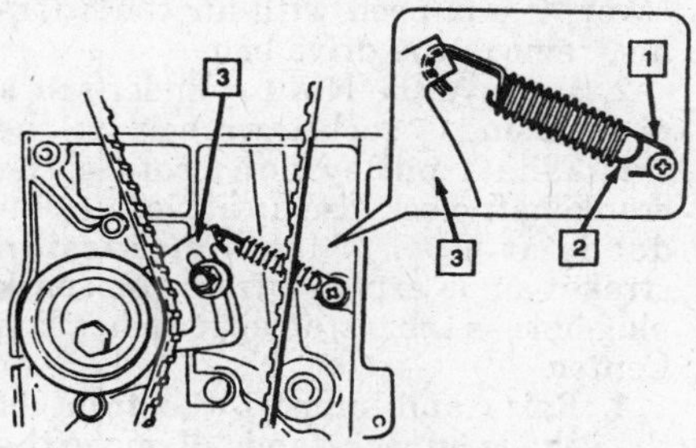

1. TENSIONER SPRING
2. SPRING DAMPER
3. TENSIONER PLATE

**Installing tensioner spring and dampner—Sprint and Metro**

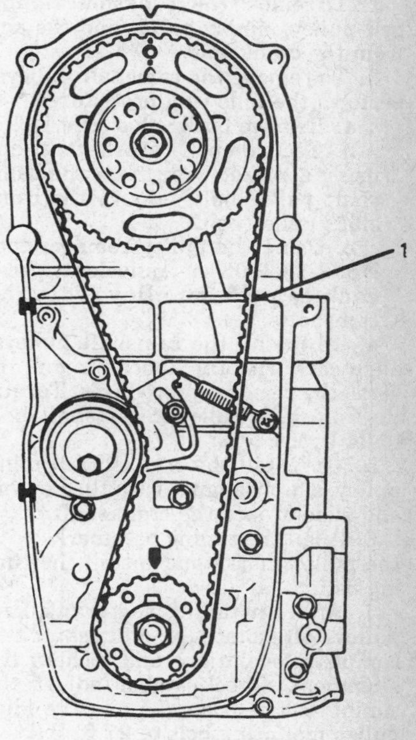

1. DRIVE SIDE OF BELT

**View of the timing belt assembly—Sprint and Metro**

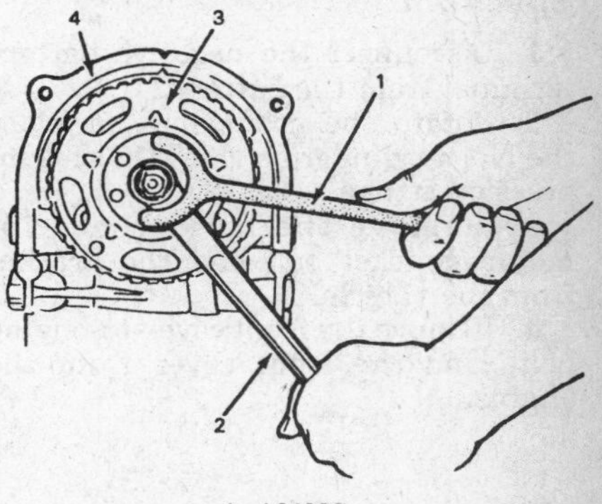

1. J-34836
2. WRENCH
3. CAMSHAFT TIMING BELT PULLEY
4. TIMING BELT INSIDE COVER

**Removing the camshaft pulley bolt using a lock holder tool—Sprint and Metro**

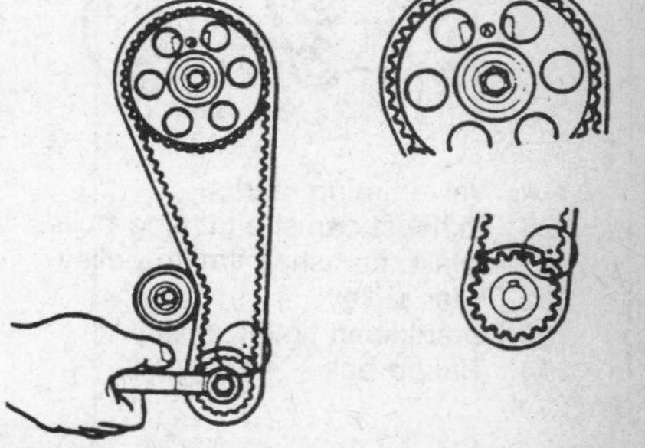

**Aligning the valve timing marks except twincam engine—Nova**

2. To remove the crankshaft timing belt pulley, simply pull it and the key from the crankshaft.

3. To remove the camshaft pulleys, perform the following procedures:

a. Remove both valve covers.

b. Secure each camshaft, then, using a socket wrench on the camshaft pulley bolt, remove the camshaft pulley bolt.

c. Using the pulley remover tool No. J-1859-03 or equivalent, press each camshaft pulley from the camshafts.

4. To install the camshaft pulleys, align each with the knock pin and reverse the removal procedures. Torque the camshaft pulley-to-camshaft bolt to 34 ft. lbs.

5. To install the crankshaft timing pulley, simply align it with the keyway and slide it onto the crankshaft.

6. Align the timing belt marks with the pulley marks and install the timing belt.

7. After installing the crankshaft pulley bolt, rotate the crankshaft two complete revolutions and recheck the alignment. Check and/or adjust the timing belt tension. Torque the idler pulley mounting bolt to 27 ft. lbs.

8. To complete the installation, reverse the removal procedures.

### *Spectrum*

1. Disconnect the negative battery terminal from the battery.

2. Rotate the crankshaft to place the No. 4 cylinder on the TDC of compression stroke.

3. Remove the front cover-to-mount bracket bolt and the bracket from the vehicle.

4. Remove the front cover-to-engine bolts and the front cover from the engine.

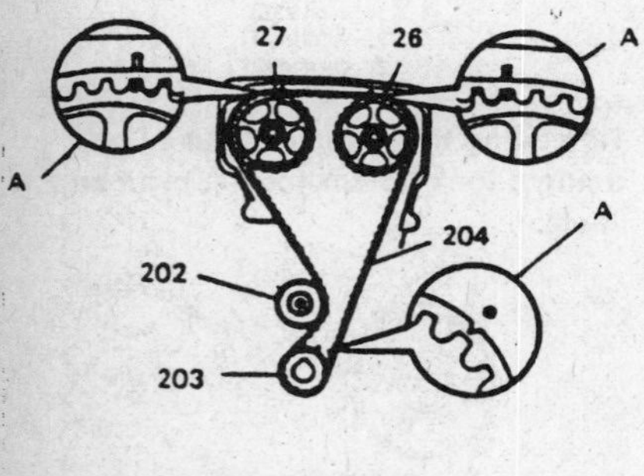


A. Valve timing marks
26. Exhaust camshaft timing pulley
27. Intake camshaft timing pulley
202. Idler pulley
203. Crankshaft timing pulley
204. Timing belt

**Aligning the valve timing marks-twincam engine—Nova**

**NOTE: Make sure that the camshaft dowel pin is positioned at the top and the mark on the cam sprocket is aligned with the upper cylinder head surface.**

5. Loosen the timing belt tension pulley-to-engine bolt, then remove the timing belt.

6. Remove the camshaft sprocket-to-camshaft bolts, the camshaft sprocket; allow the timing belt to hang.

7. If the engine has not been disturbed, reverse the removal procedures. Torque the camshaft sprocket-to-camshaft bolt to 7.2 ft. lbs. Adjust the timing belt.

8. To complete the installation, reverse the removal procedures.

# Crankshaft Pulley

## REMOVAL & INSTALLATION

### *Prizm*

1. Disconnect the negative battery cable.

2. Loosen the A/C compressor, power steering pump, and alternator and set aside. Do not disconnect hoses.

3. Remove the accessory drive belts.

4. Raise and support the vehicle safely.

5. Remove the right front wheel.

6. Remove the right lower stone shield.

7. Remove the crankshaft pulley bolt using a pulley holding tool and remove the pulley using a puller.

8. Installation is the reverse of removal. Tighten the pulley bolt to 87 ft. lbs.

# Front Crankshaft Oil Seal

## REMOVAL & INSTALLATION

### *Nova and Prizm*

#### EXCEPT TWINCAM

1. Remove the upper timing belt cover. If equipped with air conditioning, remove the drive belt.

2. Remove the No. 1 cylinder spark plug. Using a socket wrench on the crankshaft pulley bolt, rotate the crankshaft clockwise until No. 1 cylinder is at TDC of its compression stroke; air is expelled from the spark plug hole as the piston approaches Top Center.

3. Raise and support the front of the vehicle on jackstands. Remove the right-side under cover and the flywheel cover.

4. Remove the crankshaft pulley-to-crankshaft bolt and the pulley.

5. Remove the lower timing belt front cover-to-engine bolts, cover and gasket. Mark the locations of the timing belt to both timing pulleys and the rotating direction of the belt.

6. Loosen the idler pulley bolt and move the idler to relieve the belt tension, then, retighten the bolt to retain the tensioner in the released position.

7. Remove the timing belt guide, the timing belt from the crankshaft timing pulley and the timing pulley from the crankshaft.

8. Using a small pry bar, pry the oil seal from oil pump; be careful not to damage the sealing surfaces.

9. To install the new oil seal, lubricate the sealing lips with multi-purpose grease, then, using the oil seal driver tool No. J-35403 or equivalent, drive the new seal into the oil pump until it seats; make sure the seal is square in the bore (not cocked).

10. To complete the installation, adjust the timing belt tension and reverse the removal procedures. Rotate the crankshaft through two complete revolutions and recheck the timing. Start the engine and check for oil leaks.

#### TWINCAM

1. Remove the timing belt.

2. Using a small pry bar, pry the oil seal from oil pump; be careful not to damage the sealing surfaces.

3. To install the new oil seal, lubricate the sealing lips with multi-purpose grease, then, using the oil seal driver tool No. J-35403 or equivalent, drive the new seal into the oil pump until it seats; make sure the seal is square in the bore (not cocked).

4. To complete the installation, adjust the timing belt tension and reverse the removal procedures. Rotate the crankshaft through two complete revolutions and recheck the timing. Start the engine and check for oil leaks.

### *Spectrum*

1. Remove the engine.

2. Drain the crankcase.

3. Remove the alternator belt and the starter.

4. Install the flywheel holding tool No. J-35271 or equivalent, to secure the flywheel.

5. Remove the crankshaft pulley and boss.

6. Remove the timing cover bolts and the timing cover.

7. Loosen the tension pulley and remove the timing belt.

8. Remove the crankshaft timing gear and the tension pulley.

9. Remove the oil pan bolts, oil pan, oil strainer fixing bolt and the oil strainer assembly.

10. Remove the oil pump bolts and the oil pump assembly.

11. Remove the sealing material from the oil pump and engine block sealing surfaces.

**NOTE: The oil seal is part of the oil pump assembly.**

12. With the oil pump removed from the engine, pry the oil seal from the oil pump housing with a small pry bar.

13. To install the new oil seal, drive it into the housing using the seal installing tool No. J-35269 or equivalent.

14. To install the pump, lubricate the oil pump, use new gaskets, apply sealant to the sealing surfaces and reverse the removal procedures.

## Camshaft

### REMOVAL & INSTALLATION

#### *Nova*

#### EXCEPT TWINCAM

1. Remove the upper timing belt front cover and the valve cover; DO NOT remove the timing belt.
2. Disconnect the spark plug wires, then, remove the distributor-to-engine hold-down bolt, the distributor and the distributor gear bolt.
3. Disconnect the hoses from the fuel pump, then, remove the fuel pump.
4. Using a socket wrench on the crankshaft pulley bolt, rotate the crankshaft (clockwise) to position the No. 1 cylinder on the TDC of its compression stroke; the rocker arms of the No. 1 cylinder will be loose, if not, rotate the crankshaft one complete revolution.
5. Loosen the rocker arm adjusting nuts and back off the adjusting screw. Remove the rocker shaft-to-cylinder head assembly.
6. Place alignment marks on the timing belt and the timing pulleys; also, mark the direction of timing belt rotation.
7. Loosen the idler pulley bolt and push the pulley as far left as possible, then, retighten the bolt. Remove the timing belt from the camshaft timing pulleys, support it so it will remain in mesh with the crankshaft pulley; be careful not to get oil on the timing belt.
8. Use a large open-end wrench, secure the camshaft (on the flats), then, remove the camshaft pulley-to-camshaft bolt; the camshaft flats are located between the first and second cam lobes. Remove the camshaft pulley.
9. Remove the camshaft bearing cap bolts, the caps and the camshaft; keep the caps in order for reinstallation purposes.
10. Remove the distributor drive gear.
11. Inspect the camshaft for damage and/or wear; if necessary, replace the camshaft.
12. To install, insert the distributor drive gear, plate washer and bolt.
13. Using clean engine oil, coat all bearing surfaces, then, install the camshaft and No. 2, 3 and 4 bearing caps (in their proper positions and direction).
14. To install a new camshaft oil seal, apply grease the oil seal lips and sealant to the outside edge, then, slip the seal onto the camshaft; make sure it is on straight, as a crooked seal will leak.
15. Using sealant, apply it to the bottom surfaces of the No. 1 bearing cap and install it. Install all bearing cap bolts finger tight.
16. Torque the bearing cap bolts (alternately and evenly) to 8–10 ft. lbs.
17. Using a dial indicator, inspect the camshaft thrust clearance (front-to-rear movement; it should be 0.0031–0.0071 in. with a limit of 0.0098 in. Torque the distributor drive gear bolt to 22 ft. lbs.
18. To complete the installation, adjust the valves, use new gaskets, sealant (if necessary) and reverse the removal procedures. Start the engine, allow it to reach normal operating temperatures and check for leaks.

#### TWINCAM

1. Remove the cylinder head covers and the camshaft pulleys.
2. Loosen and remove the camshaft bearing caps-to-cylinder head bolts in sequence. Remove the camshaft bearing caps and camshafts; be sure to keep the parts in order for reinstallation purposes.
3. Using a putty knife, clean the gasket mounting surfaces. Inspect the camshaft for wear and/or damage, if necessary, replace the camshaft.
4. Using clean engine oil, coat all bearing surfaces, then, install the camshaft and No. 2, 3 and 4 bearing caps (in their proper positions and direction).
5. To install a new camshaft oil seal, apply grease the oil seal lips and sealant to the outside edge, then, slip the seal onto the camshaft; make sure it is on straight, as a crooked seal will leak.
6. Using sealant, apply it to the bottom surfaces of the No. 1 bearing cap and install it. Install all bearing cap bolts finger tight.
7. Torque the bearing cap bolts (alternately and evenly) to 8–10 ft. lbs.
8. Using a dial indicator, inspect the camshaft thrust clearance (front-to-rear movement; it should be 0.0031–0.0075 in. with a limit of 0.0118 in. Torque the distributor drive gear bolt to 22 ft. lbs.
9. To complete the installation, adjust the valves, use new gaskets, sealant (if necessary) and reverse the removal procedures. Start the engine, allow it to reach normal operating temperatures and check for leaks.

#### *Prizm*

1. Disconnect the negative battery cable at the battery. Drain the engine coolant.
2. Remove the spark plugs and the cylinder head cover.

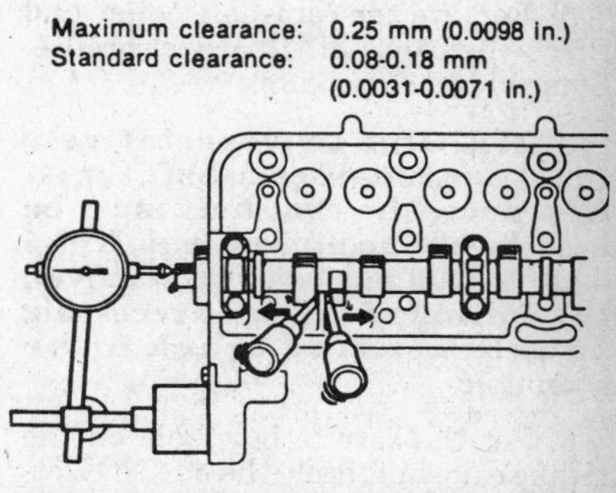


**Checking the camshaft thrust clearance-except twincam engine – Nova**

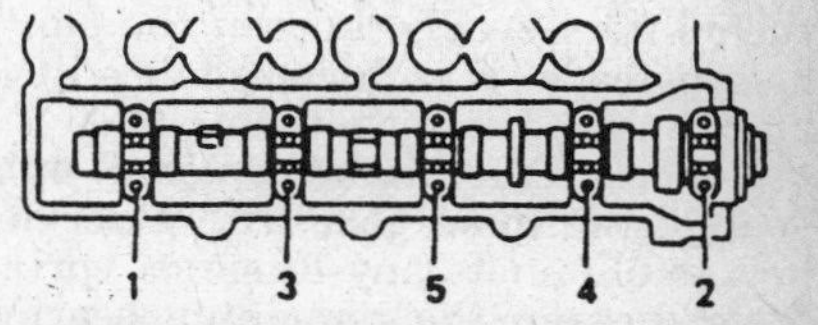


**Camshaft bearing cap removal sequence -twincam engine – Nova**

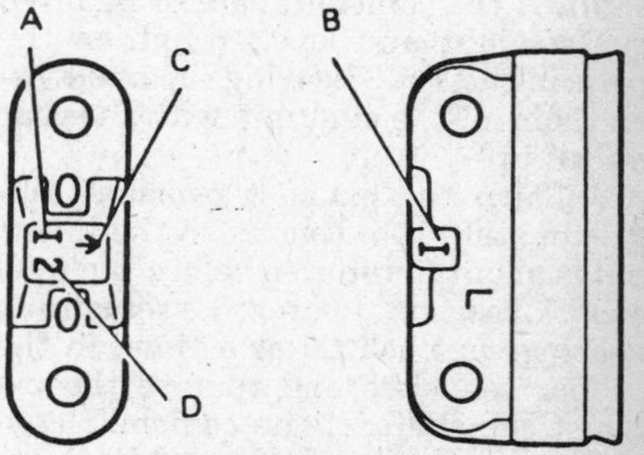


A. I = intake; E = exhaust
B. I = intake; E = exhaust
C. Front Mark
D. I.D. for bearings No. 2–5

**View of the camshaft bearing caps-twincam engine – Nova**

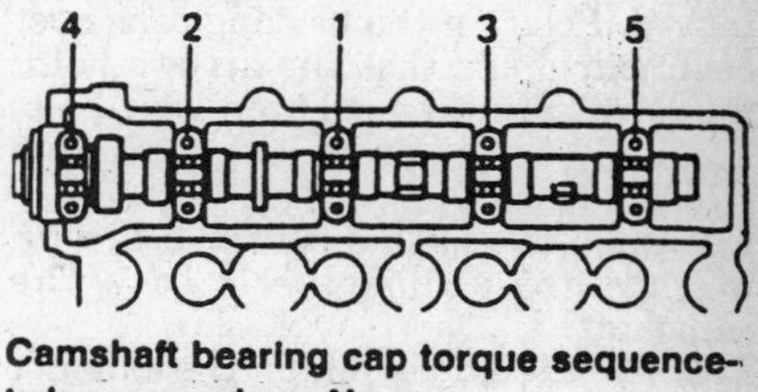


**Camshaft bearing cap torque sequence-twincam engine – Nova**

3. Remove the No. 3 and No. 2 front covers. Turn the crankshaft pulley and align its groove with the **0** mark on the No. 1 front cover. Check that the camshaft pulley hole aligns with the mark on the No. 1 camshaft bearing cap (exhaust side).

4. Remove the plug from the No. 1 front cover and matchmark the timing belt to the camshaft pulley. Loosen the idler pulley mounting bolt and push the pulley to the left as far as it will go; tighten the bolt. Slide the timing belt off the camshaft pulley and support it so it won't fall into the case.

5. Remove the camshaft pulley and check the camshaft thrust clearance. Remove the camshafts.

**NOTE: Due to the relatively small amount of camshaft thrust clearance, the camshaft must be held level during removal. If the camshaft is not level on removal, the portion of the head receiving the thrust may crack or be damaged.**

6. Set the service bolt hole on the intake camshaft gear (the one NOT attached to the timing pulley!) at the 12 o'clock position so that the Nos. 1 and 3 cylinder camshaft lobed can push their lifters evenly. Loosen the No. 1 bearing caps on each camshaft a little at a time and remove them.

7. Secure the intake camshaft sub-gear to the main gear with a service bolt to eliminate any torsional spring force. Loosen the remaining bearing caps a little at a time, in the proper sequence and remove the intake camshaft. If the camshaft cannot be lifted out straight and level, retighten the bolts in the No. 3 bearing cap and loosen them a little at a time with the gear pulled up.

8. Turn the exhaust camshaft approximately 105 degrees so the knock pin is about 5 minutes before the 6:30 o'clock position. Loosen the remaining bearing caps a little at a time, in the proper sequence and remove the exhaust camshaft. If the camshaft cannot be lifted out straight and level, retighten the bolts in the No. 3 bearing cap and loosen them a little at a time with the gear pulled up.

**To install:**

9. Position the exhaust camshaft into the cylinder head as it was removed. Position the bearing caps over each journal so that the arrows point forward and then tighten the bolts gradually, in the proper sequence to 9 ft. lbs. (13 Nm).

10. Coat the lip of a new oil seal with MP grease and drive it into the camshaft.

11. Set the knock pin on the exhaust camshaft so it is just above the edge of the cylinder head and engage the intake camshaft gear to the exhaust gear so that the mark on each gear is in alignment. Roll the intake camshaft down onto the bearing journals while engaging the gears with each other.

12. Position the bearing caps over each journal on the intake camshaft so that the arrows point forward and then tighten the bolts gradually, in the proper sequence to 9 ft. lbs. (13 Nm).

13. Remove the service bolt and install the No. 1 intake bearing cap. If it does not fit properly, pry the camshaft gear backwards until it does. Tighten the bolts to 9 ft. lbs. (13 Nm).

14. Rotate the camshafts 1 revolution (360 degrees) from TDC to TDC and check that the marks on the 2 gears are still aligned.

15. Install the camshaft timing pulley making sure that the camshaft knock pins and the matchmarks are in alignment. Lock each camshaft and tighten the pulley bolts to 43 ft. lbs. (59 Nm).

16. Align the matchmarks made during removal and then install the timing belt on the camshaft pulley. Loosen the idler pulley set bolt. Make sure the timing belt meshing at the crankshaft pulley does not shift.

17. Rotate the crankshaft clockwise 2 revolutions from TDC to TDC. Make sure that each pulley aligns with the marks made previously.

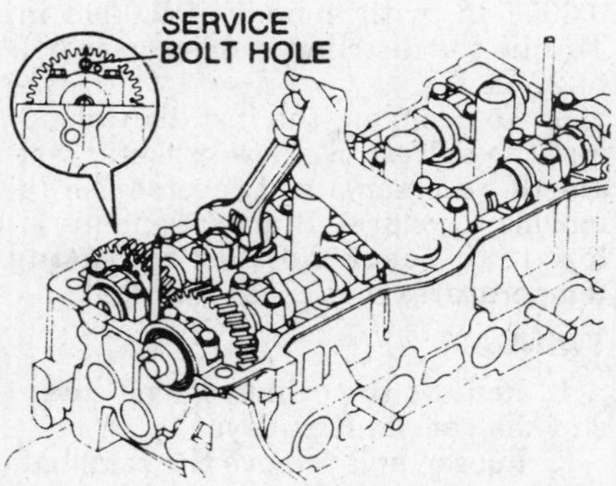


Service bolt hole positioning (intake camshaft)—Prizm

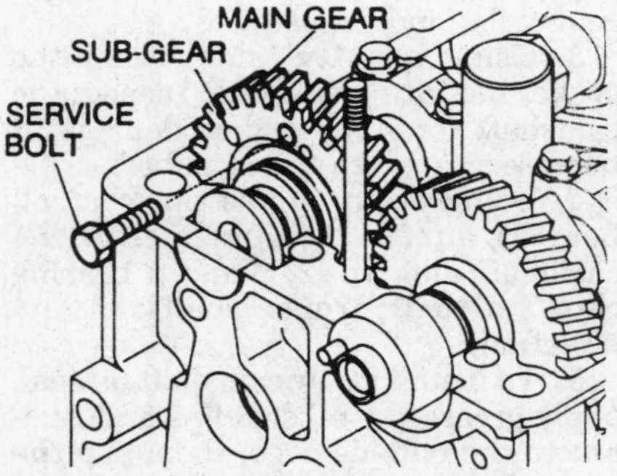


Installing the service bolt in the intake camshaft—Prizm

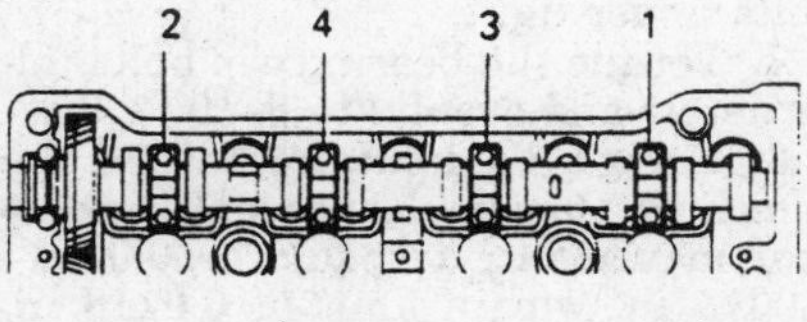


Camshaft bearing cap bolt LOOSENING sequence—Prizm

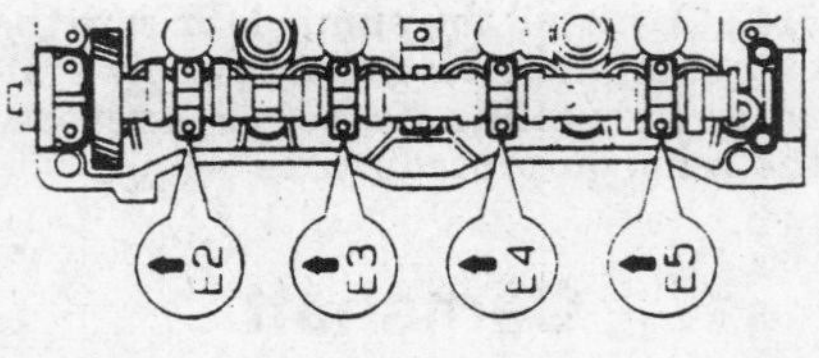


Exhaust camshaft bearing cap positioning—Prizm

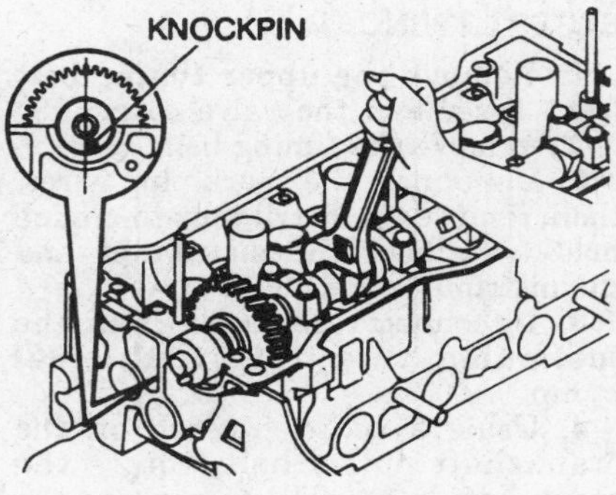


Knockpin positioning on the exhaust camshaft—Prizm

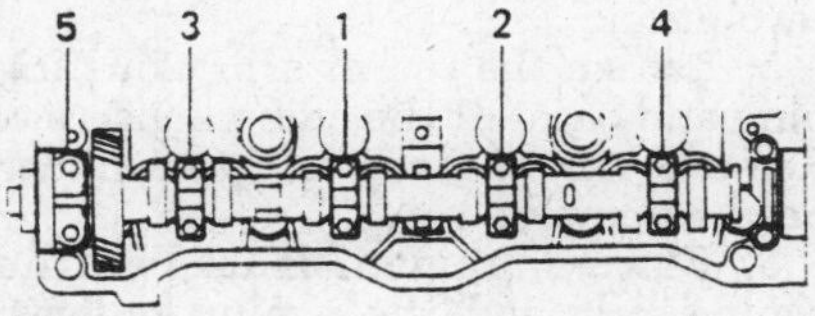


Camshaft bearing cap bolt TIGHTENING sequence—Prizm

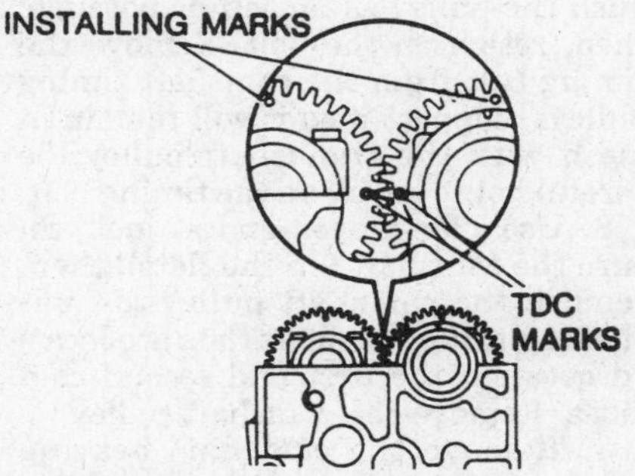


Rotate the camshaft one revolution from TDC to TDC and check that the marks are lined up—Prizm

18. Tighten the set bolt on the timing belt idler pulley to 27 ft. lbs. (37 Nm). Measure the timing belt deflection at the top span between the 2 camshaft pulleys. It should deflect no more than 0.16 in. at 4.4 lbs. of pressure. If deflection is greater, readjust by using the idler pulley.

19. Installation of the remaining components is in the reverse order of removal.

### Spectrum

1. Disconnect the negative battery terminal from the battery.
2. Align the crankshaft pulley notch with the 0 degree mark on the timing cover.
3. Remove the cylinder head cover.
4. Remove the timing cover.
5. Loosen the camshaft timing gear bolts (DO NOT rotate the engine).
6. Loosen the timing belt tensioner and remove the timing belt from the camshaft timing gear.
7. Remove the rocker arm shaft/rocker arm assembly.
8. Remove the distributor bolt and the distributor.
9. Remove the camshaft and the camshaft seal.
10. To install, drive a new camshaft seal on the camshaft using the seal installation tool No. J–35268 or equivalent, reverse the removal procedures, adjust the valves and the timing belt.

### Sprint and Metro

1. Remove the timing belt.
2. Remove the air cleaner, rocker arm cover, distributor and distributor case. Remove the rocker arm shafts and the rocker arms.
3. Remove the fuel pump and fuel pump push rod from the cylinder head.
4. Using a spanner wrench tool J-34836 to hold the camshaft pulley, remove the camshaft pulley bolt, the pulley, the alignment pin and the inside cover.
5. Carefully slide the camshaft from the rear of the cylinder head.
6. Clean the gasket mounting surfaces. Check for wear and/or damage, replace the parts as necessary.
7. To install, use new gaskets/seals and reverse the removal procedures. Torque the camshaft pulley bolt to 41–46 ft. lbs. Adjust the valve clearances and check the timing.

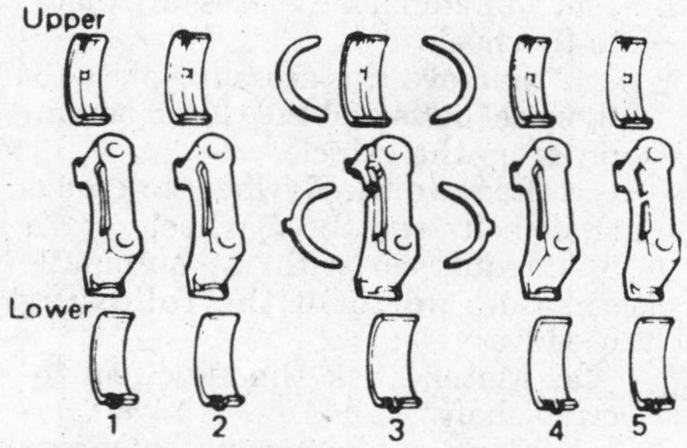


**Correct positioning of crankshaft bearing shells. Note that the grooved shells must be at the top to lubricate the connecting rods—Nova and Prizm**

## Piston and Connecting Rod

### POSITIONING

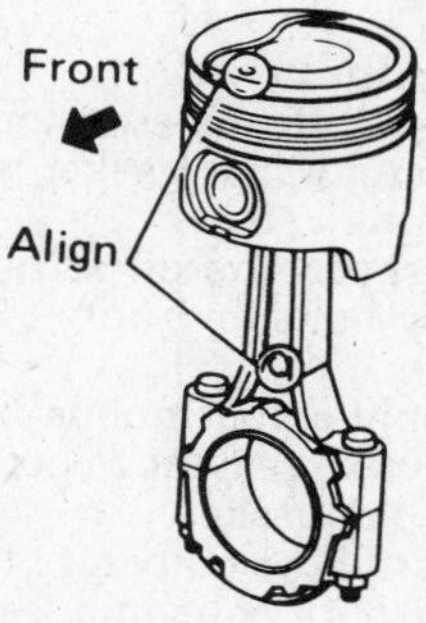


**Piston alignment marks**

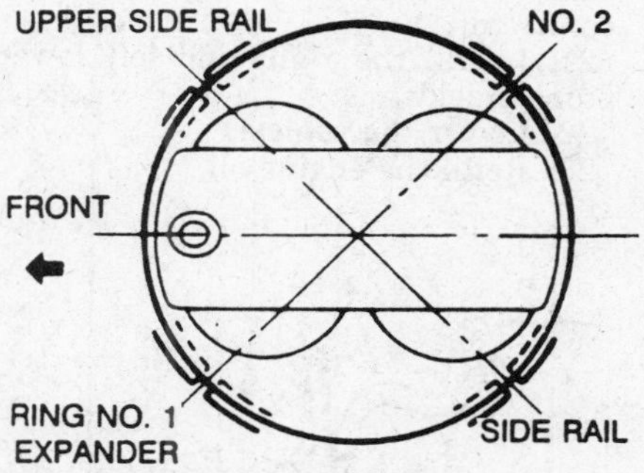


**Piston ring gap positioning—4A-F, 4A-GE engine**

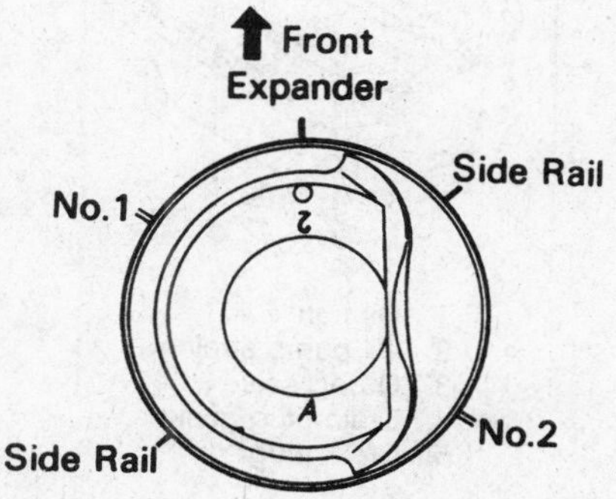


**Piston ring gap positioning—4A-LC engine**

### Nova and Prizm

Note the locations of main bearings. Upper bearings are grooved for distribution of oil to the connecting rods, while the lower mains are plain. Thrust is taken by washer shaped bearings located on both sides of the center (No. 3) bearing cap, with tabs on the lower washers which fit into notches in the lower cap. Note that both the piston crowns and connecting rods have marks which must face forward when assembling the engine. Note also the sequence of ring installation; in fact the upper outside diameter of the No. 2 compression ring is smaller than the lower O.D., while the No. 1 compression ring has an even, barrel face. Note also the positioning of the oil ring expander and side rail. **For all piston and connecting rod overhaul procedures, please refer to "Engine Rebuilding" in the Unit Repair section.**

### Spectrum

Install the piston and rod assemblies into the same cylinder bore, facing the same direction from which they were removed. Each piston has a front directional mark stamped on the top surface.

### Sprint and Metro

There are 2 sizes of pistons available: a

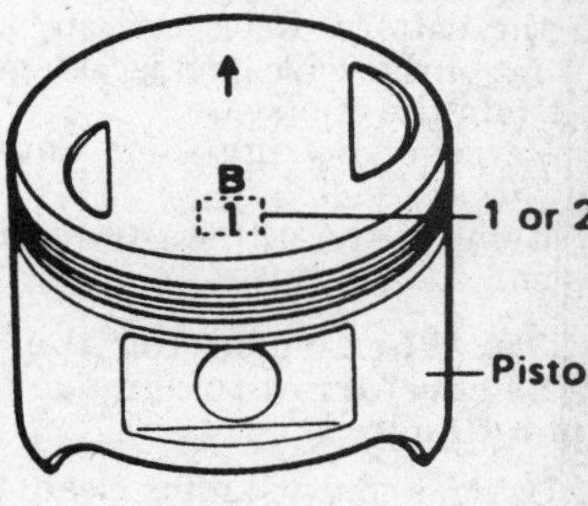


**Piston identification—Sprint and Metro**

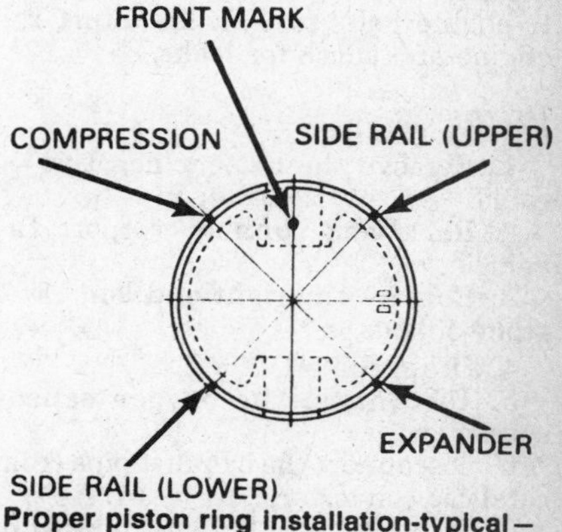


**Proper piston ring installation-typical—Spectrum**

No. 1 and a No. 2 (indicating the outside diameter of the piston), the numbers are stamped on top of each piston. An arrow is also stamped on top of each piston, indicating the front of the engine.

A number is stamped at the front right of the engine block, on the cylinder head gasket surface. The number indicates of the pistons sizes, in order, ranging from the front-to-rear cylinders. Install the correct diameter piston (with the arrow facing the front of the engine) and the connecting rod (with the oil hole facing the intake manifold) into the correct cylinder bore.

**For all piston and connecting rod overhaul procedures, please refer to the "Engine Rebuilding" in the Unit Repair section.**

# ENGINE LUBRICATION

## Oil Pan

### REMOVAL & INSTALLATION

#### *Nova*

1. Disconnect the negative terminal from the battery. Raise and support the front of the vehicle on jackstands.
2. Drain the crankcase.
3. Remove the right-side undercover.
4. Remove the oil pan-to-engine bolts and the oil pan.

**NOTE: When removing the oil pan, be careful not to damage the oil pan flange.**

5. Using a putty knife, clean the gasket mounting surfaces.
6. To install, use a new gasket, sealant (if necessary) and reverse the removal procedures. Torque the oil pan-to-engine bolts to 4 ft. lbs. Start the engine and check for leaks.

#### *Prizm*

1. Remove the battery negative (-) cable.
2. Raise and suitably support the vehicle.
3. Remove the right and left lower stone shields.
4. Drain the oil.
5. Disconnect the oxygen sensor connector.
6. Disconnect the exhaust pipe from catalytic converter.
7. Disconnect the exhaust pipe from exhaust manifold.
8. Remove the two nuts and 19 bolts from the oil pan.
9. Remove the oil pan.

**NOTE: Use caution when removing the oil pan on the oil pump body side since damage to the pump body may occur. Also be careful not to damage the oil pan flange.**

10. Remove the 2 bolts, 2 nuts, and the oil strainer/pickup assembly.
11. Remove the oil strainer/pickup assembly gasket.
12. Clean the mating surfaces of the oil pan and cylinder block of all oil residue. Clean both surfaces with a solvent that will not affect the painted surfaces.

**To install:**

13. Install the oil strainer/pickup assembly and a new gasket with 2 bolts and 2 nuts.
14. Tighten the oil strainer/pickup assembly bolts and nuts to 89 in. lbs. (10 Nm).
15. Apply a continuous bead of GM No. 1050026 sealant to both sides of a new oil pan gasket.
16. Install the oil pan to the cylinder block with 19 bolts and 2 nuts.
17. Tighten the oil pan bolts and nuts to 44 In. lbs. (5 Nm).
18. Install the exhaust pipe to exhaust manifold.
19. Install the exhaust pipe to catalytic convertor.
20. Connect the oxygen sensor connector.
21. Install the right and left lower stone shields.
22. Lower the vehicle.
23. Refill the engine oil.

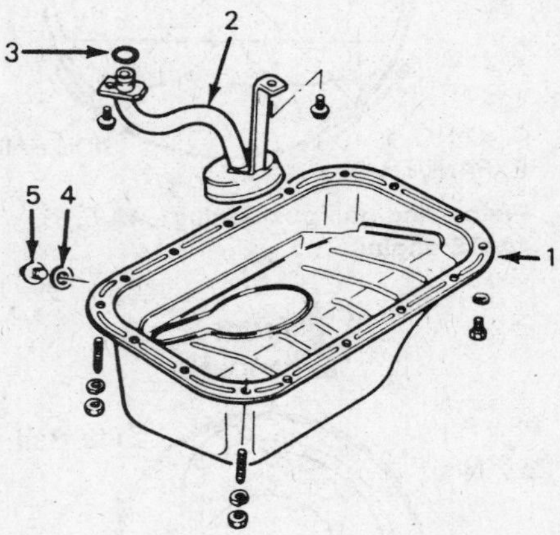


1. Oil pan
2. Oil pump strainer
3. O-ring seal
4. Drain plug gasket
5. Drain plug

**Oil pan and strainer—Sprint and Metro**

24. Install the battery negative (-) cable.
25. Start the engine and check for leaks.

#### *Spectrum*

1. Disconnect the negative battery terminal from the battery.
2. Raise and support the vehicle on jackstands, then drain the crankcase.
3. Disconnect the exhaust pipe bracket from the block and the exhaust pipe at the manifold.
4. Disconnect the right hand tension rod located under the front bumper.
5. Remove the oil pan bolts and oil pan, then clean the sealing surfaces.
6. To install, use a new gasket, apply sealant to the oil pump housing and the rear retainer housing, reverse the removal procedures.

#### *Sprint and Metro*

1. Remove the negative battery cable.
2. Raise and support the vehicle.
3. Drain the engine oil.
4. Remove the flywheel dust cover.
5. Remove the exhaust pipe at the exhaust manifold.
6. Remove the oil pan bolts, the pan and the oil pump strainer.
7. Clean the gasket mating surfaces.
8. To install, use new gaskets and reverse the removal procedures. Torque the oil pan bolts to 9–12 ft. lbs. Refill the engine oil.

## Rear Main Oil Seal

### REMOVAL & INSTALLATION

#### *Nova and Prizm*

1. Remove the transaxle from the vehicle.
2. If equipped with a manual transaxle, perform the following procedures:
   a. Matchmark the pressure plate-to-flywheel.
   b. Remove the pressure plate-to-flywheel bolts and the clutch assembly from the vehicle.
   c. Remove the flywheel-to-crankshaft bolts and the flywheel.
3. If equipped with an automatic transaxle, perform the following procedures:
   a. Matchmark the flywheel-to-crankshaft.
   b. Remove the torque converter drive plate-to-crankshaft bolts and the torque converter drive plate.
4. Remove the rear end plate-to-engine bolts and the rear end plate.
5. If removing the rear oil seal re-

tainer, perform the following procedures:

a. Remove the rear oil seal retainer-to-engine bolts, rear oil seal retainer to oil pan bolts and the rear oil seal retainer.

b. Using a small pry bar, pry the rear oil seal retainer from the mating surfaces.

c. Using a drive punch, drive the oil seal from the rear bearing retainer.

d. Using a putty knife, clean the gasket mounting surfaces.

6. To remove the rear oil seal, with the rear oil seal retainer installed, use a small pry bar and pry the seal from the rear oil seal retainer.

**NOTE: When removing the rear oil seal, be careful not to damage the seal mounting surface.**

7. Clean the oil seal mounting surface.

8. Using multi-purpose grease, lubricate the new seal lips.

9. Using an Rear Oil Seal Installation tool No. J-35388 or equivalent, tap the seal straight into the bore of the retainer.

10. If the rear oil seal retainer was removed from the vehicle, use a new gasket, sealant (if necessary) and reverse the removal procedures; be careful when installing the oil seal over the crankshaft.

11. To complete the installation, reverse the removal procedures. Torque the flywheel-to-crankshaft bolts to 58 ft. lbs. and the torque converter drive plate-to-crankshaft bolts to 61 ft. lbs.

### Spectrum

1. Remove the transaxle.
2. Remove the oil pan.
3. Remove the pressure plate and clutch (MT) or torque converter (AT), the flywheel bolts and the flywheel from the crankshaft.
4. Remove the rear oil seal retainer and remove the oil seal from the retainer. Clean the sealing surfaces.
5. Using a new oil seal, install the new seal in the oil seal retainer.
6. To install, use new gaskets, apply sealer to the mounting surfaces, apply oil to the seal lips, align the dowel pins of the retainer with the engine block and reverse the removal procedures.

### Sprint and Metro

1. Remove the transaxle.
2. Raise and support the vehicle. Remove the oil pan.
3. Remove the pressure plate, the clutch plate and the flywheel.
4. Remove the mounting bolts and the rear seal housing.
5. Pry the oil seal from the oil seal housing.
6. To install, use new gaskets/seals and reverse the removal procedures. Torque the oil seal housing to 7–9 ft. lbs. and the flywheel to 57–65 ft. lbs.

**NOTE: After installing the oil seal housing, trim the gasket flush with the bottom of the case.**

# Oil Pump

## REMOVAL & INSTALLATION

### Nova and Prizm

1. Remove the oil pan and the timing belt cover assembly.
2. Remove the oil pickup-to-engine brace bolts and the oil pickup.
3. Attach a lifting sling to the engine lift points and securely suspend the engine.
4. Mark the timing belt alignment between the camshaft and the crankshaft pulleys; also, mark the timing belt's direction of rotation. Loosen the idler pulley bolt, relieve the timing belt tension and remove the timing belt from the crankshaft sprocket; keep it engaged with the upper pulley.
5. Remove the crankshaft timing belt pulley and the timing belt idler pulley.
6. Remove the dipstick and dipstick tube.
7. Remove the oil pump-to-engine bolts and the oil pump; it may be necessary to tap lightly on the lower rear surface of the oil pump to loosen it.
8. Using a putty knife, clean the gasket mounting surfaces.
9. To replace the oil pump seal, perform the following procedures:

a. Using a small pry bar, pry the oil seal from the front of the oil pump; be careful not to damage the seal mounting surface.

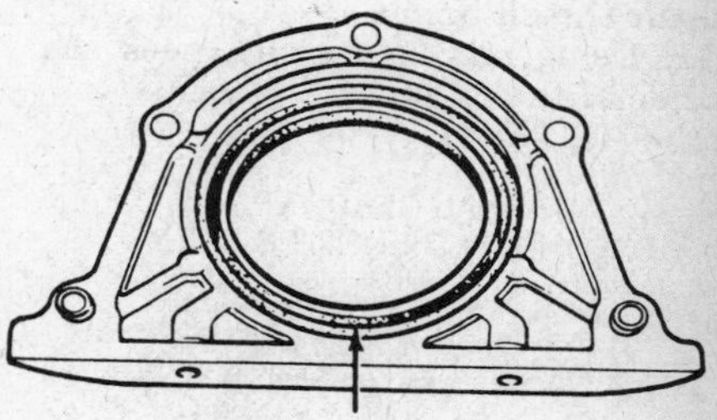

**Rear main oil seal installed in seal housing – Sprint and Metro**

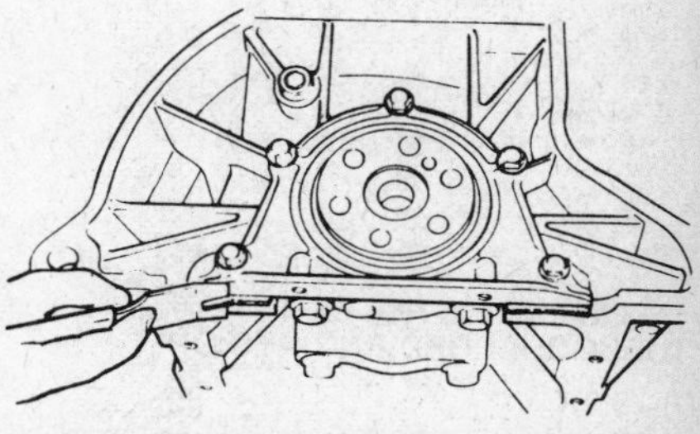

**Trimming gasket on rear main oil seal housing after installation – Sprint and Metro**

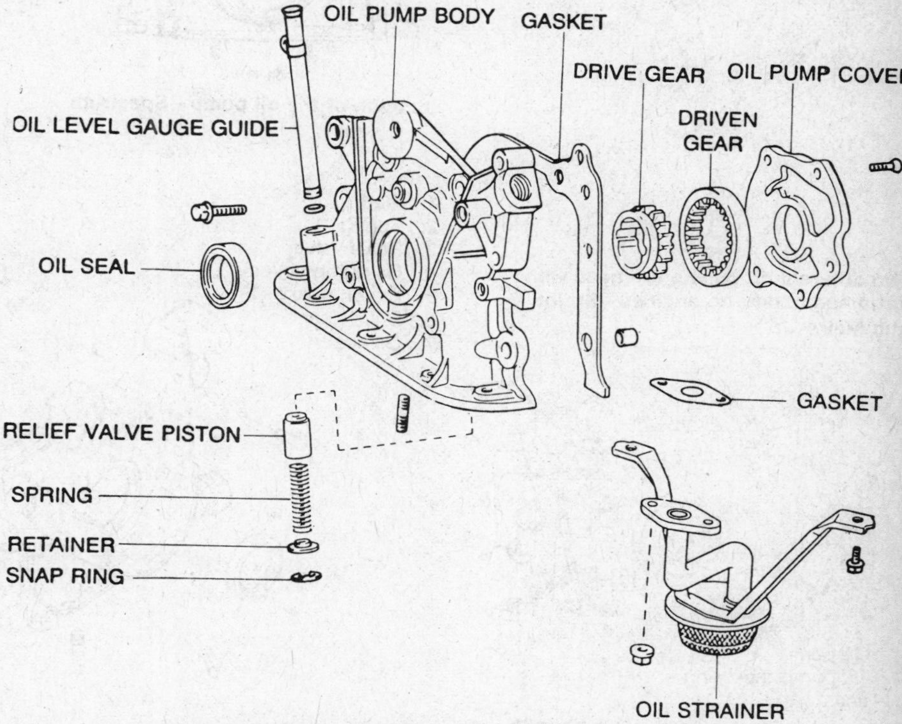


**Exploded view of the oil pump assembly – Nova and Prizm**

b. Clean the oil seal surface.

c. Using multi-purpose grease, lubricate the lips of the new oil seal.

d. Using the oil seal driver tool No. J-35403 or equivalent, drive the new oil seal into the oil pump until it seats against the seat.

10. Inspect the oil pump for wear and/or damage; if necessary, replace or repair the oil pump.

11. Using petroleum jelly, pack the inside of the oil pump.

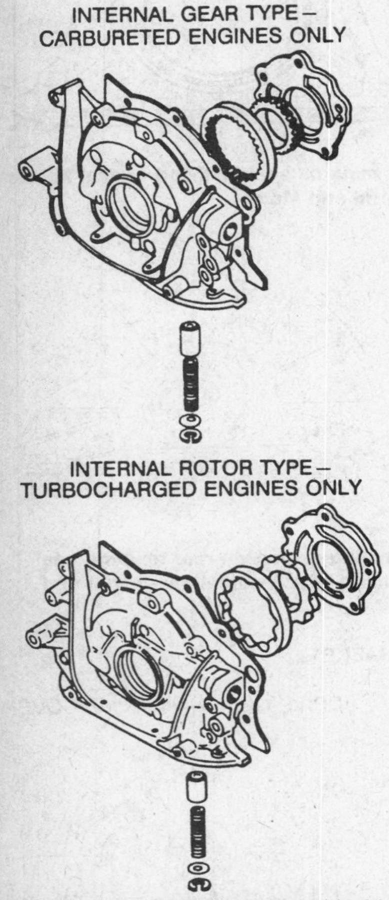


**Two different oil pumps are used with turbo and non-turbo engines – Sprint and Metro**

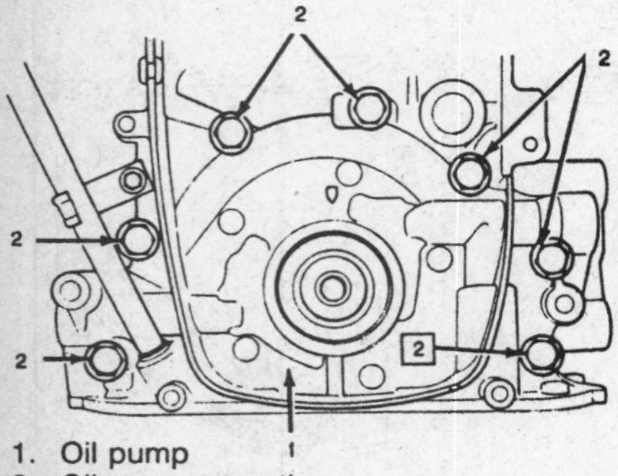


1. Oil pump
2. Oil pump mounting bolts

**Tighten the oil pump mounting bolts to 7-9 ft. lbs. – Sprint and Metro**

12. To install, use new gaskets, sealant (if necessary) and reverse the removal procedures. Engage the oil pump drive (smaller) gear with the crankshaft gear; there are both small and large spline teeth, make sure the teeth correspond properly. Torque the oil pick-up-to-engine bolts to 82 inch lbs. and the oil pump-to-engine bolts to 15 ft. lbs.

13. To complete the installation, reverse the removal procedures. Adjust the valve timing and the drive belt tensions. Refill the crankcase and the cooling system. Start the engine, allow it to reach normal operating temperatures and check for leaks.

### Spectrum

1. Remove the engine.
2. Drain the crankcase.
3. Remove the alternator belt and the starter.
4. Install the Flywheel Holding tool No. J–35271 or equivalent, to secure the flywheel.

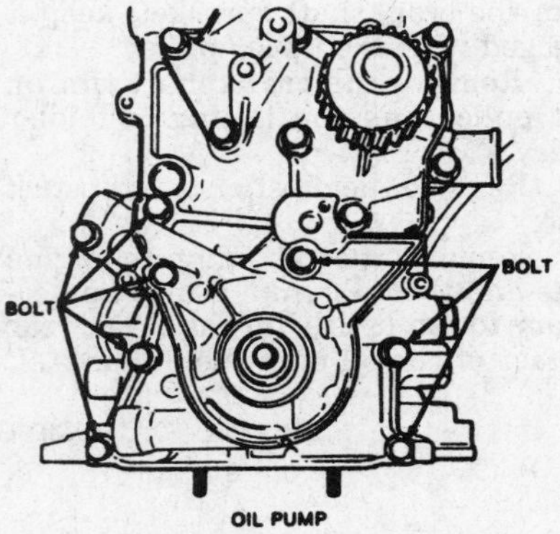


**Location of the oil pump – Spectrum**

1. Plug
2. Spring
3. Relief valve
4. Oil pump cover
5. Driven gear
6. Drive gear
7. Oil seal

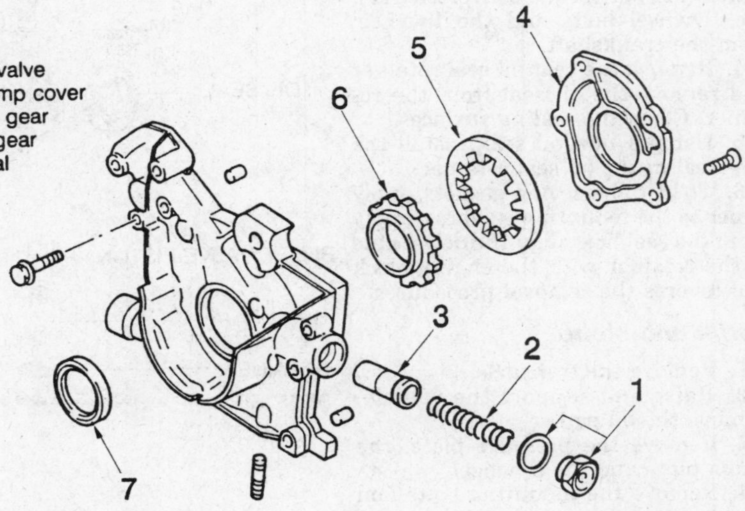


**Exploded view of the oil pump – Spectrum**

5. Remove the crankshaft pulley and boss.
6. Remove the timing cover bolts and the timing cover.
7. Loosen the tension pulley and remove the timing belt.
8. Remove the crankshaft timing gear and the tension pulley.
9. Remove the oil pan bolts, oil pan, oil strainer fixing bolt and the oil strainer assembly.
10. Remove the oil pump bolts and the oil pump assembly.
11. Remove the sealing material from the oil pump and engine block sealing surfaces.
12. To install, lubricate the oil pump, use new gaskets, apply sealant to the sealing surfaces and reverse the removal procedures.

### Sprint and Metro

1. Remove the timing belt.
2. Raise and support the vehicle. Remove the oil pan.
3. Use a suitable tool to hold the crankshaft timing belt pulley, remove the crankshaft bolt and pull the timing pulley from the shaft.
4. Remove the alternator mounting bracket and the A/C compressor bracket, if equipped.
5. Remove the alternator adjusting bolt and the upper cover bolt.
6. Remove the oil pump mounting bolts and the oil pump.
7. Pry the crankshaft oil seal from the oil pump.
8. Clean the gasket mounting surfaces. Remove the gear plate from the back of the oil pump and pack the oil pump gears with petroleum jelley.
9. To install, use new gaskets/seals and reverse the removal procedures. Torque the oil pump bolts to 7–9 ft.

lbs. and the crankshaft timing pulley bolt to 47–54 ft. lbs. Adjust the valve clearances and check the timing.

**NOTE: To install the oil pump to the engine, place the oil seal guide tool J–34853 on the crankshaft and slide the oil pump onto the alignment pins. After installing the oil seal housing, trim the gasket flush with the bottom of the case.**

# ENGINE COOLING

## Radiator

### REMOVAL & INSTALLATION

#### *Nova and Prizm*

1. Using a clean catch container, place it under the radiator, open the drain cock in the lower radiator tank and engine block, then, drain the cooling system.
2. Disconnect the electrical connector(s) from the radiator cooling fan and the A/C fan (if equipped). Remove the fan shroud, the top (4) radiator-to-chassis bolts and the bottom (2) radiator tank-to-chassis bolts (air conditioning ONLY).
3. If equipped with an a automatic transaxle, disconnect and plug the oil cooler hoses from the radiator.
4. Disconnect the overflow hose from radiator filler neck and position it high enough to keep the coolant from draining from the reservoir.
5. Remove the upper and lower radiator hoses.
6. Remove the radiator hold-down brackets and lift the radiator from the vehicle.
7. To install the radiator, reverse the removal procedures; make sure the radiator fits properly in the bottom rubber cushions. Refill both the automatic transaxle and cooling system with approved fluids. Start the engine, allow it to reach normal operating temperatures and check for leaks.

#### *Spectrum*

1. Disconnect the negative battery terminal from the battery.
2. Drain the cooling system.
3. Remove the air intake duct.
4. Remove the fan motor cable from the fan motor socket.
5. Disconnect the thermo switch cable.
6. Remove the fan motor assembly.

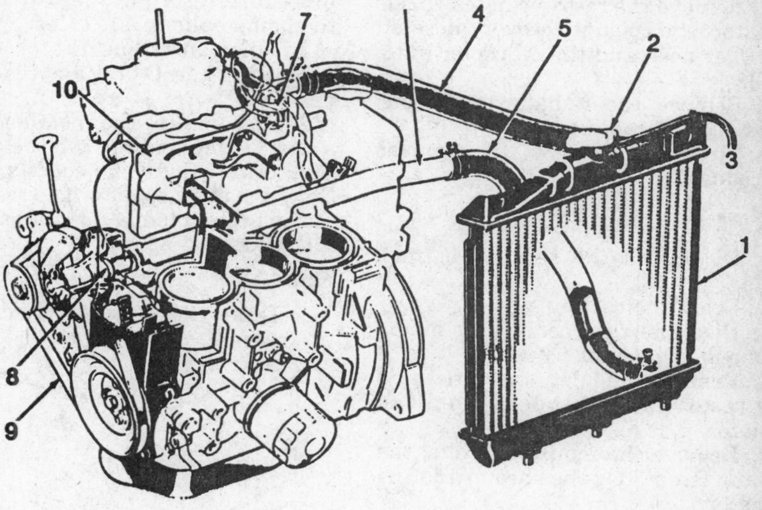


1. Radiator
2. Radiator Cap
3. To Water Reservoir Tank
4. Inlet Hose
5. Outlet Hose
6. Water Intake Pipe
7. Thermostat
8. Water Pump
9. Water Pump Belt
10. Intake Manifold

**View of the cooling system—Sprint and Metro**

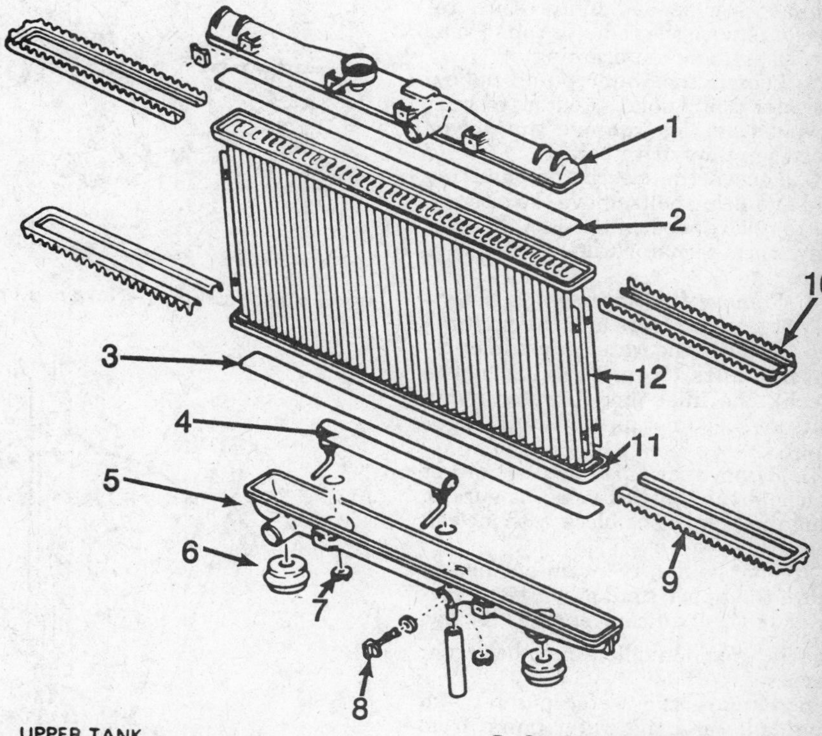


1. UPPER TANK
2. UPPER O-RING GASKET
3. LOWER O-RING GASKET
4. TRANSMISSION OIL COOLER & O-RINGS
5. LOWER TANK
6. LOWER RADIATOR SUPPORT
7. OIL COOLER NUT
8. DRAIN COCK AND GASKET
9. LOWER CLINCH RINGS
10. UPPER CLINCH RINGS
11. HEADER PLATE
12. CORE

**Exploded view radiator assembly—Nova and Prizm**

7. Remove the radiator hoses at the radiator, the coolant recovery hose at the filler neck and the oil cooler lines (AT).

8. Remove the radiator mounting bolts and the radiator.

9. To install, reverse the removal procedures.

### *Sprint and Metro*

1. Disconnect the negative battery cable.
2. Drain the cooling system.
3. Disconnect the cooling fan motor wire and the air inlet hose.
4. Remove the inlet, the outlet and the reservoir tank hoses from the radiator.
5. Remove the mounting bolts, the cooling fan motor, the shroud and the radiator.
6. To install, reverse the removal procedures and fill the cooling system.

# Water Pump

## REMOVAL & INSTALLATION

### *Nova and Prizm*

1. Place a clean container under the radiator, open the drain cocks on the radiator and engine block; once one drain cock is opened and pressure relieved, remove the radiator cap to vent the system and aid draining.
2. Loosen the water pump pulley-to-water pump bolts. If equipped with power steering, remove the power steering pump drive belt.
3. Loosen the alternator adjusting and mounting bolts, move the alternator to relieve the belt tension, then, remove the alternator/water pump drive belt.
4. Remove the water pump pulley-to-water pump bolts and the pulley.
5. Remove the water pump inlet-to-engine bolts (from the side of the block), the inlet pipe-to-water pump nuts and the inlet pipe (discard the O-ring).
6. Remove the dipstick tube bracket bolt and the dipstick tube; be sure to plug the hole in the block with a clean rag.
7. For the non-twincam engine, remove the upper timing belt front cover. For the twincam engine, remove the upper and middle timing belt front covers.
8. Remove the water pump-to-engine bolts and the water pump from the engine; discard the water pump-to-engine O-ring. Keep engine coolant off the timing belt!
9. Using a putty knife, clean the gasket mounting surfaces.
10. To install the water pump, use a new O-ring and reverse the removal procedures. Torque the water pump-to-engine bolts to 11 ft. lbs.
11. When installing the oil dipstick tube, use a new O-ring and coat it with engine oil.
12. To complete the installation, use a new O-ring and reverse the removal procedures. Refill the cooling system. Start the engine, allow it to reach normal operating temperatures and check for leaks.

### *Spectrum*

1. Drain the cooling system.

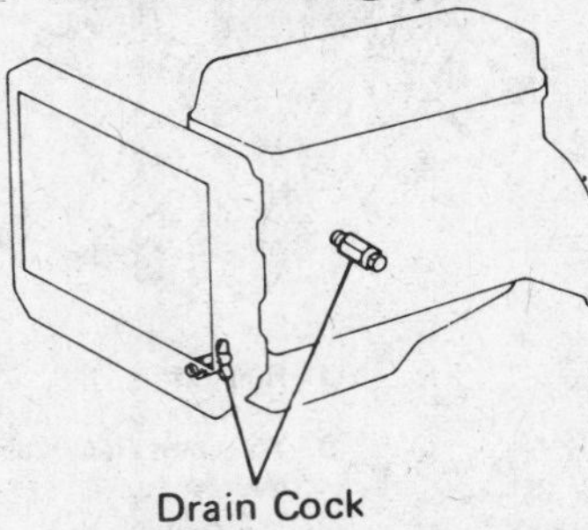


**Location of drains on radiator and engine block—Nova and Prizm**

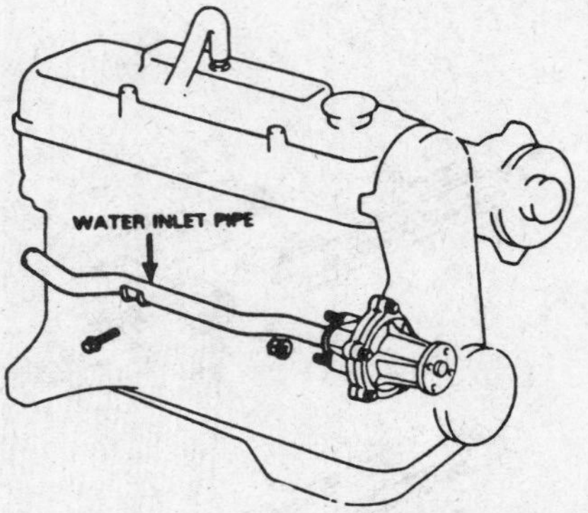


**Water pump inlet pipe—Nova and Prizm**

2. Loosen the power steering pump adjustment bolts and remove the belt.
3. Remove the timing belt.
4. Remove the tension pulley and spring.
5. Remove the water pump mounting bolts, the water pump and gasket. Clean the mounting surfaces of all gasket material.
6. To install, reverse the removal procedures. Torque the water pump to 17 ft. lbs. and the tension pulley to 30 ft. lbs.

### *Sprint and Metro*

1. Disconnect the negative battery cable.
2. Drain the cooling system.
3. Remove the water pump belt and pulley.
4. Remove the crankshaft pulley, the timing belt outside cover, the timing belt and the tensioner.
5. Remove the mounting bolts and the water pump.
6. Clean the gasket mating surfaces.
7. To install, use a new gasket/sealer and reverse the removal procedures.

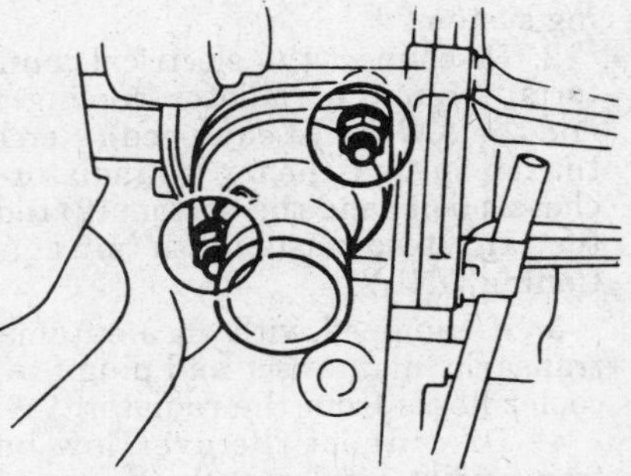

**Thermostat housing fasteners—Nova and Prizm**

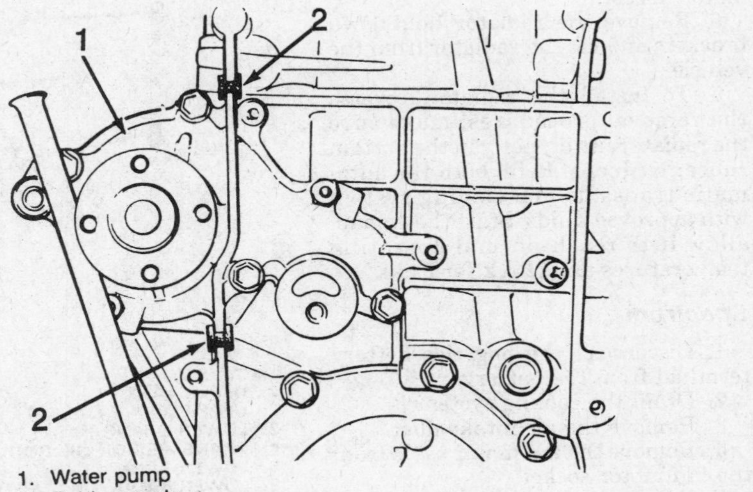


**Water pump mounting. Install rubber seals after pump installation—Sprint and Metro**

Torque the water pump bolts to 7.5–9 ft. lbs. Adjust the water pump belt deflection to 1/4 – 3/8 in. between the water pump and the crankshaft pulleys.

## Thermostat

### REMOVAL & INSTALLATION

#### *Nova and Prizm*

The thermostat is installed on the water pump inlet side.

1. Drain cooling system to a level below the water inlet housing.
2. Loosen water inlet hose clamps, then, disconnect the small and large hoses from the thermostat housing. Remove the water inlet-to-thermostat housing bolts and pull the water inlet housing from the thermostat housing (discard the O-ring).
3. To install a new thermostat, position the bellows side facing inward; make sure the thermostat fits squarely in the indented portion of the housing.
4. To complete the installation, use a new O-ring and reverse the removal procedures. Refill the cooling system. Start the engine, allow it to reach normal operating temperatures and check for leaks.

#### *Spectrum*

1. Remove the negative battery terminal. Drain the cooling system.
2. Remove the top radiator hose from the outlet pipe.
3. Remove the outlet pipe bolts, the outlet pipe, gasket and thermostat from the thermostat housing.
4. To install, reverse the removal procedures. Torque the outlet pipe-to-engine bolts to 17 ft. lbs.

#### *Sprint and Metro*

1. Disconnect the negative battery cable.
2. Drain the cooling system to a level below the thermostat.
3. Remove the air cleaner.
4. Disconnect the electrical connector at the thermostat cap.
5. Remove the inlet hose, the cap mounting bolts and the thermostat from the thermostat housing.
6. Clean the gasket mounting surfaces.

**NOTE: Make sure that the thermostat air bleed hole is clear.**

7. To install, use a new gasket, place the thermostat spring side down and reverse the removal procedures. Fill the cooling system, run the engine to normal operating temperatures and check for leaks.

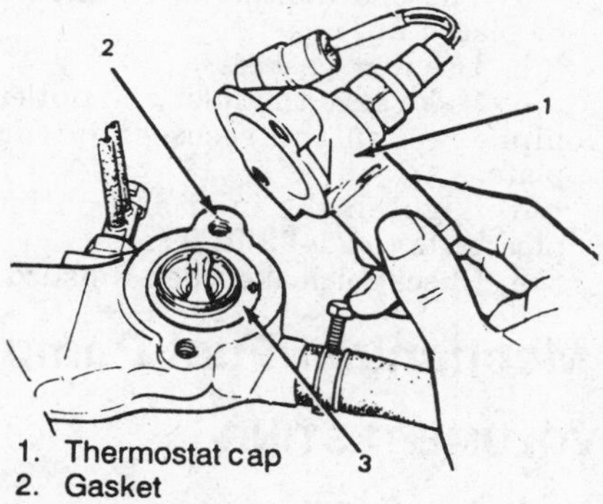


1. Thermostat cap
2. Gasket
3. Thermostat

**Thermostat installation in intake manifold – Sprint and Metro**

### COOLING SYSTEM BLEEDING

After working on the cooling system, even to replace the thermostat, it must be bled. Air trapped in the system will prevent proper filling and leave the radiator coolant level low, causing a risk of overheating.

1. To bleed the system, start with the system cool, the radiator cap off and the radiator filled to about an inch below the filler neck.
2. Start the engine and run it at slightly above normal idle speed. This will insure adequate circulation. If air bubbles appear and the coolant level drops, fill the system with an anti-freeze/water mixture to bring the level back to the proper level.
3. Run the engine this way until the thermostat opens. When this happens, coolant will move abruptly across the top of the radiator and the temperature of the radiator will suddenly rise.
4. At this point, air is often expelled and the level may drop quite a bit. Keep refilling the system until the level is near the top of the radiator and remains constant.
5. If the vehicle has an overflow tank, fill the radiator right up to the filler neck. Replace the radiator filler cap.

# EMISSION CONTROLS

**Please refer to "Emission Control" in the Unit Repair section for system maintenance procedures. Due to the complex nature of modern electronic engine control systems, comprehensive diagnosis and testing procedures fall outside the confines of this repair manual. For complete information on diagnosis, testing and repair procedures concerning all modern engine and emission control systems, please refer to "Chilton's Guide To Electronic Engine Controls".**

# FUEL SYSTEM

## Fuel System Service Precautions

- Disconnect the negative battery terminal.
- Keep a Class B dry chemical fire extinguisher available.
- Always relieve the fuel pressure before disconnecting a fuel line.
- Wrap a shop cloth around the fuel line when disconnecting a fuel line.
- Always use new O-rings.
- DO NOT replace the fuel pipes with fuel hoses.
- Always use a back-up wrench when opening or closing a fuel line.

**CAUTION**

***On fuel injected engines the fuel delivery pipe is under high pressure even after the engine is stopped. Direct removal of the fuel line, may result in dangerous fuel spray. Make sure to release the fuel pressure according to the following procedures.***

### RELIEVING FUEL SYSTEM PRESSURE

#### *Nova and Prizm*

##### TWINCAM ENGINE

**NOTE: Make sure the engine is cold before disconnecting any portion of the fuel system.**

1. Using a shop rag, wrap it around the fuel line fitting.

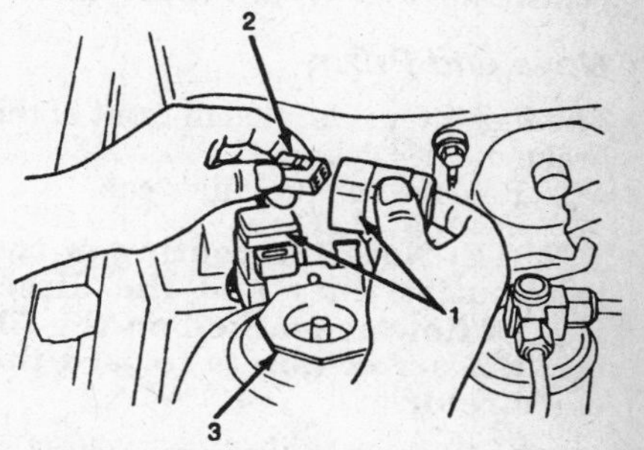


1. FUEL PUMP RELAY OR MAIN RELAY
2. FUEL PUMP RELAY LEAD WIRE (PINK, PINK/WHITE, WHITE/BLUE, WHITE/BLUE)
3. RIGHT FRONT SUSPENSION STRUT

**Fuel pump relay wire identification – Sprint and Metro**

2. Open the fuel line and absorb any excess fuel remaining in the line.

3. To install, use a new O-ring and reverse the removal procedures.

### *Spectrum*

1. Remove the fuel pump fuse from the fuse block or disconnect the harness connector at the tank.

2. Start the engine. It should run and then stall when the fuel in the lines is exhausted. When the engine stops, crank the starter for about three seconds to make sure all pressure in the fuel lines is released.

3. Install the fuel pump fuse after repair is made.

### *Sprint and Metro*

1. Release the fuel vapor pressure in the fuel tank by removing the fuel tank cap then reinstalling it.

2. With the engine running, remove the connector of the fuel pump relay and wait until the engine stops itself.

**NOTE: The main relay and fuel pump relay are identical. Which one to connect to the fuel lead wire is not specified. Identify the fuel pump relay by the color of the lead wire. The fuel pump relay lead wire is Pink, Pink/White, White/Blue, White/Blue.**

3. Once the engine is stopped, crank it a few times with the starter for about three seconds each time (with the relay connector disconnected).

4. If the fuel pressure can't be released in the above manner because the engine failed to run in Step b, disconnect the negative battery cable, cover the union bolt of the high fuel pressure line with an appropriate rag and loosen the union bolt slowly to release the fuel pressure gradually.

# Fuel Filter

## REMOVAL & INSTALLATION

### *Nova and Prizm*

The fuel filter is located in front of the brake master cylinder.

1. Remove the fuel filler cap.

**NOTE: Note the routing of the inlet/outlet lines and the direction of flow as marked on the filter; the arrow points toward the carburetor.**

2. Using a pair of pliers, move the clips on the inlet/outlet hoses back and away from the filter.

3. Disconnect the fuel lines, using a twisting motion to break them loose; be sure to plug the fuel lines to prevent the spillage of fuel and the entry of dirt. Pull the filter from its retaining clip.

4. To install, use a new fuel filter and reverse the removal procedures. When reconnecting the fuel lines, make sure the clips are installed to the inside of the bulged sections of the fuel filter connections and not at the ends of the fuel lines. Start the engine and check for leaks.

### *Spectrum*

The fuel filter is located under the Vacuum Booster of the Power Brake System and should be replaced every 15,000 miles.

1. Remove the fuel tank cap.

2. Disconnect the hoses from the fuel filter.

**NOTE: Cap the fuel hoses to prevent fuel spillage or dirt entry.**

3. Remove the fuel filter.

4. Reinstall the fuel tank cap.

5. To install, reverse the removal procedures. Securely attach the fuel filter clips and start the engine to check for leakage.

**NOTE: On fuel injected models relieve fuel system pressure before working on fuel system.**

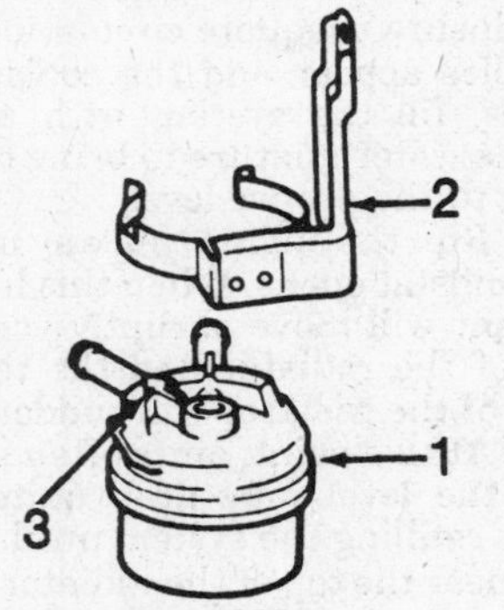


1 FUEL FILTER
2. BRACKET
3. DIRECTION OF FLOW

Fuel filter—Nova and Prizm

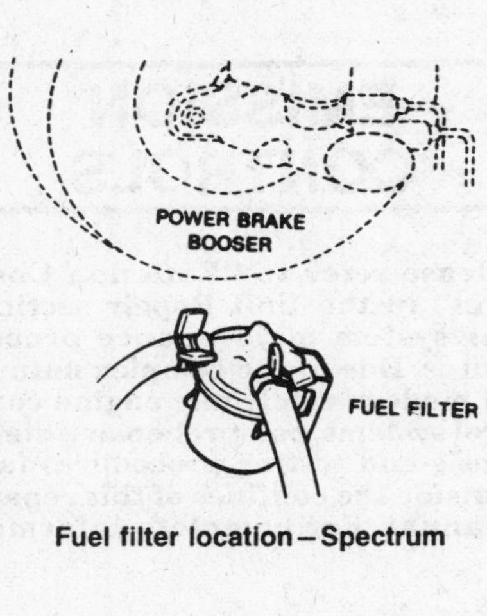


Fuel filter location—Spectrum

### *Sprint and Metro*

#### CARBURETED ENGINES

The fuel filter is located in the fuel feed line, near the fuel pump. The filter is not serviceable and must be replaced as an assembly.

1. Remove and replace the fuel tank cap, this procedure releases the pressure within the fuel system.

2. Disconnect the negative battery cable.

3. Remove the clamps from the inlet and outlet hoses and remove the hoses from the fuel filter.

4. Remove the fuel filter from the bracket.

5. To install, reverse the removal procedures. Check for leaks when finished.

#### FUEL INJECTED ENGINES

1. Release the fuel pressure as outlined under Fuel Pressure Release.

2. Place an appropriate container under the fuel filter.

3. Use a 17mm and a 19mm wrench to loosen the inlet and outlet pipes and remove the fuel filter.

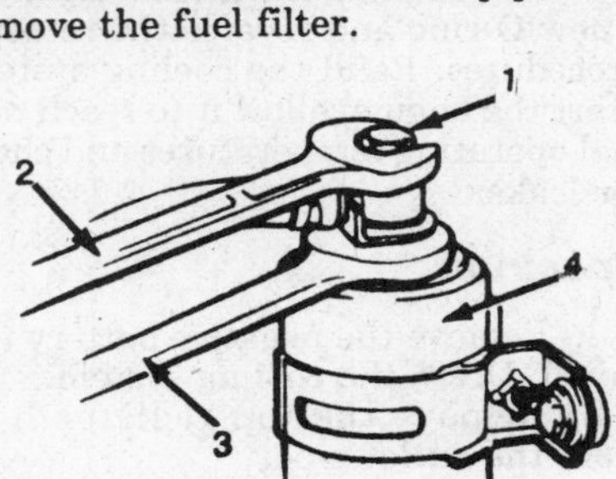


1. OUTLET PIPE BOLT
2. 17 MM (0.67 IN.) WRENCH
3. 19 MM (0.75 IN.) WRENCH
4. FUEL FILTER

Fuel filter removal,fuel injected engines

4. Installation is the reverse of removal with the following precautions:
   a. The end marked **OUT** should be placed up.
   b. Use new gaskets.
   c. Make sure the inlet and outlet pipes rest in the recesses in the plate.
   d. Tighten the inlet and outlet pipe bolts to 22–28 ft. lbs.
   e. Check for leaks when finished.

# Mechanical Fuel Pump

## VOLUME TESTING

### *Nova and Prizm*

1. Disconnect the fuel line from the carburetor. Run the fuel line into a suitable container.

2. Run the engine at idle until there is one pint of fuel in the container; one pint should be pumped in 30 seconds or less.
3. If the flow is below minimum, check for a restriction in the fuel line.
4. Tighten any loose line connections and look for any kinks or restrictions.

## PRESSURE TESTING

### Nova

1. Using a fuel pressure gauge, connect it between the fuel pump and carburetor; using a pair of vise grips, squeeze off the return hose.
2. Operate the engine at idle and note the reading on the gauge.
3. The fuel pump pressure should be 7.6 psi; if the pressure reading on the gauge is higher or lower than this specification or if the reading is sporatic with the engine at idle, the pump should be replaced.
4. Remove the gauge, reconnect the fuel lines. Start the engine and check for fuel leaks.

### Spectrum

1. Disconnect the fuel line at the carburetor. Install a rubber hose about 10 inches long. Attach a low reading pressure gauge.
2. Hold the gauge at least 16 inches above the fuel pump. If equipped, pinch the fuel return line.
3. Start the engine and run at slow idle, using the fuel that is left in the carburetor.
4. If the fuel pump is operating properly the pressure on the gauge should read a constant 3.8–4.7 psi.
5. If the pressure is too low, too high or significantly different at various engine speeds the pump should be replaced.

## REMOVAL & INSTALLATION

### Nova and Prizm

1. Note the routing of fuel lines and label (if necessary). Using a pair of pliers, slide the fuel line clips from the fuel pump connections. Disconnect the fuel lines, use a twisting motion to break them loose.
2. Remove the fuel pump-to-cylinder head bolts, then, the pump, gasket and heat shield, noting the position of the shield.
3. Using a putty knife, clean the gasket mounting surfaces; be careful not to scratch the aluminum surface of the cylinder head.
4. To install, use a new gasket and reverse the removal procedures. When reconnecting the fuel lines, make sure the clips are installed to the inside of the bulged sections of the fuel pump connections. Start the engine and check for leaks.

### Spectrum

1. Disconnect the fuel and return hoses from the fuel pump.

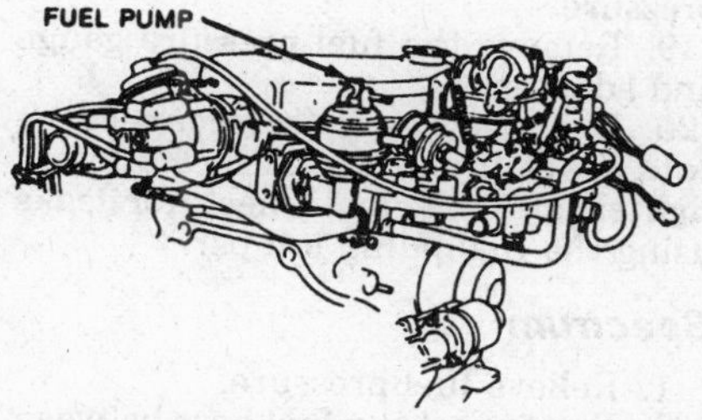


Location of the fuel pump – Spectrum

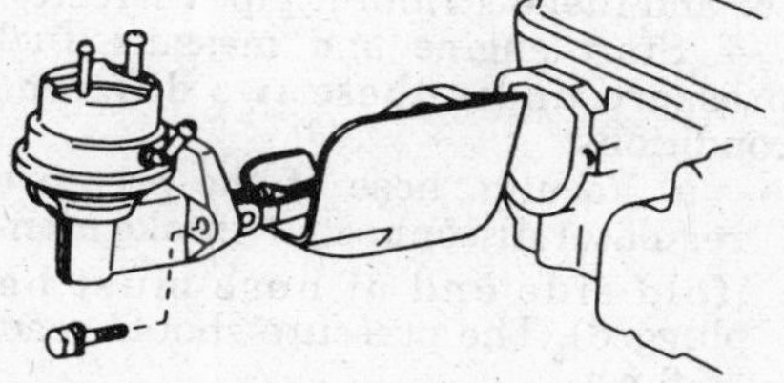

Mechanical fuel pump mounting – Nova and Prizm

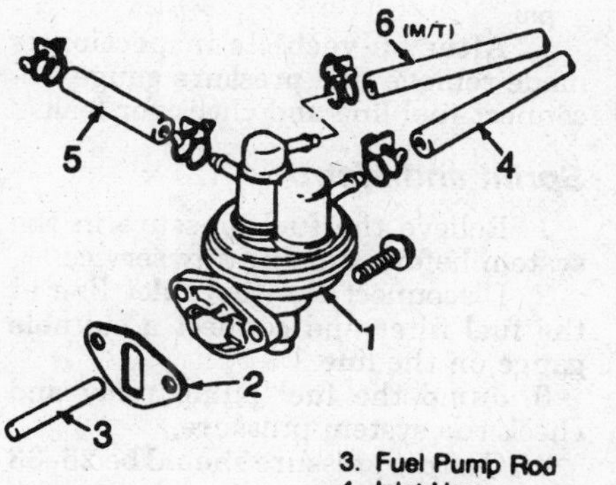


1. Fuel Pump
2. Gasket
3. Fuel Pump Rod
4. Inlet Hose
5. Outlet Hose
6. Return Hose

Fuel pump assembly, carburetted engines – Sprint and Metro

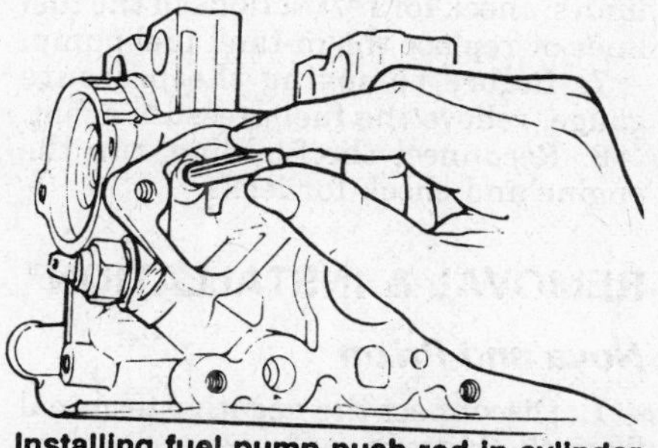

Installing fuel pump push rod in cylinder head – Sprint and Metro

2. Remove the bolts, fuel pump and heat insulator assembly.
3. After removing the fuel pump, cover the mounting face of the cylinder head to prevent oil discharge.
4. To install, reverse the removal procedures. Replace the heat insulator assembly.

### Sprint and Metro

1. Remove and replace the fuel tank cap, this procedure releases the pressure within the fuel system.
2. Disconnect the negative battery cable.
3. Remove the air cleaner from the carburetor.
4. Remove the fuel inlet, outlet and return hoses from the fuel pump.
5. Remove the fuel pump mounting bolts, the pump and the pump rod from the cylinder head.
6. To install, lubricate the pump rod, use a new gasket and reverse the removal procedures.

# Electric Fuel Pump

## PRESSURE TESTING

### Nova

1. Disconnect the negative battery terminal from the battery and the electrical connector from the cold start injector.
2. Using a shop colth, wrap it around the cold start injector pipe, loosen (slowly) the union bolt and remove the bolt; discard the gaskets.
3. Using the Pressure Gauge tools No. J-347301-1 and J-37144 or equivalent, install them onto the fuel delivery pipe.
4. Reconnect the negative battey terminal.
5. Using a jumper wire, short both terminals fo the fuel pump check connector; the connector is located near the wiper motor.
6. Turn the ignition switch **ON** and inspect the fuel pressure; it should be 38–44 psi. If the pressure is high, replace the pressure regulator. If the pressure is low, check the fuel pump, fuel filter, pressure regulator, the hoses and connections.
7. Remove the service wire from the check connector. Start the engine.
8. Disconnect the vacuum sensing hose from the pressure regulator and pinch it off.
9. The fuel pressure at idle should still be 38–44 psi.
10. Reconnect the vacuum sensing hose to the pressure regulator and allow the engine to idle for 1½ min. Recheck the fuel pressure, it should be 30–33 psi; if no pressure, inspect the vacuum sensing hose and the pressure regulator.

11. Stop the engine and inspect the fuel pressure for 5 min.; it should remain above 21 psi. If the pressure does not remain high, inspect the fuel pump, the pressure regulator and/or the injectors.
12. After inspecting the fuel pressure, disconnect the negative battery terminal and remove the fuel pressure gauge.

13. Using new gaskets, reconnect the cold start injector hose to the delivery pipe. Check for leaks.

### Prizm

1. Disconnect the negative battery cable from the battery.
2. Using a shop colth, wrap it around the cold start injector pipe, loosen (slowly) the union bolt and remove the bolt; discard the gaskets.
3. Remove the delivery pipe to cold start injector banjo fitting bolt and the two gaskets. Discard the gaskets.
4. Using the pressure gauge tools No. J-34370-1 and J-38347 or equivalent, install them onto the fuel delivery pipe using two new gaskets. Close the gauge shut of valve.
5. Reconnect the negative battey terminal.
6. Open the gauge shut off valve.
7. Turn the ignition switch to **RUN**.
8. Install a jumper wire between the **+B** and **FP** terminals fo the fuel pump check connector; the connector is located near the wiper motor.
9. Open the gauge air bleed valve and purge the air from the gauge. Use a suitable container to catch the fuel from the gauge air bleed valve.
10. The gauge reading should be 38–44 psi. If the pressure is high, replace the pressure regulator or a restricted fuel return line. If the pressure is low, check the fuel pump, fuel filter, pressure regulator, the hoses and connections and a defective fuel pressure regulator.
11. Pinch the fuel pressure regulator return hose. The pressure should be 57 psi.
12. Drain back. Remove the fuel pump jumper wire and observe the pressure gauge. A very sloe drop in pressure is normal.
13. The fuel pressure at idle should still be 30–33 psi.
14. Remove the fuel pressure regulator sensing hose, and plug the hose end. The fuel pressure gauge should read 38-44 psi.
15. Connect the vacuum sensing hose and quickly open and close the throttle valve for the air induction system. The fuel pressure gauge should show quick increases in pressure as the throttle is snapped open and decreases as it returns to idle.
16. Stop the engine. If improper pressure readings are shown, inspect the fuel pump, the pressure regulator and/or the injectors, restricted fuel lines or filter, improper injector control (thermal timer/ECM).
17. Install the negative battery cable.
18. Use the fuel pressure gauge air bleed valve to relieve the system pressure.
19. Remove the fuel pressure gauge and adapter.
20. Using new gaskets, reconnect the cold start injector fitting bolt and tighten to 13 ft. lbs. Check for leaks using the fuel pump jumper.

### Spectrum

1. Relieve fuel pressure.
2. Disconnect the fuel hose between pressure regulator and fuel distributor pipe.
3. Connect a fuel pressure gauge (J – 33945) across the pressure regulator and fuel distributor pipe correctly.
4. Start engine and measure fuel pressure under these two different conditions:
   a. Vacuum hose of the pressure regulator disconnected (intake manifold side end of hose must be plugged). The pressure should read 35.6 psi.
   b. Vacuum hose of the pressure regulator connected (at speed of 900 rpm). The pressure should read 28.4 psi.
5. After on-vechicle inspection is made remove fuel pressure gauge, reconnect fuel line and check for leaks.

### Sprint and Metro

1. Relieve the fuel pressure in the system before starting any service.
2. Disconnect the fuel inlet line at the fuel filter and connect a suitable gauge on the line.
3. Jump the fuel pump relay and check the system pressure.
4. Correct pressure should be 25–33 lbs.
5. As the pressure reaches 33 lbs., the relief valve in the pump should pulsate the pressure so it is always within the two limits.
6. If the pressure is not within the limits, check for restrictions in the fuel lines or replace the in-tank fuel pump.
7. Before removing the pressure gauge, relieve the fuel pressure again.
8. Reconnect the fuel line, run the engine and check for leaks.

## REMOVAL & INSTALLATION

### Nova and Prizm

1. Disconnect the negative terminal from the battery.
2. Drain the fuel from the fuel tank. Remove the fuel tank-to-chassis straps and lower the tank slightly. Disconnect the electrical connector and the fuel line from the fuel tube.
3. Remove the fuel pump bracket-to-fuel tank bolts and the bracket.
4. Remove the electrical connectors from the fuel pump, the fuel pump from the bracket and the fuel hose.
5. From the bottom of the fuel pump, remove the rubber cushion, the clip and pull out the filter.
6. To install, use a new bracket-to-fuel tank gasket and reverse the removal procedures. Refill the fuel tank.

### Spectrum

**NOTE: Fuel is under high pressure, if the following steps are not followed the fuel could spray out and result in a fire hazard or possible injury. The fuel pump is located inside the gas tank.**

1. Relieve fuel pressure then disconnect negative battery cable.
2. Drain fuel tank.
3. Remove all gas line hose connections and fuel pump ground wire.
4. Remove filler neck hose and clamp.
5. Remove breather hose and clamp.
6. Disconnect fuel tank hose to evaporator pipe.
7. Remove fuel tank mounting bolts and lower tank from car. At this point remove hose from pump to fuel fiter.
8. Remove fuel pump bracket plate and fuel pump as an assembly.
9. Remove pump bracket, rubber cushion and fuel pump filter.
10. To install, reverse the removal procedures. Be careful, to push the lower side of the fuel pump, together with the rubber cushion, into the fuel pump bracket.

### Sprint and Metro

**NOTE: The fuel tank must be lowered to gain access to the fuel pump which is located in the fuel tank.**

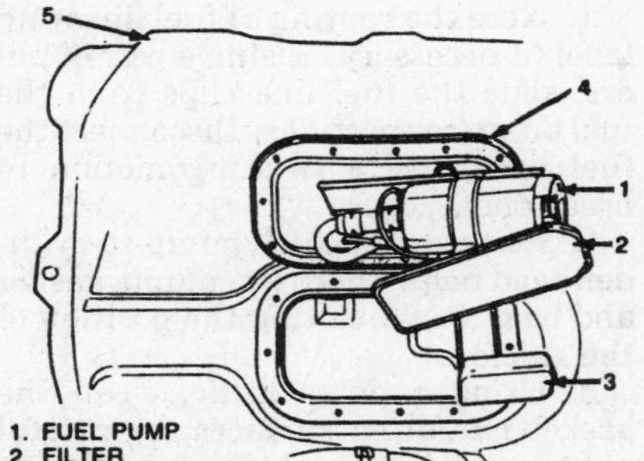


1. FUEL PUMP
2. FILTER
3. FUEL LEVER GAUGE
4. BRACKET
5. FUEL TANK

**The fuel pump is located in the fuel tank on fuel injected models - Sprint and Metro**

1. Remove the fuel tank as follows:
a. Disconnect the negative battery cable.
b. Remove the rear seat cushion and disconnect the fuel gage and fuel pump lead wires.
c. Remove the fuel filler cap and then reinstall it to release the fuel pressure in the tank.
d. Release the fuel line pressure as outlined under Fuel Pressure Release.
e. Since the tank does not have a drain plug, it must be drained by pumping or siphoning the fuel out through the fuel feed line (tank to fuel filter line).
f. Raise the vehicle on a hoist and disconnect all hoses and remove the tank from the vehicle.
2. Remove the fuel pump and fuel level gage bracket from the fuel tank.
3. Remove the fuel pump from the fuel tank.
4. Installation is the reverse of removal. Clean the fuel filter in the tank.

# Carburetor

## REMOVAL & INSTALLATION

### *Nova and Prizm*

1. To remove the air cleaner, perform the following procedures.
a. Disconnect the air intake hose.
b. Label and disconnect the emission control hoses from the air cleaner.
c. Remove the wingnut, mounting bolts and the air cleaner from the carburetor.
2. Disconnect the accelerator cable from the carburetor. If equipped with an automatic transaxle, disconnect the transaxle throttle linkage from the carburetor.
3. Disconnect the wiring connector form the carburetor solenoid valve(s).
4. Label and disconnect the emission control hoses from the carburetor. Disconnect the fuel inlet hose, draining any fuel into a metal or ceramic container (not a styrofoam cup). Disconnect the evaporative emissions canister hose.
5. Remove the cold mixture heater wire clamp and the EGR vacuum control bracket.
6. Remove the carburetor-to-intake manifold nuts, the carburetor and gasket from the intake manifold. Using a clean shop, seal off the intake manifold opening.
7. Using a putty knife, clean the gasket mounting surfaces of the carburetor and manifold.
8. To install, use a new gasket and reverse the removal procedures. Install and adjust the throttle and transaxle linkages to the carburetor. Start the engine and check for fuel leaks.

### *Spectrum*

1. Disconnect the negative battery terminal from the battery.
2. Remove the air cleaner.
3. Disconnect the harness connector and hoses.
4. Remove the accelerator cable from the carburetor.
5. Remove the bolts securing the carburetor to the intake manifold. Remove the carburetor and place a cover over the intake manifold.
6. To install, reverse the removal procedures and torque carburetor fixing bolts to 7.2 ft. lbs. then start the engine and check for leaks.

### *Sprint and Metro*

1. Remove and replace the fuel tank cap, this procedure releases the pressure within the fuel system.
2. Disconnect the negative battery cable.
3. Disconnect the warm air, the cold air, the second air, the vacuum and the EGR modulator hoses from the air cleaner case.
4. Remove the air cleaner case from the carburetor.
5. Disconnect the accelerator cable and the electrical wiring from the carburetor.
6. Remove the emission control and the fuel hoses from the carburetor.
7. Disconnect the No. 1 and No. 2 choke hoses from the carburetor.
8. Remove the mounting bolts and the carburetor from the intake manifold.
9. To install, use new gaskets and reverse the removal procedures. Torque the carburetor mounting bolts to 18 ft. lbs.

## CARBURETOR ADJUSTMENTS

### *Spectrum*

#### PRIMARY THROTTLE VALVE OPENING (FULL OPENING)

1. Inspect the angle of the primary throttle valve when the throttle valve has been fully opened. The valve angle should be 90 degrees from the horizontal plane.
2. If adjustment is needed, bend the throttle adjust arm.

#### SECONDARY THROTTLE VALVE OPENING

1. Open the throttle lever, fully open the secondary throttle valve and inspect the angle. The valve angle should be 87 degrees from the horizontal plane.
2. If needed bend the secondary shaft lever to adjust.

#### CHOKE VALVE (THIRD STAGE)

Check the choke valve in the third stage of the fast idle cam.
1. Set the choke valve to full open.
2. Slowly open the throttle lever while lightly pushing the choke valve in the closing direction with your fingers and set the choke valve to the third stage of the fast idle cam.
3. The choke valve clearance should be 0.093 in.
4. If adjustment is needed, remove the rivet of the automatic choke and adjust by bending the choke lever in the housing. Reinstall the choke lever by riveting.

#### PRIMARY THROTTLE VALVE OPENING (SECOND STAGE)

Check the clearance of the primary throttle valve in the second stage of the fast idle cam.
1. Set the choke valve to full open.
2. Open the throttle valve slowly while pushing the choke valve lightly in the closing direction with your fingers and set the choke valve to the second stage of the fast idle cam.
3. The primary throttle valve clearance should be: A/T – 0.692 in., M/T – 0.543 in.
4. Adjustment is made with the fast idle screw.

#### UNLOADER

1. Check the clearance of the choke valve when the primary throttle valve has been fully opened. The clearance should be 0.071 in.
2. If adjustment is needed remove the rivet of the automatic choke and adjust it by bending the choke lever in the housing. Reinstall the choke lever by riveting.

#### CHOKE BREAKER ADJUSTMENT

1. Apply a vacuum of about 400mm Hg to the choke breaker diaphragm unit.

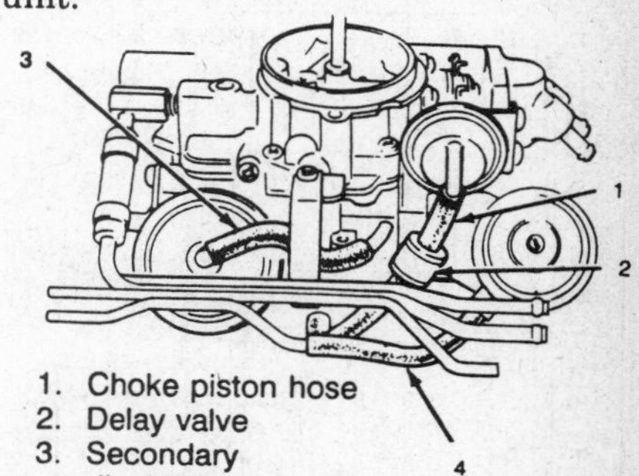


1. Choke piston hose
2. Delay valve
3. Secondary diaphragm hose
4. Idle-up actuator hose

**Carburetor vacuum hose locations – Sprint and Metro**

2. Lightly push the choke valve to the closing side. The clearance should be 1985: 0.053 in., 1986–89: 0.057 in.

3. Adjust by bending the choke lever.

### THROTTLE POSITION SENSOR (TPS) TEST AND ADJUSTMENT

**NOTE: After the connection of the ohmmeter is made to the TPS, this test should be performed in as short of time as possible.**

1. Check that the TPS bracket screws are tight.

2. Check that there is no play in the TPS arm and primary throttle valve arm.

3. Connect an ohmmeter to the green and black leads of the TPS.

4. Open the throttle lever about one-third (no continuity in this case) and then gradually close the lever and check that there is continuity when the primary slot valve reaches the the prescribed clearance of .015(A/T), .011(M/T).

5. Adjust by loosening the TPS screws. After adjustment check the clearance as in Step 4.

### SECONDARY TOUCH ANGLE

1. Measure the primary throttle valve opening at the same time the secondary throttle valve starts to open.

2. The clearance should be 0.023 in. Adjust by bending the throttle adjusting arm.

### FLOAT LEVEL

1. Measure the clearance between the float top and gasket when the float is in the raised position. The clearance should be 0.059 in.

2. Bend tab (A) to adjust.

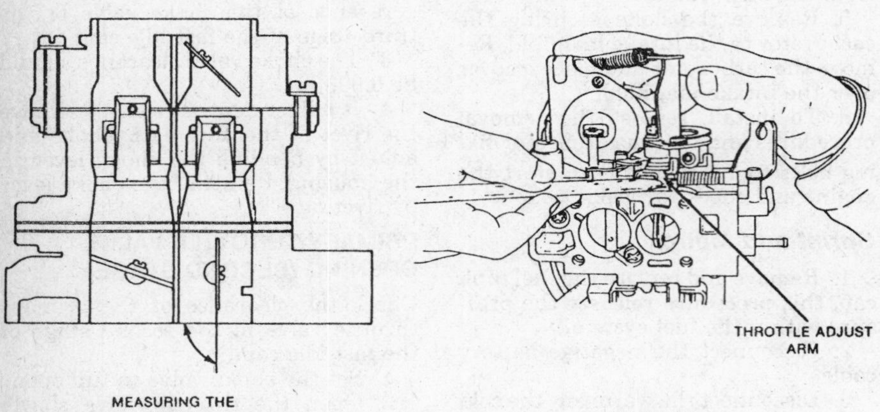


**Primary throttle valve angle (full open) – Spectrum**

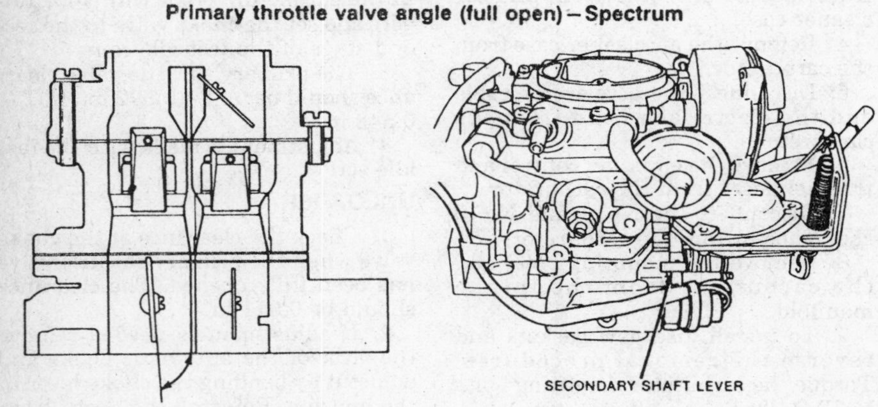


**Secondary throttle valve opening – Spectrum**

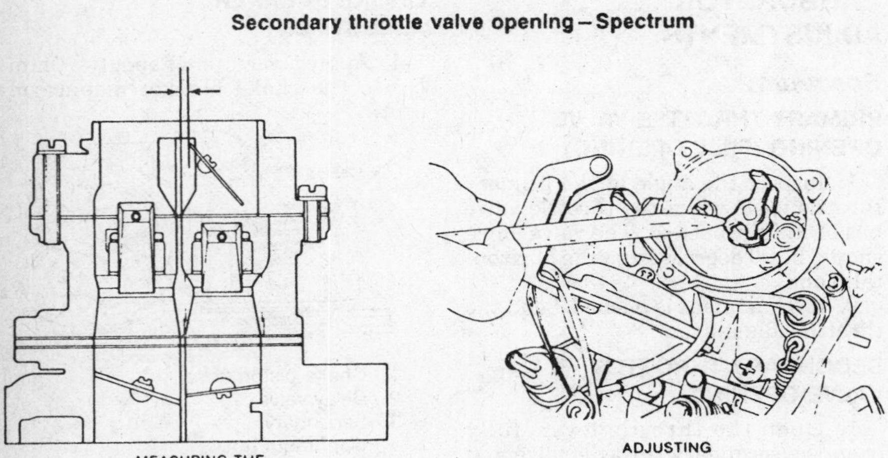


**Choke valve adjustment (third stage) – Spectrum**

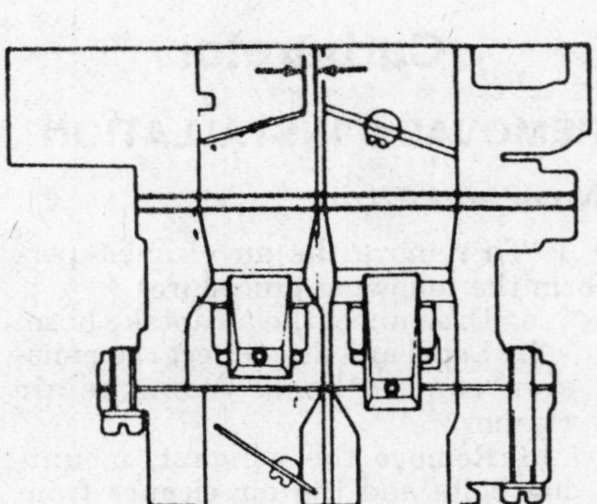

**Throttle position sensor adjustment – Spectrum**

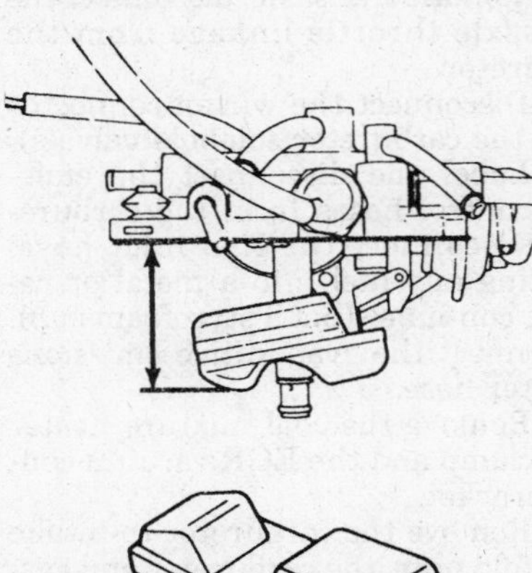

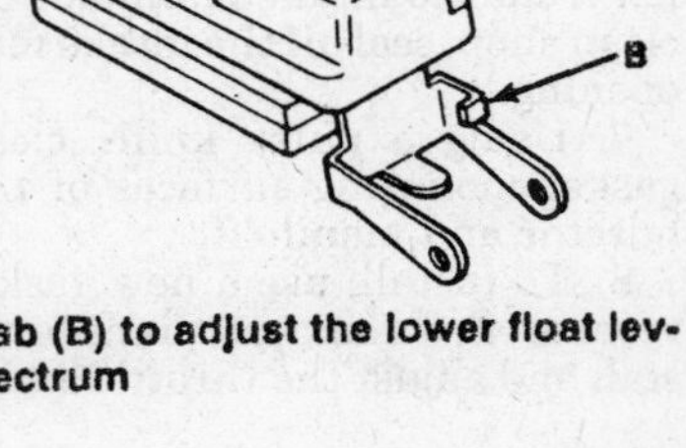


**Bend tab (B) to adjust the lower float level – Spectrum**

**NOTE: Care should be taken not to damage the needle valve when adjusting the float level.**

3. Measure the clearance between the float bottom and gasket at the lowered position of the float. the clearance should be 1.7 in. Adjust by bending (B) shown in the illustration.

### *Sprint*

#### FLOAT LEVEL

The fuel level in the float chamber should be within the round mark at the center of the level gauge. If it is not, check and adjust the float level as follows:

1. Remove and invert the air horn.
2. Measure the distance between the float and the gasketed surface of the choke chamber. The measured distance is the float level and it should be 0.21–0.24 in. The measurement should be made without the gasket on the air horn.
3. Adjustment is made by bending the tongue up and down.

#### IDLE-UP

The idle-up actuator operates even when the cooling fan is running. Therefore the idle-up adjustment must be performed when the cooling fan is not running.

##### Manual Transmission Models

1. Warm up the engine to normal operating temperature.
2. After warming up, run the engine at idle speed.
3. Check to make sure that the idle-up adjusting screw moves down (indicating that the idle-up is at work) when the lights are turned ON.
4. With the lights turned ON, check the engine rpm (idle-up speed). Be sure that the heater fan, rear defogger (if equipped), engine cooling fan and air conditioner (if equipped) are all turned OFF. The idle-up speed should be 750–850 rpm. Adjust by turning the adjusting screw.
5. After making the idle-up adjustment, make sure the idle-up adjusting screw moves as in Step 3 when only the heater fan is operated and then only the rear defogger or engine cooling fan is operated (lights should be off).

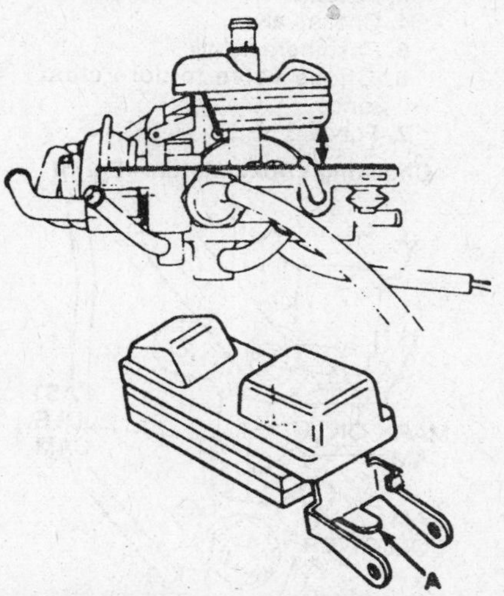


**Bend tab (A) to adjust the upper float level – Spectrum**

##### Automatic Transmission Models

1. Warm up the engine to normal operating temperature.
2. After warming up, run the engine at idle speed.
3. Apply the parking brake and block the drive wheels.
4. Turn all accessories **OFF**.
5. With the brake pedal depressed, shift the selector lever to **Drive** range.

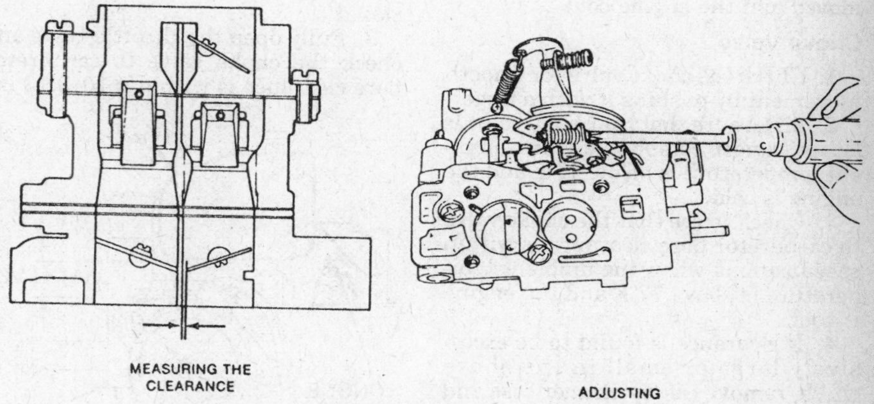


**Primary throttle valve opening (second stage) – Spectrum**

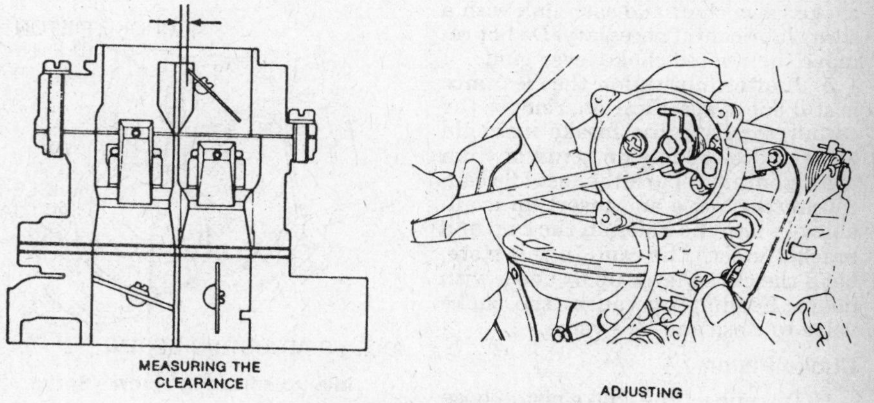


**Unloader adjustment – Spectrum**

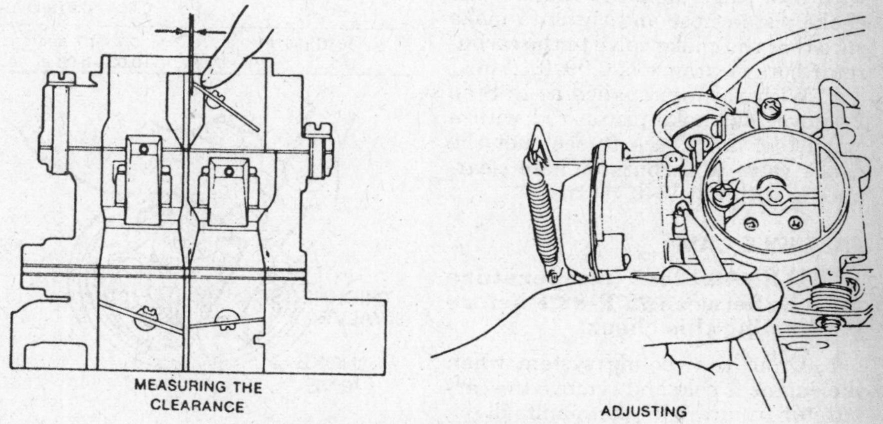


**Choke breaker adjustment – Spectrum**

Check to make sure that the idle-up adjusting screw moves down (indicating that the idle-up is at work).

6. Check the idle-up speed (do not depress the accelerator pedal). The Idle-up speed should be between 700–800 rpm. Adjustment is made by turning the adjusting screw.

### CHOKE

Perform the following check and adjustments with the air cleaner top removed and the engine cold.

#### Choke Valve

1. Check the choke valve for smooth movement by pushing it with a finger.
2. Make sure that the choke valve is closed almost completely when ambient temperature is below 77°F and the engine is cold.
3. Check to see that the choke valve to carburetor bore clearance is within specifications when the ambient temperature is above 77°F and the engine is cool.
4. If clearance is found to be excessively large or small in the above check, remove the air cleaner case and check the strangler spring, choke piston and each link in the choke system for smooth operation. Lubricate the choke valve shaft and each link with a spray lubricant if necessary. Do not remove the riveted choke lever guide.
5. If after lubrication the clearance is still out of specification, remove the carburetor from the intake manifold and remove the idle-up actuator from the carburetor. Turn the fast idle cam counterclockwise and insert an available pin into the holes on the cam and bracket to lock the cam. In this state, bend the choke lever up or down with pliers. Bending up causes the choke valve to close and vice versa.

#### Choke Piston

1. Disconnect the choke piston hose at the throttle chamber.
2. While lightly pushing down on the choke valve to the closing position with your finger, apply vacuum to the choke piston hose and check to make sure that the choke valve to the carburetor bore clearance is 0.09–0.10 in.
3. With vacuum applied as in Step 2, move the choke piston rod with a small tool and check to see that the choke valve to carburetor bore clearance is within 0.16–0.18 1n.

### FAST IDLE CAM

**NOTE: Ambient temperature must be between 72°F–82°F before performing this check.**

1. Drain the cooling system when the engine is cold and remove the carburetor from the intake manifold.
2. Leave the carburetor in a place where the ambient temperature is between 72–82°F for an hour.
3. After an hour, make sure that the mark on the cam and the center of the cam follower are in alignment.

### UNLOADER ADJUSTMENT

**NOTE: Perform this check and adjustment when the engine is cool.**

1. Remove the air cleaner cover.
2. Make sure that the choke valve is closed.
3. Fully open the throttle valve and check the choke valve to carburetor bore clearance is within 0.10–0.12 in.

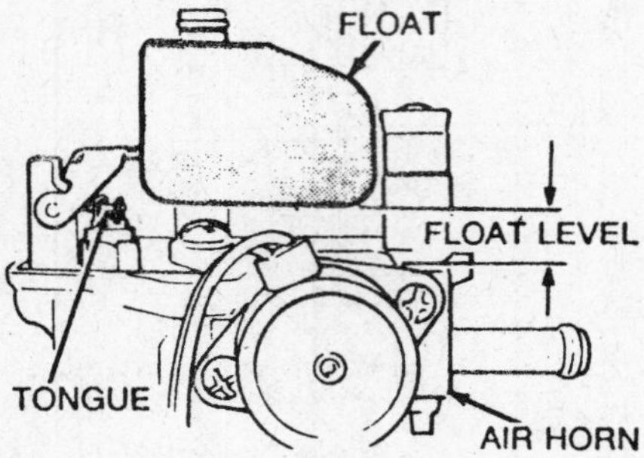


**Float level adjustment – Sprint**

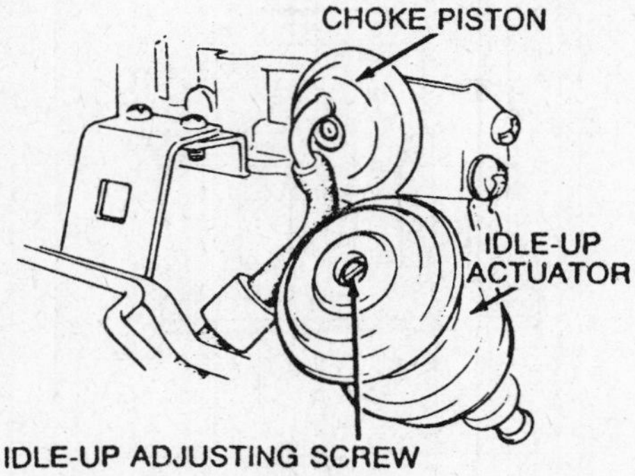


**Idle-up adjusting screw – Sprint**

| Ambient temperature | Clearance |
|---|---|
| 25°C (77°F) | 0.1—0.5 mm<br>0.004—0.019 in |
| 35°C (95°F) | 0.7—1.7 mm<br>0.03—0.06 in |

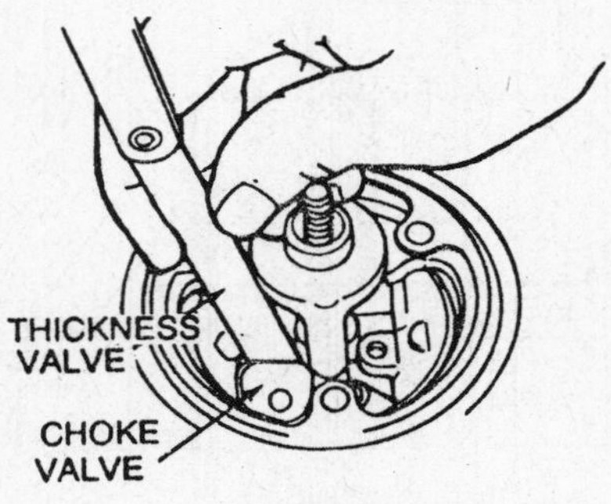


**Choke valve to bore clearance – Sprint**

4. If the clearance is out of specification adjust by bending the unloader arm.

### PUMP STROKE

1. Warm up the engine to normal operating temperature.
2. Stop the engine and remove the air cleaner.
3. Depress the accelerator pedal all the way from idle position to wide open throttle and take the measurement of the pump stroke. The pump stroke should be 0.16–0.18 in. If out of specification check the pump lever and pump rod for smooth movement.

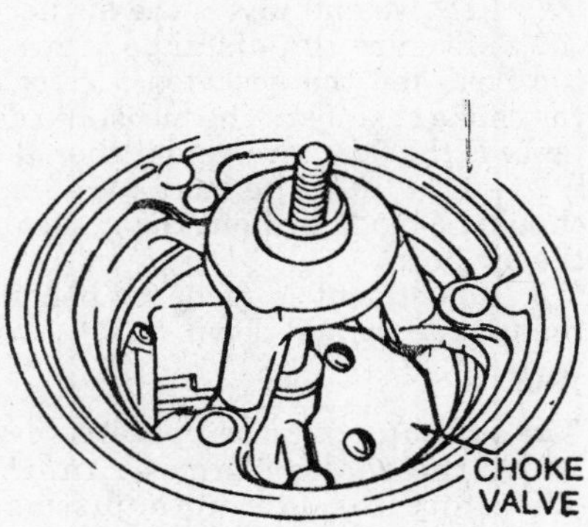


**Choke valve – Sprint**

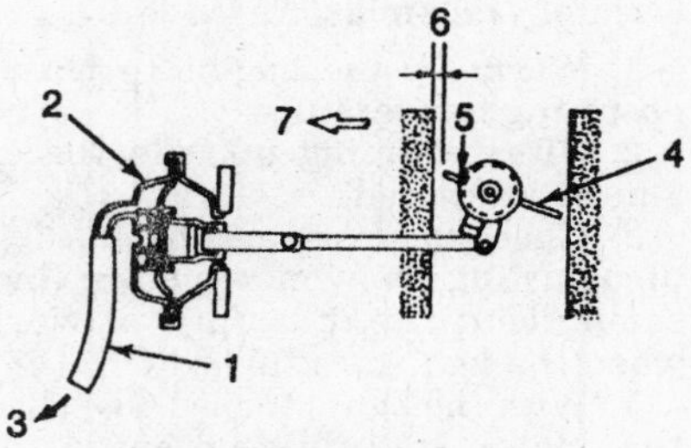


1. Choke piston hose
2. Choke piston
3. Vacuum
4. Choke valve
5. Push here lightly
6. Choke valve to bore clearance
7. Forward

**Checking choke piston – Sprint**

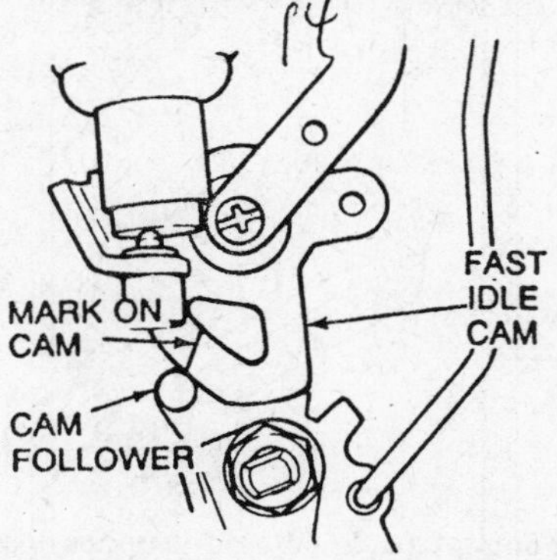


**Mark on cam and cam follower**

## *Nova*

### FLOAT

1. Allow the float the hang down by its own weight. Check the clearance between the float tip and air horn. The float level should be 0.075 in.

**NOTE: This measurement should be made without a gasket on the air horn.**

2. Adjust by bending a portion of the float lip.
3. Lift up the float and check the clearance between the needle valve plunger and the float lip. The float level in the lowered position should be 0.0657–0.0783 in.
4. Adjust by bending a portion of the float lip.

### FAST IDLE

1. Stop the engine and remove the air cleaner.
2. Disconnect and plug the hot idle compensator hose to prevent rough idle.
3. Shut off the choke opener and EGR systems by disconnecting the hose from the Thermo Vacuum Switching Valve M and plugging the M port.
4. Hold the throttle slightly open, push the choke valve closed and hold it closed while releasing the throttle valve.
5. Start the engine but do NOT depress the accelerator pedal.
6. Set the fast idle speed by turning the fast idle screw.
7. Fast idle speed should be: 3000rpm.

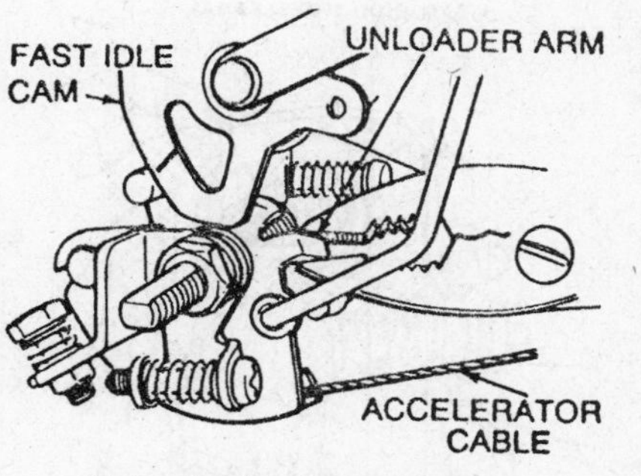


Unloader level arm Sprint

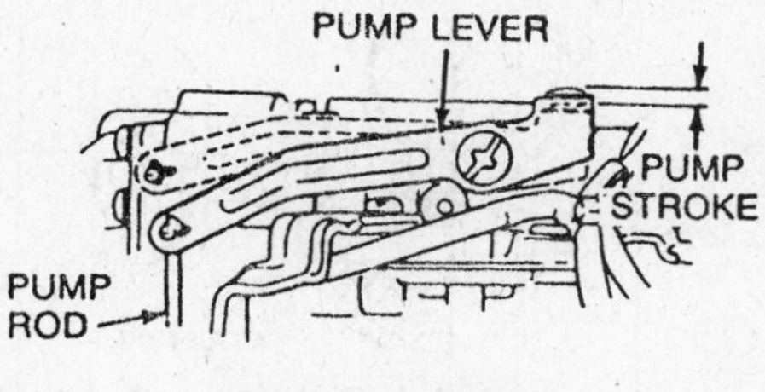


Pump stroke—Sprint

### THROTTLE VALVE OPENING

1. Check the full opening angle of the primary throttle valve, with a T scale. The standard angle should be 90 degrees from the horizontal plane.
2. Adjust by bending the 1st throttle lever stopper.
3. Check the full opening clearance between the secondary throttle valve and the body. The standard clearance should be 0.500 in.
4. Adjust by bending the secondary throttle lever stopper.

### KICK-UP ADJUSTMENT

1. With the primary throttle valve fully opened, check the clearance between the secondary throttle valve and the body. The clearance should be 0.006 in.
2. Adjust by bending the secondary throttle lever.

### SECONDARY TOUCH

1. Check the primary throttle valve opening clearance at the same time the 1st kick lever just touches the 2nd kick lever. The clearance should be 1985: 0.170 in., 1986–89: 0.230 in.
2. Adjust by bending the 1st kick lever.

### UNLOADER

1. With the primary throttle valve fully opened, check that the choke valve clearance is 0.120 in.
2. Adjust by bending the fast idle lever.

### CHOKE BREAKER

1. Set the idle cam. While holding the throttle slightly open, push the choke valve closed and hold it closed as you release the throttle valve.
2. Apply vacuum to the choke breaker 1st diaphragm.
3. Check the choke valve clearance. It should be 0.095 in.
4. Adjust by bending the relief lever.
5. Apply vacuum to choke diaphragms 1st and 2nd.
6. Check the choke valve clearance. It should be 0.245 in.
7. Adjust by turning the diaphragm adjusting screw.

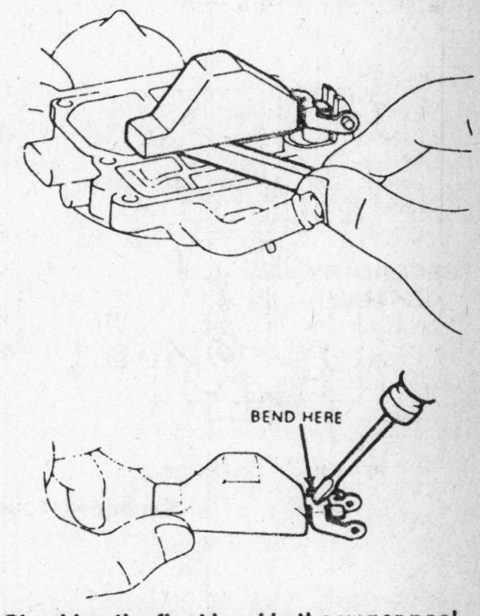


Checking the float level in the upper position—Nova

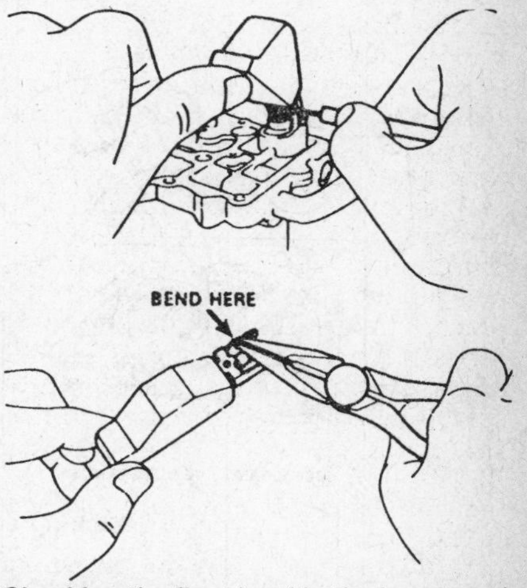


Checking the float level in the lower position—Nova

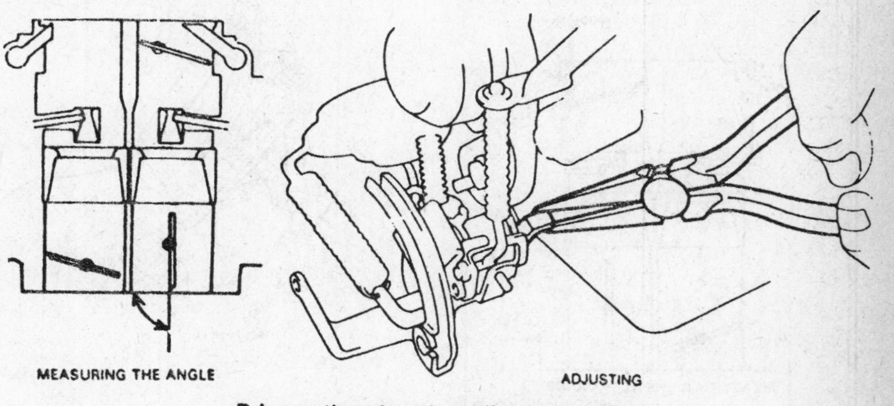


Primary throttle valve adjustment—Nova

### PUMP STROKE

1. With the choke fully opened, measure the length of the stroke. 1985: 0.157 in., 1986–89: 0.079 in.
2. Adjust the pump stroke by bending the connecting link.

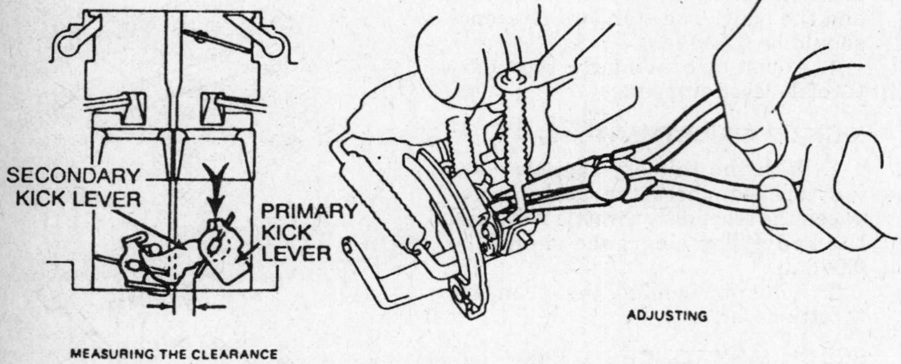


Secondary touch adjustment – Nova

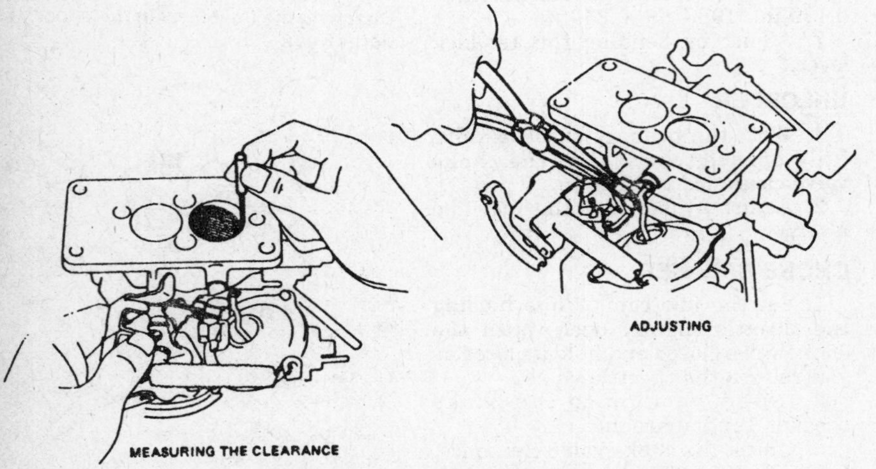


Kick-up adjustment – Nova

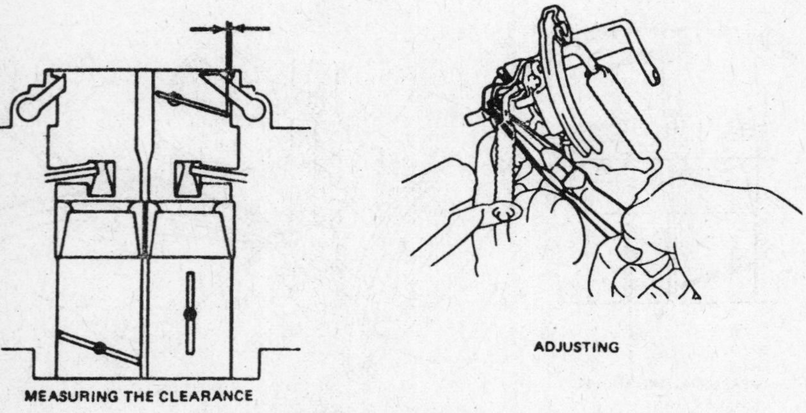


Unloader adjustment – Nova

### OVERHAUL

**For all carburetor overhaul procedures, please refer to "Carburetor Service" in the Unit Repair section.**

## Fuel Injection

**Due to the complex nature of modern fuel injection systems, comprehensive diagnosis and testing procedures fall outside the confines of this repair manual. For complete information on fuel injection diagnosis, testing and repair procedures please refer to Chilton's Guide To Fuel Injection and Feedback Carburetors.**

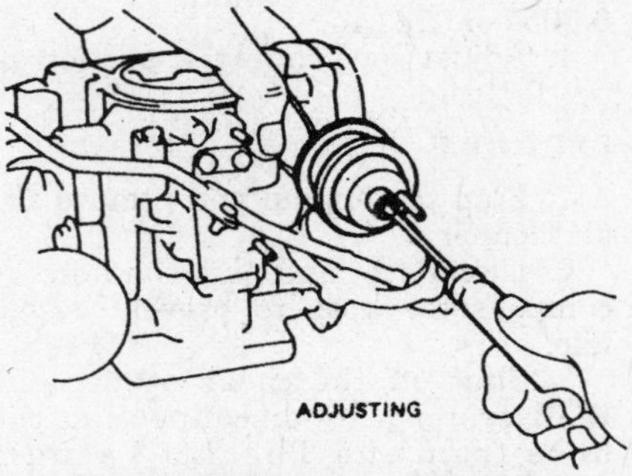


Choke breaker Ist and 2nd diaphragm adjustment – Nova

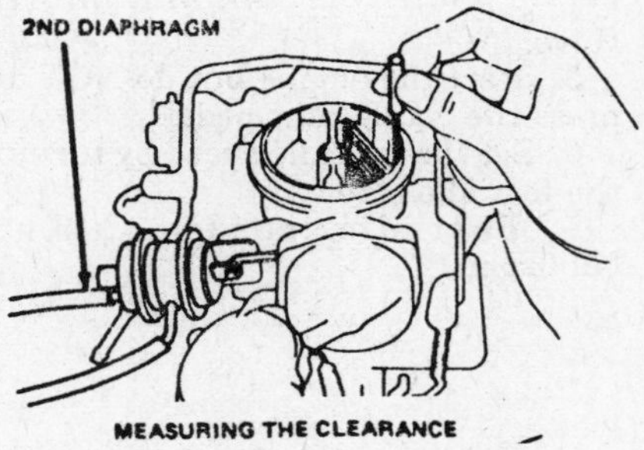


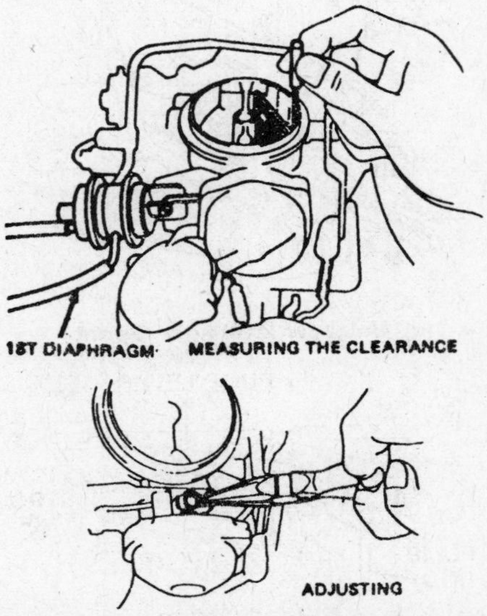


Choke breaker 1st diaphragm adjustment Nova

# MANUAL TRANSAXLE

## REMOVAL & INSTALLATION

### Nova and Prizm

1. Disconnect the negative terminal from the battery.
2. Remove the air cleaner and inlet duct.
3. From the transaxle, disconnect the back-up light switch connector, the speedometer cable, the thermostat housing and the ground wire.
4. Remove the clutch cable-to-transaxle (4) clips, the clutch slave cylinder-to-transaxle bolts and the slave cylinder.
5. Remove the (2) upper transaxle-to-engine bolts and the upper transaxle mount bolt.
6. Using an Engine Support tool or equivalent, attach it to and support the engine. Raise and support the front of the vehicle on jackstands.
7. Remove the left wheel assembly. From under the vehicle, remove the left, right and center splash shields. Remove the center beam-to-chassis bolts and the center beam.
8. Remove the flywheel cover-to-engine bolts and the cover.
9. From both sides of the vehicle, disconnect the lower control arms from the steering knuckles.
10. Disconnect both halfshaft from the transaxle.
11. Disconnect the battery cable and ignition switch wire from the starter. Remove the starter-to-engine bolts and the starter.
12. Using a floor jack, support the transaxle.
13. Remove the transaxle-to-engine bolts and the lower the transaxle from the vehicle.
14. Using a putty knife, clean the gasket mounting surfaces.
15. To install, make sure the input shaft splines align with the clutch disc splines and reverse the removal procedures. Torque the transaxle-to-engine bolts to 47 ft. lbs. (12mm) and to 34 ft. lbs. (10mm), the halfshaft-to-transaxle nuts to 27 ft. lbs., the crossmember-to-chassis nuts/bolts to 29 ft. lbs. and the left-side engine mount bolts to 38 ft. lbs. Check and/or refill the transaxle with fluid.

### Spectrum

1. Drain the oil from the transaxle.
2. Disconnect the negative battery termninal from the battery and the transaxle.
3. Disconnect the wiring connectors, speedometer cable, clutch cable and shift cables from the transaxle.
4. Remove the air cleaner heat tube.
5. Remove the upper transaxle-to-engine bolts.
6. Raise and support the vehicle on jackstands. Remove the left-front wheel assembly and splash shield.
7. Disconnect the left tie rod at the steering knuckle and the left tension rod.
8. Disconnect the drive axles and remove the shafts by pulling them straight out from the transaxle (avoid damaging the oil seals).
9. Remove the dust cover at the clutch housing.
10. Using a floor jack, support the transaxle, then remove the transaxle-to-engine retaining bolts.
11. While sliding the transaxle away from the engine, carefully lower the jack, guiding the right axle shaft out of the transaxle.

**NOTE: The right-axle shaft MUST be installed to the transaxle when the transaxle is being installed to the engine.**

12. To install, reverse the removal procedures.

### Sprint and Metro

1. Disconnect the negative battery cable and the ground strap at the transaxle.
2. Remove the air cleaner and air pipe.
3. Remove the clutch cable from the clutch release lever.
4. Remove the starter and speedometer cable. Disconnect and tag the electrical wires and wiring harness from the transaxle.
5. Remove the front and rear torque rod bolts at the transaxle.
6. Raise and support the vehicle safely.
7. Drain the transaxle fluid.
8. Remove the exhaust pipe at the exhaust manifold and at the 1st exhaust hanger.
9. Remove the clutch housing lower plate.
10. Disconnect the gear shift control shaft and the extension rod at the transaxle.
11. Remove the left front wheel.
12. Using a pry bar, pry on the inboard joints of the right and left hand axle shafts. This will detach the axle shafts from the snap rings of the differential side gears.
13. On the left side, remove the stabilizer bar mounting bolts and ball joint stud bolt. Push down on the stabilizer bar and remove the ball joint stud from the steering knuckle.
14. Pull the left axle shaft out of the transaxle.
15. Remove the front torque rod.

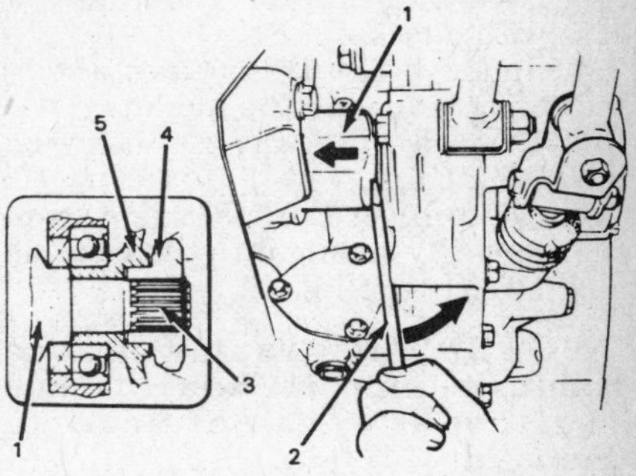


1. Inner axleshaft joint
2. Pry bar
3. Snap ring
4. Differential side gear
5. Differential carrier

**Dislocating axleshafts from snap-rings in transaxle—Sprint and Metro**

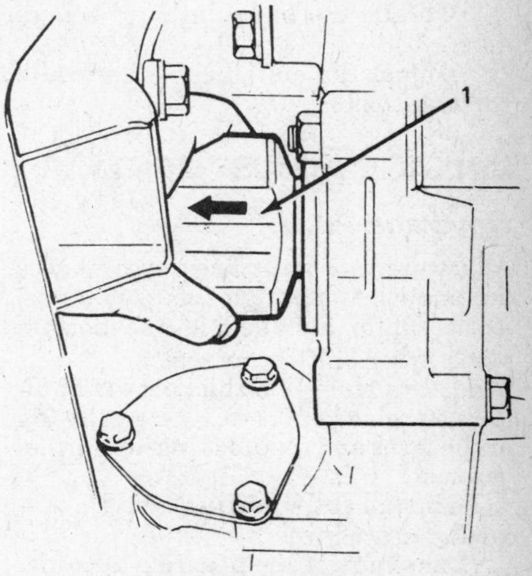


1. Inner axleshaft joint

**Grasp the inner axleshaft joint and pull outwards to remove—Sprint and Metro**

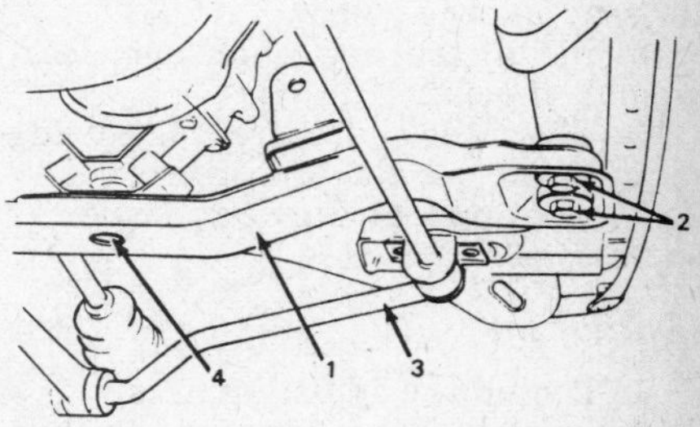


1. Mounting member
2. Mounting bolts 37–43 ft. lbs.
3. Stabilizer bar
4. Mounting nut 29–36 ft. lbs.

**Transaxle mounting bolt locations—Sprint and Metro**

16. Secure and support the transaxle case with a jack.
17. Remove the transaxle-to-body mounting bolts and the mounts.
18. Remove the transaxle-to-engine mounting bolts.
19. Disconnect the transaxle from the engine by sliding it to the left side and lower the jack.

**NOTE: When removing the transaxle, support the right axle shaft, so it does not become damaged.**

20. To install, guide the right axle shaft into the transaxle and reverse the removal procedures.

Torque the transaxle-to-engine bolts to 35 ft. lbs. Torque the transaxle-to-mount bolts to 34 ft. lbs.

Torque the mounting member bolts to 40 ft. lbs.

Torque the stabilizer bar bolts to 30 ft. lbs.

Torque the ball joint stud bolt to 44 ft. lbs.

Adjust the clutch cable and refill the transaxle.

## LINKAGE ADJUSTMENT

### *Nova and Prizm*

Adjustment of shift lever free play is accomplished through the use of a selective shim installed in the bottom ofthe lower shift lever seat.

Select a shim of a thickness that allows a preload of 0.1–0.2 lbs. at the top of the lever and install it in the shift lever seat.

To install the shim, perform the following procedures:

1. Disconnect the negative terminal from the battery.
2. Remove the console and the shifter boot.
3. Remove the shifter cover, shift support and cap.
4. Remove the shifter spacer, shifter seat and the shim.
5. Install the new shim and reassemble the shifter.
6. Check the shifter free play, using a pull scale, for the proper preload.
7. Repeat the procedure (if necessary).

### *Spectrum*

1. Loosen the adjusting nuts.
2. Place the transaxle and the shift lever in the Neutral position.
3. Turn the adjusting nuts until the shift lever is in the vertical position.
4. Tighten the adjusting nuts.

### *Sprint and Metro*

1. At the console, loosen the gear shift control housing nuts and the guide plate bolts.

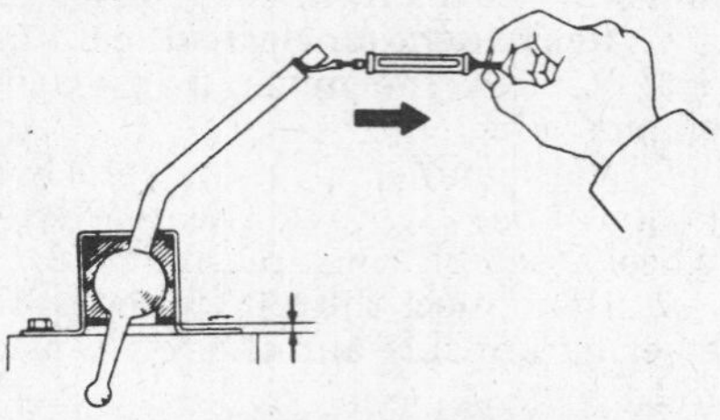

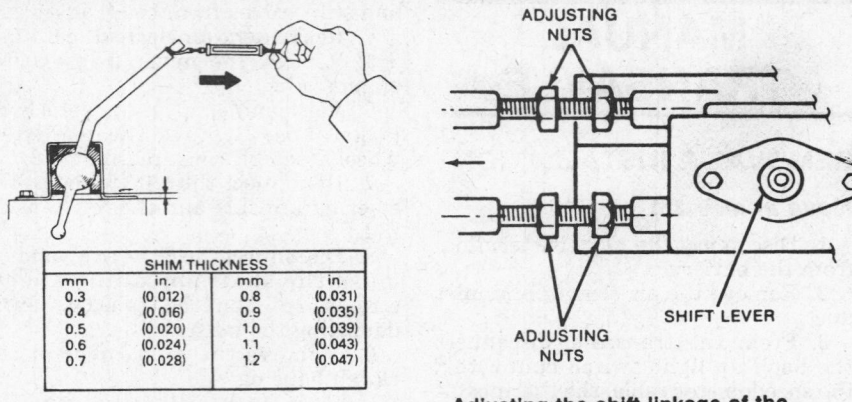

| SHIM THICKNESS | | | |
|---|---|---|---|
| mm | in. | mm | in. |
| 0.3 | (0.012) | 0.8 | (0.031) |
| 0.4 | (0.016) | 0.9 | (0.035) |
| 0.5 | (0.020) | 1.0 | (0.039) |
| 0.6 | (0.024) | 1.1 | (0.043) |
| 0.7 | (0.028) | 1.2 | (0.047) |

**Shift lever free play – Nova and Prizm**

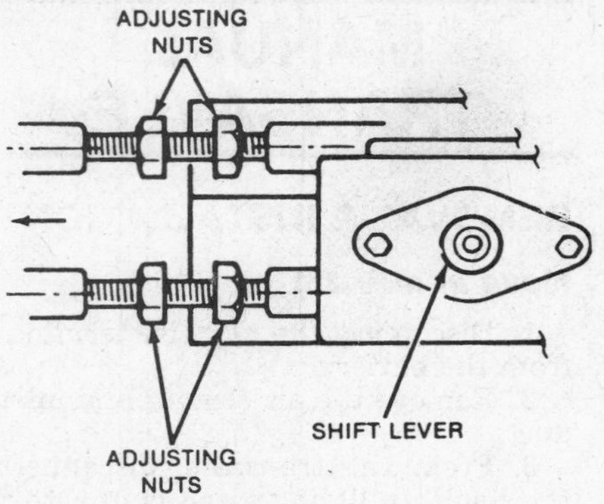


**Adjusting the shift linkage of the transaxle – Spectrum**

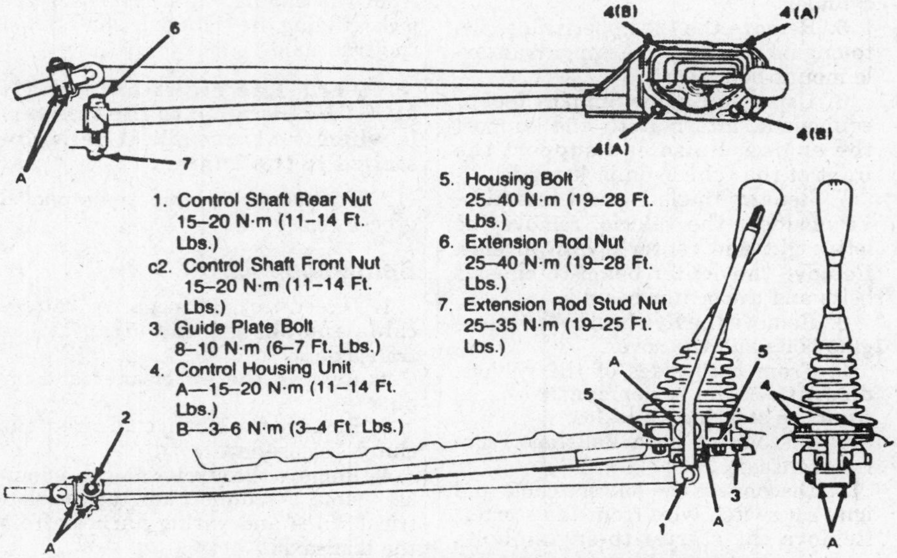


**View of the gear shift control assembly – Sprint and Metro**

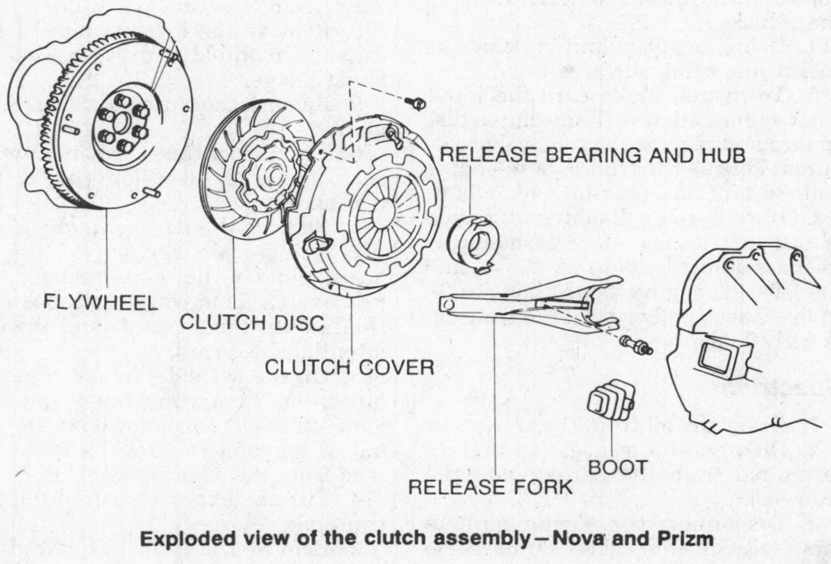


**Exploded view of the clutch assembly – Nova and Prizm**

2. Adjust the guide plate, so that the shift lever is centered and at a right angle to the plate.

3. When the guide plate is positioned correctly, torque the guide plate bolts to 7 ft. lbs. and the housing nuts to 4 ft. lbs.

# CLUTCH

## REMOVAL & INSTALLATION

### *Nova and Prizm*

**NOTE: DO NOT allow grease or oil to contaminate any of the disc, pressure plate or flywheel friction surfaces.**

1. Remove the transaxle from the vehicle.
2. Match mark the pressure plate to flywheel for realignment purposes. Remove the pressure plate-to-flywheel bolts, evenly, a little at a time until the pressure is off the springs.

**CAUTION**

***If the tension is not released in this way, the tremendous spring pressure behind the plate could be released suddenly and violently!***

3. Remove the pressure plate and the clutch disc from the flywheel.
4. To install the clutch assembly, insert the clutch alignment tool No. J-35757 or an old transaxle pilot shaft through the clutch disc, then, insert the tool or shaft into the pilot bearing.

**NOTE: The clutch disc is installed with the concave side facing the flywheel.**

5. Install the pressure plate over the disc with matchmarks aligned and install the bolts. Tighten the bolts alternately and evenly until even pressure is all around. Finally, torque the pressure plate-to-flywheel bolts to 14 ft. lbs. Remove the centering tool or input shaft.
6. To complete the installation, lubricate the release bearing hub and release fork contact points with multi-purpose grease and reverse the removal procedures.

### *Spectrum*

1. Remove the transaxle.
2. Install the Pilot Shaft tool No. J-35282 or equivalent, into the pilot bearing to support the clutch assembly during the removal procedures.

**NOTE: Observe the alignment marks on the clutch and the clutch cover and pressure plate assembly. If the markings are not present, be sure to add them.**

3. Loosen the clutch cover and pressure plate assembly retaining bolts evenly (one at a time) until the spring pressure is released.
4. Remove the clutch cover and pressure plate assembly and clutch plate.

**NOTE: Check the clutch disc, flywheel and pressure plate for wear, damage or heat cracks. Replace all damaged parts.**

5. Before installation, lightly lubricate the pilot shaft splines, pilot bearing and pilot release bearing surface with grease.

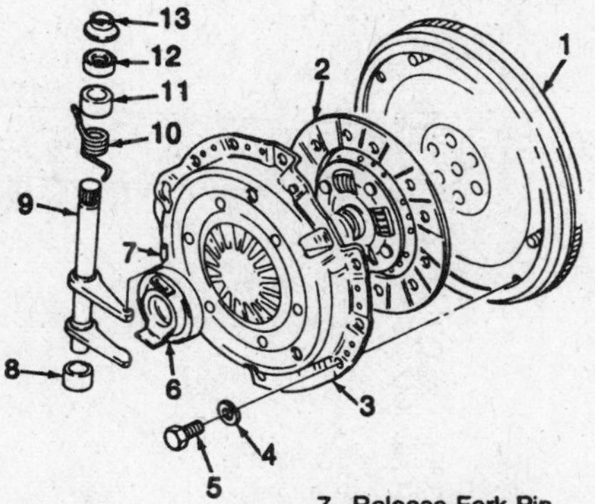


1. Flywheel
2. Disc
3. Clutch Cover
4. Lock Washer
5. Bolt
6. Release Bearing
7. Release Fork Pin
8. No. 2 Bushing
9. Release Shaft
10. Return Spring
11. No. 1 Bushing
12. Shaft Seal
13. Shaft Cover

**Exploded view of the clutch assembly – Sprint and Metro**

6. To install, reverse the removal procedures. Torque the clutch cover/pressure plate-to-flywheel bolts evenly to 13 ft. lbs., to avoid distortion.

### *Sprint and Metro*

1. Remove the transaxle.
2. Install tool J-34860 into the pilot bearing to support the clutch assembly.

**NOTE: Look for the X mark or white painted number on the clutch cover and the X mark on the flywheel. If there are no markings, mark the clutch cover and the flywheel for reassembly purposes.**

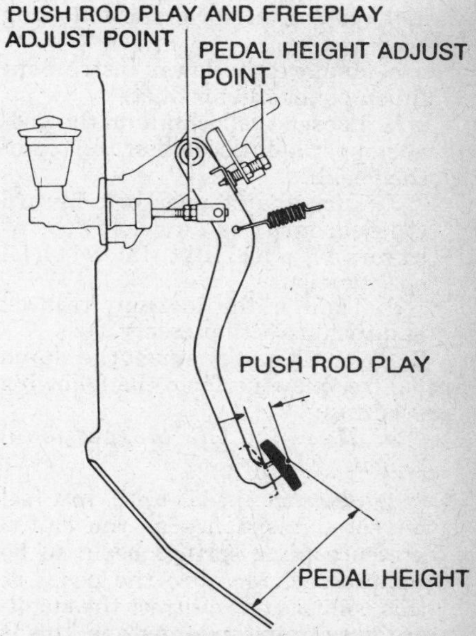


**View of the clutch pedal height and free-play adjustment – Nova and Prizm**

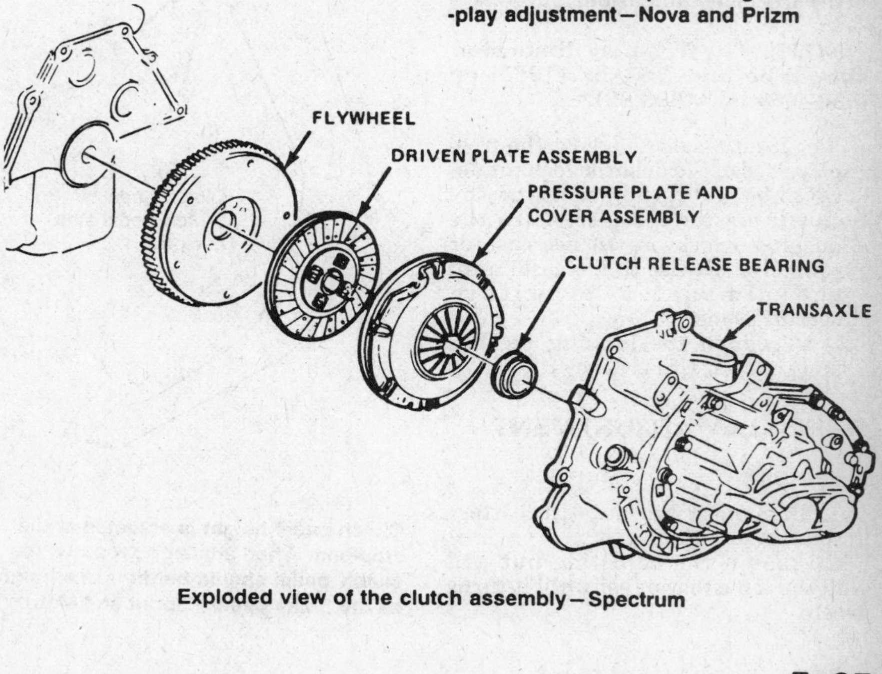


**Exploded view of the clutch assembly – Spectrum**

3. Loosen the clutch cover-to-flywheel bolts, one turn at a time (evenly) until the spring pressure is released.
4. Remove the clutch cover and clutch disc.
5. Inspect the parts for wear, if necessary, replace the parts.
6. To install, reverse the removal procedures. Torque the clutch cover bolts to 14–20 ft. lbs.

## PEDAL HEIGHT/FREE-PLAY ADJUSTMENT

### *Nova and Prizm*

1. Check pedal height as measured from the insulating sheet on the floor to the front-center of the pedal; it should be 5.65–6.043 in. If the height is not correct, perform the following procedures:
   a. Remove the lower instrument finish panel and air duct.
   b. Loosen the locknut on the pedal stopper bolt (located at the top of the pedal).
   c. Turn the stopper bolt inward (to decrease) or outward (to increase) until it is within specifications.
   d. Tighten the locknut, recheck and readjust (if necessary).
2. To check and/or adjust the clutch pedal free-play, perform the following procedures:
   a. Measure the clutch pedal height.
   b. Push the pedal until you feel increased resistance as the clutch pressure plate springs begin to be compressed. Measure the pedal at this point, then, subtract the smaller figure from the larger one; this is the free-play dimension.

**NOTE: The free-play dimension should be 0.51–0.91 in. (1985) or 0.20–0.59 in. (1986-89).**

   c. If necessary to adjust the free-play, loosen the pushrod locknut, located between the pedal and the clutch master cylinder. Turn the pushrod (clockwise to decrease or counter-clockwise to increase) until the dimension is within specifications.
   d. Tighten the locknut, recheck and readjust (if necessary).

## FREE-PLAY ADJUSTMENT

### *Spectrum*

1. Disconnect the negative battery terminal from the battery.
2. Loosen the adjusting nut and pull the cable to the rear until it turns freely.
3. Adjust the cable length by turning the adjusting nut.
4. When the clutch pedal free play travel reaches 0.39–0.79 in. release the cable.
5. When the adjustment has been completed, tighten the lock nut.

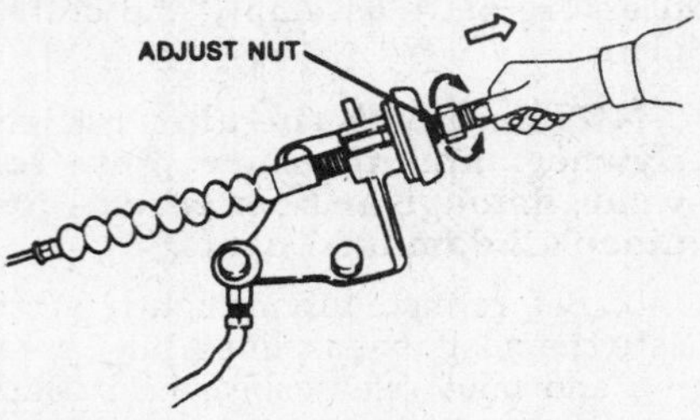


**Adjustment of the clutch cable—Spectrum**

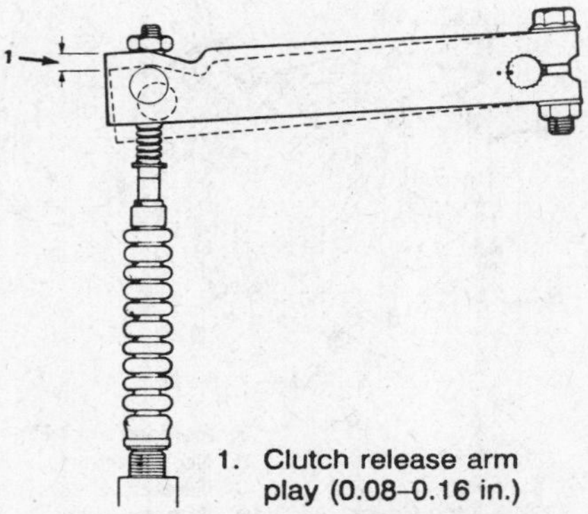


**Clutch release arm free-play adjustment—Sprint and Metro**

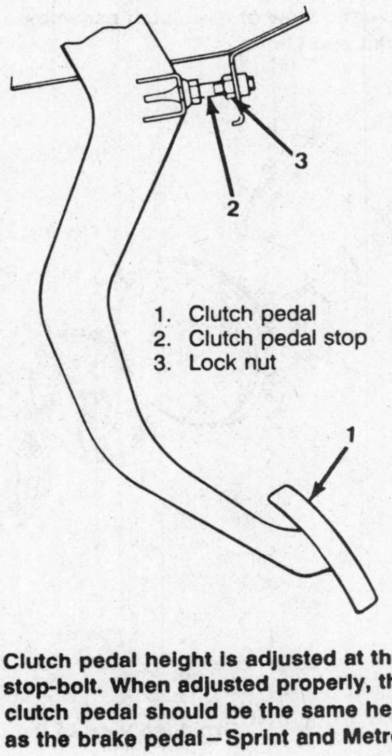


**Clutch pedal height is adjusted at the stop-bolt. When adjusted properly, the clutch pedal should be the same height as the brake pedal—Sprint and Metro**

### *Sprint and Metro*

1. At the transaxle, move the clutch release arm to check the free play, it should be 0.08–0.16 in.
2. If necessary, turn the clutch cable joint nut to adjust the cable length. The clutch pedal height should be adjusted so that the clutch pedal is the exact same height as the brake pedal. The pedal is adjusted at the stop bolt on the upper end of the pedal pivot.

# Clutch Master Cylinder

## REMOVAL & INSTALLATION

### *Nova and Prizm*

1. Drain or siphon the fluid from the master cylinder.
2. Remove the lower instrument finish panel and air duct.
3. Remove the pedal return spring, clevis pin and clip.
4. Disconnect the hydraulic line the clutch master cylinder.

**NOTE: Do not spill brake fluid on the painted surface of the vehicle.**

5. Remove the master cylinder-to-firewall nuts and withdraw the assembly.
6. To install, reverse the removal procedures. Refill the master cylinder reservoir with brake fluid. Bleed the clutch hydraulic system. Operate the clutch pedal and check the system for leaks. Check and/or adjust the clutch pedal height and free-play.

# Clutch Slave Cylinder

## REMOVAL & INSTALLATION

### *Nova and Prizm*

**NOTE: Do not spill brake fluid on the painted surface of the vehicle.**

1. Disconnect the hydraulic line from the clutch slave cylinder.
2. Remove the slave cylinder-to-engine bolts and the cylinder.
3. To install, reverse the removal procedures. Refill the clutch master cylinder reservoir with clean brake fluid. Bleed the clutch hydraulic system. Operate the clutch pedal and check for leaks.

## BLEEDING THE HYDRAULIC SYSTEM

### *Nova and Prizm*

1. Fill the clutch master cylinder reservoir with brake fluid.

**NOTE: DO NOT spill brake flu-**

**id on the painted surface of the vehicle for it will lift the finish.**

2. Fit a vinyl bleeder tube over the bleeder screw at the front of the slave cylinder and place the other end in a clean jar half filled with brake fluid.
3. Have an assistant depress the clutch pedal several times. Loosen the bleeder screw and allow the fluid to flow into the jar.
4. Tighten the screw and have the assistant release the clutch pedal.
5. Repeat bleeding procedure until no air bubbles are present in the fluid.
6. Refill the master cylinder to the specified level, check the system for leaks, then, adjust the clutch pedal height and free-play.

## Clutch Cable

### REMOVAL & INSTALLATION

#### *Spectrum*

1. Disconnect the negative battery terminal from the battery.
2. Loosen the clutch cable adjusting nuts. Disconnect the cable from the release arm and cable bracket.
3. At the clutch pedal, remove the cable retaining bolt.
4. Disconnect the cable from the front of the dash.
5. Remove the clutch cable from the vehicle.
6. To install, grease the clutch cable pin and reverse the removal procedures.
7. Adjust the clutch cable.

#### *Sprint and Metro*

1. Disconnect the negative battery cable.
2. Remove the clutch cable joint nut and disconnect the cable from the release arm.
3. Remove the clutch cable bracket mounting nuts and remove the bracket from the cable.
4. Remove the cable retaining bolts at the clutch pedal.
5. Remove the cable from the vehicle.
6. Before installation, apply grease to the hook and pin end of the cable.
7. Connect the cable to the clutch pedal and install the retaining bolts.
8. Install the clutch cable bracket on the cable.
9. Position the bracket on the transaxle and install the mounting bolts.
10. Connect the cable to the release lever and install the joint nut on the cable.
11. Adjust the clutch cable as previously outlined and connect the negative battery cable.

# AUTOMATIC TRANSAXLE

**For further information on the automatic transaxle, please refer to "Automatic Transmissions" in the Unit Repair section.**

### REMOVAL & INSTALLATION

#### *Nova and Prizm*

1. Disconnect the negative terminal from the battery and the ground cable from the transaxle. Label and disconnect the necessary electrical connectors. Drain the transaxle.
2. Remove the air intake duct. Disconnect the Throttle Valve cable from the carburetor (if equipped).
3. Disconnect the neutral safety switch, the speedometer cable and the shift control cable from the transaxle. Remove the shift cable bracket from the transaxle.
4. From the top of the transaxle, disconnect the thermostat housing-to-transaxle bolts.
5. Remove the single upper mount-to-bracket bolt. Remove the two upper bellhousing bolts.
6. Remove the upper (2) bell housing bolts.
7. Using a Engine Supporting tool, connect it to and support the engine. Raise and support the front of the vehicle on jackstands.
8. Remove the left wheel assembly, the left splash shield, the right splash shield and the center splash shield. Remove the crossmember-to-chassis bolts and the crossmember.
9. Remove the oil line cooler bracket. Disconnect and plug the oil cooler lines from the transaxle.
10. Remove the flywheel cover. Matchmark the torque converter-to-flywheel, then, remove the torque converter-to-flywheel bolts and separate the torque converter from the flywheel.

**NOTE:The crankshaft must be rotated to gain access to the other bolts.**

11. Remove both control arm-to-ball joint nuts/bolts and separate the lower control arms from the ball joints.
12. Remove both halfshaft-to-transaxle flange nuts and separate the halfshaft from the transaxle; support the halfshaft on a wire.
13. Disconnect the battery cable and ignition wire from the starter. Remove the starter-to-engine bolts and the starter.
14. Remove the lower transaxle-to-engine bolts.
15. Using a wooden block atop a floor jack, support the transaxle.
16. Remove the remaining transaxle-to-engine bolts. Separate the transaxle from the engine and lower it from the vehicle.

To install

17. Align the torque converter-to-flywheel alignment marks and reverse the removal procedures.

Torque the transaxle-to-engine bolts to 47 ft. lbs. (12mm bolt) and 34 ft. lbs. (10mm bolt)

Torque the left-side engine mount bolts to 38 ft. lbs.

Torque the torque converter-to-flywheel bolts to 13 ft. lbs. Torque the halfshaft-to-transaxle nuts/bolts to 27 ft. lbs.

Torque the crossmember-to-chassis bolts to 29 ft. lbs. Refill the transaxle with Dexron® II transmission fluid.

Start the engine, test drive it and check for leaks.

#### *Spectrum*

1. Disconnect the negative battery terminal from the battery.
2. Remove the air duct tube from the air cleaner.
3. From the transaxle, disconnect the shift cable, speedometer cable, vacuum diaphragm hose, engine wiring harness clamp and the ground cable.
4. At the left-fender, disconnect the inhibitor switch and the kickdown solenoid wiring connectors.
5. Disconnect the oil cooler lines from the transaxle.
6. Remove the three upper transax-

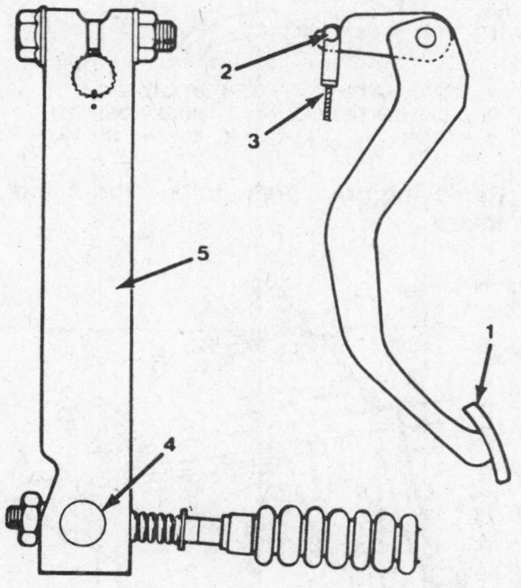


1. Clutch pedal
2. Hook on cable end (lubricate)
3. Clutch cable
4. Pin (lubricate)
5. Clutch release arm

**Clutch cable mounting on release arm and at pedal. Note the matchmarks on the release arm and shaft—Sprint and Metro**

le-to-engine mounting bolts. Raise and support the vehicle on jackstands.
7. Remove both front-wheels and the left-front fender splash shield.
8. Disconnect both tie rod ends at the steering knuckles.
9. Remove both front tension rod brackets and disconnect the rods from the control arms.
10. Disengage the axle shafts from the transaxle.
11. Remove the flywheel dust cover and the converter-to-flywheel attaching bolts.
12. Remove the transaxle rear mount through bolt.
13. Disconnect the starter wiring and the starter. Support the transaxle.
14. Remove the lower transaxle-to-engine mounting bolts and remove the transaxle.
15. To install, reverse the removal procedures. Torque the converter-to-flywheel at 30 ft. lbs., the transaxle-to-engine at 56 ft. lbs., adjust the shift linkage and fill the transaxle with Dexron® II automatic transmission fluid.

### *Sprint and Metro*

1. Disconnect the air suction guide from the air cleaner.
2. Disconnect the negative and the positive battery cables.
3. Remove the battery and the battery bracket tray.
4. Remove the negative cable from the transaxle.
5. Disconnect the solenoid wire coupler and the shift lever switch wire couplers.
6. Remove the wiring harness from the transaxle.
7. Remove the speedometer cable from the transaxle.
8. Disconnect the oil pressure control cable from the accelerator cable, and then the accelerator cable from the transaxle.
9. Remove the select cable from the transaxle.
10. Remove the starter motor.
11. Drain the transaxle fluid.
12. Disconnect the oil outlet and inlet hoses from the oil pipes. After disconnecting, plug the two oil hoses to prevent fluid in the hoses and oil cooler from draining.
13. Raise the vehicle and support it safely.
14. Remove the exhaust No. 1 pipe.
15. Remove the clutch housing lower plate.
16. Remove the six drive plate bolts. To lock the drive plate, engage a screw driver with the drive plate gear through the notch provided at the under side of the transmission case.
17. Remove the left hand front drive axle. See drive axle section for removal procedures.
18. Detach the inboard joint of the right hand drive axle from the differential.
19. Disconnect the transaxle mounting member.
20. Securely support the transaxle with a suitable jack for removal.
21. Remove the transaxle left mounting.
22. Remove the bolts fastening the engine and the transaxle.
23. Disconnect the transaxle from the engine by sliding towards the left side, and then, carefully lower the jack.

**NOTE: When removing the transaxle assembly from the engine, move it in parallel with the crankshaft and use care so as not to apply excessive force to the drive plate and torque converter. After removing the transaxle assembly, be sure to keep it so that the oil pan is at the bottom. If the transaxle is tilted, fluid in it may flow out.**

24. To install the transaxle, reverse the removal procedure noting the following important steps.
25. Before installing the transaxle assembly apply grease around the cup at the center of the torque converter.

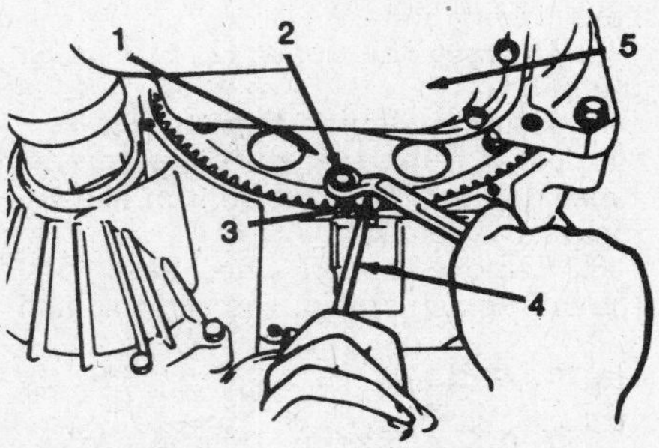


1. DRIVE PLATE
2. DRIVE PLATE BOLT
3. NOTCH
4. STANDARD SCREWDRIVER
5. ENGINE OIL PAN

**Removing drive plate bolts—Sprint and Metro**

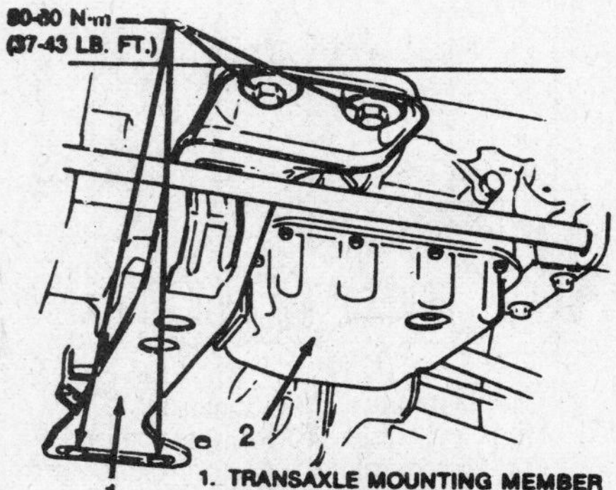


**Transaxle mounting member and oil pan—Sprint and Metro**

Then measure the distance between the torque converter flange nut and the transaxle case housing. The distance should be more than 0.85 in. (21.4mm). If the distance is less than 0.85 in. (21.4mm), the torque converter has been installed incorrectly and must be removed and reinstalled correctly.
26. When installing the transaxle, guide the right drive axle into the differential side gear as the transaxle is being raised.
27. After inserting the inboard joints of the right hand and left hand drive axles into the differential side gears, push the inboard joints into the side gears until the snap rings on the drive axles engage the side gears.
28. After connecting the oil pressure control cable to the accelerator cable, check the oil pressure control cable play and adjust if necessary.
29. Install the select cable.
30. Refill the transaxle and check the fluid level.
31. Tighten the following bolts and nuts to specifications.
   a. Drive plate bolts—14 ft. lbs. (19 Nm).
   b. Mounting member bolts—40 ft. lbs. (55 Nm).
   c. Transaxle mounting nuts—33 ft. lbs. (45 Nm).
   d. Transaxle mounting bolts (8mm)—40 ft. lbs. (55 Nm).
   e. Transaxle mounting nuts—40 ft. lbs. (55 Nm).
   f. Stabilizer shaft mounting Bolts—31 ft. lbs. (42 Nm).

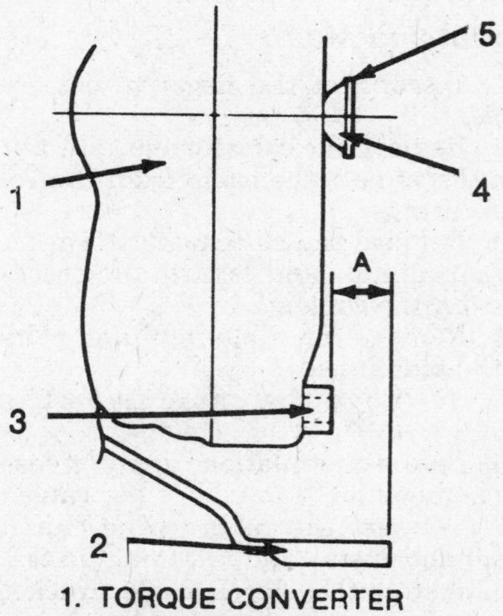


1. TORQUE CONVERTER
2. TRANSAXLE CASE HOUSING
3. FLANGE NUT
4. CUP
5. "APPLY GREASE HERE"
A: MORE THAN 21.4 mm (0.85 IN.)

**Torque converter installation—Sprint and Metro**

g. Ball stud bolt—44 ft. lbs. (60 Nm).
h. Wheel nuts—40 ft. lbs. (55 Nm).

### OIL PAN AND FILTER SERVICE

#### *Nova and Prizm*

**NOTE: The A240E 4 speed transaxle, also called Electronic Controlled Transaxle (ECT), differs from the oil pressure control type transaxle A131L 3 speed in that it is controlled by a microcomputer. On the A131L the drain and refill capacity is 2.4 U.S. qts. and the dry fill capacity is 5.8 U.S. qts. On the A240E the drain and refill capacity is 3.3 U.S. qts. and the dry fill capacity is 7.6 U.S. qts. The correct fluid specification is the use of Dexron® II automatic transmission fluid, or its equivalent.**

1. Raise the vehicle and support safely. Drain the transaxle fluid
2. Remove the oil pan retaining bolts, tap the oil pan lightly to remove.
3. Remove the oil pan gasket material and clean the surfaces thoroughly.
4. When installing the oil pan, be sure to use a new gasket.
5. Install a new filter or pick-up screen and replace the magnet into the oil cleaner.
6. Install the oil pan and fill the transaxle with the correct type of fluid and to the proper level.

#### *Spectrum*

**NOTE: Dexron®II automatic transmission fluid or its equivalent is the only recommended automatic transmission fluid to be used in this unit. The use of any other grade of fluid can lead to unsatisfactory performance or complete unit failure.**

1. Jack up the front end of the car and support it safely.
2. Remove the drain plug located at the lower part of the differential.
3. Remove the oil pan and discard the gasket.
4. Clean all gasket material from the mating surface.
5. Using a new gasket, install the gasket and pan to the transaxle.
6. Install and tighten the drain plug.
7. Fill the transaxle through the filler tube using Dexron®II Automatic Transmission Fluid.

#### *Sprint and Metro*

**NOTE: Dexron®II automatic transmission fluid or its equivalent is the only recommended automatic transmission fluid to be used in this unit. The use of any other grade of fluid can lead to unsatisfactory performance or complete unit failure.**

1. Raise the vehicle and support it safely.
2. Drain the transaxle fluid.
3. Remove the stabilizer shaft mounting bolts.
4. Remove the transaxle mounting member.
5. Remove the oil pan bolts.
6. Tap around the oil pan with a plastic hammer, and remove the oil pan.

**NOTE: Do not force the oil pan off by prying with a flat tip screwdriver, as it may cause damage to the gasket mating surfaces.**

7. Throughly remove all gasket material from the mating surface.
8. Clean the inside of the oil pan and install a new gasket.
9. Installation is the reverse of the removal procedure.

### THROTTLE CABLE ADJUSTMENT

#### *Nova and Prizm*

1. Depress the accelerator pedal completely and check that the throttle valve opens fully. If the throttle valve does not open fully, adjust the accelerator link
2. Fully depress the accelerator
3. Loosen the adjustment nuts.
4. Adjust the throttle cable housing so that the distance between the end of the boot and the stopper on the cable is correct. The distance must be 0.04 in. (0.1mm).
5. Tighten the adjusting nuts and recheck the adjustment.

### TRANSAXLE SHIFT CONTROL ADJUSTMENT

#### *Nova and Prizm*

1. Loosen the swivel nut on the lever.
2. Push the manual lever fully towards the right side of the vehicle.
3. Return the lever 2 notches to the **N** position.
4. Set the shift lever in the **N** position.
5. While holding the lever lightly towards the **R** position, tighten the swivel nut.

#### *Spectrum*

1. Loosen the two adjusting nuts at the control rod link and connect the shift cable to the link on the transaxle.
2. Shift the transaxle into the **NEUTRAL** detent.
3. Place the shifter lever into the **NEUTRAL** position.
4. Rotate the link assembly clockwise to remove slack in the cable.
5. Tighten the rear adjusting nut until it makes contact with the link. Tighten the front adjusting nut until it makes contact with the link and tighten the adjusting nuts.

## Vacuum Modulator

### REMOVAL & INSTALLATION

#### *Spectrum*

1. Disconnect the negative battery cable.
2. Disconnect the kickdown solenoid wire connector located at the left fender.
3. Raise the vehicle and suppot it safely.
4. Remove the kickdown solenoid at the transaxle.
5. Remove the vacuum modulator.
6. Installation is the reverse of the removal procedure. If a new modulator is to be installed, use the following illustration to determine the proper vacuum diaphragm rod length.

### NEUTRAL START SWITCH ADJUSTMENT

#### *Nova and Prizm*

**NOTE: If the engine will start with the shift selector in any range other than N or P positions, adjustment is required.**

1. Loosen the neutral start switch bolts and set the shift lever in the **N** position.
2. Disconnect the neutral start switch connector.
3. Connect an ohmmeter between the terminals.
4. Adjust the switch to the point where there is continuity between terminals.
5. Connect the neutral switch connector.
6. Torque the switch bolts to 48 inch lbs. (5.4 Nm).
7. Recheck the switch operation.

# DRIVE AXLE

## Halfshaft

### REMOVAL & INSTALLATION

#### *Nova and Prizm*

1. From the front wheel assemblies,

remove the grease cup, then, loosen the wheel lug nuts and the halfshaft hub nut.

2. Raise and support the front of the vehicle on jackstands, then, remove the wheel/tire assemblies, the cotter pin, the locknut cap, hub nut and washer.

3. Loosen and remove the (6) halfshaft flange-to-transaxle flange nuts

**NOTE: When removing the halfshaft-to-transaxle nuts, have an assistant depress the brake pedal to keep the shaft from turning.**

4. Remove the lower control arm-to-ball joint nuts/bolts and separate the lower control arm from the steering knuckle from lower control arm.

**NOTE: If the vehicle is equipped with a twincam engine, it may be necessary to remove the stabilizer bar from the lower control arm.**

5. Turn the steering knuckle to separate the halfshaft from the transaxle.

6. Cover the outboard CV-joint rubber boot with a cloth to prevent damage. Using the wheel puller tool No. J-25287 or equivalent, press the halfshaft from the steering knuckle and remove the driveshaft.

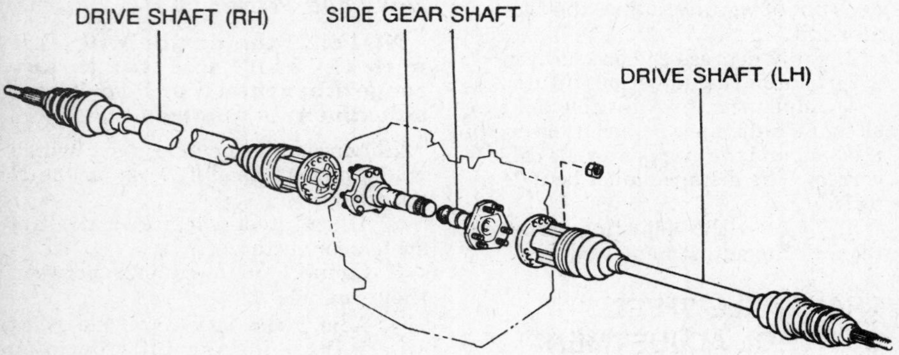


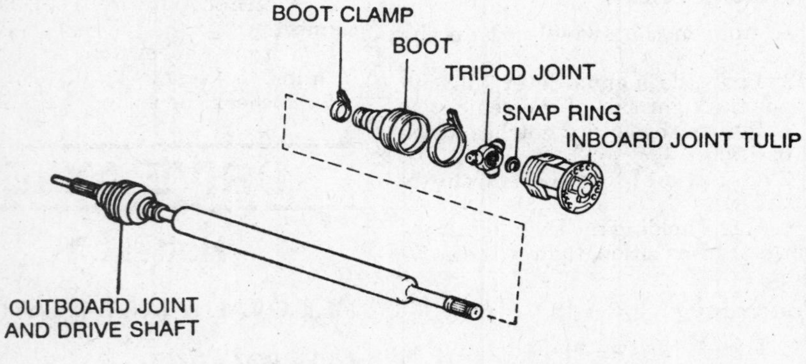


**Drive axle assembly – Nova and Prizm**

7. To install the halfshaft, lubricate the splines with multi-puprose grease, insert the it into the steering knuckle hub, install the washer and the hub nut, then, tighten the hub nut to draw the halfshaft into the steering knuckle hub until it seats.

**NOTE: When torquing the hub nut, have an assistant depress the brake pedal; it may be necessary final torque the hub nut with the vehicle resting on the ground.**

8. To complete the installation, reverse the removal procedures. Torque the lower control arm-to-ball joint nuts/bolts to 59 ft. lbs., the halfshaft-to-transaxle flange nuts to 27 ft. lbs. and the halfshaft-to-steering knuckle hub nut to 137 ft. lbs. Install a new cotter pin.

### *Spectrum*

1. Raise and support the front of the vehicle on jackstands, allowing the wheels to hang.

2. Remove the front wheel assemblies, the hub grease caps, the hub nuts and the cotter pins.

3. Install the drive axle boot seal protector tool No. J–28712 or equivalent, on the outer CV-joints and the drive axle boot seal protector tool No. J-34754 or equivalent, on the inner Tri-Pot joints.

**NOTE: Clean the halfshaft threads and lubricate them with a thread lubricant.**

4. Have an assistant depress the brake pedal, then, remove the hub nut and washer.

5. Remove the caliper-to-steering knuckle bolts and support the caliper (on a wire) out of the way.

6. Remove the rotor. Remove the drain plug and drain the oil from the transaxle.

7. Using a slide hammer puller and the puller attachment tool No. J–34866 or equivalent, pull the hub from the halfshaft.

8. Remove the tie rod-to-steering knuckle cotter pin and the nut. Using the Ball Joint Separator tool No. J–21687–02 or equivalent, press the tie rod ball joint from the steering knuckle.

9. Remove the lower ball joint-to-control arm nuts/bolts.

10. Swing the steering knuckle assembly outward and slide the halfshaft from the steering knuckle.

11. Place a large pry bar between the differential case and the inboard constant velocity joint. Pry the axle shaft from the differential case.

12. Remove the halfshaft assembly.

**NOTE: When installing the axle shaft, press it into the differential case until it locks with with snap ring.**

13. To install, use new cotter pins and reverse the removal procedures. Torque the ball joint-to-control arm nuts/bolts to 80 ft. lbs. (108 Nm), the caliper-to-steering knuckle bolts to 41 ft. lbs. (55 Nm) and the halfshaft-to-hub nut to 137 ft. lbs. (186 Nm). Check and/or adjust the front end alignment.

### *Sprint and Metro*

1. Remove the grease cap, the cotter pin and the axle shaft nut from both front wheels.

2. Loosen the wheel nuts.

3. Raise and support the front of the vehicle on jackstands.

4. Remove the front wheels.

5. Drain the transaxle fluid.

6. Using a pry bar, pry on the inboard joints of the right and left hand axle shafts to detach the axle shafts from the snap rings of the differential side gears.

7. Remove the stabilizer bar mounting bolts and the ball joint stud bolt. Pull down on the stabilizer bar and remove the ball joint stud from the steering knuckle.

8. Pull the axle shafts out of the

transaxle's side gear, first, and then from the steering knuckles.

**NOTE: To prevent the axle shaft boots from becoming damaged, be careful not to bring them into contact with any parts. If any malfunction is found in the either of the joints, replace the joints as an assembly.**

9. To install, snap the axle shaft into the transaxle, first, and then into the steering knuckle.
10. To complete the installation, reverse the removal procedures. Torque the stabilizer bar mounting bolts to 30 ft. lbs.; the ball joint stud bolt to 44 ft. lbs. and the axle shaft nut to 144 ft. lbs.

### CV-JOINT OVERHAUL

**For all CV-joint overhaul procedures, please refer to the "U/CV-Joint Overhaul" in The Unit Repair section.**

## Front Wheel Hub Knuckle and Bearings

### REMOVAL & INSTALLATION

#### *Nova and Prizm*

1. Loosen the wheel nuts and hub nut.
2. Raise and support the front of the vehicle on jackstands. Remove the wheel/tire assembly.
3. From the strut, remove the brake hose retaining clip. Disconnect the flex hose from the brake pipe.
4. Remove the caliper bracket-to-steering knuckle bolts and support the caliper on a wire. Remove the brake disc.
5. From the tie rod ball joint, remove the cotter pin and tie rod-to-steering nut. Using the ball joint removal tool No. J-24319-01 or equivalent, separate the tie rod from the steering knuckle.
6. Remove the ball joint-to-lower control arm nuts/bolts and separate the ball joint from the lower control arm.
7. Remove the halfshaft hub nut and washer. Using the wheel puller tool No. J-25287 or equivalent, press halfshaft from the steering knuckle; using a wire, support the halfshaft.
8. Match-mark the steering knuckle-to-strut relationship. Remove the (2) strut-to-steering knuckle nuts/bolts and remove the steering knuckle.
9. Mount the steering knuckle in a vise. Using a small pry bar, remove the dust deflector from the inside surface of the steering knuckle.

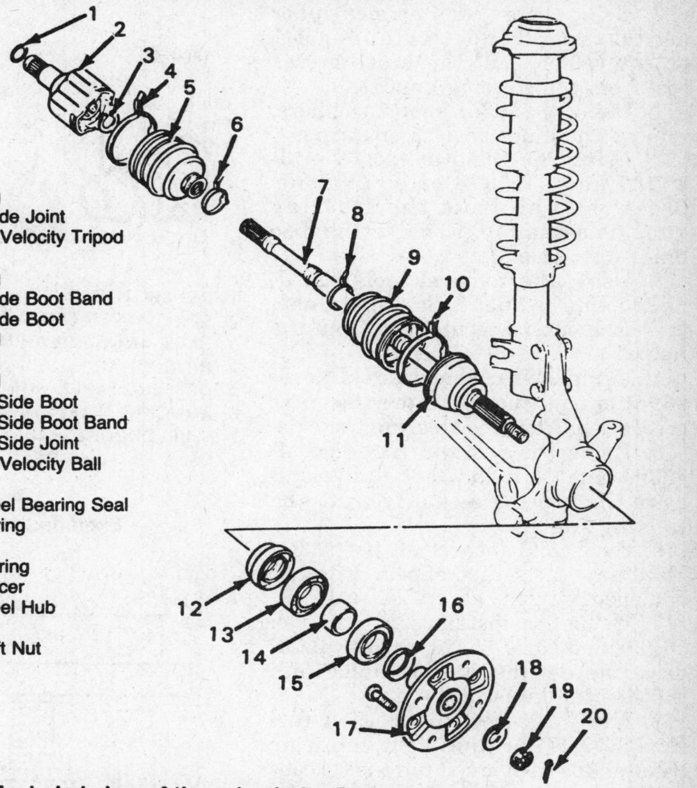

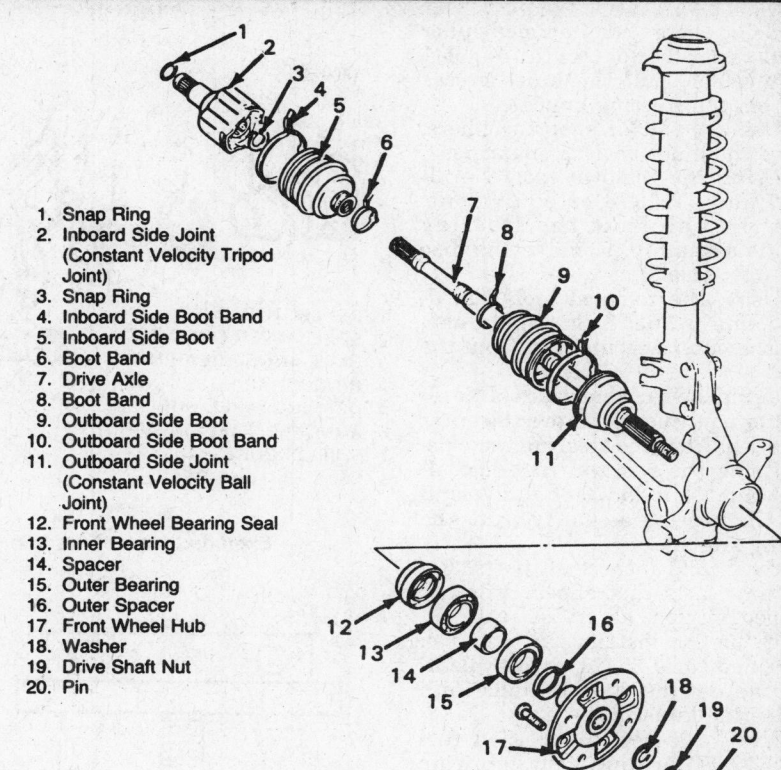

1. Snap Ring
2. Inboard Side Joint (Constant Velocity Tripod Joint)
3. Snap Ring
4. Inboard Side Boot Band
5. Inboard Side Boot
6. Boot Band
7. Drive Axle
8. Boot Band
9. Outboard Side Boot
10. Outboard Side Boot Band
11. Outboard Side Joint (Constant Velocity Ball Joint)
12. Front Wheel Bearing Seal
13. Inner Bearing
14. Spacer
15. Outer Bearing
16. Outer Spacer
17. Front Wheel Hub
18. Washer
19. Drive Shaft Nut
20. Pin

Exploded view of the axle shaft—Sprint and Metro

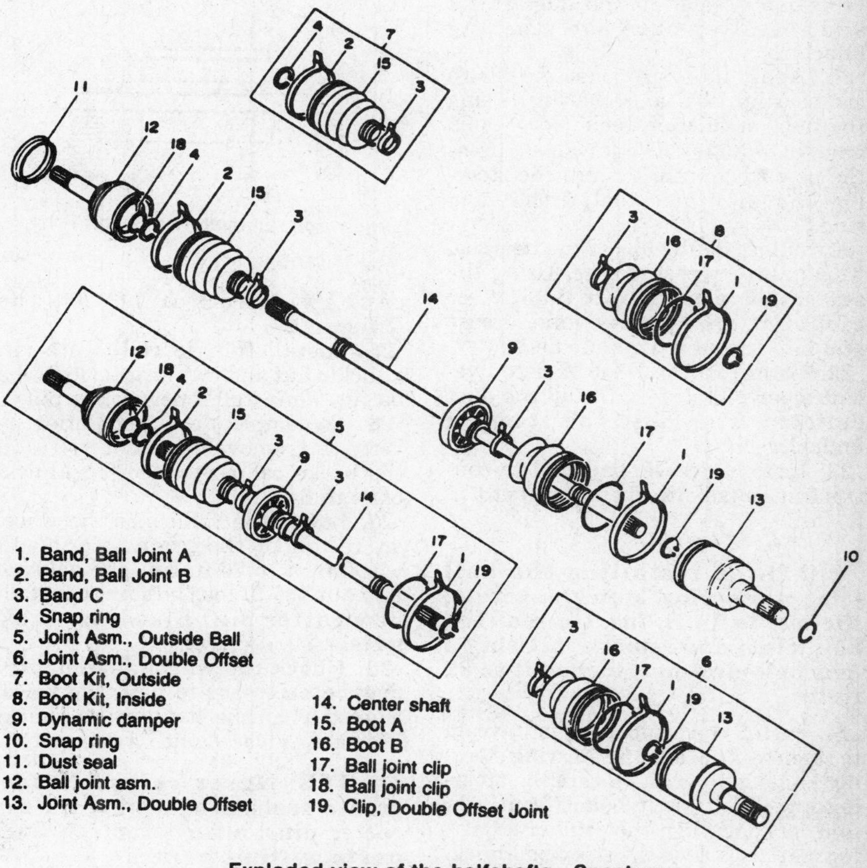

1. Band, Ball Joint A
2. Band, Ball Joint B
3. Band C
4. Snap ring
5. Joint Asm., Outside Ball
6. Joint Asm., Double Offset
7. Boot Kit, Outside
8. Boot Kit, Inside
9. Dynamic damper
10. Snap ring
11. Dust seal
12. Ball joint asm.
13. Joint Asm., Double Offset
14. Center shaft
15. Boot A
16. Boot B
17. Ball joint clip
18. Ball joint clip
19. Clip, Double Offset Joint

Exploded view of the halfshafts—Spectrum

10. Using the a slide hammer puller and the seal extractor tool No. J-26941 or equivalent, pull the inner grease seal from the steering knuckle.
11. Using a pair of snapring pliers, remove the inner bearing snapring.
12. Using the removal tools No. J-25287 and J-35378 or equivalent, press the hub from the steering knuckle assembly. Remove the disc brake dust shield.
13. Using the removal tools No. J-25287 and J-35378 or equivalent, press the outer bearing race from the hub.
14. Using the seal removal tool No. J-26941 or equivalent, remove the outer grease seal from the steering knuckle.
15. Using the removal tools No. J-35399 and No. J-35379 or equivalent, drive the bearing assembly from the steering knuckle.
16. Clean and inspect all parts. Replace any parts that appear worn or damaged. Replace all grease seals.
17. Using the installation tools No. J-8092 and No. J-35411 or equivalent, drive the new bearing assembly into the steering knuckle.
18. Using the seal installation tool No. J-35737-1 or equivalent, lubricate the seal lips with multi-purpose grease and drive the new outer grease seal into the steering knuckle.
19. Apply sealer to the dust shield and install it onto the steering knuckle.
20. Apply multi-purpose grease to the seal lip, seal and bearing. Using the hub installation tools No. J-8092 and No. J-35399 or equivalent, press the new wheel bearing into the steering knuckle, then, install the snap ring.
21. Lubricate the lips of the new seal with multi-purpose grease. Using the seal installation tool No. J-35737 or equivalent, drive the new inner grease seal into the steering knuckle.
22. Using tool No. J-35379 or equivalent (open end down), install the dust deflector ring onto the steering knuckle.
23. Install the lower ball joint-to-control arm nuts/bolts, then, torque to 59 ft. lbs.

**NOTE: If installing the ball joint-to-steering knuckle, torque the nut to 14 ft. lbs. (to seat the ball joint) and remove it. Using a new ball joint nut, torque it to 82 ft. lbs.**

24. Install the camber adjusting cam to steering knuckle, the steering steering knuckle to strut. Insert the steering knuckle-to-strut bolts (from rear to front) and align the camber adjusting marks. Torque the steering knuckle-to-strut nuts/bolts to 105 ft. lbs. (except twincam) or 166 ft. lbs. (twincam).
25. Install the tie rod-to-steering knuckle nut and torque it to 36 ft. lbs.; be sure to install a new cotter pin.
26. To complete the installation, reverse the removal procedures. Torque the brake caliper-to-steering knuckle bolts to 65 ft. lbs.
27. Lower the vehicle so the wheels are resting on the ground. Torque the wheel nuts to 76 ft. lbs., the halfshaft hub nut 137 ft. lbs.; be sure to install a new cotter pin. Bleed the brake system.
28. Check the wheel alignment; it may be necessary to have the wheels aligned when the strut or the knuckle has been replaced with a new part.

**NOTE: Never reinstall used grease seals, self locking nuts or cotter pins; always replace these parts with new ones once they have been removed.**

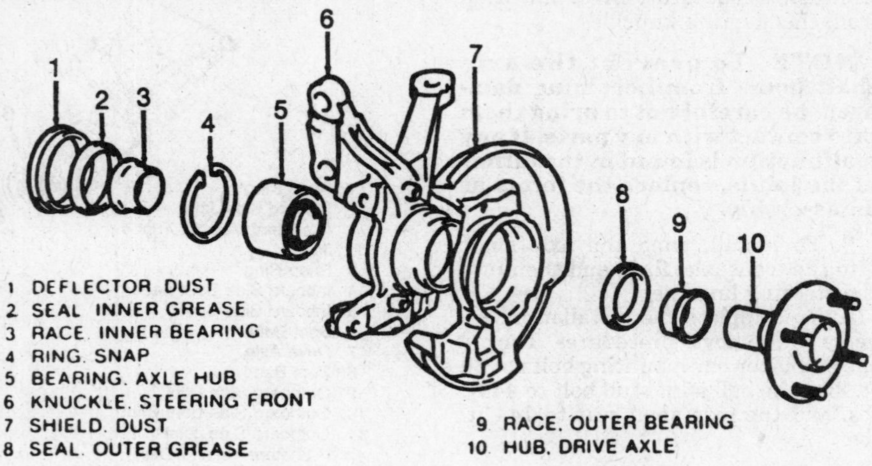


Exploded view of the hub/bearing assembly – Nova and Prizm

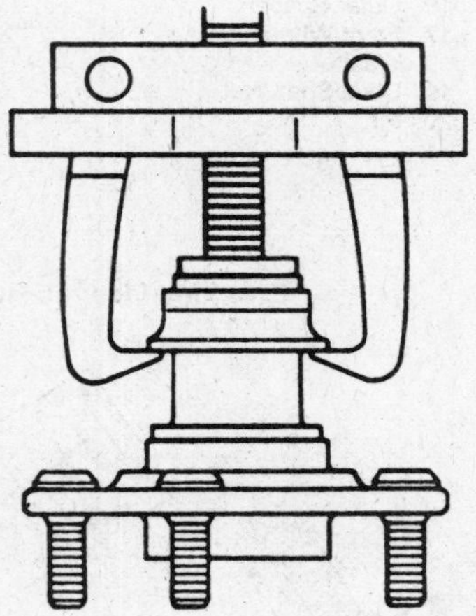

Inner race removal – Nova and Prizm

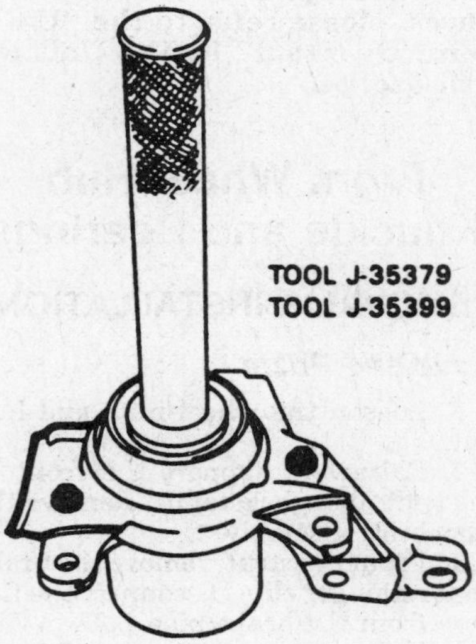


Bearing removal – Nova and Prizm

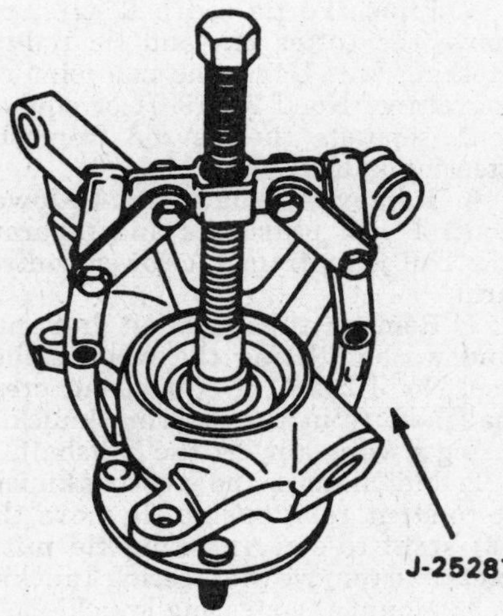


Hub removal – Nova and Prizm

29. If the cotter pin holes are not aligned, bend the tangs on the cap, slightly to align the holes; NEVER BACK OFF THE NUT.

### Spectrum

DO NOT remove the hub from the steering knuckle unless it is absolutely necessary.

1. Loosen the wheel nuts. Remove the grease cap, cotter pin, hub nut and thrust washer.
2. Remove the caliper and support it on a wire.
3. Remove the rotor.
4. Remove the tie rod nut. Using a ball joint removal tool, separate the tie rod from the steering knuckle.
5. Remove the 2 ball joint-to-control arm/tension rod retaining nuts and bolts.
6. Remove the 2 strut-to-steering knuckle retaining nuts/bolts.
7. Remove the steering knuckle. When removing the axle shaft from the steering knuckle, be careful not to drop it and support it with a wire.
8. To install, reverse the removal procedures. Bleed the brake system.

## DISASSEMBLY AND REASSEMBLY

### Spectrum

1. Remove the inner seal and snap ring.
2. Using an arbor press, press the hub from the steering knuckle. If necessary, press the spacer from the hub.
3. Remove the outer seal and snap ring.
4. Using an arbor press, press the bearing from the steering knuckle. Clean and inspect all parts.

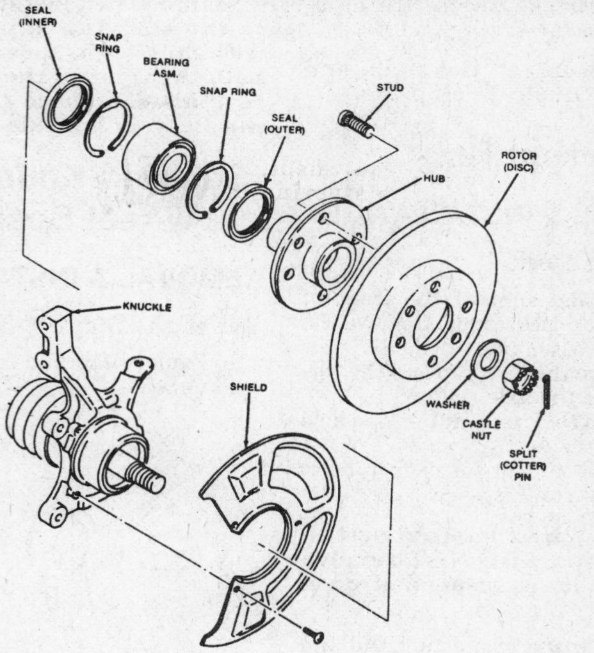


**Exploded view of the front hub assembly – Spectrum**

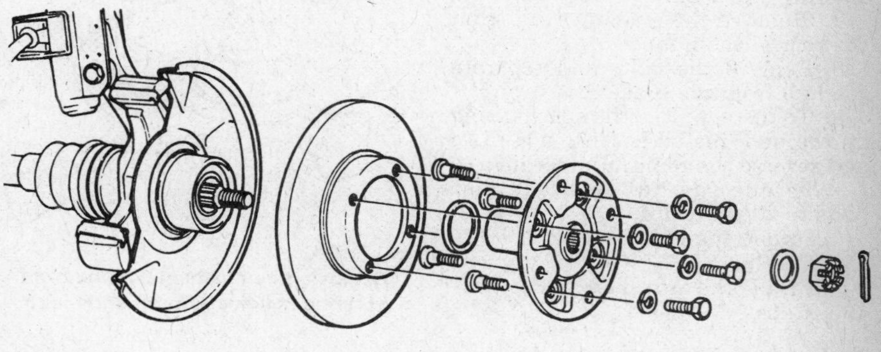

**Exploded view of the front wheel hub assembly – Sprint and Metro**

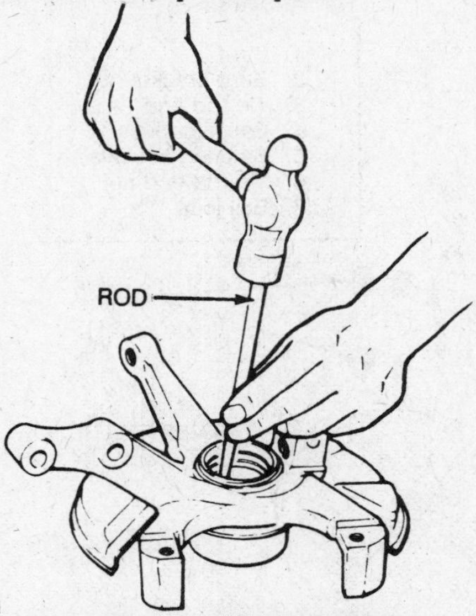


**Removing outer wheel bearing from steering knuckle – Sprint and Metro**

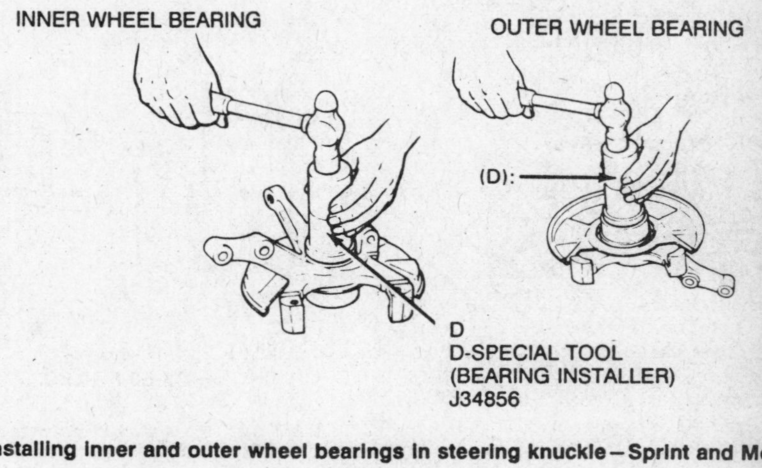


**Installing inner and outer wheel bearings in steering knuckle – Sprint and Metro**

5. To assemble, reverse the disassembly procedures.

**NOTE: Replace the seals and bearings. Lubricate all parts.**

## Front Hub

### REMOVAL & INSTALLATION

***Sprint and Metro***

1. Raise and support the front of the vehicle on jackstands. Remove the front wheel assembly.
2. Remove the dust cap and the cotter pin from the axle shaft.
3. Loosen the castle nut on the axle shaft.
4. Remove the brake caliper bolts and the brake caliper.

**NOTE: When removing the brake caliper, DO NOT remove the brake hose, suspend it on a wire.**

5. Remove the castle nut and the washer from the axle shaft.
6. Using a slide hammer tool J–2619–01 and a brake drum remover tool J–34866, pull the hub from the steering knuckle.
7. Remove the spacing ring from the rear of the hub.
8. Remove the bolts and separate the hub from the brake disc.
9. To install, place the spacing ring on the hub (install beveled side first) and reverse the removal procedures.

Torque the hub-to-brake disc bolts to 29–43 ft. lbs.

Torque the brake caliper bolts to 17–26 ft. lbs.

Torque the axle shaft nut to 108–195 ft. lbs.

**NOTE: When installing the hub to the steering knuckle, tap it with a plastic hammer to align the hub, then, using the installation tool J–34856, drive the hub into the steering knuckle.**

## Steering Knuckle and Wheel Bearings

### REMOVAL & INSTALLATION

***Sprint and Metro***

1. Remove the hub from the steering knuckle.

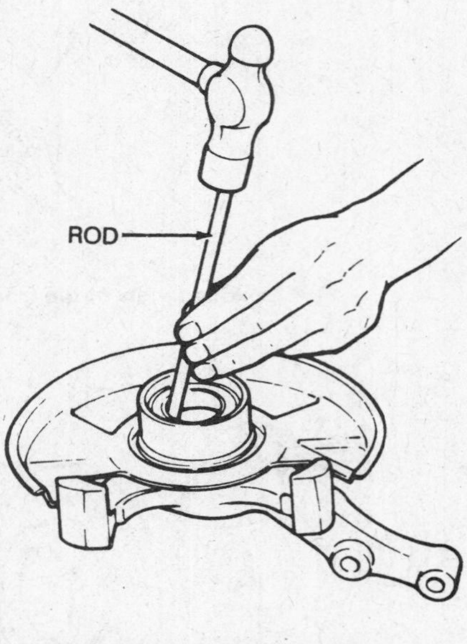


**Removing inner wheel bearing from steering knuckle – Sprint and Metro**

2. Remove the tie rod end cotter pin and nut.
3. Using the ball joint puller tool J-21687-02, remove the ball joint from the steering knuckle.
4. Remove the ball stud bolt from the steering knuckle.
5. Remove the strut-to-steering knuckle bolts.
6. Remove the steering knuckle and support the axle shaft on a wire.
7. Using a brass drift and a hammer, drive the wheel bearings from the steering knuckle.
8. Remove the spacer and clean the steering knuckle cavity.
9. Lubricate the new bearings and the steering knuckle cavity.
10. Using the installation tool J-34856, drive the new bearings (with the internal seals facing outward) into the steering knuckle.
11. Using the seal installation tool J-34881, drive the new seal into the steering knuckle (grease the seal lip).
12. To complete the installation, reverse the removal procedures. Torque the strut-to-steering knuckle bolts to 50–65 ft. lbs.; the ball joints-to-steering knuckle nuts to 22–40 ft. lbs. and the axle shaft castle nut to 108–195 ft. lbs.

# FRONT SUSPENSION

## MacPherson Strut

### REMOVAL & INSTALLATION

***Nova and Prizm***

1. From in the engine compart-

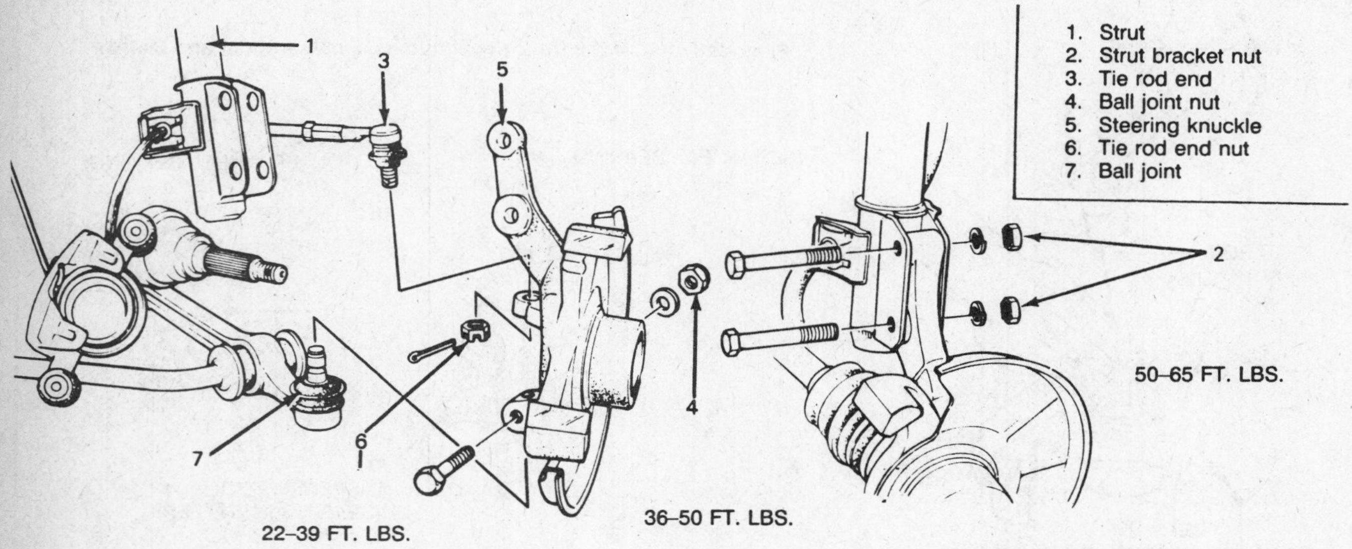


**Front steering knuckle mounting – Sprint and Metro**

ment, remove the strut-to-body nuts.
2. Loosen the wheel/tire assembly lug nuts. Raise and support the front of the vehicle so the jackstands are not under the lower control arms, then, remove the wheel/tire assemblies.
3. Detach the flexible brake line from the strut clip. Disconnect the brake hose-to-brake pipe connection from the body mount. Using a catch pan, drain the excess brake fluid. Pull the brake hose back through the opening the the strut bracket; cap both open ends of the hydraulic system.
4. Remove the brake caliper-to-steering knuckle bolts. Using a wire, support the caliper out of the way; support the caliper so that the brake hose will not be under any strain (do not disconnect the hose from the caliper).
5. Mark the adjusting cam so the camber adjustment can be restored when the strut is reassembled. Remove the steering knuckle-to-strut bolts, the strut assembly and the camber adjusting cam from the steering knuckle.
6. Using a cloth, cover the drive axle boot to protect it while the strut is removed.
7. Inspect the strut for cracks, wear, distortion and/or damage; replace the strut (if necessary).

**To install:**

8. Lubricate the upper strut bearing with multi-purpose grease and reverse the removal procedures. Align the strut-to-steering knuckle marks. Torque the steering knuckle-to-strut bolts to 105 ft. lbs. (except twincam) or 166 ft. lbs. (twincam), the strut-to-body.
9. Lower the vehicle so the strut can be aligned with body mounting holes.
10. Install and torque the strut-to-body nuts to 23 ft. lbs. (except twincam) or 29 ft. lbs. (twincam). Lower the vehicle to the ground and torque the wheel lugnuts to 76 ft. lbs. Bleed the brake system.

### *Spectrum*

1. Open the hood. Remove the nuts retaining the strut to the body.
2. Loosen the wheel nuts. Raise the vehicle and support the vehicle on jackstands.
3. Remove the wheel and tire assembly.
4. Remove the brake hose clip at the strut bracket.
5. Disconnect the brake hose at the brake caliper.
6. Tape or cap the brake hose and caliper opening.
7. Pull the brake hose through the opening in the strut bracket.
8. Remove the nuts retaining the strut to the steering knuckle.
9. Remove the strut assembly.
10. To install, reverse the removal procedures. Bleed the brake system.

### *Sprint and Metro*

1. Raise and support the front of the vehicle.
2. Remove the wheel assembly.
3. Remove the brake hose securing ring and the hose from the strut.
4. Remove the upper strut support nuts from the engine compartment.
5. Remove the strut-to-steering knuckle bolts and the strut.
6. To install, reverse the removal procedures. Torque the upper mounting nuts to 13–20 ft. lbs. and the strut-to-steering knuckle bolts to 50–65 ft. lbs.

## STRUT OVERHAUL

**For all strut overhaul procedures, please refer to the "Strut Overhaul" Unit Repair section.**

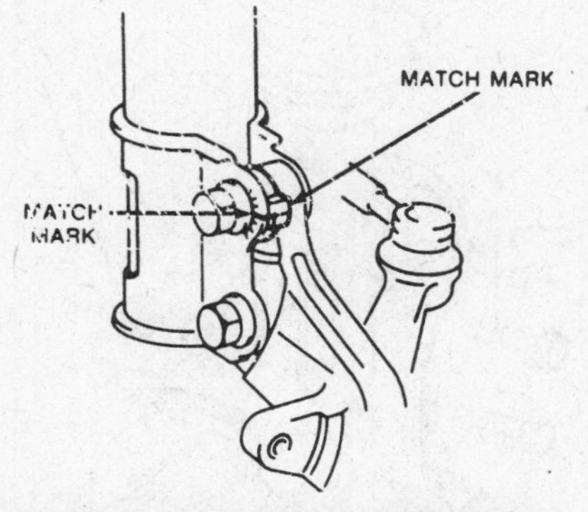


**Mark the camber adjusting cam before removing the knuckle attaching nuts and bolts so camber can be restored without rechecking alignment – Nova and Prizm**

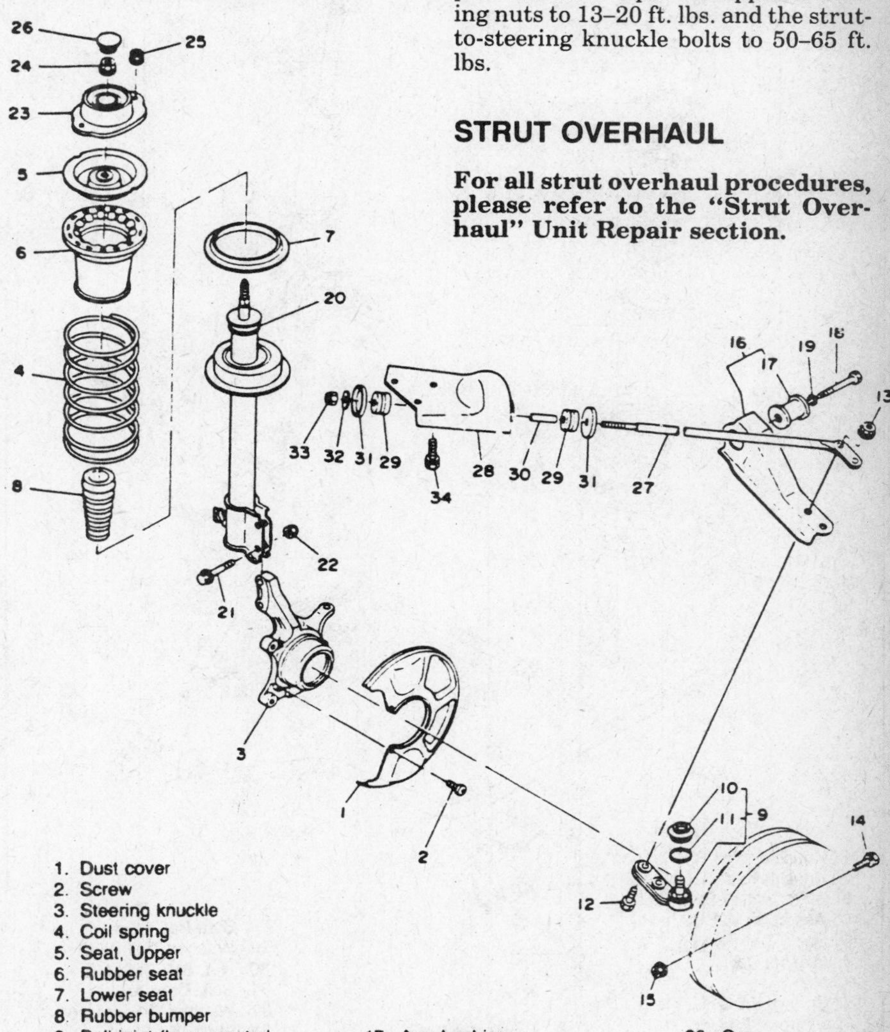

1. Dust cover
2. Screw
3. Steering knuckle
4. Coil spring
5. Seat, Upper
6. Rubber seat
7. Lower seat
8. Rubber bumper
9. Ball joint (lower control arm)
10. Ball joint boot
11. Boot clip ring
12. Control arm bolt
13. Lock nut
14. Bolt
15. Lock nut
16. Lower arm asm.
17. Arm bushing
18. Bolt
19. Lock washer
20. Front strut asm.
21. Bolt
22. Lock nut
23. Strut upper mount
24. Flange nut (strut shaft)
25. Nut
26. Cap
27. Tension rod
28. Support bracket
29. Rubber cushion
30. Tension rod spacer
31. Washer
32. Washer
33. Lock nut
34. Bolt

**Exploded view of the front suspension assembly – Spectrum**

## Stabilizer Bar

### REMOVAL & INSTALLATION

#### *Nova and Prizm*

**TWINCAM**

1. Raise and support the front of the vehicle on jackstands.
2. Disconnect the stabilizer-to-lower control arm bolts.
3. Remove the stabilizer bar-to-chassis brackets.
4. Disconnect the exhaust pipe from the exhaust manifold.
5. Remove the stabilizer bar from the vehicle.

**NOTE: Never reuse a self locking nut, always use a new one.**

6. To install, reverse the removal procedures. Torque the exhaust pipe-to-exhaust manifold to 46 ft. lbs., the stabilizer bar-to-body bolts to 14 ft. lbs. and the stabilizer bar-to-lower control arm bolts to 13 ft. lbs.

#### *Sprint and Metro*

1. Raise and support the front of the vehicle on jackstands. Remove the front wheel assemblies.
2. Remove the stabilizer bar-to-body mounting bolts.
3. Remove the cotter pin, the castle nut, the washer, the bushing and the stabilizer bar from the lower control arms.
4. To install, reverse the removal procedures. Torque the stabilizer bar-to-control arm to 29–65 ft. lbs. and the stabilizer bar-to-body bolts to 22–39 ft. lbs.

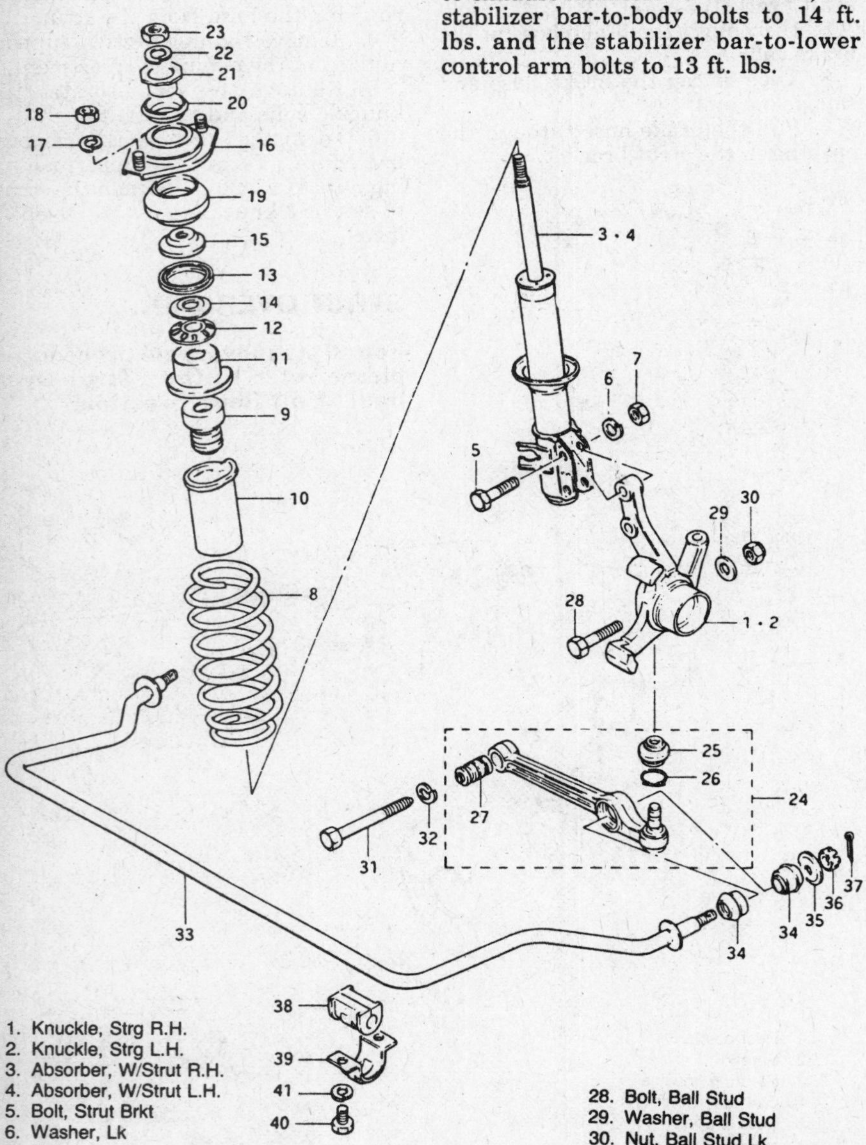

1. Knuckle, Strg R.H.
2. Knuckle, Strg L.H.
3. Absorber, W/Strut R.H.
4. Absorber, W/Strut L.H.
5. Bolt, Strut Brkt
6. Washer, Lk
7. Nut
8. Spring, Frt Coil
9. Stopper, Frt Bpr
10. Seat, Frt Spr
11. Seat, Srt Spr Upr
12. Bearing, Frt Strut
13. Seal, Frt Strut Brg Dust
14. Seat, Frt Strut Brg
15. Seat, Strut Mt
16. Support, Frt Strut
17. Washer (3/8 × 11/16)
18. Nut (M8 × 1.25 × 6)
19. Mount, Frt Strut
20. Stopper, Frt Strut Rebound
21. Support, Frt Strut Inr
22. Washer
23. Nut
24. Arm, Frt Cont
25. Seal, Ball Stud Dust
26. Clip, Dust Seal
27. Bushing, Cont Arm
28. Bolt, Ball Stud
29. Washer, Ball Stud
30. Nut, Ball Stud Lk
31. Bolt, Cont Arm
32. Washer (3/8 × 11/16)
33. Shaft, Frt Stab
34. Bushing, Stab Shf
35. Washer, Stab Shf
36. Nut (M12 × 1.25 × 10)
37. Pin
38. Mount, Stab Shf
39. Bracket, Stab Shf Mt
40. Bolt
41. Washer, Lk

**Front suspension—Sprint and Metro**

## Tension Bars

### REMOVAL & INSTALLATION

#### *Spectrum*

1. Raise and support the vehicle on jackstands.
2. If equipped with a stabilizer bar, remove the nuts, bolts and insulators retaining it to the tension rod.

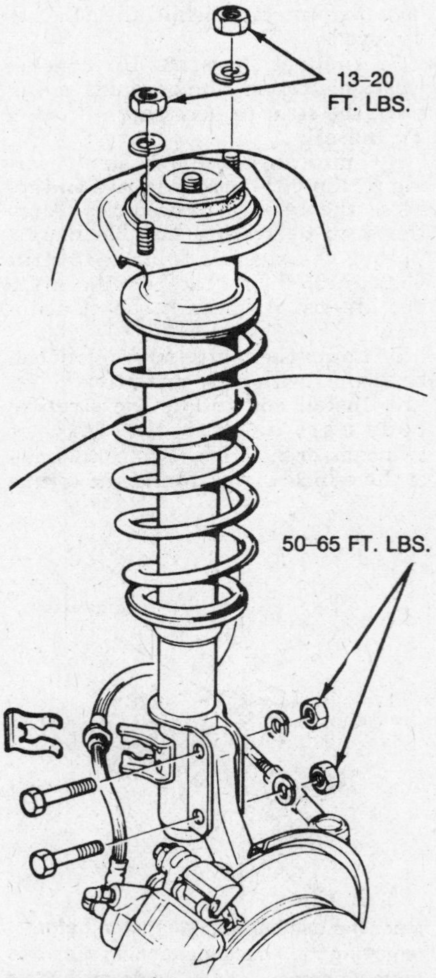


**Front suspension strut mounting—Sprint and Metro**

3. Remove the nut and washer retaining the tension rod to the body.

4. Remove the nuts and bolts retaining the tension rod to the control rod.

5. Remove the tension rod.

6. To install, reverse the removal procedures.

# Ball Joints

## INSPECTION

### Nova and Prizm

1. Turn the front wheels so they are straight and chock the rear wheels. Raise the vehicle and place a wooden block of 7–8 in. under it. Then, lower the vehicle onto the block until the spring is compressed to only about half its compression when the vehicle is resting on it.

2. Attempt to move the lower arm up and down. There should be no noticeable play.

3. If the ball joint is removed from the vehicle check the required rotating torque with and inch pound torque wrench. Flip the ball joint back and forth, several times. Install the nut and turn the stud with a torque wrench at a rate of about one turn in three seconds. At the fifth turn, measure the required torque; it should be 9–30 inch lbs. If outside these specifications, replace the ball joint.

### Spectrum

Before removing the ball joint for replacement, check it and the boot for excessive wear or damage.

## REMOVAL & INSTALLATION

### Nova and Prizm

1. Loosen the wheel lug nuts, then, raise and support the front of the vehicle using approved jacking points. Remove the front wheel assembly.

2. Remove the ball joint-to-lower control arm nuts/bolts.

3. Remove the ball joint-to-steering knuckle cotter pin and nut.

4. Using the ball joint removal tool No. J-35413 or equivalent, press the ball joint from the steering knuckle.

5. Inspect and/or replace (if necessary) the ball joint.

**NOTE: When torquing the ball joint-to-steering knuckle nut, turn it one continuous turn every 2–4 seconds; take the torque reading on the fifth turn.**

6. To install, use a new ball joint-to-steering knuckle nut and reverse the removal procedures. Torque the ball joint-to-steering knuckle nut 82 ft. lbs. (Nova), 94 ft. lbs. (Prizm) and the ball joint-to-lower control arm nuts/bolts to 57 ft. lbs. (Nova), 105 ft. lbs. (Prizm).

### Spectrum

1. Loosen the wheel nuts.

2. Raise and support the vehicle on jackstands.

3. Remove the wheel and tire assembly.

4. Remove the two nuts retaining the ball joint to the tension rod and control arm assembly.

5. Remove the pinch bolt retaining the ball joint to the steering knuckle.

6. Remove the ball joint.

7. To install, reverse the removal procedures.

### Sprint and Metro

The ball joint is part of the lower control arm.

1. Raise and support the front of the vehicle safely. Remove the front wheel assembly.

2. Remove the cotter pin, the castle nut, the washer and the bushing from the stabilizer bar.

3. Remove the stabilizer bar-to-body mounting bracket bolts.

4. Remove the ball stud and the control arm bolts.

5. Remove the control arm.

6. To install, reverse the removal procedures. Torque the control arm-to-body bolt to 36–50 ft. lbs.; the ball stud-to-steering knuckle to 36–50 ft. lbs.; the stabilizer bar-to-control arm to 29–65 ft. lbs. and the stabilizer bar-to-body to 22–39 ft. lbs.

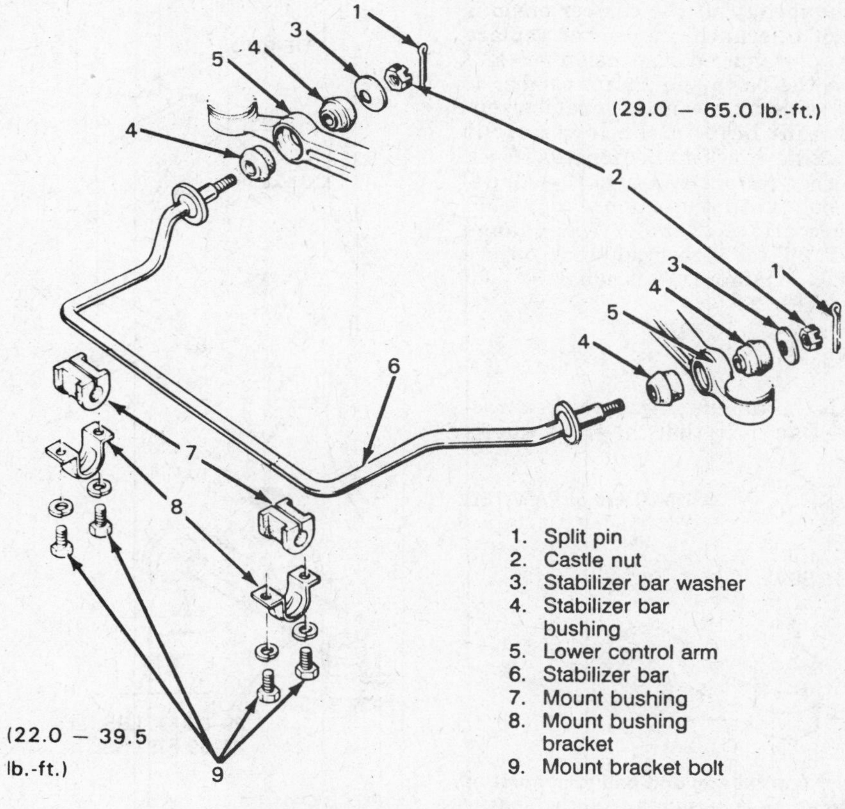


1. Split pin
2. Castle nut
3. Stabilizer bar washer
4. Stabilizer bar bushing
5. Lower control arm
6. Stabilizer bar
7. Mount bushing
8. Mount bushing bracket
9. Mount bracket bolt

Front stabilizer bar mounting—Sprint and Metro

# Lower Control Arm

## REMOVAL & INSTALLATION

### Nova

1. Raise and support the front of the vehicle using approved jacking points.

2. Remove the ball joint-to-lower control arm nuts/bolts.

**NOTE: If equipped with a twincam engine, remove the stabilizer bar-to-lower control arm nut and disconnect the stabilizer bar.**

3. Remove the control arm-to-chassis nuts/bolts and the control arm.

4. Inspect the control arm for distortion and cracking; check and/or replace the bushing.

5. If replacing the lower control arm bushing, remove the nut, the retainer and the bushing.

6. To install, use a new bushing and reverse the removal procedures. Torque the control arm bushing nut 76 ft. lbs., the control arm-to-chassis bolts to 105 ft. lbs. (front) or 72 ft. lbs. (rear), the stabilizer bar-to-lower control arm nut to 13 ft. lbs. and the ball joint-to-lower control arm nuts/bolts to 57 ft. lbs.

### *Prizm*

1. Raise and support the vehicle safely.
2. Disconnect the right and left lower control arms from the steering knuckles.
3. Remove the left and right lower arm rear brackets.
4. Remove the control arm rear bracket to crossmember nut and bolt.
5. Remove the 6 bolts and 2 nuts and remove the suspension crossmember with the lower arms.
6. To install, position the lower arm to the suspension crossmember and partially tighten bolts.
7. Install the suspension crossmember with the lower arm to the body.
8. Install the lower rear bracket and partially tighten the bolts.
9. Tighten the left and right lower arm bolts to each steering knuckle to 105 ft. lbs.
10. Lower the vehicle.
11. Bounce the vehicle up and down to stabilize the suspension.
12. Tighten the lower arm bolt 152 ft. lbs.
13. Tighten the rear bracket to crossmember bolt and nut to 14 ft. lbs.
14. Tighten the rear bracket bolts to 94 ft. lbs.
15. Check the front end alignment.

### *Spectrum*

1. Raise and support the front of the vehicle on jackstands.
2. Remove the control arm to tension arm retaining nuts and bolts.
3. Remove the nut/bolt securing the control arm to the body.
4. Remove the control arm and check for cracking or distortion.
5. To install, reverse the removal procedures.

**NOTE: Raise the control arm to a distance of 15 in. from the top of the wheel well to the center of the hub. Torque the control arm-to-body bolts to 41 ft. lbs. and the control arm-to-tension rod bolts to 80 ft. lbs. This procedure aligns the bushing arm to the body.**

### *Sprint and Metro*

1. Raise and support the front of the vehicle safely. Remove the front wheel assembly.
2. Remove the cotter pin, the castle nut, the washer and the bushing from the stabilizer bar.
3. Remove the stabilizer bar–to-body mounting bracket bolts.
4. Remove the ball stud and the control arm bolts.
5. Remove the control arm.
6. To install, reverse the removal procedures. Torque the control arm-to-body bolt to 36–50 ft. lbs.; the ball stud-to-steering knuckle to 36–50 ft. lbs.; the stabilizer bar-to-control arm to 29–65 ft. lbs. and the stabilizer bar-to-body to 22–39 ft. lbs.

## Front Wheel Alignment

### CASTER

The caster is not adjustable.

### CAMBER

Camber is the slope of the front wheels from the vertical when viewed from the front of the vehicle. When the wheels tilt outward at the top, the camber is positive (+). When the wheels tilt inward at the top, the camber is negative (−). The amount of positive and negative camber, measured in degrees from the vertical, is called camber angle. Camber is preset at the factory. If the camber angle is out of tolerance, inspect or replace worn or damaged suspension parts.

On the Nova and Prizm camber is adjustable by means of a camber adjustment bolt on the lower strut mounting bracket. Loosen the shock absorber set nut and turn the adjusting bolt until the camber is within specifications. Camber will change about 20' for each graduation on the cam. One minute (1') is equal to 1/60 of a degree.

### TOE

Toe is the amount, measured in a fraction of an inch, that the front wheels are closer together at one end than the other. Toe-in means that the front wheels are closer together at the front than at the rear of the tire; toe-out means the rear of the tires are closer together than the front.

The wheels must be dead straight ahead. The vehicle must have a full tank of gas, all fluids must be at their proper levels, all other suspension and steering adjustments must be correct and the tires must be properly inflated to their cold specifications.

1. Toe can be determined by measuring the distance between the centers of the tire threads, at the front of the tire and the rear. If the tread pattern makes this impossible, measure between the edges of the wheel rims but be sure to move the vehicle and measure in a few places to avoid errors caused by bent rims or wheel run-out.
2. If the measurement is not within specifications, loosen the boot clamps (small end) and slide from the boot. On the adjustable tie rods, loosen both tie rod end lock nuts.
3. Turn both tie rods equal amounts until the measurements are within specifications.
4. Reinstall the boot clamps, tighten the lock bolts and recheck the measurements. Make sure the rack boots are not twisted. Check that the steering wheel is in the proper position; if not, remove it and reposition it.

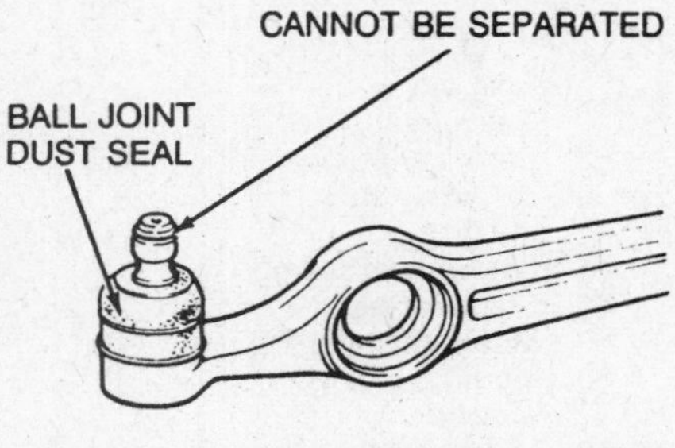


**Lower control arm and ball joint must be replaced as an assembly – Sprint and Metro**

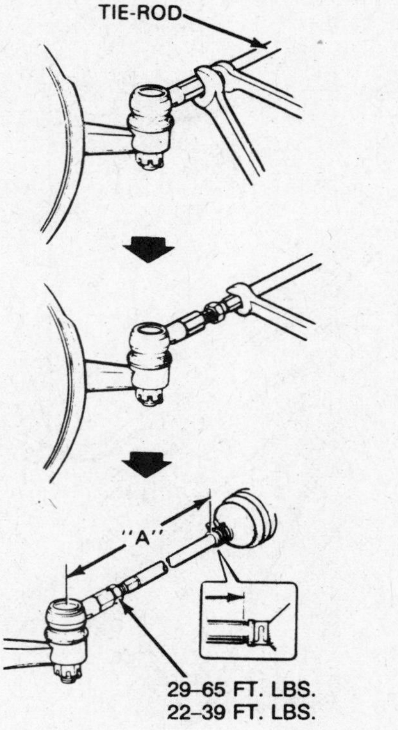


**Toe adjustment – Sprint and Metro**

# REAR SUSPENSION

## MacPherson Strut

### REMOVAL & INSTALLATION

#### *Nova*

1. Working inside the rear of the vehicle, remove the rear quarter window garnish molding, back window panel and the speaker grille (if necessary).
2. Raise and support the rear of the vehicle by placing jackstands under the frame, then, remove the rear wheel.
3. Disconnect the flexible brake hose from the strut. Remove the flexible hose and clip from the mounting point on the strut, then, reconnect the brake line to the flex hose to prevent an excessive amount of brake fluid from draining from the system.

**NOTE: Before removing the strut from the hub carrier, be sure to mark the location of the strut to the hub carrier for reinstallation purposes.**

4. Remove the strut-to-hub carrier nuts/bolts and separate the strut from the hub carrier.
5. Remove the strut-to-chassis nuts and carefully remove the strut assembly.
6. Inspect the strut for cracks, wear and/or other damage; replace it (if necessary).
7. To install, reverse the removal procedures. Torque the strut-to-chassis nuts to 17 ft. lbs., the strut-to-hub carrier nuts/bolts to 105 ft. lbs. Bleed the brake system.

#### *Prizm*

1. Remove the seat back side cushion on sedans and the rear sill side panel on hatchback models.
2. Raise and safely support the rear of the vehicle.
3. Place jack stands under the suspension support.
4. Lower the vehicle slightly so the weight rest on the jackstands and not the suspension arms.
5. Remove the wheel and tire assembly.
6. Disconnect the brake line hose and backing plate.
7. Remove the brake hose from the brake hose bracket.
8. Disconnect the stabilizer bar link from the strut assembly.
9. Remove the strut assembly mounting bolts and nuts from the rear suspension knuckle.
10. Remove the strut assembly mounting nuts holding the top of the strut support and remove the strut from the vehicle.
11. To install, reverse the removal procedures. Torque the strut-to-body nuts to 29 ft. lbs., the strut assembly-to-knuckle mounting bolts to 105 ft. lbs. and the stabilizer bar link to strut assembly to 26 ft. lbs. Bleed the brake the brake system.

**For all strut overhaul procedures, please refer to the "Strut Overhaul" in the Unit Repair section.**

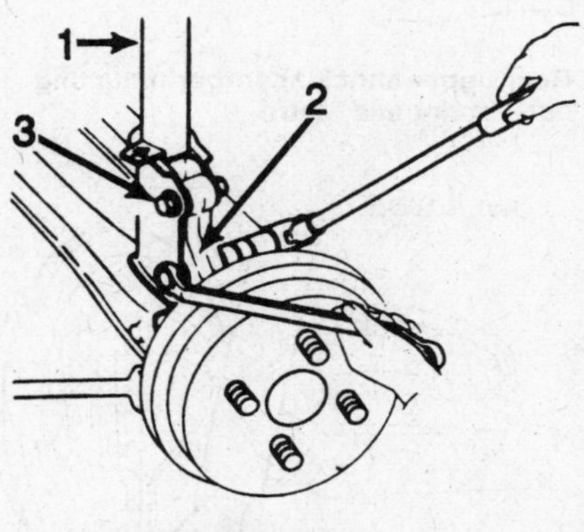


1. STRUT ASSEMBLY
2. CARRIER ASSEMBLY
3. BOLT 142 N·M (105 FT. LBS.)

**Rear strut-to-carrier bolt removal—Nova and Prizm**

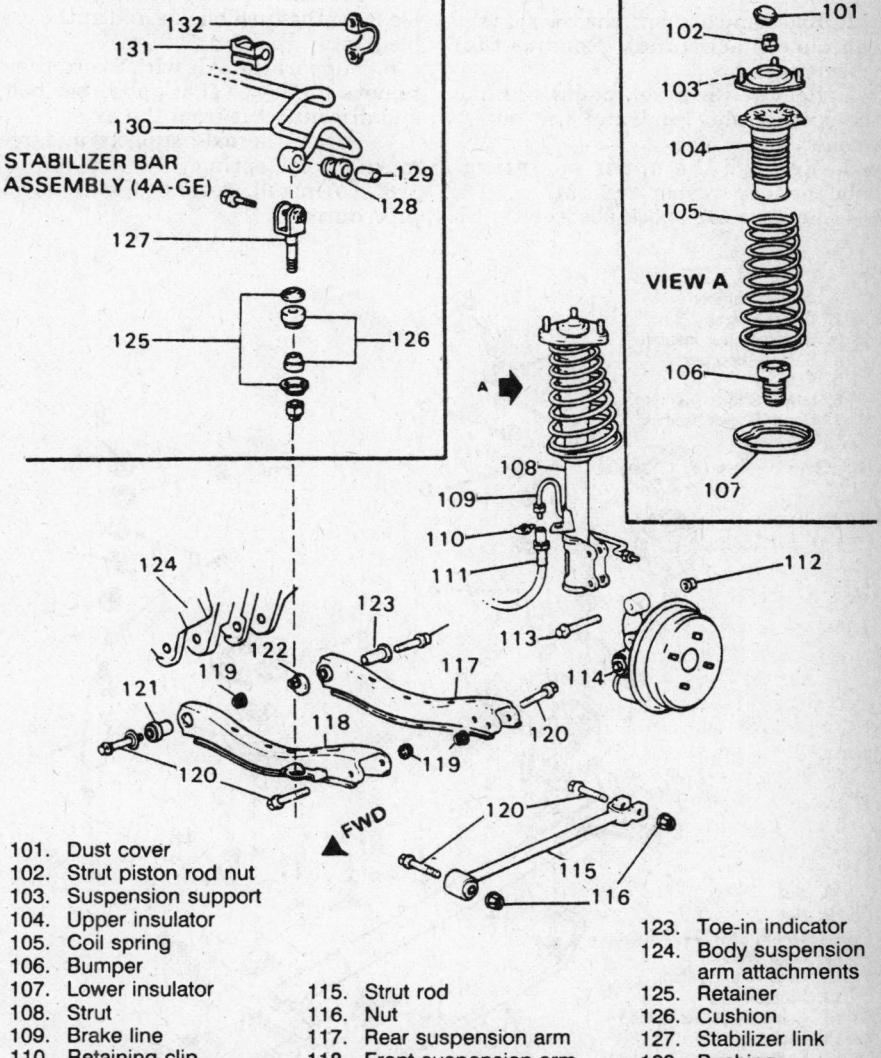

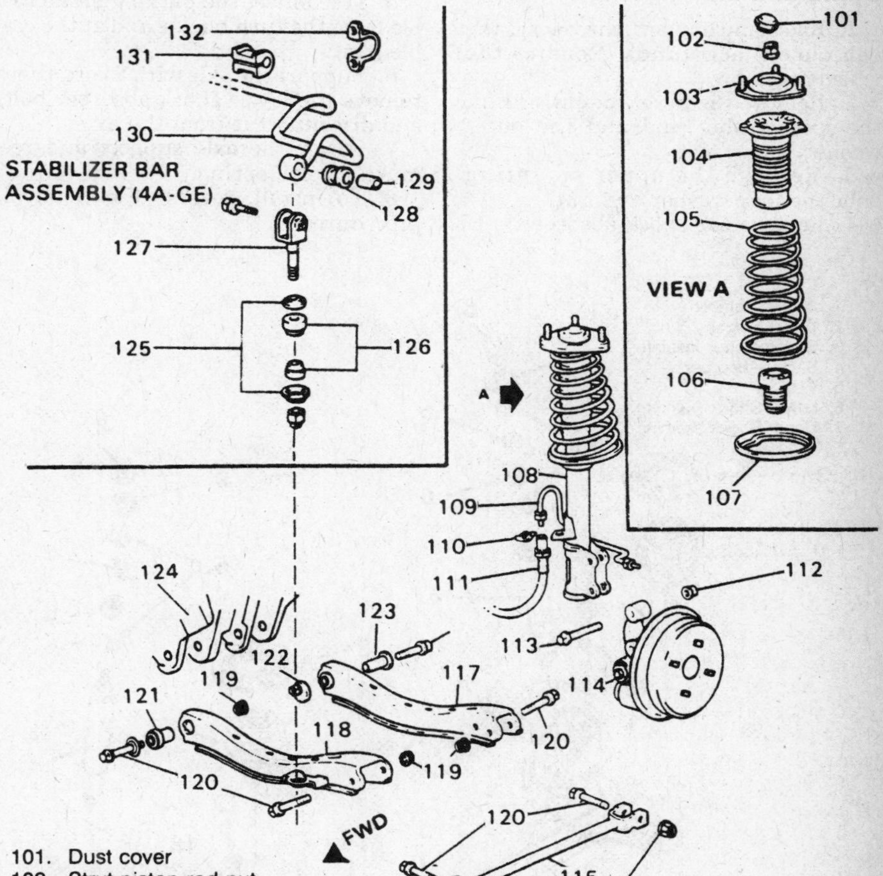


101. Dust cover
102. Strut piston rod nut
103. Suspension support
104. Upper insulator
105. Coil spring
106. Bumper
107. Lower insulator
108. Strut
109. Brake line
110. Retaining clip
111. Flexible brake hose
112. Nut (105 ft. lbs.)
113. Bolt
114. Hub carrier assembly
115. Strut rod
116. Nut
117. Rear suspension arm
118. Front suspension arm
119. Nut
120. Bolt (64 ft. lbs.)
121. Bushing
122. Toe-in adjusting cam nut
123. Toe-in indicator
124. Body suspension arm attachments
125. Retainer
126. Cushion
127. Stabilizer link
128. Bushing
129. Collar
130. Stabilizer bar
131. Bushing
132. Bracket.

**Exploded view of the rear suspension—Nova**

## Shock Absorbers

### REMOVAL & INSTALLATION

#### *Spectrum*

1. Open the trunk and lift off the trim cover (hatch back models only). Remove the upper shock absorber nut.
2. Remove the lower bolt of the shock absorber.
3. Remove the shock absorber.
4. To install, reverse the removal procedures.

**NOTE: When replacing the shock absorber, NEVER reuse the old lower bolt, ALWAYS use a new one.**

#### *Sprint and Metro*

1. Raise and support the rear of the vehicle on jackstands. Remove the wheel assembly.
2. Remove the lower mounting nut, the lock washer and and the outer washer.
3. Remove the upper mounting bolt, the lock washer and nut.
4. Remove the shock absorber.
5. To install, reverse the removal procedures. Torque the upper mounting bolt to 33–50 ft. lbs. and the lower mounting nut to 8–12 ft. lbs.

## Coil Spring

### REMOVAL & INSTALLATION

#### *Spectrum*

1. Raise and support the rear-end of the vehicle on jackstands.
2. Remove the rear wheels.
3. At the center of the rear axle, remove the brake line, retaining clip and flexible hose.
4. Remove the parking brake tension spring at the rear axle.
5. Disconnect the parking brake cable from the turn buckle and at the cable joint.
6. Support the axle with a jack, then remove the lower shock absorber bolt and disconnect it from the axle.
7. Lower the axle support and remove the coil spring.
8. To install, reverse the removal procedures.

**NOTE: Raise the axle assembly to a distance of 15.2 in. from the top of the wheel well to the center of the axle hub, then torque the fasteners. ALWAYS replace the lower shock absorber bolt with a new one.**

#### *Sprint and Metro*

1. Raise and support the rear of the vehicle on jackstands. Remove the front wheel assembly.
2. Remove the U-bolt nuts.
3. Remove the shackle and leaf spring front nuts.
4. Remove the front spring bolt.
5. Remove the spring from the vehicle.

**NOTE: Apply a thin coat of silicone grease to the springs bushings before installation.**

6. To install, align the spring pin with the hole in the axle shaft housing and reverse the removal procedures. Torque the front spring bolt to 33–50 ft. lbs.; the rear spring shackle nuts to 22–40 ft. lbs. and the U-bolt nuts to 22–33 ft. lbs.

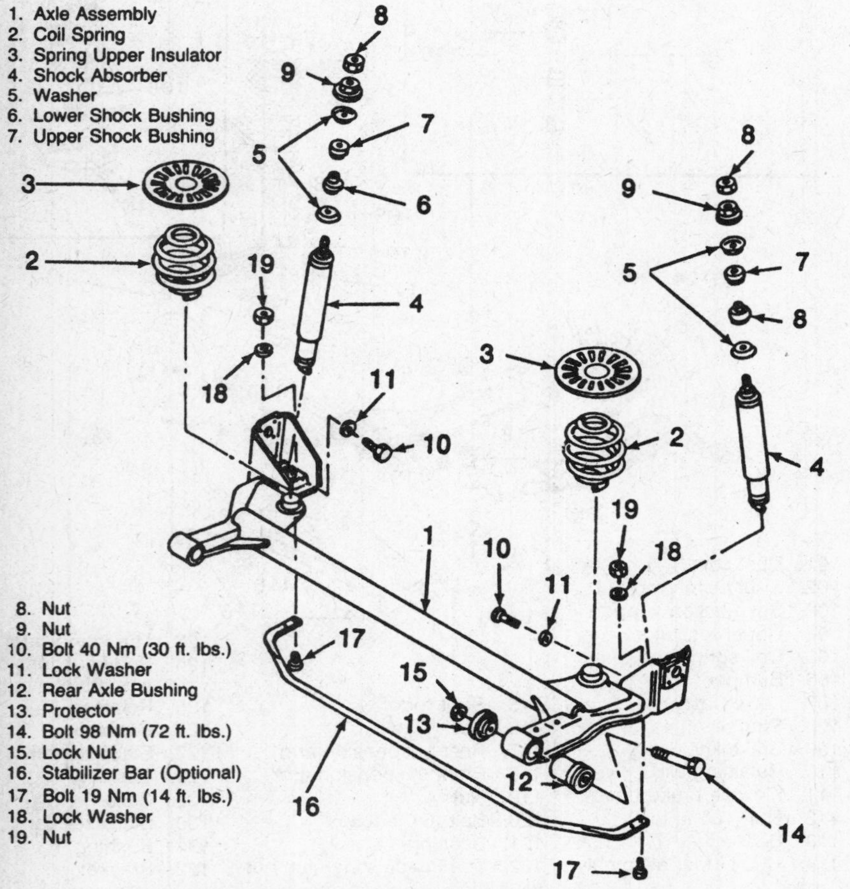


Exploded view of the rear axle assembly – Spectrum

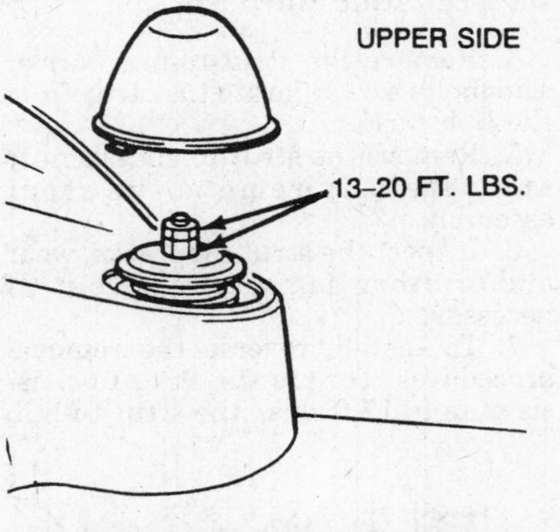


Rear upper shock absorber mounting nut – Sprint and Metro

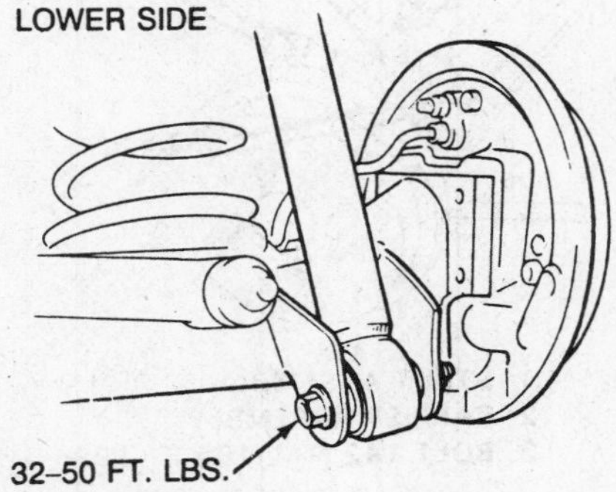


Rear lower shock absorber mounting bolt – Sprint and Metro

## Rear Suspension Arms

### REMOVAL & INSTALLATION

#### *Nova*

**FRONT**

1. Raise and support the rear of the vehicle by placing jackstands under the frame, then, remove the rear wheel.
2. If equipped with a twincam engine, remove the rear suspension arm-to-stabilizer bar nut, retainer and cushion.
3. Remove the front suspension arm-to-hub carrier nut/bolt.
4. Remove the front suspension arm-to-chassis nut/bolt and the suspension arm from the vehicle.
5. To install, use a new stabilizer link-to-suspension arm nut (twincam) and reverse the removal procedures. Torque the stabilizer bar-to-front suspension arm nut/bolt to 11 ft. lbs. (twincam).
6. Lower the vehicle, bounce the vehicle to stabilize the suspension, then, torque the front suspension arm bolts to 64 ft. lbs. Check and/or adjust the rear wheel alignment.

**REAR**

1. Raise and support the rear of the vehicle by placing jackstands under the frame, then, remove the rear wheel.
2. Remove the rear suspension arm-to-hub carrier nut/bolt.

**NOTE: Before removing the rear cam bolt, mark the alignment of the cam bolt for reinstallation purposes.**

3. Remove the rear suspension arm-to-chassis cam bolt and the suspension arm.
4. To install, reverse the removal procedures. Torque the rear suspension arm-to-chassis cam bolt to 64 ft. lbs. Check and/or adjust the rear wheel alignment.

#### *Prizm*

1. Raise and safely support the rear of the vehicle.
2. Remove the rear suspension arm to body and rear suspension knuckle mounting bolt.
3. Remove the rear suspension arm to rear suspension knuckle mounting bolts.
4. Remove the rear suspension arm.
5. Place the suspension arm into position.
6. Install the rear suspension arm to body mounting bolts and partially tighten.
7. Install the rear suspension arm to rear suspension knuckle mounting bolts and partially tighten.
8. On the No. 2 suspension arm only, align the matchmarks on the cam and body.
9. Lower the vehicle and bounce the vehicle up and down to stabilize the suspension.
10. Tighten both the No. 1 and No. 2 suspension arm mounting bolts to 87 ft. lbs.
11. Check the rear wheel alignment.

## Rear Wheel Bearings

### REMOVAL & INSTALLATION

#### *Nova and Prizm*

1. Raise and support the rear of the vehicle on jackstands.
2. Remove the rear wheel/tire assembly. Remove the brake drum (except twincam) or caliper, caliper support and disc (twincam).

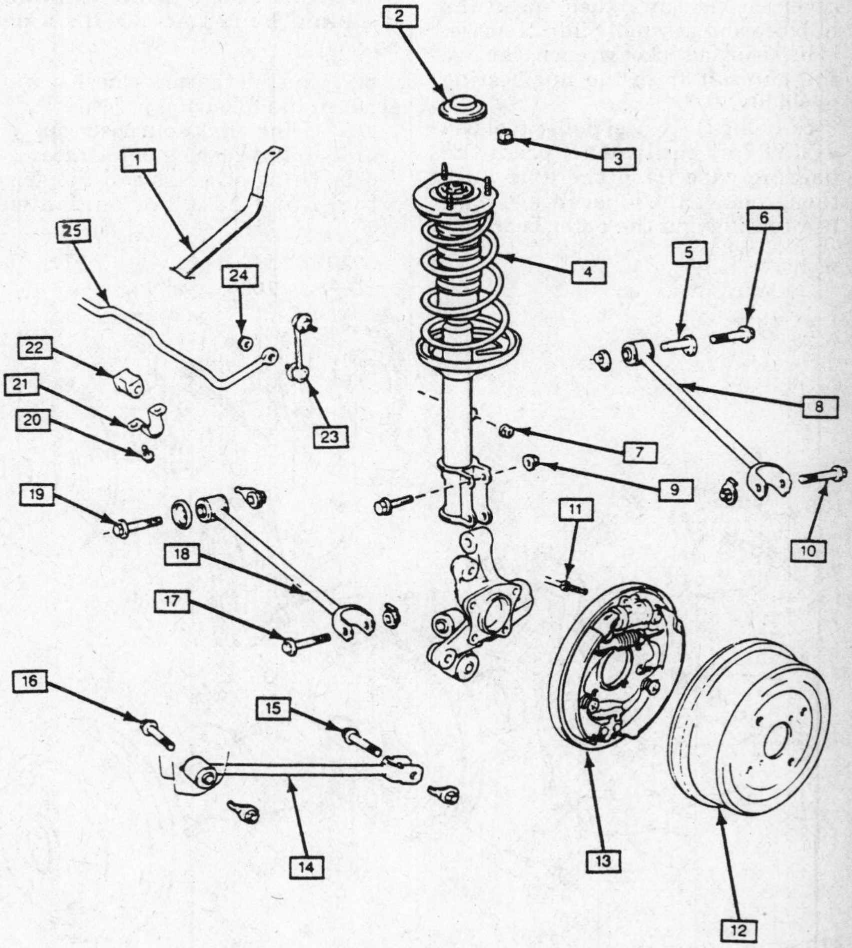


1. Fuel tank band
2. Strut tower cover
3. Strut rod piston nut
4. Strut assembly
5. Rear toe adjustment bolt
6. No 2 suspension arm to body bolt
7. Stabilizer bar link to strut assembly nut
8. No. 2 suspension arm
9. Strut assembly to knuckle nut
10. No 2 suspension arm to knuckle bolt
11. Brake line
12. Brake drum
13. Brake assembly
14. Strut rod
15. Strut rod to knuckle bolt
16. Strut rod to body bolt
17. No 1 suspension arm to knuckle bolt
18. No. 1 suspension arm
19. No 1 suspension arm to body bolt
20. Stabilizer to bracket bolt
21. Stabilizer bar bracket
22. Bushing
23. Stabilizer bar link
24. Stabilizer bar link nut
25. Stabilizer bar

**Exploded view of the rear suspension—Prizm**

3. If equipped with a drum brake, disconnect and plug the brake line from the wheel cylinder.

4. Remove the four axle hub/bearing assembly-to-carrier bolts and the hub/bearing assembly and drum brake assembly (except twincam) or dust cover (twincam). Remove and discard the O-ring.

5. To disassemble the hub/bearing assembly, perform the following procedures:

a. Using copper or aluminum, cover the vise jaws, then, insert the hub/bearing assembly into the vise.

b. Using a socket wrench, remove the hub nut from the hub/bearing assembly.

c. Using the wheel puller tool No. J-25287 or equivalent, press the bearing case from the axle hub, then, remove the inner race, the inner bearing and the outer bearing.

d. Using the wheel puller tool No. J-25287 or equivalent, press the outer bearing inner race from the axle hub.

e. Remove the seal from the axle hub.

f. Using an arbor press and the driving tool No. J-35440 or equivalent, install outer bearing inner race onto the bearing outer race and press it from the bearing case.

**NOTE: Whenever the wheel bearing assembly is disassembled, it should be replaced with a new one.**

6. To install the new wheel bearing, perform the following procedures:

a. Using multi-purpose, apply it around the bearing outer race.

b. Using an press and the driver tool No. J-35400 or equivalent, press the new bearing outer race into the bearing case.

c. Install the new bearings and inner races into the bearing case.

d. Using multi-purpose grease, lightly coat the new seal. Using the seal installation tool No. J-35736 or equivalent, drive the new seal into the bearing case until it seats.

e. Using an arbor press and the Driver tool No. J-35440 or equivalent, press the bearing case onto the hub. Torque the hub nut to 90 ft. lbs.

f. Using a chisel and a hammer, stake the hub nut.

7. To install the rear hub/bearing assembly, use a new O-ring and reverse the removal procedures. Torque the hub/bearing assembly-to-axle carrier bolts to 59 ft. lbs.

**NOTE: If equipped with drum brakes, reconnect the brake line to the wheel cylinder. Refill the brake master cylinder and bleed the brake system.**

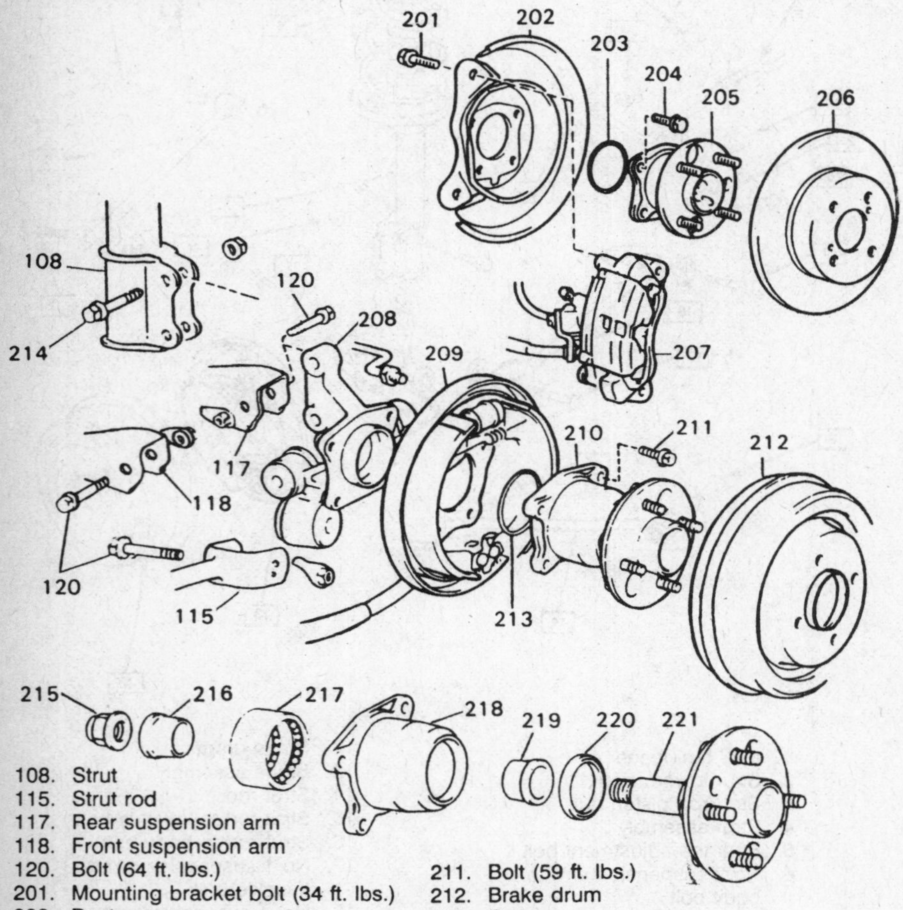

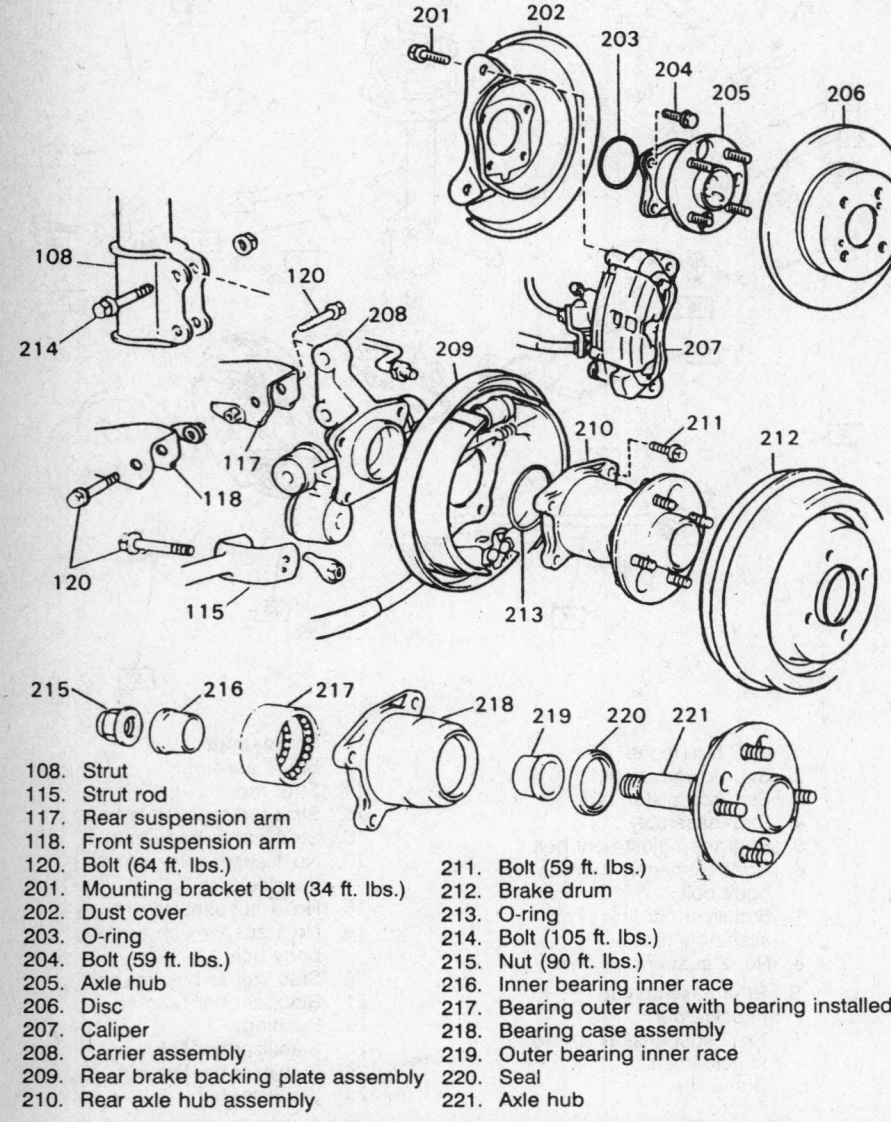

108. Strut
115. Strut rod
117. Rear suspension arm
118. Front suspension arm
120. Bolt (64 ft. lbs.)
201. Mounting bracket bolt (34 ft. lbs.)
202. Dust cover
203. O-ring
204. Bolt (59 ft. lbs.)
205. Axle hub
206. Disc
207. Caliper
208. Carrier assembly
209. Rear brake backing plate assembly
210. Rear axle hub assembly
211. Bolt (59 ft. lbs.)
212. Brake drum
213. O-ring
214. Bolt (105 ft. lbs.)
215. Nut (90 ft. lbs.)
216. Inner bearing inner race
217. Bearing outer race with bearing installed
218. Bearing case assembly
219. Outer bearing inner race
220. Seal
221. Axle hub

**Exploded view of the rear axle hub/bearing assembly—Nova and Prizm**

### *Spectrum*

1. Raise and support the front of the vehicle on jackstands.

2. Remove the rear wheel assemblies.

3. Remove the hub cap, cotter pin, hub nut, washer and outer bearing.

4. Remove the hub.

5. Using a slide hammer puller and attachment, pull the oil seal from the hub. Remove the inner bearing.

6. Using a brass drift and a hammer, drive both bearing races from the hub.

7. Clean, inspect and/or replace all parts.

8. To install, pack the bearings with grease, coat the oil seal lips with grease and reverse the removal procedures. Torque hub nut to 22 ft. lbs.

**NOTE: If the cotter pin holes are out of alignment upon reassembly, use a wrench to tighten the nut until the hole in the shaft and a slot of the nut align.**

### *Sprint and Metro*

1. Raise and support the rear of the vehicle safely.

2. Remove the wheel assembly.

3. Remove the dust cap, the cotter pin, the castle nut and the washer.

4. Loosen the adjusting nuts of the parking brake cable.

5. Remove the plug from the rear of the backing plate. Insert a screwdriver through the hole, making contact with the shoe hold down spring, then push the spring to release the parking brake shoe lever.

6. Using a slide hammer tool J-2619-01 and a brake drum remover tool J-34866, pull the brake drum from the axle shaft.

7. Using a brass drift and a hammer, drive the rear wheel bearings from the brake drum.

**NOTE: When installing the wheel bearings, face the sealed sides (numbered sides) outward. Fill the wheel bearing cavity with bearing grease.**

8. Drive the new bearings into the brake drum with the bearing installation tool J-34482.

9. To install, use a new seal and reverse the removal procedures. Torque the hub castle nut to 58–86 ft. lbs. Bleed the rear brake system. Operate the brakes 3–5 times to obtain the proper drum-to-shoe clearance. Adjust the parking brake cable.

# STEERING

## Steering Wheel

### REMOVAL & INSTALLATION

#### *Nova and Prizm*

1. Disconnect the negative terminal from the battery.

2. Remove the screw from the bottom of the steering wheel pad and pull the pad upward and off the steering wheel.

3. Remove the steering wheel-to-steering column nut. Matchmark the steering wheel-to-steering column relationship.

4. Using the Steering Wheel Puller tool No. J-1859-03 or equivalent, screw the bolts into both sides of the steering column, turn the puller center bolt to press the steering wheel from the steering shaft.

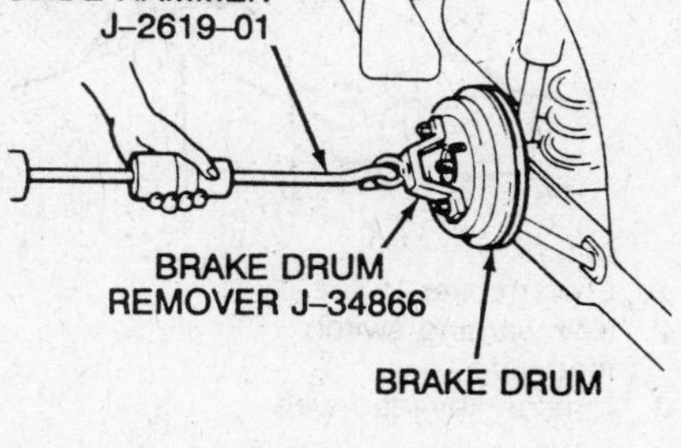


**Removing rear brake drum using a slide hammer – Sprint and Metro**

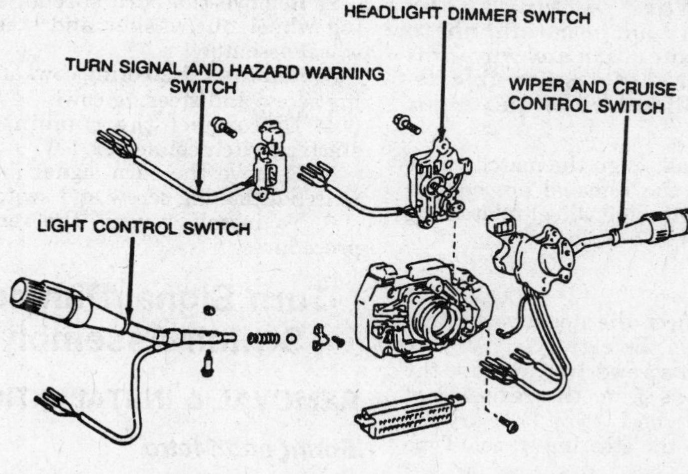


**Exploded view of combination switch – Nova and Prizm**

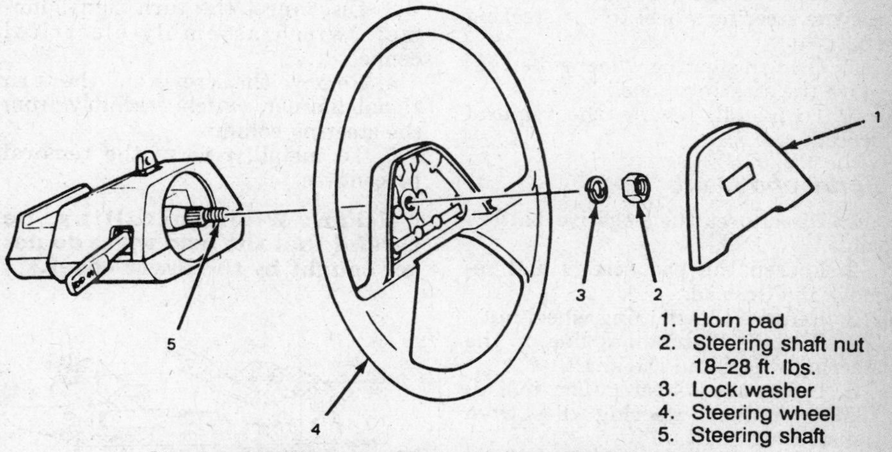


**Steering wheel and horn pad mounting – Sprint and Metro**

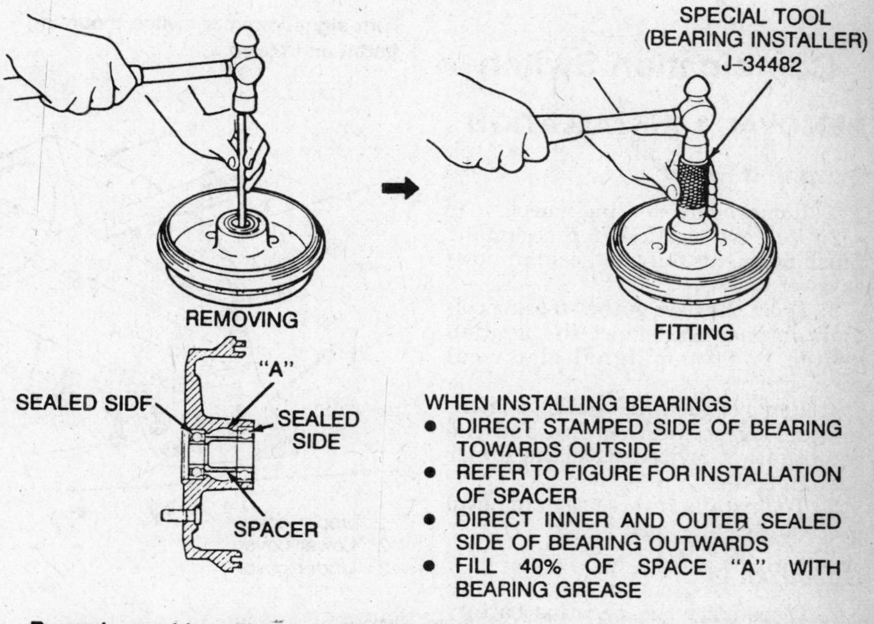


**Removing and installing rear wheel bearings in brake drum – Sprint and Metro**

**NOTE: When working on the steering column, be careful not to strike the column in any way for it is constructed of a collapsible design and will not withstand major shock.**

5. To install, align the matchmarks and reverse the removal procedures. Torque the steering wheel-to-steering column nut to 25 ft. lbs.

### *Spectrum*

1. Disconnect the negative battery terminal from the battery.
2. Using a screwdriver, remove the shroud screws from the rear-side of the steering wheel (Type 1) or pry the shroud from the steering wheel (Type 2).
3. Disconnect the horn connector and remove the shroud.
4. Remove the nut/washer retaining the steering wheel to the steering shaft.
5. Using a steering wheel puller, remove the steering wheel.
6. To install, reverse the removal procedures.

### *Sprint and Metro*

1. Disconnect the negative battery cable.
2. Loosen the pad screws and remove the the pad.
3. Remove the steering wheel nut.
4. Scribe a matchmark line on the steering wheel and the shaft.
5. Using the wheel puller tool J-1859-03, pull the steering wheel from the steering shaft.
6. To install, reverse the removal procedures. Torque the steering wheel nut to 19–29 ft. lbs.

# Combination Switch

## REMOVAL & INSTALLATION

### *Nova and Prizm*

1. Remove the steering wheel.
2. Remove the lower instrument finish panel, air duct and column lower cover.
3. From the base of the steering column shroud, disconnect the ignition switch and turn signal electrical connector.
4. Remove the combination switch-to-steering column screws and the combination switch with the upper column cover.
5. To install, reverse the removal procedures.

### *Spectrum*

1. Disconnect the negative battery terminal from the battery.
2. Remove the horn shroud, steering wheel nut/washer and steering wheel assembly.
3. Remove the steering cowl attaching screw and steering cowl.
4. Disconnect the combination/starter switch connector.
5. Remove the turn signal/dimmer switch attaching screw and switch.
6. To install, reverse the removal procedures.

# Turn Signal/Dimmer Switch Assembly

## REMOVAL & INSTALLATION

### *Sprint and Metro*

1. Remove the steering wheel.
2. Remove the upper and lower steering column covers.
3. Disconnect the turn signal/dimmer switch assembly electrical connector.
4. Remove the screws and the turn signal/dimmer switch assembly from the steering column.
5. To install, reverse the removal procedures.

**NOTE: When installing, be careful that the lead wires do not get caught by the lower cover.**

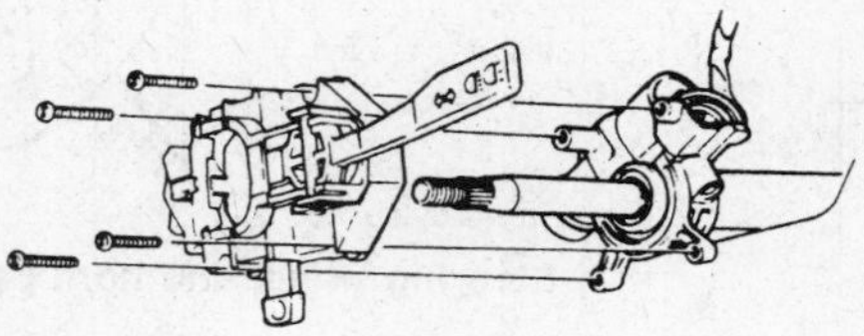

Turn signal/dimmer switch mounting—Sprint and Metro

# Ignition Lock and Switch

## REMOVAL & INSTALLATION

### *Nova and Prizm*

1. Remove the combination switch.
2. If equipped with a tilt steering column, perform the following procedures:
   a. Remove the tension springs and grommets, the tilt lever (the bolt has left-hand threads), the adjusting nut/washer.
   b. Pull out the lock bolt, then, remove the upper and lower column supports.
3. From the lower steering column, disconnect the ignition switch electrical connector.
4. Remove the retainer-to-upper bracket screws and the retainer from the upper bracket.
5. Using snap-ring pliers, remove the snap-ring from the upper bracket.
6. Insert the key into the ignition switch and release the steering lock.
7. Using a hammer and a pin punch, drive the tapered bolt from the upper bracket.
8. Remove the upper bracket-to-steering column tube bolts and the upper bracket.
9. To install, release the steering lock and install the upper bracket-to steering column bolts (tighten the bolts finger tight). Torque the upper bracket-to-steering column bolts to 14 ft. lbs.
10. If installing the tilt steering mechanism, perform the following procedures:
    a. Apply grease to the bushings and the O-rings, then, install the lower support-to-tube.

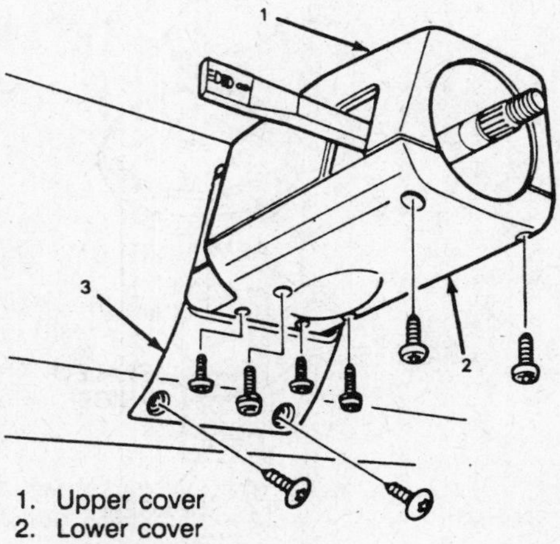


1. Upper cover
2. Lower cover
3. Under cover

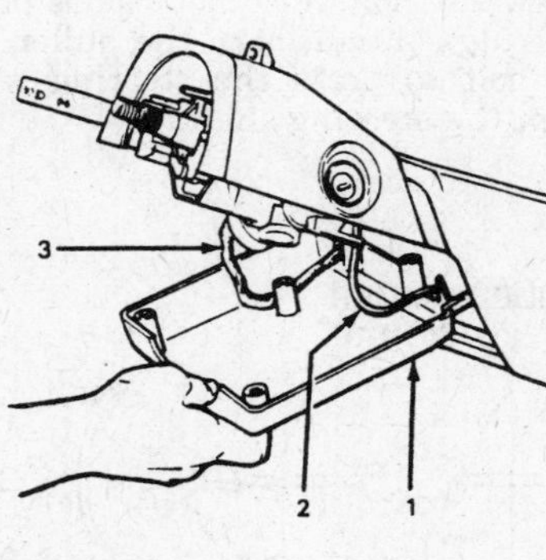


1. Lower cover
2. Key warning switch lead wire
3. Ignition key lead wire

Removing lower steering column cover—Sprint and Metro

b. Using multi-purpose grease, apply it to the tilt bracket-to-steering column mating surfaces, then, install the upper support and lock bolt.

**NOTE: If there is any play in the adjusting support, snug-up the adjusting nut.**

c. Install the tilt lever. Move the lever to loosen the bracket-to-column bolt, adjust the column height and move the lever to lock the column position; if the lever is out of position, reposition the adjusting nut.

d. Install the tilt lever retaining screw (left-hand thread) and torque it. Install the tension springs and grommets.

11. To complete the installation, reverse the removal procedures.

### *Spectrum*

1. Remove the combination switch.
2. Insert the key into the ignition and place the key in the On position (the lock bar must be pulled all the way in).
3. Remove the snap ring and rubber cushion from the steering shaft.
4. Disconnect the switch wires at the connectors.
5. Remove the 2 screws retaining the ignition/starter switch and remove the switch.
6. To install, reverse the removal procedures.

### *Sprint and Metro*

1. Remove the steering column.
2. Place the column on a bench.
3. Using a sharp point center punch and a hammer, remove the steering lock mounting bolts.
4. Turn the ignition key to **ACC** or **ON** positions and remove the lock assembly from the steering column.
5. To install, reverse the removal procedures. After installing the lock, turn the key to **LOCK** position and pull out the key. Turn the steering shaft to make sure the shaft is locked. Install new mounting bolts to the lock housing, tighten until the bolt heads break off. Torque the lower bracket bolts to 8–12 ft. lbs.; the upper bracket bolts to 10 ft. lbs. and the steering shaft bolt to 15–22 ft. lbs.

# Manual Steering Gear

## REMOVAL & INSTALLATION

### *Nova and Prizm*

1. Remove the intermediate shaft cover.
2. From the steering gear pinion shaft, loosen the upper pinch bolt, then, remove the lower pinch bolt.
3. Loosen the wheel/tire assembly lug nuts.
4. Raise and support the front of the vehicle on jackstands.
5. From the tie rod ends, remove the cotter pins and nuts. Using the ball joint removal tool No. J-24319-01 or equivalent, press the ball joint from the steering knuckle.
6. Remove the steering gear-to-chassis nuts/bolts and brackets, then, separate the universal joint from the steering gear and slide the steering gear through the access hole.
7. Inspect the steering gear for wear, and/or damage; replace or repair the damaged parts.

**NOTE: If the ball joint seal is torn or damaged, replace the ball joint. Make sure the clamps are installed squarely over the rubber insulators so they will not be damaged when the nuts and bolts are torqued.**

8. To install, reverse the removal procedures. Torque the steering gear-to-chassis nuts/bolts to 43 ft. lbs., the tie rod end-to-steering knuckle nuts to 36 ft. lbs. and the U-joint pinch clamp bolts to 26 ft. lbs.

**NOTE: If new parts have been installed, check and/or adjust the front wheel toe-in and the steering wheel center point.**

### *Spectrum*

1. Remove both tie rod ends from the steering knuckles and the left inner tie rod from the rack.
2. Remove the intermediate shaft cover.
3. Loosen the upper pinch bolt and remove the lower pinch bolt at the pinion shaft.
4. Remove the steering gear to body retaining nuts.
5. Remove the rack and pinion assembly.
6. To install, reverse the removal procedures and check the toe-in.

### *Sprint and Metro*

1. Remove the tie rod ends from the steering knuckles.
2. Under the dash, remove the steering joint cover.
3. Remove the lower steering shaft-to-steering gear clinch bolt and separate the steering shaft from the steering gear.
4. Remove the steering gear mounting bolts, the brackets and the steering gear case from the vehicle.
5. To install, reverse the removal procedures. Torque the steering gear case bolts to 14–22 ft. lbs.; the steering gear-to-steering shaft bolt to 14–22 ft. lbs. and the tie rod end-to-steering knuckle nut to 22–40 ft. lbs.

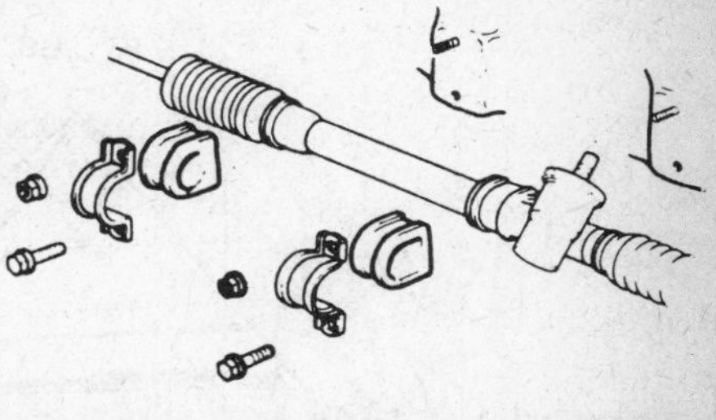

**Gear to body mounting—Nova and Prizm**

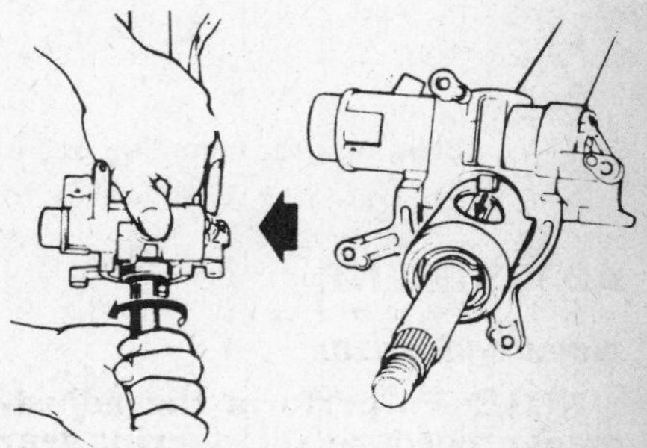

**Rotate steering shaft until tab on switch aligns with the groove in the shaft—Sprint and Metro**

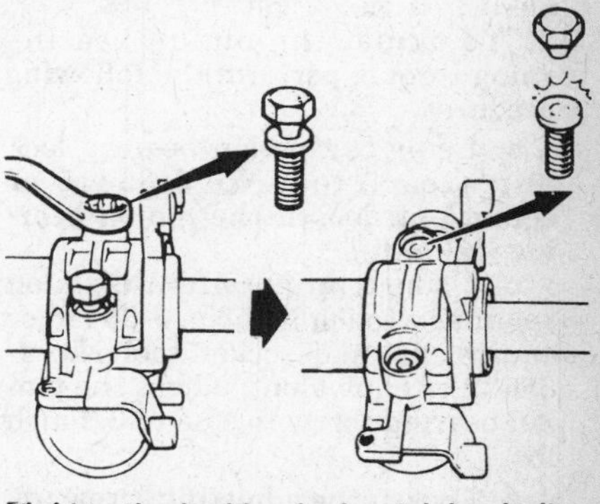

**Tighten the ignition lock retaining bolts until the head of the bolt breaks off—Sprint and Metro**

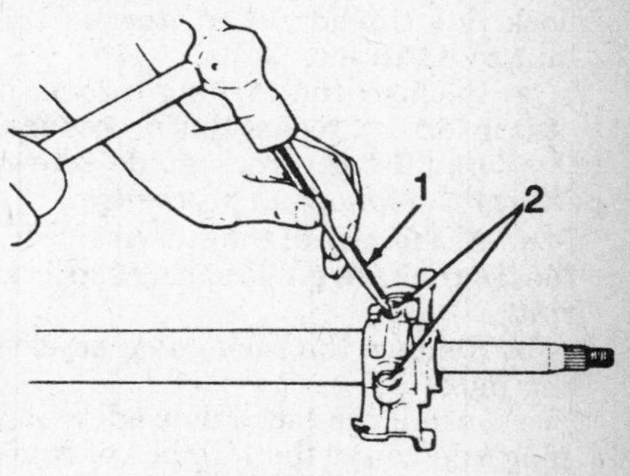


1. Center Punch (With Sharp Point)
2. Steering Lock Mounting Bolts

**Removing the ignition switch/key lock assembly—Sprint and Metro**

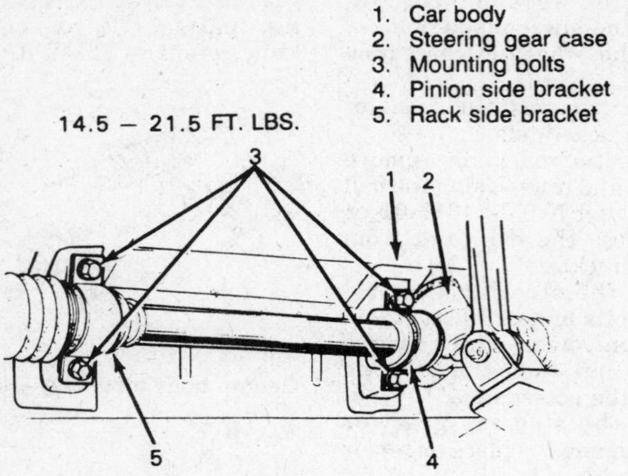


Steering gear mounting bolt locations – Sprint and Metro

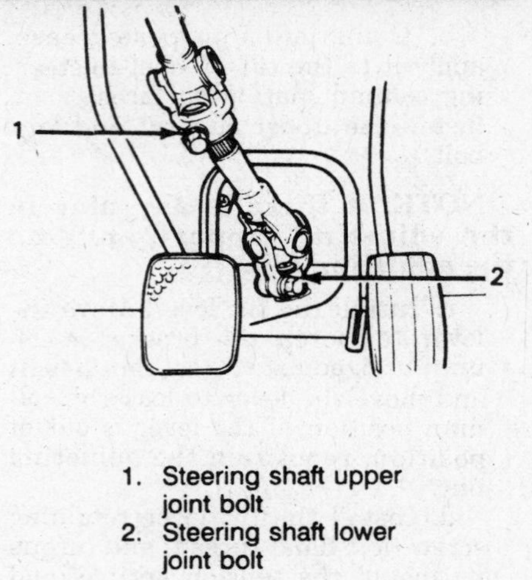


Disconnect the steering shaft from the steering gear at two locations – Sprint and Metro

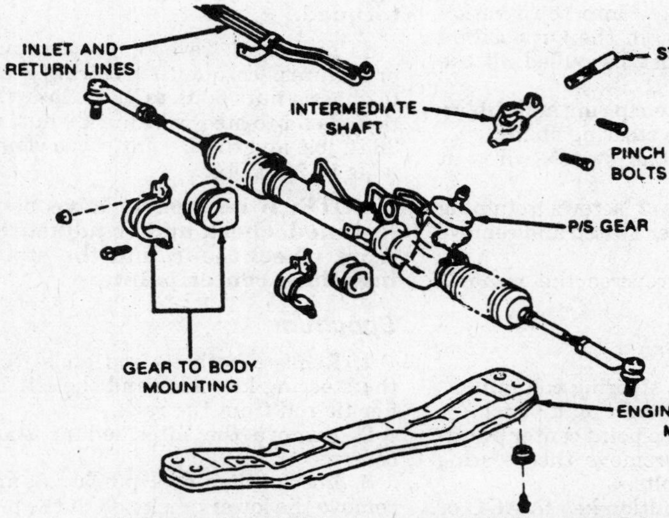


Power Rack and Pinion rack removal – Nova and Prizm

## ADJUSTMENT

### *Nova and Prizm*

**NOTE: To perform the adjustment procedure, the steering gear assembly should be removed from the vehicle.**

1. Remove the steering gear and place it in a vise.
2. To adjust the pinion bearing turning torque, perform the following procedures:
   a. Using the pinion bearing lock nut wrench tool No. J-35415 or equivalent, loosen the pinion bearing lock nut.
   b. Using a torque wrench, pinion spanner wrench tool No. J-35416 or equivalent, and socket tool No. J-35422 or equivalent, adjust the pinion bearing screw torque to 3.2 inch lbs.
   c. Loosen the adjusting screw until the turning torque is 2–2.9 inch lbs.
   d. Using sealant, coat the pinion lock nut threads, then, torque the nut to 83 ft. lbs.
   e. Recheck the turning torque, if it is incorrect, repeat this procedure.
3. To adjust the rack guide screw, perform the following procedure:
   a. At the rear of the steering gear, loosen the rack guide spring cap lock nut.
   b. Remove the rack guide adjusting plug.
   c. Install the rack guide adjusting plug and count the number of rotations, then, back-off the plug ½ the number of turns.
   d. Using a socket wrench and socket tool No. J-35423 or equivalent, hold the rack guide adjusting plug. Using a torque wrench with a lock nut wrench adapter tool No. J-35692 or equivalent, torque the rack guide lock nut to 18 ft. lbs., then, back-off the nut 25 degrees (use a compass to measure the position in degrees).
   e. Using a torque wrench and socket tool No. J-35422 or equivalent, check the pinion shaft preload; it should be 6.9–11.3 inch lbs.

**NOTE: If the preload is insufficient, retorque the lock nut and back it off 12 degrees, then, recheck the preload.**

4. Using sealant, coat the lock nut threads and torque the lock nut to 51 ft. lbs.
5. To install the steering gear, reverse the removal procedures.

# Power Steering Gear

## REMOVAL & INSTALLATION

### *Nova and Prizm*

1. Remove the intermediate steering shaft protector. Loosen the upper shaft pinch bolt and remove the lower one.
2. Open the hood and place a drain pan under the steering gear assembly. Clean the area around the inlet and return lines at the steering gear valve.
3. Loosen the wheel lugnuts, then, raise and support the front of the vehicle on jackstands. Remove both front wheel/tire assemblies.
4. Remove the cotter pins and nuts from the tie rod ends. Using the ball

joint removal tool No. J-24319-01 or equivalent, press the tie rod ends from the steering knuckles.

5. Using a floor jack, support the transaxle. Remove the rear center engine mounting member-to-chassis mounting bolts.

6. Remove the rear engine mount-to-mount bracket nut and bolt.

7. Disconnect the pressure and return lines from the steering gear. Remove the steering gear-to-chassis nuts and bolts; raise and lower the rear of the transaxle (as necessary) to gain access to the steering gear-to-chassis nuts and bolts.

8. Remove the steering gear through the access hole.

9. To install, reverse the removal procedures. Torque the steering gear-to-chassis nuts/bolts to 43 ft. lbs., the tie rod end-to-steering knuckle nuts to 36 ft. lbs. and the U-joint pinch clamp bolts to 26 ft. lbs. Add fluid to the pump reservoir and bleed the system.

**NOTE: If new parts have been installed, check and/or adjust the front wheel toe-in and the steering wheel center point.**

#### *Spectrum*

1. Remove both tie rod ends from the steering knuckles and the right inner tie rod from the rack.

2. Place a drain pan under the rack assembly and clean around the pressure lines at the rack valve.

3. Cut the plastic retaining straps at the power steering lines and hose.

4. Remove the power steering pump lines, the rack valve and drain the fluid into the pan.

5. Remove the rack and pinion.

6. To install, reverse the removal procedures, add fluid, bleed the system and check the toe-in.

### ADJUSTMENT

#### *Nova and Prizm*

**NOTE: To perform the adjustment procedure, the steering gear assembly should be removed from the vehicle.**

1. Remove the steering gear and place it in a vise.

2. To adjust the pinion bearing turning torque, perform the following procedures:

a. Using the socket wrench and socket tool No. J-35428 or equivalent, loosen the pinion bearing lock nut.

b. Using a socket wrench and socket tool No. J-35428 or equivalent, hold the pinion from turning. Using a torque wrench and socket, torque the lower pinion lock nut to 48 ft. lbs.

3. To adjust the rack guide cap, perform the following procedure:

a. At the rear of the steering gear, loosen the rack guide spring cap lock nut.

b. Using a socket wrench and socket tool No. J-35423 or equivalent, torque the rack guide lock nut to 18 ft. lbs., then, back-off the nut 12 degrees (use a compass to measure the position in degrees).

c. Using a torque wrench and socket tool No. J-35428 or equivalent, check the pinion shaft preload; it should be 7–11 inch lbs.

4. Using sealant, coat the lock nut threads and torque the lock nut to 33 ft. lbs.

5. To install the steering gear, reverse the removal procedures. Bleed the power steering system.

## Power Steering Pump

### REMOVAL & INSTALLATION

#### *Nova and Prizm*

##### EXCEPT TWINCAM

1. Place a catch pan under the power steering pump. Remove the air cleaner.

2. Remove the return hose clamp, then, disconnect the pressure and return hoses from the pump; drain the power steering fluid into the pan.

3. While pushing downward on the drive belt (to keep the belt from turning), loosen the pump pulley center nut. Remove the pump pulley and woodruff key; be sure not to loose the key.

4. Remove the pump pivot and adjusting bolts, then, move the pump to reduce the belt tension and remove the drive belt.

5. Remove the pump assembly and bracket.

6. To install, reverse the removal procedures. Torque the pressure hose-to-pump hose to 34 ft. lbs. and the power steering pump adjusting/pivot bolts to 29 ft. lbs. Refill the power steering reservoir with Dexron® II automatic transmission fluid. Bleed the power steering system. Operate the engine, then, check and/or repair the leaks.

**NOTE: If replacing the pump, switch the pulley and the mounting nut to the new pump.**

##### TWINCAM

1. Remove the air cleaner.

2. Place a catch pan under the power steering pump.

3. From the power steering pump, disconnect the pressure and return hoses.

4. Remove the under engine cover.

5. Push downward of the drive belt to keep the pulley from turning, then, remove the pump pulley set nut. Remove the drive belt.

6. Remove the pump pulley and the Woodruff key; be careful not to loose the key.

7. Remove the upper, lower and pivot bolts.

8. Disconnect the oil pressure switch connector.

9. Remove the power steering pulley, pump-to-bracket bolts and the pump.

10. To install, reverse the removal procedures. Torque the pressure hose-to-pump hose to 33 ft. lbs. and the power steering pump adjusting/pivot bolts to 29 ft. lbs. Refill the power steering reservoir with Dexron® II automatic transmission fluid. Bleed the power steering system. Operate the engine, then, check and/or repair the leaks.

#### *Spectrum*

1. Place a drain pan below the pump.

2. Remove the pressure hose clamp, pressure hose and return hose. Drain the fluid from the pump and reservoir.

3. Remove the adjusting bolt, pivot bolt and drive belt.

4. Remove the pump assembly.

5. To install, reverse the removal procedures, tighten the pressure hose to 20 ft. lbs., adjust the drive belt, fill the reservoir and bleed the system.

### BELT ADJUSTMENT

#### *Nova and Prizm*

1. Using a belt tension gauge tool BT-33-73F or equivalent, position it on the drive belt (between the longest span of 2 pulleys).

2. Loosen the power steering adjusting and pivot bolts.

3. Move the pump to adjust the drive belt tension.

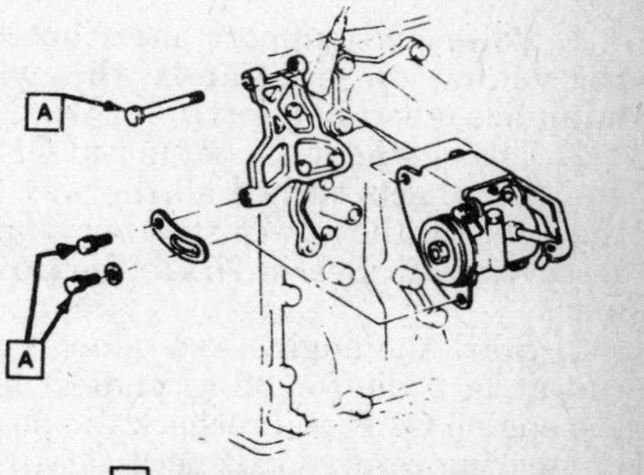


A TORQUE: 20 N·m (15 FT. LBS.)

**Power steering pump mounting and adjusting bolts – Spectrum**

**NOTE: The belt deflection should be 0.31–0.39 in. with moderate thumb pressure (about 20 lbs.) applied in the center of the span.**

4. Torque the power steering pump pivot/adjusting bolts to 29 ft. lbs.

### *Spectrum*

**NOTE: The following procedures require the use of GM belt tension gauge No. BT-33-95-ACBN (regular V-belts) or BT-33-97M (poly V-belts).**

1. If the belt is cold, operate the engine (at idle speed) for 15 minutes; the belt will seat itself in the pulleys allowing the belt fibers to relax or stretch. If the belt is hot, allow it to cool, until it is warm to the touch.

**NOTE: A used belt is one that has been rotated at least one complete evolution on the pulleys. This begins the belt seating process and it must never be tensioned to the new belt specifications.**

2. Loosen the component-to-mounting bracket bolts.
3. Using a GM belt tension gauge No. BT-33-95-ACBN (standard V-belts) or BT-33-97M (poly V-belts), place the tension gauge at the center of the belt between the longest span.
4. Applying belt tension pressure on the component, adjust the drive belt tension to the correct specifications. The belt tension should deflect about ¼ in. over a 7–10 in. span or ½ in. over a 13–16 in. span.
5. While holding the correct tension on the component, tighten the component-to-mounting bracket bolt.
6. When the belt tension is correct (70–110 inch lbs.), remove the tension gauge.

## BLEEDING THE POWER STEERING SYSTEM

### *Nova and Prizm*

1. Raise and support the front of the vehicle on jackstands (this will minimize steering effort).
2. The engine must be turned **OFF** and the wheels turned all the way to the left. Fill the power steering pump reservoir with Dexron® II to the **Cold** mark.
3. Start the engine and allow it to run at fast idle for 30 seconds. Turn the engine **OFF** and recheck the power steering reservoir; if necessary, refill the reservoir to the **Cold** mark.
4. Start the engine and turn the steering wheel from lock-to-lock several times.
5. Repeat the bleeding procedure until all the air is bled from the steering system.
6. After bleeding the system, road test the vehicle to make sure the steering is functioning properly and is free of noise.

### *Spectrum*

1. Turn the wheels to the extreme left.
2. With the engine stopped, add power steering fluid to the**MIN** mark on the fluid indicator.
3. Start the engine and run it for 15 seconds at fast idle.
4. Stop the engine, recheck the fluid level and refill to the **MIN** mark.
5. Start the engine and turn the wheels from side to side (3 times).
6. Stop the engine check the fluid level.

**NOTE: If air bubbles are still present in the fluid, the procedures must be repeated.**

# Tie Rod Ends

## REMOVAL & INSTALLATION

### *Nova and Prizm*

1. Raise and support the front of the vehicle on jacktands. Remove the wheel/tire assembly.
2. Remove the tie rod-to-steering knuckle cotter pin (discard it) and nut. Using the Ball Joint Removal tool No. J-24319-01 or equivalent, press the tie rod ends from the steering knuckles.
3. Loosen the tie rod-to-steering rack locknut. Matchmark the tie rod end-to-tie rod for installation purposes.
4. Counting the number of turns, unscrew the tie rod end from the tie rod.
5. Inspect the ball joint for wear; if necessary, replace the tie rod end.
6. To install, turn the tie rod end onto the tie rod (the same number of turns necessary to remove it), align the matchmarks and reverse the removal procedures. Torque the tie rod-to-steering rack locknut to 35 ft. lbs. and the tie rod end-to-steering knuckle nut to 36 ft. lbs. Install a new cotter pin. Check and/or adjust the front end toe.

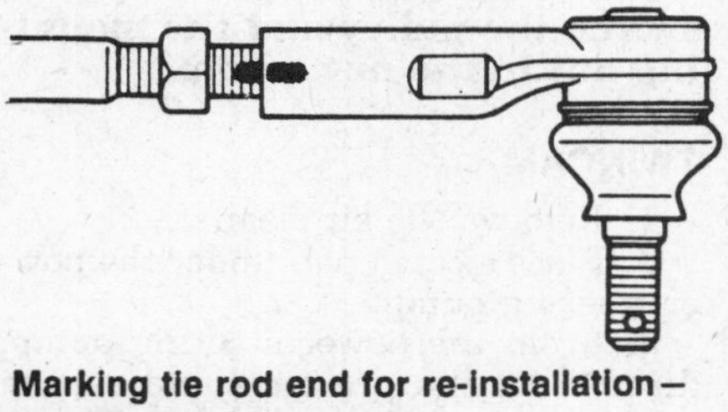

Marking tie rod end for re-installation—Nova and Prizm

### *Spectrum*

1. Raise and support the front of the vehicle on jackstands, then remove the front wheel.
2. Remove the castle nut from the ball joint. Using a ball joint removal tool, separate the tie rod from the steering knuckle.
3. Disconnect the retaining wire from the inner boot and pull back the boot.
4. Using a chisel, straighten the staked part of the locking washer between the tie rod and the rack.
5. Remove the tie rod from the rack.
6. To install, reverse the removal procedures.

### *Sprint and Metro*

1. Raise and support the front of the vehicle on jackstands. Remove the front wheel assembly.
2. Remove the cotter pin and the castle nut from the tie rod end.
3. Using the ball joint remover tool J-21687-02, remove the tie rod end ball joint from the steering knuckle.
4. Loosen the lock nut on the tie rod end.
5. Unscrew the the tie rod end from the tie rod, count the number of revolutions necessary to remove the tie rod end, for installation purposes.
6. At the steering gear, remove the boot clamps and pull the boot back over the tie rod.
7. Using a pair of pliers, bend the lock washer back from the tie rod joint.
8. Using two wrenches, hold the steering gear and unscrew the tie rod end.
9. Remove the tie rod and slide the boot from the tie rod.
10. To install, reverse the removal procedures. Torque the tie rod-to-steering gear to 51–72 ft. lbs.; the tie rod end lock nut to 26–40 ft. lbs. and

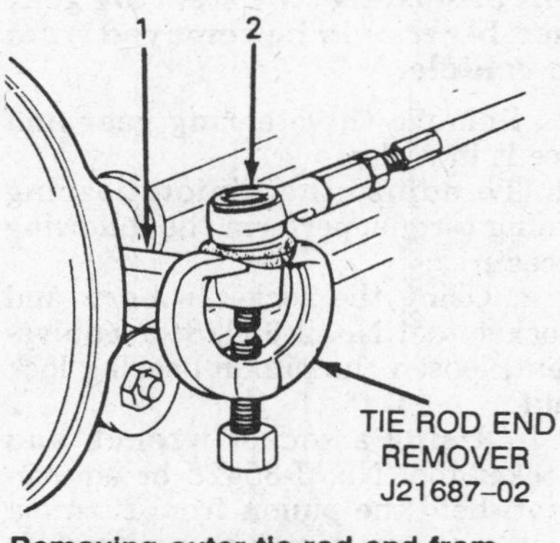


Removing outer tie rod end from steering knuckle using a puller—Sprint and Metro

the tie rod end-to-steering knuckle to 22–40 ft. lbs. With the tie rod secured to the steering gear, bend the lock washer over the flat spot on the tie rod ball end.

# BRAKES

**For all brake system repair and service procedures not detailed below, please refer to "Brakes" in the Unit Repair section.**

## Master Cylinder

### REMOVAL & INSTALLATION

**NOTE: Be careful not to spill brake fluid on the painted surfaces of the vehicle; it will damage the finish.**

#### *Nova and Prizm*

1. Using a syringe, remove the brake fluid from the master cylinder.
2. Disconnect the fluid level warning switch connector from the master cylinder.

**NOTE: If planning to disassemble the master cylinder, loosen the master cylinder reservoir mounting (or set) bolts.**

3. Disconnect the hydraulic lines from the master cylinder and plug the openings.
4. Remove the master cylinder-to-power brake booster nuts and the master cylinder; discard the gasket.
5. To install the master cylinder, use a new gasket, clean out the groove on the lower installation surface, confirm that the **UP** mark on the master cylinder boot is in the correct position (at the top), adjust the pushrod and reverse the removal procedures. Torque the master cylinder-to-power brake booster nuts to 9 ft. lbs. and the brake lines to 11 ft. lbs. Connect the level warning switch connector. Refill the fluid reservoir and bleed the brake system. Check for fluid leakage and tighten or replace fittings as necessary. Adjust the pedal height and free-play.

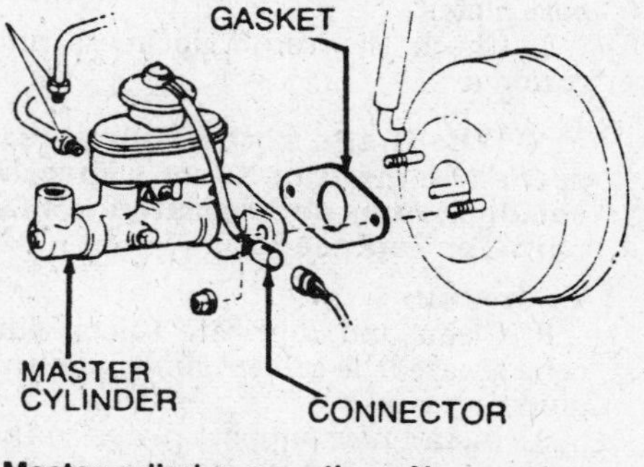


**Master cylinder mounting – Nova and Prizm**

#### *Spectrum*

1. Remove some brake fluid from the master cylinder with a syringe.
2. Disconnect and cap or tape the openings of the brake tube.
3. Disconnect the brake fluid level warning switch connector.
4. Remove the 2 nuts securing the master cylinder to the power brake booster.
5. Remove the master cylinder from the power brake booster.
6. To install, reverse the removal procedures, add fluid to the reservoir and bleed the brake system.

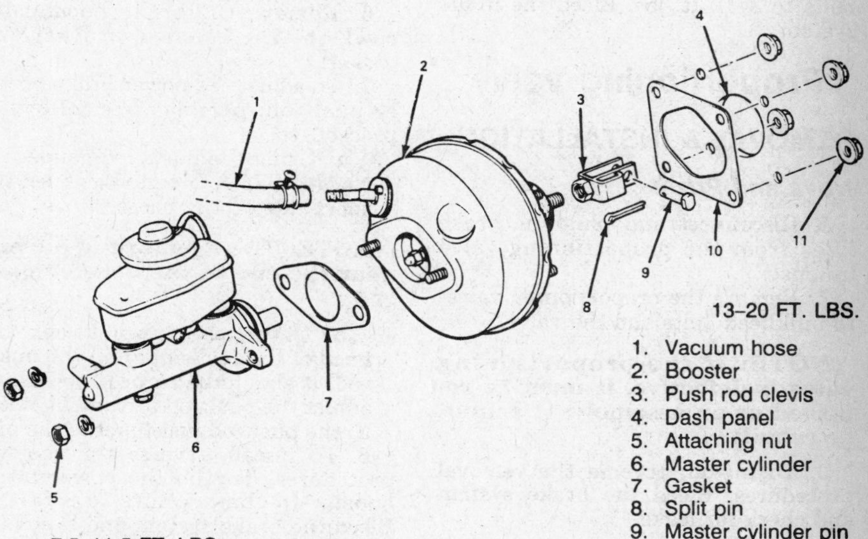


1. Vacuum hose
2. Booster
3. Push rod clevis
4. Dash panel
5. Attaching nut
6. Master cylinder
7. Gasket
8. Split pin
9. Master cylinder pin
10. Gasket
11. Attaching nut

**Master cylinder and booster mounting – Sprint and Metro**

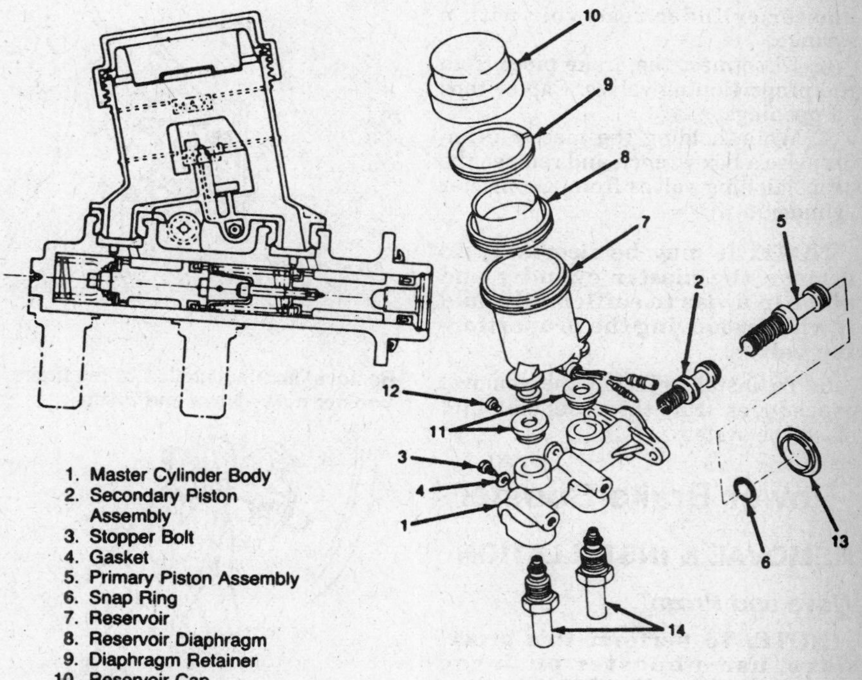


1. Master Cylinder Body
2. Secondary Piston Assembly
3. Stopper Bolt
4. Gasket
5. Primary Piston Assembly
6. Snap Ring
7. Reservoir
8. Reservoir Diaphragm
9. Diaphragm Retainer
10. Reservoir Cap
11. Reservoir Grommets
12. Reservoir Screw
13. Dust Seal
14. Proportioning Valves

**Exploded view of the master cylinder assembly – Spectrum**

### *Sprint and Metro*

1. Clean around the reservoir cap and take some of the fluid out with a syringe.
2. Disconnect and plug the brake tubes from the master cylinder.
3. Remove the mounting nuts and washers.
4. Remove the master cylinder.
5. To install, reverse the removal procedures. Torque the mounting bolts to 8–12 ft. lbs. Bleed the brake system.

# Proportioning Valve

## REMOVAL & INSTALLATION

### *Nova and Prizm*

1. Disconnect and plug the brake lines from the proportioning valve unions.
2. Remove the proportioning valve-to-bulkhead bolts and the valve.

**NOTE: If the proportioning valve is defective, it must be replaced as an assembly; it cannot be rebuilt.**

3. To install, reverse the removal procedures. Bleed the brake system and check for leaks.

### *Spectrum*

1. Clean the area around the reservoir and brake pipe connections.
2. Remove the brake fluid from the master cylinder reservoir with a syringe.
3. Disconnect the brake pipes from the proportioning valves. Cap or tape all openings.
4. While holding the master cylinder, Use a box wrench and remove the proportioning valves from the master cylinder.

**NOTE: It may be necessary to remove the master cylinder and place in a vise to sufficiently hold it while removing the proportioning valves.**

5. To install, reverse the removal procedures. Fill the reservoir and bleed the system.

# Power Brake Booster

## REMOVAL & INSTALLATION

### *Nova and Prizm*

**NOTE: To perform this procedure, use a booster push rod gauge GM part No. J-34873-A or equivalent to set the booster pushrod length.**

1. Remove the master cylinder and the 3-way union from the power brake booster.
2. Pull back the clamp and disconnect the booster vacuum line from the power brake booster.
3. Remove the instrument panel lower finish panel and the air duct.
4. Remove the brake pedal return spring.
5. Locate the clevis rod at the brake pedal (under the dash), then, pull out the clip and remove the clevis pin.
6. Remove the brake booster-to-cowl, the the booster, bracket and gasket.
7. To adjust the power brake booster pushrod, perform the following procedures:
   a. Using the push rod gauge tool No. J-34873-A or equivalent, set the short-side on the booster.

**NOTE: The head of the pin sits near the end of the booster push rod.**

   b. Check the gap between the head of the tool's pin and the pushrod; it should be zero. If necessary, adjust the pushrod by turning it until the pushrod just touches the pin.
8. To install, reverse the removal procedures. Torque the power brake booster-to-chassis nuts to 9 ft. lbs. Bleed the brake system and check for leaks in the system. Adjust the pedal height and free-play.

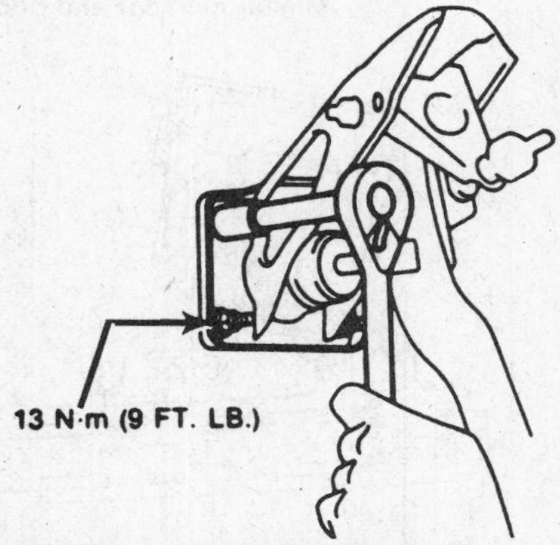


Removal and installation of the brake booster nuts—Nova and Prizm

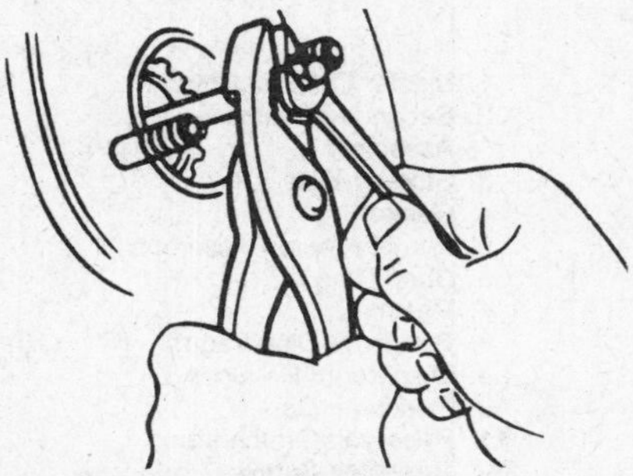

Adjusting brake booster push rod length—Nova and Prizm

### *Spectrum*

1. Remove the master cylinder.
2. Remove the vacuum hose from the vacuum servo.
3. Remove the clevis pin from the brake pedal.
4. Remove the 4 nuts from the brake assembly under the dash and remove the power booster from the engine compartment.
5. To install, reverse the removal procedures.

### *Sprint and Metro*

1. Remove the master cylinder.
2. Disconnect the push rod clevis pin from the brake pedal arm.
3. Disconnect the vacuum hose from the brake booster.
4. Remove the mounting nuts from under the dash and the booster.
5. To install, reverse the removal procedures. Torque the booster-to-cowl nuts to 14–20 ft. lbs. Bleed the brake system, if necessary.

# Disc Brake Pads

## REMOVAL & INSTALTION

### *Nova and Prizm*

#### FRONT

1. Remove ⅔ of the brake fluid from the master cylinder.
2. Raise and support the front of the vehicle on jackstands. Mark the relationship of the wheel to the axle hub. Remove the front wheel; install 2 wheel lug nuts to retain the rotor.
3. Remove the caliper-to-mounting bracket pins.
4. Lift the caliper from the mounting bracket. Using a wire, support the caliper so there is no strain on the brake hose.
5. Using a small pry bar or a C-clamp, force the piston back into the bore, being careful not to scratch the piston and/or bore. Be careful not to cut or tear the dust boots.
6. From the caliper, remove the brake pads, the wear indicator plates, the anti-squeal shims and the 4 support plates.
7. Check the rotor thickness and runnout.

**NOTE: If the rotor runout exceeds the manufacturer's specifications or has deep scratches, machine or replace it.**

**To Install:**

8. Clean and lubricate (using silicone grease) the caliper guide pins and guide surfaces.
9. Install new support plates to the mounting bracket and new pad wear indicator plates to each pad.

**NOTE: When installing the pad wear indicators, be sure the arrow on the indicator is facing in the direction of rotation.**

10. Install a new anti-squeal shim to the backside of each pad.
11. Position the new pads on the mounting bracket.

**NOTE: The inboard and outboard pads are identical and interchangeable.**

12. Position the caliper on the mounting bracket.
13. Align the guide pin holes of the adapter and the caliper. Torque the mounting bracket-to-steering knuckle bolts to 65 ft. lbs. and guide pins to 18 ft. lbs.
14. Align and install the wheel to the axle hub, then lower the vehicle.
15. Refill the master cylinder to the proper level. If necessary, bleed the brake system.

**REAR**

1. Remove ⅔ of brake fluid from the master cylinder.
2. Raise the vehicle and support it safely on jack stands.
3. Mark the position of the front wheels in relation to the axle hub and remove the wheels.
4. Remove the 2 caliper mounting bolts from the mounting bracket.

**NOTE: It is not necessary to remove the caliper hose. Remove and support the caliper.**

5. Remove the brake pads.

**To Install:**

6. Install new inner/outer pads.
7. Install new wear sensors.

**NOTE: Be sure the arrow on the pad wear indicator is pointing in the rotating direction of the disc.**

8. Install the pads onto the mounting bracket.
9. Press the caliper piston back into the bore.
10. Install the caliper onto the rotor.
11. Tighten caliper guide bolts to proper torque.
12. Install wheels and tires aligning the previous marks.
13. Torque lug nuts.
14. Lower the vehicle. With engine running pump brake pedal slowly several times to bring the pads in contact with the rotors.
15. Check the brake fluid level and add if necessary.

***Spectrum***

1. Remove ⅔ of the brake fluid from the master cylinder.
2. Loosen the wheel lugs, then raise

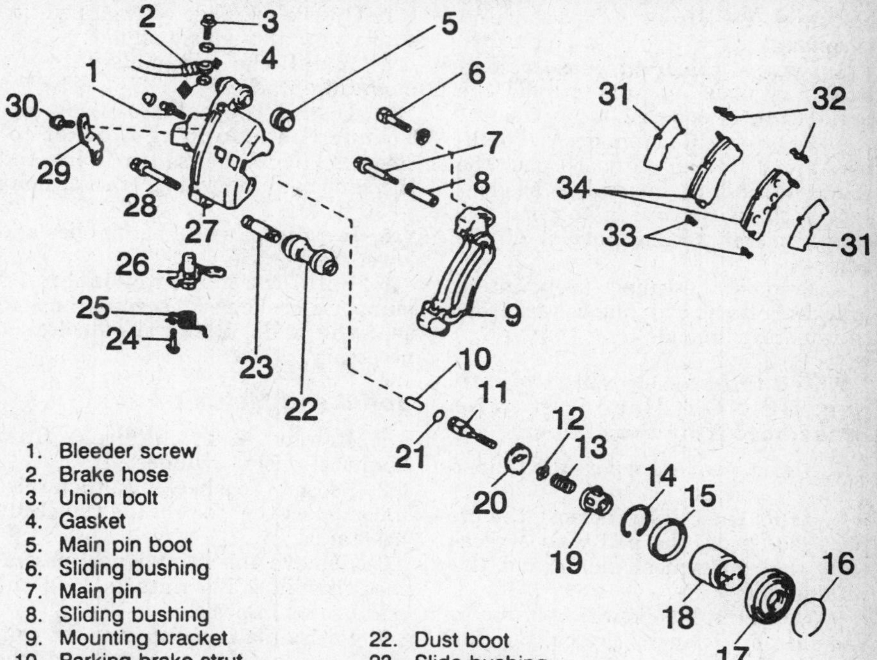

1. Bleeder screw
2. Brake hose
3. Union bolt
4. Gasket
5. Main pin boot
6. Sliding bushing
7. Main pin
8. Sliding bushing
9. Mounting bracket
10. Parking brake strut
11. Adjuster bolt
12. Adjusting bolt spring
13. Spring
14. Snap ring
15. Piston seal
16. Set ring
17. Boot
18. Piston
19. Adjusting bolt spring retainer
20. Adjusting bolt stopper
21. O-ring
22. Dust boot
23. Slide bushing
24. Stopper pin
25. Spring
26. Parking brake crank
27. Caliper housing
28. Mounting bolt
29. Cable support bracket
30. Cable support bracket bolt
31. Anti-squeal shim
32. Anti-rattle spring
33. Pad support plate
34. Pad

Exploded view of the rear caliper assembly—Nova

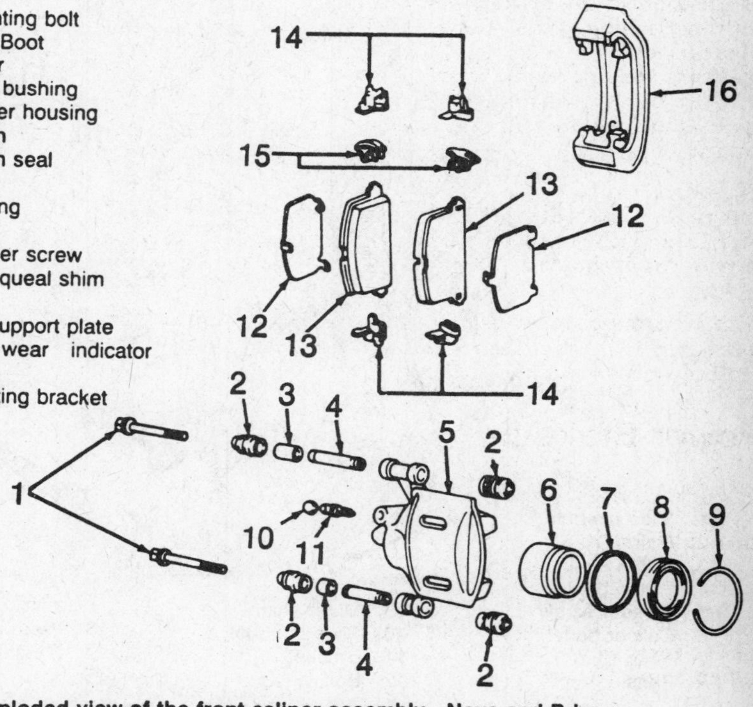

1. Mounting bolt
2. Dust Boot
3. Collar
4. Slide bushing
5. Caliper housing
6. Piston
7. Piston seal
8. Boot
9. Set ring
10. Cap
11. Bleeder screw
12. Anti-squeal shim
13. Pad
14. Pad support plate
15. Pad wear indicator plate
16. Mounting bracket

Exploded view of the front caliper assembly—Nova and Prizm

and support the front of the vehicle on jackstands.

3. Remove the front wheel assemblies. Install 2 lug nuts to hold the brake rotor in position.

4. Position a C-clamp over the caliper, 1 end on the outboard pad, the other on the inlet fitting bolt head.

5. Tighten the clamp to push the caliper piston to the bottom of the bore.

6. Remove the caliper-to-mounting bracket bolts and lift the caliper from the steering knuckle.

**NOTE: When removing the caliper, DO NOT disconnect the brake hose from the caliper.**

7. Using a wire, support the caliper from the vehicle.

8. From the caliper, remove the inner/outer pads, the pad wear indicators, the anti-squeal shims and the retainers.

9. Clean the pad mounting frame on the caliper. Inspect the caliper for signs of fluid leakage, then the rotor thickness and runout.

**To Install:**

10. Install grease inside of the slide pin bushing and the new inner/outer pads in position on the caliper.

11. Install new pad wear indicator plates to each pad.

**NOTE: When installing the pad wear indicator plates, be sure the arrow on the pad wear indicator is facing the rotating direction of the rotor.**

12. On the backside of each pad, install a new anti-squeal shim.

13. Install the new pads onto the mounting bracket.

14. Install the caliper assembly. Torque the mounting bracket-to-steering knuckle bolts to 40 ft. lbs. and the caliper to mounting bracket bolts to 36 ft. lbs.

15. Install the wheel assemblies and lower the vehicle.

16. Refill the master cylinder and pump the brake pedal several times to seat the pads. Bleed the brakes if necessary.

### *Sprint and Metro*

1. Remove ⅔ of the brake fluid from the master cylinder.

2. Loosen the wheel lugs, then raise and support the front of the vehicle on jackstands.

3. Remove the front wheel assemblies. Install 2 lug nuts to hold the brake rotor in position.

4. Position a C-clamp over the caliper, 1 end on the outboard pad, the other on the inlet fitting bolt head.

5. Tighten the clamp to push the caliper piston to the bottom of the bore.

6. Remove the caliper-to-steering knuckle bolts and lift the caliper from the steering knuckle.

**NOTE: When removing the caliper, DO NOT disconnect the brake hose from the caliper.**

7. Using a wire, support the caliper from the vehicle.

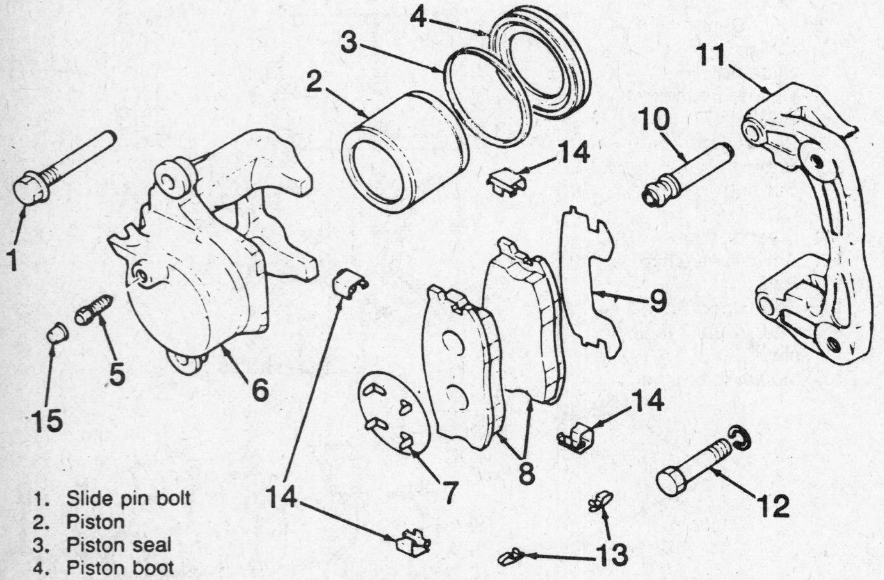


1. Slide pin bolt
2. Piston
3. Piston seal
4. Piston boot
5. Bleeder screw
6. Caliper body
7. Inner shim
8. Pads
9. Outer shim
10. Slide pin boot
11. Bracket
12. Bolt
13. Wear indicator
14. Retainer
15. Cap

**Exploded view of the caliper assembly—Spectrum**

8. From the caliper, remove the inner/outer pads and the anti-squeal shims.

9. Clean the pad mounting frame on the caliper. Inspect the caliper for signs of fluid leakage, the rotor thickness and runout. Remove and service the caliper if necessary.

**To Install:**

10. Install new inner/outer pads into position on the caliper.

11. On the backside of each pad, install a new anti-squeal shim.

12. Install the new outside pad onto the mounting bracket.

13. Install the new inside pad onto the caliper.

14. Install the caliper assembly onto the mounting bracket and the springs onto the caliper. Torque the caliper-to-mounting bracket bolts to 17–26 ft. lbs.

15. Install the wheel assemblies and lower the vehicle.

16. Refill the master cylinder and pump the brake pedal several times to seat the pads. Bleed the brakes if necessary.

# Brake Shoes

## REMOVAL & INSTALLATION

### *Nova and Prizm*

1. Raise and support the vehicle safely.

2. Remove the wheel.

3. Insert a suitable tool through the hole in the backing plate and hold the automatic adjusting lever away from the adjusting bolt.

4. With another suitable tool, turn the adjusting bolt to reduce the brake shoe adjustment.

5. Remove the drum.

6. Remove the return spring.

7. Remove the retainers, hold down springs and pins.

8. Remove the anchor spring.

9. Disconnect the parking brake cable from the parking brake lever.

10. Remove the adjuster spring.

11. Remove the shoes and the adjuster.

**To Install:**

12. Assemble the automatic adjuster lever, parking brake lever and the adjuster.

13. Install the shoes and the adjuster.

14. Install the adjuster spring.

15. Connect the parking brake cable to the parking brake lever.

16. Install the pins, hold down springs and retainers.

17. Install the anchor spring.

18. Install the return spring.

19. Adjust the brake shoes so that the outside of the lining is approxi-

mately 0.024 in. less than the inside diameter of the brake drum.

20. Install the drum and wheel and lower the vehicle.

### *Spectrum*

1. Raise and support the vehicle safely.
2. Remove the wheel.
3. Remove the cotter pin, nut and washer and remove the hub and drum.
4. Remove the return spring and the automatic adjuster spring.
5. Remove the leading shoe holding pin and remove the shoe and adjuster.
6. Remove the trailing shoe holding pin.
7. Disconnect the parking brake cable from the lever and remove the trailing shoe. Remove the lever from the shoe.

**To Install:**

8. Apply a high temperature type grease to the backing plate and shoe contact points and the anchor plate and brake shoe contact points.
9. Install the parking brake lever to the trailing shoe then connect the parking brake cable to the shoe.
10. Install the brake adjuster.
11. Install the leading shoe with the shoe holding pin and holding spring.
12. Install the automatic adjuster lever and the automatic adjuster spring.
13. Install the return spring.
14. Adjust the brake shoes so that the outside of the lining is approxi-

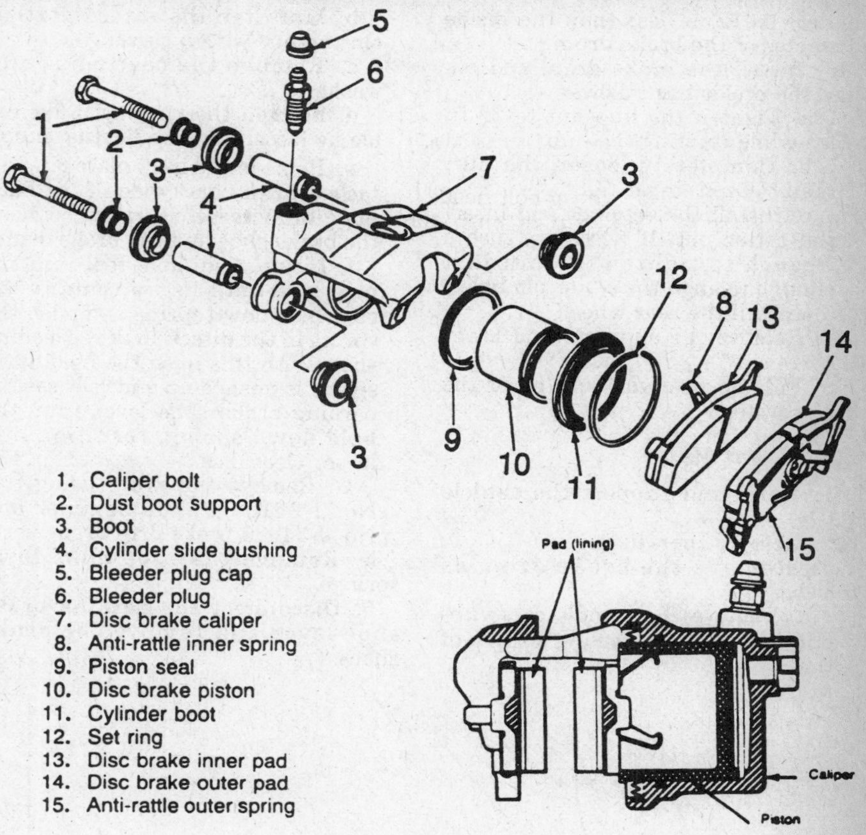


1. Caliper bolt
2. Dust boot support
3. Boot
4. Cylinder slide bushing
5. Bleeder plug cap
6. Bleeder plug
7. Disc brake caliper
8. Anti-rattle inner spring
9. Piston seal
10. Disc brake piston
11. Cylinder boot
12. Set ring
13. Disc brake inner pad
14. Disc brake outer pad
15. Anti-rattle outer spring

**Exploded view of the caliper assembly – Sprint and Metro**

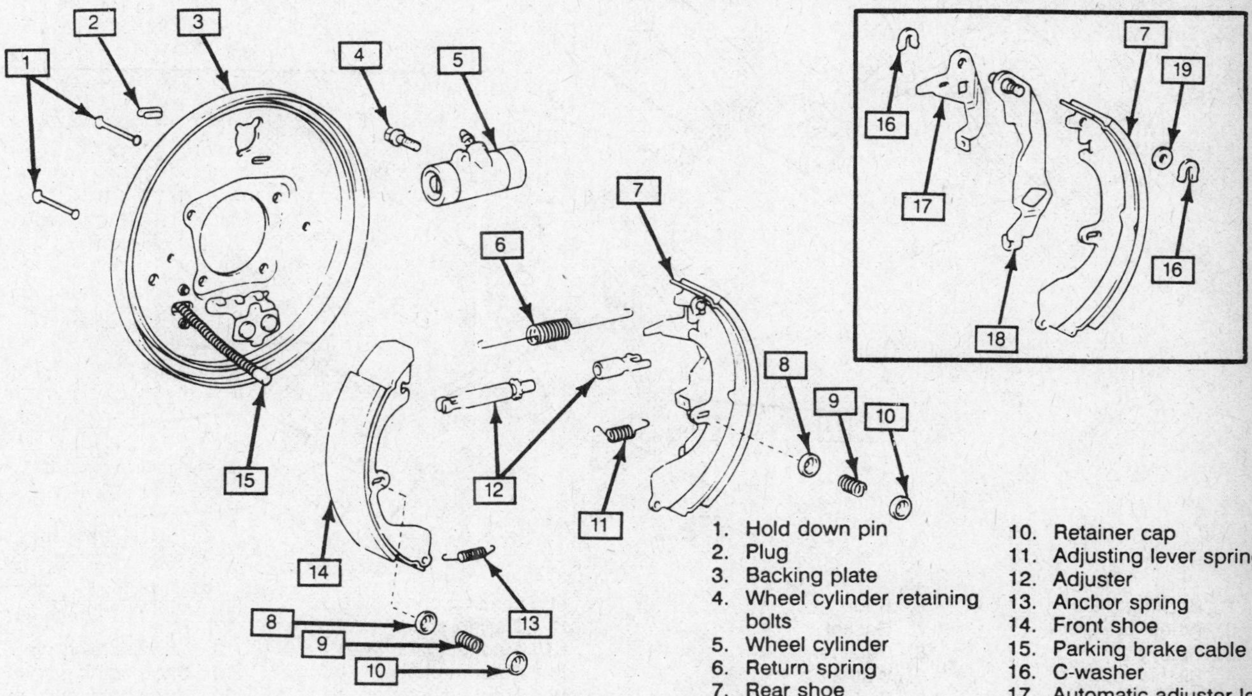

1. Hold down pin
2. Plug
3. Backing plate
4. Wheel cylinder retaining bolts
5. Wheel cylinder
6. Return spring
7. Rear shoe
8. Retainer
9. Hold down spring
10. Retainer cap
11. Adjusting lever spring
12. Adjuster
13. Anchor spring
14. Front shoe
15. Parking brake cable
16. C-washer
17. Automatic adjuster lever
18. Parking brake lever
19. Shim

**Exploded view of the rear drum brake assembly – Nova and Prizm**

mately 0.012 in. less than the inside diameter of the brake drum.

15. Install the brake drum and adjust the preload as follows:
   a. Tighten the hub nut to 22 ft. lbs while rotating the hub.
   b. Completely loosen the nut, then tighten finger tight.
   c. Install the retainer and insert the cotter pin. If necessary, use a wrench to tighten the nut just enough to align the cotter pin holes.
16. Install the rear wheel.
17. Remove the supports and lower the vehicle.
18. Fill the reservoir and bleed the brake system.

### *Sprint and Metro*

1. Raise and support the vehicle safely.
2. Remove the wheel.
3. Remove the brake drum as follows:
   a. Remove the spindle cap without damaging the sealing portion of the cap.
   b. Unfasten the staked portion om the nut with a chizel.
   c. Remove the castle nut and washer.
   d. Slacken the parking brake cable by loosening its adjusting nuts.
   e. Remove the back plate plug attached to the back side of the back plate to increase clearance between the brake shoe and the brake drum.
   f. Insert a suitable tool into the plug hole until its tip contacts the shoe hold down spring and push the spring in the direction of the leading shoe. With this push the hold down spring is pushed up and releases the parking brake shoe lever from the hold down spring, resulting in a larger clearance.
   G. Remove the drum using tool No. J-2619-01 slide hammer and No. J-34866 brake drum remover.
4. Remove the shoe hold down springs.
5. Disconnect the parking brake shoe lever and remove the brake shoes.
6. Disconnect the bottom return spring.
7. Remove the strut and upper return spring from the shoe.
8. Remove the parking brake shoe lever from the shoe.

**To Install:**

9. Assemble the springs and levers in the reverse order of removal.
10. Position the shoe assembly in place, connect the parking brake cable to the parking brake shoe lever then install the shoe hold down springs by pushing down and turning the hold down pins.
11. To minimize the measurement between the outside diameter of the shoes and the drum push down on the strut towards the back plate side (center of car) while pushing out one of the shoes.

**CAUTION**

***When pushing the shoes do not cause damage to the boots.***

12. Put the brake shoe hold down

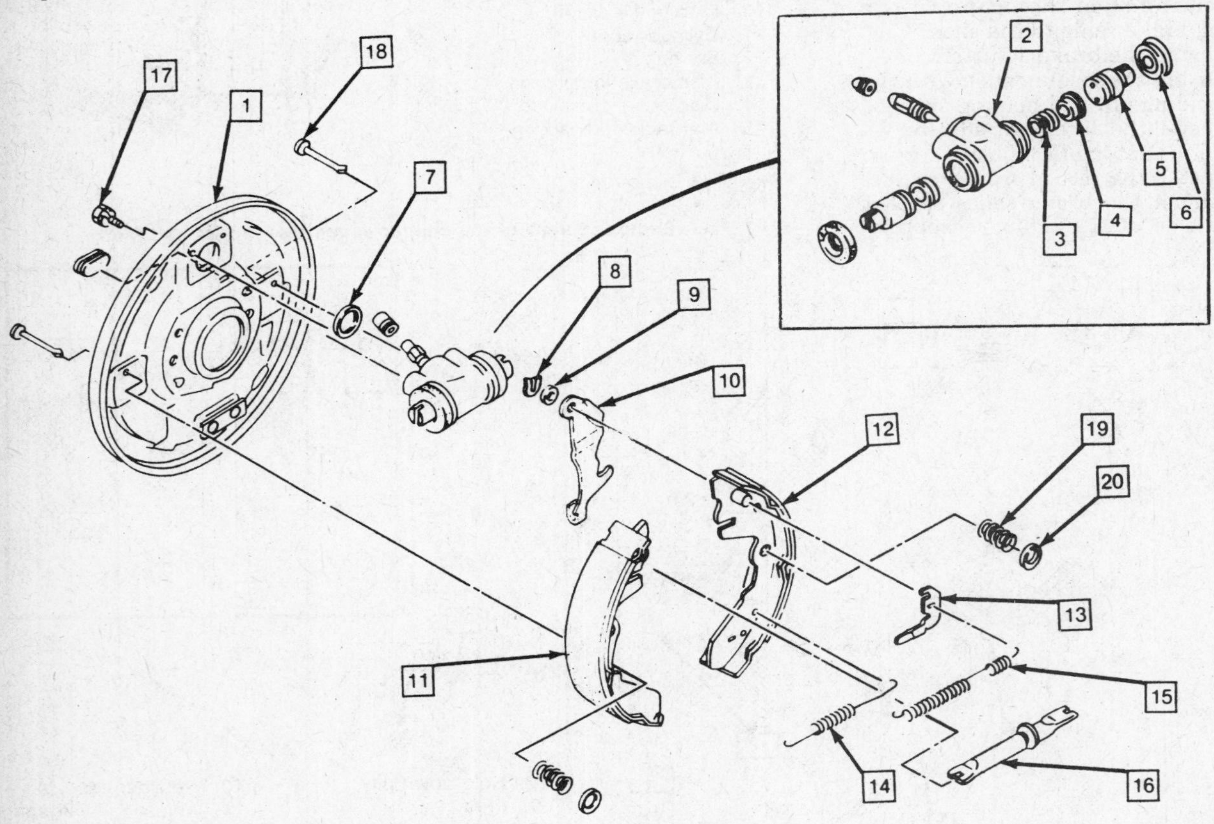


| | | | |
|---|---|---|---|
| 1. Backing plate | 6. Boot | 11. Leading shoe | 16. Brake adjuster |
| 2. Wheel cylinder | 7. Gasket | 12. Trailing shoe | 17. Bolt |
| 3. Spring | 8. Retainer | 13. Auto. adjuster lever | 18. Shoe holding pin |
| 4. Piston cup | 9. Washer | 14. Return spring | 19. Shoe holding spring |
| 5. Piston | 10. Parking brake lever | 15. Auto. adjuster spring | 20. Shoe holding seat |

**Exploded view of the rear drum brake assembly—Spectrum**

spring back to its original position. Position the hold down spring on the parking brake shoe lever so that the shoe lever comes to the side of the shoe hold down spring.

13. Install the brake drum, use a new castle nut and torque to 73 ft. lbs.
14. Stake the castle nut.
15. Install the spindle cap.
16. Install the wheel and tighten the wheel nuts to 41 ft. lbs.
17. Lower the car from its supports.
18. Depress the brake pedal 3–5 times to obtain proper drum to shoe clearance.

## Wheel Cylinder

### REMOVAL & INSTALLATION

#### *Nova and Prizm*

1. Raise and support the rear of the vehicle on jackstands. Remove the rear wheel assembly.
2. Disconnect and plug the brake line at the wheel cylinder to prevent hydraulic fluid from leaking.
3. Remove the brake drums and shoes.
4. Remove the wheel cylinder-to-backing plate bolts and the wheel cylinder.
5. To install, reverse the removal procedures. Torque the wheel cylinder-to-backing plate to 7 ft. lbs. Bleed the brake system. Check the brake operation.

#### *Spectrum*

1. Remove the brake shoe and components to gain access to the wheel cylinder.
2. Clean the area around the brake pipe and disconnect it from the wheel cylinder. Cap or tape all openings.
3. Remove the two bolts and remove the wheel cylinder.
4. To install, reverse the removal procedures. Torque the mounting nuts to 7 ft. lbs.

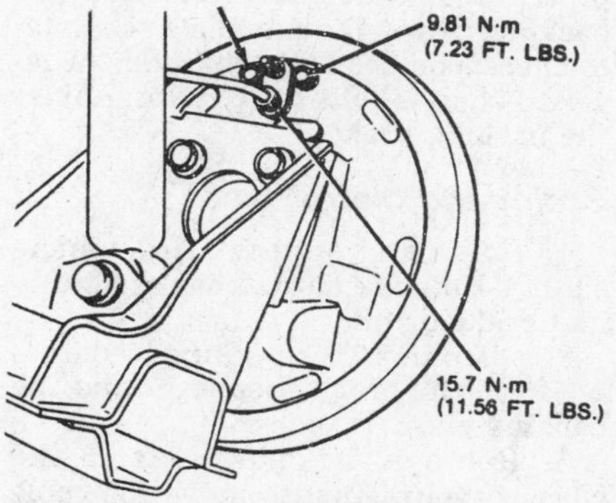


**Wheel cylinder attaching bolts – Spectrum**

1. Backing plate
2. Brake fluid tube flair nut
3. Brake fluid tube
4. Wheel cylinder mounting bolts

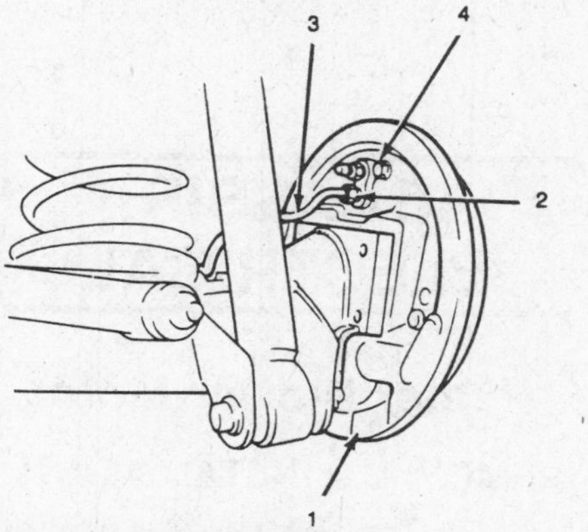


**Rear wheel cylinder mounting – Sprint and Metro**

#### *Sprint and Metro*

1. Raise and support the vehicle safely. Remove the wheel assembly.
2. Remove the brake drum. Remove the brake shoes and mounting hardware.
3. Remove ther bleeder screw from the wheel cylinder.
4. Loosen the brake pipe flare nut to the extent that the fluid will just not leak out.
5. Remove the wheel cylinder mounting bolts and remove the fluid pipe from the wheel cylinder. Plug the pipe right after removal.
6. Installation is the reverse of the removal procedure.
7. Fill the master cylinder with fluid and bleed the brake system when finished.

## Parking Brake Cable

**NOTE: Before performing this adjustment, make sure the rear brake shoe clearance is correct.**

### ADJUSTMENT

#### *Nova and Prizm*

1. Release the parking brake (all the way). Using 44 lbs. of pulling pressure,

1. Brake back plate
2. Brake shoe
3. Parking brake shoe lever
4. Brake strut
5. Quadrant spring
6. Shoe return spring
7. Anti-rattle spring
8. Shoe hold down spring
9. Shoe hold down pin
10. Packing
11. Parking lever retainer
12. Wheel cylinder
13. Bleeder plug cap
14. Rubber plug
15. Rubber plug

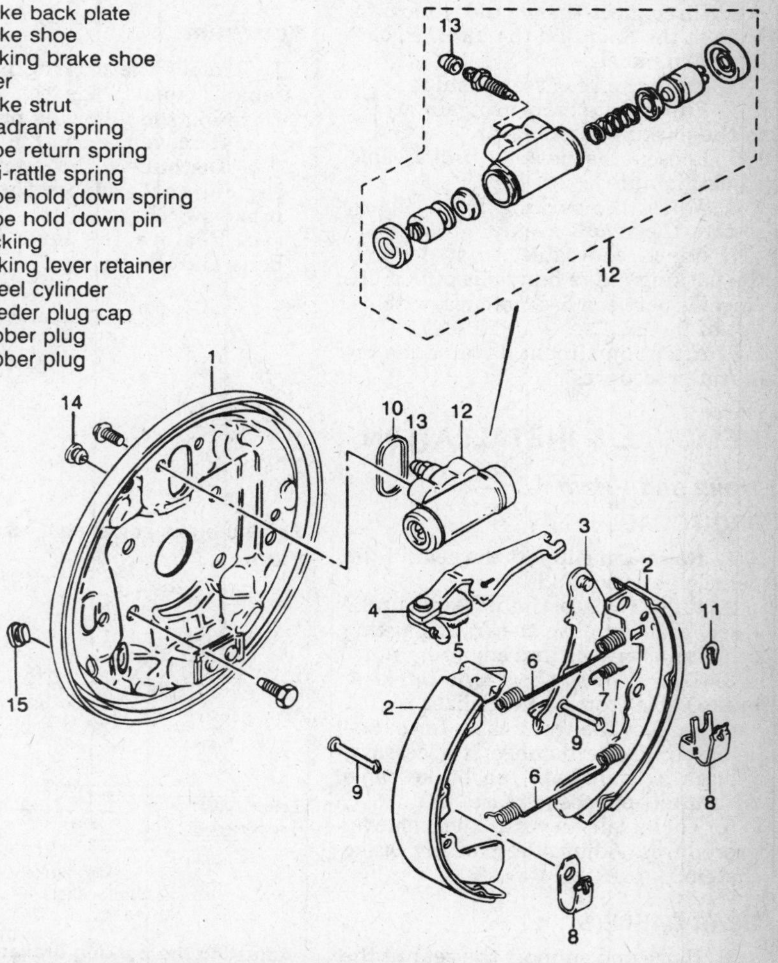


**Exploded view of the rear drum brake assembly – Sprint and Metro**

slowly pull the lever upward and count the number of clicks; 4–7 clicks (except twincam) or 5–8 (twincam).

2. If the number of clicks is incorrect, adjust the parking brake cable by performing the following procedures:

a. Remove the console box.

b. At the rear of the parking brake handle, loosen the cable nut, then, turn the adjusting nut.

3. Secure the adjusting nut position when tighten the locknut. Check the adjustment and repeat Steps 2 and 3 (if necessary). Tighten the adjusting nut securely and ensure that the adjustment is correct.

### Spectrum

The parking brake adjustment is normal when the lever moves 7–9 notches at 66 lbs. of force. If it is not within limits, adjust the rear brakes. If this adjustment does not affect the specifications, adjust the parking brake turnbuckle.

### Sprint and Metro

1. Remove both door seal plates and the seat belt buckle bolts at the floor.
2. Disconnect the shoulder harness bolts at the floor and the interior, bottom trim panels.
3. Raise the rear seat cushion.
4. Pull up the carpet to gain access to the parking brake lever.
5. Loosen the parking brake cable adjusting nuts.
6. Adjust the parking brake cables, so that they work evenly.
7. Adjust the cable, so that when the parking brake handle is pulled, its travel is between 5–8 notches, with 44 lbs. of force.
8. After adjustment, reverse the removal procedures.

## REMOVAL & INSTALLATION

### Nova and Prizm

#### FRONT CABLE

1. Raise and support the rear of the vehicle on jackstands.
2. Fully release the parking brake lever, then, remove the front parking cable-to-lever lock and adjusting nuts.
3. Disconnect the front parking brake cable from the equalizer.
4. Inspect the front cable for excessive wear and/or damage; if necessary, replace it. Lubricate the brake cable with multi-purpose grease.
5. To install, reverse the removal procedures. Adjust the parking brake system.

#### REAR CABLE(S)

1. Raise and support the rear of the vehicle on jackstands.
2. Remove the rear wheel assembly(s).
3. Fully release the parking brake lever. At the parking brake lever, back-off the front parking cable adjusting nut to provide slack on the rear cables.
4. Remove the rear brake cable(s)-to-chassis clamp bolts, then, disconnect the rear parking brake cable(s) from the equalizer.
5. If equipped with drum brakes, disassemble the rear brake assembly, then, disconnect the parking brake cable from the parking brake lever. If equipped with rear disc brakes, disconnect the brake cable from the parking brake crank.

**NOTE: If the brake disc sticks, preventing removal, it will be necessary to back-off the self adjusters. This is done through the access hole in the brake disc.**

6. Inspect the rear cable(s) for excessive wear and/or damage; if necessary, replace it (them). Lubricate the brake cable with multi-purpose grease.
7. To install, reverse the removal procedures. Adjust the parking brake system.

### Spectrum

1. Remove the parking brake lever assembly from inside the vehicle by performing the following procedures:

a. Remove the console box.

b. Disconnect the electrical wiring connector from the parking brake switch.

c. Remove the lever-to-chassis bolts and the lever.

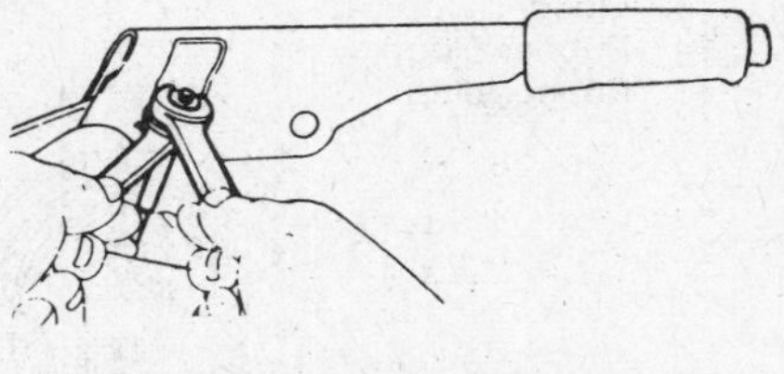

**Parking brake adjustment—Nova and Prizm**

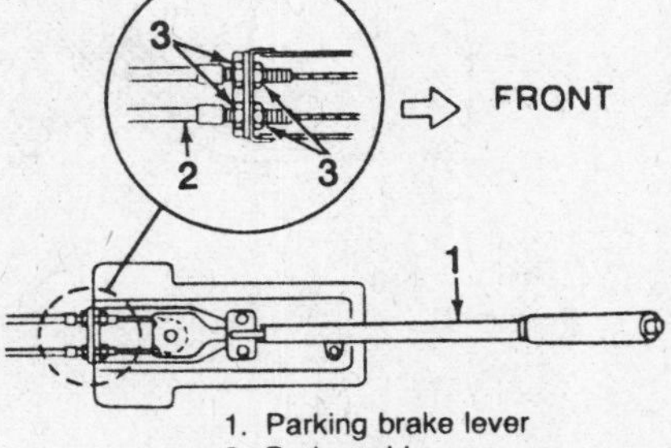


1. Parking brake lever
2. Brake cable
3. Nuts

**Adjusting the parking brakes—Sprint and Metro**

d. From the parking brake lever, remove the parking brake cable and the switch.

2. Raise and support the rear of the vehicle on jackstands.

3. To remove the parking brake cable assembly, perform the following procedures:

a. With the parking brake cable assembly in it's relaxed position, separate the front cable from the rear cable assembly.

b. Remove the tension spring from the rear axle.

c. Remove the rear wheel, the hub and the drum.

d. Disconnect the parking brake cable from the rear brake lever.

e. Remove the parking brake cable-to-chassis bolt and the cable(s) from the vehicle.

4. Inspect the parking brake lever assembly and the cable assembly for damage, wear, scoring and/or deterioration; replace the cable(s), if necessary.

5. To install, lubricate the cable(s) with grease and reverse the removal procedures. Seat the cable(s) in the backing plate. Torque the backplate-to-chassis bolt to 30 ft. lbs. and the lever-to-chassis bolts to 10 ft. lbs. Adjust the parking brake.

### Sprint and Metro

1. Raise and support the vehicle safely. Remove the wheel assembly and brake drum.
2. Disconnect the parking brake cable from the brake shoe lever and the backing plate.
3. Remove the cable(s) from the chassis mounts and remove the cable from the vehicle.
4. To install, place the white marked cable end onm the right side brakes and connect the cable to the shoe lever and backing plate.
5. Connect the cable in the chassis mounts.
6. Install the brake drum and wheel assembly.
7. Adjust the parking brake cable when finished.

# CHASSIS ELECTRICAL

## Heater Blower Motor

### REMOVAL & INSTALLATION

#### Nova

The heater blower motor is located inside the vehicle, behind the glove box.

1. Remove the three heater assembly retainer-to-chassis screws.
2. Remove the glove box-to-chassis screws and the glove box.
3. Remove the duct-to-blower/heater assemblies screws and the duct; the duct is located between the blower and heater assemblies.
4. Disconnect the blower motor wiring connector and the air source selector control cable from the blower assembly case.
5. Remove the blower assembly-to-heater case nuts/bolt and blower assembly.
6. Separate the blower motor from the blower assembly.
7. To install, reverse the removal procedures and test the motor.

### Prizm

The blower motor is located underneath the instrument panel at the far right side of the vehicle. I is accessable from below the instrument panel.

1. Disconnect the negative battery cable.
2. Disconnect the rubber air duct bttween the motor and the heater assembly.
3. Disconnect the electyrical connector from the motor.
4. Remove the three screws retaining the motor and remove the motor.
5. Installation is the reverse of removal.

### Spectrum

1. Disconnect the blower motor electrical connector at the motor case.
2. If equipped with A/C, remove the rubber hose from the blower case.
3. Rotate the blower motor case counterclockwise and remove the blower motor assembly.
4. To install, reverse the removal procedures.

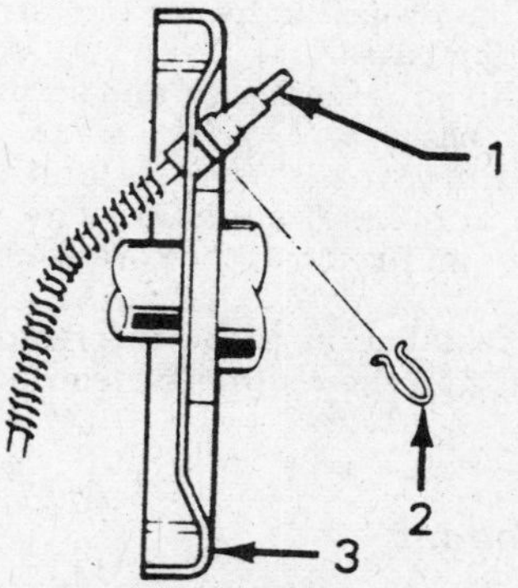


1. Parking brake cable
2. Retaining clip
3. Backing plae

**Removing parking brake cable from backing plate – Sprint and Metro**

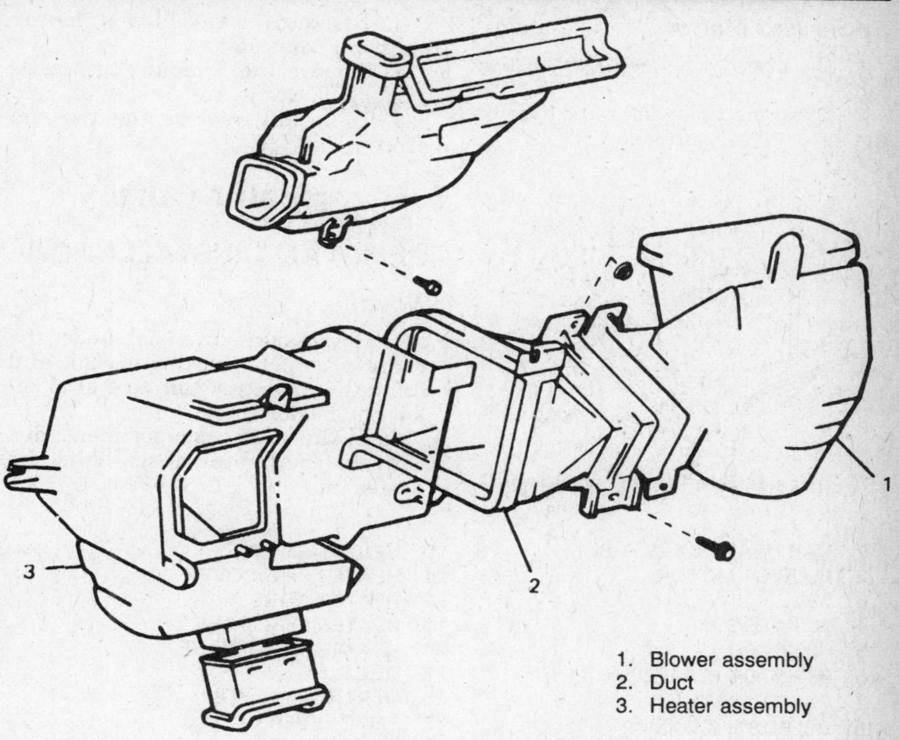


1. Blower assembly
2. Duct
3. Heater assembly

**View of the heater assembly – Nova and Prizm**

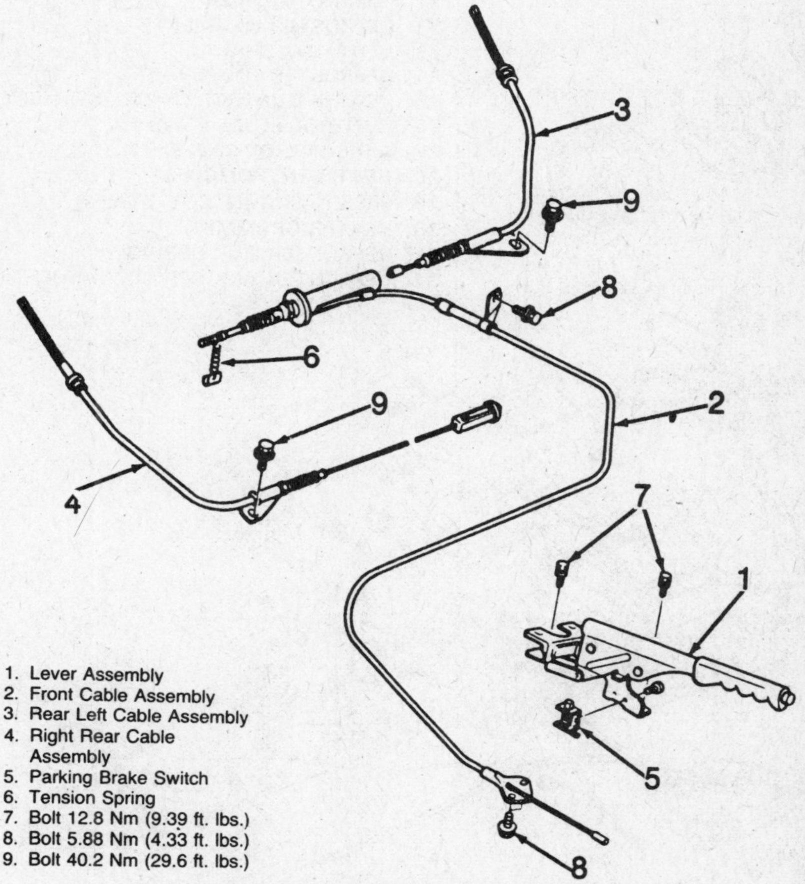


1. Lever Assembly
2. Front Cable Assembly
3. Rear Left Cable Assembly
4. Right Rear Cable Assembly
5. Parking Brake Switch
6. Tension Spring
7. Bolt 12.8 Nm (9.39 ft. lbs.)
8. Bolt 5.88 Nm (4.33 ft. lbs.)
9. Bolt 40.2 Nm (29.6 ft. lbs.)

**Exploded view of the parking brake assembly – Spectrum**

### *Sprint and Metro*

1. Disconnect the negative battery cable.
2. Disconnect the defroster hose on the steering column side.

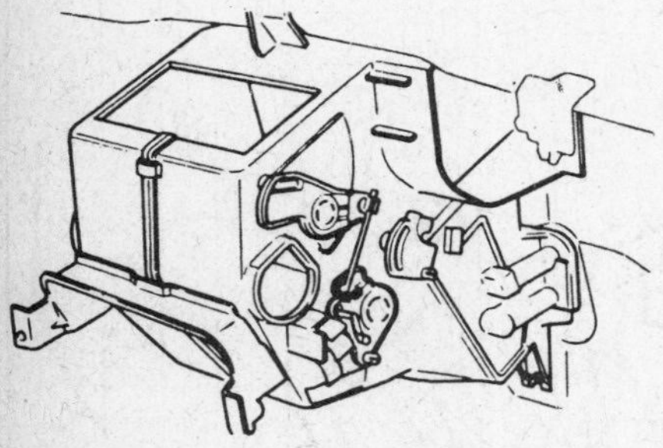

**Heater core—Nova and Prizm**

3. Disconnect the blower motor electrical connector.
4. Remove the 3 mounting screws and the blower motor.
5. To install, reverse the removal procedures.

## Heater Core

### REMOVAL & INSTALLATION

#### *Nova*

1. Place a clean drain pan under the radiator, open the drain cock and drain the cooling system to a level below the heater core.
2. In the engine compartment, disconnect the heater hoses from the heater unit.

1. CAR HEATER ASSEMBLY
2. BLOWER MOTOR
3. SEAL
4. BLOWER FAN
5. RESISTOR
6. RESISTOR PLATE
7. CASE CLAMP
8. DEFROSTER DAMPER
9. TEMP DAMPER
10. VENT DAMPER
11. HEATER PIPE COVER
12. HEATER CORE
13. HEATER LEFT CASE
14. HEATER RIGHT CASE
15. DUCT
16. VENT LINK PLATE
17. TEMP LEVER
18. TEMP PLATE
19. LINK LEVER
20. MODE LEVER
21. LINK NO. 2 LEVER
22. DEFROSTER LINK PLATE
23. VENT LINK SHAFT
24. DEFROSTER LINK SHAFT
25. HEATER CONTROL LEVER ASSEMBLY
26. CONTROL LEVER KNOB
27. AIR CONTROL CABLE
28. HEAT CONTROL CABLE
29. FRESH AIR CONTROL CABLE
30. HEATER GROMMET
31. DEFROSTER LINK SPRING
32. DEFROSTER LINK SPRING WASHER

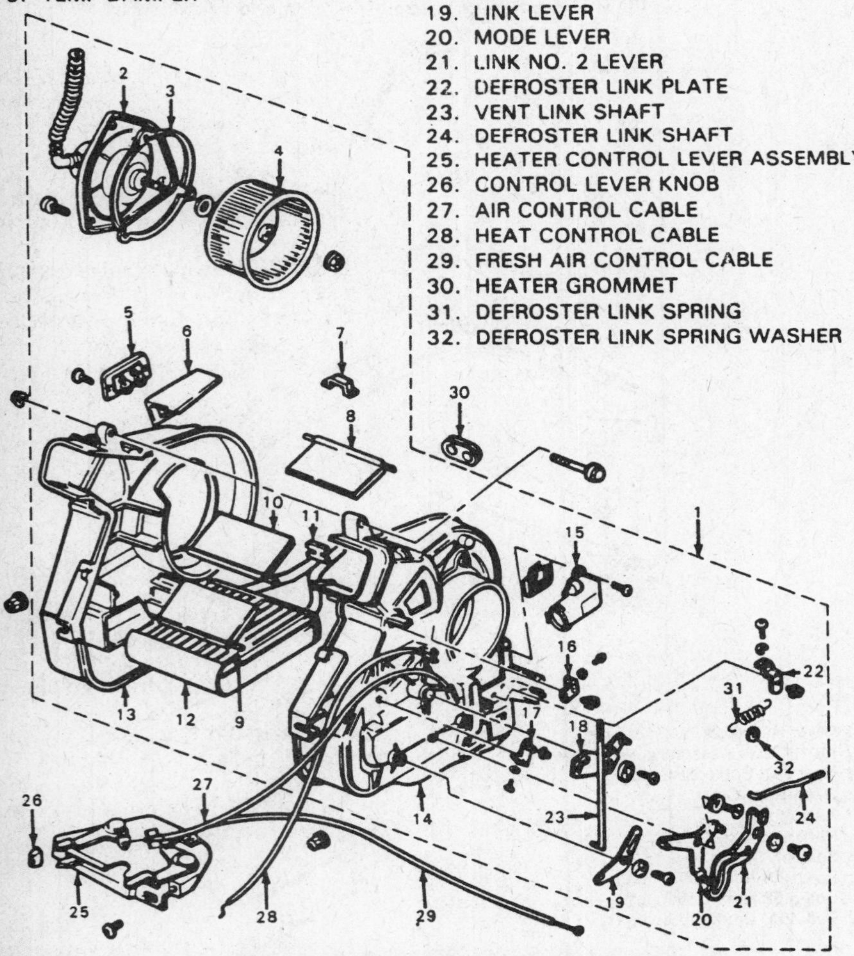

**Heater unit disassembled—Sprint and Metro**

3. From inside the vehicle (under the dash), remove the lower heater unit case-to-heater case (6) clips and remove the lower case.
4. Using a medium prybar, separate and remove the lower portion of the case from the heater case.
5. Remove the heater core from the heater case.
6. Inspect the heater hoses for cracking and deterioration, then, the heater core for leakage and corrosion; replace the items, if necessary.
7. To install, reverse the removal procedures. Refill the cooling system. Start the engine, allow it to reach normal operating temperatures and check for leaks. Turn the heater controls to Max. Heat and check the heater operation.

#### *Prizm*

The heater case and core are located directly behind the center console. The access the case and core, the entire console must be removed as well as most of the instrument panel assembly.

1. Remove the steering wheel.
2. Remove the trim bezel from the instrument panel.
3. Remove the cup holder from the console.
4. Remove the radio.
5. Remove the instrument panel assembly, cluster assembly, center console and all console trim, lower dash trim, side window air deflectors, and all instrument panel wiring harnesses.
6. Drain the coolant from the cooling system.
7. Disconnect all cables and ducts from the heater case.
8. Disconnect the blower switch harness and the heater control assembly.
9. Disconnect the two center console support braces.
10. Remove all mounting bolts, nuts and clips from the heater and air distribution cases.
11. Remove the heater and air distribution cases.
12. Remove the screws and clips from the case, separate the case halves, and remove the core from the case.
13. Installation is the reverse of removal. Fill the cooling system.

#### *Spectrum*

1. Disconnect the heater hoses in the engine compartment.
2. At the lower part of the heater unit case, remove the 6 retaining clips.
3. Using a small pry bar, pry open the lower part of the case and remove it.

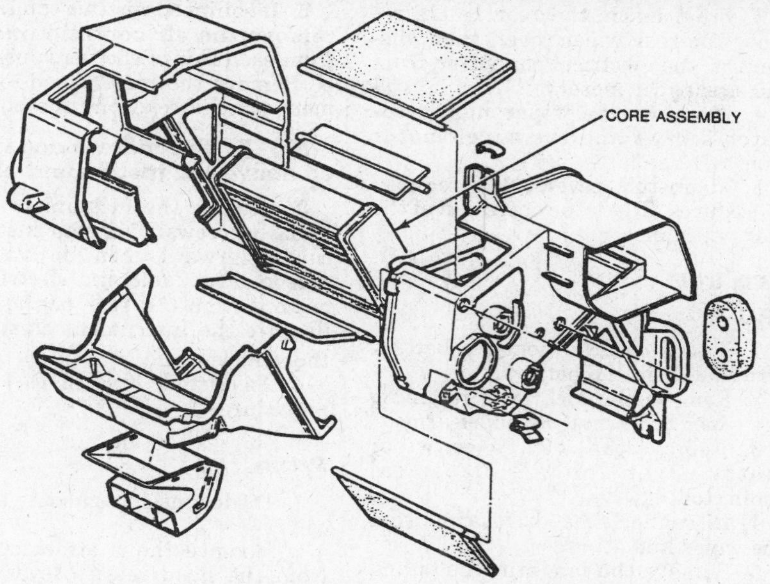


Exploded view of the heater assembly—Spectrum

4. Remove the core assembly insulator and the core assembly.
5. To install, reverse the removal procedures.

### Sprint and Metro

1. Disconnect the negative battery cable. Drain the cooling system.
2. Disconnect the two water hoses from the radiator at the heater unit.
3. Remove the glove box from the upper instrument panel.
4. Remove the defroster hoses from the heater case.
5. Disconnect the electrical connectors from the blower motor and the heater resistor.
6. Disconnect the three control cables from the heater case side levers.
7. Pull out the center vent louver.
8. Disconnect both side vent ducts from the center duct vent.
9. Remove the center duct vent and the ashtray's upper plate.
10. Remove the instrument member stay and the heater assembly mounting nuts.
11. Loosen the three heater case top mounting bolts through the glove box opening.
12. Raise the dash panel and remove the heater control assembly.
13. Separate the heater case into two sections by removing the clips.
14. Pull the heater core from the heater unit.
15. To install, reverse the removal procedures. Refill the cooling system. Start the engine, bring it to normal operating temperature and check for leaks.

# Radio

## REMOVAL & INSTALLATION

### Nova

1. Remove the ash tray, the ash tray bracket-to-center trim panel screws and the upper center trim panel-to-dash screws.
2. Move the center panel out far enough to gain access to the cigarette lighter wiring and disconnect the wiring. Remove the trim panel.
3. Remove the radio-to-instrument panel screws and braces.
4. Pull the radio out (part way), then, disconnect the antenna and electrical leads from it. Remove the radio.
5. To install, reverse the removal procedures. Check the operation of the radio.

### Prizm

1. Remove the steering column column covers by removing the 7 attaching screws.
2. Remove the trim bezel 2 attaching screws and remove the bezel.
3. Disconnect the rear wiper/washer switch, if so equipped.
4. Disconnect the cruise control/defogger switch, if so equipped.
5. Remove the 4 radio retaining screws and pull the radio from the console.
6. Disconnect the 2 electrical connections and the antenna cable from the radio.
7. Installation is the reverse of removal.

### Spectrum

1. Remove the screws retaining the radio cover and remove the cover.
2. Remove the radio and bracket.
3. Disconnect the electrical connector, speaker connectors and the antenna cable.
4. To install, reverse the removal procedures.

### Sprint and Metro

1. Disconnect the negative battery cable.
2. Remove the ash tray and the radio knobs.
3. Remove the ash tray assembly.
4. Remove the radio mounting nuts.
5. Remove the radio and disconnect the electrical connectors.
6. To install, reverse the removal procedures.

# Windshield Wiper Switch

## REMOVAL & INSTALLATION

### Nova and Prizm

#### FRONT

The front wiper switch is located on the right-side of the combination switch attached to the steering column.

1. Remove the wiper/cruise control assembly switch-to-combination switch screws and the switch assembly.
2. Trace the wiper/cruise control assembly switch wiring harness to the multi-connector. Using a scratch awl, push in the multi-connector lock levers and pull wires from the connector.
3. To install, reverse the removal procedures. Check the operation of the windshield wiper switch and the cruise control system.

#### REAR

1. Disconnect the negative terminal from the battery.
2. On the Novas, use a small pry bar and pry the rear wiper switch from the front of the instrument panel.
3. On the Prizm, remove the trim bezel.
4. Disconnect the electrical connector from the rear wiper switch.
5. To install, reverse the removal procedures. Check the operation of the rear wiper switch.

### Spectrum

#### FRONT

1. Remove the the instrument cluster bezel.

2. Remove the wiper switch electrical connector, attaching nuts and bracket.
3. Remove the wiper switch.
4. To install, reverse the removal procedures.

**REAR**

1. Using a small tool, pry the switch panel from the dash.
2. Pull the switch out and disconnect the electrical connector.
3. To install, reverse the removal procedures.

### *Sprint and Metro*

1. Disconnect the negative battery cable.
2. Remove the steering column trim panel.
3. Lower the steering column.
4. Remove the cluster bezel and the bezel.
5. Disconnect the wiper switch connector.
6. Remove the wiper switch.
7. To install, reverse the removal procedures.

# Windshield Wiper Motor

## REMOVAL & INSTALLATION

### *Nova and Prizm*

**FRONT**

1. Disconnect the negative terminal from the battery.
2. From the engine compartment, disconnect the electrical connector from the windshield wiper motor.
3. Remove the wiper motor-to-chassis screws.
4. Disconnect the wiper motor from the windshield wiper crank arm; be careful not to bend the linkage.
5. To install, reverse the removal procedures. Check the operation of the front windshield wiper motor.

**REAR**

The rear wiper motor is located in the rear hatch.

1. Disconnect the negative terminal from the battery.
2. Remove the rear wiper arm-to-wiper motor nut and wiper arm.

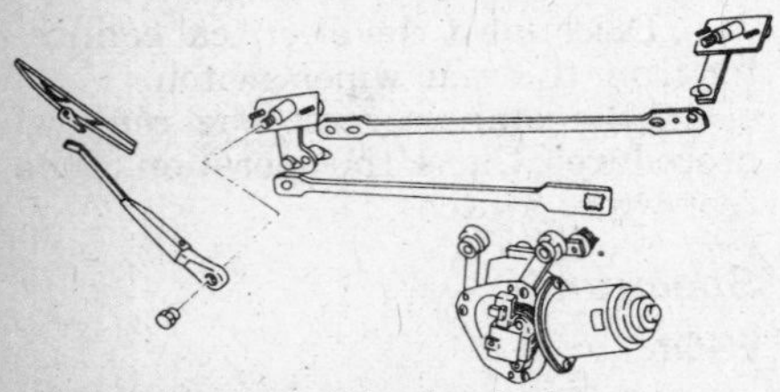

**Exploded view of the front wiper assembly—Spectrum**

3. From inside the rear hatch, remove the rear wiper cover, then, disconnect the electrical connector from the rear wiper motor.
4. Remove the wiper motor-to-hatch screws and the wiper motor from the hatch.
5. To install, reverse the removal procedures. Check the operation of the rear wiper motor.

### *Spectrum*

**FRONT**

1. Disconnect the negative battery terminal from the battery.
2. Remove the lock nuts retaining the wiper arms and the wiper arms.
3. Remove the cowl cover, wiper motor cover and the electrical connector.
4. Disconnect the drive arm from the wiper link.
5. Remove the mounting bolts and the wiper motor.
6. To install, reverse the removal procedures.

**REAR**

1. Disconnect the negative battery terminal from the battery.
2. Remove the trim pad and the wiper arm assemblies.
3. Remove the mounting bolts and the motor assembly.
4. Disconnect the electrical connector.
5. To install, reverse the removal procedures.

### *Sprint and Metro*

**FRONT**

1. Disconnect the crank arm from the wiper motor.
2. Disconnect the electrical connector from the wiper motor.
3. Remove the wiper motor from the vehicle.
4. To install, reverse the removal procedures.

**REAR**

1. Remove the electrical connector from the rear wiper motor.
2. Remove the rear motor mounting bracket.
3. Disconnect the motor from the wiper linkage.
4. Remove the motor from the vehicle.
5. To install, reverse the removal procedures.

# Instrument Cluster

## REMOVAL & INSTALLATION

### *Nova*

1. Disconnect the negative terminal from the battery.
2. If equipped with air conditioning, remove the air conditioning vents from each side of the instrument panel. Remove the meter hood-to-instrument panel screws and the hood.

**NOTE: The meter hood is located above the instrument cluster.**

3. Remove the instrument cluster-to-dash screws. Pull the instrument cluster forward, then, disconnect the speedometer cable and electrical connectors from the rear of the cluster. Remove the instrument cluster from the vehicle.
4. To install, reverse the removal procedures.

### *Prizm*

1. Disdconnect the negative battery cable.
2. Remove the 2 attaching screws from the hood release lever and remove the lever.
3. Remove the lower left dash trim by removing the 4 attaching screws.
4. Disconnect the speaker wire.
5. Remove the A/C duct from the lower A/C regester.
6. Remove the left lower dash trim.
7. Remove the steering column covers by removing the 7 retaining screws.
8. Pull out the trim bezel after removing the 2 attaching screws.
9. Disconnect the cruise control/defogger switch from the electrical connector.
10. Disconnect any electrical connections from the trim bezel and remove the trim bezel.
11. Remove the 4 attaching screws from the cluster bezel.
12. Disconnect the electrical connectors from the hazard flasher and dimmer switches.
13. Remove the cluster bezel.
14. Remove the 4 attaching screws from the cluster.
15. Disconnect the speedometer cable and electrical connections from the cluster.
16. Remove the cluster from the vehicle.
17. Installation is the reverse of removal.

### *Spectrum*

1. Disconnect the negative battery terminal from the battery.
2. Remove the instrument cluster bezel retaining screws and bezel.
3. Disconnect the windshield wiper and lighting switch connectors.
4. Remove the instrument cluster retaining screws and pull out the assembly.
5. Remove the trip reset knob and the assembly glass.

6. Remove the buzzer, sockets and bulbs.
7. Remove the speedometer assembly, fuel and temperature gauge.
8. Remove the tachometer, it equipped.
9. To install, reverse the removal procedures.

### Sprint and Metro

1. Disconnect the negative battery cable.
2. Remove the steering column trim panel.
3. Lower the steering column.
4. Remove the cluster lens and the cluster mounting screws.
5. Disconnect the speedometer cable at the transaxle and at the instrument cluster.
6. Disconnect and mark the electrical connectors at the instrument cluster.
7. Remove the instrument cluster from the vehicle.
8. To install, reverse the removal procedures.

# Headlight Switch

## REMOVAL & INSTALLATION

### Nova and Prizm

The headlight switch is located on the left-side of the combination switch which attached to the steering column.

1. Remove the combination switch screws and the switch assembly.
2. Trace the headlight/dimmer switch wiring harness to the multi-connector. Using a scratch awl, push in the multi-connector lock levers and pull wires from the connector.
3. To install, reverse the removal procedures. Check the operation of the headlight/dimmer switch.

### Spectrum

The headlight control switch is a 3-position, push type switch which is located at the left-side of the instrument panel. The dimmer/passing light switch is a part of and actuated by the turn signal switch.

1. Remove the instrument cluster bezel retaining screw and the bezel.
2. Disconnect the headlight and the windshield wiper control switch electrical connectors.
3. Place the bezel on a bench and remove the 2 nuts securing the headlight control switch.
4. Remove the headlight control switch.
5. To install, reverse the removal procedures.

### Sprint and Metro

1. Disconnect the negative battery cable.
2. Remove the steering column trim panel.
3. Lower the steering column.
4. Remove the cluster bezel and the bezel.
5. Disconnect the headlight switch connector.
6. Remove the headlight switch.
7. To install, reverse the removal procedures.

# Stoplight Switch

## REMOVAL & INSTALLATION

### Nova and Prizm

The stoplight switch is attached to a bracket at the top of the brake pedal.

1. Remove the lower instrument panel cover.
2. Disconnect the electrical connector from the stoplight switch.
3. Remove the stoplight switch-to-bracket nut and the switch.
4. To install, reverse the removal procedures. Adjust the switch so the stoplights turn with slight movement of the brake pedal.

### Spectrum

1. Remove stop light switch lock nut.
2. Remove switch by pulling straight out of pedal assembly.
3. To install push switch straight in, push the brake pedal by turning the stop light switch, so that free play in the brake pedal is eliminated, then tighten the stop light switch lock nut.

### Sprint and Metro

1. Disconnect the negative battery cable. Disconnect the stoplight switch wiring at the brake pedal.
2. Remove the switch from the plate and install the new one.
3. Adjust the switch so that there is 0.02–0.04 in. clearance between the contact plate and the end of the threads on the switch. Tighten the locknut and check the clearance again.
4. Connect the battery cable and check that the brake lights are not on with the pedal in the resting position.

# Fuses, Relays and Circuit Breakers

## LOCATION

### Nova and Prizm

The main fuse/relay/circuit breaker box is located in the engine compartment on the left-front fender; others are located at the left and right kick panels inside the vehicle. When replacing a fuse, use a fuse puller tool.

To reset a circuit breaker, unplug them, then, using a straightened paper clip, insert it into the reset hole and press inward. If this does not restore operation, check continuity between the terminals with an ohmmeter.

### Spectrum

The fuse block is located at the lower left-hand side of the instrument panel, concealed by a cover. To replace a blown fuse, pull out the fuse holder, remove the blown fuse and install one of the same amperage.

### Sprint and Metro

The main fusible link is at the battery. The wiring circuits are protected by 14 fuses in the fuse block. The fuse block is located at the lower left of the instrument panel. The cover is built into the instrument panel.

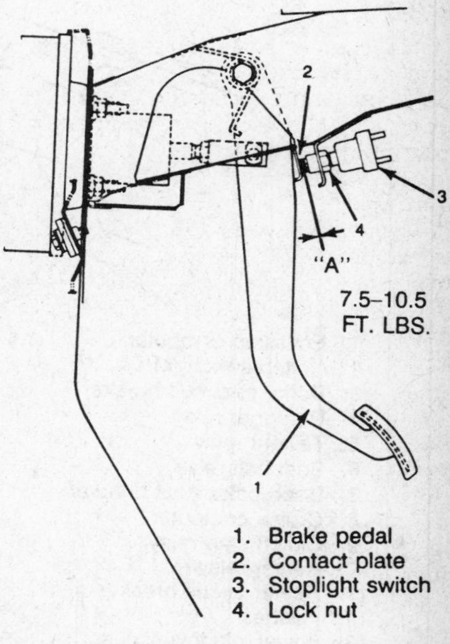


**Stoplight switch adjustment. Gap "A" must be 0.02-0.04 in.—Sprint and Metro**

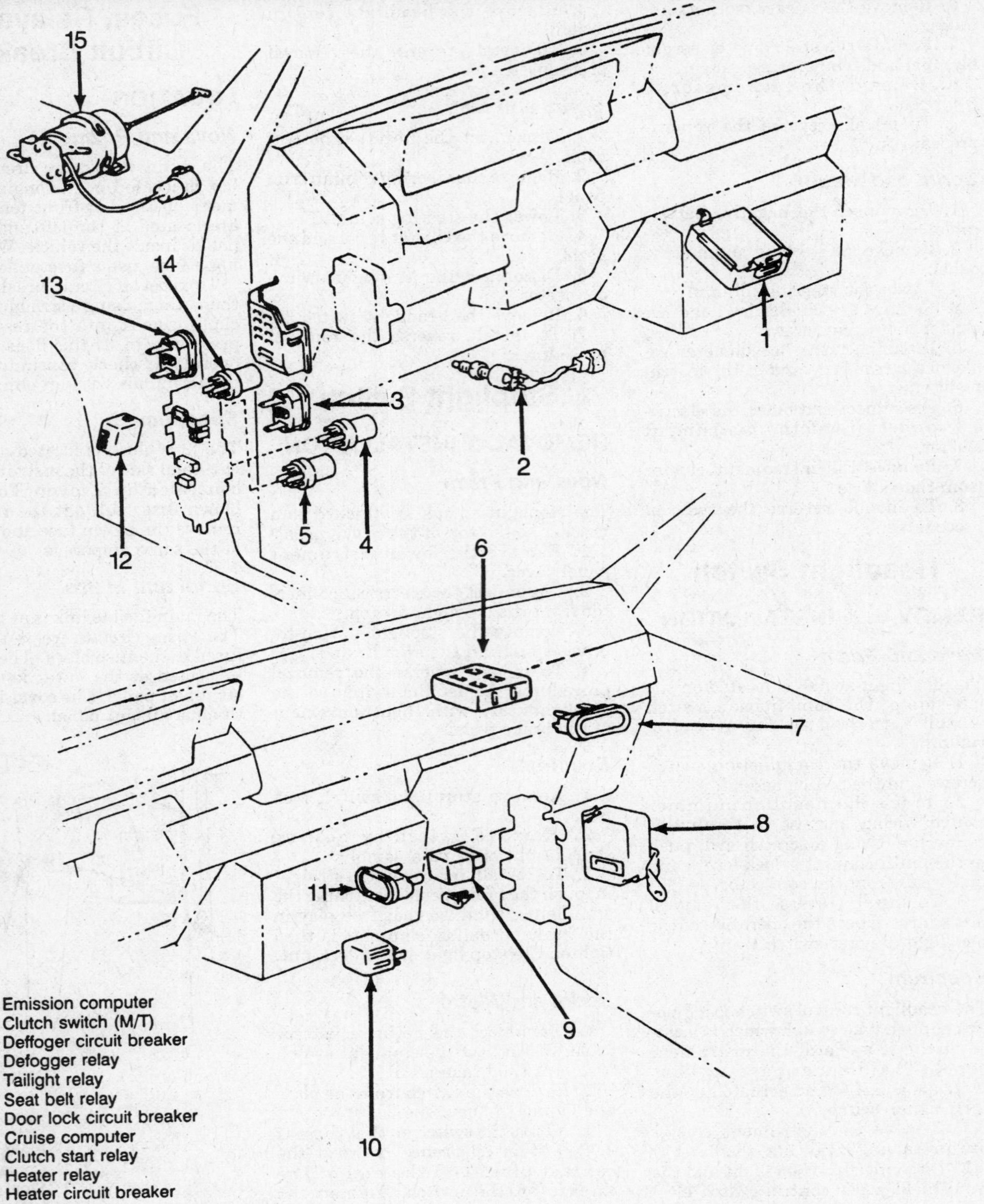


1. Emission computer
2. Clutch switch (M/T)
3. Deffoger circuit breaker
4. Defogger relay
5. Tailight relay
6. Seat belt relay
7. Door lock circuit breaker
8. Cruise computer
9. Clutch start relay
10. Heater relay
11. Heater circuit breaker
12. Flasher
13. Power window circuit breaker
14. Power window relay
15. Acuator

**Passenger compartment relays—1985–88 Nova**

# Honda 6

## Accord, Civic, CRX, Prelude—All Models

# SERIAL NUMBER IDENTIFICATION

## Vehicle Identification Plate

The vehicle identification numbers are mounted on the top edge of the instrument panel and are visible from the outside ot the vehicle. In addition, there is a vehicle/engine identification plate under the hood, on the cowl.

## Engine Number

The engine number is stamped into the clutch casing. The first 3 digits indicate engine model identification. The remaining numbers refer to production sequence.

## Vehicle Identification Label

The vehicle/engine identification plate is located on the hood bracket. It contains the engine number and other important information regarding the vehicle.

## Transaxle Number

The transaxle serial number is stamped on the top of the transaxle/clutch case.

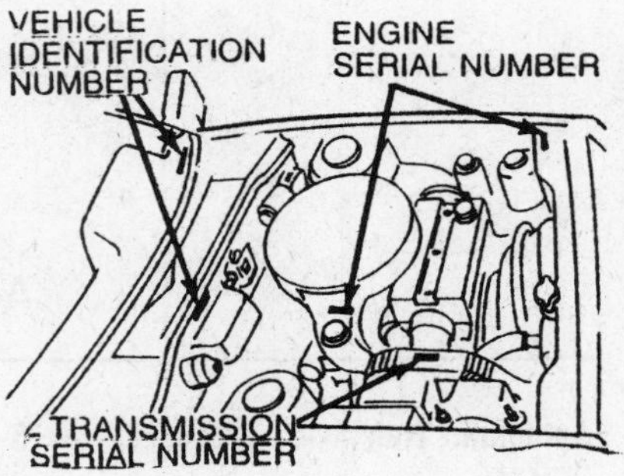


Honda identification numbers

## ENGINE IDENTIFICATION

| Year | Model | Engine Displacement cu. in. (cc/liter) | Engine Series Identification | No. of Cylinders | Engine Type |
|---|---|---|---|---|---|
| 1983 | Civic 1300 | 81.5 (1335/1.3) | EJ1 | 4 | CVCC 8-valve |
| | Civic 1500 | 90.7 (1487/1.5) | EM1 | 4 | CVCC 8-valve |
| | Accord | 106.8 (1751/1.8) | EK1 | 4 | CVCC 8-valve |
| | Prelude | 111.6 (1829/1.8) | ES1 | 4 | CVCC 12-valve |
| 1984 | Civic/CRX, 1.3 | 81.9 (1342/1.3) | EV1 | 4 | CVCC 8-valve |
| | Civic/CRX, HF,1.5 | 90.8 (1488/1.5) | EW1 | 4 | CVCC 12-valve |
| | Accord | 111.6 (1829/1.8) | ES2 | 4 | CVCC 12-valve |
| | Prelude | 111.6 (1829/1.8) | ES1 | 4 | CVCC 12-valve |
| 1985 | Civic/CRX, 1.3 | 81.9 (1342/1.3) | EV1 | 4 | CVCC 8-valve |
| | Civic/CRX, HF,1.5 | 90.8 (1488/1.5) | EW1 | 4 | CVCC 12-valve |
| | Civic/CRX, Si | 90.8 (1488/1.5) | EW3 | 4 | Non-CVCC 12-valve |
| | Accord | 111.6 (1829/1.8) | ES2 | 4 | CVCC 12-valve |
| | Accord SE-i | 111.6 (1829/1.8) | ES2 | 4 | Non-CVCC 12-valve |
| | Prelude | 111.6 (1829/1.8) | ET2 | 4 | Non-CVCC 12-valve |
| 1986 | Civic/CRX, 1.3 | 81.9 (1342/1.3) | EV1 | 4 | CVCC 8-valve |
| | Civic/CRX, HF,1.5 | 90.8 (1488/1.5) | EW1 | 4 | CVCC 12-valve |
| | Civic/CRX, Si | 90.8 (1488/1.5) | EW4 | 4 | Non-CVCC 12-valve |
| | Accord | 119.0 (1955/2.0) | BS | 4 | Non-CVCC 12-valve |
| | Accord LX-i | 119.0 (1955/2.0) | BT | 4 | Non-CVCC 12-valve |
| | Prelude | 111.6 (1829/1.8) | ET2 | 4 | Non-CVCC 12-valve |
| | Prelude Si | 119.0 (1955/2.0) | BT | 4 | Non-CVCC 12-valve |
| 1987 | Civic/CRX, 1.3 | 81.9 (1342/1.3) | D15A2 | 4 | CVCC 8-valve |
| | Civic/CRX, HF,1.5 | 90.8 (1488/1.5) | D13A2 | 4 | CVCC 12-valve |
| | Civic/CRX, Si | 90.8 (1488/1.5) | D15A3 | 4 | Non-CVCC 12-valve |
| | Accord | 119.0 (1955/2.0) | A20A1 | 4 | Non-CVCC 12-valve |

## ENGINE IDENTIFICATION

| Year | Model | Engine Displacement cu. in. (cc/liter) | Engine Series Identification | No. of Cylinders | Engine Type |
|---|---|---|---|---|---|
| 1987 | Accord LX-i | 119.0 (1955/2.0) | A20A3 | 4 | Non-CVCC 12-valve |
| | Prelude | 111.6 (1829/1.8) | A18AI | 4 | Non-CVCC 12-valve |
| | Prelude Si | 119.0 (1955/2.0) | A20A3 | 4 | Non-CVCC 12-valve |
| 1988 | Civic | 91.0 (1493/1.5) | D15B1 | 4 | Non-CVCC 16-valve |
| | Civic/CRX | 91.0 (1493/1.5) | D15B2 | 4 | Non-CVCC 16-valve |
| | Civic/CRX, HF | 91.0 (1493/1.5) | D15B6 | 4 | Non-CVCC 8-valve |
| | Civic/CRX, Si | 97.0 (1590/1.6) | D16A6 | 4 | Non-CVCC 16-valve |
| | Accord, DX/LX | 119.0 (1955/2.0) | A20A1 | 4 | Non-CVCC 12-valve |
| | Accord LX-i | 119.0 (1955/2.0) | A20A3 | 4 | Non-CVCC 12-valve |
| | Prelude | 119.0 (1955/2.0) | B20A3 | 4 | Non-CVCC 12-valve |
| | Prelude Si | 119.0 (1955/2.0) | B20A5 | 4 | Non-CVCC 12-valve |
| 1989–90 | Civic | 91.0 (1493/1.5) | D15B1 | 4 | Non-CVCC 16-valve |
| | Civic/CRX | 91.0 (1493/1.5) | D15B2 | 4 | Non-CVCC 16-valve |
| | Civic/CRX, HF | 91.0 (1493/1.5) | D15B6 | 4 | Non-CVCC 8-valve |
| | Civic/CRX, Si | 97.0 (1590/1.6) | D16A6 | 4 | Non-CVCC 16-valve |
| | Accord, DX/LX | 119.0 (1955/2.0) | A20A1 | 4 | Non-CVCC 12-valve |
| | Accord LX-i | 119.0 (1955/2.0) | A20A3 | 4 | Non-CVCC 12-valve |
| | Prelude | 119.0 (1955/2.0) | B20A3 | 4 | Non-CVCC 12-valve |
| | Prelude Si | 119.0 (1955/2.0) | B20A5 | 4 | Non-CVCC 12-valve |

## GENERAL ENGINE SPECIFICATIONS

| Year | Model | Engine Displacement cu. in. (cc) | Fuel System Type | Net Horsepower @ rpm | Net Torque @ rpm (ft. lbs.) | Bore × Stroke (in.) | Com-pression Ratio | Oil Pressure @ rpm |
|---|---|---|---|---|---|---|---|---|
| 1983 | Civic 1300 | 81.5 (1335) | 3 bbl | 60 @ 5500 | 68 @ 4000 | 2.83 × 3.23 | 9.3:1 | 50@2000 |
| | Civic 1500 | 90.7 (1487) | 3 bbl | 63 @ 5000 | 77 @ 3000 | 2.91 × 3.41 | 9.3:1 | 50@2000 |
| | Accord | 106.8 (1751) | 3 bbl | 75 @ 4500 | 96 @ 3000 | 3.03 × 3.70 | 8.8:1 | 50@2000 |
| | Prelude | 111.6 (1829) | Dual Sidedraft | 100 @ 5000 | 104 @ 4000 | 3.15 × 3.58 | 9.4:1 | 60@1500 |
| 1984 | Civic/CRX, 1.3 | 81.9 (1342) | 3 bbl | 60 @ 5500 | 73 @ 3500 | 2.91 × 3.02 | 10.0:1 | 50@2000 |
| | Civic/CRX HF, 1.5 | 90.8 (1488) | 3 bbl | 76 @ 6000 | 84 @ 3500 | 2.91 × 3.42 | 9.2:1 | 55@2000 |
| | Accord | 111.6 (1829) | 3 bbl | 86 @ 5800 | 99 @ 3500 | 3.15 × 3.58 | 9.0:1 | 50@2000 |
| | Prelude | 111.6 (1829) | Dual Sidedraft | 100 @ 5500 ① | 104 @ 4000 | 3.15 × 3.58 | 9.1:1 | 60@1500 |
| 1985 | Civic/CRX, 1.3 | 81.9 (1342) | 3 bbl | 60 @ 5500 | 73 @ 3500 | 2.91 × 3.02 | 10.0:1 | 50@2000 |
| | Civic/CRX, 1.5 | 90.8 (1488) | 3 bbl | 76 @ 6000 | 84 @ 3500 | 2.91 × 3.42 | 9.2:1 | 55@2000 |
| | Civic/CRX, HF | 90.8 (1488) | 3 bbl | 65 @ 5500 | 81 @ 3500 | 2.91 × 3.42 | 9.2:1 | 50@2000 |
| | Civic/CRX, Si | 90.8 (1488) | EFI | 91 @ 5500 | 93 @ 4500 | 2.91 × 3.42 | 8.7:1 | 50@2000 |
| | Accord | 111.6 (1829) | 2 bbl | 86 @ 5800 | 99 @ 3500 | 3.15 × 3.58 | 9.0:1 | 50@2000 |
| | Accord SE-i | 111.6 (1829) | EFI | 101 @ 5800 | 108 @ 2500 | 3.15 × 3.58 | 8.8:1 | 50@2000 |

## GENERAL ENGINE SPECIFICATIONS

| Year | Model | Engine Displacement cu. in. (cc) | Fuel System Type | Net Horsepower @ rpm | Net Torque @ rpm (ft. lbs.) | Bore × Stroke (in.) | Com-pression Ratio | Oil Pressure @ rpm |
|---|---|---|---|---|---|---|---|---|
| 1985 | Prelude | 111.6 (1829) | Dual Sidedraft | 100 @ 5500 ① | 104 @ 4000 | 3.15 × 3.58 | 9.1:1 | 55@2000 |
| 1986 | Civic/CRX, 1.3 | 81.9 (1342) | 3 bbl | 60 @ 5500 | 73 @ 3500 | 2.91 × 3.02 | 10.0:1 | 50@2000 |
| | Civic/CRX, 1.5 | 90.8 (1488) | 3 bbl | 70 @ 6000 | 84 @ 3500 | 2.91 × 3.41 | 9.2:1 | 50@2000 |
| | Civic/CRX, HF | 90.8 (1488) | 3 bbl | 58 @ 4500 | 80 @ 2500 | 2.91 × 3.41 | 8.7:1 | 50@2000 |
| | Civic/CRX, Si | 90.8 (1488) | EFI | 91 @ 5500 | 93 @ 4500 | 2.91 × 3.41 | 8.7:1 | 50@2000 |
| | Accord | 119.0 (1955) | 2 bbl | 98 @ 5500 | 110 @ 3500 | 3.25 × 3.58 | 9.1:1 | 55@2000 |
| | Accord LX-i | 119.0 (1955) | EFI | 110 @ 5500 | 114@ 4500 | 3.25 × 3.58 | 8.8:1 | 55@2000 |
| | Prelude | 111.6 (1829) | Dual Sidedraft | 100 @ 5500 | 107 @ 4000 | 3.15 × 3.58 | 9.1:1 | 50@2000 |
| | Prelude Si | 119.0 (1955) | EFI | 110 @ 5500 | 114 @ 4500 | 3.25 × 3.58 | 8.8:1 | 50@2000 |
| 1987 | Civic/CRX, 1.3 | 81.9 (1392) | 3 bbl | 60 @ 5500 | 73 @ 3500 | 2.91 × 3.07 | 10.0:1 | 50@2000 |
| | Civic/CRX, 1.5 | 90.8 (1488) | 3 bbl | 76 @ 6000 | 84 @ 3500 | 2.91 × 3.41 | 9.2:1 | 50@2000 |
| | Civic/CRX, HF | 90.8 (1488) | 3 bbl | 58 @ 4500 | 80 @ 2500 | 2.91 × 3.41 | 9.6:1 | 50@2000 |
| | Civic/CRX, Si | 90.8 (1488) | EFI | 91 @ 5500 | 93 @ 4500 | 2.91 × 3.41 | 8.7:1 | 50@2000 |
| | Accord | 119.0 (1955) | 2 bbl | 98 @ 5500 | 109 @ 3500 | 3.25 × 3.58 | 9.1:1 | 55@2000 |
| | Accord LX-i | 119.0 (1955) | EFI | 110 @ 5500 | 114 @ 4500 | 3.25 × 3.58 | 8.8:1 | 55@2000 |
| | Prelude | 111.6 (1829) | Dual Sidedraft | 100 @ 5500 | 107 @ 4000 | 3.15 × 3.58 | 9.1:1 | 50@2000 |
| | Prelude Si | 119.0 (1955) | EFI | 110 @ 5500 | 114 @ 4500 | 3.25 × 3.58 | 8.8:1 | 50@2000 |
| 1988 | Civic | 91.0 (1493) | DP-FI | 70 @ 5500 | 83 @ 3000 | 2.95 × 3.33 | 9.6:1 | 50@2000 |
| | Civic/CRX | 91.0 (1493) | DP-FI | 92 @ 6000 | 89 @ 4500 | 2.95 × 3.33 | 9.2:1 | 50@2000 |
| | Civic/CRX, HF | 91.0 (1493) | MP-FI | 62 @ 4500 | 90 @ 2000 | 2.95 × 3.33 | 9.6:1 | 50@2000 |
| | Civic/CRX, Si | 97.0 (1590) | MP-FE | 105 @ 6000 | 98 @ 5000 | 2.95 × 3.54 | 9.1:1 | 50@2000 |
| | Accord DX/LX | 119.0 (1955) | 2 bbl | 98 @ 5500 | 109 @ 3500 | 3.25 × 3.58 | 9.1:1 | 55@2000 |
| | Accord LX-i | 119.0 (1955) | MP-PFI | 110 @ 5500 | 114 @ 4500 | 3.25 × 3.58 | 9.3:1 | 55@2000 |
| | Prelude | 119.0 (1955) | Dual Sidedraft | 100 @ 5500 | 107 @ 4000 | 3.19 × 3.74 | 9.1:1 | 50@2000 |
| | Prelude Si | 119.0 (1955) | FI | 110 @ 5500 | 114 @ 4500 | 3.18 × 3.74 | 9.0:1 | 50@2000 |
| 1989-90 | Civic | 91.0 (1493) | DP-FI | 70 @ 5500 | 83 @ 3000 | 2.95 × 3.33 | 9.2:1 | 74@3000 |
| | Civic/CRX | 91.0 (1493) | DP-FI | 92 @ 6000 | 89 @ 4500 | 2.95 × 3.33 | 9.2:1 | 74@3000 |
| | Civic/CRX, HF | 91.0 (1493) | MP-FE | 62 @ 4500 | 90 @ 2000 | 2.95 × 3.33 | 9.2:1 | 74@3000 |
| | Civic/CRX, Si | 97.0 (1590) | MP-FE | 108 @ 6000 | 100 @ 5000 | 2.95 × 3.54 | 9.1:1 | 74@3000 |
| | Accord DX/LX | 119.0 (1955) | 2 bbl | 98 @ 5500 | 109 @ 3500 | 3.26 × 3.58 | 9.1:1 | 55–65 @ 3000 |
| | Accord LX-i/SE-i | 119.0 (1955) | MP-PFI | 120 @ 5800 | 122 @ 4000 | 3.26 × 3.58 | 9.3:1 | 55–65 @ 3000 |
| | Prelude | 119.0 (1955) | Dual Sidedraft | ① | 111 @ 4800 | 3.19 × 3.74 | 9.1:1 | 75–87 @ 3000 |
| | Prelude Si | 110.3 (1955) | MP-PFI | 135 @ 6200 | 127 @ 4500 | 3.19 × 3.74 | 9.0:1 | 75–87 @ 3000 |

DP-FI Dual Point Fuel Injected
MP-FI Multipoint Fuel Injected
MP-PFI Multipoint Port Fuel Injected
① Manual transaxle—104 @ 5800
Automatic transaxle—105 @ 5800

## GASOLINE ENGINE TUNE-UP SPECIFICATIONS

| Year | Model | Engine Displacement cu. in. (cc) | Spark Plugs Type | Spark Plugs Gap (in.) | Ignition Timing (deg.) MT | Ignition Timing (deg.) AT | Compression Pressure (psi) | Fuel Pump (psi) | Idle Speed (rpm) MT | Idle Speed (rpm) AT | Valve Clearance⑬ In. | Valve Clearance⑬ Ex. |
|---|---|---|---|---|---|---|---|---|---|---|---|---|
| 1983 | Civic 1300 | 81.5 (1335) | BR6EB–11 | 0.042 | 18B ⑦③ | — | 210 | 2.5 | 600–750 ① | — | 0.005–0.007 | 0.007–0.009 |
| | Civic 1500 | 90.7 (1487) | BR6EB–11 | 0.042 | 18B ③ | 18B ③ | 210 | 2.5 ① | 650–750 ② | 650–750 | 0.005–0.007 | 0.007–0.009 |
| | Accord | 106.8 (1751) | BR6EB–L11 | 0.042 | 16B ⑤③ | 16B ③ | 195 | 2.5 | 700–800 ① | 650–750 ② | 0.005–0.007 | 0.010–0.012 |
| | Prelude | 111.6 (1829) | BUR6EB–11 | 0.042 | 10B ⑤③ | 12B ③ | 215 | 2.5 | 750–850 ① | 700–800 ② | 0.005–0.007 | 0.010–0.012 |
| 1984 | Civic/CRX 1.3 | 81.9 (1342) | BUR6EB–11 | 0.042 | 21B ⑪ | — | 220 | 3.0 | 650–750 | — | 0.007–0.009 | 0.009–0.011 |
| | Civic/CRX 1.5 | 90.8 (1488) | BUR6EB–11 | 0.042 | 20B ⑪ | 15B ⑪ | 210 | 3.0 | 650–750 | 650–750 | 0.007–0.009 | 0.009–0.011 |
| | Accord | 111.6 (1829) | BUR6EB–11 | 0.042 | 22B ③ | 18B ③ | 210 | 2.5 | 700–800 | 650–750 | 0.005–0.007 | 0.010–0.012 |
| | Prelude | 111.6 (1829) | BPR6EY–11 | 0.042 | 20B ③ | 12B ③ | 210 | 2.5 | 750–850 | 750–850 | 0.005–0.007 | 0.010–0.012 |
| 1985 | Civic/CRX 1.3 | 81.9 (1342) | BUR5EB–11 | 0.042 | 21B ⑥⑪ | — | 225 | 3.0 | 650–750 | — | 0.007–0.009 | 0.009–0.011 |
| | Civic/CRX 1.5 | 90.8 (1488) | BUR5EB–11 | 0.042 | 20B ⑪ | 15B ⑪ | 210 | 3.0 | 650–750 | 650–750 | 0.007–0.009 | 0.009–0.011 |
| | Civic/CRX HF | 90.8 (1488) | BUR4EB–11 | 0.042 | 21B ⑥⑪ | — | 210 | 3.0 | 650–750 | 650–750 | 0.007–0.009 | 0.009–0.011 |
| | Civic/CRX Si | 90.8 (1488) | BPR6EY–11 | 0.042 | 16B ⑤⑪ | — | 190 | 35 | 550–650 | — | 0.007–0.009 | 0.009–0.011 |
| | Accord | 111.6 (1829) | BUR5EB–11 | 0.042 | 22B ③⑨ | 18B ③ | 190 | 2.5 | 700–800 | 650–750 | 0.005–0.007 | 0.010–0.012 |
| | Accord SE-i | 111.6 (1829) | BPR6EY–11 | 0.042 | 18B ③ | 18B ③ | 200 | 35 | 700–800 | 700–800 | 0.005–0.007 | 0.010–0.012 |
| | Prelude | 111.6 (1829) | BPR6EY–11 | 0.042 | 20B ③ | 12B ③ | 200 | 2.5 | 750–850 | 750–850 | 0.005–0.007 | 0.012–0.012 |
| 1986 | Civic/CRX 1.3 | 81.9 (1342) | BUR4EB–11 | 0.042 | 21B ⑥⑪ | — | 225 | 3.0 | 650–750 | — | 0.007–0.009 | 0.009–0.011 |
| | Civic/CRX 1.5 | 90.8 (1488) | BUR4EB–11 | 0.042 | 20B ⑪ | 15B ⑩⑪ | 200 | 3.0 | 650–750 | 650–750 | 0.007–0.009 | 0.009–0.011 |
| | Civic/CRX HF | 90.8 (1488) | BUR4EB–11 | 0.042 | 21B ⑥⑪ | — | 190 | 3.0 | 650–750 | 650–750 | 0.007–0.009 | 0.009–0.011 |
| | Civic/CRX Si | 90.8 (1488) | BPR6EY–11 | 0.042 | 16B ⑤⑪ | — | 190 | 35 | 700–800 | — | 0.007–0.009 | 0.009–0.011 |
| | Accord | 119.0 (1955) | BPR5EY–11 | 0.042 | 24B ③⑫ | 15B ③ | 200 | 3.0 | 700–800 | 650–750 | 0.005–0.009 | 0.010–0.012 |
| | Accord LX-i | 119.0 (1955) | BPR5EY–11 | 0.042 | 15B ③ | 15B ③ | 210 | 35 | 700–800 | 700–800 | 0.005–0.007 | 0.010–0.012 |

## GASOLINE ENGINE TUNE-UP SPECIFICATIONS

| Year | Model | Engine Displacement cu. in. (cc) | Spark Plugs Type | Spark Plugs Gap (in.) | Ignition Timing (deg.) MT | Ignition Timing (deg.) AT | Com-pression Pressure (psi) | Fuel Pump (psi) | Idle Speed (rpm) MT | Idle Speed (rpm) AT | Valve Clearance⑬ In. | Valve Clearance⑬ Ex. |
|---|---|---|---|---|---|---|---|---|---|---|---|---|
| 1986 | Prelude | 111.6 (1829) | BPR6EY-11 | 0.042 | 20B ③ | 12B ③ | 200 | 2.5 | 750–850 | 750–850 | 0.005–0.007 | 0.010–0.012 |
| | Prelude Si | 119.0 (1955) | BPR5EY-11 | 0.042 | 15B ③ | 15B ③ | 210 | 35 | 700–800 | 700–800 | 0.005–0.007 | 0.010–0.012 |
| 1987 | Civic/CRX 1.3 | 81.9 (1342) | BUR4EB-11 | 0.042 | 21B ⑥⑪ | — | 225 | 3.0 | 650–750 | — | 0.007–0.009 | 0.009–0.011 |
| | Civic/CRX 1.5 | 90.8 (1488) | BUR4EB-11 | 0.042 | 20B ⑪ | 15B ⑩⑪ | 200 | 3.0 | 650–750 | 650–750 | 0.007–0.009 | 0.009–0.011 |
| | Civic/CRX HF | 90.8 (1488) | BUR4EB-11 | 0.042 | 26B ⑥⑪ | — | 164 | 3.0 | 650–750 | 650–750 | 0.007–0.009 | 0.009–0.011 |
| | Civic/CRX Si | 90.8 (1488) | BPR6EY-11 | 0.042 | 16B ⑤⑪ | — | 156 | 35 | 700–800 | — | 0.007–0.009 | 0.011–0.011 |
| | Accord | 119.0 (1955) | BPR5EY-11 | 0.042 | 24B ③⑫ | 15B ③ | 171 | 3.0 | 700–800 | 650–750 | 0.005–0.007 | 0.010–0.012 |
| | Accord LX-i | 119.0 (1955) | BPR5EY-11 | 0.042 | 15B ③ | 15B ③ | 178 | 35 | 700–800 | 700–800 | 0.005–0.007 | 0.010–0.012 |
| | Prelude | 111.6 (1829) | BPR6EY-11 | 0.042 | 20B ③ | 12B ③ | 156 | 2.5 | 750–850 | 750–850 | 0.005–0.007 | 0.010–0.012 |
| | Prelude Si | 119.0 (1955) | BPR5EY-11 | 0.042 | 15B ③ | 15B ③ | 178 | 35 | 700–800 | 700–800 | 0.005–0.007 | 0.010–0.012 |
| 1988 | Civic/CRX HF, 1.5 | 91.0 (1493) | BCPR6E-11 | 0.042 | 14B | 14B | 185 | 35 | 600–700 | 700–800 | 0.005–0.007 | 0.007–0.009 |
| | Civic/CRX Std., 1.5 | 91.0 (1493) | BCPR6E-11 | 0.042 | 18B | 18B | 185 | 35 | 700–700 | 700–800 | 0.007–0.009 | 0.009–0.011 |
| | Civic/CRX Si, 1.6 | 97.0 (1590) | BCPR6E-11 | 0.042 | 18B | 18B | 185 | 35 | 700–800 | 700–800 | 0.007–0.009 | 0.009–0.011 |
| | Accord DX/LX | 119.0 (1955) | BPR5EY-11 | 0.042 | 24B ⑫ | 15B ③ | 171 | 3.0 | 800–850 | 700–800 | 0.005–0.007 | 0.010–0.012 |
| | Accord LX-i | 119.0 (1955) | BPR5EY-11 | 0.042 | 15B ③ | 15B ③ | 178 | 35 | 750–800 | 750–800 | 0.005–0.007 | 0.010–0.012 |
| | Prelude | 119.0 (1955) | BCPR5E-11 | 0.042 | 20B | 12B | 156 | 2.5 | 800–850 | 750–800 | 0.005–0.007 | 0.010–0.012 |
| | Prelude Si | 119.0 (1955) | BCPR6E-11 | 0.042 | 15B | 15B | 178 | 35 | 750–800 | 750–800 | 0.003–0.005 | 0.006–0.008 |
| 1989 | Civic/CRX | 91.0 (1493) | BCPR6E-11 | 0.042 | 18B | 18B | 185 | 36 | 700–800 | 700–800 | 0.007–0.009 | 0.009–0.011 |
| | Civic HF | 91.0 (1493) | BCPR6E-11 | 0.042 | 18B | 18B | 185 | 36 | 600–650 | 600–650 | 0.005–0.007 | 0.007–0.009 |
| | Civic/CRX Si | 97.0 (1590) | BCPR6E-11 | 0.042 | 18B | 18B | 185 | 36 | 700–800 | 700–800 | 0.007–0.009 | 0.009–0.011 |
| | Accord DX/LX | 119.0 (1955) | BPR5EY-11 | 0.042 | 24B ⑯ | 15B | 171 | 2.6–3.3 | 750–850 | 680–790 | 0.005–0.007 | 0.010–0.012 |
| | Accord LX-i | 119.0 (1955) | BPR5EY-11 | 0.042 | 15B | 15B | 178 | 33–39 | 700–800 | 700–800 | 0.005–0.007 | 0.010–0.012 |

## GASOLINE ENGINE TUNE-UP SPECIFICATIONS

| Year | Model | Engine Displacement cu. in. (cc) | Spark Plugs Type | Spark Plugs Gap (in.) | Ignition Timing (deg.) MT | Ignition Timing (deg.) AT | Compression Pressure (psi) | Fuel Pump (psi) | Idle Speed (rpm) MT | Idle Speed (rpm) AT | Valve Clearance⑬ In. | Valve Clearance⑬ Ex. |
|---|---|---|---|---|---|---|---|---|---|---|---|---|
| 1989 | Prelude | 119.0 (1955) | BCPR5E-11 | 0.042 | 20B ⑭ | 15B ⑮ | 171 | 1.3–2.1 | 750–850 | 700–800 | 0.005–0.007 | 0.010–0.012 |
| | Prelude Si | 119.0 (1955) | BCPR6E-11 | 0.042 | 15B | 15B | 178 | 36 | 700–800 | 700–800 | 0.003–0.005 | 0.006–0.008 |
| 1990 | All | SEE UNDERHOOD SPECIFICATIONS STICKER | | | | | | | | | | |

**NOTE:** The underhood specifications sticker often reflects tune-up changes made in production. Sticker figures must be used if they disagree with those in this chart.

TDC Top dead center
B Before top dead center
A After top dead center
— Not applicable
NA Not available

① In neutral, with headlights on
② In drive range, with headlights on
③ Aim timing light at red mark on flywheel or torque converter drive plate with the distributor vacuum hose connected at the specified idle speed.
④ Wagon/Sedan—4B, Calif.-2A
⑤ California—12B
⑥ Std., California—16B
MT—20B, AT—15B
⑦ 4 speed—20B
⑧ Aim timing light at white mark
⑨ California models—18B
⑩ Models with power steering—17B
⑪ Aim timing light at red mark on crankshaft pulley
⑫ California—20B
⑬ Jet valve adjustment
Except 1342cc and 1488cc—0.005–0.007
1342cc and 1488cc—0.007–0.009
⑭ California—15B
⑮ California—10B
⑯ California—20B

## FIRING ORDERS

**NOTE:** To avoid confusion, always replace spark plug wires one at a time.

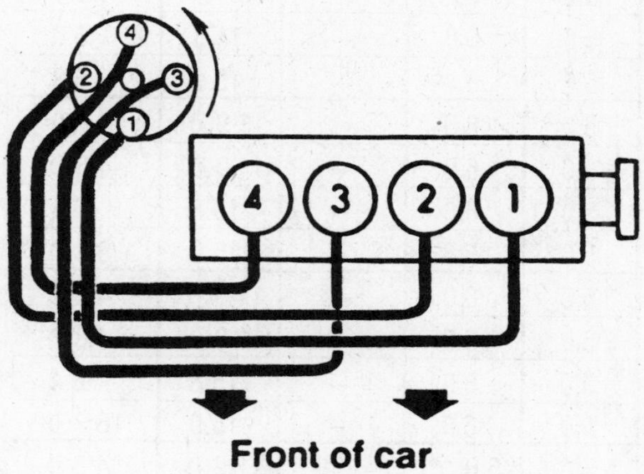


1355cc—1983 Civic, 1487cc—1983 Civic,
1751cc—1983 Accord

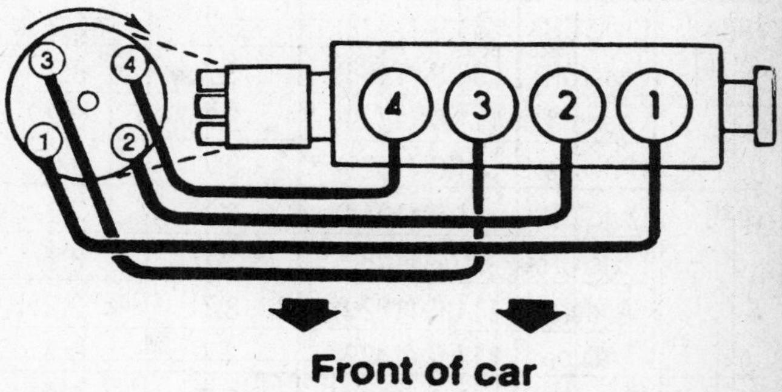


1829cc—1984 Accord & 1985 Accord SE-i
1342cc & 1488cc 1984–87 Civic
Firing order—1–3–4–2
Distributor rotation—clockwise

## FIRING ORDERS

**NOTE: To avoid confusion, always replace spark plug wires one at a time.**

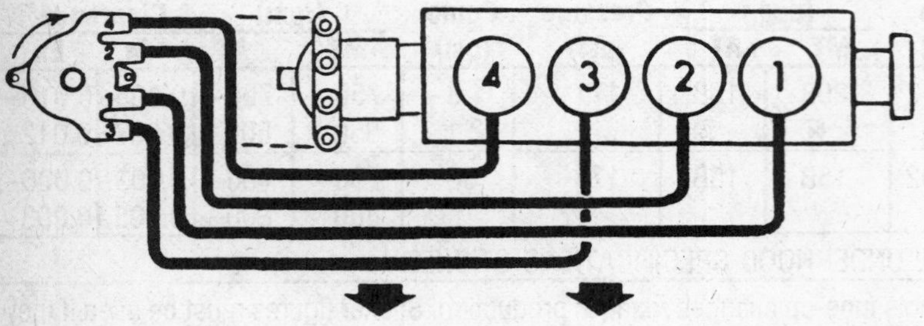


**1829cc—1985 Accord (carbureted) and 1984–87 Prelude**
**1955cc—1986–90 Accord and Prelude**
**Firing Order—1-3-4-2**
**Distributor rotation—clockwise**

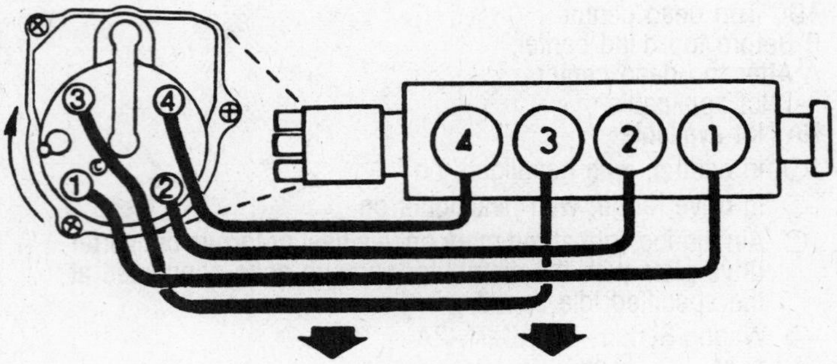


**1493cc and 1950cc—1988–90 Civic**
**Firing Order—1-3-4-2**
**Distributor rotation—clockwise**

## CAPACITIES

| Year | Model | Engine Displacement cu. in. (cc) | Engine Crankcase with Filter | Engine Crankcase without Filter | Transmission (pts.) 4-Spd | Transmission (pts.) 5-Spd | Transmission (pts.) Auto.① | Drive Axle (pts.) | Fuel Tank (gal.) | Cooling System (qts.) |
|---|---|---|---|---|---|---|---|---|---|---|
| 1983 | Civic | 81.5 (1335) | 3.7 | 3.2 | 5.2 | 5.2 | 5.2 | — | 10.4② | 4.8③ |
| | Civic | 90.7 (1487) | 3.7 | 3.2 | 5.2 | 5.2 | 5.2 | — | 10.4② | 4.8③ |
| | Accord | 106.8 (1751) | 3.7 | 3.2 | 5.0 | 5.0 | 6.0 | — | 15.8 | 6.0 |
| | Prelude | 111.6 (1829) | 3.7 | 3.2 | — | 5.0 | 5.8 | — | 15.9 | 6.3 |
| 1984 | Civic/CRX | 81.9 (1342) | 3.7 | 3.2 | 5.0 | 5.0 | 6.0 | — | 11.9④ | 4.8⑤ |
| | Civic/CRX | 90.8 (1488) | 3.7 | 3.2 | 5.0 | 5.0 | 6.0 | — | 11.9④ | 4.8⑤ |
| | Accord | 111.6 (1829) | 3.7 | 3.2 | — | 5.0 | 6.0 | — | 15.8 | 6.4 |
| | Prelude | 111.6 (1829) | 3.7 | 3.2 | — | 5.0 | 5.8 | — | 15.9 | 6.3⑥ |
| 1985 | Civic/CRX | 81.9 (1342) | 3.7 | 3.2 | 5.0 | 5.0 | 6.0 | — | 11.9④ | 4.8⑤ |
| | Civic/CRX | 90.8 (1488) | 3.7 | 3.2 | 5.0 | 5.0 | 6.0 | — | 11.9④ | 4.8⑤ |
| | Accord | 111.6 (1829) | 3.7 | 3.2 | — | 5.0 | 6.0 | — | 15.8 | 6.4 |
| | Prelude | 111.6 (1829) | 3.7 | 3.2 | — | 5.0 | 5.8 | — | 15.9 | 6.3⑥ |
| 1986 | Civic/CRX | 81.9 (1342) | 3.7 | 3.2 | 5.0 | 5.0 | 5.0⑦ | ⑨ | 11.9④ | 4.8⑤ |
| | Civic/CRX | 90.8 (1488) | 3.7 | 3.2 | 5.0 | 5.0 | 5.0⑦ | ⑨ | 11.9④ | 4.8⑤ |
| | Accord | 119.0 (1955) | 3.7 | 3.2 | — | 5.0 | 5.2 | — | 15.9 | 5.2⑧ |
| | Prelude | 111.6 (1829) | 3.7 | 3.2 | — | 5.0 | 5.8 | — | 15.9 | 6.3⑥ |
| | Prelude | 119.0 (1955) | 3.7 | 3.2 | — | 5.0 | 5.8 | — | 15.9 | 6.3⑥ |

## CAPACITIES

| Year | Model | Engine Displacement cu. in. (cc) | Engine Crankcase with Filter | Engine Crankcase without Filter | Transmission (pts.) 4-Spd | Transmission (pts.) 5-Spd | Transmission (pts.) Auto.① | Drive Axle (pts.) | Fuel Tank (gal.) | Cooling System (qts.) |
|---|---|---|---|---|---|---|---|---|---|---|
| 1987 | Civic/CRX | 81.9 (1342) | 3.7 | 3.2 | 5.0 | 5.0 | 5.0⑦ | ⑨ | 11.9④ | 4.8⑤ |
| | Civic/CRX | 90.8 (1488) | 3.7 | 3.2 | 5.0 | 5.0 | 5.0⑦ | ⑨ | 11.9④ | 4.8⑤ |
| | Accord | 119.0 (1955) | 3.7 | 3.2 | — | 5.0 | 5.2 | — | 15.9 | 5.2⑧ |
| | Prelude | 111.6 (1829) | 3.7 | 3.2 | — | 5.0 | 5.8 | — | 15.9 | 6.3⑥ |
| | Prelude | 119.0 (1955) | 3.7 | 3.2 | — | 5.0 | 5.8 | — | 15.9 | 6.3⑥ |
| 1988 | Civic/CRX | 91.0 (1493) | 3.7 | 3.2 | — | 5.0 | 5.0 | — | 11.9 | 5.8 |
| | Civic/CRX Si, 1.6 | 97.0 (1590) | 3.7 | 3.2 | — | 5.0 | 5.0 | — | 11.9⑩ | 5.8 |
| | Accord | 119.0 (1955) | 3.7 | 3.2 | — | 5.0 | 6.0 | — | 15.9 | 5.8 |
| | Prelude | 119.0 (1955) | 4.1 | 3.6 | 4.0 | 4.0 | 6.0 | — | 15.9 | 8.2 |
| 1989-90 | Civic/CRX | 91.0 (1493) | 3.7 | 3.2 | — | 4.0⑫ | 5.0⑬ | — | 11.9⑭ | ⑮ |
| | Civic/CRX | 97.0 (1590) | 3.7 | 3.2 | — | 4.0⑫ | 5.0⑬ | — | 11.9⑭ | ⑮ |
| | Accord | 119.0 (1955) | 3.7 | 3.2 | — | 4.8 | 6.4 | — | 15.9 | ⑰ |
| | Prelude | 119.0 (1955) | 4.1 | 3.6 | 4.0 | 4.0 | 6.0 | — | 15.9 | ⑯ |

① Does not include torque converter
② 4 door sedan—12.1
③ 1335cc—4.0
④ 4 door—12.1
CRX—10.8
CRX HF—10.0
CRX Si—11.9
⑤ 1342cc—3.6
⑥ Automatic transaxle—7.1
⑦ CRX—6.0
⑧ Automatic transaxle—5.8
⑨ 4WD—2.5
⑩ All others—10.6
⑪ HF—10.6
⑫ 4WD—5.0
⑬ 4WD-6.0
⑭ CRX STD and Si—11.9
All others—10.6
⑮ Automatic transaxle—5.7
Manual transaxle—5.8
⑯ Fuel injection—8.2
Carbureted with manual transaxle—7.2
Carbureted with automatic transaxle—7.9
⑰ Manual transaxle—6.9
Automatic transaxle—7.2

## CRANKSHAFT AND CONNECTING ROD SPECIFICATIONS

All measurements are given in inches.

| Year | Engine Displacement cu. in. (cc) | Crankshaft Main Brg. Journal Dia. | Crankshaft Main Brg. Oil Clearance | Crankshaft Shaft End-play | Crankshaft Thrust on No. | Connecting Rod Journal Diameter | Connecting Rod Oil Clearance | Connecting Rod Side Clearance |
|---|---|---|---|---|---|---|---|---|
| 1983 | 81.5 (1335) | 1.9676–1.9685 | 0.0009–0.0017 | 0.004–0.014 | 3 | 1.5739–1.5748 | 0.0008–0.0015 | 0.006–0.012 |
| | 90.7 (1487) | 1.9687–1.9803 | 0.0010–0.0022 | 0.004–0.014 | 3 | 1.6525–1.6535 | 0.0008–0.0015 | 0.006–0.012 |
| | 106.8 (1751) | 1.9687–1.9697 | 0.0010–0.0022 | 0.004–0.014 | 3 | 1.6525–1.6535 | 0.0008–0.0015 | 0.006–0.012 |
| | 111.6 (1829) | 1.9687–1.9697 | 0.0010–0.0022 | 0.004–0.014 | 3 | 1.7707–1.7717 | 0.0006–0.0015 | 0.006–0.012 |
| 1984 | 81.9 (1342) | 1.7707–1.7717 | 0.0009–0.0017 | 0.004–0.014 | 3 | 1.4951–1.4961 | 0.0008–0.0015 | 0.006–0.012 |
| | 90.8 (1488) | 1.9676–1.9685 | 0.0009–0.0017 | 0.004–0.014 | 3 | 1.6526–1.6535 | 0.0008–0.0015 | 0.006–0.012 |
| | 111.6 (1829) | 1.9673–1.9683 | 0.0010–0.0022 | 0.004–0.014 | 3 | 1.7707–1.7717 | 0.0006–0.0015 | 0.006–0.012 |

## CRANKSHAFT AND CONNECTING ROD SPECIFICATIONS

All measurements are given in inches.

| Year | Engine Displacement cu. in. (cc) | Crankshaft Main Brg. Journal Dia. | Crankshaft Main Brg. Oil Clearance | Crankshaft Shaft End-play | Crankshaft Thrust on No. | Connecting Rod Journal Diameter | Connecting Rod Oil Clearance | Connecting Rod Side Clearance |
|---|---|---|---|---|---|---|---|---|
| 1985 | 81.9 (1342) | 1.7707–1.7717 | 0.0009–0.0017 | 0.004–0.014 | 3 | 1.4951–1.4961 | 0.0008–0.0015 | 0.006–0.012 |
| | 90.8 (1488) | 1.9676–1.9685 | 0.0009–0.0017 | 0.004–0.014 | 3 | 1.6526–1.6535 | 0.0008–0.0015 | 0.006–0.012 |
| | 111.6 (1829) | 1.9673–1.9683 | 0.0010–0.0022 | 0.004–0.014 | 3 | 1.7707–1.7717 | 0.0006–0.0015 | 0.006–0.012 |
| 1986 | 81.9 (1342) | 1.7707–1.7717 | 0.0009–0.0017 | 0.004–0.014 | 3 | 1.4951–1.4961 | 0.0008–0.0015 | 00.06–0.012 |
| | 90.8 (1488) | 1.9676–1.9685 | 0.0009–0.0017 | 0.004–0.014 | 3 | 1.6526–1.6535 | 0.0008–0.0015 | 0.006–0.012 |
| | 111.6 (1829) | 1.9673–1.9683 | 0.0010–0.0022 ① | 0.004–0.014 | 3 | 1.7707–1.7717 | 0.0008–0.0015 | 0.006–0.012 |
| 1987 | 81.9 (1342) | 1.7707–1.7717 | 0.0009–0.0017 | 0.004–0.014 | 3 | 1.4951–1.4961 | 0.0008–0.0015 | 0.006–0.012 |
| | 90.8 (1488) | 1.9676–1.9685 | 0.0009–0.0017 | 0.004–0.014 | 3 | 1.6526–1.6535 | 0.0008–0.0015 | 0.006–0.012 |
| | 111.6 (1829) 119.0 (1955) | 1.9673–1.9683 ② | 0.0010–0.0022 ① | 0.004–0.014 | 3 | 1.7707–1.7717 | 0.0006–0.0015 | 0.006–0.012 |
| 1988 | 91.0 (1493) | 1.7707–1.7718 | 0.0010–0.0017 | 0.004–0.014 | 3 | ③ | 0.0008–0.0015 | 0.006–0.012 |
| | 97.0 (1590) | 2.1644–2.1654 | 0.0010–0.0017 | 0.004–0.014 | 3 | 1.7707–1.7717 | 0.0008–0.0015 | 0.006–0.012 |
| | 119.0 (1955) Accord | ② | 0.0010–0.0022 ① | 0.004–0.014 | 3 | 1.7707–1.7717 | 0.0008–0.0015 | 0.006–0.012 |
| | 119.0 (1955) Prelude | 2.1644–2.1654 | 0.0010–0.0017 ④ | 0.004–0.014 | 3 | 1.7707–1.7717 ⑤ | 0.0010–0.0017 | 0.006–0.012 |
| 1989 | 91.0 (1493) | 1.7707–1.7718 | ⑥ | 0.004–0.014 | 3 | 1.6526–1.6535 | 0.0008–0.0015 | 0.006–0.012 |
| | 97.0 (1590) | 2.1644–2.1654 | ⑦ | 0.004–0.014 | 3 | 1.7707–1.7717 | 0.0008–0.0015 | 0.006–0.012 |
| | 119.0 (1955) Accord | ② | 0.0010–0.0022 ① | 0.004–0.014 | 3 | 1.7707–1.7717 | 0.0008–0.0015 | 0.006–0.012 |
| | 119.0 (1955) Prelude | 2.1644–2.1654 | 0.0010–0.0017 ④ | 0.004–0.014 | 3 | 1.7707–1.7717 ⑤ | 0.0010–0.0017 ⑧ | 0.006–0.012 |

## CRANKSHAFT AND CONNECTING ROD SPECIFICATIONS

All measurements are given in inches.

| Year | Engine Displacement cu. in. (cc) | Crankshaft Main Brg. Journal Dia. | Crankshaft Main Brg. Oil Clearance | Crankshaft Shaft End-play | Crankshaft Thrust on No. | Connecting Rod Journal Diameter | Connecting Rod Oil Clearance | Connecting Rod Side Clearance |
|---|---|---|---|---|---|---|---|---|
| 1989 | 119.0 (1955) Prelude Si | 2.1644–2.1654 | 0.0010–0.0017 ④ | 0.004–0.014 | 3 | 1.8888–1.8900 ⑤ | 0.0010–0.0017 | 0.006–0.012 |

① No. 3—0.0013-0.0024
② Accord:
No. 1—1.9676–1.9685
No. 3—1.9671–1.9680
No. 2, 4, 5:1.9673–1.9683
③ HF—1.4951–1.4961
Std.—1.5739–1.5748
④ No. 3—0.0012–0.0019
⑤ Prelude Si—1.8888–1.8900
⑥ No. 2, 3, 4—0.0001–0.0017
No. 1, 5—0.0007–0.0014
⑦ No. 1, 5—0.0007–0.0014
No. 2, 4—0.0001–0.0017
No. 3—0.0012–0.0019
⑧ Prelude with fuel injection—0.0010–0.0017

## VALVE SPECIFICATIONS

| Year | Engine Displacement cu. in. (cc) | Seat Angle (deg.) | Face Angle (deg.) | Spring Test Pressure (lbs.) | Spring Installed Height (in.) | Stem-to-Guide Clearance (in.)① Intake | Stem-to-Guide Clearance (in.)① Exhaust | Stem Diameter (in.)① Intake | Stem Diameter (in.)① Exhaust |
|---|---|---|---|---|---|---|---|---|---|
| 1983 | 81.5 (1335) | 45 | 45 | NA | ② | 0.0008–0.0020 | 0.0025–0.0037 | 0.2591–0.2594 | 0.2574–0.2578 |
| | 90.7 (1487) | 45 | 45 | NA | ② | 0.0008–0.0020 | 0.0025–0.0037 | 0.2591–0.2594 | 0.2574–0.2578 |
| | 106.8 (1751) | 45 | 45 | NA | ③ | 0.001–0.002 | 0.002–0.004 | 0.2748–0.2751 | 0.2732–0.2736 |
| | 111.6 (1829) | 45 | 45 | NA | ④ | 0.001–0.002 | 0.002–0.004 | 0.2591–0.2594 | 0.2736–0.2736 |
| 1984 | 81.9 (1342) | 45 | 45 | NA | ⑤ | 0.001–0.002 | 0.002–0.003 | 0.2591–0.2594 | 0.2579–0.2583 |
| | 90.8 (1488) | 45 | 45 | NA | ⑤ | 0.001–0.002 | 0.002–0.003 | 0.2591–0.2594 | 0.2579–0.2583 |
| | 111.6 (1829) | 45 | 45 | NA | ④ | 0.001–0.002 | 0.002–0.004 | 0.2591–0.2594 | 0.2732–0.2736 |
| 1985 | 81.9 (1342) | 45 | 45 | NA | 1.896⑥ | 0.001–0.002 | 0.002–0.003 | 0.2591–0.2594 | 0.2579–0.2583 |
| | 90.8 (1488) | 45 | 45 | NA | 1.896⑥ | 0.001–0.002 | 0.002–0.003 | 0.2591–0.2594 | 0.2579–0.2583 |
| | 111.6 (1829) | 45 | 45 | NA | ④ | 0.001–0.002 | 0.002–0.004 | 0.2591–0.2594 | 0.2732–0.2736 |
| 1986 | 81.9 (1342) | 45 | 45 | NA | 1.896⑥ | 0.001–0.002 | 0.002–0.003 | 0.2591–0.2594 | 0.2579–0.2583 |
| | 90.8 (1488) | 45 | 45 | NA | 1.896⑥ | 0.001–0.002 | 0.002–0.003 | 0.2591–0.2594 | 0.2579–0.2583 |
| | 111.6 (1829) | 45 | 45 | NA | ⑦ | 0.001–0.002 | 0.002–0.004 | 0.2591–0.2594 | 0.2732–0.2736 |
| | 119.0 (1955) | 45 | 45 | NA | ⑦ | 0.001–0.002 | 0.002–0.004 | 0.2591–0.2594 | 0.2732–0.2736 |

## VALVE SPECIFICATIONS

| Year | Engine Displacement cu. in. (cc) | Seat Angle (deg.) | Face Angle (deg.) | Spring Test Pressure (lbs.) | Spring Installed Height (in.) | Stem-to-Guide Clearance (in.)① | | Stem Diameter (in.)① | |
|---|---|---|---|---|---|---|---|---|---|
| | | | | | | Intake | Exhaust | Intake | Exhaust |
| 1987 | 81.9 (1342) | 45 | 45 | NA | ⑤ | 0.001–0.002 | 0.002–0.003 | 0.2591–0.2594 | 0.2579–0.2583 |
| | 90.8 (1488) | 45 | 45 | NA | ⑤ | 0.001–0.002 | 0.002–0.003 | 0.2591–0.2594 | 0.2579–0.2583 |
| | 111.6 (1829) | 45 | 45 | NA | ⑦ | 0.001–0.002 | 0.002–0.004 | 0.2591–0.2594 | 0.2732–0.2736 |
| | 119.0 (1955) | 45 | 45 | NA | ⑦ | 0.001–0.002 | 0.002–0.004 | 0.2591–0.2594 | 0.2732–0.2736 |
| 1988 | 91.0 (1493) | 45 | 45 | NA | ⑧ | 0.001–0.002 | 0.002–0.003 | 0.2157–0.2161 | 0.2147–0.2150 |
| | 97.0 (1590) | 45 | 45 | NA | ⑧ | 0.001–0.002 | 0.002–0.003 | 0.2157–0.2161 | 0.2147–0.2150 |
| | 119.0 (1955) Accord Prelude | 45 | 45 | NA | ⑦ | 0.001–0.002 | 0.002–0.004 | 0.2591–0.2594 | 0.2732–0.2736 |
| | 119.0 (1955) Prelude Si | 45 | 45 | NA | 1.683 | 0.001–0.002 | 0.002–0.003 | 0.2591–0.2594 | 0.2579–0.2583 |
| 1989-90 | 91.0 (1493) | 45 | 45 | NA | ⑨ | 0.001–0.002 | 0.002–0.003 | 0.2157–0.2161 | 0.2147–0.2150 |
| | 97.0 (1590) | 45 | 45 | NA | ⑨ | 0.001–0.002 | 0.002–0.003 | 0.2157–0.2161 | 0.2147–0.2150 |
| | 119.0 (1955) Accord Prelude | 45 | 45 | NA | ⑦ | 0.001–0.002 | 0.002–0.004 | 0.2591–0.2594 | 0.2732–0.2736 |
| | 119.0 (1955) Prelude Si | 45 | 45 | NA | 1.683 | 0.001–0.002 | 0.002–0.003 | 0.2591–0.2594 | 0.2579–0.2583 |

NA Not Available

① Jet Valve—0.0009-0.0023

② 1335cc, 1487cc:
Intake & Exhaust inner—1.402
Intake & Exhaust outer—1.488
Auxiliary—0.906

③ 1751cc:
Intake & Exhaust inner—1.402
Intake & Exhaust outer—1.488
Auxiliary—0.984

④ 1829cc, 1955cc:
Intake—1.660
Exhaust inner—1.460
Exhaust outer—1.670
Auxiliary—0.984 (carbureted)

⑤ 1342cc, 1488cc:
Intake:1.660
Exhaust—1.690
Auxiliary—0.980 (carbureted)

⑥ Auxiliary—1.311

⑦ Intake—1.913
Exhaust—1.876

⑧ 1493cc:
Intake—1.8498–1.8880
Exhaust—1.9278–1.9463
1590cc:
Intake—1.8498–1.8683
Exhaust—1.9278–1.9263

⑨ Intake—1.8498–1.8683
Exhaust—1.9278–1.9263

## PISTON AND RING SPECIFICATIONS

All measurments are given in inches.

| Year | Engine Displacement cu. in. (cc) | Piston Clearance | Ring Gap | | | Ring Side Clearance | | |
|---|---|---|---|---|---|---|---|---|
| | | | Top Compression | Bottom Compression | Oil Control | Top Compression | Bottom Compression | Oil Control |
| 1983 | 81.5 (1335) | 0.0004–0.0020 | 0.006–0.014 | 0.006–0.014 | 0.012–0.035 | 0.0012–0.0020 ① | 0.0012–0.0020 ① | Snug |

## PISTON AND RING SPECIFICATIONS

All measurments are given in inches.

| Year | Engine Displacement cu. in. (cc) | Piston Clearance | Ring Gap Top Compression | Ring Gap Bottom Compression | Ring Gap Oil Control | Ring Side Clearance Top Compression | Ring Side Clearance Bottom Compression | Ring Side Clearance Oil Control |
|---|---|---|---|---|---|---|---|---|
| 1983 | 90.7 (1487) | 0.0004–0.0020 | 0.006–0.014 | 0.006–0.014 | 0.012–0.035 | 0.0012–0.0020 ① | 0.0012–0.0020 ① | Snug |
| | 106.8 (1751) | 0.0004–0.0024 | 0.006–0.014 | 0.006–0.014 | 0.012–0.035 | 0.0008–0.0018 | 0.0008–0.0018 | Snug |
| | 111.6 (1829) | 0.0008–0.0016 | 0.008–0.014 | 0.008–0.014 | 0.008–0.035 | 0.0008–0.0018 | 0.0008–0.0018 | Snug |
| 1984 | 81.9 (1342) | 0.0004–0.0020 | 0.006–0.014 | 0.006–0.014 | 0.006–0.024 | 0.0012–0.0024 | 0.0012–0.0022 | Snug |
| | 90.8 (1488) | 0.0004–0.0020 | 0.006–0.014 | 0.006–0.014 | 0.006–0.024 | 0.0012–0.0024 | 0.0012–0.0022 | Snug |
| | 111.6 (1829) | 0.0008–0.0016 | 0.008–0.014 | 0.008–0.014 | 0.008–0.035 | 0.0008–0.0018 | 0.0008–0.0018 | Snug |
| 1985 | 81.9 (1342) | 0.0004–0.0020 | 0.006–0.014 | 0.006–0.014 | 0.006–0.014 | 0.0012–0.0024 | 0.0012–0.0024 | Snug |
| | 90.8 (1488) | 0.0004–0.0020 | 0.006–0.014 | 0.006–0.014 | 0.006–0.014 | 0.0012–0.0024 | 0.0012–0.0024 | Snug |
| | 111.6 (1829) | 0.0008–0.0016 | 0.008–0.014 | 0.008–0.014 | 0.008–0.035 | 0.0008–0.0018 | 0.0008–0.0018 | Snug |
| 1986 | 81.9 (1342) | 0.0004–0.0020 | 0.006–0.014 | 0.006–0.014 | 0.008–0.024 | 0.0012–0.0024 | 0.0012–0.0022 | Snug |
| | 90.8 (1488) | 0.0004–0.0020 | 0.006–0.014 | 0.006–0.014 | 0.008–0.024 | 0.0012–0.0024 | 0.0012–0.0022 | Snug |
| | 111.6 (1829) | 0.0008–0.0016 | 0.008–0.014 | 0.008–0.014 | 0.008–0.035 | 0.0008–0.0018 | 0.0008–0.0018 | Snug |
| | 119.0 (1955) | 0.0008–0.0016 | 0.008–0.014 | 0.010–0.015 | 0.008–0.020 | 0.0012–0.0022 | 0.0012–0.0022 | Snug |
| 1987 | 81.9 (1342) | 0.0004–0.0020 | 0.006–0.014 | 0.006–0.014 | 0.008–0.024 | 0.0012–0.0024 | 0.0012–0.0022 | Snug |
| | 90.8 (1488) | 0.0004–0.0020 | 0.006–0.014 | 0.006–0.014 | 0.008–0.024 | 0.0012–0.0024 | 0.0012–0.0022 | Snug |
| | 111.6 (1829) | 0.0008–0.0016 | 0.008–0.014 | 0.008–0.014 | 0.008–0.035 | 0.0008–0.0018 | 0.0008–0.0018 | Snug |
| | 119.0 (1955) | 0.0008–0.0016 | 0.008–0.014 | 0.008–0.014 | 0.008–0.020 | 0.0012–0.0024 | 0.0012–0.0024 | Snug |
| 1988 | 91.0 (1493) | 0.0004–0.0016 | 0.006–0.014 | 0.006–0.014 | 0.008–0.024 | 0.0012–0.0024 | 0.0012–0.0022 | Snug |
| | 97.0 (1590) | 0.0004–0.0016 | 0.006–0.014 | 0.006–0.014 | 0.008–0.024 | 0.0012–0.0024 | 0.0012–0.0022 | Snug |
| | 119.0 (1955) | 0.0008–0.0016 | 0.008–0.014 | 0.016–0.022 | 0.008–0.028 ② | 0.0012–0.0024 ③ | 0.0012–0.0024 ④ | Snug |
| 1989-90 | 91.0 (1493) | 0.0004–0.0016 | 0.006–0.014 | 0.006–0.014 | 0.008–0.024 | 0.0012–0.0024 | 0.0012–0.0022 | Snug |

## PISTON AND RING SPECIFICATIONS

All measurments are given in inches.

| Year | Engine Displacement cu. in. (cc) | Piston Clearance | Ring Gap Top Compression | Ring Gap Bottom Compression | Ring Gap Oil Control | Ring Side Clearance Top Compression | Ring Side Clearance Bottom Compression | Ring Side Clearance Oil Control |
|---|---|---|---|---|---|---|---|---|
| 1989-90 | 97.0 (1590) | 0.0004–0.0016 | 0.006–0.014 | 0.006–0.014 | 0.008–0.024 | 0.0012–0.0024 | 0.0012–0.0022 | Snug |
| | 119.0 (1955) | 0.0008–0.0016 | 0.008–0.014 | 0.016–0.022 ⑤ | 0.008–0.028 ② | 0.0012–0.0024 ④ | 0.0012–0.0024 ④ | Snug |

① 1335cc – 0.0012-0.0024
② Prelude equipped with carburetor – 0.008–0.020
③ Prelude – 0.0012–0.0022
④ Prelude – 0.0012–0.0022
⑤ Prelude – 0.016–0.022

## TORQUE SPECIFICATIONS

All readings in ft. lbs.

| Year | Engine Displacement cu. in. (cc) | Cylinder Head Bolts① | Main Bearing Bolts | Rod Bearing Bolts | Crankshaft Pulley Bolts | Flywheel Bolts | Manifold Intake | Manifold Exhaust | Spark Plugs |
|---|---|---|---|---|---|---|---|---|---|
| 1983 | 81.5 (1335) | 43 | 29-33 | 21 | 80 | 51 | 18 | 18 | 13 |
| | 90.7 (1487) | 43 | 29-33 | 21 | 80 | 51 | 18 | 18 | 13 |
| | 106.8 (1751) | 43 | 48 | 21 | 80 | 51 | 18 | 18 | 13 |
| | 111.6 (1829) | 49 | 48④ | 23 | 83 | 76② | 16 | 22 | 13 |
| 1984 | 81.9 (1342) | 43 | 33 | 20 | 83 | 76② | 16 | 23 | 13 |
| | 90.8 (1488) | 43 | 33 | 20 | 83 | 76② | 16 | 23 | 13 |
| | 111.6 (1829) | 49 | 48④ | 23 | 83 | 76② | 16 | 22 | 13 |
| 1985 | 81.9 (1342) | 43 | 33 | 20 | 83 | 76② | 16 | 23 | 13 |
| | 90.8 (1488) | 43 | 33 | 20 | 83 | 76② | 16 | 23 | 13 |
| | 111.6 (1829) | 49 | 48④ | 23 | 83 | 76② | 16 | 22 | 13 |
| 1986 | 81.9 (1342) | 43 | 33 | 20 | 83 | 76② | 16 | 23 | 13 |
| | 90.8 (1488) | 43 | 33 | 20 | 83 | 76② | 16 | 23 | 13 |
| | 111.6 (1829) | 49 | 48④ | 23 | 83 | 76② | 16 | 22 | 13 |
| | 119.0 (1955) | 49 | 48④ | 23 | 83 | 76② | 16 | 22 | 13 |
| 1987 | 81.9 (1342) | 43 | 33 | 20 | 83 | 76② | 16 | 23 | 13 |
| | 90.8 (1488) | 43 | 33 | 20 | 83 | 76② | 16 | 23 | 13 |
| | 111.6 (1829) | 49 | 48③ | 23 | 83 | 76② | 16 | 22 | 13 |
| | 119.0 (1955) | 49 | 48③ | 23 | 83 | 76② | 16 | 22 | 13 |
| 1988 | 91.0 (1493) | 49 | 48 | 23 | 83 | 87② | 25 | 25 | 13 |
| | 97.0 (1590) | 49 | 48 | 23 | 83 | 87② | 25 | 25 | 13 |
| | 119.0 (1955) | 49 | 49 | 23④ | 83 | 76② | 20⑤ | 23⑥ | 13 |
| 1989-90 | 91.0 (1493) | 47 | ⑦⑨⑩ | 23 | 119⑦ | 87② | 16 | 23 | 13 |
| | 97.0 (1590) | 47 | ⑦⑨⑩ | 23 | 119⑦ | 87② | 16 | 23 | 13 |
| | 119.0 (1955) | 49 | 49⑦ | 23 | 108 | 76② | 16 | 23⑧ | 13 |

① 2-Step procedure; see text
② Auto Transaxle – 54
③ Fuel injected engine – 49
④ Fuel injected engine – 33
⑤ Prelude – 16
⑥ Prelude – 26
⑦ Dip bolts in clean engine oil
⑧ Prelude with fuel injection – 26
⑨ Civic and CRX except Si – 33
Civic and CRX Si – 47
⑩ Station Wagon 2WD – 33
Station Wagon 4WD – 47

## BRAKE SPECIFICATIONS

| Year | Model | Lug Nut Torque (ft. lbs.) | Master Cylinder Bore | Brake Disc | | Standard Brake Drum Diameter | Minimum Lining Thickness | |
|---|---|---|---|---|---|---|---|---|
| | | | | Minimum Thickness | Maximum Runout | | Front | Rear |
| 1983 | Civic | 51-65 | NA | 0.354① | 0.006 | 7.066⑤ | 0.063 | 0.079 |
| | Accord | 80 | NA | 0.60 | 0.006 | 7.850 | 0.063 | 0.079 |
| | Prelude | 80 | NA | 0.59 | 0.004 | 7.850 | 0.118 | 0.079 |
| 1984 | Civic/CRX | 80 | NA | ③ | 0.004 | 7.070⑤ | 0.120 | 0.080 |
| | Accord | 80 | NA | 0.67 | 0.004 | 7.850 | 0.120 | 0.080 |
| | Prelude | 80 | NA | 0.67④ | 0.004 | 7.850 | 0.120 | 0.060 |
| 1985 | Civic/CRX | 80 | NA | ③ | 0.004 | 7.070⑤ | 0.120 | 0.080 |
| | Accord | 80 | NA | 0.67 | 0.004 | 7.850 | 0.120 | 0.080 |
| | Prelude | 80 | NA | 0.67④ | 0.004 | 7.850 | 0.120 | 0.060 |
| 1986 | Civic/CRX | 80 | NA | ③ | 0.004 | 7.070⑤ | 0.120 | 0.080 |
| | Accord | 80 | NA | 0.67 | 0.004 | 7.850 | 0.120 | 0.080 |
| | Prelude | 80 | NA | 0.67④ | 0.004 | 7.750 | 0.120 | 0.060 |
| 1987 | Civic/CRX | 80 | NA | ③ | 0.004 | 7.070⑤ | 0.120 | 0.080 |
| | Accord | 80 | NA | 0.67 | 0.004 | 7.850 | 0.120 | 0.080 |
| | Prelude | 80 | NA | 0.67④ | 0.004 | 7.850 | 0.120 | 0.060 |
| 1988 | Civic/CRX | 80 | NA | ⑥ | 0.004 | 7.070⑤ | 0.120 | 0.080 |
| | Accord | 80 | NA | ④⑦ | 0.006 | 7.850 | 0.120 | 0.080 |
| | Prelude | 80 | NA | ④⑦ | 0.004 | 7.850 | 0.120 | 0.080 |
| 1989-90 | Civic | 80 | NA | 0.67 | 0.75 | 7.090 | 0.39 | 0.18 |
| | Civic SW | 80 | NA | 0.67 | 0.75 | 7.870 | ⑪ | 0.18 |
| | CRX | 80 | NA | ⑩ | ⑨ | 7.090 | ⑧ | 0.18 |
| | Accord | 80 | NA | ⑰ | ⑱ | ⑭ | ⑯ | 0.031 |
| | Prelude | 80 | NA | ⑫ | ⑬ | ⑭ | ⑮ | 0.031 |

NA Not available

① 0.394
exc 1983 1500—0.60

③ Civic 1300—0.39
Civic 1500—0.59
CRX St & Std.—0.67
1300 & HF—0.35 1984–85
1986–87—0.43

④ Rear disc—0.31

⑤ Civic Wagon—7.85

⑥ Civic/CRX HF—0.59
All others—0.67

⑦ Accord DX/LX and Prelude—0.67
Accord LX-i and Prelude Si—0.75

⑧ Std and Si—0.39
HF—0.37

⑨ Std and Si—0.75
HF—0.67

⑩ Std and Si—0.75
HF—0.67

⑪ 4WD—0.35
Except 4WD—0.39

⑫ Si—0.75
S—0.67

⑬ Si—0.83
S—0.75

⑭ Rear disc rotor—0.39

⑮ Si—0.45
S—0.35

⑯ Carburetor—0.45
Fuel injection—0.39

⑰ Carburetor—0.75
Fuel injection—0.67

## WHEEL ALIGNMENT

| Year | Model | Caster | | Camber | | Toe-in (in.) | Steering Axis Inclination (deg.) |
|---|---|---|---|---|---|---|---|
| | | Range (deg.) | Preferred Setting (deg.) | Range (deg.) | Preferred Setting (deg.) | | |
| 1983 | Civic exc. SW | 1½P–3½P | 2½P | 1N–1P | 0 | 0 | 12$^{11}/_{32}$ |
| | Civic SW | $^{5}/_{16}$P–2$^{5}/_{16}$P | 1$^{5}/_{16}$P | 1N–1P | 0 | 0 | 12$^{11}/_{32}$ |

## WHEEL ALIGNMENT

| Year | Model | Caster Range (deg.) | Caster Preferred Setting (deg.) | Camber Range (deg.) | Camber Preferred Setting (deg.) | Toe-in (in.) | Steering Axis Inclination (deg.) |
|---|---|---|---|---|---|---|---|
| 1983 | Accord | $\frac{7}{16}$P–$2\frac{7}{16}$P | $1\frac{7}{16}$ | 1N–1P | 0 | 0 | $12\frac{1}{2}$ |
| | Prelude | 1N–1P | 0 | 1N–1P | 0 | 0 | $6\frac{13}{16}$ |
| 1984 | Civic exc. SW | $1\frac{5}{16}$P–$3\frac{5}{16}$P | $2\frac{5}{16}$P | 1N–1P | 0 | 0 | $12\frac{13}{16}$ |
| | Civic SW | $1\frac{1}{8}$P–$3\frac{1}{8}$P | $2\frac{1}{8}$P | 1N–1P | 0 | 0 | 12 |
| | Accord | $\frac{7}{16}$P–$2\frac{7}{16}$P | $1\frac{7}{16}$ | 1N–1P | 0 | 0 | $12\frac{1}{2}$ |
| | Prelude | 1N–1P | 0 | 1N–1P | 0 | 0 | $6\frac{13}{16}$ |
| 1985 | Civic exc. SW | $1\frac{1}{2}$P–$3\frac{1}{2}$P① | $2\frac{1}{2}$P② | 1N–1P | 0 | 0 | 13 |
| | Civic SW | 1P–3P | 2P | 1N–1P | 0 | 0 | 12 |
| | Accord | $\frac{1}{2}$P–$2\frac{1}{2}$P | $1\frac{1}{2}$P | 1N–1P | 0 | 0 | $12\frac{1}{2}$ |
| | Prelude | 1N–1P | 0 | 1N–1P | 0 | 0 | $6\frac{13}{16}$ |
| 1986 | Civic exc. SW | $1\frac{1}{2}$P–$3\frac{1}{2}$P① | $2\frac{1}{2}$P② | 1N–1P | 0 | 0 | 13 |
| | Civic SW | 1P–3P | 2P | 1N–1P | 0 | 0 | 12 |
| | Accord | 1N–1P | 0 | 1N–1P | 0 | 0 | $6\frac{13}{16}$ |
| | Prelude | 1N–1P | 0 | 1N–1P | 0 | 0 | $6\frac{13}{16}$ |
| 1987 | Civic exc. SW | $1\frac{1}{2}$P–$3\frac{1}{2}$P ① | $2\frac{1}{2}$P ② | 1N–1P | 0 | 0 | 13 |
| | Civic SW | 1P–3P | 2P | 1N–1P | 0 | 0 | 12 |
| | Accord | 1N–1P | 0 | 1N–1P | 0 | 0 | $6\frac{13}{16}$ |
| | Prelude | 1N–1P | 0 | 1N–1P | 0 | 0 | $6\frac{13}{16}$ |
| 1988 | Civic exc. SW | 2P–4P | 3P | 1N–1P | 0 | 0 | $7\frac{5}{16}$ |
| | Civic SW | $1\frac{15}{16}$P–$3\frac{15}{16}$P | $2\frac{15}{16}$P | $\frac{11}{16}$N–$1\frac{5}{16}$P | $\frac{5}{16}$P | 0 | $7\frac{1}{4}$ |
| | Civic 4WD | $1\frac{15}{16}$P–$3\frac{15}{16}$P | $2\frac{15}{16}$P | $\frac{7}{16}$N–$1\frac{9}{16}$P | $\frac{9}{16}$P | 0 | $6\frac{15}{16}$ |
| | Accord | $\frac{1}{2}$N–$1\frac{1}{2}$P | $\frac{1}{2}$P | 1N–1P | 0 | 0 | $6\frac{13}{16}$ |
| | Prelude | $1\frac{3}{16}$P–$2\frac{13}{16}$P | $2\frac{3}{8}$P | 1N–1P | 0 | 0 | $6\frac{13}{16}$ |
| 1989-90 | Civic exc. SW | 2P–4P | 3P | 1N–1P | 0 | 0 | — |
| | Civic SW | $1\frac{15}{16}$P–$3\frac{15}{16}$P | $2\frac{15}{16}$P | $\frac{11}{16}$N–$1\frac{5}{16}$P | $\frac{5}{16}$P | 0 | — |
| | Civic 4WD | $1\frac{15}{16}$P–$3\frac{15}{16}$P | $2\frac{15}{16}$P | $\frac{7}{16}$N–$1\frac{9}{16}$P | $\frac{9}{16}$P | 0 | — |
| | Accord | $\frac{1}{2}$N–$1\frac{1}{2}$P | $\frac{1}{2}$P | 1N–1P | 0 | 0 | — |
| | Prelude | $1\frac{3}{16}$P–$2\frac{13}{16}$P | $2\frac{3}{8}$P | 1N–1P | 0 | 0 | — |

SW Station Wagon
P Positive
N Negative

① With power steering 2P-4P
② With power steering 3P

# TUNE-UP PROCEDURES

## Ignition Timing

### ADJUSTMENT

1. Stop the engine, and hook up a tachometer according to the manufacturer's instructions.

**NOTE: On some vehicles you will have to pull back the rubber ignition coil cover to reveal the terminals. On other vehicles, it will be necessary to remove the rubber cap (yellow) from the ignition timing adjusting connector, which is located in the left rear section of the engine compartment, and connect a jumper wire between the brown and green/white terminals.**

2. Connect a a timing light to the engine according to the manufacturer's instructions.
3. Make sure that all wires are clear of the cooling fan and hot exhaust manifolds. Start the engine. Check that the idle speed is set to specifications with the transaxle in Neutral (manual transaxle) or 2nd gear (automatic transaxle). If not, adjust the idle speed.

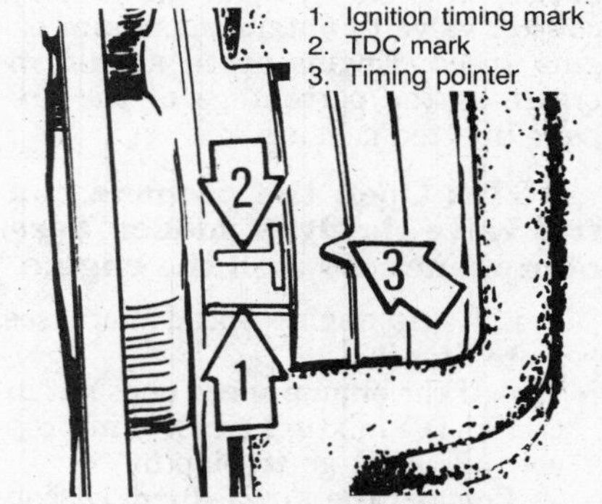


Timing marks—all except 1342 & 1488cc engines

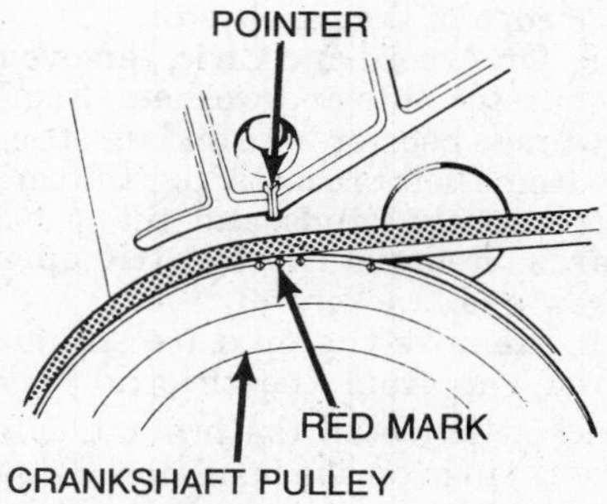


1342 and 1488cc timing marks

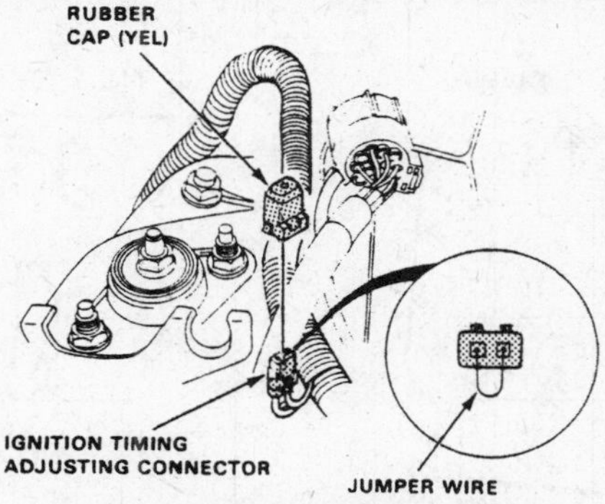


Location of ignition timing adjusting connector—1988–90 Civic

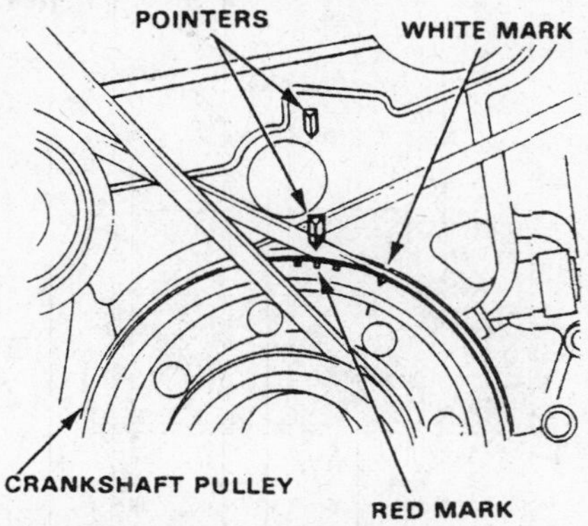


Location of ignition timing marks—1988–90 Civic

4. At any engine speed other than the specified idle speed, the distributor advance or retard mechanisms will actuate, leading to an erroneous timing adjustment.

**NOTE: Make sure that the parking brake is firmly applied and the front wheels are blocked to prevent the vehicle from rolling forward when the automatic transaxle is engaged.**

5. Disconnect and plug the vacuum hoses from the vacuum advance diaphragm. On the Accord and Prelude, be sure to remove the rubber cap from the inspection window on the cylinder block.
6. If necessary, adjust the timing by loosening the larger distributor holddown bolt and slowly rotating the distributor in the required direction while observing the timing marks.

**CAUTION**

***Do not grasp the top of the distributor cap while the engine is running as you might get a nasty shock. Instead, grab the distributor housing to rotate it.***

7. After making the necessary adjustment, tighten the holddown bolt, taking care not to disturb the adjustment.
8. Recheck the ignition timing and adjust as necessary also readjust the idle speed as necessary.

**NOTE: There are actually 2 bolts which may be loosened to adjust the ignition timing. There is a small bolt on the underside of the distributor swivel mounting plate. This smaller bolt should not be loosened unless you cannot obtain a satisfactory adjustment using the upper bolt. Its purpose is to provide an extra range of adjustment such as in cases in which the distributor was removed and then installed 1 tooth off.**

## Valve Lash

The valve clearance should be checked at 15,000 mile intervals. While all valve adjustments must be as accurate as possible, it is better to have the valves adjusted slightly loose than slightly tight, as burned valves may result from overly tight adjustments.

### ADJUSTMENT

1. Disconnect the negative battery cable. Make sure that the engine is cold.
2. Remove the valve cover.
3. Set the No. 1 cylinder to top dead center (TDC).
4. Take some white or yellow chalk or a pencil and mark where the No. 1 spark plug wire goes into the distributor cap on the distributor body.
5. Then, remove the cap and check that the rotor points toward that mark.
6. With the No. 1 cylinder at TDC adjust the valves on the No. 1 cylinder.
7. Check the valve clearance with a flat feeler gauge between the tip of the rocker arm and the top of the valve. There should be a slight drag on the feeler gauge.
8. If there is no drag or if the gauge cannot be inserted, loosen the valve adjusting screw locknut.
9. Turn the adjusting screw with a suitable tool to obtain the proper clearance. Hold the adjusting screw and tighten the locknut. Recheck the clearance.
10. Turn the crankshaft 180 degrees counterclockwise (the cam pulley will turn 90 degrees). With the No. 3 cylinder at TDC (the distributor rotor should be pointing to the No. 3 plug wire) adjust the valves on the No. 3 cylinder.
11. Turn the crankshaft 180 degrees counterclockwise (the cam pulley will turn 90 degrees). With the No. 4 cylinder at TDC (the distributor rotor now

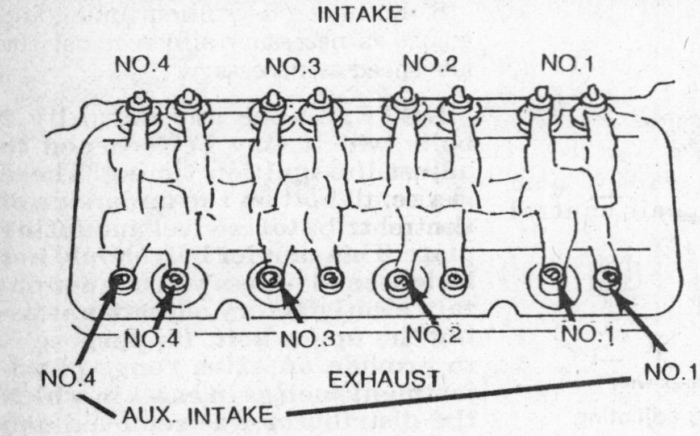

Valve locations—CVCC 12 valve engines

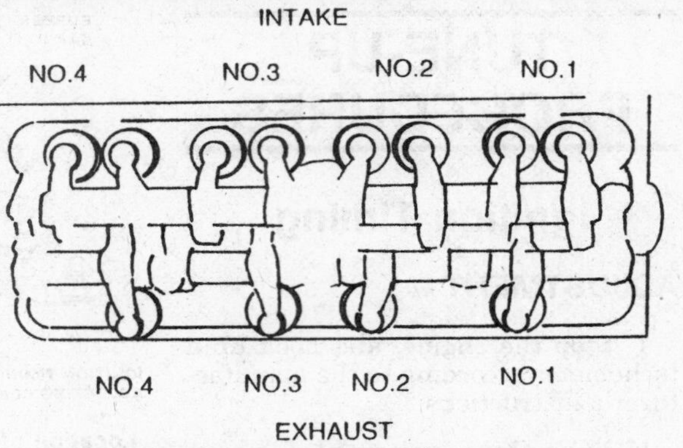

Valve locations—non-CVCC 12 valve engines

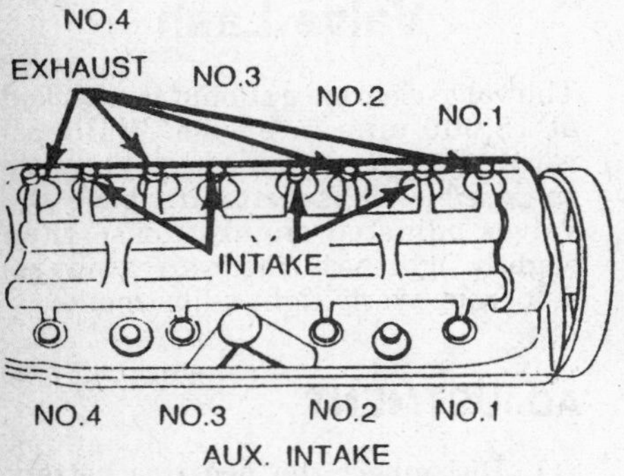

Valve locations—CVCC 8 valve engines

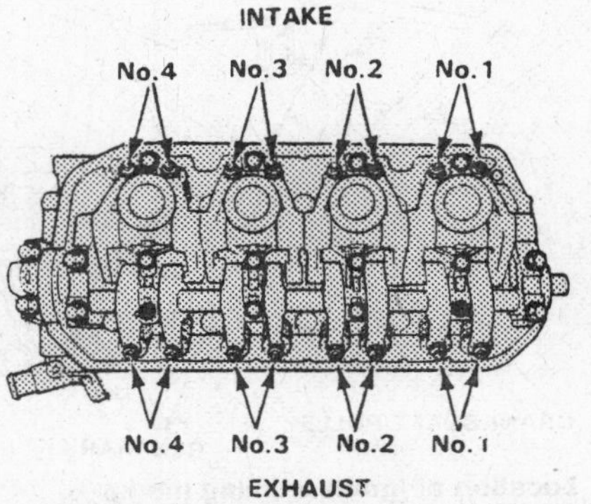

Valve adjustment—1493cc and 1590cc Std and Si engines

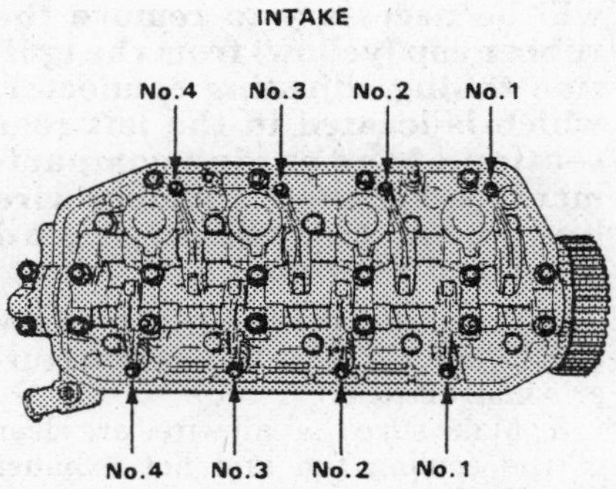

Valve adjustment—1493cc and 1590cc HF engine

pointing to the No. 4 plug wire) adjust the valves on the No. 4 cylinder.

12. Turn the crankshaft 180 degrees counterclockwise once again. The No. 2 cylinder will now be on TDC (this can be confirmed by the distributor rotor pointing to the No. 2 plug wire). The valves on the No. 2 cylinder may now be adjusted.

## Idle Speed and Mixture

### ADJUSTMENT

#### *Carbureted Vehicles*

#### EXCEPT KEIHIN 2 BBL AND DUAL SIDEDRAFT

**NOTE: This procedure requires a propane enrichment kit.**

1. Start the engine and warm it up to normal operating temperature. The cooling fan will operate.
2. Remove the vacuum hose from the intake air control diaphragm and clamp the hose end.
3. Connect a tachometer to the engine as per the manufacturer's instructions.
4. Check the idle speed with the headlights, heater blower, rear window defroster, cooling fan and the air

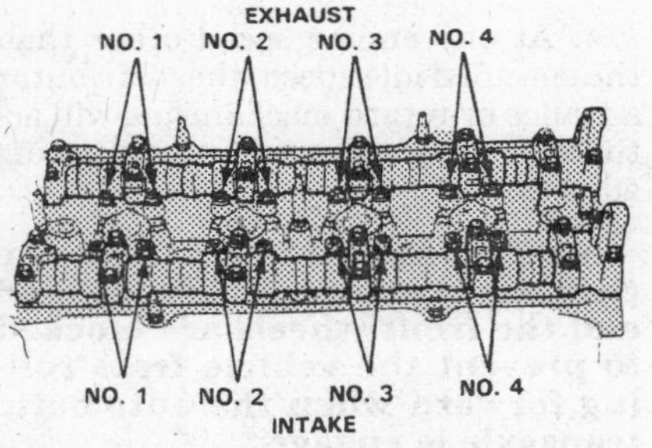

Valve location on the 1955cc DOHC engine

conditioner **OFF**. Idle speed should be set to specifications.

5. Adjust the idle speed if necessary with the throttle stop screw.
   a. On Prelude equipped with automatic transaxle, remove the frequency solenoid valve **A** and the control valve **A**. Disconnect the vacuum tubes and connect the lower hose to the air control valve **A**.
   b. On Accord equipped with automatic transaxle, remove the air filter from the frequency solenoid valve **C** and plug the opening in the solenoid valve.
   c. On all vehicles, insert the tube of the propane enrichment kit into the air intake tube about 4 in.
6. With the engine idling, depress the push button on top of the propane device, then slowly open the propane control valve to obtain maximum engine speed. Engine speed should increase as the percentage of the propane injected goes up.

**NOTE: Open the propane control valve slowly; a sudden burst of propane may stall the engine.**

   a. If the engine speed increases, go to Step 13.
   b. If the engine speed does not increase, the mixture screw is improperly adjusted; go to Step 6.
7. Remove the air cleaner. Disconnect the vacuum hose from the fast idle unloader. Remove the bolts holding the throttle opener bracket to the rear edge of the carburetor.
8. On Accord and Civic, remove the carburetor nuts and washers. Remove the brake booster hose and throttle cable from their brackets. Lift the carburetor off the studs and tilt it backwards. Remove the throttle opener screw and bracket.
9. Remove the mixture adjusting screw cap from the throttle opener bracket. Reinstall the bracket. Using new O-rings on the insulator and new gaskets on the heat shield, install the carburetor.

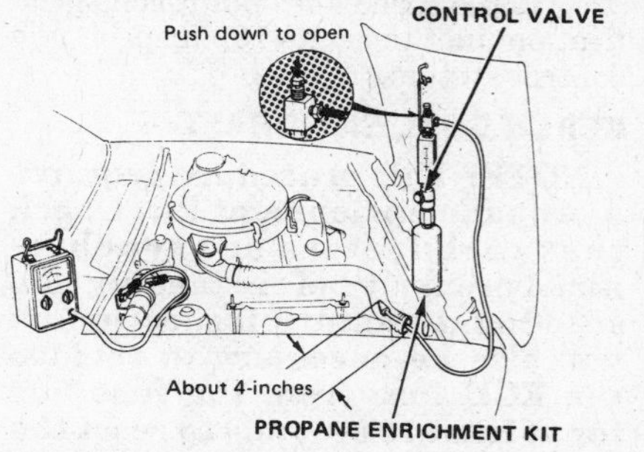


**Mixture adjustment using propane enrichment method**

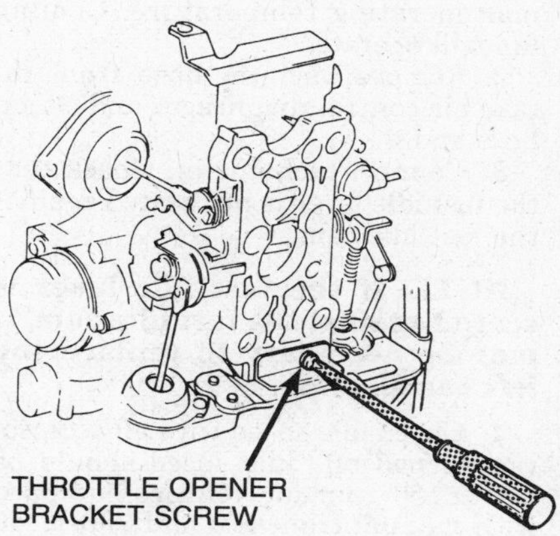


**Civic and Accord throttle opener bracket**

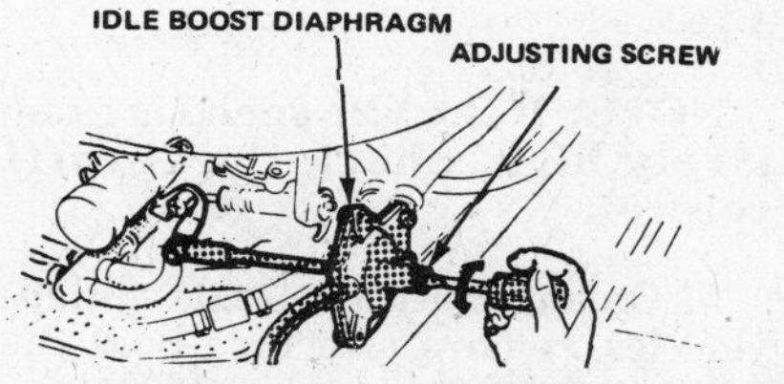


**Adjusting idle boost diaphragm**

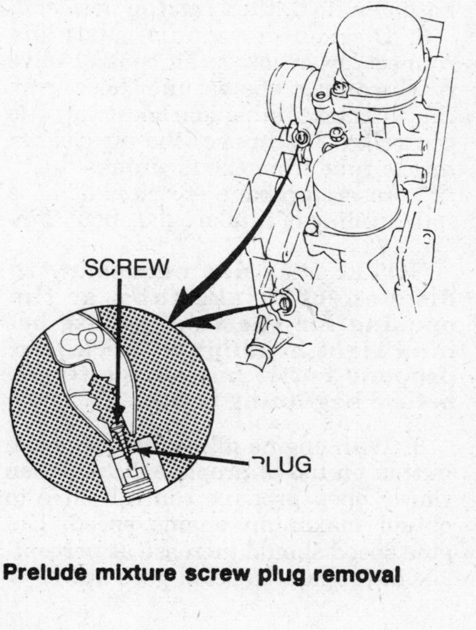


**Prelude mixture screw plug removal**

10. Reconnect the vacuum hose to the fast idle unloader.
11. Install the air cleaner, start the engine and warm it to normal operating temperature. The cooling fan will come on.
12. Disconnect and plug the vacuum hose from the intake air control diaphragm.
13. On Prelude, label and disconnect all the lines from the carburetors. Disconnect the throttle cable and the vacuum hose from the throttle opener diaphragm. Disconnect the automatic choke lead. Drain the coolant and disconnect hoses. Remove the carburetors.
14. Place a drill stop on a 3mm drill bit, 3mm from end. Drill through the center of the mixture screw plug. Screw a 5mm sheet metal screw into the plug. Grab the screw head with a pair of pliers and remove the plug. Reinstall the carburetors in the reverse order of removal and refill the cooling system.
15. On all vehicles, install the propane enrichment kit and recheck the maximum propane enriched rpm. If the enriched rpm is too low, lean out the mixture. If it is too high, enrichen the mixture. Turn the mixture screw clockwise to increase rpm; counterclockwise to decrease rpm.
16. Run the engine for about 10 seconds to stabilize the mixture. Close the propane control valve and recheck the idle speed. Repeat the procedure until the idle rpm is correct. Remove the propane enrichment kit and reconnect the air cleaner intake tube.

### KEIHIN 2 BBL

#### Except 1986–90 Accord with Automatic Transaxle

**NOTE: This procedure requires a propane enrichment kit.**

1. Place the vehicle in the **P** or **N** position, apply the emergency brake and block the drive wheels. Start the engine and warm it up to normal operating temperature. The cooling fan should come on.
2. Remove (the No. 8) vacuum hose from the intake air control diaphragm and clamp the hose end.
3. Connect a suitable tachometer to the engine using the manufacturers instructions.
4. Check the idle speed with all the accessories turned off. Adjust the idle speed by turning the throttle stop screw, if necessary.
5. Disconnect the air cleaner intake tube from the air duct on the radiator bulkhead.
6. Insert the hose from the propane kit into the intake tube approximately 4 inches.

**NOTE: Be sure that the propane bottle has an adequate supply of gas before begining going any further with this procedure.**

7. With the engine idling, depress the push button on top of the propane device, then slowly open the propane control valve to obtain the maximum engine speed. The engine speed should increase as the percentage of propane injected goes up.

**NOTE: Open the propane control valve slowly, because a sudden burst of propane may cause the engine to stall.**

8. The engine idle speed should increase as follows:
a.Civic 1342cc and 1488cc HF engine with manual transaxle – 125 ± 25 rpm
b.Civic 1488cc (except the HF engine) with manual transaxle – 100 ± 25 rpm
c.Civic 1488cc (except the HF engine) with automatic transaxle – 50 ± 20 rpm
d.1984–85 Accord with manual transaxle – 100 ± 25 rpm
e.1984–85 Accord with automatic transaxle – 50 ± 20 rpm
f.1986 Accord with manual transaxle – 35 ± 20 rpm
g.1987–90 Accord with manual transaxle – 50 ± 20 rpm
9. If the engine speed increases according to specifications, remove the propane kit, all test equipment and reconnect all disconnected vacuum hoses. If the engine speed fails to increase as specified, go on with the following steps.
10. Disconnect the vacuum hose to the fast idle unloader. Pull the throttle cable out of the bracket.
11. Remove the carburetor nuts and washers and bolts securing the steel tubing vacuum manifold. Lift the carburetor clear off the studs, then tilt it backward to obtain the access to the throttle controller bracket screws.
12. Remove the throttle controller bracket. Remove the mixture adjusting screw hole cap from the throttle controller bracket and then reinstall the bracket.
13. Reinstall the carburetor, reconnect the vacuum hose to the fast idle unloader. Reinstall the air cleaner.
14. Start the engine and let it warm up to normal operating temperature, the cooling fan will come on.
15. Remove the vacuum hose from the intake air control diaphragm and clamp the hose end. Reinstall the propane enrichment kit and recheck the maximum propane enrichment rpm.
16. If the propane enriched speed is to low, the mixture is rich. Turn the

mixture screw a 1/4 turn clockwise and recheck.

17. If the propane enriched speed is to high, the mixture is lean. Turn the mixture screw a 1/4 turn counterclockwise and recheck.

18. Close the propane control valve and recheck the idle speed. Be sure to run the engine at 2500 rpm for 10 seconds to stabilize the idle condition.

19. If the engine speed is set to specifications, remove the propane enrichment kit, all test equipment and reconnect all vacuum hoses and the air cleaner intake tube.

20. If the engine speed is not set to specifications, recheck the engine speed and if necessary adjust by turning the throttle stop screw, then repeat Steps 14–19.

21. Reinstall the mixture adjusting screw hole cap. Check the idle controller booster speed, if so equipped.

**NOTE: There is no idle controller on automatic transaxle vehicles without air conditioning and power steering. On vehicles except the 1488cc engine without automatic transaxle and power steering, check the idle speed with the headlights ON and the heater blower set on high (III). On vehicles with the 1488cc engine and automatic transaxle and with power steering, check the idle speed with the steering turned fully to the right or left.**

22. Adjust the idle speed, if necessary by turning the idle control screw.

**NOTE: On the Civic, equipped with power steering, when adjusting the idle speed, disconnect the power steering oil pressure switch wires and connect the wire terminals with a jumper wire to operate the idle controller. Keep the steering wheel pointed straight ahead.**

23. If equipped with air conditioning, make a second check with the air conditioning on. Adjust the speed if necessary by turning the adjusting screw on the idle boost diaphragm.

**NOTE: Some 1984 Accords may develope a stalling problem at idle. The cause of this stalling, is a sticking slow mixture cut-off solenoid. If this is the case the solenoid should be removed and replaced with the updated type of solenoid.**

### 1986–90 Accord with Automatic Transaxle

1. Place the vehicle in the **P** or **N** position, apply the emergency brake and block the drive wheels. Start the engine and warm it up to normal operating temperature. The cooling fan should operate.

2. Remove vacuum hose from the intake air control diaphragm and clamp the hose end.

3. Connect a suitable tachometer to the engine using the manufacturers instructions.

4. Remove air filter from frequency solenoid valve C and plug opening in solenoid valve.

5. With no engine load, lower idle speed as much as possible by turning throttle stop screw.

6. Adjust idle speed by turning idle control screw to 600 ± 50 rpm on 1986 vehicles and 630 ± 50 on 1987–90 vehicles.

7. With headlights and rear defroster ON, and heater blower to maximum, adjust idle speed by turning adjusting screw A. Idle should be 600 ± 50 rpm on 1986 vehicles and 700 ± 50 on 1987–90 vehicles.

8. If equipped with air conditioning, adjust idle speed by turning adjusting screw B to 700 ± 50 rpm with air conditioning on.

9. With no engine load, remove inside vacuum hose from idle boost throttle controller and plus hose.

10. Adjust idle speed by turning throttle stop screw to 700 ± 50 rpm (650 ± 50 rpm on high altitude vehicle).

11. Disconnect hose from frequency solenoid valve A and connect to air control valve A.

12. Check maximum engine speed by propane enrichment method, rpm increase should be 135 ± 25 rpm.

13. If engine speed does not increase per specification, adjust enriched speed by turning mixing screw.

14. Stop engine. Close propane control valve, remove all plugs, and reconnect all hoses.

15. Restart engine and recheck idle speed.

**NOTE: Raise engine speed to 2500 rpm 2 or 3 times in 10 seconds, and then check idle speed. Idle speed should be 700 ± 50 rpm on 1986 vehicles and 730 ± 50 on 1987–90 vehicles.**

16. Recheck idle speed with headlights, heater blower and rear window defroster on. Idle speed should be 700 ± 50 rpm.

17. Recheck idle speed with automatic transaxle lever in gear. Idle speed should be 700 ± 50 rpm.

18. Recheck idle speed with air conditioning on and with shift lever in **P** or **N** position. Idle speed should be 750 ± 50 rpm.

19. Recheck idle speed with air conditioning on and in gear. Idle should be 750 ± 50 rpm.

20. If idle speed does not reach specification in Steps 15–19, inspect idle control system.

### KEIHIN DUAL SIDEDRAFT

**NOTE: This procedure requires a propane enrichment kit. Check that carburetors are synchronized properly before making idle speed and mixture inspection. It will also be necessary to remove the ECU fuse from the fuse box for at least 10 seconds to reset the control unit, after this procedure is complete.**

1. Start engine and warm up to normal operating temperature. Cooling fan will operate.

2. Remove vacuum hose from intake air control diaphragm and clamp hose end.

3. Connect tachometer. Check that the fast idle lever is not seated against the fast idle cam.

**NOTE: If the fast idle lever is seated against the fast idle cam, it may be necessary to replace the left carburetor.**

4. Check idle speed with all accessories turned off. Idle speed should be 800 ± 50 rpm for vehicles equipped with manual transaxle and 750 ± 50 rpm on vehicles equipped with automatic transaxle. Adjust idle speed, if necessary, by turning throttle stop screw.

**NOTE: If the idle speed is excessively high, check the throttle control.**

5. On automatic transaxle equipped vehicles, remove attaching bolt, then remove frequency solenoid valve **A** and air control valve **A**. Disconnect the 2 prong connector from the EACV and disconnect the hose from the vacuum hose manifold, then cap the hose end.

6. Disconnect vacuum tubes and connect lower hose to air control valve **A**. Disconnect the vacuum hose from the air conditioning idle boost throttle controller. Disconnect the air cleaner intake tube from the air intake duct.

7. Insert propane enrichment hose into opening of intake tube about 4 in.

**NOTE: It is not necessary to disconnect intake tube, as the opening for the tube is just behind right headlight. Check that propane bottle has adequate gas before beginning test.**

8. With engine idling, depress push button on top of propane device, then slowly open propane control valve to obtain maximum engine speed. Engine speed should increase as percentage of propane injected goes up.

**NOTE: Open propane control valve slowly. Sudden burst of propane may stall engine.**

9. Propane enrichment maximum rpm:
a. 1983–86 Prelude with manual transaxle – 45 ± 25 rpm
b. 1983–86 Prelude with automatic transaxle – 110 ± 25 rpm (in D3 or D4)
c. 1987 Prelude with manual transaxle – 65 ± 20 rpm
d. 1987 Prelude with automatic transaxle – 130 ± 25 rpm (in D3 or D4)
e. 1988–90 Prelude with manual transaxle – 170 ± 20 rpm
f. 1988–90 Prelude with automatic transaxle – 50 ± 10 rpm

10. If engine speed does not increase per specification, remove carburetor.
11. Place a drill stop on a 1/8 in. (3mm) drill bit, then drill through center of mixture screw hole plug.

**NOTE: If drilled deeper than this measurement, damage to mixture adjusting screw may result from bit. On the later vehicles, remove the mixture adjusting screw hole caps, by pulling them straight out.**

12. Screw a 5mm sheet metal screw into hole plug.
13. Grab screw head with a pair of pliers and remove hole plug.
14. Reinstall carburetor.
15. Start engine and warm up to normal operating temperature. Cooling fan will operate.
16. Recheck maximum propane enriched rpm. If mixture is rich, turn both mixture screws 1/4 turn counterclockwise.
17. Close propane control valve.
18. Run engine at 2500 rpm for 1800 seconds to stabilize mixture conditions, then check idle speed. Adjust idle speed, if necessary.
19. On 1984–86 vehicles, remove propane enrichment kit and reconnect intake air control diaphragm hose. Install new plugs into idle mixture screw holes.
20. On 1987–90 vehicles, disconnect the No.1 5 vacuum hose from air suction valve and plug hose.
21. Disconnect upper No. 22 vacuum hose from air leak solenoid valve at air jet controller stay, and plug end of hose, than connect a vacuum gauge to solenoid valve.
22. With engine idling, depress push button on top of propane device, then slowly open propane control valve and check vacuum. Vacuum should be available.
23. If no vacuum, inspect air leak solenoid valve.
24. Inspect thermo valve **C**.
25. Remove propane enrichment kit and reconnect connector.

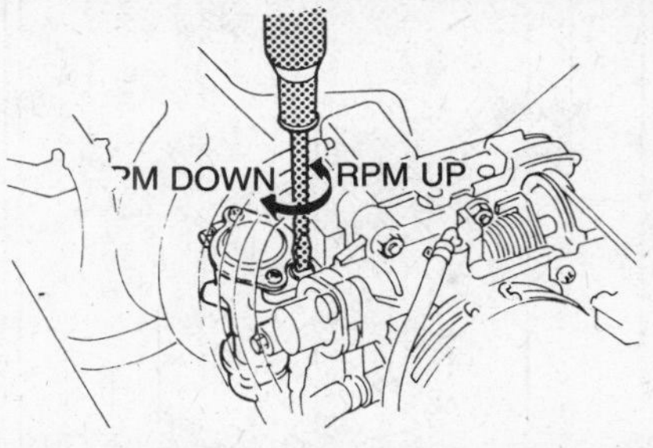

**Fuel injection idle speed adjustment screw – 1488cc and 1829cc engines**

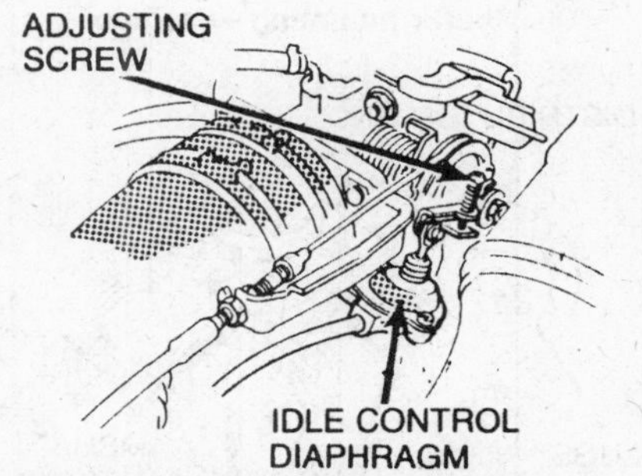

**Fuel injected engine – secondary idle speed adjustment 1488cc and 1829cc engines**

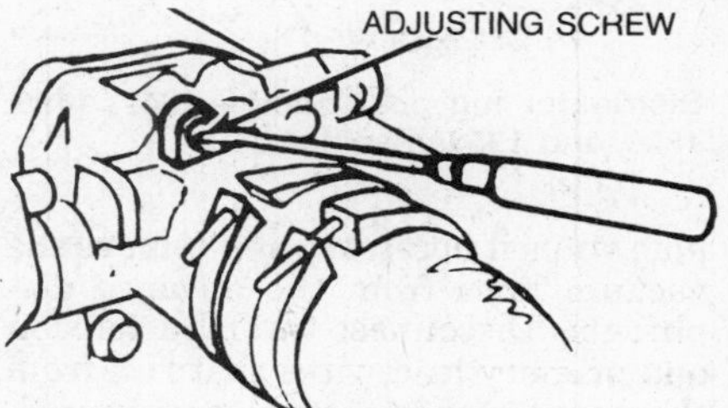

**Fuel injection idle speed adjustment screw—1955cc engine**

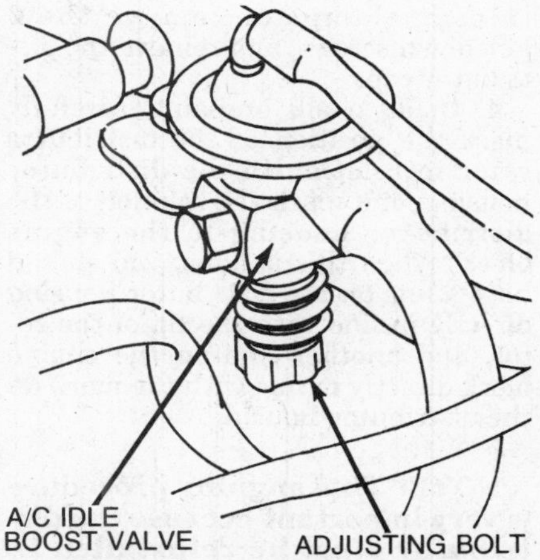

**Fuel injection secondary idle speed adjustment—1955cc engine**

26. Install new plugs into idle mixture screw holes.

**NOTE: Some 1984–85 Preludes may experience hesitation on acceleration before the engine has reached normal operating temperature. This can be corrected by installing a cold driveability kit from the manufacturer so as to hold a full vacuum advance when the engine is cold.**

### *Fuel Injected Vehicles*

**NOTE: The idle mixture is electronically controlled and is not adjustable.**

#### 1985–87 CIVIC AND 1985 ACCORD

1. Start engine and warm up to normal operating temperature; cooling fan will operate.
2. Connect a suitable tachometer using the manufacturers instructions.
3. Check idle speed with all accessories off.

**NOTE: To prevent idle control system from operating pinch vacuum hose (No. 10 on 1985–87 Civic and No. 27 on 1985 Accord).**

4. Idle speed should be 750 ± 50 rpm in **N**. Adjust idle speed, if necessary, by turning idle adjusting screw, check fast idle valve.
5. Check idle controller boosted speed with air conditioning on. Idle speed should be 750 ± 50 rpm for the Civic and 800 ± 50 rpm for the Accord.
6. Adjust idle speed, if necessary, by turning adjusting screw **B**.

#### 1986–87 ACCORD AND PRELUDE

1. Start engine and warm up to normal operating temperature; cooling fan will operate twice.
2. Connect tachometer.
3. Disconnect upper vacuum hose of idle control solenoid valve (between valve and intake manifold) from intake manifold.
4. Cap end of hose and intake manifold.
5. With all accessories off, check idle speed. Idle speed should be 750 ± 50 rpm in Neutral. Adjust idle speed, if necessary, by turning idle adjusting screw.
6. Check idle speed with heater fan switch at HI and air conditioning on. Idle speed should be 750 ± 50 rpm in Neutral. Adjust idle speed, if necessary, by turning adjusting bolt on air conditioning idle boost valve..
7. After adjustment, connect idle control solenoid valve vacuum hose.
8. On automatic transaxle equipped vehicles, after adjusting idle speed, check that it remains within specified limit when shifted in gear. Idle speed should be 750 ± 50 rpm.
9. Check idle speed with all accesso-

ries on and air conditioning off. Idle should remain 750 ± 50 rpm.

### 1988–90 CIVIC, ACCORD AND PRELUDE

1. Start engine and warm up to normal operating temperature; cooling fan will operate twice.
2. Connect tachometer.
3. Disconnect the 2 prong connector on the EACV, which is located near the throttle body.
4. Set the steering in the straight forward position and check the idle speed with all the accessories in the OFF position. The idle speed should be 625 ± 50 rpm for the Civic and 650 ± 50 rpm for the Accord and Prelude.
5. If the idle speed is out of specifications, adjust it by turning the idle adjusting screw, located on the throttle body.

**NOTE: If the idle speed is excessively high, be sure to check the throttle control system, if so equipped.**

6. Reconnect the 2 prong connector to the EACV, then remove the hazard fuse (the No. 11, 10 amp fuse on the Accord and Prelude) in the main fuse box for 10 seconds to reset the ECU.
7. Set the steering in the straight forward position and check the idle speed with all the accessories in the **OFF** position. The idle speed should be 725 ± 50 rpm for the Civic and 750 ± 50 rpm for the Accord and Prelude.
8. Idle the engine for at least a minute with all the accessories ON. If the vehicle is equipped with an automatic transaxle, block the drive wheels, apply the emergency brake and place it gear. The idle speed should now be 780 ± 50 rpm for the Civic and 750 ± 50 rpm for the Accord and Prelude.
9. Idle the engine for at least a minute with the heater fan switch on the HI position and the air conditioner ON. The idle speed should be 780 ± 50 rpm for the Civic and 750 ± 50 rpm for the Accord and Prelude.
10. After the idle speed has been set and rechecked, turn off the engine and remove all test equipment.

# ENGINE ELECTRICAL

## Distributor

### REMOVAL & INSTALLATION

1. Disconnect the nagative battery cable. Disconnect and tag the spark

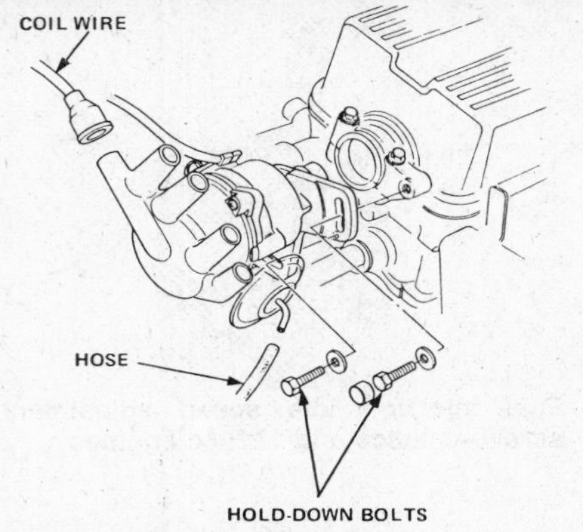


**Distributor mounting – Prelude**

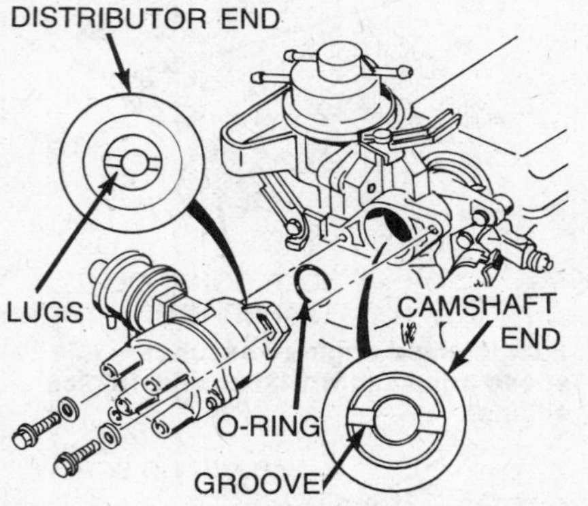


**Distributor lug positioning—1342, 1488, 1829, and 1955cc engines**

plug wires if necessary and remove the vacuum lines from the advance diaphragm. Disconnect the high tension and primary lead wires that run from the distributor to the coil, as required.

2. Disconnect the required electrical prong connectors from the distributor assembly.
3. Unsnap the 2 distributor cap retaining clamps or remove the 2 holddown screws, and remove the distributor cap.
4. Using chalk or paint, carefully mark the position of the distributor rotor in relation to the distributor housing, and mark the relation of the distributor housing to the engine block. When this is done, you should have a line on the distributor housing directly in line with the tip of the rotor, and another line on the engine block directly in line with the mark on the distributor housing.

**NOTE: This aligning procedure is very important because the distributor must be reinstalled in the exact location from which it was removed, if correct ignition timing is to be maintained.**

5. Note the position of the vacuum line(s) on the vacuum diaphragm with masking tape and then disconnect the lines from the vacuum unit.
6. Remove the bolt which attaches the distributor to the engine block, cylinder head or distributor extension housing, and remove the distributor from the engine.

**NOTE: Do not disturb the engine while the distributor is removed. If you attempt to start the engine with the distributor removed, you will have to retime the engine. The lugs on the end of the distributor and its mating grooves in the camshaft end are both offset so as to eliminate the possibility of installing the distributor 180 degrees out of time.**

7. To install, place the rotor on the distributor shaft and align the tip of the rotor with the line that you made on the distributor housing.
8. With the rotor and housing aligned, insert the distributor into the engine while aligning the mark on the housing with the mark on the block, cylinder head or extension housing.

Since the distributor pinion gear has helical teeth on some engines, the rotor will turn slightly as the gear on the distributor meshes with the gear on the camshaft. Allow for this when installing the distributor by aligning the mark on the distributor with the mark on the block, by positioning the tip of the rotor slightly to the side of the mark on the distributor.

On some engines, the distributors are equipped with a coupling that connects them to the camshaft. The lugs at the end of the coupling and its mating grooves in the end of the camshaft are offset to prevent installing the distributor 180 degrees out of time.

9. When the distributor is fully seated in the engine, install and tighten the distributor retaining bolt.
10. Align and install the distributor cap and snap the retaining clamps into place or install the 2 holddown screws.
11. Install the high tension and primary wires onto the coil, as required.
12. Connect the required electrical connectors. Check the ignition timing.

## Alternator

### PRECAUTIONS

Observe the proper polarity of the battery connections by making sure that the positive (+) and negative (–) terminal connections are not reversed. Disconnection will allow current to flow in the reverse direction, resulting in damaged diodes and an overheated wiring harness.

- Never ground or short out any alternator or alternator regulator terminals.

## ALTERNATOR BELT TENSION

| Vehicle | Old Belt in. (mm) | New Belt in. (mm) |
|---|---|---|
| Civic | 0.35–0.43 (9-11) | 0.25–0.35 (7–9) |
| Accord | 0.24–0.35 (6-9) | 0.16–0.24 (4–6) |
| Prelude | 0.39–0.47 (10-12) | 0.31–0.39 (8–10) |

- Never operate the alternator with any of its or the battery's leads disconnected.
- Always remove the battery or disconnect its output lead while charging it.
- Always disconnect the ground cable when replacing any electrical components.
- Never subject the alternator to excessive heat or dampness if the engine is being steam cleaned.

Never use arc welding equipment with the alternator connected.

### BELT TENSION ADJUSTMENT

The initial inspection and adjustment to the alternator drive belt should be performed after the first 3000 miles or if the alternator has been moved for any reason. Afterwards, you should inspect the belt tension every 12,000 miles. Before adjusting, inspect the belt to see that it is not cracked or worn. Be sure that its surfaces are free of grease and oil.

1. Push down on the belt halfway between pulleys with a force of about 24 lbs. The belt should deflect should be as specified.
2. If the belt tension requires adjustment, loosen the adjusting link bolt and move the alternator with a pry bar positioned against the front of the alternator housing.

**NOTE: Do not apply pressure to any other part of the alternator.**

3. After obtaining the proper tension, tighten the adjusting link bolt.

**NOTE: Do not overtighten the belt. Damage to the alternator bearings could result.**

### REMOVAL & INSTALLATION

1. Disconnect the negative battery cable. On some vehicles the air cleaner assembly must be removed.
2. Label and unplug the wires from the plugs on the rear of the alternator. Remove the clip from the harness bracket.

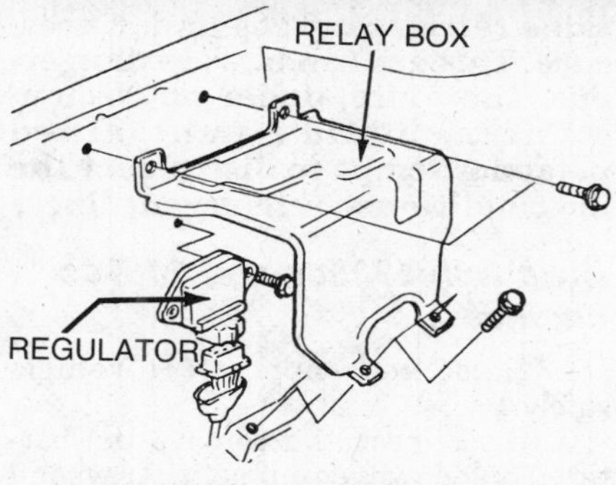

Accord voltage regulator mounting

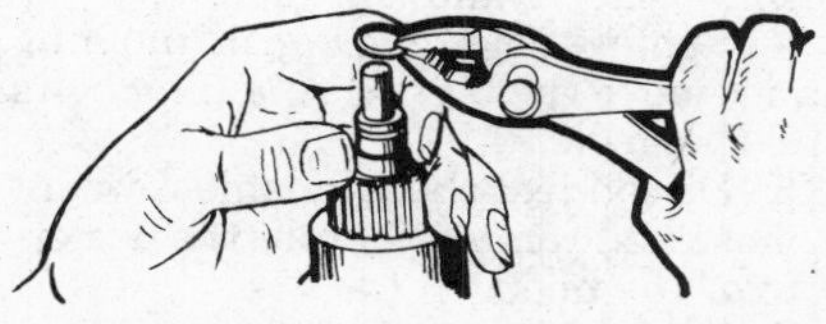
Removing pinion gear from armature

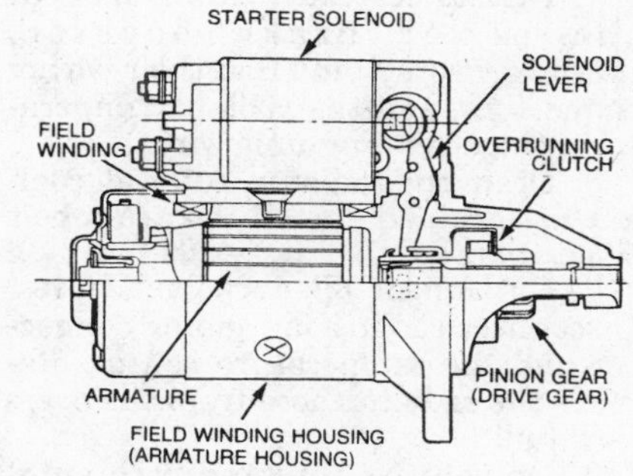

Direct drive starter—typical

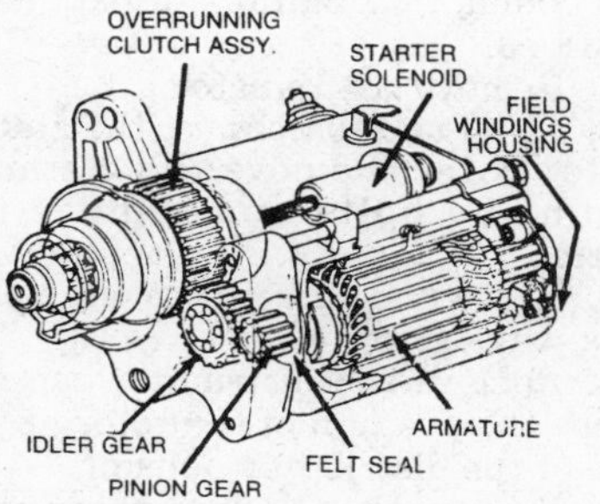

Reduction gear starter—typical

**NOTE: On Accord it may be necessary to remove the left driveshaft from the steering knuckle in order to gain enough access to remove the alternator.**

3. Loosen and remove the alternator mounting bolts and remove the drive belt. Remove the alternator assembly.
4. To install, reverse the removal procedure. Adjust the alternator belt tension.

## Voltage Regulator

### REMOVAL & INSTALLATION

#### *1983 Civic and Prelude*

1. Disconnect the negative battery cable.
2. Remove the regulator terminal lead wires.
3. Unscrew the 2 regulator retaining bolts and remove the regulator from the vehicle.
4. To install, reverse the removal procedure.

#### *1983 Accord*

1. Disconnect the negative battery cable.
2. Remove the 4 main fuse plate retaining bolts and remove the main fuse plate to gain access to the solid state regulator.
3. Remove the regulator terminal plug from the regulator.
4. Unscrew the regulator retaining bolts and remove the regulator from the vehicle.
5. To install, reverse the removal procedure.

## Starter

### REMOVAL & INSTALLATION

1. Disconnect the negative battery cable, and the starter motor cable at the positive terminal. Disconnect the engine compartment sub wiring harness from the harness clip on the starter motor, if equipped.
2. Disconnect the starter motor cable at the motor.
3. Remove the 2 attaching bolts and remove the starter.
4. Reverse the removal procedure to install the motor. Be sure to tighten the attaching bolts to 29–36 ft. lbs. and make sure that all wires are securely connected.

### STARTER DRIVE REPLACEMENT

#### *Direct Drive Type*

1. Remove the solenoid by loosening and removing the attaching bolts.
2. Remove the 2 brush holder plate retaining screws from the rear cover. Also pry off the rear dust cover along with the clip and thrust washer(s).
3. Remove the 2 through bolts from the rear cover and lightly tap the rear cover with a mallet to remove it.
4. Remove the 4 carbon brushes from the brush holder and remove the brush holder.
5. Separate the yoke from the case.

The yoke is provided with a hole for positioning, into which the gear case lock pin is inserted.

6. Pull the yoke assembly from the gear case, being sure to carefully detach the shift lever from the pinion.

7. Remove the armature unit from the yoke casing and the field coil.

8. To remove the pinion gear from the armature, first set the armature on end with the pinion end facing upward and pull the clutch stop collar downward toward the pinion. Then remove the pinion stop clip and pull the pinion stop and gears from the armature shaft as a unit.

9. To assemble the starter motor, reverse the disassembly procedure. Be sure to install new clips, and be careful of the installation direction of the shift lever.

### *Reduction Gear Type*

1. Remove the solenoid end cover. Pull out the solenoid. There is a spring on the shaft and a steel ball at the end of the shaft.

2. Remove the through bolts retaining the end frame to the motor and solenoid housing.

3. Remove the end frame. The overrunning clutch assembly complete with drive gear can be removed. The idler and motor pinion gears can be removed separately. The idler gear retains 5 steel roller bearings.

4. The clutch assembly is held together by a circlip. Push down on the gear against the spring inside the clutch assembly and remove the circlip with a circlip expander. Slide the stopper ring, gear, spring, and washer out of the clutch assembly.

5. Assembly is the reverse of disassembly. The stopper ring is installed with the smaller end lip towards the clutch. Be sure that the steel ball is in place at the end of the solenoid shaft. Grease all sliding surfaces of the solenoid before reassembly.

# ENGINE MECHANICAL

## Engine

### REMOVAL & INSTALLATION

**NOTE: If any repair operation requires the removal of a component of the air conditioning system, the system should be discharged by a trained technician. The air conditioning system contains refrigerant gas under pressure. This gas can be very dangerous. Therefore, under no circumstances should an untrained person attempt to disconnect the air conditioner refrigerant lines.**

### *Civic with 1335cc and 1487cc Engines*

1. Raise and support the vehicle safely.

2. Disconnect and remove the battery, holddown equipment, tray and mount.

3. Remove the headlight rim attaching screws and the rims.

4. Remove the lower grill molding and remove the 6 grille retaining bolts and the grille.

5. Disconnect the windshield washer hose and remove it from the underside of the hood.

6. Remove the upper torque (engine locating) arm.

7. Disconnect the vacuum hose at the power brake booster, thermosensors A and B at their wiring connectors, and the coolant temperature gauge sending unit wire.

8. Drain the radiator. After all coolant has drained, install the drain bolt finger tight.

9. Disconnect all 4 coolant hoses. Disconnect cooling fan motor connector and the temperature sensor. Remove the radiator hose from the overflow tank.

10. On vehicles equipped with automatic transaxle, remove both cooler line bolts. Replace the washers from the cooler line banjo connectors, if damaged.

11. Remove the radiator.

12. Label and disconnect the starter motor wires. Remove the 2 starter mounting bolts and remove the starter.

13. Label and disconnect the spark plug wires at the plug.

14. Remove the distributor cap and scribe the position of the rotor on the side of the distributor housing.

15. Remove the top distributor swivel bolt and remove the distributor. The rotor will rotate 30 degrees because the drive gear is beveled.

16. On vehicles equipped with manual transaxle, remove the C-clip retaining the clutch cable at the firewall. Then, remove the end of the clutch cable from the clutch release arm and bracket. First, pull up on the cable, and then push it out to release it from the bracket. Remove the end from the release arm.

17. Disconnect the back-up light switch wires.

18. Disconnect the control valve vacuum hose, the air intake hose, and the preheat air intake hose.

19. Disconnect the air bleed valve hose from the air cleaner.

20. Label and disconnect all remaining vacuum hoses from the underside of the air cleaner. Remove the air cleaner.

21. Label and disconnect all remaining emission control vacuum hoses from the engine.

22. Disconnect the emission box wiring connector and remove the black emission box from the firewall.

23. Remove the engine mount heat shield.

24. Disconnect the engine-to-body ground strap at the valve cover.

25. Disconnect the alternator wiring connector and oil pressure sensor leads.

26. Disconnect the vacuum hose from the start control and electrical leads to both cut-off solenoid leads.

27. Disconnect the vacuum hose from the charcoal canister and both fuel lines to the carburetor. Mark the adjustment and disconnect the choke and throttle cables at the carburetor.

28. On vehicles equipped with automatic transaxle, remove the center console and disconnect the gear selector control cable at the console. This may be accomplished after removing the retaining clip and pin.

29. Raise and support the vehicle safely. Drain the transaxle oil. Lower the vehicle.

30. On vehicles equipped with air conditioning, be sure to use the following procedure.:

a. Disconnect the heater hose with the heater valve cable attached.

b. Remove the compressor belt cover, then loosen the adjusting nut.

c. Loosen the belt on the compressor hose bracket at the radiator.

d. Remove the compressor mounting bolt then lift the compressor out of the bracket with the hoses attached and wire it up to the firewall.

e. Remove the compressor bracket.

31. Remove the fender well shield under the right fender, exposing the speedometer drive cable. Remove the set screw securing the speedometer drive holder. Then, slowly pull the cable assembly out of the transaxle, taking care not to drop the pin or drive gear. Finally, remove the pin, collar, and drive gear from the cable assembly.

32. Disconnect the front suspension stabilizer bar from its mounts on both sides. Also, remove the bolt retaining the lower control arm to the subframe on both sides.

33. Remove the forward mounting nut on the radius rod on both sides. Then, pry the constant velocity joint out about ½ in. and pull the stub axle

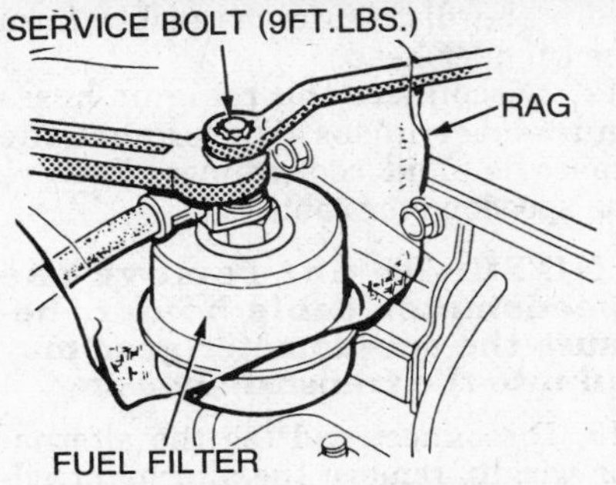

Relieving fuel system pressure

out of the transaxle case. Repeat this procedure for the other side.

34. Remove the 6 retaining bolts and remove the center beam.

35. On vehicles equipped with manual transaxle, drive out the pin retaining the shift linkage.

36. Disconnect the lower torque arm from the transaxle.

37. On vehicles equipped with automatic transaxle, remove the bolt retaining the control cable stay at the transaxle. Loosen the 2 U-bolt nuts and pull the cable out of its housing.

38. Disconnect the exhaust pipe at the manifold. Disconnect the retaining clamp also.

39. Remove the rear engine mount nut.

40. Attach a chain pulley hoist to the engine. Honda recommends using the threaded bolt holes at the extreme right and left ends of the cylinder head (with special hardened bolts) as lifting points, as opposed to wrapping a chain around the entire block and risk damaging some components.

41. Raise the engine enough to place a slight tension on the chain. Remove the nut retaining the front engine mount. Then, remove the 3 bolts retaining the front mount. While lifting the engine, remove the mount.

42. Remove the 3 retaining bolts and push the left engine support into its shock mount bracket to the limit of its travel.

43. Slowly raise the engine out of the vehicle.

44. Install the engine in the reverse order of removal, making the following checks:

a. Make sure the clip at the end of the driveshaft seats into the groove in the differential. You should hear a click as they seat themselves.

**NOTE: Always use new spring clips.**

b. Bleed the air from the cooling system.

c. Adjust the throttle cable tension.

d. Check the clutch for the correct free play.

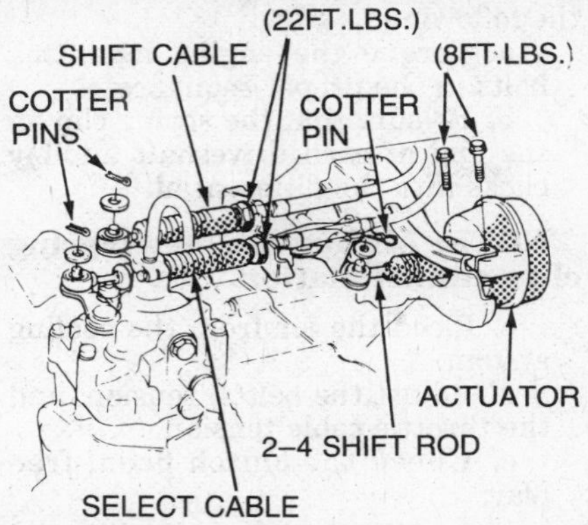

Shift and Selector control cables

e. Make sure the transaxle shifts properly.

### *Civic with 1342cc and 1488cc Engines*

1. Apply the parking brake and place blocks behind the rear wheels. Raise the vehicle and support it safely.

2. Disconnect the battery cables from the battery. Remove the battery, and then remove the battery tray from the engine compartment.

3. Scribe a line where the hood brackets meet the inside of the hood. This will help realign the hood during installation.

4. Disconnect the windshield washer fluid tubes. Unbolt and remove the hood.

5. Remove the engine and wheelwell splash shields.

6. Drain the oil from the engine, the coolant from the radiator, and the transaxle oil from the transaxle.

**NOTE: Removal of the filler plug or cap will speed the draining process.**

7. On carbureted vehicles, remove the air cleaner assembly.

8. On fuel injected vehicles, remove the intake duct and the vacuum hose. Relieve the fuel pressure by slowly loosening the service bolt on the top of the fuel filter about 1 turn.

**NOTE: Place a rag under the filter during this procedure to prevent fuel from spilling onto the engine.**

9. Disconnect the fuel return hose from the pressure regulator. Remove the special nut and then remove the fuel hoses.

10. Disconnect the following hoses and wires:

a. The engine compartment subharness connector.

b. The engine secondary cable.

c. Remove the harness cable from the fuse box.

d. The brake booster vacuum hose.

e. On vehicles equipped with air conditioning, remove the idle control solenoid hoses from the valve and remove the valve.

11. Disconnect the control box connector(s). Remove the control box(es) from the bracket(s), and let it hang next to the engine.

12. Disconnect the purge control solenoid valve vacuum hose at the charcoal canister.

13. Remove the air jet controller, if equipped.

14. Loosen the throttle cable locknut and adjusting nut, then slip the cable end out of the throttle bracket, removing the cable.

15. Disconnect the fuel line hose from the fuel pump. Remove the fuel pump cover and the pump.

16. Remove the spark plug wires and the distributor from the engine.

17. Remove the radiator and heater hoses from the engine.

18. On manual transaxle equipped vehicles, except 4WD, disconnect the transaxle ground cable. Loosen the clutch cable adjusting nut and remove the cable from the release arm. Disconnect the shift lever torque rod from the clutch housing. Slide the shift rod pin retainer out of the way, then with a pin punch, drive the pin out and remove the shift rod.

19. On 4WD vehicles, loosen the clutch adjusting nut and disconnect the clutch cable from the release arm. Disconnect the ground cable from the transaxle. Disconnect the shift control cables. Disconnect the rear axle driveshaft at the transaxle.

20. On vehicles equipped with automatic transaxle, remove the oil cooler hoses at the transaxle, let the fluid drain from the hoses then prop the hoses up out of the way near the radiator. Remove the center console from the inside of the vehicle. Put the shift lever in Reverse and remove the lock pin from the end of the shift cable. Unbolt and remove the shift cable holder. Disconnect the throttle control cable end from the throttle lever. Loosen the lower locknut on the throttle cable bracket and remove the cable from the bracket.

**NOTE: Do not move the upper locknut as it will change the transaxle shift points.**

21. Remove the speedometer cable clip, then pull the cable out of the holder.

**NOTE: Do not remove the holder from the transaxle as it may cause the speedometer gear to fall into the transaxle.**

22. Squirt penetrating oil on the nuts holding the exhaust header pipe in place. Loosen and remove the nuts and pipe.
23. Remove the driveshaft as follows:
  a. Lower the vehicle. Loosen the 32mm spindle nuts with a socket. Raise the vehicle and support it safely.
  b. Remove the front wheel, and the spindle nut.
  c. Place a floor jack under the lower control arm, then remove the ball joint cotter pin and nut.

**NOTE: Be certain the lower control arm is positioned securely on top of the floor jack so that it doesn't suddenly jump or spring off when the ball joint remover tool is used.**

  d. Using a ball joint puller, separate the ball joint from the front hub.
  e. Slowly, lower the floor jack under lower the control arm. Pull the hub outward and off the driveshaft.
  f. Using a small pry bar, pry out the inboard CV joint approximately ½ in. in order to release the spring clip from the groove in the differential.
  g. Pull the driveshaft out of the transaxle case.
24. Attach a lifting sling to the engine block and raise the hoist to remove the slack from the chain.
25. Remove the rear transaxle mount, and remove the bolts from the front transaxle mount and the engine side mount.
26. On vehicles equipped with air conditioning:
  a. Loosen the compressor drive belt adjusting bolts and remove the belt.
  b. Remove the mounting bolts from the air conditioning compressor, then wire it up out of the way on the front beam.

**NOTE: Do not disconnect the air conditioning refrigerant lines; the compressor can be moved without discharging the system.**

  c. Remove the lower compressor mounting bracket.
27. Disconnect the alternator wiring harness connectors. Remove the alternator belt. Remove the alternator mounting bolts and remove the alternator.
28. Check that the engine and transaxle are free from any hoses or electrical connectors.
29. Slowly raise the engine up and out of the vehicle.
30. To install, reverse the removal procedures. Pay special attention to the following:
  a. Torque the engine mounting bolts in the proper sequence.
  b. Be sure that the spring clip on the end of each driveshaft audibly clicks into the differential.

**NOTE: Always use new spring clips on installation.**

  c. Bleed the air from the cooling system.
  d. Adjust the belt(s) tension, and the throttle cable tension.
  e. Check the clutch pedal free play.

### *Civic with 1493cc and 1590cc Engines*

1. Disconnect the negative battery cables. Remove the battery and the battery tray.
2. Apply the parking brake and place blocks behind the rear wheels. Raise the vehicle and support it safely.
3. Scribe a line where the hood brackets meet the inside of the hood.
4. Disconnect the windshield washer fluid tubes. Unbolt and remove the hood.
5. Remove the engine and wheelwell splash shields.
6. Drain the oil from the engine, the coolant from the radiator, and the transaxle oil from the transaxle.
7. Remove the air intake duct and the front air intake duct.
8. Relieve the fuel pressure from the fuel system, by slowly loosening the banjo bolt on the fuel filler approximately 1 turn.

**NOTE: Do not smoke while working on the fuel system. Keep any and all open flames away from the work area. Before disconnecting any fuel lines, the fuel pressure should be relieved. Place a suitable shop towel over the fuel filler to prevent the pressurized fuel from spraying over the engine.**

9. Disconnect and tag the engine compartment harness connectors, battery wires and transaxle ground cable.
10. Remove the throttle cable by loosening the lock nut and the throttle cable adjust nut, then slip the throttle cable end out of the throttle bracket and accelerator linkage. Be sure not to bend the cable when removing it. Do not use pliers to remove the cable from the linkage. Always replace a kinked cable with a new one.
11. Disconnect and tag the engine wire connectors and spark plug wires. Bring the engine up to TDC on the No. 1 cylinder. Mark the distributor in relation with the engine block. Remove the distributor caps and bolts, then remove the distributor assembly from the cylinder head.
12. Disconnect the radiator hoses and heater hoses. Disconnect the transaxle fluid cooler lines. Remove the speedometer cable.

**NOTE: Do not remove the speedometer cable holder, because the speedometer gear may fall into the transaxle housing.**

13. Disconnect and tag the alternator wiring, remove the alternator adjusting bolts, mounting bolts and belt. Remove the alternator from the vehicle.
14. Loosen the air conditioning belt adjust bolt and the idler puller nut. Remove the compressor mounting bolts. Disconnect the air conditioning suction and discharge lines, only if it is necessary. Lift the compressor out of the bracket with the air conditioning hoses attached and wire the compressor to the front beam of the vehicle.

**NOTE: If it is necessary to remove the air conditioning suction and discharge lines, discharge the refrigerant from the air conditioning system. Be sure to discharge the refrigerant into a suitable container and be sure to wear safety goggles and gloves.**

15. On vehicles equipped with automatic transaxles, proceed as follows:
  a. Remove the header pipe, header pipe bracket, torque converter cover and shift control cable holder.
  b. Remove the shift control cable by removing the cotter pin, control pin and control lever roller from the control lever.
16. On vehicles equipped with manual transaxles, remove the shift lever torque rod, shift rod and clutch cable. On reassembly, slide the retainer back into place after driving in the spring pin.
17. Remove the wheelwell splash shields and engine splash shields. Remove the right and left driveshafts (halfshafts) from the transaxle and cover the shafts with a plastic bag so as to prevent the oil from spilling over the work area. Be sure to coat all precision finished surfaces with clean engine oil or grease.
18. On 4WD vehicles equipped with automatic transaxles, remove the cable clip and the control pin. Loosen the shift control cable nut and then remove the control cable.
19. On 4WD vehicles equipped with manual transaxles, remove the cotter pins and the 3 cable bracket mounting bolts. Remove the cable bracket from the rear of the transaxle mount bracket.
20. Attach a suitable chain hoist to the engine block hoist brackets and

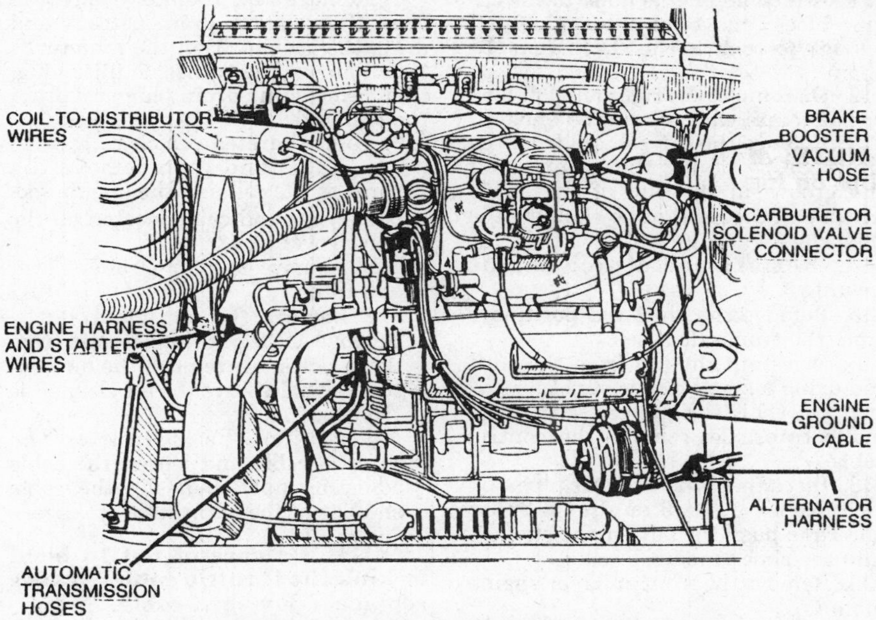


**Component removal points—Accord with 1751cc engine**

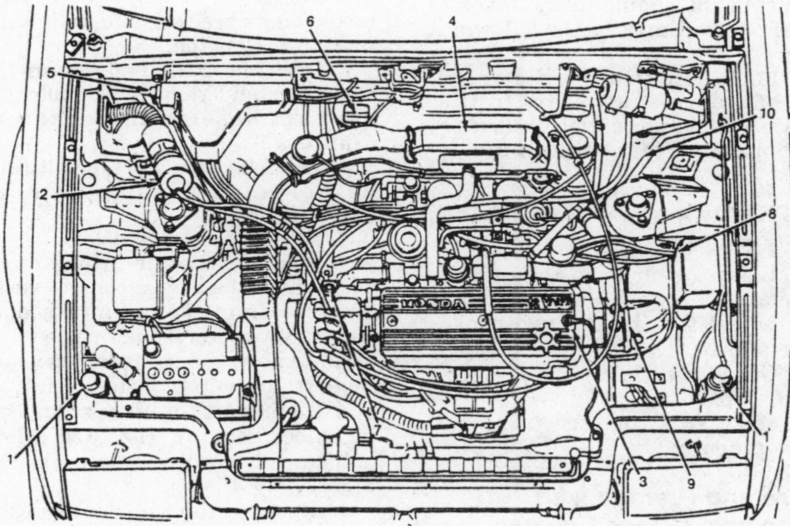

① Headlight retracting knobs
② Ignition coil wires
③ Secondary ground cable
④ Air cleaner assembly
⑤ No. 1 control box connector
⑥ Charcoal canister
⑦ Air bleed bolt for cooling system
⑧ No. 2 control box connector
⑨ Air chamber location (if so equipped)
⑩ Air jet controller location (if so equipped)

**Component removal points—Prelude with 1829cc and 1955cc engines**

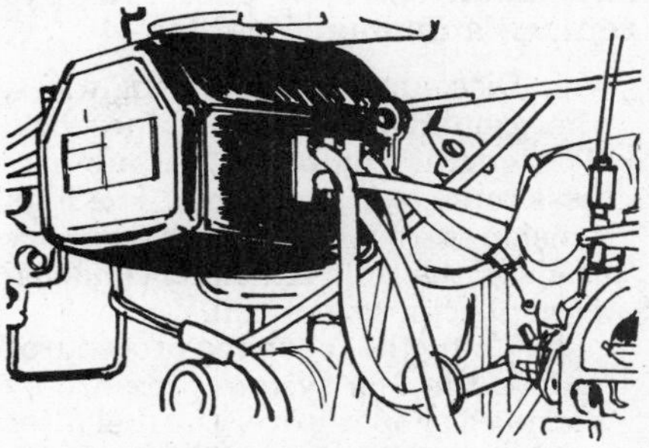

**Emission control box**

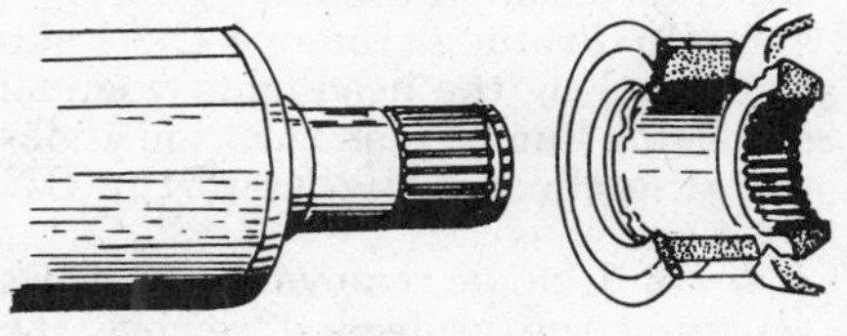

**Accord driveshaft removal**

raise the hoist just enough to remove the slack from the chain. To attach the rear engine chain, remove the plastic radiator hose bracket and hook the chain to the top of the clutch cable bracket.

21. Remove the rear transaxle mount bracket. Remove the bolts from the front transaxle bolt mount. Remove the bolts from the engine side mount. Remove the bolts from the engine side transaxle mounts.

22. Check that the engine/transaxle assembly are completely free of vacuum, fuel, coolant hoses and electrical wires.

23. Slowly raise the engine approximately 6 inches and stop. Check again that the engine/transaxle assembly are completely free of vacuum, fuel, coolant hoses and electrical wires.

24. Raise the engine/transaxle assembly all the way up and out of the vehicle, once it is clear from the vehicle, lower the assembly into a suitable engine stand.

25. Installation is the reverse order of the removal procedure. Use the following steps to aid in the installation procedure.

26. Torque the engine mount bolts in the following sequence; be sure to replace the rear transaxle bolt and the front transaxle bolt with new bolts:

a. Side transaxle mount—40 ft. lbs.

b. Rear transaxle mount bracket—43 ft. lbs.

c. Front transaxle mount—43 ft. lbs.

d. Engine side mount—40 ft. lbs.

**NOTE: Failure to tighten the bolts in the proper sequence can cause excessive noise and vibration and reduce bushing life. Be sure to check that the bushings are not twisted or offset.**

27. Check that the spring clip on the end of each driveshaft clicks into place. Be sure to use new spring clips on installation.

28. After assembling the fuel line parts, turn the ignition switch (do not operate the starter) to the **ON** position so that the fuel pump is operated for approximately 2 seconds so as to pressurize the fuel system. Repeat this procedure 2 or 3 times and check for a possible fuel leak.

29. Bleed the air from the cooling system at the bleed bolt with the heater valve open.

30. Adjust the throttle cable tension, install the air conditioning compressor and belt and adjust all belt tensions. Adjust the clutch cable free play and check that the transaxle shifts into gear smoothly.

31. Check the ignition timing.

32. Install the speedometer cable, be sure to align the tab on the cable end with the slot holder. Install the clip so the bent leg is on the groove side. After

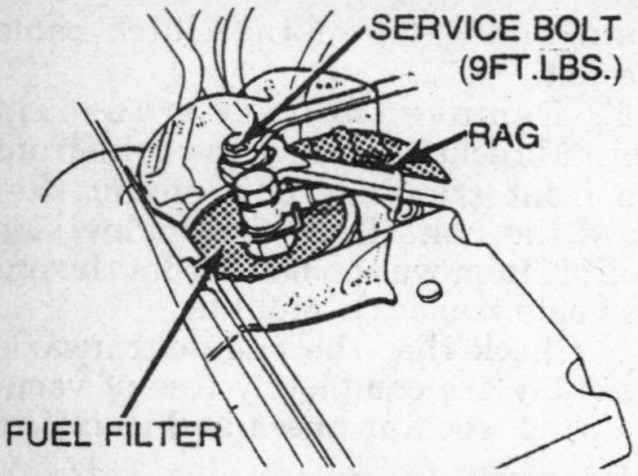

Relieving fuel system pressure

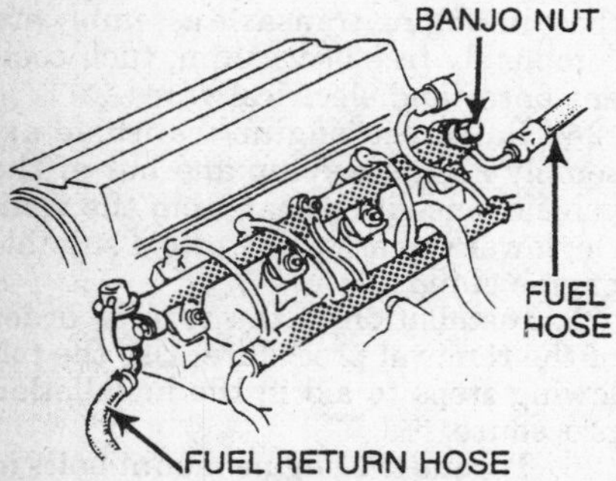

Disconnecting the fuel hoses

installing, pull the speedometer cable to make sure it is secure.

### Accord and Prelude with 1751cc Engine

1. Disconnect the negative battery cable.
2. Drain the coolant, and drain the engine oil.
3. Raise and support the vehicle safely.
4. Remove the air cleaner.
5. Remove the following wires and hoses. The coil wire and the ignition primary wire from the distributor. The engine subharness and the starter wires (mark the wires before removal to ease installation). The vacuum tube from the brake booster.
6. On automatic transaxle equipped vehicles, remove the ATF cooler hose from the transaxle. The engine ground cable. The alternator wiring harness. The carburetor solenoid valve connector. The carburetor fuel line.
7. On California and high altitude vehicles, disconnect the hoses at the air controller.
8. Remove the choke and throttle cables. Remove the radiator and heating hoses. Remove the emission control box.
9. Remove the clutch slave cylinder with the hydraulic line attached.
10. Remove the speedometer cable. Pull the wire clip from the housing, and remove the cable from the housing. Do not, under any circumstances, remove the housing from the transaxle.
11. Attach an engine hoist to the engine block, and raise the engine just enough to remove the slack from the chain.
12. Disconnect the right and left lower ball joints, and the tie rod ends.
13. Remove the driveshafts from the transaxle by prying the snapring off the groove in the end of the shaft. Then, pull the shaft out by holding the knuckle.
14. Remove the center engine mount.
15. Remove the shift rod positioner from the transaxle case.
16. Drive out the pin from the shift rod using a small pin driver.
17. On vehicles equipped with automatic transaxle, remove the control cable.
18. Disconnect the exhaust pipe.
19. Remove the 3 engine support bolts and push the left engine support into the shock mount bracket.
20. Remove the front and rear engine mounts.
21. Raise the engine carefully and remove it from the vehicle.
22. Install the engine in the reverse order of removal, making the following checks:
    a. Make sure that the clip at the end of a driveshaft seats in the groove in the differential. Failure to do so may lead to the wheels falling off.

**NOTE: Always use new spring clips.**

    b. Bleed the air from the cooling system.
    c. Adjust the throttle and choke cable tension.
    d. Check the clutch for the correct free play.
    e. Make sure that the transaxle shifts properly.

### Accord and Prelude with 1829cc and 1955cc Engines

1. Apply the parking brake and place blocks behind the rear wheels. Raise the vehicle and support it safely.
2. Disconnect both battery cables from the battery. Remove the battery, and then remove the battery tray from the engine compartment.
3. On Prelude, remove the knob caps covering the headlights' manual retracting knobs, then turn the knobs to bring the headlights to the **ON** position.
4. On Prelude, remove the 5 screws retaining the grille and remove the grille.
5. Remove the splash guard from under the engine. Unbolt and remove the hood.
6. Remove the oil filler cap and drain the engine oil.
7. Remove the radiator cap, then open the radiator drain petcock and drain the coolant from the radiator.
8. Remove the transaxle filler plug, then remove the drain plug and drain the transaxle.
9. On carbureted vehicles:
    a. Label and then remove the wires at the coil and the engine secondary ground cable located on the valve cover.
    b. Remove the air cleaner cover and filter.
    c. Remove the air intake ducts. Remove the 2 nuts and 2 bolts from the air cleaner, remove the air control valve. Remove the air cleaner as required.
    d. Loosen the locknut on the throttle cable and loosen the cable adjusting nut, then slip the cable end out of the carburetor linkage.

**NOTE: Be careful not to bend or kink the throttle cable. Always replace a damaged cable.**

    e. Disconnect the No. 1 control box connector. Remove the control box from its bracket, and let it hang next to the engine.
    f. Disconnect the fuel line at the fuel filter and remove the solenoid vacuum hose at the charcoal canister.
    g. On California and high altitude vehicles, remove the air jet controller.
10. On fuel injected vehicles:
    a. Remove the air intake duct. Disconnect the cruise control vacuum tube from the air intake duct and remove the resonator tube.
    b. Remove the secondary ground cable from the top of the engine.
    c. Disconnect the air box connecting tube. Unscrew the tube clamp bolt and disconnect the emission tubes.
    d. Remove the air cleaner case mounting nuts and remove the air cleaner case assembly.
    e. Loosen the locknut on the throttle cable and loosen the cable adjusting nut, then slip the cable end out of the bracket and linkage.

**NOTE: Be careful not to bend or kink the throttle cable. Always replace a damaged cable.**

    f. Disconnect the following wires, the ground cable at the fuse box. The engine compartment sub-harness connector and clamp. The high tension wire and ignition primary leads at the coil. The radio condenser connector at the coil.
    g. Using the following procedures relieve the fuel system pressure by placing a shop rag over the fuel filter to absorb any gasoline which may be

sprayed on the engine while relieving the pressure. Slowly loosen the service bolt approximately 1 full turn. This will relieve any pressure in the system. Using a new sealing washer, retighten the service bolt.

h. Disconnect the fuel return hose from the pressure regulator. Remove the banjo nut and then remove the fuel hose.

i. Disconnect the vacuum hose from the brake booster.

11. Disconnect the radiator and heater hoses at the engine. Label the heater hoses so they can be installed correctly.

12. On automatic transaxle equipped vehicles, disconnect the transaxle oil cooler hoses at the transaxle, let the fluid drain from the hoses, then hang the hoses up near the radiator.

13. On manual transaxle equipped vehicles, loosen the clutch cable adjusting nut and remove the clutch cable from the release arm.

14. Disconnect the battery cable at the transaxle and the starter cable at the starter motor terminal.

15. Disconnect both engine harness connectors.

16. Remove the speedometer cable clip, then pull the cable out of the holder.

**NOTE: Do not remove the holder as the speedometer gear may drop into the transaxle.**

17. On vehicles equipped with power steering:

a. Remove the speed sensor complete with hoses.

b. Remove the adjusting bolt and the drive belt.

c. Without disconnecting the hoses, pull the pump away from its mounting bracket and position it out of the way.

d. Remove the power steering hose bracket from the cylinder head.

18. Remove the center beam beneath the engine. On Accord loosen the radius rod nuts to aid in the removal of the driveshafts.

19. On vehicles equipped with air conditioning:

a. Remove the compressor clutch lead wire.

b. Loosen the belt adjusting bolt.

**NOTE: Do not remove the air conditioner hoses. The air conditioner compressor can be moved without discharging the air conditioner system.**

c. Remove the compressor mounting bolts, then lift the compressor out of the bracket with the hoses attached, and hang it on the front bulkhead with a piece of wire.

20. On vehicles equipped with manual transaxle, remove the shift rod yoke attaching bolt and disconnect the shift lever torque rod from the clutch housing.

21. On vehicles equipped with automatic transaxle:

a. Remove the center console.

b. Place the shift lever in reverse, then remove the lock pin from the end of the shift cable.

c. Unscrew the cable mounting bolts and remove the shift cable holder.

d. Remove the throttle cable from the throttle lever. Loosen the lower locknut, then remove the cable from the bracket.

**NOTE: Do not loosen the upper locknut as it will change the transaxle shift points.**

22. Disconnect the right and left lower ball joints and the tie rod ends.

23. Remove the driveshafts as follows:

a. Lower the vehicle. Loosen the 32mm spindle nuts with a socket. Raise and support the vehicle safely.

b. Remove the front wheel, and the spindle nut.

c. Remove the damper fork and the damper pinch bolts.

d. Remove the ball joint bolt and separate the ball joint from the front hub (Accord) or lower arm control (Prelude).

e. Disconnect the tie rods from the steering knuckles.

f. On Accord, remove the sway bar bolts.

g. Pull the front hub outward and off the driveshafts.

h. Using a small pry bar, pry out the inboard CV joint approximately ½ in. in order to release the spring clip from the differential, then pull the driveshaft out of the transaxle case.

**NOTE: When installing the driveshaft, insert the shaft until the spring clip clicks into the groove. Always use a new spring clip when installing driveshafts.**

24. On fuel injected vehicles, disconnect the sub-engine harness connectors and clamp.

25. Remove the exhaust header pipe.

26. Attach a chain hoist to the engine and raise it just enough to remove the slack.

27. Disconnect the No. 2 control box connector, lift the control box off its bracket, and let it hang next to the engine.

28. On vehicles equipped with air conditioning, remove the idle control solenoid valve.

29. Remove the air chamber (if so equipped).

30. Remove the 3 engine mount bolts

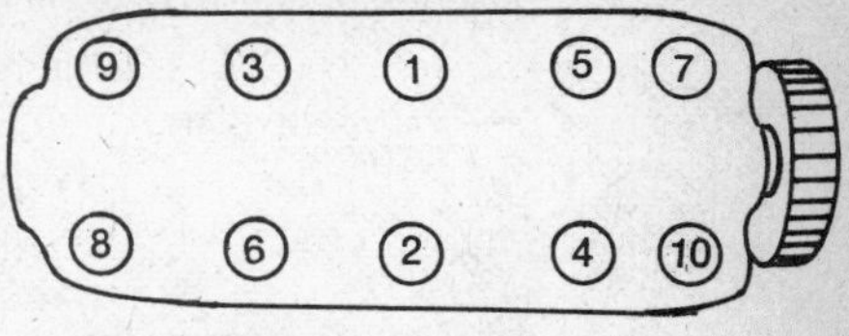


**Cylinder head torque sequence—1335cc, 1487cc and 1751cc engines**

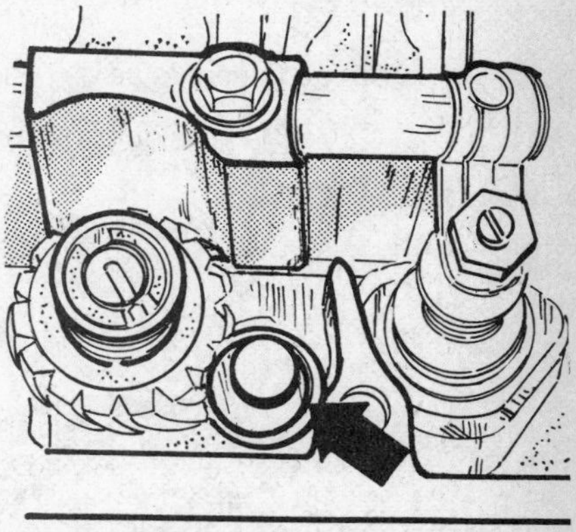

**Hidden bolt next to the oil pump gear**

located under the air chamber, then push the engine mount into the engine mount tower.

31. Remove the front engine mount nut, then remove the rear engine mount nut.

32. Loosen and remove the alternator belt. Disconnect the alternator wire harness and remove the alternator.

33. Remove the bolt from the rear torque rod at the engine, then loosen the bolt in the frame mount and swing the rod up and out of the way.

34. Raise the engine carefully from the vehicle, checking that all wires and hoses have been removed from the engine/transaxle. Raise the engine all the way up and remove it from the vehicle.

35. Installation is the reverse of removal, making the following checks:

a. Torque the engine mounting bolts in the proper sequence.

b. Bleed the air from the cooling system.

c. Adjust the clutch pedal freeplay.

d. Adjust the throttle cable tension.

e. Make sure the transaxle shifts properly.

## Cylinder Head

### REMOVAL & INSTALLATION

#### *Civic with 1335cc and 1487cc Engines*

1. Be sure that the engine is cold. Disconnect the negative battery cable.

2. Drain the radiator.

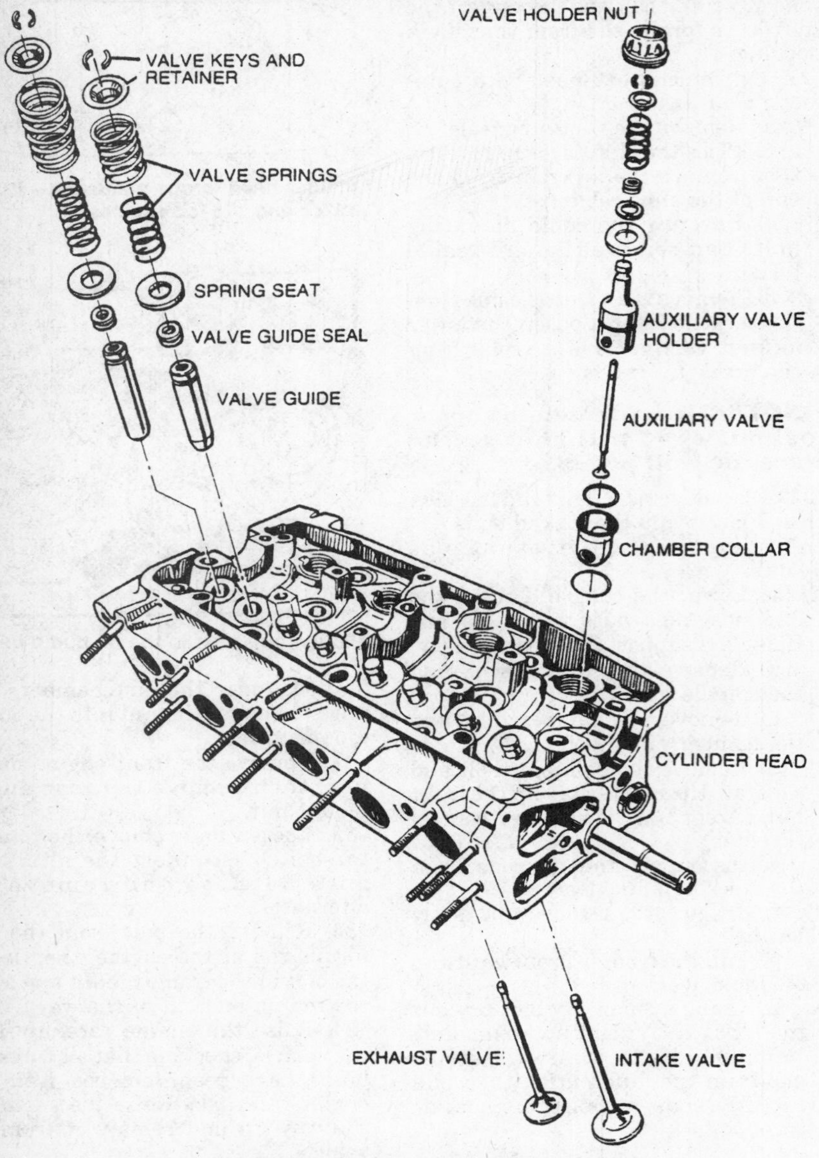

Cylinder head and valve train—8-valve engines

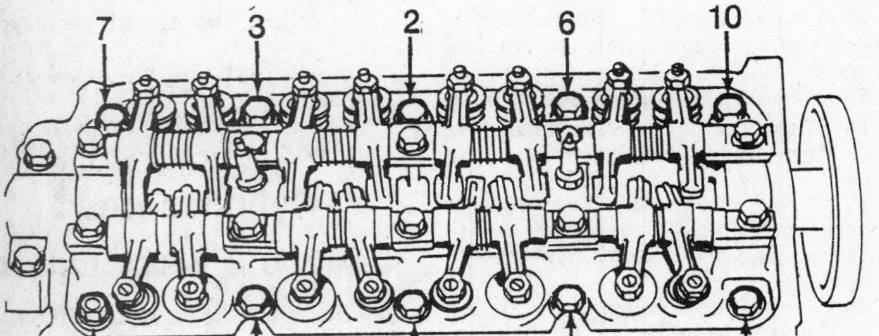

Cylinder head torque sequence—1342cc and 1488cc engines

3. Disconnect the upper radiator hose at the thermostat cover.
4. Remove the distributor cap, ignition wires and primary wire. Also, loosen the alternator bracket and remove the upper mounting bolt from the cylinder head.
5. On vehicles equipped with air conditioning, remove the compressor drive belt cover, then loosen the drive belt adjusting nut. Remove the compressor mounting bolts and move the compressor to 1 side without discharging it. Remove the compressor bracket.
6. Remove the air cleaner case.
7. Disconnect the tube running between the canister and carburetor at the canister.
8. Disconnect the throttle and choke control cables. Label and disconnect all vacuum hoses.
9. Disconnect the heater hose at the intake manifold.
10. Disconnect the wires from both thermostats.
11. Disconnect the fuel line.
12. Disconnect the temperature gauge sending unit wire, idle cut-off solenoid valve, and primary/main cut-off solenoid valve.
13. Disconnect the engine torque rod.
14. Disconnect the exhaust pipe at the exhaust manifold.
15. Remove the valve cover bolts and the valve cover.
16. Remove the 2 timing belt upper cover bolts and the cover.
17. Bring No. 1 piston to TDC. Do this by aligning the notch next to the red notch you use for setting ignition timing, with the index mark on the rear of engine block.
18. Loosen, but do not remove, the timing belt adjustment bolt and pivot bolt.

**NOTE: Use care when handling the timing belt. Do not use sharp instruments to remove the belt. Do not get oil or grease on the belt. Do not bend or twist the belt more than 90 degrees.**

19. Loosen and remove the cylinder head bolts in the reverse order of the head bolt tightening sequence. The number 1 bolt is hidden underneath the oil pump. To prevent warpage, unscrew the bolts $\frac{1}{3}$ turn each time and repeat sequence until loose.
20. Remove the cylinder head with the carburetor and manifolds attached.
21. Remove the intake and exhaust manifolds from the cylinder heads.

**NOTE: After removing the cylinder head, cover the engine with a clean cloth to prevent materials from getting into the cylinders.**

22. To install, reverse the removal procedure, being sure to pay attention to the following points:

a. Be sure that No. 1 cylinder is at top dead center before positioning the cylinder head in place.

b. Use a new head gasket and make sure the head, engine block, and gasket are clean.

c. The cylinder head aligning dowel pins should be in their proper place in the block before installing the cylinder head.

d. Tighten the head bolts in 2 progressive steps to the proper torque according to the diagram. First tighten them to 22 ft. lbs. in sequence and then to specification in the same sequence.

e. After the head bolts have been tightened, install the woodruff key and camshaft pulley, if removed, and tighten the pulley bolt according to specification. On the 1355cc engine, align the marks on the camshaft pulley so they are parallel with the top of the head and the woodruff key or cutout is facing up. On the 1487cc engine, the word **UP** or cutout should be facing upward and the mark on the cam sprocket should be aligned with the arrow on the cylinder head.

f. After installing the pulley, if removed, install the timing belt. Be careful not to disturb the timing position already set when installing the belt.

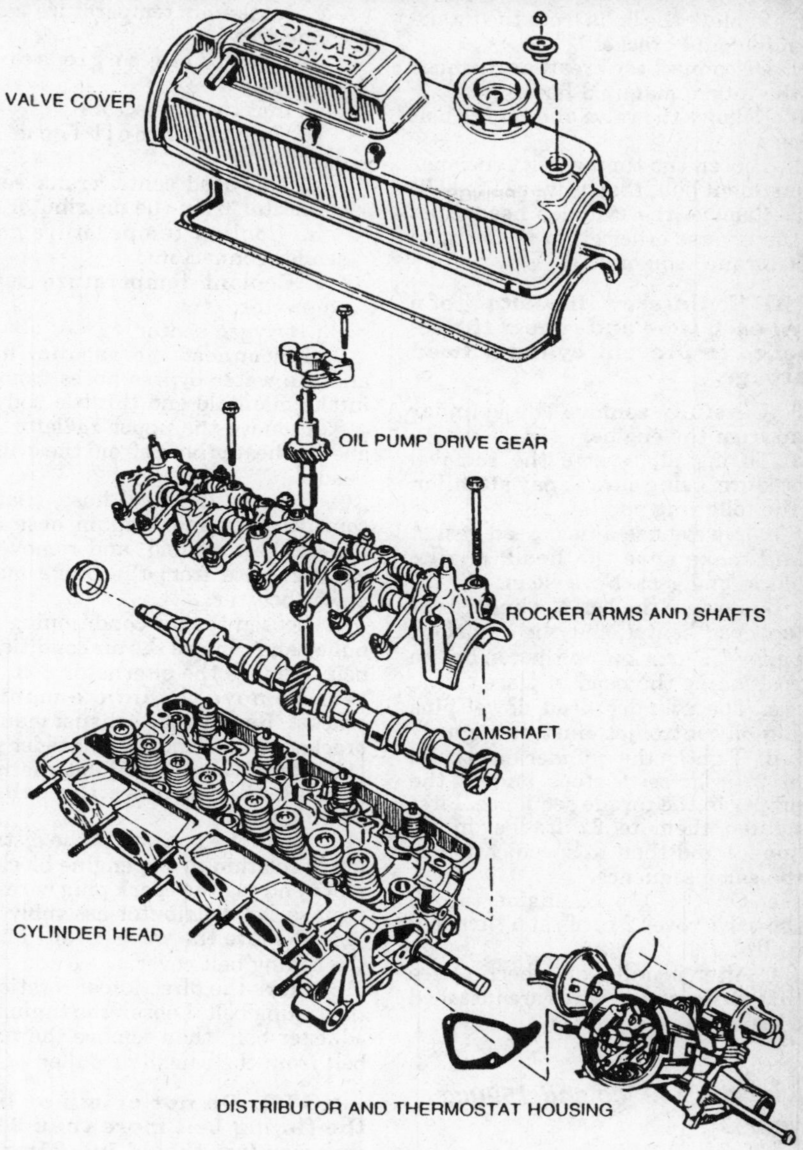


**CVCC cylinder head component**

### *Civic with 1342cc and 1488cc Engines*

1. Be sure that the engine is cold. Disconnect the negative battery cable.
2. Drain the radiator.
3. Remove the air cleaner:

a. Remove the air cleaner cover and filter.

b. Disconnect the hot and cold air intake ducts, and remove the air chamber hose.

c. Remove the 3 bolts holding the air cleaner.

d. Lift up on the air cleaner housing, then remove the remaining hoses and the air temperature sensor wire.

e. Remove the air cleaner.

4. On fuel injected vehicles, relieve the fuel pressure using the following procedures:

a. Slowly loosen the service bolt on the top of the fuel filter about 1 turn.

**NOTE: Place a rag under the filter during this procedure to prevent fuel from spilling onto the engine.**

b. Disconnect the fuel return hose from the pressure regulator. Remove the special nut and then remove the fuel hose.

5. Remove the brake booster vacuum tube from the intake manifold.
6. Remove the engine ground wire from the valve cover and disconnect the wires from the fuel cut-off solenoid valve, automatic choke and thermosensor.
7. Disconnect the fuel lines.
8. Disconnect the spark plug wires from the spark plugs, then remove the distributor assembly.
9. Disconnect the throttle cable from the carburetor.
10. Disconnect the hoses from the charcoal canister, and from the No. 1 control box at the tubing manifold.
11. Disconnect the air jet controller on California and high altitude vehicles.
12. Disconnect the idle control solenoid hoses, if the vehicle is equipped with air conditioning.
13. Disconnect the upper radiator heater and bypass hoses.
14. On fuel injected vehicles, disconnect the engine sub-harness connectors and the following couplers from the head and the intake manifold. The 4 injector couplers. The TA sensor connector. The ground connector. The TW sensor connector. The throttle sensor connector. The crankshaft angle sensor coupler.
15. Remove the thermostat housing-to-intake manifold hose.
16. Disconnect the oxygen sensor coupler.
17. Remove the exhaust manifold bracket and manifold bolts, then remove the manifold.

18. Remove the bolts from the intake manifold and bracket.
19. Disconnect the breather chamber to the intake manifold hose.
20. Remove the valve and timing belt covers.
21. Loosen the timing belt tensioner adjustment bolt, then remove the belt.
22. Remove the cylinder head bolts in the reverse order given in the head bolt torque sequence.

**NOTE: Unscrew the bolts ⅓ of a turn each time and repeat the sequence to prevent cylinder head warpage.**

23. Carefully remove the cylinder head from the engine.
24. To install, reverse the removal procedure, being sure to pay attention to the following points:
   a. Always use a new head gasket and make sure the head, engine block, and gasket are clean.
   b. Be sure the No. 1 cylinder is at top dead center and the camshaft pulley **UP** mark is on the top before positioning the head in place.
   c. The cylinder head dowel pins and oil control jet must be aligned.
   d. Tighten the cylinder head bolts in 2 progressive steps and in the proper in the torque sequence. First tighten them to 22 ft. lbs. in sequence and then to specification in the same sequence.
   e. On the 1342cc engine torque the valve cover 2 turns at a time to 9 ft. lbs.
   f. After installation, check to see that all hoses and wires are installed correctly.

### *Civic with 1493cc and 1590cc Engines*

1. Be sure that the engine is cold. Disconnect the negative battery cable. Drain the cooling system.
2. Remove the brake booster vacuum hose from the brake master power booster. Remove the engine secondary ground cable from the valve cover.
3. Remove the air intake hose and the air chamber. Relieve the fuel pressure. Disconnect the fuel hoses and fuel return hose.
4. Remove the air intake hose and resonator hose. Disconnect the throttle cable at the throttle body on vehicles equipped with automatic transaxles.
5. Disconnect the charcoal canister hose at the throttle valve.
6. Disconnect the following engine wire connectors from the cylinder head and the intake manifold:
   a. 14 prong connector from the main wiring harness
   b. EACV connector
   c. Intake air temperature sensor connector
   d. Throttle angle sensor connector
   e. Injector connectors
   f. Ignition coil from the distributor
   g. Top dead center/crank sensor connector from the distributor.
   h. Coolant temperature gauge sender connector.
   i. Coolant temperature sensor connector.
   j. Oxygen sensor.
7. Disconnect the vacuum hoses and the water bypass hoses from the intake manifold and throttle body.
8. Remove the upper radiator hose and the heater hoses from the cylinder head.
9. Remove the PCV hose, charcoal canister hose and vacuum hose from the intake manifold, and remove the vacuum hose from the brake master power booster.
10. Loosen the air conditioning idler pulley and remove the air conditioning belt. Remove the alternator belt.
11. Remove the intake manifold bracket. Remove the exhaust manifold bracket, then remove the header pipe.
12. Remove the exhaust manifold shroud, then remove the exhaust manifold.
13. Mark the position of the distributor in relation to the engine block, remove and tag the spark plug wires and remove the distributor assembly.
14. Remove the valve cover. Remove the timing belt cover.
15. Mark the direction of rotation on the timing belt. Loosen the timing belt adjuster bolt, then remove the timing belt from the camshaft pulley.

**NOTE: Do not crimp or bend the timing belt more than 90 degrees or less than 1 in. (25mm) in diameter (width).**

16. Remove the cylinder head bolts. Once the bolts are all removed, remove the cylinder head along with the intake manifold from the engine. Remove the intake manifold from the cylinder head.
17. Install the cylinder head in the reverse order of the removal procedure. Be sure to use the following steps as a guide to aid in the installation procedure:
   a. Always use a new head gasket.
   b. Be sure the cylinder head and the engine block surfaces are clean, level and straight.
   c. Be sure the **UP** mark on the timing belt pulley is at the top.
   d. Install the intake manifold and tighten the nuts in a criss cross pattern in 2 or 3 steps to 17 ft. lbs. starting with the inner nuts.
   e. Be sure the cylinder head dowel pins and control jet are aligned.
   f. Install the bolts that secure the intake manifold to its bracket but do not tighten them at this point.
   g. Position the cam correctly and install the cylinder head bolts.
   h. Tighten the cylinder head bolts

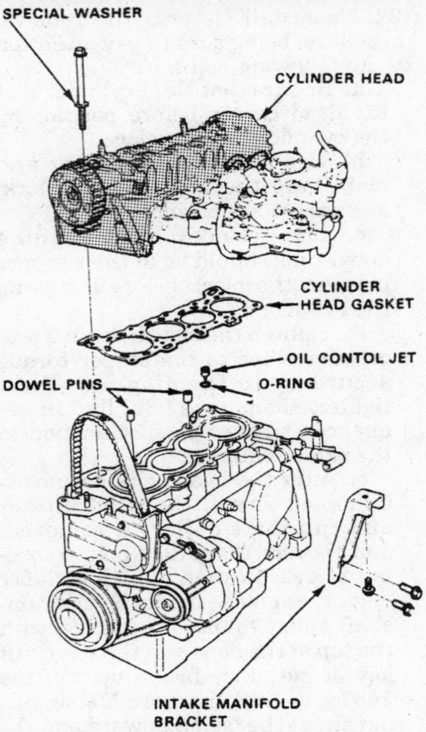

**Cylinder head removal – 1988–90 Civic**

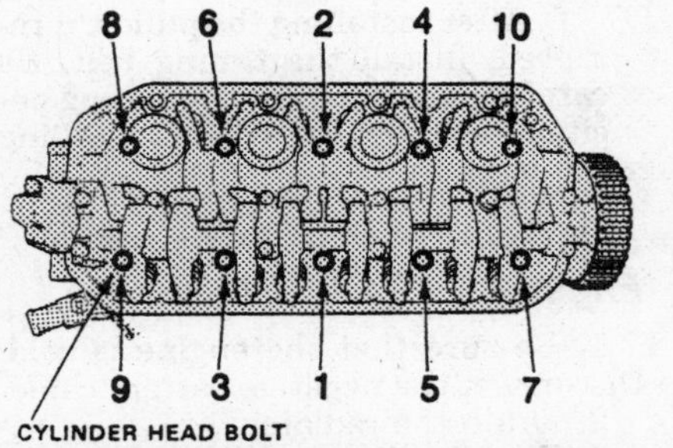

**Cylinder head torque sequence – 1493cc and 1590cc engines**

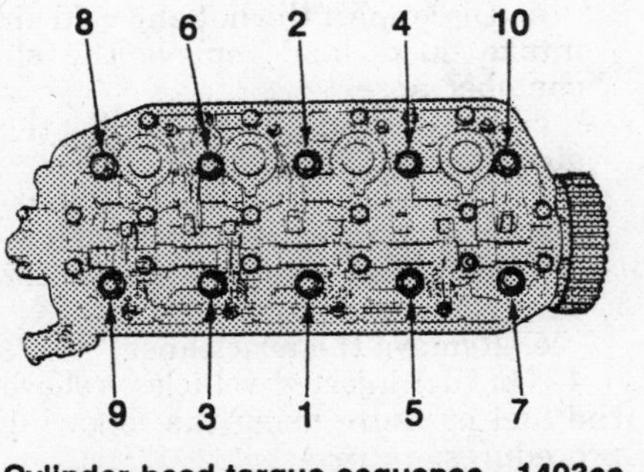

**Cylinder head torque sequence – 1493cc and 1590cc HF engines**

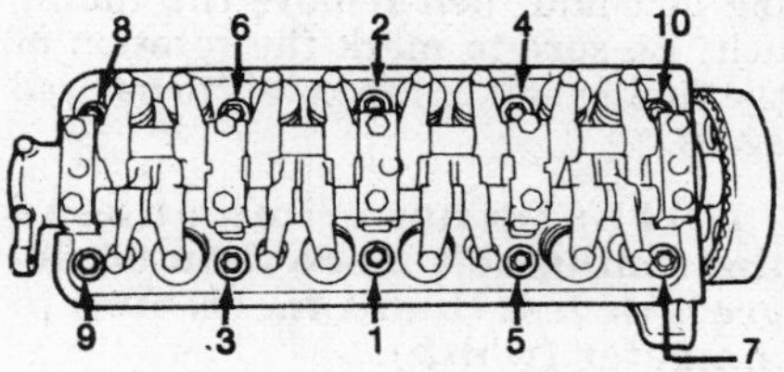


**Cylinder head torque sequence—1829cc and 1955cc engines**

in 2 steps. On the first step tighten all the bolts in the proper sequence to 22 ft. lbs. On the final step, using the same sequence, tighten the bolts to specification.

i. On the Standard and Si vehicles, install the exhaust manifold and tighten the nuts in a criss cross pattern in 2 or 3 steps to 25 ft. lbs. starting with the inner nuts.

j. On the HF vehicles, install catalytic converter to the exhaust manifold, then install the exhaust manifold assembly to 25 ft. lbs.

k. Install the header pipe onto the exhaust manifold. tighten the bolts to the intake manifold bracket. Install the header pipe on to its bracket.

18. After the installation procedure is complete, check that all tubes, hoses and connectors are installed correctly. Adjust the valve timing as outlined in this section.

### Accord and Prelude with 1751cc Engine

1. Be sure that the engine is cold. Disconnect the battery ground cable.
2. Drain the cooling system.
3. Remove the air cleaner, tagging all hoses for installation.
4. Disconnect the wires from the thermosensor temperature gauge sending unit, idle cut-off solenoid valve, primary/main cut-off solenoid valve, and the automatic choke.
5. Disconnect the fuel lines and throttle cable from the carburetor.
6. Tag all emission hoses going to the carburetor then remove them and the carburetor.
7. Disconnect all wires and hoses from the distributor, tagging them for installation, and remove the distributor.
8. Remove all coolant hoses from the head.
9. Disconnect the hot air ducts and head pipe from the head. Loosen the exhaust manifold-to-engine bracket bolts to ease assembly.
10. If equipped with power steering, loosen the adjustment bolt and remove the belt. Disconnect the hoses and plug the hoses and fitting to prevent contamination. Remove the pump mounting bolt and swing the pump to the right side of the engine.
11. On vehicles without air conditioning, remove the bolt holding the alternator bracket to the head. Loosen the adjustment bolt.
12. On vehicles equipped with air conditioning, remove the alternator and bracket from the vehicle.
13. Disconnect the brake booster vacuum hose at the one-way valve.
14. Remove the valve cover and timing bolt upper cover.
15. Loosen the timing belt pivot and adjust bolts and slide the belt off the pulley.
16. Remove the oil pump gear cover and pull the oil pump shaft out of the head.
17. Remove the head bolts in sequence working from the ends, across the head, toward the center. This is the reverse of the tightening sequence. To prevent warpage, unscrew the bolts ⅓ turn each time and repeat the sequence until loose.
18. Carefully lift the head from the block.
19. Thoroughly clean the mating surfaces to the head and block.
20. Always use a new gasket.
21. Install the head in reverse order of the removal procedure. Make sure the head dowel pins are aligned. Make sure that the **UP** mark or cut-out on the timing belt pulley is at the top. Torque the cylinder head bolts in 2 equal steps. Tighten all bolts to 22 ft. lbs. in sequence and then to specification in the final step.

### Accord and Prelude with 1829cc and 1955cc Engines Except 1955cc DOHC engine

1. Be sure that the engine is cold. Disconnect the battery ground cable.
2. Drain the cooling system.
3. Remove the vacuum hose from the brake booster.
4. Remove the air intake ducts from the air cleaner case.
5. On fuel injected vehicles, relieve the fuel pressure using the following procedure:

   a. Slowly loosen the service bolt on the top of the fuel filter about 1 turn.

   **NOTE: Place a rag under the filter during this procedure to prevent fuel from spilling onto the engine.**

   b. Disconnect the fuel return hose from the pressure regulator. Remove the special nut and then remove the fuel hose.

6. Remove the secondary ground cable from the valve cover.
7. Remove the air cleaner, tagging all hoses for installation.
8. Disconnect the wires from the automatic choke and the fuel cut-off solenoid valve.
9. Disconnect the throttle cable and the fuel lines.
10. Disconnect the connector and hoses from the distributor.
11. On fuel injected vehicles, disconnect the engine sub-harness connectors and the following couplers from the head and the intake manifold. The 4 injector couplers. The TA sensor connector. The ground connector. The TW sensor connector. The throttle sensor connector. The crankshaft angle sensor coupler.
12. Disconnect the No. 1 control box hoses from the tubing manifold.
13. On California and high altitude vehicles, disconnect the air jet controller hoses.
14. Disconnect the oxygen sensor coupler.
15. Disconnect the cooling system hoses at the cylinder head.
16. Remove the power steering pump, if equipped. Do not disconnect the pump hoses. Also, remove the hose clamp bolt on the cylinder head.
17. Remove the power steering pump bracket.
18. Disconnect the No. 2 control box connector. Lift the control box from its bracket, and let it hang next to the carburetor, if equipped.
19. Remove the air chamber. On vehicles equipped with air conditioning, disconnect the idle boost solenoid hoses.
20. Remove the engine splash guard from under the vehicle, if equipped.
21. Remove the exhaust header pipe and pull it clear of the exhaust manifold.
22. Remove the air cleaner base mount bolts and disconnect the hose from the intake manifold to the breather chamber.
23. Remove the valve cover, upper timing belt cover and then loosen the belt tensioner to remove the belt.
24. Remove the cylinder head bolts and remove the head.

**NOTE: Unscrew the cylinder head bolts ⅓ of a turn in the reverse order of the torque sequence each turn until loose to prevent warpage to the cylinder head.**

25. Installation is the reverse of the removal procedure, taking note of the following items:

   a. Make sure the cylinder head gasket surfaces are clean.
   b. Make sure the **UP** mark on the timing belt pulley is at the top.
   c. Make sure the head dowel pins are aligned.
   d. Adjust the valve timing.
   e. Torque the cylinder head bolts

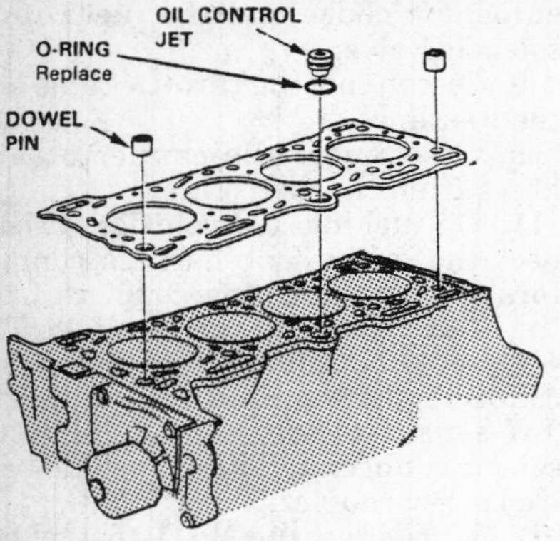

Cylinder head gasket installation—1955cc DOHC engine

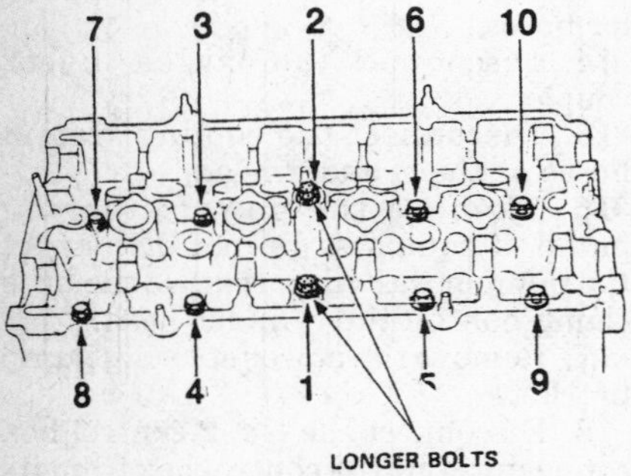

Cylinder head torque sequence—1955cc DOHC engine

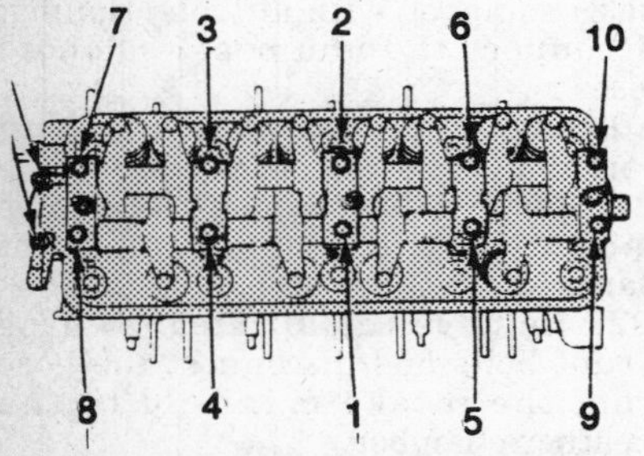

Rocker arm shaft torque sequence—1751cc, 1829cc and 1955cc engines

in 2 steps. Torque all bolts in sequence to 22 ft. lbs. and then to specification in the final step.

### *Prelude with 1955cc DOHC Engine*

1. Be sure that the engine is cold. Disconnect the battery ground cable.
2. Drain the cooling system.
3. Remove the brake booster vacuum hose from the intake manifold.
4. Remove the engine secondary ground cable from the valve cover. Disconnect the radio condenser connector and the ignition coil wire.
5. Remove the air cleaner assembly. Relieve the fuel pressure as previously outlined in this section.
6. Disconnect the fuel lines and fuel return line. Remove the air intake

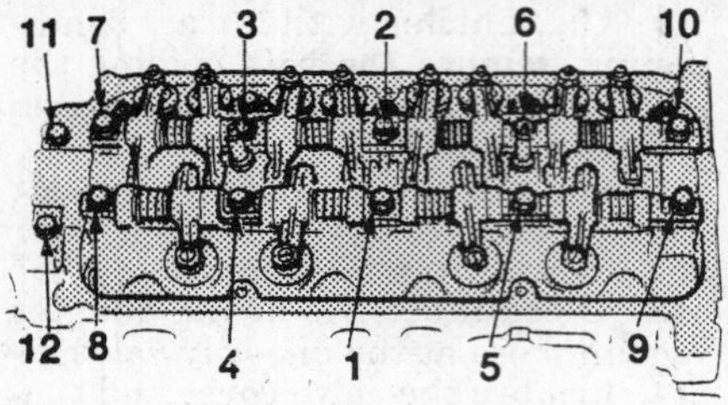

Rocker arm shaft torque sequence—Civic 1335cc, 1342cc and 1488cc engines

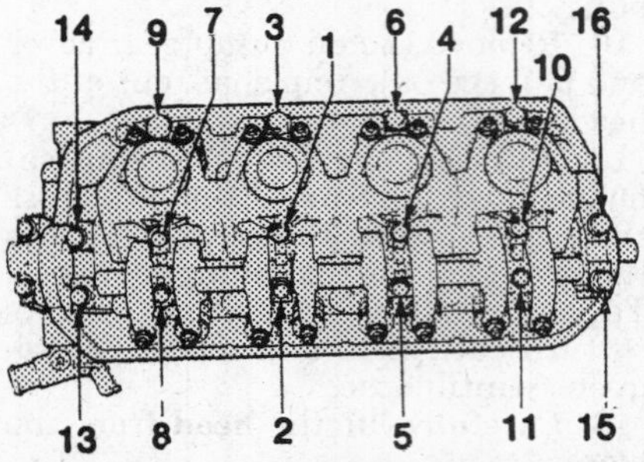

Rocker arm shaft torque sequence—1493cc and 1590cc engines

hose and the resonator hose. Disconnect the throttle cable at the throttle body.

7. Disconnect the throttle control cable at the throttle body, on vehicles equipped with automatic transaxle. Disconnect the charcoal canister hose at the throttle valve.
8. Disconnect and tag all the necessary wire harness connectors from the cylinder head. Remove the emission control box and vacuum tank, then disconnect the 2 connectors. Do not remove the emission hoses.
9. Remove the upper radiator hose. Remove the heater hoses from the cylinder head. Remove the water bypass hoses from the water pump inlet pipe.
10. Remove the power steering pump belt and the alternator belt. Also remove the air conditioning belt if so equipped.
11. Disconnect the inlet hose from the power steering pump and remove the power steering pump from the cylinder head. Remove the alternator assembly as well.
12. Remove the intake manifold bracket. Remove the exhaust manifold bracket and then the header pipe.
13. Remove and tag the ignition wires and then remove the distributor assembly. Be sure to scribe a line stating the position of the distributor assembly to the engine block for easy installation.
14. Remove the cylinder sensor. Remove the valve cover. Remove the timing belt middle cover.
15. Remove the crankshaft pulley and then remove the lower timing belt cover. Loosen the timing belt adjusting bolt and then remove the timing belt. Be sure to mark the rotation of the timing belt, if the belt is to be used again.

**NOTE: Do not crimp or bend the timing belt more than 90 degrees or less than 1 in. (25mm) in diameter (width).**

16. Remove the camshaft holders, camshafts and rocker arms. Remove the cylinder head bolts (take notice of the bolt holes that the 2 longer bolts come out of) and remove the cylinder head.
17. Remove the exhaust manifold shroud and EGR pipe, then remove the exhaust manifold from the cylinder head. Remove the intake manifold from the cylinder head.
18. Thoroughly clean the mating surfaces to the head and block.
19. Always use a new gasket.
20. Install the head in reverse order of the removal procedure. Make sure the head dowel pins and oil control jet are aligned. Make sure that the **UP** marks or cut-out on the timing belt pulleys is at the top. Torque the cylinder head bolts in 2 equal steps. Tighten all bolts to 22 ft. lbs. in sequence and then to specification in the final step.
21. Apply engine oil to all the cylinder head bolts and the washers. Place the 2 longer bolts in their proper position on the head.
22. Install the intake manifold and tighten the nuts in a criss cross pattern in 2 or 3 steps to 16 ft. lbs.
23. Install the exhaust manifold and bracket and tighten the nuts in a criss cross pattern in 2 or 3 steps to 26 ft. lbs.
24. After the installation procedure is complete, check that all tubes, hoses and connectors are installed correctly. Adjust the valve timing.

## OVERHAUL

**For all cylinder head overhaul procedures, please refer to the "Engine Rebuilding" in the Unit Repair section.**

# Camshaft and Rocker Shafts

## REMOVAL & INSTALLATION

### *Except 1955cc DOHC Engine*

1. Disconnect the negative battery cable. Position the engine at TDC on the compression stroke.
2. Remove the valve cover. Remove the upper timing belt cover. Remove

Rocker arm assembly—8-valve engines

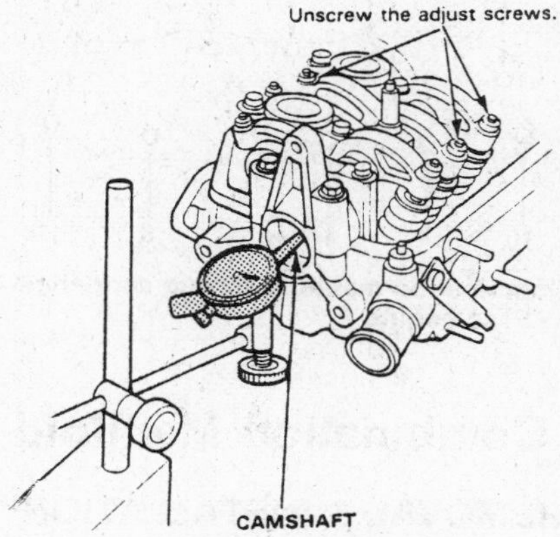
Unscrew the adjust screws.
CAMSHAFT

Checking the camshaft end play

the camshaft gear. As required, remove the distributor.

3. Remove the rocker arm assembly. Remove the camshaft from the cylinder head.

4. Installation is the reverse of the removal procedure. Be sure to use new gaskets or RTV sealant, as required.

### 1955cc DOHC Engine

1. Disconnect the negative battery cable. Position the engine at TDC on the compression stroke.

2. Remove the valve cover. Remove the upper timing belt cover. Remove the camshaft gears. As required, remove the distributor.

3. Remove the camshaft reatining caps. Remove the camshaft from the cylinder head.

4. Installation is the reverse of the removal procedure. Be sure to use new gaskets or RTV sealant, as required.

# Intake Manifold

## REMOVAL & INSTALLATION

### Carbureted Engine

1. Disconnect the negative battery cable. Drain the coolant from the radiator.

2. Remove the air cleaner and case from the carburetor(s).

3. Remove the air valve, EGR valve,

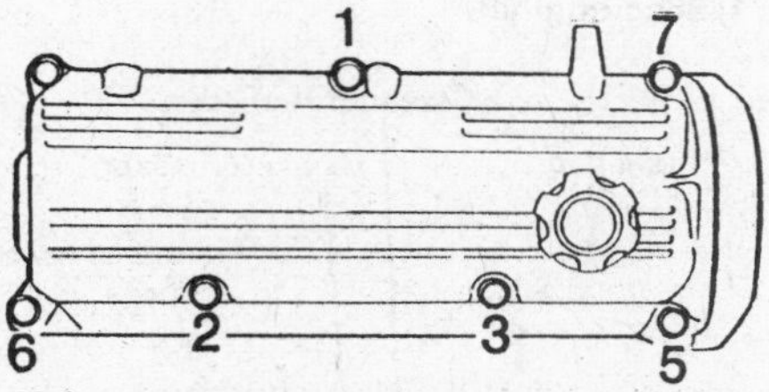
1
7
6
2
3
5

Valve cover torque sequence—1342cc engine

air suction valve and air chamber if equipped.

4. Label and remove any wires running to the intake manifold.

5. Remove the intake manifold attaching nut in a crisscross pattern, beginning from the center. Then remove the manifold.

6. Clean all the old gasket material from the manifold and the cylinder head.

7. If the intake manifold is to be replaced, transfer all the necessary components to the new manifold.

8. To install, reverse the removal procedures, being sure to observe the following points:

   a. Always use a new gasket.

   b. Tighten the nuts in a crisscross pattern in 2 or 3 steps, starting with the inner nuts.

   c. Be sure all hoses and wires are correctly connected.

### Fuel Injected Engine

1. Disconnect the negative battery cable. Drain the cooling system.

2. Label and disconnect all required electrical connectors and vacuum lines.

3. Properly relieve the fuel system pressure.

4. Remove the throttle body assembly. As required, remove the fuel injector manifold and fuel injectors.

5. As required, remove the fast idle control valve, the air bleed valve, the EGR valve and all related brackets.

6. Remove the intake manifold retaining bolts. Remove the intake manifold assembly from the vehicle. Discard the gaskets.

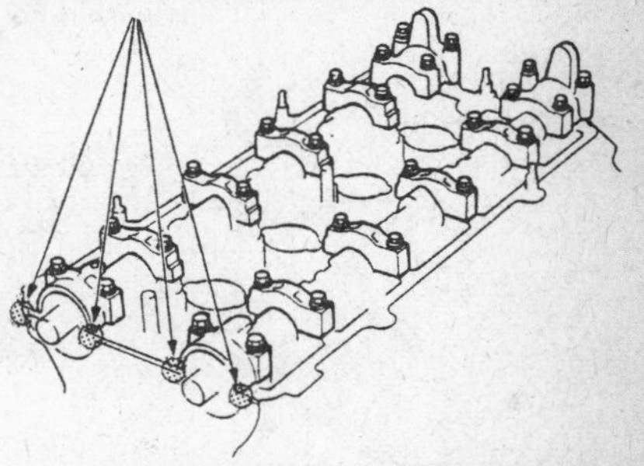

Non-hardening sealant application locations – 1955cc DOHC engine

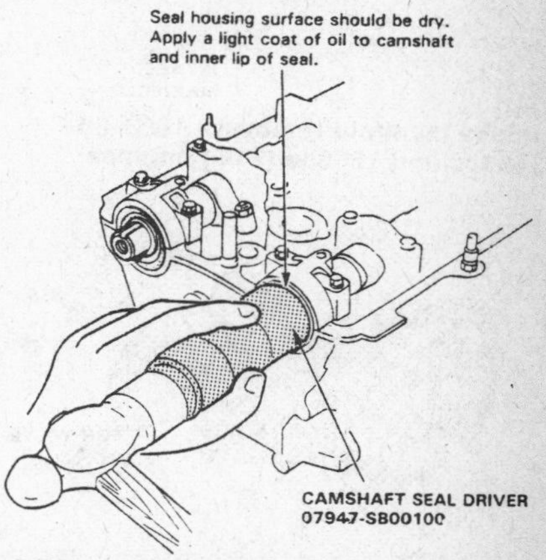
Seal housing surface should be dry.
Apply a light coat of oil to camshaft
and inner lip of seal.
CAMSHAFT SEAL DRIVER
07947-SB0010C

Installing the camshaft(s) oil seal – 1955cc DOHC engine

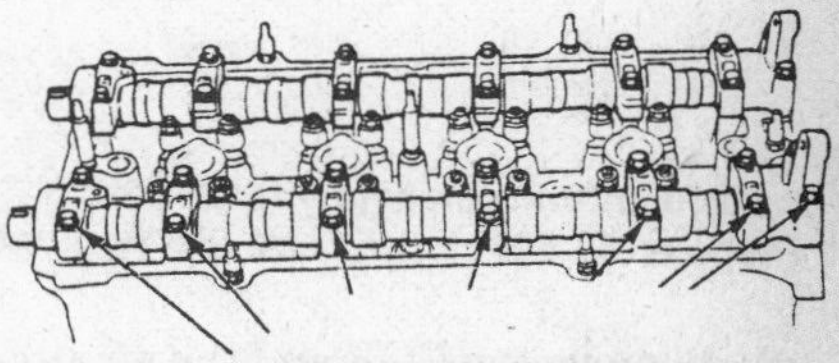

Rocker arm shaft torque sequence – 1955cc DOHC engine

**NOTE: Some vehicles use an upper and lower manifold assembly. Separate the upper manifold from the lower manifold before removing the assembly from the vehicle.**

7. Installation is the reverse of the removal procedure. Be sure to use new gaskets and RTV sealant, as required.

# Exhaust Manifold

## REMOVAL & INSTALLATION

### Carbureted Engine

1. Be sure that the engine is cold. Disconnect the negative battery cable. Remove the header pipe or catalytic converter to exhaust manifold attaching bolts.

2. Remove the oxygen sensor, if equipped.

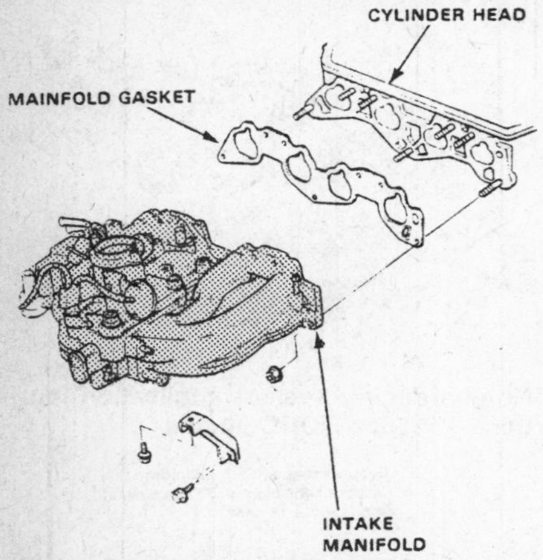


**Intake manifold removal – 1988–90 1493cc and 1590cc (STD) engines**

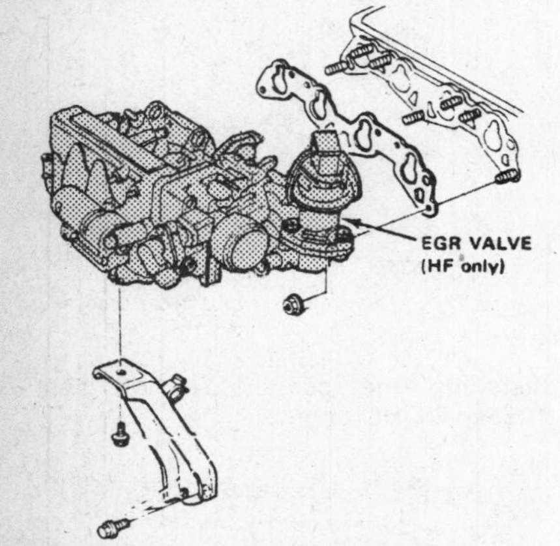


**Intake manifold removal – 1988–90 1493cc and 1590cc (HF) and (SI) engines**

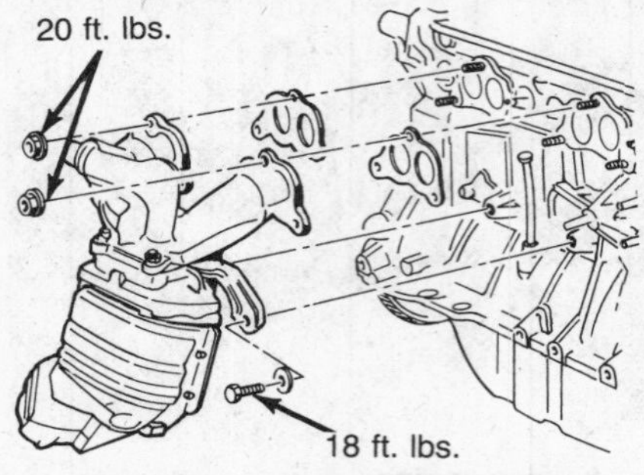


**Exhaust manifold mounting—1342 and 1488cc engines**

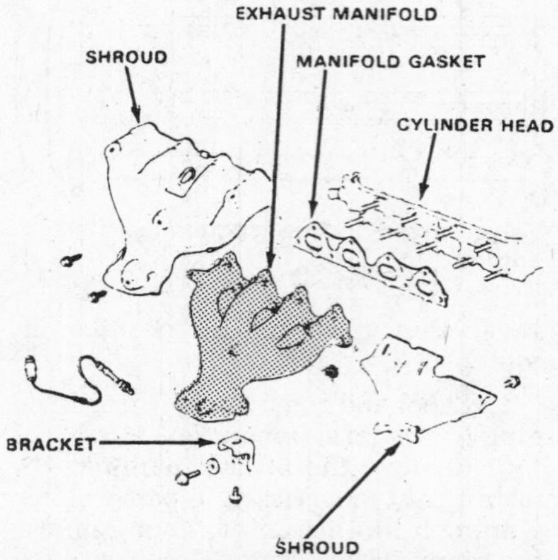


**Exhaust manifold removal – 1988–90 1493cc and 1590cc engines**

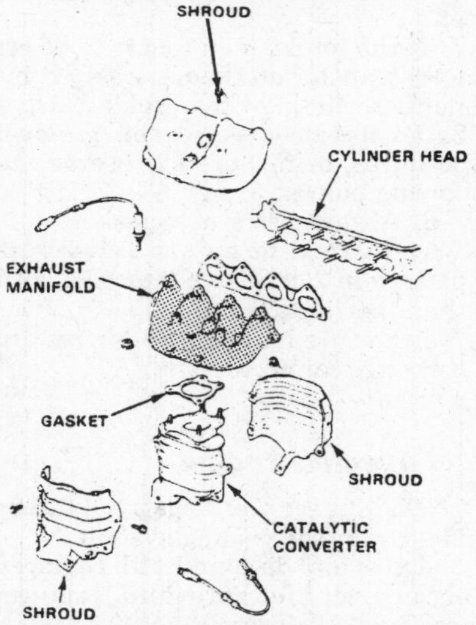


**Exhaust manifold removal – 1988–90 1493cc and 1590 (HF) engine**

3. Remove the EGR and the air suction tubes, if equipped.
4. Remove the exhaust manifold shroud.
5. Remove the exhaust manifold bracket bolts.
6. Remove the exhaust attaching nuts in a crisscross pattern starting from the center, and remove the manifold.
7. To install, reverse the removal procedure. Use new gaskets and tighten the manifold bolts in a crisscross pattern starting from the center.

### *Fuel Injected Engine*

1. Disconnect the negative battery cable.
2. As required, remove the front grille assembly.
3. Disconnect the oxygen sensor electrical connector. Disconnect the EGR tube from the exhaust manifold, if equipped.
4. As required, raise and support the vehicle safely. Disconnect the exhaust pipe from the exhaust manifold. As required, lower the vehicle.
5. Remove the shroud to exhaust manifold retaining bolt. Remove the exhaust manifold shroud.
6. Remove the exhaust manifold retaining bolts. Remove the exhaust manifold from the vehicle. Discard the gaskets.
7. Installation is the reverse of the removal procedure. Be sure to use new gaskets, as required.

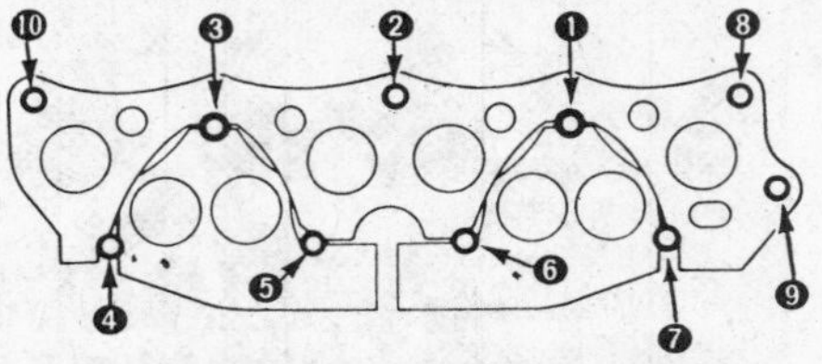


**Combination manifold torque sequence – 1335cc and 1487cc engines**

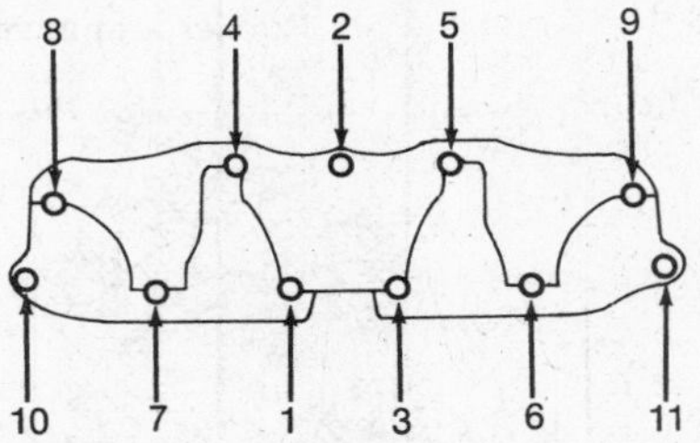


**Combination manifold torque sequence – 1751cc engine**

# Combination Manifold

## REMOVAL & INSTALLATION

1. Disconnect the negative battery cable. Drain the radiator. Disconnect the manifold coolant hoses.
2. Remove the air cleaner assembly.
3. Label and disconnect all emission control vacuum hoses and electrical leads.
4. Disconnect the fuel lines, throttle, and choke linkage.
5. Remove the carburetor from the intake manifold.
6. Remove the upper heat shield. Loosen, but do not remove the 4 bolts retaining the intake manifold to the exhaust manifold.
7. Disconnect the exhaust pipe from the exhaust manifold.
8. Remove the nuts retaining the intake and exhaust manifolds to the cylinder head. Both manifolds are removed as a unit.
9. Reverse the above procedure to install, using new gaskets. The thick washers used beneath the cylinder head-to-manifold retaining nuts must be installed with the dished (concave), side toward the engine. Tighten in sequence to specification. Adjust the choke and throttle linkage and bleed the cooling system.

# Front Cover

## REMOVAL & INSTALLATION

### *Except 1493cc, 1590cc and 1955cc DOHC Engins*

1. Align the crankshaft pulley, or

flywheel pointer, at TDC. Disconnect the negative battery cable.

2. Remove the bolt(s) which hold the timing belt upper cover and remove the cover.

3. Loosen the alternator. Loosen the air pump if equipped. Remove the pulley belts.

4. On all vehicles except the 1984–87 Civic and CRX, remove the water pump pulley bolts and the water pump pulley. As required, remove the valve cover.

5. Remove the crankshaft pulley attaching bolt. Use a puller to remove the crankshaft pulley.

**NOTE: The crankshaft bolt cannot be reused. It must be replaced whenever removed.**

6. Remove the timing gear cover retaining bolts and the timing gear cover.

7. To install, reverse the removal procedure. Make sure that the timing guide plates, pulleys and the front oil seal are properly installed on the crankshaft and before replacing the cover.

### 1493cc and 1590cc Engines

1. Disconnect the negative battery cable. Remove the driver's side wheel well splash shield.

2. Remove the air conditioning compressor adjust pulley with bracket and the belt, if equipped.

3. Remove the side engine mount bracket. Loosen the alternator adjuster bolt and through bolt then remove the belt.

4. Remove the engine support bolts and nuts, then remove the side mount rubber.

5. Remove the valve cover, if necessary. Remove the crankshaft pulley bolt and remove the crankshaft pulley.

6. Remove the timing belt upper cover and lower cover.

7. To install, reverse the removal procedure. Make sure that the timing guide plates, pulleys and the front oil seal are properly installed on the crankshaft before replacing the cover.

### 1955cc DOHC Engine

1. Disconnect the negative battery cable. Remove the engine support bolts and nuts, then remove the side mount rubber and side mount brackets.

2. Remove the lower engine splash shield. Remove the power steering pump adjust pulley nut and the adjust bolt. Remove the adjust pulley, power steering pump and power steering belt.

3. Remove the alternator through bolt, mount bolt and the adjuster nut.

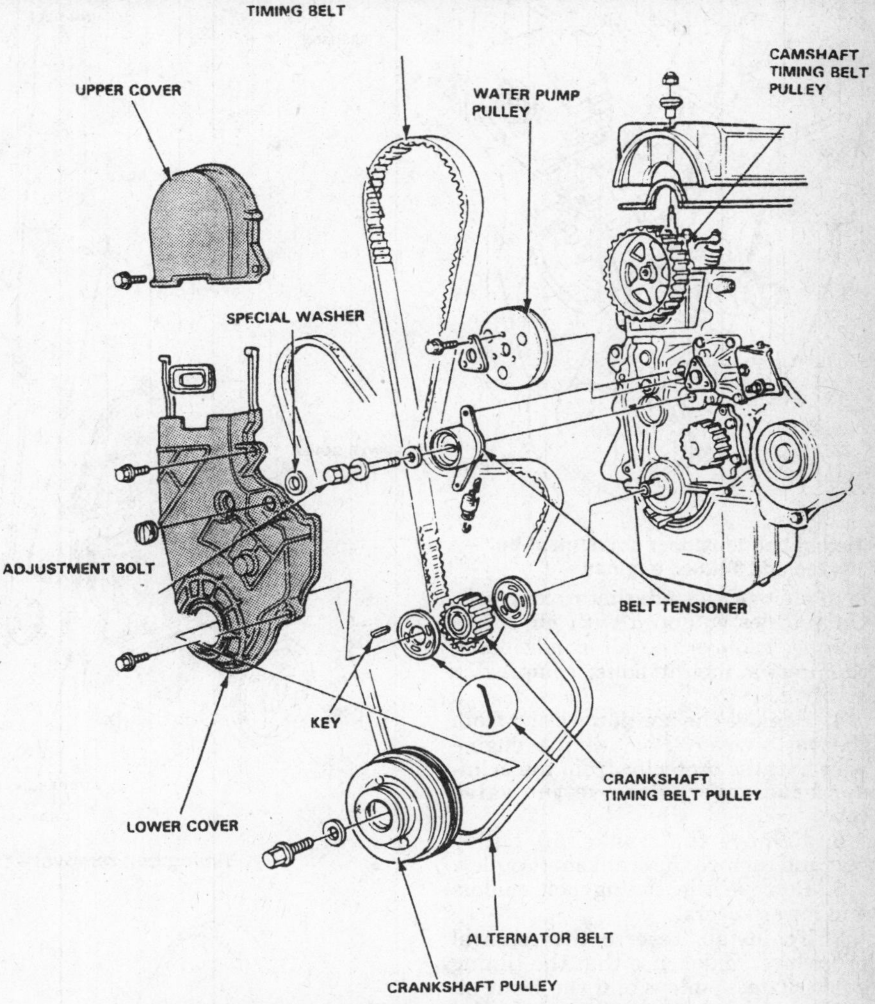


Timing belt removal – 1751cc, 1829cc and 1955cc engines

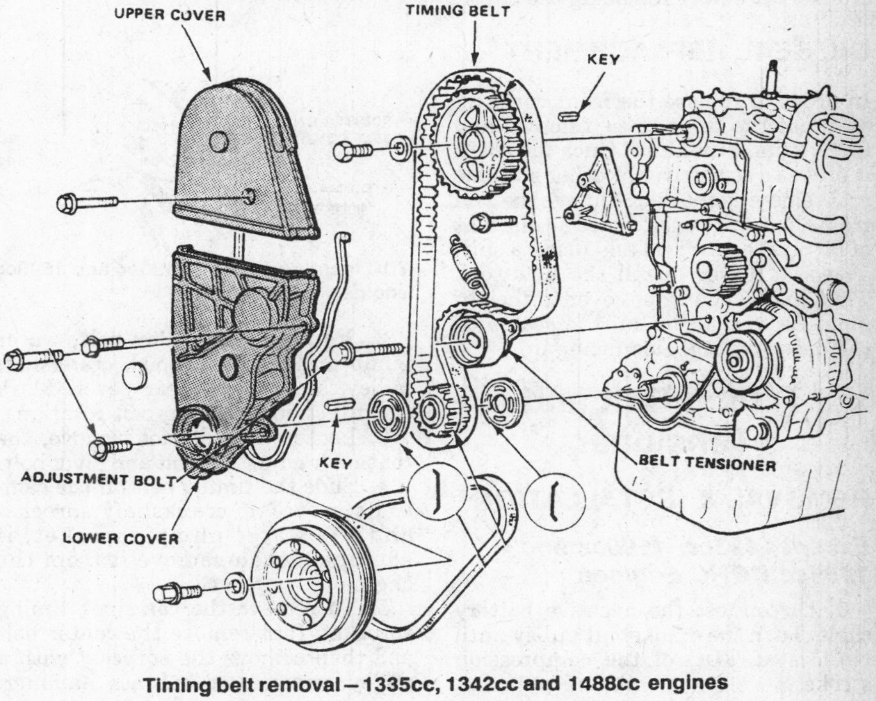


Timing belt removal – 1335cc, 1342cc and 1488cc engines

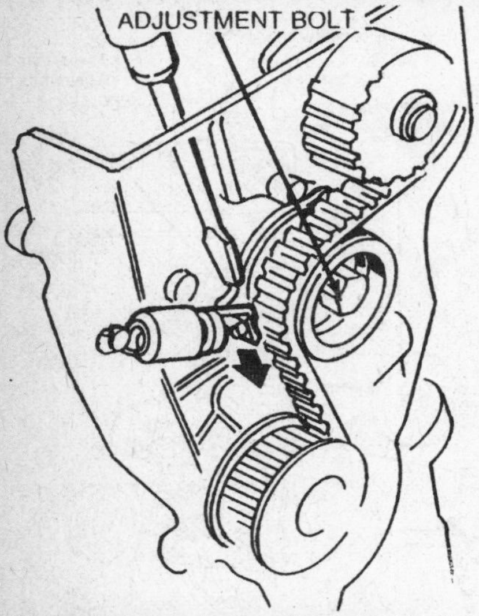


**Timing belt tensioner adjustment bolt—1342cc and 1488cc engines**

and remove the alternator and belt. On vehicles equipped with air conditioning, remove the air conditioning compressor mount bolts, compressor and belt.

4. Remove the ignition wire(s) from the valve cover. Remove the engine wire harness protector from the cylinder head cover. Remove the valve cover.

5. Remove the crankshaft pulley bolt and remove the crankshaft pulley.

6. Remove the timing belt middle and lower covers.

7. To install, reverse the removal procedure. Make sure that the timing guide plates, pulleys and the front oil seal are properly installed on the crankshaft before replacing the cover.

### OIL SEAL REPLACEMENT

In order to replace the front cover oil seal, use the front cover removal and installation procedure. Once the cover is off use a seal driver or other suitable seal removing tool and remove the seal from the front cover. Place a thin coat of oil on the new seal and using a suitable seal driver install the new seal. Then install the front cover to the engine. Be sure to install the seal with the open (spring) side facing in.

## Timing Belt and Tensioner

### REMOVAL & INSTALLATION

#### *Except 1493cc, 1590cc and 1955cc DOHC Engines*

1. Disconnect the negative battery cable. Turn the crankshaft pulley until No.1 is at TDC of the compression stroke.

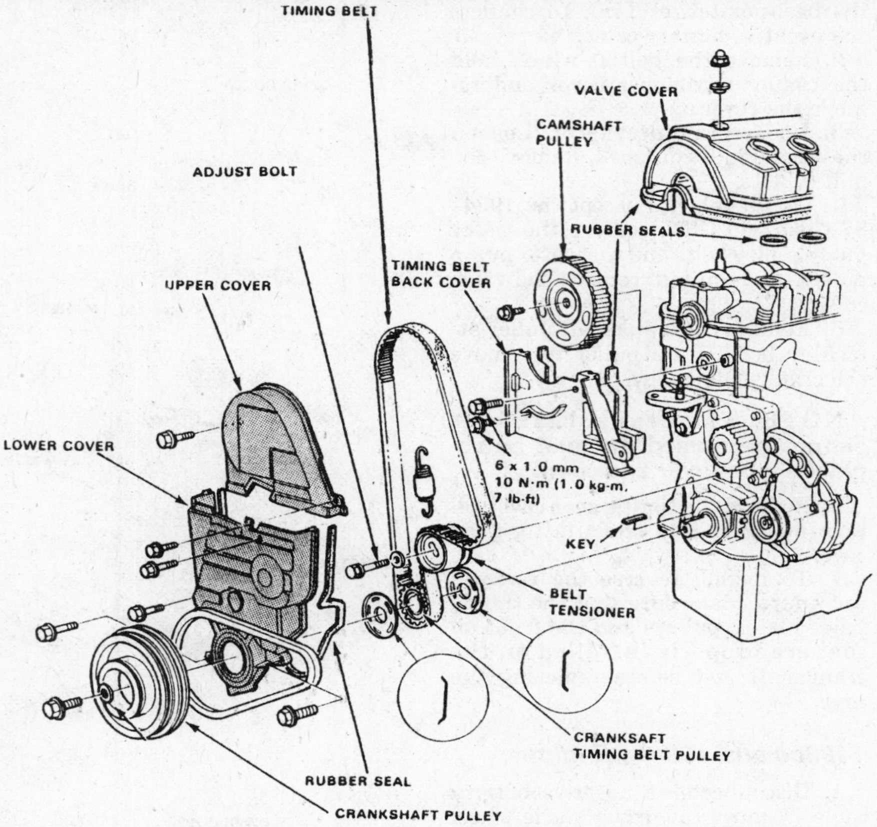


**Timing belt removal—1493cc and 1590cc engines**

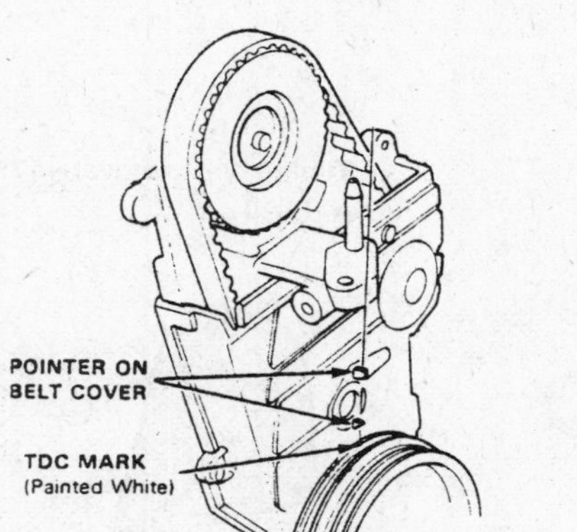


**TDC locating marks—1493cc and 1590cc engines**

2. Remove the pulley belt, water pump pulley, if equipped, crankshaft pulley, and timing gear cover. Mark the direction of timing belt rotation.

3. Loosen, but do not remove, the tensioner adjusting bolt and pivot bolt.

4. Slide the timing belt off the camshaft sprocket, crankshaft sprocket and the water pump sprocket, if equipped, then remove it from the engine.

5. To remove the camshaft timing sprocket, first remove the center bolt and then remove the sprocket with a pulley remover or a brass hammer.

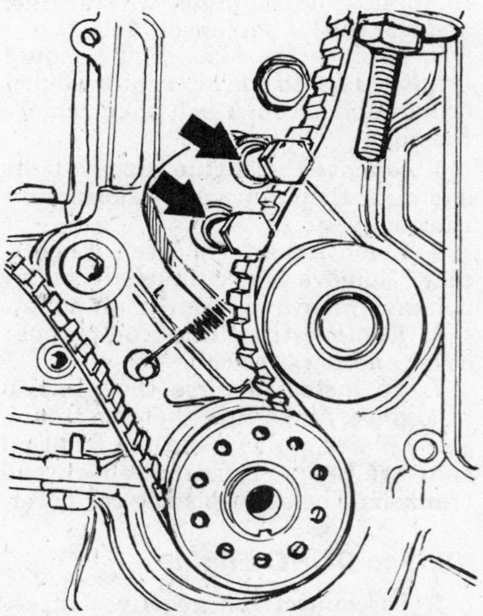

**Typical timing belt tensioner adjustment**

This can be accomplished by simply removing the timing belt upper cover, loosening the tensioner bolts, and sliding the timing belt off to expose the sprocket for removal.

**NOTE: It may be necessary to remove the valve cover, in order to gain easy access to the camshaft sprocket and accessories. If**

**you remove the timing sprocket with the timing belt cover in place, be sure not to let the woodruff key fall inside the timing cover when removing the sprocket from the camshaft.**

Inspect the timing belt. Replace it if it has been in service longer than 10,000 miles, if it is oil soaked, or if it is worn on the leading edges of the belt teeth.

6. To install, reverse the removal procedure. Be sure to position the crankshaft and camshaft timing sprockets in the TDC position.

7. When installing the timing belt, do not allow oil to come in contact with the belt. Oil will cause the rubber to swell. Be careful not to bend or twist the belt unnecessarily, nor should you use tools having sharp edges when installing or removing the belt. Be sure to install the belt with the arrow facing in the same direction it was facing during removal.

**NOTE: The tensioner is spring-loaded to apply proper tension to the timing belt automatically after making the following adjustment.**

8. After installing the timing belt, adjust the belt tension by first rotating the crankshaft counterclockwise ¼ turn or 3 teeth on the camshaft pulley. Then, retighten the adjusting bolt and finally the tensioner pivot bolt.

**NOTE: Do not remove the adjusting or pivot bolts, only loosen them. When adjusting, do not use any force other than the adjuster spring. If the belt is too tight, it will result in a shortened belt life.**

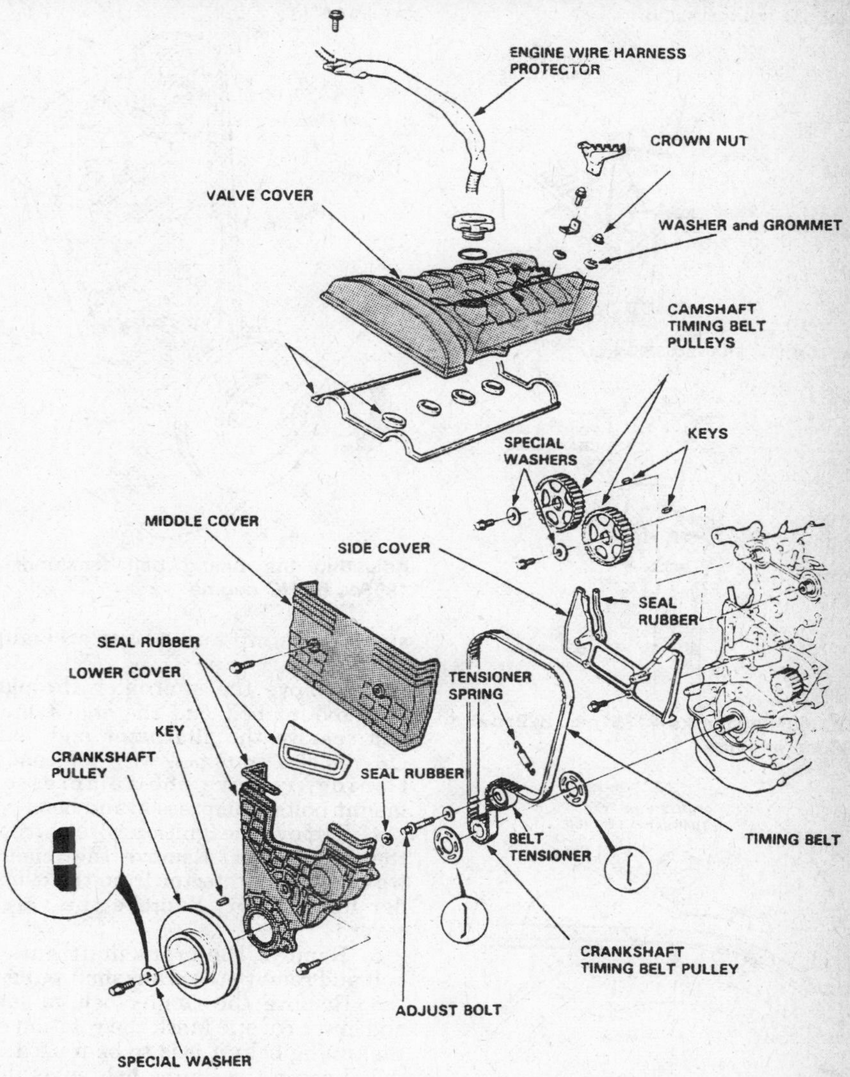


Timing belt covers removal & installation—1955cc DOHC engine

### *1493cc and 1590cc Engines*

1. Position the No. 1 cylinder at TDC on the compression stroke. Disconnect the negative battery cable. Remove the driver's side wheel well splash shield.

2. Remove the air conditioning compressor adjust pulley with bracket and the belt, if equipped.

3. Remove the side engine mount bracket. Loosen the alternator adjust bolt and through bolt then remove the belt.

4. Remove the engine support bolts and nuts, then remove the side mount rubber.

5. Remove the valve cover, if necessary. Remove the crankshaft pulley bolt and remove the crankshaft pulley.

6. Remove the timing belt upper cover and lower cover.

7. Mark the rotation of the timing belt (for easy installation). Loosen the adjusting bolt, remove the timing belt.

**NOTE: Inspect the timing belt. Replace it if it has been in service longer than 10,000 miles, if it is oil soaked, or if it is worn on the leading edges of the belt teeth.**

8. Installation is the reverse order of the removal procedure, be sure to adjust the timing belt as follows:

**NOTE: The tensioner is spring-loaded to apply proper tension to the timing belt automatically after making the following adjustment. Be sure to always adjust the timing belt tension with the engine cold.**

9. After installing the timing belt, adjust the belt tension by first rotating the crankshaft counterclockwise ¼ turn or 3 teeth on the camshaft pulley (this will put tension on the timing belt). Then, retighten the adjusting bolt and finally the tensioner pivot bolt. If the crankshaft pulley bolt broke loose while turning the crank, be sure to re-torque it to specifications.

**NOTE: Do not remove the adjusting or pivot bolts, only loosen them. When adjusting, do not use any force other than the adjuster spring. If the belt is too tight, it will result in a shortened belt life.**

### *1955cc DOHC Engine*

1. Position the No. 1 cylinder at TDC on the compression stroke. Disconnect the negative battery cable. Remove the engine support bolts and nuts, then remove the side mount rubber and side mount brackets.

2. Remove the lower engine splash shield. Remove the power steering pump adjust pulley nut and the adjust bolt. Remove the adjust pulley, power

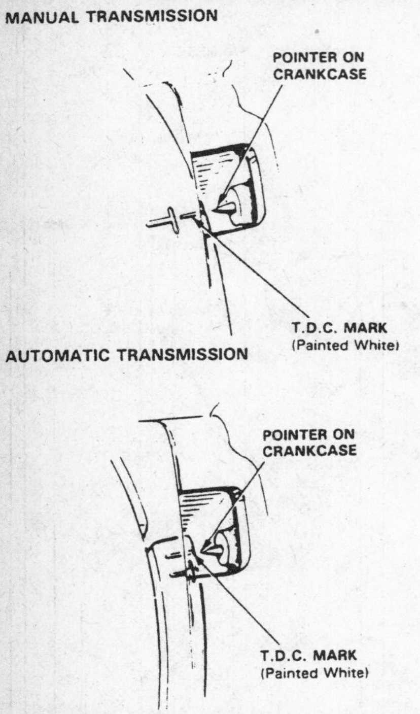


**TDC locating marks—1751cc, 1829cc and 1955cc engines**

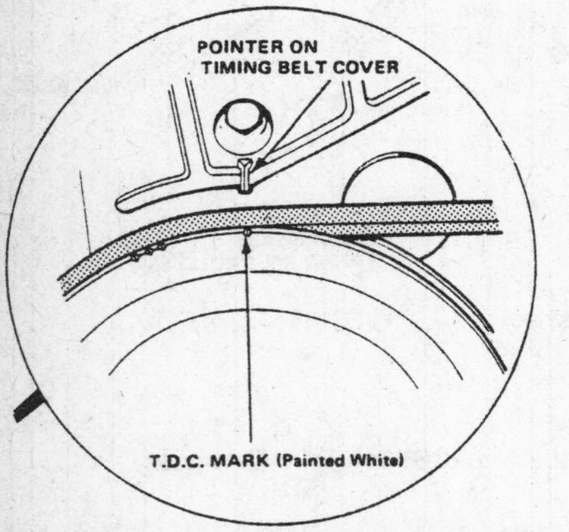


**TDC locating marks—1335cc, 1342cc and 1488cc engines**

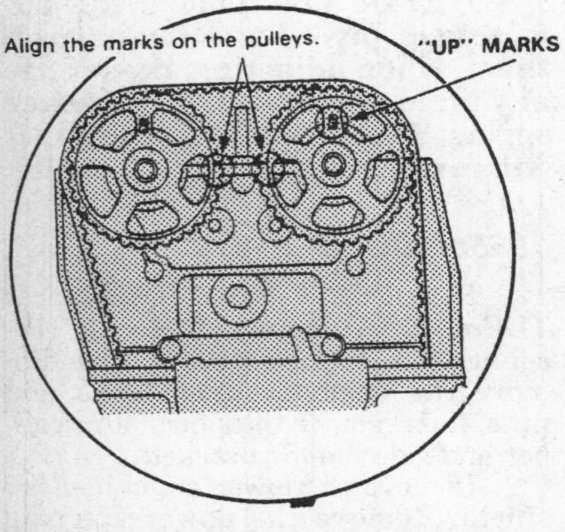


**Aligning the timing marks on the camshaft pulleys—1955cc DOHC engine**

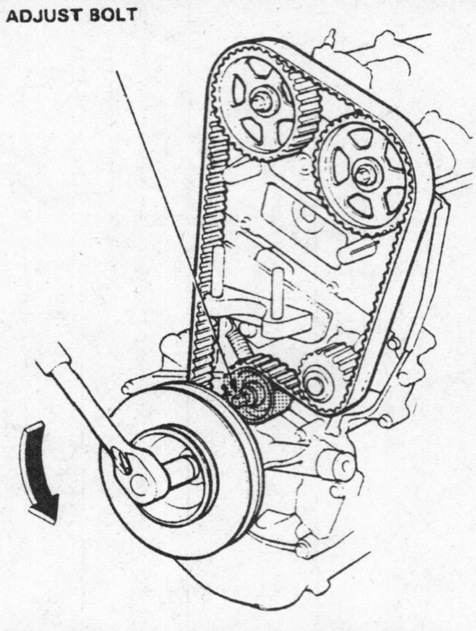


**Adjusting the timing belt tensioner—1955cc DOHC engine**

steering pump and power steering belt.

3. Remove the alternator through bolt, mount bolt and the adjust nut. and remove the alternator and belt. On vehicles equipped with air conditioning, remove the compressor mount bolts, compressor and belt.

4. Remove the ignition wire(s) from the valve cover. Remove the engine wire harness protector from the cylinder head cover. Remove the valve cover.

5. Remove the crankshaft pulley bolt and remove the crankshaft pulley.

6. Remove the timing belt middle and lower covers. Mark the rotation of the timing belt, if it is to be reused.

7. Loosen the timing belt adjusting nut and remove the timing belt.

**NOTE: Inspect the timing belt. Replace it if it has been in service longer than 10,000 miles, if it is oil soaked, or if it is worn on the leading edges of the belt teeth.**

8. Be sure to install the timing belt with the No. 1 piston at TDC on the compression stroke. Installation is the reverse order of the removal procedure, be sure to adjust the timing belt as follows:

**NOTE: The tensioner is spring-loaded to apply proper tension to the timing belt automatically after making the following adjustment. Be sure to always adjust the timing belt tension with the engine cold. To set the No. 1 cylinder at TDC, align the hole on the camshaft with the hole in the No. 1 camshaft holders and drive 5.0mm pin punches into the holes.**

9. After installing the timing belt, adjust the belt tension by first rotating the crankshaft counterclockwise 1/4 turn or 3 teeth on the camshaft pulley (this will put tension on the timing belt). Then, retighten the adjusting bolt and finally the tensioner pivot bolt. If the crankshaft pulley bolt broke loose while turning the crank, be sure to re-torque it to specifications.

**NOTE: Do not remove the adjusting or pivot bolts, only loosen them. When adjusting, do not use any force other than the adjuster spring. If the belt is too tight, it will result in a shortened belt life.**

## Timing Sprockets

### REMOVAL & INSTALLATION

**NOTE: Be sure to use the timing cover and timing belt removal and installation procedures to aid in the success of the following procedure.**

1. Turn the crankshaft pulley until No. 1 is at TDC of the compression stroke.

2. Remove the pulley belt, water pump pulley, if equipped, crankshaft pulley, and timing gear cover. Mark the direction of timing belt rotation.

3. Loosen, but do not remove, the tensioner adjusting bolt and pivot bolt.

4. Slide the timing belt off the camshaft sprocket, crankshaft sprocket and the water pump sprocket, if equipped, then remove it from the engine.

5. To remove the either camshaft or crankshaft timing sprocket, first remove the center bolt and then remove the sprocket with a pulley remover or a brass hammer.

6. To install, reverse the removal procedure. Be sure to position the crankshaft and camshaft timing sprockets in the TDC position. Torque the camshaft sprocket bolt to 30 ft. lbs.

When installing the timing belt, do not allow oil to come in contact with the belt. Oil will cause the rubber to swell. Be careful not to bend or twist the belt unnecessarily, nor should you use tools having sharp edges when installing or removing the belt. Be sure to install the belt with the arrow facing in the same direction it was facing during removal.

After installing the timing belt, adjust the belt tension by first rotating the crankshaft counterclockwise 1/4 turn or 3 teeth on the camshaft pulley. Then, retighten the adjusting bolt and finally the tensioner pivot bolt.

**NOTE: Do not remove the adjusting or pivot bolts, only loosen them. When adjusting, do not use**

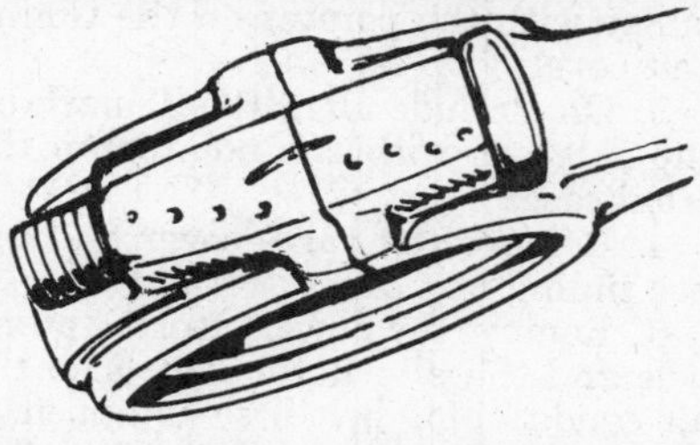

Mark the pistons and rods if they are not marked from the factory

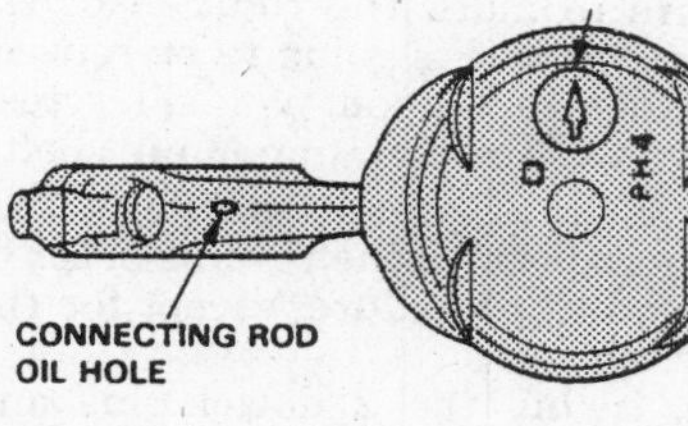


Typical piston alignment marks

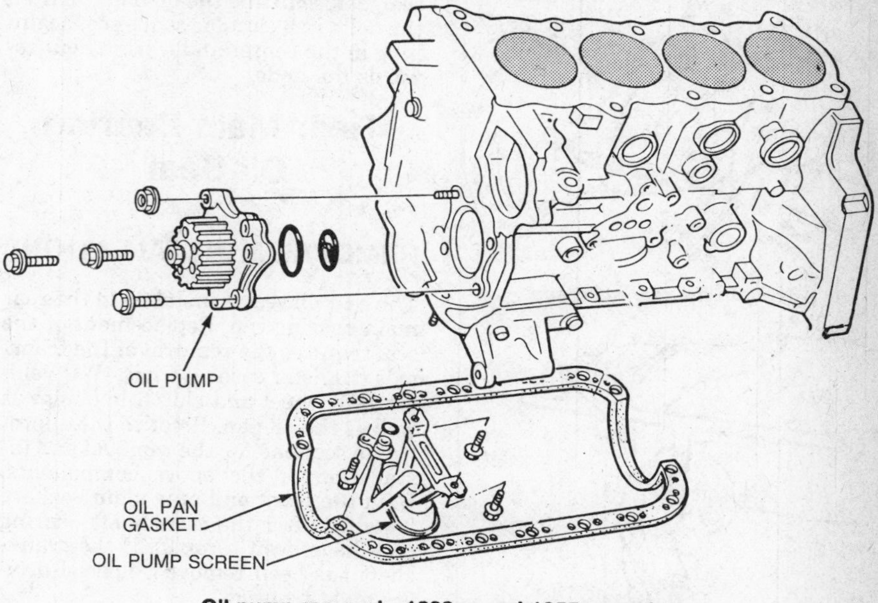


Oil pump removal – 1829cc and 1955cc engines

**For all piston and connecting rod overhaul procedures, please refer to Engine Rebuilding in the Unit Repair section.**

**any force other than the adjuster spring. If the belt is too tight, it will result in a shortened belt life.**

## Piston and Connecting Rod

### POSITIONING

**For all piston and connecting rod overhaul procedures, please refer to "Engine Rebuilding" in the Unit Repair section.**

# ENGINE LUBRICATION

## Oil Pan

### REMOVAL & INSTALLATION

**NOTE: Removal of the oil pan on the Civic 4WD requires transfer case removal.**

1. Disconnect the negative battery cable. Raise and support the vehicle safely. Drain the engine oil.
2. Remove the lower splash pan if equipped.
3. Attach a chain to the bracket on the transaxle case and raise just enough to take the load off the center

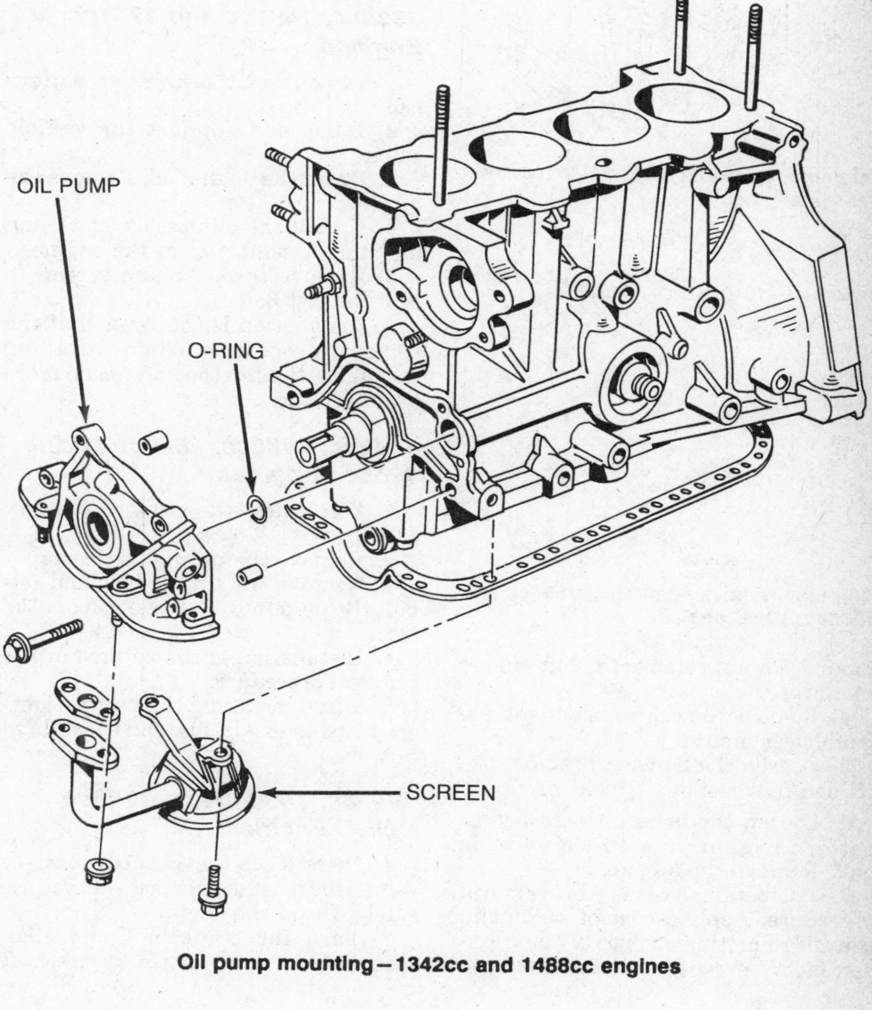


Oil pump mounting – 1342cc and 1488cc engines

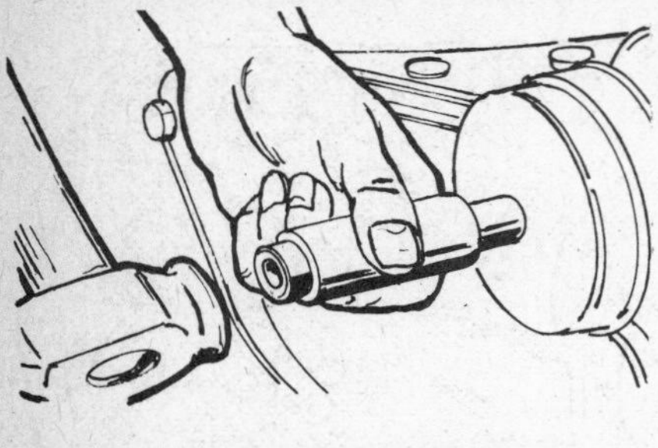

Driving in the rear main seal

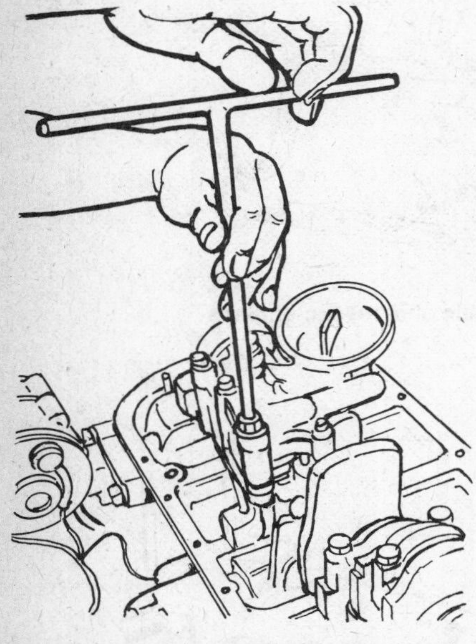

Oil pump removal—1335cc, 1487cc and 1751cc engines

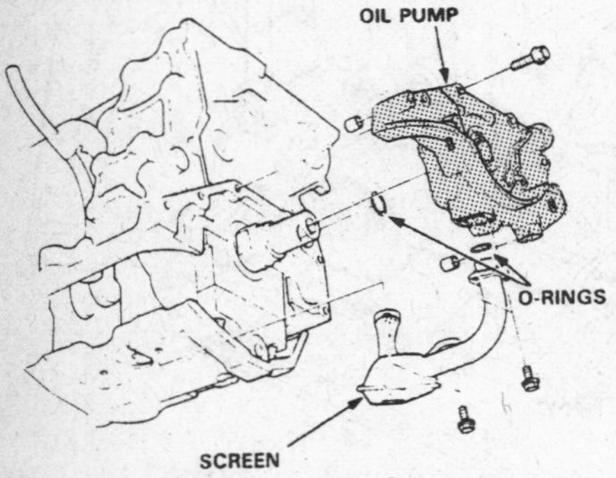


Oil pump removal— 1493cc, 1590cc and 1955cc DOHC engine

mount. Do not remove the left engine mount.

4. Remove the center beam and engine lower mount.

5. Loosen the bolts and remove the oil pan flywheel dust shield.

6. Loosen the bolts in a criss-cross pattern beginning with the outside bolt. Remove the oil pan.

7. To install, reverse the removal procedure. Apply a coat of sealant to the entire mating surface of the cylinder block, except the crankshaft oil seal, before fitting the oil pan. Tighten the bolts in a circular sequence, beginning in the center and working out towards the ends.

## Rear Main Bearing Oil Seal

### REMOVAL & INSTALLATION

The rear oil seal is installed in the rear main bearing cap. Replacement of the seal requires the removal of the transaxle (transfer case on Civic 4WD vehicles), flywheel and clutch housing, as well as the oil pan. Refer to the appropriate sections for the removal and installation of the above components. Both the front and rear main seal are installed after the crankshaft bearing caps have been torqued, if the crankshaft has been removed. Special drivers must be used.

## Oil Pump

### REMOVAL & INSTALLATION

#### *1335cc, 1487cc and 1751cc Engines*

1. Disconnect the negative battery cable.
2. Raise and support the vehicle safely.
3. Drain the engine oil. Remove the oil pan.
4. Unbolt the oil passage block and oil pump assembly from the engine.
5. Remove the oil pump screen to find the last bolt.
6. Installation is the reverse of the removal procedure. When installing the pump, tighten the bolts to no more than 8 ft. lbs.

#### *1342cc, 1488cc, 1829cc and 1955cc Engines*

1. Disconnect the negative battery cable.
2. Remove the timing belt cover.
3. Remove the timing belt and unbolt the oil pump. Remove it from the block.
4. Installation is the reverse of the removal procedure.
5. When installing the pump, tighten the bolts to 9 ft. lbs. and the nuts to 5 ft. lbs.

#### *1493cc, 1590cc and 1955cc DOHC Engines*

1. Disconnect the negative battery cable. Raise and support the vehicle safely. Drain the engine oil.
2. Turn the crankshaft and align the white groove on the crankshaft pulley with the pointer on the timing belt cover.
3. On Prelude align the **T** mark on the flywheel with the pointer on the crankcase.
4. Remove the valve cover and upper timing belt cover.
5. Remove the power steering pump belt and the alternator belt, also the air conditioning belt if so equipped.
6. Remove the crankshaft pulley and the lower timing belt cover. Remove the timing belt and drive pulley. Be sure to mark the rotation of the timing belt if it is going to be reused.
7. Remove the oil pan, oil screen and remove the oil pump mount bolts. Remove the oil pump assembly.
8. Installtion is the reverse order of the removal procedure, except for the following:
   a. Install the 2 dowel pins and new O-ring to the cylinder block.
   b. Be sure that the mating surfaces are clean and dry. Apply a suitable liquid gasket evenly, in a narrow bead centered on the mating surface.
   c. To prevent leakage of oil, apply a suitable thread sealer to the inner threads of the bolt holes.
   d. Do not allow the sealant to dry before assembling. But wait approximately 30 minutes after assembly before filling the engine with oil.

# ENGINE COOLING

## Radiator

### REMOVAL & INSTALLATION

1. Disconnect the negative battery cable. Drain the radiator.
2. Disconnect the thermo-switch wire and the fan motor wire. Remove the fan shroud if equipped.
3. Disconnect the upper coolant hose at the upper radiator tank and the lower hose at the water pump connecting pipe. Disconnect and plug the automatic transaxle cooling lines at the bottom of the radiator, if equipped.
4. Remove the hoses to the coolant reservoir, if equipped.
5. Detach the radiator mounting bolts and remove the radiator with the fan attached. The fan can be easily unbolted from the back of the radiator.
6. To install, reverse the removal procedure. Bleed the cooling system.

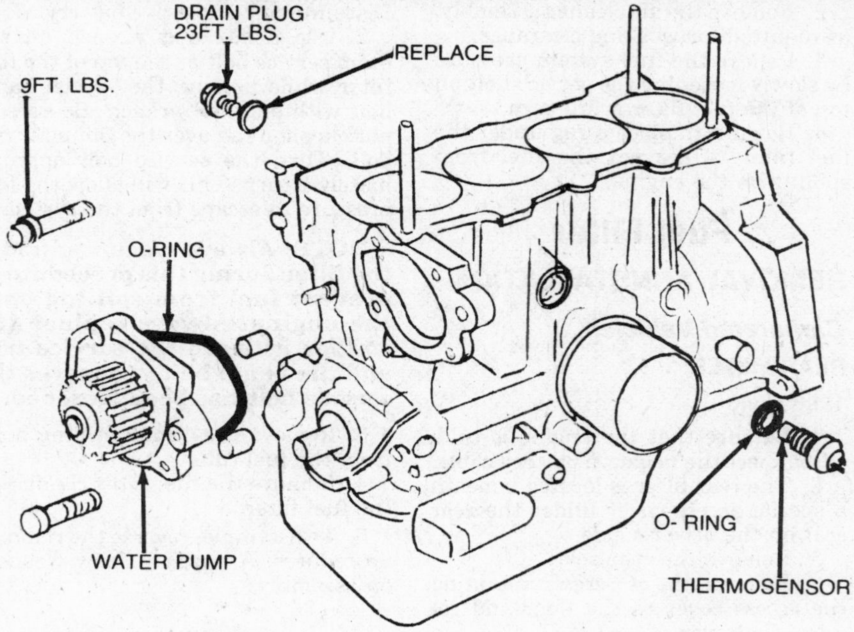


Water pump and related components—1342cc and 1488cc engines

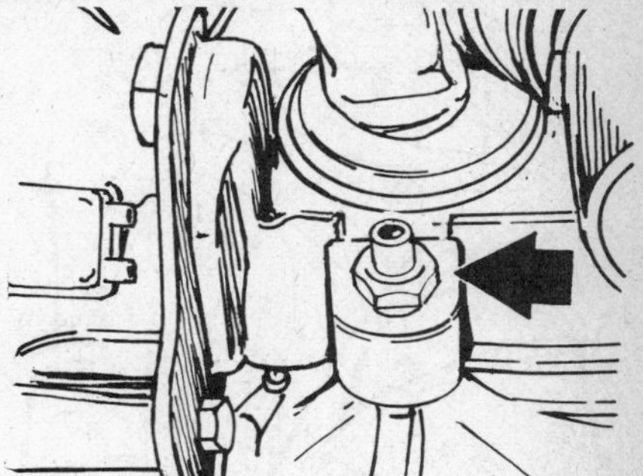

Cooling system bleed bolt

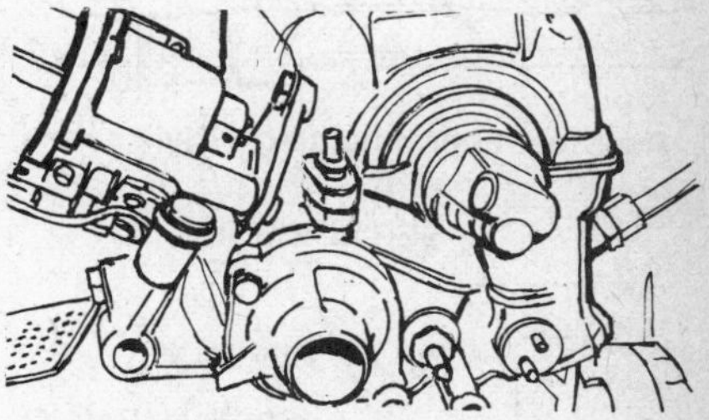

Typical thermostat housing and cooling system bleed bolt

## Water Pump

### REMOVAL & INSTALLATION

#### *Except 1342cc, 1488cc, 1493cc and 1590cc Engines*

**NOTE: On some later engines it may be necessary to remove the timing belt covers in order to gain access to the water pump assembly.**

1. Disconnect the negative battery cable. Drain the radiator.
2. Loosen the alternator bolts. Move the alternator toward the cylinder block and remove the drive belt. It may also be necessary to remove the power steering belt, air pump belt and air conditioning belt if so equipped.
3. Loosen the pump mounting bolts and remove the pump together with the pulley and the rubber seal.
4. To install, reverse the removal procedure using a new gasket. Bleed the cooling system.

#### *1342cc, 1488cc, 1493cc and 1590cc Engines*

1. Position the engine at TDC on the compression stroke. Disconnect the negative battery cable. Drain the radiator.
2. Remove the timing belt cover. Remove the timing belt from the water pump drive sprocket.
3. Loosen the water pump mounting bolts and remove together with the drive sprocket.
4. To install, reverse the removal procedure using a new O-ring. Bleed the cooling system.

## Thermostat

### REMOVAL & INSTALLATION

1. Disconnect the negative battery cable. The thermostat housing is located in the end of the cylinder head, with the exception of the 1342cc and 1488cc engines where it is located at the end of the water pump inlet tube.
2. Unbolt and remove the thermostat cover and pull the thermostat from the housing.
3. To install, reverse the removal procedure. Always install the spring end of the thermostat toward the engine. Tighten the 2 cover bolts to 7 ft. lbs. (84 inch lbs.). Always use a new gasket. Bleed the cooling system.

### COOLING SYSTEM BLEEDING

1. Loosen the air bleed bolt in the water outlet, and then fill the radiator to the bottom of the filler neck with antifreeze/coolant. Tighten the bleed bolt as soon as the coolant starts to run out in a steady stream without any air bubbles in it.
2. With the radiator cap off, start the engine and allow it to warm up (the cooling fan should go on at least twice). Then if necessary add more antifreeze/coolant to bring the level back up to the bottom of the filler neck.
3. Put the radiator cap on, restart the engine and check for any leaks.

# EMISSION CONTROLS

**Please refer to "Emission Controls", in the Unit Repair section for system maintenance procedures. Due to the complex nature of modern electronic engine control systems, comprehensive diagnosis and testing procedures fall outside the confines of this repair manual. For complete information on diagnosis, testing and repair procedures concerning all modern engine and emission control systems, please refer to "Chilton's Guide to Electronic Engine Controls".**

# FUEL SYSTEM

## Fuel System Service Precaution

### RELIEVING FUEL SYSTEM PRESSURE

1. Be sure that the engine is cold.

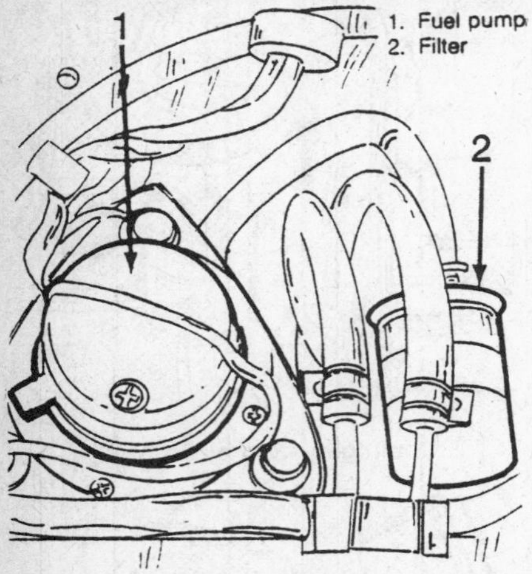


Rear fuel filter mounting—Civic sedan

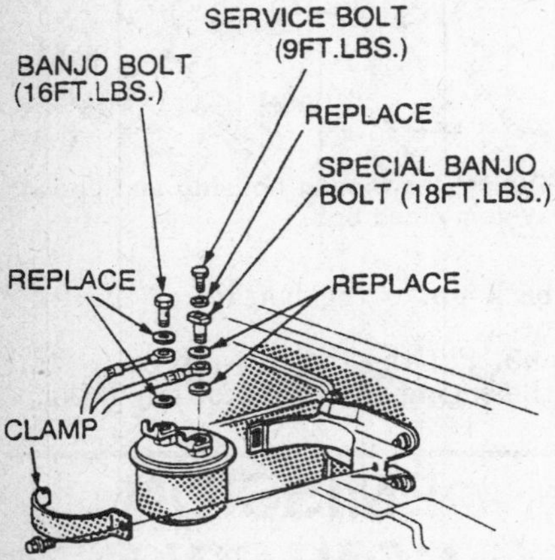


Fuel filter mounting—Accord fuel injected models

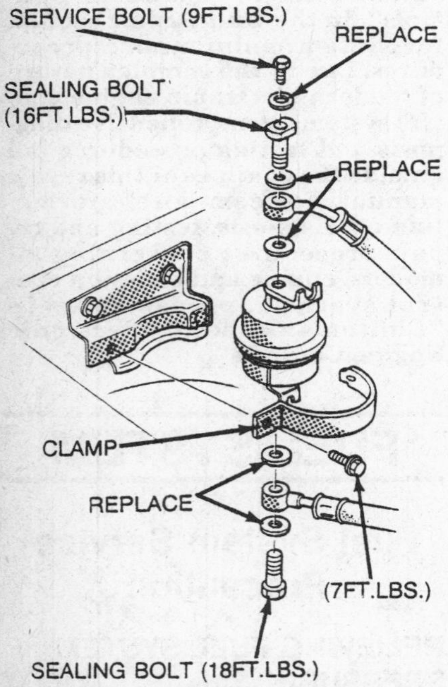


Fuel filter mounting—Civic fuel injected models

2. Remove the air cleaner assembly, as required for working clearance.
3. Relieve the fuel system pressure by slowly loosening the service bolt on top of the fuel filter a full turn.
4. Be sure to place a rag under the fuel filter to prevent the fuel from spilling on the engine.

## Fuel Filter

### REMOVAL & INSTALLATION

#### *Carbureted Vehicles*

**REAR FILTER**

**1983 Civic**

1. Be sure that the engine is cold. Disconnect the negative battery cable.
2. The rear filter is located beneath a special access cover under the rear seat on the driver's side.
3. Remove the rear seat.
4. Remove the 4 screws retaining the access cover to the floor and remove the cover.
5. The filter, together with the electric fuel pump, is located in the recess. Pinch the lines shut, loosen the hose clamps and remove the filter.
6. Installation is the reverse of the removal procedure.

**FRONT FILTER**

**1983 Civic**

1. Be sure that the engine is cold. Disconnect the negative battery cable.
2. The rear filter is located under the vehicle, in front of the spare tire.
3. Raise and support the vehicle safely. Clamp off the fuel lines leading to and from the filter.
4. Loosen the hose clamps and, taking note of which hose is the inlet and which is the outlet, remove the filter.
5. Some replacement filters have an arrow embossed or printed on the filter body, in which case you want to install the new filter with the arrow pointing in the direction of the fuel flow.
6. After installing the new filter, remember to unclamp the fuel lines. Check for leaks.

**1984–90 All Models**

1. Be sure that the engine is cold. Disconnect the negative battery cable.
2. The fuel filter is located at the carburetor.
3. Properly relieve the fuel system pressure. Disconnect the fuel lines.
4. If equipped remove the fuel filter mounting. Remove the fuel filter from the vehicle.
5. Installation is the reverse of the removal procedure.

#### *Fuel Injected Vehicles*

1. Be sure that the engine is cold. Disconnect the negative battery cable.
2. Use a box end wrench on the 6mm service bolt at the top of the fuel filter while holding the special banjo bolt with another wrench. Be sure to place a shop rag over the 6mm service bolt. Turn the service bolt approximately 1 turn. This will allow the fuel pressure to escape from the system.

**NOTE: Always place rag under the filter during this procedure to prevent fuel from spilling onto the engine. Always replace the washer between the service bolt and the banjo bolt, whenever the service bolt has been loosened.**

3. Remove the 12mm sealing bolts from the fuel filter.
4. Remove the fuel filter clamp and the fuel filter.
5. To assemble, reverse the removal procedures. Always use new washers on assembly.

## Mechanical Fuel Pump

### PRESSURE TESTING

1. To inspect the pump for operation, first disconnect the fuel line at the carburetor. Connect a fuel pressure gauge to the delivery side of the pump. Start the engine and measure the pump delivery pressure.
2. After measuring, stop the engine and check to see if the gauge drops suddenly. If the gauge drops suddenly and/or the delivery pressure is incorrect, check for a fuel or oil leak from the diaphragm or from the valves.
3. To test for volume, disconnect the fuel line from the carburetor and insert it into a 1 quart container. Crank the engine for 64 seconds at 600 rpm, or 40 seconds at 400 rpm. The bottle should be half full (1 pint).

### REMOVAL & INSTALLATION

#### *1342cc and 1488cc Engines*

1. Be sure that the engine is cold. Disconnect the negative battery cable. Pinch the fuel lines closed at the pump.
2. Remove the inlet and outlet fuel lines at the pump.

**NOTE: When removing the fuel lines, slide the clamps back and twist the lines as you pull, to avoid damaging them.**

3. Loosen and remove the mounting bolts. Remove the pump.
4. To install, reverse the removal procedure. Start the engine and check for leaks.

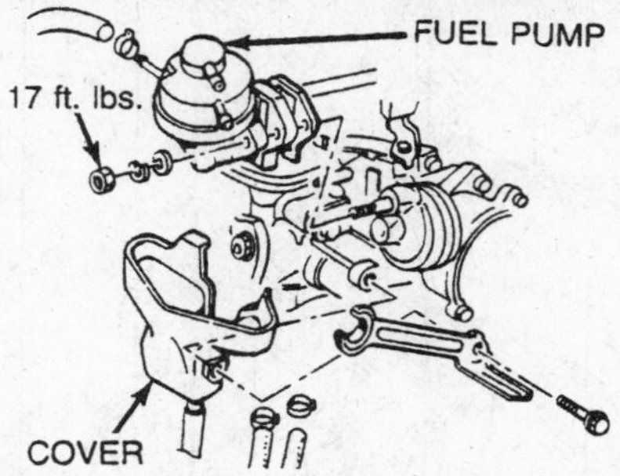


**Mechanical fuel pump mounting – 1342cc and 1488cc engines equipped with a carburetor**

## MECHANICAL FUEL PUMP SPECIFICATIONS

| Engine rpm | Delivery Pressure (lb. in.$^2$) | Vacuum (in.Hg.) | Displacement (in.$^3$/minute) |
|---|---|---|---|
| 600 | 2.56 | 17.72 | 27 |
| 3,000 | 2.56 | 7.87–11.81 | 43 |
| 6,000 | 2.56 | 7.87–11.81 | 46 |

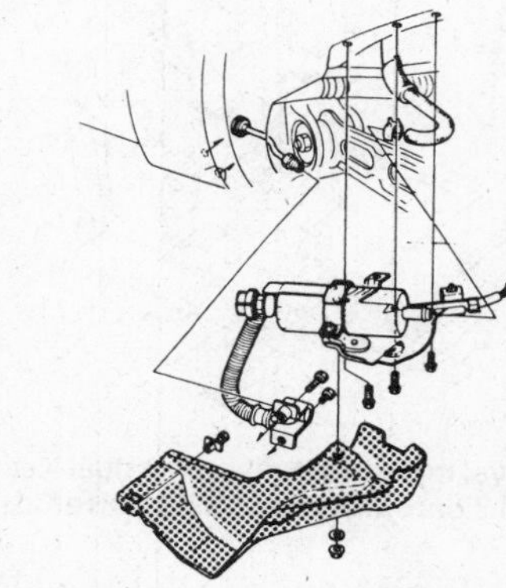

**Electric fuel pump mounting-fuel injected models**

# Electric Fuel Pump

## PRESSURE TESTING

1. Relieve the fuel pressure from the system.
2. Remove the service bolt from the fuel filter and attach a pressure gauge. On carbureted vehicles, disconnect the fuel line at the fuel filter and attach the pressure gauge to it.
3. On carbureted vehicles, remove the fuel cut off relay from the fuse box and connect a jumper wire in its place. Turn the ignition switch to **ON** until the pressure stabilizes and then turn it **OFF**. The pressure should be 2.6–3.3 psi.
4. On fuel injected vehicles, start the engine and measure the fuel pressure with the engine idling and the vacuum hose to the pressure regulator disconnected. The pressure should be 36–41 psi.
5. If the fuel pressure is not as specified, first check the fuel pump. If the fuel pump is good, check the following.
6. If the pressure is higher than specified, inspect for a pinched or clogged fuel return hose or piping and faulty pressure regulator.
7. If the pressure is lower than specified, inspect for a clogged fuel filter, pinched or clogged fuel hose from the fuel tank to the fuel pump, pressure regulator failure, leakage in the fuel line or pinched, broken or disconnected regulator vacuum hose.

## REMOVAL & INSTALLATION

### *Carbureted Vehicles*

1. Remove the gas filler cap to relieve any excess pressure in the system.
2. Obtain a pair of suitable clamps to pinch shut the fuel lines to the pump.
3. Disconnect the negative battery cable.
4. Locate the fuel pump. As required, raise and support the vehicle safely.
5. Pinch the inlet and outlet fuel lines shut. Loosen the hose clamps. As required, remove the filter mounting clip on the left hand side of the bracket.
6. Disconnect the positive lead wire and ground wire from the pump at their quick disconnect fitting.
7. Remove the 2 fuel pump retaining bolts, taking care not to loose the 2 spacers and bolt collars.
8. Remove the fuel lines and fuel pump.
9. Installation is the reverse of the removal procedure.

### *Fuel Injected Vehicles*

#### 1986–87 CIVIC AND PRELUDE

1. Disconnect the negative battery cable.
2. Relieve the fuel pressure by slowly loosening the service bolt on the top of the fuel filter about 1 turn.

**NOTE: Place a rag under the filter during this procedure to prevent fuel from spilling onto the engine. Always replace the washer between the service bolt and the banjo bolt, whenever the service bolt has been loosened.**

3. Raise the vehicle and support it safely.
4. Remove the left rear wheel.
5. Remove the fuel pump cover bolts, then remove the cover.
6. Remove the mounting bolts from the fuel pump mount, then remove the fuel pump with its mount.
7. Disconnect the fuel lines and the electrical connectors.
8. Remove the clamp and remove the fuel pump from the mounting bracket.
9. Remove the fuel line and silencer from the pump.
10. To install, reverse the removal procedures. Turn on the ignition switch and check for fuel leaks.

#### 1988–90 CIVIC

1. Disconnect the negative battery cable. Raise and support the vehicle safely.
2. Remove the fuel tank. The fuel pump is part of the fuel sending unit.
3. Remove the fuel pump from the sending unit assembly.
4. Installation is the reverse of the removal procedure.

#### 1985–90 ACCORD AND 1988–90 PRELUDE

1. Disconnect the negative battery cable.
2. Relieve the fuel pressure by slowly loosening the service bolt on the top of the fuel filter about 1 turn.

**NOTE: Place a rag under the filter during this procedure to prevent fuel from spilling onto the engine. Always replace the washer between the service bolt and the banjo bolt, whenever the service bolt has been loosened.**

3. Remove the left maintenance access cover in the luggage area. Disconnect the fuel lines and couplers.
4. Remove the fuel pump mounting nuts. Remove the fuel pump from the fuel tank. If the fuel pump is hard to remove, slightly lower the fuel tank by loosening the fuel tank mounting nuts.
5. Installation is the reverse order of the removal procedure. When installing the maintenance access cover, make sure that the seal is attached to the cover.

# Carburetor

## REMOVAL & INSTALLATION

### *Except Prelude with 1829cc Engine*

1. Disconnect the negative battery cable.
2. Disconnect and label the following. The hot air tube, all vacuum hoses and lines, the breather chamber (on air cleaner case) to intake manifold at the breather chamber, the hose from the air cleaner case to to the valve cover, the hose from the carbon canister to the carburetor, at the carburetor, the throttle opener hose, at the throttle opener.

3. On Prelude equipped with the 1829cc engine, drain the coolant and remove the coolant hoses from the thermowax valve and the right end of the intake manifold.

4. Disconnect and plug the fuel line at the carburetor. Disconnect the choke and throttle control cables. Disconnect the fuel shut-off solenoid wires.

5. Remove the carburetor retaining bolts or loosen the insulator bands and then remove the carburetor. Leave the insulator on the manifold.

**NOTE: After removing the carburetor, cover the intake manifold parts to keep out foreign materials.**

### *Prelude with 1829cc Engine*

1. Disconnect the negative battery cable. Disconnect the fresh air intake duct and hot air intake hoses from the air cleaner cover.

2. Disconnect the No. 8 vacuum hose to the hot air intake control diaphragm. Unsnap the 4 clips and remove the center bolt, then remove the air cleaner cover and element.

3. Disconnect the breather hose from the valve cover. Disconnect a tag all the hose from the air cleaner base. Disconnect and tag the connectors to the solenoids at the top of the air cleaner base.

4. Remove the 10mm bolts from under the air cleaner base. Remove the retaining nuts, air screens and flanges.

5. Remove the air cleaner base. Disconnect and tag all the necessary vacuum hoses and lines from the carburetors.

6. Disconnect the throttle cable. Disconnect the A.J.C. vacuum hoses at the vacuum tube manifold.

7. Drain coolant and remove the 3 coolant hoses at the thermowax valve. Disconnect the vent hoses from the canister to the air cut-off solenoid valve.

8. Disconnect the canister purge hose at the vacuum tube manifold. Disconnect the carburetor wire connector and choke heater wire connector.

9. Remove the main fuel line from the right side of the vacuum manifold. Loosen the insulator bands and remove the carburetor with the vacuum tube manifold assembly still attached.

10. Installation is the reverse order of the removal procedure. Be sure to check that the all the vacuum hoses are routed correctly and are not pinched or kinked. Make sure that the carburetors are fully seated in the insulator and are tight. Fill, bleed and check the coolant system. Check the idle speed/mixture and adjust as necessary.

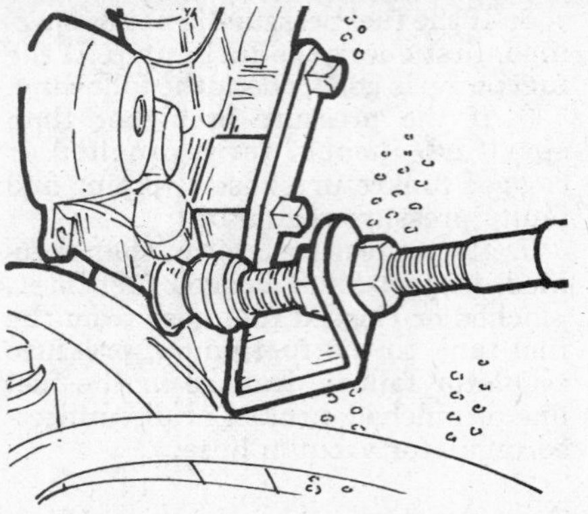

Throttle cable adjusting location

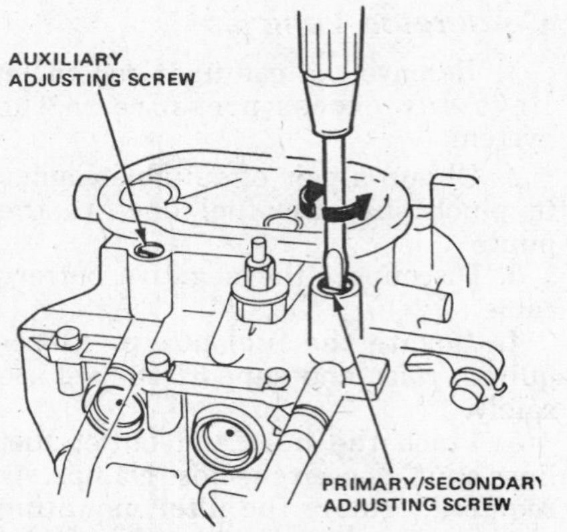


Float level adjustment—Keihn 3 bbl carburetor

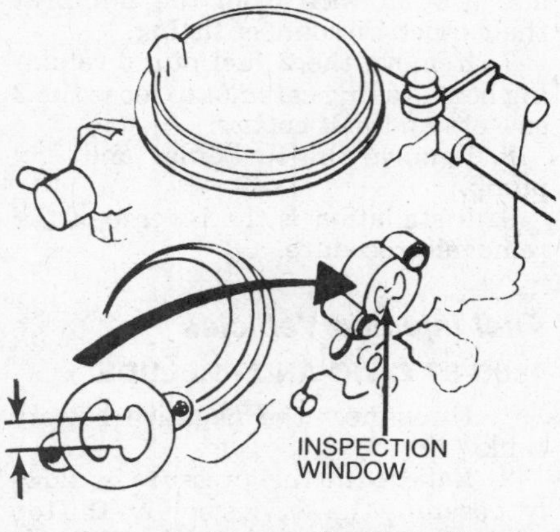


Inspection window showing the fuel level—1986 and later models with the Keihn 2 bbl. carburetor

## THROTTLE LINKAGE ADJUSTMENT

1. Remove the air cleaner assembly to provide access.

2. Check that the cable free play (deflection) is 4–10mm. This is measured right before the cable enters the throttle shaft bellcrank.

3. If the deflection is not to specifications, rotate the cable adjusting nuts in the required direction.

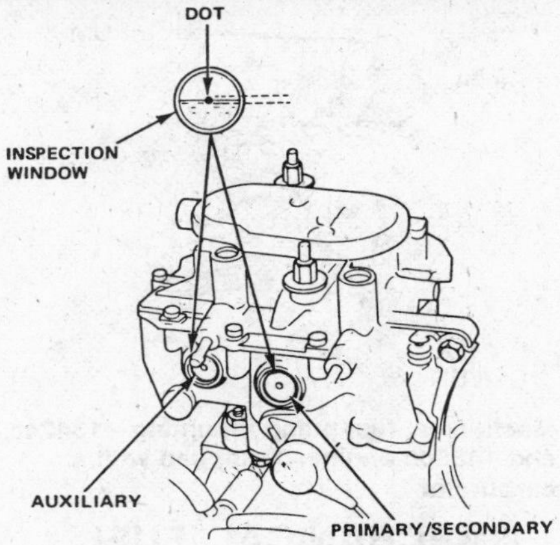


Inspection window showing the fuel level—Keihn 3 bbl carburetor

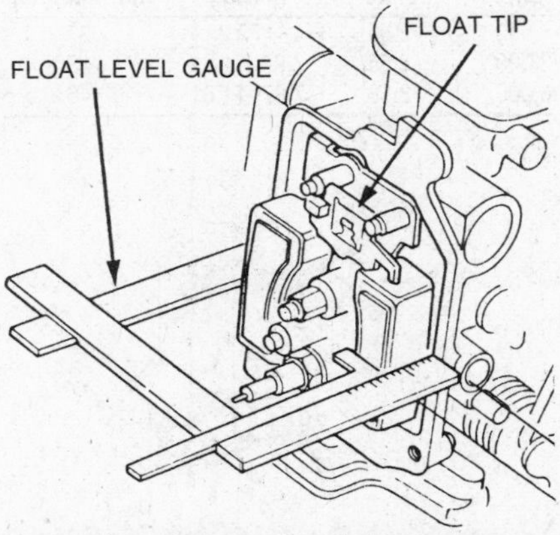


Float level measurement on the dual Keihin sidedraft carburetors—1829cc Prelude

4. As a final check, have an assistant press the gas pedal all the way to the floor, while you look down inside the throttle bore checking that the throttle plates reach the wide open throttle (WOT) vertical position.

5. Install the air cleaner.

## FLOAT AND FUEL LEVEL ADJUSTMENT

### *Except Prelude with 1829cc Engine*

With the vehicle on level ground and at normal operating temperature, check the primary and secondary fuel level inspection windows. If the fuel level is not touching the dot, adjust it by turning the adjusting screws.

**NOTE: Do not turn the adjusting screws more than 1/8 turn every 15 seconds.**

### *Prelude with 1829cc Engine*

1. Remove the side draft carburetors from the engine and remove the float chambers from the carburetors.

1. Stop tab
2. Relief lever adjusting tang
3. Actuator rod
4. Choke opener diaphragm

CVCC choke adjustment components

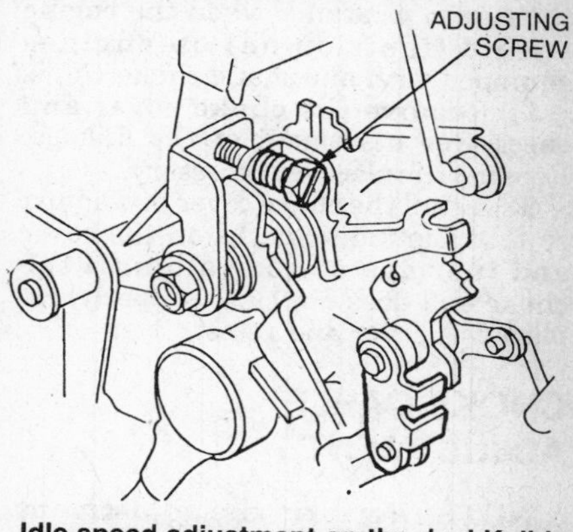


Idle speed adjustment on the dual Keihin sidedraft carburetors

1. Choke butterfly valve
2. Adjusting nut
3. Locknut

CVCC choke cable adjustment

2. Using a float level gauge, measure the float level with the float tip lightly touching the float valve and the float chamber surface tilted about 30 degrees from vertical. The float level should be 16mm.

3. To adjust the float level on the sub-carburetor, remove the float chamber. Using a float level gauge, measure the float level.

**NOTE: The float level of the sub-carburetor can't be adjusted. If the float level is incorrect the float must be replaced.**

## FAST IDLE ADJUSTMENT

### *Except Prelude with 1829cc Engine*

1. Run the engine to normal operating temperature.
2. Connect a tachometer according to the manufacturer's specifications.
3. Disconnect and plug the hose from the fast idle unloader.
4. Shut the engine off, hold the choke valve closed. Open and close the throttle to engage the fast idle cam.
5. Start the engine, run it for 1 minute. Fast idle speed should be 2300–3300 rpm for manual transaxle equipped vehicles and 2200–3200 rpm for automatic transaxle equipped vehicles.

**NOTE: Underhood specifications sticker figures must be used if they differ from those above.**

6. Adjust the idle by turning the fast idle screw.

### *Prelude with 1829cc Engine*

1. Start the engine and bring it to normal operating temperature. Shut off the engine.
2. Remove the E-clip and flat washer from the thermowax valve linkage, then slide the linkage past the fast idle cam.

**NOTE: Be careful not to bend the linkage or the fast idle speed will be changed.**

3. While holding open the throttle, turn the fast idle cam counterclockwise until the fast idle lever is on the third step.
4. Without touching the throttle, start the engine and check the idle speed. The idle speed should be 2000 rpm. Adjustment of the idle speed can be made by turning the fast idle adjusting screw.
5. Stop the engine and reconnect the thermowax valve linkage.
6. Start the engine and check that as the engine warms up, the idle speed decreases.

**NOTE: If the idle speed doesn't drop, clean the linkage along with the carburetor. If the speed still doesn't drop, check for damaged or stuck linkage.**

## CHOKE ADJUSTMENT

### *1335cc, 1487cc and 1751cc Engines*

The choke plate should close to less

than 3mm clearance when the engine is cold (ignition on) on engines equipped with automatic choke.

1. Remove the choke cover and check free movement of the linkage. Repair or replace as necessary.

2. Install the choke cover and adjust so that the index marks on the cover and thermostat body align. If the choke still does not close properly, replace the cover and retest.

## CHOKE CABLE ADJUSTMENT

**NOTE: Perform the adjustment after the throttle plate opening has been set.**

### *Civic with 1487cc Engine*

1. Remove the air cleaner assembly.
2. Push the choke knob all the way in at the dash. Check that the choke butterfly valve (choke plate) is fully open (vertical).
3. Pull out the choke knob while observing the action of the butterfly valve. When the choke knob is pulled out to the second detent position, the butterfly valve should just close. Then, when the choke knob is pulled all the way out, the butterfly valve should remain in the closed position.
4. To adjust, loosen the choke cable locknut and rotate the adjusting nut so that with the choke knob pushed flush against the dash (open position), the butterfly valve just rests against its positioning stop tab. Tighten the locknut.
5. If the choke butterfly valve is irregular in operation, or if it does not close properly, check the butterfly valve and shaft for binding. Check also the operation of the return spring.

## ACCELERATOR PUMP ADJUSTMENT

### *1335cc, 1487cc and 1751cc Engines*

1. Remove the air cleaner.
2. Make sure that the pump shaft is moving freely throughout the pump stroke.
3. Check that the pump lever is in contact with the pump shaft.
4. Measure between the bottom end of the pump lever and the lever stop tang. The gap should be 11.5–12.5mm. If not, bend the tang to adjust.

**NOTE: If the accelerator pump is not adjusted correctly, it could lead to poor acceleration, with little or no response on part throttle acceleration during warmup after a cold start.**

## OVERHAUL

**For all carburetor overhaul procedures please refer to "Carburetor Service" in the Unit Repair section.**

# Fuel Injection

**Due to the complex nature of modern fuel injection systems, comprehensive diagnosis and testing procedures fall outside the confines of this repair manual. For complete information on fuel injection diagnosis, testing and repair procedures, please refer to "Chilton's Guide to Fuel Injection and Feedback Carburetors."**

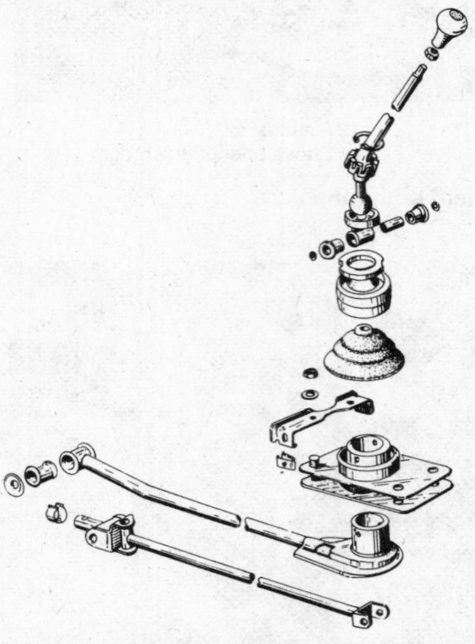

Exploded view of the gearshift mechanism

# MANUAL TRANSAXLE

## REMOVAL & INSTALLATION

### *1983–87 Civic*

**NOTE: Civic 4WD Wagon transaxle must be removed with the engine. For removal procedures please refer to Engine Removal & Installation in the Engine Mechanical section. Once the engine/transaxle assembly is removed from the vehicle, then the transaxle can be separated with the transfer case from the engine.**

1. Disconnect the negative battery cable.
2. Unlock the steering and place the transaxle in Neutral.
3. Disconnect the following wires in the engine compartment:
   a. battery positive cable.
   b. black/white wire from the solenoid.
   c. temperature gauge sending unit wire.
   d. ignition timing thermo-sensor wire.
   e. back-up light switch.
   f. distributor wiring.
   g. transaxle ground cable.
4. Unclip and remove the speedometer cable at the transaxle. Do not disassemble the speedometer gear holder.
5. Remove the clutch save cylinder with the hydraulic line attached, or disconnect the clutch cable at the release arm.
6. Remove the side and top starter mounting bolts. Loosen the front wheel lug nuts.
7. Apply the parking brake and block the rear wheels. Raise and support the vehicle safely. Remove the front wheel and tire assemblies.
8. Attach a suitable chain hoist to the rear of the engine then raise the engine slightly to take the weight off of the mounts. Drain the transaxle, then reinstall the drain plug and washer.
9. Remove the splash shields from the underside.Remove the stabilizer bar.Disconnect the left and right lower ball joints and tie end rods, using a ball joint remover.

**NOTE: Use caution when removing the ball joints. Place a floor jack under the lower control arm securely at the ball joint. Otherwise, the lower control arm may jump suddenly away from the steering knuckle as the ball joint is removed!**

10. Turn the right steering knuckle out as far as it will go. Place a prybar against the inboard CV joint, pry the right axle out of the transaxle about ½ in. This will force the spring clip out of the groove inside the differential gear splines. Pull it out the rest of the way. Repeat this procedure on the other side.
11. Disconnect the shift lever torque rod from the clutch housing.
12. Slide the pin retainer back, drive out the spring pin using a pin punch, then disconnect the shit rod. Remove the bolt from the shift rod clevis, if so equipped.
13. Place a transaxle jack under the transaxle and raise the transaxle jack securely against the transaxle to take up the weight.
14. Remove the engine torque rods

and brackets. Remove the bolts from the front transaxle mount. Remove the transaxle housing bolts from the engine torque bracket.

15. Remove the remaining starter mounting bolts. Remove the starter.

16. Remove the remaining transaxle mounting bolts and the upper bolt from the engine damper bracket. Remove the clutch housing bolts from the rear transaxle mounting bracket. Remove the 1 remaining bolt from the engine.

17. Start backing the transaxle away from the engine and remove the 2 lower damper bolts.

18. Pull the transaxle clear of the engine and lower the jack.

19. To ease installation, fabricate two 14mm diameter dowel pins and install them in the clutch housing.

20. Raise the transaxle and slide it onto the dowels. Slide the transaxle onto position aligning the mainshaft splines with the clutch plate.

21. Attach the damper lower bolts when the positioning allows. Tighten both bolts until the clutch housing is seated against the block.

22. Install 2 lower mounting bolts and torque them to 33 ft. lbs.

23. Install the front and rear torque rod brackets. Torque the front torque rod bolts to 54 ft. lbs., the front bracket bolts to 33 ft. lbs., the rear torque rod bolts to 54 ft. lbs., and the rear bracket bolts to 47 ft. lbs.

24. Remove the transaxle jack.

25. Install the starter and torque the mounting bolts to 33 ft. lbs.

26. Turn the right steering knuckle out far enough to fit the end into the transaxle. Use new 26mm spring clips on both axles. Repeat procedure for the other side.

27. Make sure that the axles bottom fully so that you feel the spring clip engage the differential.

28. Install the lower ball joints. Torque the nuts to 32 ft. lbs.

29. Install the tie rods. Torque the nuts to 32 ft. lbs.

30. Connect the shift linkage.

31. Connect the shift lever torque rod to the clutch housing and torque the bolt to 7 ft. lbs.

32. Install the stabilizer bar.

33. Install the lower shields.

34. Install the front wheels and torque the lugs to specifications.

35. Install the remaining starter bolts and torque to 33 ft. lbs.

36. Install the clutch slave cylinder and or install the clutch cable at the release arm.

37. Install the speedometer cable using a new O-ring coated with clean engine oil.

38. Connect all engine compartment wiring.

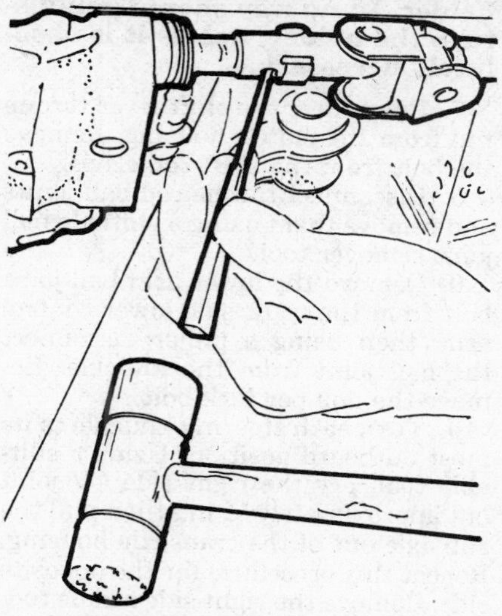

**Driving out the gearshift rod pin**

39. Fill the transaxle with SAE 10W–40 engine oil.

### *1988–90 Civic*

1. Disconnect the battery cables from the battery.

2. Remove the 3 mount bolts and loosen the 1 bolt located at the side of the battery base. Remove the intake hose band of the throttle body.

3. Remove the air cleaner case complete with the intake hose. Disconnect the starter and transaxle ground cables.

4. Disconnect the speedometer, but be sure not to disassemble the speedometer gear holder.

5. Disconnect the back-up light switch connector and the clutch cable release arm.

6. Drain the transaxle fluid into a suitable drain pan. Disconnect the connectors and remove the mount bolts.

7. Remove the distributor assembly, as required.

8. Remove the starter mounting bolts and remove the starter assembly. Remove the engine splash shield and the right wheelwell splash shield.

9. Remove the header pipe. Remove the cotter pin and the lower arm ball joint nut, separate the ball joint and lower arm.

10. Remove the bolts and nut, then remove the right radius rod. Remove the right and left driveshafts. Remove the header pipe bracket. Remove the shift lever torque rod and shift rod from the clutch housing.

11. On 4WD vehicles, remove the driveshaft and the intermediate shaft. Remove the cable bracket and the side transaxle mount from the transaxle housing and body.

12. Install a bolt at the cylinder head and attach suitable chain hoist to the bolt and the other end to the engine hanger plate. Lift the engine slightly to unload the mounts.

13. Place a suitable transaxle jack under the transaxle and raise it just enough to take the weights off of the mounts.

14. Remove the front transaxle mounting bolts. Remove the rear transaxle mounting bolts. Remove the side transaxle mount, remove the 5 remaining transaxle mounting bolts and pull the transaxle assembly far enough away from the engine to clear the 14mm dowel pins.

15. Separate the mainshaft from the clutch pressure plate and remove the transaxle by lowering the jack.

16. To install, reverse the removal procedure.

### *1983 Accord and Prelude*

1. Disconnect the battery ground cable at the battery and the transaxle case. Unlock the steering column; place the transaxle in Neutral.

2. Disconnect the following cables and wires:

a. Clutch cable at the release arm.

b. Back-up light switch wires.

c. TCS (Transaxle Controlled Spark) switch wires.

d. Black/white wire from the starter solenoid.

3. Release the engine sub wiring harness from the clamp at the clutch housing. Remove the upper 2 transaxle mounting bolts.

4. Raise the vehicle and support it safely. Drain the transaxle.

5. Remove the front wheels. Disconnect the speedometer cable.

**NOTE: When removing the speedometer cable from the transaxle, it is not necessary to remove the entire cable holder. Remove the end boot (gear holder seal), the cable retaining clip and then pull the cable out of the holder. In no way should you disturb the holder, unless it is absolutely necessary.**

6. Disconnect the shift lever torque rod from the clutch housing. Remove the bolt from the shift rod clevis.

7. Disconnect the tie rod ball joints and remove them using a suitable ball joint remover tool.

8. Remove the lower arm ball joint bolt from the right side lower control arm, then using a puller disconnect the ball joint from the knuckle. Remove the damper fork bolt.

9. Drive out the gearshift rod pin (8mm) with a drift and disconnect the rod at the transaxle case.

10. Disconnect the gearshift extension at the clutch housing.

11. Screw in the engine hanger bolts

to the engine torque rod bolt hole and to the hole just to the left of the distributor. Hook a chain onto the bolts and lift the engine just enough to take the load off the engine mounts.

12. After making sure that the engine is properly supported, remove the 2 center beam-to-lower engine mount nuts. Next, remove the center beam, followed by the lower engine mount.

13. Reinstall the center beam (without mount) and lower the engine until it rests on the beam.

14. Place a jack under the transaxle and loosen the 4 attaching bolts. Using the jack to support the transaxle, slide it away from the engine and lower the jack until the transaxle clears the vehicle.

15. To install, reverse the removal procedure. Be sure to pay attention to the following points:

a. Tighten all mounting nuts and bolts.

b. Use a new shift rod pin.

c. After installing the driveshafts, attempt to move the inner joint housing in and out of the differential housing. If it moves easily, the driveshaft end clips should be replaced.

d. Make sure that the control cables and wires are properly connected.

e. Be sure the transaxle is refilled to the proper level.

### 1984–90 Accord and 1984–87 Prelude

1. Disconnect the battery ground cable at the battery and the transaxle case. Unlock the steering column; place the transaxle in Neutral.

2. Disconnect the following cables and wires:

a. Clutch cable at the release arm

b. Back-up light switch wires

c. TCS (Transaxle Controlled Spark) switch wires

d. Black/white wire from the starter solenoid

3. Release the engine sub wiring harness from the clamp at the clutch housing. Remove the upper 2 transaxle mounting bolts.

4. Raise the vehicle and support it safely. Drain the transaxle fluid.

5. Remove the front wheels. Place a suitable transaxle jack into position under the transaxle.

6. Disconnect the speedometer cable.

**NOTE: When removing the speedometer cable from the transaxle, it is not necessary to remove the entire cable holder. Remove the end boot (gear holder seal), the cable retaining clip and then pull the cable out of the holder. In no way should you disturb the holder, unless it is absolutely necessary.**

7. Disconnect the shift lever torque rod from the clutch housing. Remove the bolt from the shift rod clevis.

8. Disconnect the tie rod ball joints and remove them using a suitable ball joint remover tool.

9. Remove the lower arm ball joint bolt from the right side lower control arm, then using a puller disconnect the ball joint from the knuckle. Remove the damper fork bolt.

10. Turn each steering knuckle to its most outboard position. Using a suitable tool, pry the right side CV joint out approximately ½ in., then pull the sub axle out of the transaxle housing. Repeat this procedure for the opposite side. Remove the right side radius rod.

11. Remove the damper bracket from the transaxle. Remove the clutch housing bolts from the front transaxle mount.

12. Remove the clutch housing bolts from the rear transaxle mounting bracket. Remove the clutch cover.

13. Remove the starter mounting bolts and remove the starter. Remove the transaxle mounting bolt.

14. Pull the transaxle away from the engine block to clear the two 14mm dowel pins and lower the transaxle jack.

15. To install, reverse the removal procedure. Be sure to pay attention to the following points:

a. Tighten all mounting nuts and bolts.

b. Use a new shift rod pin.

c. After installing the driveshafts, attempt to move the inner joint housing in and out of the differential housing. If it moves easily, the driveshaft end clips should be replaced.

d. Make sure that the control cables and wires are properly connected.

e. Be sure the transaxle is refilled to the proper level.

### 1988–90 Prelude

1. Disconnect the battery ground cable at the battery and the transaxle case. Unlock the steering column; place the transaxle in **N**.

2. Disconnect the following wires:

a. Back-up light switch wires.

b. Black/white wire from the starter solenoid.

3. On the fuel injected vehicles, remove the air cleaner assembly.

4. Remove the power steering speed sensor from the transaxle without removing the power steering hose.

5. Remove the shift cable and the select cable from the top cover of the transaxle. Remove the mounting bolt from the cable stay. Be sure not to bend or kink the cable more than necessary. Remove both cables and the stay together.

6. Remove the upper transaxle mounting bracket. Remove the 4 transaxle to block attachment bolts that must be removed from the engine compartment.

7. Raise and support the vehicle safely. Remove both front wheels and remove the undercarriage splash shield.

8. Drain the transaxle oil into a suitable drain pan. Remove the clutch slave cylinder.

9. Remove the center beam. Remove the right radius rod completely. Remove the right and left driveshafts.

10. Remove the engine stiffener. Remove the clutch cover. Support the transaxle with a suitable transaxle jack.

11. Remove the 3 lower bolts from the rear engine mounting bracket. Loosen but do not remove the top bolt. This bolt will support the weight of the engine.

12. Remove the 2 remaining engine to transaxle mounting bolts.

13. With the transaxle on a suitable transaxle jack, disengage the input shaft from the clutch disc and lower the transaxle out of the vehicle.

14. To install, reverse the removal procedure. Be sure to pay attention to the following points:

a. Tighten all mounting nuts and bolts.

b. Use a new shift rod pin.

c. After installing the driveshafts, attempt to move the inner joint housing in and out of the differential housing. If it moves easily, the driveshaft end clips should be replaced.

d. Make sure that the control cables and wires are properly connected.

e. Be sure the transaxle is refilled to the proper level.

## LINKAGE ADJUSTMENT

### Except Civic 4WD Vehicles

The shift linkage is not adjustable. However, if the linkage is binding, or if there is excessive play, check the linkage bushings and pivot points. Lubricate with light oil, or replace worn bushings as necessary.

### Civic 4WD Vehicles

#### SELECTOR CABLE ADJUSTMENT

1. Disconnect the negative battery cable. Remove the console.

2. With the transaxle in Neutral, check that the groove in the lever

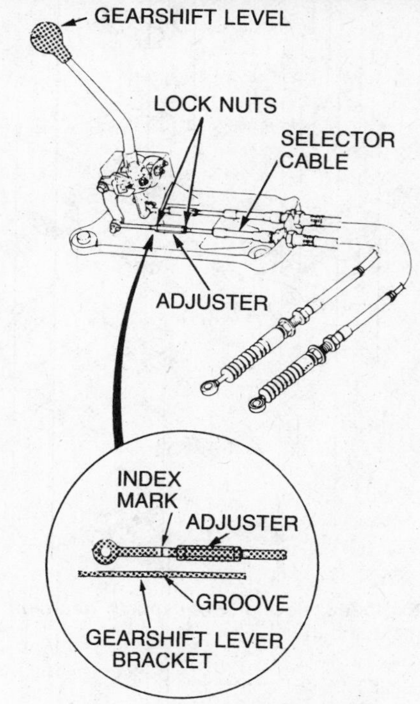


**Selector cable adjustment**

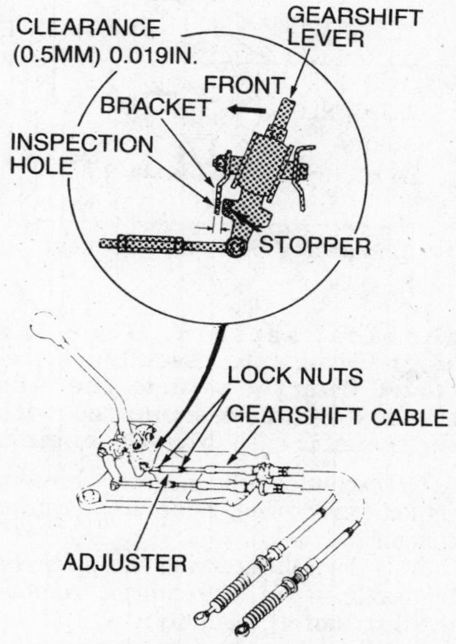


**Gearshift cable adjustment**

bracket is aligned with the index mark on the selector cable.

3. If the index mark is not aligned with the groove in the cable, loosen the locknuts and turn the adjuster as necessary.

**NOTE: After adjustment, check the operation of the gearshift lever. Also, check that the threads of the cables do not extend out of the cable adjuster by more than 10mm.**

### GEARSHIFT CABLE

1. Disconnect the negative battery cable. Remove the console.
2. Place the transaxle in 4th gear.
3. Measure the clearance between the gearshift lever bracket and the stopper while pushing the lever forward.
4. If the clearance is outside the specifications 4.3mm, loosen the locknuts and turn the adjuster in or out until the correct clearance is obtained.

**NOTE: After adjustment, check the operation of the gearshift lever. Also check that the threads of the cables do not extend out of the cable adjuster by more than 10mm.**

# CLUTCH

## REMOVAL & INSTALLATION

1. Disconnect the negative battery cable. Remove the transaxle from the vehicle. Matchmark the flywheel and clutch for reassembly.
2. Hold the flywheel ring gear with a tool made for this purpose, remove the retaining bolts and remove the pressure plate and clutch disc.

**NOTE: Loosen the retaining bolts 2 turns at a time in a circular pattern. Removing 1 bolt while the rest are tight may warp the diaphragm spring.**

3. The flywheel can now be removed, if it needs repairing or replacing. Inspect it for scoring and wear, and reface or replace as necessary. Tighten in a crisscross pattern.
4. To separate the pressure plate from the diaphragm spring, remove the 4 retracting clips.
5. To remove the release, or throwout bearing, first straighten the locking tab and remove the 8mm bolt, followed by the release shaft and release arm with the bearing attached.

**NOTE: It is recommended that the release bearing be removed after the release arm has been removed from the casing. Trying to remove or install the bearing with the release arm in the case will damage the retaining clip.**

6. If a new release bearing is to be installed, separate the bearing from the holder, using a bearing drift.
7. To assemble and install the clutch, reverse the removal procedure. Be sure to pay attention to the following points:
   a. Make sure that the flywheel and the end of the crankshaft are clean before assembling.
   b. When installing the pressure plate, align the mark on the outer edge of the flywheel with the alignment mark on the pressure plate. Failure to align these marks will result in imbalance.
   c. When tightening the pressure plate bolts, use a pilot shaft tool to center the friction disc. After centering the disc, tighten the bolts 2 turns at a time, in a crisscross pattern to avoid warping the diaphragm springs; tighten to 7 ft. lbs.
   d. When installing the release shaft and arm, place a lock tab washer under the retaining bolt.
   e. When installing the transaxle, make sure that the mainshaft is properly aligned with the disc spline and the aligning pins are in place, before tightening the case bolts to 17–22 ft. lbs.

## FREE-PLAY ADJUSTMENT

### *Except 1988–90 Prelude*

1. Measure the clutch pedal disengagement height.
2. Measure the clutch free-play.
3. Adjust the clutch free-play by turning the clutch cable adjusting nut (usually can be found by following the clutch cable from the clutch into the firewall).
4. Adjust the clutch release lever so that free-play, when you move the clutch lever at the transaxle with your hand, is:
   1983 Civic 4.4–5.4mm
   1984–90 Civic 4.0–5.0mm
   1983–90 Accord 5.2–6.4mm
   1983–87 Prelude 5.2–6.4mm
5. Adjust the pedal free-play at the outer cable housing adjuster so that pedal free-play is:
   1983 Civic 10–30mm
   1984–90 Civic 15–20mm
   1983 Accord 10–30mm
   1984–85 Accord 23–28mm
   1986–90 Accord 15–25mm
   1983–85 Prelude 23–28mm
   1986–87 Prelude 15–25mm

**NOTE: Less than 3mm of free-play may lead to clutch slippage, while more than 3mm clearance may cause difficult shifting. Make sure that the upper and lower adjusting nuts are tightened after adjustments. When replacing a clutch switch, the new switch should be adjusted to 0.02–0.06 in. (0.5–1.5mm).**

Accord slave cylinder locknut and adjusting nut

*1988–90 Prelude*

**NOTE: The clutch is self adjusting to compensate for clutch wear. The total clutch pedal free play is 0.35–0.59 in. (9–15mm). If there is no clearance between the master cylinder piston and push rod, the release bearing is held against the diaphragm spring, resulting is a slipping clutch or other faulty clutch operation.**

1. Loosen the locknut on the clutch switch and back it off till it no longer touches the clutch pedal.
2. Loosen the locknut on the clutch pedal pushrod and turn the pushrod in or out to get the specified stroke (5.3–5.5 in.) and height (8.1 in. to the floor) at the clutch pedal.
3. Tighten the push rod locknut and tighten the clutch pedal until it just makes contact. At that point turn the clutch pedal switch in further a ¼–½ in. more and then tighten the locknut.

## Clutch Cable

### REMOVAL & INSTALLATION

1. Disconnect the negative battery cable.
2. Disconnect the cable end from the brake pedal.
3. Remove the adjuster nut assembly from its mounting.
4. Raise and support the vehicle safely.
5. Disconnect the cable end from the release arm. Remove the cable from the vehicle.
6. Installation is the reverse of the removal procedure. Adjust the cable to specification.

## Clutch Master Cylinder

### REMOVAL & INSTALLATION

*Prelude*

1. Disconnect the negative battery cable. Pry out the cotter pin and pull the pedal pin out of the yoke.
2. Remove the nuts and bolts retaining the clutch master cylinder and remove the cylinder from the engine compartment.
3. Disconnect and plug the hydraulic lines from the master cylinder.
4. Installation is the reverse order of the removal procedure. Be sure to bleed the system and adjust the clutch pedal free play.

## Clutch Slave Cylinder

### REMOVAL & INSTALLATION

*Prelude*

1. Disconnect the negative battery cable. The slave cylinder is retained by 2 bolts. Disconnect and plug the hydraulic line at the slave cylinder and remove the 2 mounting bolts. Remove the return spring and remove the slave cylinder.
2. Installation is the reverse. Bleed the system after installation.

### BLEEDING THE HYDRAULIC CLUTCH SYSTEM

The hydraulic system must be bled whenever the system has been leaking or dismantled. The bleed screw is located on the slave cylinder.

1. Remove the bleed screw dust cap.
2. Attach a clear hose to the bleed screw. Immerse the other end of the hose in a clear jar half filled with brake fluid.
3. Fill the clutch master cylinder with fresh brake fluid.
4. Open the bleed screw slightly and have an assistant slowly depress the clutch pedal. Close the bleed screw when the pedal reaches the end of its travel. Allow the clutch pedal to return slowly.
5. Repeat Steps 3–4 until all air bubbles are expelled from the system.
6. Discard the brake fluid in the jar. Replace the dust cap. Refill the master cylinder.

# AUTOMATIC TRANSAXLE

### REMOVAL & INSTALLATION

*1983–87 Civic*

**NOTE: Civic 4WD Wagon transaxle must be removed with the engine. For removal procedures please refer to Engine Removal & Installation in the Engine Mechanical section. Once the engine/transaxle assembly is removed from the vehicle, then the transaxle can be separated with the transfer case from the engine.**

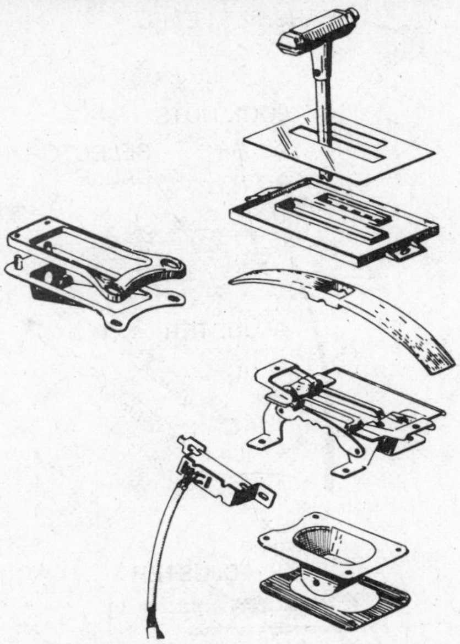

Exploded view of Hondamatic gearshift mechanism

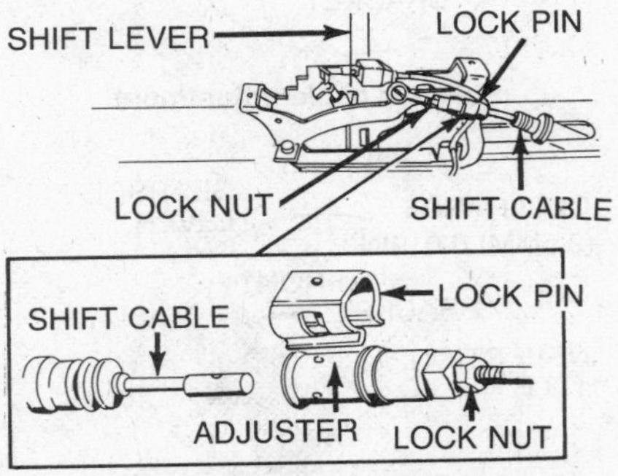


Automatic shift lever adjustment

1. Disconnect the negative battery cable. As required, remove the center console.
2. Unlock the steering and place the transaxle in **N**. As required, remove the distributor assembly.
3. Disconnect the following wires in the engine compartment:
   a. Battery positive cable
   b. Black/white wire from the solenoid
   c. Temperature gauge sending unit wire
   d. Ignition timing thermo-sensor wire
   e. Back-up light switch
   f. Distributor wiring
   g. Transaxle ground cable
   h. Throttle control cable
4. Unclip and remove the speedometer cable at the transaxle. Do not disassemble the speedometer gear holder.

5. Disconnect and plug the transaxle fluid lines.
6. Remove the side and top starter mounting bolts. Loosen the front wheel lug nuts.
7. Apply the parking brake and block the rear wheels. Raise and support the vehicle safely. Remove the front wheel and tire assemblies.
8. Attach a suitable chain hoist to the rear of the engine then raise the engine slightly to take the weight off of the mounts. Drain the transaxle, then reinstall the drain plug and washer.
9. Remove the splash shields from the underside.Remove the stabilizer bar.Disconnect the left and right lower ball joints and tie end rods, using a ball joint remover.

**NOTE: Use caution when removing the ball joints. Place a floor jack under the lower control arm securely at the ball joint. Otherwise, the lower control arm may jump suddenly away from the steering knuckle as the ball joint is removed!**

10. Turn the right steering knuckle out as far as it will go. Place a prybar against the inboard CV joint, pry the right axle out of the transaxle about ½ in. This will force the spring clip out of the groove inside the differential gear splines. Pull it out the rest of the way. Repeat this procedure on the other side.
11. Disconnect the shift lever torque rod from the clutch housing.
12. Slide the pin retainer back, drive out the spring pin using a pin punch, then disconnect the shit rod. Remove the bolt from the shift rod clevis, if so equipped.
13. Place a transaxle jack under the transaxle and raise the transaxle jack securely against the transaxle to take up the weight.
14. Remove the engine torque rods and brackets. Remove the bolts from the front transaxle mount. Remove the transaxle housing bolts from the engine torque bracket.
15. Remove the torque converter to engine retaining bolts. Remove the remaining starter mounting bolts. Remove the starter.
16. Remove the remaining transaxle mounting bolts and the upper bolt from the engine damper bracket. Remove the rear transaxle mounting bracket. Remove the 1 remaining bolt from the engine.
17. Start backing the transaxle away from the engine and remove the 2 lower damper bolts.
18. Pull the transaxle clear of the engine and lower the jack.
19. Installation is the reverse of the removal procedure.

### *1988–90 Civic*

1. Disconnect the battery cables from the battery. As required, remove the console assembly.
2. Remove the 3 mount bolts and loosen the 1 bolt located at the side of the battery base. Remove the intake hose band of the throttle body.
3. Remove the air cleaner case complete with the intake hose. Disconnect the starter and transaxle ground cables.
4. Disconnect the speedometer, but be sure not to disassemble the speedometer gear holder. Disconnect the throttle control cable.
5. Disconnect the back-up light switch connector and the clutch cable release arm. Disconnect the transaxle oil cooler lines.
6. Drain the transaxle fluid into a suitable drain pan. Disconnect the connectors and remove the mount bolts.
7. Scribe an alignment line on the distributor assembly and the cylinder head (to be used for easy installation), then remove the distributor assembly from the cylinder head.

**NOTE: It may be easier at installation, if the No. 1 engine piston is brought up to top dead center of its compression stroke before removing the distributor assembly.**

8. Remove the starter mounting bolts and remove the starter assembly. Remove the engine splash shield and the right wheelwell splash shield.
9. Remove the header pipe. Remove the cotter pin and the lower arm ball joint nut, separate the ball joint and lower arm.
10. Remove the bolts and nut, then remove the right radius rod. Remove the right and left driveshafts.
11. Remove the header pipe bracket. Remove the shift lever torque rod and shift rod from the clutch housing.
12. Install a bolt at the cylinder head and attach suitable chain hoist to the bolt and the other end to the engine hanger plate. Lift the engine slightly to unload the mounts.
13. Place a suitable transaxle jack under the transaxle and raise it just enough to take the weights off of the mounts. Remove the torque converter to engine bolts.
14. Remove the front transaxle mounting bolts. Remove the rear transaxle mounting bolts. Remove the side transaxle mount, remove the 5 remaining transaxle mounting bolts and pull the transaxle assembly far enough away from the engine to clear the 14mm dowel pins.
15. Lower the transaxle assembly from the engine.
16. Installation is the reverse of the removal procedure.

### *1983 Accord and Prelude*

1. Disconnect the battery ground cable at the battery and the transaxle case. As required, remove the console assembly.
2. Disconnect the following cables and wires:
   a. Throttle control cable
   b. Back-up light switch wires
   c. TCS (Transaxle Controlled Spark) switch wires
   d. Black/white wire from the starter solenoid
3. Release the engine sub wiring harness from the clamp at the housing. Remove the upper 2 transaxle mounting bolts. Disconnect the transaxle fluid lines.
4. Raise the vehicle and support it safely. Drain the transaxle.
5. Remove the front wheels. Disconnect the speedometer cable.

**NOTE: When removing the speedometer cable from the transaxle, it is not necessary to remove the entire cable holder. Remove the end boot (gear holder seal), the cable retaining clip and then pull the cable out of the holder. In no way should you disturb the holder, unless it is absolutely necessary.**

6. Disconnect the shift lever torque rod. Remove the bolt from the shift rod clevis.
7. Disconnect the tie rod ball joints and remove them using a suitable ball joint remover tool.
8. Remove the lower arm ball joint bolt from the right side lower control arm, then using a puller disconnect the ball joint from the knuckle. Remove the damper fork bolt.
9. Drive out the gearshift rod pin (8mm) with a drift and disconnect the rod at the transaxle case.
10. Disconnect the gearshift extension, as required.
11. Screw in the engine hanger bolts to the engine torque rod bolt hole and to the hole just to the left of the distributor. Hook a chain onto the bolts and lift the engine just enough to take the load off the engine mounts.
12. After making sure that the engine is properly supported, remove the 2 center beam-to-lower engine mount nuts. Next, remove the center beam, followed by the lower engine mount.
13. Reinstall the center beam (without mount) and lower the engine until it rests on the beam. Remove the torque conver to engine retaining bolts.
14. Place a jack under the transaxle and loosen the 4 attaching bolts. Using

the jack to support the transaxle, slide it away from the engine and lower the jack until the transaxle clears the vehicle.
15. To install, reverse the removal procedure.

### 1984–90 Accord and 1984–87 Prelude

1. Disconnect the battery ground cable at the battery and the transaxle case. As required, remove the console.
2. Disconnect the following cables and wires:
 a. Throttle control cable
 b. Back-up light switch wires
 c. TCS (Transaxle Controlled Spark) switch wires
 d. Black/white wire from the starter solenoid
3. Release the engine sub wiring harness from the clamp at the clutch housing. Remove the upper 2 transaxle mounting bolts. Disconnect the fluid cooler lines.
4. Raise the vehicle and support it safely. Drain the transaxle fluid.
5. Remove the front wheels. Place a suitable transaxle jack into position under the transaxle.
6. Disconnect the speedometer cable.

**NOTE: When removing the speedometer cable from the transaxle, it is not necessary to remove the entire cable holder. Remove the end boot (gear holder seal), the cable retaining clip and then pull the cable out of the holder. In no way should you disturb the holder, unless it is absolutely necessary.**

7. Disconnect the shift lever torque rod. Remove the bolt from the shift rod clevis.
8. Disconnect the tie rod ball joints and remove them using a suitable ball joint remover tool.
9. Remove the lower arm ball joint bolt from the right side lower control arm, then using a puller disconnect the ball joint from the knuckle. Remove the damper fork bolt.
10. Turn each steering knuckle to its most outboard position. Using a suitable tool, pry the right side CV joint out approximately ½ in., then pull the sub axle out of the transaxle housing. Repeat this procedure for the opposite side. Remove the right side radius rod.
11. Remove the damper bracket from the transaxle.
12. Remove the dust cover. Disconnect the torque converter to engine bolts.
13. Remove the starter mounting bolts and remove the starter. Remove the transaxle mounting bolt.
14. Pull the transaxle away from the engine block to clear the two 14mm dowel pins and lower the transaxle jack.
15. To install, reverse the removal procedure.

### 1988–90 Prelude

1. Disconnect the battery ground cable at the battery and the transaxle case. Remove the console, as required.
2. Disconnect the back-up light switch wires. and the black/white wire from the starter solenoid. Disconnect the throttle cable.
3. Disconnect the fluid cooler lines. On the fuel injected vehicles, remove the air cleaner assembly.
4. Remove the power steering speed sensor from the transaxle without removing the power steering hose.
5. Remove the shift cable and the select cable from the top cover of the transaxle. Remove the mounting bolt from the cable stay. Be sure not to bend or kink the cable more than necessary. Remove both cables and the stay together.
6. Remove the upper transaxle mounting bracket. Remove the 4 transaxle to block attachment bolts that must be removed from the engine compartment.
7. Raise and support the vehicle safely. Remove both front wheels and remove the undercarriage splash shield.
8. Drain the transaxle oil into a suitable drain pan.
9. Remove the center beam. Remove the right radius rod completely. Remove the right and left driveshafts.
10. Remove the engine stiffener. Remove the torque converter cover. Remove the torque converter to engine bolts. Support the transaxle with a suitable transaxle jack.
11. Remove the 3 lower bolts from the rear engine mounting bracket. Loosen but do not remove the top bolt. This bolt will support the weight of the engine.
12. Remove the 2 remaining engine to transaxle mounting bolts.
13. With the transaxle on a suitable transaxle jack, disengage the input shaft from the clutch disc and lower the transaxle out of the vehicle.
14. To install, reverse the removal procedure.

## LINKAGE ADJUSTMENT

### Carbureted Vehicles

1. Attach a weight of approximately 3 lbs. to the accelerator pedal. Raise the pedal, then release it, this will allow the weight to remove the normal free play from the throttle cable.
2. Secure the throttle control cable with clamps. Remove the air intake duct.
3. Lay the end of the throttle control cable over the the shock tower. Adjust the distance between the throttle cable end and the first locknut to 3.346–3.366 in. (85.0–85.5mm) on all vehicles except 1988–90 Prelude which is 6.22 in. (158.0mm).
4. Insert the end of the throttle control cable into the groove of the throttle control lever. Insert the throttle control cable in the bracket and secure it with the last locknut. Be sure the cable is not kinked or twisted.
5. Check the cable moves freely by depressing the accelerator. Start the engine and check the synchronization between the carburetor and the throttle control cable.
6. The throttle control lever should start to move as the engine speed is increased.
7. If the throttle control lever moves before the engine speed increases, turn the cable top locknut counterclockwise and tighten the bottom locknut.
8. If the throttle control lever moves after the engine speed increases, turn the cable top locknut clockwise and tighten the bottom locknut.

### Fuel Injected Vehicles

1. Loosen both locknuts on the throttle control cable. Press down on the throttle control cable until it stops.
2. While pressing down on the throttle control lever, pull on the throttle link to check the amount of throttle control cable free-play.
3. Remove all the throttle control cable free-play by gradually turning the top locknut.
4. Keep turning the top locknut until no movement can be felt in the throttle link, while continuing to press down on the throttle control lever, pull open the throttle link. The control lever should start to move at precisely the same time as the link. When you get to this point, tighten up the bottom locknut.

**NOTE: The adjustment of the throttle control cable is critical for proper operation of the transaxle and lockup torque converter.**

5. Depress the accelerator to the floor. While depressed, check that there is play in the throttle control lever (more than 0.08 in.). Check that the cable moves freely by depressing the accelerator pedal.

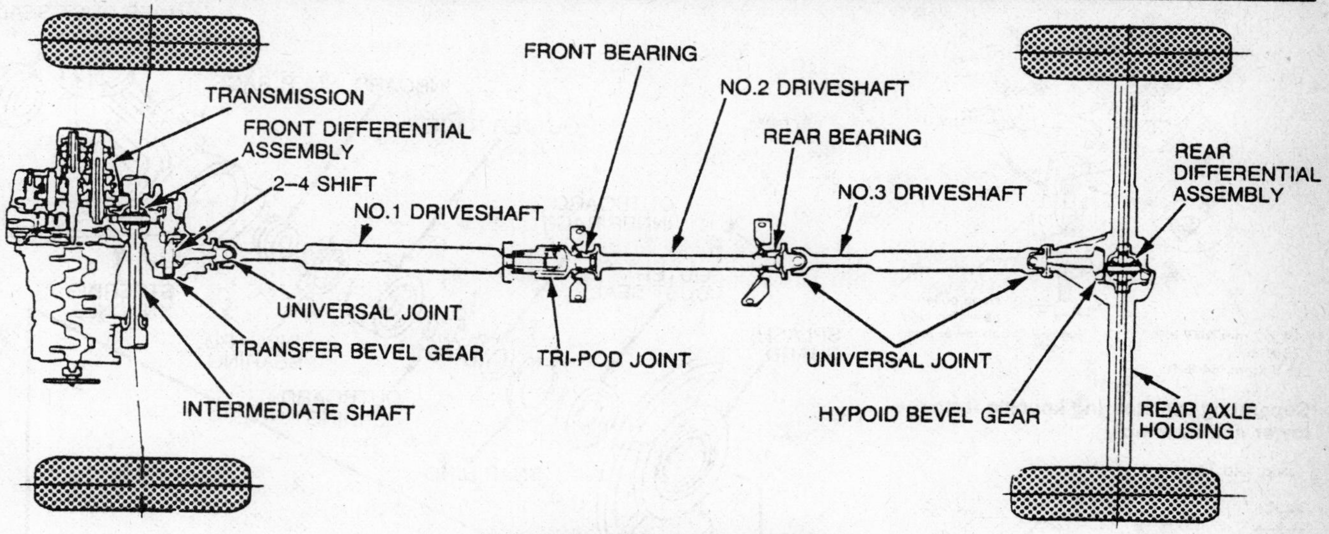


Civic 4WD Station Wagon driveline

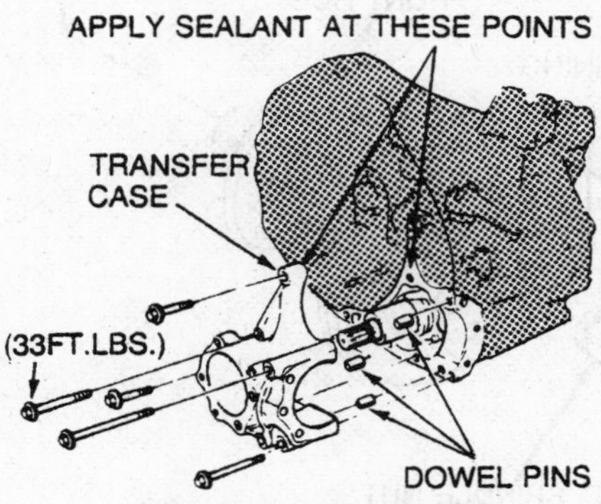


Transfer case mounting

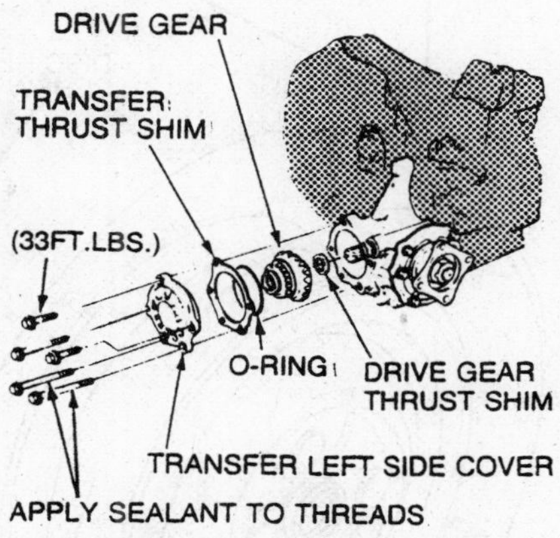


Transfer case left side assembly

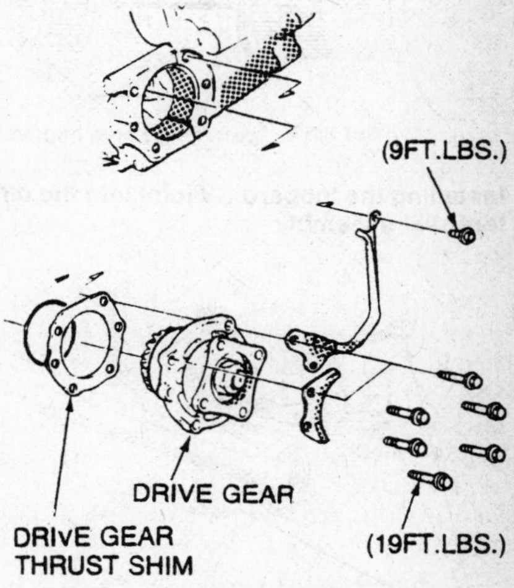


Transfer case drive gear side assembly

# TRANSFER CASE

## REMOVAL & INSTALLATION

1. Disconnect the negative battery cable. Raise the vehicle and support it safely.
2. Remove the splash shield from beneath the engine.
3. Drain the oil from both the engine and the transaxle.
4. Remove the head pipe from the engine.
5. Disconnect the driveshaft from the transaxle.
6. Remove the splash pan from beneath the transaxle.
7. Remove the left side cover from the transfer case.
8. Remove the driven gear from the transfer case.
9. Remove the transfer case from the clutch housing.
10. To install, replace the components beneath the transfer left side cover in the following order:
   a. Drive gear thrust shim
   b. Drive gear (coat with oil)
   c. O-ring
   d. Transfer thrust shim
   e. Transfer left side cover
11. Install the following components on the drive output side of the transfer case:
   a. O-ring
   b. Drive gear thrust shim
   c. Drive gear (coat with oil)

# DRIVE AXLE

## Halfshaft

### REMOVAL & INSTALLATION

#### *Except 4WD Civic Rear Halfshafts*

1. Remove the hubcap from the front wheel and then remove the center cap.
2. Pull out the 4mm cotter pin , if equipped and loosen, but do not remove, the spindle nut.
3. Loosen the front wheel lugs. Raise and support the vehicle safely.
4. Remove the wheel lug nuts and then the wheel.
5. Raise the locking tab on the spindle nut and remove the spindle nut with a suitable socket.
6. Drain the transaxle. It is not necessary to drain the transaxle oil, if just the left side is going to be removed.
7. Remove the damper fork bolt and damper pinch bolt. Remove the damper fork, if so equipped.

**NOTE: On 1984–90 Civic, make sure that a floor jack is positioned securely under the lower control arm, at the ball joint. Otherwise, the lower control arm may jump suddenly away from the steering knuckle as the ball joint is removed.**

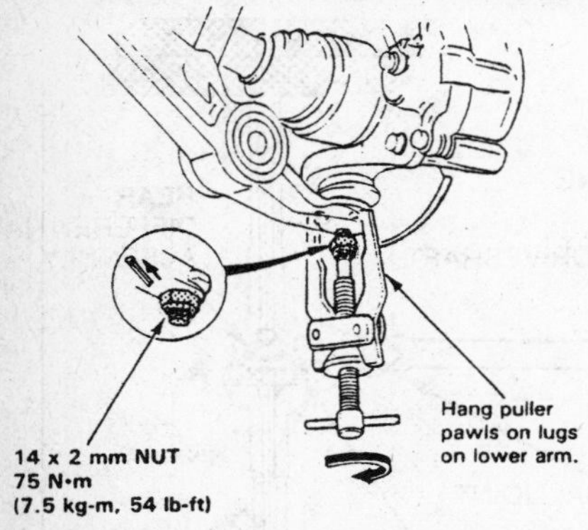


**Separating the steering knuckle from the lower arm assembly**

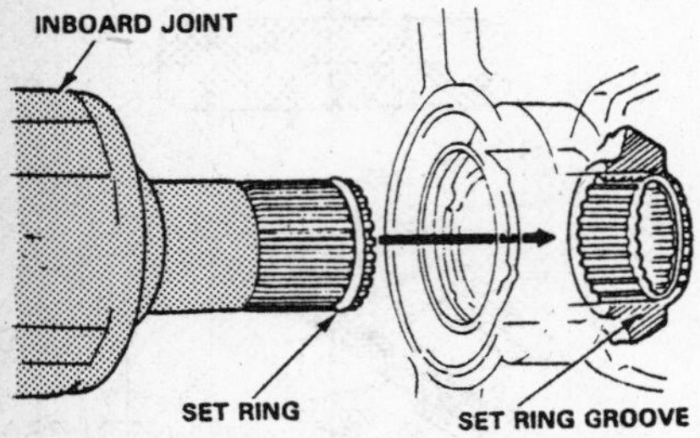


**Installing the inboard CV joint into the differential assembly**

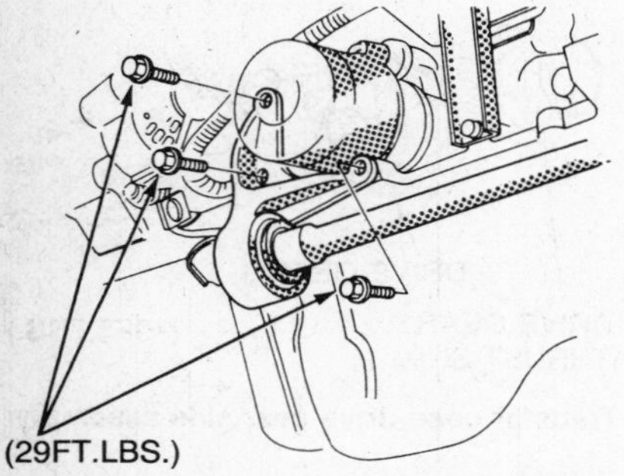


**Intermediate shaft bearing support**

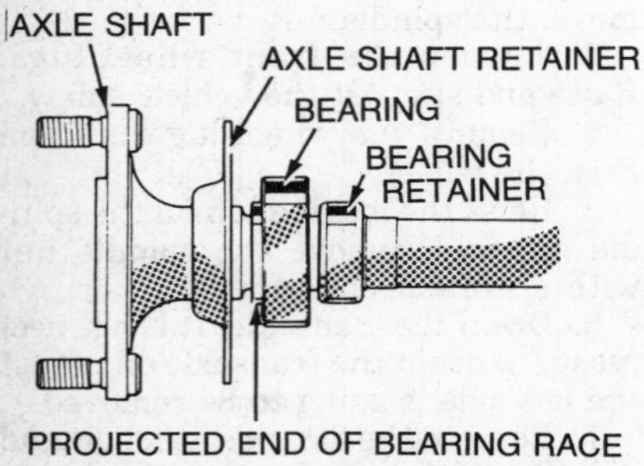


**Rear axle and bearing assembly**

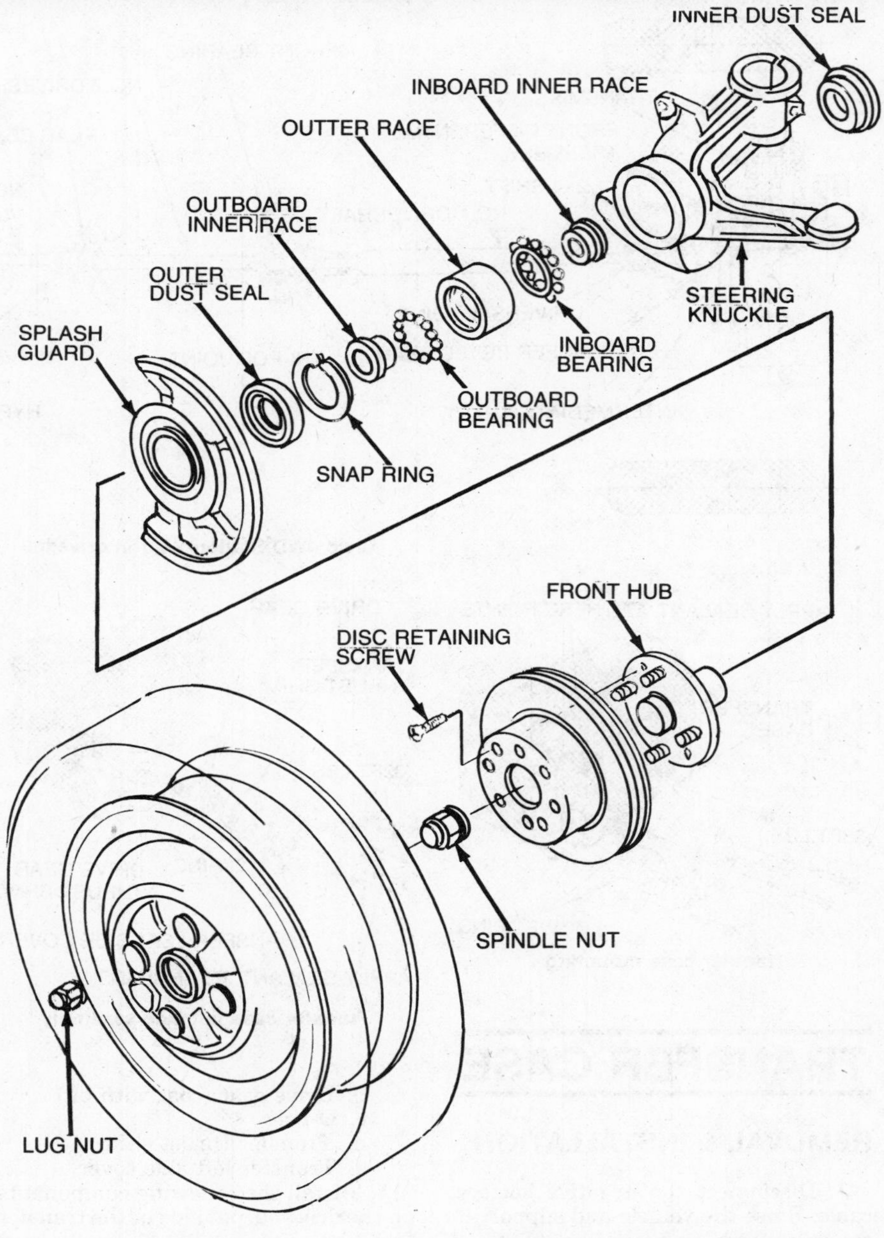


**Front steering knuckle and related components – except 1984 and later Civic, 1986 and later Accord and 1983 and later Prelude**

8. Remove the steering knuckle to lower arm castle nut, and separate the lower arm from the knuckle by using a suitable puller tool.

9. Pull the knuckle outward and remove the driveshaft outboard joint from the knuckle using a plastic hammer.

10. Using a suitable tool, pry the driveshaft assembly to force the set ring at the driveshaft end past the groove.

11. Pull the inboard joint and remove the driveshaft and CV-joint out of the differential case as an assembly.

**NOTE:Do not pull on the driveshaft as the CV-joint may come apart. Use caution when prying out the assembly and pull it straight out to avoid damaging the differential oil seal or intermediate shaft dust seal.**

12. To install, reverse the removal procedure. If either the inboard or outboard joint boot bands have been removed for inspection or disassembly of the joint (only the inboard joint can be disassembled), be sure to repack the joint with a sufficient amount of bearing grease.

13. Always use a new set ring whenever the driveshaft is being installed. Make sure that the driveshaft locks in differential side gear groove, and the CV-joint subaxle bottoms in the differential or intermediate shaft.

### *4WD Civic Rear Halfshafts*

1. Pry the spindle nut stake away from the spindle. Loosen the nut. Loosen the wheel nuts.

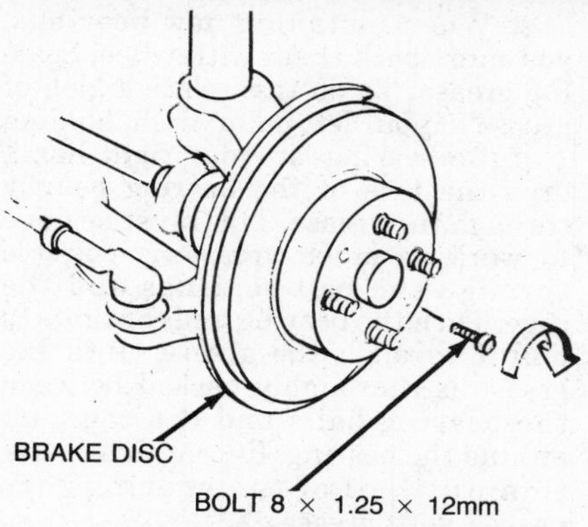


**Disc brake rotor removal**

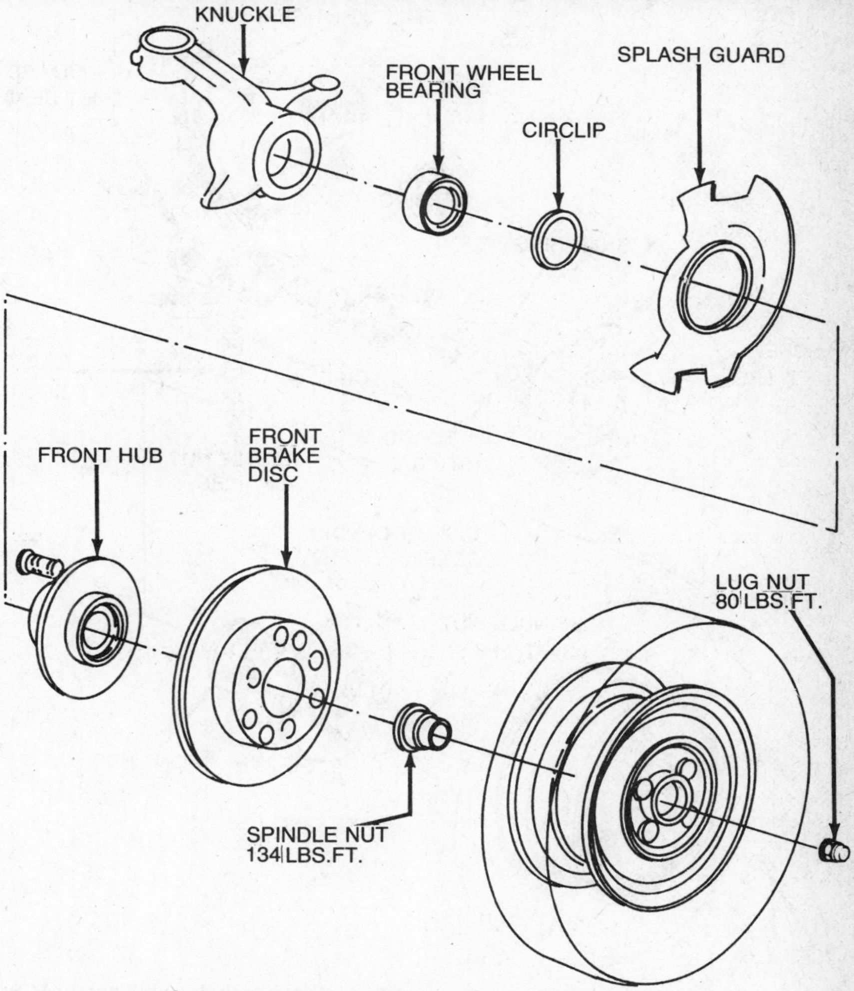


**Front steering knuckle, hub and bearing—1984 and later Civic**

2. Raise and support the vehicle safely. Remove the tire and wheel assemblies.
3. Disconnect the brake hose from the brake pipe.
4. Using a floor jack raise the rear suspension until the weight of the lower arm is relieved.
5. Remove the trailing arm bushing bolts. Disconnect the upper arm and the lower arm from the trailing arm.
6. Pull the trailing arm outward. Remove the rear driveshaft outboard joint from the trailing arm, using the proper tool.
7. Using a suitable tool, pry the driveshaft assembly to force the set ring at the driveshaft past the groove.
8. Pull the inboard joint and remove the driveshaft and the CV-joint from the differential case as an assembly.
9. Installation is the reverse of the removal procedure.

### CV-JOINT OVERHAUL

**For all CV-Joint overhaul procedures, please refer to "CV-Joint Overhaul" in the Unit Repair section.**

## Front Driveshaft

### REMOVAL & INSTALLATION

#### *Civic Wagon 4WD and Prelude 4 Wheel Steering*

1. Raise the vehicle and support it safely.
2. Drain the oil from the transaxle.
3. Remove the three 10mm bolts from the bearing support.
4. Lower the bearing support close to the steering gearbox and remove the intermediate shaft from the differential.

**NOTE: To avoid damage to the differential oil seal, keep the intermediate shaft in the horizontal position until it is clear of the differential.**

## Rear Driveshaft

### REMOVAL & INSTALLATION

#### *Civic Wagon 4WD*

1. Raise the vehicle and support it safely.
2. Mark the position of the driveshafts on both of the flanges for reassembly.
3. Remove the No. 1 driveshaft protector.
4. Remove the No. 3 driveshaft by disconnecting the U-joints.
5. Remove the bolts holding the rear bearing support, then remove the No. 2 driveshaft.
6. Remove the bolts holding the front bearing support, then remove the No. 1 driveshaft by disconnecting the U-joint.
7. To install, reverse the removal procedures.

## Front Wheel Hub, Knuckle and Bearings

### REMOVAL & INSTALLATION

**NOTE: The following procedures require the use of many special tools and a hydraulic press. Do not attempt this procedure without these special tools.**

#### *1983 Civic and 1983–85 Accord*

1. Pry the lock tab away from the spindle, then loosen the nut. Slightly loosen the lug nuts.
2. Raise the vehicle and support it safely. Remove the front wheel and spindle nut.
3. Remove the bolts retaining the brake caliper and remove the caliper from the knuckle. Do not let the caliper hang by the brake hose, support it with a length of wire.

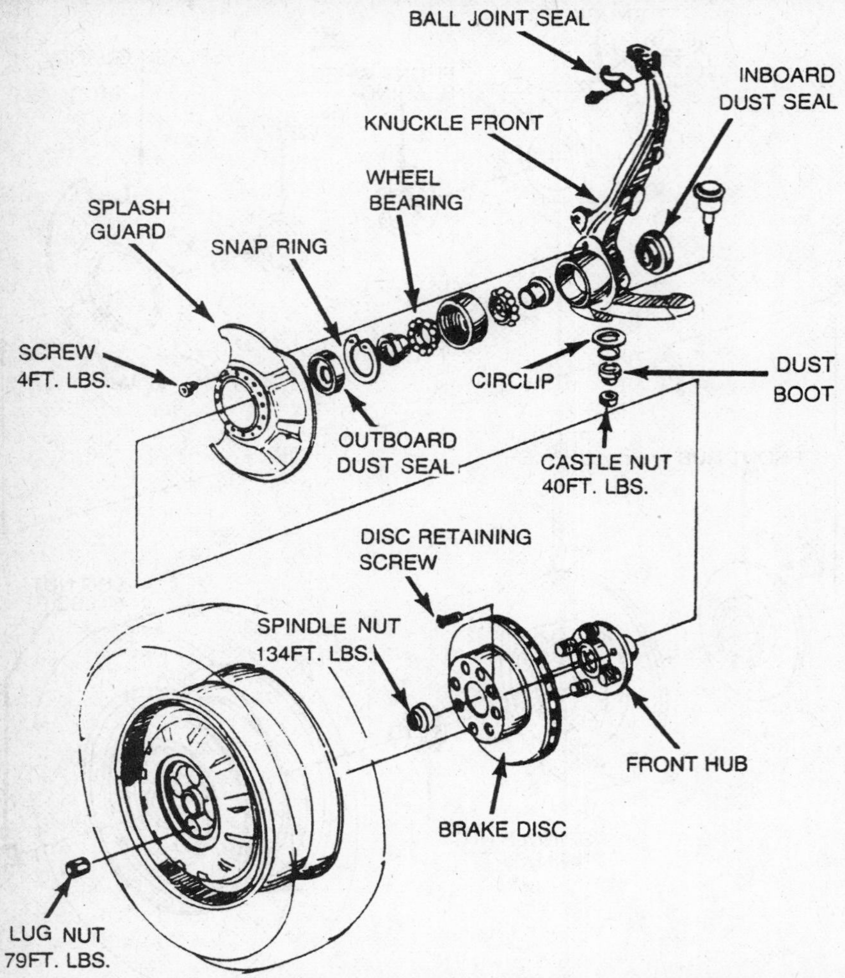


**Front steering knuckle, hub and bearing—1983 and later Prelude, 1986 and later Accord similar**

4. Remove the disc brake rotor retaining screws, if equipped. Screw two 8 × 1.25 × 12mm bolts into the disc brake removal holes, and turn the bolts to push the rotor away from the hub.

**NOTE: Turn each bolt 2 turns at a time to prevent cocking the disc excessively.**

5. Remove the tie rod from the knuckle using a tie rod end removal tool. Use care not to damage the ball joint seals.
6. Remove the cotter pin from the lower arm ball joint and remove the castle nut.
7. Remove the lower arm from the knuckle using the ball joint remover tool.
8. Loosen the lockbolt which retains the strut in the knuckle. Tap the top of the knuckle with a hammer and slide it off the shock.
9. Remove the knuckle and hub, if still attached, by sliding the assembly off the driveshaft.
10. Remove the hub from the knuckle using special tools and a hydraulic press.
11. Remove the splash guard and the snapring, then remove the outer bearing.
12. Turn the knuckle over and remove the inboard dust seal, bearing and inner race.
13. Press the bearing outer race out of the knuckle using special tools and a hydraulic press.
14. Remove the outboard bearing inner race from the hub using special tools and a bearing puller.
15. Remove the outboard dust seal from the hub.

**NOTE: Whenever the wheel bearings are removed, always replace them with a new set of bearings and outer dust seal.**

16. Clean all old grease from the driveshafts and spindles.
17. Remove all old grease from the hub and knuckle and thoroughly dry and wipe clean all components.
18. When installing new bearings, you must pack them with wheel bearing grease. To do this, place a glob of grease in your left palm, then, holding 1 of the bearings in your right hand, drag the face of the bearing heavily through the grease. This must be done to work as much grease as possible through the ball bearings and the cage. Turn the bearing and continue to pull it through the grease, until the grease is thoroughly packed between the bearing balls and the cage, all around the bearing. Repeat this operation until all of the bearings are packed with grease.
19. Pack the inside of the rotor and knuckle hub with a moderate amount of grease. Do not overload the hub with grease.
20. Apply a small amount of grease to the spindle and to the lip of the inner seal before installing.
21. To install the bearings, press the bearing outer race into the knuckle using the special tools, plus the installing base tool.
22. Install the outboard ball bearing and its inner race in the knuckle.
23. Install the snapring. Pack grease in the groove around the sealing lip of the outboard grease dust seal.
24. Drive the outboard grease seal into the knuckle, using a seal driver and hammer, until it is flush with the knuckle surface.
25. Install the splash guard, then turn the knuckle upside down and install the inboard ball bearing and its inner race.
26. Place the hub in the special tool fixture, then set the knuckle in position on the press and apply downward pressure.
27. Pack grease in the groove around the sealing lip of the inboard dust seal.
28. Drive the dust seal into the knuckle using a seal driver.
29. The remaining steps are the reverse of the removal procedure. Use a new spindle nut, and stake after torquing.

### *1984–90 Civic*

1. Pry the lock tab away from the spindle, then loosen the nut. Slightly loosen the lug nuts.
2. Raise the vehicle and support it safely. Remove the front wheel and spindle nut.
3. Remove the bolts retaining the brake caliper and remove the caliper from the knuckle. Do not let the caliper hang by the brake hose, support it with a length of wire.
4. Remove the disc brake rotor retaining screws, if equipped. Screw two 8 × 1.25 × 12mm bolts into the disc brake removal holes, and turn the bolts to push the rotor away from the hub.

**NOTE: Turn each bolt 2 turns at a time to prevent cocking the disc excessively.**

5. Remove the tie rod from the knuckle using a tie rod end removal tool. Use care not to damage the ball joint seals.
6. Use a floor jack to support the lower control arm, then remove the cotter pin from the lower arm ball joint and remove the castle nut.

**NOTE: Be sure to place the jack securely beneath the lower control arm at the ball joint. Otherwise, the tension from the torsion bar may cause the arm to suddenly jump away from the steering knuckle as the ball joint is removed.**

7. Remove the cotter pin and loosen the lower arm ball joint nut half the length of the joint threads. Separate the ball joint and lower the arm using a suitable puller.
8. Remove the knuckle protector. Remove the cotter pin and remove the upper ball pin nut. Separate the upper ball joint and knuckle using ball joint remover tool.
9. Loosen the pinchbolt which retains the shock in the knuckle. Tap the top of the knuckle with a hammer and slide it off the shock.
10. Remove the knuckle and hub, if still attached, by sliding the assembly off of the driveshaft.
11. Remove the hub from the knuckle using special tools and a hydraulic press.
12. Remove the splash guard and the snapring.
13. Press the bearing outer race of the knuckle using special tools and a hydraulic press.
14. Remove the outboard bearing inner race from the hub using special tools and a bearing puller.

**NOTE: Whenever the wheel bearings are removed, always replace with a new set of bearings and outer dust seal.**

15. Clean all old grease from the driveshafts and spindles. Remove the old grease from the hub and knuckle and thoroughly dry and wipe clean all components.
16. To install the bearings, press the bearing outer race into the knuckle using the special tools as used above, plus the installing base tool.
17. Install the snapring, then install the splash guard.
18. Place the hub in the special tool fixture, then set the knuckle in position on the press and apply downward pressure.
19. The remaining steps are the reverse of the removal procedure. Use a new spindle nut, and stake after torquing.

#### *1983–90 Prelude and 1986–90 Accord*

1. Pry the lock tab away from the spindle, then loosen the nut. Slightly loosen the lug nuts.
2. Raise the vehicle and support it safely. Remove the front wheel and spindle nut.
3. Remove the bolts retaining the brake caliper and remove the caliper from the knuckle. Do not let the caliper hang by the brake hose, support it with a length of wire.
4. Remove the disc brake rotor retaining screws, if equipped. Screw two 8 × 1.25 × 12mm bolts into the disc brake removal holes, and turn the bolts to push the rotor away from the hub.

**NOTE: Turn each bolt 2 turns at a time to prevent cocking the disc excessively.**

5. Remove the tie rod from the knuckle using a tie rod end removal tool. Use care not to damage the ball joint seals.
6. Remove the cotter pin from the lower arm ball joint and remove the castle nut.
7. Remove the lower arm from the knuckle using the ball joint remover tool.
8. Remove the cotter pin from the upper arm ball joint and remove the castle nut.
9. Remove the upper arm from the knuckle using the ball joint remover tool.
10. Remove the knuckle and hub by sliding the assembly off of the driveshaft.
11. Remove the 2 back splash guard screws from the knuckle.
12. Remove the hub from the knuckle using special tools and a hydraulic press.
13. Remove the splash guard, dust seal and the snapring, then remove the outer bearing race.
14. Turn the knuckle over and remove the inboard dust seal, bearing and inner race and bearing.
15. Press the bearing outer race out of the knuckle using special tools and a hydraulic press.
16. Remove the outboard bearing inner race from the hub using special tools and a bearing puller.
17. Remove the outboard dust seal from the hub.

**NOTE: Whenever the wheel bearings are removed, always replace with a new set of bearings and outer dust seal.**

18. Clean all old grease from the driveshafts spindles.
19. Remove all old grease from the hub and knuckle and thoroughly dry and wipe clean all components.
20. When installing new bearings, you must pack them with wheel bearing grease. To do this, place a glob of grease in your left palm, then, holding 1 of the bearings in your right hand, drag the face of the bearing heavily through the grease. This must be done to work as much grease as possible through the ball bearings and the cage. Turn the bearing and continue to pull it through the grease, until the grease is thoroughly packed between the bearing balls and the cage, all around the bearing. Repeat this operation until all of the bearings are packed with grease.
21. Pack the inside of the rotor and knuckle hub with a moderate amount of grease. Do not overload the hub with grease.
22. Apply a small amount of grease to the spindle and to the lip of the inner seal before installing.
23. To install the bearings, press the bearing outer race into the knuckle using the special tools used as above, plus the installing base tool.
24. Install the outboard ball bearing and its inner race in the knuckle.
25. Install the snapring. Pack grease in the groove around the sealing lip of the outboard grease dust seal.
26. Drive the outboard grease seal into the knuckle, using a seal driver and hammer, until it is flush with the knuckle surface.
27. Install the splash guard, then turn the knuckle upside down and install the inboard ball bearing and its inner race.
28. Place the hub in the special tool fixture, then set the knuckle in position on the press and apply downward pressure.
29. Pack grease in the groove around the sealing lip of the inboard dust seal.
30. Drive the dust seal into the knuckle using a seal driver.
31. The remaining steps are the reverse of the removal procedure. Use a new spindle nut, and stake after torquing.

# FRONT SUSPENSION

## Shock Absorbers

### REMOVAL & INSTALLATION

#### *Civic*

1. Raise the vehicle and support it

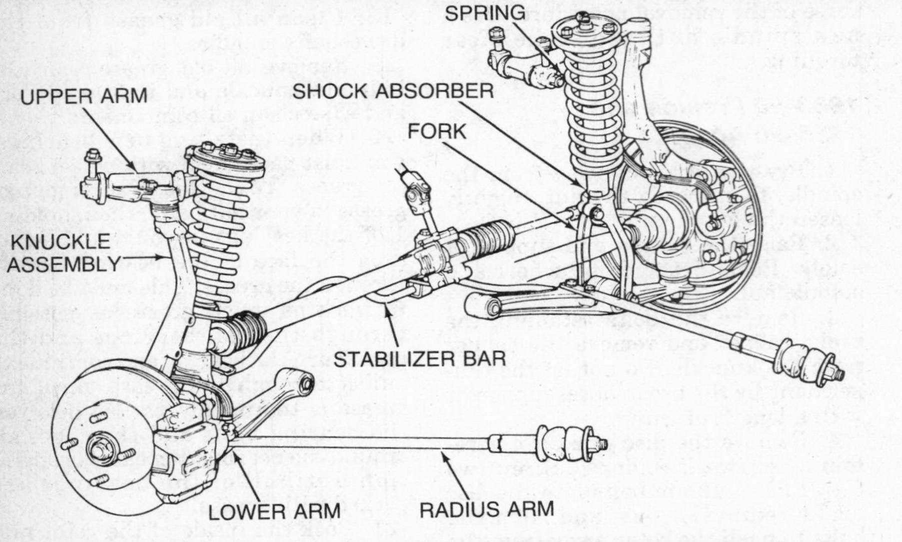


**Front suspension—1983 and later Prelude, and 1986 and later Accord**

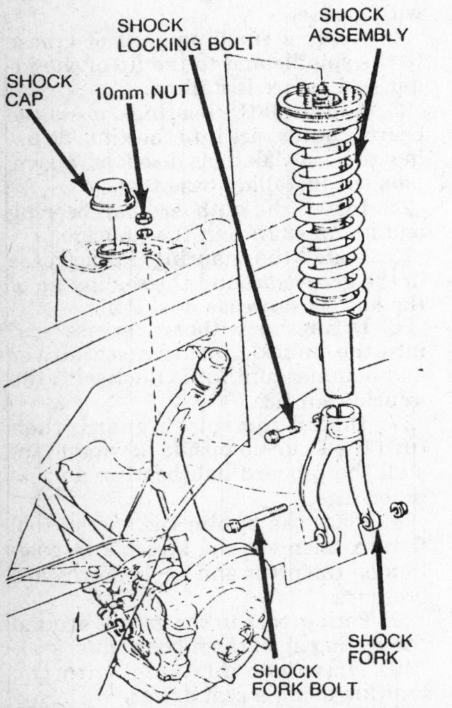


**Front shock mounting—1983 and later Prelude, and 1986 and later Accord**

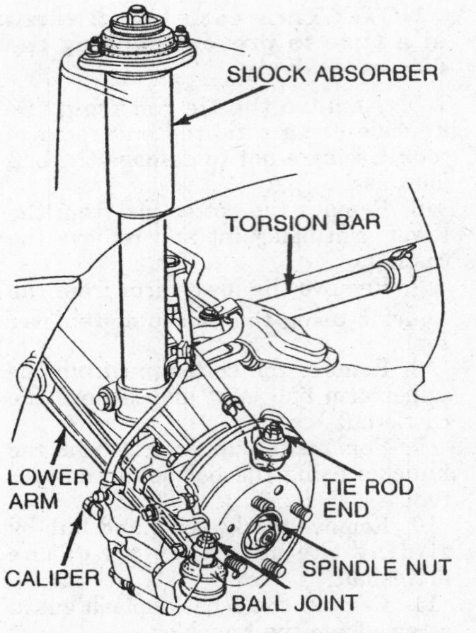


**Front suspension—1984 and later Civic**

safely. Remove the front wheels.

2. Remove the brake hose clamp bolt.

3. Place a floor jack beneath the lower control arm to support it.

4. Remove the lower shock retaining bolt from the steering knuckle, then slowly lower the jack.

**NOTE: Be sure the jack is positioned securely beneath the lower control arm at the ball joint. Otherwise, the tension from the torsion bar may cause the lower control arm to suddenly jump away from the shock absorber as the pinch bolt is removed.**

5. Compress the shock absorber by hand, then remove the 2 upper locknuts. Remove the shock absorber from the vehicle.

6. Installation is the reverse of the removal procedure, taking note of the following.

### *Accord and Prelude*

1. Raise the vehicle and support it safely. Remove the front wheels.

2. Remove the shock absorber locking bolt.

3. Remove the shock fork bolt and remove the shock fork.

4. Remove the shock absorber assembly.

5. Installation is the reverse of the removal procedure. Be sure to align the shock absorber aligning tab with the slot in the shock absorber fork.

6. The mounting base bolt should be tightened with the weight of the vehicle placed on the shock.

7. Torque the upper mounting bolts to 29 ft. lbs., the shock locking bolt to 32 ft. lbs., and the shock fork bolt to 47 ft. lbs.

# MacPherson Strut Assembly

## REMOVAL & INSTALLATION

1. Raise the vehicle and support it safely. Remove the front wheels.

2. Disconnect the brake pipe at the strut and remove the brake hose retaining clip.

3. As required, remove the caliper and carefully hang from the undercarriage of the vehicle with a piece of wire.

4. On 1983–85 Accord, disconnect the stabilizer bar from the lower arm.

5. Loosen the bolt on the knuckle that retains the lower end of the strut. Push down firmly while tapping it with a hammer until the knuckle is free of the strut.

6. Remove the 3 nuts retaining the upper end of the strut and remove the strut from the vehicle.

7. On the later vehicles, remove the damper (strut) pinch bolt, remove the damper (strut) fork bolt and remove the damper (strut) fork from the steering knuckle.

8. To install, reverse the removal procedure. Be sure to properly match the mating surface of the strut and the knuckle notch. Tighten the knuckle bolt to 47 ft. lbs.

## OVERHAUL

**For all spring and shock absorber removal and installation procedures, and all strut overhaul procedures, please refer to "Strut Overhaul" in the Unit Repair section.**

# Torsion Bars

## REMOVAL & INSTALLATION

1. Raise the vehicle and support it safely.

2. Remove the height adjusting nut and the torque tube holder.

3. Remove the 33mm circlip.

4. Remove the torsion bar cap, then remove the torsion bar clip by tapping the bar out of the torque tube.

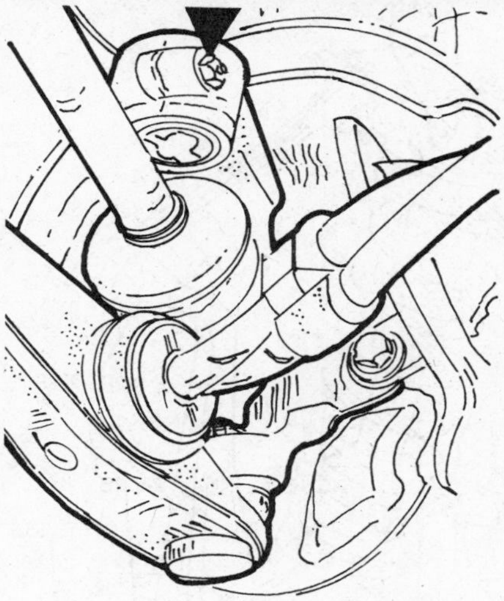

Lower strut retaining (pinch) bolt

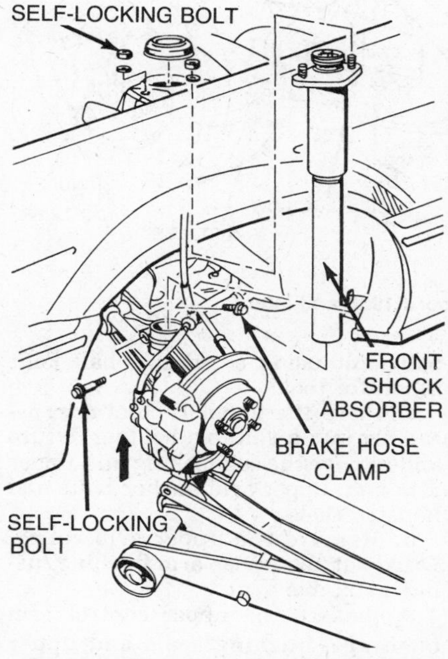


Front shock mounting—1984 and later Civic

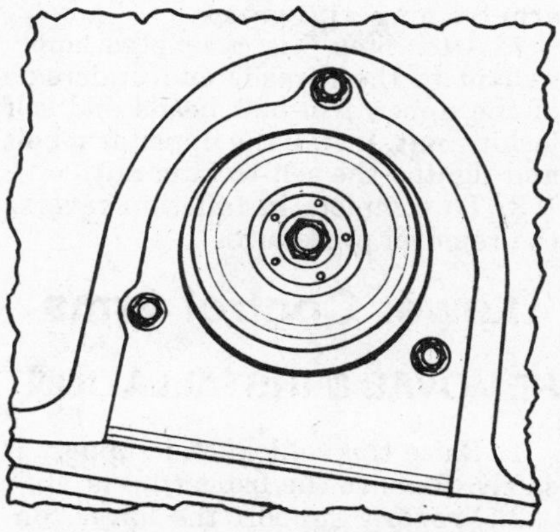

Typical strut upper mounting nuts

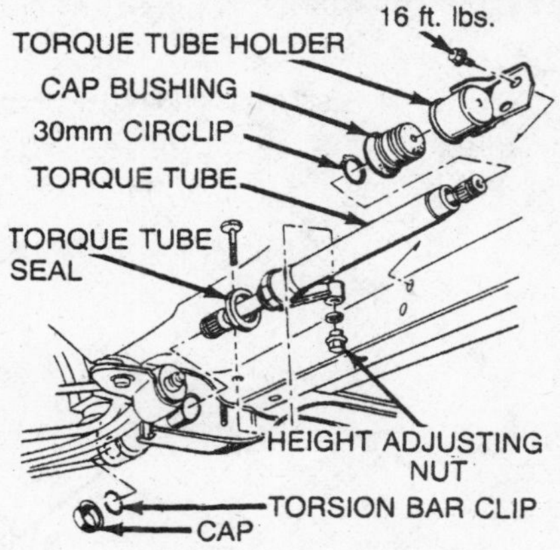


Torsion bar assembly—1984 and later Civic

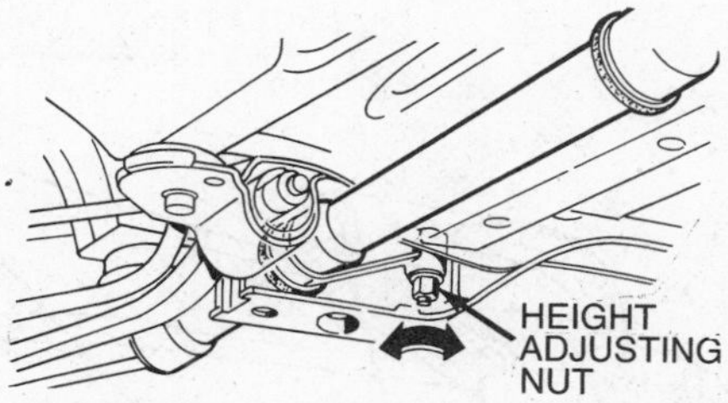


Torsion bar adjustment—1984 and later Civic

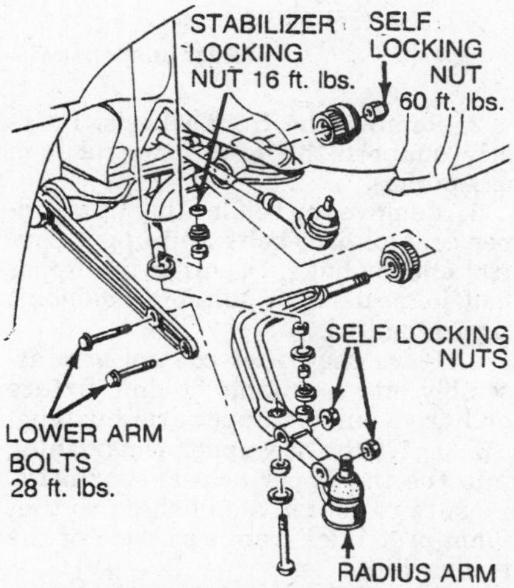


Radius arm—1984 and later Civic

**NOTE: The torsion bar will slide easier if you move the lower arm up and down.**

5. Tap the torsion bar backward, out of the torque tube and remove the torque tube.
6. Install a new seal onto the torque tube. Coat the torque tube seal and torque with grease, then install them on the rear beam.
7. Grease the ends of the torsion bar and insert into the torque tube from the back.
8. Align the projection on the torque tube splines with the cutout in the torsion bar splines and insert the torsion bar approximately 10mm.

**NOTE: The torsion bar will slide easier if the lower arm is moved up and down.**

9. Install the torsion bar clip and cap, then install the 30mm circlip and the torque tube cap.

**NOTE: Push the torsion bar to the front so there is no clearance between the torque tube and the 30mm circlip.**

10. Coat the cap bushing with grease and install it on the torque tube. Install the torque tube holder.
11. Temporarily tighten the height adjusting nut.
12. Lower the vehicle. Adjust the torsion bar spring height.

## Ball Joints

### INSPECTION

1. Raise the vehicle and support it safely.
2. Clamp a dial indicator onto the lower control arm and place the indicator tip on the knuckle, near the ball joint.
3. Place a pry bar between the lower control arm and the knuckle. Replace the lower control arm if the play exceeds 0.020 in.

## Upper Ball Joint

### REMOVAL & INSTALLATION

1. Raise and support the vehicle safely. Remove the tire and wheel assembly.
2. Remove the upper control arm from the vehicle.
3. Position the control arm assembly in a suitable holding fixture. Using the ball joint removal tool, remove the ball joint from the upper control arm.
4. Installation is the reverse of the removal procedure.

## Lower Ball Joint

### REMOVAL & INSTALLATION

#### *1983–87 Civic and 1983–85 Accord*

If the ball joint play exceeds 0.020 in. the ball joint and lower control arm or lower radius arm (1984–87 Civics) must be replaced as an assembly.

#### *Except 1983–87 Civic and 1983–85 Accord*

1. Raise and support the vehicle

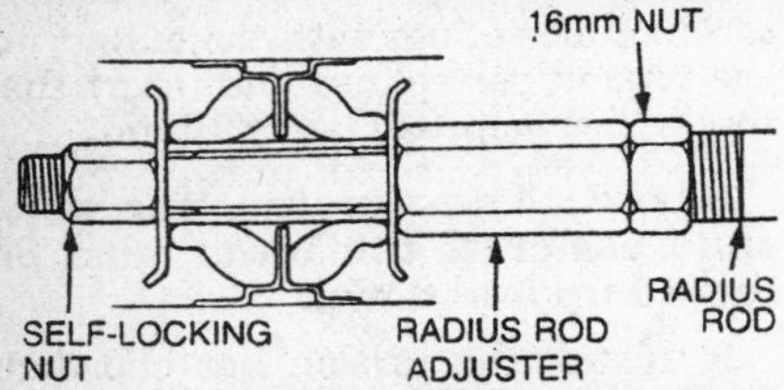


**Caster adjustment—1983 and later Prelude, and 1986 and later Accord**

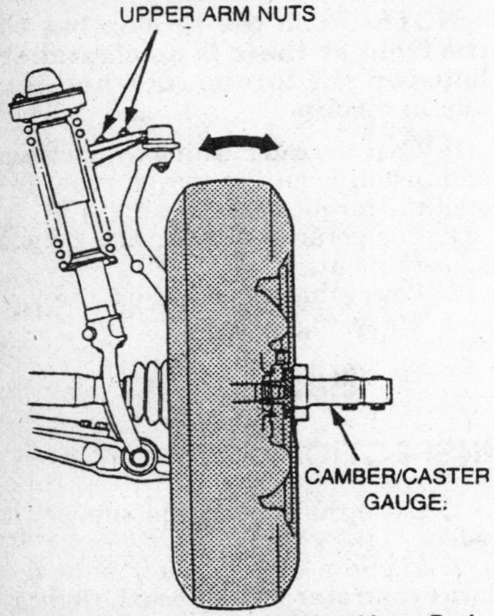


**Camber adjustment—1983 and later Prelude, and 1986 and later Accord**

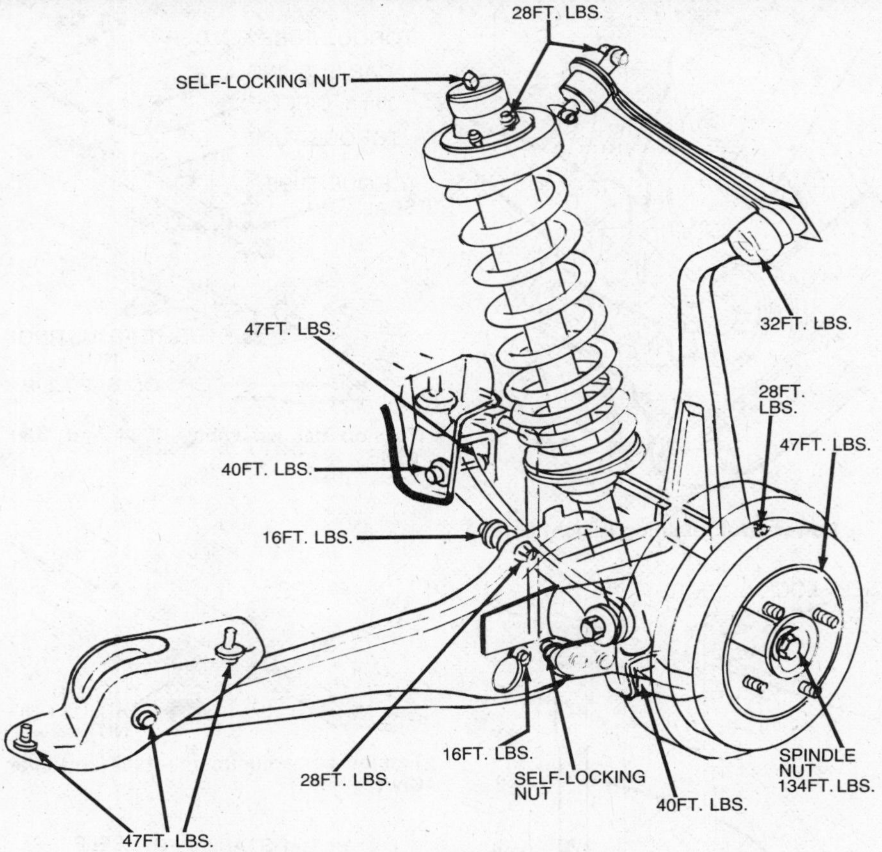


**Rear suspension—Accord 1986 and later**

safely. Remove the tire and wheel assembly.

2. Remove the steering knuckle from the vehicle.
3. Pry the snapring off and remove the boot. Pry the snapring out of the groove in the ball joint.
4. Install the ball joint removal tool with the large end facing out and tighten the ball joint nut.
5. Position the ball joint removal tool base 07965-SB00300 or equivalent on the ball joint and set the assembly in a large vise. Press the ball joint out of the steering knuckle.
6. Position the new ball joint into the hole of the steering knuckle. Install the ball joint installer tool with the small end facing out.
7. Position the ball joint installation base tool on the ball joint and set the assembly in a large vise. Press the ball joint into the steering knuckle.
8. Seat the snapring in the groove of the ball joint.
9. Install the boot and snapring using the clip guide tool.

# Upper Control Arms

## REMOVAL & INSTALLATION

### *1988–90 Civic*

1. Raise and support the vehicle safely.
2. Remove the front wheels. Properly support the lower control arm assemblies.
3. Remove the self locking nuts, upper control arm bolts and upper control anchor bolts. Separate the upper ball joint using a suitable ball joint separator tool.
4. Place the upper control arm assembly into a suitable holding fixture and drive out the upper arm bushing.
5. Drive the new upper arm bushing into the the upper arm anchor bolts. Be sure to center the bushing so that 9mm protrudes from each side of the anchor bolt.
6. Install the upper control arm assembly and install the upper arm bolts, then tighten the self locking nuts. Be sure to align the upper arm anchor bolt with the mark on the upper arm.

### *1986–90 Accord and 1983–90 Prelude*

1. Raise and support the vehicle safely.
2. Remove the front wheels. Properly support the lower control arm assemblies.
3. Remove the self locking nuts, upper control arm bolts and upper control anchor bolts. Separate the upper ball joint using a suitable ball joint separator tool.
4. Place the upper control arm assembly into a suitable holding fixture and remove the self locking nut, upper arm bolt, upper arm anchor bolts and housing seals.
5. Remove the upper arm collar. Drive out the upper arm bushing, using a suitable drift.
6. Replace the upper control arm bushings, bushing seals and upper control arm collar with new ones. Be sure to coat the ends and the insides of the upper control arm bushings, and the sealing lips of the upper control arm bushing with grease.
7. After Step 6 is completed, apply sealant to the threads and underside of the upper arm bolt heads and self locking nut. Install the upper arm bolt and tighten the self locking nut.
8. To complete installation reverse the removal procedure.

# Lower Control Arms

## REMOVAL & INSTALLATION

1. Raise the vehicle and support it safely. Remove the front wheels.
2. Properly support the lower control arm assembly. Disconnect the low-

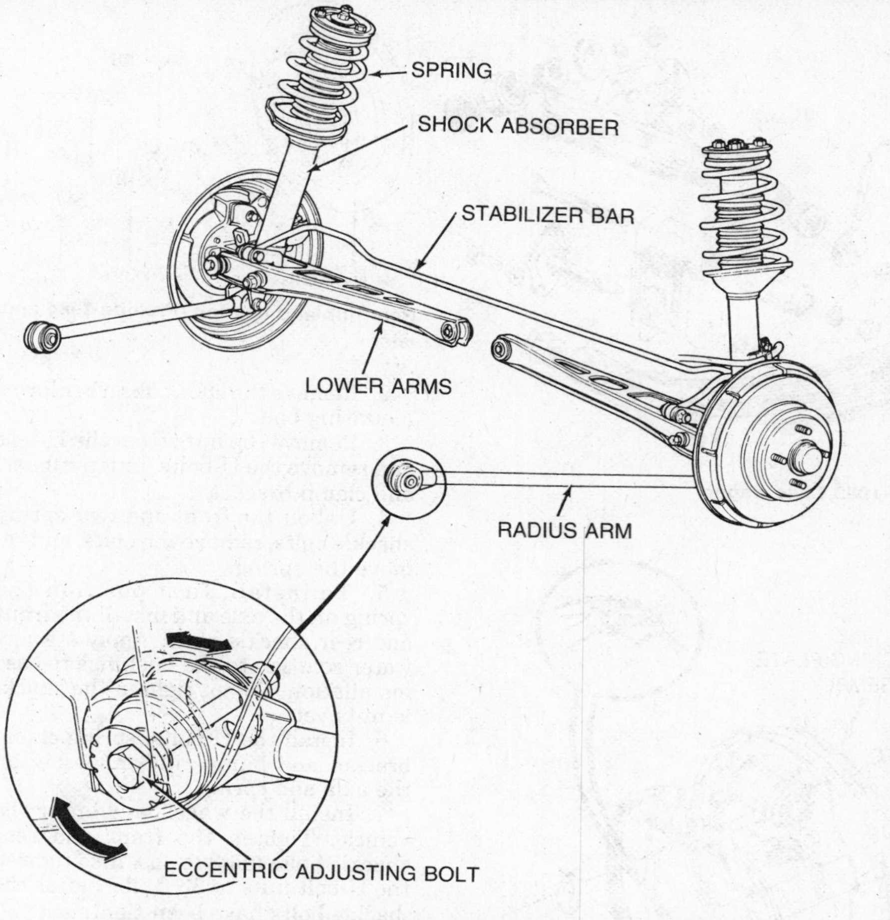


**Rear suspension—1983–85 Accord and 1983 and later Prelude**

er arm ball joint. Be careful not to damage the seal.

3. Remove the stabilizer bar retaining brackets, starting with the center brackets.
4. Remove the lower arm pivot bolt.
5. Disconnect the radius rod and remove the lower arm.
6. To install, reverse the removal procedure. Be sure to tighten the components to their proper torque.

## Front Wheel Alignment

### ADJUSTMENT

#### *Caster and Camber*

Caster and camber cannot be adjusted, except on the 1983–90 Prelude. If caster, camber or kingpin angle is incorrect or front end parts are damaged or worn, they must be replaced.

**NOTE: When adjusting the wheel alignment on the Prelude, the adjustments must be performed in the following order: camber, caster and then toe-in.**

The camber adjustment can be made by loosening the 2 nuts on the upper control arm and sliding the ball joint until the camber meets specifications. The caster adjustment can be made by loosening the 16mm nuts on the front beam radius rods and then turning the locknut to make the adjustment. Turning the nut clockwise decreases the caster and turning it counterclockwise increases the caster. After adjusting to specifications, hold the nylon locknut and lightly tighten the adjuster. Tighten the 16mm nut to 58 ft. lbs., then tighten the locknut to 32 ft. lbs. while holding the 16mm nut.

#### *Toe In*

Toe in is the difference of the distance between the forward extremes of the front tires and the distance between the rearward extremes of the front tires. The fronts of the tires are further apart than the rear to counteract the pulling together effect of front wheel drive.

Toe-out can be adjusted on all vehicles by loosening the locknuts at each end of the tie rods. To increase toe-out, turn the right tie rod in the direction of forward wheel rotation and turn the left tie rod in the opposite direction. Turn both tie rods an equal amount until toe-out meets specifications.

# REAR SUSPENSION

## MacPherson Strut

### REMOVAL & INSTALLATION

1. Remove the strut retaining bolt cover from inside of the vehicle.
2. Remove the strut retaining bolts.
3. Raise the vehicle and support it safely. Remove the rear wheels, as required.
4. Disconnect the brake line at the strut, if necessary. Remove the retaining clip and separate the brake hose from the strut.
5. As necessary, disconnect the parking brake cable at the backing plate lever. Remove the stabilizer bar from the lower arm, if so equipped. Loosen the lower arm bolt, radius rod nut and hub carrier bolt.
6. Remove the lower strut retaining bolt or pinch bolt and hub carrier pivot bolt. Remove the strut from the vehicle.
7. To install, reverse the removal procedure. Be sure to install the top of the strut in the body first. After installation, bleed the brakes, as necessary.

### OVERHAUL

**For all spring and shock absorber removal and installation procedures, and all strut overhaul procedures, please refer to "Strut Overhaul" in the Unit Repair section.**

## Rear Control Arm

### REMOVAL & INSTALLATION

1. Raise the vehicle and support it safely.
2. Remove the rear wheels and brake drums, as necessary for working clearance.
3. Disconnect the hydraulic brake line and parking brake cable, as required.
4. Remove the backing plate assembly.
5. Remove the radius arm nuts and bolts, and remove the radius arm. Unscrew the stabilizer bolt and remove the stabilizer bar, if equipped.

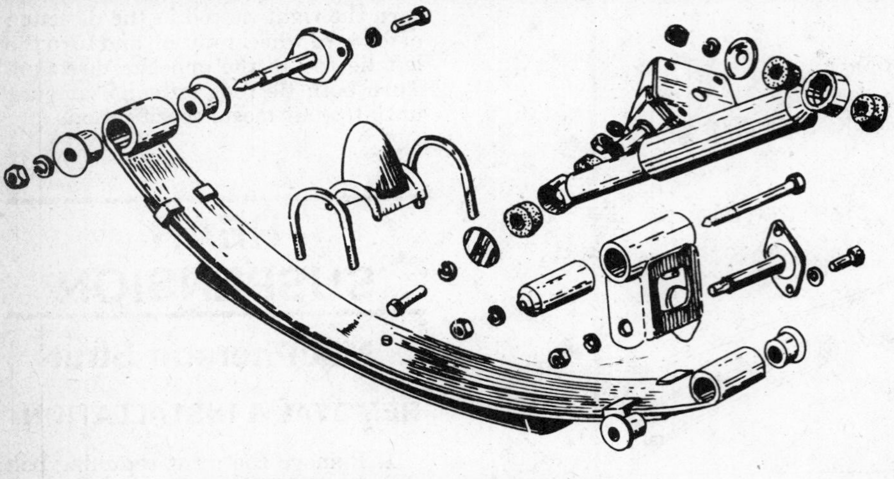

Rear suspension—1983 Civic wagon

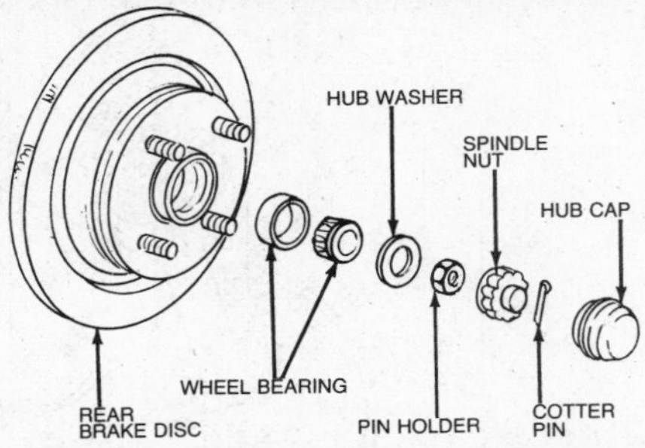


Rear hub and bearing–Prelude 1984 and later

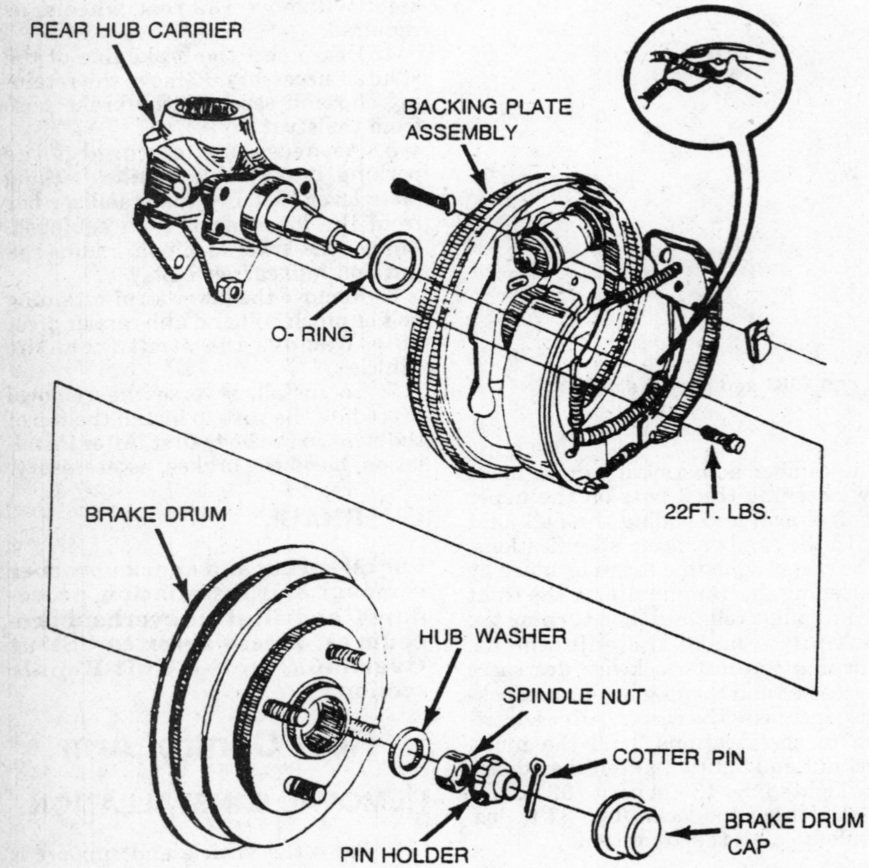


Rear hub and bearing—all except 1984 and later Civic and Prelude, and 1986 and later Accord

6. Remove the strut pinch bolt, then separate the hub carrier from the strut.
7. Remove the lower control arm retaining bolts, then remove the arm.
8. Installation is the reverse of the removal procedure.

## Spring

### REMOVAL & INSTALLATION

#### *1983 Civic Wagon*

1. Raise the vehicle and support it safely. Remove the wheels.
2. Remove the shock absorber lower mounting bolt.
3. Remove the nuts from the U-bolt and remove the U-bolts, bump rubber, and clamp bracket.
4. Unbolt the front and rear spring shackle bolts, remove the bolts, and remove the spring.
5. To install, first position the spring on the axle and install the front and rear shackle bolts. Apply a soapy water solution to the bushings to ease installation. Do not tighten the shackle nuts yet.
6. Install the U-bolts, spring clamp bracket and bump rubber loosely on the axle and spring.
7. Install the wheels and lower the vehicle. Tighten the front and rear shackle bolts to 33 ft. lbs. Also tighten the U-bolt nuts to 33 ft. lbs., after the shackle bolts have been tightened.
8. Install the shock absorber to the lower mount. Tighten to 33 ft. lbs.

## Shock Absorbers

### REMOVAL & INSTALLATION

#### *1983 Civic Wagon*

1. It is not necessary to raise the vehicle or remove the wheels unless you require working clearance.
2. Unbolt the upper mounting nut and lower bolt and remove the shock absorber. Note the position of the washers and lock washers upon removal.
3. Installation is the reverse of the removal procedure.
4. Be sure the washers and lock washers are installed correctly. Tighten the upper mount to 44 ft. lbs. and the lower mount to 33 ft. lbs.

## Rear Wheel Bearings

### ADJUSTMENT

1. Raise and support the vehicle safely. Remove the tire and wheel assembly.

2. Apply grease or oil on the spindle nut and spindle threads.

3. Install and tighten the spindle nut to 18 ft. lbs. and rotate the drum/disc 2–3 turns by hand, then retighten the spindle nut to 18 ft. lbs.

4. Repeat the above step until the spindle nut hold that torque.

5. Loosen the spindle nut to 0 ft. lbs.

**NOTE: Loosen the nut until it just breaks free, but doesn't turn.**

6. Retorque the spindle nut to 4 ft. lbs.

7. Set the pin holder so the slots will be as close as possible to the hole in the spindle.

8. Tighten the spindle nut just enough to align the slot and hole, then secure it with a new cotter pin.

## REMOVAL & INSTALLATION

### *1983 Civic and Prelude, and 1983–85 Accord*

1. Slightly loosen the rear lug nuts. Raise the vehicle and support it safely.

2. Release the parking brake. Remove the rear wheels.

3. Remove the rear bearing hub cap and cotter pin and pin holder.

4. Remove the spindle nut, then pull the hub and drum off the spindle.

5. Drive the outboard inboard bearing races out of the hub. Punch in a criss-cross pattern to avoid cocking the bearing race in the bore.

6. Clean the bearing seats thoroughly before going on to the next step.

7. Using a bearing driver, drive the inboard bearing race into the hub.

8. Turn the hub over and drive the outboard bearing race in the same way.

9. Check to see that the bearing races are seated properly.

10. When installing new bearings, pack them with wheel bearing grease. To do this, place a glob of grease in your left palm, then, holding 1 of the bearings in your right hand, drag the face of the bearing heavily through the grease. This must be done to work as much grease as possible through the ball bearings and the cage. Turn the bearing and continue to pull it through the grease, until the grease is thoroughly packed between the bearing balls and the cage, all around the bearing. Repeat this operation until all of the bearings are packed with grease.

11. Pack the inside of the hub with a moderate amount of grease. Do not overload the hub with grease.

12. Apply a small amount of grease to the spindle and to the lip of the inner seal before installing.

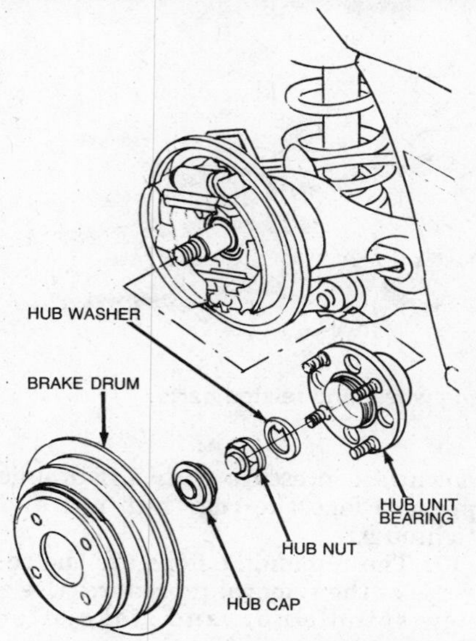


**Rear hub and bearing—Civic 1984 and later, and Accord 1986 and later**

13. Place the inboard bearings into the hub.

14. Apply grease to the hub seal, and carefully tap into place. Tap in a criss-cross pattern to avoid cocking the seal in the bore.

15. Slip the hub and drum over the spindle, then insert the outboard bearing, hub, washer, and spindle nut.

16. Adjust the bearings, as required.

### *1984–90 Civic and 1986–90 Accord*

1. Slightly loosen the rear lug nuts. Raise the vehicle and support it safely.

2. Release the parking brake. Remove the rear wheel and the brake drum.

3. Remove the rear bearing hub cap and nut.

4. Pull the hub unit off of the spindle.

5. Installation is the reverse order of removal. Tighten the new spindle nut to 134 ft. lbs., then stake the nut.

### *1984–90 Prelude Except 4 Wheel Steering*

1. Slightly loosen the rear lug nuts. Raise the vehicle and support it safely.

2. Release the parking brake. Remove the rear wheels.

3. Remove the bolts retaining the brake caliper and remove the caliper from the knuckle. Do not let the caliper hang by the brake hose, support it with a length of wire.

4. Remove the rear bearing hub cap and cotter pin and pin holder. Remove the spindle nut, then pull the hub and disc off of the spindle.

5. Drive the outboard and inboard bearing races out of the disc. Punch in a criss-cross pattern to avoid cocking the bearing race in the bore.

6. Clean the bearing seats thoroughly before going on to the next step.

7. Using a bearing driver, drive the inboard bearing race into the disc.

8. Turn the disc over and drive the outboard bearing race in the same way.

9. Check to see that the bearing races are seated properly.

10. When installing new bearings, pack them with wheel bearing grease. To do this, place a glob of grease in your left palm, then, holding 1 of the bearings in your right hand, drag the face of the bearing heavily through the grease. This must be done to work as much grease as possible through the ball bearings and the cage. Turn the bearing and continue to pull it through the grease, until the grease is thoroughly packed between the bearing balls and the cage, all around the bearing. Repeat this operation until all of the bearings are packed with grease.

11. Pack the inside of the hub with a moderate amount of grease. Do not overload the hub with grease.

12. Apply a small amount of grease to the spindle and to the lip of the inner seal before installing.

13. Place the inboard bearing into the hub.

14. Apply grease to the hub seal, and carefully tap into place. Tap in a criss-cross pattern to avoid cocking the seal in the bore.

15. Slip the hub and disc over the spindle, then insert the outboard bearing, hub washer, and spindle nut.

16. Adjust the bearings, as required.

### *1988–90 Prelude with 4 Wheel Steering*

1. Slightly loosen the rear lug nuts. Raise the vehicle and support it safely.

2. Release the parking brake. Remove the rear wheels.

3. Remove the bolts retaining the brake caliper and remove the caliper from the knuckle. Do not let the caliper hang by the brake hose, support it with a length of wire.

4. Remove the two 6mm screws from the brake disc. Tighten the 8 x 12mm bolts into the holes of the brake disc, then remove the brake disc from the rear hub.

5. Remove the cotter pin of the lower arm tie rod and remove the castle nut.

6. Separate the tie rod ball joint using a suitable ball joint removal tool.

7. Remove the cotter pin and loosen the lower arm ball joint nut half the length of the joint threads.

8. Separate the ball joint and lower arm using a suitable puller. Remove

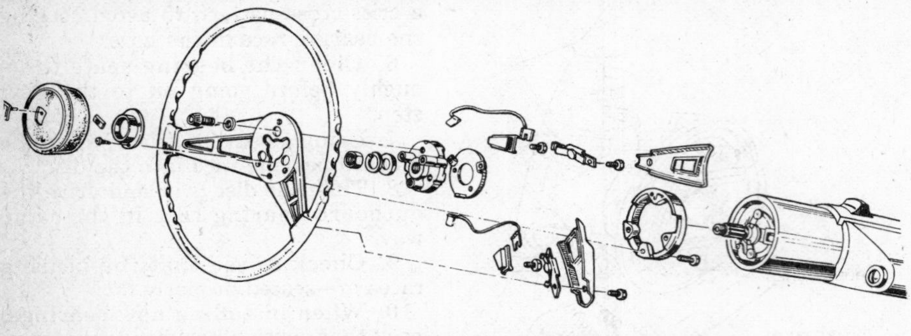

Typical exploded view of steering wheel and related parts

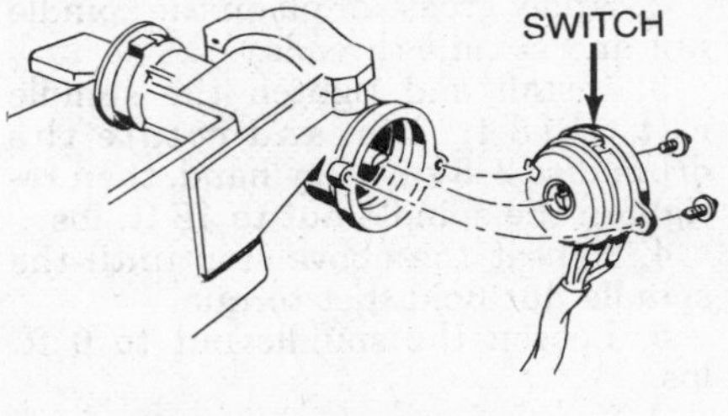


Ignition switch removal

the cotter pin and castle nut, and separate the tie rod ball joint using a ball joint removal tool.

9. Tap the outboard joint of the driveshaft to extract it from the knuckle, then remove the knuckle.

10. Remove the rear hub nut from the rear hub. Remove the splash guard mounting bolts. Using a hydraulic press, separate the hub from the knuckle.

**NOTE: Set the rear hub at the hub/disc assembly base firmly so that the knuckle will not tilt the assembly in the press. Take care not to distort the splash guard. Hold onto the hub to keep it from falling after it is pressed out.**

11. Remove the splash guard and 68mm circlip from the knuckle.

12. Using a hydraulic press and special press tools, press the wheel bearing out of the knuckle.

13. Remove the bearing inner race using a suitable bearing remover.

14. When installing new bearings, pack them with wheel bearing grease. If a bearing packer is not available or can not be used on this type of bearing, grease the bearing as follows, place a glob of grease in your left palm, then, holding 1 of the bearings in your right hand, drag the face of the bearing heavily through the grease. This must be done to work as much grease as possible through the ball bearings and the cage. Turn the bearing and continue to pull it through the grease, until the grease is thoroughly packed between the bearing balls and the cage, all around the bearing. Repeat this operation until all of the bearings are packed with grease.

15. Place the rear wheel bearing in a special tool fixture 07GAF–SE00101 or equivalent, then set the knuckle into positionand apply downward pressure with a hydraulic press. Fit the 68mm circlip into the groove of the knuckle.

16. Install the splash guard. Place the hub in a special tool fixture, then set the knuckle into position and apply downward pressure with a hydraulic press. Place the rear hub nut and tighten it.

17. The remaining steps are the reverse of the removal procedure. Use a new spindle nut, and stake after torquing.

# STEERING

## Steering Wheel

### REMOVAL & INSTALLATION

1. Disconnect the negative battery cable. Remove the steering wheel pad by lifting it off. Disconnect the necessary electrical connections under the steering wheel pad.

2. Remove the steering wheel retaining nut. Remove the steering wheel, using the proper removal tool.

3. Installation is the reverse of the removal procedure. Be sure to tighten the steering wheel nut to 22–36 ft. lbs.

## Combination Switch

### REMOVAL & INSTALLATION

1. Disconnect the negative battery cable. Remove the steering wheel.

2. Disconnect the column wiring harness and coupler. Be careful not to damage the steering column or shaft.

3. Remove the upper and lower column covers.

4. On vehicles so equipped, remove the cruise control slip ring.

5. Remove the turn signal cancelling sleeve.

6. On later vehicles, remove the switch retaining screws, then remove the switch.

7. Loosen the screw on the turn signal switch cam nut and lightly tap its head to permit the cam nut to loosen. Then remove the turn signal switch assembly and the steering shaft upper bushing.

8. To assemble and install, reverse the above procedure. When installing the turn signal switch assembly, engage the locating tab on the switch with the notch in the steering column. The steering shaft upper bushing should be installed with the flat side facing the upper side of the column. The alignment notch for the turn signal switch will be centered on the flat side of the bushing.

**NOTE: On some vehicles, if the cam nut has been removed, be sure to install it with the small end up.**

## Ignition Switch

### REMOVAL & INSTALLATION

1. Disconnect the negative battery cable. Remove the steering column housing lower cover.

2. Disconnect the ignition switch wiring at the couplers.

3. The ignition switch assembly is held onto the column by 2 shear bolts. Remove these bolts, using a drill, to separate and remove the ignition switch.

4. Install the ignition switch without the key inserted. Loosely tighten the new shear bolts. Be sure that the projection on the ignition switch is aligned with the hole in the steering column.

5. Insert the ignition key and check for proper operation of the steering wheel lock and that the ignition key turns freely.

6. Tighten the shear bolts until the hex heads twist off.

## Ignition Lock Cylinder

### REMOVAL & INSTALLATION

1. Disconnect the negative battery cable. Remove the ignition switch as outlined earlier in this section. Remove the key case cover from the ignition switch, if equipped.

2. Turn the ignition key to the **ACC** or **I** position.

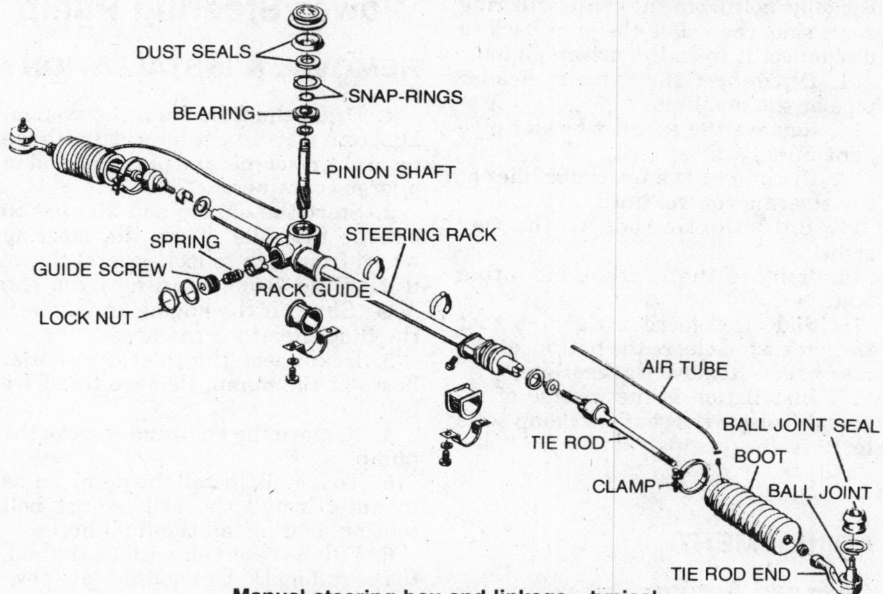

Manual steering box and linkage—typical

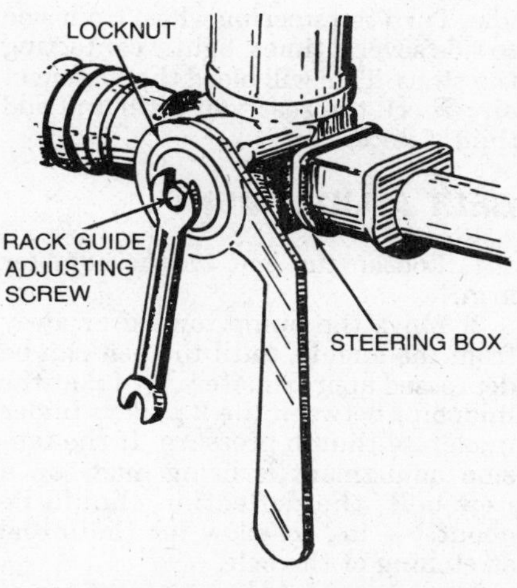

Steering box adjustment

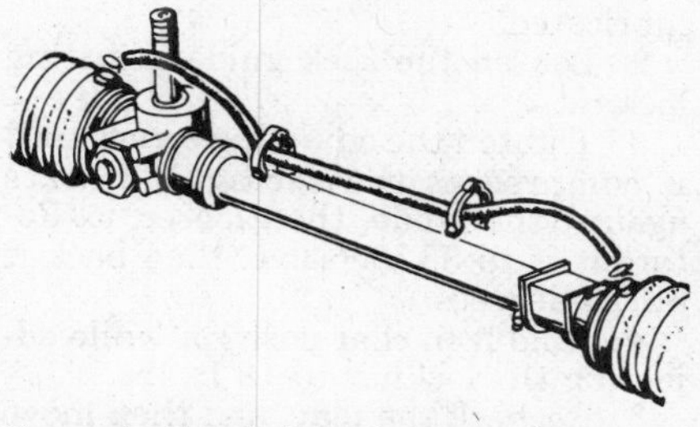
Separate the air tube from the dust boot

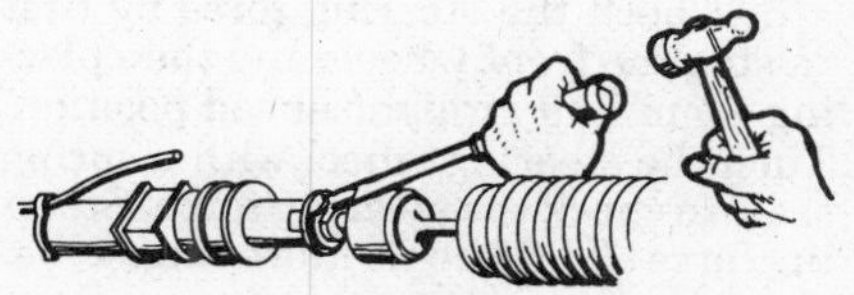
Tie rod lockwasher removal

3. Using a suitable tool, push the pin in and remove the lock cylinder from the lock body.

4. To install, turn the ignition key to the **LOCK** or **L** position and align the lock cylinder with the lock body.

5. Turn the ignition key to it is almost at the **ACC** or **I** position and insert the lock cylinder until the pin touches the lock body.

6. Turn the ignition key to the **ACC** or **I** position, push the pin and insert the lock cylinder into the lock body until the pin clicks into place.

## Manual Steering Gear

### REMOVAL & INSTALLATION

1. Raise the vehicle and support it safely.

2. Remove the cover panel and steering joint cover. Unbolt and separate the steering shaft at the coupling.

3. Remove the front wheels.

4. Remove the cotter pins and unscrew the castle nuts on the tie rod ends. Using a ball joint tool disconnect the tie rod ends. Lift the tie rod ends out out the steering knuckles.

5. On vehicles equipped with manual transaxle, disconnect the shift lever torque rod from the clutch housing. Slide the pin retainer out of the way, drive out the spring pin and disconnect the shift rod.

6. On vehicles equipped with automatic transaxles, remove the shift cable guide from the floor and pull the shift cable down by hand.

7. Remove the 2 nut connecting the exhaust header pipe to the exhaust pipe and move the exhaust pipe out of the way.

8. Push the rack all the way to the right and remove the gearbox brackets. Slide the tie rod ends all the way to the right.

9. Drop the gearbox far enough to permit the end of the pinion shaft to come out of the hole in the frame channel, then rotate it forward until the shaft is pointing rearward.

10. Slide the gearbox to the right until the left tie rod clears the exhaust pipe, then drop it down and out of the vehicle to the left.

11. Installation is the reverse of removal. Torque the mounting bracket bolts to 29 ft. lbs. On vehicles equipped with manual transaxles, reinstall the pin retainer after driving in the pin and be sure that the projection on the pin retainer is in the hole.

### ADJUSTMENT

1. Make sure that the rack is well lubricated.

2. Loosen the rack guide adjusting locknut.

3. Tighten the adjusting screw just to less than 36 inch lbs. (less than 48 inch lbs. on variable ratio steering).

4. On all vehicles except 1988–90 Civic, back off the adjusting screw 25 degrees ± 5 degrees (15 degrees ± 3 degrees on variable ratio steering) and hold it in that position while adjusting the locknut to 18 ft. lbs. (60 ft. lbs. on variable ratio steering).

5. On the 1988–90 Civic, back off the adjusting screw 50 ± 10 degrees and while holding the adjusting screw tighten the locknut to 18 ft. lbs.

6. Recheck the play, and then move the wheels lock-to-lock, to make sure that the rack moves freely.

7. Check the steering force by first raising the front wheels and then placing them in a straight ahead position. Turn the steering wheel with a spring scale to check the steering force. Steering force should be no more than 3.3 lbs.

## Power Steering Gear

### REMOVAL & INSTALLATION

#### *Civic*

1. Disconnect the negative battery cable. Raise the vehicle and support it safely.

2. Remove the cover panel and steering joint cover. Unbolt and separate the steering shaft at the coupling.

3. Drain the power steering fluid by disconnecting the return hose at the box and running the engine while turning the steering wheel lock to lock until fluid stops draining. Remove the gearbox shield. Remove the front wheels.

4. Remove the cotter pins and unscrew the castle nuts on the tie rod ends. Using a ball joint tool disconnect the tie rod ends. Lift the tie rod ends out out the steering knuckles.

5. On vehicles equipped with manual transaxle, disconnect the shift lever torque rod from the clutch housing. Slide the pin retainer out of the way, drive out the spring pin and disconnect the shift rod.

6. On vehicles equipped with automatic transaxle, remove the shift cable guide from the floor and pull the shift cable down by hand.

7. Remove the 2 nut connecting the exhaust header pipe to the exhaust pipe and move the exhaust pipe out of the way. Disconnect the 3 hydraulic lines from the control unit.

8. Push the rack all the way to the right and remove the gearbox brackets. Slide the tie rod ends all the way to the right.

9. Drop the gearbox far enough to permit the end of the pinion shaft to come out of the hole in the frame channel, then rotate it forward until the shaft is pointing rearward.

10. Slide the gearbox to the right until the left tie rod clears the exhaust pipe, then drop it down and out of the vehicle to the left.

11. Installation is the reverse of removal. Torque the mounting bracket bolts to 29 ft. lbs. On vehicles equipped with manual transaxles, reinstall the pin retainer after driving in the pin and be sure that the projection on the pin retainer is in the hole.

#### Accord and Prelude

1. Disconnect the negative battery cable. Raise the vehicle and support it safely.

2. Remove the steering shaft joint cover and disconnect the steering shaft at the coupling.

3. Drain the power steering fluid by disconnecting the return hose at the box and running the engine while turning the steering wheel lock to lock until fluid stops draining.

4. Remove the gearbox shield.

5. Remove the front wheels.

6. Using a ball joint tool, disconnect the tie rods from the knuckles.

7. On vehicles equipped with manual transaxle, remove the shift extension from the transaxle case. Disconnect the gear shift rod from the transaxle case by removing the 8mm bolt.

8. On vehicles equipped with automatic transaxle, remove the control cable clamp.

9. Remove the center beam.

10. On the 4 wheel steering vehicles, separate the joint guard cap and the joint guard. Remove the joint bolt from the driven pinion side. Remove the joint bolt from the center steering shaft side, then slide the joint back to disconnect it from the driven pinion.

11. Disconnect the exhaust header pipe at the manifold.

12. Remove the exhaust header pipe joint nuts.

13. Disconnect the hydraulic lines at the steering control until.

14. Shift the tie rods all the way right.

15. Remove the gearbox mounting bolts.

16. Slide the gearbox right so that the left tie rod clears the bottom of the rear beam. Remove the gearbox.

17. Installation is the reverse of removal. Torque the gearbox clamp bolts to 16 ft. lbs.

### ADJUSTMENT

#### Civic and Accord

1. Make sure that the rack is well lubricated.

2. Loosen the rack guide adjusting locknut.

3. Tighten the adjusting screw until it compresses the spring and seats against the guide, then loosen it. Retorque it to 35 inch lbs., then back it off 25 degrees.

4. Hold it in that position while adjusting the locknut to 18 ft. lbs.

5. Recheck the play, and then move the wheels lock-to-lock, to make sure that the rack moves freely.

6. Check the steering force by first raising the front wheels and then placing them in a straight ahead position. Turn the steering wheel with a spring scale to check the steering force. Steering force should be no more than 4 lbs.

#### Prelude

1. Make sure that the rack is well lubricated.

2. Loosen the rack guide adjusting locknut.

3. Tighten the adjusting screw until it compresses the spring and seats against the guide, then loosen it. Retorque it to 24 inch lbs. then back it off 25 degrees (3 ft. lbs. and 30–40 degrees on 4 wheel steering vehicles).

4. Hold it in that position while adjusting the locknut to 18 ft. lbs.

5. Recheck the play, and then move the wheels lock-to-lock, to make sure that the rack moves freely.

6. Check the steering force by first raising the front wheels and then placing them in a straight ahead position. Turn the steering wheel with a spring scale to check the steering force. Steering force should be no more than 4 lbs.

## Power Steering Pump

### REMOVAL & INSTALLATION

1. Drain the fluid from the system: Disconnect the cooler return hose from the reservoir and place the end in a large container.

2. Start the engine and allow it to run at fast idle. Turn the steering wheel from lock to lock several times, until fluid stops running from the hose. Shut off the engine and discard the fluid. Reattach the hose.

3. Disconnect the inlet and outlet hoses at the pump. Remove the drive belt.

4. Remove the bolts and remove the pump.

5. To install, install the pump on its mounts, install the belt, adjust belt tension, and install the fluid hoses.

6. Fill the reservoir with fresh fluid, to the full mark. Use appropriate power steering fluid.

7. Start the engine and allow to fast idle. Turn the steering wheel from side to side several times, lightly contacting the stops. This will bleed the system of air. Check the reservoir level and add fluid if necessary.

### BELT ADJUSTMENT

1. Loosen the bolt on the adjuster arm.

2. Move the pump toward or away from the engine, until the belt can be depressed approximately $^{9}/_{16}$ in. at the midpoint between the 2 pulleys under moderate thumb pressure. If the tension adjustment is being made on a new belt, the deflection should be about $^{7}/_{16}$ in., to allow for the initial stretching of the belt.

There is a raised bump on the top of the adjusting arm. If the belt has stretched to the point where the adjustment bolt is at or beyond the bump, the belt should be replaced.

3. Tighten the bolt and recheck the adjustment.

## Tie Rod Ends

### REMOVAL & INSTALLATION

1. Raise the vehicle and support it safely. Remove the front wheels.

2. Remove the cotter pins and castle nuts from the tie rod ends. Use a ball joint remover to remove the tie rod from the knuckle.

3. Disconnect the air tube at the dust seal joint. Remove the tie rod dust seal bellows clamps and move the rubber bellows on the tie rod rack joints.

4. Straighten the tie rod lockwasher tabs at the tie rod-to-rack joint and re-

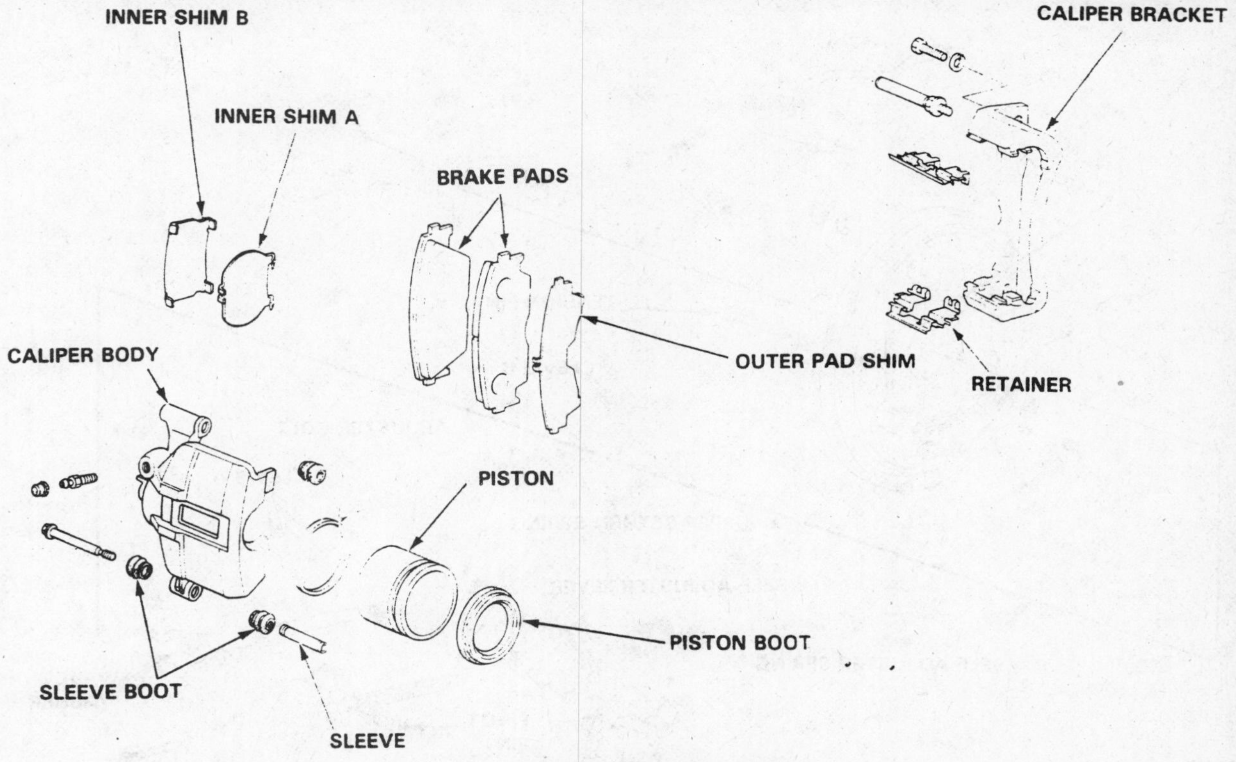


Front disc brake assembly

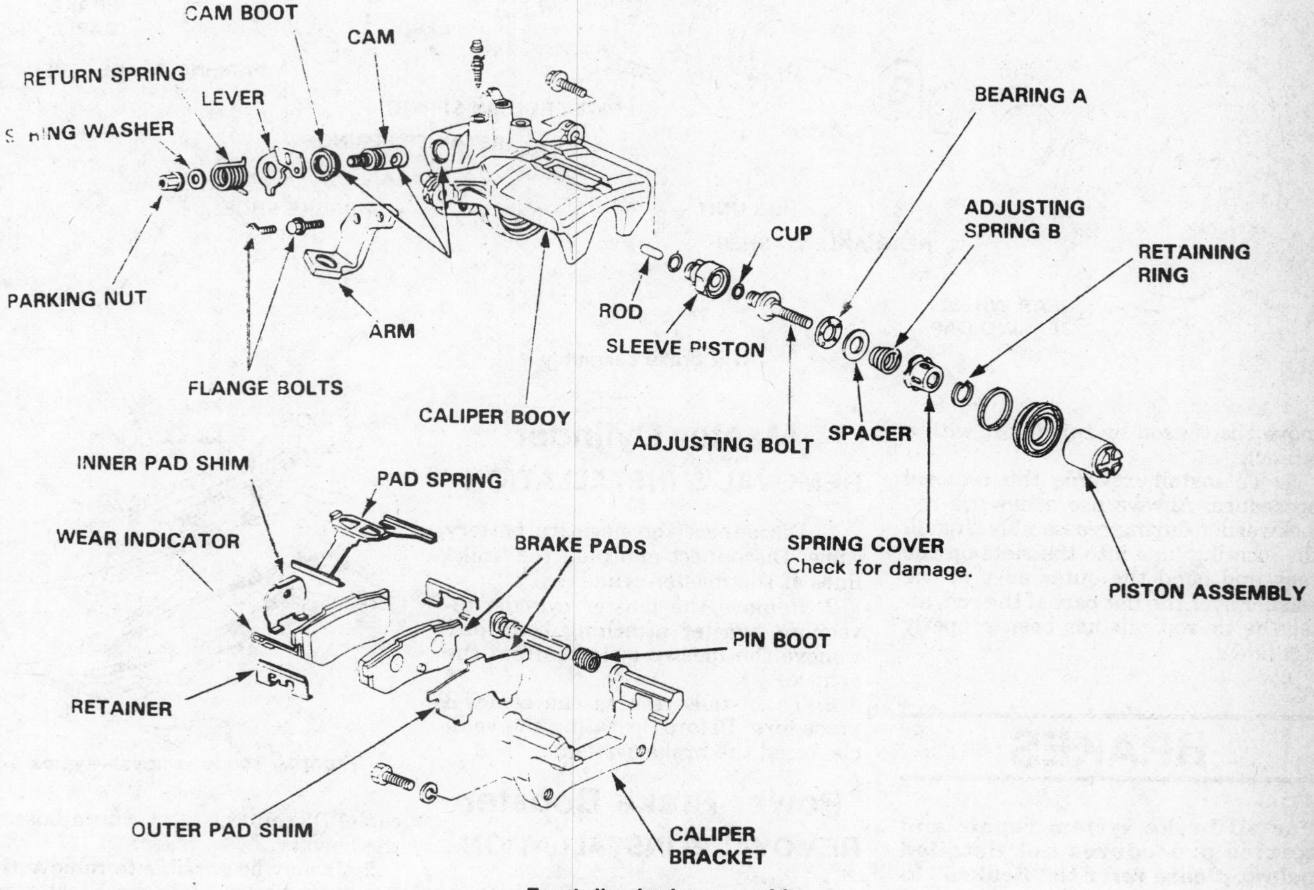


Front disc brake assembly

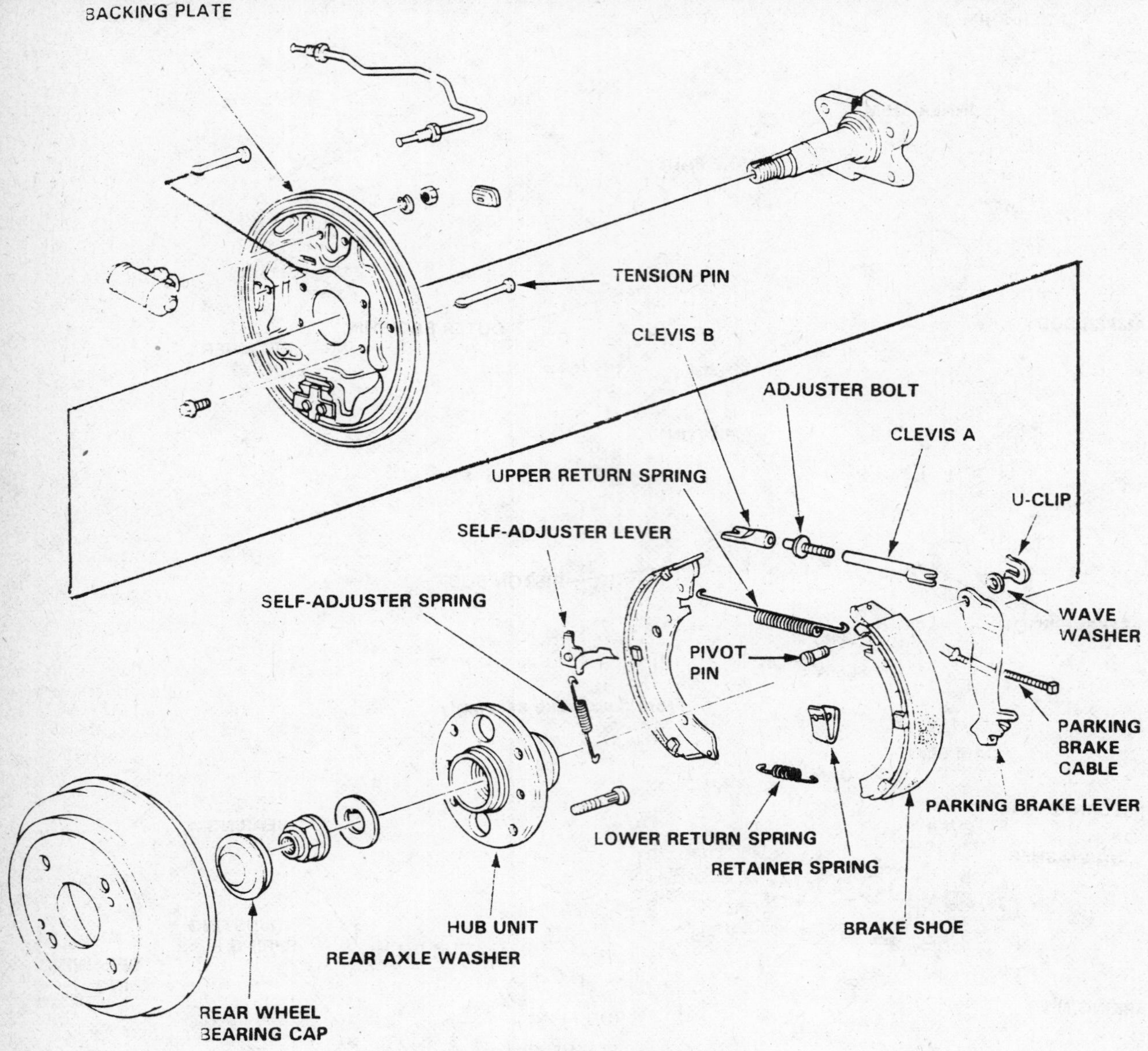


**Rear brake assembly**

move the tie rod by turning it with a wrench.

5. To install, reverse the removal procedure. Always use a new tie rod lockwasher during reassembly. Install the locating lugs into the slots on the rack and bend the outer edge of the washer over the flat part of the rod, after the tie rod nut has been properly tightened.

# BRAKES

**For all brake system repair and service procedures not detailed below, please refer to "Brakes" in the Unit Repair section.**

## Master Cylinder

### REMOVAL & INSTALLATION

1. Disconnect the negative battery cable. Disconnect and plug the brake lines at the master cylinder.

2. Remove the master cylinder-to-vacuum booster attaching bolts and remove the master cylinder from the vehicle.

3. To install, reverse the removal procedure. Before operating the vehicle, bleed the brake system.

## Power Brake Booster

### REMOVAL & INSTALLATION

1. Disconnect the negative battery cable. Disconnect the vacuum hose at the booster.

2. It may be possible to remove the master cylinder to brake booster re-

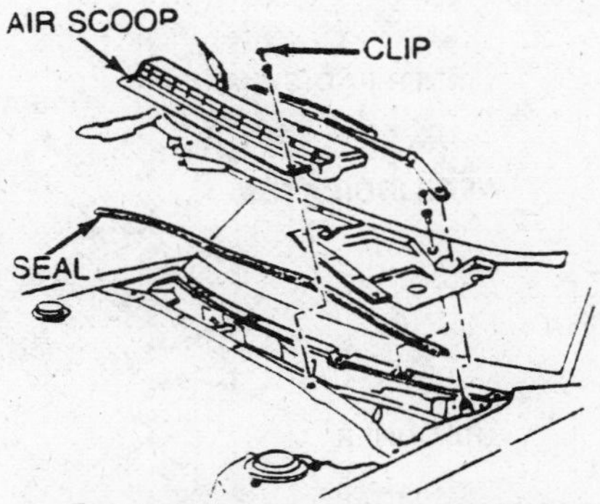


**Front air scoop removal—typical**

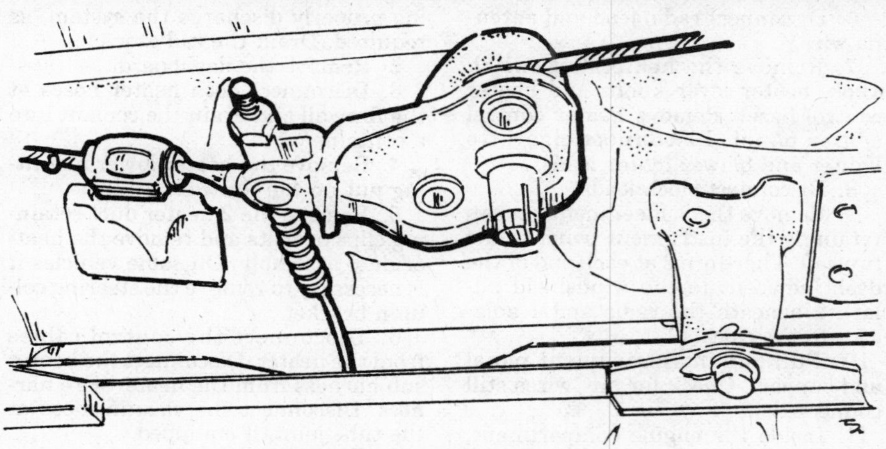

Parking brake equalizer assembly

taining nuts and than position the master cylinder assembly to the side on some vehicles. If not the master cylinder will have to be removed from the vehicle.

3. Remove the brake pedal-to-booster link pin and the 4 nuts retaining the booster. The pushrod and nuts are located inside the vehicle under the instrument panel.

4. Remove the booster assembly from the vehicle.

5. To install, reverse the removal procedure.

## Disc Brake Pads

### REMOVAL & INSTALLATION

#### *Front Wheels*

1. Raise and support the vehicle safely. Remove the tire and wheel assemblies.
2. As required, separate the brake hose clamp from the knuckle by removing the retaining bolts.
3. Remove the lower caliper retaining bolt and pivot the caliper out of the way.
4. Remove the pad shim and pad retainers. Remove the disc brake pads from the caliper.
5. Installation is the reverse of the removal procedure.

#### *Rear Wheels*

1. Raise and support the vehicle safely. Remove the tire and wheel assemblies.
2. Remove the caliper mounting bolts. Remove the caliper from the bracket.
3. Remove the disc brake pads from the caliper.
4. Installation is the reverse of the removal procedure.

## Brake Shoes

### REMOVAL & INSTALLATION

1. Raise and support the vehicle safely. Remove the tire and wheel assemblies.
2. Remove the brake drum.
3. Remove the primary brake shoe retaining hardware. Remove the secondary brake shoe hardware.
4. Remove both the primary and secondary brake shoes from their mounting.
5. Remove the springs, adjuster lever and parking brake mechanism from the brake shoes.
6. Installation is the reverse of the removal procedure.

## Wheel Cylinder

### REMOVAL & INSTALLATION

1. Raise and support the vehicle safely. Remove the tire and wheel assemblies. Remove the brake drum and shoes.
2. Disconnect the parking brake cable and brake lines at the backing plate. Be sure to have a drip pan to catch the brake fluid.
3. Remove the 2 wheel cylinder retaining nuts on the inboard side of the backing plate and remove the wheel cylinder.
4. To install, reverse the removal procedure. When assembling, apply a thin coat of grease to the grooves of the wheel cylinder piston and the sliding surfaces of the backing plate. Bleed the brakes.

## Parking Brake Cable

### ADJUSTMENT

1. Raise and support the vehicle safely.
2. Loosen the adjusting nut, located in the console on (Accord and Prelude and 1984–90 Civic) and at the equalizer, between the lower control arms on the 1983 Civic.
3. Pull the parking brake lever up 1 notch.
4. Tighten the adjusting nut until the rear brakes drag slightly.
5. Release the brake lever and check that the rear brakes do not drag.
6. The rear brakes should be locked when the handbrake lever is pulled 4–8 notches on the Civic, CRX and Prelude; 7–11 notches on the Accord.

### REMOVAL & INSTALLATION

1. Raise and support the vehicle safely. Remove the adjusting nut from the equalizer mounted on the rear axle, or in the console on (Accord, Prelude and 1984–90 Civic) and separate the cable from the equalizer.
2. Set the parking brake lever to a fully released position and remove the cotter pin from the side of the brake lever.
3. After removing the cotter pin, pull out the pin which connects the cable and the lever.
4. Detach the cable from the guides at the front and right side of the fuel tank and remove the cable.
5. To install, reverse the removal procedure, making sure that grease is applied to the cable and the guides.

# CHASSIS ELECTRICAL

## Heater Blower Motor

### REMOVAL & INSTALLATION

#### *Civic*

1. Disconnect the negative battery cable. As required, drain the cooling system and disconnect the heater hoses.
2. Remove the glove box assembly or passenger's tray. Remove the glove box frame work.
3. Remove the blower duct assembly.
4. Remove the air conditioning band and the evaporator assembly.
5. Disconnect the electrical connections at the blower motor. Remove the 3 blower motor retaining bolts and remove the blower motor.
6. Installation is the reverse order of the removal procedure.

### Accord and Prelude

1. Disconnect the negative battery cable.
2. Remove the glove box assembly and glove box frame work.
3. Remove the blower duct assembly.
4. Disconnect the wire connections at the blower motor assembly.
5. Remove the 3 blower motor retaining bolts and remove the blower motor.
6. Installation is the reverse order of the removal procedure.

# Heater Core

## REMOVAL & INSTALLATION

### Civic

1. Disconnect the negative battery cable. If equipped with air conditioning properly discharge the system. Drain the radiator.
2. Disconnect the heater valve cable from the heater valve. Remove the dashboard.
3. Disconnect both heater hoses at the firewall and drain the coolant into a container.
4. Remove the heater lower mounting nut on the firewall.
5. Remove the 2 heater duct retaining clips or bolts and remove the heater duct assembly (on the later vehicles it is necessary to remove the steering column bracket.
6. Disconnect the control cables from the heater.
7. Remove the heater valve cable cover and remove the heater assembly.
8. Remove the heater core from the heater assembly.
9. Installation is the reverse of removal. Bleed cooling system and make sure cables are properly adjusted.

### 1983–85 Accord

**NOTE: To remove the heater core, it is necessary to first remove the entire instrument panel and heater assemblies.**

1. Disconnect the negative battery cable. If equipped with air conditioning properly discharge the system. Drain the cooling system.
2. Remove the steering column lower trim cover.
3. Remove the 2 nuts and 2 bolts retaining the column to the firewall support.
4. Remove the instrument wire harnesses from cabin wire harness couples.
5. Reach behind the instrument cluster and disconnect the speedometer cable and 4 wiring harness connectors at rear of cluster. Pry out the lock tabs to disconnect.
6. Disconnect radio lead and antenna wire.
7. Remove the heater fan switch knob, heater lever knobs and heater control bezel. Remove heater control center panel. Disconnect cigarette lighter and blower motor leads.
8. Disconnect clock leads.
9. Remove the 7 sheet metal screws retaining the instrument panel to the firewall. There are 2 at each end of the dash (adjacent to the windshield pillar), 2 beneath the radio and 1 adjacent to the clock.
10. Pull out the instrument panel and support. Check for any wires still connected.
11. Inside the engine compartment, disconnect the 2 heater hoses at the firewall. Remove the nut retaining the heater unit to the firewall.
12. Disconnect the 3 heater control cables from the heater unit. Disconnect the cable clip from the heater valve.
13. Remove the heater unit lower mounting bolt and the right and left upper mounting bolts. Separate the blower hose from the heater.
14. Lay some towels underneath to catch residual coolant leakage. Remove the heater unit.
15. To service the heater core, separate the heater housing halves.
16. Reverse the above to install. Bleed the cooling system using the bleed bolt located near the ignition distributor.

### 1986–90 Accord

1. Disconnect the negative battery cable. If equipped with air conditioning properly discharge the system, as required. Drain the coolant. Disconnect the heater hoses.
2. Disconnect the heater valve cable from the heater valve. Remove the 2 lower heater mounting nuts.
3. On pushbutton type heaters, disconnect the cool vent cable at the heater. On lever type heaters, disconnect the function cable and the air mix cable at the heater.
4. Remove the dashboard.
5. Remove the heater duct (lever type) or ducts (pushbutton type).
6. On pushbutton type heaters, disconnect the air mix cable at the heater and the wiring harness at the connector.
7. Remove the 4 heater mounting bolts and pull the heater away from its mounts. Separate the heater core from the assembly.
8. Installation is the reverse of ther emoval procedure.

### Prelude

1. Disconnect the negative battery cable. If equipped with air conditioning properly discharge the system, as required. Drain the radiator.
2. Remove the dashboard.
3. Disconnect both heater hoses at the firewall and drain the coolant into a container.
4. Remove the heater lower mounting nut on the firewall.
5. Remove the 2 heater duct retaining clips or bolts and remove the heater duct assembly. On some vehicles it is necessary to remove the steering column bracket.
6. Disconnect the control cables from the heater. Disconnect the heater sub harness from the heater wire harness. Disconnect the vacuum hose at the tube joint, if equipped.
7. Remove the heater assembly mounting nuts and remove the heater assembly.
8. If equipped, remove the integrated control unit and bracket. If necessary, remove the function control motor.
9. Remove the heater core from the heater assembly.
10. Installation is the reverse of removal. Bleed cooling system and make sure cables are properly adjusted.

# Radio

## REMOVAL & INSTALLATION

### Civic

1. Disconnect the negative battery cable. Remove the screw which holds the rear radio bracket to the back tray underneath the instrument panel. Then remove the wing nut which holds the radio to the bracket and remove the bracket.
2. Remove the control knobs, hex nuts, and trim plate from the radio control shafts.
3. Disconnect the antenna and speaker leads, the bullet type radio fuse, and the white lead connected directly over the radio opening.
4. Drop the radio out, bottom first, through the package tray.
5. On later vehicles, remove the center instrument panel and then disconnect the 2 prong connector from the cigarette lighter. Remove the radio retaining screws and disconnect the electrical connections. Remove the radio.
6. To install, reverse the removal procedure. When inserting the radio through the package tray, be sure the bottom side is up and the control shafts are facing toward the engine. Otherwise, you will not be able to position the radio properly through its opening.

### Accord and Prelude

1. Disconnect the negative battery

cable. Remove the front console and the center lower trim panel beneath the radio. Then remove the 3 radio lower bracket retaining screws.

2. Pull off the radio knobs and remove the radio shaft nuts.

3. Remove the heater fan switch knob, the heater lever knobs, the heater control bezel, and the heater control center trim panel. Disconnect the cigarette lighter leads.

4. Pull out the radio from the front, and disconnect the power, speaker, and antenna leads.

5. On some vehicles, remove the ashtray and ashtray holder. Remove the 2 screws from under the center dash board, then push the radio out from behind the dash. Disconnect the electrical connectors and remove the radio.

6. Reverse the above to install.

## Windshield Wiper Motor

### REMOVAL & INSTALLATION

1. Remove the negative cable from the battery.

2. Remove the wiper arm retaining nuts and remove the wiper arms.

3. Remove the front air scoop, if equipped and hood seal located over the wiper linkage at the bottom of the windshield.

4. Disconnect the linkage from the wiper motor.

5. Remove the wiper motor water seal cover clamp, and remove the cover, if equipped.

6. Disconnect the wiper motor electrical connector, remove the motor mounting bolts and remove the motor.

7. Installation is the reverse of the removal procedure. Coat the linkage joints with grease and make sure the linkage moves smoothly.

## Windshield Wiper Switch

Refer to the Combination Switch procedure for the proper repair information

## Instrument Cluster

### REMOVAL & INSTALLATION

#### 1983 Civic

1. Disconnect the negative battery cable. Lower the steering column.

2. Remove the 4 screws and trim cover.

3. Disconnect the speedometer cable and tachometer cable if so equipped.

4. Disconnect any remaining mount screws and wire connectors and remove the instrument panel.

5. Installation is the reverse of removal.

#### 1984–88 CRX

1. Disconnect the negative battery cable. Remove the screws and clips that retain the lower dash panel and remove the panel.

2. Remove the heater lower control knob and the lower panel.

3. Remove the heater control mount screws and the upper screws in the instrument panel.

4. Pull the panel out and disconnect the wire connectors. Remove the instrument panel.

5. Remove the 4 screws, then lift out the gauge assembly so that you can disconnect the wire connectors.

6. Disconnect the speedometer cable, then remove the gauge assembly.

7. To install, reverse the removal procedure.

#### 1984–88 Civic and 1986–88 Accord

1. Disconnect the negative battery cable. Remove the upper instrument panel caps and the 4 screws, then remove the panel.

2. Remove the 4 screws retaining the gauge assembly, then lift out the gauge assembly so you can disconnect the wire connectors.

3. Disconnect the speedometer cable and remove the gauge assembly.

4. To install, reverse the removal procedure.

#### 1984–88 Civic Wagon

1. Disconnect the negative battery cable. Remove the screws and the dashboard lower panel, this allows access to the 4 instrument panel retaining bolts.

2. Remove the 4 instrument panel retaining bolts, raise the panel and disconnect the wire connectors and the speedometer cable. Remove the instrument panel with the gauge assembly.

3. The gauge assembly may be separated from the instrument panel by removing the 4 screws.

4. To install, reverse the removal procedure.

#### 1989–90 Civic, CRX and Wagon

1. Disconnect the negative battery cable.

2. On Civic and Wagon, remove the dashboard lower panel.

3. Remove the dashlight brightness controller and the rear window defoger switch by pushing the switch assembly out and than disconnecting the electrical connectors.

4. Remove the instrument panel caps and screws. remove the instrument panel cover from the dashboard.

5. On Civic, remove the gauge visor caps and screws. Remove the gauge visor.

6. Remove the instrument cluster assembly retaining screws.

7. Pull the cluster assembly forward and disconnect the speedometer cable and any electrical connections.

8. Remove the instrument cluster assembly from the vehicle.

9. Installation is the reverse of the removal procedure.

#### 1983–85 Accord

1. Disconnect the negative battery cable. Lower the steering column.

2. Remove the 3 screws at the top of the instrument panel.

3. Pull the instrument panel out, then disconnect the wire connectors and remove the panel.

4. Remove the 4 screws that hold the gauge assembly in place, then lift up on the panel so you can reach the wire connectors.

5. Disconnect the wire connectors and the speedometer cable, then remove the gauge assembly.

6. To install, reverse the removal procedure.

#### 1989–90 Accord

1. Disconnect the negative battery cable.

2. Remove each switch from the instrument panel by inserting a flat bladed tool under the bottom center of the switch and prying it loose.

3. Disconnect the electrical connectors from the switch. Remove the switch from its mounting.

4. Remove the upper lid cover and instrument panel retaining screws. Remove the instrument panel cover from the vehicle.

5. Remove the instrument panel gauge assembly retaining screws. Pull the assembly forward and disconnect the speedometer cable. Disconnect any electrical connectors.

6. Remove the assembly from the vehicle.

7. Installation is the reverse of the removal procedure.

#### 1983–88 Prelude

1. Disconnect the negative battery cable. Lower the steering column, and remove the lower dashboard panel.

2. Remove the 4 instrument panel retaining screws.

3. Pull the instrument panel out, and disconnect the wire connectors. Remove the panel.
4. Remove the 2 screws retaining the gauge assembly, then lift out the assembly and remove the wire connectors and speedometer cable.
5. Installation is the reverse of the removal procedure.

#### *1989–90 Prelude*

1. Disconnect the negative battery cable.
2. Remove the dashlight brightness controller and retractor/fog light switch from the instrument panel.
3. Remove the instrument panel screws. Separate the panel from the gauge visor.
4. Remove the cap and screws from the gauge visor. Remove the gauge visor from the dashboard.
5. Remove the dashboard lower panel. Disconnect the speedometer cable from the gauge assembly.
6. Disconnect all required electrical connectors. Remove the assembly from the vehicle.
7. Installation is the reverse of the removal procedure.

## Headlight Switch

### REMOVAL & INSTALLATION

The headlight switch is a function of the combination switch, the combination switch removal and installation procedures are outlined in this section.

## Stoplight Switch

### REMOVAL & INSTALLATION

1. Disconnect the negative battery cable.
2. The brake light switch is mounted on a bracket at the top of the brake pedal. Switch action is controlled by pedal movement.
3. Disconnect the wires, loosen the locknut and unscrew the switch from its mounting.
4. Installation is the reverse of the removal procedure.
5. The pedal height must be adjusted when the switch is installed. To adjust the pedal height, position the switch in the bracket, with the locknut loose and the plunger not touching the pedal arm.
6. Turn the plunger with pliers until the height of the pedal pad above the nearest point of the floor is:
   Civic hatchback and sedan 174mm.
   Civic wagon 168mm.
   CRX 174mm.
   Accord 205mm.
   Prelude 176mm.

## Fuses and Fusible Links

### LOCATION

All vehicles are equipped with a fusible link connected between the starter relay and the main wiring harness of the vehicle, located next to the battery.

The 1983 Civic fuse box is located below the glove compartment, on the right bulkhead. The 1984-90 Civic fuse box is located under a flip down door, under the dashboard on the left side of the instrument panel. The rating and function of each fuse is posted inside the fuse box cap for quick reference.

The 1983–85 Accord and 1983–87 Prelude fuse box is located behind a flip down door, under the dashboard on the left side of the instrument panel. The 1986–90 Accord and 1988–90 Prelude the fuse box is located in the engine compartment, near the right side shock tower.

# Hyundai

## Excel, Sonata

# 7

# SERIAL NUMBER IDENTIFICATION

## Vehicle Identification Plate

The vehicle identification number (VIN) is located on a plate attached to the left front of the dash panel so it can be seen through the windshield when you stand beside the car, in front of the driver's door.

The letters and numbers in the VIN digits can be interpreted according to their positions in the sequence as follows:

1. Manufacturing country
2. Make
3. Vehicle type
4. Type of seat belt system
5. Vehicle line
6. Trim Code/Price Class
7. Body type
8. Engine displacement
9. Check digit: a special letter or number code used to verify the serial number. This contains no useful information for the car owner.
10. Model year
11. Plant where the car was built
12. Transmission code

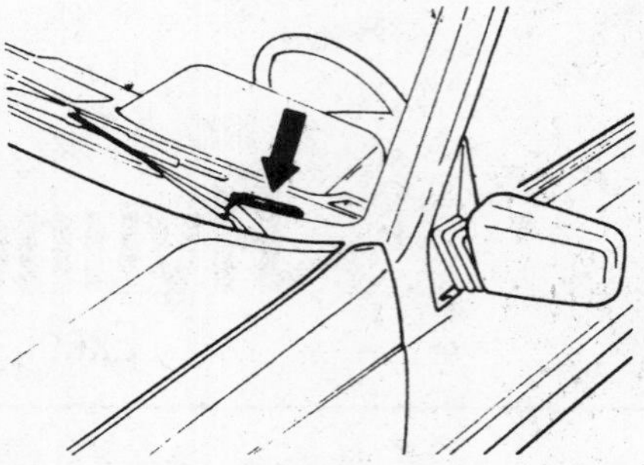

Serial number location

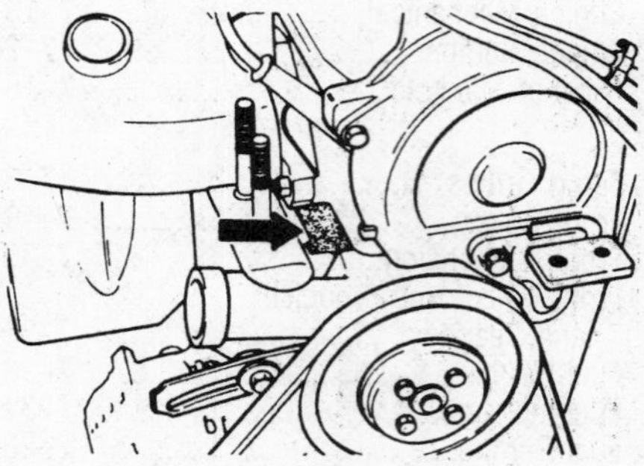

Engine number location

## Engine Identification

The engine model and serial numbers in all cases are stamped on the top edge of the block near the front of the engine. In most cases, they are located on the right side of the engine.

Engine model number

## Vehicle Identification Label

The Vehicle Identification Lable is located on the top center of the firewall in the engine compartment.

## Transmission Number

On all models, the basic transmission model number is stamped on the Vehicle Information Code Plate, located on the engine compartment side of the firewall.

The manual transaxle serial number is stamped on the clutch of the transaxle case.

On automatic transaxle models, the number is on a plate attached to the side of the transmission, or stamped on the boss of the oil pan flange.

### ENGINE IDENTIFICATION

| Year | Model | Engine Displacement cu. in. (cc/liter) | Engine Series Identification | No. of Cylinders | Engine Type |
|---|---|---|---|---|---|
| 1986 | Excel | 89.6 (1468/1.5) | – | 4 | OHC |
| 1987 | Excel | 89.6 (1468/1.5) | – | 4 | OHC |
| 1988 | Excel | 89.6 (1468/1.5) | – | 4 | OHC |
| 1989-90 | Excel | 89.6 (1468/1.5) | – | 4 | OHC |
| | Sonata | 143.5 (2351/2.4) | – | 4 | OHC |

### GENERAL ENGINE SPECIFICATIONS

| Year | Model | Engine Displacement cu. in. (cc) | Fuel System Type | Net Horsepower @ rpm | Net Torque @ rpm (ft. lbs.) | Bore × Stroke (in.) | Compression Ratio | Oil Pressure @ rpm |
|---|---|---|---|---|---|---|---|---|
| 1986 | Excel | 89.6 (1468) | 2 bbl | 77 @ 5300 | 84 @ 3000 | 2.97 × 3.23 | 9.4:1 | 45@2000 |
| 1987 | Excel | 89.6 (1468) | 2 bbl | 77 @ 5300 | 84 @ 3000 | 2.97 × 3.23 | 9.4:1 | 45@2000 |
| 1988 | Excel | 89.6 (1468) | 2 bbl | 77 @ 5300 | 84 @ 3000 | 2.97 × 3.23 | 9.4:1 | 45@2000 |
| 1989-90 | Excel | 89.6 (1468) | 2 bbl | 77 @ 5300 | 84 @ 3000 | 2.97 × 3.23 | 9.4:1 | 45@2000 |
| | Sonata | 143.5 (2351) | MPI | 126 @ 5100 | 180 @ 2600 | 3.41 × 3.94 | 8.5:1 | 45@2000 |

MPI Multi-Port Fuel Injection

## ENGINE TUNE-UP SPECIFICATIONS

| Year | Model | Engine Displacement cu. in. (cc) | Spark Plugs Type | Spark Plugs Gap (in.) | Ignition Timing (deg.) MT | Ignition Timing (deg.) AT | Compression Pressure (psi) | Fuel Pump (psi) | Idle Speed (rpm) MT | Idle Speed (rpm) AT | Valve Clearance In. | Valve Clearance Ex. |
|---|---|---|---|---|---|---|---|---|---|---|---|---|
| 1986 | Excel | 89.6 (1468) | RN9YC4 | ① | ② | ② | 164 | 2.5-3.5 | ③ | ③ | 0.006 | 0.010 |
| 1987 | Excel | 89.6 (1468) | RN9YC4 | ① | ② | ② | 164 | 2.5-3.5 | ③ | ③ | 0.006 | 0.010 |
| 1988 | Excel | 89.6 (1468) | RN9YC4 | ① | ② | ② | 164 | 2.8-3.6 | ③ | ③ | 0.006 | 0.010 |
| 1989 | Excel | 89.6 (1468) | RN9YC4 | ① | ② | ② | 164 | 2.8-3.6 | ③ | ③ | 0.006 | 0.010 |
| | Sonata | 143.5 (2351) | RN9YC4 | 0.039–0.043 | 5B | 5B | 160 | 48.0 | 750 | 750 | Hyd. | Hyd. |
| 1990 | SEE UNDERHOOD SPECIFICATIONS STICKER | | | | | | | | | | | |

**NOTE:** Valve clearance is set with the engine at normal operating temperature. On USA engines, the jet valve must be set before the intake valve. Jet valve clearance is 0.010 in.

① 1986-87 USA – 0.039–0.043; Canada: 0.027–0.031
1988–89 All models – 0.039–0.043

② 49 states – 5B
California – 3B
Canada – 4B

③ 1986-87 USA MT – 700; AT – 750
Canada – 850
1988–89 USA and Canada – 700 (1st 300 miles); 750 (after 300 miles)

## FIRING ORDERS

NOTE: To avoid confusion, always replace spark wires one at a time.

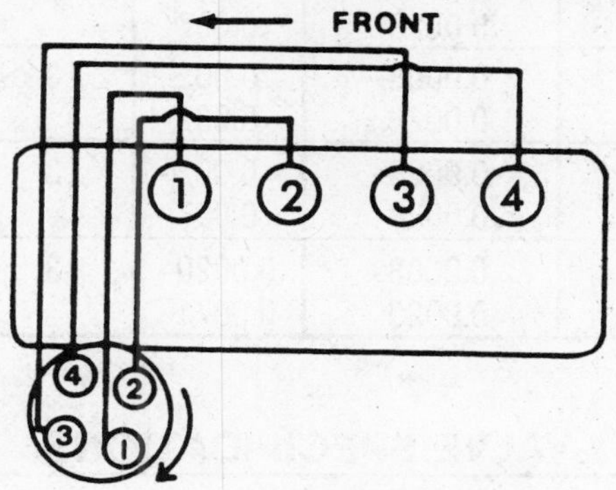


Firing order for the 1468cc and 2351cc engines

## CAPACITIES

| Year | Model | Engine Displacement cu. in. (cc) | Engine Crankcase with Filter | Engine Crankcase without Filter | Transmission (pts.) 4-Spd | Transmission (pts.) 5-Spd | Transmission (pts.) Auto. | Drive Axle (pts.) | Fuel Tank (gal.) | Cooling System (qts.) |
|---|---|---|---|---|---|---|---|---|---|---|
| 1986 | Excel | 89.6 (1468) | 4.0 | — | 4.4 | 4.4 | 12.2 | — | 10.6① | 5.3 |
| 1987 | Excel | 89.6 (1468) | 3.6 | — | 4.4 | 4.4 | 12.2 | — | 10.6① | 5.3 |
| 1988 | Excel | 89.6 (1468) | 3.6 | — | 4.4 | 4.4 | 12.2 | — | 10.6① | 5.3 |
| 1989-90 | Excel | 89.6 (1468) | 3.6 | — | 4.4 | 4.4 | 12.2 | — | 10.6① | 5.3 |
| | Sonata | 143.5 (2351) | 4.0 | — | — | 5.3 | 12.3 | — | 16.0 | 7.4 |

① Optional 13.2 gal. tank

## CAMSHAFT SPECIFICATIONS

All measurements given in inches.

| Year | Engine Displacement cu. in. (cc) | Journal Diameter 1 | 2 | 3 | 4 | 5 | Lobe Height In. | Ex. | Bearing Clearance | Camshaft End Play |
|---|---|---|---|---|---|---|---|---|---|---|
| 1986 | 89.6 (1468) | 1.338 | 1.338 | 1.338 | 1.338 | 1.338 | 1.500 | 1.504 | 0.00197–0.00354 | 0.002–0.008 |
| 1987 | 89.6 (1468) | 1.338 | 1.338 | 1.338 | 1.338 | 1.338 | 1.500 | 1.504 | 0.00197–0.00354 | 0.002–0.008 |
| 1988 | 89.6 (1468) | 1.338 | 1.338 | 1.338 | 1.338 | 1.338 | 1.500 | 1.504 | 0.00197–0.00354 | 0.002–0.008 |
| 1989-90 | 89.6 (1468) | 1.338 | 1.338 | 1.338 | 1.338 | 1.338 | 1.500 | 1.504 | 0.00197–0.00354 | 0.002–0.008 |
| | 143.5 (2351) | 1.336 | 1.336 | 1.336 | 1.336 | 1.336 | 1.753 | 1.758 | 0.00200–0.00350 | 0.004–0.008 |

## CRANKSHAFT AND CONNECTING ROD SPECIFICATIONS

All measurements are given in inches.

| Year | Engine Displacement cu. in. (cc) | Crankshaft Main Brg. Journal Dia. | Main Brg. Oil Clearance | Shaft End-play | Thrust on No. | Connecting Rod Journal Diameter | Oil Clearance | Side Clearance |
|---|---|---|---|---|---|---|---|---|
| 1986 | 89.6 (1468) | 1.8898 | 0.0008–0.0028 | 0.002–0.007 | 3 | 1.6535 | 0.0004–0.0024 | 0.004–0.010 |
| 1987 | 89.6 (1468) | 1.8898 | 0.0008–0.0028 | 0.002–0.007 | 3 | 1.6535 | 0.0004–0.0024 | 0.004–0.010 |
| 1988 | 89.6 (1468) | 1.8898 | 0.0008–0.0028 | 0.002–0.007 | 3 | 1.6535 | 0.0004–0.0024 | 0.004–0.010 |
| 1989-90 | 89.6 (1468) | 1.8898 | 0.0008–0.0028 | 0.002–0.007 | 3 | 1.6535 | 0.0004–0.0024 | 0.004–0.010 |
| | 143.5 (2351) | 2.2436 | 0.0008–0.0020 | 0.0020–0.0071 | 3 | 1.7709–1.7715 | 0.0004–0.0024 | 0.004–0.010 |

## VALVE SPECIFICATIONS

| Year | Engine Displacement cu. in. (cc) | Seat Angle (deg.) | Face Angle (deg.) | Spring Test Pressure (lbs. @ in.) | Spring Installed Height (in.) | Stem-to-Guide Clearance (in.) Intake | Exhaust | Stem Diameter (in.) Intake | Exhaust |
|---|---|---|---|---|---|---|---|---|---|
| 1986 | 89.6 (1468) | 45 | 45 | 53 @ 1.07① | 1.42② | 0.0012–0.0024 | 0.0020–0.0035 | 0.2598 | 0.2598 |
| 1987 | 89.6 (1468) | 45 | 45 | 53 @ 1.07① | 1.42② | 0.0012–0.0024 | 0.0020–0.0035 | 0.2598 | 0.2598 |
| 1988 | 89.6 (1468) | 45 | 45 | 53 @ 1.07① | 1.42② | 0.0012–0.0024 | 0.0020–0.0035 | 0.2598 | 0.2598 |
| 1989-90 | 89.6 (1468) | 45 | 45 | 53 @ 1.07① | 1.42② | 0.0012–0.0024 | 0.0020–0.0035 | 0.2598 | 0.2598 |
| | 143.5 (2351) | 45 | 45 | 73 @ 1.591① | 1.591② | 0.0012–0.0024 | 0.0020–0.0035 | 0.3150 | 0.3150 |

① Jet valve—7.7 @ 0.846
② Jet valve—0.846

## PISTON AND RING SPECIFICATIONS

All measurments are given in inches.

| Year | Engine Displacement cu. in. (cc) | Piston Clearance | Ring Gap Top Compression | Ring Gap Bottom Compression | Ring Gap Oil Control | Ring Side Clearance Top Compression | Ring Side Clearance Bottom Compression | Ring Side Clearance Oil Control |
|---|---|---|---|---|---|---|---|---|
| 1986 | 89.6 (1468) | 0.0008–0.0016 | 0.008–0.014 | 0.008–0.014 | 0.008–0.028 | 0.0012–0.0028 | 0.0008–0.0024 | Snug |
| 1987 | 89.6 (1468) | 0.0008–0.0016 | 0.008–0.014 | 0.008–0.014 | 0.008–0.028 | 0.0012–0.0028 | 0.0008–0.0024 | Snug |
| 1988 | 89.6 (1468) | 0.0008–0.0016 | 0.008–0.014 | 0.008–0.014 | 0.008–0.028 | 0.0012–0.0028 | 0.0008–0.0024 | Snug |
| 1989-90 | 89.6 (1468) | 0.0008–0.0016 | 0.008–0.014 | 0.008–0.014 | 0.008–0.028 | 0.0012–0.0028 | 0.0008–0.0024 | Snug |
| | 143.5 (2351) | 0.0004–0.0012 | 0.0098–0.0157 | 0.0079–0.0138 | 0.0079–0.0276 | 0.0012–0.0028 | 0.0008–0.0024 | Snug |

## TORQUE SPECIFICATIONS

All readings in ft. lbs.

| Year | Engine Displacement cu. in. (cc) | Cylinder Head Bolts | Main Bearing Bolts | Rod Bearing Bolts | Crankshaft Pulley Bolts | Flywheel Bolts | Manifold Intake | Manifold Exhaust | Spark Plugs |
|---|---|---|---|---|---|---|---|---|---|
| 1986 | 89.6 (1468) | ① | 36–39 | 23–25 | 9–11④ | 94–101 | 12–14 | 12–14 | 18 |
| 1987 | 89.6 (1468) | ① | 36–39 | 23–25 | 9–11④ | 94–101 | 12–14 | 12–14 | 18 |
| 1988 | 89.6 (1468) | ① | 36–39 | 23–25 | 9–11④ | 94–101 | 12–14 | 12–14 | 18 |
| 1989-90 | 89.6 (1468) | ① | 36–39 | 23–25 | 9–11④ | 94–101 | 12–14 | 12–14 | 18 |
| | 143.5 (2351) | ② | 36–40 | 36–38 | 14–22③ | 94–100 | 11–14 | 11–14 | 18 |

① Cold—51–54 ft. lbs; warm—58–61 ft. lbs.
② Cold—65–72; warm—72–80
③ Sprocket bolt—94
④ Sprocket—72

## BRAKE SPECIFICATIONS

All measurements in inches unless noted

| Year | Model | Lug Nut Torque (ft. lbs.) | Master Cylinder Bore | Brake Disc Minimum Thickness | Brake Disc Maximum Runout | Standard Brake Drum Diameter | Minimum Lining Thickness Front | Minimum Lining Thickness Rear |
|---|---|---|---|---|---|---|---|---|
| 1986 | Excel | 50-58① | 0.8125 | ② | 0.006 | 7.086 | 0.04 | 0.04 |
| 1987 | Excel | 50-58① | 0.8125 | ② | 0.006 | 7.086 | 0.04 | 0.04 |
| 1988 | Excel | 50-58① | 0.8125 | ② | 0.006 | 7.086 | 0.04 | 0.04 |
| 1989-90 | Excel | 50-58① | 0.8125 | ② | 0.006 | 7.086 | 0.04 | 0.04 |
| | Sonata | 50-60 | 1.0000 | 0.787 | 0.006 | 9.000 | 0.04 | 0.04 |

① Aluminum wheels—58–72
② Sumitomo—0.449
Tokico—0.675

## WHEEL ALIGNMENT

| Year | Model | Caster Range (deg.) | Caster Preferred Setting (deg.) | Camber Range (deg.) | Camber Preferred Setting (deg.) | Toe-in (in.) | Steering Axis Inclination (deg.) |
|---|---|---|---|---|---|---|---|
| 1986 | Excel | ½P–1⅙P | ⅚P | 0–1P | ½P | 1/16 in–5/64 out | ① |
| 1987 | Excel | ½P–1⅙P | ⅚P | 0–1P | ½P | 1/16 in–5/64 out | ① |
| 1988 | Excel | ½P–1⅙P | ⅚P | 0–1P | ½P | 1/16 in–5/64 out | ① |
| 1989-90 | Excel | ½P–1⅙P | ⅚P | 0–1P | ½P | 1/16 in–5/64 out | ① |
| | Sonata | ½P–2½P | 2P | 0–1P | ½P | ⅛ in–5/64 out | ② |

① Inside wheel—35⅔; outside wheel—29 9/32
② King pin angle—13°25'

# TUNE-UP PROCEDURES

## Ignition Timing

### ADJUSTMENT

1. Locate the timing tab line on the front of the engine and the notch on the crankshaft pulley. Mark them with chalk.
2. Run the engine until it is at normal operating temperature. This is necessary as parts dimensions, and therefore timing may change slightly with temperature.
3. Leave the engine idling, apply the handbrake and put the transmission in **NEUTRAL** (manual) or **PARK** (automatic). Turn off all accessories.

**NOTE: On High Altitude engines, the distributor vacuum hoses must be disconnected and plugged.**

4. Install a tachometer, according to the manufacturer's instructions.
5. Verify that the engine idle speed is correct. If not adjust it, because incorrect idle speed will change the timing.
6. Connect a timing light according to the manufacturer's instructions.
7. Shine the timing light at the crankshaft pulley marks. The marked line should align with the pulley notch.
8. If the marks do not align, loosen the distributor mounting nut and rotate the distributor slowly in either direction to align the timing marks. When the timing is correct, tighten the distributor holddown bolt. Recheck the timing.
9. Turn the engine off and disconnect the timing light and tachometer.

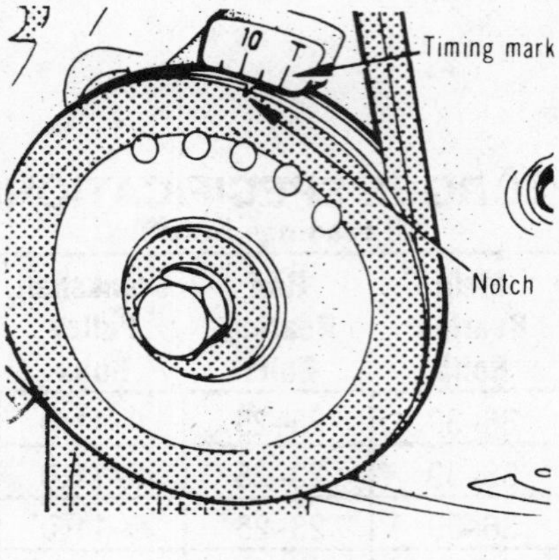

Timing marks

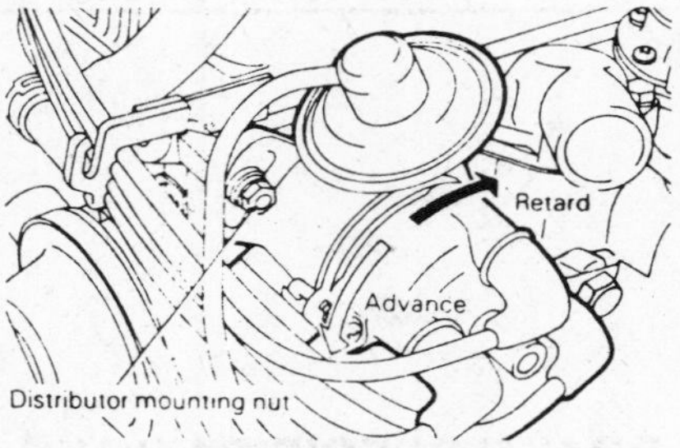

Adjusting ignition timing

## Valve Lash

### ADJUSTMENT

#### *2351cc Engine*

Valve clearance is normally adjusted with the engine stopped and at normal operating temperature. However, after the engine has been rebuilt or a valve job done, the valves should first be set and adjusted with the engine cold. The basic procedure is the same, hot or cold, the only differences being the engine temperature and the valve clearance setting. The **COLD** setting is 0.08mm (0.003 in.) for intake valves; 0.18mm (0.007 in.) for exhaust valves. The **HOT** setting is 0.15mm (0.006 in.) for intake valves; 0.25mm (0.010 in.) for exhaust valves.

**NOTE: When adjusting the valves, use, if possible, a metrically measured feeler gauge set. The English measurements are approximate equivalents and not exact!**

1. Start the engine and allow it to reach normal operating temperature.
2. Remove the air cleaner. Disconnect the large crankcase ventilation hose from the front of the air cleaner. Disconnect the two smaller hoses from the rear of the rocker arm cover and the intake manifold.
3. Loosen and remove the nuts and bracket which secure the air cleaner to the rocker arm cover.
4. Lift the bottom housing of the air cleaner off of the carburetor, with the hose from the exhaust manifold heat stove attached.
5. Unsnap the spark plug wires from their clips on the rocker arm cover.
6. Remove the two rocker arm cover bolts.
7. Carefully lift the rocker arm cover off the cylinder head. Using an 5/16 in. (8mm) allen socket and a torque wrench, torque the cylinder head bolts as detailed later in this section. Check the sequence in the accompanying illustration. Turn each bolt in the sequence back just until it breaks loose, and then torque it to 58–61 ft. lbs. After the first bolt in the sequence has been torqued, move on to the second one, repeating the procedure. Continue, in order, until all the bolts have been torqued. Make sure that the cylinder head bolts are all tightened, in sequence, to specification.
8. Remove the spark plugs.
9. Remove the distributor cap.

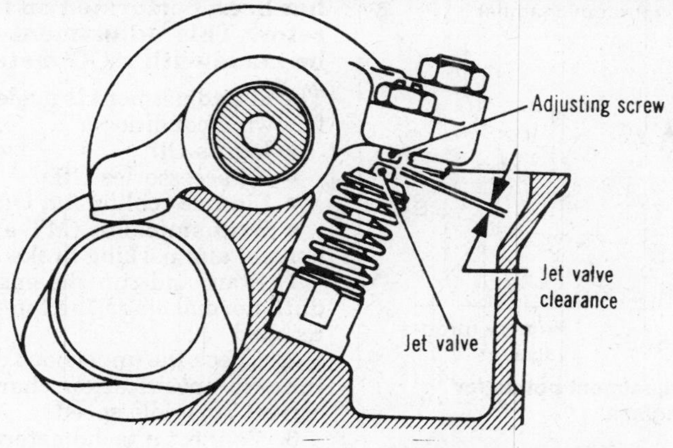


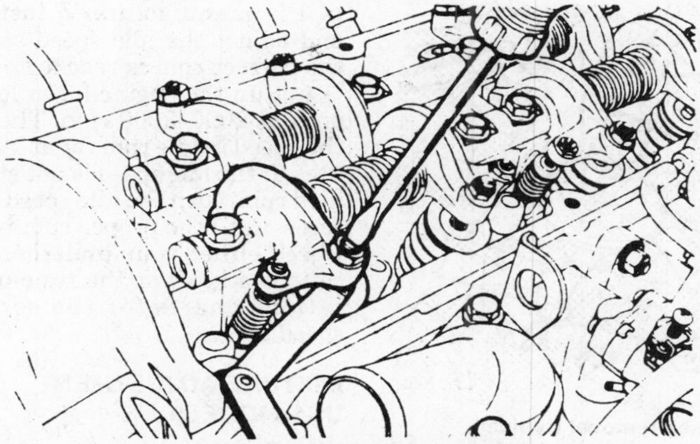
Jet valve clearance adjustment

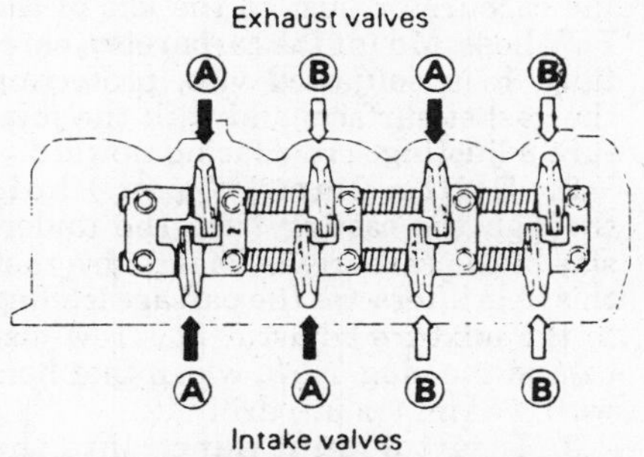

"A" and "B" valve adjusting positions

Adjusting the valves

**NOTE: A crankshaft pulley access hole is located on the left side frame member. Remove the covering plug and use a ratchet extension to turn the crankshaft when adjusting the valves.**

10. Rotate the crankshaft until the No. 1 cylinder is at TDC of the compression stroke. Turn the engine by using a wrench on the bolt in the front of the crankshaft until the **TDC** or **0** timing mark on the timing cover lines up with the notch in the front pulley. Observe the valve rockers for No. 1 cylinder. If both are in identical positions with the valves up, the engine is in the right position. If not, rotate the engine exactly 360 degrees until the **TDC** or **0** degree timing mark is again aligned. Each jet valve is associated with an intake valve that is on the same rocker lever. In this position you'll be able to adjust all the valves marked **A** in the illustration, including associated jet valves (which are located on the rockers on the intake side only).

11. To adjust the appropriate jet valves, first loosen the regular (larger) intake valve adjusting stud right nearby by loosening the locknut and backing the stud off 2 turns. Now, loosen the jet valve (smaller) adjusting stud locknut, back the stud out slightly, and insert an 0.25mm feeler gauge between the jet valve and stud. Make sure the gauge lies flat on the top of the jet valve. Being careful not to twist the gauge or otherwise depress the jet valve spring, rotate the jet valve adjusting stud back in until it just touches the gauge. Now, tighten the locknut. Make sure the gauge still slides very easily between the stud and jet valve and that they both are still just touching the gauge. Readjust if necessary. Note that, especially with the jet valve, the clearance MUST NOT be too tight. Just make sure you are not clamping the gauge in between the stud and valve, but that the parts JUST TOUCH. Repeat entire the procedure for the other jet valves associated with rockers labeled **A**. Then, repeat the procedure for the intake valves labeled **A** (0.15mm).

12. Repeat the basic adjustment procedure for exhaust valves labeled **A** using a 0.25mm feeler gauge.

13. Turn the engine exactly 360 degrees, until the timing marks are again aligned at **TDC** or **0**. First, perform the adjustment procedure for all the jet valves on rockers labeled **B** (intake side only). Complete the adjustment procedure for the regular intake valves labeled **B**. Finally, repeat the adjustment procedure for the exhaust valves labeled **B**.

**CAUTION**

***The importance of correctly setting the valve clearance cannot be overemphasized. The clearance must be right or peak performance and efficiency will never be realized. Loose valve clearances will result in excessive wear and valve train chatter; tight valve clearance will result in burnt valve seats.***

14. Apply non-hardening sealer to the rocker arm cover gasket. Always use a new gasket.

15. Install the cover, hoses, spark plug wires and the air cleaner in the reverse order of removal. Tighten the rocker arm cover bolts to 48–60 inch lbs.

16. Start the engine and check for leaks. It's best to install new gaskets and seals wherever they are used, and to observe torque specifications for the cam cover bolts.

### *1468cc Engines*

Valve clearance is adjusted with the engine off.

1. Run the engine until it reaches normal operating temperature and then turn it off.

2. Remove the air cleaner. Pull the large crankcase ventilation hose off the front of the air cleaner. Disconnect the two smaller hoses, one goes to the rear of the rocker arm cover and the other to the intake manifold.

3. Loosen and remove the nuts and bracket which attach the air cleaner to the rocker arm cover.

4. Lift the bottom housing of the air cleaner off of the carburetor and the hose coming up from the exhaust manifold heat stove.

5. Remove the spark plug wires

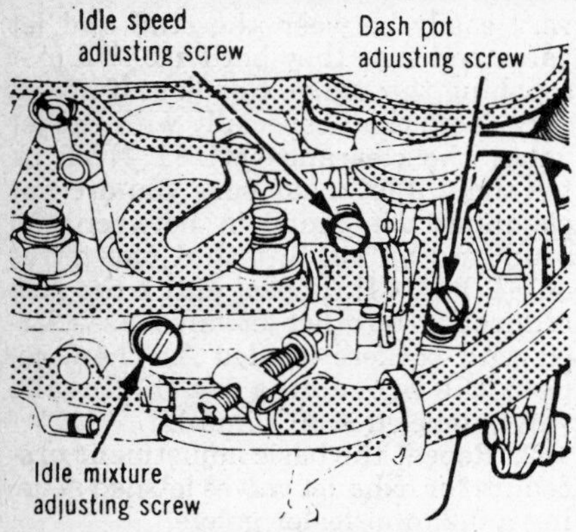

Carburetor adjustment points

from their clips on the rocker arm cover.

6. Using a deep socket or box wrench, remove the two rocker arm cover bolts.

7. Carefully lift the rocker arm cover off the cylinder head. Using an $^5/_{16}$ in. (8mm) allen socket and a torque wrench, make sure that the cylinder head bolts are all tightened to specification.

8. Hot valve clearance is 0.15mm (0.006 in.) for the intake valves and 0.25mm (0.010mm) for the exhaust.

9. Turn the crankshaft pulley to bring the piston to TDC of the compression stroke on the cylinder being adjusted.

10. Loosen the two rocker arm adjusting screw lock nuts.

11. Using the correct thickness feeler gauge, turn the adjusting screw until the gauge just snaps through the valve stem and the rocker arm.

12. Repeat the procedure to adjust the valves of each cylinder.

**CAUTION**

***Loose valve clearances will result in excessive wear and valve train chatter. Tight valve clearance will result in burnt valve seats. Make sure to set the valve clearence to the exact specifications.***

13. Apply non-hardening sealer to the rocker arm cover gasket. Always use a new gasket.

14. Install the cover, hoses, spark plug wires and the air cleaner in the reverse order of removal. Tighten the rocker arm cover bolts to 48–60 inch lbs.

15. Start the engine and check for leaks.

## Idle Speed and Mixture

### ADJUSTMENT

#### *Carbureted Engines*

Idle speed is adjusted periodically to compensate for engine wear or after

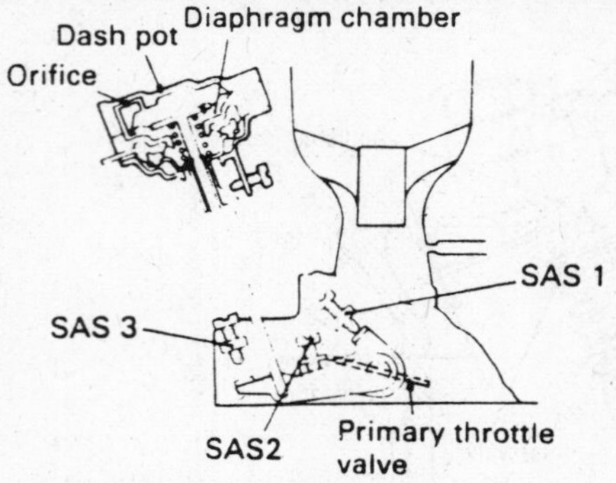

Idle speed adjustment points for carbureted engines

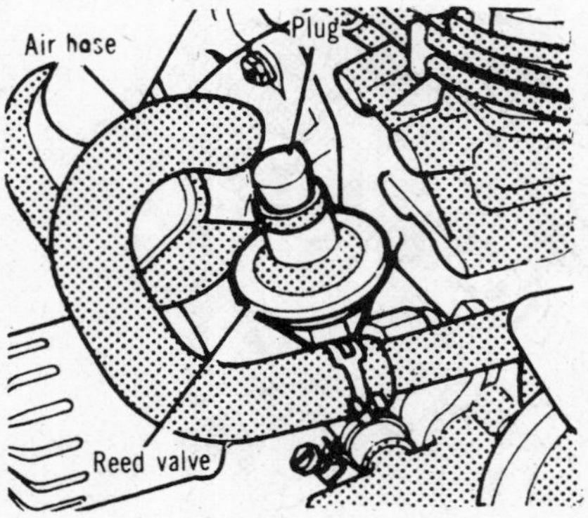

Air hose removal (typical)

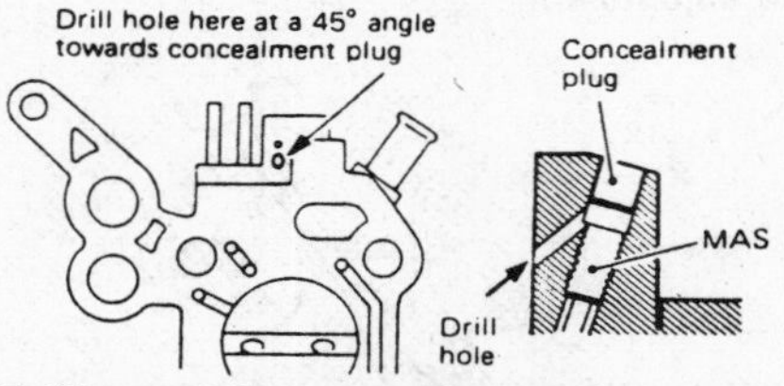

Drilling out the concealment plug to adjust CO

engine work is performed. Idle mixture adjustments are not required as a matter of routine, but only when major carburetor work is required. The emission control system compensates as required to ensure a stable idle mixture. If you suspect trouble because of a rough idle, check the idle mixture with a CO meter, if one is available.

Also, Hyundais have an idle-up solenoid that operates to prevent stalling under certain conditions. This does not require adjustment as a matter of routine either, but may be adjusted if you suspect the system is not functioning properly.

**NOTE: The idle mixture adjustment is preset at the factory. The mixture adjusting screw is inaccessible without removing and modifying the carburetor. Since this adjustment is preset, it should not be changed unless major, unscheduled maintenance has been performed on the carburetor. This adjustment can only be made with a CO meter.**

The idle adjustment is made under the following conditions:

- Lights Off
- All accessories Off
- Electric cooling fan Off
- Transmission (MT and AT) in neutral and parking brake applied

1. Start and run the engine at idle until normal operating temperature is reached.

2. Check the underhood decal or the tune-up specification charts for the correct curb idle speed.

3. Connect a tachometer, according to the manufacturer's instructions, and adjust the idle speed screw until the correct rpm is reached.

4. Run the engine for at least 5 seconds at 2000–3000 rpm. Then, reduce the speed to idle rpm for at least 2 minutes. If the idle speed is not at the specified rpm, turn the idle speed adjusting screw until the proper rpm is reached. Check either your underhood specifications sticker or the tune-up specifications charts for the correct idle speed rpm.

### MIXTURE ADJUSTMENT USA MODELS

1. Remove the carburetor. The idle mixture screw is located in the base of the carburetor, just to the left of the PCV hose. Mount the carburetor, carefully, in a softjawed vise, protecting the gasket surface, and with the mixture adjusting screw facing upward.

2. Drill a 2mm ($^5/_{64}$ in.) hole through the casting from the underside of the carburetor. Make sure that this hole intersects the passage leading to the mixture adjustment screw just behind the plug. Now, widen that hole with a 3mm (⅛ in.) drill bit.

3. Insert a blunt punch into the hole and tap out the plug. Install the carburetor on the engine and connect all hoses, lines, etc.

4. Start the engine and run it at fast idle until it reaches normal operating temperature. Make sure that all accessories are **OFF** and the transaxle is in neutral. Turn the ignition switch **OFF** and disconnect the battery ground cable for about 3 seconds, then, reconnect it. Disconnect the oxygen sensor.

5. Start the engine and run it for at least 5 seconds at 2000–3000 rpm. Then, allow the engine to idle for about 2 minutes.

6. Connect a tachometer and allow the engine to operate at the specified curb idle speed. Adjust it, if necessary, to obtain this speed. Connect a CO meter to the exhaust pipe. A reading of 0.1–0.3% is necessary. Adjust the mixture screw to obtain the reading. If,

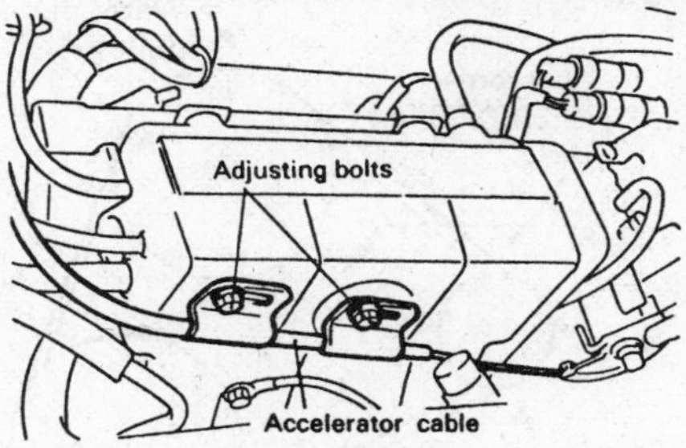


**ISC control cable adjusting points**

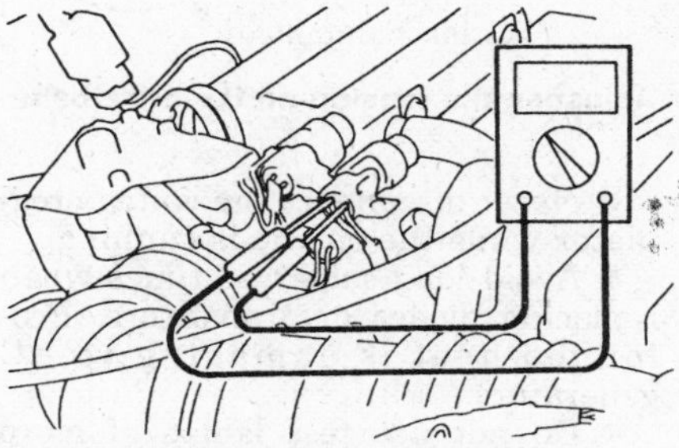

**Multi-tester connections for the ISC adjustment**

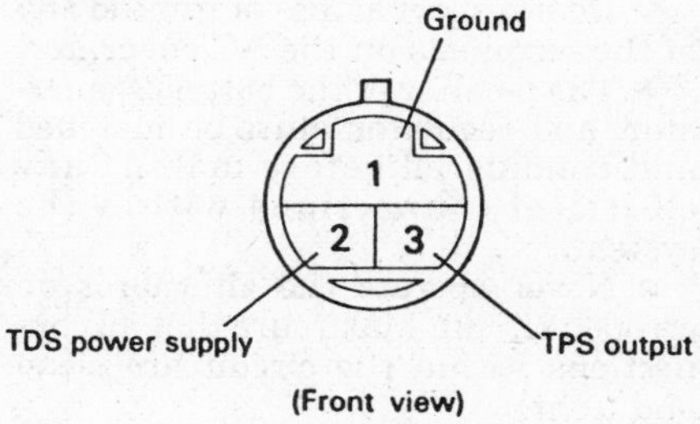


**TPS connector**

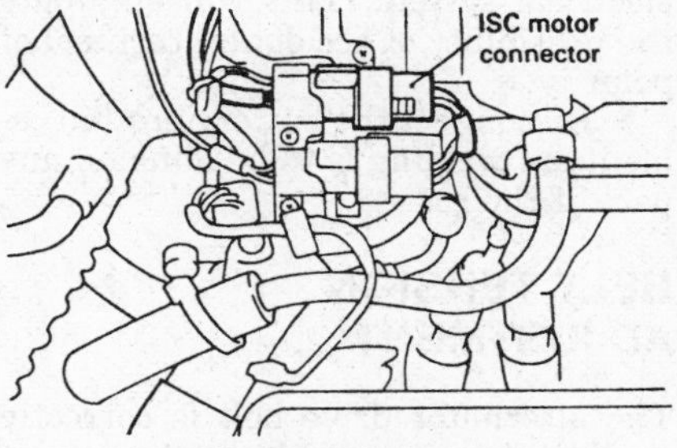


**ISC motor connector**

during this adjustment, the idle speed is varied more than 100 rpm in either direction, reset the idle speed and readjust the CO until both specifications are met simultaneously. Shut off the engine, reconnect the oxygen sensor and install a new concealment plug.

### MIXTURE ADJUSTMENT CANADIAN MODELS

1. Turn off all of the electrical accessories and place the transmission in the neutral position. Then remove the carburetor from the engine.

2. Position the carburetor in a vice with idle mixture adjusting screw facing up. Make sure that the gasket surface does not become damaged when the carburetor is placed in the the vise.

3. Drill a 2mm (5/64 in.) pilot hole in the casting surrounding the idle mixture adjusting screw, then redrill the hole to 3mm (1/8 in.). Insert a blunt punch into the hole and drive out the plug.

4. Reinstall the carburetor. Run the engine until it reaches normal operating temperature.

5. Run the engine for 5 seconds or more at 2000–3000 rpm. Allow the engine to idle for 2 minutes.

6. Set the idle CO and the engine speed to specifications, by adjusting the idle speed adjusting screw No. 1 (SAS-1) and the idle mixture adjusting screw. Idle CO should be 1.8% when the curb idle speed is set between 850–900 rpm.

7. Install the concealment plug to seal the idle mixture adjusting screw

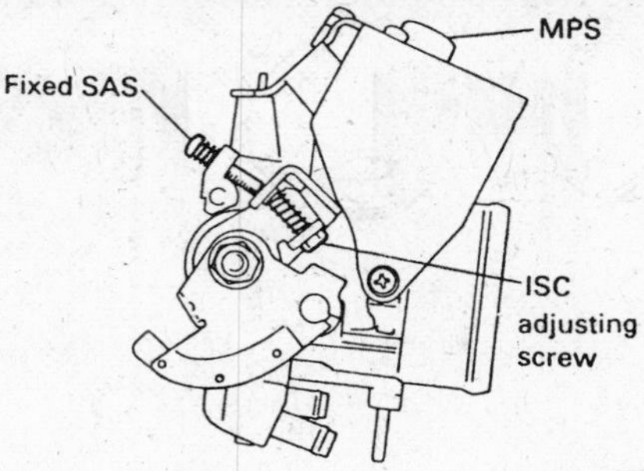


**Speed control screws for fuel injected engines**

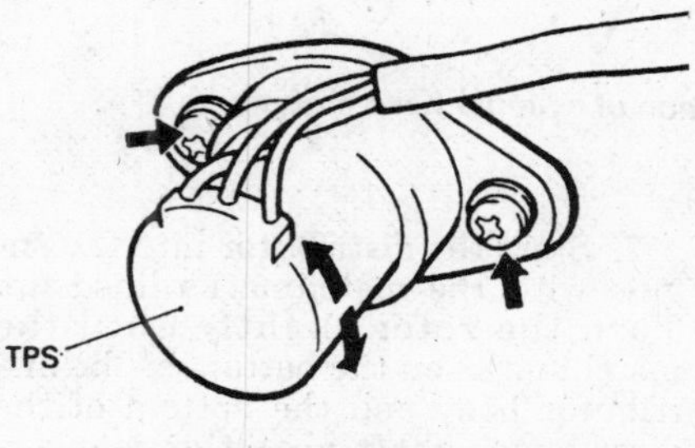


**TPS adjustment**

#### *Fuel Injected Engines*

**NOTE: This adjustment MUST be made any time the Idle Speed Control (ISC) servo, Throttle Position Sensor (TPS), mixing body or throttle body has been removed. A digital voltmeter is essential for this operation.**

1. Run the engine to normal operating temperature, then shut it off.

2. Disconnect the accelerator cable at the throttle lever on the mixing body.

3. Loosen the screws holding the TPS and turn it fully clockwise. Tighten the screws.

4. Turn the ignition switch to the ON position for at least 15 seconds, then turn it OFF. This will automatically set the ISC servo to the proper position.

5. Disconnect the ISC servo wiring connector.

6. Start the engine and check the idle speed with a tachometer. Idle speed should be 600 rpm. If not, adjust it with the adjusting screw as shown.

7. Insert the digital voltmeter test probes in the TPS connector GW and B holes as shown.

8. Turn the ignition switch to the ON position. DO NOT START THE ENGINE!

9. Read the voltage. If indicated voltage is not 0.45-0.51 volts loosen the TPS mounting screws and turn the sensor clockwise or counterclockwise until the indicated voltage is 0.48 volts. Tighten the screws and apply a thread-locking sealant.

10. Open the throttle valve fully and let it close. Recheck the indicated voltage. Adjust if necessary.

11. Remove the voltmeter and reconnect the wiring.

12. Start the engine. Recheck the idle speed. Adjust if necessary and stop the engine.

13. Turn the ignition switch to the **ON** position for at least 15 seconds, then turn it **OFF**.

14. Reconnect the cable, and adjust if necessary to remove any slack, using the adjusting nut at the throttle lever.

# ENGINE ELECTRICAL

## Distributor

### REMOVAL & INSTALLATION

1. Disconnect the battery ground cable. Remove the spark plug wires from the spark plugs and the coil wire from the coil. Then, disconnect the retaining clips or unfasten the two screws that hold on the distributor cap, and pull the distributor cap and seal off the distributor. Locate the cap and wires away from the distributor. Disconnect the vacuum advance line. Disconnect the distributor wiring connector.

2. Turn the engine until the rotor points to the No. 1 cylinder position and the timing marks on the crankshaft pulley and the timing tab are aligned at TDC or 0.

3. Mark the distributor body to the exact place the rotor points.

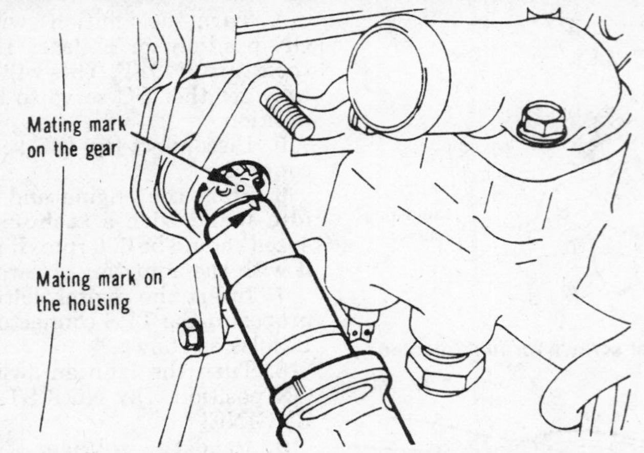


Aligning mating marks for installation of cylinder head mounted distributors

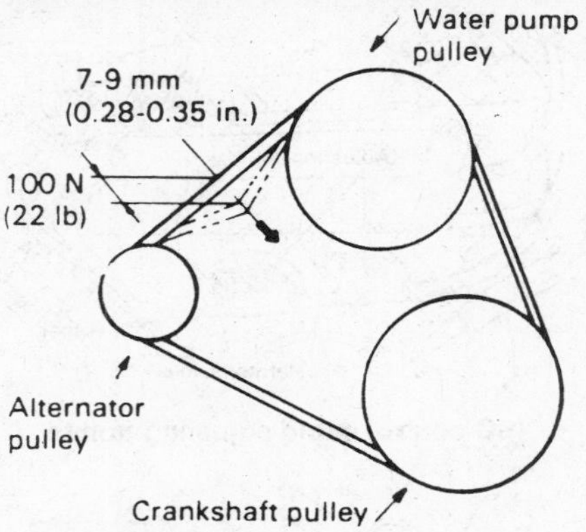


Adjusting the tension on the drive belts

Matchmark both the distributor mounting flange and the cylinder head.

4. Now, carefully pull the distributor out of the engine, noting the direction and degree to which the rotor turns as you pull it out. Mark the location of the rotor after it has turned, too.

5. If the engine has been rotated while the distributor is out, proceed to the next step. To install the distributor if the engine has been rotated, position it so the distributor and matchmarks are lined up. Now, position the rotor so it is lined up with the matchmark on the distributor body after the distributor was pulled part way out. Insert the distributor into the engine until the gears at the bottom engage and then begin turning the rotor. If there is resistance, turn the rotor back and forth slightly so the gears mesh. Once the gears engage and inserting the distributor causes the rotor to turn, push the distributor in until it seats and the rotor is lined up with the first mark made on the body.

6. If the engine has been rotated while the distributor was out, you'll have to first put the No. 1 cylinder at TDC firing position. You can either remove the valve cover or No. 1 spark plug to determine engine position. Rotate the engine with a socket wrench on the nut at the center of the front pulley in the normal direction of rotation. Either feel for air being expelled forcefully through the spark plug hole or watch for the engine to rotate up to the Top Dead Center mark without the valves moving (both valves will be closed or all the way up). If the valves are moving as you approach TDC or there is no air being expelled through the plug hole, turn the engine another full turn until you get the appropriate indication as the engine approaches TDC position.

7. Start the distributor into the engine with the matchmarks lined up. Turn the rotor slightly until the matchmarks on the bottom of the distributor body and the bottom of the distributor shaft near the gear are aligned. Then, insert the distributor all the way into the head. If you have trouble getting the distributor and camshaft gears to mesh, turn the rotor back and forth very slightly until the distributor can be inserted easily. If the rotor is not now lined up with the position of No. 1 plug terminal, you'll have to pull the distributor back out slightly, shift the position of the rotor appropriately, and then reinstall it.

8. Align the matchmarks between the distributor and. Install the distributor mounting bolt and tighten it finger tight. Reconnect the vacuum advance line and distributor wiring connector, and reinstall the gasket and cap. Reconnect the negative battery cable. Adjust the ignition timing. Then, tighten the distributor mounting bolt securely.

# Alternator

## PRECAUTIONS

To prevent damage to the alternator and regulator, the following precautions should be taken when working with the electrical system.

- Never reverse the battery connections.
- Booster batteries for starting must be connected properly: positive-to-positive and negative-to-negative.
- Disconnect the battery cables before using a fast charger; the charger has a tendency to force current through the diodes in the opposite direction for which they were designed. This burns out the diodes.
- Never use a fast charger as a booster for starting the vehicle.
- Never disconnect the voltage regulator while the engine is running.
- Avoid long soldering times when replacing diodes or transistors. Prolonged heat is damaging to AC generators.
- Do not use test lamps of more than 12 volts (V) for checking diode continuity.
- Do not short across or ground any of the terminals on the AC generator.
- The polarity of the battery, generator, and regulator must be matched and considered before making any electrical connections within the system.
- Never operate the alternator on an open circuit. Make sure that all connections within the circuit are clean and tight.
- Disconnect the battery terminals when performing any service on the electrical system. This will eliminate the possibility of accidental reversal of polarity.
- Disconnect the battery ground cable if arc welding is to be done on any part of the car.

## BELT TENSION ADJUSTMENT

The alternator drive belt is correctly tensioned when the longest span of belt between pulleys can be depressed ⅛–½ in. by moderate thumb pressure. To adjust, loosen the slotted adjusting bracket bolt on the alternator. If the alternator hinge bolts are very tight, it may be necessary to loosen them slightly to move the alternator. Move the alternator in or out by hand to get the correct tension, then tighten the adjusting bolt.

V-belts under 39 in. (100cm) in length should deflect about ⅛ in. (3mm). Belts over 40 in. (101cm) long should deflect about ½ in. (13mm).

**NOTE: Be careful not to overtighten the belt, as this may damage the alternator bearings!**

### REMOVAL & INSTALLATION

1. Turn off the ignition switch and disconnect both battery cables.
2. Loosen the support bolt and adjusting bolt, and then shift the alternator toward the engine so belt tension is relieved. Remove the belt.
3. Note the locations of all connectors. Make a drawing, if necessary. Unplug the plug type connectors and unscrew the fastening nuts for terminal type connectors. Clean any dirty connections.
4. Remove the adjusting bolt. Remove the nut from the rear of the mounting bolt.
5. Remove the alternator.
6. To install the alternator, first position it so the mounting bolt can be inserted. Install the mounting bolt loosely.

**NOTE: On models equipped with Melco alternators, spacers are required between the front leg of the alternator mounting bracket and the front case. Spacers are available in thicknesses of 0.2mm. Enough should be installed so that they do not fall out when removed.**

7. Install the adjusting bolt loosely. Install the belt and turn the alternator to put tension on the belt. Tighten the adjusting bolt 10 ft. lbs. and the mounting bolt and nut to 15–18 ft. lbs.

## Voltage Regulator

The voltage regulator is built into the alternator, if the regulator is found to be defective, the alternator and regulator must be replaced as a unit.

## Starter

### REMOVAL & INSTALLATION

1. Disconnect the negative battery cable. Then, mark and disconnect all wiring connectors at the starter.

**NOTE: It will be helpful to remove the battery and battery tray, as well as the engine underside shield.**

2. Raise and support the front end of the vehicle safely. Then remove the two starter mounting bolts and remove the starter.
3. Clean the surfaces of the starter motor flange and the flywheel housing where the starter attaches. Then, install the starter motor. Tighten the bolts to 16–23 ft. lbs.

4. Install the battery and tray if removed.
5. Reconnect the negative battery cable.

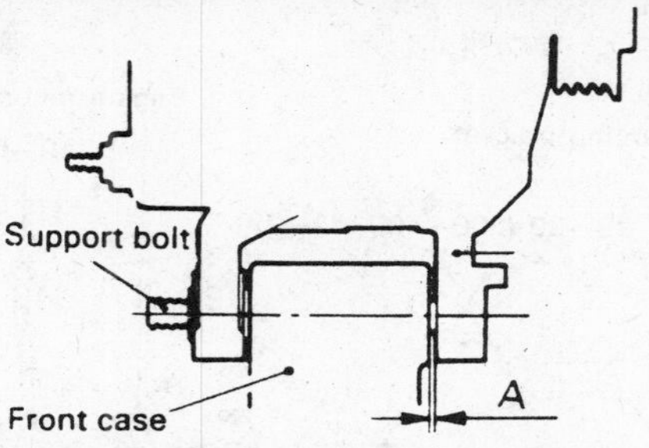


**Use shims when installing the Melco alternator**

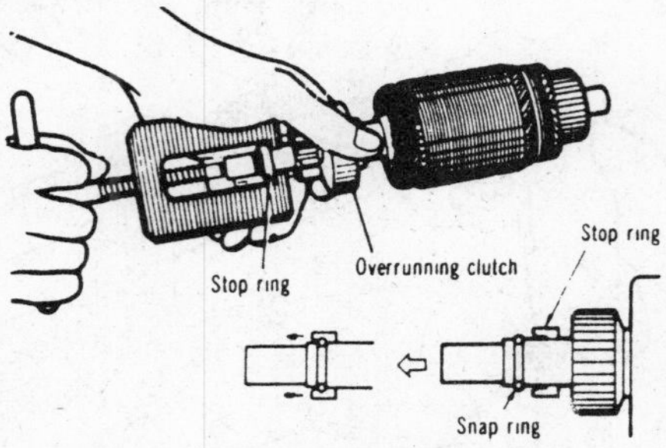


**Installing the snap-ring stopper**

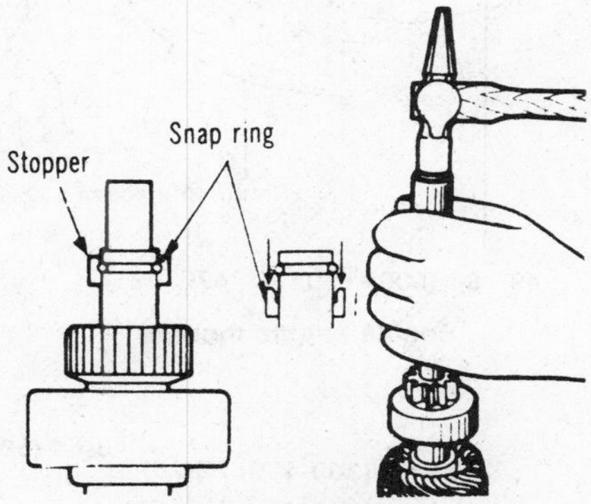


**Removing the starter drive**

### STARTER SOLENOID REPLACEMENT

1. Remove the starter from the car. Then, disconnect the starter motor wire at the M terminal of the solenoid.
2. Remove the Phillips screws from the front end of the solenoid. Disengage the solenoid plunger from the yoke inside the front of the starter and then remove the solenoid and the shims located between the solenoid and the starter front frame. If you're replacing the solenoid, make sure you get extra shims used to fit it onto the starter front frame.
3. Install the solenoid, making sure the plunger engages the drive yoke. Install the same number of shims. Then, energize the solenoid by running jumper wires from the (+) terminal of a 12 volt battery to the S terminal of the solenoid and from the (−) terminal of the battery to the M terminal. Quickly measure (in 10 seconds or less) the clearance between the front of the pinion gear and the stop in front of it in the starter front frame, and then de-energize the solenoid before it overheats. The pinion gear should be pushed back against the drive mechanism when you do this. Perform the remaining steps in reverse of the removal procedure. Make sure all connections are clean and tight.

### STARTER DRIVE REPLACEMENT

1. Remove the starter from the car.
2. Remove the solenoid.
3. Remove the two through bolts and two Phillips screws from the rear starter cover. Remove the rear cover.
4. Pry the retaining springs back and slide the two brushes out of the brush holder. Then, pull the brush holder off the rear of the starter. Remove the field coil assembly from the front frame. Remove the armature.
5. Remove the pinion shaft end cover from the center frame. Measure the clearance between the spacer and center cover and record it. If the pinion shaft is replaced, insert or subtract spacer washers until the clearance is the same as that recorded. Use a screwdriver to remove the retaining clip and then remove the washers. Remove the retaining bolt and then separate the center frame from the front frame.
6. Remove the spring retainer and spring for the yoke from the front frame. Then, remove the washer, reduction gear, shift yoke lever, and two lever supports.
7. Turn the front frame so the pinion gear is at the top and support it securely. Then, use a socket that fits tight over the pinion shaft to force the snapring collar downward. Tap the socket lightly at the top or use a press to do this. Then, use a screwdriver to work the snapring out of its groove and remove it from the shaft. Remove the collar. Remove the pinion and the spring behind it from the shaft.
8. Now, pull the overrunning clutch and pinion shaft assembly out of the rear of the front frame. Replace the pinion if its teeth are damaged (check the flywheel ring gear as well). Replace the overrunning clutch if the pinion gear is damaged or if the oneway action of the clutch is not precise.
9. To install, first coat the splines of the pinion shaft with a light coating of a high temperature grease designed for this purpose. Then, reverse all the removal procedures to install. When reassembling the washer and clip at the rear of the pinion shaft, note that the clearance must be corrected by

## COMPONENTS

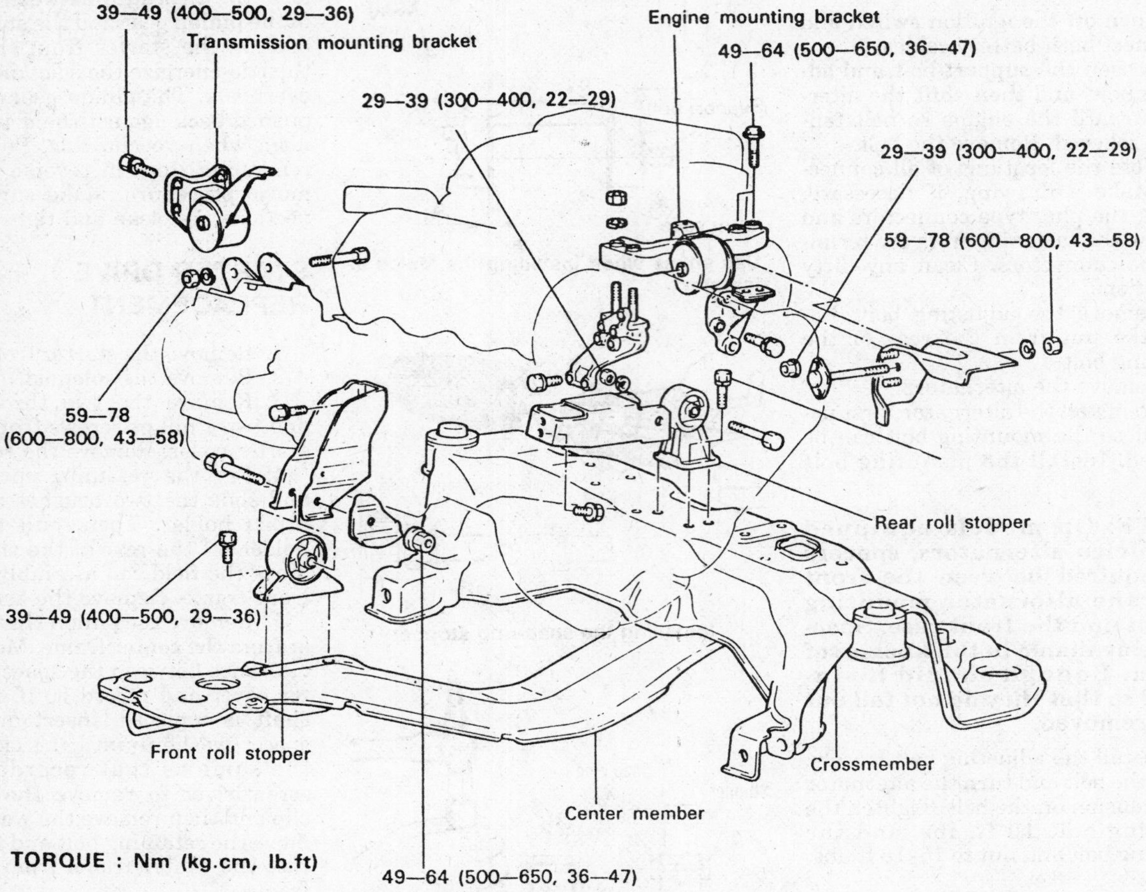
39—49 (400—500, 29—36)
Transmission mounting bracket
29—39 (300—400, 22—29)
Engine mounting bracket
49—64 (500—650, 36—47)
29—39 (300—400, 22—29)
59—78 (600—800, 43—58)
59—78
(600—800, 43—58)
Rear roll stopper
39—49 (400—500, 29—36)
Front roll stopper
Crossmember
Center member
TORQUE : Nm (kg.cm, lb.ft)
49—64 (500—650, 36—47)

**Sonata engine mounts**

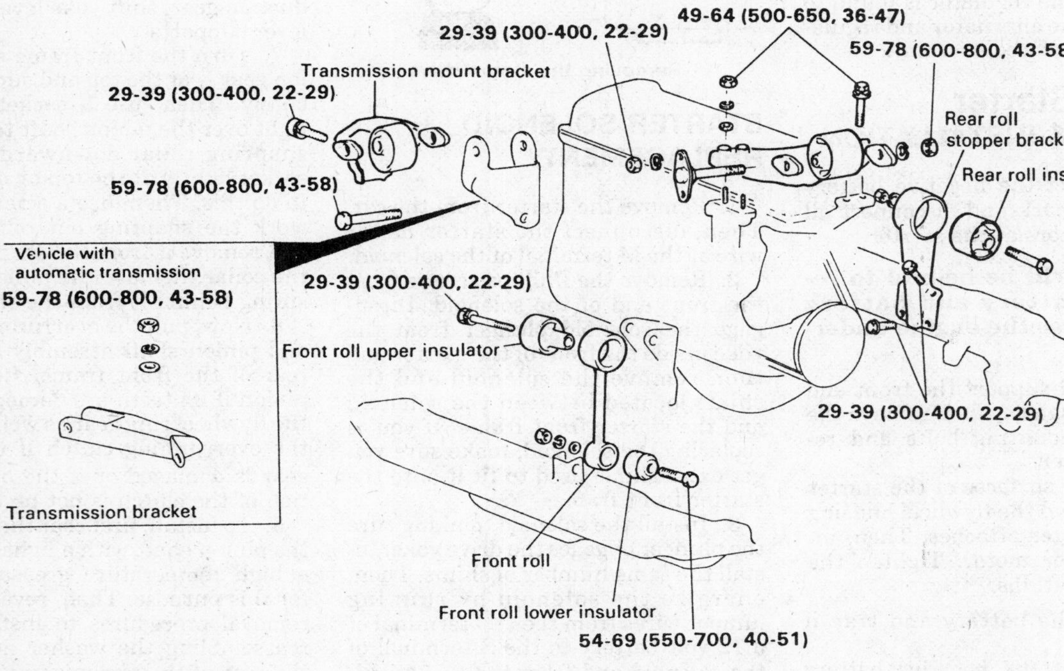
49-64 (500-650, 36-47)
29-39 (300-400, 22-29)
59-78 (600-800, 43-58)
Transmission mount bracket
29-39 (300-400, 22-29)
Rear roll
stopper bracket
Rear roll insulator
59-78 (600-800, 43-58)
Vehicle with
automatic transmission
59-78 (600-800, 43-58)
29-39 (300-400, 22-29)
Front roll upper insulator
29-39 (300-400, 22-29)
Transmission bracket
Front roll
Front roll lower insulator
54-69 (550-700, 40-51)
TORQUE : Nm (kg·cm, lb·ft)

**Excel engine mounts**

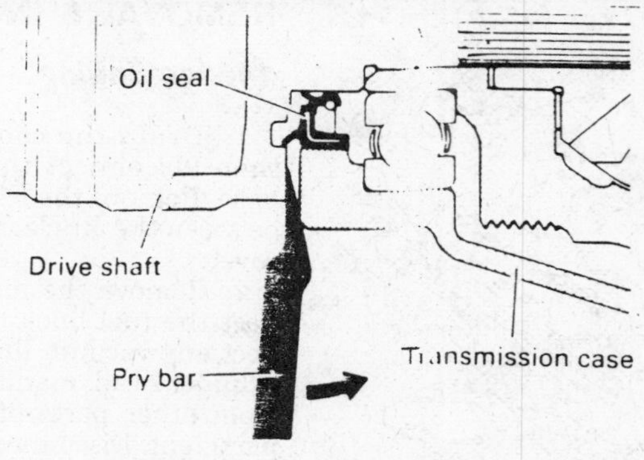


Removing the driveshafts

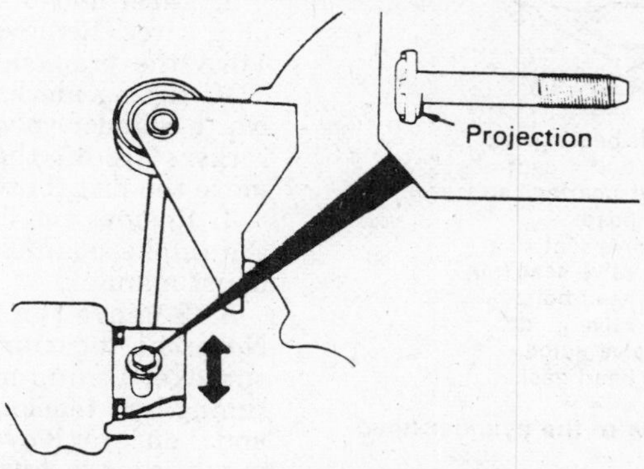


Installing the lower bolt on the roll stopper

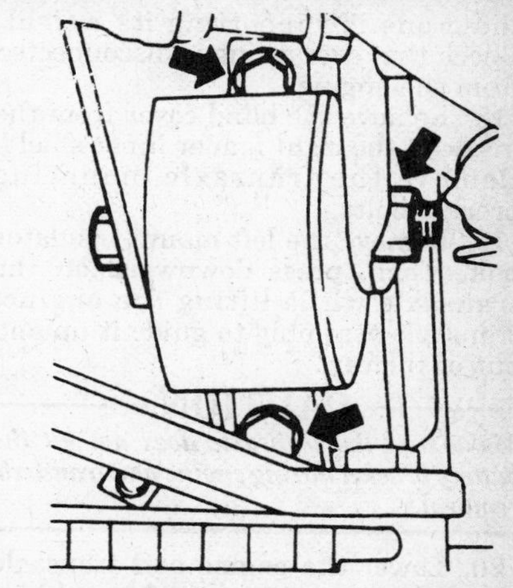

Remove the front roll stop nut and the bolt; or, you may remove the attaching bolts from the engine damper

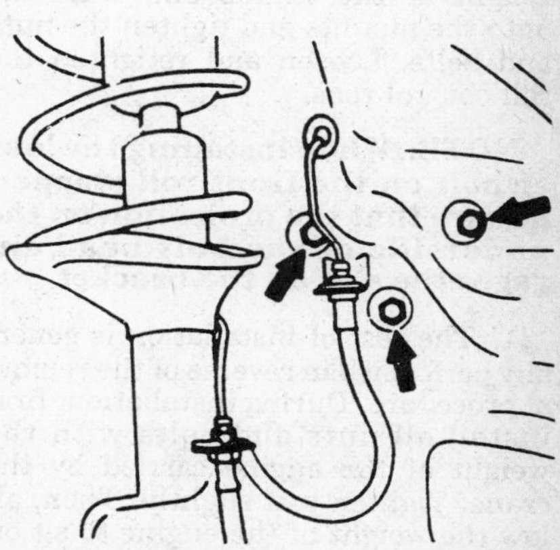

Removing the transaxle mounting bolts

changing the thickness or number of washers if the overrunning clutch and pinion shaft assembly have been replaced.

# ENGINE MECHANICAL

## Engine

### REMOVAL & INSTALLATION

**NOTE: The factory recommends that the engine and transaxle be removed as a unit.**

1. Remove the air cleaner assembly. Disconnect the purge control vacuum hose from the purge valve. Remove the purge control valve mounting bracket. Remove the windshield washer reservoir, radiator tank and carbon canister.
2. Drain the coolant from the radiator. Disconnect the upper and lower radiator hoses and then remove the radiator assembly with the electric cooling fan attached. Be sure to disconnect the fan wiring harness.
3. Disconnect the electrical connectors for the back-up lights and engine harness, located near the battery tray. If the car has a 5 speed, disconnect the select control valve connector. Disconnect the two alternator harness connectors and the oil pressure sending unit.
4. First label and then disconnect the automatic transmission oil cooler hoses. Avoid spilling oil and cap the openings.
5. Label and then disconnect all low tension wires and the one high tension wire going to the coil from the distributor. Disconnect the engine ground.
6. Disconnect the brake booster vacuum hose at the intake manifold.
7. Disconnect the fuel supply, return, and vapor hoses at the side of the engine. Avoid spilling fuel.
8. Disconnect the heater hoses from the side of the engine. Disconnect the accelerator cable at the engine side.
9. Remove the clutch control cable (manual transmission) or transmission shifter control cable (automatic transmissions) from the transaxle.
10. Unscrew and disconnect the speedometer cable at the transaxle. Disconnect the air conditioning compresser mounting bracket.
11. Raise and securely support the vehicle. Remove the splash shield. Remove the drain plug and drain the transmission fluid. Disconnect the exhaust pipe at the manifold. Then, suspend the pipe securely with wire.
12. If the car has manual transmission, remove the shift control rod and extension rod.
13. Disconnect the stabilizer bar at both lower control arms. Remove the bolts that attach the lower control arms to the body on either side. Support the arms from the body.
14. Disconnect the driveshafts at the transmission on both sides. Then, seal off the openings in the transaxle. Make sure you replace the circlips holding the driveshafts in the transaxle. Support the driveshafts from the body.
15. Attach a crane type lift, via chains or cables, to both the engine lifting hooks. Put just a little tension on the cables. Then, remove the nut and bolt from the front roll stopper; unbolt the brace from the top of the engine damper.
16. Separate the rear roll stopper from the No. 2 crossmember. Remove the attaching nut from the left mount insulator bolt, but do not remove the bolt.
17. Raise the engine just enough that

the crane is supporting its weight. Check that everything is disconnected from the engine.

18. Remove the blind cover from the inside of the right fender inner shield. Remove the transaxle mounting bracket bolts.

19. Remove the left mount insulator bolt. Then, press downward on the transaxle while lifting the engine/transaxle assembly to guide it up and out of the car.

**CAUTION**

***Make sure the transaxle does not hit the battery bracket during engine and transaxle removal.***

20. Lower the engine and transaxle carefully into position and loosely install the mounting bolts. Temporarily tighten the front and rear roll control rods mounting bolts. Lower the full weight of the engine and transaxle onto the mounts and tighten the nuts and bolts. Loosen and retighten the roll control rods.

**NOTE: When installing the lower bolt on the front roll stopper, be sure that the projection on the underside of the bolt head engages the slot on the bracket.**

21. The rest of installation is generally performed in reverse of the removal procedure. During installation, first install all nuts and bolts with the weight of the engine carried by the crane. Tighten just slightly. Then, allow the weight of the engine to sit on the mounts, and torque parts as follows:

- Left mount large insulator nut – 65–80 ft. lbs.
- Left mount small insulator nut – 22–29 ft. lbs.
- Left mount bracket-to-engine nuts/bolts – 36–47 ft. lbs.
- Transaxle mount insulator nut – 65–80 ft. lbs.
- Transaxle insulator bracket-to-side frame bolts – 22–29 ft. lbs.
- Transaxle bracket assembly-to-automatic transaxle nuts – 65–80 ft. lbs.
- Transaxle mount bracket to manual transaxle bolts – 40–43 ft. lbs.
- Rear roll insulator nut – 33–43 ft. lbs.
- Rear roll stopper bracket-to-crossmember assembly bolts – 22–29 ft. lbs.
- Front roll insulator nut – 33–43 ft. lbs.
- Front roll stopper bracket-to-crossmember assembly bolts – 33–40 ft. lbs.
- Lower roll insulator-to-roll damper bracket bolt – 22–29 ft. lbs.
- Center crossmember to body – 43–58 ft. lbs.

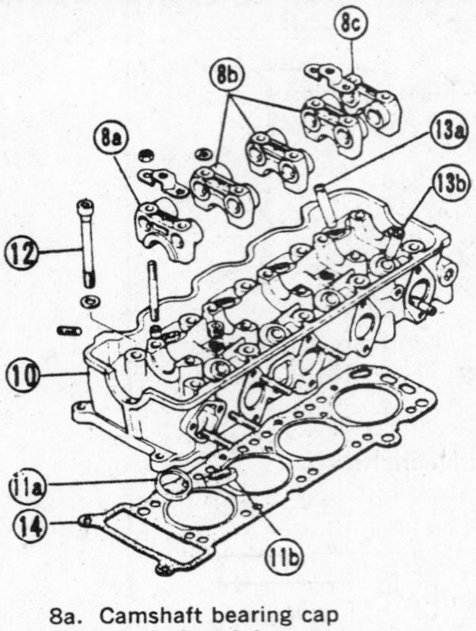


8a. Camshaft bearing cap
8b. No. 2, 3 and 4 caps
8c. Camshaft bearing cap (rear)
10. Cylinder head
11a. Intake valve seat ring
11b. Exhaust valve seat ring
12. Cylinder head bolt
13a. Exhaust valve guide
13b. Intake valve guide
14. Cylinder head gasket

**Exploded view of the cylinder head**

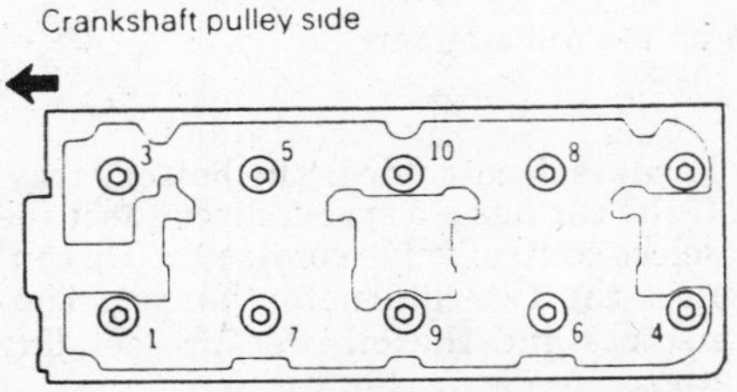


**Cylinder head removal sequence for the 1468cc engine**

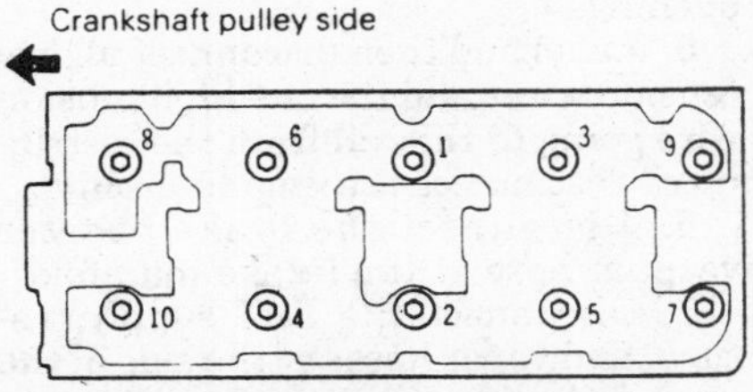


**Cylinder head torque sequence for the 1468cc engine**

22. Finally, replenish all fluids. Adjust the transmission and accelerator linkages. Start the engine and check for leaks as well as proper gauge operation. Replace the hood and have the air conditioner recharged.

## Cylinder Head

**CAUTION**

***Never remove the cylinder head unless the engine is COLD! A hot cylinder head will warp!***

### REMOVAL & INSTALLATION

#### *1468cc Engine*

1. Drain the cooling system and then disconnect the upper radiator hose. Remove the PCV hose that runs between the air cleaner and the rocker cover.

2. Remove the air cleaner. Disconnect the fuel lines. Label and disconnect any vacuum lines running to the cylinder head, manifold, or carburetor from other parts of the engine compartment. Disconnect the heater hoses going to the head.

3. Label and disconnect the spark plug wires. Remove the rocker cover. Turn the crankshaft over until the TDC timing marks line up and both No. 1 cylinder valves are closed (both rockers are off the cams). Then, remove the distributor.

4. Remove the carburetor. Remove the intake manifold. Remove the exhaust manifold.

5. Remove the timing belt cover. Note the location of the camshaft sprocket timing mark. Loosen both timing belt tensioner mounting bolts and then lever it over toward the water pump as far as it will go. Retighten the adjusting bolt to hold the tensioner in this position. Pull the timing belt off the camshaft sprocket but leave it engaged with the other sprockets.

6. Using a hex type wrench, loosen the head bolts in the sequence shown. When all have been loosened, remove them. Then, pull the head off the engine block, rocking it slightly to break it loose.

7. Inspect the head with a straightedge and a flat feeler gauge of 0.05mm (0.002 in.) thickness. The tolerance for warping of a used head is 0.05mm (0.002 in.). The block deck must be flat within the same tolerance. The height of the head should be 89mm (3.5 in.) with a maximum machining limit of 0.3mm (0.012 in.).

8. Clean the combustion chambers of carbon with a scraper that is not excessively sharp, being carefully not to damage the aluminum surface. Sharp edges in the combustion chambers can cause detonation.

9. The oil and water passages should be cleaned thoroughly, if necessary by taking the head to a machine shop that can clean it in some sort of solvent or hot tank that is compatible with aluminum. Also, blow compressed air through all the small oil passages to ensure that they are clear. Check that the EGR and air pump passages are also clear. Both gasket surfaces must be completely free of dirt.

10. Install a new head gasket (without any sealer) and then position the head on the cylinder block. Install all

the bolts finger tight. Then, torque them, in the illustrated sequence, first to 25 ft. lbs. (35 Nm). Then, torque again, in the same sequence, to 51–54 ft. lbs. (69–74 Nm).

11. Install the timing belt on the camshaft tensioner and rotate the camshaft sprocket backward so the belt is tight on what is normally the tension side. Makes sure all the timing marks are now lined up. That is, timing marks on the crankshaft sprocket and front case must line up; and the marks on the camshaft sprocket and the tab on the cylinder head must be simultaneously lined up with the side of the belt away from the tensioner under tension. Now, loosen the timing belt tensioner adjusting bolt and allow spring tension to tension the belt. Make sure all timing marks are still lined up. If not, the belt is out of time and must be shifted with the tensioner shifted back toward the water pump and locked there. Now, torque the adjusting bolt (on the right side and working through a slot) to 15–18 ft. lbs. Now, after the tensioner adjusting bolt is torqued, torque the hinged mounting bolt located on the opposite side. Don't torque the mounting bolt first, or the tension on the belt will be too great!

Turn the crankshaft one full turn in the normal direction of rotation. Loosen first the tensioner pivot bolt and then the adjusting bolt. Now torque them exactly as before, adjusting bolt (working in the slot) first! This extra step is necessary to ensure the timing belt is properly seated before final tension is adjusted.

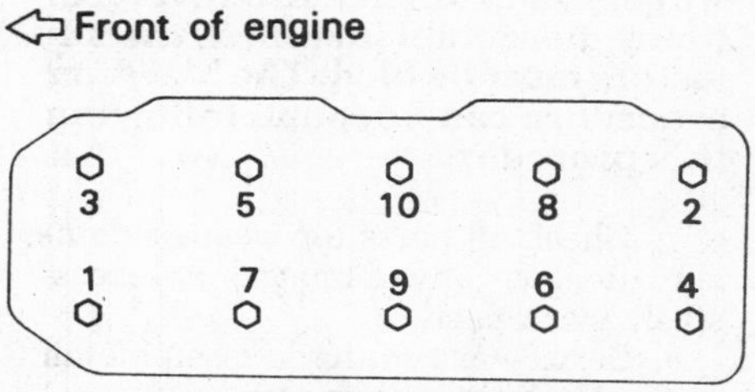


**2351cc engine cylinder head loosening sequence**

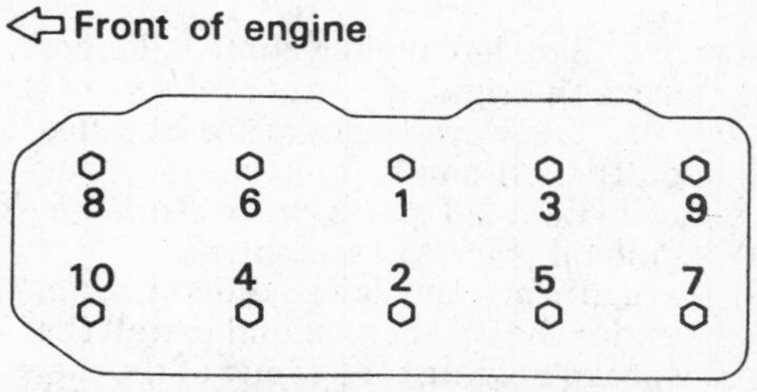


**2351cc engine cylinder head tightening sequence**

12. Install the cylinder head cover and tighten the bolts to 13–16 inch lbs. (1.5–2.0 Nm).

13. Install the timing belt cover.

14. Install the intake manifold using a new gasket and tighten the bolts and nut to 12–14 ft. lbs. (16–19 Nm).

15. Install the exhaust manifold using a new gasket and tighten the nuts to 12–14 ft. lbs. (16–19 Nm).

16. Install the carburetor.

17. Install the distributor. Connect all hoses and lines and then install the air cleaner.

18. Refill the cooling system. Operate the engine and check for leaks. After the engine has reached normal operating temperature, turn it off and remove the air cleaner and rocker cover. Retighten the cylinder head bolts to 58–61 ft. lbs. (78–83 Nm) in the sequence shown.

19. Reinstall the rocker cover and the air cleaner.

### 2351cc Engine

1. Drain the engine coolant.

2. Remove the intake and exhaust manifolds.

3. Remove the air cleaner. Detach and tag all vacuum hoses, heater hoses, and gauge connectors which connect with the cylinder head or would obstruct its removal.

4. Remove the throttle air valve body.

5. Remove the timing belt cover.

6. Remove the rocker cover.

7. Turn the engine over until the timing marks are at TDC with No. 1 cylinder at the firing position (front valves closed fully). If the rockers are not all the way off the cams, turn the engine another 360 degrees.

8. Label and disconnect all spark plug wires at the plugs.

9. Remove the distributor.

10. Remove the timing belt.

11. If you're planning to do major work on the head, rather than just replacing the head gasket, remove the rocker assembly and then remove the camshaft. Keep all parts in a clean, safe environment.

12. Using an 8mm hex socket loosen the head bolts in the order shown in three stages, alternating from bolt to bolt. Rock the head to break it loose and then remove the head and the gasket from the block.

13. Inspect the head with a straightedge and a flat feeler gauge of 0.10mm thickness. Run the gauge in every direction as shown. The tolerance for warping of a used head is 0.05mm over the entire length. The block deck must be flat within the same tolerance. The refacing limit is 0.2mm. The overall head height should be 90.0mm ± 0.1mm.

14. Clean the combustion chambers of carbon with a scraper that is not excessively sharp, and use it carefully to avoid damaging the relatively soft aluminum surface. Sharp edges in the combustion chambers can cause detonation.

15. The oil and water passages should be cleaned thoroughly, if necessary by taking the head to a machine shop that can clean it in some sort of solvent or hot tank that is compatible with aluminum. You should also blow compressed air through all the small oil passages to ensure that they are clear. Check that the EGR and air pump passages are also clear. Both gasket surfaces must be completely free of dirt.

16. Do not apply any kind of sealant to the gasket itself on any of the engines. Install the head gasket on the block deck, with the identification mark facing upward and on the cam belt end of the engine.

17. Put the head into position and install the head bolts. The bolts must be torqued to a cold specification, which is 69 ft.lb. in two equal stages. Using the sequence shown in the illustration, torque the bolts in order to 33-36 ft. lbs. Then, repeat the operation, torquing them to the full torque.

18. Perform the remaining steps in reverse of the removal procedure, referring to other procedures as necessary.

19. Start the engine, check for leaks and run the engine to normal operating temperature. Stop the engine. Remove the valve cover and torque the head bolts, warm, in sequence, to 72-80 ft. lbs. Replace the valve cover.

## OVERHAUL

**For all cylinder head overhaul procedures, please refer to "Engine Rebuilding" in the Unit Repair section.**

# Rocker Arms/Shafts

## REMOVAL & INSTALLATION

### 1468cc Engine

1. Remove the PCV hose running from the rocker cover and the air cleaner. Remove the air cleaner.

2. Remove the upper timing belt cover. Remove the rocker cover.

3. Loosen the bearing cap bolts, or the rockershaft mounting bolts, but do not remove them and remove each rocker shaft, rocker arms and springs as an assembly. Disassemble the whole assembly by progressively removing each bolt, and then the associated springs and rockers, keeping all parts in the exact order of disassembly. The left and right springs have different tension ratings and free length. Ob-

| Identification | Installation position |
|---|---|
| 1-3 | No. 1 and 3 cylinders (positions A and C in illustration shown below) |
| 2-4 | No. 2 and 4 cylinders (position B and D in illustration shown below) |

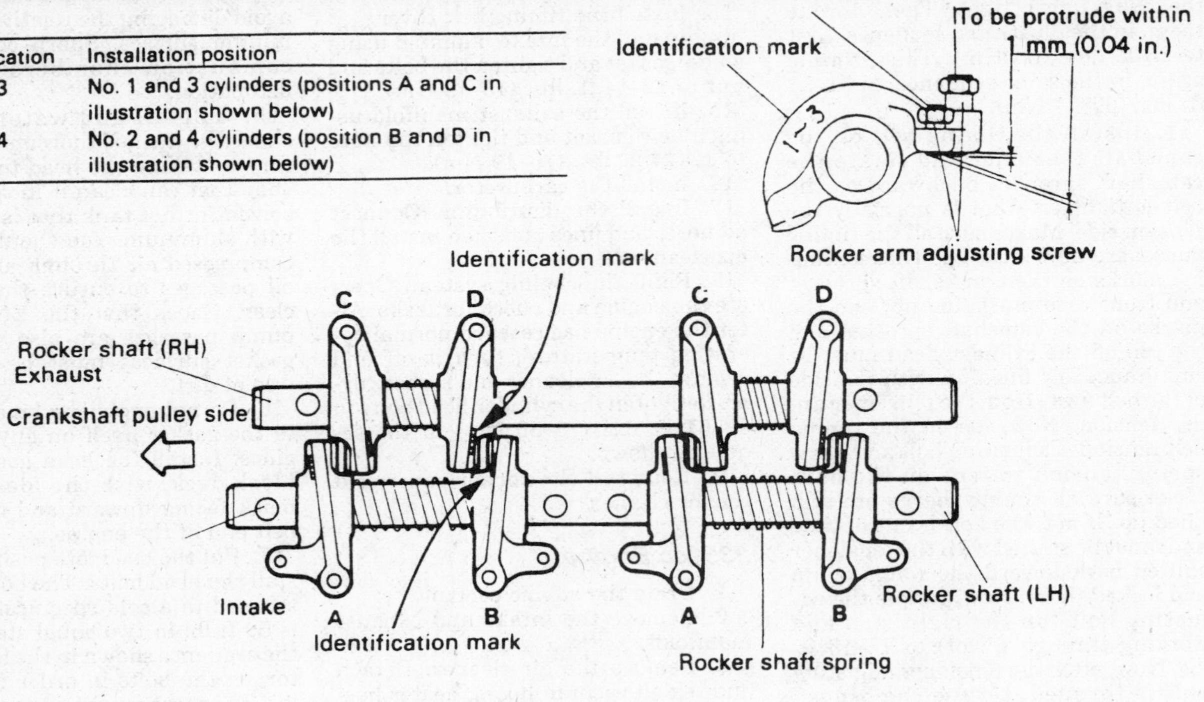


Rocker arm installation and identification

serve the location of the rocker arm as they are removed. Exhaust and intake, right and left are different. Do not mix them up.

4. Check the rocker arm face contacting the cam lobe and the adjusting screw that contacts the valve stem for excess wear. Inspect the fit of the rockers on the shaft. Replace adjusting screws, rockers, and/or shafts that show excessive wear. Pay special attention to the contact pad ends of the rocker arms and the ball surface of the adjustings studs. Check the diameter of the shaft at the rocker mounting points and subtract that number from the measured inside diameter of the corresponding rocker arm. Clearance should be 0.0005–0.0017 in. (0.013–0.043mm). The service limit is 0.004 in. (0.1mm). Check the rocker shaft bend. Total rocker shaft bend should be 0.002 in. (0.05mm). Check the spring free length. Maximum free length should be 2.1 in. (53.3mm) for the exhaust side springs; 2.6 in. (66mm) for intake side springs.

5. Assemble all the parts, noting the differences between intake and exhaust parts. The intake rocker shaft is much longer; the intake rocker shaft springs are over three in. long, while those for the exhaust side are less than 2 in. long; intake rockers have the extra adjusting screw for the jet valve; rockers are labeled **1–3** and **2–4** for the cylinder with which they are associated. See the illustration. Torque the rocker shaft mounting bolts to 15–19 ft. lbs. (20–26 Nm).

6. Adjust the valve clearances. This step may be omitted only if all parts are being reused. Install the rocker cover with a new gasket, torquing the bolts to 12–18 inch lbs. (1.5–2.0 Nm). Install the air cleaner and PCV valve. Remember that there is no timing belt cover in place, and keep your fingers clear. Run the engine at idle speed until it is hot. Then (unless valves did not require adjustment), remove the valve cover again and adjust the valve clearances with the engine hot. Finally, replace the rocker cover and timing belt cover, air cleaner, and PCV valve.

### 2351cc Engine

**NOTE: A special tool, 09246-32000, is required to retain the automatic lash adjusters in this procedure.**

1. Remove the rocker cover and gasket, and the timing belt cover.
2. Turn the crankshaft so that the No. 1 piston is at TDC compression. At this point, the timing mark on the camshaft sprocket and the timing mark on the head to the left of the sprocket will be aligned.
3. Remove the camshaft bearing cap bolts.
4. Install the automatic lash adjuster retainer tool, 09246-32000, to keep the adjuster from falling out of the rocker arms.
5. Lift off the bearing caps and rocker arm assemblies.
6. The rocker arms may now be removed from the shafts.

**NOTE: Keep all parts in the order in which they were removed. None of the parts are interchangeable! The lash adjusters are filled with diesel fuel, which will spill out if they are inverted. If any diesel fuel is spilled, the adjusters must be bled. The bleeding procedure can be found following this procedure.**

7. Check all parts for wear or damage. Replace any damaged or excessively worn part.
8. Service as required, assemble all parts. Note the following:
   a. The rocker shafts are installed with the notches in the ends facing up.
   b. The left rocker shaft is longer than the right.
   c. The wave washers are installed on the left shaft.
   d. Coat all parts with clean engine oil prior to assembly.
   e. Insert the lash adjuster from under the rocker arm and install the special holding tool. If any of the diesel fuel is spilled, the adjuster must be bled.
   f. Tighten the bearing cap bolts, working from the center towards the ends, to 15 ft. lbs.

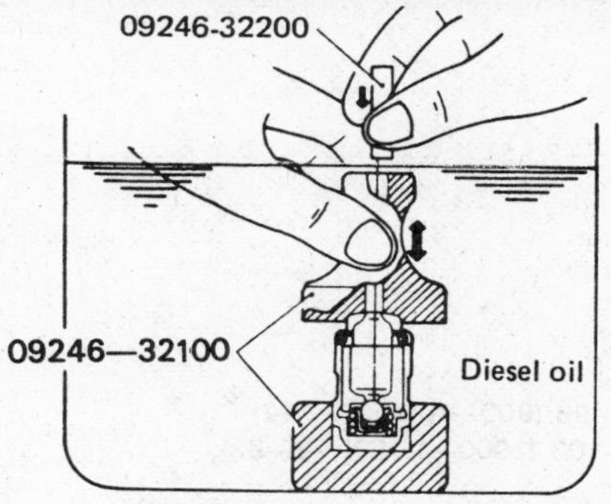

Bleeding the lash adjuster

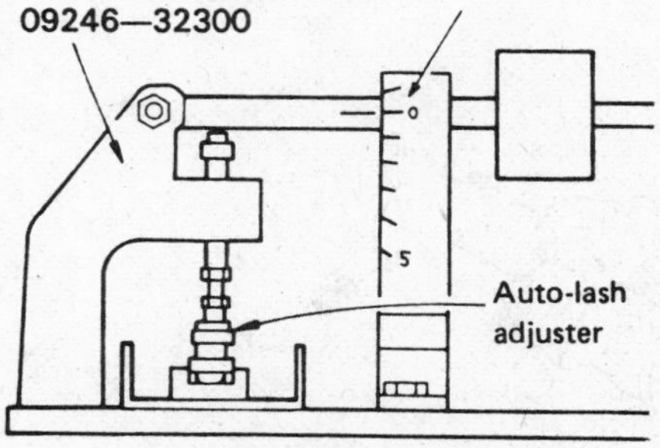

Lash adjuster leak-down

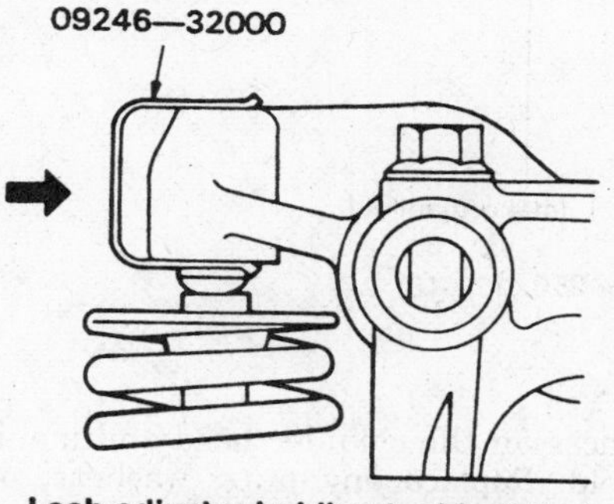

Lash adjuster holding tool installed

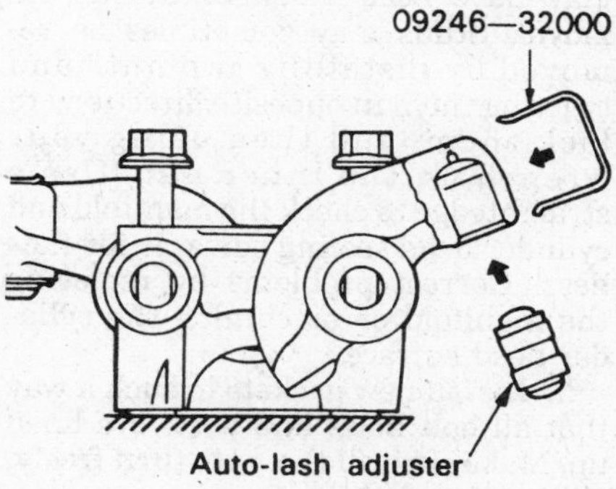

Lash adjuster installation

g. Check the operation of each lash adjuster by positioning the camshaft so that the rocker arm bears on the low, or round portion of the cam (pointed part of the can faces straight down). Insert a thin steel wire, or tool MD998442,in the hole in the top of the rocker arm, over the lash adjuster, and depress the check ball at the top of the adjuster. While holding the check ball depressed, move the arm up and down. Looseness should be felt. Full plunger stroke should be 2.2mm. If not, remove, clean and bleed the lash adjuster.

## BLEEDING THE LASH ADJUSTERS

If the lash adjuster is removed and the diesel fuel contained inside is spilled, submerge the adjuster in clean diesel fuel and compress it several times to expel the air. If air is still trapped after assembly and installation, and a clattering noise is heard when the engine is started, the air can be bled by increasing engine speed from idle to 3000 rpm and back to idle over a one minute period. Do this several times, or until the clattering stops. If this does not stop the clattering, remove and submerge the lifter in clean diesel fuel, compressing it several times. If clattering continues, replace the lash adjuster.

# Intake Manifold

## REMOVAL & INSTALLATION

**NOTE: The intake manifold is made from cast aluminum and should not be removed until the engine is cold!**

### *1468cc Engine*

1. Remove the air cleaner assembly.
2. Disconnect the fuel line and the EGR lines (models equipped with EGR) and tag and disconnect all vacuum hoses.
3. Disconnect the throttle positioner and fuel cut-off solenoid wires.

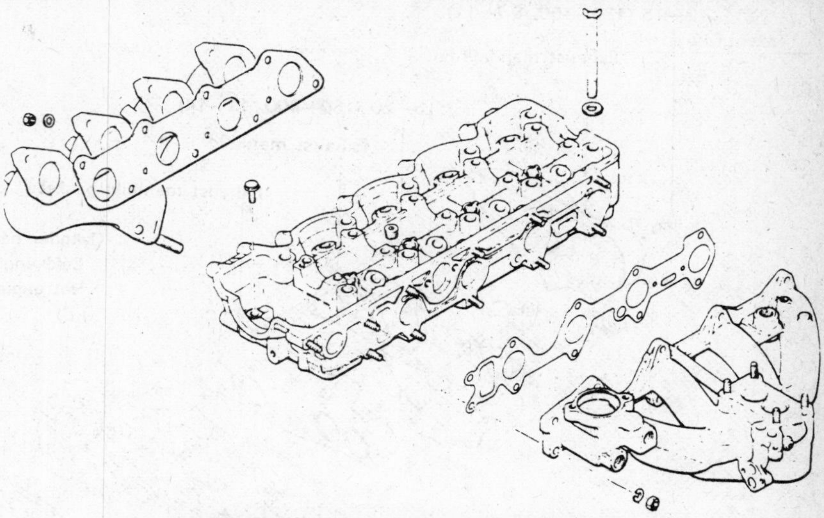
1468cc engine intake and exhaust manifolds

4. Disconnect the throttle linkage. On automatic transmission equipped cars, disconnect the shift cable linkage.
5. Disconnect the carburetor choke water hose at the manifold.
6. Disconnect the power brake booster vacuum line.
7. Drain the engine coolant.
8. Remove the water hose from the carburetor.
9. Remove the heater and water outlet hoses, disconnect the water temperature sending unit.
10. Remove the mounting nuts that hold the manifold to the cylinder head. Remove the intake manifold and carburetor as a unit.
11. Clean all mounting surfaces. Before installing the manifold, coat both sides of a new gasket with a gasket sealer.

**NOTE: If the engine is equipped with jet air system, take care not to get any sealer into the jet air intake passage!**

12. Install the intake manifold/carburetor assembly.
13. Reconnect the heater and water outlet hoses. Connect the water temperature sending unit.
14. Connect the brake booster vacuum line. Connect the choke hose at the manifold.
15. Connect the throttle and shift cable linkages, the fuel lines and all vacuum hoses. Install the air cleaner.
16. Refill the engine with coolant.

### *2351cc Engine*

1. Remove the air cleaner assembly.
2. Disconnect the fuel line (release fuel system pressure on before disconnecting any lines) and the EGR lines

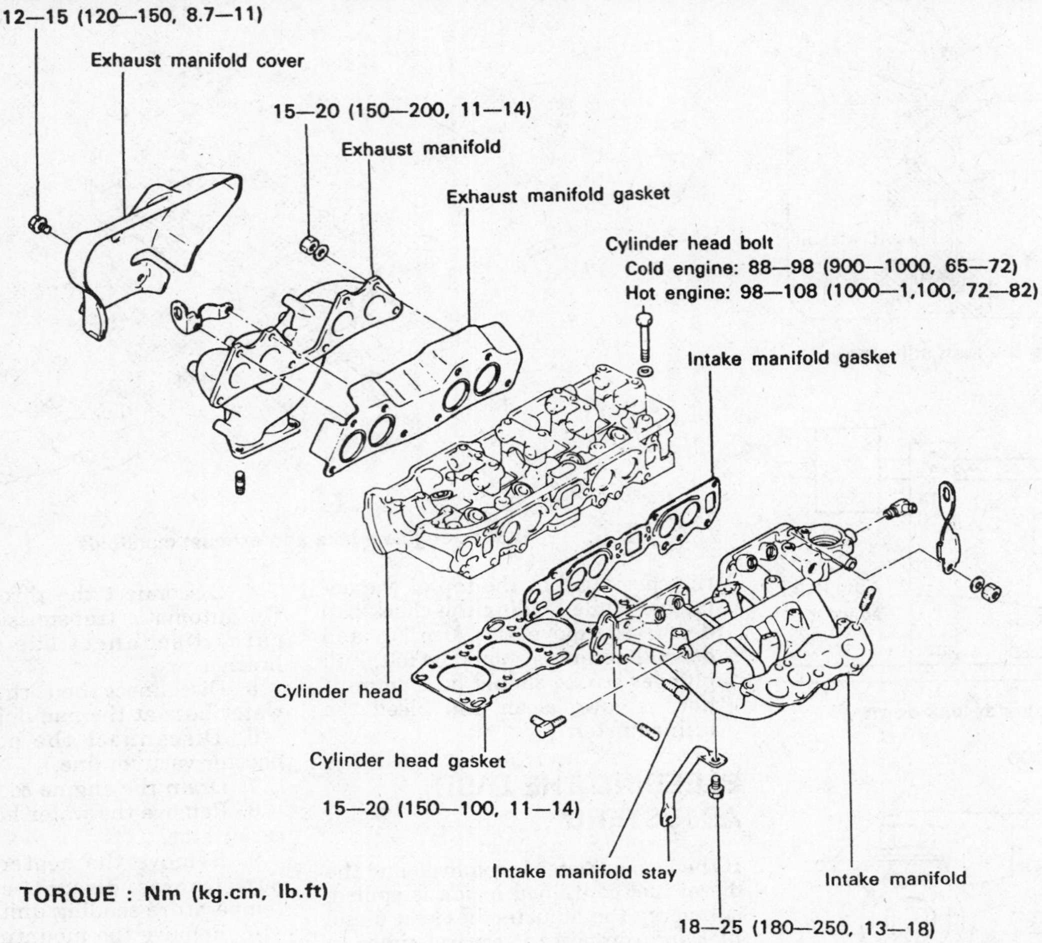


2351cc engine intake and exhaust manifolds

and tag and disconnect all vacuum hoses.

3. Disconnect the throttle positioner and fuel cut-off solenoid wires.

4. Disconnect the throttle linkage. On automatic transmission cars disconnect the shift cable linkage.

5. Drain the engine coolant and remove the water hose from the carburetor.

6. Remove the heater and water outlet hoses, disconnect the water temperature sending unit. Disconnect the oxygen sensor connecter, power transistor connecter, ISC connector, ignition coil connector, etc., and the distributor.

7. Remove the mounting nuts that hold the manifold to the cylinder head. Remove the intake manifold lower and upper sections with injector assembly as a unit.

8. Clean all mounting surfaces. Before installing the manifold, coat both sides with a gasket sealer.

**NOTE: If the engine is equipped with the jet air system, take care not to get any sealer into the jet air intake passage.**

## Exhaust Manifold

### REMOVAL & INSTALLATION

#### *1468cc Engine*

1. Remove the air cleaner. Remove the heat stove and/or heat shield on the exhaust manifold, if so equipped. With the manifold cool, soak all manifold nuts and studs with a liquid penetrant.

2. Disconnect the exhaust pipe at the exhaust manifold. Disconnect and remove the oxygen sensor. If there is a secondary air line connected to the exhaust manifold, disconnect that. First remove the exhaust pipe, then the secondary air supply pipe.

3. Now, support the manifold and re move all attaching nuts and washers. Slide the manifold from the cylinder head so you have enough room to remove the converter mounting bolts. When the converter is disconnected, remove the exhaust manifold, if necessary rock it to break it loose.

4. Thoroughly clean the sealing surfaces on the cylinder head and manifold. Replace any nuts, washers, or studs that are excessively rusted or may have been damaged during removal. Studs may sometimes be removed by installing two nuts and twisting them in opposite directions to lock them, and then using your wrench on the inner nut. Use a straightedge to check the manifold and cylinder head sealing surfaces for flatness. Correct problems by replacing the manifold or machining the cylinder head surface.

5. Install new gaskets in such a way that all bolt holes and ports are lined up. Make sure all the nuts turn freely, oiling them lightly if necessary. Also, make sure all the studs are screwed all the way into the block. Now, put the manifold in position and support it while you install all the washers and nuts hand tight. Refer to the "Torque Specifications Chart", and torque all the nuts to specification, alternately and in several stages. Install piping, heat stoves, and shields. Connect the exhaust pipe or primary catalytic converter.

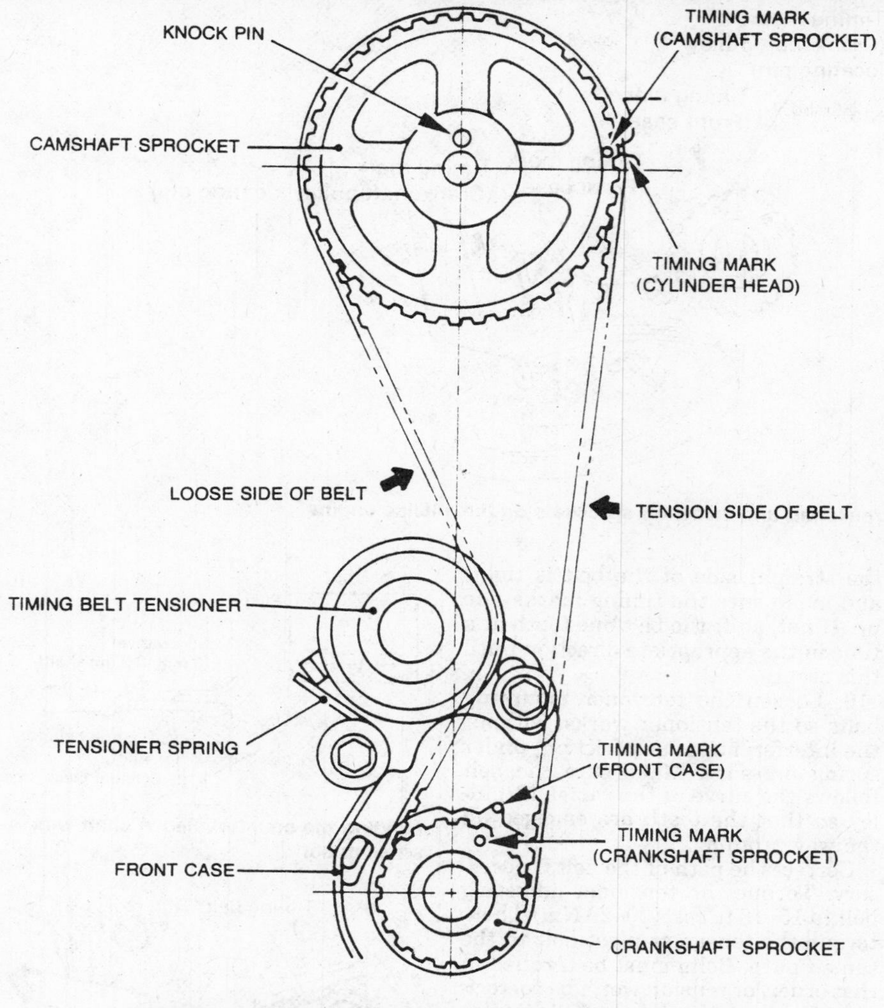

1468cc engine timing belt installation and timing mark alignment

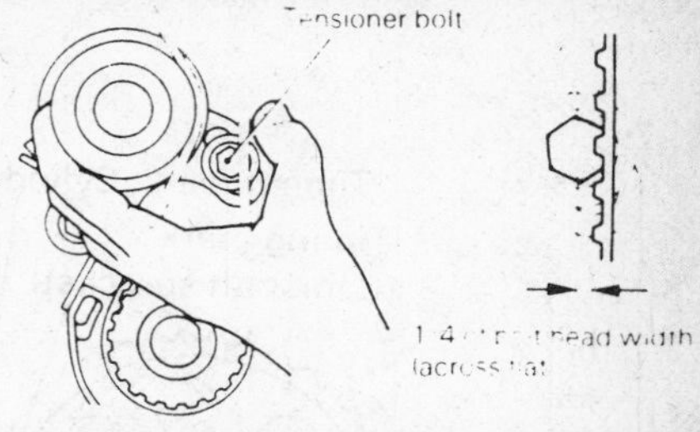

**Checking belt tension on the 1468cc engine**

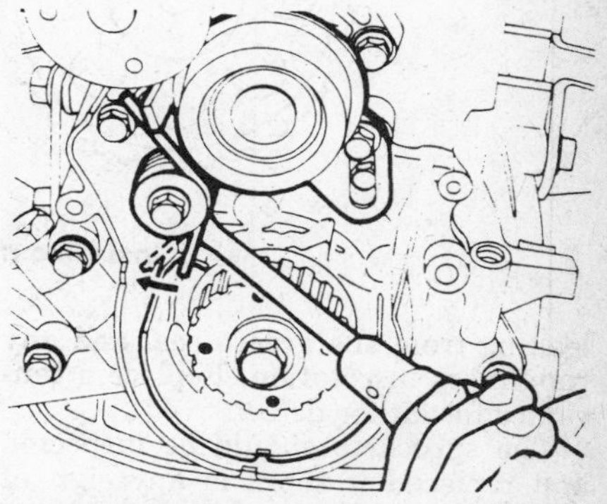
**Installing the belt tensioner spring on the 1468cc engine**

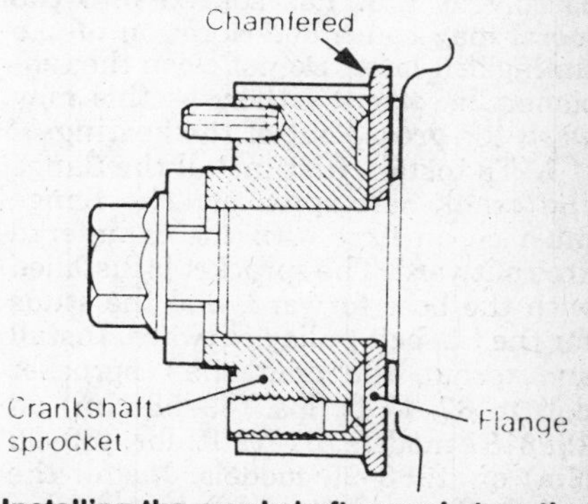

**Installing the crankshaft sprocket on the 1468cc engine**

6. Operate the engine and check for leaks.

### *2351cc Engine*

1. Remove the air cleaner assembly.
2. Disconnect any EGR or heat lines. Disconnect the reed valve (if equipped).
3. Remove the exhaust pipe support bracket from the engine block (if equipped).
4. Remove the exhaust pipe from exhaust manifold by removing the exhaust pipe flange nuts. It may be necessary to remove one nut or bolt from underneath the car. If the car is raised to perform this procedure, remember to support it on jackstands.
5. On models with a catalytic converter mounted between the exhaust manifold and exhaust pipe: first remove the exhaust pipe, then the secondary air supply pipe.
6. Remove the nuts mounting the exhaust manifold to the cylinder head. Slide the manifold from the cylinder hear so you have enough room to remove the converter mounting bolts. When the converter is disconnected, remove the exhaust manifold.
7. Install the exhaust manifold with new gaskets. New gaskets should be used, and on some engines, port liner gaskets are used.

# Timing Belt Cover, Sprockets, Tensioner and Timing Belt

## REMOVAL & INSTALLATION

### *1468cc Engine*

1. Remove the timing belt cover.
2. Turn the crankshaft until the timing marks on the camshaft sprocket and cylinder head are aligned. Loosen the tensioning bolt (it runs in the slotted portion of the tensioner) and the pivot bolt on the timing belt tensioner and lever the tensioner as far as it will go toward the water pump. Tighten the adjusting bolt. Mark the timing belt with an arrow showing direction of rotation if you may be reusing it.
3. Pull the timing belt off the camshaft sprocket. Remove the camshaft sprocket.
4. Remove the crankshaft pulley. Then, remove the timing belt.
5. Remove the crankshaft sprocket bolts and remove the crankshaft sprocket and flange, noting the direction of installation for each. Remove the timing belt tensioner.
6. Inspect the belt thoroughly. The back surface must be pliable and rough. If it is hard and glossy, the belt should be replaced. Any cracks in the belt backing or teeth or missing teeth mean the belt must be replaced. The canvas cover should be intact on all the teeth. If rubber is exposed anywhere, the belt should be replaced.

Inspect the tensioner for grease

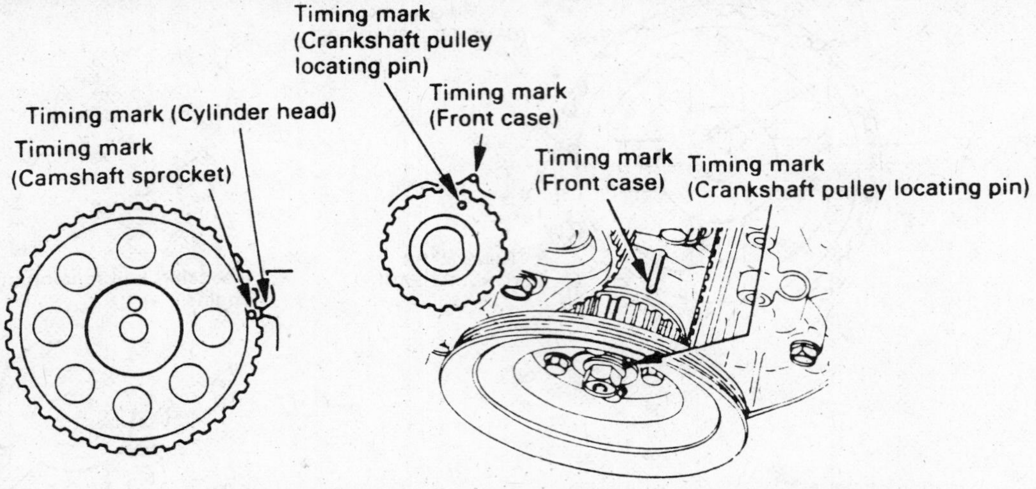


**Installing the crankshaft and camshaft sprockets on the 1468cc engine**

leaking from the grease seal and any roughness in rotation. Replace a tensioner for either defect.

The sprockets should be inspected and replaced if there is any sign of damaged teeth or cracking anywhere. Do not immerse sprockets in solvent, as solvent that has soaked into the metal may cause deterioration of the timing belt later. Do not clean the tensioner in solvent either, as this may wash the grease out of the bearing.

7. To install, first install the flange and crankshaft sprocket. The flange must go on first with the chamfered area outward. The sprocket is installed with the boss forward, and the studs for the fan belt pulley outward. Install and torque the crankshaft sprocket bolt to 37–43 ft. lbs. (49–58 Nm) on 1986–87 models; 51–72 ft. lbs. (69–98 Nm) on 1988–90 models. Install the camshaft sprocket and bolt, torquing it to 47–54 ft. lbs. (64–74 Nm).

8. Align the timing marks of the camshaft sprocket. Check that the crankshaft timing marks are still in alignment (the locating pin on the front of the crankshaft sprocket is lined up with a mark on the front case).

**To install:**

9. Mount the tensioner, spring, and spacer with the bottom end of the spring free. Then, install the bolts and tighten the adjusting bolt slightly with the tensioner moved as far as possible away from the water pump. Install the free end of the spring into the locating tang on the front case. Position the belt over the crankshaft sprocket and then over the camshaft sprocket. Make sure the belt is straight on the right side (where there's no tensioner as you do this. Slip the back of the belt over the tensioner wheel. Turn the camshaft sprocket in the opposite of its normal direction of rotation until the straight side of the belt is tight, and make sure the timing marks line up. If not, shift the belt one tooth at a time in the appropriate direction until this occurs.

10. Loosen the tensioner mounting bolts so the tensioner works, without the interference of any friction, under spring pressure. Make sure the belt follows the curve of the camshaft pulley so that the teeth are engaged all the way around.

Correct the path of the belt if necessary. Torque the tensioner adjusting bolt to 15–18 ft. lbs. (20–26 Nm).Then, torque the tensioner pivot bolt to the same figure. Bolts must be torqued in that order, or tension won't be correct.

11. Turn the crankshaft one turn clockwise until timing marks again line up to seat the belt. Then loosen both tensioner attaching bolts and let the tensioner position itself under spring tension as before. Finally, torque the bolts in the proper order exactly as before. Check belt tension by putting your fingers on the water pump side of the tensioner wheel and pull the belt toward it with your thumb. The belt should move toward the pump until the teeth are about ¼ of the way across the head of the tensioner adjusting bolt. Retension the belt if necessary.

12. Install the timing belt covers.

13. Install the crankshaft pulley, making sure the pin on the crankshaft sprocket fits through the hole in the rear surface of the pulley. Install the bolts and torque to 7.5–8.5 ft. lbs. (9–12 Nm).

### 2351cc Engine

**NOTE: An 8mm diameter metal bar is needed for this procedure.**

1. Remove the water pump drive belt and pulley.

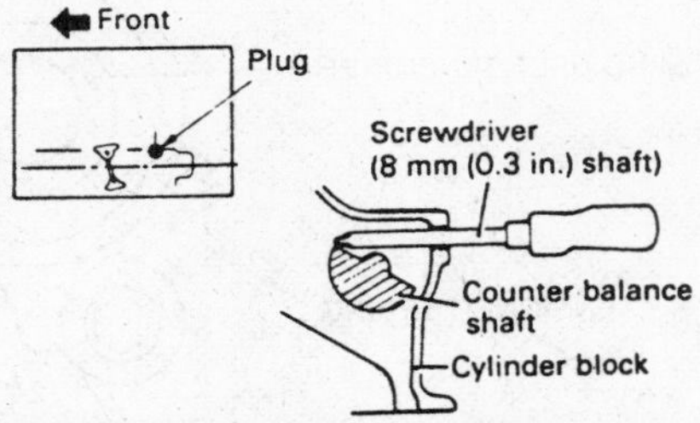


**Holding the counterbalance shaft with an 8mm bar**

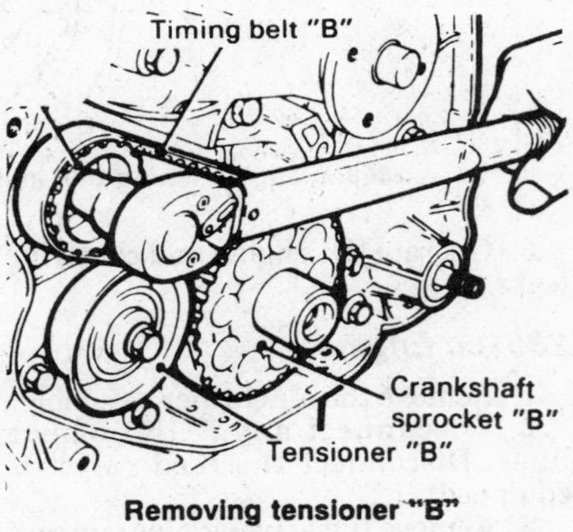


**Removing tensioner "B"**

2. Remove the crank adapter and crankshaft pulley.

3. Remove the upper and lower timing belt covers.

4. Move the tensioner fully in the direction of the water pump and temporarily secure it there.

5. If you are going to reuse the timing belt, make a paint mark on the belt to indicate the direction of rotation. Slip the belt from the sprockets.

**NOTE: Place the belt in an area where it will not be contacted by oil or other petroleum distillates.**

6. Remove the camshaft sprocket bolt and pull the sprocket from the camshaft.

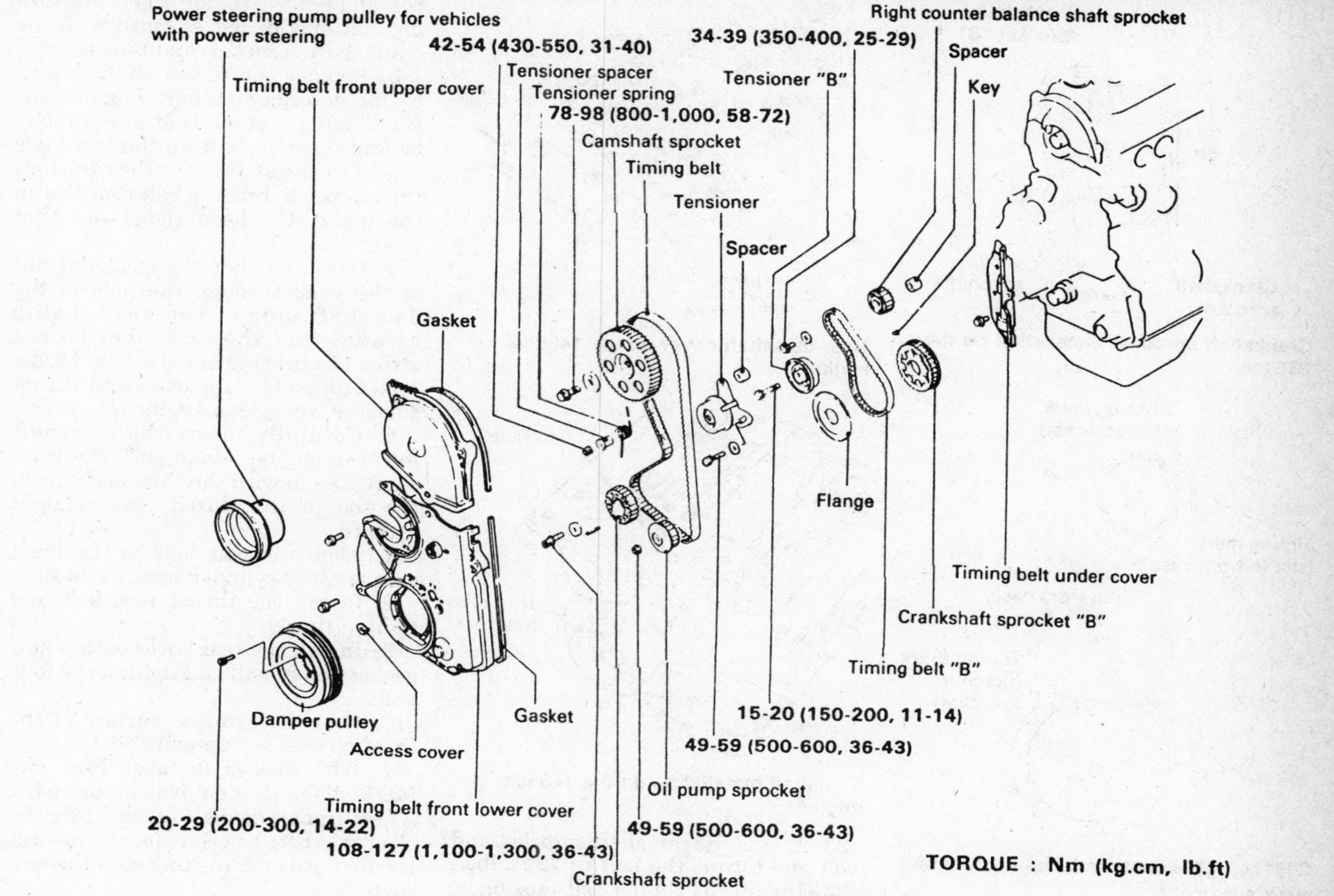


**2351cc timing belt, cover and related components**

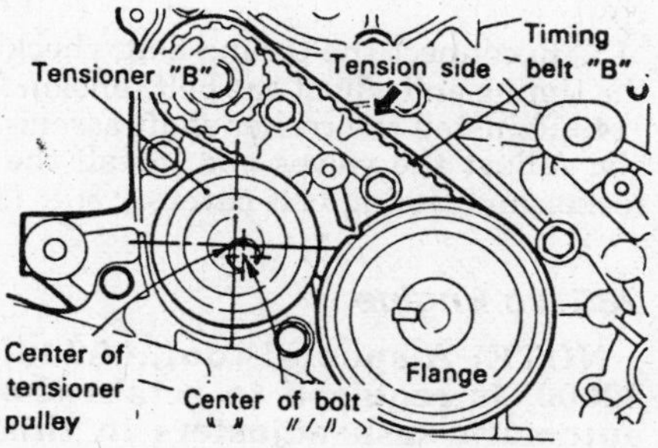


**Checking timing belt tension on the 2351cc**

7. Remove the crankshaft sprocket bolt and pull the crankshaft sprocket and flange from the crankshaft.
8. Remove the plug on the left side the block and insert an 8mm diameter metal bar in the opening to keep the silent shaft in position.
9. Remove the oil pump sprocket retaining nut and remove the oil pump sprocket.
10. Loosen the right silent shaft sprocket mounting bolt until it can be turned by hand.
11. Remove the silent shaft belt tensioner, and slip the silent shaft belt off its sprockets.

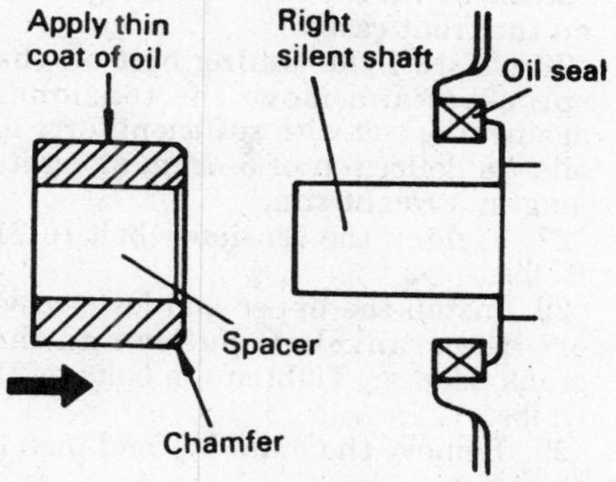


**2351cc right counterbalance shaft seal installation**

**NOTE: Do not attempt to turn the silent shaft sprocket or loosen its bolt while the belt is off.**

12. Remove the silent shaft belt sprocket from the crankshaft.
13. Check the belt for wear, damage or glossing. Replace it if any cracks, damage, brittleness or excessive wear are found.
14. Check the tensioners for a smooth rate of movement.
15. Replace any tensioner that shows

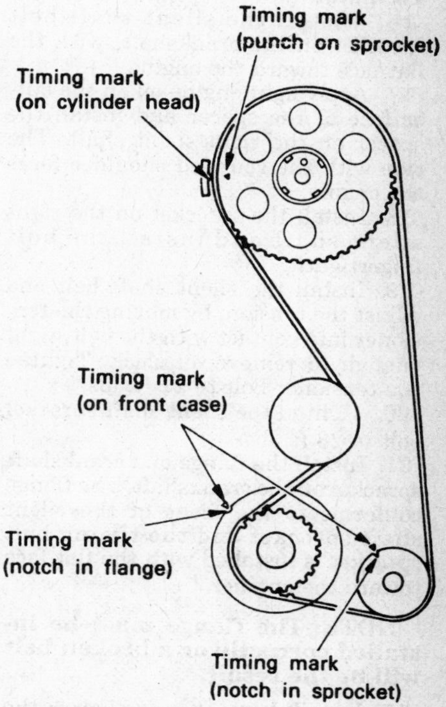


**2351cc timing belt installation**

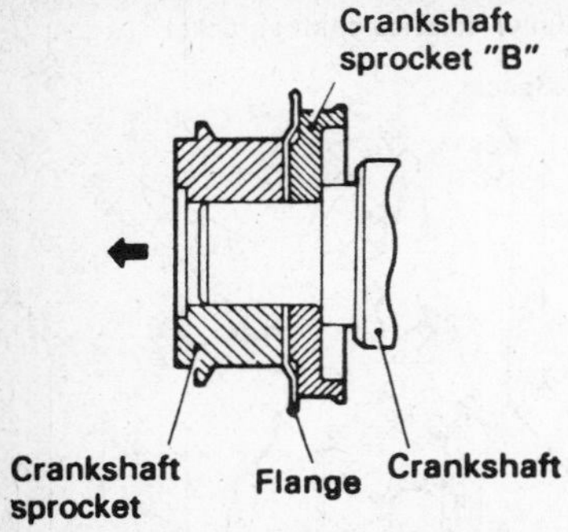


**Crankshaft sprocket installation on the 2351cc**

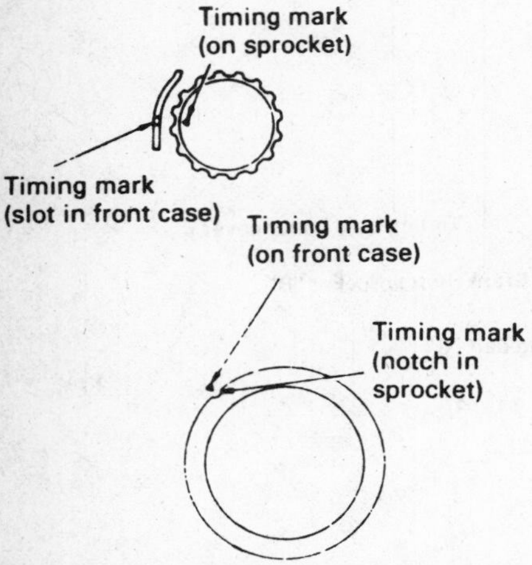


**2351cc right counterbalance shaft timing mark alignment**

grease leakage through the seal.

**To install:**

16. Install the silent shaft belt sprocket on the crankshaft, with the flat face toward the engine.

17. Apply light engine oil on the outer face of the spacer and install the spacer on the right silent shaft. The side with the rounded shoulder faces the engine.

18. Install the sprocket on the right silent shaft and install the bolt fingertight.

19. Install the silent shaft belt and adjust the tension, by moving the tensioner into contact with the belt, tight enough to remove all slack. Tighten the tensioner bolt to 21 ft. lbs.

20. Tighten the silent shaft sprocket bolt to 28 ft. lbs.

21. Install the flange and crankshaft sprocket on the crankshaft. The flange conforms to the front of the silent shaft sprocket and the timing belt sprocket is installed with the flat face toward the engine.

**NOTE: The flange must be installed correctly or a broken belt will be the result.**

22. Install the washer and bolt in the crankshaft and torque it to 94 ft. lbs.

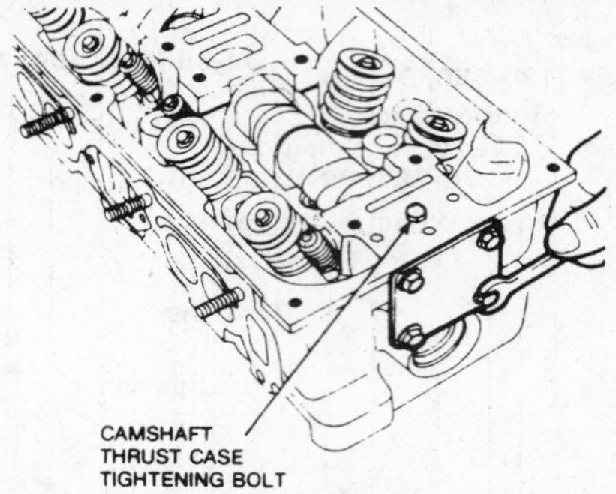


**Rear camshaft cover on the 1468cc engine**

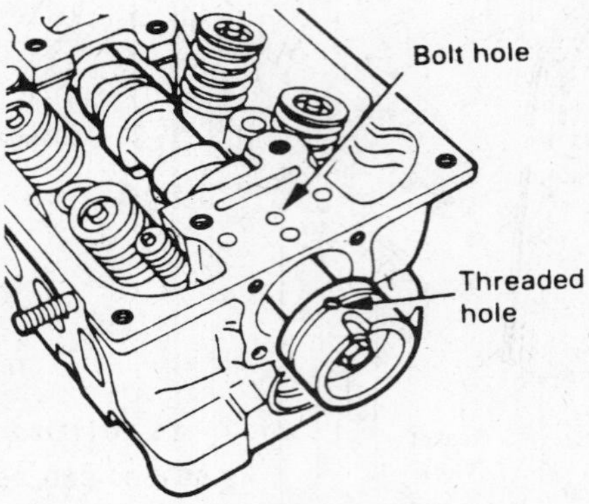


**Camshaft installation on the 1468cc engine**

23. Install the camshaft sprocket and bolt and torque the bolt to 72 ft. lbs.

24. Install the timing belt tensioner, spacer and spring.

25. Align the timing mark on each sprocket with the corresponding mark on the front case.

26. Install the timing belt on the sprockets and move the tensioner against the belt with sufficient force to allow a deflection of 5–7mm along its longest straight run.

27. Tighten the tensioner bolt to 21 ft. lbs.

28. Install the upper and lower covers, the crankshaft pulley and the crank adapter. Tighten the bolts to 21 ft. lbs.

29. Remove the 8mm bar and install the plug.

# Camshaft

## REMOVAL & INSTALLATION

### *1468cc Engine*

1. Remove the rocker cover. Remove the timing belt cover. Remove the distributor.

2. Loosen the two bolts and move the timing belt tensioner toward the water pump as far as it will go, then retighten the timing belt tensioner adjusting bolt. Disengage the timing belt from the camshaft sprocket and unbolt and remove the sprocket. The timing belt may be left engaged with the crankshaft sprocket, and tensioner.

3. Remove the rocker shaft assembly as described earlier. Remove the small, square cover that sits directly behind the camshaft on the transaxle side of the head. Remove the camshaft thrust case tightening bolt that sits on the top of the head right near that cover.

4. Carefully slide the camshaft out of the head through the hole in the camshaft side of the head, being carefull that the cam lobes do not strike the bearing bores in the head.

5. Lubricate all journal and thrust surfaces with clean engine oil.

6. Carefully insert the camshaft into the engine. Make sure the camshaft goes in with the threaded hole in the top of the thrust case straight upward.

7. Align the bolt hole in the trust case and the cylinder head surface.

8. Install the thrust case bolt and tighten firmly.

9. Install the rear cover with a new gasket and install and tighten the four bolts.

10. Coat the external surface of the front oil seal with engine oil.

11. With special installer Part No. MD 998306-01 or equivalent, drive the a new front camshaft oil seal into the clearance between the cam and head at the forward end, making sure the seal seats fully.

12. Install the camshaft sprocket and torque the bolt to 47–54 ft. lbs. (64–74 Nm)

13. Reconnect the timing belt, check the timing and adjust the belt tension.

14. Reinstall the rocker shaft assembly. Adjust the valves and install the rocker and timing belt covers.

### *2351cc Engine*

**NOTE: A special tool, 09246-32000, is required to retain the automatic lash adjusters in this procedure.**

1. Remove the rocker cover and gasket, and the timing belt cover.

2. Remove the timing belt and camshaft sprocket as described above.

3. Turn the crankshaft so that the No. 1 piston is at TDC compression. At this point, the timing mark on the camshaft sprocket and the timing mark on the head to the left of the sprocket will be aligned.

4. Remove the camshaft bearing cap bolts.

5. Install the automatic lash adjuster retainer tool, 09246-32000, to keep the adjuster from falling out of the rocker arms.

6. Lift off the bearing caps and

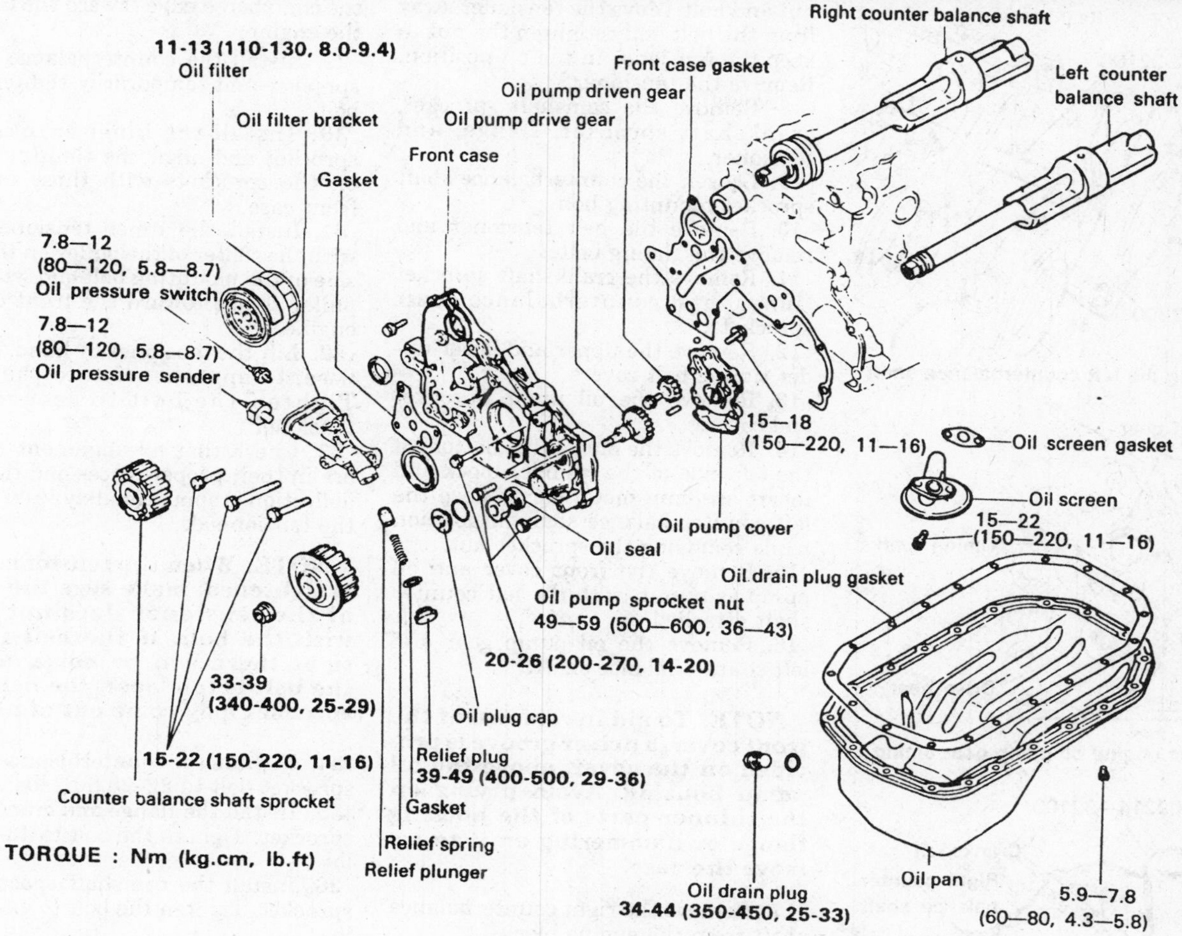


**2351cc engine front case and related components**

rocker arm assemblies.

7. Lift out the camshaft.

**NOTE: Keep all parts in the order in which they were removed. None of the parts are interchangeable! The lash adjusters are filled with diesel fuel, which will spill out if they are inverted. If any diesel fuel is spilled, the adjusters must be bled. The bleeding procedure can be found earlier in this section.**

8. Check all parts for wear or damage. Replace any damaged or excessively worn part.

9. Coat the camshaft with clean engine oil andplace it on the head.

10. Assemble all parts. Note the following:

a. The rocker shafts are installed with the notches in the ends facing up.

b. The left rocker shaft is longer than the right.

c. The wave washers are installed on the left shaft.

d. Coat all parts with clean engine oil prior to assembly.

e. Insert the lash adjuster from under the rocker arm and install the special holding tool. If any of the diesel fuel is spilled, the adjuster must be bled.

f. Tighten the bearing cap bolts, working from the center towards the ends, to 15 ft. lbs.

g. Check the operation of each lash adjuster by positioning the camshaft so that the rocker arm bears on the low, or round portion of the cam (pointed part of the can faces straight down). Insert a thin steel wire, or tool MD998442,in the hole in the top of the rocker arm, over the lash adjuster, and depress the check ball at the top of the adjuster. While holding the check ball depressed, move the arm up and down. Looseness should be felt. Full plunger stroke should be 2.2mm. If not, remove, clean and bleed the lash adjusters as described above.

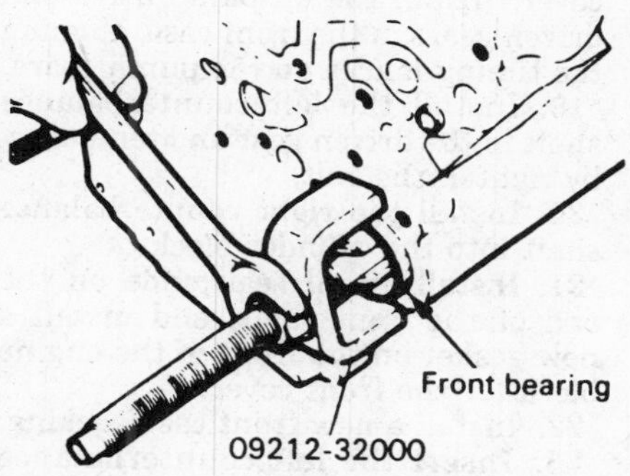


**Removing the right counterbalance shaft**

## Counterbalance Shafts

### REMOVAL & INSTALLATION

#### *2351cc Engine Only*

1. Disconnect the battery ground cable.

2. Remove the alternator and accessory belts. Remove the belt cover.

3. Rotate the crankshaft to bring No. 1 piston to TDC on the compression stroke. Align the notch on the crankshaft pulley with the T mark on the timing indicator scale and the timing mark on the upper under cover of the timing belt with the mark on the camshaft sprocket.

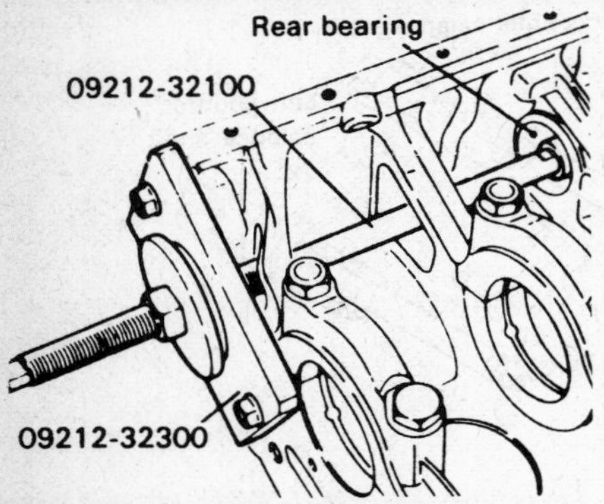


**Removing the left counterbalance shaft**

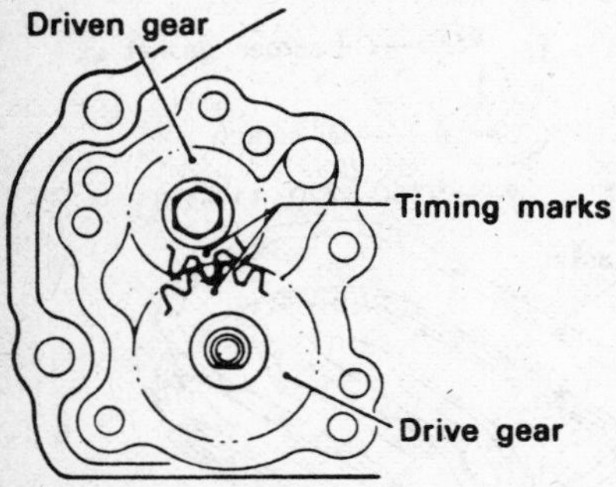


**2351cc engine oil pump gear timing**

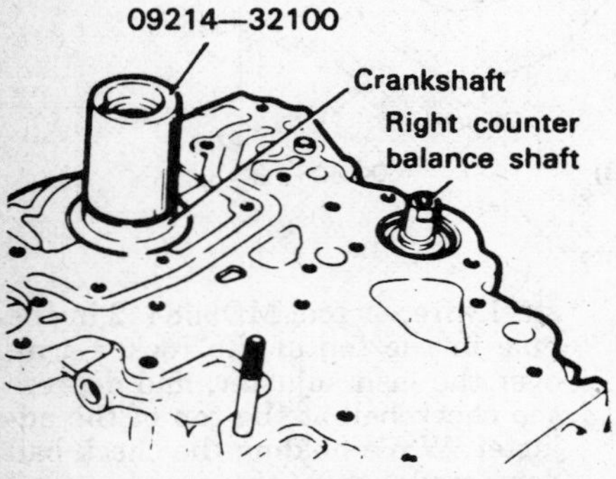


**2351cc engine timing case oil seal guide tool**

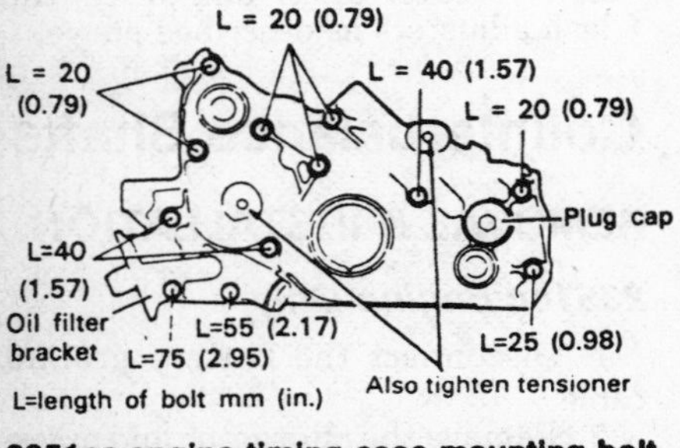


**2351cc engine timing case mounting bolt positioning**

4. Remove the crankshaft pulley and bolt.
5. Remove the timing belt covers, upper front and lower front.
6. Remove the crankshaft sprocket bolt.
7. Loosen the tensioner mounting nut and bolt. Move the tensioner away from the belt and retighten the nut to keep the tensioner in the off position. Remove the tensioner.
8. Remove the camshaft sprocket, crankshaft sprocket, flange, and tensioner.
9. Loosen the counterbalance shaft sprocket mounting bolt.
10. Remove the belt tensioner and remove the timing belt.
11. Remove the crankshaft sprocket (inner) and counterbalance shaft sprocket.
12. Remove the upper and lower under timing belt covers.
13. Remove the oil pump sprocket and cover.
14. Remove the plug at the bottom of the left side of the cylinder block and insert an 8mm metal bar to keep the left counter balance shaft in position while removing the sprocket nut.
15. Remove the front cover and oil pump as a unit, with the left counter shaft attached.
16. Remove the oil pump gear and left counterbalance shaft.

**NOTE: To aid in removal of the front cover, a driver groove is provided on the cover, above the oil pump housing. Avoid prying on the thinner parts of the housing flange or hammering on it to remove the case.**

17. Remove the right counterbalance shaft from the engine block.

**To install:**

18. Install a new front seal in the cover. Install the oil pump drive and driven gears in the front case, aligning the timing marks on the pump gears.
19. Install the left counterbalance shaft in the driven gear and temporarily tighten the bolt.
20. Install the right counterbalance shaft into the cylinder block.
21. Install an oil seal guide on the end of the crankshaft, and install a new gasket on the front of the engine block for the front cover.
22. Install a new front case packing.
23. Insert the left counterbalance shaft into the engine block and at the same time, guide the front cover into place on the front of the engine block.
24. Insert an 8mm metal bar at the bottom of the left side of the block and hold the left counterbalance shaft and tighten the bolt. Install the hole plug.
25. Install an O-ring on the oil pump cover and install it on the front cover.
26. Tighten the oil pump cover bolts and the front cover bolts to 11 to 13 ft. lbs.
27. Install the upper and lower under covers.
28. Install the spacer on the end of the right counterbalance shaft, with the chambered edge toward the rear of the engine.
29. Install the counterbalance shaft sprocket and temporarily tighten the bolt.
30. Install the inner crankshaft sprocket and align the timing marks on the sprockets with those on the front case.
31. Install the inner tensioner (B) with the center of the pulley on the left side of the mounting bolt and with the pulley flange toward the front of the engine.
32. Lift the tensioner by hand, clockwise, to apply tension to the belt. Tighten the bolt to secure the tensioner.
33. Check that all alignment marks are in their proper places and the belt deflection is approximately ¼-½ in. on the tension side.

**NOTE: When the tensioner bolt is tightened, make sure the shaft of the tensioner does not turn with the bolt. If the belt is too tight there will be noise, and if the belt is too loose, the belt and sprocket may come out of mesh!**

34. Tighten the counterbalance shaft sprocket bolt to 22–28.5 ft. lbs.
35. Install the flange and crankshaft sprocket. Tighten the bolt to 43–50 ft. lbs.
36. Install the camshaft spacer and sprocket. Tighten the bolt to 44–57 ft. lbs.
37. Align the camshaft sprocket timing mark with the timing mark on the upper inner cover.
38. Install the oil pump sprocket, tightening the nut to 25–28 ft. lbs. Align the timing mark on the sprocket with the mark on the case.

**NOTE: To be assured that the phasing of the oil pump sprocket and the left counterbalance shaft is correct, a screwdriver or a metal rod should be inserted in the plugged hole on the left side of the cylinder block. If it can be inserted more than 60mm, the phasing is correct. If the tool can only be inserted approximately 25mm, turn the oil pump sprocket through one turn and realign the timing marks. Keep the screwdriver or metal rod inserted until the installation of the timing belt is completed. Remove the tool from the hole and install the plug, before starting the engine.**

39. Install the tensioner spring and tensioner. Temporarily tighten the nut. Install the front end of the tensioner spring (bent at right angles) on the projection of the tensioner and the

other end (straight) on the water pump body.

40. If the timing belt is correctly tensioned, there should be about 12mm clearance between the outside of the belt and the edge of the belt cover. This is measured about halfway down the side of the belt opposite the tensioner.

41. Complete the assembly by installing the upper and lower front covers.

42. Install the crankshaft pulley, alternator, and accessory belts, and adjust to specifications.

43. Install the radiator, fill the cooling system, and start the engine.

## Pistons and Connecting Rods

### POSITIONING

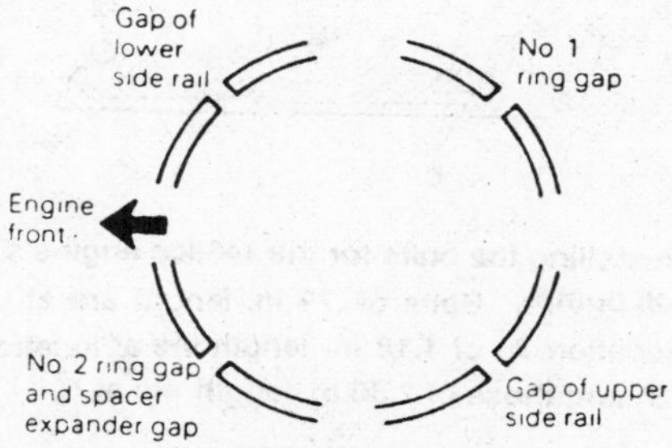


Piston ring positioning

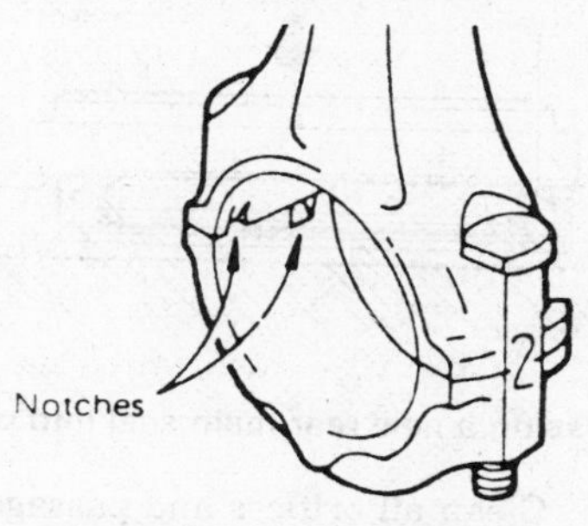


Connecting rod cap installation

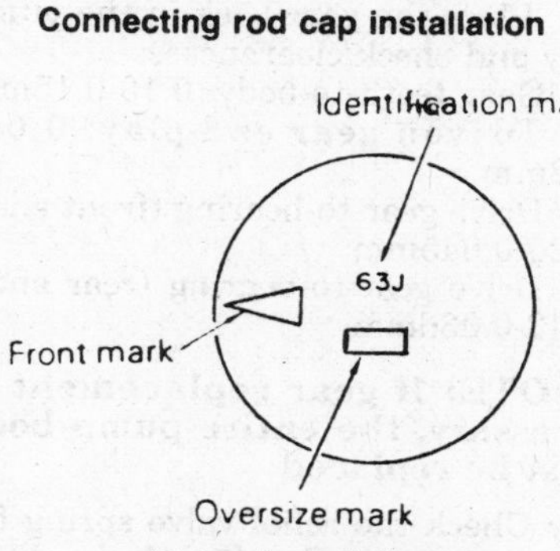


Piston installation

**For all piston and connecting rod overhaul procedures, please refer to "Engine Rebuilding" in the Unit Repair section.**

Rods and caps should be installed in numbered order. If the pistons and rods were assembled properly in the piston pin installation procedure the arrows on the piston tops will face the crankshaft pulley as will the markings on the sides of the rods. Numbers stamped on the sides of rods and caps should be on the same side; if necessary, proper positioning of the cap on the rod can be checked during assembly by making sure the two bearing notches (one on rod and one on cap) are on the same side.

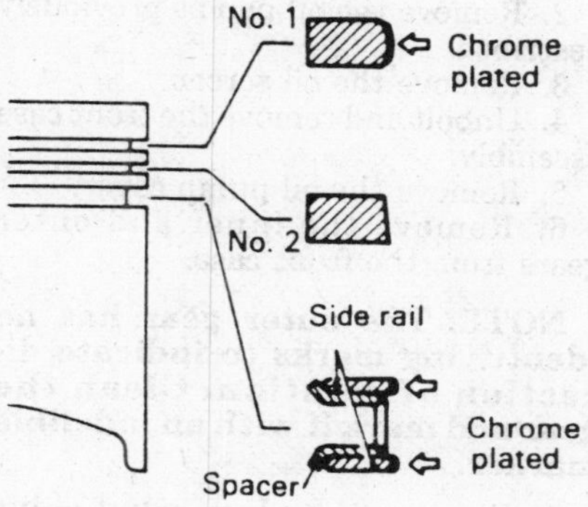


Piston ring installation

# ENGINE LUBRICATION

## Oil Pan

### REMOVAL & INSTALLATION

#### *1468cc Engine*

1. Jack up the front of the car and support it on stands.

1. Front case gasket
2. Oil pump cover
3. Oil pump outer gear
4. Oil pump inner gear
5. Plug
6. Gasket
7. Relief spring
8. Relief plunger
9. Front oil seal
10. Front case
11. Drain plug
12. Oil pan
13. Oil screen
14. Oil screen gasket

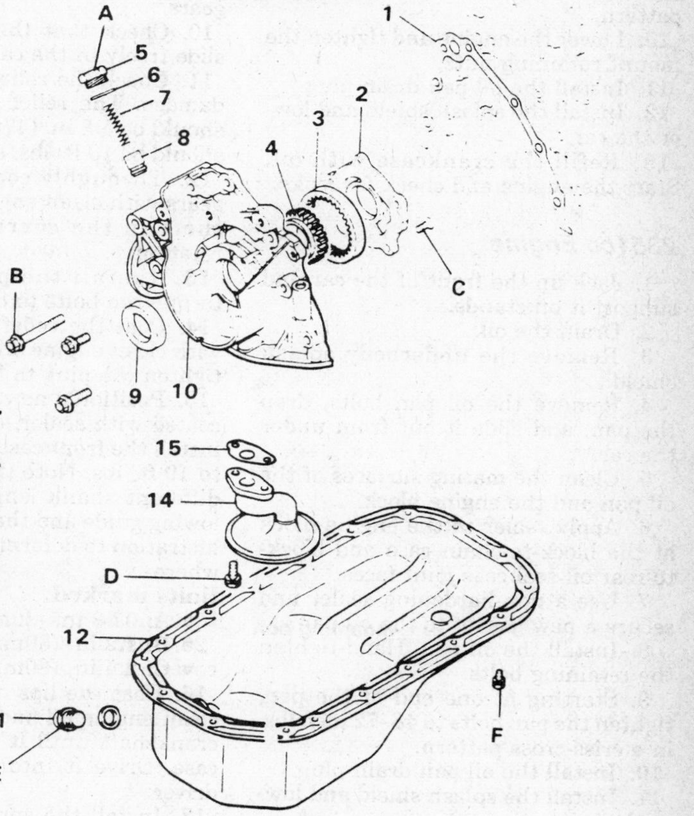


| | Nm |
|---|---|
| A | 40–49 |
| B | 12–14 |
| C | 8–9 |
| D | 18–24 |
| E | 35–44 |
| F | 6–7 |

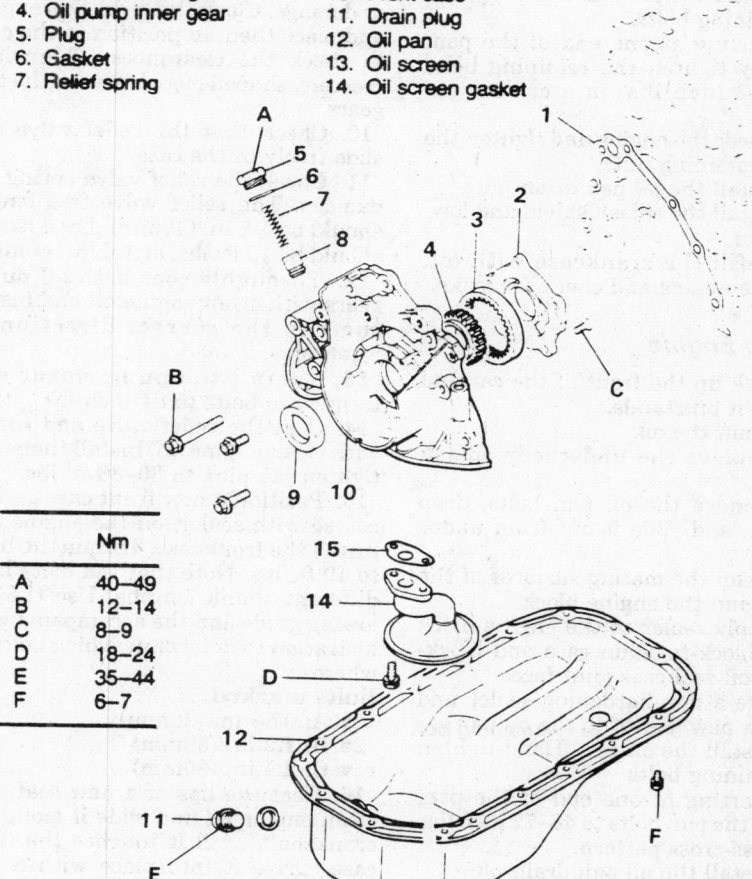

1468cc engine oil pan and front case

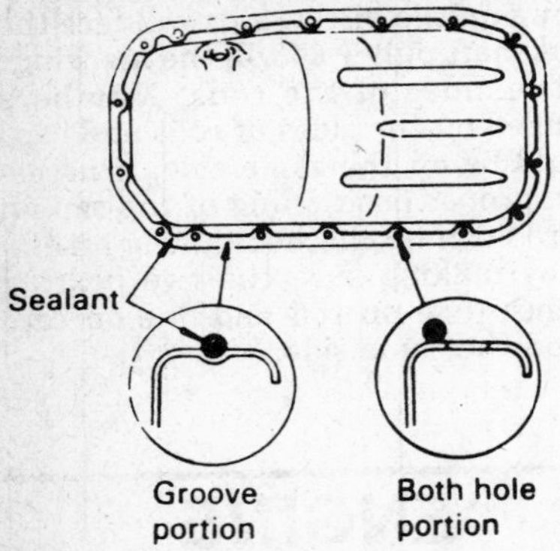


**Application guide for the formed-in-place gasket on the 2351cc engine oil pan**

2. Drain the oil.
3. Remove the underbody splash shield.
4. Remove the oil pan bolts, drop the pan, and slide it out from under the car.
5. Clean the mating surfaces of the oil pan and the engine block.
6. Apply a ⅛ in. (3mm) bead of RTV sealer along the groove in the oil pan.
7. Using non-hardening sealer, glue a new gasket to the oil pan.
8. Install the oil pan. Hand tighten the retaining bolts.
9. Starting at one end of the pan, gradually tighten the retaining bolts to 48–72 inch lbs. in a criss-cross pattern.
10. Lower the engine and tighten the mount retaining nuts.
11. Install the oil pan drain plug.
12. Install the splash shield and lower the car.
13. Refill the crankcase with oil. Start the engine and check for leaks.

### *2351cc Engine*

1. Jack up the front of the car and support it on stands.
2. Drain the oil.
3. Remove the underbody splash shield.
4. Remove the oil pan bolts, drop the pan, and slide it out from under the car.
5. Clean the mating surfaces of the oil pan and the engine block.
6. Apply sealer to the engine block at the block-to-chain case and block-to-rear oil seal case joint faces.
7. Use a non-hardening sealer and secure a new gasket to the oil pan.
8. Install the oil pan. Hand-tighten the retaining bolts.
9. Starting at one end of the pan, tighten the pan bolts to 48–72 inch lbs. in a criss-cross pattern.
10. Install the oil pan drain plug.
11. Install the splash shield and lower the car.
12. Fill the crankcase with the proper amount of oil. Start the engine and check for leaks.

# Oil Pump

## REMOVAL & INSTALLATION

### *1468cc Engine*

1. Remove the timing belt as previously described.
2. Remove the oil pan as previously described.
3. Remove the oil screen.
4. Unbolt and remove the front case assembly.
5. Remove the oil pump cover.
6. Remove the inner and outer gears from the front case.

**NOTE: The outer gear has no identifying marks to indicate direction of rotation. Clean the gear and mark it with an indelible marker.**

7. Remove the plug, relief valve spring and relief valve from the case.
8. Check the front case for damage or cracks. Replace the front seal. Replace the oil screen O-ring. Clean all parts thoroughly with a safe solvent.
9. Check the pump gears for wear or damage. Clean the gears thoroughly and place them in position in the case to check the clearances. There is a crescent-shaped piece between the two gears.
10. Check that the relief valve can slide freely in the case.
11. Check the relief valve spring for damage. The relief valve free length should be 1.8 in. (47mm). Load length should be 10 ft. lbs. at 1.6 in. (40mm).
12. Throughly coat both oil pump gears with clean engine oil and install them in the correct direction of rotation.
13. Install the pump cover and torque the bolts to 84 inch lbs.
14. Coat the relief valve and spring with clean engine oil, install them and tighten the plug to 30–36 ft. lbs.
15. Position a new front case gasket, coated with sealer, on the engine and install the front case. Torque the bolts to 10 ft. lbs. Note that the bolts have different shank lengths. Use the following guide and the accompanying illustration to determine which bolts go where.

**Bolts marked**

- A: 0.08 in. (20mm)
- B: 1.2 in. (30mm)
- C: 2.4 in. (60mm)

16. Coat the lips of a new seal with clean engine oil and slide it along the crankshaft until it touches the front case. Drive it into place with a seal driver.
17. Install the sprocket, timing belt and pulley.
18. Install the oil screen.
19. Thoroughly clean both the oil pan and engine mating surfaces. Apply a 3mm (⅛ in.) wide bead of RTV sealer in the groove of the oil pan mating surface.

**NOTE: You have only 15 minutes before the sealer sets!**

20. Tighten the oil pan bolts to 60–72 inch lbs.

### *2351cc Engine*

1. Remove the timing belt.
2. Remove the oil pump cover and gears.
3. Remove the relief valve plug, spring and plunger.
4. Thoroughly clean all parts in a safe solvent and check for wear and damage.

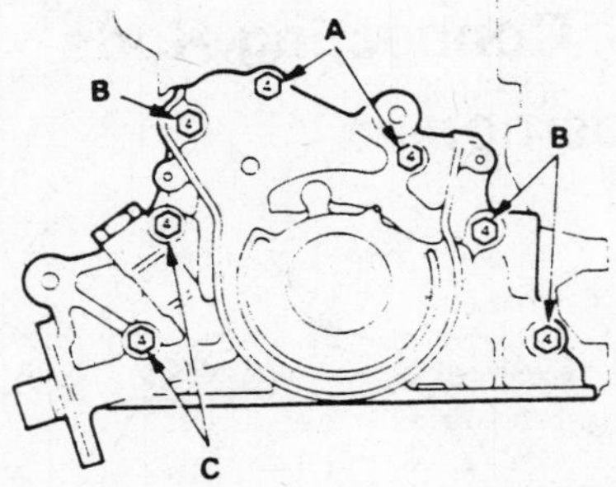


**Installing the bolts for the 1468cc engine's oil pump. Bolts of .79 in. length are at location A; of 1.18 in. length are at location B; and those of 2.36 in. length are at C.**

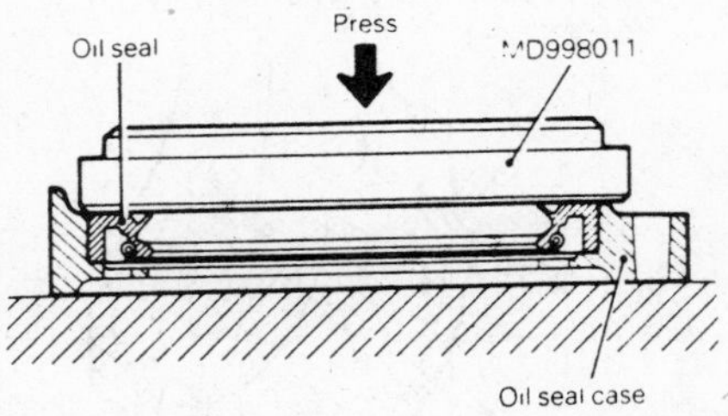


**Pressing a new rear main seal into place**

5. Clean all orifices and passages.
6. Place the gear back in the pump body and check clearances.

- Gear teeth-to-body: 0.10-0.15mm
- Driven gear end play: 0.06-0.12mm
- Drive gear-to-bearing (front end): 0.020-0.045mm
- Drive gear-to-bearing (rear end): 0.043-0.066mm

**NOTE: If gear replacement is necessary, the entire pump body must be replaced.**

7. Check the relief valve spring for wear or damage. Free length should be

47mm; load/length should be 9.5 lb @ 40mm.

8. Assembly the pump components. Make sure that the gears are installed with the mating marks aligned.

9. Install the timing belt.

## Rear Main Bearing Oil Seal

### REMOVAL & INSTALLATION

**NOTE: The rear main seal is located in a housing on the rear of the block. To replace the seal, it is necessary to remove the transmission and perform the work from underneath the car or remove the engine and perform the work on an engine stand.**

1. Unscrew the retaining bolts and remove the housing from the cylinder block.
2. Remove the separator from the housing.
3. Using a small pry bar, pry out the old seal.
4. Clean the housing and the separator.
5. Lightly oil the replacement seal. Tap the seal into the housing using a canister top or other circular piece of metal. The oil seal should be installed so that the seal plate fits into the inner contact surface of the seal case.
6. Install the separator into the housing so that the oil hole faces down.
7. Oil the lips of the seal and install the housing on the rear of the engine block.

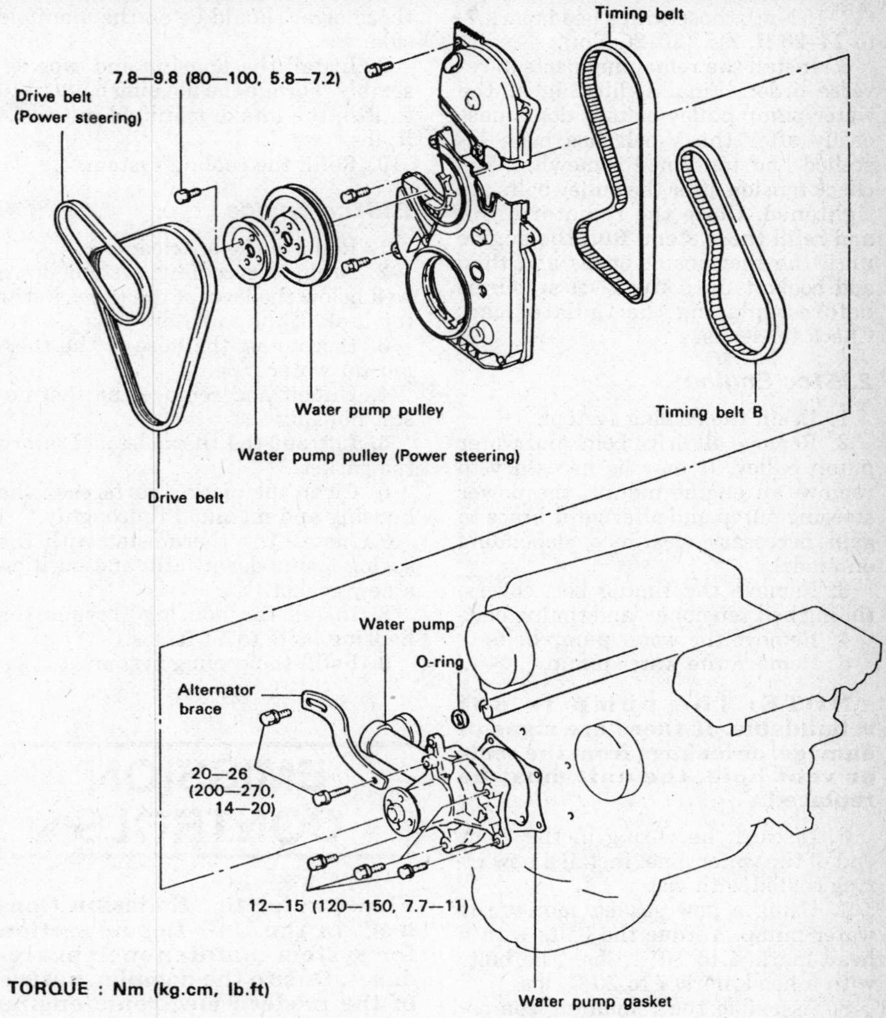


**2351cc engine water pump installation**

# ENGINE COOLING

## Radiator

### REMOVAL & INSTALLATION

1. Remove the splash shield from under the car.
2. Drain the radiator.
3. Remove the fan shroud and disconnect the fan motor wiring harness.
4. Disconnect the radiator hoses and, if equipped, the automatic transmission cooler hoses.
5. Disconnect the expansion tank hose.
6. Remove the radiator mounting bolts and lift out the radiator and fan assembly. The fan and motor may be left attached to the radiator and removed with the radiator as one unit.

**To install:**

7. Install the radiator. Tighten the retaining bolts gradually in a criss--cross pattern.
8. Connect the expansion tank hose, the radiator hoses and the automatic transmission oil cooler lines.
9. Install the fan shroud and connect the fan wiring.
10. Install the splash shield and refill the engine with coolant.

## Water Pump

### REMOVAL & INSTALLATION

#### *1468cc Engine*

1. Loosen the 4 bolts attaching the water pump pulley to the pulley flange. Loosen the alternator mounting bolts, slide the alternator toward the engine and remove the belt. Remove the radiator cap, open the drain cock at the bottom of the radiator, and drain the coolant from the radiator into a clean container.
2. Remove the timing belt covers, timing belt and tensioner.
3. Remove the water pump mounting bolts, noting the 3 different lengths and locations. Remove the pump and gasket, disconnecting the outlet at the water pipe (don't lose the O-ring).
4. Clean gasket surfaces and coat a new gasket with sealer. Then, position the gasket on the front of the block with all bolt holes lined up. Replace the O-ring for the outlet water pipe.
5. Install the pump connecting the outlet water pipe. Install the bolts with the shortest at the bottom; two just slightly longer at the one and four o'clock positions on the right side of the pump; next-to-longest bolt at the eight o'clock position just under the outlet; and the longest bolt at the eleven o'clock position and also attaching the alternator brace. Torque the bolts with a head mark, **4**, to 9–11 ft. lbs.

(12–15 Nm); those with a head mark **7**, to 14–20 ft. lbs. (20–26 Nm).

6. Install the remaining parts in reverse order. Final tightening of the water pump pulley bolts is done most easily after the V-belt has been installed and tensioned somewhat. Recheck tension after the pulley bolts are tightened. Close the radiator drain and refill the system. Run the engine until the thermostat opens and then add coolant until the level stabilizes before replacing the radiator cap. Check for leaks.

### 2351cc Engine

1. Drain the cooling system.
2. Remove all drive belts and water pump pulley. It may be necessary to remove an engine mount, the power steering pump and alternator brace to gain necessary clearance, depending on model.
3. Remove the timing belt covers, timing belt tensioner, and timing belt.
4. Remove the water pump bolts.
5. Remove the water pump.

**NOTE: The pump is not rebuildable. If there are signs of damage, or leakage from the seals or vent hole, the unit must be replaced.**

6. Discard the O-ring in the front end of the water pipe. Install a new O-ring coated with water.
7. Using a new gasket, mount the water pump. Torque the bolts with a head mark **4** to 10 ft. lbs.: the bolts with a head mark **7** to 20 ft. lbs.
8. Assemble the remaining components, install the timing belt according to the previous instructions. Fill the system with a 50% mix of antifreeze.

## Thermostat

### REMOVAL & INSTALLATION

### 1468cc Engine

1. To replace the unit, remove the air cleaner and then drain the cooling system down well below the level of the tubes in the top tank of the radiator.
2. Remove the air cleaner.
3. Disconnect the hose at the thermostat water pipe.
4. Remove the water pipe support bracket nut.
5. Unbolt and remove the thermostat housing and pipe.
6. Lift out the thermostat. Discard the gasket.
7. Clean the mating surfaces of the housing and manifold thoroughly.
8. Install the thermostat with the spring facing downward, and position a new gasket. The jiggle valve in the thermostat should be on the manifold side.
9. Install the housing and pipe assembly. Torque the housing bolts to 10 ft. lbs.; the intake manifold nut to 14 ft. lbs.
10. Refill the cooling system.

### 2351cc Engine

1. Remove the air cleaner.
2. Drain the cooling system down well below the level of the tubes in the top tank of the radiator.
3. Disconnect the hose at the thermostat water pipe.
4. Unbolt and remove the thermostat housing.
5. Lift out the thermostat. Discard the gasket.
6. Clean the mating surfaces of the housing and manifold thoroughly.
7. Install the thermostat with the spring facing downward, and position a new gasket.
8. Install the housing. Torque the housing bolts to 14 ft. lbs.
9. Refill the cooling system.

# EMISSION CONTROLS

**Please refer to "Emission Control" in the Unit Repair section for system maintenance procedures. Due to the complex nature of the modern electronic engine control systems, comprehensive diagnosis and testing procedures fall outside the confines of this repair manual. For complete information on diagnosis, testing and repair procedures concerning all modern engine and emission control systems, please refer to "Chilton's Guide to Electronic Engine Controls".**

# FUEL SYSTEM

## Fuel Filter

### REMOVAL & INSTALLATION

### 1468cc Engine

The fuel filter is of the inline type. The filter is located at low center of the firewall.

**NOTE: Remove the fuel tank cap to release pressure in the fuel lines.**

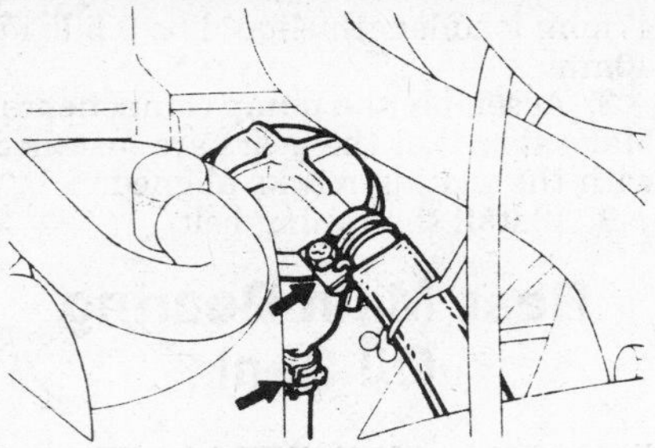

Fuel filter

1. Turn off the engine and allow it to cool. Loosen the screws in the fuel line clamps (at the filter) and then, using a pair of pliers, force open the clamps on the fuel lines and back them well away from the connections.
2. Work the fuel lines back and off the filter connections. If they are difficult to remove, it may help to pull them off with a twisting motion. Remove the filter from its mounting clip.
3. Inspect the fuel lines for cracks or breaks and replace them if necessary.
4. Install the new filter in the same position the old one was in in the clamp. Connect the inlet fuel line to the inlet fitting on the bottom of the filter. Connect the outlet to the outlet fitting on top. Make sure the hoses are fully installed over the bulged-out portions of the fittings. Then, with pliers, move the clamps over the filter fittings so they are beyond the bulged-out sections of the fittings but a small distance away from the ends of the hoses.

### 2351cc Engine

On models equipped with fuel injection, relieve fuel system pressure before replacing the filter. An electric fuel pump is used on these models and the filter is in the engine compartment. A connector, for checking the fuel function, is located under the battery tray. With the engine running, disconnect the connector, when the engine stops no pressure will remain in the system.

To remove the filter, loosen the hose clamps at both ends of the filter or unscrew the fittings and remove the fuel lines from the filter ends. Unclip the filter from the mounting bracket. Install a new filter. Start the engine and check for leaks. If a clogged filter is suspected, remove the filter and blow compressed air through the inlet and outlet fittings, reinstall the filter. Replace the old filter as soon as possible

## Mechanical Fuel Pump

### REMOVAL & INSTALLATION

The mechanical fuel pump operates di-

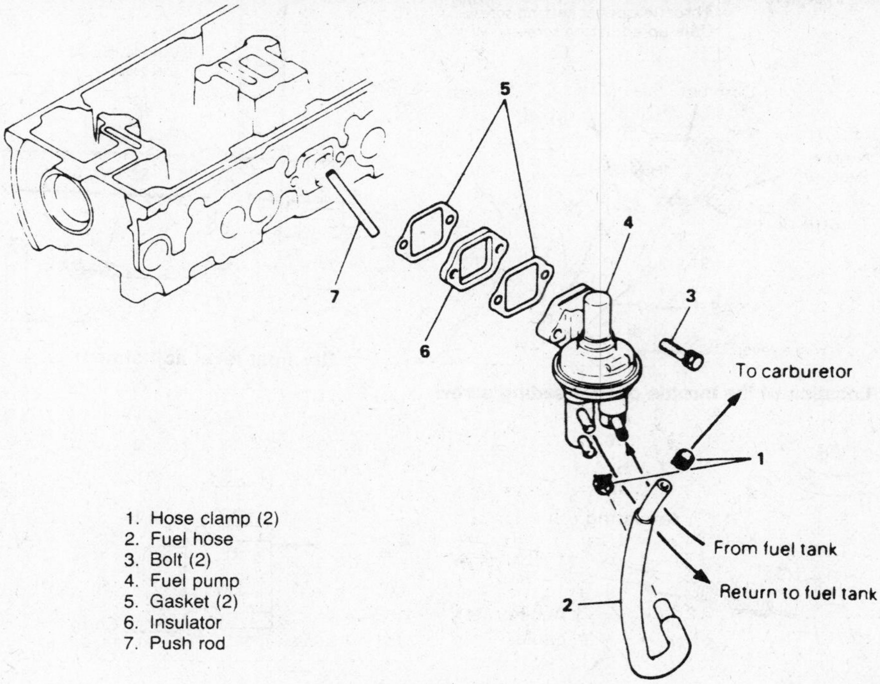


1. Hose clamp (2)
2. Fuel hose
3. Bolt (2)
4. Fuel pump
5. Gasket (2)
6. Insulator
7. Push rod

**Mechanical fuel pump**

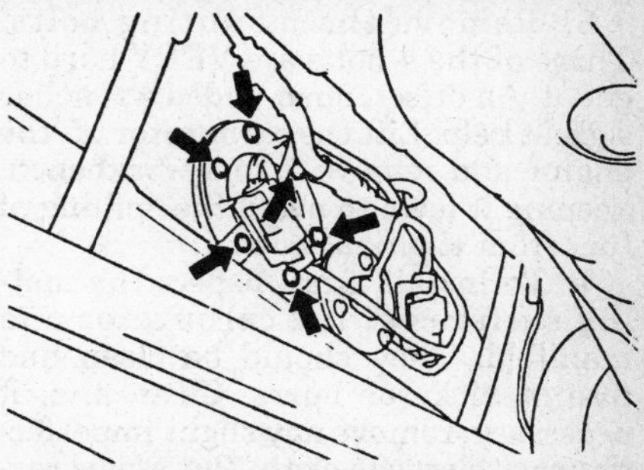

**Electric fuel pump attaching screws**

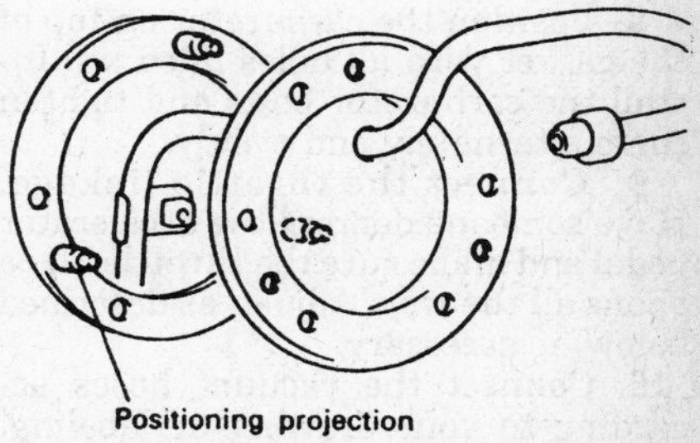


**During electric fuel pump installation, make sure that positioning studs on the packing collar are properly positioned**

rectly off of a camshaft eccentric. A fuel return valve is located in the upper body of the pump. If the fuel temperature rises above 122°F (50°C), the valve opens and routes fuel back to the tank, preventing percolation.

1. Disconnect the negative battery cable. Remove the 2 screws and remove the plastic heat shield.
2. Disconnect the three fuel pump lines.
3. Unscrew the two retaining nuts and remove the fuel pump and pushrod.
4. Remove the gasket, insulator, and gasket.
5. Clean the fuel pump.
6. Apply non-hardening sealer to both sides of the gaskets. Position a gasket, the insulator and the other gasket on the head studs.
7. Set the No. 1 piston at TDC of the compression stroke and insert the pushrod into the head. Install the pump and torque the nuts to 25 ft. lbs.

## TESTING

1. Disconnect the inlet line (coming from the filter) at the pump.
2. Connect a vacuum gauge to the pump nipple.
3. Remove the high tension cable at the coil. Then, have someone crank the engine as you watch the gauge.
4. A vacuum of 2.7–3.7 psi should be produced. If there is blowback of pressure, the inlet valve on the pump is leaking and the unit must be replaced.

# Electric Fuel Pump

All fuel injected cars are equipped with an electric fuel pump. The fuel pump is in the gas tank.

## TESTING

If the fuel pump doesn't work:

1. Check the fuse.
2. Check all wiring connections.
3. Check the control relay which is located in the engine compartment, next to the ignition coil. If the engine starts when the ignition switch is turned to **START** but stops when it is turned to **ON**, the relay is defective. Jumper terminals 1 and 2 of the test connecter, the fuel pump should operate. If the pump fails to operate when the the jumper is connected, the pump is probably defective.

## REMOVAL & INSTALLATION

**CAUTION**

***The electric fuel pump supplies fuel under high pressure. The system pressure must be relieved before servicing the fuel system. Working around gasoline is extremely dangerous unless precautions are taken! NEVER smoke! Make sure the electrical system is disconnected. Avoid prolonged contact of gasoline with the skin. Wear safety glasses. Avoid prolonged breathing of gasoline vapors.***

1. Reduce pressure in the fuel lines as follows:
   a. Disconnect the fuel pump harness connect at the fuel tank.
   b. Start the engine and let it run until. It will shut off by itself.
   c. Turn the ignition switch to **OFF**.
   d. Disconnect the battery ground cable.
2. Remove the fuel tank.
3. Disconnect the hoses at the pump.
4. Unbolt and remove the pump.
5. Install the new pump. Use a new gasket. Connect the fuel lines, inline connector and battery cable.

# Carburetor

## REMOVAL & INSTALLATION

### *USA Models*

1. Disconnect the negative battery connector. Drain the coolant down to below the level of the intake manifold.
2. Remove the air cleaner. Disconnect the throttle cable at the carburetor.
3. Make a drawing to show vacuum hose locations or label each vacuum hose, and then disconnect them all.
4. Disconnect the connectors for the solenoid valves and the Throttle Position Sensor (TPS).
5. Place a pan of some sort under the fuel connections and then disconnect them. Remove the container, avoiding the spilling of fuel.

6. Remove the mounting bolts. Three of the 4 bolts are VERY hard to get at. An offset, open-ended wrench is a great help. Lift the carburetor off the engine and remove it to a workbench, keeping it level to avoid the spilling of fuel from the float bowl.

7. To install, first inspect the mating surfaces of the carburetor and manifold. They should be clean and free of nicks or burrs. Clean and, if necessary, remove any slight imperfections with crocus cloth. Put a new carburetor gasket on the surface of the manifold.

8. Position the carburetor on top of the gasket with all holes lined up. Install the carburetor bolts and tighten them alternately and evenly.

9. Connect the throttle linkage. Have someone depress the accelerator pedal and make sure the throttle blade opens all the way. Adjust, as described below, if necessary.

10. Connect the vacuum hoses according to your drawing or labeling. Make sure all are soft and free of cracks to make a good seal. Replace hoses that are hard and cracked. Reconnect the fuel hoses.

11. Install the remaining parts in reverse order. To start the engine, merely set the choke in the usual way and operate the starter. Don't attempt to prime the engine by pouring gas into the carburetor inlet. Check for leaks with the engine running.

### *Canadian Models*

1. Disconnect the battery ground cable.
2. Drain the coolant to a level just below the intake manifold.
3. Remove the air cleaner.
4. Disconnect the wiring from the fuel cutoff solenoid.
5. Disconnect the accelerator rod and, on cars equipped with automatic transmissions, the shift rod.
6. Tag and disconnect the vacuum hoses from the carburetor.
7. Place suitable rags or a container under the fuel inlet and return hoses to catch any leaking fuel, and disconnect the hoses.
8. Disconnect the water hose which runs between the carburetor and the cylinder head.
9. Unscrew the 4 retaining nuts and remove the carburetor. Hold the carburetor level to avoid an unwanted fuel spill.
10. Mount the carburetor on the intake manifold and attach the choke water hose.
11. Reconnect the fuel lines and vacuum hoses to the carburetor.
12. Connect the accelerator or shift rod.
13. Reconnect the fuel cut-off solenoid and replace the air cleaner.
14. Refill the system with coolant.

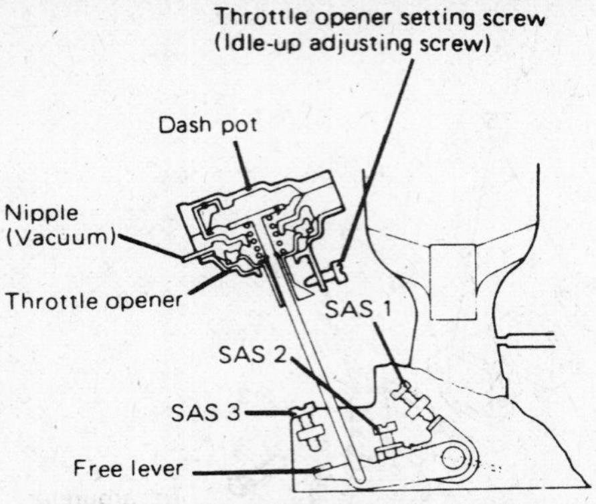

**Location of the throttle opener setting screw**

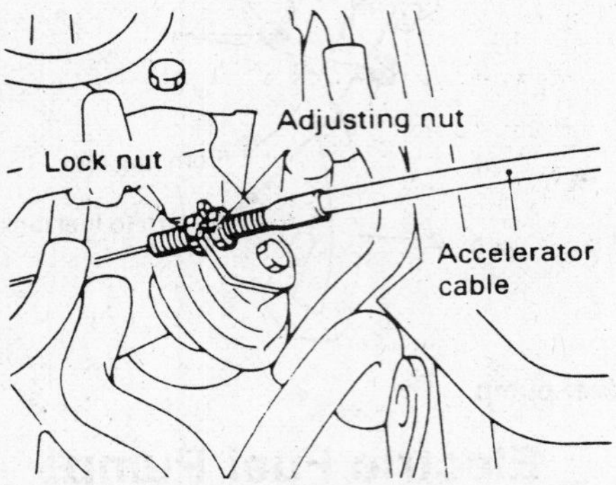

**Adjusting the accelerator cable free play**

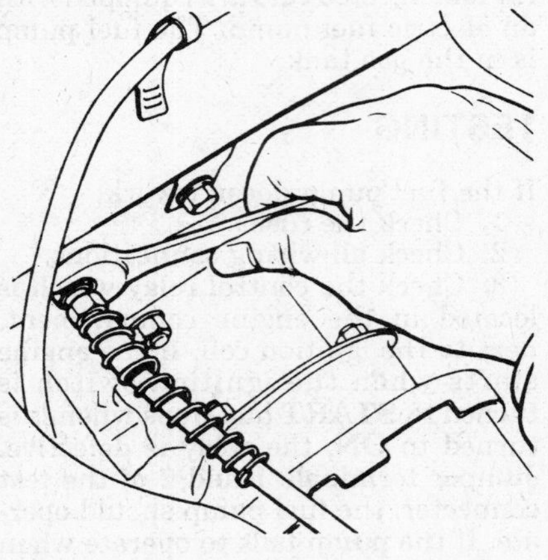
**Accelerator cable adjustment**

## THROTTLE LINKAGE ADJUSTMENT

1. Run the engine to operating temperature and allow it to idle at curb idle speed.
2. There should be no slack in the exposed part of the throttle cable near the carburetor.
3. Make sure that there are no sharp bends in the cable.
4. Loosen the cable adjusting nut lock nut and turn the adjusting nut until the throttle just starts to open.

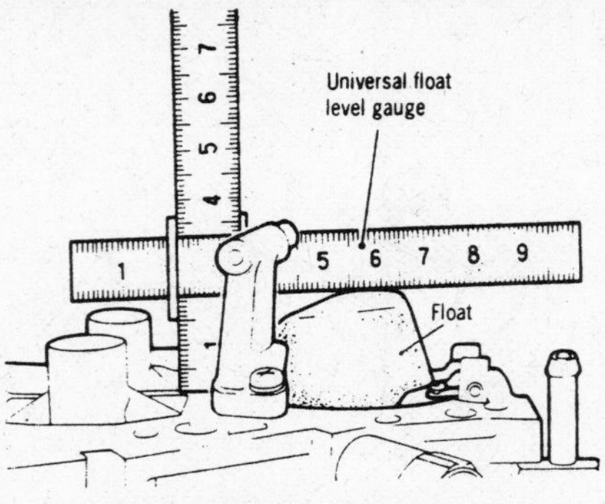

**Dry float level adjustment**

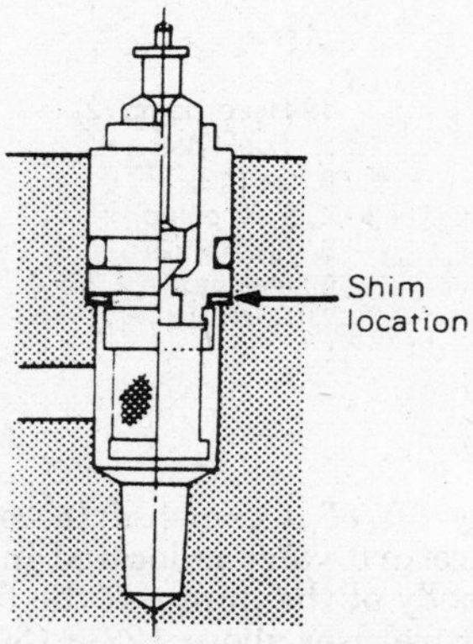

**Float needle seat shim location**

5. Back off the adjusting nut one full turn and lock it with the locknut.

## ACCELERATOR CABLE ADJUSTMENT

1. The engine must be hot so the fast idle cam will not interfere with throttle position; warm it if necessary.
2. Inspect the inner cable to see if there is slack. If there is no slack, the adjustment is ok. If there is slack, loosen the adjusting nuts until the throttle is free to assume idle position with no effect by the accelerator cable.
3. Make sure there are no sharp bends in the cable. Then, turn the adjusting nut that's farther away from the carburetor until you can see the throttle start to move; now, back the nut off one turn. Secure the locknut.

## FLOAT LEVEL ADJUSTMENT

A sight glass is fitted in the float chamber and the fuel level can be checked without disassembling the carburetor. Normal fuel level is within the level mark on the sight glass.

1. Invert the float chamber cover and remove the gasket. Use a float level gauge or depth gauge to measure the distance between what is normally the

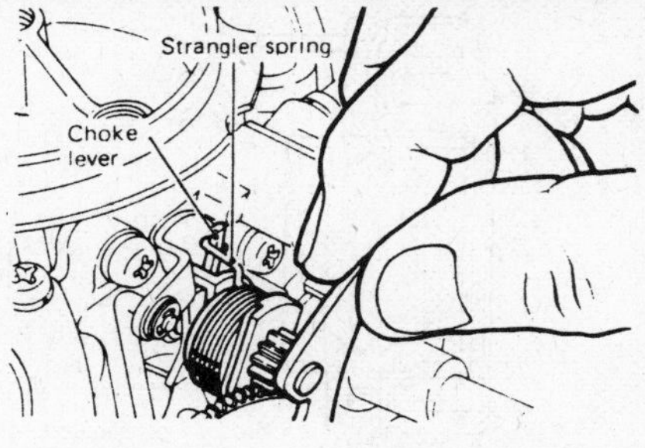

Removing the choke bracket bridge

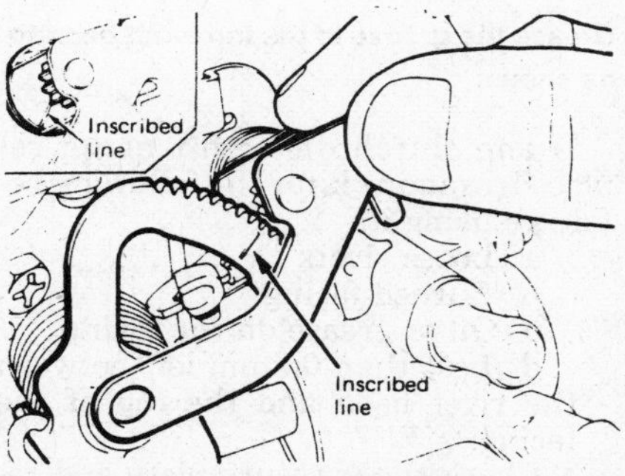

Aligning the choke gear and cam mating marks

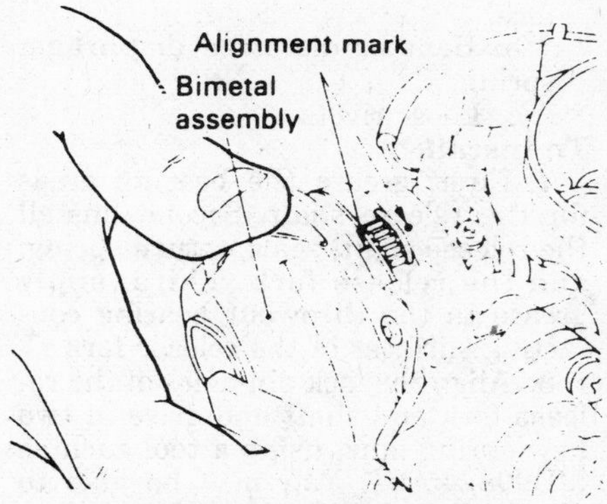

Adjusting the automatic choke

bottom of the float (the top surface in this position) and what is normally the lower surface of the float chamber cover. This dimension must be 0.79–0.82 in. (21–22mm).

2. If the dimension is not to specification, the shim under the needle seat must be changed. Use a thicker seat to raise the dimension (lower the float level). You can use a Hyundai shim kit or equivalent. The kit contains shims of 0.3mm, 0.4mm, and 0.5mm. The change in float level will be three times the change in shim thickness. You can use multiple shims if that is what is necessary to get the right dimension.

3. To change the shim, first pull out the float hinge pin. Then, remove the float and the needle. Finally, use a pair of pliers to unscrew the needle seat by the widest dimensioned area of the seat. Slip the shim(s) over the narrow portion of the seat and then reinstall it, tightening it gently by the same portion of the assembly. Reassemble the needle, float, and hinge pin and retest the dimension. Reshim if necessary.

## FUEL LEVEL ADJUSTMENT

The fuel level adjustment is corrected by increasing or decreasing the number of needle valve packings between the valve and top cover.

## FAST IDLE ADJUSTMENT

1. Run the engine until it reaches normal operating temperature. All accessories should be turned off. Place the transmission in **N** (manual transmission) or **P** (automatic transmission).
2. Disconnect the vacuum hose at the choke opener.
3. Set the lever on the second highest step of the fast idle cam.
4. Start the engine and check the fast idle speed:
   - Manual transmission – 2800 rpm
   - Automatic transmission – 2700 rpm
5. Adjust the fast idle speed by turning the screw clockwise to increase the speed or counterclockwise to decrease it.
6. Reconnect the vacuum hose at the choke opener.

## AUTOMATIC CHOKE ADJUSTMENT

### *Feedback Carburetors USA Models*

1. Remove the air cleaner.
2. Remove the choke cover.

**NOTE: Some cars might have headless screws securing the cover. These screws will have to be drilled out. To do this, you should remove the carburetor.**

3. Remove the bracket bridging the choke spring gear and the choke actuating cam.
4. Remove the choke strangler spring from the choke lever. Align the scribed mark on the choke gear with the mark below the teeth on the actuating cam, and reassemble the parts.
5. Temporarily tighten the lower bracket screw.
6. Move the arm at the upper screw to align the center line scribed in the notch on the arm with the punch mark on the float chamber.
7. Tighten the screws.
8. Install the cover with new screws (if necessary).

### *Non-Feedback Carburetors Canadian Models*

There are two sets of alignment marks on the Canadian non-feedback carburetors.

One set has inscribed lines which have to be mated to align the choke pinion gear with the choke cam lever. This algnment is performed by removing the choke cam bracket and moving the cam and gear.

The other set of marks consist of punch mark on the carburetor body and an inscribed line in the notch on the upper end of the choke cam bracket. Alignment is made by loosening the cam bracket upper end screw and moving the bracket so that the center inscribed line aligns with the punch mark.

## OVERHAUL

**For all carburetor overhaul procedures, please refer to "Carburetor Service" in the Unit Repair section.**

# Fuel Injection

**Due to the complex nature of mofern fuel injection systems, comprehensive diagnosis and testing procedure fall outside the confines of this repair manual. For complete diagnosis, testing and repair procedures, please refer to "Chilton's Guide to Fuel Injection and Feedback Carburetors."**

# MANUAL TRANSAXLE

## LINKAGE ADJUSTMENT

Hyundai manual transaxle linkages are not adjustable. If the shifter does not work properly, transmission mounting, lubrication, or parts wear problems are indicated.

## REMOVAL & INSTALLATION

1. Remove the battery and battery tray.
2. On five speed transaxles, disconnect the electrical connector for the selector control valve.

**NOTE: The actuator-to-shaft coupling pin collar is not reusable; always replace it.**

3. Disconnect and remove the speedometer and clutch cables.

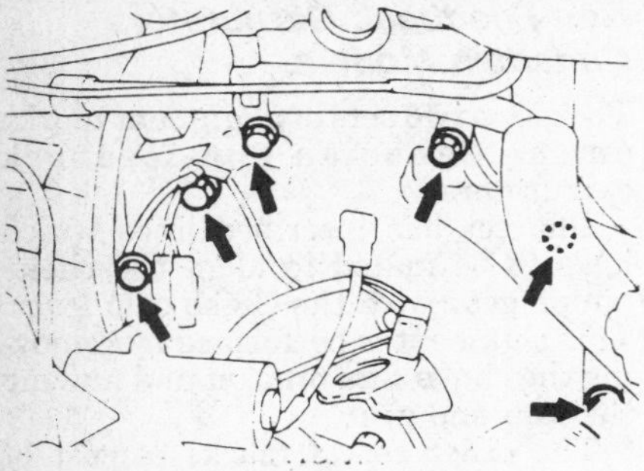

Upper transaxle bolt locations

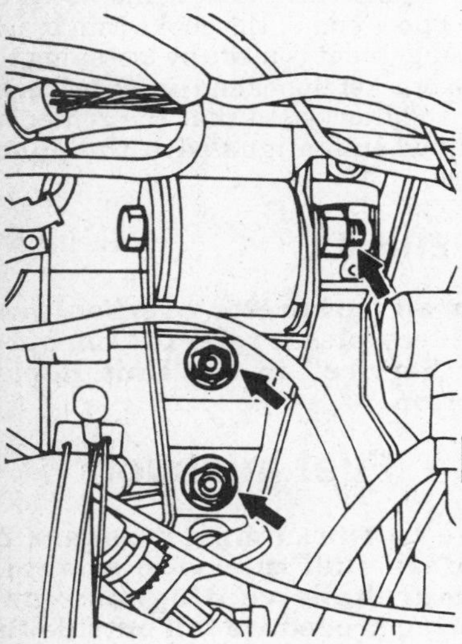

Transaxle mount insulator bolt locations

4. Disconnect the back-up lamp electrical connector. Remove the starter motor electrical harness.

5. Remove the six transaxle mounting bolts accessible from the top side of the transaxle.

6. Unbolt and remove the starter motor.

7. Raise the vehicle and support it securely on axle stands. Then, remove the splash shield from under the engine. Drain the transaxle fluid.

8. Disconnect the extension rod and the shift rod at the transmission end and lower them.

9. Disconnect the stabilizer bar at the lower control arm.

10. Remove the driveshafts.

11. Support the transaxle from below with a floor jack. Make sure the support is widely enough spread that the transmission pan will not be damaged. Then, remove the five attaching bolts and remove the bell housing cover.

12. Remove the lower bolts attaching the transaxle to the engine.

13. Remove the transaxle insulator mount bolt. Remove the cover from inside the right fender shield, and remove the transaxle support bracket.

14. Remove the transaxle mount bracket.

15. Pull the assembly away from the engine and then lower it from the vehicle.

16. Installation is the reverse of removal. Observe the following torques:

- M10–7T engine-to-transaxle bolts – 35 ft. lbs.
- M8–10T engine-to-transaxle bolts – 25 ft. lbs
- M8–20T bellhousing cover bolts – 15 ft. lbs.
- M8–14T bellhousing cover bolts – 9 ft. lbs.
- Transaxle mounting bracket bolt – 40 ft. lbs.

17. Refill the transmission pan with the specified fluid to the level of the filler plug.

18. Adjust the clutch cable. Make sure the gearshift lever works correctly.

# CLUTCH

**NOTE: The Excel employs a cable actuated clutch, while the Sonata uses a hydraulically actuated clutch.**

## REMOVAL & INSTALLATION

### CAUTION

***The clutch driven disc contains asbestos, which has been determined to be a cancer causing agent. Never clean clutch surfaces with compressed air! Avoid inhaling any dust from any clutch surface! When cleaning clutch surfaces, use a commercially available brake cleaning fluid.***

1. Remove the transaxle as described above. Insert the forward end of an old transaxle input shaft or a clutch disc guide tool into the splined center of the clutch disc, pressure plate, and the pilot bearing in the crankshaft. This will keep the disc from dropping when the pressure plate is removed from the flywheel.

2. Loosen the clutch mounting bolts alternately and diagonally in very small increments (no more than two turns at a time) so as to avoid warping the cover flange. When all bolts are free, remove the pressure plate and disc.

3. Remove the snapring. Remove the clevis pin.

4. Remove the return clip and then remove the release bearing.

5. Use a center punch and hammer to remove the spring pins from the clutch release fork and shaft. Discard the spring pins.

6. Remove the release shaft. Remove the release fork, seals, and return spring.

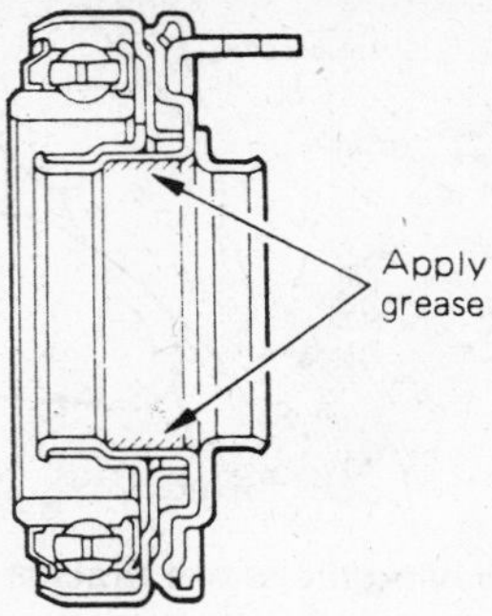


**Grease the groove in the throwout bearing as shown**

If the clutch disc isn't being replaced, examine it for the following before re-using it.

a. Loose rivets
b. Burned facing
c. Oil or grease on the facing
d. Less than 0.3mm left between the rivet head and the top of the facing.

Check the pressure plate and replace it if any of the following conditions exist:

a. Scored or excessively worn face.
b. Bent or distorted diaphragm spring.
c. Loose rivets.

**To install:**

7. First, grease the bearing areas for the release shaft. Second, install the release shaft, seals, return spring, and the release fork. Third, apply grease to the throwout bearing contacting surfaces of the release fork.

8. Align the lock pin holes of the release fork and shaft and drive in two new spring pins, using a tool such as MD998245-01. You may be able to simply fashion an appropriate tool, a device similar to a center punch with a tip the same diameter as the lock pins but flat on its front surface. Make sure the spring pin slot is a right angles to the centerline of the control shaft.

9. Apply grease into the groove in the release bearing and install it into the front bearing retainer in the transaxle. Install the return clip to the release bearing and fork.

10. Make sure the surfaces of the pressure plate and flywheel are wiped clean of grease and lightly sand them with crocus cloth. Lightly grease the clutch disc and transmission input shaft splines.

11. Locate the clutch disc on the flywheel with the stamped mark facing outward. Use a clutch disc guide or old input shaft to center the disc on the flywheel, and then install the pressure plate over it. Install the bolts and tighten them evenly. Tighten them in increments of 2 turns or less to avoid

warping the pressure plate. Torque to 11–15 ft. lbs. (15–20 Nm).

12. Remove the clutch disc centering tool. Install the transaxle. Adjust the clutch free play.

## PEDAL HEIGHT ADJUSTMENT

### *Excel*

Measure the pedal height from the top of the pedal pad to the closest point on the floor. The distance should be 7.3–7.6 in. (185–192mm). Loosen the clutch switch locknut and move the pedal stop bolt. Then, tighten the locknut.

### *Sonata*

Measure the pedal height from the face of the pedal to the floorboard. Pedal height should be 6.97–7.17 in. (177–182mm). If not:

1. Disconnect the clutch switch wiring.
2. Loosen the locknut and turn the switch as required.
3. Tighten the locknut.

## CLEVIS PIN PLAY ADJUSTMENT

### *Sonata Only*

Clevis pin play is measure at the pedal while observive the pin. Play should be 0.04–0.12 in. (1–3mm). If not, loosen the locknut and turn the pushrod as required. Tighten the locknut.

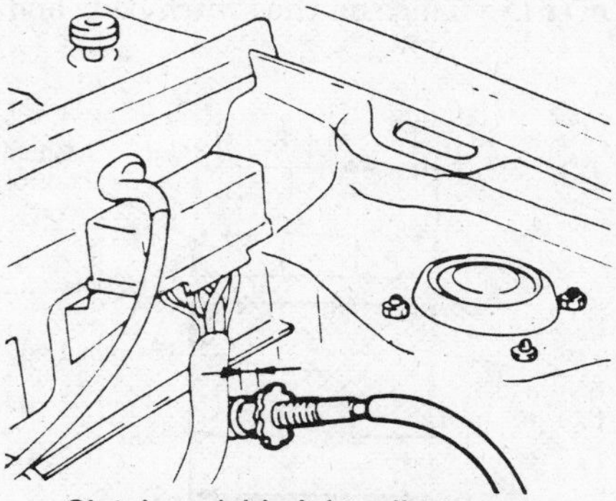

Clutch pedal height adjustment

## PEDAL PLAY ADJUSTMENT

### *Excel*

Slightly pull the cable away from the firewall. Turn the adjusting wheel on the cable until the play between the wheel and the cable retainer is 0.20–0.25 in. (5–6mm). Release the cable and make sure that the end of the tension spring engages the adjusting wheel, so that the wheel won't turn. Check the clutch pedal free-play. Free-

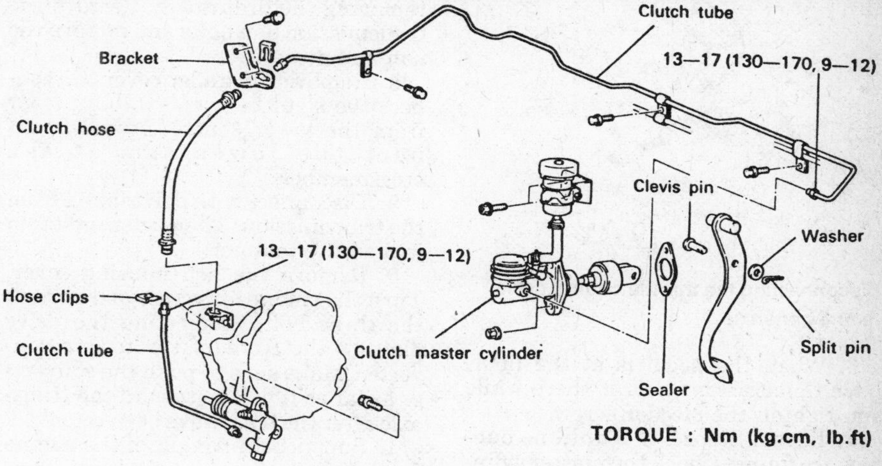


Sonata hydraulic clutch components

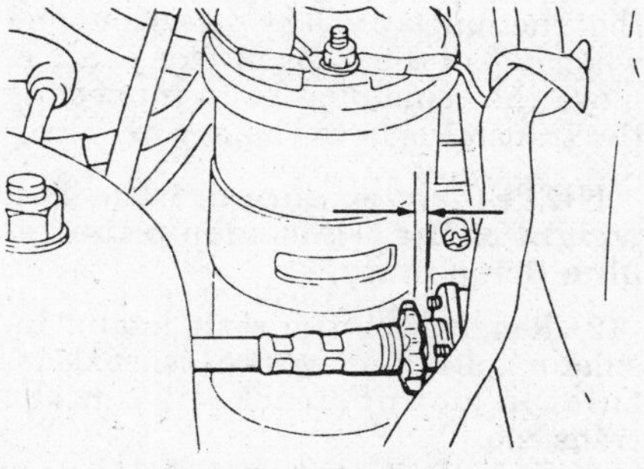

Clutch cable adjustment

play should be 0.8–1.2 in. (20–30mm). If it is outside specification, adjust it by means of the adjusting wheel on the cable.

### *Sonata*

Check this adjustment *after* checking pedal height and clevis play. Free-play should be 0.24–0.51 in. (6–13mm). If not, there is air in the system which must be bled. If air persists, there is a leak and the system must be repaired.

# Clutch Cable

## REMOVAL & INSTALLATION

### *Excel Only*

1. Completely back-off the cable adjusting wheel in the engine compartment.
2. Raise and support the front end on jackstands.
3. Pull out the split pin from the end of the clutch control lever and disconnect the cable from the lever.
4. Disconnect the cable at the clutch pedal.
5. Installation is the reverse of removal. Make sure that the cable doesn't touch any hot or moving parts. Lubricate the cable with clean engine oil. Adjust the clutch.

# Clutch Master Cylinder

## REMOVAL & INSTALLATION

### *Sonata Only*

1. Loosen the bleeder screw on the slave cylinder and drain the system.
2. Disconnect the pushrod from the clutch pedal.
3. Disconnect the clutch pedal from the pedal bracket.
4. Disconnect the fluid line from the master cylinder.
5. Unbolt and remove the master cylinder.
6. Install the master cylinder and bleed the system.

# Slave Cylinder

## REMOVAL & INSTALLATION

### *Sonata Only*

1. Disconnect the clutch hose from the slave cylinder.
2. Unbolt and remove the cylinder from the clutch housing.
3. Install the slave cylinder and bleed the system.

## SYSTEM BLEEDING

1. Raise and support the car on jackstands.
2. Loosen the bleeder screw at the slave cylinder.
3. Make sure that the master cylinder is full.
4. Attach a length of rubber hose to the bleeder screw nipple and place the other end in a glass jar half full of clean brake fluid.
5. Have your assistant push the clutch pedal down slowly to the floor. If air is in the system, bubbles will appear in the jar as the pedal is being depressed.

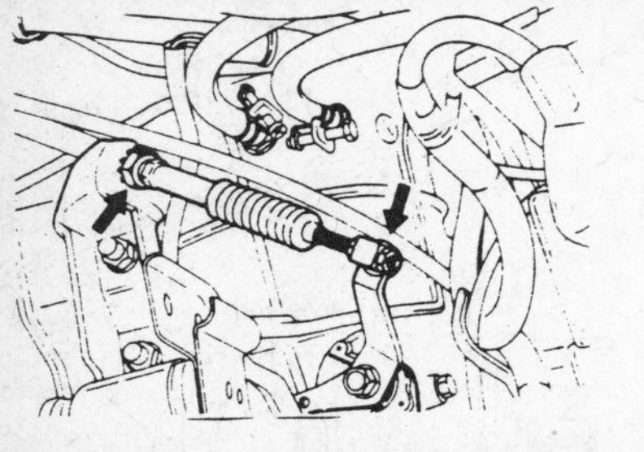

Disconnecting the throttle control cable at the transaxle

6. When the pedal is at the floor, have the assistant hold it there while you tighten the bleeder screw.
7. Repeat Steps 5 & 6 until no bubbles are found. Check the master cylinder level frequently to make sure that you don't run low on fluid.

# AUTOMATIC TRANSAXLE

## Transaxle

### REMOVAL & INSTALLATION

**NOTE: The transaxle and torque converter must be removed and installed as an assembly.**

1. Remove the battery and battery tray. Remove the air cleaner and housing.
2. Disconnect the throttle control cable at the carburetor and the manual control cable at the transaxle. To do this, loosen the locknut which uses a star washer and locates the cable housing on the bracket. Also, remove the locknut at the very end of the cable, where it connects with the neutral start switch.
3. Disconnect the inhibitor switch connector, pulse generator connector, oil cooler hoses, solenoid valve connector, and speedometer cable from the transaxle. Immediately install clean caps in the open ends of the hoses. Keep the hoses pointed up so fluid will not escape until the caps are installed.
4. Remove the five bolts attaching the converter housing to the engine that are accessible from above.
5. Jack up the car and support on jackstands. Label and then disconnect the starter motor wiring. Then, remove the mounting bolts, and the starter.
6. Remove the front wheels. Remove the engine splash shield.
7. Drain the transmission fluid by removing the drain plug. Remove the transmission pan bolts and remove the pan and drain it.
8. Remove the under cover. Disconnect the strut bars and stabilizer bar from the lower control arm. Disconnect the lower arm at the crossmember.
9. Disconnect both driveshafts from the transmission. Then, suspend them in a secure manner.
10. Remove the bell housing cover. Turn the engine for access and remove the three bolts connecting the drive plate to the front of the torque converter. Make sure to push the converter as far as it will go toward the transaxle after the bolts have been removed.
11. Support the weight of the engine from above, using a chain hoist. Support the transmission from underneath with a floor jack in such a way that the support will be spread out and will not dent the transmission pan. Remove the remaining bolts connecting the transmission to the engine.

**NOTE: Never support the full weight of the transaxle on the engine drive plate.**

12. Remove the transaxle mount insulator bolts. Remove the transaxle insulator mount bracket from the transaxle.
13. Slide the transaxle and converter away from the engine, to the right and then lower and remove it as an assembly.
14. Installation is the reverse of removal. Observe the following torques:
   - Torque converter-to-driveplate mounting bolts — 30 ft. lbs.
   - Transaxle assembly mounting bolts — 35 ft. lbs.
   - 7T engine-to-transaxle bolts — 35 ft. lbs.
   - 10T engine-to-transaxle bolts — 25 ft. lbs.
15. Adjust the throttle control cable and neutral safety switch according to the procedures above. Test the neutral safety switch.
16. Refill the transmission to the proper level and refill it, hot, according to the procedure for fluid change above. Make sure the neutral safety switch wiring does not rub against the insulator mount bracket.

### PAN REMOVAL

1. Remove the transmission pan and differential drain plugs to drain the fluid.
2. Remove the splash shield. Unbolt and remove the pan. It may be necessary to tap the pan lightly, with a soft mallet, to break the seal. Discard the gasket.
3. Clean all the gasket surfaces thoroughly. Then, put the pan and gasket in position with bolt holes lined up. Replace the bolts, tightening them with your fingers.
4. Then, tighten them diagonally in several stages to 90–102 inch lbs. Torque the drain plug to 22–25 ft. lbs. Pour 4.2 qts. of fluid into the transmission. Start the engine, put the gear selector in each of the positions for several seconds, and then go back to **PARK**. Check the fluid level again and make sure it's above the lower mark. Drive the vehicle until the transmission is hot and add fluid to the full mark.

### FILTER SERVICE

1. Remove the transmission oil pan as described above.
2. Remove the attaching bolts and remove the filter assembly. Strainers may be cleaned in a safe solvent and air dried. Foam type filters should be replaced.
3. Install the filter or strainer and torque the bolts alternately (diagonally) is several stages to 48–60 ft. lbs.

### NEUTRAL SAFETY SWITCH ADJUSTMENT

#### *Excel*

1. Apply the parking brake. Place the gearshift lever in **NEUTRAL** position.
2. Loosen the two mounting screws of the neutral switch so that it can be rotated. Now, rotate it so that the end of the operating lever (A) is directly over the flange on the switch body and

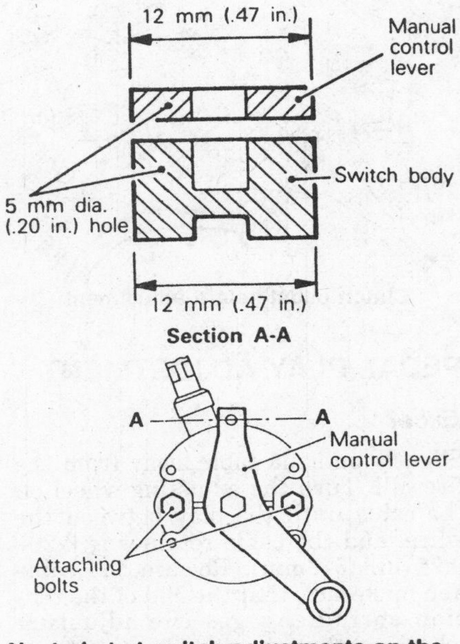


Neutral start switch adjustments on the Sonata

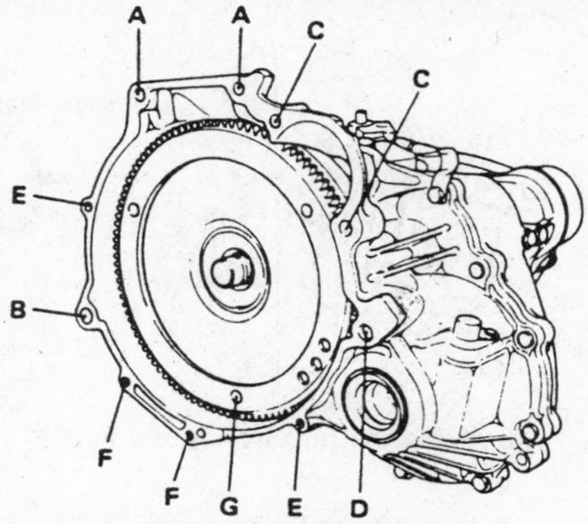

Bolt torques in ft. lbs. for the automatic transaxle: A—31-40; B—31-40; C—16-23; D—22-25; E—7-9; F—11-16; G—25-30

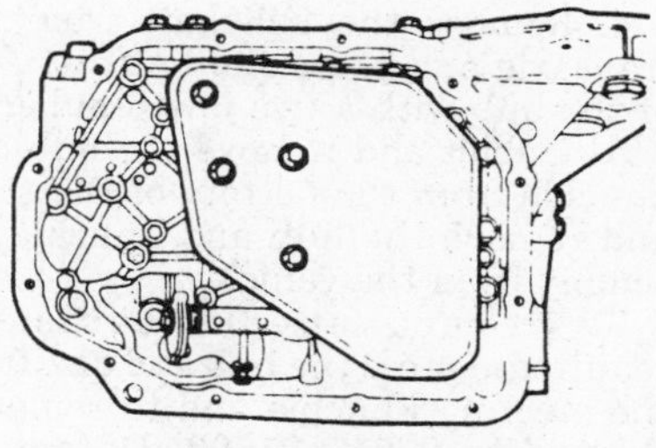
The automatic transaxle filter

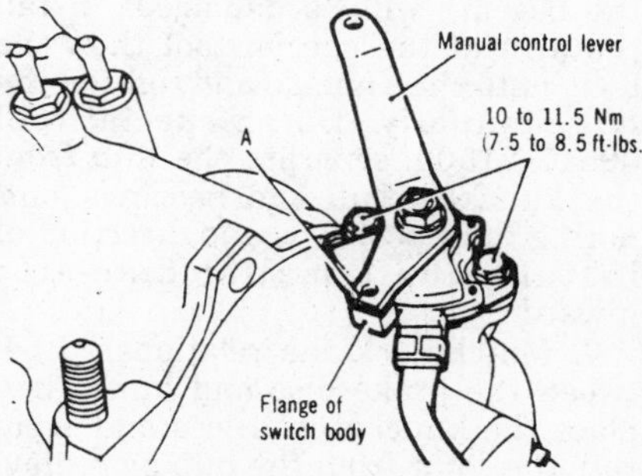

Excel neutral start switch adjustment

the holes in that flange and the outer end of the lever are lined up.

3. Hold the switch securely in place while torquing the mounting screws to 90–100 inch lbs.

4. Recheck the function of the switch by attempting to start the engine in all selector positions. It should start only in **PARK and NEUTRAL.**

### *Sonata*

1. Place the shifter in the **N** position.

2. Loosen the control cable coupler and free the cable.

3. Place the control lever in the neutral position.

4. Turn the switch body until the wide (12mm) end of the control lever aligns with the switch body's widest part, or, turn the switch body until; the 5mm hole in the control lever

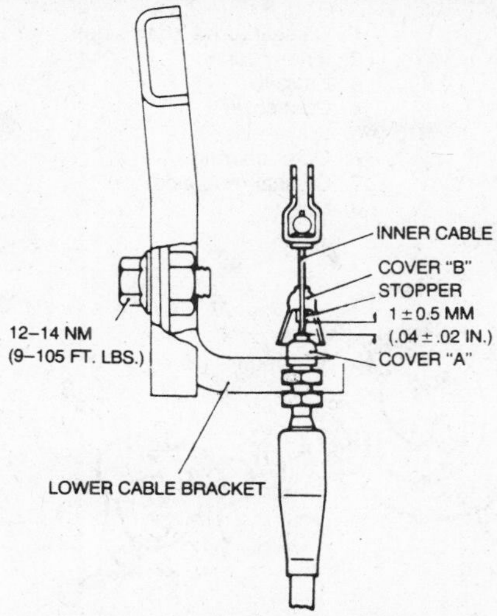

Excel throttle cable adjustment

aligns with the 5mm hole in the switch body. Tighten the nuts.

## THROTTLE CONTROL CABLE ADJUSTMENT

### *Excel Only*

1. Make sure the engine is warm with the throttle in normal idling position.

2. Loosen the lower cable bracket mounting bolt. Pull the small rubber cover located near the transmission back toward the housing to expose the nipple. Now, move the cable bracket until the distance between the nipple and the outer end of the cover next to the bracket is 0.5–1.5mm (0.02–0.06 in.). Then, torque the bracket mounting bolt to 9–10.5 ft. lbs. (12–14 Nm)

3. With the engine off, have someone open the throttle all the way and hold it there. Then, pull the cable further upward to make sure it still has freedom of movement; that it has not bottomed out. If necessary, repeat the adjustment.

## KICKDOWN SERVO ADJUSTMENT

### *Sonata Only*

1. Raise and support the front end on jackstands.

2. Clean and remove the servo cover.

3. Remove the servo switch.

4. Remove the snapring and cover.

5. Loosen the locknut.

6. Use special tool 09454-33000 to hold the servo piston while turning the adjusting screw. Tighten the screw to 86.4 inch lbs. (7.2 ft. lbs.), then back it off 2 full turns. Then, tighten it to 43.2 inch lbs. (3.6 ft. lbs.) and back it off 2¼ turns.

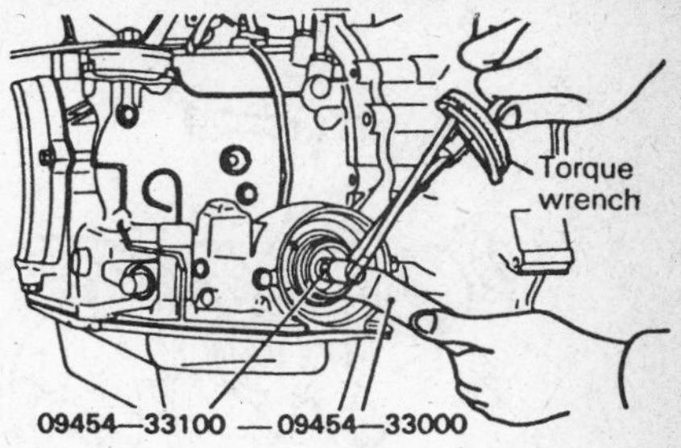

Adjusting the kickdown servo

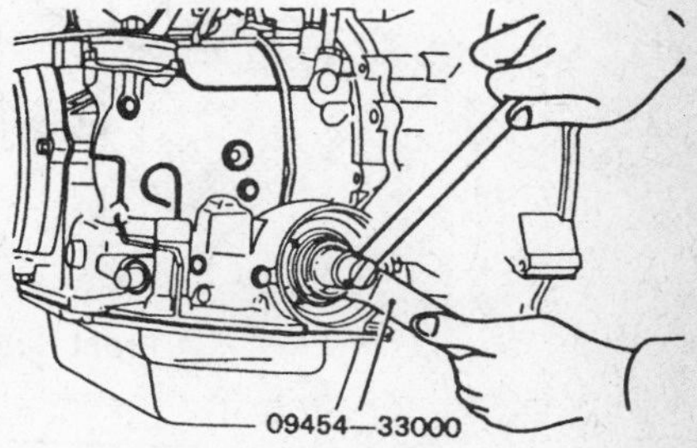

Holding the kickdown servo

7. Tighten the locknut to 18-23 ft. lbs.

8. Install a new D-ring in the cover groove and install the cover and snapring. Make sure you don't twist the D-ring.

9. Install the switch and tighten it to 12 inch lbs.

# DRIVE AXLE

## Halfshaft

### REMOVAL & INSTALLATION

1. Remove the hub center cap and loosen the driveshaft (axle) nut.

2. Loosen the wheel lug nuts.

3. Raise and support the front end on jackstands.

4. Remove the front wheels.

5. Remove the engine splash shield.

6. Remove the lower ball joint and strut bar from the lower control arm.

**NOTE: Place the lower arm ball joint on the lower arm to prevent damage to the ball joint dust boot.**

7. Drain the transaxle fluid.

8. Insert a prybar between the transaxle case (on the raised rib) and the driveshaft inner joint case. Move the bar to the right to withdraw the left driveshaft; to the left to remove the right driveshaft.

**CAUTION**

***Do not insert the pry bar too deeply (7mm) or you will damage the oil seal!***

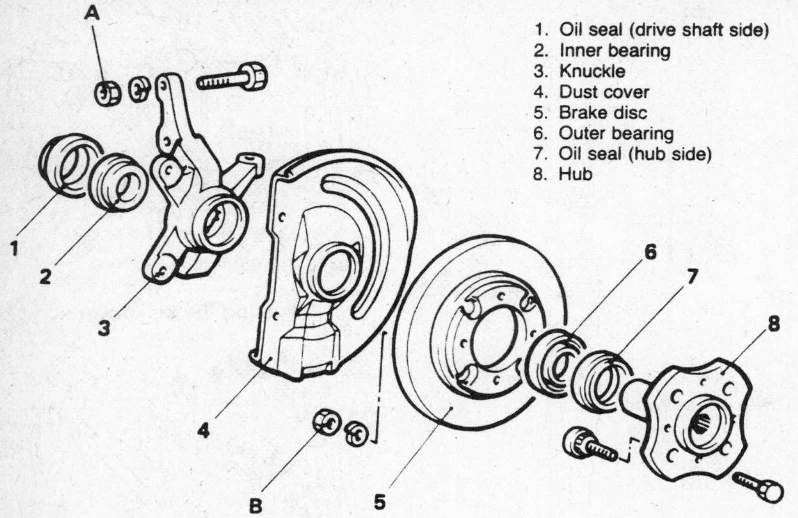


Front hub and knuckle

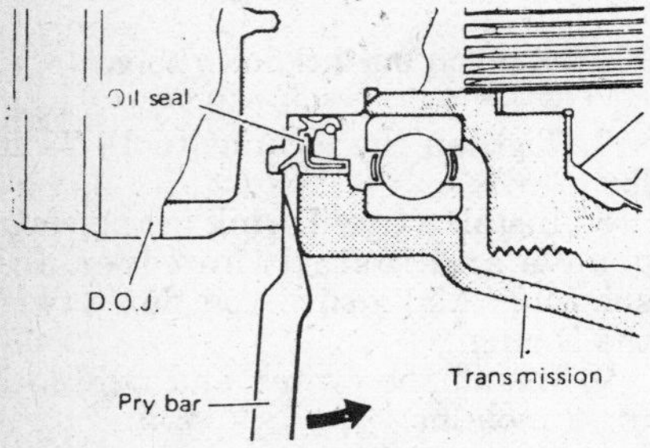


Halfshaft removal

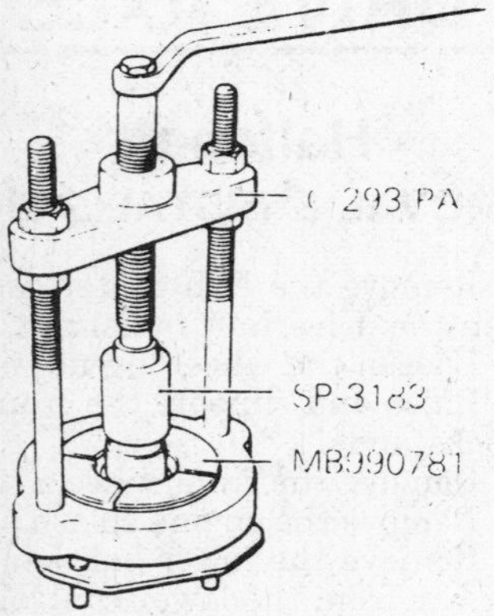


Removing the outer bearing inner race from the hub

9. Plug the transaxle case with a clean rag to prevent dirt from entering the case.
10. Use a puller/driver mounted on the wheel studs to push the driveshaft from the front hub. Take care to prevent the spacer shims from falling out of place.
11. Assembly is the reverse of removal. Insert the driveshaft into the hub, first, then install the transaxle end. Install the hub nut washer as shown in the accompanying illustration. Torque the axleshaft hub nut to 185 ft. lbs.; the lower arm-to-ball joint nuts to 87 ft. lbs.; the lower arm-to-strut bar nuts to 87 ft. lbs.

**NOTE: Always use a new inner joint retaining ring every time you remove the driveshaft.**

### CV-JOINT OVERHAUL

**For all CV-Joint overhaul procedures, please refer to "CV-Joint Overhaul", in the Unit Repair section.**

## Front Wheel Hub, Knuckle and Bearing

### REMOVAL, PACKING, INSTALLATION AND ADJUSTMENT

**NOTE: The following procedure requires the use of a number of special tools. Always replace bearings and races as a set. Never replace just an inner or outer bearing. If either is in need of replacement, both sets must be replaced.**

1. Remove the center hub cap and halfshaft nut. Then raise the vehicle and support it on floor stands, positioned so that the wheels hang freely. Then remove the front wheel.
2. Remove the brake caliper without disconnecting the hydraulic line (see the procedure above) and suspend it out of the way with a piece of wire.
3. Disconnect the stabilizer bar and

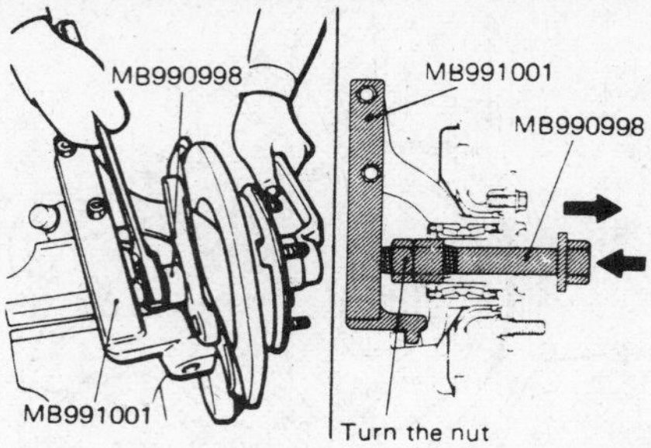


Removing the hub from the knuckle

strut bar from the lower control arm. Disconnect the ball joint at the steering knuckle. Disconnect the tie rod end ball joint at the steering knuckle as well.
4. Remove the halfshaft from the transaxle and press the halfshaft out of the hub with a two jawed puller.
5. Unbolt and remove the hub and knuckle from the bottom of the strut and remove the hub and knuckle assembly from the vehicle.
6. Several special tools are requiredto press the hub and disc from the steering knuckle and to remount them. Use 09517-21600. Do not attempt to hammer the parts apart, or the bearing will be damaged! Install the arm of the special tool then the body onto the knuckle and tighten the nut manually. Using special tool 09517-21500, separate the hub from the knuckle. Pull the bearings out, noting their positions and direction of installation (smaller diameter inward).
7. Matchmark the relationship between the brake disc and hub. Then place the knuckle in a vise and separate the rotor from the hub by removing the 4 attaching bolts.
8. Special tools 09532-1100, 09532-11301 (pulling ring and pulling collar) and 09517-21100 (stepped plate) or equivalent are needed. Fit the pulling lips of the collets onto the inner race and secure the pulling collar to the collets with the bolts provided. Then, attach the stepped plate to the hub.
9. Attach the pulling ring to the assembly, turning it and moving it up and down so the top of the pulling collar fits into the groove on the ring. Then, use an open-end wrench to keep the special tools from turning while you screw the bolt at the top of the assembly downward with another wrench. This will press the inner race out of the hub. Do this for both inner races.
10. Drive the oil seal and inner bearing inner race from the knuckle with a brass drift.
11. Using a brass drift and a ham-

mer, tap the bearing outer races out of the knuckle.

12. Thoroughly clean and inspect all parts. Any suspect part should be replaced.

13. Apply multipurpose grease to the OUTSIDE surfaces of the bearing outer races to make them easy to press in. Using special tools 09500–21000, 09517–21300, and 09517–21200, install the outer races.

14. Install rotor on the hub and torque the mounting bolts to 36–43 ft. lbs. (49–59 Nm).

15. Drive the outer bearing inner race into position. Coat the out ring and lip of the oil seal and drive the hub side oil seal into place, using a seal driver.

16. Mount the knuckle in a vise. Place the hub and knuckle together. Then use 09517–21500 to tighten the hub to the knuckle, torquing to 147–192 ft. lbs. Then, rotate the hub to seat the bearing.

17. With the hub still in the vise, check the turning torque of the bearing with an inch lbs. torque wrench and tool 09517–21500. Starting torque should be 11.5 inch lbs. If the starting torque is 0, measure the hub bearing axial play with a dial indicator. If axial play exceeds 0.004 in. (0.1mm), while the nut is tightened, the parts have been assembled incorrectly.

18. Remove the special tool. Place the outer bearing in the hub and drive the seal into place. Lower strut-to-knuckle mounting bolts are torqued to 54–65 ft. lbs. Refer to respective procedures elsewhere for the other torques. The remaining procedures are the reverse of removal except that the final torquing of the lower arm-to-ball joint connecting bolt should be accomplished after the car is on the ground.

# FRONT SUSPENSION

## MacPherson Strut

### REMOVAL & INSTALLATION

1. Raise the vehicle and support it by the body or crossmembers. Remove the front wheels. Detach the brake hose bracket at the strut.
2. Remove the nuts securing the strut to the fender well.
3. Unbolt the strut lower end from the knuckle.
4. Remove the strut from the car.
5. To install, simply reposition the strut and tighten the bolts. Observe the following torques:

- Strut-to-knuckle bolts – 55–65 ft. lbs. on the Excel; 65-76 ft. lbs. on the Sonata.
- Strut-to-fender well nuts – 7–11 ft. lbs. on the Excel; 18-25 ft. lbs. on the Sonata.

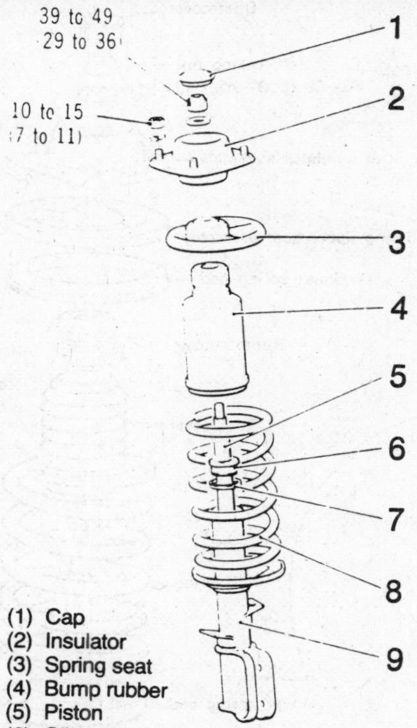


(1) Cap
(2) Insulator
(3) Spring seat
(4) Bump rubber
(5) Piston
(6) Oil seal nut
(7) Square section O-ring
(8) Spring
(9) Outer shell

Excel front strut

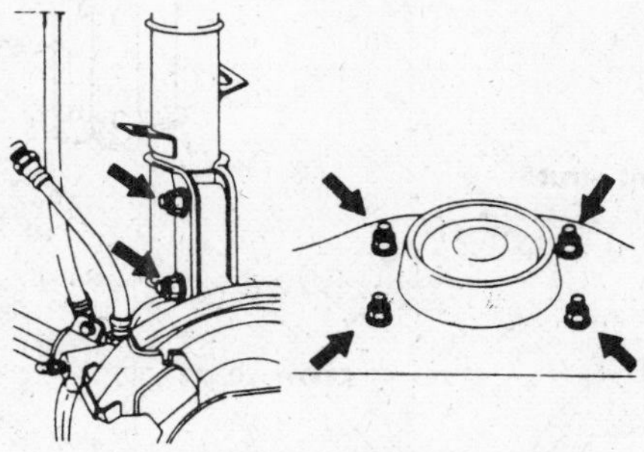

Excel strut attachment points

### OVERHAUL

**For all spring and shock absorber removal and installation procedures, and all strut overhaul procedures, please refer to "Strut Overhaul" in the Unit Repair section.**

## Stabilizer Bar

### REMOVAL & INSTALLATION

#### *Excel*

1. Raise and support the front end on jackstands.
2. Unbolt the stabilizer clamps from the crossmember.
3. Unbolt the stabilizer bar from the strut bar.
4. Examine the bushings for cracks and wear, if one is worn or cracked all the bushings must be replaced.
5. Reposition the stabilizer bar and tighten the chassis clamp bolts to 29 ft. lbs.; the strut bar clamps to 50 inch lbs.

#### *Sonata*

1. Raise and support the front end on jackstands.
2. Remove the stabilizer bar brackets from the crossmember.
3. Lower the rear of the center member and lower the stabilizer bar.
4. Disconnect the end links and remove the stabilizer.
5. Installation is the reverse of removal. Torque the end link nuts to 45 ft. lbs.; the bracket bolts to 30 ft. lbs.

## Strut Bar

### REMOVAL & INSTALLATION

#### *Excel Only*

1. Raise and support the front end on jackstands.
2. Unbolt the stabilizer bar from the strut bar.
3. Remove the bolts securing the strut bar to the control.
4. Remove the strut bar-to-frame bracket outer nut and pull the bar from the bracket.
5. Inspect all parts and replace any cracked, dry or deformed parts. The strut bar bend must not exceed 3mm over its entire length.
6. Installation is the reverse of removal. Note that the left side bar is identified with a dab of white paint. When installing the strut bar at the strut bar bracket, the distance between the inner locknut and the end of the strut bar must be 80.5mm. Torque the stabilizer bar-to-strut bar clamp bolts to 50 inch lbs.; the strut bar-to-control arm bolts to 87 ft. lbs.; the strut bar; the strut bar-to-bracket nut to 60 ft. lbs.

## Ball Joints

### INSPECTION

Support the vehicle on axle stands.

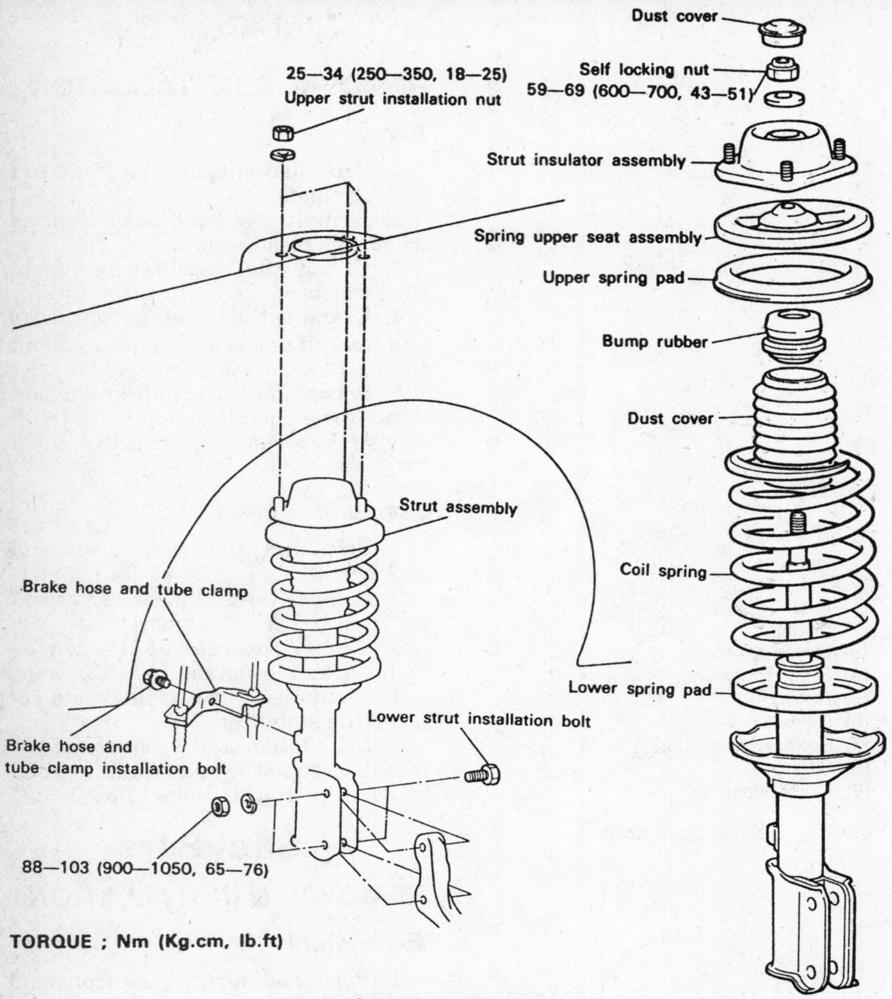


Sonata front strut

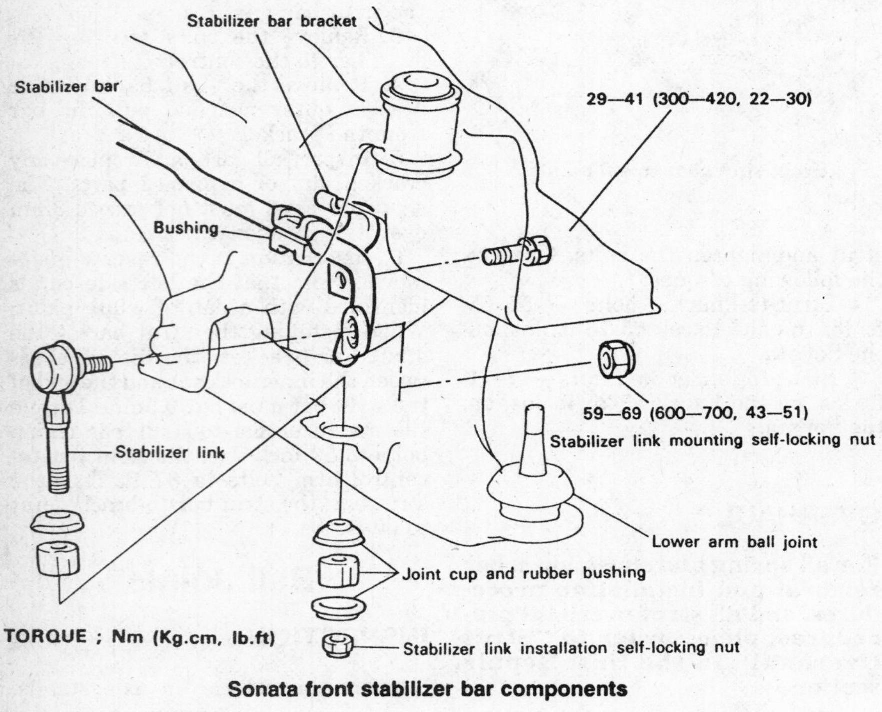


Sonata front stabilizer bar components

Disconnect the ball joint at the lower end of the strut as described below; you need not remove the lower control arm entirely. Install the nut back onto the ballstud. Then, with an inch lbs. torque wrench, measure the torque required to start the ball joint rotating. The figures are 26–86 inch lbs. If the figures are within specification, the ball joint is satisfactory. If the figure is too high, the joint should be replaced. If the figure is too low, you can still reuse the joint, provided its rotation is smooth and even. If there is roughness, or play, it must be replaced.

## REMOVAL & INSTALLATION

### Excel

1. Raise and support the front end on jackstands placed under the frame.
2. Unbolt the ball joint from the control arm.
3. Remove the stud retaining nut.
4. Use a ball joint removing tool and separate the ball joint from the steering knuckle.
5. Replace the ball joint and tighten the ball joint to control arm to 69–87 ft. lbs. (99–118 Nm). Torque the ball joint stud nut 43–52 ft. lbs. (59–71 Nm).

### Sonata

The ball joint is a press-fit in the lower arm. Remove the arm and press the ball joint out. Press a new joint in.

# Lower Control Arm

## REMOVAL & INSTALLATION

### Excel

1. Support the vehicle securely by the crossmember and remove the front wheel.
2. Remove the under cover.
3. Disconnect the stabilizer bar from the lower arm. Remove the nut from under neath the control arm and take off the washer and spacer.
4. Remove the ball joint stud nut and press the tool off with a tool such as MB991113.
5. Remove the bolts which retain the spacer at the rear and the nut and washers on the front of the lower arm shaft (at the front). Slide the arm forward, off the shaft and out of the bushing.
6. Replace the dust cover on the ball joint. The new cover must be greased on the lip and inside with No. 2 EP Multipurpose grease and pressed on with a tool such as MB990800 and a hammer until it is fully seated.
7. When installing the control arm, the nut on the stabilizer bar bolt must be torqued until the link shows 21-

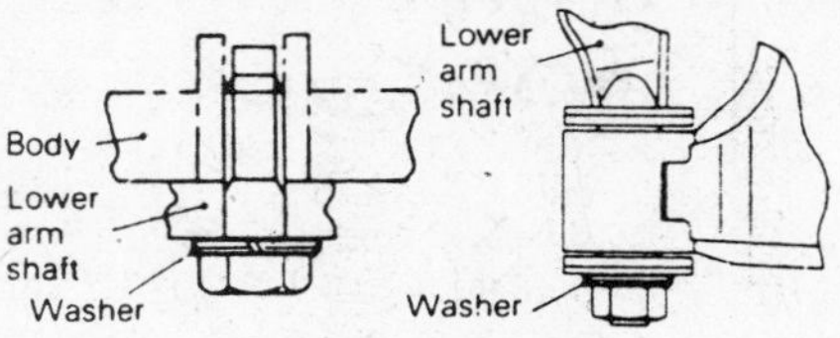


**Lower control arm installation on the Excel**

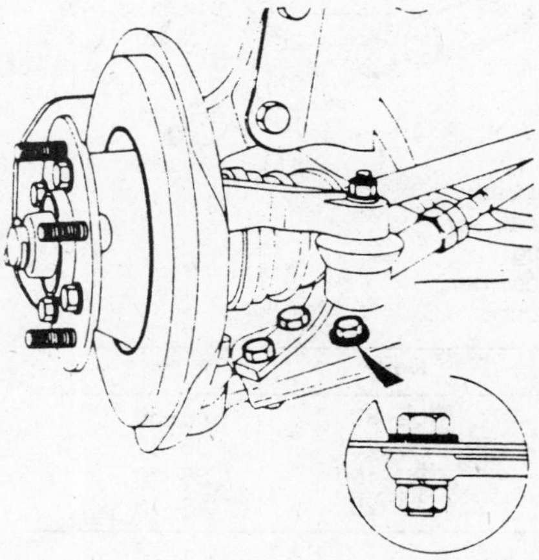

**On the Excel, install a flat washer after the ball joint is mounted in the control arm**

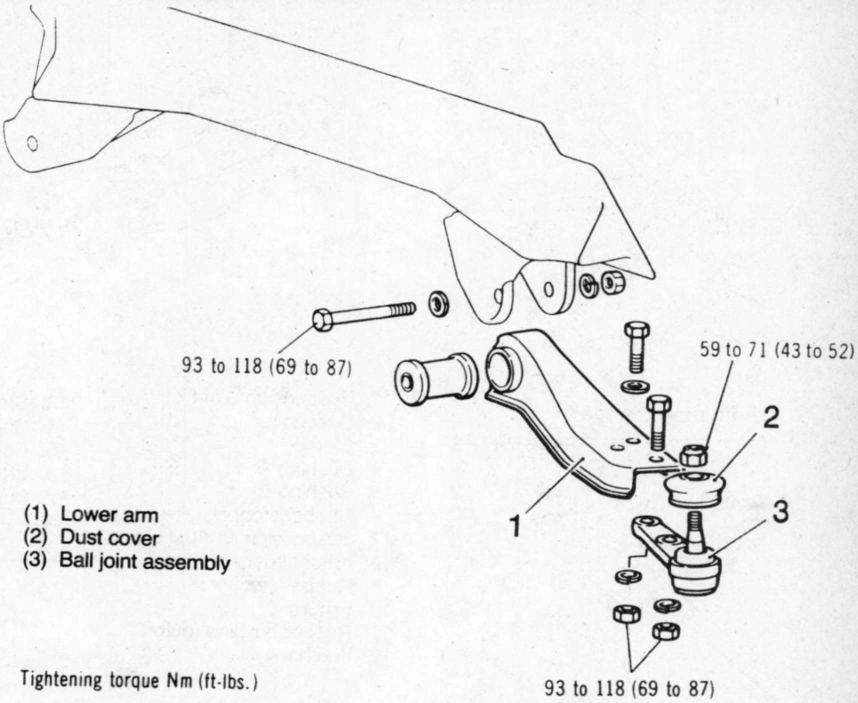


**Excel lower control arm**

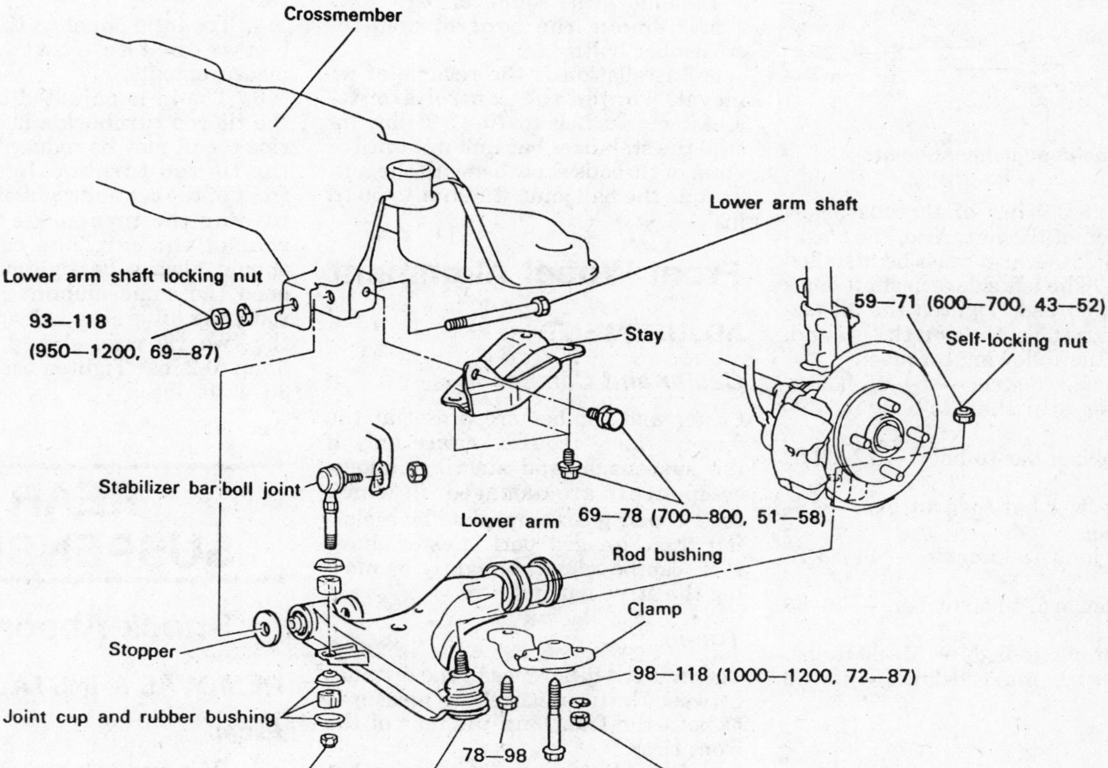


TORQUE ; Nm (kg.cm, lb.ft)

**Sonata lower control arm and related components**

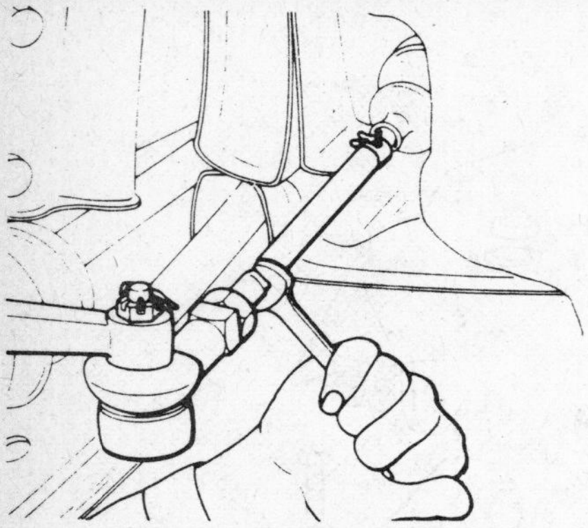

Adjusting the toe-in

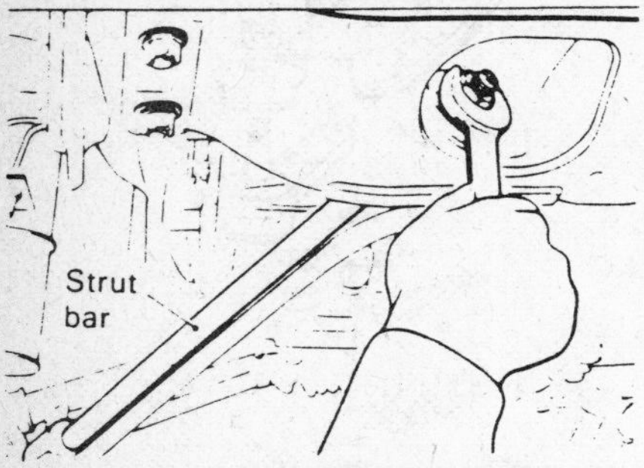


Moving the strut bar to adjust the caster

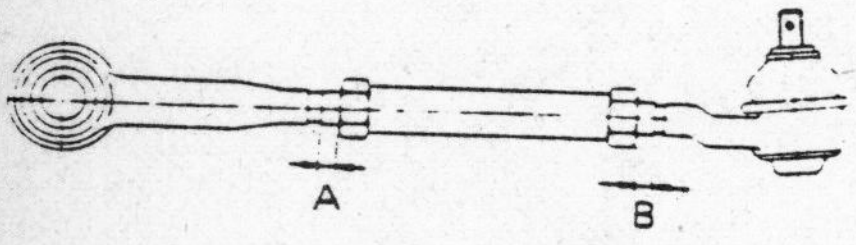


Toe-in adjustment points

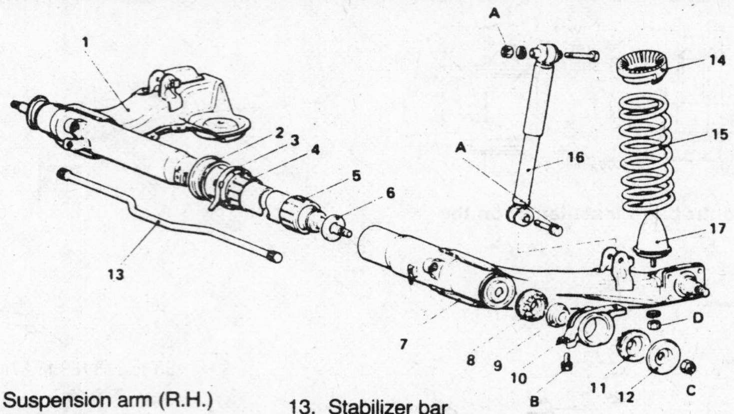


1. Suspension arm (R.H.)
2. Dust cover
3. Clamp
4. Bushing A
5. Bushing B
6. Rubber stopper
7. Suspension arm (L.H.)
8. rubber bushing (inner)
9. Rubber stopper
10. Fixture
11. Rubber bushing (outer)
12. Washer
13. Stabilizer bar
14. Spring seat
15. Coil spring
16. Shock absorber
17. Bump stopper

| | Nm | ft. lbs. |
|---|---|---|
| A | 65–80 | 46–56 |
| B | 50–70 | 36–51 |
| C | 80–100 | 56–70 |
| D | 18–25 | 13–18 |

Excel rear suspension

23mm (0.8-0.9 in.) of threads below the bottom of the nut. Also, the washer for the lower arm must be installed as shown. The left side arm shaft has a left hand thread. Tighten the all fasteners with the vehicle on the ground. Observe the following torques:

- Knuckle-to-strut – 54–65 ft. lbs.
- Lower arm shaft-to-body – 69–87 ft. lbs.
- Stabilizer bar-to-body – 22–29 ft. lbs.
- Stabilizer bar-to-strut bar – 48–60 inch lbs.
- Ball joint-to-knuckle – 44–53 ft. lbs.
- Lower arm-to-strut bar – 70–88 ft. lbs.
- Strut bar-to-body – 55–60 ft. lbs.
- Strut bar inner locknut – 55–60 ft. lbs.

### *Sonata*

1. Raise and support the front end on jackstands.
2. Loosen the ball joint nut and, using special tool 09568-3100 disconnect the joint from the knuckle. Be sure to secure the tool's cord to a nearby part!
3. Once the ball joint is free, remove the nut.
4. Remove the stabilizer bar.
5. Remove the control arm-to-crossmber bolt.
6. Installation is the reverse of removal. Torque the control arm-to-crossmember bolt to 70-87 ft. lbs. Install the stabilizer bar link nut until 5-7mm of threads show beneath the nut. Torque the ball joint stud nut to 50 ft. lbs.

## Front Wheel Alignment

### ADJUSTMENT

#### *Caster and Camber*

Caster and camber are preset at the factory. They require service only if the suspension and steering linkage components are damaged, in which case, repair is accomplished by replacing the damaged part. Caster, however, can be adjusted slightly by moving the strut bar nut.

#### *Toe-in*

Toe-in is the difference in the distance between the front wheels, as measured at both the front and the rear of the front tires.

1. Raise the front of the car so that its front wheels are just clear of the ground.
2. Use a scribing block to hold a piece of chalk at the center of each tire tread while rotating the wheels by hand.
3. Measure the distance between the marked lines at both the front and rear.
4. Toe-in is equal to the difference between the font and rear measurements.
5. Toe-in is adjusted be screwing the tie rod turnbuckle in or out. Left side toe-in may be reduced by turning the tie rod turnbuckle toward the front of the car and right side toe-in by turning the turnbuckle toward the rear of the car. The turnbuckles should always be tightened or loosened the same amount for both tie rods; the difference is length between the two tie rods should not exceed 5mm (0.2 in.). Tighten the locknuts to 36–40 ft. lbs.

# REAR SUSPENSION

## Shock Absorbers

### REMOVAL & INSTALLATION

#### *Excel*

1. Remove the wheel cover. Loosen the lug nuts.
2. Raise the rear of the car. Support the car with jackstands. Remove the wheel.
3. Remove the upper mounting bolt/nut or nut.

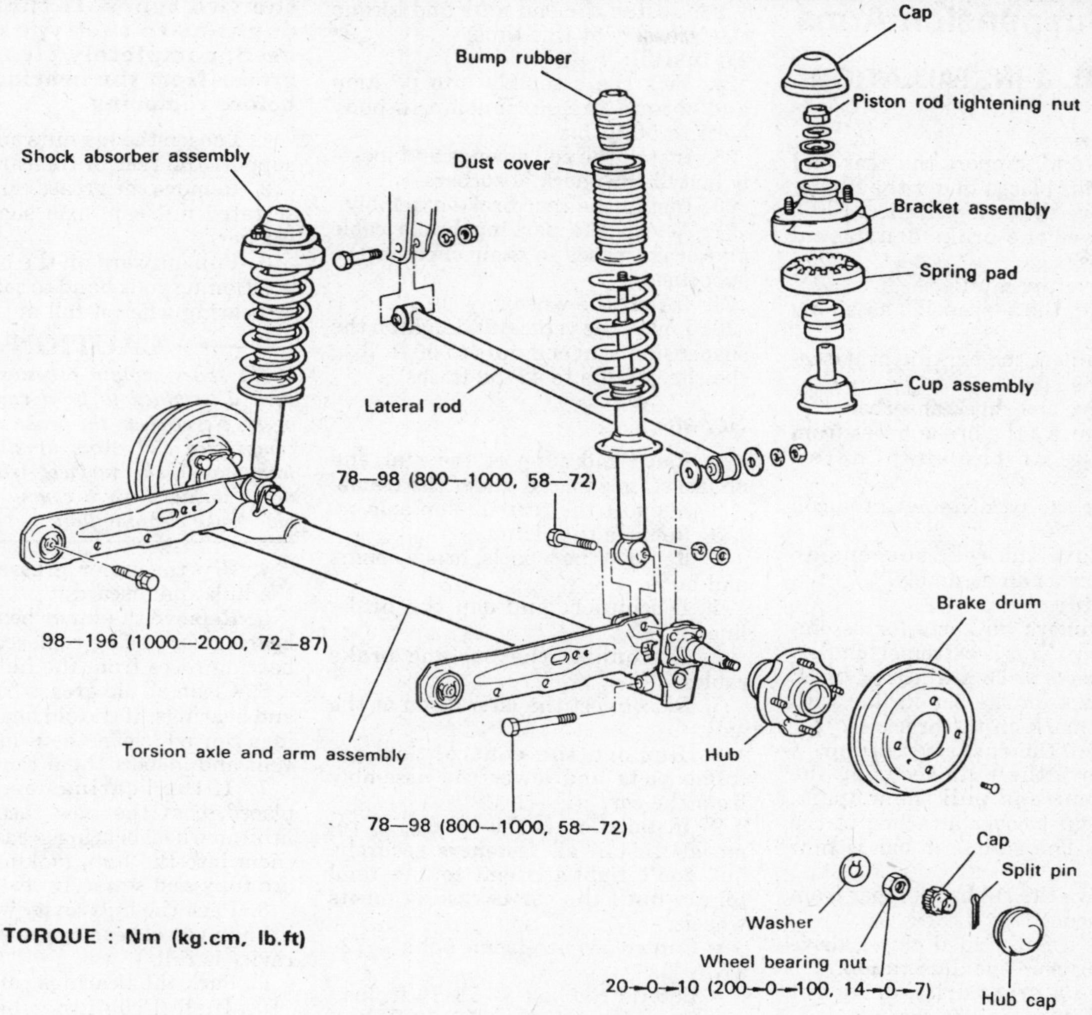


**Sonata rear suspension components**

4. While holding the bottom stud mount nut with one wrench, remove the locknut with another wrench, or on some models remove the nut and bolt from the mounting bracket.
5. Remove the shock absorber.
6. Check the shock for:
   a. Excessive oil leakage, some minor weeping is permissible;
   b. Bent center rod, damaged outer case, or other defects;
   c. Pump the shock absorber several times, if it offers even resistance on full strokes it may be considered serviceable.
7. Install the upper shock mounting nut and bolt. Hand-tighten the nut.
8. Install the bottom eye of the shock over the spring stud or into the mounting bracket and insert the bolt and nut. Tighten the nut to 52 ft. lbs. on the 1986 Excel and 47–58 ft. lbs. (64–78 Nm) on the 1987–90 Excel.
9. Tighten the upper fasteners to 52 ft. lbs. on the 1986 Excel and 47–58 ft. lbs. (64–78 Nm) on the 1987–90 Excel.

# Coil Spring

## REMOVAL & INSTALLATION

### *Excel*

1. Support the car securely at the rear of the body at approved points and remove the rear wheels.
2. Support the rear suspension arm with a floorjack. Then, remove the lower shock absorber attaching bolt, nut, and lockwasher.
3. Slowly lower the jack just to the point where the spring can be removed and remove the spring. If the spring is being replaced, transfer the spring seat to the new spring.
4. When installing the coil spring, make sure the smaller diameter is upward. Make sure the spring identification and load markings match up.
5. Torque the lower shock mounting nut/bolt to 47–58 ft. lbs. (64–78 Nm).

# Struts

## REMOVAL & INSTALLATION

### *Sonata*

1. Raise and support the rear end on jackstands.
2. Support the torsion axle.
3. Remove the upper protective cap and remove the 2 upper stud nuts.
4. Remove the lower bolt.
5. Remove the strut.
6. Installation is the reverse of removal. Tighten the upper end nuts to 18-25 ft. lbs.; the lower end bolt to 58-72 ft. lbs.

## OVERHAUL

**For all strut overhaul procedures, please refer to "Strut Overhaul" in the Unit Repair section.**

## Rear Suspension Arms

### REMOVAL & INSTALLATION

#### Excel

1. Raise and support the rear end on jackstands placed under the frame.
2. Remove the rear wheels.
3. Remove the brake drums and brake shoes.
4. Remove the muffler.
5. Jack up the suspension assembly slightly.
6. Disconnect the parking brake cable from the arm.
7. Remove the shock absorber.
8. Disconnect the brake hoses from their clips on the suspension members.
9. Lower the jack. Remove the coil spring.
10. Remove the rear suspension from the car as an assembly.

**Disassembly**

11. Matchmark all parts for assembly reference. This is extremely important! On cars with stabilizer bars, make a mark on the bar in line with the punch mark on the bracket.
12. Remove the dust cover clamp.
13. Remove the nuts securing the control arms and pull them apart. Leave the dust cover attached to the right arm. The stabilizer bar is now free.
14. Remove the rubber stopper from the right arm.
15. Using a flat bladed chisel, drive out bushing **A** in the illustration.
16. Using a brass drift, drive out bushing **B** from the left arm.

**Assembly**

17. Coat the inside of the left arm and the outside of bushing **B** with chassis lube and drive bushing **B** into place with a suitable driver such as tools 09555-21100 and 09555-21000. Drive the bushing in until the notch on 09555-21000 reaches the end of the arm.
18. Coat the inside of the arm and the outside of bushing **A** with chassis lube and drive bushing **A** into the arm until it is fully seated.
19. Install the dust cover to the center position of the right arm (about 400mm).
20. Apply chassis lube to the surface of the right arm and install the rubber stopper.
21. Align all matchmarks, including the stabilizer bar, and slowly push the suspension halves together.
22. Install all remaining bushing, washers and attaching parts.

**NOTE: The toothed sides of the washers face the bushings.**

23. Install the end nuts and torque them loosely at this time.

**To install:**

24. Jack the assembly into position and torque the suspension-to-body bolts to 50 ft. lbs.
25. Install the coil springs and loosely install the shock absorbers.
26. Install the rear brake assembly.
27. Attach the parking brake cable and brake hoses to their clips on the suspension.
28. Install the wheels.
29. Lower the vehicle and tighten the suspension arm end nuts to 50 ft. lbs.; the shock bolts to 47–58 ft. lbs.

#### Sonata

1. Raise and support the rear end on jackstands placed under the frame.
2. Support the rear torsion axle.
3. Remove the struts.
4. Remove the wheels, brake drums and hubs.
5. Disconnect and cap the brake lines.
6. Disconnect the parking brake cables.
7. Disconnect the lateral rod at the axle.
8. Remove the control arm-to-frame bolts and lower the assembly from the car.
9. Installation is the reverse of removal. Install all fasteners securely, but don't tighten them to the final torque until the car is resting on its wheels.

- Control arm-to-frame bolts – 72–87 ft. lbs.
- Lateral rod bolt – 58–72 ft. lbs.
- Strut lower bolt – 58–72 ft. lbs.

## Lateral Rod

### REMOVAL & INSTALLATION

#### Sonata

1. Raise and support the rear end on jackstands.
2. Disconnect the rod at each end and remove it.
3. Installation is the reverse of removal. Install the bolts and nuts at each end, but don't tighten them until the car is on its wheels. Torque the nuts to 58-72 ft. lbs.

## Rear Wheel Bearings

### REMOVAL, INSPECTION, PACKING, INSTALLATION & ADJUSTMENT

**NOTE: Sodium-based grease is not compatible with lithium-based grease. Read the package labels and be careful not to mix the two types. If there is any doubt as to the type of grease used, completely clean the old grease from the bearing and hub before replacing.**

1. Loosen the lug nuts and raise and support the rear of the car.
2. Remove the grease cap, cotter pin serrated nut cap, axle shaft nut and washer.
3. Pull outward on the brake drum, positioning your hand to catch the outer bearing when it fall out.

**CAUTION**

***Brake shoes contain asbestos, which has been determined to be a cancer causing agent. Never clean the brake surfaces with compressed air! Avoid inhaling any dust from any brake surface! When cleaning brake surfaces, use a commercially available brake cleaning fluid.***

4. Pry the inner grease seal from the hub and discard it.
5. Remove the inner bearing. If the bearings are being replaced, drive the bearing races from the hub.
6. Clean all old grease from the hub and bearings. If the old bearing are beings reused, clean them in a safe solvent and inspect them thoroughly.
7. If the bearings are being replaced, coat the new races with EP lithium wheel bearing grease and drive them into the hub, making sure they are fully and squarely seated.
8. Pack the hub cavity with new EP lithium wheel bearing grease, until the cavity is full.
9. Pack the bearings completely.
10. Install the inner bearing and drive a new grease seal into place.
11. Install the drum on the spindle and install the outer bearing, washer and shaft nut. Tighten the nut to 15 ft. lbs. while turning the drum, to seat the bearings. Back off on the nut until it is loose, then torque it to 48 inch lbs.
12. Install the serrated nut cap and a new cotter pin. If the cotter pin holes have to be aligned, back off on the nut no more than 15 degrees. If that won't align the holes, repeat the adjustment procedure.

# STEERING

## Steering Wheel

### REMOVAL & INSTALLATION

#### Excel

1. Pull off the horn cover at the center of the wheel by grasping the upper edge with your fingers to release it.

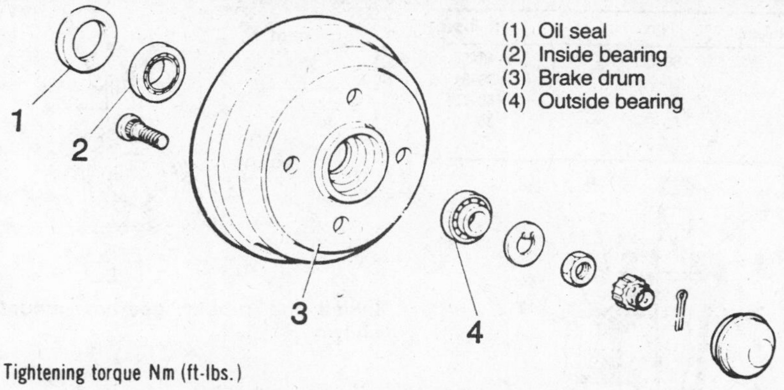


Rear wheel bearings and hub

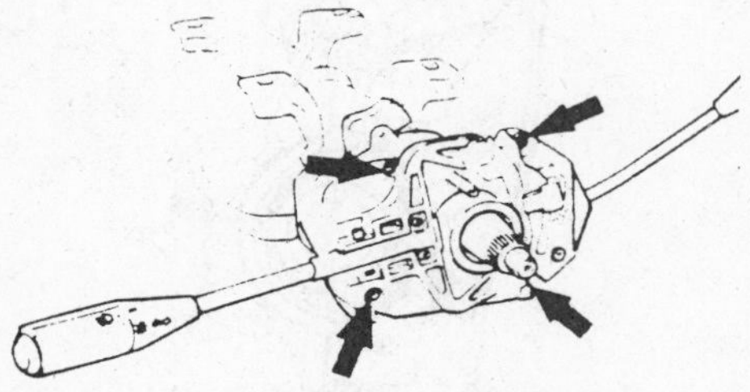

Combination switch removal

Then, disconnect the horn wire connector.

2. Remove the steering wheel retaining nut. Matchmark the relationship between the wheel and shaft.
3. Remove the steering wheel dynamic dampener.
4. Screw the 2 bolts of a steering wheel puller into the wheel. Then, turn the bolt at the center of the puller to force the wheel off the steering shaft. Do not pound on the wheel to remove it, or the collapsible steering shaft may be damaged.
5. The steering wheel can be pushed onto the shaft splines by hand far enough to start the retaining nut. Install the retaining nut and torque it to 26–32 ft. lbs. (34–44 Nm).

### *Sonata*

1. Disconnect the battery ground.
2. Remove the screws from the back of the horn pad and lift it off.
3. Disconnect the horn wire connector.
4. Pull the dynamic damper forward and off.
5. Remove the steering wheel retaining nut. Matchmark the relationship between the wheel and shaft.
6. Screw the two bolts of a steering wheel puller into the wheel. Then, turn the bolt at the center of the puller to force the wheel off the steering shaft. Do not pound on the wheel to remove it, or the collapsible steering shaft may be damaged.
7. The steering wheel can be pushed

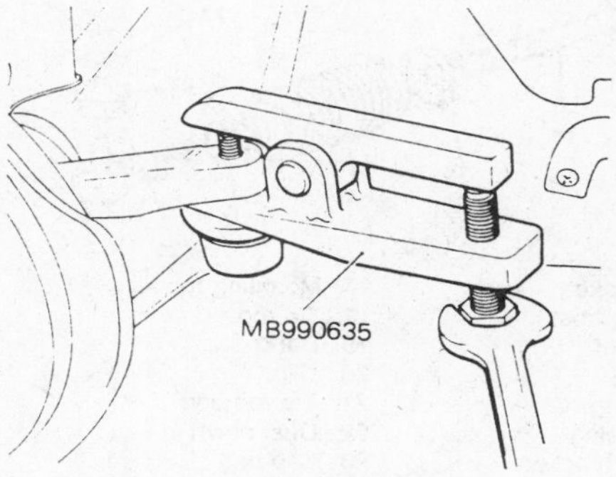


Freeing the tie rod end ball stud

onto the shaft splines by hand far enough to start the retaining nut. Install the retaining nut and torque it to 29–36 ft. lbs. (39–49 Nm).

## Combination Switch

### REMOVAL & INSTALLATION

1. Remove the steering wheel as described above. Remove the steering column cover.
2. Unplug the two electrical connectors. If necessary, remove the harness retainer.
3. Remove the retaining screws and slide the switch off the steering column.
4. Installation is the reverse of the removal procedure.

## Ignition Switch/Lock

### REMOVAL & INSTALLATION

1. Remove the steering wheel as described above. Remove the steering column cover.
2. Remove the combination switch as described above.
3. Unplug the electrical connector for the ignition lock.
4. Use a hacksaw to cut a slit in the top of each of the fastening bolts. You'll have to cut slightly into the

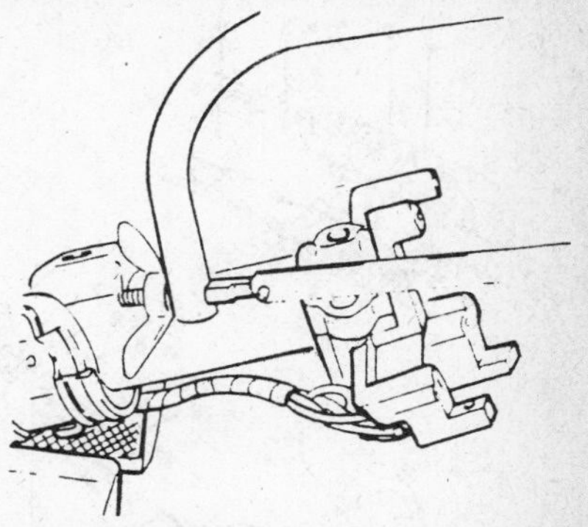

Using a hacksaw to cut screwdriver grooves into the ignition lock mounting bolts

housing for the switch to do this. Unscrew the bolts and remove the switch.

5. When installing the new switch, align the halves of the assembly around the steering column, align the assembly with the column boss, and then install the special new installation bolts just loosely. Verify that the ignition switch works and then tighten the bolts until their heads break off to prevent removal.

## Manual Steering Rack

### REMOVAL & INSTALLATION

#### *Excel Only*

1. Loosen the lug nuts.
2. Raise and support the front end on jackstands under the frame.
3. Remove the wheels.
4. Remove the steering shaft-to-pinion coupling bolt.
5. Disconnect the tie rod ends with a separator.
6. Removing the clamps securing the rack to the crossmember and remove the unit from the car. The tie rod ends can now be removed. Prior to removal, count the exact number of exposed threads on the tie rod ends, then loosen the locknut and unscrew the tie rod end. When installing new tie rod ends, oil the threads and screw them into place so that the previously noted number of threads is visible with the locknut tight. As a further reference, the distance between the end of the tie rod boot and the centerline of the tie rod ball stud should be 243.5mm (9.6 in.). Torque the locknut to 38 ft. lbs.
7. Install the rubber mount for the gear box with the slit on the downside. The remainder of installation is the reverse of removal. Observe the following torques:

- Rack-to-crossmember bolts – 22–29 ft. lbs.
- Coupling bolt – 11–14 ft. lbs.
- Tie rod nuts – 11–25 ft. lbs.

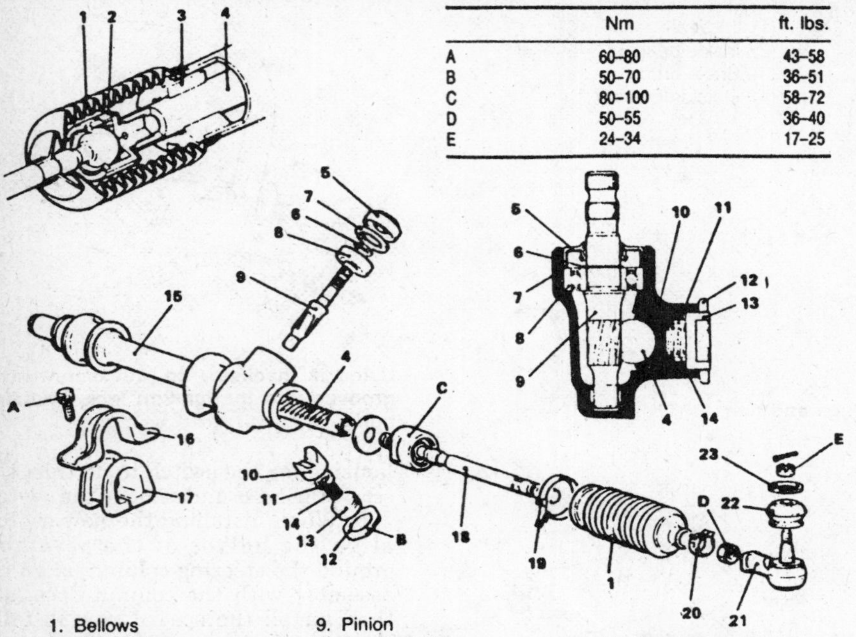

| | Nm | ft. lbs. |
|---|---|---|
| A | 60–80 | 43–58 |
| B | 50–70 | 36–51 |
| C | 80–100 | 58–72 |
| D | 50–55 | 36–40 |
| E | 24–34 | 17–25 |

1. Bellows
2. Tab washer
3. Rack bushing
4. Rack
5. Oil seal
6. Snap ring
7. Snap ring
8. Bearing
9. Pinion
10. Support yoke
11. Cushion rubber
12. Locking nut
13. Yoke plug
14. Yoke spring
15. Gear housing
16. Mounting bracket
17. Mounting rubber
18. Tie rod
19. Band
20. Clip
21. Tie rod end
22. Dust cover
23. Clip ring

**Manual rack and pinion steering assembly**

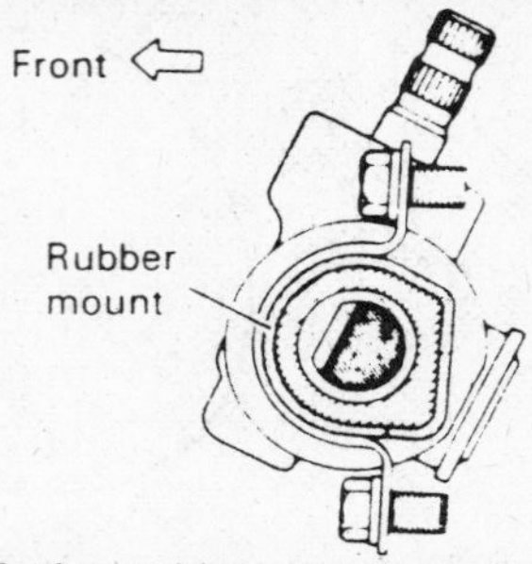


**Install the rubber gearbox mount as shown**

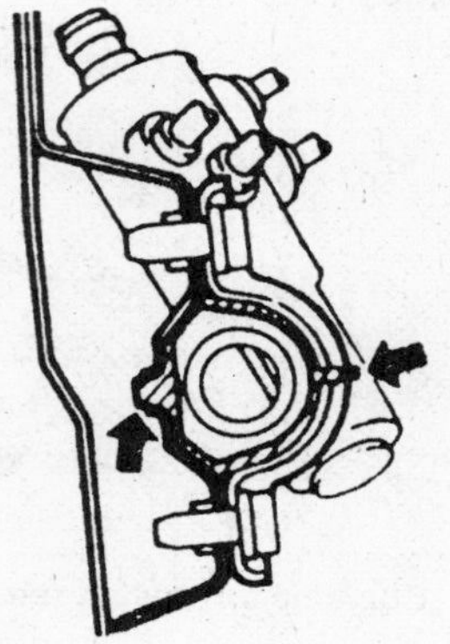

**Rubber isolator alignment on the power steering rack**

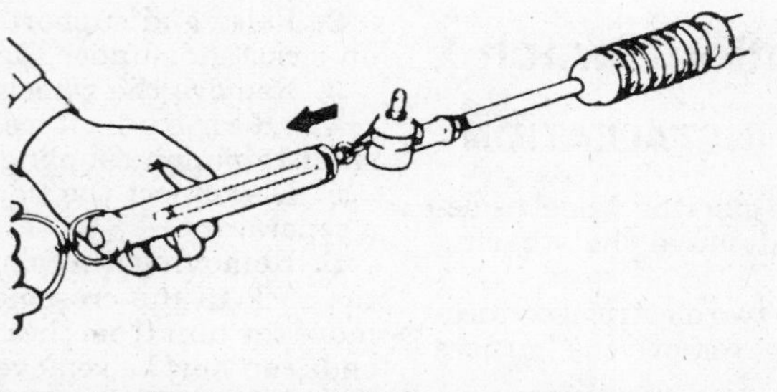

**Measuring the pinion preload on the manual steering rack**

## ADJUSTMENT

1. Mount the rack and pinion assembly in a soft jawed vise, clamping on the rack mounting area, only.
2. Using a spline adapter on an inch-pound torque wrench, turn the pinion shaft at the rate of one full turn every 4–6 seconds, turning the steering from lock-to-lock. Measure the total preload lock-to-lock. Preload should be 3.6–9.6 inch lbs.
3. Place a pull scale on each tie rod end, in turn, and pull straight away. The rack starting force should be 11–66 lbs.
4. If the specifications in either Steps 2 or 3 or not met, the rubber cushion and yoke spring behind the pinion shaft nut will have to be replaced.

# Power Steering Rack

## REMOVAL & INSTALLATION

### *Excel*

1. Loosen the lug nuts.
2. Raise and support the front end on jackstands under the frame.
3. Remove the wheels.
4. Remove the steering shaft-to-pinion coupling bolt.
5. Disconnect the tie rod ends with a separator.
6. Drain the fluid.
7. Disconnect the hoses from the gear box.
8. Remove the band from the steering joint cover.
9. Unbolt and remove the stabilizer bar.
10. Remove the rear roll stopper-to-center member bolt and move the rear roll stopper forward.
11. Remove the rack unit mounting clamp bolts and take the unit out the left side of the car. The tie rod ends can now be removed. Prior to removal, count the exact number of exposed threads on the tie rod ends, then loosen the locknut and unscrew the tie rod end. When installing new tie rod ends, oil the threads and screw them into place so that the previously noted number of threads is visible with the locknut tight. As a further reference, the distance between the end of the tie rod boot and the point at which the locknut touches the tie rod ball socket body should be 155.5–157.5mm (6.1–6.2 in.). Torque the locknut to 38 ft. lbs.
12. When installing the power steering rack, make sure that the rubber isolators have their nubs aligned with the holes in the clamps. Apply rubber cement to the slits in the gear mounting grommet. Tighten the clamp bolt to 43–58 ft. lbs., the tie rod nuts to 11–25 ft. lbs., and the coupling bolt to 22–25 ft. lbs.

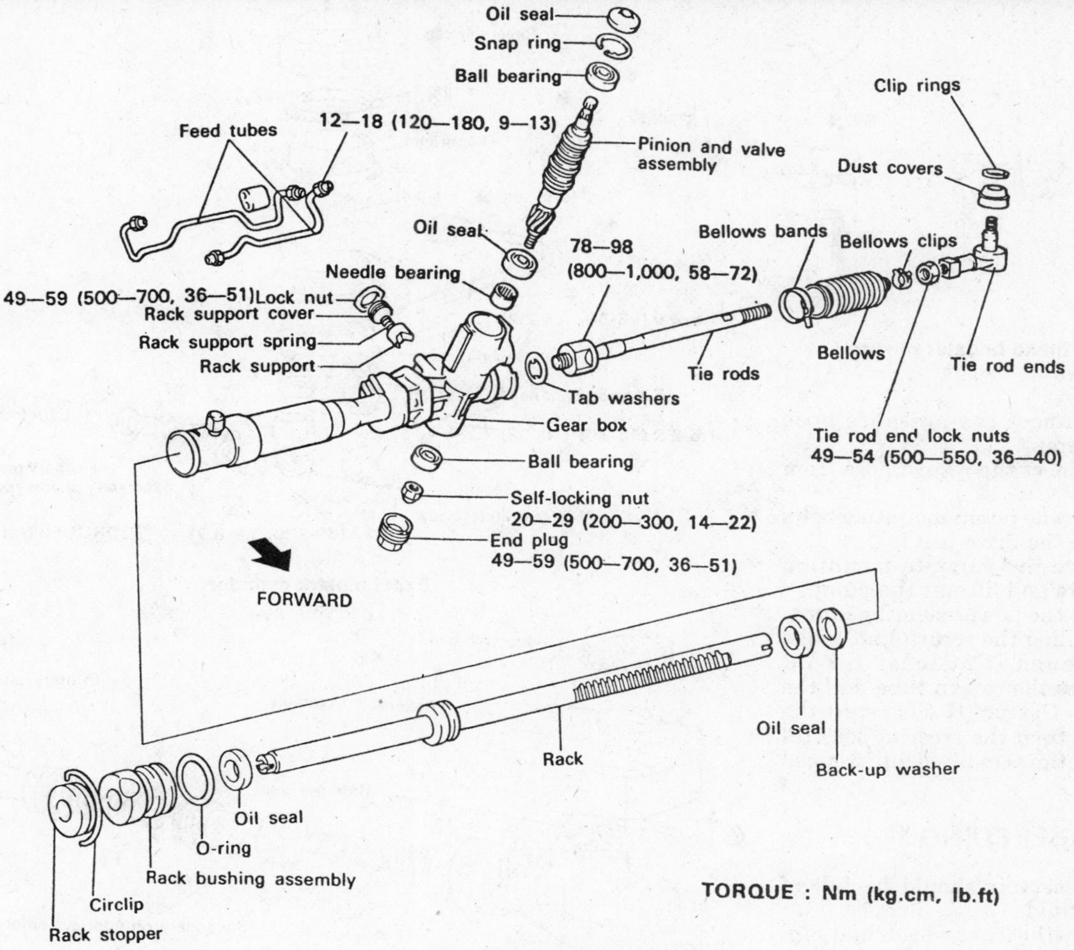


Sonata steering components

13. Fill the system with Dexron®II ATF.

### Sonata

1. Loosen the lug nuts.
2. Raise and support the front end on jackstands under the frame.
3. Remove the wheels.
4. Remove the steering shaft-to-pinion coupling bolt.
5. Disconnect the tie rod ends with a separator.
6. Drain the fluid.
7. Disconnect the hoses from the gear box.
8. Remove the center member and temporarily retighten the front muffler.
9. Unbolt and remove the stabilizer bar.
10. Remove the rack unit mounting clamp bolts and take the unit out the right side of the car. The tie rod ends can now be removed. Prior to removal, count the exact number of exposed threads on the tie rod ends, then loosen the locknut and unscrew the tie rod end. When installing new tie rod ends, oil the threads and screw them into place so that the previously noted number of threads is visible with the locknut tight. As a further reference, the distance between the end of the tie rod boot and the point at which the locknut touches the tie rod ball socket body should be 187.4mm. Torque the locknut to 38 ft. lbs.
11. When installing the power steering rack, make sure that the rubber isolators have their nubs aligned with the holes in the clamps. Apply rubber cement to the slits in the gear mounting grommet. Tighten the clamp bolt to 43–58 ft. lbs., the tie rod nuts to 11–25 ft. lbs., and the coupling bolt to 22–25 ft. lbs.
12. Fill the system with Dexron®II ATF.

## ADJUSTMENTS

### Total Pinion Preload

1. Mount the rack in a soft jawed vise, clamping the vise on the rack mounting areas, only.
2. Using a spline adapter on an inch-pound torque wrench, rotate the pinion shaft several times, lock-to-lock, and note the total pinion preload. Preload should be 5–11 inch lbs.
3. If the preload is note within specifications, adjust the position of the rack support cover and recheck the preload. If that doesn't work, the rack support cover components are defective.

### Tie Rod Swing Resistance

**EXCEL ONLY**

1. With the rack assembly mounted in a soft jawed vise, clamped on the rack mounting areas, only, give 10 hard swings on the tie rod.
2. Attach a pull scale to the tie rod end and check the swing resistance. Resistance should be 2–4½ lbs. If resistance is excessive, replace the tie rod. If resistance is below 2 lbs. the tie rod may be used if resistance is smooth and even.

# Power Steering Pump

## REMOVAL & INSTALLATION

1. Place a drain pan under the pump.

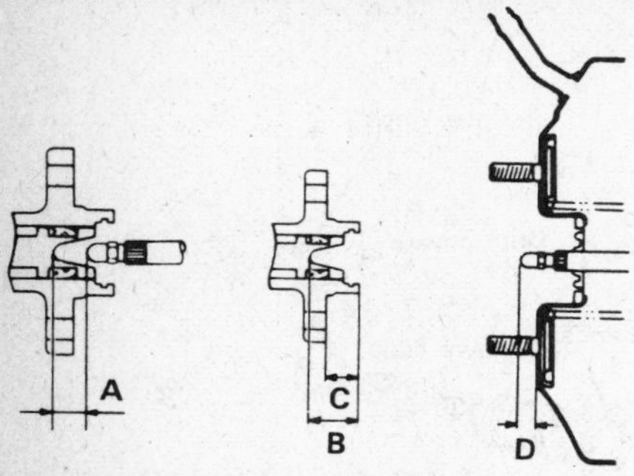


**Determining brake booster pushrod clearance**

2. Disconnect the pressure hose from the pump.
3. Disconnect the return hose from the pump.
4. Loosen the pump mounting bolts and remove the drive belt.
5. Remove the pump-to-mounting bracket bolts and lift out the pump.
6. Install the power steering pump. When installing the return line, make sure you push it at least 1.2 in. (30mm) onto the return tube. Fill the system with Dexron®II ATF, start the engine and turn the steering lock-to-lock several times to bleed any trapped air.

## SYSTEM BLEEDING

1. The reservoir should be full of Dexron®II fluid.
2. Jack up the front wheels and support the vehicle safely.
3. Turn the steering wheel fully to the right and left until no air bubbles appear in the fluid. Maintain the reservoir level.
4. Lower the vehicle and with the engine idling, turn the wheels fully to the right and left. Stop the engine.
5. Install a tube from the bleeder screw on the steering gear box to the reservoir.
6. Start the engine, turn the steering wheel fully to the left and loosen the bleeder screw.
7. Repeat the procedure until no air bubbles pass through the tube.
8. Tighten the bleeder screw and remove the tube. Refill the reservoir as needed. and check that no further bubbles are present in the fluid.

**NOTE: An abrupt rise in the fluid level after stopping the engine is a sign of incomplete bleeding. If this occures, repeat the bleeding procedure.**

# Tie Rod Ends

## REMOVAL & INSTALLATION

1. Raise the car and support it se-

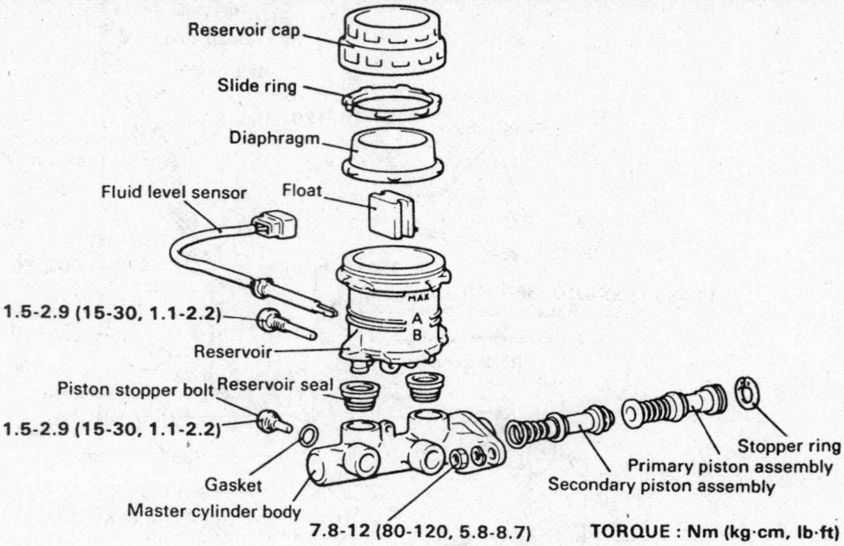


**Excel master cylinder**

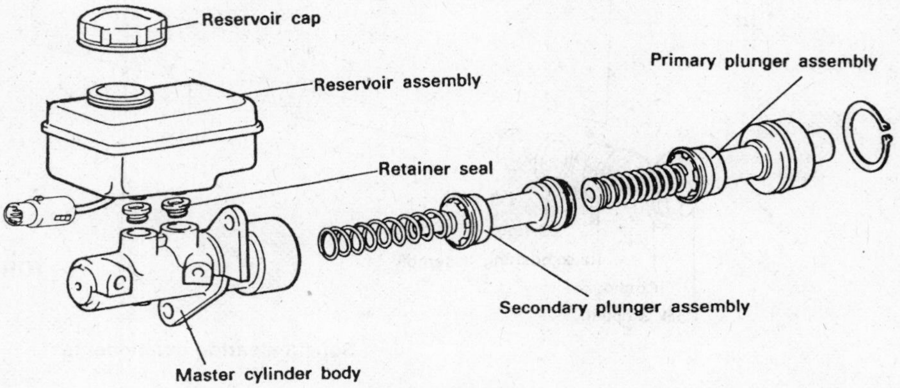


**Sonata master cylinder**

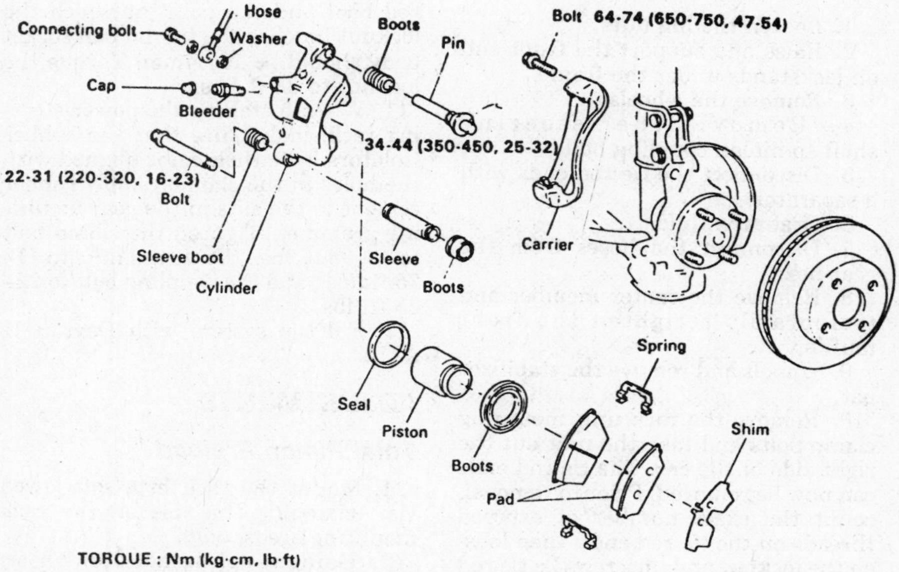


**Excel front disc brake components**

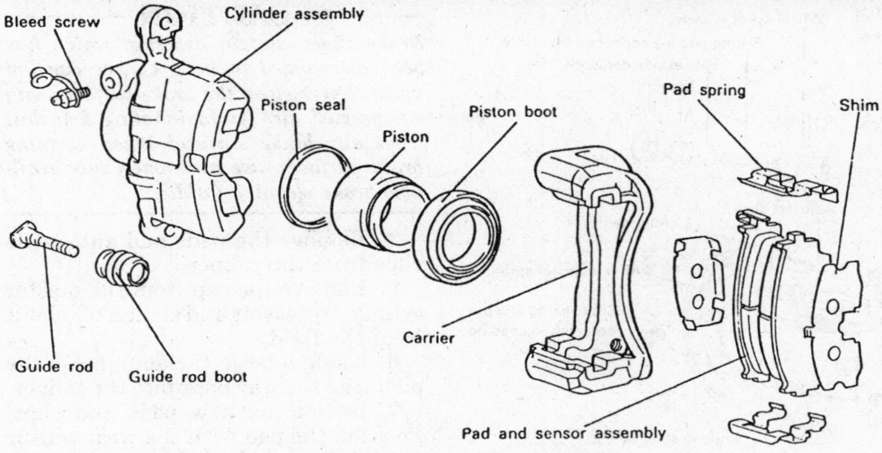


Sonata front disc brake components

curely at the front via axle stands. Remove the front wheels.

2. Remove the cotter pin and then remove the ball stud retaining nut. Use a vise-like tool (MB991113 or equivalent) to press the ball stud down and out of the steering knuckle.

3. Using a back-up wrench on the flats at the inner end of the tie rod end, loosen the nut that retains the end to the tie rod coming out of the steering box. Now, unscrew the tie rod end, counting the turns required to remove it.

4. Install the new tie rod end in reverse order. Torque the castellated nut retaining the ballstud to 11–25 ft. lbs. (15–33 Nm). Then, turn it just far enough to line up the castellations with the hole in the stud, and install a new cotter pin. Torque the inner nut to 36–40 ft. lbs. (49–54 Nm).

# BRAKES

**For all brake system repair and service procedures not detailed below, please refer to "Brakes" in the Unit Repair section.**

## Master Cylinder

### REMOVAL & INSTALLATION

1. Disconnect the fluid level sensor.
2. Disconnect the brake tubes from the master cylinder and cap them immediately.
3. Unbolt and remove the master cylinder from the booster.
4. Measure the master cylinder pushrod clearance using the accompanying illustration and the following formula: A = B − C − D. A should be 0.40–0.80mm for the Excel; 37.35–37.65mm for the Sonata.
5. Installation is the reverse of removal. Torque the mounting bolts to 72–108 inch lbs. Bleed the brake system.

## Proportioning Valve

The proportioning valve is located under the master cylinder and supported by the brake lines to which it is connected and a throughbolt. It does not require routine check or adjustment; however, if the car exhibits slightly unstable braking in a hard stop due to rear wheel lock up, it is best to have it tested with special high pressure gauges by a reputable mechanic.

### REMOVAL & INSTALLATION

1. Disconnect the brake lines at the valve.

**NOTE: Use a flare nut wrench to avoid damage to the lines and fittings.**

2. Remove the mounting bolts and remove the valve.

**NOTE: If the proportioning valve is found to be defective, it must be replaced.**

3. Install the proportioning valve and tighten the mounting bolts to 15 ft. lbs.
4. Refill the system with fluid and bleed the brakes.

## Power Brake Booster

### REMOVAL & INSTALLATION

1. Slide back the clip and disconnect the vacuum supply line at the brake booster. Pull gently in order to avoid damaging the check valve.
2. Remove the master cylinder as described above.
3. Disconnect the pushrod at the brake pedal. This requires pulling the lockpin out of the pedal clevis pin and then pulling the latter out of the pedal lever and clevis rod.
4. Remove the mounting bolts and nuts from the firewall and remove the booster.
5. Install the brake booster on the firewall and tighten the mounting nuts to 72–108 inch lbs. (8–12 Nm). Bleed the system.

## Disc Brake Pads

### REMOVAL & INSTALLATION

**CAUTION**

***Brake linings contain asbestos. Asbestos is a known cancer-causing agent. When working on brakes, remember that the dust which accumulates on the brake parts and/or in the drum contains asbestos. Always wear a protective face covering, such as a painter's mask, when working on the brakes. NEVER blow the dust from the brakes or drum! There are solvents made for the purpose of cleaning brake parts. Use them!***

#### Excel

1. Raise and support the front end on jackstands.
2. Remove the front wheels.
3. Pry off the dust shield from the caliper.
4. Depress the center of the outboard spring clip and remove the clip by slipping the ends from the pins.

**CAUTION**

***Brake shoes contain asbestos, which has been determined to be a cancer causing agent. Never clean the brake surfaces with compressed air! Avoid inhaling any dust from any brake surface! When cleaning brake surfaces, use a commercially available brake cleaning fluid.***

5. Remove the inboard spring clip with pliers.
6. Using pliers, pull the retaining pins from the caliper.
7. Lift the pads and anti-squeal shims from the caliper.
8. Clean all caliper parts, especially the torque plate shafts, with a solvent made for brake parts.

**CAUTION**

***Replace all brake pads at the same time. Never replace the pads on one wheel only!!***

9. If the dust protector or spring clips are weak, damaged or deformed, replace them.
10. Remove the cap from the master

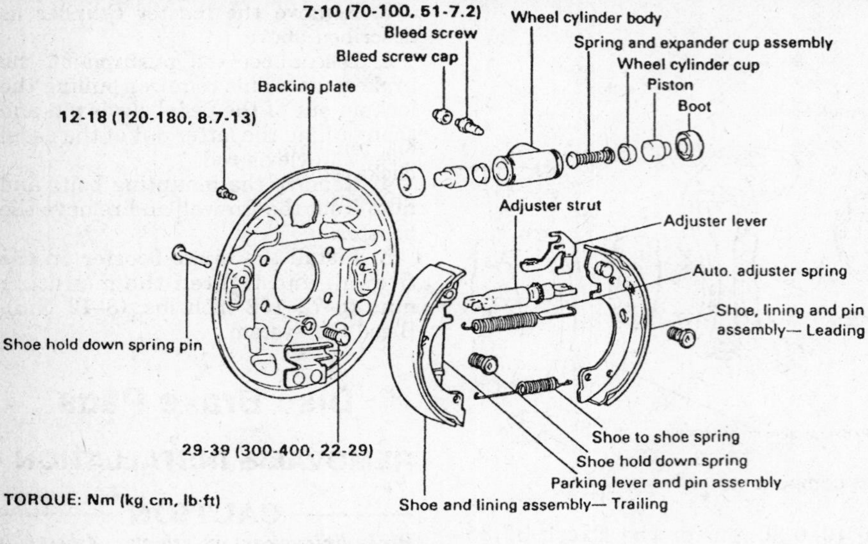


**Excel rear brake components**

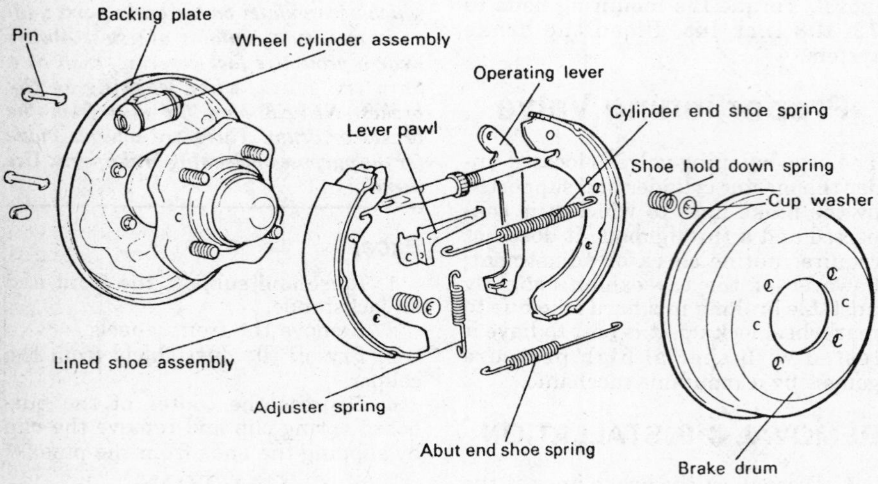


**Sonata rear brake components**

cylinder reservoir and, using a clean suction gun, remove about 6mm of fluid.

11. Using a C-clamp, force the caliper piston back into the caliper as far as it will go.

**NOTE: If the anti-squeal shims are at all rusted or deformed, discard them and use an anti-squeal compound, available at most auto parts stores. Furthermore, the anti-squeal shims may not be usable with some aftermarket brake pads due to thicker linings. The shims may preclude the proper fit of these pads. In that case, discard the shims and use the anti-squeal compound.**

12. Install the inboard pad and anti-squeal shim.

13. Install the outboard pad and anti-squeal shim.

14. Install the pins.

15. Install the two spring clips.

16. Install the dust shield.

17. Install the wheels and lower the car. Get in the car and depress the brake pedal a few times. The first couple of strokes on the pedal will feel overly long. However, the pads will set themselves and the stroke will return to normal.

### *Sonata*

1. Raise and support the front end on jackstands.

2. Remove the wheels.

3. Remove the 2 bolts from the torque plate and lift off the caliper. Suspend the caliper safely with wire. Don't stretch the brake hose.

**CAUTION**

***Brake shoes contain asbestos, which has been determined to be a cancer causing agent. Never clean the brake surfaces with compressed air! Avoid inhaling any dust from any brake surface! When cleaning brake surfaces, use a commercially available brake cleaning fluid.***

4. Remove the pads and anti-rattle clips from the caliper.

5. Remove the cap from the master cylinder reservoir and siphon off about ⅓ of the fluid.

6. Using a large C-clamp, press the piston all the way back into the caliper.

7. Install the new pads and clips. Position the pad with the wear sensor on the piston side and upwards.

8. Position the caliper and install the bolts. Torque the bolts to 23 ft. lbs.

## Brake Shoes

### REMOVAL & INSTALLATION

### *Excel*

1. Raise and support the rear end on jackstands.

2. Remove the rear wheels.

3. Pry off the hub grease cap.

4. Remove the cotter pin, lock cap and bearing adjusting nut.

5. Position your hand to catch the outer bearing and pull the hub and drum assembly from the spindle.

6. Thoroughly clean the spindle.

**CAUTION**

***Brake shoes contain asbestos, which has been determined to be a cancer causing agent. Never clean the brake surfaces with compressed air! Avoid inhaling any dust from any brake surface! When cleaning brake surfaces, use a commercially available brake cleaning fluid.***

7. Remove the lower pressed metal spring clip, the shoe return spring (the large one piece spring between the two shoes), and the two shoe holddown springs.

8. Remove the shoes and adjuster as an assembly.

9. Disconnect the parking brake cable from the lever.

10. Remove the spring between the shoes and the lever from the rear (trailing) shoe.

11. Disconnect the adjuster retaining spring and remove the adjuster, turn the star wheel in to the adjuster body after cleaning and lubricating the threads.

12. Clean the backing plate with solvent made for cleaning brakes.

13. Lubricate all contact points on the backing plate, anchor plate, wheel cylinder to shoe contact and parking

brake strut joints and contacts with lithium based grease.

14. Installation of the brake shoes, from this point, is the reverse of removal after the lever has been transferred to the new rear (trailing) shoe.

15. Pre-adjustment of the brake shoe can be made by turning the adjuster star wheel out until the drum will just slide on over the brake shoes. Before installing the drum make sure the parking brake is not adjusted too tightly, if it is, loosen it, or the adjustment of the rear brakes will not be correct.

16. Position the hub assembly on the spindle.

17. Insert the packed outer bearing, retaining washer and adjusting nut.

18. While rotating the hub, tighten the adjusting nut to 15 ft.lb., then back it off until loose.

19. Torque the nut again, this time to 48 in.lb.

20. Install the lock cap and turn the nut counterclockwise just enough to align the cap and cotter pin hole. Insert a new cotter pin. Never back the nut off more than 15 degrees to align the cotter pin hole. If more is necessary, repeat the entire adjustment procedure.

21. The brakes shoes are adjusted by pumping the brake pedal and applying and releasing the parking brake. Adjust the parking brake stroke. Road test the car.

### *Sonata*

1. Raise and support the rear end on jackstands.
2. Remove the wheels.
3. Remove the hub nut, outer bearing and brake drum.
4. Thoroughly clean the spindle.
5. Clean the brake shoes and backing plate with a commercially available solvent.

**CAUTION**

***Brake shoes contain asbestos, which has been determined to be a cancer causing agent. Never clean the brake surfaces with compressed air! Avoid inhaling any dust from any brake surface! When cleaning brake surfaces, use a commercially available brake cleaning fluid.***

6. Remove the lower spring.
7. Remove the upper spring.
8. Remove the holddown springs.
9. Remove the shoes and adjuster.
10. Disconnect the parking brake cable from the adjuster arm.
11. Apply a thin coating of lithium based grease to the backing plate pads.
12. Connect the parking brake cable to the adjuster.
13. Position the shoes on the backing plate and install the holddown springs and pins.

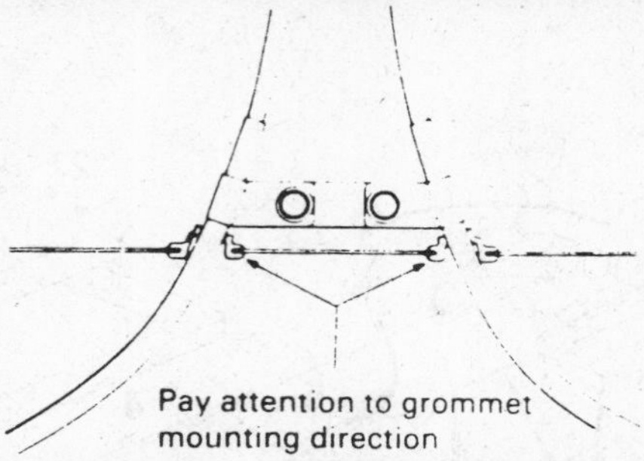
Pay attention to grommet mounting direction

Parking brake cable grommet positioning

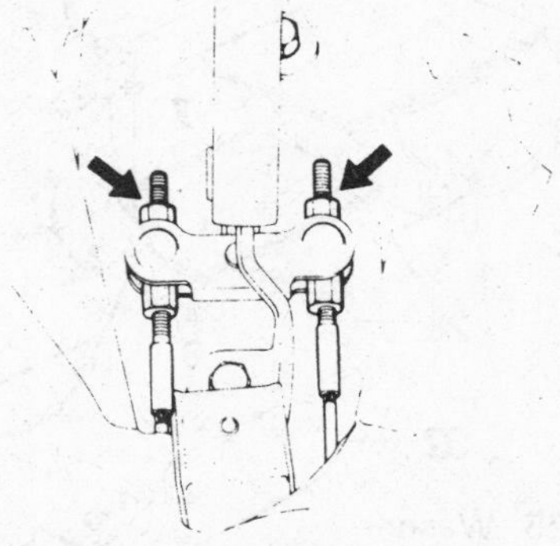

Parking brake cable adjusting nuts

14. Install the upper spring, then the lower spring and adjuster spring.
15. Install the drum and adjust the wheel bearings as described above.

## Wheel Cylinder

### REMOVAL & INSTALLATION

1. Remove the brake drums and shoes. Disconnect the brake line where it connects to the wheel cylinder behind the brake backing plate, and plug the open end of the brake line.

**CAUTION**

***Brake shoes contain asbestos, which has been determined to be a cancer causing agent. Never clean the brake surfaces with compressed air! Avoid inhaling any dust from any brake surface! When cleaning brake surfaces, use a commercially available brake cleaning fluid.***

2. Remove the two bolts that fasten the wheel cylinder to the backing plate from behind it, and remove the wheel cylinder.
3. Install the wheel cylinder and tighten the mounting bolts for the wheel cylinder to 72–108 inch lbs. (8–12 Nm). Bleed the system as described above. Make sure the self-adjusters have taken up play so the brakes actuate normally before operating the vehicle.

## Parking Brake Cable

### ADJUSTMENT

1. Apply the brake with about 45 lbs. tension and count the number of clicks required. 5–7 clicks should be required on the Excel; 8-9 clicks on the Sonata. If the number of clicks is incorrect, proceed with the remaining steps.
2. Remove the rear console box. Remove the parking brake cover and the ashtray. Then, remove the console mounting screws and remove the console.
3. Release the brake and then adjust the cable adjusting nuts until all cable slack is just removed. Then, apply the footbrake (the engine should be idling) and release it, apply the handbrake and release it, apply the footbrake and release it, etc. in a continuous cycle until the automatic adjusters stop clicking.
4. Recheck the number of clicks required to apply the brake, adjust the cable adjuster, and repeat the check until the number of clicks required is correct.
5. Reinstall the console in reverse of the removal procedure.
6. Raise the rear of the car and support it safely. Release the handbrake and rotate each rear wheel to make sure the brakes are not dragging.

### REMOVAL & INSTALLATION

#### *Excel*

1. Block the front wheels, loosen the rear lugnuts, raise the car and support it on jackstands, and remove the rear wheels and brake drums.
2. Remove the console box and rear seat (see the adjustment procedure above).
3. Release the handbrake and then disconnect the cable connectors at the equalizer. It may be necessary to loosen the cable adjusting nuts to do this.
4. Disconnect all cable clamps from the body. Remove the mounting bolts for the large mounting clamp located just forward of where the cables pass through the body grommets.
5. Pull the cables and grommets out of the body.
6. Disconnect the cables at the rear brakes.
7. When installing the cables, make sure the grommets are installed in the body completely and that the concave side faces to the rear. Adjust the handbrake mechanism as described above. Adjust the switch for the indicator light so the light comes on when the lever is pulled one notch.

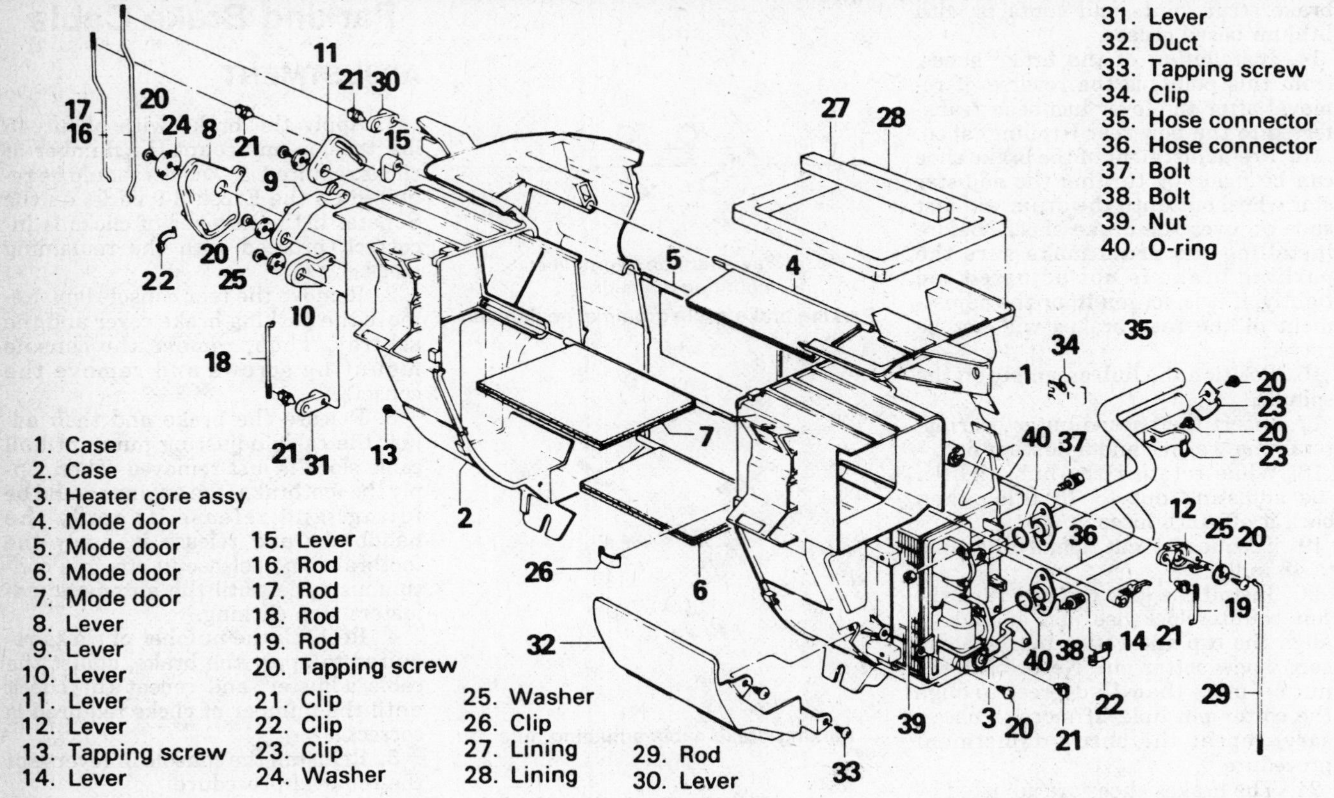


Excel heater components

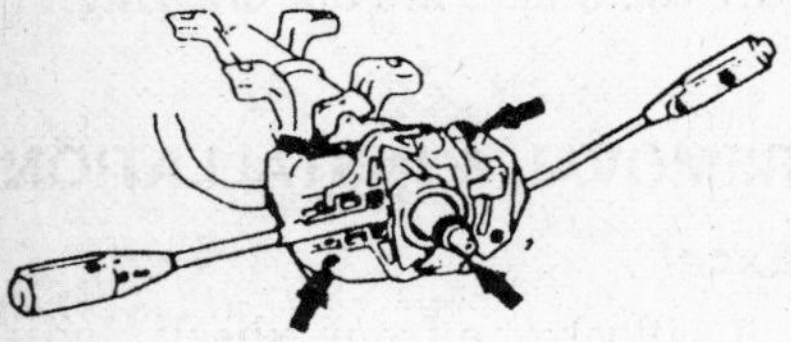

Windshield wiper switch mounting

### Sonata

1. Raise and support the rear end on jackstands.
2. Remove the console.
3. Remove the cable adjuster, pin, equalizer and nut holder.
4. Remove the parking brake switch.
5. Remove the parking brake lever.
6. Remove the rear seat cushion and roll back the carpet.
7. Remove the brake cable clamp and grommet.
8. Remove the brake drums and shoes.
9. Disconnect the brake cables from the adjusting arms.
10. Remove the retaining clips and push the cable out of the backing plates.
11. Installation is the reverse of removal.

# CHASSIS ELECTRICAL

## Heater Blower Motor

### REMOVAL & INSTALLATION

**NOTE: To remove either the blower or core, the heater case must be removed.**

#### Excel

1. Disconnect the battery ground.
2. Place the control in the HOT position.
3. Drain the cooling system.
4. Remove the heater hoses from the core tubes.
5. Remove the lower instrument panel section.
6. Remove the center console and on-board computer.
7. Loosen the heater duct mounting screw. Then, pushing downward and pulling, remove the heater ducts.
8. Disconnect the heater control cable.
9. Disconnect the wiring at the motor.
10. Remove the five heater case mounting bolts and remove the heater case from under the dash.
11. Separate the case halves and remove the blower.
12. Installation is the reverse of removal. Adjust the control cable and refill the cooling system.

#### Sonata

**CAUTION**

***The refrigerant system must be discharged. This job should be performed only by someone thoroughly familiar with refrigerant systems!***

1. Disconnect the battery ground.
2. Place the control in the HOT position.
3. Drain the cooling system.
4. Remove the heater hoses from the core tubes.
5. Discharge the air conditioning system.
6. Disconnect the suction and liquid refrigerant lines at the firewall connectors. Always use back-up wrenches! Cap all openings at once!
7. Remove the front and rear center consoles.
8. Remove the heater side covers.
9. Remove the glove box, center crash pad cover, center crash pad and the radio.

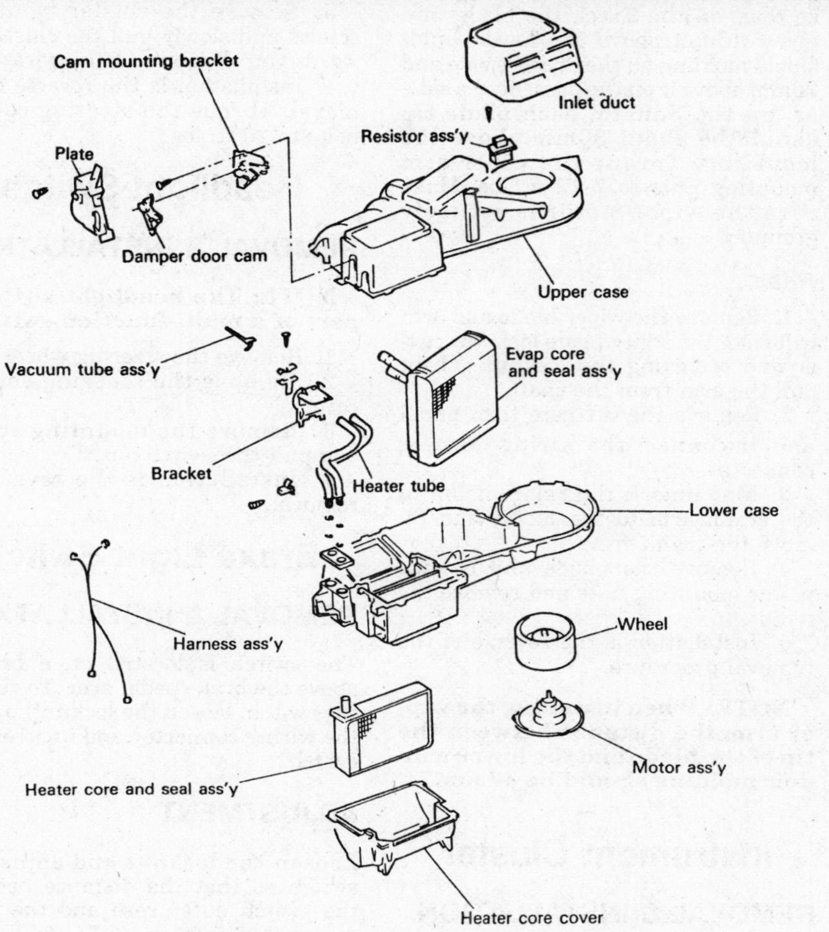


**Heater-A/C components for USA Sonatas**

3. Drain the cooling system.
4. Remove the heater hoses from the core tubes.
5. Discharge the air conditioning system.
6. Disconnect the suction and liquid refrigerant lines at the firewall connectors. Always use back-up wrenches! Cap all openings at once!
7. Remove the front and rear center consoles.
8. Remove the heater side covers.
9. Remove the glove box, center crash pad cover, center crash pad and the radio.
10. Remove the lower crash pad.
11. Remove the console mounting bracket and center support.
12. Remove the left and right rear heat duct assemblies and the rear heating joint duct.
13. Remove the control unit.
14. Disconnect the blower speed actuator connector and, in Canada, disconnect the blend door actuator connector.
15. Remove the heater-A/C unit.
16. Remove the blower motor from the case.
17. Separate the case halves and lift out the core.
18. Installation is the reverse of removal. Adjust the control cable and refill the cooling system.

10. Remove the lower crash pad.
11. Remove the console mounting bracket and center support.
12. Remove the left and right rear heat duct assemblies and the rear heating joint duct.
13. Remove the control unit.
14. Disconnect the blower speed actuator connector and, in Canada, disconnect the blend door actuator connector.
15. Remove the heater-A/C unit.
16. Remove the blower motor from the case.
17. Installation is the reverse of removal. Adjust the control cable and refill the cooling system.

# Heater Core

## REMOVAL & INSTALLATION

### Excel

1. Disconnect the battery ground cable.
2. Set the heater control to HOT and drain the cooling system.
3. Disconnect the coolant hoses at the heater core tubes, in the engine compartment.
4. Remove the lower instrument panel section.
5. Remove the center console and on-board computer.
6. Loosen the heater duct mounting screw.
7. Pushing downward and pull, remove the heater ducts.
8. Disconnect the heater control cable.
9. Disconnect the wiring at the motor.
10. Remove the five heater case mounting bolts and remove the heater case from under the dash.
11. Separate the case halves and remove the blower.
12. Installation is the reverse of removal. Refill the cooling system.

### Sonata

**CAUTION**

***The refrigerant system must be discharged. This job should be performed only by someone familiar with air conditioning systems!***

1. Disconnect the battery ground.
2. Place the control in the HOT position.

# Radio

## REMOVAL & INSTALLATION

### Excel

1. Remove the panel that surrounds the parking brake. Remove the ashtray.
2. Remove the two console mounting screws from each side, two near the handbrake, and one at the rear of the ashtray. Then, remove the console.
3. Remove the 4 mounting screws from the radio bracket, and remove the radio and bracket as an assembly. Now, separate the radio and bracket. Note that the radio fuses are located behind the radio and are now accessible.
4. Installation is the reverse of removal.

### Sonata

1. Remove the lower center instrument panel face and pad.
2. Remove the radio mounting screws and pull the radio out slowly. Disconnect the wiries.
3. Installation is the reverse of removal.

## Windshield Wiper Switch

### REMOVAL & INSTALLATION

#### *Front*

**NOTE: The windshield wiper switch is part of a combination (multi-function) switch.**

1. Remove the steering wheel.
2. Remove the steering column cover.
3. Remove the two mounting screws and pull the switch out.
4. Installation is the reverse of removal.

#### *Rear*

1. Pry the switch bezel from the panel.
2. Reach behind the panel and disconnect the wiring from the switch.
3. Depress the 2 retainers and pull the switch from the panel.
4. Installation is the reverse of removal.

## Windshield Wiper Motor

### REMOVAL & INSTALLATION

#### *Front*

1. Remove the air inlet and cowl front center trim panels. Remove the three pivot shaft mounting nuts and push the pivot shafts into the area under the cowl.
2. Remove the motor mounting bolts. Pull the motor into the best possible position for access and use a flat-bladed screwdriver to pry the linkage off the motor crank arm. Remove the motor and then the linkage.
3. If the motor is being replaced, matchmark the position of the crank arm of the motor shaft of the new motor, and then remove the nut and crank arm, transferring both to the new motor.
4. Installation is the reverse of removal. Torque the pivot shaft nuts to 4.3–5.8 ft. lbs. Position the wiper arms so that, on the Excel, the blades are about 15mm above the lower windshield molding on the driver's side and 20mm above it on the passenger's side, or, on the Sonata, each blade tip should be about 30mm above the moulding. Torque the wiper arm mounting nuts to 7–12 ft. lbs. Make sure the wiper motor is securely grounded.

#### *Rear*

1. Remove the wiper blade and arm by lifting the wiper blade lock nut cover and removing the locknut. Then, pull the arm from the shaft.
2. Remove the lift gate trim panel and disconnect the wiring harness connector.
3. Matchmark the relationship of the crank arm to the motor and remove the crank arm.
4. Remove the inside and outside motor mounting nuts and remove the motor.
5. Installation is the reverse of the removal procedure.

**NOTE: When installing the wiper arm, the distance between the tip of the blade and the lower window molding should be 40mm.**

## Instrument Cluster

### REMOVAL & INSTALLATION

#### *Excel*

1. Remove the two meter hood attaching screws, located at the bottom, and tilt the lower meter hood outward. Pull the hood downward to release the locking tangs at the top and remove it.
2. Remove the four meter assembly mounting screw (two at top and two at the bottom) and pull the unit outward. Disconnect the speedometer cable and all connectors, and remove the unit.
3. Installation is the reverse of removal.

#### *Sonata*

1. Remove the steering column support bolts and carefully lower the column on the front seat.
2. Remove the cluster trim panel.
3. Remove the cluster moutning screws and slowly pull the cluster towards you. Disconnect the wires.
4. Installation is the reverse of removal. Torque the steering column bolts to 20 ft. lbs.

## Headlight Switch

### REMOVAL & INSTALLATION

**NOTE: The headlight switch is part of a multi-function switch.**

1. Remove the steering wheel.
2. Remove the steering column cover.
3. Remove the mounting screws and pull the switch out.
4. Installation is the reverse of removal.

## Brake Light Switch

### REMOVAL & INSTALLATION

The switch is located on a bracket above the brake pedal arm. To replace the switch, loosen the locknut, unplug the wiring connector and unscrew the switch.

### ADJUSTMENT

Loosen the locknut and adjust the switch so that the distance between the switch outer case and the pedal arm is 0.02–0.04 in. (0.5–1.0mm).

## Fuses

### LOCATION

The fuse box is located behind a snap-off cover in front of the driver's left knee. The sunroof fuse is located in the electrical harness for the roof circuit, at the extreme right side of the dashboard, directly behind the right windshield pillar. The radio fuse is located behind the radio and is accessible after the radio is removed.

The hazard and turn signal flashers are located in the relay box on the left fender in the engine compartment, and are replaced by simply unplugging the burnt out flasher and plugging a new one in with all the prongs properly lined up.

# Isuzu

## I-Mark, Impulse

# 8

# SERIAL NUMBER IDENTIFICATION

## Vehicle Identification Plate

The vehicle identification number is embossed on a plate, that is attached to the top left corner of the instrument panel. The number is visible through the windshield from the outside of the vehicle. The eighth digit of the number, indicates the engine model and the tenth digit represents the model year (example is K for 1989).

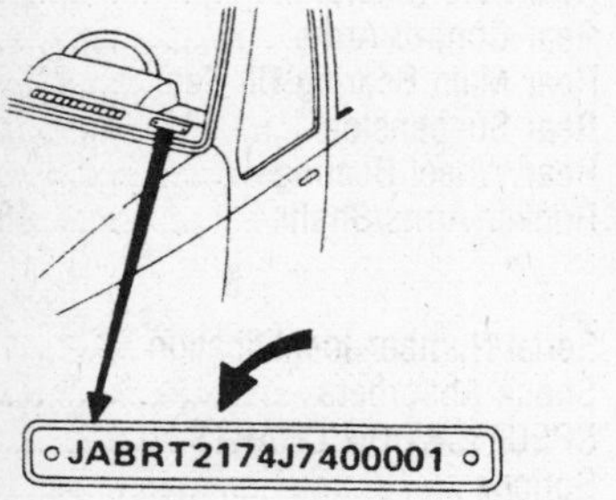


Vehicle identification plate location

## Engine Number

The Impulse equipped with the G200Z engine, has the engine serial number stamped on the top right corner of the engine block.

The Impulse equipped with the 4ZC1-T and 4ZD1 engine, has the number stamped on the left rear corner of the engine block, near the engine to transaxle mounting. On the I-Mark equipped with the G180Z engine, the number is stamped on the top right corner of the engine block. The I-Mark equipped with the 4FB1 diesel engine, has the number stamped on the left rear corner of the engine block. The I-Mark (FWD) equipped with the 4XC1-U, 4XC1-T and the 4XE1 engines, have the number stamped on the flange near the transaxle mounting, toward the front of the vehicle.

## Transmission Number

Both manual transmissions have their serial numbers on the side of the main case. The automatic location is similar.

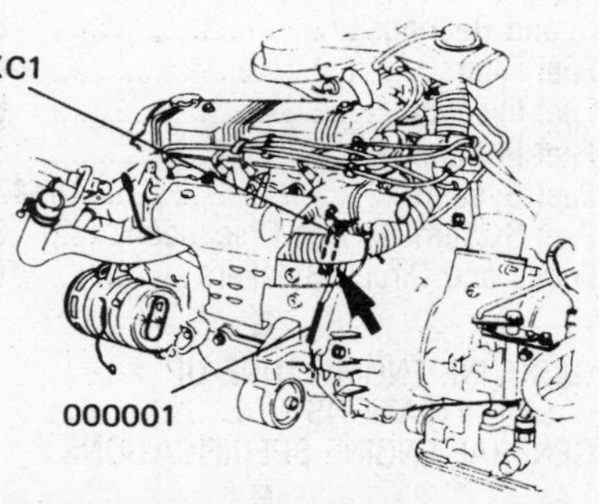


4XC1-T engine serial number location

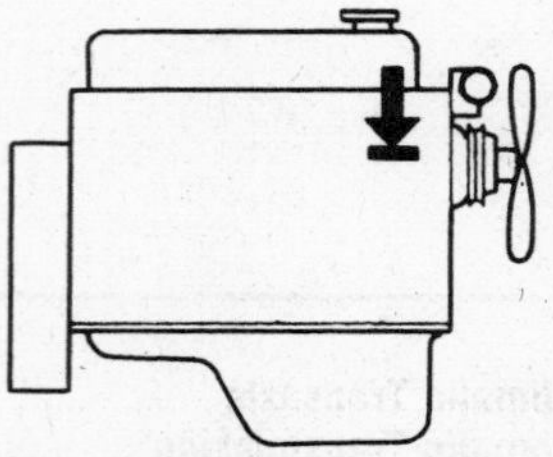

G200Z engine serial number location

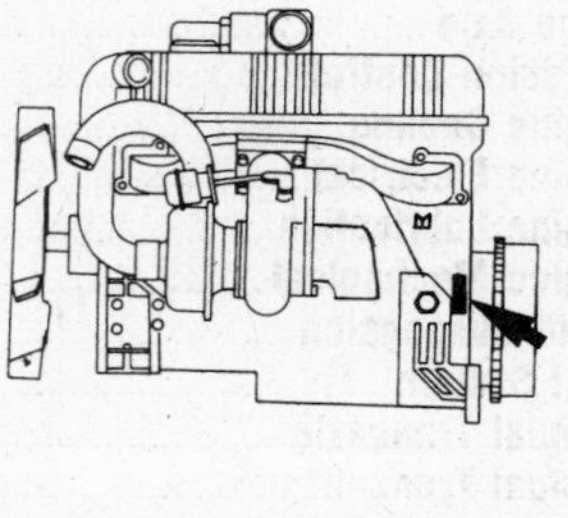

4ZC1-T and 4ZD1 engine serial number location

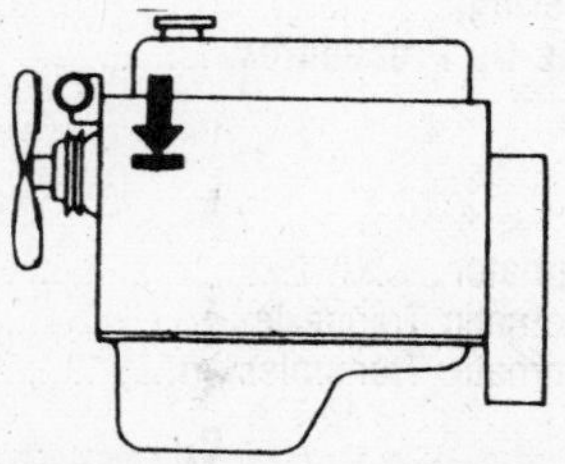

G180Z engine serial number location

### ENGINE IDENTIFICATION

| Year | Model | Engine Displacement cu. in. (cc/liter) | Engine Series Identification | No. of Cylinders | Engine Type |
|---|---|---|---|---|---|
| 1983 | I-Mark | 110.8 (1816/1.8) | G180Z | 4 | OHC |
| | I-Mark | 111 (1817/1.8) | 4FB1 Diesel | 4 | OHC |
| | Impulse | 118.9 (1949/1.9) | G200Z | 4 | SOHC |
| 1984 | I-Mark | 110.8 (1816/1.8) | G180Z | 4 | OHC |
| | I-Mark | 111 (1817/1.8) | 4FB1 Diesel | 4 | OHC |
| | Impulse | 118.9 (1949/1.9) | G200Z | 4 | SOHC |
| 1985 | I-Mark (FWD) | 90 (1471/1.5) | 4XC1-U | 4 | OHC |
| | I-Mark (RWD) | 110.8 (1816/1.8) | G180Z | 4 | OHC |
| | I-Mark (RWD) | 111 (1817/1.8) | 4FB1 Diesel | 4 | OHC |
| | Impulse | 118.9 (1949/1.9) | G200Z | 4 | SOHC |
| 1986 | I-Mark | 90 (1471/1.5) | 4XC1-U | 4 | OHC |
| | Impulse | 118.9 (1949/1.9) | G200Z | 4 | SOHC |
| | Impulse (Turbo) | 121.7 (1994/2.0) | 4ZC1-T | 4 | Turbo OHC |

## ENGINE IDENTIFICATION

| Year | Model | Engine Displacement cu. in. (cc/liter) | Engine Series Identification | No. of Cylinders | Engine Type |
|---|---|---|---|---|---|
| 1987 | I-Mark | 90 (1471/1.5) | 4XC1-U | 4 | OHC |
| | Impulse | 118.9 (1949/1.9) | G200Z | 4 | OHC |
| | Impulse (Turbo) | 121.7 (1994/2.0) | 4ZC1-T | 4 | Turbo OHC |
| 1988 | I-Mark | 90 (1471/1.5) | 4XC1-U | 4 | OHC |
| | I-Mark (Turbo) | 90 (1471/1.5) | 4XC1-T | 4 | Turbo OHC |
| | Impulse (Turbo) | 121.7 (1994/2.0) | 4ZC1-T | 4 | Turbo OHC |
| | Impulse | 138 (2254/2.3) | 4ZD1 | 4 | OHC |
| 1989-90 | I-Mark | 90 (1471/1.5) | 4XC1-U | 4 | OHC |
| | I-Mark (Turbo) | 90 (1471/1.5) | 4XC1-T | 4 | Turbo OHC |
| | Impulse (DOHC) | 92 (1588/1.6) | 4XE1 | 4 | DOHC |
| | Impulse (Turbo) | 121.7 (1994/2.0) | 4ZC1-T | 4 | Turbo OHC |
| | Impulse | 138 (2254/2.3) | 4ZD1 | 4 | OHC |

## GENERAL ENGINE SPECIFICATIONS

| Year | Model | Engine Displacement cu. in. (cc) | Fuel System Type | Net Horsepower @ rpm | Net Torque @ rpm (ft. lbs.) | Bore × Stroke (in.) | Com-pression Ratio | Oil Pressure @ rpm |
|---|---|---|---|---|---|---|---|---|
| 1983 | I-Mark | 110.8 (1816) | 2 bbl | 80 @ 4800 | 95 @ 3000 | 3.31 × 3.23 | 8.5:1 | 57 @ 1400 |
| | I-Mark | 111 (1817) | Diesel | 51 @ 5000 | 72 @ 3000 | 3.31 × 3.23 | 22.0:1 | 64 @ 1400 |
| | Impulse | 118.9 (1949) | EFI | 90 @ 5000 | 108 @ 3000 | 3.43 × 3.29 | 9.2:1 | 57 @ 1400 |
| 1984 | I-Mark | 110.8 (1816) | 2 bbl | 80 @ 4800 | 95 @ 3000 | 3.31 × 3.23 | 8.5:1 | 57 @ 1400 |
| | I-Mark | 111 (1817) | Diesel | 51 @ 5000 | 72 @ 3000 | 3.31 × 3.23 | 22.0:1 | 64 @ 1400 |
| | Impulse | 118.9 (1949) | EFI | 90 @ 5000 | 146 @ 3000 | 3.43 × 3.29 | 9.2:1 | 57 @ 1400 |
| 1985 | I-Mark (FWD) | 90 (1471) | 2 bbl | 70 @ 5400 | 87 @ 3400 | 3.03 × 3.11 | 9.6:1 | 49 @ 5200 |
| | I-Mark (RWD) | 110.8 (1816) | 2 bbl | 80 @ 4800 | 95 @ 3000 | 3.31 × 3.23 | 8.5:1 | 57 @ 1400 |
| | I-Mark) (RWD) | 111 (1817) | Diesel | 51 @ 5000 | 72 @ 3000 | 3.31 × 3.23 | 22.0:1 | 64 @ 1400 |
| | Impulse | 118.9 (1949) | EFI | 90 @ 5000 | 146 @ 3000 | 3.43 × 3.29 | 9.2:1 | 57 @ 1400 |
| 1986 | I-Mark | 90 (1471) | 2 bbl | 70 @ 5400 | 87 @ 3400 | 3.03 × 3.11 | 9.6:1 | 49 @ 5200 |
| | Impulse | 118.9 (1949) | EFI | 90 @ 5000 | 146 @ 3000 | 3.43 × 3.29 | 9.2:1 | 57 @ 1400 |
| | Impulse (Turbo) | 121.7 (1994) | EFI | 140 @ 5400 | 166 @ 3000 | 3.47 × 3.29 | 7.9:1 | 57 @ 1400 |
| 1987 | I-Mark | 90 (1471) | 2 bbl | 70 @ 5400 | 87 @ 3400 | 3.03 × 3.11 | 9.6:1 | 49 @ 5200 |
| | Impulse | 118.9 (1949) | EFI | 90 @ 5000 | 146 @ 3000 | 3.43 × 3.29 | 9.2:1 | 57 @ 1400 |
| | Impulse (Turbo) | 121.7 (1994) | EFI | 140 @ 5400 | 166 @ 3000 | 3.47 × 3.29 | 7.9:1 | 57 @ 1400 |
| 1988 | I-Mark | 90 (1471) | 2 bbl | 70 @ 5400 | 87 @ 3400 | 3.03 × 3.11 | 9.6:1 | 49 @ 5200 |
| | I-Mark (Turbo) | 90 (1471) | EFI | 110 @ 5400 | 120 @ 3400 | 3.03 × 3.11 | 8.0:1 | 49 @ 5200 |

## GENERAL ENGINE SPECIFICATIONS

| Year | Model | Engine Displacement cu. in. (cc) | Fuel System Type | Net Horsepower @ rpm | Net Torque @ rpm (ft. lbs.) | Bore × Stroke (in.) | Compression Ratio | Oil Pressure @ rpm |
|---|---|---|---|---|---|---|---|---|
| 1988 | Impulse (Turbo) | 121.7 (1994) | EFI | 140 @ 5400 | 166 @ 3000 | 3.46 × 3.29 | 7.9:1 | 57 @ 1400 |
| | Impulse | 138 (2254) | EFI | 110 @ 5000 | 127 @ 3000 | 3.52 × 3.54 | 8.6:1 | 57 @ 1400 |
| 1989-90 | I-Mark | 90 (1471) | 2 bbl | 70 @ 5400 | 87 @ 3400 | 3.03 × 3.11 | 9.6:1 | 49 @ 5200 |
| | I-Mark (Turbo) | 90 (1471) | EFI | 110 @ 5400 | 120 @ 3400 | 3.03 × 3.11 | 8.0:1 | 49 @ 5200 |
| | I-Mark (DOHC) | 92 (1588) | EFI | 125 @ 6800 | 138 @ 5400 | 3.15 × 3.11 | 9.8:1 | 49 @ 5200 |
| | Impulse (Turbo) | 121.7 (1994) | EFI | 140 @ 5400 | 166 @ 3000 | 3.46 × 3.29 | 7.9:1 | 57 @ 1400 |
| | Impulse | 138 (2254) | EFI | 110 @ 5000 | 127 @ 3000 | 3.52 × 3.54 | 8.6:1 | 57 @ 1400 |

## GASOLINE ENGINE TUNE-UP SPECIFICATIONS

| Year | Model | Engine Displacement cu. in. (cc) | Spark Plugs Type | Spark Plugs Gap (in.) | Ignition Timing (deg.) MT | Ignition Timing (deg.) AT | Compression Pressure (psi) | Fuel Pump (psi) | Idle Speed (rpm) MT | Idle Speed (rpm) AT | Valve Clearance In. | Valve Clearance Ex. |
|---|---|---|---|---|---|---|---|---|---|---|---|---|
| 1983 | I-Mark | 110.8 (1816) | BPR6ES11 | .040 | 6B | 6B | 170.6 | 3.6 | 900 | 900 | .006 | .010 |
| | Impulse | 118.9 (1949) | BPR6ES11 | .040 | 12B | 12B | 178.0 | 36① | 900② | 900② | .006 | .010 |
| 1984 | I-Mark | 110.8 (1816) | BPR6ES11 | .040 | 6B | 6B | 170.6 | 3.6 | 800 | 900 | .006 | .010 |
| | Impulse | 118.9 (1949) | BPR6ES11 | .040 | 12B | 12B | 178.0 | 36① | 900② | 900② | .006 | .010 |
| 1985 | I-Mark (FWD) | 90 (1471) | BPR6ES11 | .040 | 3B | 3B | 177.8 | 3.8–4.7 | 750 | 1000 | .006 | .010 |
| | I-Mark (RWD) | 110.8 (1816) | BPR6ES11 | .040 | 6B | 6B | 170.6 | 3.6 | 800 | 900 | .006 | .010 |
| | Impulse | 118.9 (1949) | BPR6ES11 | .040 | 12B | 12B | 178.0 | — | 900② | 900② | .006 | .010 |
| 1986 | I-Mark | 90 (1471) | BPR6ES11 | .040 | 3B | 3B | 177.8 | 3.8–4.7 | 750 | 1000 | .006 | .010 |
| | Impulse | 118.9 (1949) | BPR6ES11 | .040 | 12B | 12B | 178.0 | 36① | 900② | 900② | .006 | .010 |
| | Impulse (Turbo) | 121 (1994) | BPR6ES11 | .040 | 12B | 12B | 178.0 | 36① | 900② | 900② | .006 | .010 |
| 1987 | I-Mark | 90 (1417) | BPR6ES11 | .040 | 3B | 3B | 177.8 | 3.8–4.7 | 750 | 1000 | .006 | .010 |
| | Impulse | 118.9 (1949) | BPR6ES11 | .040 | 12B | 12B | 178.0 | 36① | 900② | 900② | .006 | .010 |
| | Impulse (Turbo) | 121.7 (1994) | BPR6ES11 | .040 | 12B | 12B | 178.0 | 36① | 900② | 900② | .006 | .010 |
| 1988 | I-Mark | 90 (1471) | BPR6ES11 | .040 | 3B | 3B | 177.8 | 3.8–4.7 | 750 | 1000 | .006 | .010 |
| | I-Mark (Turbo) | 90 (1471) | BPR6ES11 | .040 | 15B | NA | 171.0 | 28.4① | 950 | NA | .006 | .010 |
| | Impulse (Turbo) | 121.7 (1994) | BPR6ES11 | .040 | 12B | 12B | 178.0 | 35.6① | 900② | 900② | .006 | .010 |
| | Impulse | 138 (2254) | BPR6ES11 | .040 | 12B | 12B | 178.0 | 35.6① | 900② | 900② | .008 | .008 |
| 1989 | I-Mark | 90 (1471) | BPR6ES11 | .040 | 3B | 3B | 177.8 | 3.8–4.7 | 750 | 1000 | .006 | .010 |
| | I-Mark (Turbo) | 90 (1471) | BPR6ES11 | .040 | 15B | NA | 171.0 | 28.4① | 950 | NA | .006 | .010 |

## GASOLINE ENGINE TUNE-UP SPECIFICATIONS

| Year | Model | Engine Displacement cu. in. (cc) | Spark Plugs Type | Spark Plugs Gap (in.) | Ignition Timing (deg.) MT | Ignition Timing (deg.) AT | Compression Pressure (psi) | Fuel Pump (psi) | Idle Speed (rpm) MT | Idle Speed (rpm) AT | Valve Clearance In. | Valve Clearance Ex. |
|---|---|---|---|---|---|---|---|---|---|---|---|---|
| 1989 | I-Mark (DOHC) | 92 (1588) | BPR6ES11 | .040 | 16B | — | 171.0 | 28.4① | 950 | — | Hyd. | Hyd. |
| | Impulse (Turbo) | 121.7 (1994) | BPR6ES11 | .040 | 12B | 12B | 178.0 | 35.6① | 900② | 900② | .006 | .010 |
| | Impulse | 138 (2254) | BPR6ES11 | .040 | 12B | 12B | 178.0 | 35.6① | 900② | 900② | .008 | .008 |
| 1990 | SEE UNDERHOOD SPECIFICATIONS STICKER | | | | | | | | | | | |

① At 900 rpm with vacuum hose of the pressure regulator connected
② ± 50 rpm

## DIESEL ENGINE TUNE-UP SPECIFICATIONS

| Year | Engine Displacement cu. in. (cc) | Valve Clearance Intake (in.) | Valve Clearance Exhaust (in.) | Intake Valve Opens (deg.) | Injection Pump Setting (deg.) | Injection Nozzle Pressure (psi) New | Injection Nozzle Pressure (psi) Used | Idle Speed (rpm) | Cranking Compression Pressure (psi) |
|---|---|---|---|---|---|---|---|---|---|
| 1983 | 111 (1817) | 0.010 | 0.014 | 32B | 18B | 1706–1848 | — | 625① | 441 |
| 1984 | 111 (1817) | 0.010 | 0.014 | 32B | 12B | 1706–1848 | — | ② | 441 |
| 1985 | 111 (1817) | 0.010 | 0.014 | 32B | 12B | 1706–1848 | — | ② | 441 |

B Before top dead center
① Automatic transmission—725 rpm
② Manual transmision—575–675 rpm

### FIRING ORDERS

**NOTE: To avoid confusion, always replace spark plug wires one at a time.**

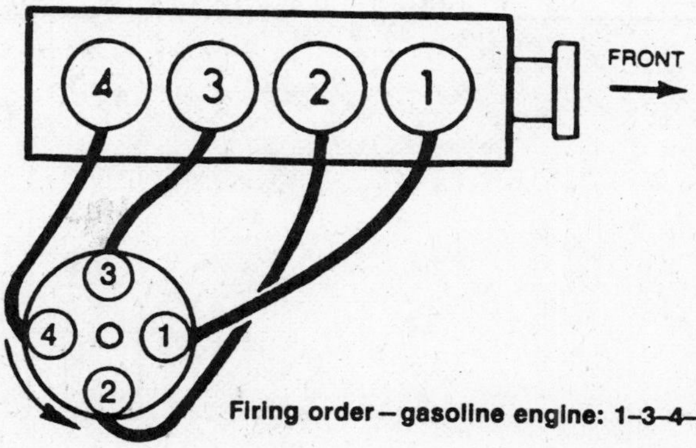


Firing order—gasoline engine: 1–3–4–2

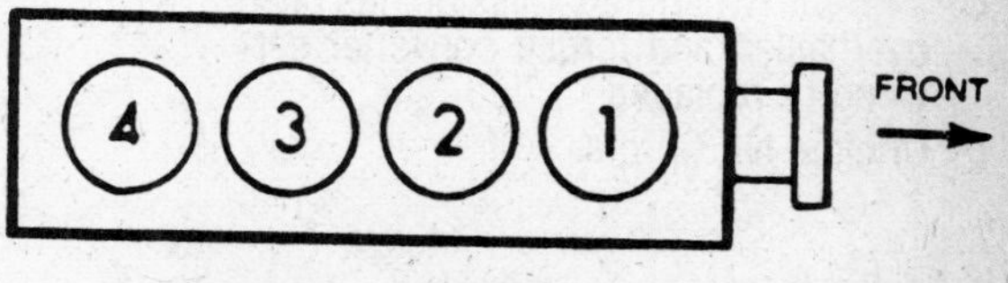


Firing order—diesel engine: 1–3–4–2

## CAPACITIES

| Year | Model | Engine Displacement cu. in. (cc) | Engine Crankcase with Filter | Engine Crankcase without Filter | Transmission (pts.) 4-Spd | Transmission (pts.) 5-Spd | Transmission (pts.) Auto. | Drive Axle (pts.) | Fuel Tank (gal.) | Cooling System (qts.) |
|---|---|---|---|---|---|---|---|---|---|---|
| 1983 | I-Mark | 110.8 (1816) | 3.8① | 3.4 | 2.8 | 3.2 | 14② | 2.1 | 13.7 | 6.8 |
| | I-Mark | 111 (1817) | 3.8① | 3.4 | 2.8 | 3.3 | 14② | 2.1 | 13.7 | 7.4 |
| | Impulse | 118.9 (1949) | 3.8① | 3.4 | — | 3.8 | 14② | 2.5 | 15.1 | 8.0 |
| 1984 | I-Mark | 110.8 (1816) | 3.8① | 3.4 | 2.8 | 3.2 | 14② | 2.1 | 13.7 | 6.8 |
| | I-Mark | 111 (1817) | 3.8① | 3.4 | 2.8 | 3.3 | 14② | 2.1 | 13.7 | 7.4 |
| | Impulse | 118.9 (1949) | 3.8① | 3.4 | — | 3.8 | 14② | 2.5 | 15.1 | 8.0 |
| 1985 | I-Mark (FWD) | 90 (1471) | 3.4③ | 3.0 | — | 5.6 | 12.6 | NA | 11.1 | 6.8 |
| | I-Mark (RWD) | 110.8 (1816) | 3.8① | 3.4 | 2.8 | 3.2 | 14② | 2.1 | 13.7 | 6.8 |
| | I-Mark | 111 (1817) | 3.8① | 3.4 | 2.8 | 3.3 | 14② | 2.1 | 13.7 | 7.4 |
| | Impulse | 118.9 (1949) | 3.8① | 3.4 | — | 3.8 | 14② | 2.5 | 15.1 | 8.0 |
| 1986 | I-Mark | 90 (1471) | 3.4③ | 3.0 | — | 5.6 | 12.6 | NA | 11.1 | 6.8 |
| | Impulse | 118.9 (1949) | 3.8① | 3.4 | — | 3.3 | 14② | 3.2 | 15.1 | 9.3 |
| | Impulse (Turbo) | 121.7 (1994) | 3.8① | 3.4 | — | 3.3 | 14② | 3.2 | 15.1 | 9.5 |
| 1987 | I-Mark | 90 (1471) | 3.4③ | 3.0 | — | 5.6 | 13.6 | NA | 11.1 | 6.8 |
| | Impulse | 118.9 (1949) | 3.8① | 3.4 | — | 3.3 | 14② | 3.2 | 15.1 | 9.3 |
| | Impulse | 121.7 (1994) | 3.8① | 3.4 | — | 3.3 | 14② | 3.2 | 15.1 | 9.5 |
| 1988 | I-Mark | 90 (1471) | 3.4③ | 3.0 | — | 5.0 | 13.6 | NA | 11.1 | 6.8 |
| | I-Mark (Turbo) | 90 (1471) | 3.4③ | 3.0 | — | 5.0 | NA | NA | 11.1 | 7.5 |
| | Impulse (Turbo) | 121.7 (1994) | 3.8① | 3.4 | — | 3.3 | 13.7 | 3.2 | 15.1 | 9.5 |
| | Impulse | 138 (2254) | 3.8① | 3.4 | — | 3.3 | 13.7 | 3.2 | 15.1 | 9.3 |
| 1989-90 | I-Mark | 90 (1471) | 3.4③ | 3.0 | — | 5.0 | 13.6 | NA | 11.1 | 6.8 |
| | I-Mark (Turbo) | 90 (1471) | 3.4③ | 3.0 | — | 5.0 | NA | NA | 11.1 | 7.5 |
| | I-Mark (DOHC) | 92 (1588) | 3.2 | 3.0 | — | 5.0 | — | — | 11.1 | 6.8 |
| | Impulse (Turbo) | 121.7 (1994) | 3.8① | 3.4 | — | 3.3 | 13.7 | 3.2 | 15.1 | 9.5 |
| | Impulse | 138 (2254) | 3.8① | 3.4 | — | 3.3 | 13.7 | 3.2 | 15.1 | 9.3 |

① The original fill is 5.0 qts., except for the diesel which is 5.5 qts.

② 21.8 pts. when transmission has been overhauled and torque converter serviced or replaced

③ Original fill 3.7 qts.

## CAMSHAFT SPECIFICATIONS

All measurements given in inches.

| Year | Engine Displacement cu. in. (cc) | Journal Diameter 1 | 2 | 3 | 4 | 5 | Lobe Lift In. | Ex. | Bearing Clearance | Camshaft End Play |
|---|---|---|---|---|---|---|---|---|---|---|
| 1983 | 110.8 (1816) | 1.3362–1.3368 | 1.3362–1.3368 | 1.3362–1.3368 | 1.3362–1.3368 | 1.3362–1.3368 | 1.451 | 1.451 | 0.0016–0.0035 | 0.0020–0.0059 |
| | 111 (1817) | 1.1004–1.1010 | 1.1004–1.1010 | 1.1004–1.1010 | 1.1004–1.1010 | 1.1004–1.1010 | 1.451 | 1.451 | 0.0008 0.0035 | — |
| | 118.9 (1949) | 1.3390 | 1.3390 | 1.3390 | 1.3390 | 1.3390 | 1.451 | 1.451 | 0.0030–0.0043 | 0.0020–0.0060 |
| 1984 | 110.8 (1816) | 1.3362–1.3368 | 1.3362–1.3368 | 1.3362–1.3368 | 1.3362–1.3368 | 1.3362–1.3368 | 1.451 | 1.451 | 0.0016–0.0035 | 0.0020–0.0059 |
| | 111 (1817) | 1.1004–1.1010 | 1.1004–1.1010 | 1.1004–1.1010 | 1.1004–1.1010 | 1.1004–1.1010 | 1.451 | 1.451 | 0.0008–0.0035 | — |
| | 118.9 (1949) | 1.3390 | 1.3390 | 1.3390 | 1.3390 | 1.3390 | 1.451 | 1.451 | 0.0030–0.0043 | 0.0020–0.0060 |
| 1985 | 90 (1471) | 1.0210–1.0220 | 1.0210–1.0220 | 1.0210–1.0220 | 1.0210–1.0220 | 1.0210–1.0220 | 1.426 | 1.426– | 0.0024–0.0044 | 0.0039–0.0071 |
| | 110.8 (1816) | 1.3362–1.3368 | 1.3362–1.3368 | 1.3362–1.3368 | 1.3362–1.3368 | 1.3362–1.3368 | 1.451 | 1.451 | 0.0016–0.0035 | 0.0020–0.0059 |
| | 111 (1817) | 1.1004–1.1010 | 1.1004–1.1010 | 1.1004–1.1010 | 1.1004–1.1010 | 1.1004–1.1010 | 1.451 | 1.451 | 0.0008–0.0035 | — |
| | 118.9 (1949) | 1.3390 | 1.3390 | 1.3390 | 1.3390 | 1.3390 | 1.451 | 1.451 | 0.0030–0.0043 | 0.0020–0.0060 |
| 1986 | 90 (1471) | 1.0210–1.0220 | 1.0210–1.0220 | 1.0210–1.0220 | 1.0210–1.0220 | 1.0210–1.0020 | 1.426 | 1.426 | 0.0024–0.0044 | 0.0039–0.0071 |
| | 118.9 (1949) | 1.3390 | 1.3390 | 1.3390 | 1.3390 | 1.3390 | 1.451 | 1.451 | 0.0030–0.0043 | 0.0020–0.0060 |
| | 121.7 (1994) | 1.3390 | 1.3390 | 1.3390 | 1.3390 | 1.3390 | 1.451 | 1.451 | 0.0026–0.0043 | 0.0002–0.0059 |
| 1987 | 90 (1471) | 1.0210–1.0220 | 1.0210–1.0220 | 1.0210–1.0220 | 1.0210–1.0220 | 1.0210–1.0220 | 1.426 | 1.426 | 0.0024–0.0044 | 0.0039–0.0071 |
| | 118.9 (1949) | 1.3390 | 1.3390 | 1.3390 | 1.3390 | 1.3390 | 1.451 | 1.451 | 0.0030–0.0043 | 0.0020–0.0060 |
| | 121.7 (1994) | 1.3390 | 1.3390 | 1.3390 | 1.3390 | 1.3390 | 1.451 | 1.451 | 0.0026–0.0043 | 0.0002–0.0059 |
| 1988 | 90 (1471) | 1.021–1.022 | 1.021–1.022 | 1.021–1.022 | 1.021–1.022 | 1.021–1.022 | 1.426 | 1.426 | 0.0024–0.0044 | 0.0039–0.0071 |
| | 138 (2254) | 1.339 | 1.339 | 1.339 | 1.339 | 1.339 | 1.451 | 1.451 | 0.0033–0.0051 | 0.0002–0.0059 |
| | 121.7 (1994) | 1.339 | 1.339 | 1.339 | 1.339 | 1.339 | 1.451 | 1.451 | 0.0033–0.0051 | 0.0002–0.0059 |
| 1989-90 | 90 (1471) | 1.021–1.022 | 1.021–1.022 | 1.021–1.022 | 1.021–1.022 | 1.021–1.022 | 1.426 | 1.426 | 0.0024–0.0044 | 0.0039–0.0071 |
| | 92 (1588) | 1.021–1.022 | 1.021–1.022 | 1.021–1.022 | 1.021–1.022 | 1.021–1.022 | 1.536 | 1.536 | 0.0024–0.0044 | 0.0039–0.0071 |
| | 138 (2254) | 1.339 | 1.339 | 1.339 | 1.339 | 1.339 | 1.451 | 1.451 | 0.0033–0.0051 | 0.0002–0.0059 |

## CAMSHAFT SPECIFICATIONS

All measurements given in inches.

| Year | Engine Displacement cu. in. (cc) | Journal Diameter 1 | 2 | 3 | 4 | 5 | Lobe Lift In. | Ex. | Bearing Clearance | Camshaft End Play |
|---|---|---|---|---|---|---|---|---|---|---|
| 1989-90 | 121.7 (1994) | 1.339 | 1.339 | 1.339 | 1.339 | 1.339 | 1.451 | 1.451 | 0.0033–0.0051 | 0.0002–0.0059 |

## CRANKSHAFT AND CONNECTING ROD SPECIFICATIONS

All measurements are given in inches.

| Year | Engine Displacement cu. in. (cc) | Crankshaft Main Brg. Journal Dia. | Crankshaft Main Brg. Oil Clearance | Crankshaft Shaft End-play | Crankshaft Thrust on No. | Connecting Rod Journal Diameter | Connecting Rod Oil Clearance | Connecting Rod Side Clearance |
|---|---|---|---|---|---|---|---|---|
| 1983 | 110.8 (1816) | 2.2016–2.2022 | 0.0008–0.0025 | 0.0024–0.0094 | 3 | 1.929 | 0.0007–0.0030 | 0.0137 |
| | 111 (1817) | 2.2016–2.2022 | 0.0012–0.0027 | 0.0024–0.0094 | 3 | 1.925 | 0.0016–0.0027 | 0.0137 |
| | 118.9 (1949) | 2.2016–2.2022 | 0.0008–0.0025 | 0.0024–0.0094 | 3 | 1.929 | 0.0007–0.0029 | 0.0078–0.0130 |
| 1984 | 110.8 (1816) | 2.2016–2.2022 | 0.0008–0.0025 | 0.0024–0.0094 | 3 | 1.929 | 0.0007–0.0030 | 0.0137 |
| | 111 (1817) | 2.2016–2.2022 | 0.0012–0.0027 | 0.0024–0.0094 | 3 | 1.925 | 0.0016–0.0027 | 0.0137 |
| | 118.9 (1949) | 2.2016–2.2022 | 0.0008–0.0025 | 0.0024–0.0094 | 3 | 1.929 | 0.0007–0.0029 | 0.0078–0.0130 |
| 1985 | 90 (1471) | 1.8865–1.8873 | 0.0008–0.0020 | 0.0024–0.0099 | 2 | 1.5720–1.5726 | 0.0010–0.0023 | 0.0079–0.0138 |
| | 110.8 (1816) | 2.2016–2.2022 | 0.0008–0.0025 | 0.0024–0.0094 | 3 | 1.929 | 0.0007–0.0030 | 0.0137 |
| | 111 (1817) | 2.2016–2.2022 | 0.0012–0.0027 | 0.0024–0.0094 | 3 | 1.925 | 0.0016–0.0027 | 0.0137 |
| | 118.9 (1949) | 2.2016–2.2022 | 0.0008–0.0025 | 0.0024–0.0094 | 3 | 1.929 | 0.0007–0.0029 | 0.0078–0.0130 |
| 1986 | 90 (1471) | 1.8865–1.8873 | 0.0008–0.0020 | 0.0024–0.0095 | 2 | 1.5720–1.5726 | 0.0010–0.0023 | 0.0079–0.0138 |
| | 118.9 (1949) | 2.2016–2.2022 | 0.0008–0.0025 | 0.0024–0.0094 | 3 | 1.929 | 0.0007–0.0029 | 0.0079–0.0130 |
| | 121.7 (1994) | 2.2032–2.2038 | 0.0009–0.0020 | 0.0024–0.0099 | 3 | 1.9276–1.9282 | 0.0012–0.0024 | 0.0078–0.0130 |
| 1987 | 90 (1471) | 1.8865–1.8873 | 0.0008–0.0020 | 0.0024–0.0095 | 2 | 1.5720–1.5726 | 0.0010–0.0023 | 0.0079–0.0138 |
| | 118.9 (1949) | 2.2016–2.2022 | 0.0008–0.0025 | 0.0024–0.0094 | 3 | 1.929 | 0.0007–0.0029 | 0.0078–0.0130 |
| | 121.7 (1994) | 2.2032–2.2038 | 0.0009–0.0020 | 0.0024–0.0099 | 3 | 1.9276–1.9282 | 0.0012–0.0024 | 0.0078–0.0130 |
| 1988 | 90 (1471) | 1.8865–1.8873 | 0.0008–0.0020 | 0.0024–0.0095 | 2 | 1.5720–1.5726 | 0.0010–0.0023 | 0.0079–0.0138 |
| | 138 (2254) | 2.2032–2.2038 | 0.0009–0.0020 | 0.0024–0.0099 | 3 | 1.9276–1.9282 | 0.0012–0.0024 | 0.0078–0.0130 |

## CRANKSHAFT AND CONNECTING ROD SPECIFICATIONS

All measurements are given in inches.

| Year | Engine Displacement cu. in. (cc) | Crankshaft: Main Brg. Journal Dia. | Crankshaft: Main Brg. Oil Clearance | Crankshaft: Shaft End-play | Crankshaft: Thrust on No. | Connecting Rod: Journal Diameter | Connecting Rod: Oil Clearance | Connecting Rod: Side Clearance |
|---|---|---|---|---|---|---|---|---|
| 1988 | 121.7 (1994) | 2.2032–2.2038 | 0.0009–0.0020 | 0.0024–0.0099 | 3 | 1.9276–1.9282 | 0.0012–0.0024 | 0.0078–0.0130 |
| 1989-90 | 90 (1471) | 1.8865–1.8873 | 0.0008–0.0020 | 0.0024–0.0095 | 2 | 1.5720–1.5726 | 0.0010–0.0023 | 0.0079–0.0138 |
| | 92 (1588) | 1.8861–1.9171 | 0.0008–0.0020 | 0.0024–0.0095 | 2 | 1.7193–1.7197 | 0.0013–0.0024 | 0.0079–0.0138 |
| | 138 (2254) | 2.2032–2.2038 | 0.0009–0.0020 | 0.0024–0.0099 | 3 | 1.9276–1.9282 | 0.0012–0.0024 | 0.0078–0.0130 |
| | 121.7 (1994) | 2.2032–2.2038 | 0.0009–0.0020 | 0.0024–0.0099 | 3 | 1.9276–1.9282 | 0.0012–0.0024 | 0.0078–0.0130 |

## VALVE SPECIFICATIONS

| Year | Engine Displacement cu. in. (cc) | Seat Angle (deg.) | Face Angle (deg.) | Spring Test Pressure (lbs.) | Spring Installed Height (in.) | Stem-to-Guide Clearance (in.) Intake | Stem-to-Guide Clearance (in.) Exhaust | Stem Diameter (in.) Intake | Stem Diameter (in.) Exhaust |
|---|---|---|---|---|---|---|---|---|---|
| 1983 | 110.8 (1816) | 45① | 45 | ② | ③ | 0.0009–0.0022 | 0.0015–0.0031 | 0.315 | 0.315 |
| | 111 (1817) | 45① | 45 | ② | ④ | 0.0015–0.0027 | 0.0020–0.0030 | 0.313 | 0.313 |
| | 118.9 (1949) | 45 | 45 | 55 @ 160 | 1.60 | 0.0009–0.0022 | 0.0015–0.0031 | 0.315 | 0.315 |
| 1984 | 110.8 (1816) | 45① | 45 | ② | ③ | 0.0009–0.0022 | 0.0015–0.0031 | 0.315 | 0.315 |
| | 111 (1817) | 45① | 45 | ② | ④ | 0.0015–0.0027 | 0.0020–0.0030 | 0.313 | 0.313 |
| | 118.9 (1949) | 45 | 45 | 55 @ 1.60 | 1.60 | 0.0009–0.0022 | 0.0015–0.0031 | 0.315 | 0.315 |
| 1985 | 90 (1471) | 45 | 45 | 49 @ 1.57 | 1.57 | 0.0009–0.0022 | 0.0012–0.0025 | 0.274–0.275 | 0.2740–0.2744 |
| | 110.8 (1816) | 45① | 45 | ② | ③ | 0.0009–0.0022 | 0.0015–0.0031 | 0.315 | 0.315 |
| | 111 (1817) | 45① | 45 | ② | ④ | 0.0015–0.0027 | 0.0020–0.0030 | 0.313 | 0.313 |
| | 118.9 (1949) | 45 | 45 | 55 @ 1.60 | 1.60 | 0.0009–0.0022 | 0.0015–0.0031 | 0.315 | 0.315 |
| 1986 | 90 (1471) | 45 | 45 | 49 @ 1.57 | 1.57 | 0.0009–0.0022 | 0.0012–0.0025 | 0.274–0.275 | 0.2740–0.2744 |
| | 118.9 (1949) | 45 | 45 | 55 @ 1.60 | 1.60 | 0.0009–0.0022 | 0.0015–0.0031 | 0.315 | 0.315 |
| | 121.7 (1994) | 45 | 45 | 55 @ 1.62 | 1.62 | 0.0009–0.0022 | 0.0015–0.0031 | 0.315 | 0.315 |

## VALVE SPECIFICATIONS

| Year | Engine Displacement cu. in. (cc) | Seat Angle (deg.) | Face Angle (deg.) | Spring Test Pressure (lbs.) | Spring Installed Height (in.) | Stem-to-Guide Clearance (in.) Intake | Stem-to-Guide Clearance (in.) Exhaust | Stem Diameter (in.) Intake | Stem Diameter (in.) Exhaust |
|---|---|---|---|---|---|---|---|---|---|
| 1987 | 90 (1471) | 45 | 45 | 49 @ 1.57 | 1.57 | 0.0009–0.0022 | 0.0012–0.0025 | 0.274–0.275 | 0.2740–0.2744 |
| | 118.9 (1949) | 45 | 45 | 55 @ 1.60 | 1.60 | 0.0009–0.0022 | 0.0015–0.0031 | 0.315 | 0.315 |
| | 121.7 (1994) | 45 | 45 | 55 @ 1.62 | 1.62 | 0.0009–0.0022 | 0.0015–0.0031 | 0.315 | 0.315 |
| 1988 | 90 (1471) | 45 | 45 | 47 @ 1.57 | 1.57 | 0.0009–0.0022 | 0.0012–0.0025 | 0.274–0.275 | 0.2740–0.2744 |
| | 138 (2254) | 45 | 45 | 55.3 @ 1.62 | 1.62 | 0.0009–0.0022 | 0.0015–0.0031 | 0.315 | 0.315 |
| | 121.7 (1994) | 45 | 45 | 55.3 @ 1.62 | 1.62 | 0.0009–0.0022 | 0.0015–0.0031 | 0.315 | 0.315 |
| 1989-90 | 90 (1471) | 45 | 45 | 47 @ 1.57 | 1.57 | 0.0009–0.0022 | 0.0012–0.0025 | 0.274–0.275 | 0.2740–0.2744 |
| | 92 (1588) | 45 | 45 | 52 @ 44 | 1.52 | 0.0009–0.0022 | 0.0018–0.0025 | 0.234–0.235 | 0.2340–0.2350 |
| | 138 (2254) | 45 | 45 | 55.3 @ 1.62 | 1.62 | 0.0009–0.0022 | 0.0015–0.0031 | 0.315 | 0.315 |
| | 121.7 (1994) | 45 | 45 | 55.3 @ 1.62 | 1.62 | 0.0009–0.0022 | 0.0015–0.0031 | 0.315 | 0.315 |

① Because of the aluminum head and valve seat inserts, cut the valve seat with 15, 45 or 75 degree cutters. Use the minimum necessary to remove dents or damage, leaving the contact width inside the 0.0472–0.063 range

② Outer – 34.5 @ 1.614
Inner – 20 @ 1.516

③ Outer – 1.61
Inner – 1.51

④ Outer – 1.85
Inner – 1.51

## PISTON AND RING SPECIFICATIONS

All measurments are given in inches.

| Year | Engine Displacement cu. in. (cc) | Piston Clearance | Ring Gap Top Compression | Ring Gap Bottom Compression | Ring Gap Oil Control | Ring Side Clearance Top Compression | Ring Side Clearance Bottom Compression | Ring Side Clearance Oil Control |
|---|---|---|---|---|---|---|---|---|
| 1983 | 110.8 (1816) | 0.0018–0.0026 | 0.0120–0.0180 | 0.0120–0.0180 | 0.0080–0.0350 | 0.0059 | 0.0059 | 0.0059 |
| | 111 (1817) | 0.0002–0.0017 | 0.0078–0.0157 | 0.0078–0.0157 | 0.0078–0.0157 | 0.0035–0.0049 | 0.0015–0.0019 | 0.0012–0.0027 |
| | 118.9 (1949) | 0.0018–0.0026 | 0.0140–0.0190 | 0.0140–0.0190 | 0.0080–0.0350 | 0.0010–0.0024 | 0.0010–0.0024 | 0.0008 |
| 1984 | 110.8 (1816) | 0.0018–0.0026 | 0.0120–0.0180 | 0.0120–0.0180 | 0.0080–0.0350 | 0.0059 | 0.0059 | 0.0059 |

## PISTON AND RING SPECIFICATIONS

All measurments are given in inches.

| Year | Engine Displacement cu. in. (cc) | Piston Clearance | Ring Gap | | | Ring Side Clearance | | |
|---|---|---|---|---|---|---|---|---|
| | | | Top Compression | Bottom Compression | Oil Control | Top Compression | Bottom Compression | Oil Control |
| 1984 | 111 (1817) | 0.0002–0.0010 | 0.0078–0.0157 | 0.0078–0.0157 | 0.0078–0.0157 | 0.0035–0.0049 | 0.0015–0.0019 | 0.0012–0.0029 |
| | 118.9 (1949) | 0.0018–0.0026 | 0.0140–0.0190 | 0.0140–0.0190 | 0.0080–0.0350 | 0.0010–0.0024 | 0.0010–0.0024 | 0.0008 |
| 1985 | 90 (1471) | 0.0110–0.0190 | 0.0098–0.0138 | NA | 0.0039–0.0236 | 0.0010–0.0026 | NA | NA |
| | 110.8 (1816) | 0.0018–0.0026 | 0.0120–0.0180 | 0.0120–0.0180 | 0.0080–0.0350 | 0.0059 | 0.0059 | 0.0059 |
| | 111 (1817) | 0.0002–0.0010 | 0.0078–0.0157 | 0.0078–0.0157 | 0.0078–0.0157 | 0.0035–0.0049 | 0.0015–0.0019 | 0.0012–0.0027 |
| | 118.9 (1949) | 0.0018–0.0026 | 0.0140–0.0190 | 0.0140–0.0190 | 0.0080–0.0350 | 0.0010–0.0024 | 0.0010–0.0024 | 0.0008 |
| 1986 | 90 (1471) | 0.0110–0.0190 | 0.0098–0.0138 | NA | 0.0039–0.0236 | 0.0010–0.0024 | NA | NA |
| | 118.9 (1949) | 0.0018–0.0026 | 0.0140–0.0190 | 0.0140–0.0190 | 0.0080–0.0350 | 0.0010–0.0024 | 0.0010–0.0024 | 0.0008 |
| | 121.7 (1994) | 0.0018–0.0026 | 0.0120–0.0180 | 0.0100–0.0160 | 0.0080–0.0280 | 0.0010–0.0024 | 0.0010–0.0024 | NA |
| 1987 | 90 (1471) | 0.0110–0.0190 | 0.0098–0.0138 | NA | 0.0039–0.0236 | 0.0010–0.0025 | NA | NA |
| | 118.9 (1949) | 0.0018–0.0026 | 0.0120–0.0180 | 0.0100–0.0160 | 0.0080–0.0280 | 0.0010–0.0024 | 0.0010–0.0024 | 0.0008 |
| | 121.7 (1994) | 0.0018–0.0026 | 0.0120–0.0180 | 0.0100–0.0160 | 0.0080–0.0280 | 0.0010–0.0024 | 0.0010–0.0024 | NA |
| 1988 | 90 (1471) | 0.0011–0.0019 | 0.0098–0.0138 | NA | 0.0039–0.0236 | 0.0010–0.0025 | NA | NA |
| | 90 (1471) Turbo | 0.0011–0.0019 | 0.0106–0.0153 | 0.0098–0.0145 | 0.0039–0.0236 | 0.0010–0.0026 | 0.0008 0.0024 | NA |
| | 138 (2254) | 0.0016–0.0024 | 0.0120–0.0180 | 0.0100–0.0160 | 0.0080–0.0280 | 0.0010–0.0024 | 0.0010–0.0024 | NA |
| | 121.7 (1994) | 0.0008 0.0016 | 0.0120–0.0180 | 0.0100–0.0160 | 0.0080–0.0280 | 0.0010–0.0024 | 0.0010–0.0024 | NA |
| 1989-90 | 90 (1471) | 0.0011–0.0019 | 0.0098–0.0138 | NA | 0.0039–0.0236 | 0.0010–0.0025 | NA | NA |
| | 90 (1471) Turbo | 0.0011–0.0019 | 0.0106–0.0153 | 0.0098–0.0145 | 0.0039–0.0236 | 0.0010–0.0026 | 0.0008 0.0024 | NA |
| | 92 (1588) | 0.0011–0.0019 | 0.0110–0.0157 | 0.0177–0.0236 | 0.0039–0.0236 | 0.0018–0.0032 | 0.0008 0.0024 | NA |
| | 138 (2254) | 0.0016–0.0024 | 0.0120–0.0180 | 0.0100–0.0160 | 0.0080–0.0280 | 0.0010–0.0024 | 0.0010–0.0024 | NA |
| | 121.7 (1994) | 0.0008 0.0016 | 0.0120–0.0180 | 0.0100–0.0160 | 0.0080–0.0280 | 0.0010–0.0024 | 0.0010–0.0024 | NA |

## TORQUE SPECIFICATIONS

All readings in ft. lbs.

| Year | Engine Displacement cu. in. (cc) | Cylinder Head Bolts | Main Bearing Bolts | Rod Bearing Bolts | Crankshaft Pulley Bolts | Flywheel Bolts | Manifold Intake | Manifold Exhaust | Spark Plugs |
|---|---|---|---|---|---|---|---|---|---|
| 1983 | 110.8 (1816) | ① | 72 | 43 | 87 | 69 | 13 | 15 | 11–14 |
| | 111 (1817) | ② | 65–72 | 54–61 | 108 | 36–43 | 25–32 | 11–18 | NA |
| | 118.9 (1949) | ① | 65–79 | 42–45 | 87 | 72–79 | 13–18 | 13–18 | 11–14 |
| 1984 | 110.8 (1816) | ① | 72 | 43 | 87 | 76 | 13 | 15 | 11–14 |
| | 111 (1817) | ② | 65–72 | 54–61 | 108 | 36–43 | 25–32 | 11–18 | NA |
| | 118.9 (1949) | ① | 65–79 | 42–45 | 87 | 72–79 | 13–18 | 13–18 | 11–14 |
| 1985 | 90 (1471) | ③ | 68 | 25 | 108 | 22④ | 17 | 17 | 11–14 |
| | 110.8 (1816) | ① | 72 | 43 | 87 | 76 | 13 | 15 | 11–14 |
| | 111 (1817) | ② | 65–72 | 54–61 | 108 | 36–43 | 25–32 | 11–18 | NA |
| | 118.9 (1949) | ① | 65–79 | 42–45 | 87 | 72–79 | 13–18 | 13–18 | 11–14 |
| 1986 | 90 (1471) | ③ | 68 | 25 | 108 | 22④ | 17 | 17 | 11–14 |
| | 118.9 (1949) | ① | 65–79 | 42–45 | 87 | 72–79 | 13–18 | 16 | 11–14 |
| | 121.7 (1994) | ① | 72 | 43 | 87 | 43 | 13–18 | 16 | 11–14 |
| 1987 | 90 (1471) | ③ | 68 | 25 | 108 | 22④ | 17 | 17 | 11–14 |
| | 118.9 (1949) | ① | 65–79 | 42–45 | 87 | 72–79 | 13–18 | 16 | 11–14 |
| | 121.7 (1994) | ① | 72 | 43 | 87 | 43 | 13–18 | 16 | 11–14 |
| 1988 | 90 (1471) | ③ | 68 | 25 | 108 | 22④ | 17 | 17 | 11–14 |
| | 138 (2254) | ① | 72 | 43 | 87 | 43 | 13–18 | 16 | 11–14 |
| | 121.7 (1994) | ① | 72 | 43 | 87 | 40 | 13–18 | 16 | 11–14 |
| 1989-90 | 90 (1471) | ③ | 68 | 25 | 108 | 22④ | 17 | 17 | 11–14 |
| | 92 (1588) | ③ | 65 | ⑤ | 123 | ⑥ | 17 | 30 | 11–14 |
| | 138 (2254) | ① | 72 | 43 | 87 | 43 | 13–18 | 16 | 11–14 |
| | 121.7 (1994) | ① | 72 | 43 | 87 | 40 | 13–18 | 16 | 11–14 |

① 1st step—62 ft. lbs.
2nd step—72 ft. lbs.

② Tighten in sequence:
New bolts—90 ft. lbs.
Used bolts—97 ft. lbs.

③ 1st step—29 ft. lbs.
2nd step—58 ft. lbs.

④ Turn the bolt an additional 45 degrees

⑤ 1st step—11 ft. lbs.
2nd step—turn an additional 45–60 degrees

⑥ 1st step—22 ft. lbs.
2nd step—turn an additional 45–60 degrees

## BRAKE SPECIFICATIONS

All measurements in inches unless noted

| Year | Model | Lug Nut Torque (ft. lbs.) | Master Cylinder Bore | Brake Disc Minimum Thickness | Brake Disc Maximum Runout | Standard Brake Drum Diameter | Minimum Lining Thickness Front | Minimum Lining Thickness Rear |
|---|---|---|---|---|---|---|---|---|
| 1983 | I-Mark | 50① | 0.875 | 0.338 | 0.0060 | 9.00 | 0.067 | 0.039 |
| | Impulse | 80–94 | 0.874 | 0.654 | 0.0051 | N/A | 0.120 | 0.120 |
| 1984 | I–Mark | 50① | 0.875 | 0.338 | 0.0060 | 9.00 | 0.067 | 0.039 |
| | Impulse | 80–94 | 0.874 | 0.654 | 0.0051 | NA | 0.120 | 0.120 |
| 1985 | I-Mark (RWD) | 50① | 0.875 | 0.338 | 0.0060 | 9.00 | 0.067 | 0.039 |
| | I-Mark (FWD) | 87 | 0.810 | 0.378 | 0.0059 | 7.09 | 0.039 | 0.039 |
| | Impulse | 80–94 | 0.874 | 0.654 | 0.0051 | NA | 0.120 | 0.120 |
| 1986 | I-Mark | 87 | 0.810 | 0.378 | 0.0059 | 7.09 | 0.039 | 0.039 |
| | Impulse | 80–94 | 0.874 | 0.654 | 0.0051 | NA | 0.120 | 0.120 |

## BRAKE SPECIFICATIONS

All measurements in inches unless noted

| Year | Model | Lug Nut Torque (ft. lbs.) | Master Cylinder Bore | Brake Disc Minimum Thickness | Brake Disc Maximum Runout | Standard Brake Drum Diameter | Minimum Lining Thickness Front | Minimum Lining Thickness Rear |
|---|---|---|---|---|---|---|---|---|
| 1987 | I-Mark | 65① | 0.810 | 0.378 | 0.0059 | 7.09 | 0.039 | 0.039 |
| | Impulse | 80–94 | 0.874 | 0.654 | 0.0051 | NA | 0.120 | 0.120 |
| 1988 | I-Mark | 65① | 0.810 | 0.378 | 0.0059 | 7.09 | 0.039 | 0.039 |
| | I-Mark (Turbo) | 65① | 0.875 | 0.378 | 0.0059 | 7.09 | 0.039 | 0.039 |
| | Impulse | 87 | 0.875 | 0.654 | 0.0051 | NA | 0.120 | 0.120 |
| | Impulse (Turbo) | 87 | 0.875 | 0.654 | 0.0051 | NA | 0.120 | 0.120 |
| 1989-90 | I-Mark | 65① | 0.810 | 0.378 | 0.0059 | 7.09 | 0.039 | 0.039 |
| | I-Mark (Turbo) | 65① | 0.875 | 0.378 | 0.0059 | 7.09 | 0.039 | 0.039 |
| | I-Mark (DOHC) | 65① | 0.875 | 0.378 | 0.0059 | 7.09 | 0.039 | 0.039 |
| | Impulse | 87 | 0.875 | 0.654 | 0.0051 | NA | 0.120 | 0.120 |
| | Impulse (Turbo) | 87 | 0.875 | 0.654 | 0.0051 | NA | 0.120 | 0.120 |

① Aluminum wheels—86 ft. lbs.

## WHEEL ALIGNMENT

| Year | Model | Caster Range (deg.) | Caster Preferred Setting (deg.) | Camber Range (deg.) | Camber Preferred Setting (deg.) | Toe-in (in.) | Steering Axis Inclination (deg.) |
|---|---|---|---|---|---|---|---|
| 1983 | I-Mark | 3 11/16P–6 3/16P | 5 3/16P | ⅞N–⅝P | ⅛P | ⅛P | 7⅞P |
| | Impulse | 3½P–6P | 4¾P | 1N–½P | 0 | 1/16P | 8 |
| 1984 | I-Mark | 3 11/16P–6 3/16P | 5 3/16P | ⅞N–⅝P | ⅛P | ⅛P | 7⅞ |
| | Impulse | 3½P–6P | 4¾P | 1N–½P | 0 | 1/16P | 8 |
| 1985 | I-Mark (RWD) | 3 11/16P–6 3/16P | 5 3/16P | ⅞N–⅝P | ⅛P | ⅛P | 7⅞ |
| | I-Mark (FWD) | 1¾P–2¾P | 2¼P | 11/16N–1 5/16P | 5/16P | 0 | 11 13/16 |
| | Impulse | 3½P–6P | 4¾P | 1N–½P | 0 | 1/16 | 8 |
| 1986 | I-Mark | 1¾P–2¾P | 2¼P | 11/16N–1 5/16P | 5/16P | 0 | 11 13/16 |
| | Impulse | 3½P–6P | 4¾P | 1N–½P | 0 | 1/16 | 8 |
| 1987 | I-Mark | 1¾P–2¾P | 2¼P | 11/16N–1 5/16P | 5/16P | 0 | 11 13/16 |
| | Impulse | 3½P–6P | 4¾P | 1N–½P | 0 | 1/16 | 8 |
| 1988 | I-Mark | 1¾P–2¾P | 2¼P | 11/16P–1 5/16P | 1P | 0 | 11 13/16 |
| | I-Mark (Turbo) | 1¾P–2¾P | 2¼P | ½P–1½P | 1P | 0 | 12⅛ |
| | Impulse | 1¾P–2¾P | 3P | ½N–½P | 0 | 0 | 8 |
| | Impulse (Turbo) | 4¾P–5¼P | 5P | ½N–½P | 0 | 0 | 8 |
| 1989-90 | I-Mark | 1¾P–2¾P | 2¼P | 11/16P–1 5/16P | 1P | 0 | 11 13/16 |
| | I-Mark (Turbo) | 1¾P–2¾P | 2¼P | ½P–1½P | 1P | 0 | 12⅛ |
| | I-Mark (DOHC) | 1¾P–2¾P | 2¼P | ½P–1½P | 1P | 0 | 12⅛ |
| | Impulse | 1¾P–2¾P | 3P | ½N–½P | 0 | 0 | 8 |
| | Impulse (Turbo) | 4¾P–5¼P | 5P | ½N–½P | 0 | 0 | 8 |

**NOTE:** Caster angle is pre-set and cannot be serviced N Negative P Positive NA Not available

# TUNE-UP PROCEDURES

All Isuzu models come equipped with a tune-up label in the engine compartment. This label has information developed during production. Should the preceding information in any way disagree with the specifications label, follow the label information for proper settings.

## Electronic Ignition

### AIR GAP ADJUSTMENT

All models of gasoline engines have electronic ignition. The only adjustment possible on this ignition system is the setting of the air gap inside the distributor.

1. Remove the distributor cap and O-ring.
2. Remove the rotor.
3. Use a feeler gauge (brass) to measure the air gap at the pick up coil projection. The gap should be 0.008–0.016 in. Adjust if necessary.
4. Loosen the screws and move the signal generator until the gap is correct. Tighten the screws and recheck the gap.

**NOTE: The electrical parts in this system are not repairable. If found to be defective they must be replaced.**

The signal generator can be checked for proper operation by using an ohmmeter to determine its resistance. It should be 140–180 ohms. If the resistance is not correct, replace the signal generator.

## Ignition Timing

### ADJUSTMENT

#### *G180Z, G200Z, 4ZC1-T and 4ZD1 Engines*

**NOTE: The timing marks are located at the front of the crankshaft pulley and consist of a graduated scale attached to the engine block and a notch in the crankshaft pulley. Check and adjust the timing every 30,000 miles.**

1. Locate and clean off the timing marks. Highlight the marks with paint or chalk.
2. Connect a timing light according to the manufacturer's instructions. The spark plug connection may be made at either No. 1 or No. 4 cylinder.
3. Start the engine and allow it to reach operating temperature. Make sure the engine idle speed is correct.

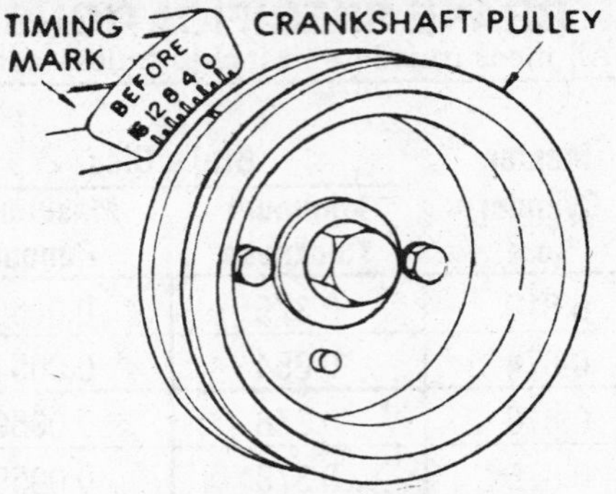


TDC timing mark alignment

4. Aim the timing light at the marks and check the position of the crankshaft pulley notch on the timing scale. If necessary, adjust the timing by loosening the distributor clamping bolt and turning the distributor to the specification in the Tune-Up chart.
5. After timing is set to specifications, tighten the distributor clamping bolt and remove the timing light connections.

#### *4XC1-U Engine*

1. Set the parking brake and block the drive wheels. Place the select lever in **NEUTRAL** if the vehicle is equipped with a manual transaxle. Place the select lever in **PARK** if the vehicle is equipped with an automatic transaxle. The air cleaner should be installed and the choke valve should be open and the engine at normal operating temperature.
2. Turn all electrical equipment off. If the vehicle is equipped with A/C it should be off also. If the vehicle is equipped with power steering the front wheels should be facing straight ahead. Wait until the engine cooling fan stops rotating.
3. The distributor vacuum line from the carburetor and intake manifold, the canister purge line, the EGR vacuum line and the ITC valve vacuum line should be disconnected and plugged.
4. Connect the timing light lead to the No.1 spark plug wire. Loosen the distributor hold down bolt (slightly).
5. Align the notched line on the crankshaft pulley with the mark on the timing cover using the timing light.
6. While aligning the notched line on the crankshaft pulley, advance or retard the timing as necessary by turning the distributor clockwise or counterclockwise.
7. After the timing has been set to specifications, tighten the distributor hold down bolt and re-check the timing.

**NOTE: Be sure the distributor body does not move together with the hold down bolt.**

8. Reconnect all vacuum lines and remove all test equipment, except for the tachometer.
9. Re-check the idle speed and adjust as necessary.

#### *4XC1-T and 4XE1 DOHC Engines*

1. Check the ECM for trouble codes. If codes are found, repair or replace the problem sensor or circuit as necessary.
2. Check all the vacuum lines for the proper routing.
3. Set the parking brake and block the drive wheels. Place the select lever in **NEUTRAL** if the vehicle is equipped with a manual transaxle. Place the select lever in **PARK** if the vehicle is equipped with an automatic transaxle. The engine should be at normal operating temperature.
4. Turn all electrical equipment off. If the vehicle is equipped with A/C it should be off also. If the vehicle is equipped with power steering the front wheels should be facing straight ahead. Wait until the engine cooling fan stops rotating.
5. Connect the timing light lead to the No.1 spark plug wire. Loosen the distributor hold down bolt (slightly).
6. Align the notched line on the crankshaft pulley with the mark on the timing cover using the timing light.
7. While aligning the notched line on the crankshaft pulley, advance or retard the timing as necessary by turning the distributor clockwise or counterclockwise.
8. After the timing has been set to specifications, tighten the distributor hold down bolt and re-check the timing.

**NOTE: Be sure the distributor body does not move together with the hold down bolt. The ignition timing is controlled by the ECM according to the engine operating conditions. Therefore, there are no external vacuum lines to the distributor.**

9. Remove all test equipment, except for the tachometer. Re-check the idle speed and adjust as necessary.

## Valve Lash

### ADJUSTMENT

1. Remove the air cleaner and rocker shaft cover.

**NOTE: Engine should be cold for adjustment. Adjust the valves every 15,000 miles.**

2. Check the rocker arm shaft bracket nuts for tightness before adjusting the valves. Torque the bracket nuts to 16 ft. lbs.

Checking rocker shaft for tightness

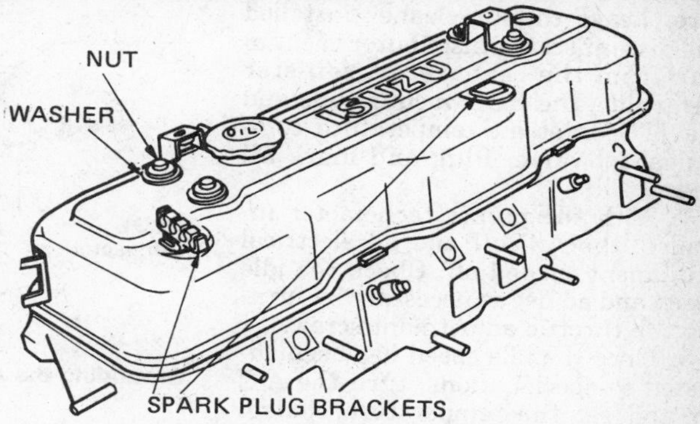


Rocker arm cover showing attaching bolts

3. Bring either No. 1 or No. 4 piston up to top dead center on the compression stroke. Align the timing mark with the pointer on the crankshaft pulley by turning the crankshaft.
4. Once the engine is set up at TDC, adjust the valves for the cylinder at TDC, the move down in order after turning the crankshaft one revolution for each cylinder.
5. Measurements should be taken at the clearance between the rocker arm and valve stem. Standard valve clearances are listed in the Tune-Up Specifications Chart.
6. To adjust the clearance, loosen the locknut and use a screwdriver to turn the adjusting stud until a slight drag is felt on the feeler gauge.

**NOTE: While all valve adjustments must be made accurately, it's better to have the valve adjustment slightly loose than slightly tight. A burned valve or warped valve stem can result from overly tight adjustments.**

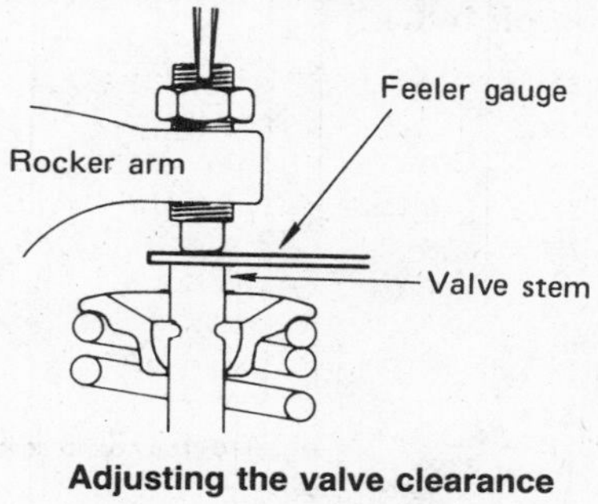


Adjusting the valve clearance

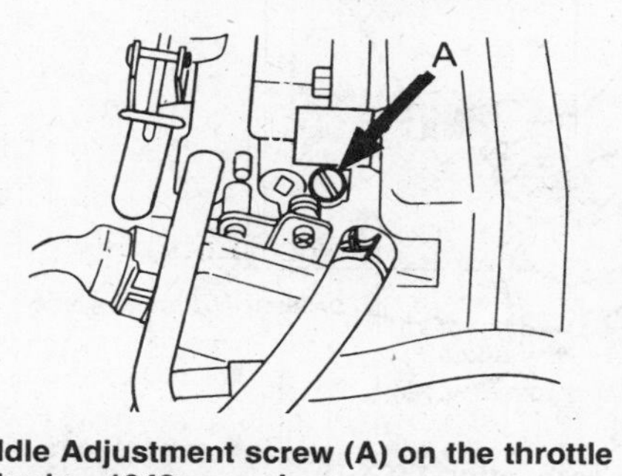


Idle Adjustment screw (A) on the throttle body—1949cc engine

| CYLINDER NO. | 1 | | 2 | | 3 | | 4 | |
|---|---|---|---|---|---|---|---|---|
| VALVES | I | E | I | E | I | E | I | E |
| STEP. 1 | ○ | ○ | ○ | | | ○ | | |
| STEP. 2 | | | | ◎ | ◎ | | ◎ | ◎ |

I : INTAKE VALVE
E : EXHAUST VALVE

Valve adjustment sequence (diesel engine)

7. Tighten the locknut and recheck the adjustment.
8. When all valves are correctly adjusted, replace the rocker arm cover using a new gasket. Check for oil leaks.

**NOTE: On the diesel engine, adjust the clearances of the valves marked with (0) when the piston in the No.1 cylinder is at TDC on its compression stroke. Turn the crankshaft one full turn to bring the piston in the No. 4 cylinder to TDC on its compression stroke (Step 2) and adjust the clearances of the valves marked with the (0) as shown in the illustration.**

**NOTE: Because the 4XE1 DOHC engine uses automatic adjust type hydraulic valve lifters, there is no need to adjust valve clearance. The torque for the camshaft bearing caps is 8 ft. lbs.**

# Idle Speed Gasoline Engines

## ADJUSTMENT

### *Carbureted Models*

#### G180Z ENGINE

**NOTE: Idle speed should be adjusted every 30,000 miles.**

1. Set the parking brake and block the drive wheels.
2. Place the transmission in **NEUTRAL**, start the engine and allow it to reach normal operating temperature.

**NOTE: If the engine is idling for more than five minutes, precede all adjustments with a clear-out blip of the throttle for a few seconds.**

3. The adjustments should be made with the choke open, air conditioner off, air cleaner installed, and distributor vacuum line, canister purge line and EGR vacuum line disconnected and plugged, and the idle compensator vacuum line closed by bending the rubber hose.
4. Turn the throttle adjusting screw to adjust the engine to 900 ± 50 rpm if the car is an automatic, and 800 ± 50 rpm the car has a manual transmission.
5. If the car has an air conditioner, turn the A/C on **Max** cold and high blower. Open the throttle to approximately ⅓ and allow the throttle to close. (This allows the speed-up solenoid to reach full travel.) Adjust the speed-up solenoid adjusting screw to set the idle at 900 ± 50 rpm.

#### 4XC1-U ENGINE

1. Set the parking brake and block the drive wheels.
2. Place the transmission in **NEUTRAL** or **PARK** and start the engine.
3. Let the engine run until it reaches normal operating tempera-

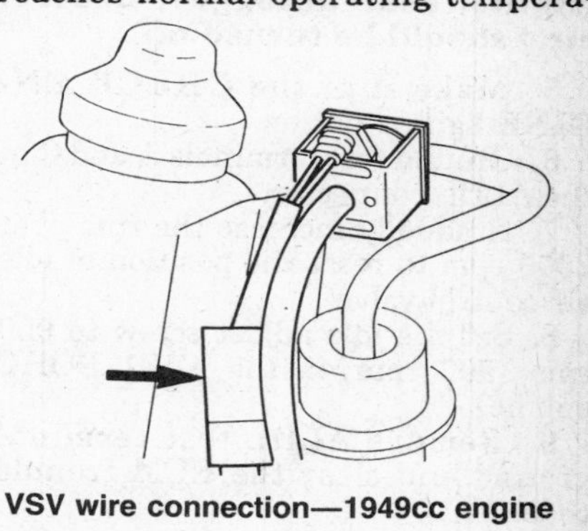

VSV wire connection—1949cc engine

ture. Leave the air cleaner installed and disconnect the distributor vacuum line from the carburetor, canister purge line, the EGR vacuum line and the ITC (inlet air temperature compensator) valve. Plug and mark all lines.

4. With the proper tachometer installed, the A/C off and all electrical equipment turned off. Check the idle speed and adjust as necessary by turning the throttle adjustment screw.

5. Once the idle speed has been adjusted to specifications, turn the A/C on and set the temperature control level to **MAX COLD**.

6. Set the blower to its highest position. Using the fast idle adjusting bolt, located at the tip of the carburetor lever set the fast idle speed to the correct specifications.

### *Fuel Injected Models*

#### G200Z, 4ZC1-T AND 4ZD1 ENGINES

1. Run the engine to the normal operating temperature and block drive wheels.

2. Check that the throttle value is fully closed.

3. Set the manual transmission in **NEUTRAL** or automatic transmission in **PARK** position.

4. With the air conditioner turned off and the harness of the pressure regulator V.S.V. disconnected, adjust the idle adjustment screw to specifications.

**NOTE: It is important to check and clean the idle port as necessary, as restrictions in the port can cause fluctuations in idle speed.**

#### 4XC1-T AND 4XE1 DOHC ENGINES

1. Set the parking brake.
2. Block the front wheels.
3. Place the select lever in **NEUTRAL.**
4. Make the idling speed adjustment with the engine at normal operating temperature, with A/C Off and front wheels facing straight ahead.

**NOTE: All electrical equipment (lights, rear defogger, heater, etc.) should be turned off.**

5. Make sure the **CHECK ENGINE** light is not on.
6. Ground test terminals **A** and **C** of the ALDL connector.
7. Gradually increase the rpm over 2000 rpm to reset the position of idle air control valve.
8. Set the idle adjust screw to 950 rpm (900 rpm on the 4XE1 DOHC engine).
9. Remove ALDL test terminal ground and clear the ECM trouble code.

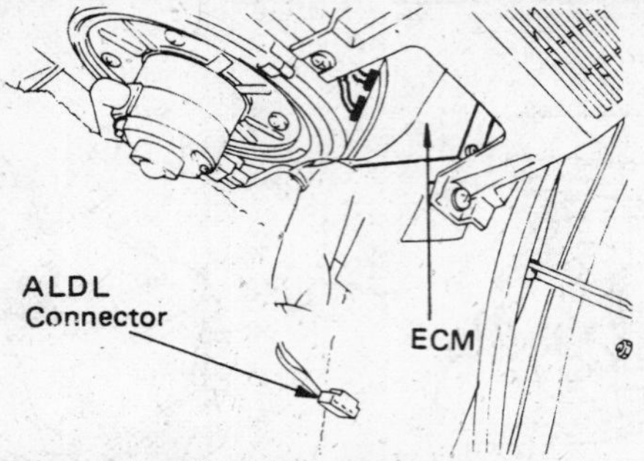


Grounding the ALDL connector

#### IDLE ADJUSTING METHOD

**After Replacing the Idle Air Control Valve**

**When the idle air contro valve has been replaced, the valve is dislocated and an idle adjustment is required.**

1. Set the parking brake.
2. Block the front wheels.
3. Place the select lever in **NEUTRAL.**
4. Make the idling speed adjustment with the engine at normal operating temperature, with A/C Off and front wheels facing straight ahead.

**NOTE: All electrical equipment (lights, rear defogger, heater, etc.) should be turned off.**

5. Make sure the **CHECK ENGINE** light is not on.
6. Ground test terminals **A** and **C** of the ALDL connector.
7. Gradually increase the rpm over 2000 rpm to reset the position of idle air control valve.
8. This will automatically reset the pintle position of the idle air control valve.
9. The idle air control valve specification should be as follows, the throttle opening should be 10% or more with the engine speed at 2000 rpm or more.

## Idle Mixture

### ADJUSTMENT

### *Carbureted Models*

#### G180Z ENGINE

1. Set the parking brake and block the drive wheels.
2. Place the transmission in **N** or **P** and remove the carburetor assembly.
3. Remove the plug for the idle mixture screw by inserting a suitable tool into the slit of the lower carburetor.
4. Turn the idle mixture screw all the way in then back the idle mixture screw out 1½ turns.
5. Adjust the idle mixture screw to set the dwell angle to 36 degrees on the 4 cylinder scale of the tachometer (24 degrees on the 6 cylinder scale.).
6. Apply a suitable adhesive to the new mixture screw concealment plug and install the new plug.
7. Re-check all adjustment. Remove all test equipment

#### 4XC1-U ENGINE

**NOTE: The idle mixture screw is adjusted and sealed at the factory and no service adjustment is required. However, if the necessity of adjustment aries for some reason, adjusting by removing plug is possible but it must be plugged again after adjustment is completed.**

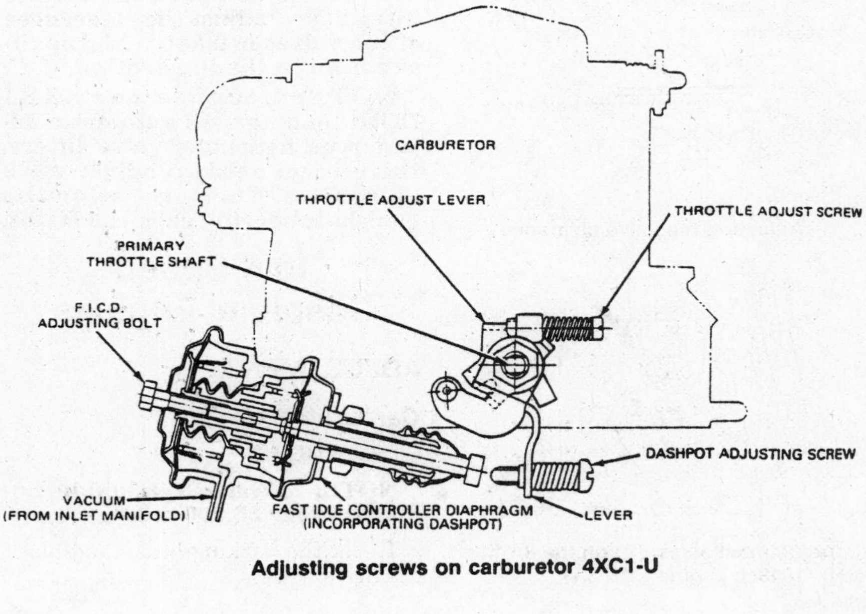


Adjusting screws on carburetor 4XC1-U

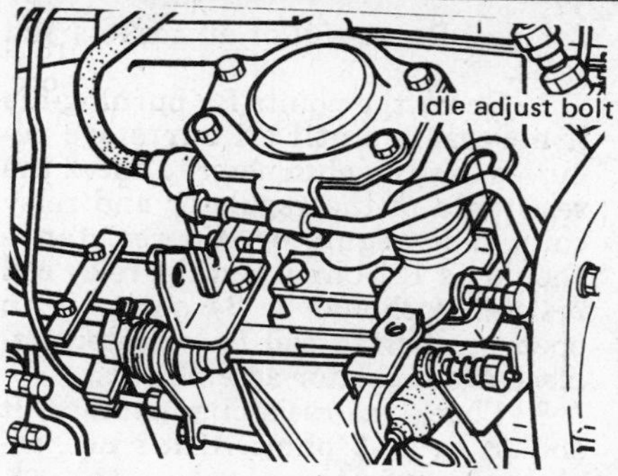


**Location of the diesel idle adjustment screw**

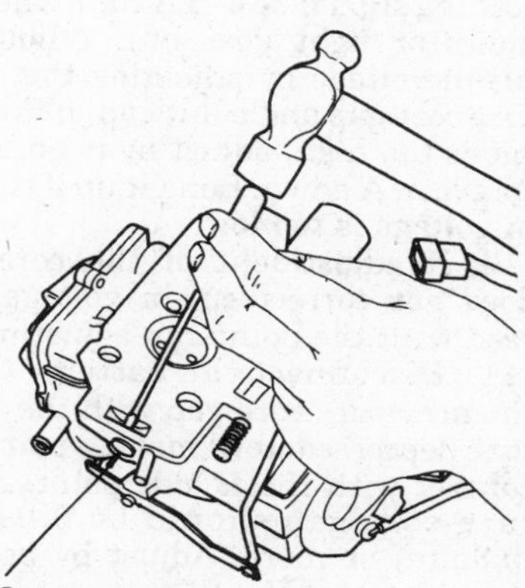


**Removing mixture plug (G180Z)**

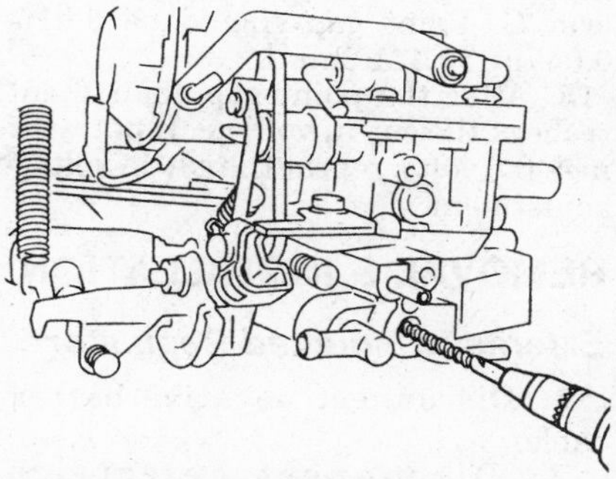

**Idle mixture screw concealment plug removal (4XC1-U engine)**

1. Remove the carburetor from the engine.
2. Using a center punch, make a punch mark on the idle mixture sealing plug. Drill a hole through the plug, insert a threaded screw and pull the plug from the throttle body. The width of the plug is about 10mm (0.39 in.).

**NOTE: If the idle mixture screw is damaged from the drilling process, replace the screw.**

3. Lightly seat the idle mixture screw, then back out 3 turns (MT) or 2 turns (AT). DO NOT overtighten the idle mixture screw.
4. Reinstall the carburetor and the air cleaner.
5. Adjust the idle speed. Disconnect the idle set connector, the **CHECK ENGINE** lamp will come on.
6. Using a dwell meter, connect the positive lead to the duty monitor and the negative lead to ground. Place the meter dial on the 4 cylinder scale. Turn the idle mixture screw until the dwell meter reads 45 degrees (4 cylinder scale) and or 30 degrees on a 6 cylinder scale. Reconnect the idle set connector, the **CHECK ENGINE** lamp should go out.
7. Readjust the throttle adjust screw to 750 rpm on vehicles with manual transaxles and 1000 rom on vehicles with automatic transaxles.
8. Check the idle speed and readjust if necessary using the throttle adjust screw. Readjust the dashpot, if necessary.
9. Turn A/C on **MAX**. Cold and blower on **HIGH** then adjust the bolt on the fast idle control device (FICD) and set the fast idle to 850 rpm (MT) or 980 (AT), if so equipped. Then stop the engine and remove the test equipment.
8. Drive a new idle mixture plug into the throttle body, flush with the throttle body apply Locktite No.262 or its equivalent to the plug.
9. Recheck all adjustments and road test.

#### *Fuel Injected Engines*

Idle mixture is controlled electronically by the Fuel Injection System. No adjustments are necessary.

## Idle Speed Diesel Engine

### ADJUSTMENT

#### *4FB1 Engine*

**NOTE: Idle speed should be adjusted every 30,000 miles.**

1. Set the parking brake and block the drive wheels.
2. Place the transmission in **NEUTRAL**.
3. Start the engine and allow it to warm up to operating temperature.
4. Connect a tachometer according to the manufacturer's instructions.
5. If the idle speed deviates from the specified range, loosen the idle adjusting screw lock nut and turn the screw in or out until the idle speed is correct.

### Fast Idle Speed

#### *Adjustment*

##### 4FB1 ENGINE

1. Start and warm up the engine.
2. Connect a tachometer according to the manufacturer's instructions.
3. Disconnect the hoses from the vacuum switch valve, then connect a pipe (4mm diameter) in position between the hoses.
4. Loosen the adjusting nut and adjust the idle speed. Fast idle should be around 900–950 rpm.
5. Tighten the adjusting nut and remove the tachometer.

# ENGINE ELECTRICAL

## Distributor

### REMOVAL & INSTALLATION

**NOTE: Every 30,000 miles, the distributor should be checked for proper operation. Check the cap and wires, rotor, air gap, vacuum advance mechanism and lubricate all working parts lightly.**

1. Turn the engine over and bring number one piston up to top dead center of its compression stroke. Disconnect the negative battery cable.
2. Tag the wires and remove the distributor cap with the ignition wires attached.
3. Disconnect the coil wires and vacuum lines. Scribe a line on the distributor housing and on the engine, use this line as a reference when reinstalling the distributor.
4. Remove the distributor clamp bolt and bracket and lift out the distributor housing from the engine.

**CAUTION**

***Never hammer on the distributor housing to tap it loose.***

5. Installation is the reverse of removal. Be sure to use the scribe line made earlier to assure correct installation. Start the engine, check the timing and adjust if necessary.

## Alternator

### PRECAUTIONS

- When installing a battery, make sure that the positive and negative cables are not reversed.
- When jump-starting the car, be sure that like terminals are connected to each other. This also applies to using a battery charger. Reversed polarity will burn out the alternator and regulator in a matter of seconds.

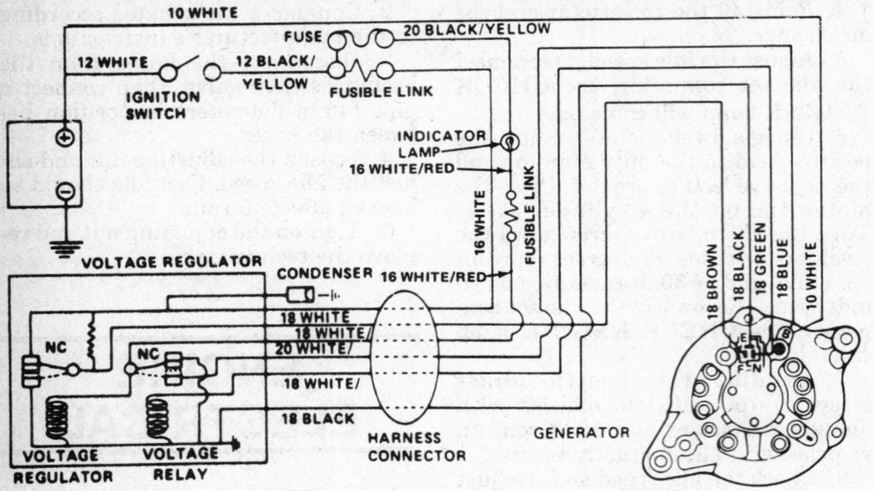

Alternator and regulator wiring schematic

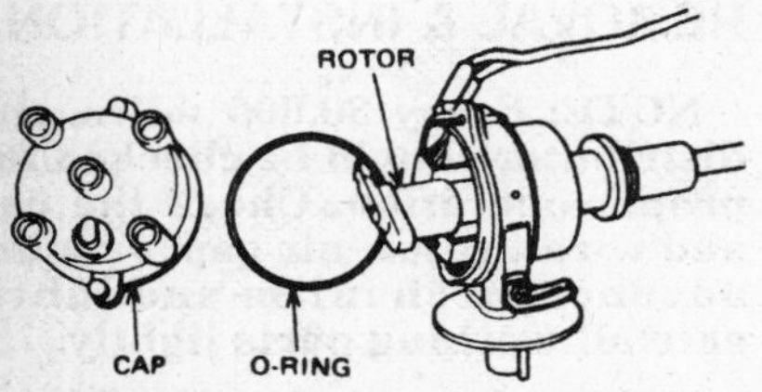

Distributor cap, O-ring and rotor

- Never operate the alternator with the battery disconnected or on an otherwise uncontrolled open circuit.
- Do not short across or ground any alternator or regulator terminals.
- Do not try to polarize the alternator.
- Do not apply full battery voltage to the field connector.
- Always disconnect the battery ground cable before disconnecting the alternator lead.
- Always disconnect the battery (negative cable first) when charging it.
- Never subject the alternator to excessive heat or dampness. If you are steam-cleaning the engine, cover the alternator.
- Never use arc welding equipment on the car with the alternator connected.

## REMOVAL & INSTALLATION

Removing the alternator is simply a matter of loosening the mounting and adjustment bolts, removing the belt and lifting out the assembly. Diesel models have a vacuum pump mounted on the front of the alternator assembly. It must be removed along with the alternator for service.

1. Disconnect the battery. Remove all necessary components in order to gain access to the alternator assembly.
2. Loosen all the mounting and adjusting bolts and remove the drive belt.
3. Remove mounting bolts and lift out the alternator.

**NOTE: Tag all wires before removing them from the alternator.**

4. Installation is the reverse of removal. Drive belt tension is 90 ± 20 lbs. using a Borroughs drive belt tension gauge.

# Voltage Regulator

## TESTING AND ADJUSTING

### *Externally Mounted Regulator*

1. Perform this test with the regulator on the car and the engine running.
2. Connect a voltmeter between the condenser lead and ground with all electrical loads disconnected, including the blower relay connector.
3. The voltage regulator is working properly when the lower side points are closed while the engine is turned off, and when the upper points are closed when the engine is running at idle. If the points are not working normally, chances are that the regulator is out of adjustment, or the voltage coil is open.
4. Check the coil resistance and replace the regulator assembly if found to be malfunctioning. If the coil resistance is normal, adjust the regulator.
5. Start the engine and increase the engine speed gradually. Voltage should increase with engine rpm up to 1400–1850 rpm. A normal condition is indicated when the voltage is within the range of 13.8–14.8 volts. Reconnect the blower relay connector.
6. Remove the regulator cover and check all internal parts for wear and damage. Be careful of all gaskets and seals.
7. Check the points for burning-file if necessary until all burrs are removed. Use an ohmmeter to check the resistance of the regulator and relay coils. The regulator coil resistance should be 102 ohms and the relay coil resistance should be 24 ohms. If an open or shorted coil is indicated, replace the regulator assembly.
8. Check the resistor resistance. It should be 10.5 ohms. If it's not, replace the resistor.
9. Connect a voltmeter between **N** terminal and ground, then increase the engine speed gradually. Voltmeter reading should be 4–5.8 volts when the indicator light goes out. Adjust the cut-in voltage by adjusting the armature core gap and point gap. If the voltage is too high, adjust by bending the core arm **A** down. Bend it up if the cut-in voltage is too low.
10. If adjustment of the core arm does not correct cut-in voltage, proceed with the point gap adjustment.
11. Disconnect the battery. Check the armature core gap with the armature depressed until moving point is in contact with the **B** side point. Armature core gap should be 0.012 in. (0.3mm) or more. Adjust by bending the point arm **B**.
12. Release the armature and adjust the gap between the **B** side point and the moving point by bending the point arm **C**. Point gap should be 0.016–0.047in. (0.4–1.2mm).
13. After the point gap adjustment, recheck the cut-in voltage. If not within 4–5.8 volts, repeat the cut-in voltage adjustment.

## REMOVAL & INSTALLATION

### *Externally Mounted Regulator*

1. Disconnect negative battery cable.
2. Disconnect electrical connections.
3. Remove hold down bolts.
4. Installation is the reverse of removal.

### *Internally Mounted Regulator*

1. Disconnect the negative battery cable.
2. Remove alternator assembly.
3. Make scribe marks on end frames to facilitate reassembly.
4. Remove thru-bolts and separate drive end frame assembly from rectifier end frame assembly.
5. Remove attaching nuts and three regulator attaching screws.
6. Separate stator, diode trio and regulator from end frame.
7. Installation is the reverse of the removal procedure.

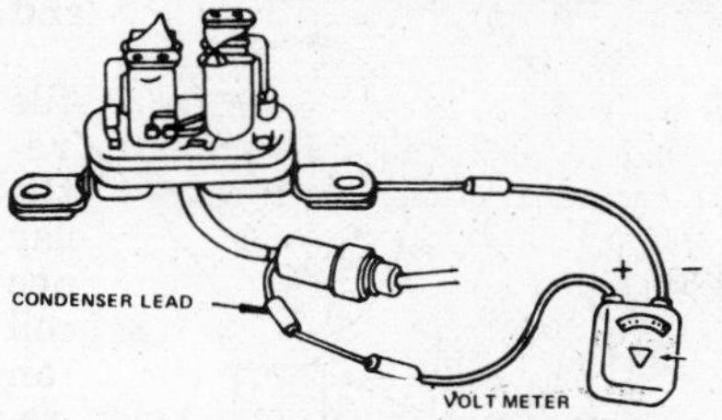


Regulator test connections

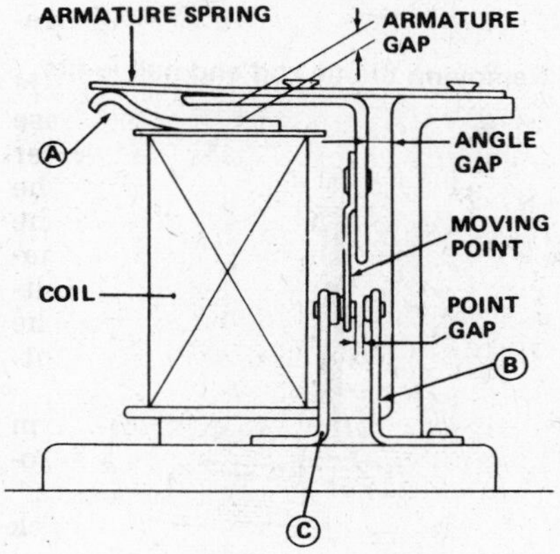


Voltage relay adjustment

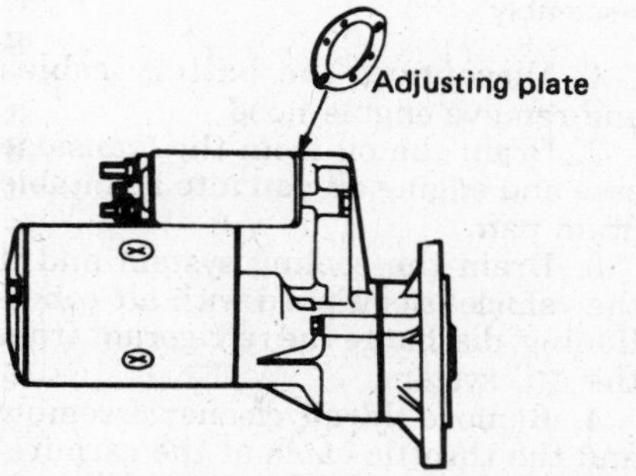


Typical diesel engine starter assembly showing adjustment shims

## Starter

### REMOVAL & INSTALLATION

#### *Gasoline Engines*

1. Disconnect the battery cables at the battery posts.
2. Disconnect the EGR pipe from the EGR valve and exhaust manifold, then remove the EGR pipe.
3. Disconnect the wiring from the starter magnetic switch.

**NOTE: Tag all wires before disconnecting.**

4. Remove the bolts and nuts attaching the starter to the motor.
5. Remove the starter assembly through the clearance under the intake manifold.
6. Installation is the reverse of removal.

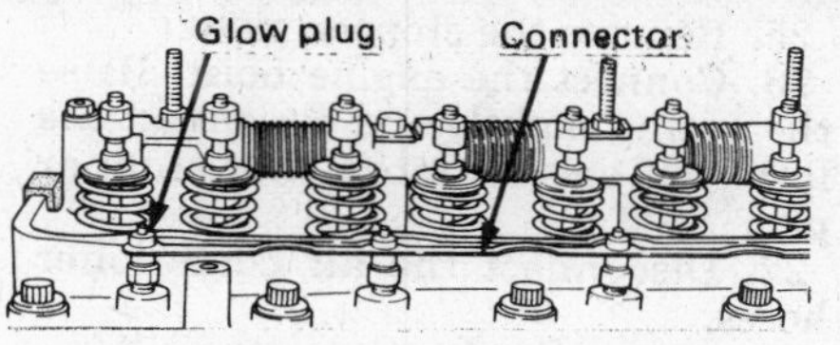


Glow plugs and connector locations

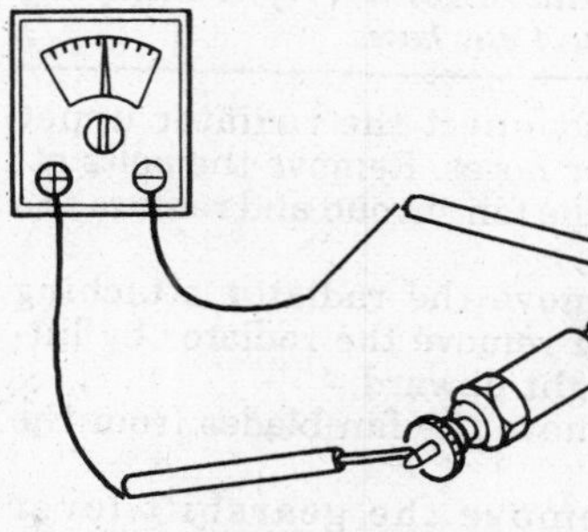

Testing continuity of glow plug

#### *Diesel Engine*

1. Open the hood and disconnect the battery cables at the posts.
2. Disconnect the magnetic switch wiring at the connector.

**NOTE: Label all wires before disconnecting.**

3. Remove the starter motor attaching nuts and bolts and remove the starter motor.
4. Installation is the reverse of removal

### STARTER DRIVE REPLACEMENT

#### *All Models*

1. Remove the starter from the vehicle.
2. Remove the starter lead wire from the solenoid. Remove the starter assembly through bolts.
3. Remove the solenoid assembly retaining nuts.
4. Remove the solenoid switch and pull out the torsion spring out of the solenoid switch (if so equipped). Remove the starter housing assembly.
5. remove the starter drive lever assembly. Remove the starter frame end cover and starter brake spring assembly. Be careful not to lose the shim from the brake assembly.
6. Remove the starter end frame, brush holder assembly and remove the starter drive and armature assembly.
7. Installation is the reverse order of the removal procedure.

### STARTER SOLENOID

1. Remove the starter from the vehicle.
2. Remove the starter lead wire from the solenoid.
3. Remove the solenoid assembly retaining nuts.
4. Remove the solenoid switch and pull out the torsion spring out of the solenoid switch (if so equipped). On some models it may be necessary to remove the starter assembly through bolts from the yoke to remove the solenoid assembly.
5. Installation is the reverse order of the removal procedure.

## Diesel Glow Plugs

### REMOVAL & INSTALLATION

The glow plugs are designed to preheat the combustion chambers so that the diesel engine will have sufficient temperature to fire the fuel on initial starting. They resemble spark plugs and are removed much the same way. Disconnect the wire leads and use a deep socket to remove the glow plug from the cylinder head. Care must be taken not to damage the glow plug in any way or to strip the threads in the cylinder head. If a tight glow plug is encountered, coat the threads with some light weight oil and allow it to soak for a while. Be sure to use the correct glow plug for the engine. They are not interchangeable.

### TESTING

**NOTE: If the glow plugs should fail to work, check the fusible link before removing the glow plugs. The fusible link wire can be found near the battery, at the left side of the engine compartment.**

1. Remove the glow plug.
2. Using a circuit tester, check for continuity across the plug terminals and the body. If no continuity exists, the glow plug should be replaced.

# GASOLINE ENGINE MECHANICAL

## Engine

### REMOVAL & INSTALLATION

#### *I-Mark (RWD)*

1. Remove the battery cables.
2. Scribe the position of the hood hinges on the underside of the hood.

Remove the four attaching bolts and lift off the hood.

3. Remove the bottom shrouds and drain the crankcase and cooling system.

4. Disconnect the PCV hose from the air cleaner body. Disconnect the air hose from the air pump and remove the air duct from the air cleaner.

5. Remove the bolts attaching the air cleaner and loosen the clamp bolt.

6. Disconnect the thermostatic air cleaner (TAC) hot air hose and remove the manifold cover.

7. Tag and disconnect the generator valves at the connector.

8. Remove the two nuts connecting the exhaust pipe to the exhaust manifold and disconnect the exhaust pipe.

9. Take the tension off the clutch control cable by loosening the adjusting nut.

10. Disconnect the heater hose from the engine to the heater control valve at the engine side.

11. Disconnect the heater hose from the heater unit and joint.

12. Disconnect the control cable from the heater temperature valve and remove the control valve together with the hose.

13. Remove the engine mounting nut.

14. Support the engine with special tool J-26555 or equivalent. Attach the engine hanger using the exhaust manifold stud bolts.

15. Disconnect the cable grounding the cylinder block to the frame.

16. Disconnect the fuel lines and vapor lines from the carburetor and charcoal canister.

17. Remove the high tension cable from the coil. Disconnect the vacuum hose from the rear of the intake manifold at the connector.

18. Disconnect the accelerator control cable from the carburetor.

19. Disconnect the starter motor wiring.

**NOTE: Tag all wires before disconnecting.**

20. Disconnect the thermo-unit, oil pressure switch and distributor wiring at the connectors.

21. Disconnect the carburetor solenoid valve and the automatic choke wiring at the connectors.

22. Disconnect the back-up light switch and transmission switch wiring at the connector on the rear part of the engine.

23. Disconnect the emission control hose from the oil pan.

24. Remove the engine mounting

**CAUTION**

***Make sure the engine is well-supported from above.***

25. Remove the stopper plate.

26. Connect the engine hoist. Raise the engine slightly and disconnect the left side engine mounting stopper plate.

27. Disconnect the air conditioner hoses.

**CAUTION**

***Discharge the A/C system before attempting to disconnect any hoses.***

28. Disconnect the radiator upper and lower hoses. Remove the bolts attaching the fan shroud and remove the shroud.

29. Remove the radiator attaching bolts and remove the radiator by lifting straight upward.

30. Remove the fan blades from the pulley.

31. Remove the gearshift lever assembly.

32. Disconnect the parking brake return spring and disconnect the cable.

33. Disconnect the propeller shaft from the transmission. Remove the clutch return spring.

34. Disconnect the clutch control cable from the clutch withdraw lever and remove it from the engine stiffener.

35. Remove the front side exhaust pipe bracket from the transmission.

36. Disconnect the front and rear side exhaust pipes at the joint, then remove the front side exhaust pipe.

37. Disconnect the speedometer cable.

38. Remove the rear engine mounting bolts.

**NOTE: Check that the engine is slightly lifted before removing the rear mounting bolts.**

39. Check to make certain all the parts have been removed or disconnected from the engine and that the parts are tied safely out of the way so as not to snag when the engine is being lifted clear.

40. Lift the engine and slide it toward the front of the car. Remove the transmission from the engine and set it on the floor.

41. Slowly lift the engine clear.

42. Installation is the reverse of removal. Fill the crankcase and cooling system. Check and adjust the clutch pedal free play and check the carburetor and clutch linkage for smooth operation if so equipped. Start the engine and check for leaks.

### *I-Mark (FWD)*

#### EXCEPT THE 4XE1 DOHC ENGINE

**NOTE: The main difference between engine removal and installation of these 2 engines is electrical wiring, vacuum hose routing and turbocharger oil and water lines.**

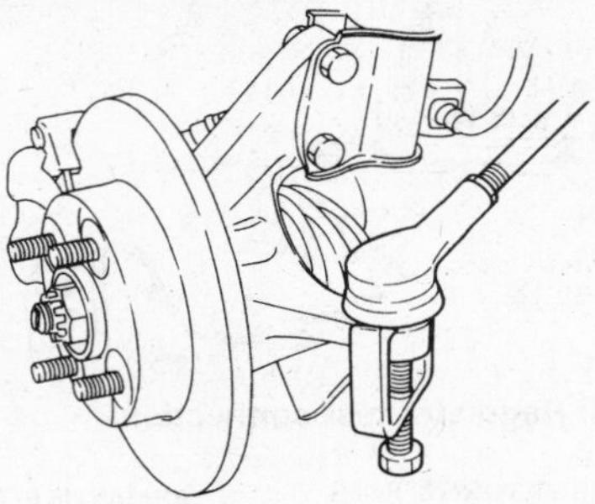

**Removing the tie rod end ball joints**

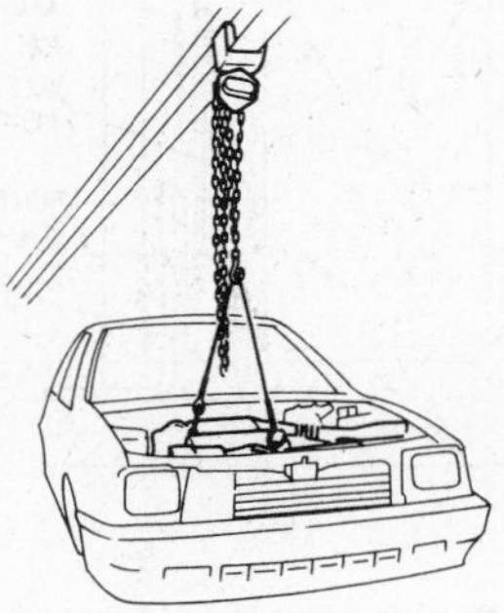

**Removing the engine with transaxle as an assembly**

1. Disconnect the battery cables and remove engine hood.

2. Drain the oil from the transaxle case and engine oil pan into a suitable drain pan.

3. Drain the cooling system and if the vehicle is equipped with air conditioning, discharge the refrigerant from the A/C system.

4. Remove the air cleaner assembly and the throttle cable at the carburetor, on non-turbocharged models.

5. Remove, plug and tag the fuel pump inlet and return hoses on non-turbocharged models.

6. Remove the power steering hoses, A/C hose assembly, radiator and heater hoses and automatic transmission cooler hoses (if so equipped).

7. Remove the brake booster hose, clutch cable and select/shift cables (if so equipped), speedometer cable and high tension cable.

8. Remove and tag all necessary electrical wires and remove the distributor from the engine.

9. Remove the battery and battery tray. Remove all the necessary wiring connectors from their respective sensor. Be sure to tag all connectors.

10. Remove and tag all necessary vacuum lines and remove the engine control cable.

11. Remove the drive shafts as follows:

a. Raise and support safely the front of the vehicle. Remove the front wheels.

b. Disconnect the tie rod end ball joints from the steering knuckles using special remover tool No. J–21687–02 or equivalent.

c. Disconnect the lower arm end ball joints from the lower arm. Loosen but do not remove the nuts attaching the strut to the body.

d. Using a suitable tool, pull out the driveshafts and be careful not to damage the transaxle oil seals when removing the driveshafts.

12. Remove the front exhaust pipe, on turbocharged engine remove exhaust pipe at wastegate manifold and vacuum line at wastegate control valve. Attach a suitable engine chain hoist to the engine hanger located on the top of the engine.

13. Raise the engine just enough to remove the weight from the engine mounts, while putting a slight tension on the rubber in the engine mounts.

14. Remove the torque rod from the side of the body.

15. Making sure that all hoses and wires are out of the way, carefully and slowly raise the engine and transaxle assembly out of the vehicle. Place the assembly on a suitable engine stand or equivalent.

16. Remove the torque rod with bracket from the engine. Remove the main wire harness assembly from the engine.

17. Place a suitable transmission jack or equivalent under the transaxle and separate the transaxle assembly from the engine.

18. Installation is the reverse order of the removal procedure. Make all necessary adjustments and refill the engine, transaxle, cooling system, power steering reservoir and recharge the A/C system with the proper lubricants and to the specified amount.

19. When installing the engine pay close attention to the following torque specifications.

a. Transaxle to engine mounting bolts 56 ft. lbs.

b. Torque rod bracket to frame bolt 40 ft. lbs.

c. Torque rod to bracket bolt 56 ft. lbs.

d. Engine mount bracket to block 28 ft. lbs.

e. Front and rear engine mounting through bolts and nuts 60 ft. lbs. (always use new bolts and nuts).

f. Right hand mounting rubber—body side 30 ft. lbs. engine side 45 ft. lbs.

g. Torque rod to body frame 42 ft. lbs.

h. Nuts attaching the strut to body 40 ft. lbs.

i. Tie rod end ball joints to steering knuckle 42 ft. lbs.

j. Front wheel lug nuts 65 ft. lbs.

20. After the installation is completed, road test the vehicle and then recheck the fluid levels and check for any leaks.

### 4XE1 DOHC ENGINE

1. Raise the hood and disconnect the battery cables.

2. Remove the battery. Scribe lines on the inside of the engine hood and remove the engine hood.

3. Drain the engine coolant into a suitable drain pan. Drain the transmission fluid into a suitable drain pan.

4. Remove the air intake duct from the common chamber. Remove the breather hose from the rear of the valve cover.

5. Remove the fast idle vacuum hose from the air intake duct. Remove the pulse air hose from the reed valve side.

6. Remove the 3 air cleaner fixing bolts. Remove the air claner and air cleaner bracket from the engine.

7. Remove and tag the following vacuum lines:

a. The EGR vacuum hoses.

b. Canister hose from the throttle valve side of the vacuun switching valve.

c. Remove the MAP sensor hose from the common chamber side.

d. Remove the pulse air hose from the common chamber side.

e. Remove the canister hoses from the common chamber side.

f. Remove the master vacuum hose from the master VAC tube at the common chamber side.

8. Disconnect the following wiring harness:

a. Electronic control gas injection harness, disconnect the 2 ECM ground connectors from the bracket located on top of the common chamber. Disconnect the 2 green and black multi-pin connectors on the top of the common chamber.

b. Remove the high tension cable from the ignition coil. Remove the 2 primary connections from the coil. Disconnect the condenser plug. Remove the ignition coil with bracket.

c. Disconnect 2 engine harness multi pin plugs, near the battery tray. Remove the engine harness ground cable from the drivers inner fender. Disconnect connector from the slow blow fuse.

d. Disconnect the connectors from the EGR temperature sensor, throttle position sensor, MAT sensor, oxygen sensor and remove the engine ground from the valve cover.

9. Working from the left hand side of the engine, remove the clutch cable by lossening the 2 adjusting nuts.

10. Remove the 2 transmission shift cables by disconnecting the cotter pin and removing the clip from the shift cable bracket.

11. Disconnect the speedometer cable from the transmission.

12. Disconnect the heater hoses from the engine. Disconnect the upper radiator hose from the engine.

13. Disconnect the accelerator cable from the throttle body and at the common chamber.

14. Disconnect the fuel feed hose at the fuel filter outlet and disconnect the return fuel line near the fuel filter.

15. Working from the front of the engine, remove the coolant reservoir.

16. Remove the 2 bolts from the power steering pump bracket, without disconnecting the feed lines and position the pump out of the way from the engine.

17. Disconnect the lower radiator hose from the radiator.

18. Remove the A/C compressor bolts and without disconnecting the A/C lines, secure the compressor away from the engine.

19. Remove the cooling fan and shroud as one assembly.

20. Raise and support the vehicle safely. Remove both front wheels.

21. Lossen the strut tower nuts on both sides, but do not remove.

22. Remove the stabilizer bar. Disconnect the control arms on both sides from the body.

23. Remove the front air deflector, if so equipped.

24. Remove the tension rod fixing nut from both sides and remove the rod out of the bracket.

25. Remove the passenger side driveshaft fixing bracket from the engine block and pull the driveshaft out of the transaxle. Pull the driveshaft on the drivers side out of the transaxle.

26. Remove the exhaust pipe from the exhaust manifold.

27. Remove the engine by using a suitable engine hoist. Remove the passenger side engine mount from the body.

28. Disconnect the torque rod at the firewall. Remove both lower engine mounting bolts.

29. Remove the engine and transaxle out of the vehicle together as an assembly.

30. Installation is the reversal of removal. Refill all fluid levels, make all adjustments as necessary then road test and check for leaks.

## *Impulse*

**NOTE: The engine removal and installation for the 4ZC1-T engine is the same as the procedure used for the G200Z and 4ZD1 engine. The main difference is the electrical wiring, vacuum hose routing**

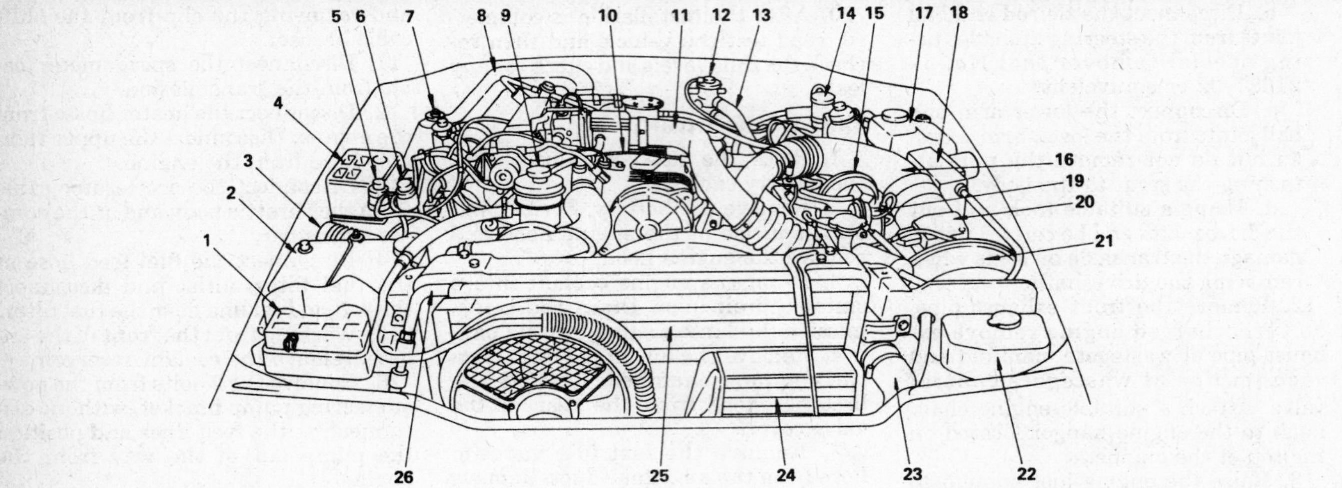


1. Relay box
2. Battery
3. Ignition coil
4. Relay box
5. Fast idel solenoid (only for models with digital meter)
6. Booster sensor (only for models with digital meter)
7. Pressure regulator
8. Blower duct
9. Power steering fluid reservoir tank
10. Accelerator cable
11. Air duct (intercoller to common chamber)
12. Air switching valve
13. Air hose-air switching valve to air manifold
14. Brake fluid reservoir tank
15. Cruise control actuator
16. Air duct (air cleaner to turbocharger)
17. Windshield washer surge tank
18. Stepping motor
19. Water valve
20. Air flow sensor
21. Air cleaner
22. Radiator reservoir
23. Air duct (to engine intercooler
24. Intercooler
25. Radiator
26. A/C pipe

**Engine parts location diagram (4ZC1-T)**

**and turbocharger oil and water lines.**

1. Remove the battery cables.
2. Disconnect the headlight cover motor harness, remove the strut-to-hood bolt and the engine hood side bolt and remove the hood.
3. Drain the crankshaft and cooling systems.
4. Disconnect the upper radiator hose.
5. Disconnect the oil cooler line for the automatic transmission (if so equipped).
6. On models with air conditioning, remove the compressor mounting bracket from the engine and position the compressor out of the way without disconnecting the refrigerant lines.

**NOTE: If the compressor lines do not have enough slack to move the compressor out of the way without disconnecting the refrigerant lines, the air conditioning system must be evacuated, using the required tools, before the refrigerant lines can be disconnected.**

**CAUTION**

***Do not disconnect any refrigerant lines unless you have experience with air conditioning systems. Escaping refrigerant will freeze any surface it contacts, including your skin and eyes.***

7. Remove the rubber air duct hose to the cylinder head cover.
8. Disconnect the accelerator cable.
9. Disconnect and tag the rubber hoses at the following connections:
   a. Between the injection pipe and the pressure regulator.
   b. Fuel pipe to injection pipe.
   c. Canister (purge) to common chamber.
   d. Canister (VC) to 3-way.
   e. VSV to common chamber.
   f. VSV to 3-way.
   g. Solenoid fast idle to common chamber.
   h. Solenoid fast idle to thermal valve.
10. Disconnect the cable harness between the fender skirt and the cylinder head.
11. Disconnect and tag the connectors at the following locations.
   a. Oil pressure switch
   b. Water temperature sensor
   c. Knock sensor
   d. I-TEC harness
   e. Crank angle distributor sensor
   f. Starter terminal
   g. Cable harness, engine rear to cross-member front
   h. Automatic transmission control
   i. $O_2$ Sensor
12. Remove the R.H. engine mounting nut.
13. Remove the air intake nut.
14. Disconnect the following rubber hoses.
   a. Radiator reservoir
   b. Auto cruise to common chamber
   c. Master vac to intake manifold
   d. Heater hoses
   e. Radiator hoses
   f. Power steering hoses
15. Remove the L.H. mounting bolt and heat shield.
16. Remove the cover from under the engine.
17. Disconnect the propeller shaft and install a plug in the transmission rear cover to prevent the oil from draining.
18. On models with automatic transmission remove the pin from the transmission select lever.
19. Disconnect the speedometer cable.
20. On models equipped with manual transmissions remove the clutch slave cylinder.
21. Remove the converter mounting bracket.
22. Remove the exhaust pipe nuts to manifold, on turbocharged engine remove exhaust pipe at wastegate manifold and control cable for turbocharger.
23. Disconnect the rear engine mounting bracket.
24. Install an engine hoist and re-

move the engine and transmission from the vehicle.

25. Installation is the reversal of removal.

26. Refill all fluid levels, make all adjustments as necessary then road test and check for leaks.

## Cylinder Head

### REMOVAL & INSTALLATION

#### *G180Z and G200Z Engines*

1. Remove the cam cover and disconnect the battery cables.
2. Remove the EGR pump clamp bolt at the rear of the cylinder head.
3. Raise the vehicle and safely support it.
4. Disconnect the exhaust pipe at the exhaust manifold.
5. Drain the cooling system.
6. Lower the car.
7. Disconnect the heater hoses at the intake manifold and at the rear of the cylinder head.
8. Disconnect the accelerator linkage, all necessary electrical connections, spark plug wires and necessary vacuum lines.

**NOTE: Tag all wires and hoses before disconnecting them from the engine.**

9. Raise the camshaft until No.4 cylinder is in firing position or compression stroke. Remove the distributor cap and mark the rotor-to-housing relationship and housing to cylinder head then remove the distributor assembly. This simple act will save untold grief when trying to get the distributor back in correctly.
10. Lock the timing chain adjuster by depressing and turning the automatic chain adjuster slide pin 90 degrees clockwise.
11. Remove the timing sprocket-to-camshaft bolt and remove the sprocket from the camshaft. Keep the sprocket on the chain damper and tensioner. Do not remove the sprocket from the chain.
12. Disconnect the air pump hose and check valve at the exhaust manifold.
13. Remove the cylinder head-to-timing cover bolts.
14. Remove the cylinder head bolts using an extension bar with socket. Remove bolts in progressive sequence, begining with the outer bolts.

**NOTE: Use light oil to free frozen bolts.**

15. With the aid of an assistant, remove the cylinder head, intake and exhaust manifolds as an assembly.
16. Clean all gasket material from the cylinder head and block surfaces. Check for nicks or heavy scratches on the mating surfaces.
17. Installation is the reverse of removal. Cylinder bolt threads in the block and threads on the bolts must be cleaned. Dirt will affect head torque.
18. Torque all head bolts to specifications according to the sequence in the illustration. Torque bolts to half normal value in sequence, then to specifications on the second pass. The torque should be 61 ft. lbs. on the first pass and 72 ft. lbs. on the second pass.

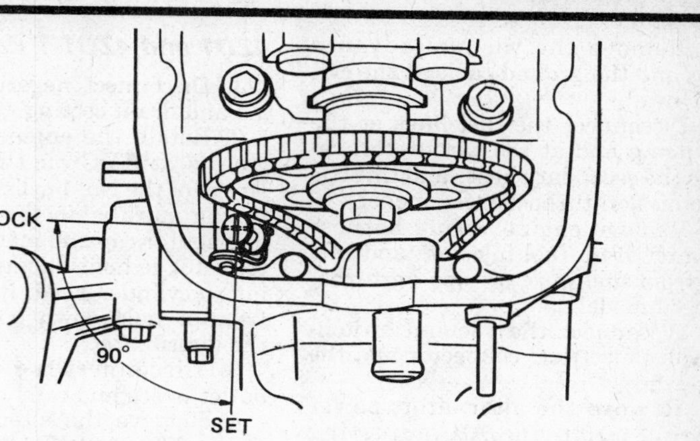

Locking the timing chain adjuster—1816cc engine

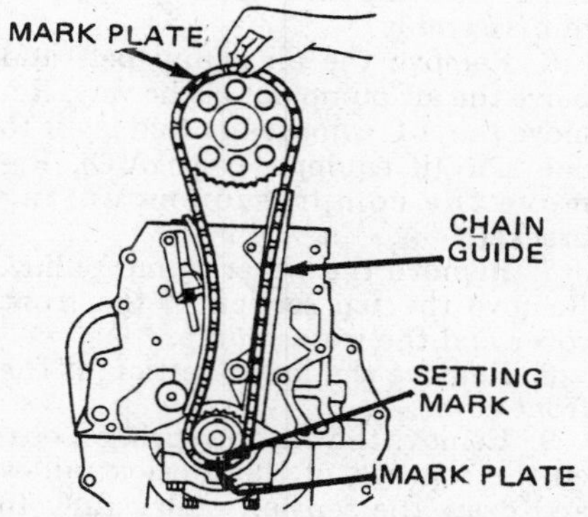

Keep the timing sprocket attached to the chain while aligning or removing

#### *4XC1-U and 4XC1-T Engines*

1. Disconnect the negative battery cable and drain the cooling system into a suitable drain pan.
2. Remove the air cleaner assembly and disconnect the flex hose along with the oxygen sensor at the exhaust manifold.
3. Disconnect the exhaust pipe bracket at the block and the exhaust pipe at the manifold. On turbocharged model remove exhaust pipe at wastegate manifold, and remove vacumm line for turbocharger control.
4. Disconnect the spark plug wires and remove the thermostat housing.
5. Rotate the engine until the engine is at TDC on the compression stroke of the No. 1 cylinder. Remove distributor cap and mark the distributor rotor to housing positon and housing to cylinder head. Remove the distributor hold down bolt and remove the distributor.

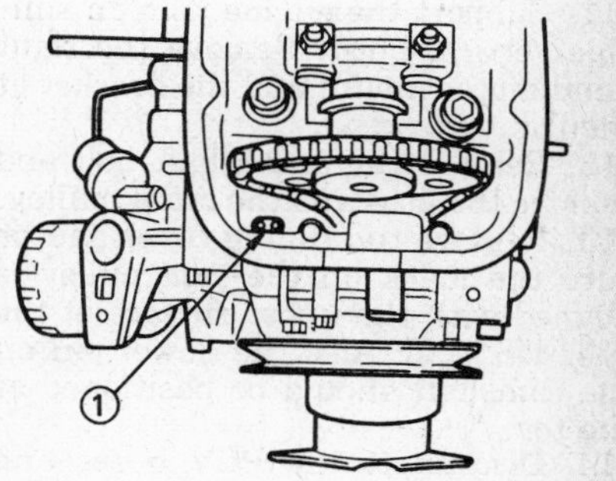

Timing chain automatic adjuster lock level—(1) 1949cc gasoline engine

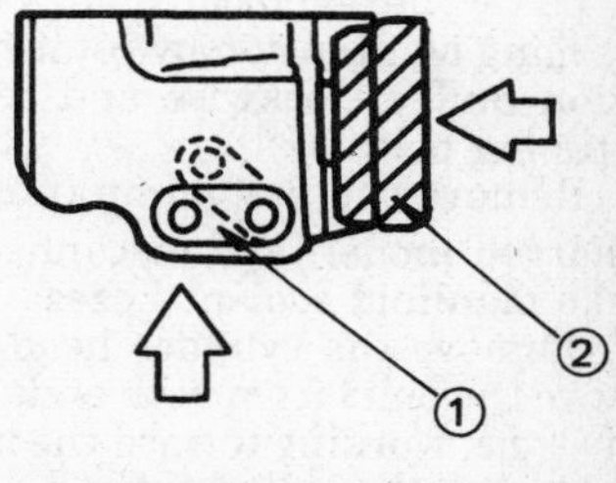

Push in on the automatic adjuster shoe (1) and lock it in the retracted position by releasing lever (2)—118.9 cu. in. gasoline engine

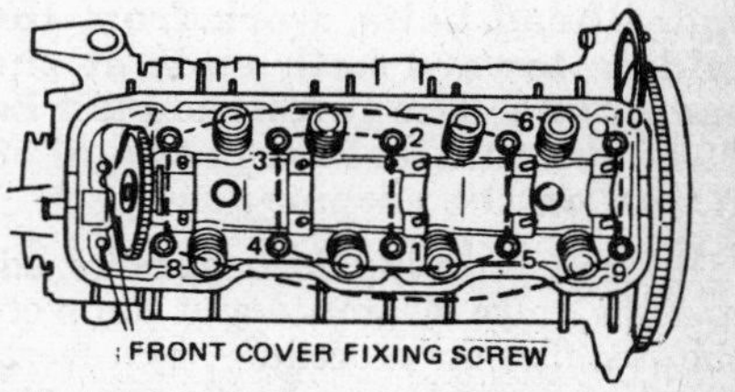

Cylinder head bolt torque sequence for the G180Z and G200Z

6. Remove the vacuum advance hoses and the ground cable at the cylinder head.
7. Disconnect the fuel lines at the fuel pump and at the carburetor, remove the secondary hoses and throttle cable on non-turbocharged model.
8. Remove engine wiring harness assembly from fuel injectors and fuel line from fuel injector pipe on turbocharged model.
9. Disconnect the vacuum switching valve electrical connector and the heater hoses.
10. Remove the alternator, power steering pump and A/C adjusting bolts, brackets and drive belts. Remove and tag all necessary electrical and vacuum lines.
11. Support the engine using a suitable vertical hoist. Remove the right hand motor mount and the bracket at the front cover.
12. Remove the crankshaft bolt and remove the boss and the crank pulley.
13. Remove the timing cover and be sure the mark on the cam pulley is aligned with the upper surface of the cylinder head. Also the dowel pin on the camshaft should be positioned at the top.
14. Disconnect the PCV hoses and remove the valve cover. If the cover sticks to the head, carefully strike the valve cover with a soft mallet.
15. Insert a hex wrench into the tension pulley hexagonical hole. Loosen the timing belt tension by rotating the tension pulley clockwise and remove the timing belt.
16. Remove the fuel pump (non-turbocharged model) and disconnect the intake manifold coolant hoses.
17. Remove the cylinder head bolts, remove the bolts from both ends at the same time, working toward the middle and remove the cylinder head.
18. To install, use new seals and gaskets, apply oil to the head bolt threads and torque the head bolts.

**NOTE: When torquing the cylinder head bolts, work from the middle toward both ends at the same time. The torque should be 29 ft. lbs. on the first pass and 58 ft. lbs. on the second pass.**

19. After torquing the head bolts, adjust the valve clearance and complete the installation procedure, by reversing the removal procedure.

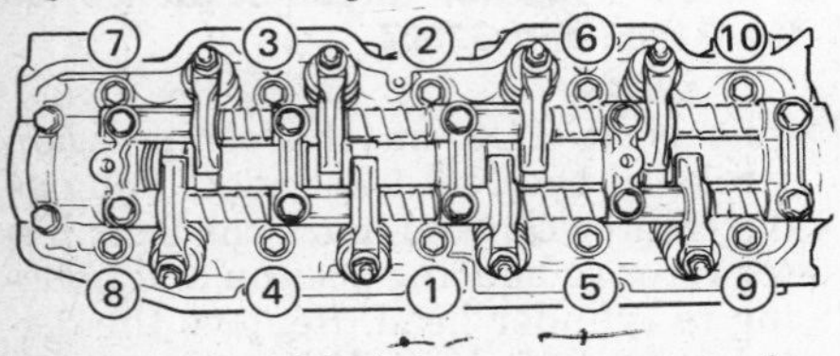

Cylinder head bolt torque sequence for the 4XC1-U and 4XC1-T engines

### *4ZD1 and 4ZC1-T Engines*

1. Disconnect negative battery cable and drain cooling system.
2. Rotate the engine until the engine is at TDC on the compression stroke of the No. 1 cylinder, make sure timing mark is on the scale. Remove distributor cap and mark the distributor rotor to housing positon and housing to cylinder head. Remove the distributor hold down bolt and remove the distributor.
3. Disconnect radiator inlet and outlet hoses and remove the radiator.
4. Remove the alternator and the air conditioner drive belts. Remove engine fan.
5. Remove the crankshaft pulley center bolt and remove the pulley and hub assembly.
6. Remove the air pump belt and move the air pump out of the way. Remove the A/C compressor and lay it to one side (if equipped with A/C). Remove the compressor mounting bracket.
7. Remove the water pump pulley. Remove the top section of the front cover and the water pump.
8. Remove the lower section of the front cover.
9. Remove the tension spring. Loosen the top bolt of the tension pulley and draw the tension pulley fully to the water pump side.
10. Remove the timing belt.
11. Remove cam cover.
12. Sequentially loosen and remove the rocker arm shaft tightening nuts from the outermost one and remove the rocker arm shaft with the bracket as an assembly.
13. Raise vehicle and disconnect the exhaust pipe at the exhaust manifold. On turbocharged model disconnect exhaust pipe from wastegate manifold and remove control cable for turbocharger.
14. Lower vehicle disconnect all lines, hoses, electrical connections and spark plug wires.

**NOTE: Tag all wires and hoses before disconnecting them from the engine.**

15. Disconnect the accelerator linkage, on turbocharged model remove engine wiring harness asembly from fuel injectors and fuel line from fuel injector pipe.
16. Remove the cylinder head bolts using an extension bar with socket. Remove bolts in progressive sequence, beginnning with the outer bolts.

**NOTE: Use light oil to free frozen bolts.**

17. With the aid of an assistant, remove the cylinder head, intake and exhaust manifolds as an assembly.

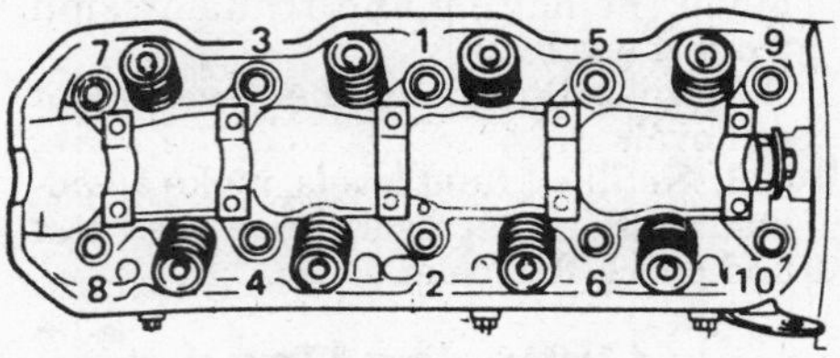

Cylinder head bolt torque sequence 4ZD1 and 4ZC1-T engines

18. Clean all gasket material from the cylinder head and block surfaces. Check for nicks or heavy scratches on the mating surfaces.
19. Installation is the reverse of removal. Cylinder bolt threads in the block and threads on the bolts must be cleaned. Dirt will affect head torque.
20. Torque in sequence and 2 steps first step 57 ft. lbs. and second step 72 ft. lbs.

### *4XE1 DOHC Engine*

**NOTE: The following procedure is the long version of cylinder head removal for I-Mark equipped with the 4XE1 DOHC engine. The instruction below may be altered as seen fit by the technician using this procedure. It may also be necessary to remove the engine from the vehicle in order to remove the cylinder head.**

1. Disconnect negative battery cable and drain cooling system. Remove the air cleaner duct hose from the common chamber.
2. Rotate the engine until the engine is at TDC on the compression stroke of the No. 1 cylinder, make sure timing mark is on the scale. Remove distributor cap and mark the distributor rotor to housing positon and housing to cylinder head. Remove the distributor hold down bolt and remove the distributor.
3. Disconnect radiator inlet and outlet hoses along with transmission oil cooler lines, if so equipped and remove the radiator.
4. Remove the power steering pump drive belt, for vehicles with air conditoners, remove the power steering pump and compressor drive belt. Loosen the 2 power steering pump adjust plates bolts.
5. Remove the alternator drive belt from the crank pulley side. Disconnect the clip securing the high pressure air conditioning line to the strut tower.
6. Disconnect and tag the following vacuum lines and wiring harness:
   a. Fast idle vacuum hose from the air duct hose.
   b. The MAP sensor vacuum hose from the common chamber.

c. Disconnect the TPC valve vacuum hose from the common chamber.

d. Disconnect the canister vacuum hose from the common chamber.

e. Electronic control gas injection harness, disconnect the 2 ECM ground connectors from the bracket located on top of the common chamber. Disconnect the 2 green and black multi-pin connectors on the top of the common chamber.

f. Remove the MAT sensor conector.

7. Disconnect the accelerator cable from the throttle body and at the common chamber. Disconnect the PCV valve hose from the valve cover.

8. Disconnect the master vacuum hose from the master vacuum tube at the common chamber side.

9. Disconnect the induction valve vacuum hose from the common chamber. Disconnect the EGR valve and the throttle valve.

10. Remove the fuel hose clips from the common chamber. Remove the common (intake) chamber retaining bolts and remove the chamber. Disconnect the fuel injection harness from the fuel injector.

11. Remove the fuel rail assembly. Disconnect the induction control vacuum switching valve harness connection. Disconnect the idle air control valve connector and vacuum hose. Remove the air induction control valve assembly.

12. Disconnect the center (valve) cover and disconnect (and tag) the high tension cables from the spark plugs and clips.

13. Remove the pulse air bracket with pipe. Remove the heat protector and the EGR pipe.

14. Disconnect the exhaust pipe from the exhaust manifold and remove the exhaust hanger. Remove the exhaust manifold bolts along with the manifold.

15. Remove the coolant bypass line and the thermostat housing.

16. Remove the engine mounting bridge.

17. Remove the upper timing belt cover.

18. Using a suitable engine hoist, slightly raise and support the engine safely.

19. Remove the passenger side engine mount from the engine. Disconnect the torque rod at the firewall.

20. Remove the passenger side engine mounting bracket from the engine. Using special crank pulley tool J-37988 or equivalent, remove the crank pulley bolt.

21. Raise the passenger side of the engine, be sure that the front wheels remain on the ground while lifting the engine. Raise the engine too high will left the front wheels off the ground and may cause damage to the drive shaft universal joint.

22. Remove the timing belt lower cover. Remove the cranking pulley and extract up through the engine compartment. Refit the crank pulley bolt. Align the crank pulley timing gear to top dead center.

23. Lossen the tension pulley bolt a ½ turn counterclockwise. If the pulley bolt is loosened more than ½ a turn, the pulley will swing too far out of adjustment amd may be difficult to readjust.

24. Mark the direction of rotation of the timing mark with a piece of chalk and remove the timing belt.

25. Loosen and remove the cylinder head bolts from the outermost one and remove the cylinder head from the engine.

26. Clean all gasket material from the cylinder head and block surfaces. Check for nicks or heavy scratches on the mating surfaces.

27. Installation is the reverse of removal. Cylinder bolt threads in the block and threads on the bolts must be cleaned. Dirt will affect head torque.

28. Torque in sequence and 2 steps first step 29 ft. lbs. and second step 58 ft. lbs.

## OVERHAUL

**For all cylinder head overhaul procedures, please refer to "Engine Rebuilding" in the Unit Repair Section.**

# Rocker Arms/Shaft

## REMOVAL & INSTALLATION

### *G180Z Engine*

**NOTE: Read entire procedure first before starting this repair and take notice to all reference marks. If no factory marks exist make marks with small punch or equivalent.**

1. Remove the cam cover and disconnect the battery cables.

2. Loosen the rocker arm shaft bracket nuts a little at a time, in sequence, starting with the outer brackets.

3. Remove the nuts from the rocker arm shaft brackets.

4. Disassemble the rocker arm shaft assembly by removing the spring from the rocker arm shaft and then removing the rocker arm brackets and arms.

5. Inspect the rocker arm shaft for runout. Support the shaft on V-blocks at each end and check runout by slowly turning it with the probe of a dial indicator, resting on the center of the shaft. Replace the shaft with a new one if the runout exceeds 0.0156 in. (0.4mm). Runout should not exceed 0.0079 in. (0.2mm).

6. Inspect the rocker arm shaft for wear. With an outside micrometer, measure shaft diameter at four arm locations. Replace the shaft if less than 0.8012 in. (20.35mm) nominal diameter is 0.8071 (20.5mm).

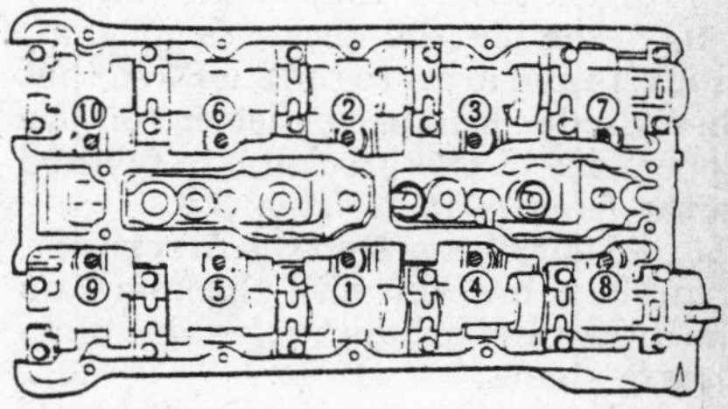

**Cylinder head bolt torque sequence—4XE1 DOHC engine**

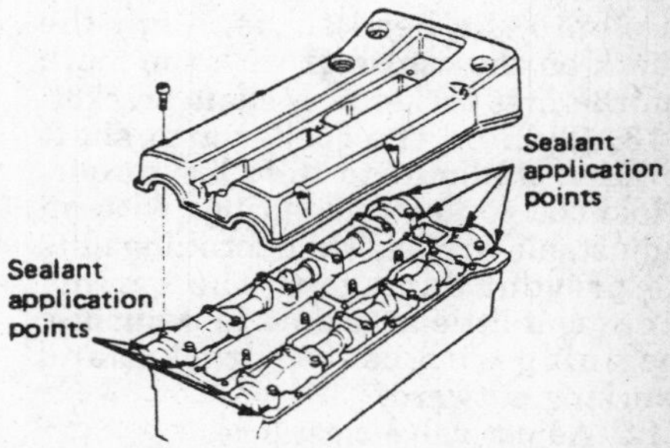


**Installing the cylinder head cover**

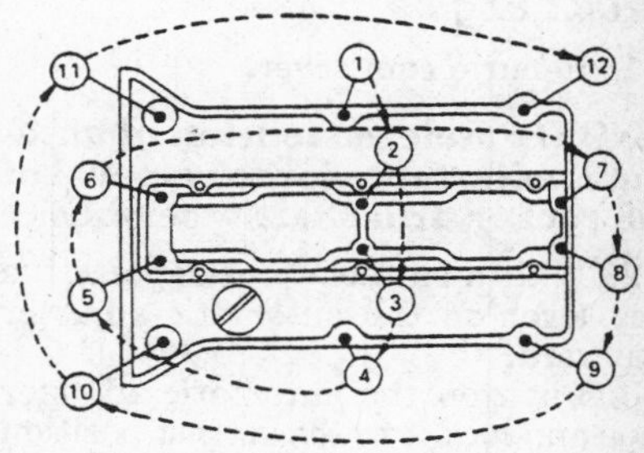

**Cylinder head cover bolt torque sequence**

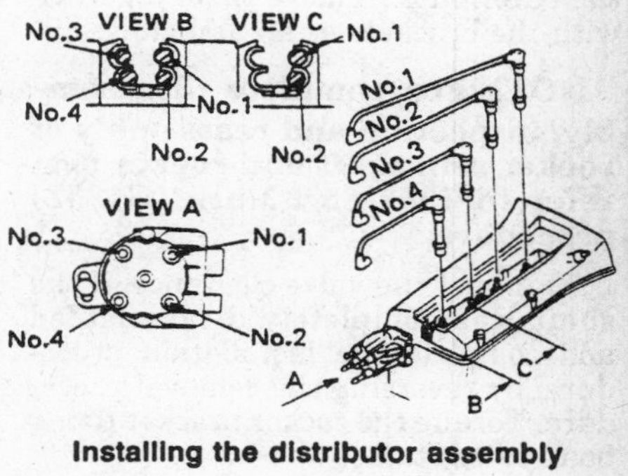


**Installing the distributor assembly**

7. With an inside micrometer, measure diameter of rocker arms. Compare the measured valve with the rocker arm shaft diameter to determine clearance if the clearance is greater than 0.0078 in. (0.2mm) replace either the arm or shaft.

8. Use a liberal amount of clean engine oil to coat the shaft, rocker arms and valve stems. Install the longer shaft on the exhaust valve side, shorter shaft on the intake side, so that the aligning marks on the shafts are turned to the front of the engine.

9. Assembly the rocker arm shaft brackets and arms to the shafts so that the cylinder number or letter (on the upper face of the brackets) is pointed to the front of the engine.

10. Align the mark on the first rocker arm shaft bracket with the mark on the intake and exhaust valve side rocker arm shafts.

11. Place the rocker arm shaft springs in position between the rocker arm shaft bracket and rocker arm.

12. Install arm shaft bracket assembly onto the head studs, align the mark on the camshaft with the mark on the first rocker arm shaft bracket.

13. Tighten the rocker arm shaft bracket stud nuts to 16 ft. lbs. torque. Hold the rocker arm springs with an adjustable wrench while torquing nuts to prevent damage to the spring. Torque a little at a time in sequence, begining with center bracket and working outward.

14. Adjust valve clearance.

15. Reinstall the cam cover. Start engine and check for proper operation.

### G200Z Engine

1. Remove cam cover.

**NOTE: Release tension of automatic adjuster prior to removal of the rocker arm shaft assembly.**

2. With a suitable tool depress the lock lever on the automatic adjuster rearward.

3. Push on the automatic adjuster shoe and lock it in the retract position by releasing the lever.

4. Loosen the rocker arm shaft bracket nuts in sequence starting with the outer ones, remove them together with the brackets as an assembly.

**NOTE:For complete disassembly, inspection and reassembly of rocker arm shaft and rocker arm refer to 1982–85 I-Mark (G180Z) procedure.**

5. Adjust the valve clearance, if the shaft was completely disassembled and complete the installation procedure, by reversing the removal procedure. Torque the rocker bracket fixing bolts to 16 ft. lbs.

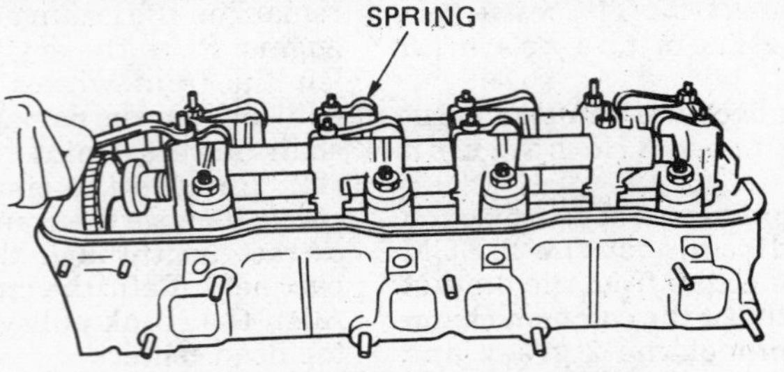


**Rocker arm assembly—gasoline engine**

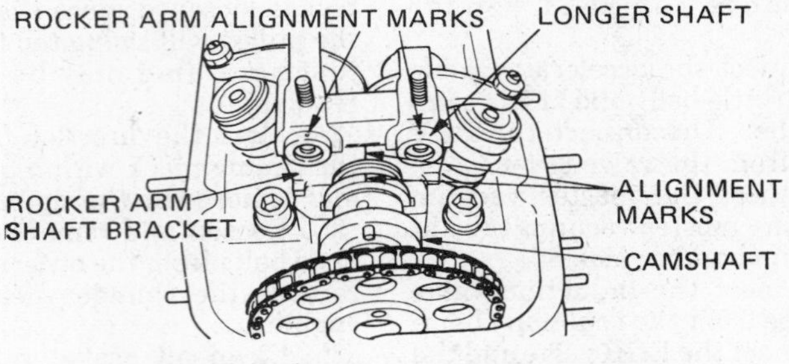


**Rocker arm shaft installation—gasoline engine**

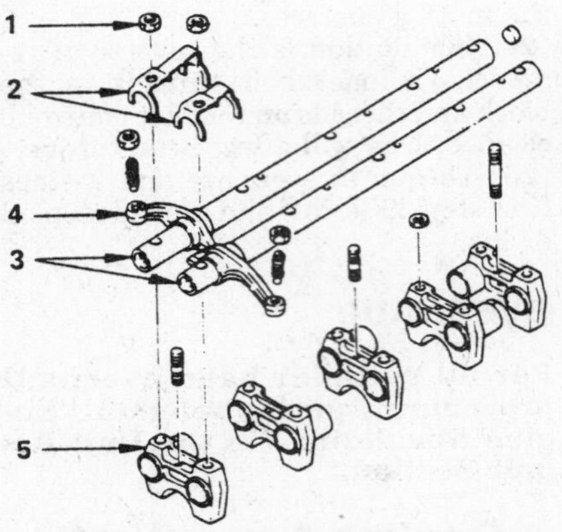


1. Rocker arm bracket nut
2. Rocker arm spring
3. Rocker arm shaft
4. Rocker arm
5. Rocker arm shaft bracket

**Rocker arm and shaft assembly—118.9 cu. in. engine**

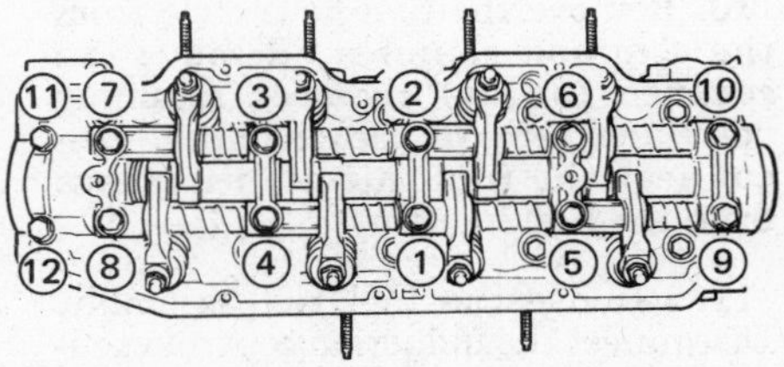


**Rocker arm bolt torque sequence for the 4XC1-U engine**

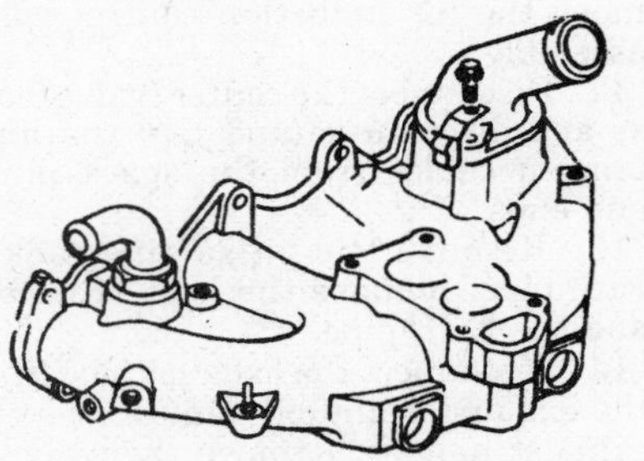

**Intake manifold—1816cc gasoline engine**

### 4ZD1 and 4ZC1-T Engines

1. Remove cam cover.

2. Loosen the rocker arm shaft bracket nuts in sequence starting with the outer ones, remove them together with the brackets as an assembly.

**NOTE:For complete disassembly, inspection and reassembly of rocker arm shaft and rocker arm refer to 1982–85 I-Mark (G180Z) procedure.**

3. Apply silicon gasket beforehand to the front side of the fitting surface of the No.1 rocker arm bracket with the cylinder. Adjust the valve clearance, if the shaft was completely disassembly and complete the installation procedure, by reversing the removal procedure. Torque the rocker bracket fixing bolts to 16 ft lbs. except the No.1 rocker arm bracket fixing bolts torque to 6.0 ft. lbs.

### 4XC1-U and 4XC1-T Engines

On the 4XC1-U and 4XC1-T engine in the (FWD) I-Mark, the rocker arm shafts are different from each other, make sure they are installed in the same position that they were removed. Install the rocker arms with the identification marks toward the front of the engine. Apply a sealant to the bracket and cylinder head mating surfaces of the front and rear rocker brackets. Torque rocker arm bolts in sequence and to 16 ft. lbs. Adjust valve clearances, reinstall the cam cover and check for leaks.

## Intake Manifold

### REMOVAL & INSTALLATION

#### *G180Z Engine*

1. Drain the cooling system and disconnect the battery cables.

**NOTE: Before removing the intake manifold, check to make certain the engine coolant is completely drained. If any water remains in the block it will flow into the cylinders when the intake manifold is removed.**

2. Remove the air cleaner assembly.
3. Disconnect the radiator hose from the front part of the intake manifold.
4. Disconnect the fuel lines, all vacuum lines and the carburetor control cable.
5. Disconnect the heater hoses from the rear part of the manifold and from the connector under the dashboard.
6. Disconnect the distributor vacuum hose and all thermo-valve wiring. Disconnect the electric choke or solenoid wires.

**NOTE: Tag all wires before disconnecting them.**

7. Disconnect the PCV hose from the rocker cover. Disconnect the EGR valve from the EGR pipe and disconnect the air injection vacuum hose from the three-way connector.
8. Remove the eight nuts attaching the intake manifold and lift it clear, being careful not to snag any loose lines.
9. Installation is the reverse of removal. Check the manifold for cracks or damage. The manifold head surfaces can be checked for distortion by using a straight edge and a feeler gauge. Distortion should be no more than 0.0157 in. (0.4mm), if it is beyond the limit, the distortion has to be corrected with a surface grinder.
10. Replace the gasket and torque all nuts in sequence to 25–32 ft. lbs.

#### *4XC1-U Engine*

1. Disconnect the negative battery cable and drain the coolant into a suitable drain pan.
2. Remove the bolt securing the alternator adjusting plate to the engine.
3. Disconnect and tag all hoses attached to the air cleaner assembly and remove the air cleaner.
4. Disconnect the air inlet temperature switch wiring connector. Disconnect and tag all the hoses, electrical connectors and control cable attached to the carburetor.
5. If equipped with A/C disconnect the fast idle control vacuum hose, the pressure tank control valve hose, the distributor/3-way connector hose and the vacuum switching valve wiring connector.
6. Remove the carburetor attaching bolts, which are located underneath the intake manifold. Remove the carburetor and the EFE heater.
7. At the intake manifold, remove the PCV hose, the water bypass hose, the two heater hoses, the EGR valve canister hose, the distributor vacuum advance hose and the ground wires.
8. Disconnect the thermometer unit switch wiring connector (if so equipped).
9. Remove the intake manifold attaching nuts and bolts and remove the intake manifold.
10. Clean the sealing surfaces of the intake manifold and the cylinder head.
11. Use a straight-edge and a feeler gauge to check the surfaces containing the cylinder head for excessive warpage. The inlet manifold must be replaced if the warpage is in excess of 0.0157 in. (0.4mm).

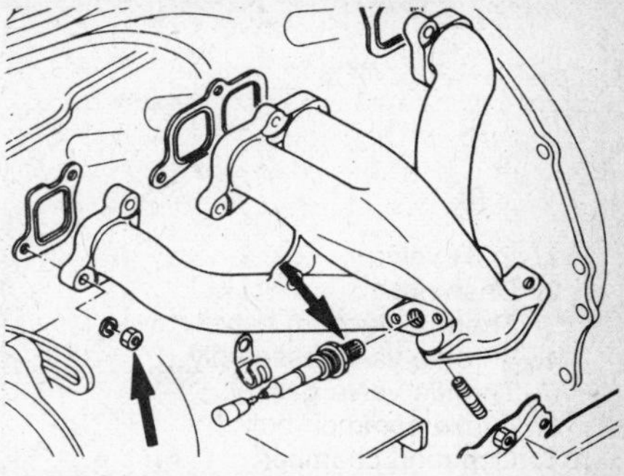

**Exhaust manifold showing oxygen sensor mounting—1949cc engine**

12. To install, use new gaskets and reverse the removal procedure. Torque the intake manifold to 17 ft. lbs; then adjust the engine control cable and the alternator belt tension. Refill the engine with coolant, run the engine and check for leaks. Make all necessary adjustments and road test the vehicle, be sure to check for and vacuum leaks around the intake manifold sealing surfaces.

#### *4XC1-T Engine*

1. Disconnect the negative battery terminal from the battery.

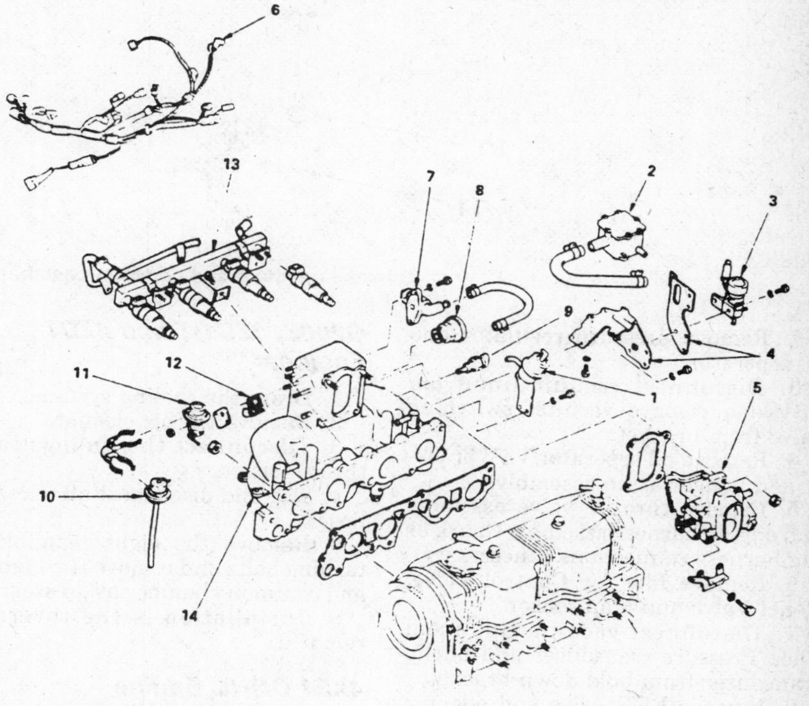

1. Pressure regulator
2. Oil separator
3. VSV
4. Bracket and hanger
5. Throttle valve assembly
6. Engine harness assembly
7. Idle air control valve
8. Relief valve
9. Map sensor
10. Back pressure transducer
11. EGR valve
12. Adaptor
13. Fuel injector with pipe
14. Intake manifold

**Exploded view of intake manifold I- Mark(4XC1-T)**

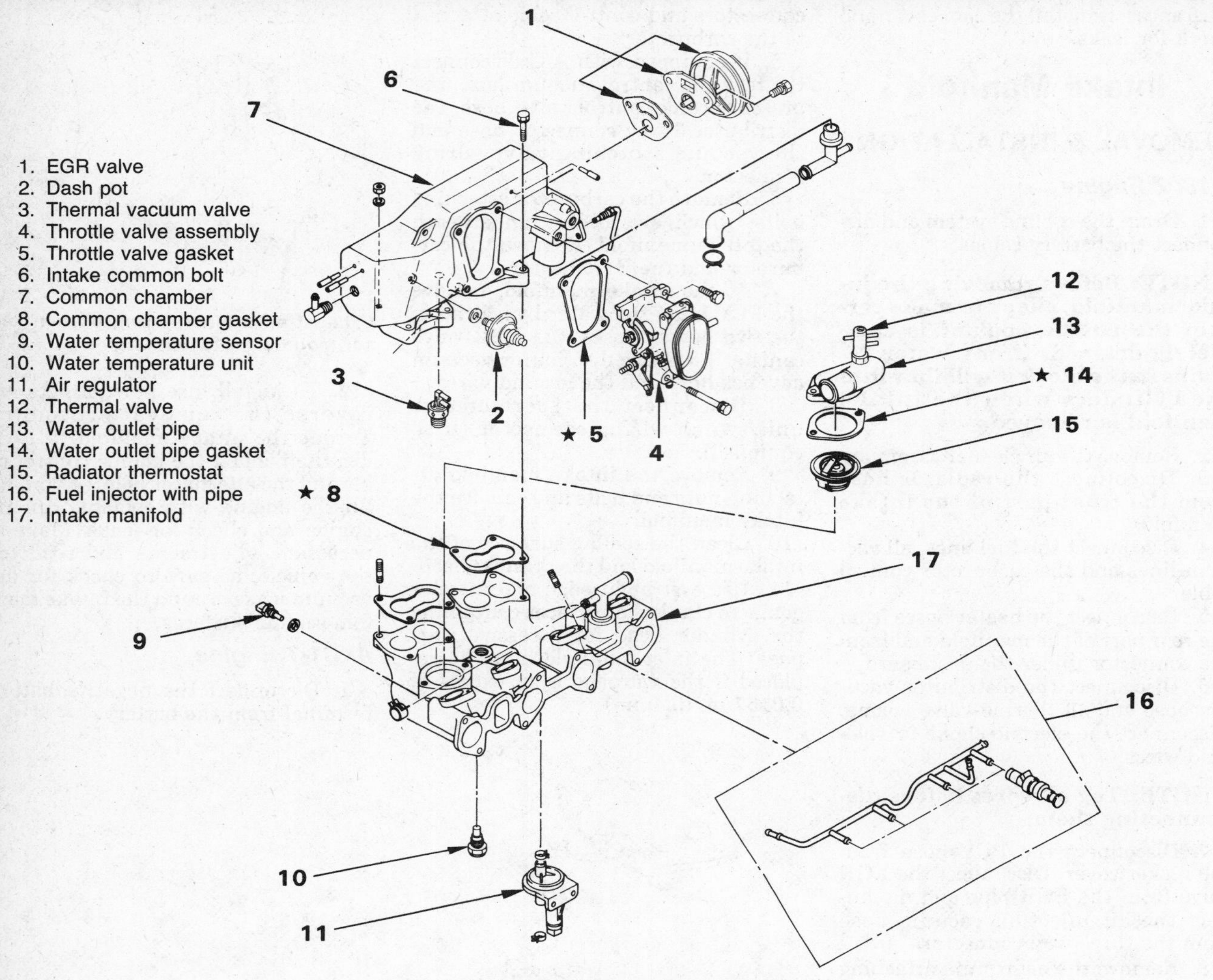


**Intake manifold and common chamber G200Z**

2. Remove pressure regulator and oil seperator.

3. Disconnect vacuum line from VSV and remove vacuum switching valve from bracket.

4. Remove oil seperator/VSV bracket and hanger as an assembly.

5. Remove throttle valve assembly and engine harness assembly (mark or tag harness connections if necessary).

6. Remove Idle Air Control Valve, Relief Valve and Map sensor.

7. Disconnect vacuum line from Back Pressure transducer and unclip transducer from hold down bracket.

8. Remove EGR valve and adaptor plate.

9. Remove fuel injectors and fuel pipe connected to rail as one unit and postion out of way then remove Intake Manifold with common chamber

10. To install, use new gaskets and reverse the removal procedures. Torque the intake manifold to 17 ft. lbs. Start and run engine check for leaks.

### G200Z, 4ZC1-T and 4ZD1 Engines

1. Drain the cooling system.
2. Remove the air cleaner.
3. Disconnect the linkage to the throttle valve.
4. Tag and disconnect all wires and hoses.
5. Remove the eight manifold attaching bolts and remove the manifold and common chamber as an assembly.
6. Installation is the reverse of removal.

### 4XE1 DOHC Engine

1. Disconnect negative battery cable and drain cooling system. Remove the air cleaner duct hose from the common chamber.

2. Disconnect and tag the following vacuum lines and wiring harness:

a. Fast idle vacuum hose from the air duct hose.

b. The MAP sensor vacuum hose from the common chamber.

c. Disconnect the TPC valve vacuum hose from the common chamber.

d. Disconnect the canister vacuum hose from the common chamber.

e. Electronic control gas injection harness, disconnect the 2 ECM ground connectors from the bracket located on top of the common chamber. Disconnect the 2 green and black multi-pin connectors on the top of the common chamber.

f. Remove the MAT sensor conector.

3. Disconnect the accelerator cable from the throttle body and at the common chamber. Disconnect the PCV valve hose from the valve cover.

4. Disconnect the master vacuum hose from the master vacuum tube at the common chamber side.

5. Disconnect the induction valve vacuum hose from the common chamber. Disconnect the EGR valve and the throttle valve.

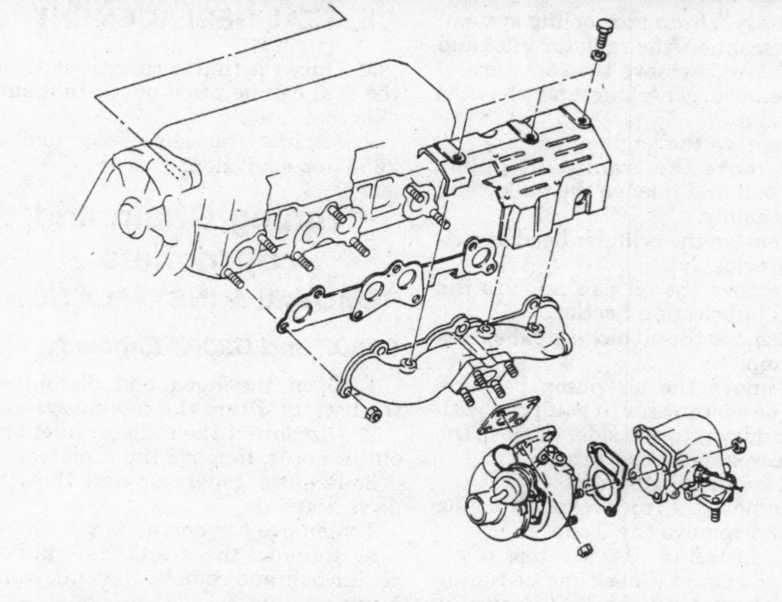

**Exploded view of exhaust manifold and turbocharger Impulse (4ZC1-T)**

3. Remove the manifold hot air cover. Raise the vehicle and support safely.
4. Disconnect the exhaust pipe from the exhaust manifold and lower the vehicle.
5. Remove the nuts and bolts securing the exhaust manifold to the cylinder head. Clean the gasket mounting surfaces.
6. Check the exhaust manifold for cracks or other damage. Use a straight-edge and a feeler gauge to check the surfaces contacting the cylinder head for excessive warpage. The exhaust manifold must be replaced if the measured warpage exceeds 0.0157 in. (0.4mm).
7. To install, use a new gasket and reverse the removal procedure. Torque the exhaust manifold to 17 ft. lbs. and the exhaust pipe to 42 ft. lbs. then start
the engine and check for any exhaust leaks.

6. Remove the fuel hose clips from the common chamber. Remove the bolt and nuts retaining the common (intake) chamber to the engine. Remove the common (intake) chamber and gasket from the engine.
7. Installation is the reverse order of the installation procedure. Be sure to use a new gasket and torque the common chamber retaining bolts and nuts to 18 ft. lbs.

## Exhaust Manifold

### REMOVAL & INSTALLATION

#### *G180Z, 4FB1 Diesel, G200Z, 4ZC1-T and 4ZD1 Engines*

1. Remove the bolts attaching the air cleaner and loosen the clamp bolt.
2. Lift the air cleaner slightly and remove the air hose.
3. Remove the bolts attaching the manifold cover and remove the manifold cover.
4. Remove the EGR pipe clip from the upper portion of the transmission and disconnect the EGR pipe from the exhaust manifold. On the 4ZC1-T engine, disconnect and tag all necessary wires, coolant hoses and pipes from the turbocharger. Also disconnect the oxygen sensor wiring connector.
5. Remove the two nuts connecting the exhaust pipe with the exhaust manifold and disconnect the exhaust pipe from the manifold on turbocharged model remove exhaust from wastegate manifold.
6. Remove the seven nuts mounting the exhaust manifold and remove the manifold.
7. Installation is the reverse of removal. Use a straightedge to check for distortion as described in the intake section. Use new gaskets and torque to specifications.

#### *4XC1-U and 4XC1-T Engines*

**NOTE: On turbocharged model refer to section on Turbocharger Removal & Installation.**

1. Disconnect the negative battery cable and the oxygen sensor wiring connector.
2. Disconnect and tag all of the hoses attached to the air cleaner assembly and remove the air cleaner.

#### *4XE1 DOHC Engine*

1. Rasie the hood and disconnect negative battery cable.
2. Raise and support the vehicle safely.
3. Remove the pulse air bracket with pipe. Remove the heat protector and the EGR pipe.
4. Disconnect the exhaust pipe from the exhaust manifold and remove the exhaust hanger. Remove the exhaust manifold bolts along with the manifold.
5. Installation is the reverse order of the removal procedure, be sure to torque the manifold bolts to 30 ft. lbs.

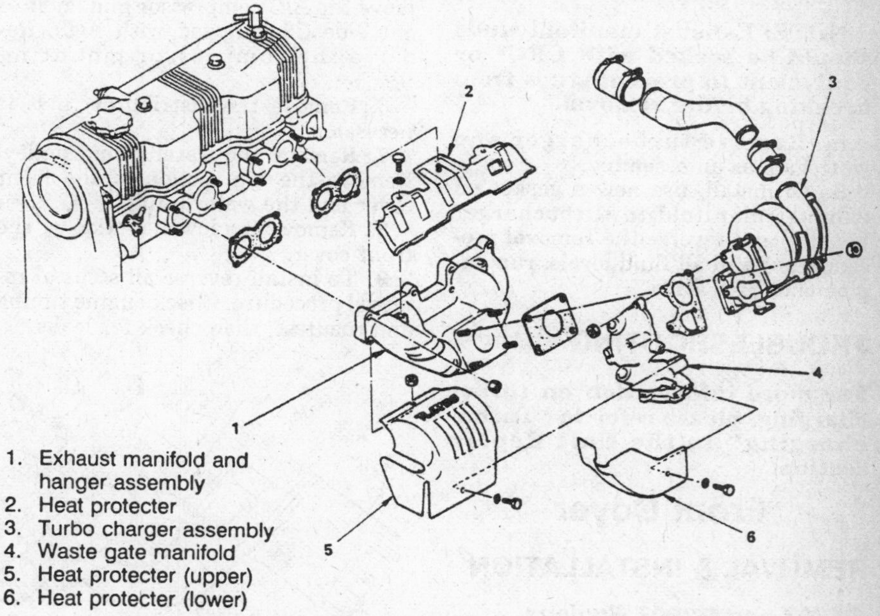


1. Exhaust manifold and hanger assembly
2. Heat protecter
3. Turbo charger assembly
4. Waste gate manifold
5. Heat protecter (upper)
6. Heat protecter (lower)

**Exploded view of exhaust manifold and turbocharger I-Mark (4XC1-T)**

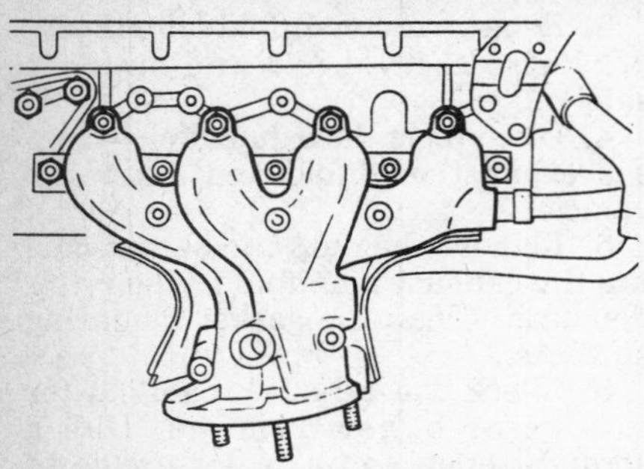

Removing the exhaust manifold

## Turbocharger

### REMOVAL & INSTALLATION

#### *4XC1-T and 4ZC1-T Engines*

1. Disconnect the negative battery terminal from the battery.

**NOTE: Turbocharger removal and installation on 4ZC1-T Impulse engine is very similar to 4XC1-T I-Mark.**

2. Remove lower and upper heat protector shield covering turbocharger assembly on 4XC1-T and on 4ZC1-T engine only one heat protector is used.
3. Remove manifold heat protecter and unplug oxygen sensor.
4. Disconnect vacuum pipe from wastegate and position out of the way on 4XC1-T and on 4ZC1-T remove control cable and position out of the way.
5. Disconnect water lines.
6. Disconnect oil lines return and delivery.
7. Disconnect exhaust pipe from wastegate manifold.

**NOTE: Exhaust manifold studs should be soaked with CRC® or equivalent to prevent studs from breaking before removal.**

8. Remove turbocharger and wastegate as an assembly.
9. To install, use new a gasket on exhaust manifold to turbocharger housing and reverse the removal procedures. Refill all fluid levels, run engine check for leaks.

### TROUBLESHOOTING

**For more information on turbocharging, please refer to "Turbocharging" in the Unit Repair section.**

## Front Cover

### REMOVAL & INSTALLATION

#### *G180Z and G200Z Engines*

1. Open the hood and disconnect the battery. Drain the cooling system.
2. Disconnect the radiator inlet and outlet hoses. Remove the radiator.
3. Remove generator and the A/C drive belts.
4. Remove the engine fan.
5. Remove the crankshaft pulley center bolt and remove the pulley and hub assembly.
6. Remove the cylinder head as outlined previously.
7. Remove the oil pan refer to the Engine Lubrication Section.
8. Remove the oil pick-up tube from the pump.
9. Remove the air pump belt, remove the compressor (if equipped with A/C) and lay it to one side. Remove the compressor mounting brackets.
10. Remove the distributor.
11. Remove the front cover attaching bolts and remove the front cover.
12. To install reverse all steps of removal procedure. Check engine timing and roadtest, then check for leaks.

#### *4ZC1-T and 4ZD1 Engines*

**NOTE: The engine may be set up with the No. 4 cylinder at TDC on its compression stroke, at the start of this procedure.**

1. Disconnect the negative battery cable and drain the coolant into a suitable drain pan.
2. Disconnect the radiator inlet and outlet hoses and remove the radiator.
3. Remove alternator and the A/C drive belts. Remove the engine fan.
4. Remove the crankshaft pulley center bolt and remove the pulley and hub assembly.
5. Remove the air pump belt and move the air pump out of the way. Remove the A/C compressor and lay it to one side (if equipped with A/C). Remove the compressor mounting bracket.
6. Remove the distributor (if it is necessary).
7. Remove the water pump pulley. Remove the top section of the front cover and the water pump.
8. Remove the lower section of the front cover.
9. To install reverse all steps of removal procedure. Check engine timing and roadtest, then check for leaks.

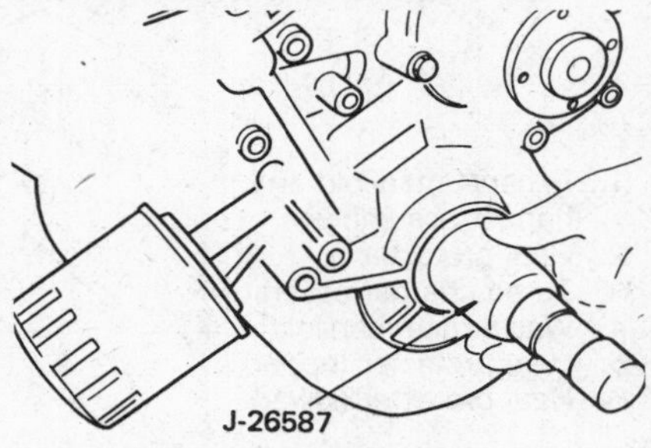


Installing timing cover seal

### OIL SEAL REPLACEMENT

1. Once the timing cover is exposed, the seal can be pried out with a suitable tool.
2. Replace the seal using tool J-26587 or equivalent.

## Timing Chain and Sprockets

### REMOVAL & INSTALLATION

#### *G180Z and G200Z Engines*

1. Open the hood and disconnect the battery. Drain the cooling system.
2. Disconnect the radiator inlet and outlet hoses. Remove the radiator.
3. Remove generator and the A/C drive belts.
4. Remove the engine fan.
5. Remove the crankshaft pulley center bolt and remove the pulley and hub assembly.
6. Remove the cylinder head.
7. Remove the oil pan.
8. Remove the oil pick-up tube from the pump.
9. Remove the air pump belt, remove the compressor (if equipped with A/C) and lay it to one side. Remove the compressor mounting brackets.
10. Remove the distributor.
11. Remove the front cover attaching bolts and remove the front cover.
12. Remove the timing chain from the crankshaft sprocket. Check sprockets for damage or wear. If the sprocket on the crankshaft must be replaced, a gear puller will be necessary to remove it.
13. Inspect the automatic chain adjuster for wear or damage. Replace any component that is doubtful. Make sure that the adjuster is freely rotating on its pin.
14. Install the timing sprocket and pinion gear (groove side toward front cover). Align the key grooves with the key on the crankshaft and then drive it into position with special tool J-26587 or equivalent.
15. Turn the crankshaft so that the key is turned toward the cylinder head side (No. 1 and No. 4 pistons at TDC).
16. Install the timing chain by aligning the mark plate on the chain with the mark on the crankshaft timing sprocket. The side of the chain with the mark plate is on the front side.

The side of the chain with the most links between mark plates is on the chain guide side.

17. Keep the timing chain engaged with the camshaft timing sprocket until the sprocket is installed on the camshaft. Install the sprocket so that the marked side faces forward and so that the triangular mark aligns with the chain mark plate.

18. Install the front cover and reverse the removal instructions.

## Timing Belt and Tensioner

### REMOVAL & INSTALLATION

#### *4ZC1-T and 4ZD1 Engines*

**NOTE: The engine may be set up with the No. 4 cylinder at TDC on its compression stroke, at the start of this procedure. But the engine must be rotated during the timing belt installation procedure. So the decision is up to the individual mechanic.**

1. Disconnect the negative battery cable and drain the coolant into a suitable drain pan.
2. Disconnect the radiator inlet and outlet hoses and remove the radiator.
3. Remove alternator and the A/C drive belts. Remove the engine fan.
4. Remove the crankshaft pulley center bolt and remove the pulley and hub assembly.
5. Remove the air pump belt and move the air pump out of the way. Remove the A/C compressor and lay it to one side (if equipped with A/C). Remove the compressor mounting bracket.
6. Remove the distributor (if it is necessary).
7. Remove the water pump pulley. Remove the top section of the front cover and the water pump.
8. Remove the lower section of the front cover.
9. Remove the tension spring. Loosen the top bolt of the tension pulley and draw the tension pulley fully to the water pump side.
10. Remove the timing belt. Inspect the timing belt for signs of cracking, abnormal wear and hardening. Check all the pulleys for cracks or chipped teeth.

**To install:**

11. Set the tension spring in its plate and temporarily tighten the top bolt on the tension pulley, after pulling the pulley fully to the water pump side.
12. Bring the matchmark of the crankshaft timing pulley into alignment with that of the front oil seal retainer.
13. Bring the matchmark of the camshaft timing pulley into alignment with that of the front plate. Keep the rocker arm altogether in a free state.
14. At this point the No. 4 cylinder will come to its compression stroke at top dead center.
15. Lay the timing belt over the crankshaft pulley, oil pump pulley , cam pulley and tension pulley (in that

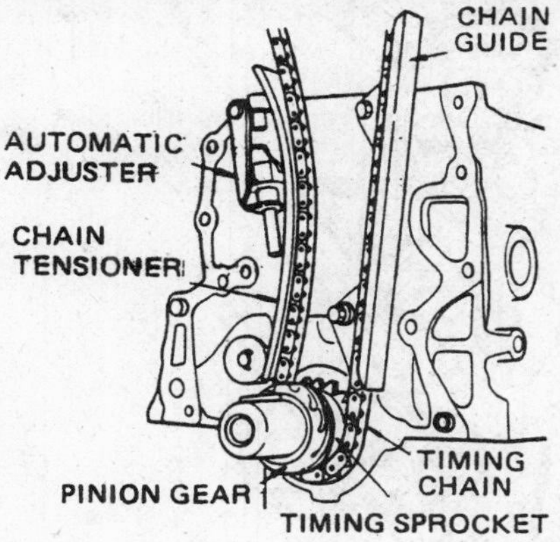

Removing the timing chain

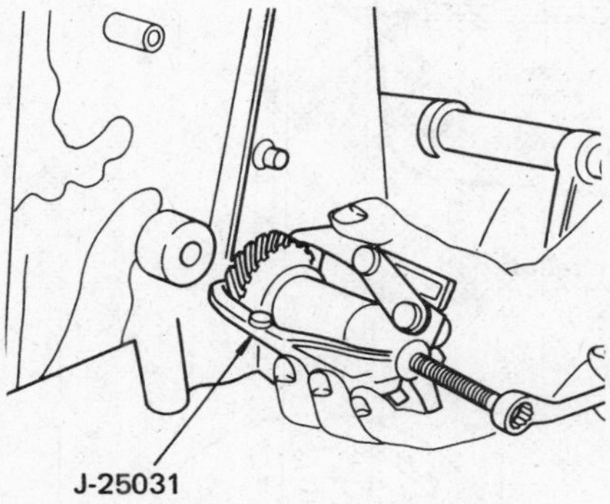

Using a puller to remove crankshaft sprocket

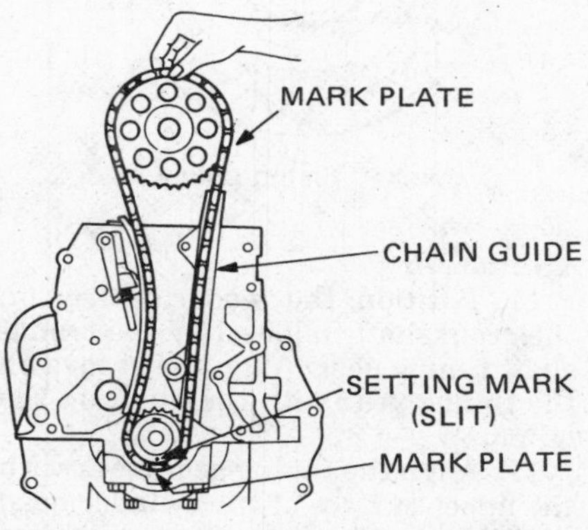

Timing chain alignment—gasoline engines

order) while avoiding loosening between them.

16. Loosen the top bolt of the tension pulley to allow the tension spring to tighten the belt and to temporarily tighten the bolt.
17. Temporarily attach the crankshaft pulley and turn the engine two complete revolutions opposite direction of normal rotation. This will bring the crankshaft matchmark into alignment with the crankshaft timing pulley matchmark.
18. Loosen the top bolt of the tension pulley and tighten the timing belt

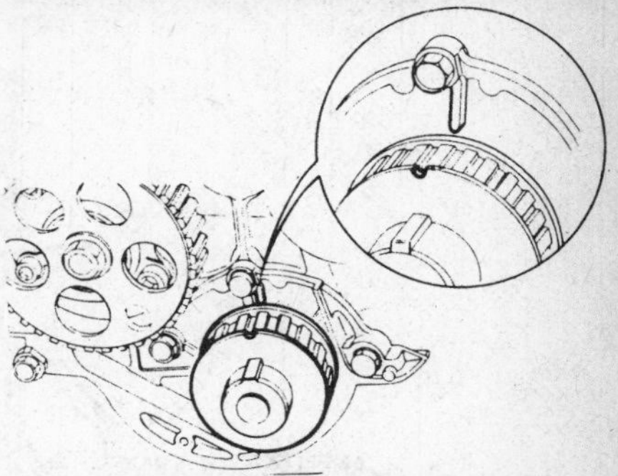
Aligning the crankshaft timing pulley—timing marks

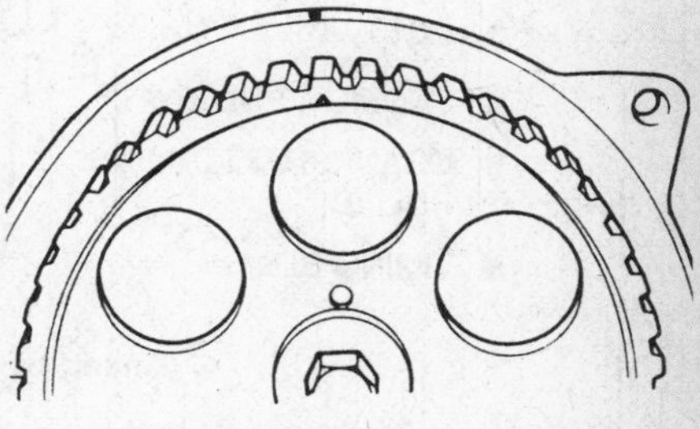
Aligning the camshaft timing pulley—timing marks

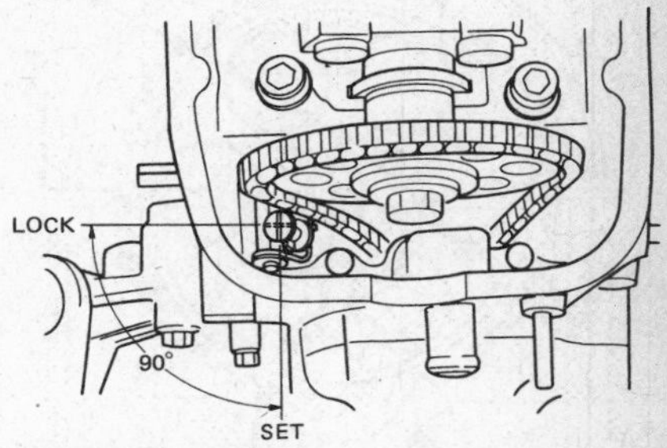

Locking the timing chain adjuster—1816cc gasoline engine

with the use of the tension pulley. Now torque the top bolt of the tension pulley to 14 ft. lbs.

19. Install the timing cover sections and torque the timing cover attaching bolts to 6 ft. lbs.
20. Install the crankshaft pulley and torque the hub bolt to 87 ft. lbs. To complete the installation, reverse the removal procedures.

#### *1985–87 4XC1-U and 4XC1-T Engines*

1. Remove the engine by referring to the Engine Removal and Installation procedure in this section. Mount the engine to an engine stand.
2. Remove the accessory drive belts.
3. Remove the engine mounting bracket from the timing cover.
4. Rotate the crankshaft until the notch on the crankshaft pulley aligns with the **0** degree mark on the timing

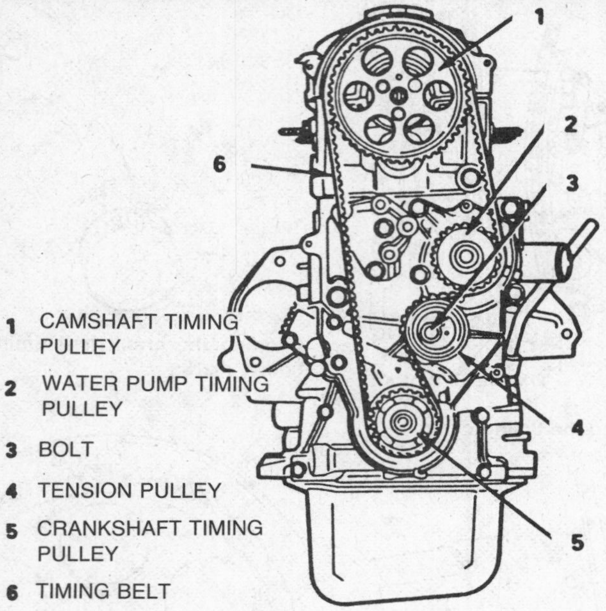


Timing belt installed

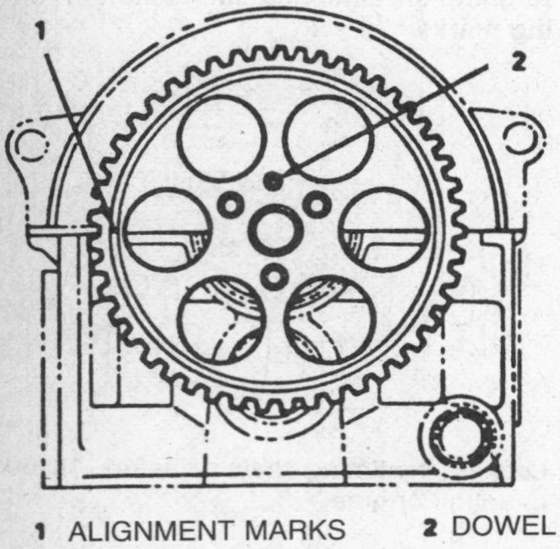


Alignment of the camshaft pulley

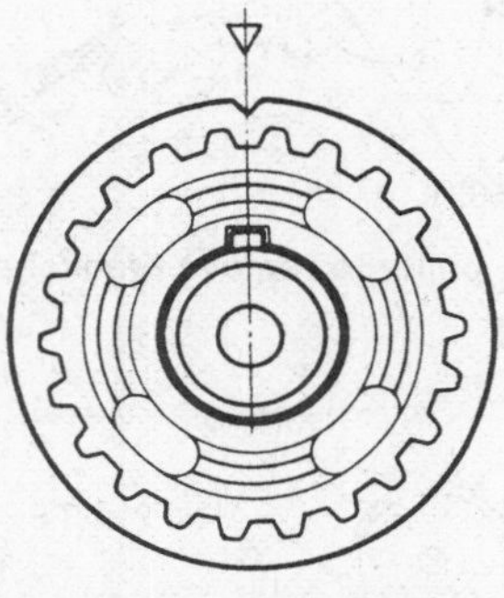

Crankshaft timing pulley mark

cover and the No. 4 cylinder is on TDC of the compression stroke.

5. Remove the starter and install the flywheel holding tool (J-35271).

6. Remove the crankshaft bolt, boss and pulley.

7. Remove the timing cover bolts and the timing cover.

8. Loosen the tension pulley bolt.

9. Insert an allen wrench into the tension pulley hexagonical hole and loosen the timing belt by turning the tension pulley clockwise.

10. Remove the timing belt.

**NOTE: Inspect the timing belt for signs of cracking, abnormal wear and hardening. Never expose the belt to oil, sunlight or heat. Avoid excessive bending, twisting or stretching.**

**To install:**

11. Position the woodruff key on the crankshaft followed by the crankshaft timing gear. Align the groove on the timing gear with the mark on the oil pump.

12. Align the timing gear mark with the upper surface of the cylinder head and the dowel pin in its uppermost position.

13. Place the timing belt arrow in the direction of the engine rotation and install the timing belt. Tighten the tension pulley bolt.

14. Insert a hex wrench into the tension pulley hexagonal hole and hold the pulley stationary while tightening the bolt temporarily.

15. Turn the crankshaft two complete reverse revolutions and align the crankshaft timing pulley groove with the mark on the oil pump. Loosen the tension pulley bolt and apply tension to the timing belt.

16. Insert a hex wrench into the tension pulley hexagonal hole and hold the pulley stationary while torquing the bolt to 37 ft. lbs.

17. Move the crankshaft back to about 50 degrees before TDC and re-adjust the timing belt. Use a drive belt tension gauge to check the timing belt tension. The tension should be 38 ± 4 ft. lbs.; if the belt is not at the proper tension it must be re-adjusted.

18. Adjust the valve clearance and to complete the installation, reverse the removal procedures.

### *1988–90 4XC1-U and 4XC1-T Engines*

1. Disconnect the negative battery cable. Drain the radiator coolant into a suitable drain pan.

2. Place a wooden block on a suitable floor jack and place the jack under the strongest point of the oil pan, slightly raise the engine.

3. Remove the rear side torque rod while the engine is slightly lifted.

4. Remove the right side engine mount, then remove the body side mount and the engine side mount.

5. Loosen the power steering oil pump retaining bolt and remove the V-belt.

6. Remove the 4 crank pulley bolts with the engine slightly lifted.

7. Remove the 6 timing cover bolts and remove the timing belt cover.

8. Be sure that the crankshaft timing mark on the crankshaft pulley hub is aligned with the top dead center mark.

9. Use special crankshaft bolt tool (J-37376 or equivalent) to turn and stop the crankshaft, then remove the bolt on the end part of the crank shaft and remove the pulley.

10. Confirm the crankshaft is at top dead center, prior to removing the timing belt. In this state, if the notch on the camshaft pulley hub is aligned with the left upper corner of the cylinder head, the number 4 cylinder is at top dead center. If the notch on the camshaft pulley is aligned with the right upper corner of the cylinder head, the No. 1 cylinder is at top dead center.

11. Loosen the bolts fixing the tension pulley. Turn the tension pulley clockwise with the allen wrench, then remove the timing belt.

**NOTE: Remove the camshaft pulley and make sure that there are no oil leaks or bolts on the oil seal section. Make sure that there are no water leaks from the water pump or oil leaks from the crankshaft oil seal. If water leaks or oil leaks appear, replace the oil seal or water pack packing with a new part.**

**To install:**

12.Install the camshaft pulley and be sure that the camshaft pulley timing mark is aligned with the upper surface of the cylinder head and the dowel pin is in the up position. Torque the retaining bolt to 7 ft. lbs.

13.Install the crankshaft timing pulley, making sure that the woodruff key is positioned correctly.

14.Install the tension spring and position the long part of the tension spring to the rear of the timing case and the short end to the rear of the tension spring retaining bolt.

15.Install the timing belt. Be sure that the belt is installed correctly, the lettering mark in the direction of the engine rotation and install the belt in the following order; over the crankshaft timing gear, camshaft timing pulley,water pump pulley and tensioner pulley.

**NOTE: There must be no slack in the timing belt after it has been installed. The teeth of the belt and the teeth of the pulley must be in perfect alignment.**

16. Loosen the tension pulley bolt. Insert an allen wrench into the tension pulley hexagonal hole. Hold the pulley stationary and temporarily tighten the bolt.

17. Turn the crankshaft 2 complete reverse revolutions and align the crankshaft timing pulley groove with the mark on the oil pump.

18. Loosen the tension pulley bolt and apply tension to the belt. Insert an allen wrench into the tension pulley hexagonal hole. Hold the pulley stationary and torque the bolt to 37 ft. lbs.

19. Move the crankshaft back to approximately 50 degrees BTDC. Once again adjust the timing belt. Set the crankshaft at that position, use a belt tension gauge to check the timing belt tension. The belt tension should be 44 lbs.

20. Attach the taper face of the crankshaft pulley to the timing belt. Fasten the crankshaft pulley center bolt and torque it to 108 ± 11 ft. lbs.

21. Install the timing cover and torque the bolts to 7 ft. lbs. Be sure to pay attention to the timing belt cover bolt length. Complete the installation procedure by reversing the remaining removal steps. Use the following torque specifications:

a. Crank pulley – 4–7 ft. lbs.

b. Engine mount bracket body side – 30 ft. lbs.

c. Engine mount bracket engine side – 45 ft. lbs.

d. Torque rod – 42 ft. lbs.

### *4XE1 DOHC Engine*

1. Disconnect negative battery cable and drain cooling system. Remove the air cleaner duct hose from the common chamber.

2. Rotate the engine until the engine is at TDC on the compression stroke of the No. 1 cylinder, make sure timing mark is on the scale.

3. Remove the power steering pump drive belt, for vehicles with air conditoners, remove the power steering pump and compressor drive belt. Loosen the 2 power steering pump adjust plates bolts.

4. Remove the alternator drive belt from the crank pulley side. Disconnect the clip securing the high pressure air conditioning line to the strut tower.

5. Remove the upper timing belt cover.

6. Using a suitable engine hoist, slightly raise and support the engine safely.

7. Remove the passenger side engine mount from the engine. Disconnect the torque rod at the firewall.

8. Remove the passenger side engine mounting bracket from the engine. Using special crank pulley tool J-37988 or equivalent, remove the crank pulley bolt.

9. Raise the passenger side of the engine, be sure that the front wheels remain on the ground while lifting the engine. Raise the engine too high will left the front wheels off the ground and may cause damage to the drive shaft universal joint.

10. Remove the timing belt lower cover. Remove the cranking pulley and extract up through the engine compartment. Refit the crank pulley bolt. Align the crank pulley timing gear to top dead center.

11. Lossen the tension pulley bolt a ½ turn counterclockwise. If the pulley bolt is loosened more than ½ a turn, the pulley will swing too far out of adjustment and may be difficult to readjust.

12. Mark the direction of rotation of the timing mark with a piece of chalk and remove the timing belt. Using and open end wrench, hole the camshaft from turning and remove the camshaft pulley(s).

**NOTE: Inspect the timing belt for signs of cracking, abnormal wear and hardening. Never expose the belt to oil, sunlight or heat. Avoid excessive bending, twisting or stretching.**

**To install:**

13. Install the camshaft pulley(s) and torque the retaining bolts to 43 ft. lbs. Align the camshaft pulley timing marks. Lock the camshaft pulley in position by inserting a 6 mm bolt through the camshaft pulleys and into the cylinder head.

**NOTE: The camshaft timing pulleys have and identification mark, the I mark for the intake side and the E mark for the exhaust side.**

14. Align the crank pulley timing gear to top dead center.

15. Install the timing belt. Be sure that the belt is installed correctly, the lettering must be able to be read while viewing it from the passenger side fender.

16. The belt must be installed in the following order; over the crankshaft timing gear, water pump pulley, idle pulley, exhaust camshaft pulley, intake camshaft pulley and tensioner pulley.

**NOTE: There must be no slack in the timing belt after it has been installed. The teeth of the belt and the teeth of the pulley must be in perfect alignment.**

17. Loosen the tensioner bolt and apply spring force to the belt. If reusing the old belt, do not tension the belt with more than spring force applied. When a new belt is being used, push the tension pulley in the direction of the belt tension. The tensioner pulley retaining bolt should be torqued to 17 ft. lbs.

18. Keep the tension pulley from turning while fastening the fixing bolt

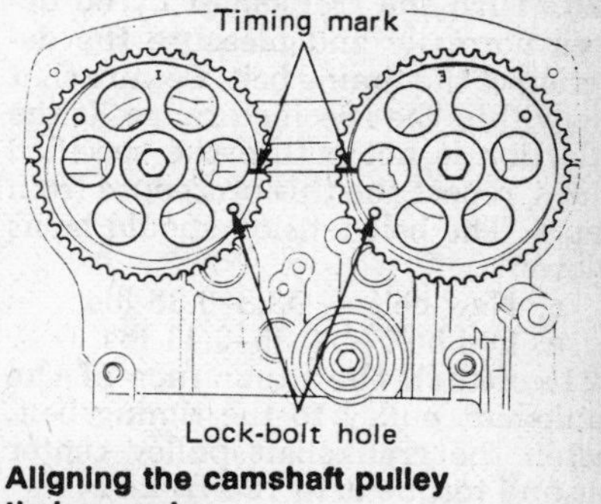

**Aligning the camshaft pulley timing marks**

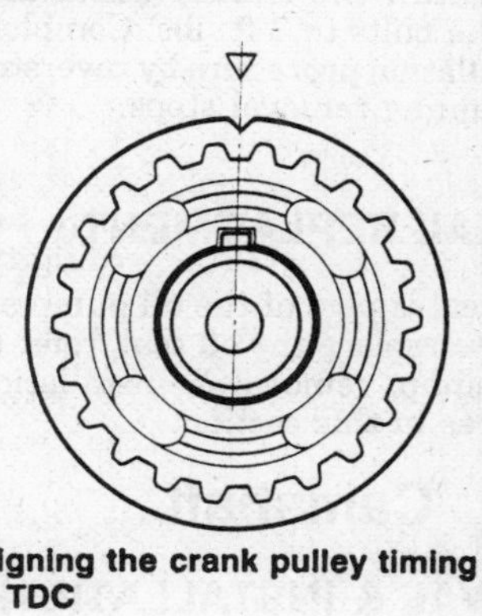
**Aligning the crank pulley timing gear to TDC**

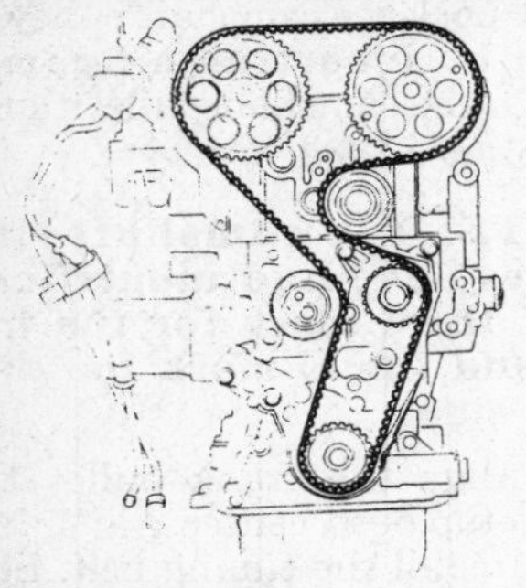

Timing belt installed properly

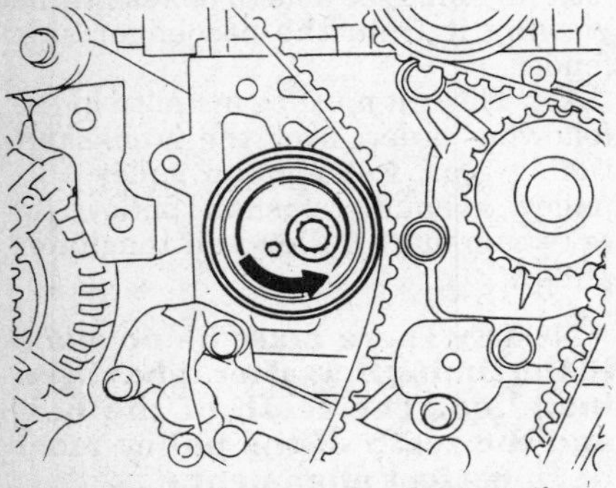

Applying tensioner spring force to the timing belt

in order to prevent excessively high low tension of the timing belt.

19. Rotate the crankshaft 2 turns normally and make sure that the notch on cylinder number 1 matches the scale on the timing cover match as well as the mark on the cam pulley. If it does not match them, repeat this procedure again from Step number 1.

20. Turn the crankshaft by 60 degrees normally and measure the deflection of the timing belt. Be sure that it is within the specified range. If the deflection is not within the specified values, repeat the this procedure from Step 4. The belt tension should be as follows:

a. New belt – 0.28–0.33 lbs.

a. Old belt – 0.35–0.41 lbs.

21. Attach the taper face of the crankshaft pulley to the timing belt. Fasten the crankshaft pulley center bolt and torque it to 123 ft. lbs.

22. Install the timing cover and torque the bolts to 7 ft. lbs. Complete the installation procedure by reversing the remaining removal steps.

## OIL SEAL REPLACMENT

The oil seal is part of the oil pump assembly; to replace the oil seal, refer to the oil pump, removal & installation procedures in this section.

# Camshaft

## REMOVAL & INSTALLATION

### *G180Z and G200Z Engines*

1. Remove the cam cover and remove the fuel pump.

2. Rotate the camshaft until No. 4 cylinder is in firing position. Remove the distributor cap and mark the rotor-to-housing position.

3. On the G180Z engine, lock the timing chain adjuster by depressing and turning the automatic adjuster slide pin 90 degrees in a clockwise direction. After locking the chain adjuster, check that the chain is loose.

4. On the G200Z engine, release the tension on the automatic adjuster as follows.

a. With a suitable tool depress the lock lever on the automatic adjuster rearward.

b. Push in the automatic adjuster shoe and lock in the retracted position by releasing the lever.

5. Remove the timing sprocket-to-camshaft bolt and remove the sprocket on the chain damper and tensioner without removing the chain from the sprocket.

6. Remove the rocker arm, shaft and the bracket assembly.

7. Remove the camshaft.

8. Installation is the reverse of removal. Use a liberal amount of clean oil to coat the camshaft before installing. Check that the mark on the No. 1 rocker arms shaft bracket is in alignment with the mark on the camshaft and that the crankshaft pulley groove is aligned with the TDC mark **0** mark on the front cover.

9. Assemble the timing sprocket to the camshaft by aligning it with the pin on the camshaft. Use care not to remove the chain from the sprocket.

10. Install the sprocket retaining bolt. Remove the half-moon seal in the front end of the head, insert a torque wrench and torque the bolt to 58 ft. lbs. Apply sealant and replace the half-moon seal in the head.

11. Set the automatic adjuster by turning the adjuster slide pin 90 degrees counterclockwise with a screwdriver.

12. Check the valve timing and the rotor mark alignment on the distributor. Reinstall the distributor cap.

### *4ZC1-T and 4ZD1 Engines*

1. Remove the cam cover.

2. Rotate the camshaft until the No. 4 cyl. is in the firing position. Remove the distributor cap and mark the rotor-to-housing position.

3. Remove the timing belt as previously outlined.

4. Apply a detention to the camshaft pulley by placing a T-bar or equivalent over the front plate fitting bolt and loosen the pulley fitting bolt. Remove the camshaft pulley, do not lose the camshaft boss or key.

5. Sequentially loosen and remove the outermost one and remove the rocker arm shaft with the bracket as an assembly.

6. Remove the camshaft.

7. Installation is the reverse of the removal procedure. Use a liberal amount of oil to coat the camshaft before installing it. Be sure that the mark on the camshaft is facing upward when it is being installed.

8. Use the timing belt removal and installation procedure previously outlined in this section to finish the installation.

### *4XC1-U and 4XC1-T Engines*

1. Disconnect the negative battery cable.

2. Align the crankshaft pulley notch with the **0** degree mark on the timing cover.

3. Remove the cylinder head cover.

4. Remove the timing cover.

5. Loosen the camshaft timing gear bolts (DO NOT rotate the engine).

6. Loosen the timing belt tensioner and remove the timing belt from the camshaft timing gear.

7. Remove the rocker arm shaft/rocker arm assembly.

8. Remove the distributor bolt and the distributor.

9. Remove the camshaft and the camshaft seal.

10. To install, drive a new camshaft seal onto the camshaft using seal installation tool No. J–35268 or equiva-

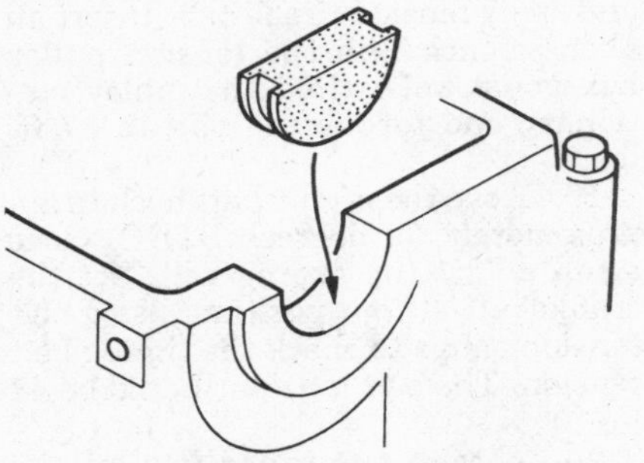

Half-moon seal

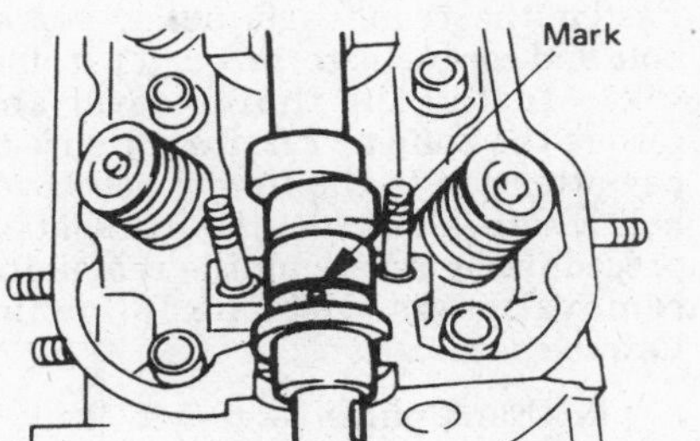


Camshaft alignment mark for the 4ZC1-T engine

lent. Place the camshaft in the cylinder head with the dowel pin in the camshaft facing forward. Reverse the removal procedure to finish this installation. Re-adjust the valves and the timing belt.

### *4XE1 DOHC Engine*

1. Disconnect the negative battery cable. Remove the engine center (head) cover from the engine.
2. Rotate the engine until the engine is at TDC on the compression stroke of the No. 1 cylinder, make sure timing mark is on the scale.
3. Remove the power steering pump drive belt, for vehicles with air conditoners, remove the power steering pump and compressor drive belt. Loosen the 2 power steering pump adjust plates bolts.
4. Remove the alternator drive belt from the crank pulley side. Disconnect the clip securing the high pressure air conditioning line to the strut tower.
5. Remove the upper timing belt cover.
6. Using a suitable engine hoist, slightly raise and support the engine safely.
7. Remove the passenger side engine mount from the engine. Disconnect the torque rod at the firewall.
8. Remove the passenger side engine mounting bracket from the engine. Using special crank pulley tool J-37988 or equivalent, remove the crank pulley bolt.
9. Raise the passenger side of the engine, be sure that the front wheels remain on the ground while lifting the engine. Raise the sngine too high will left the front wheels off the ground and may cause damage to the drive shaft universal joint.
10. Remove the timing belt lower cover. Remove the cranking pulley and extract up through the engine compartment. Refit the crank pulley bolt. Align the crank pulley timing gear to top dead center.
11. Lossen the tension pulley bolt a ½ turn counterclockwise. If the pulley bolt is loosened more than ½ a turn, the pulley will swing too far out of adjustment amd may be difficult ot readjust.
12. Mark the direction of rotation of the timing mark with a piece of chalk and remove the timing belt. Using and open end wrench, hole the camshaft from turning and remove the camshaft pulley(s).

**NOTE: Inspect the timing belt for signs of cracking, abnormal wear and hardening. Never expose the belt to oil, sunlight or heat. Avoid excessive bending, twisting or stretching.**

13. Remove the camshaft bearing cap bolts and bearing caps. Be sure to take note of the positions of the bearing caps before removing them. Lift the camshafts out of the cylinder head.
14. Installation is the reverse order of the removal procedure. Torque the bearing cap bolt to 8 ft. lbs. Be sure to install the camshaft bearing caps in their proper position.

## Piston and Connecting Rod

### POSITIONING

It is not advisable to remove the piston from the connecting rod unless part replacement is necessary. Whenever a piston is removed, the piston pin should be replaced. When examining a piston, look for scuffs, cracking or wear. The rings should be removed with a ring expander and should be kept separately to avoid interchanging parts. All clearances should be checked with a micrometer or comparable precision gauge. Assemble the piston rings to the piston so that the **NPR** or **TOP** marks are turned up. Every piston has a mark to designate proper installation, this **FRONT MARK** is located on the top edge, in line with the piston pin bore. In addition, the cylinder number that the piston came from is stamped on the connecting rod and the bearing cap.

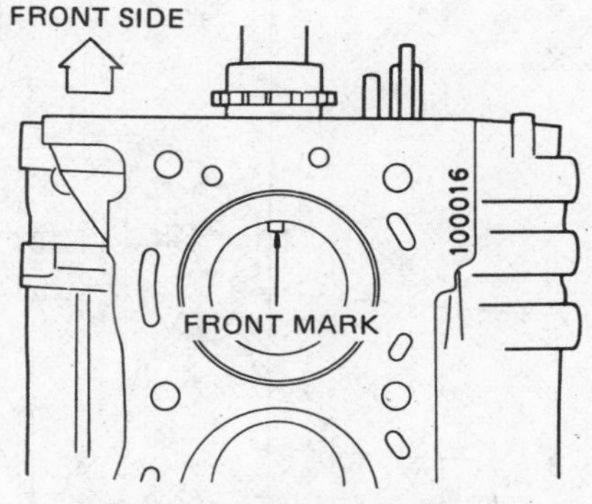

**Piston correctly installed**

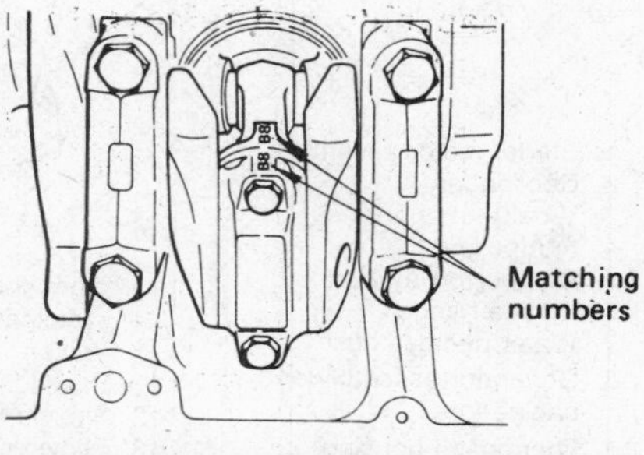

**Cylinder identification on connecting rod and bearing cap**

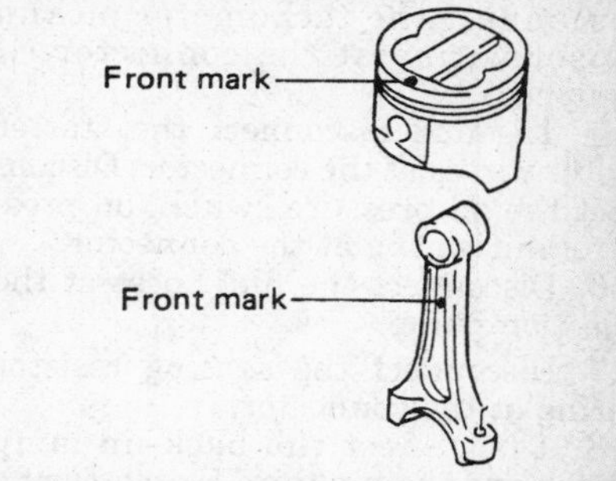

**Piston and connecting rod alignment marks**

# DIESEL ENGINE MECHANICAL

## Engine

### REMOVAL & INSTALLATION

#### *I-Mark (RWD)*

1. Open the hood and remove the battery cables at the posts. Remove the battery.
2. Scribe the position of the hinges on the underside of the hood and remove the hood.
3. Remove the bottom shrouds.
4. Drain the radiator and crankcase.
5. Remove the fan shroud attaching screws and remove the shroud. Remove the radiator attaching bolts and remove the radiator after disconnecting the upper and lower hoses.
6. Remove the air connecting hose.
7. Disconnect the heater hoses at the thermostat housing pipe and water inlet pipe.
8. Disconnect the quick start and silent idle (QSSI) thermo switch, fast idle thermo switch, thermo unit wiring at the connector on the thermostat housing.
9. Tag and disconnect the generator wiring at the connector.
10. Disconnect the vacuum hose from the connector at the rear of the vacuum pump.
11. Disconnect the vacuum hose from the actuator of fast idle.
12. Remove the two nuts connecting the exhaust pipe to the exhaust manifold and separate the pipe from the manifold, then remove the two nuts connecting the exhaust front pipe to the exhaust mounting bracket and separate the front pipe from the bracket and remove the front pipe.
13. Disconnect the accelerator cable from the injection pump lever.
14. Disconnect the fuel cut solenoid valve switch wiring at the connector.

Disconnect the tachometer pickup sensor wiring at the connector (if equipped).

15. Tag and disconnect the starter motor wiring at the connector. Disconnect the oil pressure switch, oil pressure unit wiring at the connector.

16. Disconnect the fuel hoses at the injection pump.

17. Disconnect the sensing resistor wiring at the connector.

18. Disconnect the back-up lamp switch and the top/third switch wiring at the connector on the rear of the engine.

19. Remove the return spring and disconnect the clutch control cable from the hook on the withdraw lever.

20. Disconnect the speedometer cable at the transmission side.

21. Remove the four bolts connecting the propeller shaft with the extension shaft and disconnect the propeller shaft flange yoke from the extension shaft, then pull the propeller shaft rearward. When the propeller shaft has been removed, wrap a small plastic bag around the rear transmission housing to prevent any leakage of fluid.

22. Untie the strings on the console boot and remove the screws on each side of the console box. Remove the grommets between the floor carpet and floor panel.

23. Pry off the edge of the gearshift lever dust boot and remove the gearshift lever assembly upward.

**NOTE: Plug the gearshift lever fitting hole to prevent entry of dust or foreign material.**

24. Remove the bolts and nuts attaching the rear mounting bracket, then remove the bolts attaching the exhaust mounting bracket.

25. Using a chain, engine lifting fixtures or other suitable means, lift the engine slightly.

26. Remove the engine mount nuts and disconnect the engine damper from the frame.

27. Check to make certain all parts have been removed or disconnected and tied out of the way so as not to snag on the motor when it is lifted clear.

28. Attach the engine hoist and remove the engine assembly with the transmission attached. Slowly lift the engine clear of the chassis.

29. Installation is the reverse of removal. Fill the crankcase, cooling system and check all cable adjustments.

30. Bleed the fuel system by filling the filter with diesel fuel and operating the primer pump handle several times. The force needed to operate the priming pump becomes greater as the filter fills up.

31. Start the engine and check for leaks.

## Cylinder Head

### REMOVAL & INSTALLATION

1. Drain the cooling system by opening the drain plug on the cylinder block.

2. Remove the camshaft.

3. Remove the sensing resistor assembly.

4. Remove the six screws attaching the injection pipe clip and remove the injection pipe clip.

5. Remove the eight sleeve nuts attaching the injection pipes and separate the infection pipes.

6. Remove the clip attaching the fuel leak off hose and separate the hose from the return pipe.

7. Remove the two nuts connecting the exhaust manifold to the exhaust pipe and separate the pipe from the manifold.

8. Disconnect the joint bolt attaching the oil feed line to the head side.

9. Disconnect the heater hose at the thermostat housing pipe.

10. Remove the cylinder head bolts by loosening them in sequence, then remove the cylinder head and gasket.

**NOTE: Use light oil to free stubborn bolts.**

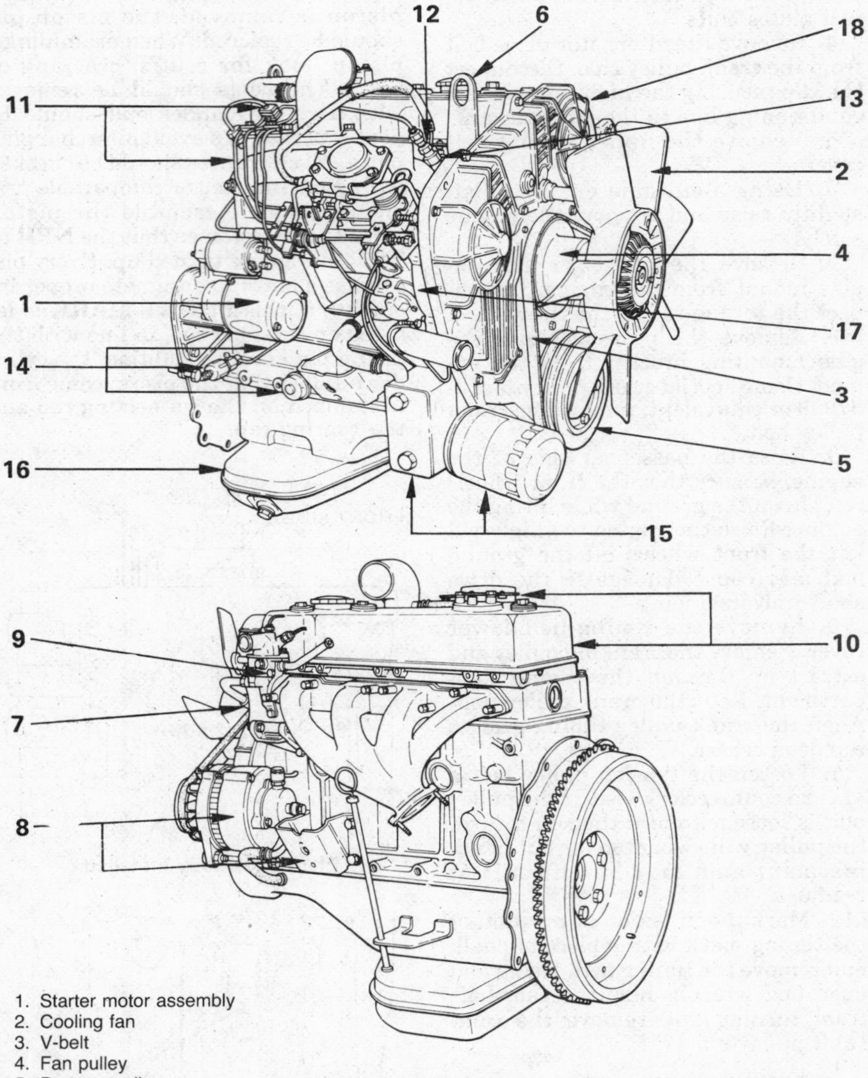


1. Starter motor assembly
2. Cooling fan
3. V-belt
4. Fan pulley
5. Damper pulley
6. Engine hanger
7. Water by-pass hose
8. Generator assembly and engine foot
9. Thermostat housing
10. Cam cover with positive crankcase ventilation valve
11. Injection pipe and clip
12. Nozzle holder assembly
13. Glow plug and connector
14. Oil pressure switch, unit and oil pipe
15. Oil cooler and oil filter
16. Oil pan
17. Tension spring
18. Dust cover

**Diesel engine major components**

11. Clean the head and block of all gasket material before reassembly.

12. Installation is the reverse of removal. Refill the cooling system. Torque all bolts in the sequence given at the front of this section. Apply oil to the bolt threads and clean them thoroughly before reinstalling them in the head. Torque the cylinder head bolts in 2 passes the first pass to 21–36 ft. lbs. and the second pass to 83–98 ft. lbs. Torque the reused bolts to 90–105 ft. lbs.

**NOTE: Make sure that the cylinder head gasket is properly placed before lowering the head. Look for the TOP mark to assure proper placement.**

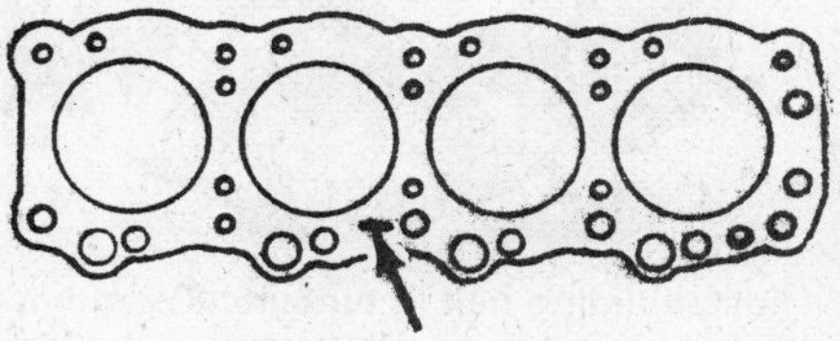

Location of TOP mark

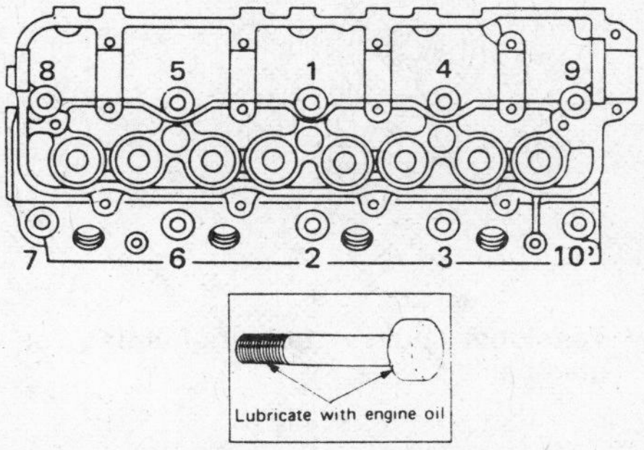


Cylinder head bolt torque sequence—diesel engine

13. Reinstall the camshaft and rocker arm assembly. Reinstall the timing belt and adjust the valve clearance.

14. Start the engine and check for leaks.

## OVERHAUL

**For all cylinder head overhaul procedures, please refer to "Engine Rebuilding" in the Unit Repair Section.**

# Rocker Arms/Shaft

## REMOVAL & INSTALLATION

1. Remove the cam cover.

2. Loosen the rocker arm shaft bracket nuts a little at a time, in sequence, commencing with the outer brackets.

3. Remove the nuts from the rocker arm shaft brackets.

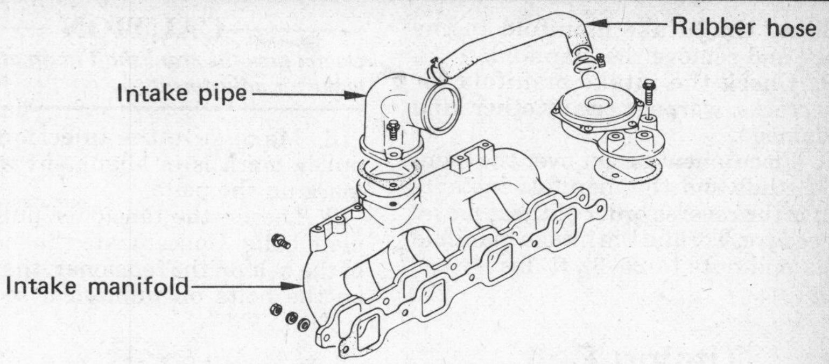


Intake manifold—diesel engine

4. Disassemble the rocker arm shaft assembly by removing the spring from the rocker arm shaft and then removing the rocker arm brackets and arms.

5. Inspect the rocker arm shaft for runout. Support the shaft on V-blocks at each end and check runout by slowly turning it with the probe of a dial indicator. Replace the shaft with a new one if the runout exceeds 0.0156 in. (0.4mm). Runout should not exceed 0.0079 in. (0.2mm).

6. Inspect the rocker arm shaft for wear, replace the shaft if obvious signs of wear are encountered.

7. Installation is the reverse of removal. Use a liberal amount of clean engine oil to coat the shaft, rocker arms and valve stems. Install the longer shaft on the exhaust valve side, shorter shaft on the intake side, so that the aligning marks on the shafts are turned to the front of the engine.

8. Torque the rocker arm shaft bracket and stud nuts to 15–22 ft. lbs. Hold the rocker arm springs with an adjustable wrench while torquing the nuts to prevent damage to the springs. Torque the nuts a little at a time in sequence, beginning with the center bracket and working outward.

9. Adjust valve clearances, reinstall the cam cover and check for leaks.

# Intake Manifold

## REMOVAL & INSTALLATION

1. Open the hood and disconnect the battery. Remove the air cleaner assembly.

2. Remove the connecting hose and PCV hose.

3. Remove the sensing resistor assembly.

4. Remove the 6 screws attaching the injection pipe clips and remove the injection pipe.

5. Remove the 10bolts attaching the upper dust cover and remove the upper dust cover.

6. Remove the 2 bolts attaching the engine hanger and remove the engine hanger.

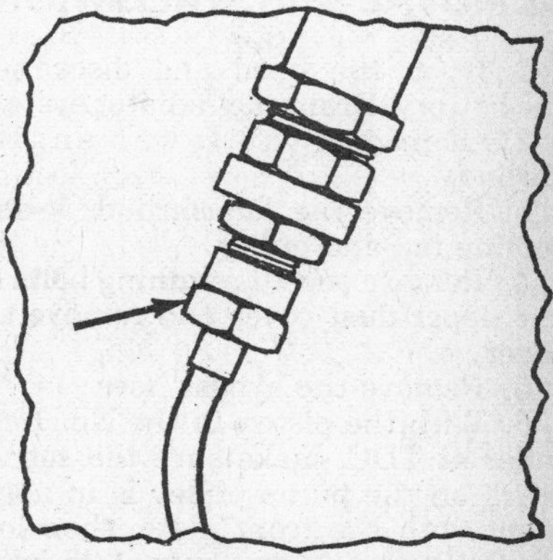

Diesel fuel injector showing injection pipe union

7. Remove the 2 bolts attaching the stay and remove the stay. Remove the three bolts and two nuts attaching the intake manifold and lift off the manifold.

8. Installation is the reverse of removal. Use a new manifold gasket. Torque to 25–32 ft. lbs.

# Exhaust Manifold

## REMOVAL & INSTALLATION

1. Disconnect the negative battery cable and remove the connecting hose plus the PCV hose from the intake manifold.

2. Remove the sensing resistor assembly.

3. Remove the 6 screws holding the injection pipe clips and remove the injection pipe clips.

4. Remove the 8 sleeve nuts holding the injection pipe and remove the injection pipe.

5. Remove the 10 bolts attaching the upper dust cover and remove the upper dust cover.

6. Remove the 2 bolts attaching the engine hanger and remove the engine hanger.

7. Remove the 2 bolts attaching the stay and remove the stay.

8. Remove the 3 bolts and two nuts

holding the intake manifold to the block and remove the manifold.

9. Check the intake manifold for any cracks, warpage or any other kind of damage.

10. Place a new gasket over the manifold studs and the manifold installation is the reverse order of the removal procedure. Torque the intake manifold bolts and nuts to 25–32 ft. lbs.

## Timing Belt

### REMOVAL & INSTALLATION

1. Open the hood and disconnect the battery. Drain the radiator system.
2. Remove the lower engine shrouds.
3. Remove the fan shroud, V-belt, cooling fan and pulley.
4. Remove the 10 retaining bolts on the upper dust cover and remove the cover.
5. Remove the bypass hose.
6. With the piston in the No. 1 cylinder at TDC, make sure the setting mark on the pump pulley is in alignment with the front plate, then lock the pulley with an 8mm 1.25 pitch bolt.
7. Remove the cam cover. Loosen the adjusting screws so that the rocker arms are held in a free state. Lock the camshaft by fitting a plate to the slit in the rear end of the camshaft.
8. Remove the damper pulley after making sure the piston in No. 1 is at TDC.
9. Remove the lower dust cover, then remove the timing belt holder.
10. Remove the tension spring. Loosen the tension pulley and plate bolts and remove the timing belt.
11. Remove the bolt locking the camshaft pulley and remove the pulley from the camshaft. Put the pulley back on the shaft, but only tighten the bolts enough to allow the pulley to be turned by hand.
12. Install the new timing belt, making sure the cogs on the pulley and the belt are engaged properly. The crankshaft should not be turned.
13. Concentrate belt looseness on the tension pulley, then depress the tension pulley with your fingers and install the tension spring. Semi-tighten the bolts in numerical sequence to prevent movement of the tension pulley.
14. Tighten the camshaft pulley bolts.
15. Remove the injection pump pulley lock bolt.
16. Remove the locking plate on the end of the camshaft.
17. Install the damper pulley on the hub and make sure the No. 1 piston is still at TDC.

**CAUTION**

***Do not turn the crankshaft in an attempt to make an adjustment.***

18. Make sure the injection pump pulley mark is in alignment with the mark on the plate.
19. Loosen the tensioner pulley and plate bolts. Concentrate the looseness of the belt on the tensioner, then tighten the bolts on numerical sequence.

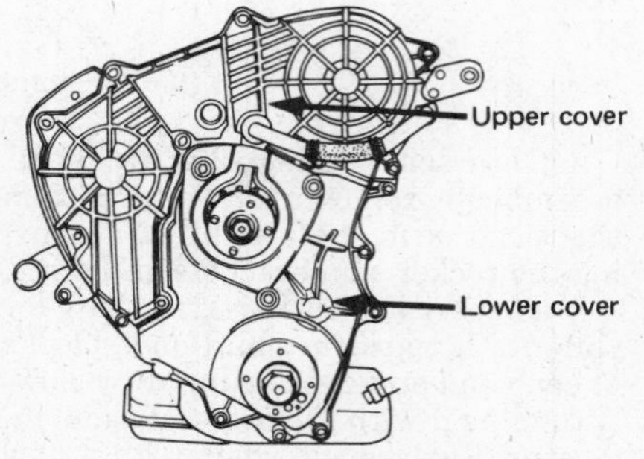

Dust covers on diesel engine

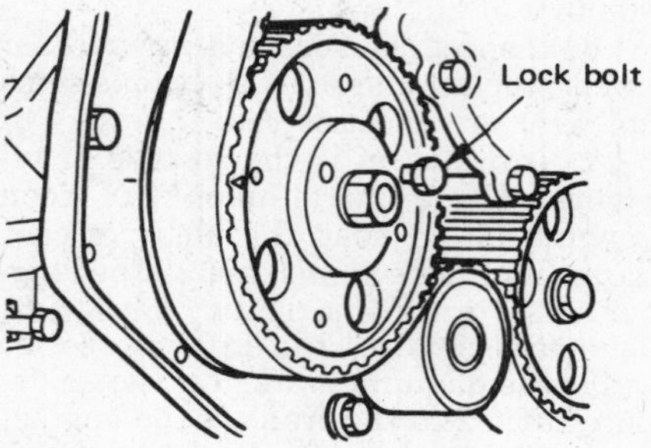

Locking the pump pulley

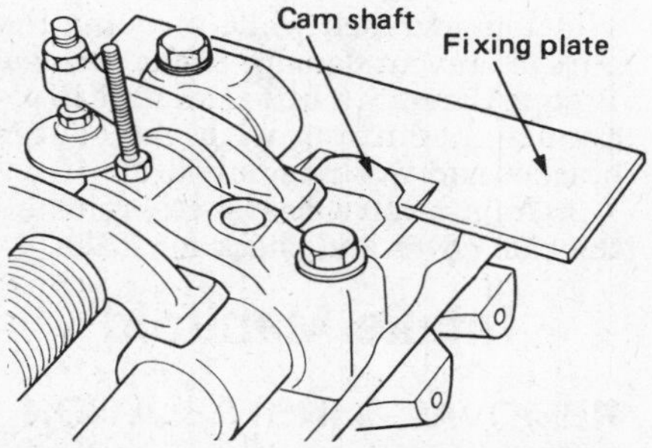

Locking the camshaft with fixing plate

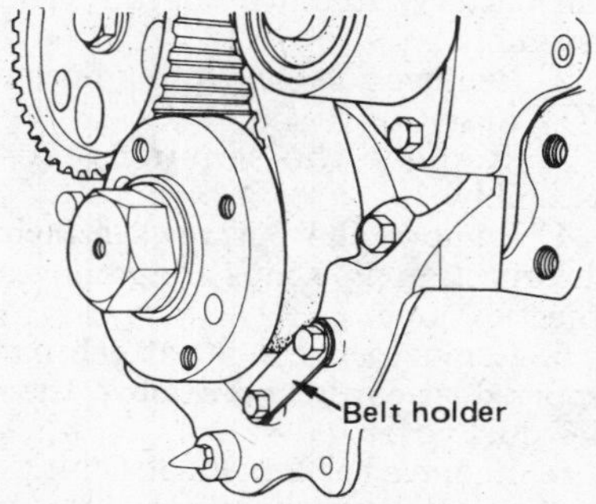

Location of timing belt holder

Torque the bolts to:
   a. Bolt No. 1 to 11–18 ft. lbs.
   b. Bolt No. 2 to 11–18 ft. lbs.
   c. Bolt No. 3 to 47–61 ft. lbs.

20. Check valve adjustment and install the cam cover.
21. Remove the damper pulley and install the belt holder in position away from the timing belt.
22. Install the bypass hose and dust covers.

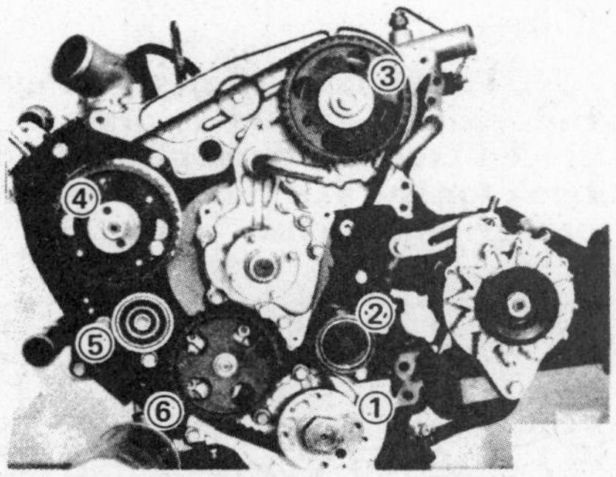

Install timing belt in numerical sequence

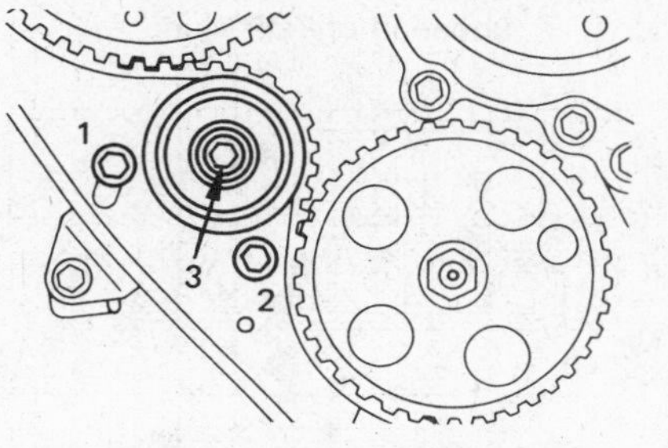

Tensioner pulley bolt tightening sequence

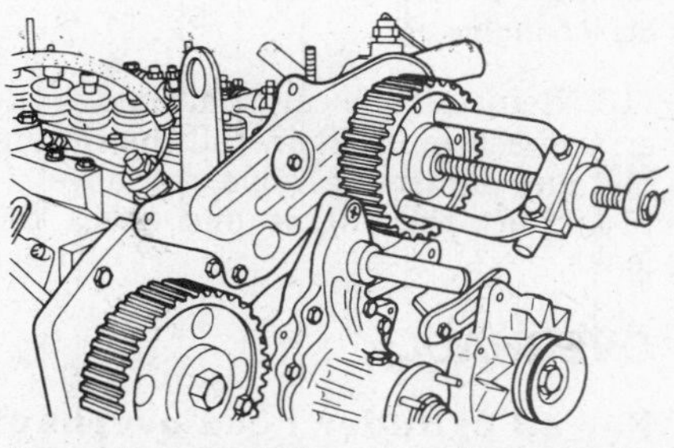
Removing camshaft pulley with gear puller

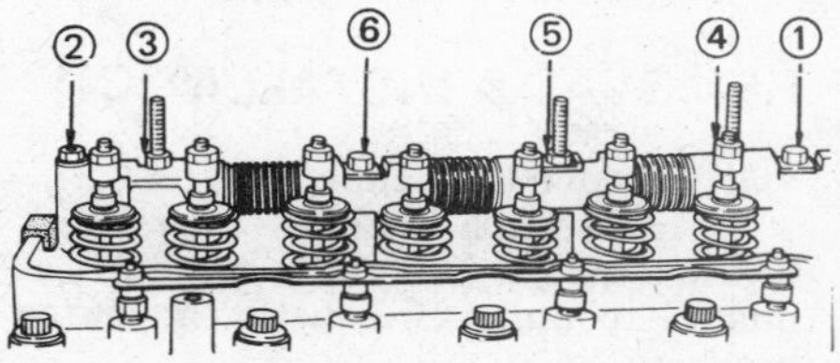

Bolt loosening sequence for removing rocker arm assembly

23. Install the damper pulley and reverse removal Steps 1–5.
24. Refill the cooling system.

## Camshaft

### REMOVAL & INSTALLATION

1. Remove the cam cover.
2. Remove the timing belt.
3. Remove the rear plug and hold the shaft by attaching the fixing plate (J–29761 or equivalent) into the slit at the rear of the camshaft.
4. Remove the camshaft pulley bolt, then remove the pulley with a gear puller.
5. Remove the rocker arms and shaft.
6. Remove the bolts attaching the front head plate and remove the plate.
7. Remove the bolts attaching the camshaft bearing caps. Remove the caps and bearings.
8. Remove the camshaft oil seal, then remove the camshaft.
9. Installation is the reverse of removal. Use a liberal amount of clean oil to coat the camshaft and journals during assembly.
10. Install a new oil seal and apply Permatex® or equivalent gasket compound to the cylinder head fitting face of the No. 1 camshaft bearing cap.
11. Torque the rocker arm shafts and camshaft bearing caps to specifications.

## Piston and Connecting Rod

### POSITIONING

It is not advisable to remove the piston from the connecting rod unless part replacement is necessary. Whenever a piston is removed, the piston pin should be replaced. When examining a piston, look for scuffs, cracking or wear. The rings should be removed with a ring expander and should be kept separately to avoid interchanging parts. All clearances should be checked with a micrometer or comparable precision gauge. Assemble the piston rings to the piston so that the NPR or TOP marks are turned up. Every piston has a mark to designate proper installation, this **FRONT MARK** is located on the top edge, in line with the piston pin bore. In addition, the cylinder number that the piston came from is stamped on the connecting rod and the bearing cap.

# ENGINE LUBRICATION

## Oil Pan

### REMOVAL & INSTALLATION

**NOTE: Isuzu recommends removing the engine (or at least raising it up) to service the oil pan. There isn't sufficient clearance to remove the pan with the engine bolted down.**

1. Remove or raise the engine to allow sufficient room to clear the oil pan.

**NOTE: On the diesel engine it may be necessary to remove the engine in order to remove the oil pan because of lack of clearance. Also on the 4XC1-U engine, disconnect the exhaust pipe bracket and the exhaust pipe at the manifold. Disconnect the right hand tension rod located under the front bumper to gain access to the oil pan.**

2. Remove the bolts and nuts attaching the oil pan to the engine block. Remove the oil pan and gasket.
3. Clean the oil pan and engine block gasket surface carefully to remove all traces of the old gasket.
4. Install in reverse order of removal, using a thin coat of Permatex® No. 2 or equivalent to hold the gasket in place while installing the bolts and to prevent any oil leaks.

**NOTE: If using a silicone sealant, apply the correct width bead of the sealant to the contact surfaces of the oil pan. There must be no gaps in the bead. The oil pan must be installed within 30 minutes after the sealant application**

5. Torque the all the oil pan bolts evenly. Check the edges of the gasket to ensure that it is sealed properly. If the gasket projects unevenly around the oil pan flange, remove the gasket and reinstall carefully.

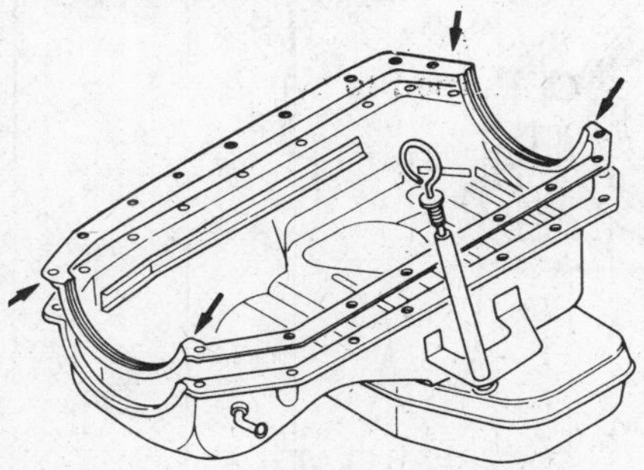

Oil pan and gasket—diesel engine

**NOTE: Do not overtighten the oil pan bolts. Bolts that are too tight cause as many leaks as bolts that are too loose.**

6. Start the engine and check for leaks.

## Rear Main Bearing Oil Seal

### REMOVAL & INSTALLATION

1. Remove the transmission, flywheel and oil pan.
2. On manual transmission models, remove the clutch cover and pressure plate assembly.
3. Remove the starter and lay to one side or wire to the frame.

**NOTE: Disconnect the battery before removing starter.**

4. Remove the 6 flywheel bolts and the flywheel assembly.
5. Remove the 4 rear crankshaft seal retainer bolts and remove the retainer seal assembly.
6. Pry the old seal out of the retainer and discard.
7. Place a new seal in position in the retainer. Fill the clearance between

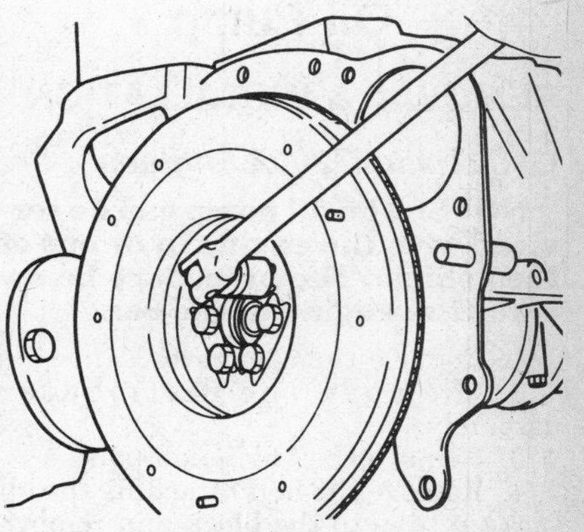

Removing flywheel assembly

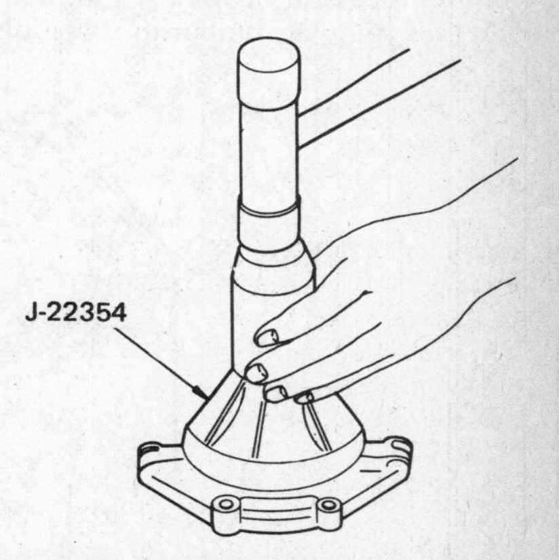


Installing crankshaft rear seal with special tool

the lips of the seal with grease and lubricate the seal lip with engine oil.

8. Place the retainer on a flat surface and drive the seal into place using installer tool No. J-35264 or equivalent.

9. Installation is the reverse of removal procedure. Be sure to apply sealant to the seal retainer mounting surface. Apply engine oil to the seal lip. Align the cylinder body dowel pin holes with the rear retainer dowel pins. Install the flywheel with the proper bolts and washers and torque to specification.

**NOTE: New bolts should be used when installing the rear seal retainer. Be very careful not to disengage the oil seal garter spring during installation of the rear seal retainer.**

10. Start the engine and check for leaks.

**NOTE: Diesel engines, 4ZD1 and 4ZC1-T use a different number seal installing tool (J-29818), and the seal is installed on the No. 5 crankshaft bearing cap. Other than that, the removal and replacement procedures are identical for all engines.**

## Oil Pump

### REMOVAL & INSTALLATION

#### *G180Z and G200Z Engines*

**NOTE: The oil pump can be serviced with the engine in or out of the vehicle. The procedure below is for the engine in the car.**

1. Remove the cam cover.
2. Remove the distributor assembly.
3. Remove the engine oil pan.
4. Remove the bolt attaching the oil pick-up tube to the block and remove the tube from the oil pump.
5. Remove the oil pump mounting bolts and remove the pump assembly.

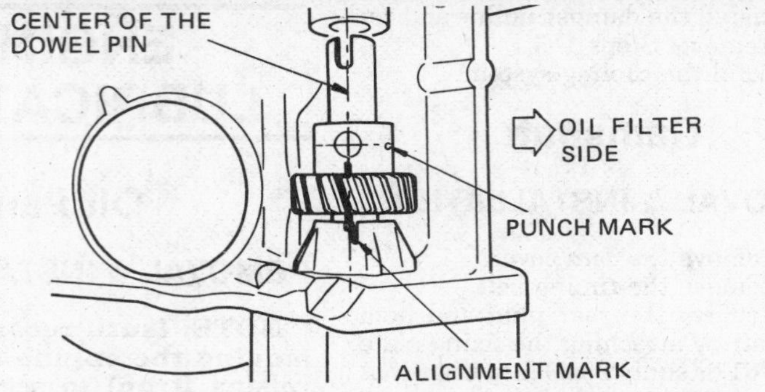


**Oil pump alignment**

6. Remove the rubber hose and relief valve from the oil pump.
7. Installation is in reverse order of removal. Align the mark on the camshaft with the mark on the No. 1 rocker arm shaft bracket. Align the notch on the crankshaft pulley with the **0** mark on the front cover. When the two sets of marks are aligned, the No. 4 cylinder is at TDC on the compression stroke.
8. Install the driven rotor so that the alignment mark lines up with the mark on the drive rotor.
9. Install the oil pump assembly by engaging the oil pump drive gear with the pinion gear on the crankshaft, so that the alignment mark on the drive gear is turned rearward and is away from the crankshaft by approximately 20 degrees in a clockwise direction.
10. When the oil pump is installed, check to assure that the mark on the oil pump drive gear is turned to the rear side as viewed from the clearance between the front cover and the cylinder block and that the slit at the end of the oil pump drive shaft is parallel with the front face of the cylinder block and is off-set forward as viewed through the distributor fitting hole.
11. Check for leaks after assembly. Measure the oil pressure by attaching a pressure gauge to the hole for the oil pressure switch. Correct oil pump pressure is 56–71 psi.

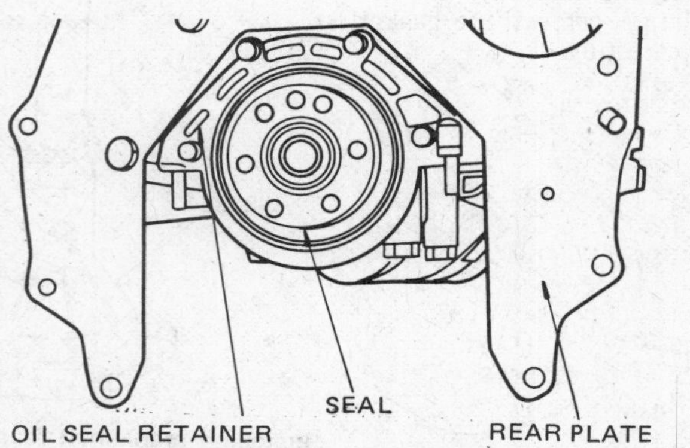


**Rear main oil seal assembly**

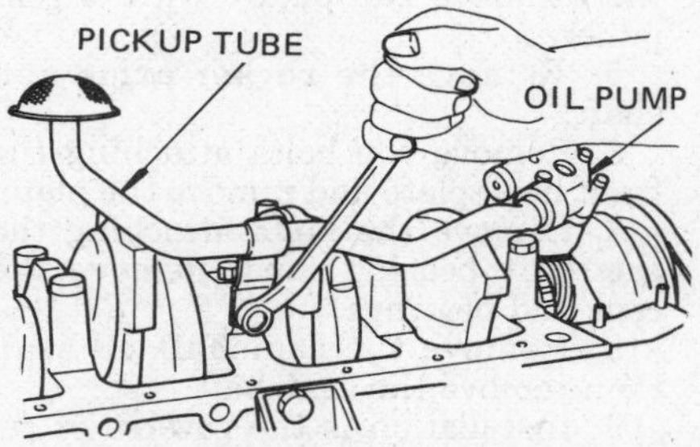


**Oil pump assembly (engine upside down)**

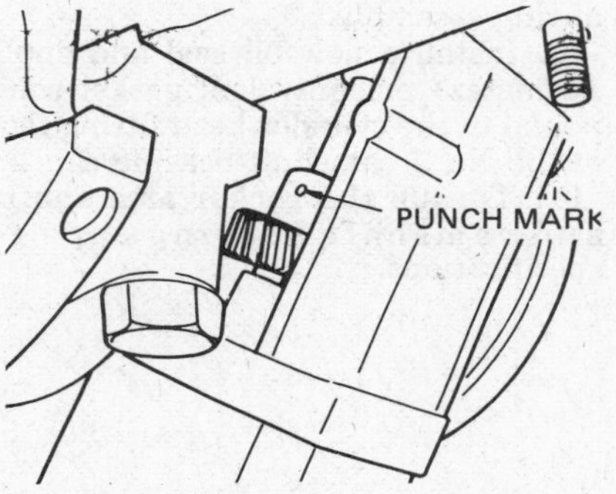


**Checking oil pump alignment**

#### *4ZC1-T and 4ZD1 Engines*

1. Remove the front cover and timing belt as previously outlined in this section.
2. Using a 6mm inner hex wrench apply a detent to the oil pump pulley and loosen the oil pump pulley bolt, remove the oil pump pulley.
3. Using the same hex head wrench, remove the allen bolts attaching the oil pump to the engine and remove the pump.
4. Installation is the reverse order of the removal procedure. Apply a liberal amount of oil to all components before installation. Install the rotor with the chamfered side turned towards the cylinder body.
5. Apply a light coat of oil to the O-ring and insert the O-ring into the groove of the oil pump housing. Install the oil pump onto the engine and torque the Allen bolts to 14 ft. lbs.
6. Check and make sure that the oil

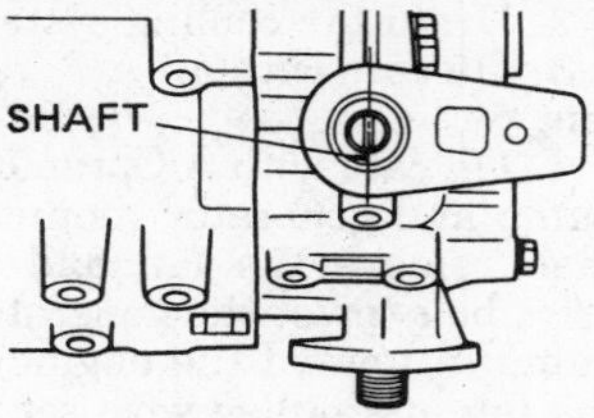


View through distributor fitting hole

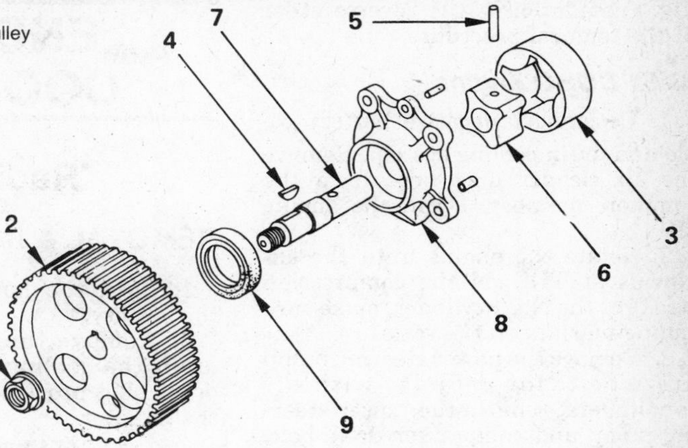


Exploded view of diesel oil pump and pulley assembly

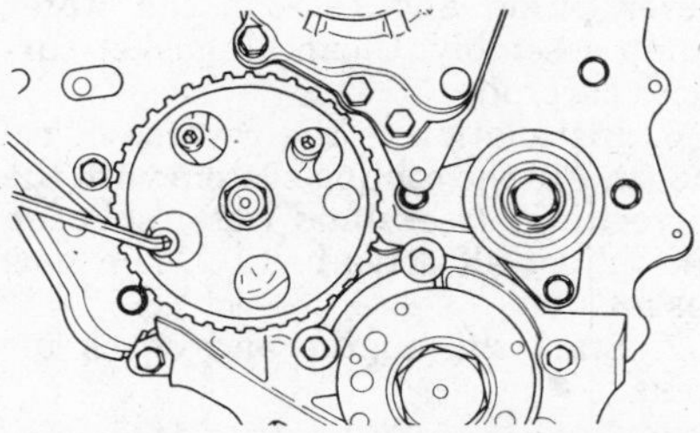

Using special tool to remove Allen bolts on oil pump

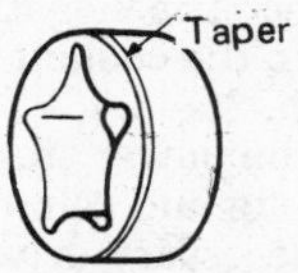


Install vane with taper side toward the cylinder body

pump turns smoothly, if it does not, replace the cartridge assembly.

7. Install the oil pump pulley and torque the pulley bolt to 58 ft. lbs. Follow the timing belt procedure previously outlined to finish the installation.

### 4FB1 Engine

1. Remove the timing belt.
2. Remove the Allen bolts attaching the oil pump and remove the pump together with the pulley.

**NOTE: The special tool for the Allen bolts is J-29767**

3. Disassemble the oil pump on the workbench. A gear puller may be necessary to remove the pulley.
4. Installation is the reverse of removal. Apply generous amounts of clean engine oil to all components before installation. Install the vane with the taper side toward the cylinder body.
5. Install a new O-ring into the groove in the housing. Lubricate with oil. Install the rotor and then the pump body together with the pulley. Torque the Allen bolts to 11–18 ft. lbs.

### 4XC1-U and 4XC1-T ENGINES

#### 1985–87

1. Remove the engine from the vehicle.
2. Drain the crankcase.
3. Remove the alternator belt and the starter.
4. Install the flywheel holding tool (J-35271) to secure the flywheel.
5. Remove the crankshaft pulley and boss.
6. Remove the timing cover bolts and the timing cover.
7. Loosen the tension pulley and remove the timing belt.
8. Remove the crankshaft timing gear and the tension pulley.
9. Remove the oil pan bolts, oil pan, oil strainer fixing bolt and the oil strainer assembly.
10. Remove the oil pump bolts and the oil pump assembly.
11. Remove the sealing material from the oil pump and engine block sealing surfaces.
12. To install, use seal installer J-35269 or equivalent and install a new oil seal in the oil pump housing, lubricate the oil pump, use new gaskets, apply sealant to the sealing surfaces and reverse the removal procedure. The final torque for the oil pump attaching bolts is 7 ft. lbs.

#### 1988–90

1. Disconnect the negative battery cable. Drain the radiator coolant into a suitable drain pan. Drain the engine oil into a suitable drain pan.
2. Place a wooden block on a suitable floor jack and place the jack under the strongest point of the oil pan, slightly raise the engine.
3. Remove the rear side torque rod while the engine is slightly lifted.
4. Remove the right side engine mount, then remove the body side mount and the engine side mount.
5. Loosen the power steering oil pump retaining bolt and remove the V-belt.
6. Remove the 4 crank pulley bolts with the engine slightly lifted.

Radiator with shroud attached

7. Remove the 6 timing cover bolts and remove the timing belt cover.
8. Be sure that the crankshaft timing mark on the crankshaft pulley hub is aligned with the top dead center mark.
9. Use special crankshaft bolt tool (J-37376 or equivalent) to turn and stop the crankshaft, then remove the bolt on the end part of the crank shaft and remove the pulley.
10. Confirm the crankshaft is at top dead center, prior to removing the timing belt. In this state, if the notch on the camshaft pulley hub is aligned with the left upper corner of the cylinder head, the number 4 cylinder is at **TDC**. If the notch on the camshaft pulley is aligned with the right upper corner of the cylinder head, the No. 1 cylinder is at top dead center.
11. Loosen the bolts fixing the tension pulley. Turn the tension pulley clockwise with the allen wrench, then remove the timing belt.
12. Remove the oil pump retaining bolts and remove the oil pump assembly.
13. Remove the old oil seal with a suitable pry tool and install a new seal with a suitable seal driver tool. Check the outside of the oil pump assembly for cracking and other damage. The oil pump must be replaced if these conditions are evident.

14. Installation is the reverse order of the removal procedure.

### 4XE1 DOHC Engine

1. Disconnect negative battery cable and drain cooling system. Remove the air cleaner duct hose from the common chamber. Drain the engine oil.
2. Rotate the engine until the engine is at TDC on the compression stroke of the No. 1 cylinder, make sure timing mark is on the scale.
3. Remove the power steering pump drive belt, for vehicles with air conditoners, remove the power steering pump and compressor drive belt. Loosen the 2 power steering pump adjust plates bolts.
4. Remove the alternator drive belt from the crank pulley side. Disconnect the clip securing the high pressure air conditioning line to the strut tower.
5. Remove the upper timing belt cover.
6. Using a suitable engine hoist, slightly raise and support the engine safely.
7. Remove the passenger side engine mount from the engine. Disconnect the torque rod at the firewall.
8. Remove the passenger side engine mounting bracket from the engine. Using special crank pulley tool J-37988 or equivalent, remove the crank pulley bolt.
9. Raise the passenger side of the engine, be sure that the front wheels remain on the ground while lifting the engine. Raise the engine too high will left the front wheels off the ground and may cause damage to the drive shaft universal joint.
10. Remove the timing belt lower cover. Remove the cranking pulley and extract up through the engine compartment. Refit the crank pulley bolt. Align the crank pulley timing gear to TDC.
11. Loosen the tension pulley bolt a ½ turn counterclockwise. If the pulley bolt is loosened more than ½ a turn, the pulley will swing too far out of adjustment and may be difficult to readjust.
12. Mark the direction of rotation of the timing mark with a piece of chalk and remove the timing belt.
13. Remove the oil pump retaining bolts and remove the oil pump assembly.
14. Remove the old oil seal with a suitable pry tool and install a new seal with a suitable seal driver tool. Check the outside of the oil pump assembly for cracking and other damage. The oil pump must be replaced if these conditions are evident.
15. Installation is the reverse order of the removal procedure.

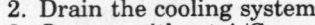

# ENGINE COOLING

## Radiator

### REMOVAL & INSTALLATION

1. Open the hood and disconnect the battery.
2. Remove the radiator cap and drain the cooling system using the drain plug provided at the bottom of the radiator.

**CAUTION**

***The engine should be cold for removal procedures.***

3. Remove the dynamic damper (if so equipped), Disconnect the electric fan connectors and the connector to the thermo switch (if so equipped). Remove the fan shroud and fan with motor assembly.
4. Loosen the top and bottom hose clamps and remove the radiator hoses. Disconnect the coolant recovery hose, rubber hose-surge tank to radiator and turbocharger coolant line.
5. Remove and plug the oil cooler lines on models equipped with automatic transmissions.
6. Remove the bolts, nuts and brackets attaching the radiator to the vehicle and remove the radiator assembly.
7. Installation is the reverse of removal. Fill the cooling system with water and the proper proportion of anti-freeze solution. Start the engine and check for leaks.

## Water Pump

### REMOVAL & INSTALLATION

### G180Z Engine

1. Open the hood and disconnect the battery. Remove the lower engine cover.
2. Drain the cooling system.
3. On cars without A/C, remove the fan.
4. On cars with A/C, remove the air pump and generator mounting bolts, then remove the fan and air pump drive belt (pivot the generator and air pump in toward the engine). Remove the fan and pulley with set plate. Remove the hoses to the pump.
5. Remove the 6 bolts attaching the water pump and remove the water pump assembly. Clean all gasket surfaces carefully.
6. Installation is the reverse of removal. Fill the cooling system with the correct anti-freeze and water solution and adjust all drive belts. Use a new gasket.
7. Start the engine and check for leaks.

### 4XC1-U, 4XC1-T and 4XE1 DOHC Engines

1. Disconnect the negative battery cable and drain the coolant into a suitable drain pan.
2. Loosen the power steering pump adjustment bolts and remove the belt. (Remove all necessary drive belts).
3. Remove the timing belt as previously outlined in this section.
4. Remove the tension pulley and spring. Remove the water pump pulley.

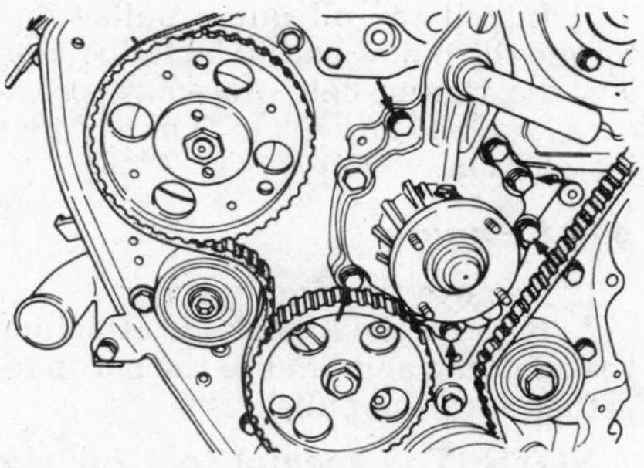

Water pump attaching bolts

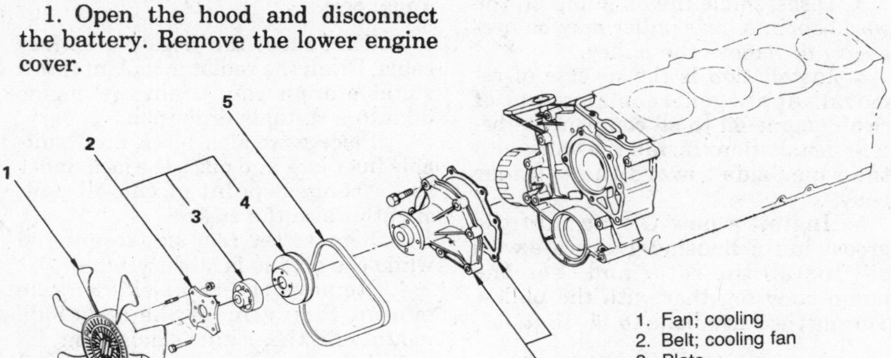


Disassembled view of water pump—118.9 cu. in. engine

5. Remove the water pump mounting bolts, water pump and gasket from the engine. Clean the mounting surfaces of all gasket material.

6. To install, reverse the removal procedures. Apply a suitable sealant to the mounting surfaces of the pump and torque the pump to 17 ft. lbs.

#### *G200Z, 4ZC1-T and 4ZD1 Engines*

1. Disconnect the battery and drain the radiator.
2. Remove the fan belt, plate, spacer, and pulley.
3. Remove the water pump and gasket.
4. Before installation, clean the gasket surfaces carefully and torque the water pump retaining bolts to 18 ft. lbs.

#### *4FB1 Engine*

1. Open the hood and disconnect the battery. Remove the radiator cap.
2. Drain the cooling system and remove the hoses from the pump.
3. Remove the fan and pulley.
4. Remove the four attaching bolts holding the damper pulley. Remove the damper pulley.
5. Remove the engine dust covers.
6. Remove the bypass hose.
7. Remove the five bolts attaching the water pump and remove the pump and gasket.
8. Clean all gasket surfaces carefully and inspect for nicks, cracks or deep scratches.
9. Installation is the reverse of removal. Use a new gasket. Torque all water pump mounting bolts to 11–18 ft. lbs.

## Thermostat

### REMOVAL & INSTALLATION

**NOTE: Engine should be cold for this procedure.**

1. Drain the cooling system and remove the air cleaner. Disconnect the electrical connections from the sensors or switches incorporated in the thermostst housing.
2. Disconnect the upper radiator hose from the thermostat housing. Remove the two attaching bolts holding the thermostat housing.
3. Lift the housing and remove the thermostat.
4. Remove all traces of old gasket.
5. Reinstall in reverse order using a new gasket. Permatex® is a good idea to avoid leaks. Torque the bolts to 14 ft. lbs. Make sure the thermostat jiggle valve is installed in the up position.

# EMISSION CONTROLS

**NOTE: Please refer to the Emission Control in the Unit Repair section for system maintenance procedures. Due to the complex nature of modern electronic engine control systems, comprehensive diagnosis and testing procedures fall outside the confines of this repair manual. For complete information on diagnosis, testing and repair procedures concerning all modern engine and emission control systems, please refer to *"Chilton's Guide to Electronic Engine Controls."***

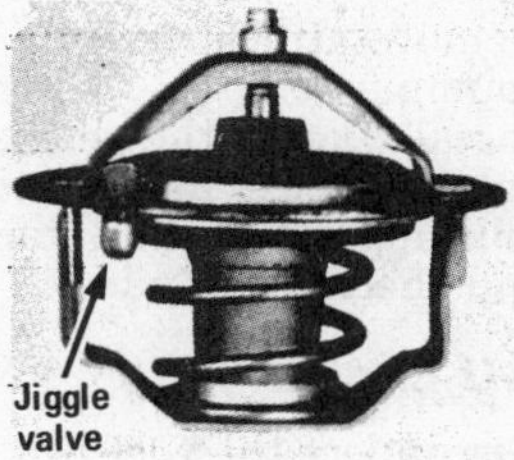


Thermostat—typical for all models

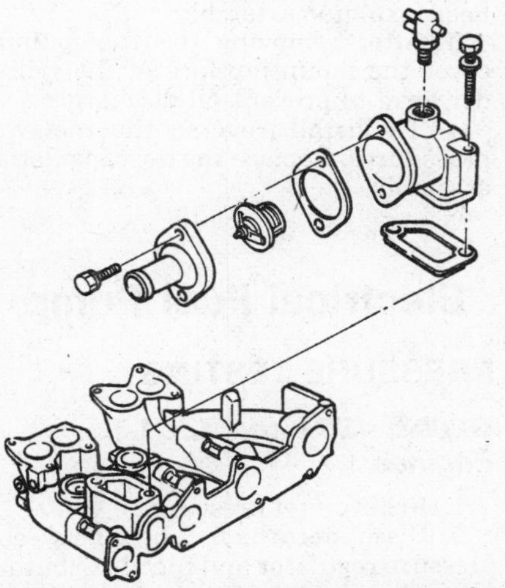

Exploded view of thermostat and housing late model I-Mark

# GASOLINE FUEL SYSTEM

## Fuel System Service Precaution

Any time the fuel system is being worked on, disconnect the negative battery cable, except for those tests where battery voltage is required and always keep a dry chemical (Class B) fire extinguisher near the work area.

### RELIEVING FUEL SYSTEM PRESSURE

1. Remove the fuel pump fuse from the fuse block or disconnect the harness connector at the tank.
2. Start the engine. It should run and then stall when the fuel in the lines is exhausted. When the engine stops, crank the starter for about three seconds to make sure all pressure in the fuel lines is released.
3. Install the fuel pump fuse after repair is made.

## Fuel Filter

### REMOVAL & INSTALLATION

#### *G180Z, G200Z, 4ZC1-T and 4ZD1 Engines*

The fuel system has a cartridge type, inline filter installed on the left side panel in the luggage compartment on all models except the Impulse. On the Impulse it is located in the engine compartment.

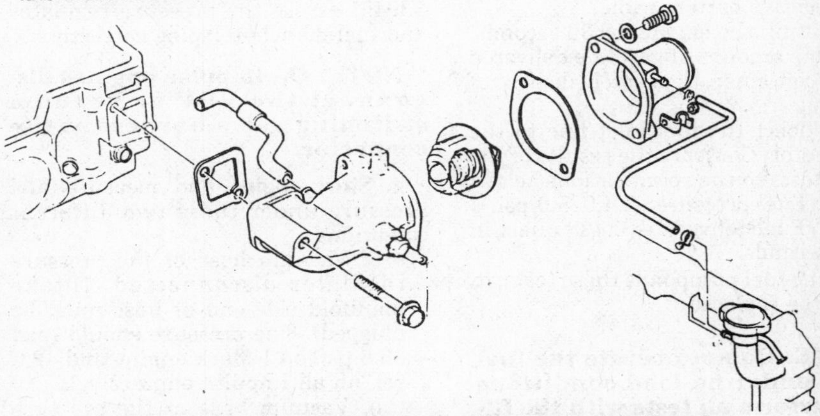

Exploded view of thermostat and housing late model Impulse

1. Remove the bolts attaching the cover on the side of the fuel tank in the luggage compartment, then remove the cover. On the impulse models, Remove the filter insulator nut and flange, disconnect the fuel filter retaining bolt.
2. Disconnect the hoses from the filter.
3. Remove the fuel filter from the clip.
4. Installation is the reverse of removal.

#### 4XC1-U, 4XC1-T and 4XE1 DOHC Engines

The fuel filter is located under the vacuum booster of the power brake system and should be replaced every 15,000 miles.

1. Relieve the fuel system pressure. Remove the fuel tank cap.
2. Disconnect and plug the fuel hoses from the fuel filter.
3. Remove the fuel filter and reinstall the fuel tank cap.
4. Installation is the reverse of the removal procedure. Be sure to securely attach the fuel filter clips and start the engine to check for any leaks.

## Mechanical Fuel Pump

### PRESSURE TESTING

#### G180Z and 4XC1-U Engines

1. Disconnect the negative battery cable.
2. Remove the fuel inlet hose from the carburetor.
3. Connect a fuel pump pressure gauge between the inlet hose and the carburetor, using a tee fitting. Reconnect the negative battery cable.
4. Start the engine and run it at fast idle, note the reading on the pressure gauge.
5. Stop the engine and disconnect the negative battery cable.
6. Place the open end of the fuel line into a graduated container. Reconnect the negative battery cable.
7. Crank the engine for 30 seconds. Note the amount of gasoline delivered to the container, then safely dispose of the fuel.
8. Conect the fuel inlet line to the carburetor. Compare the results of the these tests to the specifications below:
   a. Fuel pressure – 4.0–5.0 psi.
   b. Fuel delivery – 0.428 quart in 30 seconds.
9. If the fuel pump fails these tests, it should be replaced.

**NOTE: Do not operate the fuel pump under no-load conditions and perform all tests with the filter installed.**

### REMOVAL & INSTALLATION

**CAUTION**

***Fire hazard. Take precautions to avoid igniting any spilled fuel. Be particularly careful when using a work light around the fuel system.***

#### G180Z Engine

1. Disconnect the negative battery terminal from the battery.
2. Remove distributor assembly and spark plug wires, mark position of rotor and distributor housing.
3. Remove engine hanger if necessary.
4. Disconnect rubber hoses at pump.
5. Remove attaching bolts then remove pump assembly.
6. Installation is the reverse of the removal procedure. Be sure to replace the mounting gasket then start the engine and check for any leaks.

#### 4XC1-U Engine

1. Disconnect the fuel delivery and return hoses from the fuel pump.
2. Remove the bolts, fuel pump and heat insulator assembly.
3. After removing the fuel pump, cover the mounting face of the cylinder head to prevent oil discharge.
4. To install, reverse the removal procedures. Replace the heat insulator assembly.

## Electrical Fuel Pump

### PRESSURE TESTING

#### G200Z, 4ZD1 and 4ZC1-T Engines

1. Relieve fuel pressure.
2. Disconnect the fuel hose between pressure regulator and fuel distributor pipe.
3. Connect a fuel pressure gauge (J–33945) across the pressure regulator and fuel distributor pipe correctly.

**NOTE: On Impulse engines disconnect the VSV or vacuum switching valve harness at the connector.**

4. Start engine and measure fuel pressure under these two different conditions:
   a. Vacuum hose of the pressure regulator disconnected (Intake manifold side end of hose must be plugged). The pressure should read 35.6 psi. on I-Mark engine and 42.6 psi. on all Impulse engines.
   b. Vacuum hose of the pressure regulator connected (at speed of 900 rpm). The pressure should read 28.4 psi. on I-Mark engine and 35.6 psi. on Impulse all engines.
5. After on-vechicle inspection is made remove fuel pressure gauge, reconnect fuel line and check for leaks.

#### 4XC1-T and 4XE1 DOHC Engines

1. Relieve the fuel pressure in the system. Loosen the clip on the fuel hose between the pressure regulator and fuel delivery pipe and disconnect the fuel hose carefully.
2. Connect a suitable fuel pressure gauge across the pressure regulator and fuel distributor pipe correctly.
3. Start the engine and measure the fuel pressures under the 2 different conditions listed below:
   a. Vacuum hose of the pressure regulator disconnected, intake manifold side end of the hose plugged. The fuel pressure should be approximately 36 psi.
   b. Vacuum hose of the pressure regulator connected and idling at 900 rpm. The fuel pressure should be approximately 28 psi.

**NOTE: The following method can be used to operate the fuel pump without running the engine.**

4. Apply battery voltage to the red and brown wire (4XC1-T engine) and red and green wire (4XE1 engine) that is connected to the fuel pump relay within the right side of the engine compartment.
5. Use the same specifications as described earlier in Step 3.
6. Relieve the fuel pressure. Remove the fuel pressure gauge and reconnect the fuel line.

### REMOVAL & INSTALLATION

#### 4XC1-T and 4XE1 DOHC Engines

**NOTE: Fuel is under high pressure, if the following steps are not followed the fuel could spray out and result in a fire hazard or possible injury. The fuel pump is located inside the gas tank.**

1. Relieve fuel pressure then disconnect negative battery cable.
2. Raise and support the vehicle safely. Drain fuel tank.
3. Remove all gas line hose connections and fuel pump ground wire.
4. Remove filler neck hose and clamp.
5. Remove breather hose and clamp.
6. Disconnect fuel tank hose to evaporator pipe. Place a suitable floor

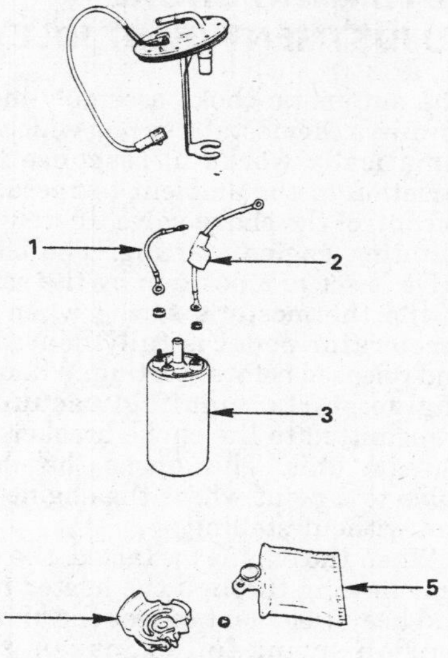


1. Ground wire
2. Lead wire
3. Fuel pump
4. Rubber cushion
5. Fuel pump filter

**Exploded view of fuel pump I-Mark (4XC1-T)**

jack with a piece of wood on it under the fuel tank.

7. Remove fuel tank mounting bolts and lower tank from car. At this point remove hose from pump to fuel filter.
8. Remove fuel pump bracket plate and fuel pump as an assembly.
9. Remove pump bracket, rubber cushion and fuel pump filter.
10. To install, reverse the removal procedures. Be careful, to push the lower side of the fuel pump, together with the rubber cushion, into the fuel pump bracket.

### G200Z and Early 1986 4ZC1-T Engines

**NOTE: Starting in early 1986, a electrical sub pump was added to the fuel system. The sub pump system pumps fuel from the fuel return line back to the main fuel pump. Removal and installation of this pump is similar to the main fuel pump.**

1. Relieve fuel pressure then disconnect negative battery cable.
2. Raise the rear seat by hand and disconnect the electrical harness connector under the right side of the seat, remove the side cover to gain access.
3. Remove the bolts connecting the fuel pump guard to the body.
4. Disconnect and cap the rubber hose at the fuel pump.
5. Remove the fuel pump bracket and fuel pump.

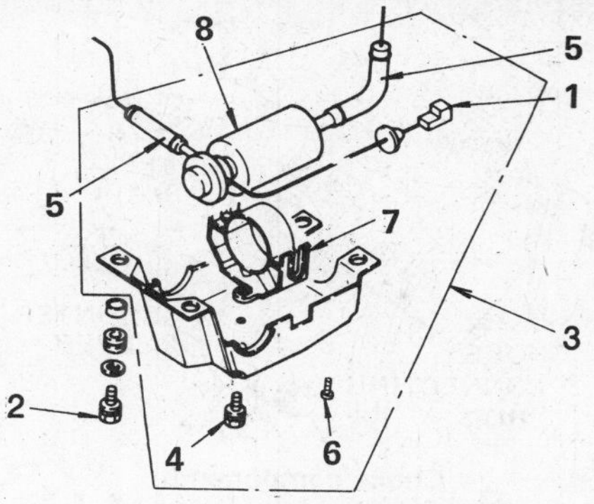


1. Connector; fuel pump harness
2. Bolt; guard to body
3. Bracket; fuel pump, guard and fuel pump assembly.
4. Bolt; guard to fuel pump bracket
5. Hose; rubber
6. Screw; fuel pump bracket
7. Bracket; fuel pump
8. Pump assembly; fuel

**Exploded view of fuel pump and attaching parts—118.9 cu. in. engine**

**NOTE: The fuel pump cannot be disassembled and must be replaced if found to be defective.**

6. Installation is the reverse of removal.

### 4ZD1 and Late 1986-90 4ZC1-T Engines

1. Relieve fuel pressure then disconnect negative battery cable.
2. Drain fuel tank.
3. Raise the rear seat by hand and disconnect the electrical harness connector under the right side of the seat, remove the side cover to gain acess.
4. Disconnect all lines.
5. Remove cap assembly, rubber fuel filler receiver and filler guard.
6. Support tank, remove tank strap holding bolts.
7. Remove tank assembly from car.
8. Remove fuel pump bracket plate and fuel pump as an assembly.
9. Remove pump bracket, rubber cushion and fuel pump sock or filter.
10. To install, reverse the removal procedures. Be careful, to push the lower side of the fuel pump, together with the rubber cushion, into the fuel pump bracket.

## Carburetor

The carburetor is a 2 barrel downdraft type composed of a low-speed side (primary) and a high-speed side (secondary) which are integrated into a single unit.

## REMOVAL & INSTALLATION

### G180Z Engine

1. Disconnect the PCV hose from the cylinder head cover.
2. Disconnect the ECS hose from the air cleaner body.
3. Disconnect the AIR hose from the air pump.
4. Remove the bolts attaching the air cleaner and loosen the clamp bolts.
5. Lift the air cleaner slightly and disconnect the TCA vacuum hose and air duct, then remove the air cleaner.
6. Disconnect the vacuum signal hose from the EGR valve.
7. Disconnect the electrical leads connector.
8. Disconnect the accelerator cable.
9. Disconnect the fuel line at the carburetor.

**CAUTION**

***Fire hazard. Use rags to catch any fuel and be careful with work light.***

10. Disconnect the ECS hose from the carburetor.
11. Remove the four nuts and lockwashers securing the carburetor to the intake manifold and remove the carburetor.
12. Installation is the reverse of removal. Clean all gasket surfaces before installation and always use a new gasket.
13. Start the engine and adjust the carburetor. Any time the carburetor is removed for inspection or overhaul, the emissions levels must be reset using an exhaust gas analyzer.

### 4XC1-U Engine

1. Disconnect the negative battery terminal from the battery.
2. Remove the air cleaner.
3. Disconnect the harness connector and hoses.
4. Remove the accelerator cable from the carburetor.
5. Remove the bolts securing the carburetor to the intake manifold. Remove the carburetor and place a cover over the intake manifold.
6. To install, reverse the removal procedures and torque carburetor fixing bolts to 7.2 ft. lbs. then start the engine and check for leaks.

## LINKAGE ADJUSTMENTS

When the primary throttle valve is opened to an angle of 47 degrees (about half way) the adjust plate, which is interlocked with the primary throttle valve, is brought into contact with the kick lever. When the primary throttle valve is opened further, the return plate is pulled apart from the stopper, allowing the secondary throttle valve to open. To measure just when the secondary is opening:

1. Measure the clearance between the primary throttle valve and the wall of the throttle chamber at the center of the throttle valve when the adjust plate is brought into contact with the kick lever.

2. Standard clearance is 0.24–0.30 in. and 0.23 in. on the I-Mark (FWD). If necessary, make adjustments by bending the kick lever.

## PRIMARY THROTTLE VALVE OPENING ADJUSTMENT

### *G180Z Engine*

Check and make necessary adjustment so that the primary throttle valve is opened, by means of the fast idle adjusting screw, to an angle of 16 degrees MT or 18 degrees AT when the choke valve is completely closed.

1. Close the choke valve completely and measure the clearance between the throttle valve and the wall of the throttle valve chamber at the center part of the valve.

2. Standard clearance is 0.059–0.069 in. for AT and 0.050–0.059 for MT.

### *4XC1-U*

Check and make necessary adjustment so that the primary throttle valve is opened, by means of the fast idle adjusting screw, to an angle of 20 degrees AT and 18 degrees MT.

1. Check the angle of the primary throttle valve in the second stage of the fast idle cam. Set the choke valve to full open.

2. Open the throttle valve slowly while pushing the choke valve lightly in the closing direction.

3. Set the choke valve to the second stage of the fast idle cam. Check the primary throttle valve angle. The valve angle and clearance's are as follows:

a. The standard angle A/T – is 20 degrees from the horizontal plane.

b. The standard angle M/T – is 18 degrees from the horizontal plane.

c. The standard clearance A/T – is 0.0272 in.

d. The standard clearance M/T – is 0.0214 in.

4. Adjust the fast idle screw if it is not at the prescribed angle.

## FLOAT LEVEL ADJUSTMENT

The fuel level is normal if it is within the marks on the window glass of the float chamber when the engine is off. If the fuel level is outside of the lines, make adjustment by bending the float seat. The needle valve should have an effective stroke of about 0.59 in. (1.5mm).

The needle valve is adjusted by bending the float stopper, but accomplishing that simple task requires the removal and disassembly of the carburetor. See the Unit Repair Section.

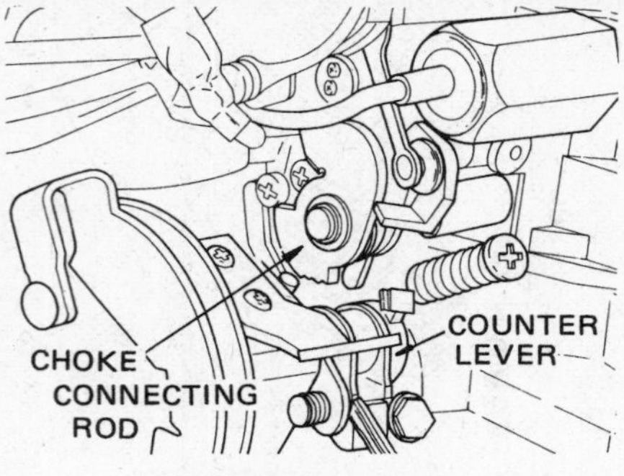

Choke components

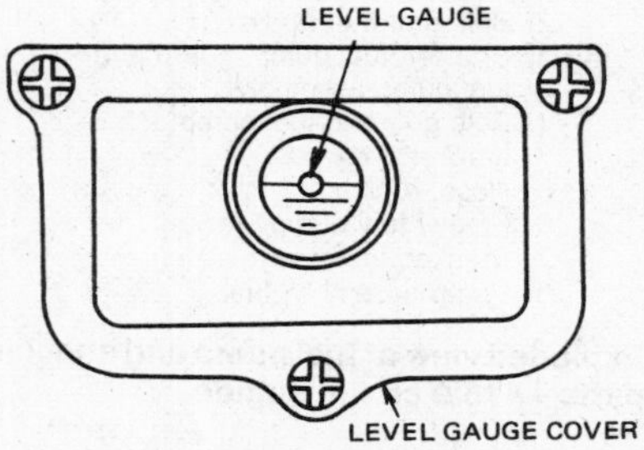

Checking float level

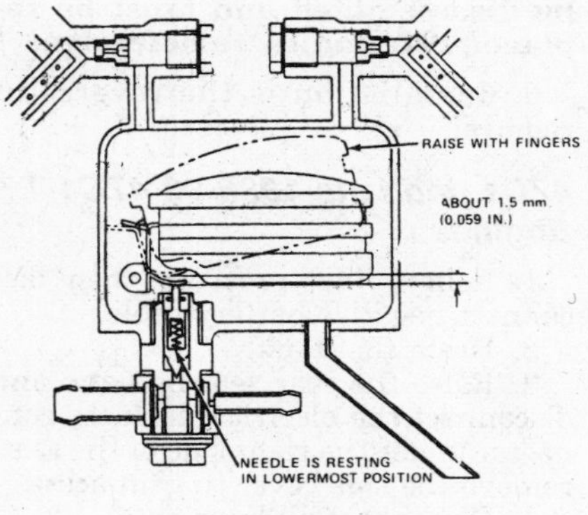

Adjusting float level

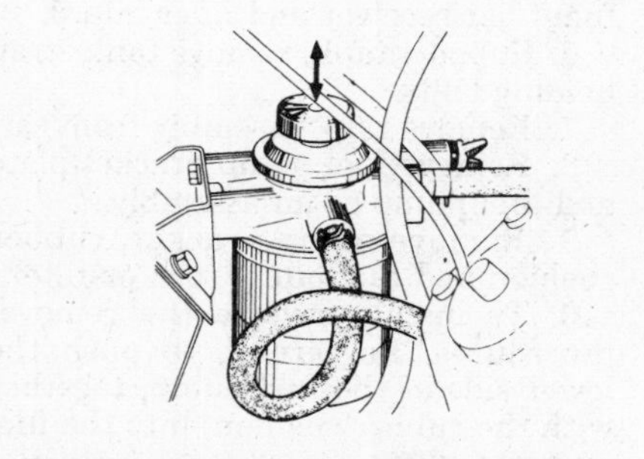
Diesel fuel filter with priming pump (arrows)

## AUTOMATIC CHOKE ADJUSTMENT (FAST IDLE)

The automatic choke assembly incorporates a themostatic spring which automatically works in response to a variation in the ambient temperature to control the choke valve, thereby facilitating engine starting. The choke valve is set to a position by the action of the thermostatic spring when the accelerator pedal is fully depressed and released before starting. When the engine starts, manifold vacuum is transmitted to the choke breaker diaphragm unit. This opens the choke valve to a point where the engine will run without stalling.

When the engine is started, the current flowing through the heater relay and heater element causes the bimetal tension spring to flex, causing the choke valve to open. The throttle valve does not return automatically to a position for engine idling but its opening angle is reduced by the action of the fast idle cam when the accelerator pedal is depressed and released while the engine is running at fast idle and finally causing the throttle valve to return to the idling position as the fast idle adjust screw releases from the fast idle cam. Thus, the engine is made to run at normal idling speed by depressing and releasing the accelerator pedal when fast idling is no longer needed.

## OVERHAUL

**For all carburetor overhaul procedures, please refer to Carburetor Service in the Unit Repair**

# Fuel Injection

**Due to the complex nature of modern fuel injection systems, comprehensive diagnosis and testing procedures fall outside the confines of this repair manual. For complete information on fuel injection diagnosis, testing and repair procedures please refer to *"Chilton's Guide To Fuel Injection And Feedback Carburetors"***

# DIESEL ENGINE FUEL SYSTEM

## Fuel Filter

### REPLACEMENT

1. Disconnect the water separator

Removing the water separator sensor

sensor wiring at the connector and the water drain hose.

2. Using special filter wrench J–22700 or equivalent, remove the fuel filter. Be careful when removing the filter cartridge so as not to spill fuel within the cartridge.

3. Drain the cartridge into a suitable drain pan and remove the sensor from the filter cartridge.

4. Install the sensor on the new filter and apply some clean diesel fuel to the O-ring before installation.

5. Apply clean diesel fuel to the filter O-ring and turn in the filter until the sealing surface is brought in contact with the O-ring. Then tighten the filter ⅔ of a turn.

6. Connect the sensor connector and install the water drain hose.

7. Fill the filter cartridge with fuel by using the priming pump handle 30–40 times. The force needed to operate the priming pump increases when the filter is full.

8. Start the engine and check for any fuel leaks.

### DRAINING THE WATER FROM THE SYSTEM

1. Place a suitable container at the end of the vinyl hose under the drain plug of the water separator.

2. Loosen the drain plug approximately four turns.

3. Pump the priming pump ten times by hand. Tighten the drain plug and continue to pump the priming pump another ten times.

4. Start the engine and check for fuel leaks. Also check to see that the filter indicator light has turned off.

## Injection Nozzle

### REMOVAL & INSTALLATION

1. Loosen the screws attaching the injection pipe clips.

2. Remove the sleeve nut attaching injection pipe and separate the injection pipe.

3. Remove the injection nozzle assembly, corrugated washer and nozzle gasket.

4. Installation is the reverse order

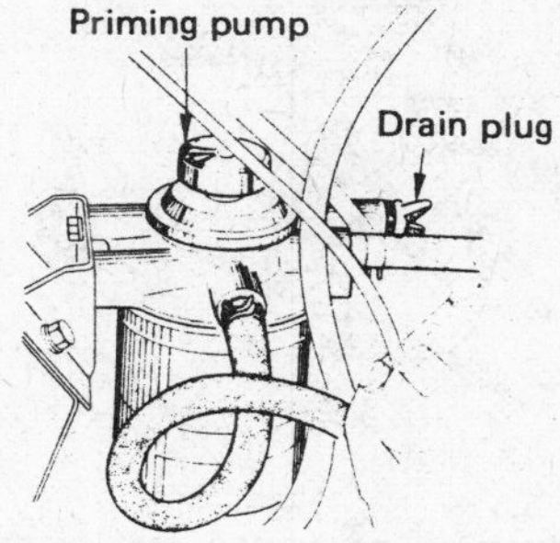


Priming pump and drain plug location

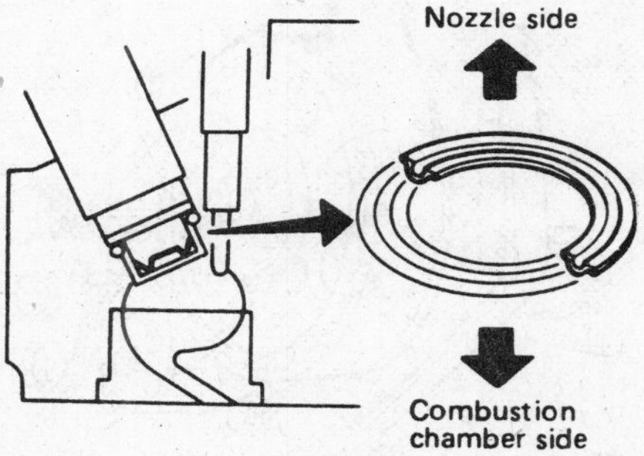


Installation of the injection nozzle

of the removal procedure. Do not reuse the old corrugated washer. The new corrugated washer should be installed with the blue collar painted side turned toward the nozzle. Torque the nozzle assembly to 47–61 ft. lbs.

**NOTE: The diesel injection pump is an extremely complicated device, built to tolerances of millionths of an inch. Servicing should be left to a qualified diesel specialist. Never use cold water to clean a hot engine or the diesel injection pump may seize.**

## Diesel Injection Pump

### REMOVAL & INSTALLATION

1. Remove the timing belt as previously described.

2. Remove the nut attaching the injection pump pulley.

3. Remove the pulley using a suitable puller and remove the lock bolt.

4. Disconnect the fuel cut-off solenoid valve switch wiring and tachometer sensor wiring, if equipped.

5. Disconnect the accelerator cable from the pump lever. (A/T models only).

6. Disconnect the vacuum hose from the actuator of the fast idle device.

7. Disconnect the fuel hoses at the injection pump.

8. Remove the 6 screws attaching the injection pipe clips and remove the clips.

9. Remove the 8 sleeve nuts attaching the injection pipes and remove the pipes.

10. Remove the 4 bolts attaching the pump rear bracket and remove the rear bracket. Disconnect the spring of the control lever.

11. Remove the 2 nuts attaching the injection pipe flange and remove the injection pump together with the fast idle device.

To install

12. Install the injection pump together with the fast idle device by aligning the notched line on the flange with the line on the front plate.

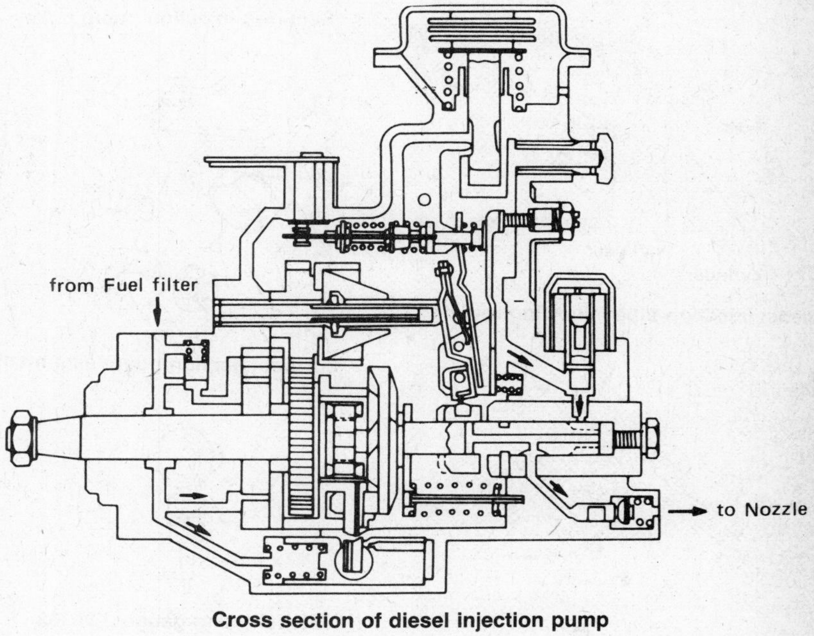


Cross section of diesel injection pump

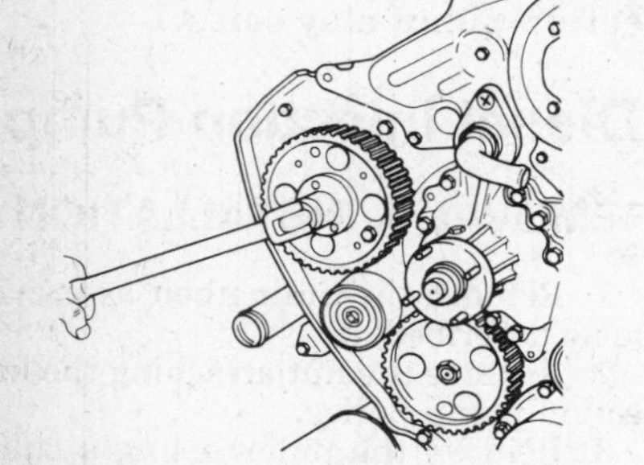

Removing nut on injection pump pulley

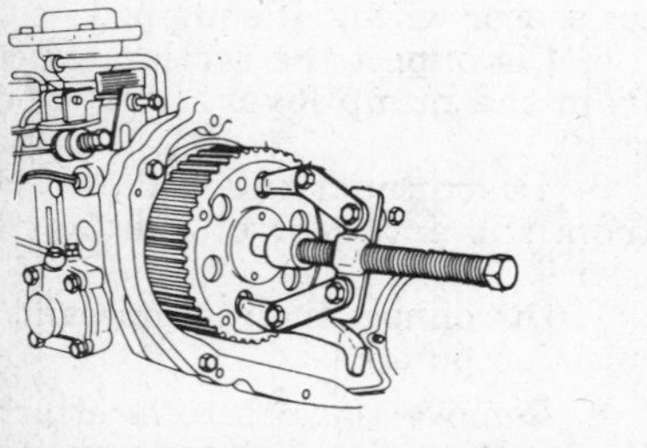

Using a puller to remove injection pump pulley

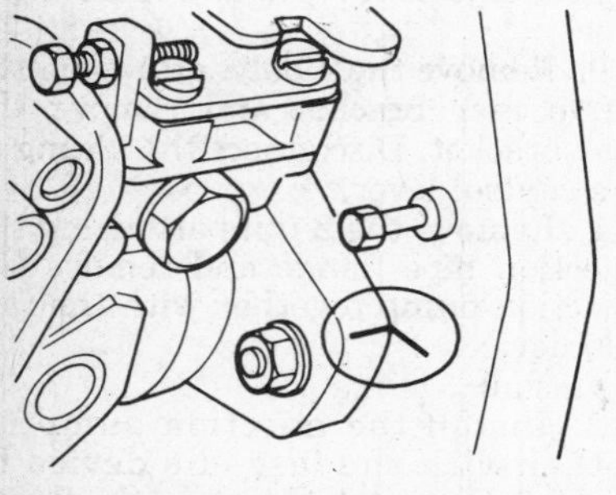

Aligning marks on injection pump and front plate

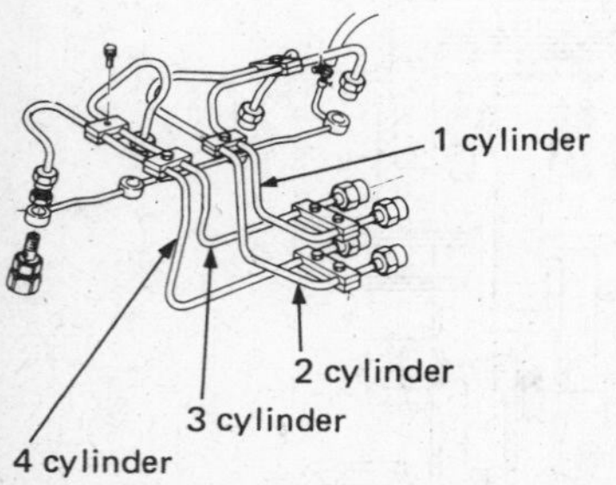


Diesel injection pipes showing routing

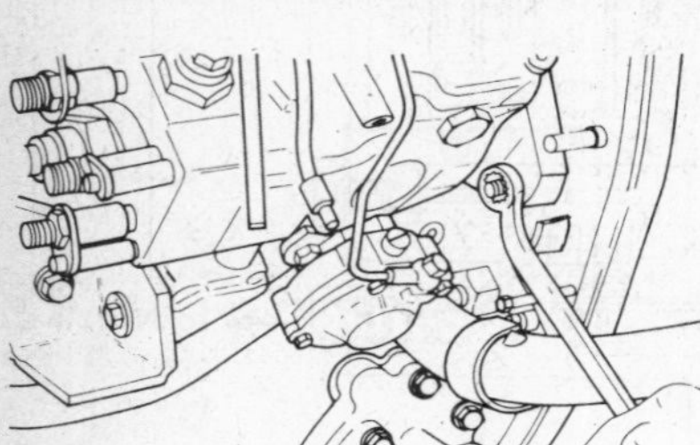

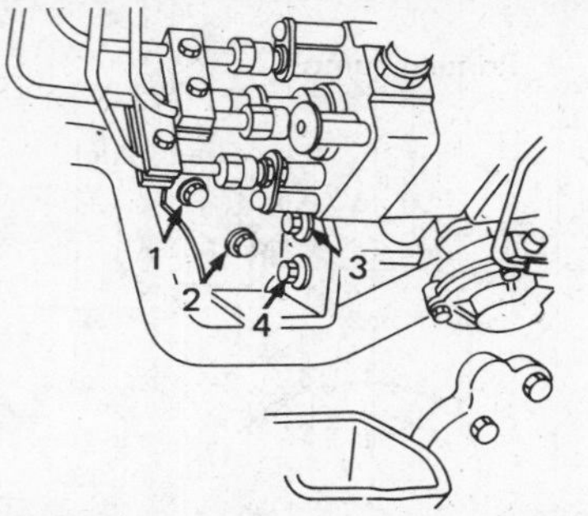


Bolt tightening sequence for injection pump mount

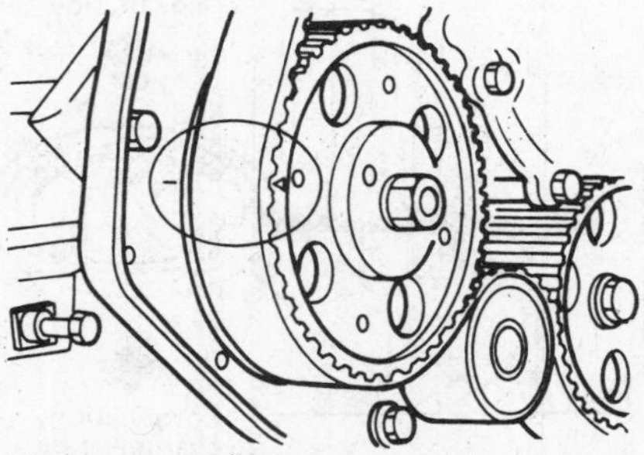

Timing mark alignment for injection pump pulley

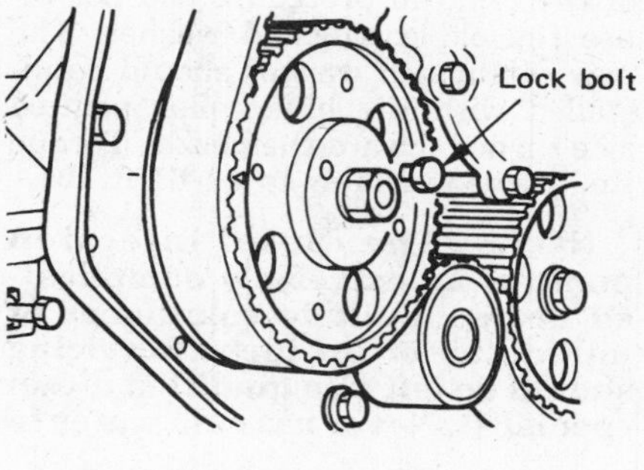


Securing injection pump pulley

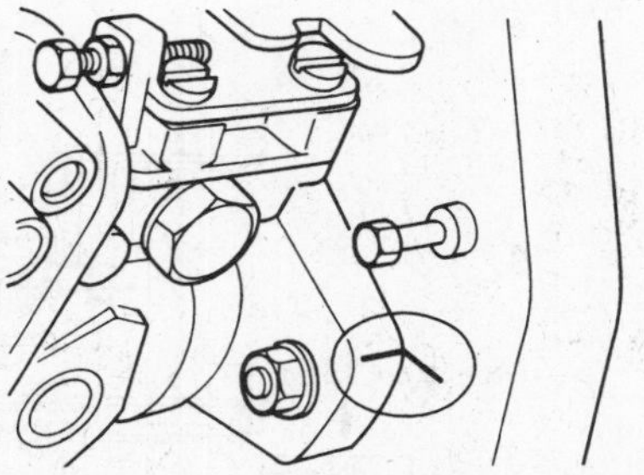

Correct injection pump alignment

Static timing gauge J-29763

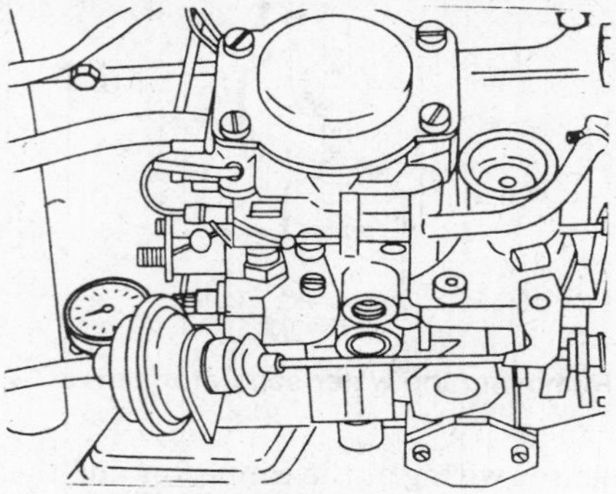

Installing the static gauge

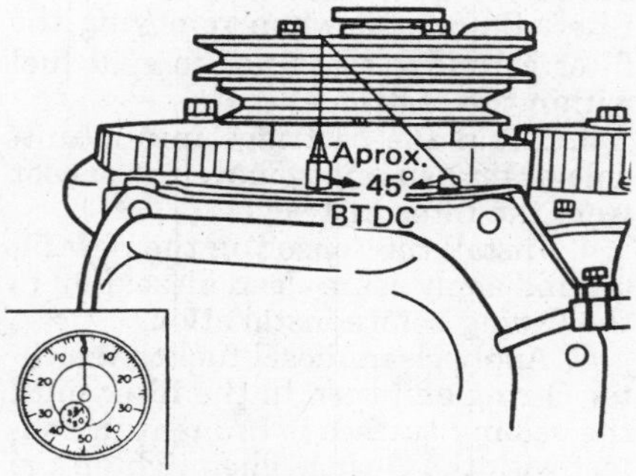


Calibrating the dial indicator

13. Tighten the bolts in sequence. No clearance should be between the rear bracket and injection pump bracket.

14. Install the injection pump pulley by aligning it with the key groove. Align the mark on the pulley with the mark on the front plate, the tighten the nut using the lock bolt to prevent the pulley from turning.

15. Reinstall the timing belt as previously described and set the injection timing.

16. Install the injection pipes, clips and the vacuum hose for the actuator. Connect all control cables and wiring.

17. Fill the filter with fuel by operating the priming handle several times. Adjust the idle speed.

## Diesel Injection Timing

### ADJUSTMENT

1. Check that the notched line on the injection pump flange is in alignment with the notched line on the injection pump front bracket.

2. Bring the piston in No. 1 cylinder to TDC on the compression stroke by turning the crankshaft as necessary.

3. With the timing pulley housing cover removed, check that the timing belt is properly tensioned and that the timing marks are aligned (see timing belt adjustment).

4. Disconnect the injection pipe from the injection pump and remove the distributor head screw, then in-

stall a static timing gauge (special tool J-29763).

5. Use a wrench to hold the delivery holder when loosening the sleeve nuts on the injection pump side.

6. Bring the piston in No. 1 cylinder to a point 45–60 degrees BTDC by turning the crankshaft, then calibrate the dual indicator to zero.

7. Turn the crankshaft pulley slightly in both directions and check that gauge indication is stable.

8. Turn the crankshaft in the normal direction of rotation (clockwise) and take the reading on the dial indicator when the timing mark on the crankshaft pulley is in alignment with the pointer.

9. If the reading on the dial indicator deviates from the specified range, hold the crankshaft in position 12 degrees BTDC and loosen the two nuts on the injection pump flange.

10. Move the injection pump to a point where the dial indicator gives a reading of 0.5mm (0.020 in.) then tighten the pump flange nuts to 42–52 ft. lbs.

# MANUAL TRANSMISSION

## REMOVAL & INSTALLATION

### *I-Mark (RWD)*

1. Disconnect the battery ground cable.
2. Remove the shift lever assembly from inside the car.
3. Loosen the clutch cable adjusting nuts at the left side of the engine compartment.
4. Remove the upper starter mounting nut and disconnect the starter wiring.
5. Raise the car and safely support it.
6. Remove the driveshaft.
7. Disconnect the speedometer cable.
8. Remove the clutch cable.
9. Remove the starter lower bolt and remove the starter.
10. Disconnect the exhaust pipe from the manifold.
11. Remove the exhaust pipe from the manifold.
12. Remove the flywheel inspection cover.
13. Remove the rear transmission support mounting bolt.
14. Support the transmission under the case and remove the rear transmission support from the frame.
15. Lower the transmission approximately four inches. Disconnect the back-up light and coasting fuel cut-off switch (gasoline models only) wires.
16. Remove the transmission housing-to-engine block bolts.

**CAUTION**

***Make sure transmission is supported by a suitable jack.***

17. Move the transmission slowly back and lower it clear of the car.
18. Installation is the reverse of removal. Lubricate the drive gear shaft spline with a light coat of grease before installing.
19. Adjust the clutch as described in the clutch section. Fill the transmission with SAE 30 engine oil until it begins to run out the filler hole.

### *Impulse*

1. Disconnect the negative battery cable. Raise and support the vehicle safely.
2. Drain the transmission oil.
3. Remove the gearshift control lever knob, cover assembly and console.
4. Disconnect the front exhaust pipe.
5. Disconnect the driveshaft.
6. Disconnect the speedometer cable assembly.
7. Disconnect the clutch slave cylinder.
8. Remove the cover under the transmission case.
9. Position a jack under the transmission case, remove the engine rear mounting nuts, lower the transmission case slightly, then remove the bolts attaching the quadrant box cover to the transmission case.
10. Disconnect all electrical harness connectors.
11. Remove the control box assembly.
12. Remove the transmission to engine retaining bolts.

**NOTE: The starter assembly is mounted in position with the bolts that are used for installing the transmission assembly to the**

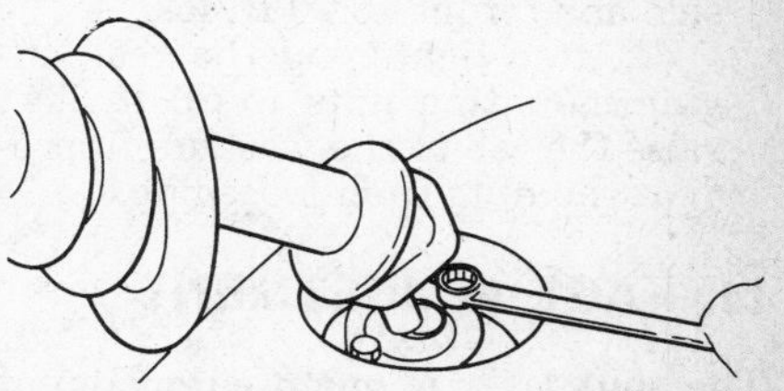

Typical removal of manual shifter assembly—except Impulse

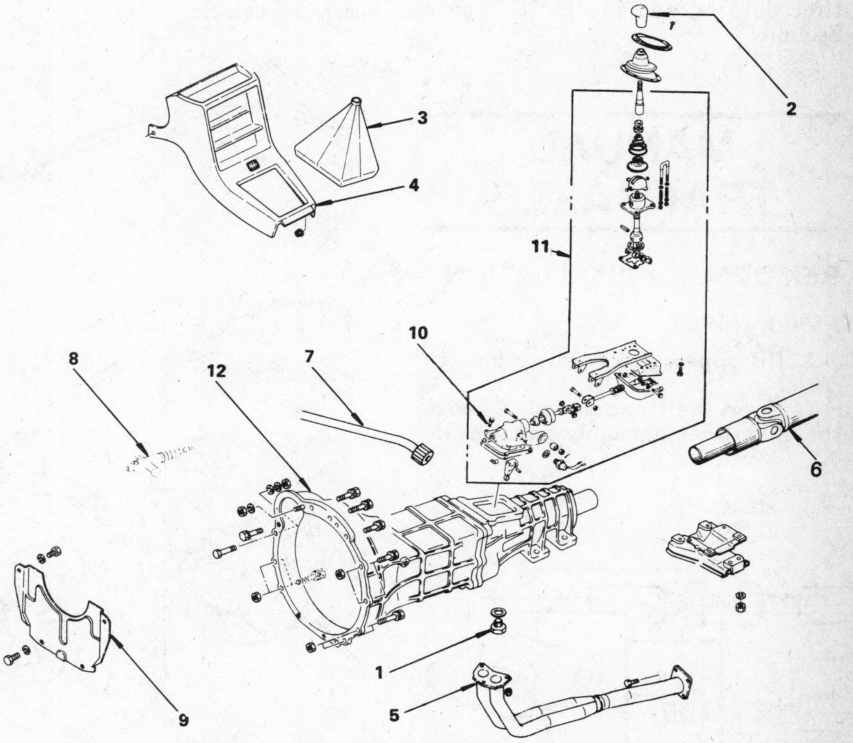


1. Plug; magnet, oil drain
2. Knob; gear shift control lever
3. Cover assembly; shift lever
4. Console assembly
5. Pipe assembly; exhaust front
6. Shaft assembly; propeller
7. Cable assembly; speedometer
8. Cylinder assembly; slave
9. Cover; under, transmission case
10. Bolts; quadrant cover to case
11. Box assembly; control
12. Transmission assembly

Transmission removal and installation—Impulse

**engine. It may be necessary to move the starter assembly forward to prevent it from falling out when the bolts are removed.**

13. Installation is the reverse of removal with the following exceptions:

a. Position the transmission assembly with the speedometer cable fitting face turned downward and slide the assembly forward, guiding the gear shaft into the pilot bearing.

b. Install and tighten the quadrant box cover to the transmission case bolts with a gasket fitted in position between the quadrant box cover and the transmission case, then install the engine rear mounting.

c. When reconnecting the propeller shaft, install the bolts from the extension shaft side and the nuts and washers on the propeller shaft side and torque to 20 ft. lbs.

d. After tightening the rear engine mounting nuts to 20 ft. lbs., raise the tab of the washers to prevent the nuts from loosening.

## LINKAGE ADJUSTMENT

The shift lever is mounted on top of the transmission extension housing and requires no adjustment. For further details, see the Unit Repair Section.

# MANUAL TRANSAXLE

## REMOVAL & INSTALLATION

### *I-Mark (FWD)*

1. Disconnect the negative battery cable.
2. Drain the transaxle oil. Remove the shift lever assembly from inside the vehicle. Remove the upper transaxle to engine retaining bolts.
3. Remove the engine hood and the negative cable from the transaxle unit.
4. Remove the air duct assembly. Disconnect and tag the wiring connectors from the transaxle.
5. Disconnect the speedometer cable from the transaxle and disconnect the clutch cable from the transaxle.
6. Disconnect the shift cables from the transaxle.
7. Raise the front of the vehicle and support it safely with suitable jack stands. Remove the front wheel assemblies.
8. Disconnect the right control arm end at the knuckle. Remove the left tension rod with bracket. Disconnect both tie rod ends at the knuckle using tool J-21687-02 or equivalent.
9. Use a suitable tool and pull out the drive shafts. Be careful with the transaxle oil seals when pulling out the drive shafts. Remove the motor mount bolts.
10. Using a suitable engine lift, raise the engine. Remove the bolts of the center beam and then lower the engine and slant the engine from the engine support fixture.
11. Remove the mounting bolts of the clutch housing to engine. Remove the transaxle assembly from underneath the vehicle.

**NOTE: In the case of the turbocharged model, removal of the transaxle assembly is made possible only after the engine foot of the engine mounting has been removed.**

12. Installation is the reverse order of the removal procedure. Use these following torque specifications during installation:

a. Clutch housing to engine bolts – 56 ft. lbs.

b. Center beam bolts – 56 ft. lbs.

c. Driveshaft/tie rod to knuckle – 42 ft. lbs.

d. Tension rod bracket bolts – 48 ft. lbs.

e. Right control arm end bolts – 80 ft. lbs.

f. Front wheel lugs aluminum – 87 ft. lbs. and steel are – 65 ft. lbs.

## LINKAGE ADJUSTMENT

### *I-Mark (FWD)*

1. Place the transaxle in neutral. Turn the adjusting nuts on the left side of the shift housing, until the shift changer lever is at the right angle to the pivot case, as viewed from the side of the gear control.
2. After the adjustment tighten those two adjusting nuts securely.

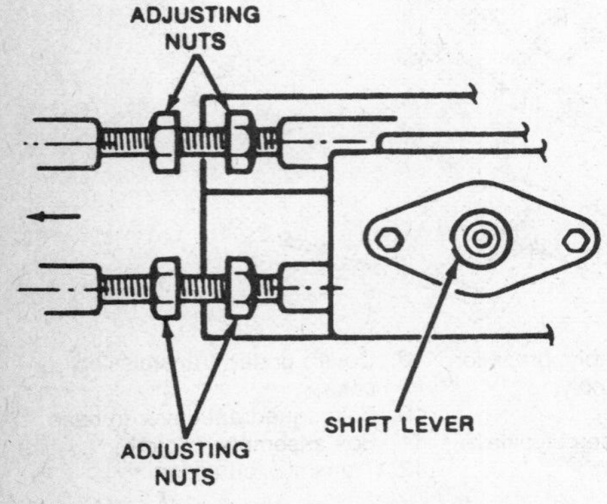


Making the shift linkage adjustment

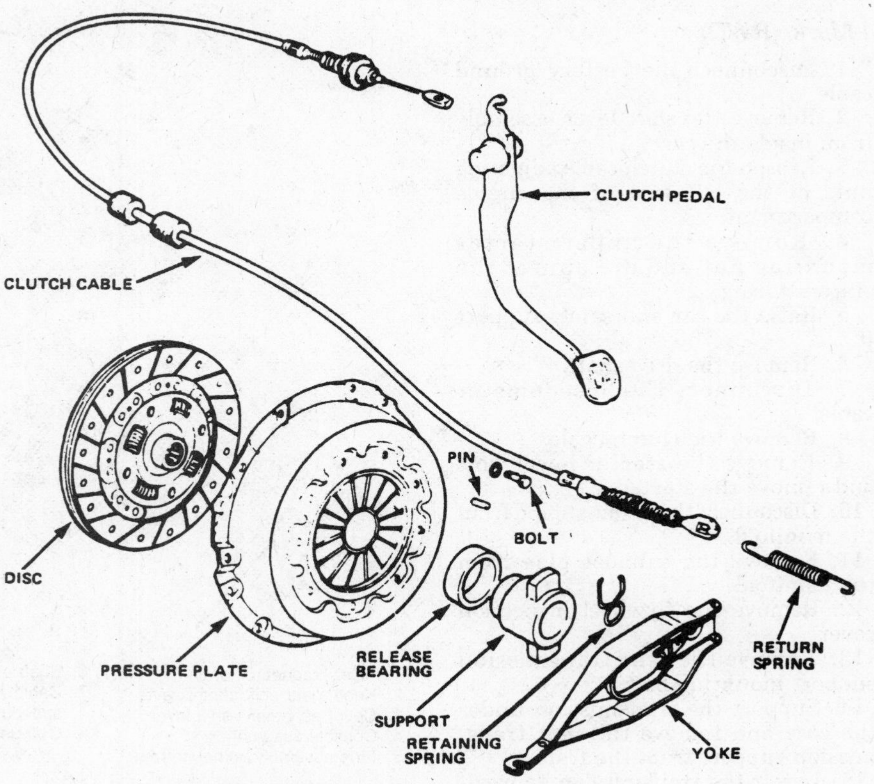


Exploded view of clutch components—all except Impulse

3. Turn the adjusting nuts on the right side of the shift housing, until the shift change lever is at right angle to the pivot case as viewed from the front or rear gear control. After the adjustment tighten those two adjusting nuts securely.

# CLUTCH

## REMOVAL & INSTALLATION

1. Remove the transmission as previously described.
2. Mark the clutch assembly position on the flywheel with paint or a scribe.
3. Install clutch aligning tool J–24547 or equivalent and remove the six retaining bolts. Remove the clutch assembly.
4. Remove the release bearing-to-yoke retaining springs, and then remove the release bearing with its support.
5. Remove the release yoke from the transmission ball stud.
6. Wash all metal parts of the clutch assembly, except the release bearing and friction plate in suitable cleaning solution.

**CAUTION**

***Soaking the release bearing in cleaning solution will ruin the bearing, soaking the clutch plate in cleaning solution will damage the facings.***

7. Inspect all parts for wear or deep scoring. Replace any parts that show excessive wear.
8. Installation is the reverse of removal. Lubricate the ball stud when installing the release yoke. Align the clutch with scribe marks and use an aligning tool to assure proper positioning of the clutch.

# Clutch Cable

## REMOVAL & INSTALLATION

### *I-Mark (RWD)*

1. Loosen the clutch lock and adjusting nuts.
2. Raise the car and support it safely with jackstands.
3. From under the car, remove the clutch cable from the release yoke and slide it forward through the retaining bracket.
4. Disconnect the cable from the pedal and remove.
5. Installation is the reverse of removal.

### *I-Mark (FWD)*

1. Disconnect the negative battery cable.
2. Raise and support safely the front of the vehicle.
3. Disconnect the clutch cable from the clutch housing and transaxle. Remove all necessary snap rings and lock nuts to free the clutch cable.
4. Remove the clutch cable from the clutch pedal and pull the cable out from the engine compartment.
5. Installation is the reverse of the removal procedure.

## ADJUSTMENT

### *I-Mark (RWD)*

1. Loosen the lock and adjusting nuts on the clutch cable.
2. Pull the cable forward toward the front of the car to take up slack.
3. Turn the adjusting nut inward until the clutch pedal free travel is 5/8 in.
4. Tighten the locknut and check the adjustment.

**NOTE: Correct pedal height from the floor is 6.2 in. (157.5mm), adjust the clutch switch to obtain, then lock the switch in position with the lock nut.**

### *I-Mark (FWD)*

1. Loosen the clutch cable adjusting nut and pull the cable to the rear of the vehicle until the adjustment nut turns freely.
2. Turn the adjusting nut either clockwise or counterclockwise to adjust the cable length.
3. When the clutch pedal free play travel reaches 0.59 ± 0.20 in. release the cable.
4. Check the adjustment and then tighten the lock nut.

# Clutch Master Cylinder

## REMOVAL & INSTALLATION

### *Impulse*

1. Disconnect the negative battery cable.
2. Disconnect clutch pedal return spring and joint pin from clutch pedal.
3. Remove oil line from rear of clutch master cylinder.
4. Remove two hold down nuts from inside of passenger compartment.
5. Remove clutch master cylinder from engine compartment.
6. Installation is the reverse order of the removal procedure. Hydraulic system must be bleed to complete installation.

# Clutch Slave Cylinder

## REMOVAL & INSTALLATION

### *Impulse*

1. Disconnect the negative battery cable.
2. Raise and support the front of the vehicle safely.
3. Remove and cap the hydraulic lines from the slave cylinder.
4. Remove the slave cylinder push rod from the clutch release bearing fork.
5. Remove the slave cylinder retaining bolts and remove the slave cylinder.
6. Installation is the reverse order of the removal procedure.

## ADJUSTMENT AND BLEEDING

1. Loosen the clutch switch lock nut, and turn the clutch switch so that the clearance between the clutch switch and the clutch pedal is 0.020–0.059 in.
2. After the adjustment, check that the push rod is in contact with the piston in the master cylinder. The clutch pedal free play and pedal stroke are self-adjusted.
3. To bleed the slave cylinder, fill the clutch fluid reservoir to the specified level with brake fluid and keep it filled during the bleeding procedure.
4. Remove the bleeder rubber cap and connect a vinyl pipe to the bleeder and hold the free end of the pipe in a transparent container.
5. Pump the clutch pedal several times and hold the pedal in the depressed stage. With the pedal depressed, loosen the bleeder on the slave cylinder a ½ of turn and then tighten it immediately.
6. Repeat the above step until the air bubbles are no longer a part of the brake fluid being bled.
7. After completion of the bleeding operation, check for pedal free play and clutch disengagement, then check the brake fluid in the clutch reservoir.

**NOTE: Removing the clutch master cylinder is only a simple matter of disconnecting the hydraulic lines and removing the retaining bolts.**

# AUTOMATIC TRANSMISSION

## REMOVAL & INSTALLATION

### *All Models*

1. Disconnect the battery cables

and raise the vehicle. Make sure it is supported safely.

2. Remove the transmission dipstick. Drain the fluid into a suitable container and discard.

3. Remove the starter toward the front of the vehicle.

4. Disconnect the drive shaft from the central joint, then slide the propeller shaft rearward and remove it.

5. Disconnect the shift control rod from the shift lever.

6. Disconnect the speedometer cable.

7. Remove the exhaust pipe bracket.

8. Disconnect the oil cooler lines by loosening the joint nuts at the transmission.

**NOTE: Secure the cooler lines closer to the body to avoid damage during transmission removal.**

9. Remove the four bolts attaching the converter housing lower cover and remove the cover.

10. Remove the lower cover on the front part of the engine to permit turning of the engine and torque converter.

11. Remove the six bolts fastening the torque converter and drive plate by turning the crankshaft pulley.

12. Remove the bolt on the center part of the rear mounting from bracket.

13. Raise the engine and transmission using a suitable jack and support the rear end of the engine to hold it in position when the transmission is removed.

14. Remove the four bolts or nuts securing the rear mounting frame bracket, then remove the bracket.

15. Lower the transmission slightly then remove the bolts and nuts fixing the converter housing, then remove the transmission toward the rear.

**CAUTION**

***When removing the transmission, exercise care so as not to let the torque converter slide out.***

16. Installation is the reverse of removal. Refill the transmission with fluid according to the capacities chart. Adjust the throttle valve control cable.

## PAN REMOVAL AND INSTALLATION

### *All Models*

1. Disconnect the battery cables and raise the vehicle. Make sure it is supported safely.

2. Place a suitable transmission jack under the transmission. Remove the bolts and nuts retaining the transmission frame support rail. Slide the support rail back so as to let the transmission tailshaft rest upon the support rail.

3. Remove several of the transmission pan retaining bolts and loosen all of the others so as to let the fluid drain out into a suitable drain pan.

**NOTE: Some models may be equipped with a drain bolt in the transmission pan. If so equipped drain the oil from it and when reinstalling it, torque it to 29 ft. lbs.**

4. Once the fluid has drained sufficiently, remove the remaining transmission pan bolts and remove the pan from the transmission.

5. Remove the filter retaining bolts and remove the transmission oil filter.

6. Install a new transmission oil filter and install the filter retaining screws. Torgue the screws to 5 ft. lbs.

7. Remove the old gasket material from the transmission pan and mating surface. Remove the oil pan magnet and clean the magnet and oil pan in a suitable solvent. Be sure to dry using compressed air.

8. Apply a suitable bead of sealant to the transmission gasket mating surface and install the transmission oil pan. Install the transmission oil pan retaining bolts and torque them to 5–10 ft. lbs.

9. Complete this procedure by reverseing the removal order.

## THROTTLE CABLE ADJUSTMENT

### *I-Mark (RWD) and Impulse*

1. Check that the throttle valve is held closed completely.

2. Adjust the setting of the adjustment nut as necessary so that the clearance between the inner cable stopper and the end of the rubber boot on the outer cable is adjusted to 0.032–0.059 in. (0.8–1.5mm) the specification for the diesel models is 0–0.04 in.

3. Open the throttle valve fully and check that the inner cable stroke is within the range of 1.30–1.36 in. (33–34mm).

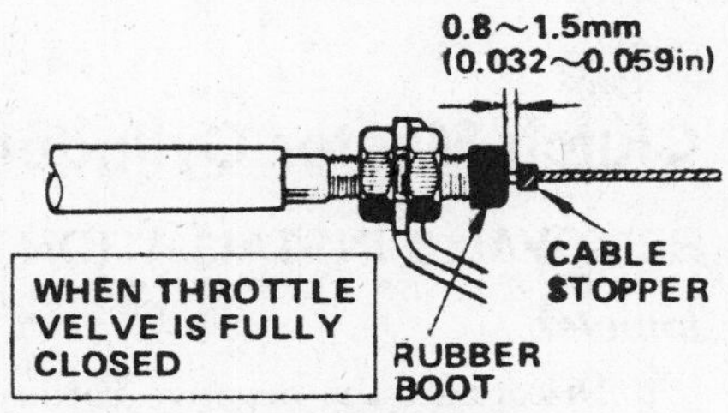


Throttle valve cable adjustment—gasoline engine

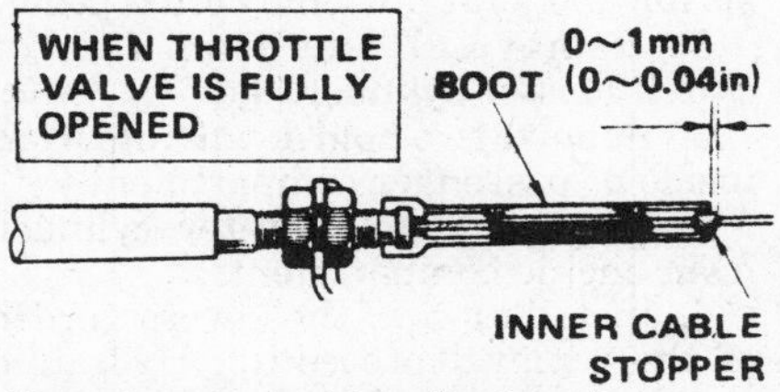


Throttle valve cable adjustment—diesel engine

## SHIFT LEVER POSITION ADJUSTMENT

### *I-Mark (RWD) and Impulse*

1. Remove the adjustment nut fastening the control lever and select lever link.

2. Move the manual valve lever forward to stop, then return to position of Neutral (third stop). With the transmission in Neutral, check to make sure the outside manual valve shift lever is in the vertical position.

3. Hold the manual shaft in that position and place the shift lever in the Neutral position.

4. To remove the play, tighten the adjusting nuts with the lower lever (control shaft lever) on the shift lever pushed rearward together with the shift control lever and tighten the adjust nut.

5. Check that the control lever moves smoothly and that position indicator works correctly.

## NEUTRAL SAFETY SWITCH OR INHIBITOR SWITCH ADJUSTMENT

### *I-Mark (RWD) and Impulse*

**NOTE: On 1988–90 Impulse models inhibitor switch is mounted on transmission instead of the shifter assembly.**

1. Loosen two screws holding switch to shift lever and set lever in Neutral position.

2. Bring the center of the switch slide bar into alignment with the line on the steel case of the switch indicating **NEUTRAL** position. Tighten the retaining screws.

3. Check adjustment by starting car it should only start in **NEUTRAL** or **PARK**.

# AUTOMATIC TRANSAXLE

## REMOVAL & INSTALLATION

### *I-Mark (FWD)*

1. Disconnect the negative battery cable.

2. Remove the air duct tube from the air cleaner.

3. At the transaxle, disconnect the shift cable, speedometer cable, vacuum diaphragm hose, engine wiring harness clamp and the ground cable.

4. At the left fender, disconnect the inhibitor switch and the kickdown solenoid wiring connectors.

5. Disconnect the oil cooler lines from the transaxle.

6. Remove the 3 upper transaxle-to-engine mounting bolts and raise and support the vehicle safely.

7. Remove both front wheels and the left front fender splash shield.

8. Disconnect the right control arm end at the knuckle. Remove the left tension rod with bracket. Disconnect both tie rod ends at the knuckle using tool J–21687–02 or equivalent.

9. Use a suitable tool and pull out the drive shafts. Be careful with the transaxle oil seals when pulling out the drive shafts. Remove the motor mount bolts.

10. Using a suitable engine lift, raise the engine. Remove the bolts of the center beam and then remove the 3 upper transaxle to engine mounting bolts.

11. Remove the flywheel dust cover and the converter-to-flywheel attaching bolts. Lower the engine and slant the engine from the engine support fixture.

12. Remove the transaxle rear mount through bolt.

13. Disconnect the starter wiring and the starter. Support the transaxle.

14. Remove the lower transaxle-to-engine mounting bolts and remove the transaxle.

15. Installation is the reverse order of the removal procedure. Use these following torque specifications during installation:

a. Transaxle assembly to engine bolts – 56 ft. lbs.

b. Center beam bolts – 56 ft. lbs.

c. Torque converter-to-flywheel bolts – 30 ft. lbs.

d. Lower engine mounts – 61 ft. lbs.

e. Driveshaft/tie rod to knuckle – 42 ft. lbs.

f. Tension rod bracket bolts – 48 ft. lbs.

g. Right control arm end bolts – 80 ft. lbs.

h. Front wheel lugs aluminum – 87 ft. lbs. and steel are – 65 ft. lbs.

### LINKAGE ADJUSTMENT

1. Loosen the adjusting nuts.

2. Place the transaxle and the shift lever in the Neutral position.

3. Turn the adjusting nuts until the shift lever is in the vertical position.

4. Tighten the adjusting nuts.

### KICKDOWN SWITCH ADJUSTMENT

1. Connect a multi-purpose tester to the kickdown switch solenoid terminals.

2. Make sure there is continuity when depressing the throttle pedal fully.

3. If continuity does not exist, adjust the kickdown switch. To adjust the switch, turn the switch so that continuity exists when depressing the throttle pedal more than ⅞ of its stroke.

### NEUTRAL SAFETY SWITCH OR INHIBITOR SWITCH ADJUSTMENT

The inhibitor switch is located on lower left side of the transmission no adjustment is possible.

# DRIVE AXLE

## Halfshafts

### REMOVAL & INSTALLATION

#### *I-Mark (FWD)*

1. Do not remove the hub assembly from the knuckle assembly unless it is absolutely necessary. Refer to the Front Hub Removal and Installation procedure in this section and remove the front hub. Disconnect the drive shaft from the knuckle using a plastic hammer. Support the axle shaft on a wire.

2. Remove the drain plug and drain the oil from the transaxle.

3. Place a large pry bar between the differential case and the inboard constant velocity joint. Pry the axle shaft from the differential case.

4. Remove the front axle assembly.

5. To install, reverse the removal procedure. When installing the axle shaft, press it into the differential case until it locks with snap ring.

### CV-JOINT OVERHAUL

**For all CV-joint overhaul procedures, please refer to CV-Joint Overhaul in the Unit Repair section.**

## Driveshaft and U-Joint

### REMOVAL & INSTALLATION

#### *I-Mark (RWD) and Impulse*

1. Raise the rear of the car and support it safely on jack stands at the rear jack brackets.

2. Disconnect the parking brake return spring from the rod.

3. Mark the mating parts of the U-joint and the drive pinion extension shaft flange.

4. Remove the bolts and nuts connecting the U-joint and the extension shaft flange.

5. Work the propeller shaft slightly forward, lower the rear end of the shaft and slide the assembly rearward. Remove the thrust spring from the front of the shaft.

6. Install a plug (or wrap a small plastic bag) on the transmission extension housing to prevent the loss of oil.

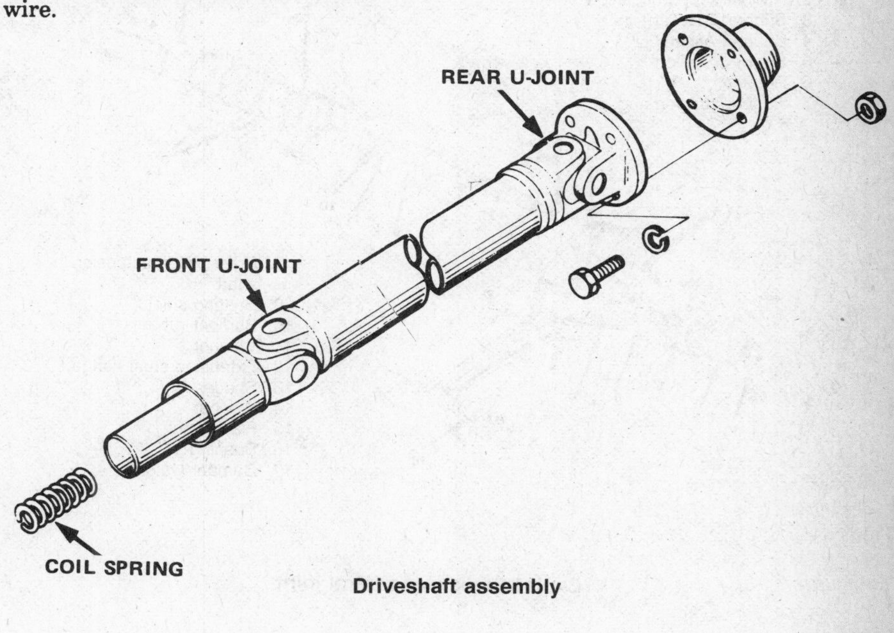


Driveshaft assembly

**CAUTION**

***When replacing any fasteners or attaching bolts, be sure to use the proper grade bolt. Substitution of lesser quality hardware could cause failure and serious damage.***

7. Installation is the reverse of removal. Make sure that the transmission rear seal is not damaged. Align all marks and torque the bolts to 18 ft. lbs.
8. Connect the parking brake return spring.

## Central Joint

### REMOVAL & INSTALLATION

#### *I-Mark (RWD) and Impulse*

1. Raise and support the rear of the car safely under the axle tubes.
2. Disconnect the parking brake return spring from the brake rod.

### BOLT TORQUE SPECIFICATIONS

| Location | Torque (ft. lbs.) |
|---|---|
| Extension shaft flange nut | 87 |
| Extension shaft flange-to-universal joint | 18 |
| Central joint support bracket-to-under body | 30 |
| Torque tube-to-carrier | 20 |
| Central joint support bracket-to-support cushion | 15 |
| Rubber cushion retainer-to-central joint support | 10 |

3. Unhook the exhaust system bracket from the central joint support bracket.
4. Mark the universal joint and flange, then disconnect the propeller shaft from the flange and support it out of the way.
5. Support the torque tube with a floor jack using minimum pressure.
6. Remove the central joint support bracket to underbody attaching bolts.
7. Allow the floor jack to lower the torque tube.
8. Disconnect the torque tube from the differential carrier by removing the attaching bolts.
9. Installation is the reverse of removal. Align all marks, torque all bolts to specifications.

## Rear Axle Shaft

### REMOVAL & INSTALLATION

#### *I-Mark (RWD) and Impulse*

1. Raise the car and support it safely with jackstands at the jack brackets.
2. Remove the wheel and brake drum assembly.
3. Working through the access holes in the axle shaft flange, remove the four nuts and washers that retain the axle shaft and bearing retainer.
4. Install an axle shaft puller (slaphammer) and remove the axle shaft.
5. To replace the bearing parts, first remove the retaining ring by cutting it off with a chisel. The bearing must be pressed off with a suitable bench press.
6. Installation is the reverse of removal. Press the new bearing on to the axle shaft with a suitable press.

1. Torque tube
2. Rubber support cushion
3. Support bracket
4. Bearing Assembly
5. Rubber cushion
6. Retainer
7. Rubber cushion ring

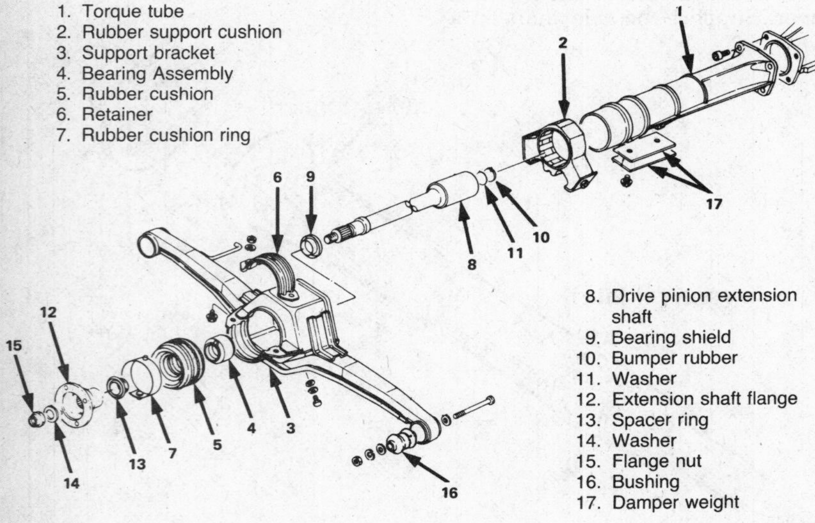


8. Drive pinion extension shaft
9. Bearing shield
10. Bumper rubber
11. Washer
12. Extension shaft flange
13. Spacer ring
14. Washer
15. Flange nut
16. Bushing
17. Damper weight

Exploded view of central joint

7. Check the axle shaft endplay by using a depth gauge to measure the depth of the rear axle bearing seat in the axle housing with the backing plate in place.
8. Measure the width of the bearing outer race. The difference between the two measurements indicates the required thickness of the shims. If necessary to increase endplay, add shims. To decrease endplay, remove shims. Standard endplay is 0–0.008 in. (0.2mm) thickness. Shims are only available in 0.006 in. (0.15mm) thickness.
9. Coat all rear axle components with gear oil before installation. Torque the lock washers and nuts to 28 ft. lbs.

## Front Wheel Hub Knuckle and Bearings

### REMOVAL & INSTALLATION

#### *I-Mark (FWD)*

DO NOT remove the hub from the steering knuckle unless it is absolutely necessary.

1. Raise and support the front of the vehicle safely and block the rear wheels. Loosen the wheel nuts. Remove the grease cap, cotter pin, hub nut and thrust washer.
2. Remove the caliper and support it on a wire.
3. Remove the rotor. With hub remover J-34866 and slide hammer J-2619–01 or eqivalents, remove the hub assembly. Remove the dust cover with a suitable pry bar.
4. Remove the tie rod nut. Using a ball joint removal tool, separate the tie rod from the steering knuckle.
5. Remove the two ball joint-to-control arm/tension rod retaining nuts and bolts.
6. Remove the strut-to-steering knuckle retaining nuts/bolts.
7. Remove the steering knuckle, bearing and oil seal. When removing the axle shaft from the steering knuckle, be careful not to drop it and support it with a wire.

**NOTE: A arbor press or equivalent is used to separate the hub and bearing from the steering knuckle.**

8. To remove the bearing from the steering knuckle, use the following procedure:
   a. Using a suitable seal puller, remove the oil seals from both sides of the hub assembly.
   b. Using suitable snap ring pliers, remove the snap rings from both sides of the hub assembly.
   c. Using a suitable arbor press

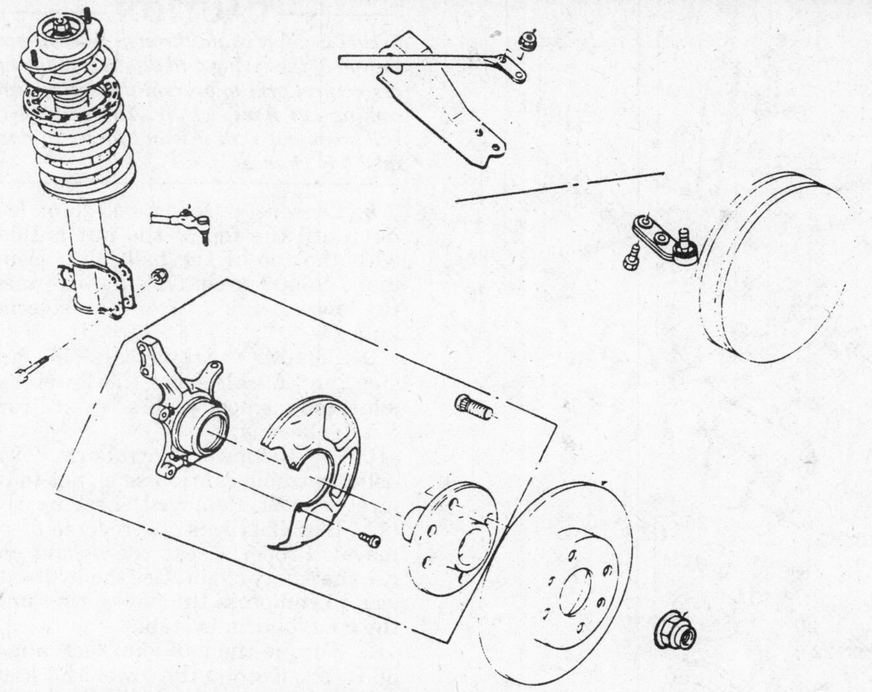

Exploded view of the front knuckle disassembly

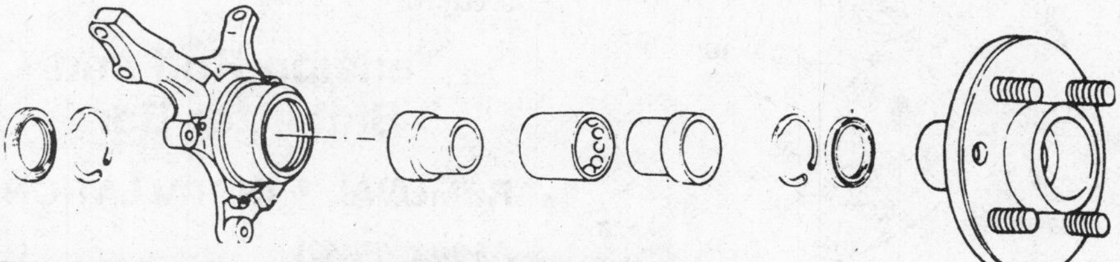

Exploded view of the disassembled front hub assembly

and the proper bearing removal tools, press the inside inner race, bearing and outside inner bearing race out of the hub assembly.

d. Reassembly is the reverse order of the disassembly procedure.

9. To install, reverse the removal procedure and bleed the brake system. Use the following torque guide.

a. Tension rod to control arm bolts – 80 ft. lbs.

b. Strut to steering knuckle – 87 ft. lbs.

c. Tie rod castle nut – 29 ft. lbs.

d. Wheel bearing nut – 137 ft. lbs.

# FRONT SUSPENSION

## Shock Absorbers

### REMOVAL & INSTALLATION

1. Raise the car and support it safely. Remove the front wheel.

2. Disconnect the shock absorber from the upper control arm using two wrenches.

3. Remove the shock absorber nuts from the engine compartment. On the Impulse models, remove the lower shock absorber through bolt from the shock absorber bushing.

4. Remove the shock absorber. Installation is the reverse of removal. Torque the control arm nut to specifications. Tighten the top nut to the end of the threads on the rod. Use lock nuts.

## MacPherson Strut

### REMOVAL & INSTALLATION

#### *I-Mark (FWD)*

1. Loosen the front wheel lug nuts, raise and support the front of the vehicle safely and remove the wheel and tire assembly.

2. Remove the brake hose clip-to-strut bolt (if so equipped). Install a drive axle cover, to protect the axle boot.

3. Remove the bolts attaching the strut to the steering knuckle.

4. Remove the two strut tower nuts and remove the strut assembly from the vehicle.

5. Installation is the reverse order of the removal procedure. The two strut tower nuts must be tightened before the lower strut bolts. The strut tower nuts should be torqued to 40 ft. lbs. and the lower strut bolts should be torqued to 86 ft. lbs.

### OVERHAUL

**For all spring and shock absorber removal and installation procedures, and all strut overhaul procedures, please refer to "Strut Overhaul" in the Unit Repair section.**

## Coil Springs

### REMOVAL & INSTALLATION

#### *All Models Except I-Mark (FWD)*

1. Raise the car and safely support

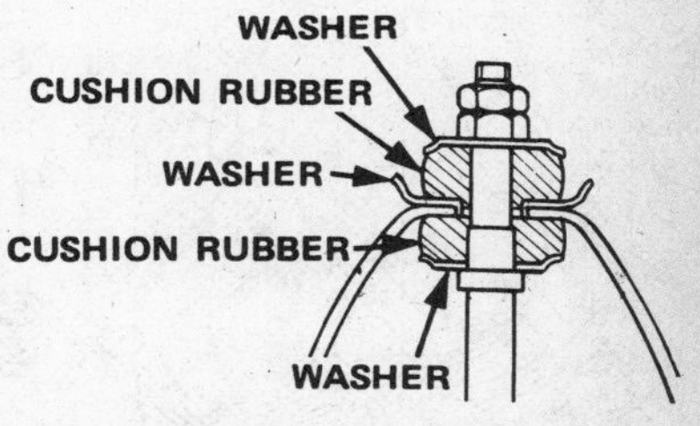


Shock absorber installation in engine compartment

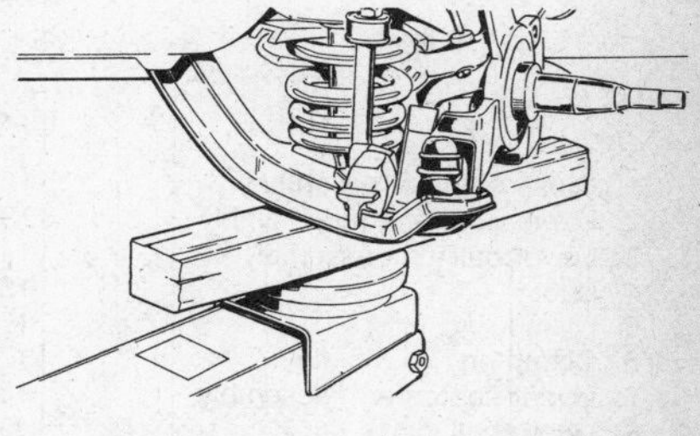

Lifting the control arm with a hydraulic jack—except Impulse

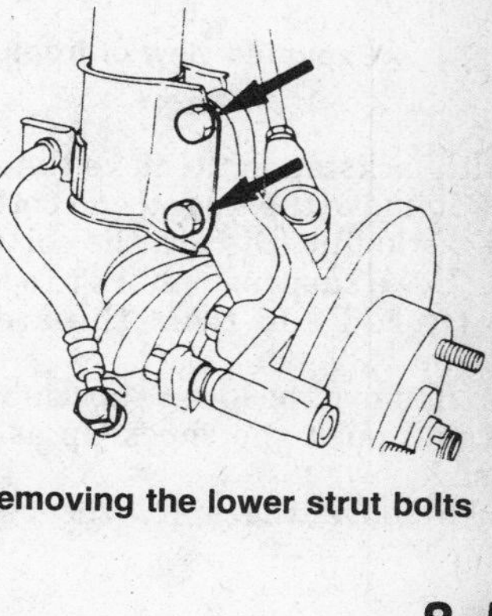

Removing the lower strut bolts

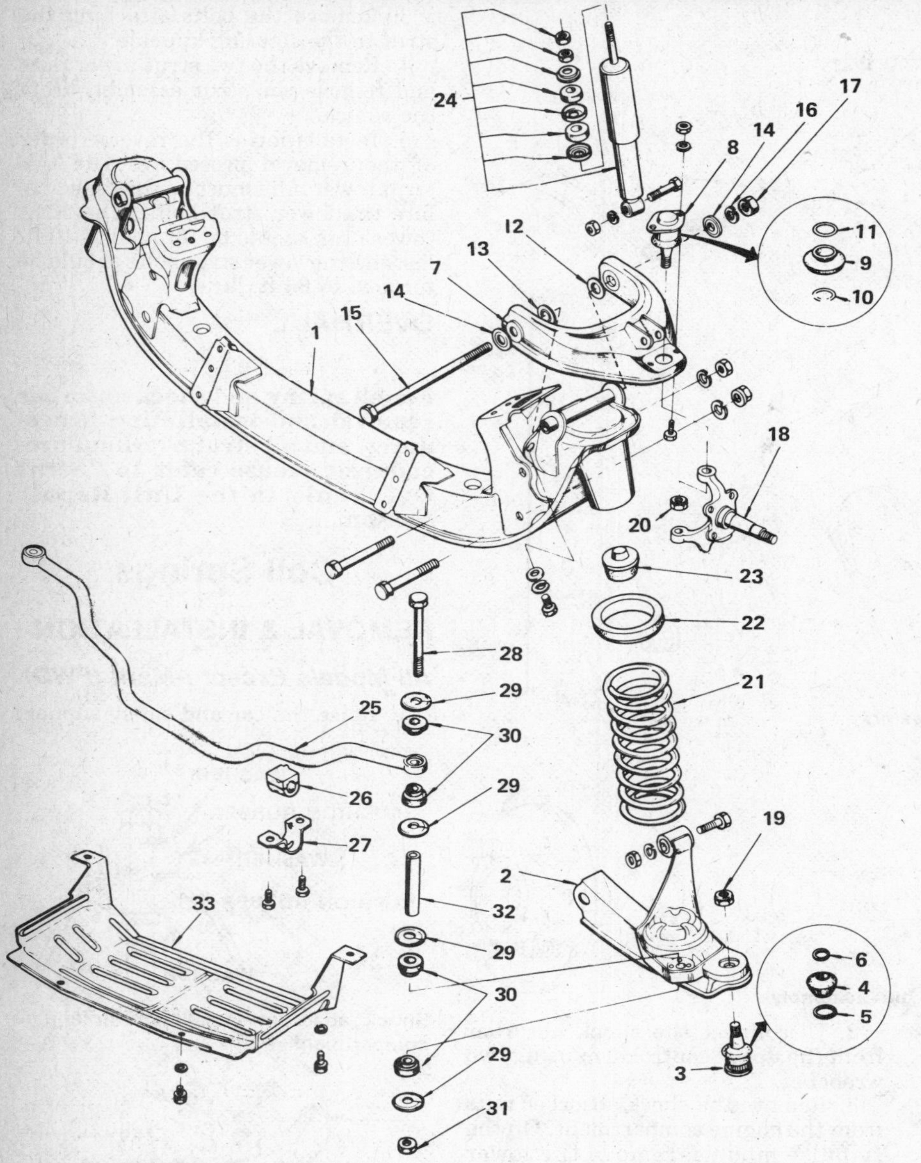


1. Cross member assembly
2. Lower control arm assembly
3. Lower ball joint assembly
4. Boot
5. Clamp ring
6. Clamp ring
7. Upper control arm assembly
8. Upper ball joint
9. Boot
10. Clamp ring
11. Clamp ring
12. Washer
13. Washer
14. Washer
15. Through-bolt
16. Spring washer
17. Nut
18. Steering knuckle
19. Nut
20. Nut
21. Front coil spring
22. Damper rubber
23. Bumper rubber
24. Shock absorber
25. Stabilizer bar
26. Rubber bushing
27. Clamp
28. Bolt
29. Retainer
30. Grommet
31. Nut
32. Distance tube
33. Under cover

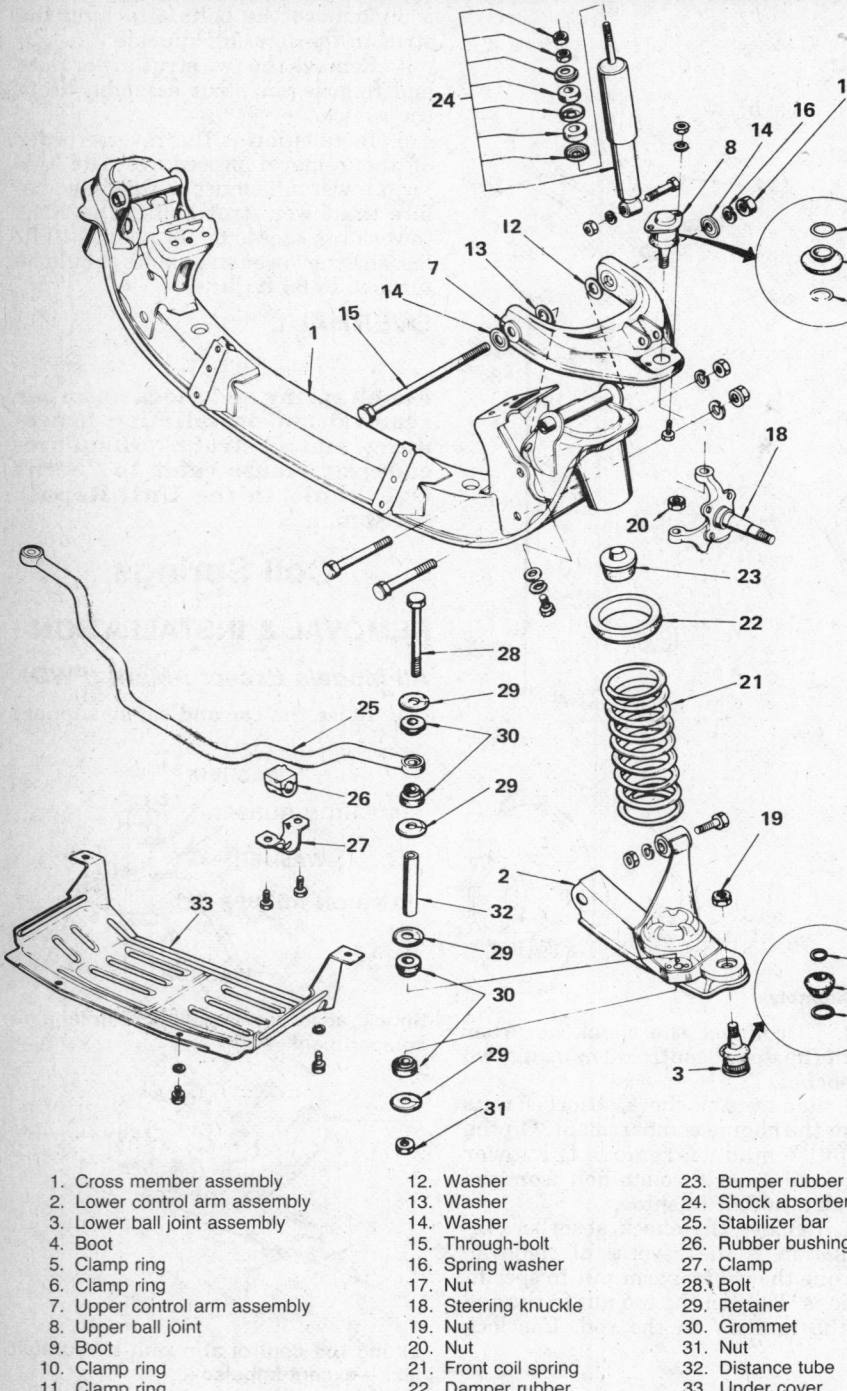

**Exploded view of front suspension system—all except Impulse**

it with jackstands. Remove the wheel.

2. Remove the tie rod end cotter pin and castle nut. Discard the cotter pin.

3. Use a suspension fork to separate the tie rod end from the steering knuckle.

4. Remove the lower shock absorber bolt and push the shock up as far as possible.

5. Remove the stabilizer bar bolt and grommet assembly from the lower control arm.

6. Remove the upper brake caliper bolt and slide the hose retaining clip back about ½ in.

7. Place the lifting pad of a hydraulic floor jack under the outer extreme of the control arm and raise the lower control arm until it is level.

**CAUTION**

***Secure a safety chain through one coil near the top of the spring and attach it to the upper control arm to prevent the spring from coming out unexpectedly. The coil spring will come out with a lethal force, so don't take any chances.***

8. Loosen the lower ball joint lock nut until the top of the nut is flush with the top of the ball joint. Using tool J-26407 or equivalent, disconnect the lower ball joint from the steering knuckle.

9. Remove the hub assembly and steering knuckle from the lower ball joint and support with a wire or rope out of the way.

10. Pry the lower control arm down, using extreme caution so as not to injure yourself. Remove the spring.

11. Installation is the reverse of removal. Properly seat the spring and use the safety chain. Use the hydraulic jack to compress the new spring until the control arm is stable.

12. Torque the ball joint lock nut to 58 ft. lbs. Torque the lower shock absorber mounting nuts and all other attaching hardware according to the specifications chart at the end of the section.

## Tension Rod and Stabilizer Bar

### REMOVAL & INSTALLATION

#### *I-Mark (FWD)*

1. Raise and support the vehicle on jackstands.

2. If equipped with a stabilizer bar, remove the nuts, bolts and insulators retaining it to the tension rod.

3. Remove the nut and washer retaining the tension rod to the body.

4. Remove the nuts and bolts retaining the tension rod to the control rod. Remove the washers, rubber cushion spacer, rubber cushion and 2 more washers.

5. Remove the tension rod.

6. To install, reverse the removal procedure. Torque the tension rod nut to 51 ft. lbs. and torque the tension rod to control arm nuts to 80 ft. lbs.

## Ball Joints

### INSPECTION

The maximum permissible axial play in the ball joint is 0.008 in. (0.2mm). Replace any joint that exceeds this value.

**NOTE: The lower ball joint is splined to the lower control arm.**

**The upper ball joints are offset to allow for camber setting.**

## REMOVAL & INSTALLATION

**NOTE: For Impulse models please refer to Control Arms, Knuckles And Coil Springs. The ball joints must be replaced with the control arms.**

### *I-Mark (RWD)*

#### UPPER BALL JOINT

1. Raise the car and support it safely. Remove the wheel.
2. Remove the upper brake caliper bolt and slide the hose retaining clip back about ½ in.
3. Remove the lower shock absorber nut and bolt and push the shock absorber up.
4. Place a hydraulic jack under the outer extreme of the lower control arm and raise until level.
5. Loosen the upper ball joint nut until the top of the nut is flush with the top of the ball joint.
6. Using special tool J-26407 or equivalent, disconnect the upper ball joint from the steering knuckle.
7. Remove the two bolts connecting the upper ball joint to the upper control arm. Remove the ball joint.
8. Installation is the reverse of removal. Install the new ball joint in the control arm so that the cut-off portion is facing outward. Torque all attaching nuts and bolts. For specifications, see the torque chart at the end of the section.

**NOTE: The car should be aligned whenever any suspension components are replaced.**

#### LOWER BALL JOINT

1. Raise the car and support it safely. Remove the front wheel.
2. Remove the tie rod end cotter pin and castle nut. Discard the pin and separate the tie rod end with a suspension fork. Remove the tie rod from the steering knuckle.
3. Remove the stabilizer bar bolt and grommet assembly from the lower control arm.

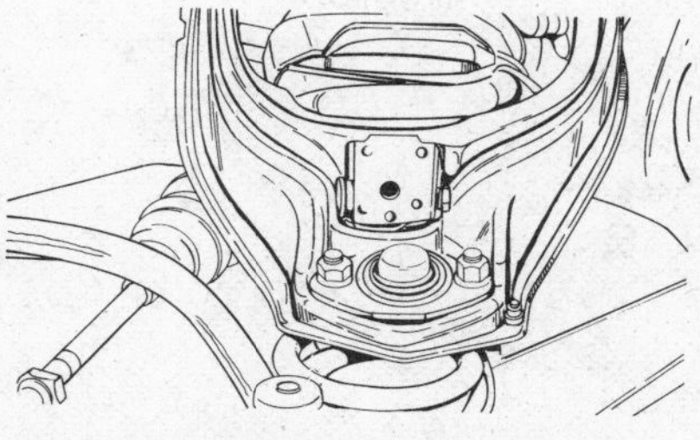

Installing the upper ball joint in the control arm—except Impulse

4. Remove the upper brake caliper bolt and slide the brake hose retaining clip back about ½ in.
5. Remove the shock absorber lower bolt and push the shock up.

**CAUTION**

***Secure a safety chain through the upper and lower control arms to prevent the possibility of the spring coming out and causing serious damage or injury. Allow enough room to get the ball joint out.***

6. Place a hydraulic jack under the outer extremity of the lower control arm and raise it until level.
7. Loosen the ball joint lock nut until the top of the nut is flush with the top of the ball joint.
8. Using special tool J-26407 or equivalent, disconnect the lower ball joint from the steering knuckle.
9. Remove the hub assembly and steering knuckle from the lower ball joint and support with a wire or rope.
10. Remove the lower ball joint from the control arm using tool J-9519-03 or equivalent.
11. Installation is the reverse of removal. Do not strike the ball joint bottom. Torque the ball joint nut to 50 ft. lbs.
12. Torque all bolts to specifications as listed in the chart at the end of the section.

### *I-Mark (FWD)*

1. Loosen the wheel nuts.
2. Raise the vehicle and support it on jackstands.
3. Remove the wheel and tire assembly.
4. Remove the two nuts retaining the ball joint to the tension rod and control arm assembly.
5. Remove the pinch bolt retaining the ball joint to the steering knuckle.
6. Remove the ball joint.
7. To install, reverse the removal procedure. Torque the steering knuckle arm nut to 51 ft. lbs. and the tension rod nut to 80 ft. lbs.

# Control Arms

## REMOVAL & INSTALLATION

### *I-Mark (RWD)*

#### UPPER

1. Raise the car and support it safely. Remove the front wheel.
2. Remove the upper brake caliper bolt and slide the brake hose retainer clip back about ½ in.
3. Remove the lower shock bolt and push the shock absorber up.
4. Place a hydraulic jack under the control arm on the outer extreme and raise the control arm until it is level.
5. Loosen the upper ball joint lock nut until the top of the nut is flush with the top of the ball joint. Disconnect the upper ball joint from the

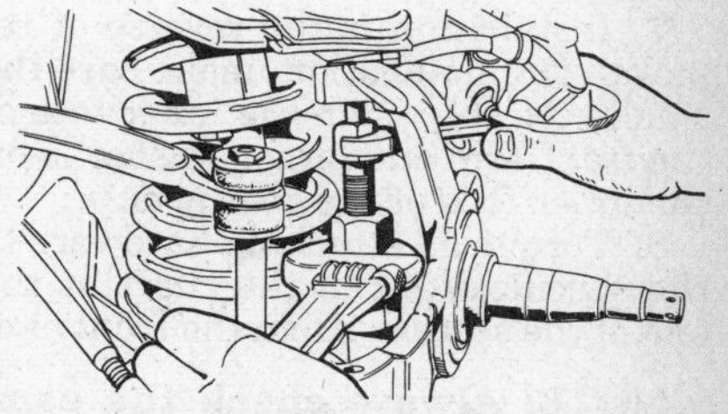

Disconnecting the lower ball joint with the special tool—except Impulse

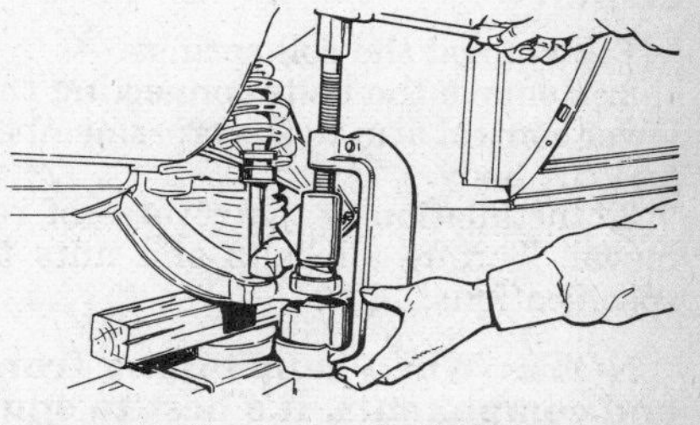

Removing the lower ball joint from the control arm—except Impulse

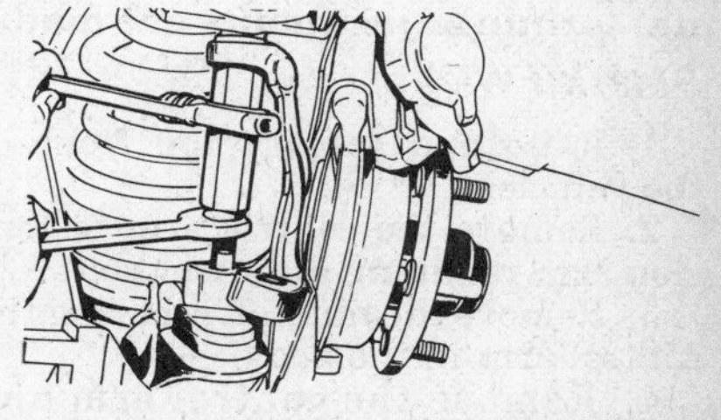

Removing the lower ball joint from the steering knuckle—except Impulse

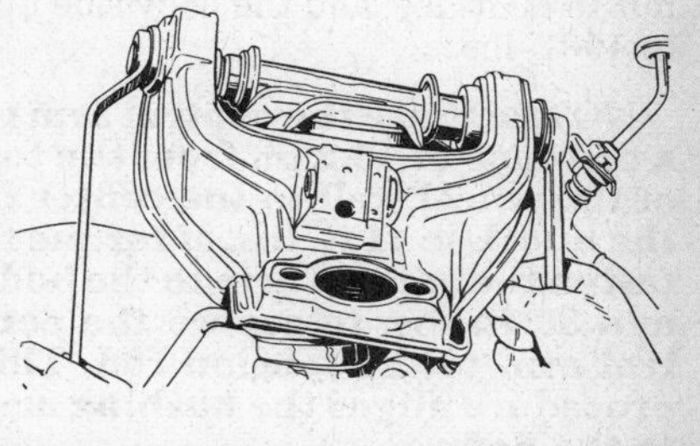

Removing the upper control arm from the crossmember—except Impulse

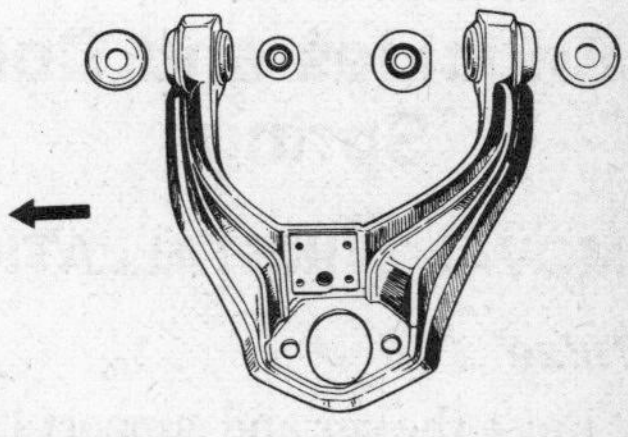

Installation of the upper control arm—except Impulse

steering knuckle using tool J–26407 or equivalent.

6. Disconnect and remove the through bolt connecting the upper control arm to the crossmember. Remove the upper control arm.

7. Installation is the reverse of removal. On installation, make sure the smaller washer is on the inner face of the front arm and larger washer is on the inner face of the rear arm.

8. Torque all attaching hardware to the specifications in the chart at the end of the section. Align the front end.

**NOTE: Always check the camber when working around the upper control arm area.**

#### LOWER

1. Removal the coil springs.
2. Remove the bolts connecting the lower control arm to the crossmember and the body.
3. Installation is the reverse of removal. Torque all bolts and nuts to specifications.

**NOTE: When reinstalling front end components, it's best to snug all the bolts and nuts first, then lower the car so that there is weight on the suspension when final torque adjustments are made.**

#### *I-Mark(FWD)*

1. Raise and support the front of the vehicle.
2. Remove the control arm to tension arm retaining nuts and bolts.
3. Remove the nut/bolt securing the control arm to the body.
4. Remove the control arm and check for cracking or distortion.
5. To install, reverse the removal procedure. Torque the knuckle side nut to 80 ft. lbs. and the body side nut to 40 ft. lbs.

**NOTE: Raise the control arm to a distance of 15.2 in. from the top of the wheel well to the center of the hub. Use 41 ft. lbs. of torque to fasten the control arm to the body and 80 ft. lbs. to secure the control arm to the tension rod. This procedure aligns the bushing arm to the body.**

## Control Arms, Knuckles and Coil Springs

### REMOVAL & INSTALLATION

#### *Impulse*

1. Raise the car and support it safely. Remove the front wheel.
2. Remove the brake caliper assembly and wire it up out of the way. Mark the position of the nuts on the front of the strut bar for reassembly (these nuts control caster). Then remove the strut bar.
3. Remove the stabilizer bar brackets on both sides of the vehicle. Remove the bolt, tube and grommets holding the stabilizer bar to the lower link. Move the end of the stabilizer bar out of the way.
4. Remove the tie rod end cotter pin and castle nut and remove the tie rod end using tool J–21687–02.
5. Put the top plate of the coil spring compressor tool J-36567 or equivalent on the top of the upper link. The safety chain is welded to a square projection on the plate. Run on end of the safety chain throuigh the spring, about 3 coils from the top and secure the ends of the chain together. Be sure when setting this up, not to interfere with the brake pipe.

**CAUTION**

***During all the following Steps, do not work directly beside the coil spring. Although it is held by the upper and lower links and should not come loose. it is a good idea to stay out its direct line of removal.***

6. Place a floor jack under the lower link an apply slight upward pressure. Remove the knuckle and rotor assembly from the upper and lower ball joints. Reinstall the old nuts on the ball joint studs to prevent damage to the threads.
7. Lower the floor jack slowly. The lower link will swing down to its lowest point. The spring ends will be held by the upper and lower seats. Remove the floor jack completely.
8. Set the lower plate of the special coil compressing tool into the coil spring. On the right hand side of the vehicle, put the plate into the 3rd space between the coils counting from the lower link. On the left hand side of the vehicle, put the plate into the 2nd space between the coils counting from the lower link. Install the threaded rods, bearing spacers and t-handles to the top of the lower plate.

**NOTE: Do not allow the spring to angle toward the front or rear of the vehicle.**

9. Press downward and inward on the lower link until the spring end is free of the lower seat. If necesary, loosen the lower link pivot bolt to allow more link travel. Remove the lower link bolt, then remove the coil spring together with the lower link.
10. After the spring has cleared the lower spring seat, turn the t-handle of the tool equal amounts to release the spring tension.
11. Press out the lower link bushing.
12. Press out the upper link bushings.

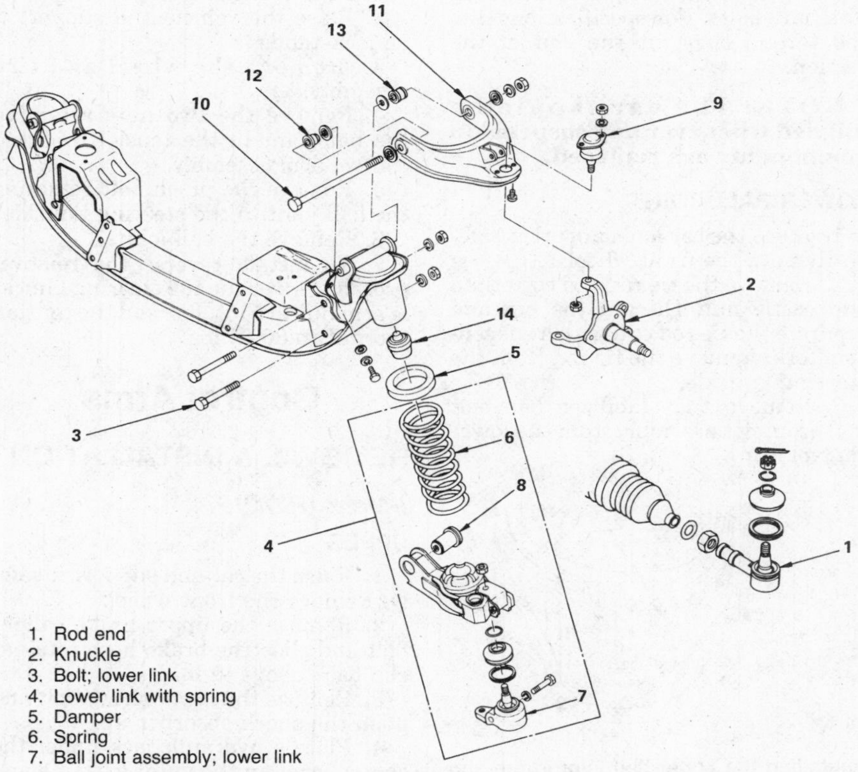


1. Rod end
2. Knuckle
3. Bolt; lower link
4. Lower link with spring
5. Damper
6. Spring
7. Ball joint assembly; lower link

Exploded view of front suspension—Impulse

13. Installation is the reverse of removal with the following precautions:
a. When installing the upper control arm washers install the small washer on the inboard side of the rear end.
b. Leave the upper and lower control arm link bolts semi-tight as they are to be torqued to specifications after completion of installation with the wheels lowered to the floor.
c. When installing the upper ball joint to the control arm the cutaway portion of the ball joint should be turned outward.
14. Use the following torque guide:
a. Upper link retaining bolt—47 ft. lbs.
b. Upper link ball joint retaining nut—41 ft. lbs.
c. Lower link retaining bolt—68 ft. lbs.
d. Lower link ball joint retaining nut—top bolt—76 ft. lbs.—lower bolt—47 ft. lbs.
e. Upper ball joint retaining nut—39 ft. lbs.
f. Lower ball joint retaining nut—58 ft. lbs.
g. Stabilizer self lock nut—19 ft. lbs.
h. Stabilizer bracket bolt—14 ft. lbs.
i. Strut bar bolt—72 ft. lbs.
j. Strut bar front nut—47 ft. lbs.
k. Strut bar rear nut—114 ft. lbs.
l. Tie rod end nut—61 ft. lbs.
m. Brake caliper assembly bolt—36 ft. lbs.

## Front Wheel Bearing

### ADJUSTMENT

#### *I-Mark (RWD)*

1. Raise and support the front of the vehicle safely.
2. Remove the bearing dust cap, cotter key and spindle nut. Discard the cotter key.
3. Torque the front wheel bearing spindle nut to 22 ft. lbs. while rotating the wheel. This will allow the bearing to seat the spindle.
4. Back off the spindle nut completely, then turn it back until it is finger tight. If the slots in the nut is not aligned with the holes in the spindle tighten only enough to align.
5. Install a new cotter key. A properly adjusted wheel bearing has a small amount of end play and looseness at the nut when adjusted in the above manner.

### REMOVAL & INSTALLATION

1. Lossen the front wheel lug nuts. Raise and support the front of the vehicle safely.
2. Remove the bearing dust cap, cotter key and spindle nut. Discard the cotter key.
3. Remove the front wheels. Remove the disc brake caliper assembly and support it out of the way with a piece of wire.
4. Remove the front bearing and then remove the hub with disc plate from the steering knuckle.
5. Drive the inner bearing and seal from the rear of the hub assembly with a suitable hammer and punch.
6. It necessary, drive out the inner and outer bearing races with a suitable punch and hammer.
7. Install new races and bearings along with a new grease seal. Be sure to pack the bearing and lubricate the bearing race with suitable bearing grease before assembly.
8. Installation is the reverse order of the removal procedure. Be sure to adjust the wheel bearing end play upon completion of the installation.

## Front Wheel Alignment

**NOTE: Steering problems are not always the result of improper alignment. Before aligning the car, check the tire pressure and check all suspension components for damage or excessive wear.**

#### *Camber*

On all I-Mark (RWD) and late model Impulse, camber angle can be increased approximately 1 degree by removing the upper ball joint, rotating it ½ turn and reinstalling it with the cut-off portion of the upper flange on the inboard side of the control arm. On early Impulse models, camber is not adjustable. Replace parts as necessary to correct alignment. On I-Mark (FWD) camber cannot be adjusted it preset at the factory.

#### *Caster*

On I-Mark (RWD) caster angle can be changed by realigning the washers located between the legs of the upper control arm. Washers come in two sizes 3mm and 9mm. On I-Mark and Impulse caster angle is built into the front end and is not itself adjustable.

**NOTE: On 1988–90 Impulse, caster angle can be adjusted by varying length of the strut bar (adjust with lock nut).**

#### *Toe In Angle*

Toe in is controlled by adjusting the tie rod. To adjust the toe in setting loosen the nuts at the steering knuckle end of the tie rod. Rotate the rod as required to adjust the toe in. Retighten the cover and locknuts, check that the rubber bellows is not twisted. For all specifications, see the Alignment Specs in the front of the section.

# REAR SUSPENSION

## Shock Absorbers

### REMOVAL & INSTALLATION

1. Raise the car and support it safely under the axle housing. Disconnect the parking brake cable clip and the brake line retaining clip if so equipped.
2. Disconnect the lower end of the shock absorber from the axle.
3. Remove the shock tower cover from inside the trunk on all models except the Impulse and disconnect the upper end of the shock absorber.
4. Working from under the car, remove the shock absorber.
5. Installation is the reverse of removal. Use lock nuts at each end. Torque all shock absorber lower bolts/nuts to 30 ft. lbs.

## Coil Springs

### REMOVAL & INSTALLATION

1. Raise the rear of the car on the axle housing and support it at the jack side brackets with jackstands.
2. Position a hydraulic jack under the differential housing, but use a light contact pressure.
3. Disconnect the shock absorber lower mounting bolts.
4. Slowly lower or separate the axle assembly from the car body to the point where the spring becomes loose enough to allow removal.

**CAUTION**

***Do not stress the brake hoses when lowering the axle.***

5. Installation is the reverse of removal. Position the spring correctly. Make sure that the insulator is in position on top of the spring.
6. Torque the shock absorber lower bolts to 29 ft. lbs.

## Rear Control Arm

### REMOVAL & INSTALLATION

1. Raise the car and support it safely.

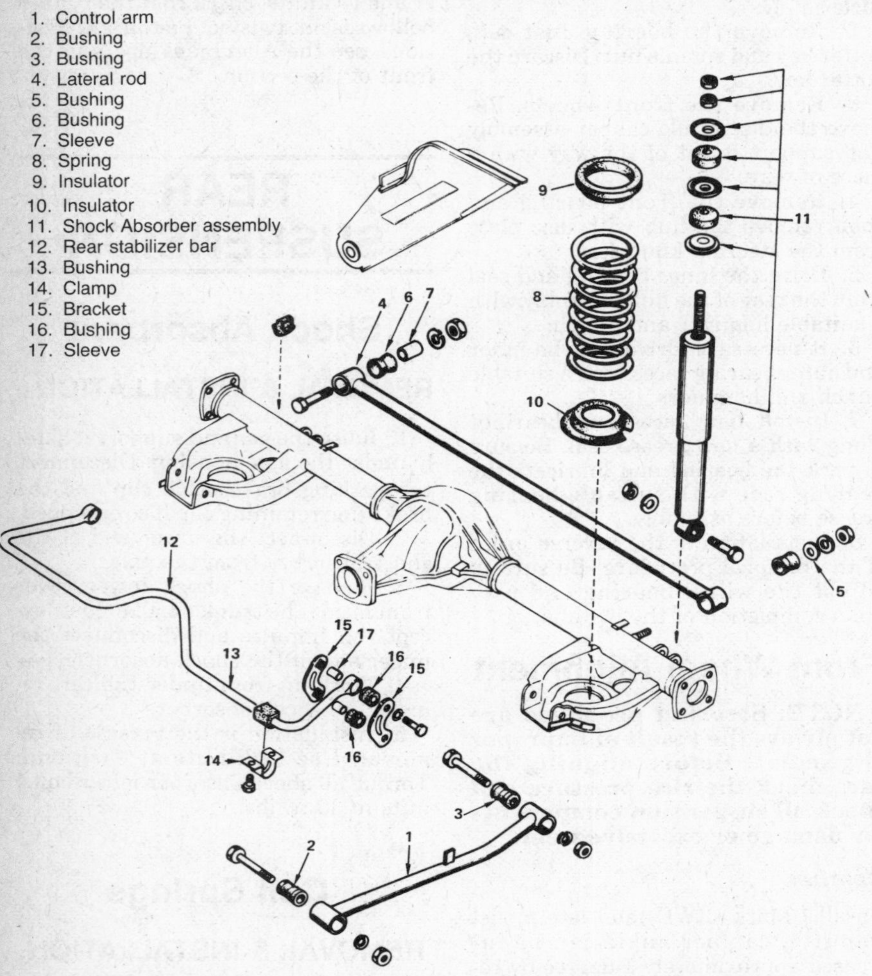

Exploded view of rear suspension system—all except Impulse

2. Remove the bolt connecting the control arm to the axle case.

3. Remove the bolt connecting the control arm to the body.

4. Remove the control arm assembly.

5. Installation is the reverse of removal. Torque the bolts to specifications.

**NOTE: When reinstalling the control arm assembly, leave the bolts semi-tight. Lower the car before torquing any nuts. The vehicle weight should be on all suspension components when torquing the nuts.**

## Rear Axle Hub

### REMOVAL & INSTALLATION

#### *I-Mark (FWD)*

1. Raise the rear end of the vehicle and support it on jackstands. Remove the rear wheels.

2. Remove the hub cap, cotter pin, hub nut, washer and outer bearing.

3. Disconnect the parking brake cable from the turnbuckle at the center of the rear axle. Disconnect the parking brake cable from the parking brake joint at the left side of the rear axle.

4. Disconnect the brake line from the wheel cylinder.

5. Remove the parking brake inner cable from the brake lever and outer cable from the rear axle case.

6. Remove the bolts attaching the brake assembly (backing plate) and rear axle hub (knuckle) to the rear axle. Separate the hub (knuckle) from the backing plate.

7. To install, reverse the removal procedure. Torque the rear axle hub (knuckle) retaining bolts to 41 ft. lbs.

**NOTE: If the cotter pin holes are out of alignment upon reassembly, use a wrench to tighten the nut until the hole in the shaft and a slot of the nut align.**

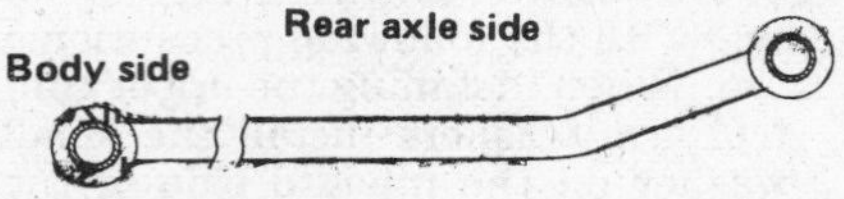

Installing rear control arm—all except Impulse

## Rear Wheel Bearings

### REMOVAL & INSTALLATION

#### *I-Mark (FWD)*

1. Remove the rear axle hub.

2. Using a slide hammer puller and attachment , pull the oil seal from the hub. Remove the inner bearing.

3. Using a brass drift and a hammer, drive both bearing races from the hub.

4. Clean, inspect and/or replace all parts.

5. To install, pack the bearings with grease, coat the oil seal lips with grease and reverse the removal procedure.

### ADJUSTMENT

#### *I-Mark (FWD)*

1. Torque the rear hub nut to 22 ft. lbs.

2. Rotate the hub 2 or 3 times, to seat bearing.

3. If the cotter pin holes are not aligned, tighten the nut just enough to align the holes.

# STEERING

## Steering Wheel

### REMOVAL & INSTALLATION

1. Raise the hood and disconnect the battery ground cable.

2. On models with the 2-spoke wheel, remove the two screws retaining the horn shroud and disconnect the horn contact.

3. On models with the 3-spoke wheel, remove the medallion cover from the center of the wheel by prying lightly around the edge with a small screwdriver.

4. Remove the steering wheel nut and washer. Mark the steering wheel and shaft to assure proper positioning later.

5. Using a steering wheel puller, remove the steering wheel. Installation is the reverse of removal. Align the marks you made earlier.

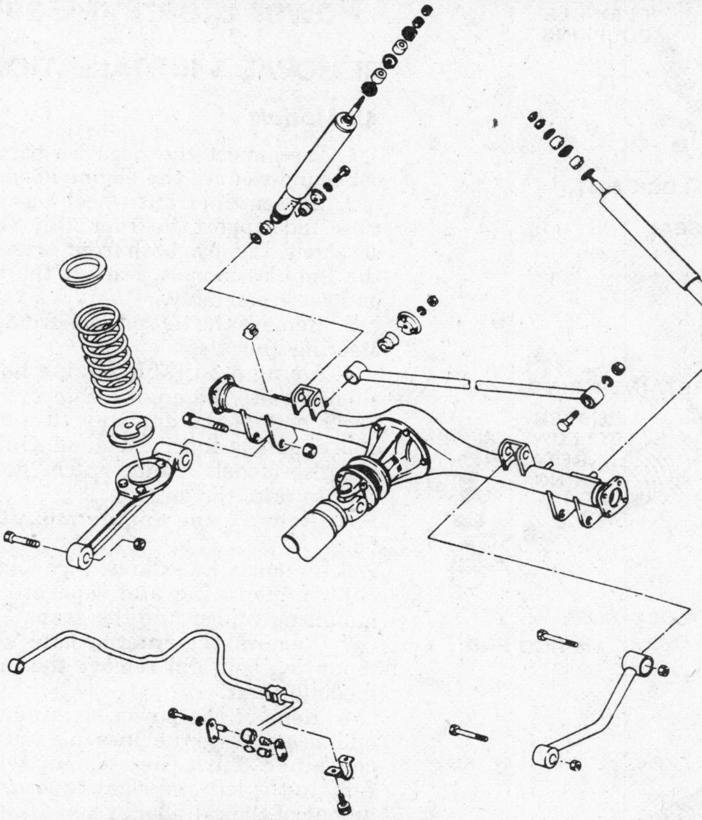

**Exploded view of the Impulse rear suspension**

6. Torque the steering wheel nut to specifications.

# Combination Switch

## REMOVAL & INSTALLATION

### *All Except Impulse*

1. Remove the steering wheel as previously described.
2. Remove the steering column covers and disconnect the electrical connectors to the switches.
3. Remove the washer/wiper switch by removing the two retaining screws.
4. Remove the turn signal/headlight switch and hazard switch by removing the four retaining screws.
5. Installation is the reverse of removal. Make sure the connectors are tight and properly connected.

**NOTE: The light, wiper/washer, turn signal switches etc. on the Impulse, are contained in a control panel which is removed as an assembly. Refer to the procedure under Chassis Electrical.**

# Ignition Lock/Switch

## REMOVAL & INSTALLATION

### *All Models*

1. Disconnect the negative battery cable. Using the steering wheel removal procedure, (as previously outlined), remove the steering wheel.
2. Remove the screws retaining the upper and lower steering column covers.
3. Disconnect all the electrical connectors.
4. On the I-Mark models, remove the combination windshield wiper and washer switch by removing the two retaining screws. Then remove the combination turn signal, headlight dimmer and hazard warning switch by removing the two retaining screws.
5. Remove the ignition lock cylinder housing by removing the snap ring and washer, along with the lock cylinder housing retaining bolts on the column flange. On Impulse models, remove the ignition lock cylinder in position except for the **LOCK** position.
6. Remove the lock cylinder housing from the steering column shaft.
7. Installation is the reverse order of the removal procedure.

# Manual Steering Gear

## REMOVAL & INSTALLATION

### *I-Mark (RWD)*

1. Raise the car and safely support

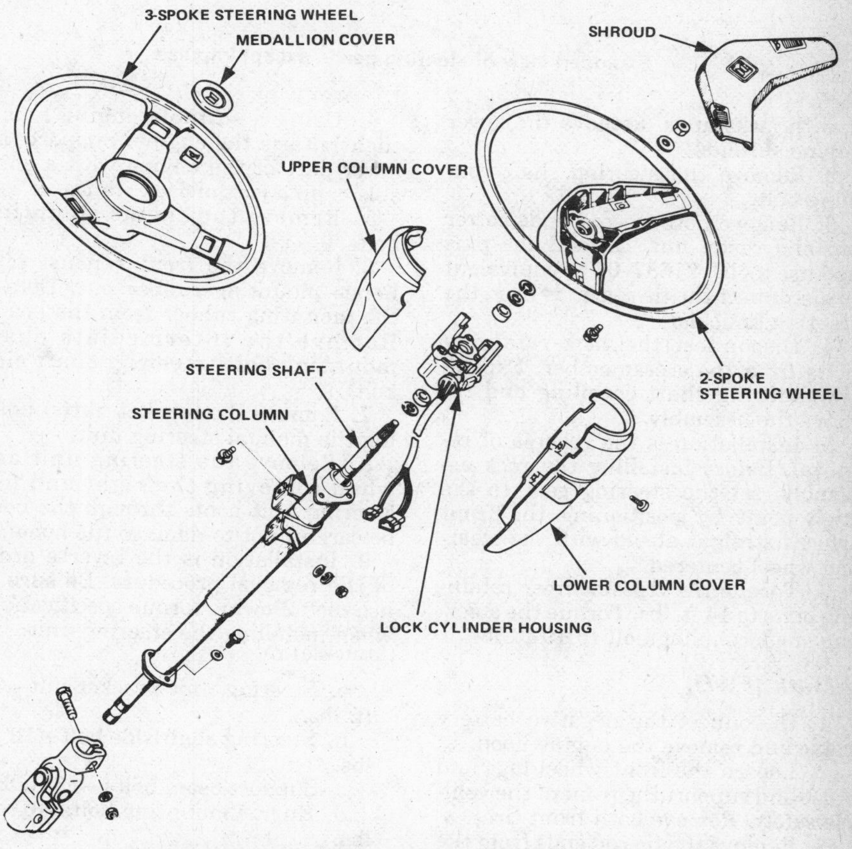


**Exploded view of steering column assembly—except Impulse**

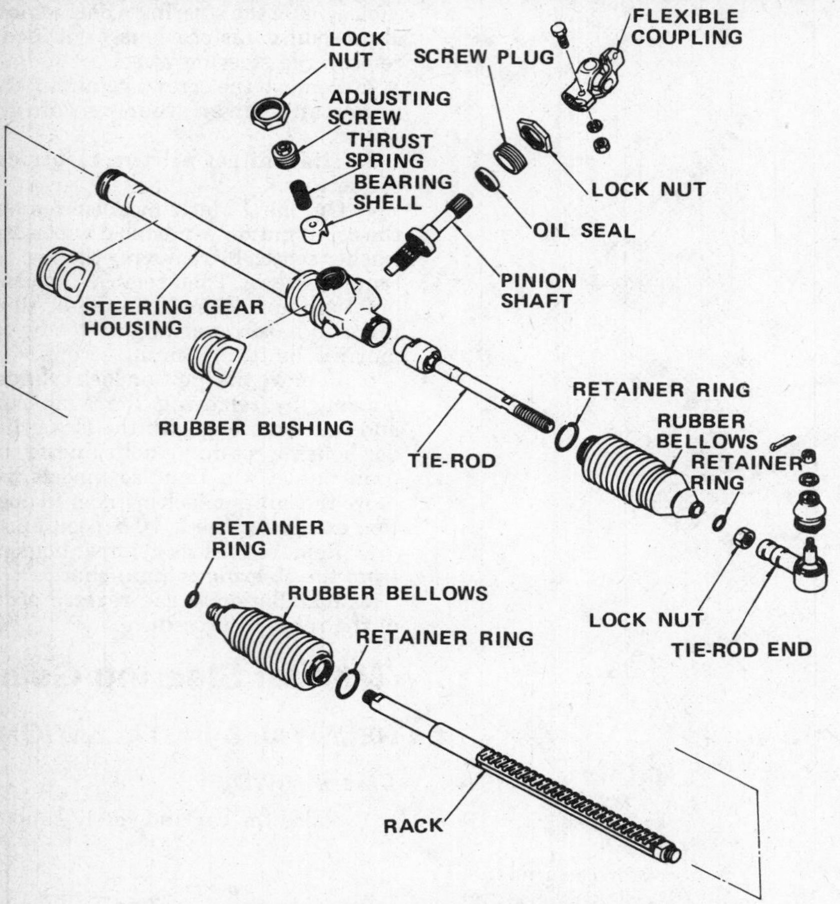


Exploded view of steering gear—except Impulse

it with jackstands. Remove the lower engine shrouds.

2. Remove the steering shaft coupling bolt.

3. Remove both tie rod ends cotter pin and castle nut. Discard the pins and use tool J-21687-02 or equivalent to disconnect the tie rod ends from the steering knuckles.

4. Disconnect the rack retaining bolts from the crossmember. Expand the steering shaft coupling and remove the assembly.

5. Installation is the reverse of removal. Before installing the rack assembly, set the steering gear to the high point by positioning the front wheels straight ahead with the steering wheel centered.

6. Torque the crossmember retaining bolts to 14 ft. lbs. Torque the steering shaft coupling bolt to 19 ft. lbs.

### I-Mark (FWD)

1. Disconnect the negative battery cable and remove the engine hood.

2. Loosen the front wheel lugs and raise and support the front of the vehicle safely. Remove both front tires.

3. Remove the tie rod ends from the steering knuckles.

4. Using a suitable engine hoist, slightly raise the engine. Support the lower part of the engine with a suitable engine jack or jack stand.

5. Remove the engine mounting bolts.

6. Remove the front exhaust pipe hange mounting rubber nut. Detach the mounting rubber from the beam. Remove the intermediate shaft mounting bolt (steering shaft side bolt).

7. Remove the bracket nut(s) holding the manual steering unit.

8. Remove the steering unit and when removing the right and left steering unit boots through the body be careful not to damage the boots.

9. Installation is the reverse order of the removal procedure. Be sure to use the following torque specifications when installing the steering unit.

a. Steering unit bracket nut – 30 ft. lbs.

b. Steering shaft side bolt – 19 ft. lbs.

c. Support beam bolts – 56 ft. lbs.

d. Engine mounting bolts – 61 ft. lbs.

e. Tie rod end nut – 29 ft. lbs.

# Power Steering Gear

## REMOVAL & INSTALLATION

### All Models

1. Disconnect the negative battery cable and remove the engine hood.

2. Loosen the front wheel lugs and raise and support the front of the vehicle safely. Remove both front tires. On the Impulse models, remove the hub and rotor assembly.

3. Remove the tie rod ends from the steering knuckles.

4. Using a suitable engine hoist, slightly raise the engine. Support the lower part of the engine with a suitable engine jack or jack stand. On the Impulse models it may not be necessary to raise the engine.

5. Remove the engine mounting bolts.

6. Remove the exhaust pipe hanger rubber mounting and separate the mounting rubber and the beam.

7. Remove the intermediate shaft mounting bolt and remove the intermediate shaft.

8. Remove the power steering unit oil line and place the lines in a suitable container. Turn the steering wheel fully to the left and right to force the oil out of the cylinder.

9. Remove the bracket nut(s) holding the power steering unit in the vehicle. Remove the unit from the vehicle and be careful not to damage the boots.

10. Installation is the reverse order of the removal procedure. Use the same torque specifications as the manual steering unit. The feed oil line is torqued to 25 ft. lbs. and the return line is torqued to 33 ft. lbs.

11. After installation is completed, realign the front end.

## ADJUSTMENTS

Adjustment of the steering gear assembly is accomplished by turning the adjusting screw in or out.

1. Set the steering to the high point by positioning the front wheels straight ahead with the steering wheel centered.

2. Thread the adjusting screw into the steering gear housing and torque the adjusting screw to 11 ft. lbs.

3. Back off the adjusting screw slightly, then torque the locknut to 58 ft. lbs.

# Power Steering Pump

## REMOVAL & INSTALLATION

### All Models

1. Disconnect the negative battery

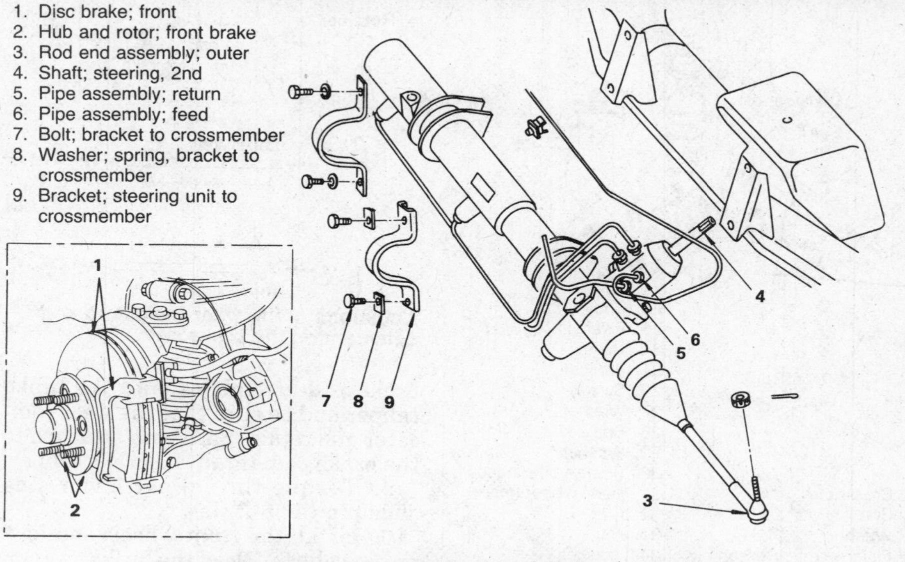


**Power steering unit removal and installation—Impulse**

cable. Remove all necessary drive belts.

2. Disconnect the high pressure lines from the power steering pump and let them and the pump drain out into a suitable drain pan. On the Impulse G200Z engine it is necessary to remove the under the engine dust cover in order to reach the high pressure lines and to remove the drive belt.

3. In the I-Mark models, remove the power steering pump adjusting plate, brackets and retaining bolts. Then remove the power steering pump from the vehicle.

4. On the G200Z Impulse, remove the power steering pump pulley, brackets and retaining bolts and remove the pump from the vehicle.

5. On the 4ZCI-T Impulse, remove the V-belt, pump pulley, idler pulley, brackets and retaining bolts. Then remove the pump from the vehicle.

6. Installation is the reverse order of the removal procedure. Tighten the drive belts to specifications, refill the power steering reservoir, bleed the system and start the car and check for leaks.

### BLEEDING

1. Turn the wheels to the extreme left.

2. With the engine stopped, add power steering fluid to the **MIN** mark on the fluid indicator.

3. Start the engine and run it for 15 seconds at fast idle.

4. Stop the engine, recheck the fluid level and refill to the **MIN** mark.

5. Start the engine and turn the wheels from side to side (3 times).

6. Stop the engine check the fluid level.

**NOTE: If air bubbles are still present in the fluid, the procedure must be repeated.**

## Tie Rod Ends

### REMOVAL & INSTALLATION

#### *All Models*

1. Raise the vehicle and remove the front wheel.

2. Remove the castle nut from the ball joint. Using a ball joint removal tool, separate the tie rod from the steering knuckle.

3. Disconnect the retaining wire from the inner boot and pull back the boot.

4. Using a chisel, straighten the staked part of the locking washer between the tie rod and the rack.

5. Remove the tie rod from the rack.

6. To install, reverse the removal procedure.

# BRAKES

**For all brake system repair and service not detailed below, please refer to "Brakes" in the Unit Repair section.**

## Master Cylinder

### REMOVAL & INSTALLATION

1. Set the parking brake and chock the wheels to prevent the car from rolling.

2. Open the hood and disconnect the front and rear brake lines from the master cylinder.

3. Remove the nuts securing the master cylinder to the power brake unit and the support bracket.

4. Remove the nuts securing the fluid reservoir bracket and remove the master cylinder and fluid reservoir as an assembly (remove the fluid hoses, too).

**NOTE: Be careful not to spill brake fluid on any painted surface. Brake fluid acts exactly like paint remover.**

5. Installation is the reverse of removal.

**For information on bleeding the master cylinder and brake system, see Brakes in the Unit Repair section.**

## Power Brake Booster

### REMOVAL & INSTALLATION

1. Wipe the master cylinder, power unit and lines clean with a clean rag. Use rags to catch any leaking fluid.

2. Disconnect the hydraulic lines at the master cylinder, and cover the lines with a clean, lint-free material to prevent dirt from contaminating the system. Remove the air hose from the air duct connector, if so equipped.

3. Remove the master cylinder bracket bolts to the cylinder and fender skirt and remove the bracket.

4. Remove the bolts securing the fluid reservoir bracket.

5. Remove the vacuum hose clip and the hose from the check valve.

6. Remove the clevis pin from the brake pedal and separate the clevis and pedal.

7. Remove the power unit retaining nuts holding it to the dash panel and lift out the power unit and master cylinder/reservoir as an assembly.

8. Installation is the reverse of removal. Bleed the brake system and top up the fluid level.

## Disc Brake Pads

### REMOVAL & INSTALLATION

#### *Front*

##### I-MARK (RWD)

1. Loosen the lug nuts. Raise and support the front of the vehicle safely.

2. Remove the front wheels.

3. Remove the clips, pins, **M** type spring, brake pad shims and brake pads.

4. Remove any dirt or forgien material from the shoe recess of the caliper.

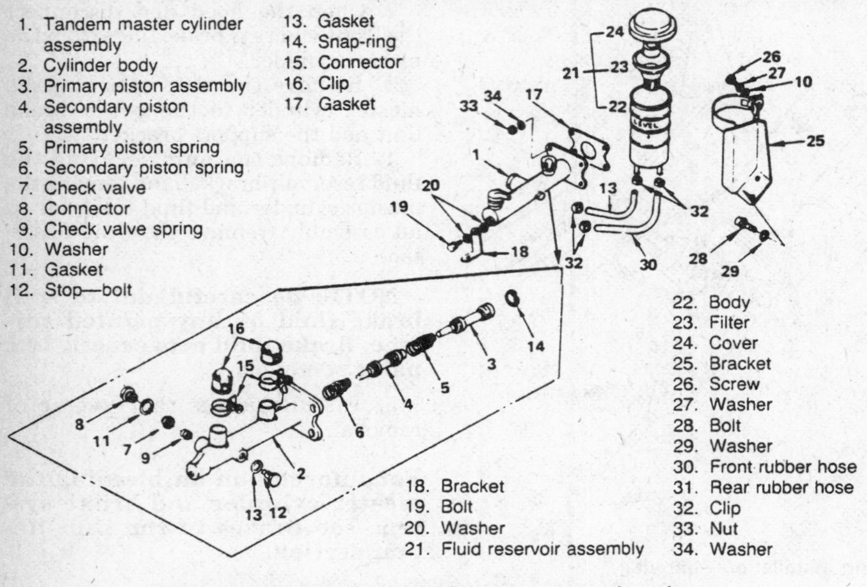


**Exploded view of master cylinder—except Impulse**

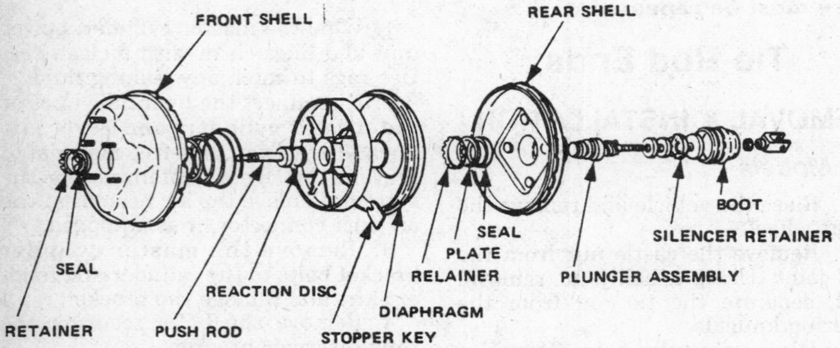


**Exploded view of power brake unit—typical**

Visually inspect the piston seals for leakage.

5. Apply a suitable multi-purpose grease to the back of the brake pad shims.

6. Push the caliper pistons back into their bores. While pressing in the piston assemblies, be sure to crack the bleed valve on the caliper so as to prevent brake fluid from overflowing in the reservoir. Once the pistons are bottomed out, tighten the bleeder screw.

7. Assemble the brake pad shims to the brake pads with the arrow marks pointing in the direction of normal disc rotation and install them in the caliper.

8. Install the **M** type springs, pins and clips. Install the front wheels and lower the vehicle. Bleed the brake system, if necessary.

### I-MARK (FWD)

1. Loosen the lug nuts. Raise and support the front of the vehicle safely.

2. Remove the front wheels.

3. Remove the lower side slide pin. Lift up the brake caliper and remove it by pulling it towards the inside of the vehicle. Tie the caliper back up out of the way.

4. Remove the pads, shims, wear indicators, retainers and pad return spring.

5. Remove any dirt or forgien material from the shoe recess of the caliper. Visually inspect the piston seals for leakage.

6. Apply a suitable multi-purpose grease to the back of the brake pad shims.

7. Push the caliper pistons back into their bores. While pressing in the piston assemblies, be sure to crack the bleed valve on the caliper so as to prevent brake fluid from overflowing in the reservoir. Once the pistons are bottomed out, tighten the bleeder screw.

8. Install the brake pad shims and brake pad assemblies onto the brake caliper and be sure that the wear indicator and retainer are both attached to the brake pad. Intall the brake caliper.

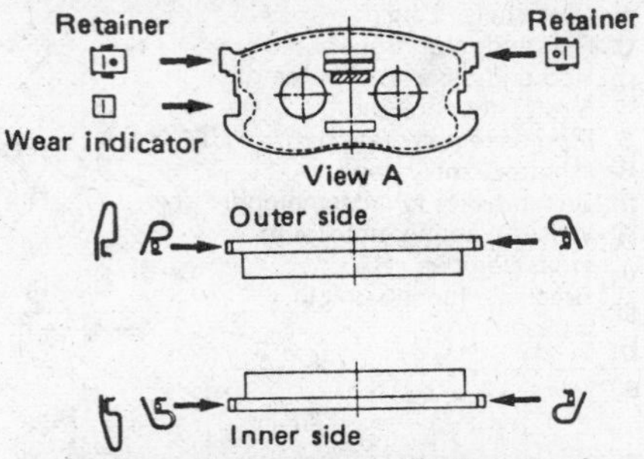


**Locations of the wear indicators and retainers on the brake pad**

9. Torque the caliper lower side slide pin to 36 ft. lbs.

10. Install the front wheels and lower the vehicle. Bleed the brake system, if necessary.

### IMPULSE

1. Loosen the lug nuts. Raise and support the front of the vehicle safely.

2. Remove the front wheels.

3. Remove the upper and lower brake caliper retaining bolts. Tie the caliper back up out of the way.

4. Remove the brake pads from the support bracket on the caliper.

5. Remove any dirt or forgien material from the shoe recess of the caliper. Visually inspect the piston seals for leakage.

6. Apply a suitable multi-purpose grease to the back of the brake pad shims.

7. Push the caliper pistons back into their bores. While pressing in the piston assemblies, be sure to crack the bleed valve on the caliper so as to prevent brake fluid from overflowing in the reservoir. Once the pistons are bottomed out, tighten the bleeder screw.

8. Install the brake pad shims and brake pad assemblies onto the brake caliper and intall the brake caliper.

9. Torque the caliper retaining bolt to 27 ft. lbs.

10. Install the front wheels and lower the vehicle. Bleed the brake system, if necessary.

## *Rear*

### IMPULSE

1. Loosen the lug nuts. Raise and support the rear of the vehicle safely.

2. Remove the rear wheels.

3. Remove the flexible brake line. Remove the lower caliper lock pin.

4. Raise the brake caliper up from the bottom and remove it from the rotor. Tie back out of the way.

5. Remove the brake pads and clips.

6. Remove any dirt or forgien mate-

rial from the shoe recess of the caliper. Visually inspect the piston seals for leakage.

7. Push the caliper pistons back into their bores. While pressing in the piston assemblies, be sure to crack the bleed valve on the caliper so as to prevent brake fluid from overflowing in the reservoir. Once the pistons are bottomed out, tighten the bleeder screw.

8. Install the clips and brake pad assemblies onto the brake caliper. Install the brake caliper. Be sure to apply a suitable multi-purpose grease to the entire circumference of the guide pin.

9. Torque the caliper lower lock pin to 15 ft. lbs.

10. Install the rear wheels and lower the vehicle. Bleed the brake system, if necessary.

## Brake Shoes

### REMOVAL & INSTALLATION

#### *I-Mark*

1. Loosen the lug nuts. Raise and support the rear of the vehicle safely.
2. Remove the rear wheels.
3. Remove the wheel and drum assembly. On I-Mark (FWD) models, to remove the brake drum, remove the bearing cap, cotter pin, castle nut, spacer and bearing.
4. Remove the brake return springs, brake shoe holding pins, cups and springs.
5. Move the automatic adjuster lever all the way in the direction of exspansion and disconnect the brake shoe strut. Then remove the primary shoe.
6. Disconnect the parking brake cable from the parking brake lever and remove the secondary brake shoe.
7. Clean and inspect the backing plate. Apply a suitable high temperature type grease to the 6 spots on the backing plate over which the brake shoes slide.
8. Assemble the automatic adjuster lever and latch the primary shoe, then connect the parking brake cable lever to the secondary shoe.
9. Install the secondary shoe and install the parking brake cable to the parking brake lever.
10. Install the primary shoe, the brake shoe strut and the automatic adjuster lever. The automatic adjuster lever, ratchet springs and ratchet stopper on the right and left side are not interchangeable.
11. Install the return springs, shoe holding pins, cups and springs. Install the drum and adjust the brake lining in sets.
12. Install the wheels and bleed the brake system if necessary.

**NOTE: The Impulse models are equipped with rear dics brakes, but to use a drum type parking brake assembly. These parking brake shoes can be removed in the same manner as the drum brakes on the I-Mark models.**

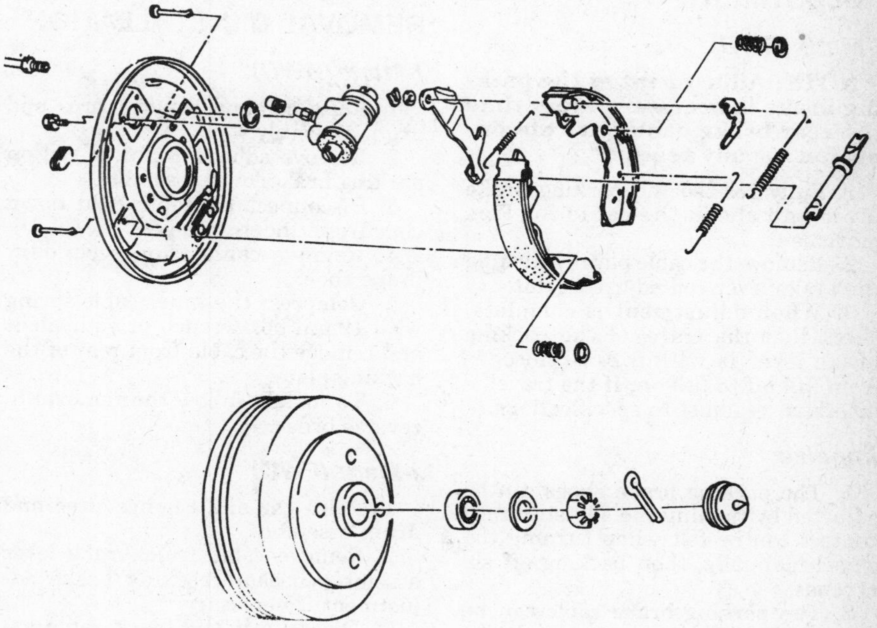

**Exploded view of a typical drum brake assembly**

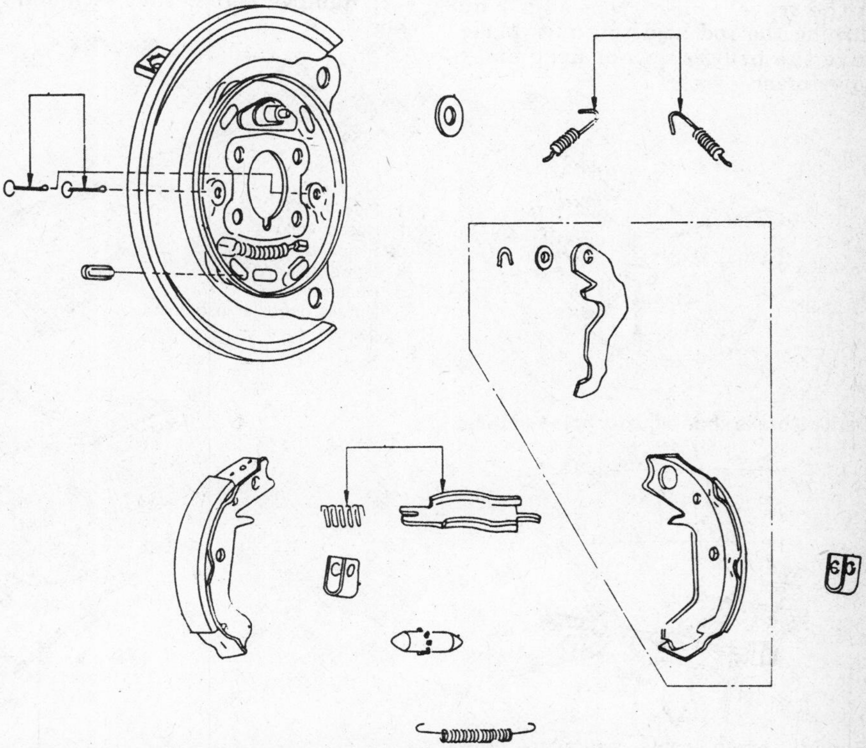

**Exploded view of the parking drum brake assembly—Impulse**

## Wheel Cylinder

### REMOVAL & INSTALLATION

1. Remove the brake shoes.
2. Disconnect the hydraulic brake line at the wheel cylinder.

3. Remove the wheel cylinder attaching bolts from the backing plate.
4. Cap or tape the openings of the brake line and wheel cylinders.
5. Installation is the reverse of removal. Bleed the brake system.

## Parking Brake Cable

### ADJUSTMENT

#### *I-Mark (RWD)*

**NOTE: Adjustment of the parking brake is necessary every time the rear brake cables are disconnected for any reason.**

1. Fully release the parking brake lever and check the cable for free movement.
2. Remove the cable play by turning the brake lever rod adjusting nut.
3. When adjustment is complete, check that the travel of the parking brake lever is within 8–10 notches from full off to full on. If the travel is incorrect, readjust to specifications.

#### *Impulse*

1. The parking brake shoes can be adjusted by turning the adjuster until contact can be felt when turning the wheel manually, then backing off six notches.
2. The parking brake cable can be adjusted by pulling the parking brake lever from full off to full on. The lever travel should be within 11–13 notches. If the travel is incorrect adjust by turning the rod adjusting nut. Make sure the brakes do not drag after adjustment.

#### *I-Mark (FWD)*

1. Release the parking brake lever.
2. Adjust the length of the cable by turning the turnbuckle.
3. Tighten the lock nut securely. The parking brake lever stroke is normal if the lever comes within 7–9 notches when pulled with a force of 60 ft. lbs.

### REMOVAL & INSTALLATION

#### *I-Mark (RWD)*

1. Raise car and remove tires and drum assembly.
2. Remove adjusting nut at rod on parking brake lever assembly.
3. Disconnect all cable hold down clips from undercarriage.
4. Remove cable from secondary brake shoe.
5. Compress the inner cable spring with 12mm box wrench or equivalent and remove the cable from rear of the backing plate.
6. To install, follow the removal in reverse order.

#### *I-Mark (FWD)*

1. Raise car and remove tires and drum assembly.
2. Remove cable from brake lever assembly backoff parking brake adjustment if necessary.
3. Disconnect the front cable assembly from the rear cable assembly and the tension spring from rear axle.
4. Remove cable from secondary shoe.

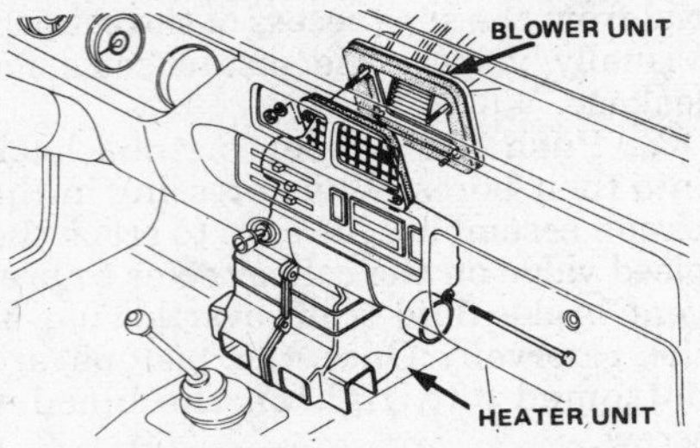


Heater installation—except Impulse

5. Remove cable housing from backing plate.
6. To install, follow the removal in reverse order.

#### *Impulse*

1. Raise car and remove tires and drum assembly.
2. Remove cable from brake lever.

**NOTE: The bolt that holds cable to lever assembly has left-handed threads.**

3. Disconnect all cable hold down clips from undercarriage.
4. Remove cable housing from backing plate.
5. To install, follow the removal in reverse order.

# CHASSIS ELECTRICAL

## Heater Blower Motor

### REMOVAL & INSTALLATION

#### *I-Mark (RWD)*

1. Disconnect the battery cables.

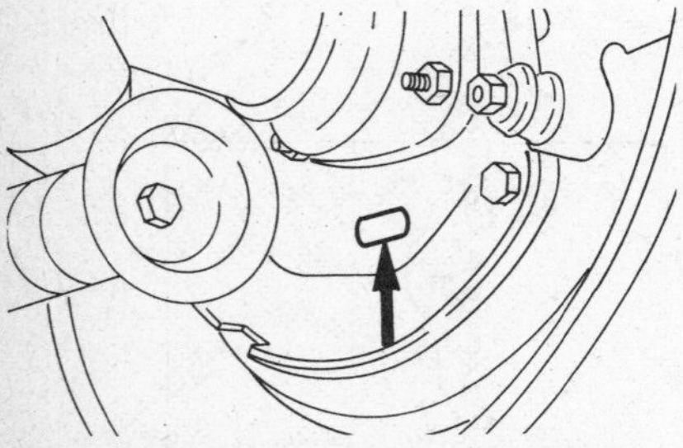

Parking brake shoe adjuster hole—Impulse

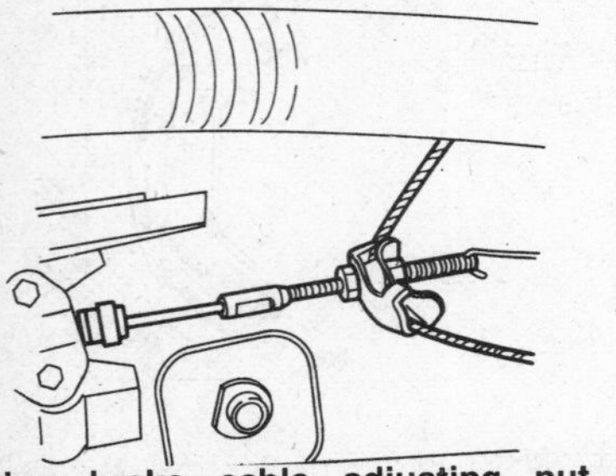

Parking brake cable adjusting nut—Impulse

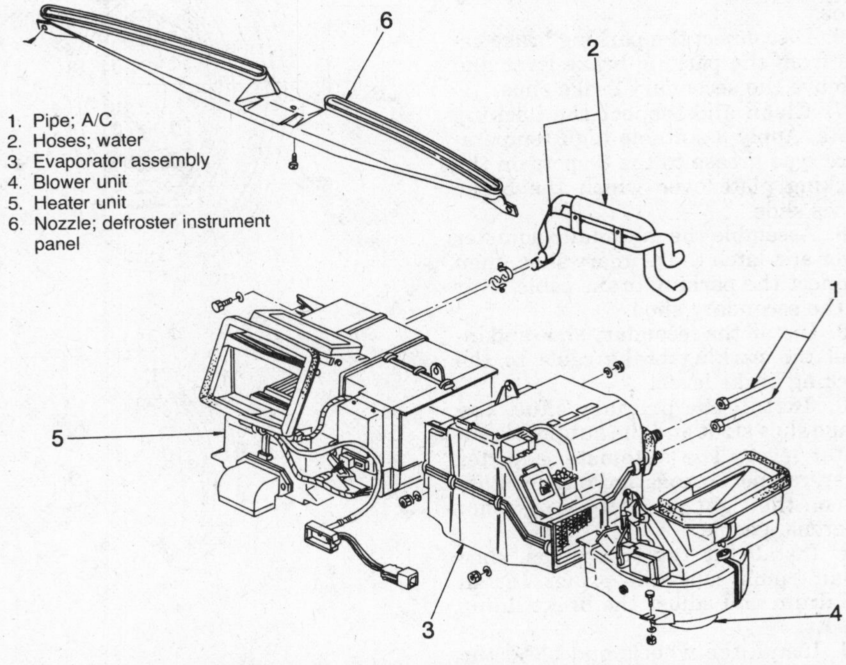


Heater and evaporator assembly removal and installation—Impulse

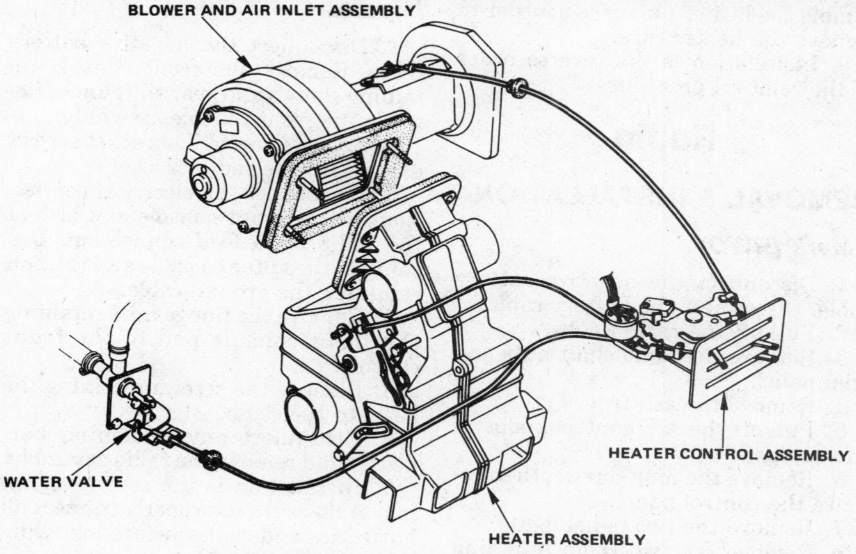


Heater system components—except Impulse

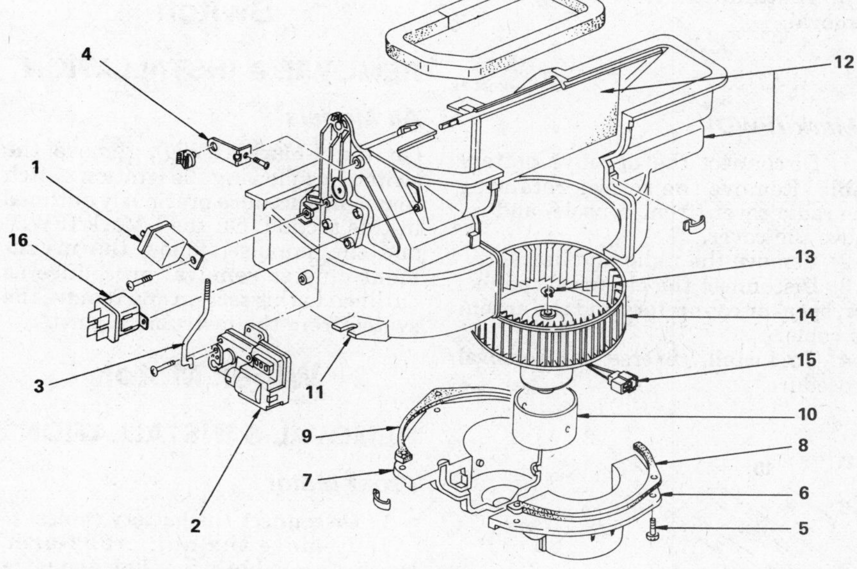


1. Relay; fresh-circulation
2. Actuator; blower unit
3. Rod; actuator
4. Lever; shutter
5. Screw; cover to case
6. Cover; blower unit
7. Cover; blower unit
8. Lining; blower unit
9. Lining; blower unit
10. Isolator; blower unit
11. Case; blower unit rear
12. Case; blower unit front
13. Ring; snap
14. Impeller; motor
15. Motor assembly; fan
16. Relay; blower unit

Blower motor removal—Impulse

2. Disconnect the wiring at the blower motor.
3. Remove the retaining screws and pull out the blower motor and squirrel cage.
4. Remove the retaining clip holding the squirrel cage to the motor and separate the two.
5. Installation is the reverse of removal.

### *I-Mark (FWD)*

1. Disconnect the blower motor electrical connector at the motor case.
2. If equipped with A/C, remove the rubber hose from the blower case.
3. Rotate the blower motor case counterclockwise and remove the blower motor assembly.
4. To install, reverse the removal procedure.

### *Impulse*

1. Disconnect the negative battery cable.
2. Remove the instrument panel and glove compartment box.
3. Discharge the A/C system , if so equipped. Disconnect the A/C lines.
4. Remove the foot air duct.
5. Remove the evaporator housing assembly.
6. Remove the blower unit. Disassemble the blower unit in order to remove the blower motor.
7. Installation is the reverse order of the removal procedure.

## Heater Core

### REMOVAL & INSTALLATION

### *I-Mark (RWD)*

1. Disconnect the battery cables.
2. Drain the radiator.

**CAUTION**

***This operation should only be carried out on a cold engine.***

3. Disconnect the heater hoses at the core connections and plug the core tubes to prevent the spillage of coolant when removing the core inside the car.
4. Remove the outer blower unit case cover and disconnect the fresh air door control cable.
5. Disconnect the temperature cable at the water valve.
6. Remove the steering wheel as previously described.
7. Remove the instrument cluster as described.
8. Disconnect the wiring for the console gauges, remove the console retaining screws, untie the shift lever leather boot and remove the console.
9. Remove the heater control and radio face plate.
10. Remove the glovebox.
11. Remove the radio as described.
12. Disconnect the selector mode cable from the driver's side of the heater assembly.
13. Carefully pull the temperature and fresh air door cables through the cowl and remove the control panel through the cluster opening.
14. Remove the instrument panel assembly as described.
15. Remove the heater unit assembly through-bolt located at the rear and bottom of the heater.
16. Remove the four attaching nuts holding the heater unit and blower unit together and remove the heater unit assembly.
17. Remove the bolts holding the heater unit case halves together and remove the heater core.
18. Installation is the reverse of removal. Refill and bleed the cooling system.

### *I-Mark (FWD)*

1. Drain radiator and disconnect

the heater hoses in the engine compartment.

2. At the lower part of the heater unit case, remove the six retaining clips.

3. Using a small pry bar, pry open the lower part of the case and remove it.

4. Remove the core assembly insulator and the core assembly.

5. To install, reverse the removal procedure.

### Impulse

1. Disconnect the negative battery cable and drain the cooling system.

2. Discharge the A/C system, if so equipped.

**NOTE: The air conditioning system must be discharged and evacuated, using the required tools, before the refrigerant lines can be disconnected.**

**CAUTION**

*Do not disconnect any refrigerant lines unless you have experience with air conditioning systems. Escaping refrigerant will freeze any surface it contacts, including your skin and eyes.*

3. Remove the instrument panel and compartment box. Mark or tag all electrical connections.

4. Disconnect the A/C lines at the evaporator.

5. Disconnect and plug the heater hoses.

6. Remove the foot air duct.

7. Remove the evaporator housing assembly.

8. Remove the heater unit. Disassemble the heater unit case in order to remove the heater core.

9. Installation is the reverse order of the removal procedure.

# Radio

## REMOVAL & INSTALLATION

### I-Mark (RWD)

1. Disconnect the negative battery cable. Disconnect the battery cables.

2. Pull off the radio knobs.

3. Remove the radio shaft nuts and trim panel.

4. Remove the ash tray.

5. Pull off the A/C control knobs, if so equipped.

6. Remove the four screws, then remove the control panel.

7. Remove the two panel lights.

8. Remove the two radio retaining screws.

9. Disconnect the electrical connectors and lead-in cable.

10. Installation is the reverse of removal.

### I-Mark (FWD)

1. Disconnect the negative battery cable. Remove the screws retaining the radio cover (front console) and remove the cover.

2. Remove the radio and bracket.

3. Disconnect the electrical connector, speaker connectors and the antenna cable.

4. To install, reverse the removal procedure.

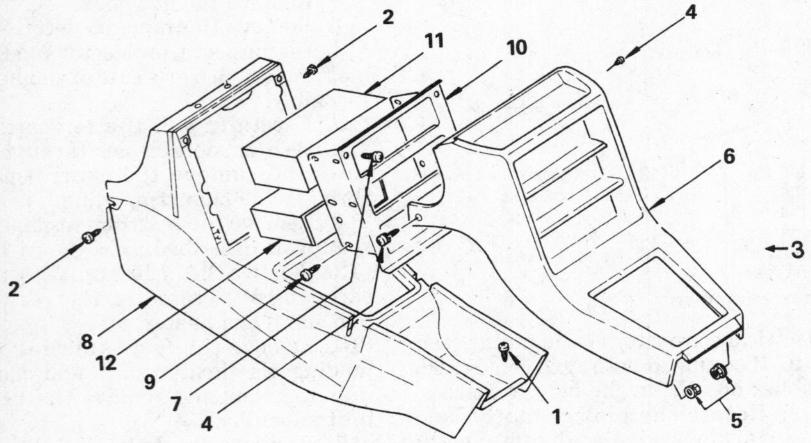


1. Screw; front console to body
2. Screws; front console to bracket
3. Console assembly
4. Screws; front console pad to front console
5. Flange nuts; front console pad to front console
6. Front console pad
7. Screws; bezel to front console
8. Front console
9. Screws; bezel to radio
10. Bezel
11. Cassette deck with FM/AM radio or FM/AM radio
12. Graphic equalizer or cassette deck

**Radio and front console removal and installation—Impulse**

### Impulse

1. Disconnect the negative battery cable. Remove the front console retaining screws and gear shift knob. Remove the front console assembly.

2. Remove the radio bracket screws along with the radio bracket.

3. Disconnect the electrical connections at the front console and also at the radio main feed connection. Disconnect the antenna cable and the bolt retaining the ground cable.

4. Remove the flange nuts retaining the front console pad to the front console.

5. Remove the screws retaining the bezel to the radio.

6. Disconnect any remaining harnesses and remove the radio assembly.

7. Installation is the reverse of removal . Be sure to properly connect all harnesses and cables before installing the console assembly.

# Windshield Wiper Switch

## REMOVAL & INSTALLATION

### All Models

On the I-Mark (RWD), remove the switch by following the ignition switch removal procedure previously outlined in this section. On the I-Mark (FWD) and the Impulse, follow the instrument cluster removal procedure as outlined in this section and remove the switch from the instrument cluster.

# Wiper Motor

## REMOVAL & INSTALLATION

### Front Motor

1. Disconnect the battery cables.

2. Remove the nut, crank-arm, bracket assembly, wiper link and pivot assembly from motor.

3. Disconnect the wiring connector.

4. Remove the three nuts securing the wiper motor and remove the motor.

5. Installation is the reverse of removal.

### Rear Motor

1. Disconnect the negative battery cable.

2. Remove the trim pad and the wiper arm assemblies.

3. Remove the mounting bolts and the motor assembly.

4. Disconnect the electrical connector.

5. To install, reverse the removal procedure.

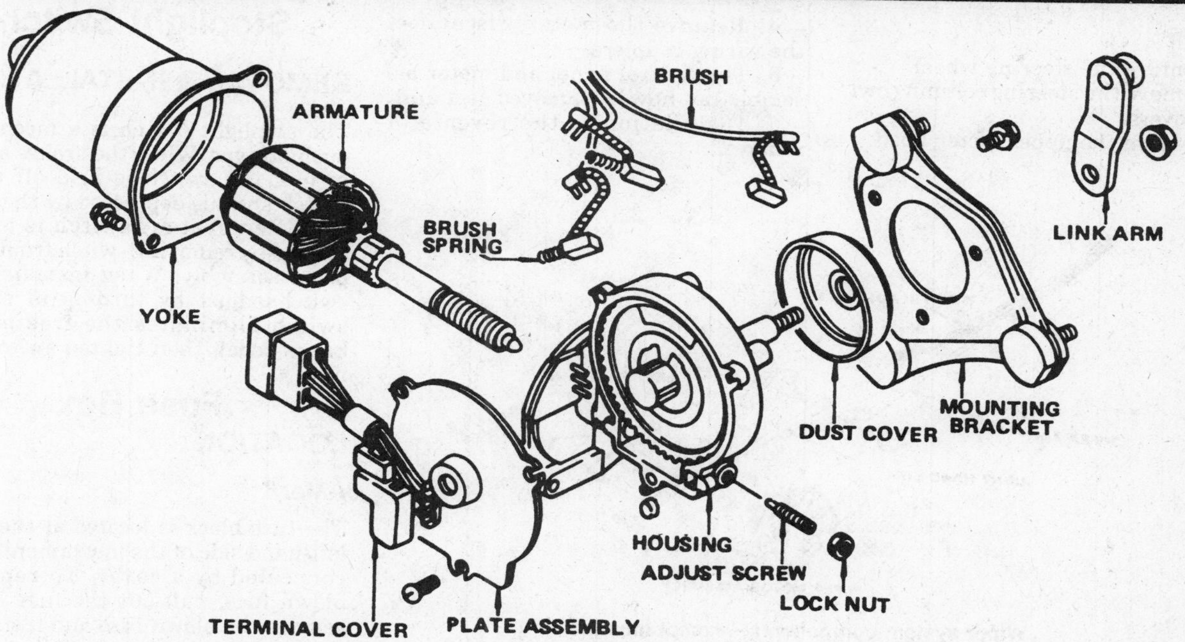

Exploded view of wiper motor components-except Impulse

## Instrument Cluster

### REMOVAL & INSTALLATION

#### *I-Mark (RWD)*

1. Disconnect the battery.
2. Remove the cluster panel.
3. Remove the instrument cluster attaching screws.
4. Rotate the cluster outwards and disconnect the electrical connectors and the speedometer cable.
5. Installation is the reverse of removal.

#### *I-Mark (FWD)*

1. Disconnect the negative battery cable.
2. Remove the instrument cluster bezel retaining screws and bezel.
3. Disconnect the windshield wiper and lighting switch connectors.
4. Remove the instrument cluster retaining screws and pull out the assembly.
5. Remove the trip reset knob and the assembly glass.
6. Remove the buzzer, sockets and bulbs.
7. Remove the speedometer assembly, fuel and temperature gauge.
8. Remove the tachometer, if equipped.
9. To install, reverse the removal procedure.

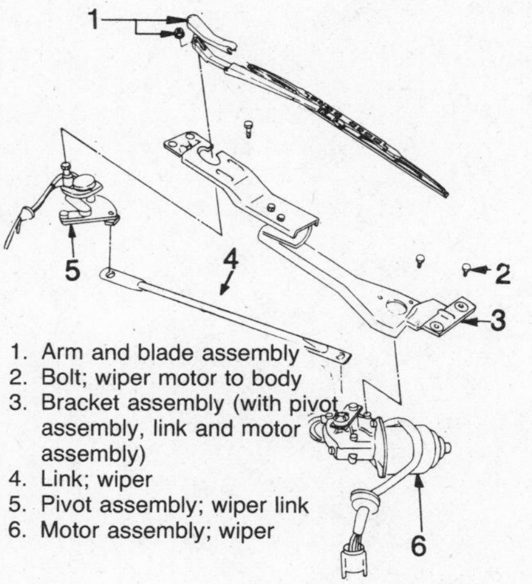

1. Arm and blade assembly
2. Bolt; wiper motor to body
3. Bracket assembly (with pivot assembly, link and motor assembly)
4. Link; wiper
5. Pivot assembly; wiper link
6. Motor assembly; wiper

Front wiper motor and linkage—Impulse

1. Be sure to disconnect the negative battery before working on the instrument panel.
2. Meter hood attaching screws
3. Meter hood
4. Winshield wiper switch
5. Lighting switch connectors
6. Meter assembly attaching screws
7. Meter assembly
8. Trip meter reset knob
9. Meter glass
10. Window plate

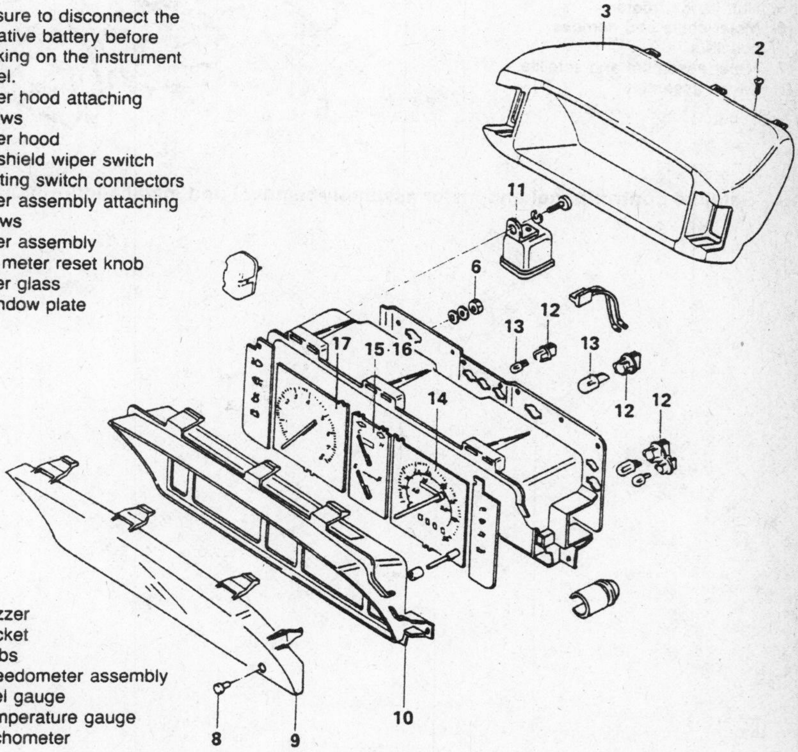

11. Buzzer
12. Socket
13. Bulbs
14. Speedometer assembly
15. Fuel gauge
16. Temperature gauge
17. Tachometer

Exploded view of the I-Mark (FWD) instrument cluster

*Impulse*

1. Remove the steering wheel.
2. Remove the steering column cowl set or covers.
3. Remove the upper meter hood.
4. Remove the meter, disconnect the wiring couplers.
5. The control panel and meter assembly can now be removed as a unit.
6. Installation is the reverse of removal.

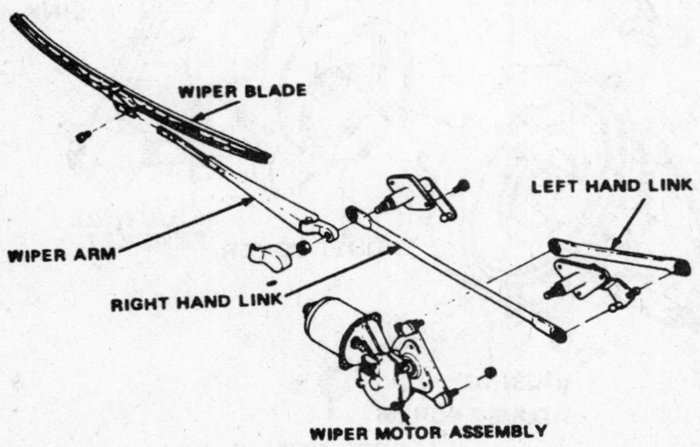


**Wiper system components—except Impulse**

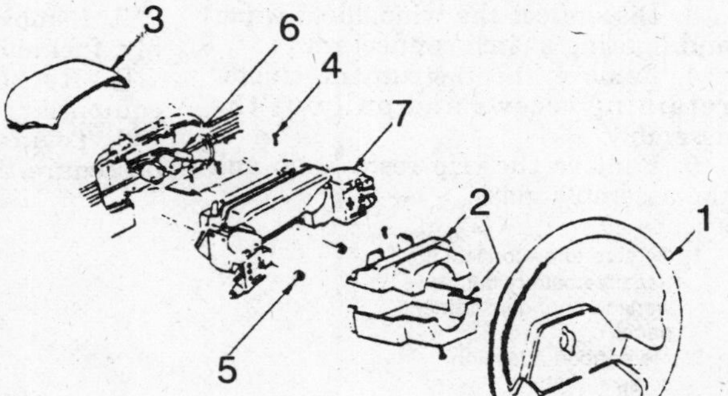


**Satellite control panel and meter assembly removal and installation—Impulse**

# Stoplight Switch

## REMOVAL & INSTALLATION

The stoplight switch is a mechanical push/off type. When the brakes are not in use, the switch is held off as the switch shaft is depressed by the brake arm. Removal off switch is accomplished by removing switch from brake pedal assembly. When installing new switch adjust by turning in so that switch eliminates the free play in brake pedal, then tighten switch lock nut.

# Fuse Box

## LOCATION

### *I-Mark*

The fuse block is located at the lower left-hand side of the instrument panel, concealed by a cover. To replace a blown fuse, pull out the fuse holder, remove the blown fuse and install one of the same amperage. On older rear wheel drive models a second fuse box was located in the engine compartment.

### *Impulse*

The fuse block is located at the lower left-hand side of the instrument panel, concealed by a cover. To replace a blown fuse, pull out the fuse holder, remove the blown fuse and install one of the same amperage. A second fuse box is located in the engine compartment.

**NOTE: On I-Mark (FWD) a 10 amp fuse for A/C compressor is located under dash on left hand side. On an late model Impulse a third fuse holder is located beneath the blower fan case.**

# Mazda 9

## 323, 626, 929, GLC, MX-6, RX-7

# SERIAL NUMBER IDENTIFICATION

## Vehicle Identification Plate

The serial number is on a plate located on the driver's side windshield pillar and is visible through the glass.
A vehicle identification number (VIN) plate, bearing the serial number and other data, is attached to the cowl.

## Engine Number

The engine number is located on a plate which is attached to the engine housing, just behind or below the distributor or on a machined pad at the right front side of the engine block. The engine number consists of an identification number followed by a 6-digit production number.

The 626, MX-6 and RX-7 engine serial number is located on the rear of the alternator bracket, stamped on the engine block. The 626 diesel engine serial number is located between the first and second fuel injectors, stamped on the engine block. The GLC and 323 engine serial number is stamped on the left hand side of the engine block, just below the cylinder head. The 929 engine serial number is stamped on the cylinder block, just below the distributor.

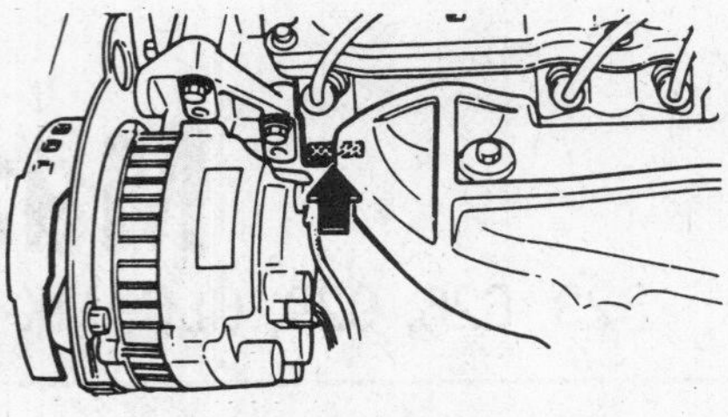

Engine number location

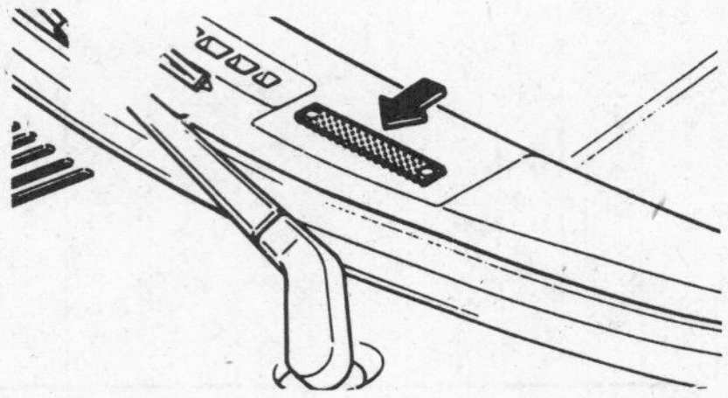

Vehicle identification plate location

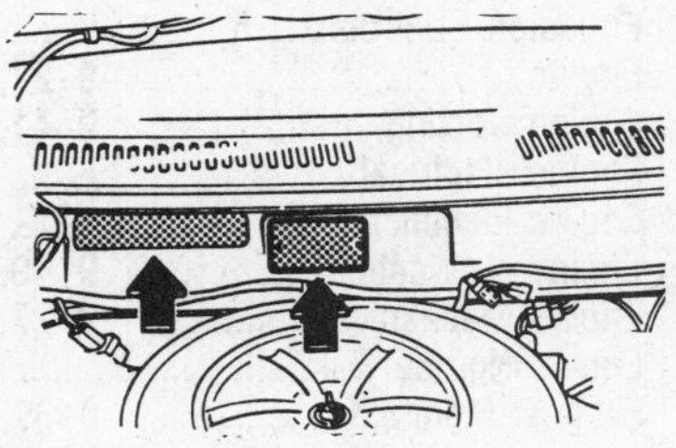

Chassis number (left) and model plate (right) location

## Vehicle Identification Label

In addition to the serial numbers, other important vehicle information and specifications can be found on the underhood emission sticker, vacuum hose routing diagram, tire pressure label and motor vehicle safety certification label.

## Transmission/ Transaxle Number

The transmission/transaxle model and serial number are either stamped on a plate that is bolted to the transmission case or stamped directly on the case itself. The location varies from model to model.

### ENGINE IDENTIFICATION

| Year | Model | Engine Displacement cu. in. (cc/liter) | Engine Series Identification | No. of Cylinders | Engine Type |
|---|---|---|---|---|---|
| 1983 | GLC | 90.9 (1490/1.5) | E5 | 4 | SOHC |
| | 626 | 121.9 (1998/2.0) | FE | 4 | SOHC |
| | RX7 | 70 (1146/1.1) | 12A | — | Rotary |
| 1984 | GLC | 90.9 (1490/1.5) | E5 | 4 | SOHC |
| | 662 | 121.9 (1998/2.0) | FE | 4 | SOHC |
| | RX7 | 70 (1146/1.1) | 12A | — | Rotary |
| 1985 | GLC | 90.9 (1490/1.5) | E5 | 4 | SOHC |
| | 626 | 121.9 (1998/2.0) | FE | 4 | SOHC |
| | 626 | 121.9 (1998/2.0) | RF | 4 | Diesel |
| | RX7 | 70 (1146/1.1) | 12A | — | Rotary |
| | RX7 | 80 (1308/1.3) | 13B | — | Rotary |
| 1986 | 323 | 97.4 (1597/1.6) | B6 | 4 | SOHC |
| | 626 | 121.9 (1998/2.0) | FE | 4 | SOHC |
| | 626 | 121.9 (1998/2.0) | FE | 4 | SOHC-Turbo |
| | RX7 | 80 (1308/1.3) | 13B | 2 | Rotary |

## ENGINE IDENTIFICATION

| Year | Model | Engine Displacement cu. in. (cc/liter) | Engine Series Identification | No. of Cylinders | Engine Type |
|---|---|---|---|---|---|
| 1987 | 323 | 97.4 (1597/1.6) | B6 | 4 | SOHC |
| | 626 | 121.9 (1998/2.0) | FE | 4 | SOHC |
| | 626 | 121.9 (1998/2.0) | FE | 4 | SOHC-Turbo |
| | RX7 | 80 (1308/1.3) | 13B | – | Rotary |
| | RX7 | 80 (1308/1.3) | 13B | – | Rotary-Turbo |
| 1988 | 323 | 97.4 (1597/1.6) | B6 | 4 | SOHC |
| | 323 | 97.4 (1597/1.6) | B6 | 4 | DOHC |
| | 626 | 133.2 (2184/2.1) | F2 | 4 | SOHC |
| | 626 | 133.2 (2184/2.1) | F2 | 4 | SOHC-Turbo |
| | MX6 | 133.2 (2184/2.1) | F2 | 4 | SOHC |
| | MX6 | 133.2 (2184/2.1) | F2 | 4 | SOHC-Turbo |
| | RX7 | 80.0 (1308/1.3) | 13B | – | Rotary |
| | RX7 | 80.0 (1308/1.3) | 13B | – | Rotary-Turbo |
| | 929 | 180.2 (2954/2.9) | JE | 6 | DOHC |
| 1989-90 | 323 | 97.4 (1597/1.6) | B6 | 4 | SOHC |
| | 323 | 97.4 (1597/1.6) | B6 | 4 | DOHC-Turbo |
| | 626 | 133.2 (2184/2.1) | F2 | 4 | SOHC |
| | 626 | 133.2 (2184/2.1) | F2 | 4 | SOHC-Turbo |
| | MX6 | 133.2 (2184/2.1) | F2 | 4 | SOHC |
| | MX6 | 133.2 (2184/2.1) | F2 | 4 | SOHC-Turbo |
| | RX7 | 80.0 (1308/1.3) | 13B | – | Rotary |
| | RX7 | 80.0 (1308/1.3) | 13B | – | Rotary-Turbo |
| | 929 | 180.2 (2954/2.9) | JE | 6 | SOHC |

SOHC Single Overhead Cam
DOHC Dual Overhead Cam

## GENERAL ENGINE SPECIFICATIONS

| Year | Model | Engine Displacement cu. in. (cc) | Fuel System Type | Net Horsepower @ rpm | Net Torque @ rpm (ft. lbs.) | Bore × Stroke (in.) | Compression Ratio | Oil Pressure @ 3000 rpm |
|---|---|---|---|---|---|---|---|---|
| 1983 | GLC | 90.9 (1490) | 2 bbl | 68 @ 5000 | 82 @ 3000 | 3.03 × 3.15 | 9.0:1 | 50-64 |
| | 626 | 121.9 (1998) | 2 bbl | 83 @ 4800 | 110 @ 2500 | 3.39 × 3.39 | 8.6:1 | 43-57 |
| 1984 | GLC | 90.9 (1490) | 2 bbl | 68 @ 5000 | 82 @ 3000 | 3.03 × 3.15 | 9.0:1 | 50-60 |
| | 626 | 121.9 (1998) | 2 bbl | 83 @ 4800 | 110 @ 2500 | 3.39 × 3.39 | 8.6:1 | 43-51 |
| 1985 | GLC | 90.9 (1490) | 2 bbl | 68 @ 5000 | 82 @ 3000 | 3.03 × 3.15 | 9.0:1 | 50-60 |
| | 626 | 121.9 (1998) | 2 bbl | 83 @ 4800 | 110 @ 2500 | 3.39 × 3.39 | 8.6:1 | 43-57 |
| | 626 Diesel | 121.9 (1998) | DFI | 72 @ 4650 | 100 @ 2750 | 3.39 × 3.39 | 22.7:1 | 58-70 |

## GENERAL ENGINE SPECIFICATIONS

| Year | VIN | No. Cylinder Displacement cu. in. (liter) | Fuel System Type | Net Horsepower @ rpm | Net Torque @ rpm (ft.lbs.) | Bore × Stroke (in.) | Com-pression Ratio | Oil Pressure @ rpm |
|---|---|---|---|---|---|---|---|---|
| 1986 | 323 | 97.4 (1597) | EFI① | 82 @ 5000 | 92 @ 2500 | 3.07 × 3.29 | 9.3:1 | 43-57 |
| | 626 | 121.9 (1998) | EFI | 93 @ 5000 | 115 @ 2500 | 3.39 × 3.39 | 8.6:1 | 43-57 |
| | 626 Turbo | 121.9 (1998) | EFI | 120 @ 5000 | 150 @ 3000 | 3.39 × 3.39 | 7.8:1 | 43-57 |
| 1987 | 323 | 97.4 (1597) | EFI① | 82 @ 5000 | 92 @ 2500 | 3.07 × 3.29 | 9.3:1 | 43-57 |
| | 626 | 121.9 (1998) | EFI | 93 @ 5000 | 115 @ 2500 | 3.39 × 3.39 | 8.6:1 | 43-57 |
| | 626 Turbo | 121.9 (1998) | EFI | 120 @ 5000 | 115 @ 3000 | 3.39 × 3.39 | 7.8:1 | 43-57 |
| 1988 | 323 | 97.4 (1597) | EFI | 82 @ 5000 | 92 @ 2500 | 3.07 × 3.29 | 9.3:1 | 50-64 |
| | 323 Turbo | 97.4 (1597) | EFI | 132 @ 6000 | 136 @ 3000 | 3.07 × 3.29 | 7.9:1 | 50-64 |
| | 626 | 133.2 (2184) | EFI | 97 @ 5000 | 120 @ 2500 | 3.39 × 3.70 | 8.6:1 | 43-57 |
| | 626 Turbo | 133.2 (2184) | EFI | 125 @ 5000 | 155 @ 3500 | 3.39 × 3.70 | 7.8:1 | 43-57 |
| | MX6 | 133.2 (2184) | EFI | 97 @ 5000 | 120 @ 2500 | 3.39 × 3.70 | 8.6:1 | 43-57 |
| | MX6 Turbo | 133.2 (2184) | EFI | 125 @ 5000 | 155 @ 3500 | 3.39 × 3.70 | 7.8:1 | 43-57 |
| | 929 | 180.2 (2954) | EFI | 158 @ 5500 | 170 @ 4000 | 3.54 × 3.05 | 8.5:1 | 50-64 |
| 1989-90 | 323 | 97.4 (1597) | EFI | 82 @ 5000 | 92 @ 2500 | 3.07 × 3.29 | 9.3:1② | 50-64 |
| | 323 Turbo | 97.4 (1597) | EFI | 132 @ 6000 | 136 @ 3000 | 3.07 × 3.29 | 7.9:1 | 50-64 |
| | 626 | 133.2 (2184) | EFI | 110 @ 4700 | 130 @ 3000 | 3.39 × 3.70 | 8.6:1 | 43-57 |
| | 626 Turbo | 133.2 (2184) | EFI | 145 @ 4300 | 190 @ 3500 | 3.39 × 3.70 | 7.8:1 | 43-57 |
| | MX6 | 133.2 (2184) | EFI | 110 @ 4700 | 130 @ 3000 | 3.39 × 3.70 | 7.8:1 | 43-57 |
| | MX6 Turbo | 133.2 (2184) | EFI | 145 @ 4300 | 110 @ 3500 | 3.39 × 3.70 | 8.6:1 | 43-57 |
| | 929 | 180.2 (2954) | EFI | 158 @ 5500 | 170 @ 4000 | 3.54 × 3.05 | 8.5:1 | 41-61 |

NA Not available
DFI Diesel Fuel Injection
EFI Electronic Fuel Injection
① Canadian models use 2 bbl carburetor

## GENERAL ENGINE SPECIFICATIONS—ROTARY ENGINE

| Year | Model | Engine Displacement cu. in. (cc) | Fuel System Type | Net Horsepower @ rpm | Net Torque @ rpm (ft. lbs.) | Rotor Displacement (cu. in.) | Com-pression Ratio | Oil Pressure @ 3000 rpm |
|---|---|---|---|---|---|---|---|---|
| 1983 | RX7 | 70 (1146) | 4 bbl | 101 @ 6000 | 105 @ 4000 | 35 | 9.4:1 | 64-78 |
| 1984 | RX7 | 80 (1308) | EFI | 135 @ 2750 | 133 @ 2750 | 40 | 9.4:1 | 64-78 |
| | RX7 | 70 (1146) | 4 bbl | 101 @ 6000 | 105 @ 4000 | 35 | 9.4:1 | 64-78 |
| 1985 | RX7 | 80 (1308) | EFI | 135 @ 2750 | 133 @ 2750 | 40 | 9.4:1 | 64-78 |
| | RX7 | 70 (1146) | 4 bbl | 101 @ 6000 | 105 @ 4000 | 35 | 9.4:1 | 64-78 |

## GENERAL ENGINE SPECIFICATIONS—ROTARY ENGINE

| Year | Model | Engine Displacement cu. in. (cc) | Fuel System Type | Net Horsepower @ rpm | Net Torque @ rpm (ft. lbs.) | Rotor Displacement (cu. in.) | Com-pression Ratio | Oil Pressure @ 3000 rpm |
|---|---|---|---|---|---|---|---|---|
| 1986 | RX7 | 80 (1308) | EFI | 146 @ 6500 | 138 @ 3500 | 40 | 9.4:1 | 64-78 |
| | Turbo | 80 (1308) | EFI | 182 @ 6500 | 183 @ 3500 | 40 | 8.5:1 | 64-78 |
| 1987 | RX7 | 80 (1308) | EFI | 146 @ 6500 | 138 @ 3500 | 40 | 9.4:1 | 64-78 |
| | Turbo | 80 (1308) | EFI | 182 @ 6500 | 183 @ 3500 | 40 | 8.5:1 | 64-78 |
| 1988 | RX7 | 80 (1308) | EFI | 146 @ 6500 | 138 @ 3500 | 40 | 9.4:1 | 64-78 |
| | Turbo | 80 (1308) | EFI | 182 @ 6500 | 183 @ 3500 | 40 | 8.5:1 | 64-78 |
| 1989-90 | RX7 | 80 (1308) | EFI | 146 @ 6500 | 138 @ 3500 | 40 | 8.5:1 | 64-78 |
| | Turbo | 80 (1308) | EFI | 182 @ 6500 | 183 @ 3500 | 40 | 9.4:1 | 64-78 |

EFI Electronic Fuel Injection

## GASOLINE ENGINE TUNE-UP SPECIFICATIONS

| Year | Model | Engine Displacement cu. in. (cc) | Spark Plugs Type | Spark Plugs Gap (in.) | Ignition Timing (deg.) MT | Ignition Timing (deg.) AT | Com-pression Pressure (psi) | Fuel Pump (psi) | Idle Speed (rpm) MT | Idle Speed (rpm) AT | Valve Clearance In. | Valve Clearance Ex. |
|---|---|---|---|---|---|---|---|---|---|---|---|---|
| 1983 | GLC | 90.9 (1490) | BPR5ES | 0.031 | 8B | 8B | NA | 2.8-3.8 | 850 | 750 | ④ | ⑤ |
| | 626 | 121.9 (1998) | BPR5ES | 0.031 | 6B | 6B | NA | 2.8-3.5 | 750 | 700 | 0.012 | 0.012 |
| 1984 | GLC | 90.9 (1490) | BPR5ES | 0.031 | 6B | 6B | NA | 4.2-6.0 | 850 | 750 | ④ | ⑤ |
| | 626 | 121.9 (1998) | BPR5ES | 0.031 | 6B | 6B | NA | 2.8-4.3 | 750 | 700 | 0.012 | 0.012 |
| 1985 | GLC | 90.9 (1490) | BPR5ES | 0.031 | 6B | 6B | NA | 4.2-6.0 | 850 | 750 | ④ | ⑤ |
| | 626 | 121.9 (1998) | BPR5ES | 0.031 | 6B | 6B | NA | 2.8-4.3 | 750 | 700 | 0.012 | 0.012 |
| 1986 | 323 | 9.74 (1597) | BPR5ES-11 | 0.040 | 2B① | 2B | NA | ② | 800–900 | 900–1050 | ③ | ③ |
| | 626 | 121.9 (1998) | BPR5ES | 0.031 | 6B | 6B | NA | 64-85 | 750 | 900 | ③ | ③ |
| | 626 Turbo | 121.9 (1998) | BPR6ES | 0.031 | 6B | 6B | NA | 64-85 | 750 | 900 | ③ | ③ |
| 1987 | 323 | 97.4 (1597) | BPR5ES-11 | 0.040 | 2B① | 2B | NA | ② | 800–900 | 900–1050 | ③ | ③ |
| | 626 | 121.9 (1998) | BPR5ES | 0.031 | 6B | 6B | NA | 64-85 | 750 | 900 | ③ | ③ |
| | 626 Turbo | 121.9 (1998) | BPR6ES | 0.031 | 6B | 6B | NA | 64-85 | 750 | 900 | ③ | ③ |
| 1988 | 323 | 97.4 (1597) | BPR5ES-11 ⑥ | 0.040 | 2B⑦ | 2B⑦ | NA | 64-85 | 850 | 850 | Hyd. | Hyd. |
| | 626 | 133.2 (2184) | ZFR5A-11 | 0.040 | 6B | 6B | NA | 64-85 | 750 | 750 | Hyd. | Hyd. |
| | 626 Turbo | 133.2 (2184) | ZFR5A-11 | 0.040 | 9B | 9B | NA | 64-85 | 750 | 750 | Hyd. | Hyd. |
| | MX6 | 133.2 (2184) | ZFR5A-11 | 0.040 | 6B | 6B | NA | 64-85 | 750 | 750 | Hyd. | Hyd. |
| | MX6 Turbo | 133.2 (2184) | ZFR5A-11 | 0.040 | 9B | 9B | NA | 64-85 | 750 | 750 | Hyd. | Hyd. |
| | 929 | 180.2 (2954) | ZFR5A-11 | 0.040 | 15B | 15B | NA | 64-85 | 650 | 650 | Hyd. | Hyd. |
| 1989 | 323 | 97.4 (1597) | BPR5ES-11 | 0.041 | 2B | 2B | 135-192 | 64-85 | 650 | 650 | Hyd. | Hyd. |

## GASOLINE ENGINE TUNE-UP SPECIFICATIONS

| Year | Model | Engine Displacement cu. in. (cc) | Spark Plugs Type | Spark Plugs Gap (in.) | Ignition Timing (deg.) MT | Ignition Timing (deg.) AT | Com-pression Pressure (psi) | Fuel Pump (psi) | Idle Speed (rpm) MT | Idle Speed (rpm) AT | Valve Clearance In. | Valve Clearance Ex. |
|---|---|---|---|---|---|---|---|---|---|---|---|---|
| 1989 | 323 Turbo | 97.4 (1597) | BCPR-6ES11 | 0.041 | 12B | 12B | 109-156 | 64-85 | 850 | 850 | Hyd. | Hyd. |
| | 626 | 133.2 (2184) | ZFR5A-11 | 0.041 | 6B | 6B | 114-162 | 64-85 | 750 | 750 | Hyd. | Hyd. |
| | 626 Turbo | 133.2 (2184) | ZFR5A-11 | 0.041 | 9B | 9B | 98-139 | 64-85 | 750 | 750 | Hyd. | Hyd. |
| | MX6 | 133.2 (2184) | ZFR5A-11 | 0.041 | 6B | 6B | 114-162 | 64-85 | 750 | 750 | Hyd. | Hyd. |
| | MX6 Turbo | 133.2 (2184) | ZFR5A-11 | 0.041 | 9B | 9B | 98-139 | 64-85 | 750 | 750 | Hyd. | Hyd. |
| | 929 | 180.2 (2954) | ZFR5A-11 | 0.041 | 15B | 15B | 114-164 | 64-85 | 650 | 650 | Hyd. | Hyd. |
| 1990 | SEE UNDERHOOD SPECIFICATION STICKER | | | | | | | | | | | |

NA Not available
B Before top dead center
① 7B with the vacuum hose connected on EFI models
② Carburetor—4.0-5.0 psi
EFI—64-85 psi
③ Valve side—0.012 in.
Cam side—0.008 in.
④ Intake valve side—0.0010 in.
Intake cam side—0.007 in.
⑤ Exhaust valve side—0.012 in.
Exhaust cam side—0.009 in.
⑥ DOHC turbocharged engine—DCPR6E11
⑦ DOHC turbocharged engine—12 degrees BTDC

## TUNE-UP SPECIFICATIONS—ROTARY ENGINE

| Year | Engine Displacement cu. in. (cc) | Spark Plugs Type | Spark Plugs Gap (in.) | Distributor | Ignition Timing (degrees) Leading | Ignition Timing (degrees) Trailing | Idle Speed (rpm) MT | Idle Speed (rpm) AT① |
|---|---|---|---|---|---|---|---|---|
| 1983 | 70 (1146) | ② | 0.053 | Electronic④ | 0 | 20A | 725–775 | 725–775 |
| 1984 | 70 (1146) | ③ | 0.053 | Electronic | 0 | 20A | 750 | 750 |
| | 80 (1308) | ③ | 0.053 | Electronic④ | 5A | 20A | 800 | 800 |
| 1985 | 70 (1146) | ③ | 0.053 | Electronic④ | 0 | 20A | 750 | 750 |
| | 80 (1308) | ③ | 0.055 | Electronic | 5A | 20A | 800 | 800 |
| 1986 | 80 (1308) | S-29A⑤, S-31⑥ | 0.080 | Electronic | 5A | 20A | 750 | 750 |
| 1987 | 80 (1308) | S-29A⑤, S-31⑥ | 0.080 | Electronic | 5A | 20A | 750 | 750 |
| 1988 | 80 (1308) | SD10A⑤, SD11A⑥ | 0.080 | Electronic | 5A | 20A | 750 | 750 |
| 1989-90 | 80 (1308) | SD10A⑤ SD11A⑥ | 0.080 | Electronic⑤ | 5A | 20A | 750 | 750 |
| | 80 (1308) | SD10A⑤ SD11A⑥ | 0.080 | Electronic⑤ | 5A | 20A | 750 | 750 |

A After top dead center
① Transmission in Drive
② BR7ET, BR8ET, BR9ET
③ BR7EQ14, BR8EQ14, BR9EQ14
④ Air gap—0.20-0.35
⑤ Leading
⑥ Trailing

## DIESEL ENGINE TUNE-UP SPECIFICATIONS

| Year | Engine Displacement cu. in. (cc) | Valve Clearance Intake (in.) | Valve Clearance Exhaust (in.) | Intake Valve Opens (deg.) | Injection Pump Setting (deg.) | Injection Nozzle Pressure (psi) New | Injection Nozzle Pressure (psi) Used | Idle Speed (rpm) | Cranking Compression Pressure (psi) |
|---|---|---|---|---|---|---|---|---|---|
| 1985 | 121.9 (1998) | 0.008–0.012 | 0.012–0.016 | 13B | 0 ① | 1920 | NA | 800-850 | 426 @ 200 |

B Before top dead center
① @ 0.039 in. lift of cam

## FIRING ORDERS

**NOTE: To avoid confusion, always replace spark plug wires one at a time.**

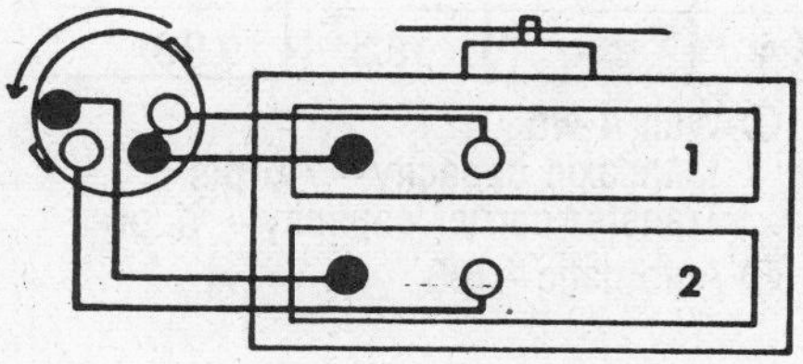


Rotary engine

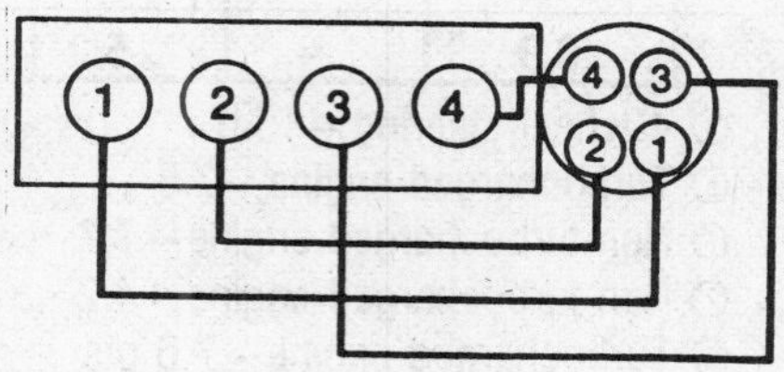


**1490cc engine – 1983–85 GLC**
**1597cc engine – 1986–90 323**
**1998cc engine – 1983–90 626 and MX-6**
**Firing order – 1-3-4-2**

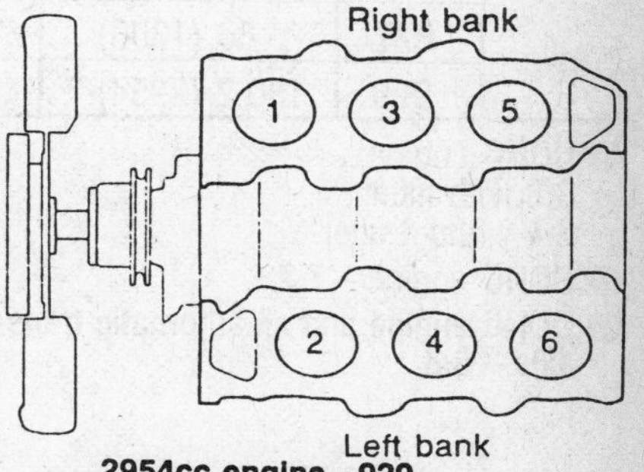


**2954cc engine – 929**
**Firing order – 1-2-3-4-5-6**

## CAPACITIES

| Year | Model | Engine Displacement cu. in. (cc) | Engine Crankcase with Filter | Engine Crankcase without Filter | Transmission (pts.) 4-Spd | Transmission (pts.) 5-Spd | Transmission (pts.) Auto. | Drive Axle (pts.) | Fuel Tank (gal.) | Cooling System (qts.) |
|---|---|---|---|---|---|---|---|---|---|---|
| 1983 | GLC | 90.9 (1490) | 4.0 | 3.5 | 2.8 | 6.8 | 12.0 | — | 11.1 | 5.8 |
| | 626 | 121.9 (1998) | 5.0 | 4.5 | — | 7.0 | 12.0 | — | 15.6 | 7.4 |
| | RX7 | 70 (1146) | 5.0 | 4.5 | — | 4.2 | 13.2 | 2.6 | 16.4 | 10.0 |
| 1984 | GLC | 90.9 (1490) | 4.0 | 3.5 | 2.8 | 6.8 | 12.0 | — | 11.1 | 5.8 |
| | 626 | 121.9 (1998) | 5.0 | 4.5 | — | 7.0 | 12.0 | — | 15.6 | 7.4 |
| | RX7 | 70 (1146) | 5.0 | 4.5 | — | 4.2 | 15.8 | 2.6 | 16.4 | 10.0 |
| 1985 | GLC | 90.9 (1490) | 4.0 | 3.5 | 2.8 | 6.8 | 12.0 | — | 11.1 | 5.8 |
| | 626 | 121.9 (1998) | 5.0 | 4.5 | — | 7.0 | 12.0 | — | 15.6 | 7.4 |
| | 626 Diesel | 121.9 (1998) | 6.8 | 6.3 | — | 7.0 | 12.0 | — | 15.8 | 9.5 |
| | RX7 | 70 (1146) | 5.0 | 4.5 | — | 4.2 | 15.8 | 2.6 | 16.4 | 10.0 |
| | RX7 | 80 (1308) | 5.0 | 4.5 | — | 4.2 | 15.8 | 2.8 | 16.6 | 9.2 |
| 1986 | 323 | 97.4 (1597) | 3.2 | 2.9 | 6.8 | 6.8 | 12.0 | — | 11.9 | 6.3 |
| | 626 | 121.9 (1998) | 5.0 | 4.5 | — | 7.0 | 12.0 | — | 15.6 | 7.4 |
| | RX7 | 80 (1308) | 5.0 | 4.5 | — | 4.2 | 15.8 | 2.8 | 16.6 | 9.2 |
| 1987 | 323 | 97.4 (1597) | 3.2 | 2.9 | 6.8 | 6.8 | 12.0 | — | 11.9 | 6.3 |
| | 626 | 121.9 (1998) | 5.0 | 4.5 | — | 7.0 | 12.0 | — | 15.6 | 7.4 |
| | RX7 | 80 (1308) | 5.0 | 4.5 | — | 4.2 | 15.8 | 2.8 | 16.6 | 9.2 |

## CAPACITIES

| Year | Model | Engine Displacement cu. in. (cc) | Engine Crankcase with Filter | Engine Crankcase without Filter | Transmission (pts.) 4-Spd | Transmission (pts.) 5-Spd | Transmission (pts.) Auto. | Drive Axle (pts.) | Fuel Tank (gal.) | Cooling System (qts.) |
|---|---|---|---|---|---|---|---|---|---|---|
| 1988 | 323 | 97.4 (1597) | 3.6① | 3.2① | — | 6.8② | 13.2 | 2.8 | 12.7 | 5.3② |
| | 626 | 133.2 (2184) | 4.9 | 4.1 | — | 7.2⑤ | 13.2 | NA | 15.9④ | 7.9 |
| | MX6 | 133.2 (2184) | 4.9 | 4.1 | — | 7.2⑤ | 13.2 | NA | 15.9④ | 7.9 |
| | RX7 | 80 (1308) | 6.1 | 4.7 | — | 5.2 | 15.8 | 2.8 | 16.6 | 9.2⑥ |
| | 929 | 180.2 (2954) | 5.7 | 4.8 | — | 5.2 | 15.4 | 2.8 | 18.5 | 9.9 |
| 1989-90 | 323 | 97.4 (1597) | 3.6① | 3.2① | — | 7.6⑧⑨ | 13.4 | — | 12.7 | 5.3⑩ |
| | 626 | 133.2 (2184) | 4.9 | 4.1 | — | 7.0⑤ | 14.4 | — | 15.9④ | 7.9 |
| | MX6 | 133.2 (2184) | 4.9 | 4.1 | — | 7.0⑤ | 14.4 | — | 15.9④ | 7.9 |
| | RX7 | 80 (1308) | 6.1 | 4.7 | — | 5.2 | 15.8 | 1.3 | 16.6 | 9.2⑥ |
| | 929 | 180.2 (2954) | 5.7 | 9.8 | — | 5.2 | 15.4 | — | 18.5 | 9.9④ |

① DOHC engine
3.8 with filter
3.4 without filter
② DOHC engine—7.2
③ DOHC engine and all automatic transaxle—6.3
④ 4 wheel steering—15.0
⑤ Turbocharged engine—7.8
⑥ Non-turbocharged engine—7.7
⑦ Non-turbocharged engine—4.2
⑧ Turbocharged engine—7.6 pts
⑨ With 4 wd
Transaxle capacity—7.6 pts
Transfer carrier capacity— 1 pt
⑩ Automatic—6.3

## CAMSHAFT SPECIFICATIONS

All measurements given in inches.

| Year | Engine Displacement cu. in. (cc) | Journal Diameter 1 | Journal Diameter 2 | Journal Diameter 3 | Journal Diameter 4 | Journal Diameter 5 | Lobe Lift In. | Lobe Lift Ex. | Bearing Clearance | Camshaft End Play |
|---|---|---|---|---|---|---|---|---|---|---|
| 1983 | 90.9 (1490) ④ | 1.6515–1.6522 | 1.6504–1.6510 | 1.6504–1.6510 | 1.6504–1.6510 | 1.6515–1.6522 | 1.7368 | 1.7368 | 0.014–0.030 ② | 0.001–0.007 ① |
| | 121.9 (1998) | 1.257–1.258 | 1.256–1.257 | 1.256–1.257 | 1.256–1.257 | 1.257–1.258 | 1.5023 | 1.5024 | 0.014–0.033 ② | 0.003–0.007 ① |
| 1984 | 90.9 (1490) ④ | 1.6515–1.6522 | 1.6504–1.6510 | 1.6504–1.6510 | 1.6504–1.6510 | 1.6515–1.6522 | 1.7368 | 1.7368 | 0.014–0.030 ② | 0.001–0.001 ① |
| | 121.9 (1998) | 1.2570–1.6522 | 1.2560–1.6510 | 1.2560–1.6510 | 1.2560–1.6510 | 1.2570–1.6522 | 1.5023 | 1.5024 | 0.014–0.030 ③ | 0.003–0.007 ① |
| 1985 | 90.9 (1490) | 1.6515–1.6522 | 1.6504–1.6510 | 1.6504–1.6510 | 1.6504–1.6510 | 1.6515–1.6522 | 1.7368 | 1.7368 | 0.014–0.030 ③ | 0.001–0.007 ① |
| | 121.9 (1998) | 1.257–1.258 | 1.256–1.257 | 1.256–1.257 | 1.256–1.257 | 1.257–1.258 | 1.5023 | 1.5024 | 0.014–0.030 ② | 0.03–0.007 ① |
| | 121.9 (1998) Diesel | 1.258–1.259 | 1.258–1.259 | 1.258–1.259 | 1.258–1.259 | 1.258–1.259 | 1.744 | 1.783 | 0.0098–0.0026 | 0.006–0.008 |
| 1986 | 97.4 (159) | 1.710–1.711 | 1.709–1.710 | 1.709–1.710 | 1.709–1.710 | 1.710–1.711 | 1.439–1.443 | 1.439–1.443 | 0.001–0.003 ③ | 0.002–0.007 |

## CAMSHAFT SPECIFICATIONS

All measurements given in inches.

| Year | Engine Displacement cu. in. (cc) | Journal Diameter 1 | 2 | 3 | 4 | 5 | Lobe Lift In. | Ex. | Bearing Clearance | Camshaft End Play |
|---|---|---|---|---|---|---|---|---|---|---|
| 1986 | 121.9 (1998) | 1.257–1.258 | 1.256–1.257 | 1.256–1.257 | 1.256–1.257 | 1.257–1.258 | 1.5023 | 1.5024 | 0.0014–0.0033 ② | 0.003–0.006 ① |
| 1987 | 97.4 (1597) | 1.710–1.711 | 1.709–1.710 | 1.709–1.710 | 1.709–1.710 | 1.710–1.711 | 1.439–1.443 | 1.439–1.443 | 0.001–0.003 ⑤ | 0.002–0.007 |
| | 121.9 (1998) | 1.257–1.258 | 1.256–1.257 | 1.256–1.257 | 1.256–1.257 | 1.257–1.258 | 1.5023 | 1.5024 | 0.0014–0.0033 ② | 0.003–0.006 ① |
| 1988 | 97.4 (1597) | 1.710–1.711 | 1.709–1.710 | 1.709–1.710 | 1.709–1.710 | 1.710–1.710 | 1.434–1.438 | 1.434–1.438 | 0.001–0.003 ⑤ | 0.002–0.007 |
| | 97.4 (1597) ⑥ | 1.021–1.022 | 1.021–1.022 | 1.021–1.022 | 1.021–1.022 | 1.021–1.022 | 1.6098 | 1.6098 | 0.0014–0.0032 | 0.0028–0.0075 |
| | 133.2 (2184) | 1.2575–1.2585 | 1.2563–1.2573 | 1.2563–1.2573 | 1.2563–1.2573 | 1.2575–1.2585 | 1.6256–1.6295 | 1.6455–1.6495 | 0.0014–0.0033 ⑦ | 0.003–0.006 |
| | 180.2 (2954) | 1.9268–1.9274 | 1.9258–1.9266 | 1.9258–1.9266 | 1.9258–1.9274 | — | 1.6163 | 1.6257 | 0.0024–0.0035 ⑧ | 0.002–0.007 |
| 1989-90 | 97.4 (1597) | 1.710–1.711 | 1.710–1.711 | 1.709–1.711 | 1.710–1.711 | 1.710–1.711 | 1.4321–1.4380 | 1.4321–1.4380 | 0.0013–0.0045 ⑤ | 0.0020–0.0071 |
| | 97.4 (1597) ⑥ | 1.0213–1.0222 | 1.0213–1.0222 | 1.0213–1.0222 | 1.0213–1.0222 | 1.0213–1.0222 | 1.6098 | 1.6098 | 0.0014–0.0032 | 0.0028–0.0075 |
| | 133.2 (2184) | 1.2575–1.2585 | 1.2563–1.2573 | 1.2563–1.2573 | 1.2563–1.2573 | 1.2575–1.2585 | 1.6256–1.6295 | 1.6197– | 0.0014–0.0033 ⑦ | 0.003–0.006 |
| | 180.2 (2954) | 1.9268–1.9274 | 1.9258–1.9266 | 1.9255–1.9266 | 1.9268–1.9274 | — | 1.6163 | 1.6257 | 0.0024–0.0035 ⑧ | 0.0020–0.0071 |

① Wear limit—0.008
② Center clearance—0.0026–0.0043
③ Center clearance—0.0011–0.0031
④ Includes GLC wagon
⑤ Center clearance—0.026–0.0045
⑥ DOHC engine
⑦ Nos. 2, 3 & 4—0.0026–0.0045
⑧ Nos. 2 & 3—0.0031–0.0045

## CRANKSHAFT AND CONNECTING ROD SPECIFICATIONS

All measurements are given in inches.

| Year | Engine Displacement cu. in. (cc) | Crankshaft Main Brg. Journal Dia. | Crankshaft Main Brg. Oil Clearance | Crankshaft Shaft End-play | Crankshaft Thrust on No. | Connecting Rod Journal Diameter | Connecting Rod Oil Clearance | Connecting Rod Side Clearance |
|---|---|---|---|---|---|---|---|---|
| 1983 | 90.9 (1490) | 1.9661–1.9668 | 0.0009–0.0017 | 0.004–0.006 | 5 | 1.5724–1.5734 | 0.0009–0.0019 | 0.004–0.101 |
| | 121.9 (1998) | 2.359–2.360 | 0.0012–0.0019 | 0.0031–0.0071 | 3 | 2.005–2.006 | 0.0010–0.0026 | 0.004–0.010 |
| 1984 | 90.9 (1490) | 1.9661–1.9668 | 0.0009–0.0017 | 0.004–0.006 | 5 | 1.5724–1.5734 | 0.0009–0.0019 | 0.004–0.010 |
| | 121.9 (1998) | 2.359–2.360 | 0.0012–0.0019 | 0.0031–0.0071 | 3 | 2.005–2.006 | 0.0010–0.0026 | 0.004–0.010 |

## CRANKSHAFT AND CONNECTING ROD SPECIFICATIONS

All measurements are given in inches.

| Year | Engine Displacement cu. in. (cc) | Crankshaft Main Brg. Journal Dia. | Crankshaft Main Brg. Oil Clearance | Crankshaft Shaft End-play | Crankshaft Thrust on No. | Connecting Rod Journal Diameter | Connecting Rod Oil Clearance | Connecting Rod Side Clearance |
|---|---|---|---|---|---|---|---|---|
| 1985 | 90.9 (1490) | 1.9661–1.9668 | 0.0009–0.0017 | 0.004–0.006 | 5 | 1.5724–1.5734 | 0.0009–0.0019 | 0.004–0.010 |
| | 121.9 (1998) | 2.359–2.360 | 0.0012–0.0019 | 0.0031–0.0071 | 3 | 2.005–2.006 | 0.0010–0.0026 | 0.004–0.010 |
| | 121.9 (1998) Diesel | 2.360–2.361 | 0.0012–0.0019 | 0.0016–0.0110 | 3 | 2.0055–2.0063 | 0.0012–0.0024 | 0.0043–0.0102 |
| 1986 | 97.4 (1597) | 1.9662–1.9668 | 0.0011–0.0027 | 0.0031–0.0071 | 4 | 1.7693–1.7699 | 0.0011–0.0027 | 0.0043–0.0103 |
| | 121.9 (1998) | 2.359–2.360 | 0.0012–0.0019 | 0.0031–0.0071 | 3 | 2.005–2.006 | 0.0010–0.0026 | 0.004–0.010 |
| 1987 | 97.4 (1597) | 1.9662–1.9668 | 0.0011–0.0027 | 0.0031–0.0071 | 4 | 1.7693–1.7699 | 0.0011–0.0027 | 0.0043–0.0103 |
| | 121.9 (1998) | 2.359–2.360 | 0.0012–0.0019 | 0.0031–0.0071 | 3 | 2.005–2.006 | 0.0010–0.0026 | 0.004–0.010 |
| 1988 | 97.4 (1597) | 1.9961–1.9668 | 0.0009–0.0017 ② | 0.0031–0.0111 | 4 | 1.7693–1.7699 | 0.0011–0.0027 | 0.0043–0.0103 |
| | 132.2 (2184) | 2.3597–2.3604 | 0.0010–0.0017 ① | 0.0031–0.0071 | 3 | 2.0055–2.0061 | 0.0011–0.0026 | 0.004–0.010 |
| | 180.2 (2954) | 2.4385–2.4392 | 0.0010–0.0015 | 0.0031–0.0111 | NA | 2.0842–2.0848 | 0.0009–0.0025 | 0.007–0.013 |
| 1989-90 | 97.4 (1597) | 1.9961–1.9668 | 0.0009–0.0017 ② | 0.0031–0.0111 | 4 | 1.8898–1.8904 | 0.0011–0.0027 | 0.0043–0.0103 |
| | 132.2 (2184) | 2.3597–2.3604 | 0.0010–0.0017 ① | 0.0031–0.0071 | 3 ③ | 2.1261–2.1266 | 0.0011–0.0026 | 0.012– |
| | 180.2 (2954) | 2.4385–2.4392 | 0.0010–0.0015 | 0.0031–0.0111 | NA | 2.2047–2.2053 | 0.0009–0.0025 | 0.007–0.013 |

① Bearing No. 3—0.0012–0.0019 ② DOHC engine—0.0010-0.0017

## VALVE SPECIFICATIONS—PISTON ENGINE

All measurements in inches unless noted.

| Year | Engine Displacement cu. in. (cc) | Seat Angle (deg.) | Face Angle (deg.) | Spring Squareness Limit | Spring Free Length Outer | Spring Free Length Inner | Stem-to-Guide Clearance Intake | Stem-to-Guide Clearance Exhaust | Stem Diameter Intake | Stem Diameter Exhaust |
|---|---|---|---|---|---|---|---|---|---|---|
| 1983 | 90.0 (1490) | 45 | 45 | 0.059 | 1.705 | 1.705 | 0.0007–0.0021 | 0.0007–0.0021 | 0.3164 | 0.3163 |
| | 121.9 (1998) | 45 | 45 | 0.071 | 2.047 | 1.732 | 0.0010–0.0185 | 0.0010–0.0165 | 0.3177 | 0.3159 |
| 1984 | 90.0 (1490) | 45 | 45 | 0.059 | 1.705 | 1.705 | 0.0007–0.0021 | 0.0007–0.0021 | 0.3164 | 0.3163 |

## VALVE SPECIFICATIONS—PISTON ENGINE

All measurements in inches unless noted.

| Year | Engine Displacement cu. in. (cc) | Seat Angle (deg.) | Face Angle (deg.) | Spring Squareness Limit | Spring Free Length | | Stem-to-Guide Clearance | | Stem Diameter | |
|---|---|---|---|---|---|---|---|---|---|---|
| | | | | | Outer | Inner | Intake | Exhaust | Intake | Exhaust |
| 1984 | 121.9 (1998) | 45 | 45 | 0.071 | 2.047 | 1.732 | 0.0010–0.0185 | 0.0010–0.0165 | 0.3177 | 0.3159 |
| 1985 | 90.0 (1490) | 45 | 45 | 0.059 | 1.705 | 1.705 | 0.0007–0.0021 | 0.0007–0.0021 | 0.3164 | 0.3163 |
| | 121.9 (1998) | 45 | 45 | 0.071 | 2.047 | 1.732 | 0.0010–0.0185 | 0.0010–0.0165 | 0.3177–0.3138 | 0.3159–.3165 |
| | 121.9 (1998) Diesel | 45 | 45 | 0.071 | 2.047 | 1.732 | 0.0016–0.0031 | 0.0020–0.0031 | 0.3138–0.3144 | 0.3136–0.3142 |
| 1986 | 97.4 (1597) | 45 | 45 | 0.059 | 1.717 | 1.717 | 0.0018–0.0051 | 0.0019–0.0053 | 0.2740–0.2750 | 0.2740–0.2750 |
| | 121.9 (1998) | 45 | 45 | 0.071 | 2.047 | 1.732 | 0.0010–0.0024 | 0.0010–0.0024 | 0.3177–0.3185 | 0.3159–0.3165 |
| 1987 | 97.4 (1597) | 45 | 45 | 0.059 | 1.717 | 1.717 | 0.0018–0.0051 | 0.0019–0.0053 | 0.2740–0.2750 | 0.2740–0.2750 |
| | 121.9 (1998) | 45 | 45 | 0.071 | 2.047 | 1.732 | 0.0010–0.0024 | 0.0010–0.0024 | 0.3177–0.3185 | 0.3159–0.3165 |
| 1988 | 97.4 (1597) | 45 | 45 | 0.059 | 1.720 | 1.720 | 0.0010–0.0024 | 0.0011–0.0026 | 0.2744–0.275 | 0.2744–0.275 |
| | 97.4 (1597) ② | 45 | 45 | NA | 1.858 | 1.858 | 0.0010–0.0024 | 0.0012–0.0026 | 0.2350–0.2360 | 0.2350–0.2360 |
| | 133.2 (2184) | 45 | 45 | 0.067 | 1.949 | 1.949 | 0.0010–0.0024 | 0.0012–0.0026 | 0.2740–0.2750 | 0.2740–0.2750 |
| | 180.2 (2954) | 45 | 45 | ④ | ③ | ③ | 0.0010–0.0024 | 0.0012–0.0026 | 0.2740–0.2750 | 0.2760–0.2770 |
| 1989-90 | 97.4 (1597) | 45 | 45 | 0.059 | 1.720 | 1.720 | 0.0010–0.0024 | 0.0011–0.0026 | 0.274–0.275 | 0.274–0.275 |
| | 97.4 (1597) ② | 45 | 45 | 0.062 | 1.858 | 1.858 | 0.0010–0.0024 | 0.0012–0.0026 | 0.2350–0.2356 | 0.2348–0.2354 |
| | 133.2 (2184) | 45 | 45 | 0.067 | 1.949 | 1.984 | 0.0010–0.0024 | 0.0012–0.0026 | 0.2744–0.2750 | 0.2742–0.2748 |
| | 180.2 (2954) | 45 | 45 | ④ | ⑤ | ⑤ | 0.0010–0.0024 | 0.0012–0.0026 | 0.2744–0.2750 | 0.3159–0.3165 |

① Test pressure
Outer—31.4 @ 1.339
Inner—17.9 @ 1.260
Installed height
Outer—1.339
Inner—1.260

② DOHC engine

③ Intake
Outer—2.0000
Inner—1.9835
Exhaust
Outer—2.382
Inner—2.130

④ Intake
Outer—0.070
Inner—0.064

⑤ Intake
Outer—2.000
Inner—1.835
Exhaust
Outer—2.295
Inner—2.091

## PISTON AND RING SPECIFICATIONS

All measurments are given in inches.

| Year | Engine Displacement cu. in. (cc) | Piston Clearance | Ring Gap Top Compression | Ring Gap Bottom Compression | Ring Gap Oil Control | Ring Side Clearance Top Compression | Ring Side Clearance Bottom Compression | Ring Side Clearance Oil Control |
|---|---|---|---|---|---|---|---|---|
| 1983 | 90.9 (1990) | 0.0010–0.0026 | 0.008–0.016 | 0.008–0.016 | 0.012–0.035 | 0.0012–0.0028 | 0.0012–0.0028 | — |
| | 121.9 (1998) | 0.0014–0.0030 | 0.008–0.014 | 0.006–0.012 | 0.012–0.035 | 0.0012–0.0028 | 0.0012–0.0028 | — |
| 1984 | 90.9 (1490) | 0.0010–0.0026 | 0.008–0.016 | 0.008–0.016 | 0.012–0.035 | 0.0012–0.0028 | 0.0012–0.0028 | — |
| | 121.9 (1998) | 0.0014–0.0030 | 0.008–0.014 | 0.006–0.012 | 0.012–0.035 | 0.0012–0.0028 | 0.0012–0.0028 | — |
| 1985 | 90.9 (1490) | 0.0010–0.0026 | 0.008–0.016 | 0.008–0.016 | 0.012–0.035 | 0.012–0.0028 | 0.0012–0.0028 | — |
| | 121.9 (1998) | 0.0014–0.0030 | 0.008–0.014 | 0.006–0.012 | 0.012–0.035 | 0.0012–0.0028 | 0.0012–0.0028 | — |
| | 121.9 (1998) Diesel | 0.0012–0.0020 | 0.0079–0.0157 | 0.0079–0.0157 | 0.0079–0.0157 | 0.0020–0.0035 | 0.0016–0.0031 | — |
| 1986 | 97.4 (1597) | 0.0015–0.0020 | 0.0080–0.0160 | 0.0060–0.0120 | 0.0120–0.0350 | 0.0010–0.0030 | 0.0010–0.0030 | — |
| | 121.9 (1998) | 0.0014–0.0030 | 0.008–0.014 | 0.006–0.012 | 0.012–0.035 | 0.0012–0.0028 | 0.0012–0.0028 | — |
| 1987 | 97.4 (1597) | 0.0015–0.0020 | 0.0080–0.0160 | 0.0060–0.0120 | 0.0120–0.0350 | 0.0010–0.0030 | 0.0010–0.0030 | — |
| | 121.9 (1998) | 0.0014–0.0030 | 0.008–0.014 | 0.006–0.012 | 0.012–0.035 | 0.0012–0.0028 | 0.0012–0.0028 | — |
| 1988 | 97.4 (1597) | 0.0010–0.0026 | 0.0079–0.0157 | 0.059–0.0118 | 0.008–0.028 | 0.0012–0.0026 | 0.0012–0.0026 | — |
| | 133.2 (2184) | 0.0014–0.0030 | 0.0080–0.0138 | 0.006–0.012 | 0.0080–0.0276 ① | 0.0012–0.0028 | 0.0012–0.0028 | — |
| | 180.2 (2954) | 0.0019–0.0026 | 0.0080–0.0138 | 0.006–0.012 | 0.008–0.028 | 0.0012–0.0028 | 0.0012–0.0028 | — |
| 1989-90 | 97.4 (1597) | 0.0010–0.0026 | 0.0079–0.0157 | 0.00579–0.0587 | 0.008–0.028 | 0.0012–0.0026 | 0.0012–0.0026 | — |
| | 133.2 (2184) | 0.0014–0.0030 | 0.008–0.0138 | 0.006–0.012 | 0.008–0.0276 ① | 0.0012–0.0028 | 0.0012–0.0028 | — |
| | 180.2 (2954) | 0.0019–0.0026 | 0.008–0.014 | 0.006–0.012 | 0.008–0.028 | 0.001–0.003 | 0.001–0.003 | — |

① Turbocharged engine — 0.012 — 0.0354

## TORQUE SPECIFICATIONS

All readings in ft. lbs.

| Year | Engine Displacement cu. in. (cc) | Cylinder Head Bolts | Main Bearing Bolts | Rod Bearing Bolts | Crankshaft Pulley Bolts | Flywheel Bolts | Manifold Intake | Manifold Exhaust | Spark Plugs |
|---|---|---|---|---|---|---|---|---|---|
| 1983 | 90.9 (1490) | 56-59 | 48-51 | 22-26 | 80-87 | 65-69① | 14-19 | 14-19 | 11-17 |
| | 121.9 (1998) | 59-64② | 61-65 | 37-41 | 80-87 | 71-76 | 14-19 | 16-20 | 11-17 |
| 1984 | 90.9 (1490) | 56-59 | 48-51 | 22-26 | 80-87 | 65-69① | 14-19 | 14-19 | 11-17 |
| | 121.9 (1998) | 59-64② | 61-65 | 37-41 | 80-87 | 71-76 | 14-19 | 16-20 | 11-17 |
| 1985 | 90.9 (1490) | 56-59 | 48-51 | 22-26 | 80-87 | 65-69① | 14-19 | 14-19 | 11-17 |
| | 121.9 (1998) | 59-64② | 61-65 | 37-41 | 108-112 | 71-76 | 14-19 | 16-20 | 11-17 |
| | 121.9 (1998) Diesel | ③ | 61-65 | 51-54 | 116-123 | 130-137 | 14-19 | 16-20 | NA |
| 1986 | 121.9 (1998) | 59-64② | 61-65 | 37-41 | 108-112 | 71-76 | 14-19 | 16-20 | 11-17 |
| | 97.4 (1597) | 56-60 | 40-43 | 37-41 | 36-45 | 71-76 | 14-19 | 12-17 | 11-17 |
| 1987 | 97.4 (1597) | 56-60 | 40-43 | 37-41 | 36-45 | 71-76 | 14-19 | 12-17 | 11-17 |
| | 121.9 (1998) | 59-64② | 61-65 | 37-41 | 108-112 | 71-76 | 14-19 | 16-20 | 11-17 |
| 1988 | 97.4 (1597) | 56-60 | 40-43 | 35-38④ | 36-45 | 71-76 | 14-19 | 12-17⑤ | 11-17 |
| | 133.2 (2184) | 59-64 | 61-65 | 48-51 | 36-45 | 71-76 | 14-22 | 14-22 | 11-17 |
| | 180.2 (2954) | ⑥ | ⑦ | ⑧ | 116-123 | 76-81 | 14-19 | 16-21 | 11-17 |
| 1989-90 | 97.4 (1597) | 56-60 | 40-43 | 35-38④ | 9-13 | 71-76 | 14-19 | 12-17⑤ | 11-17 |
| | 133.2 (2184) | 59-64 | 61-65 | 48-51 | 36-45 | 71-76 | 14-22 | 14-22 | 11-17 |
| | 180.2 (2954) | ⑥ | ⑦ | ⑧ | 7-11 | 76-81 | 14-19 | 16-21 | 11-17 |

① Automatic Transmission—51–61

② Warm—69–80

③ Torque to 22 ft. lbs. Then turn 90 degrees more

④ DOHC Engine—48-51

⑤ DOHC Engine—29-42

⑥ 14 ft. lbs.
Paint a mark on each bolt head. Using the mark as a reference, tighten the bolts 90 degrees in the proper sequence. Retighten each bolt another 90 degrees in the proper sequence

⑦ 14 ft. lbs.
Paint a mark on each bolt head. Using the mark as a reference, tighten the bolts 90 degrees. Tighten the bolts again 45 degrees

⑧ 22 ft. lbs.
Paint a mark on each bolt head. Using the mark as a reference, tighten the bolts 90 degrees

## TORQUE SPECIFIACTIONS—ROTARY ENGINE

| Engine Displacement cu. in. (cc) | Front Cover | Bearing Housing | Rear Stationary Gear | Eccentric Shaft Pulley Bolt | Flywheel-to-Eccentric Shaft Nut | Manifolds Intake | Manifolds Exhaust | Oil Pan | Tension Bolts |
|---|---|---|---|---|---|---|---|---|---|
| 70 (1146) | 15 | 15 | 15 | 72-87 | 289-362 | 14-19 | 23-34 | 6-8 | 23-27 |
| 80 (1308) | 12-17 | 12-17 | 12-17 | 80-98 | 290-360 | 14-19 | 23-34 | 6-8 | 23-29 |

## BRAKE SPECIFICATIONS

All measurements in inches unless noted

| Year | Model | Lug Nut Torque (ft. lbs.) | Master Cylinder Bore | Brake Disc | | Standard Brake Drum Diameter | Minimum Lining Thickness | |
|---|---|---|---|---|---|---|---|---|
| | | | | Minimum Thickness | Maximum Runout | | Front | Rear |
| 1983 | GLC | 65–80 | 0.8125 | 0.390 | 0.0040 | 7.0900 | 0.118 | 0.040 |
| | 626 | 65–80 | 0.8750 | 0.550 | 0.0040 | 7.8741 | 0.040 | 0.040 |
| | RX7 | 65–87 | 0.8130 | 0.6693① | 0.0039 | 7.8741 | 0.039 | 0.039 |
| 1984 | GLC | 65–80 | 0.8125 | 0.390 | 0.0040 | 7.0900 | 0.118 | 0.040 |
| | 626 | 65–80 | 0.8750 | 0.550 | 0.0040 | 7.8741 | 0.040 | 0.040 |
| | RX7 | 65–80 | 0.8130 | 0.6693① | 0.0039 | 7.8741 | 0.039 | 0.039 |
| 1985 | GLC | 65–80 | 0.8125 | 0.390 | 0.0040 | 7.0900 | 0.118 | 0.040 |
| | 626 | 65–80 | 0.8750 | 0.550 | 0.0040 | 7.8741 | 0.040 | 0.040 |
| | 626 Diesel | 65–80 | 0.8750 | 0.710 | 0.0040 | 7.8741 | 0.040 | 0.040 |
| | RX7 | 65–87 | 0.8130 | 0.6693① | 0.0039 | 7.8741 | 0.039 | 0.039 |
| 1986 | 323 | 65–87 | 0.8750 | 0.630② | 0.0030 | 7.8700 | 0.120 | 0.040 |
| | 626 | 65–87 | 0.8750 | 0.710② | 0.0040 | 7.8700 | 0.118 | 0.040 |
| | RX7 | 65–87 | 0.8750 | 0.790③ | 0.0040 | – | 0.120 | 0.040 |
| 1987 | 323 | 65–87 | 0.8750 | 0.630② | 0.0030 | 7.8700 | 0.120 | 0.040 |
| | 626 | 65–87 | 0.8750 | 0.710② | 0.0040 | 7.8700 | 0.118 | 0.040 |
| | RX7 | 65–87 | 0.8750 | 0.790③ | 0.0040 | – | 0.120 | 0.040 |
| 1988 | 323 | 65–87 | 0.8750 | 0.390④ | 0.0030 | 7.8700 | 0.120 | 0.040 |
| | 626 | 65–87 | 0.8750 | 0.940 | 0.0040 | 9.0000 | 0.039 | 0.031 |
| | MX6 | 65–87 | 0.8750 | 0.940 | 0.0040 | 9.0000 | 0.039 | 0.031 |
| | 929 | 65–87 | 0.8750 | 0.870 | 0.0040 | – | 0.039 | 0.031 |
| | RX7 | 65–87 | 0.8750 | 0.870 | 0.0040 | – | 0.035③ | 0.031 |
| 1989-90 | 323 | 65–87 | 0.8750 | 0.390⑥ | 0.0040 | 7.8700 | 0.039 | 0.039④ |
| | 626 | 65–87 | 0.8750 | 0.870⑥ | 0.0040 | 9.0000 | 0.039 | 0.040 |
| | MX6 | 65–87 | 0.8750 | 0.870⑥ | 0.0040 | 9.0000 | 0.039 | 0.040 |
| | 929 | 65–87 | 0.8750 | 0.870⑥ | 0.0040 | – | 0.039 | 0.031 |
| | RX7 | 65–87 | 0.8750 | 0.870⑦ | 0.0040 | – | 0.035③ | 0.031 |

**NOTE:** Minimum lining thickness is as recommended by the manufacturer. Due to variations in state inspection regulations, the minimum allowable thickness may be different than specified

① Rear rotor
  Solid – 0.3543
  Ventilated – 0.7870

② Rear disc – 0.350

③ Rear disc
  14 in. wheels – 0.310
  15 in. wheels – 0.710

④ Rear disc – 0.31

⑤ Except 14 in. wheel
  14 in. wheel – 0.43

⑥ Rear disc – 0.39

⑦ Rear disc – 14 in. wheel – 0.40
  15 in. wheel – 0.79

## WHEEL ALIGNMENT

| Year | Model | Caster Range (deg.) | Caster Preferred Setting (deg.) | Camber Range (deg.) | Camber Preferred Setting (deg.) | Toe-in (in.) | Steering Axis Inclination (deg.) |
|---|---|---|---|---|---|---|---|
| 1982 | GLC Waon | ¾P-1¾P | 1¼P | ¾P-2¼P | 1½P | 0-¼ | 8¼ |
| | GLC | 7/16P-1 7/16P | 15/16P | 1 3/16P-2 11/16P | 1 15/16P | ⅛-⅛ | 12 3/16 |
| | 626 | ¾P-1¾P | 1¼P | 2 15/16P-3 15/16P | 3 7/16P | 0-¼ | 10 9/16 |
| | RX7 | ½P-1½P | 1P | ① | ② | 0-¼ | 10¾ |
| 1983 | GLC Wagon | ¼P-1¼P | ¾P | 13/16P-2 5/16P | 1 9/16P | 0-¼ | 8¼ |
| | GLC | 7/16P-1 7 16P | 15/16P | 1 3/16P-2 11/16P | 1 15/16P | ⅛-⅛ | 12 3/16 |
| | 626 | 3/16N-13/16P | 5/16P | 15/16P-2 7/16P | 1 11/16P | 0-¼⑤ | 12 15/16 |
| | RX-7 | ½P-1½P | 1P | ① | ② | 0-¼ | 10¾ |
| 1984 | GLC | 7/16P-1 7/16P | 15/16P | 1 3/16P-2 11/16P | 1 15/16P | ⅛-⅛ | 12 3/16 |
| | 626 | 3/16N-13/16P | 5/16P | 15/16P-2 7/16P | 1 11/16P | 0-¼⑤ | 12 15/16 |
| | RX-7③ | ½P-1½P | 1P | ① | ② | 0-¼ | 10¾ |
| | RX-7④ | 1/16P-1 1/16P | 9/16P | ① | ② | 0-¼ | 11 5/16 |
| 1985 | GLC | 7/16P-1 7/16P | 15/16P | 1 3/16P-2 11/16P | 1 15/16P | ⅛-⅛ | 12 3/16 |
| | 626 | 3/16N-11/16P | 5/16P | 15/16P-2 7/16P | 1 11/16P | 0-¼⑤ | 12 15/16 |
| | RX-7③ | ½P-1½P | 1P | ① | ② | 0-¼ | 10¾ |
| | RX-7④ | 1/16P-1 1/16P | 9/16P | ① | ② | 0-¼ | 11 5/16 |
| 1986 | 323 | 1/16P-1 9/16P | 13/16P | 13/16P-2 5/16P | 1 9/16P | 3/64-13/16 | 12⅜ |
| | 626 | 3/16N-11/16P | 5/16P | 15/16P-2 7/16P | 1 11/16P | 0-¼⑤ | 12 15/16 |
| | RX-7 | ⑦ | 5/16P | 4⅝P | – | 0-¼⑧ | 13¾ |
| 1987 | 323 | 1/16P-1 9/16P | 13/16P | 13/16P-2 5/16P | 1 9/16P | 3/64-13/16 | 12⅜ |
| | 323 Wagon | ¾N-¾P | 0 | – | – | 3/64-13/64 | 12⅜ |
| | 626 | 3/16N-11/16P | 5/16P | 15/16P-2 7 16P | 1 11/16P | 0-¼⑤ | 12 15/16 |
| | RX-7 | ⑦ | 5/16P | 4⅝P | – | 0-¼⑧ | 13¾ |
| 1988 | 323 (2WD) | 13/16P-2 5/16P | 1 9/16P | 5/16P-1 5/16P | 13/16P | 3/64-13/64 | 12⅜ |
| | 323 (4WD) | 1 1/16P-2 9/16P | 1 13/16P | 9/16P-1 9/16P | 1 1/16P | 3/64-13/64 | 12 |
| | 626⑨ | 5/16P-1 5/16P | 1 3/16P | 7/16N-1 1/16P | 5/16P | 0-¼ | 12 13/16 |
| | MX6⑨ | 5/16P-1 15/16P | 1 3/16P | 7/16N-1 1/16P | 5/16P | 0-¼ | 12 13/16 |
| | 929 | 3¾P-5¼P | 4½P | ¼P-1¾P | 1P | 0-¼ | 12 11/16 |
| | RX-7 | 3 15/16P-5 7/16P | 4⅝P | 3/16N-13/16P | 5/16P | 0-¼ | 13¾ |
| 1989-90 | 323 (2WD) | 13/16P-2 5/16P | 1 9/16P | 5/16P-1 5/16P | 13/16P | 3/64-13/36 | 12⅜ |
| | 323 (4WD) | 1 1/16P-2 9/16P | 1 13/16P | 9/16P-1 9/16P | 1 1/16P | 3/64-13/64 | 12 |
| | 626⑨ | 5/16P-1 5/16P | 1 3/16P | 7/16N-1 1/16P | 5/16P | 0-¼ | 12 13/16 |
| | MX6⑥ | 5/16P-1 15/16P | 1 3/16P | 7/16N-1 1/16P | 5/16P | 0-¼ | 12 13/16 |
| | 929 | 3¾N-5¼P | 4½P | ¼P-1¾P | 1P | 0-¼ | 12 11/16 |
| | RX-7 | 3 15/16P-5 7/16P | 4⅝P | 3/16N-13/16P | 5/16P | 0-¼ | 13¾ |

① Right side wheel—3 11/16P-4 11/16P
Left side wheel—3 3/16P-4 3/16P
② Right side wheel—4 13/16P
Left side wheel—3 11/16P
③ 13 in. tires
④ 14 in. tires
⑤ Rear—⅛ in.
⑥ Rear—7/16N–9/16P
⑦ Rear—1¼N-¼N-¾ preferred
⑧ Rear—0 in.
⑨ Rear Alighment
2 Wheel Steering
Camber—1¼N–¼P
Toe In—¼N–¼P
4 Wheel Steering
Camber—¾N–¾P
Toe In—0–½P

## ECCENTRIC SHAFT SPECIFICATIONS—ROTARY ENGINE

All measurements are given in inches.

| Engine Type | Journal Diameter Main Bearing | Journal Diameter Rotor Bearing | Oil Clearance Main Bearing | Oil Clearance Rotor Bearing | Eccentric Shaft End-play Normal | Eccentric Shaft End-play Limit | Minimum Shaft Run-out |
|---|---|---|---|---|---|---|---|
| 12A | 1.6929 | 2.9134 | 0.0016–0.0028 | 0.0016–0.0031 | 0.0016–0.0028 | 0.0035 | 0.0024 |
| 13B | 1.6918–1.6923 | 2.9122–2.9128 | 0.0016–0.0031 | 0.0016–0.0031 | 0.0016–0.0028 | 0.0035 | 0.0047 |

## ROTOR AND HOUSING SPECIFICATIONS—ROTARY ENGINE

All measurements are given in inches.

| Engine Type | Rotor Side① Clearance | Rotor Width | Housings Front and Rear Distortion Limit | Housings Front and Rear Wear Limit | Housings Rotor Width | Housings Rotor Distortion Limit | Housings Intermediate Distortion Limit | Housings Intermediate Wear Limit |
|---|---|---|---|---|---|---|---|---|
| 12A | 0.0047–0.0075 | 2.7481 | 0.0016 | 0.0039 | 2.7559 | 0.0024 | 0.0016 | 0.0039 |
| 13B | 0.0047–0.0083 | 3.142–3.144 | 0.0016 | 0.0039 | 3.1485–3.1500 | 0.0024 | 0.0016 | 0.0039 |

① New

## SEAL CLEARANCES—ROTARY ENGINE

All measurements are given in inches.

| Engine Type | Apex Seals To Side Housing Normal | Apex Seals To Side Housing Limit | Apex Seals To Rotor Groove Normal | Apex Seals To Rotor Groove Limit | Side Seal To Rotor Groove Normal | Side Seal To Rotor Groove Limit | Side Seal To Corner Seal Normal | Side Seal To Corner Seal Limit |
|---|---|---|---|---|---|---|---|---|
| 12A | 0.0051–0.0075 | — | 0.0020–0.0035 | 0.0059 | 0.0012–0.0031 | 0.0039 | 0.0020–0.0059 | 0.0157 |
| 13B | 0.0051–0.0075 | — | 0.0024–0.0040 | 0.0059 | 0.0011–0.0031 | 0.0039 | 0.0020–0.0059 | 0.0160 |

# TUNE-UP PROCEDURES

## Ignition Timing

### ADJUSTMENT

#### *1983–85 RX-7*

**NOTE: The rotary engine uses 2 distributor circuits to set the leading and trailing timing. Only the front rotor is used to time the engine.**

1. Warm up the engine to normal operating temperature.

2. Stop the engine and connect a tachometer.

3. Connect a timing light to the wire of the leading (lower) spark plug on the front rotor.

4. To check/adjust the **leading** timing:

a. Start the engine and run it at the specified idle speed. Verify that the engine is running at its normal idle speed. If not, adjust idle speed to specification.

b. Aim the timing light at the timing indicator pin on the front cover.

c. If the timing pointer does not line up with the first (yellow) notch on the pulley, loosen the locknut and rotate the distributor either way until the timing is correct. Tighten the locknut and check that the timing is still correct.

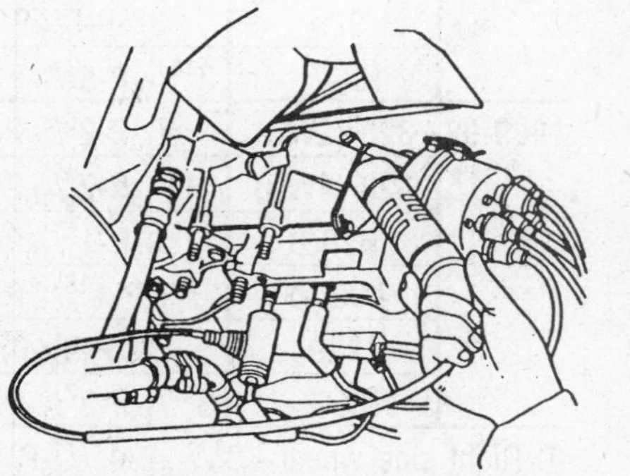

**Checking rotary engine ignition timing with a timing light on 1983–85 models. Connect the timing light to the leading (lower) spark plug wire first. When checking and adjusting the trailing timing, connect the timing light to the upper spark plug**

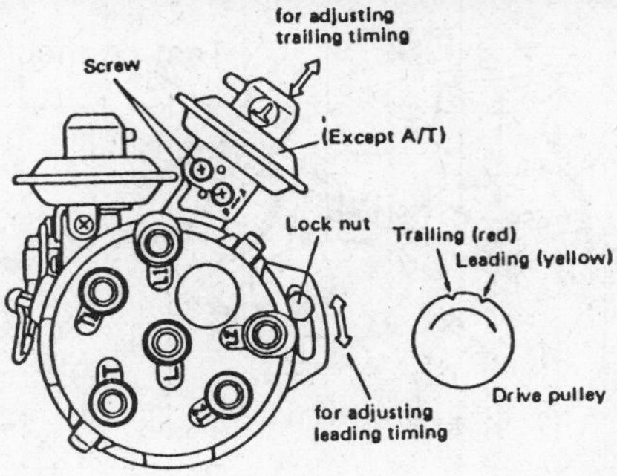


Ignition timing adjustment nn 1983–85 rotary engines

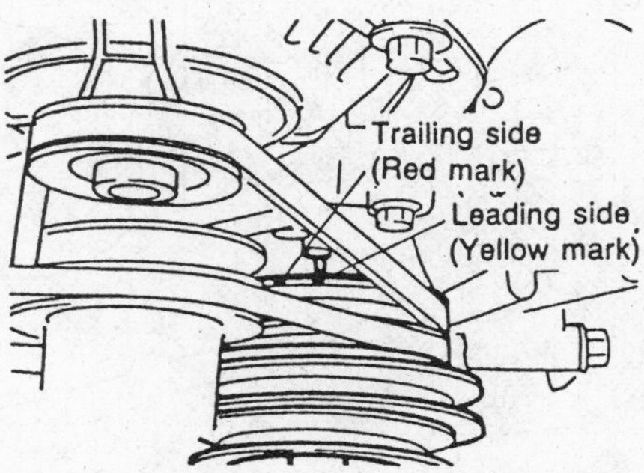


Rotary engine timing marks – all models

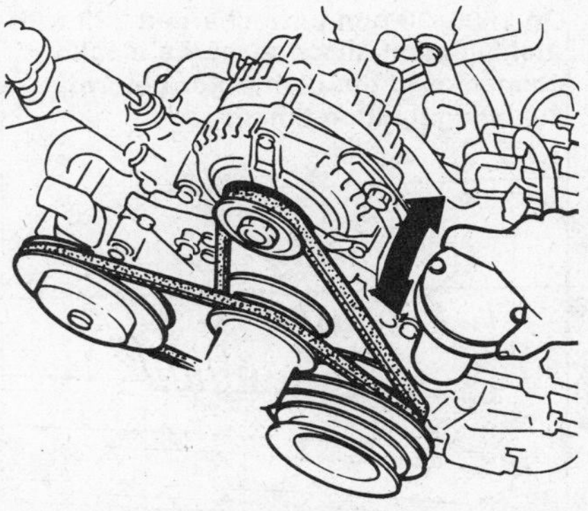

Turn the crank angle sensor to adjust the ignition timing – 1986–90 RX-7

5. To check/adjust the **trailing** timing:

a. Stop the engine and connect the timing light to the trailing (upper) spark plug on the front rotor. Start the engine position the detent lever in Drive for automatic transmission vehicles, and check the trailing timing. The timing pointer should line up with the second (red) notch in the pulley.

b. If the trailing timing is not correct, loosen the vacuum unit attaching screws on vehicles equipped with manual transmission or the adjusting lever attaching screws on vehicles equipped with automatic transmission. Move the proper component in or out until the timing pointer lines up with the second mark on the pulley, then tighten the screws and recheck the trailing timing.

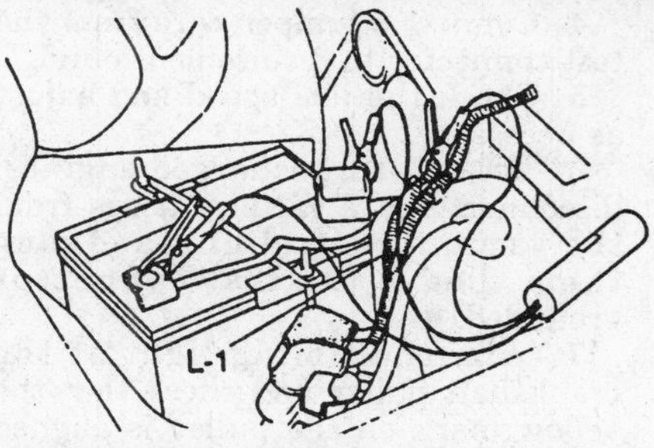


When checking 1986–90 rotary engine timing, connect the timing light to the "L-1" high tension lead

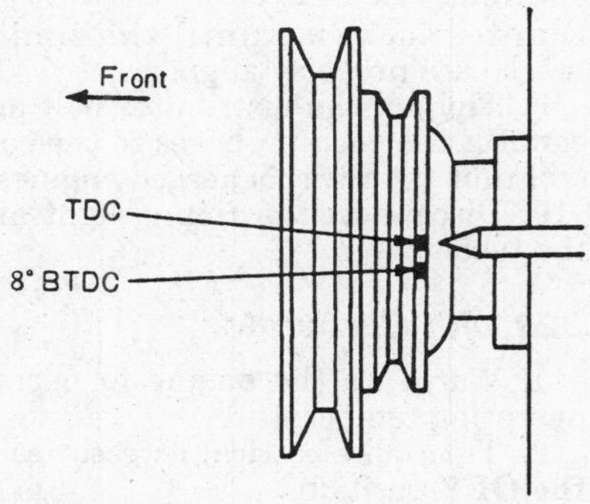

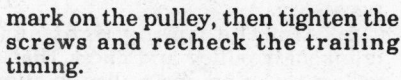

Timing marks – 1983–84 GLC Wagon

### *1986–90 RX-7*

**NOTE: The rotary engine uses 2 distributor circuits to set the leading and trailing timing. Only the front rotor is used to time the engine. 1986–90 models do not have a distributor. Instead, ignition timing is adjusted by means of a crank angle sensor.**

1. Warm up the engine to normal operating temperature.

2. Stop the engine and connect a tachometer. Turn all the electrical accessories to the **OFF** position.

3. Start the engine and verify that the engine is running at its normal idle speed. If not, adjust idle speed to specification.

4. To check/adjust the **leading** timing:

a. Connect a timing light to the lower wire on the front rotor.

b. Aim the timing light at the pulley and verify that the yellow timing mark on the pulley is aligned with the indiactor pin.

c. If the marks are not aligned, remove the rubber cap that covers the crank angle sensor adjusting bolt.

d. Loosen the bolt and move the crank angle sensor to adjust the leading timing.

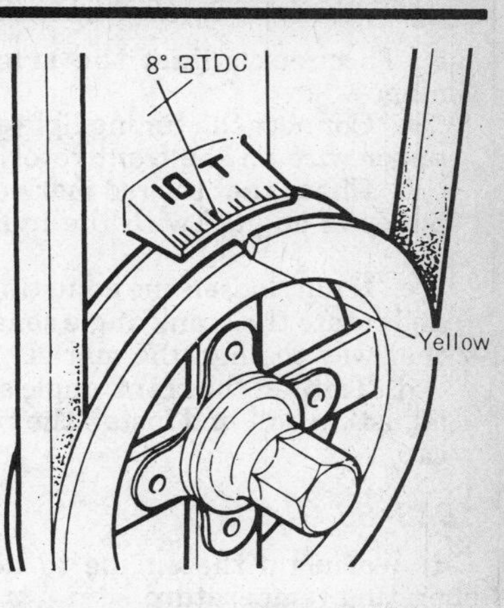


Timing marks – 1983–85 GLC

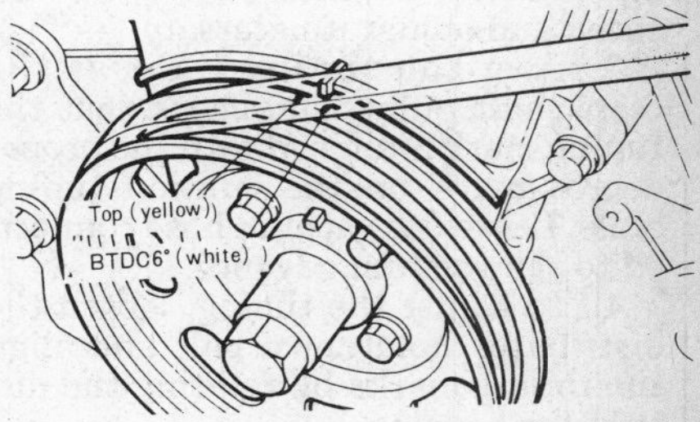


Timing marks—1983–85 626

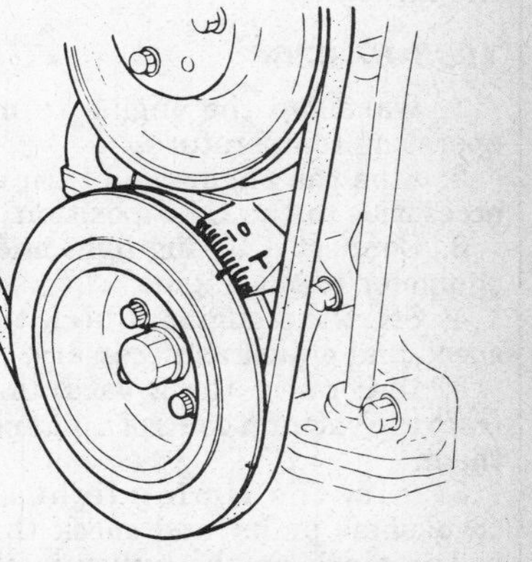

Tming marks – 1986–90 323

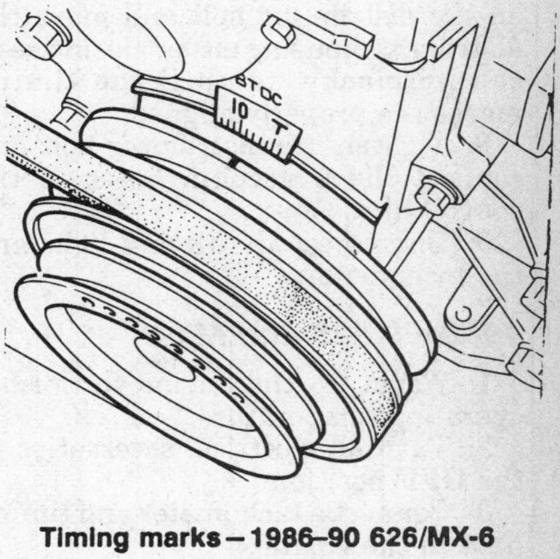


Timing marks – 1986–90 626/MX-6

5. To check/adjust the **trailing** timing:

a. Connect the timing light to the upper wire on the front rotor.

b. Check that the red mark on the pulley is aligned with the indicator pin.

c. If not, loosen the adjusting bolt and rotate the crank angle sensor either way to align the marks.

d. Tighten the crank angle sensor adjusting bolt and install the rubber cap.

### 1983–85 GLC

1. Warm up the engine to normal operating temperature.
2. Connect a tachometer and timing light to the engine. Check the idle speed and adjust if necessary.
3. Aim the timing light at the crankshaft pulley and check that the timing mark is aligned with the proper degree mark on the ignition timing scale. Leave the vacuum hose connected to the vacuum advance.
4. To adjust the timing, loosen the distributor hold down bolt and align the timing marks by rotating the distributor housing.
5. When the timing is within specification, tighten the distributor bolt.
6. Disconnect the timing light and the tachometer.

### 1983–87 626

1. Warm up the engine to normal operating temperature.
2. Stop the engine and turn all the accesories to the **OFF** position.
3. Connect a timing light and a tachometer to the engine.
4. Start the engine. Check the idle speed and adjust as necessary.
5. Disconnect the 2 vacuum hoses from the vacuum control unit and plug them.
6. Aim the timing light at the crankshaft pulley and check that the yellow mark on the pulley is aligned with the mark on the timing belt cover.
7. If the marks are not aligned, loosen the distributor bolt and move the distributor housing either clockwise or counterclockwise until the timing marks are properly aligned.
8. Tighten the distributor bolt and connect the 2 vacuum hoses to the control unit.
9. Disconnect the timing light and the tachometer.

### 1988–90 626 and MX-6

1. Warm up the engine to normal operating temperature.
2. Turn all electrical accessories to the **OFF** position.
3. Connect a tachometer and timing light to the engine.
4. Connect a jumper wire from the test connector to a suitable ground.
5. Check the idle speed and adjust as necessary.
6. On non-turbocharged engines, disconnect the 2 vacuum hoses from the vacuum control unit and plug them. Leave the test connector grounded.
7. Aim the timing light at the crankshaft pulley and check that the yellow mark on the pulley is aligned with the mark on the timing belt cover.
8. If the marks are not aligned, loosen the distributor bolt and move the distributor housing either clockwise or counterclockwise until the timing marks are properly aligned.
9. Tighten the distributor bolt and connect the vacuum hoses to the control unit (non-turbocharged engines).
10. Disconnect the timing light and the tachometer.

### 323 with Carburetor

1. Warm up the engine to normal operating temperature.
2. Turn all electrical accessories to the **OFF** position.
3. Connect a tachometer and timing light to the engine.
4. Check the idle speed and adjust if necessary.
5. Aim the timing light at the crankshaft pulley and check that the yellow mark on the pulley is aligned with the mark on the timing belt cover.
6. If the marks are not aligned, loosen the distributor bolt and move the distributor housing either clockwise or counterclockwise until the timing marks line up.
7. Tighten the distributor bolt and connect the vacuum hose to the control unit.
8. Disconnect the timing light and the tachometer.

### 323 with Fuel Injection

1. Warm up the engine to normal operating temperature.
2. Turn all electrical accessories to the **OFF** position.
3. On both turbo and non-turbocharged engines, disconnect the vacuum hose(s) from the vacuum control unit and plug them.
4. Connect a tachometer and timing light to the engine.
5. On turbocharged engines, connect a jumper wire from the test connector to a suitable ground.
6. Check the idle speed and adjust as necessary.
7. On turbocharged engines, disconnect the jumper wire from the test connector.
8. On non-turbocharged engines, disconnect the black connector at the distributor before checking the timing.
9. Aim the timing light at the crankshaft pulley and check that the yellow mark on the pulley is aligned with the mark on the timing belt cover.
10. If the marks are not aligned, loosen the distributor bolt and move the distributor housing either way until the timing marks are properly aligned.
11. Tighten the distributor bolt and connect the vacuum hoses to the control unit. On non-turbocharged engines, connect the black wire connector at the distributor.

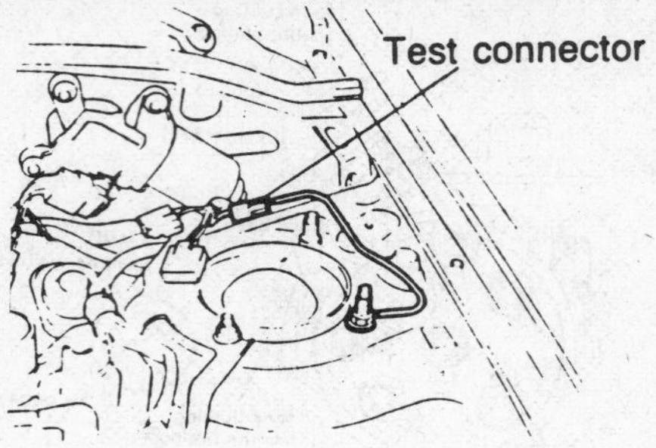


**Grounding the test connector for ignition timing adjustment – 1988–90 626 and MX-6**

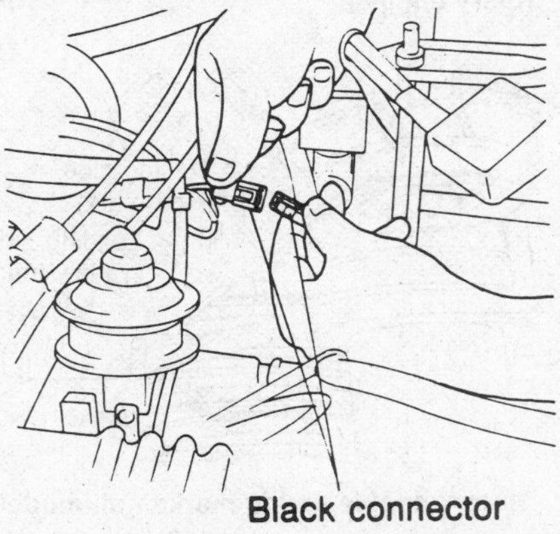


**On 1986–90 non-turbocharged 323 with fuel injection, disconnect the black connector at the distributor before adjusting ignition timing**

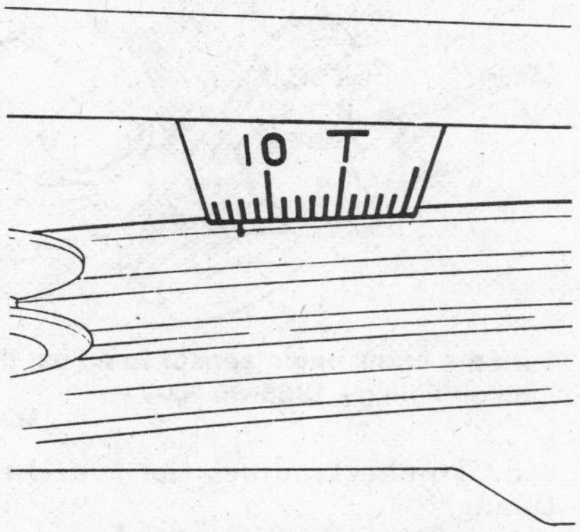


**Tming marks – 1988–90 929**

**Grounding the test connector for ignition timing adjustment—1988–90 929**

12. Disconnect the timing light and tachometer.

### *1988–90 929*

1. Warm up the engine to normal operating temperature.
2. Stop the engine and turn all electrical accessories to the OFF position.
3. Ground the green test connector pin with a jumper wire.
4. Start the engine and allow it to run at idle speed.
5. Connect a timing light to the No. 1 spark plug wire.
6. Illuminate the timing marks on the crankshaft pulley and the ignition timing scale with the timing light and check the timing.
7. If the timing is not within specification, loosen the distributor bolt and rotate the distributor housing to adjust the timing.
8. When the timing is correct, tighten the distributor bolt.
9. Disconnect the timing light and remove the jumper wire from the test connector.

# Valve Lash

## ADJUSTMENT

### *Gasoline Piston Engine*

#### 1983–87

1. Run the engine until normal operating temperature is reached.
2. Remove the valve cover.
3. Rotate the engine until the No. 1 piston TDC. Adjust No. 1 and No. 2 cylinder intake valve clearance. Adjust No. 1 and No. 3 cylinder exhaust valve clearance.
4. Rotate the engine one turn, so that the No. 4 piston is at TDC. Adjust the No. 3 and No. 4 cylinder intake valve clearance. Adjust the No. 2 and No. 4 cylinder exhaust valve clearance.
5. Install the valve cover with a new valve cover gasket.

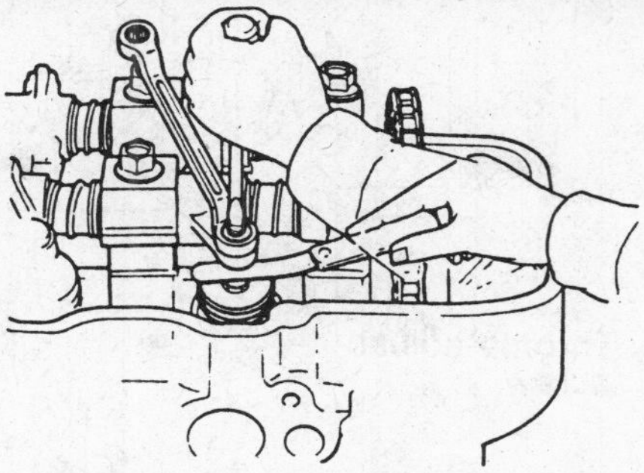

**Adjusting engine valve clearance**

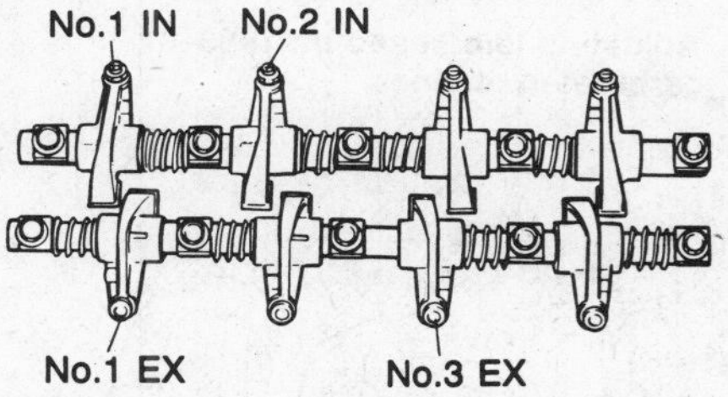


**Intake and exhaust valve arrangement**

#### 1988–90

Hydraulic valve lifters are used on all engines. These engines do not require periodic valve adjustment, as the hydraulic valve lifter automatically compensates for any required adjustment.

### *Diesel Engine*

The camshaft lobes are in direct contact with the valves. The adjustment of the valves is performed by removing the tappet discs and replace the discs with ones of the appropriate thickness. To perform the valve adjustment, special tappet holder tool 49–S210–220 or its equivalent is required along with an array of dics of varying dimensions.

1. Remove the valve cover.
2. Turn the engine over by the crankshaft pulley bolt until the valve cams of the No. 1 cylinder are both pointing upward and the timing marks indicate that No. 1 cylinder is at TDC on the firing stroke.
3. Measure the clearance between the top surface of the tappet and the cam's lower surface with the appropriate thickness feeler gauge. Check the intake valves of No. 1 and No. 2 and the exhaust valves of No. 1 and No. 3. The clearances are, Intake: 0.008–0.012 in., Exhaust: 0.012–0.016 in. Record the clearance on a sheet of paper.
4. If the clearance is outside the specified range, determine the thickness of the new disc required. Thicknesses range from 0.146–0.169 in. in intervals of 0.002 in. Figure the required thickness of the new disc with the following formula: Thickness of the original disc + (the clearance measured minus the standard clearance specification) = the required thickness for the new disc. For example, if the intake valve clearance was measured at 0.012 in. and the disc was 4.00mm or 0.157 in. thick, you would figure it this way: 0.157 in. + (0.012–0.010 in.) = 0.159 in.

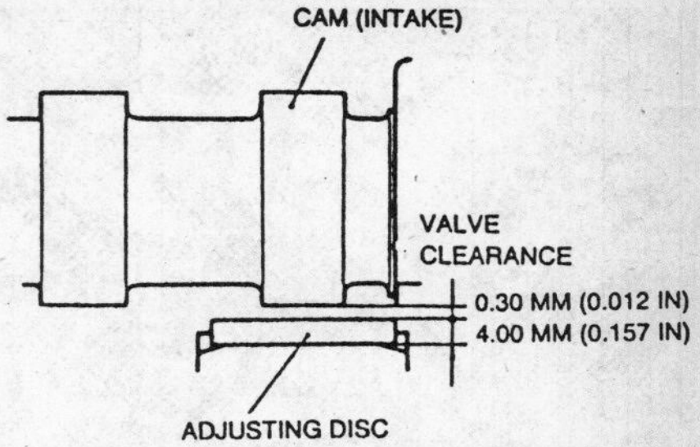


**Measuring valve clearance—626 diesel**

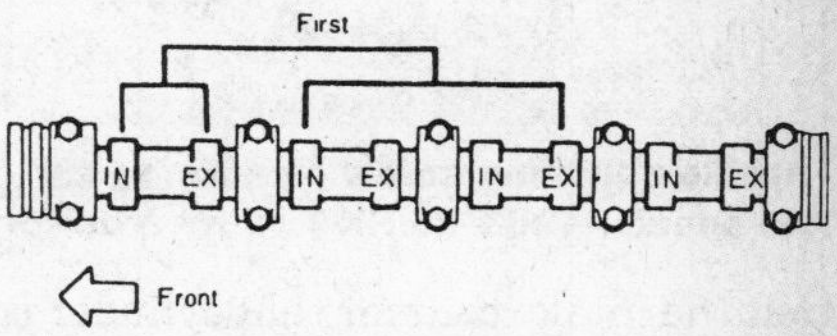


**On 626 diesel, check and adjust these valves FIRST**

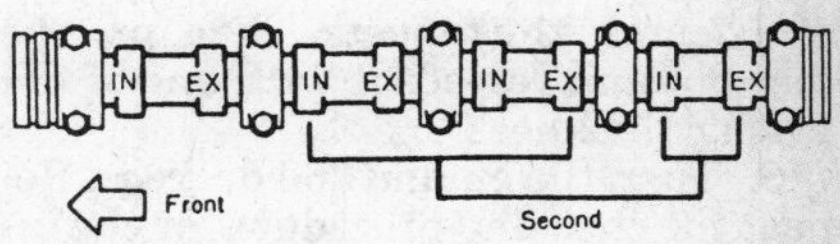


**On 626 diesel, check and adjust these valves SECOND**

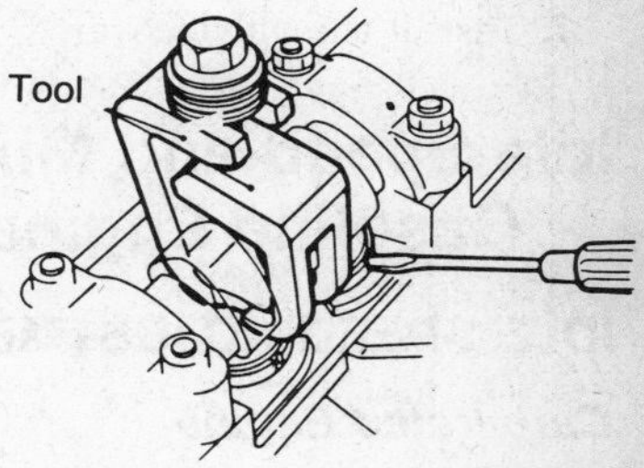


**Compressing the valve tappets—626 diesel**

**NOTE: The engine must be positioned so that the cam above each valve is positioned upward before installing the special tool. Attempting to depress the valve without properly positioning the engine can damage the valve by bending it.**

5. If the valves you have checked require adjustment, turn each of the tappets around so one of the notches is facing toward the left side of the car for access to the discs. Before working on each valve, turn the engine over so

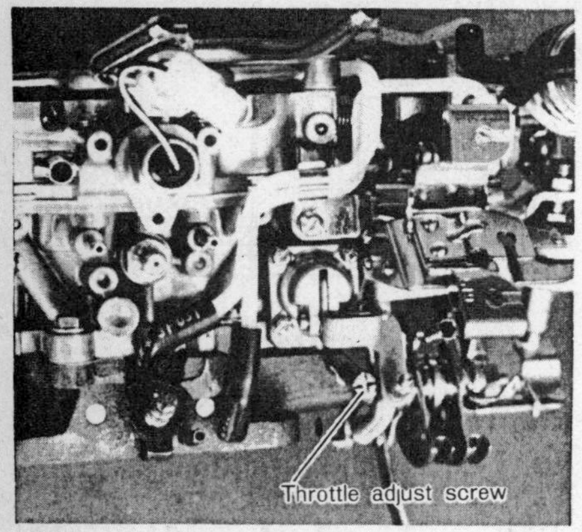


**Throttle adjusting screw location to set idle speed—1983–85 RX-7 with carburtor**

that the intake cam for that cylinder is pointing straight upward. Then, install the tool in the position shown (right between the cams). Tighten the bolt to force the tool halves together and depress the tappets. Then, pry the disc out and replace it with one of the proper thickness.

6. Turn the engine 360 degrees. Repeat the checking procedure for the intake valves of cylinders No. 2 and 4 and the exhaust valves of Nos. 3 and 4. Then, adjust those valves, as necessary.

7. Install the valve cover.

## Idle Speed and Mixture Gasoline Engines

### IDLE SPEED ADJUSTMENT

#### *Carbureted Engine*

**1983–85 RX-7**

1. If possible, set up an extra cooling fan to blow air into the engine compartment.
2. Set the parking brake and block the wheels.
3. Switch off all accessories to the **OFF** position.
4. Remove the fuel tank filler cap.
5. On 1983–84 models, disconnect the tube at the idle compensator in the air cleaner and plug the end of the tube. On 1985 vehicles, disconnect the richer solenoid connector.

**NOTE: On 1983–84 models, make sure the throttle opener (if equipped with A/C) and dashpot does not prevent the idle lever from returning the idle stop.**

6. Connect a tachometer to the engine.
7. Start the engine and allow it to reach normal operating temperature.
8. Check the idle speed with the tachometer. If the idle speed is not correct, adjust it by turnng the throttle adjust screw in the carburetor.
9. Reconnect the hose at the idle compensator on the air cleaner, richer solenoid connector (1985) and replace the fuel tank filler cap.

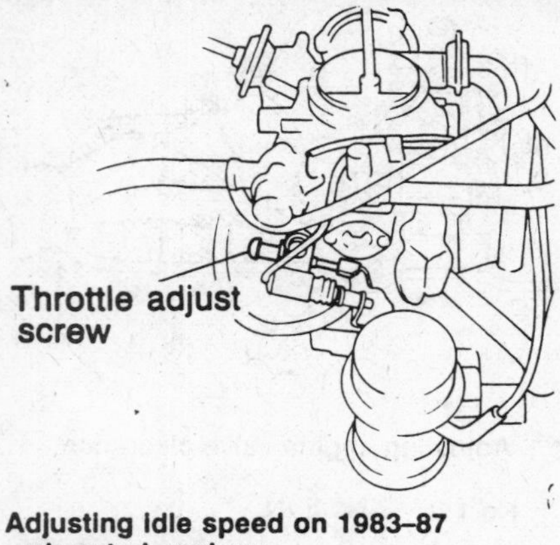


**Adjusting idle speed on 1983–87 carbureted engines**

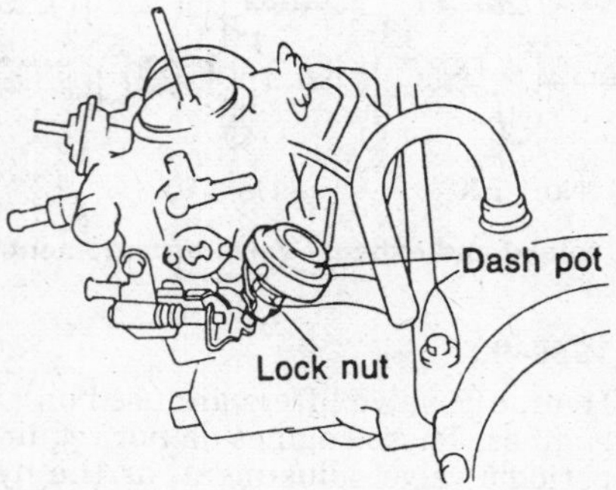


**Dash pot adjustment on 1986–87 323**

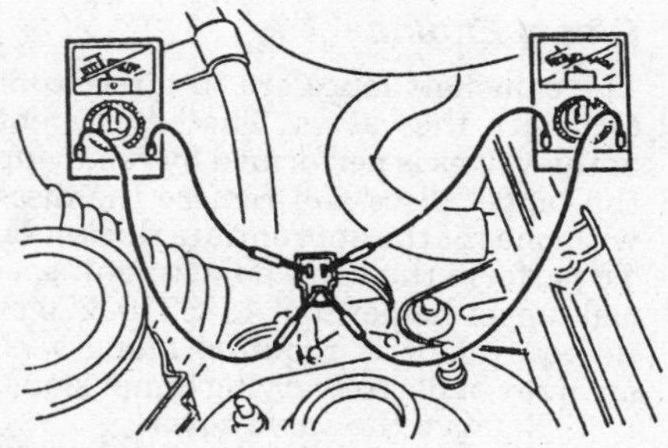

**Checking throttle sensor current on fuel injected RX-7**

**1983–87 EXCEPT RX-7**

1. Warm up the engine. Turn off the headlights and other accessories to the **OFF** position.
2. Make sure that the check valve is fully open. Check the ignition timing, and adjust as required. Disconnect the electric cooling fan motor before setting the idle speed.
3. Connect a tachometer to the engine. Apply the parking brake and block the wheels. The transmission should be in **NEUTRAL**.

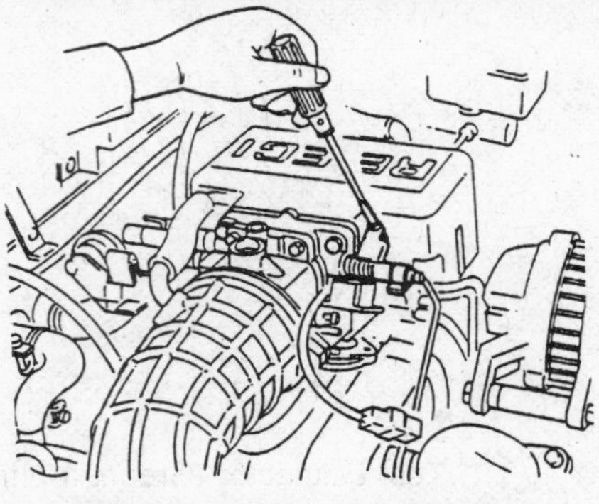

**Adjusting the throttle sensor on 1985 fuel injected RX-7**

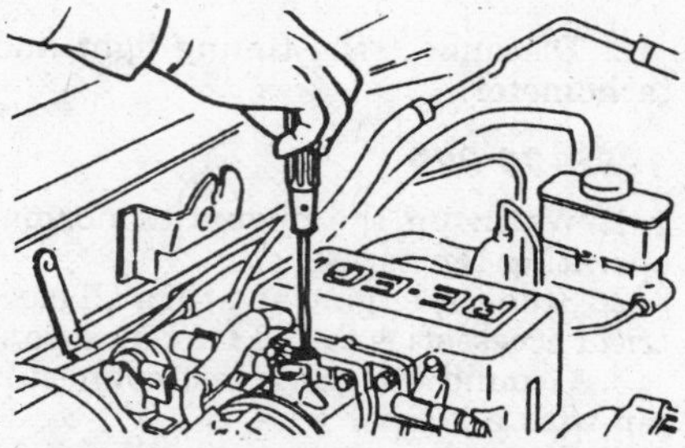

**Idle speed adjustment screw location on fuel injected RX-7—1985**

4. Turn the throttle adjusting screw to adjust the idle speed.
5. On 1986–87 323, the dash pot must be adjusted as follows:
   a. Start the engine and warm up to normal operating temperature. Leave the tachometer connected.
   b. Increase the engine speed to 3000 rpm.
   c. Slowly reduce the engine speed and make sure the dash pot rod contacts the lever at 2400–2600 rpm.
   d. If not as described, loosen the locknut and adjust the rod by turning the dash pot.

#### *Fuel Injected Engines*

**1985 RX-7**

1. Switch all the electrical accessories to the **OFF** position, remove the fuel filler cap and connect a tachometer to the engine.
2. Start the engine and let it run until it reaches normal operating temperature, connect a tachometer to the engine.
3. Inspect/adjust the throttle sensor by performing the following:
   a. With the engine off, connect a pair of voltmeters to the greencheck connector.
   b. Turn the ignition switch to the **ON** position and check to see if current flows to one of the voltmeters.
   c. If there is no current, remove the rubber cap and turn the adjusting screw clockwise until a current flow can be read on one of the volt-

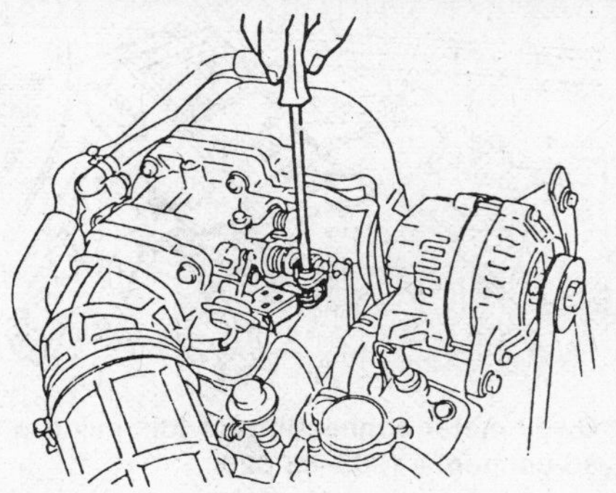

Adjusting the throttle sensor on non-turbocharged RX-7 – 1986–90

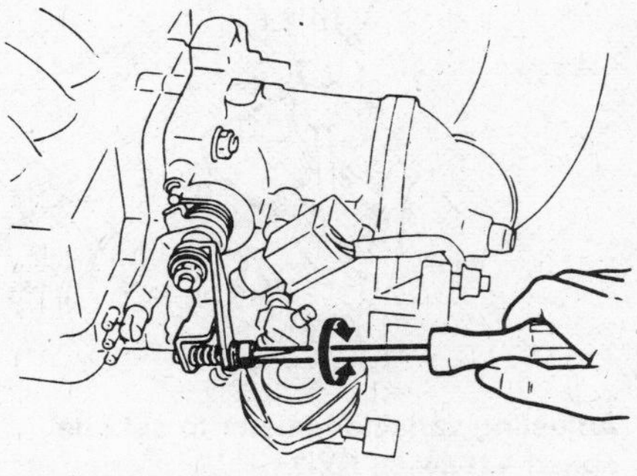

Adjusting the throttle sensor on turbo charged RX-7 – 1986–90

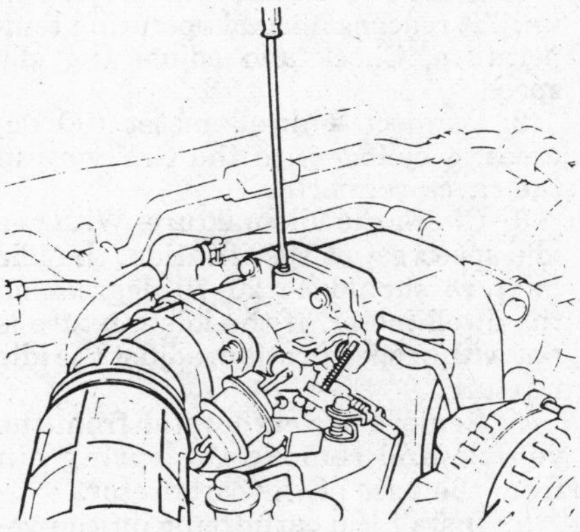

Idle speed adjustment screw location on non-turbochrged RX-7 – 1986–90

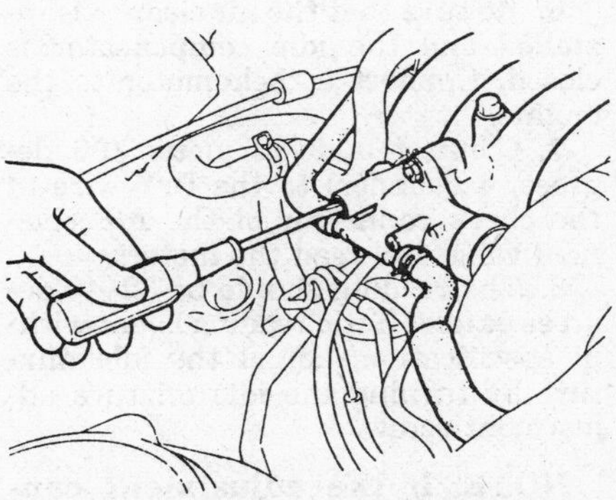

Idle speed adjustmemt screw location on turbocharged RX-7 – 1986–90

meters. If both voltmeters show current, turn the screw counterclockwise. Do not use excessive pressure on the screw.

d. Install the rubber cap and disconnect the voltmeters.

**NOTE: Instead of 2 voltmeters, a test light checker may be used to determine current flow.**

4. Once the throttle sensor is adjusted, disconnect the vent and vacuum solenoid connector.

5. Adjust the idling speed by turning the air adjust screw.

### 1986–90 RX-7

1. Switch off all accessories engine. Start the engine and let it run until it reaches normal operating temperature, then shut off the engine.

2. Connect a jumper wire to the terminals of the initial set coupler. Before adjusting the idle speed complete the following.

a. Connect a tachometer to the service coupler (black/white wire with a black connector) at the trailing side coil with igniter.

b. If the tachometer does not function correctly on the trailing side coil with igniter, reconnect at the leading side coil with igniter (black/white terminal).

c. If using an inductive (secondary pick-up type tachometer), connect it only at the trailing side of the spark plug wires. If connected on the leading side coil with igniter, it will not function properly.

3. Inspect and adjust the throttle sensor by performing the following:

a. With the engine off, connect a dual test light to the greenconnector.

b. Turn the ignition switch to the **ON** position and check that one of the lamps illuminate.

c. If both lamps illuminate or neither one does, turn the throttle sensor adjusting screw until one of the lamps illuminate. If both of the lamps illuminate, remove the rubber cap and turn the screw counterclockwise. If both lamps illuminate, turn the screw clockwise.

d. Reinstall the rubber cap.

4. On 1986–90 models without turbocharging, remove the blind cap and adjust the idle speed by turning the air adjust screw. On 1987–90 models without turbocharging, remove the blind cap from the by-pass air control (BAC) valve and adjust the idle speed by turning the air adjust screw.

5. Install the blind cap and disconnect the jumper wire from the initial coupler. Be sure to remove the jumper wire, otherwise the engine performance will be reduced.

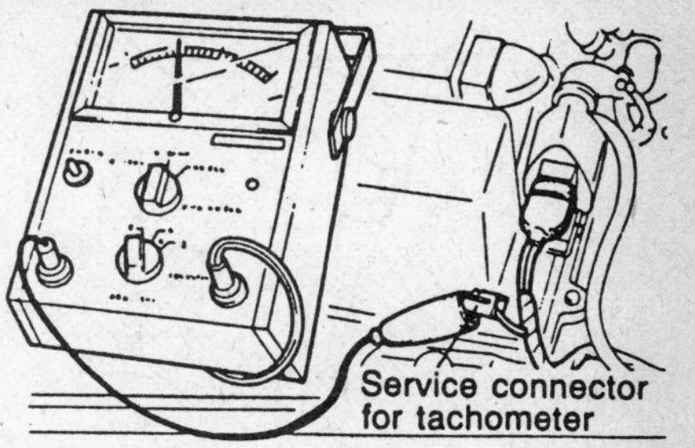



Connecting the tachometer to the check connector – 1986–90 323, 626, MX-6

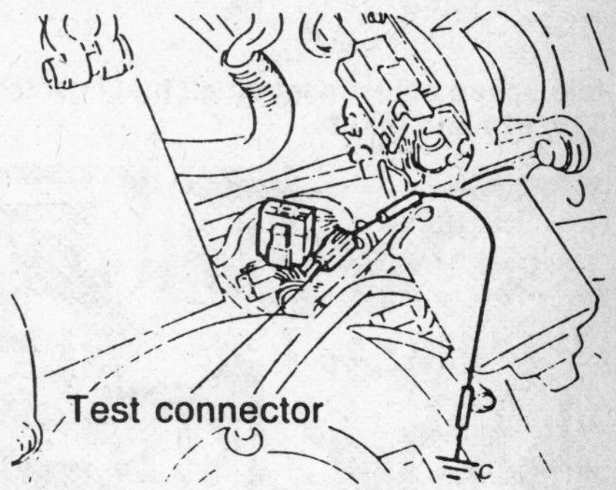



Grounding the green test connector for idle speed adjustment – 1988–90 323, 626, MX-6

### 1986–90 323, 626 and MX-6

1. Connect a tachometer to the white engine check connector. Start the engine and let it run until it for 3 minutes in neutral (manual transmissions/transaxles) or park (automatic transmissions/transaxles) in the 2500–3000 rpm range.

2. Make sure all accessories are switched to the **OFF** position. On 1986–87 models, make sure the electric cooling fan is off, if not run the engine at idle until the cooling fan stops.

3. Check the initial ignition timing and adjust as necessary.

4. On 1988–90 models, connect a jumper wire from pin 1 of the green test connector to ground.

5. Check to see if the idle speed is within specification.

6. If the idle speed is not within specification, remove the blind cap and adjust it by turning the air adjusting screw in the throttle body.

7. Install the blind cap. On 1988–90 models, disconnect the jumper wire.

8. Disconnect the tachometer.

## MIXTURE ADJUSTMENT

### *Carbureted Engines*

### 1983–85 RX-7

1. Remove the carburetor from the vehicle. Separate the the main body from the throttle body.

2. Use a hack saw and cut through the limiter cap and mixture screw

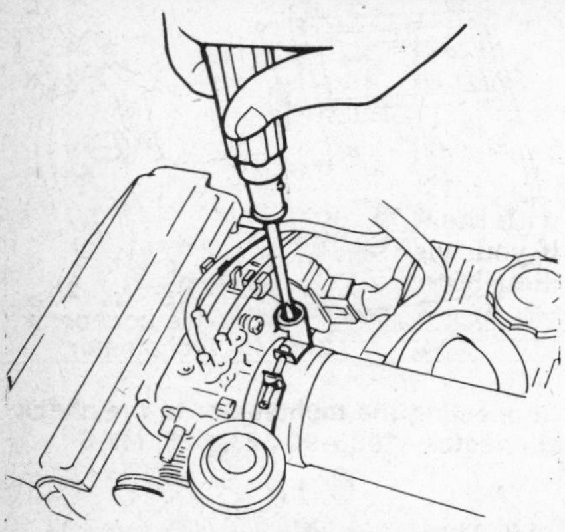

**Idle speed adjustment on all fuel injected 323, 626 and MX-6**

**Mixture adjusting screw – 1983–85 RX-7 with carburetor**

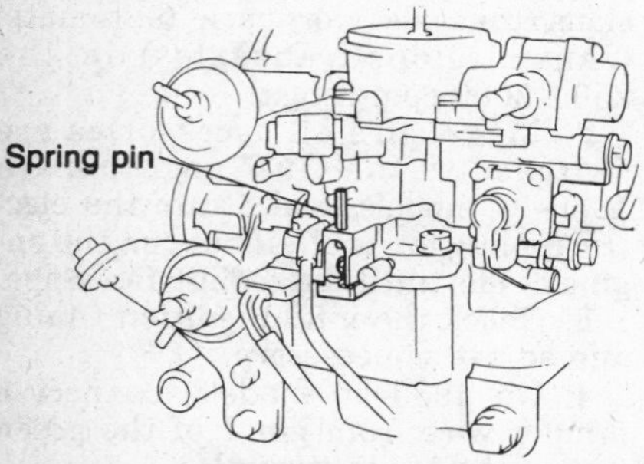


**Location of spring pin on carburetor**

about 0.4 in. from the end of the cap.

3. Remove the mixture screw. Install a new mixture screw and tighten it until it is fully seated. Back the screw out three turns.

4. Install the carburetor. Run the engine until normal operating temperature is reached. Check the idle speed and adjust as necessary by turning the throttle adjust screw.

5. Set the idle speed at the highest rpm by backing out the mixture adjusting screw.

6. Reset the idle speed by turning the throttle adjust screw, 770 rpm in Neutral for manual transmission and 870 rpm in **DRIVE** for automatic transmission.

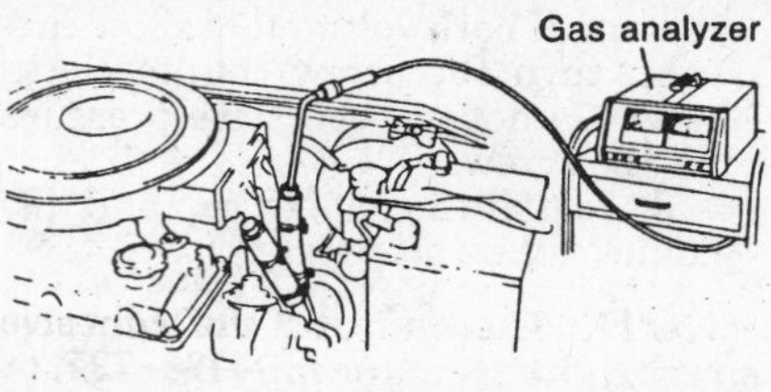


**Adjusting idle mixture on 323 models. Insert the probe into the secondary air hose as shown**

7. Screw in the idle mixture screw and adjust the idle speed to 750 rpm for manual transmission and 840 rpm for automatic transmission.

8. On vehicles equipped with automatic transmission, shift the selector to the Drive position and adjust the idle speed to 750 rpm by turning the throttle adjust screw.

9. After the idle mixture adjustment is completed, fit an idle limiter cap onto the mixture adjust screw securely.

10. After adjusting the idle speed, the throttle sensor on the carburetor should be adjusted.

### 1983–85 GLC AND 1986–87 323

**NOTE: Do not fix the spring pin to lock the mixture adjust screw until the adjustment is performed. Before adjusting the idle mixture, check/adjust the idle speed.**

1. Start the engine and allow it run until it reaches normal operating temperature. Connect a tachometer to the engine. On the 323, disconnect and plug the secondary hoses from the reed valves.

2. Connect a dwell meter (90 degrees, 4 cylinder) to the Y wire in the check connector of the A/F solenoid valve and read the meter.

3. The reading should be 32–40 degrees at idle. If the reading is not within specification, adjust the idle mixture by turning the idle mixture adjustment screw.

**NOTE:If the adjustment cannot be made, it is probably because of a faulty oxygen sensor, or either a broken wire or a short in the wiring between the oxygen sensor and the control unit.**

4. On the 323, insert an exhaust gas analyzer probe into the secondary air hose and seal the opening to prevent exhaust gas leakage. Adjust the CO to 1.5–2.5% by turning the idle mixture screw.

5. Be sure that the idle speed is set at specification. If not, adjust as necessary by using the throttle adjust screw. Fix the spring pin to lock the mixture adjustment screw.

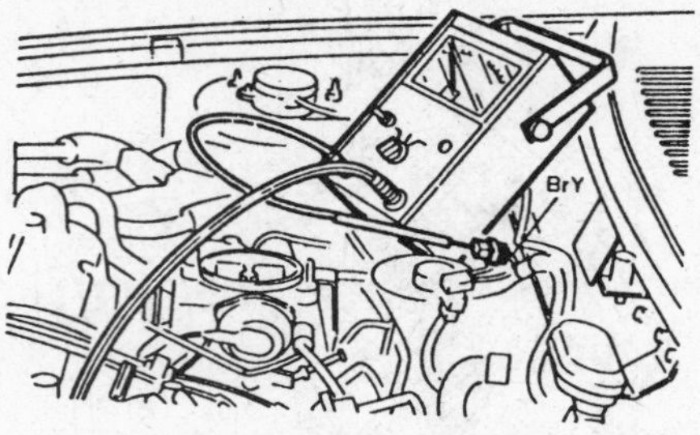


**Dwell meter connection for idle mixture adjustment – 1983–85 626**

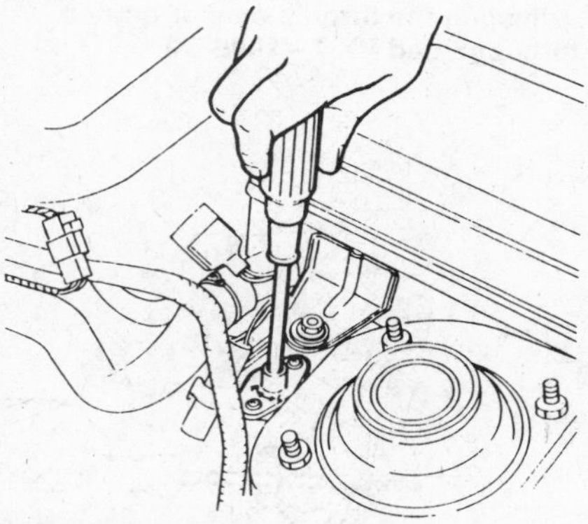

**Adjusting variable resistor to set idle speed – 1984–85 RX-7**

### 1983–85 626

1. Start the engine and let it run until it reaches normal operating temperature. Check and adjust the idle speed.

2. Connect a dwell meter (90 degrees, 4 cylinder) to the BrY wire in the check connector.

3. Check the idle mixture. With the idle speed set at specification, the idle mixture should be 20–70 degrees on the dwell meter. If the idle mixture is not within specification, adjust the idle mixture.

4. Remove the carburetor from the vehicle and remove the spring pin from the base of the carburetor.

5. Install the carburetor on the vehicle and start the engine. Let it run until it reaches normal operating temperature.

6. Be sure that the air cleaner is installed and the idle compensator is closed. Connect a tachometer to the engine.

7. Connect a dwell meter (90 degrees, 4 cylinder) to the BrY wire in the check connector of the A/F solenoid valve and read the meter.

8. The reading should be 32–40 degrees at idle. If the reading is not within specification, adjust the idle mixture by turning the idle mixture adjustment screw.

**NOTE: If the adjustment cannot be made, it is possible the oxygen sensor is not operating prop-**

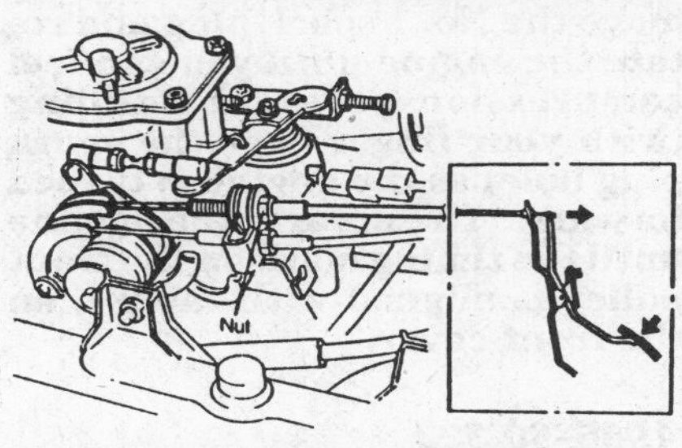

Adjusting the throttle pedal free-play

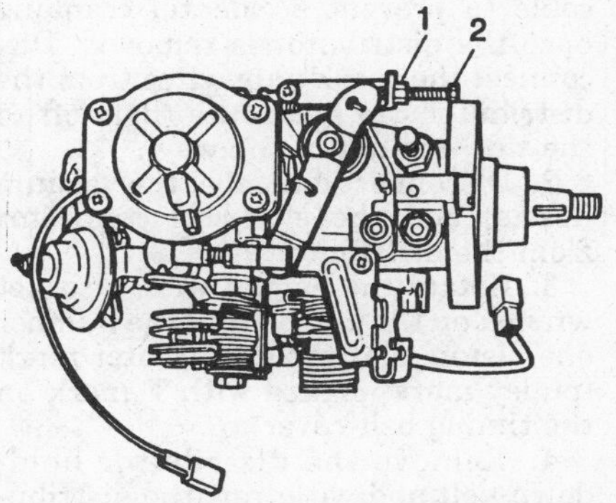

Adjusting the idle speed on the 626 diesel engine

**erly or either a broken wire or short in the the wiring between the oxygen sensor and the control unit.**

9. Drive the spring pin back into to position in the carburetor.

### *Fuel Injected Engine*

#### 1984–85 RX-7

**NOTE: The idle mixture adjustment usually is not necessary. The idle mixture adjustment should be adjusted when the variable resistor is replaced. Disconnect the variable resistor connector and connect an ohmmeter to the variable resistor. If continuity does not exist, replace the variable resistor and adjust the idle mixture. Resistance from terminal A to C should be 0.5–4.5 ohms and from terminal B to C, 0.5–4.5 ohms.**

1. Start the engine and let it run until it reaches normal operating temperature, connect a tachometer to the engine. Switch all accessories to the **OFF** position. Remove the fuel filler cap.
2. Check and adjust the throttle sensor as necessary. Disconnect the vent and vacuum solenoid connector.
3. Adjust the idling speed to 800 rpm by turning the air adjust screw (AAS).
4. Set the idle speed at the highest by turning the variable resistor and then readjust the idle speed to 800 rpm by turning the air adjust screw (AAS).
5. Turn the variable resistor counterclockwise until the engine speed reaches 780 rpm then turn it clockwise until the engine speed reaches 800 rpm.
6. Connect the vent and vacuum solenoid connector, fill up the head of the adjustment screw with the adhesive agent part number N304–23–795 or equivalent.

#### EXCEPT 1984–85 RX-7

Because a automatic compensation function of the air fuel mixture has been built into the the Electronic Gasoline Injection (EGI) control unit, it is not necessary to check and adjust the idle mixture.

## Idle Speed Diesel Engine

### ADJUSTMENT

**NOTE: Adjusting the idle speed on the diesel requires you to have a special tachometer which measures idle speed off a special sensor on the injection pump.**

1. Warm the engine to normal operating temperatures.
2. Connect a tachometer to the engine. The idle speed should be 800–850 rpm.
3. If the idle speed is incorrect, check the throttle pedal free play, it should be 0.04–0.12 in. If the free play is not within specification, adjust the cable by loosening the locknut on the cable bracket and turning the adjusting nut. Tighten the locknut.
4. Check the idle speed. Adjust the idle speed to 800–850 rpm, by loosening the locknut on the idle adjusting bolt. Turn the bolt clockwise to increase the idle speed and counterclockwise to decrease the idle speed. Tighten the locknut.
5. Remove the tachometer.

# ENGINE ELECTRICAL

## Distributor

### REMOVAL & INSTALLATION

#### *1983–85 RX-7*

1. Disconnect the negative battery cable. Rotate the engine in the normal direction of rotation until the first TDC or "Leading" timing mark aligns with the pin on the front cover. Matchmark the body of the distributor, or crank angle sensor, and the engine rotor housing.
2. The easiest way to clear the high tension wires out of the way is to simply remove the cap and set it aside with the wires still attached. However, if you wish to keep the cap with the distributor, tag the wires and then pull the wires out of the cap, observing markings.
3. Disconnect the vacuum advance and, if equipped, retard hoses. Disconnect the primary electrical connector.
4. Remove the distributor adjusting bolt. Pull the distributor vertically out of the engine.
5. To install the distributor, first make sure the engine has not been disturbed. If it has been moved, turn the crankshaft until the first timing mark (yellow) aligns with the pin on the front cover. Then align the dimple in the distributor gear with the notch or line cast into the body of the distributor.
6. Insert the distributor carefully and slowly into the engine with the distributor body and rotor housing matchmarks aligned. Avoid allowing the shaft to turn and be careful not to damage the housing when inserting the hear into it.
7. Install the adjusting bolt, but do not tighten. Turn the distributor until the protrusion of the signal rotor aligns with the core of the pick-up coil, and then tighten the locking bolt.
8. Install vacuum hoses, electrical connectors and high tension wires in reverse of the removal procedure.
9. Set the ignition timing.

#### *1986–89 RX-7*

A new distributorless ignition system was introduced to the RX-7 in 1986 which replaced the conventional electronic ignition system used on earlier models. The distributorless igntion system does not use a distributor, pick-up coil, reluctor or ignition module to control the timing. This computerized system uses a crank angle sensor, 2 coil/igniter assemblies, and an electronic control unit.

1. Rotate the engine so that the leading (yellow) timing mark on the pulley is aligned with the timing indicator pin.
2. Matchmark the crank angle sensor with the front rotor housing. The matchmarks must be neatly and accurately placed.
3. Disconnect the connector from the sensor.
4. Loosen the locknut and pull the sensor straight out of the rotor housing.
5. Remove the O-ring from the sensor and purchase a new one.

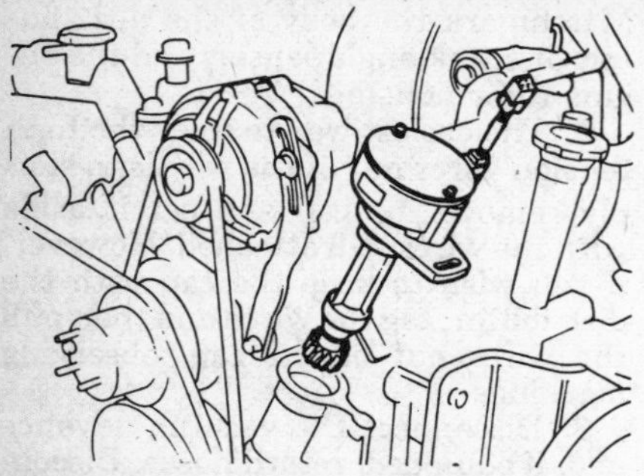

**RX-7 crank angle sensor removal and installation—1986–90**

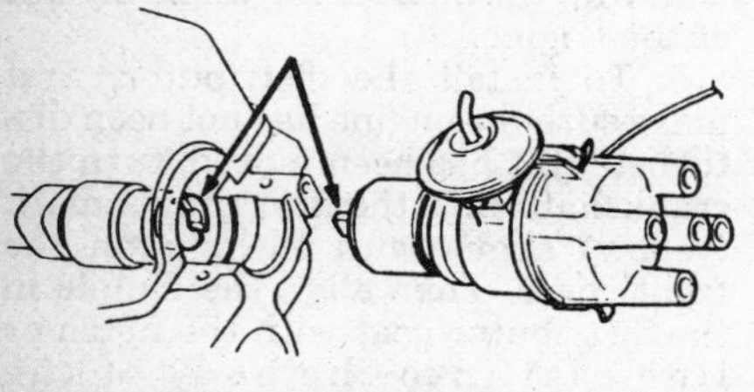

**When installing the distributor on the 1490 cc engine front wheel drive, make sure the distributor shaft fits into the groove in the camshaft**

6. To install the crank angle sensor, coat the new O-ring with a light film of clean engine oil and install it on the sensor.
7. Insert the crank angle sensor into the front rotor housing opening and align the matchmarks, then install the locknut.
8. Reconnect the sensor connector.
9. Set the ignition timing. Tighten the locknut to 70–96 inch lbs.

### *1983–85 GLC and 626*

1. Disconnect the negative battery cable. Unfasten the clips or screws which hold the distributor cap to the top of the distributor, and remove the cap. Note the location of the wire going to the No. 1 cylinder where it enters the cap.
2. Rotate the engine until the timing mark on the pulley is aligned with the pin on the front cover. Check to see if the contact on the rotor is pointing toward the No. 1 spark plug wire. If the rotor is half a turn away from the No. 1 plug wire, turn the crankshaft ahead 1 full turn until the timing mark is again aligned with the pin. Match mark the distributor body with the cylinder head.
3. If equipped, disconnect the vacuum advance line at the advance unit. Disconnect the primary wire at the connector near the distributor.
4. Remove the adjusting bolt and pull the distributor out of the engine.
5. To install the distributor, first align the dimple on the distributor drive gear with the mark cast into the base of the distributor body by rotating the shaft. Then, being careful not to rotate the shaft, insert the distributor back into the cylinder head with the distributor body and cylinder head match marks aligned and seat it.
6. Install the mounting bolt, but do not tighten it. Install the distributor cap, reconnect the vacuum advance line and the primary connector. Set the timing.

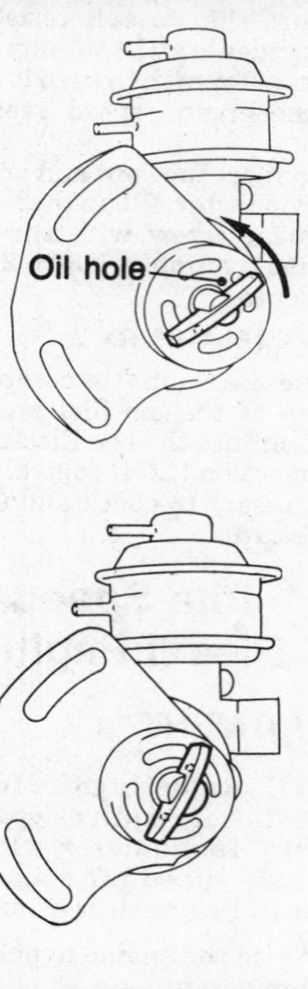


**Align the blade with the oil hole before installing the distributor—1986–90 323 without turbo**

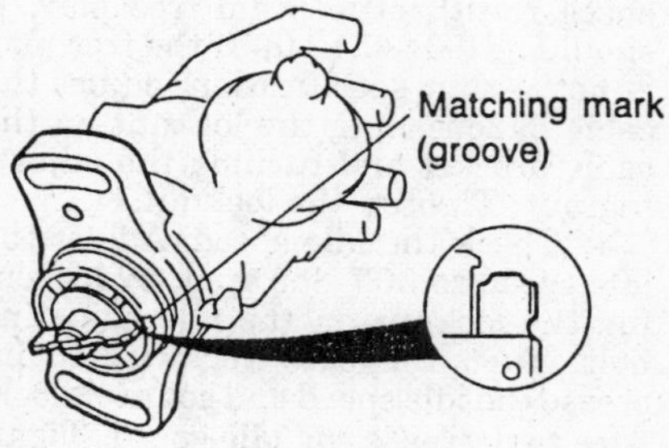


**Align the distribtor blade with the groove in the housing—1988–90 323 with turbo charger**

**NOTE: If the engine has been rotated while the distributor was removed, it will be necessary to turn the crankshaft until the point where the No. 1 cylinder is just about to fire. To do this, remove the No. 1 spark plug and rotate the engine until you can feel compression pressure building (with your finger over the spark plug hole) as the engine is turned forward. Then, turn the engine until the timing mark on the front pulley is aligned with the pin on the front cover.**

### *1986–90 323*

1. Disconnect the negative battery cable to prevent accidental cranking once the distributor is removed. Disconnect the spark plug wires from the distributor cap and route them off to the side and out of the way.
2. Disconnect and label the vacuum hose(s) and the electrical connector from the distributor.
3. Rotate the engine with a socket wrench on the pulley until the number one piston is at top dead center mark (pulley mark aligned with **T** mark on the timing belt cover).
4. Remove the distributor hold-down bolt and withdraw the distributor from the cylinder head.
5. Remove the O-ring seal and discard it.

**NOTE: Do not turn the crankshaft after the distributor is removed.**

6. Coat the new O-ring seal with a light film of clean engine oil and fit it into the cylinder head opening.

**NOTE: Make sure that the number one piston is at top dead center before installing the distributor.**

7. On non-turbocharged engines, turn the distributor blade so that it aligns with the small oil holes in the bottom of the distributor. On turbocharged engines, align the distributor blade with the grooved matchmark on the body.
8. Install the distributor and reconnect the wiring connector, vacuum hose(s) ad spark plug wires. Connect the negative battery cable.
9. Set the ignition timing.

### *1986–89 626 and MX-6*

1. Disconnect the negative battery cable to prevent accidental cranking once the distributor is removed. Disconnect the spark plug wires from the distributor cap.
2. On the non-turbocharged engine, disconnect the vacuum hoses and wiring. On the turbocharged engine, disconnect the electrical coupler.
3. Rotate the engine with a socket wrench on the pulley until the number one piston is at top dead center.

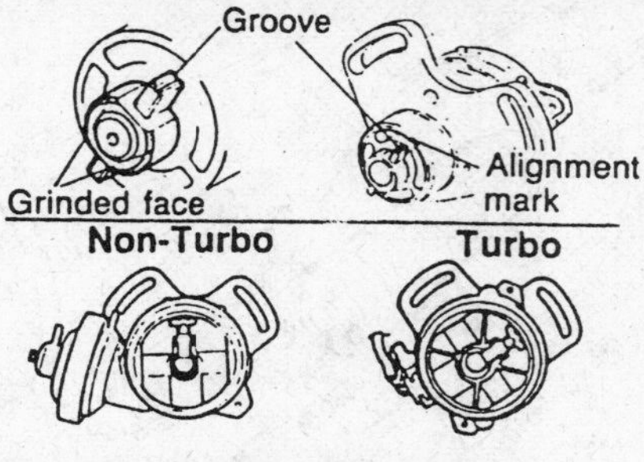


**Distributor shaft coupling and rotor alignment—1986–90 626 and MX-6**

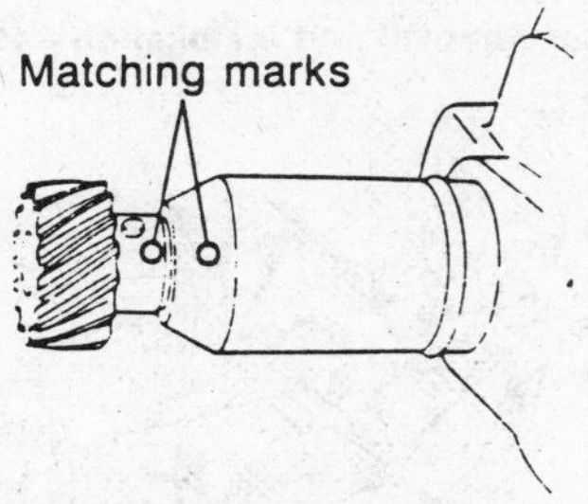


**Distributor housing and drive gear alignment marks—929**

4. Loosen the lock bolts and remove the distributor.
5. Remove the O-ring from the coupling shaft and discard it.

**NOTE: Make sure that the number one piston is at top dead center before installing the distributor.**

6. Install a new O-ring onto the coulpling shaft and apply a coat of clean engine oil to the O-ring to the driven gear.
7. On 1986–87 models, first align the dimple on the distributor drive gear with the mark cast into the base of the distributor body by rotating the shaft. On 1988–90 models, align the shaft coupling blade with the alignment marks on the distributor body, and turn the distributor over and check that the rotor is properly aligned.
8. Install the distributor and connect the wiring connector, vacuum hose(s) and spark plug wires. Connect the negative battery cable.
9. Set the ignition timing.

### *1988–90 929*

1. Disconnect the negative battery cable to prevent accidental cranking once the distributor is removed. Disconnect the spark plug wires from the distributor cap.
2. Disconnect the distributor electrical connector.
3. Rotate the engine with a socket wrench on the pulley until the number one piston is at top dead center (yellow mark on pulley aligned with **T** mark on the timing scale).
4. Loosen the lock bolt and remove the distributor. Remove the O-ring from the distributor shaft and discard it.

**NOTE: Do not turn the crankshaft once the distributor is removed.**

5. Install the new O-ring over the distributor shaft and lightly oil both the O-ring and the driven gear with clean engine oil.
6. Align the match marks on the distributor housing with the driven gear.
7. Install the distributor and connect the electrical connector and the spark plug wires. Connect the negative battery cable.
8. Set the ignition timing. Torque the lock bolt to 14–18 ft. lbs. once the timing is set.

# Alternator

## PRECAUTIONS

There are several precautions which must be strictly observed in order to avoid damaging the unit. They are:

- Reversing the battery connections will result in damage to the diodes.
- Booster batteries should be connected from negative to negative, and positive to positive.
- Never use a fast charger as a booster to start the vehicle.
- When servicing the battery with a fast charger, always disconnect the vehicle battery cables.
- Never attempt to polarize an alternator.
- Avoid long soldering times when replacing diodes or transistors. Prolonged heat is damaging to alternators.
- Do not use test lamps of more than 12 volts (V) for checking diode continuity.
- Do not short across or ground any of the terminals on the alternator.
- The polarity of the battery, alternator, and regulator must be matched and considered before making any electrical connections within the system.
- Never operate the alternator on an open circuit. Make sure that all connections within the circuit are clean and tight.
- Disconnect the battery terminals when performing any service on the electrical system. This will eliminate the possibility of accidental reversal of polarity.
- Disconnect the battery ground cable if arc welding is to be done on any part of the vehicle.

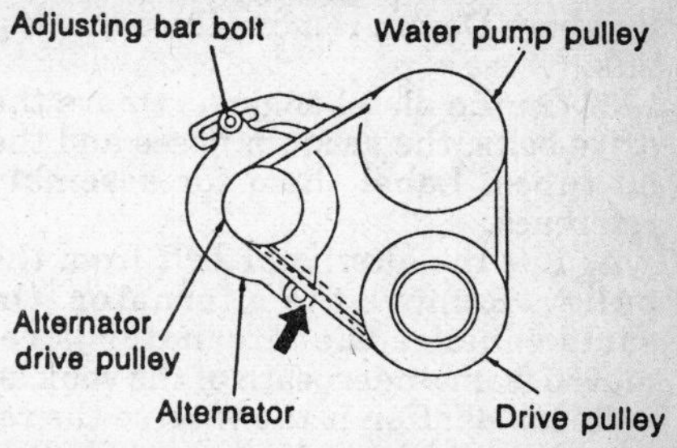


**Alternator belt adjustment—piston engines**

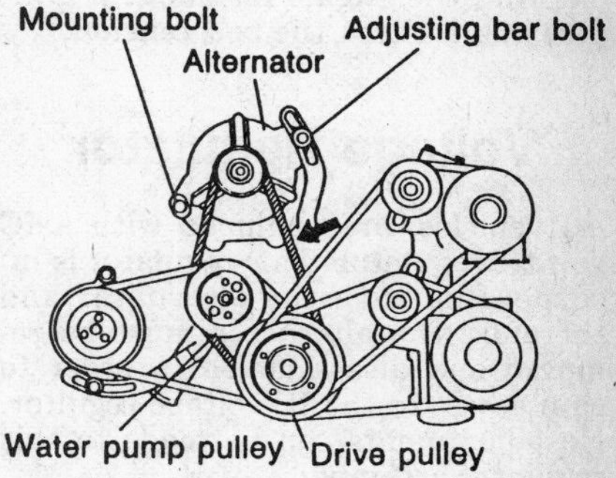


**Alternator belt adjustment—rotary engines**

## BELT TENSION ADJUSTMENT

Check tension by applying thumb pressure to the belt, midway between the eccentric shaft and alternator pulleys. Used belts should deflect about 0.55–67 in. for rotary engines and 0.31–0.35 in. for piston engines. New belts should deflect slightly less.

1. To adjust the alternator drive belt, loosen the alternator mounting bolt and adjusting bar bolt. Move the alternator to obtain the correct belt tension and tighten the bolts. Run the engine for about 5 minutes and recheck the belt tension.
2. To adjust the power steering pump drive belt, loosen the mounting bolt and locknut. Turn the adjusting bolt, if equipped or manually move the pump until the correct belt tension is obtained. Tighten the locknut, run the engine for about 5 minutes and recheck the belt tension.
3. To adjust the air conditioning drive belt, loosen the locknut on the idler pulley, if equipped and turn the adjusting bolt until the correct belt tension is obtained. Tighten the locknut, run the engine for about 5 minutes and recheck the belt tension.

## REMOVAL & INSTALLATION

1. Disconnect the negative battery cable. Label and disconnect all electrical leads from the alternator.
2. Remove the alternator adjusting

link bolt. Do not remove the adjusting link.

3. On the diesel engine, remove the drive belts, the vacuum hoses and the oil tubes. Label them for assembly reference.

4. Lift the alternator belt from the pulley. Remove the alternator. On some vehicles the alternator is removed from underneath of the vehicle.

5. Installation is the reverse the removal procedure. Adjust the drive belt tension.

6. Connect the negative battery cable. Run the engine for about 5 minutes and recheck the belt tension.

## Voltage Regulator

All vehicles, are equipped with a IC voltage regulator. This regulator is incorporated with the alternator and therefore the alternator must be removed and disassembled in order to gain access to the IC voltage regultor. No adjustments can be made to this regulator assembly.

## Starter

### REMOVAL & INSTALLATION

#### *All Except RX-7 and 1988–90 626 and MX-6*

1. Disconnect the negative battery cable from the battery.

2. If the car is equipped with the lower mounted starter, remove the gravel shield from underneath the engine. On automatic transmission equipped vehicles, remove the 2 bolts attaching the starter bracket to the transmission.

3. Raise and support the vehicle safely as required.

4. On 1989–90 323 with 4WD, remove the differential lock assembly from the transaxle by removing the sensor switch and removing the retaining bolts. Insert a suitable tool into the shift rod housing and turn the shift rod 90 degrees clockwise to disengage the differential lock assembly from the transaxle.

5. Remove the battery cable from the starter terminal.

6. Label and disconnect the leads from the magnetic switch terminals.

7. Remove the starter retaining bolts and withdraw the starter assembly.

8. To install, position the starter onto the flywheel housing and install the retaining bolts. On 1986–90 323, 1986–87 626 and 1988–90 929 torque the starter mounting bolts to 23–34 ft. lbs.

9. Connect the leads to the appropriate terminals on the magnetic switch.

10. Connect the battery cable to the starter terminal.

11. On 1989–90 323 with 4WD, install the center differential lock assembly onto the transaxle by positioning the assembly onto the transaxle and turning the shift rod 90 degrees counterclockwise. Install the attaching bolts and torque them to 78–122 ft. lbs. Install the sensor switch and torque it to 14–22 ft. lbs.

12. Install the gravel shield if it was removed.

13. Connect the negative battery cable to the battery.

#### *1988–90 626 and MX-6*

1. Disconnect the negative battery cable from the battery.

2. Disconnect the starter wiring.

3. Raise the front of the vehicle and support it safely.

4. Unbolt and remove the intake manifold bracket.

5. Remove the upper starter bolts and leave the lower bolt loose to support the starter.

6. Remove the lower bolt and withdraw the starter out from the lower side of the vehicle.

7. Position the starter onto the flywheel housing and install the lower bolt for support. Install the remaining bolts and torque all bolts to 27–38 ft. lbs.

8. Install the intake manifold bracket. Torque the bracket bolt to 27–38 ft. lbs. and the nut to 14–19 ft. lbs.

9. Lower the vehicle.

10. Connect the starter wiring.

11. Connect the negative battery cable.

#### *RX-7*

The starter is mounted on the driver's side bottom of the engine.

1. Disconnect the negative battery cable.

2. Raise the vehicle and support it safely.

3. Disconnect the heavy battery cable from the terminal marked **B** on the magnetic switch.

4. Disconnect the thinner ignition switch wire from the terminal marked **S** on the solenoid.

5. On vehicles with automatic transmissions, remove the front starter motor bracket bolts and the bracket. Remove the 2 starter retaining bolts and remove the starter.

6. To install, support the starter by and hand and position it onto the flywheel housing. Install the two mounting bolts. On 1986–90 RX-7, torque the bolts to 24–33 ft. lbs. Install the front starter bracket, if removed.

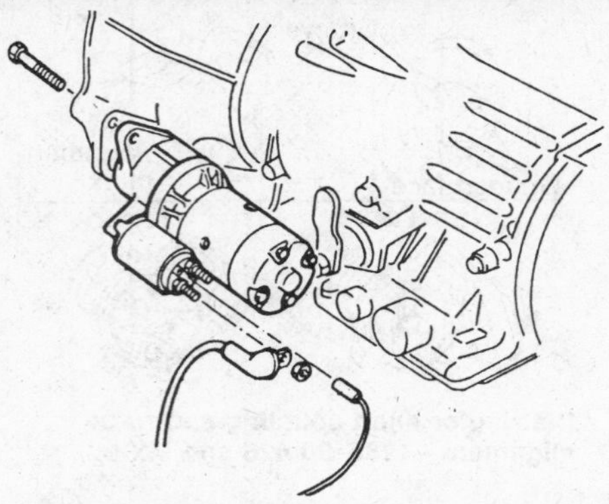

**Starter removal and installation – 1983–85 RX-7**

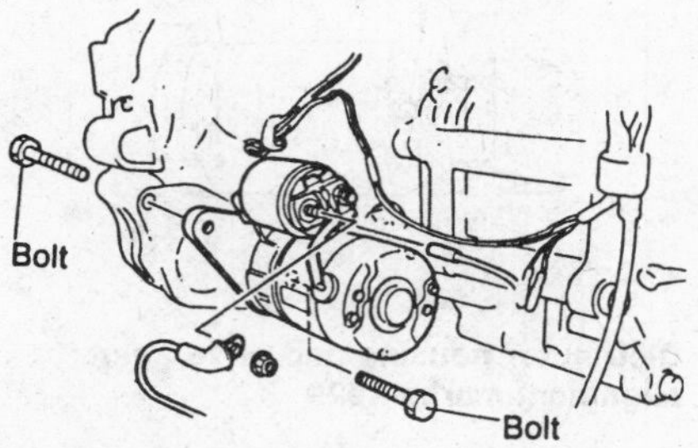


**Starter removal and installation – 1986–90 RX-7**

7. Connect the starter wiring to the appropriate terminals on the magnetic switch. On 1986–90 models, torque the "B" terminal (battery cable) nut to 8 ft. lbs.

8. Lower the vehicle.

9. Connect the negative battery cable.

### STARTER DRIVE REPLACEMENT

#### *Direct Drive Type*

1. Remove the solenoid.

2. Remove the plunger from the drive engagement fork.

3. Remove the nuts from the thru bolts.

4. Remove the drive housing.

5. Remove the engagement fork, spring and spring seat.

6. Place a deep socket over the drive end of the armature shaft and drive the over running clutch stopper toward the clutch.

7. Remove the spring retainer from the armature.

8. Withdraw the over running clutch from the armature shaft.

9. To assemble, reverse the disassembly procedure. Check the clearance between the pinion and the stop collar with the solenoid closed. It should be 0.020–0.079 in. If the pinion gap is not to specification, adjust the gap by altering the number of washers between the solenoid and the front bracket.

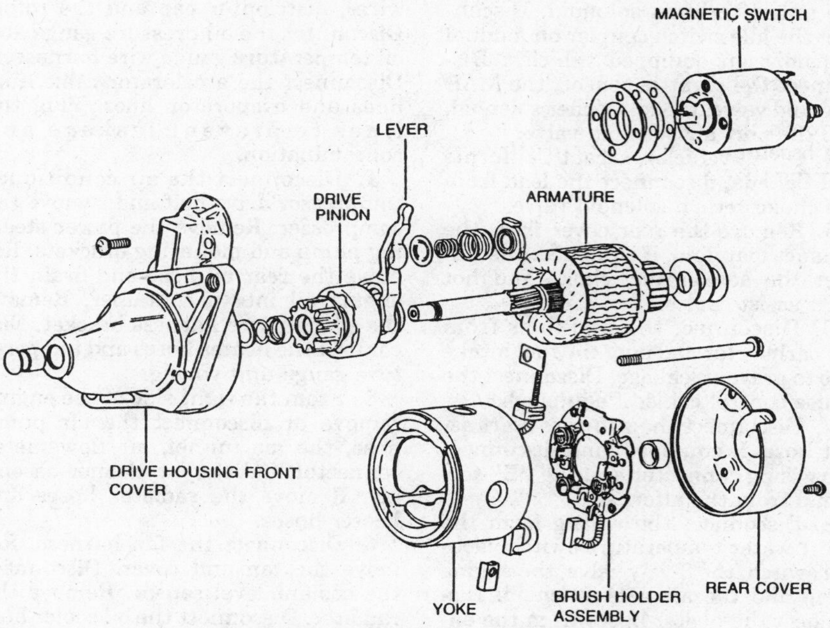


**Exploded view of a conventional type of starter**

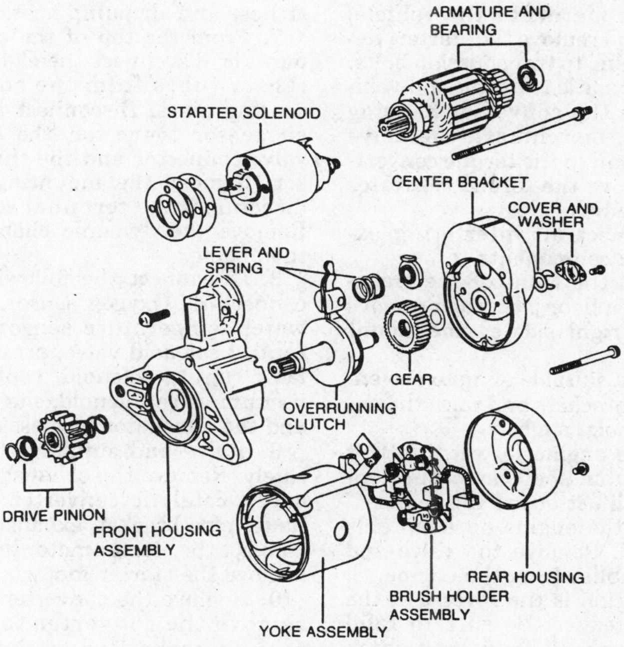


**Exploded view of a reduction type of starter**

### *Reduction Type*

1. Remove the solenoid and the plunger from the drive engagement fork.
2. Remove the thru housing bolts and separate the front housing from the armature housing.
3. At the rear of the center bracket, remove the 2 cover screws, the cover, the C-washer and the adjustment washer.
4. Remove the center bracket bolts and separate the center bracket from the front housing. Remove the reduction gear and washer.
5. Remove the packing, the spring, and the lever.
6. At the front housing, tap the stop ring to reveal the retaining ring. Remove the retaining ring from the driveshaft.
7. Remove the gear assembly from the driveshaft and remove the drive assembly from the front housing.
8. To install, reverse the removal procedure. Adjust the pinion shaft thrust gap to 0.020 in. max., by adjust the washer numbers at the center bracket housing.

## Diesel Glow Plugs

### REMOVAL & INSTALLATION

1. Disconnect the negative battery cable.
2. Remove the glow plug connector nut, lockwasher and flatwasher, then remove the glow plug connector wire from its terminal.
3. Using a suitable tool, remove the glow plug from the engine.
4. Installation is the reverse order of the removal procedure.

### TESTING

#### *Glow Plug Inspection*

1. Disconnect the wiring from the glow plug.
2. Using an ohmmeter, check the continuity between each terminal of the glow plug and the cylinder head.
3. If continuity does not exist, remove and replace the glow plug.

#### *Glow Plug Relay Inspection*

1. Disconnect the glow plug relay connector. Using a suitable jumper wire, connect the wire to the battery and the relay connector. Also connect a suitable ohmmeter to the relay connector.
2. If the ohmmeter shows continuity when the battery is connected. The relay is good.
3. If the ohmmeter shows no continuity when the battery is connected then the relay is not good and should be replaced.

# ROTARY ENGINE MECHANICAL

## Engine

### REMOVAL & INSTALLATION

#### *RX-7*

#### 1983–85 WITH CARBURETOR

1. Properly relieve the fuel system pressure. Disconnect the negative battery cable. Scribe matchmarks on the hood and hinges and remove the hood.

2. Working from underneath the vehicle, remove the gravel shield then drain the cooling system and the engine oil.

3. Disconnect the high tension wires from the center towers of the ignition coils.

**NOTE: A good rule of thumb when disconnecting the engine wiring and vacuum hoses, it to put a piece of masking tape on the wire or hose and on the connection you remove the wire or hose from, then mark both pieces of tape, 1, 2, 3, etc. When replacing the wiring and hoses, simply match the pieces of tape.**

4. Disconnect the distributor wiring, the oil level sensor lead, the water temperature lead and, on all except California vehicles, the coupler from the oil thermo sensor.

5. On all California vehicles and vehicles equipped with automatic transmission, disconnect the vacuum sensing tube from the vacuum switch. Disconnect the evaporative hose.

6. Disconnect the hoses from the oil cooler, located beneath the radiator. Disconnect the radiator coolant level sensor lead from the top of the radiator and disconnect the coolant reservoir hose.

7. Remove the bolts holding the coolant fan and drive unit to the drive pulley and remove. Remove the air cleaner.

**NOTE: On vehicles equipped with air conditioning it will be necessary to remove the compresser and the condenser from their mounts. Do not unfasten the refrigerant lines. Tie the units off to a convenient place on the body or engine compartment.**

8. On all vehicles, except California and Canada, disconnect the connectors from the No. 2 water temperature sensor, located on the radiator next to the radiator cap.

9. Remove the lower and upper radiator hoses. Disconnect the automatic transmission fluid pipes from the radiator, if equipped.

10. Remove the cooling fan, the drive assembly, the radiator and shroud assembly.

11. Remove the vacuum hose for the brake booster. Disconnect the heat exchanger pipe from the rear of the intake manifold.

12. Disconnect the coupler from the power valve solenoid on all vehicles, except Canadian vehicles equipped with manual transmission.

13. Disconnect the coasting enrichment connector on vehicles equipped with manual transmission. Disconnect the leads from the choke heater and the anti-afterburn solenoid. Disconnect the idle switch coupler on manual transmission equipped vehicles. Disconnect the throttle sensor, the MAB solenoid valve, the idle richer solenoid, and the port air solenoid valve.

14. On all vehicles, except California and Canada, disconnect the lead from the choke return solenoid valve.

15. Remove the rear cover from the exhaust manifold, if equipped. Disconnect the accelerator, choke and hot start assist cables.

16. Disconnect the fuel lines from the carburetor and plug the fuel intake line to prevent leakage. Disconnect the cruise control cable, if equipped.

17. Disconnect the sub-zero start assist hose, if equipped, and disconnect the wiring connector and the "B" terminal from the alternator.

18. Disconnect the wiring from the No. 1 water temperature switch vacuum switch, the 3-way valve, the engine strap and the air vent solenoid. Disconnect the heater hoses from the engine. If equipped with air conditioning, disconnect the compressor bolts and move aside.

19. From underneath the vehicle, disconnect and remove the starter. Remove the engine to transmission bolts.

20. On automatic transmission vehicles, remove the converter housing lower cover, matchmark the drive plate in relation to the torque converter, then remove the torque converter to drive plate bolts.

21. Disconnect all interfering exhaust system components.

22. Support the front of the transmission with a floor jack, then remove the left and right side engine mount bolts.

23. Attach a suitable sling to the engine hanger brackets and raise the engine with a hoist slightly.

24. Pull the engine forward until it clears the clutch shaft or torque converter, then lift it out of the vehicle.

25. Mount the engine on a suitable engine stand. Remove the valve and piping assemblies from the engine.

26. Installation is the reverse of the removal procedure. Be sure to refill the engine with all fluids and check the engine timing.

### 1985–90 WITHOUT TURBOCHARGER

1. Properly relieve the fuel system pressure. Disconnect the negative battery cable. Scribe mark the hinge locations and remove the hood. Drain the coolant and engine oil.

2. As required, discharge the air conditioning system, using the proper equipment.

3. From the left side of the engine compartment, remove the spark plug wires, distributor cap and the rotor. Disconnect the oil pressure gauge and oil temperature gauge wire harnesses. Disconnect the accelerator cable, fuel lines and evaporator lines. Plug the lines to prevent leakage and contamination.

4. Disconnect the air conditioner compressor drive belt and remove the compresser. Remove the power steering pump and mounting brackets. Remove the rear oil hose and drain the engine oil into a container. Remove the starter wire harness bracket. Disconnect the heater hoses and temperature gauge unit wiring.

5. From the right side of the engine remove or disconnect the air pump hose, the air funnel, air flow meter connector and the air cleaner assembly. Remove the radiator hoses and heater hoses.

6. Disconnect the fan harness. Remove the fan and cover. Disconnect the coolant level sensor. Remove the radiator. Disconnect the oil cooler hoses. Disconnect the cruise control cable and the oil pump metering rod connector. Remove water hoses, brake booster hose and air pump hoses.

7. From the top of the engine, remove or disconnect the eight vacuum sensor tubes from the chamber to sensing pipes. Disconnect the intake air sensor connector, the air supply valve connector and the throttle sensor. Remove the mounting nut and disconnect the terminal cover wire. Remove the dynamic chamber from the engine.

8. Disconnect the following wiring connectors. Oxygen sensor, injectors, water temperature sensor, vacuum control solenoid valve, pressure regulator control solenoid, vent solenoid, vacuum valve solenoid, engine ground and the alternator harness and wires.

9. Raise and support the vehicle safely. Remove the exhaust pipe front cover, catalytic converter cover, exhaust pipe bracket, exhaust pipe, disconnect the starter motor harness and remove the starter motor.

10. Remove the converter cover and remove the converter to flywheel mounting bolts. Remove the transmission to engine mounting bolts and engine mount nuts.

11. Lower the vehicle, attach a suitable lifting sling to a hoist and carefully remove the engine after pulling it forward slightly to disengage the transmission.

12. Installation is the reverse of the removal procedure. Replace the coolant and lubricant. Check the ignition timing.

### 1985–90 WITH TURBOCHARGER

1. Properly relieve the fuel system

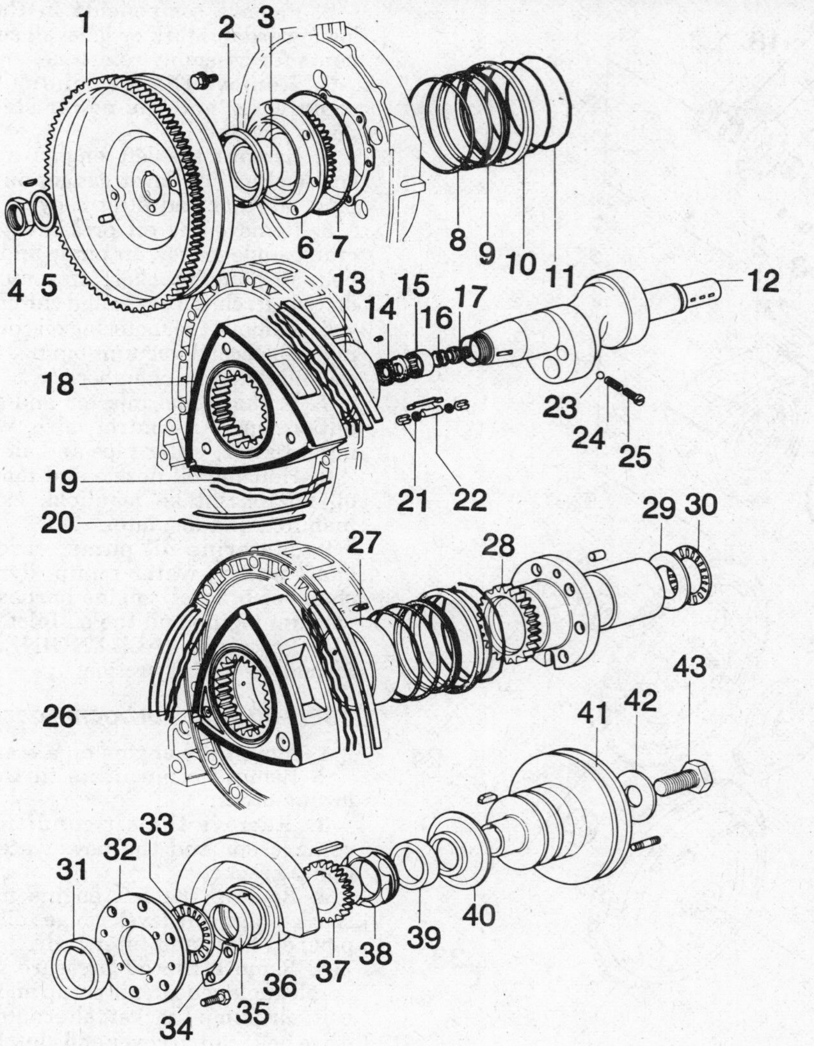


1. Flywheel
2. Oil seal
3. Main bearing
4. Locknut
5. Washer
6. Rear stationary gear
7. O-ring
8. Oil seal O-ring
9. Oil seal
10. Oil seal
11. Oil seal spring
12. Eccentric shaft
13. Rotor bearing
14. Grease seal
15. Needle bearing
16. O-ring
17. Blind plug
18. Front rotor
19. Side seal spring
20. Side seal
21. Corner seal and spring
22. Apex seal and spring
23. Ball
24. Spring
25. Oil nozzle
26. Rear rotor
27. Rotor bearing
28. Front stationary gear
29. Thrust washer
30. Thrust bearing
31. Spacer
32. Bearing housing
33. Needle bearing
34. Washer
35. Thrust plate
36. Balance weight
37. Oil pump drive sprocket
38. Distributor drive gear
39. Spacer
40. Oil slinger
41. Eccentric shaft pulley
42. Washer
43. Pulley bolt

**Typical rotor and eccentric shaft components—12A engine shown**

pressure. Disconnect the negative battery cable. Drain the engine oil and coolant into suitable containers.

2. Starting from the front and right side of the engine, remove the following components.

a. Air intake pipe and air cleaner assembly

b. Battery and battery box

c. Cooling fan and upper and lower radiator hoses

d. Heater return hose. Coolant level sensor connector and radiator switch connector. ATF hose (1987–90 vehicles only)

e. Radiator, cowling and intercooler

f. Accelerator cable and cruise control cable, if equipped. Brake vacuum hose, pressure sensor vacuum hose, relief silencer hose and spilt air pipe

g. Oxygen sensor connector. Insulator covers, front converter upper nut and engine harness connector

3. Working from the left side of the engine, remove the following components.

a. Power steering pump and drive belt. Leave the hoses connected to the power steering pump and secure it out of the way.

b. Air conditioning compressor and drive belt. Leave the hoses connected to the compressor and secure it out of the way.

c. Remove the spark plug wires, crank angle sensor connector and alternator connector.

d. Remove the canister hose. Remove and plug the fuel hose.

e. Remove the oil pressure connector, heater hose, clutch release cylinder, engine ground and oil cooler pipe and bracket.

4. Raise and support the vehicle safely. Remove the under cover, catalytic converter insulator, split air pipe, exhaust pipe bracket and catalytic converter. Remove the exhaust pipe and front converter, starter, transmission attaching bolts and engine mounting nuts.

5. Lower the vehicle, attach a suitable lifting sling to a hoist and carefully remove the engine after pulling it forward slightly to disengage the transmission.

6. Installation is the reverse of the removal procedure. Replace the coolant and lubricant. Check the ignition timing.

## DISASSEMBLY

**NOTE: Because of the design of the rotary engine, it is not practical to attempt component removal and installation. It is best to disassemble and assemble the entire engine, or go as far as necessary with the disassembly and assembly procedure as needed.**

### *1983–85 Carbureted Engine*

1. Mount the engine on a stand.
2. Remove the oil hose support bracket from the front housing.
3. Disconnect the vacuum hoses, air hoses and remove the decel valve.
4. Remove the air pump and drive belt. Remove the air pump adjusting bar.
5. Remove the alternator and drive belt.
6. Disconnect the metering oil pump connecting rod, oil tubes and vacuum sensing tube from the carburetor.
7. Remove the exhaust manifold

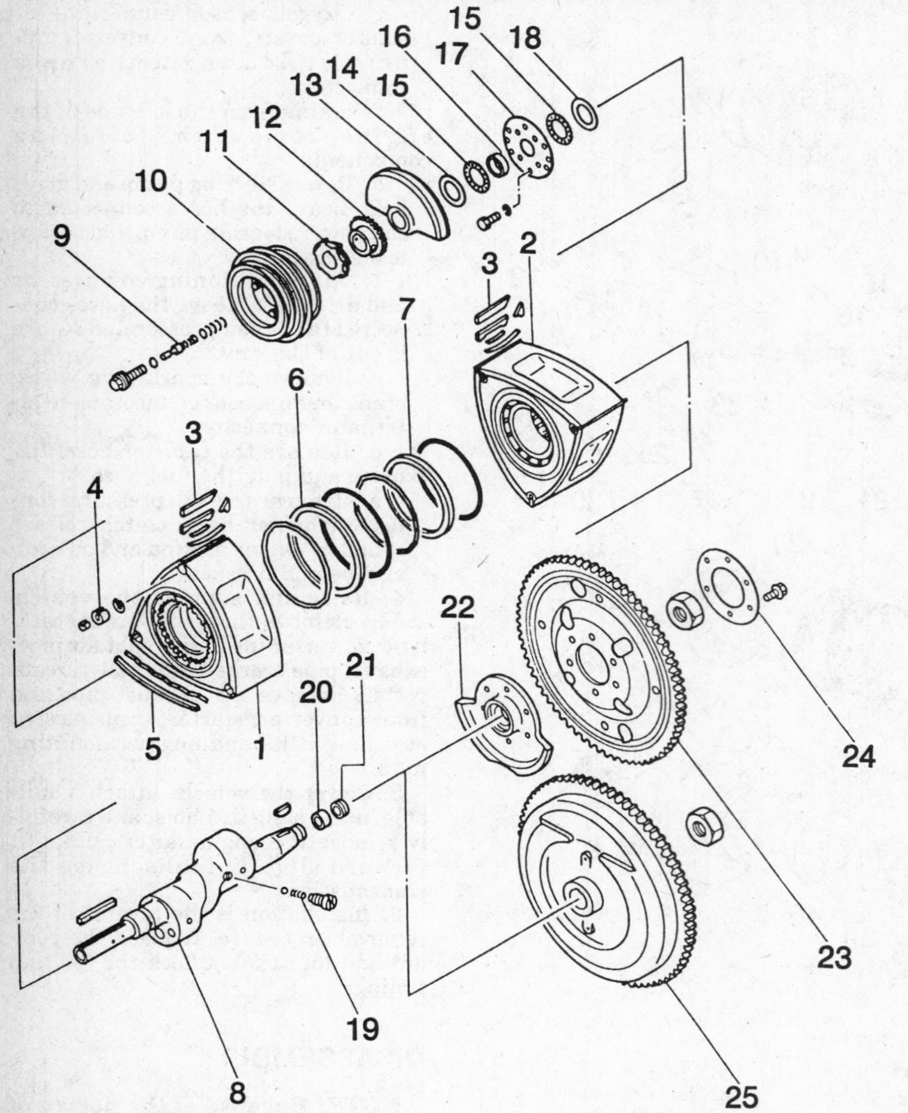


1. Front rotor
2. Rear rotor
3. Apex seal
4. Corner seal
5. Side seal
6. Outer oil seal
7. Inner oil seal
8. Eccentric shaft
9. Oil bypass valve
10. Eccentric shaft pulley
11. Distributor drive gear
12. Oil pump drive sprocket
13. Balance weight
14. Thrust washer
15. Thrust needle bearing
16. Spacer
17. Plate
18. Thrust plate
19. Oil jet valve
20. Pilot bearing (M/T)
21. Oil seal (M/T)
22. Counter weight (A/T)
23. Drive plate (A/T)
24. Back plate (A/T)
25. Flywheel (M/T)

**Engine rotating components – 13B engine**

cover, if equipped. Remove the carburetor and intake manifold as an assembly.

8. Remove the gasket and two rubber rings.

9. Remove the thermal reactor and gaskets, if equipped. Remove the exhaust manifold and engine mount.

10. Remove the distributor.

11. Disconnect and remove the oil pipe from the cooler. Remove the water hose. Remove the oil cooler, filter and O-rings. Do not remove the oil filter from the cooler housing unless replacement is necessary.

12. Unbolt the A/C compressor pulley and remove the water pump.

13. Proceed to "ALL ENGINES" information in this section.

### *1985–90 without Turbocharger*

1. Mount the engine on a stand.

2. Remove components in the following order. Mark or label all components for assembly reference.

3. Remove the air conditioning compresser and the power steering pump bracket.

4. Remove the left engine mount, spark plugs, oil level gauge, oil filler pipe, oil filter and filter body.

5. Remove the oil pressure gauge, crank angle sensor, air pump and drive belt, air pump bracket, alternator and drive belt, clutch cover and clutch disc.

6. Remove the metering oil connecting rod, second vacuum piping, throttle and dynamic chamber.

7. Primary fuel injector and distribution pipe. Air control valve, switching actuator, water pipe and air hose.

8. Housing oil nozzle and manifold oil nozzle, intake manifold, exhaust manifold and insulator.

9. Metering oil pump, eccentric shaft pulley, water pump, dynamic chamber bracket, engine harness and vacuum piping and the oil inlet pipe.

10. Proceed to "ALL ENGINES" information in this section.

### *1986–90 with Turbocharger*

1. Mount the engine on a stand.

2. Remove components in the following order.

3. Remove the air conditioning compressor and the power steering pump bracket.

4. Remove the left engine mount, spark plugs, oil level gauge, oil filler pipe, oil filter and filter body.

5. Remove the oil pressure gauge, crank angle sensor, air pump and drive belt, air pump bracket, alternator and drive belt, clutch cover and clutch disc.

6. Remove the metering oil connecting rod, second vacuum piping, throttle and dynamic chamber.

7. Primary fuel injector and distribution pipe. Air control valve, switching actuator, water pipe, turbocharger and insulator and air hose. Cover the intake and exhaust port openings with masking tape to prevent the prevent the entry of dirt and foreign matter.

8. Housing oil nozzle and manifold oil nozzle, intake manifold, exhaust manifold and insultor.

9. Metering oil pump, eccentric shaft pulley, water pump, dynamic chamber bracket, engine harness and vacuum piping and the oil inlet pipe.

10. Proceed to "ALL ENGINES" information in this section.

### *All Engines*

1. Invert the engine.

2. Remove right engine mount and the oil pan.

3. Remove the oil strainer and gasket.

4. Identify the front and rear rotor

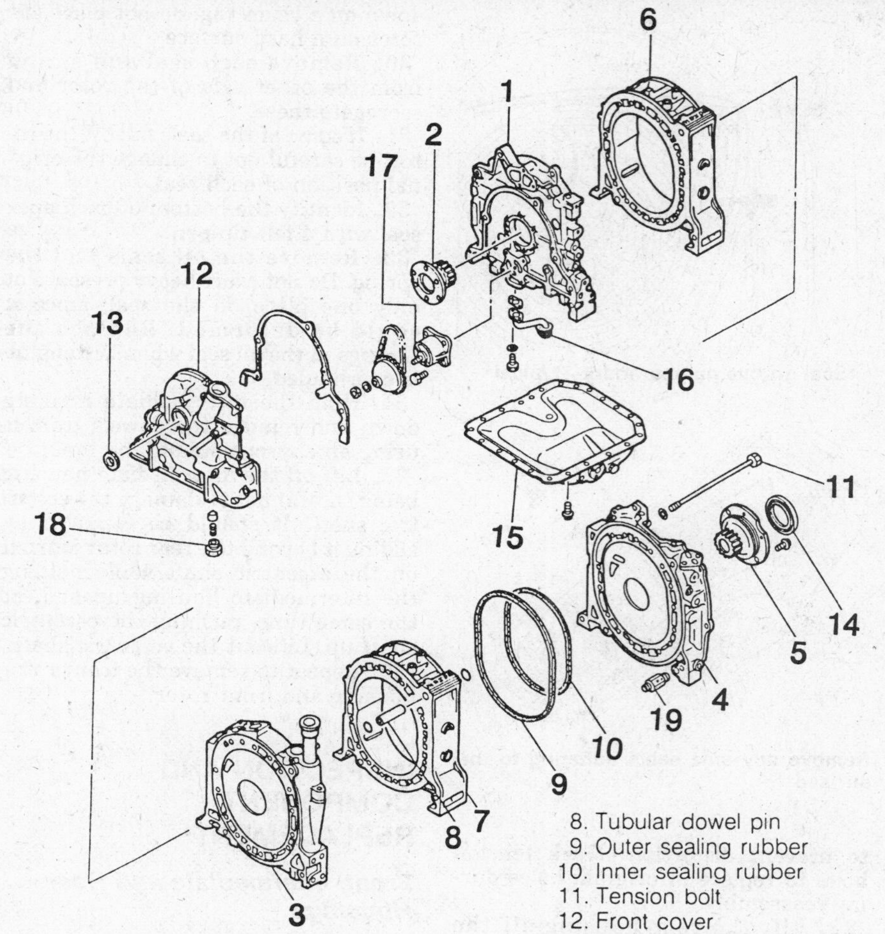


1. Front housing
2. Front stationary gear
3. Intermediate housing
4. Rear housing
5. Rear stationary gear
6. Front rotor housing
7. Rear rotor housing
8. Tubular dowel pin
9. Outer sealing rubber
10. Inner sealing rubber
11. Tension bolt
12. Front cover
13. Front oil seal
14. Rear oil seal
15. Oil pan
16. Oil strainer
17. Oil pump
18. Oil pressure control valve
19. Oil pressure regulator valve

**Engine housing components—13B engine**

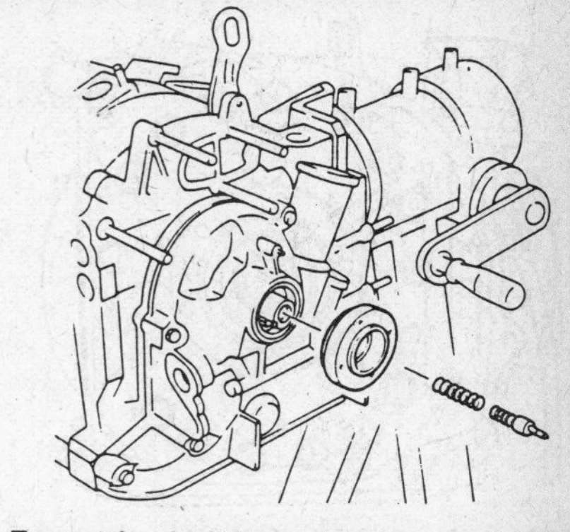

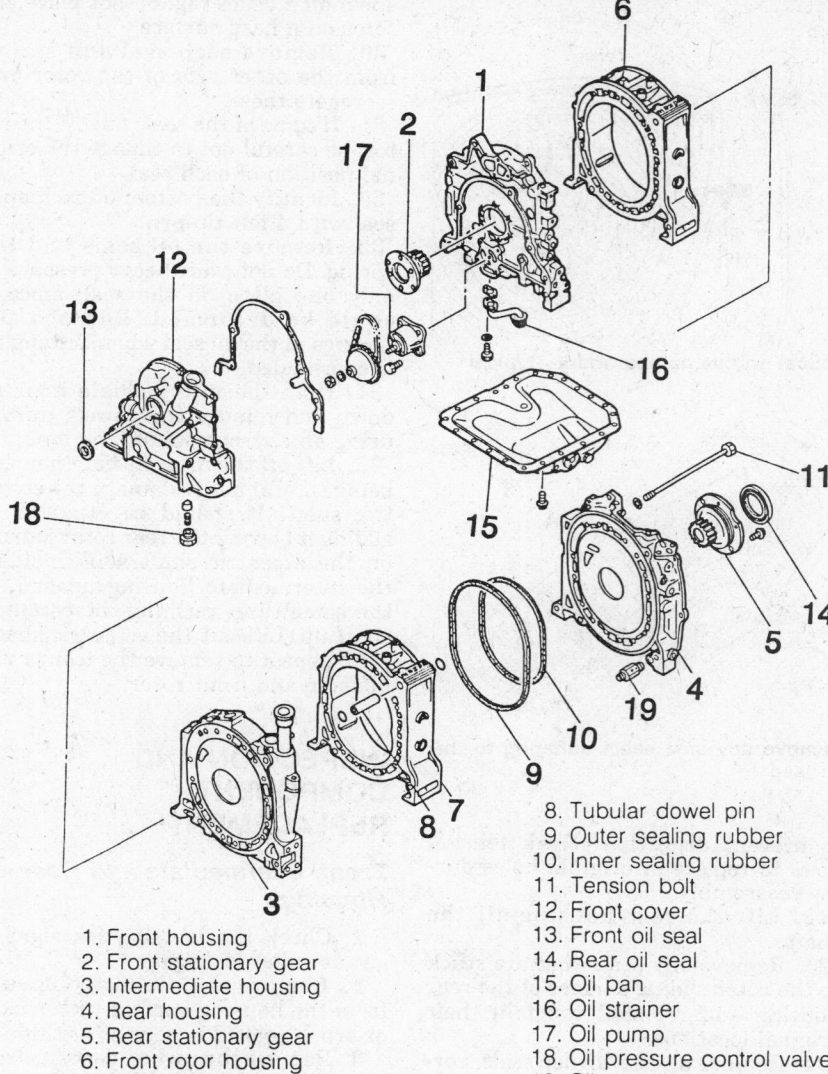

**Eccentric shaft bypass valve, spring and pulley boss removal and installation—13B engines**

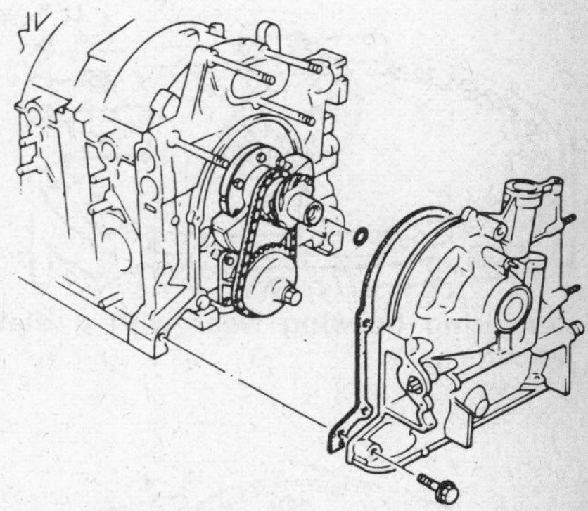

**Front cover removal and installation—13B engines**

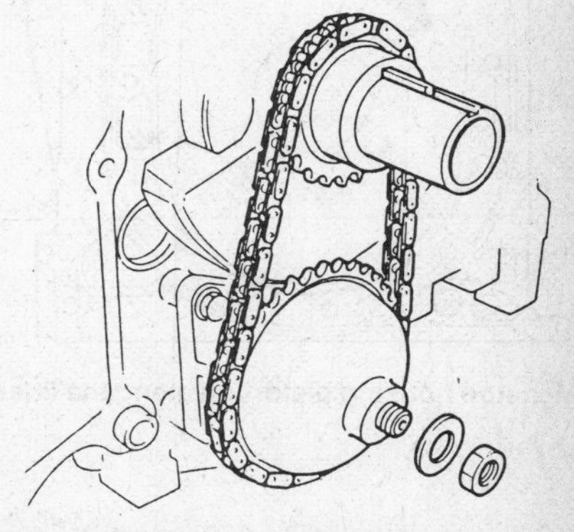

**Oil pump drive gear, driven gear and chain removal and installation—13B engines**

housing with a felt tip pen. These are common parts and must be identified to be assembled in their respective locations.

5. Turn the engine on the stand so that the top of the engine is up.

6. Remove the engine mounting bracket from the front cover.

7. Remove the eccentric shaft pulley. Remove the eccentric shaft bypass valve and spring. Remove the O-ring from the eccentric shaft lock bolt and discard it. Remove the eccentric shaft pulley boss.

8. Turn the engine on a stand so that the front end of the engine is up.

9. Remove the front cover with the oil pressure control valve..

10. Remove the O-ring from the oil passage on the front housing.

11. Remove the oil slinger and distributor drive gear from the shaft.

12. Unbolt and remove the chain adjuster.

13. Remove the locknut and washer from the oil pump driven sprocket.

14. Slide the oil pump drive sprocket and driven sprocket, together with the drive chain off the eccentric shaft and oil pump, simultaneously.

15. Remove the baffle plate (turbocharged engines only). Remove the keys from the eccentric and oil pump shaft. Remove the oil pump.

16. Slide the balance weight, thrust washer and needle bearing from the shaft.

17. Unbolt the bearing housing and slide the bearing housing, needle bearing, spacer and thrust plate off the shaft.

18. Turn the engine on the stand so that the top of the engine is up.

19. If equipped with a manual transmission, remove the clutch pressure plate and clutch disc. Remove the flywheel with a puller. Remove the key from the shaft.

20. If equipped with an automatic transmission, remove the drive plate. Remove the counterweight. Block the weight and remove the mounting nut. Remove the counterweight with a suitable puller.

21. Working at the rear of the engine, loosen the tension bolts. Do not loosen the tension bolts one at a time. Loosen the bolts evenly in small stages

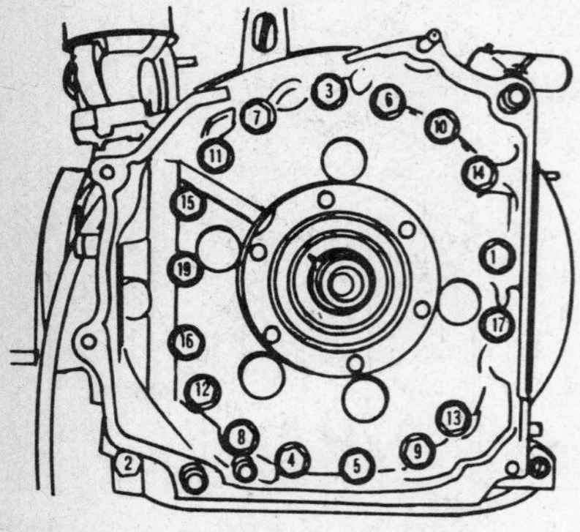

12A engine tension bolt loosening sequence

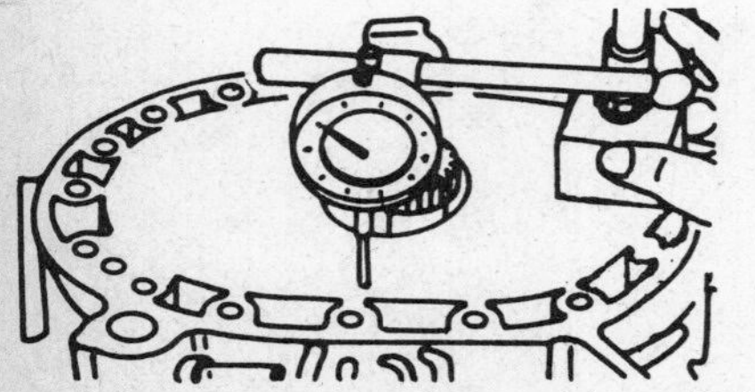

Measuring housing wear with a dial ndicator

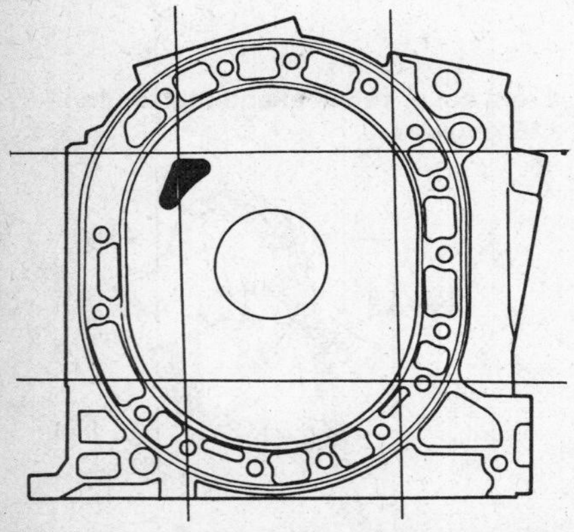

Measure housing distortion along the lines

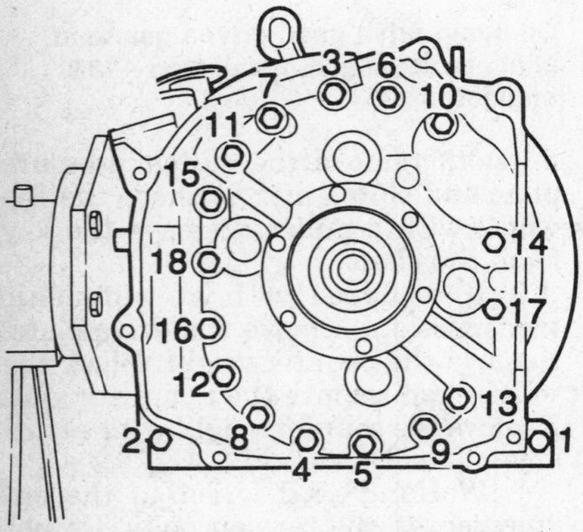


13B engine tension bolt loosenting sequence

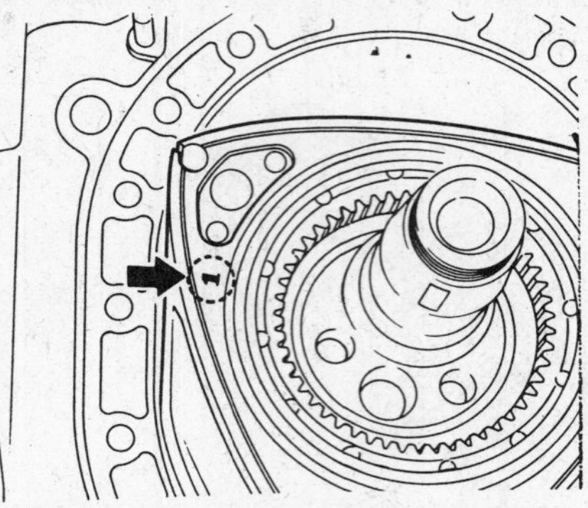

Seal groove number mark—typical

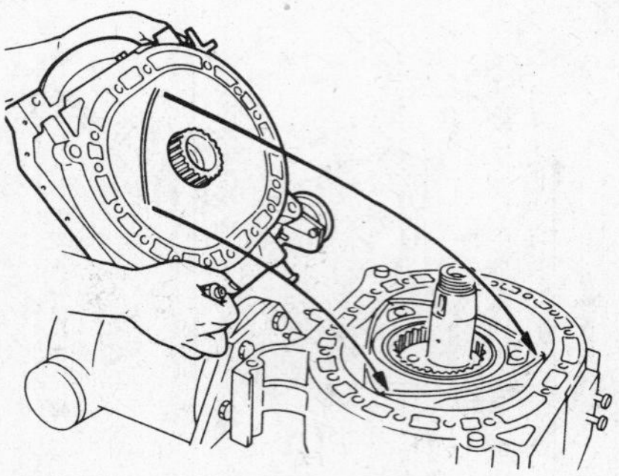

Remove any side seals adhering to the surface

to prevent distortion. Mark tension bolts to replace in original holes during reassembly.

22. Lift the rear housing off the shaft.

23. Remove any seals that are stuck to the rotor sliding surface of the rear housing and reinstall them in their original locations.

24. Remove all the corner seals, corner seal spring, side seal and side seal springs from the rear side of the rotor. Mazda has a special tray which holds all the seals and keeps them segregated to prevent mistakes during reassembly. Each seal groove is marked with numbers near the grooves on the rotor face to prevent confusion.

25. Remove the two rubber seals, two O-rings or oil seal from the rear rotor housing. Remove the pressure regulator and the rear rotor housing side pieces.

26. Remove the tubular dowels from the rear rotor housing using the appropriate puller.

27. Lift the rear rotor housing away from the rear rotor, being very careful not to drop the apex seals on the rear rotor. Remove the O-ring from the upper dowel hole.

28. Remove each apex seal, side piece and spring from the rear rotor and segregate them.

29. Remove the rear rotor from the eccentric shaft and place it upside down on a clean rag. do not place the rotor on a hard surface.

30. Remove each seal and spring from the other side of the rotor and segregate these.

31. If some of the seals fall off the rotor, be careful not to change the original position of each seal.

32. Identify the bottom of each apex seal with a felt tip pen.

33. Remove the oil seals and the spring. Do not exert heavy pressure at only one place on the seal, since it could be deformed. Replace the O-rings in the oil seal when the engine is overhauled.

34. Hold the intermediate housing down and remove the dowels from it using an appropriate pulling tool..

35. Lift off the intermediate housing being careful not to damage the eccentric shaft. It should be removed by sliding it beyond the rear rotor journal on the eccentric shaft while holding the intermediate housing up and, at the same time, pushing the eccentric shaft up. Lift out the eccentric shaft.

36. Repeat to remove the front rotor housing and front rotor.

## INSPECTION AND COMPONENT REPLACEMENT

### *Front, Intermediate and Rear Housings*

1. Check the housing for signs of gas or water leakage.

2. Remove the sealing compound from the housing surface with a cloth or brush soaked in solvent or thinner.

3. Remove the carbon deposits from the front housing with extra fine emery cloth. Be careful when using a carbon scraper.

4. Check for distortion by placing a straightedge on the surface of the housing. Measure the clearance between the straightedge and the housing with a feeler gauge. If the clearance is greater than 0.0016 in. at any point, replace the housing.

5. Use a dial indicator to check for wear on the rotor contact surfaces of the housing. If the wear is greater than 0.004 in., replace the housing.

**NOTE: The wear at either end of the minor axis is greater than at any other point on the housing. However, this is normal and should be not cause for concern.**

### *Front Stationary Gear and Main Bearing*

1. Examine the teeth of the stationary gear for wear or damage.

2. Be sure that the main bearing

shows no signs of excessive wear, scoring, or flaking.

3. Check the main bearing to eccentric journal clearance by measuring the journal with a vernier caliper and the bearing with a pair of inside calipers. The standard clearance is between 0.0016–0.0031 in.

### Main Bearing Replacement

1. Unfasten the securing bolts, if used. Remove stationary gear and main bearing assembly, out of the housing, using puller tool 49-0813-235, or equivalent.
2. Press the main bearing out of the stationary gear.
3. Press a new main bearing into the stationary gear so that it is in the same position that the old bearing was.
4. Align the slot in the stationary gear flange with the dowel pin in the housing and press the gear into place. On later engines, align the bearing lug with the slot in the gear. Install the securing bolts, if required.

### Rear Stationary Gear and Main Bearing

Inspect the rear stationary gear and main bearing in a similar manner to the front. In addition, examine the O-ring, which is located in the stationary gear, for signs of wear or damage. Replace the O-ring, if necessary. To replace the stationary gear, use the following procedure.

1. Remove the rear stationary gear securing bolts.
2. Drive the stationary gear out of the rear housing with a brass drift.
3. Apply a light coating of grease to a new O-ring and fit it into the groove on the stationary gear.
4. Apply sealer to the flange of the stationary gear.
5. Install the stationary gear on the housing so that the slot on its flange aligns with the pin on the rear housing. On later engines align the bearing lug with the housing slot. Use care not to damage the O-ring during installation.
6. Tighten the stationary gear bolts evenly, in several stages, to 12–17 ft. lbs.

### Rotor Housings

1. Examine the inner margin of both housings for signs of gas or water leakage.
2. Wipe the inner surface of each housing with a clean cloth to remove the carbon deposits.
3. Clean all of the rust deposits out of the cooling passages of each rotor housing.
4. Remove the old sealer using the proper removal solvent.

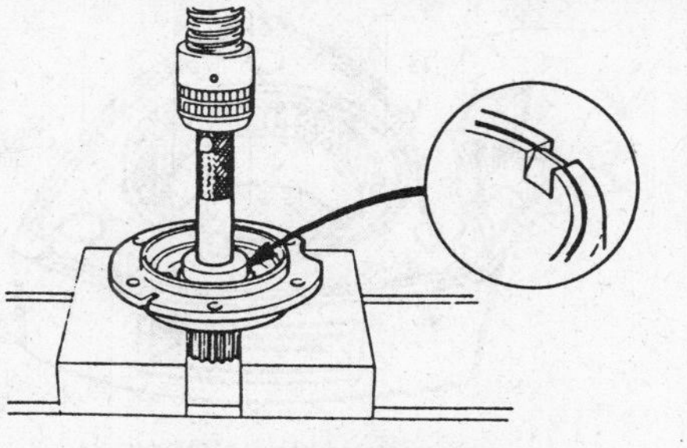

Main bearing replacement

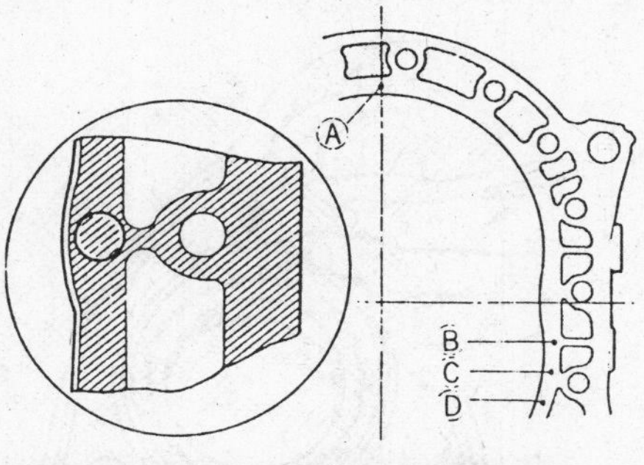


Measure the rotor housing width at the indicated points

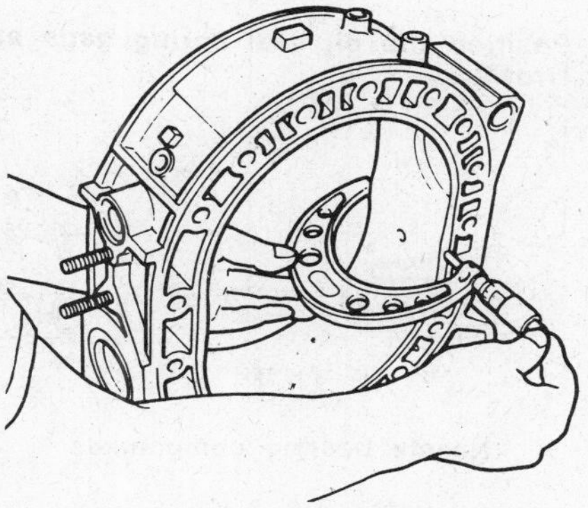

Checking rotor housing width

5. Examine the chromium plated inner surfaces for scoring, flaking, or other signs of damage. If any are present, the housing must be replaced.
6. Check the rotor housings for distortion by placing a straightedge on the axes.
7. If distortion exceeds 0.002 in., replace the rotor housing.
8. Check the widths of both rotor housings, at a minimum of eight points near the trochoid surfaces of each housing, using a vernier caliper.
9. If the difference between the maximum and minimum values obtained is greater than 0.0024 in., replace the housing. A housing in this condition will be prone to gas and coolant leakage.

### Rotors

1. Check the rotor for signs of blowby around the side and corner seal areas.

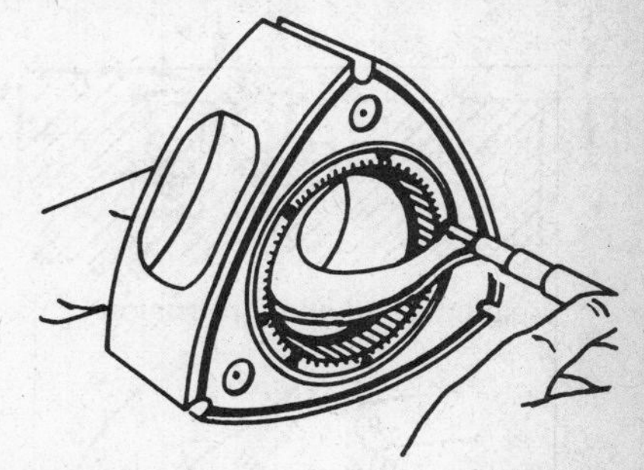

Measure the rotor width at the point indicated

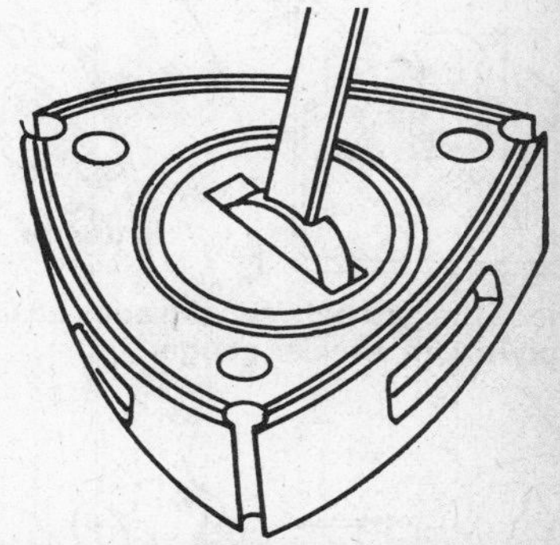

Insert the special bearing expander into the rotor

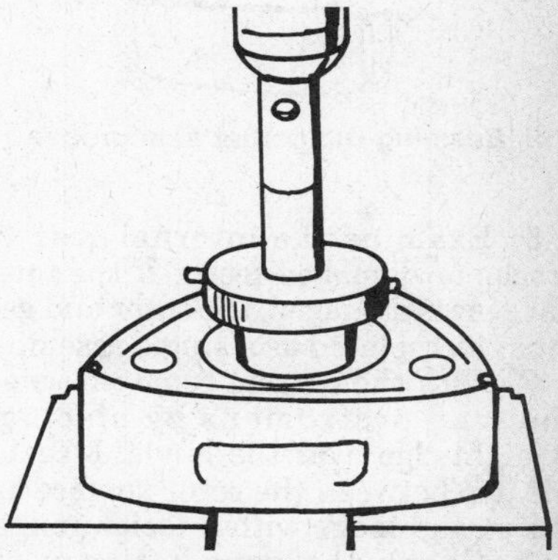

Installing a new rotor bearing

2. The color of the carbon deposits on the rotor should be brown, just as in a piston engine. Usually the carbon deposits on the leading side of the rotor are brown, while those on the trailing side tend toward black, as viewed from the direction of rotation.
3. Remove the carbon on the rotor with a scraper or extra fine emery paper. Use the scraper carefully when doing the seal grooves so that no damage is done to them.
4. Wash the rotor in solvent and blow it dry with compressed air.

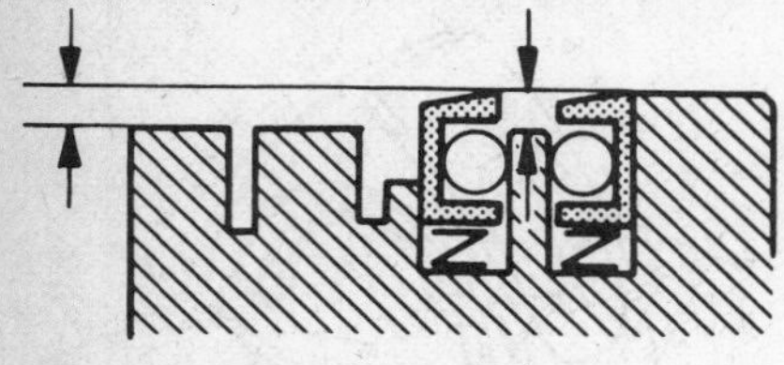

Measuring oil seal protrusion

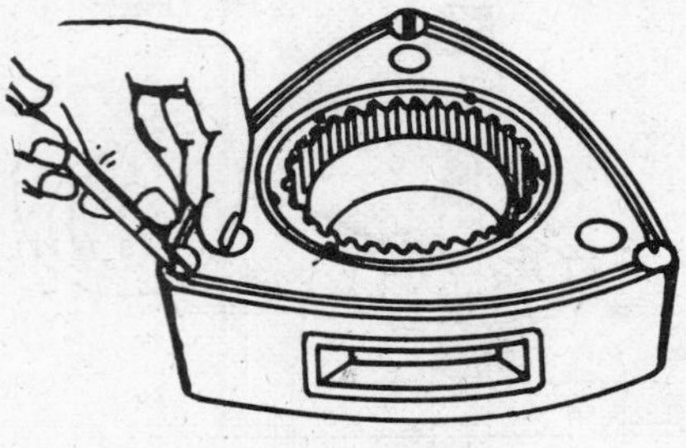

Corner seal installation

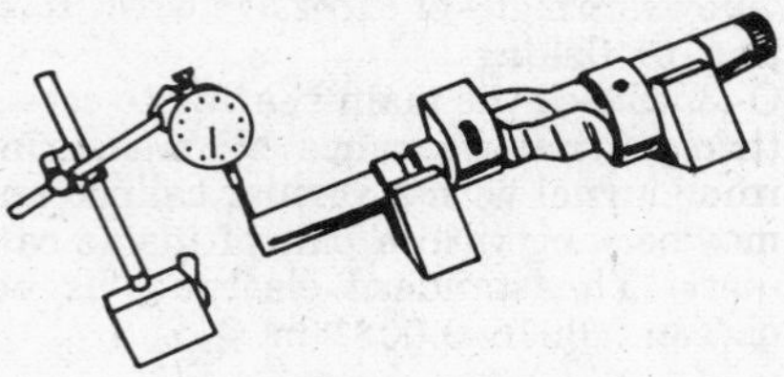

Position the dial indicator as shown to measure shaft run-out

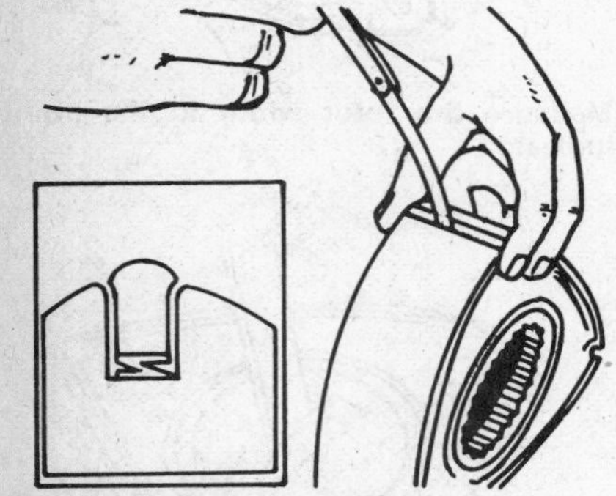

Check the gap between the apex seal and groove with a feeler gauge

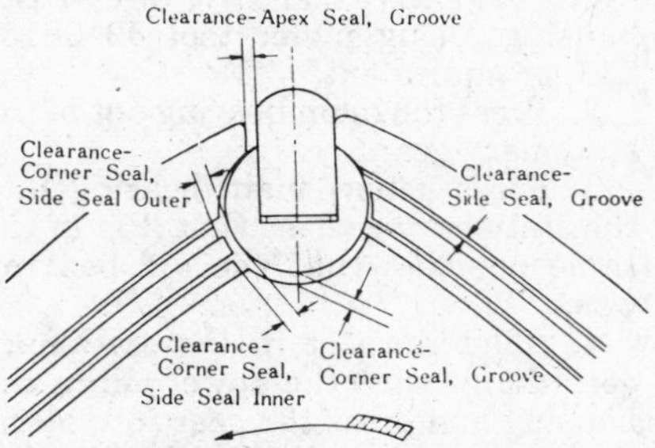


Check the clearance of the seals at the points indicated

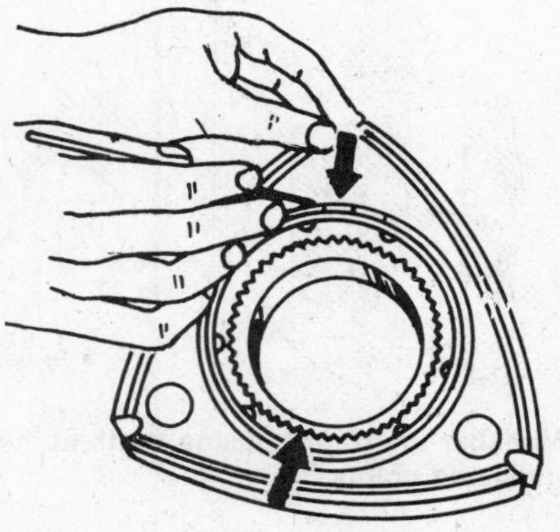

Position the oil seal spring gaps at arrows

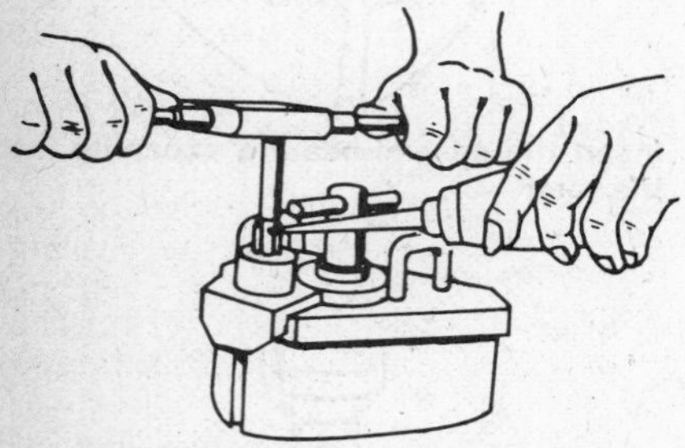

Reaming the corner seal groove

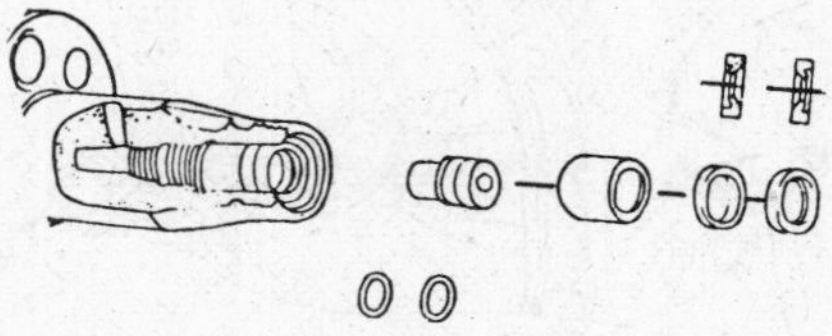

Needle bearing components

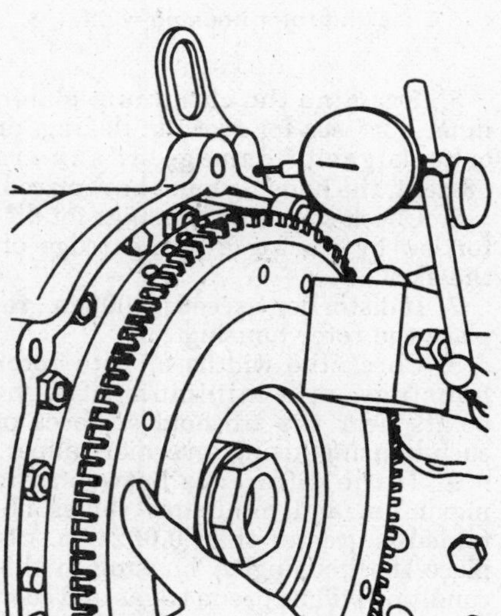

Use a dial indicator attached to the flywheel to measure eccentric shaft end-play

5. Examine the internal gear for cracks or damaged teeth. If the internal gear is damaged, the rotor and gear must be replaced as a single assembly.

6. With the oil seal removed, check the land protrusions by placing a straightedge over the lands. Measure the gap between the rotor surface and the straightedge with a feeler gauge.

7. Check the gaps between the housings and the rotor on both of its sides.

a. Measure the rotor width with a vernier caliper.

b. Compare the rotor width against the width of the rotor housing which was measured above.

c. Replace the rotor, if the difference between the two measurements is not within 0.0047–0.0074 in. for the 1983–85 engine and 0.0047–0.0083 in. for the 1985–90 engine.

8. Check the rotor bearing for flaking, wearing, or scoring.

### Rotor Bearing Replacement

1. Check the clearance between the rotor bearing and the rotor journal on the eccentric shaft. Measure the inner diameter of the rotor bearing and the outer diameter of the journal. The wear limit is 0.0039 in., replace the bearing if it exceeds specification.

2. Place the rotor on the support so that the internal gear is facing downward. Using the puller tool 49–0813–240 without adaptor ring, press the bearing out of the rotor. Being careful not to damage the internal gear.

3. Place the rotor on the support with internal gear faced upward. Place the new rotor bearing on the rotor so that the bearing lug is in line with the slot of the rotor bore.

4. Remove the screws attaching the adaptor ring to the special tool. Using the special tool and adaptor ring, press fit the new bearing until the bearing is flush with the rotor boss.

### Oil Seal Inspection

1. Examine the oil seal while it is mounted in the rotor.

2. If the width of the oil seal lip is greater than 0.020 in., replace the oil seal.

3. If the protrusion of the oil seal is greater then 0.020 in., replace the seal.

### Oil Seal Replacement

1. Pry the seal out by inserting a small prybar into the slots on the rotor. Be careful not to deform the lip of the oil seal if it is to be reinstalled.

2. Fit both the oil seal springs into their respective grooves, so that their ends are facing upward and their gaps are opposite each other on the rotor.

3. Insert a new O-ring into each of the oil seals. Before installing the O-rings into the oil seals, fit each of the seals into its proper groove on the rotor. Check to see that all of the seals move smoothly and freely.

4. Coat the oil seal groove and the oil seal with engine oil.

5. Gently press the oil seal into the groove with your fingers. Be careful not to distort the seal. Be sure that the white mark is on the bottom side of each seal when it is installed.

6. Repeat the installation procedure for the oil seals on both sides of each rotor.

### Apex Seals

1. Remove the carbon deposits from the apex seals and their springs. Do not use emery cloth on the seals as it will damage their finish.

2. Wash the seals and the springs in cleaning solution.

3. Check the apex seals for cracks.

4. Test the seal springs for weakness.

5. Use a micrometer to check the seal height.

6. With a feeler gauge, check the side clearance between the apex seal and the groove in the rotor. Insert the gauge until its tip contacts the bottom of the groove. If the gap is greater than 0.0035 in. for the 1983–85 engine, or .0059 in. for the 1985–90 engine, replace the seal.

7. Check the gap between the apex seals and the side housing by using a vernier caliper to measure the length of each apex seal. Compare this measurement to the minimum figure obtined when the rotor housing width was being measured.

8. If the seal is too long, sand the ends of the seal with emery cloth until the proper length is reached. Do not use the emery cloth on the faces of the seal.

### Side Seals

1. Remove the carbon deposits from the side seals and their springs.

2. Check the side seals for cracks.

3. Check the clearance between the side seals and their grooves with a feeler gauge.

4. Check the clearance between the side seals and the corner seals with both installed in the rotor. Insert a feeler gauge between the end of the side seal and the corner seal. Insert the gauge against the direction of the rotor's rotation. Check the side seal protrusion. Acceptable minimum protrusion is 0.020 in.

5. Replace the side seal if the clearance is greater than 0.016 in.

6. If the side seal is replaced, adjust the clearance between it and the corner seal as follows. File the side seal on its reverse side, in the same rotational direction of the rotor, along the outline made by the corner seal.

7. The clearance obtained should be 0.002–0.006 in. If it exceeds this, the performance of the seals will deteriorate.

**NOTE: There are 4 different types of side seals, depending upon location. Do not mix the seals up and be sure to use the proper type of seal for replacement.**

### Corner Seals

1. Clean the carbon deposits.

2. Examine each of the seals.

3. Measure the clearance between the corner seal and its groove. The clearance should be 0.008–0.0019 in. The wear limit of the gap is 0.031 in.

4. If the wear between the corner seal and the groove is uneven, check the clearance with special tool 49–0839–165. This tool has a go/no go function.

5. If neither end of the gauge goes into the groove, the clearance is within specification.

6. If the go end of the gauge fits into the groove, but the no go end does not, replace the corner seal with one that is 0.0012 in. oversize.

7. If both ends of the gauge fit into the groove, then the groove must be reamed out. Replace the corner seal with one which is 0.0072 in. oversize, after reaming. Take the measurement of the groove in the direction of maximum wear, i.e., that of rotation.

### Seal Springs

Check the seal springs for damage or weakness. Be exceptionally careful when checking the spring areas which contact either the rotor or the seal.

### Eccentric Shaft

1. Wash the eccentric shaft in solvent and blow the oil passages dry with compressed air.

2. Check the shaft for wear, cracks, or other signs of damage. Make sure that none of the oil passages are clogged.

3. Measure the shaft journals. Replace the shaft if any of its journals shows excessive wear.

4. Check eccentric shaft run-out. Rotate the shaft slowly and note the dial indicator reading. If run-out is greater than specification, replace the eccentric shaft.

5. Check the blind plug at the end of the shaft. If it is loose or leaking, remove it with an Allen wrench and replace the O-ring.

6. Check the operation of the needle roller bearing for smoothness by inserting a mainshaft into the bearing and rotating it. Examine the bearing for signs of wear or damage. Check the oil jet for spring weakness, sticking or ball damage.

7. Replace the bearings, if necessary, with the special bearing replacer tools 49–0823–073 and 49–0823–072.

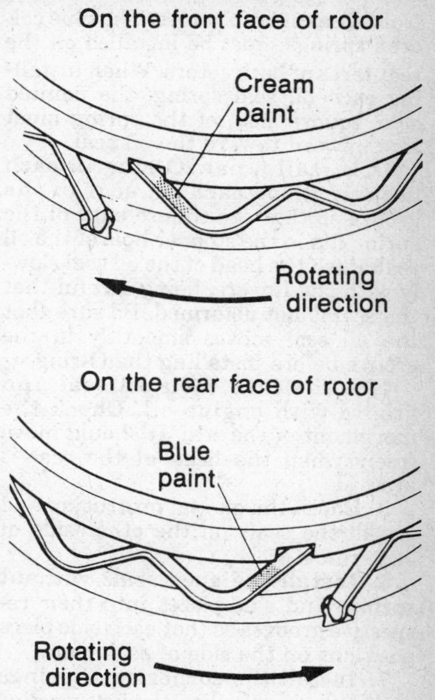


**The oil seal springs are iddentified by a painted mark**

### Needle Bearing and Thrust Plate

1. Inspect the needle bearing for wear and damage.

2. Inspect the bearing housing and the thrust plate for wear and damage.

### Oil Pump Drive Chain and Sprocket

1. Lay the chain on a flat surface and check the entire length for broken links.

2. Check the oil pump drive and driven sprockets for missing and broken teeth.

3. Make replacements as necessary.

## ASSEMBLY

1. Replace all O-rings, rubber seals and gaskets with new parts. Place the rotor on a rubber pad or cloth.

2. Install the oil seal rings in their respective grooves in the rotors with the edge of the spring in the stopper hole. The oil seal springs are painted cream or blue in color. The cream colored springs must be installed on the

front faces of both rotors. The blue colored springs must be installed on the rear faces of both rotors. When installing each oil seal spring, the painted side, square side, of the spring must face upward toward the oil seal.

3. Install a new O-ring in each groove. Place each oil seal in the groove so that the square edge of the spring fits in the stopper hole of the oil seal. Push the head of the oil seal slowly with the fingers, being careful that the seal is not deformed. Be sure that the oil seal moves smoothly in the groove before installing the O-ring.

4. Lubricate each oil seal and groove with engine oil. Check the movement of the seal. It should move freely when the head of the seal is pressed.

5. Check the oil seal protrusion and install the seals on the other side of each rotor.

6. Install the apex seals without springs and side pieces into their respective grooves so that each side piece positions on the side of each rotor.

7. Install the corner seal springs and corner seals into their respective grooves.

8. Install the side seal springs and side seals into their respective grooves.

9. Apply engine oil to each spring and check each spring for smooth movement.

10. Check each seal protrusion.

11. Invert the rotor being careful that the seals do not fall out, and install the oil seals on the other side of the same manner.

12. Mount the front housing on a workstand so that the top of the housing is up.

13. Lubricate the internal gear of the rotor with engine oil.

14. Hold the apex seals with used O-ring to keep the apex seals installed and place the rotor on the front housing. Be careful not to drop the seals. Turn the front housing so that the sliding surface faces upward.

15. Mesh the internal and stationary gears so that one of the rotor apexes is at any one of the 4 places shown and remove the old O-ring which is holding the apex seals in position.

16. Lubricate the front rotor journal of the eccentric shaft with engine oil and lubricate the eccentric shaft main journal.

17. Insert the eccentric shaft. Be careful that you do not damage the rotor bearing and main bearing.

18. Apply sealing agent to the front side of the front rotor housing.

19. Apply a light coat of petroleum jelly onto new O-rings and rubber seals and install the O-rings and rubber seals on the front side of the rotor housing.

**NOTE: The inner rubber seal is of the square type. The wider white line of the rubber seal should face the combustion chamber and the seam of the rubber seal should be positioned as such. Do not stretch the rubber seal.**

20. If the engine is being overhauled, install the seal protector to only the inner rubber seal to improve durability.

21. Invert the front rotor housing, being careful not to let the rubber seals and O-rings fall from their grooves, and mount it on the front housing.

22. Lubricate the dowels with the engine oil and insert them through the front rotor housing holes and into the front housing.

23. Apply sealer to the front side of the rotor housing.

24. Install new O-rings and rubber seals on the front rotor housing in the same manner as for the other side.

25. Insert each apex spring seal, making sure that the seal is installed in the proper direction.

26. Install each side piece in its original position and be sure that the springs seat on the side piece.

27. Lubricate the side pieces with engine oil. Make sure that the front rotor housing is free of foreign matter and lubricate the sliding surface of the front housing with engine oil.

28. Turn the front housing assembly with the rotor, so that the top of the housing is up. Pull the eccentric shaft about 1 in.

29. Position the eccentric portion of the eccentric shaft diagonally, to the upper right.

30. Install the intermediate housing over the eccentric shaft onto the front rotor housing. Turn the engine so that the rear of the engine is up.

31. Install the rear rotor and rear rotor housing following the same steps as for the front rotor and the front housing.

32. Lubricate the stationary gear and main bearing.

33. Install the rear housing onto the rear rotor housing.

34. If necessary, turn the rear rotor slightly to mesh the rear housing stationary gear with the rear rotor internal gear.

35. Install a new washer on each tension bolt, and lubricate each bolt with engine oil.

36. Install the tension bolts and tighten them evenly, in several stages and in the proper sequence. The specified torque is 23–27 ft. lbs. Be sure bolts are installed in their original positions. Longer bolts are used in later engines and are not interchangeable.

37. After tightening the bolts, turn the eccentric shaft to be sure that the shaft and rotors turn smoothly and easily.

38. Lubricate the oil seal in the rear housing.

39. On vehicles equipped with manual transmission, install the flywheel on the rear of the eccentric shaft so that the keyway of the flywheel fits the key on the shaft.

40. Apply sealer to both sides of the flywheel lockwasher and install the lockwasher.

41. Install the flywheel locknut. Hold the flywheel securly and tighten the nut to 350 ft. lbs.

42. On vehicles with automatic transmission, install the key, counterweight, lockwasher and nut. Tighten the nut to 350 ft. lbs. Install the drive plate on the counterweight and tighten the attaching nuts.

**NOTE: 350 ft. lbs. is a great deal of torque. In actual practice, it is practically impossible to accurately measure that much torque on the nut. At least a 3 ft. bar will be required to generate sufficient torque. Tighten it as tight as possible, with no longer than 3 ft. of leverage. Be sure the engine is held securly.**

43. Turn the engine so that the front faces up.

44. Install the thrust plate with the tapered face down, and install the needle bearing on the eccentric shaft. Lubricate with engine oil.

45. Install the bearing housing on the front housing. Tighten the bolts and bend up the lockwasher tabs. The spacer should be installed so that the center of the needle bearing comes to the center of the eccentric shaft and the spacer should be seated on the thrust plate.

46. Install the needle bearing on the shaft and lubricate it with engine oil.

47. Install the balancer and thrust washer on the eccentric shaft.

48. Install the oil pump drive chain over both of the sprockets. Install the sprocket and chain assembly over the eccentric shaft and oil pump shaft simultaneously. Install the key on the eccentric shaft. Be sure that both of the sprockets are engaged with the chain before install them over the shafts.

49. Install the distributor drive gear onto the eccentric shaft with the **F** mark on the gear facing the front of the engine. Slide the spacer and oil slinger onto the eccentric shaft.

50. Align the keyway and install the eccentric shaft pulley. Tighten the pulley bolt to 72–87 ft. lbs.

51. Turn the engine until the top of the engine faces up.

52. Check the eccentric shaft endplay in the following manner.

a. Attach a dial indicator to the flywheel. Move the flywheel forward and backward.

b. Note the reading on the dial indicator, it should be 0.0016–0.0028 in.

c. If the endplay is not within specification, adjust it by replacing the front spacer. Spacers come in 4 sizes, ranging from 0.3150–0.3181 in. If necessary, a spacer can be ground on a surface plate with emery paper.

d. Check the endplay again and, if it is now within specification, proceed with the next Step.

53. Remove the pulley from the front of the eccentric shaft. Tighten the oil pump drive sprocket nut and bend the locktabs on the lockwasher.

54. Fit a new O-ring over the front cover oil passage.

55. Install the chain tensioner, if equipped, and tighten its securing bolts.

56. Position the front cover gasket and the front cover on the front housing, then secure the front cover with its attachment bolts.

57. Install the eccentric shaft pulley again. Tighten its bolt to required torque.

58. Turn the engine so that the bottom faces up.

59. Cut off the excess gasket on the front cover along the mounting surface of the oil pan.

60. Install the oil strainer gasket and strainer on the front housing and tighten the attaching bolts.

61. Apply sealer to the joint surfaces of each housing.

62. Install the oil pan.

63. Turn the engine so that the top is up. On 1985–90 engines, go to Step 74.

64. Install the water pump.

65. Rotate the eccentric shaft until the yellow mark (leading side mark) aligns with the pointer on the front cover.

66. Align the marks on the distributor gear and housing and install the distributor so that the lockbolt is in the center of the slot.

67. Rotate the distributor until the leading points start to separate and tighten the distributor locknut.

68. Install the gaskets and thermal reactor.

69. Install the hot air duct.

70. Install the carburetor and intake manifold assembly.

71. Connect the oil tubes, vacuum tube and metering oil pump connecting rod to the carburetor.

72. Install the decel valve and connect the vacuum lines, air hoses and wires.

73. Install the alternator bracket, alternator and bolt and check the clearance. If the clearance is more than 0.006 in., adjust the clearance using a shim. Shims are available in three sizes, 0.0059 in., 0.0118 in., and 0.0197 in.

74. On 1985–90 engines, install the water pump and tighten the nuts in a crisscross sequence. Tighten to 13–20 ft. lbs. Be sure to use shims on the side housing contact surfaces. If shims are not used, coolant will leak.

75. Attach two O-rings to the oil filter body. Install the oil filter body.

76. Align the leading timing mark (yellow painted) on the eccentric shaft pulley with the indicator pin on the front cover.

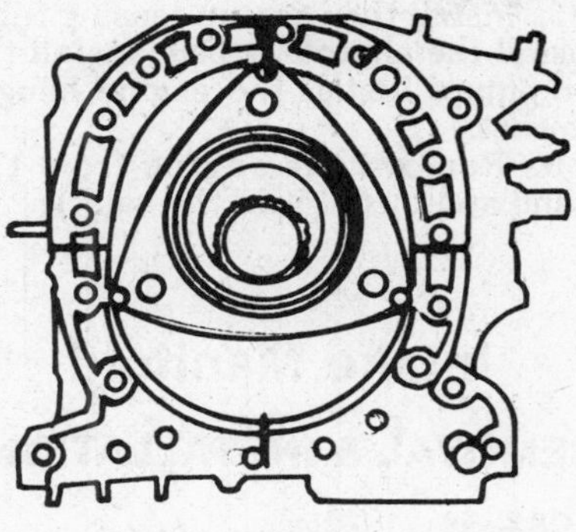

The rear rotor must be positioned as shown during engine assembly

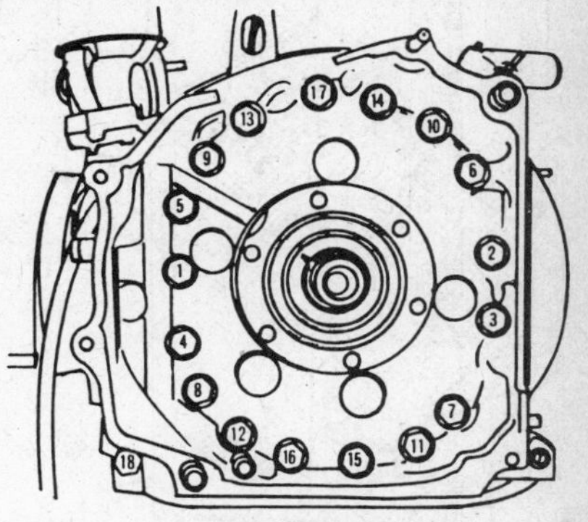

12A engine tension bolt tightening sequence

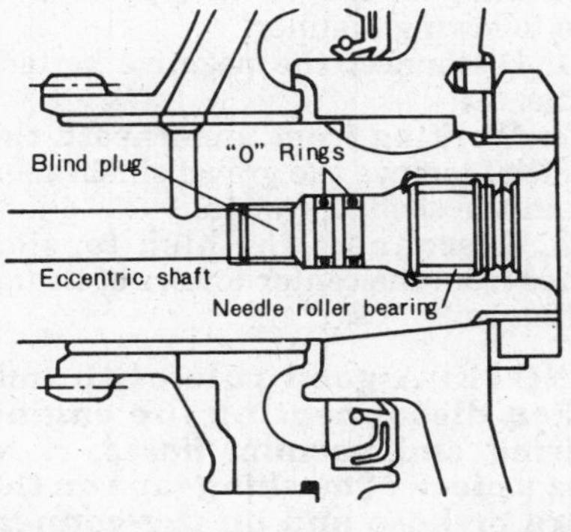


Eccentric shaft blind plug assembly

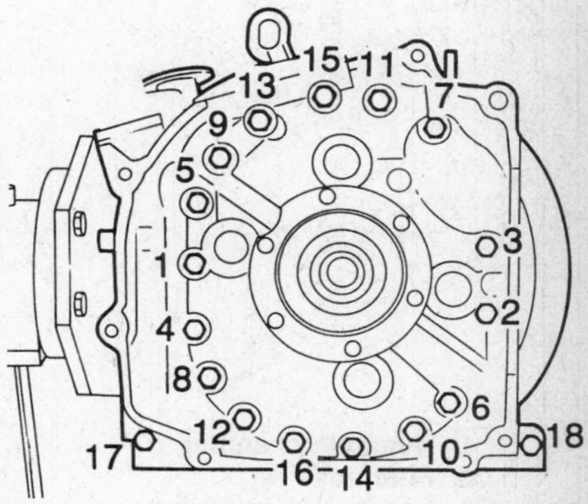

13B engine tension bolt tightening sequence

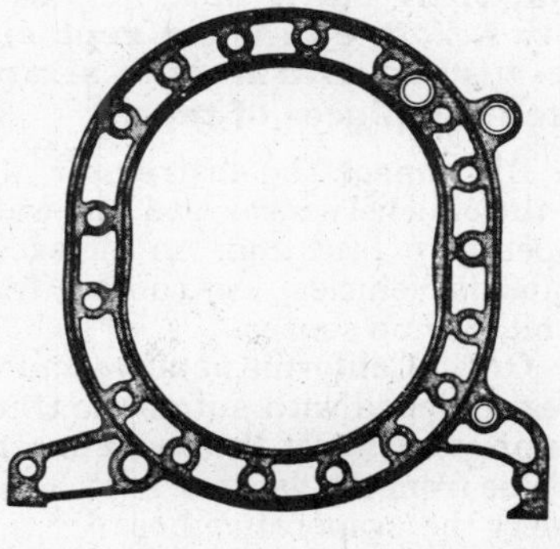

Apply sealer to the grey shadowed areas of the rotor housing

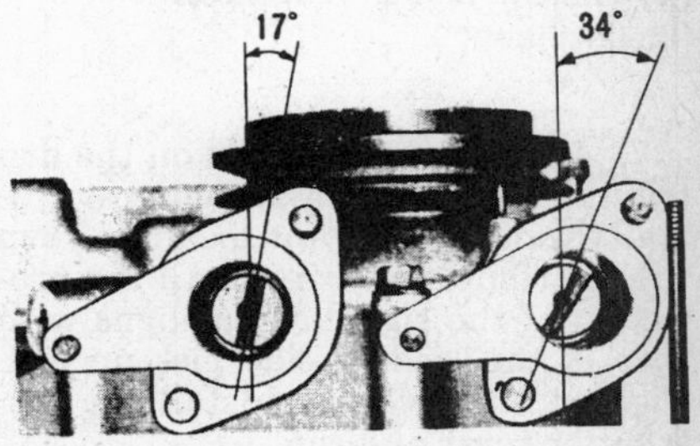


Position the slots in the distributor drive as shown

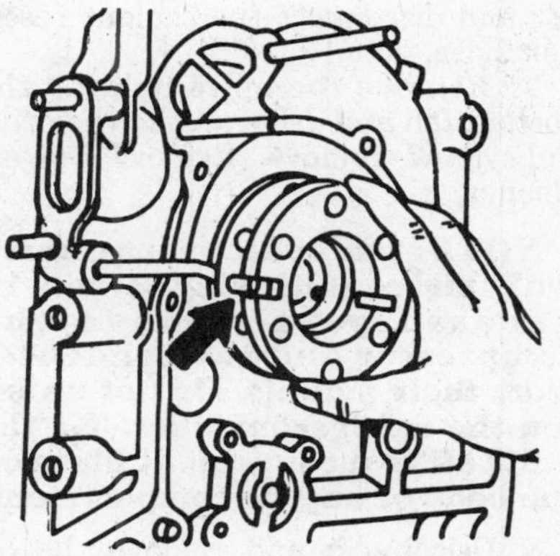

Align the slot in the stationary gear flange with the pin in the housing (arrow)

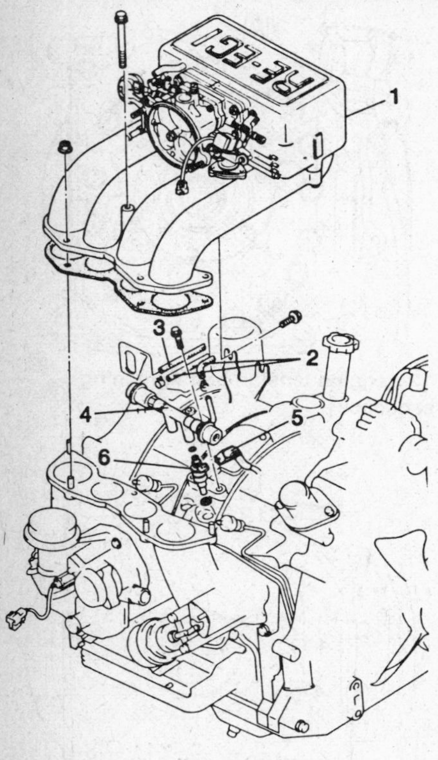


1. Dynamic chamber
2. Fuel hose
3. Vacuum sensing tube
4. Injector connector
5. Delivery pipe
6. Injector

Dynamic chamber, removal and installation

77. Align the tally marks on the distributor housing and driven gear. Install the distributor and locknut. Turn the distributor housing until the projection of the signal rotor aligns with core of the leading side pick-up coil. Tighten the locknut. Install the distributor rotor and cap.
78. Place the exhaust manifold gasket in position and install the exhaust manifold. Tighten to 23–34 ft. lbs.
79. Install the hot air duct and absorber plate.
80. Install the intake manifold auxiliary ports. Installation should be made so that the bigger sides of the auxiliary port valve shaft align the matching mark on the gasket as shown in the figure.
81. Install the O-rings. Install the intake manifold and gasket.
82. Connect the metering oil pump pipes. Tighten to 14–19 ft. lbs.
83. Install the fuel injection nozzles.
84. Install the delivery pipe assembly, the chamber, and the emission device assembly as one piece. Tighten delivery pipe body to 14–19 ft. lbs., emission device assembly to 14–19 ft. lbs.
85. Install the vacuum sensing tube. Install the alternator belt. Install the air pump. Install the engine hanger bracket.
86. Remove the engine from the stand and install it in the vehicle.

## Intake Manifold

### REMOVAL & INSTALLATION

#### *1983–85*

To remove the intake manifold and carburetor assembly with the engine remaining in the vehicle, proceed in the following manner.

1. Disconnect the negative battery cable.
2. Working from underneath the vehicle, remove the gravel shield then drain the cooling system.
3. Disconnect the high tension wires from the center towers of the ignition coils.

**NOTE: A good rule of thumb when disconnecting the engine wiring and vacuum hoses, it to put a piece of masking tape on the wire or hose and on the connection you remove the wire or hose from, then mark both pieces of tape, 1, 2, 3, etc. When replacing the wiring and hoses, simply match the pieces of tape.**

4. Disconnect the distributor wiring, the oil level sensor lead, the water temperature lead and, on all except California vehicles, the coupler from the oil thermo sensor.
5. On all California vehicles and vehicles equipped with automatic transmission, disconnect the vacuum sensing tube from the vacuum switch. Disconnect the evaporative hose.
6. Disconnect the hoses from the oil cooler, located beneath the radiator. Disconnect the radiator coolant level sensor lead from the top of the radiator and disconnect the coolant reservoir hose.
7. Remove the bolts holding the coolant fan and drive unit to the drive pulley and remove. Remove the air cleaner.

**NOTE: On vehicles equipped with air conditioning it will be necessary to remove the compresser and the condenser from their mounts. Do not unfasten the refrigerant lines. Tie the units off to a convenient place on the body or engine compartment.**

8. Dsiconnect and remove the oil hose support bracket from the front housing.

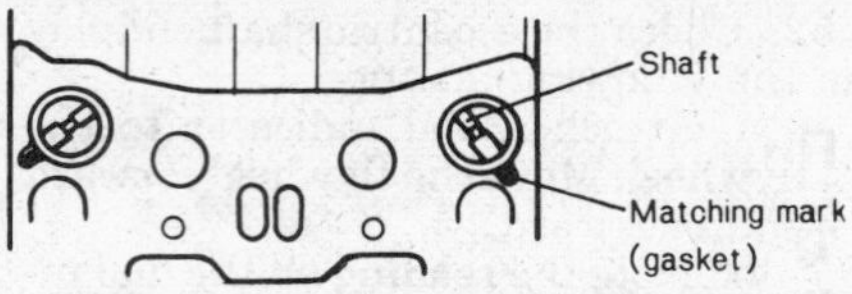


Auxiliary port valve and mounting gasket marks must match

9. Disconnect the vacuum hoses, air hoses and remove the decel valve.
10. Remove the air pump and drive belt. Remove the air pump adjusting bar. Remove the air outlet pipe from the end of the manifold. Disconnect the vacuum sensing tube.
11. Remove the exhaust manifold cover, then unbolt and remove the inlet manifold complete with carburetor.
12. Inspect the intake manifold for cracks and a smooth surface. Complete the installation in reverse of the removal procedure. Tighten the inlet manifold bolts evenly and in an alternate sequence to 14-19 ft. lbs.

#### *1985–90*

1. Remove the dynamic chamber by removing or disconnecting the following parts.
   a. On turbocharged engines, drain the cooling system.
   b. Negative battery cable, air funnel, intercooler (turbo only), oil filler pipe (turbo only), accelerator cable and throttle sensor connector.
   c. Metering oil pump connecting rod and water hoses.
   d. Terminal cover, vacuum sensing tubes.
   e. Air supply connector, intake air temperature sensor connector.
   f. Retaining bolts and nuts and the dynamic chamber.
2. Cover the intake manifold port opening with a clean cloth to prevent dust or dirt from entering the engine.
3. Remove the incline check valve assemblies and vacuum lines.
4. Remove the air hoses from the manifold mounted solenoids.
5. Remove the actuator from the intake manifold.
6. Remove the nuts and bolts that mount the intake manifold to the engine, remove the manifold. Clean all gaskets mounting surfaces.
7. Remove the auxiliary port valve. Check the valve for cracks and breakage.
8. Install the auxiliary valve. Make sure that the bigger side of the valve shafts align with the matching mark on the mounting gasket.
9. Install the remaining parts in the reverse order of removal. Fill the cooling system and perform all the necessary adjustments.

## Thermal Reactor

### REMOVAL & INSTALLATION

The thermal reactor/heat exchanger system is replaced by two catalytic converters and a special reactive exhaust manifold. See "Emission Control" section for details.

## Exhaust Manifold

### REMOVAL & INSTALLATION

#### *1983–85 12A Engine*

1. Remove the air cleaner and hot air duct hose. Remove the air injection pump.
2. Disconnect the thermal reactor-to-air control valve air pipe.
3. Remove the thermal reactor uper side nuts. Mazda makes a special angled T-bar wrench for this job (tool number 49–8501–125).
4. Raise the vehicle and support it on jackstands. Disconnect the air pipe, running between the inlet manifold and the heat exchanger, from the inlet manifold.
5. Remove the air pipe running between the thermal reactor and the air duct.
6. Disconnect the air duct hanger bracket from the transmisson housing.
7. Disconnect the air duct from the thermal reactor.
8. Remove the thermal reactor lower side nuts.
9. Remove the thermal reactor.
10. Install the reactor gasket, then tighten the nuts in several steps, to avoid putting a strain on the reactor, to 33–40 ft. lbs.

#### *1985–90 13B Non-Turbo Engine*

1. Disconnect the negative battery cable.
2. Remove the air intake manifold (throttle and dynamic chamber).
3. Remove the exhaust absorber plate.
4. Disconnect the oxygen sensor connector and route the wiring so that it will be readily removed with the exhaust manifold.
5. Raise and support the front end on jackstands. Remove the exhaust pipe front cover, catalytic converter cover, exhaust pipe bracket and disconnect the exhaust exhaust pipe from the exhaust manifold.
6. Loosen and remove the exhaust manifold retaining nuts and lock washers.
7. Separate the manifold and insulator from the engine and pull the manifold from the engine mounting studs. Remove the gasket and discard it.
8. Throughly clean the exhaust manifold contact surfaces and check the exhaust manifold for warpage with a metal straight edge.
9. Install a new manifold gasket onto the engine and install the exhaust manifold assembly over the mounting studs and make it flush with the gasket. Install the mounting nuts and lock washers and torque them to 23–34 ft. lbs.
10. Connnect all the exhaust manifold components using new gaskets as required.
11. Connect the oxygen sensor connector. Install the absorber plate and torque the retaining screws to 6–8 ft. lbs.
12. Complete the installation of the intake manifold in reverse of the removal procedure.
13. Start the engine and allow it to reach normal operating temperature and check for exhaust leaks.

#### *1987–90 13B Turbo Engine*

1. Remove the turbocharger from the engine. Seal all the turbocharger openings to prevent the entry of foreign matter.
2. Remove the insulator covers from the exhaust manifold. Loosen and remove the exhaust manifold retaining nuts and lock washers.
3. Remove the exhaust manifold and waste gate actuator assembly from the engine. Remove the gasket and discard it.
4. Throughly clean the exhaust manifold and turbocharger contact surfaces and check the exhaust manifold for warpage with a metal straight edge.
5. Install a new manifold gasket onto the engine and install the exhaust manifold/actuator assembly over the mounting studs and make it flush with the gasket. Install the mounting nuts and lock washers and torque them to 23–34 ft. lbs.
6. Install a new turbocharger gasket onto the exhaust manifold and carefully guide the turbo over the mounting studs and onto the gasket. Install the mounting nuts and lockwashers. Torque the mounting nuts to 33–40 ft. lbs. Once the nuts are torqued, crimp the tabs on the nut retaining plate to prevent the nuts from loosening.
7. Complete the remainder of the turbocharger installation procedure in reverse of the removal procedure. Use new gaskets where required. Fill the cooling system and connect the negative battery cable. Start the engine and check for leaks. Make all the necessary adjustments.

## Turbocharger

### REMOVAL AND INSTALLATION

1. Disconnect the negative battery cable. Drain the cooling system.
2. Disconnect the air hoses from the air pump and remove the air pump from the engine.
3. Loosen the hose clamps and disconnect the air funnel and air hose from the air cleaner and the turbocharger. Remove the air funnel and air hose from the engine.
4. Disconnect the connector from the air control valve and remove the valve from the engine.
5. Disconnect the split air pipe from the engine and remove the pipe along with the gasket.
6. Disconnect the water hose and the water pipe from the engine and remove them.
7. Disconnect the supply and return oil pipes from the turbo and cover the openings.
8. Remove the front converter insulator covers and disconnect the front converter from the exhaust manifold. Remove the gasket and discard it.
9. Unstake the retainer tabs from the retainer plate with a small prying tool. Remove the nuts and washers that secure the turbocharger to the exhaust manifold studs and remove the turbocharger from the engine. Cover all the turbo openings to prevent the entry of dirt and foreign matter. Remove the turbocharger gasket and discard it.
10. Remove the insulator covers from the exhaust manifold. Loosen and remove the exhaust manifold retaining nuts and lock washers.
10. Remove the exhaust manifold and waste gate actuator assembly from the engine. Remove the gasket and discard it.
11. Throughly clean the exhaust manifold and turbocharger contact surfaces and check the exhaust manifold for warpage with a metal straight edge.
12. Install a new manifold gasket onto the engine and install the exhaust manifold/actuator assembly over the mounting studs and make it flush with the gasket. Install the mounting nuts and lock washers and torque them to 23–34 ft. lbs.
13. Install a new turbocharger gasket onto the exhaust manifold and carefully guide the turbo over the mounting studs and onto the gasket. Install the mounting nuts and lockwashers. Torque the mounting nuts to 33–40 ft. lbs. Once the nuts are torqued, crimp the tabs on the nut retaining plate to prevent the nuts from

loosening. Remove the protective covers from the turbo openings.

14. Connect the front converter to the exhaust manifold with a new gasket. Torque the nuts to 33–40 ft. lbs.

15. Install the remaining components in reverse of the removal procedure. If any part requires a new gasket, install one:

a. Insulator covers.
b. Oil pipes.
c. Water pipe and water hose.
d. Split air pipe.
e. Air control valve.
f. air funnel and air hose.
g. air pump and air hoses.

16. Fill the cooling system and connect the negative battery cable. Start the engine and check for leaks. Make all the necessary adjustments.

# ROTARY ENGINE LUBRICATION

## Oil Pan

### REMOVAL & INSTALLATION

1. Disconnect the negative battery cable. Drain the engine oil.

2. Disconnect the oil level sensor and oil thermo unit, if so equipped. On the 1985–90 13B engine, raise and support the vehicle safely and remove the engine under cover. Support the engine from above, remove the engine mount nuts and lift the engine slightly (about 2–3 in.) to gain working clearance.

3. Disconnect the oil level sensor connector. Remove the pan bolts. Separate the pan from the housing using an appropriate prying tool and lower the pan from the engine.

4. To install, clean all of the old gasket material off the pan and engine mating surfaces then, apply a continuous bead sealer, part no. 8527 77 739 to the pan surface. The bead should be from 0.16–0.24 in. wide and should overlap at the end. Make sure the bolt holes are properly encircled by the sealant bead.

5. Install the gasket on the pan, then apply an identical bead of sealer on top of the gasket. Install the gasket and torque the bolts to 6–8 ft. lbs. Fill the crankcase with oil. The oil pan must be installed no more than 30 minutes after the sealant is applied.

**NOTE: Some engines are not equipped with an oil pan gasket. On these engines, apply the sealant in the same manner described above, but only apply the sealant to the pan surface.**

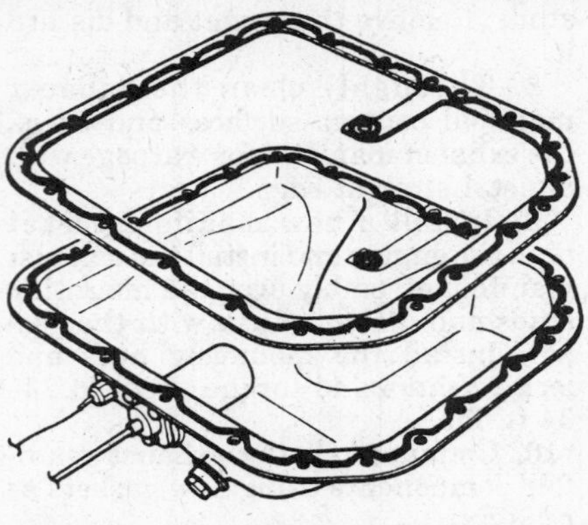

Oil pan sealing on RX-7. Oil pan with gasket shown

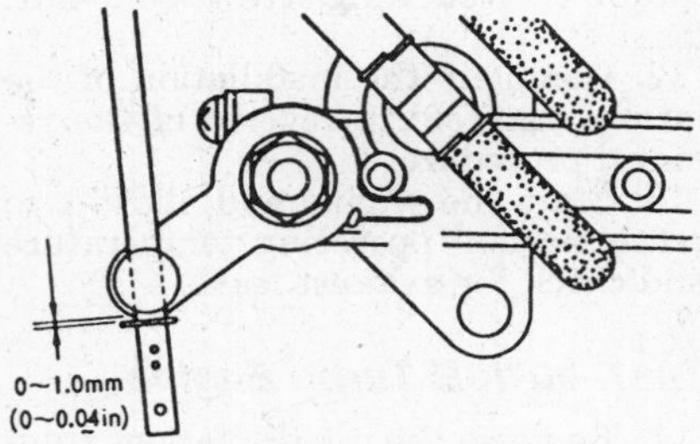


Metering oil pump lever and washer clearance – 12A engines

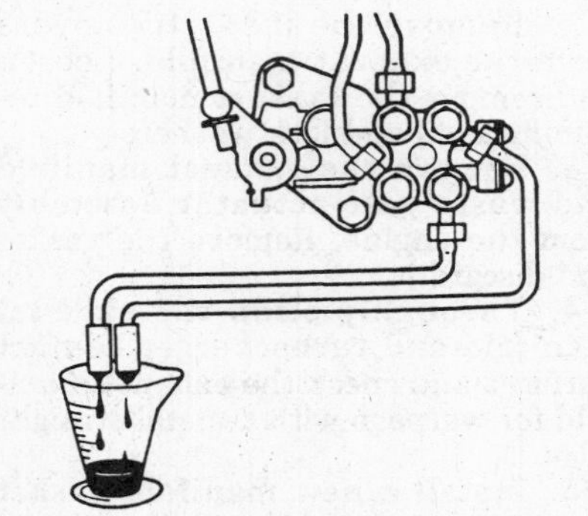

Measuring oil metering pump discharge on 13B engines

## Oil Pump

### REMOVAL & INSTALLATION

Oil pump removal and installation is contained in the engine overhaul section above. Perform only those steps needed to remove the oil pump.

## Metering Oil Pump

### OPERATION

A metering oil pump, mounted on the top of the engine, is used to provide additional lubrication to the engine when it is operating under a load.

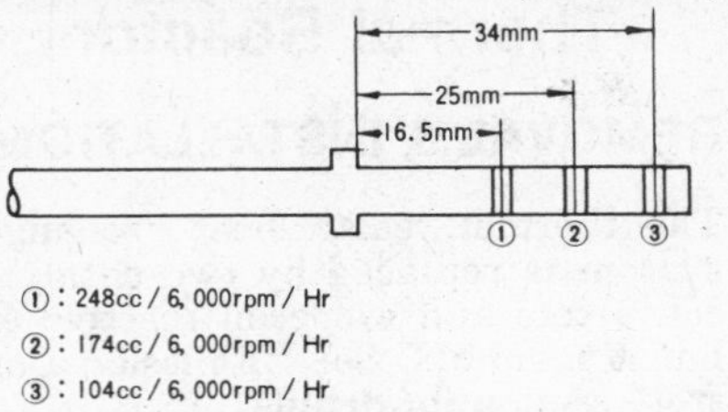


Connecting rod adjusting holes

The metering pump is a plunger type and is controlled by throttle opening. A cam arrangement, connected to the throttle lever, operates a plunger. The plunger, in turn, acts as a differential plunger, the stroke of which determines the amount of oil flow. When the throttle opening is small, the amount of the plunger stroke is small, as the throttle opening increases, so does the amount of the plunger stroke.

### TESTING

#### *1983–85 with 12A Engine*

1. Before measuring the oil pump discharge, check the oil pump and oil pump hoses for leaks. Make sure that the clearance between the metering oil pump lever and the washer is 0–0.04 in.

2. At the carburetor, disconnect the oil lines which run from the metering oil pump to the carburetor.

3. Use a container which has a scale calibrated in cubic centimeters (cc) on its side to catch the pump discharge from the oil lines.

3. Run the engine at 2000 rpm for 6 minutes.

4. At the end of this time, 1.8–2.2cc should be collected in the container. If not, replace the pump.

**NOTE: While measuring the oil pump discharge, make sure that a proper amount of clean engine oil is added to the carburetor to compensate for the oil lost during the test.**

#### *1985–90 With 13B Engine*

1. Start the engine and allow it to reach normal operating temperature. Shut off the engine.

2. Connect a tachometer to the engine according to the manufacturer's instructions.

3. Disconnect the 2 housing oil hoses from the metering oil pump. Only disconnect two hoses at one time.

4. Fabricate and connect suitable hoses to the metering oil pump for measurement.

5. Pull the metering pump rod up to its maximum stop. Make sure to lift

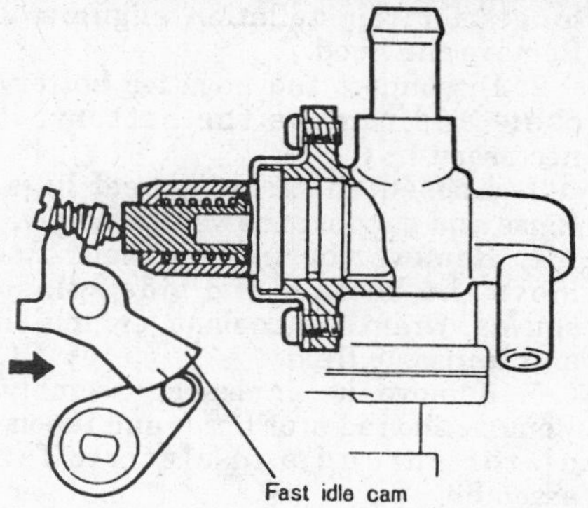


**Push the fast idle cam in the direction of the arrow**

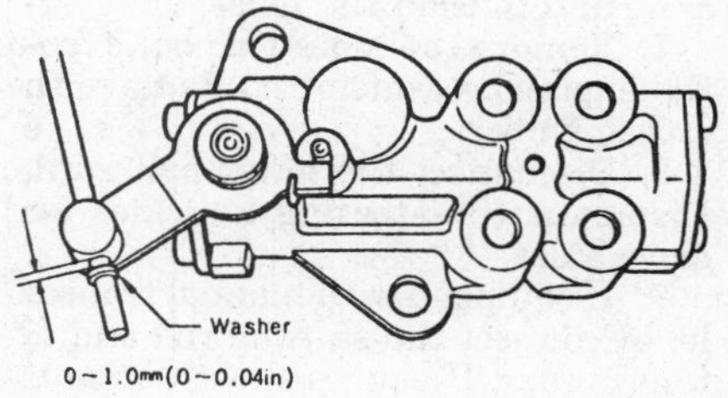


**Adjusting metering rod and lever clearance on 13B engines**

the rod fully while the engine is running.

6. Start and run the engine at 2000 rpm for 5 minutes and measure the oil discharge, it should be 4.2–5.6cc for non-turbocharged engines and 5.2–6.6cc for turbocharged engines. If not, replace the pump.

7. Install the housing hoses and measure the manifold metering oil discharge in the same manner.

**NOTE: While measuring the oil pump discharge, make sure that a proper amount of clean engine oil is added to the carburetor to compensate for the oil lost during the test.**

### ADJUSTMENT

#### *1983–85 with 12A Engine*

Rotate the adjusting screw on the metering oil pump to obtain the proper oil flow. Clockwise rotation of the screw increases the flow, counterclockwise rotation decreases the oil flow.

If necessary, the oil discharge rate may be further adjusted by changing the position of the cam in the pump connecting rod. The shorter the rod throw, the more oil will be pumped. Adjust the throw by means of the three holes provided.

#### *1985–90 with 13B Engine*

1. Rotate the fast idle cam to separate the cam and the roller.

2. Check the clearance between the adjusting rod and the lever. If the clearance is not between 0–0.04 in., adjust it by adding the proper amount of washers to create the proper clearance.

## Oil Cooler

### REMOVAL & INSTALLATION

1. Drain the crankcase and cooling system.
2. Raise the front of the vehicle and support it safely. Block the rear wheels.
3. Remove the gravel shield and the radiator grill upper cover.
4. Disconnect the inlet and outlet lines from the oil cooler. Drain the lines completely and plug the ends.
5. Disconnect the oil by-pass outlet line. Discard the sealing washer.
6. Unbolt and remove the oil cooler and the filter assembly as a unit. Discard the O-rings and the filter cartridge.
7. Assemble the oil cooler with a new cartridge, new O-rings and a new sealing washer.
8. Install the unit onto its mounting and tighten the mounting nuts.
9. Connect the inlet and outlet lines and tighten the union bolts. Connect the oil by-pass line and tighten the fitting. Once the unit is in place, adjust it so that it makes a 40–50 degree angle with the under cover to ensure proper air flow across the fins.
10. Install the radiator grill upper cover and the gravel shield.
11. Refill the crankcase and the cooling system to the proper levels.
12. Start the engine and check for leaks.

# ROTARY ENGINE COOLING

## Radiator

### REMOVAL & INSTALLATION

#### *1983–85*

1. Disconnect the negative battery cable. Drain the coolant by disconnecting the lower radiator hose.
2. Remove the cooling fan, air intake pipe, battery and bracket.
3. Remove the lower radiator hose, heater hoses and upper radiator hose.
4. Disconnect the coolant level sensor connector, radiator switch connector and the automatic transmission lines from the radiator (if equipped).
5. Remove the radiator attaching bolts and remove the radiator along with the radiator cowling.
6. Installation is the reverse order of the removal procedure.
7. Connect all hoses and fill the radiator to the proper level.
8. Start the engine and check for leaks.

#### *1986–90*

1. Position a drain under the radiator, loosen the drain plug and drain the radiator.
2. Remove the cooling fan from the water pump pulley.
3. Remove the air inlet pipe.
4. Disconnect the cables from the battery and remove the battery and bracket.
5. Disconnect the heater and uppper hose from the radiator.
6. Disconect the coolant level sensor and the radiator switch connectors.
7. If equipped with automatic transmission, disconnect the radiator cooling hoses from the bottom of the radiator and plug the ends to prevent leakage.
8. Remove the radiator and the radiator cowling.
9. Install the radiator cowling and the radiator. Leave the cowling bolts snug and complete the installation of the remaining components in reverse of installation.
10. Once the cooling fan is bolted to the water pump pulley, check the clearance between the blades of the cooling fan and the fan shroud. If the clearance is not sufficient to allow the blades to turn without contacting the cowling, adjust the cowling as required and then properly tighten the cowling bolts.
11. Fill the cooling system to the proper level. Start the engine and check for coolant leaks.

## Water Pump

### REMOVAL & INSTALLATION

1. Disconnect the negative battery cable. Remove the air cleaner and disconnect the water temperature switch wiring from the radiator.
2. Remove the air conditioner, air pump, power steering, and alternator drive belts. Remove the alternator and the air pump.
3. Remove the cooling fan and drive assembly. On the 1985–90 13B engine, turn the eccentric shaft so that the top mark of the pulley is aligned with the indicator pin.
4. Remove the drive pulley for the air conditioner compresser from in

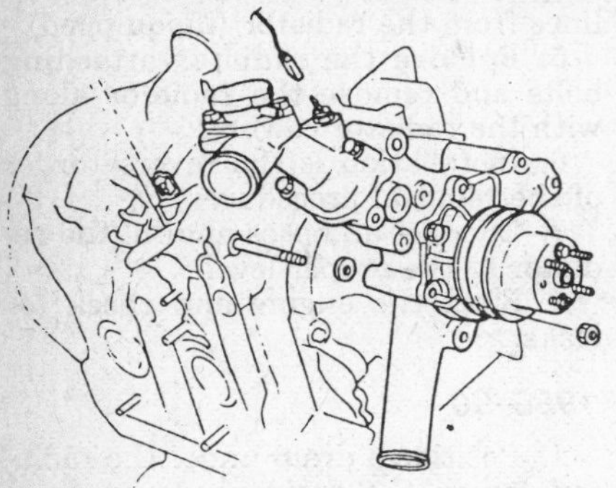

RX-7 water pump removal and installation

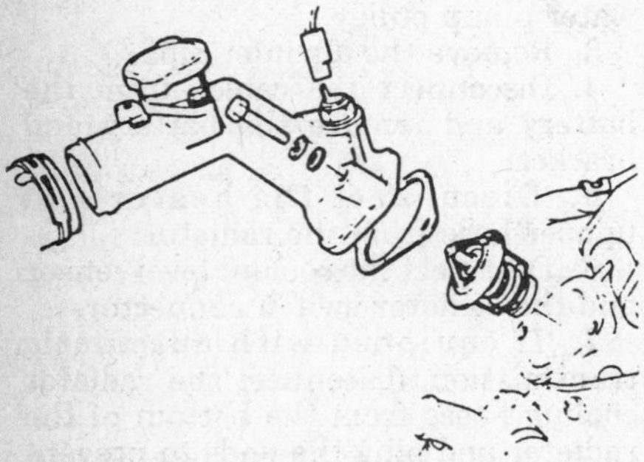

Thermostat removal and installation—1986–90 RX-7

front of the alternator/air pump drive pulleys. It is the pulley on the eccentric shaft, not the one on the front of the compresser.

5. Place a pan under the lower radiator hose then disconnect the hose, or remove the drain plug, and allow the coolant to drain out of the system.

6. Remove the upper radiator hose, coolant reservoir hose and coolant bypass hose. Disconnect the water thermo sensor connector and the water thermo switch connector, if the vehicle is equipped with automatic transmission.

7. Remove the attaching bolts and remove the water pump along with the cooling fan pulley. Retrieve the spacers or shims from the two studs where the gasket does not mount.

8. When installing, clean the old gasket from the mating surfaces, and install a new gasket with sealer. Install the spacers or shims and torque the attaching bolts evenly to 13–20 ft. lbs. Continue the installation is the reverse of the removal procedure. Check the clearance between the tip of the cooling fan blades and the cowling. Adjust the cowling until there is between 0.63–0.94 in. clearance.

## Thermostat

### REMOVAL & INSTALLATION

The thermostat is equipped with a plunger which covers and uncovers a bypass hole at its bottom. Because of this unusual construction, only the specified Mazda thermostat should be used for replacement. A standard thermostat will cause the engine to overheat.

1. Disconnect the negative battery cable. Drain the engine coolant. Remove the upper hose from thermostat housing.

2. Disconnect the water thermo switch connector. Remove the thermostat housing and the thermostat.

3. Installation is the reverse or removal procedure, always install a new mounting gasket. When installing the thermostat, make sure the jiggle pin is facing up. On 1986–90 models, align the marks on the upper hose with the cover marks during installation.

# GASOLINE PISTON ENGINE MECHANICAL

## Engine

### REMOVAL & INSTALLATION

#### *1983 GLC Wagon*

1. Properly relieve the fuel system pressure. Disconnect the negative battery cable. Remove the hood.
2. Remove the engine splash shield.
3. Drain the coolant.
4. Drain the engine oil.
5. Disconnect all electrical wires and leads. Remove the battery.
6. Disconnect all fluid lines and hoses.
7. Remove the air cleaner.
8. Unbolt and remove the radiator and cowling.
9. Disconnect the throttle cable from the carburetor and remove the throttle linkage from the rocker cover.
10. Disconnect the choke cable.
11. Remove the starter.
12. Disconnect the exhaust pipe.
13. Remove the clutch cover plate. Support the transmission.
14. Unbolt the right and left engine mounts.
15. Attach a lifting sling to the engine and pull the engine forward until it clears the clutch shaft.
16. Lift the engine from the vehicle.
17. Installation is the reverse of removal.

#### *1983–85 GLC Except Wagon*

1. Properly relieve the fuel system pressure. Mark the outline of the hood hinges for reinstallation alignment. Remove the hood.

2. Disconnect the negative battery cable and remove the battery, if necessary.

3. Loosen the front wheel lugs. Raise and support the vehicle safely.

4. Remove the front wheels. Remove the bottom and side splash shields. Drain the coolant, engine oil and transaxle fluid.

5. Remove the air cleaner assembly. Remove the radiator hoses and the radiator shroud and electric fan assembly.

6. Connect an engine lifting sling to the engine. Connect a chain hoist or portable engine crane to the lifting sling and tension the hoist.

7. Remove the mounting bolts from the engine crossmember. Remove the crossmember.

8. Disconnect the lower ball joints. Dismount the steering knuckles and drive axles.

9. If equipped with manual transaxle, disconnect the shifting rod and extension bar. If equipped with an automatic transaxle, disconnect the selector rod and counter rod.

10. Remove the front and rear transaxle mounting bushings. Disconnect the exhaust pipe from the catalytic converter. Remove the transaxle crossmember.

11. Disconnect all wires and hoses from under the engine and transaxle. Label them for identification.

12. Disconnect all wires, heater hoses and vacuum hoses from the upper side of the engine and transaxle. Label them for correct installation.

13. Disconnect the accelerator cable, speedometer cable, clutch cable, power brake booster line and fuel lines.

14. Check to be sure all remaining hoses and wiring are disconnected. remove the evaporative canister. Remove the right side upper engine mount through bolt.

15. Lift the engine and transaxle assembly from the vehicle. Take care not to allow the assembly to swing forward into the radiator.

16. Installation is in the reverse order of removal.

#### *1986–90 323 Except Turbo*

1. Properly relieve the fuel system pressure. Disconnect the negative battery cable. Drain the engine oil, transaxle oil and coolant into suitable drain pans.

2. Remove the battery and battery box. Remove the air cleaner assembly, oil level gauge and cooling fan with the radiator assembly. On vehicles equipped with automatic transaxle, just remove the radiator shroud, do not remove the radiator.

3. Remove the accelerator cable and cruise control cable, if equipped. Remove the speedometer cable and fuel hoses. On vehicles equipped with automatic transaxle, remove the upper and lower radiator hoses.

4. Remove the heater hose, brake vacuum hose, 3-way solenoid vacuum hoses, canister hose and the engine harness connectors along with the engine ground.

5. Remove the upper and lower radiator hoses. Remove the exhaust pipe. If equipped with automatic transaxle, remove the secondary air pipe.

6. Rempove the air conditioning compresser and power steering pump, if equipped. Do not disconnect the high and low pressure hoses from the compresser. Secure the compresser in the fender well area with a piece of wire or rope. Do not remove the pressure and return hoses from the pump. Raise the pump and move it out of the way.

7. Remove the driveshafts, clutch control cable, shift control rod, engine under cover and side cover.

8. Install a suitable engine hoist to the engine and lift the engine slightly. Remove the engine mounts.

9. Carefully remove the engine and transaxle from the vehicle.

10. Installation is the reverse of removal. Refill the engine coolant, engine oil and transaxle fluid.

### 1988–90 323 with Turbo

1. Properly relieve the fuel system pressure. Disconnect the negative battery cable. Remove the hood. Drain the cooling system. Drain the engine oil.

2. Remove the battery and battery holder. Remove the air cleaner assembly. Disconnect the body-to-transaxle ground wire, back-up light and engine harness connectors.

3. Disconnect all the necessary vacuum hoses. Disconnect the clutch release cylinder.

4. Disconnect the shift control cables. Disconnect the speedometer cable. Disconnect the accelerator cable.

5. Disconnect the heater hoses from the engine. Remove the radiator hoses. Remove the radiator. Remove the intercooler assembly.

6. Remove the air conditioning compresser mounting bolts and position the comprerssor to the side, as required. Do not disconnect the refrigerant lines.

7. Remove the power steering pump retaining bolts. Remove the power steering pump and position it to the side, as required.

8. Raise and support the vehicle safely. Remove the tire and wheel assemblies. Remove the engine under cover and side cover. Remove the control unit.

9. Disconnect the exhaust system at the exhaust manifolds. Remove the driveshafts. If equipped with 4WD, remove the propeller shaft.

10. Remove the engine crossmember assembly. Remove the number two and three engine mounts. If equipped with 4WD, remove the number four engine mount.

11. Properly support the transaxle assembly, using the required equipment. Properly support the engine using the required equipment.

12. Remove the engine to transaxle retaining bolts. Lower the vehicle. Remove any and all retaining brackets required for engine removal.

13. Install the engine lifting device and carefully remove the engine from the vehicle.

14. Installation is the reverse of the removal procedure. Fill the engine, tranaxle and cooling system to the proper levels.

### 1983–84 626

1. Remove the hood.

2. Disconnect the negative battery cable.

3. Drain the cooling system.

4. Remove the upper and lower radiator hoses.

5. On cars equipped with an automatic transmission, disconnect the cooler lines.

6. Remove the radiator cowling and fan.

7. Remove the radiator.

8. Remove the air hoses from the air cleaner and remove the air cleaner.

9. Disconnect the wiring from the distributor primary, coil wire, oil pressure gauge unit, alternator wiring and the right side engine mounting nut.

10. Disconnect the wiring from the water temperature gauge unit, fuel cut solenoid, automatic choke, starter motor.

11. Disconnect the air hoses (reed valve), vacuum hoses (3 way solenoid valve), fuel hoses, acceleration wire, master vacuum hose, and the left side engine mounting nut.

12. Raise the front of the vehicle and support safely.

13. Remove the under cover.

14. Disconnect the exhaust pipe and support it.

15. Remove the clutch under cover plate.

16. On cars equipped with automatic transmission, remove the torque converter and driving plate support bolts.

17. Support the transmission with a suitable jack and remove the transmission support bolts and nuts.

18. Remove the starter motor and the clutch release cylinder.

19. Connect a suitable lifting sling to the engine hanger brackets and to a hoist, and remove the slack.

20. Pull the engine forward until it clears the clutch shaft, then lift the engine from the vehicle.

21. Installation is the reverse of the removal procedure. Fill the engine, transmission and the cooling system to the proper levels.

### 1985–89 626 and MX-6

1. Properly relieve the fuel system pressure. Remove the hood. Disconnect the negative battery cable. Remove the battery, if necessary.

2. Loosen the front wheel lugs. Drain the coolant, engine oil and transaxle fluid.

3. Remove the air cleaner assembly. Remove the radiator hoses. Remove the radiator shroud and electric fan assembly. Remove the washer tank and the radiator overflow.

4. Remove the fuel hose, fuel return hose, accelerator cable and speedometer cable. If equipped with a turbocharger, remove the inner cooler pipe and hose.

5. On vehicles with a manual transaxle, remove the clutch cable along with the clutch slave cylinder, and on those with an automatic transaxle, remove the control cable.

6. Remove the engine ground wire, engine harness, power brake vacuum hose and three-way valve vacuum switch with bracket. Remove the heater hoses, duty solenoid valve and the vacuum sensor.

7. Remove any additional engine or transaxle wiring. Remove the air vent hose and vacuum canister hose.

8. On air conditioned vehicles, remove the air conditioning compressor and position it to the side. Do not disconnect the high and low pressure hoses from the compressor.

9. Raise and support the vehicle safely. Remove the splash shield. Remove the tire and wheel assembly.

10. Remove the power steering pump and position it to the side. Do not remove the pressure and return hoses from the pump.

11. Remove the drive axles and change rod, using the proper tools.

12. Disconnect the shift control rod on vehicles equipped with manual transaxle. Remove the shift control extension bar. Install a suitable engine hoist to the engine and lift the engine slightly.

13. Remove the transaxle and engine mounting bolts and nuts. Disconnect the exhaust pipe and turbocharger, if equipped.

14. Remove the torque stopper mount from the right wheel housing

area and inside the engine compartment.

15. Carefully remove the engine and transaxle from the vehicle. Separate the engine from the transaxle.

16. Installation is the reverse of removal. Refill the engine coolant, engine oil and transaxle fluid.

### *1988–90 929*

1. Relieve the fuel system pressure. Disconnect the negative battery cable and drain the engine oil and the cooling system.
2. Matchmark and remove the hood.
3. Remove the fresh air duct and the air cleaner assembly.
4. Disconnect the accelerator cable from the throttle body.
5. Remove the cooling fan pulley bolts and remove the cooling fan and cowling.
6. Remove the drive belts, spark plug wires and spark plugs.
7. Disconnect the evaporative canister and brake hoses.
8. Disconnect the fuel hoses the fuel rails. Plug the ends.
9. Remove the heater hoses and disconnect the engine harness.
10. Working from underneath the vehicle, remove the engine undercover.
11. Remove the upper and lower radiator hoses.
12. On models equipped with automatic transmission, disconnect the automatic transmission fluid hoses from the radiator.
13. Disconnect the radiator harness and remove the radiator.
14. Remove the alternator and the alternator strap.
15. If equipped, disconnect the air conditioning compressor and bracket from it's mounting and tie the unit off to side of the vehicle with the lines in tact and connected. Position the power steering pump in the same manner as the air conditioner, if equipped.
16. Remove the section of exhaust pipe that runs from the catalytic converter to the exhaust manifold.
17. Connect a lifting strap to the engine lifting bracket and attach a hoist to the sling and tension the hoist. Support and remove the transmission.
18. Remove the engine mounting nuts and lift the engine out of the vehicle.
19. Installation is the reverse of the removal procedure. Fill the engine, transmission and cooling system to the proper levels.

## Cylinder Head

**NOTE: As required, refer to the "Front Cover, Timing Belt, Tensioner and Timing Pulleys, Removal and Installation" procedure in this section for the correct camshaft pulley removal and timing belt installation procedure.**

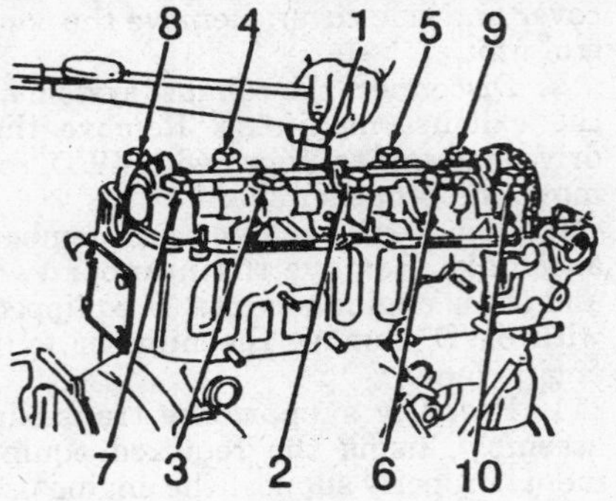


**Cylinder head bolt torque sequence—GLC and 1982 626**

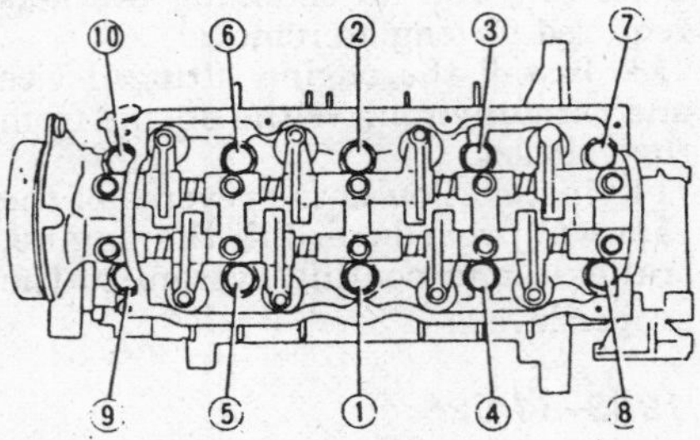


**Cylinder head bolt torque sequence—1983–85 626**

## REMOVAL & INSTALLATION

### *1983–85 GLC and 1983 626*

Be sure that the cylinder head is cold before removal. This will prevent warpage. Do not remove the cam gear from the timing chain.

1. Disconnect the negative battery cable. Drain the cooling system.
2. Remove the air cleaner.
3. Disconnect all applicable electrical wires and leads.
4. Rotate the crankshaft to put the No. 1 cylinder at TDC on the compression stroke.
5. Remove the distributor.
6. Remove the rocker arm cover.
7. Raise and support the vehicle safely. Disconnect the exhaust pipe from the manifold.
8. Remove the accelerator linkage.
9. Remove the nut, washer and the distributor gear from the camshaft.
10. Remove the nut, washer and camshaft gear. On front wheel drive vehicles equipped with the 1490cc engine, remove the tensioner from the timing case cover. Fasten the gear and chain together.
11. Remove the cylinder head bolts and cylinder head to front cover bolt. Loosen the head bolts in reverse of the torque sequence.
12. Remove the rocker arm assembly.
13. Remove the camshaft from the camshaft gear.
14. Lift off the cylinder head.
15. Installation is the reverse of the removal procedure. Adjust the chain tension. Torque the cylinder head/camshaft bolts to 56–59 ft. lbs. on the GLC and to 65–69 ft. lbs on the 626. Adjust the valve clearance.

### *1983–85 626*

1. Disconnect the negative battery cable. Turn the crankshaft so that the piston of the number one cylinder is at top dead center. Drain the coolant into a suitable drain pan.
2. Remove the air cleaner, distributor, thermostat, fuel pump and accelerator cable.
3. Remove the intake manifold and carburetor. Remove the alternator and alternator strap. Remove the air conditioning compressor and alternator bracket installation bolts. Do not disconnect the high and low pressure hoses from the compressor. Secure the compressor in the fender well area with a piece of wire or rope.
4. Remove the engine ground wire. Remove the upper timing belt cover and timing belt.

**NOTE: Before removing the timing belt, turn the crankshaft to align the timing mark (A) of the camshaft pulley with the front timing mark. Be sure to mark the direction of rotation on the timing belt so that the belt can be reinstalled in the same direction. If the camshaft pulley has to be removed, use a suitable tool to lock the pulley in place so as to keep it from turning and remove the pulley retaining nut or bolt.**

5. Remove the secondary pipes and disconnect the oxygen sensor connector.
6. Remove the insulator assembly along with the nuts and gaskets. Remove the exhaust pipe from the exhaust manifold.
7. Remove the rear housing and gaskets. Remove the cylinder head cover and gaskets.
8. Remove the cylinder head bolts. Loosen the head bolts in reverse of the torque sequence.
9. Remove the cylinder head and exhaust manifold as an assembly. Remove the cylinder head gasket.
10. Clean and inspect the gasket mating surfaces. Check for wear and damage, replace defective parts as necessary.

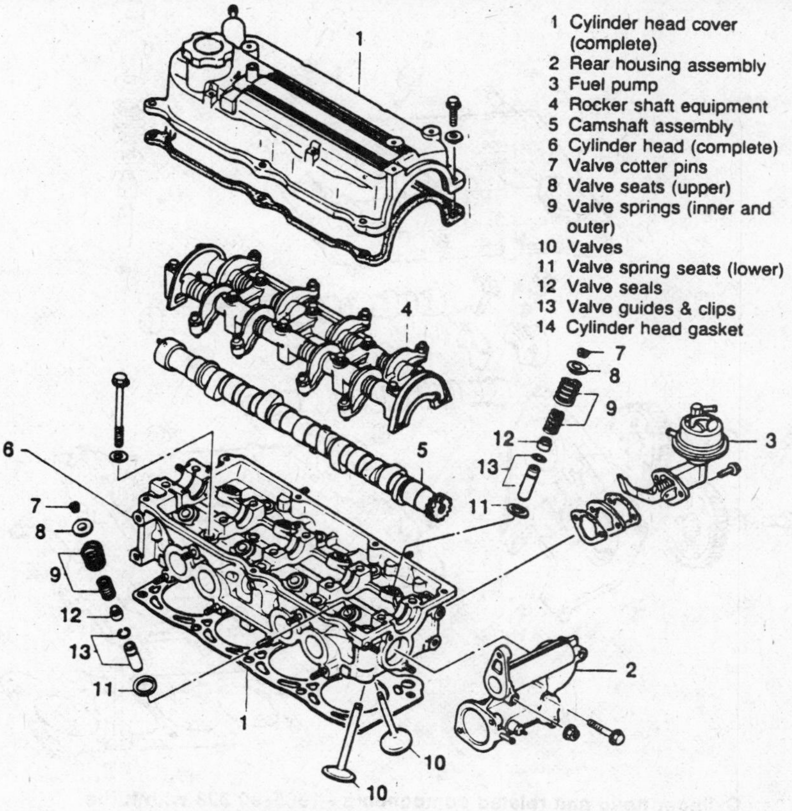


**Cylinder head components – 1986–87 626**

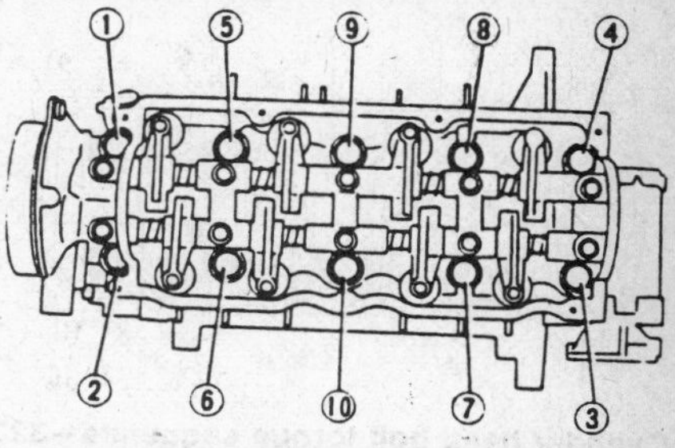


**Cylinder head bolt loosening sequence – 626 and MX-6**

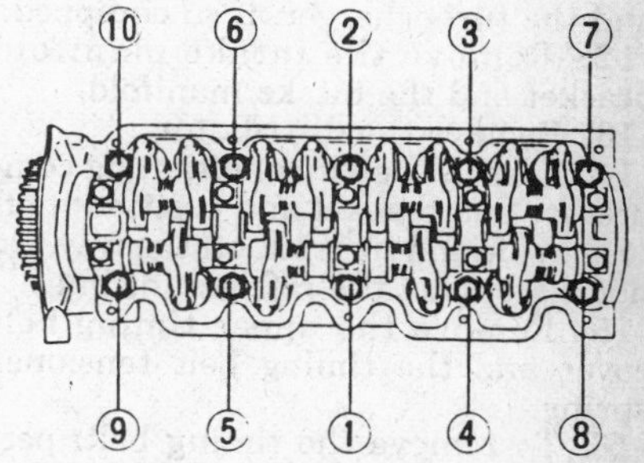


**Cylinder head bolt torque sequence – 1988–90 626 and MX-6**

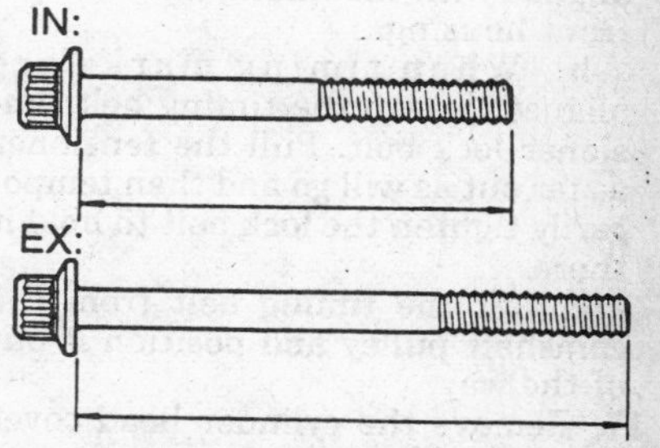


**On 929, measure the length of each cynder head bolt before installation**

11. To install, use new gaskets and reverse the removal procedure. Torque the cylinder head bolts in sequence to 59–65 ft. lbs. Do not forget to insert the plain washer. Torque the rocker arm assembly to 13–19 ft. lbs. Adjust the valve clearance and check the timing. Refill the cooling system.

### *1986–87 626*

1. Disconnect the negative battery cable. Turn the crankshaft so that the piston of the number one cylinder is at top dead center. Drain the coolant.
2. Remove the accelerator cable, secondary air pipe, distributor and rear housing.
3. Remove the air hose, secondary air pipe, oil pipe and insulator number one, two and three.
4. If equipped, remove the turbocharger bracket and the front catalytic converter.
5. Remove the oil return hose, wa ter inlet hose, water outlet hose an the EGR pipe.
6. Remove the exhaust manifold retaining bolts. Remove the exhaust manifold. If equipped with a turbocharger, remove the exhaust manifold and the turbocharger as an assembly.
7. Remove the intake manifold retaining bolts. Remove the intake manifold assembly and gasket.
8. Remove the timing belt cover and timing belt.

**NOTE: Before removing the timing belt, turn the crankshaft to align the timing mark (A) of the camshaft pulley with the front timing mark. Be sure to mark the direction of rotation on the timing belt. The reason to mark the belt is so that the belt can be reinstalled in the same direction. If the camshaft pulley has to be removed, use a suitable tool to lock the pulley in place so as to keep it from turning and remove the pulley retaining nut or bolt.**

9. Remove the cylinder head cover and gaskets. Remove the cylinder head bolts. Loosen the head bolts in reverse of the torque sequence.
10. Remove the cylinder head and cylinder head gasket.
11. Clean and inspect the gasket mating surfaces and check the cylinder head for warpage. Check for wear and damage, replace defective parts as necessary.
12. To install, use new gaskets and reverse the removal procedure. Torque the cylinder head bolts specification. Do not forget to insert the plain washer, as necessary. Adjust the valves, as required.

### *1988–90 626 and MX-6*

1. Disconnect the negative battery cable and drain the cooling system.
2. Disconnect the spark plug wires and remove the spark plugs.
3. Disconnect the accelerator cable. If equipped with automatic transaxle, disconnect the throttle cable.
4. Remove the air intake pipe.
5. Remove the air intake pipe and fuel hose. Cover the fuel hose to prevent leakage.
6. Remove the upper radiator hose, water by-pass hose, heater hose, oil cooler hose (turbo only) and brake vacuum hose.
7. Remove the 3-way and EGR solenoid valve assemblies.
8. Disconnect the engine harness connector and ground wire.
9. Remove the vacuum chamber and exhaust manifold insulator.
10. Remove the EGR pipe, turbo oil pipes (if so equipped) and exhaust pipe.

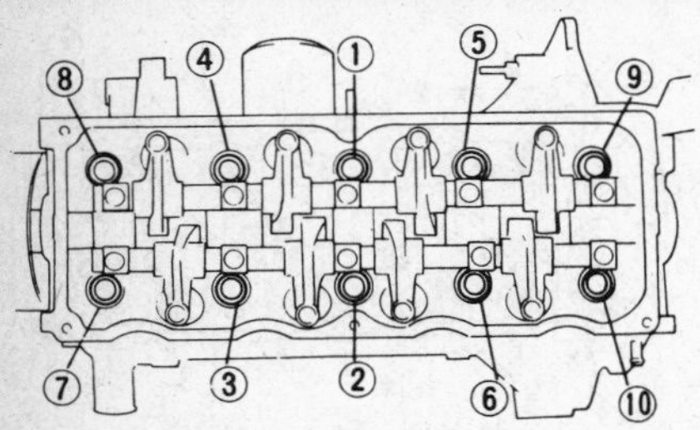


**Cylinder head bolt torque sequence—323 without turbo**

11. Remove the exhaust manifold and the turbocharger, if so equipped.
12. Remove the intake manifold bracket and the intake manifold.
13. Remove the distributor.
14. Loosen the air conditioning compressor and bracket and position it off to the side and tie it out off the way. Do not disconnect the refrigerant lines.
15. Remove the upper timing belt cover and the timing belt tensioner spring.
16. To remove the timing belt, perform the following:
    a. Rotate the crankshaft so that the 1 on the camshaft pulley is aligned with the timing mark on the front housing.
    b. When timing marks are aligned, loosen the timing belt tensioner lock bolt. Pull the tensioner as far out as will go and then temporarily tighten the lock bolt to hold it there.
    c. Lift the timing belt from the camshaft pulley and position it out of the way.
17. Remove the cylinder head cover and cover gasket.
18. Loosen the cylinder head bolts in the proper sequence and remove the cylinder head and head gasket.
19. Thoroughly clean the cylinder head and cylinder block contact surfaces to remove any dirt or oil. Check the cylinder head for warpage and cracks. The maximum allowable contact distortion is 0.006 in. Inspect the cylinder head bolts for damaged threads and make sure they are free from grease and dirt.
20. Lay the new gasket on the surface of the block.

**NOTE: Turbocharged and non-turbocharged engines use different cylinder head gaskets. To ensure proper sealing and compression, make sure that the proper type gasket is being installed.**

21. Set the cylinder head on the gasket.
22. Coat the bolt threads and seat surfaces with clean engine oil and torque the bolts in the proper sequence to 59–64 ft. lbs. in 3 stages.
23. Apply a suitable sealant to the 4 corners of the cylinder head and install the cover with a new gasket. Torque the cover nuts to 52–69 inch lbs.
24. Make sure that the camshaft pulley and front housing timing marks are still aligned and install the timing belt.
25. Complete the remainder of the installation by reversing the removal procedure. Fill the cooling system to the proper level and connect the negative battery cable.

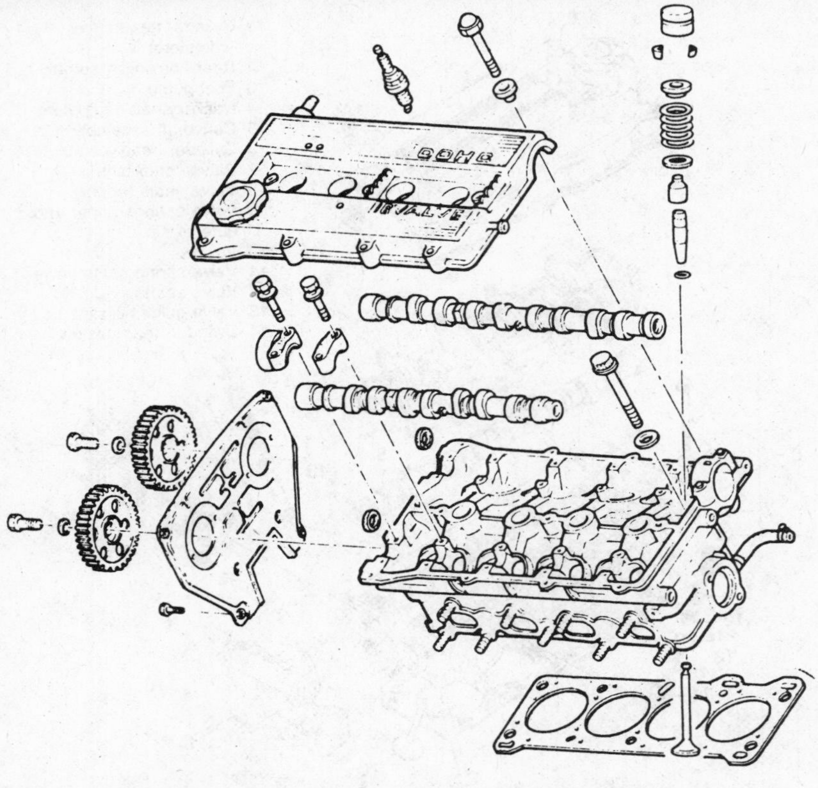

**Cylinder head and related components—1988–90 323 with turbo**

### *1986–90 323 without Turbo*

1. Disconnect the negative battery cable. Turn the crankshaft so that the piston of the number one cylinder is at TDC. Drain the coolant.
2. Remove the air cleaner assembly, and remove the following components.
    a. Remove the oil level gauge, accelerator cable and cruise control cable if equipped.
    b. Remove the fuel hoses, heater hoses, brake vacuum hose and canister hose. If equipped with a carburetor, remove the fuel pump.
    c. Remove the engine harness connectors, spark plug wires, distributor, spark plugs and secondary air pipe assembly for carbureted vehicles.
    d. Remove the front hanger and engine ground wire. Remove the upper radiator hose, water bypass hose and bracket.
    e. Remove the intake manifold assembly. Remove the exhaust manifold insulator and the exhaust manifold.
    f. Remove the engine side cover. Remove the upper and lower timing belt cover. Remove the timing belt tensioner with spring and remove the timing belt.

**NOTE: Before removing the timing belt, turn the crankshaft to align the timing matching mark on the camshaft pulley with the matching mark on the cylinder head cover. Be sure to mark the direction of rotation on the timing belt. The reason to mark the belt is so that the belt can be reinstalled in the same direction.**

    g. To remove the camshaft pulley, use a suitable tool to lock the pulley in place so as to keep it from turning and remove the pulley retaining nut or bolt.
    h. Remove the rear engine hanger and cylinder head cover and gaskets.
    i. Remove the cylinder head bolts. Loosen the head bolts in reverse of the torque sequence.
    j. Remove the cylinder head and cylinder head gasket.

3. Clean and inspect the gasket mating surfaces. Check for wear and damage, replace defective parts, as necessary.

4. To install, use new gaskets and reverse the removal procedure. Torque the cylinder head bolts to specification. Do not forget to insert the plain washer. Adjust the valve clearance, as required. Check the timing. Refill the cooling system.

5. Be sure to install the camshaft pulley onto the dowel pin and keyway with the matching mark straight up, so that the timing marks on the camshaft pulley and cylinder head align. Tighten the camshaft pulley to 36–45 ft. lbs.

### *1988–90 323 with Turbo*

1. Properly relieve the fuel system pressure. Disconnect the negative battery cable. Drain the cooling system. Remove the air cleaner assembly. Remove the distributor, distributor wires and spark plugs.

2. Remove the air intake pipe, air pipe, air bypass valve and hoses.

3. Remove the radiator.

4. Remove the engine side cover and the engine under cover. .

5. Disconnect the exhaust pipe at the exhaust manifold. Remove the turbocharger mounting bracket and the exhaust manifold and turbocharger insulators. Remove the exhaust manifold retaining bolts. Remove the exhaust manifold and the turbocharger assembly from the engine.

6. Remove the radiator hose and coolant bypass pipe. Disconnect the accelerator cable. Disconnect all required electrical connections, vacuum hoses and fuel line couplings.

7. Remove the surge tank and bracket.

8. Remove the cylinder head cover retaining bolts. Remove the cylinder head cover from the engine.

9. Remove the timing cover assembly retaining bolts. Remove the timing cover assembly. Remove the timing belt.

10. Remove the cylinder head retaining bolts. Remove the cylinder head and the intake manifold assembly from the engine. Remove the thermostat and the thermostat cover.

11. Thoroughly clean the cylinder head and cylinder block contact surfaces to remove any dirt or oil. Check the cylinder head for warpage and cracks. The maximum allowable contact distortion is 0.006 in. Inspect the cylinder head bolts for damaged threads and make sure they are free from grease and dirt.

12. Installation is essentially the reverse of the removal procedure, but pay attention to the following:

a. Install the thermostat with the jiggle pin facing upward and the printed side of the gasket facing the thermostat.

b. Be sure to torque the cylinder head bolts to specification and in the proper sequence to 56–60 ft. lbs. Torque the bolts in several stages.

c. Use a new cylinder head cover gasket and apply sealant to the cover. Torque the cover bolts to 26–35 inch lbs.

d. Fill the cooling system to the proper level and perform the necessary tune-up adjustments.

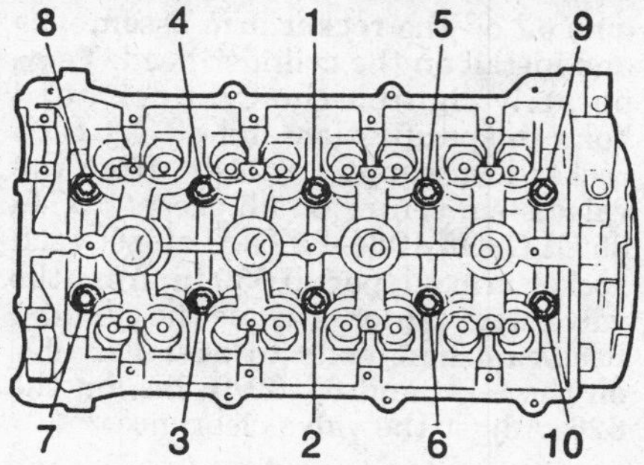


**Cylinder head bolt torque sequence–1988–90 323 with turbo**

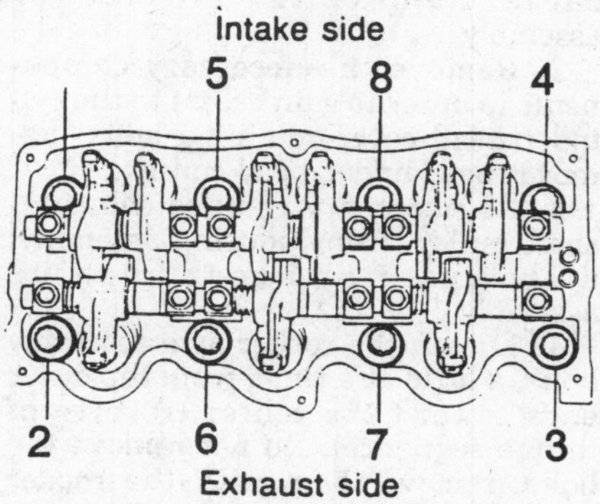


**Cylinder head bolt removal sequence–929**

### *1988–90 929*

1. Properly relieve the fuel system pressure. Disconnect the negative battery cable. Remove the air cleaner assembly. Drain the coolant.

2. Position the engine at TDC on the compression stroke so that all the pulley matchmarks are aligned. Remove the timing cover assembly. Remove the timing belt and mark the direction of rotation if it is to be re-used.

3. Disconnect and plug canister, brake vacuum and fuel hoses. If equipped with automatic transmission, disconnect the A/T vacuum hose.

4. Remove the 3-way solenoid valve assembly and disconnect all engine harness connector and grounds.

5. If equipped with automatic transmission, remove the dipstick. Disconnect the required vacuum hoses. Disconnect the accelerator linkage.

6. Remove the distributor and the EGR pipe.

7. Remove the extension manifold. Remove the intake manifold by loosening the retaining bolts in the proper sequence.

8. Remove the cylinder head cover.

9. Remove the center exhaust pipe insulator and pipe. Disconnect the exhaust manifold retaining bolts. Remove the exhaust manifold with insulator.

10. Remove the seal plate.

11. Remove the cylinder head retaining bolts in the proper sequence in 2 or 3 stages. Remove the cylinder head from the vehicle.

12. Thoroughly clean the cylinder head and cylinder block contact surfaces to remove any dirt or oil. Check the cylinder head for warpage and cracks. The maximum allowable con-

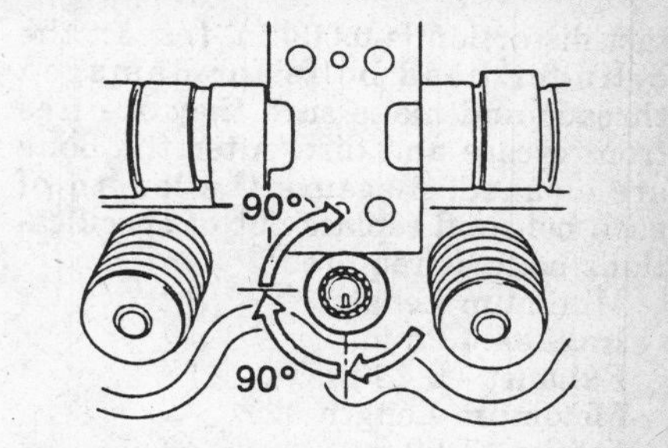


**On 929 use paint mark as a reference, then torque cylinder head bolts by using the angular method**

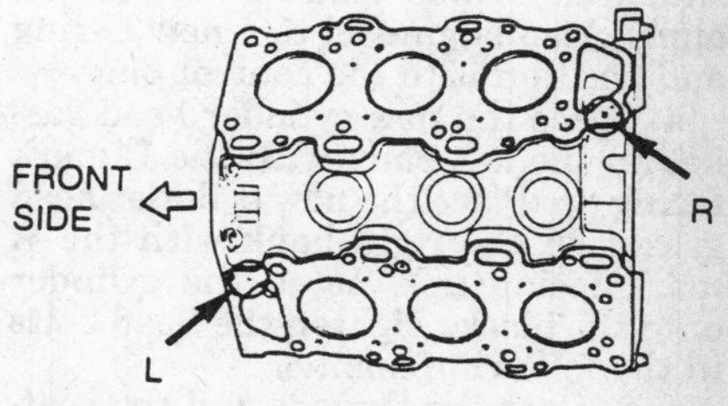


**Cylinder head gasket installation–929**

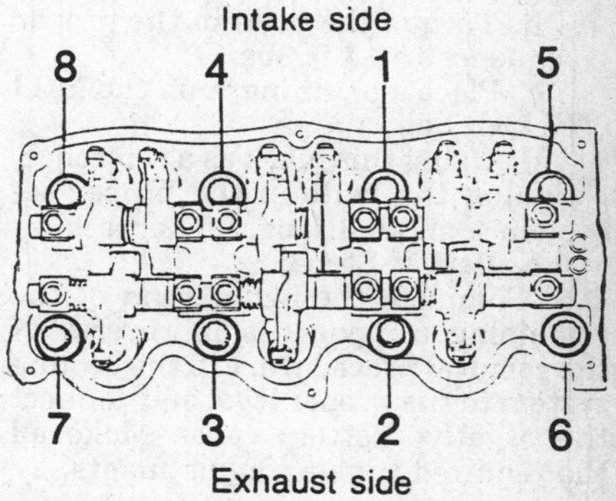


**Cylinder head bolt removal sequence 1988–89 929**

tact distortion is 0.004 in. Inspect the cylinder head bolts for damaged threads and make sure they are free from grease and dirt. After the bolts are cleaned, measure the length of each bolt and replace out of specifications bolts as required.

Minimum Length
Intake – 4.25 in.
Exhaust – 5.43 in.
Maximum Length
Intake – 4.29 in.
Exhaust – 5.47 in.

13. Check the oil control plug projection at the cylinder block. Projection should be 0.0209–0.224 in. If correct, apply clean engine oil to a new O-ring and position it to the control plug.

14. Place the new cylinder head gasket on the left bank with the **L** mark facing up. Place the new cylinder head gasket on the right bank with the **R** mark facing up. Install the cylinder onto the block. Tighten the head bolts in the following manner:

a. Coat the threads and the seating faces of the head bolts with clean engine oil.

b. Torque the bolts in the proper sequence to 14 ft. lbs.

c. Place a paint mark on the head of each bolt.

d. Using this mark as a reference, tighten the bolts in the proper sequence an additional 90 degrees.

e. Repeat Step d.

15. Complete the installation of the remaining components in reverse of the removal procedure. Fill the cooling system to the proper level and connect the negative battery cable. Make all the required tune-up adjustments.

## OVERHAUL

**For all cylinder head overhaul procedures, please refer to "Engine Rebuilding" in the Unit Repair section.**

# Rocker Shafts

## REMOVAL & INSTALLATION

### *1983–85 GLC*

This operation should only be performed on a cold engine. The bolts which hold the rocker shafts in place also hold the cylinder head to the block.

1. Disconnect the negative battery cable. Disconnect the choke cable.

2. If equipped, disconnect the air bypass valve cable.

3. Remove the rocker cover.

4. Remove the rocker arm shaft attaching bolts and the rocker arm assemblies.

5. Installation is the reverse of removal. Place a light film of clean engine oil on the rocker arm assemblies and install on the cylinder head. Temporarily tighten the cylinder head bolts to specification and off set each rocker arm support 0.04 in. from the valve stem center on all except 1984–85 GLC. On 1984–85 GLC off set each rocker arm support 0.039 in. from the valve stem center. Torque the cylinder head/camshaft bolts to 56–59 ft. lbs. on the GLC and 65–69 ft. lbs. on the 626. Adjust the valve clearance.

### *1983–90 626 and MX-6*

1. Disconnect the negative battery cable. Remove the air cleaner assembly.

2. Remove the necessary components in order to gain access to the cylinder head cover retaining bolts. Remove the cylinder head cover.

3. As necessary remove the camshaft pulley, front housing assembly, distributor and rear housing assembly.

4. Loosen the rocker arm assembly bolts, a little at a time, from the outer ends toward the center (reverse of torque sequence). Do not remove the bolts, remove them with the rocker arm assembly.

5. Inspect the parts for wear and damage, replace as necessary. Clean and inspect the gasket mounting surfaces.

6. Installation is the reverse of the removal procedure. Use new gaskets or RTV sealant, as required. Adjust the valve clearance if not equipped with hydraulic lash adjusters. Check the timing.

### *1986–90 323 without Turbo*

1. Disconnect the negative battery cable. Remove the air cleaner assembly.

2. Remove the necessary components in order to gain access to the cylinder head cover retaining bolts. Remove the cylinder head cover.

3. Remove the rocker arm and rocker shaft assembly from its mounting. Tag and bag all the components as what cylinder they belong to and whether they are for intake or exhaust service.

4. Installation is the reverse of the removal procedure with attention to the following:

a. Be sure to use new gaskets or RTV sealant, as required.

b. Torque the rocker arm bolts in sequence to 16–21 ft. lbs.

c. Make sure both rocker arm shaft bolt holes face downward when installing.

d. The bolt holes spacing is different for the exhaust and intake shafts.

e. There are 2 types of rocker arms with different offsets. One type of rocker is for No.1 and No. 2 cylinder intake and exhaust and the other type belongs to No. 3 and 4 cylinders.

f. Adjust the valves, as required.

### *1988–90 929*

1. Properly relieve the fuel system pressure. Disconnect the negative battery cable.

2. Remove the necessary components in order to gain access to the cylinder head cover retaining bolts. Remove the cylinder head cover.

3. It may be necessary to remove the distributor in order to remove the left cylinder head cover. If so, position the engine at TDC on the compression stroke before removing the distributor.

4. Carefully remove the rocker arm retaining bolts. Remove the rocker arm assemblies from the cylinder head.

5. Installation is the reverse of the removal procedure. Be sure to use new gaskets or RTV sealant, as required. Torque the rocker arm assembly retaining bolts in the proper sequence.

# Intake Manifold

## REMOVAL & INSTALLATION

### *Except 626, MX-6, 323 and 929*

1. Disconnect the negative battery cable. Drain the cooling system.

2. Remove the air cleaner, air intake, or turbocharger ducts. Remove the accelerator linkage. Disconnect the PCV valve.

3. Disconnect the choke cable and fuel line on carbureted vehicles. On engines with fuel injection, disconnect the fuel line, vacuum hoses and electrical connectors. Disconnect the heater return hose and bypass hose.

4. Remove the intake manifold retaining bolts. Remove the manifold and carburetor or throttle body and injectors as an assembly.

5. Installation is the reverse of the removal procedure. Torque the intake manifold retaining bolts to specification. Use a new gasket, as required.

### *323*

**CAUTION**

***Before removing the intake manifold, release the fuel system pressure.***

1. Disconnect the negative battery cable and drain the cooling system.

2. Disconnect the accelerator cable from the throttle body. Disconnect all air and vacuum hoses from the dynamic chamber and the throttle body.

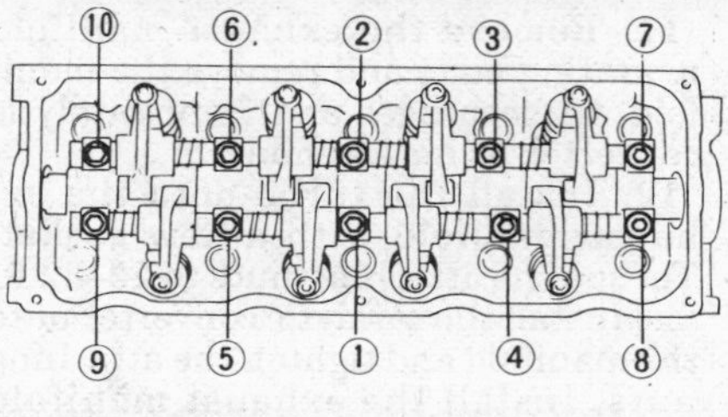


**Rocker shaft torque sequence—323, 626 and MX6**

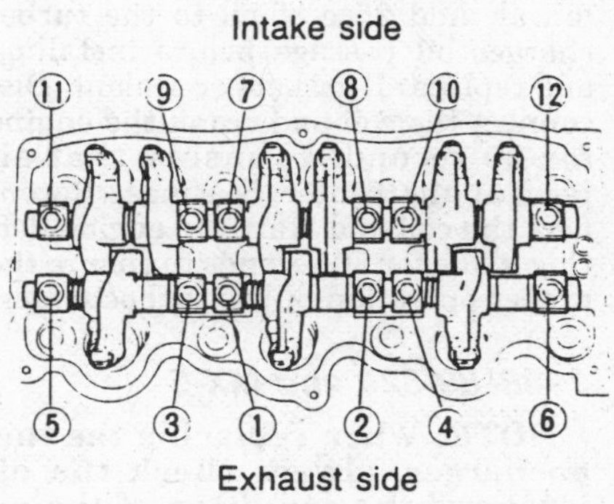


**Rocker arm bolt torque sequnce—929**

3. Loosen the hose clamps and disconnect the air funnel from the airflow meter and the throttle body. On turbocharged engines, disconnect the air funnel from the throttle body and the intercooler.

4. Disconnect the spark plug wires from the distributor and disconnect the connector from the ignition coil. Disconnect the hose from the air cleaner assembly. Remove the air cleaner/airflow meter assembly from the vehicle.

5. Disconnect the water hoses. Disconnect the throttle sensor connector. Remove the retaining nuts and bolts from the throttle body and separate the throttle body from the intake manifold.

6. Disconnect the hoses and remove the BAC valve. On turbocharged engines, disconnect the water hose for the oil cooler. Plug the opening to prevent leakage.

7. On turbocharged engines, unbolt the intake manifold and dynamic chamber assembly from the cylinder block and lift it out of the vehicle. On non-turbocharged engines, unbolt the dynamic chamber from the intake manifold and remove it along with the gasket, then remove the intake manifold. Remove the intake manifold gasket from the cylinder block. Cover or plug the intake ports to prevent anything from falling into the engine.

8. Thorouhly clean the intake manifold and cylinder block gasket mating surfaces. Visually inspect the intake manifold and dynamic chamber for cracks.

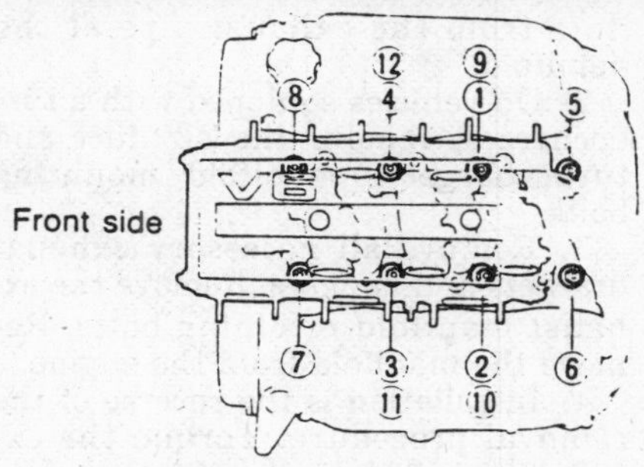


**Intake manifold torque sequence—929**

9. Place a new gasket on the cylinder block and lower the intake manifold onto the gasket. On turbo-charged engines, attach the dynamic chamber to the intake manifold with a new gasket. Install the retaining nuts and bolts and torque to 14–19 ft. lbs.

10. Install the remaining components in the reverse order of removal.

11. Refill the cooling system to the proper level and connect the negative battery cable.

### 1983–90 626 and MX-6

**CAUTION**

***Before removing the intake manifold, release the fuel system pressure.***

1. Disconnect the negative battery cable and drain the cooling system.

2. Disconnect the airflow meter connector. Remove the air cleaner duct (1987 only), secondary air hoses, air control vacuum hoses and remove the air cleaner. On 1988–89 models, remove the air duct and disconnect and No. 1 resonance chamber.

3. Remove the air flow meter and attendant air hoses. On 1988–89 non-turbocharged engines, disconnect and remove the No. 2 resonator which is connected to the bottom of the flex air hose.

4. On 1988–89 turbocharged engines, trace the upper hose on the intercooler to the air by-pass valve and disconnect the hoses. Unbolt and remove the valve from its mounting bracket. Remove the intercooler.

5. Disconnect the electrical connectors from the throttle body. Disconnect the water and vacuum hoses and plug the openings.

6. Disconnect the accelerator cable from the throttle body and remove the throttle body and gasket from the dynamic chamber. Disconnect the PCV hose and the vacuum pipe assembly. Remove the nuts and bolts that attach the dynamic chamber to the intake manifold and remove it along with the gasket.

7. Disconnect connectors from the fuel injectors and route the wiring harness off to the side and out of the way. Disconnect the fuel hose from the injector rail and remove the rail assembly with the injectors attached. Plug all the fuel openings.

8. Disconnect the remaining vacuum hoses and remove the EGR pipe.

9. Remove the intake manifold bracket. Remove the intake manifold and the gasket. Cover or plug the intake ports to prevent anything from falling into the engine.

10. Thoroughly clean the intake manifold and cylinder block gasket mating surfaces with a gasket scraper and solvent. Visually inspect the intake manifold and dynamic chamber for cracks.

11. Place a new gasket on the cylinder block and lower the intake manifold onto the gasket. Install the retaining nuts and torque them to 14–22 ft. lbs.

12. Install the remaining components in the reverse order of removal.

13. Refill the cooling system to the proper level and connect the negative battery cable. Check the accelerator cable deflection.

### 1988–90 929

**CAUTION**

***Before removing the intake manifold, release the fuel system pressure.***

1. Disconnect the negative battery cable. Disconnect the water hoses and plug them. The coolant will be drained from the radiator just before the intake manifold is ready to be removed.

2. Disconnect the air inlet duct from the air cleaner and disconnect the air flow meter connector.

3. Disconnect the vacuum hoses from the TICS and purge air control soleniod valves. These valves are bolted to the front of the air cleaner assembly.

4. Remove the air cleaner, air cleaner element, air flow meter and air funnel.

5. Disconnect the by-pass air control (BAC) valve connector, water hoses and remove the valve.

6. Disconnect the throttle sensor connector and the accelerator cable. Remove the throttle body and gasket.

7. Disconnect all vacuum hoses, EGR pipe, EGR position sensor connector, water hose and ground wire.

8. Remove the wiring harness bracket.

9. Disconnect the air intake pipe from the dynamic chamber with the gasket.

10. Mark the extension manifolds right and left for assembly reference as they are not interchangable. Remove the 6 extension manifolds with their gaskets from the dynamic chamber.

11. Disconnect the intake air thermo

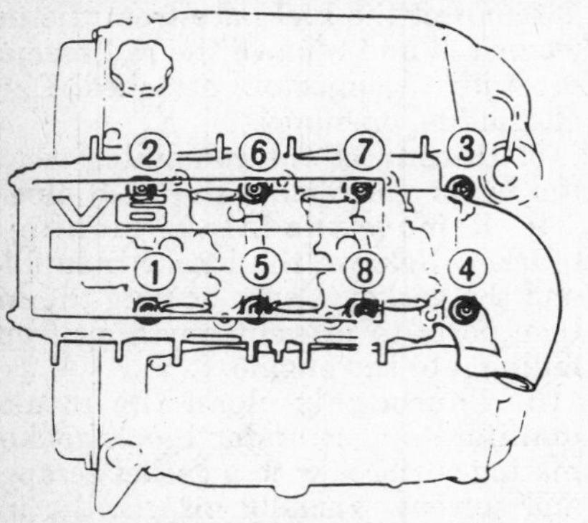

Intake manifold loosening sequence—929

sensor connector, vacuum hoses and ground connectors.

12. Remove the attaching nuts and lift the dynamic chamber straight up from the intake manifold studs. Drain the radiator and disconnect all remaining connectors, fuel hoses, water hoses.

13. Using the proper sequence, loosen the intake manifold nuts in 2 stages. Lift the intake manifold from the engine and remove the 2 intake manifold gaskets. Cover the intake ports to prevent anything from falling into the engine.

14. Visually inspect the intake manifold for cracks, warpage or any other type of damage and replace as necessary. Remove all gasket material from the seating surface on the manifold and the engine.

**NOTE: Forward of one of the studs that secure the dynamic chamber is an O-ring that seals the manifold to the chamber. Remove this O-ring and replace it with a new one.**

15. Place the new intake manifold gaskets onto the cylinder block and lower the manifold over the gaskets. Install the intake manifold washers with the white paint marks facing up. Install the retaining nuts and torque in two stages to 14–18 ft. lbs. using the proper sequence.

16. Install the remaining components in reverse of the removal procedure. Fill the cooling system to the proper level. Connect the negative battery cable. Start the engine and check for leaks.

## Exhaust Manifold

### REMOVAL & INSTALLATION

#### *All Except 929*

1. Disconnect the negative battery cable. Remove the heat shield cover, if equipped. Remove the 2 attaching nuts from the exhaust pipe at the manifold.

2. On vehicles equipped with a turbocharger, remove the air duct and turbocharger-to-manifold mounting bolts.

3. Remove all necessary exhaust brackets and hangers. Remove the exhaust manifold retaining bolts. Remove the manifold from the engine.

4. Installation is the reverse of the removal procedure. Torque the exhaust manifold to specification. Use new gaskets.

#### *929*

1. Properly relieve the fuel system pressure. Disconnect the negative battery cable. Remove the air cleaner assembly.

2. Raise and support the vehicle safely. Disconnect the exhaust manifold from the exhaust flange. Lower the vehicle.

3. Remove the necessary components in order to gain access to the exhaust manifold retaining bolts. Remove the exhaust manifold heat shields. Remove the exhaust manifold retaining bolts.

4. Remove the exhaust manifold from its mounting. Remove and discard the exhaust manifold gasket.

5. Installation is the reverse of the removal procedure. Torque the exhaust manifold nuts to specification. Be sure to use new gaskets, as required.

## Turbocharger

### REMOVAL & INSTALLATION

#### *1986–87 626*

1. Be sure that the engine is cold. Disconnect the negative battery cable. Drain the cooling system.

2. Align the No. 1 cylinder at TDC on the compression stroke. Remove the distributor and the spark plug wires.

3. Remove the turbocharger air duct and secondary air pipe from the exhaust manifold.

4. Remove the lower insulator cover. Remove the secondary air pipe and nipple.

5. Disconnect the oil feed pipe from the turbocharger.

6. Remove the upper insulator cover.

7. Disconnect the exhaust pipe from the front catalytic converter.

8. Disconnect the EGR pipe and water hoses.

9. Remove the oxygen sensor from the exhaust manifold. Remove the front pipe from the catalytic converter.

10. Unbolt the turbo from the mounting bracket.

11. Remove the exhaust manifold mounting bolts and remove the manifold, turbocharger and front catalytic converter as an assembly.

12. Install the turbo onto the exhaust manifold with a new gasket. Torque the attaching nuts to 23–32 ft. lbs. Install the catalytic converter onto the manifold and tighten the attaching nuts. Install the exhaust manifold onto the block with new gaskets and torque the nuts to 16–21 ft.lbs.

13. Installation is the reverse or removal. Add 25cc of oil to the turbocharger oil passage before installing and replace all gaskets or sealant. Disconnect the coil and crank the engine for 20 seconds to insure that oil reaches the center bearings. Reconnect the coil and start the engine, letting it idle for 30 seconds to ensure the proper operation of the turbocharger.

#### *1988–89 626 and MX-6*

**NOTE: When replacing the turbocharger, always check the oil level and the condition of the oil and the turbo oil inlet and outlet lines. If the oil is dirty or the lines are damaged, replace them.**

1. Disconnect the negative battery cable and drain the cooling system.

2. Remove the air hoses and the air bypass hose.

3. Remove the exhaust manifold insulators.

4. Disconnect the oil inlet and return pipes from the turbocharger and plug the ends.

5. Disconnect the water hoses from the water pipe and plug the ends.

6. Disconnect the EGR pipe from the exhaust manifold.

7. Remove the oxygen sensor.

8. Disconnect the front pipe from the turbocharger and set the gasket aside. Remove the bolt from the turbocharger joint pipe.

9. Support the turbocharger by hand and remove the exhaust manifold retaining nuts. Remove the turbo and the manifold as an assembly. Cover the exhaust manifold ports with a clean rag or masking tape to prevent the entry of foreign matter.

**CAUTION**

***Do not drop the turbocharger or carry it around by the actuating handle. When laying the unit down, do so with the turbine shaft in the horizontal position. Do not bend the actuator mounting or rod.***

10. Remove all the sealant and gasket material from the turbocharger and exhaust manifold mating surfaces. Use all new gaskets.

11. Pour 25 cc of clean engine oil into the opening for the turbo oil line.

12. Attach the turbo to the exhaust

manifold and torque the nuts to 20–29 ft. lbs. Attach the assembly to the engine using new gaskets and torque the nuts to specification. Torque the turbocharger joint pipe bolt to 27–46 ft. lbs. and the turbocharger bracket bolts to 23–30 ft. lbs.

13. Install the front pipe and the oxygen sensor.

14. Connect the EGR pipe to the exhaust manifold and the water hose to the inlet pipe.

15. Connect the oil inlet and return pipes to the turbo connections. Install the exhaust manifold insulators.

16. Install the air bypass valve and air hoses.

17. Fill the cooling system to the proper level and connect the negative battery cable.

18. Disconnect the connector from the igniter and crank the engine for 20 seconds. Reconnect the connector and start the engine. Run the engine at idle for 20 seconds. Stop the engine and disconnect the negative battery cable. Depress and hold the brake pedal in for 5 seconds to clear the malfunction code from the control unit.

### *1988–90 323*

**NOTE: When replacing the turbocharger, always check the oil level and the condition of the oil and the turbo oil inlet and outlet lines. If the oil is dirty or the lines are damaged, replace them.**

1. Disconnect the negative battery cable.

2. From underneath the vehicle, remove the engine undercover.

3. Disconnect the 2 air hoses attached to the throttle body inlet hose and remove the air pipe.

4. Remove the exhaust manifold insulator covers.

5. Remove the water hoses.

6. Remove the oil pipe and the oil return hose.

7. Support the turbocharger by hand and remove the nuts and bolts from the exhaust manifold. Remove the turbocharger and the exhaust manifold as an assembly. Remove the mounting gasket.

8. Remove the nuts and lift the turbocharger from the exhaust manifold studs. Cover the exaust manifold ports to prevent the entry of foreign matter. If the gasket is bent or cracked, replace it with a new one. If the turbocharger mounting nuts are damaged, replace them with factory made replacement nuts only.

**CAUTION**

*Be careful to avoid dropping the turbocharger or handling it roughly. Be careful not to bend the wastegate actuator mounting and rod.*

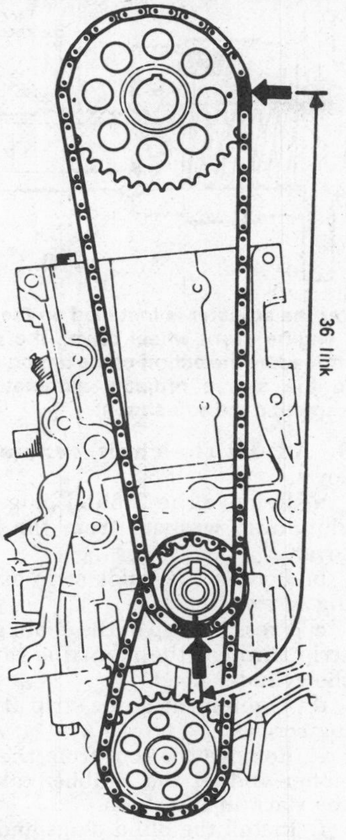


**Timing chain alignment marks—1983 GLC Wagon**

9. Installation is the reverse or removal.

## TROUBLESHOOTING

**For more information on turbocharging, please refer to "Turbocharging" in the Unit Repair Section.**

# Timing Chain

## REMOVAL & INSTALLATION

### *1983–85 GLC*

**NOTE: On front wheel drive GLC, the engine must be removed from the vehicle. Start procedure at Step 5.**

1. Disconnect the negative battery cable. Position the No. 1 piston at TDC. Drain the cooling system. Remove the radiator hoses, thermostat housing, thermostat, fan, water pump and radiator.

2. Remove all lower and side splash or skid shields. Remove the crankshaft pulley. Remove the alternator, air pump and any component that will interfere with front cover removal.

3. Remove the blind cover, small plate retained by 2 or 3 bolts that covers the chain adjuster. Install the special clamping tool or make a simple device to prevent the slipper head of the chain adjuster from popping out.

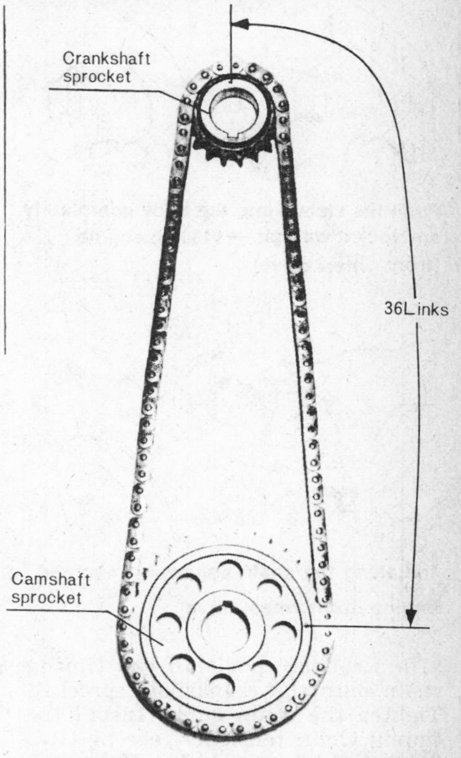


**Timing chain alignment marks—1983–85 GLC sedan**

4. Remove the cylinder head, oil pan and timing chain front cover.

5. On GLC front wheel drive, remove the chain tensioner which is located on the left upper corner of the timing cover, before removing the cylinder head. Remove the crankshaft pulley.

6. If equipped, remove the oil slinger from the crankshaft. Depending on the engine, remove the oil pump pulley and chain or the timing chain with sprockets first, the remaining sprockets and chain second. Loosen the timing chain guide strip and remove the chain tensioner, if necessary.

7. When installing the oil pump sprocket and chain, check for excessive slack. Replace the chain if necessary. On the 626, the chain slack should be 0.015 in. Adjusting shims positioned between the oil pump and mounting are available in thicknesses of 0.006 in.

8. Inspect the slipper head of the chain adjuster, the chain guide strip and the vibration damper for wear or damage. Check the adjuster spring for loss of tension. Replace parts as necessary.

9. Place the camshaft sprocket into the timing chain. Wire the sprocket and chain in position.

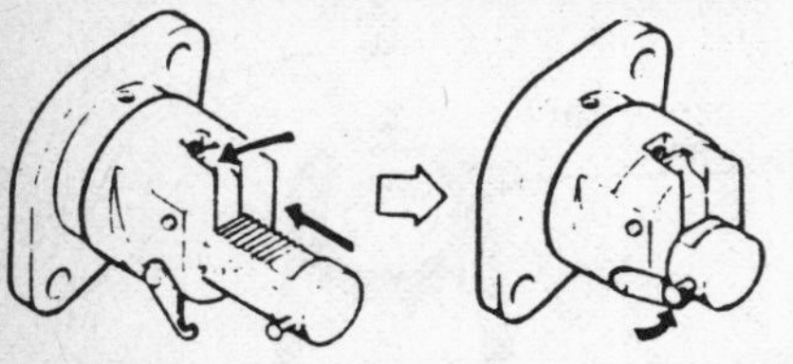

Push the sleeve into the body completely and lock it with pin—1490 cc engine (front wheel drive)

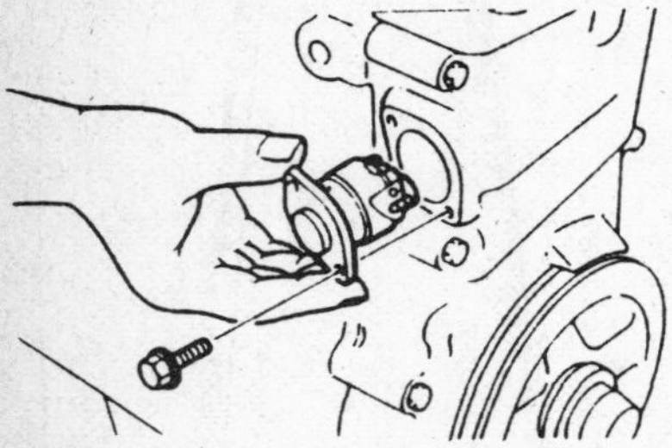

Installing the chain adjuster—1490 cc engine (front wheel drive)

10. Properly position the timing chain onto the crankshaft sprocket. Tighten the chain guide. Install the timing chain tensioner, except GLC front wheel drive vehicles. Make sure the snubber spring is fully compressed. Install the clamping tool.

11. Install a new timing cover oil seal. Install the timing chain front cover, oil pan and cylinder head. When installing the front cover, be sure tension is applied to the timing chain to prevent it from coming off of the crankshaft sprocket. If the chain comes off of the sprocket, incorrect timing and engine damage will occur.

12. Install the sprocket and timing chain on the camshaft. Adjust the timing chain tension.

13. Complete the installation in the reverse order of the removal procedure.

# Timing Chain Tensioner

## REMOVAL, INSTALLATION AND ADJUSTMENT

### *1983 GLC Wagon*

1. Disconnect the negative battery cable. Remove the water pump, if necessary.
2. Remove the tensioner cover.
3. Remove the attaching bolts from the tensioner. Remove the tensioner.
4. Fully compress the snubber spring. Insert a suitable tool into the tensioner release mechanism.
5. Without removing the tool, insert the tensioner and align the bolt holes. Install and torque the bolts.

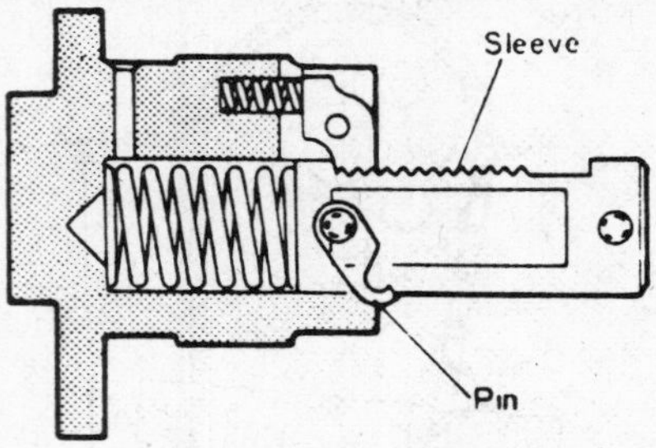


After the adjuster is installed on the 1490 cc engine (front wheel drive), the pin is removed by the action of the timing chain and the sleeve projects automatically, completing the adjustment

6. Adjust the chain tension as follows.
   a. Remove the 2 blind plugs and aluminum washers from the front cover.
   b. Loosen the guide strip attaching screws.
   c. Press the top of the chain guide strip through the adjusting hole in the cylinder head.
   d. Tighten the guide strip attaching screws.
   e. Remove the tool from the tensioner and let the snubber take up the slack in the chain.
   f. Install the blind plugs and aluminum washers.
   g. Install the tensioner cover and gasket.
   h. Install a new gasket and water pump, if removed. Install the crankshaft pulley and drive belt and adjust the tension. Check the cooling system level.

### *1983–85 GLC Except Wagon*

The chain tensioner is located on the left upper side of the timing case cover. It is operated by spring plug hydraulic pressure. The tensioner has a one way locking system and an automatic release device. After assembly, it will automatically adjust when the engine is rotated 1 or 2 times. No disassembly of the tensioner is required.

1. The tensioner is retained by 2 bolts. Remove the bolts and the tensioner.
2. Check the number of teeth showing on the sleeve of the tensioner. If 13 or more notches are showing the timing chain is stretched and must be replaced.
3. To install the tensioner, push the sleeve back into the body and lock it with the swivel catch on the tensioner body. Install the tensioner into the timing cover. After installation, the catch is released by the action of the timing chain when the engine is rotated one to two revolutions. The sleeve projects automatically providing the proper chain adjustment.

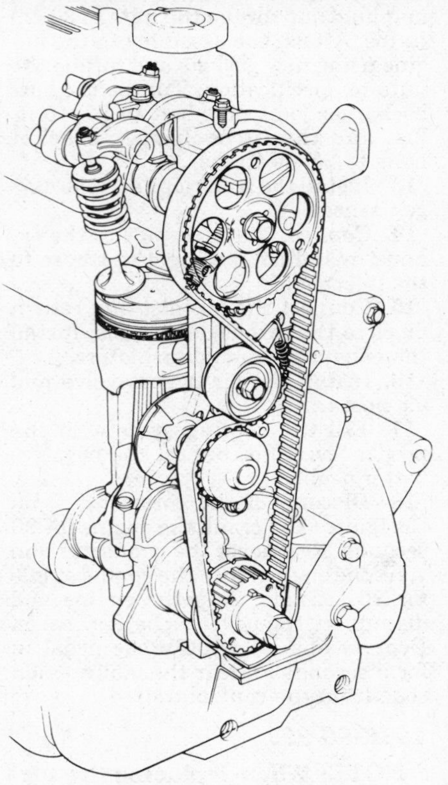

Typical timing belt assembly

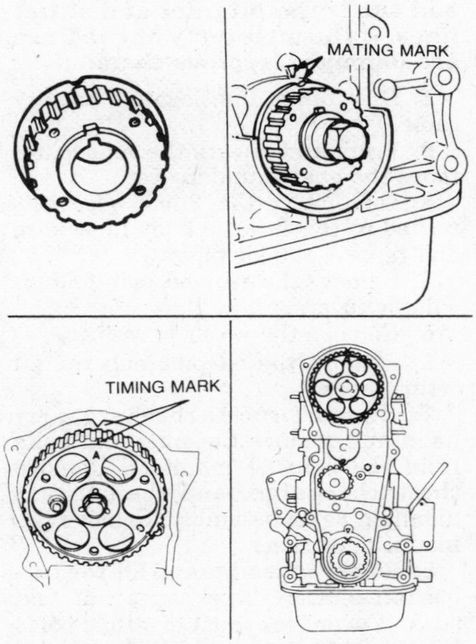


Timing belt alignmnt marks—1983–87 626

# Timing Belt

## REMOVAL & INSTALLATION

### *1983–87 626*

1. Disconnect the negative battery cable. Remove the alternator belt and the power steering pump belt. Remove

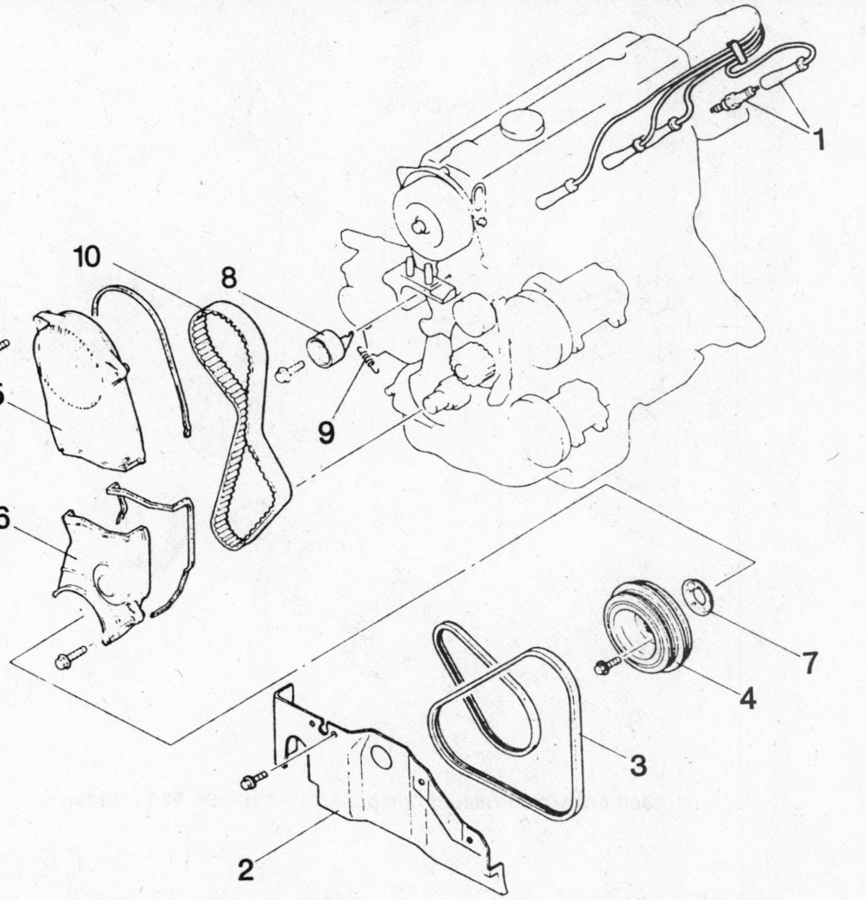


1. High-tension lead and spark plug
2. Engine side cover
3. Drive belt
4. Crankshaft pulley
5. Upper timing belt cover
6. Lower timing belt cover
7. Baffle plate
8. Timing belt tensioner
9. Timing belt tensioner spring
10. Timing belt

**Timing belt and related components – 1988–90 626 and MX-6**

the upper and the lower timing belt cover.

2. Turn the crankshaft to position the **A** mark on the camshaft pulley with the mark on the housing. Remove the crankshaft pulley mounting bolts and the pulley.

3. Remove the tensioner pulley lock bolt, the pulley and the spring. Remove the timing belt and mark an arrow in the direction of rotation on the timing belt.

4. To remove the camshaft pulley, insert a T-wrench through the camshaft pulley onto a housing bolt, place another wrench on the pulley center bolt, hold the T-wrench securely and remove the pulley center bolt.

5. Pull the camshaft pulley from the camshaft. To remove the crankshaft pulley, remove the center bolt and the pulley.

6. Install the timing belt and be sure the timing mark on the timing belt pulley is aligned with the matching mark. Make sure that the mark (A) of the camshaft pulley is aligned with the timing mark. If it is not, turn the camshaft to align it.

7. Install the timing belt tensioner and spring. Temporarily secure it as the spring is fully extended.

8. Install the timing belt, if using the old timing belt, be sure it is reinstalled in the same direction of previous rotation. Also make sure there is no oil, grease or dirt on the timing belt.

9. Loosen the tensioner lock bolt. Turn the crankshaft twice in the direction of rotation. Align the timing marks. Tighten the timing belt tensioner lock bolt to 28–38 ft. lbs. Check the timing belt tension. The timing belt deflection should be 0.43–0.51 in. at 22 lbs.

### *1988–89 626 and MX-6*

1. Disconnect the negative battery cable and remove the spark plug wires and spark plugs.

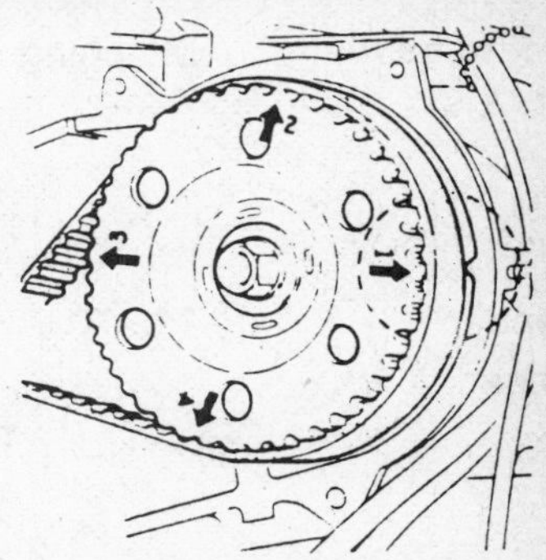

**Camshaft pulley and front housing timing mark alignment – 1988–90 626 and MX-6**

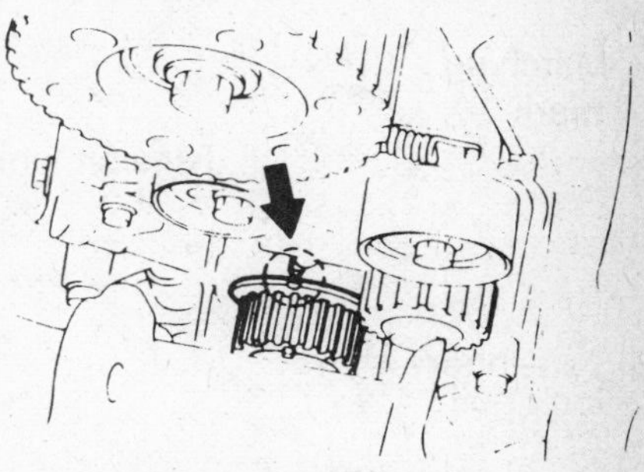

**Timing belt pulley and front housing alignment marks – 1989–90 626 and MX-6**

2. Remove the engine side cover and the drive belts.

3. Unbolt the crankshaft pulley and remove the upper and lower timing belt covers. Remove the crankshaft pulley baffle plate and make a note of how it is installed. The curved side should be facing out.

4. Turn the crankshaft until the **1** mark on the camshaft is aligned with the mark on top of the front housing. Unbolt and remove the tensioner and the tensioner spring.

5. Remove the timing belt. If the timing belt is to be re-used, mark the direction of rotation, prior to removal.

6. Inspect the belt and replace it if it is oil soaked, or shows excessive wear, peeling, cracking, or hardening. Inspect the tensioner for free and smooth rotation and replace it if it does not turn smoothly. Replace all damaged components as necessary.

7. Align the timing mark on the timing belt pulley with the matchmark on the lower front housing. Recheck the camshaft pulley and and front housing alignment marks. Turn the camshaft as necessary to re-align the marks.

8. Install the spring and tensioner with the attaching bolt. Move the tensioner until the spring is fully extended and temporarily tighten the tensioner bolt to hold it in place.

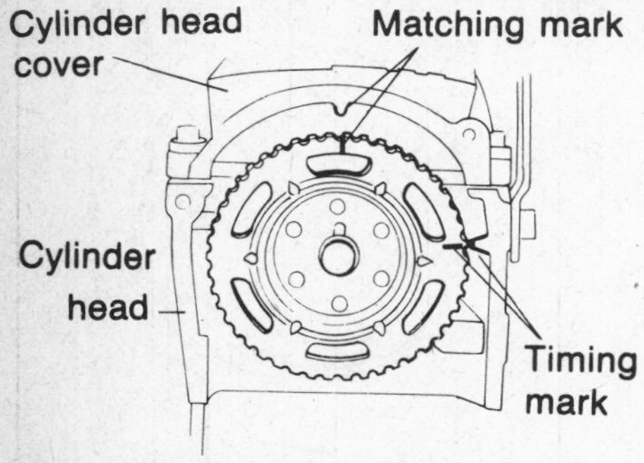


**Timing mark alignment on 323 without turbo**

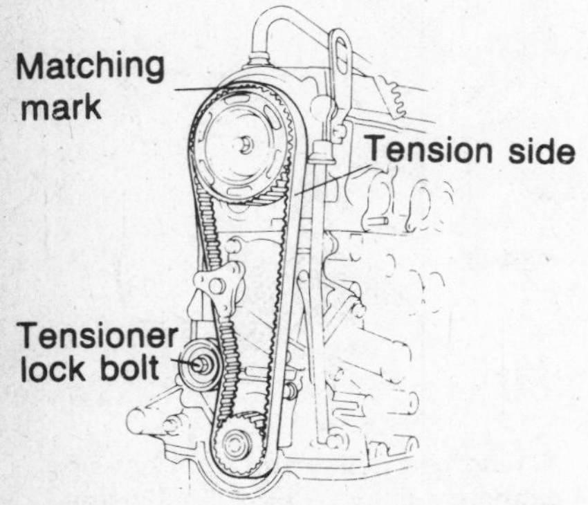


**Timing belt and tensioner on 323 without turbo**

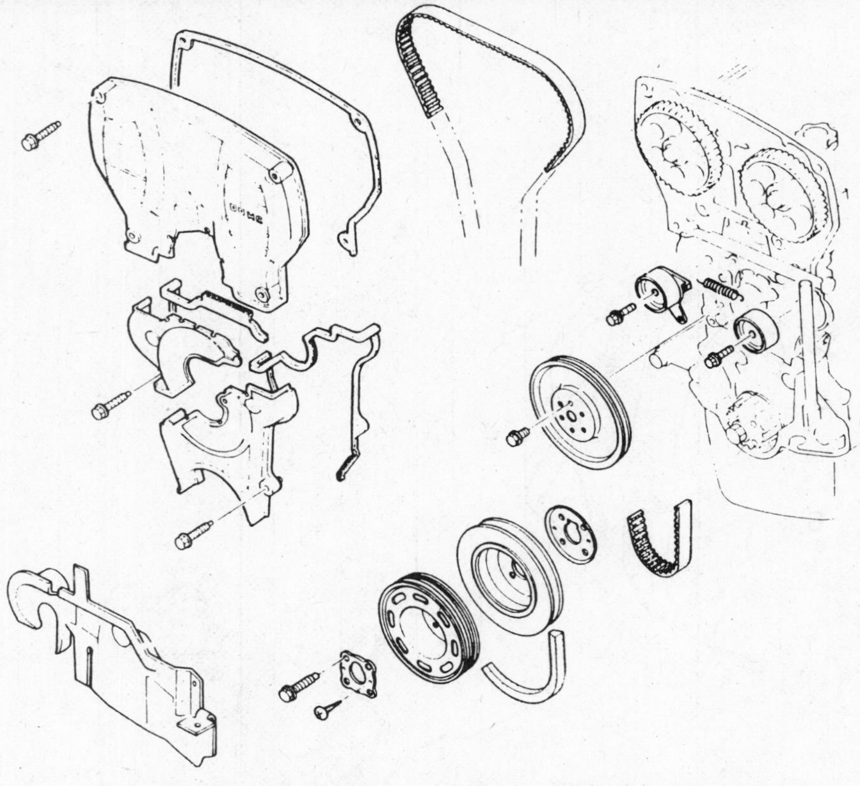

**Timing belt cover and related components – 1988–90 323 with turbo**

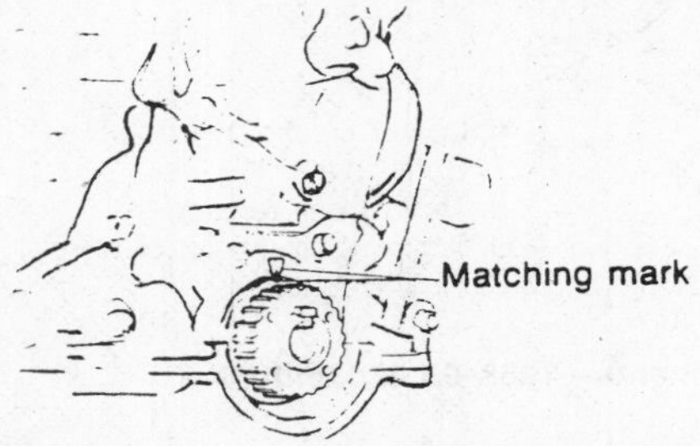

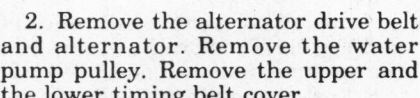

**Crankshaft gear timing mark alignmemt – 1988–90 323 with turbo**

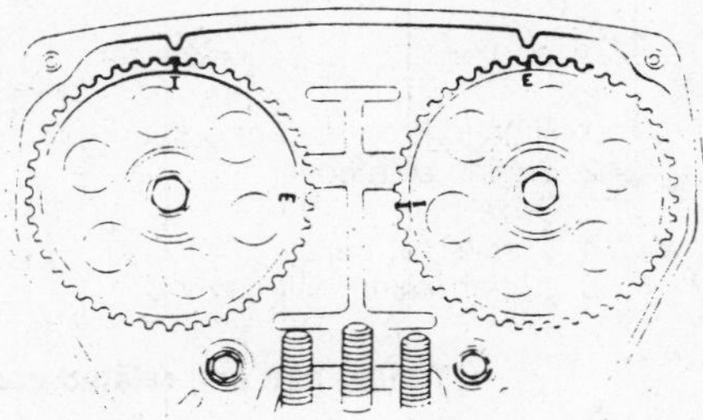

**Camshaft gear timing mark alignment – 1988–90 323 with turbo**

9. Install the timing belt. Make that there is no slack at the side of the water pump and idler pulleys. Old belts should be installed in the original direction of rotation.
10. Loosen the tensioner lock bolt and turn the crankshaft twice in the direction of engine rotation to align all the timing marks.
11. Make sure all timing marks are aligned correctly. If not, remove the timing belt tensioner and timing belt and repeat Steps 7–10 until all the timing marks are correctly aligned. Torque the tensioner lock bolt to 27–38 ft. lbs. Check the timing belt deflection. Correct deflection is 0.30–0.33 in. If the deflection is not correct, loosen the tensioner lock bolt and adjust the tension by repeating Steps 10 and 11 or replace the tensioner spring.
12. Install the baffle plate so that the curved side faces outward. Torque the pulley screws to 9–13 ft. lbs.
13. Complete the installation of the remaining components in reverse of the removal procedure. Connect the negative battery cable, check and/or adjust the ignition timing and the idle speed.

### *1986–90 323 without Turbo*

1. Disconnect the negative battery cable. Remove the engine side cover. Remove the air conditioning belt and the power steering pump belt.
2. Remove the alternator drive belt and alternator. Remove the water pump pulley. Remove the upper and the lower timing belt cover.
3. Turn the crankshaft to position the matching mark of the camshaft pulley is aligned with the cylinder head and the cylinder head cover timing mark.
4. Remove the crankshaft pulley mounting bolts and the pulley along with the baffle plate.
5. Remove the tensioner pulley lock bolt, the pulley and the spring.
6. Remove the timing belt and mark an arrow in the direction of rotation on the timing belt.
7. To remove the camshaft (water pump) pulley, use a suitable tool to lock the pulley in place so as to keep it from turning and remove the pulley retaining nut or bolt. To remove the crankshaft pulley, remove the center bolt and the pulley.
8. Reinstall the camshaft and crankshaft pulleys if they where removed. Install the timing belt as follows, be sure the timing mark on the timing belt pulley is aligned with the matching mark. Make sure that the matching mark of the camshaft pulley is aligned with the cylinder head and the cylinder head cover timing mark. If it is not, turn the camshaft to align it.
9. Install the timing belt tensioner and spring. Temporarily secure it as the spring is fully extended.
10. Install the timing belt, if using the old timing belt, be sure it is reinstalled in the same direction of previous rotation. Also make sure there is

no oil, grease or dirt on the timing belt.

11. Loosen the tensioner lock bolt. Turn the crankshaft twice in the diretion of rotation. Align the timing marks.

12. Make sure the timing marks are correctly aligned, if they are not aligned, remove the timing belt tensioner and timing belt and repeat Steps 8–12.

13. Tighten the timing belt tensioner lock bolt to 14–19 ft. lbs. Check the timing belt tension. The timing belt deflection should be 0.35–0.51 in. at 22 lbs.

14. Complete the installation by reversing the removal procedure.

### *1988–90 323 with Turbo*

1. Disconnect the negative battery cable. Remove the engine side cover. Remove the required drive belts. Remove the water pump pulley and crankshaft pulley.

**NOTE: Remove the number three engine mount installation bolts, then lower the engine in order to remove the air conditioning pulley, power steering pulley and the crankshaft pulley.**

2. Position the engine at TDC on the compression stroke.

3. Remove the timing cover assembly retaining bolts. Remove the upper, middle and lower timing covers from their mountings.

4. Remove the baffle plate. Remove the timing belt tensioner and spring. Remove the timing belt from the engine. If the old belt is being reused, mark the direction of rotation. Be sure that the timing mark on the timing belt pulley is aligned with the mark on the engine. Be sure that the camshaft pulleys are properly aligned.

5. Install the spring and tensioner with the attaching bolt. Move the tensioner until the spring is fully extended and temporarily tighten the tensioner bolt to hold it in place.

6. Install the timing belt by keeping the right side of the belt as tight as possible. Old belts must be installed in the original direction of rotation.

7. Turn the crankshaft twice in the normal direction of rotation and make sure that all the timing marks are aligned. Loosen the tensioner lock bolt and apply tension to the belt.

8. Torque the tensioner lock bolt to 27–38 ft. lbs. and turn the crankshaft twice in the normal direction of rotation to ensure all the timing marks are aligend correctly.

9. Measure the tension between the camshaft pulleys. The deflection should be between 0.33–0.45 in. between the pulleys. If not correct, repeat Steps 5–8 or replace the tensioner

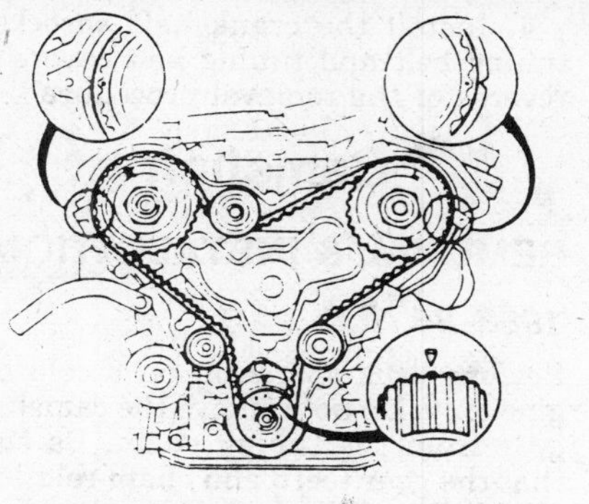

**Timing belt alignment marks – 929**

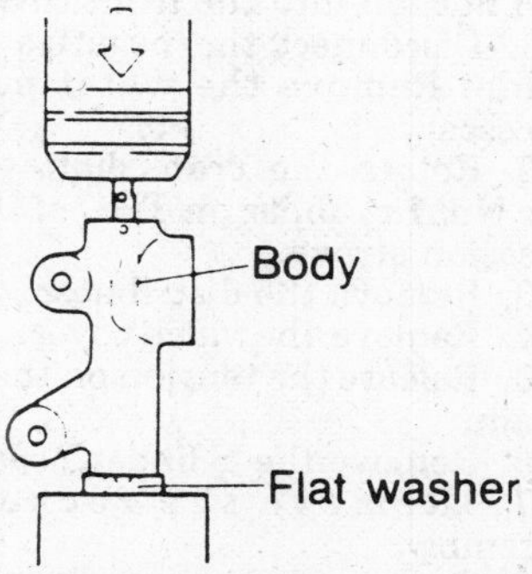


**Pressing the rod into the auto tesnioner body – 929**

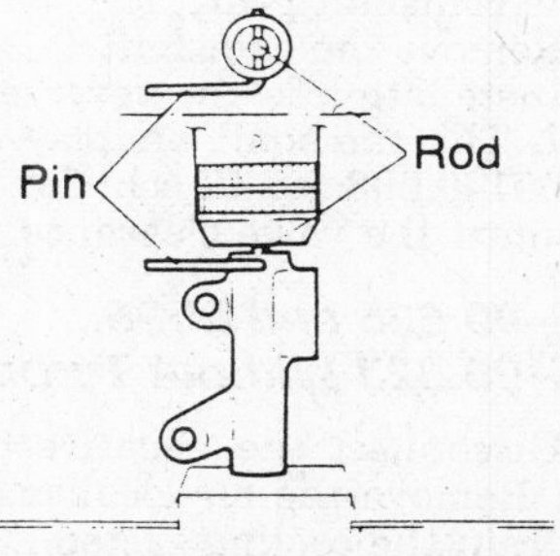


**Using pin to hold auto tensioner rod in place during installation – 929**

spring to adjust the tension to specification.

10. Installation of the remaining components is reverse of the removal procedure. During installation, make sure that the curved surface of the baffle plate faces outward. Torque the crankshaft pulley bolts to 109–152 inch lbs. and the No. 3 engine mount bracket to 44–63 ft. lbs. Adjust the drive belt tension and check the ignition timing.

### *1988–90 929*

1. Position the engine at TDC on the compression stroke. Properly relieve the fuel system pressure. Disconnect the negative battery cable. Remove the air cleaner assembly. Drain the cooling system and remove the spark plug wires.

2. Remove the fresh air duct assembly. Remove the cooling fan and radiator cowling. Remove the drive belts.

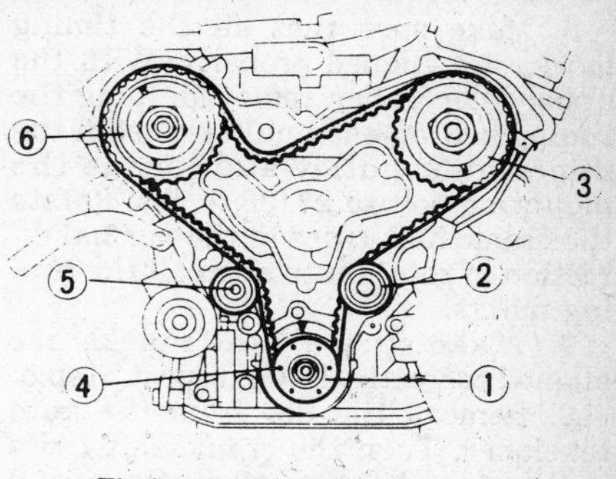


**Timing belt installation – 929**

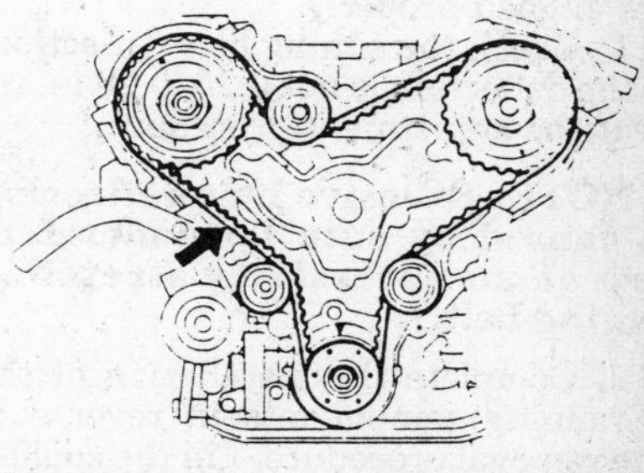

**Checking timing belt deflection on 929**

3. Remove the air conditioning compressor idler pulley. If necessary, remove the compresser and position it to the side.

4. Remove the crankshaft pulley and baffle plate. Remove the coolant bypass hose. Remove the upper radiator hose.

5. Remove the timing belt cover assembly retaining bolts. Remove the timing belt cover assembly and gasket. Turn the crankshaft to align the mating marks of the pulleys.

6. Remove the upper idler pulley. Remove the timing belt from the pulleys. If reusing the belt be sure to mark the direction of rotation. Unbolt and remove the timing belt automatic tensioner.

**NOTE: Prior to installation of the timing belt, the automatic tensioner must be loaded. For this operation a press that is capable of producing 2000 lbs. of force will be required.**

7. To load the tensioner, place a flat washer on the bottom of the tensioner body to prevent damage to the body. Press the rod into the tensioner body using an arbor press or vise. Do not use more than 2000 lbs of pressure. Once the rod is fully inserted into the body, insert a bent pin or small Allen wrench through the body to hold the rod in place. Remove the unit from the press and install onto the block and torque the mounting bolt to 14–19 ft. lbs. Leave the pin in place.

8. Make sure that all the timing marks are aligned properly. With the upper idler pulley removed, hang the timing belt on each pulley. Install the upper idler pulley and torque the mounting bolt to 27–38 ft. lbs. Rotate the crankshaft twice in the normal direction of rotation to align all the timing marks.
9. Make sure all the marks are aligned correctly. If not, repeat Step 8.
10. Remove the pin from the auto tensioner. Turn the crankshaft twice in the normal direction of rotation and make sure that all the timing marks are aligned properly.
11. Check the timing belt deflection. If the deflection is not 0.20–0.28 in. repeat the adjustment procedure.

**NOTE: Excesive belt deflection is caused by auto tensioner failure or an excessively stretched timing belt.**

12. Complete the installation of the remaining components in reverse of the removal procedure. Fill the cooling system to the proper level. Adjust the belt tension. Check and/or adjust the ignition timing and the idle speed.

## Front Cover Oil Seal

### REMOVAL & INSTALLATION

#### *1983–85 GLC*

1. Disconnect the negative battery cable. Drain the cooling system, except GLC front wheel drive.
2. Remove the radiator, except GLC front wheel drive.
3. Remove the drive belts and crankshaft pulley.
4. Pry the front oil seal carefully from the timing case cover.
5. Installation is the reverse of the removal procedure.

#### *Except 1983–85 GLC*

1. Remove the timing belt covers, timing belt, and crankshaft sprocket as described above and below.
2. With a flat bladed screwdriver, carefully pry the seal out of the front cover being careful not to damage the bore of the oil pump housing with the screwdriver blade. Clean the seal bore out thoroughly. No dirt or grease should be allowed to remain inside the bore, as such foreign matter will cause premature failure of the new oil seal.
3. Coat the lip of the new seal with engine oil. Using a piece of pipe that is just slightly smaller than the bore of the oil pump and about the diameter of the seal itself, tap a new seal in place. Position the seal so its front edge is aligned with the front edge of the oil pump body.
4. Install the crankshaft sprocket, timing belt and timing belt covers in reverse of the removal procedure.

## Camshaft

### REMOVAL & INSTALLATION

#### *1983–85 GLC*

Perform this operation on a cold engine only. Do not remove the camshaft gear from the timing chain. Be sure that the gear teeth and chain relationship is not disturbed. Wire the chain and cam gear to a place so that they will not fall into the front cover.

1. Disconnect the negative battery cable. Remove the water pump, if necessary.
2. Rotate the crankshaft to place the No. 1 cylinder on TDC of the compression stroke.
3. Remove the distributor.
4. Remove the valve cover.
5. Release the tension on the timing chain.
6. Remove the cylinder head bolts.
7. Remove the rocker arm assembly.
8. Remove the nut, washer and distributor gear from the camshaft.
9. Remove the nut and washer holding the camshaft gear.
10. Remove the camshaft.
11. Installation is the reverse of removal. The camshaft endplay should be 0.001–0.008 in. Check the timing and adjust the valve clearance.

#### *1983–90 626 and MX-6, 1986–90 323 Without Turbo*

1. Disconnect the negative battery cable. Remove the air cleaner assembly. Drain the cooling system.
2. Remove the front cover assembly. Remove the cam gear. As required remove the thermostat housing.
3. Remove the distributor assembly. Remove the cylinder head cover. On 1983–85 626, remove the fuel pump. On the 1986–89 626 and MX-6, remove the rear housing.
4. Remove the rocker arm assembly. If equipped, remove the thrust plate.
5. Remove the camshaft from the cylinder head.
6. Installation is the reverse of the removal procedure. Install a new seal in the front cover housing and new gaskets as necessary.

#### *1988–90 323 with Turbo*

1. Disconnect the negative battery cable. Position the engine at TDC on the compression stroke. Remove the air cleaner assembly. Remove the spark plugs.
2. Remove the cylinder head cover.

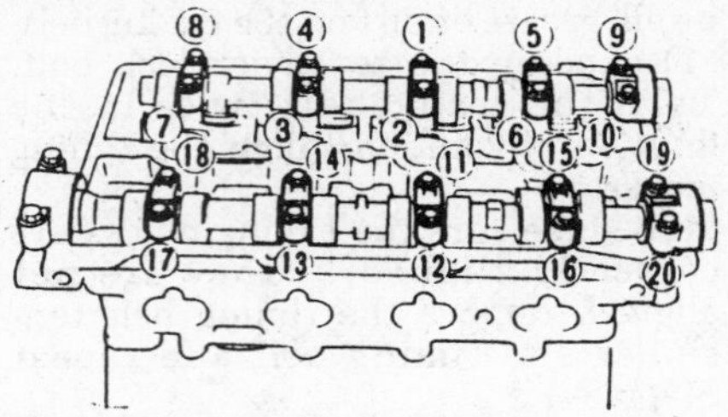


**Camshaft bolt torque sequence – 1988–90 323 with turbo**

3. Remove the distributor. Remove the timing cover assembly. Remove the timing belt and camshaft pulleys. Remove the seal plate.
4. Remove the camshaft retaining bolts. Remove the camshafts from the cylinder head. Remove the camshaft oil seals and discard. Keep the exhaust and the intake camshaft parts separate.
5. Coat the camshaft journal with a liberal amount clean engine oil and lay the camshafts into the cylinder head.
6. Coat the new camshaft oil seals with clean engine oil and install them. Coat the front surface of the camshaft caps with a thin coat of sealant. Install the camshaft caps and torque the retaining bolts to specification and in the proper sequence. Camshaft caps must be installed according to the number stamped on the caps.
7. Install the seal plate and torque the retaining bolts to 69–95 inch lbs.
8. Install the exhaust side camshaft pulley with the **E** mark straight up. Install the intake side camshaft pulley with the **I** mark straight up. Hold the camshaft journal stationary with the proper tool and torque the pulley bolts to 36–45 ft. lbs.
9. Complete the installation of the remaining components in reverse of the removal preocedure. Be sure to use new gaskets or RTV sealant, as required.

#### *1988–90 929*

**NOTE: The following procedure is given for camshaft removal after the cylinder head has been removed from the engine. If removal is attempted without removing the cylinder head from the engine, refer to the appropriate sections for component removal procedures necessary to gain access to the camshaft.**

1. Properly relieve the fuel system pressure. Disconnect the negative battery cable. Remove the air cleaner assembly.
2. Remove the cylinder head from the engine. Position the cylinder head assembly in a suitable holding fixture.
3. Remove the rocker arm shaft re-

taining bolts. Remove the rocker arm shafts.

4. Remove the camshaft sprocket and and gently pry the oil seals from the cylinder head. Carefully withdraw the camshaft from the cylinder head.

5. Coat the camshaft journals, lobes and bearings with a liberal amount of clean engine oil and slide the camshaft into the cylinder head. Install the thrust plate and torque the mounting bolt to 69–95 inch lbs.

6. Coat the lip of the new camshaft oil seals with clean engine oil and drive the seals into the head using an appropriate seal installation tool.

7. Complete the installation of the cylinder head in reverse of the removal procedure. When installing the camshaft pulleys, align the left and right camshaft so that the keyways are facing up, The camshaft pulleys are stamped **L** and **R** for the left and right banks respectively. Make sure that these marks are facing outward during installation. Torque the pulley bolts to 52–59 ft. lbs. Be sure to use new gaskets or RTV sealant, as required. Torque the cylinder head to specification and in the proper sequence.

## Piston and Connecting Rod

### POSITIONING

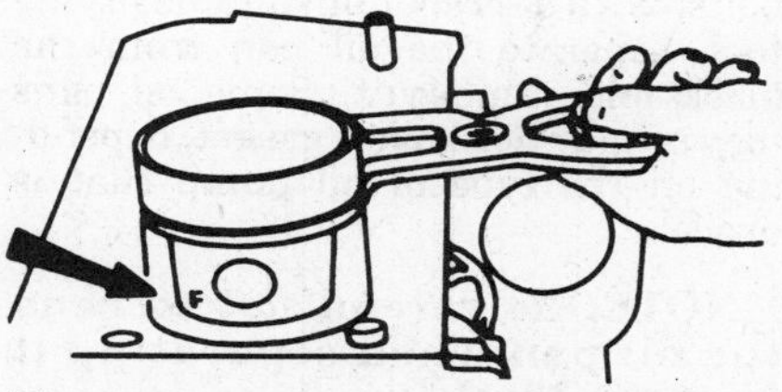

The "F" marks (arrow) face the front of the engine

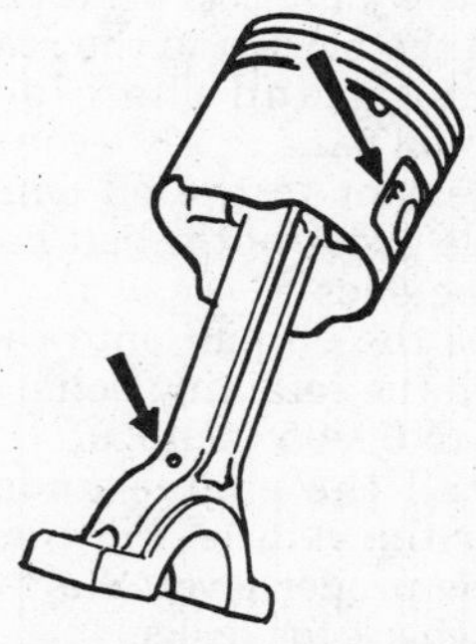

Piston and connecting rod positioning

#### Except 1988–90 929

When assembling the piston and connecting rod, the big end of the rod and the **F** mark on the piston must face in the same direction. The pistons should be installed in the block with the **F** facing the front of the engine. The oil hole of the connecting rod must face the intake manifold.

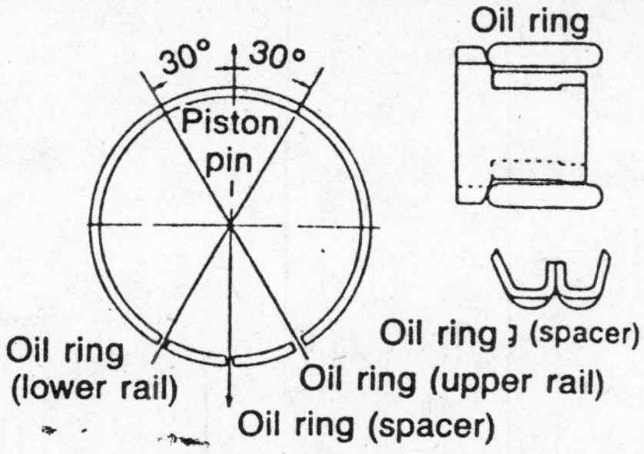


Oil control ring positioning – 323

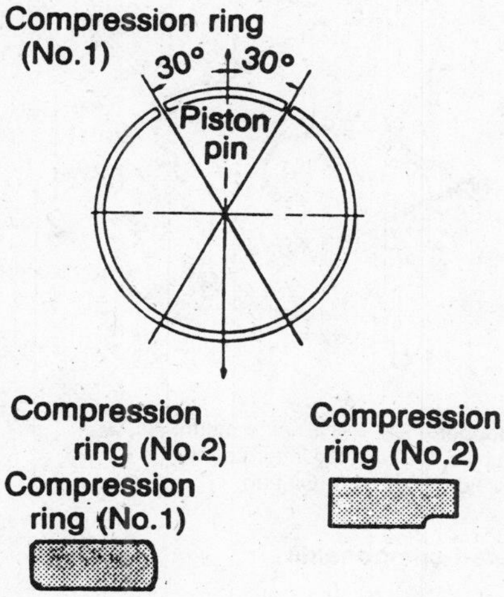


Compression ring positioning – 323

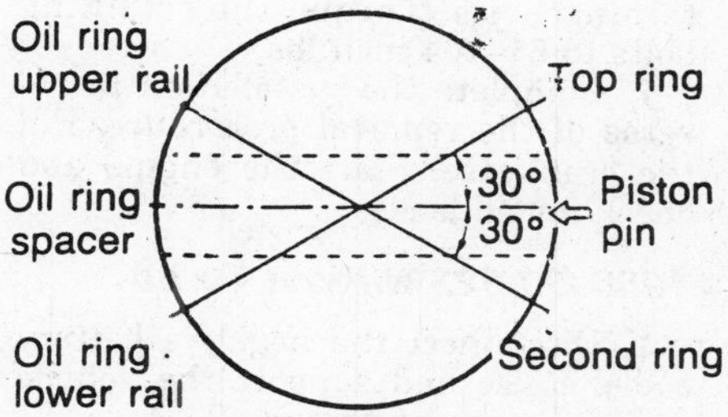


Piston ring positioning – 626, MX-6 and 929

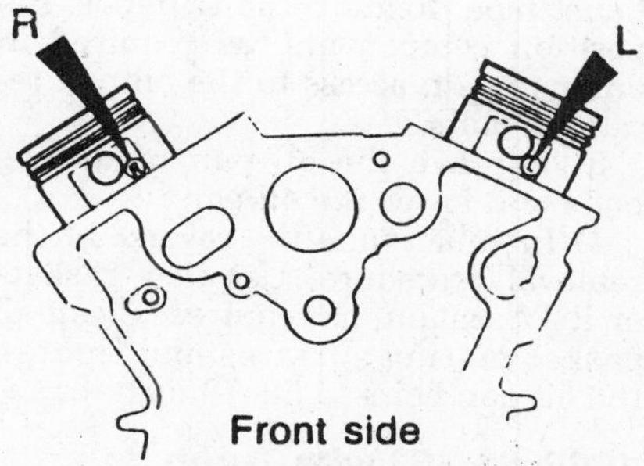


Piston positioning – 929

#### 1988–90 929

On the 929, inert each piston assembly into the cylinder block with the **L** mark (left bank) and the **R** (right bank) facing the front of the engine. The left and right bank pistons are the same.

# GASOLINE PISTON ENGINE LUBRICATION

## Oil Pan

### REMOVAL & INSTALLATION

#### 1983–85 GLC

1. Raise and support the vehicle safely. Disconnect negative battery cable. Remove the engine splash shield or skid plate.
2. Remove the engine rear brace attaching bolts and loosen the bolts on the left side, if equipped.
3. Loosen the front motor mounts, raise the front of the engine and block up to gain clearance, if necessary (except on GLC front wheel drive).
4. Remove the oil pan. Remove the oil pump pickup tube, if necessary, to remove the oil pan.
5. Installation is the reverse of the removal procedure. Thoroughly scrape the gasket contact surfaces and use new gaskets or RTV sealant, as required. Torque the oil pan bolts to 6 ft. lbs. Refill the crankcase.

#### 1983–87 626

1. Disconnect the negative battery cable. Raise and support the vehicle, safely. Drain the engine oil. Remove the torque stopper. Remove the right wheel and splash shield.
2. Remove the front exhaust pipe and raise the passenger side of the engine slightly, using the proper lifting equipment. Remove engine mount No. 3.
3. Remove the front engine lower cover. Remove the oil pan retaining bolts and lower the oil pan.
4. Installation is the reverse of the removal procedure. Be sure to use new gaskets or RTV sealant, as required.

#### 1988–89 626 and MX-6

1. Disconnect the negative battery cable. Raise and support the vehicle safely. Drain the engine oil.

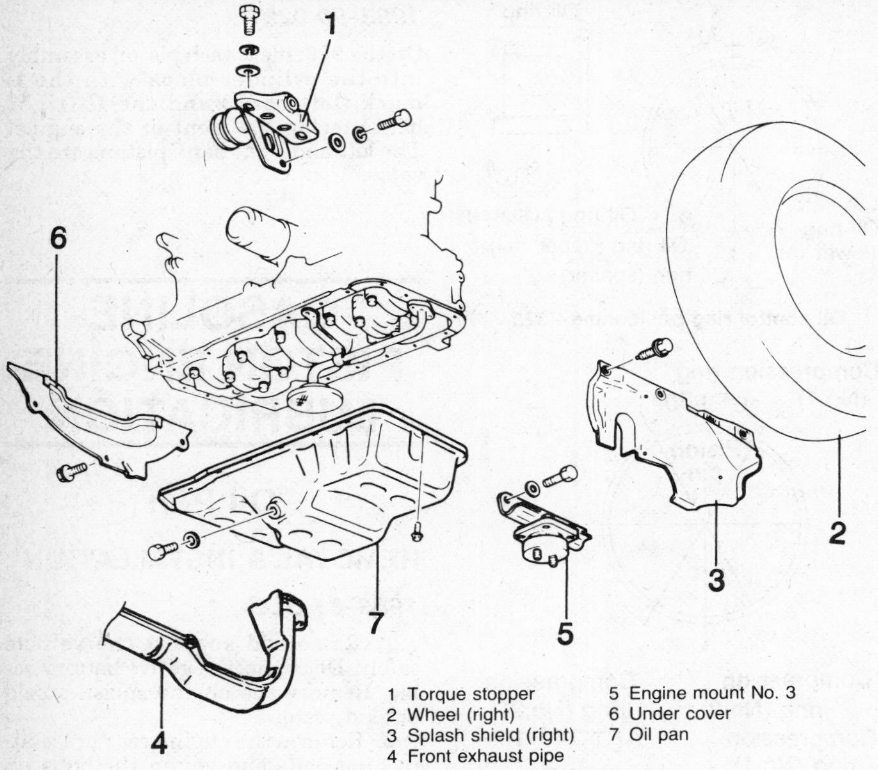


1 Torque stopper
2 Wheel (right)
3 Splash shield (right)
4 Front exhaust pipe
5 Engine mount No. 3
6 Under cover
7 Oil pan

**Typical oil pan and related components**

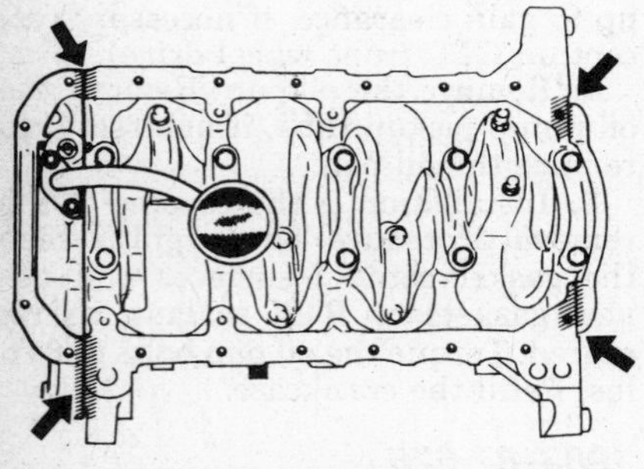

**Use sealer at these locations when installing the oil pan**

2. Unbolt and remove the exhaust pipe and gusset plate. Remove the clutch housing cover.
3. Remove the right hand subframe.
4. Remove the oil pan retaining bolts and lower the oil pan. Remove the oil stainer and stiffener.
5. To install, thoroughly clean all contact surfaces and apply a continuous bead of sealnt to the stiffener around the inside of the bolt holes. Raise the stiffener up onto the bottom of the block and install the retaining bolts. Torque the retaining bolts to 61–104 inch lbs. Install a new strainer and torque the bolts to 61–104 inch lbs.
6. Apply sealant to the oil pan contact surface in the same manner as the stiffener. Raise the oil pan up and against the stiffener and install the retaining bolts. Torque the retaining bolts to 61–104 inch lbs.
7. Complete the installation in reverse of the removal procerdure. Fill the crankcase. Start the engine and check for oil leaks.

### *1986–90 323 without Turbo*

1. Disconnect the negative battery cable. Raise and support the vehicle safely. Drain the engine oil.
2. Remove the engine splash shields. Disconnect and lower the exhaust pipe. Remove the stiffener. Reposition components, as required in order to gain access to the oil pan retaining bolts.
3. Remove the oil pan mounting bolts and lower the oil pan.
4. Installation is the reverse of the removal procedure. Use new gaskets or RTV sealant, as required. Clean all gasket mating surfaces and tighten the oil pan bolts to 52–78 inch lbs.

### *1988–90 323 with Turbo*

1. Disconnect the negative battery cable. Mount engine support tool 49B0175A0, and suspend the engine. Raise and support the vehicle safely.
2. Drain the engine oil. Remove the engine under cover assembly. Remove the exhaust pipe bracket. Remove the exhaust pipe.
3. Remove the turbocharger bracket. Remove the oil pan retaining bolts. Remove the oil pan from the engine by prying gently on the area where the pan mates with the transaxle and nowhere else. Loosen the mounting member bolts until the pan can be removed. Clean all the gasket contact surfaces thoroughly.
4. Apply sealant to the block and install the gaskets onto the oil pump body and the rear cover making sure that the projections are properly positioned in the notches.
5. Apply a continuous bead of silicone sealant to the oil pan inside the bolt holes. Position the oil pan onto the transaxle and install the transaxle mounting bolts. Torque the upper bolt to 27–38 ft. lbs. and the lower bolt to 14–19 ft. lbs. Install the oil pump retaining bolts and torque to 69–95 inch lbs. in several steps.
6. Complete the installation in reverse of the removal procedure. Be sure to use new gaskets or RTV sealant, as required.

### *1988–90 929*

1. Disconnect the negative battery cable. Raise and support the vehicle safely.
2. Drain the engine oil. Remove the engine under cover.
3. Remove the oil pan retaining bolts. With a scraper or suitable prying tool, separate the oil pan from the block and remove it. Some oil pans may or may not have a gasket, depending on the type of oil pump that is used.

**NOTE: Be careful not to bend the oil pan when separating it from the block.**

4. On oil pans with a gasket, apply sealer to the joints between the front cover and the block and the rear main seal housing and the block. On gasketless oil pans, apply a continuous bead of sealant to the oil pan flange around the inside of the bolt holes and overlap the ends.
5. Raise the oil pan onto the block and install the retaining bolts. Torque the bolts to 69–95 inch lbs.
6. Install the engine undercover and lower the vehicle. Fill the crankcase to the proper level. Start the engine and check for leaks.

## Rear Main Bearing Oil Seal

### REMOVAL & INSTALLATION

### *1983–85 GLC*

If the rear main oil seal is being replaced independently of any other parts, it can be done with the engine in place. If the rear main oil seal and the rear main bearing are being replaced together, the engine must be removed.

1. Refer to the "Transmission Or Transaxle, Removal and Installation" procedure and remove the transmission/transaxle.

2. Remove the clutch disc, pressure plate and flywheel if equipped with manual transmission/transaxle. Remove the drive plate if equipped with automatic transmission/transaxle.

3. Punch 2 holes in the crankshaft rear oil seal. They should be punched on opposite sides of the crankshaft, just above the bearing cap to cylinder block split line.

4. Install a sheet metal screw in each hole. Pry against both screws at the same time to remove the oil seal.

5. Clean the oil recess in the cylinder block and bearing cap. Clean the oil seal surface on the crankshaft.

6. Coat the oil seal surfaces with oil. Coat the oil surface and the seal surface on the crankshaft with Lubriplate®. Install the new oil seal and make sure that it is not cocked. Be sure that the seal surface was not damaged.

7. Install the flywheel. Coat the threads of the flywheel attaching bolts with oil resistant sealer.

8. To complete the installation, reverse the removal procedure.

### *1986–90 323 and 1983–90 626 and MX-6*

1. Disconnect the negative battery cable. Raise and support the vehicle safely. Remove the transaxle.

2. If equipped with a manual transaxle, remove the pressure plate, the clutch disc and the flywheel. If equipped with an automatic transaxle, remove the drive plate from the crankshaft.

3. Remove the rear oil pan-to-seal housing bolts.

4. Remove the rear main seal housing bolts and the housing from the engine.

5. Remove the oil seal from the rear main housing.

6. Clean the gasket mounting surfaces.

7. To install, use a new seal, coat the seal and the housing with oil. Press the seal into the housing, using an arbor press.

8. To complete the installation, use new gaskets, apply sealant to the oil pan mounting surface and reverse the removal procedure. Torque the rear seal housing bolts to 6–8 ft. lbs.

### *1988–90 929*

1. Raise and support the vehicle safely. Remove the transmission from the vehicle.

2. If equipped with manual transmission, remove the clutch pressure plate and flywheel.

3. If equipped with automatic transmission, remove the flywheel assembly.

4. Drain the engine oil. Remove the engine oil pan.

5. Remove the rear main seal cover retaining bolts. Remove the rear main seal cover. Remove the seal from the rear cover.

6. Installation is the reverse of the removal procedure. Apply clean engine oil to the seal before pressing it into the cover.

7. After installing the rear cover cut away the portion of the gasket that projects out toward the oil pan side.

# Oil Pump

## REMOVAL & INSTALLATION

### *1983–85 GLC*

1. Disconnect the negative battery cable. Raise and support the vehicle safely. Remove the oil pan.

2. Remove the lock washer, nut, sprockets and chain, if equipped.

3. Remove the oil pump attaching bolts and adjusting shims.

4. Remove the oil pump assembly.

5. To install, use new gaskets, sealant and O-ring and reverse the removal procedure.

### *1983–90 626 and MX-6 and 1986–90 323 Without Turbo*

1. Disconnect the negative battery cable. Remove the front cover assembly. Remove the timing belt, tensioner and required pulleys.

2. Raise and support the vehicle safely. Drain the engine oil. Remove the oil pan. Remove the oil pump strainer and pickup tube.

3. On the 1986–90 626 and 1988–90 MX-6, remove the number three engine bracket.

4. As required lower the vehicle. Remove the oil pump retaining bolts. Remove the oil pump from its mounting.

5. Replace the oil seal in the oil pump and coat the lip with clean engine oil. Fill the oil pump cavity with vasoline.

6. Installation is the reverse of the removal procedure. On 323 torque the pump bolts to 14–19 ft. lb. and the pan bolts to 6–6.5 ft. lb. On 1988–89 626 and MX-6 torque the M8 (smaller) bolts to 14–19 ft. lbs. and the M10 (larger) bolts to 27–38 ft. lbs.

### *1988–90 323 with Turbo*

1. Disconnect the negative battery cable. Remove the timing cover assembly. Remove the timing belt pulley.

2. Raise and support the vehicle safely. Drain the engine oil. Remove the oil pan.

3. Remove the oil strainer. Remove the oil pump retaining bolts. Remove the oil pump from its mounting.

4. Installation is the reverse of the removal procedure. Torque the oil pump retaining bolts to 14–19 ft. lbs. Be sure to use new gaskets or RTV sealant, as required. Adjust the timing.

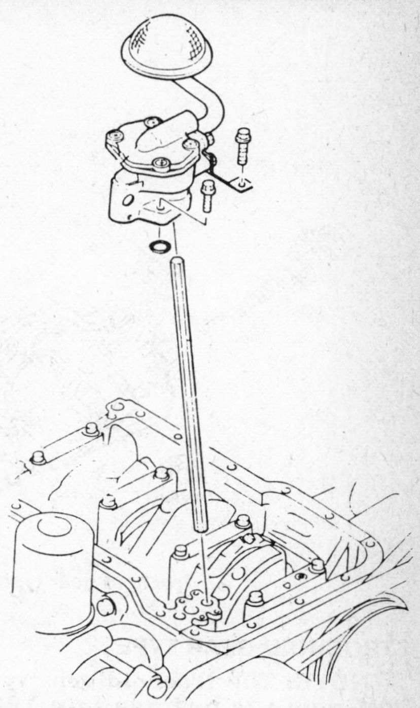

**Positive displacement gear type oil pump 1988–90 929**

### *1988–90 929*

#### POSITIVE DISPLACEMENT GEAR TYPE

1. Disconnect the negative battery cable. Raise and support the vehicle safely.

2. Drain the engine oil. Remove the engine under cover. Remove the oil pan retaining bolts. Remove the oil pan from the engine.

3. Remove the oil pump and strainer retaining bolts. Remove the oil pump assembly from its mounting.

4. Remove the oil pump drive shaft and O-ring.

5. Installation is the reverse of the removal procedure. Torque the oil pump retaining bolts to 6–8 ft. lbs. Be sure to use new gaskets or RTV sealant, as required. Engage the oil pump driveshaft and check for freedom of rotation.

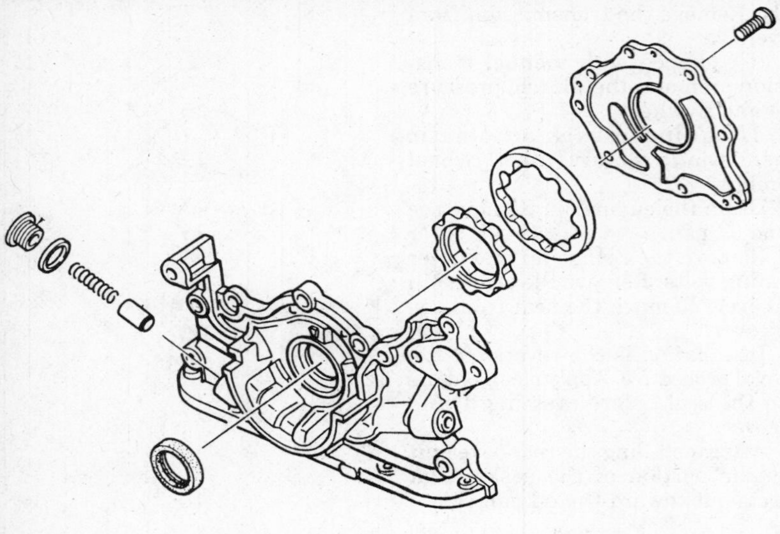

Trochoid gear type oil pump on 1989–90 929

### TROCHOID GEAR TYPE

**NOTE: The trochoid gear type oil pump is not used on 1988 models.**

1. Disconnect the negative battery cable. Raise and support the vehicle safely.
2. Drain the engine oil and the cooling system.
3. Remove the timing belt and the timing belt pulley and key. Remove the thermostat and gasket.
4. Remove the oil pan, oil strainer and O-ring.
5. Unbolt and remove the oil pump and gasket.
6. Installation is the reverse of the removal procedure. Press in a new oil seal and coat the seal lip with oil. Use a new gasket, O-ring and sealant as required. Torque the oil pump retaining bolts to 14–19 ft. lbs.

# GASOLINE PISTON ENGINE COOLING

## Radiator

### REMOVAL & INSTALLATION

1. Disconnect the negative battery cable. Drain the radiator.
2. Remove the fan blades and shroud or disconnect the electrical harness from the electric fan motor and remove the fan and cowling mount. On 929, disconnect the vacuum hoses from the fresh air duct and remove the duct.
3. Remove the upper and lower hoses and coolant reservoir tank hose. Disconnect the transmission cooler lines, if equipped.
4. Remove the radiator mounting bolts and remove the radiator.
5. Install the radiator by reversing the removal procedure. Refill the cooling system.

## Water Pump

### REMOVAL & INSTALLATION

#### *1983–85 GLC*

1. Disconnect the negative battery cable. Drain the coolant.
2. On GLC front wheel drive, raise the front of the vehicle and safely support it safely. Remove the splash shield. Remove the drive belt, lower hose and bypass pipe with O-ring. Remove the water pump.
3. On all other vehicles, remove all drive belts. Remove the cooling fan and fan drive assembly. Remove the radiator cowling. Remove the air pump, if necessary. Remove the radiator lower hose, heater hose as required and bypass hose.
4. Loosen and remove the water pump mounting bolts, remove the water pump.

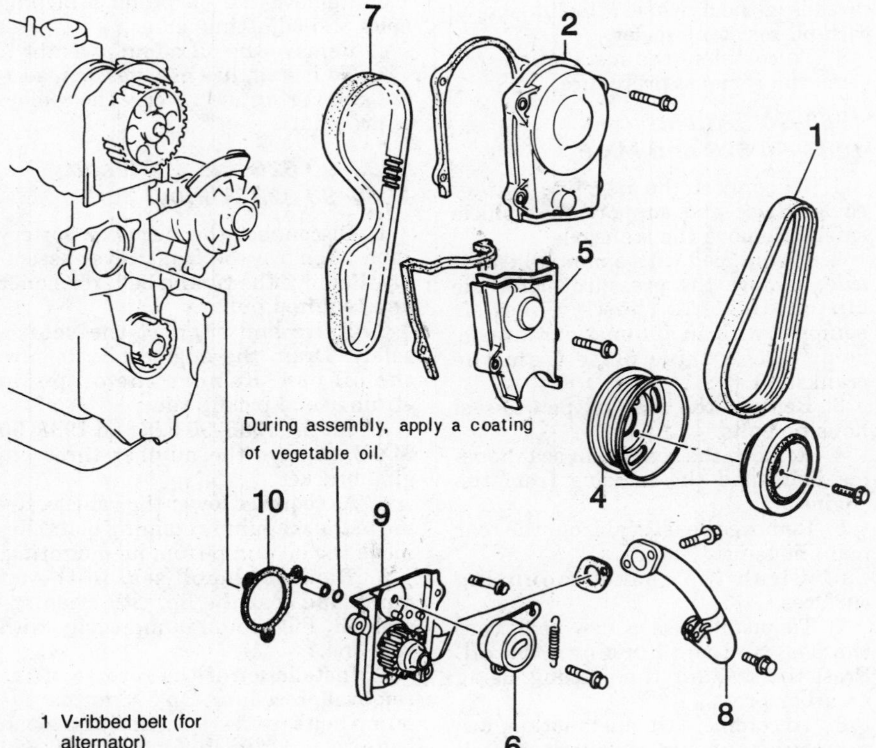


1 V-ribbed belt (for alternator)
2 Timing belt cover (upper)
3 Splash shield
4 Crankshaft pulley
5 Timing belt cover (lower)
6 Tensioner
7 Timing belt
8 Inlet pipe
9 Water pump
10 Gasket

Typical water pump and related components

5. Clean all gasket surfaces. Mount the new water pump and gasket. Tighten the mounting bolts evenly in several stages. The rest of the installation is in the reverse order of removal.

### *1983–90 626 and MX-6 and 1986–90 323 without Turbo*

**NOTE: Use special tool No. 49E301060 or equivalent on the engine flywheel gear to stop the engine from rotating during removal and installation of the crankshaft pulley.**

1. Disconnect the negative battery cable. Drain the cooling system. Turn the crankshaft so that the No. 1 cylinder piston is at TDC on the compression stroke.
2. Remove the front cover assembly, timing belt and required pulleys.
3. Remove the water inlet pipe from the water pump.
4. Remove the water pump retaining bolts. Remove the water pump from its mounting.
5. Installation is the reverse of the removal procedure. Use new O-rings and gaskets. 1988–90 626 and MX-6 use an O-ring and 3 rubber seals which must be replaced. Fill the cooling system and check the timing.

### *1988–90 323 with Turbo*

1. Disconnect the negative battery cable. Drain the cooling system. Position the engine at TDC on the compression stroke.
2. Remove the drive belts. Remove the water pump pulley. Remove the crankshaft pulley. Remove the baffle plate.
3. Remove the middle and lower timing belt covers. Remove the belt tensioner. Remove the tensioner spring. Remove the timing belt.
4. Remove the coolant inlet pipe. Remove the water pump retaining bolts. Remove the water pump from its mounting.
5. Installation is the reverse of the removal procedure. Be sure to use new gaskets or RTV sealant, as required. Torque the water pump retaining bolts to 14–19 ft. lbs.

### *1988–90 929*

1. Disconnect the negative battery cable. Drain the cooling system. Position the engine at TDC on the compression stroke.
2. Remove the drive belts. Remove the timing belt cover assembly. Remove the timing belt.
3. Remove the water pump retaining bolts. Remove the water pump from its mounting.
4. Installation is the reverse of the removal procedure. Be sure to use new gaskets or RTV sealant, as required.

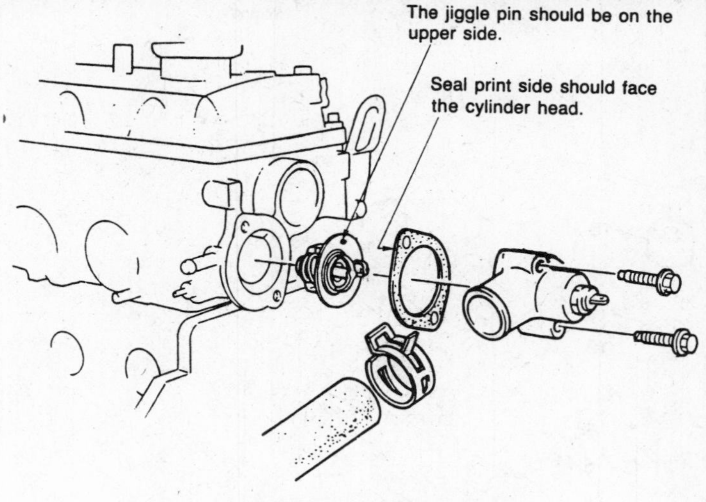


**Thermostat assembly—323**

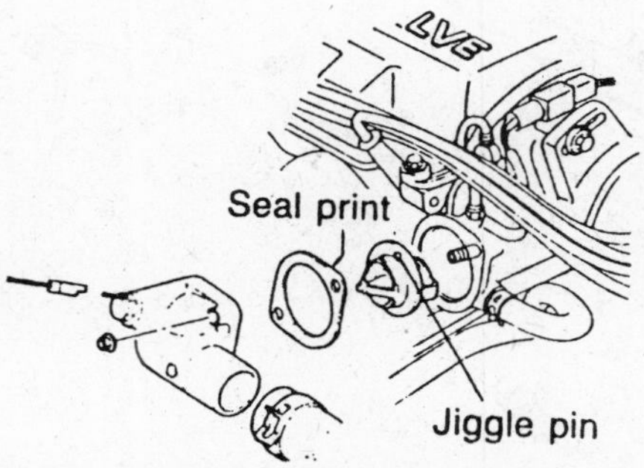


**Thermostat assembly—626 and MX-6**

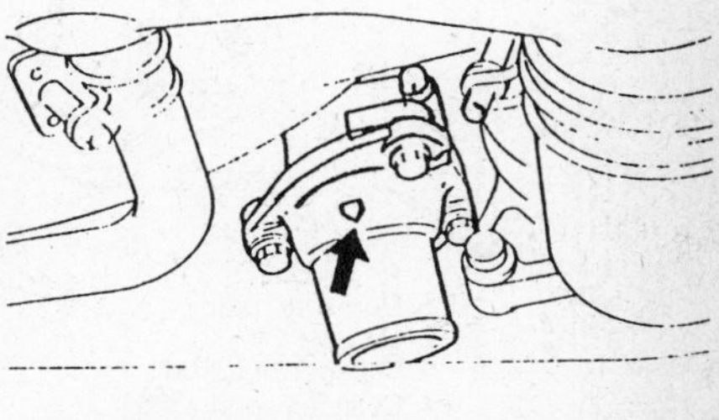

**Thermostat housing positioning—929**

## Thermostat

### REMOVAL & INSTALLATION

1. Disconnect the negative battery cable. Drain the cooling system.
2. Disconnect the radiator hose and the coolant temperature switch lead from the thermostat housing.
3. Remove the thermostat housing mounting bolts, housing, gasket and thermostat.
4. Clean all gasket surfaces. Install the new thermostat with the temperature sensing pellet downwards or toward the engine block. Use a new mounting gasket and install the housing.
5. To complete the installation, reverse the removal procedure. When installing the thermostat into the housing, be sure the jiggle pin is positioned upward. On 929, install the thermostat housing so that the mark is facing the front of the engine. Fill the cooling system.

# DIESEL ENGINE MECHANICAL

## Engine

### REMOVAL & INSTALLATION

1. Disconnect the negative battery cable.
2. Drain the engine oil, the transaxle oil and the engine coolant. Remove the hood.
3. Raise and support the vehicle safely. Remove both front wheels.
4. Disconnect the wires from the starter, the alternator, the cooling fan and the backup light switch connector at the transaxle.
5. Remove the oil pressure switch connector, the OSS and the after flow relays from the air cleaner bracket.
6. Disconnect the water level sensor and the temperature switch wiring connectors.
7. Disconnect the glow plug, the revolution sensor, the fuel cut relay and the water temperature sensor wiring connectors.

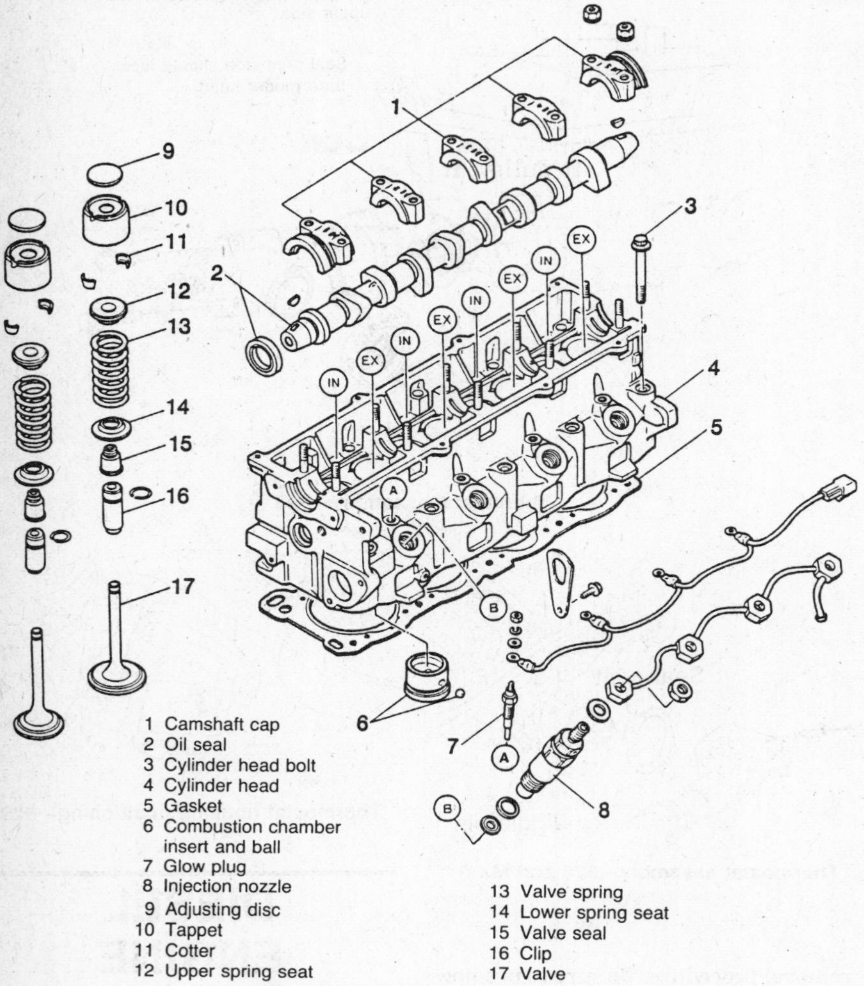


**Exploded view of the cylinder head—626 diesel**

8. Remove the air cleaner assembly and the air cleaner bracket.
9. Remove the radiator hoses, the heater hoses, the radiator coolant tank hose, the radiator and the mounts.
10. Remove the two fuel hoses from the fuel injection pump.
11. Remove the vacuum hose from the brake vacuum pipe, the two heater and the two oil bypass hoses from the oil cooler.
12. Remove the accelerator cable and the CSD wire from the fuel injection pump.
13. Remove the clutch release cylinder, the ground cable and speedometer cable from the transaxle.
14. Remove the exhaust pipe rubber supports, the brackets and the exhaust pipe from the exhaust manifold.
15. Separate the shift rods and the extension bars from the transaxle.
16. Remove the lower ball joint clamp bolts and separate the control arms from the steering knuckles.
17. Remove the tie rod ends from the steering knuckles.
18. Separate the axleshafts from the front wheels.
19. Place a pry bar between the right axleshaft to disconnect it from the joint shaft, pull out the axleshaft.
20. Remove the mounting nuts from the engine/transaxle mounts. Lower the vehicle.
21. Place a pry bar between the left axleshaft and the transaxle. Pry on the axleshaft to disconnect it from the transaxle. Be careful not to damage the oil seal of the axleshaft.
22. Connect a differential side gear holder tool 49–G030–455 to the transaxle case.
23. Properly position a suitable engine lifting device to the engine.
24. Remove the torque stopper from the front of the engine, the engine mounting bolts and the engine/transaxle assembly from the vehicle.
25. Installation is the reverse of the removal procedure.

## Cylinder Head

### REMOVAL & INSTALLATION

1. Disconnect the negative battery cable.
2. Remove the air cleaner tube. Drain the engine coolant and the engine oil.
3. Disconnect the heater outlet hose from the oil cooler and the upper radiator hose.
4. Remove the fuel inlet and return hoses from the fuel injection pump.
5. Disconnect the water temperature gauge wire, the flow plug connector and the ground strap from the engine.
6. Remove the fuel injection pipes.
7. Disconnect the exhaust pipe from the exhaust manifold.
8. Remove the right splash shield and the drive belts.
9. Remove the cylinder head cover with the gasket.
10. Remove the rear timing belt cover, the timing belt and the rear camshaft pulley bolt. Using the puller tool 49–S120–215A, pull the rear pulley from the camshaft.
11. Install two bolts (M8 × 1.25 × 45mm) through the injection pump pulley to bracket, to lack the pulley. Remove the injection pump pulley bolt, the two holding bolts and the pulley using tool 49–S120–215A.
12. Remove the tensioner, the spring, the lock bolt and the rear seal plate.
13. Remove the right timing belt cover and the top bolt of the left timing belt cover.
14. Align the camshaft pulleys mark with the mark on the front seal plate and turn the crankshaft 45 degrees in the direction of rotation.
15. Loosen the tensioner pulley lock bolt, push on the timing belt, between the camshaft and the water pump pulley, then straighten.
16. Rotate the camshaft pulley slightly and remove the timing belt from the pulley.
17. Using an adjustable wrench to hold the camshaft, remove the camshaft pulley bolt.
18. Using the puller tool 49–S120–215A, pull the camshaft pulley from the camshaft.
19. Remove the front seal plate lock bolts.
20. Loosen the camshaft bearing cap bolts, a little at a time, working from the outer caps, towards the center caps.
21. Remove the camshaft bolts, the camshaft bearing caps, the oil seals and the camshaft.
22. Loosen the cylinder head bolts, a little at a time, working from the outer

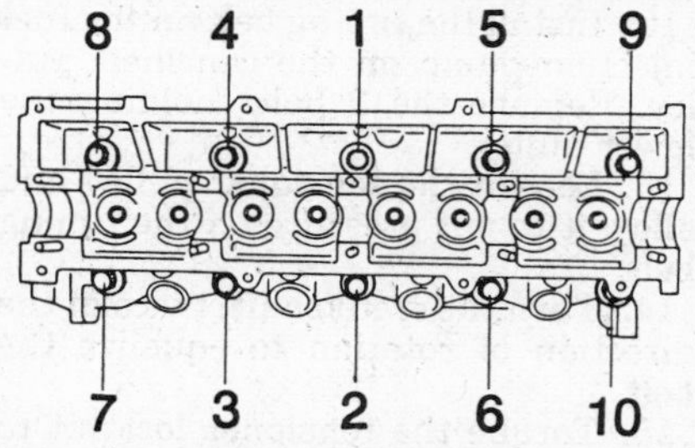


Cylinder head torquing sequence—diesel

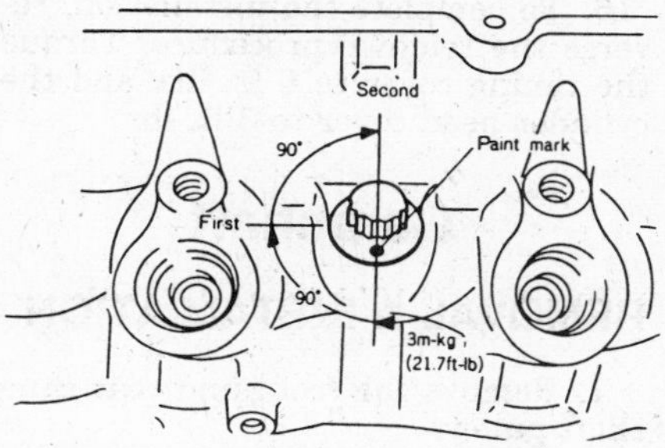


Cylinder bolt torquing procedure—diesel

bolts, towards the center bolts.

23. Remove the cylinder head from the engine. Remove the intake and the exhaust manifolds, if necessary. Clean the gasket mating surfaces.

24. To install, use a new head gasket, measure the cylinder head bolt lengths they should be 4.4371–4.4607 in. and make sure that the crankshaft is turned 45 degrees past the TDC of the No. 1 cylinder firing position.

25. Apply engine oil to the cylinder head bolt threads and torque them in sequence to 22 ft. lbs. Apply a paint or punch mark to the bolt heads. Retorque the bolts by turning 90 degrees and after the sequence, add another 90 degree turn.

26. Lubricate the camshaft and the bearing caps. Install the camshaft, the bearing caps and new oil seals. Torque the camshaft bearing caps bolts to 15–20 ft. lbs., starting at the center, tighten towards both ends.

27. Install the front seal plate, the front camshaft key and the pulley. Torque the pulley lock bolt to 41–48 ft. lbs.

28. Align the camshaft pulley mark with the alignment mark of the front seal plate.

29. Remove the inspection hole cover on the clutch housing. Position the timing indicator to the 45 degree mark on the flywheel.

30. Position the tensioner pulley near the water pump pulley and tighten the lock bolt.

31. Install the timing belt. Release the tensioner lock bolt.

32. Turn the crankshaft clockwise, twice and torque the tensioner lock bolt to 28 ft. lbs. Recheck the timing marks on the camshaft pulley and the flywheel.

33. Check the timing belt deflection, by pressing between the water pump pulley and the camshaft pulley, it should be 0.4434 in.

34. Install the rear camshaft and the fuel injection pump pulleys and torque the pulleys to 45 ft. lbs.

35. Install the rear tensioner pulley assembly, align the timing marks on the rear camshaft and the fuel injection pulleys, and install the rear timing blet. Adjust the rear timing belt deflection to ³⁄₈ in., between the longest span between the two pulleys.

36. Install the rear timing cover and adjust the valve clearance.

37. Continue the installation in the reverse order of the removal procedure.

### OVERHAUL

**For all cylinder head overhaul procedures, please refer to "Engine Rebuilding" in the Unit Repair Section.**

## Intake Manifold

### REMOVAL & INSTALLATION

1. Disconnect the negative battery cable. Drain the coolant. Remove the air cleaner assembly tube, the top radiator hose and the oil cooler hose from the intake manifold.
2. Remove the exhaust manifold insulator from the exhaust manifold.
3. Disconnect the cylinder head cover to intake manifold PCV hose.
4. Remove the intake manifold mounting bolts, the manifold, the gasket and the engine hanger.
5. Clean the gasket mounting surfaces.
6. To install, use a new gasket and reverse the removal procedure. Torque the manifold nuts/bolts to 15 ft. lbs. and the engine hanger to 20 ft. lbs.

## Exhaust Manifold

### REMOVAL & INSTALLATION

1. Disconnect the negative battery cable. Remove the exhaust manifold insulator from the exhaust manifold.
2. Disconnect the exhaust pipe from the exhaust manifold.
3. Remove the exhaust manifold bolts and the manifold.
4. Clean the gasket mounting surfaces.
5. To install, use a new gasket and reverse the removal procedure. Torque the manifold to 18 ft. lbs.

## Front Timing Covers, Belt, Tensioner and Pulleys

### REMOVAL & INSTALLATION

1. Disconnect the negative battery cable.
2. Loosen the alternator and remove the drive belts.
3. Remove the right side splash shield, the cylinder head cover and the crankshaft pulley. Remove the right and left timing belt covers and gaskets.
4. Before loosening the tensioner pulley, turn the crankshaft to align the camshaft pulley with the seal plate timing mark.
5. Loosen the tensioner, push it back and tighten place.
6. Remove the torque stopper and the timing belt. If reusing the timing belt, mark the direction of rotation on the belt.
7. Turn the crankshaft 45 degrees in the direction of rotation, from the timing mark of the oil pump, this will prevent damage to the pistons and valves.
8. Place an adjustable wrench on a camshaft lobe, hold the camshaft and loosen the camshaft pulley lock bolt and back out of the bolt a few turns.
9. Using the puller tool 49–S120–215, pull the camshaft pulley from the camshaft.
10. Remove the crankshaft timing belt pulley, by holding the flywheel ring gear and removing the pulley bolt, washer and the pulley.
11. To install, torque the camshaft pulley bolt to 45 ft. lbs. and the crankshaft pulley bolt to 120 ft. lbs.
12. Align the camshaft pulley mark with the seal plate mark and the crankshaft pulley mark with the mark on the oil pump housing.
13. Install the tensioner pulley in the retracted position.
14. Install the timing belt with the directional arrow aligned with the rotation of the engine.
15. Release the tensioner pulley to put spring pressure on the timing belt.
16. Turn the crankshaft, twice in the direction of rotation to equalize the belt. Do not turn in reverse.
17. Torque the tensioner pulley bolt to 28 ft. lbs. Check the belt deflection between the camshaft pulley and the water pump pulley, it should be ⁷⁄₁₆ in.
18. To complete the installation and reverse the removal procedure. Torque the timing cover bolts to 6 ft. lbs.

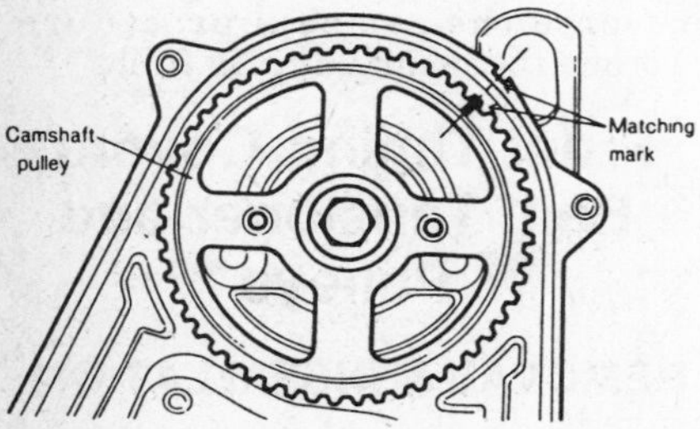


Timing the front camshaft pulley— diesel

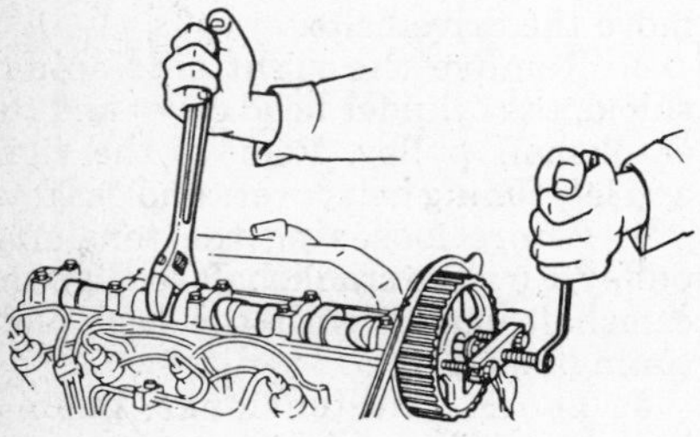


Removing the rear camshaft pulley— diesel

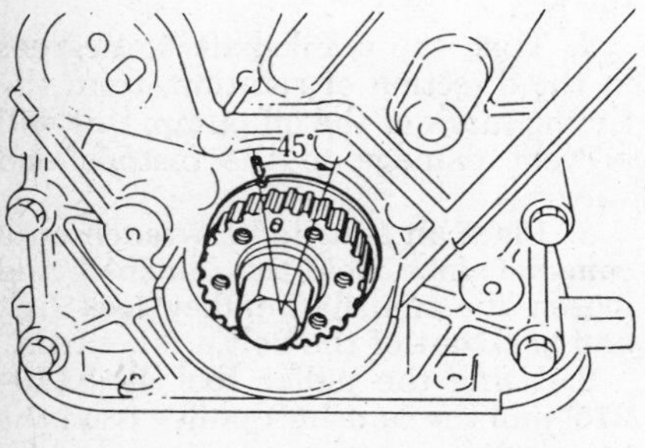


Turning the crankshaft 45 degrees— diesel

Removing the front camshaft pulley— diesel

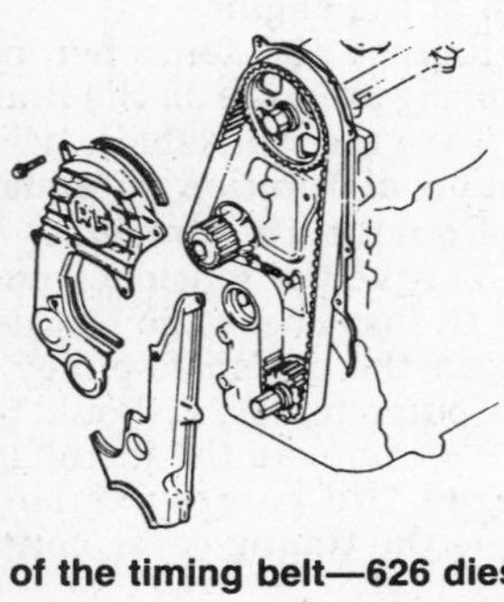

View of the timing belt—626 diesel

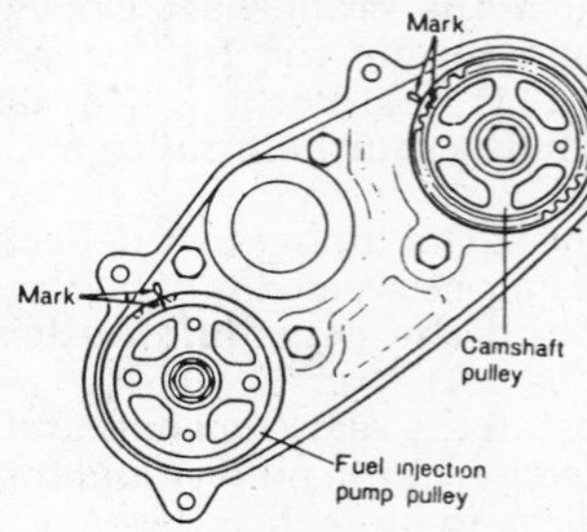


Aligning the rear timing belt pulley marks- 626 diesel

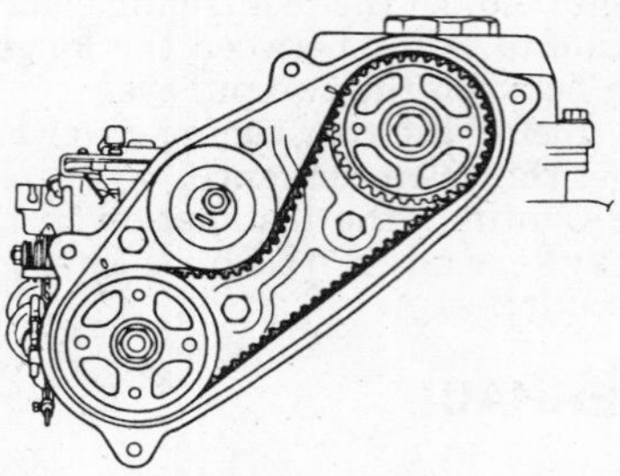

Installing the timing belt—626 diesel

## Rear Timing Cover, Belt, Tensioner and Pulleys

### REMOVAL & INSTALLATION

1. Disconnect the negative battery cable.
2. Remove the rear timing belt cover, the cylinder head cover and gasket.
3. Turn the crankshaft to align the rear camshaft pulley mark the timing on the rear seal plate.
4. Loosen the tensioner pulley locknut. Using a small pry bar, rotate the pulley away from the timing belt and tighten in place.
5. Remove the rear timing belt. If reusing the belt, mark it with a arrow, indicating the direction of rotation.
6. Using an adjustable wrench, hold the camshaft lobe and loosen the rear camshaft pulley bolt and back out the bolt a few turns.
7. Using puller tool 49–S120–215A, remove the camshaft pulley.
8. Install 2 bolts (M8 × 1.25 × 45mm) to fasten the fuel injection pump pulley to the bracket. Loosen the pulley lock bolt.
9. Using puller tool 49–S120–215A, pull the pulley from the fuel injection pump.
10. Install the pulleys and torque to 45 ft. lbs.
11. Align the pulley marks with the timing marks on the rear seal plate.
12. Install the timing belt on the fuel injection pump on the camshaft pulley. Remove the 2 bolts holding the lower pulley.
13. Loosen the tensioner pulley and allow it to put pressure on the timing belt.
14. Turn the crankshaft, twice in the direction of rotation to equalize the belt.
15. Torque the tensioner locknut to 18 ft. lbs. and check the belt deflection, it should be ⅜ in. between the longest span of the 2 pulleys.
16. To complete the installation, reverse the removal procedure. Torque the timing cover to 6 ft. lbs. and the cylinder head cover to 6 ft. lbs.

## Camshaft

### REMOVAL & INSTALLATION

1. Remove the front and rear camshaft pulleys.
2. Loosen each camshaft cap bolt, a little at a time, working from both ends, towards the center.
3. Remove the bearing caps, the oil seals and the camshaft.
4. Check for wear and distortion, replace the parts, if necessary.
5. To install, lubricate the parts, use new gaskets and seals and reverse the removal procedure. Torque the camshaft bearings, starting at the center, working toward both ends, to 18 ft. lbs.

## Piston and Connecting Rods

**For all piston and connecting rod service procedures, please refer to "Engine Rebuilding" in the Unit Repair section.**

# DIESEL ENGINE LUBRICATION

The diesel engine uses a crescent type oil pump that is directly driven by the front of the crankshaft. An oil bypass filter is provided to eliminate carbon/sludge in the engine oil and to improve efficiency. A water cooled oil cooler, attached to the right side of the engine, and oil jets, built into the engine crankcase, enable the pistons to run cooler.

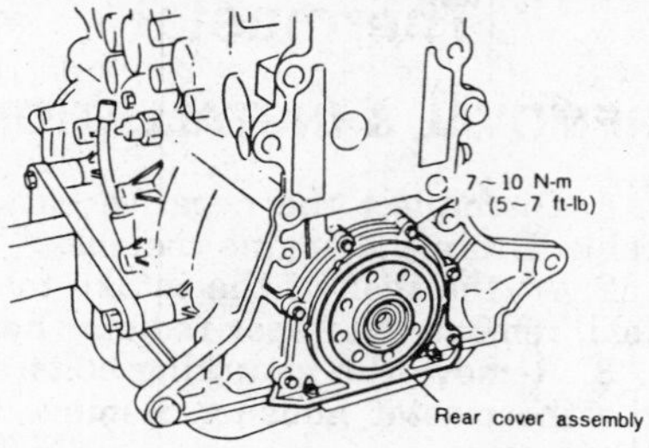

View of the rear main oil seal—diesel

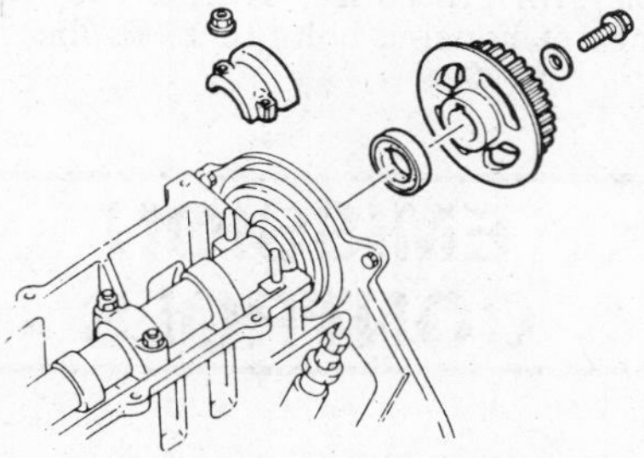
View of the rear oil seal—626 diesel

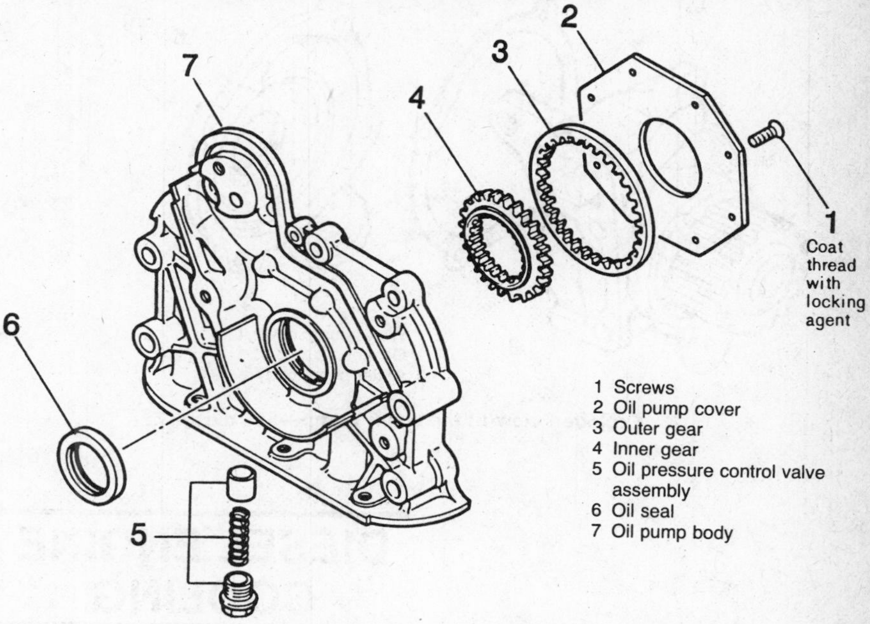

Exploded view of the oil pump assembly—626 diesel

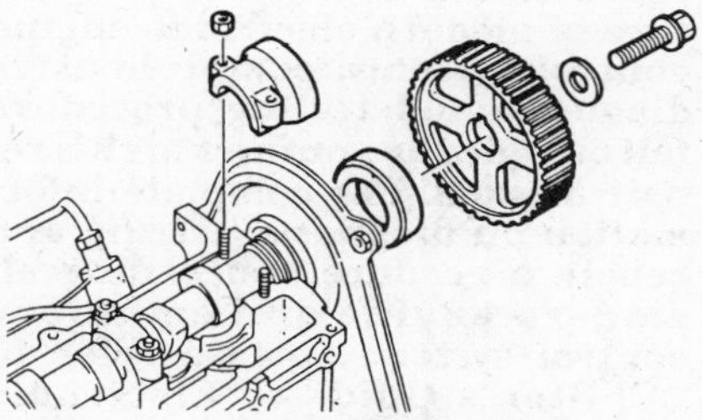
View of the front oil seal—626 diesel

## Oil Pan

### REMOVAL & INSTALLATION

1. Disconnect the negative battery cable.
2. Drain the engine oil and the coolant.
3. Raise and support the vehicle safely.
4. Remove the No. 3 engine mount nuts.
5. Remove the engine hanger at the front of the engine and attach it to the right front top corner. Using the engine support tool 49–G030–025, take the weight off of the engine.
6. Remove the right front wheel and the splash shield.
7. Remove the 5 crossmember bolts, the crossmember, the No. 3 engine mount and bracket.
8. Remove the under cover, the water return pipe and the oil pan.
9. Clean the gasket mating surfaces.
10. To install, use a new gasket and sealer and reverse the removal procedure. Torque the oil pan bolts to 6 ft. lbs. Fill the engine with oil and coolant, check for leaks. Lower the vehicle.

## Rear Main Oil Seal

### REMOVAL & INSTALLATION

1. Remove the transaxle.
2. Attach the clutch disc center tool 49–SE01–310 to the clutch assembly and the flywheel ring gear brake tool 49–V101–060 to the flywheel.
3. Remove the mounting bolts, the clutch cover assembly and the clutch disc.
4. Remove the flywheel mounting bolts and the flywheel.
5. Using a seal removal tool, place a rag to protect the end of the flywheel, pry the oil seal from the oil seal housing.
6. To install, use a new seal, lubricate the seal with engine oil, place the new seal over the end of the crankshaft, place a piece of pipe, the same diameter as the seal, against the seal and drive it into the oil seal housing. To complete the installation, reverse the removal procedure.

## Camshaft Oil Seal

### REMOVAL & INSTALLATION

The camshaft has an oil seal located at each end of the shaft, the seals are of 2 sizes and are not interchangeable.

1. Remove the necessary camshaft pulley and the oil seal.
2. It may be necessary to remove the end camshaft bearing cap, to remove the oil seal.
3. To install the new seal, lubricate the seal and press onto the end of the camshaft. Replace the bearing cap, if it was removed.
4. To complete the installation, reverse the removal procedure.

## Front Main Bearing Oil Seal

### REMOVAL & INSTALLATION

1. Remove the timing belt.
2. Remove the crankshaft pulley bolt and the crankshaft pulley.
3. Using a suitable tool, pry the oil seal from the front of the oil pump.
4. To install, lubricate the new seal, place it on the crankshaft, use a piece of pipe of the same diameter to drive the seal into the oil pump housing and reverse the removal procedure.

## Oil Jet

### REMOVAL & INSTALLATION

1. Remove the oil pan.
2. At the base of each cylinder bore, an oil jet is located. Remove the mounting bolt and the oil jet.
3. Make sure that the oil passage is not clogged.
4. To install, use new mounting

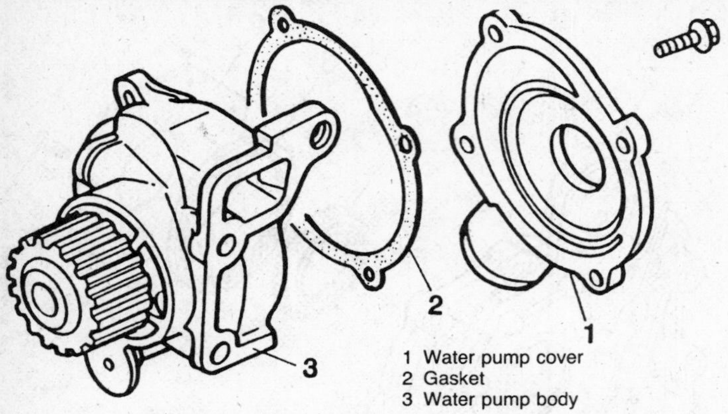


Exploded view of the water pump—626 diesel

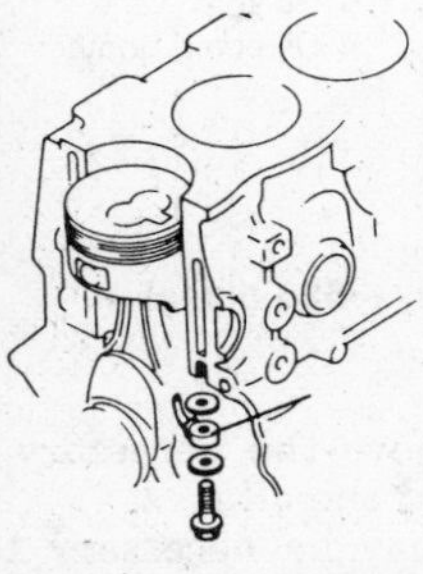

Oil jet assembly—626 diesel

washers and reverse the removal procedure.

## Oil Pump

### REMOVAL & INSTALLATION

1. Remove the timing belt.
2. Remove the oil pan and the oil pick up tube from the oil pump.
3. Remove the crankshaft pulley center bolt, the washer and the pulley.
4. Remove the oil pump mounting bolt and the oil pump.
5. If necessary, remove the oil pump cover plate, using a impact driver to loosen the screws. Remove the cover plate, the inner ring and the outer ring.
6. Check for wear and replace the parts as necessary.
7. To assembly, pack the oil pump cavity with vasoline and install the outer gear ring with the punch marks facing forward.
8. When installing the cover plate, coat the locking screws with a locking agent.
9. To install the oil pump, use new gaskets and O-ring. Continue the installation in the reverse order of the removal procedure. Fill the engine with oil and coolant.

# DIESEL ENGINE COOLING

## Radiator

### REMOVAL & INSTALLATION

1. Disconnect the negative battery cable. Drain the engine coolant.
2. Remove the upper and the lower radiator hoses.
3. Remove the fan motor assembly and the shroud.
4. Remove the mounting bolts and the radiator.
5. To install, reverse the removal procedure. Fill the coolant system with fluid.

## Water Pump

### REMOVAL & INSTALLATION

1. Disconnect the negative battery cable.
2. Drain the cooling system.
3. Remove the top timing belt cover and the installation bolt from the lower timing belt cover.
4. Turn the crankshaft to align the camshaft pulley mark with the mark on the sealing plate.
5. Loosen the tensioner pulley lock bolt, push the pulley out of the way and tighten it.
6. Move the camshaft pulley slightly to remove the timing belt.
7. Disconnect the heater and the radiator return hoses.
8. Remove the mounting bolts, the water pump and gaskets.
9. Clean the gasket mounting surfaces.
10. To install, use new gaskets and reverse the removal procedure.

## Thermostat

### REMOVAL & INSTALLATION

1. Disconnect the negative battery cable. Drain the engine coolant.
2. At the rear of the intake manifold, remove the upper radiator hose.
3. Remove the mounting bolts and the thermostat housing. Remove the thermostat.
4. Clean the gasket mounting surfaces.
5. Installation is the reverse of the removal procedure. Torque the thermostat housing bolts to 18 ft. lbs.

# EMISSION CONTROLS

**Please refer to the "Emission Control" in the unit repair section for system maintenance procedures. Due to the complex nature of modern electronic engine control systems, comprehensive diagnosis and testing procedure fall outside the confines of this repair manual. For complete information on diagnosis, testing and repair procedure concerning all modern engine and emissions control systems, please refer to "Chilton's Guide to Electronic Engine Controls.**

# GASOLINE ENGINE FUEL SYSTEM

## Fuel System Service Precaution

Failure to conduct fuel system maintenance and repairs in a safe manner may result in serious personal injury. Maintenance and testing of the vehicle's fuel system components can be accomplished safely and effectively by adhering to the following rules and guidelines.

### GENERAL PRECAUTIONS

- To avoid the possibility of fire and personal injury, always disconnect the negative battery cable unless the repair or test procedure specifically requires that battery voltage be applied.

- Always relieve the fuel system pressure prior to disconnecting any fuel system component (injector, fuel rail, pressure regulator, etc...), fitting or fuel line connection. To relieve pressure wrap a shop rag around the fitting or connection being opened, and slowly open the system. Wait for pressure to relieve itself, then remove the rag and wipe up any spilled fuel. Exercise extreme caution whenever relieving fuel system pressure to avoid exposing skin, face and eyes to fuel spray. Be advised that fuel under pressure may penetrate the skin or any part of the body that it comes in contact with.
- Always place a shop towel or cloth around the fitting or connection prior to loosening to absorb any excess fuel due to spillage. Ensure that all fuel spillage (should it occur) is quickly removed from engine surfaces. Ensure that all fuel soaked cloths or towels are deposited into a suitable waste container.
- Always have a properly charged fire extinguisher in the vicinity of the work area and always ensure work areas are adequately ventilated.
- Do not allow fuel spray or fuel vapors to come in contact with spark or open flame. Remember that smoking and fuel maintenance do not mix!
- Always use a backup wrench when loosening and tightening fuel line connection fittings. This will prevent unnecessary stress and torsion to fuel line piping. Always follow the proper torque specifications.
- Always replace worn fuel fitting O-rings with new ones. Do not substitute fuel hose or equivalent where rigid fuel pipe is called for.
- Always use common sense.

### RELIEVING FUEL SYSTEM PRESSURE

**CAUTION**

***Vehicles equipped with fuel injection are subjected to high fuel line pressure. The fuel injection system is under high pressure even when the engine is not operating. Excercise extreme care when diconnecting and relieving fressure from the fuel lines.***

1. Disconnect the fuel pump connector at the fuel pump, while the engine is running.
2. Allow the engine to stall. Turn the ignition switch to the **OFF** position.
3. Disconnect the negative battery cable. Allow the engine to cool.
4. Carefully loosen, but do not remove, the fuel hose clamp located at the distribution pipe inlet.
5. Place a rag around the end of the fuel inlet hose and slide the clamp away from the distribution pipe inlet opening.
6. With the rag still in place, carefully work the fuel hose from the inlet opening to relieve any system pressure. Drain excess fuel ina suitable container.

## Fuel Filter

### REMOVAL & INSTALLATION

#### *1983 GLC Wagon*

1. Properly relieve the fuel system pressure. Disconnect the negative battery cable. The flter is the inline type and is located under the hood in the engine compartment.
2. Detach both hoses from the filter.
3. Unfasten the filter from its mounting bracket.
4. To install, reverse the removal procedure. Start the engine and check for leaks.

#### *RX-7*

1. Properly relieve the fuel system pressure. Disconnect the negative battery cable. Raise and support the vehicle safely.
2. Loosen the clips at both ends of the filter and place a collection pan beneath it to catch any of the fuel that is in the lines.
3. Disconnect the fuel filter lines and remove the filter from its retainer.
4. Install the new filter, paying close attention to the direction of the filter in relation to the direction of the fuel flow.
5. Turn the starter to **ON** to activate the fuel pump and check the fuel filter connections for leaks.

#### *All Except GLC Wagon and RX-7*

1. Properly relieve the fuel system pressure. Disconnect the negative battery cable. Remove the screw and wire retainer bracket.
2. Remove the inlet and outlet fuel lines.
3. Remove the fuel filter. On some vehicles it may be necessary to remove the bracket with the fuel filter.
4. Installation is the reverse of the removal procedure. Install the filter in the proper direction. If the fuel filter is equipped with union bolt fittings, use new metal crush gaskets. Start the engine and check for leaks.

## Mechanical Fuel Pump

### REMOVAL & INSTALLATION

1. Disconnect the negative battery cable. Remove the 2 fuel line clips from the pump inlet and outlet hoses. Remove the hoses.
2. Remove the fuel pump mounting bolts. Remove the fuel pump from the engine.
3. Installation is the reverse of the removal procedure. Use new gaskets as required.

### PRESSURE TESTING

Connect a suitable fuel pressure gauge to the main fuel feed from the fuel pump, then crank the engine and read the fuel pressure. It should be 4–6 psi.

## Electric Fuel Pump

### REMOVAL & INSTALLATION

#### *External Chassis Mounted*

##### EXCEPT RX-7

1. Properly relieve the fuel system pressure. Disconnect the negative battery cable.
2. Disconnect the fuel pump lead wire in the luggage compartment.
3. Raise and support the vehicle safely.
4. Disconnect the fuel pump bracket.
5. Disconnect the fuel inlet and outlet hoses and remove the fuel pump.
6. Installation is the reverse of removal. Use new gaskets as required.

##### RX-7

1. Properly relieve the fuel system pressure. Disconnect the negative battery cable. Remove the rear floor mat and floor plate.
2. Disconnect the fuel pump electrical connection under the floor plate.
3. Raise and support the vehicle safely.
4. Remove the fuel pump protecting cover. Remove inlet and outlet lines. Remove the pump. Installation is the reverse of removal.

#### *Internal Tank Mounted*

1. Properly relieve the fuel system pressure. Disconnect the negative battery cable. Depending on the vehicle, lifting of the rear mat or removal of the rear seat will be required in order to gain access to the fuel pump cover plate.
2. Disconnect the electrical connector.
3. Remove the fuel pump cover screws and lift off the cover.

4. Disconnect the fuel feed and return hoses. Wrap a clean rag around the fuel lines when disconnect to catch any fuel spray, then plug the lines to prevent leakage.

5. Remove the mounting screws and lift the fuel pump and gauge assembly from the fuel tank.

6. Installation is the reverse of the removal procedure. Be careful not to allow any dirt or other foreign material to contaminate the fuel tank while the unit is removed. Use a new cover plate gasket as required.

## PRESSURE TESTING

1. On electric fuel pumps with carburetor engines, connect a suitable tee connection to the fuel filter hose and attach a pressure gauge. Install a jumper wire to connect the terminals of the fuel pump test connection, then turn the ignition **ON** and read the fuel pressure. Compare it to specification.

2. On electric fuel pumps with fuel injection, connect a suitable pressure gauge to the main fuel line from the fuel pump. Install a jumper wire to connect the terminals of the test connector, then turn the ignition ON and read the fuel pump output pressure. Compare it to specification.

3. Install a tee connector in the fuel line from the filter and attach the pressure gauge. Remove the jumper wire from the test connector and disconnect the vacuum line at the fuel pressure regulator. Start the engine and read the fuel pressure at idle. Compare it to specification.

4. Reconnect the vacuum hose to the pressure regulator and again read the fuel pressure. Compare it to specification.

5. Stop the engine and allow it to cool before disconnecting the pressure regulator after testing.

# Carburetor

## REMOVAL & INSTALLATION

### *RX-7*

1. Disconnect the negative battery cable. Remove the air cleaner.

2. Detach the choke and accelerator cables.

3. Label and disconnect the fuel and vacuum lines and plug the main fuel line to prevent leakage.

4. Remove the oil line.

5. Remove all electrical wiring from carburetor.

6. Remove the carburetor.

7. To install, reverse the removal procedure.

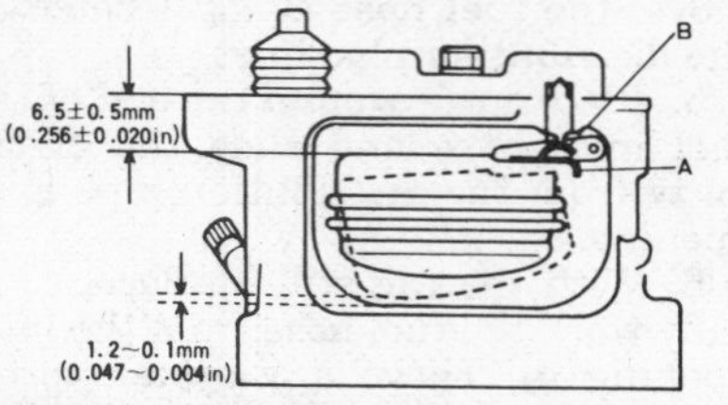


**Piston engine float adjustment: bend tab "A" to adjust float drop and bend tab "B" to adjust float level**

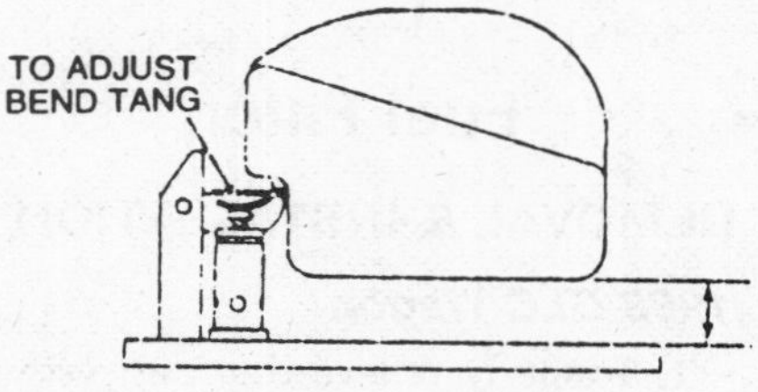


**Float level adjustment, float bowl inverted and gasket installed**

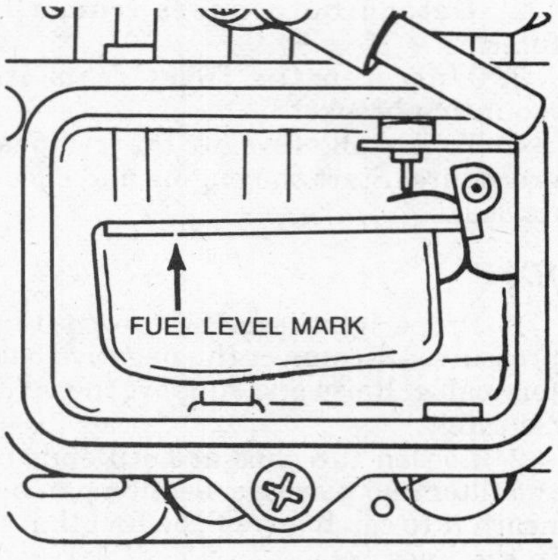


**Fuel level mark on sight glass: piston engine**

### *Except RX-7*

1. Disconnect the negative battery cable. Remove the air cleaner assembly.

2. Disconnect the accelerator cable assembly. Disconnect the cruise control cable if necessary. Remove all necessary wiring and vacuum lines.

3. Disconnect the fuel supply and fuel return lines. As required, disconnect the air/fuel solenoid harness at the wiring connector and the bullet connector.

4. Remove the connector for the bimetal choke heater, if equipped. Disconnect the choke cable, if equipped.

5. Disconnect the leads from the throttle solenoid and deceleration valve at the quick disconnects. Disconnect the throttle return spring.

6. Remove the carburetor retaining bolts. Remove the carburetor assembly from the engine.

7. Installation is the reverse of the removal procedure. Be sure to use a new carburetor base gasket.

## THROTTLE LINKAGE ADJUSTMENT

1. Check the accelerator pedal position, it should be lower than the brake pedal.

2. If necessary, adjust the nut on the linkage above the pedal to obtain the proper height.

3. Check the free play of the cable at the carburetor. It should be 0.04–0.12 in. If not, adjust by turning the clevis nut.

4. The accelerator pedal distance below the brake pedal should be 2.0 ± 0.2 in. for the 1983–85 GLC, 1.7 ± 0.2 in. for the 1983–85 RX-7.

5. On all other vehicles depress the accelerator pedal to the floor and confirm that the throttle valve is fully open. Adjust as necessary, by using the adjusting bolt or nut on the linkage above the accelerator pedal.

## FLOAT AND FUEL LEVEL ADJUSTMENTS

### *GLC and 626*

1. Remove the carburetor air horn assembly.

2. Invert the air horn and allow the float to hang so that the needle valve contacts the seat.

3. Measure the clearance between the float and the air horn without the air horn gasket in place.

4. The clearance should be:
1983 626 – 0.394 in.
1984–85 626 – 0.530 in.
1984 GLC – 0.476 in.
1985 GLC – 0.390 in.
All other vehicles – 0.433 in.

5. Adjust by bending the float seat lip.

6. Reassemble and recheck idle.

### *RX-7*

1. Remove the carburetor air horn assembly.

2. Invert the air horn to a position with the float facing upward. The air horn gasket surface must be level. Place the air horn on a carburetor work stand, if available, in order to insure a level position.

3. The distance between the float and the air horn gasket should be 0.63 ± 0.02 in., measured at the top of the float.

4. Install the air horn assembly.

### *323*

1. Remove the carburetor air horn assembly.

2. Invert the air horn and allow the float to hang so that the needle valve contacts the seat.

3. Measure the clearance between the float and the air horn without the air horn gasket in place.

4. The clearance should be 1.811–1.890 in.

5. Turn the air horn upside down on a stand and allow the float to lower by its own weight. measure the clearance between the float and the air horn, the clearnace shouls be 0.236–0.276 in.

6. If the clearance is not correct, bend the arm until the proper clearnace is obtained.

## FLOAT DROP ADJUSTMENTS

### *RX-7*

1. Remove the carburetor air horn assembly.

2. Position the air horn in the normal installed position. The air horn gasket surface should be level.

3. The float should be in a fully dropped position. Measure the distance between the lowest part of the float and the air horn gasket.

4. The measured distance should be 2.0 ± 0.02 in. If the distance is not correct, bend the tab on the float to obtain the correct distance.

5. Install the air horn.

### *Except RX-7*

1. Remove the carburetor air horn and hold it in its normal position.

2. Measure the distance between the air horn without the gasket and the bottom of the float.

3. The distance should be 1.929 in. for 1983–85 626 and 1.77 in. for 1983–85 GLC front wheel drive.

4. If the distance is not correct, bend the float stopper until the distance is correct.

5. To install, use new gaskets and remove the removal procedure.

## FAST IDLE CAM ADJUSTMENT

### *RX-7*

1. Disconnect the negative battery cable. Remove the carburetor from the engine.

2. With the choke valve fully closed, adjust the clearance between the primary throttle valve and the wall of the throttle bore by bending the connecting rod between the choke valve and the throttle valve.

### *1983–85 GLC*

1. On the 1415cc engine, remove the bimetal cover.

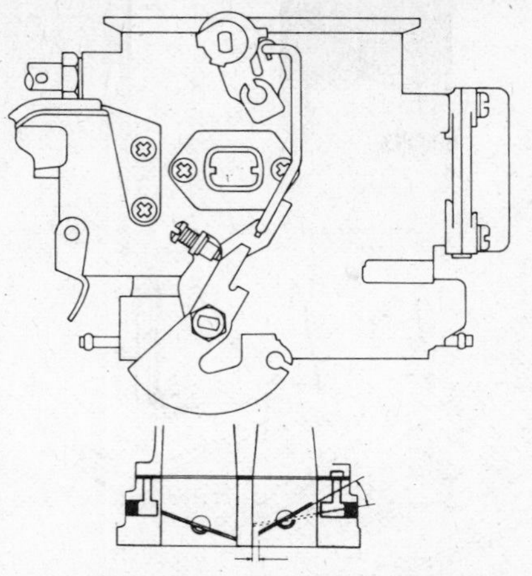

**Fast idle adjustments: measure the angle "A" and clearance "B"—rotary engines**

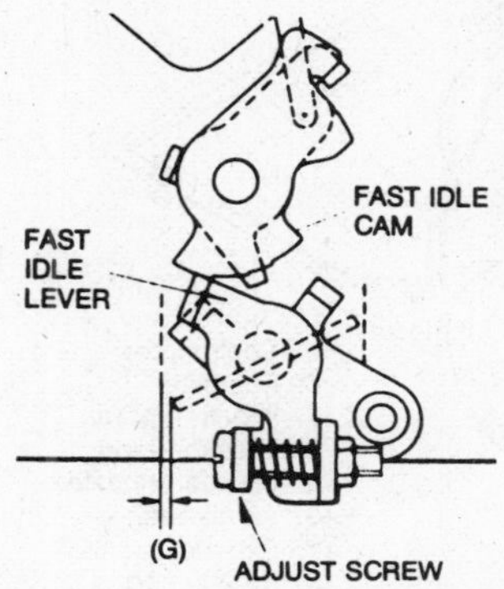


**Fast idle cam adjustment—1970 cc engine**

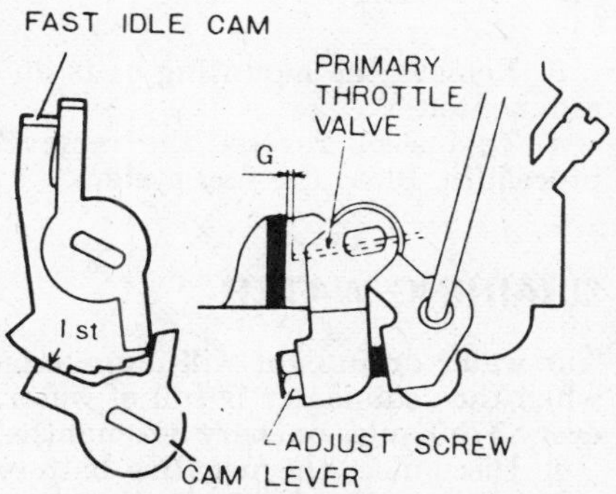


**Fast idle cam adjustment—1415cc and 1490cc engines**

2. Using your fingers, close the choke valve fully.

3. Make sure the fast idle cam is on the first position on all vehicles except the GLC. On the GLC make sure that the fast idle cam is on the third position

4. Check the clearance at the throttle valve opening and adjust by turning the adjustment screw.

### *1983–85 626*

1. Set the fast idle cam on the second position.

2. Adjust the throttle valve clearance by turning the adjusting screw.

### *1986–87 323*

1. Set the fast idle cam to the third position.

2. Adjust the throttle valve clearance, between the primary throttle valve and wall by turning the adjusting screw. The standard clearance should be 0.011–0.023 in. on manual transmission equipped vehicles and 0.014–0.026 in. on automatic transmission equipped vehicles.

## CHOKE ADJUSTMENT

1. Set the fast idle cam select arm on the second position.

2. Make sure that the choke valve clearance is as follows:

a. 1983–85 GLC – 0.043 ± 0.008.

b. 1983–85 RX-7 – 0.057–0.070 in.

c. 1986–87 323 – 0.026–0.046 in.

3. If necessary, adjust the choke valve clearance, by bending the choke Starting arm. If a large adjustment is required, the choke rod should be bent.

## OVERHAUL

**For all carburetor overhaul procedures please refer to "Carburetor Service" in the Unit Repair section.**

# Fuel Injection

**Due to the complex nature of modern fuel injection systems, comprehensive diagnosis and testing procedures fall outside the confines of this repair manual. For complete information on fuel injection diagnosis, testing and repair procedures please refer to "Chilton's Guide To Fuel Injection and Feedback Carburetors".**

# DIESEL FUEL SYSTEM

## Fuel Filter

The fuel filter installed between the sedimenter and the fuel injection pump. The filter is constructed of a paper element with the priming pump to bleed the air from the fuel line.

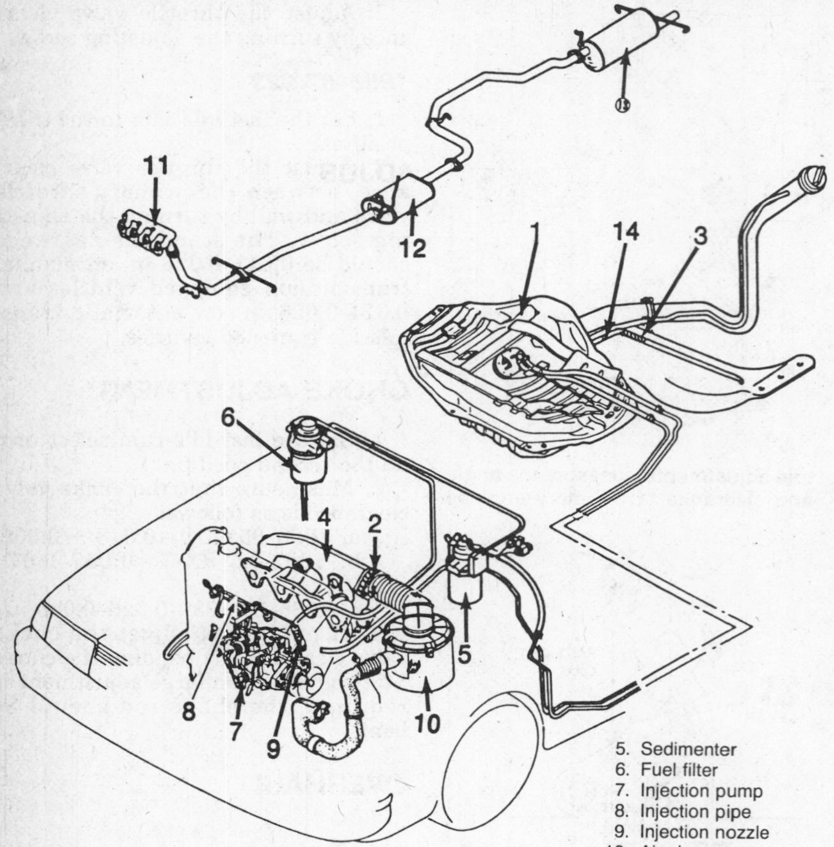


5. Sedimenter
6. Fuel filter
7. Injection pump
8. Injection pipe
9. Injection nozzle
10. Air cleaner
11. Exhaust manifold
12. Pre-silencer
13. Main silencer
14. Orifice

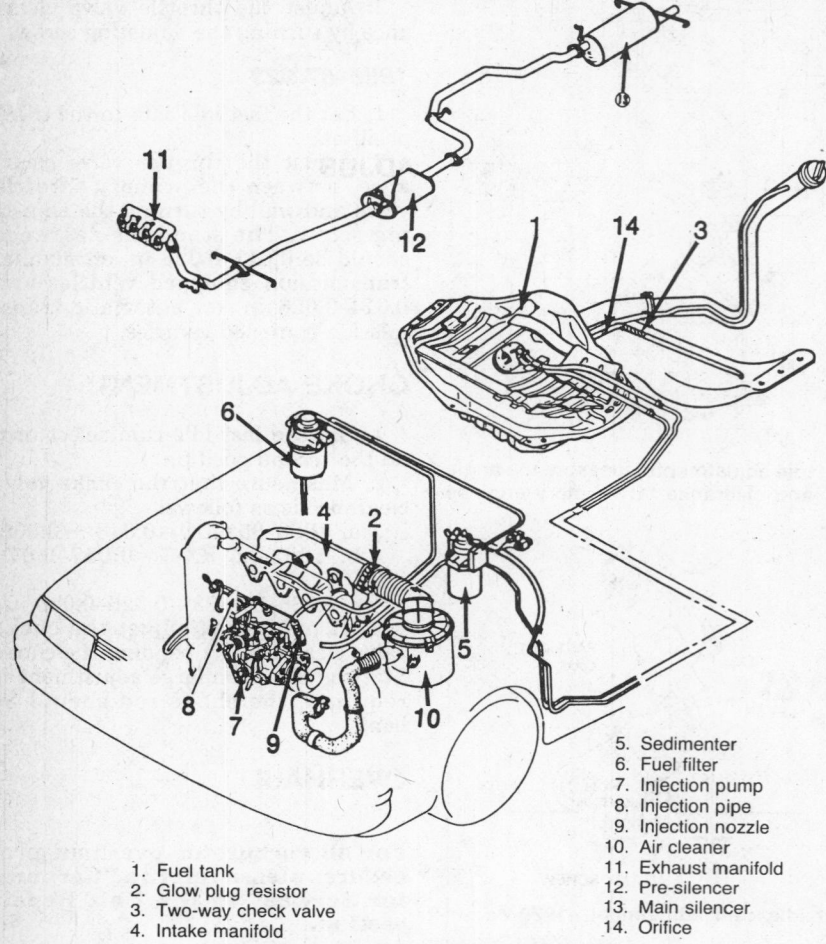

1. Fuel tank
2. Glow plug resistor
3. Two-way check valve
4. Intake manifold

**View of the fuel system—626 diesel**

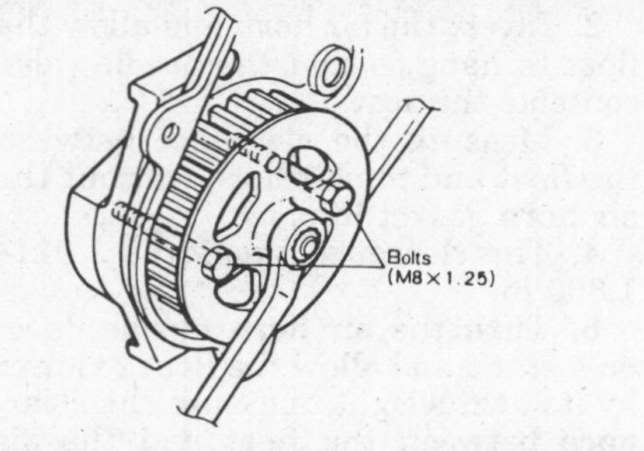


**Removing the fuel injection pump pulley-626 diesel**

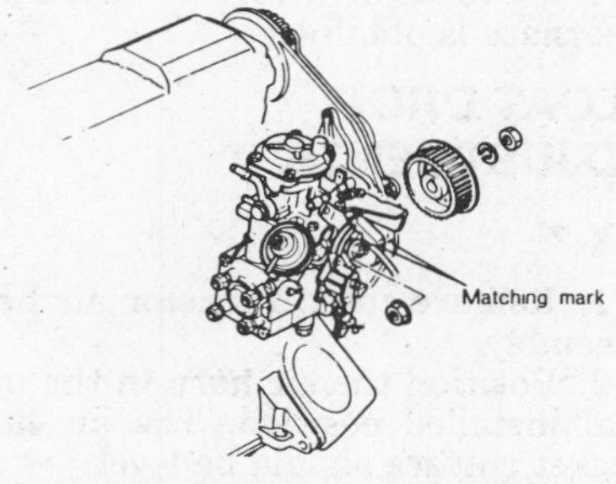


**Removing the fuel injection pump—diesel**

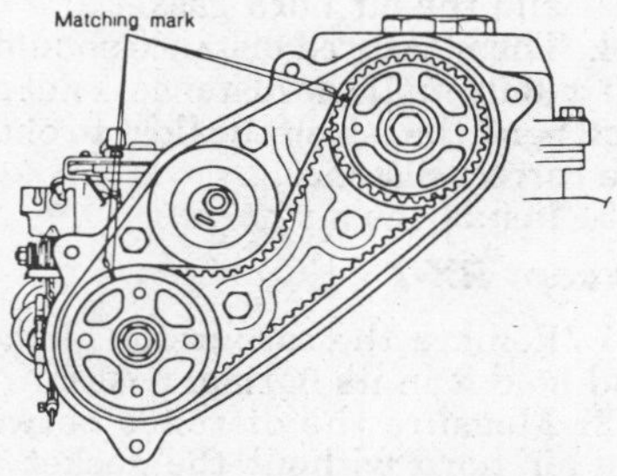


**Aligning the timing marks—626 diesel**

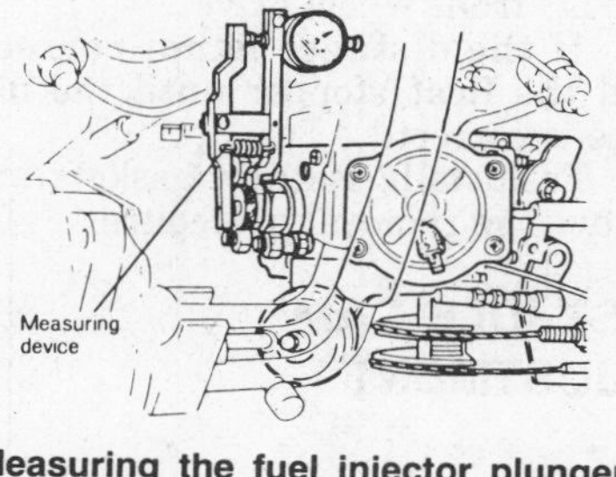


**Measuring the fuel injector plunger—diesel**

### REPLACEMENT

1. Release the pressure in the fuel line. Disconnect the negative battery cable.
2. Using a fuel filter wrench, remove the filter from the fuel filter housing.
3. To install, apply fuel to the O-ring and turn the filter onto the fuel filter housing, tighten by hand. Bleed the air from the fuel system.

## Sedimenter

The sedimenter, mounted on the left suspension mounting block, is installed between the fuel tank and the fuel filter, it is used to separate the water from the fuel.

### REMOVAL & INSTALLATION

1. Release the pressure in the fuel system. Disconnect the negative battery cable.
2. Remove the fuel lines and the electrical connectors from the sedimenter.
3. Remove the mounting bolts and sedimenter.
4. To install, reverse the removal procedure. Bleed the fuel system.

### DRAINING WATER

The water drain light will illuminate, when the sedimenter is full of water, every 3750 miles or every 3¾ months.

1. Disconnect the negative battery cable. Loosen the drain plug.
2. Loosen the air bleed screw, if it is hard to drain the water.
3. After the water is drained, tighten the drain plug.
4. If the air bleed screw has been opened, bleed the air from the fuel line.
5. Make sure the plugs of the sedimenter are closed and the fuel hoses are connected.
6. Loosen the fuel filter air vent plug. Pump the fuel filter head in and up and down motion, until solid fuel flows from the air vent plug hole.
7. Depress the fuel filter pump head and close the air vent plug.

## Diesel Injection Pump

The injection pump is a distributor (VE) type, located at the left rear of the engine and driven by the rear camshaft timing belt, it is manufactured by Nippondenso.

### REMOVAL & INSTALLATION

1. Properly relieve the fuel system

pressure. Disconnect the negative battery cable.

2. Disconnect the accelerator control, the cold start device control and the cruise control cable if equipped..

3. Disconnect the fuel out valve and the pickup coil couplers.

4. Remove the fuel injection tubes, the fuel and vacuum hoses from the pump.

5. Remove the rear timing belt cover, the tensioner and the timing belt.

6. Remove the fuel injection pulley from the fuel injection pump. Use puller tool 49–S120–215, to remove the pulley. Be careful not to drop the semi circular (Woodruff) key.

7. If the matching marks are not present on the pump flange and the rear seal plate, use a cold chisel to mark them.

8. Remove the mounting bolts and the fuel injection pump from the rear seal plate.

9. To install, align the matching marks of the pump flange and the rear seal plate. Install the pump mounting bolts and the pulley.

10. To complete the installation, reverse the removal procedure. Time the rear timing belt. Torque the pump mounting nuts to 16 ft. lbs. and the bolt to 28 ft. lbs. Torque the fuel pump pulley to 46 ft. lbs. Bleed the air from the fuel injection pump and system.

### BLEEDING THE FUEL INJECTION PUMP

1. At the fuel filter, open the air vent plug.

2. Use a pumping motion on top of the fuel filter to bleed air from the fuel line, until a steady stream of fluid flows.

3. Close the air bleed valve and continue to pump, about 15 times, until the pump works hard.

## Diesel Injection Timing

### ADJUSTMENT

1. Remove the fuel injection pipes and remove the service hole cover on the clutch housing.

2. Align the timing mark (TDC) on the flywheel with the indicator pin by turning the crankshaft.

3. Remove the hydraulic head plug on the injection pump, mount the measuring device tool 49–9140–074 or equivalent into the plug hole on the hydraulic head, so the tip of the dial gauge touches the plunger end of the pump and the dial gauge indicates approximately 0.008 in. (2.0mm).

**NOTE: The delivery valve should be removed as an assembly shown in order to mount the measuring device. When installing the delivery valve, the gasket should be replaced and the valve should be torqued 3–4 ft. lbs.**

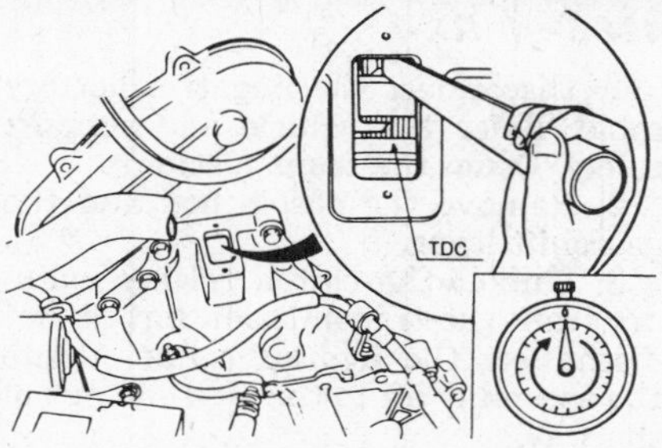

Timing the engine—626 diesel

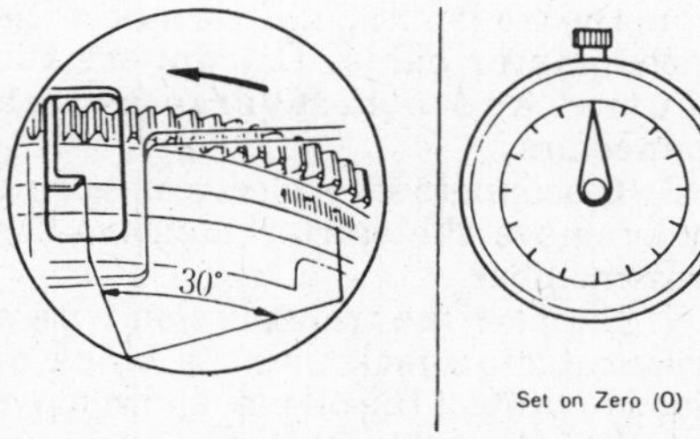

Adjusting the timing—626 diesel

4. Turn the flywheel slowly counterclockwise, until the timing mark on the crankshaft pulley moves from the original position (TDC) to the counterclockwise side by 30–50 degrees and make sure the dial indicator pointer stops.

5. Set the dial indicator to zero. When setting the dial indicator to zero, confirm that the pointer does not deviate from the scale mark of zero, by slightly turning the crankshaft to the right and left.

6. Turn the flywheel clockwise, to align the timing mark (TDC) on the flywheel with the indicator pin.

7. If the dial indicator pointer indicates 0.004 ± 0.0008 in. (1.0 ± 0.02mm) when the timing mark (TDC) is aligned with the indicator pin, the injection timing is correctly adjusted. If it does not, adjust the pump timing as outlined in Steps 8 and 9.

8. Start the engine and run it until it reaches normal operating temperature.

9. Stop the engine and loosen the injection pump attaching nuts and bolts. Adjust the injection timing by moving the pump until the cam lift becomes 0.004 ± 0.0008 in. (1.0 ± 0.02mm) on the dial indicator.

10. Tighten the injection pump nuts and bolts, recheck the cam lift and remove all test equipment.

## Cold Start Device

When pulling the cold start device knob, the injection timing is advanced and the idle speed is increased.

### ADJUSTMENT

1. Check the CSD cable deflection of 0.04–0.12 in. If the deflection is not correct, turn the cable adjusting nuts of the CSD.

2. Warm the engine to the normal operating temperatures.

3. Connect a tachometer to the engine.

4. Pull the CSD knob fully out.

5. The engine speed should be 1350–1650 rpm.

6. If the engine speed is not correct, turn the connecting lever on the fuel injection pump, to adjust.

7. Remove the tachometer and push the CSD knob in.

## Fast Idle Control Device

When the air conditioning and blower motor switches, are in the **ON** position, the vacuum from the vacuum pump goes to the actuator and a control lever is pulled, causing the engine speed to increase.

### ADJUSTMENT

1. Warm the engine to the normal operating temperature.

2. Connect a tachometer to the engine.

3. Apply vacuum directly to the actuator and check the engine speed, it should be 900–950 rpm.

4. If the speed is not correct, turn the adjusting screw on the end of the actuator.

5. Reconnect the vacuum hose, turn on the air conditioning and the blower motor switches and confirm the engine speed.

6. Disconnect the tachometer and turn the air conditioning switches off.

## Injection Nozzle

### REMOVAL & INSTALLATION

1. Relieve the fuel line pressure. Disconnect the negative battery cable. Remove the fuel injection tubes, the fuel return tube locknuts and the tubes.

2. Remove the fuel injector nozzles, the nozzle washers and the corrugated gasket from the cylinder head.

3. To install, use new

copper/corrugated washers and face the red side of the corrugated washer toward the nozzle. Reverse the removal procedure and torque the nozzles to 48 ft. lbs.

# MANUAL TRANSMISSION

## REMOVAL & INSTALLATION

### 1983–85 RX-7

1. Disconnect the negative battery cable. Remove the clutch release cylinder and tie the clutch release cylinder up out of the way. Do not disconnect the hydraulic line from the clutch release cylinder.
2. Remove the air cleaner assembly, on 12A engines only.
3. Remove the bolts attaching the transmission to the rear end of the engine. Unscrew and remove the gear shift lever knob. Remove the console box, so equipped.
4. Remove the gear shift lever boot and boot plate. Remove the gear shift lever and retainer assembly.
5. Raise the vehicle and support it safely. Remove the front engine under cover and rear engine under cover. Remove the converter under cover and disconnect the air pipe.
6. Remove the converter brackets. Remove the rear exhaust pipe and converter assembly. Remove the front exhaust pipe and monolith converter assembly.
7. Remove the floor under covers. Drain the transmission oil into a suitable drain pan. Remove the driveshaft.
8. Disconnect the wiring and remove the starter motor. Remove the bolts attaching the transmission to the rear end of the engine. Disconnect the couplers from the back-up lamp switch.
9. Place a suitable transmission jack under the transmission. Disconnect the speedometer. Remove the nuts attaching the transmission support to the vehicle. Place a suitable piece of wood approximately 1 in. in height between the oil pan and the center link. This will prevent the engine from interfering with the dash panel.
10. Slide the transmission rearward until the main shaft clears the clutch disc and carefully remove the transmission from under the vehicle.
11. Installation is the reverse order of the removal procedure. Adjust the clutch and shift linkage. Refill the transmission and road test the vehicle.

### 1986–90 RX-7

1. Disconnect the negative battery cable. Raise the vehicle and support safely. Drain the transmission.
2. Remove the cosole box and the gearshift lever.
3. Unbolt the clutch release cylinder from the transmission but do not disconnect the hydraulic line. Route the assembly off to the side and out of the way.
4. Disconnect the exhaust pipe and remove the converter covers.
5. Disengage the propeller shaft from the transmission. Disconnect the speedometer cable. Disconnect the neutral and 5th/reverse switch connectors.
6. Disconnect the electrcal wiring and remove the starter. Remove the crossmember.
7. Support the transmission with a transmission jack using a block of wood to protect the oil pan and remove the transmission case-to-engine attaching bolts.
8. Slide the transmission rearward until the main shaft clears the clutch disc and carefully remove the transmission from under the vehicle.
9. Installation is the reverse order of the removal procedure. Adjust the clutch and shift linkage. Refill the transmission and road test the vehicle.

### 1983 GLC Wagon

1. Disconnect the negative battery cable.
2. Put the transmission in **NEUTRAL** and remove the shift lever.
3. Remove the 2 upper bolts from the clutch housing.
4. Raise the vehicle and support it safely.
5. Drain the transmission oil and replace the plug.
6. Remove the driveshaft, and plug or cover the hole in the extension housing.
7. Disconnect the speedometer cable and back-up light switch wires.
8. Disconnect the exhaust pipe hanger from the bracket on the clutch housing.
9. Remove the exhaust pipe support bracket from the clutch housing. Disconnect the clutch cable at the release lever.
10. Remove the lower clutch housing cover.
11. Remove the starter electrical connections, the bolts, and the starter.
12. Disconnect the exhaust pipe hanger at the extension housing.
13. Place a jack under the engine, using a block of wood to protect the oil pan. Make sure the jack can securely support the weight of the engine.
14. Disconnect the transmission support member at the transmission.
15. Remove transmission to engine attaching bolts.
16. Carefully slide the transmission rearward until the input shaft has cleared the clutch disc, and lower it from the vehicle.
17. To install, reverse the removal procedure. Adjust clutch and shift linkage. Refill the transmission with the proper grade of gear oil.

### 1988–90 929

1. Disconnect the negative battery cable. Remove the console. Remove the gearshift lever.
2. Raise and support the vehicle safely. Drain the transmission fluid. Disconnect the speedometer cable.
3. Disconnect the required electrical connectors. Disconnect the exhaust pipe and bracket assembly. Remove the heat insulator.
4. Remove the driveshaft. Remove the starter. Remove the clutch release cylinder.
5. Support the engine, using the proper equipment. Support the transmission, using the proper equipment.
6. Remove the transmission crossmember retaining bolts. Remove the crossmember.
7. Remove the transmission to clutch housing retaining bolts. Carefully remove the transmission assembly from the vehicle.
8. Installation is the reverse of the removal procedure.

## SHIFT LEVER ADJUSTMENT

The shift lever may be adjusted during transmission installation by means of the adjusting shims on the 3 bolts between the cover plate and the packing. The force required to move the shift knob should be 4.4–8.8 lbs.

# MANUAL TRANSAXLE

## REMOVAL & INSTALLATION

### 1983–85 GLC

1. Disconnect the negative battery cable. Raise the vehicle and support it safely. Disconnect the speedometer cable.
2. Disconnect all electrical wiring and connections, control linkages from the transaxle. Mark these units for assembly reference.
3. Remove the water pipe bracket and the harness clips. Remove the front wheels. Remove the under cover

and side cover. Disconnect the lower ball joints from the steering knuckles. Pull the axleshafts from the differential gears as follows.

a. The driveshaft can be removed by puling the caliper toward the operator, appling impact to the shaft.

b. Never give a sharp impact, just gradually increase the force. Pull the shaft straight out of the axle, be careful not to damage the oil seal.

c. Be sure the driveshaft's ball joint is bent to its maximum extent.

**NOTE: Do not allow the axleshafts to drop. Damage may occur to the ball and socket joints and to the rubber boots. Wire the shafts to the vehicle body when released from the differential.**

4. Support the engine with the support tool 49-E301-025.
5. At the transaxle, separate the shift control rod from the shift rod.
6. Remove the extension bar from the transaxle. Remove the crossmember.
7. Remove the transaxle rubber mounts.
8. Remove the starter.
9. Properly support the transaxle assembly using the proper equipment.
10. Remove the mounting bolts and the transaxle.
11. Installation is the reverse of the removal procedure. Be sure the rubber mounts are not twisted or distorted and not in contact with the body.
12. To properly install the axleshafts in the differential side gears, position the axleshaft in a horizontal position, push the axleshaft into the side gear. To be sure the axleshaft engages the groove, a sound may be head or attempt to pull the driveshaft from the differential. Reconnect the ball joints at the lower arms.

### 1983–87 626

1. Disconnect the negative battery cable. Remove the speedometer cable from the transaxle.
2. Remove the clutch cable bracket mounting bolts and disconnect the clutch cable from the release lever.
3. Remove the ground wire and wiring harness clip. Remove any pipe brackets attached to the case.
4. Remove the starter.
5. Install the engine support tool 49-G030-025, and support the weight of the engine.
6. Remove all of the transaxle to engine mounting bolts, except the 2 lower ones.
7. Raise and support the vehicle safely. Drain the transaxle oil.
8. Remove the front wheels and the splash shields.
9. Remove the stabilizer bar control link. Remove the under cover if equipped.
10. Remove the lower arm ball joint and the knuckle coupling bolt, pull the arm downward and separate the lower arm from the knuckle.
11. Remove the left side axleshaft from the transaxle. Insert a lever between the axleshaft and the transaxle case. Tap the end of the lever to uncouple the axleshaft from the differential side gear. Pull the front hub forward and separate the axleshaft from the transaxle.

**NOTE: Do not insert the lever too deeply between the shaft and the case or the oil seal lip could be damaged. To avoid damage to the oil seal, hold the CV-joint at the differential with one hand and pull the axleshaft straight out.**

12. Remove the right side axleshaft and joint shaft. Insert a lever between the driveshaft and the joint shaft. Pry the lever to uncouple the shafts.
13. Pull the front hub forward and then separate the axleshaft from the joint shaft.
14. Remove the joint shaft bracket mounting bolts. Remove the joint shaft and bracket from the transaxle as an assembly.
15. Remove the transaxle mounting bracket nuts at the crossmember.
16. Remove the crossmember and the left lower arm as an assembly.
17. Separate the shift change control rod from the shift change rod.
18. Remove the shift control extension bar from the transaxle. Remove the transaxle undercover.
19. Position the proper removal equipment under the transaxle assembly.
20. Remove the two remaining transaxle to engine bolts and separate the transaxle from the engine. Lower the assembly to the floor.
21. Remove the transaxle mounting brackets from the transaxle.
22. Installation is the reverse of the removal procedure.

### 1988–90 626 and MX-6

1. Remove the battery and battery carrier.
2. Disconnect the main fuse block, distributor lead and air flow meter connector. Remove the air cleaner assembly.
3. On turbocharged engines, disconnect the intercooler hoses. On nonturbocharged engines, remove the resonance chamber.
4. Disconnect the speedometer cable and the transaxle grounds.
5. Raise and support the vehicle safely and remove the front wheels and splash shield. Drain the transaxle oil.
6. Remove the clutch release cylinder and disconnect the tie rod ends using the proper tool.
7. Remove the stabilizer control links. Remove the nuts and bolts from the lower control arm ball joints and pull the lower control arms downward to separate them from the steering knuckles. Be careful not to damage the ball joint dust boots.
8. Insert a small pry bar between the left driveshaft and the transaxle case and tap the end of the lever to uncouple the driveshaft from the differential side gear. Pull the front hub forward and separate the driveshaft from the transaxle. Remove the left joint shaft bracket. Separate the right driveshaft and joint shaft in the same manner as the left.

**NOTE: Do not insert the lever too deeply between the shaft and the case or the oil seal lip could be damaged. To avoid damage to the oil seal, hold the CV-joint at the differential with one hand and pull the driveshaft straight out.**

9. Once both drive and joint shafts are removed, install differential side gear holders 49-G030-455 (turbo), 49-G027-003 or their equivalents in the differential side gears to hold them in place and prevent misalignemnt.
10. Remove the gusset plates and under cover. Remove the extension bar and the control rod. Remove the surge tank bracket and the starter.
11. Suspend the engine from the engine hanger with a suitable lifting device or engine support fixture.
12. Remove the No. 4 and No. 2 engine mounts and bracket. Disconnect the rubber hanger from the crossmember, then remove the crossmember and left side lower control arm as an assembly.
13. Lean the engine towards the transaxle and support the transaxle with a jack. Remove the trasaxle-to-engine mounting bolts and slide the transaxle from underneath the vehicle.
14. Installation is the reverse of the removal procedure. Fill the transaxle to the proper level.

### 1986–90 323 without 4WD

1. Disconnect the negative battery cable. Remove the air cleaner. Loosen the front wheel lug nuts.
2. Disconnect the speedometer from the transaxle. Disconnect the clutch cable from the release lever and remove the clutch cable bracket mounting bolts.
3. Remove the ground wire installation boot. Remove the water pipe

bracket. Remove the secondary air pipe and the EGR pipe bracket.

4. Remove the wire harness clip. Disconnect the coupler for the neutral switch and back-up lamp switch. Disconnect the body ground connector.

5. Remove the 2 upper transaxle mounting bolts. Mount the engine support tool 49-ER301-025A or equivalent to the engine hanger.

6. Raise and support the vehicle safely. Drain the transaxle oil into a suitable container and remove the front wheels.

7. Remove the engine under cover and side covers. Remove the front stabilizer.

8. Remove the lower arm ball joints and the knuckle clinch bolts, pull the lower arm downward and separate the lower arms from the knuckles.

9. Separate the driveshaft by pulling the front hub outward. Make sure not to use too much force at once, increase the force gradually. Be sure the driveshaft's ball joint is bent to its maximum extent. Do not allow the axleshafts to drop. Damage may occur to the ball and socket joints and to the rubber boots. Wire the shafts to the vehicle body when released from the differential.

10. Remove the transaxle crossmember. Separate the change control rod from the transaxle. Remove the extension bar from the transaxle. Remove the wiring and the starter motor.

11. Remove the end plates. Lean the engine toward the transaxle side to lower the transaxle by loosening the engine support hook bolt. Support the transaxle with a suitbale transaxle jack.

12. Remove the necessary engine brackets. Remove the remaining transaxle mounting bolt and No. 2 engine bracket. Lower the jack and slide the transaxle out from under the vehicle.

13. To install, reverse the removal procedure. Adjust clutch and shift linkage. Refill the transaxle with the proper grade of gear oil.

### *1988–90 323 with 4WD*

1. Remove the battery and the air cleaner assembly. Disconnect the speedometer cable in the center. Remove the clutch release cylinder retaining bolt and clip and remove the clutch release cylinder. Raise and support the vehicle safely and drain the tranaxle and engine oil.

2. Disconnect the neutral safety switch, back-up lamp switch, differential lock sensor switch and differential lock motor electrical connectors. Disconnect the transaxle shift and select control cables from the transaxle by removing the pins and cable retaining

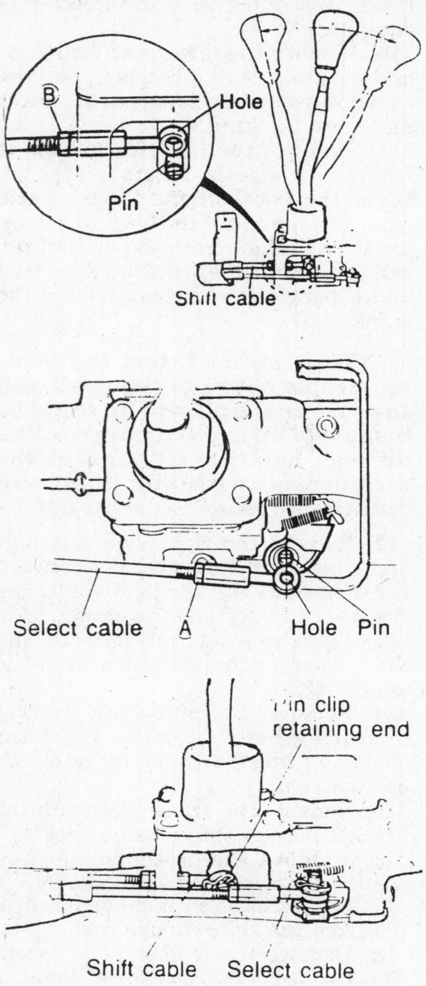


**Shift control cable adjustment—1988–89 323 with 4WD**

clips. Route the cables off to the side and out of the way.

3. Mount the engine support tool 49-8017-5A0 or equivalent to the engine hanger. Remove the No. 4 engine mount bracket and remove the the front wheels.

4. Remove the side cover and under cover. Remove the oil filter and differential lock assembly. Disconnect the starter wiring and remove the starter and stabilizer bar.

5. Disconnect the tie rod end from the lower control arm. Insert a small pry bar between the driveshaft and the transaxle case and tap the end of the lever to uncouple the driveshaft from the differential side gear. Remove the remaining driveshaft in the same manner. Insert differential side gear holder 49-B027-001 or its equivalent to hold the side gears in place and prevent misalignment.

6. Remove the end plate bolts and connect a suitable hoist and lifting strap to the transaxle. Lift the transaxle and transfer carrier assembly out of the engine.

7. Installation is the reverse of the removal procedure. Fill the crankcase. Fill the transaxle to the proper level through the speedometer drive gear opening. Adjust the shift and select control cables as described in "Linkage Adjustment".

## LINKAGE ADJUSTMENT

### *1988–90 323 with 4WD Only*

1. Set the transaxle shift lever to the **NEUTRAL** position.

2. On the transaxle make sure the shift and select levers are also in the **NEUTRAL** position.

3. Remove the shift lever console.

4. Disconnect the shift and select cables from the control levers by remvong the pins, flatwashers and spring clips. The clips must be replaced.

5. Make sure the select cable end hole aligns with the select lever pin. If not aligned, loosen cable adjusting nut "A" and rotate the cable end until the holes are aligned.

6. Place the shift lever at the center of its front-to-rear stoke.

7. Make sure the select cable end hole aligns with the select lever pin. If not aligned, loosen cable adjusting nut "B" and rotate the cable end until the holes are aligned.

8. Connect the cables.

# CLUTCH

## REMOVAL & INSTALLATION

1. Disconnect the negative battery cable. Remove the transmission or transaxle.

2. Remove the clutch cover, if equipped. Remove the pressure plate retaining bolts. Remove the pressure plate and clutch disc from the engine flywheel.

3. Remove the flywheel only if the flywheel surface is damaged or there is trouble in removing the pilot bearing. On the RX-7, use the flywheel box wrench tool 49-0820-035, to remove the flywheel nut and the flywheel. On all others, remove the bolts and the flywheel.

4. From the clutch housing, unhook the return spring from the throw out bearing and remove the bearing.

5. Remove the bolt holding the release fork and release lever together. Pull the release lever and remove the key and the release fork. until the retaining spring frees itself from the ball stud.

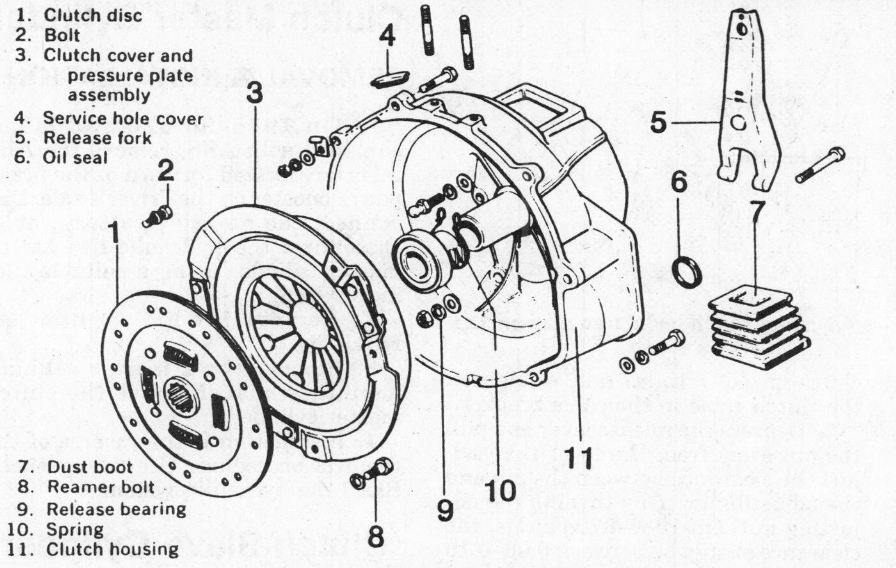

Clutch components (typical)

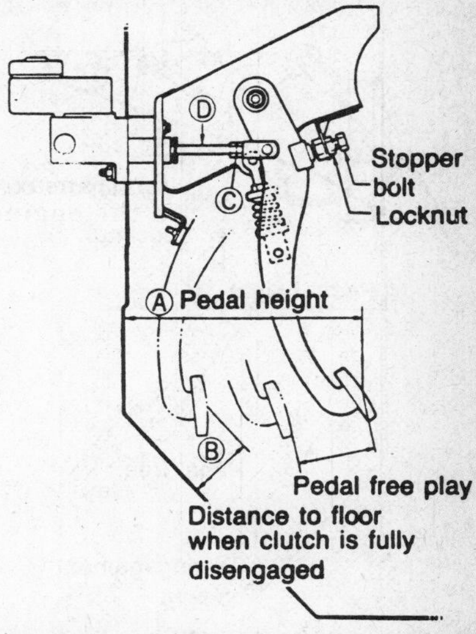

Clutch pedal height adjustment – 1988–89 626 and MX-6

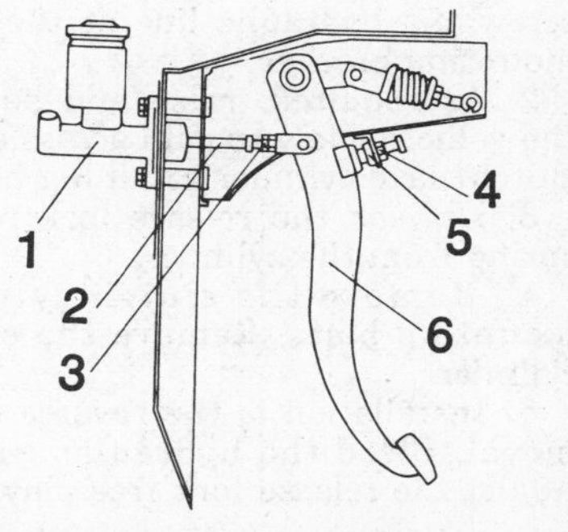

1. Master cylinder
2. Rod
3. Locknut
4. Adjusting bolt
5. Locknut
6. Clutch pedal

Clutch pedal height adjustment

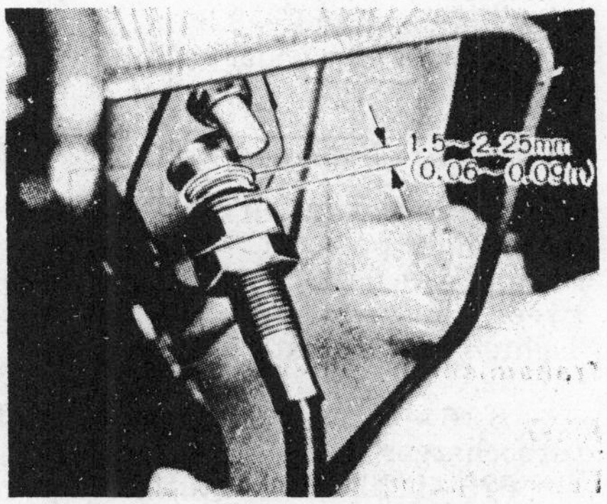

GLC clutch cable adjustment

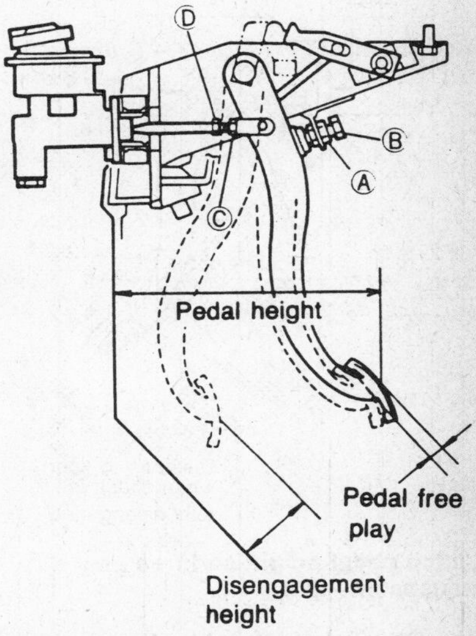

Clutch pedal height and free play adjustment – 323 cable type

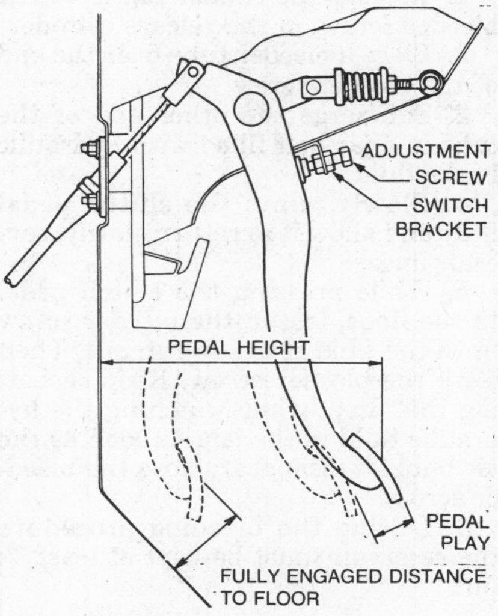

Clutch pedal height and free-play adjustments – 1983–87 626

6. Installation is the reverse of removal. If removed, install the flywheel and torque to specfication. The flywheel nut on vehicles equipped with a rotary engine is torqued to 289–362 ft. lbs. with no more than a 3 foot extension on the wrench.

## PEDAL HEIGHT ADJUSTMENT

1. Remove the floor mat.
2. Loosen the locknut on the adjusting, stopper bolt or clutch switch.
3. Turn the adjusting bolt until the clearance between the upper surface of the pedal pad and the firewall is within specification.
4. After adjustment, tighten the locknut.
5. Pedal height is as follows:
   1982–83 GLC – 7.48 ± 0.20 in.
   1984–85 GLC – 9.05–9.25 in.
   1982–85 RX-7 – 7.5 ± 0.20 in.
   1986–90 RX-7 – 8.66 ± 0.20 in.
   1982–88 626 – 8.44–8.64 in.
   1988–90 626 and MX-6 – 8.52–8.72 in.
   1986–90 323 (cable type) – 8.44–8.64 in.
   1988–90 323 (hydraulic type) – 9.02–9.22 in.
   1988–90 929 – 8.46–8.66 in.

## PEDAL FREE PLAY ADJUSTMENT

### *Cable Clutch*

#### EXCEPT 323

1. Depress the clutch pedal lightly by hand and measure the free play.
2. Loosen the locknut and pull the outer cable away from the engine side of the firewall.

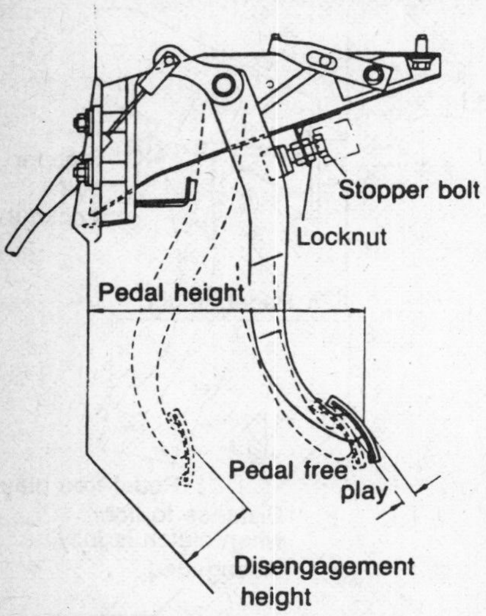


Clutch pedal height and free play adjustment—323 hydraulic type

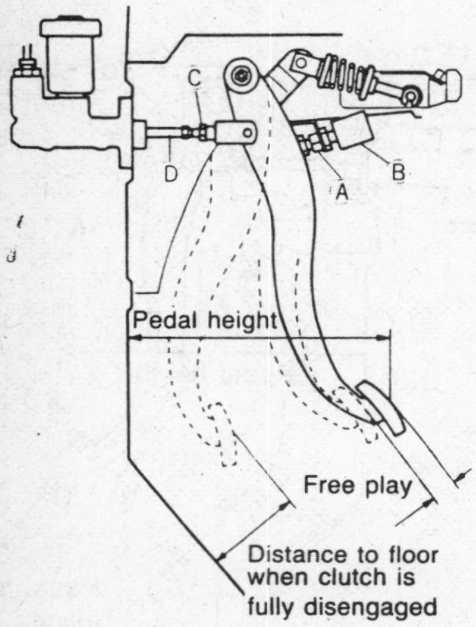


Clutch pedal height and free play adjustment—929

2. Turn the adjusting nut on the cable to obtain a 0.06–0.010 in. clearance between the adjusting nut and the firewall.
3. Tighten the locknut. Adjust the free play to specification.
4. Pedal free play is as follows:
   GLC—0.43–0.67 in.
   626—0.43–0.67 in. non turbocharged vehicles
   626—0.20–0.51 in. turbocharged vehicles
   MX-6—0.20–0.51 in.
   RX-7—0.02–0.12 in. at the pedal

**323**

Depress the pedal lightly and measure the free play. The free play should be from 0.35–0.59 in. If not within specification, adjust the free play as follows:
1. On 1988–90 vehicles, depress the clutch pedal 7 times and straighten the clutch cable in the cable bracket.

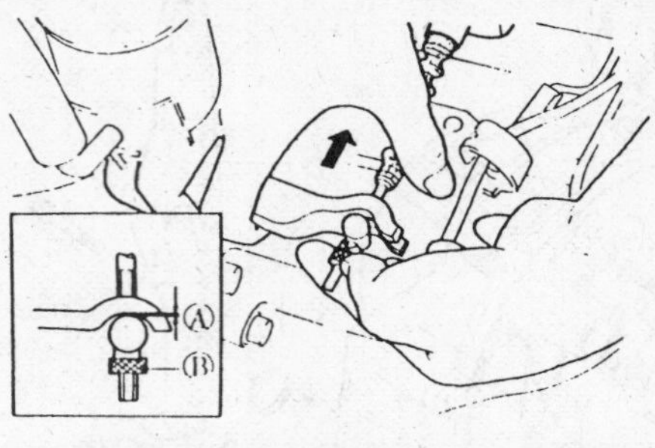


Adjusting clutch pedal free play on 323

2. Depress the release lever and pull the pin away from the lever then adjust the clearance between the pin and the adjusting lever by turning the adjusting nut. On 1986–87 vehicles, the clearance should be between 0.06–0.10 in. On 1988–89 vehicles, the clearance should be between 0.08 in.
3. After adjustment, ensure that when the clutch is disengaged, the distance between the floor and the upper center of the pedal is 3.3 in.
4. Recheck the pedal height and adjust if necessary.

### *Hydraulic Clutch*

Loosen the locknut on the clutch master cylinder pushrod. Turn the pushrod to obtain 0.02–0.12 in. free play between the pedal and the pushrod. Tighten the locknut on the pushrod.
   323—0.20–0.51 in.
   626—0.08–0.12 in. except turbocharger
   626—0.20–0.51 in. turbocharger
   MX-6—0.20–0.51 in.
   GLC—0.08–0.12 in.
   RX-7—0.02–0.12 in.
   929—0.02–0.12 in.

# Clutch Cable

## REMOVAL AND INSTALLATION

1. Remove the adjusting nut and pin.
2. Unbolt and remove the clutch cable bracket.
3. Disconect the cable from the clutch pedal.
4. Withdraw the cable from the engine compartment.
5. Installation is the reverse of the removal procedure. Coat the pedal cable hook and the joint between the release lever and pin with lithium grease.

# Clutch Master Cylinder

## REMOVAL & INSTALLATION

1. On 1988–90 626 and MX-6 equipped with ABS, remove the ABS relay box located forward of the brake power booster on the driver's side. Disconnect the negative battery cable. Disconnect the hydraulic line at the master cylinder using a suitable tubing wrench.
2. Remove the blower duct, as required.
3. Remove the 2 master cylinder mounting nuts. Remove the clutch master cylinder.
4. Installation is the reverse of the removal procedure. Use new gaskets. Bleed the hydraulic system.

# Clutch Slave Cylinder

## REMOVAL & INSTALLATION

1. Disconnect the negative battery cable. Remove the air cleaner. Unscrew the hydraulic line at the body mounting bracket.
2. As required, raise and support the vehicle safely to gain access to the clutch slave cylinder retaining bolts.
3. Unhook the release fork return spring from the cylinder.
4. Remove the clutch cylinder mounting bolts. Remove the clutch cylinder.
5. Installation is the reverse of removal. Bleed the hydraulic system. Adjust the release fork free play.

## BLEEDING THE CLUTCH HYDRAULIC SYSTEM

1. Remove the rubber cap from the bleeder screw on the release cylinder.
2. Place a bleeder tube over the end of the bleeder screw.
3. Submerge the other end of the tube in a jar half filled with hydraulic brake fluid.
4. Slowly pump the clutch pedal fully and allow it to return slowly, several times.
5. While pressing the clutch pedal to the floor, loosen the bleeder screw until the fluid starts to run out. Then close the bleeder screw. Keep repeating this Step, while watching the hydraulic fluid in the jar. As soon as the air bubbles disappear, close the bleeder screw.
6. During the bleeding procedure the reservoir must be kept at least ¾ full.

# AUTOMATIC TRANSMISSION

## REMOVAL & INSTALLATION

### *1983–85 RX-7*

1. Disconnect the negative battery cable.
2. Disconnect the inhibitor switch connector.
3. Apply the parking brake and block the wheels.
4. Remove the converter housing upper cover.
5. Disconnect the vacuum sensing tube from the vacuum diaphragm.
6. Remove the air cleaner assembly and the converter housing side cover.
7. Remove the bolts attaching the transmission to the rear end of the engine. Raise and support the vehicle safely.
8. Remove the front, the rear and the converter under covers.
9. Remove the air pipe and the converter brackets.
10. Remove the rear of the exhaust pipe and the pellet converter assembly.
11. Remove the front exhaust pipe and the monolith converter assembly.
12. Remove the floor under covers.
13. Remove the driveshaft and install the turning holder tool 49–0259–440 to the extension housing, to prevent the fluid from leaking from the housing.
14. Disconnect the starter wiring connectors.
15. Remove the starter and the lower converter housing cover.
16. Place an alignment mark on the drive pate and the torque converter, for reinstallation purposes.
17. Remove the bolts securing the torque converter to the drive plate.
18. Remove the transmission to engine bolts.
19. Properly support both the engine and the transmission assemblies.
20. Disconnect the speedometer cable and the selector rod at the selector lever.
21. Remove the transmission to body nuts.
22. Using a transmission removal jack, lower the transmission slightly and remove the fluid coolant tubes.
23. Slide the transmission rearward, until the input shaft clears the eccentric shaft, then remove the transmission/torque converter assembly from under the vehicle.
24. To install, reverse the removal procedure.

### *1986–90 RX-7*

1. Disconnect the negative battery cable. Raise the vehicle and support safely.
2. Remove the exhaust pipe with the heat insulator.
3. Matchmark and disconnect the propeller shaft. Install the turning holder tool 49–0259–440 to the extension housing, to prevent the fluid from leaking from the housing.
4. Remove the vacuum and oil pipes and plug the ends to prevent leakage.
5. Remove the starter bracket and starter.
6. Disconnect the speedometer cable.
7. Disconnect the shift rod from the transmission.
8. Remove the oil level gauge and filler pipe.
9. Disconnect the harness coupler.
10. Remove the service hole coupler.
11. Support the transmission with a jack and remove the transmission mounting bolts. Slide the transmission rearward, until the input shaft clears the eccentric shaft, then remove the transmission/torque converter assembly from under the vehicle.
12. Installation is the reverse of the removal procedure.

### *1983 GLC Wagon*

1. Disconnect the negative battery cable. Raise and support the vehicle safely. Drain the transmission.
2. Remove the heat insulator.
3. Disconnect the exhaust pipe.
4. Disconnect the driveshaft at the rear axle flange.
5. Matchmark and remove the driveshaft.
6. Disconnect the speedometer cable.
7. Disconnect the shift rod.
8. Remove all vacuum hoses.
9. Disconnect all wiring.
10. Disconnect the oil cooler lines and plug the ends.
11. Remove the access cover from the lower end of the converter housing.
12. Matchmark the drive plate and torque converter for realignment and remove the converter bolts.
13. Support the transmission using the proper equipment. Remove the crossmember.
14. Remove the converter housing to engine bolts.
15. Remove the filler tube.
16. Separate the flexplate and the converter.
17. Remove the transmission and converter as an assembly.
18. To install the transmission, reverse the removal procedure.

### *1988–90 929*

1. Disconnect the negative battery cable. Remove the transmission oil dipstick.
2. Raise and support the vehicle safely. Disconnect the shift rod. Remove the front exhaust pipe. Remove the heat insulator.
3. Matchmark and remove the driveshaft. Remove the starter. Disconnect the speedometer cable.
4. Disconnect the inhibitor switch connector, the turbine sensor connector, the lock up solenoid connector and the solenoid valve connector.
5. Remove the oil pipe and the vacuum pipe. Remove the undercover assembly.
6. Support the engine using the proper equipment. Support the transmission assembly, using the proper equipment. Remove the crossmember assembly.
7. Remove the flywheel cover. Remove the transmission to torque converter retaining bolts.
8. Remove the transmission to engine retaining bolts. Carefully remove the transmission from the vehicle.
9. Installation is the reverse of the removal procedure.

## PAN REMOVAL AND INSTALLATION

1. Raise and support the vehicle safely.
2. Place a suitable container to catch the transmission fluid when the pan is loosened.
3. Slowly loosen the oil pan mounting bolts and allow the pan to tip downward.
4. Support the oil pan and slowly remove the mounting bolts as the fluid drains from the edge of the pan.
5. Remove the oil pan and clean all gasket mating surfaces. Wipe the inside of the oil pan with a clean rag. Remove any deposits with solvent and dry the inside of the pan.
6. Installation is the reverse of removal. Use a new gasket and torque the oil pan mounting bolts to 5 ft. lbs.

## FILTER SERVICE

1. Raise and support the vehicle safely. Drain the transmission fluid.
2. Remove the transmission oil pan.
3. Remove the transmission filter from the valve body.
4. Installation is the reverse of the removal procedure. Be sure to use a new O-ring and valve body to filter gasket, as required.
5. Use a new transmission pan gasket or RTV sealant, as required. Fill the transmission with the proper grade and type transmission fluid.

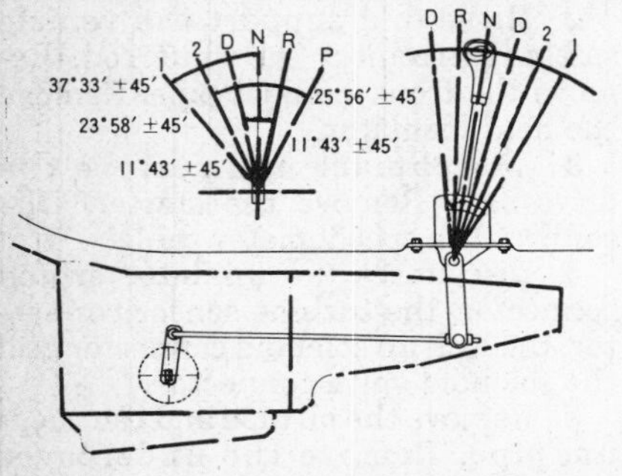


Transmission linkage adjustment

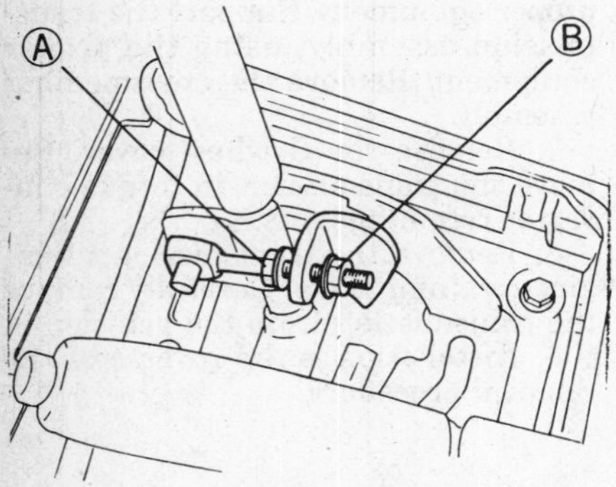


1986–90 RX-7 shifter adjustment

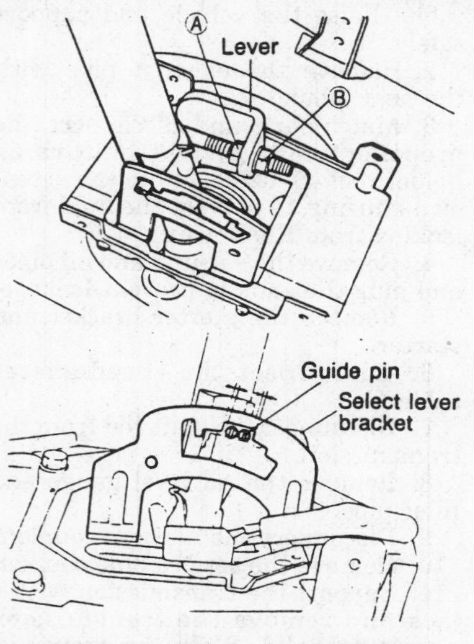


Shift lever adjustment—1988–90 929

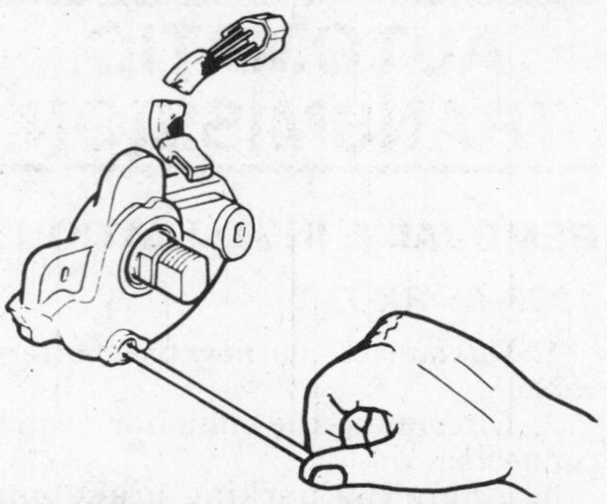

Align the neutral safety switch by inserting a drill through the holes on it.

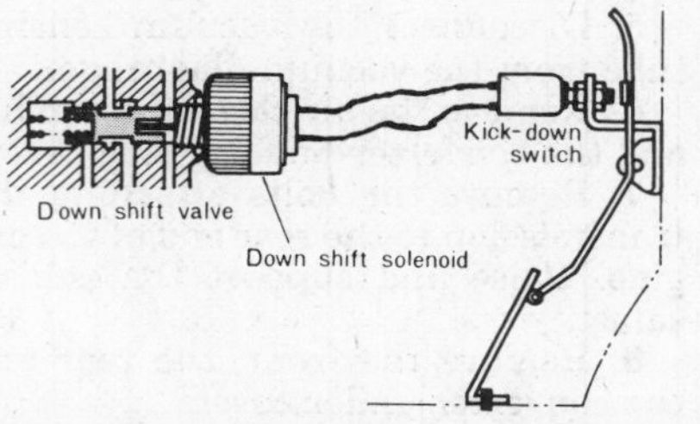


Kickdown switch the downshift solenoid circuit

## SHIFT LINKAGE ADJUSTMENT

### *1983–85 RX-7*

1. Before adjusting the linkage, check and adjust the idle speed. Remove the boot plate.
2. Place the shifting lever in the **PARK** position.
3. Loosen the selector lever plate setting bolt.
4. Raise and support the vehicle safely.
5. Place the selector rod at the Park position, the 1st detent position from the rear of the transmission.
6. Torque the selector lever plate setting bolt to 30 ft. lbs. Check the operation after adjustment.

### *1986–90 RX-7*

1. Remove the shifter cover.
2. Turn locknuts A and B to the proper adjusting position.
3. Move the shifter level to the **PARK** position.
4. Shift the transmission. Make sure the vehicle is supported safely when working underneath.
5. Turn locknut A by hand until it just touches the shifter lever, then back it off 1 full turn.
6. Torque locknut B to 8 ft. lbs.
7. Move the shifter and make sure there is a click at each gear when shifting from **PARK** through **FIRST**. The positions of the selector lever and the indicator should be exact. The release button should return smoothly when used to shift the selector.

### *1983 GLC Wagon*

1. Place the transmission selector lever in **NEUTRAL**.
2. Disconnect the clevis from the lower end of the selector arm.
3. Move the manual lever to the **NEUTRAL** position. The Neutral position is the third detent from the back.
4. Loosen the 2 clevis retaining nuts and adjust the clevis so that it freely enters the lever hole.
5. Tighten the retaining nuts.
6. Connect the clevis to the lever and secure with the spring washer, flat washer and retaining clip.

### *1988–90 929*

1. Remove the console shifter cover assembly. Position the transmission selector lever in the **PARK** detent.
2. Loosen the locknuts A and B. Move the selector from the **PARK** range and than back to the **PARK** range.
3. Using a feeler gauge, check the clearance between the first locknut, behind the shifter bracket. Adjust the shift lever and locknut to 0.039 in.
4. Remove the feeler gauge and tighten the locknut B.
5. Move the selector lever through the other gear ranges and check to be sure that there is clearance between the selector lever bracket and the guide pin.
6. If clearance does not exist, readjust both locknuts.

## NEUTRAL SAFETY SWITCH ADJUSTMENT

### *RX-7 and 929*

1. Shift the selector lever to the **NEUTRAL** position.
2. Raise the vehicle and support safely.
3. Loosen the inhibitor switch mounting bolts.
4. Unfasten the screw underneath the switch body.
5. Move the switch body so that the screw hole in the case aligns with the small hole inside the switch.
6. Check the alignment by inserting an 0.08 in. diameter pin through the holes. Once the proper alignment is obtained, remove the pin and tighten the switch mounting bolts. Install the screw and lightly tighten.
7. Check the system for proper operation.

### *1983 GLC Wagon*

1. Place the manual lever in **NEUTRAL**. Neutral is the third detent from the back.
2. Remove the manual lever.
3. Loosen the neutral switch attaching bolts and remove the screws from the alignment hole at the bottom of the switch.
4. Rotate the switch so that the hole in the switch aligns with the hole in the internal rotor. The 0.078 in. diameter pin should be inserted while tightening switch.

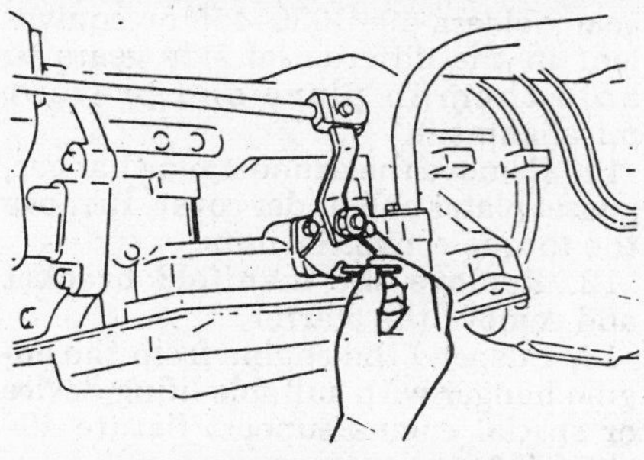

Adjusting inhibitor switch on RX-7 and 929

5. Install the alignment hole screw and manual lever.

## KICKDOWN SWITCH AND DOWNSHIFT SOLENOID ADJUSTMENT

### *1983–85 RX-7 Only*

1. Disconnect the wiring connectors from the kickdown switch.
2. Screw out the kickdown switch, a few turns.
3. Fully depress the accelerator pedal.
4. Gradually screw in the kickdown switch until you hear a clicking sound then screw it in ½ turn more.

**NOTE: On the 1984–85 RX-7 screw the switch stopper just to where it makes contact with the accelerator pedal.**

5. Tighten the locknut and connect the wiring connectors.

### *1983 GLC Wagon*

1. Check the accelerator linkage for smooth operation.
2. Turn the ignition on but do not start the engine.
3. Depress the accelerator pedal fully to the floor. As the pedal nears the end of its travel, a light click should be heard from the downshift solenoid.
4. If the kickdown switch operates too soon, loosen the locknut on the switch shaft. Adjust the shaft so that the accelerator linkage make contact with it when the pedal is depressed $^7/_8$–$^{15}/_{16}$ of the way to the floor. Tighten the locknut.
5. If no noise comes from the solenoid at all, then check the wiring for the solenoid and the switch.
6. If the wiring is in good condition, remove the wire from the solenoid and connect it to a 12 volt power source. If the solenoid does not click when connected, it is defective and should be replaced.
7. When the solenoid is removed, about two pints of transmission fluid will leak out.

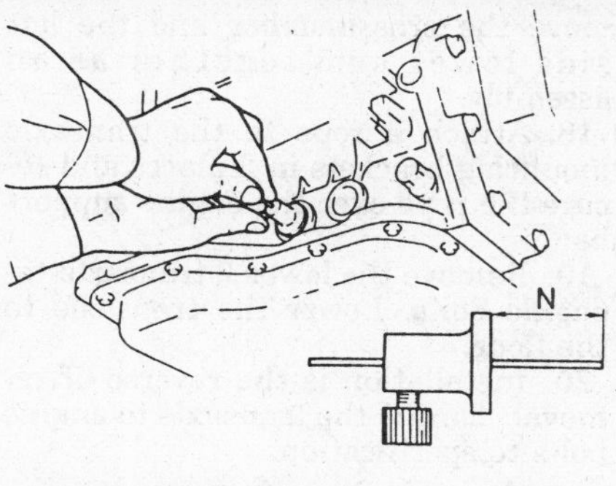


Measuring vacuum diaphragm rod length with special tool—929 and 1986–90 RX-7

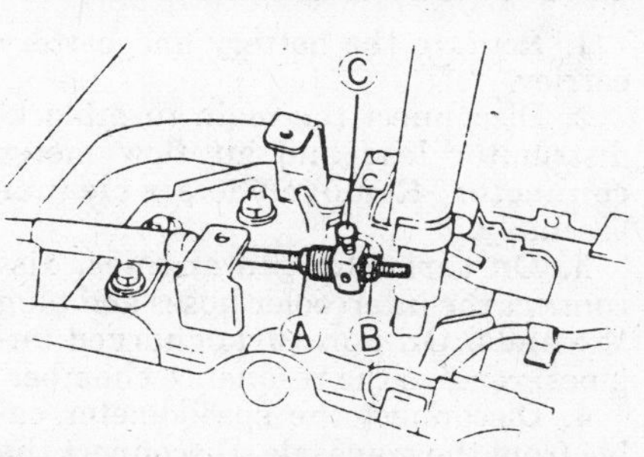


Vacuum diaphargm rod length selection chart

## VACUUM DIAPHRAGM ADJUSTMENT

### *1986–90 RX-7 and 929*

1. Drain approximately 1 quart of fluid from the transmission prior to removing the vacuum diaphragm.
2. Remove the vacuum diaphragm rod and O-ring from the transmission.
3. Using special measuring tool 49–G032–355 and a machinists scale, measure the "N" dimension of the rod. Use the dimension and the selection chart to select the correct length rod.
4. Install the vacuum diaphragm with a new O-ring and fill the transmission to the proper level.

## BAND ADJUSTMENT

### *Jatco 3N71B and 14N71B*

1. Raise the vehicle and support it safely.
2. Drain the transmission fluid and remove the transmission pan.
3. Loosen the locknut and torque the servo adjusting bolt to 9–11 ft. lbs.
4. Back off the servo bolt 2 turns for the 3N71B unit or 3 turns for the L4N71B unit. Tighten the locknut.
5. On the L4N71B, an overdirve brake band is used. Loosen the locknut and torque the stem to 5–7 ft. lbs., then back off the stem two full turns.
6. Install the pan assembly and fill with fluid.

### *JATCO R3A*

1. Raise the vehicle and support safely.
2. Locate the servo cover and remove it from the right side of the case.
3. Loosen locknut and tighten the servo adjusting bolt to 9–11 ft. lbs. torque.
4. Loosen the servo bolt two full turns and tighten the locknut.
5. Install the servo cover and lower the vehicle.

# AUTOMATIC TRANSAXLE

## REMOVAL & INSTALLATION

### *1983–85 GLC*

1. Disconnect the negative battery cable. Raise and support the vehicle safely. When removing or installing the transaxle assembly the rear end of the engine must be lifted and secured with the aid of a chain, or special engine support.
2. Disconnect all electrical wiring and connections, control linkages from the transaxle. Mark these units to aid in reassembling.
3. Remove the front wheels. Disconnect the lower ball joints from the steering knuckles. Pull the driveshafts from the differential gears.

**NOTE: Separate the driveshaft by pulling the front hub outward. Make sure not to use too much force at once, increase the force gradually. Be sure the driveshafts ball joint is bent to its maximum extent. Do not allow the axleshafts to drop. Damage may occur to the ball and socket joints and to the rubber boots. Wire the shafts to the vehicle body when released from the differential.**

4. Remove the undercover. Hook the engine support tool 49-E301-025 or equivalent on the engine hanger and hoist the engine up slightly. Disconnect the control cable. Remove the crossmember and disconnect the cooler lines.
5. Disconnect the oil hose from the oil pipe, plug both the pipe and the hose to prevent fluid lose. Remove the starter motor. Remove the end covers and remove the bolts holding the torque converter to the drive plate.
6. Using the proper equipment, support the transaxle. Remove the transaxle to engine mounting bolts. Remove the unit from the vehicle.

7. Installation is the reverse of removal. Be sure the rubber mounts are not twisted or distorted and not in contact with the body.

8. To properly install the axleshafts in the differential side gears, position the axleshaft in a horizontal position, push the driveshafts into the side gears. To be sure the axleshaft engages the groove, attempt to pull the axleshaft from the differential. Reconnect the ball joints at the lower arms.

### *1983–87 626*

1. Disconnect the negative battery cable and drain the transaxle. Disconect the speedometer cable.

2. Remove the shift control cable from the transaxle.

3. Disconnect the ground wire, the inhibitor switch and the kickdown solenoid.

4. Remove the starter motor.

5. Attach the engine support tool 49–G030–025 and suspend the engine.

6. Remove the line connected to the vacuum diaphragm.

7. Remove the 5 upper transaxle-to-engine attaching bolts.

8. Remove the transmission cooler lines from the transaxle. Plug the ends to prevent leakage.

9. Raise and support the vehicle safely.

10. Remove the front wheels and the left and right splash shields.

11. Remove the stabilizer bar control link. Remove the undercover.

12. Remove the pinch bolt and separate the ball joint from the steering knuckle.

13. Pull the left axleshaft from the transaxle by inserting a chisel between the driveshaft and the bearing housing. Tap the end of the chisel lightly in order to separate the axleshaft and differential side gear. Do not insert the chisel too far between the shaft and the housing, doing so might damage the lip of the oil seal or the dust cover.

14. Pull the front hub outward and remove the axleshaft from the transaxle. Support the axleshaft during and after removal to avoid damaging the CV-joints and boots.

15. Pull the right axleshaft from the transaxle by inserting a prybar between the axleshaft and the joint shaft and force the axleshaft coupling open.

16. Pull the front hub out and remove the axleshaft from the joint shaft. Support the axleshaft during and after removal to avoid damaging the CV-joints and boots. Remove the joint shaft assembly from the transaxle.

17. Remove the transaxle undercover and torque converter to drive plate bolts. Using the proper equipment, support the transaxle assembly. Remove the crossmember and the left side lower arm together as an assembly.

18. Attach a rope to the transaxle mounting brackets in 2 places and secure the rope over the engine support bar.

19. Remove the lower 2 transaxle-to-engine bolts. Lower the transaxle to the floor.

20. Installation is the reverse of removal. Torque the transaxle to engine bolts to specification.

### *1988–90 626 and MX-6*

1. Remove the battery and battery carrier.

2. Disconnect the main fuse block, distributor lead and air flow meter connector. Remove the air cleaner assembly.

3. On turbocharged engines, disconnect the intercooler hoses and plug the ends. On non-turbocharged engines, remove the resonance chamber.

4. Disconnect the speedometer cable from the transaxle. Disconnect the inhibitor switch, soleniod valve, pulse generator and fluid temperature switch. Disconnect the transaxle ground wires.

5. Disconnect the selector and throttle cables from the transaxle selector lever.

6. Raise and support the vehicle safely and remove the front wheels and splash shield. Drain the transaxle fluid. Disconnect the inlet and outlet hoses from the oil cooler and plug the ends to prevent leakage.

7. Separate the tie rod ends using the proper tool.

8. Remove the stabilizer control links. Remove the nuts and bolts from the lower control arm ball joints and pull the lower control arms downward to separate them from the steering knuckles. Be careful not to damage the ball joint dust boots.

9. Insert a small pry bar between the left drivehshaft and the transaxle case and tap the end of the lever to uncouple the driveshaft from the differential side gear. Pull the front hub forward and separate the driveshaft from the transaxle. Remove the left joint shaft bracket. Separate the right driveshaft and joint shaft in the same manner as the left.

**NOTE: Do not insert the lever too deeply between the shaft and the case or the oil seal lip could be damaged. To avoid damage to the oil seal, hold the CV-joint at the differential with one hand and pull the axleshaft straight out.**

10. Once both drive and joint shafts are removed, install differential side gear holders 49–G030–455 or equivalent in the differential side gears to hold them in place and prevent misalignment.

11. Remove the exhaust pipe hanger, gusset plates and under cover. Remove the torque converter nuts.

12. Remove the manifold bracket and remove the starter.

13. Suspend the engine from the engine hanger with suitable lifing device or special engine support fixture 49–G017–5A0.

12. Remove the No. 4 and No. 2 engine mounts and bracket. Remove the crossmember and left side lower control arm as an assembly.

13. Lean the engine towards the transaxle and support the transaxle with a jack. Remove the transaxle-to-engine mounting bolts and slide the transaxle from underneath the vehicle.

14. Installation is the reverse of the removal procedure. Fill the transaxle to the proper level. Adjust the throttle cable and selector cables.

### *1986–87 323*

1. Disconnect the negative battery cable. Remove the air cleaner and loosen the front wheel lug nuts.

2. Disconnect the speedometer and throttle cable from the transaxle. Disconnect the change control cable from the transaxle.

3. Remove the ground wire installation boot. Remove the water pipe bracket. Remove the secondary air pipe and the EGR pipe bracket.

4. Remove the wire harness clip. Disconnect the coupler for the inhibitor switch, the kickdown solenoid and any other necessary solenoids or switches. Disconnect the body ground connector and selector cable.

5. Remove the two or four upper transaxle mounting bolts. Disconnect the neutral switch connector and ther vacuum line from the vacuum diaphragm. Disconnect the transaxle oil cooler lines. Mount the engine support tool 49-ER301-025A or equivalent to the engine hanger.

6. Raise and support the vehicle safely. Drain the transaxle oil into a suitable container and remove the front wheels.

7. Remove the engine under cover and side covers. Remove the front stabilizer.

8. Remove the lower arm ball joints and the knuckle clinch bolts, pull the lower arm downward and separate the lower arms from the knuckles.

9. Separate the driveshaft from the transaxle by prying with a suitable pry bar inserted between the shaft and the case. Be sure not to damage the oil seals.

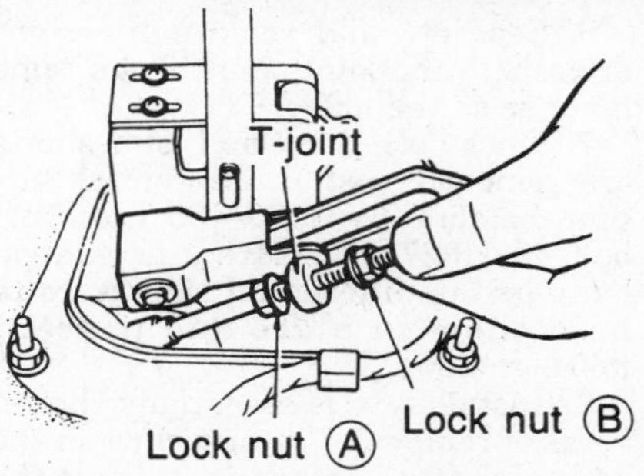


**Shifter adjustment on 323 and 626 models**

10. Using the proper equipment, support the transaxle assembly. Remove the transaxle crossmember. Remove the wiring and the starter motor.
11. Remove the end plates. Lean the engine toward the transaxle side to lower the transaxle by loosening the engine support hook bolt. Support the transaxle with a suitbale transaxle jack.
12. Remove the necessary engine brackets. Remove the remaining transaxle mounting bolt. Lower the jack and slide the transaxle out from under the vehicle.
13. To install, reverse the removal procedure. Adjust the shift linkage. Refill the transaxle with the proper grade of gear oil.

### *1888–90 323*

1. Disconnect the negative battery cable. Raise the vehicle and support safely. Drain the transxle.
2. Disconnect the lead wire from the distributor. Disconnect the air flow meter connector and remove the air cleaner assembly.
3. Disconnect the speedometer and throttle selector cables from the selector lever.
4. Disconnect the inhibitor switch and overdrive release sloniod connectors. Disconnect the transaxle case grounds and route the wiring off to the side and out of the way.
5. Unbolt and remove the selector cable from the transaxle case.
6. Remove the heater pipe and disconnect the oil hose from the conection on the transaxle. Plug the end of the hose to prevent leakage.
7. Suspend the engine from the hanger bracket with special support fixture 49-G017-5A0 or its equivalent.
8. Remove the front wheels. Remove the splash shield and engine under cover.
9. Remove the lower arm ball joints and the knuckle clinch bolts, pull the lower arm downward and separate the lower arms from the knuckles.
10. Separate the driveshaft from the transaxle by prying with a suitable pry bar. Install special differential side gear holding tool 49-B027-006 or equivalent to prevent misalignment of the side gears. Disconnect the other driveshaft in the same manner. Remove the clips from the ends of the driveshafts and replace with new.
11. Remove the starter, No. 2 engine mount and the crossmember. Remove the gusset and end plates.
12. Lock the flywheel with the proper tool and remove the torque converter bolts. Lean the engine towards the transaxle by loosening the support hook bolt on the support fixture.
13. Support the transaxle with a jack and remove the transaxle mounting bolts. Remove the transaxle from nderneath the engine.
14. Installation is essentially the reverse of the removal procedure. Torque the transaxle mounting bolts to 41–59 ft. lbs., torque converter and drive plate bolts to 25–36 ft. lbs. Adjust the throttle and selector cables.

## PAN REMOVAL & INSTALLATION

1. Raise and support the vehicle safely. Remove splash shields, ect. as required to gain pan removal clearance.
2. Drain the transaxle fluid..
3. Slowly loosen the oil pan mounting bolts and allow the pan to tip downward.
4. Support the oil pan and slowly remove the mounting bolts as the fluid drains from the edge of the pan.
5. Remove the oil pan and clean all gasket mating surfaces. Wipe the inside of the oil pan with a clean rag. Remove any deposits with solvent and dry the inside of the pan. If equipped, remove the pan magnets, clean them off and install them in their original positions.
6. Installation is the reverse of removal. Use a new gasket and torque the oil pan mounting bolts to specification.

## FILTER SERVICE

1. Raise and support the vehicle safely. Drain the transaxle fluid.
2. Remove the transaxle fluid pan.
3. Remove the transaxle filter from the valve body.
4. Installation is the reverse of the removal procedure. Be sure to use a new O-ring and valve body to filter gasket, as required.
5. Use a new transaxle pan gasket or RTV sealant, as required. Fill the transaxle with the proper grade and type transmission fluid.

## SHIFT LEVER ADJUSTMENT

1. Set the parking brake.
2. Loosen locknuts A and B.
3. Move the gearshaft to the **Park** position.
4. Shift the selector lever on the transaxle to the **Neutral** position. This is the third detent from the rear of the transaxle.
5. Turn locknut A by hand until it lightly contacts the T-joint or spacer.
6. Tighten locknut B or lcoking screw C on 1988–89 626 8 ft. lbs.
7. Move the selector lever through all gear positions and make sure it operates smoothly.

## KICKDOWN SWITCH ADJUSTMENT

1. Connect an ohmmeter between the terminals of the kickdown switch.
2. Depress the accelerator to the floor and check for continuity.
3. To adjust, loosen the switch locknuts and depress the accelerator cable fully.
4. Turn the switch until the threaded portion of the case contacts the stopper. Back off the switch ½ revolution and tighten the locknuts.

## DOWNSHIFT SOLENOID

When the accelerator pedal is fully depressed, the kickdown switch becomes active and the downshift solenoid gets power. The downshift valve in the control valve is pushed up to kickdown position 3-to-2 and position 2-to-1 at an given speed.

## NEUTRAL SAFETY/REVERSE LAMP SWITCH ADJUSTMENT

The switch contacts should operate when the switch plunger is moved into its respective operating positions. The switch operates from the closed to the neutral position and then to the reverse light position. The switch plunger must operate smoothly otherwise the gear selector will be affected.
1. Turn the manual shaft to the **NEUTRAL** position.
2. loosen the inhibitor switch mounting bolts.
3. Remove the screw and move the inhibitor switch so that the small hole aligns with the screw hole. Check this alignment by inserting a 0.079 in. pin through the 2 holes.
4. Tighten the switch mounting bolts and remove the pin. Install and tighten he screw.

# DRIVE AXLE

## Halfshaft

### REMOVAL & INSTALLATION

#### *1983–85 GLC*

1. Raise and support the vehicle safely. Remove both front wheels and splash shields. Drain the transaxle fluid.
2. Loosen the drive axle locknut at the center of the disc brake hub after raising the lock tab. Apply brake pressure while loosening.
3. Remove the lower ball joint from the steering knuckle.
4. Remove the axleshaft from the transaxle case by pulling the brake caliper outward with increasing force. While applying outward force, hit the driveaxleshaft with a brass hammer, if necessary, to help in removal.
5. Remove the locknut and pull the axleshaft from the steering knuckle. Remove the axleshaft and plug the transaxle case with a clean rag to prevent dirt from entering.
6. Installation is in the reverse order of removal. Before installing the axleshaft into the transaxle case, check the oil seals for cuts or damage. Replace the oil seals if necessary. Insert the axle into the transaxle case by pushing on the wheel hub assembly.

#### *1983–87 626 and 1986–90 323*

1. Raise and support the vehicle safely. Drain the transaxle fluid and remove the splash shield.
2. Operate the brakes to secure the wheel hub and loosen the axleshaft locknut, but do not remove it. Remove the front wheels. Raise the tabs before loosening the locknut.
3. Remove the stabilizer bar control link from the lower arm.
4. Remove the pinch bolt and remove the ball joint from the steering knuckle.
5. Remove the left side axleshaft.
   a. On manual transaxles, insert a prybar between the axleshaft and the transaxle case. Remove the axleshaft from the side gear by lightly tapping the end of the prybar. Do not insert the prybar too far, doing so, could damage the lip of the oil seal or the dust cover.
   b. For automatic transaxle, insert a prybar between the axleshaft and the bearing housing. Tap the end of the prybar in order to uncouple the axleshaft and differential side gear.
   c. After removing the axleshaft locknut, pull the front hub outward and toward the rear. Disconnect the axleshaft from the wheel and the transaxle.
6. Remove the right side axleshaft and joint shaft.
   a. Insert a prybar between the axleshaft and the joint shaft and separate them.
   b. Remove the axleshaft locknut and pull the front hub outward and to the rear, disconnecting the axleshaft from the front hub. Remove the axleshaft from the joint shaft.
   c. If the driveshaft is stuck to the front hub and cannot be removed, install bearing puller tool 49-0839-425C or equivalent, to push the shaft out. After removing the driveshaft, install differential side gear holder tool 49G-030-455 into the transaxle, this prevents dirt from getting into the transaxle.
7. Install differential side gear holder 49–G030–455 to prevent misalignment of the side gears.
8. Installation is the reverse of removal.

#### *1988–90 626 and MX-6*

**NOTE: Removal and installation of the driveshafts is the same for manual and automatic transaxles.**

1. Drain the transaxle oil. Raise the the vehicle and support safely.
2. Remove the front wheels and the splash shields. Apply the brakes and unstake the driveshaft locknut using a small cold chisel. Loosen the locknut but do not remove it.
3. Using the proper tool, disconnect the tie rod ends. Remove the stabilizer control links.
4. Remove the nuts and bolts from the lower control arm ball joints and pull the lower control arm downward to separate it from the steering knuckle. Be careful not to damage the ball joint dust boots.
5. Remove the locknut and insert a small pry bar between the left driveshaft and the transaxle case. Tap the end of the lever to uncouple the driveshaft from the differential side gear. Pull the front hub forward and separate the driveshaft from the transaxle. If the hub is difficult to remove, use a puller to separate it from the driveshaft. Remove the left joint shaft bracket and shaft.

**NOTE: Do not insert the lever too deeply between the shaft and the case or the oil seal lip and the boot could be damaged. To avoid damage to the oil seal and the boot, hold the CV-joint at the differential with one hand and pull the driveshaft straight out.**

6. Separate and remove the right driveshaft and joint shaft in the same manner as the left.
7. Once both drive and joint shafts are removed, install differential side gear holders 49–G030–455 (non-turbo), 49–H027–003 (turbo) or equivalents in the differential side gears to hold them in place and prevent misalignment.
8. Installation is essentially the reverse of removal. Use new clips on the spline shafts. Before installing the driveshafts, inspect the oil seal for damage. Coat the seal with clean transaxle oil prior to installation. Lock the stabilizer nut so that approximately 0.8 in. of the through bolt thread is exposed. Torque the wheel hub locknut to 174–235 ft. lbs.

### CV-JOINT OVERHAUL

**For all CV-joint overhual procedures, please refer to "CV-Joint Overhaul" in the Unit Repair Section.**

## Driveshaft and U-Joints

### REMOVAL & INSTALLATION

#### *1983–90 RX-7, 1988–90 929 and 1983 GLC Wagon*

Do not remove the oil seals from vehicles with a center bearing unless they are defective.

1. Raise and support the vehicle safely. Matchmark the flanges on the driveshaft and pinion so that they may be installed in their original position.
2. Remove all necessary exhaust components. On 929, remove the all the nuts, bolts, lockwashers, spacers and bushings from the center support bearing. Remove the nuts that attach the driveshaft to the companion flange of the rear axle. Lower the back end of the driveshaft and slide the front end out of the transmission.
3. Plug up the hole in the transmission with the main shaft turning holder tool 49–0259–440 or 49–S120–440, to prevent fluid from leaking.
4. Driveshaft installation is the reverse of removal. On RX-7, if the driveshaft was replaced and unusual noise and vibration is noticed, correct the problem with balance washers positioned on various places on the companion flange. If noise and vibration is exhibited on the 929, the problem may be corrected by using different size bolts and spacers on the center bearing support. On 929, torque the center bearing bolts to 28–38 ft. lbs.

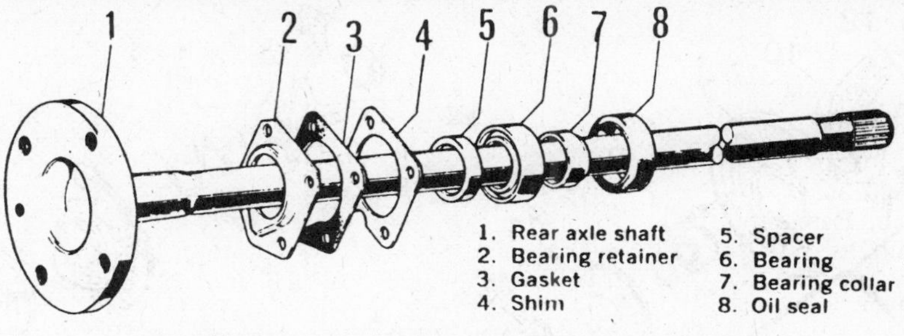


**Components of the rear wheel drive axle shaft assembly**

### *1988–90 323 with 4WD*

1. Raise and support the vehicle safely.
2. Matchmark the front and rear flanges for assembly reference. Stuff a rag in the double offset joint to prevent damage to the boot by the propeller shaft. Remove the front and rear retaining bolts and nuts.
3. Remove the nuts, bolts, shims and bushings from the center bearing support and remove the support bracket.
4. Lower and remove the driveshaft from the vehicle.
5. Installation is the reverse of the removal procedure. Torque the rear flange bolts to 27–38 ft. lbs. Torque the front flange bolts to 20–22 ft. lbs. Check that the front and rear shafts are aligned. If not, adjust the height of the center bearing support with shims. Both shims must be the same thickness.

# Rear Axle Shafts

## REMOVAL & INSTALLATION

### *1983–85 All Models Except RX-7*

1. Raise and support the vehicle safely.
2. Remove the rear wheel assembly.
3. If equipped with brake drums, remove the brake drum, the return spring, the brake shoe assembly, the parking brake cable, the brake tube and the backing plate nuts.
4. If equipped with disc brakes, remove the brake caliper, the disc rotor and the dust cover retaining nuts.
5. Connect the axleshaft puller tool 49-0223-630B and attachment tool 49-8501-631 to the axleshaft, then pull the backing plate assembly from the housing.
6. To install, reverse the removal procedure.

### *1983–85 RX-7*

1. If the vehicle is equipped with rear drum brakes, perform the following:
   a. Raise and support the vehicle safely. Remove the tire and wheel assembly.
   b. Remove the brake drum. Remove the brake shoes. Remove the brake line clip. Remove the backing plate assembly and position it to the side.
   c. Loosen, but do not remove the hub spindle to shock absorber through bolts. Remove the lateral link through bolt.
   d. Remove the hub spindle to shock absorber through bolts. Remove the hub spindle assembly from its mounting.
   e. Installation is the reverse of the removal procedure.
2. If the vehicle is equipped with rear disc brakes, perform the following:
   a. Raise and support the vehicle safely. Remove the tire and wheel assembly.
   b. Disconnect the brake line from the shock absorber. Remove the disc brake caliper and position it to the side.
   c. Remove the locknut and the dust cover. Remove the lateral link through bolt.
   d. Remove the hub spindle to shock absorber through bolts. Remove the hub spindle assembly from its mounting.
   e. Installation is the reverse of the removal procedure.

### *1986–90 RX-7*

1. Raise the vehicle and support it safely.
2. Remove the rear tire. Using a blunt drift or small cold chisel, uncrimp the locknut on the axleshaft. Depress the brake pedal to hold the hub secure and then remove the axle nut.
3. Remove the caliper assembly and tie it back with a piece of rope. Remove the setting screws and the disc plate.
4. Remove the knuckle assembly.
5. Remove the nuts attaching the driveshaft to the companion flange ot the transaxle and remove the driveshaft.
6. When installing, insert the wheel side of the driveshaft to the axle flange and then install the differential side of the driveshaft. Tighten the driveshaft attaching nuts 40–47 ft. lbs.
7. The rest of the installation procedure is the reverse order of the removal procedure. On ABS equipped vehicles, check the clearance between the speed sensor and the rotor. The clearance should be between 0.016–0.039 in. Torque the locknut to 174–231 ft. lbs. Be sure to measure the play of the wheel bearing. If the play exceeds the 0.004 in. or less, replace the wheel bearing. Crimp the driveshaft locknut to the driveshaft groove.

### *1988–90 929*

1. Raise and support the vehicle safely. Remove the rear tire and wheel assembly. Remove the rear driveshaft.
2. Remove the caliper and position it to the side. Remove the locknut and washer. Remove the rotor.
3. Remove the brake shoes. Disconnect the parking brake cable. Remove the wheel speed sensor assembly (ABS equipped vehicles only).
4. Disconnect and remove the rear trailing arm. Remove the rear shock absorber.
5. Disconnect the stabilizer control link. Disconnect the upper control link using the proper tool. Disconnect the lower link in front of the assembly using the proper tool. Disconnect the lower link behind the assembly.
6. Matchmark the driveshaft and flange for asembly reference and remove the rear hub and support assembly from its mounting.
7. Installation is the reverse of the removal procedure. Torque the lower front and rear and upper links to 40–55 ft. lbs, rear hub support to 69–86 ft. lbs., caliper assembly to 33–50 ft. lbs. and driveshaft flange bolts to 40–47 ft. lbs. Check the rear bearing end play. Maximum allowable endplay is 0.08 in. Torque the disc plate lock nut to 174–231 ft. lbs. Use a new locknut. Adjust the rear toe-in.

### *1988–90 323 with 4WD*

1. Raise and support the vehicle safely. Remove the rear tire and wheel assembly.
2. Remove the dust cap. Unstake the locknut and remove. To remove the right rear locknut, turn it clockwise.
3. Remove the caliper and position it to the side. Remove the driveshaft, using tool 490-8394-25C.
4. Disconnect the lateral link. Disconnect the trailing link. Remove the lower arm retaining bolts that hold the strut assembly to the lower arm.
5. Remove the hub and knuckle assembly from its mounting.

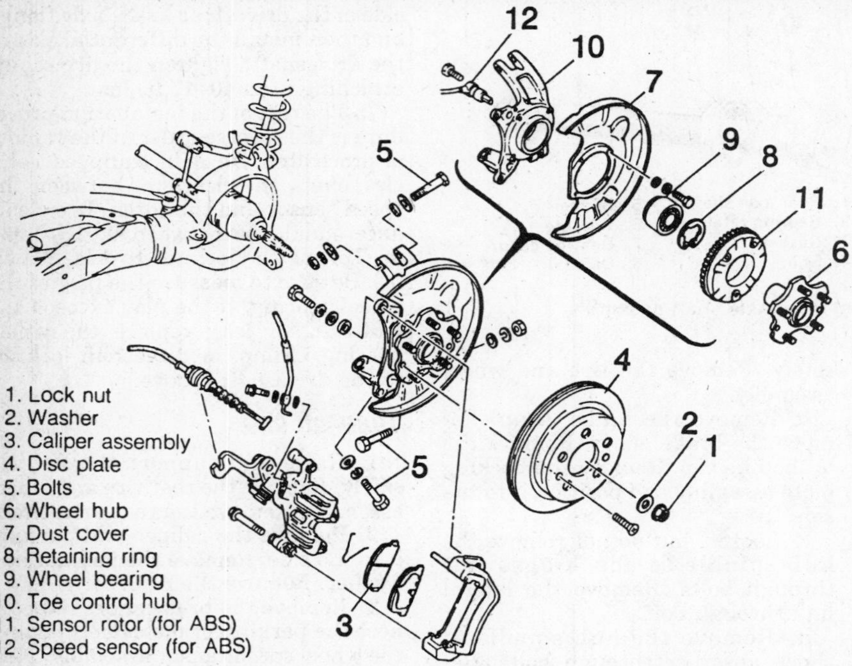


1. Lock nut
2. Washer
3. Caliper assembly
4. Disc plate
5. Bolts
6. Wheel hub
7. Dust cover
8. Retaining ring
9. Wheel bearing
10. Toe control hub
11. Sensor rotor (for ABS)
12. Speed sensor (for ABS)

Rear axle hub components – 1986–90 RX-7

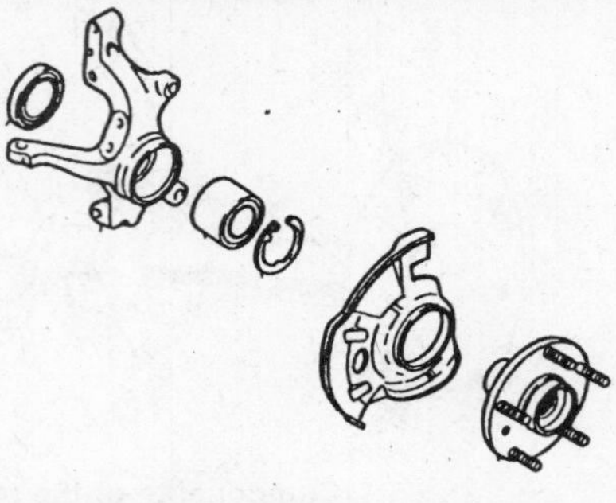

Front axle hub compoents on 1988–90 626 and MX-6

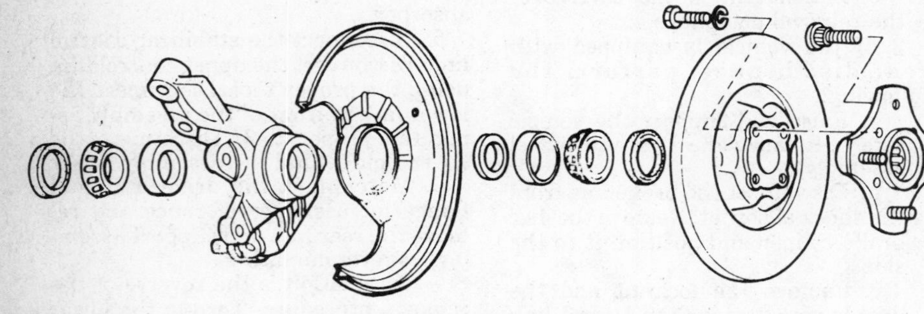

Rear axle hub components – 323 with 4WD

6. Installation is the reverse of the removal procedure. Check the rear wheel bearing endplay. There must be no endplay. Torque the locknuts to 116–174 ft. lbs.

## Front Wheel Drive Axle Hub and Bearing

### REMOVAL & INSTALLATION

1. Loosen the lug nuts. Raise the vehicle and support it safely. Remove the tire and wheel.
2. Raise the staked tab from the hub center nut, remove the nut from the axle. Apply the brake to help hold the rotor while loosening the nut.
3. Using ball joint puller tool 49-0118-850C or equivalent, separate the tie rod end from the steering knuckle. Disconnect the horseshoe clip that retains the brake line to the strut. On the 626 and MX-6, remove the stabilizer bar control link from the control arm.
4. Remove the mounting bolts that hold the caliper assembly to the knuckle. Wire the caliper out of the way, do not allow the caliper to be supported by the brake hose, support it with wire.
5. Remove the thrubolt and nut that retains the lower ball joint to the steering knuckle and disconnect the ball joint.
6. Remove the 2 bolts and nuts retaining the strut to the steering knuckle. Separate the steering knuckle and hub from the strut and axleshaft. On 626 and MX-6 with ABS, remove the speed sensor from the strut bracket.
7. The hub is pressed through the wheel bearings into the knuckle. Replacement of the hub and removal requires wheel hub puller tool 49-B001-726 for the GLC and tool 49-G030-725/49-G030-727 or equivalent pulley assembly for the 1983–87 626 and 323, and G49-G033-102, 104 and 105 for 1988–90 626 and MX-6 in order to separate the hub from the steering knuckle.

**NOTE:On 1988–90 626 and MX-6, if there is an inner race on the front wheel hub, grind or machine a section of the bearing inner race to approximately 0.0197 in. and remove it with a small cold chisel.**

8. Remove the inner oil seal and bearing. Remove the outer bearing using a press and tool 49-F401-368/49-F401-365 for the GLC and tool 49-G030-725/49-G030-728 for the 1983–87 626 and 323 in order to remove the bearing from the steering knuckle. Drive the outer and inner race from the knuckle with a brass drift and hammer. On 1988–90 323, remove the outer bearing race with tools 49-B092-372 and 49-F401-366A and then withdraw the outer oil seal from the front hub. On 1988–90 323, remove the bearing outer race with tool 49-FT01-361 and a press and remove the wheel bearing. On 1988–89 626 and MX-6, press the bearing from the hub using tools, 49-G033-102, 104 and 106.
9. Install new inner and outer races as required. Make sure that the edge of the race contact the steering knuckle. Pack the inner and outer bearing and install in knuckle. Use tool 49-B001-727 for the GLC and tool 49-G030-728 for the 1983–87 626 and 323 to press the hub into the steering knuckle. On 1988–90 323, use tool 49-V001-795 to seat the bearing in the hub. On 1988–90 626 and MX-6, use tools 49-G030-797, 49-F027-007 and 49-H026-103 to install the wheel bearing.
10. On 1983–87 models, measure the preload with a scale connected to the caliper mounting hole on the knuckle.

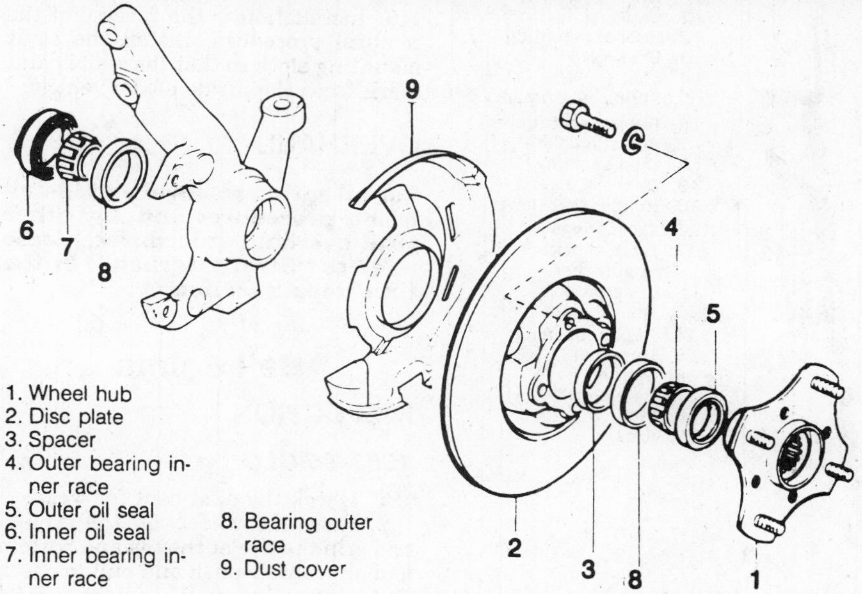


Front axle hub compoents on 323

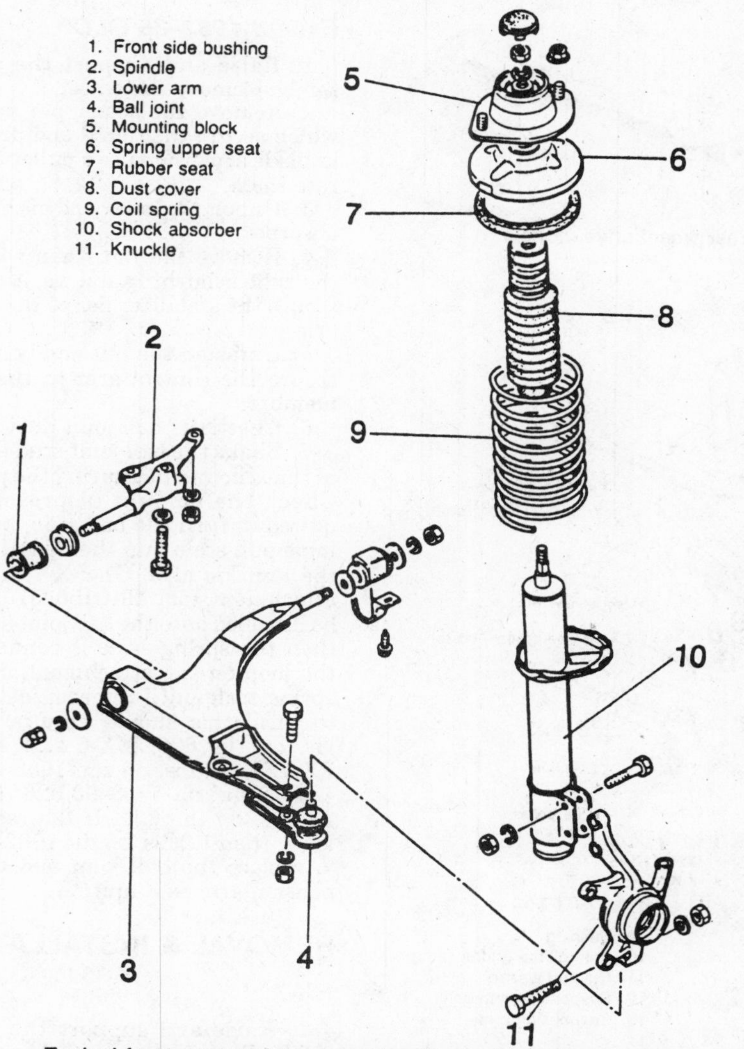


Typical front suspension assembly—front wheel drive models

Various spacers are available to increase or decrease the preload. Preload should be 1.7–6.9 ft. lbs.

11. On 1988–90 323, measure/adjust the preload as follows:

a. Insert the bearing and spacer into the steering knuckle and install tool 49-B001-727. Tighten the tool to 145 ft. lbs.

b. Connect a spring scale to cailper mounting bolt hole on the dust cover and pull on the scale to measure the bearing preload (starting rotation torque). This preload should be 0.53–2.55 lbs. for 13 inch wheels and 0.48–2.35 lbs. for 14 inch wheels. When tightening the preload tool, torque in 36 ft. lb. increments.

c. If the preload is not within specification, spacers are available in a variety of thicknesses to adjust it. Increase the the spacer thicknes when the preload is too high and decrease the thickness if too low.

12. Install the inner and outer grease seals. Press fit the hub through the bearings into the knuckle.

13. Installation of the knuckle and hub is in the reverse order of removal. Always use a new axle locknut. On the GLC and 323, torque axleshaft locknut to 116–174 ft. lbs. On the 626 and MX-6 torque the locknut to 116–124 ft. lbs. Stake the locknut after tightening.

# FRONT SUSPENSION

## MacPherson Struts

### REMOVAL & INSTALLATION

1. Unfasten the nuts which secure the upper strut mount to the top of the wheel arch. If so equipped, remove the ASA (adjustable shock aborbers) rubber cap, electrical connectors and actuator assembly from its mounting before removing the strut retaining nuts.

2. Raise and support the vehicle safely. Remove the tire and wheel assembly.

3. As required, remove the disc brake caliper. Remove the brake line clip from the strut assembly. If equipped, remove the ABS harness bracket.

4. Unfasten the two bolts that secure the lower end of the strut to the steering knuckle arm.

5. Remove the strut assembly from the vehicle.

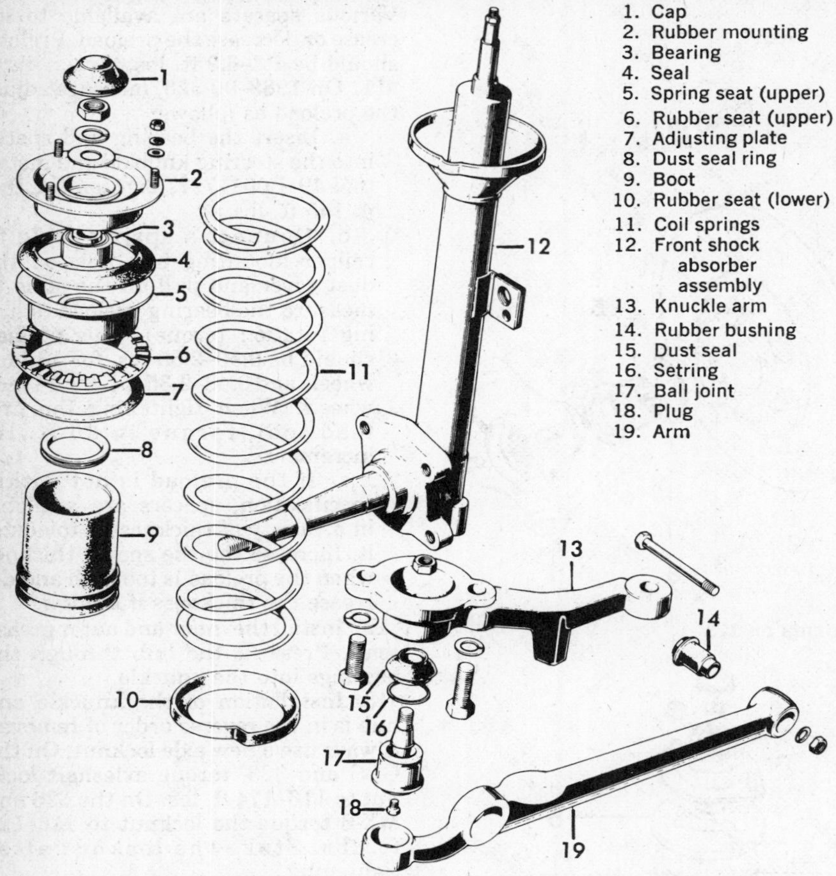

1. Cap
2. Rubber mounting
3. Bearing
4. Seal
5. Spring seat (upper)
6. Rubber seat (upper)
7. Adjusting plate
8. Dust seal ring
9. Boot
10. Rubber seat (lower)
11. Coil springs
12. Front shock absorber assembly
13. Knuckle arm
14. Rubber bushing
15. Dust seal
16. Setring
17. Ball joint
18. Plug
19. Arm

Typical front suspension assembly—rear wheel drive models

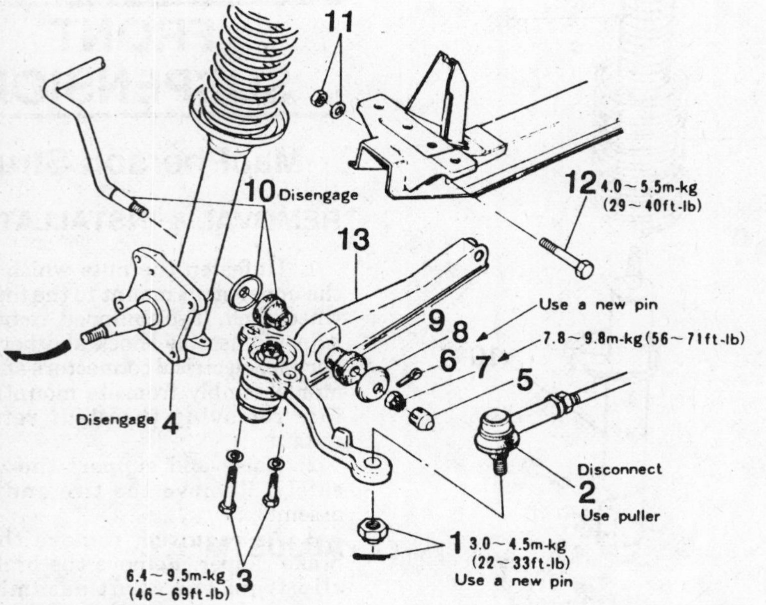


1. Castle nut and cotter pin
2. Tie-rod end
3. Strut to lower arm bolts
4. Strut and wheel spindle
5. Cap nut
6. Cotter pin
7. Castle nut
8. Washer
9. Bushing
10. Anti-roll bar and bushing
11. Nut and washer
12. Suspension arm bolt
13. Suspension arm

GLC rear wheel drive—strut and lower control arm

6. Installation is the reverse of the removal procedure. Install the strut mounting block so that the white paint mark faces the inside of the vehicle.

### OVERHAUL

**For all spring removal and installation procedures and any other strut overhaul procedures, please refer to "Strut Overhaul" in the Unit Repair section.**

## Ball Joints

### INSPECTION

#### *1983–85 GLC*

1. Check the dust boot for wear.
2. Raise the wheels off the ground and grip the tire at the top and bottom and alternately push and pull to check ball joint end play. Wear limit is 0.04 in. If necessary, replace the ball joint and control arm assembly.

#### *Except 1983–85 GLC*

1. Raise and support the vehicle safely. Remove the wheel.
2. Remove the cotter pin and nut, which secure the tierod end, from the knuckle arm, then use a puller to separate them.
3. Unbolt the lower end of the shock absorber.
4. Remove the nut, then withdraw the rubber bushing and washer which secure the stabilizer bar to the control arm.
5. Unfasten the nut and bolt which secure the control arm to the frame member.
6. Check the ball joint dust boot.
7. Shake the ball joint stud a couple of times before measuring the preload. Check the amount of pressure required to turn the ball stud, by hooking a pull scale into the tie rod hole in the knuckle arm. On RX-7, a special attachment tool 49-0180-510B must be installed onto the ball joint stud and then the spring scale is connected to the loop on the attachment. Pull the spring scale until the arm just begins to turn, this should require 4.4–7.7 lbs. on the 626, MX-6 and 1986–90 RX-7, 1–2.2 lbs. on the 1983–87 323, 4.0–6.8 lbs. on 1988–90 323 and 1.1–2.6 lbs. on the 929. If the reading is lower than 1.2 lbs. on the 1982–85 RX-7, replace the ball joint and the suspension arm as a unit.

### REMOVAL & INSTALLATION

#### *RX-7*

1. Raise and support the vehicle safely. Remove the control arm.

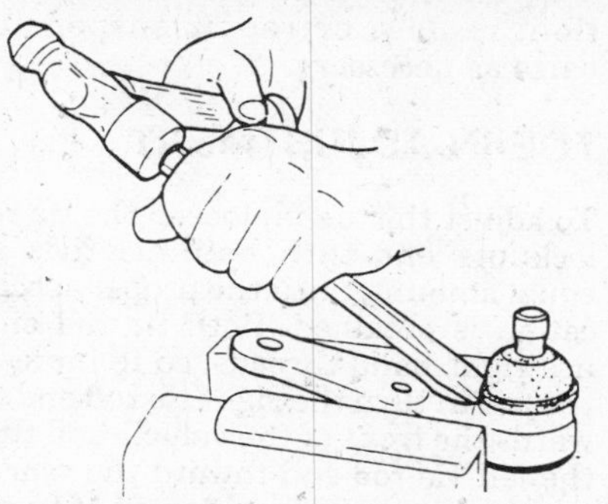

Ball joint dust boot removal

2. Remove the set ring and the dust boot.
3. Press the ball joint out of the control arm.
4. Clean the ball joint mounting bore and coat the inside of the new ball joint dust boot with lithium grease.
5. Press the ball joint into the control arm use the appropriate tool.

**NOTE: If the pressure required to press the new ball joint into place is less than 3300 lbs., the bore is worn and the control arm must be replaced.**

#### *1983–85 GLC*

1. Raise and support the vehicle safely. Remove the wheel.
2. Remove the cotter pin and nut, which secure the tie rod end, from the knuckle arm, then use a puller to separate them.
3. Unbolt the lower end of the shock absorber. Properly support the control arm assembly.
4. Remove the nut, then withdraw the rubber busing and washer which secure the stabilizer bar to the control arm.
5. Push outward on the strut assembly while removing the end of the control arm from the frame member.
6. Remove the control arm and steering knuckle arm as an assembly.
7. Separate the knuckle arm from the control arm with a puller.
8. Remove the ball joint from its mounting, using the proper removal tools.
9. Installation is the reverse of the removal procedure.

#### *1886–90 323, 1988–90 929 and 1983–90 626 and MX-6*

Replacement of the ball joint dust boot is accomplished by removing the lower control arm from the vehicle and chiseling the off old boot. Coat the inside of the new dust boot with lithium grease and press it into the ball joint using the proper tool. Check the ball joint stud threads for damage and repair as necessary. Check the ball joint preload and install the lower control arm by reversing the removal procedure.

**NOTE: If replacement of the ball joint is required, the entire lower control arm assembly must be replaced.**

## Lower Control Arm

### REMOVAL & INSTALLATION

#### *1983–85 Rear Wheel Drive*

1. Raise and support the vehicle safely. Remove the wheel.
2. Remove the cotter pin and nut, which secure the tie rod end, from the knuckle arm, then use a puller to separate them.
3. Unbolt the lower end of the shock absorber.
4. Remove the nut, then withdraw the rubber bushing and washer which secure the stabilizer bar to the control arm.
5. Unfasten the nut and bolt which secures the control arm to the frame member.
6. Push outward on the strut assembly while removing the end of the control arm from the frame member.
7. Remove the control arm and steering knuckle arm as an assembly.
8. Separate the knuckle arm from the control arm with a puller.
9. Installation of the control arm is the reverse of removal.

#### *1983–85 GLC Except Wagon*

1. Loosen the wheel lugs, raise the vehicle and safely support it safely. Remove the front wheel.
2. Remove the thrubolt connecting the lower arm to the steering knuckle.
3. Remove the bolts and nuts mounting control arm to the body.
4. Remove the lower control arm. The ball joint can be serviced at this time if necessary.
5. Installation is in the reverse order or removal. Torque the ball Joint to steering knuckle 32–40 ft. lbs. The outer bolts 43–54 ft. lbs. and the inner bolts 69–86 ft. lbs.

#### *1986–90 RX-7*

1. Raise the vehicle and support it safely.
2. Remove the lower splash shield.
3. Disconnect the front stabilizer link from the control arm.
4. Remove the pinch bolt, then separate the lower ball joint from the steering knuckle.
5. Remove the front control arm mounting bolt.
6. Remove the control arm bushing bracket bolts and lower the control arm from the vehicle.
7. Installation is the reverse of removal. Check the ball joint preload and inspect the dust boot for damage. Check the front end alignment after the installation is complete.

#### *1986–90 323 and 1983–90 626 and MX-6*

1. Raise and support the vehicle safely. Remove the tire and wheel assembly.
2. Remove the splash shield. If equipped, remove the compression rod retaining bolts.
3. Remove the stabilizer link from the control arm through bolt. Remove the lower control arm to frame attaching bolts.
4. Properly support the control arm assembly. Remove the pinch bolt and separate the ball joint from the steering knuckle.
5. Remove the lower control arm. On 1988–90 626 and MX-6, disconnect the lower arm spindle from the lower arm first and then remove the lower arm.
6. Installation is the reverse of the removal procedure. When tightening of the lower control bolts and nuts is required, lower the vehicle and then tighten the bolts and nuts. The vehicle must be unloaded. On 1988–90 626 and MX-6, tighten the link nut until approximately 0.8 in. of the through bolt is exposed.

#### *1988–90 929*

1. Raise and support the vehicle safely. Remove the tire and wheel assembly.
2. Remove the stabilizer link assembly. Remove the tie rod end from its mounting.
3. Remove the compression rod retaining bolts. Position the compression rod assembly out of the way.
4. Remove the knuckle arm. Properly support the lower control arm.
5. Remove the lower control arm retaining bolt. Remove the lower control arm from the vehicle.
6. Installation is the reverse of the removal procedure.

## Front Wheel Bearings

### ADJUSTMENT

**NOTE:The preload adjustment procecdures described here apply only to rear wheel drive vehicles.**

#### *All Except 929*

1. Raise and support the vehicle safely. Remove the tire and wheel as-

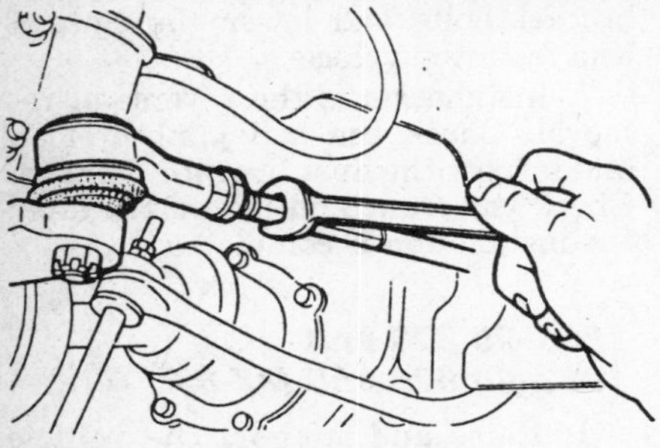

Adjusting toe-in

Front rotor components and bearing—929

sembly. Remove the brake caliper assembly and support it properly.

2. To seat the bearings, back off on the adjusting nut three turns and then rotate the hub/dics assembly while tightening the adjusting nut.

3. Back off on the adjusting nut about ⅙ of a turn. Hook a spring scale in one of the bolt holes on the hub.

4. Pull the spring scale squarely, until the hub just begins to rotate. The scale reading should be 0.9–2.2 lbs on all vehicles except GLC and and 1983–85 RX-7. The GLC reading should be 0.33–1.32 lbs. The 1983–85 RX-7 reading should be 0.99–1.43 lbs. Tighten the adjusting nut until the proper spring scale reading is obtained.

5. Place the castellated nut lock over the adjusting nut. Align one of the slots on the nutlock with the hole in the spindle and fit the cotter pin into place.

#### *1988–90 929*

1. Raise and support the vehicle safely. Remove the tire and wheel assembly.

2. Remove the caliper assembly and position it to the side.

3. Position a dial indicator gauge against the dust cap. Push and pull the disc plate by hand in the axial direction.

4. Measure the endplay of the wheel bearing. If end play is greater than specification, replace the wheel bearing.

5. Wheel bearing endplay is a maximum of 0.002 in.

### REMOVAL & INSTALLATION

#### *1983–85 Rear Wheel Drive*

1. Raise and support the vehicle safely. Remove the tire and wheel assembly. Remove the brake disc caliper.

2. Remove the locknut and washer. Remove the outer bearing assembly. Remove the rotor.

3. Drive the inner seal out of the rotor and remove the inner bearing assembly. Drive the outer bearing races out.

4. Installation is the reverse of removal. Repack the bearings and the hub cavity with lithium grease. Adjust the wheel bearings.

#### *929*

1. Raise the front of the vehicle and support safely. Remove the front wheels.

2. Unbolt the caliper assembly and support it with a piece of wire.

3. Pry the dust cap loose from the rotor disc.

4. Unstake the locknut and remove it and the washer from the axle shaft.

5. Pull the rotor disc from the front axle.

**6. On vehicles equipped with ABS, pull the ABS sensor rotor from the disc using a two-jawed puller. Remove the oil seal.**

7. Remove the bearing retaining ring. Using tools 49–B001–797 and 49–H033–101, press the front wheel bearing from the disc.

8. Press the ABS sensor rotor into the disc using the proper tool. Press the rotor in evenly to avoid damaging the teeth.

9. Press the bearing into the disc using the proper tool. Install the bearing retainer.

**10. Install a new oil seal and coat the lip of the seal with grease. Complete the installation of the disc in reverse of the removal procedure. Torque the disc locknut to 72–130 ft. lbs. Adjust the bearing preload and check the endplay. Wheel bearing endplay is a maximum of 0.002 in.**

## Front Wheel Alignment

### CASTER AND CAMBER

Caster and camber are preset by the manufacturer. They require adjustment only if the suspension and steering linkage components are damaged. In this case, adjustment is accomplished by replacing the damaged part.

On certain vehicles, the caster and camber may be changed by rotating the shock absorber support. If alignment cannot be brought to specification, replace or repair suspension parts as necessary.

### TOE-IN ADJUSTMENT

To adjust the toe-in, loosen the tie rod locknuts and turn both tie rods an equal amount, until the proper specification is obtained. Both tie rod ends use right-hand threads, so to increase the toe-in turn the right tie rod end towards the front of the vehicle and turn the left tie rod end toward the rear of the vehicle the same number of turns. One turn of the tie rod end changes the toe-in approximately 0.24 in.

# REAR SUSPENSION

## Shock Absorbers

### REMOVAL & INSTALLATION

#### *1983–85 RX-7*

1. Remove the trim panel from the rear of the luggage compartment.

2. Raise the rear of the vehicle and support it safely. Remove the rear wheel. Unfasten the nuts, then remove the washers and rubber bushings from the upper shock absorber mounts.

3. Unfasten the nut and bolt which secure the end of the rear shock to the axle housing. Remove the shock.

4. Installation is the reverse of removal. Torque the shock absorber bolts to 54 ft. lbs.

#### *1983 GLC Wagon*

1. Raise and support the vehicle safely.

2. Remove the rear wheel.

3. Remove the upper and lower shock absorber bolts. Remove the shock absorber.

4. Install the shock absorber in the reverse order of removal.

## MacPherson Strut

### REMOVAL & INSTALLATION

#### *Except RX-7*

1. As required, remove the side trim panels from the inside of the trunk, or the rear seat and trim and then loosen and remove the top mounting nuts from the strut mounting block assembly.

2. Raise the vehicle and safely sup-

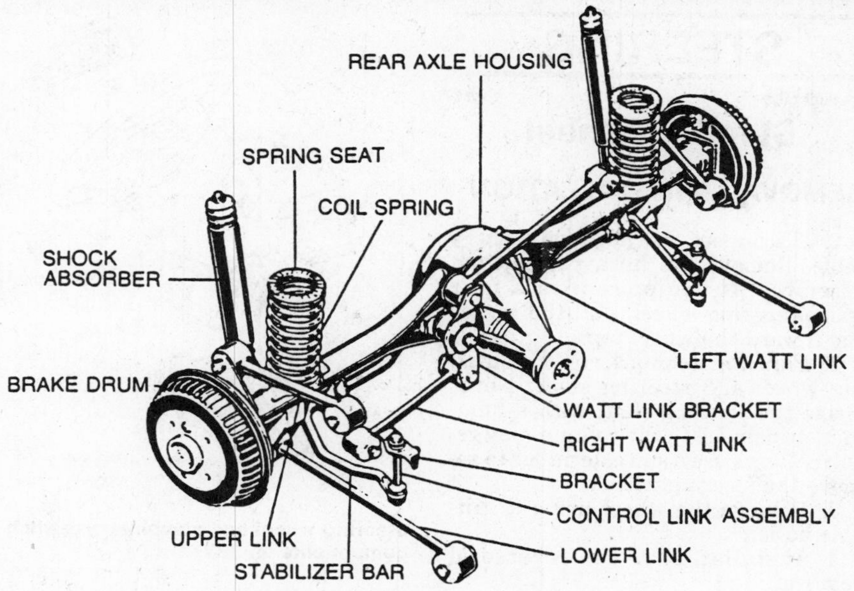


Rear suspension assembly—1983–85 RX-7

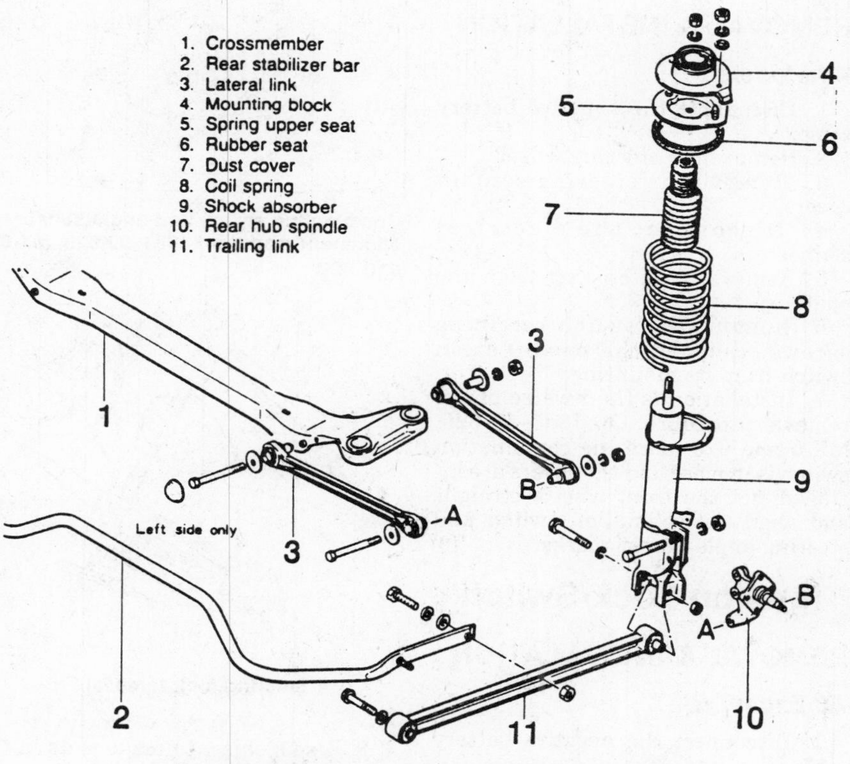


Rear suspension assembly—GLC front wheel drive

port it safely. Remove the tire and wheel assemblies, as required to gain working clearance.

3. Remove the rubber protective cover and than disconnect and remove the adjustable shock absorber (ASA) assembly. Remove the top strut retaining bolts. Disconnect the flexible brake hose and clip from the strut. On 1988–90 626 and MX-6, remove the ABS harness/bracket assembly and the trunk side trim.

4. As required, disconnect the trailing arm from the lower side of the strut. Separate the lateral link and strut by removing the bolt assembly. On 1988–89 626 and MX-6 disconnect the strut bar from the strut bar bracket and remove the strut bar bracket from the strut cap.

5. Remove the lower strut retaining bolts. On 1988–90 626 and MX-6 with 2 wheel steering, remove the upper cap nuts also. Remove the strut assembly from the vehicle.

6. Installation is the reverse of the removal procedure.

### *1986–90 RX-7*

1. Raise the the vehicle and support it safely.

2. Remove the two top strut flange mounting bolts, actuator, nut and actuator bracket.

3. Remove the bottom strut absorber mounting bolt and remove the strut and spring assembly from the vehicle. If equipped, disconnect the electrical connector from the strut assembly.

4. Installation is the reverse of the removal procedure.

## OVERHAUL

**For all strut overhaul procedures, please refer to "Strut Overhaul" in the Unit Repair section.**

# Springs

## REMOVAL & INSTALLATION

### *1983 GLC Wagon*

1. Raise and support the vehicle safely.

2. Remove the rear wheel.

3. Remove the upper and lower shock absorber bolts and nuts and remove the shock absorber.

4. Place a jack under the lower arm to support it.

5. Remove the pivot bolt and nut that secures the rear end of the lower arm to the axle housing.

6. Slowly lower the jack to relieve the spring pressure on the lower arm, then remove the spring.

7. Install the spring in the reverse order of removal.

### *1983–85 RX-7*

1. Raise the vehicle and support it safely.

2. Remove the rear wheel.

3. Position a floor jack under the rear axle housing.

4. Disconnect the shock absorber lower end of the lower link bolt. Remove the rear bolt from the upper link. The trailing control arm links run parallel from the front to rear on the vehicle, with the smaller watt links running side to side on the vehicle.

5. Disconnect the front ends of the stabilizer bar, if equipped.

6. Remove the right and left watt links at the rear axle housing.

7. Carefully lower the rear axle

housing and remove the coil spring and the rubber seat.

8. The installation is the reverse of the removal.

## Rear Wheel Bearings

**NOTE: The adjustment procedures described here apply only to front wheel drive vehicles. For rear wheel bearing service procedures refer to "Rear Axle Shafts" in the Drive Axle section.**

### ADJUSTMENT

#### *1983–90 626 and MX-6*

1. Raise and support the vehicle safely. Remove the tire and wheel assembly.
2. Remove and properly support the caliper assembly.
3. Position a dial indicator gauge against the dust cap. Push and pull the disc brake rotor or brake drum in the axial direction and measure the endplay of the wheel bearing.
4. Endplay should be 0.0079 in. Correct by replacing the wheel bearing.

#### *1986–90 323*

1. Raise and support the vehicle safely. Remove the tire and wheel assembly.
2. Remove the dust cap and torque the locknut to 18–21 ft. lbs.
3. Turn the wheel assembly to seat the bearing properly. Loosen the locknut until it can be turned by hand.
4. Hook a spring seal to a wheel lug stud in order to measure the oil seal drag. Pull the spring scale squarely.
5. Take the oil seal drag value when the wheel hub starts to turn and record the measurement.
6. Add the oil seal drag value to the standard bearing preload of 0.6–1.9 lb. Turn the locknut slowly until the standard bearing preload is obtained.

### REMOVAL & INSTALLATION

1. Raise and support the vehicle safely. Remove the tire and wheel assembly.
2. Remove the rear brake drum or rotor and lift out the bearing cage assembly. Remove the bearing retainer as required.
3. Use a blunt drift to knock the bearing race out, then press in a new race using a bench press and suitable mandrel.
4. Continue the installation in the reverse of the removal procedure. Renew oil seal as required.

# STEERING

## Steering Wheel

### REMOVAL & INSTALLATION

1. Disconnect the negative battery cable. Remove the horn pad buttom assembly. If equipped with a four spoke steering wheel, pull the center cap toward the wheel top.
2. Punch matchmarks on the steering wheel and steering shaft. Never strike the steering shaft with a hammer, as damage to the column may result. Always use a suitable puller to remove the steering wheel.
3. Remove the wheel using a suitable puller.
4. Installation is the reverse of removal.

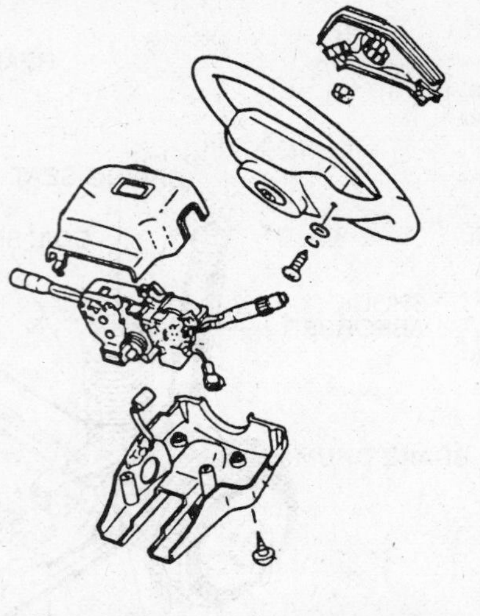

**Steering wheel and combination switch components on 323**

## Combination Switch

### REMOVAL & INSTALLATION

#### *All Models*

1. Disconnect the negative battery cable.
2. Remove the steering wheel.
3. Remove the steering column covers.
4. Disconnect the electrical connectors.
5. Remove the stop ring from the shaft.
6. Remove the switch retaining screws. Remove the combination switch from its mounting.
7. Installation is the reverse of the removal procedure. On 1988–89 626, MX-6 and 929, once the combination switch is in place and the covers are installed, set the front wheels straight and align the cobination switch and steering angle sensor marks.

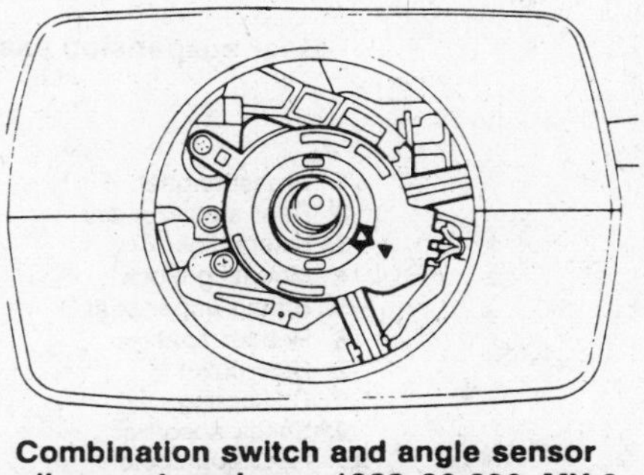

**Combination switch and angle sensor alignment marks on 1988–90 626, MX-6 and 929**

## Ignition Lock/Switch

### REMOVAL & INSTALLATION

#### *All Except RX-7*

1. Disconnect the negative battery cable.
2. Remove the steering wheel.
3. Remove the steering column covers.
4. Disconnect the electrical connectors.
5. Remove the stop ring from the shaft.
6. Remove the switch retaining screws. Remove the combination switch from its mounting.
7. Remove the instrument frame brace. Disconnect the switch wires.

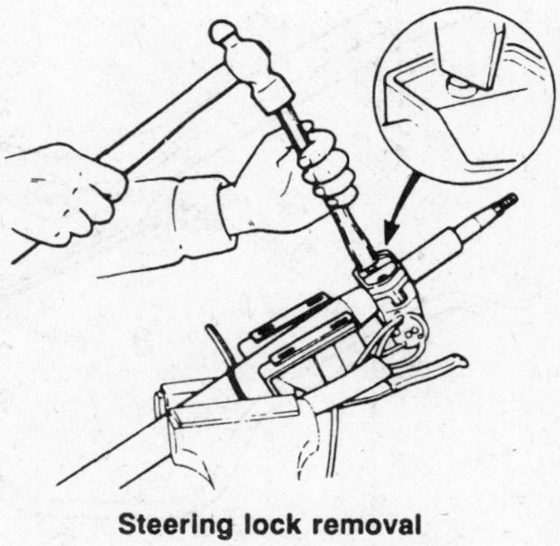

**Steering lock removal**

8. Use a chisel to make slots in the lockscrews. Remove the screws.
9. Installation is the reverse of the removal procedure. Install the new screws until the head twists off. Make sure that the lock operates properly while tightening the new locking screws.

#### *RX-7*

1. Disconnect the negative battery cable.
2. Remove the steering wheel.

3. Remove the steering wheel covers.
4. Remove the air duct and disconnect the couplers of the combination switch.
5. Remove the combination switch assembly.
6. Place a protector under the steering lock assembly to protect the steering shaft from the shock of the hammer blows.
7. Using a chisel, make grrooves in the heads of the lock installation screws and remove the screws from the column jacket.
8. To install, use new screws and tighten the switch's retaining bolts, until their heads break off. Make sure that the lock operates properly while tightening the new locking screws.
9. To complete the installation, reverse the removal procedure.

## Steering Gear

### REMOVAL & INSTALLATION

#### *1983–85 RX-7*

1. Remove the steering wheel.
2. Remove the column covers.
3. Remove the combination switch assembly.
4. Remove the steering lock and ignition switch assembly.
5. Remove the steering column support bracket.
6. Raise and support the vehicle safely.
7. Remove the front wheel.
8. Remove the cotter pin and nut and disconnect the center link from the pitman arm using a ball joint puller.
9. Unbolt the steering gear from the frame, taking note of the presence of any shim for realigning the gear with the shaft.
10. Remove the steering column dust cover and remove the gear housing, column jacket and aligning shim.
11. Reverse the removal for installation. Place the shim in its original position for realignment. Gear housing to frame bolt torque is 32–40 ft. lbs.

#### *1986–90 RX-7*

1. Disconnect the battery cables and remove the battery. Drain the cooling system.
2. Remove the radiator cooling fan, shroud and radiator.
3. Raise and support the vehicle safely. If equipped with power steering, disconnect and plug the fluid lines.
4. Disconnect the front stabilizer bar from the steering rack assembly.
5. Remove the cotter pin and tie rod end castle nut. Separate the tie rod from the steering knuckle.
6. Remove the pinch bolt at the steering column U-joint.
7. Remove the steering rack mounting bolts and power steering hoses, if equipped with power steering.
8. Remove the rack and separate the steering column U-joint.
9. Installation is the reverse of removal. If equipped with power steering, bleed the system as required. Check the front end alignment.

#### *1983–85 GLC Except Wagon*

1. Raise and support the vehicle safely.
2. Remove the wheels. Disconnect the tie rod ends from the knuckles.
3. On vehicles eqiuipped with power steering, place a pan underneath to catch fluid and disconnect the return and pressure lines.
4. Remove the boot band and attaching bolts and remove the gear and linkage from the engine compartment through the tie rod hole.
5. Installation is the reverse of removal. Make sure the steering wheel is straight forward and tighten the following torques. Mounting bracket bolts, 23–34 ft. lbs., tie rod end and knuckle bolts, 21–35 ft. lbs., Intermediate shaft and pinion connecting bolt, 13–19.5 ft. lbs.

#### *1986–90 323 and 1983–90 626 and MX-6*

**NOTE: The following information does not pertain to 1988–90 626 and MX-6 equipped with four wheel steering.**

1. Disconnect the negative battery cable. Raise the vehicle and support it safely. On the 323 equipped with 4WD, remove the battery and battery tray.
2. Raise and support the vehicle safely. Remove the tire and wheel assemblies. Remove the under covers.
3. Remove the steering gear to steering column coupler pinch bolt and separate the coupler from the steering gear. Disconnect the tie rod end nuts and cotter pin. Remove the knuckle arm/tie rod connections.
4. On vehicles equipped with power steering, remove and plug the pressure hose going to the power steering pump. Matchmark the pressure pipe union nuts to ensure proper installation and sealing. Oil will lak from the pressure and return pipes. Have a container on hand to collect the excess fluid.
5. Remove the boot band and all attaching and retaining bolts from the steering gear. Remove the gear and linkage from the engine compartment through the tie rod hole.
6. Installation is the reverse of removal. Be sure to bleed the air out of the system if equipped with a power steering pump.

#### *1988–90 626 and MX-6 with FWS*

##### FRONT STEERING GEAR

1. Disconnect the negative battery cable. Raise and support the vehicle safely. Remove the tire and wheel assemblies.
2. Disconnect and plug the required power steering lines. Remove the bolt retaining the unit to the firewall.
3. Disconnect the exhaust pipe at the muffler assembly. Remove the undercover support assembly.
4. Remove the steering angle transfer shaft retaining bolts. Remove, or position out of the way, the steering angle assembly.
5. Remove the stabilizer link bolts and nuts. Remove the stabilizer assembly from the vehicle.
6. Remove the steering assembly retaining nuts. Remove the left side lower engine mount.
7. Remove the front frame nuts and bolts and the rear frame nuts and bolts. Remove the frame assembly, as required or allow the crossmember to hang freely.
8. Remove the remaining steering assembly bolt from its mounting. Remove the steering gear assembly from the vehicle.
9. Installation is the reverse of the removal procedure. Bleed the system, as required.

##### REAR STEERING GEAR

1. Disconnect the negative battery cable. Raise and support the vehicle safely. Remove the rear tire assemblies, as required for working clearance.
2. Disconnect the electrical connector from the steering gear assembly. Remove the lectrical harness retaining bolts.
3. Remove the steering angle transfer shaft cover. Disconnect the universal joint and bolts from the steering angle transfer shaft assembly. Remove the lower cover and the brake line joint block.
4. Disconnect and cap all required fluid lines. Disconnect the lower spring link retaining bolts. Remove the solenoid valve, which is mounted on the steering gear assembly.
5. Using the proper tool, disconnect the tie rod ends from the knuckles. Remove the mounting bolts from the left and right sub frames. Allow the components to hang freely.
6. Remove the rear steering gear mounting bolts. Remove the rear steering gear assembly from the vehicle.

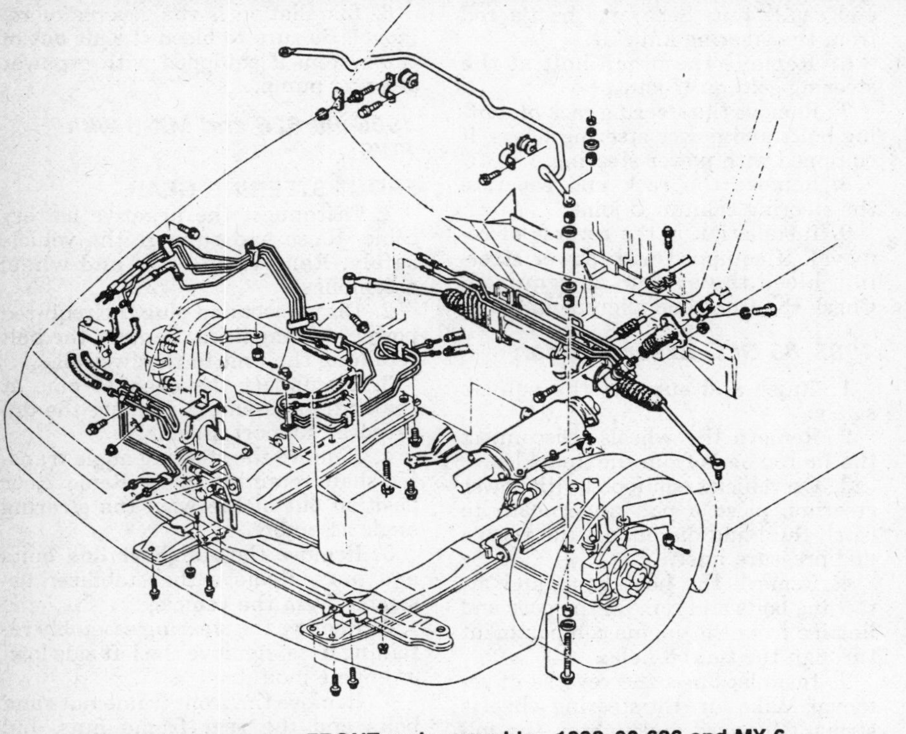

Front wheel steering FRONT rack assembly—1998–90 626 and MX-6

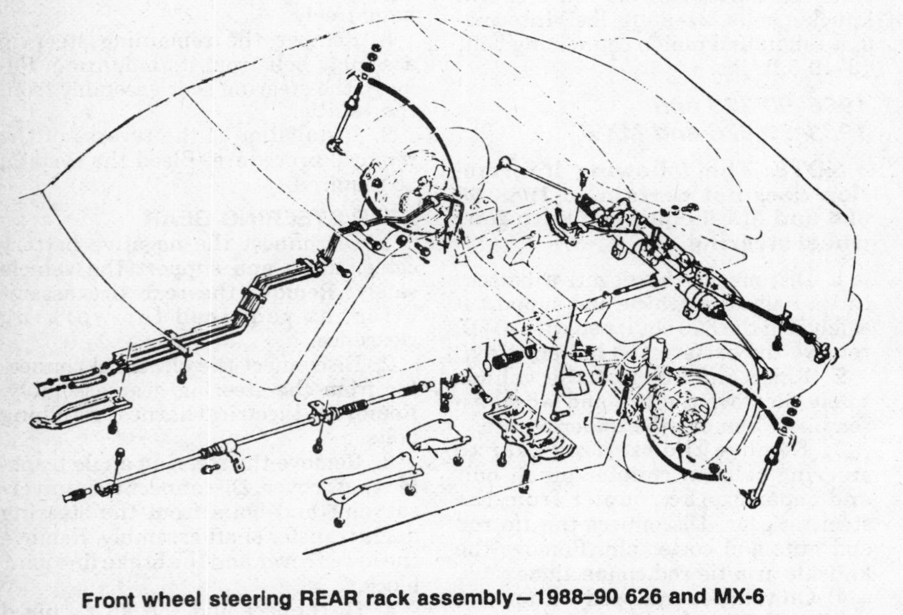

Front wheel steering REAR rack assembly—1988–90 626 and MX-6

7. Installation is the reverse of the removal procedure. Bleed the system, as required.

*1988–90 929*

1. Disconnect the negative battery cable. Raise and support the vehicle safely. Remove the tire and wheel assemblies.
2. Remove the lower steering gear assembly cover. Remove the steering damper.
3. Disconnect and plug the power steering fluid lines. Remove the control valve assembly. Remove the pressure switch.
4. Separate the tie rod ends from their mountings. Remove the steering gear from the vehicle.
5. Installation is the reverse of the removal procedure. Bleed the system, as required.

## Power Steering Pump

### REMOVAL & INSTALLATION

1. Disconnect the negative battery cable. Disconnect and plug the fluid hoses from the pump.
2. Remove all necessary drive belts. Remove the alternator and or the air conditioning compresser if necessary.
3. Loosen the pump belt adjusting bolt, slide the pump to one side and remove the belt. On some vehicles it may be necessary to remove the pump pulley before removing the pump. On 1988–89 626, MX-6 and 929 use tool 49–W023–585 or equivalent to hold the pullley stationary while the pulley lock bolt is removed.
4. Support the pump, remove the mounting bolts and lift out the pump.
5. Installation is the reverse of removal. Adjust belt to give a ½ in. deflection at the midpoint of its longest stretch. Fill the reservoir and bleed the system.

### SYSTEM BLEEDING

1. Check the fluid level. Add fluid as required.
2. Turn the steering wheel full cyle in both directions 5 times with the engine off.
3. Recheck the fluid level again and add as required.
4. Start the engine and allow to warm up at idle. Turn the steering wheel full cyle in both directions 5 times with the engine running.
5. Turn the steering wheel completely to the left and the right, several times until the air bubbles leave the oil.
6. Top off the fluid reservoir.

## Tie Rod Ends

### REMOVAL & INSTALLATION

1. Raise and support the vehicle safely.
2. Place alignment marks on the tie rod end, adjusting nut and shaft. Disconnect the tie rod end from the center link and knuckle arm, using the proper removal tool.
3. Remove the tie rod end from the vehicle.
4. Install the tie rod end to the center link and knuckle arm. Be sure to use new cotter pins.

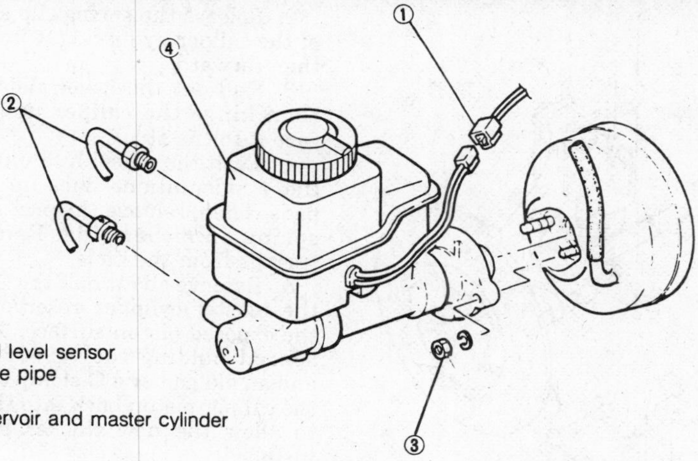


1. Fluid level sensor
2. Brake pipe
3. Nut
4. Reservoir and master cylinder

**Master cylinder removal and installation on 323**

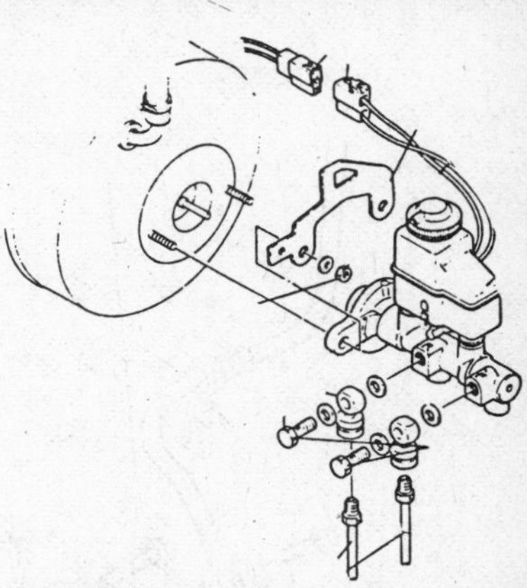

**Master cylinder removal and installation on 929**

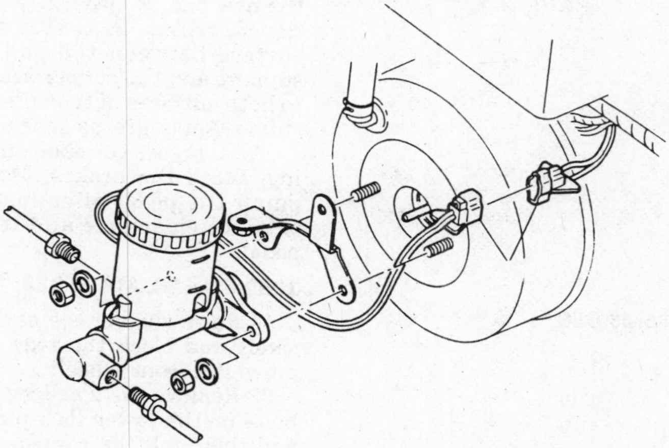

**Master cylinder removal and installation on 626 and MX-6**

# BRAKES

**For all brake system repair and service procedures not detailed below, please refer to "Brakes" in the Unit Repair section.**

## Master Cylinder

### REMOVAL & INSTALLATION

**NOTE: On vehicles that have a fluid reservoir located separately from the master cylinder, remove the lines which run between the two and plug the lines to prevent leakage.**

1. Disconnect the negative battery cable. Disconnect the oil level sensor if so equipped. Id equipped, disconnect the electrical connector from the assembly.
2. Using a suitable wrench, disconnect and plug the brake fluid lines from the master cylinder. On ABS equipped vehicles, "banjo" type fittings are used. Collect all the excess fluid in a small container.
3. Remove the proportioning bypass valve attaching bolts and valve, if equipped.
4. Remove the bolts attaching the master cylinder to the power brake unit. Remove the master cylinder from the vehicle. Remove the clutch piep holder, if so equipped.
5. Installation is the reverse of removal. Bleed the brake system. On ABS equipped vehicles, use new crush washers on the banjo fitings.

## Proportioning Valve

### REMOVAL & INSTALLATION

1. Disconnect the negative battery cable. Disconnect and plug the brake lines at the valve assembly. The 323, 626 and the MX-6 use a dual proportioning valve.
2. Remove the valve retaining bolts. Remove the valve from its mounting.
3. Installation is the reverse of the removal procedure. Bleed the system. Inspect the fluid lines for leakage.

## Power Brake Booster

### REMOVAL & INSTALLATION

1. Disconnect the negative battery cable. Remove the blower air duct, if so equipped. Disconnect the vacuum hose from the power booster assembly.
2. On some vehicles it may be possible to remove the power brake booster without disconnecting the brake fluid lines from the master cylinder. If so remove the cylinder and position it to the side.
3. As required, disconnect the master cylinder fluid lines and remove it from the vehicle.
4. Remove the cotter pin and disconnect the clevis pin from the booster yoke at the brake pedal.
5. Remove the booster mounting nuts and remove the booster from the vehicle.
6. Installation is the reverse of removal. Use a new gasket. Bleed the system.

## Disc Brake Pads

### REMOVAL AND INSTALLATION

#### *Front*

**1983–85 GLC**

1. Raise the front of the vehicle, support it with safety stands, and remove the front wheels. Unclip the brake hose at the shock absorber by pressing the lower clip outward with a suitable prying tool and then forcing the clip downward.

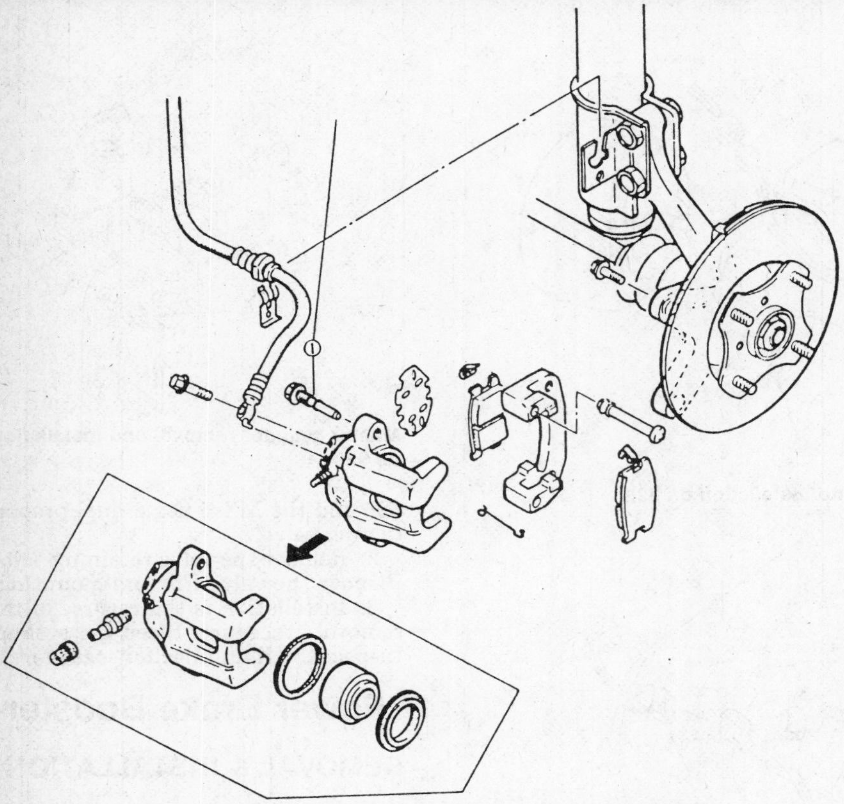

Front disc brake components – 1983–85 GLC

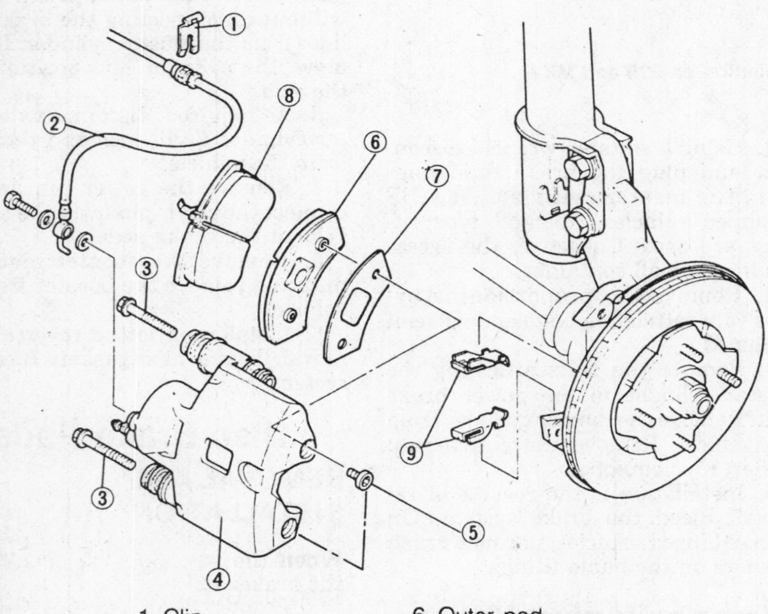

1. Clip
2. Flexible hace
3. Bolts
4. Caliper assemble
5. Screws
6. Outer pad
7. Outer shim
8. Inner pad
9. Guide plates

Front disc brake components – 1983–87 626 and 323

2. Release the spring clip at the top of the caliper by forcing it inward and then forward.

3. Pull out the lower slide pin and then hinge the caliper upward and wire it to the strut.

4. Turn the wheel hub until one of the 4 indentations lines up with the pads. Then, remove the pad, shim and spring on either side. Remove the springs from the pads.

5. Remove about half the fluid from the master cylinder reservoir. Clean the exposed piston surface. Then, use special holding tool 49–0221–600C and an old pad or a C-clamp to depress the caliper piston back into the caliper to allow the new thicker pad to be installed.

6. Install in reverse order, making sure to transfer the shim and spring to the new pad. If either is warped or fatigued, replace it. Grease the contact surface between the pad mounting support and the caliper assembly, and to both surfaces of the outer and inner shims. Apply grease sparingly.

Also, grease the slide pin and bushing. Bleed the brakes. Make sure to pump the pedal after installation to take up clearance and test for full pedal.

### 1983–90 626, MX-6, 323, 929

1. Raise the vehicle and support it safely and block the rear wheels. Remove the front wheels.

2. Remove the 2 caliper installation bolts or the lower lock pin bolt (929) and then pull the caliper off the disc. Tie the caliper up to prevent putting tension and stress on the brake hose.

3. Remove the outer pad by using a suitable prying tool to release the clip. Then, remove the inner pad.

4. Remove about half the brake fluid from the reservoir in the master cylinder. Use a C-clamp or special holding tool 49–0221–600C with an old pad to depress the caliper piston back into the caliper to allow the new thicker pad to be installed.

5. Reverse the removal procedure to install. If either or both pads shows excessive wear, replace both pads. Before reattaching the caliper, push the sleeve toward the outside of the caliper so the sleeve boot does not get pinned between the caliper and steering knuckle and get torn. On 929 torque the lower lock pin bolt to 61–69 ft. lbs.

### RX-7

1. Raise the front of the car and support it safely.

2. Remove the wheels.

3. On 1983–85 modles, remove the lower caliper attaching bolt and flip the caliper up to expose the pads. On 1986–90 models, remove the lock pin bolt and lift up the caliper. Tie the cali-

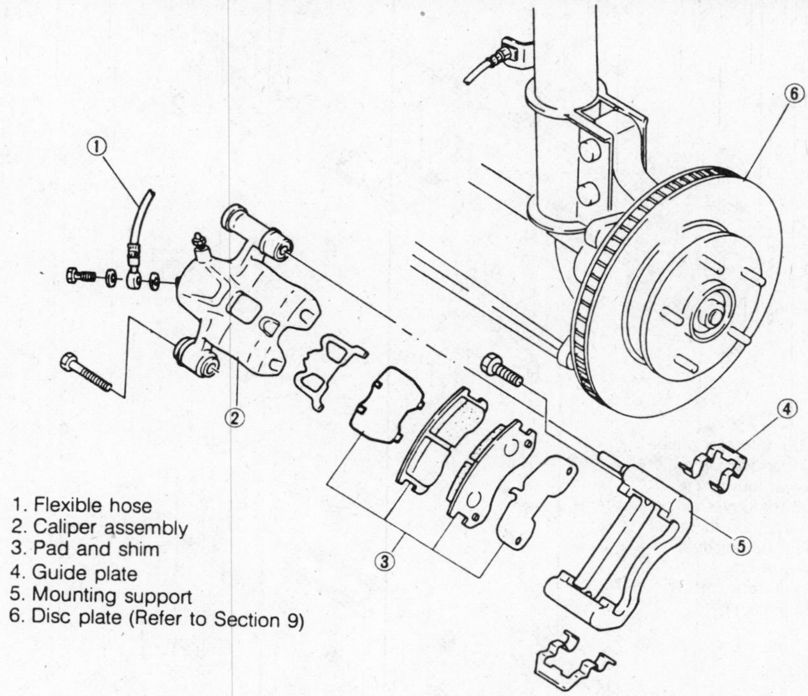


**Front disc brake components – 1988–90 626 and MX-6**

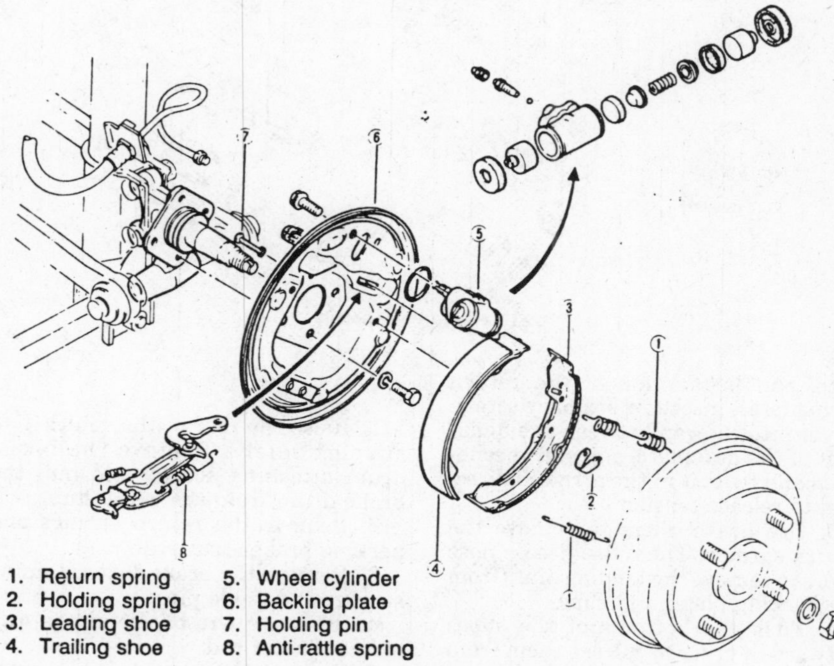


**Rear brake components – 1983–85 GLC**

per up to prevent putting tension and stress on the brake hose.

4. Remove the anti-rattle spring and remove the brake pads and their shims.

5. Use special tool 49–0221–600C to push the piston inward and hold it in place to accept the new thicker pad.

6. Install new brake pads. Be sure to fit the shims in the proper positions and attach the anti-rattle spring.

7. Fit the caliper in place. If the piston in the caliper is out too far to allow installation of the caliper with the new brake pads, remove master cylinder reservoir cap and syphen some (by not

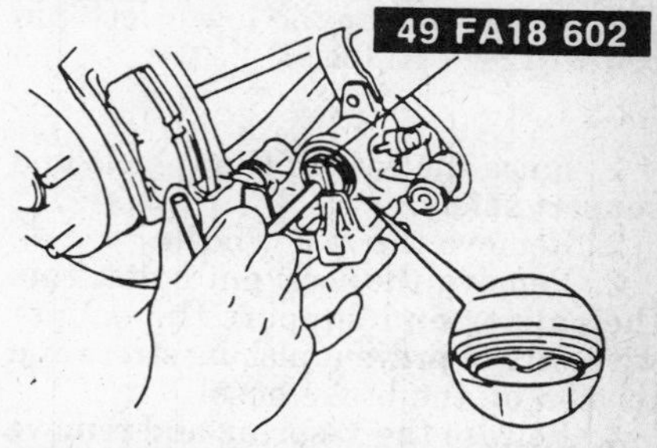


**Aligning the piston groove using special tool**

all) of the brake fluid out of the reservoir, then press in the piston. If the piston will not press in, submerge one end of a piece of hose in brake fluid, attach the other end of the caliper bleeder valve, open the valve and push in the piston. When the piston is in far enough, close the valve.

8. Remaining assembly is the reverse of removal. On 1986–90 RX-7, torque the lock bolt to 23–30 ft. lbs.

### Rear

#### 1988–90 626, MX-6 and 323

1. Loosen the rear wheel lug nuts and raise the rear of the vehicle and support safely. Release the parking brake and remove the rear wheels.
2. Disconnect the parking brake cable mounting bracket and the cable operating lever.
3. Remove the upper caliper mounting bolt and pivot the caliper assembly downward and position it out of the way.
4. Release the V-springs and remove the inner and outer pads with the shims.
5. Coat the new shims with grease then attach them to the pads.
6. Using special tool 49–FA18–602 turn the piston fully inward in a clockwise rotation. Install the inner pad and align the piston groove with the inner pad alignment pin using the special tool. Again, this alignment must be accomplished with the inner pad installed.
7. Complete the installation in reverse of the removal procedure. Torque the caliper mounting bolt to 12–17 ft. lbs. When connecting the parking brake cable on 626 and MX-6, there must be no clearance between the cable end and the operating lever. When the wheels are installed apply the brakes a few times and check that there is no excessive brake drag when the wheels are turned.

#### 929

Rear disc brake pad removal and installation is essentally the same as for the front disc brake pads except for the lower lock pin bolt torque. For rear disc brakes, torque the lower lock pin bolt to 12–17 ft. lbs.

**RX-7**

1. Raise the rear of the vehicle and support safely.
2. Remove the rear wheels.
3. Remove the lock pin bolts from the caliper and support the caliper with wire to prevent placing stress and tension on the brake hose.
4. Release the V-spring and remove the brake pads from the mounting support.
5. Complete the installation in reverse of the removal procedure. Torque the caliper lock pin bolts to 2–30 ft. lbs. Depress the brake pedal to adjust the parking brake cable play.

## Brake Shoes

### REMOVAL & INSTALLATION

#### *1983–85 GLC*

1. Loosen the rear wheel lugs, raise the rear of the car and support it safely on jackstands. Remove the rear tire and wheel.
2. Remove the rear brake drum. Clean the dirt from the brake components with a dry brush.
3. Disconnect the parking brake cable from the lever at the rear of the brake mounting plate.
4. Remove the lower return spring from between the two brake shoes. Disconnect the upper return spring from the front brake shoe. Remove the clip that holds the front shoe to the mounting plate and remove the front shoe.
5. Disconnect the adjuster spring from the rear brake shoe. Remove the mounting clip and the rear brake shoe.
6. Disconnect the adjuster spring from the rear brake shoe. Remove the mounting clip and the rear brake shoe.
7. Push on the adjuster lever while rotating a screwdriver between and quadrant and the knurled pin to retract the self adjuster.
8. Apply a small amount of grease to the mounting plate brake shoe contact points. Install the shoes, mounting clips and springs in the reverse order of removal.
9. Install the brake drum using a new hub nut (be sure to stake the nut). Connect the parking brake cables. Bleed the brakes if necessary. Pump the pedal several times to adjust the drum to shoe clearance.

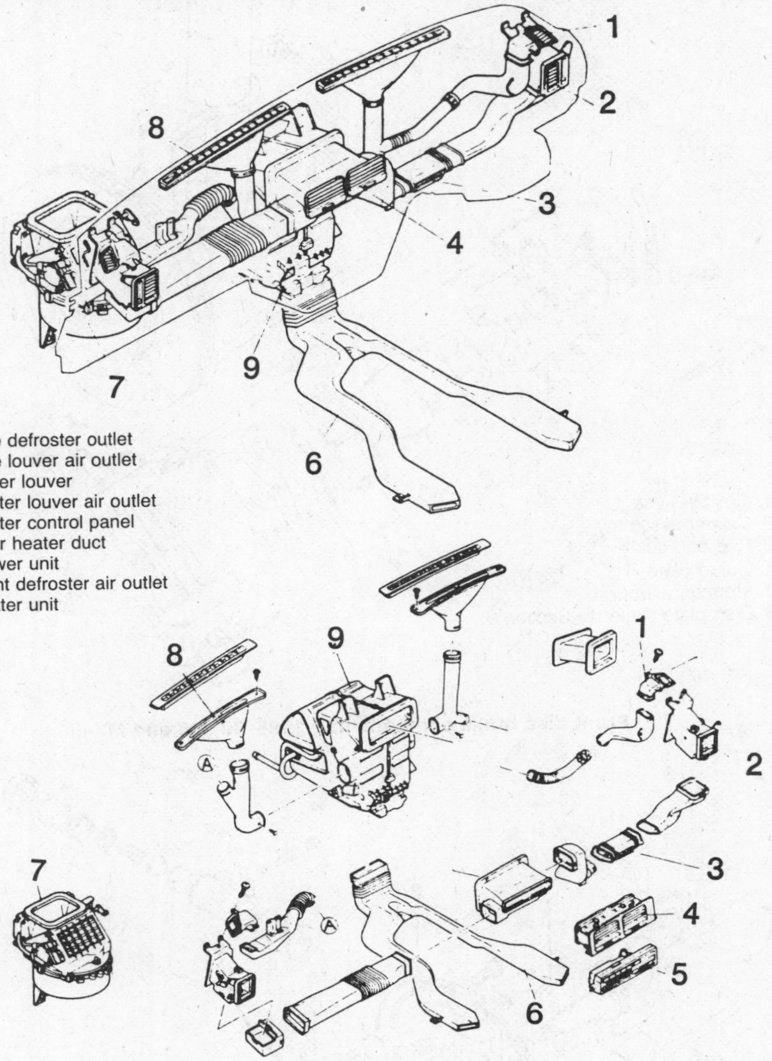

1 Side defroster outlet
2 Side louver air outlet
3 Lower louver
4 Center louver air outlet
5 Heater control panel
6 Rear heater duct
7 Blower unit
8 Front defroster air outlet
9 Heater unit

**323 Heater assembly**

#### *1983–90 626, MX-6 and 323*

1. Raise the vehicle and suppport safely. Remove the wheels and the brake drum. Clean the dirt from the brake components with a dry brush.
2. To ease removal of the leading shoe, and installation of the return spring later, insert an ordinary screwdriver into the gap between the quadrant of the automatic adjuster mechanism and twist it in the arrowed direction to release tension.
3. Use brake pliers to remove the return springs. Then, use needle nose pliers to remove the holding pins (from the backing plate) and clips.
4. Push the bottoms of the shoes outward in order to release them from the anchors and then unhook them at the wheel cylinder. Remove the leading shoe first. Both rear wheels should be done if either side shows excessive wear.
5. Apply grease to the shoe and cylinder contact points, shoe anchor points and backing plate projections.
6. Reverse the removal procedure to install. Make sure to apply the brakes several times to take up the adjustment before the vehicle is driven.

#### *RX-7*

1. Raise the rear of the vehicle and support safely. Remove the brake drum attaching screws and pull the brake drum from the wheel hub.
2. Remove the return springs and parking brake strut rod.
3. Remove the brake shoe retaining springs and guide pins.
4. Remove the brake shoes and strut adjuster rod.
5. Remove the parking brake cable from the operating lever on the brake shoe.
6. Installation is the reverse of removal. When installing new brake shoes, apply multi-purpose grease between the brake shoe metal and the backing plate, the brake shoe and wheel cylinder piston, and between the brake shoe metal and the anchor pin. Do not allow grease to come in contact with the brake shoe lining at any time.

## Wheel Cylinder

### REMOVAL & INSTALLATION

1. Raise and support the vehicle safely. Remove the tire and wheel assembly.
2. Remove the brake drum and brake shoes.
3. Disconnect and plug the brake lines.
4. Remove the stud nuts and bolt attaching the wheel cylinder to the backing plate and remove the wheel cylinder.
5. Installation is the reverse of removal. Be sure to bleed the system after installation.

## Parking Brake Cable

### ADJUSTMENT

#### *Except 1988–90 626, MX-6 and 929*

1. Raise and support the vehicle safely. Adjust the rear brakes.
2. Adjust the front cable with the nut located at the rear of the parking brake handle. The handle should require 6–8 notches for 1983–85 RX-7 and 5–9 for the 1982–85 GLC to apply the parking brake. Adjust the remaining models as follows:
   a. 1983–87 626 – 7–9 notches.
   b. 1986–87 323 – 7–11 notches for drum brakes and 9–15 notches for disc brakes.
   c. 1988–90 323 – 5–7 notches for rear disc brakes and 6–8 notches for rear drum brakes.
   d. 1986–90 RX-7, the adjustment is 4–5 notches.
4. Operate the parking brake several times, check to see that the rear wheels do not drag when it is fully released.

#### *1988–90 626 and MX-6*

The proper parking brake lever stroke for these models is 5–7 notches.

1. Before beginning the adjustment, start the engine and depress the brake pedal several times.
2. Remove the adjusting nut clip at the front of the parking brake cable and rotate the adjusting nut until the lever stroke is within specification.
3. After adjustment, turn the ignition switch On and pull the parking brake lever back 1 notch and make sure that the parking brake reminder light illuminates. Check that the rear brakes do not drag.

#### *1988–90 929*

1. Raise and support the vehicle safely. Remove the rear tire and wheel assembly.
2. Remove the brake service hole plug. Turn the adjuster in the direction of the arrow, on the disc plate, until the plate locks.
3. Turn the adjuster 3–5 notches in the opposite direction to set the adjustment.
4. Make sure that the brakes do not drag. Check the functions of the parking brake assembly.

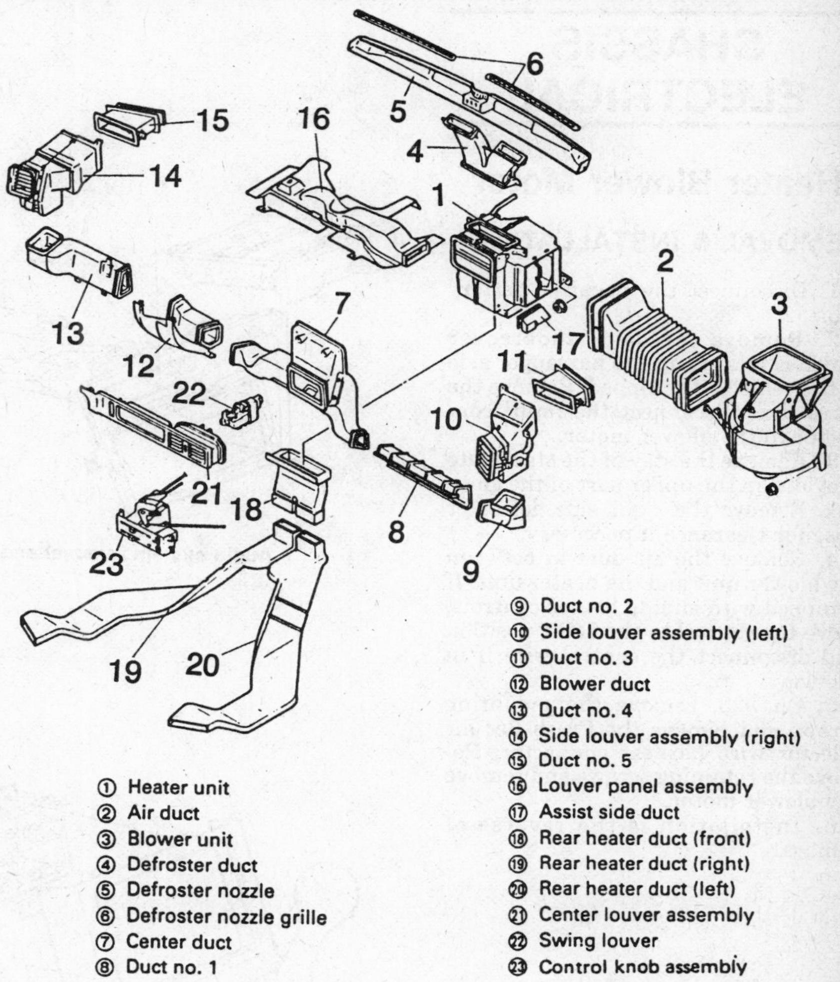


**Heater assembly 626**

### REMOVAL & INSTALLATION

#### *Front Cable*

1. Disconnect the negative battery cable. Remove the console assembly, as required.
2. Remove the adjusting nut. Remove the mounting bracket assembly.
3. Remove the parking brake lever assembly.
4. Remove the front cable.
5. Installation is the reverse of the removal procedure. Adjust the parking brake cable, as required.

#### *Rear Cable*

1. Disconnect the negative battery cable. Remove the rear console assembly, as required.
2. Remove the bracket assembly. Disconnect the cable from its mounting.
3. Raise and support the vehicle safely. Remove the rear tire and wheel assembly.
4. On all except 929, disconnect the brake cable from its mounting and remove it from the vehicle.
5. On the 929, remove the disc brake caliper assembly and position it to the side. Remove the rotor. Remove the parking brake shoe assembly, then remove the cable from its mounting.
6. Installation is the reverse of the removal procedure. Adjust the parking brake, as required.

# CHASSIS ELECTRICAL

## Heater Blower Motor

### REMOVAL & INSTALLATION

1. Disconnect the negative battery cable.
2. Remove the dash undercover which is located on the passenger side of the vehicle, if equipped. Remove the glove box. Disconnect the multi connector to the blower motor.
3. Remove the stay of the steel plate provided in the upper part of the glove box. Remove the right side defroster hose for clearance if necessary.
4. Remove the air duct in between the blower unit and the heater unit. If equipped with sliding heater controls, move the control to the **HOT** position and disconnect the control wire if in the way.
5. On 323, remove the mounting screws and remove the Fresh-Rec air selector wire harness connector. Remove the retaining screws and remove the blower motor.
6. Installation is the reverse of removal.

## Heater Core

### REMOVAL & INSTALLATION

1. Disconnect the negative battery cable. Drain the coolant.
2. Disconnect the heater hoses at the engine firewall.
3. On 1988–90 323, 626 and MX-6 disconnect the duct which runs between the heater box and the blower motor or, depending on the vehicle, remove the crash pad and instrument panel pad from the dash.
4. Disconnect the defroster hoses if necessary, set the control to the **DEF** and **HOT** position and disconnect the control wires if they are in the way.
5. Unfasten the retaining screws that secure the halves of the heater box together or remove the heater unit and bracket. Separate the heater box for access to the heater core.
6. Detach the hoses if not already disconnected. Remove the mounting clips and the heater core. Plugs the open inlet and outlet connections to prevent the leakage of coolant onto the interior. Installation is the reverse of the removal procedure.

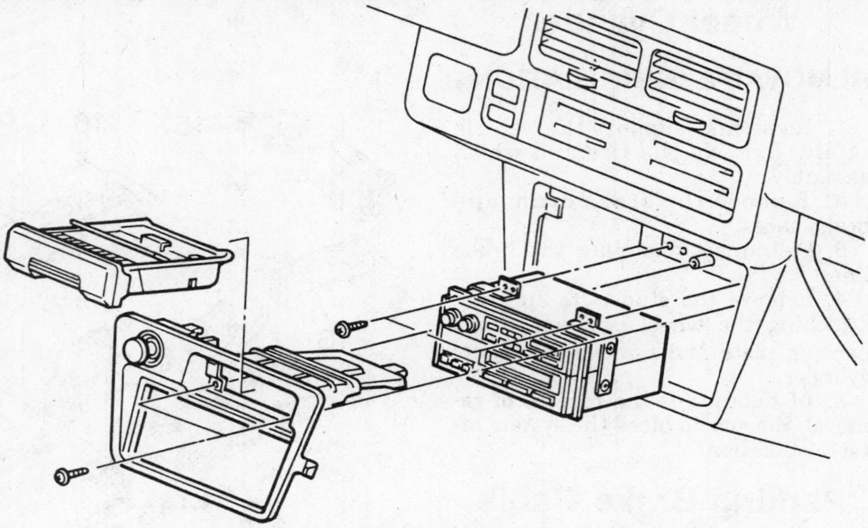

Audio system removal and installation on 323 without 4WD

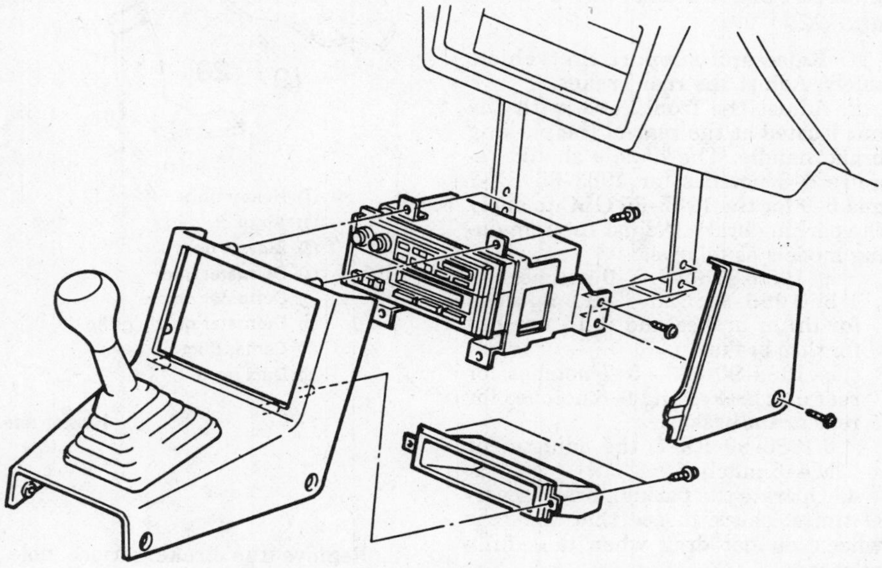

Audio system removal and installation on 323 with 4WD

## Radio

### REMOVAL & INSTALLATION

#### *1983–85 GLC*

1. Disconnect the negative battery cable. Pull off the switch knobs.
2. Remove the mounting bolts and pull the radio backward and out of the dash.
3. Disconnect the antenna feeder and wiring connector and remove the radio.
4. Install in reverse order.

#### *1983–87 626*

1. Disconnect the negative battery cable.
2. Remove the ashtray, radio knobs, heater control lever knob, and the fan control switch knob.
3. Remove the center panel attaching screws and pull the center panel rearward.
4. Remove the radio attaching screws and disconnect the antenna.
5. Installation is the reverse of removal.

#### *1988–90 626 and MX-6*

1. Disconnect the negative battery cable.
2. Remove the ashtray. On vehicles equipped with a compact disc player, gently pry the ornament plate from the center panel. On conventional sound systems, withdraw the box from the center panel. Remove the lower

center panel attaching screws and remove the panel by releasing the upper retaining clips.

3. Remove the audio unit bracket retaining screws and carefully slide the unit out from the dash until the electrical connections are visible and accessible.

4. Disconnect all the electrical connections and antenna leads from the rear of the unit and pull it out of the dash. Installation is the reverse of the removal procedure.

### *323*

1. Pull the ash tray out, depress the tang in back, and remove it from its slot in the dash.

2. Remove the two fastening screws from the area of the panel fascia behind the ash tray, and remove the panel, disconnecting the cigarette lighter when you can reach in behind it and unplug it.

3. Remove the two screws from the tops of the two mounting brackets, slide the radio out, disconnect the aerial and electrical connector plug, and remove it.

4. If the unit is actually being replaced, transfer the mounting brackets to the new radio. Install in reverse order.

### *929*

**NOTE: On vehicles equipped with automatic transmision, apply the hand brake and move the lever to the L position to gain sufficient removal and installation clearance. Protect the console and trim surfaces with soft cloth and do not attempt to pry the trim from the face of the audio system.**

1. Disconnect the negative battery cable.

2. Remove the 3 plastic Phillips head screws from the duct panel under cover located on the passenger's side. Locate and remove the single large plastic hex nut that holds the duct panel under cover in place.

3. Reach in behind the audio unit and remove the two attaching nuts. Push on the mounting studs and pull the unit from the dash until the electrical connections are visible and accessible. Disconnect the electrical connections and antenna leads from the rear of the unit and pull the unit from the dash. Installation is the reverse of the removal procedure. Make sure that the duct panel under cover on the passenger's side is aligned properly with the ducting under the dash.

# Windshield Wiper Switch

## REMOVAL & INSTALLATION

The windshield wiper switch is incorporated in the multifunction combination switch. To remove the switch the combination switch must also be removed. Refer to the combination switch removal and installation procedure in this section.

# Windshield Wiper Motor

## REMOVAL & INSTALLATION

1. Disconnect the negative battery cable. Remove the wiper arms.

2. Remove the cowl plate screws, move the cowl plate up at the front and disconnect the washer hose. Remove the cowl plate.

3. Disconnect the wires from the wiper motor.

4. Unbolt and remove the motor.

5. Installation is the reverse of removal. Check the system for proper operation.

# Instrument Cluster

## REMOVAL & INSTALLATION

### *1983–85 RX-7*

1. Disconnect the negative battery cable. Remove the knob from the headlight switch. Remove the halves of the steering column shroud.

2. Open the left hand door, to gain access to the screw located on the side of the instrument cluster.

3. Remove the 3 retaining screws which are located underneath the instrument cluster.

4. Tip the top of the cluster toward the steering wheel.

5. Disconnect the wiring and the speedometer cable from the back of the instrument cluster.

6. Remove the cluster.

7. Installation is the reverse of removal.

### *1986–90 RX-7*

The instrument cluster front bezel contains the switches for headlamps and lighting, cruise control, turn signals and high beams, windshield wiper controls and dimmer knobs. The bezel and switch assembly is removed by unscrewing the seven attaching screws, then pulling the cluster gently and disconnecting the instrument cluster wiring harness from the switch assemblies. Once the bezel is removed, the switch assemblies can be removed from the rear of the unit. The gauges can be removed once the bezel is clear by simply unscrewing the mounting screws and disconnecting the speedometer cable and wiring connectors.

### *GLC and GLC Wagon with Standard Dash*

1. Disconnect the negative battery terminal. Cover the instrument panel pad directly below the instrument cluster to prevent damage to the pad during the procedure.

2. Remove the meter hood by removing the screw above either dial, and pulling the hood off the dash.

3. Remove the wood grain center panel cover by removing the screw from the left side and unclipping the panel on the right.

4. Remove the three screws located under the front edge of the crash pad, and remove the pad.

5. Reach behind the speedometer and disconnect the cable by pressing on the flat surface of the connector.

6. Remove the 3 screws from the instrument cluster, and pull the cluster out of the dash.

7. Disconnect the multiple connectors.

8. Installation is the reverse of removal.

### *GLC with Sport Dash*

1. Disconnect the negative battery cable.

2. Put masking tape along the panel just below where the cluster will come out to protect it.

3. Remove the meter hood by removing the tripmeter knob, screws, clips, and the hood.

4. Remove the wood grain center panel cover in the same manner as the meter hod.

5. Remove the instrument panel pad by removing the three screws located under the front edge of removing the pad.

6. Remove the screws from the top of the combination instrument cluster, and pull the cluster outward.

7. Disconnect the speedometer cable by pressing on the flat surface of the plastic connector. Disconnect the wiring connectors. Remove the cluster.

8. Installation is the reverse of the removal procedure.

### *1983–84 626*

1. Disconnect the negative battery cable.

2. Remove the steering wheel and the column cover.

3. Disconnect the speedometer cable.

4. Remove the meter hood.

5. Remove the combination meter attaching screws, disconnect the wire connections and remove the combination meter assembly.

6. Installation is the reverse of removal.

### 1985 626

1. Disconnect the negative battery cable. Tilt the steering wheel downward.

2. Remove the cover from the top of the meter hood. Remove the 2 screws from the top of the meter assembly.

3. Remove the 2 attaching screws from the underside of the meter hood. Then, remove the 4 screws from the underside of the assembly.

4. Remove the 4 screws attaching the meter assembly to the hood. Pull the assembly out slightly and disconnect the plugs and speedometer cable, and remove the light (to disconnect the plugs, it is necessary to depress the retaining clip). Pull the assembly out.

5. Install the instrument cluster in reverse order.

### 1986–87 626

1. Disconnect the negative battery cable. Tilt the steering wheel downward.

2. Disconnect the speedometer cable from the rear of the cluster by reaching up behind the cluster and unscrewing the collar.

3. Remove the 4 screws from the underside of the instrument cluster assembly where it attaches to the underside of the dash and the three from the underside of the hood.

4. Remove the 2 screws attaching the cluster to the hood at the top. Then, pull the assembly slightly outward and disconnect the wiring connectors (to disconnect the plugs, it is necessary to depress the retaining clip). Then, the cluster assembly may be removed.

5. Install the instrument cluster in reverse order.

### 1988–90 626 and MX-6

1. Disconnect the negative battery cable.

2. On vehcles equipped with automatic transaxle, remove the 2 attaching screws that hold the shift knob to the shaft. Remove the shift lever knob.

3. Remove the rear console mounting screws and pull the console rearward and remove it.

4. Remove the front console mounting screws and pry the ornament from the steering wheel pad. Remove the steering wheel.

5. Remove the attaching screws and separate the upper and lower column covers. Remove the under cover attaching screws and remove the under cover. Reach behind hood release and remove the nut and the hood release knob.

6. Remove the meter hood attaching screws and pull the meter hood out until the electrical connectors are visible. Disconnect the speedometer cable at the speedometer. Disconnect all the connectors from the rear of the meter hood and remove it.

7. Remove the attaching screws and pull the meter assembly outward. Disconnect the speedometer cable, meter connectors and remove the meter assembly.

8. Remove the switch panel retaining screws and pull the switch panel forward untill the connectors are accessible. Disconnect the connectors and remove the switch panel.

9. Remove the glove box and disconnect the glove box light connector.

10. Remove the center panel. Remove the retaining screws and slide the heater control assembly from the instrument panel. On lever control type instrument panels, disconnect the control cables from the **DEF**, **MAX-COLD** and **REC** lever positions. On Logicon type panels, disconnect the electrical connectors from the rear of the panel.

11. Remove the protective cap that covers the instrument panel center mounting bolt. Remove the center and side instrument panel mounting and bracket bolts. Remove the steering shaft mounting bolts.

12. Disconnect the harness connectors from the rear of the dash and remove the intrument panel.

13. Installation is the reverse of the removal procedure.

### 1986–87 323

1. Disconnect the negative battery cable. Remove the three screws from under the top edge of the instrument hood.

2. Pull the hood out for access, unplug the electrical connectors to the cluster switches on either side, and remove it.

3. Remove the screw located near the bottom of the cluster on either side, and remove the cluster from the dash, unplugging connectors when you can reach them.

4. Installation is the reverse of removal.

### 1988–90 323

1. Remove the steering wheel, upper and lower column covers and the combination switch assembly.

2. Remove the attaching screws and remove the meter hood.

3. Remove the meter hood attaching screws and pull the meter hood out until the electrical connectors are visible. Disconnect the speedometer cable at the speedometer. Disconnect all the connectors from the rear of the meter hood and remove it.

4. Remove the attaching screws and separate the side wall from the front gear shift console on both sides. Remove the rear console (1 bolt) and remove the front console and slide it forward. Disconnect the antenna feeder wire from the back of the radio.

5. Remove the atttching hardware and remove the passenger's and driver's side under covers.

6. Remove the lower panel attaching screws. Remove the lower louver with the reinforcement. Remove the duct and disconnect the hood release wire.

7. Remove the covers from the center and side panel bolts. Remove the driver's and passenger's side covers along with the attaching bolts.

8. Remove the glove box insert and remove the bolts from the center bracket.

9. Remove the nut from both sides of the side bracket and remove the ashtray retaining screws.

10. Unscrew and remove the center panel. Disconnect the cigarette lighter conector and remove the light.

11. Disconnect and remove the cables from the heater control and blower units.

12. Unscrew and remove the lower cover. Remove the bolts from the instrument panel support bracket. Pull the instrumnent panel forward and disconnect the harness connectors from the rear of the unit. Remove the instrument panel from the rear of the vehcle.

13. Installation is the reverse of the removal procedure.

### 1988–90 929

1. Disconnect the negative battery cable. Disconnect the speedometer cabkle at the transmission. Remove the shifter knob and dash upper plate.

2. Remove the ashtray and disconnect the cigarette lighter connector. On vehicles equipped with manual transmission, apply the parking brake and remove the support bracket. Remove the attaching screws and pull the console rearward and remove it.

3. Remove the steering wheel. Remove the steering wheel upper and lower cover assemblies.

4. Unscrew and pull the switch panel out and away from the dash. Disconnect the electrical connectors and remove the switch panel.

5. Remove the meter hood attach-

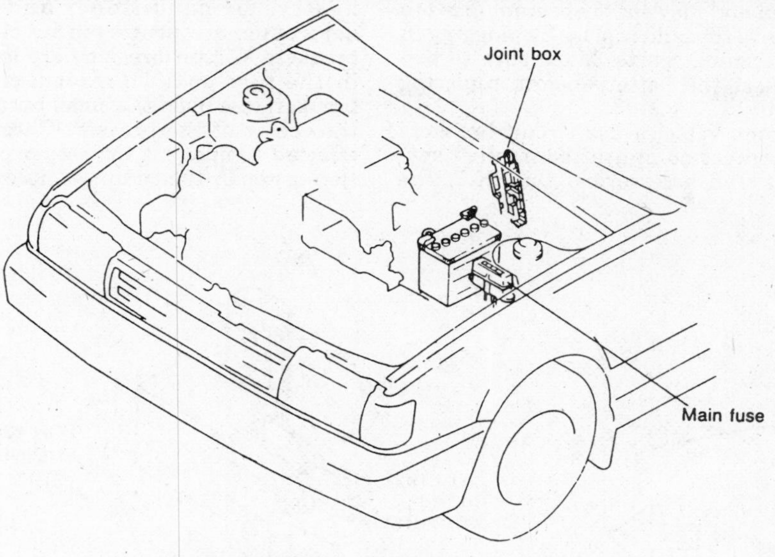


Main fuse box and joint box location on 323

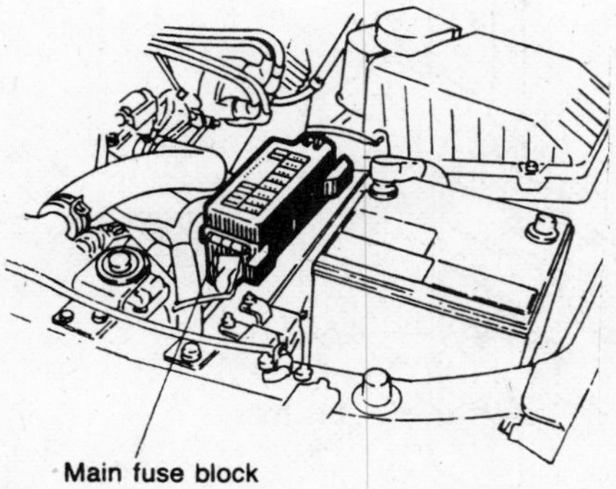


Main fuse box location on 626 and MX-6

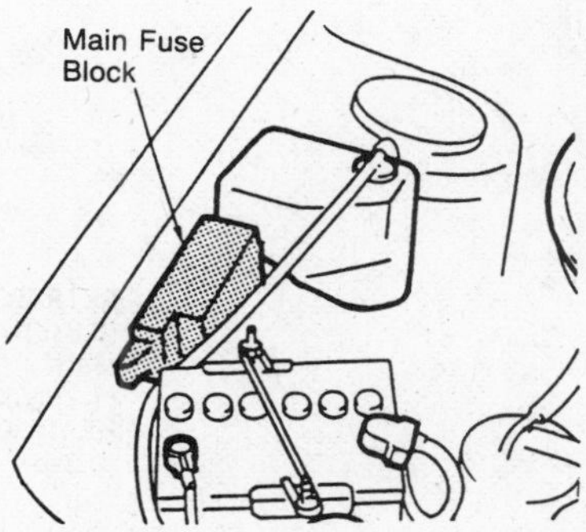


Main fuse box location on 929

ing screws and pull the meter hood out until the electrical connectors are visible. Disconnect the speedometer cable at the speedometer. Disconnect all the connectors from the rear of the meter hood and remove it.

6. Remove the left and right ducts by releasing the clips and fasteners.

7. Unscrew and remove the center lower panel. Remove the hood release knob.

8. On vehicles equipped with automatic transmission, remove the locking screw and remove the parking brake release knob and remove the nut from the parking brake release cable.

9. Unscrew and slide the air conditioning panel from the dash. Disconnect the connectors from the rear of the panel.

10. Remove the front header, left and right side trim. Remove the protective cap from the center intrument panel bolt and remove the bolt. Pull the side panel out carefully until the installation bolts are visible. Remove the side panel installation bolts.

11. Locate the bolts at the instrument panel center bracket and remove them. Remove the bolts from the steering shaft. Pull the instrument panel forward and disconnect the connectors that bridge the instruments and the harnesses. Remove the intrument panel from the vehicle.

12. Installation is the reverse of the removal procedure.

# Stoplight Switch

## REMOVAL & INSTALLATION

1. Disconnect the negative battery cable.

2. Disconnect the stoplamp switch wire connector from the switch.

3. Remove the switch retainer and outer washer from the pedal pin. Slide the stoplight switch out of the brake pedal bracket and remove the switch.

4. Installation is the reverse of removal.

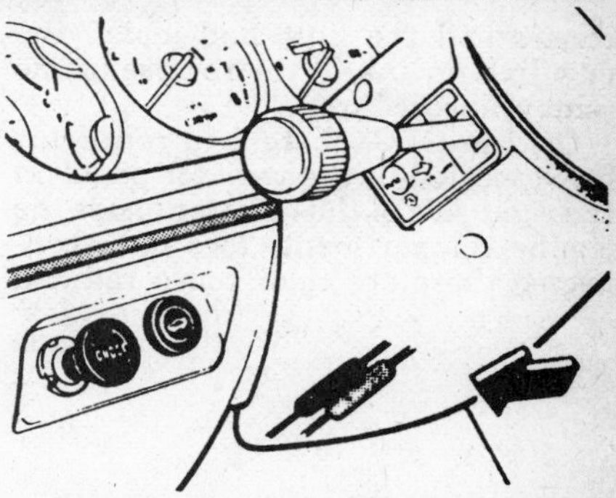

Fusible links in the steering column—RX-7

# Fuse Box

## LOCATION

On the 1983–87 GLC and 626, the fuse box is located underneath the left hand side of the dash panel or on the left side kick panel. All covers have the location, amperage, and the circuit protected by each individual fuse, stamped on them. On the 1988–89 626 and MX-6, the main fuse block is between the battery and the distributor cap on the driver's side of the engine compartment.

On the 323, the fuse joint box is located under the dash, in front of the driver. The main fuse block is located in the engine compartment in front of the driver's side strut and next to the battery.

On the 929, the main fuse block is located on the passengers side of the engine compartemnt between the battery and the window washer reservoir. The fuse panel is located in the passenger compartment on the driver's side just above the brake pedal.

On RX-7, the fuse block is located under the dash on the driver's side of the car. Remove the plastic cover to gain access to the fuses. On 1986–89 models only, there is a main fuse box located in the driver's side of the engine compartment.

# Fusible Links

## LOCATION

On all rotary engine vehicles, these are located in either 1 or 2 boxes next to the battery in the engine compartment. If these links blow, they may be replaced with the specified parts by disconnecting the battery, disconnecting wiring to each link requiring replacement, removing the attaching screws and the link, and install the new link or link in the reverse of the removal procedure.

On the GLC, there is a connector block located in the radiator panel on the right side of the radiator inside the engine compartment. Two links connected there are color coded red and green and may simply be unplugged to remove the, and replace by plugging in replacement parts. Make sure to disconnect the battery before replacing them.

Some vehicles use circuit breakers to protect computer controlled systems and accessories. On RX-7, the heater, air conditioner and rear derfroster are protected by circuit breakers. Circuit breakers are located in the fuse box. To reset a circuit breaker, just push the small button in the center of the breaker. Check the affected component for proper operation or repair the circuit as necessary.

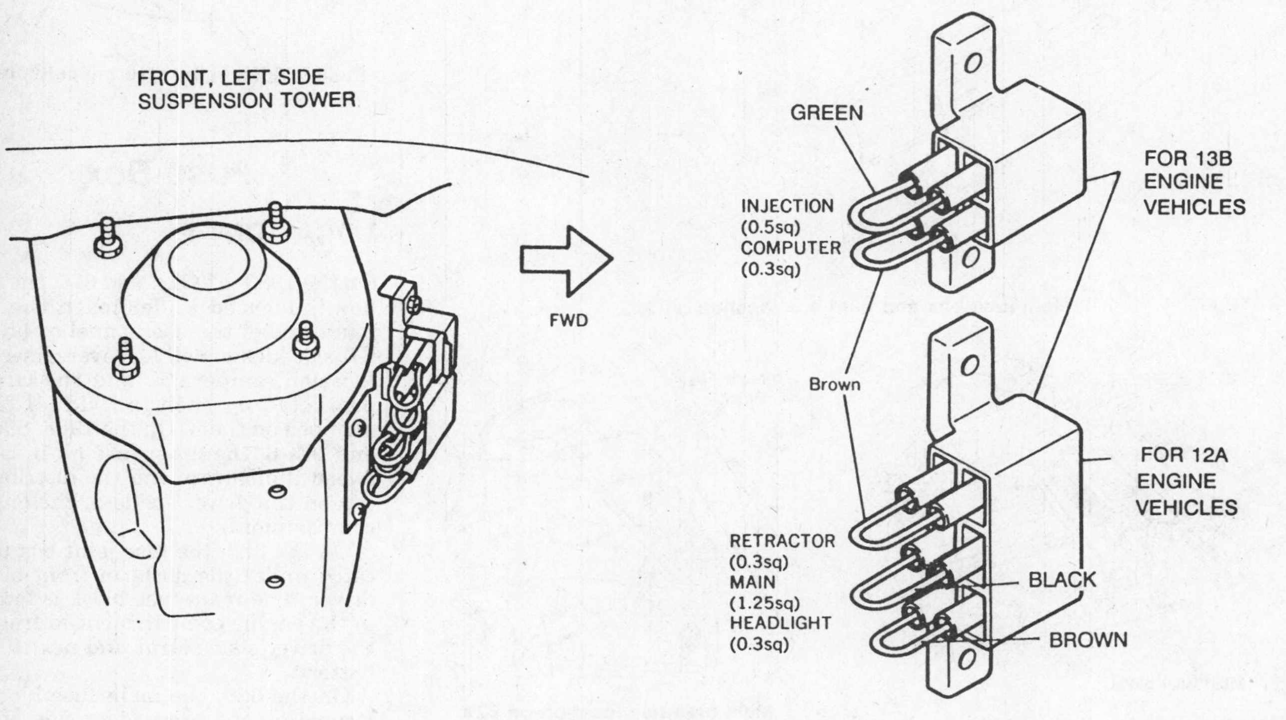


**Fusible link location on 1983–85 RX-7**

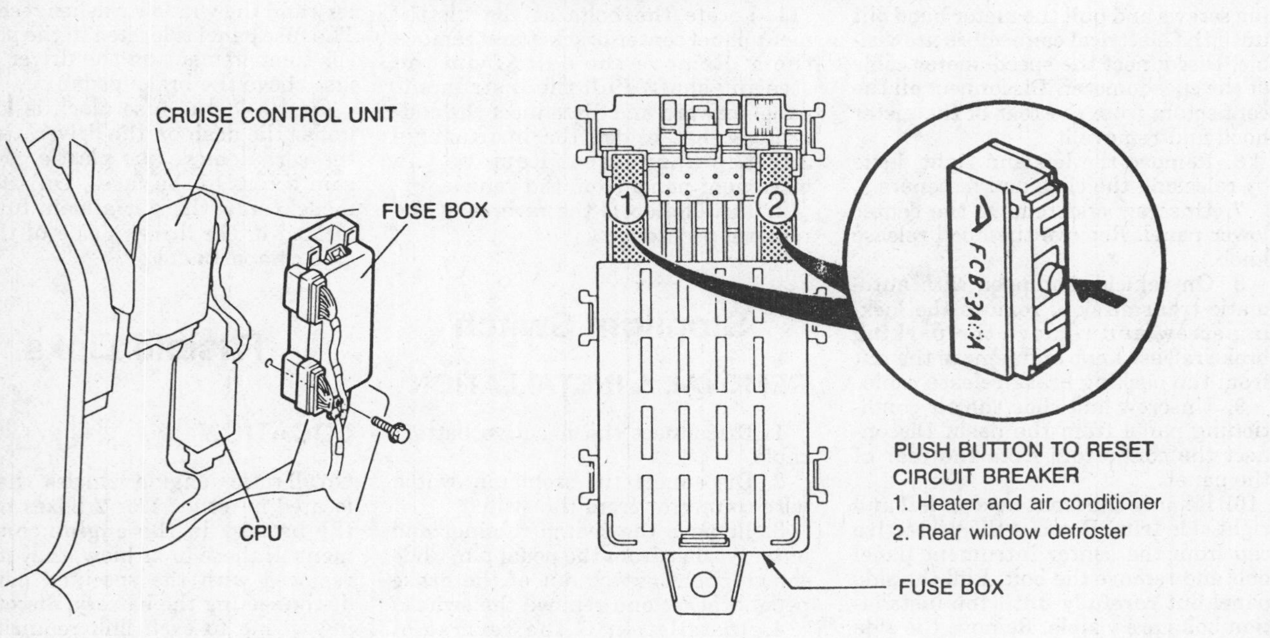


**Main fuse and circuit breaker location on 1986–90 RX-7**

# Mercedes-Benz

## 190, 240, 260, 300, 380, 420, 500, 560—All Models

# 10

# SERIAL NUMBER IDENTIFICATION

## Vehicle Identification Plate

The Vehicle Identification Plate is located in the left window post and consists of a 17 digit number.

## Engine Number

The Engine Number is located in rear of the engine block and consists of a 10 digit number.

## Transmission Number

Mercedes-Benz cars for the U.S. market have been equipped with either a 4 or 5 speed manual transmission or with a fully automatic 4 speed unit. The automatic transmissions are equipped with a torque converter.

Serial numbers on the manual transmission are located on a pad on the side cover of the transmission (left side).

Automatic transmission serial numbers are located on a metal plate which is attached to the driver's side of the transmission.

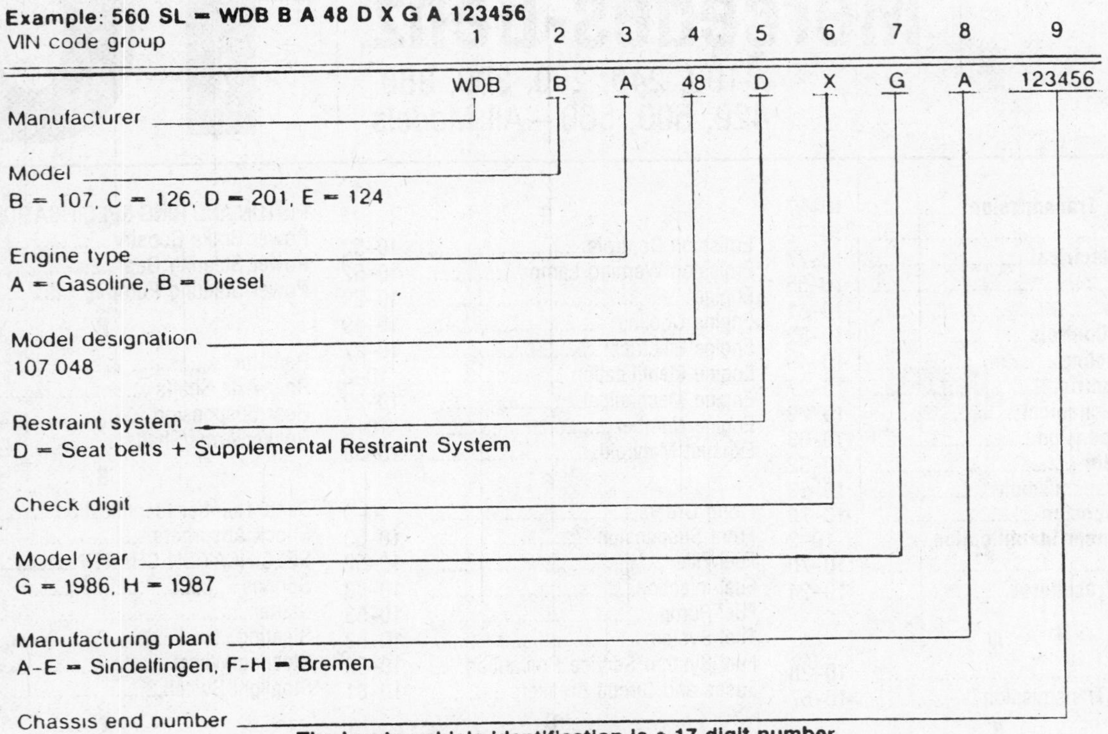

The key to vehicle identification is a 17 digit number

## ENGINE IDENTIFICATION

| Year | Model | Engine Displacement cu. in. (cc/liter) | Engine Series Identification | No. of Cylinders | Engine Type |
|---|---|---|---|---|---|
| 1983 | 240D | 146 (2399/2.4) | OM616 | 4 | 616.912 |
| | 300D | 183 (2996/3.0) | OM617 | 5 | 617.912 |
| | 300CD | 183 (2996/3.0) | OM617 | 5 | 617.912 |
| | 300SD | 183 (2996/3.0) | OM617 | 5 | 617.951 |
| | 300TD | 183 (2996/3.0) | OM617 | 5 | 617.952 |
| | 380SEC | 234 (3839/3.8) | M116 | 8 | 116.963 |
| | 380SEL | 234 (3839/3.8) | M116 | 8 | 116.961 |
| | 380SL | 234 (3839/3.8) | M116 | 8 | 116.962 |
| 1984 | 190D | 134 (2197/2.2) | OM601 | 4 | 601.921 |
| | 190E | 140 (2299/2.3) | M102 | 4 | 102.912 |

## ENGINE IDENTIFICATION

| Year | Model | Engine Displacement cu. in. (cc/liter) | Engine Series Identification | No. of Cylinders | Engine Type |
|---|---|---|---|---|---|
| 1984 | 300D | 183 (2996/3.0) | OM617 | 6 | 617.912 |
| | 300CD | 183 (2996/3.0) | OM617 | 5 | 617.912 |
| | 300SD | 183 (2996/3.0) | OM617 | 5 | 617.951 |
| | 300TD | 183 (2996/3.0) | OM617 | 5 | 617.952 |
| | 380SE | 234 (3839/3.8) | M116 | 8 | 116.963 |
| | 380SL | 234 (3839/3.8) | M116 | 8 | 116.962 |
| | 500SEC | 303 (4973/5.0) | M117 | 8 | 117.963 |
| | 500SEL | 303 (4973/5.0) | M117 | 8 | 117.963 |
| 1985 | 190D | 134 (2197/2.2) | OM601 | 4 | 601.921 |
| | 190E | 140 (2299/2.3) | M102 | 4 | 102.961 |
| | 300D | 183 (2996/3.0) | OM617 | 5 | 617.912 |
| | 300CD | 183 (2996/3.0) | OM617 | 5 | 617.912 |
| | 300SD | 183 (2996/3.0) | OM617 | 5 | 617.951 |
| | 300TD | 183 (2996/3.0) | OM617 | 5 | 617.952 |
| | 380SE | 234 (3839/3.8) | M116 | 8 | 116.963 |
| | 380SL | 234 (3839/3.8) | M116 | 8 | 116.962 |
| | 500SEC | 303 (4973/5.0) | M117 | 8 | 117.963 |
| | 500SEL | 303 (4973/5.0) | M117 | 8 | 117.963 |
| 1986 | 190D | 152 (2497/2.5) | OM602 | 5 | 602.911 |
| | 190E | 140 (2299/2.3) | M102 | 4 | 102.961 |
| | 190E-16 | 140 (2299/2.3) | M102 | 4 | 102.983 |
| | 300E | 181 (2962/3.0) | M103 | 6 | 103.983 |
| | 300SDL | 183 (2996/3.0) | OM603 | 6 | 603.961 |
| | 420SEL | 256 (4196/4.2) | M116 | 8 | 116.965 |
| | 560SL | 338 (5547/5.6) | M117 | 8 | 117.967 |
| | 560SEC | 338 (5547/5.6) | M117 | 8 | 117.968 |
| | 560SEL | 338 (5547/5.6) | M117 | 8 | 117.968 |
| 1987 | 190D | 152 (2497/2.5) | OM602 | 5 | 602.911 |
| | 190D | 152 (2497/2.5) | OM602 | 5 | 602.961 |
| | 190E | 140 (2299/2.3 | M102 | 4 | 102.985 |
| | 190E | 159 (2599/2.6) | M103 | 6 | 103.942 |
| | 190E-16 | 140 (2299/2.3) | M102 | 4 | 102.983 |
| | 260E | 159 (2599/2.6) | M103 | 6 | 103.940 |
| | 300D | 183 (2996/3.0) | M603 | 6 | 603.962 |
| | 300SDL | 183 (2996.3.0) | M603 | 6 | 603.961 |
| | 300TD | 183 (2996/3.0) | M603 | 6 | 603.962 |
| | 300E | 181 (2962/3.0) | M103 | 6 | 103.983 |
| | 420SEL | 256 (4196/4.2) | M116 | 8 | 116.965 |
| | 560SL | 338 (5547/5.6) | M117 | 8 | 117.967 |
| | 560SEC | 338 (5547/5.6) | M117 | 8 | 117.968 |
| | 560SEL | 338 (5547/5.6) | M117 | 8 | 117.968 |

## ENGINE IDENTIFICATION

| Year | Model | Engine Displacement cu. in. (cc/liter) | Engine Series Identification | No. of Cylinders | Engine Type |
|---|---|---|---|---|---|
| 1988 | 190E | 140 (2299/2.3) | M102 | 4 | 102.985 |
| | 190E | 159 (2599/2.6) | M103 | 6 | 103.942 |
| | 190D | 152 (2497/2.5) | OM602 | 5 | 602.911 |
| | 260E | 159 (2599/2.6) | M103 | 6 | 103.940 |
| | 300E | 181 (2962/3.0) | M103 | 6 | 103.983 |
| | 300CE | 181 (2962/3.0) | M103 | 6 | 103.983 |
| | 300TE | 181 (2962/3.0) | M103 | 6 | 103.983 |
| | 300SE | 181 (2962/3.0) | M103 | 6 | 103.981 |
| | 300SEL | 181 (2962/3.0) | M103 | 6 | 103.981 |
| | 420SEL | 256 (4196/4.2) | M116 | 8 | 116.965 |
| | 560SEL | 338 (5547/5.6) | M117 | 8 | 117.967 |
| | 560SEC | 338 (5547/5.6) | M117 | 8 | 117.968 |
| | 560SL | 338 (5547/5.6) | M117 | 8 | 117.968 |
| 1989-90 | 190E | 159 (2599/2.6) | M103 | 6 | 103.942 |
| | 190D | 152 (2497/2.5) | OM602 | 5 | 602.911 |
| | 260E | 159 (2599/2.6) | M103 | 6 | 103.940 |
| | 300E | 181 (2962/3.0) | M103 | 6 | 103.983 |
| | 300CE | 181 (2962/3.0) | M103 | 6 | 103.983 |
| | 300TE | 181 (2962/3.0) | M103 | 6 | 103.983 |
| | 300SE | 181 (2962/3.0) | M103 | 6 | 103.981 |
| | 300SEL | 181 (2962/3.0) | M103 | 6 | 103.981 |
| | 420SEL | 256 (4196/4.2) | M116 | 8 | 116.965 |
| | 560SEL | 338 (5547/5.6) | M117 | 8 | 117.967 |
| | 560SEC | 338 (5547/5.6) | M117 | 8 | 117.968 |
| | 560SL | 338 (5547/5.6) | M117 | 8 | 117.968 |

## GENERAL ENGINE SPECIFICATIONS

| Year | Model | Engine Displacement cu. in. (cc) | Fuel System Type | Net Horsepower @ rpm | Net Torque @ rpm (ft. lbs.) | Bore × Stroke (in.) | Compression Ratio | Oil Pressure @ 2000 rpm |
|---|---|---|---|---|---|---|---|---|
| 1983 | 240D | 147 (2399) | DFI | 64 @ 4000 | 97 @ 2400 | 3.58 × 3.64 | 21:1 | 55 |
| | 300D | 183 (2996) | Turbo | 120 @ 4350 | 170 @ 2400 | 3.58 × 3.64 | 21:1 | 55 |
| | 300SD | 183 (2996) | Turbo | 115 @ 4200 | 169 @ 2400 | 3.58 × 3.64 | 21:1 | 55 |
| | 300CD | 183 (2996) | Turbo | 120 @ 4350 | 170 @ 2400 | 3.58 × 3.64 | 21:1 | 55 |
| | 300TD | 193 (2996) | Turbo | 120 @ 4350 | 170 @ 2400 | 3.58 × 3.64 | 21:1 | 55 |
| | 380SEC | 234 (3839) | CIS | 155 @ 4750 | 196 @ 2750 | 3.46 × 3.11 | 8.3:1 | 55 |
| | 380SEL | 234 (3839) | CIS | 155 @ 4750 | 196 @ 2750 | 3.46 × 3.11 | 8.3:1 | 55 |
| | 380SL | 234 (3839) | CIS | 155 @ 4750 | 196 @ 2750 | 3.46 × 3.11 | 8.3:1 | 55 |

## GENERAL ENGINE SPECIFICATIONS

| Year | Model | Engine Displacement cu. in. (cc) | Fuel System Type | Net Horsepower @ rpm | Net Torque @ rpm (ft. lbs.) | Bore × Stroke (in.) | Com-pression Ratio | Oil Pressure @ 2000 rpm |
|---|---|---|---|---|---|---|---|---|
| 1984 | 190D | 134 (2197) | DFI | 72 @ 4200 | 96 @ 2800 | 3.43 × 3.64 | 22:1 | 55 |
| | 190E | 140 (2299) | CIS | 113 @ 5000 | 133 @ 3500 | 3.76 × 3.16 | 8.0:1 | 55 |
| | 300D | 183 (2996) | Turbo | 120 @ 4350 | 170 @ 2400 | 3.58 × 3.64 | 21:1 | 55 |
| | 300SD | 183 (2996) | Turbo | 115 @ 4200 | 169 @ 2400 | 3.58 × 3.64 | 21:1 | 55 |
| | 300CD | 183 (2996) | Turbo | 120 @ 4350 | 170 @ 2400 | 3.58 × 3.64 | 21:1 | 55 |
| | 300TD | 183 (2996) | Turbo | 120 @ 4350 | 170 @ 2400 | 3.58 × 3.64 | 21:1 | 55 |
| | 380SE | 234 (3839) | CIS | 155 @ 4750 | 196 @ 2750 | 3.46 × 3.11 | 8.3:1 | 55 |
| | 380SL | 234 (3839) | CIS | 155 @ 4750 | 196 @ 2750 | 3.46 × 3.11 | 8.3:1 | 55 |
| | 500SEC | 303 (4973) | CIS | 184 @ 4500 | 247 @ 2000 | 3.80 × 3.35 | 8.0:1 | 55 |
| | 500SEL | 303 (4973) | CIS | 184 @ 4500 | 247 @ 2000 | 3.80 × 3.35 | 8.0:1 | 55 |
| 1985 | 190D | 134 (2197) | DFI | 72 @ 4200 | 96 @ 2800 | 3.43 × 3.64 | 22:1 | 55 |
| | 190E | 140 (2299) | CIS | 113 @ 5000 | 133 @ 3500 | 3.76 × 3.16 | 8.0:1 | 55 |
| | 300D | 193 (2996) | Turbo | 120 @ 4350 | 170 @ 2400 | 3.58 × 3.64 | 21:1 | 55 |
| | 300SD | 183 (2996) | Turbo | 115 @ 4200 | 169 @ 2400 | 3.58 × 3.64 | 21:1 | 55 |
| | 300CD | 183 (2996) | Turbo | 120 @ 4350 | 170 @ 2400 | 3.58 × 3.64 | 21:1 | 55 |
| | 300TD | 183 (2996) | Turbo | 120 @ 4350 | 170 @ 2400 | 3.58 × 3.64 | 21:1 | 55 |
| | 380SE | 234 (3839) | CIS | 155 @ 4750 | 196 @ 2750 | 3.46 × 3.11 | 8.3:1 | 55 |
| | 380SL | 234 (3839) | CIS | 155 @ 4750 | 196 @ 2750 | 3.46 × 3.11 | 8.3:1 | 55 |
| | 500SEC | 303 (4973) | CIS | 184 @ 4500 | 247 @ 2000 | 3.80 × 3.35 | 8.0:1 | 55 |
| | 500SEL | 303 (4973) | CIS | 184 @ 4500 | 247 @ 2000 | 3.80 × 3.35 | 8.0:1 | 55 |
| 1986 | 190D | 152 (2497) | DFI | 93 @ 4600 | 122 @ 2400 | 3.43 × 3.31 | 22:1 | 55 |
| | 190E | 140 (2299) | CIS | 113 @ 5000 | 133 @ 3500 | 3.76 × 3.16 | 8.0:1 | 55 |
| | 190E-16 | 140 (2299) | CIS | 167 @ 5800 | 162 @ 4750 | 3.76 × 3.16 | 9.7:1 | 55 |
| | 300D | 183 (2996) | Turbo | 148 @ 4600 | 201 @ 2400 | 3.43 × 3.31 | 22:1 | 55 |
| | 300SDL | 183 (2996) | Turbo | 148 @ 4600 | 201 @ 2400 | 3.43 × 3.31 | 22:1 | 55 |
| | 300TD | 183 (2996) | Turbo | 148 @ 4600 | 201 @ 2400 | 3.43 × 3.31 | 22:1 | 55 |
| | 420SEL | 256 (4196) | CIS | 201 @ 5200 | 228 @ 3600 | 3.62 × 3.11 | 9.0:1 | 55 |
| | 560SL | 338 (5547) | CIS | 227 @ 4750 | 279 @ 3250 | 3.80 × 3.73 | 9.0:1 | 55 |
| | 560SEC | 338 (5547) | CIS | 238 @ 4800 | 287 @ 3500 | 3.80 × 3.73 | 9.0:1 | 55 |
| | 560SEL | 338 (5547) | CIS | 238 @ 4800 | 287 @ 3500 | 3.80 × 3.73 | 9.0:1 | 55 |
| 1987 | 190D | 152 (2497) | DFI | 93 @ 4600 | 122 @ 2400 | 3.43 × 3.31 | 22:1 | 55 |
| | 190D | 152 (2497) | Turbo | 123 @ 4600 | 168 @ 2400 | 3.43 × 3.31 | 22:1 | 55 |
| | 190E | 140 (2299) | CIS | 130 @ 5100 | 146 @ 3600 | 3.76 × 3.16 | 9.0:1 | 55 |
| | 190E | 159 (2599) | CIS | 158 @ 5800 | 162 @ 4600 | 3.26 × 3.16 | 9.2:1 | 55 |
| | 190E-16 | 140 (2299) | CIS | 167 @ 5800 | 162 @ 4750 | 3.76 × 3.16 | 9.7:1 | 55 |
| | 260E | 159 (2599) | CIS | 158 @ 5800 | 162 @ 4600 | 3.26 × 3.16 | 9.2:1 | 55 |
| | 300D | 183 (2996) | Turbo | 148 @ 4600 | 201 @ 2400 | 3.43 × 3.31 | 22:1 | 55 |
| | 300E | 181 (2962) | CIS | 177 @ 5700 | 188 @ 4400 | 3.16 × 3.48 | 9.2:1 | 55 |
| | 300SDL | 183 (2996) | Turbo | 148 @ 4600 | 201 @ 2400 | 3.43 × 3.31 | 22:1 | 55 |
| | 300TD | 183 (2996) | Turbo | 148 @ 4600 | 201 @ 2400 | 3.43 × 3.31 | 22:1 | 55 |

## GENERAL ENGINE SPECIFICATIONS

| Year | Model | Engine Displacement cu. in. (cc) | Fuel System Type | Net Horsepower @ rpm | Net Torque @ rpm (ft. lbs.) | Bore × Stroke (in.) | Com-pression Ratio | Oil Pressure @ 2000 rpm |
|---|---|---|---|---|---|---|---|---|
| 1987 | 420SEL | 256 (4196) | CIS | 201 @ 5200 | 228 @ 3600 | 3.62 × 3.11 | 9.0:1 | 55 |
| | 560SEL | 338 (5547) | CIS | 227 @ 4750 | 279 @ 3250 | 3.80 × 3.73 | 9.0:1 | 55 |
| | 560SEC | 338 (5547) | CIS | 238 @ 4800 | 287 @ 3500 | 3.80 × 3.73 | 9.0:1 | 55 |
| | 560SEL | 338 (5547) | CIS | 238 @ 3500 | 287 @ 3500 | 3.80 × 3.73 | 9.0:1 | 55 |
| 1988 | 190D | 152 (2497) | DFI | 93 @ 4600 | 122 @ 2400 | 3.43 × 3.31 | 22:1 | 55 |
| | 190E | 140 (2299) | CIS | 130 @ 5100 | 146 @ 3500 | 3.76 × 3.16 | 9.0:1 | 55 |
| | 190E | 159 (2599) | CIS | 158 @ 5800 | 162 @ 4600 | 3.26 × 3.16 | 9.2:1 | 55 |
| | 260E | 159 (2599) | CIS | 158 @ 5800 | 162 @ 4600 | 3.26 × 3.16 | 9.2:1 | 55 |
| | 300E | 181 (2962) | CIS | 177 @ 5700 | 188 @ 4400 | 3.16 × 3.48 | 9.2:1 | 55 |
| | 300CE | 181 (2962) | CIS | 177 @ 5700 | 188 @ 4400 | 3.16 × 3.48 | 9.2:1 | 55 |
| | 300SE | 181 (2962) | CIS | 177 @ 5700 | 188 @ 4400 | 3.16 × 3.48 | 9.2:1 | 55 |
| | 300SEL | 181 (2962) | CIS | 177 @ 5700 | 188 @ 4400 | 3.16 × 3.48 | 9.2:1 | 55 |
| | 300TE | 181 (2962) | CIS | 177 @ 5700 | 188 @ 4400 | 3.16 × 3.48 | 9.2:1 | 55 |
| | 420SEL | 256 (4196) | CIS | 201 @ 5200 | 228 @ 3600 | 3.62 × 3.11 | 9.0:1 | 55 |
| | 560SEC | 338 (5547) | CIS | 238 @ 4800 | 287 @ 3500 | 3.80 × 3.73 | 9.0:1 | 55 |
| | 560SEL | 338 (5547) | CIS | 238 @ 4800 | 287 @ 3500 | 3.80 × 3.73 | 9.0:1 | 55 |
| | 560SL | 338 (5547) | CIS | 227 @ 4750 | 279 @ 3250 | 3.80 × 3.73 | 9.0:1 | 55 |
| 1989-90 | 190D | 152 (2497) | DFI | 93 @ 4600 | 122 @ 2400 | 3.43 × 3.31 | 22:1 | 55 |
| | 190E | 159 (2599) | CIS | 158 @ 5800 | 162 @ 4600 | 3.26 × 3.16 | 9.2:1 | 55 |
| | 260E | 159 (2599) | CIS | 158 @ 5800 | 162 @ 4600 | 3.26 × 3.16 | 9.2:1 | 55 |
| | 300E | 181 (2962) | CIS | 177 @ 5700 | 188 @ 4400 | 3.16 × 3.48 | 9.2:1 | 55 |
| | 300CE | 181 (2962) | CIS | 177 @ 5700 | 188 @ 4400 | 3.16 × 3.48 | 9.2:1 | 55 |
| | 300SE | 181 (2962) | CIS | 177 @ 5700 | 188 @ 4400 | 3.16 × 3.48 | 9.2:1 | 55 |
| | 300SEL | 181 (2962) | CIS | 177 @ 5700 | 188 @ 4400 | 3.16 × 3.48 | 9.2:1 | 55 |
| | 300TE | 181 (2962) | CIS | 177 @ 5700 | 188 @ 4400 | 3.16 × 3.48 | 9.2:1 | 55 |
| | 420SEL | 256 (4196) | CIS | 201 @ 5200 | 228 @ 3600 | 3.62 × 3.11 | 9.0:1 | 55 |
| | 560SEC | 338 (5547) | CIS | 238 @ 4800 | 287 @ 3500 | 3.80 × 3.73 | 9.0:1 | 55 |
| | 560SEL | 338 (5547) | CIS | 238 @ 4800 | 287 @ 3500 | 3.80 × 3.73 | 9.0:1 | 55 |
| | 560SL | 338 (5547) | CIS | 227 @ 4750 | 279 @ 3250 | 3.80 × 3.73 | 9.0:1 | 55 |

CIS Continuous Fuel Injection
DFI Diesel Fuel Injection
Turbo Turbocharged

## GASOLINE ENGINE TUNE-UP SPECIFICATIONS

| Year | Model | Engine Displacement cu. in. (cc) | Spark Plugs Type | Spark Plugs Gap (in.) | Ignition Timing (deg.) MT | Ignition Timing (deg.) AT | Com-pression Pressure (psi) | Fuel Pump (psi) | Idle Speed (rpm) MT | Idle Speed (rpm) AT | Valve Clearance In. | Valve Clearance Ex. |
|---|---|---|---|---|---|---|---|---|---|---|---|---|
| 1983 | 380SEL | 234 (3839) | N10Y | .032 | — | TDC | 125 | 8 | 550 | 550 | Hyd. | Hyd. |
| | 380SL | 234 (3839) | N10Y | .032 | — | TDC | 125 | 8 | 550 | 550 | Hyd. | Hyd. |
| | 380SLC | 234 (3839) | N10Y | .032 | — | TDC | 125 | 8 | 550 | 550 | Hyd. | Hyd. |

## GASOLINE ENGINE TUNE-UP SPECIFICATIONS

| Year | Model | Engine Displacement cu. in. (cc) | Spark Plugs Type | Spark Plugs Gap (in.) | Ignition Timing (deg.) MT | Ignition Timing (deg.) AT | Com-pression Pressure (psi) | Fuel Pump (psi) | Idle Speed (rpm) MT | Idle Speed (rpm) AT | Valve Clearance In. | Valve Clearance Ex. |
|---|---|---|---|---|---|---|---|---|---|---|---|---|
| 1984 | 190E | 140 (2299) | S12YC | .032 | 5B | 5B | 125 | 8 | 650 | 650 | Hyd. | Hyd. |
| | 380SEL | 234 (3839) | N10Y | .032 | — | TDC | 125 | 8 | 550 | 550 | Hyd. | Hyd. |
| | 380SL | 234 (3839) | N10Y | .032 | — | TDC | 125 | 8 | 550 | 550 | Hyd. | Hyd. |
| | 380SLC | 234 (3839) | N10Y | .032 | — | TDC | 125 | 8 | 550 | 550 | Hyd. | Hyd. |
| | 500SEC | 303 (4973) | N10Y | .032 | — | TDC | 124 | 8 | 650 | 650 | Hyd. | Hyd. |
| | 500SEL | 303 (4973) | N10Y | .032 | — | TDC | 125 | 8 | 650 | 650 | Hyd. | Hyd. |
| 1985 | 190E | 140 (2299) | S12YC | .032 | 5B | 5B | 125 | 8 | 650 | 650 | Hyd. | Hyd. |
| | 380SEL | 234 (3839) | N10Y | .032 | — | TCD | 125 | 8 | 550 | 550 | Hyd. | Hyd. |
| | 380SL | 234 (3839) | N10Y | .032 | — | TDC | 125 | 8 | 550 | 550 | Hyd. | Hyd. |
| | 380SLC | 234 (3839) | N10Y | .032 | — | TDC | 125 | 8 | 550 | 550 | Hyd. | Hyd. |
| | 500SEC | 303 (4973) | N10Y | .032 | — | TDC | 125 | 8 | 650 | 650 | Hyd. | Hyd. |
| | 500SEL | 303 (4973) | N10Y | .032 | — | TDC | 125 | 8 | 650 | 650 | Hyd. | Hyd. |
| 1986 | 190E | 140 (2299) | S12YC | .032 | 5B | 5B | 125 | 8 | 650 | 650 | Hyd. | Hyd. |
| | 190E-16 | 140 (2299) | S7YC | .032 | TDC | TDC | 125 | 8 | 890 | 890 | .006 | .012 |
| | 300E | 181 (2962) | S9YC | .032 | TDC | TDC | 125 | 8 | 650 | 650 | Hyd. | Hyd. |
| | 420SEL | 256 (4196) | N9YC | .032 | — | 5B | 125 | 8 | 650 | 650 | Hyd. | Hyd. |
| | 560SL | 338 (5547) | N9YC | .032 | — | 5B | 125 | 8 | 650 | 650 | Hyd. | Hyd. |
| | 560SEC | 338 (5547) | N9YC | .032 | — | 5B | 125 | 8 | 650 | 650 | Hyd. | Hyd. |
| | 560SEL | 338 (5547) | N9YC | .032 | — | 5B | 125 | 8 | 650 | 650 | Hyd. | Hyd. |
| 1987 | 190E | 140 (2299) | S9YC | .032 | 10B | 10B | 125 | 8 | 750 | 750 | Hyd. | Hyd. |
| | 190E | 159 (2599) | S12YC | .032 | 9B | 9B | 125 | 8 | 700 | 700 | Hyd. | Hyd. |
| | 190E-16 | 140 (2299) | S7YC | .032 | TDC | TDC | 125 | 8 | 890 | 890 | .006 | .012 |
| | 260E | 159 (2599) | S12YC | .032 | 9B | 9B | 125 | 8 | 700 | 700 | Hyd. | Hyd. |
| | 300E | 181 (2962) | S9YC | .032 | TDC | TDC | 125 | 8 | 650 | 650 | Hyd. | Hyd. |
| | 420SEL | 256 (4196) | N9YC | .032 | — | 5B | 125 | 8 | 650 | 650 | Hyd. | Hyd. |
| | 560SL | 338 (5547) | N9YC | .032 | — | 5B | 125 | 8 | 650 | 650 | Hyd. | Hyd. |
| | 560SEC | 338 (5547) | N9YC | .032 | — | 5B | 125 | 8 | 650 | 650 | Hyd. | Hyd. |
| | 560SEL | 338 (5547) | N9YC | .032 | — | 5B | 125 | 8 | 650 | 650 | Hyd. | Hyd. |
| 1988 | 190E | 140 (2299) | S9YC | .032 | 10B | 10B | 125 | 8 | 750 | 750 | Hyd. | Hyd. |
| | 190E | 159(2599) | S12YC | .032 | 9B | 9B | 125 | 8 | 700 | 700 | Hyd. | Hyd. |
| | 260E | 159 (2599) | S12YC | .032 | 9B | 9B | 125 | 8 | 700 | 700 | Hyd. | Hyd. |
| | 300E | 181 (2962) | S9YC | .032 | TDC | TDC | 125 | 8 | 650 | 650 | Hyd. | Hyd. |
| | 300CE | 181 (2962) | S9YC | .032 | — | TDC | 125 | 8 | — | 650 | Hyd. | Hyd. |
| | 300SE | 181 (2962) | S9YC | .032 | — | TDC | 125 | 8 | — | 650 | Hyd. | Hyd. |
| | 300SEL | 181 (2962) | S9YC | .032 | — | TDC | 125 | 8 | — | 650 | Hyd. | Hyd. |
| | 300TE | 181 (2962) | S9YC | .032 | — | TDC | 125 | 8 | — | 650 | Hyd. | Hyd. |
| | 420SEL | 256 (4196) | N9YC | .032 | — | TDC | 125 | 8 | — | 650 | Hyd. | Hyd. |
| | 560SEC | 338 (5547) | N9YC | .032 | — | TDC | 125 | 8 | — | 650 | Hyd. | Hyd. |
| | 560SEL | 338 (5547) | N9YC | .032 | — | TDC | 125 | 8 | — | 650 | Hyd. | Hyd. |
| | 560SL | 338 (5547) | N9YC | .032 | — | TDC | 125 | 8 | — | 650 | Hyd. | Hyd. |

## GASOLINE ENGINE TUNE-UP SPECIFICATIONS

| Year | Model | Engine Displacement cu. in. (cc) | Spark Plugs Type | Spark Plugs Gap (in.) | Ignition Timing (deg.) MT | Ignition Timing (deg.) AT | Compression Pressure (psi) | Fuel Pump (psi) | Idle Speed (rpm) MT | Idle Speed (rpm) AT | Valve Clearance In. | Valve Clearance Ex. |
|---|---|---|---|---|---|---|---|---|---|---|---|---|
| 1989-90 | 190E | 159 (2599) | S12YC | .032 | 9B | 9B | 125 | 8 | 700 | 700 | Hyd. | Hyd. |
| | 260E | 159 (2599) | S12YC | .032 | 9B | 9B | 125 | 8 | 700 | 700 | Hyd. | Hyd. |
| | 300E | 181 (2962) | S9YC | .032 | TDC | TDC | 125 | 8 | 650 | 650 | Hyd. | Hyd. |
| | 300CE | 181 (2962) | S9YC | .032 | — | TDC | 125 | 8 | — | 650 | Hyd. | Hyd. |
| | 300SE | 181 (2962) | S9YC | .032 | — | TDC | 125 | 8 | — | 650 | Hyd. | Hyd. |
| | 300SEL | 181 (2962) | S9YC | .032 | — | TDC | 125 | 8 | — | 650 | Hyd. | Hyd. |
| | 300TE | 181 (2962) | S9YC | .032 | — | TDC | 125 | 8 | — | 650 | Hyd. | Hyd. |
| | 420SEL | 256 (4196) | N9YC | .032 | — | TDC | 125 | 8 | — | 650 | Hyd. | Hyd. |
| | 560SEC | 338 (5547) | N9YC | .032 | — | TDC | 125 | 8 | — | 650 | Hyd. | Hyd. |
| | 560SEL | 338 (5547) | N9YC | .032 | — | TDC | 125 | 8 | — | 650 | Hyd. | Hyd. |
| | 560SL | 338 (5547) | N9YC | .032 | — | TDC | 125 | 8 | — | 650 | Hyd. | Hyd. |

Hyd. Hydraulic lifters
TDC Top dead center

## DIESEL ENGINE TUNE-UP SPECIFICATIONS

| Year | Engine Displacement cu. in. (cc) | Valve Clearance Intake (in.) | Valve Clearance Exhaust (in.) | Intake Valve Opens (deg.) | Injection Pump Setting (deg.) | Injection Nozzle Pressure (psi) New | Injection Nozzle Pressure (psi) Used | Idle Speed (rpm) | Cranking Compression Pressure (psi) |
|---|---|---|---|---|---|---|---|---|---|
| 1983 | 147 (2399) 240D | .004 | .012 | 13.5B | 24B | 1564–1706 | 1422–1706 | 750–800 | 284–327 |
| | 183 (2996) 300D | .004 | .014 | 13.5B | 24B | 1958–2074 | 1740 | 650–850 | 284–327 |
| | 183 (2996) 300CD | .004 | .014 | 13.5B | 24B | 1958–2074 | 1740 | 650–850 | 284–327 |
| | 183 (2996) 300SD | .004 | .014 | 13.5B | 24B | 1958–2074 | 1740 | 650–850 | 284–327 |
| | 183 (2996) 300TD | .004 | .014 | 13.5B | 24B | 1958–2074 | 1740 | 650–850 | 284–327 |
| 1984 | 134 (2197) 190D | Hyd. | Hyd. | 12A | 15A | 1564–1706 | 1422–1706 | 700–800 | 284–327 |
| | 183 (2996) 300D | .004 | .014 | 13.5B | 24B | 1958–2074 | 1740 | 650–850 | 284–327 |
| | 183 (2996) 300D | .004 | .014 | 13.5B | 24B | 1958–2074 | 1740 | 650–850 | 284–327 |
| | 183 (2996) 300SD | .004 | .014 | 13.5B | 24B | 1958–2074 | 1740 | 650–850 | 284–327 |
| | 183 (2996) 300TD | .004 | .014 | 13.5B | 24B | 1958–2074 | 1740 | 650–850 | 284–327 |
| 1985 | 134 (2197) 190D | Hyd. | Hyd. | 12A | 15A | 1564–1706 | 1422–1706 | 700–800 | 284–327 |

## DIESEL ENGINE TUNE-UP SPECIFICATIONS

| Year | Engine Displacement cu. in. (cc) | Valve Clearance Intake (in.) | Valve Clearance Exhaust (in.) | Intake Valve Opens (deg.) | Injection Pump Setting (deg.) | Injection Nozzle Pressure (psi) New | Injection Nozzle Pressure (psi) Used | Idle Speed (rpm) | Cranking Compression Pressure (psi) |
|---|---|---|---|---|---|---|---|---|---|
| 1985 | 183 (2996) 300D | .004 | .014 | 13.5B | 24B | 1958–2074 | 1740 | 650–850 | 284–327 |
| | 183 (2996) 300D | .004 | .014 | 13.5B | 24B | 1958–2074 | 1740 | 650–850 | 284–327 |
| | 183 (2996) 300SD | .004 | .014 | 13.5B | 24B | 1958–2074 | 1740 | 650–850 | 284–327 |
| | 183 (2996) 300TD | .004 | .014 | 13.5B | 24B | 1958–2074 | 1740 | 650–850 | 284–327 |
| 1986 | 152 (2497) 190D | Hyd. | Hyd. | 12A | 15A | 1564–2103 | 1740 | 660–700 | 284–327 |
| | 183 (2996) 300SDL | Hyd. | Hyd. | 12A | 15A | 1958–2103 | 1740 | 610–650 | 284–327 |
| 1987 | 152 (2497) 190D | Hyd. | Hyd. | 12A | 15A | 1564–2103 | 1740 | 660–700 | 284–327 |
| | 152 (2497) 190D | Hyd. | Hyd. | 12A | 15A | 1564–2103 | 1740 | 660–700 | 284–327 |
| | 183 (2996) 300D | Hyd. | Hyd. | 12A | 15A | 1958–2103 | 1740 | 610–650 | 284–327 |
| | 183 (2996) 300TD | Hyd. | Hyd. | 12A | 15A | 1958–2103 | 1740 | 610 650 | 284–327 |
| | 183 (2996) 300SDL | Hyd. | Hyd. | 12A | 15A | 1958–2103 | 1740 | 610–650 | 248–327 |
| 1988 | 152 (2497) | Hyd. | Hyd. | 12A | 15A | 1564–2103 | 1740 | 660–700 | 284–327 |
| 1989-90 | 152 (2497) | Hyd. | Hyd. | 12A | 15A | 1564–2103 | 1740 | 660–700 | 284–327 |

Hyd. Hydraulic lifters

## FIRING ORDERS

**NOTE: To avoid confusion, always replace spark wires one at a time.**

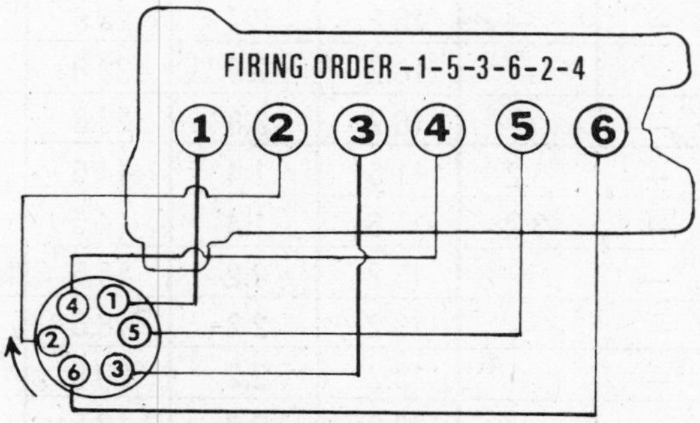


**6 cylinder gasoline engine**

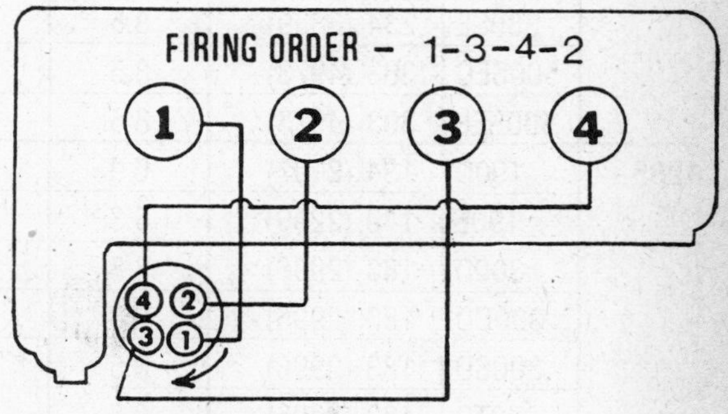


**4-cylinder gas engine**

## FIRING ORDERS

**NOTE: To avoid confusion, always replace spark plug wires one at a time.**

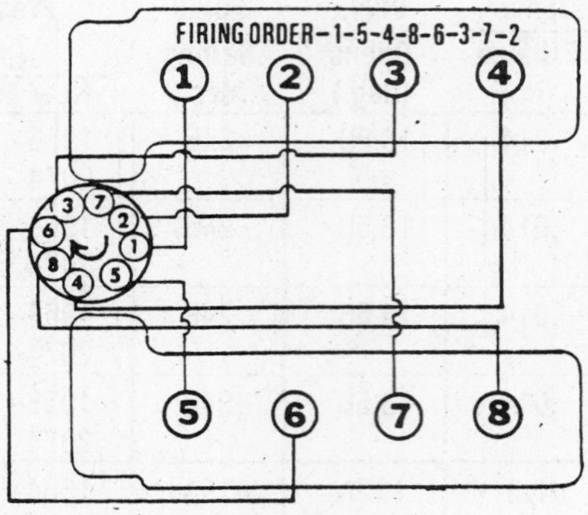


V8 gasoline engines

## CAPACITIES

| Year | Model | Engine Displacement cu. in. (cc) | Engine Crankcase with Filter | Engine Crankcase without Filter | Transmission (pts.) 4-Spd | Transmission (pts.) 5-Spd | Transmission (pts.) Auto. | Drive Axle (pts.) | Fuel Tank (gal.) | Cooling System (qts.) |
|---|---|---|---|---|---|---|---|---|---|---|
| 1983 | 240D | 147 (2399) | 6.3 | 5.3 | — | — | 11.5 | 2.1 | 18.5 | 10.5 |
| | 300D | 183 (2996) | 6.9 | 5.3 | — | — | 13.2 | 2.2 | 18.5 | 13.2 |
| | 300CD | 183 (2996) | 6.8 | 5.3 | — | — | 13.2 | 2.2 | 18.5 | 13.2 |
| | 300SD | 183 (2996) | 8.5 | 8.0 | — | — | 13.2 | 2.2 | 20.3 | 13.2 |
| | 300TD | 183 (2996) | 8.5 | 8.0 | — | — | 13.2 | 2.2 | 18.5 | 13.2 |
| | 380SL | 234 (3839 | 8.5 | 8.0 | — | — | 16.2 | 2.7 | 22.4 | 13.2 |
| | 380SEL | 234 (3839) | 8.5 | 8.0 | — | — | 13.0 | 2.7 | 23.8 | 13.2 |
| | 380SEC | 234 (3839) | 8.5 | 8.0 | — | — | 13.0 | 2.7 | 23.8 | 13.2 |
| 1984 | 190D | 134 (2197) | 6.9 | 6.4 | — | 3.2 | 12.5 | 1.5 | 14.5 | 9.0 |
| | 190D | 140 (2299) | 4.8 | 4.3 | — | 3.2 | 11.6 | 1.5 | 14.5 | 9.0 |
| | 300D | 183 (2996) | 6.8 | 5.3 | — | — | 13.2 | 2.2 | 18.5 | 13.2 |
| | 300CD | 183 (2996) | 6.8 | 5.3 | — | — | 13.2 | 2.2 | 18.5 | 13.2 |
| | 300SD | 183 (2996) | 8.5 | 8.0 | — | — | 13.2 | 2.2 | 20.3 | 13.2 |
| | 300TD | 183 (2996) | 8.5 | 8.0 | — | — | 13.2 | 2.2 | 18.5 | 13.2 |
| | 380SL | 234 (3839) | 8.5 | 8.0 | — | — | 16.2 | 2.7 | 22.5 | 13.2 |
| | 380SE | 234 (3839) | 8.5 | 8.0 | — | — | 16.2 | 2.7 | 23.8 | 13.2 |
| | 500SEC | 303 (4973) | 8.5 | 8.0 | — | — | 16.2 | 2.8 | 23.8 | 13.7 |
| | 500SEL | 303 (4973) | 8.5 | 8.0 | — | — | 16.2 | 2.8 | 23.8 | 13.7 |
| 1985 | 190D | 134 (2197) | 6.9 | 6.4 | — | 3.2 | 11.6 | 1.4 | 14.5 | 9.0 |
| | 190E | 140 (2299) | 5.3 | 4.8 | — | 3.2 | 11.6 | 1.4 | 14.5 | 9.0 |
| | 300D | 183 (2996) | 6.8 | 5.3 | — | — | 13.2 | 2.2 | 18.5 | 13.2 |
| | 300CD | 183 (2996) | 6.8 | 5.3 | — | — | 13.2 | 2.2 | 18.5 | 13.2 |
| | 300SD | 183 (2996) | 8.5 | 8.0 | — | — | 13.2 | 2.2 | 20.3 | 13.2 |
| | 300TD | 183 (2996) | 8.5 | 8.0 | — | — | 13.2 | 2.2 | 18.5 | 13.2 |

## CAPACITIES

| Year | Model | Engine Displacement cu. in. (cc) | Engine Crankcase with Filter | Engine Crankcase without Filter | Transmission (pts.) 4-Spd | Transmission (pts.) 5-Spd | Transmission (pts.) Auto. | Drive Axle (pts.) | Fuel Tank (gal.) | Cooling System (qts.) |
|---|---|---|---|---|---|---|---|---|---|---|
| 1985 | 380SL | 234 (3839) | 8.5 | 8.0 | – | – | 16.2 | 2.7 | 22.4 | 13.2 |
| | 380SE | 234 (3839) | 8.5 | 8.0 | – | – | 16.2 | 2.7 | 23.8 | 13.2 |
| | 500SEC | 303 (4973) | 8.5 | 8.0 | – | – | 16.2 | 2.8 | 23.8 | 13.7 |
| | 500SEL | 303 (4973) | 8.5 | 8.0 | – | – | 16.2 | 2.8 | 23.8 | 13.7 |
| 1986 | 190D | 152 (2497) | 7.5 | 7.0 | – | 3.2 | 11.6 | 1.5 | 14.5 | 8.5 |
| | 190E | 140 (2299) | 5.3 | 4.8 | – | 3.2 | 11.6 | 1.4 | 14.5 | 9.0 |
| | 190E-16 | 140 (2299) | 5.3 | 4.8 | – | 3.4 | 12.6 | 2.3 | 18.5 | 8.5 |
| | 300E | 181 (2962) | 6.4 | 5.9 | – | 3.2 | 13.1 | 2.3 | 18.5 | 8.5 |
| | 300SDL | 183 (2996) | 8.5 | 8.0 | – | 3.2 | 13.1 | 2.3 | 23.8 | 13.3 |
| | 420SEL | 256 (4196) | 8.5 | 8.0 | – | – | 16.2 | 2.7 | 18.5 | 13.8 |
| | 560SL | 338 (5547) | 8.5 | 8.0 | – | – | 16.2 | 2.7 | 22.4 | 13.8 |
| | 560SEL | 338 (5547) | 8.5 | 8.0 | – | – | 16.2 | 2.7 | 23.8 | 13.8 |
| | 560SEC | 338 (5547) | 8.5 | 8.0 | – | – | 16.2 | 2.7 | 23.8 | 13.8 |
| 1987 | 190D | 152 (2497) | 8.0 | 7.5 | – | 3.2 | 11.6 | 1.5 | 14.5 | 8.5 |
| | 190E | 140 (2299) | 4.8 | 4.3 | – | 3.2 | 12.7 | 2.3 | 14.5 | 9.0 |
| | 190E | 159 (2599) | 6.4 | 5.9 | – | 3.2 | 12.7 | 2.3 | 14.5 | 9.5 |
| | 190E16 | 140 (2299) | 5.3 | 4.8 | – | 3.4 | 12.6 | 2.3 | 18.5 | 8.5 |
| | 260E | 159 (2599) | 6.4 | 5.9 | – | 3.2 | 13.1 | 2.3 | 18.5 | 9.5 |
| | 300E | 181 (2962) | 6.4 | 5.9 | – | 3.2 | 13.1 | 2.3 | 18.5 | 8.5 |
| | 300D | 183 (2996) | 8.5 | 8.0 | – | – | 13.1 | 2.3 | 18.5 | 10.6 |
| | 300TD | 183 (2996) | 8.5 | 8.0 | – | – | 13.1 | 2.3 | 19.0 | 10.6 |
| | 300SDL | 183 (3996) | 8.5 | 8.0 | – | 3.2 | 13.1 | 2.3 | 23.8 | 13.3 |
| | 420SEL | 256 (4196) | 8.5 | 8.0 | – | – | 16.2 | 2.7 | 23.8 | 13.8 |
| | 560SL | 338 (5547) | 8.5 | 8.0 | – | – | 16.2 | 2.7 | 22.4 | 13.8 |
| | 560SEL | 338 (5547) | 8.5 | 8.0 | – | – | 16.2 | 2.7 | 23.8 | 13.8 |
| | 560SEC | 338 (5547) | 8.5 | 8.0 | – | – | 16.2 | 2.7 | 23.8 | 13.8 |
| 1988 | 190D | 152 (2497) | 8.0 | 7.5 | – | – | 11.6 | 1.5 | 14.5 | 8.5 |
| | 190E | 140 (2299) | 4.8 | 4.3 | – | 3.2 | 12.7 | 2.2 | 14.5 | 9.0 |
| | 190E | 159 (2599) | 6.4 | 5.9 | – | 3.2 | 12.7 | 2.3 | 14.5 | 9.5 |
| | 260E | 159 (2599) | 6.4 | 5.9 | – | 3.2 | 13.1 | 2.3 | 18.5 | 9.5 |
| | 300E | 181 (2962) | 6.4 | 5.9 | – | 3.2 | 13.1 | 2.3 | 18.5 | 8.5 |
| | 300CE | 181 (2962) | 6.4 | 5.9 | – | – | 13.1 | 2.3 | 18.5 | 10.6 |
| | 300SE | 181 (2962) | 6.4 | 5.9 | – | – | 13.1 | 2.3 | 23.8 | 10.6 |
| | 300SEL | 181 (2962) | 6.4 | 5.9 | – | – | 13.1 | 2.3 | 23.8 | 10.6 |
| | 300TE | 181 (2962) | 6.4 | 5.9 | – | – | 13.1 | 2.3 | 19 | 10.6 |
| | 420SEL | 256 (4196) | 8.5 | 8.0 | – | – | 16.2 | 2.7 | 23.8 | 13.8 |
| | 560SEC | 338 (5547) | 8.5 | 8.0 | – | – | 16.2 | 2.7 | 23.8 | 13.8 |
| | 560SEL | 338 (5547) | 8.5 | 8.0 | – | – | 16.2 | 2.7 | 23.8 | 13.8 |
| | 560SL | 338 (5547) | 8.5 | 8.0 | – | – | 16.2 | 2.7 | 22.4 | 13.8 |

## CAPACITIES

| Year | Model | Engine Displacement cu. in. (cc) | Engine Crankcase with Filter | Engine Crankcase without Filter | Transmission (pts.) 4-Spd | Transmission (pts.) 5-Spd | Transmission (pts.) Auto. | Drive Axle (pts.) | Fuel Tank (gal.) | Cooling System (qts.) |
|---|---|---|---|---|---|---|---|---|---|---|
| 1989-90 | 190D | 152 (2497) | 8.0 | 7.5 | — | — | 11.6 | 1.5 | 14.5 | 8.5 |
| | 190E | 159 (2599) | 6.4 | 5.9 | — | 3.2 | 12.7 | 2.3 | 14.5 | 9.5 |
| | 260E | 159 (2599) | 6.4 | 5.9 | — | 3.2 | 13.1 | 2.3 | 18.5 | 9.5 |
| | 300E | 181 (2962) | 6.4 | 5.9 | — | 3.2 | 13.1 | 2.3 | 18.5 | 8.5 |
| | 300CE | 181 (2962) | 6.4 | 5.9 | — | — | 13.1 | 2.3 | 18.5 | 10.6 |
| | 300SE | 181 (2962) | 6.4 | 5.9 | — | — | 13.1 | 2.3 | 23.8 | 10.6 |
| | 300SEL | 181 (2962) | 6.4 | 5.9 | — | — | 13.1 | 2.3 | 23.8 | 10.6 |
| | 300TE | 181 (2962) | 6.4 | 5.9 | — | — | 13.1 | 2.3 | 19 | 10.6 |
| | 420SEL | 256 (4196) | 8.5 | 8.0 | — | — | 16.2 | 2.7 | 23.8 | 13.8 |
| | 560SEC | 338 (5547) | 8.5 | 8.0 | — | — | 16.2 | 2.7 | 23.8 | 13.8 |
| | 560SEL | 338 (5547) | 8.5 | 8.0 | — | — | 16.2 | 2.7 | 23.8 | 13.8 |
| | 560SL | 338 (5547) | 8.5 | 8.0 | — | — | 16.2 | 2.7 | 22.4 | 13.8 |

## CAMSHAFT SPECIFICATIONS

All measurements given in inches.

| Year | Engine Displacement cu. in. (cc) | Journal Diameter 1 | Journal Diameter 2 | Journal Diameter 3 | Journal Diameter 4 | Journal Diameter 5 | Lobe Lift In. | Lobe Lift Ex. | Bearing Clearance | Camshaft End Play |
|---|---|---|---|---|---|---|---|---|---|---|
| 1983 | 147 (2399) | 1.378 | 1.831 | 1.831 | 1.831 | 1.831 | .394 | .413 | .002 | .004 |
| | 183 (2996) | 1.378 | 1.831 | 1.831 | 1.831 | 1.831 | .394 | .413 | .002 | .004 |
| | 234 (3839) | 1.377 | 1.936 | 1.936 | 1.944 | 1.944 | NA | NA | .0016 | .004 |
| 1984 | 134 (2197) | 1.218 | 1.218 | 1.218 | 1.218 | 1.218 | NA | NA | NA | NA |
| | 140 (2299) | 1.260 | 1.260 | 1.260 | 1.260 | 1.260 | NA | NA | NA | NA |
| | 183 (2996) | 1.378 | 1.831 | 1.831 | 1.831 | 1.831 | .394 | .413 | .002 | .004 |
| | 234 (3839) | 1.377 | 1.936 | 1.936 | 1.944 | 1.944 | NA | NA | .0016 | .004 |
| | 303 (4973) | 1.377 | 1.936 | 1.936 | 1.944 | 1.944 | NA | NA | .0016 | .004 |
| 1985 | 134 (2197) | 1.218 | 1.218 | 1.218 | 1.218 | 1.218 | NA | NA | NA | NA |
| | 140 (2299) | 1.260 | 1.260 | 1.260 | 1.260 | 1.260 | NA | NA | NA | NA |
| | 183 (2996) | 1.378 | 1.831 | 1.831 | 1.831 | 1.831 | .394 | .413 | .002 | .004 |
| | 234 (3839) | 1.377 | 1.936 | 1.936 | 1.944 | 1.944 | NA | NA | .0016 | .004 |
| | 303 (4973) | 1.377 | 1.936 | 1.936 | 1.944 | 1.944 | NA | NA | .0016 | .004 |
| 1986 | 140 (2299) | 1.260 | 1.260 | 1.260 | 1.260 | 1.260 | NA | NA | NA | NA |
| | 140 (2299) | 1.102 | 1.102 | 1.102 | 1.102 | 1.102 | NA | NA | NA | NA |
| | 152 (2497) | 1.260 | 1.260 | 1.260 | 1.260 | 1.260 | NA | NA | NA | NA |
| | 181 (2962) | 1.378 | 1.831 | 1.831 | 1.831 | 1.831 | .394 | .413 | .002 | .004 |
| | 183 (2996) | 1.378 | 1.831 | 1.831 | 1.831 | 1.831 | .394 | .413 | .002 | .004 |
| | 256 (4196) | 1.377 | 1.936 | 1.936 | 1.944 | 1.944 | NA | NA | .0016 | .004 |
| | 338 (5547) | 1.377 | 1.936 | 1.936 | 1.944 | 1.944 | NA | NA | .0016 | .004 |
| 1987 | 140 (2299) | 1.260 | 1.260 | 1.260 | 1.260 | 1.260 | NA | NA | NA | NA |
| | 140 (2299) | 1.102 | 1.102 | 1.102 | 1.102 | 1.102 | NA | NA | NA | NA |

## CAMSHAFT SPECIFICATIONS

All measurements given in inches.

| Year | Engine Displacement cu. in. (cc) | Journal Diameter 1 | 2 | 3 | 4 | 5 | Lobe Lift In. | Ex. | Bearing Clearance | Camshaft End Play |
|---|---|---|---|---|---|---|---|---|---|---|
| 1987 | 159 (2599) | 1.378 | 1.831 | 1.831 | 1.831 | 1.831 | .394 | .413 | .002 | .004 |
| | 152 (2497) | 1.260 | 1.260 | 1.260 | 1.260 | 1.260 | NA | NA | NA | NA |
| | 159 (2599) | 1.378 | 1.831 | 1.831 | 1.831 | 1.831 | .394 | .413 | .002 | .004 |
| | 181 (2962) | 1.378 | 1.831 | 1.831 | 1.831 | 1.831 | .394 | .413 | .002 | .004 |
| | 183 (2996) | 1.378 | 1.831 | 1.831 | 1.831 | 1.831 | .394 | .413 | .002 | .004 |
| | 256 (4196) | 1.377 | 1.936 | 1.936 | 1.944 | 1.944 | NA | NA | .0016 | .004 |
| | 338 (5547) | 1.377 | 1.936 | 1.936 | 1.944 | 1.944 | NA | NA | .0016 | .004 |
| 1988 | 140 (2299) | 1.260 | 1.260 | 1.260 | 1.260 | 1.260 | NA | NA | NA | NA |
| | 152 (2497) | 1.260 | 1.260 | 1.260 | 1.260 | 1.260 | NA | NA | NA | NA |
| | 159 (2599) | 1.378 | 1.831 | 1.831 | 1.831 | 1.831 | .394 | .413 | .002 | .004 |
| | 181 (2962) | 1.378 | 1.831 | 1.831 | 1.831 | 1.831 | .394 | .413 | .002 | .004 |
| | 256 (4196) | 1.377 | 1.936 | 1.936 | 1.944 | 1.944 | NA | NA | .0016 | .004 |
| | 338 (5547) | 1.377 | 1.936 | 1.936 | 1.944 | 1.944 | NA | NA | .0016 | .004 |
| 1989-90 | 152 (2497) | 1.260 | 1.260 | 1.260 | 1.260 | 1.260 | NA | NA | NA | NA |
| | 159 (2599) | 1.378 | 1.831 | 1.831 | 1.831 | 1.831 | .394 | .413 | .002 | .004 |
| | 181 (2962) | 1.378 | 1.831 | 1.831 | 1.831 | 1.831 | .394 | .413 | .002 | .004 |
| | 256 (4196) | 1.377 | 1.936 | 1.936 | 1.944 | 1.944 | NA | NA | .0016 | .004 |
| | 338 (5547) | 1.377 | 1.936 | 1.936 | 1.944 | 1.944 | NA | NA | .0016 | .004 |

NA Not available

## CRANKSHAFT AND CONNECTING ROD SPECIFICATIONS

All measurements are given in inches.

| Year | Engine Displacement cu. in. (cc) | Crankshaft Main Brg. Journal Dia. | Main Brg. Oil Clearance | Shaft End-play | Thrust on No. | Connecting Rod Journal Diameter | Oil Clearance | Side Clearance |
|---|---|---|---|---|---|---|---|---|
| 1983 | 147 (2399) | 2.754–2.755 | 0.002–0.003 | 0.004–0.009 | ① | 2.045–2.046 | 0.001–0.002 | 0.004–0.010 |
| | 183 (2996) | 2.754–2.755 | 0.002–0.003 | 0.004–0.009 | ① | 2.045–2.046 | 0.001–0.002 | 0.004–0.010 |
| | 234 (3839) | 2.517–2.518 | 0.002–0.003 | 0.004–0.009 | ① | 1.887–1.888 | 0.004–0.009 | 0.009–0.014 |
| 1984 | 134 (2198) | 2.281–2.282 | 0.001–0.003 | 0.004–0.010 | ① | 1.887–1.888 | 0.001–0.003 | 0.003–0.012 |
| | 140 (2299) | 2.281–2.282 | 0.001–0.003 | 0.004–0.010 | ① | 1.887–1.888 | 0.001–0.003 | NA |
| | 183 (2996) | 2.754–2.755 | 0.002–0.003 | 0.004–0.009 | ① | 2.045–2.046 | 0.001–0.002 | 0.004–0.010 |
| | 234 (3839) | 2.517–2.518 | 0.002–0.003 | 0.004–0.009 | ① | 1.887–1.888 | 0.004–0.009 | 0.009–0.014 |
| | 303 (4973) | 2.517–2.518 | 0.002–0.003 | 0.004–0.009 | ① | 1.887–1.888 | 0.004–0.009 | 0.009–0.014 |

## CRANKSHAFT AND CONNECTING ROD SPECIFICATIONS

All measurements are given in inches.

| | Engine | Crankshaft | | | | Connecting Rod | | |
|---|---|---|---|---|---|---|---|---|
| Year | Displacement cu. in. (cc) | Main Brg. Journal Dia. | Main Brg. Oil Clearance | Shaft End-play | Thrust on No. | Journal Diameter | Oil Clearance | Side Clearance |
| 1985 | 134 (2197) | 2.281–2.282 | 0.001–0.003 | 0.004–0.010 | ① | 1.887–1.888 | 0.001–0.003 | 0.003–0.012 |
| | 140 (2299) | 2.281–2.282 | 0.001–0.003 | 0.004–0.010 | ① | 1.887–1.887 | 0.001–0.003 | NA |
| | 183 (2996) | 2.754–2.755 | 0.002–0.003 | 0.004–0.009 | ① | 2.045–2.046 | 0.001–0.002 | 0.004–0.010 |
| | 234 (3839) | 2.517–2.518 | 0.002–0.003 | 0.004–0.009 | ① | 1.887–1.888 | 0.004–0.009 | 0.009–0.014 |
| | 303 (4973) | 2.517–2.518 | 0.002–0.003 | 0.004–0.009 | ① | 1.887–1.888 | 0.004–0.009 | 0.009–0.014 |
| 1986 | 140 (2299) | 2.281–2.282 | 0.001–0.003 | 0.004–0.010 | ① | 1.887–1.888 | 0.001–0.003 | NA |
| | 152 (2497) | 2.281–2.282 | 0.001–0.003 | 0.004–0.010 | ① | 1.887–1.888 | 0.001–0.003 | NA |
| | 183 (2996) | 2.754–2.755 | 0.002–0.003 | 0.004–0.009 | ① | 2.045–2.046 | 0.001–0.002 | 0.004–0.010 |
| | 256 (4196) | 2.517–2.518 | 0.002–0.003 | 0.004–0.009 | ① | 1.887–1.888 | 0.004–0.009 | 0.009–0.014 |
| | 338 (5547) | 2.517–2.518 | 0.002–0.003 | 0.004–0.009 | ① | 1.887–1.888 | 0.004–0.009 | 0.009–0.014 |
| 1987 | 140 (2299) | 2.281–2.282 | 0.001–0.003 | 0.004–0.010 | ① | 1.887–1.888 | 0.001–0.003 | NA |
| | 159 (2599) | 2.360–2.361 | NA | NA | ① | 2.031–2.032 | 0.001–0.002 | NA |
| | 152 (2497) | 2.281–2.282 | 0.001–0.003 | 0.004–0.010 | ① | 1.887–1.888 | 0.001–0.003 | NA |
| | 181 (2962) | 2.360–2.361 | NA | NA | ① | 2.031–2.032 | 0.001–0.002 | NA |
| | 183 (2996) | 2.754–2.755 | 0.002–0.003 | 0.004–0.009 | ① | 2.045–2.046 | 0.001–0.002 | 0.004–0.010 |
| | 256 (4196) | 2.517–2.518 | 0.002–0.003 | 0.004–0.009 | ① | 1.887–1.888 | 0.004–0.009 | 0.009–0.014 |
| | 338 (5547) | 2.517–2.518 | 0.002–0.003 | 0.004–0.009 | ① | 1.887–1.888 | 0.004–0.009 | 0.009–0.014 |
| 1988 | 140 (2299) | 2.281–2.282 | 0.001–0.003 | 0.004–0.010 | ① | 1.887–1.888 | 0.001–0.003 | NA |
| | 152 (2497) | 2.281–2.282 | 0.001–0.003 | 0.004–0.010 | ① | 1.887–1.888 | 0.001–0.003 | NA NA |
| | 159 (2599) | 2.360–2.361 | NA | NA | ① | 2.031–2.032 | 0.001–0.002 | NA |
| | 181 (2962) | 2.360–2.361 | NA | NA | ① | 2.031–2.032 | 0.001–0.002 | NA |
| | 256 (4196) | 2.517–2.518 | 0.002–0.003 | 0.004–0.009 | ① | 1.887–1.888 | 0.004–0.009 | 0.009–0.014 |

## CRANKSHAFT AND CONNECTING ROD SPECIFICATIONS

All measurements are given in inches.

| Year | Engine Displacement cu. in. (cc) | Crankshaft Main Brg. Journal Dia. | Crankshaft Main Brg. Oil Clearance | Crankshaft Shaft End-play | Crankshaft Thrust on No. | Connecting Rod Journal Diameter | Connecting Rod Oil Clearance | Connecting Rod Side Clearance |
|---|---|---|---|---|---|---|---|---|
| 1988 | 338 (5547) | 2.517–2.518 | 0.002–0.003 | 0.004–0.009 | ① | 1.887–1.888 | 0.004–0.009 | 0.009–0.014 |
| 1989-90 | 152 (2497) | 2.281–2.282 | 0.001–0.003 | 0.004–0.010 | ① | 1.887–1.888 | 0.001–0.003 | NA NA |
| | 159 (2599) | 2.360–2.361 | NA | NA | ① | 2.031–2.032 | 0.001–0.002 | NA |
| | 181 (2962) | 2.360–2.361 | NA | NA | ① | 2.031–2.032 | 0.001–0.002 | NA |
| | 256 (4196) | 2.517–2.518 | 0.002–0.003 | 0.004–0.009 | ① | 1.887–1.888 | 0.004–0.009 | 0.009–0.014 |
| | 338 (5547) | 2.517–2.518 | 0.002–0.003 | 0.004–0.009 | ① | 1.887–1.888 | 0.004–0.009 | 0.009–0.014 |

NA Not available

① Center main on 5 main bearing engines; rear main on 7 mian bearing engines; 3rd from front on 300D (5 cylinder)

## VALVE SPECIFICATIONS

| Year | Engine Displacement cu. in. (cc) | Seat Angle (deg.) | Face Angle (deg.) | Spring Test Pressure (lbs.) | Spring Installed Height (in.) | Stem-to-Guide Clearance (in.) Intake | Stem-to-Guide Clearance (in.) Exhaust | Stem Diameter (in.) Intake | Stem Diameter (in.) Exhaust |
|---|---|---|---|---|---|---|---|---|---|
| 1983 | 147 (2399) | 30① | 30① | 12.90 | 1.178 | 0.004 | 0.004 | 0.390 | 0.391 |
| | 183 (2996) | 30① | 30① | 119 | 2.008 | 0.004 | 0.004 | 0.391 | 0.391 |
| | 234 (3839) | 45 | 45 | 194 | 1.200 | 0.004 | 0.004 | 0.353 | 0.352 |
| 1984 | 134 (2197) | 45① | 45① | 169 | 2.000 | 0.004 | 0.004 | 0.314 | 0.353 |
| | 140 (2299) | 45① | 45① | 191 | 1.929 | 0.004 | 0.004 | 0.314 | 0.353 |
| | 183 (2996) | 30① | 30① | 119 | 2.008 | 0.004 | 0.004 | 0.391 | 0.391 |
| | 234 (3939) | 45 | 45 | 194 | 1.200 | 0.004 | 0.004 | 0.353 | 0.352 |
| | 303 (4973) | 45 | 45 | 194 | 1.200 | 0.004 | 0.004 | 0.353 | 0.352 |
| 1985 | 134 (2197) | 45① | 45① | 169 | 2.000 | 0.004 | 0.004 | 0.314 | 0.353 |
| | 140 (2299) | 45① | 45① | 191 | 1.929 | 0.004 | 0..004 | 0.314 | 0.353 |
| | 183 (2996) | 30① | 30① | 119 | 2.008 | 0.004 | 0.004 | 0.391 | 0.391 |
| | 234 (3839) | 45 | 45 | 194 | 1.200 | 0.004 | 0.004 | 0.353 | 0.352 |
| | 303 (4973) | 45 | 45 | 194 | 1.200 | 0.004 | 0.004 | 0.353 | 0.352 |
| 1986 | 140 (2299) | 45① | 45① | 191 | 1.929 | 0.004 | 0.004 | 0.314 | 0.353 |
| | 140 (2299) | 45 | 45 | 191 | 1.929 | 0.004 | 0.004 | 0.274 | 0.313 |
| | 152 (2497) | 45① | 45① | 169 | 2.000 | 0.004 | 0.004 | 0.314 | 0.353 |
| | 183 (2996) | 45 | 45 | 191 | 1.929 | 0.004 | 0.004 | 0.314 | 0.353 |
| | 181 (2962) | 45 | 45 | NA | NA | 0.004 | 0.004 | 0.314 | 0.352 |
| | 256 (4196) | 45 | 45 | 194 | 1.200 | 0.004 | 0.004 | 0.353 | 0.352 |
| | 338 (5547) | 45 | 45 | 194 | 1.200 | 0.004 | 0.004 | 0.353 | 0.352 |

## VALVE SPECIFICATIONS

| Year | Engine Displacement cu. in. (cc) | Seat Angle (deg.) | Face Angle (deg.) | Spring Test Pressure (lbs.) | Spring Installed Height (in.) | Stem-to-Guide Clearance (in.) Intake | Stem-to-Guide Clearance (in.) Exhaust | Stem Diameter (in.) Intake | Stem Diameter (in.) Exhaust |
|---|---|---|---|---|---|---|---|---|---|
| 1987 | 140 (2299) | 45① | 45① | 191 | 1.929 | 0.004 | 0.004 | 0.314 | 0.353 |
| | 140 (2299) | 45 | 45 | 191 | 1.929 | 0.004 | 0.004 | 0.274 | 0.313 |
| | 152(2497) | 45① | 45① | 169 | 2.000 | 0.004 | 0.004 | 0.314 | 0.353 |
| | 159 (2599) | 45 | 45 | NA | NA | 0.004 | 0.004 | 0.314 | 0.353 |
| | 183 (2996) | 45 | 45 | 191 | 1.929 | 0.004 | 0.004 | 0.314 | 0.353 |
| | 181 (2962) | 45 | 45 | NA | NA | 0.004 | 0.004 | 0.314 | 0.352 |
| | 256 (4196) | 45 | 45 | 194 | 1.200 | 0.004 | 0.004 | 0.353 | 0.352 |
| | 338 (5547) | 45 | 45 | 194 | 1.200 | 0.004 | 0.004 | 0.353 | 0.352 |
| 1988 | 140 (2299) | 45① | 45① | 191 | 1.929 | 0.004 | 0.004 | 0.314 | 0.353 |
| | 152 (2497) | 45① | 45① | 169 | 2.000 | 0.004 | 0.004 | 0.314 | 0.353 |
| | 159 (2599) | 45 | 45 | NA | NA | 0.004 | 0.004 | 0.314 | 0.353 |
| | 181 (2962) | 45 | 45 | NA | NA | 0.004 | 0.004 | 0.314 | 0.352 |
| | 256 (4196) | 45 | 45 | 194 | 1.200 | 0.004 | 0.004 | 0.353 | 0.352 |
| | 338 (5547) | 45 | 45 | 194 | 1.200 | 0.004 | 0.004 | 0.353 | 0.352 |
| 1989-90 | 152 (2497) | 45① | 45① | 169 | 2.000 | 0.004 | 0.004 | 0.314 | 0.353 |
| | 159 (2599) | 45 | 45 | NA | NA | 0.004 | 0.004 | 0.314 | 0.353 |
| | 181 (2962) | 45 | 45 | NA | NA | 0.004 | 0.004 | 0.314 | 0.352 |
| | 256 (4196) | 45 | 45 | 194 | 1.200 | 0.004 | 0.004 | 0.353 | 0.352 |
| | 338 (5547) | 45 | 45 | 194 | 1.200 | 0.004 | 0.004 | 0.353 | 0.352 |

NA Not available
① Plus 15"

## PISTON AND RING SPECIFICATIONS

All measurments are given in inches.

| Year | Engine Displacement cu. in. (cc) | Piston Clearance | Ring Gap Top Compression | Ring Gap Bottom Compression | Ring Gap Oil Control | Ring Side Clearance Top Compression | Ring Side Clearance Bottom Compression | Ring Side Clearance Oil Control |
|---|---|---|---|---|---|---|---|---|
| 1983 | 147 (2399) | 0.001–0.002 | 0.008–0.016 | 0.008–0.016 | 0.010–0.016 | 0.004–0.005 | 0.003–0.004 | 0.001–0.002 |
| | 183 (2996) | 0.001–0.002 | 0.008–0.016 | 0.008–0.016 | 0.010–0.016 | 0.004–0.005 | 0.003–0.004 | 0.001–0.002 |
| | 234 (3839) | 0.001 | 0.010–0.017 | 0.010–0.017 | 0.010–0.016 | 0.004–0.005 | 0.001–0.002 | 0.001–0.002 |
| 1984 | 134 (2197) | 0.001–0.002 | 0.008–0.016 | 0.008–0.016 | 0.008–0.016 | 0.004–0.005 | 0.002–0.003 | 0.001–0.003 |
| | 140 (2299) | 0.001–0.002 | 0.008–0.016 | 0.008–0.016 | 0.008–0.016 | 0.004–0.005 | 0.002–0.003 | 0.001–0.002 |
| | 183 (2996) | 0.001–0.002 | 0.008–0.016 | 0.008–0.016 | 0.010–0.016 | 0.004–0.005 | 0.003–0.004 | 0.001–0.002 |
| | 234 (3839) | 0.001 | 0.010–0.017 | 0.010–0.017 | 0.010–0.016 | 0.004–0.005 | 0.001–0.002 | 0.001–0.002 |
| | 303 (4973) | 0.001 | 0.010–0.017 | 0.010–0.017 | 0.010–0.016 | 0.004–0.005 | 0.001–0.002 | 0.001–0.002 |

## PISTON AND RING SPECIFICATIONS

All measurments are given in inches.

| Year | Engine Displacement cu. in. (cc) | Piston Clearance | Ring Gap Top Compression | Ring Gap Bottom Compression | Ring Gap Oil Control | Ring Side Clearance Top Compression | Ring Side Clearance Bottom Compression | Ring Side Clearance Oil Control |
|---|---|---|---|---|---|---|---|---|
| 1985 | 134 (2197) | 0.001–0.002 | 0.008–0.016 | 0.008–0.016 | 0.008–0.016 | 0.004–0.005 | 0.001–0.003 | 0.001–0.003 |
| | 140 (2299) | 0.001–0.002 | 0.008–0.016 | 0.008–0.016 | 0.008–0.016 | 0.004–0.005 | 0.002–0.003 | 0.001–0.002 |
| | 183 (2996) | 0.001–0.002 | 0.008–0.016 | 0.008–0.016 | 0.010–0.016 | 0.004–0.005 | 0.003–0.004 | 0.001–0.002 |
| | 234 (3839) | 0.001 | 0.010–0.017 | 0.010–0.017 | 0.010–0.016 | 0.004–0.005 | 0.001–0.002 | 0.001–0.002 |
| | 303 (4973) | 0.001 | 0.010–0.017 | 0.010–0.017 | 0.010–0.016 | 0.004–0.005 | 0.001–0.002 | 0.001–0.002 |
| 1986 | 140 (2299) | 0.001–0.002 | 0.008–0.016 | 0.008–0.016 | 0.008–0.016 | 0.004–0.005 | 0.002–0.003 | 0.001–0.003 |
| | 152 (2497) | 0.001–0.002 | 0.008–0.016 | 0.008–0.016 | 0.010–0.016 | 0.004–0.005 | 0.003–0.004 | 0.001–0.002 |
| | 181 (2962) | 0.001–0.002 | 0.008–0.016 | 0.008–0.016 | 0.010–0.016 | 0.004–0.005 | 0.003–0.004 | 0.001–0.002 |
| | 183 (2996) | 0.001–0.002 | 0.008–0.016 | 0.008–0.016 | 0.010–0.016 | 0.004–0.005 | 0.003–0.004 | 0.001–0.002 |
| | 256 (4196) | 0.001 | 0.008–0.016 | 0.008–0.016 | 0.010–0.016 | 0.004–0.005 | 0.003–0.004 | 0.001–0.002 |
| | 338 (5547) | 0.001 | 0.010–0.017 | 0.010–0.017 | 0.010–0.016 | 0.004–0.005 | 0.001–0.002 | 0.001–0.002 |
| 1987 | 140 (2299) | 0.001–0.002 | 0.008–0.016 | 0.008–0.016 | 0.008–0.016 | 0.004–0.005 | 0.002–0.003 | 0.001–0.003 |
| | 152 (2497) | 0.001–0.002 | 0.008–0.016 | 0.008–0.016 | 0.010–0.016 | 0.004–0.005 | 0.003–0.004 | 0.001–0.002 |
| | 159 (2599) | 0.001–0.002 | 0.008–0.016 | 0.008–0.016 | 0.008–0.016 | 0.004–0.005 | 0.003–0.004 | 0.001–0.002 |
| | 181 (2962) | 0.001–0.002 | 0.008–0.016 | 0.008–0.016 | 0.010–0.016 | 0.004–0.005 | 0.003–0.004 | 0.001–0.002 |
| | 183 (2996) | 0.001–0.002 | 0.008–0.016 | 0.008–0.016 | 0.010–0.016 | 0.004–0.005 | 0.003–0.004 | 0.001–0.002 |
| | 256 (4196) | 0.001 | 0.008–0.016 | 0.008–0.016 | 0.010–0.016 | 0.004–0.005 | 0.003–0.004 | 0.001–0.002 |
| | 338 (5547) | 0.001 | 0.010–0.017 | 0.010–0.017 | 0.010–0.016 | 0.004–0.005 | 0.001–0.002 | 0.001–0.002 |
| 1988 | 140 (2299) | 0.001–0.002 | 0.008–0.016 | 0.008–0.016 | 0.008–0.016 | 0.004–0.005 | 0.002–0.003 | 0.001–0.003 |
| | 152 (2497) | 0.001–0.002 | 0.008–0.016 | 0.008–0.016 | 0.010–0.016 | 0.004–0.005 | 0.003–0.004 | 0.001–0.002 |
| | 159 (2599) | 0.001–0.002 | 0.008–0.016 | 0.008–0.016 | 0.010–0.016 | 0.004–0.005 | 0.003–0.004 | 0.001–0.002 |
| | 181 (2962) | 0.001–0.002 | 0.008–0.016 | 0.008–0.016 | 0.010–0.016 | 0.004–0.005 | 0.003–0.004 | 0.001–0.002 |

## PISTON AND RING SPECIFICATIONS

All measurments are given in inches.

| Year | Engine Displacement cu. in. (cc) | Piston Clearance | Ring Gap Top Compression | Ring Gap Bottom Compression | Ring Gap Oil Control | Ring Side Clearance Top Compression | Ring Side Clearance Bottom Compression | Ring Side Clearance Oil Control |
|---|---|---|---|---|---|---|---|---|
| 1988 | 256 (4196) | 0.001 | 0.008–0.016 | 0.008–0.016 | 0.010–0.016 | 0.004–0.005 | 0.003–0.004 | 0.001–0.002 |
| | 338 (5547) | 0.001 | 0.010–0.017 | 0.010–0.017 | 0.010–0.016 | 0.004–0.005 | 0.001–0.002 | 0.001–0.002 |
| 1989-90 | 152 (2497) | 0.001–0.002 | 0.008–0.016 | 0.008–0.016 | 0.010–0.016 | 0.004–0.005 | 0.003–0.004 | 0.001–0.002 |
| | 159 (2599) | 0.001–0.002 | 0.008–0.016 | 0.008–0.016 | 0.010–0.016 | 0.004–0.005 | 0.003–0.004 | 0.001–0.002 |
| | 181 (2962) | 0.001–0.002 | 0.008–0.016 | 0.008–0.016 | 0.010–0.016 | 0.004–0.005 | 0.003–0.004 | 0.001–0.002 |
| | 256 (4196) | 0.001 | 0.008–0.016 | 0.008–0.016 | 0.010–0.016 | 0.004–0.005 | 0.003–0.004 | 0.001–0.002 |
| | 338 (5547) | 0.001 | 0.010–0.017 | 0.010–0.017 | 0.010–0.016 | 0.004–0.005 | 0.001–0.002 | 0.001–0.002 |

## TORQUE SPECIFICATIONS

All readings in ft. lbs.

| Year | Engine Displacement cu. in. (cc) | Cylinder Head Bolts | Main Bearing Bolts | Rod Bearing Bolts | Crankshaft Pulley Bolts | Flywheel Bolts | Manifold Intake | Manifold Exhaust | Spark Plugs |
|---|---|---|---|---|---|---|---|---|---|
| 1983 | 147 (2399) | ④① | 65 | 33 | 155 | ⑥ | NA | 20 | — |
| | 183 (2996) | 65⑨ | 65 | 33 | 218 | ⑥ | NA | 18 | — |
| | 234 (3839) | 44⑧ | ③ | 33 | 289 | ⑥ | NA | NA | 15 |
| 1984 | 134 (2197) | ④① | 65 | ⑤ | 218 | 25 | 18 | NA | — |
| | 140 (2299) | 51⑦ | 65 | ⑥ | 218 | 25 | NA | NA | 15 |
| | 183 (2996) | 65⑨ | 65 | 33 | 218 | ⑥ | 18 | 18 | — |
| | 234 (3839) | 44⑧ | ③ | 33 | 289 | ⑥ | NA | NA | 15 |
| | 303 (4973) | 44⑧ | ② | 33 | 187 | ⑥ | NA | 20 | 15 |
| 1985 | 134 (2197) | ④① | 40 | ⑤ | 218 | 25 | 18 | NA | — |
| | 140 (2299) | 51⑦ | 65 | ⑥ | 145 | 25 | NA | NA | 15 |
| | 183 (2996) | 65⑨ | 65 | 33 | 218 | ⑥ | 18 | 18 | — |
| | 234 (3839) | 44⑧ | ③ | 33 | 289 | ⑥ | NA | NA | 15 |
| | 303 (4973) | 44⑧ | ② | 33 | 187 | ⑥ | NA | 20 | 15 |
| 1986 | 140 (2299) | 51⑦ | 65 | ⑥ | 145 | 25 | NA | NA | 15 |
| | 152 (2497) | ④① | 40 | ⑤ | 218 | 25 | 18 | NA | — |
| | 181 (2962) | 65⑨ | 65 | 33 | 218 | ⑥ | 18 | 18 | 15 |
| | 183 (2996) | 65⑨ | 65 | 33 | 218 | ⑥ | 18 | 18 | — |
| | 256 (4196) | 44⑧ | ③ | 33 | 289 | ⑥ | NA | NA | 15 |
| | 338 (5547) | 44⑧ | ② | 33 | 187 | ⑥ | NA | 20 | 15 |
| 1987 | 140 (2299) | 51⑦ | 65 | ⑥ | 145 | 25 | NA | NA | 15 |
| | 152 (2497) | ④① | 40 | ⑤ | 218 | 25 | 18 | NA | — |

## TORQUE SPECIFICATIONS

All readings in ft. lbs.

| Year | Engine Displacement cu. in. (cc) | Cylinder Head Bolts | Main Bearing Bolts | Rod Bearing Bolts | Crankshaft Pulley Bolts | Flywheel Bolts | Manifold Intake | Manifold Exhaust | Spark Plugs |
|---|---|---|---|---|---|---|---|---|---|
| 1987 | 159 (2599) | 70⑩ | 65 | 22 | 217 | 22 | NA | NA | 15 |
| | 181 (2962) | 65⑨ | 65 | 33 | 218 | ⑥ | NA | 18 | 15 |
| | 183 (2996) | 65⑨ | 65 | 33 | 218 | ⑥ | 18 | 18 | — |
| | 256 (4196) | 44⑧ | ③ | 33 | 289 | ⑥ | NA | NA | 15 |
| | 338 (5547) | 44⑧ | ② | 33 | 187 | ⑥ | NA | 20 | 15 |
| 1988 | 140 (2299) | 51⑦ | 65 | ⑥ | 145 | 25 | NA | NA | 15 |
| | 152 (2497) | ④① | 40 | ⑤ | 218 | 25 | 18 | NA | — |
| | 159 (2599) | 70⑩ | 65 | 22 | 217 | 22 | NA | NA | 15 |
| | 181 (2962) | 65⑨ | 65 | 33 | 218 | ⑥ | NA | 18 | 15 |
| | 256 (4196) | 44⑧ | ③ | 33 | 289 | ⑥ | NA | NA | 15 |
| | 338 (5547) | 44⑧ | ② | 33 | 187 | ⑥ | NA | 20 | 15 |
| 1989-90 | 152 (2497) | ④① | 40 | ⑤ | 218 | 25 | 18 | NA | — |
| | 159 (2599) | 70⑩ | 65 | 22 | 217 | 22 | NA | NA | 15 |
| | 181 (2962) | 65⑨ | 65 | 33 | 218 | ⑥ | NA | 18 | 15 |
| | 256 (4196) | 44⑧ | ③ | 33 | 289 | ⑥ | NA | NA | 15 |
| | 338 (5547) | 44⑧ | ② | 33 | 187 | ⑥ | NA | 20 | 15 |

NA Not available

① See text

② M 10 bolts—37 ft. lbs.
M 12 bolts—72 ft. lbs.

③ M 10 bolts—43 ft. lbs.
M 12 bolts—58 ft. lbs.

④ M 10 bolts:
1st step—18 ft. lbs.
2nd step—29 ft. lbs., setting time 10 minutes
3rd step—90 degrees torquing angle
4th step—29 degrees torquing angle
M 8 bolts—18 ft. lbs.

⑤ 1st step—22–25 ft. lbs.
2nd step—90–100 degrees torqing angle

⑥ 1st step—22—25 ft. lbs.
2nd step—90–100 degrees torqing angle

⑦ M 12 bolts:
1st step—29 ft. lbs.
2nd step—51 ft. lbs., setting time 10 minutes
3rd step—90 degrees torquing angle
4th step—90 degrees torquing angle
M 8 bolts—18 ft. lbs.

⑧ 1st step—22 ft. lbs.
2nd step—44 ft. lbs., setting time 10 minutes
3rd step—Loosen bolts and retighten to 44 ft. lbs.

⑨ 1st step—29 ft. lbs.
2nd step—51 ft. lbs., setting time 10 minutes
3rd step—90 degrees torquing angle
4th step—90 degrees torquing angle

⑩ 1st step—70 ft. lbs.
2nd step—90 degrees torquing angle
3rd step—90 degrees torquing angle

## BRAKE SPECIFICATIONS

All measurements in inches unless noted

| Year | Model | Lug Nut Torque (ft. lbs.) | Master Cylinder Bore | Brake Disc Minimum Thickness | Brake Disc Maximum Runout | Standard Brake Drum Diameter | Minimum Lining Thickness Front | Minimum Lining Thickness Rear |
|---|---|---|---|---|---|---|---|---|
| 1983 | 240D | 75 | ② | ①⑤ | 0.005⑦ | — | 0.08 | 0.08 |
| | 300D | 75 | ② | ①⑤ | 0.005⑦ | — | 0.08 | 0.08 |
| | 300CD | 75 | ② | ①⑤ | 0.005⑦ | — | 0.08 | 0.08 |
| | 300SD | 75 | ② | ③⑤ | 0.005 | — | 0.08 | 0.08 |
| | 300TD | 75 | ② | ①⑤ | 0.005⑦ | — | 0.08 | 0.08 |
| | 380SL | 75 | ② | ③⑤ | 0.005 | — | 0.08 | 0.08 |

## BRAKE SPECIFICATIONS

All measurements in inches unless noted

| Year | Model | Lug Nut Torque (ft. lbs.) | Master Cylinder Bore | Brake Disc | | Standard Brake Drum Diameter | Minimum Lining Thickness | |
|---|---|---|---|---|---|---|---|---|
| | | | | Minimum Thickness | Maximum Runout | | Front | Rear |
| 1983 | 380SEC | 75 | ② | ③⑤ | 0.005 | — | 0.08 | 0.08 |
| | 380SEL | 75 | ② | ③⑤ | 0.005 | — | 0.08 | 0.08 |
| 1984 | 190D | 75 | ④ | 0.35⑥ | 0.005⑦ | — | 0.08 | 0.08 |
| | 190E | 75 | ④ | 0.35⑥ | 0.005⑦ | — | 0.08 | 0.08 |
| | 300D | 75 | ② | ①⑤ | 0.005⑦ | — | 0.08 | 0.08 |
| | 300CD | 75 | ② | ①⑤ | 0.005⑦ | — | 0.08 | 0.08 |
| | 300SD | 75 | ② | ③⑤ | 0.005 | — | 0.08 | 0.08 |
| | 300TD | 75 | ② | ①⑤ | 0.005⑦ | — | 0.08 | 0.08 |
| | 380SE | 75 | ② | ③⑤ | 0.005 | — | 0.08 | 0.08 |
| | 380SL | 75 | ② | ③⑤ | 0.005 | — | 0.08 | 0.08 |
| | 500SEC | 75 | ② | ③⑤ | 0.005 | — | 0.08 | 0.08 |
| | 500SEL | 75 | ② | ③⑤ | 0.005 | — | 0.08 | 0.08 |
| 1985 | 190D | 75 | ④ | 0.35⑥ | 0.005⑦ | — | 0.08 | 0.08 |
| | 190E | 75 | ④ | 0.35⑥ | 0.005⑦ | — | 0.08 | 0.08 |
| | 300D | 75 | ② | ①⑤ | 0.005⑦ | — | 0.08 | 0.08 |
| | 300CD | 75 | ② | ①⑤ | 0.005⑦ | — | 0.08 | 0.08 |
| | 300SD | 75 | ② | ③⑤ | 0.005 | — | 0.08 | 0.08 |
| | 300TD | 75 | ② | ①⑤ | 0.005⑦ | — | 0.08 | 0.08 |
| | 380SE | 75 | ② | ③⑤ | 0.005 | — | 0.08 | 0.08 |
| | 380SL | 75 | ② | ③⑤ | 0.005 | — | 0.08 | 0.08 |
| | 500SEC | 75 | ② | ③⑤ | 0.005 | — | 0.08 | 0.08 |
| | 500SEL | 75 | ② | ③⑤ | 0.005 | — | 0.08 | 0.08 |
| 1986 | 190D | 75 | ④ | 0.35⑥ | 0.005⑦ | — | 0.08 | 0.08 |
| | 190E | 75 | ④ | 0.35⑥ | 0.005⑦ | — | 0.08 | 0.08 |
| | 190E-16 | 75 | ④ | 0.35⑥ | 0.005⑦ | — | 0.08 | 0.08 |
| | 300D | 75 | ② | ①⑤ | 0.005⑦ | — | 0.08 | 0.08 |
| | 300TD | 75 | ② | ①⑤ | 0.005⑦ | — | 0.08 | 0.08 |
| | 300SDL | 75 | ② | ③⑤ | 0.005 | — | 0.08 | 0.08 |
| | 420SEL | 75 | ② | ③⑤ | 0.005 | — | 0.08 | 0.08 |
| | 560SL | 75 | ② | ③⑤ | 0.005 | — | 0.08 | 0.08 |
| | 560SEC | 75 | ② | ③⑤ | 0.005 | — | 0.08 | 0.08 |
| | 560SEL | 75 | ② | ③⑤ | 0.005 | — | 0.08 | 0.08 |
| 1987 | 190D | 75 | ④ | 0.35⑥ | 0.005⑦ | — | 0.08 | 0.08 |
| | 190E | 75 | ④ | 0.35⑥ | 0.005⑦ | — | 0.08 | 0.08 |
| | 190E-16 | 75 | ④ | 0.35⑥ | 0.005⑦ | — | 0.08 | 0.08 |
| | 260E | 75 | ② | ①⑤ | 0.005⑦ | — | 0.08 | 0.08 |
| | 300D | 75 | ② | ①⑤ | 0.005⑦ | — | 0.08 | 0.08 |
| | 300E | 75 | ② | ①⑤ | 0.005⑦ | — | 0.08 | 0.08 |
| | 300TD | 75 | ② | ①⑤ | 0.005⑦ | — | 0.08 | 0.08 |

## BRAKE SPECIFICATIONS

All measurements in inches unless noted

| | | Lug Nut | Master | Brake Disc | | Standard Brake | Minimum Lining Thickness | |
|---|---|---|---|---|---|---|---|---|
| Year | Model | Torque (ft. lbs.) | Cylinder Bore | Minimum Thickness | Maximum Runout | Drum Diameter | Front | Rear |
| 1987 | 300SDL | 75 | ② | ③⑤ | 0.005 | — | 0.08 | 0.08 |
| | 420SEL | 75 | ② | ③⑤ | 0.005 | — | 0.08 | 0.08 |
| | 560SL | 75 | ② | ③⑤ | 0.005 | — | 0.08 | 0.08 |
| | 560SEC | 75 | ② | ③⑤ | 0.005 | — | 0.08 | 0.08 |
| | 560SEL | 75 | ② | ③⑤ | 0.005 | — | 0.08 | 0.08 |
| 1988 | 190D | 75 | ④ | 0.35⑥ | 0.005⑦ | — | 0.08 | 0.08 |
| | 190E | 75 | ④ | 0.35⑥ | 0.005⑦ | — | 0.08 | 0.08 |
| | 260E | 75 | ② | ①⑤ | 0.005⑦ | — | 0.08 | 0.08 |
| | 300E | 75 | ② | ①⑤ | 0.005⑦ | — | 0.08 | 0.08 |
| | 300CE | 75 | ② | ①⑤ | 0.005⑦ | — | 0.08 | 0.08 |
| | 300SE | 75 | ② | ③⑤ | 0.005 | — | 0.08 | 0.08 |
| | 300SEL | 75 | ② | ③⑤ | 0.005 | — | 0.08 | 0.08 |
| | 300TE | 75 | ② | ①⑤ | 0.005⑦ | — | 0.08 | 0.08 |
| | 420SEL | 75 | ② | ③⑤ | 0.005 | — | 0.08 | 0.08 |
| | 560SEC | 75 | ② | ③⑤ | 0.005 | — | 0.08 | 0.08 |
| | 560SEL | 75 | ② | ③⑤ | 0.005 | — | 0.08 | 0.08 |
| | 560SL | 75 | ② | ③⑤ | 0.005 | — | 0.08 | 0.08 |
| 1989-90 | 190D | 75 | ④ | 0.35⑥ | 0.005⑦ | — | 0.08 | 0.08 |
| | 190E | 75 | ④ | 0.35⑥ | 0.005⑦ | — | 0.08 | 0.08 |
| | 260E | 75 | ② | ①⑤ | 0.005⑦ | — | 0.08 | 0.08 |
| | 300E | 75 | ② | ①⑤ | 0.005⑦ | — | 0.08 | 0.08 |
| | 300CE | 75 | ② | ①⑤ | 0.005⑦ | — | 0.08 | 0.08 |
| | 300SE | 75 | ② | ③⑤ | 0.005 | — | 0.08 | 0.08 |
| | 300SEL | 75 | ② | ③⑤ | 0.005 | — | 0.08 | 0.08 |
| | 300TE | 75 | ② | ①⑤ | 0.005⑦ | — | 0.08 | 0.08 |
| | 420SEL | 75 | ② | ③⑤ | 0.005 | — | 0.08 | 0.08 |
| | 560SEC | 75 | ② | ③⑤ | 0.005 | — | 0.08 | 0.08 |
| | 560SEL | 75 | ② | ③⑤ | 0.005 | — | 0.08 | 0.08 |
| | 560SL | 75 | ② | ③⑤ | 0.005 | — | 0.08 | 0.08 |

① Caliper with 57mm piston diameter—0.44 in.
Caliper with 60mm piston diameter—0.42 in.

② Pushrod circuit—15/16 in.
Floating circuit—3/4 in.

③ Caliper with 57mm piston diameter—0.81 in.
Caliper with 60mm piston diameter—0.79 in.

④ Pushrod circuit—7/8 in.
Floating circuit—11/16 in.

⑤ Rear disc—0.33 in.

⑥ Rear disc—0.30 in.

⑦ Rear disc—0.006 in.

## WHEEL ALIGNMENT SPECIFICATIONS

| | | Caster | | Camber | | | Steering Axis |
|---|---|---|---|---|---|---|---|
| Year | Model | Range (deg.) | Preferred Setting (deg.) | Range (deg.) | Preferred Setting (deg.) | Toe-in (in.) | Inclination (deg.) |
| 1983 | 240D | 8¼–9¼ | 8¾ | 5/16N–3/16P | 0 | ⅛ | NA |
| | 300D | 8¼–9¼ | 8¾ | 5/16N–3/16P | 0 | ⅛ | NA |
| | 300CD | 8¼–9¼ | 8¾ | 5/16N–3/16P | 0 | ⅛ | NA |
| | 300SD | 10¾–9¾ | 10¼ | 5/16N–3/16P | 0 | ⅛ | NA |
| | 300TD | 8¼–9¼ | 8¾ | 5/16N–3/16P | 0 | ⅛ | NA |
| | 380SL | 4–3⅜ | 3 11/16 | 5/16N–3/16P | 0 | 1/16 | NA |
| | 380SEC | 10¾–9¾ | 10¼ | 5/16N–3/16P | 0 | ⅛ | NA |
| | 380SEL | 10¾–9¾ | 10¼ | 5/15N–3/16P | 0 | ⅛ | NA |
| 1984 | 190D | 9 11/16–10 11/16 | 10 3/16 | 0–½P | 5/16 | 3/16 | NA |
| | 190E | 9 11/16–10 11/16 | 10 3/16 | 0–½P | 5/16 | 3/16 | NA |
| | 300D | 8¼–9¼ | 8¾ | 5/16N–3/16P | 0 | ⅛ | NA |
| | 300CD | 8¼–9¼ | 8¾ | 5/16N–3/16P | 0 | ⅛ | NA |
| | 300SD | 10¾–9¾ | 10¼ | 5/16N–3/16P | 0 | ⅛ | NA |
| | 300TD | 8¼–9¼ | 8¾ | 5/16N–3/16P | 0 | ⅛ | NA |
| | 380SL | 4–3⅜ | 3 11/16 | 5/16N–3/16P | 0 | 1/16 | NA |
| | 380SE | 10¾–9¾ | 10¼ | 5/16N–3/16P | 0 | ⅛ | NA |
| | 500SEC | 10¾–9¾ | 10¼ | 5/16N–3/16P | 0 | ⅛ | NA |
| | 500SEL | 10¾–9¾ | 10¼ | 5/16N–3/16P | 0 | ⅛ | NA |
| 1985 | 190D | 9 11/16–10 11/16 | 10 3/16 | 1/16N–9/16P | 5/16 | 3/32 | NA |
| | 190E | 9 11/16–10 11/16 | 10 3/16 | 1/16N–9/16P | 5/16 | 3/32 | NA |
| | 300D | 8¼–9¼ | 8¾ | 5/16N–3/16P | 0 | ⅛ | NA |
| | 300CD | 8¼–9¼ | 8¾ | 5/16N–3/16P | 0 | ⅛ | NA |
| | 300SD | 10¾–9¾ | 10¼ | 5/16N–3/16P | 0 | ⅛ | NA |
| | 300TD | 8¼–9¼ | 8¾ | 5/16N–3/16P | 0 | ⅛ | NA |
| | 380SL | 4–3⅜ | 3 11/16 | 5/16N–3/16P | 0 | 1/16 | NA |
| | 380SE | 10¾–9¾ | 10¼ | 5/16N–3/16P | 0 | ⅛ | NA |
| | 500SEC | 10¾–9¾ | 10¼ | 5/16N–3/16P | 0 | ⅛ | NA |
| | 500SEL | 10¾–9¾ | 10¼ | 5/16N–3/16P | 0 | ⅛ | NA |
| 1986 | 190D | 10–11 | 10½ | ½N–0 | 3/16N | 3/32 | NA |
| | 190E | 10–11 | 10½ | ½N–0 | 3/16N | 3/32 | NA |
| | 190E–16 | 10–11 | 10½ | 11/16N–3/16N | 5/16N | 3/32 | NA |
| | 300D | 9 11/16–10 11/16 | 10 3/16 | 5/16N–3/16P | 0 | 3/16 | NA |
| | 300E | 9 11/16–10 11/16 | 10 3/16 | 5/16N–3/16P | 0 | 3/16 | NA |
| | 300SDL | 10–11 | 10½ | ½N–0 | 3/16N | 3/32 | NA |
| | 420SEL | 10–11 | 10½ | ½N–0 | 3/16N | 3/32 | NA |
| | 560SL | 10–11 | 10½ | ½N–0 | 3/16N | 3/32 | NA |
| | 560SEC | 10–11 | 10½ | ½N–0 | 3/16N | 3/32 | NA |
| | 560SEL | 10–11 | 10½ | ½N–0 | 3/16N | 3/32 | NA |
| 1987 | 190D | 10–11 | 10½ | ½N–0 | 3/16N | 3/32 | NA |
| | 190E | 10–11 | 10½ | ½N–0 | 3/16N | 3/32 | NA |

## WHEEL ALIGNMENT SPECIFICATIONS

| Year | Model | Caster Range (deg.) | Caster Preferred Setting (deg.) | Camber Range (deg.) | Camber Preferred Setting (deg.) | Toe-in (in.) | Steering Axis Inclination (deg.) |
|---|---|---|---|---|---|---|---|
| 1987 | 190E-16 | 10–11 | 10½ | 11/16N–5/16P | 5/16N | 3/32 | NA |
| | 300D | 9 11/16–10 11/16 | 10 3/16 | 5/16N–3/16P | 0 | 3/16 | NA |
| | 300E | 9 11/16–10 11/16 | 10 3/16 | 5/16N–3/16P | 0 | 3/16 | NA |
| | 300SDL | 10–11 | 10½ | ½N–0 | 3/16N | 3/32 | NA |
| | 300TD | 10–11 | 10½ | ½N–0 | 3/16N | 3/32 | NA |
| | 420SEL | 10–11 | 10½ | ½N–0 | 3/16N | 3/32 | NA |
| | 560SL | 10–11 | 10½ | ½N–0 | 3/16N | 3/32 | NA |
| | 560SEC | 10–11 | 10½ | ½N–0 | 3/16N | 3/32 | NA |
| | 560SEL | 10–11 | 10½ | ½N–0 | 3/16N | 3/32 | NA |
| 1988 | 190D | 10–11 | 10½ | ½N–0 | 3/16N | 3/32 | NA |
| | 190E | 10–11 | 10½ | ½N–0 | 3/16N | 3/32 | NA |
| | 260E | 9 11/16–10 11/16 | 10 3/16 | 5/16N–3/16P | 0 | 3/16 | NA |
| | 300E | 9 11/16–10 11/16 | 10 3/16 | 5/16N–3/16P | 0 | 3/16 | NA |
| | 300CE | 9 11/16–10 11/16 | 10 3/16 | 5/16N–3/16P | 0 | 3/16 | NA |
| | 300SE | 10–11 | 10½ | ½N–0 | 3/16N | 3/32 | NA |
| | 300SEL | 10–11 | 10½ | ½N–0 | 3/16N | 3/32 | NA |
| | 300TE | 9 11/16–10 11/16 | 10 3/16 | 5/16N–3/16P | 0 | 3/16 | NA |
| | 420SEL | 10–11 | 10½ | ½N–0 | 3/16N | 3/32 | NA |
| | 560SEC | 10–11 | 10½ | ½N–0 | 3/16N | 3/32 | NA |
| | 560SEL | 10–11 | 10½ | ½N–0 | 3/16N | 3/32 | NA |
| | 560SL | 10–11 | 10½ | ½N–0 | 3/16N | 3/32 | NA |
| 1989-90 | 190D | 10–11 | 10½ | ½N–0 | 3/16N | 3/32 | NA |
| | 190E | 10–11 | 10½ | ½N–0 | 3/16N | 3/32 | NA |
| | 260E | 9 11/16–10 11/16 | 10 3/16 | 5/16N–3/16P | 0 | 3/16 | NA |
| | 300E | 9 11/16–10 11/16 | 10 3/16 | 5/16N–3/16P | 0 | 3/16 | NA |
| | 300CE | 9 11/16–10 11/16 | 10 3/16 | 5/16N–3/16P | 0 | 3/16 | NA |
| | 300SE | 10–11 | 10½ | ½N–0 | 3/16N | 3/32 | NA |
| | 300SEL | 10–11 | 10½ | ½N–0 | 3/16N | 3/32 | NA |
| | 300TE | 9 11/16–10 11/16 | 10 3/16 | 5/16N–3/16P | 0 | 3/16 | NA |
| | 420SEL | 10–11 | 10½ | ½N–0 | 3/16N | 3/32 | NA |
| | 560SEC | 10–11 | 10½ | ½N–0 | 3/16N | 3/32 | NA |
| | 560SEL | 10–11 | 10½ | ½N–0 | 3/16N | 3/32 | NA |
| | 560SL | 10–11 | 10½ | ½N–0 | 3/16N | 3/32 | NA |

NA Not available
P Positive
N Negative

# TUNE-UP PROCEDURES

## Ignition Timing

### ADJUSTMENT

Before attempting to set the timing, read the "Ignition Timing Specifications" chart carefully and determine at what speed the timing should be set and whether the vacuum should be connected or disconnected.

**NOTE: It is a good idea to paint the appropriate timing mark with dayglow or white paint to make it quickly and easily visible.**

On engines with transistorized coil ignition, the timing light may or may not work depending on the construction of the light.

#### *All Gasoline Engines*

**NOTE: All 1986–90 gasoline engines as of utilize the new EZL electronic ignition system. Although service checking of ignition timing is possible, no adjustment is either possible or necessary.**

The typical vibration damper is marked like this (note the pin)

1. Raise the hood and connect a tachometer.
2. Connect a timing light.
3. Run the engine at the specified speed and read the firing point on the balancing plate or vibration damper while shining the light on it.

**NOTE: The balancer on some engines has 2 timing scales. If in doubt as to which scale to use, rotate the crankshaft (in the direction of rotation only) until the distributor rotor is aligned with the notch on the distributor housing (No. 1 cylinder). In this position, the timing pointer should be at TDC on the proper timing scale.**

4. Adjust the ignition timing by loosening the distributor clamp bolt and rotating the distributor. To advance the timing, rotate the distributor in the opposite direction of normal rotation. To retard the timing, rotate the distributor in the direction of normal rotation.
5. Once the timing has been adjusted, recheck the timing once more to be sure that it has not been disturbed.
6. Remove the timing light and tachometer and connect any wires that were removed.

#### *Diesel Engines*

The diesel uses no distributor, so requires no ignition timing adjustment.

## Valve Lash

### ADJUSTMENT

#### *4 Cylinder Gasoline Engines*

**190 SERIES**

The 190E (SOHC) utilizes hydraulic valve clearance compensation. No adjustment is either possible or necessary. The 190E-16 (DOHC) uses mechanical lash adjusters, adjustable by means of tappets and thrust washers.

Valve clearance on the 190E-16 is measured between the cam base circle and the cup-type valve tappet (see illustration).

1. Tag and disconnect the spark plug wires and position them out of the way.
2. Remove the spark plugs and then remove the cylinder head cover.
3. Note the position of the intake and exhaust valves. Viewed from the front of the vehicle, the exhaust valves are on the left and the intake valves are on the right.
4. Using a wrench on the crankshaft pulley bolt, rotate the crankshaft until the heel of the camshaft lobe is in the position shown in the illustration.

**NOTE: Do not rotate the engine using the camshaft sprocket bolt. The strain will distort the timing chain tensioner rail. Always rotate the engine in the direction of normal rotation only.**

5. To measure the valve clearance, insert a feeler gauge of the specified thickness between the heel of the camshaft lobe and the top of the valve tappet. Clearance is correct if the blade can be inserted and withdrawn with a very slight drag.
6. If all measured clearances are within specifications, install the cylinder head cover, spark plugs and their wires; you're done!

If any clearances are not within specifications, continue checking until you find what the actual clearance is. Write it down, you'll need it later.

7. Remove the camshafts as detailed later in this section.
8. Lift out the valve tappet. Directly under the tappet is a thrust plate. The thrust plate is held in place by means of the valve keepers; it is also your means of changing the tappet height and thus the valve clearance.

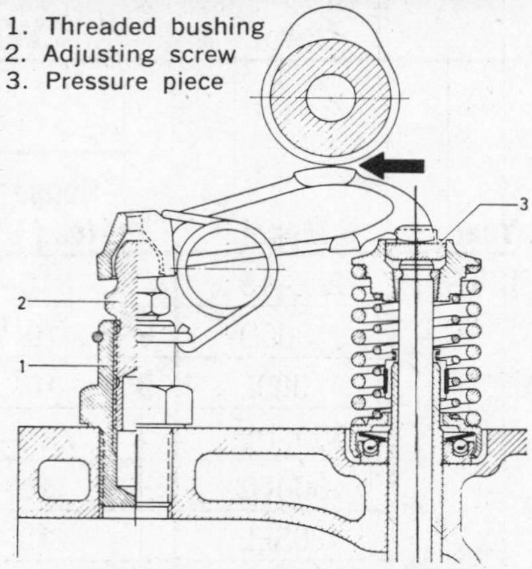


Measure the valve clearance between the sliding surface of the rocker arm and the heel of the camshaft lobe on 4 cylinder engines (except 190)

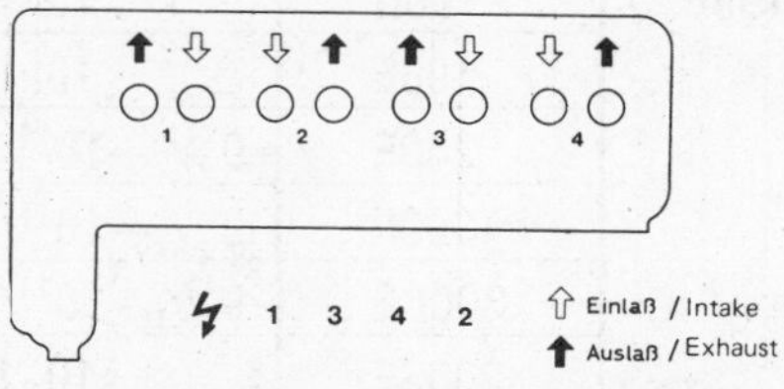


Valve location—SOHC 4 cylinder engines

9. Pry the thrust plate from the valve keepers and check to see what thickness it is; it should be stamped on the surface.
10. Check what the clearance was from Step 6 for the valve that is being worked on. The difference between the measured clearance and the specified clearance is amount by which the existing thrust plate thickness must be increased to obtain the proper valve clearance. New thrust plates are available in increments of 0.05mm.
11. When the proper thickness of the new thrust plate has been determined, press it into the valve keepers and drop the tappet into position over the valve stem/spring.
12. Install the camshafts and then recheck the valve clearance.
13. Installation of the remaining components is as detailed in Step 6.

#### *6 Cylinder Gasoline Engines*

**NOTE: The 190E with 2.6L engine, 260E, 300E, 300CE, 300SE, 300TE and 300SEL utilizes hydraulic valve clearance compensation. No adjustment is either possible or necessary.**

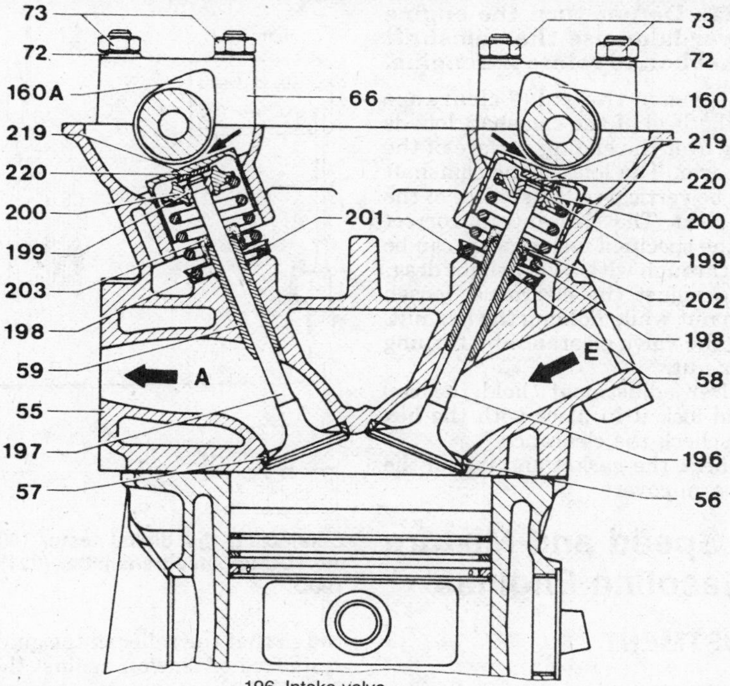


55 Cylinder head
56 Valve seat ring, intake
57 Valve seat ring, exhaust
58 Valve guide, intake
59 Valve guide, exhaust
160E Camshaft, intake
160A Camshaft, exhaust
196 Intake valve
197 Exhaust valve
198 Valve spring
199 Valve keeper
200 Valve spring retainer
201 Thrust ring
202 Valve stem seal, intake valve
203 Valve stem seal, exhaust valve
219 Valve tappet
220 Thrust plate
E Intake
A Exhaust

**On the 190E-16 (DOHC), measure valve clearance between the valve tappet and the heal of the camshaft lobe (small arrow)**

**A valve adjusting wrench (crow's foot) is required to accurately measure torque on all models**

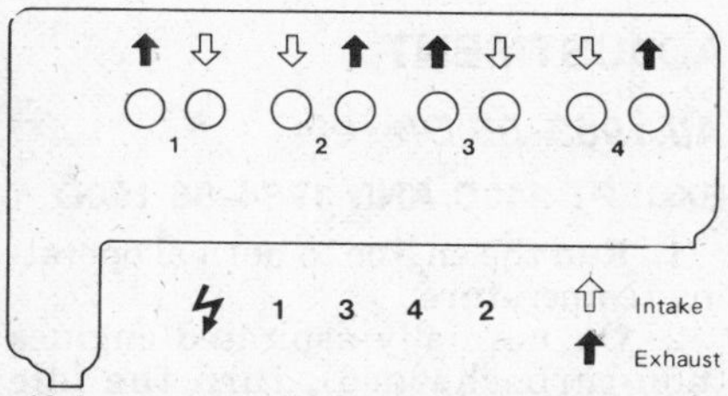


**Valve arrangement—4-cylinder diesels**

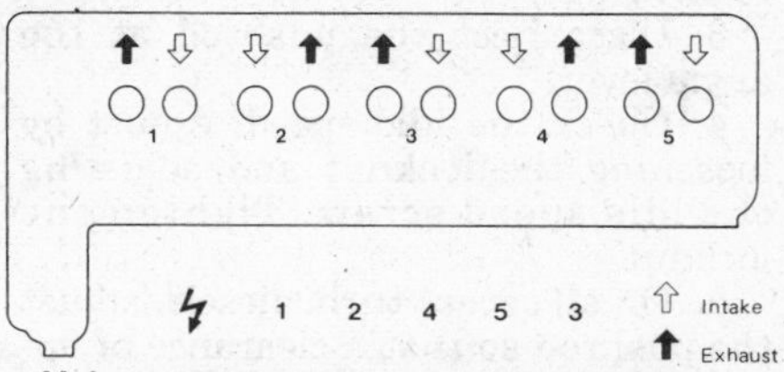


**Valve arrangement—5-cylinder diesels**

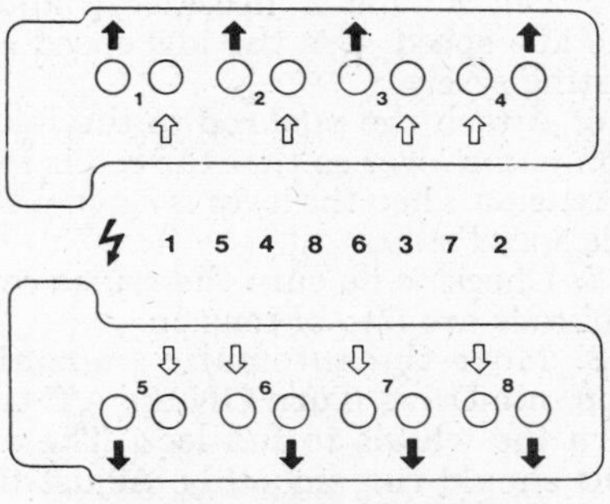


**Valve location – V8 engines**

### *V8 Gasoline Engines*

**NOTE: V8 engines use hydraulic valve lifters and require no periodic adjustment.**

The valve clearance is measured between the sliding surface of the rocker arm and the heel of the camshaft lobe. The highest point of the camshaft lobe should be at a 90 degree angle to the sliding surface of the rocker arm.

1. Disconnect the negative battery cable. Loosen the venting line and remove the regulating linkage. Remove the valve cover.
2. Disconnect the cable from the ignition coil.
3. Identify all of the valves as intake or exhaust.
4. Beginning with the No. 1 cylinder, crank the engine with the starter to position the heel of the camshaft approximately over the sliding surface of the rocker arm.
5. Rotate the crankshaft by means of a socket wrench on the crankshaft pulley bolt until the heel of the camshaft lobe is perpendicular to the sliding surface of the rocker arm.

**NOTE: Do not rotate the engine using the camshaft sprocket bolt. The strain will distort the timing chain tensioner rail. Always rotate the engine in the direction of normal rotation only.**

6. Some models have holes in the vibration damper plate to assist in crankshaft rotation. In this case, a small prybar can be used to carefully rotate the crankshaft.
7. To measure the valve clearance, insert a feeler blade of the specified thickness between the heel of the camshaft lobe and the sliding surface of the rocker arm. The clearance is correct if the blade can be inserted and withdrawn with a very slight drag.
8. If adjustment is necessary, it can be done by turning the ball pin head at the hex collar. If the clearance is too small, increase it by turning the ball pin head in. If the clearance is too large, turn the ball pin head out.

**NOTE: If the adjuster turns very easily, or it the proper clearance can't be obtained, check the torque on the adjuster using a special adapter (crow's foot).**

9. When the ball pin head is turned, the adjusting torque should be 14–29 ft. lbs. (19–39 Nm). If the torque is lower, either the adjusting screw, the threaded bolt, or both will have to be replaced. If the valve clearance is too small, and the ball pin head cannot be screwed in far enough to correct it, a thinner pressure piece should be installed in the spring retainer. To replace the pressure piece, the rocker arm must be removed.
10. Install the regulating linkage, valve cover gasket, and valve cover. Be sure the gasket is seated properly.
11. Connect the cable to the coil and the venting line. Run the engine and check for leaks at the valve cover.

7. Capnut
8. Locknut
14. Holding wrench
16. Adjusting wrench

**Adjusting valve clearance on diesel engine**

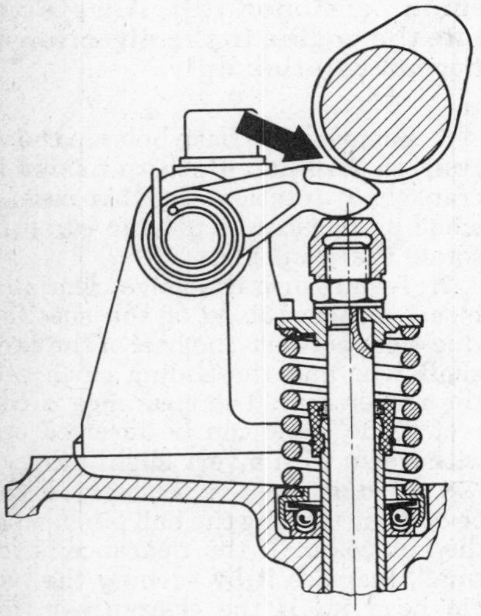

**Measure valve clearance on diesel engines at arrow**

### All Diesel Engines

**NOTE: The 190D and the 1987 300D, 300TD and 300SDL utilize hydraulic valve clearance compensators. No adjustment is either necessary or possible.**

1. Disconnect the negative battery cable. Remove the valve cover and note the position of the intake and exhaust valves.

2. Turn the engine with a socket and breaker bar on the crankshaft pulley or by using a remote starter, hooked to the battery (+) terminal and the large, uppermost starter solenoid terminal. Due to the extremely high compression pressures in the diesel engine, it will be considerably easier to use a remote starter. If a remote starter is not available, the engine can be bumped into position with the normal starter.

**NOTE: Do not turn the engine backwards or use the camshaft sprocket bolt to rotate the engine.**

3. Measure the valve clearance when the heel of the camshaft lobe is directly over the sliding surface of the rocker arm. The lobe of the camshaft should be vertical to the surface of the rocker arm. The clearance is correct when the specified feeler gauge can be pulled through with a very slight drag.

4. To adjust the clearance, loosen the cap nut while holding the hex nut. Adjust the valve clearance by turning the hex nut.

5. After adjustment, hold the cap nut and lock it in place with the hex nut. Recheck the clearance.

6. Check the gasket and install the rocker arm cover.

## Idle Speed and Mixture Gasoline Engines

### ADJUSTMENT

These engines have electronically controlled idle speed, using a solenoid connected to terminals 1 and 5 of the control unit. Idle speed and mixture adjustments are not recommended.

## Idle Speed Diesel Engine

### ADJUSTMENT

#### All 1983–85 Diesels

##### EXCEPT 240D AND 1984–85 190D

1. Run the engine to normal operating temperature.

2. On normally aspirated engines (non-turbocharged), turn the idle speed adjuster on the dash completely to the right.

3. Disconnect the pushrod at the angle lever.

4. Check the idle speed. Adjust by loosening the locknut and adjusting the idle speed screw. Tighten the locknut.

5. On all except turbodiesels, adjust the pushrod so that a clearance of approximately 0.2 in. exists between the cam on the lever and the actuator on the switchover valve. The lever on the fuel injection pump must rest against the idle stop.

6. Depress the stop lever as far as possible. The cruise control Bowden cable should be free of tension against the angel lever. Use the adjusting screw to alter the tension. Let go of the stop lever. The Bowden cable should have a slight amount of play.

7. On turbodiesels, adjust the pushrod so that the roller in the guide lever rests free of tension against the stop.

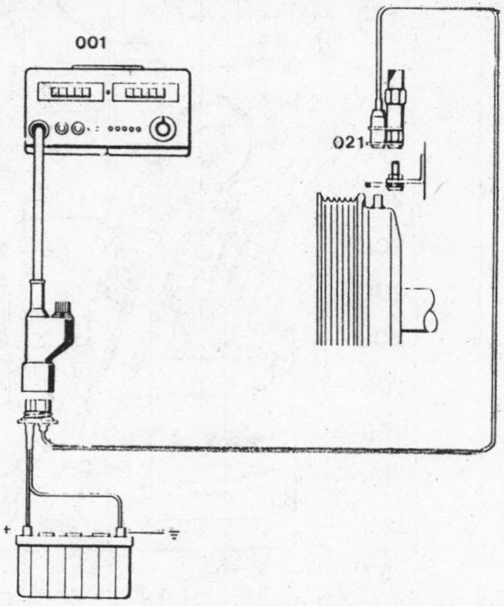


**Connecting the digital tester (001) and the TDC impulse transmitter (021) on the 190D**

8. Put the automatic transmission in Drive and turn the steering wheel to full lock. The engine should run smoothly. If not, adjust the idle speed. Disconnect the cruise control connecting rod, and push the lever clockwise to the idle stop. Attach the connecting rod, making sure the lever is about 0.04 in. from the idle speed stop.

**CAUTION**

***If the engine speed is adjusted higher, it will be above the controlled idle speed range of the governor and the engine can increase in speed to maximum rpm.***

##### 1983 240D

1. Run the engine to normal operating temperature.

2. Turn the idle speed adjuster knob on the dashboard completely to the right.

3. Disconnect the pushrod at the operating lever.

4. Move the guide lever to the idle speed position. Set the edge of the guide lever at the mark (arrow) on the cap.

5. Check, and if necessary, adjust the idle speed. Use the idle speed adjusting screw.

6. Attach the pushrod to the injection pump lever so that the rod is free of tension when the lever is against the idle speed stop.

7. Check to be sure the cruise control rods are free of tension.

8. Move the automatic transmission into Drive. Turn **ON** the A/C and turn the wheels to full lock. The engine should run smoothly. Adjust the idle speed if necessary.

Clearance between cam and actuator on switch-over valve—all except turbodiesel

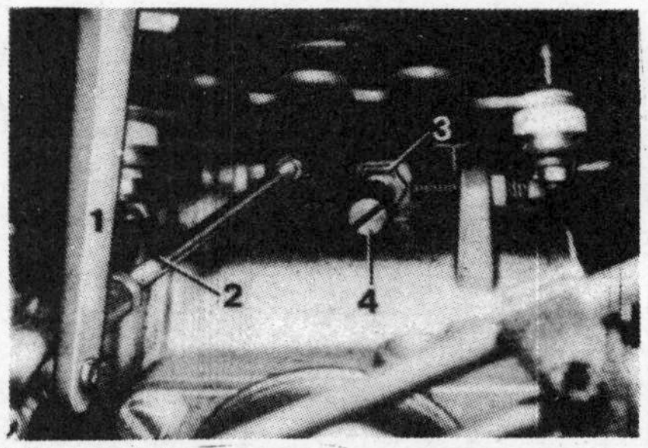


Idle speed adjustment—1983–85 5 cylinder engines

Idle speed adjustment—240D

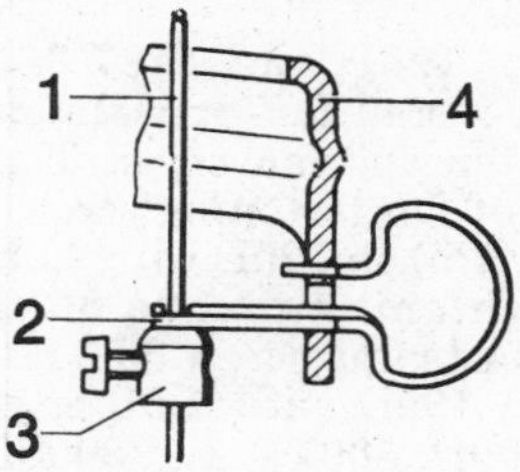


1. Cable
2. Spring
3. Adjusting barrel
4. Lever

Be sure the specially shaped spring is installed as shown

### 1984–85 190D

**NOTE: Testing the idle speed on the 190D will require 2 special tools. They are a digital tester (SUN®-1019, 2110 or All-Test® 3610-MB) and a TDC impulse transmitter, not commonly available tools. Without these special tools, idle speed adjustment is impossible and should not be attempted.**

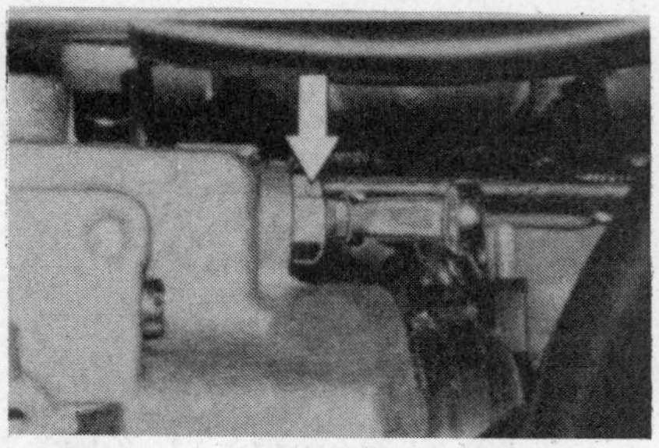

Adjusting the idle—1985 190D

Idle speed trimming plug—190D (2.5L) shown, other similar

1. Run the engine until it reaches normal operating temperature.
2. Connect the digital tester and the TDC impulse transmitter as indicated in the illustration.
3. Check all linkages for ease of operation.
4. Disconnect the pushrod from the adjusting lever.
5. Start the engine and check the idle speed. If required, adjust by loosening the locknut on the vacuum control unit and turning the unit itself in or out.

**NOTE: 1985 models with electronic idle speed control have no vacuum control unit. To adjust idle speed, loosen the locknut and turn the shaft until the idle speed is 670 rpm.**

6. After the idle speed is correct, tighten the vacuum control unit locknut and reconnect the pushrod so that it is tension-free when the lever is against the idle speed stop.
7. Switch **ON** all auxiliary power accessories and check that the engine continues to run smoothly. Readjust the idle speed if necessary.
8. Disconnect the 2 special tools and turn **OFF** the engine.

Loosen the locknut (4A) and turn the vacuum control unit (4) to adjust the idle speed on the 1984–85 190D

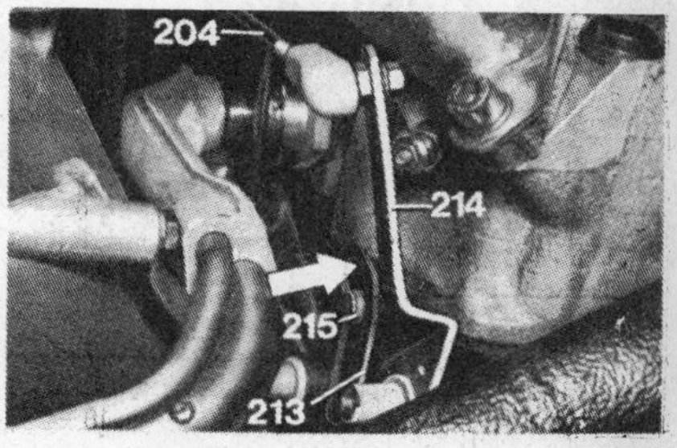


Throttle linkage on the 1984–85 190D

# ENGINE ELECTRICAL

## Distributor

### REMOVAL & INSTALLATION

**NOTE: The distributor on the 190E with 2.6L engine, 260E, 300E, 300CE, 300SE, 300TE and 300SEL is part of the cylinder head. With the exception of the cap and rotor, it is not readily removable.**

The removal and installation procedures for all distributors on Mercedes-Benz vehicles are basically similar. Certain minor differences may exist from model to model.

1. The distributor is usually located on the front side or front of the engine.
2. Disconnect the negative battery cable. Remove the dust, cover, distributor cap, cable plug connections, and vacuum line.
3. Rotating the engine in the normal direction, crank it around until the distributor rotor points to the mark on the rim of the distributor housing. This indicates the No. 1 cylinder.
4. The engine can be cranked with a socket wrench on the balancer bolt or with a pry bar inserted in the balancer.
5. Matchmark the distributor body and the engine so that the distributor can be returned to its original position.

6. Remove the distributor hold-down bolt and withdraw the distributor from the engine.

**NOTE: Do not crank the engine while the distributor is removed.**

7. Installation is the reverse of removal. Insert the distributor so that the matchmarks on the distributor and engine are aligned.

8. Tighten the clamp bolt and check the dwell angle and ignition timing.

## Alternator

### PRECAUTIONS

Some precautions that should be taken into consideration when working on this, or any other, AC charging system are as follows:

- Never switch battery polarity.
- When install a battery, always connect the grounded terminal first.
- Never disconnect the battery while the engine is running.
- If the molded connector is disconnected from the alternator, do not ground the hot wire.
- Never run the alternator with the main output cable disconnected.
- Never electric weld around the car without disconnecting the alternator.
- Never apply any voltage in excess of battery voltage during testing.
- Never "jump" a battery for starting purposes with more than 12 volts.

### REMOVAL & INSTALLATION

Viewing the engine from the front, the alternator is located on either side, usually down low. Because of the location, it is sometimes easier to remove the alternator from below the vehicle. The following is a general procedure for all models.

1. Disconnect the negative battery cable. Locate the alternator and disconnect and identify all wires.
2. Loosen the adjusting (pivot) bolt or the adjusting mechanism and swing the alternator in toward the engine.
3. Remove the drive belt from the alternator pulley.
4. The alternator can now be removed from its mounting bracket or the bracket and alternator can be removed from the engine.
5. Installation is the reverse of removal.
6. Tighten all of the drive belts that were loosened.

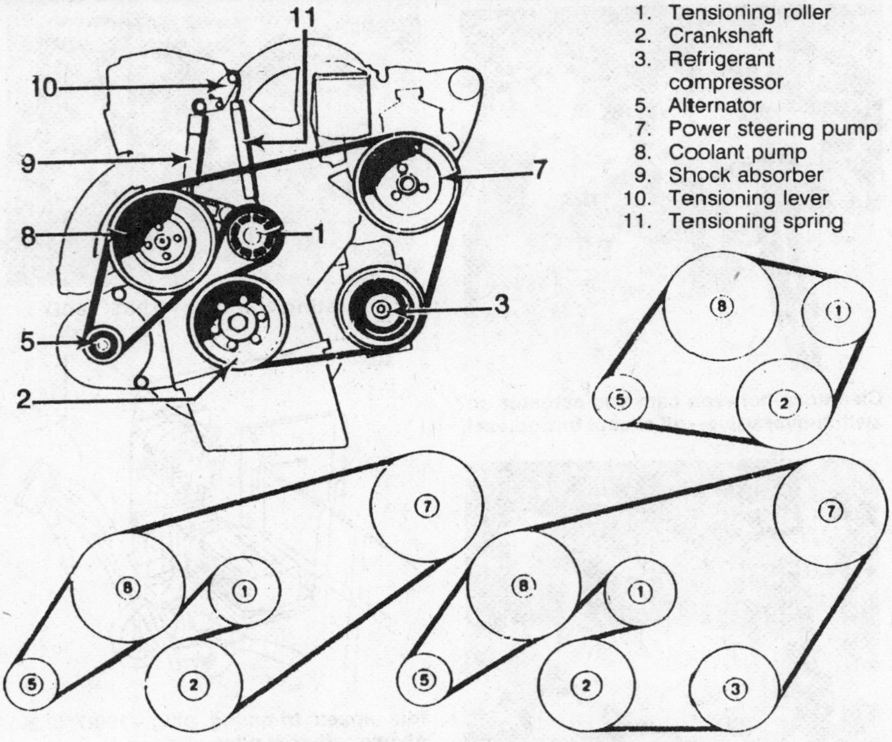


Poly V-belt and accessories—190D, 300D and 300SDL

## Poly V-Belt

### REMOVAL & INSTALLATION

#### *190D and 1987 300D, 300TD and 300SDL*

1. Disconnect the negative battery cable. On 190D with 2.2L engines, loosen fan cover and place on fan. Remove fan and remove together with fan cover.
2. On 190D with 2.5L engine, remove radiator with one-piece fan cover.
3. On 190D with 2.5L engine with split fan cover, open cover and remove. For this purpose, place rear part on fan. Pull holding clamp form front part. Remove both parts one after the other.
4. On 190D with 2.5L engine and 1987 300D, 300TD and 300SDL, loosen fan cover and place above fan. Remove viscofan clutch, using screwdriver element 103 589 01 09 00 or equivalent, torque wrench 001 589 72 21 00 or equivalent and counterholder 603 589 00 40 00 or equivalent, for this purpose.
5. Remove nut.
6. Slacken draw spring. For this purpose, swivel lever clockwise.
7. Remove poly V-belt. For this purpose, push back tensioning roller.
8. Check pulley profiles and tensioning device for damage and contamination and replace, if required (ie, worn out bearing points of tensioning device, dents in pulleys, etc.).
9. Mount poly V-belt. Slightly pull up tensioning roller. Turn poly V-belt on its back, make a small loop and slip in-between coolant pump pulley and crankshaft pulley.

To install:

10. Press poly V-belt with left hand tightly against coolant pump pulley and rotate pulley counterclockwise, until the poly V-belt has run up on tensioning roller.
11. Place poly V-belt on tensioning roller and on crankshaft pulley. Then turn free poly V-belt part around and place on refrigerant compressor-, power steering pump-, coolant pump- and alternator pulley.
12. Tension poly V-belt and mount tensioning device reverse order of removal.
13. On 190D and 1987 300D and 300TD, install fan or viscofan clutch with a fan and fan cover. Tightening torque of fan fastening screw 18.5 ft. lbs. (25 Nm) on 190D with 2.2L engine and tightening torque of viscofan clutch fastening screw 33.2 ft. lbs. (45 Nm) on 190D with 2.5L engine and 1987 300D, 300TD and 300SDL. For tightening viscofan clutch fastening screw, screwdriver element 103 589 01 09 00 or equivalent, torque wrench 001 589 72 21 00 or equivalent and counterholder 603 589 00 40 00 or equivalent.

## Poly V-belt Tensioner

### REMOVAL & INSTALLATION

#### *190D and 1987 300D, 300TD and 300SDL*

1. Disconnect the negative battery

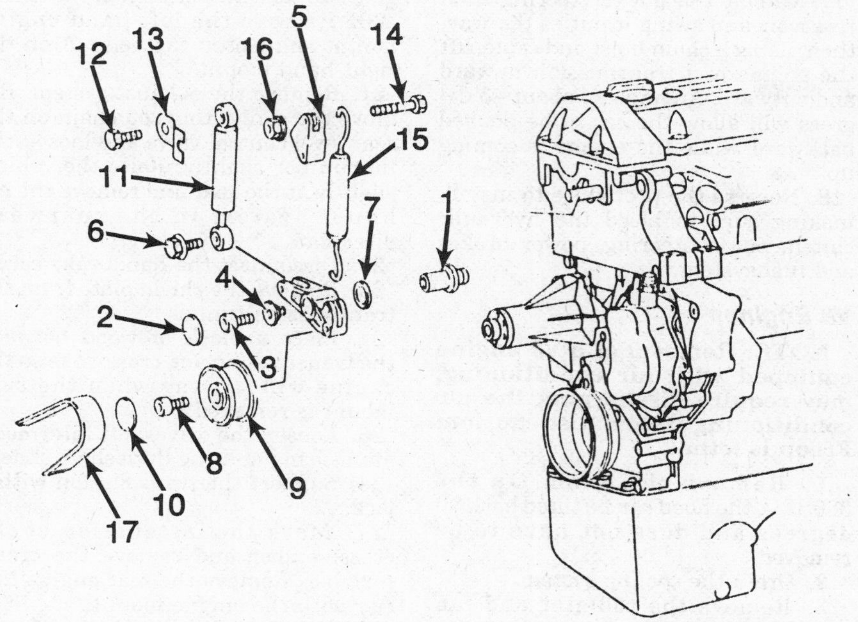


1. Bearing bolt (Tightening torque 74 ft. lbs. (100 Nm))
2. Closing cap
3. Hex head socket screw (M 6 × 25) (Tightening torque 7 ft. lbs. (10 Nm))
4. Lock washer
5. Tensioning lever
6. Screw (M 7× 35) (Tightening torque 7 ft. lbs. (10 Nm))
7. Sealing disk
8. Hex head socket screw (M 8 × 40) (Tightening torque 22 ft. lbs. (30 Nm))
9. Tensioning roller
10. Closing cap
11. Shock absorber
12. Hex head screw (M 8 × 30) (Tightening torque 19 ft. lbs. (25 Nm))
13. Holder
14. Hex head screw (8 × 100) (Tightening torque 19 ft. lbs. (25 Nm))
15. Draw spring
16. Collar nut
17. Poly-V-belt

**Poly V-belt tensioning device servicing—190D, 300D and 300SDL**

cable. Remove poly V-belt.

2. Remove tensioning roller. For this purpose, remove closing cap and remove hex head socket screw.
3. Remove pulley for coolant pump.
4. Remove hex head screws and remove shock absorber.
5. Disengage draw spring.
6. On first version, remove closing cover on tensioning lever. Take off hex head socket screw and remove together with lock washer and tensioning lever.
7. Remove bearing bolt.
8. On second version, remove closing cap.
9. Remove fitted screw together with tensioning lever.
10. Check bearing bolt and tensioning lever for wear. If one part is worn out replace both parts.
11. Clean threads in timing housing cover and on bearing bolt with activator. Then coat threads on bearing bolt with adhesive Omnifit 100 M orange 002 989 23 71 or equivalent and tighten bearing bolt to 73.8 ft. lbs. (100 Nm).

**To install:**

12. Reverse removal procedure.
13. Check shock absorber for function prior to installation.
14. Install poly V-belt.

### BELT TENSION ADJUSTMENT

All alternator dive belts should be tensioned to approximately ½ in. deflection under thumb pressure at the middle of the longest span.

**NOTE: The 190D, 1985–90 190E and all 1986–90 models utilize a single V-belt with automatic tensioning. No adjustment is necessary.**

## Starter

### REMOVAL & INSTALLATION

#### *260E, 300E, 300CE and 300TE*

1. Disconnect negative battery terminal.
2. Remove complete air cleaner.
3. Remove holder on intake manifold.
4. Remove engine compartment enclosure.
5. Disconnect electric wires for oil level and oil pressure sensor.
6. Remove starter.

**To install:**

7. Reverse removal procedure.

#### *All Other Models*

1. Remove all wires from the starter and tag them for location.
2. Disconnect the battery cable.
3. Unbolt the starter from the bellhousing and remove the ground cable.
4. Remove the starter from underneath the car.
5. Installation is the reverse of removal. Be sure to replace all wires and washers in their original location.

# ENGINE MECHANICAL

**NOTE: Care should be taken when working on Mercedes-Benz engines, since there are many aluminum parts which can be damaged if carelessly handled.**

## Engine

### REMOVAL & INSTALLATION

**NOTE: In all cases, Mercedes-Benz engines and transmissions are removed as a unit.**

**CAUTION**

***Air conditioner lines should not be indiscriminately disconnected without taking proper precautions. It is best to swing the compressor out of the way while still connected to its hoses. Never do any welding around the compressor-heat may cause an explosion. Also, the refrigerant, while inert at normal room temperature, breaks down under high temperature into hydrogen fluoride and phosgene (among other products), which are highly poisonous.***

#### *All 4, 5 and 6 Cylinder Engines*

1. First, remove the hood, then drain the cooling system and disconnect the battery. While not strictly necessary, it is better to remove the battery completely to prevent breakage by the engine as it is lifted out.
2. Remove the fan shroud, radiator, and disconnect all heater hoses and oil cooler lines. Plug all openings to keep out dirt.
3. Remove the air cleaner and all fuel, vacuum and oil hoses (e.g., power

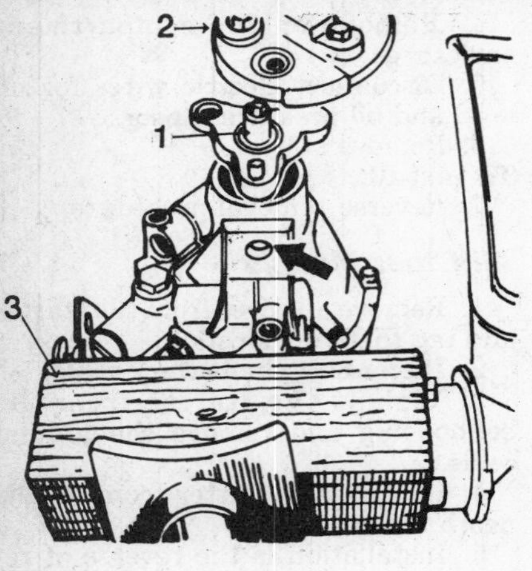


1 U-joint flange
2 U-joint plate
3 Wooden block

**Supporting a V8 engine**

steering and power brakes). Plug all openings to keep out dirt.

4. Remove the viscous coupling and fan.

5. On diesel engines, disconnect the idle control starting cables. On the 300SD, loosen the oil filter cover slightly; siphon off the power steering fluid and disconnect the hoses.

6. On all engines, disconnect the accelerator linkage.

7. Disconnect all ground straps and electrical connections. It is a good idle to tag each wire for easy reassembly.

8. Detach the gearshift linkage and the exhaust pipes from the manifolds.

9. Loosen the steering relay arm and pull it down out of the way, along with the center steering rod and hydraulic steering damper.

10. The hydraulic engine shock absorber should be removed.

11. Remove the hydraulic line from the clutch housing and the oil line connectors from the automatic transmission.

12. Unbolt the clutch slave cylinder from the bellhousing after removing the return spring.

13. Remove the exhaust pipe bracket attached to the transmission and place a woodpadded jack under the bellhousing, or place a cable sling under the oil pan, to support the engine. On turbocharged models, disconnect the exhaust pipes at the turbocharger.

14. Mark the position of the rear engine support and unbolt the 2 outer bolts, then remove the top bolt at the transmission and pull the support out.

15. Disconnect the speedometer cable and the front driveshaft U-joint. Push the driveshaft back and wire it out of the way.

16. Unbolt the engine mounts on both sides and, on 4 cylinder engines, the front limit stop.

17. Unbolt the power steering fluid reservoir and swing it out of the way; then, using a chain hoist and cable, lift the engine and transmission upward and outward. An angle of about 45 degrees will allow the car to be pushed backward while the engine is coming up.

18. Reverse the procedure to install, making sure to bleed the hydraulic clutch, power steering, power brakes and fuel system.

### V8 Engines

**NOTE: Removal of a V8 engine equipped with air conditioning, may require discharging the air conditioning system. Use caution; Freon is lethal.**

1. Remove the hood. On the 380SEC, the hood can be tilted back 90 degrees and does not have to be removed.

2. Drain the cooling system.

3. Remove the radiator and fan shroud.

4. Remove the cable plug from the temperature switch.

5. Remove the battery, battery frame and air filter.

6. Drain the power steering reservoir and windshield washer reservoir.

7. Disconnect and plug the high pressure and return lines on the power steering pump.

8. Detach the fuel lines from the fuel filter, pressure regulator, and pressure sensor.

9. If equipped, loosen the line to the supply and anti-freeze tanks. On models so equipped, disconnect the lines to the hydro-pneumatic suspension.

10. Disconnect the cables from the ignition coil and transistor ignition switchbox.

11. Disconnect the brake vacuum lines.

12. Detach the cable connections for the following:
 a. Venturi control unit
 b. Temperature sensor
 c. Distributor
 d. Temperature switch
 e. Cold starting valve
 f. Speedometer inductance transmitter (3.8L only)

13. Remove the regulating shaft by pushing it in the direction of the firewall.

14. Disconnect the thrust and pullrods.

15. Disconnect the heater lines.

16. Detach the lines to the oil pressure and temperature gauges.

17. Remove the ground strap from the vehicle.

18. Detach the cables from the alternator, terminal bridge, and battery. Remove the battery.

19. Position a lifting sling on the engine and take up the slack in the chain.

20. Remove the left-hand engine mount and loosen the hex nut on the right-hand mount.

21. Remove the exhaust system. Remove the connecting rod chain on the rear level control valve and loosen the torsion bar slightly. Raise the vehicle slightly at the rear and remove the exhaust system in the rearward direction.

22. Disconnect the handbrake cable.

23. Remove the shield plate from the transmission tunnel.

24. Place a block of wood between the transmission and cross-yoke so the engine will not sag when the rear mount is removed.

25. Loosen the driveshaft intermediate bearing and the driveshaft slide.

26. Support the transmission with a jack.

27. Mark the installation of the crossmember and remove the crossmember. Remove the rear engine carrier with the engine mount.

28. Unbolt the front U-joint flange on the transmission and push it back. Do not loosen the clamp nut on the intermediate bearing. Support the driveshaft.

29. Disconnect the speedometer shaft, shift rod, control pressure rod, regulating linkage (on automatic transmissions), kickdown switch cable, starter lockout switch cable, and the cable for the back-up light switch.

30. Remove the front engine mounting bolt and remove the engine at approximately a 45 degree angle.

31. Installation is the reverse of removal. Lower the engine until it is behind the front axle carrier. Place a jack under the transmission and lower the engine into its compartment. While lowering the engine, install the right-hand shock mount.

32. Fill the engine with all required fluids and start the engine. Check for leaks.

# Cylinder Head

## REMOVAL & INSTALLATION

### 4 and 5 Cylinder Engines

#### EXCEPT 190E-16 (DOHC)

This is fairly straightforward but some caution must be observed to ensure that the valve timing is not disturbed.

1. Disconnect the negative battery cable. Drain the radiator and remove all hoses and wires. Tag all wires to ensure easy reassembly.

2. Remove the camshaft cover and associated throttle linkage, then press out the spring clamp from the notch in the rocker arm (all except 190).

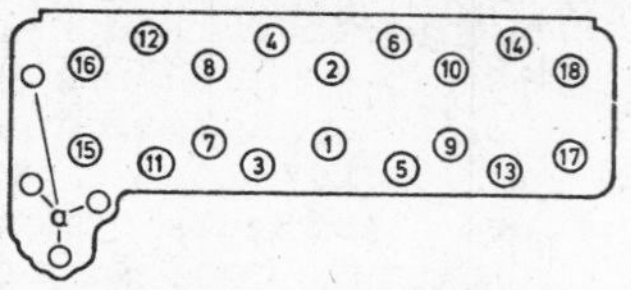

Cylinder head torque sequence—4 cylinder diesel engines (except 190D)

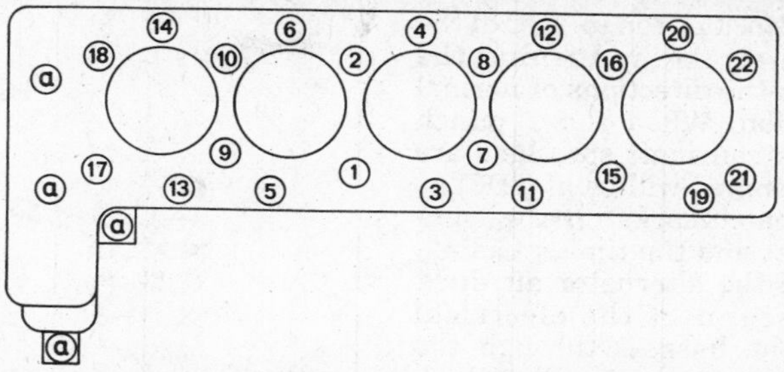

Cylinder head torque sequence—1983–85 5 cylinder engines (bolts marked "A" are tightened with a Hex bit)

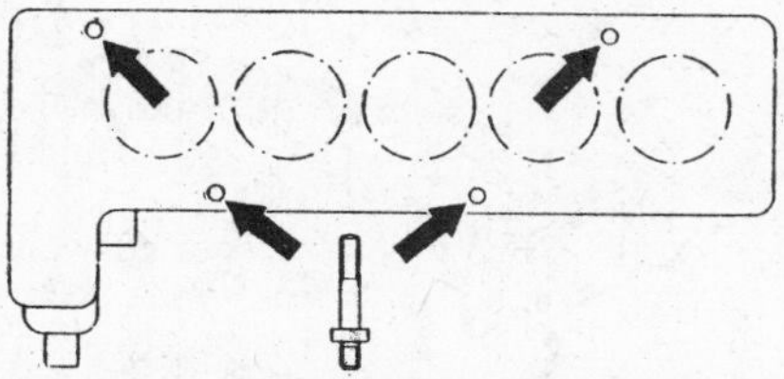

Studs (arrows) on the 1983–85 5 cylinder engine are for attaching the rocker cover

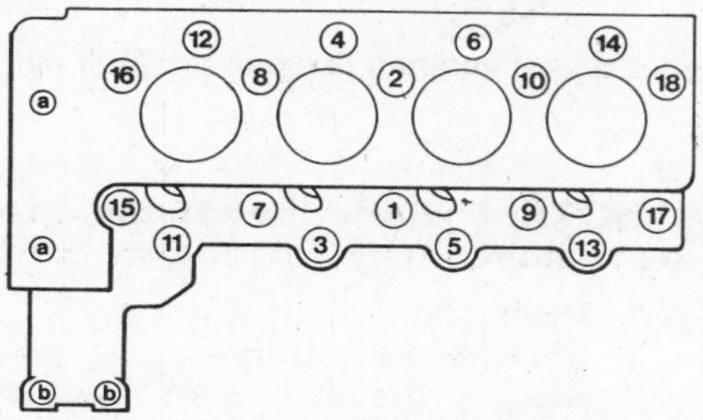

Cylinder head torque sequence—190E SOHC (bolts "A" are tightened to 25 Nm)

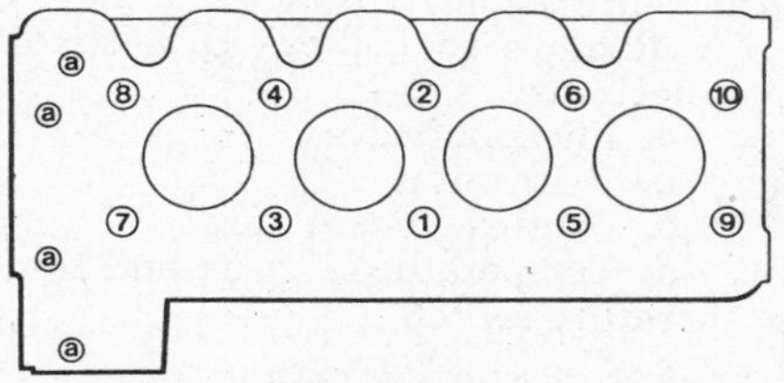

Cylinder head torque sequence—1984–85 190D (bolts "A" and "B" are tightened to 25 Nm)

**NOTE: The cylinder head cover on the 190E is removed with the spark plug cables and distributor cap still attached to it.**

3. Push the clamp outward over the ball cap of the rocker, then depress the valve with a large prying tool and lift the rocker arm out of the ball pin head (all except 190).

4. Remove the rocker arm supports (all except 190) and the camshaft sprocket nut.

5. On all 5 cylinder engines and the 190E, the rockers and their supports must be removed together.

6. Using a suitable puller, remove the camshaft sprocket, after having first marked the chain, sprocket and cam for ease of assembly.

7. Remove the sprocket and chain and wire it out of the way.

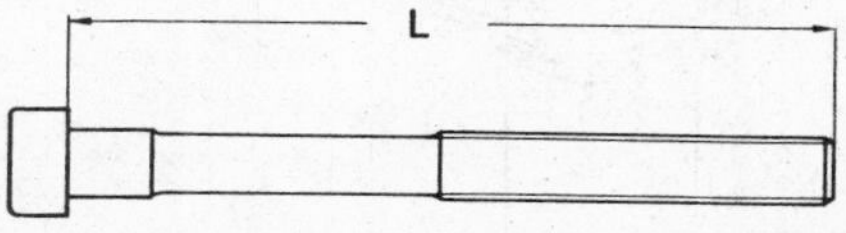


Cylinder head bolt stretch is measured at "L"

**CAUTION**

***Make sure the chain is securely wired so that it will not slide down into the engine.***

8. Unbolt the manifolds and exhaust header pipe and push them out of the way.

9. Loosen the cylinder head holddown bolts in the reverse order of that shown in torque diagrams for each model. It is good practice to loosen each bolt a little at a time, working around the head, until all are free. This prevents unequal stresses in the metal.

10. Reach into the engine compartment and gradually work the head loose from each end by rocking it. Never, under any circumstances, use a screwdriver between the head and block to pry, as the head will be scarred badly and may be ruined.

11. Installation is the reverse of removal.

**CAUTION**

***The dowel pin used for cylinder head alignment has been moved in 1985–90 190D models. Due to this change, the cylinder head and/or the gasket are NOT interchangeable with the 1984 190D.***

**NOTE: All diesel engines utilize cylinder head stretch-bolts. These bolts undergo a permanent stretch each time they are tightened. When a maximum length is reached, they must be discarded and replace with new bolts. When tightening the head bolts on these engines, it is imperative that the steps listed under "Torque Specifications" are followed exactly.**

### 190E-16 (DOHC)

1. Disconnect the negative battery cable. Drain the engine coolant and disconnect the radiator and heater hoses at the cylinder head.

| Model | Length when new (mm) | Maximum (mm) |
|---|---|---|
| 190E | 119 | 122 |
| 190D | 80 | 83.6 |
| | 102 | 105.6 |
| | 115 | 118.6 |
| 240D, 300D, | 104 | 105.6 |
| 300CD, 300SD, | 119 | 120.5 |
| 300TD (1980-85) | 144 | 145.6 |

Under no circumstances may the older type cylinder head bolts be exchanged with the newer "stretch" bolts.

2. Tag and disconnect the intake air temperature sensor lead and the crankcase ventilation hose where they connect to the air cleaner.

3. Remove the 2 air cleaner mounting nuts. Lift the housing at the rear until it releases from its holding studs, slide it backwards slightly and then remove it from the air flow sensor.

4. Loosen the oil dipstick mounting bracket screw and pull the dipstick out of the crankcase.

5. Loosen the screw in the center of the serpentine belt tensioner ¼–½ turn, loosen the tensioning nut by turning it counterclockwise and then remove the belt.

6. Remove the exhaust manifold.

7. Remove the 4 screws holding the ignition cable cover to the cylinder head cover. Remove the cover, tag and disconnect the cables and position them out of the way.

8. Loosen the clamp on the rear heater hose and pull it off the water outlet.

9. Disconnect the breather line at the cylinder head cover.

10. Remove the 6 mounting nuts and lift up the cylinder head cover.

**CAUTION**

***If the cylinder head cover sticks to the head, DO NOT use a hammer to loosen it as it may crack. Try to break the seal by pushing at both corners on one side or the other with your hands.***

11. Set the No. 1 piston to TDC of the compression stroke by turning the crankshaft in the directions of normal engine rotation. When the 2 punch marks in the camshaft sprockets are aligned, the engine will be at TDC.
12. Place matchmarks on the camshaft sprocket and the timing chain.
13. Remove the alternator air duct. Tag and disconnect the electrical leads. Pull the harness through the component compartment wall and position it out of the way. Remove the alternator.
14. Using a 32mm wrench, unscrew the chain tensioner.
15. Tag and disconnect the tow pump lines and then remove the pump from the exhaust-side camshaft. Remove the 3 screws and pull the pump flange from the end of the camshaft.
16. Remove the 2 mounting nuts and lift the chain slide from the front of the engine.

**NOTE: If so equipped, remove the sheet metal bracket that is attached to the 2 front cylinder head bolts and the 2 eyes at the timing chain housing cover.**

17. Remove the 4 mounting screws from each camshaft sprocket. Knock the camshaft back slightly with a rubber mallet. Be careful! Remove the front bearing caps and pull off the 2 sprockets.

**CAUTION**

***Secure the timing chain in such a way that it will not slip down into the crankcase.***

18. Loosen the water by-pass hose clamp. Remove the mounting screws and pull out the water inlet/thermostat housing.
19. Use a Allen wrench to remove the 2 return pipe mounting screws and then pull it out of the cylinder head. If the pipe sticks, rotate it clockwise slightly and force it out with a suitable prybar.
20. Unbolt the intake manifold and push it out of the way.
21. Loosen the cylinder head bolts in the reverse order of the tightening sequence. Loosen each bolt a little at a time, working around the head until all are free; this will prevent unequal stress on the aluminum head.
22. Reach into the engine compartment and gradually work the head loose from the cylinder block. NEVER, under any circumstances, use a screwdriver or the like to pry the head free.
23. Installation is in the reverse order of removal. Please note the following:

a. Measure the cylinder head bolts prior to installation. A new bolt is 110mm long from the bottom of bolt head to the end of the bolt. If it has stretched to more than 113mm, replace it.

b. Tighten the cylinder head bolts a little at a time, in the order shown in the illustration.

c. Use new O-rings and a new flange gasket when installing the return pipe.

d. Install the intake camshaft sprocket first (right side when facing the vehicle). Be certain that the matchmarks made earlier are aligned.

e. Make sure that the 2 punch marks in the sprockets are in alignment.

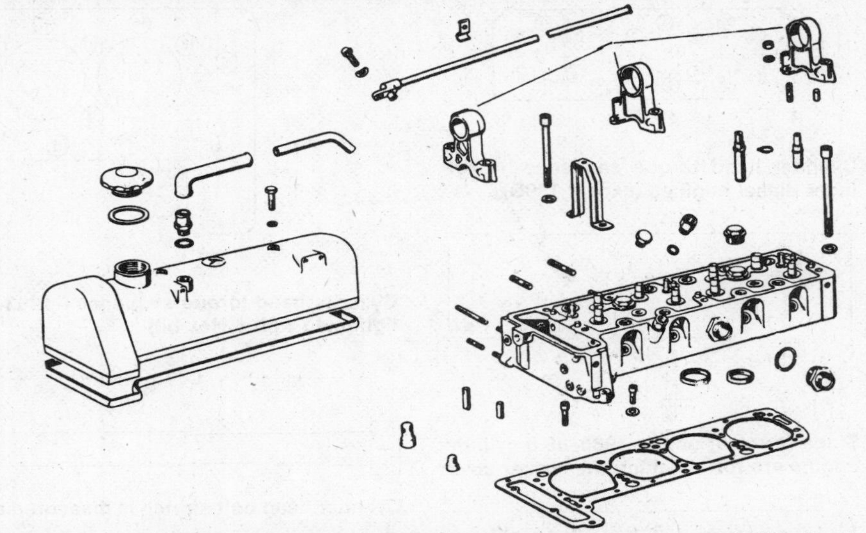

**Exploded view of the cylinder head—4 cylinder diesel engines (except 190D); 5 cylinder engines similar**

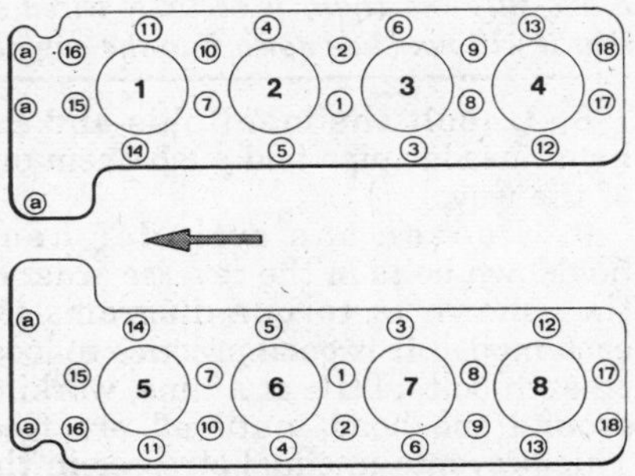

**Cylinder head torque sequence—V8 engines**

### *V8 Engines*

**NOTE: Before removing the cylinder head from a V8, be sure you have the 4 special tools necessary to torque the head bolts; without them it will be impossible. Do not confuse the left and right-hand head gaskets the left side has 2 attaching holes in the timing chain cover, the right side has only 1 hole. Cylinder heads on 3.8L and 5.0L V8's are not interchangeable.**

**NOTE: Cylinder heads can only be removed with the engine cold.**

1. Drain the cooling system.
2. Remove the battery.
3. Remove the air cleaner. Remove the fan and fan shroud.
4. Pull the cable plug from the temperature sensor.
5. Detach the vacuum hose from the venturi control unit.
6. Remove the following electrical connections:

a. Injection valves.

b. Distributor

c. Venturi control unit

d. Temperature sensor and temperature switch

e. Starting valve

f. Temperature switch for the auxiliary fan.

7. Loosen the ring line on the fuel distributor.
8. Loosen the screws on the injection valves and pressure regulator or mixture regulator. Remove the ring line with the injection valves and pressure regulator.
9. Plug the holes for the injection valves in the cylinder head.
10. Remove the regulating shaft by disconnecting the pull rod and the thrust rod.
11. Remove the ignition cable plug.
12. Loosen the vacuum connection on the intake manifold.
13. Loosen the vacuum connection for the central lock at the transmission.
14. Remove the oil filler tube from the right hand cylinder head and remove the temperature connector.
15. Remove the oil pressure gauge line from the left hand cylinder head.
16. Loosen the coolant connection on the intake manifold.

Return pipe – 190E-16 (DOHC)

Be careful removing the cylinder head bolts on a V8. The inner row of cam bolts are the only bolts NOT holding the head on. Note the angle of the bolts.

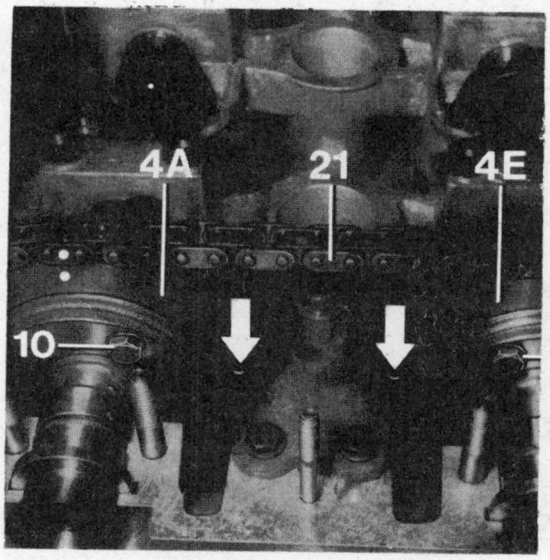


When the two punch marks are in alignment on the 190E-16 camshaft sprockets, the engine is at TDC

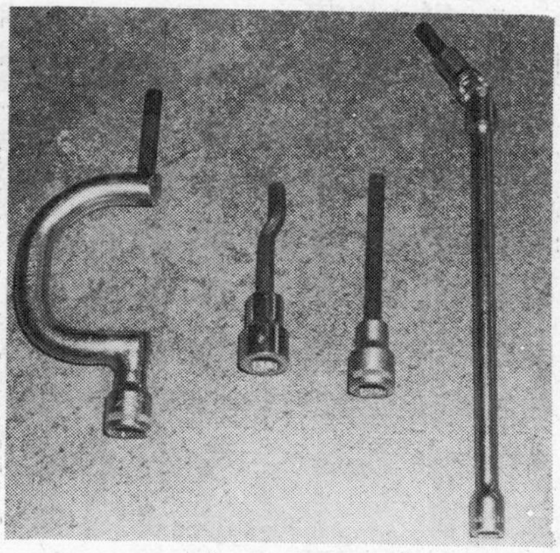

You need these tools to remove or install the V8 cylinder head. Without them it is practically impossible.

The timing marks on the camshaft bearing cap (1) and the camshaft (2) should be in alignment when the No. 1 cylinder is at TDC

17. Remove the intake manifold bolts.

18. Loosen the alternator belt and remove the alternator and mounting bracket.

19. Remove the electrical connections from the distributor and electronic ignition switch-gear.

20. Drain some fluid from the power steering reservoir and disconnect and plug the return hose and high pressure supply line.

21. Disconnect the exhaust system and remove the exhaust manifolds.

22. Loosen the right hand holder for the engine damper.

23. Remove the right hand chain tensioner.

24. Matchmark the camshaft, camshaft sprocket, and chain. Remove the camshaft sprocket and chain after removing the cylinder head cover. Be sure to hang the chain and sprocket to prevent it from falling into the timing chain case.

25. Remove the upper slide rail. Remove the distributor and remove the inner slide rail on the left cylinder head. Remove the rail after the camshaft sprocket.

26. Unscrew the cylinder head bolts. This should be done with a cold engine. Unscrew the bolts in the reverse order of the torque sequences. Unscrew all the bolts a little at a time and proceed in this manner until all the bolts have been removed.

**NOTE: Cylinder head bolts on the 3.8L and 5.0L V8's are nickel plated and 10mm longer than those for previous engines.**

27. Remove the cylinder head. Do not pry on the cylinder head.

28. Remove the cylinder head gasket.

29. Clean the cylinder head and cylinder block joint faces.

**To install:**

30. Position the cylinder head gasket.

31. Do not confuse the cylinder head gaskets. The left hand head has 2 attaching holes in the timing chain cover while the right hand has 3.

32. Install the cylinder head and torque the bolts according to the illustrated torque sequence.

33. Further installation is the reverse of removal. Insert the rear cam bearing cylinder head bolt before positioning the cylinder head. Also, install the exhaust manifold only after the cylinder head bolts have been tightened. The camshaft sprocket should be installed so that the flange faces the camshaft. Check the valve clearance and fill the engine with oil. Top up the power steering tank and bleed the power steering system.

34. Run the engine and check for leaks.

### *6 Cylinder SOHC (1986–90)*

**NOTE: The cylinder head on the 190E with 2.6L engine, 260E, 300E, 300CE, 300SE, 300TE and 300SEL should be removed cold, with the camshaft, intake and exhaust manifolds attached.**

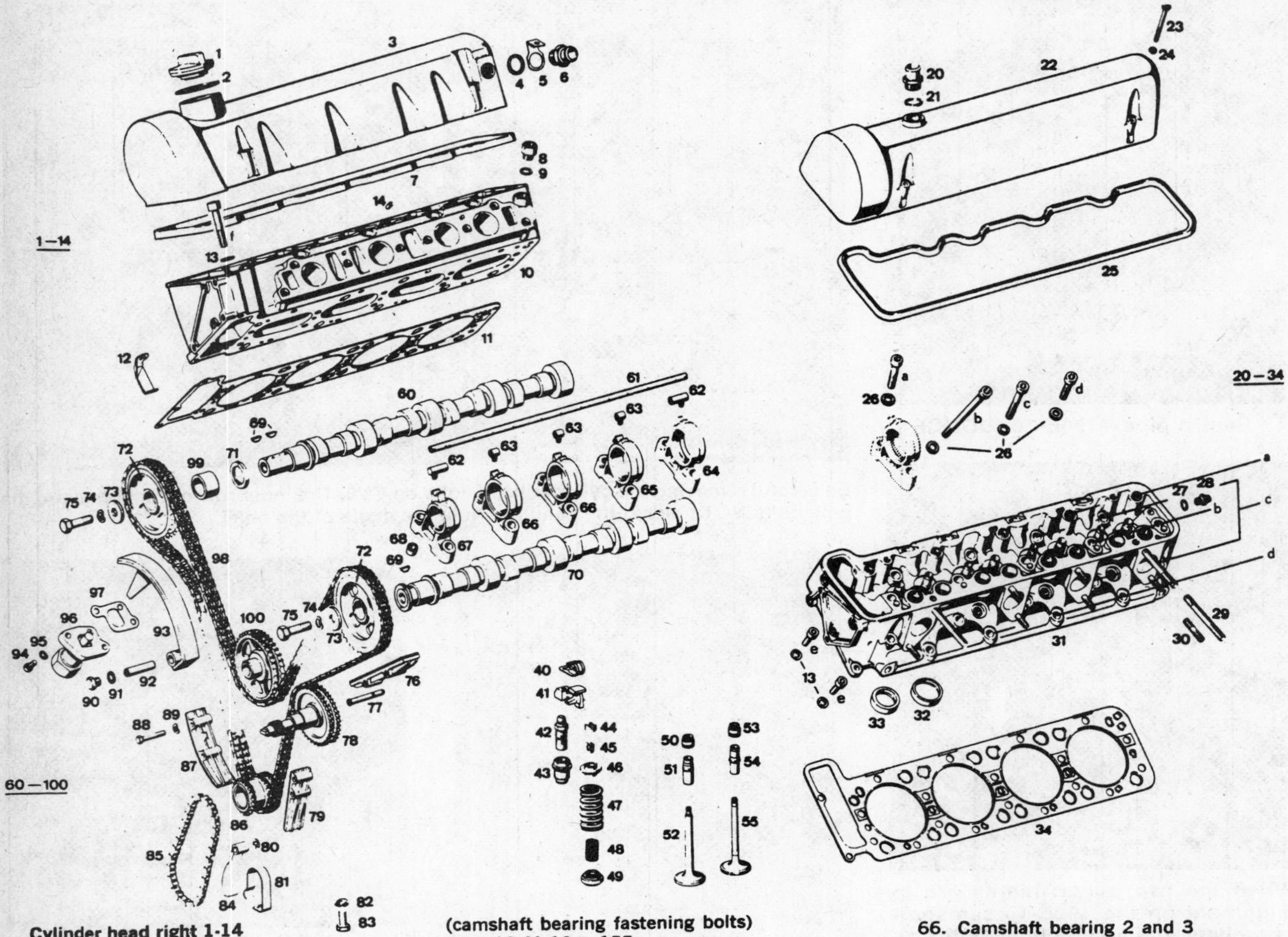


**Cylinder head right 1-14**

1. Filler plug
2. Sealing ring
3. Cylinder head cover
4. Sealing ring
5. Holder for cable to injection valves
6. Connection
7. Valve cover gasket
8. Connection to temperature sensor
9. Sealing ring
10. Cylinder head
11. Cylinder head gasket
12. Cable holder
13. 5 Washers
14. Hollow dowel pins

**Cylinder head left 20-34**

20. Connection
21. Sealing ring
22. Cylinder head cover
23. 8 Screws
24. 8 Sealing rings
25. Cylinder head cover gasket
26. 36 Washers
27. Sealing ring
28. Screw connection oil pressure gauge
29. 3 Studs
30. 13 Studs
31. Cylinder head
32. Valve seat ring—intake
33. Valve seat ring—exhaust
34. Cylinder head gasket

**Cylinder head bolts**

(a)—10 M 10 x 50chrauben)
(camshaft bearing fastening bolts)
(b)—10 M 10 x 155
(c)—18 M 10 x 80
(d)—8 M 10 x 55
(e)—4 M 8 x 30
(f)—1 M 8 x 70

**Valve arrangement 40-55**

40. Tensioning spring
41. Rocker arm
42. Adjusting screw
43. Threaded bushing
44. Thrust piece
45. Valve cone piece
46. Valve spring retainer
47. Outer valve spring
48. Inner valve spring
49. Rotator
50. Intake valve seal
51. Exhaust valve guide
52. Intake valve
53. Exhaust valve seal
54. Exhaust valve guide
55. Exhaust valve

**Engine timing 60-100**

60. Camshaft-right
61. Oil pipe (external lubrication)
62. Connecting piece
63. Connecting piece
(61–63: Oil pipe to camshaft bearing)
64. Camshaft bearing-flywheel end
65. Camshaft bearing 4
66. Camshaft bearing 2 and 3
67. Camshaft bearing-cranking end
68. 5 Hollow dowel pins
69. Spring washer
70. Camshaft-left
71. Compensating washer
72. Camshaft gear
73. Washer-camshaft gear
74. Spring washer
75. Bolt
76. 3 Slide rails
77. 6 Bearing bolts
78. Drive gear ignition distributor
79. Guide rail
80. Lockwasher
81. Spring—chain tensioner, oil pump
82. Washer
83. Screw
84. Clamp
85. Single roller chain (oil pump drive)
86. Crankshaft gear
87. Slide rail
88. 4 Screws
89. 4 Spring washers
90. Plug
91. Sealing ring
92. Bearing bolt
93. Tensioning lever
94. 2 Bolts
95. 2 Spring washers
96. Chain tensioner
97. Gasket
98. Double roller chain
99. Spacer ring
100. Idler gear

**Exploded view of the V8 cylinder head**

1. Disconnect the negative battery cable. Remove the engine undercovers from below.
2. Drain the engine coolant. Drain the engine oil.
3. Remove the air filter.
4. Remove the distributor cap mounting bolts. Unbolt the cylinder head cover and remove it with the ignition wires and distributor cap still attached.

**NOTE: Distributor cap removal will require a 5mm T-shaped Allen wrench about 80mm in length.**

5. Loosen the 3 Allen screws and lift off the distributor rotor.
6. Using a 6mm Allen wrench, unscrew the distributor driver and remove it. Carefully pry off the protective cover.
7. Remove the mounting screws for the cylinder head front cover and carefully knock the cover off with a rubber mallet.
8. Rotate the crankshaft so that the No. 1 cylinder is set at TDC of the compression stroke.
9. Unscrew the timing chain tensioner plug and remove the compression spring.
10. Use a 17mm Allen-head socket and unscrew the tensioner threaded ring.
11. Insert an M8 screw into the tensioner bore, tilt it slightly and ease the tensioner out of the bore. If the tensioner is difficult to remove (or install for that matter), loosen the socket head screw above the tensioner bore slightly; this should facilitate removal (or installation).
12. Matchmark the camshaft sprocket to the camshaft by putting a dab of paint next to the hole in the sprocket with the dowel pin.
13. Matchmark the camshaft sprocket to the timing chain.
14. Remove the mounting screws and pull off the camshaft sprocket. Secure the timing chain in such a way that it will not slip down into the crankcase.
15. Remove the slide rail bolt with an impact puller.
16. Unscrew the oil dipstick guide tube bracket and then pull out the dipstick and tube.
17. Unscrew the upper intake manifold mounting bolt. Loosen the lower bolt.
18. Loosen the hose clamp and remove the coolant hose at the water pump.
19. Unscrew the exhaust pipe at both flanges.
20. Disconnect the automatic transmission dipstick tube at the cylinder head and position it out of the way.
21. Tag and disconnect all wiring, electrical leads and vacuum hoses connected to, or in the way of the cylinder head.
22. Disconnect the fuel feed and return lines, plug them and position them out of the way.
23. Disconnect the accelerator pedal Bowden cable.
24. Loosen the cylinder head bolts in the reverse order of the tightening sequence. Loosen each bolt a little at a time, working around the head until all bolts are free; this will prevent unequal stress on the aluminum head.
25. Reach into the engine compartment and gradually work the head loose from the cylinder block. NEVER, under any circumstances, use a screwdriver or the like to pry the head free.

**To install:**

26. Position a new cylinder head gasket on the cylinder block.
27. Connect the water pump coolant hose to the head and then position the head on the block. There are 2 dowel pins for locating purposes.
28. Measure the length of the cylinder head bolts from the underside of the bolt head to the end of the bolt. If the length exceeds 108.4mm, the bolts must be replaced with new stretch bolts.
29. Install the cylinder head bolts and tighten them a little at a time, in the order shown.
30. Install the camshaft sprocket and tighten the bolts to 8 ft. lbs. (11 Nm). Be sure the dowel pin is in the hole marked previously and that the matchmarks on the timing chain and sprocket are in alignment.
31. Slide the chain tensioner housing into the bore. Screw in the threaded ring and tighten it to 22 ft. lbs. (30 Nm). Install the thrust bolt with the detent spring. Position the compression spring and a new seal. Tighten the plug to 37 ft. lbs. (50 Nm).
32. Check the alignment of the timing marks on the camshaft bearing cap and the camshaft. When they are aligned, the engine should be at TDC of the compression stroke.
33. Install a new elastic gasket into the groove of the timing chain housing cover and then mount the front cover. Tighten the 2 lower screws first. Torque all screws to 15.5 ft. lbs. (21 Nm).
34. Install the protective cover with a new seal. Install the distributor driver so that the groove engages the pin on the camshaft. Tighten the screw to 15.5 ft. lbs. (21 Nm).
35. Installation of the remaining components is in the reverse order of removal.

**The groove (arrow) on the driver (5) must engage the pin in the camshaft—260E, 300E, 300CE, 300SE, 300SEL and 300TE**

**Removing the chain tensioner on the 260E, 300E, 300CE, 300SE, 300SEL and 300TE**

**Matchmark the camshaft sprocket on the 260E, 300E, 300CE, 300SE, 300SEL and 300TE**

**NOTE: When refilling the coolant system on the 300E, 300CE, 300SE, 300TE and 300SEL, always remove the hexhead plug on the left side of the cylinder head and fill the hole with coolant until it overflows. Install the plug and then fill the coolant system. When filling the coolant system on the 190E with 2.6L engine and 260E, open the vent screw approximately 2 turns, start the engine and run at idle.**

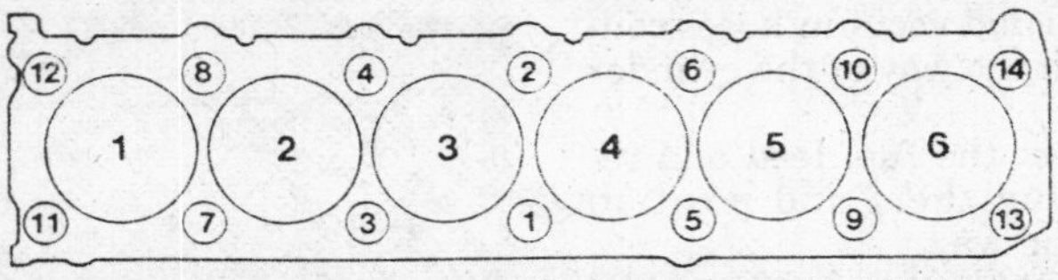


Cylinder head tightening sequence on 260E, 300E, 300CE, 300SE, 300SEL and 300TE

## OVERHAUL

**For all cylinder head procedures, please refer to "Engine Rebuilding" in the Unit Repair Section.**

## Rocker Arms

### REMOVAL & INSTALLATION

#### *Gasoline Engines*

**ALL EXCEPT 190E, 260E, 300E, 300CE, 300SE, 300TE AND 300SEL**

**NOTE: All V8's use hydraulic valve lifters.**

Before removing the rocker arm(s), be sure that they are identified as to their position relative to the camshaft lobe. They should be installed in the same place as they were before disassembly.

Be very careful removing the thrust pieces. They can easily fall into the engine.

1. Disconnect the negative battery cable. Remove the rocker arm cover or covers.
2. Force the clamping spring out of the notch in the top of the rocker arm. Slide it in an outward direction across the ball socket or the rocker arm.

**NOTE: Turn the engine over each time to relieve any load from the rocker arm.**

3. On V8 models, the clamping spring must be forced from the adjusting screw with a small prybar.
4. Force the valve down to remove load from the rocker arm.

**NOTE: Don't depress the spring too far. When the piston is up as it should be, the valve will hit the piston. As the spring goes down, the thrust piece will fall off into the engine.**

5. Lift the rocker arm from the ball pin and remove the rocker arm.

**To install:**

6. Force the rocker arm down until the rocker arm and its ball socket can be installed in the top of the pin.
7. Install the rocker arms.
8. Slide the clamping spring across the ball socket of the rocker arm until it rests in the notch of the rocker arm.
9. On V8 models, engage the clamping spring into the recess of the adjusting screw.
10. Check and, if necessary, adjust the valve clearance.
11. After completion of the adjustment, check to be sure that the clamping springs are correctly seated.
12. Install the rocker arm cover and connect any hoses or lines that were disconnected.
13. Run the engine and check for leaks at the rocker arm cover.

**190E, 260E, 300E, 300CE, 300SE, 300TE AND 300SEL**

**NOTE: The 190E-16 utilizes double overhead camshafts acting directly on valve tappets. There are no rocker arms on this engine.**

Rocker arms on this engine are individually mounted on rocker arm shafts that fit into either side of the camshaft bearing brackets.

1. Disconnect the negative battery cable. Remove the cylinder head cover. The cover is removed with the spark plug wires and distributor cap still connected.
2. Tag each rocker arm and shaft so that they are identified as to their position relative to the camshaft. They should always be install in the same place as they were before disassembly.
3. The rocker arm shaft is held axially and rotationally by a bearing bracket fastening bolt. Remove the bolt on the side of the bearing bracket that allows access to the exposed end of the rocker shaft.
4. Thread a bolt (M8) into the end of the rocker arm shaft and slowly ease the shaft out of the bearing bracket.

**CAUTION**

***Support the rocker arm/lifter assembly while removing the shaft so it will not drop onto the cylinder head.***

**NOTE: Carefully forcing the valve down with a small prybar will remove the load on the hydraulic valve tappet and ease the removal of the shaft. Don't depress the spring too far. When the piston is up as it should be, the valve will hit the piston. As the spring goes down the thrust piece will fall off into the engine.**

5. Replace the bearing bracket bolt and tighten it to 11 ft. lbs. (15 Nm) until ready to replace the rocker shaft.

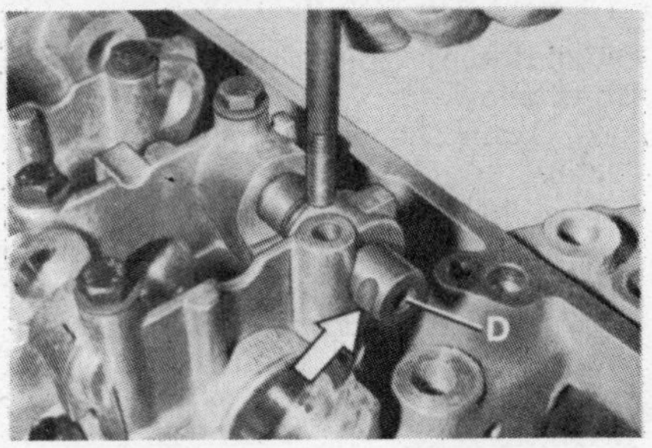


To remove the rocker shaft on the 190E SOHC,thread a bolt into the hole (D). On installation, the dished groove (arrow) must always line up with the mounting bolt shank

**To install:**

6. Position the rocker arm between the 2 bearing brackets and slide the shaft into place.

**NOTE: The circular groove on the end of the rocker shaft must line up with the mounting bolt shank to ensure proper positioning.**

7. Replace the bearing bracket mounting bolt.
8. Repeat Steps 3–7 for all remaining rocker arm/shaft assemblies. Turn the engine over each time to relieve any load from the rocker arm.
9. Replace the cylinder head cover.

#### *Diesel Engines*

**NOTE: The 190D does not use rocker arms. The camshaft acts directly on the hydraulic valve tappet.**

Rocker arms on diesel engines can only be removed as a unit with the respective rocker arm blocks.

1. Disconnect the negative battery cable. Detach the connecting rod for the venturi control unit from the bearing bracket lever and remove the bearing bracket from the rocker arm cover.
2. Remove the air vent line from the rocker arm cover and remove the rocker arm cover.
3. Remove the stretch-bolts from the rocker arm blocks and remove the blocks with the rocker arms. Turn the crankshaft in each case so that the camshaft does not put any load on the rocker arms.

**NOTE: Turn the crankshaft with a socket wrench on the crankshaft pulley bolt. Do not rotate the engine by turning the camshaft sprocket.**

4. Before installing the rocker arms, check the sliding surfaces of the ball cup and rocker arms. Replace any defective parts.

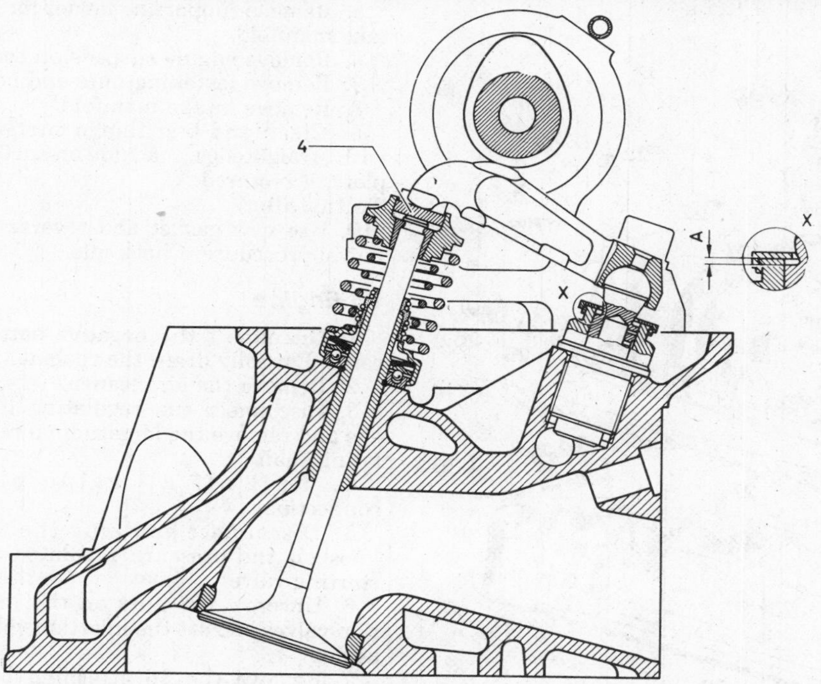


Cutaway of valve train showing hydraulic valve lifter. Dimension "A" is base setting clearance.

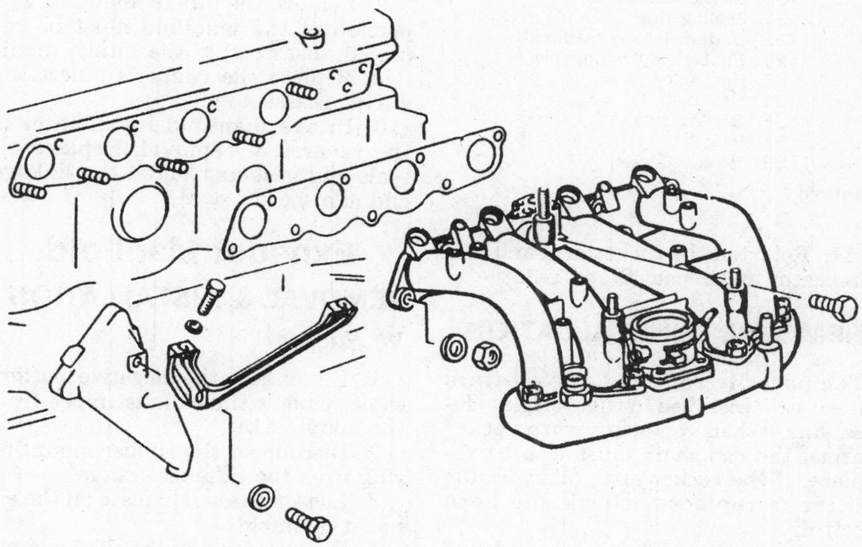

Intake manifold servicing – 190E with 2.3L or 2.3-16 engine

**To install:**

5. Assembly the rocker arm blocks and insert new stretch-bolts.
6. Tighten the stretch-bolts. In each case, position the camshaft so that there is no load on the rocker arms. See the previous NOTE.
7. Check to be sure that the tension clamps have engaged with the notches of the rocker arm blocks.
8. Adjust the valve clearance.
9. Reinstall the rocker arm cover, air vent line, and bearing bracket for the reverse lever. Attach the connecting rod for the venturi control unit to the reversing lever.
10. Make sure that during acceleration, the control cable can move freely without binding.
11. Start the engine and check the rocker arm cover for leaks.

### SELECTIVE THRUST PIECES

| Measured Value (in.) | Thrust Piece Thickness(s) (in.) |
|---|---|
| 0–0.002 | 0.2146/0.2283 |
| 0.002–0.034 | 0.2008 |
| 0.035–0.066 | 0.1870 |
| 0.067–0.099 | 0.1732 |
| 0.099–0.131 | 0.1594 |
| above 0.131 | 0.1457 |

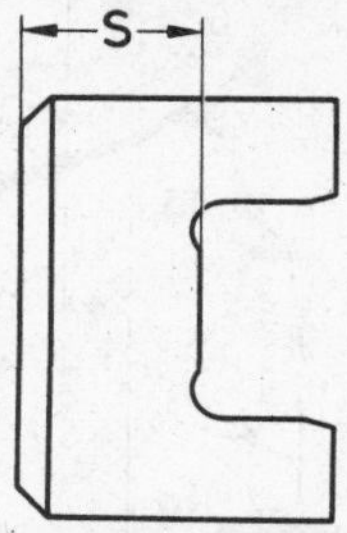


Thrust piece thickness

## Hydraulic Valve Lifters

### *V8 Engines*

Hydraulic valve lifters are used with overhead cams. The rocker arm is always in contact with the cam, reducing noise and eliminating operating clearance.

### CHECKING BASE SETTING

The base setting is the clearance between the upper edge of the cylindrical part of the plunger and the lower edge of the retaining cap (dimension A) when the cam lobe is vertical.

**NOTE: A dial indicator with an extension and a measuring thrust piece (MBNA *100 589 16 63 00), 0.187 in. thick are necessary to perform this adjustment.**

1. Turn the cam lobe to a vertical position, relative to the rocker arm.
2. Attach a dial indicator and tip extension and insert the extension through the bore in the rocker arm onto the head plunger. Preload the dial indicator by 0.08 in. and zero the instrument.
3. Depress the valve with a valve spring compressor. The lift on the dial indicator should be 0.028–0.075 in.
4. If the lift is excessive, the base setting can be changed by installing a new thrust piece.
5. Remove the dial indicator.
6. Remove the rocker arm.
7. Remove the thrust piece and insert the measuring disc.

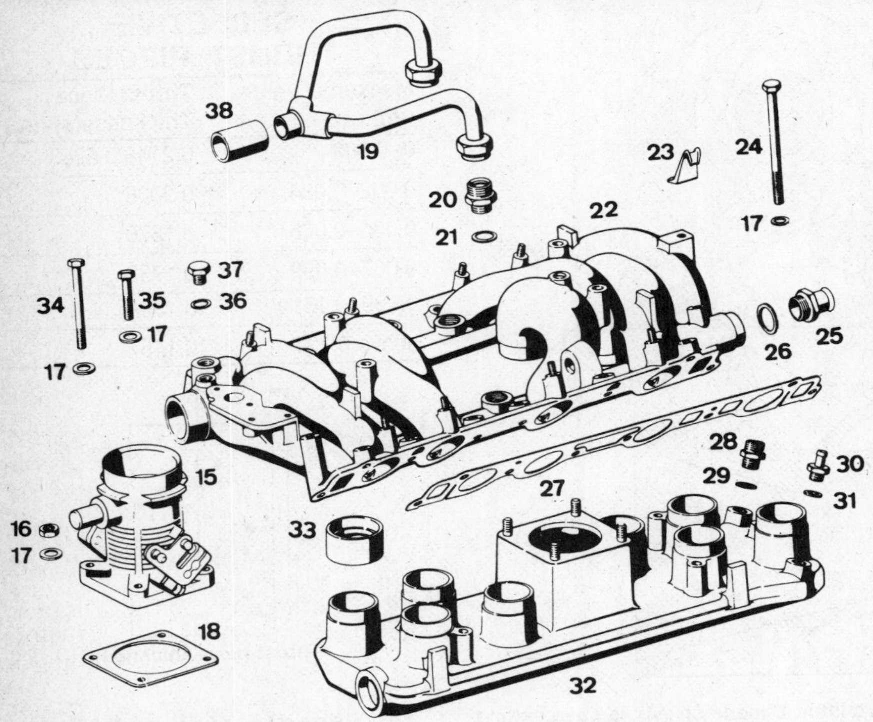

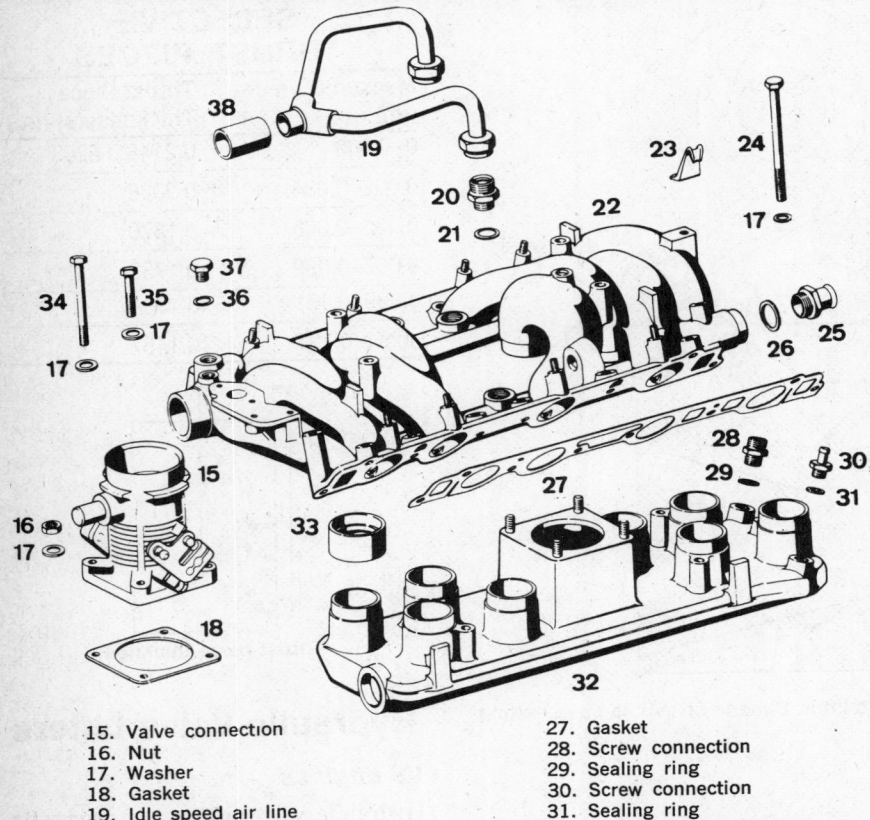

15. Valve connection
16. Nut
17. Washer
18. Gasket
19. Idle speed air line
20. Screw connection
21. Sealing ring
22. Upper Intake manifold
23. Holder
24. Hex bolt
25. Connection
26. Sealing ring
27. Gasket
28. Screw connection
29. Sealing ring
30. Screw connection
31. Sealing ring
32. Bottom intake manifold
33. Rubber connecting piece
35. Hex bolt
34. Hex bolt
36. Sealing ring
37. Plug
38. Hose

V8 intake manifold

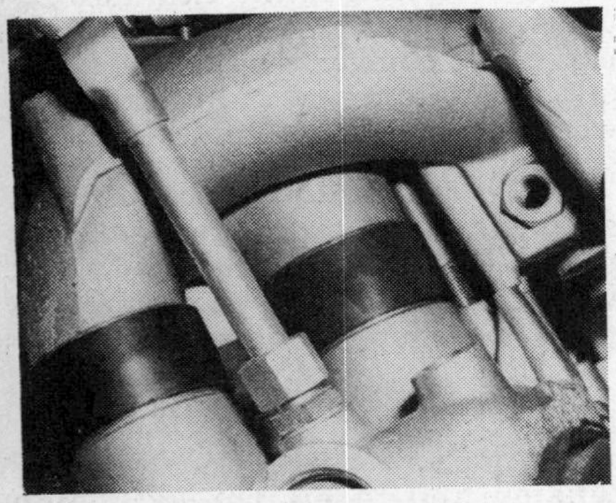

**Replace the rubber connecting pieces on the intake manifold, anytime the manifold is removed.**

8. Install the rocker arm and repeat Steps 1–3.
9. Select a thrust piece according to the table. If the measured valve was 0–0.002 in. and the 0.2146 in. thrust piece will not give the proper base setting, use the 0.2283 in. thrust piece.
10. Remove the dial indicator and the rocker arm. Install the selected thrust piece.
11. Reinstall the rocker arm and dial indicator and repeat Steps 1–3.

### REMOVAL & INSTALLATION

Temporarily removed valve lifters must be reinstalled in their original locations. When replacing worn rocker arms, the camshaft must also be replace. If the rocker arm, or hydraulic lifter is replaced, check the base setting.

Remove the rocker arm and unscrew the valve lifter with a 24mm socket.

## Intake Manifold

### REMOVAL & INSTALLATION

#### *190E with 2.3L Engine*

1. Disconnect the negative battery cable. Remove mixture control unit with air guide housing.
2. Disconnect fuel lines.
3. Remove holder for starter cable.
4. Remove electric lines and vacuum lines.
5. Remove supporting holder for intake manifold.
6. Remove engine suspension eye.
7. Remove fastening nuts and bolt.
8. Remove intake manifold.
9. Clean and test flange surfaces with straightedge, machine on surface plate, if required.

**To install:**

10. Use new gasket and reverse removal procedure. Check idle.

#### *V8 Engine*

1. Disconnect the negative battery cable. Partially drain the coolant.
2. Remove the air cleaner.
3. Disconnect the regulating linkage and remove the longitudinal regulating shaft.
4. Pull off all cable plug connections.
5. Disconnect and plug the fuel lines on the pressure regulator and starting valve.
6. Unscrew the nuts on the injection valves and set the injection valves aside.
7. Remove the 16 attaching bolts from the intake manifold.
8. Loosen the hose clip on the thermostat housing hose and disconnect the hose.
9. Remove the intake manifold. If a portion of the manifold must be replaced, disassembly the intake manifold. Replace the rubber connections during reassembly.
10. Intake manifold installation is the reverse of removal. Replace all seals and gaskets. Adjust the linkage and idle speed.

## Exhaust Manifold

### REMOVAL & INSTALLATION

#### *V8 Engine*

1. Disconnect the negative battery cable. Unbolt the exhaust pipes from the manifolds.
2. Disconnect the rubber mounting ring from the exhaust system.
3. Loosen the shield plate on the exhaust manifold.
4. When removing the lift hand exhaust manifold, remove the shield plate for the engine mount together with the engine damper.
5. Unbolt the manifold from the engine.
6. Pull the manifold off of the mounting.
7. Installation is the reverse of removal.

## Turbocharger

### REMOVAL & INSTALLATION

1. Disconnect the negative battery

1. Mounting bracket
2. Intermediate flange
3. Turbocharger

**Remove the mounting nuts (arrow) to remove the turbocharger**

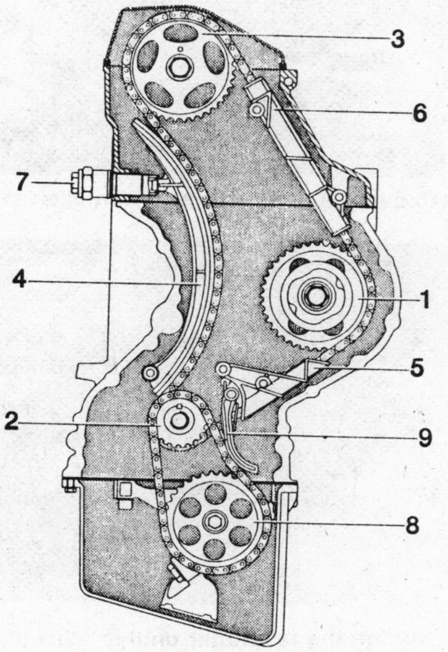


1. Injection timing advance mechanism
2. Crankshaft sprocket
3. Camshaft sprocket
4. Tensioning rail
5. Slide rail
6. Slide rail
7. Chain tensioner
8. Oil pump drive gear
9. Tensioning lever, chain, oil pump drive

**Timing chain assembly—1984–85 190D**

cable. Remove the air filter.

2. Disconnect the electrical cable from the temperature switch.

3. Loosen the lower hose clamp on the air duct that connects the air filter with the compressor housing.

4. Remove the vacuum line and crankcase breather pipe.

5. Remove the air filter and air intake duct.

6. Disconnect the oil line at the turbocharger.

7. Remove the air filter mounting bracket.

8. Disconnect the turbocharger at the exhaust flange.

9. Disconnect and remove the pipe bracket on the automatic transmission.

10. Push the exhaust pipe rearward.

11. Remove the mounting bracket at the intermediate flange.

12. Unbolt and remove the turbocharger.

13. Remove the intermediate flange and oil return line at the turbocharger.

14. Installation is the reverse of removal. Before installing the turbocharger, install the oil return line and intermediate flange. Install the flange gasket between the turbocharger and exhaust manifold with the reinforcing bead toward the exhaust manifold. Use only heat proof nuts and bolts and fill a new turbocharger with 1/4 pint of engine oil through the engine oil supply bore before operating.

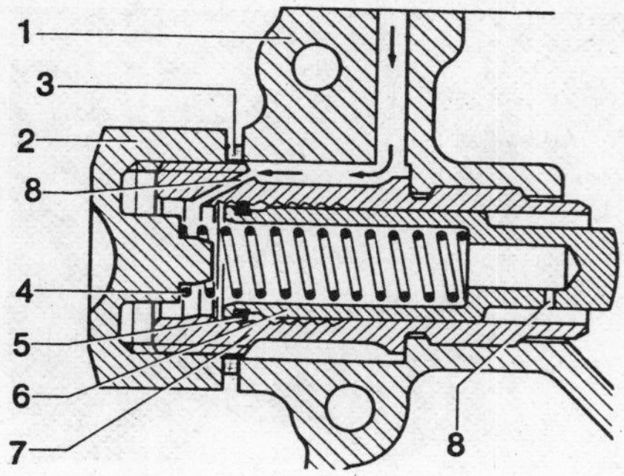


1. Crankcase
2. Cap nut
3. Seal ring
4. Compression
5. Detent spring
6. Thrust pin
7. Chain tensioner housing
8. Supply hole 1.1 mm dia.
9. Orifice 1.2 mm dia.

**Cross section of the timing chain tensioner—190E (190D similar)**

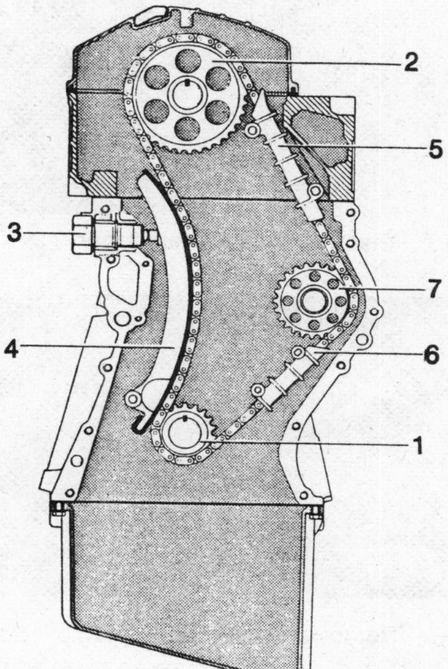


1. Crankshaft sprocket
2. Camshaft sprocket
3. Chain tensioner
4. Tensioning rail
5. Slide rail
6. Slide rail
7. Idler gear

**Timing chain assembly—190E SOHC**

## TROUBLESHOOTING

**For more information on turbocharging, please refer to "Turbocharging" in the Unit Repair section.**

# Timing Chain Tensioner

## FILLING

### *190D and 1987 300D, 300TD and 300SDL*

1. Place chain tensioner with thrust pin in downward direction in engine oil SAE 10 up to above collar on hex head.

2. Slowly press thrust pin 7–10 times up to stop by means of a press or an upright drill press.

3. Upon filling, the chain tensioner should permit compressing very slowly only, uniformly and at considerable force.

4. To prevent peak pressures of chain tensioner against tensioning rail, a modified valve disk will be installed in chain tensioner.

**NOTE: This chain tensioner can also be installed in vehicles manufactured at an earlier date.**

## REMOVAL & INSTALLATION

### *4 and 5 Cylinder Engines*

There are 2 kinds of timing chain tensioners. One uses an O-ring seal and the other a flat gasket. Do not install a flat gasket on a tensioner meant to be use with an O-ring.

Chain tensioners should be replaced as a unit if defective.

1. Disconnect the negative battery cable. Drain the coolant. If the car has air conditioning, disconnect the compressor and mounting bracket and lay it aside. Do not disconnect the refrigerant lines. On diesel engines, drain the coolant from the block.

2. Remove the thermostat housing.

3. Loosen and remove the chain tensioner. Be careful of loose O-rings. On the 190, you must first remove the tensioner capnut and the tension spring. The tensioner body can then be unscrewed with an Allen wrench.

4. Check the O-rings or gasket and replace if necessary.

5. To fill the chain tensioner, place the tensioner (pressure bolt down) in a container of SAE 10 engine oil, at least up to the flat flange. Using a drill press, depress the pressure bolt slowly, about 7–10 times. Be sure this is done slowly and uniformly.

The inside bolt (arrow) on the V8 chain tensioner can only be reached by inserting a long, straight allen key underneath the exhaust manifold.

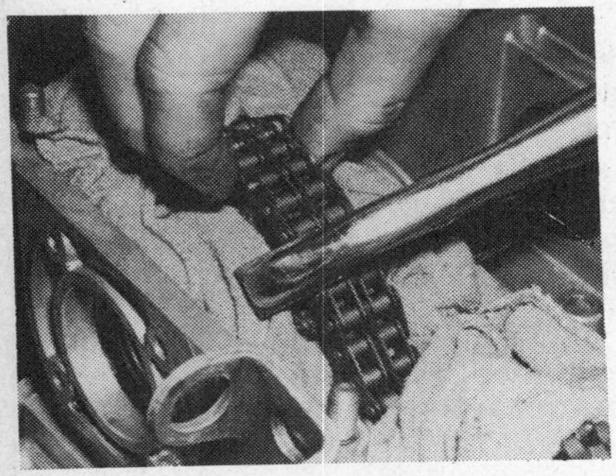

Clamp the chain to the gear and cover the opening with rags

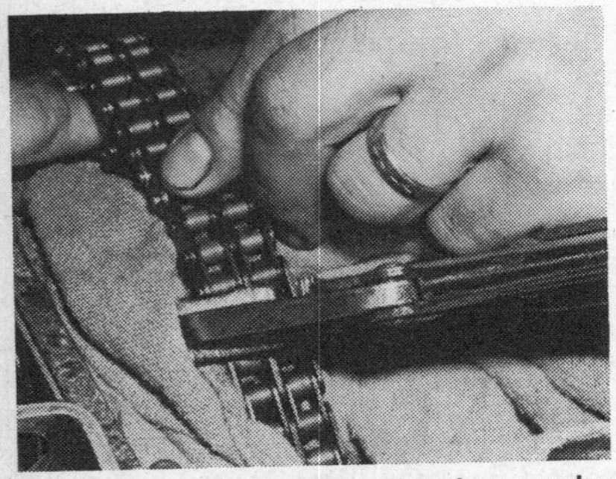

Clamp the chain again, cover the opening and remove the old chain from the master link. Connect both ends of the new chain.

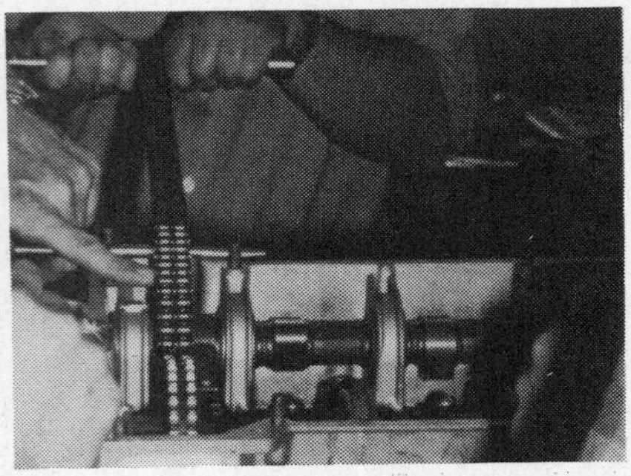

Crank the engine by hand until the new chain has come all the way through the engine. Be sure to keep tension on chain.

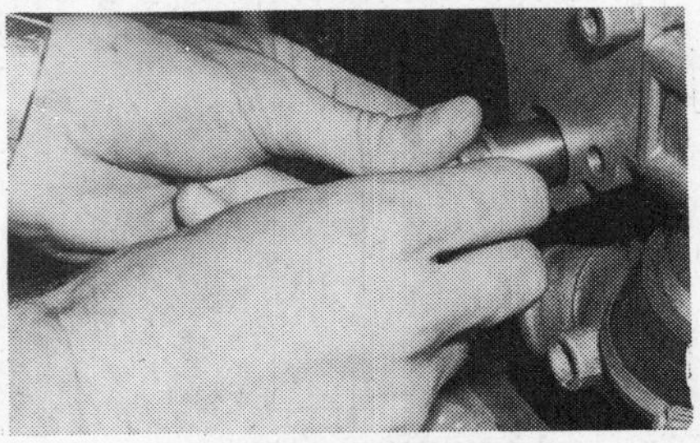

Install the chain tensioner

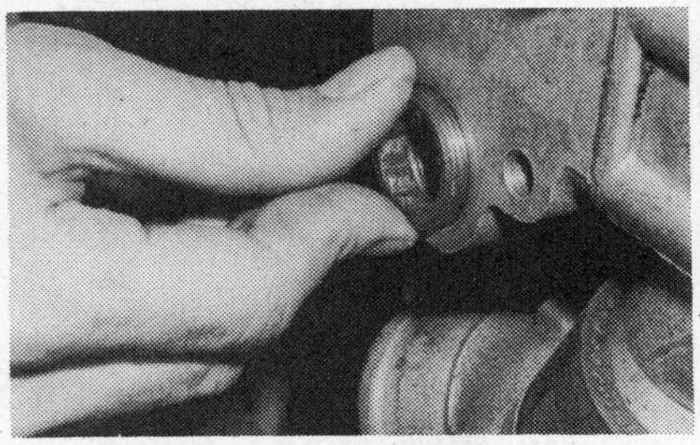

Remove the threaded plug.

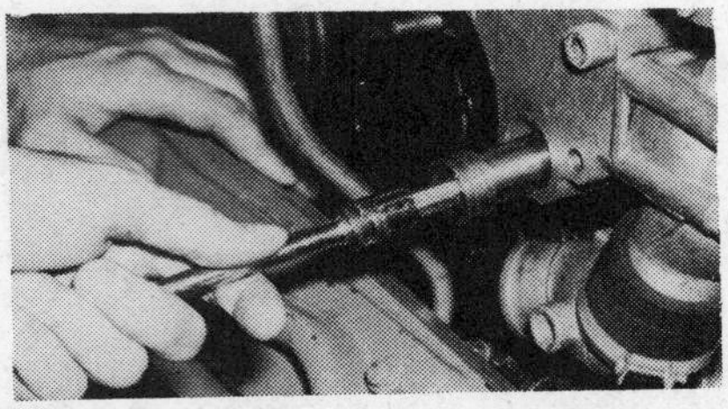

Remove the chain tensioner with a 10 mm allen key

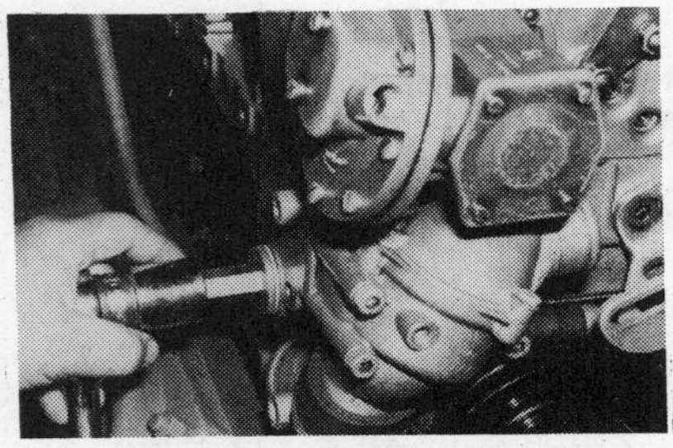

Remove the plug with a 17 mm allen key

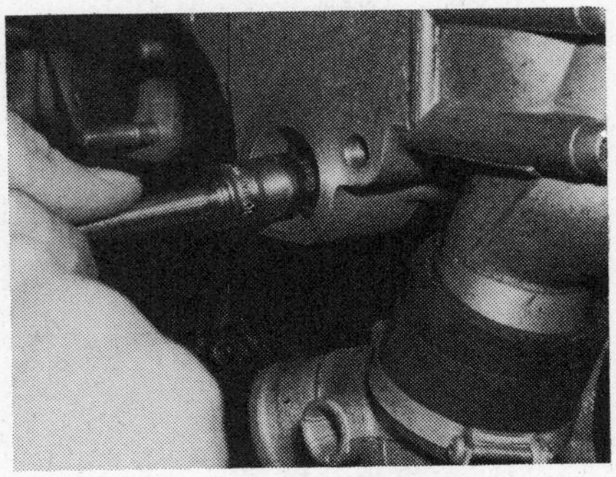

Tighten the tensioner until it "clicks"

6. Install the chain tensioner. Tighten the bolts evenly. Tighten the capnut on the 190 to 51 ft. lbs. (70 Nm).

### *V8 Engines*

The chain tensioner is connected to the engine oil circuit. Bleeding occurs once oil pressure has been established and the tensioner is filling with oil.

A venting hole has been installed in the tensioner to prevent oil foaming. If there is a lot of timing chain noise, use this type of tensioner, which is identified by a white paint dot on the cap.

Service procedures for tensioners and rails on the different V8's are similar. Arrangement and shape and size of parts however, is slightly different.

1. Disconnect the negative battery cable. On California models, disconnect the line from the tensioner.
2. Remove the attaching bolts and remove the tensioner. The inside bolts will probably require a long, straight 6mm Allen key to bypass the exhaust manifold. It is a tight fit.
3. Place the tensioner vertically in a container of engine oil. Operate the pressure bolt to fill the tensioner. After filling, it should permit compression very slowly under considerable force. If not, replace the tensioner with a new unit.
4. Install the tensioner and tighten the bolts evenly.

## Timing Chain

### REPLACEMENT

#### *All Models Except 190D and 1987 300D and 300SDL*

An endless timing chain is used on production engines, buy a split chain with a connecting link is used for service. The endless chain can be separated with a "chain breaker." Only one master link (connecting link) should be used on a chain.

1. Disconnect the negative battery cable. Remove the spark plugs.
2. Remove the valve cover(s).
3. Clamp the chain to the camshaft gear and cover the opening of the timing chain case with rags. On 6 cylinder and V8 engines, remove the rocker arms from the right hand camshaft.
4. Separate the chain with a chain breaker.

**To install:**

5. Attach a new timing chain to the old chain with a master link.
6. Using a socket wrench on the

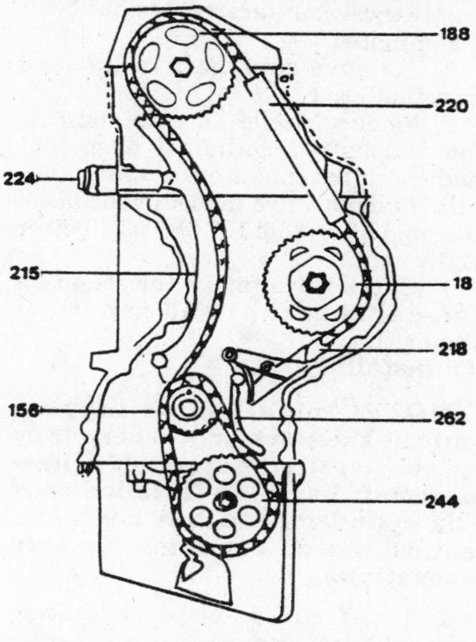


Timing chain—190D, 300D and 300SDL

crankshaft. slowly rotate the engine in the direction of normal rotation. Simultaneously, pull the old chain through until the master link is uppermost on the camshaft sprocket. Be sure to keep tension on the chain throughout this procedure.

7. Disconnect the old timing chain and connect the ends of the new chain with the master link. Insert the new connecting link from the rear so that the lockwashers can be seen from the front.

8. Rotate the engine until the timing marks align. Check the valve timing. Once the new chain is assembled, rotate the engine (by hand) through a least one complete revolution to be sure everything is OK.

#### *190D and 1987 300D, 300TD and 300SDL*

1. Disconnect the negative battery cable. Remove cylinder head cover.
2. Remove injection nozzles.
3. Remove chain tensioner.
4. Remove fan and fan cover.
5. Connect new timing chain with connecting link to old timing chain.
6. Slowly rotate crankshaft in rotating direction of engine, while simultaneously pulling up the old timing chain until the connecting link comes to rest against uppermost point of camshaft timing gear.

**NOTE: Timing chain should remain in mesh while rotating camshaft and crankshaft timing gears.**

7. Take off old timing chain and connect ends of new timing chain with connecting link. For this purpose, secure chain ends with wire on camshaft timing gear.

**To install:**

**NOTE: Use only a rivet-type connecting link. Do not use connecting link that use a retaining spring.**

8. Insert connecting link from the rear into timing chain.
9. Put separately enclosed outer flange of connecting link (with punched in IWIS identification) into pressing-on tool. The outer flange is held magnetically.
10. Place pressing-on tool on connecting link and press on flange up to stop, while holding pressing-on tool on vertical level.
11. Rearrange plunger of assembly tool in such a manner that the notch is pointing forward.
12. Hold assembly tool on handle and rivet chain bolts individually. Tightening torque of spindle approximately 22–26 ft. lbs. (30–35 Nm).
13. Check chain bolt rivet and rivet again, if required.
14. Install chain tensioner.
15. Rotate crankshaft and check adjusting mark at TDC position of engine.

**NOTE: If the adjusting mark is wrong, check timing of camshaft and begin of delivery of injection pump.**

16. Install cylinder head cover and tighten to 7.5 ft. lbs. (10 Nm).
17. Install fan and fan cover.

## Camshaft

### REMOVAL & INSTALLATION

#### *4 and 5 Cylinder Engines*

#### EXCEPT 190D AND 190E

When the camshaft is replaced, be sure the rocker arms are also replaced.

1. Disconnect the negative battery cable. Remove the valve cover.
2. Remove the chain tensioner.
3. Remove the rocker arms.
4. Set the crankshaft at TDC for the No. 1 cylinder and be sure that the camshaft timing marks are aligned.
5. Hold the camshaft and loosen the cam gear bolt. Remove the cam gear and wire it securely so that the chain does not lose tension nor slip down into the chain case.
6. Remove the camshaft.
7. Installation is the reverse of removal. Be sure to check that the valve timing marks align when the No. 1 cylinder is at TDC. Check the valve clearance.

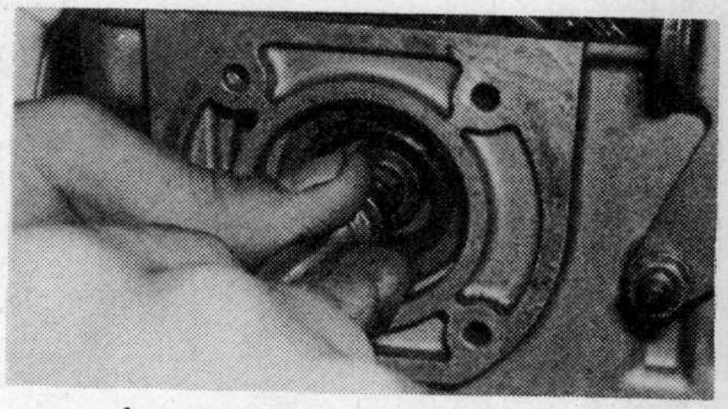

Loosen the camshaft bolts.

On the 190E SOHC, the mark (arrow) on the camshaft collar (B) must always be aligned

Remove the vacuum pump and camshaft cover.

#### 190E MODELS

**NOTE: On the 190E it is always a good idea to replace the rocker arms and shafts whenever the camshaft is replaced.**

1. Disconnect the negative battery cable. Remove the valve cover.
2. Remove the chain tensioner.
3. Remove the rocker arms and shafts.
4. Set the crankshaft at TDC for the No. 1 piston and make sure that the timing marks on the camshaft are in alignment.
5. Using a 24mm open-end wrench, hold the rear of the camshaft (flats are provided) and then loosen and remove the camshaft retaining bolt. Carefully slide the gear and chain off the shaft and wire them securely so they won't slip down into the case.

Using a puller, remove the pins from the slide rails and remove the slide rails.

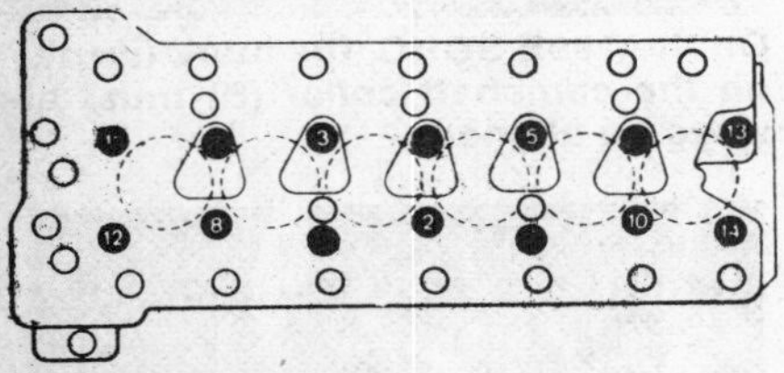

○ Unscrew M 8 bolts

① Unscrew cylinder head bolts in reverse order

● Do not loosen bolts

**Bolts to be removed during the camshaft housing removal**

**NOTE: Be careful not to lose the Woodruff key while removing the gear.**

6. The camshaft is secured on the cylinder head by means of the bearing caps. Remove them and keep them in their proper order. Each cap is marked by a number punched into its side; this number must match the number cast into the cylinder head.

**CAUTION**

***When removing the bearing caps on the 190D, always loosen the center 2 first and then move on to the outer ones.***

7. Remove the camshaft.
8. Installation is in the reverse order of removal. Always make sure that the No. 1 cylinder is at TDC and all timing marks are aligned. Tighten the bearing caps to 15 ft. lbs. (21 Nm). The camshaft gear retaining bolt should be tightened to 58 ft. lbs. (80 Nm).

**NOTE: Be certain not to forget the Woodruff key.**

**NOTE: The camshaft on the 1985–90 190D utilizes a new lobe design, allowing the valves to close softer. The code number is "06" and it can be retrofitted to 1984 engines. The timing has not changed.**

### 190D AND 1987 300D, 300TD AND 300SDL

1. Disconnect the negative battery cable. Remove cylinder head cover.
2. Set crankshaft to TDC of No.1 cylinder.

**NOTE: Do not rotate the engine on the fastening screw of the camshaft timing gear. Do not rotate engine in reverse.**

3. Remove chain tensioner.
4. Mark camshaft timing gear and timing chain in relation to each other.
5. Remove camshaft timing gear. To loosen screws, apply counterhold on camshaft by means of a mandrel.
6. On vehicles with level control, remove pressure oil pump and put aside with lines connected.
7. To prevent damage to camshafts, be sure to apply the following sequence during assembly:
   a. 190D with 2.2L engine – Remove both screws on camshaft bearing 1, 3 and 5. Loosen both screws on camshaft bearing 2 and 4 alternately and in steps until counterpressure has been eliminated.
   b. 190 with 2.5L engine – Remove both screws on camshaft bearing 1, 2, 3 and 6. Loosen both screws on camshaft bearing 4 and 5 alternately and in steps only until counterpressure has been eliminated.
   c. 1987 300D, 300TD and 300SDL – Remove both screws on camshaft bearing 1, 5, 6 and 7. Loosen both screws for camshaft bearing 2, 3, and 4 alternately and in steps only until counterpressure has been eliminated.
8. Remove camshaft in upward direction.
9. Remove circlip for axial locating for camshaft longitudinal alignment and check for condition.
10. Pull out valve tappet by means of solenoid lifter, tool 102 589 03 40 00 or equivalent.
11. Check valve tappet for condition (visual checkup) and renew, if required.

**To install:**

**NOTE: Install valve tappets only at the same spot where they were installed before. If a new camshaft has been installed or if the cylinder head has been machined, check camshaft for easy operation.**

12. Insert circlip for axial locating into cylinder head.
13. Lubricate camshaft and place into cylinder head (without valve tappet).
14. Tighten camshaft bearing caps uniformly to 18.5 ft. lbs. (25 Nm). Pay attention to identification of bearing caps.
15. When checking for easy operation, the camshaft can be rotated by means of a hex socket screw M 10 × 30, which is screwed in through camshaft timing gear instead of fastening screw. If the camshaft can be rotated with effort only, proceed as follows:
   a. Loosen camshaft bearing caps individually. Then turn camshaft if required.
   b. Repeat until tight bearing point has been found.
   c. Check camshaft for runout.
16. Lubricate valve tappets and insert. Pay attention to sequence.
17. Lubricate camshaft and place into cylinder head in such a manner that the TDC mark is vertical.
18. Install camshaft bearing caps.

**NOTE: Screw in camshaft bearing screws 2 and 4 on 190D with 2.2L engine, 4 and 5 on 190D with 2.5L engine, 2, 3, and 4 on 1987 300D, 300TD and 300SDL engine in steps only and alternately. The remaining camshaft bearing caps can then be installed at will. Pay attention to tightening torques.**

19. Mount camshaft timing gear. Pay attention to color marks. Tighten fastening screw for camshaft timing gear to 48 ft. lbs. (65 Nm). For this purpose, apply counterhold to camshaft timing gear by means of a steel pin or suitable tool.
20. Install chain tensioner.
21. On vehicles with level control, mount pressure oil pump and driver.

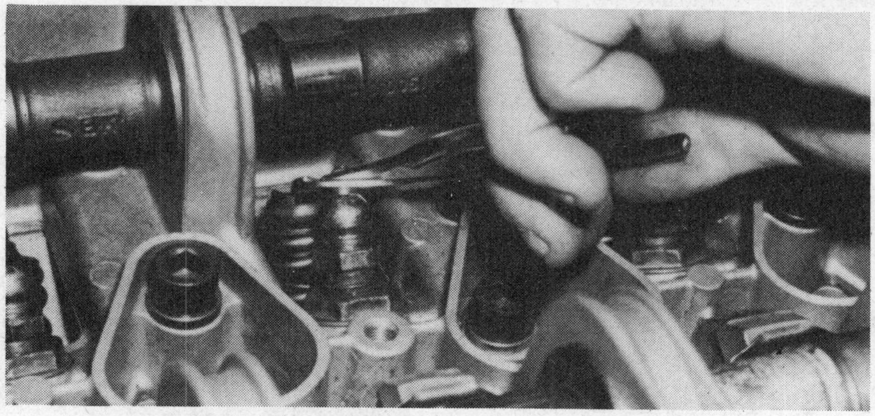

Remove the rocker arm springs, rocker arms and thrust pieces.

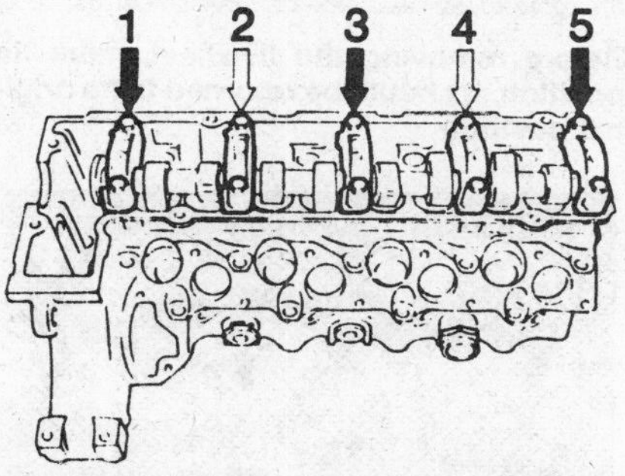


**Camshaft bearing cap servicing sequence – 190D with 2.2L engine**

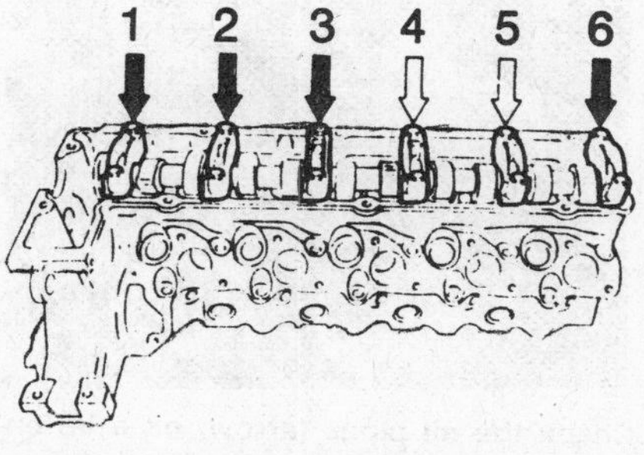


**Camshaft bearing cap servicing sequence – 190D with 2.5L or 2.5L Turbo engine**

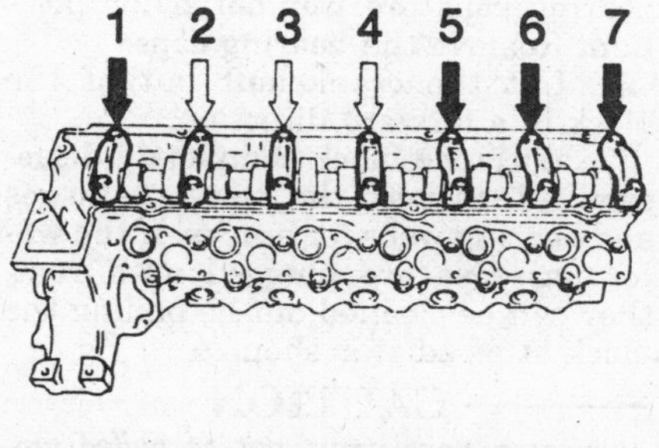


**Camshaft bearing cap servicing sequence – 300D and 300SDL**

22. Check engine for TDC marks.
23. Mount cylinder head cover.
24. Run engine, check for leaks.

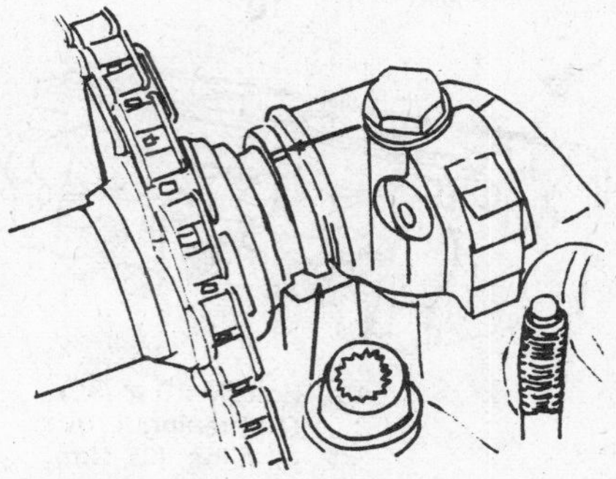

**Camshaft alignment marks – 190D, 300D and 300SDL**

### *V8 Engines*

Experience shows that the right hand camshaft is always the first one to require replacement. When the V8 camshaft is removed, keep the pedestals with the camshaft. In particular, make sure that the 2 left hand rear cam pedestals are not swapped. The result will be no oil pressure. Always replace the oil gallery pipe with the camshaft.

**NOTE: Arrangement of parts on the 3.8L and 5.0L V8 is slightly different compared to other V8 engines. Service procedures are the same.**

1. Disconnect the negative battery cable. Remove the valve cover.
2. Remove the tensioning springs and rocker arms.
3. Using a wrench on the crankshaft pulley, crank the engine around until the No. 1 piston is at TDC on the compression stroke. Using some stiff wire, hang the camshaft gear so that the chain will not slip off the gears.
4. Remove the camshaft gear.
5. Unbolt the camshaft, camshaft bearing pedestals and the oil pipe. Note the angle of the bolts that do not hold the head to the block.
6. Install the bearing pedestals and camshaft. On the left hand camshaft, the outer bolt on the rear bearing must be inserted prior to installing the bearings or it will not clear the power brake until. Tighten the bolts from the inside out. Torque camshaft bearing cap bolts to 37 ft. lbs. (50 Nm). When finished tightening, the camshaft should rotate freely.
7. Check the oil pipes for obstructions and replace if necessary.
8. When install the oil pipes, also check the 3 inner connecting pipes.
9. Install the compensating washer so that the keyway below the notch slides over the Woodruff key of the camshaft.
10. Install the rocker arms and tensioning springs.
11. Adjust the valve clearance and check the valve timing.

## Engine Overhaul

### DISASSEMBLY

**NOTE: This procedure is general and intended to apply to all Mercedes-Benz engines. It is suggested, however, that you be entirely familiar with Mercedes-Benz engines and be equipped with the numerous special tools before attempting an engine rebuild.**

1. Remove the engine and support it on an engine stand or other suitable support.
2. Set the engine at TDC and matchmark the timing chain and timing gear(s). Remove the cylinder head(s) and gasket(s).
3. Remove the oil pan bolts and the pan and, on most models, the lower crankcase section.
4. Remove the oil pump.
5. Matchmark the connecting rod bearing caps to identify the proper cylinder for reassembly. Matchmark the sides of the connecting rod and side of the bearing cap for proper alignment. Pistons should bear an arrow indicating the front. If not, mark the front of the piston with an arrow using a magic marker. Also identify pistons as to cylinder so they may be replaced in their original location.
6. Remove the connecting rod nuts, bearing caps and lower bearing shells.
7. Place small pieces of plastic tubing on the rod bolts to prevent crankshaft damage.
8. Inspect the crankshaft journals for nicks and roughness and measure diameters.
9. Turn the engine and ream the ridge from the top of the cylinders to remove all carbon deposits.
10. Using a hammer handle or other piece of hardwood, gently tap the pistons and connecting rods out from the bottom.

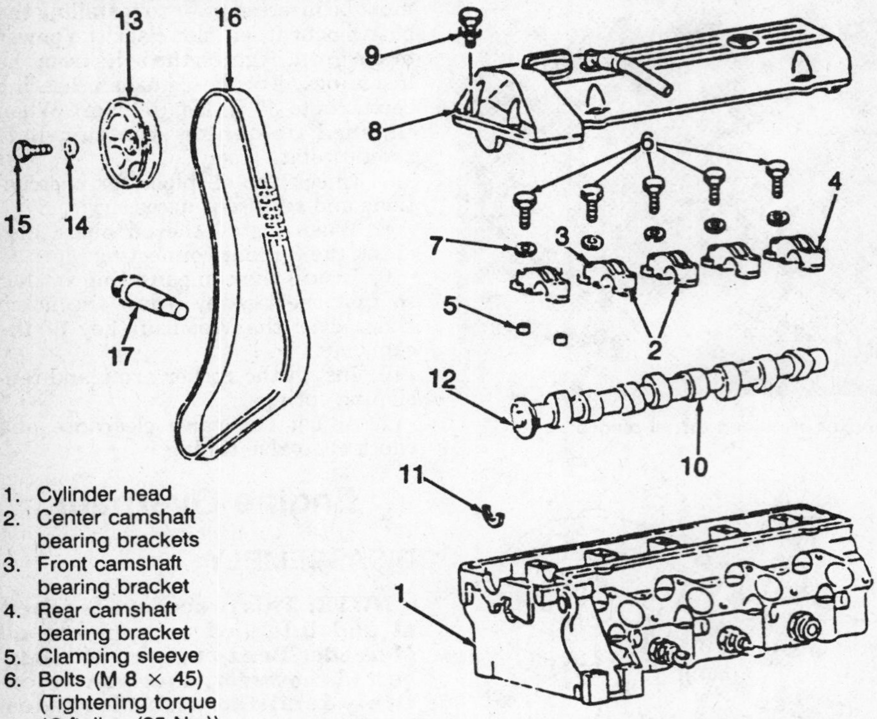

1. Cylinder head
2. Center camshaft bearing brackets
3. Front camshaft bearing bracket
4. Rear camshaft bearing bracket
5. Clamping sleeve
6. Bolts (M 8 × 45) (Tightening torque 19 ft. lbs. (25 Nm))
7. Washer B 8,4
8. Cylinder head cover
9. Bolts (M 6 × 30) (Tightening torque 7 ft. lbs. (10 Nm)
10. Camshaft
11. Lock washer
12. Cylinder pin
13. Camshaft sprocket
14. Washer B 10
15. Bolt (M 10 × 50) (Tightening torque 48 ft lbs. (65 Nm))
16. Timing chain
17. Chain tensioner

**Camshaft servicing—190D, 300D and 300SDL**

**Before removing the flywheel, mark its position. It should be returned to its original position**

**Check the oil pipes (arrow) on a V8 engine.**

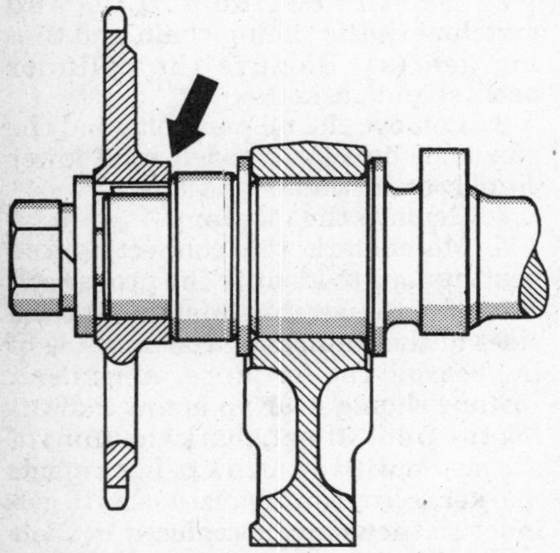

**The camshaft flange (arrow) on 3.8 liter V-8's faces rearward**

11. The cylinder bores can be inspected at this time for taper and general wear.

12. Check the pistons for proper size and inspect the ring grooves. If any rings are cracked, it is almost certain that the grooves are no longer true, because broken rings work up and down. It is best to replace any such worn pistons.

13. The pistons, pins and connecting rods are marked with a color dot assembly code. Only parts having the same color may be used together.

14. If the cylinders are bored, make sure the machinist has the pistons before hand, cylinder bore sizes are nominal, and the pistons must be individually fitted to the block. Maximum piston weight deviation in any one engine is 4 grams.

15. The flywheel and crankshaft are balanced together as a unit. Matchmark the location of the flywheel relative to the crankshaft, then remove the flywheels and can be identified by their hourglass shape. Once used, they should be discarded and replaced at assembly.

16. Remove the water pump, alternator, and fuel pump, if not done previously.

17. Unbolt and remove the vibration damper and crankshaft pulley. On certain models, it is necessary to clamp the vibration damper with C-clamps before removing the bolts. Otherwise, the vibration damper will come apart.

18. Remove the timing chain tensioner and chain cover.

19. Matchmark the position of the timing chain on the timing gear of the crankshaft.

20. Matchmark the main bearing caps for number and position in the block. It is important that they are installed in their original positions. Most bearing caps are numbered for position. Remove the bearing caps.

21. Lift the crankshaft out of the block in a forward direction.

22. With the block completely disassembled, inspect the water passages and bearing webs for cracks. If the water passages are plugged with rust, they can be cleaned out be boiling the block at a radiator shop.

**CAUTION**

***Aluminum parts must not be boiled out. They will be eroded by chemicals.***

23. Measure piston ring end gap by sliding a new ring into the bore and measuring. Measure the gap at the top, bottom, and midpoint of piston

1. Screw
2. Cup washers
3. Screw
4. Pulley
6. Vibration damper
7. Hub
8. Crankshaft sprocket
9. Crankshaft
10. Woodruff key
11. Crankshaft bearing shell in cylinder crankcase
12. Crankshaft bearing shell in bearing cap

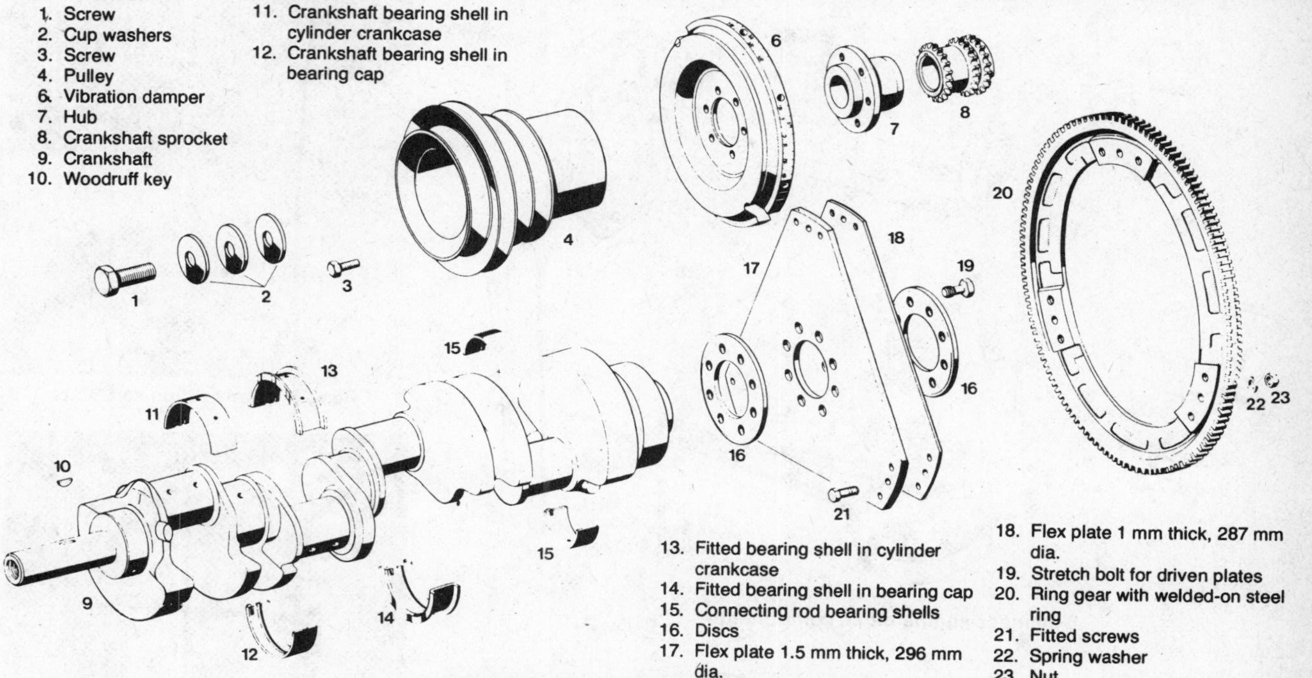

13. Fitted bearing shell in cylinder crankcase
14. Fitted bearing shell in bearing cap
15. Connecting rod bearing shells
16. Discs
17. Flex plate 1.5 mm thick, 296 mm dia.
18. Flex plate 1 mm thick, 287 mm dia.
19. Stretch bolt for driven plates
20. Ring gear with welded-on steel ring
21. Fitted screws
22. Spring washer
23. Nut

**Exploded view of the V8 crankshaft assembly**

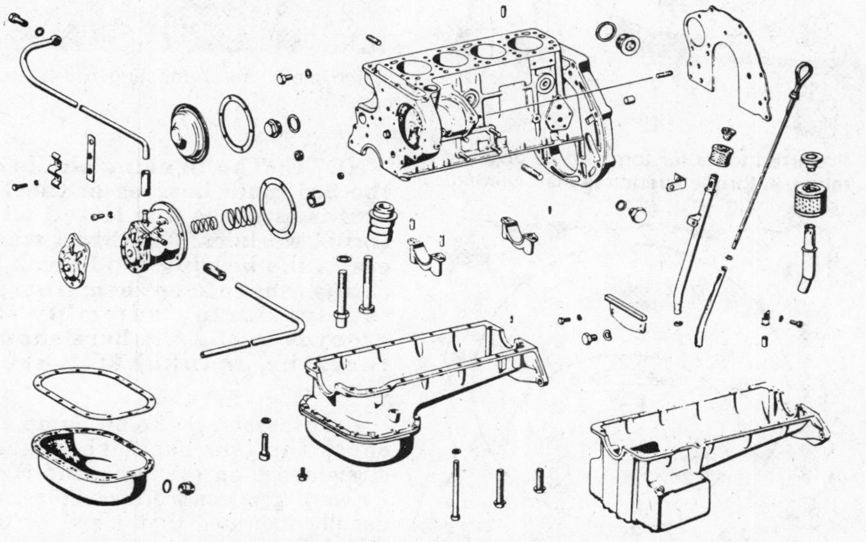

**4-cylinder diesel engine cylinder block components (5-cylinder 300D is similar)**

travel and correct by filling or grinding the ring ends.

24. To check bearing clearances, use Plastigage® inserted between the bearing and the crankshaft journal. Blow out all crankshaft oil passages before measuring; torque the bolts to specification. Plastigage® is a thin plastic strip that is crushed by the bearing end cap and spreads out an amount in proportion to clearance. After torqueing the bearing cap, remove the cap and compare the width of the Plastigage® with the scale.

**NOTE: Do not rotate the crankshaft. Bearing shells of various thicknesses are available and should be used to correct clearance; it may be necessary to machine the crankshaft journals undersize to obtain the proper oil clearance.**

**CAUTION**

*Use a shim stock between bearings and caps to decrease clearance is not a good practice.*

25. Check crankshaft end-play using a feeler gauge.

26. When installing new piston rings, ring grooves must be cleaned out, preferably using a special groove cleaner, although a broken ring will work as well. After installing the ring, check ring side clearance.

## ASSEMBLY

1. Assemble the engine using all new gaskets and seals and make sure all parts are properly lubricated. Bearing shells and cylinder walls must be lubricated with engine oil before assembly. Make sure no metal clips remain in the cylinder bores or crankcase.

2. To install pistons and rods, turn the engine right side up and insert the rods into the cylinders. Clamp the rings to the piston, with their gaps equally spaced around the circumference, using a piston ring compressor. Gently tap the piston into the bore, using a hammer handle or similar hard wood, making sure the rings clear the edge.

**NOTE: Pistons on the 3.8L and 5.0L V8 are installed with the arrow facing in the driving direction.**

3. Torque the connecting rod bearing and main bearing caps to specification and try to turn the crankshaft by hand. It should turn with moderate resistance, not spin freely or be locked up. Main bearing caps use standard

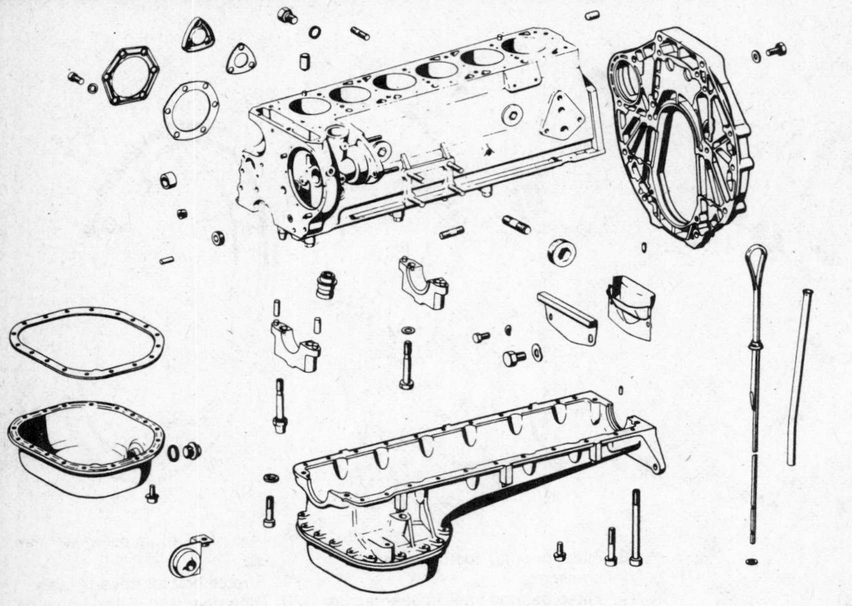

6-cylinder engine block components

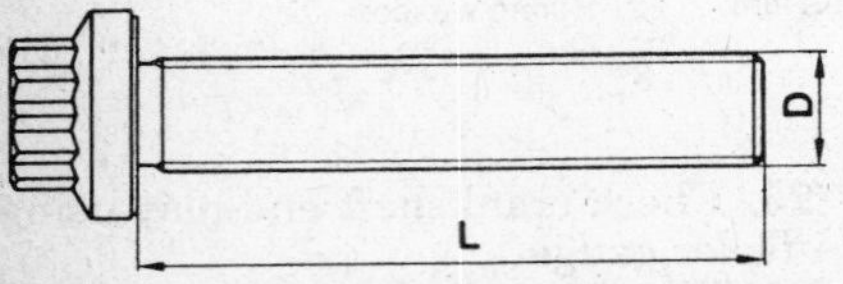


**Measure the distance (L) to determine the main bearing cap bolt "stretch" on the 1985–88 190D**

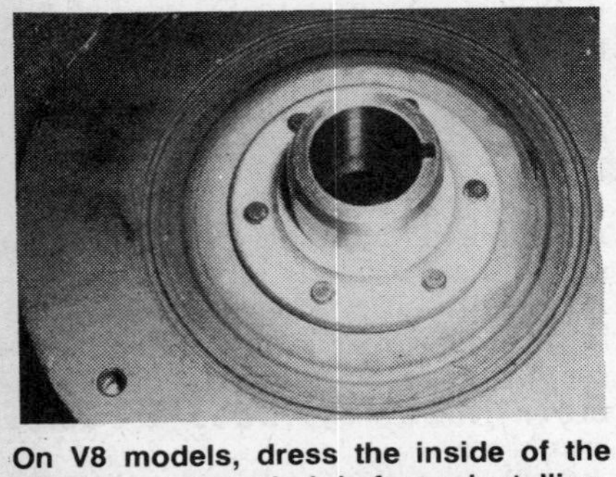

On V8 models, dress the inside of the vibration damper hub before reinstalling. This will allow you to "feel" the key when installing. On early models, the key extends only 1/3 of the length of the keyway; on later models, ½ the length of the keyway.

bolts (except 1985–90 190D; see **NOTE** below); stretch-bolts are used for the connecting rods (see this step for torquing procedure). These bolts are tightened by angle of rotation rather than by use of a torque wrench.

**NOTE: Bearing cap bolts on 1985–90 190D's undergo a permanent stretch and must be replaced if the length (L) exceeds 2.5 in. (63.8mm)**

Make sure the stretch section diameter is greater than 0.35 in. (0.003 in.).

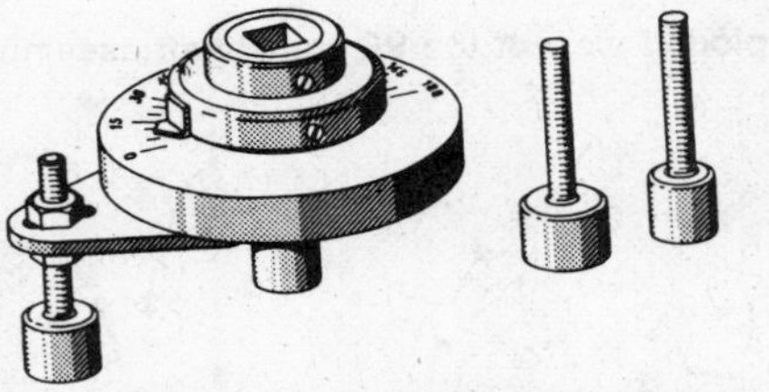

Preferred tools for torquing by angle rotation. A torque wrench is also needed.

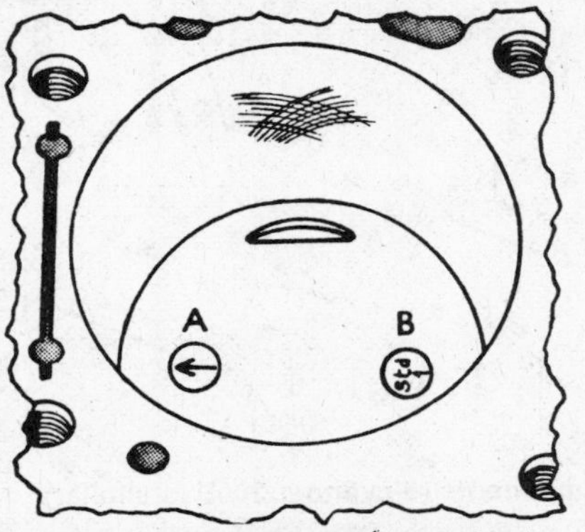


**Pistons normally are marked with an arrow (a) indicating front and a weight or size marking (b).**

Remove the bolt from the rod and measure the diameter at the point normally covered by the rod; it should be at least 0.31 in. For reasons of standardization, the angle of rotation for all the screw connections tightened according to angle of rotation has been set to 90 degrees + 10 degrees. Initially the bolts should be torqued to 22–35 ft. lbs. (30–47 Nm), then an additional 90 degrees.

Check the connecting rod bolts

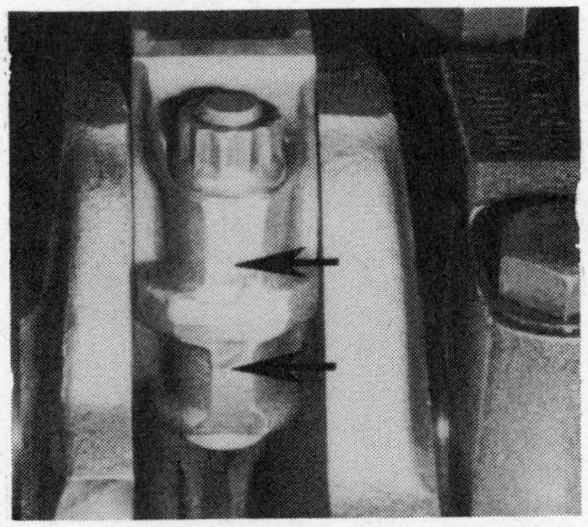

Match mark the connecting rod bearing caps.

**NOTE: The bearing shells on the 3rd main bearing of the 190 series engines are fitted with thrust washers. The thrust washers in the bearing cap have 2 locating tabs to keep them from rotating. During assembly the grooves in the washers should face the crankshaft thrust surfaces.**

4. Disassembly the oil pump and check the gear backlash. Place a straightedge on the cover and check for warpage. Deep scoring on the cover usually indicates that metal or dirt particles have been circulating through the oil system. Covers can be machined, but it is best to replace them is damaged.

5. Install the oil pump.

6. Install the oil pan and lower crankcase and tighten the bolts evenly all around, then turn the engine right side up and install the cylinder head gasket and head. Make sure the gasket surfaces are clean before installation; a small dirt particle could cause gasket failure. Tighten the cylinder head bolt in sequence, in stages, to insure against distortion. Don't forget the small bolts at the front of the head.

7. Install the engine into the vehicle.

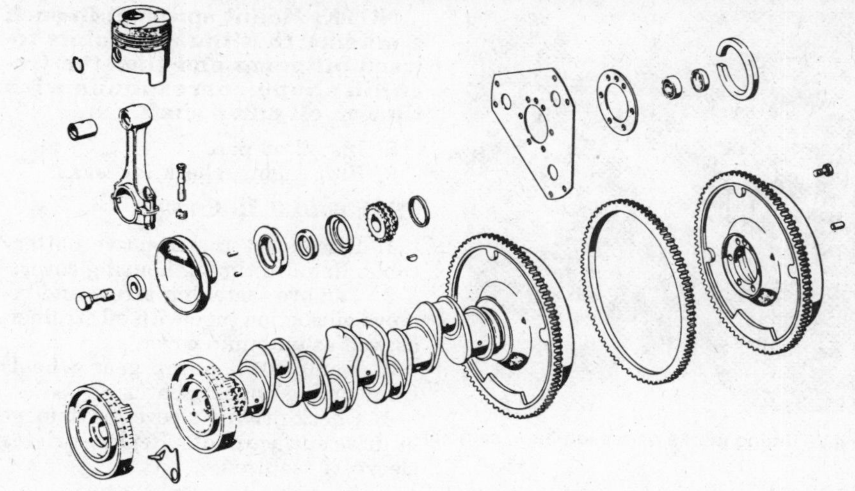

4-cylinder diesel engine components (5-cylinder is similar).

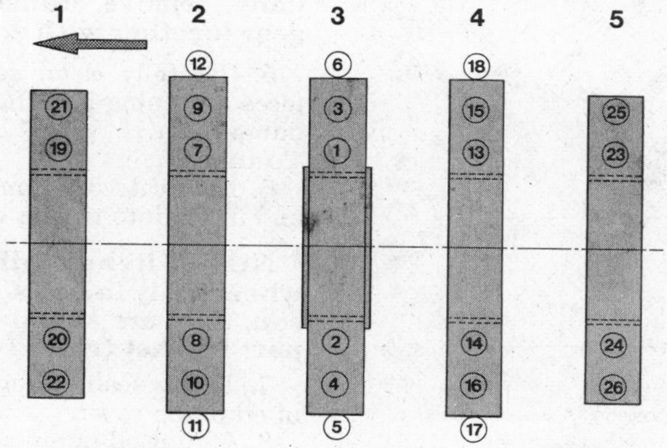


Main bearing cap torque sequence—3.8 liter V-8's

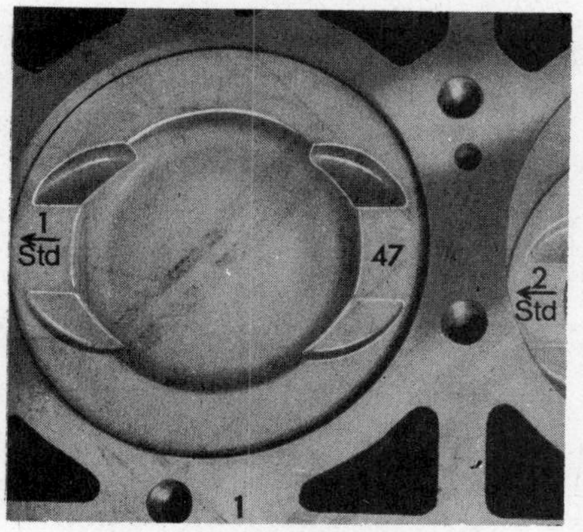


Piston marking on 3.8 V8

**NOTE: It is a good practice to use a good break-in oil after an engine overhaul. Be sure that all fluids have been replaced and perform a general tune-up. Check the valve timing.**

## Valve Timing

Ideally, this operation should be performed by a dealer who is equipped with the necessary tools and knowledge to do the job properly.

Checking valve timing is too inaccurate at the standard tappet clearance; therefore timing values are given for an assumed tappet clearance of 0.4mm. The engines are not measured at 0.4mm but rather at 2mm.

1. To check the timing, remove the rocker arm cover and spark plugs. Remove the tensioning springs. On the 6 cylinder engine install the testing thrust pieces. Eliminate all valve clearance.

2. Install a degree wheel.

**NOTE: If the degree wheel is attached to the camshaft as shown, values read from it must be doubled.**

3. A pointer must be made out of a bent section of $^3/_{16}$ in. brazing rod or coathanger wire, and attached to the engine.

4. With a 22mm wrench on the crankshaft pulley, turn the engine in the direction of rotation until the TDC mark on the vibration damper registers with the pointer and the distributor rotor points to the No. 1 cylinder mark on the housing. The camshaft timing marks should align at this point.

**NOTE: Due to the design of the chain tensioner on V8 engines, the right side of the chain travels slightly farther than the left side. This means the right-side cam will be almost 7 degrees retarded compared to the left side, and both marks will not simultaneously align.**

5. Turn the loosened degree wheel until the pointer lines up with the 0 degree (OT) mark, then tighten it in this position.

6. Continue turning the crankshaft in the direction of rotation until the camshaft lobe of the associated valve is vertical (e.g., point away from the rocker arm surface). To take up tappet clearance, insert a feeler gauge (thick enough to raise the valve slightly from its seat) between the rocker arm cone and the pressure piece.

7. Attach the indicator to the cylinder head so that the feeler rests against the valve spring retainer of the No. 1 cylinder intake valve. Preload the indicator at least 0.008 in. then set to zero, making sure the feeler is exactly perpendicular on the valve spring retainer. It may be necessary to bleed down the chain tensioner at this time to facilitate readings.

8. Turn the crankshaft in the normal direction of rotation, again using a wrench on the crankshaft pulley, until the indicator reads 0.016 in. less than zero reading.

9. Note the reading of the degree wheel at this time, remembering to double the reading if the wheel is mounted to the camshaft sprocket.

10. Again turn the crankshaft until the valve is closing and the indicator again reads 0.016 in. less than zero reading. Make sure, at this time, that preload has remained constant, then note the reading of the degree wheel. The difference between the 2 degree wheel reading is the timing angle (number of degrees the valve is open) for that valve.

11. The other valves may be checked in the same manner, comparing them against each other and the opening values given in "Tune-Up Specifications." It must be remembered that turning the crankshaft contrary to the normal direction of rotation results in inaccurate readings and damage to the engine.

12. If valve timing is not to specification, the easiest way of bringing it in line is to install an offset Woodruff key in the camshaft sprocket. This is far simpler than replacing the entire timing chain and it is the factory-recommended way of changing valve timing

## VALVE TIMING OFFSET KEYS

| Offset | Part No. | For a Correction at Crankshaft of |
|---|---|---|
| 2° (0.7) | 621 991 04 67 | 4° |
| 3°20⁺ (0.9) | 621 991 02 67 | 6½° |
| 4 ° (1.1) | 621 991 01 67 | 8° |
| 5° (1.3) | 621 991 00 67 | 10° |

Note that the timing marks on the right-hand cam do not exactly align. This is because the timing chain travels farther on the right side than on the left.

provided the timing chain is not stretched too far or worn out. Offset keys are available in the following sizes:

13. The Woodruff key must be installed with the offset toward the right, in the normal direction of rotation, to effect advanced valve opening; toward the left to retard.

14. Advancing the intake valve opening too much can result in piston and/or valve damage (the valve will hit the piston). To check the clearance between the valve head and the piston, the crankshaft must be positioned at 5 degrees ATDC (on intake stroke). The procedure is essentially the same as for measuring valve timing.

15. As before, the dial indicator is set to zero after being preloaded, then the valve is depressed until it touches the top of the piston. As the normal valve head-to-piston clearance is approximately 0.035 in., you can see that the dial indicator must be preloaded at least 0.042 in. so there will be enough movement for the feeler.

If the clearance is much less than 0.035 in., the cylinder head must be removed and checked for carbon deposits. If none exist, the valve seat must be cut deeper into the head. Always set the ignition timing after installing an offset key.

The V8 timing marks on the left-hand cam

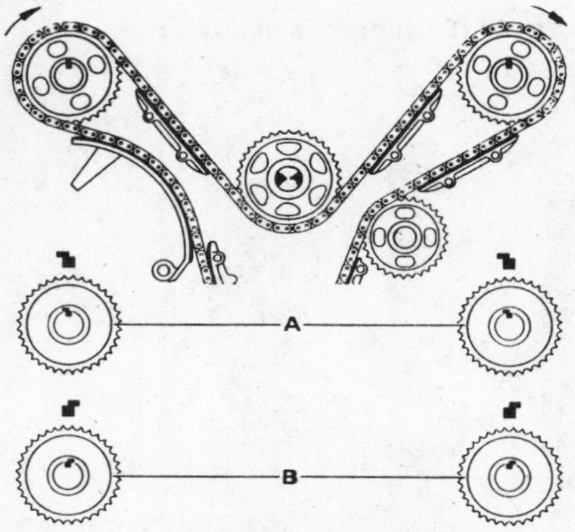


With installation position "A" opening begins earlier
With installation position "B" opening begins later

Offset woodruff keys for V8 engine

# Oil Pump

## REMOVAL & INSTALLATION

### *190D and 1987 300D, 300TD and 300SDL*

1. Disconnect the negative battery cable. Remove oil pan.
2. Remove screw from sprocket and remove sprocket from drive shaft.
3. Remove screws and remove oil pump.
4. On 190D with 2.5L engine and 1987 300D, 300TD and 300SDL, additional screw on intake manifold holder.

**To install:**

5. Position oil pump and torque screw to 18.5 ft. lbs. (25 Nm).
6. On 190D with 2.5L engine and 1987 300D, 300TD and 300SDL, the additional screw is torqued to 7.5 ft. lbs. (10 Nm).
7. Engage sprocket in chain and mount on drive shaft.

**NOTE: Mount sprocket in such a manner that the rise points toward oil pump and that the trochoid shape corresponds with that on oil pump shaft.**

8. Install oil pan.
9. Run engine, check for leaks.

### *190E with 2.3L Engine*

1. Disconnect the negative battery cable. Remove timing housing cover.
2. Remove fastening screw and remove oil suction pipe with oil strainer, as well as oil pump cover.
3. Remove oil pump gear wheels from timing housing cover.
4. Check driving sleeve for damage or drive surface dents. Replace driving sleeve, if required.

**NOTE: If driving sleeve cannot be pulled from crankshaft manually, remove crankshaft timing gear together with driving sleeve.**

5. Carefully clean separating surfaces on timing housing cover and oil pump cover.

**To install:**

6. Lubricate oil pump gear wheels and insert into timing housing cover.

**NOTE: Renew oil pump gear wheels only in pairs. For this reason, they are supplied as a spare part in a set (rotor set) only.**

7. Renew sealing ring on connection of oil pump cover.
8. Mount oil pump cover on timing housing cover. Position oil suction pipe with oil strainer and with new gasket on oil pump cover. Screw in fastening screws and tighten to 7.5 ft. lbs. (10 Nm).

**NOTE: Pay attention to correct installation of gasket between flange of oil suction pipe and oil pump cover.**

9. Check oil pump for easy operation.
10. Slip driving sleeve on crankshaft.
11. Install timing housing cover.
12. Check for leaks with engine running.

### *380SL and 560SL*

1. Disconnect the negative battery cable. Drain engine oil.
2. Remove oil pan.
3. Place compensating weight of first crankpin in horizontal position.
4. Remove fastening screw, tilt oil pump forward, remove drive chain from drive sprocket and remove oil pump.

**To install:**

5. Tilt oil pump forward and place drive chain on drive sprocket, screw-in fastening screw and tighten to 18.5 ft. lbs. (25 Nm).

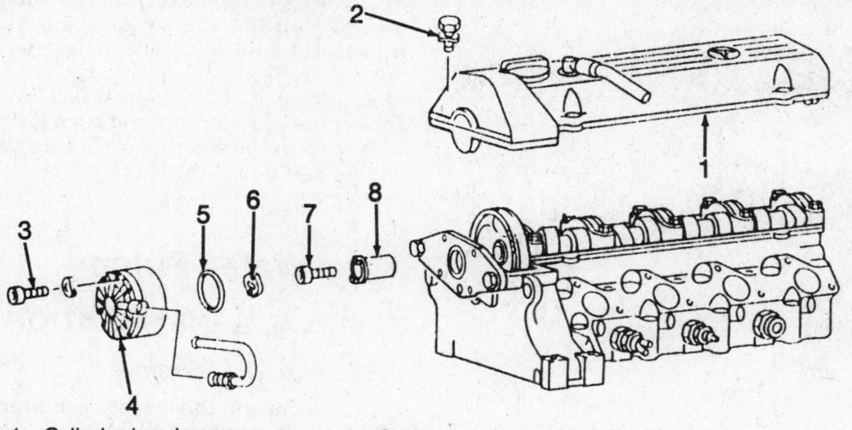

1. Cylinder head cover
2. Screw (Tightening torque 7 ft. lbs. (10 Nm))
3. Screw
4. Hydraulic oil pump
5. O-ring
6. Driven plate
7. Hex, head socket screw
8. Drive sleeve

**Hydraulic oil pump servicing – 190D, 300D and 300SDL**

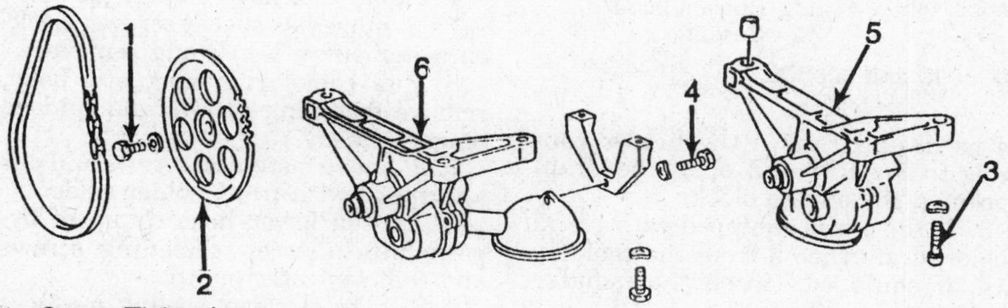

1. Screw (Tightening torque 19 ft. lbs. (25 Nm)
2. Oil pump sprocket
3. Screw (Tightening torque 19 ft. lbs. (25 Nm)
4. Screw (engines 602 and 603 only) (Tightening torque 7 ft. lbs. (10 Nm)
5. Oil pump (engine 601)
6. Oil pump (engine 602 and 603)

**Oil pump servicing – 190D, 300D and 300SDL**

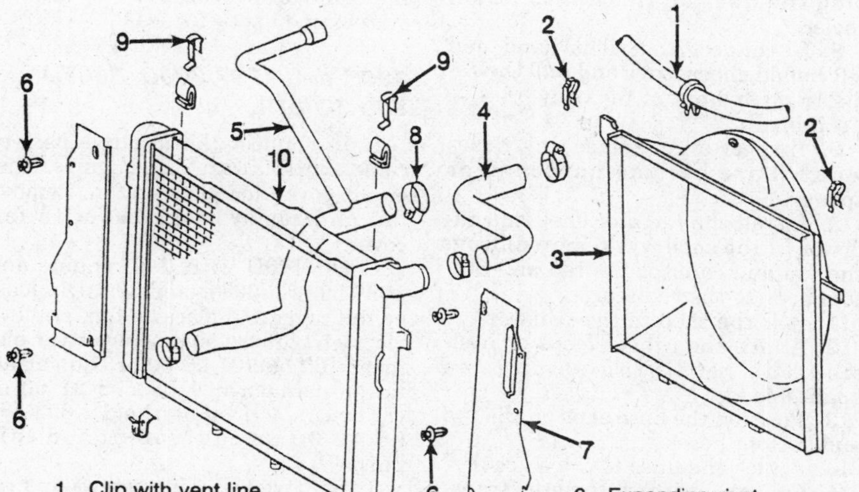

1. Clip with vent line
2. Clamps
3. Fan cover
4. Upper coolant hose
5. Lower coolant hose
6. Expanding rivet
7. Radiator cover left
8. Radiator cover right
9. Holding clamps
10. Radiator

**Radiator servicing – 190D, 300D and 300SDL**

6. Install oil pan with new gasket and tighten fastening screws to 7.5 ft. lbs. (10 Nm) (threads M6) or 18.5 ft. lbs. (25 Nm) (threads M8).
7. Fill with engine oil.
8. Run engine and check for leaks.

#### *420SEL, 500SEL, 500SEC, 560SEL and 560SEC*

1. Disconnect the negative battery cable. Drain engine oil.
2. Remove oil pan lower half.
3. Place compensating weight of first crankpin in horizontal position.
4. Remove screws.
5. Loosen screw on drive sprocket, tilt oil pump toward rear and remove screw.
6. Push drive sprocket away from oil pump by means of a suitable tool and remove oil pump.
7. Lift drive sprocket out of drive chain.
8. Engage drive sprocket in drive chain.
9. Push oil pump on drive sprocket. Dowel sleeve in drive sprocket should enter cutout in drive shaft.
10. Tilt oil pump to rear, screw-in screw and tighten to 21 ft. lbs. (28 Nm).
11. Screw-in fastening screws and tighten to 18.5 ft. lbs. (25 Nm).
12. Install oil pan lower half with new gasket and tighten fastening screw to 7.5 ft. lbs. (10 Nm) (threads M6) or 18.5 ft. lbs. (25 Nm) (threads M8).
13. Fill with engine oil.
14. Run engine and check for leaks.

# ENGINE COOLING

## Radiator

### REMOVAL & INSTALLATION

#### *190D and 1987 300D, 300TD and 300SDL*

1. Disconnect the negative battery cable. On vehicles with automatic transmission, pinch oil lines from or to transmission with special tool 000 589 40 37 00 or equivalent, displacing coil spring slightly laterally and removing from radiator for this purpose.
2. Disconnect coolant hoses on radiator.
3. Pull out flat contour springs for fan cover, slightly lift fan cover and place over fan.
4. On 300D and 300TD models, remove expanding rivets for lateral radi-

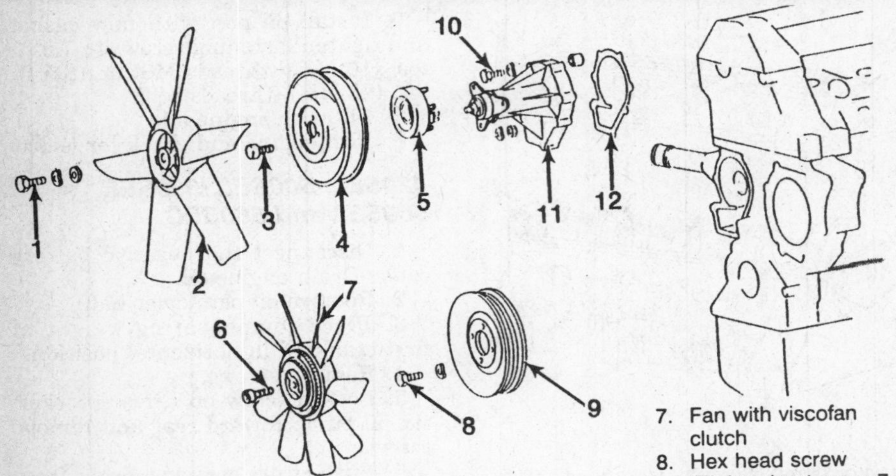


1. Hex head screw (engine 601) (Tightening torque 19 ft. lbs. (25 Nm)
2. Fan
3. Hex head socket screw (Tightening torque 7 ft. lbs. (10 Nm)
4. Pulley
5. Magnet, body
6. Hex head socket screw (engines 602,603) (Tightening torque 33 ft. lbs. (45 Nm)
7. Fan with viscofan clutch
8. Hex head screw (Tightening torque 7 ft. lbs. (10 Nm)
9. Pulley
10. Hex head screw (Tightening torque 7 ft. lbs. (10 Nm)
11. Coolant pump
12. Gasket

**Water pump servicing – 190D, 300D and 300SDL**

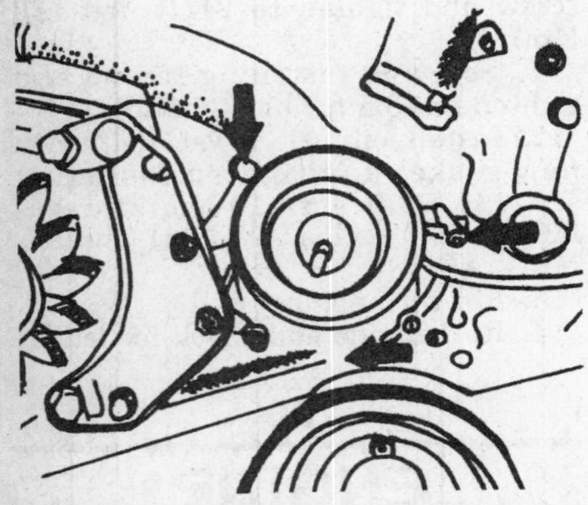

**Water pump servicing – 190E with 2.3L or 2.3-16 engine**

ator panelling right and left.

5. On some models, pull off holding clamps at right and left below.

6. Pull out flat contour springs for radiator and lift out radiator.

**To install:**

7. Reverse the removal procedure. Take note that the fastening mounts of the radiator are correctly introduced into rubber grommets of lower holders, and the holders of the fan cover into holding lugs on radiator.

8. Fill with coolant, pressure test cooling system with tester and check for leaks.

### *All Other Models*

1. Disconnect the negative battery cable. Remove the radiator cap.

2. Unscrew the radiator drain plug and drain the coolant from the radiator. If all of the coolant in the system is to be drained, move the heater controls to **WARM** and open the drain cocks on the engine block.

3. If the car is equipped with an oil cooler, drain the oil from the cooler.

4. If equipped, loosen the radiator shell.

5. Loosen the hose clips on the top and bottom radiator hoses and remove the hoses from the connections on the radiator.

6. Unscrew and plug the bottom line on the oil cooler.

7. If the car is equipped with an automatic transmission, unscrew and plug the lines on the transmission cooler.

8. Disconnect the right hand and left hand rubber loops and pull the radiator up and out of the body.

**To install:**

9. Inspect and replace any hoses which have become hardened or spongy.

10. Install the radiator shell and radiator (if the shell was removed) from the top and connect the top and bottom hoes to the radiator.

11. Bolt the shell to the radiator.

12. Attach the rubber loops or position the retaining spring, as applicable.

13. Position the hose clips on the top and bottom hoses.

14. Attach the lines to the oil cooler.

15. On cars with automatic transmission, connect the lines to the transmission cooler.

16. Move the heater levers to the **WARM** position and slowly add coolant, allowing air to escape.

17. Check the oil level and fill if necessary. Run the engine for about one minute at idle with the filler neck open.

18. Add coolant to the specified level. Install the radiator cap and turn it until it seats in the second notch. Run the engine and check for leaks.

# Water Pump

## REMOVAL & INSTALLATION

### *190E with 2.3L Engine*

1. Disconnect the negative battery cable. Drain coolant.

2. Remove air cleaner.

3. Remove radiator.

4. Loosen hose clamps and disconnect heater return line and coolant hose from coolant pump.

5. Remove fan.

6. Remove pulley of water pump.

7. Remove hex socket screws, slacken water pump V-belt and remove.

8. Pull cable from magnetic body, remove fastening screws and remove magnetic body.

9. Remove fastening screws and put alternator with front holder aside.

10. Loosen lower hose clamp of bypass line, unscrew fastening screws and remove water pump.

11. Carefully clean sealing surfaces on water pump housing and timing housing cover.

**To install:**

12. Apply gasket adhesive to gasket and pump.

13. Install pump and torque bolts to 7.5 ft. lbs. (10 Nm).

14. Complete installation by reversing removal procedure. Fill coolant system and check for leaks.

### *190D and 1987 300D, 300TD and 300SDL*

1. Disconnect the negative battery cable. On 190 with 2.2L engines, loosen fan cover and place on fan. Remove fan and remove together with fan cover.

2. On 190D with 2.5L engine and 1987 300D, 300TD and 300SDL, loosen fan cover and place on fan. Remove viscofan clutch using screwdriver element 103 589 01 09 00 or equivalent, torque wrench 001 589 72 21 00 or equivalent and counterholder 603 589 00 40 00 or equivalent for this purpose.

3. Remove fastening screws and remove pulley.

4. On 190D with 2.2L engine, pull cable from magnet body.

5. Remove hex nuts and remove magnet body.

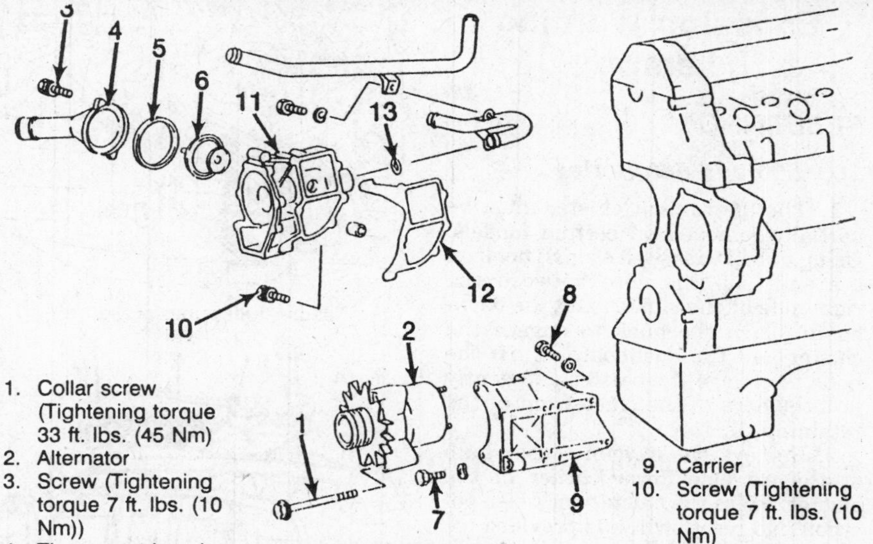


1. Collar screw (Tightening torque 33 ft. lbs. (45 Nm)
2. Alternator
3. Screw (Tightening torque 7 ft. lbs. (10 Nm))
4. Thermostat housing cap
5. Sealing ring
6. Thermostat
7. Screw (Tightening torque 19 ft. lbs. (25 Nm)
8. Screw (Tightening torque 19 ft. lbs. (25 Nm)
9. Carrier
10. Screw (Tightening torque 7 ft. lbs. (10 Nm)
11. Coolant pump housing
12. Gasket
13. O-ring

**Water pump housing servicing—190D, 300D and 300SDL**

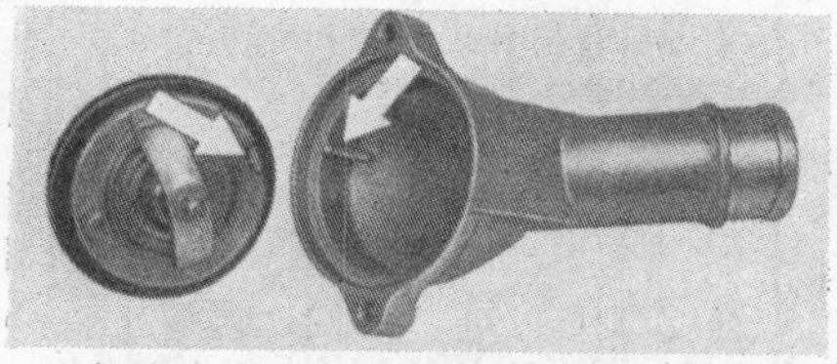

**Aligning the thermostat on the 190D**

**NOTE: The magnet carrier is glued to the water pump housing and should not be pulled off.**

6. Remove water pump housing.
7. Clean sealing surfaces.

**To install:**

8. Insert water pump with a new gasket and tighten combination screws to 7.5 ft. lbs. (10 Nm).
9. Mount water pump with a new gasket and tighten combination screws to 7.5 ft. lbs. (10 Nm).
10. Mount magnet body and plug on cable.
11. Mount pulley and tighten fastening screws to 7.5 ft. lbs. (10 Nm).
12. Complete installation by reversing removal procedure.

### *V8 Models*

1. Disconnect the negative battery cable. Drain the water from the radiator and block.
2. Remove the air cleaner.
3. Loosen and remove the drive belt.
4. Disconnect the upper water hose from the radiator and thermostat housing.
5. Remove the fan and coupling.
6. Remove the hose from the intake (top) connection of the water pump.
7. Set the engine at TDC. Matchmark the distributor and engine and remove the distributor. Crank the engine with a socket wrench on the crankshaft pulley bolt or with a small prybar inserted in the balancer. Crank in the normal direction of rotation only.
8. Turn the balancer so that the recesses provide access to the mounting bolts. Remove the mounting bolts. Rotate the engine in the normal direction of rotation only.
9. Remove the water pump.

**To install:**

10. Clean the mounting surfaces of the water pump and block.
11. Installation is the reverse of removal. Always use a new gasket. Set the engine at TDC and install the distributor rotor points to the notch on the distributor housing. Fill the cooling system and check and adjust the ignition timing.

### *All Other Models*

1. Disconnect the negative battery cable. Drain the water from the radiator.
2. Loosen the radiator shell and remove the radiator.
3. Remove the fan with the coupling and set it aside in an upright position.
4. Loosen the belt around the water pump pulley and remove the belt.
5. Remove the bolts from the harmonic balancer and remove the balancer and pulley.
6. Unbolt and remove the water pump.
7. Installation is the reverse of removal. Tighten the belt and fill the cooling system.

## Water Pump Housing

### REMOVAL & INSTALLATION

#### *190D and 1987 300D, 300TD and 300SDL*

1. Disconnect negative terminal on battery.
2. Remove alternator and put aside.
3. Remove carrier for alternator.
4. Remove return line on crankcase and pull out of water pump housing.
5. Remove water pump housing.
6. Clean sealing surfaces.

**To install:**

7. Renew O-ring on return line.

**NOTE: Keep O-ring free of grease. For better assembly, immerse O-ring into coolant.**

8. Plug coolant pump housing on return line and screw with a gasket to crankcase, tighten to 7.5 ft. lbs (10 Nm).
9. Screw return line to crankcase.
10. Mount carrier for alternator and tighten screws to 18.5 ft. lbs. (25 Nm).
11. Mount alternator and tighten screw to 33 ft. lbs. (45 Nm). Connect negative terminal to battery.

## Thermostat

### REMOVAL & INSTALLATION

#### *All Except V8 Engines*

The thermostat housing is a light metal casting attached directly to the cylinder head, except on the 190D where it is attached to the side of the water pump housing; and the 190E with the 2.6L engine, 260E, 300E, 300CE, 300SE, 300TE and 300SEL where it is under a plastic cover atop the water pump.

1. Disconnect the negative battery cable. Open the radiator cap and depressurize the system.
2. Open the radiator drain cock and partially drain the coolant. Drain enough coolant to bring the coolant level below the level of the thermostat housing.
3. Remove the 4 bolts on the thermostat housing cover and remove the cover.
4. Note the installation position of the thermostat and remove it.

**To install:**

5. Installation is the reverse of removal. Be sure that the thermostat is positioned with the ball valve at the highest point and that the 4 bolts are tightened evenly against the seal. On

the 190D, the recess in the thermostat casing should be located above the lug in the thermostat housing. On the 190E with 2.6L engine, 260E, 300E, 300CE, 300SE, 300TE and 300SEL, the ball valve must be at its highest point in the housing to allow complete venting of gas bubbles.

6. Refill the cooling system and check for leaks.

**NOTE: When refilling the coolant system on the 300E, 300CE, 300SE, 300TE and 300SEL, always remove the hex-head plug on the left side of the cylinder head and fill the hole with coolant until it overflows. Install the plug and then fill the coolant system. When filling the coolant system on the 190E with 2.6L and the 260E, open the vent screw on top of the thermostat housing approximately 2 turns, start the engine run the engine at idle.**

#### *V8 Engines*

1. Drain the coolant from the radiator and block.
2. Remove the air cleaner.
3. Disconnect the battery and remove the alternator.
4. Unscrew the housing cover on the side of the water pump and remove the thermostat.
5. If a new thermostat is to be installed, always install a new sealing ring.
6. Installation is the reverse of removal. Be sure to tighten the screws on the housing cover evenly to prevent leaks. Refill the cooling system and check of leaks.

# EMISSION CONTROLS

**Please refer to "Emission Control" in the Unit Repair section for system maintenance procedures. Due to the complex nature of modern electronic engine control systems, comprehensive diagnosis and testing procedures fall outside the confines of this repair manual. For complete information on diagnosis, testing and repair procedures concerning all modern engine and emission control systems, please refer to "Chilton's Guide to Electronic Engine Controls".**

## Emission Warning Lamps

### RESETTING

#### *380, 500 and 560 Series*

1. The instrument cluster must be partially removed on certain models. Using a steel wire with a small hook on the end, slip the wire between the right side of the cluster and the dashboard. Turn the hook to engage the cluster and the dashboard. Turn the hook to engage the cluster and gently pull the edge of the cluster out of the retaining clips.
2. Remove the oxygen sensor bulb at the extreme lower corner of the cluster. Press the cluster back into position. No reset switch is provided.

# GASOLINE FUEL SYSTEM

## Fuel System Service Precaution

When working around any part of the fuel system, take precautionary steps to prevent fire and/or explosion:

- Disconnect negative terminal from battery (except when testing with battery voltage is required).
- When ever possible, kuse a flashlight instead of a drop light.
- Keep all open flame and smoking material out of the area.
- Use a shop cloth or similar to catch fuel when opening a fuel system.
- Relieve fuel system pressure before servicing.
- Use eye protection.
- Always keep a dry chemical (class B) fire extinguisher near the area.

## Fuel Filter

### REMOVAL & INSTALLATION

Two types of filters are used, depending on the car model. Both are located between the rear axle and the fuel tank.

1. Unscrew the cover box.
2. Remove the pressure hoses.
3. Loosen the attaching screws and remove the filter. Remove the connecting plug from the old filter and install it on a new filter using a new gasket.

**To install:**

4. Install a new filter in the direction of flow.

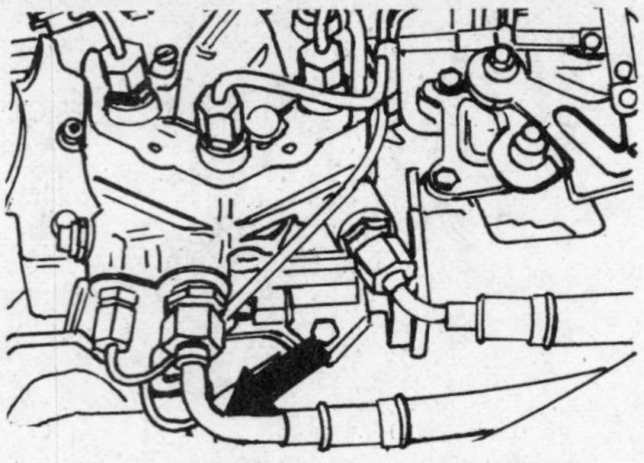

Testing fuel pump pressure

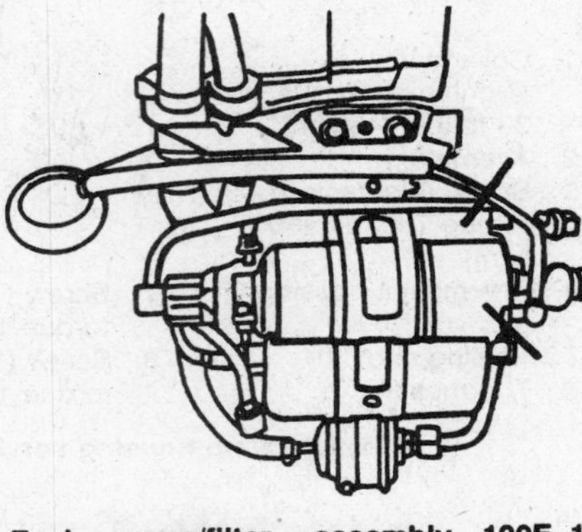

Fuel pump/filter assembly—190E-16 shown, others similar

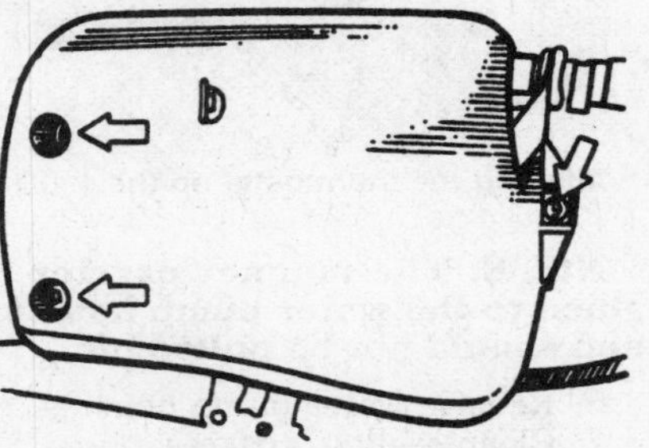

Fuel pump package cover—190 series, 260E, 300E, 300CE, 300SE, 300SEL and 300TE

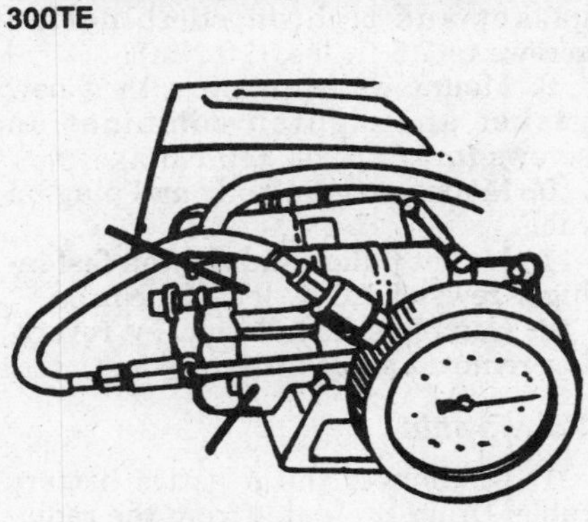

Fuel pump pressure test

5. Replace the attaching screws.
6. Install the pressure hoses.
7. Install the fuel filter in the holder by positioning it in the center of the transparent holder. Be sure the plastic sleeve between the fuel filter and fuel pump is installed. Galvanic corrosion

may occur in cases of direct contact between these components.

8. Replace the cover box and check for proper sealing.

### TESTING DELIVERY

1. Remove the wire from the coil to prevent starting.
2. Connect a pressure gauge into the output line of the fuel pump.
3. Crank the engine and read the delivery pressure on the pressure gauge. The pressure should be a constant 1.5–2.5 psi.
4. If the pressure is not within specifications or is erratic, remove the pump for service or for replacement with a new or rebuilt unit. No adjustment is provided.

## Electric Fuel Pump

**NOTE: Do not confuse the electric fuel pump with the injection pump.**

All Mercedes-Benz fuel injected engines are equipped with electric fuel pumps. The electric fuel pump is located underneath the rear floor panel. The fuel return line was also eliminated and a check ball installed in its place. The fuel pump uses a replaceable check valve on the outside of the pump which can be replaced separately.

Two types of fuel pumps have been used. One, the large pump, has been replaced with a new small design which has a bypass system to prevent vapor lock.

### REMOVAL & INSTALLATION

1. Disconnect the negative battery cable. Jack the left rear of the car and support it on jack stands. This will provide sufficient working clearance.
2. Remove and plug the intake, outlet and bypass lines from the pump.
3. Disconnect the electrical leads.
4. Unbolt and remove the fuel pump and vibration pads.

**NOTE: 1986–90 V8s utilize 2 fuel pumps connected in series.**

5. Install the fuel pump in the reverse order of removal. Be sure that the electrical leads are connected to the proper terminals. The negative wire (brown) is connected to the negative terminal (brown plastic plate) and the positive wire (black/red) is connect to the positive terminal (red plastic plate). If the terminals are reversed, the pump will operate in the reverse direction of normal rotation and will deliver no fuel.

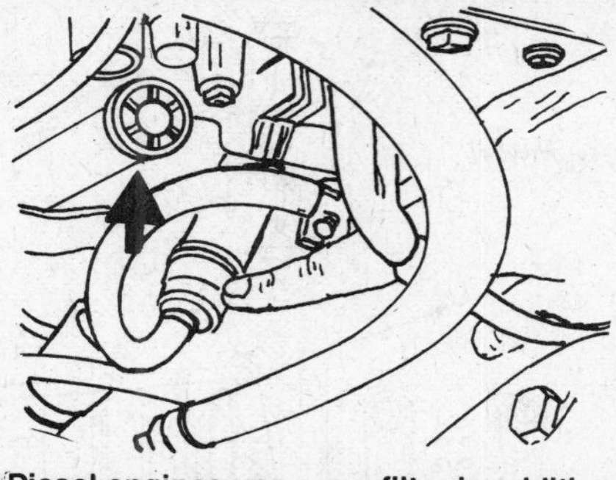

Diesel engines use a pre-filter in addition to the main fuel filter. The arrow indicates the hard operated delivery pump

Some diesel injection pumps have a manually operated delivery pump (1)

### TESTING FUEL PUMP DELIVERY PRESSURE

Remove the fuel return hose from the fuel distributor. Connect a fuel line and hold the end in the measuring cup. Disconnect the plug from the safety switch on the mixture regulator and turn **ON** the ignition for 30 seconds. If the delivery rate is less than 1 liter in 30 seconds, check the voltage at the fuel pump (11.5v) and the fuel lines for kinks. Disconnect the leak off line between the fuel accumulator and the suction damper. Check the delivery rate again. If it is low, replace the accumulator.

Replace the fuel filter and test again. If still low, replace the fuel pump.

## Fuel Injection

**Due to the complex nature of modern fuel injection systems, comprehensive diagnosis and testing procedures fall outside the confines of this repair manual. For complete information of fuel injection diagnosis, testing and repair procedures, please refer to Chilton's Guide To Fuel Injection And Feedback Carburetors.**

# DIESEL FUEL SYSTEM

## Main Fuel Filter

Loosen the center attaching bolt and remove the filter cartridge downward. Lubricate the new filter gasket with clean diesel fuel and install a new filter cartridge.

To bleed the fuel filter: Loosen the bleed bolt on the fuel filter housing and release the manually operated delivery pump. Operate the delivery pump until the fuel emerges free of bubbles at the bleed screw. Close the bleed bolt and operate the pump until the overflow valve on the injection pump opens (a buzzing noise will be heard). Close the manual pump before starting the engine. To bleed the injection pump on 4 cylinder diesels, loosen the bleed screw on the injection pump and keep pumping the hand pump until fuel emerges free of bubbles.

**NOTE: The 190D uses a self-bleeding fuel pump, therefore the hand pump has been eliminated. No bleeding is necessary.**

### *Diesel Pre-filter*

Diesel engines use a pre-filter in addition to the main fuel filter, since even the most minute particle of dirt will clog the injection system. The pre-filter is located in the line just before it enters the injection pump.

To replace it, simply unscrew the clamps on each end and remove the old filter. Install a new filter and bleed the system (see Main Fuel Filter).

# MANUAL TRANSMISSION

### REMOVAL & INSTALLATION

#### *With Engine*

**ALL MODELS**

The transmission should only be removed with the engine as a unit, since the transmission-to-clutch housing bolts can only be reached from the inside. Once the engine/transmission unit has been removed from the vehicle, the transmission and bellhousing must be separated from the engine, as follows:

See the "Engine" section to remove the engine/transmission.

1. After removing the engine/transmission unit, unbolt the bellhousing from the engine. The bolts which hold the transmission to the bellhousing cannot be reached except from inside the bellhousing.

2. Remove the starter from its mounting position and pull the transmission and bellhousing from the engine.

3. The bolts which secure the bellhousing to the transmission are now visible and can be removed to separate the bellhousing and transmission.

**To install:**

4. Connect the engine, bellhousing, and transmission, after coating the splines of the mainshaft with grease.

5. Install the starter.

6. Further installation is the reverse of removal.

### *Without Engine*

#### 1983 240D

1. Disconnect the battery.

2. Disconnect the regulating shaft in the engine compartment.

3. Support the transmission with a floor jack.

4. Unbolt the rear engine mount.

5. Unbolt each side of the engine carrier on the floor frame.

6. Unscrew the exhaust mounting bracket on the transmission. Note the number and positioning of all washers.

7. Unbolt the retaining strap and remove the exhaust pipe bracket.

8. Loosen the clamp nut on the driveshaft.

9. Loosen, but do not remove, the intermediate bearing bolts.

10. Unbolt the driveshaft on the transmission so that the companion plate remains with the driveshaft.

11. Carefully push the driveshaft as far to the rear as permitted.

12. Loosen and remove the tachometer drive shaft on the rear transmission case cover. Unclip the clip for the tachometer drive shaft from its holder.

13. Unscrew the holder for the line to the clutch housing. Unscrew the clutch slave cylinder and move it toward the rear until the pushrod is clear of the housing.

14. Push off the clip locks and then remove the shift rods from the intermediate levers on the shift bracket. Note the position of the disc springs.

**CAUTION**

***When the shift rods are disconnected, do not move the shift lever into reverse or you risk damaging the back-up light switch.***

15. Unbolt the starter and remove it.

16. Remove all transmission-to-intermediate flange screw. Remove the upper 2 last.

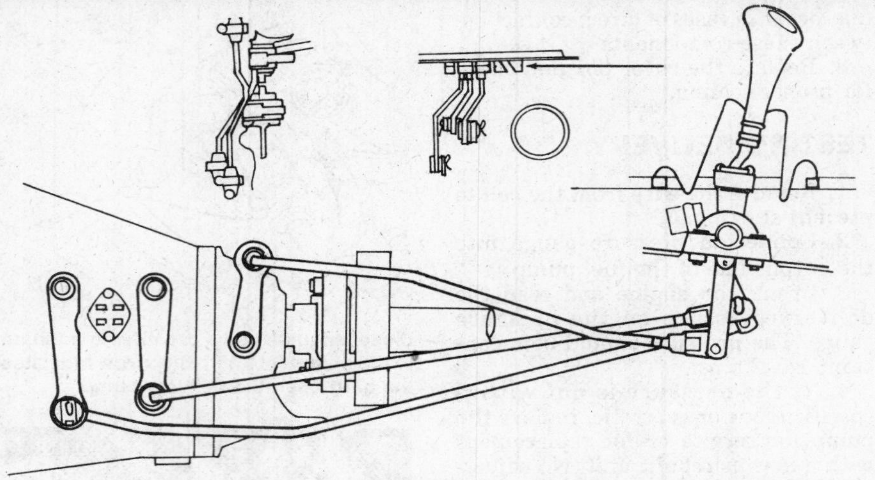

**Transmission linkage – 1983 240D. Arrow at top shows locking rod installed prior to adjustment**

17. Carefully pull the transmission toward the rear of the vehicle and then remove it downward.

**CAUTION**

***Make sure that the input shaft has cleared the clutch plate before tilting the transmission.***

**To install:**

18. Lightly grease the centering lug and splines on the transmission input shaft.

**NOTE: Position the clutch slave cylinder and line above the transmission before beginning installation.**

19. Move the transmission into the clutch so that one gear step engages. Rotate the mainshaft back and forth until the splines on the input shaft and clutch plate are aligned.

20. Move the transmission all the way in and then tighten the transmission-to-intermediate flange screws.

21. Install the starter.

22. Install the clutch slave cylinder with the proper plastic shims.

23. Installation of the remaining components is in the reverse order of removal. Please note the following:

   a. After installing the driveshaft, roll the car back and forth and then tighten the intermediate bearing free of tension.

   b. Tighten the driveshaft clamp nut to 22–29 ft. lbs. (30–40 Nm).

   c. Make sure of the proper positioning of all washers, spacers and shims.

#### 190D, 190E, 260E, 300E, 300CE, 300SE, 300TE AND 300SEL

1. Disconnect the battery.

2. Cover the insulation mat in the engine compartment to prevent damage.

3. On vehicles equipped with a auxiliary heater, be sure that the water hose is out of the way.

4. Support the transmission with a floor jack.

5. Unbolt the engine mounts at the rear transmission cover.

6. Unbolt the engine carrier on the floor frame.

7. Unscrew the exhaust holder at the transmission. Note the number and positioning of all washers.

8. Unscrew the clamping strap and remove the exhaust pipe holder.

9. Remove the intermediate bearing shield plate.

10. Loosen the clamp nut on the driveshaft.

11. Loosen, but do not remove, the intermediate bearing bolts.

12. Unbolt the driveshaft on the transmission so that the companion plate remains with the driveshaft.

13. Carefully push the driveshaft as far to the rear as permitted.

**NOTE: On the 190E, the fitted sleeves on the universal flange must be loosened before separating the flange from the companion plate. This will require a cylindrical mandrel.**

14. Disconnect the exhaust system at the rear suspension and suspend it with wire.

15. Loosen and remove the input shaft for the tachometer.

16. Loosen and remove the tachometer drive shaft on the rear transmission case cover. Unclip the clip for the tachometer drive shaft from its holder.

17. Unscrew the holder for the line to the clutch housing. Unscrew the clutch slave cylinder and move it toward the rear until the pushrod is clear of the housing.

18. Push off the clip locks and then remove the shift rods from the inter-

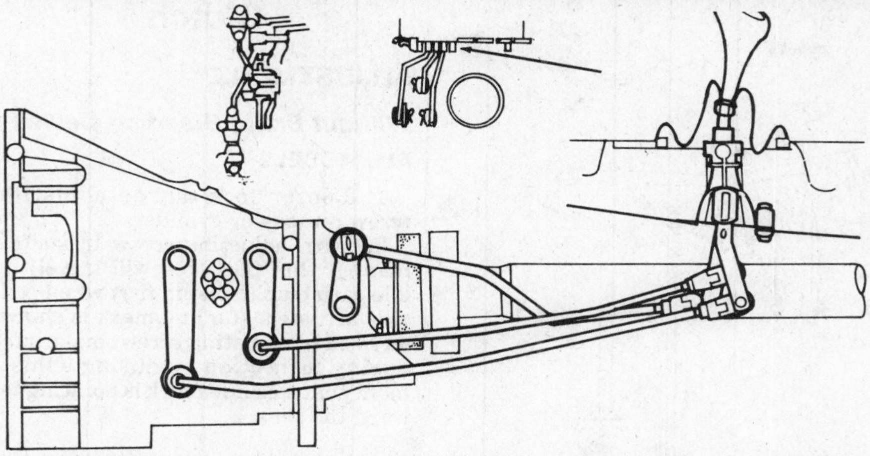

Transmission linkage—190 (4 speed shown, 5 speed similar). Arrow at top shows locking rod installed prior to adjustment

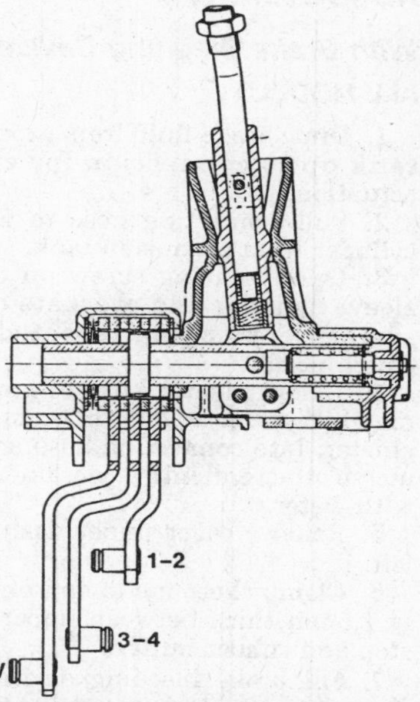


Intermediate lever positioning on the 5 speed 190.

mediate levers on the shift bracket. Note the position of the disc springs.

**CAUTION**

***When the shift rods are disconnected, do not move the shift lever into reverse or you risk damaging the back-up light switch.***

19. Unbolt the starter and remove it.
20. Remove all transmission-to-intermediate flange screw. Remove the upper 2 last.
21. Rotate the transmission approximately 45 degrees to the left, slide it out of the clutch plate and then remove it downward.

**CAUTION**

***Make sure that the input shaft has cleared the clutch plate before tilting the transmission.***

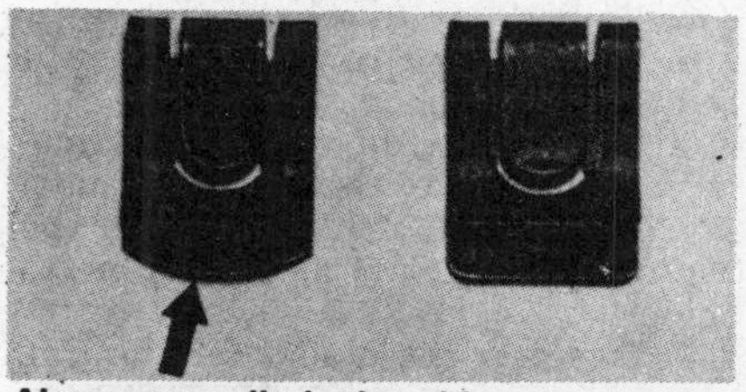

Always use clip locks with curved edges when installing the shift rods on the 190

**To install:**

22. Lightly grease the centering lug and splines on the transmission input shaft.

**NOTE: Position the clutch slave cylinder and line above the transmission before beginning installation.**

23. Move the transmission into the clutch so that one gear step engages. Rotate the mainshaft back and forth until the splines on the input shaft and clutch plate are aligned.
24. Move the transmission all the way in and then tighten the transmission-to-intermediate flange screws.
25. Install the starter.
26. Install the clutch slave cylinder with the proper plastic shims.
27. Installation of the remaining components is in the reverse order of removal. Please note the following:
   a. After installing the driveshaft, roll the car back and forth and then tighten the intermediate bearing free of tension.
   b. Tighten the driveshaft clamp nut to 22–29 ft. lbs. (30–40 Nm).
   c. Make sure of the proper positioning of all washers, spacers and shims.

## LINKAGE ADJUSTMENT

The only type of shifter used is a floor mounted type.

**CAUTION**

***On all types of transmissions, never hammer or force a new shift knob on with the shifter installed, as the plastic bushing connected to the lever will be damaged and caused hard shifting.***

Proper adjustment of the shift linkage is dependent on both the position of the shift levers at the transmission and the length of the shift rods. The shift levers, rods and bearing block are all located underneath the floor tunnel; the driveshaft shield may have to be removed to gain access to them.

1. With the transmission in **N** and the driveshaft shield removed (if so equipped), remove the clip locks and disconnect the shift rods from the intermediate shift levers under the floor shift bearing bracket.
2. With the shifter still in the **N** position, lock the 3 intermediate shift levers by inserting a 0.2156 in. rod (a No. 3 drill bit will do, or any other tool of approximately the same diameter) through the levers and the holes in the bearing bracket.
3. Check the position of the shift levers at the transmission (see illustrations). Adjust by loosening the clamp bolts and moving the levers.
4. With the intermediate levers locked and the shift levers adjusted properly, try hooking the shift rods back onto their respective intermediate levers. The shift rods may be adjusted by loosening the locknut and turning the ball socket on the end until they are the proper length.

**NOTE: When hooking up the shift rods to the intermediate levers, be very careful not to move the transmission shift levers out of their adjusted position.**

**When reattaching the shift rods on 190 models, use only clip locks which have a radius edge. If the old style clip locks with a square edge are used, there is a possibility that the locks will pop out and the shift rods will drop down.**

5. Remove the locking rod from the bearing bracket, start the engine and then shift through the gears a few times. Occasionally slight binding may call for VERY slight further adjustments.

# CLUTCH

## REMOVAL & INSTALLATION

1. To remove the clutch, first remove the transmission.
2. Loosen the clutch pressure plate

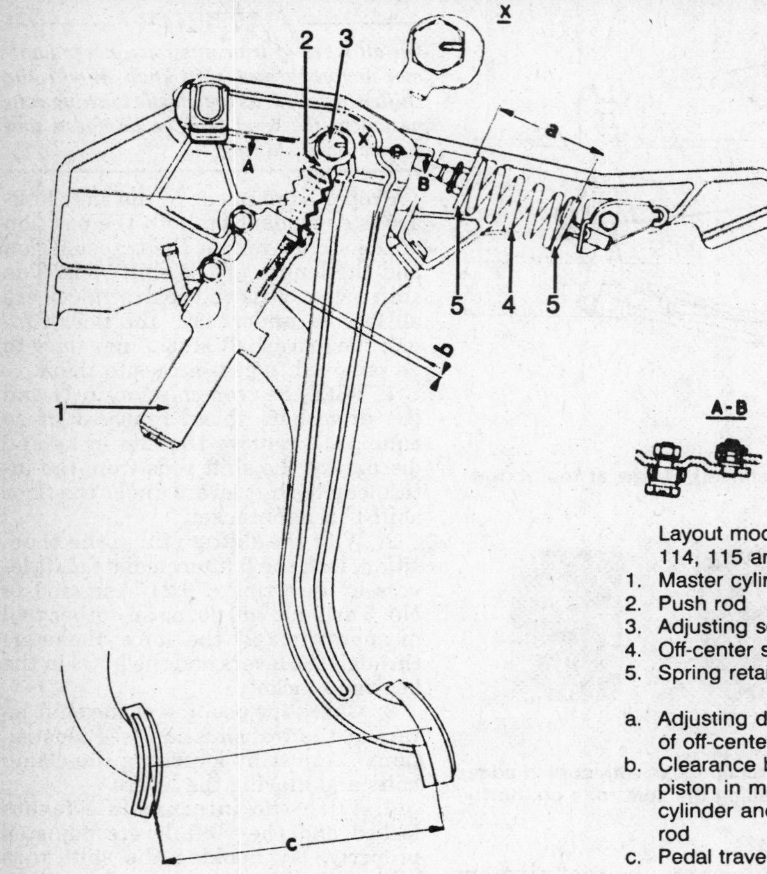


Layout model 107, 114, 115 and 116

1. Master cylinder
2. Push rod
3. Adjusting screw
4. Off-center spring
5. Spring retainer

a. Adjusting dimension of off-center spring
b. Clearance between piston in master cylinder and push rod
c. Pedal travel (lash)

Clutch adjustment

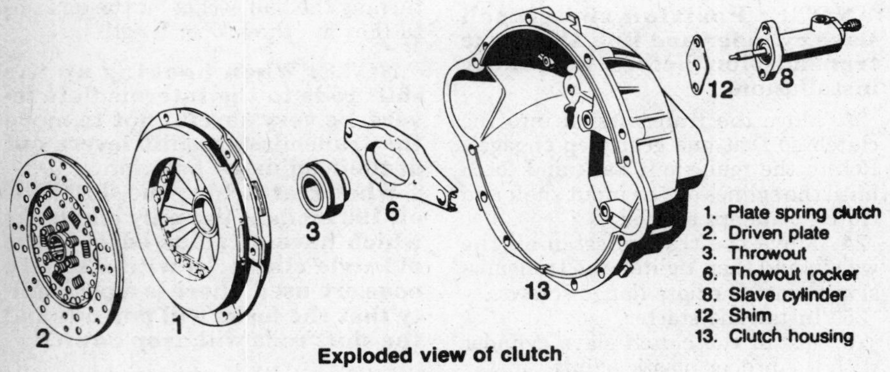


1. Plate spring clutch
2. Driven plate
3. Throwout
6. Thowout rocker
8. Slave cylinder
12. Shim
13. Clutch housing

Exploded view of clutch

holddown bolts evenly, 1–1½ turns at a time, until tension is relieved. Never remove one bolt at a time, as damage to the pressure plate is possible.

3. Examine the flywheel surface for blue heat marks, scoring, or cracks. If the flywheel is to be machined, always machine both sides.

**To install:**

4. Coat the splines with high temperature grease and place the clutch disc against the flywheel, centering it with a clutch pilot shaft. A wooden shaft, available at automotive jobbers, is satisfactory, but an old transmission mainshaft works best.

5. Tighten the pressure plate holddown bolts evenly, 1–1½ turns at a time, until tight, then remove the pilot shaft.

**CAUTION**

***Most clutch plates have the flywheel side marked as such (Kupplungsseite). Do not assume that the pressure springs always face the transmission.***

## Clutch

### ADJUSTMENT

#### *Without Brake Bleeding Device*

**ALL MODELS**

1. Loosen lock nut on adjusting screw on master cylinder.

2. Turn adjusting screw in such a manner that push rod will travel the idle path **b** up to piston first when pedal is actuated. If a line mark is shown on head of adjusting screw, make sure during inspection or during adjustment that this line mark is pointing toward the rear.

### ADJUSTMENT

#### *With Brake Bleeding Device*

**ALL MODELS**

1. Draw brake fluid from expansion tank up to connection for clutch actuation.

2. Pull connecting hose to master cylinder from expansion tank.

3. Open venting screw on clutch sleeve cylinder and evacuate clutch system by stepping repeatedly on clutch pedal.

4. Insert plastic hose of approximately 1 meter in length, 8mm in diameter, into connecting hose and immerse other end into a container filled with water.

5. Remove cover under dash panel left.

6. Clamp sheet metal approximately 1.5mm thick between upper pedal stop and rubber buffer.

7. Fill brake bleeding device with air and set working pressure to 0.5 bar gauge pressure.

8. Adjust brake bleeding device depending on make in such a manner that air is blown from clutch system and bubbles will rise in water tank.

**NOTE: Place water tank into lefthand leg room to gain advantage.**

9. Turn adjusting screw on clutch pedal only until airflow is interrupted and no more bubbles are rising in water tank. Then tighten locking nut on adjusting screw.

10. Remove sheet metal at upper pedal stop. Bubbles should rise again in water tank. Then set brake bleeding device to 0.

11. Attach connecting hose to expansion tank.

12. Vent clutch actuation.

13. Check clutch actuation for function with engine running.

## Clutch Master Cylinder

### REMOVAL & INSTALLATION

1. Disconnect the negative battery cable. Remove cover under instrument panel at left.
2. Remove floor mat at left.
3. To prevent contamination inside vehicle, draw fluid from respective chamber of combination clutch and expansion tank.
4. Unscrew line on master cylinder.
5. Pull off connecting hose on combination brake and clutch expansion tank.
6. Loosen piston rod for brake unit (brake booster) on brake pedal.
7. Pull cable plug from stop light switch.
8. Unscrew nuts for attaching pedal carrier to fire wall.
9. Move pedal assembly to the rear until screw plate of pedal carrier is free from threaded bolt of brake unit (brake booster) and holder at top on water tank.
10. Remove pedal assembly in downward direction, while paying attention to connecting hose for master cylinder and remove master cylinder.

**To install:**

11. Return any fallen rubber mounts, reverse removal procedure and bleed clutch actuation.

## Clutch Slave Cylinder

### REMOVAL & INSTALLATION

1. Detach and plug the pressure line from the slave cylinder.
2. Remove the attaching screws from the slave cylinder.
3. Remove the slave cylinder, pushrod, and spacer.

**To install:**

4. Place the grooved side of the spacer in contact with the housing and hold it in position.
5. Install the slave cylinder and pushrod into the housing. Be sure that the dust cap is properly seated.
6. Install the attaching screws.
7. Connect the pressure line to the slave cylinder.
8. Bleed the slave cylinder.

### BLEEDING THE SLAVE CYLINDER

The same principle is used as in bleeding the brakes.

1. Check the brake fluid level in the compensating tank and fill to maximum level.
2. Put a hose on the bleeder screw of the right front caliper and open the bleeder screw.
3. Have a helper depress the brake pedal until the hose is full and there are no air bubbles. Be sure that the bleeder screw is closed each time the pedal is released.
4. Put the free end of the hose on the bleeder screw of the slave cylinder and open the bleeder screw.
5. Keep stepping on the brake pedal. Close the bleeder screw on the caliper and release the brake pedal. Open the bleeder screw and repeat the process until no air bubbles show up at the mouth of the inlet line of the compensating tank. Between operations, check and, if necessary, refill the compensating tank.
6. Close the bleeder screws on the caliper and slave cylinder and remove the hose.
7. Check the clutch operation and the fluid level.

# AUTOMATIC TRANSMISSION

### REMOVAL & INSTALLATION

#### *722.3 (W4A040) Transmission*

**ALL EXCEPT 190D, 190E AND 260E**

1. Disconnect negative terminal of battery.
2. Remove holder for oil filler pipe on cylinder head.
3. Disengage engine longitudinal regulating shaft.
4. Force off ball socket.
5. Disconnect control wire for control pressure.
6. On vehicles with injection engines, pull out lock and loosen control wire.
7. On vehicles with carburetor engines, compress both plates on plastic clip with pliers and pull out control wire.
8. Jack up vehicles and support safely.
9. Remove cross yoke center place.
10. Remove drain plug on oil pan and drain oil.
11. Remove drain plug on torque converter and drain oil.
12. Remove cover plate.
13. Remove screws for driving plate torque converter.
14. Place a fitting wooden block inbetween engine oil pan and cross yoke.
15. Loosen exhaust system on plug connection and remove.
16. Remove crossbeam together with rear engine mount.
17. Remove cable strap and remove cable on kickdown solenoid valve. Remove fastening screw for impulse transmitter and pull out impulse transmitter.

**NOTE: Disconnect tachometer shaft on vehicles with mechanical tachometer.**

18. Remove exhaust support.
19. Remove exhaust shielding plate.
20. Loosen propeller shaft clamping nut and contract propeller shaft as much as possible.
21. Remove plug for starter lockout switch.

**NOTE: Starter lockout switch plug is secured by a lock (white plastic ring). Prior to pushing off plug, turn lock in upward direction. Carefully push off plug at cable outlet and tongue by means of 2 suitable tools.**

22. Pull off plug.
23. Disconnect control rod on range selector lever.
24. Remove holder and pull off vacuum line.
25. Remove oil cooler feed line.
26. Remove oil cooler return line.
27. Remove fastening screw for oil filler pipe and push oil filler pipe in upward direction.
28. Remove all fastening screw except for two lateral screws.
29. Slightly lift transmission with mount 116 589 06 62 00 or equivalent for pit lift.
30. Remove lateral screws.
31. Push transmission to rear as far as propeller shaft permits and lower carefully.

**To install:**

32. Reverse removal procedure taking attention to the following:
    a. Replace sealing rings for forward and return flow lines.
    b. Torque propeller shaft clamping nuts to 22 ft. lbs. (30 Nm).
    c. Torque driving plate screw to 31 ft. lbs. (42 Nm).
    d. Screw in drain plug on oil pan and on torque converter and torque to 10.5 ft. lbs. (14 Nm).
    e. Replace self-locking screws on cross yoke center piece and torque to 33 ft. lbs. (45 Nm).
    f. Adjust cable for control pressure.

#### *722.4 (W4A020) Transmission*

**190D, 190E AND 260E**

**NOTE: Attach a 300mm square sheet metal panel to unit compartment wall to protect insulating mat during all jobs where the transmission is lowered at the rear. Disconnect exhaust assembly at rear mounting bracket and fasten by means of a wire approximately 50cm lower. On vehicles**

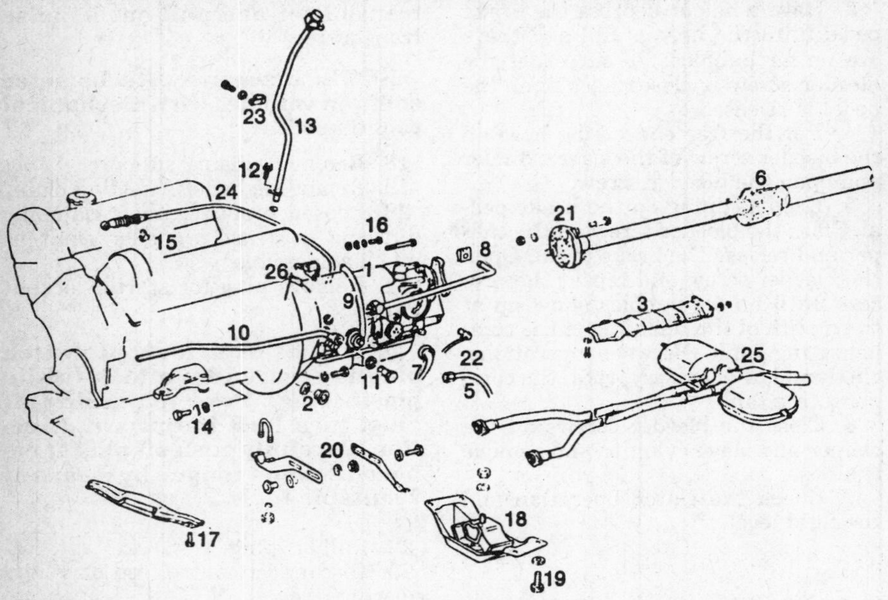


1. Transmission
2. Oil drain plug front, torque converter (Tightening torque 10 ft. lbs. (14 Nm)
3. Shielding plate
4. Cross member-center piece
5. Cable for kickdown solenoid valve
6. Clamping nut of propeller shaft (Tightening torque 22 ft. lbs. (30 Nm)
7. Plug starter lockout switch
8. Shiftrod and clips
9. Vacuum line
10. Oil lines to oil cooler
11. Hollow screw and sealing rings
12. Fastening screw
13. Oil filling pipe
14. Screws for fastening converter (Tightening torque 31 ft. lbs. (42 Nm))
15. Fuse, comtrol pressure cable
16. Fastening screws
17. Self-locking hex head screws
18. Cross member with rear engine mount
19. Fastening screws
20. Exhaust support
21. Unscrew companion plate on flexible flange
22. Impulse sensor, speedometer
23. Holder, oil filling pipe
24. Control pressure cable
25. Exhaust system
26. Cover position sensor EZL

**Automatic transmission servicing—300D, 300E, 300CE, 300TE, 300SE, 300SEL, 300CD, 300TD, 300SD, 380SL, 380SEL, 380SEC, 500SEC, 500SEL, 420SEL, 560SL, 560SEL and 560SEC**

**with auxiliary heater, make sure that the water hose is not damaged when lowering transmission. On 123 models, disconnect engine throttle control.**

1. Disconnect negative cable on battery.

2. Remove holder for oil filling pipe on cylinder head and holder on valve cover.

3. On vehicles with injection engines:

a. Force off ball socket.

b. Disconnect cable control for control pressure. Pull out lock and remove cable control.

c. Force plastic ball socket apart by means of a screwdriver and pull holding bracket from slotted lever.

4. On models with carburetor engine, force off ball socket. Compress holding clips and disengage cable control for control pressure.

5. On 190D and 1987 300D and 300TD, force off ball socket, remove holding clips and disengage control pressure cable control.

6. Jack up vehicle and support safely.

7. Remove drain plug on oil pan as well as torque converter and drain oil.

8. Install drain plug with new seals and tighten to 10.5 ft. lbs. (14 Nm).

9. Remove screw for driven plate torque converter.

10. Remove cross member with rear engine mount.

11. Remove exhaust support. Remove companion plate with articulated flange-transmission.

**NOTE: Remove tangentially soft companion plate installed at transmission end with a mandrel.**

12. Disconnect exhaust system on rear suspension.

13. Remove shielding plate.

14. Remove propeller shaft clamping nut and run together propeller shaft as much as possible.

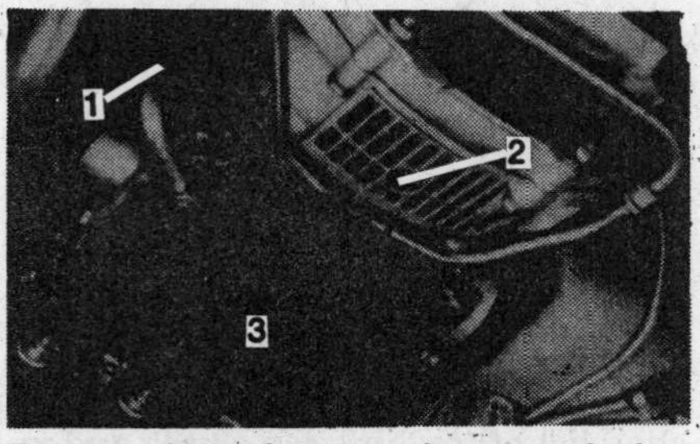


**Bottom view of automatic transmission showing dipstick tube (1), converter drain plug (2) and pan (3)**

15. Pull off cable on kickdown solenoid valve.

16. Remove speedometer shaft. On vehicles with electronic speedometer, remove impulse transmitter.

17. Disconnect control rod on floor shift.

18. Remove fastening clip for speedometer shaft.

19. Swivel locking bracket in upward direction and pull plug from starter lockout switch.

20. Pull vacuum line form vacuum control unit.

21. Remove socket screw from oil filler pipe and pull out oil filler pipe in upward direction.

22. Remove oil cooler lines and fastening clamps.

23. Remove all fastening screws on transmission-to-engine except the 2 screws at left and right.

24. On 190D, insert holding device for torque converter into vent grille cutout and screw in stud until it is entering the socket of oil drain plug.

25. Slightly lift transmission with mounting for pit lift.

26. Remove remaining screws.

27. Slide transmission—to the extent propeller shaft permits—to the rear and carefully let down.

**To install:**

28. Reverse the removal procedure and pay particular attention to the following:

a. Install new sealing rings on oil cooler line.

b. Torque driven plate-to-converter screws to 31 ft. lbs. (42 Nm).

## PAN AND FILTER REPLACEMENT

1. Disconnect the negative battery cable. Drain the transmission of all fluid by loosening the dipstick tube.

2. Remove the transmission pan.

3. Remove the bolt or bolts which retain the filter to the transmission.

4. Remove the filter and replace it with a new one.

5. Install the transmission pan, using a new gasket.

6. Refill the transmission to the

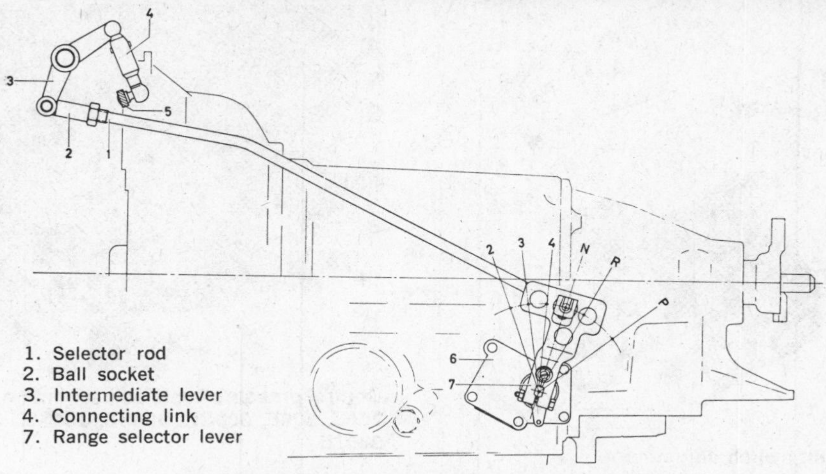


1. Selector rod
2. Ball socket
3. Intermediate lever
4. Connecting link
7. Range selector lever

**Column mounted selector rod linkage—W3A 040**

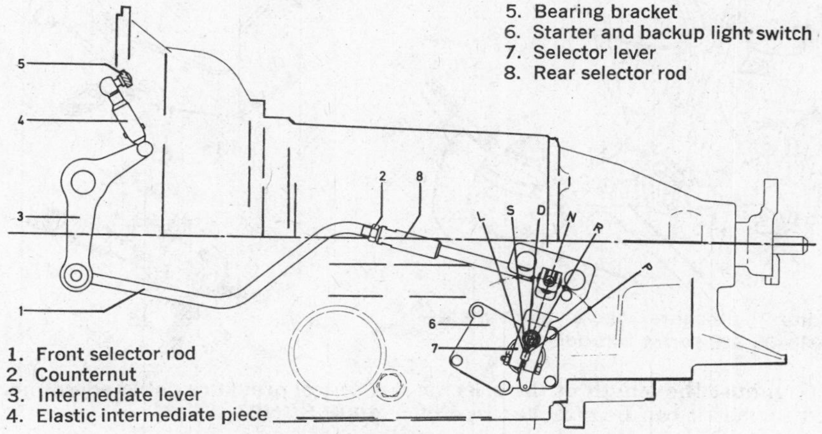


5. Bearing bracket
6. Starter and backup light switch
7. Selector lever
8. Rear selector rod

1. Front selector rod
2. Counternut
3. Intermediate lever
4. Elastic intermediate piece

**Selector rod linkage on the W4A 040 and W4B 025**

proper level with the specified brand of fluid.

## SELECTOR ROD LINKAGE ADJUSTMENT

**NOTE: Before performing this adjustment on any Mercedes-Benz vehicle, be sure that the vehicle is resting on its wheels. No part of the vehicle may be jacked for this adjustment.**

### *Column Mounted Linkage*

#### W3A 040 (380SEL ONLY) AND W4A 040

1. Loosen the counternut on the rear selector rod while holding both recesses of the front selector rod with an open end wrench.
2. Disconnect the selector rod from the selector lever.
3. Set the selector lever on the transmission and on the column to **N**.
4. Adjust the selector rod until the bearing pin is aligned with the bearing bushing in the selector lever.
5. Connect the rear selector lever to

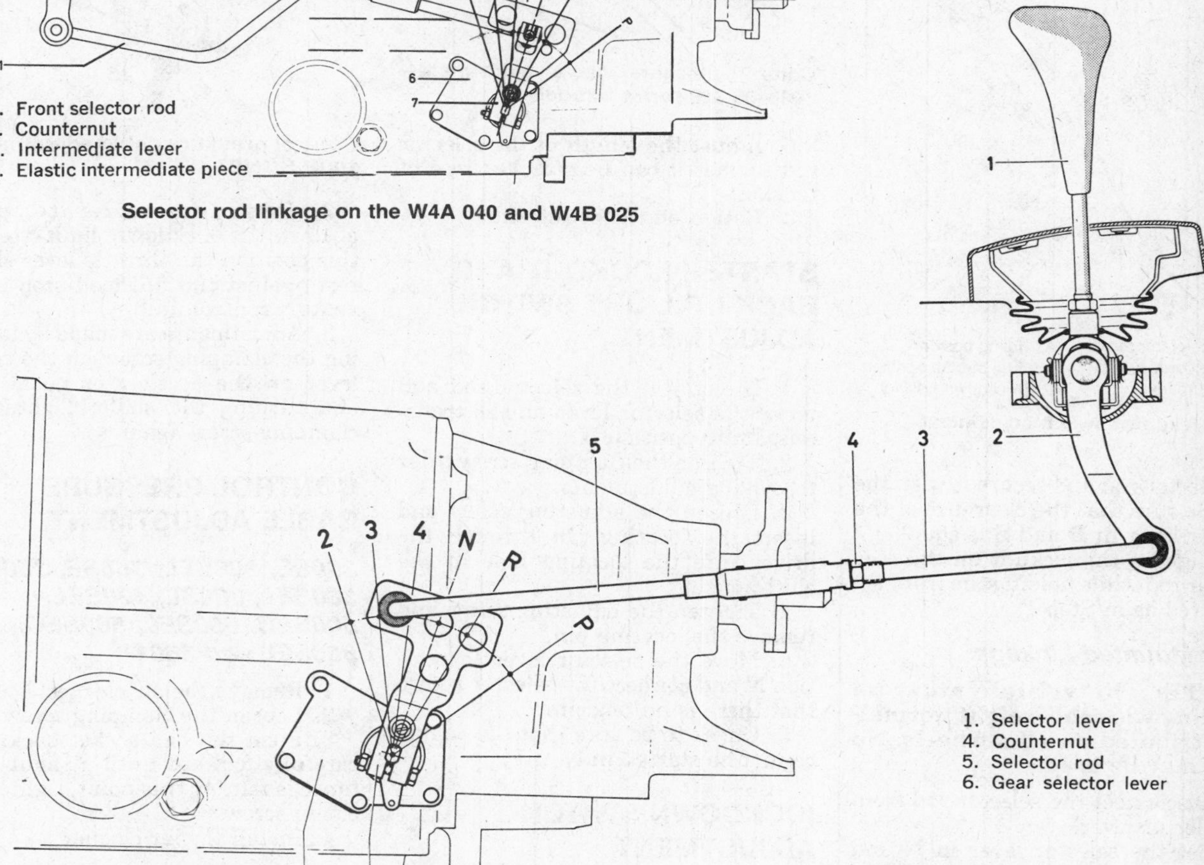


1. Selector lever
4. Counternut
5. Selector rod
6. Gear selector lever

**Floor mounted selector rod linkage**

1. Selector range lever
2. Washer
3. Adjusting screw
4. Shaft
5. Locating pin
6. Clamping screw

(a)—Column shift for left-hand and right-hand drive vehicles 220/8, 220 D/8, 230/8, 280 S/8, 280 SE/8 and 300 SEL/8.

(b)—Steering wheel shift for left-hand drive vehicles (220/8, 220 D/8, 230/8, 250/8)

(c)—Steering wheel shift for right-hand drive vehicles (220/8, 220 D/8, 230/8, 250/8)

(d)—Steering wheel shift for left-hand drive vehicles (280S/8, 280 SE/8, 300 SEL/8, 280 SE/3.5 and 300 SEL/3.5)

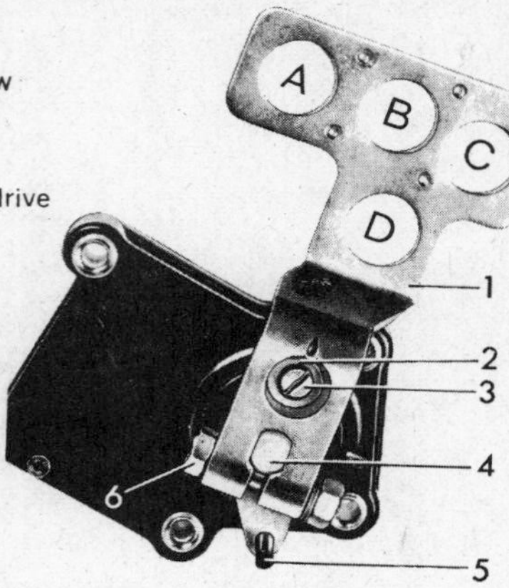


**Starter lockout and backup light switch adjustment**

**Control pressure cable adjustment on the 260E, 300E, 300CE, 300SE, 300SEL and 300TE**

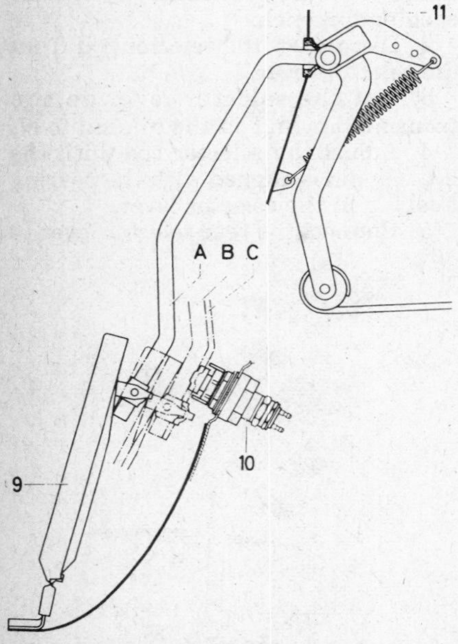


9. Accelerator pedal
10. Kickdown switch
11. Return lever

A. Idling position
B. Full throttle position
C. Kickdown position

**Kickdown switch adjustment**

the selector rod and secure it with the lock. Be sure that the clearance of the selector lever in **D** and **S** is equal.

6. Tighten the locknut on the rear selector rod while holding the front selector rod as in Step 1.

### *Floor Mounted Linkage*

**NOTE: The vehicle must be standing with the weight normally distributed on all 4 wheels. No jacks may be used.**

1. Disconnect the selector rod from the selector lever.
2. Set the selector lever in **N** and make sure that there is approximately 1mm clearance between the selector lever and the **N** stop of the selector gate.

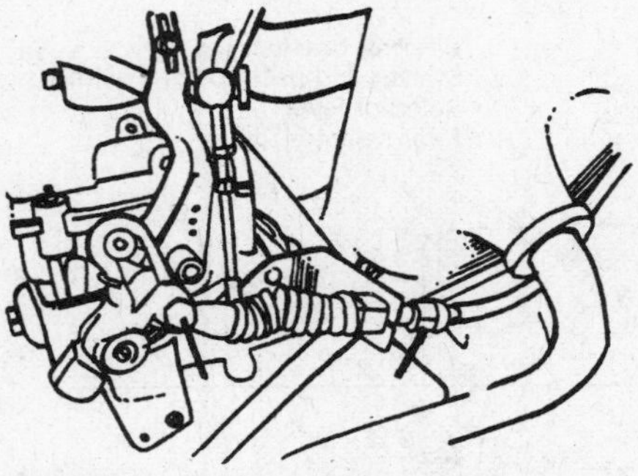

**Control pressure cable adjustment—1986–88 300 series turbodiesel**

3. Adjust the length of the selector rod so that it can be attached free of tension.
4. Retighten the counternut.

## STARTER LOCKOUT AND BACK-UP LIGHT SWITCH ADJUSTMENT

1. Disconnect the selector rod and move the selector lever on the transmission to position **N**.
2. Tighten the clamping screw prior to making adjustments.
3. Loosen the adjusting screw and insert the locating pin through the driver into the locating hole in the shift housing.
4. Tighten the adjusting screw and remove the locating pin.
5. Move the selector lever to position **N** and connect the selector rod so that there is no tension.
6. Check to be sure that the engine cannot be started in **N** or **P**.

## KICKDOWN SWITCH ADJUSTMENT

1. The kickdown position of the solenoid valve is controlled by the accelerator pedal.

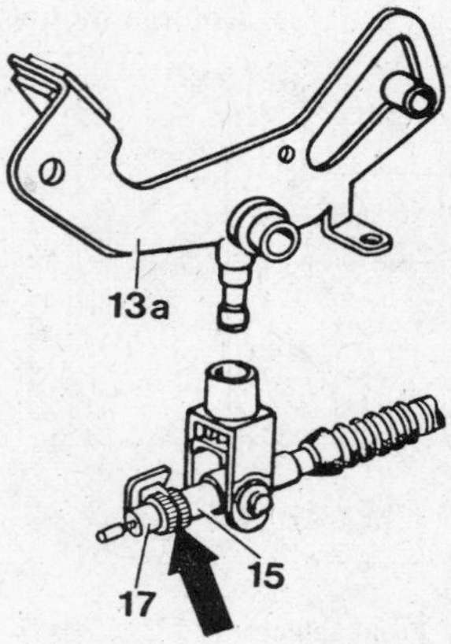


**Control pressure cable adjustment—190E SOHC**

2. Push the accelerator pedal against the kickdown limit stop. In this position the throttle lever should rest against the full load stop of the venturi control unit.
3. Adjustments are made by loosening the clamping screw on the return lever on the accelerator pedal shaft and turning the shaft. Tighten the clamping screw again.

## CONTROL PRESSURE CABLE ADJUSTMENT

### *300SE, 300SEL, 380SE, 380SEC, 380SEL, 380SL, 420SEL, 500SEC, 500SEL, 560SEC, 560SEL and 560SL*

1. Remove the air cleaner.
2. Loosen the clamping screw.
3. Push the ball socket back, then carefully forward until a slight resistance is felt. At this point, tighten the clamp screw.
4. Install the air cleaner.

### *Turbodiesels*

1. Pry off the ball socket.
2. Push the ball socket back, then

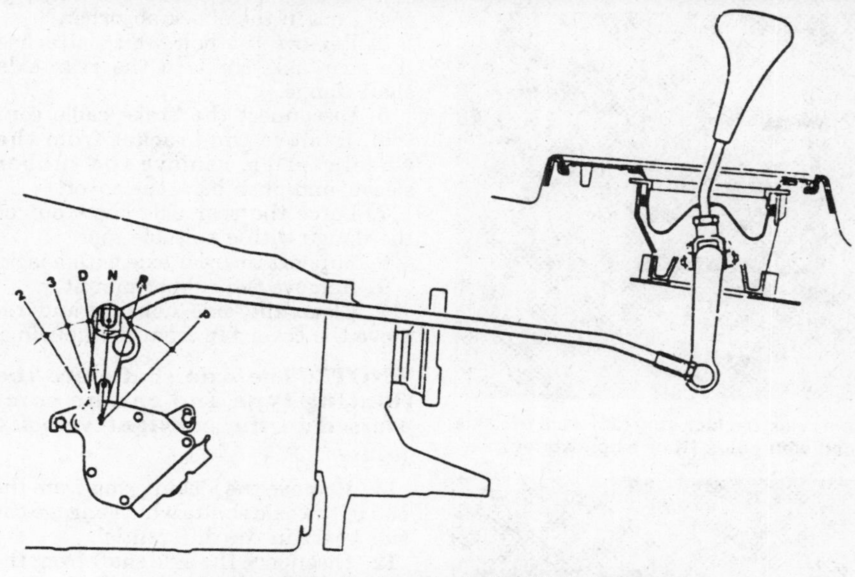

Control rod adjustment—190D, 190E AND 260E

Control pressure cable adjustment—1984–85 190D

pull carefully forward until a slight resistance is felt.

3. Hold the ball socket above the ball head. The drag lever should rest against the stop.

4. Adjust the cable at the adjusting screw so that the ball socket can be attached with no strain.

### 190D

1. Remove the ball socket and extend the telescoping rod to its full length.

2. Pull the control cable forward until a slight resistance is felt. Hold the ball socket over the ball head and engage tension free.

3. Adjust by using the telescoping rod if so required.

### 190E and 190E-16

1. Turn the adjusting screw inward until the compression nipple on the spacing sleeve has approximately 1mm of play left.

2. Unscrew the adjusting screw until the tip of the pointer rests directly above the groove on the adjusting screw.

### 260E, 300E, 300CE and 300TE

1. Disconnect the ball socket.

2. Pull the control pressure cable forward until a slight resistance is felt. In this position, hold the ball socket above the ball and engage the 2, free of tension.

3. Adjust by turning the screw if required.

# DRIVE AXLE

Mercedes-Benz automobiles use either 2 or 3 piece driveshaft to connect the transmission to a hypoid independent rear axle. All models covered in this book use independent rear suspension with open or enclosed driveshaft to the rear wheels.

## Driveshaft and U-Joints

### REMOVAL & INSTALLATION

#### 1983–85 240D, 300D, 300CD and 300TD

Matchmark all driveshaft connections prior to removal.

1. Remove the equalizer and disconnect the parking brake cables.

2. Remove the bolts which secure the two brackets to the chassis at the front and rear and remove the brackets. It may be necessary to lower the exhaust system slightly to allow access to the left hand bolts on the rear bracket.

3. Loosen the nut on the driveshaft about 2 turns without pushing the rubber sleeve back (it slides along). On a two-piece shaft, only loosen the front clamp nut.

4. Remove the nuts which secure the attaching plate to the transmission flange and rear axle.

5. Remove the bolts which secure the intermediate bearing (s) to the chassis. Push the driveshaft together and slightly down, and remove the driveshaft from the vehicle.

**NOTE: If possible, do not separate the parts of the driveshaft since each driveshaft is balanced at the factory. If separation is necessary, all parts must be marked and reassembled in the same relative positions to assure that the driveshafts will remain reasonably well balanced.**

**To install:**

6. Installation is the reverse of removal.

7. Pack the cavities of the 2 centering sleeves with special Mercedes-Benz grease.

8. Install the driveshaft and attach the intermediate bearing(s) to the chassis.

9. Rock the car backward and forward several times to be sure that the driveshaft is properly centered without forcing.

10. Prior to tightening the clamp nuts on the 3 piece driveshaft, be sure that the intermediate shaft does not contact either the front or rear intermediate bearing. The clearance between the intermediate shaft and the bearing should be the same at both ends.

#### All Other Models

**NOTE: Steps 1–3 apply to 4 cylinder and V8 models. Matchmark all driveshaft connections prior to removal.**

1. Fold the torsion bar down after disconnecting the level control linkage (if equipped).

2. Remove the exhaust system.

3. Remove the heat shield from the frame.

4. Support the transmission with a jack and completely remove the rear engine mount crossmember.

5. Without sliding the rubber sleeve back, loosen the clamp nut approximately 2 turns (the rubber sleeve will slide along).

**NOTE: On 3 piece driveshafts, only the front clamp nut need be loosened.**

6. Unscrew the U-joint mounting flange from the U-joint plate.

**NOTE: The 1983 380SEL and 380SEC uses a new design coupling flange with thinner washers**

**under a new hex nut. The previous design used thicker washers. Do not mix the 2 types.**

7. Bend back the locktabs and remove the bolts that attach the driveshaft to the rear axle pinion yoke.
8. Remove the bolts which attach the intermediate bearing(s) to the frame. Push the driveshaft together slightly and remove it from the vehicle.
9. Try not to separate the driveshafts. If it is absolutely necessary, matchmark all components so that they can be reassembled in the same order.
10. Installation is the reverse of removal. Always use new self-locking nuts. After the driveshaft is installed, rock the car back and forth several times to settle the driveshaft. Make sure that neither intermediate shaft is binding against either intermediate bearing, and that the clearance between the intermediate bearing and the driveshaft is the same at both ends.

## Rear Axle Shafts

**NOTE: The rubber covered joints are filled with special oil. If they are disassembled for any reason, they must be refilled with special oil.**

### REMOVAL & INSTALLATION

#### *All Except 190D, 190E, 260E, 300E, 300CE, 300SE, 300TE, 300SEL, 300SDL, 420SEL, 380SEC, 500SEC, 560SEC, 560SEL, 1987 300D and 300TD*

#### MODELS WITHOUT TORQUE COMPENSATOR (TORSION BAR)

Most models do not use a torque compensator (torsion bar) which is actually a steel bar used to locate the rear axle under acceleration. In general, only the large sedans use a torque compensator, but it is wise to check for one prior to servicing the axle shaft. The illustrations apply to either type.

1. Jack up the rear of the car and remove the wheel and center axle hold-down bolt (in hub).
2. Remove the brake caliper and suspend it from a hook.
3. Drain the differential oil and place a jack under the differential housing.
4. Unbolt the rubber mount from the chassis and the differential housing, then remove the differential housing cover to expose the ring and pinion gears.
5. Press the shaft from the axle flange. If necessary, loosen the shock absorber.
6. Using a pry bar, remove the axle lock ring inside the differential case.
7. Pull the axle from the housing by pulling the splined end from the side gears, with the spacer.

Removing the lock-ring (26) from the axle shaft with pliers (1) or a screwdriver

Lock the collar nut on the 190 at the crush flange (arrow)

**NOTE: Axle shafts are stamped R and L for right and left units. Always use new lockrings.**

8. Installation is the reverse of removal. Fill the rear axle. New radial seal rings are used on all models. Lubricate the outside diameter of rubber covered radial sealing rings with hypoid gear lubricant prior to installation.

**CAUTION**

*Check endplay of the lockring in the groove. If necessary, install a thicker lockring or spacer to eliminate all endplay, while still allowing the lockring to rotate. Do not allow the joints in the axle shaft to hang free or the joint bearing may be damaged and leak.*

#### MODELS WITH TORQUE COMPENSATOR (TORSION BAR)

1. Drain the oil from the rear axle.
2. Disconnect and plug the brake lines.
3. Loosen the connecting rod and unscrew the torsion bar bearing bracket. Lower the exhaust system slightly and remove the torsion bar.
4. Loosen the shock absorber.
5. Remove the bolt which attaches the rear axle shaft to the rear axle shaft flange.
6. Disconnect the brake cable control. Remove the bracket from the wheel carrier, remove the rubber sleeve, and push back the cover.
7. Force the rear axle shaft out of the flange with a suitable tool.
8. Support the rear axle with a jack.
9. Remove the rubber mount.
10. Clean the axle housing and remove the cover fan from the housing.

**NOTE: The axle shafts are the floating type and can be compressed in the constant velocity joints.**

11. Remove the locking ring from the end of the axle shafts which engage the side gears in the differential.
12. Disengage the axle shaft from the side gear and remove the axle shaft together with the spacer.

**CAUTION**

*Do not hang the outer constant velocity joint in a free position (without any support) as the shaft may be damaged and the constant velocity joint housing may leak.*

13. Installation is the reverse of removal.
14. If either axle shaft is replace, be sure that the proper replacement shaft is installed. Axle shafts are marked L and R for left and right.
15. Check the end-play between the lock-ring on the axle shaft and the side gear. There should be no noticeable end-play, but the lock-ring should be able to turn in the groove.
16. Be sure to bleed the brakes and fill the rear axle with the proper quantity and type of lubricant. New radial seal rings are used on all models. Lubricate the outside diameter of rubber covered radial seal rings with hypoid gear lubricant prior to installation.

#### *190D, 190E, 260E, 300E, 300CE, 300SE, 300TE, 300SEL, 300SDL, 380SEC, 420SEL, 500SEC, 560SEC, 560SEL, 1987 300D and 300TD*

1. Loosen, but do not remove, the axle shaft collar nut.
2. Raise the rear of the vehicle and support it on jackstands.
3. Disconnect the axle shaft from the hub assembly. On the 190, make sure that while loosening the locking screws, the bit is seated properly in the multi-tooth profile of the screws.
4. Remove the self-locking screws that attach the inner CV-joint to the connecting flange on the differential. Always loosen the screws in a crosswise manner.

Axle shaft markings (r)

**NOTE: Make sure that the end cover on the inner CV-joint is not damaged when separated from the connecting flange.**

5. While supporting the axle shaft, use a slide hammer or the like and press the axle shaft out of the hub assembly.
6. Tilt the axle shaft down and remove it.

**CAUTION**

***Make sure that the CV-joint boots are not damaged during the removal process.***

7. Installation is in the reverse order of removal. Please note the following:
   a. Always clean the connecting flanges before installation.
   b. Always use new self-locking screws. Lubricate the screw threads and contact faces with oil before installing.
   c. 190, 260E, 300E, 300CE and 300TE – tighten the screws to 51 ft. lbs. (70 Nm).
   d. 300D, 300SE, 300SEL, 300TD, 300SDL, 420SEL, 560SEC and 560SEL – tighten the screws to 51 ft. lbs. (70 Nm) M10 bolts, 100 ft. lbs. (135 Nm) (M12 × 1.5 bolts).
   e. All other models – Tighten the screws to 90–105 ft. lbs. (125–145 Nm). Always tighten the screws in a crosswise pattern.
   f. Tighten the axle shaft collar nut to 203–230 ft. lbs. (280–320 Nm) on the 190 and 22 ft. lbs. (30 Nm) on the others. On the 190, lock the collar nut at the crush flange.

### CV-JOINT OVERHAUL

**For all CV-joint overhaul procedures, please refer to "CV-Joint Overhaul" in the Unit Repair section.**

# FRONT SUSPENSION

## Shock Absorbers

### REMOVAL & INSTALLATION

#### *380SL, 380SLC and 560SL*

1. Jack up the front of the car until the weight is off of the wheels and support the car securely on jack stands.
2. When removing the shock absorbers, it is also wise to draw a simple diagram of the location of parts such as lockrings, rubber stops, locknuts and steel plates, since many shock absorbers require their own peculiar installation of these parts.
3. Raise the hood and locate the upper shock absorber mount.
4. Support the lower control arm with a jack.
5. Unbolt the mount for the shock absorber at the top. Remove the coolant expansion tank to allow access to the right front shock absorber.
6. Remove the nuts which secure the shock absorber to the lower control arm.
7. Push the shock absorber piston rod in, install the stirrup, and remove the shock absorber.
8. Remove the stirrup, since this must be install on replacement shock absorber.
9. Installation is the reverse of removal. Always use new bushing when installing replacement shock absorber.

#### *All Other Models Except 190D, 190E, 260E, 300E, 300CE, 300SE, 300TE and 300SEL*

1. Jack and support the car. Support the lower control arm.
2. Loosen the nuts on the upper shock absorber mount. Remove the plate and ring.
3. Place the shock absorber vertical to the lower control arm and remove the lower mounting bolts.
4. Remove the shock absorber. Be sure to disconnect and plug the pressure line on models with level control.
5. Installation is the reverse or removal. On Bilstein shocks, do not confuse the upper and lower plates.

**NOTE: The 380SEL shock absorber uses a protective plastic sleeve that must be installed between the lower retainer and lower rubber ring. Also, a slot is provided for holding the piston rod, in place of the 2 flats used previously.**

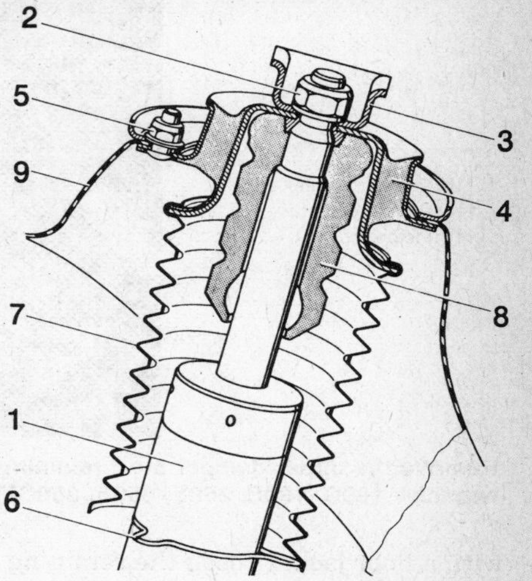


1. Damper strut
2. Hex. nut
3. Rebound stop
4. Rubber mount
5. Hex. nuts
6. Stop ring
7. Sleeve
8. Additional PU spring
9. Front end

**Upper damper strut mounting – 190D, 190E, 260E, 300E, 300CE and 300TE**

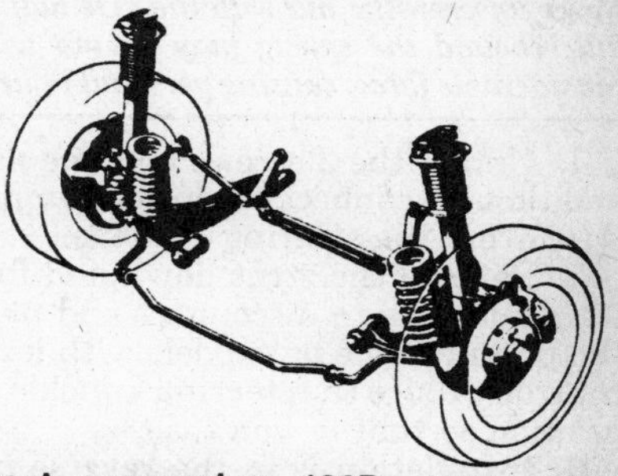

**Front suspension – 190D, 190E, 260E 300E, 300CE and 300TE**

**NOTE: 380SEC shock absorbers have the same part number regardless of manufacturer. However, the shock absorbers of these cars have a larger diameter and narrower lower mounting eye than other models.**

## Damper Strut

### REMOVAL & INSTALLATION

#### *190D, 190E, 260E, 300E, 300CE, 300SE, 300TE and 300SEL*

1. Raise the front of the vehicle and support it with jackstands. Remove the wheel.
2. Using a spring compressor, compress the spring until any load is removed from the lower control arm.

**NOTE: When using a spring compressor, be sure that a least 7½ coils are engaged before applying tension.**

3. Support the lower control arm

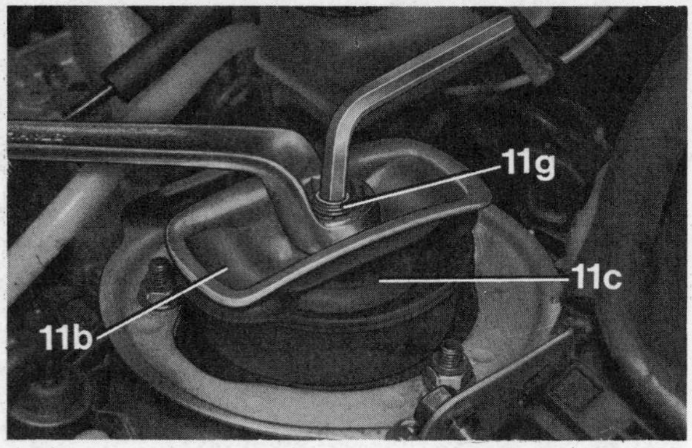


11b Rebound limiter
11c Rubber mount
11g Piston rod

**Remove the upper damper strut retaining nut by locking the piston rod with an Allen wrench—190D, 190E, 260E, 300E, 300CE and 300TE**

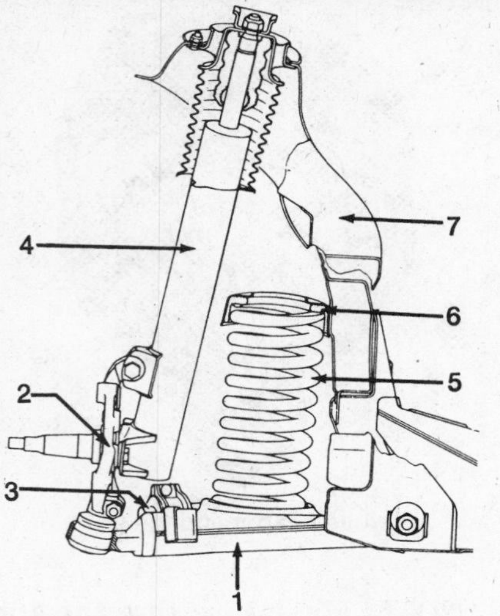


1. Wishbone
2. Steering knuckle
3. Torsion bar
4. Damper strut
5. Front spring
6. Spring-rubber mount
7. Front end

**Front spring—190D, 190E, 260E, 300E, 300CE and 300TE**

with a floor jack. Loosen the retaining bolt for the upper end of the damper strut by holding the inner piston rod with an Allen wrench and then unscrewing the nut. NEVER use an impact wrench on the retaining nut.

**CAUTION**

***Never unscrew the nut with the axle half at full rebound the spring may fly out with considerable force. causing personal injury.***

4. Unbolt the 2 screws and one nut and then disconnect the lower damper strut from the steering knuckle.
5. Remove the strut down and forward. Be sure to disconnect and plug the pressure line on models with level control. Secure the steering knuckle in position so that it won't tilt.
6. Installation is in the reverse order of removal. Please note the following:
 a. When attaching the lower end of the damper strut to the steering knuckle, first position all 3 screws; next tighten the 2 lower screws to 72 ft. lbs. (100 Nm); finally, tighten the nut on the upper clamping connection screw to 54 ft. lbs. (75 Nm).
 b. Tighten the retaining nut on the upper end of the damper strut to 44 ft. lbs. (60 Nm).

## Springs

### REMOVAL & INSTALLATION

#### *190D, 190E, 260E, 300E, 300CE, 300SE, 300TE and 300SEL*

1. Raise the front of the vehicle and support it jackstands. Remove the wheel.
2. Remove the engine compartment lining underneath the vehicle (if so equipped).
3. Install a spring compressor so that at least 7½ coils are engaged.
4. Support the lower control arm with a floor jack and then loosen the retaining nut at the upper end of the damper strut.

**CAUTION**

***NEVER loosen the damper strut retaining nut unless the wheels are on the ground, the control arm is supported or the springs have been removed.***

5. Lower the jack under the control arm slightly and then remove the spring toward the front.
6. On installation, position the spring between the control arm and the upper mount so that when the control arm is raised, the end of the lower coil will be seated in the impression in the control arm.
7. Use the jack and raise the control arm until the spring is held securely.
8. Using a new nut, tighten the upper end of the damper strut to 44 ft. lbs. (60 Nm).
9. Slowly ease the tension on the spring compressor until the spring is seated properly and then remove the compressor.
10. Installation of the remaining components is in the reverse order of removal.

#### *380SL and 560SL*

**NOTE: Be extremely careful when attempting to remove the front springs as they are compressed and under considerable load.**

1. Raise the front of the vehicle and support it with jackstands. Remove the wheels.
2. Remove the front shock absorber and disconnect the sway bar.
3. First punchmark the position of the eccentric adjusters, then loosen the hex bolts.
4. Support the lower control arm with a jack.
5. Knock out the eccentric pins and gradually lower the arm until spring tension is relieved.
6. The spring can now be removed.

1. Front axle carrier
3. Lower control arm
4. Upper control arm
10. Front spring
11. Front shock absorber
12. Torsion bar
29. Rubber mounting
31. Rubber mounting for front spring

**Front spring removal—380SL and 560SL**

**NOTE: Check caster and camber after installing a new spring.**

7. Installation is the reverse of removal.
8. For ease of installation, tape the rubber mounts to the springs.
9. If the eccentric adjusters were not matchmarked, install the eccentric bolts as illustrated under "Front End Alignment".

#### *All Other Models*

1. Raise and support the front of the car and support the lower control arm.
2. Remove the wheel. Unbolt the upper shock absorber mount.
3. Install a spring compressor and compress the spring.

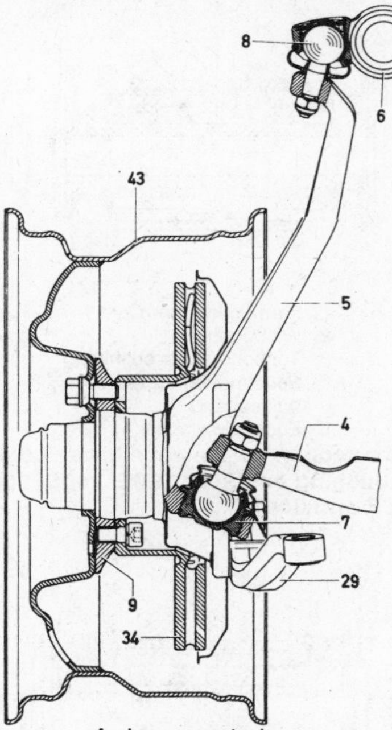


4. Lower control arm
5. Steering knuckle
6. Upper control arm
7. Support joint
8. Guide joint
9. Front wheel hub
29. Steering knuckle arm
34. Brake disc
43. Wheel

**Steering knuckle/ball joint—all except 190 series, 260E, 300 series (1986–90), 380SL and 560SL**

4. Remove the front spring with the lower mount.

5. Installation is the reverse of removal. Tighten the upper shock absorber suspension.

## Steering Knuckle and Ball Joints

### INSPECTION

1. To check the steering knuckles or ball joints, jack up the car, placing a jack directly under the front spring plate. This unloads the front suspension to allow the maximum play to be observed.

2. Late model ball joints need to be replaced only if dried out with plainly visible wear and/or play.

### REMOVAL & INSTALLATION

#### *190D, 190E, 260E, 300E, 300CE, 300SE, 300TE and 300SEL*

1. Raise the front of the vehicle and support it with jackstands. Remove the wheel.

2. Install a spring compressor on the spring.

1. Wishbone
2. Steering knuckle
3. Bolt with nut
4. Ball joint

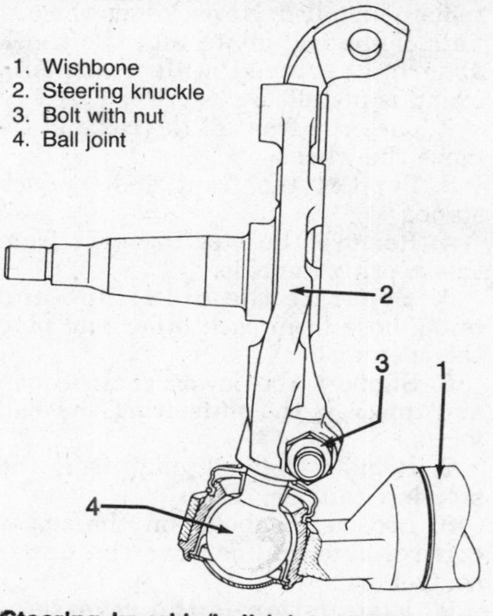


**Steering knuckle/ball joint—190D, 190E, 260E, 300E, 300CE and 300TE**

3. Remove the brake caliper and then wire it out of the way. Be careful not to damage the brake line.

4. Remove the brake disc and wheel hub.

**NOTE: On vehicles equipped with ABS, remove the speed sensor.**

5. Unscrew the 3 socket-head bolts and then remove the brake backing plate from the steering knuckle.

6. Tighten the spring compressor until all tension and/or lead has been removed from the lower control arm.

7. Disconnect the steering knuckle arm from the steering knuckle (this is the arm attached to the tie rod).

**CAUTION**

***There must be no tension on the lower control arm.***

8. Unscrew the 3 bolts and disconnect the lower end of the damper strut from the steering knuckle.

9. Remove the hex-head clamp nut at the supporting joint (lower ball joint).

10. Remove the steering knuckle.

11. Installation is in the reverse order of removal. Please note the following:

 a. Tighten the supporting joint clamp nut to 70 ft. lbs. (125 Nm).

 b. Refer to the "Damper Strut Removal and Installation" procedure when connecting the lower end of the damper strut to the steering knuckle.

#### *380SL and 560SL*

1. This should only be done with the front shock absorber installed. If, however, the front shock absorber has been removed, the lower control arm

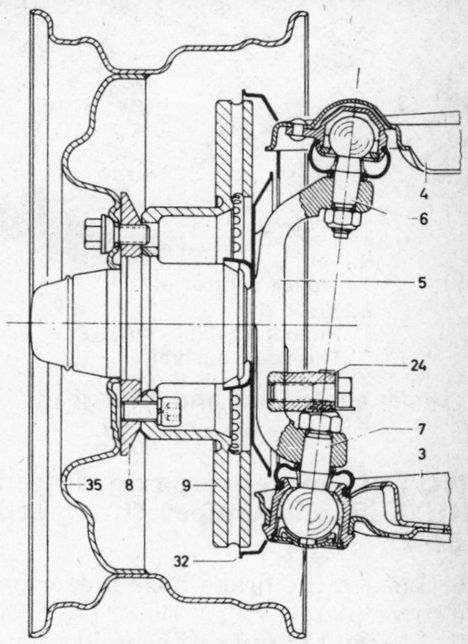


3. Lower control arm
4. Upper control arm
5. Steering knuckle
6. Guide joint
7. Supporting joint
8. Front wheel hub
9. Brake disc
24. Steering knuckle arm
32. Cover plate
35. Wheel

**Steering knuckle/ball joint—380SL and 560SL**

should be supported with a jack and the spring should be clamped with a spring tensioner. In this case, the hex nut on the guide joint should not be loosened without the spring tensioner installed.

2. Jack up the front of the car and support it on jack stands.

3. Remove the wheel.

4. Remove the brake caliper.

5. Unbolt the steering relay lever from the steering knuckle. For safety, install spring clamps on the front springs.

6. Remove the hex nuts from the upper and lower ball joints.

7. Remove the ball joints from the steering knuckle with the aid of a puller.

8. Remove the steering knuckle.

9. Installation is the reverse of removal. Be sure that the seats for the pins of the ball joints are free of grease.

10. Bleed the brakes.

#### *All Other Models*

1. Raise and support the car. For safety, it's a good idea to install some type of clamp on the front spring. Position jack stands at the outside front against the lower control arms.

2. Remove the wheel.

3. Remove the steering knuckle arm from the steering knuckle.

4. Remove and suspend the brake caliper.

5. Remove the front wheel hub.

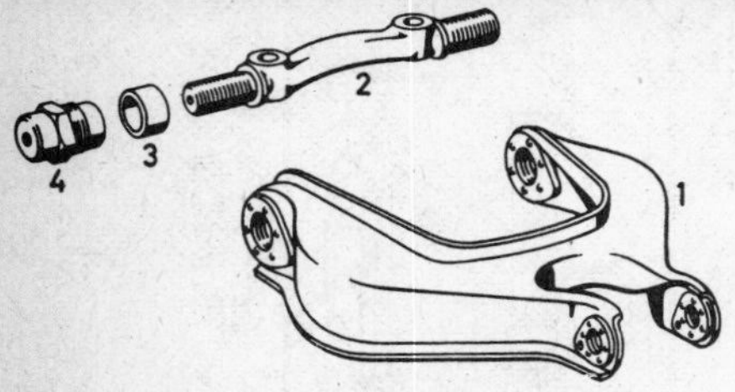


1. Upper control arm
2. Pivot pin
3. Rubber sealing ring
4. Threaded bushing

**Upper control arm and pivot shaft**

**NOTE: On vehicles equipped with ABS, disconnect the speed sensor.**

6. Loosen the brake hose holder on the cover plate.
7. Loosen the nut on the guide joint and remove the joint from the steering knuckle.
8. Loosen the nut on the support joint.
9. Swivel the steering knuckle outward and force the ball joint from the lower control arm.
10. Remove the steering knuckle.
11. If necessary, remove the cover plate from the steering knuckle.
12. Installation is the reverse of removal. Use self-locking nuts and adjust the wheel bearings.

## Upper Control Arm

**NOTE: The 190D, 190E, 260E, 300E, 300CE, 300SE, 300TE and 300SEL models have no upper control arm.**

### REMOVAL & INSTALLATION

#### *All Models Except 380SL and 560SL*

1. Raise and support the car. Position jack stands at the outside front against the lower control arms.
2. Remove the wheel.
3. Loosen the nut on the guide joint.
4. Remove the guide joint from the steering knuckle.
5. Secure the steering knuckle with a hook on the upper control arm stop to prevent it from tilting.
6. Loosen the clamp screw and separate the upper control arm from the torsion bar.
7. Loosen the upper control arm bearing at the front and remove the upper control arm.
8. Installation is the reverse of removal. Use new self-locking nuts and check the front wheel alignment.

#### *380SL, 380SLC and 560SL*

1. The front shock absorbers should remain installed. Never loosen the hex nuts of the ball joints with the shock absorber removed, unless a spring clamp is installed.
2. Jack the front of the car and remove the wheel.
3. Support the front end on jack stands.
4. Remove the steering arm from the steering knuckle.
5. Separate the brake line and brake hose from each other and plug the openings.
6. Support the lower control arm and unscrew the nuts from the ball joints.
7. Remove the ball joints from the steering knuckle.
8. Loosen the bolts on the upper control arm and remove the upper control arm.
9. Installation is the reverse of removal.

**CAUTION**

***Mount the front hex bolt from the rear in a forward direction, and the rear hex bolt from the front in a rearward direction.***

10. Bleed the brakes.

## Lower Control Arm

### REMOVAL & INSTALLATION

#### *All Models Except 190D, 190E, 260E, 300E, 300CE, 300SE, 300TE, 300SEL, 380SL and 560SL*

The lower control arm is the same as the front axle half. For safety install a spring compressor on the coil spring.

1. Raise and support the front of the car and remove the wheels.
2. Remove the front shock absorber. Loosen the top mount first.
3. Remove the front springs.
4. Separate and plug the brake lines.
5. Remove the track rod from the steering knuckle arm.
6. Matchmark the position of the eccentric bolts on the bearing of the lower control arm in relation to the crossmember.
7. Remove the shield from the cross yoke.
8. Support the front axle half.
9. Loosen the eccentric bolt on the front and rear bearing of the lower control arm and knock them out.
10. Remove the bolt from the cross yoke bearing.
11. Loosen the screw at the opposite end of the cross yoke bearing.
12. Pull the cross yoke bearing down slightly.
13. Loosen the support of the upper control arm on the torsion bar. Remove the clamp screw from the clamp.

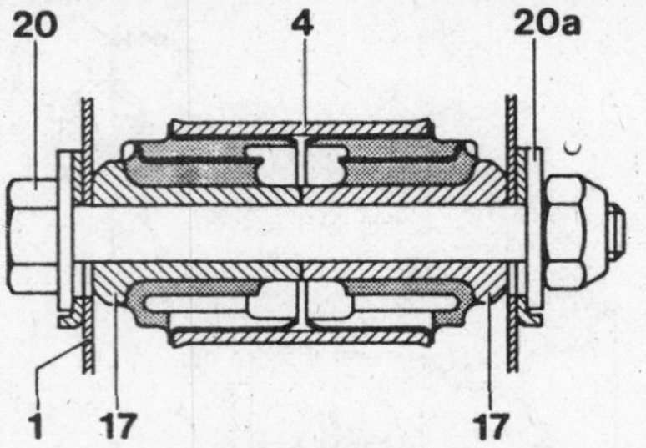


1. Frame side member
2. Wishbone
3. Torsion rubber bushing
4. Eccentric bolt (caster adjustment)
5. Eccentric washer

**Cross section of the rear lower control arm bushing on 190D, 190E, 260E, 300E, 300CE and 300TE**

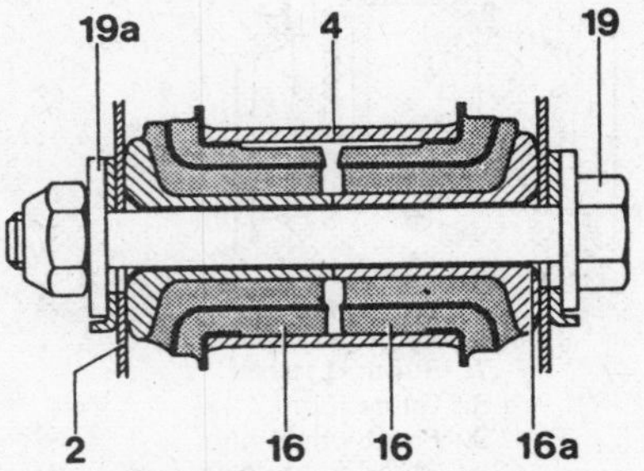


1. Frame cross member
2. Wishbone
3. Torsion rubber bushing
4. Clamping sleeve
5. Eccentric bolt (camber adjustment)
6. Eccentric washer

**Cross section of the front lower control arm bushing on 190D, 190E, 260E, 300E, 300CE and 300TE**

14. Remove the upper control arm bearing on the front end.
15. Remove the front axle half.
16. Installation is the reverse of removal. Tighten the eccentric bolts on the lower control arm bearing with the car resting on the wheels. Bleed the brakes and check the front end alignment.

#### *190D, 190E, 260E, 300E, 300CE, 300SE, 300TE and 300SEL*

1. Remove the engine compartment lining at the bottom of the vehicle (if so equipped).
2. Raise the front of the vehicle and support it with jackstands. Remove the wheel.
3. Support the lower control arm with jackstands and then disconnect the torsion bar bearing at the control arm.
4. Remove the spring as detailed earlier in this chapter.
5. Disconnect the tie rod at the steering knuckle and then press out the ball joint with the proper tool.
6. Remove the brake caliper and position it out of the way. Be sure that you do not damage the brake line.

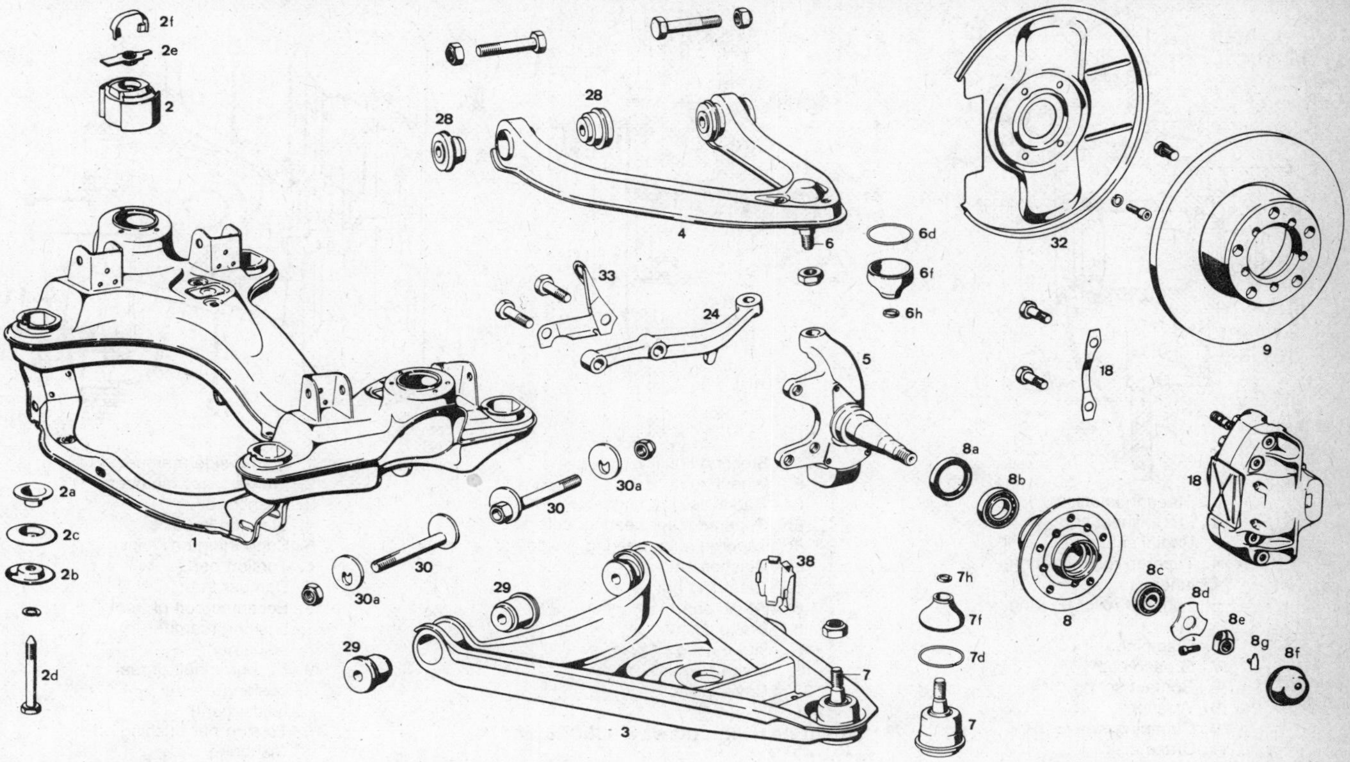


1. Front axle carrier
2. Rubber mount for suspension of front axle
2a. Stop buffer for inward deflection
2b. Stop plate
2c. Stop buffer for outward deflections
2d. Hex. bolt with snap-ring
2e. Fastening nut
2f. Nut holder
3. Lower control arm
4. Upper control arm
5. Steering knuckle
6. Guide joint
6d. Circlip
6f. Sleeve
6h. Clamping ring
7. Supporting joint
7d. Circlip
7f. Sleeve
7h. Clamping ring
8. Front wheel hub
8a. Radial sealing ring
8b. Inside tapered roller bearing
8c. Outside tapered roller bearing
8d. Washer
8e. Clamp nut
8f. Wheel cap
8g. Contact spring
9. Brake disc
18. Brake caliper
18a. Lockwasher
24. Steering knuckle arm
28. Rubber slide bearing
29. Rubber bearing (torsion bearing)
30. Cam bolt
30a. Cam washer
32. Cover plate
33. Holder for brake hose
38. Protective cap for steering lock

**Lower control arm and pivot shaft**

7. Remove the brake disc/wheel hub assembly.

8. Disconnect the lower end of the damper strut from the steering knuckle and then remove the knuckle.

9. Mark the position of the inner eccentric pins, relative to the frame, on the bearing of the control arm.

10. Unscrew and remove the pins.

11. Remove the jackstands and remove the lower control arm.

12. Installation is in the reverse order of removal. Please note the following:

a. Tighten the eccentric bolts on the inner arm to 130 ft. lbs. (180 Nm).

b. To facilitate torsion bar installation, raise the opposite side of the lower control arm with a jack.

c. Tighten the clamp nut on the tie rod ball joint to 25 ft. lbs. (35 Nm).

d. When installing the rear torsion bar bushing, on the 300E, 300CE, 300SE, 300TE and 300SEL, the flats on the cone must be vertical.

### 380SL and 560SL

1. Since the front shock absorber acts as a deflection stop for the front wheels, the lower shock absorber attaching point should not be loosened unless the vehicle is resting on the wheels or unless the lower control arm is supported.

2. Jack up the front of the vehicle and support it on jack stands.

3. Support the lower control arm.

4. Loosen the lower shock absorber attachment.

5. Unscrew the steering arm from the steering knuckle.

6. Separate the brake line and brake hose and plug the openings.

7. Remove the front spring.

8. Unscrew the hex nuts on the ball joints.

9. Remove the lower ball joint and remove the lower control arm.

10. Installation is the reverse of removal. Bleed the brakes and check the front end alignment.

# Front Wheel Bearings

## REMOVAL & INSTALLATION

If the wheel bearing play is being checked for correct setting only, it is not necessary to remove the caliper. It is only necessary to remove the brake pads.

1. Remove the brake caliper.

2. Pull the cap from the hub with a pair of channel-lock pliers. Remove the radio suppression spring, if equipped.

3. Loosen the socket screw of the clamp nut on the wheel spindle. Remove the clamp nuts and washer.

4. Remove the front wheel hub and brake disc.

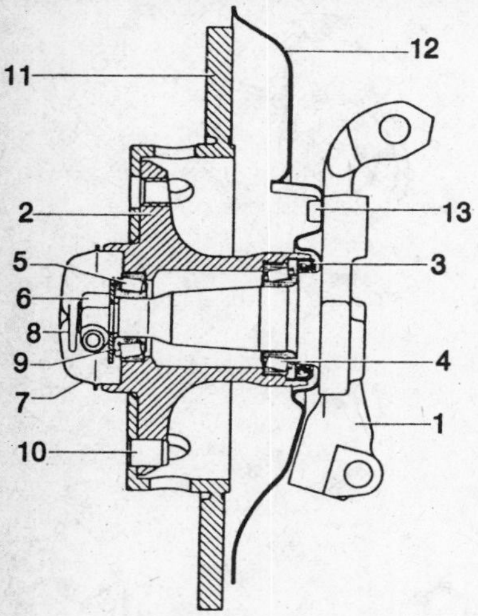


1. Steering knuckle
2. Front wheel hub
3. Radial seal ring
4. Tapered roller bearing, inner
5. Tapered roller bearing, outer
6. Clamping nut
7. Greaso cap
8. Contact spring
9. Washer
10. Clamping sleeve
11. Brake disk
12. Brake backing plate
13. Allen screws

**Wheel bearing cutaway—190D, 190E, 260E, 300E, 300CE and 300TE**

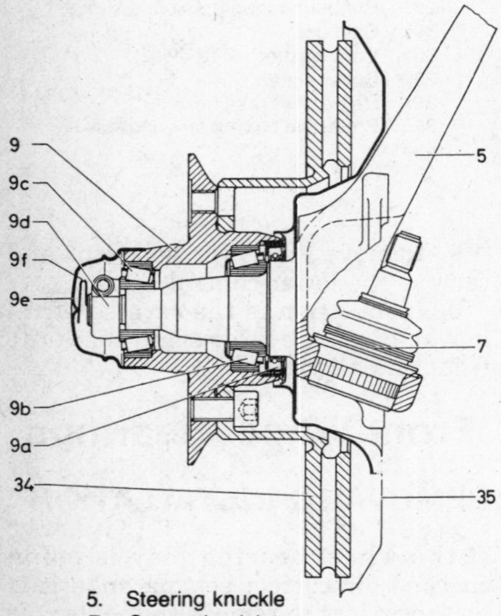


5. Steering knuckle
7. Supporting joint
9. Front wheel hub
9a. Radial sealing ring
9b. Tapered roller bearing, inside
9c. Tapered roller bearing, outside
9d. Clamping nut
9e. Wheel cap
9f. Contact spring
34. Brake disc
35. Cover plate

**Wheel bearing cutaway—all except 190D, 190E, 260E, 300E, 300CE, 300TE, 380SL and 560SL**

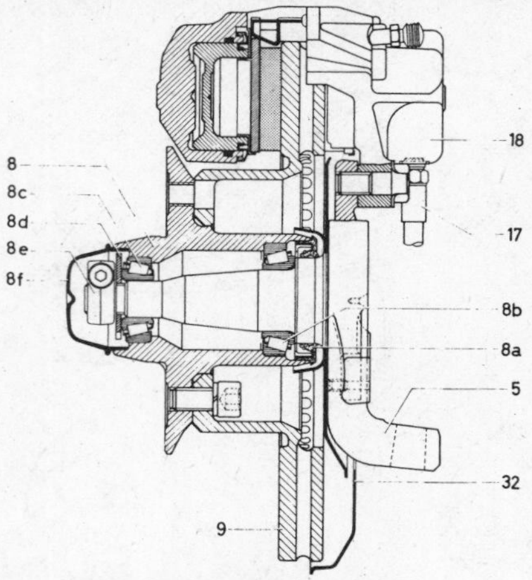


5. Steering knuckle
8. Wheel hub
8a. Radial sealing ring
8b. Tapered roller bearing, outside
8c. Tapered roller bearing, inside
8d. Washer
8e. Clamping nut
8f. Wheel cap
9. Brake disc
17. Brake hose
18. Brake caliper
32. Cover plate

**Wheel bearing cutaway—380SL and 560SL**

**Dial indicator set-up for checking wheel bearing play**

5. Remove the inner race with the roller cage of the outer bearing.

6. Using a brass or aluminum drift, carefully tap the outer race of the inner bearing until it can be removed with the inner race, bearing cage, and seal.

7. In the same manner, tap the outer race of the bearing out of the hub.

8. Separate the front hub from the brake disc.

9. To assemble, press the outer races into the front wheel hub.

10. Pack the bearing cage with bearing grease and insert the inner race with the bearing into the wheel hub.

11. Coat the sealing ring with sealant and press it into the hub.

12. Pack the front wheel hub with 45–55 grams of wheel bearing grease. The races of the tapered bearing should be well packed and also apply grease to the front faces of the rollers.

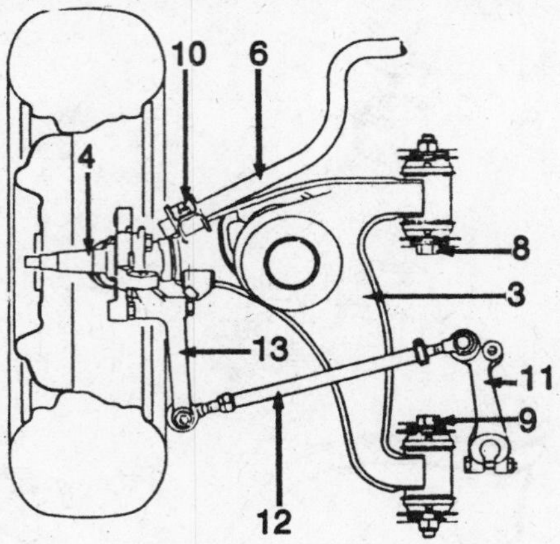


1. Frame side member
2. Frame cross member
3. Wishbone
4. Steering knuckle
5. Supporting ball joint
6. Torsion bar
7. Damper strut
8. Eccentric bolt of front bushing (camber adjusment)
9. Eccentric bolt of rear bushing (caster adjustment)
10. Torsion bar bushing on wishbone
11. Pitman arm
12. Tie rod
13. Steering knuckle arm

**Caster and camber adjustment points—190D, 190E, 260E, 300E, 300CE and 300TE**

Pack the front bearings with the specified amount of grease. Too much grease will cause overheating of the lubricant and it may lose its lubricity. Too little grease will not lubricate properly.

13. Coat the contact surface of the sealing ring on the wheel spindle with Molykote paste.

14. Press the wheel hub onto the wheel spindle.

15. Install the inner race and cage of the outer bearing.

16. Install the steel washer and the clamp nut.

## ADJUSTMENT

1. Tighten the clamp nut until the hub can just be turned.

2. Slacken the clamp nut and seat the bearings on the spindle by rapping the spindle sharply with a hammer.

3. Attach a dial indicator, with the pointer indexed, onto the wheel hub.

4. Check the end-play of the hub by pushing and pulling on the flange. The end-play should be approximately 0.0004–0.0008 in.

5. Make an additional check by rotating the washer between the inner

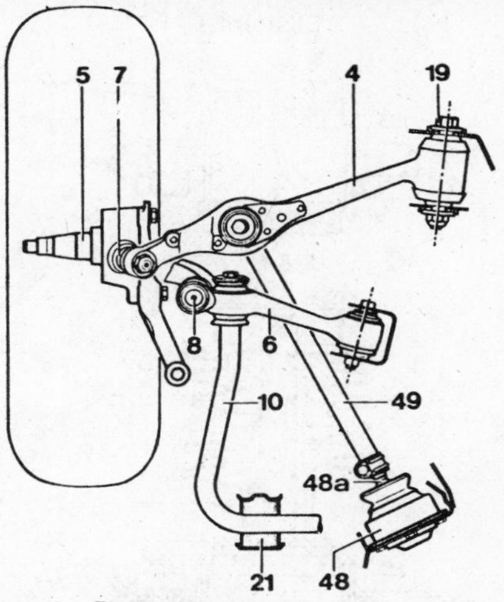


1. Frame side member
2. Frame cross member for front axle
4. Lower control arm
5. Steering knuckle
6. Upper control arm
7. Supporting joint
8. Guide joint
10. Torsion bar
19. Eccentric bolt (camber adjustment)
21. Torsion bar mounting on front end
48. Supporting joint
48a. Ball pin (caster adjustment)
49. Supporting tube

**Caster and camber adjustment points on all other models**

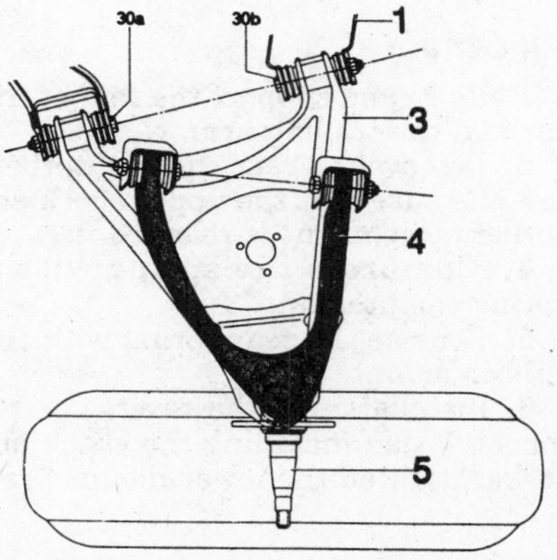


1. Front axle carrier
3. Lower control arm
4. Upper control arm
5. Steering knuckle
30a. Cam bolt front
30b. Cam bolt rear

**Caster and camber adjustment points—380SL and 560SL**

race of the outer bearing and the clamp nut. It should be able to be turned by hand.

6. Check the position of the suppressor pin in the wheel spindle and the contact spring in the dust cap.

7. Pack the dust cap with 20–25 grams of wheel bearing grease and install the cap.

8. Install the brake caliper and bleed the brakes.

# Front Wheel Alignment

Caster and camber are critical to proper handling and tire wear. Neither adjustment should be attempted without the specialized equipment to accurately measure the geometry of the front end.

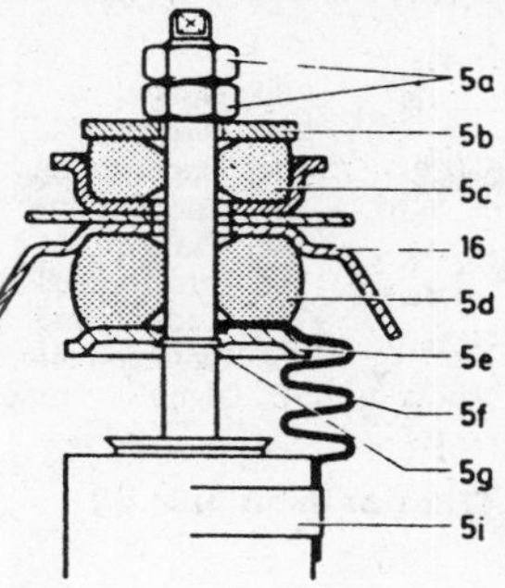


5a. Nut
5b. Washer
5c. Upper rubber ring
5d. Lower rubber ring
5e. Plate
5f. Dust protection
5g. Lockring
5i. Clamping strap
16. Dome on frame floor

**Rear shock absorber upper mount—190D, 190E, 260E, 300E, 300CE and 300TE**

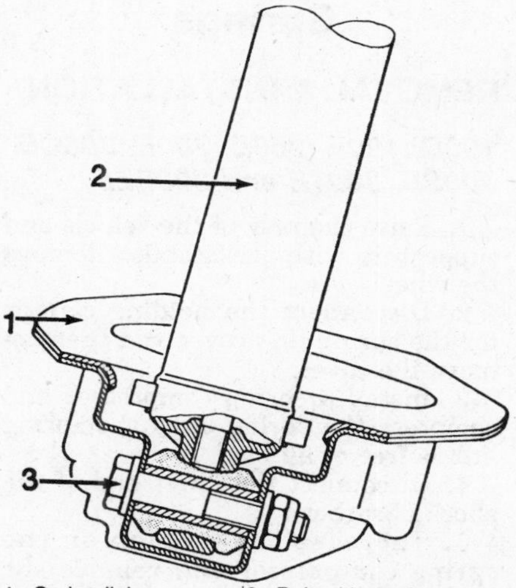


1. Spring link
2. Shock absorber
3. Bolt with washers and self- locking nut

**Rear shock absorber lower mount—190D and 190E**

## CASTER/CAMBER ADJUSTMENT

### *All Models Except 380SL and 560SL*

The front axle provides for caster and camber adjustment, but both wheel adjustments can only be made together. Adjustment are made with cam bolts on the lower control arm bearings.

The front bearing cam bolt is used to set caster, while the rear bearing cam bolt is used for camber.

### *380SL and 560SL*

Caster and camber are dependent upon each other and cannot be adjusted independently. They can only be adjusted simultaneously.

Caster is adjusted by turning the lower control arm around the front mounting, using the eccentric bolt.

Camber is adjusted by turning the lower control arm about the rear mounting, using the eccentric bolt. Bear in mind that caster will be changed accordingly.

When the camber is adjusted in a positive direction, caster is changed in a negative camber by 0° 15' results in a caster change of approximately 0° 20'. Adjustment of the caster by 1 degrees results in a camber change of approximately 0° 7'.

## TOE-IN ADJUSTMENT

Toe-in is the difference of the distance between the front edges of the wheel rims and the rear edges of the wheel rims.

To measure toe-in, the steering

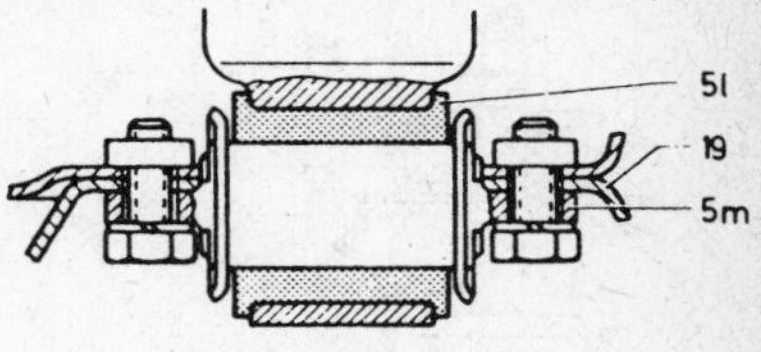


5l. Rubber mounting
5m. Fastening clip
19. Semi-trailing arm

**Rear shock absorber upper mount—1983–85 300SD, 300SDL, 300SE, 300SEL, 380SE, 380SEC, 380SEL, 380SL, 420SEL, 500SEC, 500SEL, 560SEC, 560SEL and 560SL**

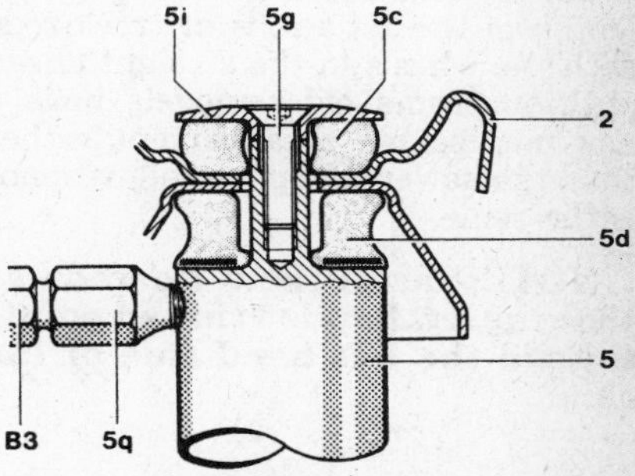

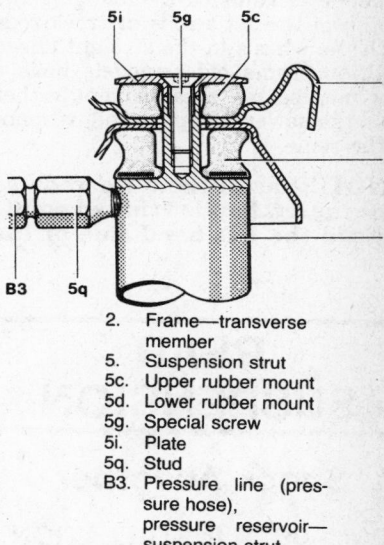

2. Frame—transverse member
5. Suspension strut
5c. Upper rubber mount
5d. Lower rubber mount
5g. Special screw
5i. Plate
5q. Stud
B3. Pressure line (pressure hose), pressure reservoir—suspension strut

**Rear shock absorber upper mount—1983–85 300TD. Retrofitting is not possible**

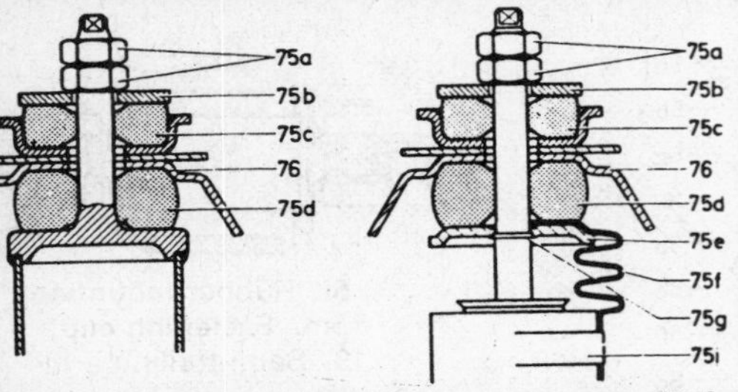

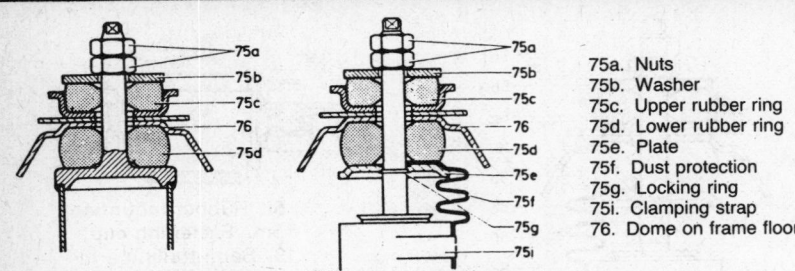

75a. Nuts
75b. Washer
75c. Upper rubber ring
75d. Lower rubber ring
75e. Plate
75f. Dust protection
75g. Locking ring
75i. Clamping strap
76. Dome on frame floor

**Rear shock absorber upper mount—240D (75f not used in U.S.)**

should be in the straight ahead position and the marks on the pitman arm and pitman shaft should be aligned.

Toe-in is adjusted by changing the length of the 2 tie rods or track rods with the wheels in the straight ahead position. Some older models have a hex nut locking arrangement rather than the newer clamp, but adjustment is the same.

**NOTE: Install new tie rods so that the left handed thread points toward the left hand side of the car.**

# REAR SUSPENSION

## Shock Absorber

### REMOVAL & INSTALLATION

#### *190D, 190E, 260E, 300E, 300CE, 300SE, 300TE, 300SEL, 380SL and 560SL*

1. Jack up the rear of the car and support the control arm.
2. From inside the trunk (sedans), remove the rubber cap, locknut, and hex nut from the upper mount of the shock absorber. On 380SL, the upper mount of the rear shock absorber is accessible after removing the top, top flap, rear seat, backrest and lining. On the 380SLC, remove the rear seat, backrest and cover plate.
3. Unbolt the mounting for the rear shock absorber at the bottom and remove the shock absorber. Be sure to disconnect and plug the pressure line on the 190E-16.
4. Installation is the reverse of removal.

#### *All Other Models*

1. Remove the rear seat and backrest.
2. Remove the cover from the rear wall.
3. Raise and support the car and the trailing arm.
4. Loosen the nuts on the upper mount. Remove the washer and rubber ring.
5. Loosen the lower mount and remove the shock absorber downward.
6. Installation is the reverse of removal. Tighten the upper mounting nut to the end of the threads.

## Springs

### REMOVAL & INSTALLATION

#### *190D, 190E, 260E, 300E, 300CE, 300SE, 300TE and 300SEL*

1. Raise the rear of the vehicle and support it with jackstands. Remove the wheel.
2. Disconnect the holding clamps for the spring link cover and then remove the cover.
3. Install a spring compressor and compress the spring until the spring link is free of all load.
4. Disconnect the lower end of the shock absorber.
5. Increase the tension on the spring compressor and remove the spring.
6. Installation is in the reverse order of removal. Please note the following:
   a. Position the spring so that the end of the lower coil is seated in the impression of the spring seat and the upper coil seats properly in the rubber mount in the frame floor.
   b. Do not release tension on the spring compressor until the lower end of the shock absorber is connected and tightened to 47 ft. lbs. (65 Nm).

#### *380SL and 560SL*

1. Jack up the rear of the car.
2. Remove the rear shock absorber.
3. With a floor jack, raise the control arm to approximately a horizontal position. Install a spring compressor to aid in this operation.
4. Carefully lower the jack until the control arm contacts the stop on the rear axle support.
5. Remove the spring and spring compressor with great care.

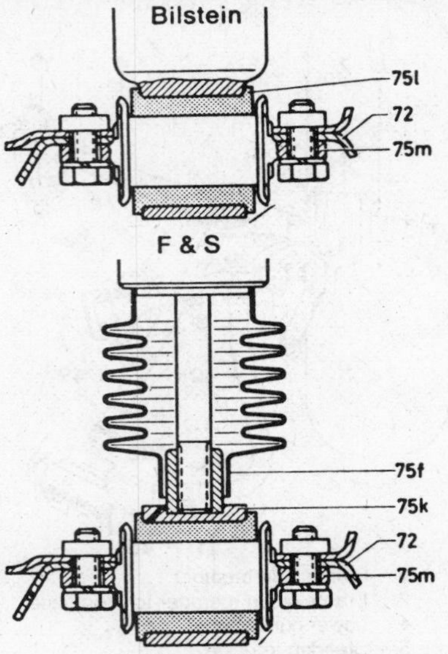


72. Semi-trailing arm
75f. Dust protection
75k. Suspension eye
75l. Rubber mounting
75m. Fastening stirrup

**Rear shock absorber lower mount—240D**

6. Installation is the reverse of removal. For ease of installation, attach the rubber seats to the springs with masking tape.

#### *All Others*

1. Raise and support the rear of the car and the trailing arm.
2. Remove the rear shock absorber.
3. Be sure that the upper shock absorber attachment is released first.
4. Compress the spring with a spring compressor.
5. Remove the rear spring with the rubber mount.
6. Installation is the reverse or removal. When installing the shock absorber, tighten the lower mount first.

# STEERING

## Steering Wheel

### REMOVAL & INSTALLATION

**CAUTION**

***Some Mercedes-Benz are equipped with a Supplemental Restraint System (SRS). Improper maintenance, including incorrect removal and installation of related components, can lead to personal injury caused by unintentional activation of the Airbag. Related components on these models should be serviced only by authorized service technicians.***

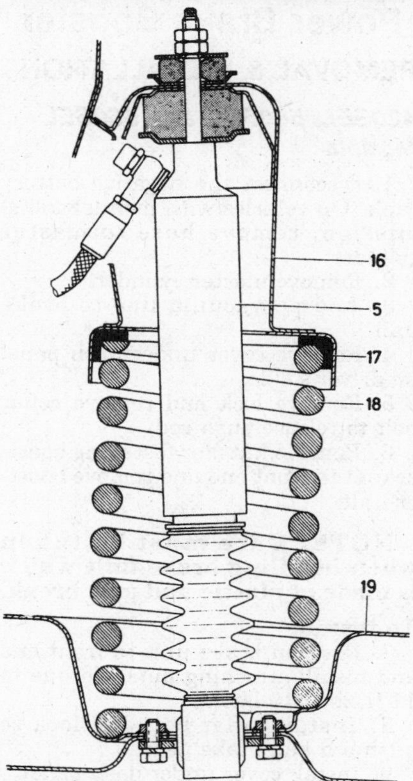


5. Spring strut
16. Dome on frame floor
17. Rubber mount
18. Rear spring
19. Semi-trailing arm

**Rear spring—380SL**

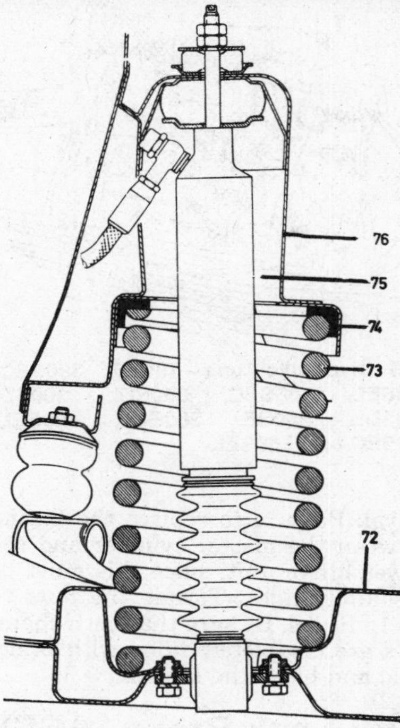


72. Semi-trailing arm
73. Rear spring
74. Rubber mounting
75. Shock absorber or spring strut
76. Dome on frame floor

**Rear spring—all models except 190D, 190E, 260E, 300E, 300CE, 300TE, 380SL and 560SL**

### *Models without SRS*

**NOTE: 380SEC uses a bolt and spring that pushes the power piston into the teeth of the Pitman shaft when the steering is in the center position. Any backlash (play at the steering wheel) is taken up.**

1. Disconnect the negative battery cable. On 380SL and 560SL, pry the 3-pointed star trademark from the center padding. On all other models, remove the padded plate. Pull at one corner near the wheel spokes.
2. Unscrew the hex nut from the steering shaft and remove the spring washer and the steering wheel.

**NOTE: All models use an Allen screw in place of the hex nut. The Allen screw must be replaced if removed.**

3. Installation is the reverse of removal. Be sure that the alignment mark on the steering shaft is pointing upward and be sure that the slightly curved spoke of the steering wheel is down.

# Power Steering Gear

## REMOVAL & INSTALLATION

1. Suck the oil from the power steering reservoir using a syringe.
2. Detach the high-pressure hose and oil return hose from the steering assembly.
3. Cap both lines to prevent entry of dirt, then remove the clamp screw from the lower part of the coupling flange.
4. Remove the rubber plug from the cover plate and remove the U-joint socket screw. On LS90 power steering units, remove the steering spindle. Pull the steering spindle up only until the coupling is no longer engaged with the worn gear.
5. The tailpipe and left side exhaust pipe may have to be removed for access.
6. Detach the tie rod and center tie rod (or drag link and track rod). from the pitman arm, using pullers or a tie rod splitter.
7. Remove the hex-head bolts that hold the gearbox to the frame, then press the worm shaft stub from the steering coupling and remove the gearbox from underneath the car.

**To install:**

8. First install the pitman arm (if it has been removed) aligning the matchmarks. Tighten the pitman arm nut to 110 ft. lbs. and install the cotter pin. Use new self-locking nuts to attach the gear to the frame.
9. Remove the screw plug from the steering box. Turn the wormshaft until the center of the power piston is directly below the bore in the housing. Check dimension (a) which can be altered by changing the position of the pitman arm on its shaft.
10. Center the steering wheel.
11. Press the worm shaft stub into the steering shaft coupling, making sure not to damage the serrations.

**NOTE: Install assembly pin as for manual steering.**

12. Install and tighten the hex-head screws that hold the gearbox to the chassis, then install and tighten the coupling clamp screw.
13. Install the plug in the gearbox, using a new gasket; attach the tie rods to the pitman arm and make sure that the steering knuckle arms rest against their stops at full left and right lock.
14. Check toe-in and correct if necessary. Remove the dust covers from the fluid lines, then reconnect the high and low pressure lines.
15. Fill the reservoir and connect a hose between the bleed screw on the steering and the reservoir.
16. Open the bleed screw and, with engine running, bleed the system and top up.

# Power Steering Pump

## REMOVAL & INSTALLATION

### *All Models*

1. Disconnect the negative battery cable. Remove the nut from the supply tank.
2. Remove the spring and damping plate.
3. Drain the oil from the tank with a syringe.
4. Loosen and remove the expanding and return hoses from the pump. Plug all connections and pump openings.
5. If necessary for clearance, loosen the radiator shell. Loosen the mounting bolts, and move the pump toward the engine by using the toothed wheel. Remove the belt. Remove the pulley, and then remove the pump.
6. Loosen the nut on the attaching plate and the bolt on the support.
7. Push the pump toward the engine and remove the belts from the pulley.
8. Unscrew the mounting bolts and remove the pump and carrier.
9. Installation is the reverse of removal.

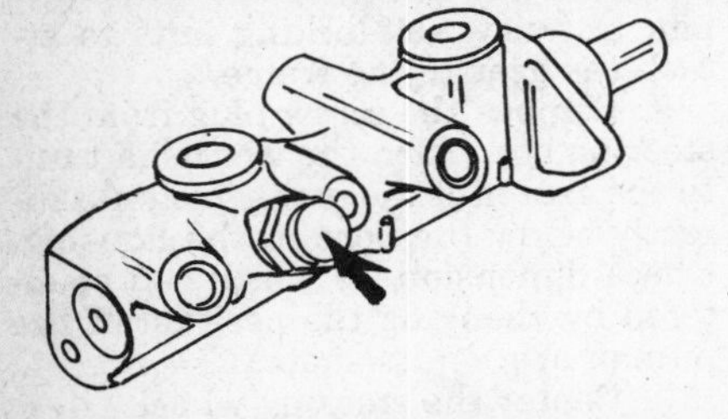

Reset pin (arrow) on master cylinder with pressure warning differential

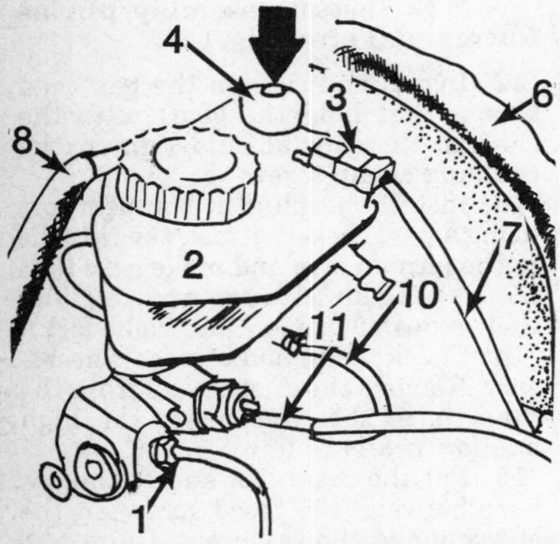


Master cylinder servicing—380SE, 380SEC, 380SEL, 500SEC, 500SEL, 300SD, 300SDL, 300SE, 300SEL, 420SEL, 560SEC and 560SEL

# BRAKES

**For all brake system service and repair procedures not detailed below, please refer to "Brakes" in the Unit Repair section.**

## Master Cylinder

### REMOVAL & INSTALLATION

1. Disconnect the negative battery cable. To remove the master cylinder, first open a bleed screw at one front, and one rear, wheel.
2. Pump the pedal to empty the reservoir completely. Make sure both reservoirs are completely drained.
3. Disconnect the switch connectors using a small screwdriver. Disconnect the brake lines at the master cylinder. Plug the ends with bleed screw caps or the equivalent.
4. Unbolt the master cylinder from the power brake unit and remove. Be careful you do not lose the O-ring in the flange groove of the master cylinder.
5. Installation is the reverse of removal. Be sure to replace the O-ring between the master cylinder and the power brake unit, since this must be absolutely tight. Torque the nuts to 12–15 ft. lbs. Be sure that both chambers are completely filled with brake fluid and bleed the brakes.

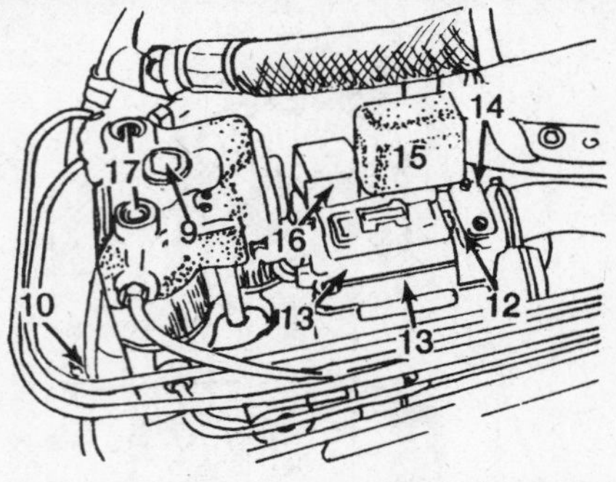


ABS hydraulic unit—380SE, 380SEC, 380SEL, 500SEC, 500SEL, 300SD, 300SDL, 300SE, 300SEL, 420SEL, 560SEC and 560SEL

## Anti-Lock Brake (ABS) Hydraulic Unit

### REMOVAL & INSTALLATION

#### *420SEL, 560SEC and 560SEL Models*

1. With ignition switch **OFF**, disconnect battery negative terminal.
2. Disconnect brake lines from hydraulic unit and seal open lines with blind plugs.

**NOTE: Do not loosen sealed center bolt and 2 socket screws.**

3. Remove cover fastening screw and remove cover.
4. Disconnect grounding strap from pump motor.
5. Disconnect stress relief and remove plug.

**NOTE: Two relays for pump motor or for solenoid valves can be replaced.**

6. Remove mounting nuts and remove hydraulic unit.

**To install:**

7. Mount hydraulic unit on mounting bracket and attach 12 terminal plug and attach stress relief.
8. Install hydraulic unit cover and screw.
9. Connect brake lines to hydraulic unit. Torque line nuts to 10 ft. lbs. (14 Nm).

**NOTE: Do not interchange brake lines.**

10. Connect ground terminal of battery.

## Power Brake Booster

### REMOVAL & INSTALLATION

#### *420SEL, 560SEC and 560SEL Models*

1. Disconnect the negative battery cable. On vehicles with manual transmission, remove hose to master cylinder.
2. Remove master cylinder.
3. Loosen vacuum line to brake unit.
4. Remove cover under dash panel on driver's side.
5. Remove lock and remove collar bolt to release push rod.
6. Remove nuts for fastening booster unit to front end and remove booster unit.

**NOTE: Care must be taken when handling brake unit which is made of plastic and may break.**

**To install:**

7. Position brake unit to front end and install attaching nuts. Torque to 11 ft. lbs. (15 Nm).
8. Install collar bolt and lock to push rod and brake pedal.
9. Install cover under dash panel.
10. Connect vacuum line to brake unit and torque nut to 22 ft. lbs. (30 Nm).
11. Install master cylinder.
12. On vehicles with manual transmission, connect hose to master cylinder on expansion tank.

## Disc Brake Pads

### REMOVAL & INSTALLATION

#### *190D, 190E, 260E, 300E, 300CE and 300TE*

**FRONT AXLE**

1. Raise the front of the vehicle and support safely.
2. Remove the front wheel assemblies.
3. Lift the 2 holding lugs located laterally on the cover of the plug connection by means of a suitable tool and open the cover. Do not use force. Remove the cable of clip sensor from the plug connection on the floating caliper. Do not pull on the cable.
4. Remove the lower caliper bolt while applying counterhold to the sliding bolt.
5. Swing the cylinder housing upward and engage with a suitable hook to the wheelhousing. Remove both brake pads from the brake carrier.
6. Pull the clip sensor out of the backplate of the lining.
7. Draw some brake fluid out of the expansion tank.

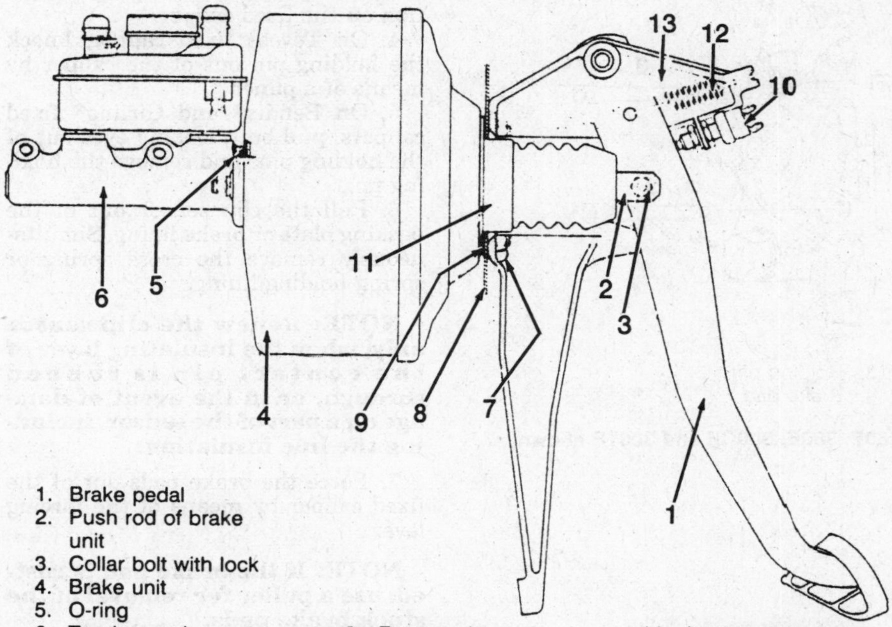


1. Brake pedal
2. Push rod of brake unit
3. Collar bolt with lock
4. Brake unit
5. O-ring
6. Tandem-main cylinder
7. Hex nut
8. Front end
9. Gasket
10. Stop lamp switch
11. Intermediate flange
12. Restoring spring
13. Carrier

**Power braking system – 380SE, 380SEC, 380SEL, 500SEC, 500SEL, 300SD, 300SDL, 300SE, 300SEL, 420SEL, 560SEC and 560SEL**

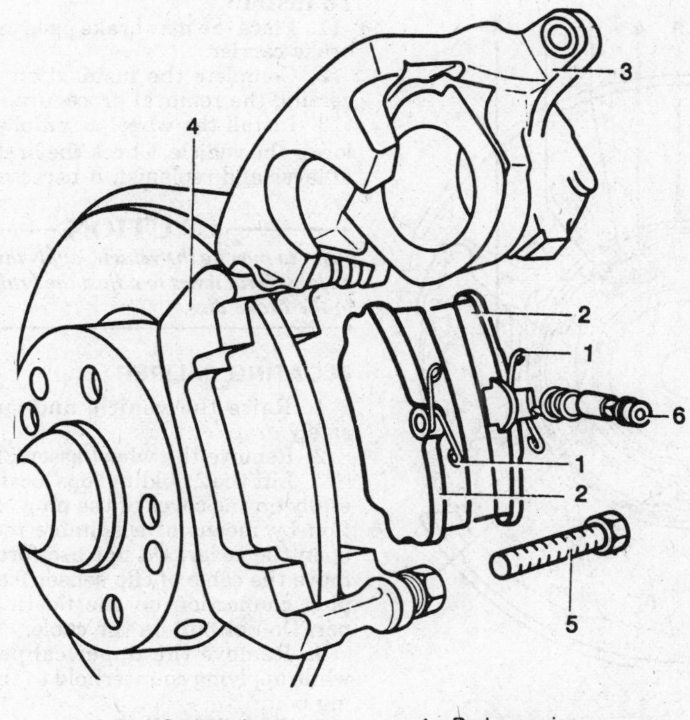


1. Spring clamp
2. Brake pad
3. Cylinder housing
4. Brake carrier
5. Self-locking bolt
6. Clip sensor

**Fixed front caliper assembly – 190D, 190E, 260E, 300E, 300CE and 300TE shown, others similar**

8. Push the piston back with resetting device 000 589 52 43 00 or equivalent.

**To install:**

9. Place the new brake pads into the brake carrier. Make sure that the spring clamp is located in parallel with the upper edge of the lining.

10. Complete the installation by reversing the removal procedure. Torque the caliper bolt to 26 ft. lbs. (35 Nm).

11. Install the wheel assemblies and lower the vehicle. Check the brake fluid lever and replenish if necessary.

**CAUTION**

***Prior to moving the vehicle, apply the brake pedal several times to adjust the brake pads to the brake disc.***

### REAR AXLE

1. Raise the rear of the vehicle and support safely.

2. Remove the rear wheel assemblies.

3. Knock the holding pin out of the fixed caliper by means of a punch. Remove the cross spring.

4. Push the brake pads out of the fixed caliper by means of a pushing lever.

**NOTE: If the brake pads are rusted, use a puller for removal of the stuck brake pads.**

5. Clean the guide surface for the brake pad in the fixed caliper with a brake caliper brush.

6. Draw some brake fluid from the expansion tank.

7. Push both the pistons back with a resetting device.

**To install:**

8. Place the new brake pads into the brake carrier.

9. Complete the installation by reversing the removal procedure.

10. Install the wheel assemblies and lower the vehicle. Check the brake fluid lever and replenish if necessary.

**CAUTION**

***Prior to moving the vehicle, apply the brake pedal several times to adjust the brake pads to the brake disc.***

## *240D, 300D, 300CD, 300SD, 300TD 300SE, 300SEL, 380SEC, 380SEL, 380SL, 420SEL, 500SEC, 500SEL, 560SEC, 560SEL AND 560SL*

### FIXED CALIPER

1. Raise the vehicle and support safely.

2. Remove the wheel assemblies.

3. On fixed calipers with a brake lining wear indicator, pull the cables of

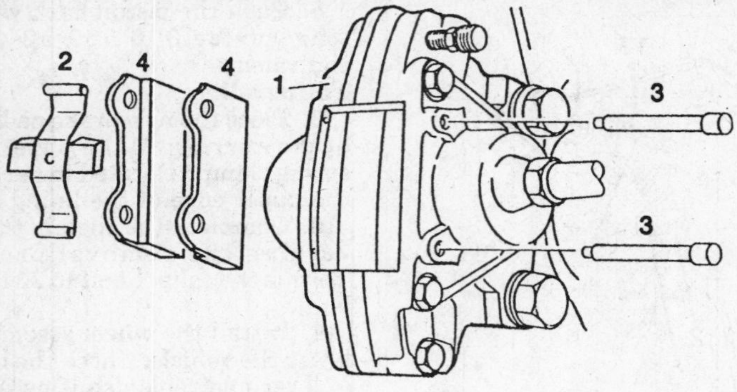


1. Fixed caliper
2. Cross spring
3. Holding pin
4. Brake pad

**Fixed rear caliper assembly—190D, 190E, 260E, 300E, 300CE and 300TE shown, others similar**

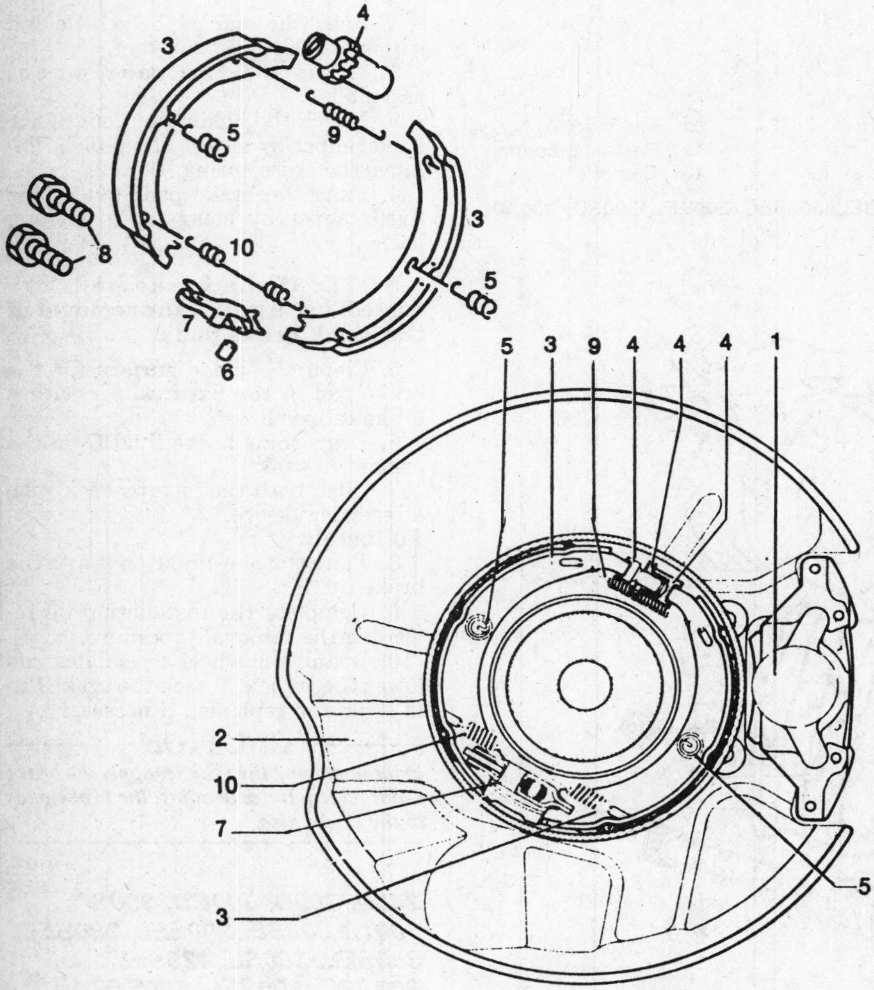


1. Fixed caliper
2. Backing plate
3. Brake shoes
4. Adjusting device
5. Spring
6. Bolt
7. Expanding lock
8. Bolts
9. Return spring
10. Return spring

**Parking brake assembly—190D, 190E, 260E, 300E, 300CE and 300TE shown, others similar**

the clip sensors out of the plug connection on the fixed caliper.

4. On Teves® fixed caliper, knock the holding pin out of the caliper by means of a punch.

5. On Bendix® and Girling® fixed calipers, pull both locking eyes out of the holding pins and remove the holding pins.

6. Pull the clip sensor out of the backing plate or brake lining. Simultaneously remove the cross spring or spring holding lining.

**NOTE: Renew the clip sensor only, when the insulating layer of the contact pin is rubbed through, or in the event of damage on a part of the sensor, including the line insulation.**

7. Force the brake pads out of the fixed caliper by means of the forcing lever.

**NOTE: If the brake pad is rusted, use a puller for removal of the stuck brake pads.**

8. Clean the guide for the brake pad in the fixed caliper with a brake caliper brush.

9. Draw a slight amount of brake fluid from the expansion tank.

10. Push both the pistons back with a resetting device.

**To install:**

11. Place the new brake pads into the brake carrier.

12. Complete the installation by reversing the removal procedure.

13. Install the wheel assemblies and lower the vehicle. Check the brake fluid lever and replenish if necessary.

**CAUTION**

***Prior to moving the vehicle, apply the brake pedal several times to adjust the brake pads to the brake disc.***

### FLOATING CALIPER

1. Raise the vehicle and support safely.

2. Remove the wheel assemblies.

3. Lift the 2 holding lugs located laterally on the cover of the plug connection by means of a suitable tool and open the cover. Do not use force. Remove the cable of clip sensor from the plug connection on the floating caliper. Do not pull on the cable.

4. Remove the upper caliper bolt while applying counterhold to the sliding bolt.

5. Fold the cylinder housing in a downward direction and attach to the torsion bar by means of a suitable hook. Remove both brake pads from the brake carrier.

6. Pull the clip sensor out of the lining backup plate.

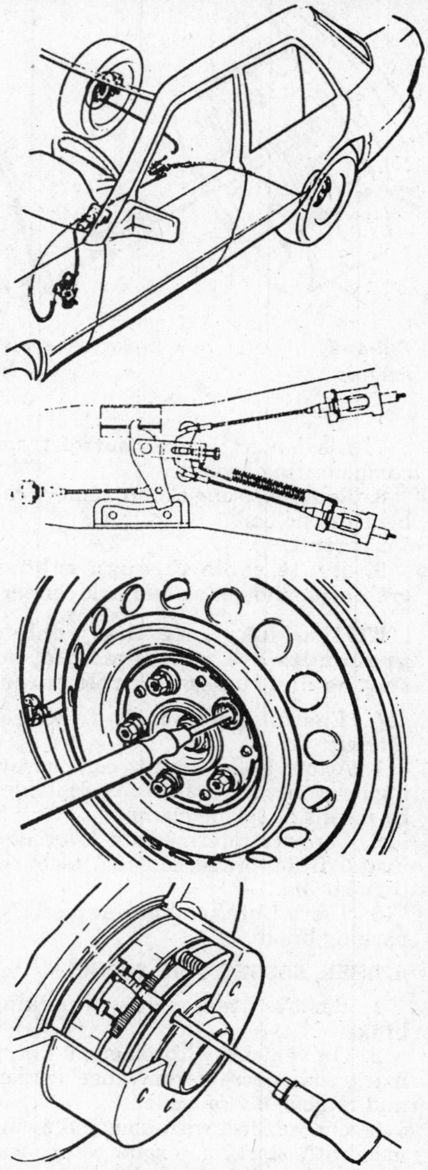

Parking brake adjustment—190D, 190E, 260E, 300E, 300CE and 300TE shown, others similar

**NOTE: The wear indicator on the floating caliper is at inside the brake pad only. Renew the clip sensor only, when the insulating layer of the contact pin is rubbed through, or in the event of damage on a part of the sensor, including the line insulation.**

7. Clean the contact surface of the brake pads in the brake carrier.

8. Draw a slight amount of brake fluid from the expansion tank.

9. Push the piston back with resetting device.

**To install:**

10. Place the new brake pads into the brake carrier. Make sure that the spring clamp is located in parallel with the upper edge of the lining.

11. Complete the installation by reversing the removal procedure. Torque the caliper bolt to 26 ft. lbs. (35 Nm).

12. Install the wheel assemblies and lower the vehicle. Check the brake fluid lever and replenish if necessary.

**CAUTION**

***Prior to moving the vehicle, apply the brake pedal several times to adjust the brake pads to the brake disc.***

## Brake Shoes

### REMOVAL & INSTALLATION

#### *All Models*

1. Raise the rear of the vehicle and support safely.

2. Remove the rear wheel assemblies.

3. Remove the caliper bolts and remove the floating caliper from the wheel carrier.

4. Hang the floating caliper (including the brake hose) on the rear spring by means of a suitable hook.

**NOTE: The hook is fabricated. The brake hose should not undergo tensile stress.**

5. Turn the rear axle shaft flange in such a manner that 1 tapped hole faces the spring. Then compress the spring slightly with installer, turn the tool by approximately 90 degrees, disconnect the spring from the covering ring and remove it.

6. Remove the spring on the other brake shoe.

7. Disconnect the return spring with the remover and installer from the brake shoes.

8. Pull both brake shoes apart until they can be removed over the rear axle flange.

9. Disconnect the return spring from the brake shoes and remove the adjusting device.

10. Push the bolt out of the expanding lock and remove the expanding lock from the brake cable control.

**To install:**

11. Reverse the removal procedure. Torque the caliper bolts to 38 ft. lbs. (50 Nm).

## Parking Brake Cable

### REMOVAL & INSTALLATION

#### *Front Cable*

**190D, 190E, 260E, 300E, 300CE, 300SE, 300TE AND 300SEL**

1. Disconnect the return spring at the cable control compensator.

2. Unbolt the brake cable from the intermediate lever and pull the cable away.

3. Remove the parking brake lever.

4. Loosen the brake cable at the lever and then pull it out toward the rear, through the floor.

5. Installation is in the reverse order of removal.

**240D, 300D, 300CD AND 300TD**

1. Remove the spring from the equalizer.

2. Back off the adjusting screw completely.

3. Detach the relay lever from the bracket on the frame and from the adjusting shackle.

4. Detach the cable from the relay lever by pulling the cotter pin out of the bolt.

5. Remove the clip from the cable guide. Remove the clips from the chassis.

6. Detach the brake cable from the parking brake link. Remove the clip from the cable guide and detach the brake cable from the parking brake.

7. Pull the cable downward from the chassis.

8. Installation is in the reverse of removal.

**380SL AND 560SL**

1. Remove the exhaust system.

2. Disconnect the return spring.

3. Remove the bolts which attach the guide to the intermediate lever and pull the cotter pin from the flange bolt. Remove the flange bolt.

4. Remove the spring clamp from the cable guide and remove the cable control from the bracket.

5. Remove the tunnel cover.

6. Disconnect the brake control from the parking brake and remove the spring clamp from the cable guide. Remove the cable control from the parking brake.

7. Remove the brake control cable out of the frame toward the rear.

8. Installation is the reverse of removal.

**420SEL, 560SEC AND 560SEL**

1. Disconnect return spring on bracket and back-off adjusting screw on adjusting bracket.

2. Loosen brake cable on intermediate lever, while pulling cotter pin out of flange bolt and remove flange bolt.

3. Remove spring clip from cable guide on frame floor.

4. Remove floor mat and cover under dash panel.

5. Remove center console.

6. Disconnect brake cable from pedal plate. Remove spring clip from cable guide. Remove brake cable.

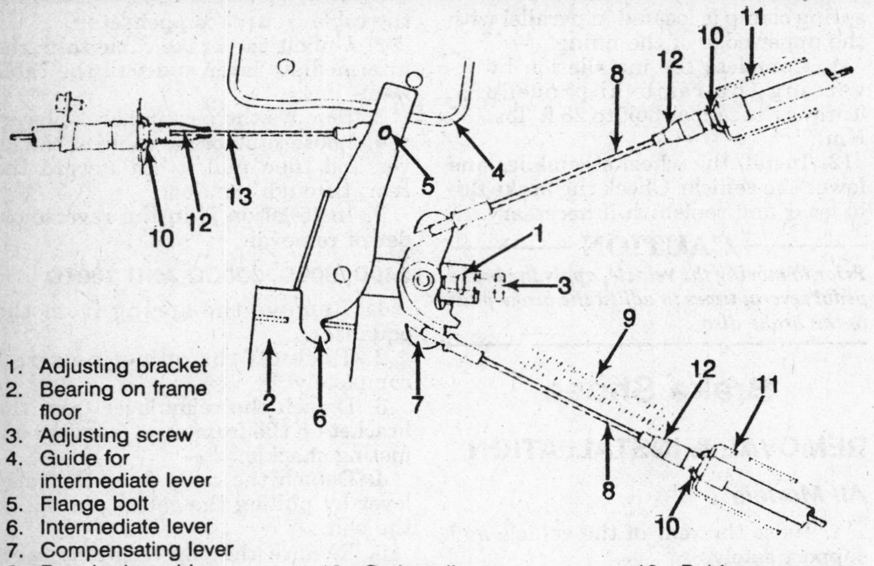


1. Adjusting bracket
2. Bearing on frame floor
3. Adjusting screw
4. Guide for intermediate lever
5. Flange bolt
6. Intermediate lever
7. Compensating lever
8. Rear brake cable control
9. Draw spring
10. Spring clip
11. Bracket for rear brake cable control
12. Rubber grommet
13. Front brake cable control

**Front brake cable control assembly—380SE, 380SEC, 380SEL, 500SEC, 500SEL, 300SD, 300SDL, 300SE, 300SEL, 420SEL, 560SEC and 560SEL**

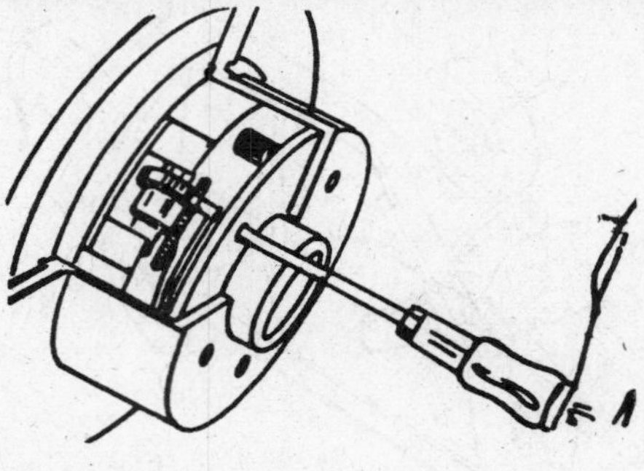

Cut-away view of rear brake shoe ad justment

7. Loosen pipe clamp on pedal assemble.
8. Remove brake cable from accelerator pedal bearing.
9. Fold back passenger compartment carpet until cable is exposed. Slightly raise passenger compartment seat. Loosen plate and pipe clamp. Pull out brake cable.
10. Open cable band on shift bracket and pull brake cable out of heater box toward rear.

**To install:**

11. Route brake cable at rear past heater box and pull up to pedal of parking brake.
12. Attach brake cable to cable draw link of pedal and insert spring clamp.
13. Attach brake cable to accelerator pedal bearing and by means of pipe clamp to pedal assemble.
14. Route brake cable to rear through frame floor and attach to tunnel by means of plate, pipe clamp and by means of cable band to shift bracket.
15. Attach cable to frame floor by means of spring clamp.
16. Attach brake cable to intermediate lever by means of flange bolt and secure.
17. Attach return spring to bracket.
18. Adjust parking brake.
19. Install carpet and install center console.
20. Install cover under dash panel.
21. Install floor mat.

#### ALL OTHER MODELS

1. Remove the floor mat.
2. Remove the leg room cover (upper and lower).
3. Remove the air duct.
4. Disconnect the 4 rubber rings and lower and support the exhaust system.
5. Remove the shield above the exhaust pipes.
6. Disconnect and return spring from the bracket.
7. Back off the adjusting screw on the bracket.
8. Disconnect the intermediate lever from the adjusting bracket.
9. Loosen the brake cable controls on the intermediate lever while pulling the cotter pin from the flange bolt. Remove the flange bolt.
10. Remove the spring clip from the cable guide on the floor pan.
11. Disconnect the brake cable control from the parking brake bracket.
12. Remove the spring clip from the cable and remove the cable control from the parking brake.
13. Pull the cable away upward.
14. Installation is the reverse of removal. Adjust the parking brake.

### *Rear Brake Cable*

#### 190D AND 190E MODELS

1. Remove brake shoes of parking brake.
2. Remove hex head screw from wheel carrier and remove brake cable.
3. Disconnect return spring from holder.
4. Back-off adjusting screw of adjusting bracket.
5. Remove front brake cable from intermediate lever.
6. Disconnect intermediate lever on bearing of frame floor.
7. Disconnect brake control from compensating lever.
8. Remove spring clamp, remove cable from holder.

**To install:**

9. Route cable through rubber grommet of holder on rear axle carrier.

**NOTE: Make sure that rubber grommets are not damaged, so that no dirt can enter cable guide.**

10. Fasten brake cable to wheel carrier.
11. Attach brake cable to compensating lever. Secure brake cable to holder by means of spring clamp.
12. Connect intermediate lever and install front brake cable. Attach return spring.
13. Install brake shoes and adjust parking brake.

#### 420SEL, 560SEC AND 560SEL

1. Remove brake shoes of parking brake.
2. On vehicles with diagonal swing axle, remove screw from wheel carrier and remove brake cable.
3. On vehicles with diagonal swing axle with starting torque compensation, remove both socket screws from wheel carrier and remove cable.
4. Disconnect return spring an bracket and back-off adjusting screw on adjusting bracket.
5. Disconnect intermediate lever on bearing of frame floor and remove adjusting bracket.
6. Disconnect brake cable from compensating lever.
7. Remove spring clamp, take cable out of bracket.
8. Pull out brake cable toward rear through rubber grommet in semi-trailing arm.

**To install:**

9. Make sure that rubber grommets are not damaged, so that no dirt can enter cable guide.
10. Route brake cable through rubber grommet in semi-trailing arm and attach to wheel carrier or bracket, respectively.

11. Attach brake cable to compensating lever. Then mount intermediate lever into bearing on frame floor.
12. Install brake shoes and adjust parking brake.

#### 240D, 300D, 300CD AND 300TD

1. Remove the parking brake shoes after removing the wheel.
2. Remove the screws from the wheel support and detach the brake cable.
3. Back off the adjusting screw from the adjusting shackle.
4. Remove the spring clips, detach the cable, and remove the equalizer.
5. Installation is the reverse of removal.

#### ALL OTHER MODELS

1. Remove the parking brake shoes.
2. Remove the bolt from the wheel carrier and remove the cable.
3. Remove the exhaust system. On some models the exhaust system can be lowered and supported after removing the rubber rings. If equipped, remove the heat shield from above the exhaust pipes.
4. Disconnect the draw spring from the holder.
5. Detach the guide from the intermediate lever.
6. Remove the adjusting screw from the bracket.
7. Disconnect the intermediate lever on the bearing and remove it from the adjusting bracket.
8. Remove the holder, compensating lever, cable control plates and intermediate lever from the tunnel.
9. Remove the spring clamps and disconnect the cable from the plate.
10. Installation is the reverse of removal.

### ADJUSTMENT

#### 260E, 300E, 300CE, 300SE, 300TE AND 300SEL

1. Loosen the parking brake cable slack adjusting screw. The expanders in the rear wheel should not be preloaded via the cable.
2. Raise the rear of the vehicle and support it with jackstands.
3. Remove one of the wheel bolts and then rotate the wheel until you have access to the star wheel adjuster through the hole. Positioning of the hole should be around 2 o'clock.
4. Use a screwdriver to run the star wheel adjuster until wheel locks. Turn the adjuster back about 4 or 5 teeth until the wheel turns freely.

**NOTE: To tighten the star wheel adjuster on the left wheel, move the screwdriver upwards; on the right wheel, move it downwards.**

5. Turn the parking brake cable slack adjuster screw into the bracket until the cables have no slack.
6. Depress the parking brake hand (400 N), several times.
7. Turn the adjusting screw until the brake pedal can be depressed by one tooth at a force of approximately 170–200 N.

#### ALL OTHER MODELS

1. If the floor pedal can be depressed more than 2 notches before actuating the brakes, adjust by jacking up the rear of the car, then removing one lug bolt and adjusting the star wheel with a screwdriver.
2. Move the screwdriver upward on the left (driver's) side, downward on the right (passenger's) side to tighten the shoes.
3. When the wheel is locked, back off about 2–4 clicks.
4. With this type system, the adjusting bolt on the cable relay lever only serves to equalize cable length; therefore, do not attempt to adjust the brakes by turning this bolt.

# CHASSIS ELECTRICAL

## Heater Blower Motor

### REMOVAL & INSTALLATION

#### *240D, 260E, 300D, 300E, 300CE, 300SE, 300TE, 300SEL, 300CD and 300TD*

1. Disconnect the negative battery cable. Remove the cover from under the right side of the instrument panel.
2. Disconnect the plug from the blower motor.
3. Unscrew the contact plate screw, lift the contact plate and disconnect both wires to the series resistor.
4. Loosen the blower motor flange screws and lift out the blower motor.
5. Installation is in the reverse order or removal.

#### *380SL and 560SL*

1. Disconnect the negative battery cable. Working in the engine compartment, unscrew the 8 mounting screws and remove the panel which covers the blower motor.
2. Disconnect the plug from the series resistor at the firewall.
3. Remove the mounting bolts and then remove the series resistor.
4. Unscrew the 4 blower motor retaining nuts and lift out the motor.
5. Installation is in the reverse order of removal. Be sure that the rubber sealing strip is not damaged.

#### *300SD, 380SE, 380SEL, 380SEC, 420SEL, 500SEL, 500SEC, 560SEC and 560SEL*

1. Disconnect the negative battery cable. Remove the cover from under the right side of the instrument panel.
2. Remove the cover for the blower motor and disconnect the two-prong plug.
3. Remove the retaining bolts on the blower motor flange and then remove the blower motor.
4. Installation is in the reverse order of removal.

#### *190D and 190E*

1. Disconnect the negative battery cable. Open the hood to a 90 degree position and then remove the wiper arms.
2. Disconnect the retaining clips for the air intake cover at the firewall.
3. Remove the rubber sealing strip from the cover and then remove the retaining screw. Slide the cover out of the lower windshield trim strip and remove it.
4. Disconnect the vacuum line from the heater valve.
5. Remove the heater cover retaining screws.
6. Pull up the rubber sealing strip from the engine side of the defroster plenum (firewall), unscrew the retaining screws and pull up and out on the blower motor cover.
7. Loosen the cable straps on the connecting cable and then disconnect the plug.
8. Unscrew the mounting bolts and then remove the blower motor.
9. Installation is in the reverse order of removal.

## Instrument Cluster

### REMOVAL & INSTALLATION

#### *380SL*

1. Disconnect the negative battery cable. Remove the steering wheel.

**NOTE: The instrument cluster is held in the instrument panel by means of a molded rubber strip. When pulling out the cluster, the panel can be slightly raised above the cluster. NEVER force the cluster with a screwdriver or the like.**

2. Pull the instrument cluster out as much as possible and loosen or remove the tachometer shaft, all electrical connections and the oil pressure line.

Recess slot in the instrument cluster

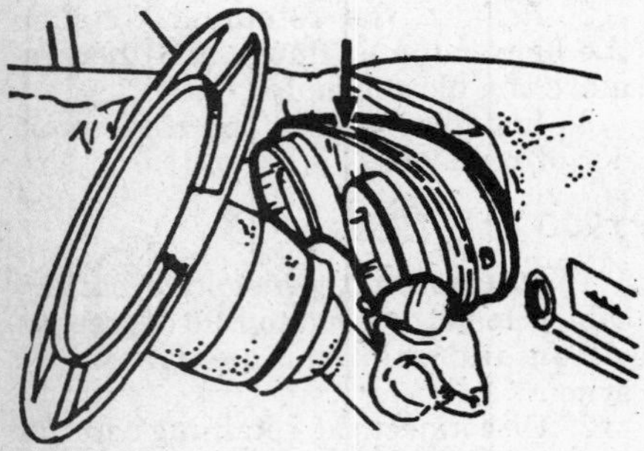
Instrument panel removal showing rubber retaining strip

3. Remove the instrument cluster to the left.

**CAUTION**

*Do not bend the oil pressure line.*

4. Installation is in the reverse order of removal. Make sure that the speedometer cable is not bent excessively or it will vibrate when running.

### *190D, 190E, 420SEL, 560SEC, 560SEL and 560SL*

1. Disconnect the negative battery cable. Remove the cover under the left side of the instrument panel.
2. Disconnect the defroster ducting which runs behind the instrument cluster.
3. Unscrew the speedometer cable from below and then push the cluster out far enough to disconnect all connections on the back of the instrument cluster.
4. Remove the 5 clips which secure the instrument cluster and then remove it.
5. Installation is in the reverse order of removal.

### *260E, 300E, 300CE, 300SE, 300TE and 300SEL*

1. Disconnect the negative battery cable. Remove the instrument panel undercover.
2. Remove the speedometer cable from the slips on the panel under the instrument cluster. This will allow the cable come out when the cluster is removed.

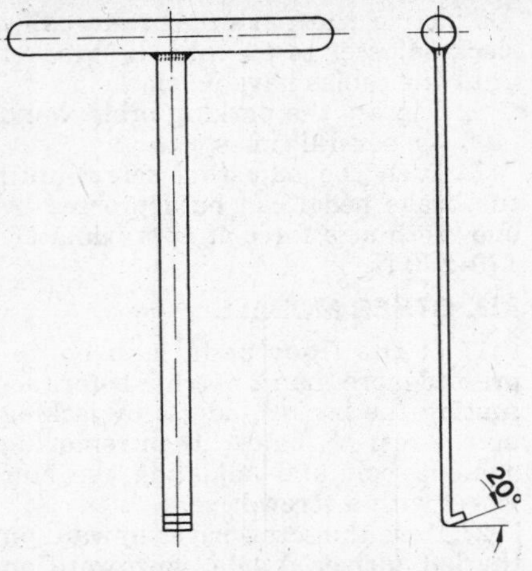

Fabricated tool for removing the instrument cluster

3. Fabricate a removal tool (hook) and insert it between the padding and the cluster at the top of the left side of the cluster. Rotate the tool and then pull out until it rests against the detent.
4. Pull the instrument cluster out evenly on both sides. Be sure the speedometer cable slides into the recess on the brake pedal cover.
5. Reach behind the cluster, unscrew the speedometer cable and disconnect all electrical leads (don't forget to tag them).
6. Remove the instrument cluster.
7. When installing, position the cluster and reconnect the speedometer cable and all electrical leads.
8. Push the cluster backwards into its recess.

**NOTE: Be certain that the speedometer cable slides back into the footwell area without buckling behind the cluster.**

### *240D, 300D, 300CD, 300SD (1983–85), 300TD, 380SE, 380SEC, 380SEL, 500SEC and 500SEL*

1. Disconnect the negative battery cable. Remove the steering wheel (300SD, 380SE, 380SEC, 380SEL, 500SEC and 500SEL only).
2. Remove the instrument cluster slightly by hand. Don't pull on the edge of the glass.
3. A removal hook can be fabricated and inserted between the instrument cluster and the dashboard.
4. Guide the removal hook up to the right to the recess (arrow) and pull the instrument cluster out.

**NOTE: The 1983–85 300SD, 380SE, 380SEC, 380SEl, 500SEC and 500SEL models use 5 clips to hold the instrument cluster in place.**

5. Pull it out as far as possible and disconnect the speedometer cable, electrical connections and oil pressure line.

**To install:**

6. Reconnect the electrical connections, oil pressure line and speedometer cable. To avoid speedometer cable noise, guide it into the largest radius possible.
7. Push the instrument cluster firmly into the dashboard.

# Combination Switch

## REMOVAL & INSTALLATION

### *190D, 190E, 240D, 260E, 300D, 300E, 300CE, 300SE, 300TE, 300SEL, 300CD, 300TD, 380SL, 380SLC and 560SL*

1. Disconnect the negative battery cable. Remove the rubber sleeve on the switch and then unscrew the retaining screws.
2. Pull the switch out slightly, loosen the screws for the cable connection of the twin carbon contacts and pull out the cable.
3. Remove the cover underneath the left side of the instrument panel.
4. Disconnect the plug and then remove the switch.
5. Installation is in the reverse order of removal.

### *300SD (1983–85), 380SE, 380SEC, 380SEL, 420SEL, 500SEC, 500SEL, 560SEC and 560SEL*

1. Disconnect the negative battery cable. Remove the steering wheel.
2. Remove the cover underneath the left side of the instrument panel.
3. Unscrew the switch retaining screws.
4. Disconnect the 14-prong plug underneath the instrument panel.
5. Remove the switch.
6. Installation is in the reverse order of removal.

# Ignition Switch

## REMOVAL & INSTALLATION

### *All Models with Ignition Switch In Dashboard*

#### EXCEPT 190D, 190E, 260E, 300E, 300CE, 300SE, 300TE AND 300SEL

1. Disconnect the negative battery cable. Remove the instrument cluster.
2. Remove the right-hand cover plate under the dashboard.
3. Remove the plug connection from the ignition switch.

4. Remove the screws which hold the ignition switch to the rear of the lock cylinder and remove the ignition switch.

**To install:**

5. Attach the plug connection, after fastening the switch to the steering lock.
6. Install the instrument cluster.
7. Check the switch for proper function and install the lower cover.

**190D, 190E, 260E AND 300E**

1. Disconnect the negative battery cable. Remove the cover plate under the left side of the instrument panel.
2. Remove the steering wheel. Remove the instrument cluster.
3. Pry the cylinder rosette (trim ring) upwards and then remove it.
4. Insert the ignition key and turn it to position **1**.
5. Disconnect the plug at the rear of the ignition switch.

**NOTE: The plug can only be disconnected when the key is in position 1.**

6. Loosen the screws and then remove the steering column jacket (upper and lower halves).
7. Release the clamp on the jacket tube. Press in the lock-pin in position **1** and then pull the steering lock out slightly from the jacket tube holder.
8. Pull off the ignition key at the right bottom section, slightly to the rear. Swivel the steering lock so that the lock cylinder clears its hole in the instrument panel.
9. Unscrew the retaining screws and remove the ignition switch from the back of the steering lock.
10. Installation is in the reverse order of removal. Remember to reconnect the switch to the steering lock.

## Lock Cylinder

### REMOVAL & INSTALLATION

#### *Key can be removed in Position No. 1*

1. Disconnect the negative battery cable. Turn the key to position **1** and remove the key.
2. Pry the cover sleeve from the lock cylinder with a small screwdriver.
3. Using a bent paper clip, hook onto the cover sleeve and remove the sleeve. Be sure that you do not remove the rosette in the dashboard also.
4. Insert the paper clip between the rosette and the steering lock and push in the lock pin. Remove the lock cylinder slightly with the key.
5. Insert the paper clip into the locking hole and pull the lock cylinder completely out.

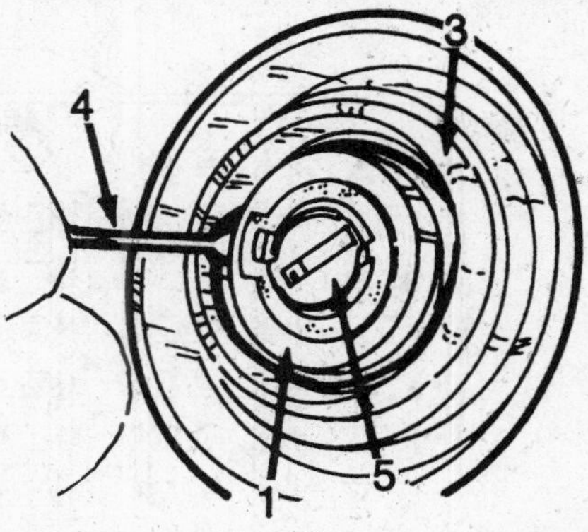


1. Steering lock 3. Rosette 4. Steel wire (paper clip) 5. Locking cylinder

**Ignition lock cylinder removal from the instrument panel (both types)**

6. Installation is the reverse or removal. Turn the lock cylinder to position **1** and insert it into the steering lock, making sure that the lock pin engages. Push the cover sleeve into position **1**.
7. Make sure that the cylinder operates properly.

## Lock Cylinder

### REMOVAL & INSTALLATION

#### *Key cannot be removed in Position No. 1*

**All Models Except 190D, 190E, 260E, 300E, 300CE, 300SE, 300TE and 300SEL**

Because of legal requirements, the lock was changed from the previous version, so that the key can only be removed in position **0**.

1. Disconnect the negative battery cable. Turn the key to position **1**.
2. Lift the cover sleeve to the edge of the key and turn the key to position **0**.
3. Remove the key and cover sleeve.
4. Insert the key into the lock cylinder and turn to position **1** (90 degrees to the right), push in the lock pin and remove the lock cylinder.

**To install:**

5. Turn the lock cylinder to position **1** and insert the lock cylinder, making sure that the locking pin engages.
6. Turn the key to position **0** and remove the key.
7. Place the cover sleeve on the steering lock, insert and turn the key, and push in the cover sleeve in position **1**.
8. Check the locking cylinder for proper function.

#### *190D, 190E, 260E, 300E, 300CE, 300SE, 300TE and 300SEL*

1. Disconnect the negative battery cable. Pry the cylinder rosette (trim ring) upwards and then remove it.
2. Insert the ignition key and turn it to position **1**.
3. Using a bent paper clip, insert each end into the holes on either side of the lock cylinder. Press the clip ends inward; the pressure will unlock the cylinder from the steering lock.
4. Grasp the key and with pressure still on the paper clip, pull the ignition key/lock cylinder assembly out of the steering lock.
5. Remove the paper clip, turn the key to position **0** and remove it. Slide the lock cylinder out of the cover.

**To install:**

6. Insert the lock cylinder just enough so that the ridge on the cylinder body engages the groove in the steering lock.
7. Slide the cover onto the lock cylinder so that the detent is on the left side.
8. Insert the ignition key, turn it to position **1** and then push the lock cylinder and its cover into the steering lock.

**NOTE: When the ignition key is in position 1** and is aligned with the mark on the cover, the detent on the cover is also aligned with the ridge on the steering lock. This is the only manner in which the lock cylinder/cover can be installed in the steering lock.

9. Check that the lock cylinder functions properly, if so, install the rosette.

## Steering Lock

### REMOVAL & INSTALLATION

#### *All Models Except 190D, 190E, 260E, 300E, 300CE, 300SE, 300TE and 300SEL*

1. Disconnect the ground cable from the battery.
2. Remove the instrument cluster.
3. Remove the plug connection from the ignition switch behind the dashboard.
4. Pull the ignition key to position **1**.
5. Loosen the attaching screw for the steering lock.
6. Remove the cover sleeve from the steering lock.
7. On vehicles with the latest version of the steering lock, pull the connection for the warning buzzer.
8. Push in the lock pin with a small punch.
9. Turn the steering lock and remove it from the holder in the column jacket. Be sure that the rosette is not damaged.

**CAUTION**

***The lock pin can only be pushed in when the cylinder is in position 1.***

**To install:**

10. Connect the warning buzzer if so equipped.
11. Place the steering lock in position 1 and insert the lock into the steering column while pushing the lock pin in. Be sure that the lock pin engages.
12. Tighten the attaching clamp screw.
13. Attach the plug connection to the ignition switch.
14. Push the cover sleeve onto the lock in position 1.
15. Install the instrument cluster.
16. Check to be sure that the steering lock works properly.

### 190D, 190E, 260E, 300E, 300CE, 300SE, 300TE and 300SEL

1. Disconnect the negative battery cable. Remove the cover plate under the left side of the instrument panel.
2. Remove the steering wheel. Remove the instrument cluster.
3. Pry the cylinder rosette (trim ring) upwards and then remove it.
4. Insert the ignition key and turn it to position 1.
5. Disconnect the plug at the rear of the ignition switch.

**NOTE: The plug can only be disconnected when the key is in position 1.**

6. Loosen the screws and then remove the steering column jacket (upper and lower halves).
7. Release the clamp on the jacket tube. Press in the lock-pin in position 1 and then pull the steering lock out slightly from the jacket tube holder.
8. Pull off the ignition key at the right bottom section, slightly to the rear. Swivel the steering lock so that the lock cylinder clears its hole in the instrument panel.
9. Unscrew the retaining screws and remove the ignition switch from the back of the steering lock.
10. Unplug the switch and remove the steering lock.
11. Installation is in the reverse order of removal.

# Wiper Motor and Linkage

## REMOVAL & INSTALLATION

### 240D, 300D, 300CD and 300TD

1. Disconnect the negative battery cable. Remove the wiper arms.
2. Remove the air intake grille on the right side.

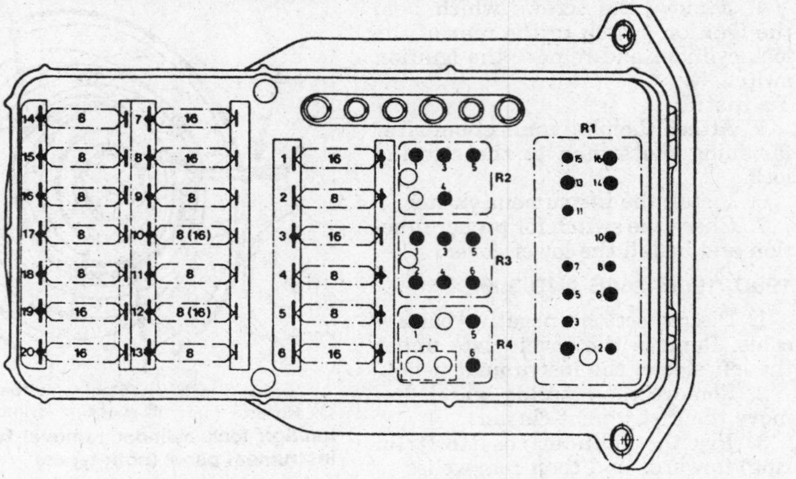


Fuse and relay panel locatins – 190 models

3. Remove the covering cap and nut on the left and right side bearing shafts.
4. Remove the 4 expanding rivets and then remove the left side air intake grille.
5. Remove the center air plenum cover (4 expanding rivets and a Phillips screw).
6. Carefully pull the left and right side connecting rods off of the wiper motor crank.
7. Remove the water drain tube from the right side bearing shaft.
8. Disconnect the coupler plug in the engine compartment. Unclip the plug from the firewall and pull it all the way through.
9. Unbolt the wiper motor and remove it toward the right side.
10. Installation is in the reverse order of removal.

### 300SD (1983–85), 300SE, 380SEC, 380SEL, 420SEL, 500SEC, 500SEL, 560SEC and 560SEL

1. Disconnect the negative battery cable. Remove the wiper arms.
2. Remove the air intake cover. Unscrew the fastening screws and then disconnect the front plug connector.
3. Compress the mounting flange on the rear plug connector. Push the plug out of the firewall toward the front of the car, twist it and then insert it toward the rear of the car.
4. Remove the wiper motor and linkage.
5. Unscrew the nut on the wiper motor shaft.
6. Swivel the wiper linkage and then unscrew the bolts for the wiper motor underneath.
7. Remove the wiper motor.

**To install:**

8. Mount the wiper motor in the base plate.
9. Push the crank arm on the wiper motor shaft and position the nut. Make sure that the lever on the right hand wiper shaft is pointing down.
10. Align the crank arm so that the upper edge is parallel with the wiper motor shaft.
11. Tighten the nut on the wiper motor shaft.
12. Attach the wiper motor and linkage assembly to the vehicle.
13. Installation of the remaining components is in the reverse order of removal.

### 260E, 300E, 300CE, 300SE, 300TE and 300SEL

1. Disconnect the negative battery cable. Open the hood.
2. Remove the air inlet cover.
3. Pry open the cover plate on the lower end of the wiper arm and remove the Allen screw.
4. Pull the wiper arm off the shaft.
5. Remove the motor assembly mounting nuts and clamp.
6. Disconnect the electrical lead and then remove the wiper assembly.
7. Unscrew the nut on the motor shaft and pry off the driver lever.
8. Unbolt the wiper motor and remove it.
9. Tighten the wiper motor-to-mount bracket nuts to 4 ft. lbs. (5 Nm). The motor must be in the **PARK** position; if unsure, connect the electrical lead temporarily and operate the switch to the **PARK** position. Disconnect the lead.
10. Position the drive arm onto the motor shaft and tighten the nut to 14 ft. lbs. (19 Nm).
11. Installation of the remaining components is the reverse order of removal.

### 190D and 190E

1. Open the hood all the way and

disconnect the battery.

2. Remove the wiper arm.
3. Remove the round cover from the wiper shaft.
4. Remove the 2 clips, the rubber seal and the 2 screws and then remove the air intake cover.
5. Pull the 3-piece air intake pan from the windshield and remove it.
6. Unscrew the wiper motor/linkage assembly.
7. Remove the cover and unscrew the 4 mounting bolts for the fuse box. Pull the fuse box slightly forward and up and then unplug the wiper motor connection.
8. Remove the wiper motor/linkage assembly.
9. Remove the nut on the wiper motor shaft and then pull off the crank arm and linkage.
10. Unscrew and remove the wiper motor.

**To install:**

11. Attach the wiper motor to the base plate.
12. Press the crank arm onto the wiper motor shaft. Make sure that the crank arm and the pushrod are parallel.
13. Attach the crank arm to the wiper motor and install the wiper motor/linkage assembly.
14. Installation of the remaining components is in the reverse order of removal.

## Stoplight Switch

### REMOVAL & INSTALLATION

1. Disconnect the negative battery cable. Disconnect electrical connector from stop switch.
2. Remove locking nut.
3. Remove stop switch.

**To install:**

4. Screw switch into bracket.
5. Adjust switch so the stop lamp lights between 7–20mm measured to center of pedal plate and tighten locking nuts.

## Fuses

A listing of the protected equipment and the amperage of the fuse is printed in the lid of the fuse box. Spare fuses and a tool for removing and installing fuses are contained in the vehicle tool kit.

Fuses cannot be repaired; they must be replaced. Always determine the cause of the blown fuse before replacing it with a new one.

### LOCATION

#### *240D, 300D, 300CD and 300TD*

On early models, the fuse box may be found in the kick panel on the driver's side. On later models, the fuse box is located in the engine compartment on the driver's side, next the brake master cylinder. Some models have separate fuse boxes or inline fuses for additional equipment. The radio is usually fused with a separate inline glass fuse behind the radio and the ignition is unfused.

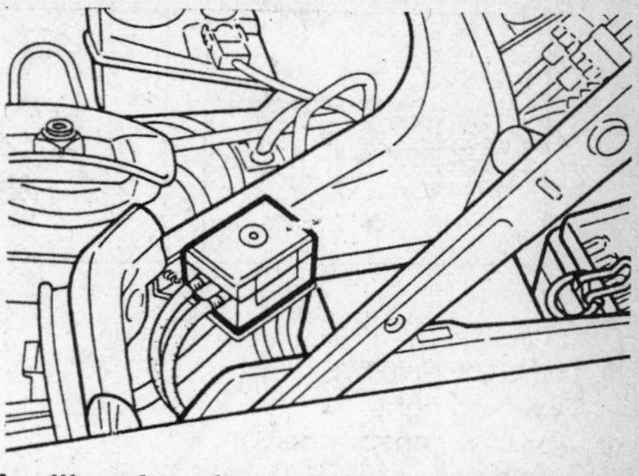

**Auxiliary fuse box—190D with 2.5L engine**

#### *190D, 190E, 260E, 300E, 300CE, 300SE, 300TE, 300SEL, 300SD, 380SE, 380SEC, 380SEL, 420SEL, 500SEC, 500SEL, 560SEC, 560SEL, and 560SEC*

The fuse box is located in the engine compartment, on the driver's side, next to the brake master cylinder. Some models may have separate fuse boxes or inline fuses in the engine compartment for additional equipment. The radio is usually fused with a separate inline glass fuse behind the radio and the ignition is unfused. The fuse box also contains various relays.

#### *380SL*

The fuse box is located in the right-hand (passenger's side) kick panel, behind a cover plate. There may also be separate fuse boxes or inline fuses in the engine compartment for additional equipment. The radio is usually fused with a separate inline glass fuse behind the radio and the ignition is unfused. The kick panel area also contains various relays and switches.

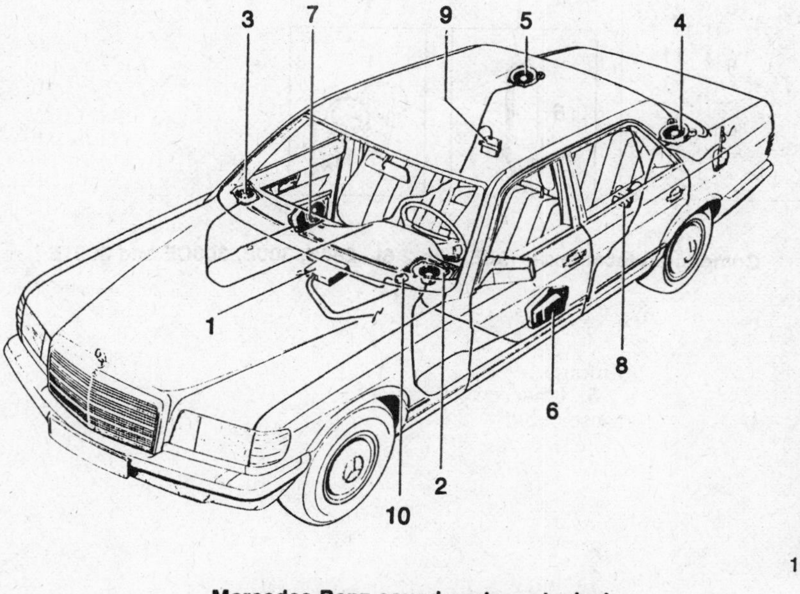


1. Radio with coupling amplifier attached
2. Left front speaker—midrange/tweeter
3. Right front speaker—midrange/tweeter
4. Left rear speaker—full range/2 tweeters
5. Right rear speaker—full range/2 tweeters
6. Left front door speaker—woofer
7. Right front door speaker—woofer
8. Left amplifier
9. Right amplifier
10. Fader switch

**Mercedes-Benz sound system—typical**

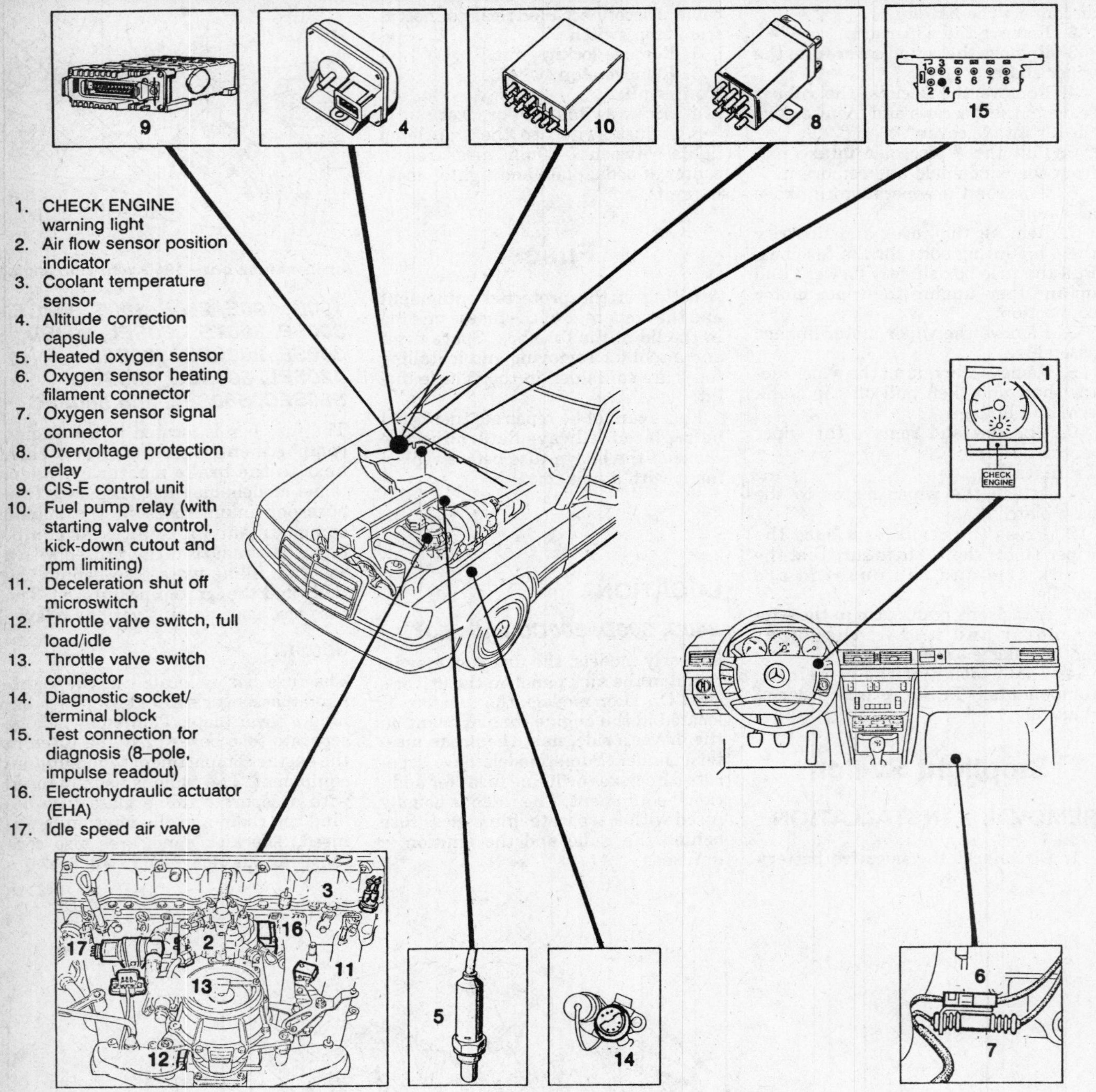
1. CHECK ENGINE warning light
2. Air flow sensor position indicator
3. Coolant temperature sensor
4. Altitude correction capsule
5. Heated oxygen sensor
6. Oxygen sensor heating filament connector
7. Oxygen sensor signal connector
8. Overvoltage protection relay
9. CIS-E control unit
10. Fuel pump relay (with starting valve control, kick-down cutout and rpm limiting)
11. Deceleration shut off microswitch
12. Throttle valve switch, full load/idle
13. Throttle valve switch connector
14. Diagnostic socket/ terminal block
15. Test connection for diagnosis (8–pole, impulse readout)
16. Electrohydraulic actuator (EHA)
17. Idle speed air valve
9
4
10
8
15
1
CHECK ENGINE
3
2
16
17
11
13
12
5
14
6
7

**Component locations – 190E with 2.6L, 260E, 300E, 300CE and 300TE**

# Merkur

XR4Ti, Scorpio

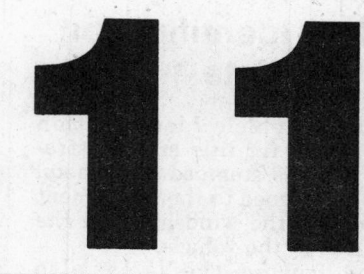

# 11

# SERIAL NUMBER IDENTIFICATION

## Vehicle Identification Plate

The official Vehicle Identification Number (VIN) for title and registration purposes is stamped on a metal tab that is fastened to the instrument panel close to the windshield on the driver's side of the vehicle.

On the Scorpio, the VIN is also stamped on the floor pan of the passenger's door.

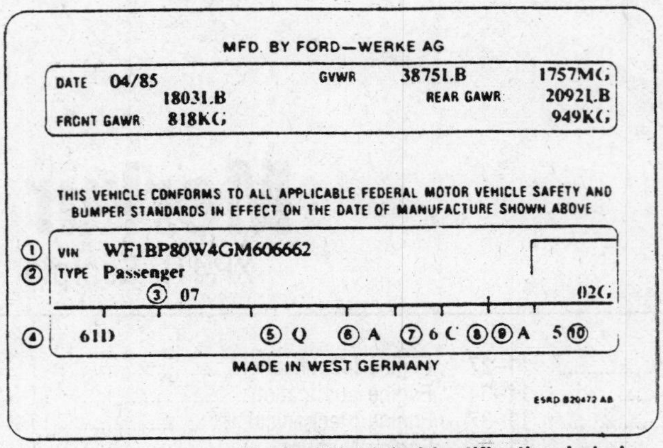


1. Vehicle identification number
2. Vehicle type
3. Paint
4. Body type code
5. Interior trim
6. Air conditioning
7. Radio
8. Sunroof
9. Axle ratio
10. Transmission

Typical Vehicle Identification Label

## Engine Number

Refer to Vehicle Certification Label for engine identification and consecutive unit numbers. The engine calibration number is located on a sticker affixed to the front of the engine. Engine code information is also contained on this sticker.

On the 2.9L engine, the last 8 digits of the VIN number are stamped on the front, left side, next to the exhaust port and the upper right, rear side of the engine.

## Vehicle Identification Label

The vehicle identification/certification label is attached to the left front door lock panel. The upper half of the label contains the name of the manufacturer, gross vehicle weight (GVWR) and gross axle weight (GAWR) ratings, and the certification statement. A 17 character VIN number is also shown. The number indicates; manufacturer, type of restraint system, line, series, body type, engine (8th position), model year (10th position) and consecutive unit number. The last 6 digits of the VIN label indicate the consecutive unit number of each vehicle built at each assembly plant. Also shown on the label are the color code, body type and interior trim codes. The remaining numbers are special equipment, axle and transmission codes.

### ENGINE IDENTIFICATION

| Year | Model | Engine Displacement cu. in. (cc/liter) | Engine Series Identification | No. of Cylinders | Engine Type |
|---|---|---|---|---|---|
| 1985 | XR4Ti | 140 (2300/2.3) | W | 4 | SOHC |
| 1986 | XR4Ti | 140 (2300/2.3) | W | 4 | SOHC |
| 1987 | XR4Ti | 140 (2300/2.3) | W | 4 | SOHC |
| 1988 | XR4Ti | 140 (2300/2.3) | W | 4 | SOHC |
| | Scorpio | 177 (2900/2.9) | V | 6 | OHV |
| 1989-90 | XR4Ti | 140 (2300/2.3) | W | 4 | SOHC |
| | Scorpio | 177 (2900/2.9) | V | 6 | OHV |

SOHC Single Overhead Camshaft
OHV Overhead Valves

### GENERAL ENGINE SPECIFICATIONS

| Year | Model | Engine Displacement cu. in. (cc) | Fuel System Type | Net Horsepower @ rpm | Net Torque @ rpm (ft. lbs.) | Bore × Stroke (in.) | Compression Ratio | Oil Pressure @ rpm |
|---|---|---|---|---|---|---|---|---|
| 1985 | XR4Ti | 140 (2300) | EFI | 175 @ 5000① | 200 @ 3000② | 3.78 x 3.12 | 8.0:1 | 50 @ 2000 |
| 1986 | XR4Ti | 140 (2300) | EFI | 175 @ 5000① | 200 @ 3000② | 3.78 x 3.12 | 8.0:1 | 50 @ 2000 |
| 1987 | XR4Ti | 140 (2300) | EFI | 175 @ 5000① | 200 @ 3000② | 3.78 x 3.12 | 8.0:1 | 50 @ 2000 |
| 1988 | XR4Ti | 140 (2300) | EFI | 175 @ 5000① | 200 @ 3000② | 3.78 x 3.12 | 8.0:1 | 50 @ 2000 |
| | Scorpio | 177 (2900) | EFI | 144 @ 5500 | 162 @ 3000 | 3.66 x 2.83 | 9.0:1 | 50 @ 2000 |

## GENERAL ENGINE SPECIFICATIONS

| Year | Model | Engine Displacement cu. in. (cc) | Fuel System Type | Net Horsepower @ rpm | Net Torque @ rpm (ft. lbs.) | Bore × Stroke (in.) | Com-pression Ratio | Oil Pressure @ rpm |
|---|---|---|---|---|---|---|---|---|
| 1989-90 | XR4Ti | 140 (2300) | EFI | 175 @ 5000① | 200 @ 3000② | 3.78 x 3.12 | 8.0:1 | 50 @ 2000 |
| | Scorpio | 177 (2900) | EFI | 144 @ 5500 | 162 @ 3000 | 3.66 x 2.83 | 9.0:1 | 50 @ 2000 |

EFI Electronic Fuel Injection
① 145 @ 4400 with automatic transaxle
② 180 @ 3000 with automatic transaxle

## GASOLINE ENGINE TUNE-UP SPECIFICATIONS

| Year | Model | Engine Displacement cu. in. (cc) | Spark Plugs Type | Spark Plugs Gap (in.) | Ignition Timing (deg.) MT | Ignition Timing (deg.) AT | Com-pression Pressure (psi) | Fuel Pump (psi) | Idle Speed (rpm) MT | Idle Speed (rpm) AT | Valve Clearance In. | Valve Clearance Ex. |
|---|---|---|---|---|---|---|---|---|---|---|---|---|
| 1985 | XR4Ti | 140 (2300) | AWSF-32C | 0.034 | 13B① | 10B① | NA | 39② | 900① | 900① | Hyd. | Hyd. |
| 1986 | XR4Ti | 140 (2300) | BSFC-32 | 0.034 | 13B① | 10B① | NA | 39② | 900① | 900① | Hyd. | Hyd. |
| 1987 | XR4Ti | 140 (2300) | BSFC-32 | 0.034 | 13B① | 10B① | NA | 39② | 900① | 900① | Hyd. | Hyd. |
| 1988 | XR4Ti | 140 (2300) | AWSF-32C | 0.034 | 13B① | 10B① | NA | 39② | 900① | 900① | Hyd. | Hyd. |
| | Scorpio | 177 (2900) | AWSF-42C | ③ | ③ | ③ | NA | 43.5 | ③ | ③ | Hyd. | Hyd. |
| 1989 | XR4Ti | 140 (2300) | AWSF-32C | 0.034 | 13B① | 10B① | NA | 39② | 900① | 900① | Hyd. | Hyd. |
| | Scorpio | 177 (2900) | AWSF-42C | ③ | ③ | ③ | NA | 43.5 | ③ | ③ | Hyd. | Hyd. |
| 1990 | SEE UNDERHOOD SPECIFICATIONS STICKER | | | | | | | | | | | |

**NOTE:** The Underhood Specifications sticker often reflects tune-up specification changes made in production. Sticker figures must be used if they disagree with those in this chart.
MT—Manual transmission
AT—Automatic transmission
NA—Not available at time of publication
B—Before Top Dead Center
Hyd.—Hydraulic valve lash adjusters

① Ignition timing and idle speed are computer-controlled by the EEC-IV enginecontrol system. See text for details

② Specification is fuel system pressure. Two fuel pumps are used. See text for details

③ Refer to emissions decal

## FIRING ORDERS

NOTE: To avoid confusion, always replace spark plug wires one at a time.

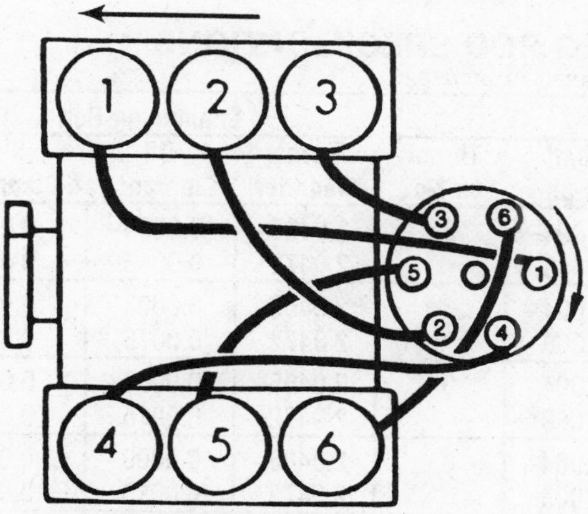


**Ford Motor Co. 2900cc V6**
**Engine firing order: 1-4-2-5-3-6**
**Distributor rotation: clockwise**

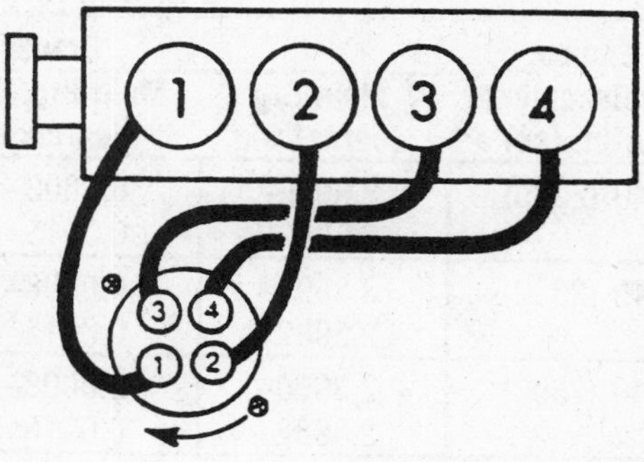


**FORD MOTOR CO. 2300 cc 4-cyl.**
**Engine firing order: 1-3-4-2**
**Distributor rotation: clockwise**

## CAPACITIES

| Year | Model | Engine Displacement cu. in. (cc) | Engine Crankcase with Filter | Engine Crankcase without Filter | Transmission (pts.) 4-Spd | Transmission (pts.) 5-Spd | Transmission (pts.) Auto. | Drive Axle (pts.) | Fuel Tank (gal.) | Cooling System (qts.) |
|---|---|---|---|---|---|---|---|---|---|---|
| 1985 | XR4Ti | 140 (2300) | 5.0 | 4.5 | — | 2.6 | 16① | 1.9 | 15 | 10.5 |
| 1986 | XR4Ti | 140 (2300) | 5.0 | 4.5 | — | 2.6 | 16① | 1.9 | 15 | 10.5 |
| 1987 | XR4Ti | 140 (2300) | 5.0 | 4.5 | — | 2.6 | 16① | 1.9 | 15 | 10.5 |
| 1988 | XR4Ti | 140 (2300) | 5.0 | 4.5 | — | 2.6 | 16① | 2.7 | 15 | 10.5 |
| | Scorpio | 177 (2900) | 5.0 | 4.5 | — | 2.4 | 19① | 2.8 | 17 | 9.0 |
| 1989-90 | XR4Ti | 140 (2300) | 5.0 | 4.5 | — | 2.6 | 16① | 2.7 | 15 | 10.5 |
| | Scorpio | 177 (2900) | 5.0 | 4.5 | — | 2.4 | 19① | 2.8 | 17 | 9.0 |

① Specification is for total refill. Check fluid level with dipstick

## CAMSHAFT SPECIFICATIONS

All measurements given in inches.

| Year | Engine Displacement cu. in. (cc) | Journal Diameter 1 | Journal Diameter 2 | Journal Diameter 3 | Journal Diameter 4 | Journal Diameter 5 | Lobe Lift In. | Lobe Lift Ex. | Bearing Clearance | Camshaft End Play |
|---|---|---|---|---|---|---|---|---|---|---|
| 1985 | 140 (2300) | 1.7713–1.7720 | 1.7713–1.7720 | 1.7713–1.7720 | 1.7713–1.7720 | — | 0.400 | 0.400 | 0.001–0.003 | 0.001–0.007 |
| 1986 | 140 (2300) | 1.7713–1.7720 | 1.7713–1.7720 | 1.7713–1.7720 | 1.7713–1.7720 | — | 0.400 | 0.400 | 0.001–0.003 | 0.001–0.007 |
| 1987 | 140 (2300) | 1.7713–1.7720 | 1.7713–1.7720 | 1.7713–1.7720 | 1.7713–1.7720 | — | 0.400 | 0.400 | 0.001–0.003 | 0.001–0.007 |
| 1988 | 140 (2300) | 1.7713–1.7720 | 1.7713–1.7720 | 1.7713–1.7720 | 1.7713–1.7720 | — | 0.400 | 0.400 | 0.001–0.003 | 0.001–0.007 |
| | 177 (2900) | 1.7285–1.7293 | 1.7135–1.7143 | 1.6985–1.6992 | 1.6835–1.6842 | — | 0.373 | 0.373 | 0.0010–0.0026 | 0.0008–0.0040 |
| 1989-90 | 140 (2300) | 1.7713–1.7720 | 1.7713–1.7720 | 1.7713–1.7720 | 1.7713–1.7720 | — | 0.400 | 0.400 | 0.001–0.003 | 0.001–0.007 |
| | 177 (2900) | 1.7285–1.7293 | 1.7135–1.7143 | 1.6985–1.6992 | 1.6835–1.6842 | — | 0.373 | 0.373 | 0.0010–0.0026 | 0.0008–0.0040 |

## CRANKSHAFT AND CONNECTING ROD SPECIFICATIONS

All measurements are given in inches.

| Year | Engine Displacement cu. in. (cc) | Crankshaft Main Brg. Journal Dia. | Crankshaft Main Brg. Oil Clearance | Crankshaft Shaft End-play | Crankshaft Thrust on No. | Connecting Rod Journal Diameter | Connecting Rod Oil Clearance | Connecting Rod Side Clearance |
|---|---|---|---|---|---|---|---|---|
| 1985 | 140 (2300) | 2.3990–2.3982 | 0.0008–0.0015 | 0.004–0.008 | 3 | 2.0465–2.0472 | 0.0008–0.0015 | 0.004–0.011 |
| 1986 | 140 (2300) | 2.3990–2.3982 | 0.0008–0.0015 | 0.004–0.008 | 3 | 2.0465–2.0472 | 0.0008–0.0015 | 0.004–0.011 |
| 1987 | 140 (2300) | 2.3990–2.3982 | 0.0008–0.0015 | 0.004–0.008 | 3 | 2.0465–2.0472 | 0.0008–0.0015 | 0.004–0.011 |
| 1988 | 140 (2300) | 2.3990–2.3982 | 0.0008–0.0015 | 0.004–0.008 | 3 | 2.0465–2.0472 | 0.0008–0.0015 | 0.004–0.011 |
| | 177 (2900) | 2.2433–2.2441 | 0.0008–0.0015 | 0.004–0.008 | 3 | 2.1252–2.1260 | 0.0006–0.0016 | 0.004–0.011 |

## CRANKSHAFT AND CONNECTING ROD SPECIFICATIONS

All measurements are given in inches.

| Year | Engine Displacement cu. in. (cc) | Crankshaft Main Brg. Journal Dia. | Crankshaft Main Brg. Oil Clearance | Crankshaft Shaft End-play | Crankshaft Thrust on No. | Connecting Rod Journal Diameter | Connecting Rod Oil Clearance | Connecting Rod Side Clearance |
|---|---|---|---|---|---|---|---|---|
| 1989-90 | 140 (2300) | 2.3990–2.3982 | 0.0008–0.0015 | 0.004–0.008 | 3 | 2.0465–2.0472 | 0.0008–0.0015 | 0.004–0.011 |
| | 177 (2900) | 2.2433–2.2441 | 0.0008–0.0015 | 0.004–0.008 | 3 | 2.1252–2.1260 | 0.0006–0.0016 | 0.004–0.011 |

## VALVE SPECIFICATIONS

| Year | Engine Displacement cu. in. (cc) | Seat Angle (deg.) | Face Angle (deg.) | Spring Test Pressure (lbs.) | Spring Installed Height (in.) | Stem-to-Guide Clearance (in.) Intake | Stem-to-Guide Clearance (in.) Exhaust | Stem Diameter (in.) Intake | Stem Diameter (in.) Exhaust |
|---|---|---|---|---|---|---|---|---|---|
| 1985 | 140 (2300) | 45 | 44 | 71–79① | 1.5313–1.5938 | 0.0010–0.0027 | 0.0015–0.0032 | 0.3416–0.3423 | 0.3411–0.3418 |
| 1986 | 140 (2300) | 45 | 44 | 71–79① | 1.5313–1.5938 | 0.0010–0.0027 | 0.0015–0.0032 | 0.3416–0.3423 | 0.3411–0.3418 |
| 1987 | 140 (2300) | 45 | 44 | 71–79① | 1.5313–1.5938 | 0.0010–0.0027 | 0.0015–0.0032 | 0.3416–0.3423 | 0.3411–0.3418 |
| 1988 | 140 (2300) | 45 | 44 | 71–79① | 1.5313–1.5938 | 0.0010–0.0027 | 0.0015–0.0032 | 0.3416–0.3423 | 0.3411–0.3418 |
| | 177 (2900) | 45 | 44 | 60–68② | 1.5781–1.6093 | 0.0008–0.0025 | 0.0018–0.0035 | 0.3159–0.3167 | 0.3149–0.3156 |
| 1989-90 | 140 (2300) | 45 | 44 | 71–79① | 1.5313–1.5938 | 0.0010–0.0027 | 0.0015–0.0032 | 0.3416–0.3423 | 0.3411–0.3418 |
| | 177 (2900) | 45 | 44 | 60–68② | 1.5781–1.6093 | 0.0008–0.0025 | 0.0018–0.0035 | 0.3159–0.3167 | 0.3149–0.3156 |

① @ 1.52 in.
② @ 1.585 in.

## PISTON AND RING SPECIFICATIONS

All measurments are given in inches.

| Year | Engine Displacement cu. in. (cc) | Piston Clearance | Ring Gap Top Compression | Ring Gap Bottom Compression | Ring Gap Oil Control | Ring Side Clearance Top Compression | Ring Side Clearance Bottom Compression | Ring Side Clearance Oil Control |
|---|---|---|---|---|---|---|---|---|
| 1985 | 140 (2300) | 0.0030–0.0038 | 0.010–0.020 | 0.010–0.020 | 0.015–0.055 | 0.002–0.004 | 0.002–0.004 | Snug |
| 1986 | 140 (2300) | 0.0030–0.0038 | 0.010–0.020 | 0.010–0.020 | 0.015–0.055 | 0.002–0.004 | 0.002–0.004 | Snug |
| 1987 | 140 (2300) | 0.0030–0.0038 | 0.010–0.020 | 0.010–0.020 | 0.015–0.055 | 0.002–0.004 | 0.002–0.004 | Snug |
| 1988 | 140 (2300) | 0.0030–0.0038 | 0.010–0.020 | 0.010–0.020 | 0.015–0.055 | 0.002–0.004 | 0.002–0.004 | Snug |
| | 177 (2900) | 0.0011–0.0019 | 0.015–0.023 | 0.015–0.023 | 0.015–0.055 | 0.0020–0.0033 | 0.0020–0.0033 | Snug |
| 1989-90 | 140 (2300) | 0.0030–0.0038 | 0.010–0.020 | 0.010–0.020 | 0.015–0.055 | 0.002–0.004 | 0.002–0.004 | Snug |
| | 177 (2900) | 0.0011–0.0019 | 0.015–0.023 | 0.015–0.023 | 0.015–0.055 | 0.0020–0.0033 | 0.0020–0.0033 | Snug |

## TORQUE SPECIFICATIONS

All readings in ft. lbs.

| Year | Engine Displacement cu. in. (cc) | Cylinder Head Bolts | Main Bearing Bolts | Rod Bearing Bolts | Crankshaft Pulley Bolts | Flywheel Bolts | Manifold Intake | Manifold Exhaust | Spark Plugs |
|---|---|---|---|---|---|---|---|---|---|
| 1985 | 140 (2300) | 80–90① | 80–90① | 30–36② | 100–120 | 56–64 | 14–21 | 16–23 | 7–15 |
| 1986 | 140 (2300) | 80–90① | 80–90① | 30–36② | 100–120 | 56–64 | 14–21 | 16–23 | 7–15 |
| 1987 | 140 (2300) | 80–90① | 80–90① | 30–36② | 100–120 | 56–64 | 14–21 | 16–23 | 7–15 |
| 1988 | 140 (2300) | 80–90① | 80–90① | 30–36② | 100–120 | 56–64 | 14–21 | 16–23 | 7–15 |
| | 177 (2900) | ④ | 65–75 | 19–24 | 85–96 | 47–52 | ⑤ | 20–30 | 18–28 |
| 1989-90 | 140 (2300) | 80–90① | 80–90① | 30–36② | 100–120 | 56–64 | 14–21 | 16–23 | 7–15 |
| | 177 (2900) | ④ | 65–75 | 19–24 | 85–96 | 47–52 | ⑤ | 20–30 | 18–28 |

① Torque in 2 steps – 1st to 50–60 and 2nd to 80–90
② Torque in 2 steps – 1st to 25–30 and 2nd to 30–36
③ Torque in 2 steps – 1st to 5–7 and 2nd to 16–23
④ Torque in 3 steps – 1st to 22; 2nd to 51–55; 3rd an additional 90 degrees

⑤ Intake manifold (in sequence)
Step 1 – 3–6 ft. lbs.
Step 2 – 6–11 ft. lbs.
Step 3 – 11–15 ft. lbs.
Step 4 – 15–18 ft. lbs.
Step 5 – warm engine and recheck torque

Uppere intake (plenum)
Step 1 – 7 ft. lbs.
Step 2 – 15–18 ft. lbs.

## BRAKE SPECIFICATIONS

All measurements in inches unless noted

| Year | Model | Lug Nut Torque (ft. lbs.) | Master Cylinder Bore | Brake Disc Minimum Thickness | Brake Disc Maximum Runout | Standard Brake Drum Diameter | Minimum Lining Thickness Front | Minimum Lining Thickness Rear |
|---|---|---|---|---|---|---|---|---|
| 1985 | XR4Ti | 75–105 | 0.940 | 0.900 | 0.003 | 10.0 | ① | ① |
| 1986 | XR4Ti | 75–105 | 0.940 | 0.900 | 0.003 | 10.0 | ① | ① |
| 1987 | XR4Ti | 75–105 | 1.000 | 0.900 | 0.003 | 10.0 | ① | ① |
| 1988 | XR4Ti | 75–105 | 1.000 | 0.900 | 0.003 | 10.0 | ① | ① |
| | Scorpio | 52–73 | – | ② | 0.0039 | – | ① | ① |
| 1989-90 | XR4Ti | 75–105 | 1.000 | 0.900 | 0.003 | 10.0 | ① | ① |
| | Scorpio | 52–73 | – | ② | 0.0039 | – | ① | ① |

① $^{1}/_{8}$ in. above metal shoe
$^{1}/_{16}$ in. above rivets

② Front – 0.900
Rear – 0.350

## WHEEL ALIGNMENT

| Year | Model | Caster Range (deg.) | Caster Preferred Setting (deg.) | Camber Range (deg.) | Camber Preferred Setting (deg.) | Toe-in (in.) | Steering Axis Inclination (deg.) |
|---|---|---|---|---|---|---|---|
| 1985 | XR4Ti | $^{15}/_{16}$P–2$^{15}/_{16}$P | 1$^{15}/_{16}$P | 1$^{1}/_{2}$N–$^{1}/_{2}$P | $^{1}/_{2}$N ① | ② | 13$^{11}/_{16}$ |
| 1986 | XR4Ti | $^{15}/_{16}$P–2$^{15}/_{16}$P | 1$^{15}/_{16}$P | 1$^{1}/_{2}$N–$^{1}/_{2}$P | $^{1}/_{2}$N ① | ② | 13$^{11}/_{16}$ |
| 1987 | XR4Ti | $^{15}/_{16}$P–2$^{15}/_{16}$P | 1$^{15}/_{16}$P | 1$^{1}/_{2}$N–$^{1}/_{2}$P | $^{1}/_{2}$N ① | ② | 13$^{11}/_{16}$ |
| 1988 | XR4Ti | $^{15}/_{16}$P–2$^{15}/_{16}$P | 1$^{15}/_{16}$P | 1$^{1}/_{2}$N–$^{1}/_{2}$P | $^{1}/_{2}$N ① | ② | 13$^{11}/_{16}$ |
| | Scorpio | 1P–3P | 2P | 1$^{1}/_{4}$N–1$^{1}/_{4}$P | 0 ③ | ④ | – |
| 1989-90 | XR4Ti | $^{15}/_{16}$P–2$^{15}/_{16}$P | 1$^{15}/_{16}$P | 1$^{1}/_{2}$N–$^{1}/_{2}$P | $^{1}/_{2}$N ① | ② | 13$^{11}/_{16}$ |
| | Scorpio | 1P–3P | 2P | 1$^{1}/_{4}$N–1$^{1}/_{4}$P | 0 ③ | ④ | – |

① Rear – 2$^{3}/_{4}$N–2$^{3}/_{16}$P; dependent upon ride height
② Front – $^{1}/_{16}$N–$^{3}/_{4}$P; dependent upon ride height
Rear – $^{1}/_{32}$N–$^{5}/_{16}$P; dependent upon ride height
③ Rear – 4$^{5}/_{16}$N–1$^{7}/_{8}$P; dependent upon ride height
④ Rear – $^{1}/_{2}$N–$^{5}/_{8}$P; combined wheel-to-wheel

# TUNE-UP PROCEDURES

## Ignition Timing

### BASE TIMING ADJUSTMENT

**NOTE: Make all adjustments with the engine at normal operating temperature, transmission in N (manual) or P (automatic), parking brake applied, wheels blocked and all accessories turned OFF.**

1. With engine turned **OFF**, clean and highlight the timing marks on the crankshaft pulley and front cover. Connect a timing light and tachometer to the engine. The ignition coil connector allows a tachometer connection using an alligator clip without removing the coil connector.
2. Disconnect the single wire spark output (SPOUT) connector near (within 6 inches of the TFI module) the distributor. Restart the previously warmed up engine.
3. Check the idle rpm. The engine is equipped with an electronic idle speed control and the idle should be between 825–975 rpm (manual transmission) or 925–1075 rpm (automatic transmissions). If idle adjustment is necessary, turn **OFF** the engine and disconnect the electrical connector at the idle bypass valve. Restart the engine and run at approximately 2000 rpm, briefly. Allow the engine to return to idle and adjust the idle speed to 725–775 rpm by turning the throttle plate stop screw. Turn **OFF** the engine and reconnect the electrical connector to the bypass valve. Restart engine and proceed with ignition timing check.

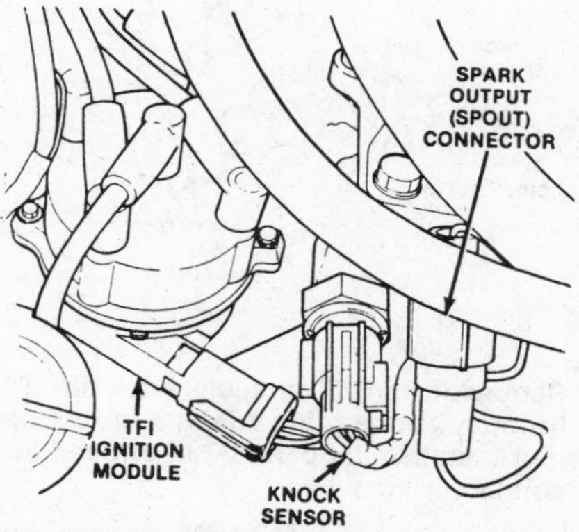

The SPOUT connector must be disconnected to set base timing

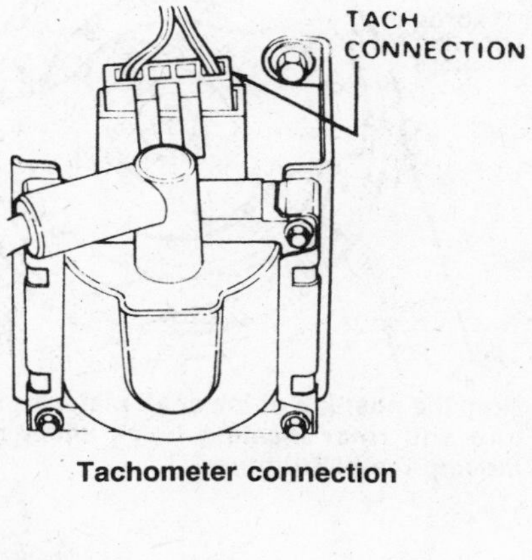

Tachometer connection

**NOTE: If the underhood calibration/emissions sticker specifications differ from this procedure, follow the specs and directions on the sticker as they will reflect product changes. If the cooling fan turns ON during idle speed adjustment, wait until turns shuts OFF or disconnect it temporarily before making adjustment. On Scorpio models, loosen the throttle camplate roller bolt prior to adjustment of the throttle stop adjusting screw. Torque the camplate roller bolt when adjustment is completed.**

4. Point the timing light at the marks. Timing should be 13 degrees BTDC (before top dead center) for manual transmission models, or 10 degrees BTDC for automatic transmission models. Refer to the Emissions Control Decal, if the information on the decal differs from the specs mention here, set the timing according to the decal. Loosen the distributor hold-down bolt and adjust the timing as required by twisting the distributor assembly clockwise or counterclockwise. Torque the hold-down bolt and recheck timing.

**NOTE: Some distributor hold-down bolts made have a special Torx® head which requires a special wrench.**

5. After base timing has been set, turn **OFF** the engine and remove all test equipment. Reconnect the single SPOUT wire harness at the distributor.

### INITIAL TIMING CHECK

#### *2.3L Engine*

An initial timing check should be performed if there is reason to believe the distributor is no longer timed to the engine. This condition can result from incorrect installation of the distributor or a timing belt that has jumped timing.

1. Remove the No. 1 spark plug from the engine.
2. Install a compression gauge in the No. 1 spark plug hole.
3. Connect a remote starter switch between the battery positive terminal and the starter relay **S** terminal.

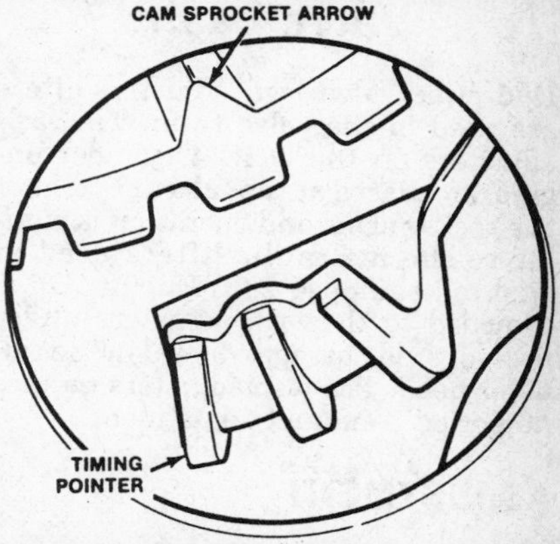

Correct timing mark alignment as viewed through the access plug on the timing belt outer cover

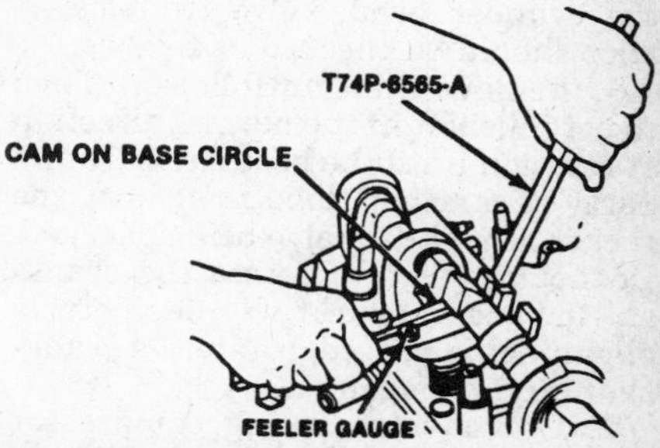

Measuring clearance between the base circle of the camshaft and the follower with a feeler gauge and spring compressor tool

4. Using the starter switch, bump the engine around until the compression gauge indicates the No. 1 piston is on its compression stroke.
5. Continue bumping the engine with the starter switch until the timing mark on the crankshaft (pulley notch) is aligned with the Top Dead Center (TDC) mark on the timing scale.
6. Remove the distributor cap and check that the rotor tip is pointing to the No. 1 spark plug wire terminal in the distributor cap. If the rotor and cap are correctly aligned, the initial timing is OK, proceed to the next step. If the rotor and distributor cap do not align, remove the distributor and reinstall it so the rotor is pointing to No. 1 plug tower.
7. Remove the access plug from the timing belt outer cover and check that the timing mark on the cam sprocket is aligned with the timing pointer. If the cam sprocket timing mark is aligned with the pointer, the engine is properly timed. If the cam sprocket timing mark does not align with the pointer, the timing belt has jumped time and must be replaced.
8. Check and/or readjust the base ignition timing.

## Valve Lash

Hydraulic valve lash adjusters/lifters are used in the valve train. The lash adjusters on the OHC 4 cylinder engine, are placed at the fulcrum point of the rocker arms and operation is similar to the hydraulic lifters used in pushrod equipped 2.9L Engine. Oil is provided to the lash adjusters under pressure via passages drilled in the cylinder head. The lash adjusters require no periodic manual adjustment.

### ADJUSTMENT

#### *2.3L Engine*

If a lash adjuster becomes noisy or valve service has been performed on the cylinder head, valve train clearance should be checked as follows:

1. Remove the cam follower. Turn the crankshaft in the normal direction of rotation until the base circle (round part) of camshaft lobe is against the rocker arm of the valve being checked. Do not attempt to rotate the crankshaft backwards; if the base circle alignment is missed, rotate the crankshaft and try again.
2. Use a valve spring compressor tool No. T74P-6565-A or equivalent, to slowly apply pressure to the cam follower, until the lash adjuster is completely collapsed. Hold the rocker arm in this position and check the clearance between the base circle of the cam lobe and the rocker arm with a feeler gauge. Allowable clearance is 0.035–0.055 in. (0.89–1.4mm). Desired clearance is 0.040–0.050 in. (1.0–1.27mm).
3. If the clearance is excessive, remove the cam follower and inspect for wear. If the follower is not worn, measure the assembled height of the valve spring. If the assembled height of the spring is correct, check for camshaft wear. If the camshaft is not worn, the lash adjuster should be removed and checked.
4. Replace worn parts as required and recheck clearance.

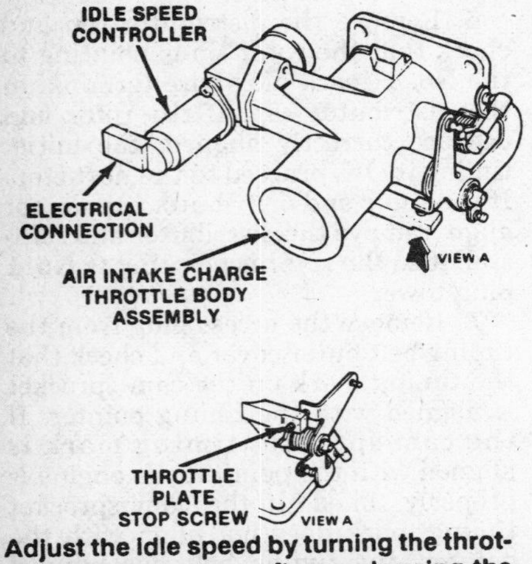


**Adjust the idle speed by turning the throttle plate stop screw after unplugging the idle speed controller connector. Disconnect or reconnect all electrical connections with the ignition switch off.**

#### *2.9L Engine*

1. Turn the crankshaft (in normal direction of rotation) until the lifters, of the cylinder to be adjusted, are in the base circle location of the camshaft; that is, after the intake valve has opened and closed. Both the intake and exhaust valves should now be fully closed.
2. Loosen the adjusting screws until distinctive lash (clearance) between the rocker arm and valve tip is noticed.
3. Slowly, torque the adjusting screw until all clearance is taken out and the rocker arm is just touching the valve tip.
4. Torque the adjusting screw an additional 1½ turns to set the normal working position of the lifter plunger. Proceed to the next valve. Turn the crankshaft to the correct position for the next cylinder and adjust.

## Idle Speed and Mixture

### ADJUSTMENT

Refer to the ignition timing procedure for checking and adjusting the idle speed. Mixture is controlled by the EEC IV (electronic engine control) system and is not adjustable. EEC IV system testing is required if an ignition or air/fuel mixture problem is suggested.

**NOTE: If the engine speed is excessive while driving the vehicle with the throttle at the idle position, turn the ignition switch OFF and restart it. If the engine speed is still excessive, do not drive the vehicle until the condition is repaired.**

# ENGINE ELECTRICAL

## Distributor

### REMOVAL & INSTALLATION

#### *2.3L Engine*

1. Disconnect the negative battery cable. Rotate the crankshaft until the No. 1 cylinder is on the TDC of it's compression stroke.
2. Disconnect the wiring harness to the TFI module on the side of the distributor. Disconnect the coil wire.
3. Loosen the hold-down screws, remove the distributor cap and position it aside with the spark plug wires attached.
4. Using chalk or paint, matchmark the rotor-to-distributor and the distributor housing-to-engine position.
5. Remove the rotor-to-distributor screws and the rotor.
6. Remove the distributor hold-down bolt and clamp, located under the distributor bowl between the distributor base and cylinder block. If the hold-down bolt has a Torx® head, a special wrench will be required.
7. Remove the distributor from the engine by grasping the base and pulling straight out. Check that the base O-ring is in position and not damaged or cut. Once the distributor is removed, the TFI module can be replaced by simply removing the mounting bolts and working the module back and forth until the pin connectors are free. Make sure there are no bent pin connectors when installing the TFI module.

**NOTE: When installing a new TFI module, coat the metal base plate uniformly with a $^1/_{32}$ in.**

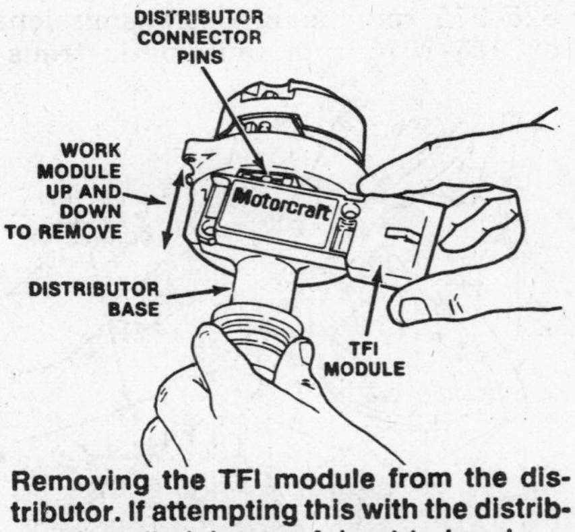


**Removing the TFI module from the distributor. If attempting this with the distributor installed, be careful not to bend any connector pins**

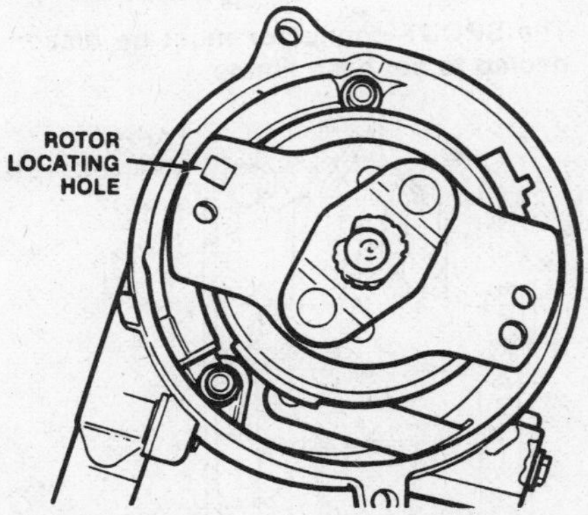


**Note the position of the shaft plate, armature and rotor locating holes when removing the distributor.**

**thick cover of silicone dielectric compound. Failure to do so will result in premature module failure due to excessive heat buildup.**

**To install:**

8. Lubricate the base O-ring lightly with engine oil. To install, align the matckmarks and reverse the removal procedures.
9. Install the hold-down clamp and bolt. Torque the bolt until the distributor can barely be rotated.
10. Install the rotor and distributor cap. Reconnect the coil wire and TFI harness connector, then reconnect the negative battery cable.
11. Start the engine, check and/or adjust the ignition timing as required. Once the ignition timing is set, torque the hold-down bolt to 6–8 ft. lbs. (8–11 Nm).

### *2.9L Engine*

1. Disconnect the negative battery cable.
2. Remove the distributor cap, with plug wires attached and position the assembly aside.
3. Using chalk or paint, matchmark the rotor-to-distributor and the distributor housing-to-engine positions.
4. Rotate the crankshaft, in the normal direction of rotation, until No. 1 piston is at TDC on the compression stroke and the timing marks are aligned.
5. Remove the distributor rotor and disconnect the TFI electrical harness connector.
6. Remove the distributor hold-down bolt and the distributor.

**To install:**

7. Verify that the No. 1 piston is still at TDC of the compression stroke and the timing marks are aligned.
8. Rotate the distributor shaft until the rotor is pointing about 20 degrees counterclockwise from the No. 1 spark plug tower mark on the distributor body.
9. Install the rotor to the distributor. Hold the distributor with the TFI module parallel with the rear of the engine block and install it into the engine slowly. The rotor should be pointing to the distributor body mark after the drive gear is engaged and the distributor is seated into the engine.
10. Rotate the distributor in the engine until the leading edge of the vane is aligned with the vane switch. Make sure the rotor is pointing to the matchmark on the distributor body.
11. If the vane and vane switch cannot be aligned, pull the distributor out of the block enough to disengage the drive gear and rotate the shaft slightly until another drive tooth is engaged. Repeat as necessary to get proper alignment.
12. Install the bracket and mounting bolt, but do not tighten completely. Connect the TFI harness connector. Install the distributor cap and wires.
13. Start the engine, check and/or adjust the engine timing and secure the distributor.

## Alternator

### PRECAUTIONS

Several precautions must be observed with alternator equipped vehicles to avoid damage to the unit.

- If the battery is removed for any reason, make sure it is reconnected with the correct polarity. Reversing the battery connections may result in damage to the 1 way rectifiers.
- When utilizing a booster battery as a starting aid, always connect the positive to positive terminals, and the negative terminal from the booster battery to a good engine ground on the vehicle being started.
- Never use a fast charger as a booster to start vehicles with alternating current (AC) circuits.
- Disconnect the battery cables when charging the battery with a fast charger.
- Avoid long soldering times when making alternator repairs. Prolonged heat will damage the alternator.
- Do not use test lamps of more than 12 volts when checking diode continuity.
- Do not short across or ground any of the alternator terminals.
- The polarity of the battery, alternator and regulator must be matched and considered before making any electrical connections within the system.
- Never separate the alternator on an open circuit. Make sure all connections within the circuit are clean and tight.
- Disconnect the battery ground terminal when performing any service on electrical components.
- Disconnect the battery if arc welding is to be done on the vehicle.

### BELT TENSION ADJUSTMENT

Adjust the drive belt tension so there is approximately 1/8–3/8 in. of deflection on the longest span of belt between pulleys. Apply pressure to the square rib on the alternator housing using the proper size open end wrench to maintain pressure when adjusting belt tension. Torque the:

Adjuster pivot bolt – 44–60 ft. lbs. (60–81 Nm)

Adjuster nut – 30–46 ft. lbs. (40–62 Nm)

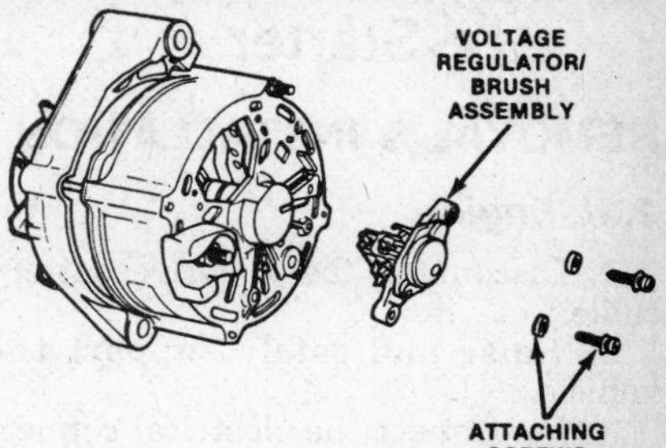


**Voltage regulator mounting at rear of alternator housing**

### REMOVAL & INSTALLATION

1. Disconnect the negative battery cable. Remove other drive belts that interfere with alternator removal.
2. Loosen the alternator pivot bolt and remove the adjustment arm-to-alternator bolt. Pivot the alternator to release belt tension.
3. Remove the drive belts.
4. Label and disconnect the wiring terminals from the alternator.
5. Remove the alternator pivot bolt and the alternator.
6. To install, reverse the removal procedures. Adjust the drive belt tension.

## Voltage Regulator

### REMOVAL & INSTALLATION

The voltage regulator is mounted to the rear of the alternator and contains the brushes as well as circuit control components. It is replaced as a unit by simply removing the mounting bolts and disconecting the wiring connector.

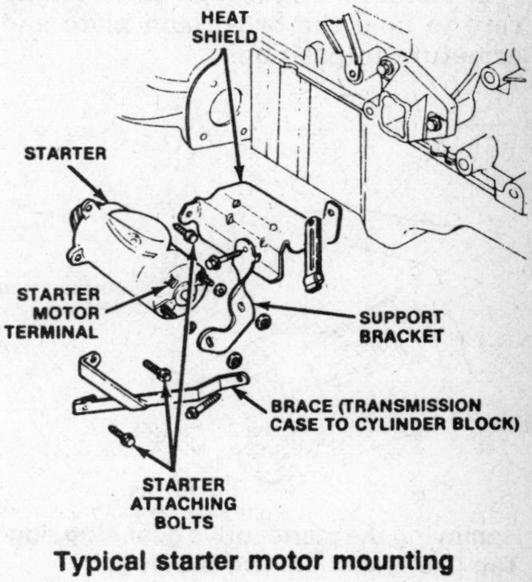


**Typical starter motor mounting**

## Starter

### REMOVAL & INSTALLATION

#### 2.3L Engine

1. Disconnect the negative battery cable.
2. Raise and safely support the vehicle.
3. Disconnect the electrical connectors from the starter.
4. Remove the heat shield-to-engine bolt.
5. Remove the starter-to-engine bolts, the heat shield rear support bracket, transmission-to-engine brace and the starter.
6. To install, reverse the removal procedures. Torque the mounting bolts to 15–20 ft. lbs. (20–27 Nm). Check the starter operation.

#### 2.9L Engine

1. Disconnect the negative battery cable.
2. Raise and safely support the vehicle.
3. Disconnect the electrical connectors from the starter.
4. Disconnect the starter motor relay-to-solenoid wire.
5. Remove the starter-to-housing bolts and the starter.

**To install:**

6. Position the starter into the bell housing and torque the bolts to 20–25 ft. lbs. (27–34 Nm).
7. To complete the installation, reverse the removal procedures. Check the starter operation.

### STARTER DRIVE REPLACEMENT

#### 2.3L Engine

1. Remove the starter and place it in a vise.
2. Remove the top (drive yoke) cover from the starter.
3. Remove the through bolts, taking care to hold the brush end plate and armature in position.

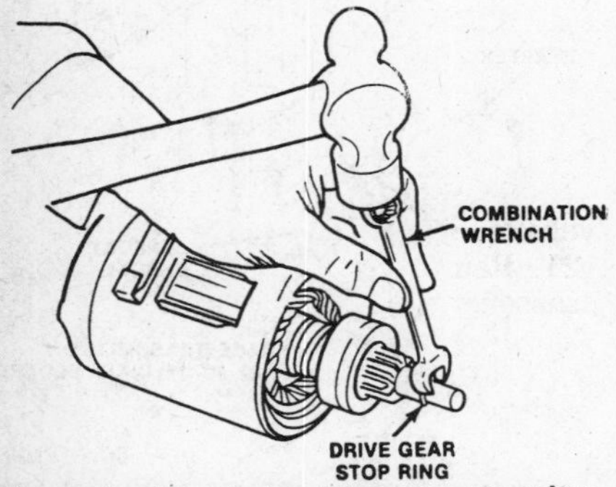


**Removing the starter drive gear stop ring. Tap lightly and discard the ring.**

4. Remove the pivot pin that retains the drive yoke, using a 0.218 in. (5.5mm) pin punch or small drift.
5. Remove the drive end housing, yoke return spring and drive yoke from the starter.
6. Remove the thrust washer and stop ring retainer from the armature shaft.
7. Remove the drive gear stop ring using a combination wrench and hammer. Discard the stop ring and slide the starter drive gear off the armature shaft.

**To install:**

8. Apply Lubriplate® on the armature splines and reverse the removal procedures. Install a new stop ring by holding it with needle nosed pliers and tapping it onto the armature shaft with a hammer. Install the starter and check it's operation.

#### 2.9L Engine

1. Remove the starter and place it in a vise.
2. Remove the screws, washers and end cap from the front nose of the starter. Remove the C-clip and spacer from the armature tip.
3. Remove the through bolts and lift off the commutator end plate.
4. Remove the nut and brush wiring from the solenoid connection.
5. Separate the main starter housing and armature assembly from the drive end housing.
6. Remove the solenoid mounting screws from the drive end housing and remove the solenoid.
7. Remove the starter drive assembly from the housing. Disconnect the solenoid plunger from the actuating arm.
8. Remove the C-clip retainer from the end of the drive pinion shaft and remove the drive.

**To install:**

9. Slide the drive and thrust collar on the pinion shaft and mount the C-clip.
10. Install the drive assembly into the drive end housing. ensure the correct location of the ring gear carrier. Install the rubber block. Connect the solenoid plunger and install the solenoid to the housing.
11. Make sure the brushplate is installed correctly on the armature. Install the armature and starter housing assembly after carefully aligning the sun gear with the planet gears. Torque the bolts to 3.3–4.4 ft. lbs. (4.5–6 Nm).
12. Install the end cap assembly. Connect the brush wire to the solenoid.

### STARTER SOLENOID REPLACEMENT

1. Disconnect the negative battery cable and remove the starter.
2. Disconnect the brush wire from the end of the solenoid.
3. Remove the solenoid bolts and the solenoid from the starter.

**To install:**

4. Align the yoke plunger in the solenoid bore and push the solenoid into position on the starter.
5. Secure the solenoid-to-starter bolts and connect the brush wire to the front of the solenoid.
6. Install the starter motor and check it's operation.

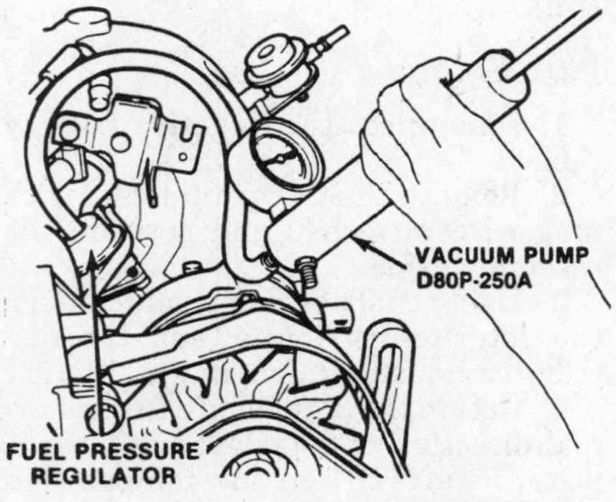


**Depressurize the fuel system by applying vacuum to the fuel pressure regulator**

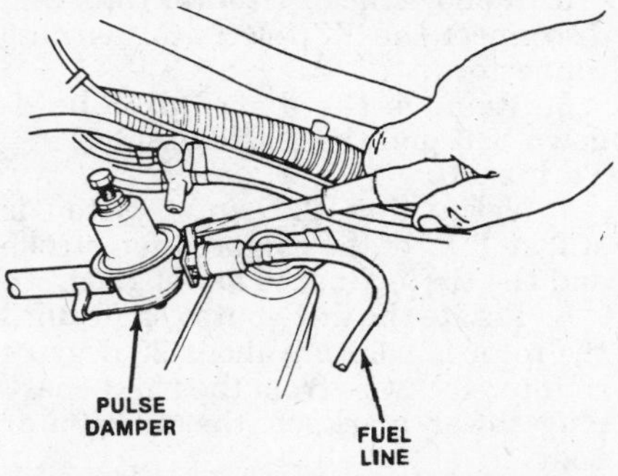


**Disconnect the fuel line at the pulse damper**

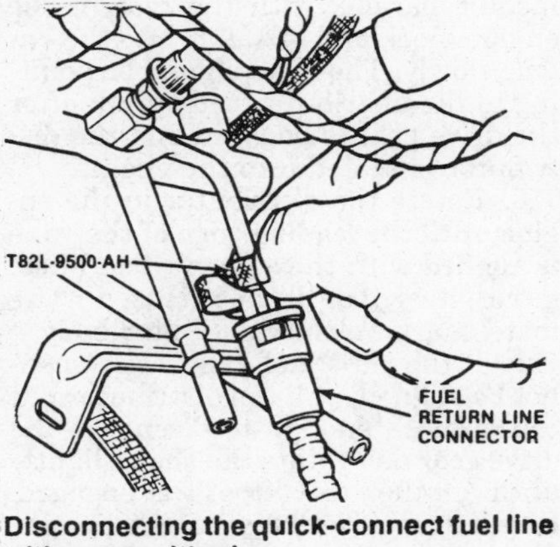


**Disconnecting the quick-connect fuel line with removal tool**

# ENGINE MECHANICAL

## Engine

### REMOVAL & INSTALLATION

*2.3L Engine*

1. Depressurize the fuel system and disconnect the negative battery cable.
2. Label and disconnected the hoses, vacuum lines and wires.
3. Mark the hood hinge positions on the hood. Make sure the ground strap near the right hinge is disconnected, then remove the hood.
4. Disconnect the battery and remove it from the vehicle. Drain the cooling system.
5. Remove the air cleaner and duct assembly from the turbocharger.
6. Remove the upper and lower radiator hoses. If equipped with an automatic transmission, disconnect and plug the transmission fluid cooler lines from the radiator. If equipped with a manual transmission, disconnect the radiator air vent hose at the radiator.
7. Disconnect the electric cooling fan wire harness and remove the fan and shroud as an assembly. Remove the radiator.
8. Disconnect the heater hoses from the engine. Separate the oil level sensor wiring connector and remove the engine oil level dipstick.
9. Disconnect the wiring form the alternator and starter motor. Disconnect the air bypass valve connector and throttle position sensor connector from the throttle body. Disconnect the vacuum hose at the EGR valve, then separate the fuel injection wiring harness connector located between the upper intake manifold and the engine oil dipstick.
10. Disconnect the throttle cable and transmission kickdown cable (if equipped) at the pivot ball connections on the bracket. Remove the accelerator cable bracket attaching screws and the bracket from the upper intake manifold, then place the bracket and the accelerator and kickdown cables aside.
11. Depressurize the fuel system, if not already done, and disconnect the fuel line at the pulse damper. Disconnect the fuel return line using quick connector removal tool T82L-9500-A or equivalent. Plug the fuel line and rail immediately to prevent contamination of the fuel system by dirt or grease during service.
12. Disconnect the wiring to the ignition coil, TFI module, oil pressure switch, temperature sending unit and all other sensors. Label all connectors for installation. Label and disconnect the supply hose at the vacuum tree mounted on the dash panel.
13. Remove the turbocharger air inlet tube, then disconnect the orange ground wire and vacuum hose at the turbocharger air inlet elbow.
14. Raise and safely support the front of the vehicle. Remove the air conditioner compressor from the mounting brackets and move it aside.
15. Drain the engine oil. Remove the starter motor. Remove the flywheel or converter housing upper mounting bolts and the side braces.
16. Disconnect the muffler inlet pipe from the turbocharger. Disconnect any exhaust system mounting brackets from the engine. Remove the right and left side engine mount-to-crossmember studs and nuts.
17. Remove the flywheel or converter housing lower plate cover.
18. If equipped with a manual transmission, remove the lower flywheel housing mounting bolts. If equipped with an automatic transmission, disconnect the converter from the driveplate (turn the engine in normal direction of rotation to gain access to the mountings). Remove the converter housing lower mounting bolts.
19. Lower the vehicle. Support the transmission with a jack.
20. Attach an engine lifting sling to the existing engine lifting brackets. Slowly raise the engine and separate it from the transmission. Be sure the converter (automatic transmission) remains on the input shaft.
21. Slowly raise the engine from the vehicle, being careful not to snag any hoses, lines or wire harness connectors on the way out. Watch for any engine sensor connectors that may not have been disconnected.

**To install:**

22. Reverse the removal procedures. If equipped with an automatic transmission, be sure the converter mounts are aligned with the flexplate and the converter hub fits flush into the crank pilot. If equipped with a manual transmission be sure the transmission mainshaft is aligned with the clutch disc. If necessary turn the engine with the transmission in gear until the shaft splines engage the disc.

**NOTE: Whenever self-locking motor mount bolts are nuts are removed, they must be replaced with new self-locking nuts or bolts. Clean old locking adhesive from the bolt or hole threads prior To installation.**

*2.9L Engine*

1. Disconnect the negative battery cable.
2. Drain the cooling system.
3. Disconnect the underhood lamp connector (black-to-gray), located on the inboard side of the battery.
4. Disconnect the windshield washer hose from the reservoir. Plug the reservoir.
5. Disconnect the hood ground strap. Mark the hood hinge locations and remove the hood.
6. Loosen the clamps and disconnect the inlet air hoses at the throttle body. Remove the air cleaner cover, air box and inlet air hoses.
7. Remove the upper radiator shroud and cooling fan.
8. Remove the power steering pump mounting bolts and position the pump aside.
9. Remove the alternator and thermactor pump (if equipped).
10. Disconnect the heater hoses from the firewall bulkhead.
11. Disconnect the coolant hoses at the water pump and thermostat housing.
12. Disconnect the throttle cable from the linkage on the throttle body. Remove the cable bracket from the upper manifold. Set the bracket to the side.
13. Release fuel system pressure at the pressure regulator. Disconnect the fuel supply and return lines.
14. Remove the distributor cap, rotor, distributor and plug wires. Label and disconnect the ignition coil electrical connectors.
15. Label and disconnect the vacuum hoses from the front and rear of the upper intake manifold and EGR fitting.
16. Remove the carbon canister, bracket and vacuum line.
17. Label and disconnect the air charge temperature (ACT) sensor; idle speed control valve; throttle position (TP) sensor; air conditioning compressor clutch wiring; fuel injectors; engine coolant (ECT) sensor and the oil pressure switch.
18. Remove the ground wire from the spade connector located on the left fender apron.
19. Lift the cowl weatherstrip and unclip the manifold absolute sensor (MAP) and set it to the side.
20. Raise and safely support the vehicle.
21. Remove the exhaust manifold to crossover pipe retaining nuts.
22. If equipped with an automatic transmission, disconnect and plug the transmission lines from the radiator.
23. Remove the radiator-to-chassis bolts, disengage the upper radiator clips by depressing the tabs and re-

move the radiator from under the vehicle.

24. Disconnect the starter motor wiring and remove the starter motor.

25. Remove the engine insulator lower retaining nuts and washers. Remove the lower side and lower clutch or converter housing to engine mounting bolts.

26. If equipped with an automatic transmission, remove the inspection plate. Remove the converter to flywheel mounting nuts.

27. Loosen the air conditioning compressor retaining and pivot bolts.

28. Lower the vehicle.

29. Attach an appropriate engine sling to the lifting brackets provided on the engine. Attach a hoist. Support the transmission with a suitable floor jack.

30. Remove both upper bell housing-to-engine bolts. Raise the engine slightly and remove the air conditioning compressor from the mounting brackets and wire the compressor (with hoses attached) aside.

31. Raise the engine enough to clear the mounts and pull the engine forward to clear the transmission. If equipped with an automatic transmission, make sure the converter is pushed back onto the transmission. Carefully raise the engine out of the vehicle to prevent damage to the engine compartment and engine components.

**To install:**

32. When installing the engine, remove the left engine support bracket to gain clearance.

33. Lower the engine into the compartment carefully. Make sure the exhaust manifolds are aligned with the exhaust pipe. If equipped with a manual transmission, start the transmission mainshaft into the clutch disc. It may be necessary to adjust the angle of the transmission with the floor jack if the mainshaft binds. Turn the engine slightly to engage the clutch disc splines. If equipped with an automatic transmission, align the converter studs with the flywheel mounting holes and start the converter pilot into the crankshaft.

34. Install the engine in the reverse order of removal. Torque the:

Upper bell housing-to-engine bolts – 23–26 ft. lbs. (30–36 Nm) – automatic

Upper bell housing-to-engine bolts – 30–38 ft. lbs. (40–51 Nm) – manual

35. Before lowering the engine completely, install the air conditioning compressor and install the left engine bracket. Proceed with the rest of the engine installation. Torque the remaining bell housing bolts to the same value as the upper.

# Cylinder Head

## REMOVAL & INSTALLATION

### 2.3L Engine

**NOTE: The engine should be COLD before removing the cylinder head to prevent warpage or distortion.**

1. Relieve the fuel pressure. Disconnect the negative battery cable. Drain the cooling system.

2. Disconnected hoses and electrical connectors to assure proper assembly.

3. Rotate the crankshaft to position the No. 1 cylinder on TDC (top dead center) on the compression stroke with the timing marks aligned.

4. Disconnect the air intake cast tube from the turbocharger to the throttle body. Remove the valve rocker cover.

5. Remove the upper radiator hose and disconnect the heater hose if it interferes with cylinder head removal. Remove the alternator drive belts and the alternator and mounting brackets.

6. Remove the intake and exhaust manifolds from the cylinder head.

7. Remove the camshaft drive belt cover.

8. Loosen the drive belt tensioner and remove the drive belt.

9. Remove the water outlet from the cylinder head.

10. Remove the cylinder head bolts evenly, and remove the cylinder head.

**To install:**

11. Using a new cylinder head gasket, position it on the block. Rotate the camshaft so the drive sprocket locating pin is at the 5 o'clock position, to avoid valve or piston damage when reinstalling the cylinder head on the engine.

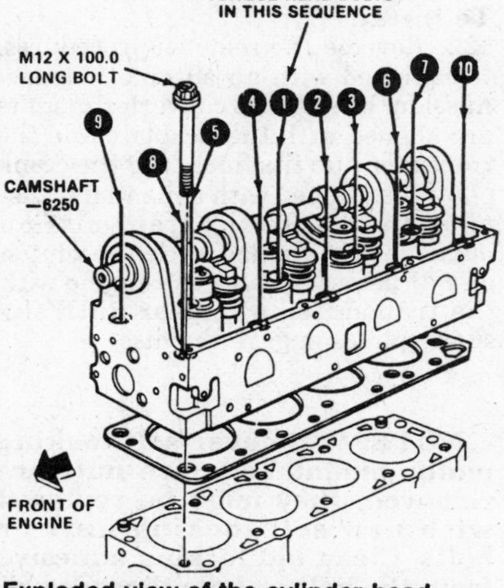


**Exploded view of the cylinder head and torquing sequence – 2.3L engine**

12. Position the cylinder head and camshaft assembly on the block. Install the bolts finger tight, then torque to specifications in 2 stages. The 1st to 50–60 ft. lbs. (68–81 Nm), the 2nd step to 80–90 ft. lbs. (108–122 Nm).

**NOTE: If difficulty in positioning the head on the block is encountered, guide pins may be fabricated by cutting the heads off 2 extra cylinder head bolts.**

13. Set the crankshaft at TDC (if rotated) and be sure the camshaft drive gear is positioned correctly.

14. Install the camshaft drive belt and release the tensioner. Rotate the crankshaft 2 full turns clockwise (facing the engine) to remove all slack from the belt. The timing marks should again be aligned. Torque the tensioner lockbolt and pivot bolts.

15. Install the camshaft drive belt cover.

16. Apply sealer to the water outlet and new gasket, and install.

17. Install the intake and exhaust manifolds and torque the mounting nuts and bolts to specifications.

18. Install a new valve cover gasket and install the valve cover.

19. Install all removed components, hoses and wiring.

20. To complete the installation, reverse the removal procedures.

### 2.9L Engine

1. Relieve the fuel pressure. Disconnect the negative battery cable.

2. Disconnected hoses and electrical connectors to assure proper assembly.

3. Rotate the crankshaft to position the No. 1 cylinder on TDC on the compression stroke with the timing marks aligned.

4. Drain the engine coolant.

5. Remove the intake hoses from the throttle body and disconnect the throttle linkage. Remove the distributor.

6. Remove the upper radiator hose. Remove the rocker arm (valve) covers Remove the rocker arm and shaft assemblies.

7. Remove the fuel line from the fuel rail. Remove the intake manifold.

8. Remove the pushrods. Keep the pushrods in correct sequence for proper assembly in the same position as removed.

9. Remove the exhaust manifolds from the cylinder heads.

10. Remove the cylinder head mounting bolts, starting from the outer edges toward the center. A No. 55 Torx® drive bit/socket is required.

11. Remove the cylinder heads.

**To install:**

12. Clean the gasket mounting surfaces.

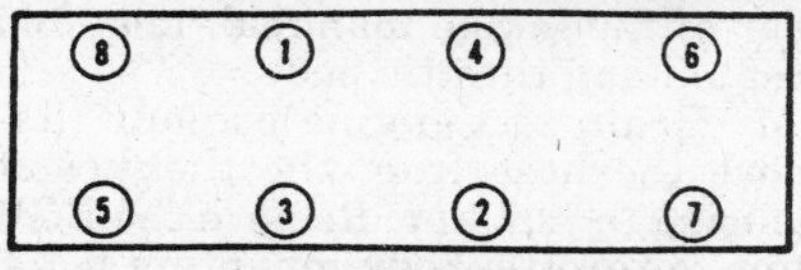


STEP 1: TIGHTEN IN SEQUENCE TO 22 FT. LBS (30 Nm)
STEP 2: TIGHTEN IN SEQUENCE TO 51–55 FT. LBS. (70–75 Nm)
STEP 3: WAIT 5 MINUTES
STEP 4: IN SEQUENCE, TURN ALL BOLTS 90 DEGREES

**Cylinder head torquing sequence – 2.9L engine**

13. Using new head gaskets, position them on the cylinder block; the gaskets are marked top and front and are not interchangeable.
14. Using old head bolts, cut the tops off and make alignment studs. Torque the cylinder head bolts, in sequence, using the following 4 steps:
Step 1 – torque to 22 ft. lbs. (30 Nm)
Step 2 – torque to 51–55 ft. lbs. (70–75 Nm)
Step 3 – wait 5 minutes
Step 4 – torque an additional 90 degrees
15. To complete the installation, reverse the remove procedures. Adjust the valves. Check and adjust the ignition timing.

### OVERHAUL

**For all cylinder head overhaul procedures, please refer to "Engine Rebuilding" in the Unit Repair Section.**

## Cam Follower

### REMOVAL & INSTALLATION

#### *2.3L Engine*

1. Loosen the clamp on the PCV hose at the oil separator on the rocker arm cover and disconnect the hose. Do not attempt to remove the oil separator from the valve cover; it is pressed into the cover and sealed with Loctite®.
2. Disconnect the coolant hose that passes over the rear of the rocker arm cover. Remove the coolant pipe retaining clip screw from the right, front side of the valve cover.
3. Remove the throttle body from the upper intake manifold. Label all connectors, hoses and linkage for installation in their original locations.
4. Disconnect the spark plug wires at the spark plugs and at the valve cover studs, then lay the wires aside.
5. Remove the remaining valve cover bolts, then lift the valve cover and gasket off the cylinder head. Tap the valve cover with a rubber mallet to break it loose, if necessary.
6. Rotate the camshaft so the base circle of the cam is against the cam follower you intend to remove.
7. Using a valve spring compressor tool No. T74P-6565-A or equivalent, depress the valve spring and slide the cam follower over the lash adjuster and out from under the camshaft.
8. Once the cam follower is removed, the hydraulic lash adjuster can be lifted out, if necessary. Make sure the lash adjuster bore is clean before installing the adjuster into the cylinder head.
9. To install the cam follower, reverse the removal procedures. Make sure the lash adjuster is collapsed and released before rotating the camshaft.

## Rocker Arms/Shaft

### REMOVAL & INSTALLATION

#### *2.9L Engine*

1. Remove the rocker arm (valve) covers.
2. Remove the rocker arm stand mounting bolts from the ends, working toward the center. Loosen each bolt 2 turns at a time in sequence.
3. When all the bolts are loose, lift off the rocker arm shaft assembly.
4. Loosen each rocker arm adjusting screw several turns.

**To install:**

5. Clean the gasket mounting surfaces.
6. Install the oil baffle and guide the rocker arms into their pushrod sockets. Torque the rocker stand bolts, in sequence, starting from the center working toward the ends. Torque, 2 turns at a time, to 43–50 ft. lbs. (59–67 Nm).
7. Adjust the valves. Install the rocker arm (valve) covers. Apply a bead of RTV sealer to the covers. The covers must be installed within 15 minutes after RTV is applied.

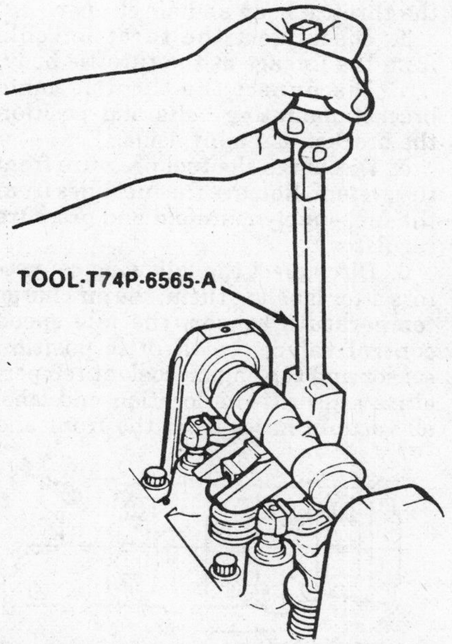


**Compress the valve spring with spring compressor as shown to remove cam follower**

## Intake Manifold

### REMOVAL & INSTALLATION

#### *2.3L Engine*

**UPPER MANIFOLD**

1. Disconnect the negative battery cable. Label and disconnect the electronic connectors at the air bypass valve, the throttle position sensor, injector wiring harness, knock sensor, fan temperature sensor and coolant temperature sensor.
2. Label and disconnect the upper intake manifold vacuum fitting connections at the manifold fitting, the rear vacuum line at the dash panel tree, the vacuum line to the EGR valve, and the vacuum line to the fuel pressure regulator. Disconnect the PCV hose at the intake manifold fitting.
3. Disconnect the accelerator cable and kickdown cable (automatic only) from the throttle linkage at the pivot ball connection. Unbolt the accelerator cable bracket from the upper intake manifold, then lay the bracket and cables aside.
4. Loosen the hose clamps and remove the turbocharger outlet hose flexible connection to the throttle body.

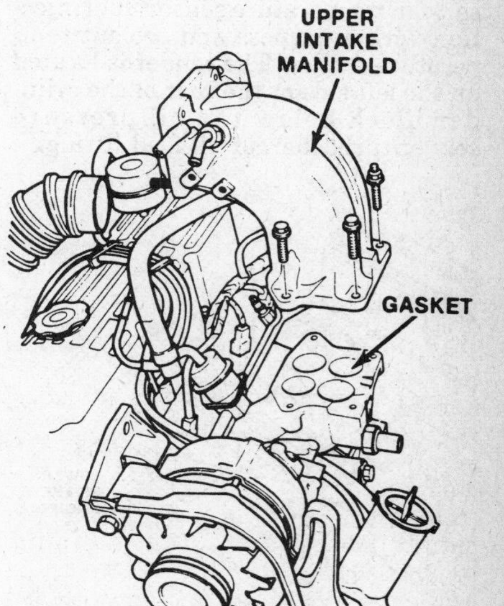


**Exploded view of the upper intake mainfold – 2.3L engine**

5. Remove the EGR flange attaching bolts, then remove the flange and EGR valve as an assembly. Remove the flange gasket and discard.

6. Remove the nut attaching the pulse damper to its bracket, then disconnect the low oil level sensor and remove the engine oil level dipstick.

7. Remove the engine oil dipstick bracket mounting bolt. If necessary, cut the fuel injection wiring harness routing strap at the pulse damper bracket.

8. Remove the pulse damper bracket attaching nuts and remove the bracket.

9. The throttle body can either be removed at this point by removing the mounting bolts, or left attached and removed with the upper intake manifold as an assembly.

10. Loosen and remove the upper intake manifold mounting bolts. Lift the upper intake manifold upward and off the lower intake manifold. Remove the gasket.

**To install:**

11. Clean the gasket mounting surfaces.

12. Reverse the removal procedures. Torque the:

Upper intake manifold mounting nuts and bolts, in the sequence – 15–22 ft. lbs. (18–26 Nm)

EGR flange bolts – 13–19 ft. lbs. (18–26 Nm)

Throttle body bolts – 12–15 ft. lbs. (16–20 Nm)

13. To complete the installation, reverse the removal procedures.

### LOWER MANIFOLD

1. Drain the cooling system and disconnect the negative battery cable.

2. Label and disconnect the wire harness connectors at the knock sensor, fan temperature sensor, fuel injection wiring harness and coolant temperature sender. The sender is located on the left side at the rear of the cylinder block below the oil pressure sender/turbocharger oil feed fitting.

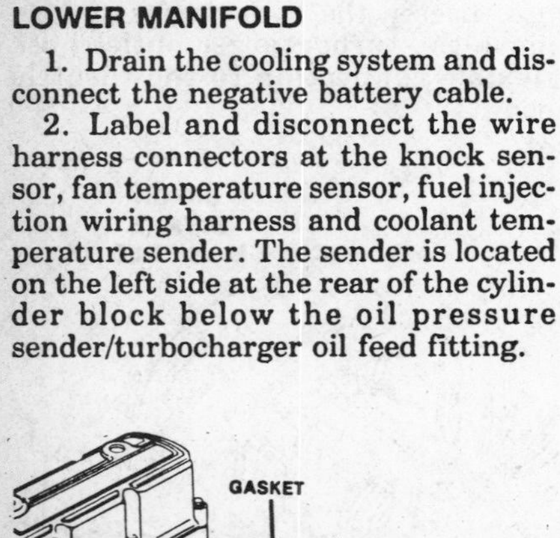

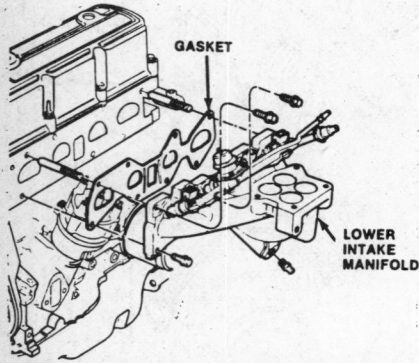


**Exploded view of the lower intake manifold – 2.3L engine**

3. Disconnect the coolant bypass line from the lower intake manifold.

4. Depressurize the fuel system by connecting a hand vacuum pump to the fuel pressure regulator and applying 25 in. Hg. Disconnect the fuel supply line from the fuel supply manifold, then disconnect the push connect fuel return line.

5. Remove the nut attaching the pulse damper to its bracket and place the pulse damper and fuel supply line aside.

6. Remove the upper intake manifold as previously described.

7. Disconnect the coolant temperature sensor, then remove the upper and lower mounting bolts from the lower intake manifold and lift the manifold off the engine with the fuel injectors and fuel supply manifold installed.

8. Remove the manifold-to-cylinder head bolts and the manifold; the injectors can be removed at this time by exerting a slight twisting/pulling motion.

**To install:**

9. Clean the gasket mounting surfaces. Inspect the parts for damage.

10. Clean and oil all stud threads. Install a new mounting gasket over the studs.

11. Install the lower manifold-to-cylinder head, with lift bracket in position, and torque the bolts, in sequence, to 12–15 ft. lbs. (16–20 Nm).

12. To complete the installation, reverse the removal procedures.

### *2.9L Engine*

1. Disconnect the negative battery cable.

2. Remove the air inlet hoses from the throttle body and air cleaner.

3. Disconnect the throttle cable from the linkage at the throttle body.

4. Disconnect the throttle cable bracket mounting bolts and position the bracket assembly aside.

5. Discharge the fuel pressure from the system. Remove the fuel lines from the fuel supply manifold and pressure regulator.

6. Disconnect the following connectors after labeling them: the air charge temperature sensor, the idle speed control valve, the throttle position sensor and the engine coolant temperature sensor. Note location and label all vacuum hoses from the front and rear of the intake manifold, manifold plenum and throttle body.

7. Drain the engine coolant. Remove the hose from the thermostat housing to radiator. Remove the EGR tube-to-throttle body mounting bolts. Remove the EGR tube from the throttle body.

8. Remove the plenum-to-intake manifold Torx® bolts and the throttle body/plenum assembly.

9. Remove the distributor. Remove the rocker arm (valve) covers.

10. Remove the intake manifold mounting bolts. Note the length and position of each bolt. Tap the manifold lightly with a plastic hammer to break the gasket seal and remove the intake manifold.

**To install:**

11. Clean the gasket mounting surfaces; make sure no gasket material falls into the intake passages.

12. Apply sealing compound to the gasket mounting joint surfaces.

13. Position a new gasket on the intake manifold and ensure the tab on the right cylinder head fits the cutout of the gasket.

14. Place the manifold carefully onto the engine. Install and hand tighten the mounting bolts. Follow the tightening sequence provides and progressively tighten the mounting bolts and nuts to the torque values shown.

15. To complete the installation, reverse the removal procedures.

## Exhaust Manifold

### REMOVAL & INSTALLATION

### *2.3L Engine*

1. Loosen the cap on the coolant expansion tank and drain the cooling system.

2. Remove the heater return hose at the water pump. Remove the bolt attaching the coolant pipe routing bracket to the right, front side of the valve cover.

3. Disconnect the coolant pipe-to-expansion tank hose at the coolant pipe.

4. Disconnect the turbocharger oil supply line at the turbocharger. Disconnect the turbocharger coolant supply and return line at the turbocharger.

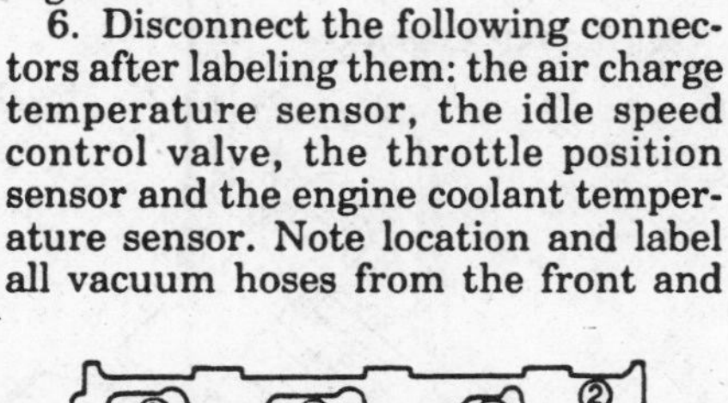


STEP 1: TIGHTEN ALL BOLTS/NUTS IN SEQUENCE TO 3–6 FT. LBS. (4–8 Nm)
STEP 2: TIGHTEN ALL BOLTS/NUTS IN SEQUENCE TO 6–11 FT. LBS.(8–15 Nm)
STEP 3: TIGHTEN ALL BOLTS/NUTS IN SEQUENCE TO 11–15 FT. LBS. (15–21 Nm)
STEP 4: TIGHTEN ALL BOLTS/NUTS IN SEQUENCE TO 15–18 FT. LBS. (21–25 Nm)

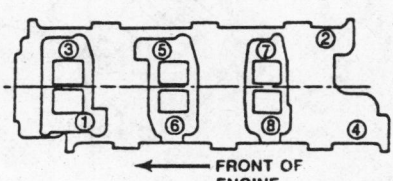

**V6 intake manifold installation**

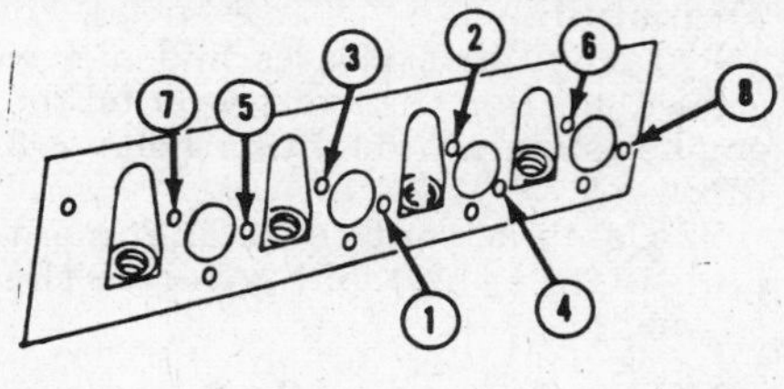


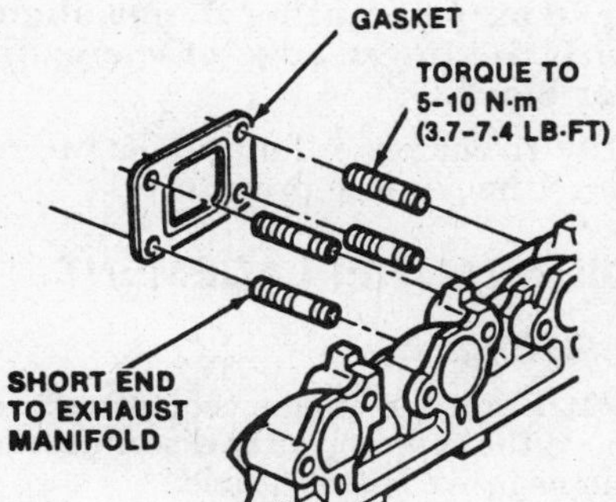


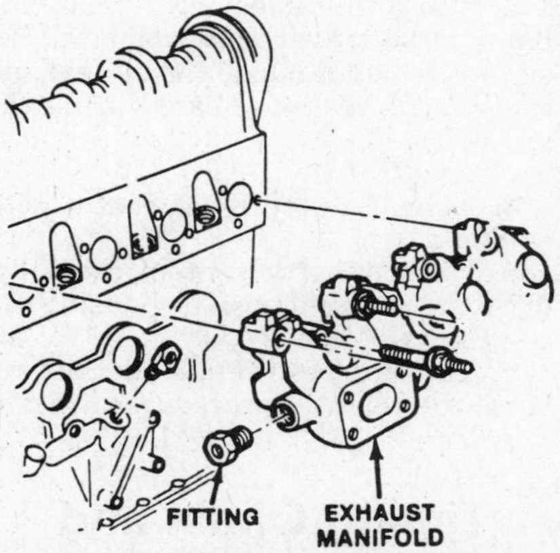


**Exploded view of the exhaust manifold —2.3L engine**

5. Disconnect the PCV tube at the turbo air inlet adapter, then remove the turbo-to-exhaust manifold nuts.
6. Remove the turbocharger support bracket.
7. Remove the exhaust manifold-to-cylinder head nuts/bolts and the manifold.

**To install:**

8. Clean the gasket mounting surfaces.
9. Install the exhaust manifold-to-cylinder head nuts and torque, in sequence, in 2 steps, to:
   Step 1 – 14–17 ft. lbs. (20–23 Nm)
   Step 2 – 20–30 ft. lbs. (27–41 Nm)
10. To complete the installation, reverse the removal procedures. Refill the cooling system and crank the engine a few times without starting to build oil pressure back up in the turbocharger. Start the engine and check for leaks.

### *2.9L Engine*

#### RIGHT SIDE

1. Disconnect the negative battery cable.
2. Remove the heat shield mounting bolts and remove the heat shield.
3. Remove the nuts that retain the crossover pipe. Remove the pipe.
4. Remove the thermactor air pipe to manifold, on models equipped.
5. Remove the manifold-to-cylinder head nuts and the manifold.

**To install:**

6. Clean the gasket mounting surfaces.
7. Using new gaskets, reverse the removal procedures. Torque the manifold mounting nuts to 20–30 ft. lbs. (26–40 Nm). Start the engine and check for leaks.

#### LEFT SIDE

1. Disconnect the negative battery cable.
2. Remove the EGR valve-to-manifold bolts. Remove the EGR tube-to-throttle body attaching screws and detach the tube.
3. Remove the heat shield. Remove the crossover pipe-to-manifold mounting nuts. Remove thermactor pipe, if equipped.
4. Remove the manifold-to-cylinder head nuts and the manifold.

**To install:**

5. Clean all gasket mounting surfaces.
6. Using new gaskets, reverse the removal procedures. Torque the exhaust manifold-to-cylinder head nuts to 20–30 ft. lbs. (26–40 Nm). Start the engine and check for leaks.

# Turbocharger

## REMOVAL & INSTALLATION

Turbocharger servicing is by replacement only. Maintain clean as possible working conditions while removing and installing the turbocharger. When disconnecting lines and feed pipes always cover or plug openings to prevent contamination by dirt or grease.

1. Disconnect the negative battery cable. Drain the cooling system.
2. Clean the turbocharger and area around the turbo with a noncaustic solution.
3. Disconnect the oxygen sensor wiring connector from the harness.
4. Remove the air tube-to-turbocharger bolts. Loosen the clamp on the intake hose-to-throttle body bolts and disconnect the flexible hose.
5. Label and disconnect all vacuum hoses and tubes that will interfere with turbocharger removal. Disconnect the boost control solenoid hose from the turbocharger outlet fitting.
6. Disconnect the PCV tube from the turbocharger air inlet elbow and the boost control solenoid hose from the turbocharger inlet fitting.
7. Remove the cast air tube and hose assembly from between the turbo and throttle body assembly.
8. Disconnect the electrical ground wire from the turbocharger outlet fitting.
9. Disconnect the oil supply line routing bracket and line from the turbocharger. Disconnect the coolant outlet line from the turbocharger housing. Loosen the hose clamp and disconnect the coolant inlet line from the turbocharger fitting.
10. Loosen the heat shield-to-upper right engine mount nut.
11. Raise and safely support the front of the vehicle. Remove the transmission mount center plate.
12. Disconnect the exhaust pipe from the turbocharger. Disconnect the oil return line from the bottom of the turbocharger; be careful not kink or damage the line. Remove and discard the gasket.
13. Remove the lower turbocharger nuts/bolts, the lower turbocharger support bracket bolt and the bracket.
14. Lower the vehicle. If equipped with an automatic transmission, remove the nut and disconnect the dipstick tube support bracket from the cast tube flange.
15. Remove the upper turbocharger nuts.
16. Loosen the other turbocharger nuts, a little at a time, and slide the turbo on the mounting studs until the nuts can be removed. Remove the turbocharger, gasket, outlet tube and hose as an assembly. Continue disassembly on a clean workbench to transfer components to the new turbocharger.

**To install:**

17. Clean the gasket mounting surfaces.

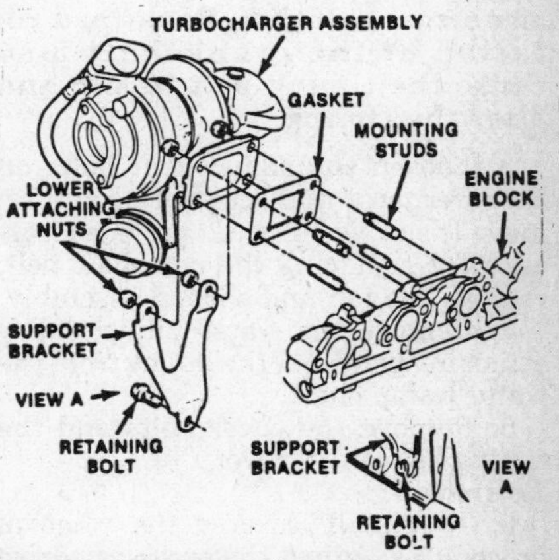


**Exploded view of the turbocharger-to-exhaust manifold assembly—2.3L engine**

18. To install, reverse the removal procedures. Use new mounting gasket on the turbo and oil return line. Use new mounting nuts when installing the turbocharger. Torque the:

Lower bracket bolt—28–40 ft. lbs. (38–54 Nm)

Oil return line—14–21 ft. lbs. (19–28 Nm)

Exhaust pipe—25–35 ft. lbs. (34–47 Nm)

Turbo mounting nuts—28–40 ft. lbs. (38–54 Nm)

Cast air pipe to turbo—15–22 ft. lbs. (20–30 Nm)

## TROUBLESHOOTING

**For more information on turbocharging, please refer to "Turbocharging" in the Unit Repair Section.**

# Front Cover

## REMOVAL & INSTALLATION

### 2.3L Engine

1. Disconnect the negative battery cable.

**NOTE: An access plug is provided in the cam drive belt cover so the camshaft timing can be checked without removing the drive belt cover.**

2. Remove the access plug, turn the crankshaft until the timing mark on the crankshaft damper indicates TDC, and observe that the timing mark on the camshaft drive sprocket is aligned with the pointer on the inner belt cover. Also, the rotor of the distributor must align with No. 1 cylinder firing position.

**NOTE: Never turn the crankshaft of any of the overhead cam engines in the opposite direction of normal rotation. Backward rotation of the crankshaft may cause the timing belt to slip and alter the timing.**

3. Loosen the adjustment bolts on the alternator and accessories and remove the drive belts. To provide clearance for removing the camshaft belt, remove the fan and shroud assembly.
4. Remove the water pump pulley attaching bolts and the pulley from the water pump shaft.
5. Remove the cover bolts and the timing belt outer cover.

**To install:**

6. To install, reverse the removal procedures. Adjust the accessory drive belt tension. Start the engine and check the ignition timing.

### 2.9L Engine

1. Disconnect the negative battery cable. Drain the engine coolant and remove the radiator.
2. Drain the engine oil. Remove the engine oil pan.
3. Remove the air conditioning compressor. Thermactor air pump and bracket.
4. Remove the power steering pump and bracket. Remove the alternator and drive belts.
5. Remove the radiator cooling fan assembly. Remove the water pump, heater hose and radiator hoses.
6. Remove the drive pulley from the crankshaft.
7. Remove the front cover mounting bolts. Tap the cover with a plastic hammer to loosen the gasket seal. Remove the front cover. Replace the oil seal after cleaning the cover and removing all gasket material from the mounting surfaces.

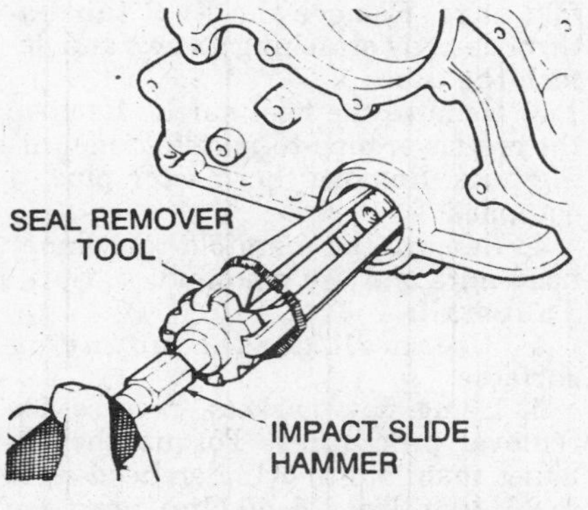


Scorpio front crankshaft seal removal

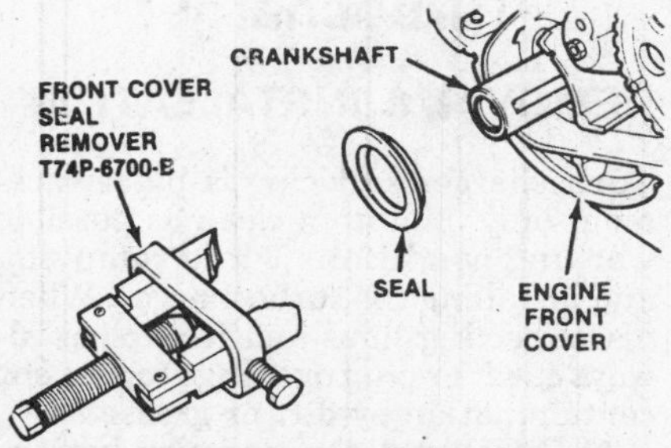


Front crankshaft oil seal showing remover tool

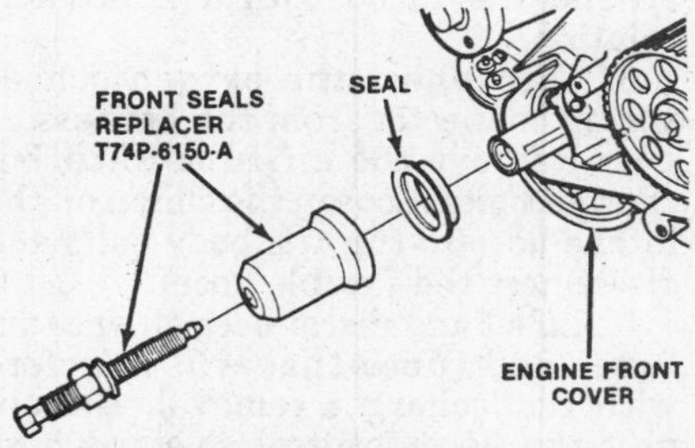


Install front cover oil seal using tool as shown

**To install:**

8. Using guide sleeves and a new gasket, position the front cover on the engine, start all mounting bolts 2–3 turns.
9. Using a front cover alignment tool, install the front cover to the engine.

**NOTE: Make sure the front cover to oil pan mating flange aligns with the lower edge of the cylinder block.**

10. To complete the installation, reverse the removal procedures.

## OIL SEAL REPLACEMENT

### 2.9L Engine

1. Drain the engine coolant and remove the radiator after disconnecting the negative battery cable.
2. Remove the crankshaft pulley, the water pump and drive belt.
3. Use a suitable long jawed slide hammer puller with internal jaws. Position the puller inside the oil seal and remove the seal. Use care during the procedure.

**To install:**

4. Using a new oil seal, coat it with engine oil.
5. Using a seal driver tool, carefully, drive the new seal into the housing until it seats.
6. To complete the installation, reverse the removal procedures.

# Timing Chain and Sprockets

## REMOVAL & INSTALLATION

### 2.9L Engine

1. Disconnect the negative battery cable. Drain the cooling system and the crankcase.
2. Rotate the engine until No. 1 cylinder is at TDC of it's compression stroke. Align the timing marks.
3. Remove the radiator and engine oil pan.
4. Remove the water pump and engine front cover.
5. With the sprockets aligned with their timing marks, release chain tensioner.
6. Remove the camshaft sprocket, timing chain and crankshaft sprocket.

**To install:**

7. Position the sprockets with the timing chain and install the sprocket/chain assembly onto the engine. Make sure the sprocket marks are aligned and apply tensioner pressure.
8. To complete the installation, reverse the removal procedures.

## Timing Belt and Tensioner

### ADJUSTMEMT

#### *2.3L Engine*

1. Disconnect the negative battery cable and remove the front cover.
2. Loosen the belt tensioner adjustment and pivot bolts.
3. Loosen the tensioner adjustment bolt, allowing it to spring back against the belt.
4. Rotate the crankshaft 2 complete revolutions in the normal rotation direction to remove any belt slack. Turn the crankshaft until the timing marks are aligned.
5. Torque the tensioner adjustment bolt to 14–21 ft. lbs. (19–28 Nm).
6. To complete the installation, reverse the removal procedures. Adjust the accessory drive belt tension. Start the engine and check the ignition timing.

### REMOVAL & INSTALLATION

#### *2.3L Engine*

Should the camshaft drive belt jump timing by a tooth or two, the engine could still run; but very poorly. To visually check for correct timing of the crankshaft, auxiliary shaft and the camshaft, follow this procedure.

An access plug is provided in the cam drive belt cover so the camshaft timing can be checked without removing the drive belt cover. Remove the access plug, turn the crankshaft until the timing mark on the crankshaft damper indicates TDC, and observe that the timing mark on the camshaft drive sprocket is aligned with the pointer on the inner belt cover. Also, the rotor of the distributor must align with No. 1 cylinder firing position.

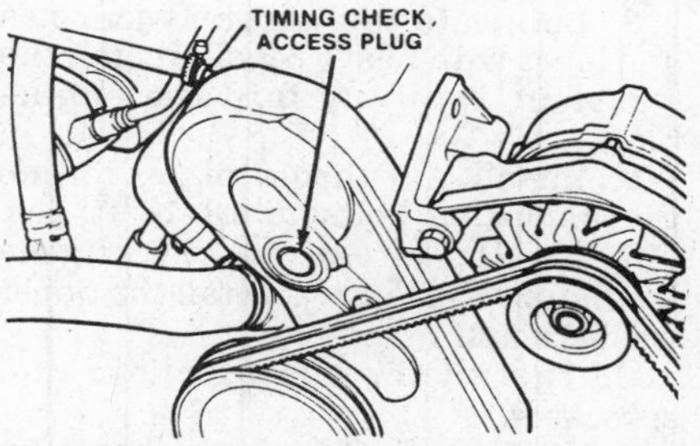


**Location of access plug for checking valve timing visually**

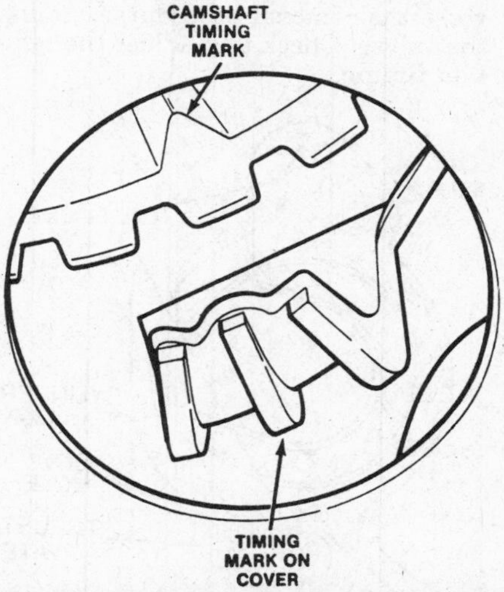


**Correct timing mark alignment as viewed through the access hole**

**CAUTION**

***Never turn the crankshaft of any of the overhead cam engines in the opposite direction of normal rotation. Backward rotation of the crankshaft may cause the timing belt to slip and alter the timing.***

1. Set the engine at TDC as described above for checking valve timing. The crankshaft and camshaft timing marks should align with their respective pointers and the distributor rotor should point to the No. 1 plug tower.
2. Loosen the adjustment bolts on the alternator and accessories and remove the drive belts. To provide clearance for removing the camshaft belt, remove the fan and shroud assembly.
3. Remove the water pump pulley attaching bolts and the pulley from the water pump shaft. Remove the cover bolts and the timing belt outer cover.
4. Remove the crankshaft damper and pulley center bolt. Using a crankshaft damper puller tool No. T74P-6312-A or equivalent, remove the crankshaft damper from the crankshaft.
5. Loosen the belt tensioner adjustment and pivot bolts. Using the tensioner tool No. T74P-6254-A or equivalent, lever the tensioner away from the belt and retighten the adjustment bolt to hold it away.
6. Remove the camshaft drive belt.

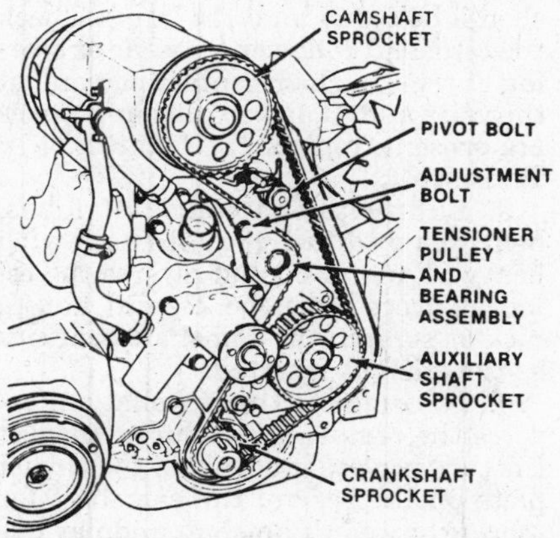


**Location of timing belt tensioner, adjustment and pivot bolts**

**To install:**

7. Install the belt over the crankshaft pulley, then, counterclockwise over the auxiliary shaft sprocket and the camshaft sprocket. Adjust the belt so it is centered on the sprockets.
8. Loosen the tensioner adjustment bolt, allowing it to spring back against the belt.
9. Rotate the crankshaft 2 complete revolutions in the normal rotation direction to remove any belt slack. Turn the crankshaft until the timing marks are aligned. If the timing has slipped, remove the belt and repeat the procedure.
10. Torque the:
    Tensioner adjustment bolt – 14–21 ft. lbs. (19–28 Nm)
    Pivot bolt – 28–40 ft. lbs. (38–54 Nm)
11. Replace the belt guide and crankshaft pulley, belt outer cover, fan and pulley, drive belts and accessories. Adjust the accessory drive belt tension. Start the engine and check the ignition timing.

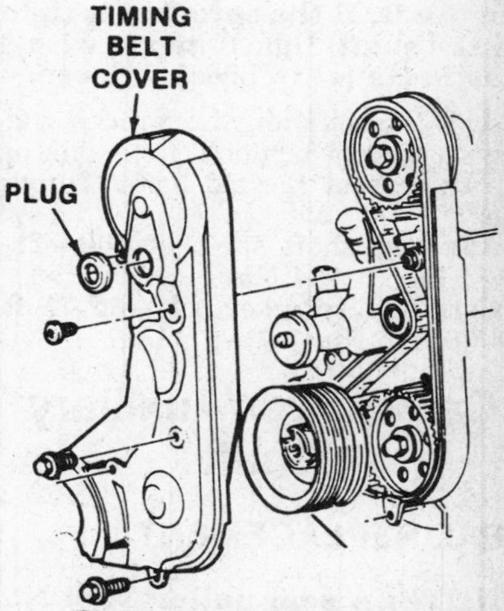


**Timing belt cover assembly**

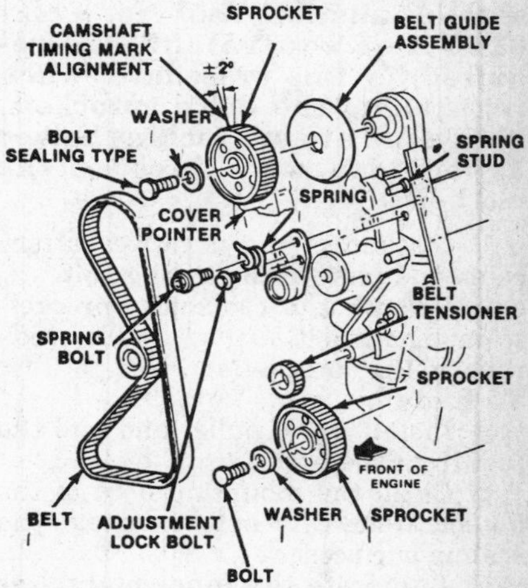


**Exploded view of timing belt and sprocket assemblies**

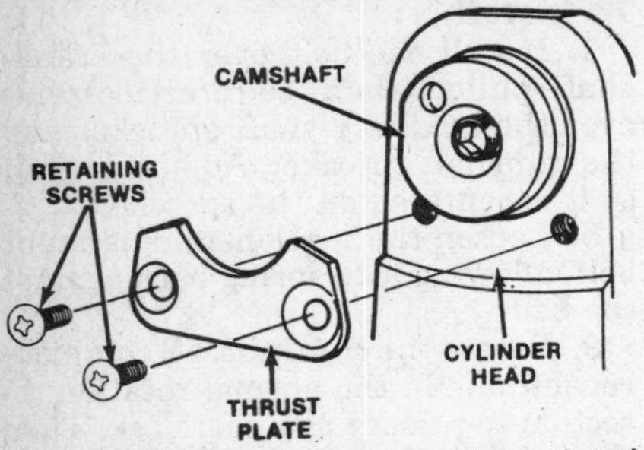

Camshaft retainer at rear of cylinder head

## Timing Belt Sprockets

### REMOVAL & INSTALLATION

#### *2.3L Engine*

1. Disconnect the negative battery cable and remove the timing belt.
2. Using a sprocket holding/removal tool No. T74P-6256-B or equivalent, secure the sprockets and remove the sprocket center bolts.

**NOTE: Do not hammer on the sprocket or use a jawed puller to remove it. If the sprocket is tight on the shaft, lightly tap it with a plastic mallet to break it loose.**

3. When installing the sprockets, always use a new bolt or Teflon® tape on the threads of the old bolts. Torque the:

Auxiliary shaft sprocket bolt – 28–40 ft. lbs. (38–54 Nm)

Camshaft sprocket bolt – 50–71 ft. lbs. (68–96 Nm)

## Cam Cover/Auxiliary Shaft

### SEAL REPLACEMENT

**NOTE: A seal puller Tool No. T74P-6700-B or equivalent, and a seal installation Tool No. T74P-6150-A or equivalent, are required for this procedure. When reinstalling the drive sprockets, always use a new attaching bolt or Teflon® tape on the threads of the old bolts.**

1. Disconnect the negative battery cable and remove the timing belt.
2. Remove the camshaft sprocket-to-camshaft bolt. Using a puller tool, remove the sprocket(s).

**To install:**

3. Install a seal puller and pull the seal from the bore.
4. Clean the mounting bore of the oil seal, take care not to damage the sealing surfaces.
5. Lubricate the inner and outer surfaces of the seal. Install the seal using the appropriate installation tool.
6. Reinstall the drive sprocket(s) and timing belt. Start the engine and check it's operation.

## Camshaft

### REMOVAL & INSTALLATION

#### *2.3L Engine*

1. Disconnect the negative battery cable. Drain the cooling system.
2. Remove the camshaft drive belt, and the rocker arm (valve) cover (see various procedure sections).
3. Remove the fan and shroud assembly (if not previously removed). Remove the upper and lower radiator hoses. If equipped with an automatic transmission, disconnect and plug the transmission fluid cooler lines.
4. Raise and support the front of the vehicle.
5. If clearance is a problem when removing the camshaft from the cylinder head, remove the front motor mount upper center nut. Position a piece of wood on a floor jack and raise the engine slowly as high as it will go. Place a piece of wood between the engine and mount brackets to support the engine in the raised position.
6. Lower the vehicle.
7. Remove the camshaft followers by compressing the valve springs and sliding them out from under the camshaft. Keep the followers in order so they may be installed in their original locations. Remove the camshaft sprocket and oil seal. Remove the camshaft retainer from the rear of the camshaft.
8. Slide the camshaft through the head supports carefully. Support the camshaft or bearing and lobe damage can occur. Inspect the camshaft for wear or damage and check the lobes and journals with a micrometer. All of the camshaft bearing journals are the same size. The allowable out-of-round limit on any journal is 0.0005 in. (0.0127mm) and the total runout should be 0.005 in. (0.127mm). Check the camshaft follower for wear or scoring at the camshaft contact pad and at the valve end. If any scoring or grooves are present, replace the follower.

**To install:**

9. Lubricate the camshaft lobes, bearings and bearing journals with heavy SF motor oil and reverse the removal procedures: be careful not to nick or scratch the camshaft bearings as the shaft is inserted.
10. To complete the installation, reverse the removal procedures. Inspect the thrust plate groove and the thrust plate on the rear of the camshaft for scoring or wear. Camshaft endplay has a maximum service limit of 0.009 in. (0.229mm).

**NOTE: After any procedure requiring removal of the rocker arms, each lash adjuster must be fully collapsed after assembly and released; this must be done before the camshaft is turned.**

#### *2.9L Engine*

1. Disconnect the negative battery cable. Drain the cooling system.
2. Remove the radiator and engine oil pan.
3. Remove the front cover. Remove the timing chain and sprockets.
4. Loosen the air conditioning condenser mounting bolts. Remove the upper and lower engine insulator retaining nuts and washers.
5. Remove the grille retaining screws. Lift the grille upward to disengage the lower locating tabs and remove the grille.
6. Remove the air conditioning condenser retaining bolts and lower the condenser and electric fan assembly to the floor.
7. Remove the intake manifold, cylinder heads and valve tappets. Raise the engine enough, with a floor jack, to permit the camshaft to clear the upper edge of the front bumper. Remove the camshaft thrust plate mounting bolts and the camshaft.

**To install:**

8. Lubricate the camshaft journals and lobes with heavy SF oil. Install the camshaft carefully into the engine block.
9. Install the thrust plate, torque the mounting bolts to 13–16 ft. lbs. (17–21 Nm). Position the engine insulators and loosely install the upper washers and nuts.
10. Install the timing chain and sprockets.
11. Install the front cover, water pump etc.
12. To complete the installation, reverse the removal procedures. Adjust the valves. Check and adjust the ignition timing.

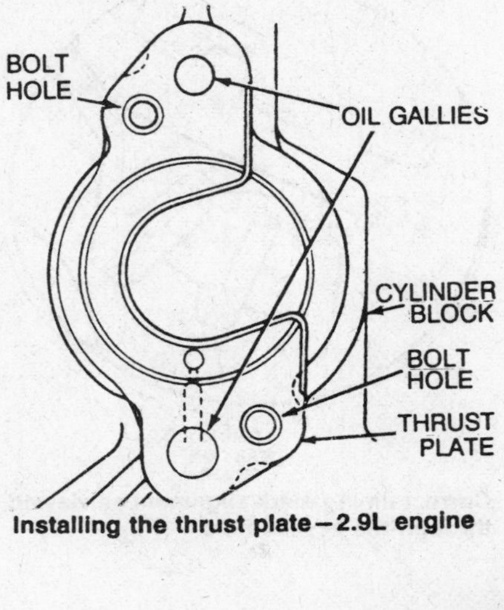

Installing the thrust plate – 2.9L engine

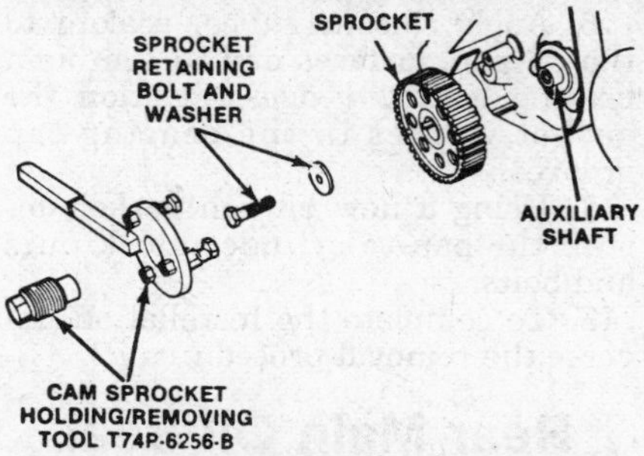

Auxiliary shaft sprocket removal showing puller/holder tool

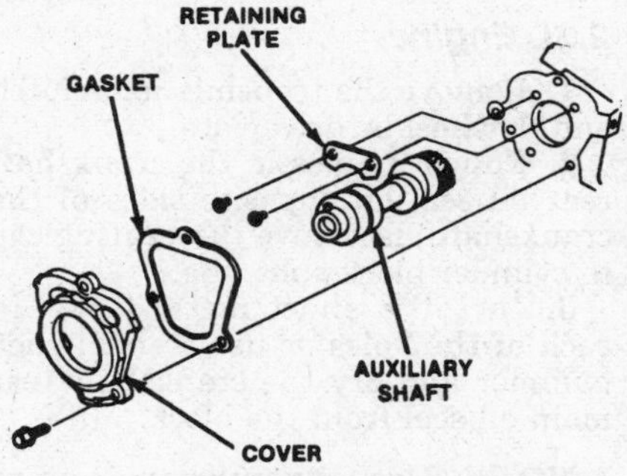

Auxiliary shaft and cover assembly

## Auxiliary Shaft

### REMOVAL & INSTALLATION

#### *2.3L Engine*

1. Remove the camshaft drive belt cover.
2. Remove the drive belt. Using a puller/holding tool, remove the auxiliary shaft sprocket.
3. Using a front cover seal remover tool No. T74P-6700-B or equivalent, remove the auxiliary shaft seal.
4. Remove the auxiliary shaft cover and thrust plate.
5. Withdraw the auxiliary shaft from the block, being careful not to damage the bearing surfaces or shaft journals during removal.

**NOTE: The distributor drive gear and the fuel pump eccentric on the auxiliary shaft must not be allowed to touch the auxiliary shaft bearings during removal and installation.**

**To install:**

6. Lubricate the shaft with heavy SF engine oil before sliding it into place.
7. Slide the auxiliary shaft into the housing and insert the thrust plate to hold the shaft.
8. Using a new gasket and auxiliary shaft cover, torque the cover bolts to 6–9 ft. lbs. (8–12 Nm).

**NOTE: Install the auxiliary shaft cover without the oil seal. Once the cover is in place, install a new oil seal using installer tool No. T74P-6150-A or equivalent. Lubricate the seal and cover seat with engine oil and make sure the seal bottoms in its bore.**

9. Align the timing marks and install the drive belt.
10. Install the drive belt cover.
11. To complete the installation, reverse the removal procedures. Start the engine and check the ignition timing.

## Pistons and Connecting Rods

**For all piston and connecting rod overhaul procedures, please refer to "Engine Rebuilding" in the Unit Repair section.**

### POSITIONING

The connecting rods should be factory marked with cylinder location numbers on the rod and bearing cap edges. If factory marks are not present, match mark both the rod and cap numerically and in sequence from the front to the back of the engine. The numbers not only tell from which cylinder the piston and rod came from but also insures that the rod caps are installed in correct matching position with the connecting rod. The piston is marked with a notch indicating front position for installation. Ring gaps should be spaced with the compression rings approximately 2 in. (50mm) apart on opposite sides of the oil ring gaps.

# ENGINE LUBRICATION

## Oil Pan

### REMOVAL & INSTALLATION

#### *2.3L Engine*

1. Disconnect the negative battery cable. Raise and safely support the vehicle.
2. Separate the oil level sensor wiring connector and remove the engine oil level dipstick.
3. Drain the crankcase. Using an engine support fixture tool, install it to take the weight off of the motor mounts.
4. Remove the right and left engine mount through bolts and/or nuts.
5. Remove the starter and the pinch bolt from the steering column-to-steering gear coupling.
6. Raise the engine as high as it will go with the support fixture. Be careful if using a shop crane not to raise the engine too high.
7. Remove the steering gear-to-crossmember bolts.
8. Disengage the steering gear from the steering column and pull forward,

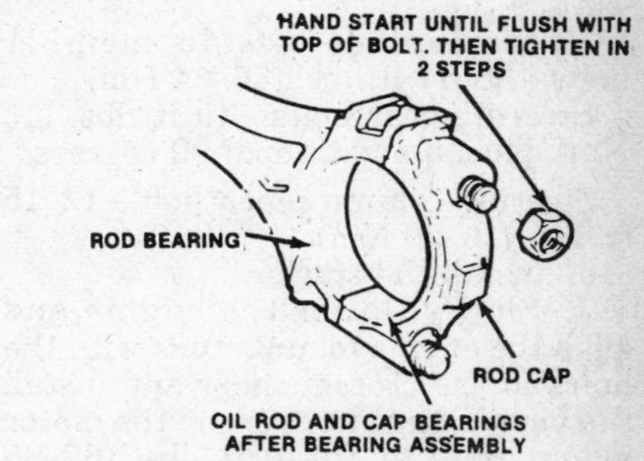


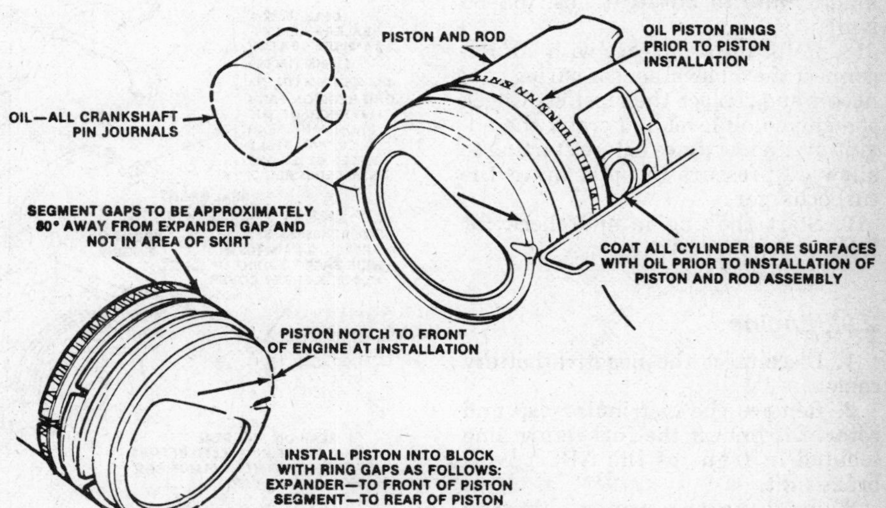

View of the piston and connecting rod positioning

away from the crossmember. Exercise caution to prevent stretching or bending the power steering gear hoses and lines.

9. Position a transmission jack under the crossmember and remove the crossmember-to-side rail bolts.

10. Carefully lower the transmission jack and crossmember.

11. Remove the oil pan bolts and lower the pan. Remove the pan, turn the engine in normal direction of rotation if the pan hangs up on the crankshaft throws.

**To install:**

12. Clean the gasket mounting surfaces. Inspect the for cracks and damage.

13. Using new oil pan gasket and seals, apply a ¼ in. bead of sealant along the cylinder block and the front cover. Apply another ¼ in. bead of sealer along the cylinder block and the rear main bearing cap.

14. Position the oil pan on the cylinder block and install the retaining bolts. Torque the:

Oil pan-to-front cover bolts—8–10 ft. lbs. (11–13 Nm)

Oil pan-to-cylinder block bolts—6–8 ft. lbs. (8–11 Nm)

Oil pan plug—15–25 ft. lbs. (20–34 Nm)

15. Raise the crossmember back into position and install the crossmember-to-side member mounting bolts. Torque the:

Crossmember-to-side member bolts—38–47 ft. lbs. (56–64 Nm)

Steering gear bolts—10 ft. lbs. (15 Nm), plus, an additional 90 degrees

Steering column pinch bolt—12–15 ft. lbs. (16–20 Nm)

16. Install the starter.

17. Slowly, lower the engine and align the engine mount studs with the holes in the crossmember and install the mounting bolts. Torque the motor mount nuts to 50–70 ft. lbs. (68–95 Nm).

18. Refill the crankcase with oil. Reconnect the oil level sensor wiring connector and replace the dipstick. Check the engine oil level and crank the engine over a few times before starting to allow oil pressure to build up in the turbocharger.

19. Start the engine and check for leaks.

### *2.9L Engine*

1. Disconnect the negative battery cable.

2. Remove the distributor cap and rotor. Disconnect the fuel return line located in front of the ABS power brake unit.

3. Remove the upper radiator shroud.

4. Raise and safely support the vehicle.

5. Remove the both lower engine insulator-to-crossmember nuts and washers.

6. Remove the starter motor and the exhaust crossover pipe. Lower the vehicle.

7. Connect a engine cross support bar and raise the engine until the bell housing touches the firewall.

8. Raise and safely support the vehicle.

9. Remove the lower heater hose bolts. Drain the engine oil. Remove the lower transmission bolts.

10. Remove the lower steering shaft flange coupler retaining nuts and bolts.

11. Place a floor jack under the No. 1 crossmember. Remove the front flexible brake line attaching clips.

12. Remove the crossmember bolts and lower the crossmember 2 inches.

13. Remove the oil pan attaching nuts/bolts and the oil pan.

**To install:**

14. Clean the gasket mounting surfaces.

15. Apply sealant to the cylinder block. Install the bearing cap; be sure the bearing cap is installed flush with the cylinder block rear face.

16. Apply silicone rubber sealant to the oil pan surfaces and to the main bearing gasket wedges. Position the gasket wedges in the bearing cap grooves.

17. Using a new oil pan gasket, install the pan-to-cylinder block nuts and bolts.

18. To complete the installation, reverse the removal procedures.

# Rear Main Oil Seal

## REMOVAL & INSTALLATION

### *2.3L Engine*

1. Remove the transmission, clutch and flywheel or driveplate.

2. Punch 2 holes in the crankshaft rear oil seal on opposite sides of the crankshaft just above the bearing cap to cylinder block split line.

3. Install a sheet metal screw in each of the holes or use a small slide hammer and pry the crankshaft rear main oil seal from the block.

**NOTE: Use extreme caution not to scratch the crankshaft oil seal surface. Clean the oil seal recess in the cylinder block and main bearing cap.**

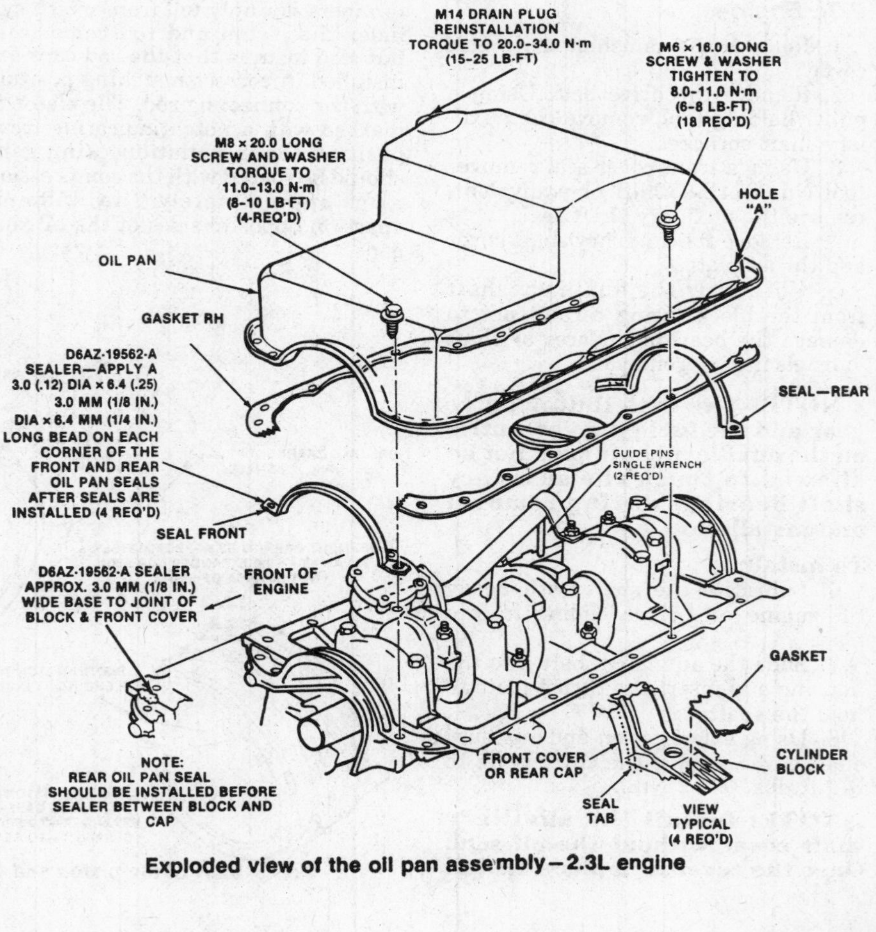


Exploded view of the oil pan assembly—2.3L engine

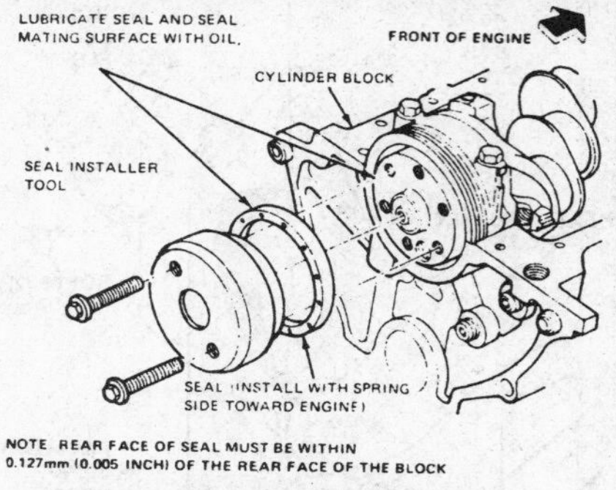


**Rear main oil seal installation**

**To install:**

4. Lubricate the seal and the seal mounting surfaces with oil.
5. Install the seal in the recess, driving it in place with an oil seal installation tool or a large socket.
6. To complete the installation, reverse the removal procedures.

### *2.9L Engine*

1. Remove the transmission and clutch assembly (if equipped with a manual transmission).
2. Remove the flywheel, the flywheel housing and the rear plate.
3. Use an awl or icepick, punch 2 holes in the rear main seal; punch the holes on opposite sides of the seal, just above the bearing cap split line.
4. Install a sheet metal screw into each of the holes.
5. Using 2 small prybars, pry outward on the screws, at the same time to remove the seal; be careful not to scratch the crankshaft seal surface.

**To install:**

6. Clean the oil seal recess an the block and bearing cap. Carefully clean the crankshaft seal surface.
7. Lubricate the oil seal block surface with SF motor oil.
8. Start the seal into the mounting recess and carefully tap the seal into position.
9. To complete the installation, reverse the removal procedures.

# Oil Pump

## REMOVAL & INSTALLATION

### *2.3L Engine*

1. Remove the oil pan.
2. Remove the oil pump inlet tube and screen support bracket nut from the No. 4 main bearing cap.
3. Remove the oil pump bolts, the gasket, the intermediate shaft and the oil pump.

**To install:**

4. Prime oil pump by filling inlet and outlet port with engine oil and rotating shaft of pump to distribute it.
5. Position intermediate driveshaft and retaining clip into the cylinder block guide hole or into the oil pump.
6. Position new gasket on pump body and insert intermediate driveshaft into pump body.
7. Install pump and intermediate shaft as an assembly.

**NOTE: Do not force pump if it does not seat readily. The driveshaft may be misaligned with the distributor shaft. To align, rotate the intermediate driveshaft into a new position.**

8. Install and torque the:
Oil pump bolts—14–21 ft. lbs. (19–28 Nm)
Strap nut—28–40 ft. lbs. (38–54 Nm)
9. To complete the installation, reverse the removal procedures.

### *2.9L Engine*

1. Remove the engine oil pan.
2. Remove the oil pump-to-engine bolt, the oil pump and pump driveshaft.

**To install:**

3. Prime the oil pump by filling it with oil while turning the pump shaft to distribute the oil inside the pump.
4. Install the pump driveshaft into the engine block; make sure the pointed end of the shaft is facing inward.
5. Using a new gasket, position the oil pump and install the mounting bolts.

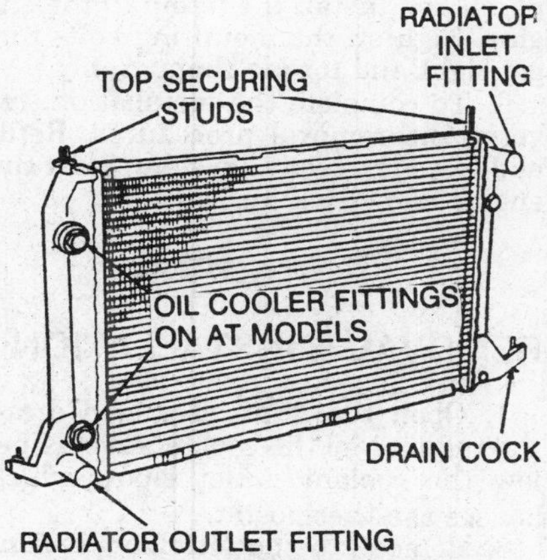


**Crossflow radiator components**

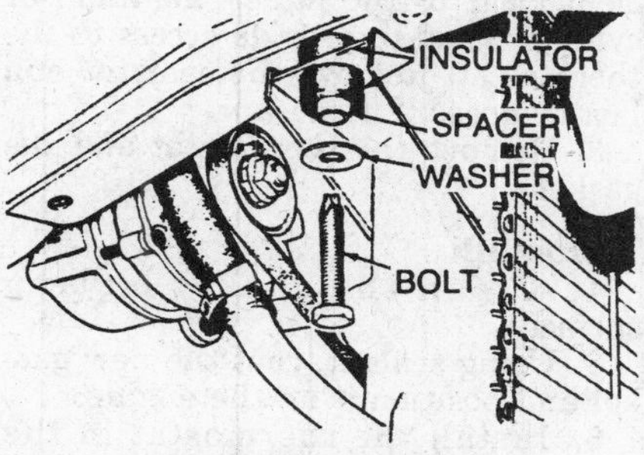


**Lower radiator mounting**

6. To complete the installation, reverse the removal procedures. Refill the crankcase.

# ENGINE COOLING

# Radiator

## REMOVAL & INSTALLATION

### *XR4Ti*

1. Drain the cooling system.
2. Disconnect the upper, lower and overflow hoses at the radiator and overflow reservoir.
3. If equipped with an automatic transmission, disconnect and plug the fluid cooler lines at the radiator.
4. Remove the fan and shroud assembly. If the air conditioner condenser is attached to the radiator, remove the retaining bolts and position the condenser aside. DO NOT disconnect the refrigerant lines.
5. Remove the radiator attaching bolts or top brackets and lift out the radiator.

**To install:**

6. If a new radiator is to be installed, transfer the petcock from the old radiator to the new one. If equipped with an automatic transmission, transfer the fluid cooler line fittings from the old radiator.
7. Position the radiator and install, but do not torque, the radiator support bolts. If equipped with an automatic transmission, connect the fluid cooler lines. Then, torque the radiator support bolts and install the fan and shroud assembly.
8. To complete the installation, reverse the removal procedures. Refill and bleed the cooling system.
9. Start the engine, allow it to reach normal operating temperatures and check for leaks.
10. If equipped with automatic transmission, check the cooler lines for leaks and interference. Check transmission fluid level.

### *Scorpio*

1. Disconnect the negative battery cable. Drain the cooling system.
2. Disconnect the upper and lower radiator hoses from the radiator.
3. If equipped with an automatic transmission, disconnect and plug the transmission oil cooler lines.
4. Disconnect the air conditioning cooling fan switch connector. Remove the upper fan shroud bolts and rivets.

Drive out the center pin from the plastic shroud attaching rivets and remove the rivets. Remove the upper shroud.

5. Raise and safely support the vehicle.

6. Remove both bolts and washers from the lower radiator mounts. Disengage the upper securing studs by depressing the tabs. Remove the radiator from underneath the vehicle.

**To install:**

7. Make sure the mounting insulators are in position on the radiator studs. Position the radiator from below and install the upper mounting studs.

8. Install the mounting bolts from below. Position the insulating bushings, spacer and washers both above and below the brackets as the bolts are installed. Torque the bolts to 6–8 ft. lbs. (8–12 Nm).

9. To complete the installation, reverse the removal procedures. Refill and bleed the cooling system, run the engine and check for leaks.

## Water Pump

### REMOVAL & INSTALLATION

#### *2.3L Engine*

1. Drain the cooling system.
2. Disconnect the negative battery cable.
3. Remove all drive belts and the outer timing belt cover.
4. Disconnect the lower radiator hose and heater hose from the water pump.
5. Remove the electric fan and shroud assembly if necessary for clearance.
6. Remove the water pump retaining bolts and the water pump.

**To install:**

7. Clean the gasket mounting surfaces.

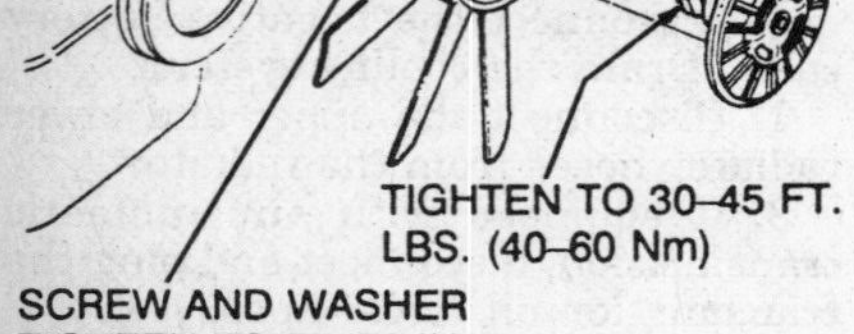


**Scorpio cooling fan and clutch assembly**

8. Using water resistant sealant, coat both sides of the new gasket.
9. To complete the installation, reverse the removal procedures. Torque the water pump mounting bolts to 14–21 ft. lbs. (19–29 Nm).

#### *2.9L Engine*

1. Disconnect the negative battery cable. Drain the cooling system.
2. Disconnect the radiator and heater hose from the water pump.
3. Remove the fan and clutch assembly. Special tool No. T88M-6312B fan hub wrench and T88M-6312A fan clutch wrench or equivalents are required.

**NOTE The fan clutch attaching nut is equipped with left hand threads; turn the nut clockwise to remove.**

4. Loosen the alternator mounting bolts. Remove the drive belt and the alternator.
5. Remove the water pump drive pulley. Remove the water pump-to-engine bolts and the water pump.

**NOTE: Two different length bolts are used, note their locations.**

**To install:**

6. Clean all gasket mounting surfaces.
7. Using sealant, apply it to both sides of the new mounting gasket.
8. Position the gasket on the water pump and install the pump to the engine. Tighten the mounting bolts finger tight and torque them evenly.
9. To complete the installation, reverse the removal procedures. Refill and bleed the cooling system. Start the engine and check for leaks.

## Thermostat

### REMOVAL & INSTALLATION

1. Open the drain cock and drain the radiator so the coolant level is below the coolant outlet elbow which houses the thermostat.
2. Remove the outlet elbow retaining bolts and position the elbow sufficient clear of the intake manifold or cylinder head to provide access to the thermostat. Remove the radiator and heater hoses if necessary.
3. Remove the thermostat and the gasket.

**To install:**

4. Clean the gasket mating surfaces.
5. Using sealant, coat the new gasket and position it on the engine.
6. Install the thermostat in the coolant elbow; be sure the full width of

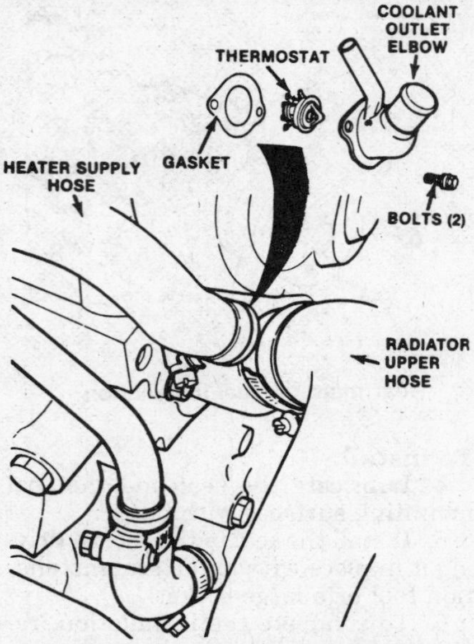


**Thermostat and housing assembly**

the heater outlet tube is visible within the thermostat port.

7. Install the outlet elbow and torque the bolts to 14–21 ft. lbs. (19–28 Nm).
8. Refill the radiator. Operate the engine, until normal operating temperatures are reached and check for leaks. Recheck the coolant level.

### COOLING SYSTEM BLEEDING

1. Check all hose clamps for proper tightness.
2. Make sure the radiator draincock is closed. Place the heater control temperature selector in the **MAX HEAT** position.
3. Remove the pressure cap and refill the expansion tank to the **MAX** mark on the reservoir.
4. Leave the pressure cap off. Start and run the engine until normal operating temperatures are reached.
5. Stop the engine and add coolant to the expansion tank as necessary. Install the pressure cap.

# EMISSION CONTROLS

**Please refer to "Emission Control" in the Unit Repair section for system maintenance prodedures. Due to the complex nature of modern electronic engine control systems, comprehensive diagnosis and testing procedures fall outside the confines of**

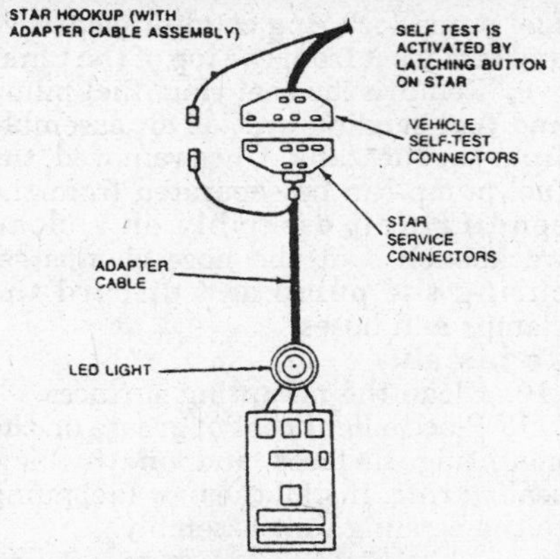


**View of the STAR tester and the voltmeter connections for the electronic quick test**

**this repair manual. For complete information on diagnosis, testing and repair procedures concerning all modern engine and emission control systems, please refer to "Chilton's Guide To Electronic Engine Controls".**

## Emission Warning Lamps

### RESETTING

1. Firmly apply the parking brake. Place the transmission into **P** (automatic) or **N** (manual).
2. Turn **OFF** all electrical loads.
3. Make sure the ignition switch is turned **OFF**.
4. Using a STAR tester, connect the color coded adapter leads to the tester. Connect the adapter leads to the 2 service connectors to the vehicle self-test connectors.
5. Place the ignition switch in the **RUN** position, to activate the self-test; do not depress the throttle during the test.

**NOTE: The memory will activate the service code lists.**

6. When the service codes begin, disconnect the STAR tester; this will the clear the memory of all codes.

# FUEL SYSTEM

## Fuel System Service Precaution

### RELIEVING FUEL SYSTEM PRESSURE

Depressurize the fuel system before

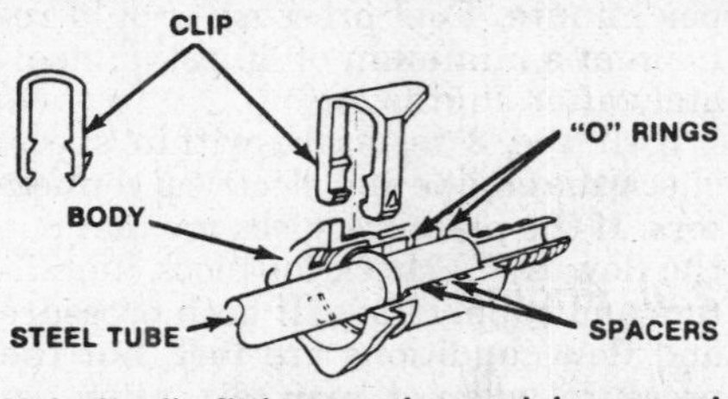


**Hairpin clip fitting used on quick connect fuel lines**

disconnecting any fuel system lines or components or attempting any service procedures.

1. Connect a hand vacuum pump to the fuel pressure regulator vacuum connection.
2. Apply 25 in. Hg. for at least 3 minutes to allow the fuel system to depressurize.
3. Never replace high pressure fuel line with ordinary fuel hose and replace all clamps.

### *Quick Connect Fittings*

"Quick Connect" (push) type fuel fittings are used on all models equipped with a pressurized fuel system. The fittings must be disconnected using proper procedures or the fitting may be damaged. Two types of retainers are used on the push connect fittings. Line sizes of 3/8 in. and 5/16 in. use a "hairpin" clip retainer. 1/4 in. line connectors use a "duck bill" clip retainer. In either case, a special connector tool must be used to separate the quick connect fittings or they may be damaged.

### REMOVAL & INSTALLATION

#### *Hairpin Clip*

1. Clean all dirt and/or grease from the fitting. Spread the 2 clip legs about an 1/8 in. each to disengage from the fitting and pull the clip outward from the fitting. Use finger pressure only, do not use any tools.
2. Grease the fitting and hose assembly and pull away from the steel line. Twist the fitting and hose assembly slightly while pulling, if necessary, when a sticking condition exists.

**To install:**

3. Inspect the hairpin clip for damage; replace the clip, if necessary. Reinstall the clip in position on the fitting.
4. Inspect the fitting and inside of the connector to insure freedom of dirt or obstruction. Install fitting in to the connector and push together. A click will be heard when the hairpin snaps into proper connection. Pull on the line to insure full engagement.

#### *Duck Bill Clip*

1. A special tool is available for removing the retaining clips (Ford Tool No. T82L-9500-AH). If the tool is not available, see the next step. Align the slot on the push connector disconnect tool with either tab on the retaining clip. Pull the line from the connector.
2. If the special clip tool is not available, use a pair of narrow 6 in. channel lock pliers with a jaw width of 0.2 in. or less. Align the jaws of the pliers with the openings of the fitting case and compress the part of the retaining clip that engages the case. Compressing the retaining clip will release the fitting which may be pulled form the connector. Both sides of the clip must be compressed at the same time to disengage.

**To install:**

3. Inspect the retaining clip, fitting end and connector; replace the clip, if necessary.
4. Push the line into the steel connector until a click is heard, indicating clip is in place. Pull on line to check engagement.

## Fuel Filter

### REMOVAL & INSTALLATION

Models equipped with EFI have 4 fuel filters: a nylon mesh "sock" at the fuel pump inlet in the fuel tank, a large paper element filter mounted in the fuel line under the vehicle, a small canister filter mounted in the engine compartment and an individual mesh filters at each injector fuel inlet. Of these, only the undercar paper element filter is scheduled for regular replacement.

1. Filter replacement requires discharging of the fuel injection system pressure prior to filter change.
2. Discharge pressure, disconnect the fuel lines and remove the fuel filter retainer from it's mounting bracket beneath the fuel pump. Note the direction of the fuel flow arrow on filter.
3. To install the new filter, reverse the removal procedures; make sure the arrow points in the direction of fuel flow (toward the engine).
4. Start the engine and check for leaks.

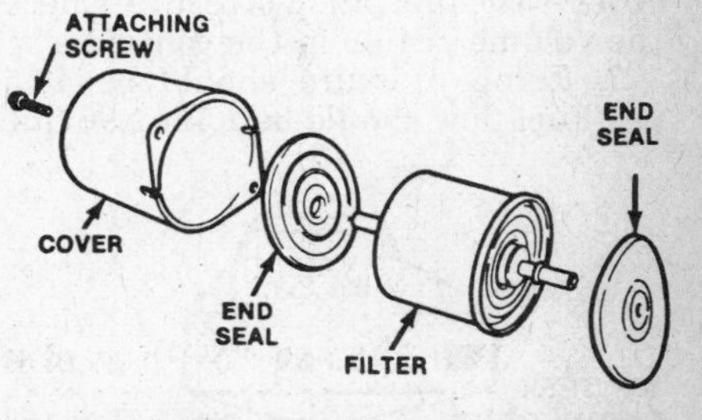


**Exploded view of fuel filter showing location on fuel pump bracket**

## Electric Fuel Pump

### TESTING

#### 2.3L Engine

1. Connect a compatible fuel pressure gauge to the Schrader valve on the fuel supply manifold. An adapter may be required to tap into the valve.
2. Start the engine. If the engine will not start, remove the fuel pump relay from the circuit protection panel.

**NOTE: If equipped with a 2.3L engine, connect a jumper wire from relay panel terminal 87 to the alternator output terminal.**

3. With the pump running, check the pressure reading on the gauge. Normal fuel pressure is 35–45 psi at idle.
4. Insert the test volume hose in a graduated container and open the flow control valve for 10 seconds; if the pump delivers 7.5 oz. in 10 seconds, the fuel volume is correct.
5. Disconnect the jumper wire to stop the pumps and observe the pressure gauge. If the pressure holds at a minimum of 30 psi, the system is holding pressure. Install the fuel pump relay and disconnect the pressure gauge.

#### 2.9L Engine

1. Disconnect the electrical connector at the inertia switch (located at the rear center of the luggage compartment near the tailgate striker).
2. Crank the engine for at least 15 seconds to reduce the fuel pressure in the fuel lines.
3. Disconnect the fuel return line at the pressure regulator. Avoid fuel spillage.
4. Connect a hose from the fuel return fitting to a calibrated 2 quart container. Attach a fuel pressure gauge to the Schrader valve fitting on the fuel rail.
5. Connect a jumper wire to circuit 9-25 at the VIP test connector which is located on the **BLUE/red** wire near the ECA module.
6. Turn the ignition switch to the **RUN** position; do not start the engine. Touch the jumper wire to ground and observe the fuel pump pressure. Check the volume of fuel in the container.
7. Pump pressure should be 43.5 psi. Fuel flow should be 1.18–1.96 qts. per minute. Fuel pressure should remain at a minimum of 30 psi immediately after shutdown.
8. If the 3 tests are within specs, check the engine and electrical connectors. If the pressure specs are met but the flow is off; check for block fuel filters and supply lines. If both pressure and flow conditions are met, but the pressure will not maintain after de-energization, check for leaking injectors or pressure regulator. If both are all right, replace the fuel pump.

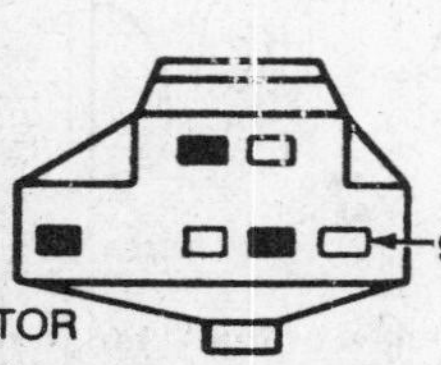

Scorpio VIP test connector identification

### REMOVAL & INSTALLATION

#### XR4Ti

##### LOW PRESSURE TANK PUMP

1. Run the vehicle until the fuel tank is about ¼ full. Disconnect the negative battery cable.
2. Depressurize the fuel system and drain as much gas from the tank by pumping it out through the filler neck into an approved safety container, then seal the can(s) tightly for temporary storage during service procedures. Place the gasoline away from the work area and take precautions to avoid the risk of fire.
3. Chock the front wheels. Raise and safely support the rear of the vehicle. Rock the vehicle a bit to make sure the vehicle is firmly supported before working underneath it.
4. Working under the vehicle at the rear frame rails near the fuel tank, disconnect the fuel supply, return and vent lines at the right and left side of the frame.
5. Disconnect the wiring to the fuel pump.
6. Support the fuel tank, loosen and remove the mounting straps, then lower the tank carefully.
7. Disconnect the fuel and vapor lines and wire harness connectors at the pump flange.
8. Clean the outside of the mounting flange and retaining ring. Turn the fuel pump lock ring counter-clockwise and remove it from the top of the tank.
9. Remove the seal ring, fuel pump and fuel sending unit as an assembly from the fuel tank. Once removed, the fuel pump can be separated from the sending unit assembly on a clean workbench. Cut the hose clamps securing the pump and discard the clamps and hoses.

**To install:**

10. Clean the mounting surfaces.
11. Place a light coat of grease on the mounting surfaces and on the new sealing ring. Install the new fuel pump to the sending unit assembly.

**NOTE: If the low pressure fuel pump is removed from the sending unit assembly for any reason, the rubber hoses and clamps must be replaced along with any gaskets.**

12. To install, reverse the removal procedures. Coat the seal ring with heavy duty grease before installing the pump and sending unit and make sure the lock ring lugs are engaged properly.
13. After the tank is secured and all connections are complete, refill the tank with at least 10 gals. of fuel. Turn the ignition key **ON** for 3 seconds. Repeat 6–7 times until the fuel system is pressurized. Check for any fitting leaks.
14. Start the engine and check for leaks.

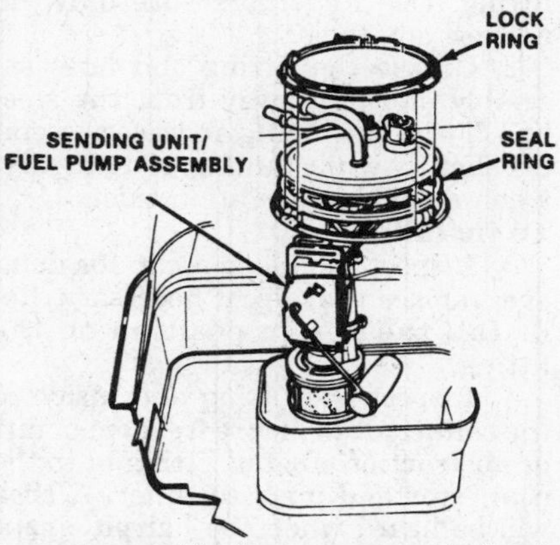

Low pressure fuel pump assembly located in the fuel tank

#### XR4Ti

##### HIGH PRESSURE CHASSIS PUMP

1. Disconnect the negative battery cable.
2. Depressurize the fuel system by attaching a hand vacuum pump to the fuel pressure regulator and applying 25 in. Hg. of vacuum for 3 minutes.
3. Chock the front wheels, raise and safely support the vehicle. Rock the vehicle a bit to make sure the vehicle is firmly supported before working underneath it.
4. Working under the vehicle at the rear frame rail just ahead of the fuel

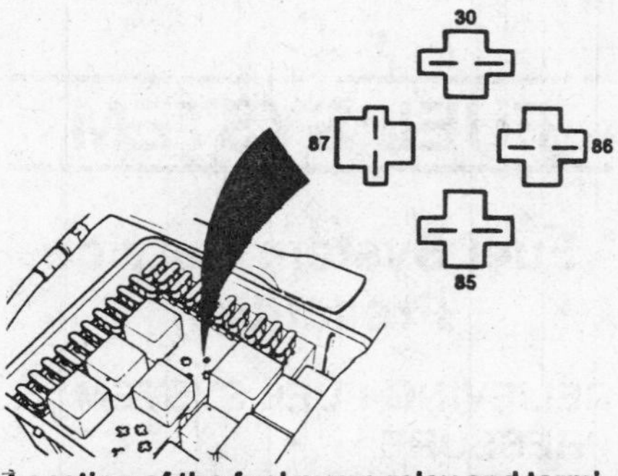

Location of the fuel pump relay and terminal identification for testing – XR4Ti

tank, locate the external fuel pump and filter bracket and disconnect the inlet and outlet fuel lines. Separate the fuel pump electrical connector.

5. Remove the fuel pump bracket attaching screws and lower the fuel pump and bracket as an assembly. Working on a clean workbench, remove the pump and foam insulator from the mounting bracket. Disconnect the wiring harness from the pump.

**To install:**

6. To install, reverse the removal procedures; make sure the pump is indexed correctly in the mounting bracket insulator.

7. Position the insulator ends in the opening at the base of the mounting bracket. Route the wire harness between the insulator ends, then position the pump on the body mounting bracket and install the attaching bolts.

8. Reconnect the fuel lines and harness connectors. Refill the tank with at least 10 gals. of fuel. Turn the ignition key **ON** for 3 seconds.

9. Repeat 6–7 times until the fuel system is pressurized. Check for any fitting leaks. Start the engine and check for leaks.

### *Scorpio*

#### FUEL TANK PUMP

1. Relieve the fuel system pressure. Disconnect the negative battery cable.

2. From in the luggage compartment, disconnect the fuel pump electrical connector (located near the right rear lamp assembly). Push the grommet and wiring harness from the luggage compartment.

3. Remove the fuel tank.

4. Clean any dirt that has built up from the fuel pump mounting flange. Remove the mounting clamp. Unscrew the fuel pump locking ring and remove.

5. Remove the fuel pump and sender assembly. Remove the sealing ring.

**To install:**

6. Clean the fuel tank pump mounting surface.

7. Install a new seal onto the fuel pump flange by assembling the seal around the fuel pump locking ring threads.

8. Lower the pump carefully into the tank; make sure the location arrows on the pump and tank are aligned.

9. Push the pump downward against the loading spring; visually make sure the sealing ring edges can be seen all around the flange.

10. Turn the locking ring clockwise while holding the pump in position.

11. Tighten the locking ring and install the lock ring. Install the fuel tank.

# FUEL INJECTION

**Due to the complex nature of modern fuel injection systems, comprehensive diagnoses and testing procedures fall outside the confines of this repair manual. For complete information on fuel injection diagnoses, testing and repair procedures please refer to "Chilton's Guide to Fuel Injection and Feedback Carburetors".**

# MANUAL TRANSMISSION

## REMOVAL & INSTALLATION

### *2.3L Engine*

1. Wedge a block of wood approximately 7 in. long under the clutch pedal. Holding the pedal above its normal position will disengage the clutch cable self adjuster. Disconnect the negative battery cable, then raise and safely support the vehicle. Allow enough working clearance to remove the transmission from below the vehicle.

2. Drain the transmission fluid. Matchmark the driveshaft and rear companion flange so the driveshaft may be installed in the same position for proper balance.

3. Disconnect and remove the driveshaft. Install a suitable plug in the extension housing seal to prevent fluid leakage during service.

4. Remove the nuts attaching the catalytic converter inlet pipe to the turbocharger. Remove the catalytic converter outlet-to-muffler inlet flange nuts and the catalytic converter support bracket. Remove the catalytic converter and inlet pipe as an assembly.

**NOTE: If the engine is started for any reason just prior to transmission removal, allow sufficient time for the catalytic converter to cool before attempting removal procedures. The normal converter operating temperature can cause severe burns.**

5. Remove the starter.

6. Remove the front stabilizer bar to body U-brackets and the body stiffener rod.

7. Remove the transmission air baffle, if equipped. Position a block of wood between the stabilizer bar and the body side rail.

8. Support the transmission with a floor jack. Remove the rear transmission mount to transmission mounting bolts. Remove the transmission support member.

9. Loosen the engine mount attaching nuts until only 2–3 threads are visible on the end of the stud. Position a block of wood against the engine oil pan and raise the front of the engine. Raise the engine until the stud nuts on the engine mounts contact the crossmember.

10. As the engine tilts downward, lower the transmission jack slightly and remove the Torx® bolts that mount the shift lever. Remove the shift lever from the extension housing.

11. Disconnect the back-up light and neutral safety switch wiring harness connectors. Remove the snapring and pull the speedometer cable out of the extension housing.

12. Remove the clutch release lever cover and pull rearward on the clutch release cable to disengage it from the release lever.

13. Remove the speedometer cable routing clip screws (2 places) and move the cable aside on the left side of the vehicle. Remove the transmission-to-flywheel housing bolts.

14. Slide the transmission rearward until the flywheel housing contacts the body. Raise the rear of the transmission and pull it rearward to clear the body, then, back and away from the engine and lower to the ground. Lower the engine slightly, if necessary for clearance.

**To install:**

15. Align the transmission input shaft with the clutch pressure plate and push the transmission forward until the flywheel housing contacts the body. Raise the rear of the transmission as necessary to clear the body, lower it and push it into position. Rock the transmission slightly to align the input shaft and clutch disc splines.

**NOTE: Exercise caution to prevent damage to the transmission pilot bearing in the end of the crankshaft.**

16. Install the shifter into the extension housing and torque the mounting bolts to 16–19 ft. lbs. (21–26 Nm).

17. Continue installation and make sure the mounting surface of the transmission and flywheel housing are free of dirt and burrs.

18. Install 2 guide pins in the lower flywheel housing bolt holes (bolts with the heads cut off). Raise the transmission and move it forward on the guide pins until the input shaft splines enter the clutch hub splines and the case is

against the flywheel housing. Torque the:

Flywheel housing-to-engine bolts—28–38 ft. lbs. (38–51 Nm)

Engine mount stud nuts—50–70 ft. lbs. (68–95 Nm)

Rear transmission mount—25–35 ft. lbs. (34–48 Nm)

### 2.9L Engine

1. Disconnect the negative battery cable. Wedge a wood block approximately 7 inches long under the clutch pedal. Holding it the above its normal position will disengage the clutch cable self adjuster.
2. Disconnect the negative battery cable. Remove the distributor cap and rotor.
3. Unscrew and remove the gear shift lever knob. Remove the center console screws and the console. Remove the shift lever boot, the center console bracket, frame and noise dampening pad.
4. Remove the gear lever-to-extension housing screws and the gear shift lever assembly.
5. Disconnect the oxygen sensor wiring connector located in the engine compartment. Remove the wiring from the retaining clip.
6. Raise and safely support the vehicle. Drain the transmission fluid. Remove the stabilizer bar-to-side members bolts.
7. Remove the ground strap from the exhaust pipe. Remove the exhaust system from the exhaust manifolds to the front muffler. Remove the converter heat shield.
8. Scribe a mark on the rear driveshaft and differential yokes for installation reference. Remove the rear shaft mounting bolts. Remove the driveshaft center support bolts and slide the driveshaft from the back of the transmission.
9. Support the engine by placing a block of wood between the oil pan and floor jack. Remove the radio ground strap, the transmission rear mount nuts and the mount.
10. Disconnect the speedometer sensor, speedometer sensor ground strap, neutral gear start switch and the back-up lamp switch.
11. Disconnect the electrical connectors from the starter and remove the starter.
12. Pull the clutch lever dust boot aside and disconnect the clutch cable from the release lever. Remove the clutch cable and dust boot from the housing.
13. Remove the rear engine cover plate from the bell housing. Support the transmission with a jack. Remove the engine-to-bell housing bolts and the starter heat shield.
14. Lower the engine and transmission jacks slightly. Pull the transmission rearward. Adjust the jacks and pull the transmission until it separates from the engine. Lower the transmission and remove it from the vehicle.

**To install:**

15. Position the transmission and start the mainshaft into the clutch disc; adjust the supporting jacks, as necessary. Turn the engine slightly, if necessary, to engage the mainshaft with the clutch disc splines. Torque the:

Transmission-to-engine bolts—28–38 ft. lbs. (38–51 Nm)

Transmission mount—25–35 ft. lbs. (34–48 Nm)

Center driveshaft mount bolts—13–17 ft. lbs. (18–23 Nm)

Rear driveshaft mounting bolts—42–55 ft. lbs. (57–75 Nm)

# CLUTCH

## REMOVAL & INSTALLATION

1. Lift the clutch pedal to it's uppermost position to disengage the pawl and quadrant. Push the quadrant forward, unhook the clutch cable and allow the quadrant to slowly swing rearward.
2. Disconnect the negative battery cable. Raise and safely support the vehicle.
3. Disconnect the cable from the clutch release lever.
4. Remove the clutch cable from the flywheel housing.
5. Disconnect the starter motor cable and remove the starter motor. Remove the lower shield from the flywheel housing.
6. Remove the transmission.
7. Remove the flywheel housing. If the pressure plate is being reused, paint or scribe alignment marks on the pressure plate and flywheel so they may be assembled in their original positions.
8. Loosen the pressure plate-to-flywheel bolts, evenly, in rotation, to release the spring pressure gradually. Remove the pressure plate and clutch disc.
9. Remove the clutch release bearing from the release lever. Inspect the lever and bearing for wear and replace as necessary.

**NOTE: The clutch release bearing is lubricated and permanently sealed during manufacture. Never wash or soak the bearing in cleaning solvent or it will ruin the bearing.**

**To install:**

10. Using an alignment tool, install and align the clutch disc and pressure plate; make sure the clutch disc is installed with the correct side facing the flywheel.

**NOTE: A new disc will be stamped flywheel to indicate the correct installation, but the disc is installed properly if the damper springs face away from the flywheel. The 3 dowel pins on the flywheel must be properly aligned with the pressure plate. Avoid touching the disc surface and start the pressure plate mounting bolts slowly and evenly to avoid distortion.**

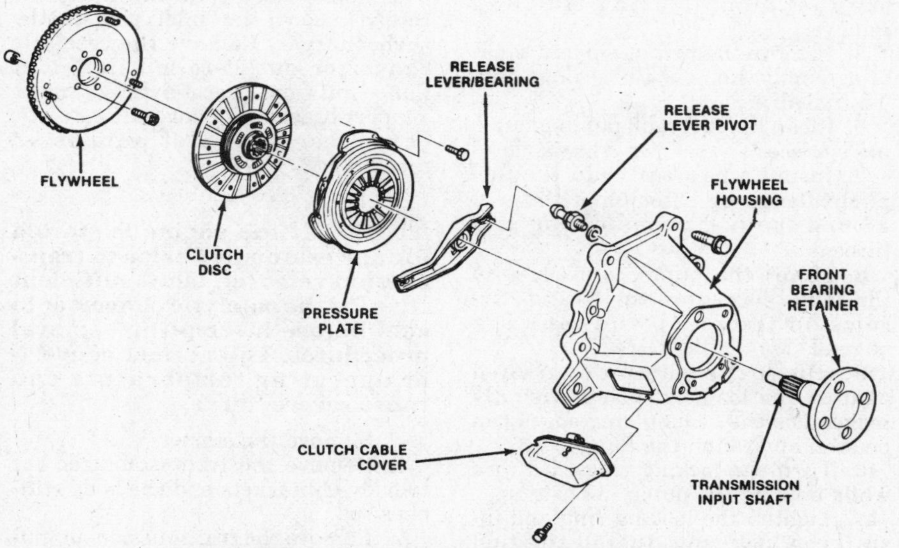


Exploded view of the clutch assembly—2.3L engine

11. Torque the pressure plate-to-flywheel bolts, evenly, in sequence, to 15–19 ft. lbs. (20–25 Nm).
12. To complete the installation, reverse the removal procedures. Check and/or adjust the clutch operation.

### ADJUSTMENTS

The clutch free play is self adjusting during normal operation. The self adjusting feature should be checked every 5000 miles. This is accomplished by insuring that the clutch pedal travels to the top of it's upward position.
1. Grasp the clutch pedal with your hand or put your foot under the pedal, then pull up on the pedal until it stops. Very little effort is required (about 10 lbs.).
2. During the application of upward pressure, a click may be heard which means an adjustment was necessary and has been accomplished.

## Clutch Cable

### REMOVAL & INSTALLATION

1. Hold the clutch pedal above it's normal position to disengage the clutch cable self adjuster.
2. Raise and safely support the vehicle. Remove the clutch release lever cover.
3. Pull rearward on the cable to disengage it from the release lever. The sound panels under the left side of the dashboard must be removed to gain access to the clutch cable routing through the body.
4. Install the replacement cable using the same routing as the old cable, unless the reason for cable replacement was binding or wear due to sharp turns in the cable.

# AUTOMATIC TRANSMISSION

### REMOVAL & INSTALLATION

1. Disconnect the negative battery cable and remove the transmission dipstick. Raise and safely support the vehicle.
2. Place a drain pan under the transmission fluid pan. Starting at the rear of the pan and working forward, loosen the bolts and allow the fluid to drain. Remove all of the oil pan bolts except 2 at the front, to allow the fluid to further drain. After all the fluid has drained, install 2 bolts on the rear side of the pan to temporarily hold it in place.
3. Disconnect the oxygen sensor harness and unclip the wires from the securing clip. Remove the starter motor. On 4 cylinder engines, remove the catalytic converter inlet pipe-to-turbocharger nuts. Remove the support bracket bolt and the catalytic converter and inlet pipe as an assembly. On V6 models remove the exhaust system from the exhaust manifolds to the front muffler. Remove the converter heat shield.
4. Remove the stabilizer bar U-brackets and the body stiffener rod, then, position a block of wood between the stabilizer bar and the body side rail.
5. Remove the torque converter drain plug access cover and adapter plate bolts from the lower end of the converter housing.
6. Remove the torque converter-to-drive plate nuts through the starter opening. Remove the converter drain plug and drain the converter. Reinstall the plug. Turn the engine in normal direction of rotation to gain access to the converter nuts and drain plug, using a wrench on the crankshaft pulley bolt.

**NOTE: If equipped with a 2.3L engine, do not turn the engine counter-clockwise; backward rotation may cause the valve timing belt to jump time.**

7. Remove the driveshaft and plug the extension housing to prevent dirt entry and fluid loss during service.
8. Using a floor jack, support the transmission and secure it with a safety chain. Remove the rear mount-to-transmission support bracket bolts. Remove the nuts attaching the rear mount to the body and remove the mount.
9. Disconnect the shift rod from the transmission lever and the downshift rod from the transmission downshift lever.
10. Disconnect the neutral start switch wires and the speedometer cable from the transmission.
11. Remove the vacuum line from the transmission vacuum modulator and the transmission filler tube.
12. Disconnect the transmission cooler lines using quick connect removal tool No. T82L-9500-AH or equivalent.
13. Remove the upper converter housing bolts.
14. Remove the crossmember-to-frame side support bolts and the crossmember.
15. Lower the transmission slightly. Place a piece of wood on a floorjack and support the engine.
16. Pull the transmision back and away from the engine slowly. Make sure the converter is mounted fully on the transmission and not stuck on the driveplate.
17. Lower the transmission and converter and remove it from beneath the vehicle.

**To install:**

18. Reverse the removal procedures: make sure the torque converter hub is fully engaged in the pump gear. Torque the:
Converter housing-to-engine bolt—28–38 ft. lbs. (38–51 Nm)
Torque converter-to-flywheel nuts—12–16 ft. lbs. (27–46 Nm)—2.3L engine
Torque converter-to-flywheel nuts—22–30 ft. lbs. (29–41 Nm)—2.9L engine
19. If the transmission was completely drained, add 2 quarts of fluid before starting the engine. Start the engine, check the fluid level with the dipstick and top off as necessary.

### PAN AND FILTER SERVICE

1. Raise and safely support the vehicle.
2. Place a drain pan under the oil pan, then start at the rear of the pan and work forward loosening the pan bolts until the fluid starts to drain. Slowly remove the pan bolts, leaving 2 on 1 side for last, until the pan tilts down and the remaining fluid drains.
3. Remove the remaining bolts and lower the oil pan.
4. Remove the transmission filter attaching screws and lower the filter from the valve body.

**To install:**

5. Clean the gasket mating surfaces.
6. Install the oil filter gasket and the new oil filter. Torque the bolts to 6–8 ft. lbs. (8–11 Nm).
7. Install the oil pan and gasket. Torque the attaching bolts to 12–17 ft. lbs. (16–23 Nm). Refill the transmission.

### LINKAGE ADJUSTMENTS

#### *XR4Ti*

#### C3 TRANSMISSION

1. Raise and safely the vehicle.
2. Remove the retaining clip and disengage the shift rod from the selector lever.
3. Rotate the transmission shift lever forward, as far as possible; this is the **DRIVE 1** or **LOW** position.
4. Rotate the transmission shift lever 2 detent positions rearward; this is the **DRIVE** position.
5. Move the gearshift lever to the **DRIVE** position as indicated by the shifter. Without moving the transmission or gearshift levers, attempt to

slide the shift rod clevis over the selector lever pin. If the clevis slides on the pin, the linkage is properly adjusted.

6. If the clevis does not slide onto the pin, loosen the locknut and thread the clevis in or out to obtain the proper fit. After making the adjustment, tighten the clevis locknut.

7. Install the selector rod retaining clip and lower the vehicle.

8. Check transmission in each selector position.

**NOTE: Make sure the linkage adjustment has not affected the operation of the neutral safety switch. With the parking brake set and service brakes applied firmly, try to start the engine in each gearshift position. The engine should crank only in N and P positions; if the engine cranks in any other shifter position, check the linkage adjustment and neutral safety switch.**

#### *Scorpio*

#### A4LD TRANSMISSION

1. Position the selector lever in the **D** position.

2. Raise and safely support the vehicle.

3. Remove the retaining clip and disengage the shift rod from the selector lever.

4. Rotate the transmission shift lever forward, as far as possible; this is the **DRIVE 1** or **LOW** position.

5. Rotate the lever 3 detent positions rearward; this is the **DRIVE** or **D** position.

6. Without moving the transmission shift lever or selector lever, attempt to slide the shift rod clevis over the selector lever pin. If the clevis slides onto the pin, the linkage is in proper adjustment. If the clevis does not slide onto the pin, loosen the locknut and thread the clevis in or out to obtain proper fit.

7. After making the adjustment, tighten the locknut and install the selector rod retaining clip.

### KICKDOWN ADJUSTMENT

1. Using a pair of pliers, remove the kickdown cable retaining clip located near the throttle body routing bracket.

2. Rotate the throttle body lever to the wide open position and hold it there.

3. While holding the throttle open, install the cable retaining clip, then release the throttle lever.

### NEUTRAL SAFETY SWITCH

The neutral safety switch is threaded into the transmission housing and torqued to 7–10 ft. lbs. (10–14 Nm). Aside from this, there is no adjustment. The neutral safety switch O-ring should be replaced every time the switch is removed or replaced. A special deep socket is necessary to remove the switch without damage. The twisting force from an open end wrench will collapse the switch housing. Make sure the electrical connector is clean and tight.

### FRONT BAND ADJUSTMENT

#### *XR4Ti*

#### C3 TRANSMISSION

1. Raise and safely support the vehicle.

2. Clean all of the dirt and grease from around the band adjusting screw area.

3. Remove and discard the band adjusting screw locknut. Install a new locknut on the screw, but do not tighten it.

4. Using an accurate torque wrench, torque the adjusting screw to 10 ft. lbs. (14 Nm) and back it off 2 turns.

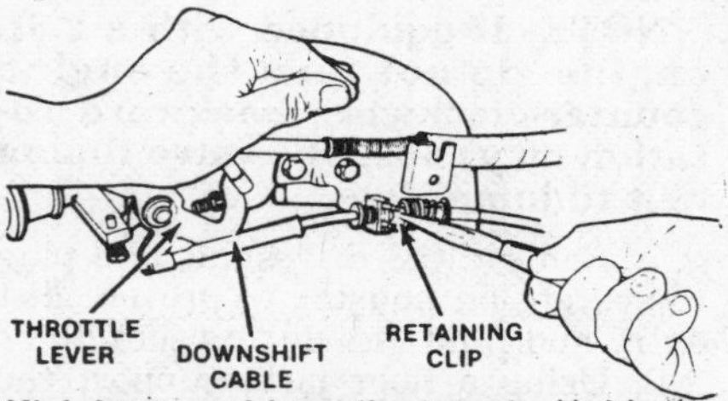


**Kickdown cable adjustment. Hold the throttle lever in the wide open position and install the cable clip, then release the lever**

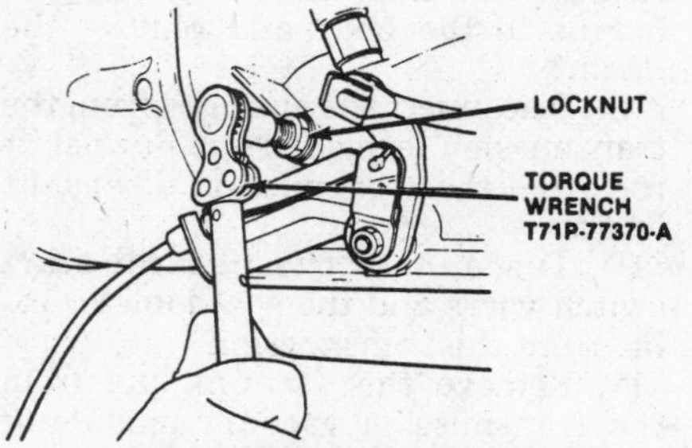


**Front band adjustment**

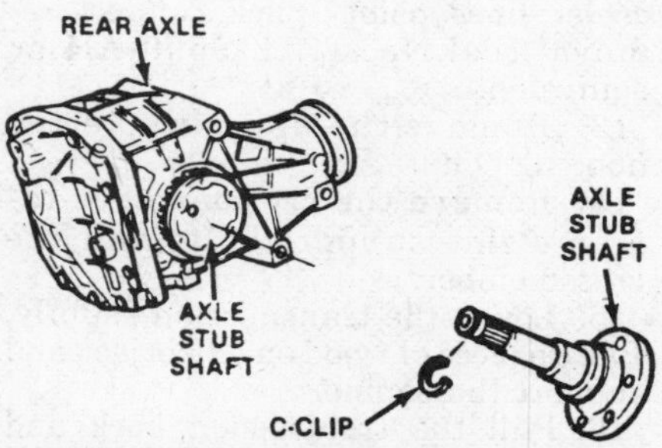


**The axle shafts are held in position by C-clips installed on the end of the shaft**

5. Hold the adjusting screw from turning and torque the locknut to 35–45 ft. lbs. (48–61 Nm).

## DRIVE AXLE

### Halfshafts

Power is transferred to the rear wheels by independent axle halfshafts. Each shaft is equipped with both an inner and an outer constant velocity joint. CV-joints require care during servicing to avoid causing damage to machined surfaces and splines. Never allow a CV-joint to hang by it's own weight; wire the shaft to the underbody to support it during service procedures.

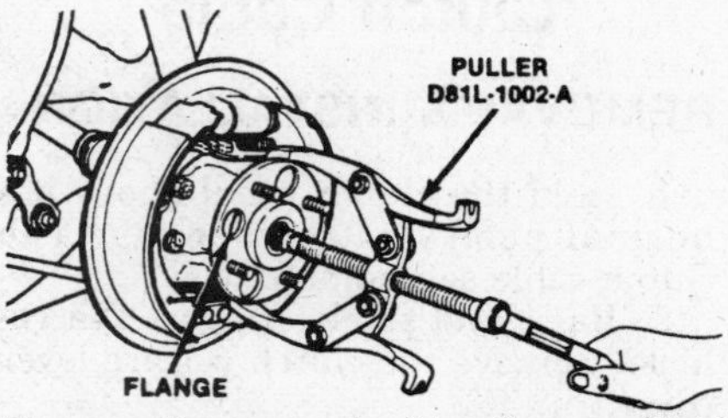


**Remove the rear axle drive flange with a puller**

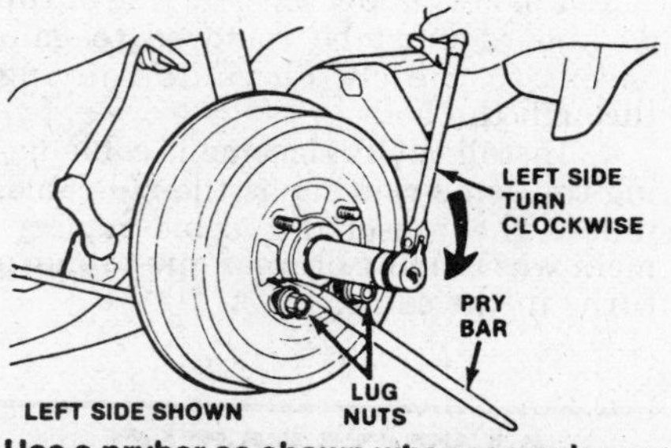


**Use a prybar as shown when removing or installing the rear axle flange locknut.**

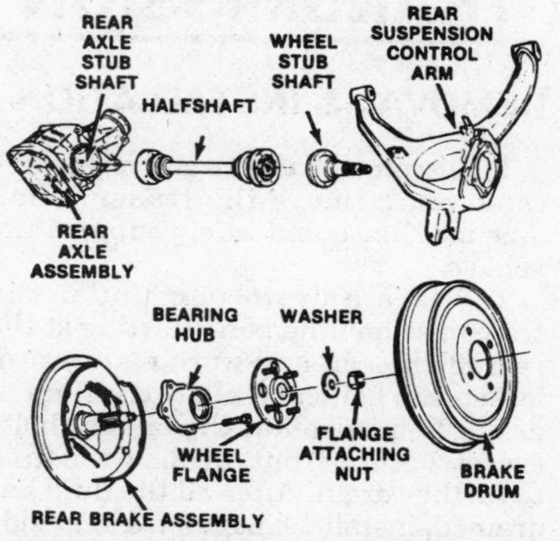


**Exploded view of the rear axle, halfshaft and hub assembly.**

### REMOVAL & INSTALLATION

1. Raise and safely support the vehicle with the rear wheels hanging freely. Make sure the transmission is in **N** and the parking brake is fully released.

2. Remove the flange bolts on the outside joint at the wheel stub shaft. Rotate the halfshaft to bring the flange bolts around.

3. Remove the flange bolts at the differential stub shaft only after securing the outer end of the halfshaft with wire or rope to the vehicle underbody.

4. Use a wide, flat-bladed prybar to separate the flanges, if necessary, but be careful not to damage any mating surfaces.

5. Carefully lower the axle driveshaft down and out. Handle the CV-joints with care; they can be damaged if dropped.

**NOTE: The halfshafts are different lengths, so they must be installed on the correct side of the vehicle. Be careful not to confuse the 2; the longer shaft is installed on the right side of the vehicle.**

6. Pack the constant velocity joints with grease before installation.

7. To install, reverse the removal procedures. Torque the halfshaft flange bolts to 28–31 ft. lbs. (38–43 Nm).

### CV-JOINT OVERHAUL

**For all CV-Joint overhaul procedures, please refer to "CV-Joint Overhaul" in the Unit Repair section.**

## Driveshaft and U-Joints

### REMOVAL & INSTALLATION

1. Raise and safely support the vehicle.

2. Scribe alignment marks on the driveshaft and pinion flanges before removal.

**NOTE: If the driveshaft is indexed improperly when installed, it could ruin driveline balance and cause vibrations.**

3. Place the transmission gear selector in **N** to allow rotation of the driveshaft.

4. Detach any exhaust system components interfering with driveshaft removal.

5. Remove the pinion flange-to-driveshaft bolts.

6. Remove the center bearing support-to-floorpan bolts; be careful not to lose the spacers that are installed between the support bearing bracket and the floor pan.

**NOTE: Note the position and number of the spacers so they may be installed in their original location. Failure to do so could result in driveline vibration.**

7. Remove the driveshaft-to-transmission flange bolts.

8. To install the driveshaft, reverse the removal procedures. Torque the:

Flange bolts – 42–49 ft. lbs. (57–67 Nm)

Center bearing support mounting bolts – 13–17 ft. lbs. (18–23 Nm)

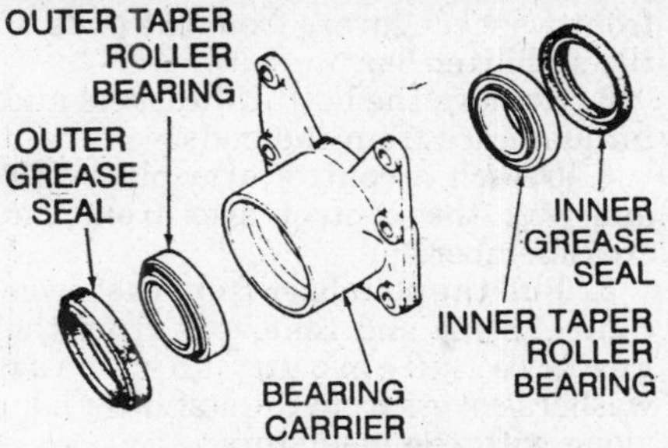

Rear axle bearing carrier components

## Rear Axle Shaft and Bearing

### REMOVAL & INSTALLATION

**NOTE: The rear axle flange locknuts are not interchangeable; they have different threads. The right side has right handed threads and the left side has left handed threads. Be sure to turn the nuts in the proper direction when removing or installing.**

1. Prior to raising the rear of the vehicle, loosen the rear axle locknut and wheel lugs. Raise and safely support the rear of the vehicle.

2. Remove the rear wheel and the brake drum or rotor. If equipped with drum brakes, there is a drum retaining clip which must be removed. The self adjusters may have to be backed off in order to allow drum removal.

3. Remove the axle locknut. Using a 3 jawed puller and slide hammer, remove the rear axle flange from the halfshaft.

4. Remove the bearing hub bolts and the bearing hub.

5. The hub contains a set of inner and outer bearings and races similar to conventional front wheel bearings. The cups are replaceable and the inner and outer bearings should be packed with grease in the normal manner. A grease seal is installed on either side of the hub.

**To install:**

6. To install, reverse the removal procedures. Torque the hub mounting bolts to 45–48 ft. lbs. (52–64 Nm). Install the axle flange and brake drum.

7. Install a new locknut on the axle, being careful not to mix sides. Torque the locknuts to 185–214 ft. lbs. (250–290 Nm).

# FRONT SUSPENSION

## MacPherson Strut

### REMOVAL & INSTALLATION

#### *XR4Ti*

1. Raise and safely support the front of the vehicle, after loosening the front wheel lug nuts.

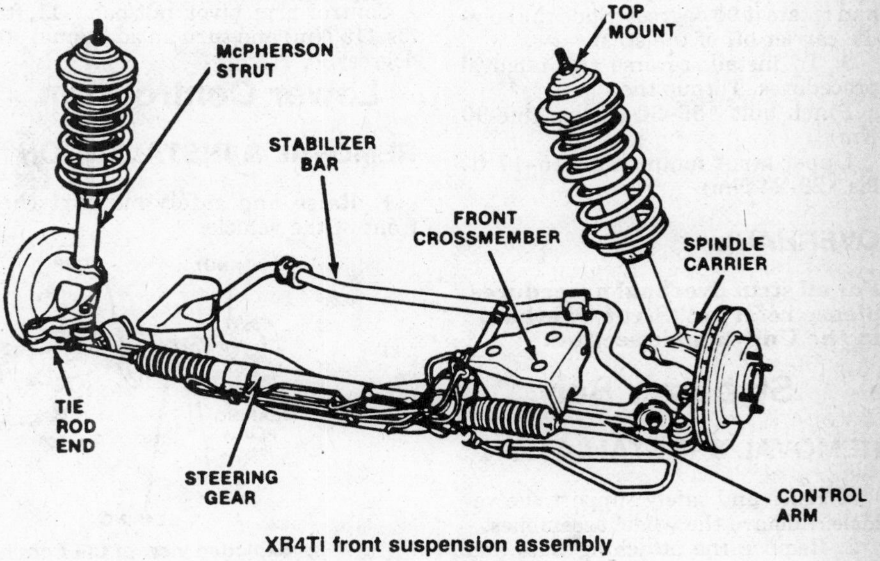

XR4Ti front suspension assembly

2. Remove the tire assembly and the caliper/anchor assembly. Position a floor jack under the lower control arm and raise it until it is slightly lower than the control arm.
3. Remove the strut-to-lower control arm pinch bolt. Use a small pry bar to spread the mounting flange ears and push down on the lower control arm to separate the arm and strut. Lower the jack (if necessary) but do not allow the brake hose to stretch. When separated, rest the control arm on the jack.
4. Hold the top of the strut by inserting a 6mm hex wrench in the slot provided and remove the locknut.
5. Remove the strut assembly from the vehicle.
6. To install, reverse the removal procedures.

### *Scorpio*

1. Disconnect the negative battery cable. Loosen the wheel lugs, raise and safely support the vehicle.
2. Remove the front wheel. Remove the caliper and support it on a wire.
3. Remove the wheel sensor from the spindle carrier. Separate the tie rod end from the spindle.
4. To separate the control arm ball joint from the spindle, use a small pry bar to pry down on the control arm and stabilizer bar. Pull the strut clear of the control arm.
5. Remove the brake pad sensor wire from the strut clip and the dust cover from the top strut mount on the inner fender.
6. Support the strut and spindle carrier. Remove the upper locknuts and washers. Lower the strut assembly from the upper mount.
7. Remove the pinch bolt from the spindle carrier. Insert Tool No. T85M-3206A or the equivalent (Spindle Carrier Lever) into the spindle carrier slot and rotate it 90 degrees. Slide the spindle carrier off of the strut.
8. To install, reverse the removal procedures. Torque the:

Pinch bolt – 59–66 ft. lbs. (80–90 Nm)

Upper strut mounting – 15–17 ft. lbs. (20–24 Nm)

### OVERHAUL

**For all strut overhaul procedures, please refer to "Strut Overhaul" in the Unit Repair section.**

## Stabilizer Bar

### REMOVAL & INSTALLATION

1. Raise and safely support the vehicle. Remove the wheel assemblies.
2. Remove the attaching nuts and front washers/covers from the ends of the stabilizer bar.
3. Remove the both U-brackets and torque brace from the body.
4. Detach a control arm pivot bolt and pull the control arm from the crossmember.
5. Pull the stabilizer from the lower control arms and remove it from the vehicle. Remove the rear washers/covers from the stabilizer bar, along with the insulators.

**To install:**

6. Coat the inside of the stabilizer bar bushings and the bushing surfaces on the stabilizer bar with rubber lube; do not use engine oil. Install the insulators on the stabilizer bar.
7. Install the rear washers/covers on the stabilizer bar. The rear washer is black and has a shallower dish than the front washer, which is yellow. When the washer is installed, make sure the plastic cover is in place between the dished steel washer and the bushing. The dished side of the steel washer faces away from the bushing.
8. Install the stabilizer bar into the control arm bushings. Install the control arm into the crossmember with the pivot bolt, washer and nut. Snug the attaching nut but do not tighten.
9. Install the U-bolts on the insulators and install the attaching bolts. Torque the bolts to 42–52 ft. lbs. (57–70 Nm).
10. Install the front washers/covers on the stabilizer bar, making sure the dished side of the steel washer faces away from the bushing, with the plastic cover in place between the bushing and steel washer.
11. Install the stabilizer bar attaching nuts but just snug them; do not tighten to specifications.
12. Lower the vehicle and torque the:

Stabilizer bar nut – 52–81 ft. lbs. (70–110 Nm)

Control arm pivot nut/bolt – 11 ft. lbs. (15 Nm) and turn an additional 90 degrees

## Lower Control Arm

### REMOVAL & INSTALLATION

1. Raise and safely support the front of the vehicle.
2. Remove the front tire.
3. Remove the cotter pin and attaching nut. Separate the control arm from the spindle carrier.

**NOTE: With the spindle carrier and control arm disconnected, the spindle carrier can easily cause damage to the control arm ball joint boot. The control arm and ball joint are replaced as an assembly if the ball joint is worn or damaged.**

4. Remove the control arm-to-crossmember pivot bolt.
5. Remove the stabilizer bar-to-control arm nut.
6. Remove the front washer/cover from the end of the stabilizer bar.
7. Remove the control arm and bushing as an assembly. Remove the rear washer/cover from the end of the stabilizer bar. Remove the bushings if replacement is necessary; the bushings are pressed into the control arm.

**To install:**

8. Reverse the removal procedures.

**NOTE: The stabilizer bar bushings are designed to allow the control arm to move forward and rearward somewhat; this movement should not be interpreted as a suspension problem.**

9. Torque the control arm ball joint stud nut to 48–63 ft. lbs. (65–85 Nm) and install a new cotter pin; the castle nut may be tightened slightly to align the cotter pin hole with the castellations but do not loosen the nut for alignment.
10. If equipped with a 2.3L engine, torque the control arm pivot bolt to 11 ft. lbs. (15 Nm), plus, an additional 90 degrees.
11. If equipped with a 2.9L engine, install the front wheel and lower the vehicle. Torque the control arm pivot bolt to 22 ft. lbs. (30 Nm), plus, an additional ¼ turn.

## Front Wheel Bearing

### REMOVAL & INSTALLATION

1. Raise and safely support the vehicle. Remove the front wheels and

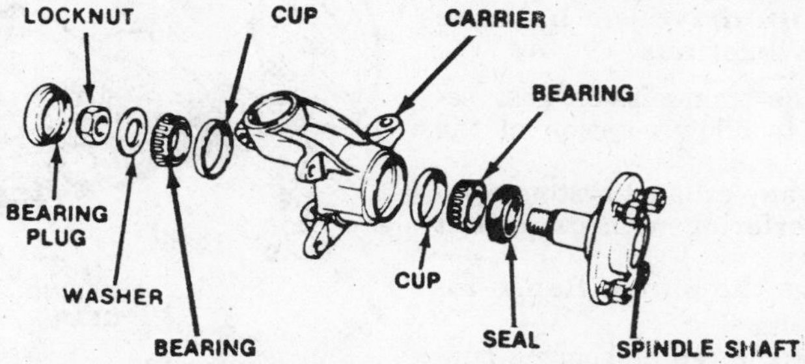


Exploded view of the front hub and bearing assembly

brake calipers; suspend the calipers on wire to prevent brake hose damage.

2. Matchmark the rotor and wheel stud. The unit is balanced by the factory and must be installed in the same position to maintain balance.

3. Remove the cotter pin and the tie rod end nut. Separate the tie rod from the steering knuckle.

4. Remove the cotter pin, the control arm nut and the control arm from the steering knuckle.

5. Separate the strut from the steering knuckle.

6. Place the spindle and hub in a vise, wheel studs pointing downward, clamped between 2 pieces of wood and the vise jaws.

7. Using a flat drift, remove the bearing plug from the rear of the steering knuckle.

8. Remove the spindle bearing locknut.

**NOTE: Spindles form the right side of the vehicle are equipped with left handed threads and are loosened by turning clockwise. Spindles from the left side of the vehicle are equipped with right handed threads which are loosened by turning counterclockwise. The spindles are marked with an R or L on the large hexagonal recess.**

9. Lift the spindle carrier and inner bearing off the (hub) spindle shaft. Remove the inner bearing and splined washer. If the bearing is to be reused, label for location identification.

10. Clamp the spindle carrier (knuckle) in a vise and remove the grease seal using a flat prybar. Remove the outer bearing and label for location identification.

11. Remove bearing cups from the spindle, if necessary, using a bearing puller jaws on a slide hammer.

**To install:**

12. Clean and inspect all parts. Press new bearing cups into the spindle. Pack the wheel bearing with high temperature grease.

13. Install the outer bearing and grease seal in the spindle (knuckle). Install the spindle shaft (hub).

14. Install the inner bearing and splined washer. Install the spindle bearing locknut and torque to:

2.3L engine – 202–232 ft. lbs. (274–315 Nm)

2.9L engine – 288–331 ft. lbs. (390–450 Nm)

15. Install the bearing cover plug.

**NOTE: Be sure the spindle is mounted secure in the vise but do not damage the studs. The amount of torque required for the locknut is extremely important. If a higher or lower torque is applied bearing failure is likely to occur.**

16. To complete the removal procedures. Reverse the removal procedures. Torque the:

Strut-to-spindle pinch bolt – 59–66 ft. lbs. (80–90 Nm)

Lower control arm nut – 48–63 ft. lbs. (65–85 Nm)

Tie rod end nut – 15–23 ft. lbs. (20–32 Nm)

## Front Wheel Alignment

### ADJUSTMENT

#### *Caster and Camber*

Caster and camber are not adjustable. If out of specifications, the vehicle body should be checked for distortion at suspension mounting points. The tires should be properly inflated and any abnormal loads removed from the vehicle when checking or adjusting alignment.

#### *Toe*

To adjust the toe, loosen the jam nuts at the tie rod ends and release the clips at the small ends of the steering gear boots. Make sure the boots are free on the tie rods so they won't be twisted when the tie rods are turned.

Turn the tie rods in or out an equal amount on each side. Turning the tie rods in (shortening) will increase the toe, while moving the tie rods out (lengthening) decreases toe. When the toe setting is correct, torque the jam nuts to 42–50 ft. lbs. (57–68 Nm). Make sure the steering gear boot ends are positioned correctly and install the boot clips.

# REAR SUSPENSION

## Shock Absorber

### REMOVAL & INSTALLATION

1. Remove the rear parcel shelf or luggage compartment cover and remove the upper shock mount trim cover.

2. Raise and safely support the rear of the vehicle.

3. Position a floor jack under the lower control arm of the side requiring shock replacement. Raise the jack until it contacts the control arm.

4. Remove the upper shock mount through bolt and nut.

5. Remove the cap from the lower shock mount. Remove the through bolt/nut and the shock absorber.

**To install:**

6. Install the replacement shock and reverse reverse the removal procedures. Install the lower through bolt with the head facing inboard, then, torque the:

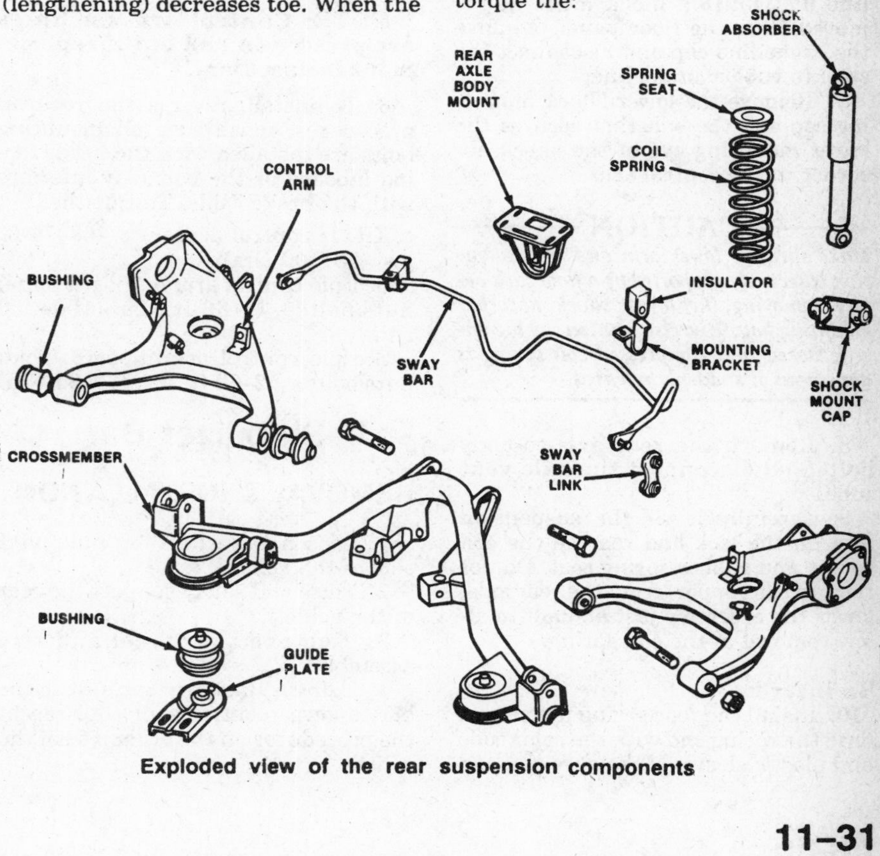


Exploded view of the rear suspension components

Lower mounting head bolt—33–40 ft. lbs. (45–55 Nm)
Lower mounting head nut—30–37 ft. lbs. (40–50 Nm)
Upper mounting bolt and nut—30–37 ft. lbs. (40–50 Nm)

## Coil Spring

### REMOVAL & INSTALLATION

1. Loosen the rear wheel lug nuts. Raise and safely support the rear of the vehicle, with the rear suspension hanging freely. Remove the rear tire and the brake drum or rotor and caliper.

**NOTE: The rear brake self adjusters may have to be backed off in order to remove the brake drum.**

2. Position a floor jack under the rear control arm and take a slight amount of weight off of the spring.
3. Disconnect the rear brake hose at the body bracket (rubber line from steel line).
4. Remove the rear axle flange/brake backing plate-to-control arm bolts.
5. Remove the halfshaft. Secure the backing plate in it's installed position with 2 bolts to prevent damage to the steel brake line.
6. On Scorpio models, detach the stabilizer bar from the link rod. When removing the left spring, the brake line distribution block must be removed from the floor panel. Remove the brake line clip and disconnect the steel to rubber brake line.
7. Remove the lower shock mounting cap and the bolt that secures the lower mounting eye of the shock absorber to the control arm.

**CAUTION**

***Make sure the lower arm and spring tension is securely supported by a floor jack before removing the lower shock absorber mounting bolt. Exercise caution, as the energy stored in a compressed coil spring is dangerous if suddenly released.***

8. Remove the rear axle-to-body bolts and disconnect the axle vent tube.
9. Carefully lower the suspension arm on the jack and remove the coil spring and rubber spring seat. Do not remove the support from the rear axle; lower the assembly just enough to allow removal of the coil spring.

**To install:**
10. Install the rear spring upper seat onto the spring end with the color code and plastic sleeve. Make sure the end of the coil seats against the step in the spring seat and the seat tabs are positioned between the 1st and 2nd coil.

**NOTE: The coil spring and seat must be installed dry. Do not lubricate with spray silicone or any other type of lubricant.**

11. Raise the jack slowly and make sure the spring and seat are correctly located. Raise the rear axle into position and install the body mount attaching bolts. Clean the body mount bolts and apply Loctite®, then, torque to:
XR4Ti—14–18 ft. lbs. (20–25 Nm)
Scorpio—31–37 ft. lbs. (41–51 Nm)
12. To complete the install, reverse the removal procedures.

## Lower Control Arm

### REMOVAL & INSTALLATION

1. Remove the coil spring.
2. Use a small prybar to open the routing clamp and disengage the parking brake cable from the control arm.
3. Disconnect the sway stabilizer link from the control arm.
4. Remove the rear bearing hub and suspend the brake backing plate or caliper assembly on a length of wire.
5. Pull the wheel stub shaft out of the control arm. Remove the control arm inner and outer bolts and the control arm from the vehicle.

**NOTE: Control arm bushings are pressed in and out if replacement is necessary.**

6. To install, reverse the removal procedures; make sure all mounting bolts are installed with the heads facing inboard or the bolt may interfere with the brake cable. Torque the:
XR4Ti control arm nuts—63–74 ft. lbs. (85–100 Nm)
Scorpio control arm outboard (blue) nuts/bolts—74–88 ft. lbs. (100–120 Nm)
Scorpio control arm inboard (gold) nuts/bolts—52–63 ft. lbs. (70–85 Nm)

## Stabilizer Bar

### REMOVAL & INSTALLATION

1. Loosen the wheel lug nuts on 1 side of the vehicle.
2. Raise and safely support the rear of the vehicle.
3. Remove the wheel and tire assembly.
4. Using a small pry bar, unclip the bar-to-lower control arm clip; repeat the procedures on the other side of the vehicle.

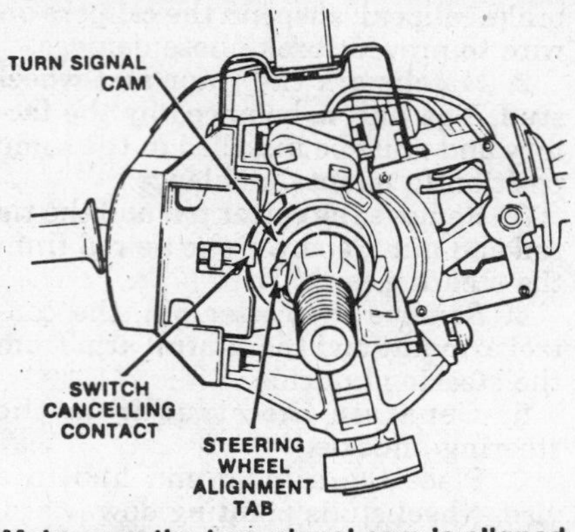

**Make sure the turn signal cam is aligned with the cancelling lever before installing the steering wheel**

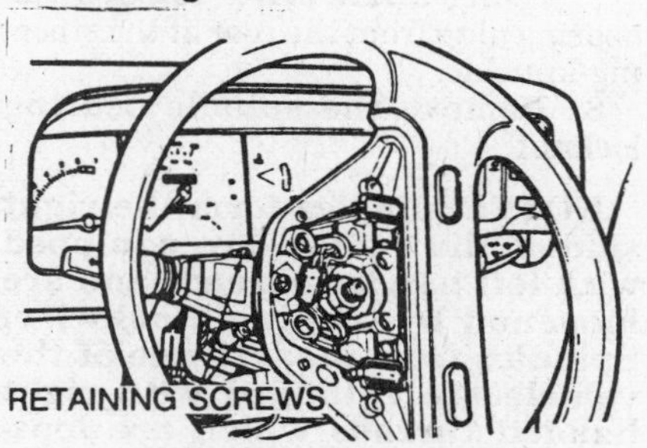

**Combination switch mounting**

5. Remove the stabilizer bracket-to-floor pan bolts and the stabilizer bar assembly. Place a piece of tape on the stabilizer bar next to the U-bracket and insulator for alignment reference during assembly.
6. To install, reverse the removal procedures. Torque the U-bracket mounting bolts to 15–18 ft. lbs. (20–25 Nm).

# STEERING

## Steering Wheel

### REMOVAL & INSTALLATION

1. Disconnect the negative battery cable.
2. Turn the ignition switch to the **RUN** position and center the steering wheel with the front tires in a straight ahead position.
3. Remove the steering wheel hub cover assembly by carefully prying it up with a small prybar.
4. Loosen the center hub nut a few turns and pull the steering wheel straight up to release it from the tapered steering shaft.
5. Remove the wheel hub nut and lift off the steering wheel.
6. Make sure the turn signal cam is

aligned with the turn signal switch cancelling lever.

**To install:**

7. Position the steering wheel over the column shaft and align the slot on the underside of the steering wheel hub with the tab on the turn signal switch. Install the center hub nut on the shaft and torque it to 33–40 ft. lbs. (45–55 Nm).

8. Turn the ignition key to **LOCK** and remove it, then check that the steering wheel locks properly. Install the hub trim pad and connect the negative battery cable. Verify that the horn functions.

## Turn Signal and Combination Switch

The combination switch contains the controls for windshield wiper/washer and headlamp high beam operation. Although mounted next to each other in the steering column, the turn signal and combination switches are replaced separately.

### REMOVAL & INSTALLATION

1. Disconnect the negative battery cable.
2. Remove the steering wheel and the upper/lower steering column shrouds; there is a screw near the hazard flasher switch and 2 under the column, on either side of the hood release lever.
3. Remove the sound panels from the underside of the dash. Be careful to disconnect courtesy lights and radio speaker connectors before removing the column completely.
4. Remove the switch-to-column screws. Disengage the switch from the column, disconnect the wire connectors and remove the switch from the steering column.
5. To install, align the switch mounting holes with the corresponding holes in the housing and continue in the reverse order of removal.

## Ignition Lock/Switch

### REMOVAL & INSTALLATION

1. Disconnect the negative battery cable.
2. Remove the steering wheel, sound panels and column shrouds.
3. Turn the ignition key switch to the **I** (ignition) position. Use a suitable tool and depress the lock spring (hole provided) and remove the lock cylinder from the ignition switch.
4. Remove the ignition switch mounting screws and disengage the switch from the steering column.

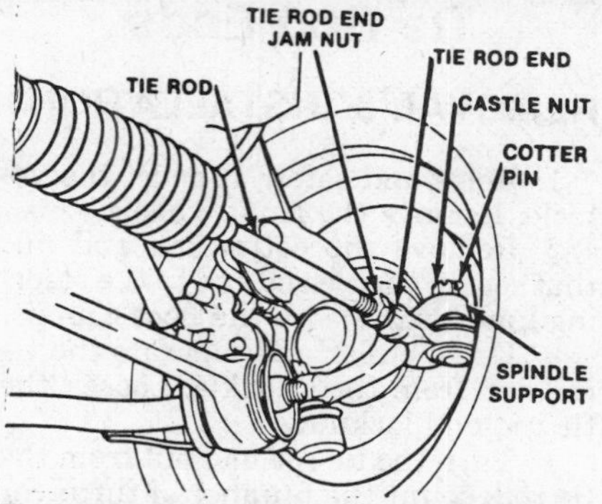


**Tie rod end and steering knuckle assembly**

5. To install, reverse the removal procedures.

## Power Steering Gear

### REMOVAL & INSTALLATION

1. Disconnect the negative battery cable and turn the ignition switch to the **ON** position. Center the steering wheel with the front tires in the straight ahead position.
2. Raise and safely support the front of the vehicle.
3. Remove the lower flexible coupler-to-steering gear input shaft pinch bolt.
4. Remove the front wheels.
5. Remove the cotter pin and castle nut from the tie rod ends. Disconnect the tie rod ends from the steering knuckles, using a puller.
6. Position a drain pan, then, disconnect the power steering pressure and return lines from the steering gear assembly by removing the routing clamp and the washer head pump line plate assembly-to-gear housing screw. Plug the lines and connections at the steering gear to prevent the entry of dirt or contaminants during service.
7. Remove the steering gear-to-crossmember bolts and the gear.

**To install:**

8. Reverse the removal procedures. Torque the:

Mounting bolts – 11 ft. lbs. (15 Nm), plus, an additional 90 degrees

Steering shaft pinch bolt – 18–22 ft. lbs. (25–30 Nm)

**NOTE: Tie rod ends may be replaced by separating them from the steering knuckle after releasing the boot, loosening the locknut and unscrewing the tie rods from the gear assembly. Always count the number of turns for reinstallation reference.**

9. Bleed the power steering system.

### ADJUSTMENT

This procedure is not a servicable adjustment; it is to be done only as part of a complete overhaul of the rack/pinion assembly.

1. Remove the rack/pinion assembly from the vehicle and position it in a soft jawed vise in the horizontal position. Position the rack/pinion in the straight ahead position.
2. Remove the yoke plug from the front side of the rack/pinion assembly.
3. Lubricate the yoke plug threads with Loctite® activator No. 764 or equivalent, and reinstall the yoke plug.
4. Using the yoke plug hex adapter tool No. T85M-3504-C or equivalent, torque the yoke plug to 30–35 inch lbs. (3.4–3.9 Nm).
5. Using the pinion shaft replacer/torque adapter tool, position it on the pinion shaft so the lock screws engage the shaft splines. Turn the pinion in 1 direction and then the opposite direction, until the rack has moved, twice, from stop-to-stop.
6. Retorque the yoke plug to 30–35 inch lbs. (3.4–3.9 Nm).
7. Using the pinion shaft torque adapter tool No. T85M-3504-B or equivalent, check the pinion shaft turning force; it should be at least 12 inch lbs. (1.35 Nm). If the turning force is less than 12 inch lbs. (1.35 Nm), repeat the torquing procedure.
8. When the pinion shaft rotation torque meets the specification, back off the yoke plug 22–27 degrees and recheck the turning force; it should not exceed 15 inch lbs. (1.7 Nm).
9. If the torque exceeds 15 inch lbs. (1.7 Nm), back off the yoke cover 5 degrees.
10. Using Loctite® 290 penetrating anerobic sealant or equivalent, apply it to the yoke cover threads.
11. Stake the rack/pinion assembly housing in 3 places around the yoke plug; do not use the original staking positions.
12. Reinstall the rack/pinion assembly into the vehicle. Bleed the power steering system.

## Power Steering Pump

### REMOVAL & INSTALLATION

**NOTE: Special power steering pump pulley removal and installer tools are required for this procedure. The pulley remover is tool No.T69L-10300-B and the installer is tool No. T65P-3A733-E.**

1. Disconnect the power steering fluid return line from the pump fitting and drain the fluid into a suitable container.

2. Remove the pressure line from the pump.

3. Remove the drive belts from the pump.

4. Remove the pump drive pulley using a suitable puller. Unbolt the pump from the mounting bracket and lift it clear.

**To install:**

5. Reverse the removal procedures; a pulley installer tool will be necessary to attach the pump pulley. Torque the:

Pump mounting bolts – 30–45 ft. lbs. (41–61 Nm)

Pressure and return hose fittings – 10–25 ft. lbs. (14–34 Nm)

6. Hose swivel and/or end play in the fitting is normal and does not indicate a loose fitting. Overtorquing the tube nut can result in a leak and require replacement of the hose assembly.

7. Bleed the power steering system.

### BELT ADJUSTMENT

Adjust the drive belt tension so that there is approximately 1/8–3/8 in. of deflection on the longest span of belt between pulleys. Apply pressure to the square rib on the alternator housing using the proper size open end wrench to maintain pressure when adjusting belt tension. Torque the:

Adjuster pivot bolt – 44–60 ft. lbs. (60–81 Nm)

Adjuster nut – 30–46 ft. lbs. (40–62 Nm)

### SYSTEM BLEEDING

After any service procedure that requires draining the power steering pump, perform the following procedure to remove any trapped air in the system. Failure to bleed the power steering pump can cause excessively noisy operation.

1. Disconnect the ignition coil wire. Raise and safely support the front of the vehicle with the front wheels off the ground.

2. Fill the power steering pump reservoir to the specified level with Type F power steering and transmission fluid.

3. Crank the engine with the starter while rotating the steering wheel from lock-to-lock. Crank the engine briefly and keep checking the fluid level in the pump reservoir. Keep adding fluid until the level remains constant.

4. Reconnect the coil wire.

5. Start the engine and allow it to idle for several minutes. Rotate the steering wheel from lock-to-lock several times, then turn **OFF** the engine and recheck the fluid level. Add fluid as necessary.

## Tie Rod Ends

### REMOVAL & INSTALLATION

1. Raise and safely support the vehicle. Remove the front wheels.

2. Remove the cotter pin and nut that secure the tie rod end to the steering knuckle. Release the boot clamps.

3. Use a puller and separate the tie rod end from the knuckle. Loosen the tie rod end locknut.

4. Turn the tie rod end out from the tie rod; count the number of turns for installation reference.

**To install:**

5. Screw in the new tie rod end, approximately the same number of turns as removed. Tighten the lock nut.

6. To complete the installation, reverse the removal procedures. Check and/or adjust the alignment.

# BRAKES

**For all brake system repair and service procedures not detailed below, please refer to "Brakes" in the Unit Repair Section.**

## Master Cylinder

### REMOVAL & INSTALLATION

#### XR4Ti

1. Disconnect the low fluid indicator connector from the filler cap.

2. Disconnect the brake lines from the master cylinder.

3. Remove the master cylinder-to-brake booster nuts and lockwashers.

4. Remove the master cylinder from the booster.

**To install:**

5. Reverse the removal procedures. Torque the master cylinder mounting nuts to 16–20 ft. lbs. (21–27 Nm).

6. Refill the master cylinder reservoir with brake fluid and bleed the brake system.

#### Scorpio

**CAUTION**

***Before servicing any components of the 4 Wheel Anti-Lock Brake System (ABS), it is mandatory that the high pressure in the system be discharged. To discharge the system: Turn the ignition switch to the OFFposition and pump the brake pedal a minimum of 20 times until an increase in brake pedal force is clearly experienced.***

1. Disconnect the negative battery cable.

2. Disconnect all of the electrical connectors from the reservoir cap, main valve, pressure switch, valve block, electric pump and ground connection.

3. Disconnect the hydraulic lines from the valve body and plug the lines to prevent dirt entry.

4. Remove the under dash trim panel and disconnect the brake pedal to unit pushrod by removing the retainer clip.

5. Support the hydraulic unit and remove the mounting nuts. Remove the unit from the vehicle and drain the reservoir.

6. Remove and replace the seal gasket (always use a new gasket) between the hydraulic unit and the dash panel.

**To install:**

7. Place the hydraulic unit into position and support it. Install the mounting nuts and torque them to 30–40 ft. lbs. (41–51 Nm.).

8. Install the pushrod to brake pedal retaining clip. Connect the fluid lines and electrical wiring to the unit. Refill the reservoir with new brake fluid. Bleed the front brake system.

9. Connect the negative battery cable. Turn the ignition switch to the **RUN** position and check the electric pump operation.

10. Do not operate the electric pump for more than 2 minutes at a time or it will overheat. Bleed the rear brake system. Install the under dash panel. Road test the vehicle to check brake operation.

## Proportioning Valve

### REMOVAL & INSTALLATION

#### XR4Ti

1. Raise and safely support the vehicle.

2. Disconnect the brake lines from the proportioning valve, located just under the master cylinder/booster assembly.

3. Remove the attaching bolt and remove the proportioning valve from the vehicle.

4. To install, reverse of removal. Bleed the brake system.

## Power Brake Booster

The 1985–86 XR4Ti models are equipped with a single diaphragm brake booster, while 1987–89 XR4Ti models use a dual diaphragm booster. Although different in appearance, both boosters function the same way and service procedures are similar.

### REMOVAL & INSTALLATION

1. Depress the brake pedal several times to deplete the vacuum reserve in the brake booster. Depressurize the fuel system by connecting a hand vacuum pump to the fuel pressure regulator and applying 25 in. Hg. of vacuum for about 3 minutes.
2. Disconnect the fuel line at the pulse damper. Disconnect the fuel return line using a quick disconnect tool.
3. Disconnect the low oil level sensor connector and remove the engine oil level dipstick. The dipstick connector is only used on 1985–86 models.
4. Remove the screw attaching the engine oil dipstick tube to the pulse damper bracket. Remove the pulse damper bracket-to-intake manifold stud nuts. Disconnect the pulse damper from the fuel manifold and remove the damper/bracket assembly.
5. Label and disconnect the vacuum lines at the vacuum tree. Disconnect the low fluid warning light connector from the master cylinder cap and pull the vacuum check valve from the booster body.
6. Working inside, below the instrument panel, disconnect booster valve operating rod from the brake pedal assembly. To do this, disconnect the stop light switch wires at the connector. Remove the hairpin retainer and nylon washer from the pedal pin. Slide the switch off, just enough for the outer arm to clear the pin. Remove the switch. Slide the booster push rod, bushing and inner nylon washer off the pedal pin.
7. Disconnect the brake lines at the master cylinder outlet fittings.
8. If equipped with speed control, remove the left cowl screen in the engine compartment. Remove speed control servo-to-firewall nuts and move the servo aside.
9. Remove the bracket-to-firewall bolts.
10. Remove the booster and bracket assembly from the firewall, sliding the valve operating rod out from the engine side.
11. To install, reverse of removal. Bleed the brakes system.

## Disc Brake Pads

### REMOVAL & INSTALLATION

#### *Front*

1. Remove approximately ⅓ of the brake fluid from the master cylinder.
2. Raise and safely support the front of the vehicle. Remove the front wheels.
3. Disconnect the electrical connector from the wear sensor; to disconnect, press the harness connector pads and pull apart.
4. Using a prybar, place it between the caliper and the outer pad, then, force the piston into the caliper.
5. Remove the caliper-to-caliper support bolts and the caliper; support it on a wire.

**NOTE: When removing the caliper, the anti-rattle spring will fall out.**

6. Remove the outboard pad and the inboard pad.
7. If the piston has not seated in the caliper, use a C-clamp to force it into the caliper.

**To install:**

8. Install the pads onto the caliper.
9. Position the caliper over the rotor; make sure the pads are properly engaged on the anchor plate.

**NOTE: Make sure the sensor wire is positioned between the caliper and the anchor before install the caliper bolts.**

10. Install the caliper-to-caliper support bolts and torque to 18–23 ft. lbs. (25–30 Nm).
11. Install the anti-rattle spring. Connect the wear sensor electrical connector; make sure the O-ring is in position before making the connection.

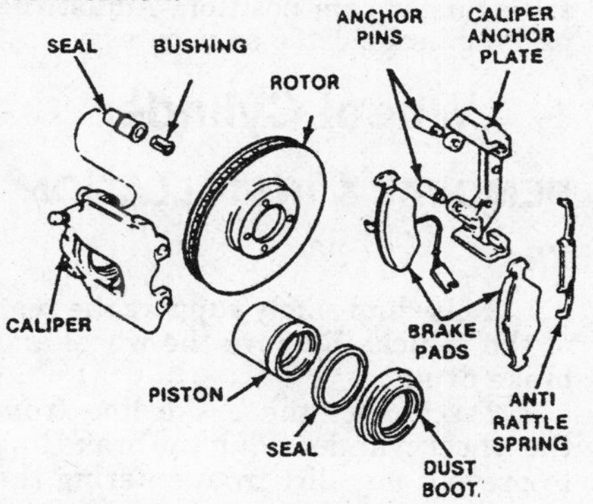


**Exploded view of the front disc brake assembly**

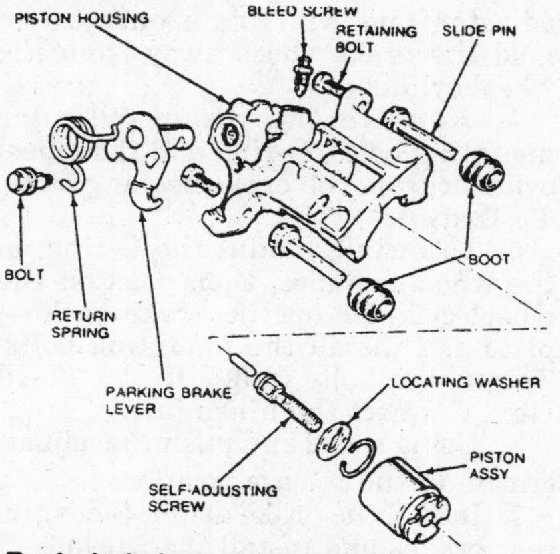


**Exploded view of the rear disc brake assembly—Scorpio**

12. To complete the installation, reverse the removal procedures. Refill the master cylinder reservoir.

#### *Rear*

##### SCORPIO

1. Raise and safely support the rear of the vehicle. Remove the rear wheels.
2. Disengage the parking brake cable from the retaining bracket.
3. Using a prybar, place it between the caliper and the outer pad, then, force the piston into the caliper.
4. Remove the front caliper piston housing-to-anchor bracket slide pin bolt and lift the piston assembly up and away from the rotor.
5. Remove the brake pads from the carrier bracket.
6. If the piston has not seated in the caliper, use a C-clamp to force it into the caliper.

**To install:**

7. Install the brake pads onto the carrier bracket and the caliper over the rotor; position the piston's slot over the tab in the brake pad backing plate. Make sure the anti-rattle spring are correctly positioned in the piston housing.
8. Install the caliper-to-caliper bracket slide pin bolt and torque it to 23–25 ft. lbs. (31–35 Nm).
9. Connect the parking brake cable to the retainer bracket.
10. To complete the installation, reverse the removal procedures. Turn the ignition switch to the **RUN** position and pump the brake pedal prior to moving the vehicle, to pressurize the system and position the brake pads.

## Brake Shoes

### REMOVAL & INSTALLATION

#### *XR4Ti*

1. Raise and safely support the rear of the vehicle. Remove the rear wheels.
2. Remove the brake drum and discard the retaining clip.
3. Should the brake drum be difficult to remove, perform the following procedures:
   a. Remove the wheel cylinder bolts
   b. Push the wheel cylinder away from the backing plate to provide access.
   c. Using a thin blade tool, insert it through the backing plate and rotate the self-adjuster cam to released position.
   d. Remove the brake drum and retorque the wheel cylinder bolts to 5–7 ft. lbs. (7–10 Nm).
4. Remove both brake drum hold-down springs.
5. Pry the lower end of the primary

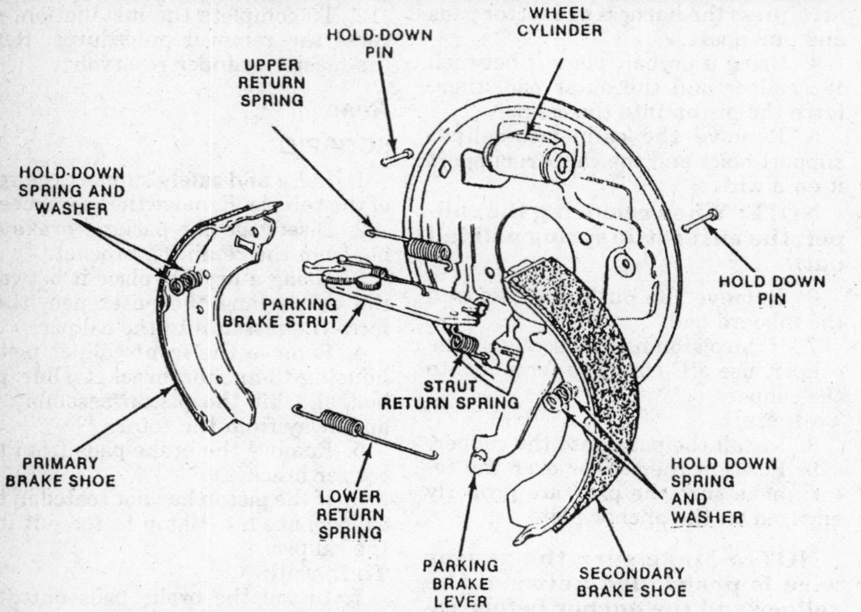


**Exploded view of the rear drum brake assembly—Merkur**

shoe from it's anchor and remove the lower spring.

6. Remove the shoes and strut by passing the strut between the wheel cylinder and the hub.

7. Pull the top of the primary shoe away from the secondary shoe to disconnect the strut from the secondary shoe.

8. Disconnect the parking brake cable from the secondary shoe lever.

9. Remove the strut return spring from the secondary shoe.

10. Remove the adjuster cam spring, pull the primary shoe away from the strut while rotating the cam to the fully released position.

11. Remove the primary shoe spring and the primary shoe spring from the strut.

**To install:**

12. Using high temperature brake grease, lubricate the 6 support ledges (where the brake shoes contact the backing plate).

13. Connect the parking brake cable to the secondary shoe lever.

**NOTE: When properly installed, the plastic washer will be between the spring and the lever.**

14. Position the secondary shoe and install the hold-down spring. Install the strut and cam assembly onto the primary shoe.

15. Rotate the cam to the fully released position. Install the cam adjuster spring and the primary shoe spring.

16. Install the strut spring onto the secondary shoe and the strut.

17. Position the strut onto the parking brake lever and move the primary shoe toward the backing plate.

**NOTE: The strut will "click" into place over the parking brake lever and the secondary shoe web.**

18. To complete the installation, reverse the removal procedures. Depress the brake pedal, twice, hard, to set the self-adjuster cam position. Adjust the parking brake cable as necessary.

## Wheel Cylinder

### REMOVAL & INSTALLATION

#### *XR4Ti*

1. Raise and safely support the rear of the vehicle. Remove the wheel and brake drum.

2. Disconnect the brake line from the wheel cylinder. Plug the brake line to prevent any dirt from entering the system.

3. Pull the primary (front) shoe away from the wheel cylinder. The self adjuster cam will rotate outward to hold the brake shoes away from the wheel cylinder.

4. Remove the wheel cylinder mounting bolts, O-ring and the wheel cylinder from the brake backing plate.

**To install:**

5. To install, mount the O-ring on the wheel cylinder, then position the wheel cylinder on the brake backing plate and install the mounting bolts. Torque the bolts to 5–7 ft. lbs. (7–10 Nm). Connect the brake line.

6. Using a tool and push the adjuster cam to the release position.

7. Install the brake drum. Bleed the rear brakes and install the wheel.

**NOTE: If a pressure bleeder is used, push the brake pedal hard twice to set the self adjuster cam position. The cam will make a ratcheting sound as it resets.**

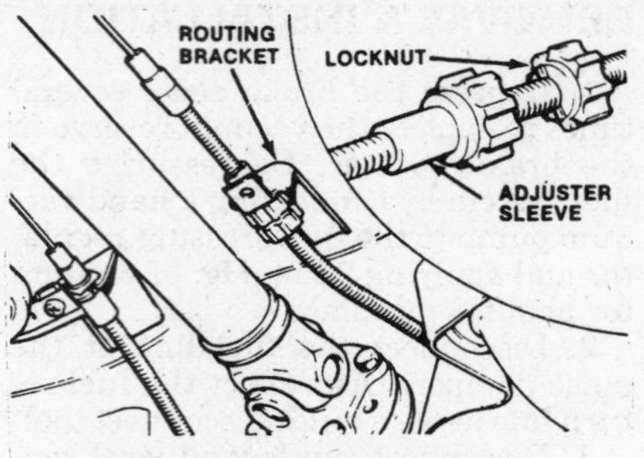


**Parking brake adjustment**

## Parking Brake Cable

### ADJUSTMENT

#### *XR4Ti*

**NOTE: Parking brake stop plungers are installed in both rear backing plates. These plungers are used to determine correct parking brake cable adjustments.**

1. Fully release the parking brake. Pump the brake pedal to make sure the brake lining self adjuster is properly set.

2. Place the transmission in **N** and raise the rear axle until the rear wheels clear the floor.

3. Loosen the adjuster locknut, located on the cable at the routing bracket under the vehicle, and rotate the adjuster sleeve along the cable casing until in and out movement can be felt at both parking brake stop plungers.

**CAUTION**

***Both the adjuster and locknut are threaded onto the cable casing. Any attempt to pry them apart will result in damage to the sleeve and/or locknut. To loosen the locknut, hold the adjuster with pliers and turn the locknut counterclockwise with another set of pliers.***

4. Tighten the adjuster against the retaining bracket until a slight movement is felt at each stop plunger. When added together, the total movement of the plungers should not exceed 0.16 in. (4mm).

5. Tighten the locknut by hand against the sleeve as much as possible, then tighten the locknut an additional 2 clicks using suitable pliers. Turn the rear wheels by hand to make sure the brake linings are not dragging against the drum.

6. Lower the rear of the vehicle and check the operation of the parking brake.

*Scorpio*

1. Raise and safely support the vehicle. Release the parking brake lever.
2. Remove the adjusting locknut retainer. Loosen the adjuster locknut and adjuster nut until both parking brake levers have fully returned to the caliper stops.
3. Paint reference marks on both the caliper lever and housing for position reference.
4. Turn the adjuster nut until the parking brake levers start to move away from their stops. Finger tighten the locknut against the adjuster nut. Use a wrench and tighten the locknut to a minimum of 3 clicks and no more than 6 clicks. A complete revolution of the locknut equals 6 clicks.
5. Install the locknut retainer. Lower the vehicle. Check parking brake application.

### REMOVAL & INSTALLATION

*XR4Ti*

1. Release the parking brake. Raise and safely support the vehicle.
2. Loosen the brake cable adjuster locknut.
3. Remove the rear wheels and brake drums. Remove the brake shoes on both sides of the vehicle.
4. Using a screwdriver, spread the retaining clip and pull the cable out of the backing plate.
5. Remove the clip and clevis pin attaching the cable equalizer to the parking brake lever in the passenger compartment.
6. Using a prybar, open the routing clamps and disengage the cable from both control arms, then, thread the cable through the body brackets and remove it from the vehicle.
7. To install, reverse the removal procedures; make sure the cable adjuster is on the left (driver's) side of the vehicle. Adjust the parking brake cable.

*Scorpio*

1. Raise and safely support the vehicle. Remove both rear wheels.
2. Remove the adjuster locknut retainer. Loosen the adjuster nut.
3. Remove the circlip and clevis pin that attaches the cable yoke to the parking brake lever rod.
4. Remove the circlip that attaches the cable to the caliper levers. Remove the cable from the calipers and guide sleeves.
5. Remove the cable from the lower arm retaining clips.
6. Remove the circlip that retains the outer cable (non adjusting) to the retaining bracket. Remove the cable from the bracket.
7. Pull the cable through the lower arm and remove the cable.
8. To install, reverse the removal procedures. Adjust the parking brake cable.

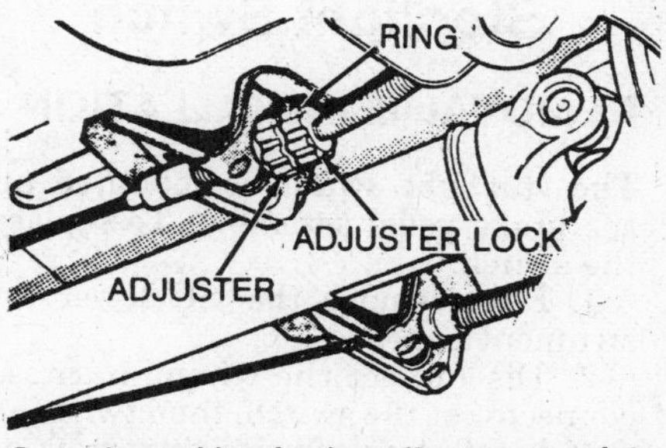

**Scorpio parking brake adjustment points**

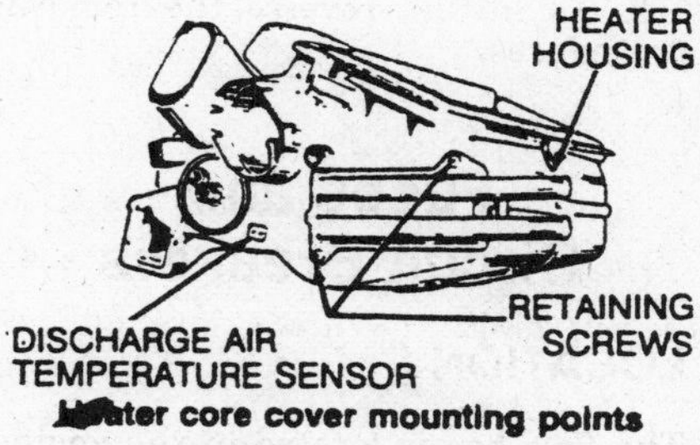

**Heater core cover mounting points**

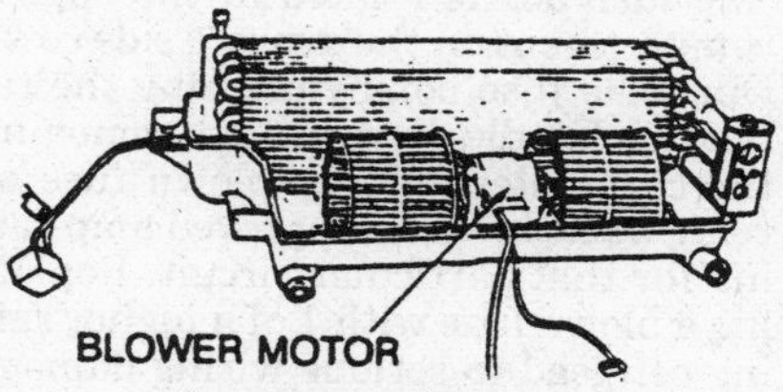

**Blower motor location**

# CHASSIS ELECTRICAL

## Heater Blower Motor

### REMOVAL & INSTALLATION

**NOTE: Evaporator case removal is required for blower motor replacement.**

1. Remove the evaporator case from the vehicle.
2. Remove the access cover screws and the cover.
3. Remove the screws retaining the scrolls to the lower case assembly. Remove the screws retaining the thermostat.
4. Separate the evaporator case halves after removing the retaining clips.
5. Remove the blower motor mounting screw and the blower motor.
6. To install, reverse the removal procedures; be sure to align the thermostat sensor during installation.

## Heater Core

### REMOVAL & INSTALLATION

1. Disconnect the negative battery cable.
2. Drain the cooling system. Remove the heater hoses from the heater core tubes at the firewall. Plug the core tubes.
3. Remove the tube cover screws, the cover and the plate from the firewall.
4. From inside the vehicle, remove the center console and move it rearward. Remove the right side footwell trim panel.
5. Disconnect the heater control lever. Disconnect the electrical leads from the glove compartment lamp, air conditioning blower switch and cigarette lighter.
6. Remove the ash tray, radio, ECA and anti-lock module (if equipped). Remove the right hand dash panel.
7. Remove all duct hoses from the heater housing.
8. Detach the control cables from the heater housing.
9. Remove the heater housing-to-firewall screws. Pull the heater into the vehicle until the core tubes are clear of the firewall and pull the housing toward the right side of the vehicle for removal.
10. Remove the heater core from the housing.
11. To install, reverse order of removal. Refill the cooling system. Start the engine, allow it to reach normal operating temperatures and check for leaks.

## Radio

### REMOVAL & INSTALLATION

1. Disconnect the negative battery cable.
2. Insert 2 radio removal tools T85M-19061-A, 1 on each side, into the access holes on the front of the radio until a click is heard.
3. Apply an outward side pressure to release the locking tangs and slide the radio forward from the dash.
4. Disconnect the antenna, speaker, ground and power leads from the radio.
5. Disengage the special removal tools by depressing the locking tangs on the side of the radio while applying a slight inward pressure on the tool, then, pull the tool from the access holes.
6. To install, reverse the removal

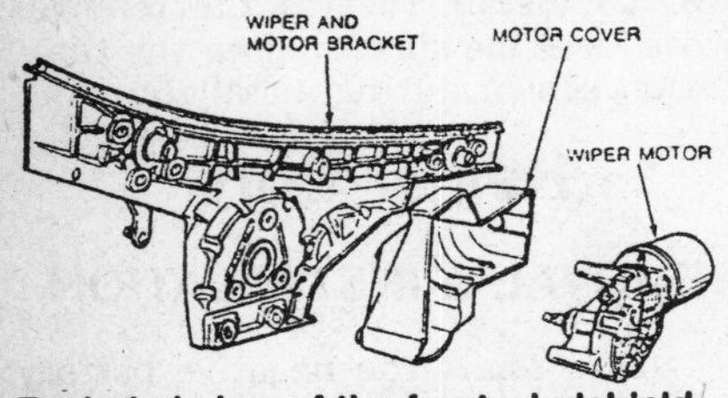


**Exploded view of the front windshield wiper motor assembly**

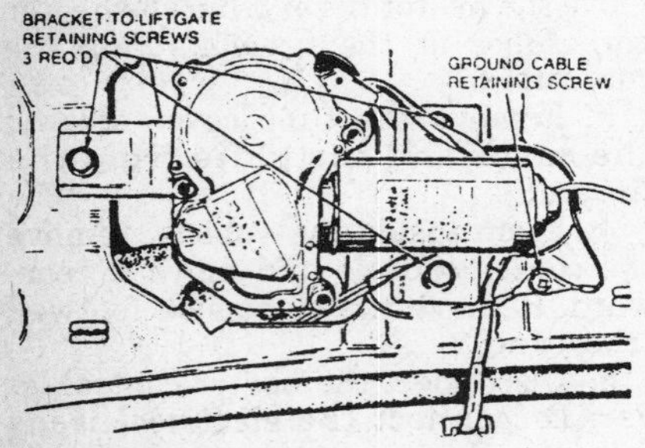


**Exploded view of the rear wiper motor assembly**

procedures. Remove the plastic support bracket from the rear of the radio and install it on the replacement unit.

## Windshield Wiper Switch

### REMOVAL & INSTALLATION

The windshield wiper/washer is a part of the combination switch.

### REMOVAL & INSTALLATION

1. Disconnect the negative battery cable.
2. Remove the steering wheel and the upper/lower steering column shrouds; there is a screw near the hazard flasher switch and 2 under the column, on either side of the hood release lever.
3. Remove the sound panels from the underside of the dash. Be careful to disconnect courtesy lights and radio speaker connectors before removing the column completely.
4. Remove the switch-to-column screws. Disengage the switch from the column, disconnect the wire connectors and remove the switch from the steering column.
5. To install, align the switch mounting holes with the corresponding holes in the housing and reverse the removal procedures.

## Windshield Wiper Motor

### REMOVAL & INSTALLATION

#### *Front Motor*

The internal magnets used in the wiper motor are a ceramic material. Exercise care when handling the motor to avoid damaging the magnets by dropping or striking with metal tools. The ceramic magnets cannot tolerate sharp impacts.

1. Operate the wiper motor and turn **OFF** key when the linkage mounting nut is exposed, then, remove the arm and blade assembly.
2. Disconnect the negative battery cable.
3. Remove the linkage-to-motor locknut and disconnect the linkage from the motor shaft.
4. Remove the motor-to-chassis bolts and the motor. Disconnect the electrical harness plug.
5. To install, reverse the removal procedures. Torque the:
   Motor bolts – 7–9 ft. lbs. (10–12 Nm)
   Linkage locknut – 13–15 ft. lbs. (18–20 Nm)

#### *Rear Motor*

1. Lift the plastic cover at the base of the wiper arm to expose the mounting nut. Remove the nut, then, lift the wiper arm and blade assembly from the pivot shaft.
2. Open the hatch and remove the trim panel by carefully prying out the panel clips from their locations.
3. Remove the wiper motor bracket-to-liftgate bolts. Remove the ground lead screw and disconnect the wire harness plug. Remove the motor and bracket as an assembly. Disconnect the rear washer supply hose from the wiper.
4. To install, reverse the removal procedures. Torque the:
   Wiper motor bracket bolts – 4–5 ft. lbs. (6–7 Nm)
   Wiper arm attaching nut – 7–9 ft. lbs. (10–12 Nm)

## Instrument Cluster

### REMOVAL & INSTALLATION

1. Disconnect the negative battery cable.
2. Remove the upper steering column shroud screws and the shroud.
3. Remove the rheostat and intermittent wiper control from the instrument panel, if equipped.
4. Remove the bezel screws and the bezel.
5. Remove the cluster panel-to-dash screws.
6. Pull the cluster forward and disconnect the speedometer cable and wiring harness connectors from the instrument cluster. Remove the cluster.
7. To install, reverse the removal procedures.

## Headlight Switch

The headlight switch is a part the of the combination switch.

### REMOVAL & INSTALLATION

1. Disconnect the negative battery cable.
2. Remove the steering wheel and the upper/lower steering column shrouds; there is a screw near the hazard flasher switch and 2 under the column, on either side of the hood release lever.
3. Remove the sound panels from the underside of the dash. Be careful to disconnect courtesy lights and radio speaker connectors before removing the column completely.
4. Remove the switch-to-column screws. Disengage the switch from the column, disconnect the wire connectors and remove the switch from the steering column.
5. To install, align the switch mounting holes with the corresponding holes in the housing and continue in the reverse order of removal.

## Stoplight Switch

### REMOVAL & INSTALLATION

The stoplight switch is mounted on the brake pedal assembly. To replace the switch:

1. First remove the left lower instrument panel.
2. Disconnect the wiring harness connector at the switch, then twist the switch counterclockwise to remove it from its mounting bracket.
3. To install, reverse the removal procedures.

## Fuses and Circuit Breakers

### LOCATION

The fuse box is located in the engine compartment on the driver's side cowl. Open the fuse box by pressing the retaining handle inward and removing the cover. Replace any blown fuse or relay with the same approved amp rating for that particular circuit. Replacing a blown fuse with 1 of a higher rating can lead to serious wiring damage and a possible fire.

# Mitsubishi

## Cordia, Galant, Mirage, Precis, Sigma, Starion, Tredia

# 12

# SERIAL NUMBER IDENTIFICATION

## Vehicle Identification Plate

The vehicle identification number (VIN) is mounted on the instrument panel, adjacent to the lower corner of the windshield on the driver's side and is visible through the windshield.
A standard 17 digit VIN code is used, the tenth digit identifies model year:

**D** represents 1983
**E** represents 1984
**F** represents 1985
**G** represents 1986
**H** represents 1987
**I** represents 1988
**J** represents 1989
**K** represents 1990

The eighth digit identifies the installed engine.
A vehicle information code plate is riveted onto the front of the right side wheelhouse or onto the firewall (depending on model). The plate shows model code, engine model, transaxle model and body color code.
A chassis number plate is located on the top center of the firewall in the engine compartment.

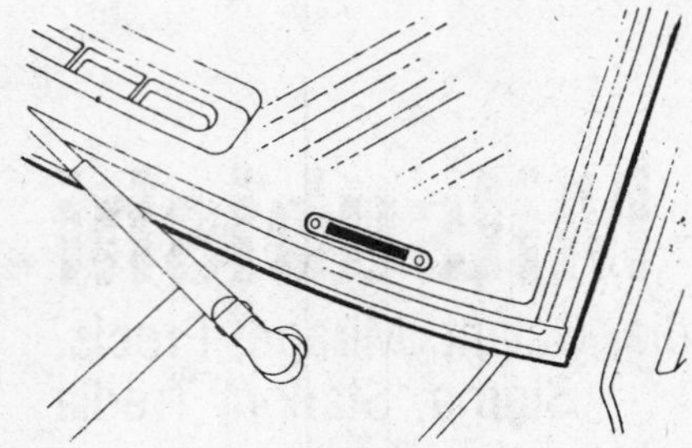

VIN location

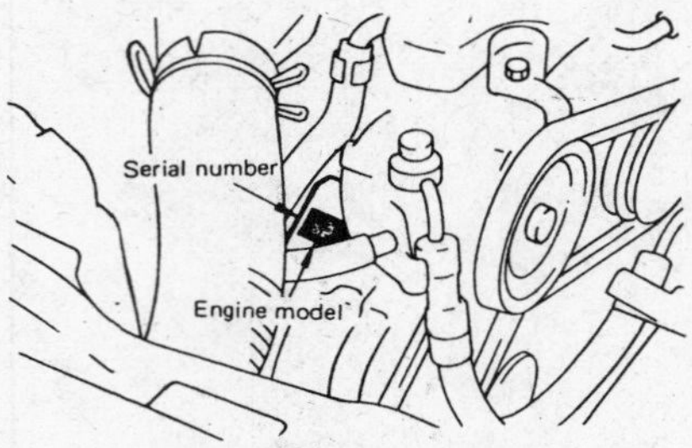


Engine number location

## Engine Number

The engine model and serial numbers in all cases are stamped on the block near the front of the engine. In most cases, they are located on the right side.

Engine codes for all years are as follows:

**6G72** for the 2972cc (181.4 CID) engine
**G45B** for the 2555cc (155.9 CID) engine
**G62B** for the 1795cc (109.5 CID) engine
**G63B** for the 1997cc (121.9 CID) engine
**G15B** for the 1468cc (89.6 CID) engine
**G32B** for the 1597cc (97.4 CID) engine
**G64B** for the 2350cc (143.4 CID) engine

## Transmission Number

The transmission identification number is located below the engine number on the vehicle information code plate.

### ENGINE IDENTIFICATION

| Year | Model | Engine Displacement cu. in. (cc/liter) | Engine Series Identification | No. of Cylinders | Engine Type |
|---|---|---|---|---|---|
| 1983 | Cordia | 109.5 (1795/1.8) | G62B | 4 | OHC |
| | Tredia | 109.5 (1795/1.8) | G62B | 4 | OHC |
| | Starion | 155.9 (2555/2.5) | G54B | 4 | OHC |
| 1984 | Cordia | 109.5 (1795/1.8 | G62B | 4 | OHC |
| | Cordia | 121.9 (1997/2.0) | G63B | 4 | OHC |
| | Tredia | 109.5 (1795/1.8) | G62B | 4 | OHC |
| | Tredia | 121.9 (1997/2.0) | G63B | 4 | OHC |
| | Starion | 155.9 (2555/2.5) | G54B | 4 | OHC |

## ENGINE IDENTIFICATION

| Year | Model | Engine Displacement cu. in. (cc/liter) | Engine Series Identification | No. of Cylinders | Engine Type |
|---|---|---|---|---|---|
| 1985 | Cordia | 109.5 (1795/1.8) | G62B | 4 | OHC |
| | Cordia | 121.9 (1997/2.0) | G63B | 4 | OHC |
| | Tredia | 109.5 (1795/1.8) | G62B | 4 | OHC |
| | Tredia | 121.9 (1997/2.0) | G63B | 4 | OHC |
| | Starion | 155.9 (2555/2.5) | G54B | 4 | OHC |
| | Mirage | 89.6 (1468/1.5) | G15B | 4 | OHC |
| | Mirage | 97.4 (1597/1.6) | G32B | 4 | OHC |
| | Galant | 143.4 (2350/2.3) | G64B | 4 | OHC |
| 1986 | Cordia | 109.5 (1795/1.8) | G62B | 4 | OHC |
| | Cordia | 121.9 (1997/2.0) | G63B | 4 | OHC |
| | Tredia | 109.5 (1795/1.8) | G62B | 4 | OHC |
| | Tredia | 121.9 (1997/2.0) | G63B | 4 | OHC |
| | Starion | 155.9 (2555/2.5) | G54B | 4 | OHC |
| | Mirage | 89.6 (1468/1.5) | G15B | 4 | OHC |
| | Mirage | 97.4 (1597/1.6) | G32B | 4 | OHC |
| | Galant | 143.4 (2350/2.3) | G64B | 4 | OHC |
| 1987 | Cordia | 109.5 (1795/1.8) | G62B | 4 | SOHC |
| | Cordia | 121.9 (1997/2.0) | G63B | 4 | SOHC |
| | Tredia | 109.5 (1795/1.8) | G62B | 4 | SOHC |
| | Tredia | 121.9 (1997/2.0) | G63B | 4 | SOHC |
| | Starion | 155.9 (2555/2.5) | G54B | 4 | SOHC |
| | Mirage | 89.6 (1468/1.5) | G15B | 4 | SOHC |
| | Mirage | 97.4 (1597/1.6) | G32B | 4 | SOHC |
| | Galant | 143.4 (2350/2.3) | G64B | 4 | SOHC |
| | Precis | 89.6 (1468/1.5) | G15B | 4 | SOHC |
| 1988 | Cordia | 109.5 (1795/1.8) | G62B | 4 | SOHC |
| | Cordia | 121.9 (1997/2.0) | G63B | 4 | SOHC |
| | Tredia | 109.5 (1795/1.8) | G62B | 4 | SOHC |
| | Tredia | 121.9 (1997/2.0) | G63B | 4 | SOHC |
| | Starion | 155.9 (2555/2.5) | G54B | 4 | SOHC |
| | Mirage | 89.6 (1468/1.5) | G15B | 4 | SOHC |
| | Mirage | 97.4 (1597/1.6) | G32B | 4 | SOHC |
| | Galant | 143.4 (2350/2.3) | G64B | 4 | SOHC |
| | Galant | 181.4 (2972/3.0) | 6G72 | 6 | SOHC |
| | Precis | 89.6 (1468/1.5) | G15B | 4 | SOHC |
| 1989-90 | Starion | 155.9 (2555/2.5) | G64B | 4 | SOHC |
| | Mirage | 89.6 (1468/1.5) | 4G61 | 4 | SOHC |
| | Mirage | 97.4 (1597/1.6) | 4G61 | 4 | DOHC |
| | Galant | 122 (1997/2.0) | 4G63 | 4 | SOHC & DOHC |
| | Sigma | 181.4 (2972/3.0) | 6G72 | 6 | SOHC |
| | Precis | 89.6 (1468/1.5) | G15B | 4 | SOHC |

## GENERAL ENGINE SPECIFICATIONS

| Year | Model | Engine Displacement cu. in. (cc) | Fuel System Type | Net Horsepower @ rpm | Net Torque @ rpm (ft. lbs.) | Bore × Stroke (in.) | Com-pression Ratio | Oil Pressure @ rpm |
|---|---|---|---|---|---|---|---|---|
| 1983 | Cordia | 109.5 (1795) | Carb. | 82 @ 5000 | 93 @ 3000 | 3.17 × 3.46 | 7.5:1 | 63① |
| | Tredia | 109.5 (1795) | Carb. | 82 @ 5000 | 93 @ 3000 | 3.17 × 3.46 | 7.5:1 | 63① |
| | Starion | 155.9 (2555) | ECI② | 145 @ 5000 | 185 @ 2500 | 3.59 × 3.86 | 7.0:1 | 63① |
| 1984 | Cordia | 109.5 (1795) | ECI② | 120 @ 5500 | 110 @ 2600 | 3.17 × 3.46 | 7.5.1 | 63① |
| | Cordia | 121.9 (1997) | Carb. | 110 @ 5000 | 117 @ 3000 | 3.35 × 3.46 | 8.5:1 | 63① |
| | Tredia | 109.5 (1795) | ECI② | 120 @ 5500 | 110 @ 2600 | 3.17 × 3.46 | 7.5:1 | 63① |
| | Tredia | 121.9 (1997) | Carb. | 110 @ 5000 | 117 @ 3000 | 3.35 × 3.46 | 8.5:1 | 63① |
| | Starion | 155.9 (2555) | ECI② | 145 @ 5000 | 185 @ 2500 | 3.59 × 3.86 | 7.0:1 | 63① |
| 1985 | Cordia | 109.5 (1795) | ECI② | 116 @ 5500 | 129 @ 3000 | 3.17 × 3.46 | 7.5:1 | 63① |
| | Cordia | 121.9 (1997) | Carb. | 88 @ 5000 | 108 @ 3500 | 3.35 × 3.46 | 8.5:1 | 63① |
| | Tredia | 109.5 (1795) | ECI② | 116 @ 5500 | 129 @ 3000 | 3.17 × 3.46 | 7.5:1 | 63① |
| | Tredia | 121.9 (1997) | Carb. | 88 @ 5000 | 108 @ 3500 | 3.35 × 3.46 | 8.5:1 | 63① |
| | Starion | 155.9 (2555) | ECI② | 145 @ 5000 | 185 @ 2500 | 3.59 × 3.86 | 7.0:1 | 63① |
| | Mirage | 89.6 (1468) | Carb. | 68 @ 5500 | 82 @ 3500 | 2.97 × 3.23 | 9.4:1 | 63① |
| | Mirage | 97.4 (1597) | ECI② | 102 @ 5500 | 122 @ 3000 | 3.03 × 3.39 | 7.6:1 | 63① |
| | Galant | 143.4 (2350) | ECI② | 101 @ 5000 | 131 @ 2500 | 3.41 × 3.94 | 8.5:1 | 63① |
| 1986 | Cordia | 109.5 (1795) | ECI② | 116 @ 5500 | 129 @ 3000 | 3.17 × 3.46 | 7.5:1 | 63① |
| | Cordia | 121.9 (1997) | Carb. | 88 @ 5000 | 108 @ 3500 | 3.35 × 3.46 | 8.5:1 | 63① |
| | Tredia | 109.5 (1795) | ECI② | 116 @ 5500 | 129 @ 3000 | 3.17 × 3.46 | 7.5:1 | 63① |
| | Tredia | 121.9 (1997) | Carb. | 88 @ 5000 | 108 @ 3500 | 3.35 × 3.46 | 8.5:1 | 63① |
| | Starion | 155.9 (2555) | ECI② | 145 @ 5000 | 185 @ 2500 | 3.59 × 3.86 | 7.0:1 | 63① |
| | Mirage | 89.6 (1468) | Carb. | 68 @ 5000 | 82 @ 3500 | 2.97 × 3.23 | 9.4:1 | 63① |
| | Mirage | 97.4 (1597) | ECI② | 102 @ 5500 | 122 @ 3000 | 3.03 × 3.39 | 7.6:1 | 63① |
| | Galant | 143.4 (2350) | MPI③ | 110 @ 4500 | 138 @ 3500 | 3.41 × 3.94 | 8.5:1 | 63① |
| 1987 | Cordia | 109.5 (1795) | ECI② | 116 @ 5500 | 129 @ 3000 | 3.17 × 3.46 | 7.5:1 | 63① |
| | Cordia | 121.9 (1997) | Carb. | 88 @ 5000 | 108 @ 3500 | 3.35 × 3.46 | 8.5:1 | 63① |
| | Tredia | 109.5 (1795) | ECI② | 116 @ 5500 | 129 @ 3000 | 3.17 × 3.46 | 7.5:1 | 63① |
| | Tredia | 121.9 (1997) | Carb. | 88 @ 5000 | 108 @ 3500 | 3.35 × 3.46 | 8.5:1 | 63① |
| | Starion | 155.9 (2555) | ECI② | 145 @ 5000 | 185 @ 2500 | 3.59 × 3.86 | 7.0:1 | 63① |
| | Mirage | 89.6 (1468) | Carb. | 68 @ 5000 | 82 @ 3500 | 2.97 × 3.23 | 9.4:1 | 63① |
| | Mirage | 97.4 (1597) | ECI② | 102 @ 5500 | 122 @ 3000 | 3.03 × 3.39 | 7.6:1 | 63① |
| | Galant | 143.4 (2350) | MPI③ | 110 @ 4500 | 138 @ 3500 | 3.41 × 3.94 | 8.5:1 | 63① |
| | Precis | 89.6 (1468) | Carb. | 68 @ 5000 | 82 @ 3500 | 2.97 × 3.23 | 9.4:1 | 63① |
| 1988 | Cordia | 109.5 (1795) | ECI② | 116 @ 5500 | 129 @ 3000 | 3.17 × 3.46 | 7.5:1 | 63① |
| | Cordia | 121.9 (1997) | Carb. | 88 @ 5000 | 108 @ 3500 | 3.35 × 3.46 | 8.5:1 | 63① |
| | Tredia | 109.5 (1795) | ECI② | 116 @ 5500 | 129 @ 3000 | 3.17 × 3.46 | 7.5:1 | 63① |
| | Tredia | 121.9 (1997) | Carb. | 88 @ 5000 | 108 @ 3500 | 3.35 × 3.46 | 8.5:1 | 63① |
| | Starion | 155.9 (2555) | ECI② | 145 @ 5000 | 185 @ 2500 | 3.59 × 3.86 | 7.0:1 | 63① |

## GENERAL ENGINE SPECIFICATIONS

| Year | Model | Engine Displacement cu. in. (cc) | Fuel System Type | Net Horsepower @ rpm | Net Torque @ rpm (ft. lbs.) | Bore × Stroke (in.) | Com-pression Ratio | Oil Pressure @ rpm |
|---|---|---|---|---|---|---|---|---|
| 1988 | Mirage | 89.6 (1468) | Carb. | 68 @ 5000 | 82 @ 3500 | 2.97 × 3.23 | 9.4:1 | 63① |
| | Mirage | 97.4 (1597) | ECI② | 102 @ 5500 | 122 @ 3000 | 3.03 × 3.39 | 7.6:1 | 63① |
| | Galant | 143.4 (2350) | MPI③ | 110 @ 4500 | 138 @ 3500 | 3.41 × 3.94 | 8.5:1 | 63① |
| | Galant | 181.1 (2972) | MPI③ | 142 @ 5000 | 168 @ 2500 | 3.59 × 2.99 | 8.9:1 | 63① |
| | Precis | 89.6 (1468) | Carb. | 68 @ 5500 | 82 @ 3500 | 2.97 × 3.23 | 9.4:1 | 63① |
| 1989-90 | Starion | 155.9 (2555) | ECI② | 145 @ 5000 | 185 @ 2500 | 3.59 × 3.86 | 7.0:1 | 63① |
| | Mirage | 86.6 (1468) | Carb. | 68 @ 5000 | 82 @ 3500 | 2.97 × 3.23 | 9.4:1 | 63① |
| | Mirage | 97.4 (1597) | ECI② | 102 @ 5500 | 122 @ 3000 | 3.03 × 3.39 | 7.6:1 | 63① |
| | Galant | 122 (1997)④ | MPI③ | 120 @ 5000 | 116 @ 4500 | 3.35 × 3.46 | 8.5:1 | 11.4 @ 750 |
| | Galant | 122 (1997)⑤ | MPI③ | 135 @ 6000 | 125 @ 5000 | 3.35 × 3.46 | 9.0:1 | 11.4 @ 750 |
| | Sigma | 181.1 (2972) | MPI③ | 142 @ 5000 | 168 @ 2500 | 3.59 × 2.99 | 8.9:1 | 63① |
| | Precis | 89.6 (1468) | Carb. | 68 @ 5500 | 82 @ 3500 | 2.97 × 3.23 | 9.4:1 | 63① |

① Relief valve opening pressure
② Electronic controlled injection
③ Multi-point injection
④ Single overhead camshaft
⑤ Double overhead camshaft

## TUNE-UP SPECIFICATIONS

| Year | Model | Engine Displacement cu. in. (cc) | Spark Plugs Type | Spark Plugs Gap (in.) | Ignition Timing (deg.) MT | Ignition Timing (deg.) AT | Com-pression Pressure (psi) | Fuel Pump (psi) | Idle Speed (rpm) MT | Idle Speed (rpm) AT | Valve Clearance① In. | Valve Clearance① Ex. |
|---|---|---|---|---|---|---|---|---|---|---|---|---|
| 1983 | Cordia | 109.5 (1795) | BUR6EA-11 | 0.039-0.043 | 5B | 5B | 170③ | 2.4-3.4 | 650 | 750 | 0.006 | 0.010 |
| | Tredia | 109.5 (1795) | BUR6EA-11 | 0.039-0.043 | 5B | 5B | 170③ | 2.4-3.4 | 650 | 750 | 0.006 | 0.010 |
| | Starion | 155.9 (2555) | BUR6EA-11 | 0.039-0.043 | 10B | — | 170③ | 35-47 | 850 | — | 0.006 | 0.010 |
| 1984 | Cordia | 109.5 (1795) | BPR7ES-11 | 0.039-0.043 | 5B | 5B | 170③ | 35-47 | 750 | — | 0.006 | 0.010 |
| | Cordia | 121.9 (1997) | BPR6ES-11 | 0.039-0.043 | 5B | 5B | 170③ | 2.4-3.4 | 700② | 750② | 0.006 | 0.010 |
| | Tredia | 109.5 (1795) | BPR7ES-11 | 0.039-0.043 | 5B | 5B | 170③ | 35-47 | 750 | — | 0.006 | 0.010 |
| | Tredia | 121.9 (1997) | BPR6ES-11 | 0.039-0.043 | 5B | 5B | 170③ | 2.4-3.4 | 700② | 750② | 0.006 | 0.010 |
| | Starion | 155.9 (2555) | BUR6EA-11 | 0.039-0.043 | 10B | 10B | 170③ | 35-47 | 750 | 850 | 0.006 | 0.010 |
| 1985 | Cordia | 109.5 (1795) | BPR7ES-11 | 0.039-0.043 | 5B | 5B | 170③ | 35-47 | 750 | 750 | 0.006 | 0.010 |
| | Cordia | 121.9 (1997) | BPR6ES-11 | 0.039-0.043 | 5B | 5B | 170③ | 2.4-3.4 | 700② | 750② | Hyd. | Hyd. |
| | Tredia | 109.5 (1795) | BPR7ES-11 | 0.039-0.043 | 5B | 5B | 170③ | 35-47 | 750 | 750 | 0.006 | 0.010 |
| | Tredia | 121.9 (1997) | BPR6ES-11 | 0.039-0.043 | 5B | 5B | 170③ | 2.4-3.4 | 700② | 750② | Hyd. | Hyd. |
| | Starion | 155.9 (2555) | BUR6EZ-11 | 0.039-0.043 | 10B | 10B | 170③ | 35-47 | 750 | 850 | 0.006 | 0.010 |
| | Mirage | 89.6 (1468) | W20EP-U10 | 0.039-0.043 | 3B | 3B | 170③ | — | 700 | 750 | 0.006 | 0.010 |
| | Mirage | 97.4 (1597) | BUR7EA-11 | 0.039-0.043 | 8B | 8B | 170③ | 36 | 700 | — | 0.006 | 0.010 |
| | Galant | 143.4 (2350) | BPR6ES-11 | 0.039-0.043 | — | 5B | 170③ | 36 | — | 750 | Hyd. | Hyd. |

## TUNE-UP SPECIFICATIONS

| Year | Model | Engine Displacement cu. in. (cc) | Spark Plugs Type | Spark Plugs Gap (in.) | Ignition Timing (deg.) MT | Ignition Timing (deg.) AT | Compression Pressure (psi) | Fuel Pump (psi) | Idle Speed (rpm) MT | Idle Speed (rpm) AT | Valve Clearance① In. | Valve Clearance① Ex. |
|---|---|---|---|---|---|---|---|---|---|---|---|---|
| 1986 | Cordia | 109.5 (1795) | BUR7EZ-11 | 0.035–0.039 | 5B | 5B | 170③ | 35–47 | 750 | 750 | 0.006 | 0.010 |
| | Cordia | 121.9 (1997) | BPR6ES-11 | 0.035–0.039 | 5B | 5B | 170③ | 2.4–3.4 | 700② | 750② | Hyd. | Hyd. |
| | Tredia | 109.5 (1795) | BUR7EZ-11 | 0.035–0.039 | 5B | 5B | 170③ | 35–47 | 750 | 750 | 0.006 | 0.010 |
| | Tredia | 121.9 (1997) | BPR6ES-11 | 0.035–0.039 | 5B | 5B | 170③ | 2.4–3.4 | 700② | 750② | Hyd. | Hyd. |
| | Starion | 155.9 (2555) | BP6ES-11 | 0.039–0.043 | 10B | 10B | 170③ | 35–47 | 750 | 850 | 0.006 | 0.010 |
| | Mirage | 89.6 (1468) | W20EP-U10 | 0.039–0.043 | 3B | 3B | 170③ | — | 700 | 750 | 0.006 | 0.010 |
| | Mirage | 97.4 (1597) | BUR7EZ-11 | 0.035–0.039 | 8B | 8B | 170③ | 36 | 700 | — | 0.006 | 0.010 |
| | Galant | 143.4 (2350) | BPR6ES-11 | 0.039–0.043 | — | 5B | 170③ | 36 | — | 750 | Hyd. | Hyd. |
| 1987 | Cordia | 109.5 (1795) | BUR7EZ-11 | 0.035–0.039 | 5B | 5B | 170③ | 35–47 | 750 | 750 | 0.006 | 0.010 |
| | Cordia | 121.9 (1997) | BPR6ES-11 | 0.035–0.039 | 5B | 5B | 170③ | 2.4–3.4 | 700② | 750② | Hyd. | Hyd. |
| | Tredia | 109.5 (1795) | BUR7EZ-11 | 0.035–0.039 | 5B | 5B | 170③ | 35–47 | 750 | 750 | 0.006 | 0.010 |
| | Tredia | 121.9 (1997) | BPR6ES-11 | 0.035–0.039 | 5B | 5B | 170③ | 2.4–3.4 | 700② | 750② | Hyd. | Hyd. |
| | Starion | 155.9 (2555) | BP6ES-11 | 0.039–0.043 | 10B | 10B | 170③ | 35–47 | 750 | 850 | 0.006 | 0.010 |
| | Mirage | 89.6 (1468) | W20EP-10 | 0.039–0.043 | 3B | 3B | 170③ | — | 700 | 750 | 0.006 | 0.010 |
| | Mirage | 97.4 (1597) | BUR7EZ-11 | 0.035–0.039 | 8B | 8B | 170③ | 36 | 700 | — | 0.006 | 0.010 |
| | Galant | 143.4 (2350) | BPR6ES-11 | 0.039–0.043 | — | 5B | 170③ | 36 | — | 750 | Hyd. | Hyd. |
| | Precis | 89.6 (1468) | W20EP-10 | 0.039–0.043 | 3B | 3B | 170③ | — | 700 | 750 | 0.006 | 0.010 |
| 1988 | Cordia | 109.5 (1795) | BUR7EZ-11 | 0.035–0.039 | 5B | 5B | 170③ | 35–47 | 750 | 750 | 0.006 | 0.010 |
| | Cordia | 121.9 (1997) | BPR6ES-11 | 0.035–0.039 | 5B | 5B | 170③ | 2.4–3.4 | 700② | 750② | Hyd. | Hyd. |
| | Tredia | 109.5 (1795) | BUR7EZ-11 | 0.035–0.039 | 5B | 5B | 170③ | 35–47 | 750 | 750 | 0.006 | 0.010 |
| | Tredia | 121.9 (1997) | BPR6ES-11 | 0.035–0.039 | 5B | 5B | 170③ | 2.4–3.4 | 700② | 750② | Hyd. | Hyd. |
| | Starion | 155.9 (2555) | BP6ES-11 | 0.039–0.043 | 10B | 10B | 170③ | 35–47 | 750 | 850 | 0.006 | 0.010 |
| | Mirage | 89.6 (1468) | W20EP-10 | 0.039–0.043 | 3B | 3B | 170③ | — | 700 | 750 | 0.006 | 0.010 |
| | Mirage | 97.4 (1597) | BUR7EZ-11 | 0.035–0.039 | 8B | 8B | 170③ | 36 | 700 | — | 0.006 | 0.010 |
| | Galant | 143.4 (2350) | BPR6ES-11 | 0.039–0.043 | — | 5B | 170③ | 36 | — | 750 | Hyd. | Hyd. |
| | Galant | 181.4 (2972) | PGR5A-11 | 0.039–0.043 | 5B | 5B | 170③ | 38 | 700 | 700 | Hyd. | Hyd. |
| | Precis | 89.6 (1468) | W20EP-10 | 0.039–0.043 | 3B | 3B | 164③ | — | 700 | 750 | 0.006 | 0.010 |
| 1989 | Starion | 155.9 (2555) | BP6ES-11 | 0.039–0.043 | 10B | 10B | 170③ | 35–47 | 750 | 850 | 0.006 | 0.010 |
| | Mirage | 89.6 (1468) | W20EP-10 | 0.039–0.043 | 3B | 3B | 170③ | — | 700 | 750 | 0.006 | 0.010 |
| | Mirage | 97.4 (1597) | BUR7EZ-11 | 0.035–0.039 | 8B | 8B | 170③ | 36 | 700 | — | 0.006 | 0.010 |
| | Galant | 122 (1997) | BPR6ES | 0.039–0.043 | — | 5B | 125 | 64–85 | — | 750 | 0.0004–0.0016 | 0.0004–0.0016 |
| | Galant | 122 (1997) | BPR6ES | 0.039–0.043 | — | 5B | 125 | 64–85 | — | 750 | 0.0004–0.0016 | 0.0004–0.0016 |
| | Sigma | 181.4 (2972) | PGR5A-11 | 0.039–0.043 | 5B | 5B | 170③ | —38 | 700 | 700 | Hyd. | Hyd. |
| | Precis | 89.6 (1468) | W20EP-10 | 0.039–0.043 | 3B | 3B | 164③ | — | 700 | 750 | 0.006 | 0.010 |
| 1990 | ALL | SEE UNDERHOOD SPECIFICATIONS STICKER | | | | | | | | | | |

① Jet Valve—0.010
② With air conditioning
Manual transaxle—750
Automatic transaxle—850
③ Standard Valve—136 Limit

## FIRING ORDERS

**NOTE: To avoid confusion, always replace spark wires one at a time.**

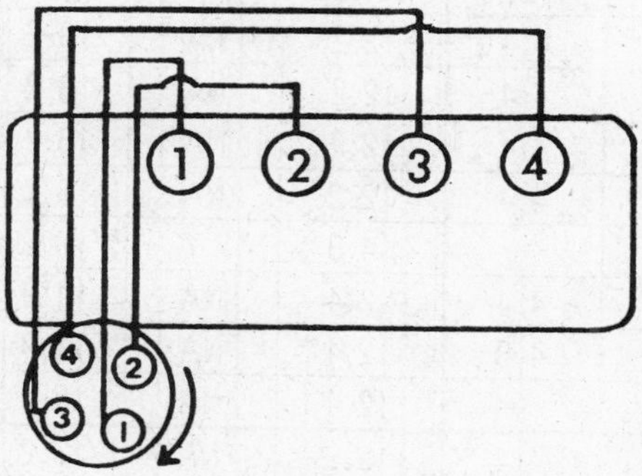


1468, 1597, 1795, 1997 and 2350cc engines

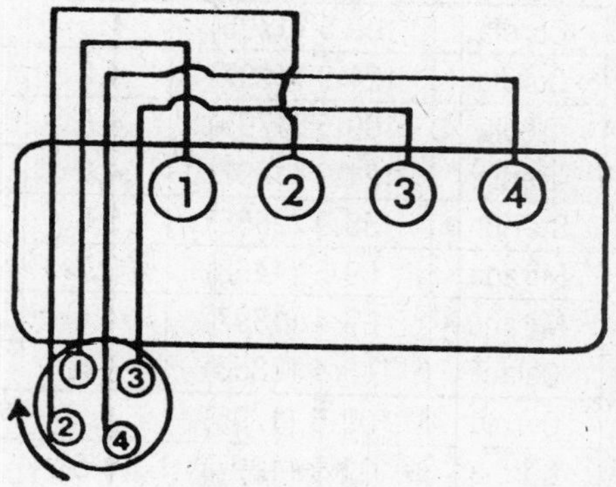


2555cc engine

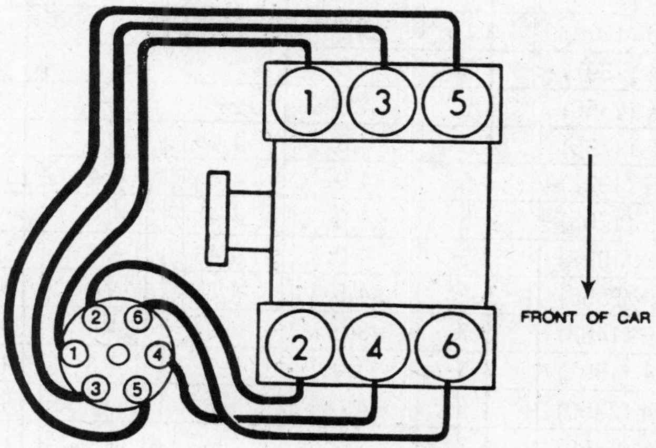


2972 (181.4) V6 engine
Firing order:1-2-3-4-5-6

## CAPACITIES

| Year | Model | Engine Displacement cu. in. (cc) | Engine Crankcase with Filter | Engine Crankcase without Filter | Transmission (pts) 4-Spd | Transmission (pts) 5-Spd | Transmission (pts) Auto. | Drive Axle (pts.) | Fuel Tank (gal.) | Cooling System (qts.) |
|---|---|---|---|---|---|---|---|---|---|---|
| 1983 | Cordia | 109.5 (1795) | 4.5 | 4.0 | 4.4 | 4.4 | 12.2 | NA | 13.2 | 7.4 |
| | Tredia | 109.5 (1795) | 4.5 | 4.0 | 4.4 | 4.4 | 12.2 | NA | 13.2 | 7.4 |
| | Starion | 155.9 (2555) | 5.0 | 4.5 | 4.8 | — | 14.8 | 2.7 | 19.8 | 9.7 |
| 1984 | Cordia | 109.5 (1795) | 4.5 | 4.0 | 4.4 | 4.4 | 12.2 | NA | 13.2 | 7.4 |
| | Cordia | 121.9 (1997) | 4.5 | 4.0 | 4.4 | 4.4 | 12.2 | NA | 13.2 | 7.4 |
| | Tredia | 109.5 (1795) | 4.5 | 4.0 | 4.4 | 4.4 | 12.2 | NA | 13.2 | 7.4 |
| | Tredia | 121.9 (1997) | 4.5 | 4.0 | 4.4 | 4.4 | 12.2 | NA | 13.2 | 7.4 |
| | Starion | 155.9 (2555) | 5.0 | 4.5 | 4.8 | — | 14.8 | 2.7 | 19.8 | 9.7 |

## CAPACITIES

| Year | Model | Engine Displacement cu. in. (cc) | Engine Crankcase with Filter | Engine Crankcase without Filter | Transmission (pts) 4-Spd | Transmission (pts) 5-Spd | Transmission (pts) Auto. | Drive Axle (pts.) | Fuel Tank (gal.) | Cooling System (qts.) |
|---|---|---|---|---|---|---|---|---|---|---|
| 1985 | Cordia | 109.5 (1795) | 4.5 | 4.0 | 4.4 | 4.4 | 12.2 | NA | 13.2 | 7.4 |
| | Cordia | 121.9 (1997) | 4.5 | 4.0 | 4.4 | 4.4 | 12.2 | NA | 13.2 | 7.4 |
| | Tredia | 109.5 (1795) | 4.5 | 4.0 | 4.4 | 4.4 | 12.2 | NA | 13.2 | 7.4 |
| | Tredia | 121.9 (1997) | 4.5 | 4.0 | 4.4 | 4.4 | 12.2 | NA | 13.2 | 7.4 |
| | Starion | 155.9 (2555) | 5.5 | 5.0 | 4.8 | — | 14.8 | 2.7 | 19.8 | 9.7 |
| | Mirage | 89.6 (1468) | 3.7 | 3.2 | — | 4.4 | 12.4 | NA | 11.9 | 5.3 |
| | Mirage | 97.4 (1597) | 4.5 | 4.0 | — | 4.8 | 12.4 | NA | 11.9 | 5.3 |
| | Galant | 143.4 (2350) | 4.5 | 4.0 | — | — | 12.4 | NA | 15.9 | 7.4 |
| 1986 | Cordia | 109.5 (1795) | 4.5 | 4.0 | 4.4 | 4.4 | 12.2 | NA | 13.2 | 7.4 |
| | Cordia | 121.9 (1997) | 4.5 | 4.0 | 4.4 | 4.4 | 12.2 | NA | 13.2 | 7.4 |
| | Tredia | 109.5 (1795) | 4.5 | 4.0 | 4.4 | 4.4 | 12.2 | NA | 13.2 | 7.4 |
| | Tredia | 121.9 (1997) | 4.5 | 4.0 | 4.4 | 4.4 | 12.2 | NA | 13.2 | 7.4 |
| | Starion | 155.9 (2555) | 5.0 | 4.5 | 4.8 | — | 14.8 | 2.7 | 19.8 | 9.7 |
| | Mirage | 89.6 (1468) | 3.7 | 3.2 | — | 4.4 | 12.4 | NA | 11.9 | 5.3 |
| | Mirage | 97.4 (1597) | 4.5 | 4.0 | — | 4.8 | 12.4 | NA | 11.9 | 5.3 |
| | Galant | 143.4 (2350) | 4.5 | 4.0 | — | — | 12.4 | NA | 15.9 | 7.4 |
| 1987 | Cordia | 109.5 (1795) | 4.5 | 4.0 | 4.4 | 4.4 | 12.2 | NA | 13.2 | 7.4 |
| | Cordia | 121.9 (1997) | 4.5 | 4.0 | 4.4 | 4.4 | 12.2 | NA | 13.2 | 7.4 |
| | Tredia | 109.5 (1795) | 4.5 | 4.0 | 4.4 | 4.4 | 12.2 | NA | 13.2 | 7.4 |
| | Tredia | 121.9 (1997) | 4.5 | 4.0 | 4.4 | 4.4 | 12.2 | NA | 13.2 | 7.4 |
| | Starion | 155.9 (2555) | 5.0 | 4.5 | 4.8 | — | 14.8 | 2.7 | 19.8 | 9.7 |
| | Mirage | 89.6 (1468) | 3.7 | 3.2 | — | 4.4 | 12.4 | NA | 11.9 | 5.3 |
| | Mirage | 97.4 (1597) | 4.5 | 4.0 | — | 4.8 | 12.4 | NA | 11.9 | 5.3 |
| | Galant | 143.4 (2350) | 4.5 | 4.0 | — | — | 12.4 | NA | 15.9 | 7.4 |
| | Precis | 89.6 (1468) | 3.7 | 3.2 | — | 4.4 | — | NA | 11.9 | 5.3 |
| 1988 | Cordia | 109.5 (1795) | 4.5 | 4.0 | 4.4 | 4.4 | 12.2 | NA | 13.2 | 7.4 |
| | Cordia | 121.9 (1997) | 4.5 | 4.0 | 4.4 | 4.4 | 12.2 | NA | 13.2 | 7.4 |
| | Tredia | 109.5 (1795) | 4.5 | 4.0 | 4.4 | 4.4 | 12.2 | NA | 13.2 | 7.4 |
| | Tredia | 121.9 (1997) | 4.5 | 4.0 | 4.4 | 4.4 | 12.2 | NA | 13.2 | 7.4 |
| | Starion | 155.9 (2555) | 5.0 | 4.5 | 4.8 | — | 14.8 | 2.7 | 19.8 | 9.7 |
| | Mirage | 89.6 (1468) | 3.7 | 3.2 | — | 4.4 | 12.4 | NA | 11.9 | 5.3 |
| | Mirage | 97.4 (1597) | 4.5 | 4.0 | — | 4.8 | 12.4 | NA | 11.9 | 5.3 |
| | Galant | 143.4 (2350) | 4.5 | 4.0 | — | — | 12.4 | NA | 15.9 | 7.4 |
| | Galant | 181.4 (2972) | 4.5 | 4.0 | — | 5.3 | 12.3 | NA | 15.9 | 9.7 |
| | Precis | 89.6 (1468) | 3.7 | 3.2 | — | 4.4 | — | NA | 11.9 | 5.3 |
| 1989-90 | Starion | 155.9 (2555) | 5.0 | 4.5 | 4.8 | — | 14.8 | 2.7 | 19.8 | 9.7 |
| | Mirage | 89.6 (1468) | 3.7 | 3.2 | — | 4.4 | 12.4 | NA | 11.9 | 5.3 |
| | Mirage | 97.4 (1597) | 4.5 | 4.0 | — | 4.8 | 12.4 | NA | 11.9 | 5.3 |
| | Galant | 122 (1997) | ① | ① | — | 3.8 | 12.9 | NA | 15.9 | 7.6 |
| | Sigma | 181.4 (2972) | 4.5 | 4.0 | — | 5.3 | 12.3 | NA | 15.9 | 9.7 |
| | Precis | 89.6 (1468) | 3.7 | 3.2 | — | 4.4 | — | NA | 11.9 | 5.3 |

① SOHC
Without filter—4 qts.
With filter—4.5 qts.

DOHC
Without filter—5 qts.
With filter—5.5 qts.

## CRANKSHAFT AND CONNECTING ROD SPECIFICATIONS

All measurements are given in inches.

| Year | Engine Displacement cu. in. (cc) | Crankshaft Main Brg. Journal Dia. | Main Brg. Oil Clearance | Shaft End-play | Thrust on No. | Connecting Rod Journal Diameter | Oil Clearance | Side Clearance |
|---|---|---|---|---|---|---|---|---|
| 1983 | 109.5 (1795) | 2.244 | 0.0008–0.0020 | 0.0020–0.0071 | 3 | 1.772 | 0.0008–0.0020 | 0.004–0.010 |
| | 155.9 (2555) | 2.362 | 0.0008–0.0020 | 0.0020–0.0071 | 3 | 2.087 | 0.0008–0.0024 | 0.004–0.010 |
| 1984 | 109.5 (1795) | 2.244 | 0.0008–0.0020 | 0.0020–0.0071 | 3 | 1.772 | 0.0008–0.0020 | 0.004–0.010 |
| | 121.9 (1997) | 2.244 | 0.0008–0.0020 | 0.0020–0.0071 | 3 | 1.772 | 0.0008–0.0020 | 0.004–0.010 |
| | 155.9 (2555) | 2.362 | 0.0008–0.0020 | 0.0020–0.0071 | 3 | 2.087 | 0.0008–0.0024 | 0.004–0.010 |
| 1985 | 109.5 (1795) | 2.244 | 0.0008–0.0020 | 0.0020–0.0071 | 3 | 1.772 | 0.0008–0.0020 | 0.004–0.010 |
| | 121.9 (1997) | 2.244 | 0.0008–0.0020 | 0.0020–0.0071 | 3 | 1.772 | 0.0008–0.0020 | 0.004–0.010 |
| | 155.9 (2555) | 2.362 | 0.0008–0.0020 | 0.0020–0.0071 | 3 | 2.087 | 0.0008–0.0024 | 0.004–0.010 |
| | 89.6 (1468) | 1.889 | 0.0008–0.0020 | 0.0020–0.0071 | 3 | 1.653 | 0.0004–0.0024 | 0.004–0.010 |
| | 97.4 (1597) | 2.244 | 0.0008–0.0020 | 0.0020–0.0071 | 3 | 1.772 | 0.0004–0.0024 | 0.004–0.010 |
| | 143.4 (2350) | 2.244 | 0.0008–0.0020 | 0.0020–0.0071 | 3 | 2.087 | 0.0008–0.0024 | 0.004–0.010 |
| 1986 | 109.5 (1795) | 2.244 | 0.0008–0.0020 | 0.0020–0.0071 | 3 | 1.772 | 0.0008–0.0020 | 0.004–0.010 |
| | 121.9 (1997) | 2.244 | 0.0008–0.0020 | 0.0020–0.0071 | 3 | 1.772 | 0.0008–0.0020 | 0.004–0.010 |
| | 155.9 (2555) | 2.362 | 0.0008–0.0020 | 0.0020–0.0071 | 3 | 2.087 | 0.0008–0.0024 | 0.004–0.010 |
| | 89.6 (1468) | 1.889 | 0.0008–0.0020 | 0.0020–0.0071 | 3 | 1.653 | 0.0004–0.0024 | 0.004–0.010 |
| | 97.4 (1597) | 2.244 | 0.0008–0.0020 | 0.0020–0.0071 | 3 | 1.772 | 0.0004–0.0024 | 0.004–0.010 |
| | 143.4 (2350) | 2.244 | 0.0008–0.0020 | 0.0020–0.0071 | 3 | 2.087 | 0.0008–0.0024 | 0.004–0.010 |
| 1987 | 109.5 (1795) | 2.244 | 0.0008–0.0020 | 0.0020–0.0071 | 3 | 1.772 | 0.0008–0.0020 | 0.004–0.010 |
| | 121.9 (1997) | 2.244 | 0.0008–0.0020 | 0.0020–0.0071 | 3 | 1.772 | 0.0008–0.0020 | 0.004–0.010 |
| | 155.9 (2555) | 2.362 | 0.0008–0.0020 | 0.0020–0.0071 | 3 | 2.087 | 0.0008–0.0024 | 0.004–0.010 |
| | 89.6 (1468) | 1.889 | 0.0008–0.0020 | 0.0020–0.0071 | 3 | 1.653 | 0.0004–0.0024 | 0.004–0.010 |
| | 97.4 (1597) | 2.244 | 0.0008–0.0020 | 0.0020–0.0071 | 3 | 1.772 | 0.0004–0.0024 | 0.004–0.010 |
| | 143.4 (2350) | 2.244 | 0.0008–0.0020 | 0.0020–0.0071 | 3 | 2.087 | 0.0008–0.0024 | 0.004–0.010 |

## CRANKSHAFT AND CONNECTING ROD SPECIFICATIONS

All measurements are given in inches.

| Year | Engine Displacement cu. in. (cc) | Crankshaft: Main Brg. Journal Dia. | Crankshaft: Main Brg. Oil Clearance | Crankshaft: Shaft End-play | Crankshaft: Thrust on No. | Connecting Rod: Journal Diameter | Connecting Rod: Oil Clearance | Connecting Rod: Side Clearance |
|---|---|---|---|---|---|---|---|---|
| 1988 | 109.5 (1795) | 2.244 | 0.0008–0.0020 | 0.0020–0.0071 | 3 | 1.772 | 0.0008–0.0020 | 0.004–0.010 |
| | 121.9 (1997) | 2.244 | 0.0008–0.0020 | 0.0020–0.0071 | 3 | 1.772 | 0.0008–0.0020 | 0.004–0.010 |
| | 155.9 (2555) | 2.362 | 0.0008–0.0020 | 0.0020–0.0071 | 3 | 2.087 | 0.0008–0.0024 | 0.004–0.010 |
| | 89.6 (1468) | 1.889 | 0.0008–0.0020 | 0.0020–0.0071 | 3 | 1.653 | 0.0004–0.0024 | 0.004–0.010 |
| | 97.4 (1597) | 2.244 | 0.0008–0.0020 | 0.0020–0.0071 | 3 | 1.772 | 0.0004–0.0024 | 0.004–0.010 |
| | 143.4 (2350) | 2.244 | 0.0008–0.0020 | 0.0020–0.0071 | 3 | 2.087 | 0.0008–0.0024 | 0.004–0.010 |
| | 181.4 (2972) | 2.362 | 0.0008–0.0019 | 0.0020–0.0098 | 3 | 1.969 | 0.0006–0.0018 | 0.008–0.016 |
| 1989-90 | 121.9 (1997) | 2.244 | 0.0008–0.0020 | 0.0020–0.0071 | 3 | 1.772 | 0.0008–0.0020 | 0.004–0.010 |
| | 155.9 (2555) | 2.362 | 0.0008–0.0020 | 0.0020–0.0071 | 3 | 2.087 | 0.0008–0.0024 | 0.004–0.010 |
| | 89.6 (1468) | 1.889 | 0.0008–0.0020 | 0.0020–0.0071 | 3 | 1.653 | 0.0004–0.0024 | 0.004–0.010 |
| | 97.4 (1597) | 2.244 | 0.0008–0.0020 | 0.0020–0.0071 | 3 | 1.772 | 0.0004–0.0024 | 0.004–0.010 |
| | 181.4 (2972) | 2.362 | 0.0008–0.0019 | 0.0020–0.0981 | 3 | 1.969 | 0.0006–0.0018 | 0.008–0.016 |
| | 181.4 (2972) | 2.362 | 0.0008–0.0019 | 0.0020–0.0098 | 3 | 1.969 | 0.0006–0.0018 | 0.008–0.016 |

## VALVE SPECIFICATIONS

| Year | Engine Displacement cu. in. (cc) | Seat Angle (deg.) | Face Angle (deg.) | Spring Test Pressure (lbs. @ in.) | Spring Installed Height (in.) | Stem-to-Guide Clearance (in.) Intake | Stem-to-Guide Clearance (in.) Exhaust | Stem Diameter (in.) Intake | Stem Diameter (in.) Exhaust |
|---|---|---|---|---|---|---|---|---|---|
| 1983 | 109.5 (1795) | 45 | 45 | 62 @ 1.591 | 1.591 | 0.0010–0.0022 | 0.0020–0.0035 | 0.315 | 0.315 |
| | 155.9 (2555) | 45 | 45 | 62 @ 1.591 | 1.591 | 0.0012–0.0024 | 0.0020–0.0035 | 0.315 | 0.315 |
| 1984 | 109.5 (1795) | 45 | 45 | 62 @ 1.591 | 1.591 | 0.0010–0.0022 | 0.0020–0.0035 | 0.315 | 0.315 |
| | 121.9 (1997) | 45 | 45 | 62 @ 1.591 | 1.591 | 0.0010–0.0022 | 0.0020–0.0035 | 0.315 | 0.315 |
| | 155.9 (2555) | 45 | 45 | 62 @ 1.591 | 1.591 | 0.0012–0.0024 | 0.0020–0.0035 | 0.315 | 0.315 |
| 1985 | 109.5 (1795) | 45 | 45 | 62 @ 1.591 | 1.591 | 0.0010–0.0022 | 0.0020–0.0035 | 0.315 | 0.315 |
| | 121.9 (1997) | 45 | 45 | 62 @ 1.591 | 1.591 | 0.0010–0.0022 | 0.0020–0.0035 | 0.315 | 0.315 |

## VALVE SPECIFICATIONS

| Year | Engine Displacement cu. in. (cc) | Seat Angle (deg.) | Face Angle (deg.) | Spring Test Pressure (lbs. @ in.) | Spring Installed Height (in.) | Stem-to-Guide Clearance (in.) | | Stem Diameter (in.) | |
|---|---|---|---|---|---|---|---|---|---|
| | | | | | | Intake | Exhaust | Intake | Exhaust |
| 1985 | 155.9 (2555) | 45 | 45 | 62 @ 1.591 | 1.591 | 0.0012–0.0024 | 0.0020–0.0035 | 0.315 | 0.315 |
| | 89.6 (1468) | 45 | 45 | 53 @ 1.469 | 1.417 | 0.0012–0.0024 | 0.0020–0.0035 | 0.315 | 0.315 |
| | 97.4 (1597) | 45 | 45 | 62 @ 1.469 | 1.469 | 0.0012–0.0024 | 0.0020–0.0035 | 0.315 | 0.315 |
| | 143.4 (2350) | 45 | 45 | 72 @ 1.591 | 1.591 | 0.0012–0.0024 | 0.0024–0.0035 | 0.322 | 0.315 |
| 1986 | 109.5 (1795) | 45 | 45 | 62 @ 1.591 | 1.591 | 0.0010–0.0022 | 0.0020–0.0035 | 0.315 | 0.315 |
| | 121.9 (1997) | 45 | 45 | 72 @ 1.591 | 1.591 | 0.0010–0.0022 | 0.0020–0.0035 | 0.315 | 0.315 |
| | 155.9 (2555) | 45 | 45 | 72 @ 1.591 | 1.591 | 0.0012–0.0024 | 0.0020–0.0035 | 0.315 | 0.315 |
| | 89.6 (1468) | 45 | 45 | 53 @ 1.469 | 1.417 | 0.0008–0.0020 | 0.0020–0.0035 | 0.315 | 0.315 |
| | 97.4 (1597) | 45 | 45 | 62 @ 1.469 | 1.469 | 0.0012–0.0024 | 0.0020–0.0035 | 0.315 | 0.315 |
| | 143.4 (2350) | 45 | 45 | 72 @ 1.591 | 1.591 | 0.0012–0.0024 | 0.0020–0.0035 | 0.322 | 0.315 |
| 1987 | 109.5 (1795) | 45 | 45 | 62 @ 1.591 | 1.591 | 0.0010–0.0022 | 0.0020–0.0035 | 0.315 | 0.315 |
| | 121.9 (1997) | 45 | 45 | 72 @ 1.591 | 1.591 | 0.0010–0.0022 | 0.0020–0.0035 | 0.315 | 0.315 |
| | 155.9 (2555) | 45 | 45 | 72 @ 1.591 | 1.591 | 0.0012–0.0024 | 0.0020–0.0035 | 0.315 | 0.315 |
| | 89.6 (1468) | 45 | 45 | 53 @ 1.469 | 1.417 | 0.0008–0.0020 | 0.0020–0.0035 | 0.315 | 0.315 |
| | 97.4 (1597) | 45 | 45 | 62 @ 1.469 | 1.469 | 0.0012–0.0024 | 0.0020–0.0035 | 0.315 | 0.315 |
| | 143.4 (2350) | 45 | 45 | 72 @ 1.591 | 1.591 | 0.0012–0.0024 | 0.0020–0.0035 | 0.322 | 0.315 |
| 1988 | 109.5 (1795) | 45 | 45 | 62 @ 1.591 | 1.591 | 0.0010–0.0022 | 0.0020–0.0035 | 0.315 | 0.315 |
| | 121.9 (1997) | 45 | 45 | 72 @ 1.591 | 1.591 | 0.0010–0.0022 | 0.0020–0.0035 | 0.315 | 0.315 |
| | 155.9 (2555) | 45 | 45 | 72 @ 1.591 | 1.591 | 0.0012–0.0024 | 0.0020–0.0035 | 0.315 | 0.315 |
| | 89.6 (1468) | 45 | 45 | 53 @ 1.469 | 1.417 | 0.0008–0.0020 | 0.0020–0.0035 | 0.315 | 0.315 |
| | 97.4 (1597) | 45 | 45 | 62 @ 1.469 | 1.469 | 0.0012–0.0024 | 0.0020–0.0035 | 0.315 | 0.315 |
| | 143.4 (2350) | 45 | 45 | 72 @ 1.591 | 1.591 | 0.0012–0.0024 | 0.0020–0.0035 | 0.322 | 0.315 |
| | 181.4 (2972) | 44 | 45 | 74 @ 1.591 | 1.591 | 0.0012–0.0024 | 0.0020–0.0035 | 0.314 | 0.313 |

## VALVE SPECIFICATIONS

| Year | Engine Displacement cu. in. (cc) | Seat Angle (deg.) | Face Angle (deg.) | Spring Test Pressure (lbs. @ in.) | Spring Installed Height (in.) | Stem-to-Guide Clearance (in.) | | Stem Diameter (in.) | |
|---|---|---|---|---|---|---|---|---|---|
| | | | | | | Intake | Exhaust | Intake | Exhaust |
| 1989-90 | 121.9 (1997) | 45 | 45 | 72 @ 1.591 | 1.591 | 0.0010–0.0022 | 0.0020–0.0035 | 0.315 | 0.315 |
| | 155.9 (2555) | 45 | 45 | 72 @ 1.591 | 1.591 | 0.0012–0.0024 | 0.0020–0.0035 | 0.315 | 0.315 |
| | 89.6 (1468) | 45 | 45 | 53 @ 1.469 | 1.417 | 0.0008–0.0020 | 0.0020–0.0035 | 0.315 | 0.315 |
| | 97.4 (1597) | 45 | 45 | 62 @ 1.469 | 1.469 | 0.0012–0.0024 | 0.0020–0.0035 | 0.315 | 0.315 |
| | 143.4 (2350) | 45 | 45 | 72 @ 1.591 | 1.591 | 0.0012–0.0024 | 0.0020–0.0035 | 0.322 | 0.315 |
| | 181.4 (2972) | 44 | 45 | 74 @ 1.591 | 1.591 | 0.0012–0.0024 | 0.0020–0.0035 | 0.314 | 0.313 |

## PISTON AND RING SPECIFICATIONS

All measurements are given in inches.

| Year | Engine Displacement cu. in. (cc) | Piston Clearance | Ring Gap | | | Ring Side Clearance | | |
|---|---|---|---|---|---|---|---|---|
| | | | Top Compression | Bottom Compression | Oil Control | Top Compression | Bottom Compression | Oil Control |
| 1983 | 109.5 (1795) | 0.0008–0.0016 | 0.0100–0.0180 | 0.0080–0.0160 | 0.0080–0.0200 | 0.002–0.004 | 0.001–0.002 | — |
| | 155.9 (2555) | 0.0008–0.0016 | 0.0120–0.0200 | 0.0100–0.0160 | 0.0120–0.0310 | 0.002–0.004 | 0.001–0.002 | — |
| 1984 | 109.5 (1795) | 0.0008–0.0016 | 0.0100–0.0180 | 0.0080–0.0160 | 0.0080–0.0200 | 0.002–0.004 | 0.001–0.002 | — |
| | 121.9 (1997) | 0.0008–0.0016 | 0.0100–0.0180 | 0.0080–0.0160 | 0.0080–0.0200 | 0.002–0.004 | 0.001–0.002 | — |
| | 155.9 (2555) | 0.0008–0.0016 | 0.0120–0.0200 | 0.0100–0.0160 | 0.0120–0.0310 | 0.002–0.004 | 0.001–0.002 | — |
| 1985 | 109.5 (1795) | 0.0008–0.0016 | 0.0100–0.0180 | 0.0080–0.0160 | 0.0080–0.0200 | 0.002–0.004 | 0.001–0.002 | — |
| | 121.9 (1997) | 0.0008–0.0016 | 0.0100–0.0180 | 0.0080–0.0160 | 0.0080–0.0200 | 0.002–0.004 | 0.001–0.002 | — |
| | 155.9 (2555) | 0.0008–0.0016 | 0.0120–0.0200 | 0.0100–0.0160 | 0.0120–0.0310 | 0.002–0.004 | 0.001–0.002 | — |
| | 89.6 (1468) | 0.0008–0.0016 | 0.0080–0.0160 | 0.0080–0.0160 | 0.0080–0.0280 | 0.0012–0.0028 | 0.0008–0.0024 | — |
| | 97.4 (1597) | 0.0008–0.0016 | 0.0080–0.0160 | 0.0080–0.0160 | 0.0080–0.0280 | 0.0012–0.0028 | 0.0008–0.0024 | — |
| | 143.4 (2350) | 0.0008–0.0016 | 0.0100–0.0180 | 0.0080–0.0160 | 0.0080–0.0280 | 0.002–0.004 | 0.001–0.002 | — |
| 1986 | 109.5 (1795) | 0.0008–0.0016 | 0.0100–0.0180 | 0.0080–0.0160 | 0.0080–0.0200 | 0.002–0.004 | 0.001–0.002 | — |
| | 121.9 (1997) | 0.0008–0.0016 | 0.0100–0.0180 | 0.0080–0.0160 | 0.0080–0.0200 | 0.002–0.004 | 0.001–0.002 | — |
| | 155.9 (2555) | 0.0008–0.0016 | 0.0120–0.0200 | 0.0100–0.0160 | 0.0120–0.0310 | 0.002–0.004 | 0.001–0.002 | — |

## PISTON AND RING SPECIFICATIONS

All measurements are given in inches.

| Year | Engine Displacement cu. in. (cc) | Piston Clearance | Ring Gap | | | Ring Side Clearance | | |
|---|---|---|---|---|---|---|---|---|
| | | | Top Compression | Bottom Compression | Oil Control | Top Compression | Bottom Compression | Oil Control |
| 1986 | 89.6 (1468) | 0.0008–0.0016 | 0.0080–0.0160 | 0.0080–0.0160 | 0.0080–0.0280 | 0.0012–0.0028 | 0.0008–0.0024 | — |
| | 97.4 (1597) | 0.0008–0.0016 | 0.0080–0.0160 | 0.0080–0.0160 | 0.0080–0.0280 | 0.0012–0.0028 | 0.0008–0.0024 | — |
| | 143.4 (2350) | 0.0008–0.0016 | 0.0100–0.0180 | 0.0080–0.0160 | 0.0080–0.0280 | 0.002–0.004 | 0.001–0.002 | — |
| 1987 | 109.5 (1795) | 0.0008–0.0016 | 0.0100–0.0180 | 0.0080–0.0160 | 0.0080–0.0200 | 0.002–0.004 | 0.001–0.002 | — |
| | 121.9 (1997) | 0.0008–0.0016 | 0.0100–0.0180 | 0.0080–0.0160 | 0.0080–0.0200 | 0.002–0.004 | 0.001–0.002 | — |
| | 155.9 (2555) | 0.0008–0.0016 | 0.0120–0.0200 | 0.0100–0.0160 | 0.0120–0.0310 | 0.002–0.004 | 0.001–0.002 | — |
| | 89.6 (1468) | 0.0008–0.0016 | 0.0080–0.0160 | 0.0080–0.0160 | 0.0080–0.0280 | 0.0012–0.0028 | 0.0008–0.0024 | — |
| | 97.4 (1597) | 0.0008–0.0016 | 0.0080–0.0160 | 0.0080–0.0160 | 0.0080–0.0280 | 0.0012–0.0028 | 0.0008–0.0024 | — |
| | 143.4 (2350) | 0.0008–0.0016 | 0.0100–0.0180 | 0.0080–0.0160 | 0.0080–0.0280 | 0.0012–0.0028 | 0.0008–0.0024 | |
| 1988 | 109.5 (1795) | 0.0008–0.0016 | 0.0100–0.0180 | 0.0080–0.0160 | 0.0080–0.0200 | 0.002–0.004 | 0.001–0.002 | — |
| | 121.9 (1997) | 0.0008–0.0016 | 0.0100–0.0180 | 0.0080–0.0160 | 0.0080–0.0200 | 0.002–0.004 | 0.001–0.002 | — |
| | 155.9 (2555) | 0.0008–0.0016 | 0.0120–0.0200 | 0.0100–0.0160 | 0.0120–0.0310 | 0.002–0.004 | 0.001–0.002 | — |
| | 89.6 (1468) | 0.0008–0.0016 | 0.0080–0.0160 | 0.0080–0.0160 | 0.0080–0.0280 | 0.0012–0.0028 | 0.0008–0.0024 | — |
| | 97.4 (1597) | 0.0008–0.0016 | 0.0080–0.0160 | 0.0080–0.0160 | 0.0080–0.0280 | 0.0012–0.0028 | 0.0008–0.0024 | — |
| | 143.4 (2350) | 0.0008–0.0016 | 0.0100–0.0180 | 0.0080–0.0160 | 0.0080–0.0280 | 0.0012–0.0028 | 0.0008–0.0024 | |
| | 181.4 (2972) | 0.0008–0.0016 | 0.0118–0.0177 | 0.0098–0.0157 | 0.0079–0.0276 | 0.0012–0.0035 | 0.0008–0.0024 | |
| 1989-90 | 121.9 (1997) | 0.0008–0.0016 | 0.0100–0.0180 | 0.0080–0.0160 | 0.0080–0.0200 | 0.002–0.004 | 0.001–0.002 | — |
| | 155.9 (2555) | 0.0008–0.0016 | 0.0120–0.0200 | 0.0100–0.0160 | 0.0120–0.0310 | 0.002–0.004 | 0.001–0.002 | — |
| | 89.6 (1468) | 0.0008–0.0016 | 0.0080–0.0160 | 0.0080–0.0160 | 0.0080–0.0280 | 0.0012–0.0028 | 0.0008–0.0024 | — |
| | 97.4 (1597) | 0.0008–0.0016 | 0.0080–0.0160 | 0.0080–0.0160 | 0.0080–0.0280 | 0.0012–0.0028 | 0.0008–0.0024 | — |
| | 143.4 (2350) | 0.0008–0.0016 | 0.0100–0.0180 | 0.0080–0.0160 | 0.0080–0.0280 | 0.0012–0.0028 | 0.0008–0.0024 | |
| | 181.4 (2972) | 0.0008–0.0016 | 0.0118–0.0177 | 0.0098–0.0157 | 0.0079–0.0276 | 0.0012–0.0035 | 0.0008–0.0024 | |

## TORQUE SPECIFICATIONS

All readings in ft. lbs.

| Year | Engine Displacement cu. in. (cc) | Cylinder Head Bolts① | Main Bearing Bolts | Rod Bearing Bolts | Crankshaft Pulley Bolts | Flywheel Bolts | Manifold Intake | Manifold Exhaust | Spark Plugs |
|---|---|---|---|---|---|---|---|---|---|
| 1983 | 109.5 (1795) | 73–79 | 38 | 37 | 80–94 | 94–101 | 11–14 | 11–14 | NA |
| | 155.9 (2555) | 73–79② | 55–61 | 33 | 80–94 | 94–101 | 11–14 | 11–14 | NA |
| 1984 | 109.5 (1795) | 73–79 | 38 | 37 | 80–94 | 94–101 | 11–14 | 11–14 | NA |
| | 121.9 (1992) | 73–79 | 38 | 37 | 80–94 | 94–101 | 11–14 | 11–14 | NA |
| | 155.9 (2555) | 73–79② | 55–61 | 33 | 80–94 | 94–101 | 11–14 | 11–14 | NA |
| 1985 | 109.5 (1795) | 73–79 | 38 | 37 | 80–94 | 94–101 | 11–14 | 11–14 | NA |
| | 121.9 (1997) | 73–79 | 38 | 37 | 80–94 | 94–101 | 11–14 | 11–14 | NA |
| | 155.9 (2555) | 73–79② | 55–61 | 33 | 80–94 | 94–101 | 11–14 | 11–14 | NA |
| | 89.6 (1468) | 58–61 | 38 | 24 | 51–72 | 94–101 | 11–14 | 11–14 | NA |
| | 97.4 (1597) | 58–61 | 38 | 24 | 80–93 | 94–101 | 11–14 | 11–14 | NA |
| | 143.4 (2350) | 73–79 | 38 | 33 | 80–94 | 94–101 | 11–14 | 11–14 | NA |
| 1986 | 109.5 (1795) | 73–79 | 38 | 37 | 80–94 | 94–101 | 11–14 | 11–14 | NA |
| | 121.9 (1997) | 73–79 | 38 | 37 | 80–94 | 94–101 | 11–14 | 11–14 | NA |
| | 155.9 (2555) | 73–79② | 55–61 | 33 | 80–94 | 94–101 | 11–14 | 11–14 | NA |
| | 89.6 (1468) | 58–61 | 38 | 24 | 51–72 | 94–101 | 11–14 | 11–14 | NA |
| | 97.4 (1597) | 58–61 | 38 | 24 | 80–93 | 94–101 | 11–14 | 11–14 | NA |
| | 143.4 (2350) | 73–79 | 38 | 33 | 80–94 | 94–101 | 11–14 | 11–14 | NA |
| 1987 | 109.5 (1795) | 73–79 | 38 | 37 | 80–94 | 94–101 | 11–14 | 11–14 | NA |
| | 121.9 (1997) | 73–79 | 38 | 37 | 80–94 | 94–101 | 11–14 | 11–14 | NA |
| | 155.9 (2555) | 73–79② | 55–61 | 33 | 80–94 | 94–101 | 11–14 | 11–14 | NA |
| | 89.6 (1468) | 58–61 | 38 | 24 | 51–72 | 94–101 | 11–14 | 11–14 | NA |
| | 97.4 (1597) | 58–61 | 38 | 24 | 80–93 | 94–101 | 11–14 | 11–14 | NA |
| | 143.4 (2350) | 73–79 | 38 | 33 | 80–94 | 94–101 | 11–14 | 11–14 | NA |
| 1988 | 109.5 (1795) | 73–79 | 38 | 37 | 80–94 | 94–101 | 11–14 | 11–14 | NA |
| | 121.9 (1997) | 73–79 | 38 | 37 | 80–94 | 94–101 | 11–14 | 11–14 | NA |
| | 155.9 (2555) | 73–79② | 55–61 | 33 | 80–94 | 94–101 | 11–14 | 11–14 | NA |
| | 89.6 (1468) | 58–61 | 38 | 24 | 51–72 | 94–101 | 11–14 | 11–14 | NA |
| | 97.4 (1597) | 58–61 | 38 | 24 | 80–93 | 94–101 | 11–14 | 11–14 | NA |
| | 143.4 (2350) | 73–79 | 38 | 33 | 80–94 | 94–101 | 11–14 | 11–14 | NA |
| | 181.4 (2972) | 73–79 | 55–61 | 38 | 109–115 | 53–55 | 11–14 | 11–16 | NA |
| 1989-90 | 155.9 (2555) | 73–79② | 55–61 | 33 | 80–94 | 94–101 | 11–14 | 11–14 | NA |
| | 89.6 (1468) | 58–61 | 38 | 24 | 51–72 | 94–101 | 11–14 | 11–14 | NA |
| | 97.4 (1597) | 58–61 | 38 | 24 | 80–93 | 94–101 | 11–14 | 11–14 | NA |
| | 122 (1997)③ | 72–80 | 36–40 | 36–38 | 80–94 | 94–101 | 13–18 | 18–22 | NA |
| | 122 (1997)④ | 72–80 | 47–51 | 36–38 | 80–94 | 94–101 | 18–22 | 18–22 | NA |
| | 181.4 (2972) | 73–79 | 55–61 | 38 | 109–115 | 53–55 | 11–14 | 11–16 | NA |

① All figures are hot torques. For cold engine figures see text
② No. 11 in text diagram 11-15
③ Single overhead camshaft
④ Double overhead camshaft

## BRAKE SPECIFICATIONS

All measurements in inches unless noted.

| Year | Model | Lug Nut Torque (ft. lbs.) | Master Cylinder Bore | Brake Disc Minimum Thickness | Brake Disc Maximum Runout | Maximum Brake Drum Diameter | Minimum Lining Thickness Front | Minimum Lining Thickness Rear |
|---|---|---|---|---|---|---|---|---|
| 1983 | Cordia | 50–57① | 0.87 | — | 0.450 | 8.000 | 0.040 | 0.040 |
| | Tredia | 50–57① | 0.87 | — | 0.450 | 8.000 | 0.040 | 0.040 |
| | Starion | 50–57① | 0.94 | — | 0.880 | — | 0.040 | — |
| 1984 | Cordia | 50–57② | 0.87 | — | 0.650 | 8.000 | 0.040 | 0.040 |
| | Tredia | 50–57② | 0.87 | — | 0.650 | 8.000 | 0.040 | 0.040 |
| | Starion | 50–57② | 0.94 | — | 0.880 | — | 0.040 | — |
| 1985 | Cordia | 50–57② | 0.87 | — | 0.650 | 8.000 | 0.040 | 0.040 |
| | Tredia | 50–57② | 0.87 | — | 0.650 | 8.000 | 0.040 | 0.040 |
| | Starion | 50–57② | 0.94 | — | 0.880 | — | 0.040 | — |
| | Mirage | 50–57② | 0.81④ | — | 0.450③ | 7.100 | 0.040 | 0.040 |
| | Galant | 50–57② | 0.94 | — | 0.650 | 08.000 | 0.040 | 0.040 |
| 1986 | Cordia | 50–57② | 0.87 | — | 0.650 | 8.000 | 0.040 | 0.040 |
| | Tredia | 50–57② | 0.87 | — | 0.650 | 8.000 | 0.040 | 0.040 |
| | Starion | 50–57② | 0.94 | — | 0.880 | — | 0.040 | — |
| | Mirage | 50–57② | 0.81④ | — | 0.450③ | 7.100 | 0.040 | 0.040 |
| | Galant | 50–57② | 0.94 | — | 0.650 | 8.000 | 0.040 | 0.040 |
| 1987 | Cordia | 50–57② | 0.87 | — | 0.650 | 8.000 | 0.040 | 0.040 |
| | Tredia | 50–57② | 0.87 | — | 0.650 | 8.000 | 0.040 | 0.040 |
| | Starion | 50–57② | 0.94 | — | 0.880 | — | 0.040 | — |
| | Mirage | 50–57② | 0.81④ | — | 0.450③ | 7.100 | 0.040 | 0.040 |
| | Galant | 50–57② | 0.94 | — | 0.650 | 8.000 | 0.040 | 0.040 |
| | Precis | 51–58① | 0.81 | — | 0.450 | 7.100 | 0.040 | 0.040 |
| 1988 | Cordia | 50–57② | 0.87 | — | 0.650 | 8.000 | 0.040 | 0.040 |
| | Tredia | 50–57② | 0.87 | — | 0.650 | 8.000 | 0.040 | 0.040 |
| | Starion | 50–57② | 0.94 | — | 0.880 | — | 0.040 | — |
| | Mirage | 50–57② | 0.81④ | — | 0.450③ | 7.100 | 0.040 | 0.040 |
| | Galant | 43–52② | 0.94 | — | 0.650 | — | 0.040 | 0.040 |
| | Precis | 51–58① | 0.81 | — | 0.450 | — | 0.040 | 0.040 |
| 1989–90 | Starion | 50–57② | 0.94 | — | 0.880 | — | 0.040 | — |
| | Mirage | 50–57② | 0.81④ | — | 0.450③ | 7.100 | 0.040 | 0.040 |
| | Galant | 43–52② | 0.94 | — | 0.650 | — | 0.040 | 0.040 |
| | Precis | 51–58① | 0.81 | — | 0.450 | — | 0.040 | 0.040 |
| | Sigma | 43–52② | 0.94 | — | 0.004 | — | 0.079 | 0.039 |

① With aluminum wheels—57–72
② With aluminum wheels—66–81
③ Turbo 0.650
④ Turbo 0.87

## WHEEL ALIGNMENT

| Year | Model | Caster Range (deg.) | Caster Preferred Setting (deg.) | Camber Range (deg.) | Camber Preferred Setting (deg.) | Toe-in (in.) | Steering Axis Inclination (deg.) |
|---|---|---|---|---|---|---|---|
| 1983 | Cordia | 5/16–1 5/16P | 13/16P | 1/16N–15/16P | 7/16P① | 1/8N–1/8P | 7 1/16 |
| | Tredia | 5/16–1 5/16P | 13/16P | 1/16N–15/16P | 7/16P① | 1/8N–1/8P | 7 1/16 |
| | Starion | — | 5 1/3P | — | 0P② | 5/64N–13/64P | — |
| 1984 | Cordia | 5/16–1 5/16P | 13/16P | 1/16N–15/16P | 7/16P① | 1/8N–1/8P | 7 1/16 |
| | Tredia | 5/16–1 5/16P | 13/16P | 1/16N–15/16P | 7/16P① | 1/8N–1/8P | 7 1/16 |
| | Starion | — | 5 1/3P | — | 0P② | 5/64N–13/64P | — |
| 1985 | Cordia | 5/16–1 5/16P | 13/16P | 1/16N–15/16P | 7/16P③ | 1/8N–1/8P | 7 1/16 |
| | Tredia | 5/16–1 5/16P | 13/16P | 1/16N–15/16P | 7/16P③ | 1/8N–1/8P | 7 1/16 |
| | Starion | — | 5 1/3P | — | 0P | 5/64N–13/64P | — |
| | Mirage | 7/32–1 7/32P | 23/32P | 1/2N–1/2P | 0P④ | 1/8N–1/8P | 5 3/4 |
| | Galant | 5/32–1 5/32P | 21/32P | 0–1P | 1/2P | 1/8N–1/8P | 6 5/8 |
| 1986 | Cordia | 5/16–1 5/16P | 13/16P | 1/16N–15/16P | 7/16P⑤ | 1/8N–1/8P | 7 1/16 |
| | Tredia | 5/16–1 5/16P | 13/16P | 1/16N–15/16P | 7/16P⑤ | 1/8N–1/8P | 7 1/16 |
| | Starion | — | 5 1/3P | — | 0P | 5/64N–13/64P | — |
| | Mirage | 7/32–1 7/32P | 23/32P | 1/2N–1/2P | 0P④ | 1/8N–1/8P | 5 3/4 |
| | Galant | 5/32–1 5/32P | 21/32P | 0–1P | 1/2P | 1/8N–1/8P | 6 5/8 |
| 1987 | Cordia | 5/16–1 5/16P | 13/16P | 1/16N–5/16P | 7/16P⑤ | 1/8N–1/8P | 7 1/16 |
| | Tredia | 5/16–1 5/16P | 13/16P | 1/16N–15/16P | 7/16P⑤ | 1/8N–1/8P | 7 1/16 |
| | Starion | 5 5/16–6 5/16P | 5 13/16P | 1N–0P | 1/2N | 13/64P–13/64P | — |
| | Mirage | 1/2–1 1/2P⑥ | 1P | 1/2N–1/2P | 0P① | 1/8N–1/8P | 5 3/4 |
| | Galant | 5/32–1 5/32P | 21/32P | 0–1P | 1/2P | 1/8N–1/8P | 6 5/8 |
| | Precis | 1/2–1/8P | 3/16P | 0–1P | 1/2P⑦ | 1/16P–5/32P | 12 11/16 |
| 1988 | Cordia | 5/16–1 5/16P | 13/16P | 1/16N–5/16P | 7/16P⑤ | 1/8N–1/8P | 7 1/16 |
| | Tredia | 5/16–1 5/16P | 13/16P | 1/16N–15/16P | 7/16P⑤ | 1/8N–1/8P | 7 1/16 |
| | Starion | 5 5/16–6 5/16P | 5 13/16P | 1N–0P | 1/2N | 13/64P–13/64P | — |
| | Mirage | 1/2–1 1/2P⑥ | 1P | 1/2N–1/2P | 0P① | 1/8N–1/8P | 5 3/4 |
| | Galant | 5/32–1 5/32P | 21/32P | 0–1P | 1/2P⑧ | 1/8N–1/8P | 6 5/8 |
| | Precis | 1/2–1/8P | 3/16P | 0–1P | 1/2P⑦ | 1/16P–5/32P | 12 11/16 |
| 1989–90 | Starion | 5 5/16–6 5/16P | 5 13/16P | 1N–0P | 1/2N | 13/64P–13/64P | — |
| | Mirage | 1/2–1 1/2P⑥ | 1P | 1/2N–1/2P | 0P① | 1/8N–1/8P | 5 3/4 |
| | Galant | 5/32–1 5/32P | 21/32P | 0–1P | 1/2P⑧ | 1/8N–1/8P | 6 5/8 |
| | Precis | 1/2–1/8P | 3/16P | 0–1P | 1/2P⑦ | 1/16P–5/32P | 12 11/16 |
| | Sigma | 3 1/16–1 3/16P | 11/16P | 0–1P⑨ | 1/2P⑩ | 1/8N–1/8P | NA |

N Negative
P Positive
① Rear—11/16N
② Rear—5/16P
③ Rear—9/16N
④ Rear—21/32N
⑤ Rear—11/16P
⑥ With power steering—11/16–2 3/16
⑦ Rear—5/8N
⑧ Rear—3/4N
⑨ Rear—1N–1/4N
⑩ Rear—3/4N

# TUNE-UP PROCEDURES

## Ignition Timing

### ADJUSTMENT

1. Run the engine until operating temperature is reached.
2. Leave the engine idling, apply the handbrake and position the gear selector in **N** if equipped with a manual transmission or **P** if equipped with an automatic transmission. Turn off all accessories and stop the engine.
3. Install a tachometer, connecting the red lead to the (–) terminal of the coil and the black lead to a clean ground. On all models except the following:
   a. 1986 Galant – connect special tool MD998439 or equivalent to the tachometer connector between the ignition coil promary line connector and the distributor connctor.
   b. 1988–90 Starion and Mirage with the 1.6L engine – disconnect the female connector from the ignition timing connector, connect a suitable jumper wire with an alligator clip to the ignition timing adjusting terminal to ground it.
   c. 1988–90 Galant and Sigma – insert a suitable jumper wire (from the harness side) to the 1 pin connector located between the noise filter and the primary side of the ignition coil, and connect the tachometer. Be sure to insert the jumper wire along the terminal surface. If the connector is a male connector, the jumper wire should be inserted to the lock tab side. If the connector is a female connector, the jumper wire should be inserted opposite the lock tab side. Also using a alligator clip, connect a suitable jumper wire to the terminal for the ignition timing adjustment (locatd in the engine compartment) and ground it.
4. Disconnect and plug the vacuum lines to the sub vacuum chamber at the distributor, if so equipped. On the Cordia and Tredia 1.8L engine, disconnect the boost sensor connector, located in the engine compartment.
5. Start the engine and let it reach normal operating temperature. Check and verify that the engine idle speed is correct. If it is not within specifications, adjust it.
6. Stop the engine and connect the timing light according to manufacturers instructions. Disconnect and plug the vacuum advance hose, as required.
7. Start the engine and allow it to idle. Point the timing light at the mark on the front cover and read the timing by noting the position of the groove in the front pulley in relation to the timing mark or scale on the front cover. If the timing is incorrect, loosen the distributor mounting bolt. Turn the distributor slightly clockwise to retard the timing or counterclockwise to advance it.
8. When the reading is correct, tighten the distributor mounting bolt back up and then verify that the setting has not changed.
9. Turn the engine off, disconnect the timing light and tachometer and, if necessary, reconnect all the vacuum lines and disconnect connectors. Remove all jumper wires. Recheck the idle speed and adjust as necessary.

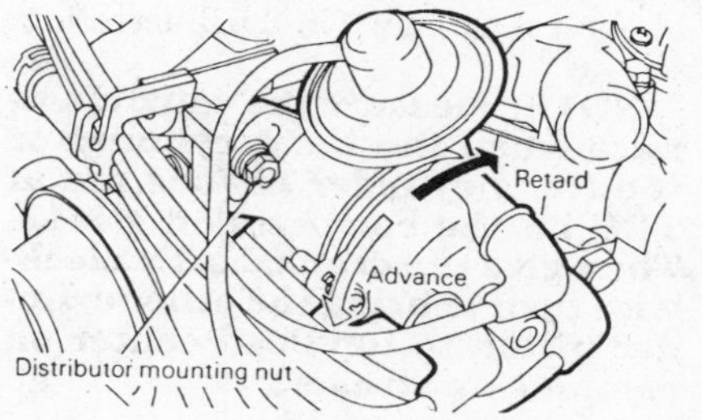


Adjusting ignition timing

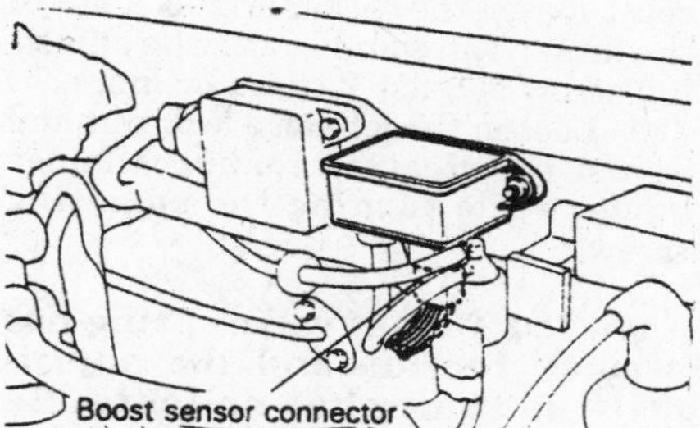


**Boost sensor connector location – Cordia/Tredia**

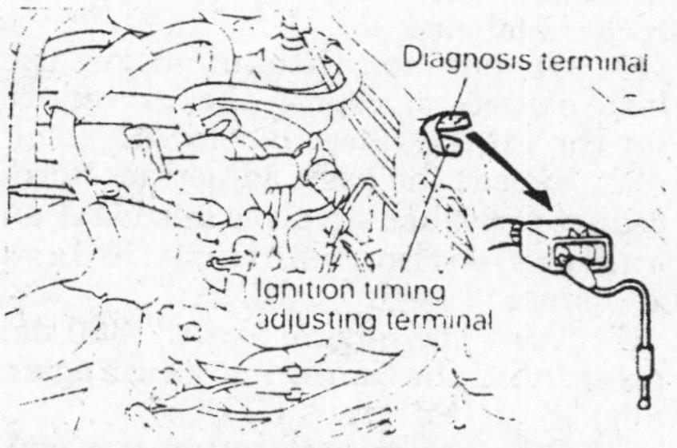


**Jumping the ignition timing adjusting terminal – Mirage**

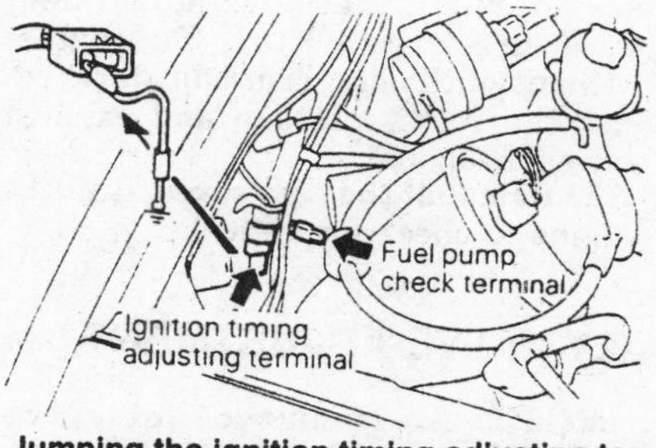


**Jumping the ignition timing adjusting terminal – Starion**

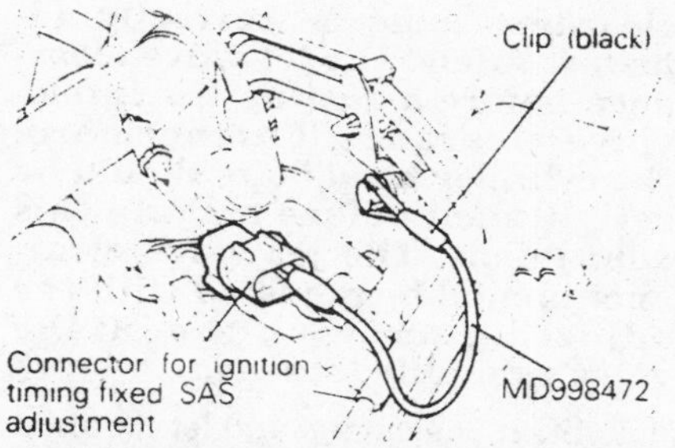


**Jumping the ignition timing adjusting terminal – Galant**

## Valve Lash

### ADJUSTMENT

Valve lash must be adjusted on all engines not equipped with automatic lash adjusters. Some engines have an unusual third valve of very small size called a jet valve. The jet valve must be adjusted, whether the engine uses automatic lash adjusters for the normal intake and exhaust valves or not. Thus, on some engines, there are 3 valves per cylinder that must be adjusted.

1. Run the engine until operating temperature is reached.
2. Turn off the engine and block the wheels.
3. Remove all necessary components in order to gain access to the rocker cover.
4. Remove the spark plugs from the cylinder head for easy operations.
   a. On Starion models – remove the air intake pipe and remove the rocker cover.
   b. On Cordia and Tredia models – disconnect the oxygen sensor connecting joint. Remove the engine bracket mounting, be sure to place a block of wood on the oil pan and jack it up into to place for the duration of the operation. Remove the upper front timing belt cover, remove the air cleaner assembly (2.0L) and the air intake pipe (1.8L) and remove the rocker cover.
   c. On all other models – remove the air cleaner or air intake pipe assembly and remove the rocker cover.
5. Turn each cylinder head bolt in the sequence back just until it is loose. Torque the cylinder head bolts in the proper sequence to specification.
6. Position the engine at **TDC** with No. 1 cylinder at the firing position. Turn the engine by using a wrench on the bolt in the front of the crankshaft until the **0** degree timing mark on the

timing cover lines up with the notch in the front pulley. On some models turn the crankshaft clockwise unitl the notch on the pulley is lined up with the **T** mark on the timing belt lower cover.

7. Observe the valve rockers for No. 1 cylinder. If both are in identical positions with the valves up, the engine is in the right position. If not, rotate the engine exactly 360 degrees until the **0** degree timing mark is again aligned. Each jet valve is associated with an intake valve that is on the same rocker lever. In this position you'll be able to adjust all the valves marked **A** in the illustration, including associated jet valves which are located on the rockers on the intake side only.

Adjusting valve clearance

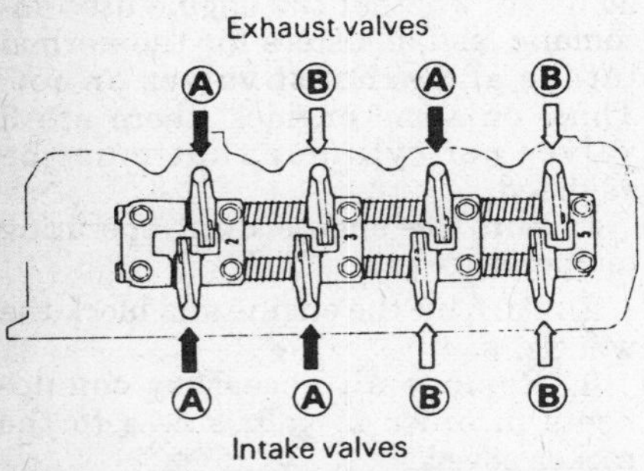


"A" and "B" valve adjusting positions

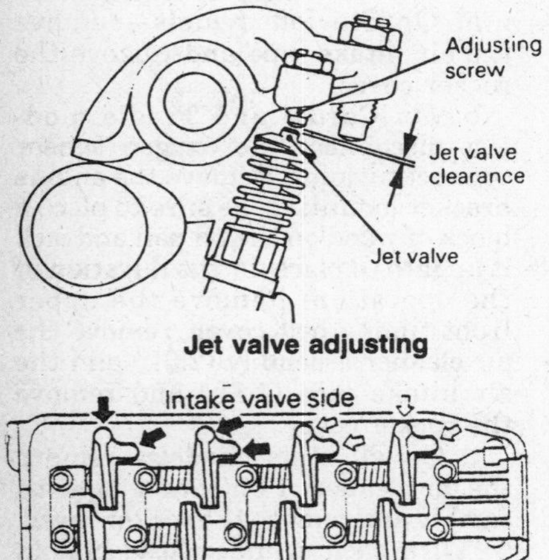


Jet valve adjusting

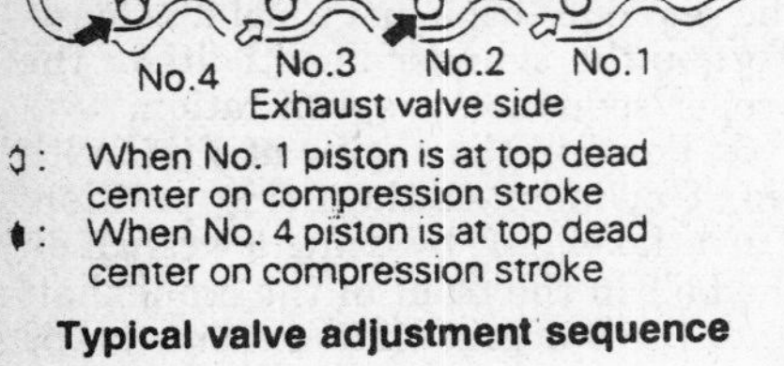


◊: When No. 1 piston is at top dead center on compression stroke

♦: When No. 4 piston is at top dead center on compression stroke

Typical valve adjustment sequence

8. To adjust the appropriate jet valves, first loosen the regular (larger) intake valve adjusting stud by loosening the locknut and backing the stud off 2 turns. Note that this particular step is not required on engines that have automatic lash adjusters.

9. Loosen the jet valve (smaller) adjusting stud locknut, back the stud out slightly and insert the feeler gauge between the jet valve and stud. Make sure the gauge lies flat on the top of the jet valve. Be careful not to twist the gauge or otherwise depress the jet valve spring, rotate the jet valve adjusting stud back in until it just touches the gauge. Tighten the locknut. Make sure the gauge still slides very easily between the stud and jet valve and that they both are still just touching the gauge.

**Note: The clearances must not be too tight.**

10. Repeat the entire procedure for the other jet valves associated with rockers labeled **A**.

11. On engines without automatic lash adjusters, repeat the procedure for the intake valves labeled **A**.

12. Repeat the basic adjustment procedure for exhaust valves labeled **A** on engines without automatic lash adjusters.

13. Turn the engine exactly 360 degrees, until the timing marks are again aligned at **O** degrees BTDC.

14. On engines with automatic lash adjusters, after the jet valves and rockers on the intake side and labeled **B** are adjusted, the valve adjustment procedure is completed. On engines without automatic lash adjusters, adjust the regular intake and exhaust valves labeled **B**.

15. Reinstall the cam cover. Run the engine to check for oil leaks.

## JET VALVE ADJUSTMENT

**NOTE: An incorrect jet valve clearance would affect the emission levels and could also cause engine troubles, so the jet valve clearance must be correctly adjusted. Adjust the jet valve clearance before adjusting the intake valve clearance. Furthermore, the cylinder head bolts should be retightened before making this adjustment. The jet valve clearance should be adjusted with the adjusting screw on the intake valve side fully loosened.**

1. Start the engine and let it run at idle until it reaches normal operating temperature.

2. Remove all spark plugs from the cylinder head for easy operation.

3. On Starion models—remove the air intake pipe and remove the rocker cover.

4. On Cordia and Tredia models—disconnect the oxygen sensor connecting joint. Remove the engine bracket mounting, be sure to place a block of wood on the oil pan and jack it up into to place for the duration of the operation. Remove the upper front timing belt cover, remove the air cleaner assembly (2.0L) and the air intake pipe (1.8L) and remove the rockewr arm.

5. On all other models—remove the air cleaner or air intake pipe assembly and remove the rocker cover.

6. Now, put the engine at TDC with No. 1 cylinder at the firing position. Turn the engine by using a wrench on the bolt in the front of the crankshaft until the **0** degree timing mark on the timing cover lines up with the notch in the front pulley (on some models turn the crankshaft clockwise until the notch on the pulley is lined up with the **T** mark on the timing belt lower cover). This will bring both No. 1 and No. 4 cylinder pistons up to **TDC**.

**NOTE: Never turn the crankshaft counterclockwise.**

7. Move the rocker arms on the number 1 and number 4 cylinders up and down by hand to determine if the piston in that cylinder is at top dead center on the compression stroke. If the intake and exhaust rocker arms do not move, the piston in that cylinder is not at **TDC** on the compression stroke.

8. Measure the jet valve clearance at point **A** as shown in the illustration.

**NOTE: Measure the valve clearance when the No. 1 cylinder or the No. 4 cylinder pistons are at TDC on the compression stroke. Then give the crankshaft 1 clockwise turn to bring the other cylinder piston to top dead center on compresion stroke.**

9. If the jet valve clearance is not as specified (0.010 in. hot and 0.007 in. cold), loosen the rocker arm lock nut of the intake valve and loosen the adjusting screw at least 2 turns or more.

10. Loosen the jet valve lock-nut and adjust the clearance using a feeler gauge while turning the adjusting screw.

**NOTE: The jet valve spring has a small tension and the adjustment is somewhat delicate. Be careful not to push in the jet valve by turning the adjusting screw in too much.**

11. Tighten the adjusting screw until it touches the feeler gauge. Turn the locknut to secure it, while holding the rocker arm adjusting screw with a suitable tool to keep it from turning.

12. Check the intake and exhaust valve clearance, if it is not within specifications, adjust the valves as follows:

a. Loosen the locknut on the adjusting screw for the valve. Turn the adjusting screw counterclockwise and insert the proper size feeler gauge between the valve stem and the adjusting screw.

b. Tighten the adjusting screw until it touches the feeler gauge. Turn the locknut to secure it, while holding the rocker arm adjusting screw with a suitable tool to keep it from turning.

13. Turn the engine by using a wrench on the bolt in the front of the crankshaft 360 degrees until the **0** degree timing mark on the timing cover lines up with the notch in the front pulley (on some models turn the crankshaft clockwise until the notch on the pulley is lined up with the **T** mark on the timing belt lower cover).

14. Repeat Steps 9 through 13 on the other valves (marked **B**) for clearance adjustment.

15. Reinstall all the remove components in the reverse order of the removal procedure.

## Idle Speed and Mixture

### IDLE SPEED ADJUSTMENT

#### *Carbureted Engines*

**NOTE: The throttle valve adjusting screw should not be tampered with unless the carburetor has been rebuilt. This screw is preset and determines the relationship between the throttle valve and the free lever, and has been accurately set at the factory. If this setting is disturbed, the throttle opener adjustment and or dashpot adjustment cannot be done accurately. Also the improper setting (throttle valve opening) will increase the exhaust gas temperature and deceleration, which in turn will reduce the life of the catalyst greatly and deteriorate the exhaust gas cleaning performance. It will also effect the fuel consumption and the engine braking.**

#### 1983–84

1. Run the engine at fast idle until normal operating temperature is reached. Turn off all lights and accessories. The electric cooling fan must

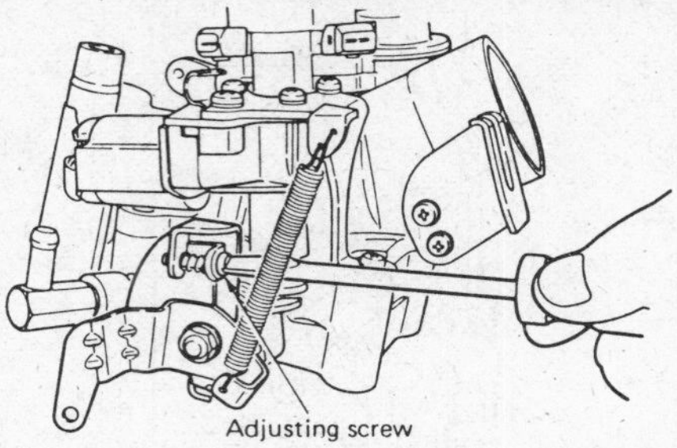


**Idle Speed adjusting screw for '84 Cordia/Tredia**

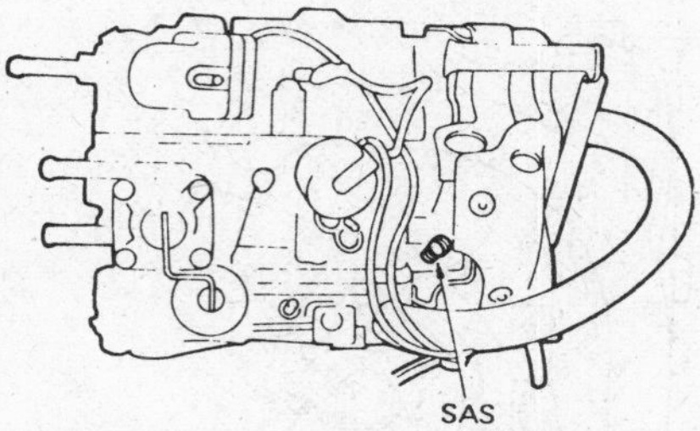


**Idle speed adjusting screw (SAS)**

not be operating. Set the parking brake, block the wheels and position the gear selector in neutral.

2. Run the engine between 2000 and 3000 rpm for about 5 seconds, then allow it to idle for 2 minutes.

3. Check the idle speed adjustment screw on the carburetor linkage arm.

#### 1985–90

1. With the vehicle in park, the drive wheels blocked and all the accessories off. Run the engine until it reaches normal operating temperature.

2. Bring the engine rpm up to 2000–3000 rpm for about 10 seconds, then let the engine idle for at least 2 minutes.

3. Connect a tachometer to the engine and check the idling speed. If it does not meet specifications, readjust the idle speed to the nominal specification, using the idle speed adjusting screw, which is located closest to the primary throttle valve shaft.

#### *Fuel Injected Engines*

1. Run the engine until normal operating temperature is reached. Make sure all lights and accessories are turned off.

2. Apply the parking brake and block the wheels. Posstion the gear selector in neutral and stop the engine.

3. Attach a tachometer and timing light. Start the engine and increase the engine speed to 2000–3000 rpm several times, return to idle and check the ignition timing, adjust if necessary.

4. Remove the rubber cap covering the idle speed adjuster switch, leaving the cable connector connected. The idle adjuster switch is located on the throttle linkage. Adjust the idle speed.

5. If the idle adjustment screw must be turned more than 1 turn during adjustment, disconnect the connector from the speed adjust switch and plug it into the dummy terminal on the injector base. Adjust to correct idle speed and reconnect to the idle switch. Remove the tachometer and timing light.

### IDLE SPEED CONTROL ADJUSTMENT

#### *1984 Cordia and Tredia*

1. Run the engine at fast idle until it reaches normal operating temperature. Turn the engine off at that point.

2. Turn the ignition switch on for at least 15 seconds, then turn it off. Disconnect the ISC servo harness connector.

3. Start the engine. Connect a tachometer and check the idle speed. Adjust it to 600 rpm, using the adjusting screw on the ISC servo. Reconnect the servo.

#### *1985–88 Cordia and Tredia*

**NOTE: When replacing the ISC servo, the engine speed should be adjusted.**

1. With the vehicle in park, the drive wheels blocked and all the accessories off. Run the engine until it reaches normal operating temperature.

2. Remove the carburetor from the engine. Remove the concealment plug from the carburetor.

3. Reinstall the carburetor onto the engine and relax the tension on the accelerator cable.

4. Place the ignition switch to the one position and wait for at least 18 seconds. Turn the ignition switch off and disconnect the ISC actuator connector and the oxygen sensor connector.

5. Start the engine check the ignition timing and adjust if necessary. Increase the engine speed between 2000–3000 rpm, 2 or 3 times and then let the engine idle for 30 seconds.

6. Adjust the mixture adjusting screw for a concentration of 0.1–0.3%. Adjust the engine rpm to the specified speed by using the ISC adjustment screw.

7. Turn the idle mixture screw (secondary air supply screw) until the engine reaches its highest rpm. Turn the screw ⅔ of turn in the reverse direction from that point.

8. Race the engine 2 or 3 times.

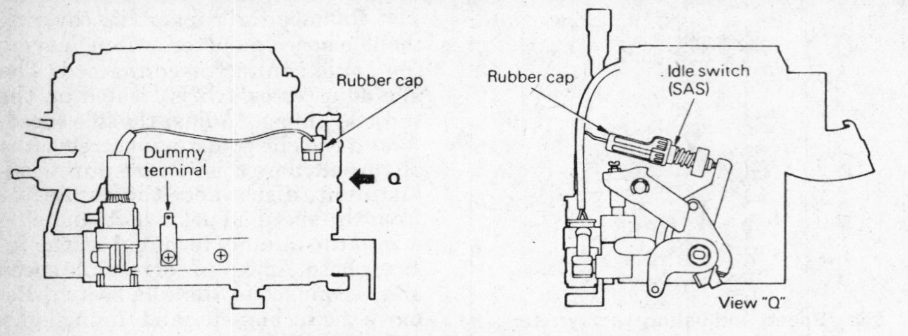


**Idle speed adjustment for fuel injection**

Check to be sure that the CO and engine rpm are still adjusted to specifications. If they are not, readjust as necessary.

9. Adjust the tension of the accelerator cable. The cable should have enough play so as not to interfere with idle switch.

10. Reconnect the ISC actuator connector and the oxygen sensor connector.

### *Precis*

1. Make sure the gear selector is in **N** or **P**. Run the engine at fast idle until the cooling system reaches 185°F or more (not to exceed 205°F). Then, race the engine at 2000–3000 rpm for more than 5 seconds. Release the throttle. All accessories including the electric cooling fan must be off.

2. Idle the engine for a full 2 minutes. Connect a tachometer between the (–) terminal of the coil and a good ground while the engine is idling. If the idle speed is not to the specification, adjust the idle speed screw (which is located closest to the primary throotle valve shaft) to obtain the propr idle speed specifications.

3. The idle speed should be as follows:

a. Manual Transaxle – 700 ±100 rpm

b. Automatic Transaxle – 750 ±100 rpm

c. Canada – 850 ±30 rpm

## IDLE SPEED CONTROL (ISC) THROTTLE POSITION SENSOR (TPS) AND SERVO ADJUSTMENT

### *1985–90 Turbocharged Engines*

**NOTE: This adjustment is very important, since the vehicle driveability depends upon it. If the ISC servo, throttle position sensor, mixing body, or throttle body has been replaced or removed for any reason, use the following procedure to make the adjustments.**

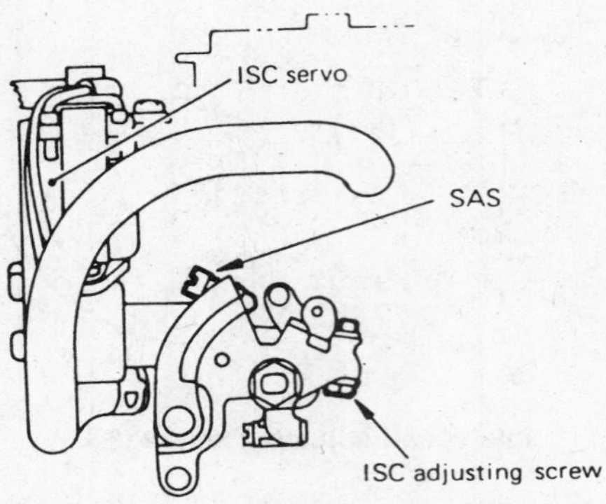


**Adjusting the Idle Speed Control and CO on the 2.0L automatic. Adjust the ISC adjusting screw and then the SAS (Speed Adjusting Screw)**

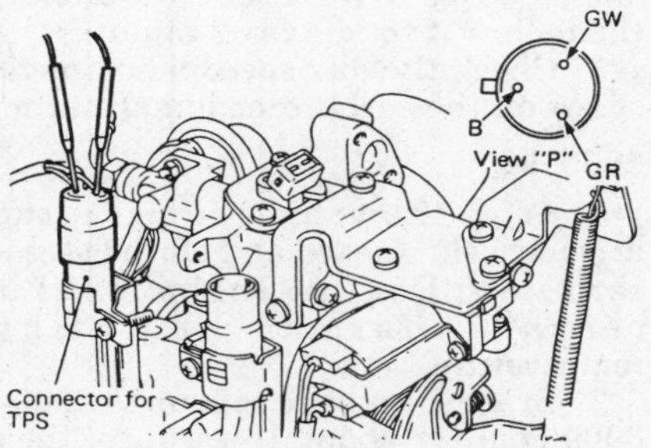


**Connect the digital voltmeter to the "GW" and "B" pins of the Throttle Position sensor connector—1985 and later turbocharged vehicles**

1. With the vehicle in **PARK**, the drive wheels blocked and all the accessories off, run the engine until it reaches normal operating temperature.

2. Stop the engine and disconnect the accelerator cable from the throttle lever of the injection mixer. Loosen the 2 throttle position sensor mounting screws, turn the throttle position sensor clockwise as far as it will go and then temporarily tighten the screws.

3. Turn the ignition switch to the on position for 15 seconds and then turn it off. This will set the ISC servo to the specified position.

4. Disconnect the ISC servo harness connector. Start the engine, check the engine speed and adjust to specifications.

5. Stop the engine and disconnect the throttle position sensor harness connector.

6. Connect an adapter and a digital voltmeter between the throttle position sensor connector. Insert the probes of the digital voltmeter into the GW lead (TPS outlet) and the **B** lead (ground) of the body side harness. Place the ignition switch to the **ON** position, but do not start the engine.

7. Read the throttle position sensor output voltage.

8. If the measurement of the output voltage does not agree with the 0.48–0.52 volts, loosen the throttle position sensor screws and turn the sensor left or right to bring the sensor into specifications. After applying sealant to the sensor, tighten the mounting screws.

9. Fully open the throttle valve one and confirm that the output voltage is correct when it is returned.

10. Remove the adapter and the digital voltmeter, reconnect the ISC servo harness connector and confirm that the curb idle is correct.

## IDLE-UP SPEED ADJUSTMENT

### *1985–88 Cordia, Tredia, Mirage and 1987–90 Precis*

#### CARBURETED ENGINES WITHOUT AIR CONDTIONING

**NOTE: Adjustment condition – lights, electric cooling fan and all accessories are off and transaxle is in neutral.**

1. Make sure the curb idle speed is within specifications, adjust if necessary.

2. By using the auxiliary lead wire, activate the idle up solenoid valve. Apply the intake manifold vacuum to the throttle opener and activate the throttle opener.

3. Open the throttle slightly (to engine speed of about 2000 rpm) and then slowly close it.

4. Adjust the engine speed to the specifications with the idle-up adjusting screw.

5. After repeating Step 3, check the engine speed.

6. Remove the auxiliary lead wire used in Step 2 and reconnect the idle-up solenoid valve wiring.

### *1985–88 Cordia, Tredia, Mirage and 1985–90 Precis*

#### CARBURETED ENGINES WITH AIR CONDITIONING

1. With the vehicle in park, the

drive wheels blocked and all the accessories off. Run the engine until it reaches normal operating temperature.

2. Disconnect the electric cooling fan connector. On vehicles equipped with power steering, set the tires in the straight ahead position to prevent the pump from being loaded. Set the steering wheel in the stationary position.

3. Be sure that the curb idle speed is within the specifications, adjust if necessary.

4. With the air conditioner on, adjust the engine speed to the specified speed with the throttle opener setting screw (idle-up adjusting screw).

5. Reconnect the electric cooling fan connector and turn the A/C on and off several times to check the operation of the throttle opener.

## THROTTLE POSITION SENSOR ADJUSTMENT

### *1985–90 1.5L and 1.6L Engines and 1985–88 2.0L Engine with Manual Transaxle*

1. Start the engine and let it run until the engine reaches normal operating temperature. Be sure that the fast idle cam is released.

2. Stop the engine. Back off the secondary air supply screws sufficiently and close the throttle valve fully. Make sure to count the number of turns taken on the screws.

3. Connect a digital voltmeter the bottom 2 slots of the TPS connector. Turn the ignition switch on the adjust the TPS outlet voltage to 250 millivolts with the adjusting screw.

4. Tighten the secondary air supply screws by giving the same number of turns to the screws as recorded in Step 2.

**NOTE: The Cordia and Tredia 2.0L engine with automatic transaxle TPS adjustment is the same except for making the idle speed control adjustment first. The TPS outlet voltage should be 445 millivolts.**

### *Galant and Sigma Multi-Port Injected Models*

1. Disconnect the throttle position sensor connector.

2. Measure the resistance between terminal 1 (sensor ground) and terminal 3 (sensor power). The standard resistance should be 3.5–6.5 kilo – ohms.

3. Connect a pointer type ohmmeter, between terminal 1 and 2 (sensor output terminal).

4. Operate the throttle valve slowly from the idle position to the full open position and check that the resistance changs smoothly from inproportion with the throttle valve opening angle.

## IDLE MIXTURE ADJUSTMENT

### *Carbureted Engines*

#### EXCEPT 1987–90 PRECIS AND 1985–88 CORDIA, TREDIA AND MIRAGE WITH AUTOMATIC TRANSAXLE

1. Remove the carburetor from the engine. The idle mixture screw is located in the base of the carburetor, just to the left of the PCV hose. Mount the carburetor, carefully, in a softjawed vise, protecting the gasket surface and with the mixture adjusting screw facing upward.

2. Drill a $^5/_{64}$ in. hole through the casting from the underside of the carburetor. Make sure that this hole intersects the passage leading to the mixture adjustment screw just behind the plug. Now, widen that hole with a ⅛ in. drill bit.

3. Insert a blunt punch into the hole and tap out the plug. Install the carburetor on the engine and connect all hoses, lines, etc.

4. Start the engine and run it at fast idle until it reaches normal operating temperature. Make sure that all accessories are off and the transaxle is in Neutral. Turn the ignition switch off and disconnect the battery ground cable for about 3 seconds, then, reconnect it. Disconnect the oxygen sensor.

5. Start the engine and run it for at least 5 seconds at 2000–3000 rpm. Then, allow the engine to idle for about 2 minutes.

6. Connect a tachometer and allow the engine to operate at the specified curb idle speed. Adjust it if necessary, to obtain this speed. Connect a CO meter to the exhaust pipe. A reading of 0.1–0.3% is necessary. Adjust the mixture screw to obtain the reading. If, during this adjustment, the idle speed is varied more than 100 rpm in either direction, reset the idle speed and readjust the CO until both specifications are met simultaneously. Shut off the engine, reconnect the oxygen sensor and install a new concealment plug.

#### 1985–88 CORDIA, TREDIA AND MIRAGE WITH AUTOMATIC TRANSAXLE

1. Remove the carburetor from the engine and place the carburetor in a suitable fixture in order to remove the concealment plug.

2. Drill a $^5/_{64}$ in. (2mm) pilot hole in the casting surrounding the idle mixture adjusting screw. Then redrill the hole to ⅛ in. (3mm) and insert a punch into the hole to drive out the concealment plug.

3. Reinstall the carburetor on the engine without the concealment plug.

4. With the vehicle in park, the drive wheels blocked and all the accessories off, run the engine until it reaches normal operating temperature.

5. Turn off the engine and disconnect the negative battery cable for about 3 seconds and reconnect the cable.

6. Disconnect the connector of the exhaust oxygen sensor. Run the vehicle for 5 minutes at a speed of 30 rpm or run the engine for more than 5 minutes at the engine speed of 2000–3000 rpm.

7. Run the engine at idle for 2 minutes and set the idle CO and the engine speed to specification (the idle CO: 0.1–0.3% at nominal curb idle speed).

8. Reconnect the oxygen sensor connector. Readjust the engine speed, if necessary and install the concealment plug into the hole to seal the idle mixture adjusting screw.

#### 1987–90 PRECIS

1. Remove the carburetor. The idle mixture screw is located in the base of the carburetor, just to the left of the PCV hose. Mount the carburetor, carefully, in a soft jawed vise, protecting the gasket surface, and with the mixture adjusting screw facing upward.

2. Drill a small hole through the casting from the underside of the carburetor. Make sure that this hole intersects the passage leading to the mixture adjustment screw just behind the plug. Now, widen that hole with a ⅛ in. drill bit.

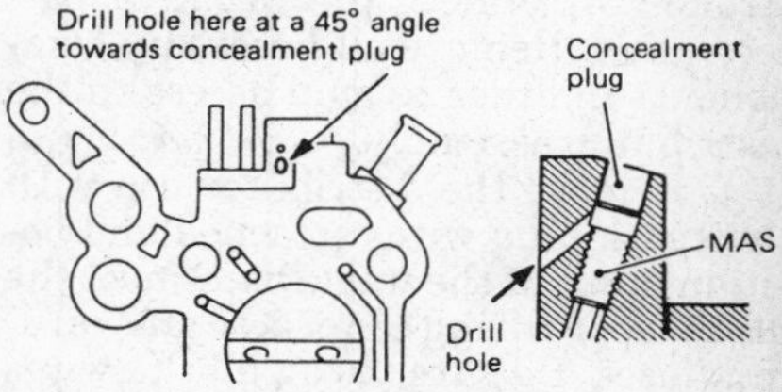


**Drilling out the concealment plug to adjust CO on carbureted models**

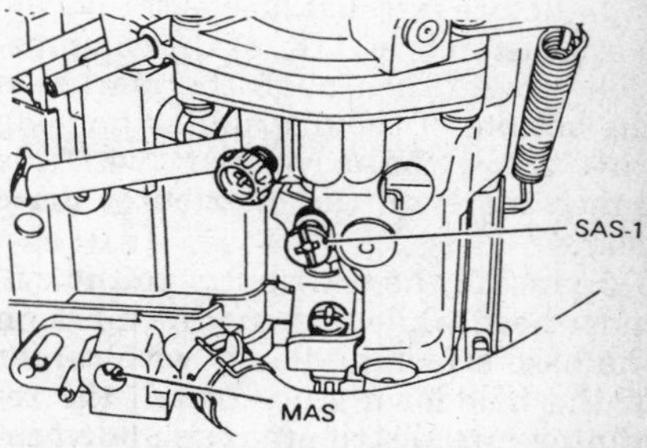


**The location of the MAS (Mixture Adjusting Screw**

3. Insert a blunt punch into the hole and tap out the plug. Install the carburetor on the engine and connect all hoses, lines, etc.

4. Start the engine and run it at fast idle until it reaches normal operating temperature. Make sure that all accessories are off and the transaxle is in neutral. Turn the ignition switch off and disconnect the battery ground cable for about 3 seconds, then, reconnect it. Disconnect the oxygen sensor.

5. Start the engine and run it for at least 5 seconds at 2000–3000 rpm. Then, allow the engine to idle for about 2 minutes.

6. Connect a tachometer and allow the engine to operate at the specified curb idle speed. Adjust it, if necessary, to obtain this speed. Connect a CO meter to the exhaust pipe. A reading of 0.1–0.3% is necessary. Adjust the mixture screw to obtain the reading. If, during this adjustment, the idle speed is varied more than 100 rpm in either direction, reset the idle speed and readjust the CO until both specifications are met simultaneously. Shut off the engine, reconnect the oxygen sensor and install a new concealment plug.

# ENGINE ELECTRICAL

## Distributor

### REMOVAL & INSTALLATION

1. Rotate the engine until the No. 1 piston is at TDC of the compression stroke. Disconnect the negative battery cable. Remove all necessary components in order to gain access to the distributor assembly.

2. Remove the distributor cap with the spark plug wires attached and position it out of the way. Disconnect the distributor wiring connector and vacuum hoses. Be sure to tag all the wires and vacuum lines for easy installation.

3. Remove the distributor base retaining nut. Remove the distributor.

4. Before installation check that the No. 1 piston is at TDC of the compression stroke, then align the marks on the bottom of the distributor housing (just above the drive gear) with the punch mark on the distributor drive gear.

5. Install the distributor to the cylinder head while aligning the mark on the base attaching flange with center of the holddown stud. Install the retaining nut, distributor cap and vacuum hoses. Start the engine and adjust the ignition timing.

## Alternator

### PRECAUTIONS

In order to prevent damage to the alternator observe the following precautions:

- Reversing the battery connections will result in damage to the diodes.
- Booster cables should be connected from positive to positive and the negative cable from the booster battery connected to a good ground on the engine of the vehicle with the dead battery.
- Never use a fast charger as a booster to start the vehicle.
- When servicing the battery with a fast charger always disconnect the battery cables.
- Never attempt to polarize an alternator.
- Avoid long soldering times when replacing diodes or transistors. Prolonged heat is damaging to alternators.
- Do not use test lamps of more than 12V (volts) for checking diode continuity.
- Do not short across or ground any of the alternator terminals.
- The polarity of the battery, alternator and regulator must be matched and considered before making any electrical connections within the system.
- Never operate the alternator on an open circuit. Make sure all connections within a circuit are clean and tight.
- Disconnect the negative (or both) battery terminals when performing any service on the electrical system.
- Disconnect the negative battery cable if arc welding is to be done on any part of the vehicle.

### BELT TENSION ADJUSTMENT

#### *Except Sigma*

1. Check the drive belt(s) for cracking, fraying or any other deterioration. Replace the drive belt if suspect.
2. Loosen the alternator pivot nut.
3. Loosen the lock bolt of the belt tension adjuster.
4. Using the adjustment bolt, adjust the belt tension to specification. Belt tension is proper when the belt can be deflected at midpoint $^9/_{32}$–$^{11}/_{32}$ in.
5. Tighten the lock bolt.
6. Tighten the alternator pivot nut.

#### *Sigma*

1. Check the drive belt(s) for cracking, fraying or any other deterioration. Replace the drive belt if suspect.

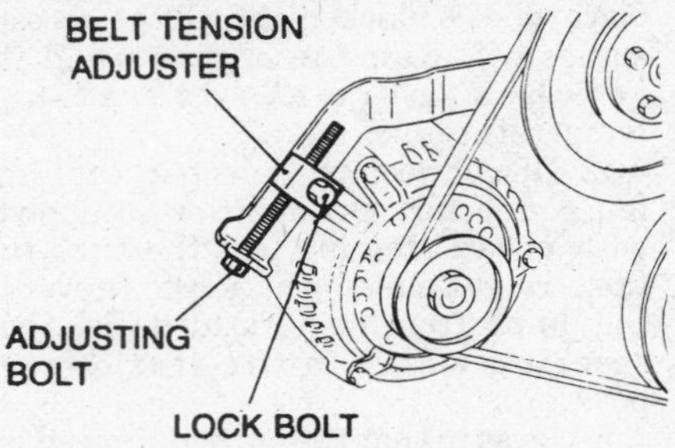


**Alternator belt adjustment—except Sigma**

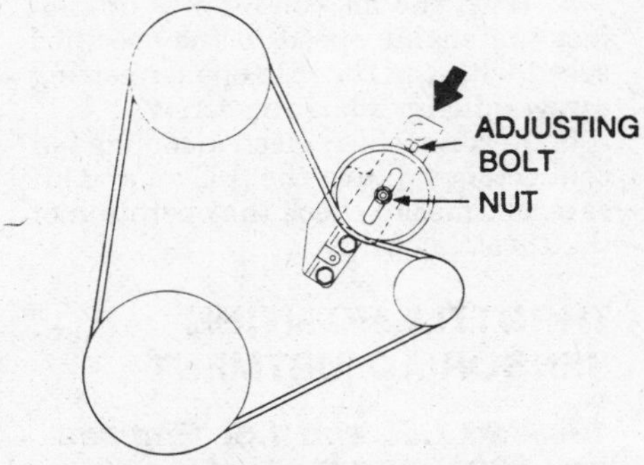


**Alternator belt adjustment—Sigma**

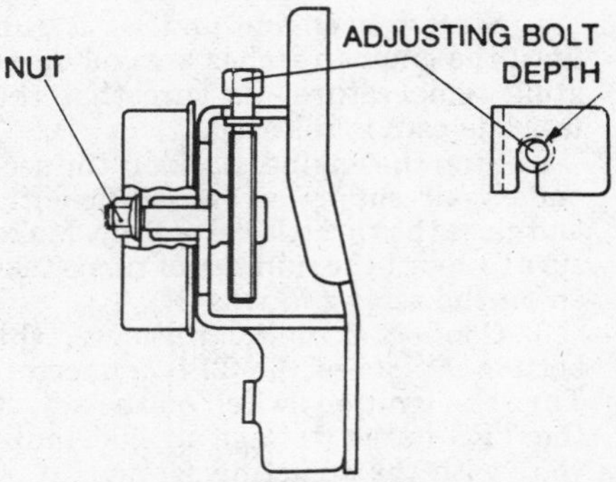


**Tension pulley adjustment bolt**

2. To increase the belt tension, loosen the nut 1/8 turn, turn the left hand threaded adjusting bolt clockwise and displace the tension pulley slightly.

**CAUTION**

*Put the adjusting bolt into the recess at the far depth of the elongated hole on the tension bracket.*

3. Tighten the nut to 28–43 ft. lbs. (39–60 Nm).

### REMOVAL & INSTALLATION

#### *Except Galant and Sigma V6*

1. Disconnect the negative battery cable.
2. Remove all necessary components in order to gain access to the alternator assembly.

3. On some models it may be necessary to remove the A/C compressor and position it out of the way in order to gain access to the alternator.

4. On the 1985-88 Mirage, it will be necessary to remove the A/C condenser fan motor and the power steering pump with bracket. On the 1985-88 Tredia and Cordia, it will be necessary to remove the power steering pump.

**NOTE: After removing the engine bracket mounting, be sure to place a block of wood on the oil pan and jack up the engine into to place for the duration of the operation.**

5. Disconnect the alternator electrical. Note or tag the wires so that you can reinstall them correctly.

6. Remove the top mounting bolt. Loosen the lower mounting nut. Slide the alternator over in its attaching bracket and remove the fan belt.

7. Remove the lower mounting nut and bolt. Remove the alternator from the vehicle.

8. Installation is the reverse of the removal procedure. Replace shims as required in their respective places. Adjust the drive belt as required.

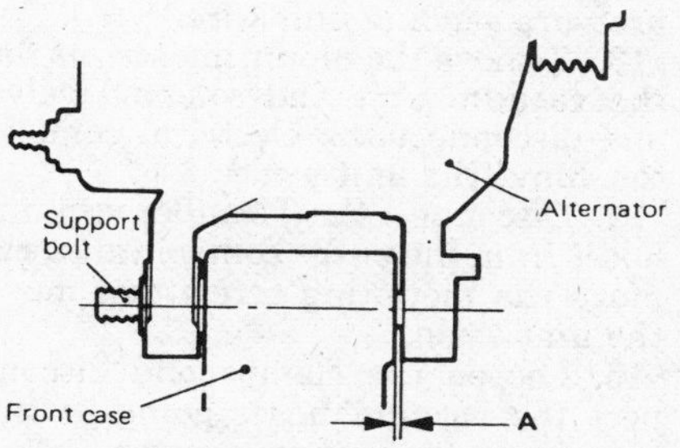


**Gap "A" shows where you should measure the clearance for installation of alternator mounting shims**

### *Galant and Sigma V6*

1. Disconnect the negative battery cable.
2. Remove the front engine mounting bracket.
3. Remove the power steering pressure hose nut.
4. Remove the A/C low pressure line mounting bolt.
5. Remove the drive belt tensioner with bracket.
6. Disconnect high tension spark plug wires 2, 4, 6.
7. Remove the distributor cap and timing belt cover cap.
8. Disconnect the alternator electrical connections and remove the alternator.
9. To install reverse the removal procedure.
10. Adjust the alternator belt to specifications.

# Voltage Regulator

The voltage regulator is of solid state design and built into the alternator. No normal maintenance is necessary.

# Starter

## REMOVAL & INSTALLATION

1. Disconnect the negative battery cable.
2. Remove the necessary components in order to gain access to the starter assembly.
3. Disconnect the electrical connections from the starter motor.
4. Remove the starter motor to engine mounting bolts. Remove the starter motor from the vehicle.
5. If various components make starter motor removal difficult from the top of the engine compartment, raise and support the vehicle, then remove the starter from underneath after removing the splash shield.
6. Installation is the reverse of the removal procedure.

## STARTER DRIVE REPLACEMENT

### *Direct Drive Starter*

1. Remove the starter. Remove the solenoid.
2. Remove the through-bolts and screws from the rear bracket. Remove the rear bracket.
3. Pry back the retaining rings and slide the brushes out of the brush holder. Remove the brush holder and the yoke assembly.
4. Remove the washer from the rear of the armature. Remove the field coil assembly from the front frame. Remove the spring retainer, spring and

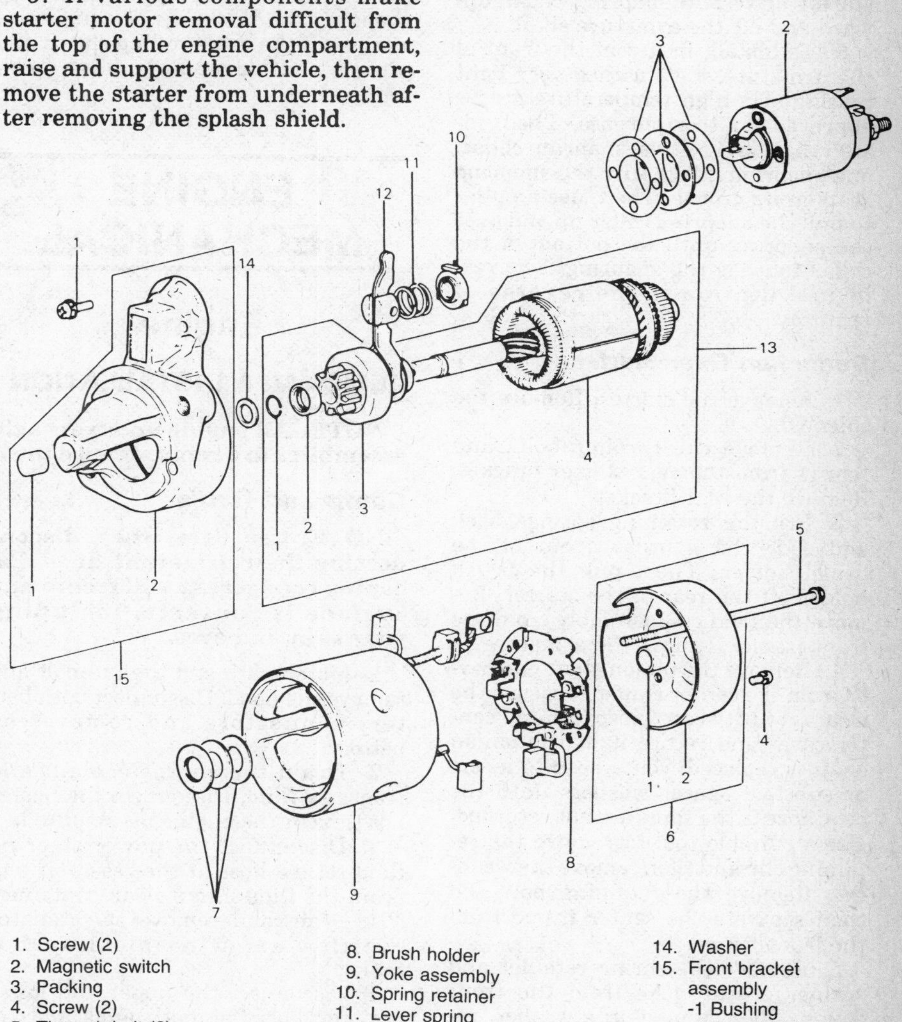


1. Screw (2)
2. Magnetic switch
3. Packing
4. Screw (2)
5. Through bolt (2)
6. Rear bracket assembly
   -1 Bushing
   -2 Rear bracket
7. Washer
8. Brush holder
9. Yoke assembly
10. Spring retainer
11. Lever spring
12. Lever
13. Armature assembly
    -1 Snap ring
    -2 Stop ring
    -3 Overrunning clutch
    -4 Armature
14. Washer
15. Front bracket assembly
    -1 Bushing
    -2 Front bracket

NOTE
Numbers show order of disassembly.
For reassembly, reverse order of disassembly.

**Typical starter motor components**

spring seat from the starter front frame. Separate the armature from the front bracket by first pulling the armature back out of the front bearing and then shifting the armature so the starter drive is pulled out of the yoke. Make sure you don't lose the washer located in the front frame.

5. Invert the armature so the starter drive is on top and rest the rear of the armature on a solid surface. Use a deep well socket wrench that is just slightly larger than the diameter of the armature shaft to press the snapring collar back. Install the socket over the top of the shaft and then press it downward or tap it very lightly to force the ring downward. Once the snapring is exposed, use snapring pliers to open it until it will slide upward, out of the groove and off the shaft. Now, pull the starter drive and snapring collar upward and off the armature shaft.

6. To install, first coat the front of the armature shaft with a very light coating of a high temperature grease approved for this purpose. Then, install the starter drive, snapring collar, and snapring. Make sure the snapring seats in its groove. Then, use a puller to pull the snapring collar up and over the snapring until the bottom of the collar touches the snapring. The rest of installation is the reverse of removal.

#### *Reduction Gear Starter*

1. Remove the starter. Remove the solenoid.
2. Remove the through-bolts and screws from the rear starter bracket. Remove the rear bracket.
3. Pry the retaining springs back and slide the 2 brushes out of the brush holder. Then, pull the brush holder off the rear of the starter. Remove the field coil assembly from the front frame. Remove the armature.
4. Remove the pinion shaft end cover from the center frame. Measure the clearance between the spacer and center cover and record it. If the pinion shaft is replaced, you'll have to insert or subtract spacer washers until the clearance is the same as that recorded. Use a suitable tool to remove the retaining clip and then remove the washers. Remove the retaining bolt and then separate the center frame from the front frame.
5. Remove the spring retainer and spring for the yoke from the front frame. Then, remove the washer, reduction gear, shift yoke lever and 2 lever supports.
6. Turn the front frame so the pinion gear is at the top and support it securely. Then, use a socket that fits tight over the pinion shaft to force the snapring collar downward. Tap the socket lightly at the top or use a press to do this. Then, use a suitable tool to work the snapring out of its groove and remove it from the shaft. Remove the collar. Remove the pinion and the spring behind it from the shaft.
7. Now, pull the overrunning clutch and pinion shaft assembly out of the rear of the front frame. Replace the pinion of its teeth are damaged (check the flywheel ring gear as well). Replace the overrunning clutch if the pinion gear is damaged or if the one way action of the clutch is not precise.
8. To install, first coat the splines of the pinion shaft with a light coating of a high temperature grease designed for this purpose. Then, reverse all the removal procedures to install. When reassembling the washer and clip at the rear of the pinion shaft, note that the clearance must be corrected by changing the thickness or number of washers if the overrunning clutch and pinion shaft assembly have been replaced.

# ENGINE MECHANICAL

## Engine

### REMOVAL & INSTALLATION

**NOTE: All engine and transaxle assemblies are removed as a unit.**

#### *Cordia and Tredia*

**NOTE: Use care when disconnecting the refrigerant lines. Escaping refrigerant will freeze any surface it contacts, including your skin and eyes.**

1. Matchmark and then unbolt and remove the hood. Disconnect both battery connectors and remove the battery.
2. Drain the engine coolant and transaxle fluid. Disconnect the heater hoses from the engine, as required.
3. Disconnect the power steering fluid return hose at the reservoir and drain the fluid into a clean container.
4. Drain and remove the radiator overflow and windshield washer tanks.
5. Disconnect the upper and lower radiator hoses at both ends and remove them. If the vehicle has air conditioning, disconnect the hoses as close as possible to the condenser unit in front of the radiator and cap the openings securely. Then, remove the radiator or radiator and condenser assemble.
6. Remove the battery tray. Disconnect both heater hoses from the side of the engine.
7. Remove the air cleaner. On turbocharged vehicles, disconnect the turbocharger intake hose.
8. Disconnect the brake booster vacuum hose. On turbocharged vehicles only, disconnect the oil cooler hoses at the engine. On vehicles with A/T, disconnect the cooler lines.
9. On vehicles with M/T, disconnect the clutch cable, on vehicles with A/T, disconnect the shift control cable. On all vehicles, disconnect the speedometer cable from the transaxle.
10. Disconnect the accelerator cable at the side of the engine. Disconnect the engine ground strap at the right front fender. On vehicles with an air conditioner, disconnect the hoses at the compressor and cap all openings securely.
11. Disconnect the power steering hoses at the side of the pump. Cap all openings. Disconnect the coil low and high tension wires. Label the low tension wires for reassembly to the proper terminals. Disconnect the battery negative cable from the engine.
12. Label and disconnect the alternator connectors. Disconnect the oil pressure sending unit wire.
13. Remove the mounting screws for the vacuum unit and solenoid valve and disconnect the electrical connector. Move the unit aside.
14. Disconnect the 2 smaller vacuum hoses from the purge control valve, remove the mounting screw and move the unit aside.
15. Loosen the clamps and disconnect the vacuum hoses going to the evaporative emissions canister.
16. Disconnect the fuel return hose from the carburetor or injection mixer. Disconnect the fuel supply hose at the fuel filter.
17. Raise the vehicle and support it safely. Then, disconnect the exhaust pipe at the manifold. Fasten the exhaust pipe with wire to keep it from falling.
18. On M/T vehicles, disconnect the shift control rod and extension and remove them.
19. Disconnect the left and right side strut bars and stabilizer bars where they connect to the lower control arms. Then, remove the bolts fastening the control arms on both sides to the rearward crossmember.
20. Disconnect the lower arm ball joint at the steering knuckle on both sides. Then, disconnect the strut bar and stabilizer bar at the lower control arm. Now, using a prybar inserted between the transaxle case and driveshaft, carefully pry the halfshaft out of the transaxle on each side. Plug the

openings in the transaxle to prevent dirt from getting in.

21. Carefully lower all parts to the crossmember. Discard the retaining clips for the halfshafts. They must be replaced.

22. Attach a cable securely supported by a lift and pulley arrangement to each engine lifting point. Put tension on all the cables to support the engine securely.

23. Remove the nut from the left side engine mount insulator. Remove the 4 front roll bracket mounting bolts located on the side of the front crossmember.

24. Remove the mounting bolt from the rear roll insulator. Remove the nuts attaching the left engine mount insulator to the fender.

25. From inside the right fender shield, detach the protective cap and then remove the transaxle insulator bracket mounting bolts. Remove the bolts connecting the transaxle mount insulator.

26. Remove the bolts to the shift control selector. Remove the wiring connector going to the transaxle. Disconnect vacuum hoses.

27. Remove the transaxle insulator bracket. Now, increase the tension on the lifting cables so the engine weight is supported entirely by the cables and none of the weight is on the mounts. Remove the bolts passing through the insulators of the rear roll stop and left mounting bracket.

28. Check to make sure that all items are disconnected from the engine/transaxle assembly. Press downward on the transaxle to guide the assembly and lift it carefully out of the vehicle.

29. Installation is the exact reverse of removal. When installing the engine, be careful to ensure that engine compartment wiring and hoses do not catch on engine wiring and hoses do not catch on engine parts. Torque mounting bolts as follows:

Left engine mount insulator nut (large) – 43–58 ft. lbs.

Left engine mount insulator nuts (small) – 22–29 ft. lbs.

Left engine mount bracket-to-engine bolts/nuts – 36–47 ft. lbs.

Transaxle mount insulator nut – 43–58 ft. lbs.

Transaxle insulator bracket-to-fender shield bolts – manual 40–43 ft. lbs.

Transaxle insulator bracket-to-fender shield bolts – automatic 22–29 ft. lbs.

Transaxle mounting bracket-to-automatic transaxle nuts – 43–58 ft. lbs.

Transaxle mounting bracket bolts – 22–29 ft. lbs.

Rear roll stop insulator nut – 22–29 ft. lbs.

Rear roll stop-to-rear crossmember nuts – 43–58 ft. lbs.

Rear roll stop bracket-to-rear roll stop stay bolt – 22–29 ft. lbs.

Front roll stop insulator nut – 36–47 ft. lbs.

Front roll bracket-to-front crossmember nuts – 29–36 ft. lbs.

After the engine is securely mounted, replenish all fluids. Operate the engine checking carefully for leaks. Check all gauges for proper readings. Adjust clutch and shift linkage. Adjust the accelerator cable. Have the air conditioner recharged.

### Starion

**NOTE: Use care when disconnecting the refrigerant lines. Escaping refrigerant will freeze any surface it contacts, including your skin and eyes.**

1. Matchmark and then unbolt and remove the hood. Drain the cooling system. Disconnect the accelerator cable at the injection mixer. Disconnect both battery cables.

2. Disconnect the 2 heater hoses at the block and the brake booster vacuum hose at the intake manifold.

3. Disconnect the fuel hoses at the injection system.

4. Disconnect the high tension wire at the center of the distributor. Disconnect the temperature sensor wire. Disconnect the intake manifold ground cable connector. First label the wires for reassembly and then disconnect the starter motor wiring harness.

5. Disconnect the power steering pump hoses. Remove the power steering pump.

6. Unbolt and disconnect the 2 engine oil cooler hoses at the oil filter adapter. Plug all openings to prevent the entry of dirt and leakage of oil.

7. Label and then disconnect the alternator wiring. Disconnect the engine ground cable. Disconnect the 2 plugs for the electronic injection wiring harness.

8. Disconnect the vacuum hose from the boost sensor, located on the firewall.

9. Remove the rear catalytic converter.

10. Unscrew and disconnect the speedometer cable at the transmission. Disconnect the wiring for the oil pressure gauge sending unit on the block.

11. On A/T equipped vehicles, disconnect both oil cooler hoses and plug all openings. On all vehicles, disconnect the back-up light switch harness at the plug located under the transmission.

12. Remove the propeller shaft.

13. Remove the clutch slave cylinder.

14. Put the gearshift in neutral. Unbolt the gearshift lever assembly.

15. Securely support the engine using a suitable engine crane. Support the transmission with a jack. Then, remove the front and rear engine mounting nuts and bolts, and the rear crossmember. Raise the assembly slightly and remove all the front support brackets and insulators. Then, gradually lower the transmission jack and pull the engine and transmission assembly out by raising the front of the engine so the transmission will clear the firewall.

16. Install in exact reverse order. When reassembling mounts, make sure all holes are properly aligned and that mounts are not distorted. On both front insulators, make sure the locating boss and hole in the insulator

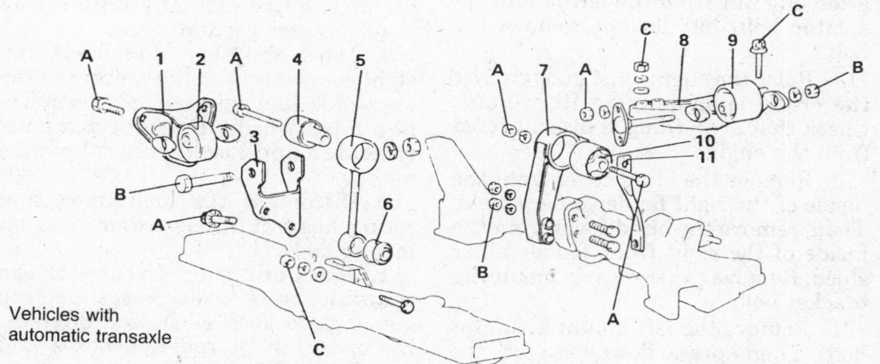


Vehicles with automatic transaxle

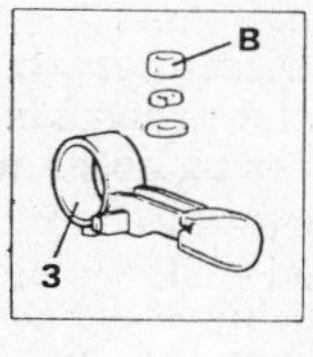


1. Transaxle insulator bracket
2. Transaxle mount insulator
3. Transaxle mount bracket
4. Upper roll insulator
5. Front roll rod
6. Lower roll insulator
7. Rear roll stopper bracket
8. Left mount bracket
9. Left mount insulator
10. Rear roll insulator
11. Rear roll stopper stay

| | Nm | ft.lbs. |
|---|---|---|
| A | 30–40 | 22–29 |
| B | 60–80 | 43–58 |
| C | 50–65 | 36–47 |

Cordia, Tredia engine/transaxle mounting

are in alignment. Torques are as follows.

| Mounts | ft. lbs. |
|---|---|
| Crossmember mounting belts | 7.2 |

| Mounts | ft. lbs. |
|---|---|
| Bolts assm. front mounting brackets to front crossmember | 22–29 |
| Nuts assm. front mounts and bolt attaching rear mounts to rear crossmember | 9.4–14 |
| Nuts atop rear mount, attaching it to transmission | 14–17 |

17. On the rear crossmember insulators torque the bolts to the following specifications:
Turn them until a flat will line up with lockwasher tabs and then bend the tabs up against the flats to keep the bolts from unscrewing. Refill all fluids and adjust all linkages.

### Mirage

**NOTE: Use care when disconnecting the refrigerant lines. Escaping refrigerant will freeze any surface it contacts, including your skin and eyes.**

1. Remove the hood. Remove the air cleaner assembly. Disconnect both battery cables and then remove the batter. Unbolt and remove the battery tray.
2. Disconnect the electrical connectors for the backup lights and engine harness, located near the battery tray. If the vehicle has a 5 speed, disconnect the select control valve connector. Disconnect the 2 alternator harness connectors and the oil pressure sending unit.
3. First label and then disconnect the A/T oil cooler hoses. Avoid spilling oil and cap the openings.
4. Drain the cooling system. Then disconnect and remove the upper and lower hoses and remove them. Remove the radiator.
5. Label and then disconnect all low tension wires and the one high tension wire going to the coil from the distributor. Disconnect the engine ground.
6. Disconnect the brake booster vacuum hose at the intake manifold. Disconnect the cap power steering lines, as required. Remove pump as needed.
7. Disconnect the fuel supply, return and vapor hoses at the side of the engine.
8. If the vehicle has a turbocharger, the 3 electrical connectors must be disconnected – 1 for the idle speed control system and 2 for the injection system. All are located on the injection mixer.
9. Disconnect the heater hoses from the side of the engine. Disconnect the accelerator cable at the side of the injection mixer and the block.
10. On vehicles equipped with M/T, disconnect the clutch control cable. On vehicles equipped with A/T, disconnect the shift control cable from the transaxle.
11. Unscrew and disconnect the speedometer cable at the transaxle.
12. Raise and securely support the vehicle. Remove the drain plug and drain the transmission fluid. Disconnect the exhaust pipe at the manifold. Then, suspend the pipe securely with wire.
13. On vehicles equipped with M/T, remove the shift control rod and extension rod.
14. Disconnect the stabilizer bar at both lower control arms. Remove the bolts that attach the lower control arms to the body on either side. Support the arms from the body.
15. If the vehicle is turbocharged, disconnect and remove the oil cooler tube from the side of the engine.
16. Disconnect the halfshaft at the transaxle on both sides. Then, seal off the openings in the transaxle. Make sure you replace the circlips holding the driveshafts in the transaxle. Support the halfshafts from the body.
17. Attach a crane-type lift, via chains or cables, to both the engine lifting hooks. Put just a little tension on the cables. Then, remove the nut and bolt from the front roll stopper; unbolt the brace from the top of the engine damper.
18. Separate the rear roll stopper from the crossmember. Remove the attaching nut from the left mount insulator bolt, but do not remove the bolt.
19. Raise the engine just enough that the crane is supporting its weight. Check that everything is disconnected from the engine.
20. Remove the blind cover from the inside of the right fender inner shield. Then, remove the blind cover from the inside of the right front fender inner shied. Remove the transaxle mounting bracket bolts.
21. Remove the left mount insulator bolt. Then, press downward on the transaxle while lifting the engine/transaxle assembly to guide it up and out of the vehicle.
22. Installation is generally performed in reverse of the removal procedure. During installation, first install all nuts and bolts with the weight of the engine carried by the crane. Tighten just slightly. Then, allow the weight of the engine to sit on the mounts and torque parts as follows.
23. Finally, replenish all fluids. Adjust the transaxle and accelerator linkages. Start the engine and check for leaks as well as proper gauge operation. Replace the hood and recharge the air conditioner if necessary.

### Galant 4 Cylinder Engine

**NOTE: Use care when disconnecting the refrigerant lines. Escaping refrigerant will freeze any surface it contacts, including your skin and eyes.**

1. Matchmark the position of the hood hinges on the hood and remove it. Drain the engine coolant. Remove the drain plug and drain the transaxle fluid.
2. Remove the air cleaner. Disconnect the battery cables, remove the battery and then unbolt and remove the battery tray.
3. Carefully label and then disconnect each of 3 connectors of the engine wiring harness.
4. Disconnect the ground wire at the right side wheelhouse. Drain the power steering fluid by disconnecting a hose at the low point of the system. Plug all openings.
5. On vehicles with the electronically controlled suspension, remove the compressor and reserve tank.
6. Disconnect the transaxle control cable by moving the adjusting nut on the transaxle end of the cable and pulling the cable out of the fitting on the transaxle. Keep the rearward nut from moving to preserve the adjustment.
7. Disconnect the alternator connectors and the oil pressure sending unit. Disconnect the high tension cable at the coil.
8. Disconnect the engine ground cable at the firewall. Disconnect the brake booster vacuum hose.
9. Label and then disconnect the eight connectors for the sensors of the electronic fuel injection at the injection mixing body. Disconnect the accelerator and speed control cables nearby.
10. Disconnect the fuel supply and return hoses at the electronic injection mixing body.
11. Mark and then disconnect the transmission oil cooler hoses. Cap the openings to keep oil in and dirt out. Disconnect both radiator hoses and both heater hoses at the engine.
12. Unscrew and then disconnect the speedometer cable at the transaxle. Disconnect the power steering hoses at the pump and cap all openings.
13. Raise and securely support the vehicle. Disconnect the exhaust pipe at the exhaust manifold. Then, hang the pipe to the body with wire.

14. Disconnect the steering knuckles from the lower arm ball joints. Disconnect the tie rods from the steering knuckle. Remove the halfshafts from the transaxle. Make sure to cap all openings to keep fluid in and dirt out. Discard the retaining clips that hold the shafts in the transaxle and replace them.

15. Attach your lifting crane to both engine lifting hooks and put very slight tension on the chains or cables. Then remove the nut, but not the bolt, coupling the engine mount bracket to the body. Remove the upper installation nuts of the front and rear roll stopper brackets.

16. Detach the protective cap from inside the right fender shield and then remove the transaxle mounting bracket bolts. Then, remove the bolts connecting the transaxle mount insulator to the bracket and remove the bracket.

17. Now, increase the tension on the engine lifting mechanism until the weight of the engine is borne by the lift instead of its mounts. Now, remove the bolts of the rear roll stopper bracket, the engine mount bracket and the front roll stopper bracket. Confirm that all cable, wires and linkages are disconnected.

18. Tilting the transaxle side downward, carefully life the engine/transaxle assemble out of the vehicle.

19. Install in exact reverse order. Make sure that nothing gets pinched or bent as you're putting the engine back in position. When installing rubber insulators, make sure they are not twisted. Observe the following torques:

| Mounts | ft. lbs. |
|---|---|
| Left mount large insulator nut | 65–80 |
| Left mount small insulator nut | 22–29 |
| Left mount bracket-to-engine nuts/bolts | 36–47 |
| Transaxle mount insulator nut | 65–80 |
| Transaxle insulator bracket-to-side frame bolts | 22–29 |
| Transaxle bracket assem.-to-auto. transaxle nuts | 65–80 |
| Transaxle mount bracket to manual transaxle bolts | 40–43 |
| Rear roll insulator nut | 33–43 |
| Rear roll stopper bracket-to-crossmember assem. bolts | 22–29 |
| Front roll insulator nut | 33–43 |
| Front roll stopper bracket-to-crossmember assem. bolts | 33–40 |
| Lower roll insulator-to-roll damper bracket bolt | 22–29 |
| Center crossmember to body | 43–58 |
| Transaxle mount bracket bolts and front roll stopper mounting bracket bolts | 29–36 |
| Transaxle mount bracket through bolts and nuts | 43–58 |
| Front roll stopper bracket through bolts and nuts, and engine mount bracket attaching nuts and bolts | 36–47 |
| Rear roll stopper bracket through bolt, and engine mount bracket through bolt flange attaching nut | 22–29 |

20. Check the operation of all linkages, adjusting if necessary, Replenish all fluids and then operate the engine, checking for leaks.

### *Galant and Sigma V6 Engine*

**NOTE: Use care when disconnecting the refrigerant lines. Escaping refrigerant will freeze any surface it contacts, including your skin and eyes.**

1. Matchmark the position of the hood hinges on the hood and remove it. Drain the engine coolant. Remove the drain plug and drain the transaxle fluid.

2. Remove the air cleaner. Disconnect the battery cables, remove the battery and then unbolt and remove the battery tray.

3. Carefully label and then disconnect each of the connectors of the engine wiring harness.

4. Remove the accelerator cable bracket mounting screws. Remove the accelerator cable and cruise control cable from the throttlebody linkage.

5. Disconnect and plug the high pressure fuel lines and fuel return lines from the engine.

6. Open the cover of the fusible link box and disconnect the alernator wiring. Disconnnect and tag all necessary wiring including the pulse generator connector (used on models with automatic transaxles),

7. On models equipped with automatic transaxles, disconnect the transaxle control cables. Remove the control cable bracket mounting bolts and disconnect the transaxle control cables from the transaxle. Disconnect and pplug the oil cooler lines.

8. On models equipped with electronic controlled suspension, remove the air compressor.

9. On models equipped with manual transaxles, remove the mounting bolts of thr clutch release cylinder. Remove the mounting bracket of the clutch oil tube and secure the the clutch release cylinder and the clutch oil tube assembly on the chassis side with some suitable wire.

10. Disconnect the speedometer. Disconnect and plug the heater hoses. Remove all the radiator hoses and remove the radiator.

11. Disconnect and plug the A/C lines from the compressor. Release the engine block section clamp and disconnect the discharge flexible hose. Remove the clip from the power steering oil pump section and disconnect the suction flexible hose.

12. Remove the engine under cover panels. Remove the stabilizer mounting nut and tie rod end cotter pin. Using the special tie rod tool, disconnect the tie rod end from the steering knuckle. Using the suitable tool, disconnect the lower arm ball joint from the knuckle. Loosen the nut but do not remove it.

13. Remove the left side halfshaft (after removing the circlip, cotter pin and halfshaft nut) by inserting a suitable tool between the bearing bracket and the halfshaft and then pry the halfshaft from the bearing bracket. Be sure to pull the halfshaft out from the bearing bracket as an assembly with the hub knuckle and other parts. Suspend the removed halfshaft with a wire to prevent the joint section from bending sharply.

14. Remove the right side halfshaft circlip and lock nut, then remove the halfshaft from the hub by using the special hub removal tool. Once the hub is remove, use a suitable tool and pull the halfshaft out from the transaxle.

15. Remove the rubber hangers from the exhaust system. Disconnect the oxygen sensor connector. Remove the bolts or nuts from the front exhaust pipe and remove the pipe from the the engine. Be sure to suspend the disconnected exhaust pipe with a wire to keep it from bending sharply.

16. Remove the distributor cap and connect a suitable engine lifting device to the proper locations on the engine and raise the lifting device just enough to take the slack out of the cable.

17. Remove the front roll stopper bracxket mount bolt, engine damper and rear roll stopper bracket mount bolt. Remove the bolts and nuts that fasten the engine mount bracket to the body.

18. To remove the transaxle mount bracket, first remov the 4 plugs from the fender shield. Remove the mounting bolts of the transaxle mount bracket with care to prevent them from falling into the fender shield.

19. Check that all cables, hoses, electrical harness connections and wires are disconnected from the side of the engine. Slowly remove the engine and

transaxle assembly upwards from the engine compartment with the engine lift. Once the engine and transaxle assembly has cleared the vehicle, place it on a suitable engine stand.

20. Installation is the reverse order of the removal procedure, except for the following:

a. When installing the halfshaft nut, install the washer and wheel bearing nut in the proper direction. If the position of the cotter pin holes does not match, tighten the nut up to 188 ft. lbs. and then install the cotter pin in the first matching holes and bend it securely.

b. After the installation is complete, check all the remove and disconnect components for proper operation and adjust or repair as necessary.

### Precis

**NOTE: Use care when disconnecting the refrigerant lines. Escaping refrigerant will freeze any surface it contacts, including your skin and eyes.**

1. Remove the air cleaner assembly by disconnecting all hoses, unbolting it and removing it. Disconnect both battery cables and then remove the battery. Unbolt and remove the battery tray.
2. Disconnect the electrical connectors for the back-up lights and engine harness, located near the battery tray. If the vehicle has a 5 speed, disconnect the select control valve connector. Disconnect the 2 alternator harness connectors and the oil pressure sending unit.
3. First label and then disconnect the transmission oil cooler hoses. Avoid spilling oil and cap the openings.
4. Drain the cooling system through the cock on the bottom of the radiator and the plug in the block. Then disconnect and remove the upper and lower hoses and remove them. Remove the radiator.
5. Label and then disconnect all low tension wires and the 1 high tension wire going to the coil from the distributor. Disconnect the engine ground.
6. Disconnect the brake booster vacuum hose at the intake manifold.
7. Disconnect the fuel supply, return, and vapor hoses at the side of the engine. Avoid spilling fuel.
8. Disconnect the heater hoses from the side of the engine.
9. On vehicles equipped with M/T, disconnect the clutch control cable. On vehicles equipped with A/T, disconnect the shifter control cable from the transaxle.
10. Unscrew and disconnect the speedometer cable at the transaxle.
11. Raise and securely support the vehicle. Remove the drain plug and drain the transmission fluid. Disconnect the exhaust pipe at the manifold. Then, suspend the pipe securely with wire.
12. If the vehicle has manual transaxle, remove the shift control rod and extension rod.
13. Disconnect the stabilizer bar at both lower control arms. Remove the bolts that attach the lower control arms to the body on either side. Support the arms from the body.
14. Disconnect the halfshafts at the transaxle on both sides. Then, seal off the openings in the transaxle. Make sure you replace the circlips holding the halfshafts in the transaxle. Support the halfshafts from the body.
15. Attach a crane-type lift, via chains or cables, to both the engine lifting hooks. Put just a little tension on the cables. Then, remove the nut and bolt from the front roll stopper; unbolt the brace from the top of the engine damper.
16. Separate the rear roll stopper from the crossmember. Remove the attaching nut from the left mount insulator bolt, but do not remove the bolt.
17. Raise the engine just enough that the crane is supporting its weight. Check that everything is disconnected from the engine.
18. Remove the blind cover from the inside of the right fender inner shield. Remove the transaxle mounting bracket bolts.
19. Remove the left mount insulator bolt. Then, press downward on the transaxle while lifting the engine/transaxle assembly to guide it up and out of the vehicle.
20. Installation is generally performed in reverse of the removal procedure. During installation, first install all nuts and bolts with the weight of the engine carried by the crane. Tighten just slightly. Then, allow the weight of the engine to sit on the mounts, and torque parts as follows:

Left mount large insulator nut – 65–80 ft. lbs.

Left mount small insulator nut – 22–29 ft. lbs.

Left mount bracket-to-engine nuts/bolts – 36–47 ft. lbs.

Transaxle mount insulator nut – 65–80 ft. lbs.

Transaxle insulator bracket-to-side frame bolts – 22–29 ft. lbs.

Transaxle bracket assembly-to-automatic transaxle nuts – 65–80 ft. lbs.

Transaxle mount bracket-to-manual transaxle bolts – 40–43 ft. lbs.

Rear roll insulator nut – 33–43 ft. lbs.

Rear roll stopper bracket-to-crossmember assembly bolts – 22–29 ft. lbs.

Front roll insulator nut – 33–43 ft. lbs.

Front roll stopper bracket-to-crossmember assembly bolts – 33–40 ft. lbs.

Lower roll insulator roll-to-damper bracket bolt – 22–29 ft. lbs.

Center crossmember body – 43–58 ft. lbs.

21. Finally, replenish all fluids. Adjust the transaxle and accelerator linkages. Start the engine and check for leaks as well as proper gauge operation. Replace the hood and have the air conditioner recharged.

## Cylinder Head

### REMOVAL & INSTALLATION

#### 4 Cylinder Except 1.5L and 1.6L Engines

1. Turn the engine until the No. 1 piston is at TDC on the compression stroke. Disconnect the negative battery cable. Remove the air cleaner assembly.
2. Drain the engine coolant. Remove the upper radiator hose and disconnect the heater hoses.
3. Disconnect the fuel lines, wiring harnesses, distributor vacuum lines, spark plug wires (from plugs), purge valves, accelerator linkage and water temperature unit wire.
4. Remove the distributor and (if necessary) the fuel pump from the cylinder head.
5. Remove the nuts connecting the exhaust pipe to the manifold or turbocharger. Lower the exhaust pipe.
6. Remove the turbocharger and/or exhaust manifold.
7. Remove the intake manifold assembly.
8. On 1795, 1997cc and 2350cc engines:

a. Remove the upper, outer front cover. Align the timing mark on the cylinder head with the mark on the camshaft sprocket (engine should already be on the No. 1 piston TDC of the compression stroke).

b. Matchmark the timing belt with the timing mark on the camshaft sprocket using a felt tip marker.

c. Remove the sprocket and insert a 2 in. piece of rubber or other material between the camshaft sprocket and sprocket holder on the lower front cover, to hold the sprocket and belt so that the valve timing will not be changed.

d. Remove the timing belt upper under cover and the rocker arm cover.

9. On 2555cc engines:

a. Remove the rocker arm cover.

b. Position the camshaft sprocket dowel pin at the 12 o'clock position with the timing mark TDC at the front of the timing case cover (engine should already be on the No. 1 piston TDC of the compression stroke).

c. Match the timing chain with the timing mark on the camshaft sprocket. Take a soft piece of wire and secure the chain and sprocket together at the timing mark and opposite side.

d. Remove the camshaft sprocket bolt, gear and sprocket from the camshaft.

10. Except on the Starion, a special hex head wrench will be needed. Mitsubishi part no. MD998051-01 or equivalent. Loosen and remove the cylinder head bolts in 2 or 3 stages to avoid cylinder head warpage. Follow the sequence shown in the appropriate illustration.

11. Remove the cylinder head from the engine.

12. Clean the cylinder head and block mating surfaces and install a new cylinder head gasket.

13. Position the cylinder head on the engine block, engage the dowel pins front and rear and install the cylinder head bolts.

14. The bolts must be torqued to cold specification, which is 65–72 ft. lbs. in 2 equal stages. Using the sequence shown in the appropriate illustration, torque the bolts in order to 32.5–36 ft. lbs. then, repeat the operation torquing them to the full torque. Note that on the Starion, the front head bolts, attaching the head only to the timing cover, are torqued to 11–15 ft. lbs. Torque them to about 7 ft. lbs. the first time around.

15. Install the timing belt upper under cover (1775 and 1997cc engines).

16. Locate the camshaft in original position. Pull the camshaft sprocket and belt or chain upward and install on the camshaft.

**NOTE: If the dowel pin and the dowel pin hole does not line up between the sprocket and the spacer or camshaft, move the camshaft by bumping either of the 2 projections provided at the rear of No. 2 cylinder exhaust cam of the camshaft, with a light hammer or other tool, until the hole and pin align. Be certain the crankshaft does not turn.**

17. Install the camshaft sprocket bolt and the distributor gear and tighten.

18. Install the timing belt upper front cover and spark plug cable support.

19. Apply sealant to the intake manifold gasket on both sides. Position the gasket and install the intake manifold. Tighten the nuts to specifications. Be sure that no sealant enters the jet air passages, when equipped

20. Install the exhaust manifold gaskets and the manifold assembly. Tighten the nuts to specifications.

21. Connect the exhaust pipe to the exhaust manifold and install the fuel pump. Install the purge valve.

22. Install the water temperature gauge wire, heater hoses and the upper radiator hose.

23. Connect the fuel lines, accelerator linkage, vacuum hoses and the spark plug wires.

24. Fill the cooling system and connect the batter ground cable. Install the distributor.

25. Temporarily adjust the valve clearance to the cold engine specifications.

26. Install the gasket on the rocker arm cover and temporarily install the cover on the engine.

27. Start the engine and bring it to normal operating temperature. Stop the engine and remove the rocker arm cover.

28. Adjust the valves to hot engine specifications.

29. Reinstall the rocker arm cover and tighten securely.

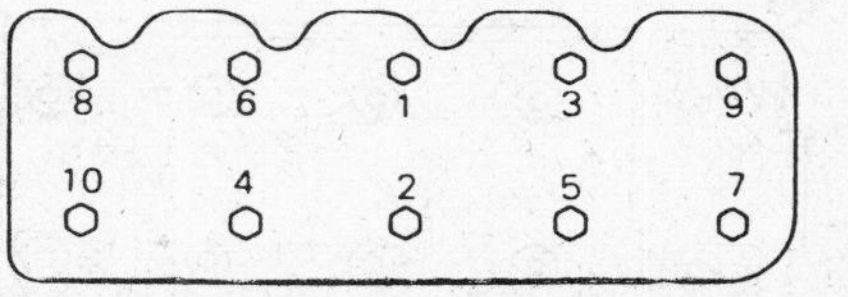

**Engine head bolt torque sequence for 1795, 1997 and 2350cc engines**

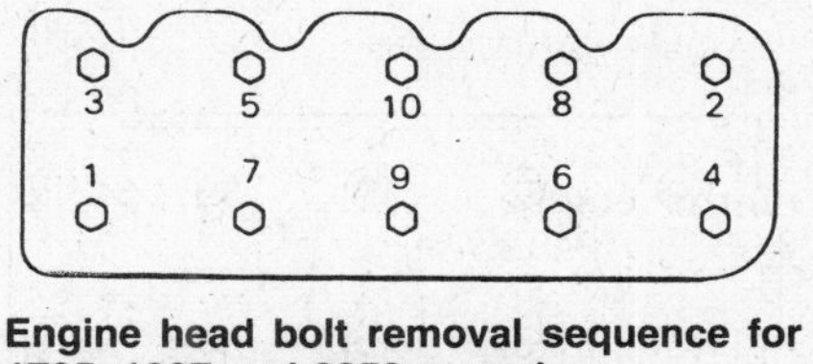

**Engine head bolt removal sequence for 1795, 1997 and 2350cc engines**

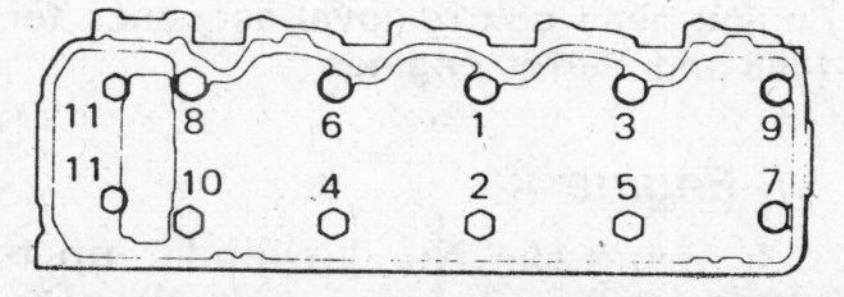

**Engine head bolt torque sequence for the 2555cc engine**

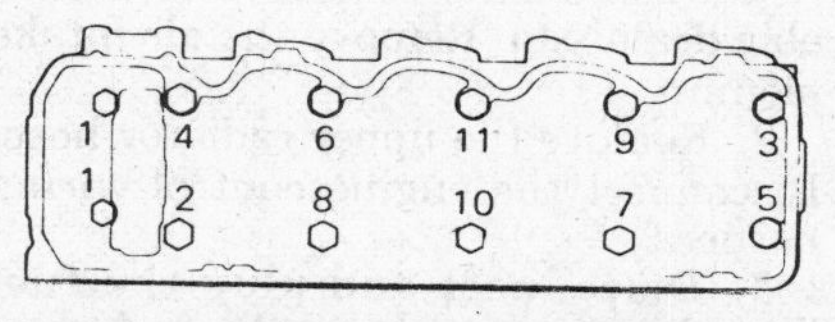

**Engine head bolt removal sequence for the 2555cc engine**

30. Install the air cleaner, hoses, purge valve hose, and any other removed unit.

### *1.5L Engine*

1. Disconnect the negative battery cable. Drain the cooling system and then disconnect the upper radiator hose. Remove the PCV hose that runs between the air cleaner and the rocker cover.

2. Remove the air cleaner. Disconnect the fuel lines. Label and disconnect any vacuum lines running to the cylinder head, manifold, or carburetor from other parts of the engine compartment. Disconnect the heater hoses going to the head.

3. Label and disconnect the spark plug wires. Remove the rocker cover. Turn the crankshaft over until the TDC timing marks line up and both No. 1 cylinder valves are closed (both rockers are off the cams). Then, remove the distributor.

4. Remove the carburetor, intake manifold and the exhaust manifold.

5. Remove the timing belt cover. Note the location of the camshaft sprocket timing mark. Loosen both timing belt tensioner mounting bolts and then lever it over toward the water pump as far as it will go. Retighten the adjusting bolt to hold the tensioner in this position. Pull the timing belt off the camshaft sprocket but leave it engaged with the other sprockets.

6. Using a hex-type wrench, part No. MD998360 loosen the head bolts in the sequence shown. When all have been loosened, remove them. Then, pull the head off the engine block, rocking it slightly to break it loose, if necessary.

7. Remove the gasket. If pieces of the gasket adhere to the head or block deck, scrape them off carefully, using a scraper that will not scratch the surfaces. Make sure none of the pieces gets into the engine.

8. Install a new head gasket (without any sealer) and then position the head on the block deck. Install all the bolts finger tight. Then, torque them, in the illustrated sequence, first to 25 ft. lbs. Then, torque again, in the same sequence, to 58–61 ft. lbs.

9. Install the timing belt on the camshaft tensioner and rotate the camshaft sprocket backward so the belt is tight on what is normally the tension side. Make sure all the timing marks are now lined up.

10. Loosen the timing belt tensioner adjusting bolt and allow spring tension to tension the belt. Make sure all timing marks are still lined up. If not, the belt is out of time and must be shifted with the tensioner shifted back toward the water pump and locked there.

Torque the adjusting bolt (on the right side and working through a slot) to 15–18 ft. lbs. After the tensioner adjusting bolt is torqued, torque the hinged mounting bolt located on the opposite side. Don't torque the mounting bolt first, or the tension on the belt will be too great.

11. Now, turn the crankshaft 1 full turn in the normal direction of rotation. Loosen first the tensioner pivot bolt and then the adjusting bolt. Now torque them exactly as before – adjusting bolt (working in the slot) first. This extra step is necessary to ensure the timing belt is properly seated before final tension is adjusted.

12. Install the intake and exhaust manifolds, carburetor, distributor, air cleaner, rocker cover, timing belt cover, and all hoses in reverse of the above procedures. Refill the cooling system. Operate the engine and check for leaks.

### 1.6L Engine

1. Disconnect the negative battery cable. Drain engine coolant and then disconnect the upper radiator hose at the thermostat. Remove PCV and canister purge hoses.

2. Remove the air cleaner. Disconnect the fuel line. Disconnect vacuum hoses at the distributor and canister purge control valve.

3. Label and then disconnect the spark plug wires. Remove the rocker cover. Turn the crankshaft over until the TDC timing marks line up and both No. 1 cylinder valves are closed (both rockers are off the cams). Then, remove the distributor.

4. Disconnect the heater hose at the intake manifold. Disconnect the water hose leading from the cylinder head and carburetor water jacket.

5. Disconnect the temperature gauge sending unit wire at the head. Remove the fuel pump.

6. Remove the exhaust manifold. Turn the crankshaft until No. 1 piston is at TDC of its compression stroke. Align the timing mark on the upper cover at the rear of the timing belt with the mark on the camshaft sprocket to do this. Use some sort of marker to mark the relationship between the timing belt and the mark on the cam sprocket.

7. Loosen and remove the bolt fastening the sprocket to the camshaft, holding the sprocket in position as you work to keep the belt from slipping off. Then, rest the sprocket on the sprocket holder provided on the lower front cover. If necessary, slip a short piece of used timing belt or other thin, flexible object between the holder and the sprocket to keep tension and avoid losing belt timing. Be sure not to turn the crankshaft throughout this work.

8. Remove the bolts from the timing belt rear cover and remove the cover.

9. Remove the cylinder head bolts. Loosen in three stages, going from bolt to bolt in the sequence shown. This requires a special hex wrench, Part No. MD998360 or equivalent.

10. Once the bolts are removed, the head may be rocked to break it loose. Do not slide it as there are dowel pins on the block deck.

11. Install a new head gasket without sealant, and install the head over the dowel pins. Install the cylinder head bolts. Then, in the sequence shown, torque the bolts first to 25 ft. lbs. Then, repeat the sequence, torquing to 51–54 ft. lbs.

12. Install the intake manifold, exhaust manifold and carburetor. Install the fuel pump and reconnect all fuel lines.

13. Install the distributor. Reconnect the plug wires in the proper firing order. Reconnect the temperature gauge wire and all water hoses. Reconnect the distributor, PCV and evaporative emissions system vacuum hoses.

14. Reconnect the top radiator hose and refill the cooling system. Operate the engine and check for leaks.

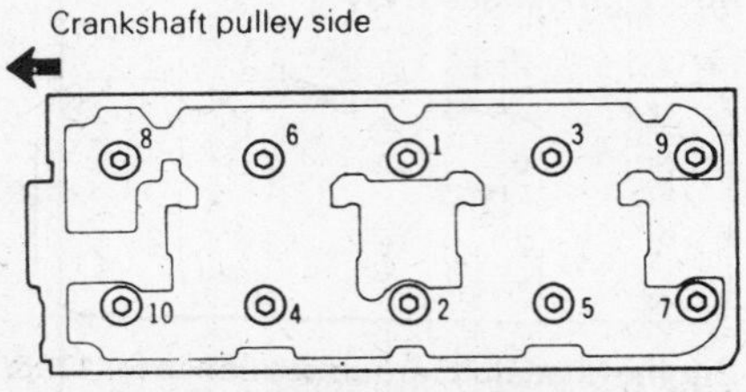


**Engine head bolt torque sequence for 1468 and 1597cc engines**

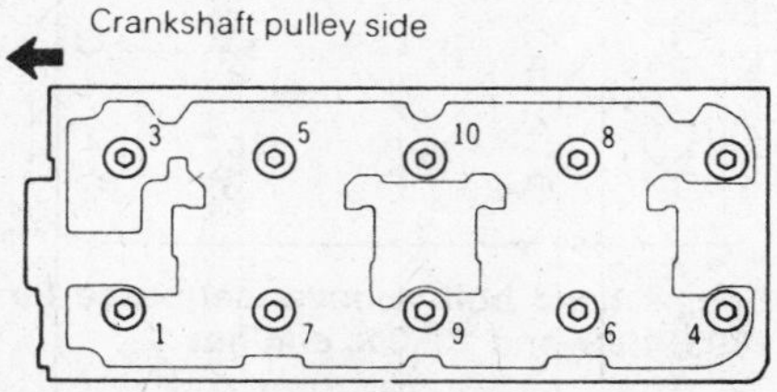


**Engine head bolt removal sequence for 1468 and 1597cc engines**

### V6 Engine

1. Bring the No. 1 cylinder up to TDC of its compression stroke. Disconnect the negative battery cable. Drain the engine coolant into a suitable drain pan. Remove the air intake plenum.

2. Remove the upper radiator hose. Disconnect the engine control wiring harness.

3. Disconnect and plug the fuel lines, be sure to release the fuel pressure in the fuel system first. Remove the intake manifold and manifold gasket.

4. Disconnect and tag the spark plug wires. Disconnect the oxygen sensor connector.

5. Remove the self-locking nuts from the exhaust pipe and then suspend the exhaust pipe with a piece of wire.

6. Remove the distributor assembly and the air intake plenum stay. Remove any bolts that attach hoses or pipes to the cylinder heads.

7. Remove the heat protector mounting bolts, then remove the heat protector along with the exhaust manifolds.

8. Remove the oil level gauge guide and the exhaust manifold gaskets.

9. Remove the timing belt and camshaft sprocket. You will need camshaft special tool MB990767 or equivalent ot hold the camshaft sprocket still so as to break loose the camshaft sprocket mounting bolt.

10. Remove the timing belt rear cover. Remove the small retaining bolt from the side of the cylinder heads.

11. Remove the rocker arm cover and rocker arm cover gasket.

12. Remove the cylinder head bolts (in the proper sequence in 2 or 3 cycles) and remove the cylinder heads and gaskets from the engine.

13. Installation is the reverse order of the removal procedure, except for the following:

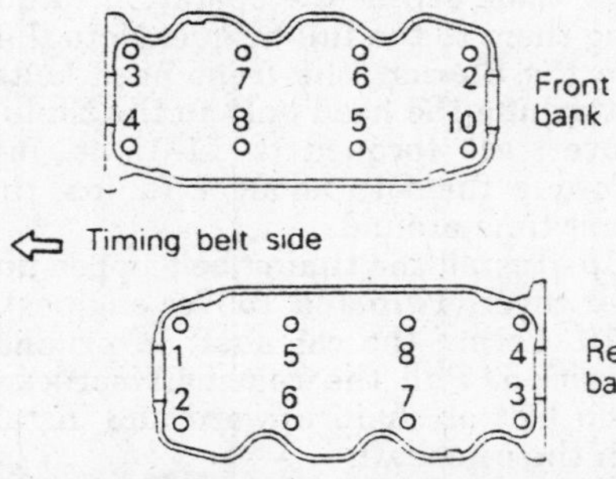


**Cylinder head bolt removal sequence – 1988–89 Galant**

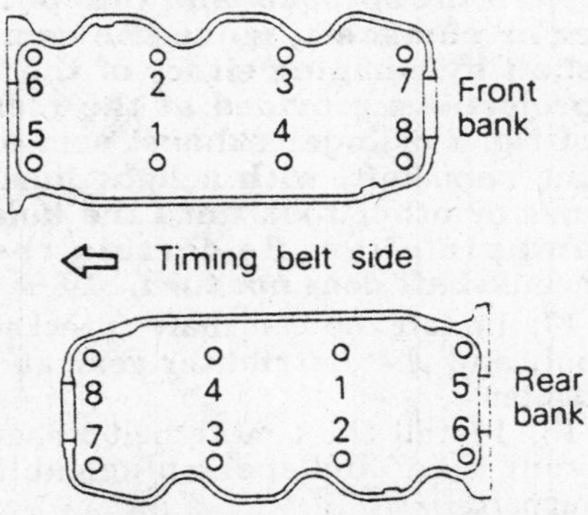


**Cylinder head bolt torque sequence – 1988–89 Galant**

a. Using a suitable torque wrench, torque the head bolts in the proper sequnce in 2 or 3 steps to a final torque of 73–79 ft. lbs. (hot) or 65–72 ft. lbs. (cold).

b. Be sure to coat all O-rings with clean engine oil and apply a suitable sealant to the cut-out ends of the rocker arm covers.

c. Be sure to use special tool MB990767 or equivalent to hold the camshaft sprocket still so as to torque the camshaft sprocket mounting bolt to 58–72 ft. lbs.

## OVERHAUL

**For all cylinder head procedures, please refer to "Engine Rebuilding" in the Unit Repair section.**

# Rocker Arms/Shafts

## REMOVAL & INSTALLATION

### *4 Cylinder Except 1.5L and 1.6L Engines*

**NOTE: On 1985–90 models which have hydraulic lash adjusters, 8 special holders, tool NO. MD998443, are required to retain the hydraulic lash adjusters when disassembling the valve train.**

1. Disconnect the negative battery cable.
2. Remove the rocker cover and, on Cordia, Tredia and Galant the upper timing belt cover.
3. Loosen the camshaft sprocket bolt until it can be turned by hand.
4. Turn the engine over until the camshaft sprocket timing mark lines up with the timing mark on the cylinder head on the Cordia, Tredia and Galant. On the Starion, the timing mark on the sprocket ends up on the extreme right of the sprocket bolt as viewed from the front. In both cases the TDC mark on the front crankshaft pulley must line up with the timing scale on the front cover.
5. Remove the camshaft sprocket bolt and without allowing tension on the timing chain or belt to be lost, place the sprocket in the sprocket holder of the front cover or lower timing belt cover. Make sure that the crankshaft is not turned throughout the work.
6. On 1985–88 Cordia, Tredia and 1985–90 Galant with hydraulic lash adjusters, put the special clips on the eight hydraulic adjusters at the outer ends of all eight rocker arms. Note that these clips go over the lash adjusters that actuate the large intake valves, not on the small adjusting screw for the smaller jet valves.

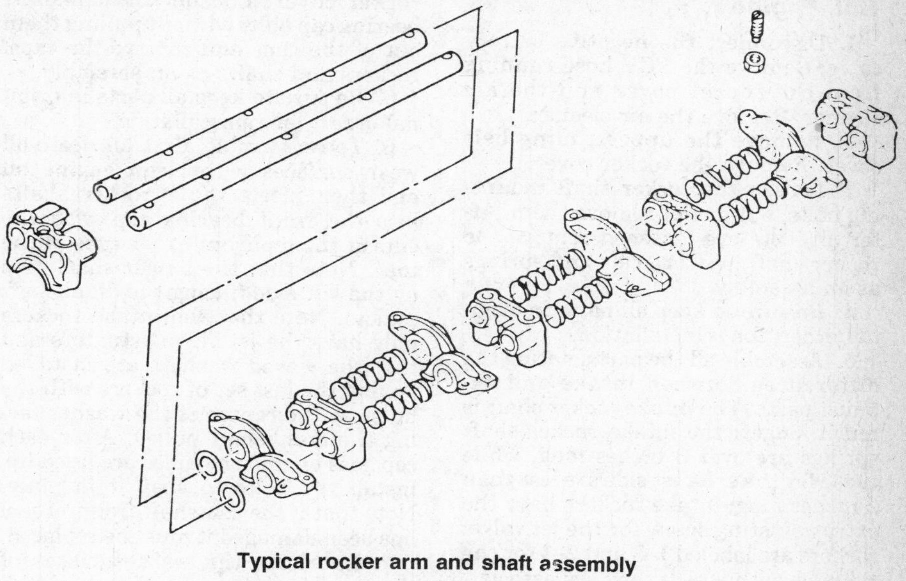

Typical rocker arm and shaft assembly

7. Loosen but do not remove the camshaft bearing cap bolts. After all bolts have been loosened, remove them and then, holding the ends so the assembly stays together, remove the rocker shaft assembly from the cylinder head. Note that the rearmost cam bearing cap is not associated with the rocker shafts on the Starion and need not be removed.
8. Keep all parts in original order. Assemble the parts of the rocker assembly as follows:

a. Cordia, Tredia and Galant install left and right side rocker shafts into the front bearing cap. Notches in the ends of the shaft must be upward.

b. Install the bolts for the front cap to retain the shafts in place. Note that the left rocker shaft is longer than the right rocker shaft.

c. Install the wave washer onto the left rocker shaft with the bulge forward.

d. Coat the inner surfaces of the rockers and the upper bearing surfaces of the bearing caps with clean engine oil and assemble rockers, springs and the remaining bearing caps in the order in which removed. The intake rockers are the only ones with the jet valve actuators.

**Note: The rockers are labeled for cylinders 1–3 and 2–4 because the direction the jet valve actuator faces changes. Use mounting bolts to hold the caps in place after each is assembled.**

9. When the assembly is complete, install it onto the head and start all mounting bolts into the head and tighten finger tight.
10. On the Starion install the right and left rocker shafts into the front bearing cap. Note that shafts can be identified by the fact that the rear end of the left side shaft has a notch. Align the mating marks of the front of the rocker shaft with that on the front bearing cap. Insert the front bolts.
11. Install the waved washers on both sides with the bulge in the washers facing forward.
12. Install the rockers, shafts, caps and bolts in their original positions, using the bolts to hold each cap in place after it is installed.
13. Oil the inner surfaces of the rockers and the upper bearing surfaces of the caps with clean engine oil prior to assembly. Note that the valve actuating ends of the rockers must face outward and that only the intake side rockers have the jet valve actuator.
14. When the assembly is complete, install it onto the head and start all the bolts into the threads, tightening them finger tight.
15. Torque the attaching bolts for the rocker assembly 14–15 ft. lbs. going from the center outward.
16. Without removing tension from the timing chain or belt, lift the sprocket out of the holder and position it against the front of the cam. Make sure the locating tang on the sprocket goes into the hole in the front of the cam.
17. Install the bolt. Torque it to 37–43 ft. lbs. on the Starion and 59–72 ft. lbs. on the Cordia, Tredia and Galant.
18. Adjust the valves.
19. Apply sealant to the top surface of the semicircular seals in the head and then install the valve cover. Install the upper timing belt cover on the Cordia, Tredia and Galant.

### 1.5L Engine

1. Disconnect the negative battery cable. Remove the PCV hose running from the rocker cover and the air cleaner. Remove the air cleaner.
2. Remove the upper timing belt cover. Remove the rocker cover.
3. Loosen the rocker shaft mounting bolts, but do not remove them. After all bolts are loosened remove the rocker shaft, rocker arms and springs as an assembly.
4. Be sure to keep all parts in original order, for reinstallation.
5. Assemble all the parts, noting the differences between intake and exhaust parts. The intake rocker shaft is much longer; the intake rocker shaft springs are over 3 inches long, while those for the exhaust side are less than 2 inches long; intake rockers have the extra adjusting screw for the jet valve; rockers are labeled 1–3 and 2–4 for the cylinder with which they are associated. Torque the rocker shaft mounting bolts to 15–19 ft. lbs.
6. Adjust the valve clearances. This step may be omitted only if all parts are being reused. Install the rocker cover with a new gasket, torquing the bolts to 1–1.5 ft. lbs. Install the air cleaner and PCV valve. Remember that there is no timing belt cover in place and keep your fingers clear. Run the engine at idle speed until it is hot. Then remove the valve cover again and adjust the valve clearances with the engine hot. Finally, replace the rocker cover and timing belt cover, air cleaner and PCV valve.

### 1.6L Engine

1. Disconnect the negative battery cable. Remove the air cleaner assembly. Label and then disconnect the spark plug high tension wires. Remove the upper front timing belt cover.
2. Turn the crankshaft until No. 1 piston is at TDC of its compression stroke. Align the timing mark on the upper cover at the rear of the timing belt with the mark on the camshaft sprocket to do this. Use some sort of marker to mark the relationship between the timing belt and the mark on the cam sprocket.
3. Loosen and remove the bolt fastening the sprocket to the camshaft, holding the sprocket in position as you work to keep the belt from slipping off. Then, rest the sprocket on the sprocket holder provided on the lower front cover. If necessary, slip a short piece of used timing belt or other thin, flexible object between the holder and the sprocket to keep tension and avoid losing belt timing. Be sure not to turn the crankshaft throughout this work.
4. Remove the upper cover located behind the timing belt. Remove the rocker cover. Loosen the camshaft bearing cap bolts without pulling them out of the caps and remove the caps, rockers and shafts as an assembly.
5. Be sure to keep all parts in original order, for reinstallation.
6. To reassemble, first lubricate all wear surfaces with clean engine oil and then insert the 2 rocker shafts into the front bearing cap with the cuts at the top/front of the caps at the tops. Note that the longer shaft goes on the left side (facing the crankshaft pulley). Note that the intake rockers only have the jet valve actuators and that the waved washers are installed behind the last set of rockers with the bulge at the center of the washer facing the crankshaft pulley. After each cap goes on and the holes are lined up, install the bolts to keep it in place. Note that if the camshaft front oil seal has been damaged it must be replaced.
7. Lubricate the wear surfaces of the cam bearing caps and then install them. Torque the bolts to 14–15 ft. lbs.
8. Install the timing belt rear cover. Pull the camshaft sprocket upward and install it to the camshaft. Turn the camshaft slightly if necessary to make the dowel pin fit into the hole in the sprocket. Make sure that the mating mark made when these parts were disassembled are still aligned so the camshaft will be in time. Make corrections as necessary. Install the sprocket attaching bolt, torquing it to 44–57 ft. lbs.
9. Install the timing belt upper cover and spark plug high tension wire supports. Adjust the valve clearances. Apply sealant to the top of the front bearing cap and rear of the head where the rocker cover seals and then install the rocker cover. Install new gaskets and install the rocker cover, torquing the bolts to 4–5 ft. lbs. Reconnect the spark plug wires and install the air cleaner and PCV and evaporative emissions hoses. Run the engine at idle speed until it is hot. Then, remove the rocker cover and again set the valves with the engine hot.

### V6 Engine

1. Disconnect the negative battery cable. Remove the rocker arm covers. It may be necessary to refer to the cylinder head removal procedure as an aid in the rocker arm cover removal.
2. To remove the rocker arm assembly, remove the camshaft bearing cap retaining bolts and remove the rocker arm assembly from the cylinder head. Be sure to install the tool MD998443–

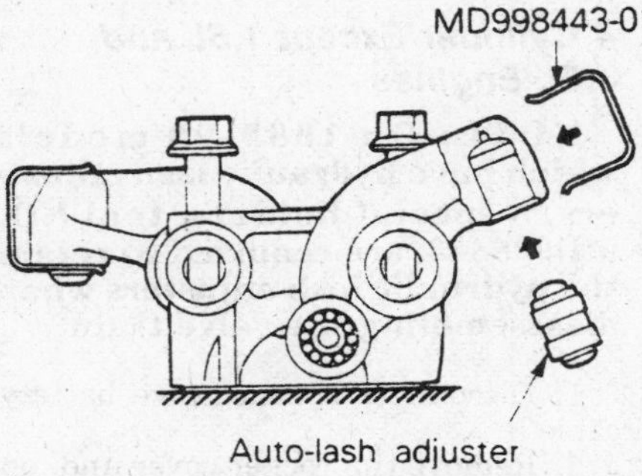


**Auto lash adjuster installation – 1988–89 Galant**

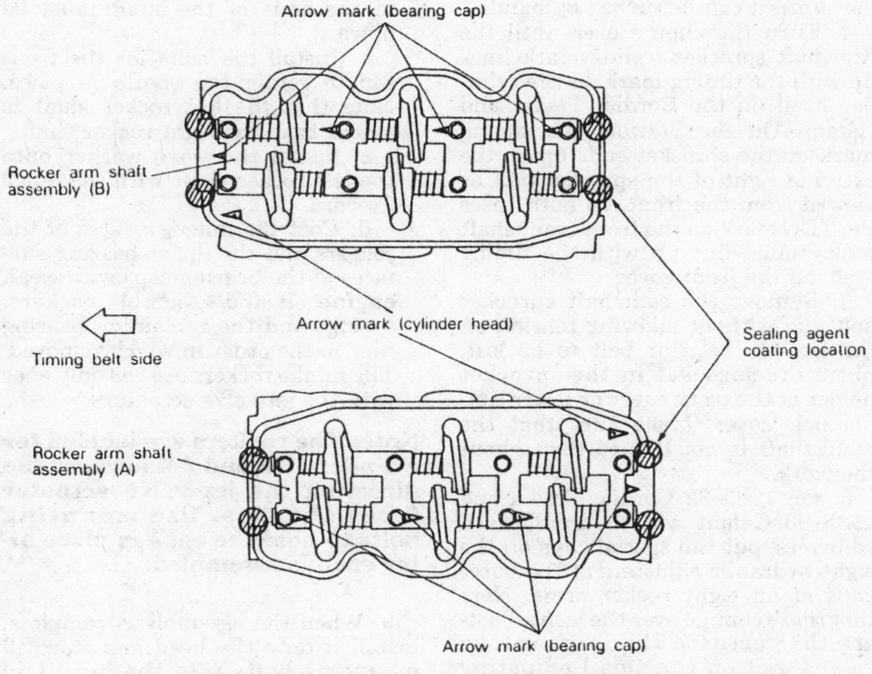


**Rocker arm shaft assemblies installation – 1988–89 Galant**

01 or equivalent over the auto lash adjuster to keep it from falling out.

3. When disassembling the rocker arm shaft assembly, be sure to remove one rocker arm and spring at a time and keep all the parts in their original order.

4. Check the rocker arms and rocker arm shafts for any cracks, distortion, wear or heat damage and replace as necessary.

5. Reassemble the rocker arm shaft assemblies in the reverse order of disassembly. If the auto lash adjuster should fall out during disassembly, reinstall it from underneath the rocker arm, using caution so as not to spill the diesel fuel inside the adjuster. Then be sure to install tool MD998443-01 or equivalent over the auto lash adjuster to keep it from falling out.

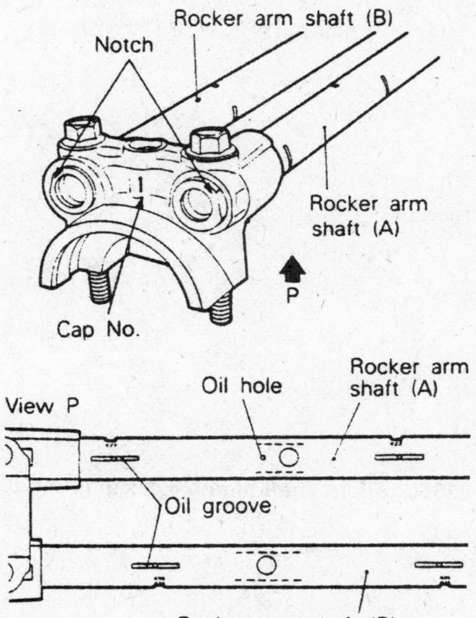


**Installing the bearing cap number one—1988–89 Galant**

6. Apply a small amount of a suitable sealant on the 4 corners of the cylinder head just in front of the bearing caps at the end of the rocker arm shaft.

**NOTE: Be sue that the sealant does not swell out onto the cam journal surrface of the cylinder head. If it swells out, immediately wipe it off before it can dry.**

7. Attach the rocker arm shaft assemblies so that the arow mark on the bearing cap faces in the same direction as the arow on the cylinder head.

**NOTE: The arrow marks face each other on the rocker arm shaft assemblies. Since bearing caps number 1 and 4 look alike, check the number stamped on the cap. Be sure to coat the inside of the bearing cap and rocker arm with clean engine oil before assembling them.**

8. Insert bearing cap No. 1 so that the notch on the end of the shaft faces in the direction as shown in the illustration provided and insert the mounting bolts. Be sure that the oil groove faces downward and the oil port is located on the rocker shaft side **A**.

9. Install al the bearing cap bolts and torque them to 15 ft.lbs. Remove the auto lash adjuster special tool.

10. Apply a suitable sealant to the rocker arm covers and install the covers to the cylinder head. Reinstall any other removed components and reconnect the negative battery cable.

## Intake Manifold

### REMOVAL & INSTALLATION

1. Disconnect the negative battery cable. Remove the air cleaner and duct hose assembly. Disconnect the air plenum assembly on fuel injected models.

2. Disconnect the fuel line(s), EGR lines and other vacuum hoses and wire harness connectors. On the fuel injected models, it is necessary to remove the fuel delivery pipe, fuel injectors and pressure regulator.

3. Disconnect the throttle positioner solenoid and fuel cutoff solenoid wires.

4. Disconnect the accelerator linkage and, if equipped with A/T, the shift cables at the carburetor/injector.

5. Drain the coolant.

6. Remove the water hose from carburetor and cylinder head. On some models it may be necessary to disconnect the upper radiator hose.

7. Remove the heater and water outlet hoses. On some models it may be ecessay to remove the water outlet housing.

8. Disconnect the water temperature sending unit.

9. Remove the mounting nuts/bolts from the ends toward the middle. Remove the manifold and carburetor/injector assembly. Remove the insulators and gaskets at this time as well, if so equipped.

10. Clean all mounting surfaces. Before reinstalling the manifold, coat both sides with gasket sealer. Install mounting nuts/bolts starting from the center toward the ends.

## Exhaust Manifold

### REMOVAL & INSTALLATION

1. Disconnect the negative battery cable. Remove the air cleaner and duct hose assembly. Disconnect the oxygen sensor connection, if so equipped. On some fuel injected models, it may be necessary to emove the air plenum assembly.

2. Remove the manifold heat stove, heat protector and hose. Disconnect the EGR lines and reed valve, if equipped. On the 1988–90 Galant, when removing the front exhaust gasket, remove the oil level gauge guide. In order to remove the rear manifold, the air plenum assembly must be removed.

3. Disconnect the exhaust pipe bracket from the engine block.

4. Remove the exhaust pipe flange bolts from the manifold. It may be necessarry to remove the exhaust pipe flange bolts from under the vehicle.

5. Remove the manifold flange stud nuts starting from the ends toward the middle and remove the manifold from the cylinder head.

6. Installation is the reverse of removal. Install mounting nuts starting from the middle toward the ends. On the 1988–90 Galant, when installing the front exhaust manifold and be sure

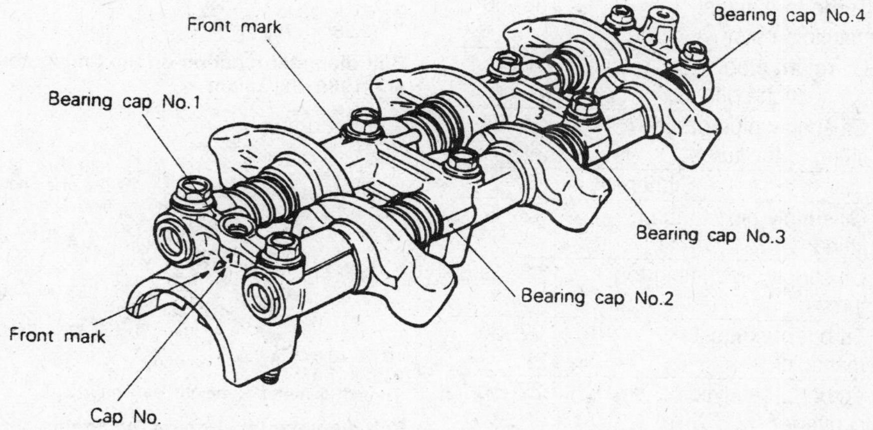


**Rocker arm assembly for the 1988–89 Galant**

to coat the O-ring of the oil level gauge guide with clean engine oil, before inserting it into the cylinder block.

## Turbocharger

### REMOVAL & INSTALLATION

1. Disconnect the negative battery cable. Remove the air cleaner and turbocharger inlet ducting. Unbolt the turbocharger discharge hose going to the injection mixer.
2. Disconnect the oxygen sensor at the catalytic converter to protect it.
3. Unbolt and remove the large heat shield that covers the top of the turbocharger.
4. Remove the nuts fastening the turbo to the catalytic converter. On Cordia, Tredia and Mirage, disconnect the oil return pipe at the oil pan. On Starion, disconnect the oil return hose at the oil return pipe and the timing chain cover.
5. Disconnect the oil supply line at the turbo and at the oil filter bracket.
6. Disconnect the turbocharger from the exhaust manifold and remove the unit from the vehicle.
7. Installation is the reverse of the removal procedure. Replace all gaskets as required. Pour clean engine oil into the oil supply fitting before connecting the oil supply pipe.

### TROUBLESHOOTING

**For more information on turbocharging, please refer to "Turbocharging" in the Unit Repair section.**

| | ft. lbs. |
|---|---|
| Cordia, Tredia and Mirage | |
| Oil supply pipe banjo fitting at the block | 10–13 |
| Turbo-to-converter bolts | 36–50 |
| Turbo-to-exhaust manifold nuts | 36–50 |
| Oil return pipe connection bolts | 6–7 |
| Oil supply pipe banjo fitting at the turbo | 21–24 |
| Starion | |
| Oil supply pipe to turbo fitting | 13–17 |
| Oil supply pipe fitting to turbo | 16.5–19.5 |
| Turbo-to-exhaust manifold | 37–50 |
| Turbo-to-catalytic converter | 37–50 |
| Oil drain pipe to turbo | 6–7 |

## Front Cover

### REMOVAL & INSTALLATION

#### *Except 2.5L and V6 Engines*

1. Disconnect the negative battery cable. Remove the alternator drive belt.
2. Unbolt and remove the water pump drive pulley. Remove the bolt from the crankshaft pulley. Using a suitable puller, remove the crankshaft pulley.
3. Remove the bolts from the cover (1468cc—Mirage and Precis) or upper and lower covers and remove them. If the engine has 2 covers, the upper cover comes off first.
4. Install in reverse order, using new gaskets under the cover(s).

#### *2.5L Engine*

1. Disconnect the negative battery cable. Unbolt the clutch fan. Unbolt the fan shroud and then remove the shroud and clutch fan together. Remove the pulley and belt.
2. Remove the crankshaft bolt. With a puller, remove the crankshaft pulley.
3. Remove the rocker cover. Then, remove the 2 front bolts from the cylinder head; these screw into and seal the top of the timing cover.
4. Remove the oil pan bolts (front and side) that screw into the timing cover.
5. Drain the cooling system and remove the coolant hose leading to the water pump. Remove the alternator or other accessories that are in the way of the timing cover.
6. Unbolt and remove the timing cover.
7. Clean all the gasket surfaces. If the oil pan gasket was damaged in removing the front cover, carefully cut the oil pan gasket off flush with the front of the block on both sides and remove the cut off pieces of gasket.
8. Carefully pry the old oil seal out of the cover without scratching the bore into which the seal fits. Then, install a new seal with an installer such as Part Nos. MD998376-01 and MB990938-01.
9. Install new gaskets to the cylinder block. Cut an exact replacement for the section of oil pan gasket you removed from a new pan gasket, if necessary. Insert this piece of gasket onto the front of the pan in the exact position of the old piece and then use liquid sealer on the joint between the 2 sections of gasket on both sides. Install the chain cover. Install the cover bolts and torque them to 9–10.5 ft. lbs. Lightly coat the outside diameter of the crankshaft pulley boss with clean engine oil. Then install the pulley onto the crankshaft, install the bolt and turn it to force the pulley all the way on. Torque it to 80–94 ft. lbs.
10. Install the front head bolts (2) and torque to 11–15 ft. lbs. Install the oil pan bolts and torque them to 4.5–5.5 ft. lbs.
11. Install all hoses and accessories and refill the cooling system.

#### *V6 Engine*

1. Disconnect the negative battery cable. Disconnect the power steering oil pump pressure switch connector.
2. Remove the power steering pump hose bracket bolts from the engine.

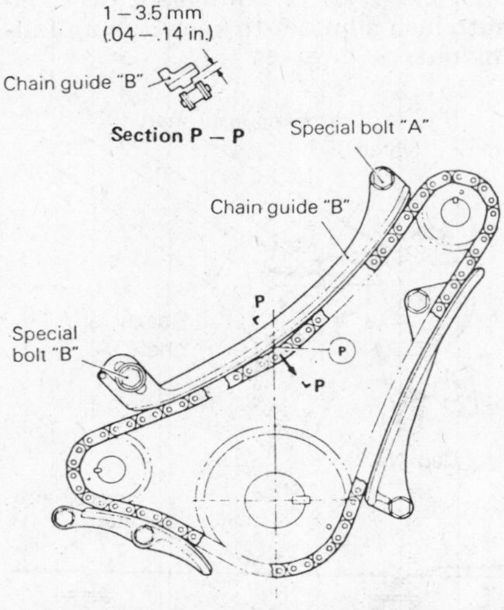


**2555cc silent shaft timing mark alignment**

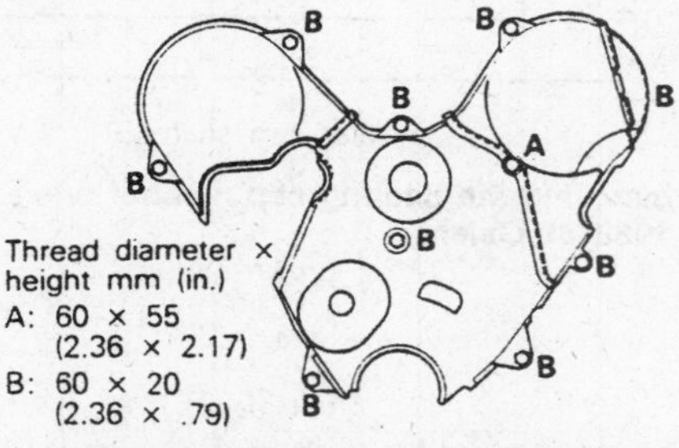


**Bolt diameter location on the timing cover—1988–89 Galant**

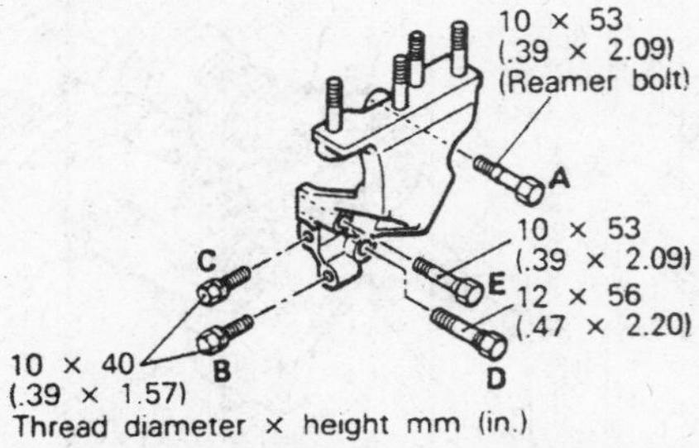


**Bolt diameter location on the engine support bracket—1988–89 Galant**

3. Slightly jack up the engine and support it safely and remove the engine mounting bolt(s) from the engine mounting bracket and remove the bracket.

4. Remove the A/C compressor belt and tension pulley bracket.

5. Remove the power steering pump and place it out of the way with the pressure lines still attached. Remove the tensioner pulley and pulley bracket.

6. Remove the outer upper timing belt cover and gaskets.

7. Remove the engine mounting bolt(s) from the engine support bracket and remove the bracket. Be sure to take note of the different bolt sizes and the holes in which they came out of.

8. Remove the timing belt cover cap and the other outer upper timing belt cover with gaskets.

9. Remove the under cover panel. Remove the crankshaft pulley bolt and using a suitable pulley, remove the crankshaft pulley. Remove the front flange and then remove the lower timing belt cover(s). Be sure to take note of the different bolt sizes in the lower cover and the holes in which they came out of.

10. Installation is the reverse order of the removal procedure. Torque the crankshaft pulley bolt to 108–116 ft. lbs.

## Timing Chain and Sprockets

### REMOVAL & INSTALLATION

#### *2.5L Engine*

1. Disconnect the negative battery cable.

2. Remove the rocker cover.

3. Put the engine on TDC No. 1 cylinder firing position by turning the crankshaft until the TDC timing marks line up and both front valves are fully closed (rockers off the cams).

4. Remove the timing cover.

5. Unbolt and remove the three silent shaft chain guides.

6. Unscrew and remove the oil pump drive sprocket bolt and the left silent shaft sprocket bolt.

7. When the bolts are removed, pull these 2 sprockets off and then disengage the chain from the crankshaft sprocket. Note that the 2 sprockets are identical, but that the oil pump drive sprocket is installed with the concave side toward the engine while the left silent shaft sprocket has the concave side out.

8. Remove the sprockets and the chain. Remove the crankshaft sprocket for the silent shaft chain.

9. The timing chain tensioner maintains constant spring pressure on the chain. Fasten the follower plunger so it will not be forced out of the body of the oil pump. Securely run wire around the follower and the left side of the oil pump.

10. Remove the camshaft sprocket bolt and pull the sprocket off the camshaft. Separate the chain from the sprockets and remove it. Pull the sprocket for the camshaft timing chain that is on the crankshaft off, keeping it and the silent shaft drive sprockets in order for correct installation.

11. Inspect the tensioner follower and replace it if the follower shows a deep grooving where the chain was ridden against it. To replace it, remove the wire holding it in place and allow the spring to gradually push it out of the oil pump body.

12. Replace the rubber seal that goes in the oil pump body and the spring behind it when replacing the tensioner follower. Make sure the thinner part of the follower faces downward. Wire the new follower in place just as the old one was.

13. If the timing chain right and left guides show heavy grooving, they should be replaced by unbolting them. Sprockets should be replaced if the teeth are deformed from wear or there are any obvious cracks.

14. To install first install the crankshaft sprocket for the camshaft timing chain onto the crankshaft. Install the sprocket so that the teeth are on the crankshaft or inner end of the sprocket. Engage the camshaft timing chain with the camshaft sprocket so the chrome plated link straddles the timing mark on the front of the sprocket.

15. Wrap the lower end of the chain around the crankshaft sprocket so the chrome link straddles the timing mark there and make sure the chain rides inside the chain guides on both sides.

16. Rest the camshaft sprocket on the sprocket holder and get the camshaft bolt. Engage the cam shaft sprocket with the front of the camshaft so the prong on the camshaft flange fits into the hole in the sprocket, install the bolt and torque to 37–43 ft. lbs. Remove the wire holding the tensioner follower.

17. Install the crankshaft silent shaft chain sprocket, facing so that the teeth are on the outer end of the sprocket.

18. Assemble the oil pump drive gear and left silent shaft sprockets to the left silent shaft chain with the chrome plated links straddling the timing marks on each. Make sure the concave side of the oil pump sprocket is toward the oil pump, but that the concave side of the left silent shaft sprocket faces outward.

19. Engage the chain with the crankshaft sprocket so the chrome plated link straddles the timing mark on the front of the sprocket. Install each sprocket on its shaft. Install and tighten the bolts finger tight.

20. Install the 3 chain guides, turning bolts finger tight. Then torque the sprocket bolts. Tighten the right side and bottom chain guide bolts fully.

21. Rotate the silent shaft sprockets slightly, the oil pump sprocket clockwise and the left silent shaft sprocket counter clockwise so the slack in the chain all goes to the span between the oil pump and left silent shaft sprockets, near the adjustable guide that is still loose.

22. Adjust the position of the chain guide **B**, the adjustable guide, by positioning it and then tightening the bolts until the play in the center of the chain near the adjustable guide is 0.04–1.4 in. Pull the chain away from the guide at the center of the guide at the center of the guide and measure the distance between the outer edge of the guide and edge of the chain to do this. When the play is correct, torque, first, the guide adjusting bolt (the one that runs in the slot) to 11–15 ft. lbs. Then, torque the upper guide bolt to 6–7 ft. lbs.

23. Install the timing chain cover and front pulley.

24. Continue the installation in the reverse order of the removal.

## Timing Belt and Sprockets

### REMOVAL & INSTALLATION

#### *4 Cylinder Except 1.5L and 1.6L Engines*

**NOTE: Timing belt and sprocket removal procedures are combined because the procedures are interrelated. Belts are kept in place to permit sprocket bolts to be loosened. If you intention is to replace only the belt(s) simply skip the steps related to removing or replacing the sprockets, unless it is noted that a sprocket must be removed to gain access to a belt related part.**

1. Disconnect the negative battery cable. Remove the timing belt cover. Rotate the engine until the timing marks on the camshaft sprocket and cylinder head or rear belt cover and the crankshaft sprocket and front cover are perfectly aligned.

2. Loosen the timing belt tensioner adjusting bolt and the mounting bolt, shift the tensioner as far as it will go

toward the left or water pump side (so belt tension is lost) and then retighten the adjusting bolt. If the belt is to be reused, draw an arrow on it in the direction of rotation. Now, remove the belt. Then, hold the tensioner in position as you remove the tensioner adjusting bolt. Slowly release tension, remove the mounting bolt, and then remove the tension, spring and spacer.

3. Remove the bolt and remove the camshaft sprocket.

4. If you need to replace the inner timing belt which drives the oil pump and right silent shaft or need to remove the sprockets, proceed as follows; otherwise, proceed with Step 5:

a. Remove the crankshaft front sprocket bolt and remove the front crankshaft sprocket and flange. Remove the plug from the left side of the block. Insert a suitable tool about 0.3 inches in diameter and

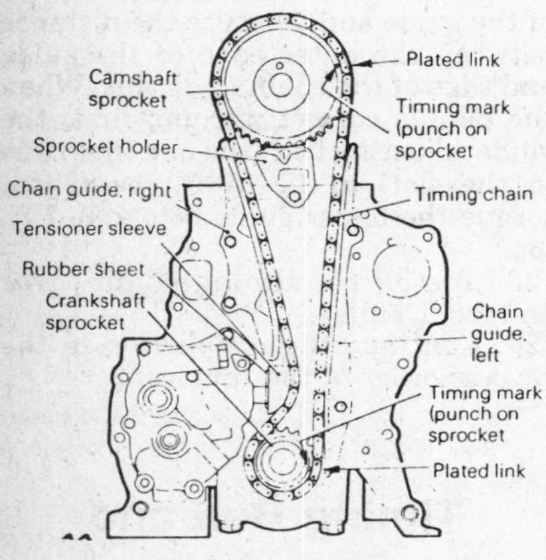


**2555cc cam drive timing marks**

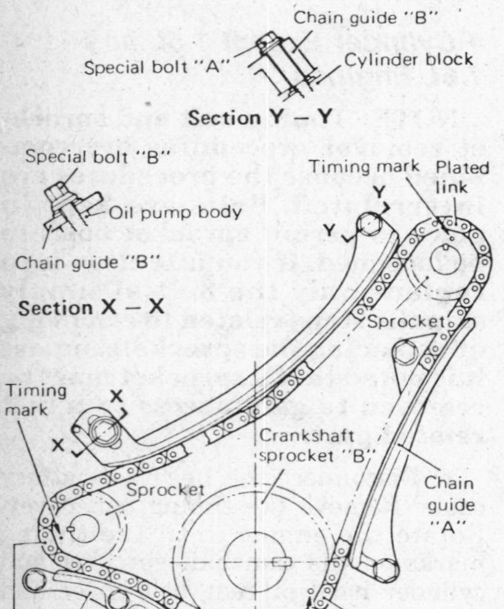


**2555cc silent shaft chain timing marks**

about 2.5 inches long or longer into the hole to keep the left silent shaft in position.

b. Remove the oil pump sprocket retaining nut and remove the nut and the sprocket. Loosen the right silent shaft sprocket bolt until you can turn it with your fingers.

c. Then, remove the inner tensioner bolts and remove the tensioner. Remove the inner timing belt. Then, remove the large crankshaft sprocket from the crankshaft and the right silent shaft bolt, sprocket and spacer.

5. Inspect all components as required. Replace defective parts as needed.

**To install**

6. Install the larger crankshaft sprocket onto the crankshaft with the flatter or flanged side forward and the boss which is there to extend the sprocket forward from the front of the crankshaft at the rear. Align the timing mark on the sprocket with the mark on the front case. Apply a light coating of engine oil to the inner surface of the right silent shaft spacer and install the spacer. The chamfer must face inward, toward the engine. Then, install the right silent shaft sprocket and bolt and tighten the bolt finger tight. Align the timing mark on this sprocket also with the timing mark on the front case.

7. Install the inner belt over the sprockets so that the timing marks are in alignment and the upper side is under slight tension. Then, install the inner belt tensioner with the center of the pulley on the left side of the mounting bolt and the flange of the pulley facing the front of the engine. Lift the tensioner with the tips of your fingers until there is tension on the inner belt's upper length. Hold the tensioner in exactly this position and tighten the tensioner mounting bolt. Make sure the turning of the bolt does not alter the position of the tensioner, or belt tension will be excessive. Then, tighten the right silent shaft retaining flange bolt to 25–28 ft. lbs.

8. Now, check to make sure the timing marks effected by this belt are in alignment. Shift the position of the belt's teeth and retension if necessary. Depressing the belt's upper span with your index finger should enable you to depress it about 0.2–0.3 in. Adjust the tension again to product this amount of deflection if necessary.

9. Now, torque the right silent shaft mounting bolt to 25–28 ft. lbs. Then, install the flange and crankshaft sprocket onto the crankshaft. The concave (inner) side of the flange must face to the rear so as to fit the curved front of the inner crankshaft sprocket. The flat side of the outer crankshaft sprocket must face the flange, to the rear. Finally, install the washer and bolt to the front of the crankshaft and torque it to 80–94 ft. lbs.

10. Install the camshaft sprocket to the camshaft and torque the bolt to 58–72 ft. lbs.

11. Install the spacer and main timing belt tensioner, installing the bolts finger tight. Now, install the spring between the locking tang on the right side of the tensioner and the tang on the right side of the water pump, just above the tensioner. This will force the tensioner to turn counterclockwise on the pivot bolt. Push the tensioner all the way toward the water pump and lock it by tightening the adjusting bolt.

12. Check alignment of all timing marks: the mark on the camshaft sprocket must align with the mark on the head; the mark on the crankshaft sprocket must align with that on the front case; and the mark on the oil pump sprocket must align with that on the front case.

13. Install the timing belt. The belt should be fitted over the sprockets in order: first the crankshaft, then the oil pump and then the camshaft sprocket. The (right) side of the belt which is normally straight must be straight during installation so the timing marks will remain lined up when the belt is actually tensioned. Remove the suitable tool installed to keep the silent shaft in position and replace the plug. Making sure there is no tension on the pivot bolt, loosen the tensioner adjusting bolt so the spring applies tension to the belt. Make sure the belt

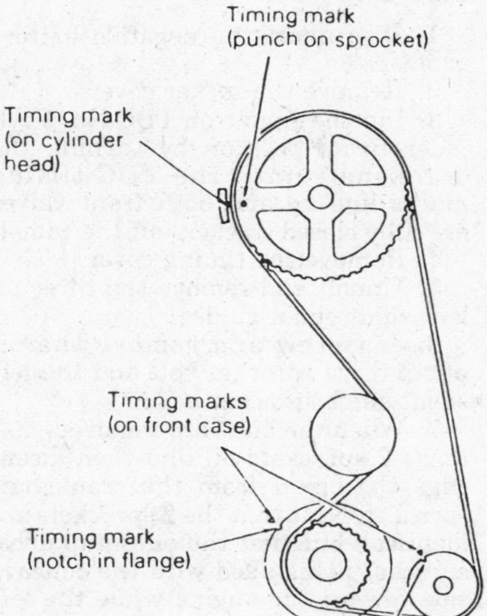


**1795 and 1997cc camshaft drive belt timing marks**

remains completely engaged with the teeth on the camshaft sprocket and that all timing marks remain aligned. Correct if necessary. Then, tighten the adjusting bolt. Finally, tighten the pivot bolt. Make sure to tighten the bolts in that order, or tension will not be correct. Recheck alignment of the timing marks.

14. Now, turn the engine one full turn clockwise only. Loosen the tensioner pivot bolt and then the adjusting bolt. Allow the tensioner spring to again position the tensioner without interference from bolt friction. Then, tighten the adjusting bolt. Tighten the pivot bolt. Try to pry the belt outward by placing your thumb under the belt and your fingers on the seal line at the right side of the timing belt rear cover. The distance between the back of the belt and seal line will be about 0.55 in. if the tension is correct.

15. Continue the installation in the reverse order of the removal procedure.

### 1.5L Engine

1. Disconnect the negative battery cable. Remove the cooling fan, spacer, water pump pulley and belt. Remove the timing belt cover.

2. Turn the crankshaft until the timing marks on the camshaft sprocket and cylinder head are aligned. Loosen the tensioning bolt (it runs in the slotted portion of the tensioner) and the pivot bolt on the timing belt tensioner and lever the tensioner as far as it will go toward the water pump. Tighten the adjusting bolt. Mark the timing belt with an arrow showing direction of rotation if you may be reusing it.

3. Pull the timing belt off the camshaft sprocket. Remove the camshaft sprocket.

4. Remove the crankshaft pulley. Then, remove the timing belt.

5. Remove the crankshaft sprocket bolts and remove the crankshaft sprocket and flange, noting the direction of installation for each. Remove the timing belt tensioner.

6. Inspect all components, as required. Replace defective parts as needed.

**To install**

7. To install, first reinstall the flange and crankshaft sprocket. The flange must go on first with the chamfered area outward. The sprocket is installed with the boss forward and the studs for the fan belt pulley outward. Install and torque the crankshaft sprocket bolt to 51–72 ft. lbs. Install the camshaft sprocket and bolt, torquing it to 47–54 ft. lbs.

8. Align the timing marks of the camshaft sprocket. Check that the crankshaft timing marks are still in alignment (the locating pin on the front of the crankshaft sprocket is lined up with a mark on the front case).

9. To install the tensioner assembly, mount the tensioner, spring and spacer with the bottom end of the spring free. Then, install the bolts and tighten the adjusting bolt slightly with the tensioner moved as far as possible away from the water pump. Install the free end of the spring into the locating tang on the front case. Position the belt over the crankshaft sprocket and then over the camshaft sprocket. Make sure the belt is straight on the right side (where there's no tensioner as you do this. Slip the back of the belt over the tensioner wheel. Turn the camshaft sprocket in the opposite of its normal direction of rotation until the straight side of the belt is tight and make sure the timing marks line up. If not, shift the belt one tooth at a time in the appropriate direction until this occurs.

10. Install the crankshaft pulley, making sure the pin on the crankshaft sprocket fits through the hole in the rear surface of the pulley. Install the bolts and torque to specification.

11. Loosen the tensioner mounting bolts so the tensioner works, without the interference of any friction, under spring pressure. Make sure the belt follows the curve of the camshaft pulley so that the teeth are engaged all the way around. Correct the path of the belt if necessary. Torque the tensioner adjusting bolt to 15–18 ft. lbs. Then, torque the tensioner pivot bolt to the same figure. Bolts must be torqued in that order, or tension won't be correct.

12. Turn the crankshaft 1 turn clockwise until timing marks again line up to seat the belt. Then loosen both tensioner attaching bolts and let the tensioner position itself under spring tension as before. Finally, torque the bolts in the proper order exactly as before. Check belt tension by putting your fingers on the water pump side of the tensioner wheel and pull the belt toward it with your thumb. The belt should move toward the pump until the teeth are about ¼ of the way across the head of the tensioner adjusting bolt. Retension the belt if necessary.

13. Install the timing belt covers and remaining cooling system parts in the reverse of the removal procedure.

### 1.6L Engine

1. Disconnect the negative battery cable. Remove the crankshaft pulley. Remove the upper and lower timing belt covers. Rotate the crankshaft until all timing marks are lined up. There is a pin on the crankshaft sprocket which serves as the timing mark. It lines up with a pin protruding from the block behind the sprocket.

2. Remove the crankshaft sprocket bolt and loosen the other sprocket bolts.

3. Loosen the tensioner mounting and adjusting bolts, shift the tensioner all the way to the left and retighten the adjusting bolt. Mark the timing belt with an arrow in the direction of rotation if it may be reused. Remove the timing belt.

4. Remove the camshaft sprocket, crankshaft sprocket and flange. If necessary, the crankshaft sprocket may be pulled off with a puller such as Mitsubishi part No. MD998311.

5. Remove the tensioner.

6. Inspect all components, as required. Replace defective parts as required.

7. Install the spacer, flange and crankshaft sprocket. The spacer is installed with the larger opening to the rear, so it fits tightly over the crankshaft at the front. Then install the flange with the slightly concave side backward. Finally, install the sprocket with the flat side rearward and boss forward. Install the sprocket bolt and torque to 80–93 ft. lbs. Make sure the sprocket and block timing marks are still lined up. Also check the timing marks for the oil pump drive sprocket and make sure they are lined up.

8. Apply a thin coating of clean engine oil to the outer circumference of the camshaft spacer and install the spacer onto the camshaft. Install the camshaft sprocket and bolt to 44–57 ft. lbs. Make sure the timing marks are aligned. Then install the crankshaft pulley so the engine can be turned. The bolts may be finger tight.

9. Install the tensioner by first installing the spring, then the tensioner itself and then by installing and tightening the nut (finger tight) used for adjusting the tensioner. Make sure the bent end of the spring goes to the right. Then, rock the tensioner as necessary until the pivot hole and bolt hole in the block align and install the pivot bolt. The spring must be installed so the bent end will work against the tab on the tensioner and the straight end works against the tab on the water pump body. Engage the ends of the spring with the tabs. Push the tensioner as far as it will go toward the water pump and then tighten the adjusting nut.

10. Install the timing belt, first over the crankshaft sprocket and then onto the oil pump sprocket. With the right side straight, engage the belt with the camshaft sprocket. Then, loosen the tensioner adjusting nut so the tensioner will tension the belt.

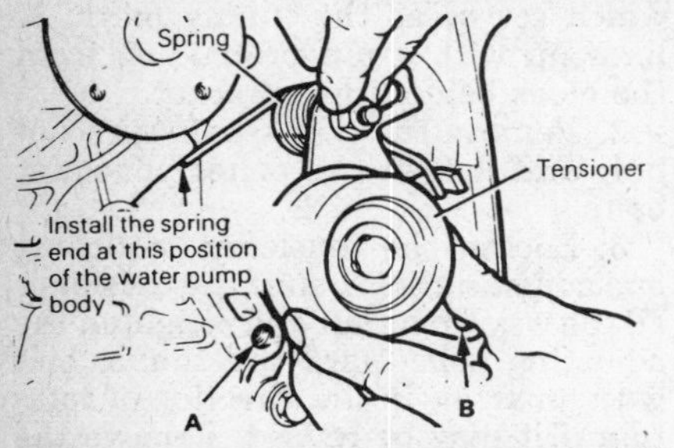

**Installing belt tensioner spring—1597 engine**

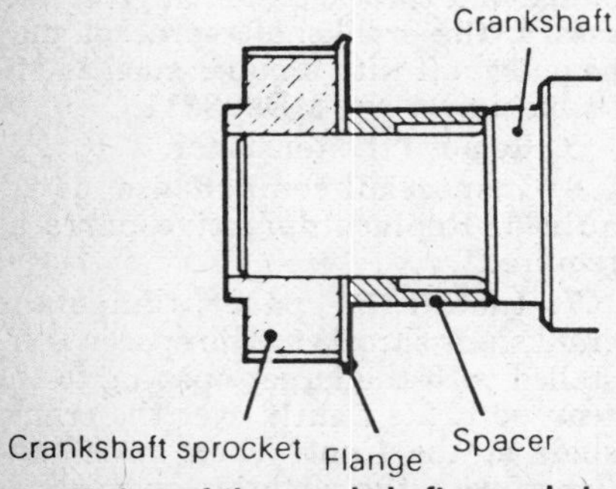

**Installation of the crankshaft sprocket—1597 engine**

11. Push the tensioner slightly toward the adjusting nut so that the belt teeth will be forced to mesh with the sprocket teeth. Check to make sure that all teeth have meshed. Finally, with the tensioner under spring tension only, tighten the adjusting nut and then the pivot bolt. Check to make sure all timing marks are in alignment and make corrections if necessary.

12. Turn the crankshaft one full turn in the normal direction of rotation, until all timing marks again align. Turn the engine smoothly and do not allow it to turn backwards. Don't grab the belt to test tension during this procedure. Again loosen the tensioner adjusting nut and mounting bolt, again allowing it to adjust under spring pressure along. Then, torque the tensioner adjusting nut to 16–21 ft. lbs. Finally, tighten the mounting bolt.

13. Test the tension on the belt by grasping the right edge of the rear timing belt cover and using your thumb to pull the center of the belt span toward it. With reasonable pressure, the belt should move to within just under half an inch (0.47 in.) from the seal line. Repeat Steps 11 and 12 if the tension isn't correct.

14. Remove the crankshaft pulley. Install the timing belt lower front cover. Then install the upper cover.

### *V6 Engine*

1. Bring the No. 1 piston up to top dead center of its compression stroke. Disconnect the negative battery cable. Disconnect the power steering oil pump pressure switch connector.

2. Remove the power steering pump hose bracket bolts from the engine.

3. Slightly jack up the engine and support it safely and remove the engine mounting bolt(s) from the engine mounting bracket and remove the bracket.

4. Remove the A/C compressor belt and tension pulley bracket.

5. Remove the power steering pump and place it out of the way with the pressure lines still attached. Remove the tensioner pulley and pulley bracket.

6. Remove the outer upper timing belt cover and gaskets.

7. Remove the engine mounting bolt(s) from the engine support bracket and remove the bracket. Be sure to take note of the different bolt sizes and the holes in which they came out of.

8. Remove the timing belt cover cap and the other outer upper timing belt cover with gaskets.

9. Remove the under cover panel. Remove the crankshaft pulley bolt and using a suitable pulley, remove the crankshaft pulley. Remove the front flange and then remove the lower timing belt cover(s) and gaskets. Be sure to take note of the different bolt sizes in the lower cover and the holes in which they came out of.

10. Loosen the timing belt tensioner bolt and turn the timing belt tensioner counterclockwise along the elongated hole. Remove the tensioner bolt, tensioner and timing belt.

**NOTE: If the old timing belt is going to be reused, the direction of rotation should be marked on the belt brefore removing it.**

11. Attach the tension and the timing bolt tensioner. Engage the top of the tensioner sping onto the water pump pin. Be sure the hook on the spring is facing outward. Turn the timing belt tensioner to the extreme counterclockwise along the elongated hole and temporarily fix the timing belt tensioner.

**To install**

12. Install the timing belt as follows:

   a. Align the timing marks of the camshaft sprockets (on the front and rear sides) and the crankshaft sprocket. At the top dead point on the number 1 cylinder compression stroke.

   b. Route the timing belt on the crankshaft sprocket then on the camshaft sprocket on the side without slackness in the tight side.

   c. Run the timing belt onto the water pump pulley, the camshaft sprocket on the front side, and the timing belt tensioner.

   d. Apply force counteclockwise to the camshaft sprocket on the rear side. When the tight side of the belt is felt, check that the timing marks are aligned.

13. Attach the flange. Back off the fixing bolts of the temporarily tighten tension 1 or 2 turns and tighten the timing belt with tensioner spring force.

14. Using a suitable tool, tun the crankshaft 2 turns in the normal (clockwise) rotating direction. Never turn the engine counterclockwise.

15. Re-align the sprockets timing marks and tighten the tensioner fixing bolts. Using a belt tension gauge, check the belt tension. The belt tension should be 57–84 lbs.

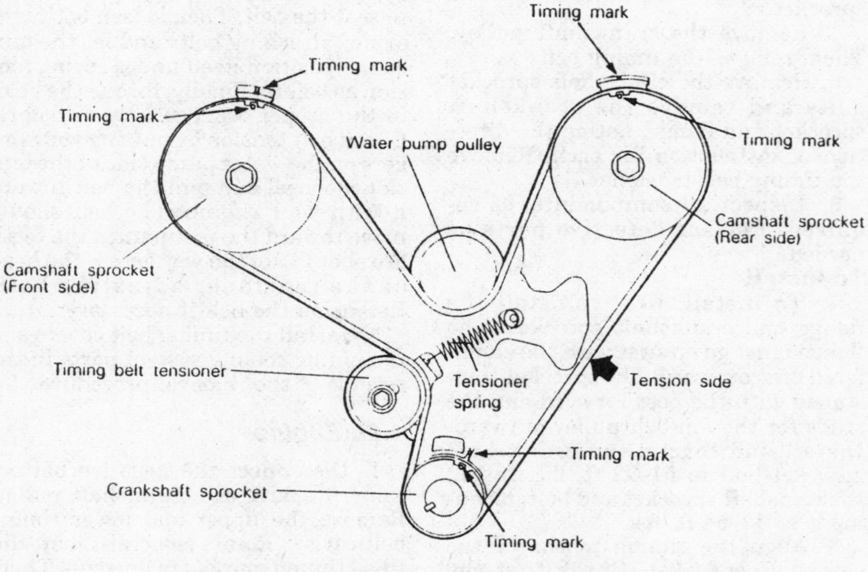

**Timing belt installation – 1988–89 Galant**

16. Complete installation by reversing the order of the removal procedure. Torque the crankshaft pulley bolt to 108–116 ft. lbs.

## Silent Shafts

### REMOVAL & INSTALLATION

#### *4 Cylinder Except 2.5L Engine*

**NOTE: A special oil seal guide MD998285 or equivalent is needed to complete this operation.**

1. Disconnect the negative battery cable. Remove the timing belt covers, timing belts and sprockets.
2. Drain the oil and remove the oil filter. Then, remove the oil pan and gasket. Remove the oil pick-up and gasket.
3. Remove the oil pressure relief plunger plug and gasket, and then remove the spring and plunger from the oil filter bracket. Remove the 4 bracket mounting bolts and remove the oil filter mount and its gasket.
4. Remove the cap and gasket that cover the oil pump driven gear shaft. This is located on the right side of the front case as you look at the front of the engine, just above the protruding silent shaft.
5. Using a long socket, remove the retaining bolt from the oil pump driven gear (behind the plug removed earlier).
6. Remove the mounting bolts for the front case and remove it from the block. Remove the front case gasket. Then, slide the silent shafts from the block, noting their installation angles.
7. Inspect the silent shaft bearing journals for signs of excessive wear of seizure. If there are signs of critical wear problems, the bushings should also be inspected. The bushings may be replaced by pulling them out and pressing new ones in, using special tools. This is done with the crankshaft removed, since it normally is required only at time of major engine overhaul.
8. Lubricate the silent shaft bearing journals with clean engine oil and install the shafts into the block. Insert the shafts so they are positioned as they were when you removed them ( a suitable tool in the left side of the block will ensure that the left side shaft will be in position).
9. Install a special seal guide to the crankshaft (MD998285–01 or equivalent) so the smaller diameter faces outward. Coat the outer diameter of the seal with clean engine oil. Install a new front case gasket. Then, install the front case by carefully positioning its crankshaft seal over the seal guide and lining up all bolt holes; then, install all eight mounting bolts. Tighten the bolts just finger tight.
10. Install the oil filter mounting bracket gasket and then the mounting bracket and 4 bolts; torque the front case bolts to 15–19 ft. lbs. and the oil filter mounting bracket bolts to 11–15 ft. lbs.
11. Install the remaining parts in reverse of the removal procedure.

#### *2.5L Engine*

**NOTE: Two long, 8mm bolts are needed to pull out the silent shaft thrust plates and 2 guides, made by cutting the heads off 6mm bolts about 2 in. long.**

1. Disconnect the negative battery cable. Remove the timing cover, chains and sprockets. Before removing the 2 sprocket bolts, put a wrench on the flange bolt which attaches the upper oil pump gear to the center of the right side silent shaft and turn it just enough to break it loose.
2. Screw 8mm bolts into the bolt holes in the thrust plate and turn them evenly to pull the thrust plate out of the block. Then, remove the left silent shaft.
3. Remove the oil pump mounting bolts. Then, pull the oil pump and gasket straight off the front of the block. The right side silent shaft will come out with the pump. Be careful to support the pump and shaft in such a way that the rear shaft bearing will not be damaged. Remove the bolt from the center of the oil pump driven (upper) gear. Now, separate the silent shaft and key from the oil pump driven gear by sliding it out. Remove the oil pump gasket.
4. Inspect the silent shaft bearing journals for signs of excessive wear or seizure. If there are signs of critical wear problems, the bushings should also be inspected. The busings may be replaced by pulling them out and pressing new ones in , using special tools. This is done with the crankshaft removed, since it normally is required only at time of major engine overhaul.
5. Lubricate the left silent shaft bearing journals with clean engine oil and install the shaft into the block. Insert the shaft so it is positioned as it was when you removed it (a suitable tool in the left side of the block will ensure that the shaft will be in position).
6. Screw the 2 guides (made from 6mm headless bolts) into the holes in the block above and below the left side silent shaft. Install a new O-ring with engine oil. Then, install the thrust plate over the guides and into the block. Finally, remove the guides and install the thrust plate mounting bolts, torquing to 7.5–8.5 ft. lbs.

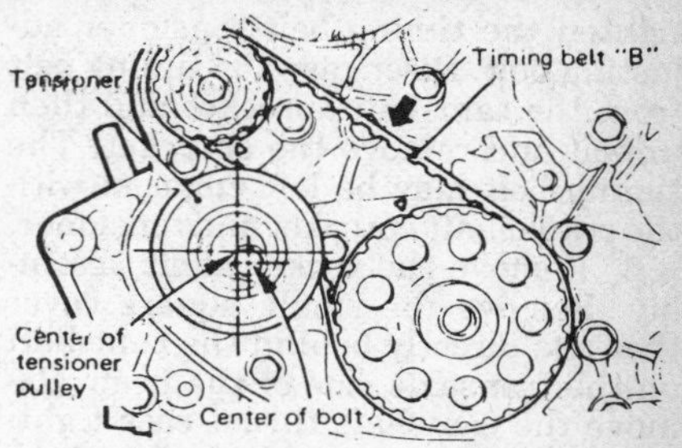

**1795 and 1997cc silent shaft timing marks**

7. Pull the cover off the oil pump housing and verify that the oil pump gears still positioned so the timing marks are aligned. Install the cover over the guide pins and pour about 0.6 cu. in. of clean engine oil into the oil pump outlet (which is at top right as you look at the pump cover). Install the oil pump gasket to the rear of the pump (you may want to use grease to hold it in position). Then, position the pump in its installed direction and engage the key of the right silent shaft to the slot in the oil pump driven gear. Slide the shaft all the way into the pump driven gear and then install the bolt and torque to 44–50 ft. lbs. Lubricate the right side silent shaft bearing journals with clean engine oil and then insert the shaft into the block and install the oil pump. Install the oil pump mounting bolts and torque to 7.5–8.5 ft. lbs.
8. Install the sprockets, timing chains, tensioners and front cover.

## Camshaft

### REMOVAL & INSTALLATION

#### *1.8L, 2.0L and 2.3L Engines*

1. Disconnect the negative battery cable. Remove the distributor. Remove the rocker cover, disconnect the camshaft sprocket and remove the rocker arm shaft and cam bearing assembly. The camshaft may then be lifted off the top of the cylinder head.
2. Check and replace defective components as required.
3. Thoroughly lubricate the camshaft bearing journals, the bearing saddles in the cylinder head and the inner surfaces of the caps with clean engine oil. Then continue the installation in the reverse order of the removal procedure.

#### *1.5L Engine*

1. Disconnect the negative battery cable. Remove the rocker cover, timing belt cover and the distributor.
2. Loosen the 2 bolts, move the timing belt tensioner toward the water pump as far as it will go and then re-

tighten the timing belt tensioner adjusting bolt. Disengage the timing belt from the camshaft sprocket and then unbolt and remove the sprocket. The timing belt may be left engaged with the crankshaft sprocket and tensioner.

3. Remove the rocker shaft assembly. Remove the small, square cover that sits directly behind the camshaft on the transaxle side of the head. Remove the camshaft thrust case tightening bolt that sits on the top of the head right near that cover.

4. Now, very carefully slide the entire camshaft out of the head through the hold in the camshaft side of the head, being sure the cam lobes do not strike the bearing bores in the head.

5. Check and replace defective components as required.

6. Lubricate all journal and thrust surfaces with clean engine oil and then insert the camshaft into the engine, again keeping the cam lobes from touching the bearing bores. Make sure the camshaft goes in with the threaded hole in the top of the thrust case straight upward and align the bolt hole in the thrust case and the cylinder head surface once the camshaft is all the way inside the head. Install the thrust case bolt and tighten firmly. Finally, install the rear cover with a new gasket and install and tighten the 4 bolts.

7. Coat the external surface of the front oil seal with engine oil. With a special installer part No. MD998306-01 or equivalent, drive the reusable or new front camshaft oil seal into the clearance between the cam and head at the forward end. Make sure the seal seats fully.

8. Install the camshaft sprocket and torque the bolt to 47–54 ft. lbs. Reconnect the timing belt, check timing and adjust the belt tension. Reinstall the rocker shaft assembly. Adjust the valves. Install the rocker and timing belt covers.

### 1.6L Engine

1. Disconnect the negative battery cable. Remove the distributor and remove the rocker cover. Remove the upper timing cover. Turn the engine over until the timing mark on the rear timing belt cover aligns with the mark on the camshaft sprocket. It's a good idea to mark the timing belt itself to align with the marks on the sprocket and rear timing belt cover to make precise reassembly easier. Now, remove the camshaft sprocket from the camshaft and remove the rocker arms and shafts assembly.

2. Pull the camshaft front oil seal off the front of the camshaft. Remove the camshaft.

3. Check and replace defective components as required.

4. Thoroughly lubricate the camshaft bearing journals, the bearing saddles in the cylinder head and the inner surfaces of the caps with clean engine oil.

5. Then, install the camshaft onto the cylinder head, being careful not to damage any of the camshaft journals. Install the rocker arm and shaft assembly to the head, torquing the bolts to 14–15 ft. lbs.

6. Coat the outside diameter of the front end of the camshaft with clean engine oil. Then, with a special tool such as MD998354-01 or equivalent, tap a new front seal in, using a hammer. Install the rear timing belt cover.

7. Turn the camshaft so the dowel pin on the front lines up with the hole in the sprocket. If you need to turn the cam, you can do so by exerting force on either of the 2 projections behind the No. 2 cylinder exhaust valve cam. Reconnect the camshaft drive sprocket by lifting it off the rest and installing it to the camshaft with the dowel pin going through the hole in the sprocket. Torque the sprocket bolt to 44–57 ft. lbs.

8. Install the remaining parts and adjust the valves.

### 2.5L Engine

1. Disconnect the negative battery cable. Remove the distributor. Remove the rocker cover and rocker shaft assembly. Remove also the rear bearing cap bolts and the cap.

2. Remove the camshaft from the head.

3. Check and replace defective components as required.

4. Thoroughly lubricate the camshaft bearing journals, the bearing saddles in the cylinder head and the inner surfaces of the caps with clean engine oil. Then, install the camshaft onto the cylinder head, being careful not to damage any of the camshaft journals. Apply a sealer to the outside diameter of the circular seal for the rear bearing and install it in the head with one side directly in contact with the rear of the camshaft. The packing will end up under the rearmost portion of the rear bearing cap. Then, install and torque the rocker shaft/bearing cap assembly. Include the rear bearing cap, using the same torque. Refit the cam sprocket and chain to the camshaft.

5. Also inspect the semicircular seal that goes in the front of the timing chain cover and seal the top with an adhesive such as 3M Super Weatherstrip Adhesive 801k or equivalent.

6. Adjust the valve clearances. Install the rocker cover and all other parts removed earlier. Start the engine and idle it until after the temperature gauge indicates normal operating temperature. Then, remove the rocker cover again and adjust the valves with the engine hot.

### V6 Engine

1. Remove the rocker arm covers as previously outlined in this section.

2. Using special tool MD9990767-01 or equivalent, remove the camshaft sprockets.

3. Remove the rocker arm shaft and cam bearing assemblies. Be sure to intall the special tool MD99843-01 or equivalent to assure that the auto lash adjuster does not fall out.

4. Carefully lift out the camshafts from their prospective heads, be sure to keep all removed parts in the proper order.

5. Check and replace defective components as required.

6. Thoroughly lubricate the camshaft bearing journals, the bearing saddles in the cylinder head and the inner surfaces of the caps with clean engine oil.

7. Installation is the reverse order of the removal procedure. Torque the camshaft sprocket bolts to 58–72 ft. lbs. and the bearing cap retaining bolts to 15 ft. lbs. It may be necessary to use the cylinder head and the rocker arm procedure already outlined in this section as guide for an easier installation.

## Piston and Connecting Rod

**For all piston and connecting rod overhaul procedures, please refer to "Engine Rebuilding" in the Unit Repair section.**

### POSITIONING

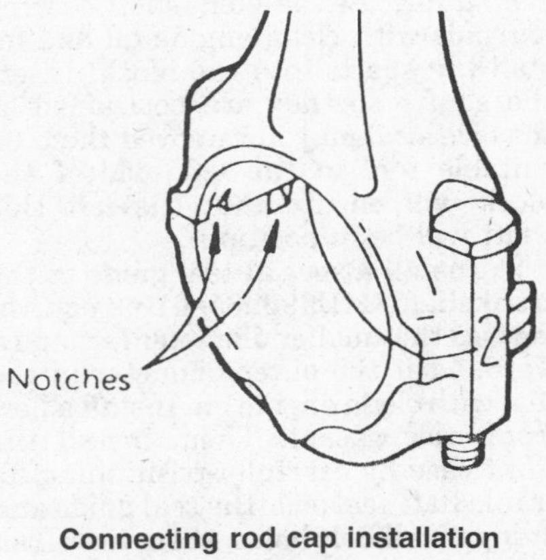


Connecting rod cap installation

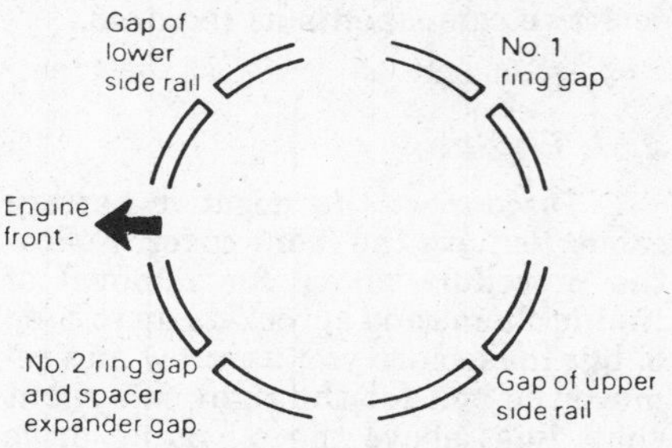


**Piston ring positioning**

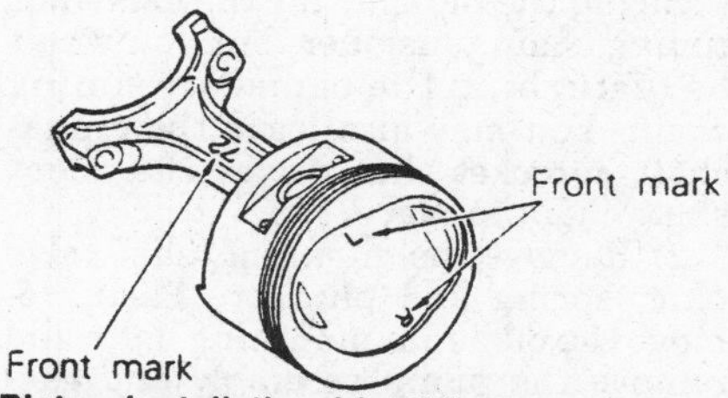


**Piston installation identification marks—1988–89 Galant**

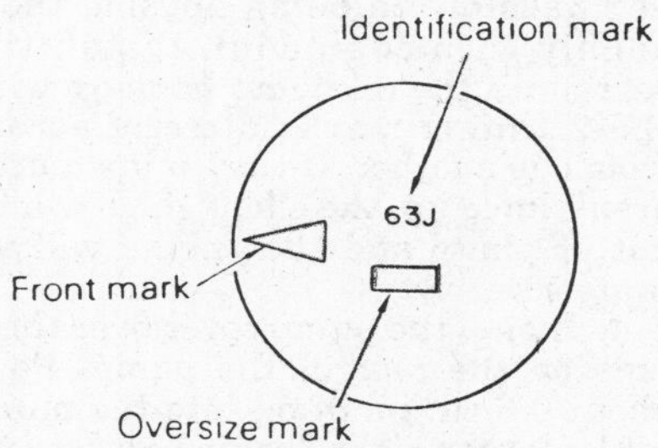


**Piston installation**

# ENGINE LUBRICATION

## Oil Pan

### REMOVAL & INSTALLATION

1. The oil pan must be pulled downward as much as 6 in. to clear the oil pickup. In nearly all applications, this requires that the engine mounts be disconnected and the engine raised to clear a crossmember underneath the shallower section of the pan. First, survey the area under the engine to determine whether or not there is clearance, in case, in your particular model the engine can be left in place.

2. Disconnect the negative battery cable. Drain the oil pan into a suitable container. Disconnect all those hoses and wires that would prevent the engine from being lifted the required distance for removal of the pan. On some models it will be necessary to remove the stater, transaxle mounts, bell housing and oil filter.

3. Support the vehicle in a secure manner far enough above ground for you to get underneath and remove the oil pan bolts. Hook a lift to the hooks on the cylinder head and support the engine.

4. Remove the attaching through bolts from the engine mounts. Raise the engine far enough to gain clearance, as necessary. Remove the oil pan from the vehicle.

5. Installation is the reverse of the removal procedure.

6. On the Mirage 1597cc engine, coat the 4 seams on the gasket surface for the block with a liquid sealer. These are the joints between the front cover and block on the front and the rear oil seal case and the block at the rear.

7. On the vehicles using gasketless pans, you'll need a tube of liquid sealer part No. MD997110 or equivalent. Cut the end of the tube off at the smallest diameter and run a bead of sealer around the entire groove in the oil pan. It should be about 0.16 in. thick. Run the head in back of the bolt holes. The pan should be installed within 15 minutes of the time you apply the sealer. Position the pan, install the bolts and tighten finger tight.

8. Torque the bolts alternately and in several stages.

## Rear Main Bearing Oil Seal

### REMOVAL & INSTALLATION

#### *Cordia, Tredia, Galant, Starion and Sigma*

1. Remove the transaxle or transmission and clutch from the vehicle. Remove the flywheel or driveplate and adapter plate.

2. Unbolt and remove the lower bell housing cover from the rear of the engine. Remove the rear plate from the upper portion of the rear of the block.

3. The lower surface of the oil seal case seals against the oil pan gasket or sealer at the rear. On engines with a gasket, carefully separate the gasket from the bottom of the seal case with a moderately sharp instrument. You may want to loosen the oil pan bolts slightly at the rear to make it easier to separate the 2 surfaces. If the gasket is damaged, the oil pan will have to be removed and the gasket replaced. On vehicles employing sealer, you'll have to unbolt and lower the oil pan now, and then clean both surfaces, apply new sealer and reinstall the oil pan after Step 7 is completed.

4. Remove the oil seal case bolts and pull it straight off the rear of the crankshaft. Remove the case gasket.

5. Remove the seal retainer or oil separator from the case, and then pry out the seal. Inspect the sealing surface at the rear of the crankshaft. If a deep groove is worn into the surface, the crankshaft will have to be replaced. Lubricate the sealing surface with clean engine oil.

6. Using a seal installer such as MD998376-01 and MD990938-01, install the new seal into the bore of rear oil seal case in such a way that the flat side of the seal will face outward when the case is installed on the engine. The inside of the seal must be flush with the inside surface of the seal case.

7. Install the retainer or oil separator directly over the seal with the small hole located directly at the bottom. Then, install a new gasket onto the block surface and install the seal case to the rear of the block. Retorque pan bolts, as necessary. Refill the oil pan if necessary.

8. Install the rear plate and bell housing cover. Install the flywheel or drive plate and the transaxle in reverse of the removal procedure.

#### *Mirage and Precis*

1. Remove the transaxle or manual transaxle and clutch from the vehicle. Remove the flywheel or driveplate and adapter plate.

2. Unbolt and remove the rear plate from the rear of the block. On the Mirage with the 1597cc engine, use a moderately sharp instrument and separate the rear portion of the oil pan gasket from the lower surface of the rear main seal case on the back of the block. You may want to loosen the oil pan bolts slightly at the rear to make it easier to separate the 2 surfaces. If the gasket is damaged, drain the oil pan and remove it. On the 1468cc engine, drain the oil pan and remove it, as the sealing surfaces must be cleaned and new sealer applied all around.

3. Unbolt the oil seal case and then pull it straight back and off the crankshaft. Remove the case gasket. Pry the old seal out of the case.

4. Inspect the sealing surface at the rear of the crankshaft. If a deep groove is worn into the surface, the crankshaft will have to be replaced. Press a new seal into the case with a special seal installing tool such as MD998011. The seal must be pressed in square until it bottoms in the case.

5. Oil the crankshaft sealing surfaces and the lips of the new seal. On

the Mirage with the 1597cc engine spread a liquid sealer thoroughly around those areas which butt up against the block and oil pan gasket at the bottom surface and on the front at both sides. Then, install the seal, gasket and seal case straight over the crankshaft sealing surface. Install and tighten the 5 case bolts.

6. On the 1468cc engine, install sealer and reinstall the oil pan. On the Mirage with the 1597cc engine reinstall the pan with a new gasket, if necessary, or retorque pan bolts, as necessary.

7. Reinstall the transaxle. Make sure the engine oil pan is refilled with clean engine oil, if necessary.

# Oil Pump

## REMOVAL & INSTALLATION

### *1.8L, 2.0L and 2.3L Engines*

1. Disconnect the negative battery cable. Remove the timing belt cover, timing belts and sprockets. Drain the oil pan.

2. The front oil pan bolts screw into the front case, onto which the oil pump is mounted. On 1983–84 models, you may be able to loosen the oil pan bolts, use a sharp instrument to separate the gasket and front cover and remove the cover without replacing the gasket. This avoids lifting the engine. On 1985–90 models using sealer, you'll have to remove the oil pan.

3. Remove the oil filter. Remove the oil screen and gasket. Remove the oil relief plunger plug and gasket. Then, remove the relief spring and plunger from the oil filter bracket.

4. Remove the 4 oil filter bracket mounting bolts and remove the bracket.

5. Remove the cap from the oil pump area of the front case. This is slightly to the right and above the silent shaft on the driver's side of the vehicle. Remove the plug from the left side of the block (near the front case) and insert a suitable tool at least 2.4 in. long to retain the position of the silent shaft.

6. Remove the retaining bolt for the left silent shaft retaining bolts. Use a deep well socket. Now, remove the mounting bolts and remove the front case from the front of the block.

7. Remove the oil pump cover mounting bolts from the rear of the front case and remove the oil pump cover. Remove the gears from the front case.

8. Install the oil pump cover to the front case and torque the 5 bolts to 11–13 ft. lbs.

9. Install a special oil seal guide, Part No. MD998285-01 to the front of the crankshaft, with the smaller diameter facing outward. Install a new front case gasket to the block. Install the front case and install and tighten the eight mounting bolts just slightly. Remove the seal guide.

10. Install the oil pump gear and left silent shaft retaining bolt and torque to 25–28 ft. lbs.

11. Install the oil filter bracket and gasket. Tighten all the front case mounting bolts to 15–19 ft. lbs. and those going through the oil filter bracket to 11–15 ft. lbs. Install the cap that covers the oil pump shaft.

12. Coat the oil pressure relief plunger with clean engine oil and insert it into the bore, followed by the spring. Install the plug and gasket and torque the plug to 29–36 ft. lbs.

13. Install the oil screen and gasket.

14. Install the oil pan in reverse of removal. Install the sprockets, tensioners and timing belts and tension them to specification. Install the timing covers and engine accessories. Make sure to refill the oil pan with the full capacity of clean engine oil. Idle the engine and make sure oil pressure builds up within a reasonable length of time.

### *1.5L and 1.6L Engines*

**NOTE: On the 1468cc engine, the front case must be removed to gain access to the oil pump. On the Mirage with the 1597cc engine, the oil pump is bolted to the front of the front case. You may wish to leave the front case in place and simply remove the timing belt covers and belts to gain access to the pump. If you are doing a complete overhaul, you may want to follow the procedure as written in order to replace the oil pan gasket and other parts.**

1. Disconnect the negative battery cable. Remove the timing belt cover and timing belt.

2. Drain the oil and then remove the oil pan. Unbolt the oil pick-up and screen from the front case and remove it.

3. Remove the front cover with the oil pump assembled to it. On the 1468cc engine, pull the cover straight off to avoid damaging the crankshaft seal.

4. Put the cover on a clean bench. Remove the oil pump relief valve plug and gasket, spring and plunger.

5. Remove the attaching nut and then remove the oil pump sprocket on the Mirage with the 1597cc engine. On the 1468cc engine, turn the cover over. Then, remove the bolts and remove the oil pump cover from the case.

6. Installation is the reverse of the removal procedure. Repair or replace defective components as required.

### *2.5L Engine*

1. Disconnect the negative battery cable. Remove the front cover. Follow the procedure above for removal of timing chains and sprockets up to Step 3, but make sure you unscrew and remove the bolt for the right side silent shaft (just above the oil pump drive sprocket) before you remove the chain. In other words, you'll be removing the timing chain for the silent shafts and securing the plunger for the camshaft timing chain tensioner, but you won't be disturbing the camshaft timing chain. You may also leave the crankshaft sprocket that drives the silent shaft chain in place.

2. Remove the oil pump relief valve plug, spring and plunger. Then, remove the oil pump mounting bolts and remove the pump assembly and gasket. Remove the cover from the rear of the oil pump.

3. Oil the oil pump gears and the inner walls of the pump housing thoroughly with engine oil. Install the gears into the oil pump housing with the 2 timing marks directly across from one another. If the timing marks aren't lined up, the silent shaft will be out of phase and the engine will vibrate severely.

4. Install the pump cover over the 2 pins on the rear of the pump. Pour about 0.6 cu. in. of oil into the pump outlet (at top right, looking at the rear cover). Place the gasket over the 2 locator pins.

5. Install the pump onto the front of the block, engaging the keyway slot in the upper oil pump gear with the key on the right silent shaft and fitting the locating pins into the holes in the front of the block. Install the oil pump mounting bolts and torque in several stages and alternately to 7.5–8.5 ft. lbs. Install the bolt that attaches the right silent shaft to the upper oil pump gear.

6. Remove the securing wire from the timing chain tensioner. Reinstall the oil pump relief valve spring, plunger and cap and torque the cap to 22–32 ft. lbs.

7. Install the timing chains and sprockets. When the timing chain for the silent shafts is installed, torque the bolt that attaches the right silent shaft gear to 44–50 ft. lbs.

8. Install the front cover. Make sure the engine oil pan is full to the correct level. Start the engine, idling it and making sure oil pressure is built up within a reasonable length of time. Check for leaks and repair as necessary.

### 1988–90 Galant and Sigma

1. Drain the engine coolant into a suitable container, remove the radiator cap while draining the coolant.
2. Remove the battery, coolant overflow tube and coolant reserve tank bracket and tank.
3. Remove the upper radiator hose. Disconnect the electrical fan motor connection, thermosensor conections on the condenser fan and the radiator fan.
4. Remove the oil cooler lines from the radiator, if the vehicle is equipped with an automatic transaxle.
5. Remove the radiator fan motor, lower radiator hose and radiator backet.
6. Remove any remaining radiator retaining bolts and remove the radiator.
7. Installation is the reverse order of the removal procedure. Replace the radiator bushings, if necessary.

### Starion

1. Disconnect and remove the battery. Drain the coolant into a clean container.
2. Remove the 2 bolts on either side of the radiator and remove the upper and lower fan shrouds. Disconnect the upper and lower hoses at the radiator. Disconnect the overflow tank hose at the filler cap opening.
3. Then, remove the 4 radiator mounting bolts, 2 on either side and remove the radiator.
4. Install the unit in reverse order. Refill the radiator with clean coolant and run the engine until the thermostat opens. Refill the radiator with coolant as necessary, install the cap and then fill the overflow tank.

### Precis

1. Disconnect the negative battery cable. Remove the splash shield from under the vehicle.
2. Drain the radiator.
3. Remove the fan shroud and disconnect the fan motor wiring harness.
4. Disconnect the radiator hoses and, if equipped, the A/T cooler hoses.
5. Disconnect the expansion tank hose.
6. Remove the radiator mounting bolts and lift out the radiator and fan assembly.
7. Installation is the reverse of removal.

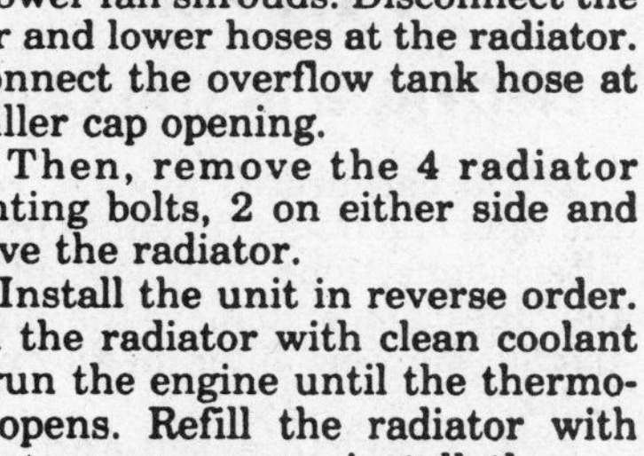

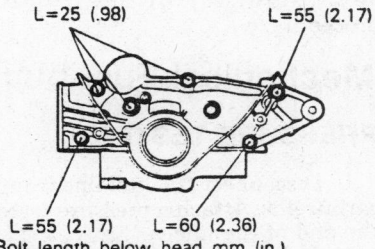


**Bolt diameter location on the oil pump assembly – 1988–89 Galant**

## Water Pump

### REMOVAL & INSTALLATION

### Cordia, Tredia, 1985–87 Galant, Mirage and Precis

1. Disconnect the negative battery cable. Loosen the 4 bolts attaching the water pump pulley to the pulley flange. Loosen the alternator mounting bolts, slide the alternator toward the engine and remove the belt. Drain the radiator.
2. Remove the 4 bolts attaching the water pump pulley to the pump flange and remove the pulley. Remove the timing belt covers and timing belt tensioner.
3. Remove the 5 water pump mounting bolts. Remove the pump and gasket, disconnecting the outlet at the water pipe (don't lose the O-ring).
4. Install the unit in reverse order, making sure the prongs on the lower tank fit securely into the bushings on the crossmember. Refill the radiator with clean coolant and run the engine until the thermostat opens. Refill the radiator with coolant as necessary, install the cap and then fill the overflow tank. If the vehicle has an automatic transaxle, check the fluid level and if necessary refill.

### V6 Engine

1. Bring the No. 1 piston up to top dead center of its compression stroke. Disconnect the negative battery cable and drain the engine oil into a suitable container.
2. Remove the timing belt covers, timing belt and sprockets as previously outlined in this section.
3. Connect a suitable engine lift to the engine and take up the slack in the chain.
4. Remove the crankshaft sprocket. Remove the front 2 transaxle mounts.
5. Remove the oil pressure switch, oil filter, oil filter bracket and bracket gasket.
6. Remove the oil pan, oil pan gasket, oil pump screen and screen gasket.
7. Remove the oil pump pressure relief valve assembly. Remove the crankshaft front oil seal.
8. Remove the oil pump case, oil pump gasket, oil pump cover, oil pump oute rotor and oil pump inner rotor.
9. Installation is the reverse order of the removal procedure. Be sure to check all moving parts and replace as necessary. Use new gaskets and O-rings when necessary, replace the front crankshaft seal with a new one. Apply a suitable sealant to the oil pan gasket and coat the threads of the oil pressue switch with a suitable sealant. Torque the oil pump bolts to 10 ft. lbs.

# ENGINE COOLING

## Radiator

### REMOVAL & INSTALLATION

### Cordia, Tredia, Mirage and 1985–87 Galant

1. Disconnect the negative battery cable. Disconnect the electrical connector for the fan motor. Drain the coolant into a clean container.
2. Disconnect the upper and lower radiator hoses and the overflow tank at the radiator. If the vehicle has an automatic transaxle, disconnect the 2 hoses for the cooler at the lower tank and plug all openings. Then, remove the 2 mounting bolts from the rear of the radiator, lift the unit out of the bushings at the front crossmember and remove it. On Galant note that the radiator is held at the top by 2 brackets which must be unbolted from the top of the panel in front of the radiator.
3. Remove the fan and electric motor from the radiator, transferring it to a new unit, if necessary.
4. Clean gasket surfaces and coat a new gasket with sealer. Then, position the gasket on the front of the block with all bolt holes lined up. Replace the O-ring for the outlet water pipe.
5. Install the pump over a new gasket, connecting the outlet water pipe.
6. Install the remaining parts in reverse order. Final tigtening of the water pump pulley bolts is done most easily after the V belt has been installed and tensioned somewhat. Recheck tension after the pulley bolts are tightened. Close the radiator drain and refill the system. Run the engine until the thermostat opens and then add coolant until the level stabilizes before replacing the radiator cap. Check for leaks.

### 1988–90 Galant and Sigma

1. Bring the No. 1 piston up to top dead center of its compression stroke. Disconnect the negative battery cable and drain the engine oil and coolant into a suiatble containers.

2. Remove the timing belt covers, timing belt and sprockets and crankshaft sprocket as previously outlined in this section.

3. Remove the water pump mounting bolts. Remove the pump and gasket, disconnecting the outlet at the water pipe (don't lose the O-ring).

4. Clean gasket surfaces and coat a new gasket with sealer. Then, position the gasket on the front of the block with all bolt holes lined up. Replace the O-ring for the outlet water pipe.

5. Install the pump over a new gasket, connecting the outlet water pipe.

6. Complete the installation by reversing the order of the removal procedure. Torque the water pump bolts to 14–19 ft. lbs.

#### *Starion*

1. Disconnect the negative battery cable. Drain the radiator.

2. Loosen the 4 nuts attaching the clutch fan to the water pump studs; then, loosen the adjusting and mounting bolts for the alternator, rock it toward the engine and remove the belt. Remove the 4 bolts for the fan shrouds from the rear of the radiator and remove the upper and lower shrouds. Now, loosen the nuts and remove them together with the lockwashers. Then, remove the fan clutch unit, storing the fan clutch in its normal altitude to keep the fluid from migrating to the wrong portions of the unit. Remove the pulley from the studs.

3. Disconnect the lower radiator hose at the pump by loosening the clamp and pulling the hose off. Then, remove the mounting bolts from the pump and then remove the pump and gasket from the front of the block.

4. Clean both gasket surfaces thoroughly and coat both sides of a new gasket and both gasket surfaces with sealer.

5. Install the gasket onto the block and then position the water pump over the gasket. Install the bolts in the proper positions.

6. Install the remaining parts in reverse order.

7. Refill the radiator with clean antifreeze and water mixed 50/50. Run the engine until the thermostat opens, refill the radiator as necessary, install the cap and check for leaks.

## Thermostat

### REMOVAL & INSTALLATION

1. Disconnect the negative battery cable. Drain the coolant below the level of the thermostat.

2. Remove the 2 retaining bolts and lift the thermostat housing off the intake manifold with the hose still attached. If you are careful, it is not necessary to remove the upper radiator hose.

3. Lift the thermostat out of the manifold.

4. Installation is the reverse of the removal procedure.

# EMISSION CONTROLS

**Please refer to "Emission Control" in the unit repair section for system maintenance procedures. Due to the complex nature of modern electronic engine control systems, comprehensive diagnosis and testing procedures fall outside the confines of this repair manual. For complete information on diagnosis, testing and repair procedures concerning all modern engine and emission control systems, please refer to "Chilton's Guide to Electronic Engine Controls".**

# FUEL SYSTEM

## Fuel System Service Precautions

To reduce the risk of a fire and personal injury, it is necessary to relieve the fuel system pressure before servicing any fuel related components. It is also not advisble to smoke while working on any fuel related components. Be sure to remove the negative battery cable before starting any procedure and never remove or attach the wiring harness connectors, with the ignition switch in the **ON** position.

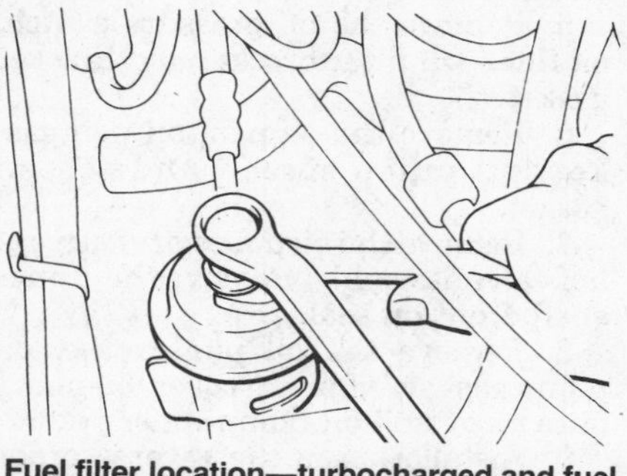

Fuel filter location—turbocharged and fuel injected engines

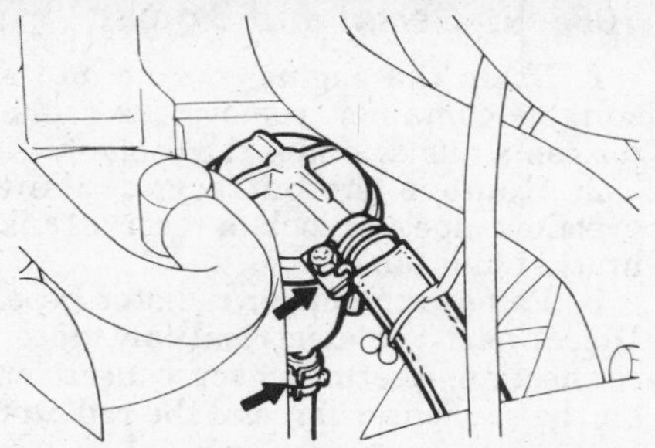

Fuel filter with carbureted engines

### RELIEVING FUEL SYSTEM PRESSURE

#### *Fuel Injected Models*

1. Disconnect the fuel pump harness connector at the fuel tank side.

2. Start the engine and after it stops by itself, turn the ignition switch to the **OFF** position.

3. Disconnect the negative battery terminal. Reconnect the fuel pump haress connector and then reconnect the negative battery terminal.

## Fuel Filter

### REMOVAL & INSTALLATION

1. On carbureted models, remove the inlet and outlet fuel lines from the filter connections after loosening the fuel line clamps. Remove the old filter. Install the new filter in the reverse order.

2. On fuel injected and turbocharged models, the underhood filter is replaced after first reducing fuel line pressure. Hold the side filter nut securely and remove the mounts. Disconnect the lines and remove the filter.

3. On the 1988–90 Galant models, remove the air cleaner assembly and the compressor for the electronic controlled suspension, if so equipped.

4. Disconnect the fuel lines and remove the fuel filter mounting bolt and then remove the fuel filter assembly.

5. Install the new fuel filter in the reverse order of the removal procedure.

## Mechanical Fuel pump

### PRESSURE TESTING

1. Disconnect the fuel line from the carburetor. Attach a pressure tester to the end of the line.

2. Crank the engine. If fuel pump pressure is not within specification replace the fuel pump.

## REMOVAL & INSTALLATION

1. Disconnect the negative battery cable. Remove the distributor cap to check the direction of the rotor, and then turn the engine over until the pointer near the front pulley is at Top Dead Center and the rotor points to the ignition wire for No. 1 cylinder, indicating that No. 1 is at firing position. Disconnect the negative battery cable.

2. Disconnect the fuel lines by using a pair of pliers to shift clamps away from the nipples on the pump and then pulling the lines off with a twisting motion. Note the locations at which lines connect.

3. Remove the 2 mounting bolts from the head, and then remove the pump, spacer, and gasket(s) from the head. As you pull the pump off the head, catch the pushrod which is located just behind the pump.

4. Inspect the pump as follows: There is a small breather hole in the area of the pump above the diaphragm which vents the pump's upper chamber. Leakage of fuel or oil here indicates that the pump's diaphragm or oil seal is leaking and that the unit should be replaced. Also, inspect the end of the pushrod and the wear surface where the pushrod engages with the pump operating lever. Replace the pushrod or pump if there is obvious wear. If the camshaft end of the pushrod is badly worn you should remove the cam cover and inspect the camshaft eccentric which operates the fuel pump for excessive wear.

5. Clean the gasket surfaces of the insulator, pump and cylinder head. Insert the 2 bolts through the pump's mounting base. Slide a new gasket, the insulator, and a second new gasket into position over the 2 bolts. Turn the pump so its mounting surface faces the cylinder head.

6. Locate the pump pushrod against the cupped surface of the operating lever and angle it upward in the position it was in during removal. Hold the pushrod at that angle as you insert it into the bore in the head. Once the pushrod is in the bore in the cylinder head, you can release it with your fingers and move the pump toward the head following the installation angle of the pushrod. Start the 2 bolts into the bores in the head and tighten them finger tight.

7. Tighten the mounting bolts alternately and evenly. Inspect the hoses for cracks (even hairline cracks can leak) and replace if necessary. Then, reconnect the fuel hoses. Make sure the hoses are installed all the way onto the nipples and then work the clamps into position. Make sure the clamps are located well past the bulged portion of the nipples but do not sit at the extreme inner ends of the hoses. Replace the distributor cap. Start the engine and check for leaks.

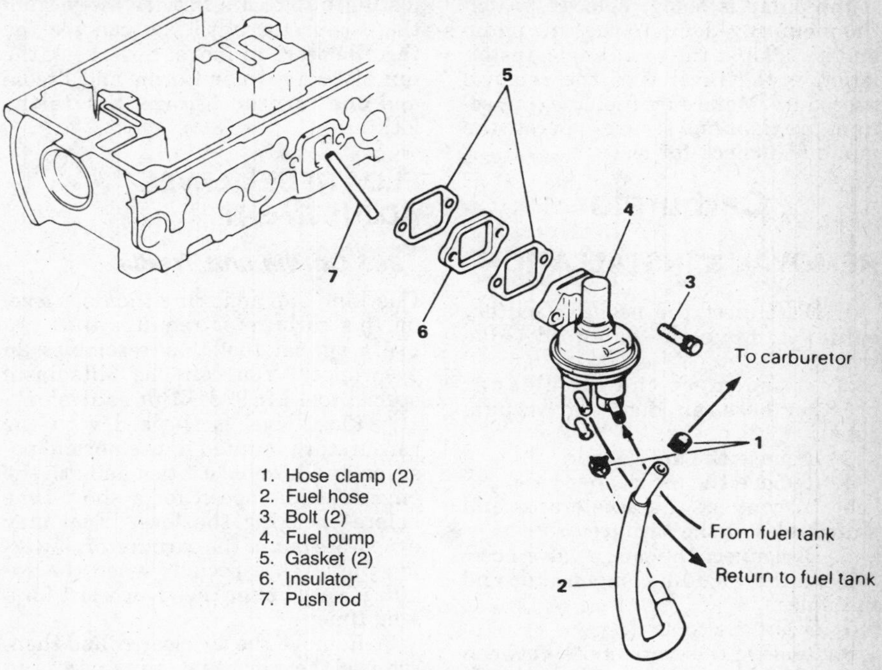


Mechanical fuel pump

# Electric Fuel Pump

## PRESSURE TESTING

1. Relieve the fuel pressue as follows:
   a. Disconnect the fuel pump harness connector at the fuel tank side.
   b. Start the engine and after it stops by itself, turn the ignition switch to the **OFF** position.
   c. Disconnect the negative battery terminal. Reconnect the fuel pump haress connector and then reconnect the negative battery terminal.

2. Install a suitable fuel pressure gauge to the fuel delivery pipe, be sure to tighten the bolt at 18–25 ft. lbs.

3. Apply voltage to the terminal for the fuel pump drive and activate the fuel pump; then, with fuel pressure thus applied, check the there is no fuel leakage from the pressure gauge or the special tool connection pipe.

4. Disconnect the vacuum hose from the pressure regulator and plug the hose end. Measure the fuel pressure during idling. The standard value is 36–36 psi (245–264 kPa).

5. Measue the fuel pressure when the vacuum hose is connected to the pressure regulator. The standard value is 28 psi (196 kPa).

6. If the fuel pressure readings are not within specifications, determine the proable cause and make the necessary repairs.

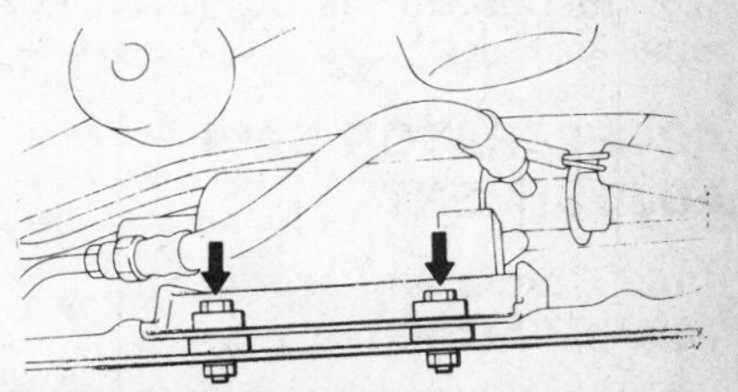

Externally mounted electric fuel pump mounting bolts

7. Remove all test equipment, use a new gasket and tighten the bolt on the delivery pipe to 18–25 ft. lbs. Start the engine and check for fuel leaks.

## REMOVAL & INSTALLATION

1. Start the engine and allow it to idle. Disconnect the electric fuel pump connector (accessible by removing a panel in the floor of the trunk). Allow the engine to continue running until it stalls to relieve the pressure in the fuel lines.

2. If the vehicle is equipped with a drain plug remove it and drain the fuel into a suitable container. Support the vehicle safely. Remove the left rear wheel.

3. Support the fuel tank with a floor jack. Loosen the fuel tank band mounting nuts and lower the tank for access to the pump support. Then, remove the nut and bolt attaching the pump clamp to the support.

4. Disconnect the fuel lines, noting their locations and remove the pump.

If the pump is being replaced, switch the mounting clamp to the new pump and install it at the same angle. Installation is the reverse of the removal procedure. Make sure fuel line connections are tight and secure. Operate the pump and check for leaks.

## Carburetor

### REMOVAL & INSTALLATION

1. Disconnect the negative battery cable. Remove the solenoid valve wiring.
2. Disconnect the air cleaner breather hose, air duct and vacuum tube.
3. Remove the air cleaner.
4. Remove the air cleaner case.
5. Disconnect the accelerator and shift cables at the carburetor.
6. Disconnect the purge valve hose; remove the vacuum compensator and fuel lines.
7. Drain the coolant.
8. Remove the water hose between the carburetor and the cylinder head.
9. Remove the carburetor.
10. Installation is the reverse of removal.

### ACCELERATOR CABLE ADJUSTMENT

#### *1983 Cordia and Tredia and 1983–87 Starion*

1. Run the engine until it is hot so the fast idle cam will not effect the throttle setting.
2. Check the action of the accelerator pedal. There should be minimal play between the normal, resting position of the pedal and the point where play in the cable is taken up and the throttle starts to move 0–0.08 in. (0–0.04 in. for Starion).
3. If there is excessive play, loosen the cable adjusting nuts located on the cable mount on the carburetor and shift their position on the outer cable as necessary to remove the play. Then, tighten them together in opposite directions on the cable mount.

#### *1984–88 Cordia and Tredia and 1985–90 Mirage and Precis*

1. The engine must be hot so the fast idle cam will not interfere with throttle position; warm it if necessary.
2. Inspect the inner cable to see if there is slack. If there is no slack, the adjustment is okay. If there is slack, loosen the adjusting nuts until the throttle is free to assume idle position with no effect by the accelerator cable.
3. Make sure there are no sharp bends in the cable. Then, turn the adjusting nut that's farther away from the carburetor until you can see the throttle start to move; now, back the nut off ½ a turn on Cordia and Tredia and one turn on Mirage. Secure the locknut.

### FLOAT/FUEL LEVEL ADJUSTMENT

#### *1983 Cordia and Tredia*

Checking and adjusting the float level on this carburetor requires that you use a special tool that resembles an eyedropper. You can use Mitsubishi special tool MD998161 or equivalent.

1. Float level is checked with the carburetor mounted in the normal position on the vehicle. Start and run the engine at idle speed for a short time before checking the level. Fuel may evaporate out of the carburetor, lowering the level, especially when the engine is very hot or the vehicle sits for a long time.
2. Remove the air cleaner and then, remove the plug that gives access to the float bowl. The plug is located just to one side of the fuel inlet fitting.
3. Hold the top of the special tool and turn the lower portion, the guide collar. The top of the threads inside the guide collar must be 4 lines (0.16 in.) below the bold line on the upper portion of the tool.
4. Now, insert the gauge into the level checking hole until the bottom end of the guide collar touches the plug seat. Make sure it goes in straight. Push the top of the rubber squirt head down a little to verify that fuel is being drawn up. If there is no gasoline in the gauge, remove it and turn the collar half a turn upward and reinsert the tool into the carburetor. When gas comes up into the tool, remove it, turn the collar half a turn downward to permit you to read the fuel level and read it. It should be between 0.08 in. below the bold line and 0.04 in. above it. If the fuel level is correct, replace the plug. Otherwise, proceed with the steps that follow.
5. Remove the screws and remove the float chamber cover. Invert it, pull out the float lever pin and remove it and the float. Remove the needle valve.
6. Remove the float seat retainer and then gently pull out the seat with a pair of pliers (squeezing the seat too hard could distort it). You'll need a shim set, Mitsubishi part MD606952. To raise the float level, use a thinner shim; to lower it, increase the thickness of the shim. Shims in the kit are 0.008, 0.012 and 0.02 in. in thickness.
7. Install the parts in reverse order, including the cover plug and air cleaner. Start the engine and allow it to idle briefly. Recheck the float level with the special tool and make further adjustments as necessary.

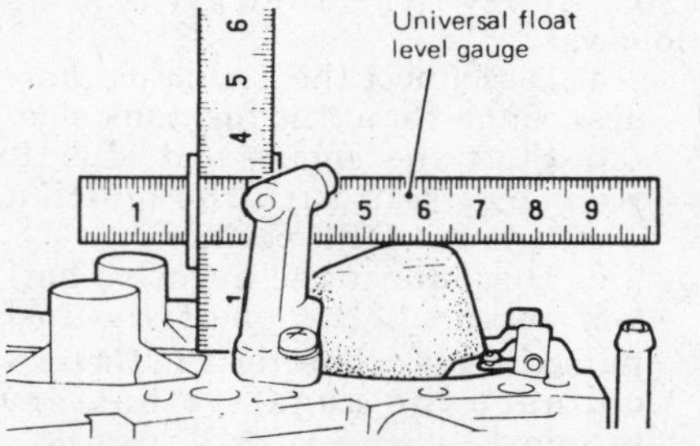

Adjusting the float level—1984 and later models

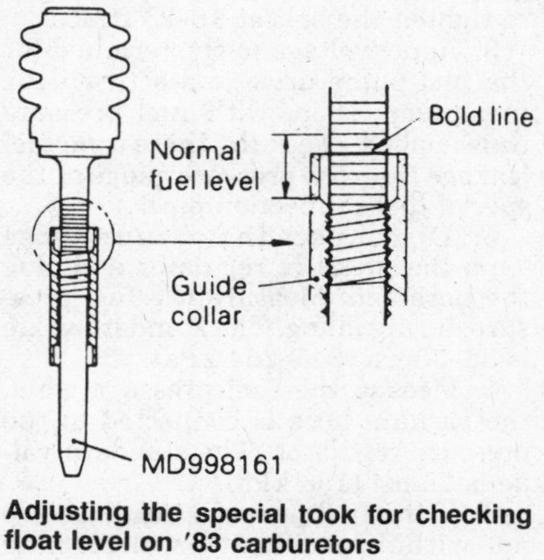

Adjusting the special took for checking float level on '83 carburetors

#### *1984–88 Cordia and Tredia and 1985–90 Mirage and Precis*

1. Invert the float chamber cover and remove the gasket. Use a float level gauge or depth gauge to measure the distance between that is normally the bottom of the float (the top surface in this position) and what is normally the lower surface of the float chamber cover. This dimension must be 0.7476–0.8204 in.
2. If the dimension is not to specification, the shim under the needle seat must be changed. Use a thicker seat to raise the dimension (lower the float level). You can use a Mitsubishi shim kit MD606952 or equivalent. The kit contains shims of 0.0118, 0.0157 and 0.0196 in. The change in float level will be 3 times the change in shim thickness. You can use multiple shims if that is what is necessary to get the right dimension.
3. To change the shim, first pull out the float hinge pin. Then, remove the float and the needle. Finally, use a pair of pliers to unscrew the needle seat by the widest dimensioned area of the seat. Slip the shim(s) over the narrow portion of the seat and then reinstall it, tightening it gently by the same portion of the assembly. Reassemble the needle, float and hinge pin and re-

test the dimension. Reshim if necessary.

## THROTTLE OPENER ADJUSTMENT

### *1984–88 Cordia and Tredia with 2.0L Engine and Manual Transaxle and 1985–90 Mirage and Precis with 1.5L Engine*

1. Check and if necessary adjust the normal idle speed.
2. Locate the throttle opener on the top of the carburetor. The throttle return spring is attached to a bracket right on top of the throttle opener. Follow the vacuum line leading out of the throttle opener to the throttle opener to the throttle opener solenoid. The engine should be idling at normal operating temperature with the transaxle in neutral. Connect a tachometer.
3. Connect a jumper wire to the positive battery terminal. Then, disconnect the electrical lead at the throttle opener solenoid and connect the other end of the jumper wire to the solenoid connector. Open the throttle until the engine reaches about 200 rpm and then slowly release the throttle.
4. Check the engine speed. It should be:
   1985–88 Cordia and Tredia 750 rpm
   Mirage and Precis 850 rpm
   1984 Cordia and Tredia 700 rpm with manual transaxle and 750 automatic
   Mirage 850 rpm
5. Adjust the throttle opener adjusting screw to achieve the correct rpm. This screw has finger grips on it and is located on the lower portion of the throttle opener.
6. Check that the rpm remains at the correct level. Readjust it, as necessary, until it remains at the correct level.
7. Disconnect the jumper wire and reconnect the throttle opener solenoid wire.

## IDLE-UP ADJUSTMENT

### *1984 Cordia and Tredia with 2.0L Engine and Air Conditioning*

1. The engine must be at normal operating temperature. Wheels must be in straight ahead position so there is no load on the power steering pump. Disconnect the electric fan motor connector. Apply the parking brake and make sure the transaxle is in neutral. Turn the air conditioner on.
2. Connect a tachometer. Using the throttle opener adjust screw located near the throttle return spring mount on top of the carburetor, adjust the rpm to 850. Make sure the rpm stays steady at this level, readjusting it if necessary. Reconnect the cooling fan electrical connector.

## AUTOMATIC CHOKE ADJUSTMENT

All carburetors have a tamper proof choke assembly which is factory adjusted. Choke adjustment is not required during service, except when major carburetor overhaul or choke calibration is required.

## OVERHAUL

**For all carburetor overhaul procedures, please refer to "Carburetor Service" in the Unit Repair section.**

# Fuel Injection

**Due to the complex nature of modern fuel injection systems, comprehensive diagnosis and testing procedures fall outside the confines of this repair manual. For complete information on fuel injection diagnosis, testing and repair procedures please refer to "Chilton's Guide to Fuel Injection and Feedback Carburetors".**

# MANUAL TRANSMISSION

## REMOVAL & INSTALLATION

1. Disconnect the negative battery cable. Remove the air cleaner. Remove the starter.
2. Remove the top transmission mounting bolts from the bell housing.
3. From inside the vehicle, raise the console assembly and remove the dust cover retaining plate at the shift lever.
4. Place the transmission in the neutral position. Remove the control lever assembly.
5. Raise the vehicle and support it safely. Drain the transmission. Disconnect the speedometer and the back-up light switch.
6. Remove the driveshaft. Disconnect the exhaust pipe. Remove the clutch cable or slave cylinder and linkage.
7. Support the engine and transmission and remove the engine rear support bracket. Drain the transmission, as required.
8. Remove the bell housing cover and bolts, move the transmission rearward and lower it carefully to the floor. Remove the transmission from under the vehicle.

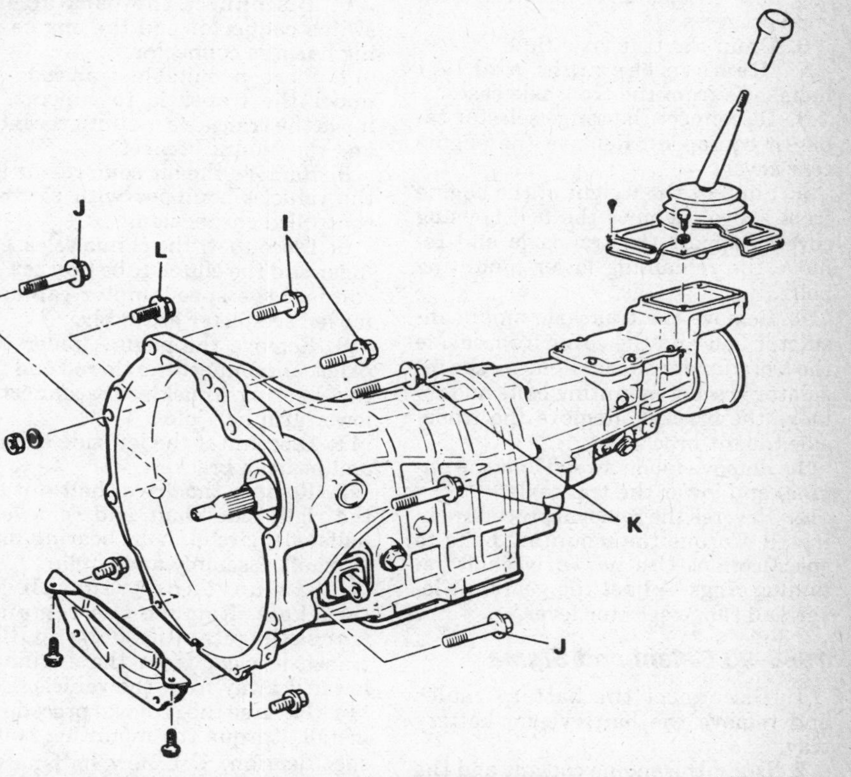


Torque labeled bolts as follows on the Starion transmission: I and J—31-40 ft. lbs; K—16-23 ft. lbs.; L—14-20 ft. lbs.

9. To install the transmission, reverse the removal procedure. Torque the transmission to engine bolts to the figures shown in the illustration. Make sure the transmission is in the proper gear before installing the gear shift lever.

# MANUAL TRANSAXLE

## REMOVAL & INSTALLATION

### *Cordia, Tredia and 1985–87 Galant*

1. Disconnect the negative battery cable. Remove the battery and battery tray. Remove the coolant and windshield reservoir tanks. Remove the air cleaner and housing.
2. Disconnect from the transaxle; the clutch cable or slave cylinder, speedometer cable, back-up light harness, starter motor and the upper bolts connecting the engine to the transaxle.
3. Raise and support the vehicle safely.
4. Remove the front wheels, Remove the engine splash shield.
5. Remove the shift rod and extension. It may be necessary to remove any heat shields that interfere with your progress.
6. Drain the transaxle fluid.
7. Remove the right and left halfshafts from the transaxle case.
8. Disconnect the range selector cable (if equipped). Remove the engine rear cover.
9. Support the weight of the engine from above. Remove the bell housing cover. Support the transaxle and remove the remaining lower mounting bolts.
10. Remove the transaxle mount insulator bolt and the cover from inside the front fender shield. Remove the insulator bracket mounting bolts and remove the bracket. Remove the transaxle mount bracket.
11. Remove (slide away from the engine) and lower the transaxle.
12. Reverse the removal procedure in install. Torque the mounting bolts to specification. Use new driveshaft retaining rings. Adjust the gearshift lever and range selector lever.

### *1988–90 Galant and Sigma*

1. Disconnect the battery cables and remove the battery and battery tray.
2. Drain the engine coolant and the transaxle fluid into suitable containers.

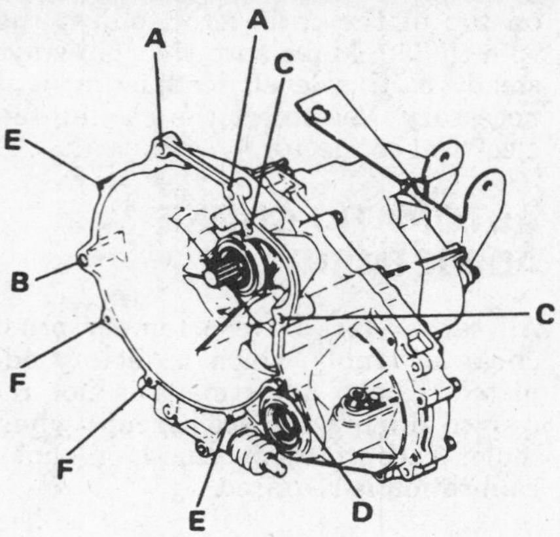


**Torque Cordia/ Tredia and Mirage transaxle bolts as follows (all figs. in ft. lbs.): A—31-40; B—31-40; C—16-23; D—22-25; E—7-9; F—11-16.**

3. Disconnect the connections for the air flow sensor, purge control solenoid valve and air cleaner assembly.
4. Disconnect the air intake hose and breather hose and emove the air cleaner assembly. Raise and support the vehicle safely.
5. Disconnect the transaxle control cables. Disconnect the lower radiator hose and the water inlet pipe **B**. Disconnect all the connections on the water pipe assembly.
6. Disconnect the back-up light switch connector and the engine wiring harness connector.
7. Place a suitable transaxle jack under the transaxle to support. Remove the transaxle mount bracket cap and the mount bracket.
8. Remove the air compressor from the vehicles equipped with electronic controlled suspension.
9. Disconnect the clutch release cylinder and the clutch tube bracket. Disconnect the speedometer cable. Remove the starter assembly.
10. Remove the engine under cover panel. Disconnect the tie rod end from the steering knuckle. Disconnect the lower arm ball joint.
11. Disconnect the left side halfshaft and bearing bracket.
12. Remove the drive shaft nut from the right side shaft and remove the halfshaft, circlip, bolt, bearing bracket, shaft assembly and circlip.
13. Remove the transaxle stay (bracket). Remove the remaining transaxle retaining bolts, pull the transaxle clear from the engine and lower it away from the vehicle.
14. Reverse the removal procedure in install. Torque the mounting bolts to specification. Use new halfshaft retaining rings. Adjust the gearshift lever and range selector lever.

### *Mirage and Precis*

1. Remove the battery and battery tray. On turbocharged vehicles, remove the air cleaner housing assembly.
2. On 5 speed transaxles, disconnect the electrical connector for the selector control valve. On turbocharged vehicles, remove the actuator mounting bolts, remove the actuator to shaft pin and then remove the actuator. Replace the collar with a new part.
3. Disconnect and remove the speedometer and clutch cables.
4. Disconnect the back-up lamp electrical connector. Remove the starter motor electrical harness.
5. Remove the 6 transaxle mounting bolts accessible from the top side of the transaxle.
6. Unbolt and remove the starter motor.
7. Raise the vehicle and support it safely. Then, remove the splash shield from under the engine. Drain the transaxle fluid.
8. Disconnect the extension rod and the shift rod at the transaxle end and lower them.
9. Disconnect the stabilizer bar at the lower control arm.
10. Remove the halfshaft.
11. Support the transaxle from below with a floorjack or similar device. Make sure the support is widely enough spread that the transaxle pan will not be damaged. Then, remove the 5 attaching bolts and remove the bell housing cover.
12. Remove the lower bolts attaching the transaxle to the engine.
13. Remove the transaxle insulator mount bolt. Remove the cover from inside the right fender shield and remove the transaxle support bracket.
14. Remove the transaxle mount bracket.
15. Pull the assembly away from the engine and then lower it from the vehicle.
16. Installation is the reverse of removal. Refill the transaxle with the specified fluid to the level of the filler plug. Adjust the clutch cable. Make sure the gearshift lever works correctly.

# CLUTCH

## REMOVAL & INSTALLATION

1. Disconnect the negative battery cable.
2. Remove the transmission. It is recommended that a clutch aligning tool be inserted in the clutch disc during disassembly.

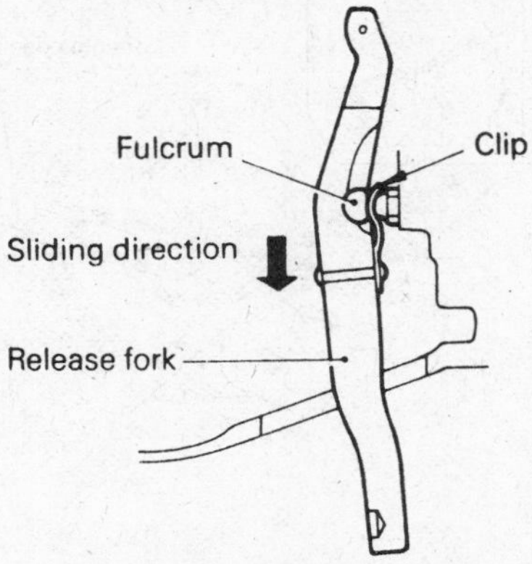


**Release fork removal—Starion**

3. Diagonally remove pressure plate bolts a little at a time each. Then remove the pressure plate and driven disc.

4. From inside the bell housing, remove the return spring clip and remove the release bearing assembly. On the Starion, remove the release fork by sliding it in the direction of the arrow to disengage the fulcrum from the clip. Attempting to remove it any other way will damage the clip.

5. If necessary, remove the release control lever and spring pin with a $^{3}/_{16}$ in. punch. Always replace spring pins, as they should not be reused. Remove the control lever shaft assembly and clutch shift arm, 2 felt packings and 2 return springs.

6. Installation is the reverse of removal. Torque the pressure plate bolts, diagonally, to 11–15 ft. lbs.

## FREE PLAY ADJUSTMENT

### *Cable Type*

1. Depress the clutch pedal by hand, freeplay (until tension is felt) should be 0.8–1.2 in. on 1983 models and 0.6–0.8 in. on 1984–90 models.

2. If the free play is too great or too little, turn the outer cable adjusting nut for adjustment.

3. After adjustment is made, depress the clutch pedal several times and recheck.

### *Hydraulic Type*

1. Measure the clutch pedal clevis pin play at the pedal pad, it should be 6.9–7.1 in. for Cordia and Tredia and 7.4–7.6 in. for Starion.

2. Measure the clutch pedal height from the surface of the pad to the floor, it should be 0.04–0.12 in.

3. If adjustment is required, turn the clutch switch to adjust the pedal height then tighten the locknut.

4. To adjust the clevis pin play turn the pushrod and then tighten the locknut.

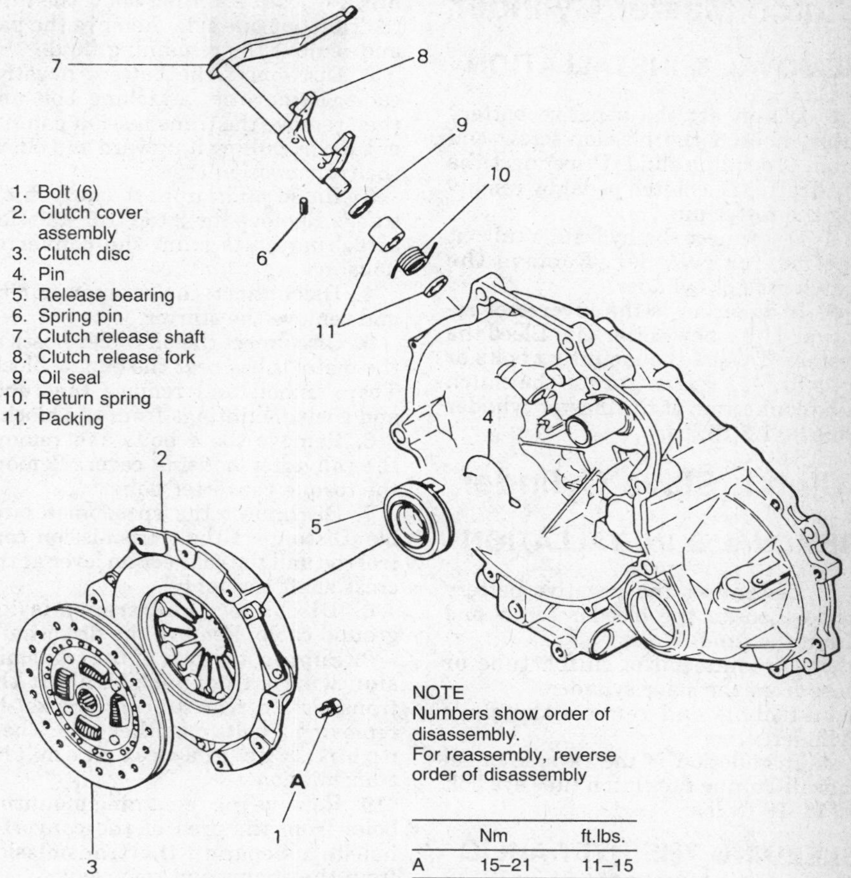


| | Nm | ft.lbs. |
|---|---|---|
| A | 15–21 | 11–15 |

**Clutch assembly—front wheel drive**

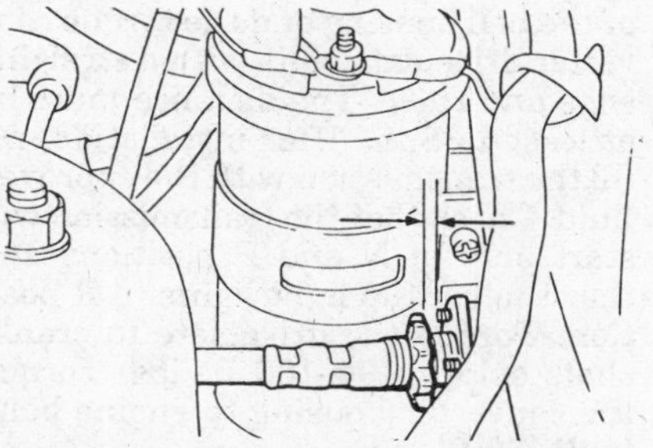

**Clutch cable adjustment—front wheel drive**

5. If adjustment can not be made there is probably either air in the system or the clutch cylinder or clutch disc is defective.

6. Bleed the air from the system as follows.

7. Loosen the bleeder screw at the clutch slave cylinder.

8. Push the clutch pedal down slowly while the bleeder screw is opened.

9. Hold the pedal down and tighten the bleeder screw.

10. Check the clutch master cylinder and refill with fluid if necessary. Repeat the bleeding procedure several times until all air is dispelled from the system.

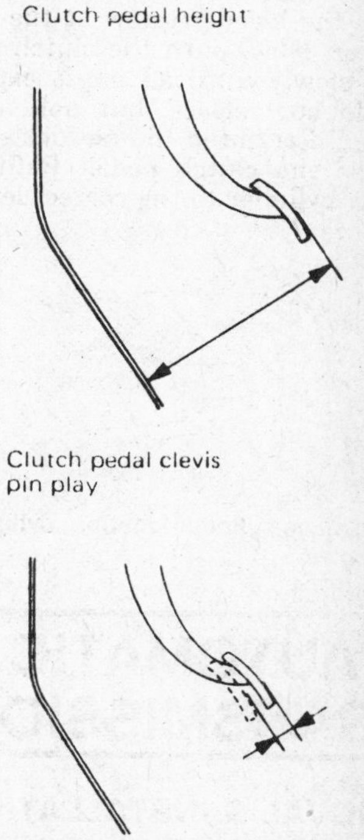


**Adjustment measurments—hydraulic type clutch**

## Clutch Master Cylinder

### REMOVAL & INSTALLATION

1. Disconnect the negative battery cable. Loosen the bleeder screw and drain the clutch fluid. Disconnect the pushrod at the clutch pedal by removing the cotter pin.
2. Disconnect the hydraulic tube at the master cylinder. Remove the clutch master cylinder.
3. Installation is the reverse of removal. Use a new cotter pin. Bleed the system. Torque the mounting bolts or nuts to 7–11 ft. lbs. Torque the clutch tube connection at the master cylinder to 9.4–12.3 ft. lbs.

## Clutch Slave Cylinder

### REMOVAL & INSTALLATION

1. Disconnect the negative battery cable. Loosen the bleeder screw and drain the fluid.
2. Disconnect the clutch tube or hose from the slave cylinder.
3. Unbolt and remove the slave cylinder.
4. Installation is the reverse of removal. Torque the clutch tube eye bolt to 14–18 ft. lbs.

### BLEEDING THE HYDRAULIC CLUTCH SYSTEM

Make sure the clutch master cylinder is filled with the correct fluid. Then, loosen the bleeder screw at the slave cylinder. Now, push the clutch pedal down slowly until all air is expelled and do not release, but hold it depressed. Retighten the bleeder screw. Release the clutch pedal. Refill the master cylinder to the correct level.

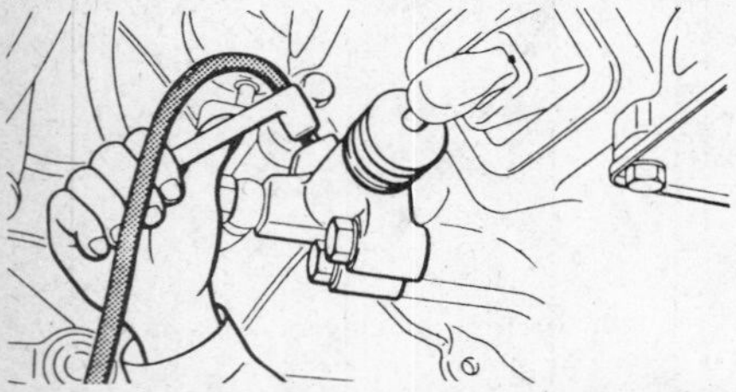

Clutch slave cylinder location; cylinder is being bled

# AUTOMATIC TRANSMISSION

### REMOVAL & INSTALLATION

1. Loosen the oil pan mounting screws, tap the oil pan at one corner to break it loose and then allow the fluid to drain out one side. Remove the pan and remove the remaining fluid.
2. Disconnect the battery negative cable. Remove its attaching bolt and then remove the transmission pan filler tube by pulling it upward and out of the transmission case.
3. Raise and support the vehicle safely. Remove the 2 top transmission attaching bolts from the converter housing.
4. Disconnect the starter wiring and remove the starter.
5. Disconnect the oil cooler hoses at the metal tubes near the engine block. Then, unbolt and remove the tubes and their mountings from the block.
6. Remove the 4 bolts and remove the converter housing cover. Remove the torque converter bolts.
7. Disconnect the speedometer cable. Disconnect the transmission control rod and the connection lever at the cross shaft assembly.
8. Disconnect the transmission ground cable. Remove the driveshaft.
9. Support the rear of the transmission with a floor jack. Unbolt the transmission rear support bracket by removing 2 bolts on either side. Then, unbolt the bracket from the transmission.
10. Remove the remaining mounting bolts from the area of the converter housing. Separate the transmission from the engine and remove it.
11. Installation is the reverse of the removal procedure. Before beginning, check the distance between the front of the bell housing and the torque converter driveplate bolts with a straightedge and ruler. The distance must be at least 1.38 in. After installation, refill the transmission with the approved fluid. Check that the transmission will start only in N and P positions and that the backup light lights in R position. Torque the driveplate to crankshaft bolts to 94–100 ft. lbs. Torque the converter housing to engine bolts to 31–39 ft. lbs.

### PAN AND FILTER REPLACEMENT

1. Raise and support the vehicle safely..
2. Loosen and remove the transmission pan drain plug. As required, remove the splash shield.
3. Remove the pan mounting bolts and pan. Remove the filter.
4. Install a new filter, as required. Reinstall the oil pan using a new gasket. Add the proper amount of transmission fluid after. Start the engine and move the selector lever through all positions. Allow the engine to run until normal operating temperature is reached.

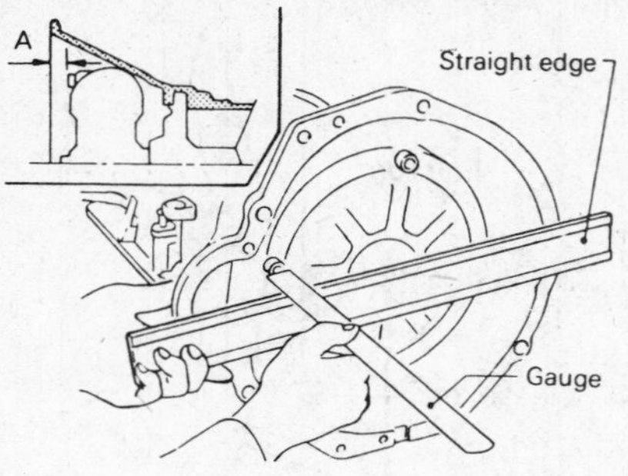


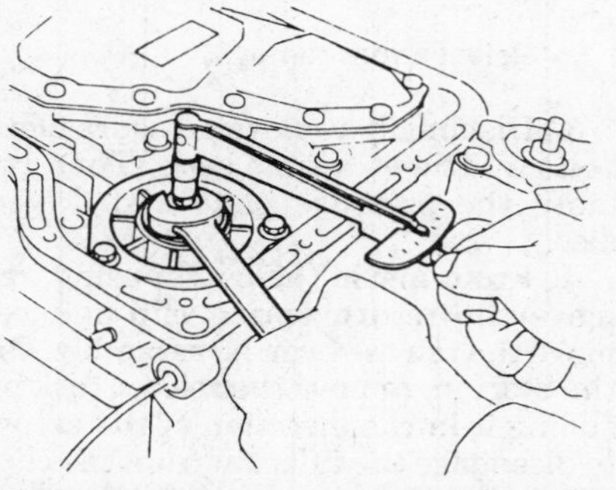

Adjusting the Starion automatic transmission band

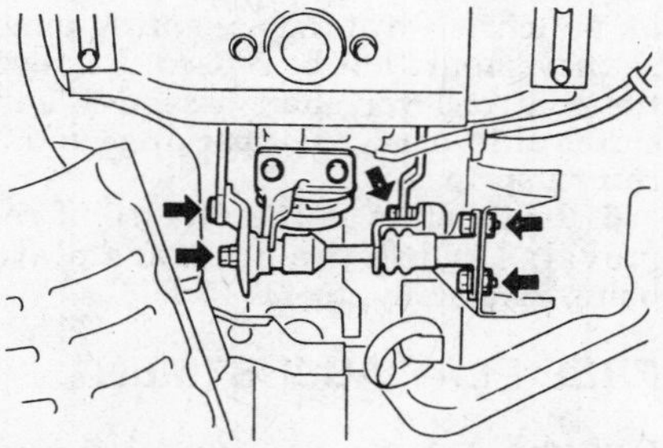

Disconnecting the control rod and connection lever from the crosshaft—Starion

5. Recheck the fluid level with the dipstick, add fluid if necessary.

### KICKDOWN BAND ADJUSTMENT

1. Remove the transmission oil pan.
2. Loosen the band adjusting stem locknut and turn the stem outward. Then, turn the stem inward with a torque wrench until the required torque reaches 5–7 ft. lbs. Then, back the stem off exactly 2 turns.
3. Hold the adjustment and torque the locknut to 11–29 ft. lbs.

### NEUTRAL SAFETY SWITCH ADJUSTMENT

1. Place the control lever in the **N** position.

2. Make sure the short end of the manual control lever covers the switch body flange. Loosen the control cable to manual control lever couplin adjusting nuts (2 pcs) to set the cable and lever free.

3. Turn the body of the switch until the wide end of the manual control lever aligns with the switch body flange, or turn the switch body until the hole in the manual control lever aligns with the hole in the switch body.

4. Tighten the attaching bolts being careful not to disturb the switch adjustment. Remove the slackness of the cotrol cable by usig the adjusting nut and then check that the selector moves smoothly.

5. Check the switch operation by attempting to start engine in gears other than the Park and Neutral positions.

# AUTOMATIC TRANSAXLE

## REMOVAL & INSTALLATION

**NOTE: The transaxle and converter must be removed and installed as an assembly.**

1. Disconnect the negative battery cable. Remove the battery tray. Remove the coolant reservoir and windshield washer tank. Remove the air cleaner and housing. Where so equipped, disconnect also the pulse generator connector and solenoid valve connector.

2. Disconnect the throttle control cable at the carburetor and the manual control cable at the transaxle.

3. Disconnect from the transaxle; the neutral safety switch connector, fluid cooler hose and the 4 upper bolts connecting the engine to the transaxle.

4. Raise and support the vehicle safely.

5. Remove the front wheels. Remove the engine splash shield.

6. Drain the transaxle fluid.

7. Remove the right and left halfshafts from the transaxle case. Remove the strut bars and the stabilizer bar from the lower arms.

8. Disconnect the speedometer cable. Disconnect and plug the oil cooler hoses. Remove the starter motor.

9. Remove the lower cover from the converter housing. Remove the 3 bolts that connect the converter to the engine drive plate.

**NOTE: Never support the full weight of the transaxle on the engine drive plate.**

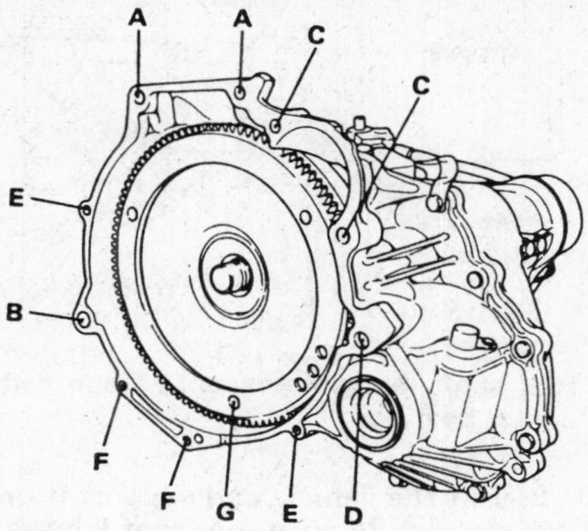


**Bolt torques in ft. lbs. for the automatic transaxle: A—31-40; B—31-40; C—16-23; D—22-25; E—7-9; F—11-16; G—25-30**

10. Turn and force the converter back and away from the engine drive plate.

11. Support the weight of the engine from above. Support the transaxle and remove the remaining mounting bolts.

12. Remove the transaxle mount insulator bolt.

13. Remove and lower the transaxle and converter as an assembly.

14. To install reverse the removal procedure. Torque the converter housing bolts according to the illustration. Torque the drive plate bolts to 25–30 ft. lbs. Be sure to connect all controls, wiring and hoses. Use new retaining rings when installing the drive axles. Refill the transaxle to the proper level with the recommended fluid.

## PAN AND FILTER REPLACEMENT

1. Raise and support the vehicle safely.

2. Loosen and remove the transaxle pan drain plug. As required, remove the splash shield.

3. Remove the pan mounting bolts and pan. Remove the filter.

4. Install a new filter, as required. Reinstall the oil pan using a new gasket. Add the proper amount of transmission fluid. Start the engine and move the selector lever through all positions. Allow the engine to run until norml operating temperature is reached.

5. Recheck the fluid level with the dipstick, add fluid if necessary.

## THROTTLE CABLE ADJUSTMENT

1. Run the engine to normal operating temperature and make sure that the throttle lever on the carburetor is in the curb idle position.

2. Raise the cover on the throttle cable to expose the nipple.

3. Loosen the lower cable mounting bolt.

4. Move the lower cable bracket until the distance between the nipple and the top of the cable end is 0.5mm.

5. Tighten the lower cable bracket mounting bolt and check the adjustment by pulling the cable upward with the throttle plate in the wide open position. The cable should move freely.

## KICKDOWN BAND ADJUSTMENT

1. Wipe all dirt and other contamination from the kickdown servo cover and surrounding area.

2. Remove the snapring and then the cover.

3. Loosen the locknut.

4. Holding the kickdown servo piston from turning tighten the adjusting screw to 7 ft. lbs. and then back it off. Repeat the tightening and backing off 2 times in order to ensure seating of the band on the drum.

5. Tighten the adjusting screw to 3.5 ft. lbs. and back it off 3.5 turns (counterclockwise).

6. Holding the adjusting screw against rotation, tighten the locknut to 11–15 ft. lbs.

7. Install a new seal ring (D shaped) in the groove in the outside surface of the cover. Use care not to distort the seal ring.

8. Install the cover and then install the snapring.

## NEUTRAL SAFETY SWITCH ADJUSTMENT

1. Place the control lever in the Neutral position.

2. Make sure the short end of the manual control lever covers the switch body flange. Loosen the control cable to manual control lever couplin adjusting nuts (2 pcs) to set the cable and lever free.

3. Turn the body of the switch until the wide end of the manual control lever aligns with the switch body flange,

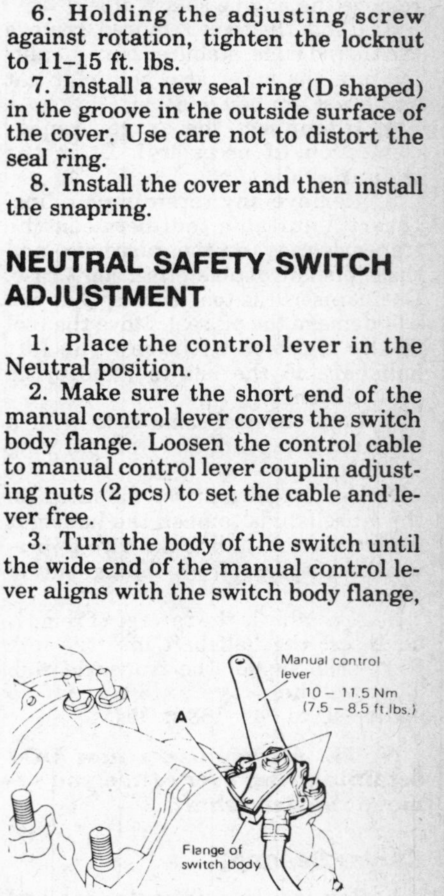


**Neutral start switch adjustment. "A" denotes the small end of the lever**

or turn the switch body until the hole in the manual control lever aligns with the hole in the switch body.

4. Tighten the attaching bolts being careful not to disturb the switch adjustment. Remove the slackness of the cotrol cable by usig the adjusting nut and then check that the selector moves smoothly.

5. Check the switch operation by attempting to start engine in gears other than the Park and Neutral positions.

# DRIVE AXLE

## Halfshaft

### REMOVAL & INSTALLATION

#### *Except Center Bearing*

1. Remove the hub center cap and remove the cotter pin, then loosen the driveshaft (axle) nut. Loosen the wheel lug nuts.
2. Lift the vehicle and support it on jack stands. Remove the front wheels. Remove the drive axle (hub) nut and remove the engine splash shield.
3. Using the tools required, remove the tie rod ends, stabilzer barr mounting nut, the lower arm ball joint nut and lower am ball joint.
4. Disconnect the oxygen sensor connection (if necessary). Drain the transaxle fluid.
5. Remove any retaining circlips. Insert a suitable tool between the transaxle case (on the raised rib) and the halfshaft double offset joint case. Do not insert the tool too deeply or you will damage the oil seal. Move the tool to the right to withdraw the left halfshaft; to the left to remove the right halfshaft.
6. Plug the transaxle case with a clean rag to prevent dirt from entering the case.
7. Use a puller driver mounted on the wheel studs to push the halfshaft from the front hub. Take care to prevent the spacer from falling out of place.
8. Assembly is the reverse of removal. Insert the halfshaft into the hub first, then install the transaxle end. Torque the drive axle nut (if so equipped) to 144–188 ft. lbs.

**NOTE: Always use a new DOJ retaining ring every time you remove the driveshaft.**

#### *Center Bearing*

1. Remove the hub center cap and loosen the halfshaft (axle) nut. Loosen the wheel lug nuts.

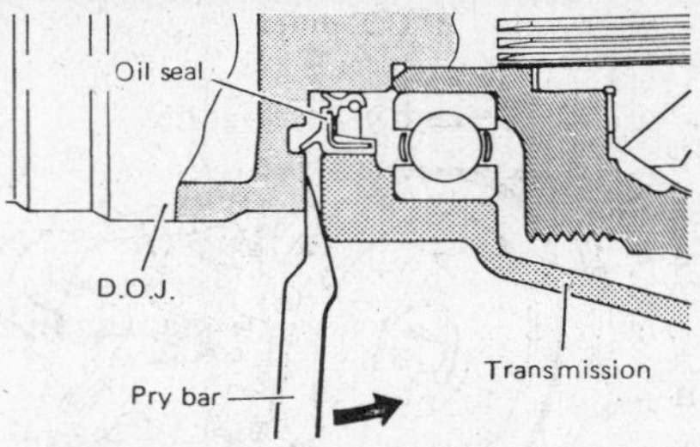


**Half shaft removal—except Mirage with center bearing**

2. Lift the vehicle and support it on jack stands. Remove the front wheels. Remove the engine splash shield.
3. Remove the lower ball joint and strut bar from the lower control arm.
4. Drain the transaxle fluid.
5. Before removing the halfshaft remove the center bearing snapring.
6. Remove the halfshaft from the transaxle by lightly tapping the outer race with a plastic hammer.
7. Do not insert a pry bar between the transaxle case and the halfshaft, as damage to the dust cover of the shaft will occur.
8. If the halfshaft is pulled out from the birthfield joint side there is danger of causing damage to the joint.
9. Drive the shaft out of the hub by lightly tapping the halfshaft end with a plastic hammer.
10. Plug the transaxle case with a clean rag to prevent dirt from entering the case.
11. Use a puller driver mounted on the wheel studs to push the halfshaft from the front hub. Take care to prevent the spacer from falling out of place.
12. Assembly is reverse of removal. Insert the halfshaft into the hub first, then install the transaxle end. Always use a new DOJ retaining ring every time you remove the halfshaft.

### CV-JOINT OVERHAUL

**For all CV-joint overhaul procedures, please refer to "CV-Joint Overhaul" in the Unit Repair section.**

## Driveshaft and U-Joints

### REMOVAL & INSTALLATION

1. Raise and support the vehicle safely. Matchmark the rear flange yoke and the differential pinion flange.
2. Remove the bolts from the rear flange. Remove the driveshaft by pulling it from the rear of the transmission extension housing. Place a container under the transmission extension housing to collect any oil leakage when the driveshaft is removed.
3. To install the shaft, align the front sleeve yoke with the splines of the transmission output shaft and push the driveshaft into the extension housing.

**NOTE: Be careful not to damage the rear transmission seal lip upon installation**

4. Align the matchmarks on the rear yokes, install the bolts, and Torque to 36–43 ft. lbs.
5. Inspect the oil level of the transmission.

## Rear Axle/Shafts

### REMOVAL & INSTALLATION

#### *Except Starion*

1. Raise and support the vehicle safely. Remove the tire and wheel.
2. Remove the brake drum and brake shoes. Remove the 4 wheel side flange mounting nuts and bolts.
3. Connect a flanged slide hammer to the axle flange and "pull" the axle from the differential. Take care not to damage the side differential seals.
4. Repair or replace defective components, as required. Install a new circlip on the differential side and install the axle shaft in the reverse order of removal. Tighten the mounting nuts and bolts to 36–43 ft. lbs.

#### *Starion*

1. Raise and support the vehicle safely. Remove the tire and wheel.
2. Disconnect the parking brake cable and remove the disc brake pads and caliper. Leave the brake line connected to the caliper and use a piece of wire to suspend the caliper out of the way.
3. Remove the halfshaft mounting bolts. Remove the lower control arm-to- knuckle bolt.
4. Remove the strut assembly retaining bolts and remove the axle housing assembly.
5. Remove the axle shaft from the axle housing as follows:
   a. Remove the companion flange mounting nut. Now using a plastic hammer tap the axle shaft out of the axle housing.
   b. Remove the spacer, outer bearing, dust cover, companion flange, dust cover, oil seal, inner bearing, axle housing and dust cover.
6. Reassemble the axle shaft into the axle housing and install the axle housing by reversing the removal procedure. Torque the companion flange mounting nut to 188–217 ft. lbs. Torque the strut mounting bolts

to 36–51 ft. lbs., the halfshaft mounting bolt/nuts to 40–47 ft. lbs. and the lower control arm bolt/nut to 51–58 ft. lbs.

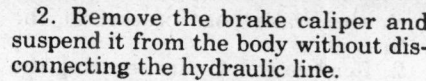

## Front Wheel Hub Knuckle and Bearings

### REMOVAL & INSTALLATION

1. Raise and support the vehicle safely. Remove the tire and wheel. Remove the grease cap and halfshaft nut.

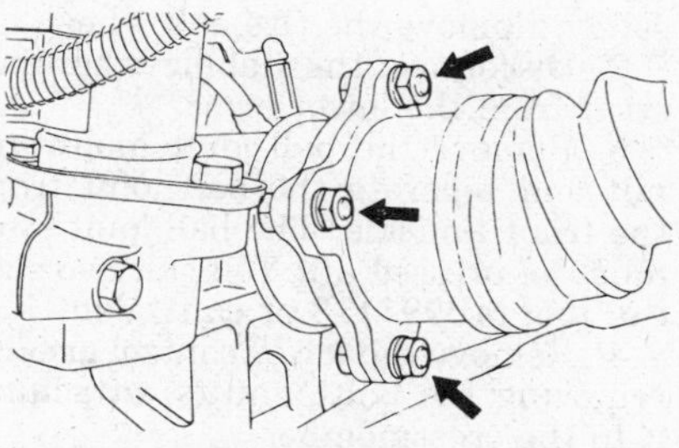

Rear drive axle flange mounting

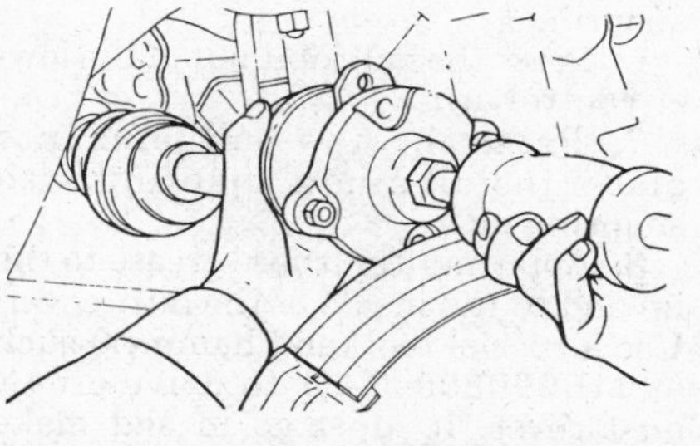

Rear axle removal with slide hammer

2. Remove the brake caliper and suspend it from the body without disconnecting the hydraulic line.
3. Disconnect the stabilizer bar and strut bar from the lower arm.
4. Loosen but do not remove the ball joint stud nut and press the ball joint stud out of the knuckle; then remove the nut.
5. Press the halfshaft out of the hub.
6. Disconnect the tie rod end ball joint from the knuckle in the same way as the lower ball joint was disconnected.

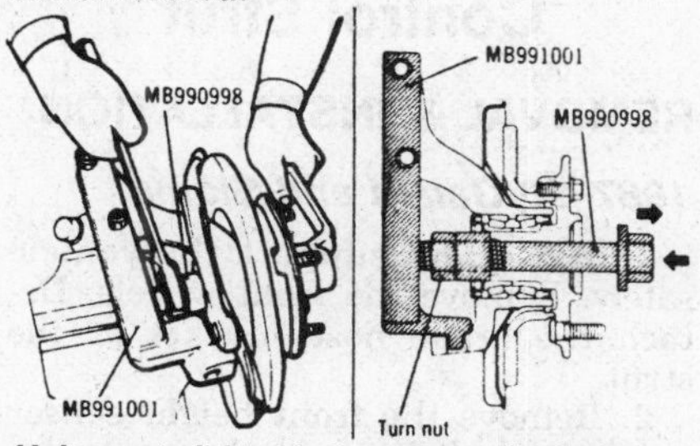


Using special tools to remove the hub from the knuckle

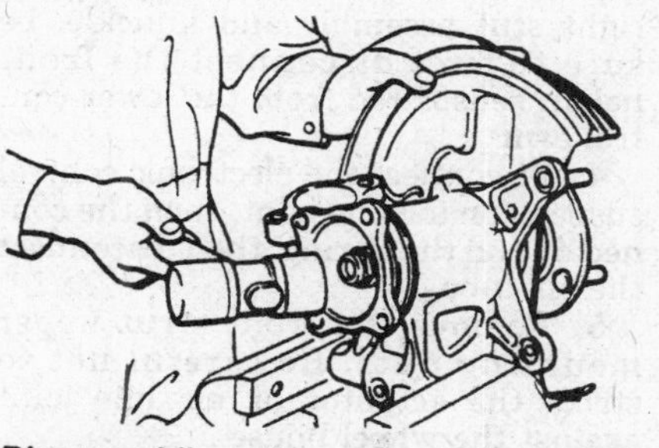

Disassembling the rear axle shaft–Starion

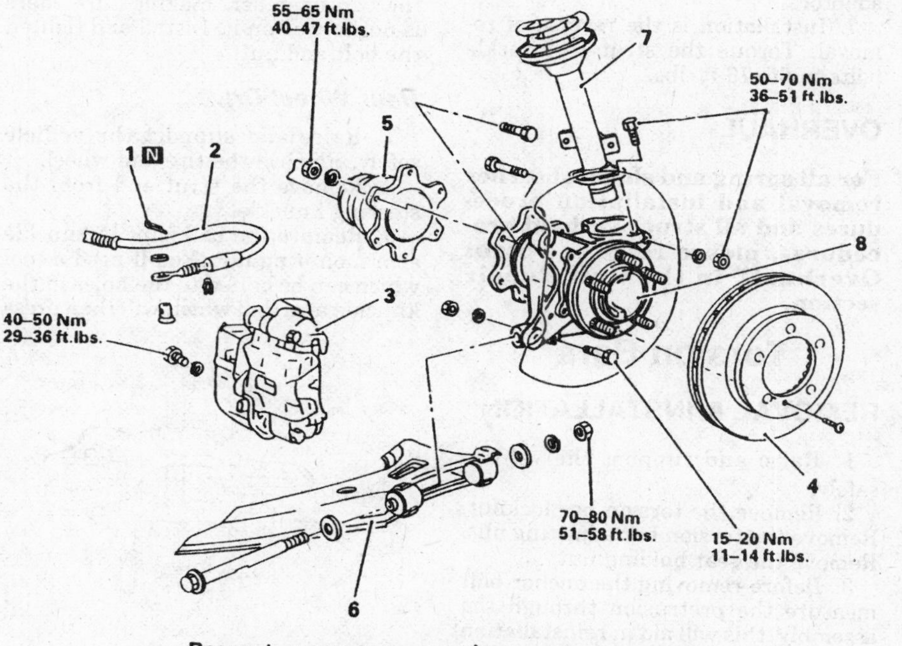


Rear axle assembly removal & installation–Starion

7. Remove the nuts and bolts connecting the knuckle to the strut and remove the hub and knuckle.
8. The hub must now be pressed out of the knuckle using a special tool set such as MB990998-01 and MB991001.
9. Assembly is the reverse of removal.
10. Front wheel drive models require no bearing adjustment. The axle washer must be installed, "taper side" facing out. Tighten the axle nut to 144–188 ft. lbs. Align the nearest cotter pin hole and install cotter pin.

# FRONT SUSPENSION

## Shock Absorbers

### REMOVAL & INSTALLATION

#### *Except Cordia and Tredia*

1. Disconnect the negative battery cable. Remove the shock absorber retaining nut from the upper control arm.
2. Raise and support the vehicle safely. Remove the front under cover spoiler.
3. Remove the shock absorber retaining nut and bolt from the lower control arm.
4. Remove the shock absorber from the vehicle.
5. Installation is the reverse of the removal procedure.

## MacPherson Strut

### REMOVAL & INSTALLATION

#### *Cordia and Tredia*

1. Raise and support the vehicle safely.
2. Remove the front wheel. Remove the brake line from the strut.
3. Disconnect the strut assembly from the steering knuckle by removing the 2 bolts/nuts. Support the strut and remove the 2 nuts and washers fastening it to the wheel well. Remove the strut.
4. Installation is the reverse of the removal procedure. When installing the strut, apply a non hardening sealer to the mating surfaces of the strut and knuckle arm.

#### *Starion*

1. Raise and support the vehicle safely. Remove the tire and wheel. Re-

move the caliper. Remove the front hub with disc and dust cover.

2. Disconnect the stabilizer linkage and the lower. Remove the strut assembly, knuckle arm and strut insulator retaining bolts and remove the strut assembly from the wheelhouse.

3. Installation is the reverse of the removal procedure. When installing the strut, apply a non hardening sealer to the mating surfaces of the strut and knuckle arm.

#### *Mirage and Galant*

1. Raise and support the vehicle safely. Remove the front wheels. On the Mirage, detach the brake hose bracket at the strut.

2. Remove the 2 nuts, bolts and lockwashers attaching the lower end of the strut to the steering knuckle.

3. Remove the dust cover from the top of the strut on the wheel well. Support the strut from underneath. Install the socket wrench on the nut at the top of the strut and a box or open end wrench on the socket. Then, install the Allen wrench through the center of the socket, long part downward. Hold the Allen wrench in place, if necessary by using a small diameter pipe as a cheater. Turn the socket to loosen the nut. Remove the nut and the lower and remove the strut.

4. To install, reverse the removal procedure. Torque the bolts attaching the bottom of the strut to the knuckle to 53–63 ft. lbs. on the Mirage and 65–76 ft. lbs. on the Galant. The nut at the top of the strut must be torqued with the shaft of the shock held from turning with the Allen wrench, as during the loosening process. Since it is not usually possible to use a torque wrench on the flats of a socket, you'll have to estimate the torque you're applying. It should be 36–43 ft. lbs.

#### *Precis*

1. Raise and support the vehicle safely. Remove the front wheels. Detach the brake hose bracket at the strut.

2. Remove the 4 nuts securing the strut to the fender well.

3. Unbolt the strut lower end from the knuckle.

4. Remove the strut from the vehicle.

5. Installation is the reverse of removal. Torque the strut to knuckle bolts to 55–65 ft. lbs.; the strut to fender well nuts to 7–11 ft. lbs.

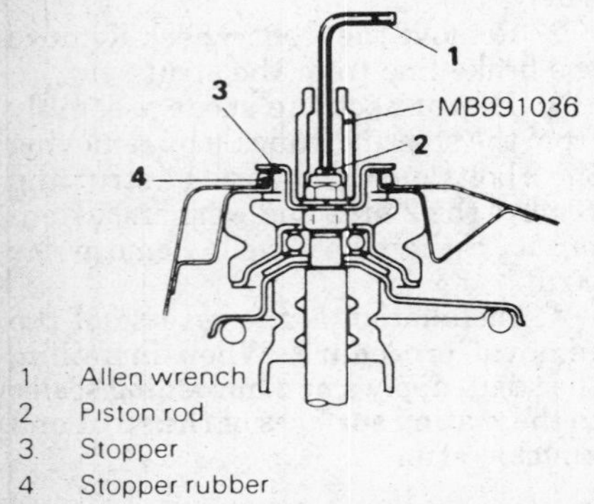


**Removing the upper strut attaching nut with a socket wrench and Allen wrench on the Galant and Mirage**

## Electronic Control Strut

### REMOVAL & INSTALLATION

#### *1987–90 Galant and Sigma*

1. Raise and support the vehicle safely. Remove the front wheels. Detach the brake hose bracket at the strut.

2. Remove the front height sensor mounting bolt.

3. Remove the front strut lower mounting bolts. When uncoupling the right stut assembly and knuckle, be sure to first disconnect the front height sensor rod from the lower control arm.

4. Disconnect the electronic control suspension air line joint, then the connector and the O-ring, then disconnect the air tube.

5. Remove the front strut upper mounting nuts. Be careful not to strike the actuator or air line joint against the wheel house.

6. Remove the front strut assembly along with the actuator and the adaptor.

7. Installation is the reverse of removal. Torque the strut to knuckle bolts to 65–76 ft. lbs.

### OVERHAUL

**For all spring and shock absorber removal and installation procedures and all strut overhaul procedures, please refer to "Strut Overhaul" in the Unit Repair section.**

## Torsion Bars

### REMOVAL & INSTALLATION

1. Raise and support the vehicle safely.

2. Remove the torsion bar locknut. Remove the torsion bar adjusting nut. Remove the seat holding nut.

3. Before removing the anchor bolt measure the protrusion through the assembly, this will aid in reinstallation of the assembly. Remove the anchor bolt that retains the torsion bar to its mouinting on the frame.

4. Remove the nuts that retain the torsion bar to the control arm.

5. Remove the torsion bar from the vehicle.

6. Installation is the reverse of the removal procedure. Adjust the alignment and the torsion bar, as required.

## Ball Joints

### REMOVAL & INSTALLATION

#### *Front Wheel Drive*

1. Raise and support the vehicle safely. Remove the tire and wheel.

2. Disconnect the stabilizer bar and strut from the lower arm.

3. Remove the ball joint mounting nut and separate the ball joint from the front knuckle. The ball joint stud must be pressed off. You can use special tool MB991113 or equivalent.

4. Remove the lower control arm by removing the bolt(s)/nut(s) attaching it to the crossmember.

5. Remove the dust cover from the ball joint. Remove the mounting snapring.

6. Press the ball joint out of the lower control arm.

7. Press the new ball joint into place. Install a new snapring with snapring pliers.

8. Apply multipurpose grease to the lip and to the inside of the dust cover. Use a special tool (and hammer) such as MB990800-3-01 to drive a new dust cover. It must go in and make contact with the snapring.

9. Install the lower control arm to the corssmember, making sure there is not torque on it. Install and tighten the bolt and nut.

#### *Rear Wheel Drive*

1. Raise and support the vehicle safely. Remove the tire and wheel.

2. Remove the strut end from the steering knuckle.

3. Remove the ball joint to knuckle arm mounting nut. You'll need a tool which can be bolted to the holes in the knuckle arm and which will then press

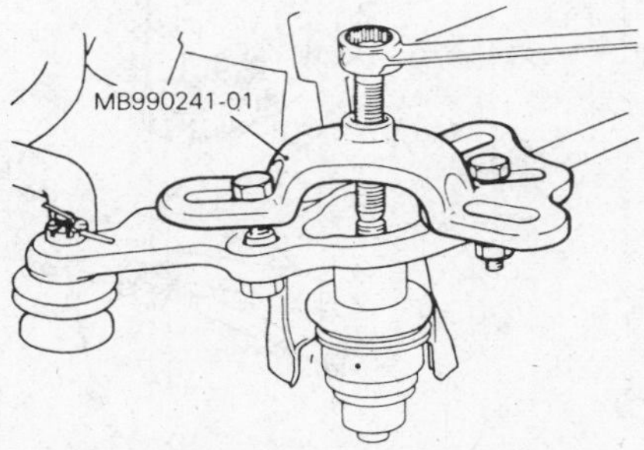


**Pressing the ball joint off—Starion**

downward on the center of the Ball Stud – MB990241-01 or equivalent.

4. Remove the ball joint to control arm nuts and bolts and remove the ball joint.

5. Install in reverse order. Torques in ft. lbs.: Ball joint mounting bolts 43–51 ft. lbs., strut to knuckle arm bolts 58–72 ft. lbs., ballstud nut 43–52 ft. lbs.

## Lower Control Arm

### REMOVAL & INSTALLATION

#### *Cordia and Tredia*

1. Raise and support the vehicle. Remove the tire and wheel.

2. Disconnect the stabilizer bar and strut bar from the lower control arm by removing the 1 attaching bolt for the stabilizer bar and the 2 bolts for the strut bar.

3. Remove the ballstud nut and then press the ball joint stud out of the knuckle with a tool such as MB991113.

4. Remove the nut and bolt attaching the inner end of the stabilizer bar to the crossmember and pull the stabilizer bar and bushing out of the crossmember.

5. Installation is the reverse of removal. Install all parts and tighten nuts and bolts just snug. Then, complete tightening, torquing the lower arm to crossmember attaching nut/bolt to 87–108 ft. lbs. and the ball joint stud nut to 43–52 ft. lbs. Torque the strut rod to stabilizer bar bolt/nut to 43–50 ft. lbs.

#### *Starion*

1. Raise and support the vehicle safely. Remove the tire and wheel.

2. Disconnect the stabilizer bar where the link bolts to the control arm by removing the nut underneath the arm. Remove the nut and bolt attaching the strut bar to the control arm.

3. Disconnect the tie rod at the knuckly arm. Use a fork like tool such as MB990778-01, a standard type tool for pulling ball joint studs. First, loosen the stud nut until it is near the top of the threads and then hammer the tool between the ball joint of the tie rod end and the knuckle arm. When the ballstud comes loose, remove the nut and disconnect the stud.

4. Unbolt the MacPherson strut from the knuckle arm.

5. Unbolt the inner end of the ball joint assembly to disconnect it from the outer end of the control arm.

6. Remove the nut, bolt and lockwasher and pull the inner end of the control arm out of the crossmember.

7. Installation is the reverse of removal. Torque the bolt fastening the control arm to the crossmember to 58–69 ft. lbs.; the bolts attaching the ball joint to the outer end to 43–51 ft. lbs.; the ballstud nut to 43–52 ft. lbs.; and the strut attaching bolts to 58–72 ft. lbs. Tighten the nut for the stabilizer bar link until 0.59–0.67 in. of thread shows below the bottom of the nut.

#### *Mirage, Galant and Sigma*

1. Raise and support the vehicle safely. Remove the tire and wheel.

2. On the Mirage, remove the under cover.

3. Disconnect the stabilizer bar from the lower arm. On the Galant, remove the nut at the top and remove the washer and bushing, keeping them in order. On the Mirage, you can remove the nut from underneath the control arm and take off the washer and spacer.

4. On the Galant with electronically controlled suspension, if you're removing the right arm, disconnect the height sensor rod from the lower arm. Loosen the ball joint stud nut and then press the stud out of the control arm, using a fork like tool (MB990778-01) and hammer on the Galant; on the Mirage, remove the stud nut and press the tool off with a tool such as MB991113.

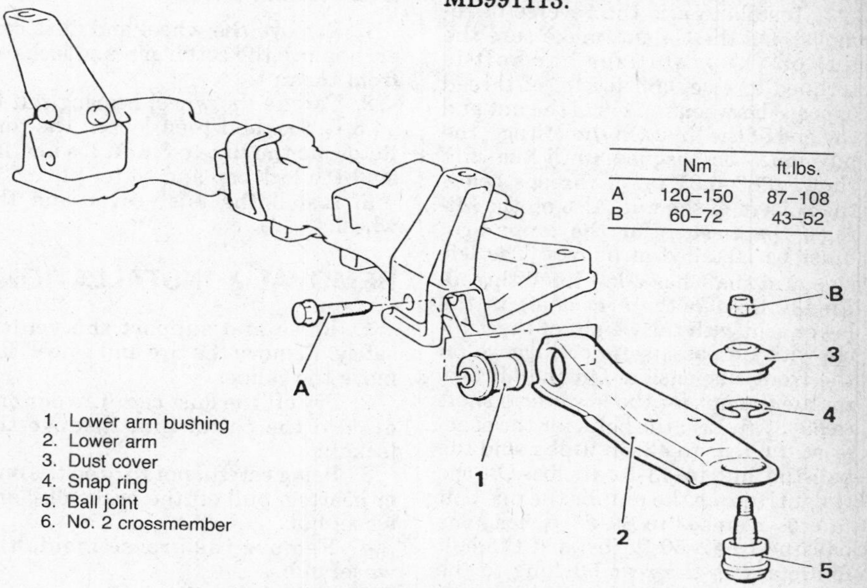


1. Lower arm bushing
2. Lower arm
3. Dust cover
4. Snap ring
5. Ball joint
6. No. 2 crossmember

| | Nm | ft.lbs. |
|---|---|---|
| A | 120–150 | 87–108 |
| B | 60–72 | 43–52 |

Cordia, Tredia lower front control arm and ball joint

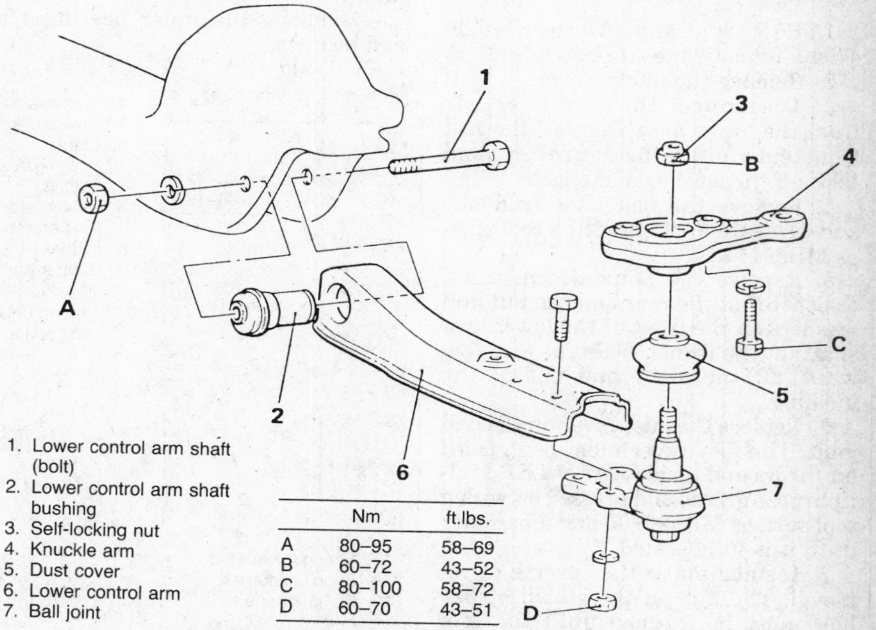


1. Lower control arm shaft (bolt)
2. Lower control arm shaft bushing
3. Self-locking nut
4. Knuckle arm
5. Dust cover
6. Lower control arm
7. Ball joint

| | Nm | ft.lbs. |
|---|---|---|
| A | 80–95 | 58–69 |
| B | 60–72 | 43–52 |
| C | 80–100 | 58–72 |
| D | 60–70 | 43–51 |

Starion lower front control arm and ball joint

5. On the Galant, remove the nuts and bolts which retain the bushings to the crossmember at the front and which retain the bushing retainer to the crossmember at the rear and pull the arm out. On the Mirage, remove the bolts which retain the spacer at the rear and the nut and washers on the front of the lower arm shaft (at the front). Slide the arm forward, off the shaft and out of the busing.

6. Replace the dust cover on the ball joint. The new cover must be greased on the lip and inside with #2 EP Multipurpose grease and pressed on with a tool such as MB990800 and a hammer until it is fully seated.

7. Installation is the reverse of removal. On the Galant, make sure the nut on the stabilizer bar bolt is torqued to give 0.63–0.7 in. of thread exposed between the top of the nut and the end of the link. On the Mirage, the nut must be torqued until the link shows 0.83–0.91 in. of threads below the bottom of the nut. Also on the Mirage, the washer for the lower arm must be installed as shown. The left side arm shaft has a left hand thread. Finally tighten the arm shaft to the lower arm with the weight of the vehicle with no passengers or luggage on the front suspension. On the Mirage, torque the nut for the lower arm shaft to 69–87 ft. lbs.; the bolts for the spacer at the rear to 43–58 ft. lbs. and the ballstud nut to 43–52 ft. lbs. On the Galant, torque the nut for the nut/bolt to crossmember to 69–87 ft. lbs., the ballstud to 42–50 ft. lbs. and the bolt for retaining the rear bushing to the body to 58–72 ft. lbs.

### *Precis*

1. Raise and support the vehicle safely. Remove the tire and wheel.

2. Remove the under cover.

3. Disconnect the stabilizer bar from the lower arm. Remove the nut from under neath the control arm and take off the washer and spacer.

4. Remove the ball joint stud nut and press the tool off with a tool such as MB991113.

5. Remove the bolts which retain the spacer at the rear and the nut and washers on the front of the lower arm shaft (at the front). Slide the arm forward, off the shaft and out of the bushing.

6. Replace the dust cover on the ball joint. The new cover must be greased on the lip and inside with #2 EP Multipurpose grease and pressed on with a tool such as MB990800 and a hammer until it is fully seated.

7. Installation is the reverse of removal. The nut on the stabilizer bar bolt must be torqued until the link shows 21–23mm of threads below the bottom of the nut. Also, the washer for the lower arm must be installed as shown. The left side arm shaft has a left hand thread. Finally, tighten the arm shaft to the lower arm with the weight of the car with no passengers or luggage on the front suspension. Torque the nut for the lower arm shaft to 69–87 ft. lbs.; the bolts for the spacer at the rear to 43–58 ft. lbs.; the ball stud nut to 43–52 ft. lbs.

## Front Wheel Bearings

### ADJUSTMENT

#### *Rear Wheel Drive*

1. Remove the wheel and dust cover. Remove the cotter pin and lock cap from the nut.

2. Torque the wheel bearing nut to 14.5 ft. lbs. and then loosen the nut. Retorque the nut to 3.6 ft. lbs and install the lock cap and cotter pin.

3. Install the dust cover and the wheel.

### REMOVAL & INSTALLATION

1. Raise and support the vehicle safely. Remove the tire and wheel. Remove the caliper.

2. Pry off the dust cap. Tap out and discard the cotter pin. Remove the locknut.

3. Being careful not to drop the outer bearing, pull off the brake disc and wheel hub.

4. Remove the grease inside the wheel hub.

5. Using a brass drift, carefully drive the outer bearing race out of the hub.

6. Remove the inner bearing seal and bearing.

7. Check the bearings for wear or damage and replace them if necessary.

8. Coat the inner surface of the hub with grease.

9. Grease the outer surface of the bearing race and drift it into place in the hub.

10. Pack the inner and outer wheel bearings with grease. If the brake disc has been removed and/or replaced, tighten the retaining bolts to specification.

11. Install the inner bearing in the hub. Being careful not to distort it, install the oil seal with its lip facing the bearing. Drive the seal on until its outer edge is even with the edge of the hub.

12. Install the hub/disc assembly on the spindle, being careful not to damage the oil seal.

13. Install the outer bearing, washer and spindle nut. Adjust the bearing.

## Front Wheel Alignment

### ADJUSTMENT

Camber is preset at the factory and cannot be adjusted. Caster should not require adjustment, although adjustment (to a certain extent) is possible by adjusting the length of the strut bar. Loosen both nuts and turn in or out as required. Toe adjustment is possible by adjusting both tie rod end turnbuckles (the same amount) on Cordia and Tredia, or the left tierod end turnbuckle on Starion.

Before turning the turnbuckles on Cordia and Tredia, unfasten the clips for the rubber boots on the inner ends of the turnbuckles. Using a wrench from below on the flats in the middle of the turnbuckle, the toe will move

| | Nm | ft.lbs. |
|---|---|---|
| A | 65–80 | 47–58 |
| B | 70–90 | 51–65 |
| C | 80–100 | 58–72 |
| D | 18–25 | 13–18 |

1. Suspension arm (R.H.)
2. Dust cover
3. Clamp
4. Bushing A
5. Bushing B
6. Rubber stopper
7. Suspension arm (L.H.)
8. Fixture
9. Rubber bushing
10. Washer
11. Spring upper seat
12. Coil spring

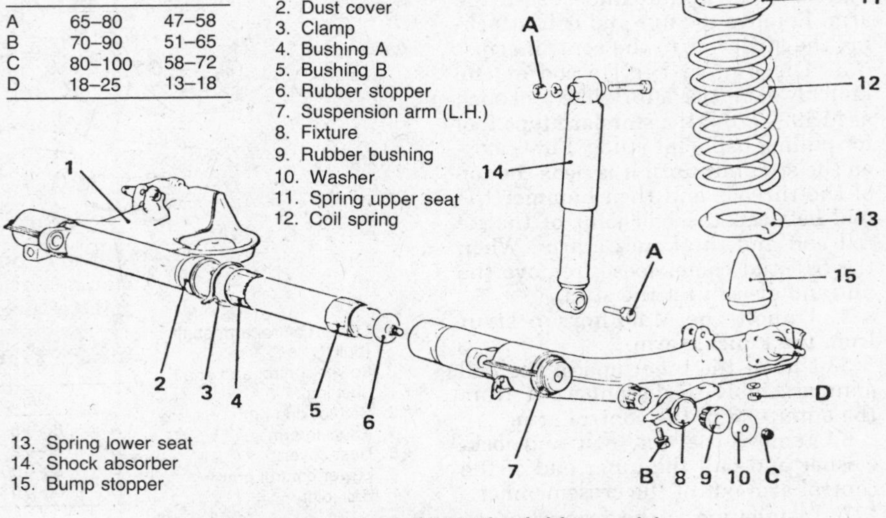


13. Spring lower seat
14. Shock absorber
15. Bump stopper

**Rear suspension—front wheel drive models**

out as the left side turnbuckle is turned toward the front of the vehicle and the right toward the rear.

On the Mirage, Galant, Precis and Sigma toe in is adjusted as for Cordia and Tredia, neither caster nor camber can be adjusted.

On the Starion, toe in can usually be adjusted by turning the 1 turnbuckle. You should, however, check to make sure that the difference between the length of right and left tie rods is not greater than 0.2 in. If it is, you should remove the tight tie rod at the knuckle and bring the length within specifications; and then toe-in is brought to correct values also.

# REAR SUSPENSION

## Shock Absorbers

### REMOVAL & INSTALLATION

#### *All Models*

1. Raise and support the vehicle safely. Remove the tire and wheel.
2. Position a floor jack under the lower control arm. Remove the upper shock mounting bolt and nut.
3. Compress the shock slightly and remove the lower mounting bolt.
4. Remove the shock absorber.
5. Installation is the reverse of the removal procedure.

## MacPherson Strut

### REMOVAL & INSTALLATION

#### *Starion*

1. Support the rear of vehicle on jackstands at the frame rails. Position a floor jack under the lower control arm and raise it slightly.
2. Disconnect the rear brake hose from the strut assembly.
3. Disconnect the axle shaft from the wheel side flange.
4. Remove the strut assembly to axle housing mounting bolts. Separate the strut assembly from the axle housing. Lower the floor jack and push down on the housing while opening the coupling with a small pry bar.
5. Remove the upper strut mounting nuts from under the side trim in rear hatch.
6. Remove the strut assembly.
7. Install in reverse order. Tighten the top mounting nuts to 18–25 ft. lbs. and the lower mounting to 36–51 ft. lbs.

#### *Galant*

1. Support the vehicle on jackstands. Remove the rear wheels.
2. Place a floor jack under the axle/arm assembly and raise it slightly. Then, remove the forward trim from the trunk and remove the cap and strut mounting nuts and washers.
3. Remove the nut, pull the throughbolt out where the strut connects with the axle/arm assembly and remove the strut assembly.
4. Installation is the reverse of removal. Torque the upper strut mounting nuts to 33–40 ft. lbs. (18–25 ft.lbs. on ELC models) and the lower throughbolt to 72–87 ft. lbs. (58–72 ft.lbs. on ELC models).

### OVERHAUL

**For all spring and shock absorber removal and installation procedures and all strut overhaul procedures, please refer to the "Strut Overhaul" in the Unit Repair section.**

## Coil Spring

### REMOVAL & INSTALLATION

#### *All Models*

1. Raise and support the vehicle safely allowing the rear axle to hang unsupported.
2. Place a jack under the work side control arm and remove the bottom bolts of the shock absorbers.
3. Lower the arm and remove the coil spring.
4. Installation is the reverse of removal.

## Rear Control Arm

### REMOVAL & INSTALLATION

#### *Except The Starion*

1. Raise and support the vehicle. Remove the rear wheels. Remove the rear brake assemblies. As required, remove the muffler.
2. Disconnect the parking brake cable from the suspension arm on both sides.
3. Jack up the suspension arm on both sides just slightly. Then remove both lower shock absorber attaching bolts. Then, lower the jack carefully and, when it can be disengaged, remove the spring. Keep the spring in the position it was in when installed so it can be installed in the same direction.
4. Disconnect the brake hoses at the suspension arms. Then, support the rear suspension assembly while you remove the 2 mounting bolts on either side and remove the assembly.
5. Installation is the reverse of removal. Lower shock mounting bolts are torqued to 47–58 ft. lbs. Suspension assembly to body mounting bolts are torqued to 51–65 ft. lbs. on Cordia and Tredia and to 36–51 ft. lbs. on Mirage.

#### *Starion*

1. Raise and support the vehicle safely.
2. Disconnect the parking brake from the control arm brackets. Disconnect the stabilizer bar.
3. Remove the nut and bolt connecting the lower control arm to the front support.
4. Matchmark the relationship between the crossmember and the eccentric bushing so alignment can be restored at assembly. Remove the nut and bolt connecting the lower control arm to the crossmember.
5. Remove the lower control arm from the vehicle.
6. Install in reverse order.

## Rear Wheel Bearings

### REMOVAL & INSTALLATION

#### *All Models Except the Mirage*

1. Raise and support the vehicle safely. Inspect the play of the bearing, if there is excessive play in the wheel bearing, remove the hub cap, cotter pin and lock cap.
2. Loosen the lock-nut. Using a suitable torque wrench, tighten the lock nut to 14 ft. lbs. and then loosen to 0 ft. lbs. Then re-torque the lock-nut to 4–7 ft. lbs.
3. Install the lock cap and the cotter pin.
4. If the position of the cotter pin is not matched with the holes in the lock cap, reposition the lock cap so that the holes align. If this cannot be accomplished, back off the lock nut 15°. Align the lock cap and install the cotter pin.

#### *Mirage*

1. Raise and support the vehicle safely. Loosen the lug nuts.
2. Remove the tire and wheel. Remove the grease cap. Remove the nut.
3. Pull the drum off. The outer bearing will fall out while the drum is coming off, so position your hand to catch it.
4. Pry out the oil seal. Discard it. Remove the inner bearing.
5. Check the bearing races and bearings. If any scoring, heat checking or damage is noted, they should be replaced. When bearings or races need replacement, replace them as a set.

6. If the bearings and races are to be replaced, drive out the race with a brass drift.

7. Before installing new races, coat them with lithium based wheel bearing grease. The races are most easily installed using a driver made for that purpose. They can, however, be driven into place with a brass drift. Make sure that they are fully seated.

8. Thoroughly pack the bearings with lithium based wheel bear grease. Pack the hub with grease.

9. Install the inner bearing and coat the lip and rim of the grease seal with grease. Drive the seal into place with a seal driver.

10. Mount the drum on the axleshaft. Install the outer bearing. Don't install the nut at this point.

11. Using a pull scale attached to one of the lugs, measure the starting force necessary to get the drum to turn. Starting force should be 5 lbs. If the starting torque is greater than specified, replace the bearings.

12. Install the nut on the axleshaft. Thread the nut on, by hand, to a point at which the back face of the nut is 2–3mm from the shoulder of the shaft (where the threads end).

13. Using an inch lb. torque wrench, turn the nut counterclockwise 2–3 turns, noting the average force needed during the turning procedure. Turning torque for the nut should be about 48 inch lbs. If turning torque is not within 5 inch lbs., either way, replace the nut.

14. Tighten the nut to 75–110 ft. lbs. Using a stand mounted gauge, check the axial play of the wheel bearings. Play should be less than 0.0079 in. If play cannot be brought within that figure, you probably have assembled the unit incorrectly. Pack the grease cap with wheel bearing grease and install it.

# STEERING

## Steering Wheel

### REMOVAL & INSTALLATION

1. Disconnect the negative battery cable. Pry off the steering wheel center foam pad or remove the mounting screws from the back (depending on model). Disconnect the electrical connector for the horn.

2. Remove the steering wheel retaining nut after marking the wheel and shaft position.

3. Using a steering wheel puller, remove the steering wheel.

4. Installation is the reverse of the removal procedure. Be sure the front wheels are in a straight ahead position.

## Combination Switch

### REMOVAL & INSTALLATION

1. Disconnect the negative battery cable. Remove the steering wheel and have the tilt handle in the lowest position.

2. Remove the combination meter and column covers.

3. Remove the connectors from the column switch and the column switch from the column tube.

**NOTE: Some models may have the turn signal and hazard switches mounted on a base plate. Removal of the attaching screws will allow these switches to be removed without removal of the remaining switches.**

4. Switch installation is the reverse of removal. Be sure that the switch is centered in the column or self cancelling will be affected.

## Ignition Switch

### REMOVAL & INSTALLATION

1. Disconnect the negative battery cable. Cut a notch in the lock bracket bolt head with a hacksaw.

2. Remove the bolt and lock.

3. Remove the column cover and unbolt and remove the ignition switch.

4. Install both lock and switch in reverse of removal.

**NOTE: When installing lock, the bolt should be tightened until the head is crushed. When installing switch, install the switch bolt loosely and insert and work the key a few times to make sure everything checks out before tightening the bolt.**

## Manual Steering Gear

### REMOVAL & INSTALLATION

#### *Cordia and Tredia*

1. Raise and support the vehicle safely. Remove the front wheels.

2. Remove the bolt connecting the steering shaft universal joint with the steering gear. Before removing the bolt, mark its location and be sure the wheels are pointed straight.

3. Remove the tie rod ends from the hub knuckles. Disconnect mounting bolts located near the inner tie rods on the crossmember. Remove right side submember from the No. 2 crossmember. Remove the gearbox from the No. 2 crossmember. Pull the gear box out from the right side of the vehicle.

4. Installation is the reverse of removal. Observe the following torques:

Gear box to No. 2 crossmember–43–58 ft. lbs.

Tie rod to rack–58–72 ft. lbs.

Tie rod end locknut–36–40 ft. lbs.

Tie rod to knuckle–17–25 ft. lbs.

#### *Mirage*

1. Support the vehicle. Remove front wheels.

2. Uncouple the shaft assembly from the gearbox from inside the passenger compartment.

3. Press the tie rod ends off the steering knuckles.

4. Cut the retaining band off the rubber boot that covers the joint connecting the box with the steering shaft.

5. Remove the 4 attaching bolts for the 2 main steering box clamps. Pull the gearbox out toward the left side of the vehicle.

6. Install in reverse order, making sure that the projections on the rubber mounting fit into the holes in the housing bracket and clamps.

7. Replace the band attaching the steering joint rubber boot. Make sure the steering wheel rotates smoothly throughout its travel. Adjust toe-in. Torque the steering box mounting bolts to 43–58 ft. lbs. and the tie rod end attaching nuts to 11–25 ft. lbs.

#### *Precis*

1. Raise and support the vehicle safely. Remove the bolt which secures the universal joint in the steering shaft to the gearbox. It's just inside the car where the steering linkage passes through the toeboard.

2. Remove the cotter pin from the tie rod end ballstud and loosen the nut. Press the ballstud out of the steering knuckle with a vice like tool such as MB991113 or equivalent; then remove the nut. Do the same on the other side.

3. Cut the band off the steering joint rubber boot.

4. Remove the 2 attaching bolts from the gearbox housing clamp on either side and pull the gearbox out the left side of the vehicle. Work slowly to keep the unit from being damaged.

5. Install the unit in reverse order. There are rubber tabs on the inside and outside of the sleeve. The larger tab must go on the inside. Use a new band for the steering joint rubber boot. Adjust toe-in. Use the following

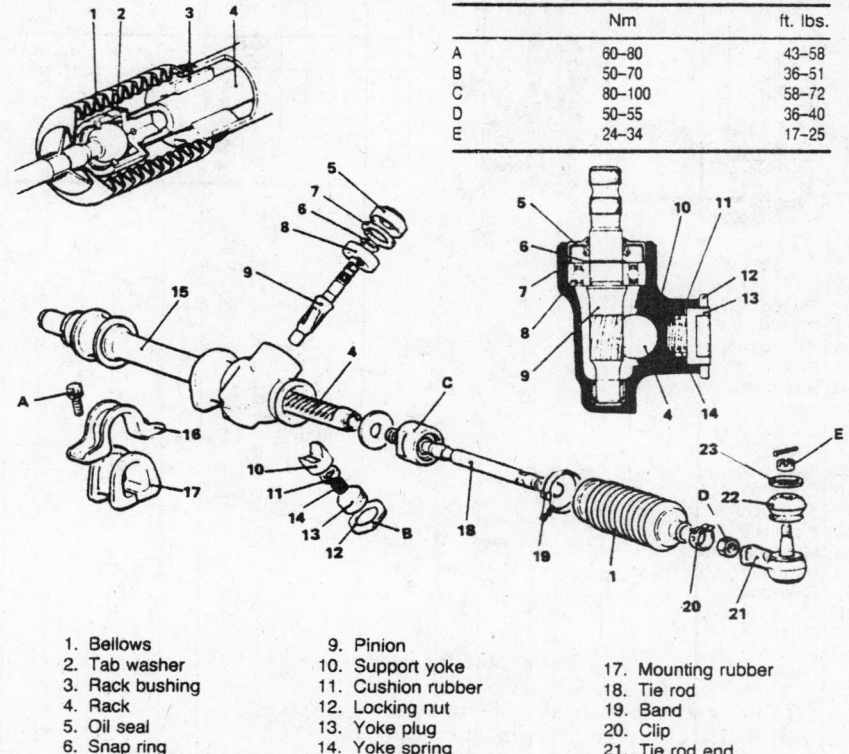

| | Nm | ft. lbs. |
|---|---|---|
| A | 60–80 | 43–58 |
| B | 50–70 | 36–51 |
| C | 80–100 | 58–72 |
| D | 50–55 | 36–40 |
| E | 24–34 | 17–25 |

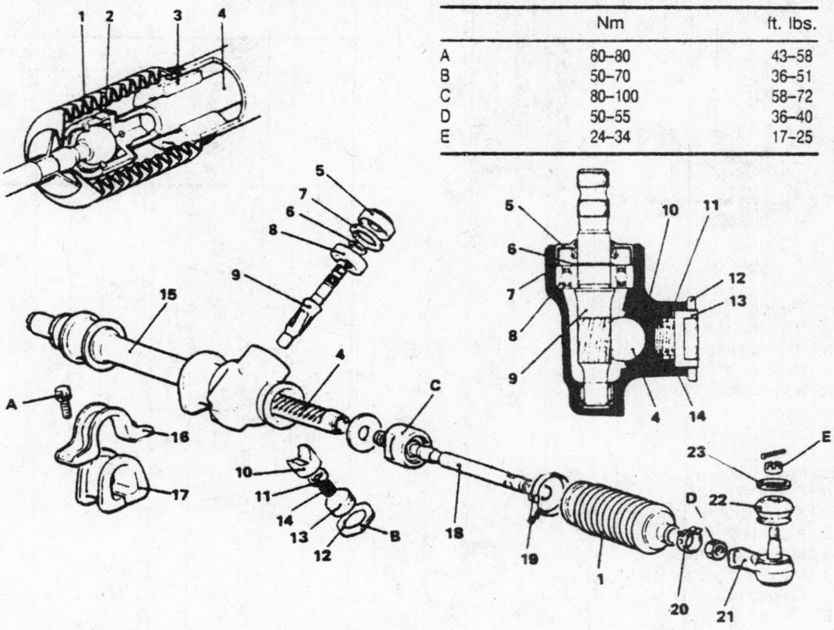

1. Bellows
2. Tab washer
3. Rack bushing
4. Rack
5. Oil seal
6. Snap ring
7. Snap ring
8. Bearing
9. Pinion
10. Support yoke
11. Cushion rubber
12. Locking nut
13. Yoke plug
14. Yoke spring
15. Gear housing
16. Mounting bracket
17. Mounting rubber
18. Tie rod
19. Band
20. Clip
21. Tie rod end
22. Dust cover
23. Clip ring

**Manual steering gear assembly**

torques: mounting bracket attaching bolts, 43–58 ft. lbs.; ball stud nut, 17 ft. lbs. (then turn farther to align castellations with the cotter pin hole and install a new cotter pin). Turn the steering wheel back and forth to test steering and support the vehicle safely.

## Power Steering Gear

### REMOVAL & INSTALLATION

#### *Cordia and Tredia*

1. Raise and support the vehicle safely. Remove the bolt attaching the steering shaft universal joint to the gearbox.
2. Remove the cotter pin from the tie rod end ballstud and then loosen the nut. Press the ballstud out of the steering knuckle with a vice like tool such as MB991113 or equivalent. Remove the nut and pull the stud out of the knuckle.
3. Place a drain pan under the gearbox and then disconnect the pressure and return hose connectors with a flare nut wrench and allow the fluid to drain.
4. Disconnect the hose from the bottom of the fuel filter and plug it.
5. Remove the fuel line clips to permit the fuel line to move.
6. Remove the brace from the rear engine roll stop.
7. Remove the crossmember support bracket from the No. 2 crossmember, located on the right side of the vehicle.
8. Unbolt and remove the 2 bolts in each gearbox mounting clamp, working from the engine compartment side.
9. Pull the gearbox out the right side of the vehicle, working carefully to keep the unit from being damaged.
10. Installation is the reverse of the removal procedure.

#### *Starion*

1. Raise and support the vehicle safely. Remove the clamp bolt which connects the steering box input shaft to the steering shaft.
2. Place a drain pan underneath and then disconnect the pressure and return hoses at the gearbox.
3. Press the pitman arm off the gearbox with the special tool.
4. Remove the 4 attaching nuts and remove the steering box.
5. Install in reverse order, torquing the steering box mounting nuts/bolts to 25–29 ft. lbs. and the pitman arm shaft retaining nut to 25–33 ft. lbs. Fill the power steering pump with fluid, as required.

#### *Mirage*

1. Raise and support the vehicle safely. Remove the bolt which secures the universal joint in the steering shaft to the gearbox. It's just inside the vehicle where the steering linkage passes through the toeboard.
2. Remove the cotter pin from the tie rod end ballstud and loosen the nut. Press the ballstud out of the steering knuckle with a vice like tool such as MB991113 or equivalent; then remove the nut. Do the same on the other side.
3. Cut the bad off the steering joint rubber boot. Place a drain pan under the steering box. Then, disconnect the pressure and return hoses at the gearbox.

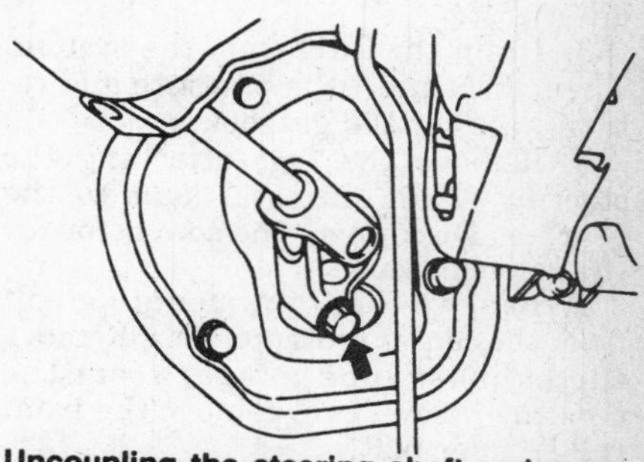

**Uncoupling the steering shaft and gearbox on the Mirage**

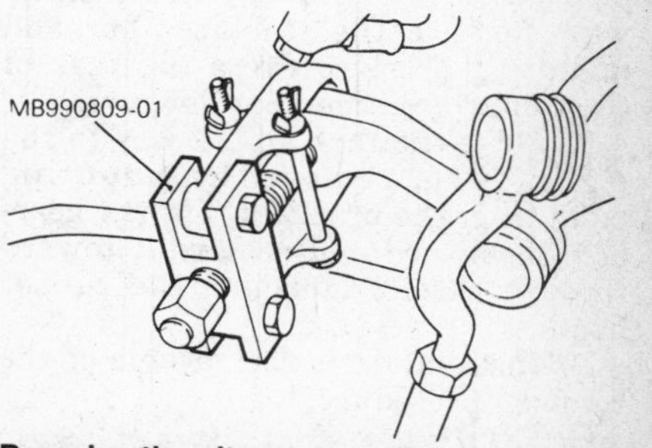


**Pressing the pitman arm off to remove the Starion steering box**

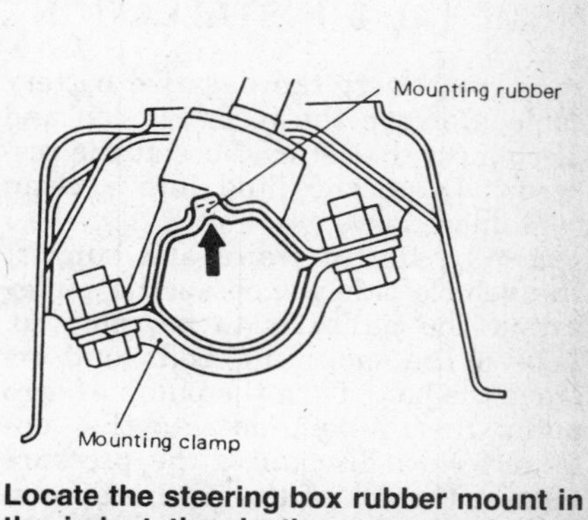


**Locate the steering box rubber mount in the indentation in the crossmember as shown—Mirage**

4. Remove the stabilizer bar.

5. Remove the rear roll stopper to center member bolt and then move the rear roll stopper forward.

6. Remove the 2 mounting bolts in the clip on either side of the gearbox and remove the unit carefully out the left of the vehicle. Avoid damaging the rubber boots.

7. Installation is the reverse of the removal procedure.

### *Galant and Sigma*

1. Raise and support the vehicle safely. If the vehicle has electronically controlled suspension, remove the stabilizer bar.

2. Remove the cotter pin from the tie rod and ballstud and loosen the nut. Press the ballstud out of the steering knuckle with a vice like tool such as MB991113 or equivalent; then remove the nut. Do the same on the other side.

3. Drain the fluid from the system. Then, disconnect the pressure and return hoses at the gearbox.

4. Remove the bolt attaching the steering shaft universal joint to the gearbox. Disconnect the connector for the solenoid valve.

5. Remove the front mounting bolt from the center crossmember. Remove the exhaust pipe hanger from the crossmember. Then, remove the front roll stopper bolt.

6. Disconnect the oxygen sensor connection. Disconnect the exhaust pipe at the front and lower it out of the way. Remove the stabilizer bar and mounting bracket. Press the rear of the center crossmember downward.

7. Move the rack all the way to the right. Then, remove the mounting bolts from the brackets. Tilt the gearbox downward and remove it toward the left. Avoid damaging the rubber boots.

8. Installation is the reverse of the removal procedure.

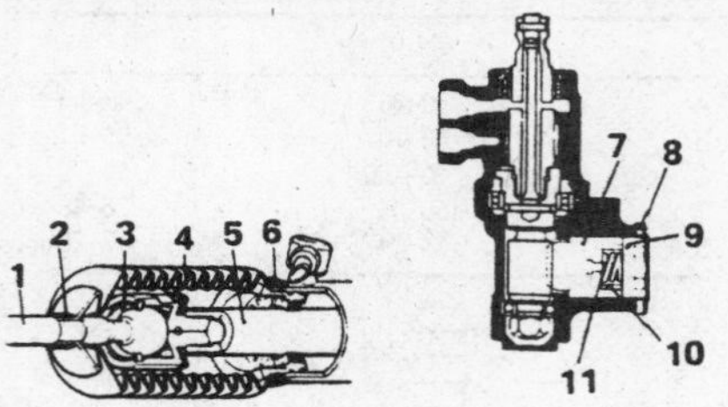


| | Nm | ft. lbs. |
|---|---|---|
| A | 60–80 | 43–58 |
| B | 50–70 | 36–51 |
| C | 80–100 | 58–72 |
| D | 50–55 | 36–39 |
| E | 24–34 | 17–25 |

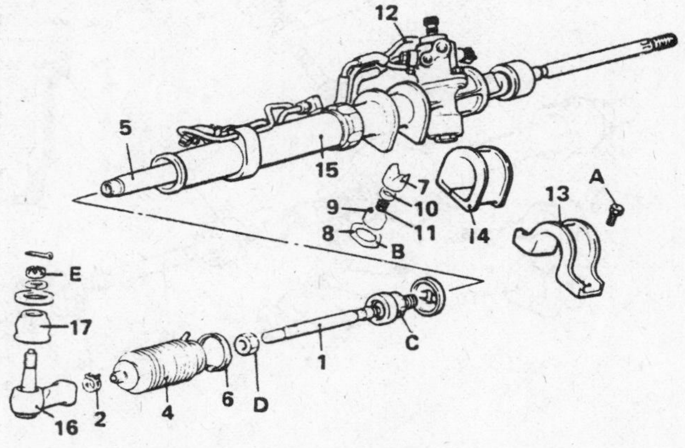


1. Tie rod
2. Clip
3. Tab washer
4. Bellows
5. Rack
6. Band
7. Support yoke
8. Locking nut
9. Yoke plug
10. Cushion rubber
11. Yoke spring
12. Air tube
13. Mounting bracket
14. Mounting rubber
15. Gear box
16. Tie rod end
17. Dust cover

**Power steering gear assembly**

## Power Steering Pump

### REMOVAL & INSTALLATION

1. Disconnect the negative battery cable. Remove the reservoir cap and disconnect the return hose at the reservoir. Drain the fluid into a clean container.

2. As required, raise and support the vehicle safely. Loosen the pulley nut if the pulley is to be removed. Loosen the mounting bolts and remove the belt. Turn the pump over to pump remaining fluid into the container. Now disconnect the pressure hose at the top of the pump. Disconnect the suction hose at the side of the pump and drain the fluid.

3. Remove the pump attaching bolts and lift the pump from the brackets.

4. Make sure the bracket bolts are tight and install the pump to the brackets.

5. If pulley had been removed, install it and tighten the nut securely. Bend the lock tab over the nut.

6. Install the drive belt and adjust to a tension of 22 lbs. at a deflection of 0.28–0.39 in. at the top center of the belt. Tighten the pump bolts securely to hold the tension.

7. Connect the pressure and return lines and fill the reservoir with approved fluid.

### SYSTEM BLEEDING

1. The reservoir should be full with the proper grade and type power steering fluid.

2. Jack up the front wheels and support the vehicle safely.

3. Turn the steering wheel fully to the right and left until no air bubbles appear in the fluid. Maintain the reservoir level.

4. Lower the vehicle and with the engine idling, turn the wheels fully to the right and left. Stop the engine.

5. If equipped, install a tube from the bleeder screw on the steering gear box to the reservoir.

6. Start the engine, turn the steering wheel fully to the left and loosen the bleeder screw.

7. Repeat the procedure until no air bubbles pass through the tube.

8. Tighten the bleeder screw and remove the tube. Refill the reservoir as needed and check that no further bubbles are present in the fluid. An abrupt rise in the fluid level after stopping the engine is a sign of incomplete bleeding. This will cause noise from the pump or control valve.

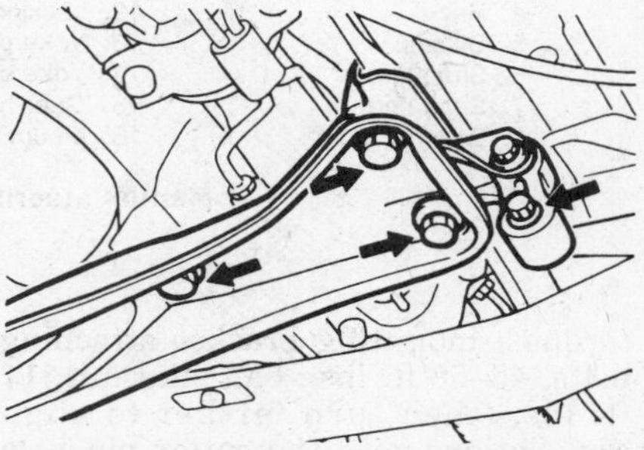

**Removing the center memberfront mounting bolts to remove the steering box—Galant**

## Tie Rod Ends

### REMOVAL & INSTALLATION

### *Starlon*

1. Raise and support the vehcile safely.

2. Remove the cotter pin and locknut from the tie rod end.

3. Using the proper tools separate the tie rod end from its mounting.

4. Unscrew the tie rod end from the relay rod.

5. Installation is the reverse of the removal procedure. Adjust the toe in as required.

# BRAKES

**For all brake system repair and service procedures not detailed below, please refer to "Brakes" in the Unit Repair section.**

## Master Cylinder

### REMOVAL & INSTALLATION

1. Disconnect the negative battery cable. On the Starion, Mirage with turbocharger and Precis, the brake fluid reservoir is separate from the master cylinder. Disconnect the hoses at the master cylinder and plug them or drain the fluid into a container.
2. Disconnect the electrical connector for the fluid level sensor. Remove the proportioning valve bracket, if so equipped.
3. Disconnect all the brake tubes. Remove the nuts and lockwashers attaching the master cylinder to the booster. Remove the master cylinder from the vehicle.
4. Install the reverse order, torquing the attaching nuts to 6–9 ft. lbs. Refill the reservoirs with approved, new fluid and bleed the system thoroughly.

## Power Brake Booster

### REMOVAL & INSTALLATION

1. Disconnect the negative battery cable. Disconnect the vacuum supply line from the brake booster.
2. Remove the master cylinder. It may be possible to position the master cylinder out of the way rather then disconnect the fluid lines.
3. Disconnect the pushrod from the brake pedal.
4. Remove the mounting bolts from the firewall. Remove the power brake booster.
5. Installation is the reverse of the removal procedure. Bleed the brake system.

## Disc Brake Pads

### REMOVAL & INSTALLATION

1. Raise the vehicle and support it safely.
2. Remove the wheel and tire assembly.
3. Disconnect the brake hose from the caliper.
4. Remove the bolts connecting the caliper and support to the backing plate. Slide the caliper off of the rotor.
5. Remove the pads from the caliper support.
6. Remove and check the rotor.

**To Install**

7. Install the rotor.
8. Install the caliper support with the new pads in position, on the knuckle.
9. Use a piston expander to expand the piston and install the caliper body.
10. Connect the brake hose to the caliper.
11. Fill the system with new brake fluid and bleed the system.
12. Lower the vehicle and install the tire and wheel assembly.

## Brake Shoes

### REMOVAL & INSTALLATION

1. Raise the vehicle and support it safely.
2. Remove the wheel and tire assembly.
3. Remove the brake drum.
4. Remove the shoe-to-strut spring and the shoe-to-shoe spring.
5. Remove the shoe holddown spring and the shoe retainer spring.
6. Remove the leading shoe.
7. Remove the parking brake cable from the lever and then remove the trailing shoe.
8. Install in the reverse order of removal.

## Wheel Cylinder

### REMOVAL & INSTALLATION

1. Raise and support the rear of the vehicle. Remove the wheel and brake drum. Remove the brake shoes.
2. Place a container under the brake backing plate to catch the brake fluid that will run out of the wheel cylinder.
3. Disconnect the brake line and remove the cylinder mounting bolts. Remove the cylinder from the backing plate.
4. Installation is the reverse of the removal procedure. Bleed the brake system.

## Parking Brake Cable

### ADJUSTMENT

1. Remove the center console, rear seat and rear console box if necessary.
2. Apply the parking brake and count the number of clicks (notches) until fully applied.
3. Proper adjustment is 5–7 notches for front wheel drive and 4–5 for rear wheel drive models.
4. Adjust the parking lever stroke by turning the cable adjusting nut after attempting to tighten by applying the brake lever several times to adjust the rear brakes.
5. Raise the rear of the vehicle and safely support. Release the parking brake and turn the rear wheels to confirm that the brakes are not dragging.

### REMOVAL & INSTALLATION

#### *Front Wheel Drive*

1. Raise rear of vehicle and support it safely.
2. Remove the console and rear seat. Disconnect the brake cable at the parking brake lever (brakes released). Remove the cable clamps inside the driver's compartment (2 bolts). Disconnect the clamps on the rear suspension arm.
3. Remove the rear brake drums and the brake shoe assemblies. Disconnect the parking brake cable from the lever on the trailing (rear) brake shoe by removing the snapring. Remove the brake cables.
4. Installation is the reverse of removal. Make sure the grommets through which the cables pass into the passenger compartment are installed with the concave side outward. Adjust the parking brake. Adjust the switch so the indicator light comes on when the parking brake lever is pulled 1 notch.

#### *Rear Wheel Drive*

1. As required, remove the console and rear seat.

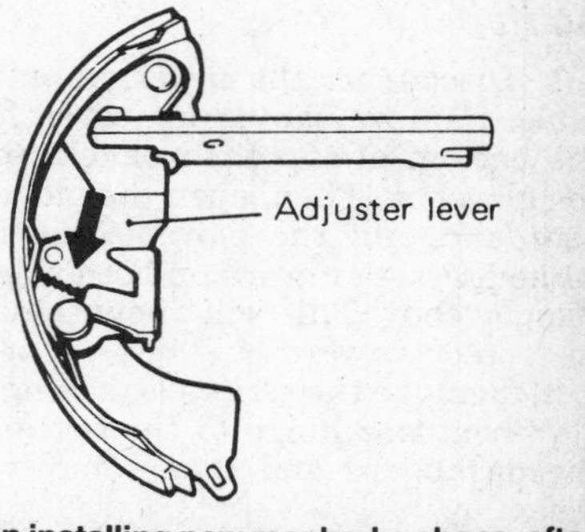


**When installing new rear brake shoes, after the springs are installed, move the adjuster level all the way back, as shown**

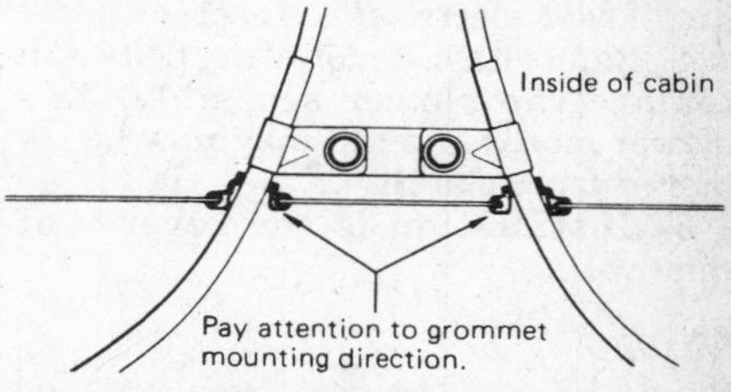


**Install the grommets through which the parking brake cable passes into the car in the direction shown**

2. Raise and support the rear of the vehicle.
3. Disconnect all clevis pin connecting and the cable ends.
4. Pull the cable through the floor.
5. Install in reverse order.
6. Adjust the cable. Apply sealer to the edge of the grommet at the floor opening. Check the parking brake indicator, the light should come on when the brake is applied 1 notch.

# CHASSIS ELECTRICAL

## Heater Blower Motor

### REMOVAL & INSTALLATION

#### *Cordia and Tredia*

1. Disconnect the negative battery cable. Unscrew the 1 attaching bolt and remove the lower cover from under the right side of the instrument panel. Remove the mounting screws at the front and remove the glovebox. Remove the cowl side trim.
2. Disconnect the air selector control wire. Disconnect the discharge duct at the blower.
3. Disconnect the electrical connector. Remove the 4 mounting bolts and remove the blower assembly.
4. Installation is the reverse of the removal procedure.

#### *Starion*

1. Disconnect the negative battery cable. Remove the under cover from the bottom of the dash panel, under the glovebox. Then, open the glovebox door and pull the glovebox forward while pressing inward on both sides of the glovebox. This will allow the door to drop downward.
2. Remove the screws attaching the glovebox door hinge to the bottom of the dashboard and then remove the assembly.
3. Disconnect the fresh air/recirculated air changeover cable from the blower housing. Disconnect the blower electrical connector.
4. Remove the 3 mounting bolts and remove the blower assembly. The blower motor and fan may now be removed from the case.
5. Installation is the reverse of removal.

#### *Mirage*

1. Disconnect the negative battery cable. Open the glovebox door, release the hinges and remove the glovebox.
2. Remove the 4 Phillips screws and remove the parcel tray.
3. Disconnect the recirculation/fresh air changeover control wire. Disconnect the electrical connector. Disconnect the duct leading out of the blower assembly.
4. Remove the 3 mounting bolts and remove the blower assembly. You can now remove the blower motor mounting screws and remove the motor from the blower assembly.
5. Installation is the reverse of the removal procedure.

#### *Galant and Sigma*

1. Disconnect the negative battery cable. Remove the screw covers and then remove the 2 screws from the under cover (located at the bottom of the instrument panel on the right side). Remove the under cover.
2. Remove the installation screws and remove the instrument under cover (located under the steering column). Then, remove the underframe installation screws located under that cover and remove the passenger side underframe.
3. Remove the 2 stops from the bottom of the glovebox at the front. Then, remove the glovebox installation screws and remove the glovebox. Remove the duct leading into the blower unit, which is accessible through the glovebox door.
4. Remove the 4 mounting bolts and remove the blower assembly. Disconnect the electrical connector and the inside/outside air changeover control vacuum hose before pulling the unit all the way out.
5. Installation is the reverse of removal.

#### *Precis*

**NOTE: To remove either the blower or core, the heater case must be removed.**

1. Disconnect the battery ground.
2. Place the control in the **HOT** position.
3. Drain the cooling system.
4. Remove the heater hoses from the core tubes.
5. Remove the lower instrument panel section.
6. Remove the center console.
7. Disconnect the ducts at the heater case.
8. Disconnect the heater control cable at the case.
9. If equipped with air conditioning, discharge the system and remove the evaporator.
10. Unbolt and remove the heater case.
11. Installation is the reverse of removal. Adjust the control cable. If, necessary, charge the refrigerant system.

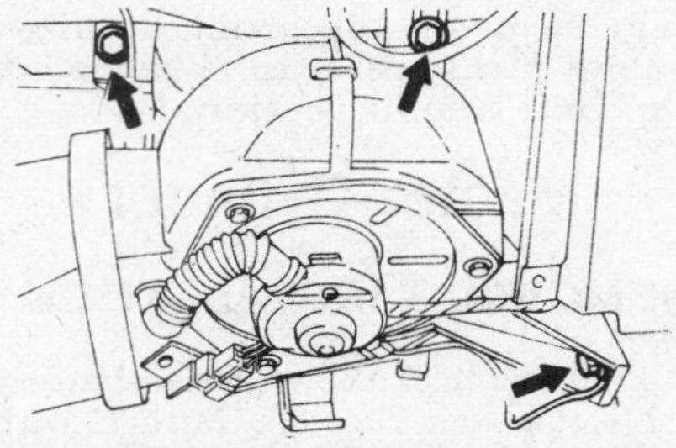

Remove the arrowed bolts and remove the blower motor (Cordia and Tredia)

## Heater Core

### REMOVAL & INSTALLATION

#### *Cordia, Tredia, Mirage, Galant and Sigma*

1. Disconnect the battery ground cable.
2. Set the heater control lever to **WARM**.
3. Drain the cooling system.
4. Remove the instrument panel.
5. Remove the duct from between the heater unit and the blower case.
6. Disconnect the coolant hoses at the heater case.
7. Unbolt and remove the heater case.
8. Remove the hose and pipe clamps and remove the water valve, if equipped.
9. Remove the core from the case.
10. Set the mixing damper to the closed position and, with the damper in that position, install the rod so that the water valve is fully closed.
11. Place the damper lever in the **VENT** position and adjust the linkage so that the **FOOT/DEF** damper opens to the **DEF** side and the **VENT** damper is level with the separator.
12. Install the hoses. They are marked for flow direction.
13. The remainder of assembly is the reverse of disassembly.

#### *Starion*

1. Drain the cooling system and disconnect the negative battery cable.
2. Place the heater control in the **WARM** position.
3. Disconnect the heater hose at the engine firewall.
4. Remove the instrument panel and the center console.
5. Remove the center ventilator duct, defroster duct and lap duct.

6. Remove the center reinforcement and heater control assembly.
7. Remove the heater assembly mounting bolts and the heater assembly.
8. Remove the heater core.
9. Install in reverse order.

## Radio

### REMOVAL & INSTALLATION

#### Cordia and Tredia

1. Disconnect the negative battery cable. Pry the radio cover panel out with a thin object. Pry from the right on Cordia and the left on Tredia.
2. Remove the mounting screws, disconnect the antenna and electrical connector and remove the radio.
3. Installation is the reverse of removal.

#### Starion

1. Disconnect the negative battery cable. Insert a flat tool between the tray in the rear console and its cover and twist it to release the tray. Then, remove it. Now, remove the side console cover screws. Push the cover downward and slightly forward to release it and then remove it.
2. Remove the radio mounting screws from the center reinforcement. Put the shift lever into fourth gear and then unscrew and remove the gearshift knob.
3. Pull the front console box slightly to the rear. Then, disconnect the electrical connector and antenna at the radio. Now, pull the front console box out toward the passenger seat.
4. Now, remove the 4 Phillips screws and then remove the radio panel. Remove the radio and bracket as a assembly. Remove the bracket from the radio.
5. Installation is the reverse of removal.

#### Mirage

1. Disconnect negative battery cable. Remove the panel that surrounds the parking brake. Remove the ashtray.
2. Remove the 2 console mounting screws from each side, 2 near the hand brake and 1 at the rear of the ashtray. Then, remove the console.
3. Remove the 4 mounting screws from the radio bracket, and remove the radio and bracket as an assembly. Now, separate the radio and bracket. Note that the radio fuses are located behind the radio and are now accessible.
4. Installation is the reverse of removal.

#### Galant and Sigma

1. Disconnect the negative battery cable. Use a suitable tool to pry on the lower part of the radio panel and remove it. Then, remove the 4 Phillips screws from the sides of the radio (and tape player) mounting bracket and pull the units out. Disconnect the electrical connectors and the antenna and then remove the unit.
2. Installation is the reverse of the removal procedure.

#### Precis

1. Disconnect the negative battery cable.
2. Remove the trim cover retaining screws. Remove the trim cover.
3. Remove the radio retaining screws. Remove the radio support brace, if equipped.
4. Pull the radio forward and disconnect the electrical connectors and the antenna wire. Remove the radio from the vehicle.
5. Installation is the reverse of the removal procedure.

## Windshield Wiper Switch

### REMOVAL & INSTALLATION

#### Except Galant, Mirage and Sigma

1. Disconnect the negative battery cable.
2. Remove the steering column lower trim panel.
3. Remove the steering wheel. Remove the steering column cable band.
4. Disconnect the electrical connections from the switch assembly.
5. Remove the switch retaining screws. Remove the switch assembly from the vehicle.
6. Installation is the reverse of the removal procedure.

#### Galant, Mirage and Sigma

1. Disconnect the negative battery cable.
2. If equipped with tilt wheel lower the steering wheel to its lowest position.
3. Remove the steering wheel. Remove the steering column lower trim panel. Remove the steering column upper trim panel. Remove the steering column cable band.
4. Disconnect the electrical connections from the switch assembly.
5. Remove the switch retaining screws. Remove the switch assembly from the vehicle.
6. Installation is the reverse of the removal procedure.

## Windshield Wiper Motor

### REMOVAL & INSTALLATION

#### Cordia and Tredia

1. Remove the wiper blade and arm assembly.
2. Remove the cover from the access hole or the deck panel, guide panel and garnish depending on mode.
3. Remove the wiper drive mounting bolts at the arm pivots. On the Tredia, remove the washer nozzle.
4. Loosen the wiper motor mounting bolts. Disconnect the wiper motor and linkage and remove. Install in reverse order.

#### Starion

1. Remove the wiper arms. Remove the pivot shaft mounting nuts and washers and push the pivot shafts into the area behind the cowl.
2. Remove the cover from the access hole for the wiper motor on the right side of the cowl, underneath the hood. Then, remove the motor mounting bolts. Pull the motor into the best possible position for access and use a flat suitable tool to pry the linkage off the motor crank arm.
3. If the linkage is being replaced, it can be worked out of the cowl at this time. If the motor is being replaced, matchmark the position of the crank arm of the motor shaft of the new motor and then remove the nut and crank arm, transferring both to the new motor.
4. Installation is the reverse of removal. Make sure the wiper blades stop about 0.5 in. from the lower windshield molding. Torque the wiper arm attaching nuts to 7–12 ft. lbs.

#### Mirage and Precis

1. Remove the wiper ar{ms. Remove the air inlet and cowl front center trim panels. Remove the 3 pivot shaft mounting nuts and push the pivot shafts into the area under the cowl.
2. Remove the motor mounting bolts. Pull the motor into the best possible position for access and use a flat suitable tool to pry the linkage off the motor crank arm. Remove the motor and then the linkage.
3. If the motor is being replaced, matchmark the position of the crank arm of the motor shaft of the new motor and then remove the nut and crank arm, transferring both to the new motor.
4. Installation is the reverse of removal. Torque the pivot shaft nuts to 4.3–5.8 ft. lbs. Position the wiper arms so the blades are about 0.6 in. above

the lower windshield molding on the driver's side and 0.8 in. above it on the passenger's side. Torque the wiper arm mounting nuts to 7.2–12 ft. lbs. Make sure the wiper motor is securely grounded.

### *Galant and Sigma*

1. Remove the wiper arms. Remove the front deck and inlet trim.
2. Then, remove the 3 mounting bolts for each pivot shaft and push the shafts into the area behind the panel. Disconnect the electrical connector. Loosen and remove the 3 motor mounting bolts and then remove the motor and linkage as an assembly.
3. If the motor is being replaced, matchmark the relationship between linkage and motor, as it is critical. If the linkage only is being replaced, pry the connection off the end of the motor crank arm with a flat suitable tool.
4. Install in reverse order. Make sure the wiper arms sit in their original positions when in parked position. Make sure the wiper motor is securely grounded.

# Instrument Cluster

## REMOVAL & INSTALLATION

### *Cordia and Tredia*

1. Disconnect the negative battery cable.
2. Remove the screws at the top of the instrument cluster trim panel. Remove the trim panel.
3. Disconnect the speedometer cable from the back of the speedometer.
4. Remove the cluster mounting screws and pull the cluster forward.
5. Disconnect the electrical connectors and remove the cluster. Install in reverse order.

### *Starion*

1. Disconnect the negative battery cable.
2. Remove the meter trim hood mounting screws. Pull out and down on the side of the hood.
3. Disconnect the plug connectors on both sides of the cluster.
4. Remove the cluster mounting screws and nuts. Pull the lower sides of the cluster up and disconnect the speedometer cable.
5. Disconnect the plug connectors at the rear of the cluster and remove the cluster. Install in reverse order.

### *Mirage*

1. Disconnect the negative battery cable. Remove the 2 meter hood attaching screws, located at the bottom and tile the lower meter hood outward. Pull the hood downward to release the locking tangs at the top and remove it.
2. Remove the 4 meter assembly mounting screws (2 at top and 2 at the bottom) and pull the unit outward. Disconnect the speedometer cable and all connectors and remove the unit.
3. Installation is the reverse of removal.

### *Galant and Sigma*

1. Disconnect the negative battery cable. Remove the 2 meter hood mounting screw covers located along the bottom of the hood using a suitable tool. Then, remove the screws and pull off the hood.
2. Remove the 4 meter assembly mounting screws (2 on each side), pull the assembly outward slightly and then disconnect the electrical connectors, speedometer cable and adapter. Remove the assembly.
3. Installation is the reverse of removal.

# Headlight Switch

## REMOVAL & INSTALLATION

### *Except Galant, Mirage and Sigma*

1. Disconnect the negative battery cable.
2. Remove the steering column lower trim panel.
3. Remove the steering wheel. Remove the steering column cable band.
4. Disconnect the electrical connections from the switch assembly.
5. Remove the switch retaining screws. Remove the switch assembly from the vehicle.
6. Installation is the reverse of the removal procedure.

### *Galant, Mirage and Sigma*

1. Disconnect the negative battery cable.
2. If equipped with tilt wheel lower the steering wheel to its lowest position.
3. Remove the steering wheel. Remove the steering column lower trim panel. Remove the steering column upper trim panel. Remove the steering column cable band.
4. Disconnect the electrical connections from the switch assembly.
5. Remove the switch retaining screws. Remove the switch assembly from the vehicle.
6. Installation is the reverse of the removal procedure.

# Stoplight Switch

## REMOVAL & INSTALLATION

1. Disconnect the negative battery cable.
2. Remove the trim panel from underneath of the brake pedal, if equipped.
3. Disconnect the electrical and vacuum connections from the switch assembly.
4. Remove the switch assembly from the vehicle.
5. Installation is the reverse of the removal procedure.

# Fuses and Circuit Breakers

## LOCATION

The fuse box on every model is located under the instrument panel on the left (driver's side) above the cowl side trim. On the Galant and most of the later models, there are also secondary fuses in the relay box in the engine compartment. The sunroof fuse is located in the electrical harness for the roof circuit at the extreme right side of the dashboard, directly behind the right windshield pillar. The radio fuse is located behind the radio and is accessible after the radio is removed.

There is a checker knob in the fuse box that make it easy to find a blown fuse. Slide the check knob until it is lined up with the fuse you want to check. Turn on the ignition switch and lighting switch and the light will cone on, indicating the fuse is functioning.

# Nissan/Datsun 13

## 200SX, 240SX, 280ZX, 300ZX, 810, Maxima, Pulsar, Sentra, Stanza

# SERIAL NUMBER IDENTIFICATION

## Vehicle Identification Plate

The vehicle identification plate is attached to the hood ledge or the firewall. The VIN plate is mounted on the front of the left strut housing on the 300ZX and on the right side of the firewall, behind the battery, on the 280ZX. The identification plate gives the vehicle model, engine displacement in cc., SAE horsepower rating, wheelbase, engine number and chassis number.

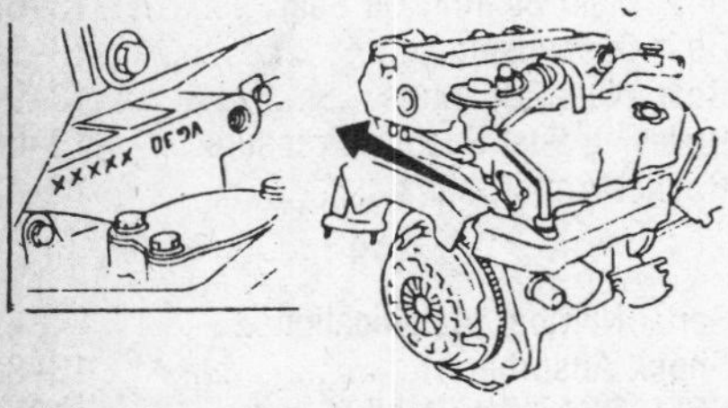

Engine identification number location–VG30E and VG30ET

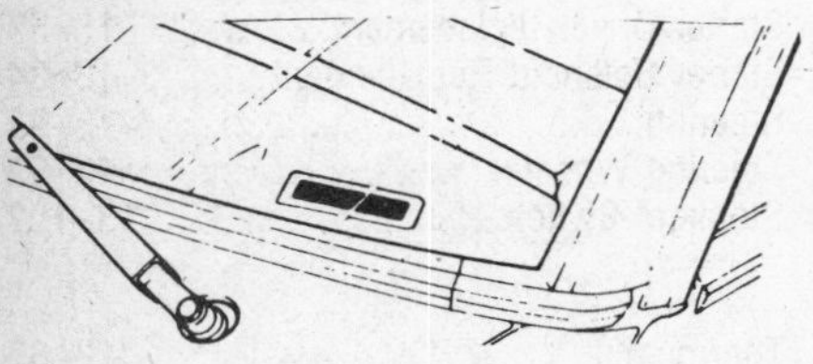

VIN location

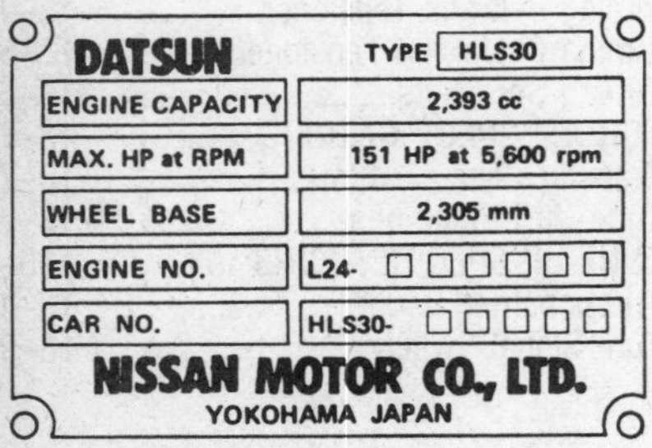

DATSUN
TYPE HLS30
ENGINE CAPACITY
2,393 cc
MAX. HP at RPM
151 HP at 5,600 rpm
WHEEL BASE
2,305 mm
ENGINE NO.
L24- □□□□□□
CAR NO.
HLS30- □□□□□
NISSAN MOTOR CO., LTD.
YOKOHAMA JAPAN


Vehicle identification plate

## Engine Number

The engine number is stamped on the right side top edge of the cylinder block, except on the 1984–90 200SX, 300ZX and 1985–90 Maxima. On the 300ZX, the number is stamped on the right rear edge of the right cylinder bank, looking from driver side seat. On the Maxima, the number can be found on the driver's side edge of the front cylinder bank, looking from driver side seat. On the 1984–88 200SX (CA20E and CA18ET engines), the number is stamped on the left rear edge of the block, next to the bell housing, looking from driver side seat. The engine serial number is preceded by the engine model code.

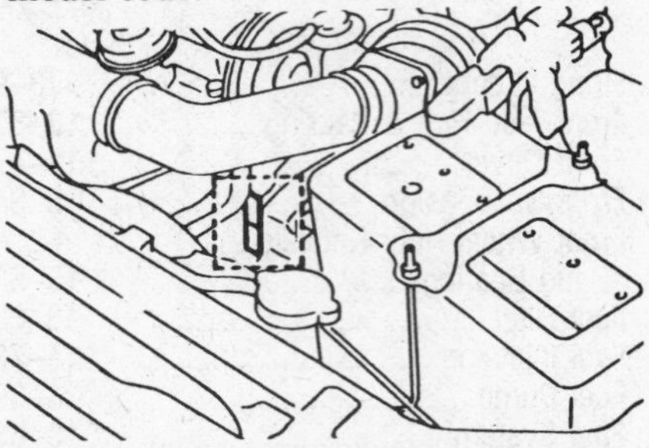

CD17 1.7L diesel engine serial number location

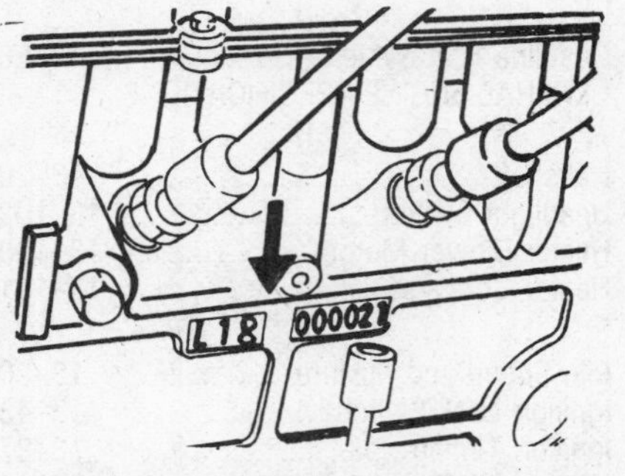


Engine serial and code number, all except V6, CD17 and CA20/CA18ET

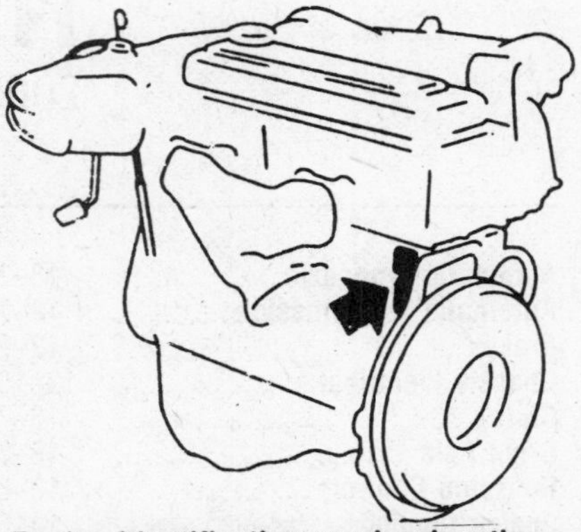

Engine identification number location–CA18ET, CA20E, E16i, GA16i, CA16DE, CA18DE

## Chassis Number

The chassis number is on the firewall under the hood on all models. On the 1989–90 240SX, the chassis number plate is affixed to the firewall next to the wiper motor on the passenger's side of the engine compartment. All vehicles also have the chassis number (also known as the vehicle identification number) on a plate attached to the top of the instrument panel on the driver's side, visible through the windshield. The chassis serial number is preceded by the model designation. All models have an Emission Control information label on the firewall or on the underside of the hood.

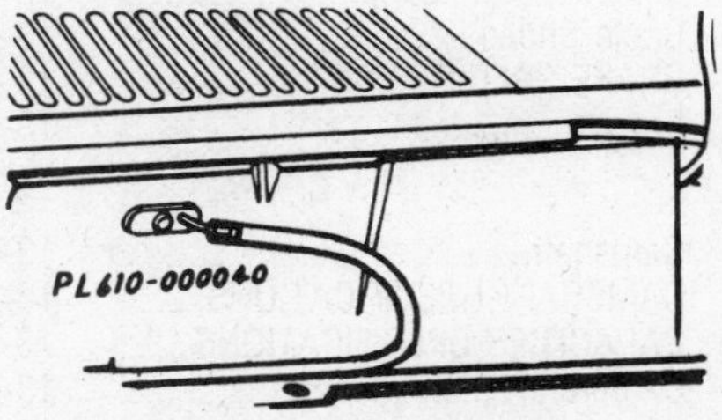


Chassis number location

## ENGINE IDENTIFICATION

| Year | Model | Engine Displacement cu. in. (cc/liter) | Engine Series Identification | No. of Cylinders | Engine Type |
|---|---|---|---|---|---|
| 1983 | 810 | 146 (2393/2.4) | L24E | 6 | SOHC |
| | 200SX | 133.4 (2181/2.2) | Z22, Z22E | 4 | SOHC |
| | 280ZX | 168 (2753/2.8) | L28E | 6 | SOHC |
| | | 168 (2753/2.8) | L28ET (Turbo) | 6 | SOHC |
| | Pulsar | 97.4 (1597/1.6) | E16 | 4 | SOHC |
| | Sentra | 90.8 (1488/1.5) | E15 | 4 | SOHC |
| | | 97.4 (1597/1.6) | E16 | 4 | SOHC |

## ENGINE IDENTIFICATION

| Year | Model | Engine Displacement cu. in. (cc/liter) | Engine Series Identification | No. of Cylinders | Engine Type |
|---|---|---|---|---|---|
| 1983 | Stanza | 120.4 (1974/2.0) | CA20 | 4 | SOHC |
| 1984 | 200SX | 120.4 (1974/2.0) | CA20E | 4 | SOHC |
| | | 110.3 (1809/1.8) | CA18ET (Turbo) | 4 | SOHC |
| | 300ZX | 180.6 (2960/3.0) | VG30E | V6 | SOHC |
| | | 180.6 (2960/3.0) | VG30ET (Turbo) | V6 | SOHC |
| | Maxima | 146 (2393/2.4) | L24E | 6 | SOHC |
| | Pulsar | 90.8 (1488/1.5) | E15ET (Turbo) | 4 | SOHC |
| | | 97.4 (1597/1.6) | E16S | 4 | SOHC |
| | Sentra | 97.4 (1597/1.6) | E16, E16S | 4 | SOHC |
| | Stanza | 120.4 (1974/2.0) | CA20S, CA20E | 4 | SOHC |
| 1985 | 200SX | 120.4 (1974/2.0) | CA20E | 4 | SOHC |
| | | 110.3 (1809/1.8) | CA18ET (Turbo) | 4 | SOHC |
| | 300ZX | 180.6 (2960/3.0) | VG30E | V6 | SOHC |
| | | 180.6 (2960/3.0) | VG30ET (Turbo) | V6 | SOHC |
| | Maxima | 180.6 (2960/3.0) | VG30E | V6 | SOHC |
| | Pulsar | 90.8 (1488/1.5) | E15ET (Turbo) | 4 | SOHC |
| | | 97.4 (1597/1.6) | E16S | 4 | SOHC |
| | Sentra | 97.4 (1597/1.6) | E16, E16S | 4 | SOHC |
| | Stanza | 120.4 (1974/2.0) | CA20S, CA20E | 4 | SOHC |
| 1986 | 200SX | 120.4 (1974/2.0) | CA20E | 4 | SOHC |
| | | 110.3 (1809/1.8) | CA18ET (Turbo) | 4 | SOHC |
| | 300ZX | 180.6 (2960/3.0) | VG30E | V6 | SOHC |
| | | 180.6 (2960/3.0) | VG30ET (Turbo) | V6 | SOHC |
| | Maxima | 180.6 (2960/3.0) | VG30E | V6 | SOHC |
| | Pulsar | 97.4 (1597/1.6) | E16S | 4 | SOHC |
| | Sentra | 97.4 (1597/1.6) | E16, E16S | 4 | SOHC |
| | Stanza | 120.4 (1974/2.0) | CA20E | 4 | SOHC |
| 1987 | 200SX | 110.3 (1809/1.8) | CA18ET (Turbo) | 4 | SOHC |
| | | 120.4 (1974/2.0) | CA20E | 4 | SOHC |
| | | 180.6 (2960/3.0) | VG30E | V6 | SOHC |
| | 300ZX | 180.6 (2960/3.0) | VG30E | V6 | SOHC |
| | | 180.6 (2960/3.0) | VG30ET (Turbo) | V6 | SOHC |
| | Maxima | 180.6 (2960/3.0) | VG30E | V6 | SOHC |
| | Pulsar | 97.4 (1597/1.6) | E16i | 4 | SOHC |
| | | 97.5 (1598/1.6) | CA16DE | 4 | DOHC |
| | Sentra | 97.4 (1597/1.6) | E16S, E16i | 4 | SOHC |
| | Stanza | 120.4 (1974/2.0) | CA20E | 4 | SOHC |
| 1988 | 200SX | 120.4 (1974/2.0) | CA20E | 4 | SOHC |
| | | 180.6 (2960/3.0) | VG30E | V6 | SOHC |
| | 300SX | 180.6 (2960/3.0) | VG30E | V6 | SOHC |
| | | 180.6 (2960/3.0) | VG30ET (Turbo) | V6 | SOHC |

## ENGINE IDENTIFICATION

| Year | Model | Engine Displacement cu. in. (cc/liter) | Engine Series Identification | No. of Cylinders | Engine Type |
|---|---|---|---|---|---|
| 1988 | Maxima | 180.6 (2690/3.0) | VG30E | V6 | SOHC |
| | Pulsar | 97.4 (1597/1.6) | E16i | 4 | SOHC |
| | | 110.3 (1809/1.8) | CA18DE | 4 | DOHC |
| | Sentra | 97.4 (1597/1.6) | E16i | 4 | SOHC |
| | Stanza | 120.4 (1974/2.0) | CA20E | 4 | SOHC |
| 1989-90 | 240SX | 145.6 (2389/2.4) | KA24E | 4 | SOHC |
| | 300ZX | 180.6 (2960/3.0) | VG30E | V6 | SOHC |
| | | 180.6 (2960/3.0) | VG30ET (Turbo) | V6 | SOHC |
| | Maxima | 180.6 (2690/3.0) | VG30E | V6 | SOHC |
| | Pulsar | 97.4 (1597/1.6) | GA16i | 4 | SOHC |
| | | 110.3 (1809/1.8) | CA18DE | 4 | DOHC |
| | Sentra | 97.4 (1597/1.6) | GA16i | 4 | SOHC |
| | Stanza | 120.4 (1974/2.0) | CA20E | 4 | SOHC |

OHV—Pushrod-activated overhead valves SOHC—Single overhead camshaft DOHC—Double overhead camshaft

## GENERAL ENGINE SPECIFICATIONS

| Year | Model | Engine Displacement cu. in. (cc) | Fuel System Type | Net Horsepower @ rpm | Net Torque @ rpm (ft. lbs.) | Bore × Stroke (in.) | Compression Ratio | Oil Pressure @ rpm |
|---|---|---|---|---|---|---|---|---|
| 1983 | 810 | 146 (2393) | EFI | 120 @ 5200 | 134 @ 2800 | 3.27 × 2.90 | 8.9:1 | 43 @ 2000 |
| | 200SX | 133.4 (2181) | EFI | 102 @ 5200 | 129 @ 2800 | 3.43 × 3.62 | 8.5:1 | — |
| | 280ZX | 168 (2753) | EFI | 145 @ 5200 | 156 @ 4000 | 3.39 × 3.11 | 8.8:1 | 43 @ 2000 |
| | | 168 (2753) | EFI① | 180 @ 5600 | 202 @ 2800 | 3.39 × 3.11 | 7.4:1 | 43 @ 2000 |
| | Pulsar | 97.4 (1597) | 2 bbl | 69 @ 5200 | 93 @ 3200 | 2.99 × 3.46 | 9.4:1 | 43 @ 1700 |
| | Sentra | 90.8 (1488) | 2 bbl | 67 @ 5200 | 85 @ 3200 | 2.92 × 3.23 | 9.0:1 | 43 @ 1700 |
| | | 97.4 (1597) | 2 bbl | 69 @ 5200 | 93 @ 3200 | 2.99 × 3.46 | 9.4:1 | 43 @ 1700 |
| | Stanza | 120.4 (1974) | 2 bbl | 88 @ 5200 | 112 @ 2800 | 3.33 × 3.46 | 8.5:1 | 43 @ 2000 |
| 1984 | 200SX | 120.4 (1974) | EFI | 102 @ 5200 | 116 @ 3200 | 3.33 × 3.46 | 8.5:1 | 43 @ 2000 |
| | | 110.3 (1809) | EFI① | 120 @ 5200 | 134 @ 3200 | 3.27 × 3.29 | 8.0:1 | 43 @ 2000 |
| | 300ZX | 180.6 (2960) | EFI | 160 @ 5200 | 174 @ 4000 | 3.43 × 3.27 | 9.0:1 | 43 @ 2000 |
| | | 180.6 (2960) | EFI① | 200 @ 5200 | 227 @ 3600 | 3.43 × 3.27 | 7.8:1 | 43 @ 2000 |
| | Maxima | 146 (2393) | EFI | 120 @ 5200 | 134 @ 2800 | 3.27 × 2.90 | 8.9:1 | 43 @ 2000 |
| | Pulsar | 90.8 (1488) | EFI① | 100 @ 5200 | 152 @ 3200 | 2.92 × 3.23 | 7.8:1 | 43 @ 1700 |
| | | 97.4 (1597) | 2 bbl | 69 @ 5200 | 93 @ 3200 | 2.99 × 3.46 | 9.4:1 | 43 @ 1700 |
| | Sentra | 97.4 (1597) | 2 bbl | 69 @ 5200 | 93 @ 3200 | 2.99 × 3.46 | 9.4:1 | 43 @ 1700 |
| | Stanza | 120.4 (1974) | 2 bbl | 88 @ 5200 | 112 @ 2800 | 3.33 × 3.46 | 8.5:1 | 43 @ 2000 |
| | | 120.4 (1974) | EFI | 97 @ 5200 | 114 @ 3200 | 3.33 × 3.46 | 8.5:1 | 43 @ 2000 |
| 1985 | 200SX | 120.4 (1974) | EFI | 102 @ 5200 | 116 @ 3200 | 3.33 × 3.46 | 8.5:1 | 43 @ 2000 |
| | | 110.3 (1809) | EFI① | 120 @ 5200 | 134 @ 3200 | 3.27 × 3.29 | 8.0:1 | 43 @ 2000 |
| | 300ZX | 180.6 (2960) | EFI | 160 @ 5200 | 174 @ 4000 | 3.43 × 3.27 | 9.0:1 | 43 @ 2000 |
| | | 180.6 (2960) | EFI① | 200 @ 5200 | 227 @ 3600 | 3.43 × 3.27 | 7.8:1 | 43 @ 2000 |
| | Maxima | 180.6 (2960) | EFI | 152 @ 5200 | 167 @ 3600 | 3.43 × 3.27 | 9.0:1 | 43 @ 2000 |

## GENERAL ENGINE SPECIFICATIONS

| Year | Model | Engine Displacement cu. in. (cc) | Fuel System Type | Net Horsepower @ rpm | Net Torque @ rpm (ft. lbs.) | Bore × Stroke (in.) | Com-pression Ratio | Oil Pressure @ rpm |
|---|---|---|---|---|---|---|---|---|
| 1985 | Pulsar | 90.8 (1488) | EFI① | 100 @ 5200 | 152 @ 3200 | 2.92 × 3.23 | 7.8:1 | 43 @ 1700 |
| | | 97.4 (1597) | 2 bbl | 69 @ 5200 | 93 @ 3200 | 2.99 × 3.46 | 9.4:1 | 43 @ 1700 |
| | Sentra | 97.4 (1597) | 2 bbl | 69 @ 5200 | 93 @ 3200 | 2.99 × 3.46 | 9.4:1 | 43 @ 1700 |
| | Stanza | 120.4 (1974) | 2 bbl | 88 @ 5200 | 112 @ 2800 | 3.33 × 3.46 | 8.5:1 | 43 @ 2000 |
| | | 120.4 (1974) | EFI | 97 @ 5200 | 114 @ 3200 | 3.33 × 3.46 | 8.5:1 | 43 @ 2000 |
| 1986 | 200SX | 120.4 (1974) | EFI | 102 @ 5200 | 116 @ 3200 | 3.33 × 3.46 | 8.5:1 | 43 @ 2000 |
| | | 110.3 (1809) | EFI① | 120 @ 5200 | 134 @ 3200 | 3.27 × 3.29 | 8.0:1 | 43 @ 2000 |
| | 300ZX | 180.6 (2960) | EFI | 160 @ 5200 | 174 @ 4000 | 3.43 × 3.27 | 9.0:1 | 43 @ 2000 |
| | | 180.6 (2960) | EFI① | 200 @ 5200 | 227 @ 3600 | 3.43 × 3.27 | 7.8:1 | 43 @ 2000 |
| | Maxima | 180.6 (2960) | EFI | 152 @ 5200 | 167 @ 3600 | 3.43 × 3.27 | 9.0:1 | 43 @ 2000 |
| | Pulsar | 97.4 (1597) | 2 bbl | 69 @ 5200 | 93 @ 3200 | 2.99 × 3.46 | 9.4:1 | 43 @ 1700 |
| | Sentra | 97.4 (1597) | 2 bbl | 69 @ 5200 | 93 @ 3200 | 2.99 × 3.46 | 9.4:1 | 43 @ 1700 |
| | Stanza | 120.4 (1974) | 2 bbl | 88 @ 5200 | 112 @ 2800 | 3.33 × 3.46 | 8.5:1 | 43 @ 2000 |
| | | 120.4 (1974) | EFI | 97 @ 5200 | 114 @ 3200 | 3.33 × 3.46 | 8.5:1 | 43 @ 2000 |
| 1987 | 200SX | 120.4 (1974) | EFI | 102 @ 5200 | 116 @ 3200 | 3.33 × 3.46 | 8.5:1 | 43 @ 2000 |
| | | 110.3 (1809) | EFI① | 120 @ 5200 | 134 @ 3200 | 3.27 × 3.29 | 8.0:1 | 43 @ 2000 |
| | | 180.6 (2960) | EFI | 160 @ 5200 | 174 @ 4000 | 3.43 × 3.27 | 9.0:1 | 43 @ 2000 |
| | 300ZX | 180.6 (2960) | EFI | 160 @ 5200 | 174 @ 4000 | 3.43 × 3.27 | 9.0:1 | 43 @ 2000 |
| | | 180.6 (2960) | EFI① | 200 @ 5200 | 227 @ 3600 | 3.43 × 3.27 | 7.8:1 | 43 @ 2000 |
| | Maxima | 180.6 (2960) | EFI | 160 @ 5200 | 174 @ 4000 | 3.43 × 3.27 | 9.0:1 | 43 @ 2000 |
| | Pulsar | 97.4 (1597) | EFI | 70 @ 5000 | 94 @ 2800 | 2.99 × 3.46 | 9.4:1 | 43 @ 1700 |
| | | 97.5 (1598) | EFI | 113 @ 6400 | 99 @ 4800 | 3.07 × 3.29 | 10.0:1 | 67 @ 2000 |
| | Sentra | 97.4 (1597) | 2 bbl | 70 @ 5000 | 92 @ 2800 | 2.99 × 3.46 | 9.4:1 | 43 @ 1700 |
| | Stanza | 120.4 (1974) | EFI | 97 @ 5200 | 114 @ 3200 | 3.33 × 3.46 | 8.5:1 | 43 @ 2000 |
| 1988 | 200SX | 120.4 (1974) | EFI | 99 @ 5200 | 116 @ 2800 | 3.33 × 3.46 | 8.5:1 | 60.5@3200 |
| | | 180.6 (2960) | EFI | 165 @ 5200 | 168 @ 3600 | 3.43 × 3.27 | 9.0:1 | 59 @ 3200 |
| | 300ZX | 180.6 (2960) | EFI | 165 @ 5200 | 174 @ 3600 | 3.43 × 3.27 | 9.0:1 | 59 @ 3200 |
| | | 180.6 (2690) | EFI① | 205 @ 5200 | 227 @ 3600 | 3.43 × 3.27 | 8.3:1 | 58.5@3200 |
| | Maxima | 180.6 (2960) | EFI | 157 @ 5200 | 168 @ 3600 | 3.43 × 3.27 | 9.0:1 | 59 @ 3200 |
| | Pulsar | 97.4 (1597) | EFI | 70 @ 5000 | 94 @ 2800 | 2.99 × 3.46 | 9.4:1 | 64 @ 3200 |
| | | 110.3 (1809) | EFI | 125 @ 6400 | 115 @ 4800 | 3.27 × 3.29 | 10:01 | 67 @ 2000 |
| | Sentra | 97.4 (1597) | EFI | 70 @ 5000 | 94 @ 2800 | 2.99 × 3.46 | 9.4:1 | 64 @ 3000 |
| | Stanza | 120.4 (1974) | EFI | 97 @ 5200 | 114 @ 2800 | 3.33 × 3.46 | 8.5:1 | 58 @ 3000 |
| 1989-90 | 240SX | 145.6 (2389) | EFI | 140 @ 5600 | 152 @ 4400 | 3.50 × 3.78 | 9.1:1 | 65 @ 3000 |
| | 300ZX | 180.6 (2960) | EFI | 165 @ 5200 | 174 @ 4000 | 3.43 × 3.27 | 9.0:1 | 59 @ 3200 |
| | | 180.6 (2960) | EFI① | 205 @ 5200 | 227 @ 3600 | 3.43 × 3.27 | 8.3:1 | 58 @ 3200 |
| | Maxima | 180.6 (2690) | EFI | 160 @ 5200 | 182 @ 2800 | 3.43 × 3.27 | 9.0:1 | 59 @ 3200 |
| | Pulsar | 97.4 (1597) | EFI | 90 @ 6000 | 96 @ 3200 | 2.99 × 3.46 | 9.4:1 | 64 @ 3000 |
| | | 110.3 (1809) | EFI | 96 @ 3200 | 115 @ 4800 | 3.27 × 3.29 | 9.5:1 | 67 @ 2000 |
| | Sentra | 97.4 (1597) | EFI | 90 @ 6000 | 96 @ 3200 | 2.99 × 3.47 | 9.4:1 | 64 @ 3000 |
| | Stanza | 120.4 (1974) | EFI | 94 @ 5400 | 114 @ 2800 | 3.33 × 3.47 | 8.5:1 | 61 @ 3200 |

NA Not available ① Turbocharged

## GASOLINE ENGINE TUNE-UP SPECIFICATIONS

| Year | Model | Engine Displacement cu. in. (cc) | Spark Plugs Type | Spark Plugs Gap (in.) | Ignition Timing (deg.) MT | Ignition Timing (deg.) AT | Com-pression Pressure (psi) | Fuel Pump (psi) | Idle Speed (rpm) MT | Idle Speed (rpm) AT | Valve Clearance In. | Valve Clearance Ex. |
|---|---|---|---|---|---|---|---|---|---|---|---|---|
| 1983 | 810 | 146 (2393) | BP6ES | 0.041 | 8B | 8B | 171 | 36 | 700 | 650 | 0.010 | 0.012 |
| | 200SX | 133.4 (2181) | BPR6ES ① | 0.033 | 8B | 8B | 171 | 37 | 750 | 700 | 0.012 | 0.012 |
| | 280ZX | 168 (2753) | BPR6ES-11 | 0.041 | 8B | 8B | 171 | 36 | 700 | 700 | 0.010 | 0.012 |
| | | 168 (2753) ② | BPR6ES-11 | 0.041 | 24B | 24B | 171 | 36 | 650 | 650 | 0.010 | 0.012 |
| | Pulsar | 97.4 (1597) | BPR5ES-11 ④ | 0.041 | ⑤ | ⑤ | 181 | 3.8 | 750 | 650 | 0.011 | 0.011 |
| | Sentra | 90.8 (1488) | BPR5ES-11 | 0.041 | 2A | 2A | 181 | 3.8 | 750 | 750 | 0.011 | 0.011 |
| | | 97.4 (1597) | BPR5ES-11 ④ | 0.041 | ⑤ | ⑤ | 181 | 3.8 | 750 | 650 | 0.011 | 0.011 |
| | Stanza | 120.4 (1974) | BPR6ES-11 ③ | 0.041 | 0 | 0 | 171 | 3.8 | 750 | 700 | 0.012 | 0.012 |
| 1984 | 200SX | 120.4 (1974) | BCPR6ES-11 ⑥ | 0.041 | 0⑳ | 0 | 171 | 37 | 750 ⑦ | 700 ⑧ | 0.012 | 0.012 |
| | | 110.3 (1809) ② | BCPR6ES-11 ⑥ | 0.041 | 15B | 15B | 171 | 37 | 750 | 700 ⑧ | 0.012 | 0.012 |
| | 300ZX | 180.6 (2960) | BCPR6ES-11 | 0.041 | 20B | 20B | 173 | 37 | 700 | 650 | Hyd. | Hyd. |
| | | 180.6 (2960) ② | BCPR6E-11 | 0.041 | 20B | 20B | 165 | 37 | 700 | 650 | Hyd. | Hyd. |
| | Maxima | 146 (2393) | BPR6ES-11 | 0.041 | 8B | 8B | 171 | 36 | 700 | 650 | 0.010 | 0.012 |
| | Pulsar | 97.4 (1597) | BPR5ES-11 ④ | 0.041 | ⑤ | ⑤ | 181 | 3.8 | 750 | 650 | 0.011 | 0.011 |
| | | 90.8 (1488) ② | BPR6ES-11 | 0.041 | 15B | 15B | 181 | 37 | 750 | 650 | 0.011 | 0.011 |
| | Sentra | 97.4 (1597) | BPR5ES-11 ④ | 0.041 | ⑤ | ⑤ | 181 | 3.8 | 750 | 650 | 0.011 | 0.011 |
| | Stanza | 120.4 (1974) ⑨ | BPR6ES-11 ③ | 0.041 | 0 | 0 | 171 | 3.8 | 750 | 700 | 0.012 | 0.012 |
| | | 120.4 (1974) ⑩ | BCPR6ES-11 ⑥ | 0.041 | 0 | 0 | 171 | 37 | 750 ⑦ | 700 ⑧ | 0.012 | 0.012 |
| 1985 | 200SX | 120.4 (1974) | BCPR6ES-11 ⑥ | 0.041 | 4B | 0 | 171 | 37 | 750 | 700 | 0.012 | 0.012 |
| | | 110.3 (1809) ② | BCPR6ES-11 ⑥ | 0.041 | 15B | 15B | 171 | 37 | 750 | 750 ⑧ | 0.012 | 0.012 |
| | 300ZX | 180.6 (2960) | BCPR6ES-11 | 0.041 | 20B | 20B | 173 | 37 | 700 ⑧ | 700 ⑧ | Hyd. | Hyd. |
| | | 180.6 (2960) ② | BCPR6E-11 | 0.041 | 20B | 20B | 165 | 37 | 700 | 650 | Hyd. | Hyd. |
| | Maxima | 180.6 (2960) | BCPR6ES-11 | 0.041 | 20B | 20B | 173 | 37 | 700 ⑧ | 700 ⑧ | Hyd. | Hyd. |
| | Pulsar | 90.8 (1488) ② | BPR6ES-11 | 0.041 | 15B | 15B | 181 | 37 | 750 | 650 | 0.011 | 0.011 |

## GASOLINE ENGINE TUNE-UP SPECIFICATIONS

| Year | Model | Engine Displacement cu. in. (cc) | Spark Plugs Type | Spark Plugs Gap (in.) | Ignition Timing (deg.) MT | Ignition Timing (deg.) AT | Compression Pressure (psi) | Fuel Pump (psi) | Idle Speed (rpm) MT | Idle Speed (rpm) AT | Valve Clearance In. | Valve Clearance Ex. |
|---|---|---|---|---|---|---|---|---|---|---|---|---|
| 1985 | Pulsar | 97.4 (1597) | BPR5ES-11 ④ | 0.041 | ⑤ | ⑤ | 181 | 3.8 | 750 | 650 | 0.011 | 0.011 |
| | Sentra | 97.4 (1597) | BPR5ES-11 ④ | 0.041 | ⑤ | ⑤ | 181 | 3.8 | 750 | 650 | 0.011 | 0.011 |
| | Stanza | 120.4 (1974) ⑨ | BPR6ES-11 ③ | 0.041 | 0 | 0 | 171 | 3.8 | 650 | 650 | 0.012 | 0.012 |
| | | 120.4 (1974) ⑩ | BCPR6ES-11 ⑥ | 0.041 | 4B | 0 | 171 | 37 | 750 | 700 | 0.012 | 0.012 |
| 1986 | 200SX | 120.4 (1974) | BCPR6ES-11 ⑥ | 0.041 | 4B ⑪ | 0 ⑪ | 171 | 37 | 750 | 700 | 0.012 ⑰ | 0.012 ⑰ |
| | | 110.3 (1809) ② | BCPR6ES-11 ⑥ | 0.041 | 15B | 15B | 171 | 37 | 750 ⑧ | 750 ⑧ | 0.012 | 0.012 |
| | 300ZX | 180.6 (2960) | BCPR6ES-11 | 0.041 | 20B | 20B | 173 | 37 | 700 ⑧ | 700 ⑧ | Hyd. | Hyd. |
| | | 180.6 (2960) ② | BCPR6E-11 | 0.041 | 20B | 20B | 165 | 37 | 700 | 650 | Hyd. | Hyd. |
| | Maxima | 180.6 (2960) | BCPR6ES-11 | 0.041 | 20B | 20B | 173 | 37 | 700 ⑧ | 700 ⑧ | Hyd. | Hyd. |
| | Pulsar | 97.4 (1597) | BPR5ES-11 ④ | 0.041 | ⑪ | ⑪ | 181 | 3.8 | 800 | 650 | 0.011 | 0.011 |
| | Sentra | 97.4 (1597) | BPR5ES-11 ④ | 0.041 | ⑪ | ⑪ | 181 | 3.8 | 800 | 650 | 0.011 | 0.011 |
| | Stanza | 120.4 (1974) | BCPR6ES-11 ⑥ | 0.041 | 4B | 0 | 171 | 37 | 750 | 700 | 0.012 | 0.012 |
| 1987 | 200SX | 120.4 (1974) | BCPR6ES-11 ⑥ | 0.041 | 15B | 15B | 171 | 37 | 750 | 700 | Hyd. | Hyd. |
| | | 110.3 (1809) ② | BCPR5ES-11 ⑥ | 0.041 | 15B | 15B | 171 | 37 | 750 | — | 0.012 | 0.012 |
| | | 180.6 (2960) | BCPR6ES-11 | 0.041 | 20B | 20B | 173 | 37 | 700 | 700 | Hyd. | Hyd. |
| | 300ZX | 180.6 (2960) | BCPR6ES-11 | 0.041 | 20B | 20B | 173 | 37 | 700 | 650 | Hyd. | Hyd. |
| | | 180.6 (2960) ② | BCPR6E-11 | 0.041 | 15B | 15B | 165 | 37 | 700 | 650 | Hyd. | Hyd. |
| | Maxima | 180.6 (2960) | BCPR6ES-11 | 0.041 | 20B | 20B | 173 | 37 | 750 | 700 | Hyd. | Hyd. |
| | Pulsar | 97.4 (1597) | BPR5ES-11 | 0.041 | 7B | 7B | 181 | 14 | 800 | 700 | 0.011 | 0.011 |
| | | 97.5 (1598) | PFR6A-11 | NA | 15B | — | 199 | 28 | 800 | — | Hyd. | Hyd. |
| | Sentra | 97.4 (1597) | BPR5ES-11 | 0.041 | 7B | 7B | 181 | 14 ⑭ | 800 | 700 | 0.011 | 0.011 |
| | Stanza | 120.4 (1974) | BCPR6ES-11 ⑥ | 0.041 | 15B | 15B | 171 | 37 | 750 | 700 | Hyd. ⑲ | Hyd. ⑲ |
| 1988 | 200SX | 120.4 (1974) | BCPR6ES-11 ⑥ | 0.041 | 15B | 15B ⑰ | 171 | 36 ⑲ | 750 | 750 ⑰ | Hyd. | Hyd. |
| | | 180.6 (2690) | BCPR6ES-11 | 0.041 | 20B | 20B | 173 | 37 ⑳ | 700 | 700 ⑰ | Hyd. | Hyd. |

## GASOLINE ENGINE TUNE-UP SPECIFICATIONS

| Year | Model | Engine Displac000024 cu. in. (cc) | Spark Plugs Gap Type | (deg.) (in.) | Ignition Timing Pressure MT | AT | Com-pression Pump (psi) | Fuel (rpm) (psi) | Idle Speed Clearance MT | AT | Valve In. | Ex. |
|---|---|---|---|---|---|---|---|---|---|---|---|---|
| 1988 | 300ZX | 180.6 (2960) | BCPR6ES-11 | 0.041 | 15B | 20B | 173 | 37 ⑳ | 700 ⑰ | 700 ⑰ | Hyd. | Hyd. |
| | | 180.6 (2690) ② | BCPR6E-11 | 0.041 | 10B | 15B | 169 | 44 ⑳ | 700 | 650 ⑰ | Hyd. | Hyd. |
| | Maxima | 180.6 (2960) | BCPR6ES-11 | 0.041 | 15B | 20B | 173 | 30 ⑱ | 750 | 700 ⑰ | Hyd. | Hyd. |
| | Pulsar | 97.4 (1597) | BPR6ES-11 | 0.041 | 7B | 7B | 181 | 14 ⑱ | 800 | 700 ⑰ | 0.011 | 0.011 |
| | | 110.3 (1809) | PFR6A-11 | NA | 15B | 15B | 199 | 36 ㉑ | 800 | 700 ⑰ | Hyd. | Hyd. |
| | Sentra | 97.4 (1597) | BPR6ES-11 | 0.041 | 7B | 7B | 181 | 14 ㉒ | 800 | 700 ⑰ | 0.011 | 0.011 |
| | Stanza | 120.4 (1974) | BCPR6ES-11 ⑥ | 0.041 | 15B | 15B | 171 | 43.4 | 750 | 700 | Hyd. ⑲ | Hyd. ⑲ |
| 1989-90 | 240SX | 145.6 (2389) | ZFR5D-11 | 0.041 | 15B | 15B | 192 | 33 ㉑ | 750 | 750 | Hyd. | Hyd. |
| | 300ZX | 180.6 (2690) | BCPR6ES-11 | 0.041 | 15B | 20B | 173 | 37 ⑳ | 700 | 700 ⑰㉓ | Hyd. | Hyd. |
| | | 180.6 (2960) | BCPR6ES-11 | 0.041 | 10B | 15B | 169 | 44 ⑳ | 700 | 650 | Hyd. | Hyd. |
| | Maxima | 180.6 (2960) | BKRES-11 | 0.041 | 15B | 15B | 181 | 36 ㉑ | 750 | 700 | Hyd. | Hyd. |
| | Pulsar | 97.4 (1597) | BCPR5ES-11 | 0.041 | 7B | 7B ㉕ | 181 ㉕ | 43 ⑱ | 800 ⑰㉖ | 750 ⑰㉖ | 0.011 | 0.011 |
| | | 110.3 (1809) | PFR6A-11 | ㉔ | 15B | 15B | 199 | 36 ㉑ | 800 | 700 ⑰ | Hyd. | Hyd. |
| | Sentra | 97.4 (1597) | BCPR5ES-11 | 0.041 | 7B | 7B | 181 | 43 ⑱ | 800 ㉖ | 700 ⑰㉖ | Hyd. | Hyd. |
| | Stanza | 120.4 (1974) | BCPR5ES-11 | 0.041 | 15B | 15B | 171 | 37 ㉑ | 750 | 700 ⑰ | Hyd. | Hyd. |
| 1990 | SEE UNDERHOOD SPECIFICATIONS STICKER | | | | | | | | | | | |

**NOTE:** The Underhood Specifications sticker often reflects tune-up specification changes made in production. Sticker figures must be used if they disagree with those in this chart

MT Manual transmission
AT Automatic transmission
NA Not adjustable
A After Top Dead Center
B Before Top Dead Center
Hyd. Hydraulic valve lash adjusters
① Intake side; Exhaust side—BPR5ES
② Turbocharged model
③ Intake side; Exhaust side—BPR5ES-11
④ Canada—BPR5ES; Gap—0.033
⑤ 5A @ 750 rpm MT; Calif. & Can.
5A @ 650 rpm AT; Calif. & Can.
15B @ 800 rpm MT; 49 States
8B @ 650 rpm AT; 49 States
⑥ Intake side; Exhaust side—BCPR5ES-11
⑦ 49 States Stanza—800 rpm
⑧ High Altitude Models—680 rpm
⑨ CA20S
⑩ CA20E
⑪ 5A @ 800 rpm MT; Calif. & Can.
5A @ 650 rpm AT; Calif. & Can.
10B @ 800 rpm MT; 49 States
10B @ 650 rpm AT; 49 States
⑫ Mid-year models—15B
⑬ Mid-year models—Hyd.
⑭ E16S—3.8
⑮ Station wagon—0.012
⑯ Models built after 6/1/84: 4B
⑰ In drive position

## GASOLINE ENGINE TUNE-UP SPECIFICATIONS

(18) At idle speed
(19) Measuring point: between fuel filter and injection body at idle speed
(20) The moment gas pedal is fully depressed
(21) Measuring point: between fuel filter and fuel pipe with vacuum hose connected at pressure regulator valve and at idle speed
(22) 4WD Model 36.6 psi. All readings at idle speed
(23) 600 at high altitudes
(24) Spark plug gap not adjustable
(25) With throttle harness disconnected
(26) Feedback controlled; not adjustable

## FIRING ORDERS

NOTE: To avoid confusion, always replace spark plug wires one at a time.

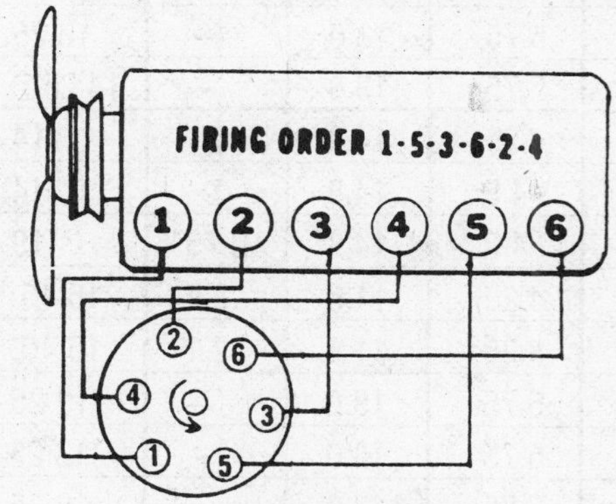


L24, L28 engines

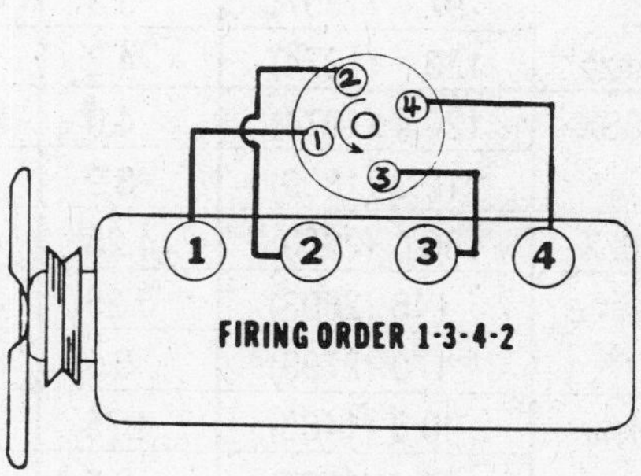


A-series engines

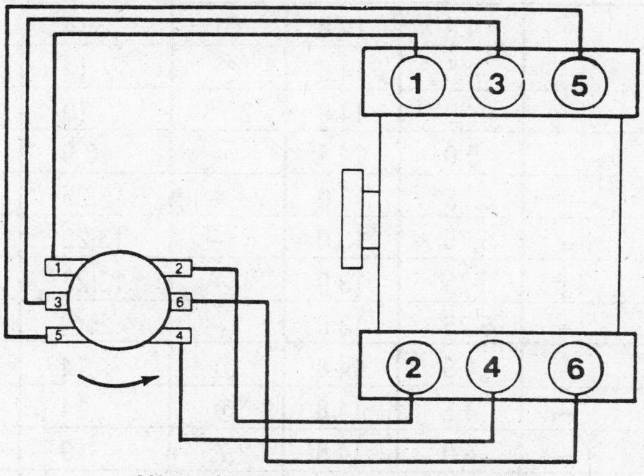

V6 engine firing order: 1–2–3–4–5–6

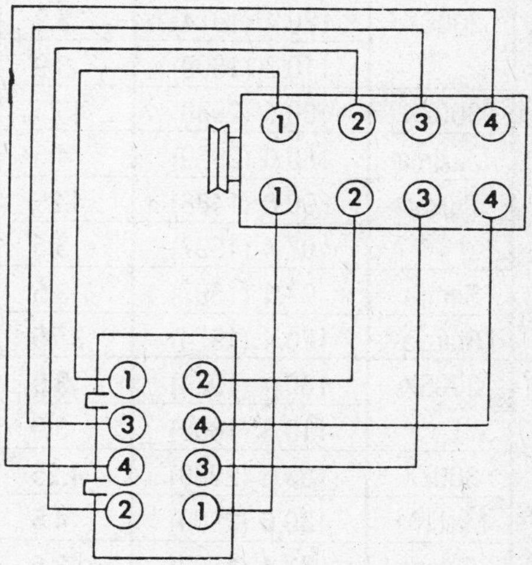

C-Series engines

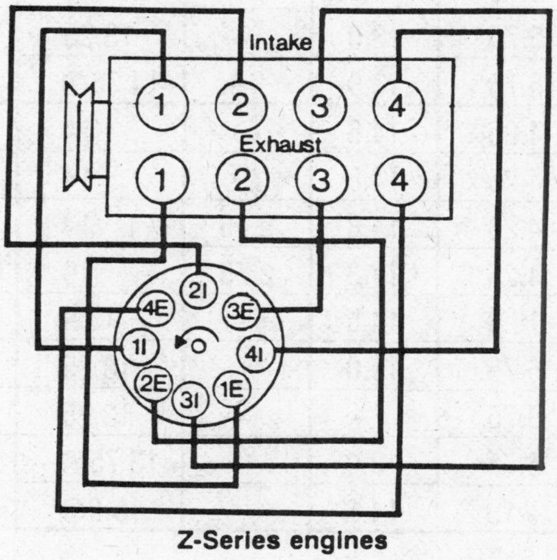


Z-Series engines

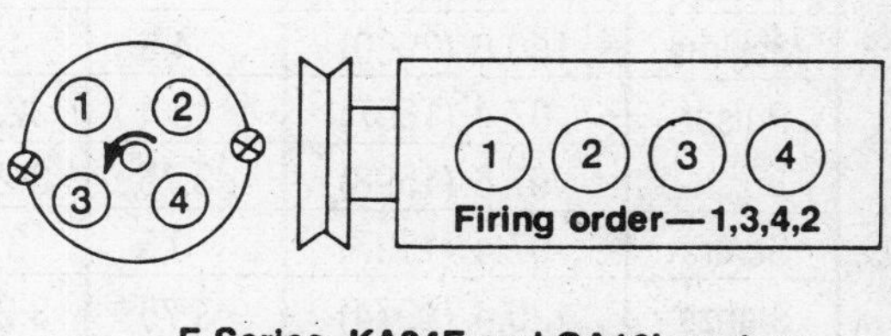


E-Series, KA24E and GA16I engines

## CAPACITIES

| Year | Model | Engine Displacement cu. in. (cc) | Engine Crankcase with Filter | Engine Crankcase without Filter | Transmission (pts.) 4-Spd | Transmission (pts.) 5-Spd | Transmission (pts.) Auto.■ | Drive Axle (pts.) | Fuel Tank (gal.) | Cooling System (qts.) |
|---|---|---|---|---|---|---|---|---|---|---|
| 1983 | 810 | 146 (2393) | 5.25 | 4.75 | — | 4.25 | 11.8 | 2.1 | 16.4① | 11.0 |
| | 200SX | 133.4 (2181) | 4.4 | 4.1 | — | 4.25 | 11.8 | 2.4 | 14① | 10.0 |
| | 280ZX | 168 (2753) | 4.75 | 4.25 | — | 4.25 | 11.8 | 2.75 | 21.12 | 11.12 |
| | Pulsar | 97.4 (1597) | 3.9 | 3.5 | — | 5.75 | 13.0 | — | 13.25 | 5.5 |
| | Sentra | 90.8 (1488) | 4.1 | 3.6 | 4.9 | 5.75 | 13.0 | — | 13.25 | 5.5 |
| | | 97.4 (1597) | 3.5 | 3.0 | 4.9 | 5.75 | 13.0 | — | 13.25 | 5.5 |
| | Stanza | 120.4 (1974) | 4.2 | 3.5 | — | 5.75 | 13.0 | — | 14.25② | 7.2 |
| 1984 | 200SX | 120.4 (1974) | 4.0 | 3.75 | — | 4.25 | 14.8 | ③ | 14 | 9.1 |
| | | 110.3 (1809) | 3.9 | 3.4 | — | 4.5 | 14.8 | ③ | 14 | 9.1 |
| | 300ZX | 180.6 (2960) | 4.25 | 3.9 | — | 4.0 | 14.8 | 2.75 | 19 | 11.1④ |
| | Maxima | 146 (2393) | 5.25 | 4.75 | — | 4.25 | 11.8 | 2.1 | 16.4① | 11.0 |
| | | 170 (2793) | 6.5 | 6.0 | — | 4.25 | 11.8 | 2.1 | 16.4① | 10.0 |
| | Pulsar | 90.8 (1488) | 4.75 | 4.25 | — | 5.75 | 13.0 | — | 13.25 | 5.5 |
| | | 97.4 (1597) | 3.9 | 3.5 | — | 5.75 | 13.0 | — | 13.25 | 5.5 |
| | Sentra | 97.4 (1597) | 3.5 | 3.0 | 4.9 | 5.75 | 13.0 | — | 13.25 | 5.5 |
| | Stanza | 120.4 (1974) | 4.2 | 3.75 | — | 5.75 | 13.0 | — | 14.25② | 7.2 |
| 1985 | 200SX | 120.4 (1974) | 3.9 | 3.4 | — | 4.5 | 14.8 | ③ | 14 | 9.1 |
| | | 110.3 (1809) | 3.9 | 3.4 | — | 4.5 | 14.8 | ③ | 14 | 9.1 |
| | 300ZX | 180.6 (2960) | 4.25 | 3.9 | — | 4.0 | 14.8 | 2.75 | 19 | 11.1④ |
| | Maxima | 180.6 (2960) | 4.5 | 4.1 | — | 10.0 | 14.5 | — | 15.9 | 9.75 |
| | Pulsar | 90.8 (1488) | 4.25 | 3.85 | — | 5.75 | 13.0 | — | 13.25 | 5.5 |
| | | 97.4 (1597) | 3.5 | 3.1 | — | 5.75 | 13.0 | — | 13.25 | 5.5 |
| | Sentra | 97.4 (1597) | 3.5 | 3.0 | 4.9 | 5.75 | 13.0 | — | 13.25 | 5.5 |
| | Stanza | 120.4 (1974) | 3.75 | 3.25 | — | 5.75 | 13.0 | — | 14.25② | 7.2 |
| 1986 | 200SX | 120.4 (1974) | 3.9 | 3.4 | — | 4.5 | 14.8 | ③ | 14 | 9.1 |
| | | 110.3 (1809) | 3.9 | 3.4 | — | 4.5 | 14.8 | ③ | 14 | 9.1 |
| | 300ZX | 180.6 (2960) | 4.25 | 3.9 | — | 4.0 | 14.8 | 2.75 | 19 | 11.1④ |
| | Maxima | 180.6 (2960) | 4.5 | 4.1 | — | 10.0 | 14.5 | — | 15.9 | 9.75 |
| | Pulsar | 97.4 (1597) | 3.5 | 3.1 | — | 5.75 | 13.0 | — | 13.25 | 5.5 |
| | Sentra | 97.4 (1597) | 3.5 | 3.0 | 4.9 | 5.75 | 13.0 | — | 13.25 | 5.5 |
| | Stanza | 120.4 (1974) | 3.75 | 3.25 | — | 5.75 | 13.0 | — | 14.25② | 7.2 |
| 1987 | 200SX | 120.4 (1974) | 3.9 | 3.4 | — | 4.25 | 14.8 | ③ | 14 | 9.1 |
| | | 110.3 (1809) | 3.9 | 3.4 | — | 4.25 | 14.8 | ③ | 14 | 9.1 |
| | | 180.6 (2960) | 4.5 | 4.0 | — | 4.25 | 14.8 | 2.75 | 14 | 9.6 |
| | 300ZX | 180.6 (2960) | 4.25 | 3.9 | — | 4.25 | 14.8 | 2.75 | 19 | 11.1④ |
| | Maxima | 180.6 (2960) | 4.5 | 4.1 | — | 10.0 | 14.5 | — | 15.9 | 9.75 |
| | Pulsar | 97.4 (1597) | 3.4 | 2.9 | — | 5.75 | 13.0 | — | 13.25 | ⑤ |
| | | 97.5 (1598) | 3.75 | 3.25 | — | 5.75 | — | — | 13.25 | 5.9 |
| | Sentra | 97.4 (1597) | 3.5 | 3.0 | — | 5.75 | 13.0 | — | 13.75⑥ | ⑤ |
| | Stanza | 120.4 (1974) | 3.75 | 3.25 | — | 10 | 14.5 | — | 15.9⑦ | 7.75 |

## CAPACITIES

| Year | Model | VIN | No. Cylinder Displacement cu. in. (liter) | Engine Crankcase with Filter | Engine Crankcase without Filter | Transmission (pts.) 4-Spd | 5-Spd | Auto. | Drive Axle (pts.) | Fuel Tank (gal.) | Cooling System (qts.) |
|---|---|---|---|---|---|---|---|---|---|---|---|
| 1988 | 200SX | | 120.4 (1974) | 3.9 | 3.4 | — | 4.25 | 14.8 | ③ | 14 | 9.1 |
| | | | 180.6 (2690) | 4.5 | 4.0 | — | 4.25 | 14.8 | 2.75 | 14 | 9.6 |
| | 300ZX | | 180.6 (2960) | 4.25 | 3.9 | — | 4.25 | 14.8 | 2.75 | 19 | 11.1④ |
| | Maxima | | 180.6 (2960) | 4.5 | 4.1 | — | 10.0 | 14.5 | — | 15.9 | 9.75 |
| | Pulsar | | 97.4 (1597) | 3.4 | 2.9 | — | 5.75 | 13.2 | — | 13.25 | ⑤ |
| | | | 110.3 (1809) | 3.7 | 3.3 | — | 10.0 | 14.4 | — | 13.25 | ⑨ |
| | Sentra | | 97.4 (1597) | 3.4 | 3.0 | 5.7 | 5.9 | 13.2 | ⑩ | 13.25⑪ | ⑤ |
| | Stanza | | 120.4 (1974) | 3.75 | 3.25 | — | 10 | 14.4 | ⑩ | 15.9⑦ | 7.75⑫ |
| 1989-90 | 240SX | | 145.6 (2389) | 3.75 | 3.4 | — | 5.1 | 17.5 | ⑬ | 16 | 7.1⑭ |
| | 300ZX | | 180.6 (2960) | 4.25 | 3.8 | — | 4.25⑮ | 14.8 | ⑬ | 19 | 11.1⑯ |
| | Maxima | | 180.6 (2960) | 4.5 | 4.1 | — | 10.0 | 15.5 | — | 15.9 | 8.75 |
| | Pulsar | | 97.4 (1597) | 3.4 | 3.0 | — | 5.75 | 6.6 | — | 13.25 | ⑰ |
| | | | 110.3 (1809) | 3.75 | 3.25 | — | 10.0 | 7.25 | — | 13.25 | 5.9 |
| | Sentra | | 97.4 (1597) | 3.4 | 3.0 | 5.75 | 5.9 | 13.2 | ⑩ | 13.25⑪ | 5.3⑱ |
| | Stanza | | 120.4 (1974) | 3.75 | 3.25 | — | 10.0 | 7.25 | — | 15.9 | 7.75 |

■ Figure is for drain and refill
— Not applicable
① Hatchback or station wagon—15.9
② Station wagon—15.9
③ Solid rear axle—2.1
IRS—2.75
④ Turbo—11.5
⑤ MT—4.9; AT—5.5
⑥ 4WD—12.4
⑦ 4WD—13.25
⑧ With rear heater—9.7
⑨ MT—5.9; AT—6.1
⑩ Rear differential carrier on 4WD—2.1
⑪ 4WD—12.4
⑫ Station wagon with heater 7.1
and without heater 6.1
⑬ Rear differential carrier on
4WD—2.75
⑭ Reservoir Capacity—.75
⑮ Turbo—5.1
⑯ Turbo—11.6
⑰ MT—5.75
AT—6.25
⑱ 4WD w/AT—5.75

## CAMSHAFT SPECIFICATIONS

All measurements given in inches.

| Year | Engine Displacement cu. in. (cc) | Journal Diameter 1 | 2 | 3 | 4 | 5 | Lobe Lift In. | Ex. | Bearing Clearance | Camshaft End Play |
|---|---|---|---|---|---|---|---|---|---|---|
| 1983 | CA20 120.4 (1974) | 1.8085–1.8092 | 1.8085–1.8092 | 1.8085–1.8092 | 1.8085–1.8092 | 1.8077–1.8085 | 0.354 | 0.354 | 0.0040 ② | 0.0028–0.0055 |
| | E15 90.8 (1488) | 1.6515–1.6522 | 1.6498–1.6505 | 1.6515–1.6522 | 1.6498–1.6505 | 1.6515–1.6522 | NA | NA | 0.0014–0.0030 ③ | 0.0160 |
| | E16 97.4 (1597) | 1.6515–1.6522 | 1.6498–1.6505 | 1.6515–1.6522 | 1.6498–1.6505 | 1.6515–1.6522 | NA | NA | 0.0014–0.0030 ③ | 0.0059–0.0114 |
| | L-Series 146 (2393) 168 (2753) | 1.8878–1.8883 | 1.8878–1.8883 | 1.8878–1.8883 | 1.8878–1.8883 | 1.8878–1.8883 | 0.262 | 0.262 | 0.0015–0.0026 | 0.0031–0.0150 |
| | Z-Series 119.1 (1952) | 1.2967–1.2974 | 1.2967–1.2974 | 1.2967–1.2974 | 1.2967–1.2974 | — | NA | NA | 0.0018–0.0035 | 0.0080 |

## CAMSHAFT SPECIFICATIONS

All measurements given in inches.

| Year | Engine Displacement cu. in. (cc) | Journal Diameter 1 | 2 | 3 | 4 | 5 | Lobe Lift In. | Ex. | Bearing Clearance | Camshaft End Play |
|---|---|---|---|---|---|---|---|---|---|---|
| 1984 | C-Series 110.3 (1809) 120.4 (1974) | 1.8085–1.8092 | 1.8085–1.8092 | 1.8085–1.8092 | 1.8085–1.8092 | 1.8077–1.8085 | 0.354 | 0.354 | 0.0040 ② | 0.0028–0.0055 |
| | E15ET 90.8 (1488) | 1.6515–1.6522 | 1.6498–1.6505 | 1.6515–1.6522 | 1.6498–1.6505 | 1.6515–1.6522 | NA | NA | 0.0014–0.0030 ③ | 0.0160 |
| | E16, E16S 97.4 (1597) | 1.6515–1.6522 | 1.6498–1.6505 | 1.6515–1.6522 | 1.6498–1.6505 | 1.6515–1.6522 | NA | NA | 0.0014–0.0030 ③ | 0.0059–0.0114 |
| | L-Series 146 (2393) | 1.8878–1.8883 | 1.8878–1.8883 | 1.8878–1.8883 | 1.8878–1.8883 | 1.8878–1.8883 | 0.262 | 0.262 | 0.0015–0.0026 | 0.0031–0.0150 |
| | V-Series 180.6 (2960) | 1.8472–1.8480 | 1.8472–1.8480 | 1.8472–1.8480 | 1.8472 1.8480 | 1.8472–1.8480 | NA | NA | 0.0024–0.0041 | 0.0012–0.0024 |
| 1985 | C-Series 110.3 (1809) 120.4 (1974) | 1.8085–1.8092 | 1.8085–1.8092 | 1.8085–1.8092 | 1.8085–1.8092 | 1.8077–1.8085 | 0.354 | 0.354 | 0.0040 ② | 0.0028–0.0055 |
| | E15ET 90.8 (1488) | 1.6515–1.6522 | 1.6498–1.6505 | 1.6515–1.6522 | 1.6498–1.6505 | 1.6515–1.6522 | NA | NA | 0.0014–0.0030 ③ | 0.0160 |
| | E16, E16S 97.4 (1597) | 1.6515–1.6522 | 1.6498–1.6505 | 1.6515–1.6522 | 1.6498–1.6505 | 1.6515–1.6522 | NA | NA | 0.0014–0.0030 ③ | 0.0059–0.0114 |
| | V-Series 180.6 (2960) | 1.8472–1.8480 | 1.8472–1.8480 | 1.8472–1.8480 | 1.8472 1.8480 | 1.8472–1.8480 | NA | NA | 0.0024–0.0041 | 0.0012–0.0024 |
| 1986 | C-Series 110.3 (1809) 120.4 (1974) | 1.8085–1.8092 | 1.8085–1.8092 | 1.8085–1.8092 | 1.8085–1.8092 | 1.8077–1.8085 | 0.354 | 0.354 | 0.0040 ② | 0.0028–0.0055 |
| | E16, E16S 97.4 (1597) | 1.6515–1.6522 | 1.6498–1.6505 | 1.6515–1.6522 | 1.6498–1.6505 | 1.6515–1.6522 | NA | NA | 0.0014–0.0030 ③ | 0.0059–0.0114 |
| | V-Series 180.6 (2960) | 1.8472–1.8480 | 1.8472–1.8480 | 1.8472–1.8480 | 1.8472 1.8480 | 1.8472–1.8480 | NA | NA | 0.0024–0.0041 | 0.0012–0.0024 |
| 1987 | CA16DE 97.5 (1598) | 1.0998–1.1006 | 1.0998–1.1006 | 1.0998–1.1006 | 1.0998–1.1006 | 1.0998–1.1006 | 0.335 | 0.335 | 0.0018–0.0035 | 0.0028–0.0059 |
| | C-Series 110.3 (1809) 120.4 (1974) | 1.8085–1.8092 | 1.8085–1.8092 | 1.8085–1.8092 | 1.8085–1.8092 | 1.8077–1.8085 | 0.354 | 0.354 | 0.0040 ② | 0.0028–0.0055 |
| | E-Series 97.4 (1597) | 1.6515–1.6522 | 1.6498–1.6505 | 1.6515–1.6522 | 1.6498–1.6505 | 1.6515–1.6522 | NA | NA | 0.0014–0.0030 ③ | 0.0059–0.0114 |
| | V-Series 180.6 (2960) | 1.8472–1.8480 | 1.8472–1.8480 | 1.8472–1.8480 | 1.8472 1.8480 | 1.8472–1.8480 | NA | NA | 0.0024–0.0041 | 0.0012–0.0024 |
| 1988 | CA20E 120.4 (1974) | 1.8085–1.8092 | 1.8085–1.8092 | 1.8085–1.8092 | 1.8085–1.8092 | 1.8077–1.8055 | 0.335 | 0.374 | 0.0040 ② | 0.0028–0.0055 |
| | V-Series 180.6 (2960) | 1.8866–1.8874 | 1.8472–1.8480 | 1.8472–1.8480 | 1.8472–1.8480 | 1.6701–1.6709 | NA | NA | 0.0018–0.0035 | 0.0012–0.0024 |

## CAMSHAFT SPECIFICATIONS

All measurements given in inches.

| Year | Engine Displacement cu. in. (cc) | Journal Diameter 1 | 2 | 3 | 4 | 5 | Lobe Lift In. | Ex. | Bearing Clearance | Camshaft End Play |
|---|---|---|---|---|---|---|---|---|---|---|
| 1988 | E16i 97.4 (1597) | 1.6515–1.6522 | 1.6498–1.6505 | 1.0515–1.6522 | 1.6498–1.6505 | 1.6515–1.6522 | NA | NA | 0.0014–0.0030 | 0.0059–0.0114 |
| | CA18DE 110.3 (1809) | 1.0998–1.1006 | 1.0998–1.1006 | 1.0998–1.1006 | 1.0998–1.1006 | 1.0998–1.1006 | 0.335 | 0.335 | 0.0018–0.0035 | 0.0028–0.0059 |
| 1989-90 | CA20E 120.4 (1974) | 1.8085–1.8092 | 1.8085–1.8092 | 1.8085–1.8092 | 1.8085–1.8092 | 1.8077–1.8055 | 0.335 | 0.374 | 0.0040 ② | 0.0028–0.0055 |
| | KA24E 145.6 (2389) | 1.2967–1.2974 | 1.2967–1.2974 | 1.2967–1.2974 | 1.2967–1.2974 | 1.2967–1.2974 | 0.409 | 0.409 | 0.0018–0.0035 | 0.0028–0.0059 |
| | V-Series 180.6 (2960) | 1.8866–1.8874④ | 1.8472–1.8480 | 1.8472–1.8480 | 1.8472–1.8480 | 1.6701–1.6709 | NA | NA | 0.0018–0.0035 | 0.0012–0.0024 |
| | GA16i 97.4 (1597) | 1.6510–1.6518 | 1.6510–1.6518 | 1.6510–1.6518 | 1.6510–1.6518 | 1.6510–1.6518 | NA | NA | 0.0018–0.0035 | 0.0012–0.0059 |
| | CA18DE 110.3 (1809) | 1.0998–1.1006 | 1.0998–1.1006 | 1.0998–1.1006 | 1.0998–1.1006 | 1.0998–1.1006 | 0.335 | 0.335 | 0.0018–0.0035 | 0.0028–0.0059 |

NA Not available

① No. 1 & 5: 0.0015–0.0024
No. 2 & 4: 0.0011–0.0020
No. 3: 0.0016–0.0025

② Clearance limit

③ Journals No. 1, 3 & 5
No. 2 & 4: 0.0031–0.0047

④ Front of engine, left hand camshaft only

## CRANKSHAFT AND CONNECTING ROD SPECIFICATIONS

All measurements are given in inches.

| Year | Engine Displacement cu. in. (cc) | Crankshaft Main Brg. Journal Dia. | Main Brg. Oil Clearance | Shaft End-play | Thrust on No. | Connecting Rod Journal Diameter | Oil Clearance | Side Clearance |
|---|---|---|---|---|---|---|---|---|
| 1983 | CA20 120.4 (1974) | 2.0847–2.0852 | 0.0016–0.0024 | 0.0120 | 3 | 1.7701–1.7706 | 0.0008–0.0024 | 0.0080–0.0120 |
| | E-Series 97.4 (1597) | 1.9663–1.9671 | ① | 0.0020–0.0070 | 3 | 1.5730–1.5738 | 0.0012–0.0024 | 0.0040–0.0146 |
| | L24E 146 (2393) | 2.1631–2.1636 | 0.0010–0.0030 | 0.0020–0.0070 | Center | 1.7701–1.7706 | 0.0010–0.0030 | 0.0080–0.0120 |
| | L28E, L28ET 168 (2753) | 2.1631–2.1636 | 0.0008–0.0026 | 0.0020–0.0070 | Center | 1.9670–1.9675 | 0.0009–0.0026 | 0.0079–0.0118 |
| | Z-Series 119.1 (1952) | 2.1631–2.1636 | 0.0008–0.0024 | 0.0020–0.0071 | 3 | 1.9670–1.9675 | 0.0010–0.0022 | 0.0080–0.0120 |
| 1984 | C-Series 110.3 (1809) 120.4 (1974) | 2.0847–2.0852 | 0.0016–0.0024 | 0.0120 ② | 3 | 1.7701–1.7706 | 0.0008–0.0024 | 0.0080–0.0120 |
| | E-Series 90.8 (1488) 97.4 (1597) | 1.9663–1.9671 | ① | 0.0020–0.0070 | 3 | 1.5730–1.5738 | 0.0012–0.0024 | 0.0040–0.0146 |
| | L24E 146 (2393) | 2.1631–2.1636 | 0.0010–0.0030 | 0.0020–0.0070 | Center | 1.7701–1.7706 | 0.0010–0.0030 | 0.0080–0.0120 |
| | V-Series 180.6 (2960) | 2.4790–2.4793 | 0.0011–0.0022 | 0.0020–0.0067 | 4 | 1.9670–1.9675 | 0.0004–0.0020 | 0.0079–0.0138 |

## CRANKSHAFT AND CONNECTING ROD SPECIFICATIONS

All measurements are given in inches.

| Year | Engine Displacement cu. in. (cc) | Crankshaft Main Brg. Journal Dia. | Crankshaft Main Brg. Oil Clearance | Crankshaft Shaft End-play | Crankshaft Thrust on No. | Connecting Rod Journal Diameter | Connecting Rod Oil Clearance | Connecting Rod Side Clearance |
|---|---|---|---|---|---|---|---|---|
| 1985 | C-Series 110.3 (1974) 120.4 (1974) | 2.0847–2.0852 | 0.0016–0.0024 | 0.0120 ② | 3 | 1.7701–1.7706 | 0.0008–0.0024 | 0.0080–0.0120 |
| | E-Series 90.8 (1488) 97.4 (1597) | 1.9663–1.9671 1.9671 | ① | 0.0020–0.0070 0.0070 | 3 | 1.5730–1.5738 1.5738 | 0.0012–0.0024 0.0024 | 0.0040–0.0146 0.0146 |
| | V-Series 180.6 (2960) | 2.4790–2.4793 | 0.0011–0.0022 | 0.0020–0.0067 | 4 | 1.9670–1.9675 | 0.0004–0.0020 | 0.0079–0.0138 |
| 1986 | C-Series 110.3 (1809) 120.4 (1974) | 2.0847–2.0852 | 0.0016–0.0024 | 0.0120 ② | 3 | 1.7701–1.7706 | 0.0008–0.0024 | 0.0080–0.0120 |
| | E-Series 97.4 (1597) | 1.9663–1.9671 | ① | 0.0020–0.0070 | 3 | 1.5730–1.5738 | 0.0004–0.0017 | 0.0040–0.0146 |
| | V-Series 180.6 (2960) | 2.4790–2.4793 | 0.0011–0.0022 | 0.0020–0.0067 | 4 | 1.9670–1.9675 | 0.0004–0.0020 | 0.0079–0.0138 |
| 1987 | CA16DE 97.5 (1598) | 2.0847–2.0856 | 0.0008–0.0019 | 0.0120 | 3 | 1.7698–1.7706 | 0.0007–0.0018 | 0.0007–0.0018 |
| | C-Series 110.3 (1809) 120.4 (1974) | 2.0847–2.0852 | 0.0016–0.0024 | 0.0120 ② | 3 | 1.7701–1.7706 | 0.0008–0.0024 | 0.0080–0.0120 |
| | E-Series 97.4 (1597) | 1.9661–1.9671 | ① | 0.0020–0.0071 | 3 | 1.5730–1.5738 | 0.0004–0.0017 | 0.0040–0.0146 |
| | V-Series 180.6 (2960) | 2.4790–2.4793 | 0.0011–0.0022 | 0.0020–0.0067 | 4 | 1.9670–1.9675 | 0.0004–0.0020 | 0.0079–0.0138 |
| 1988 | CA20E 120.4 (1974) | 2.0847–2.0852 | 0.0016–0.0024 | 0.0120 | 3 | 1.7701–1.7706 | 0.0008–0.0024 | 0.0080–0.0120 |
| | V-Series 180.6 (2960) | 2.4790–2.4793 | 0.0011–0.0022 | 0.0020–0.0067 | 4 | 1.9760–1.9675 | 0.0006–0.0021 | 0.0079–0.0138 |
| | E16i 97.4 (1597) | 1.9661–1.9671 | ③ | 0.0020–0.0065 | 3 | 1.5733–1.5738 | 0.0004–0.0017 | 0.0040–0.0146 |
| | CA18DE 110.3 (1809) | 2.0847–2.0856 | 0.0008–0.0019 | 0.0020–0.0091 | 3 | 1.7698–1.7706 | 0.0007–0.0018 | 0.0079–0.0138 |
| 1989-90 | CA20 120.4 (1974) | 2.0847–2.0852 | 0.0008–0.0019 | 0.0020 0.0071 | 3 | 1.7701–1.7706 | 0.0004–0.0017 | 0.0080–0.0120 |
| | KAE24 145.6 (2389) | 2.3609–2.3612 | 0.0008–0.0019 | 0.0020–0.0071 | 3 | 1.9672–1.9675 | 0.0004–0.0017 | 0.0080–0.0160 |
| | V-Series 180.6 (2960) | 2.4790–2.4793 | 0.0011–0.0022 | 0.0020–0.0067 | 4 | 1.9667–1.9675 | 0.0006–0.0021 | 0.0079–0.0138 |
| | GA16i 97.4 (1597) | 1.9668–1.9671 | 0.0008–0.0017 | 0.0024–0.0071 | 3 | 1.5731–1.5738 | 0.0004–0.0014 | 0.0079–0.0185 |
| | CA18DE 110.3 (1809) | 2.0847–2.0856 | 0.0008–0.0019 | 0.0020–0.0071 | 3 | 1.7698–1.7706 | 0.0007–0.0018 | 0.0079–0.0138 |

① No. 1 & 5—0.0012–0.0022
No. 2, 3 & 4—0.0012–0.0036
② CA18ET—0.0020–0.0071
③ No. 1, 3, & 5—0.0012–0.0022
No. 2 & 4—0.0012–0.0036

## VALVE SPECIFICATIONS

| Year | Engine Displacement cu. in. (cc) | Seat Angle (deg.) | Face Angle (deg.) | Spring Test Pressure (lbs.) | Spring Installed Height (in.) | Stem-to-Guide Clearance (in.) | | Stem Diameter (in.) | |
|---|---|---|---|---|---|---|---|---|---|
| | | | | | | Intake | Exhaust | Intake | Exhaust |
| 1983 | CA20 120.4 (1974) | 44°30′ | 45°30′ | 108 @ 1.16 ④ | 1.575 ② | 0.0008–0.0021 | 0.0016–0.0029 | 0.2742–0.2748 | 0.2734–0.2740 |
| | E-Series 90.8 (1488) 97.4 (1597) | 44°30′ | 45°30′ | — | 1.543 | 0.0008–0.0020 | 0.0018–0.0030 | 0.2744–0.2750 | 0.2734–0.2740 |
| | L24E 146 (2393) | 44°30′ | 45°30′ | ① | 1.575 ② | 0.0010–0.0020 | 0.0020–0.0030 | 0.3136–0.3142 | 0.3128–0.3134 |
| | L28E,L28ET 168 (2753) | 45 | 45 | 108 @ 1.16 ③ | 1.575 ② | 0.0008–0.0021 | 0.0016–0.0029 | 0.3136–0.3142 | 0.3128–0.3134 |
| | Z-Series 119.1 (1952) | 45 | 45 | 115.3 @ 1.16 ④ | 1.575 ② | 0.0008–0.0021 | 0.0016–0.0029 | 0.3136–0.3142 | 0.3128–0.3134 |
| 1984 | C-Series 110.3 (1809) 120.4 (1974) | 44°30′ | 45°30′ | 108 @ 1.16 ④ | 1.575 ② | 0.0008–0.0021 | 0.0016–0.0029 | 0.2742–0.2748 | 0.2734–0.2740 |
| | E-Series 90.8 (1488) 97.4 (1597) | 44°30′ | 45°30′ | — | 1.543 | 0.0008–0.0020 | 0.0018–0.0030 | 0.2744–0.2750 | 0.2734–0.2740 |
| | L24E 146 (2393) | 44°30′ | 45°30′ | ① | 1.575 ② | 0.0010–0.0020 | 0.0020–0.0030 | 0.3136–0.3142 | 0.3128–0.3134 |
| | V-Series 180.6 (2960) | 44°30′ | 45°30′ | 118 @ 1.18 ④ | 1.575 ② | 0.0008–0.0021 | 0.0016–0.0029 | 0.2742–0.2748 | 0.3128–0.3134 |
| 1985 | C-Series 110.3 (1809) 120.4 (1974) | 44°30′ | 45°30′ | 108 @ 1.16 ④ | 1.575 ② | 0.0008–0.0021 | 0.0016–0.0029 | 0.2742–0.2748 | 0.2734–0.2740 |
| | E-Series 90.8 (1488) 97.4 (1597) | 44°30′ | 45°30′ | — | 1.543 | 0.0008–0.0020 | 0.0018–0.0030 | 0.2744–0.2750 | 0.2734–0.2740 |
| | V-Series 180.6 (2960) | 44°30′ | 45°30′ | 118 @ 1.18 ④ | 1.575 ② | 0.0008–0.0021 | 0.0016–0.0029 | 0.2742–0.2748 | 0.3128–0.3134 |
| 1986 | C-Series 110.3 (1809) 120.4 (1974) | 44°30′ | 45°30′ | 108 @ 1.16 ④ | 1.575 ② | 0.0008–0.0021 | 0.0016–0.0029 | 0.2742–0.2748 | 0.2734–0.2740 |
| | E-Series 97.4 (1597) | 44°30′ | 45°30′ | — | 1.543 | 0.0008–0.0020 | 0.0018–0.0030 | 0.2744–0.2750 | 0.2734–0.2740 |
| | V-Series 180.6 (2960) | 44°30′ | 45°30′ | 118 @ 1.18 ④ | 1.575 ② | 0.0008–0.0021 | 0.0016–0.0029 | 0.2742–0.2748 | 0.3128–0.3134 |
| 1987 | CA16DE 97.5 (1598) | 44°30′ | 45°30′ | — | — | 0.0008–0.0021 | 0.0016–0.0021 | 0.2348–0.2354 | 0.2341–0.2346 |
| | C-Series 110.3 (1809) 120.4 (1974) | 44°30′ | 45°30′ | 108 @ 1.16 ④ | 1.575 ② | 0.0008–0.0021 | 0.0016–0.0029 | 0.2742–0.2748 | 0.2734–0.2740 |
| | E-Series 97.4 (1597) | 44°30′ | 45°30′ | — | 1.543 | 0.0008–0.0020 | 0.0018–0.0030 | 0.2744–0.2750 | 0.2734–0.2740 |
| | V-Series 180.6 (2960) | 44°30′ | 45°30′ | 118 @ 1.18 ④ | 1.575 ② | 0.0008–0.0021 | 0.0016–0.0029 | 0.2742–0.2748 | 0.3128–0.3134 |

## VALVE SPECIFICATIONS

| Year | Engine Displacement cu. in. (cc) | Seat Angle (deg.) | Face Angle (deg.) | Spring Test Pressure (lbs.) | Spring Installed Height (in.) | Stem-to-Guide Clearance (in.) | | Stem Diameter (in.) | |
|---|---|---|---|---|---|---|---|---|---|
| | | | | | | Intake | Exhaust | Intake | Exhaust |
| 1988 | CA20E 120.4 (1974) | 45° | 45°30′ | 129.9⑤ | 1.959 ⑥ | 0.0008–0.0021 | 0.0016–0.0029 | 0.2742–0.2748 | 0.2734–0.2740 |
| | V-Series 180.6 (2960) | 45° | 45°30′ | 118 @ 1.18 ④ | 1.575 ② | 0.0008–0.0021 | 0.0016–0.0029 | 0.2742–0.2748 | 0.3136–0.3138 |
| | E16i 97.4 (1597) | 45° | 45°30′ | — | 1.543 | 0.0008–0.0020 | 0.0018–0.0030 | 0.2744–0.2750 | 0.2734–0.2740 |
| | CA18DE 110.3 (1809) | 45° | 45°30′ | ⑦ | ⑧ | 0.0008–0.0021 | 0.0016–0.0029 | 0.2348–0.2354 | 0.2341–0.2346 |
| 1989-90 | CAE20 120.4 (1974) | 45° | 45°30′ | 129.9⑥ | 1.959 ⑦ | 0.0008–0.0021 | 0.0016–0.0029 | 0.2742–0.2748 | 0.2734–0.2740 |
| | KAE24 145.6 (2389) | 45° | 45°30′ | 135.8 @ 1.480 ⑩ | ⑪ | 0.0008–0.0021 | 0.0016–0.0028 | 0.2742–0.2748 | 0.3129–0.3134 |
| | V-Series 180.6 (2960) | 45° | 45°30′ | 117.7 @ 1.181 ⑫ | 2.016 ⑦ | 0.0008–0.0021 | 0.0016–0.0029 | 0.2742–0.2748 | 0.3136–0.3138⑬ |
| | GA16i 97.4 (1597) | 45° | 45°30′ | — | 1.634 ⑭ | 0.0008–0.0020 | 0.0008–0.0020 | 0.2348–0.2354 | 0.2582–0.2587 |
| | CA18DE 110.3 (1809) | 45° | 45°30′ | — ⑭ | 1.634 ⑧ | 0.0008–0.0020 | 0.0008–0.0020 | 0.2348–0.2354 | 0.2582–0.2587 |

① Exhaust:
Outer—108 @ 1.16
Inner—56 @ 0.965
Intake:
Outer—105.2 @ 1.18
Inner—54.9 @ 0.984

② Outer; Inner—1.378

③ Outer; Inner—56 @ 0.965

④ Outer; Inner—57 @ 0.98

⑤ Outer; Inner—66.6

⑥ Outer; Inner—1.736

⑦ 0.650 in. @ 121 lbs. of load

⑧ 1.697 in. free Height

⑨ Outer; Inner—63.9 @ 1.146

⑩ Intake:
Outer—2.2614
Inner—2.1000
Exhaust:
Outer—2.949
Inner—1.8878

⑫ Outer; Inner—57.3 @ 0.9840

⑬ Maxima; 300ZX—0.3128–0.3134

## PISTON AND RING SPECIFICATIONS

All measurments are given in inches.

| Year | Engine Displacement cu. in. (cc) | Piston Clearance | Ring Gap | | | Ring Side Clearance | | |
|---|---|---|---|---|---|---|---|---|
| | | | Top Compression | Bottom Compression | Oil Control | Top Compression | Bottom Compression | Oil Control |
| 1983 | CA20 120.4 (1974) | 0.0009–0.0017 | 0.0079–0.0138 | 0.0059–0.0118 | 0.0118–0.0354 | 0.0016–0.0029 | 0.0012–0.0025 | 0.0020–0.0057 |
| | E-Series 90.8 (1488) 97.4 (1597) | 0.0009–0.0017 | 0.0079–0.0138 | 0.0059–0.0118 | 0.0118–0.0354 | 0.0016–0.0029 | 0.0012–0.0025 | 0.0020–0.0057 |
| | L24E 146 (2393) | 0.0010–0.0020 | 0.0090–0.0150 | 0.0060–0.0120 | 0.0120–0.0350 | 0.0020–0.0030 | 0.0010–0.0030 | 0.0010–0.0030 |
| | L28E 168 (2753) | 0.0010–0.0018 | 0.0098–0.0157 | 0.0050–0.0118 | 0.0120–0.0350 | 0.0016–0.0029 | 0.0012–0.0025 | — |
| | L28ET 168 (2753) | 0.0010–0.0018 | 0.0075–0.0130 | 0.0050–0.0118 | 0.0120–0.0350 | 0.0016–0.0029 | 0.0012–0.0025 | 0.0009–0.0028 |
| | Z-Series 119.1 (1952) | 0.0010–0.0020 | 0.0098–0.0160 | 0.0060–0.0120 | 0.0120–0.0350 | 0.0020–0.0030 | 0.0010–0.0025 | 0 |

## PISTON AND RING SPECIFICATIONS

All measurments are given in inches.

| Year | Engine Displacement cu. in. (cc) | Piston Clearance | Ring Gap Top Compression | Ring Gap Bottom Compression | Ring Gap Oil Control | Ring Side Clearance Top Compression | Ring Side Clearance Bottom Compression | Ring Side Clearance Oil Control |
|---|---|---|---|---|---|---|---|---|
| 1984 | CA18ET 110.3 (1809) | 0.0010–0.0018 | ② | 0.0059–0.0098 | 0.0079–0.0236 | 0.0016–0.0029 | 0.0012–0.0025 | — |
| | CA20S, CA20E 120.4 (1974) | 0.0010–0.0018 | 0.0098–0.0138 | 0.0059–0.0098 | 0.0079–0.0236 | 0.0016–0.0029 | 0.0012–0.0025 | — |
| | E15ET 90.8 (1488) | 0.0016–0.0024 | ③ | 0.0059–0.0098 | 0.0079–0.0236 | 0.0016–0.0029 | 0.0012–0.0025 | 0.0020–0.0049 |
| | E16, E16S 97.4 (1597) | 0.0009–0.0017 | 0.0079–0.0138 | 0.0059–0.0118 | 0.0118–0.0354 | 0.0016–0.0029 | 0.0012–0.0025 | 0.0020–0.0057 |
| | L24E 146 (2393) | 0.0010–0.0020 | 0.0090–0.0150 | 0.0060–0.0120 | 0.0120–0.0350 | 0.0020–0.0030 | 0.0010–0.0030 | 0.0010–0.0030 |
| | V-Series 180.6 (2960) | 0.0010–0.0018 | 0.0083–0.0173 | 0.0071–0.0173 | 0.0079–0.0299 | 0.0016–0.0029 | 0.0012–0.0025 | 0.0006–0.0075 |
| 1985 | CA18ET 110.3 (1809) | 0.0010–0.0018 | ② | 0.0059–0.0122 | 0.0079–0.0299 | 0.0016–0.0029 | 0.0012–0.0025 | — |
| | CA20S,CA20E 120.4 (1974) | 0.0010–0.0018 | 0.0098–0.0201 | 0.0059–0.0122 | 0.0079–0.0299 | 0.0016–0.0029 | 0.0012–0.0025 | — |
| | E15ET 90.8 (1488) | 0.0016–0.0024 | ③ | 0.0059–0.0098 | 0.0079–0.0236 | 0.0016–0.0029 | 0.0012–0.0025 | 0.0020–0.0049 |
| | E16,E16S 97.4 (1597) | 0.0009–0.0017 | 0.0079–0.0138 | 0.0059–0.0118 | 0.0118–0.0354 | 0.0016–0.0029 | 0.0012–0.0025 | 0.0020–0.0057 |
| | V-Series 180.6 (2960) | 0.0010–0.0018 | 0.0083–0.0173 | 0.0071–0.0173 | 0.0079–0.0299 | 0.0016–0.0029 | 0.0012–0.0025 | 0.0006–0.0075 |
| 1986 | CA18ET 110.3 (1809) | 0.0010–0.0018 | ② | 0.0059–0.0122 | 0.0079–0.0299 | 0.0016–0.0029 | 0.0012–0.0025 | — |
| | CA20E 120.4 (1974) | 0.0010–0.0018 | 0.0098–0.0201 | 0.0059–0.0122 | 0.0079–0.0299 | 0.0016–0.0029 | 0.0012–0.0025 | — |
| | E16, E16S 97.4 (1597) | 0.0009–0.0017 | 0.0079–0.0138 | 0.0059–0.0118 | 0.0118–0.0354 | 0.0016–0.0029 | 0.0012–0.0025 | 0.0020–0.0057 |
| | V-Series 180.6 (2960) | 0.0010–0.0018 | 0.0083–0.0173 | 0.0071–0.0173 | 0.0079–0.0299 | 0.0016–0.0029 | 0.0012–0.0025 | 0.0006–0.0075 |
| 1987 | CA16DE 97.5 (1598) | 0.0006–0.0014 | 0.0087–0.0154 | 0.0075–0.0177 | 0.0079–0.0299 | 0.0016–0.0029 | 0.0012–0.0025 | 0.0010–0.0033 |
| | CA18ET 110.3 (1809) | 0.0010–0.0018 | ② | 0.0059–0.0122 | 0.0079–0.0299 | 0.0016–0.0029 | 0.0012–0.0025 | — |
| | CA20E 120.4 (1974) | 0.0010–0.0018 | 0.0098–0.0201 | 0.0059–0.0122 | 0.0079–0.0299 | 0.0016–0.0029 | 0.0012–0.0025 | — |
| | E16i 97.4 (1597) | 0.0009–0.0017 | ④ | ⑤ | 0.0079–0.0236 | 0.0016–0.0029 | 0.0012–0.0025 | ⑥ |
| | E16S 97.4 (1597) | 0.0009–0.0017 | 0.0079–0.0138 | 0.0059–0.0118 | 0.0118–0.0354 | 0.0016–0.0029 | 0.0012–0.0025 | 0.0020–0.0057 |
| | V-Series 180.6 (2960) | 0.0010–0.0018 | 0.0083–0.0173 | 0.0071–0.0173 | 0.0079–0.0299 | 0.0016–0.0029 | 0.0012–0.0025 | 0.0006–0.0075 |
| 1988 | CA20E 120.4 (1974) | 0.0010–0.0018 | 0.0098–0.0201 | 0.0059–0.0122 | 0.0079–0.0299 | 0.0016–0.0029 | 0.0012–0.0025 | — |

## PISTON AND RING SPECIFICATIONS

All measurments are given in inches.

| Year | Engine Displacement cu. in. (cc) | Piston Clearance | Ring Gap | | | Ring Side Clearance | | |
|---|---|---|---|---|---|---|---|---|
| | | | Top Compression | Bottom Compression | Oil Control | Top Compression | Bottom Compression | Oil Control |
| 1988 | V-Series 180.6 (1960) | 0.0010–0.0018 | 0.0083–0.0173 ⑦ | 0.0071–0.0173 | 0.0079–0.0299 | 0.0016–0.0029 | 0.0012–0.0025 | 0.0006–0.0075 |
| | E16i 97.4 (1597) | 0.0009–0.0017 | ④ | ⑤ | 0.0079–0.0236 | 0.0016–0.0029 | 0.0012–0.0025 | ⑥ |
| | CA18DE 110.3 (1809) | 0.0006–0.0014 | 0.0087–0.0154 | 0.0075–0.0177 | 0.0079–0.0299 | 0.0016–0.0029 | 0.0012–0.0025 | 0.0010–0.0033 |
| 1989-90 | CA20E 120.4 (1974) | 0.0010–0.0018 | 0.0098–0.0201 | 0.0059–0.0122 | 0.0079–0.0299 | 0.0016–0.0029 | 0.0012–0.0025 | — |
| | KAE24 145.6 (2389) | 0.0008–0.0016 | 0.0110–0.0169 ⑦ | 0.0177–0.0236 | 0.0079–0.0236 | 0.0016–0.0031 | 0.0012–0.0028 | 0.0026–0.0053 |
| | V-Series 180.6 (2960) | 0.0010–0.0018 | 0.0083–0.0173 ⑦ | 0.0071–0.0173 | 0.0079–0.0299 | 0.0016–0.0029 | 0.0012–0.0025 | 0.0006–0.0075 |
| | GA16i 97.4 (1597) | 0.0006–0.0014 | 0.0079 0.0138 | 0.0146 0.0205 | 0.0079–0.0236 | 0.0016–0.0031 | 0.0012–0.0028 | |
| | CA18DE 110.3 (1809) | 0.0010–0.0018 | 0.0098–0.0201 | 0.0059–0.0122 | 0.0079–0.0299 | 0.0016–0.0029 | 0.0012–0.0025 | — |

① Without mark—0.0079–0.0114
With mark—0.0055–0.0087

② Piston grades No.1 & No. 2:
1984—0.0098–0.0126
1985-88—0.0098–0.0150
Piston grades No.3, 4, & 5
1984—0.0075–0.0102
1985-88—0.0110–0.0165

③ Piston grades No.1 & No. 2
0.0079–0.0102 (yellow)
Piston grades No.3, 4, & 5
0.0055–0.0079

④ Type 1: 0.0055–0.0102
Type 2: 0.0079–0.0118

⑤ Type 1: 0.0110–0.0146
Type 2: 0.0059–0.0098

⑥ Type 1: 0.0026–0.0055
Type 2: 0.0002–0.0069

⑦ Turbocharged engine
0.0083–0.0122

## TORQUE SPECIFICATIONS

All readings in ft. lbs.

| Year | Engine Displacement cu. in. (cc) | Cylinder Head Bolts | Main Bearing Bolts | Rod Bearing Bolts | Crankshaft Pulley Bolts | Flywheel Bolts | Manifold | | Spark Plugs |
|---|---|---|---|---|---|---|---|---|---|
| | | | | | | | Intake | Exhaust | |
| 1983 | CA20 120.4 (1974) | 51–61 ⑥ | 33–40 | 22–27 | 90–98 | 72–80 | 13–16 | 13–17 | 11–14 |
| | E15, E16 90.8 (1488) 97.4 (1597) | 51–54 ① | 36–43 | 23–27 | 83–108 | 58–65 | 11–14 | 11–14 | 11–14 |
| | L24E 146 (2393) | 51–61 | 33–40 | 33–40 | 101–116 | 94–108 | ② | ② | 11–14 |
| | L28E, L28ET 168 (2753) | 54–61 ③ | 33–40 | 33–40 | 101–116 | 94–108 | ④ | ④ | 11–14 |
| | Z-Series 119.1 (1952) | 51–58 | 33–40 | 33–40 | 87–116 | 101–116 | 12–15 | 12–15 | 11–14 |

## TORQUE SPECIFICATIONS

All readings in ft. lbs.

| Year | Engine Displacement cu. in. (cc) | Cylinder Head Bolts | Main Bearing Bolts | Rod Bearing Bolts | Crankshaft Pulley Bolts | Flywheel Bolts | Manifold Intake | Manifold Exhaust | Spark Plugs |
|---|---|---|---|---|---|---|---|---|---|
| 1984 | CA18ET,CA20E<br>110.3 (1809) | ⑤ | 33–40 | 24–27 | 90–98 | 72–80 | 14–19 | 14–22 | 14–22 |
| | CA20S<br>120.4 (1974) | 51–61<br>⑤ | 33–40 | 22–27 | 90–98 | 72–80 | 13–16 | 13–17 | 14–22 |
| | E-Series<br>90.8 (1488)<br>97.4 (1597) | 51–54<br>① | 36–43 | 23–27 | 83–108 | 58–65 | 12–15 | 12–15 | 14–22 |
| | L24E<br>146 (2393) | 51–61 | 33–40 | 33–40 | 101–116 | 94–108 | ② | ② | 11–14 |
| | V-Series<br>180.6 (2960) | 40–47<br>⑥ | 67–74 | 33–40 | 90–98 | 72–80 | ⑦ | 13–16 | 14–22 |
| 1985 | CA18ET,CA20E<br>110.3 (1809) | ⑤ | 33–40 | 24–27 | 90–98 | 72–80 | 14–19 | 14–22 | 14–22 |
| | CA20S<br>120.4 (1974) | 51–61<br>⑤ | 33–40 | 22–27 | 90–98 | 72–80 | 13–16 | 13–17 | 14–22 |
| | E-Series<br>90.8 (1488)<br>97.4 (1597) | 51–54<br>① | 36–43 | 23–27 | 83–108 | 58–65 | 12–15 | 12–15 | 14–22 |
| | V-Series<br>180.6 (2960) | 40–47<br>⑦ | 67–74 | 33–40 | 90–98 | 72–80 | ⑦ | 13–16 | 14–22 |
| 1986 | C-Series<br>110.3 (1809)<br>120.4 (1974) | ⑤ | 33–40 | 24–27 | 90–98 | 72–80 | 14–19 | 14–22 | 14–22 |
| | E-Series<br>97.4 (1597) | 51–54<br>① | 36–43 | 23–27 | 80–94 | 58–65 | 12–15 | 12–15 | 14–22 |
| | V-Series<br>180.6 (2960) | 40–47<br>⑥ | 67–74 | 33–40 | 90–98 | 72–80 | ⑧ | 13–16 | 14–22 |
| 1987 | CA16DE<br>97.5 (1598) | 76<br>⑥ | 33–40 | 30–33 | 105–112 | 61–69 | 14–19 | 27–35 | 14–22 |
| | CA18ET,CA20E<br>110.3 (1809)<br>120.4 (1974) | ⑤ | 33–40 | 24–27 | 90–98 | 72–80 | 14–19 | 14–22 | 14–22 |
| | E-Series<br>97.6 (1597) | 51–54<br>① | 36–43 | 23–27 | 80–94 | 58–65 | 12–15 | 12–15 | 14–22 |
| | V-Series<br>180.6 (2960) | 40–47<br>⑥ | 67–74 | 33–40 | 90–98 | 72–80 | ⑧ | 13–16 | 14–22 |
| 1988 | CA20E<br>120.4 (1974) | ⑧ | 33–40 | 24–27 | 90–98 | 72–80 | 14–19 | 14–22 | 14–22 |
| | V-Series<br>180.6 (2960) | 40–47<br>⑥ | 67–74 | ⑨ | 90–98 | 72–80 | ⑦ | 13–16 | 14–22 |
| | E16i<br>97.4 (1597) | ⑩ | 36–43 | 23–27 | 80–94 | 58–65<br>⑪ | 12–15 | 12–15 | 14–22 |
| | CA18DE<br>110.3 (1809) | ⑫ | 33–40 | ⑨ | 105–112 | 61–69 | 14–19 | 27–35 | 14–22 |

## TORQUE SPECIFICATIONS

All readings in ft. lbs.

| Year | Engine Displacement cu. in. (cc) | Cylinder Head Bolts | Main Bearing Bolts | Rod Bearing Bolts | Crankshaft Pulley Bolts | Flywheel Bolts | Manifold Intake | Manifold Exhaust | Spark Plugs |
|---|---|---|---|---|---|---|---|---|---|
| 1989-90 | CA20E 120.4 (1974) | ⑧ | 33–40 | 24–27 | 90–98 | 72–80 | 14–19 | 14–22 | 14–22 |
| | KAE24 145.6 (2389) | ⑬ | 34–38 | ⑨ | 87–116 | 105–112 | 12–15 | 12–15 | 14–22 |
| | V-Series 180.6 (2960) | ⑥ | 67–74 | ⑨ | 90–98 | 72–80 ⑭ | ⑦ | 13–16 | 14–22 |
| | GA16i 97.4 (1597) | ⑥ | 34–38 | ⑮ | 132–152 | 69–76 | 12–15 | 12–15 | 14–22 |
| | CA18DE 110.3 (1809) | ⑫ | 33–40 | ⑯ | 105–112 | 61–69 | 12–15 | 12–15 | 14–22 |

① Tighten in two steps:
1st – 33 ft. lbs.
2nd – 51–54 ft. lbs.

② 8mm bolts: 11–18 ft. lbs.
8mm nut: 9–12 ft. lbs.
10mm bolts: 25–33 ft. lbs.

③ Tighten in three steps:
1st – 30 ft. lbs.
2nd – 44 ft. lbs.
3rd – 54–61 ft. lbs.

④ 8mm bolts: 10–13;
10mm bolts: 25–36 ft. lbs.

⑤ Tighten in 2 steps
1st – 22 ft. lbs.
2nd – 58 ft. lbs.
Then loosen all bolts completely.
Final torque is in 2 steps
1st – 22 ft. lbs.
2nd – 54–61 ft. lbs.
If angle torquing, turn all bolts 90–95 degrees clockwise

⑥ See text

⑦ Intake bolt: 12–14 ft. lbs.
Intake nut: 17–20 ft. lbs.

⑧ Tighten in 2 steps
1st – 22 ft. lbs.
2nd – 58 ft. lbs.
Then loosen all botls completely.
Final torque is in 2 steps
1st – 22 ft. lbs.
2nd – 54–61 ft. lbs.
(If angle torquing, tighten bolt 8 to 83–88 degrees and all other bolts to 75–80 degrees clockwise.)
NOTE: No. 8 bolt is the longest bolt.

⑨ Tighten in 2 steps
1st – 10–12 ft. lbs.
2nd – 28–33 ft. lbs.
(If angle torquing, tighten bolts to 60–65 degrees clockwise.)

⑩ Tighten in 2 steps
1st – 22 ft. lbs.
2nd – 51 ft. lbs.
Then loosen all bolts completely.
Final torque in 2 steps
1st – 22 ft. lbs.
2nd – 51–54 ft. lbs.

⑪ A/T Drive Plate: 69–76 ft. lbs.

⑫ Tighten in 2 steps
1st – 22 ft. lbs.
2nd – 76 ft. lbs.
Then loosen all bolts completely.
Final torque in 2 steps
1st – 22 ft. lbs.
2nd – 76 ft. lbs.
(If angle torquing, tighten all bolts to 85–90 degrees clockwise.)

⑬ Tighten in 2 steps
1st – 22 ft. lbs.
2nd – 58ft. lbs.
Then loosen all bolts completely.
Final torque is in 2 steps
1st – 22 ft lbs.
2nd – 54–61ft lbs.
(If angle torqueing in 2nd step, turn all bolts 80 to 85 degrees clockwise with an angle torque wrench).

⑭ 300ZX Maxima – 61 to 69

⑮ Tighten in 2 steps
1st – 10 to 12 ft. lbs.
2nd – 17 – 21 ft. lbs.
(If angle torqueing in 2nd step, turn all nuts 35 – 40 degrees with an angle torque wrench.

⑯ Tighten in 2 steps
1st – 10–12 ft. lbs.
2nd – 30–33 ft. lbs
(If angle torqueing in 2nd step, turn all nuts. 60 to 65 degrees with an angle torque wrench).

## BRAKE SPECIFICATIONS

All measurements in inches unless noted

| Year | Model | Lug Nut Torque (ft. lbs.) | Master Cylinder Bore | Brake Disc Minimum Thickness | Brake Disc Maximum Runout | Standard Brake Drum Diameter | Minimum Lining Thickness Front | Minimum Lining Thickness Rear |
|---|---|---|---|---|---|---|---|---|
| 1983 | 810 | 58–72 | 0.8125 | 0.630 ① | 0.0059 ② | 9.000 | 0.079 | 0.059 |
| | 200SX | 58–72 | 0.8750 | 0.413 ③ | 0.0047 ④ | – | 0.079 | 0.079 |
| | 280ZX | 58–72 | 0.9375 | 0.709 ① | 0.0039 ② | – | 0.080 | 0.080 |
| | Pulsar | 58–72 | 0.7500 | 0.394 | 0.0028 | 7.09 | 0.079 | 0.059 |

## BRAKE SPECIFICATIONS

All measurements in inches unless noted

| Year | Model | Lug Nut Torque (ft. lbs.) | Master Cylinder Bore | Brake Disc | | Standard Brake Drum Diameter | Minimum Lining Thickness | |
|---|---|---|---|---|---|---|---|---|
| | | | | Minimum Thickness | Maximum Runout | | Front | Rear |
| 1983 | Sentra | 58–72 | 0.7500 | 0.394 | 0.0028 | 7.09 | 0.079 | 0.059 |
| | Stanza | 58–72 | 0.8125 | 0.633 | 0.0028 | 8.000 | 0.080 | 0.059 |
| 1984 | 200SX | 58–72 | 0.9380 | 0.630 ⑤ | 0.0028 ⑥ | 9.000 | 0.079 | 0.059 ⑦ |
| | 300ZX | 58–72 | 0.9380 | 0.787 ⑤ | 0.0028 ⑥ | — | 0.080 | 0.080 |
| | Maxima | 58–72 | 0.8125 | 0.630 ① | 0.0059 ② | 9.000 | 0.079 | 0.059 |
| | Pulsar | 58–72 | 0.7500 | 0.394 | 0.0028 | 8.000 | 0.079 | 0.059 |
| | Sentra | 58–72 | 0.7500 | 0.394 | 0.0028 | 8.000 | 0.079 | 0.059 |
| | Stanza | 58–72 | 0.8125 | 0.633 | 0.0028 | 8.000 | 0.080 | 0.059 |
| 1985 | 200SX | 58–72 | 0.9380 | 0.630 ⑤ | 0.0028 ⑥ | — | 0.080 | 0.080 |
| | 300ZX | 58–72 | 0.9380 | 0.787 ⑤ | 0.0028 ⑥ | — | 0.080 | 0.080 |
| | Maxima | 58–72 | 0.9380 | 0.787 ⑤ | 0.0028 ⑥ | — | 0.079 | 0.079 |
| | Pulsar | 58–72 | 0.7500 | 0.394 | 0.0028 | 8.000 | 0.079 | 0.059 |
| | Sentra | 58–72 | 0.7500 | 0.394 | 0.0028 | 8.000 | 0.079 | 0.059 |
| | Stanza | 58–72 | 0.8125 | 0.633 | 0.0028 | 8.000 | 0.080 | 0.059 |
| 1986 | 200SX | 58–72 | 0.9380 | 0.630 ⑤ | 0.0028 ⑥ | — | 0.080 | 0.080 |
| | 300ZX | 58–72 | 0.9380 | 0.787 ⑤ | 0.0028 ⑥ | — | 0.080 | 0.080 |
| | Maxima | 58–72 | 0.9380 | 0.787 ⑤ | 0.0028 ⑥ | — | 0.079 | 0.079 |
| | Pulsar | 58–72 | 0.7500 | 0.433 | 0.0028 | 8.000 | 0.079 | 0.059 |
| | Sentra | 58–72 | 0.7500 | 0.394 | 0.0028 | 8.000 | 0.079 | 0.059 |
| | Stanza | 58–72 | 0.8125 ⑪ | 0.630 ⑫ | 0.0028 | 8.000 ⑬ | 0.079 | 0.059 |
| 1987 | 200SX | 87–108 | 0.9380 | 0.630 ⑤ | 0.0028 ⑥ | — | 0.080 | 0.080 |
| | 300ZX | 72–87 | 0.9380 | 0.787 ⑧ | 0.0028 ⑥ | — | 0.079 | 0.079 |
| | Maxima | 72–87 | 1.0000 | 0.787 ⑤ | 0.0028 ⑥ | — | 0.079 | 0.079 |
| | Pulsar | 72–87 | ⑨ | ⑩ | 0.0028 | 8.000 | 0.079 | 0.059 |
| | Sentra | 72–87 | ⑨ | ⑩ | 0.0028 | 8.000 ⑭ | 0.079 | 0.059 |
| | Stanza | 72–87 | ⑨ | 0.787 | 0.0028 | 10.24 ⑮ | 0.079 | 0.059 |

## BRAKE SPECIFICATIONS

All measurements in inches unless noted

| Year | Model | Lug Nut Torque (ft. lbs.) | Master Cylinder Bore | Brake Disc Minimum Thickness | Brake Disc Maximum Runout | Standard Brake Drum Diameter | Minimum Lining Thickness Front | Minimum Lining Thickness Rear |
|---|---|---|---|---|---|---|---|---|
| 1988 | 200SX | 87–108 | 0.9380 | 0.630⑤ | 0.0028⑥ | — | 0.080 | 0.080 |
| | 300SX | 72–87 | 0.9380 | 0.787⑧ | 0.0028⑥ | — | 0.080 | 0.080 |
| | Maxima | 72–87 | 1.0000 | 0.787⑤ | 0.0028⑥ | — | 0.079 | 0.079 |
| | Pulsar | 72–87 | ⑨ | ⑩ | 0.0028 | 8.000 | 0.079 | 0.059 |
| | Sentra | 72–87 | ⑯ | ⑩ | 0.0028 | 8.000⑭ | 0.079 | 0.059 |
| | Stanza | 72–87 | ⑨ | 0.787 | 0.0028 | 9.000 | 0.079 | 0.059 |
| 1989-90 | 240SX | 87–108 | 0.875 | 0.709⑰ | 0.0028⑥ | — | 0.079 | 0.079 |
| | 300ZX | 72–87 | 0.9375 | 0.787⑧ | 0.0028⑥ | — | 0.079 | 0.079 |
| | Maxima | 72–87 | 1.0000 | 0.787⑤ | 0.0028⑥ | 9.06 | 0.079 | 0.059 |
| | Pulsar | 72–87 | ⑱ | ⑲ | 0.0028 | 8.05 | 0.079 | 0.059 |
| | Sentra | 72–87 | ⑳ | ⑩ | 0.0028 | 8.05㉑ | 0.079 | 0.059 |
| | Stanza | 72–87 | 1.0000 | 0.7870 | 0.0028 | 9.06 | 0.079 | 0.059 |

**NOTE:** Minimum lining thickness is as recommended by the manufacturer. Due to variation in state inspection regulations, the minimum allowable thickness may be different than recommended.

— Not applicable

① Rear disc – 0.339

② Rear disc – 0.0059

③ Rear disc – 0.339

④ Rear disc – 0.0059

⑤ Front disc on V6 models – 0.787
Rear disc on all models – 0.354

⑥ Rear disc – 0.0028

⑦ Rear disc – 0.0079

⑧ Front disc on Turbo – 0.945
rear disc on all models – 0.709

⑨ Pulsar
with CA16DE – 1.0000
with E16i – 0.9380
with CA18DE – 1.0000
Sentra
with gasoline engine – 0.9380
Stanza
All except 2WD wagon – 1.0000
2WD wagon – 0.9380

⑩ Pulsar
with CA16DE – 0.630
with E16i – 0.394
with CA18DE – 0.630
Sentra
Gasoline engine except wagon
0.394
Gasoline engine wagon – 0.630
4WD wagon – 0.630

⑪ 2WD wagon – 0.9380
4WD wagon – 1.0000

⑫ Wagon – 0.787

⑬ 2WD wagon – 9.000
4WD wagon – 10.24

⑭ 4WD – 9.000

⑮ Wagon – 9.000

⑯ 2WD wagon – 0.9380
4WD wagon – 1.0000

⑰ Front; Rear – 0.079

⑱ Pulsar
with CA18DE
large – 1.0000
small – 0.8125
With GA16i
large – 0.9375
Small – 0.7500

⑲ Pulsar
with CA18DE 0.630
with GA16i 0.394

⑳ Sentra 2WD and 4WD
large – 1.0000
small – 0.8125

㉑ 4WD – 9.06

## WHEEL ALIGNMENT

| Year | Model | Caster Range (deg.) | Caster Preferred Setting (deg.) | Camber Range (deg.) | Camber Preferred Setting (deg.) | Toe-in (in.) | Steering Axis Inclination (deg.) |
|---|---|---|---|---|---|---|---|
| 1983 | 810 (Front) | 2 15/16P–4 7/16P | 3 11/16P | 5/16N–1 3/16P | 7/16P | 1/32 | 12 1/8 |
| | (Rear) | — | — | 15/16P–2 7/16P | 1 11/16P | 7/32 | — |
| | 200SX | 1 3/4P–3 1/4P | 2 1/2P | 11/16N–13/16P | 1/16P | 3/64 | 8 5/32 |
| | 280ZX (Front) | 4 3/16P–5 11/16P | 4 15/16P | 9/16N–15/16P | 3/16P | 3/64–1/8 | 9 11/32 |
| | (Rear) | — | — | 1/16N–1 7/16P | 3/4P | 5/64–5/32 | — |
| | Pulsar | 3/4P–2 1/4P | 1 1/2P | 9/16N–1 1/16P | 1/4P | 0–5/64 | 12 3/4 |
| | Sentra | 3/4P–2 1/4P | 1 1/2P | 9/16N–1 1/16P | 1/4P | 1/8–3/16 | 12 15/16 |
| | Stanza (Front) | 11/16P–2 3/16P | 1 3/8P | 3/4N–3/4P | 0 | 0–5/64 | 14 13/32 |
| | (Rear) | — | — | 0–1 1/2P | 3/4P | 0–5/64 | — |
| 1984 | 200SX (Front) | 2 3/4P–4 1/4P | 3 1/2P | 7/16N–1 1/16P | 1/4P | 1/32N–1/32P | 11 11/16 |
| | (Rear) | — | — | 1 1/4N–1/4P | 1/2N | 1/16N–0 | — |
| | 300ZX (Front) | 5 13/16P–7 5/16P | 6 9/16P | 9/16N–15/16P | 3/16P | 1/32–1/8 | 13 |
| | (Rear) | — | — | 1 15/16N–7/16N | 1 3/16N | 1/16–1/16 | — |
| | Maxima (Front) | 2 15/16P–4 7/16P | 3 11/16P | 5/16N–1 3/16P | 7/16P | 1/32 | 12 1/8 |
| | (Rear) | — | — | 1 1/4P–2 3/4P | 2P | 5/32 | — |
| | Pulsar | 3/4P–2 1/4P | 1 1/2P | 9/16N–1 1/16P | 1/4P | 0–5/64 | 12 3/4 |
| | Sentra (Front) | 3/4P–2 1/4P | 1 1/2P | 7/16N–1 1/16P | 1/4P | 1/16–3/32 | 12 3/16 |
| | (Rear) | — | — | 1 3/4N–1/4N | 1N | 1/8N–1/8P | — |
| | Stanza (Front) | 11/16P–2 3/16P | 1 3/8P | 3/4N–3/4P | 0 | 0–5/64 | 14 13/32 |
| | (Rear) | — | — | 0–1 1/2P | 3/4P | 0–5/64 | — |
| 1985 | 200SX (Front) | 2 3/4P–4 1/4P | 3 1/2P | 7/16N–1 1/16P | 1/4P | 1/32N–1/32P | 11 11/16 |
| | (Rear) | — | — | 1 1/4N–1/4P | 1/2N | 1/16N–0 | — |
| | 300ZX (Front) | 5 13/16P–7 5/16P | 6 9/16P | 9/16N–15/16P | 3/16P | 1/32–1/8 | 13 |
| | (Rear) | — | — | 1 15/16N–7/16N | 1 3/16N | 1/16–1/16 | — |
| | Maxima (Front) | 1 1/4P–2 3/4P | 2P | 7/16N–1 1/16P | 5/16P | 1/32–1/8 | 13 3/4 |
| | (Rear—Sedan) | — | — | 1/2N–1P | 1/4P | 15/64–5/64 | — |
| | (Rear—Wagon) | — | — | 23/64N–1 5/32P | — | 9/32–1/8 | — |

## WHEEL ALIGNMENT

| Year | Model | Caster Range (deg.) | Caster Preferred Setting (deg.) | Camber Range (deg.) | Camber Preferred Setting (deg.) | Toe-in (in.) | Steering Axis Inclination (deg.) |
|---|---|---|---|---|---|---|---|
| 1985 | Pulsar (Front) | 3/4P–2 1/4P | 1 1/2P | 7/16N–1 1/16P | 1/4P | 1/16–3/32 | 12 3/16 |
| | (Rear) | — | — | 1 3/4N–1/4N | 1N | 1/8N–1/8P | — |
| | Sentra (Front) | 3/4P–2 1/4P | 1 1/2P | 7/16N–1 1/16P | 1/4P | 1/16–3/32 | 12 3/16 |
| | (Rear) | — | — | 1 3/4N–1/4N | 1N | 1/8N–1/8P | — |
| | Stanza (Front) | 11/16P–2 3/16P | 1 3/8P | 7/16N–1 1/16P | 1/4P | 0–5/64 | 14 13/32 |
| | (Rear) | — | — | 0–1 1/2P | 3/4P | 0–5/64 | — |
| 1986 | 200SX (Front) | 2 3/4P–4 1/4P | 3 1/2P | 7/16N–1 1/16P | 1/4P | 1/32N–1/32P | 11 11/16 |
| | (Rear) | — | — | 1 1/4N–1/4P | 1/2N | 1/16N–0 | — |
| | 300ZX (Front) | 5 13/16P–7 5/16P | 6 9/16P | 9/16N–15/16P | 3/16P | 1/32–1/8 | 13 |
| | (Rear) | — | — | 1 15/16N–7/16N | 1 3/16N | 1/16N–3/32P | — |
| | Maxima (Front) | 1 1/4P–2 3/4P | 2P | 7/16N–1 1/16P | 5/16P | 1/32–1/8 | 13 3/4 |
| | (Rear, Sdn) | — | — | 1/2N–1P | 1/4P | 15/64–5/64 | — |
| | (Rear—Wgn) | — | — | 23/64N–1 5/32P | — | 9/32–1/8 | — |
| | Pulsar (Front) | 3/4P–2 1/4P | 1 1/2P | 7/16N–1 1/16P | 1/4P | 1/16–3/32 | 12 3/16 |
| | (Rear) | — | — | 1 3/4N–1/4N | 1N | 1/8N–1/8P | — |
| | Sentra (Front) | 3/4P–2 1/4P | 1 1/2P | 7/16N–1 1/16P | 1/4P | 1/16–3/32 | 12 3/16 |
| | (Rear) | — | — | 1 3/4N–1/4N | 1N | 1/8N–1/8P | — |
| | Stanza (Front) | 11/16P–2 3/16P | 1 3/8P | 7/16N–1 1/16P | 1/4P | 0–5/64 | 14 13/32 |
| | (Rear) | — | — | 0–1 1/2P | 3/4P | 9/32N–1/4P | — |
| | Stanza Wagon (Front 2WD) | 3/4P–2 1/4P | 1 1/2P | 1/4N–1 1/4P | 1/2P | 1/16–1/8 | 12 |
| | (Front 4WD) | 9/16P–2 1/16P | 1 5/16P | 9/16N–1 1/16P | 5/16P | 1/32N–1/16P | 11 3/4 |
| | (Rear 2WD) | — | — | 1N–1P | 0 | 5/64–5/16 | — |
| | (Rear 4WD) | — | — | 0–1 1/2P | 3/4P | 5/32N–0 | — |
| 1987 | 200SX (Front) | 2 3/4P–4 1/4P | 3 1/2P | 7/16N–1 1/16P | 1/4P | 1/32N–1/32P | 11 11/16 |
| | (Rear) | — | — | 1 1/4N–1/4P | 1/2N | 5/64N–0 | — |
| | 300ZX (Front) | 5 13/16P–7 5/16P | 6 9/16P | 9/16N–15/16P | 3/16P | 1/32–1/8 | 13 |
| | (Rear) | — | — | 1 15/16N–7/16N | 1 3/16N | 1/16N–3/32P | — |
| | Maxima (Front) | 1 1/4P–2 3/4P | 2P | 7/16N–1 1/16P | 5/16P | 1/32–1/8 | 13 3/4 |
| | (Rear) | — | — | 1 3/16N–5/16P | 7/16N | 5/64–15/64 | — |

## WHEEL ALIGNMENT

| Year | Model | Caster Range (deg.) | Caster Preferred Setting (deg.) | Camber Range (deg.) | Camber Preferred Setting (deg.) | Toe-in (in.) | Wheel Turning Angle (deg.) |
|---|---|---|---|---|---|---|---|
| 1987 | Pulsar (Front) | 1 3/16P–2 11/16P | 1 15/16P | 1 1/4N–1/4P | 1/2N | 1/32N–1/32P | 14 7/16 |
| | (Rear) | — | — | 2N–1/2N | 1 1/4N | 1/16N–3/32P | — |
| | Sentra – 2wd (Front exc Cpe) | 1 1/16P–2 9/16P | 1 13/16P | 15/16N–9/16P | 3/16N | 1/32N–1/32P | 14 |
| | (Front – Cpe) | 1 1/4P–2 3/4P | 2P | 1 1/16N–1/4P | 7/16N | 1/32N–1/32P | 14 1/4 |
| | (Rear exc Cpe) | — | — | 1 3/4N–1/4N | 1N | 1/32–3/16 | — |
| | (Rear Cpe) | — | — | 1 15/16N–7/16N | 1 3/16N | 1/32–3/16 | — |
| | Sentra 4WD (Front) | 3/16P–1 11/16 | 15/16P | 13/16N–11/16P | 1/16N | 1/32N–1/16P | 13 9/16 |
| | (Rear) | — | — | 15/16N–9/16P | 3/16N | 0–5/32 | — |
| | Stanza (Front) | 1 1/4P–2 3/4P | 2P | 1/4N–1 1/2P | 5/8P | 1/32–1/8 | 14 9/16 |
| | (Rear) | — | — | 1 3/16N–5/16P | 7/16N | 5/64–16/64 | — |
| | Stanza Wagon (Front 2WD) | 3/4P–2 1/4P | 1 1/2P | 1/4N–1 1/4P | 1/2P | 1/16–1/8 | 12 |
| | (Front 4WD) | 9/16P–2 1/16P | 1 5/16P | 7/16N–1 1/16P | 3/16P | 1/32N–1/16P | 11 3/4 |
| | (Rear 2WD) | — | — | 1N–1P | 0 | 5/64–5/16 | — |
| | (Rear 4WD) | — | — | 0–1 1/2P | 3/4P | 5/32N–0 | — |
| 1988 | 200SX (Front) | 2 3/4P–4 1/4P | — | 3/8N–1 1/16P | — | 1/64P–1/10P | 12 3/4 |
| | (Rear) | — | — | 1 1/4N–1/4P | — | 5/64P–0 | — |
| | 300SX (Front) | 5 13/16P–7 5/16P | — | 9/16N–15/16P | — | 1/32P–1/8P | 13 11/16 |
| | (Rear) | — | — | 1 15/16N–7/16N | — | ① | — |
| | Maxima (Front) | 1 1/4P–2 3/4P | — | 7/16N–1 1/16P | — | 1/16P – 1/4P | 14 1/2 |
| | (Rear) | — | — | 1 3/16N–5/16P | — | 3/32P–1/4P | — |
| | Pulsar (Front) | 1 3/16P–2 11/16P | — | 1 1/4N–1/4P | — | ② | 14 13/16 |
| | (Rear) | — | — | 2N–1/2N | — | ① | — |
| | Sentra 2WD (Front – Cpe) | 7/8P–2 3/8P | — | 1 1/16N–7/16P | — | ③ | 14 3/4 |
| | (Rear – Cpe) | — | — | 1 15/16N–7/16N | — | 1/32P–1/8P | — |
| | (Front exc Cpe) | 3/4P–2 1/4P | — | 15/16N–9/16P | — | ③ | 14 1/2 |
| | (Rear exc Cpe) | — | — | 1 7/8N–3/8N | — | 0–3/16P | — |
| | Sentra 4WD (Front) | 1/8P–1 5/8P | — | 7/8N–5/8P | — | ④ | 13 15/16 |
| | (Rear) | — | — | 7/8N–5/8P | — | 0–3/16P | — |

## WHEEL ALIGNMENT

| Year | Model | Caster Range (deg.) | Caster Preferred Setting (deg.) | Camber Range (deg.) | Camber Preferred Setting (deg.) | Toe-In (in.) | Steering Axis Inclination (deg.) |
|---|---|---|---|---|---|---|---|
| 1988 | Stanza (Front) | 1¼P–2¾P | — | 7/16N–1 1/16P | — | 1/32P–⅛P | 14⅝ |
| | (Rear) | — | — | 1 3/16N–5/16P | — | 3/32P–¼P | — |
| | Stanza Wagon (Front 2WD) | ¾P–2¼P | — | ¼N–1¼P | — | 1/16P–9/64P | 12 |
| | (Rear 2WD) | — | — | 1N–1P | — | ⑤ | — |
| | (Front 4WD) | 9/16P–2 1/16P | — | ½N–1 1/16P | — | 1/64P–1/16P | 11¾ |
| | (Rear 4WD) | — | — | 0–1½P | — | ⑥ | — |
| 1989-90 | 240SX (Front) | 6P–7½P | — | 1½N–0 | — | 0–3/16P | 13¼ |
| | (Rear) | — | — | 2N–½N | — | 1/16–3/32 | — |
| | 300ZX (Front) | 5 13/16P | — | 9/16N–15/16P | — | 1/32–⅛ | 13 7/16 |
| | (Rear) | — | — | 1 15/16N–7/16N | — | 1/16–3/32 | — |
| | Maxima (Front) | ½P–2P | — | 1N–½P | — | 1/32–⅛ | 14⅜ |
| | (Rear) | — | — | 1 5/16N–3/16 | — | 1/32–⅛P | — |
| | Pulsar (Front) | 1 3/16P–2 11/16P | — | 1¼N–¼P | — | ⑦ | 14 13/16 |
| | (Rear) | — | — | 2N–½N | — | 1/16–3/32 | — |
| | Sentra 2WD (Front—Cpe) | ⅞P–2⅜P | — | 1 1/16N–7/16P | — | 1/32–1/16⑧ | 14¾ |
| | (Rear—Cpe) | — | — | 1 15/16N–7/16N | — | 1/32P–⅛P⑨ | — |
| | (Front exc Cpe) | ¾P–2¼P | — | 15/16N–9/16P | — | 1/32–1/16⑧ | 14½ |
| | (Rear exc Cpe) | — | — | 1⅞N–⅜N | — | 0–3/16P | — |
| | Sentra 4WD (Front) | ⅛P–1⅝P | — | ⅞N–⅝P | — | ③ | 13 15/16 |
| | (Rear) | — | — | ⅞N–⅝P | — | 0–3/16 | — |
| | Stanza (Front) | 1 5/16P–2 13/16P | — | 7/16N–1 1/16P | — | 1/16–5/32 | 14⅝ |
| | (Rear) | — | — | 1 3/16N–5/16P | — | 3/32–5/16⑤ | — |

N—Negative
P—Positive
① 1/16 Toe Out—3/32 Toe In
② 1/16 Toe Out—1/16 Toe In
③ 1/32 Toe Out—1/16 Toe In
④ 1/32 Toe Out—1/32 Toe In
⑤ 3/32 Toe Out—5/16 Toe In
⑥ 5/32 Toe Out—0
⑦ 1/16 Toe Out—1/16 Toe In
⑧ 1/32 Toe Out—1/16 Toe In
⑨ 1/32 Toe Out—⅛ Toe In

# TUNE-UP PROCEDURES

## Ignition Timing

**NOTE: The 200SX, 200SX Turbo and Stanza models use a dual electronic ignition. The firing order is 1-3-4-2 and the rotor is designed with a 135 degree offset to fire both spark plugs at the same time.**

**NOTE: Nissan/Datsun does not give ignition timing adjustments for any models (U.S.), except those specified below as the timing is continually adjusted by the engine control system. These models (except below) are not covered in this section. If the ignition timing requires adjustment, please refer to the underhood specifications sticker for applicable procedures.**

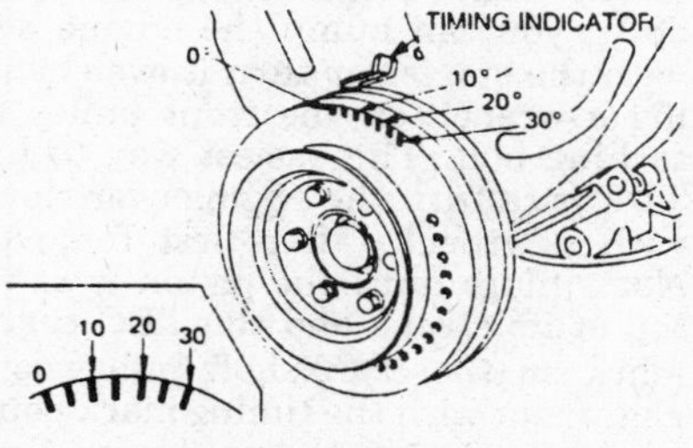


300ZX V6 timing marks

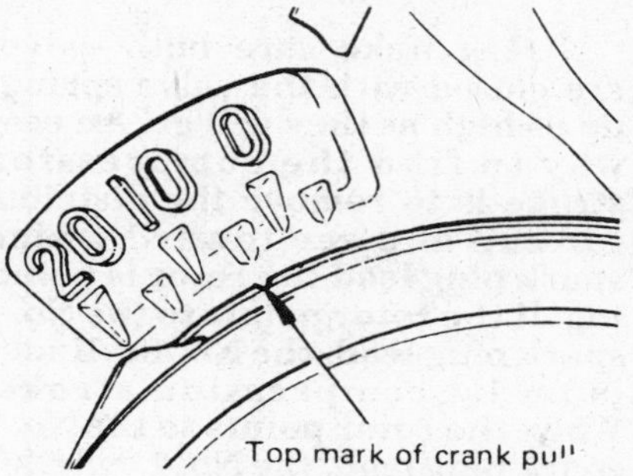


Typical timing marks

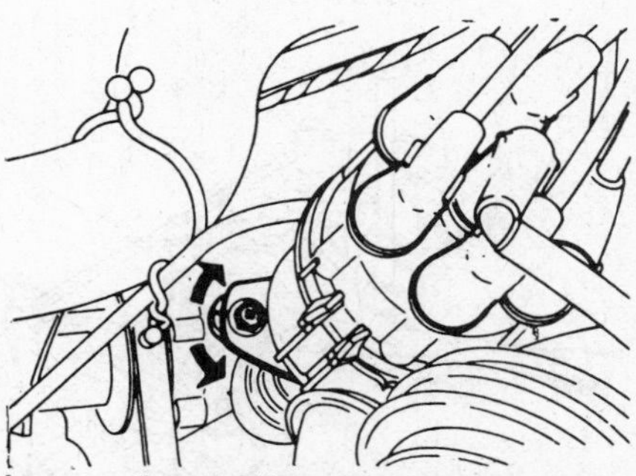

Loosen the distributor lockbolt and turn the distributor slightly to advance (upper arrow) or retard (lower arrow) the timing

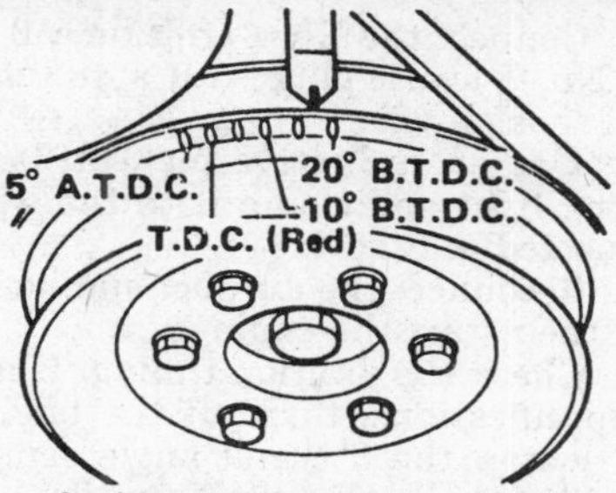


Ignition timing marks–240SX

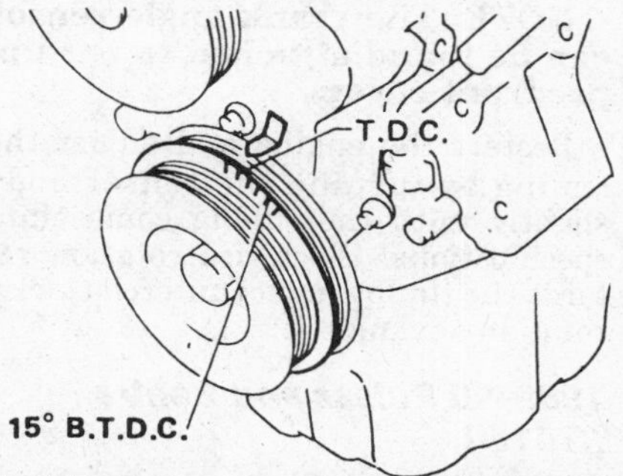


Ignition timing marks–CA18DE engines

### ADJUSTMENT

#### *All Except 1983–86 200SX and 1987–90 Pulsar (CA16DE and CA18DE)*

**NOTE: This is general procedure model and year vary. Please refer to the underhood specifications sticker for applicable procedures.**

1. Locate the timing marks on the crankshaft pulley and the front of the engine.
2. Clean off the timing marks so that you can see them.
3. Use chalk or white paint to color the mark on the crankshaft pulley and the mark on the scale which will indicate the correct timing when aligned with the notch on the crankshaft pulley.
4. Attach a tachometer to the engine.
5. Attach a timing light to the engine, according to the manufacturer's instructions.
6. Leave the vacuum line connected to the distributor vacuum diaphragm and disconnect and plug the hose on those models.
7. Check to make sure that all of the wires clear the fan and then start the engine. Allow the engine to reach normal operating temperature.
8. Check that the idle speed is set to specifications.
9. Aim the timing light and illuminate the timing marks. If the marks that you put on the pulley and the engine are aligned when the light flashes, the timing is correct. Turn off the engine and remove the tachometer and the timing light. If the marks are not in alignment, proceed with the following steps.
10. Turn off the engine.
11. Loosen the distributor lockbolt(s) just enough so that the distributor can be turned with a little effort.
12. Start the engine. Keep the wires of the timing light clear of the fan.
13. With the timing light aimed at pulley and the marks on the engine, turn the distributor in the direction of rotor rotation to retard the spark, and in the opposite direction of rotor rotation to advance the spark. Align the marks on the pulley and the engine with the flashes of the timing light. Tighten the hold-down bolt.

#### *1983–86 200SX*

**NOTE: When checking ignition timing on air conditioner-equipped cars, make sure that the air conditioner is OFF when proceding with the check.**

**CAUTION**

***Automatic transmission-equipped models should be shifted into D for idle speed checks. When in DRIVE the parking brake must be fully applied and both front and rear wheels chocked. When racing the engine on automatic transmission-equipped models, make sure that the shift lever is in the N or P position, and always have an assistant in the driver's seat with his or her foot on the brake pedal. After all adjustments are made, shift the car to the P position and remove the wheel chocks.***

1. Run the engine until it reaches normal operating temperature.
2. Open the hood, and run the engine up to 2000 rpm for about 2 minutes under no-load (all accessories "off").
3. Run the engine at idle speed. Disconnect the hose from the air induction pipe, and cap the pipe.
4. Race the engine two or three times under no-load, then run the engine for one minute at idle.
5. Check idle speed. Adjust the idle

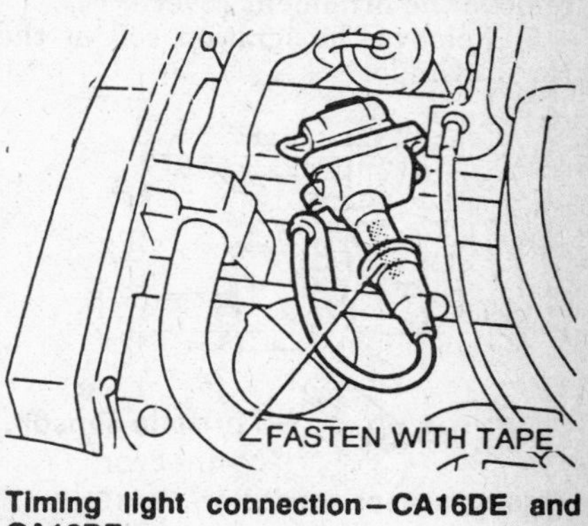


Timing light connection–CA16DE and CA18DE

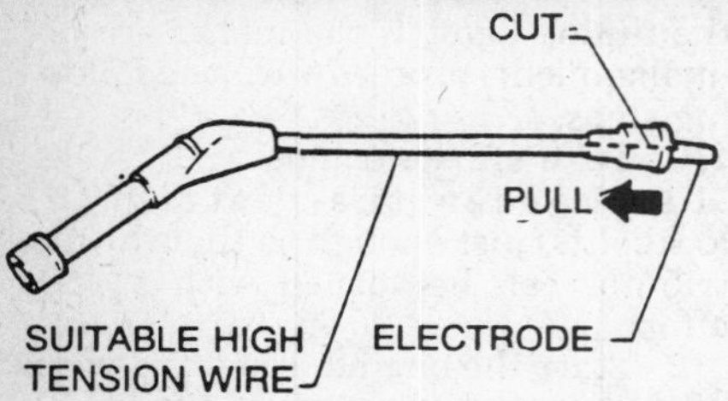


**Suitable high tension wire for timing adjustment—CA16DE and CA18DE**

speed by turning the idle speed adjusting screw if necessary.

6. Connect the timing light according to the manufacturer's instructions. Ignition timing should be adjusted to correct specifications. Adjust the timing by loosening the distributor hold-down bolts and turning the distributor clockwise to advance and counter-clockwise to retard.
7. Reconnect the air induction pipe hose.
8. Roadtest the vehicle for proper operation.

### *1987–90 Pulsar (CA16DE and CA18DE)*

**NOTE: The CA16DE and CA18DE engines do not utilize a conventional distributor and high tension wires. Instead they use 4 small ignition coils fitted directly to each spark plug. The ECU controls the coils by means of a crankangle sensor from which it receives piston position and engine speed information. The ECU takes the information from the crank angle sensor and sends it to the power transistor which controls the engine timing.**

1. Run the engine until it reaches normal operating temperature.
2. Check that the idle speed is at specifications.
3. Disconnect the air duct and both air hoses at the throttle chamber.
4. Remove the ornament cover between the camshaft covers. It has 8 screws and says "Twin Cam". The acceleration wire need not be removed to remove the ornament cover.
5. Remove the ignition coil at the No. 1 cylinder.

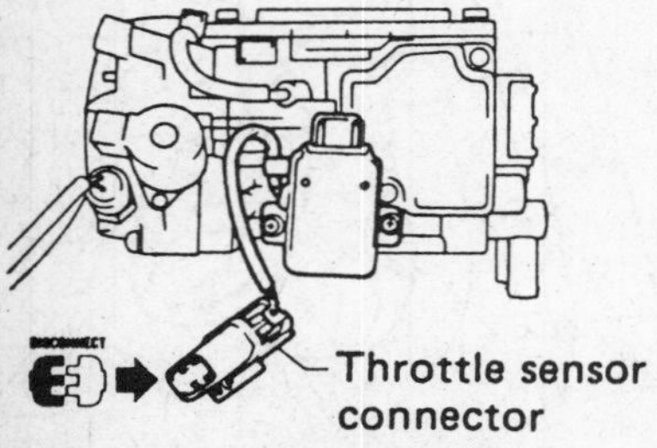


**Throttle sensor connector—GA16I engines**

6. Connect the No. 1 ignition coil to the No. 1 spark plug with a suitable high tension wire.
7. Use an inductive pick-up type timing light and clamp it to the wire connected in Step 6.
8. Reconnect the air duct and hoses and then start the engine.
9. Check the ignition timing. If not to specifications, turn off the engine and loosen the 3 crank angle sensor mounting bolts slightly.

**NOTE: The crank angle sensor can be found attached to the upper front cover.**

Restart the engine and adjust the timing by turning the sensor body slightly until the timing comes into specifications. Clockwise rotation retards the timing and counterclockwise rotation advances it.

### *1989–90 Pulsar and Sentra (GA16I)*

1. Run the engine until the water temperature indicator points to the middle of the gauge.
2. Run the engine for 2 minutes with no load (all electrical accessories in the **OFF** position).
3. Connect a timing light to the engine and illuminate the timing marks. If the timing is not within specification, proceed to adjust.
4. To adjust the timing, stop the engine and disconnect the throttle sensor connector. Loosen the distributor hold down bolt just enough to allow the distributor to be turned by hand.
5. Start the engine and race it 2 or 3 times with no load and then allow the engine to run at idle speed.
6. Adjust the ignition timing by rotating the distributor either clockwise or counterclockwise.
7. Tighten the distributor hold down bolt and stop the engine.
8. Connect the throttle sensor connector and remove the timing light.

# Valve Lash

Hydraulic valve lifters are used on all engines from 1984–90 except those models listed below. Engines with hydraulic lifter do not require periodic valve adjustment, as the hydraulic valve lifter automatically compensates for any required adjustment. Hydraulic valve lifters are best maintained through regular, scheduled engine oil and filter changes.

## ADJUSTMENT

### *Pulsar and Sentra*

**NOTE: The CA16DE, CA18DE and GA16i engines utilize hydraulic lash adjusters. No adjustment is either necessary or possible.**

1. Run the engine until it reaches normal operating temperature. Oil temperature, not water temperature, is critical to valve adjustment. With this in mind, make sure the engine is fully warmed up since this is the only way to make sure the parts have reached their full expansion. Generally speaking, this takes around 15 minutes. After the engine has reached normal operating temperature, shut if off.
2. Purchase a new valve cover gasket before removing the valve cover. The new silicone gasket sealers are just as good or better if you can't find a gasket.
3. Note the location of any hoses or wires which may interfere with valve cover removal, tag and disconnect them and move them aside. Then, remove the bolts which hold the valve cover in place.
4. After the valve cover has been removed, the next step is to get the No. 1 piston at TDC on the compression stroke. There are at least two ways to do it; you can bump the engine over with the starter or turn it over by using a wrench on the front pulley attaching bolt. The easiest way to find TDC is to turn the engine over slowly with a wrench (after first removing No. 1 plug) until the piston is at the top of its stroke and the TDC timing mark on the crankshaft pulley is in alignment with the timing mark pointer. At this point, the valves for No. 1 should be closed.

**NOTE: Make sure both valves are closed with the valve springs up as high as they will go. An easy way to find the compression stroke is to remove the distributor cap and see toward which spark plug lead the rotor is pointing. If the rotor points to the No. 1 spark plug lead, the No. 1 cylinder is on its compression stroke. When the rotor points to the No. 2 spark plug lead, the No. 2 cylinder is on its compression stroke etc.**

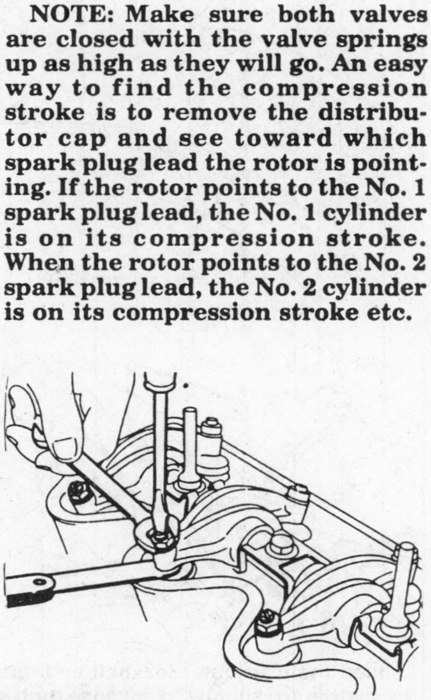

**Adjusting the valves on the E-series engine**

5. With No. 1 piston at TDC of the compression stroke, check the clearance on valves No. 1, 2, 3 and 5 (counting from the front to the rear). Adjust valves No. 1, 2, 3 and 6 on 1983–87 Pulsar and Sentra.

6. To adjust the clearance, loosen the locknut and turn the adjuster with a screwdriver while holding the locknut. The correct size feeler gauge should pass with a slight drag between the rocker arm and the valve stem.

7. Turn the crankshaft one full revolution to position the No. 4 piston at TDC of the compression stroke. Adjust valves No. 4, 6, 7 and 8 in the same manner as the first four. Adjust valves No. 4, 5, 7 and 8 on 1983–89 Pulsar and Sentra.

8. Replace the valve cover with a new cover gasket or sealing compound.

### 280ZX and 1983–84 810 and Maxima

1983–84 810 and Maxima engines and all 280ZX engines are adjusted hot. The engine must be warmed up until the temperature gauge indicator needle is in the middle of the scale and then shut off.

1. Note the locations of all hoses or wires that would interfere with valve cover removal disconnect them and move them aside. Then, remove the 6 bolts which hold the valve cover in place.

2. Bump one end of the cover sharply to loosen the gasket and then pull the valve cover off the engine vertically.

3. Place a wrench on the crankshaft pulley bolt and turn the engine over until the first cam lobe is pointing straight up. The timing marks on the crankshaft pulley should be lined up approximately where they would be when the No. 1 spark plug fires.

**NOTE: If you decide to turn the engine by "bumping" it with the starter, be sure to disconnect the high tension wire from the coil to prevent the engine from accidentally starting.**

**CAUTION**

*Never attempt to turn the engine by using a wrench on the camshaft sprocket bolt; this would put a tremendous strain on the timing chain.*

4. On the 1983 280ZX and 1983–84 810 and Maxima, adjust valves 1, 2, 3, 6, 8 and 9. The feeler gauge should pass between the cam and the cam follower with a very slight drag. Insert the feeler gauge straight, not at an angle.

5. If the clearance is not within the specified limits, loosen the pivot locking nut and then insert the feeler

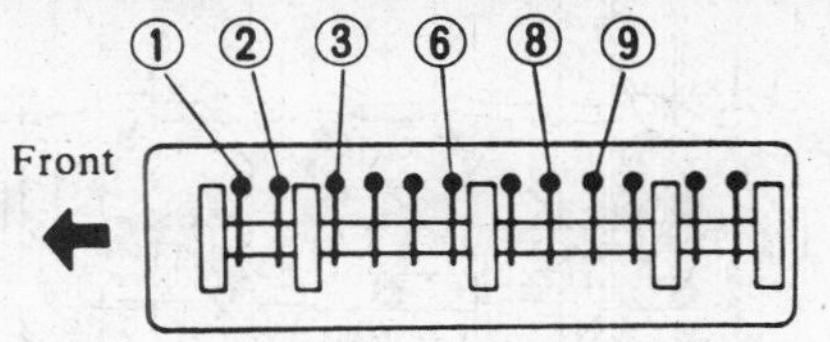


**Primary valve adjustment—1983–84 810/Maxima and 1983 280ZX**

gauge between the cam and the cam follower. Adjust the pivot screw until there is a very slight drag on the gauge, tighten the locking nut, recheck the adjustment and correct as necessary.

6. Turn the engine over so that the first cam lobe is pointing straight down. On the 1983 280ZX and the 1983–84 810 and Maxima, adjust valves 4, 5, 7, 10, 11 and 12. If clearance is not within specifications, adjust as detailed in Step 5.

### 1983 200SX (Z-Series engine) and 1983 Stanza

1. The valves must be adjusted with the engine warm, so start the car and run the engine until the needle on the temperature gauge reaches the middle of the gauge. After the engine is warm, shut it off.

2. Purchase either a new gasket or some silicone gasket sealer before removing the camshaft cover. Counting on the old gasket to be in good shape is a losing proposition; always use new gaskets. Note the location of any wires and hoses which may interfere with

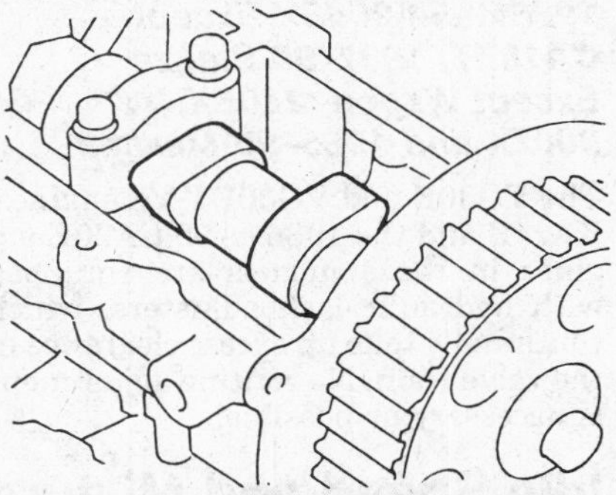

**Position of No. 1 cylinder camshaft lobes at TDC**

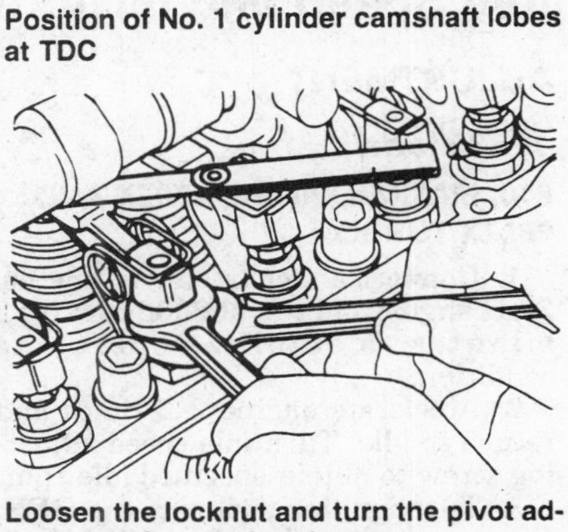

**Loosen the locknut and turn the pivot adjuster to change the clearance**

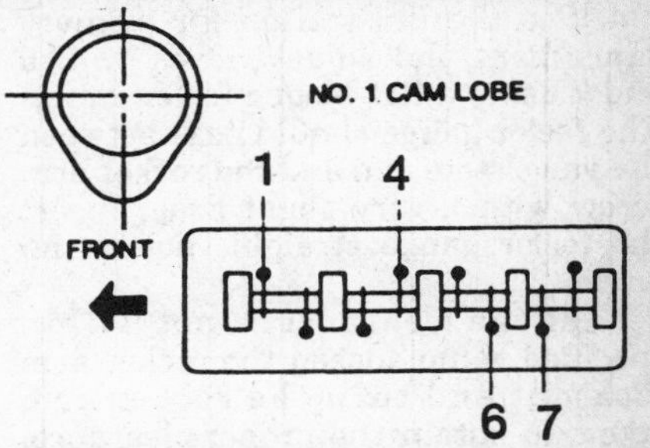


**Primary valve adjustment, No.1 cam lobe pointing down—1983 Z-series and CA20**

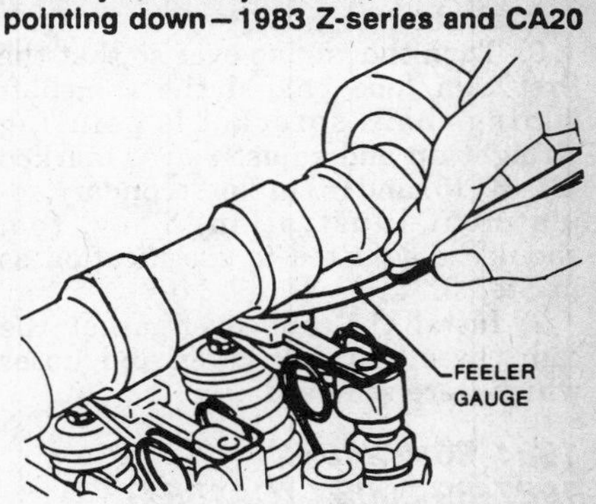


**Checking lash with feeler gauge**

cam cover removal, tag and disconnect them and move them to one side. Remove the bolts holding the cover in place and remove the cover. Remember, the engine will be hot, so be careful.

3. Place a wrench on the crankshaft pulley bolt and turn the engine over until the first cam lobe behind the camshaft timing chain sprocket is pointing straight down.

**NOTE: If you decide to turn the engine by "bumping" it with the starter, be sure to disconnect the high tension wire from the coil(s) to prevent the engine from accidentally starting.**

**CAUTION**

*Never attempt to turn the engine by using a wrench on the camshaft sprocket bolt; there is a 1:2 turning ratio between the camshaft and the crankshaft which will put a tremendous strain on the timing chain.*

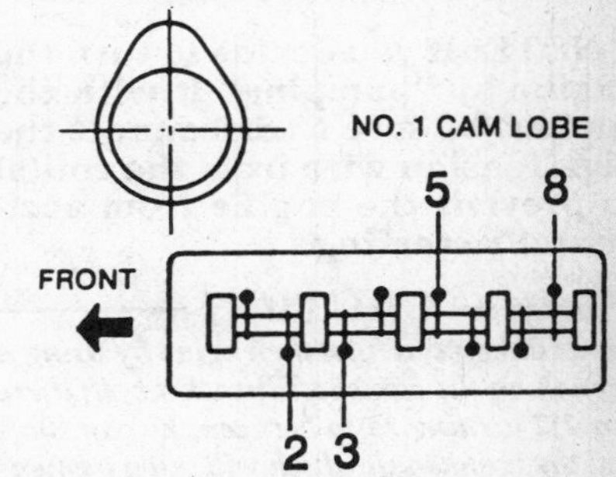


**Secondary valve adjustment, No.1 cam lobe pointing up—1983 Z-series and CA20**

4. See the illustration for primary adjustment and adjust valves 1, 4, 6 and 7 using a flat-bladed feeler gauge. The feeler gauge should pass between the valve stem end and the rocker arm screw with a very slight drag. Insert the feeler gauge straight, not on an angle.

5. If the clearance is not within specified value, loosen the rocker arm lock nut and turn the rocker arm screw to obtain the proper clearance. After correct clearance is obtained, tighten the lock nut.

6. Turn the engine over so that the first cam lobe behind the camshaft timing chain sprocket is pointing straight up and adjust valves marked (2), (3), (5) and (8) in the secondary adjustment illustration. They, too, should be adjusted to specification as in Step 5.

7. Install the cam cover gasket, the cam cover and any wires and hoses which were removed.

### *1984–86½ 200SX 1987–89 200SX (CA18ET) 1984–86 Stanza and 1986–88 Stanza Wagon*

1. The valves must be adjusted with the engine warm, so start the car and run the engine until the needle on the temperature gauge reaches the middle of the gauge. After the engine is warm, shut it off.

2. Purchase either a new gasket or some silicone gasket sealer before removing the camshaft cover. Counting on the old gasket to be in good shape is a losing proposition; always use new gaskets. Note the location of any wires and hoses which may interfere with cam cover removal, tag and disconnect them and move them to one side. Remove the bolts holding the cover in place and remove the cover. Remember, the engine will be hot, so be careful.

3. Place a wrench on the crankshaft pulley bolt and turn the engine over until the first cam lobe behind the camshaft timing chain sprocket is pointing straight down.

**NOTE: If you decide to turn the engine by "bumping" it with the starter, be sure to disconnect the high tension wire from the coil(s) to prevent the engine from accidentally starting.**

**CAUTION**

*Never attempt to turn the engine by using a wrench on the camshaft sprocket bolt; there is a 1:2 turning ratio between the camshaft and the crankshaft which will put a tremendous strain on the timing chain.*

4. Check and adjust the clearance on valves 1, 2, 4 and 6 as shown in the accompanying illustration. This is with No. 1 cylinder at TDC on compression. The feeler gauge should pass between the valve stem end and the rocker arm screw with a very slight drag. Insert the feeler gauge straight, not on an angle.

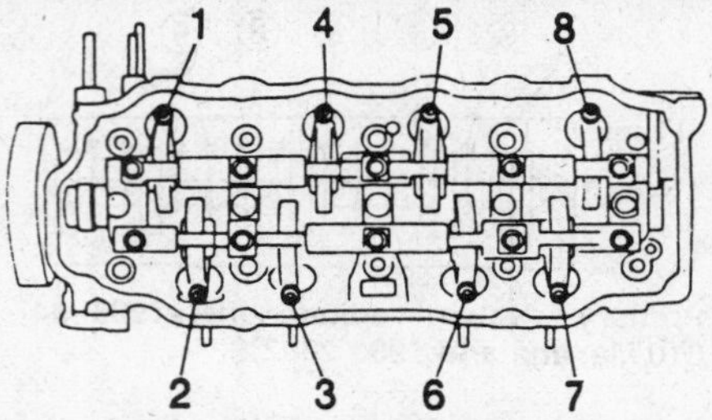

**Valve adjustment sequence – 1984–88 200SX, CA18ET, 1984–86 Stanza and 1986–88 Stanza Wagon**

5. If the clearance is not within specified value, loosen the rocker arm lock nut and turn the rocker arm screw to obtain the proper clearance. After correct clearance is obtained, tighten the lock nut.

6. Turn the engine over so that the first cam lobe behind the camshaft timing chain sprocket is pointing straight up and adjust the clearance on valves 3, 5, 7 and 8 with the No. 4 cylinder at TDC on compression.

7. Install the cam cover gasket, the cam cover and any wires and hoses which were removed.

Follow the procedure above for 1983 models, with the following exceptions:

### *1986½–88 200SX Except CA18ET, 1987–90 Stanza Except Wagon, 240SX, 300ZX and 1985–90 Maxima*

The VG30E and VG30ET V6 engines, KA24E and the 1986½–89 CA20E engines in these models are equipped with hydraulic lash adjusters, which continually take up excess clearance in the valve train. No routine adjustment is necessary or possible.

## Idle Speed and Mixture

### ADJUSTMENT

### *1983 Models*

#### 810, MAXIMA, 200SX, 280ZX AND 280ZX TURBO

1. Connect a tachometer to engine. Start engine and run at 2000 rpm for 2 minutes to stabilize operating condition.

2. Accelerate engine 2–3 times and return to idle. Turn idle speed adjusting screw to obtain specified idle rpm.

3. Turn ignition switch to the **OFF**. Disconnect throttle valve switch harness connector. Disconnect and plug distributor vacuum hose.

4. Disconnect air injection hose and canister purge hose at intake manifold. Plug air induction pipe and purge hose fitting on intake manifold.

5. Start engine, accelerate 2–3 times and allow to idle for 1 minute. Check and, if necessary, adjust ignition timing.

6. Connect a jumper wire between throttle valve switch harness connector terminals No. 24 and No. 30. Install CO meter probe into tailpipe at least 16 inches.

7. With engine idling, check CO level. If necessary to adjust CO, remove air flow meter and drill a small hole in plug covering air by-pass screw. Do not allow drill to contact screw.

8. Clean up all metal shavings from the drilling. Install self tapping screw into hole and remove plug from bore. Install air flow meter. Adjust CO level by turning air bypass screw clockwise to enrich mixture and counterclockwise to lean mixture.

9. Remove air flow meter. Tap new seal plug, with convex side up, into air by-pass screw bore. Install air flow meter.

10. Stop engine. Remove jumper wire from throttle valve switch harness connector. Reconnect harness and all hoses. Reset idle speed to specified rpm.

#### PULSAR, SENTRA AND STANZA

1. Connect a tachometer to the engine and run the engine at idle speed or at 2000 rpm for the Stanza for at least 2 minutes.

2. Install the CO meter probe 16 inches or more into the tailpipe and disconnect and plug the distributor vacuum and air induction hoses. Accelerate the engine to 2000–3000 rpm several times under a no load condition (all electrical accessories in the **OFF** position).

3. Let the engine return to and run at idle speed for at least a minute. Check the ignition timing and adjust if necessary, reconnect the distributor vacuum hoses.

4. Check the idle speed and adjust if necessary and on the Sentra MPG models, disconnect the air/fuel ratio solenoid harness connector. Accelerate the engine several times and return it to idle speed, then check the CO level.

5. If the CO level has to be adjusted, remove the carburetor and drill a small hole in the plug covering the mixture adjustment screw. Be sure that the drill bit does not hit the mixture screw, remove the plug and reinstall the carburetor. All drill shavings must be completely removed.

6. Adjust the CO level by turning the mixture adjustment screw inward

to enrich the mixture and outward to lean the mixture.

7. Reconnect all hoses and install the new plug in the mixture adjusting screw hole.

**NOTE: On 1983 Sentras and Pulsars a rough or uneven idle after engine warm-up may be caused by a loose connection at the fusible link connector at the battery positive terminal or at the carburetor electrical connection.**

### *1984–90 Models*

#### 200SX EXCEPT TURBO, STANZA AND 1984 MAXIMA

1. Connect tachometer and timing light. Turn accessories and air conditioner off. Warm engine to normal operating temperature. On Maxima and 200SX models, open hood and run engine at 2000 rpm for 10 minutes.
2. Stop engine, disconnect and plug vacuum hose at distributor. On Maxima models, disconnect the gray harness connector at distributor. Accelerate engine 2–3 times and return to idle. Adjust idle speed by turning idle speed adjusting screw.
3. On Stanza and 200SX models, turn diagnostic mode selector on ECU (behind left kick panel) to **OFF** position and reconnect vacuum hose at distributor. On Maxima, move passenger seat so ECU is visible.
4. On all models, run engine at 2000 rpm for 2 minutes. The green ECU inspection lamp on Stanza and 200SX should flash on and off at least 9 times in 10 seconds at 2000 rpm. The lamp on Maxima should flash at least 5 times in 10 seconds. If lamp flashed, go to next step.
5. On Maxima models, turn ignition **OFF** and reconnect the gray connector and vacuum hose at distributor. Start and race engine 2–3 times and return to idle. Recheck idle speed and remove test equipment.
6. On Stanza and 200SX models, accelerate engine 2–3 times and return to idle. If red and green ECU inspection lamps flash together, mixture is okay and adjustment is complete. Recheck idle speed and remove test equipment

#### 200SX TURBO, 1985–88 MAXIMA, 300ZX AND 300ZX TURBO

1. Connect the tachometer (coil adapter must be used on most models) and timing light. Turn accessories and air conditioner off. Start and warm engine to operating temperature.
2. On 300ZX and Maxima models, disconnect harness connect at idle-up solenoid valve. Accelerate engine 2–3 times and return to idle. Check and adjust idle speed and ignition timing. To adjust idle speed on all models except 300ZX Turbo, turn idle speed adjusting screw. Reconnect idle-up solenoid on 300ZX and Maxima models.
3. To adjust idle speed on 300ZX Turbo models, stop engine and disconnect harness connect at auxiliary air control valve. Start engine and adjust idle speed to specifications. Stop engine and reconnect control valve. Start engine and ensure idle speed is correct.
4. Locate ECU behind left kick panel on 200SX Turbo, and right kick panel on other models. Turn diagnostic mode selector screw on ECU fully counterclockwise. Start and run engine at 2000 rpm for two minutes. Green ECU inspection lamp should flash on and off at least 9 times in 10 seconds at 2000 rpm and 200SX Turbo and at least 5 times in other models. If lamp flashes, go to next step.
5. On Maxima, 300ZX and 300ZX Turbo models, disconnect harness connector at throttle valve switch. On all models, accelerate engine 2–3 times and return to idle. If Red and Green ECU inspection lamps flash together, mixture adjustment is okay. Recheck idle speed and remove test equipment.

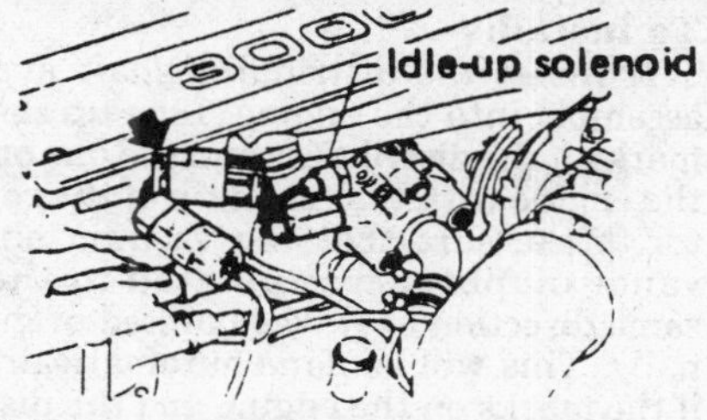

**Idle-up solenoid location on VG30E engines**

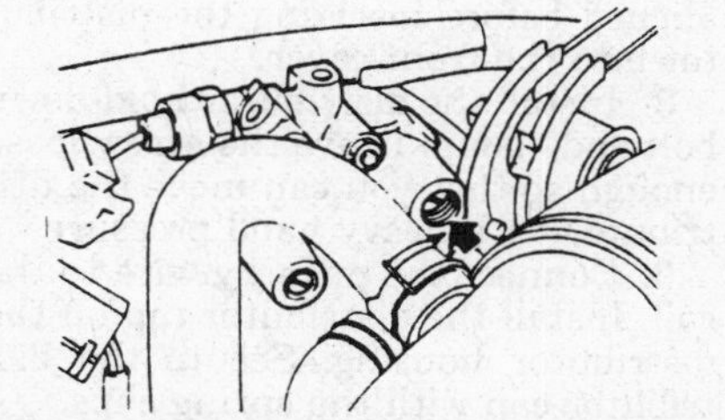
**Idle speed adjustment screw location on VGE30 engines**

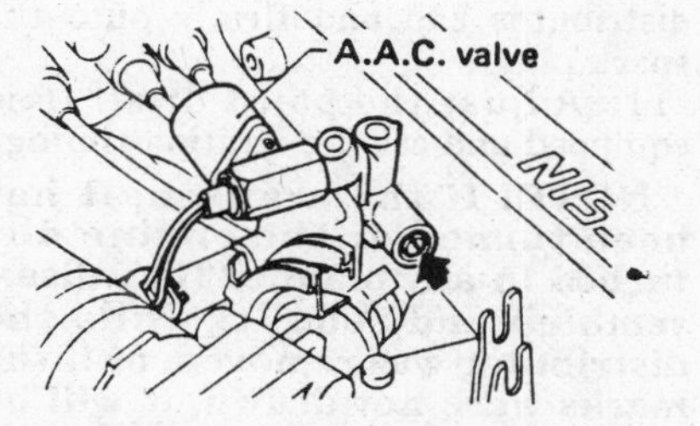

**AAC valve location on 300ZX turbo engines**

#### 1989–90 MAXIMA

1. Before adjusting the idle speed on the engine you must visually check the following items first: air cleaner for clogging, hoses and ducts for leaks, EGR valve for proper operation, all electrical connectors, gaskets and idle switch.
2. Start the engine and warm the engine so it reaches normal operating temperature. The water temperature indicator should be in the middle of the gauge.
3. Then, race the engine to 2000-3000 rpm a few times under no load (all electrical accessories in the **OFF** position) and then allow it to return to the idle speed.
4. Connect a tachometer to the engine.
5. Check the idle speed in the **N** position for both manual and automatic transaxle models.
6. To adjust the idle speed, close the AAC valve (Auxiliary Air Control) by turning the diagnostic mode selector on the ECU. fully clockwise.
7. Adjust the idle speed by turning the idle speed adjusting screw with transaxle in the **N** position.
8. Operate the AAC. valve by turning the diagnostic mode selector on the ECU. fully conterclockwise.
9. Stop the engine. Remove the tachometer and road test vehicle for proper operation.

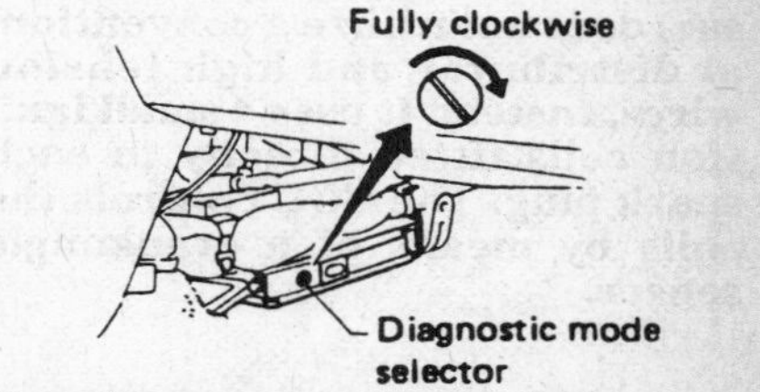

**Turn diagnostic mode selector fully clockwise to close AAC valve – 1989–90 Maxima**

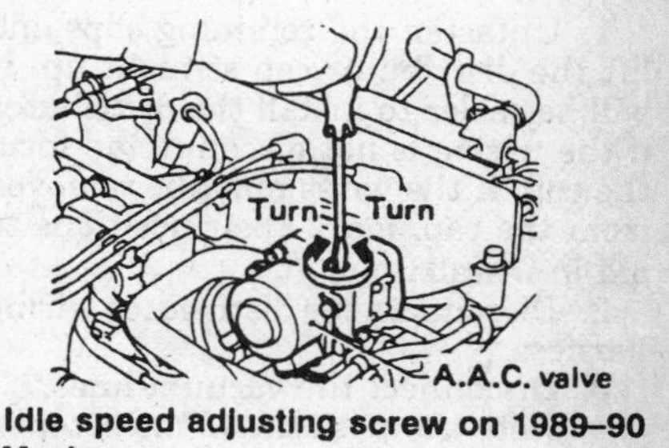

**Idle speed adjusting screw on 1989–90 Maxima**

#### 240SX

1. Before adjusting the idle speed on the engine you must visually check the following items first: air cleaner for clogging, hoses and ducts for leaks, EGR valve for proper operation, all electrical connectors, gaskets and the

throttle valve and throttle valve switch operation.

2. Start the engine and warm the engine so it reaches normal operating temperature. The water temperature indicator should be in the middle of the gauge.

3. Then race the engine to 2000–3000 rpm a few times under no load (all electrical accessories in the **OFF** position and then allow it to return to the idle speed.

4. Connect a tachometer to the engine. Check the idle speed in the **N** position for both manual and automatic transmission models.

5. To adjust the idle speed, first disconnect the throttle sensor harness connector.

6. Adjust the idle speed by turning the idle speed adjusting screw.

7. Stop the engine. Connect the the throttle sensor harness connector.

8. Remove the tachometer.

# ENGINE ELECTRICAL

## Distributor

**NOTE: The CA16DE and CA18DE (used in the 1987–90 Pulsar) does not utilize a conventional distributor and high tension wires. Instead it uses 4 small ignition coils fitted directly to each spark plug. The ECU controls the coils by means of a crankangle sensor.**

### REMOVAL & INSTALLATION

#### *Undisturbed*

1. Unfasten the retaining clips and lift the distributor cap straight up. It will be easier to install the distributor if the wiring is not disconnected form the cap. If the wires must be removed from the cap, mark their positions to aid in installation.

2. Disconnect the distributor wiring harness.

3. Disconnect the vacuum lines.

4. Note the position of the rotor in relation to the base. Scribe a mark on the base of the distributor and on the engine block to facilitate reinstallation. Align the marks with the direction the metal tip of the rotor is pointing.

5. Remove the bolt(s) which hold the distributor to the engine.

6. Lift the distributor assembly from the engine.

**To install:**

7. Insert the distributor shaft and assembly into the engine. Line up the mark on the distributor and the one on the engine with the metal tip of the rotor. Make sure that the vacuum advance diaphragm is pointed in the same direction as it was pointed originally. This will be done automatically if the marks on the engine and the distributor are lined up with the rotor. On 1989–90 240SX, make sure the distributor driving spindle is properly aligned before inserting the distributor into the front cover.

8. Install the distributor hold-down bolt and clamp. Leave the screw loose enough so that you can move the distributor with heavy hand pressure.

9. Connect the primary wire to the coil. Install the distributor cap on the distributor housing. Secure the distributor cap with the spring clips.

10. Install the spark plug wires if removed. Make sure that the wires are pressed all the way into the top of the distributor cap and firmly onto the spark plug.

11. Adjust the point dwell if so equipped and set the ignition timing.

**NOTE: If the crankshaft has been turned or the engine disturbed in any manner (i.e., disassembled and rebuilt) while the distributor was removed, or if the marks were not drawn, it will be necessary to initially time the engine. Follow the procedure given below.**

#### *Disturbed*

1. It is necessary to place the No. 1 cylinder in the firing position to correctly install the distributor. To locate this position, the ignition timing marks on the crankshaft front pulley are used.

2. Remove the No. 1 cylinder spark plug. Turn the crankshaft until the piston in the No. 1 cylinder is moving up on the compression stroke. This can be determined by placing a thumb over the spark plug hole and feeling the air being forced out of the cylinder. Stop turning the crankshaft when the timing marks that are used to time the engine are aligned. On 1989–90 240SX, the driving spindle must be properly aligned to accept the distributor.

3. Oil the distributor housing lightly where the distributor bears on the cylinder block.

4. Install the distributor so that the rotor, which is mounted on the shaft, points toward the No. 1 spark plug terminal tower position when the cap is installed. Of course, you won't be able to see the direction in which the rotor is pointing if the cap is on the distributor. Lay the cap on the top of the distributor and make a mark on the side of the distributor housing just below the No. 1 spark plug terminal. Make sure that the rotor points toward that mark when you install the distributor.

5. When the distributor shaft has reached the bottom of the hole, move the rotor back and forth slightly until

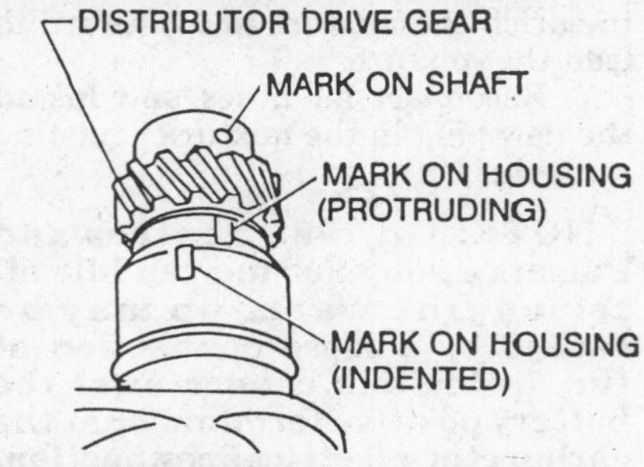


**Distributor shaft and housing alignment marks – 300ZX**

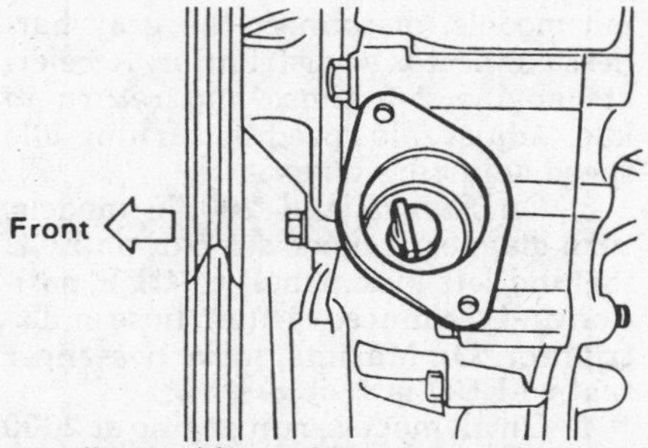


**Distributor drive spidle alignment – 240SX**

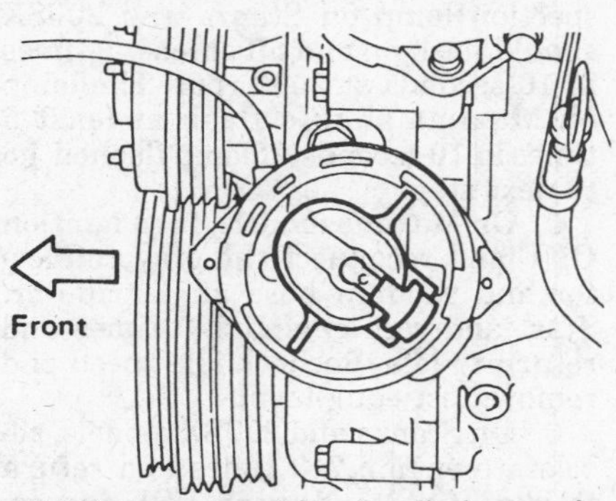


**Distributor rotor at No. 1 cylinder spark position – 240SX**

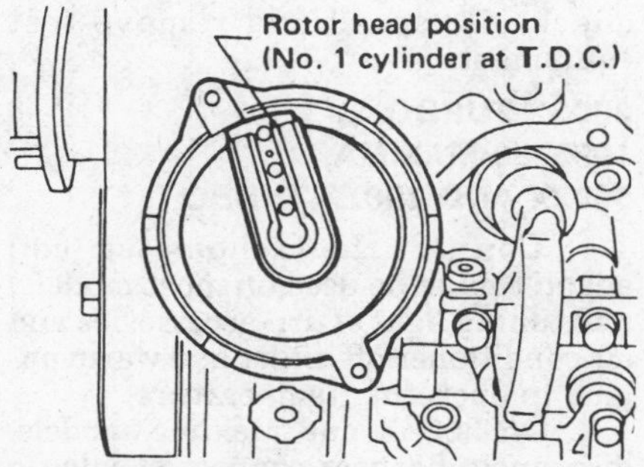


**Distributor rotor at No. 1 cylinder spark position – 300ZX**

the driving lug on the end of the shaft enters the slots cut in the end of the oil pump shaft and the distributor assembly slides down into place.

6. When the distributor is correctly installed, the reluctor teeth should be aligned with the pick-up coil. This can be accomplished by rotating the distributor body after it has been installed in the engine. Once again, line up the marks that you made before the distributor was removed.

7. Install the distributor hold-down bolt.

8. Install the spark plug into the No. 1 spark plug hole and continue from Step 3 of the preceding distributor installation procedure.

## Alternator

### PRECAUTIONS

An alternator is used on all models. The following precautions must be observed to prevent alternator and regulator damage:

- Be absolutely sure of correct polarity when installing a new battery, or connecting a battery charger.
- Do not short across or ground any alternator or regulator terminals.
- Disconnect the battery ground cable before replacing any electrical unit.
- Never operate the alternator with any of the leads disconnected.
- When steam cleaning the engine, be careful not to subject the alternator to excessive heat or moisture.
- When charging the battery, remove it from the car or disconnect the alternator output terminal.

### BELT TENSION ADJUSTMENT

The correct belt tension for all alternators is about ½ in. play on the longest span of the belt.

1. Loosen the alternator pivot and mounting bolts.

2. Pry the alternator toward or away from the engine until the tension is correct. Use a hammer handle or wooden prybar.

3. When the tension is correct, tighten the bolts and check the adjustment. Be careful not to over-tighten the belt, which will lead to alternator bearing failure.

### REMOVAL & INSTALLATION

1. Disconnect the negative battery terminal.

2. Disconnect the 2 lead wires and connector from the alternator.

3. Loosen the drive belt adjusting bolt and remove the belt.

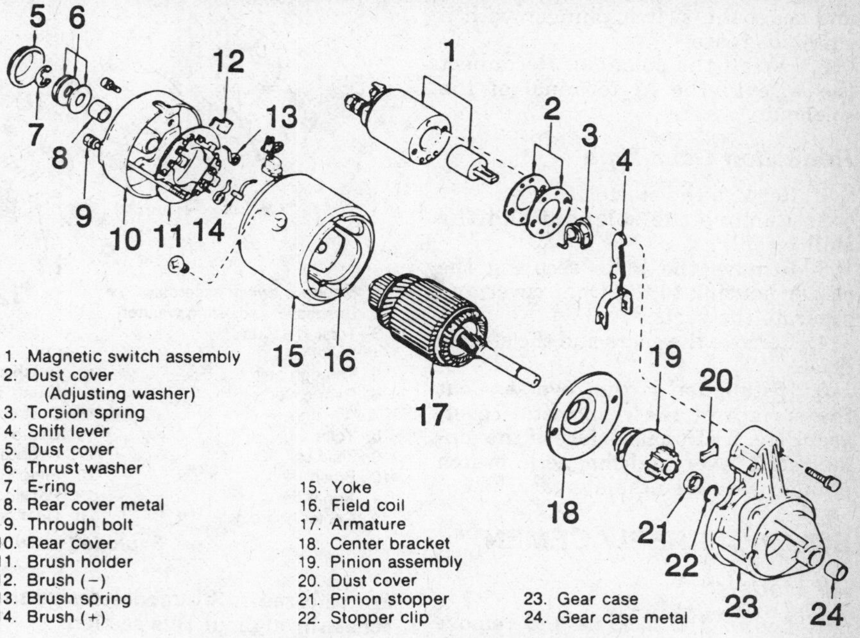


Exploded view of a non-reduction gear starter

4. Unscrew the alternator attaching bolts and remove the alternator from the vehicle. On the 300ZX, first remove the front stabilizer bar bolts and pull the stabilizer bar down.

5. Installation is in the reverse order of removal.

## Voltage Regulator

### REMOVAL & INSTALLATION

**NOTE: All models covered here are equipped with integral regulator alternators. Since the regulator is part of the alternator, no adjustments are possible or necessary.**

## Starter

### REMOVAL & INSTALLATION

1. Disconnect the negative battery cable.

2. Disconnect and label the wires from the terminals on the solenoid.

3. Remove the 2 bolts which secure the starter to the flywheel housing and pull the starter forward and out. To install, reverse the removal procedure. Check the starter for proper operation.

### DRIVE REPLACEMENT

#### *Non-Reduction Gear Type*

1. Remove the starter from the vehicle. Loosen the locknut and remove the connection going to the **M** terminal of the solenoid. Remove the securing screws and remove the solenoid.

2. Remove the dust cover, E-ring, thrust washers, and the 2 screws retaining the brush holder assembly. Remove the brush cover thru-bolts and remove the cover assembly (all models).

3. Lift the brushes to free them from the commutator and remove the brush holder.

4. Tap the yoke assembly lightly with a wooden hammer and remove it from the field and case.

5. Remove the nut and bolt which serve as a pin for the shift lever, carefully retaining the associated washers.

6. Remove the armature assembly and shift lever.

7. Push the stop ring (located at the end of the armature shaft) toward the clutch and remove the snap ring. Remove the stop ring.

8. Remove the clutch assembly from the armature shaft.

**To install the drive:**

9. Install the clutch assembly onto the armature shaft.

10. Put the stop ring on and hold it toward the clutch while installing the snapring.

11. Install the armature assembly and shift lever into the yoke.

12. Install the washers, nut and bolt which serve as a shift lever pivot pin.

13. Install the field back onto the yoke assembly.

14. Life the brushes and install the brush holder. Install the brush cover and thru-bolts.

15. Replace the brush holder set screws, the thrust washers, E-ring, and the dust cover. Coat the surface of the rear metal cover, gear case, frictional surface of the pinion, shift lever

and magnetic switch plunger with a suitable grease.

16. Install the solenoid. Reconnect the wire to the **M** terminal of the solenoid.

### *Reduction Gear Type*

1. Remove the starter.
2. Remove the solenoid and the shift lever.
3. Remove the bolts securing the center housing to the front cover and separate the parts.
4. Remove the gears and the starter drive.
5. Installation is the reverse. Coat the surface of the rear metal cover, gear case, frictional surface of the pinion, shift lever and magnetic switch plunger with a suitable grease.

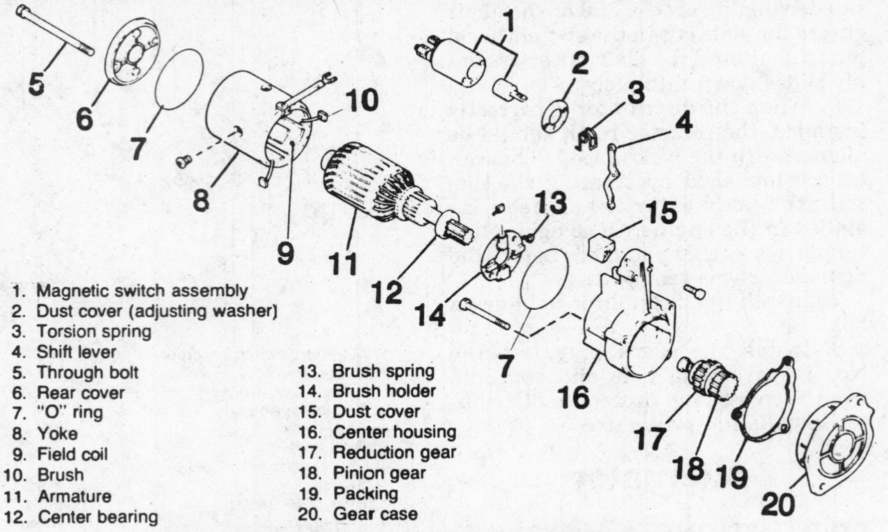


**Exploded view of a reduction gear starter**

## SOLENOID REPLACEMENT

### *All Models*

1. Loosen the locknut and remove the connection going to the **M** terminal of the solenoid.
2. Remove the 3 securing screws and remove the solenoid.
3. To install, reverse the removal procedures. Check the starter for proper operation.

# ENGINE MECHANICAL

## Engine

## REMOVAL & INSTALLATION

Refer to the "Engine Identification" chart for identification of engines by model, number of cylinders, displacement, and camshaft location. Engines are referred to by model designation codes throughout this section.

### *Rear Wheel Drive*

It is best to remove the engine and transmission as a unit, except on 300ZX and 240SX; the engine and transmission are separated before engine removal.

1. Mark the location of the hinges on the hood. Unbolt and remove.
2. Release the fuel system pressure. Disconnect the battery cable. Remove the battery on California models with the Z22E engine with air conditioning.
3. Drain the coolant and automatic transmission fluid, if so equipped.
4. Remove the radiator after disconnecting the automatic transmission coolant tubes. Plug the tubes to prevent leakage.
5. Remove the air cleaner.
6. Remove the fan and pulley.
7. Disconnect:
   a. water temperature gauge wire
   b. oil pressure sending unit wire
   c. ignition distributor primary wire
   d. starter motor connections
   e. fuel hose
   f. alternator leads
   g. heater hoses
   h. throttle and choke connections
   i. engine ground cable

**NOTE: A good rule of thumb when disconnecting the rather complex engine wiring of today's cars is to put a piece of masking tape on the wire and on the connection you removed the wire from, then mark both pieces of tape 1, 2, 3, etc. When replacing wiring, simply match the pieces of tape.**

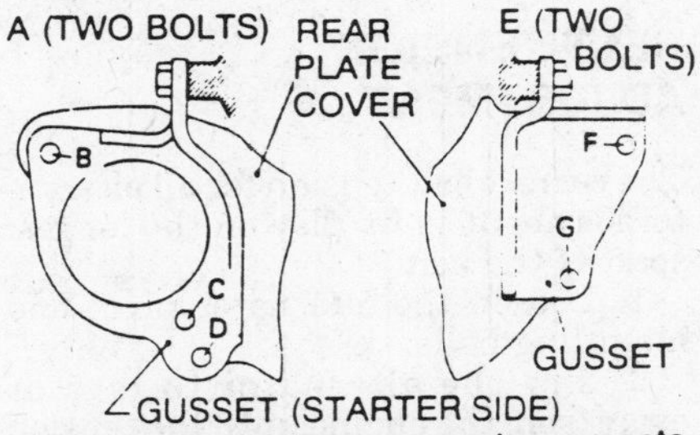


**Torquing the 200SX (V6) engine gussets**

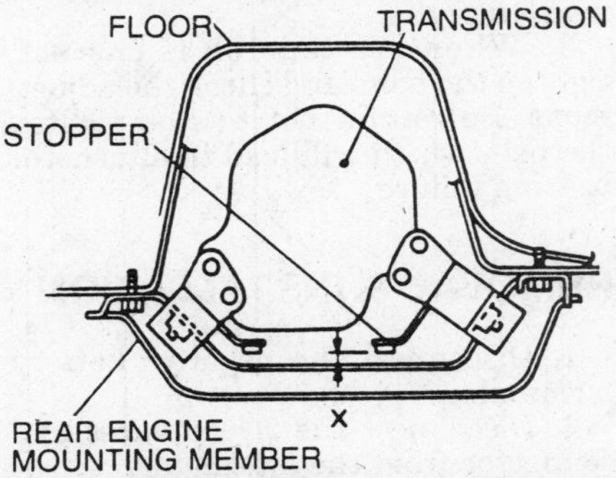


**Adjust the rear mount stopper clearance (X) to 13±1.5mm–200SX (4 cyl.) with AT**

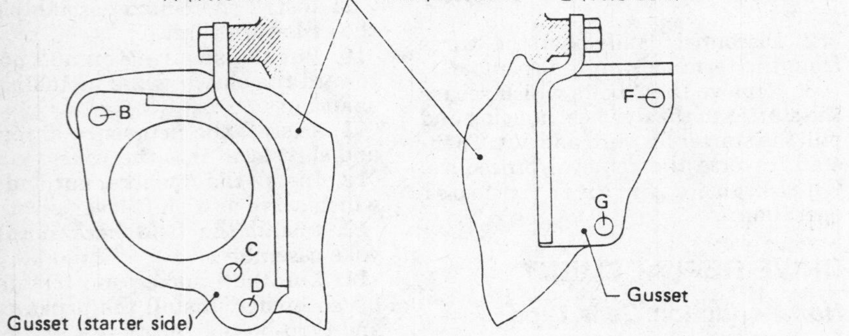


| 1st | 2nd | 3rd | 4th | 5th | 6th |
|---|---|---|---|---|---|
| A*1 | D*2 | A*2 | F*2 and G*2 | E*2 | B*2 and C*2 |

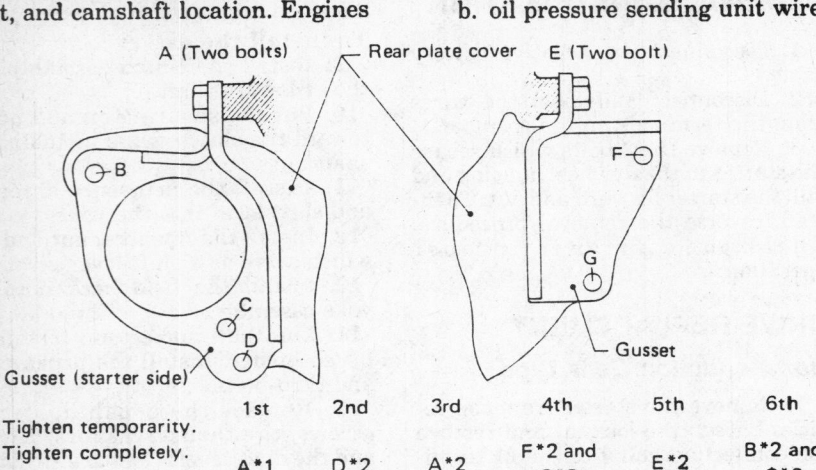

*1: Tighten temporarity.
*2: Tighten completely.

**Torquing 300ZX engine gussets**

## CAUTION

***On models with air conditioning, it is necessary to remove the compressor and the condenser from their mounts. DO NOT ATTEMPT TO UNFASTEN ANY OF THE AIR CONDITIONER HOSES.***

8. Disconnect the power brake booster hose from the engine.
9. Remove the clutch operating cylinder and return spring.
10. Disconnect the speedometer cable from the transmission. Disconnect the back up light switch and any other wiring or attachments to the transmission.
11. Disconnect the column shift linkage. Remove the floorshift lever. On the Z22E model, remove the boot, withdraw the lock pin, and remove the lever from inside the car.
12. Detach the exhaust pipe from the exhaust manifold. Remove the front section of the exhaust system.
13. Mark the relationship of the driveshaft flanges and remove the driveshaft.
14. Place a jack under the transmission to support it. Remove the rear crossmember.
15. Attach a hoist to the lifting hooks on the engine (at either end of the cylinder head). Support the engine.
16. Unbolt the front engine mounts. Tilt the engine by lowering the jack under the transmission and raising the hoist.
17. Reverse the procedure to install the engine.

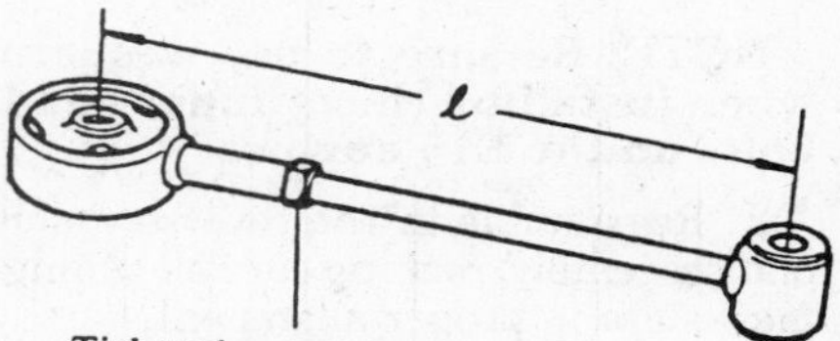


**Adjusting the buffer rod length – 310**

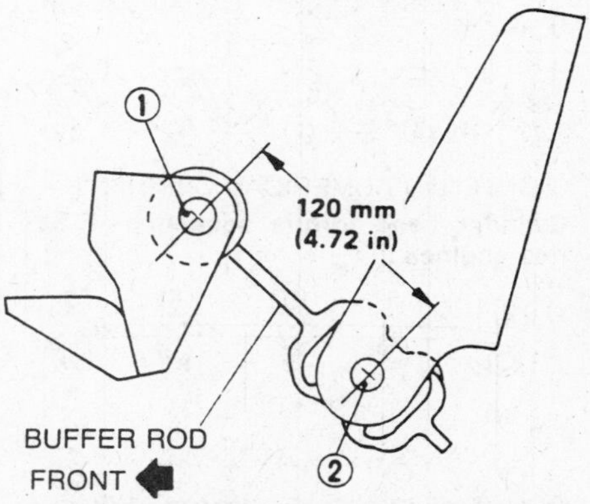


**On the 1986 Stanza wagon (4wd), tighten the buffer rod and the sub-mounting bolts in the order shown**

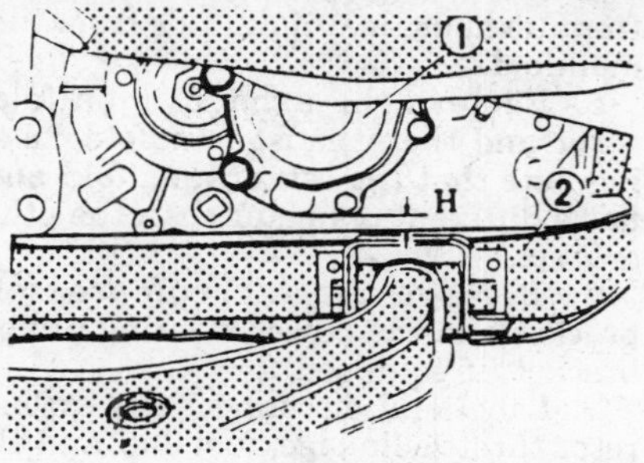


1. Clutch housing
2. Sub-frame

**Clearance between the frame and clutch housing – 310**

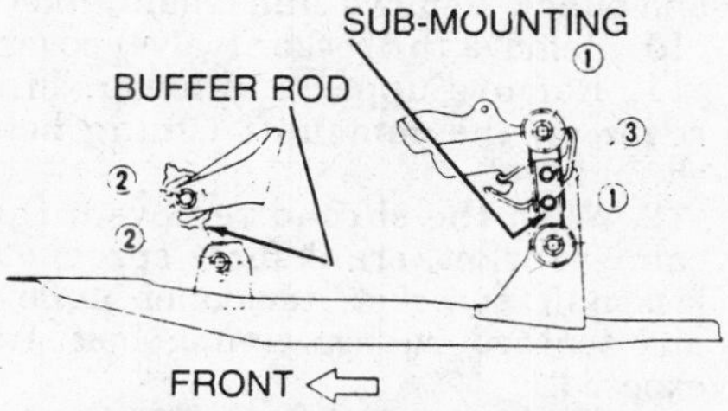


**On the 1986 Stanza Wagon (2WD) and all 1987–89 models, tighten the buffer rod and the sub-mounting bolts in the order shown**

On the 200SX (V6) and 300ZX, torque the engine gusset bolts in six stages, as shown in the accompanying illustration. When installing the engine on A/T equipped 200SXs (4 cyl.), adjust the rear mounting insulator to 0.51±0.059 in. (13±1.5mm) **X** in the illustration.

## CAUTION

***Never loosen the front engine mount insulator cover nuts on a 200SX (4 cyl.); if removed, the insulator will malfunction due to oil loss.***

### Front Wheel Drive

It is recommended that the engine and transmission be removed as a unit. If need be, the units may be separated after removal. Always release the fuel pressure in the system before disconnecting the fuel lines. Situate the vehicle on as flat and solid a surface as possible. Place chocks or equivalent at front and rear of rear wheels to stop vehicle from rolling while working on the vehicle.

**NOTE: On the 1989–90 Sentra, the engine cannot be removed separately from the tranaxle. Remove the engine and the transaxle as a unit. If equipped with 4WD, remove the engine, transaxle and transfer case together.**

1. Mark the location of the hinges on the hood. Remove the hood by holding at both sides and unscrewing bolts. This requires two people.

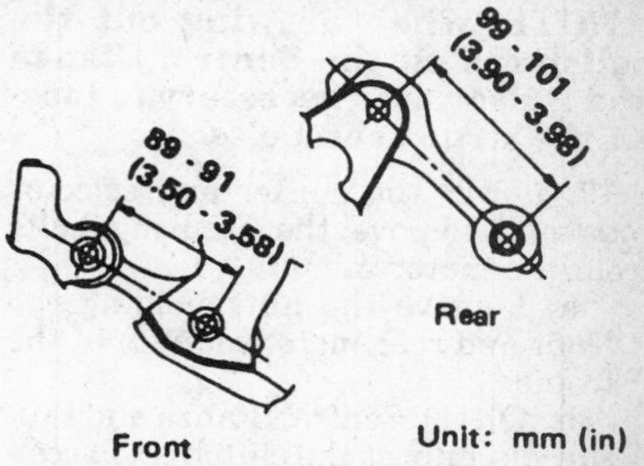


**Front and rear buffer rod length adjustment on 1987–90 Pulsar (E16I and GA16I), 1989–90 Maxima and 1989–90 Sentra**

2. Remove the battery and drain radiator coolant.
3. Remove the air cleaner and disconnect the accelerator wire from the carburetor.
4. Disconnect the following wires and hoses:
   a. Ignition wire from the coil to the distributor
   b. Ignition coil ground wire and the engine ground cable
   c. Disconnect the block connector from the distributor
   d. Remove fusible links
   e. Unplug all engine harness connectors
   f. Remove the fuel and fuel return hoses
   g. Disconnect the upper and lower radiator hoses
   h. Detach the heater inlet and outlet
   i. Remove the master-vac vacuum hose
   j. Disconnect the carbon canister hoses and the air pump air cleaner hose
5. Remove the air pump air cleaner.
6. Remove the carbon canister.
7. Remove the auxiliary fan and the washer tank.
8. Remove the grille and radiator with the fan assembly.
9. Remove the clutch cylinder from the clutch housing.
10. Remove both buffer rods (do not alter the length of the rods) and disconnect the speedometer cable.
11. Remove the spring pins from the transmission gear selection rods.
12. Attach suitable engine slingers to the block and attach chain or cable. Keep the lifting source slack at this point.
13. Disconnect the exhaust pipe at both the manifold connection and the clamp holding the pipe to the engine.
14. On the Sentra, Stanza and Pulsar, remove the lower ball joint.
15. Drain the gear oil.
16. Disconnect the right and left side drive shafts from their side flanges and remove the bolt holding the radius link support.

**NOTE: When drawing out the halfshafts on the Sentra, Stanza and Pulsar, it is necessary to loosen the strut head bolts.**

17. Lower the shifter and selector rods and remove the securing bolts from the motor mounts.

a. Remove the nuts holding the front and rear motor mounts to the frame.

b. On the Sentra, Stanza and Pulsar, disconnect the clutch and accelerator wires and remove the speedometer cable with its pinion from the transaxle.

18. Lift the engine up and away from the car.

**Installation is the reverse of removal with the following cautions and observations.**

19. When lowering the engine into the car and onto the frame, make sure to keep it as level as possible.

20. Check the clearance between the frame and clutch housing and make sure that the engine mount bolts are seated in the groove of the mounting bracket.

21. After installing the motor mounts, adjust and install the buffer rods. On the 1987–90 Pulsar with E16i and GA16i engines, 1989–90 Maxima and 1989–90 Sentra: front should be 3.50–3.58 in., and the rear, 3.90–3.98 in.

22. On the 1986 Stanza Wagon and all 1987–90 Stanzas, tighten the engine mount bolts first, then apply a load to the mounting insulators before tightening the buffer rod and sub-mounting bolts. See illustrations for tightening order.

## Cylinder Head

### REMOVAL & INSTALLATION

**NOTE: To prevent distortion or warping of the cylinder head, allow the engine to cool completely before removing the head bolts.**

#### *E15, E15ET, E16, E16S, E16i Single Overhead Camshaft Engines*

1. Crank the engine until the No. 1 piston is at Top Dead Center on its compression stroke and disconnect the negative battery cable. Drain the cooling system and remove the air cleaner assembly.

2. Remove the alternator.

3. Number all spark plug wires as to their respective cylinders and remove the distributor, with all wires attached.

4. Remove the EAI pipes bracket and EGR tube at the right (EGR valve) side. Disconnect the same pipes on the front (exhaust manifold) side from the manifold.

5. Remove the exhaust manifold cover and the exhaust manifold, taking note that the center manifold nut has a different diameter than the other nuts.

6. Remove the A/C compressor bracket and the power steering pump bracket (if equipped).

7. Label and disconnect the carburetor throttle linkage, fuel line, and all vacuum and electrical connections.

8. Remove the intake manifold with carburetor or throttle body.

9. Remove water pump drive belt and pulley. Remove crankshaft pulley.

10. Remove the rocker (valve) cover.

11. Remove upper and lower dust cover on the camshaft timing belt shroud.

12. With the shroud removed, the cam sprocket, crankshaft sprocket, jackshaft sprocket, tensioner pulley, and toothed rubber timing belt are exposed.

13. Mark the relationship of the camshaft sprocket to the timing belt and the crankshaft sprocket to the timing belt with paint or a grease pencil. This will make setting everything up during reassembly much easier if the engine is disturbed during disassembly.

14. Remove the belt tensioner pulley.

15. Mark an arrow on the timing belt showing direction of engine rotation, because the belt wears a certain way and should be replaced the way it was removed. Slide the belt off the sprockets.

16. Carefully remove the cylinder head from the block, pulling the head up evenly from both ends. If the head seems stuck, DO NOT pry it off. Tap lightly around the lower perimeter of the head with a rubber mallet to help break the seal. Label all head bolts with tape, as they must go back in their original positions.

**To install:**

17. Thoroughly clean both the cylinder block and head mating surfaces. Avoid scratching either.

18. Turn the crankshaft and set the No. 1 cylinder at TDC on its compression stroke. This causes the crankshaft timing sprocket mark to be aligned with the cylinder block cover mark.

19. Align the camshaft sprocket mark with the cylinder head cover mark. This causes the valves for No. 1 cylinder to position at TDC on the compression stroke.

20. Place a new gasket on the cylinder block.

21. **E15 engines:** Install the cylinder head on the block and tighten the bolts in two stages: first 29–33 ft. lbs. on all bolts, then go around again and torque them all up to 51–54 ft. lbs. After the engine has been warmed up, check all bolts and re-torque if necessary.

**E16 engines:**

**NOTE: There are 3 different size head bolts used on the E16i engine. Their location is shown in the accompanying illustration.**

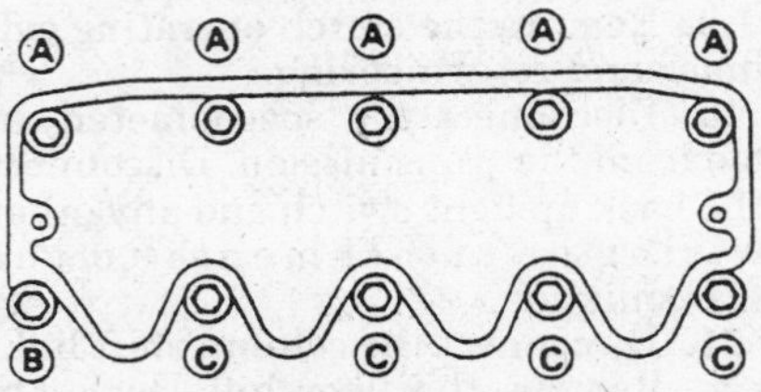


**Cylinder head bolt location on E16i engines**

**Bolt (A) is 3.74 in., bolt (B) is 4.33 in. and bolt (C) is 3.15 in. Measure the length of each bolt prior to installation and make sure they are installed in their proper locations on the head.**

Install the cylinder head on the block and tighten the bolts in 2 stages: first tighten all bolts to 22 ft. lbs. (29 Nm), then retighten them all to 51 ft. lbs. (69 Nm). Next, loosen all bolts completely, and then retighten them again to 22 ft. lbs. (29 Nm). Tighten all bolts to a final torque of 51–54 ft. lbs. (69–74 Nm); or if an angle wrench is available, turn each bolt until they have achieved the specified number of degrees—bolts 1, 3, 6, 8 & 9: 45–50 degrees; bolt 7: 55–60 degrees and bolts 2, 4, 5 & 10: 40–45 degrees.

**NOTE: Be sure to use washers when installing the cylinder head bolts on the E16 engines.**

22. Reassemble in the reverse order of disassembly, making sure all timing marks are in proper alignment.

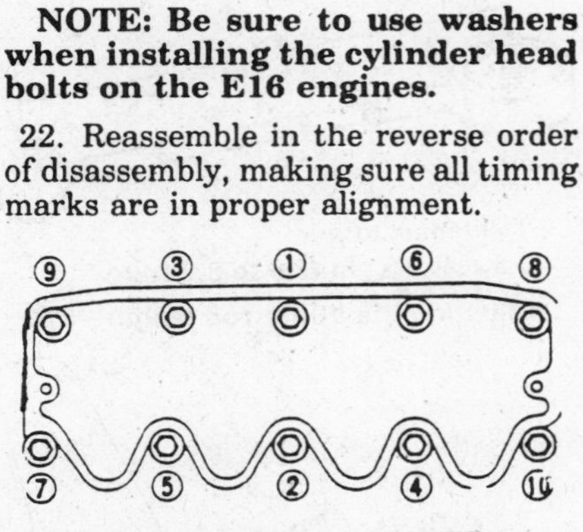


TIGHTEN IN NUMERICAL ORDER

**Cylinder head torque sequence—E-Series engines**

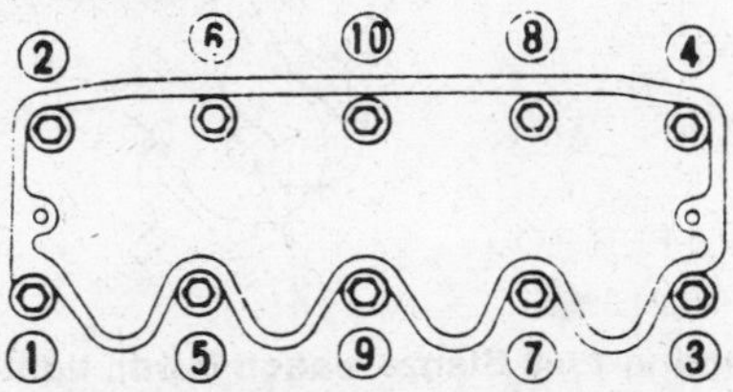


**Loosen the cylinder head bolts, in stages, in the order shown—E-series engines**

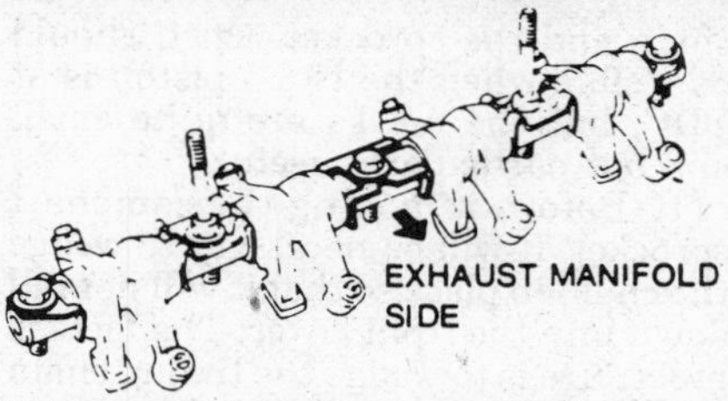


Make sure the cutout on the E-series engine rocker shaft faces the exhaust manifold

### GA16i Single Overhead Camshaft Engines

1. Drain the coolant from the radiator and the cylinder block. Don't allow coolant to spill on the drive belts.
2. Remove the intake manifold suppport bracket and remove the air cleaner assembly. Release the fuel system pressure and disconnect the center wire from the distributor cap.
3. Remove the rocker arm cover retaining screws and lift the cover from the head.
4. Matchmark then remove the distributor from the cylinder head. Remove all the spark plugs.
5. Set the No. 1 cylinder at TDC of the compresion stroke by rotating the engine until the cut out machined in the rear of the camshaft is aligned as shown in the illustration.
6. Hold the camshaft sprocket stationary with the proper tool and loosen the sproket bolt. Place highly visible and accurate paint or chalk alignment marks on the camshaft sprocket and the timing chain, then slide the sprocket from the camshaft and lift the timing chain from the sprocket. Remove the sprocket. The timing chain will not fall off the crankshaft sprocket unless the front cover is removed. This is due to the cast portion of the front cover located on the lower side of the crankshaft sprocket which acts a stopper mechanism. For this reason a chain stopper (wedge) is not required to remove the cylinder head.
7. Loosen the cylinder bolts in 2 or 3 stages to prevent warpage and cracking of the head. One of the cylinder head bolts is longer than the rest. Mark this bolt bolt with masking tape and make a note of its location.
8. Carefully remove the cylinder head from the block, pulling the head up evenly from both ends. If the head seems stuck, DO NOT pry it off. Tap lightly around the lower perimeter of the head with a rubber mallet to help break the seal. The cylinder head and the intake and exhaust manifolds are removed together. Remove the cylinder head gasket.

**To install:**

9. Thoroughly clean both the cylinder block and head mating surfaces. Avoid scratching either.
10. Turn the crankshaft and set the No. 1 cylinder at TDC on its compression stroke. This is done by aligning the timing pointer with the appropriate timing mark on the pulley as shown in the illustration. To ensure that the No. 1 piston is at TDC, verify that the knock pin in the front of the camshaft is set at the top.
11. Place a new gasket on the block and lay the head onto the gasket.

**NOTE: These engines use 2 different length cylinder head bolts. Bolt (1) as shown in the tightening sequence is 5.24 in. while bolts (2) thru (10) are 4.33 in. Do not confuse the location of these bolts.**

12. Coat the threads and the seating surface of the head bolts with clean engine oil and use a new set of washers. Install the cylinder head bolts in their proper locations and tighten as follows: tighten all the bolts in sequence to 22 ft. lbs, then tighten all bolts in sequence to 47 ft. lbs. Loosen all bolts in reverse of the tightening sequence. Tighten all bolts again to 22 ft. lbs. If an angle torque wrench is available, tighten bolt (1) 80–85 degrees clockwise and bolts (6) thru (10) 60–65 degrees clockwise. If an angle torque wrench is not available, torque the bolts in sequence to 43–51 ft. lbs. Finally, tighten bolts (11) thru (15) to 4.6 to 6.1 ft. lbs.
13. Place the timing chain on the camshaft sprocket using the alignment marks. Slide the sprocket and timing chain onto the camshaft and install the center bolt.
14. Complete the remainder of the installation in reverse of the removal procedure.

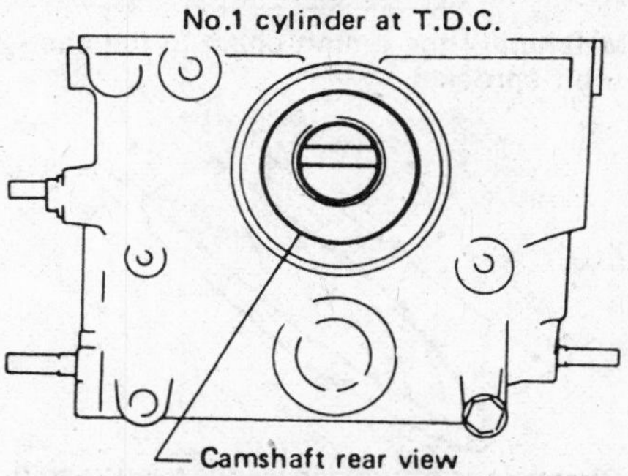


When camshaft is aligned as shown, the No. 1 piston is at TDC – GA16i engines

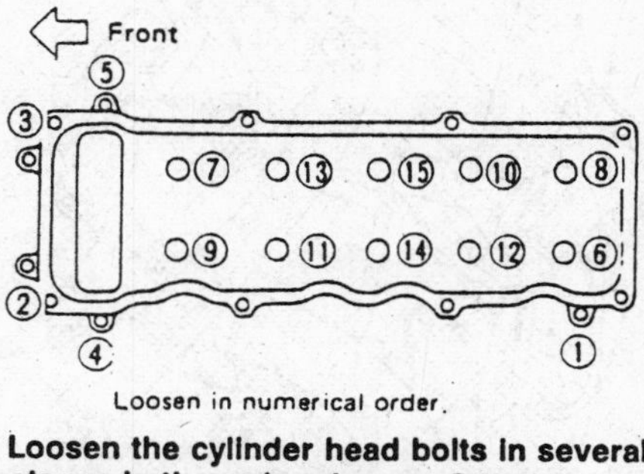


Loosen the cylinder head bolts in several stages in the order shown – GA16i engines

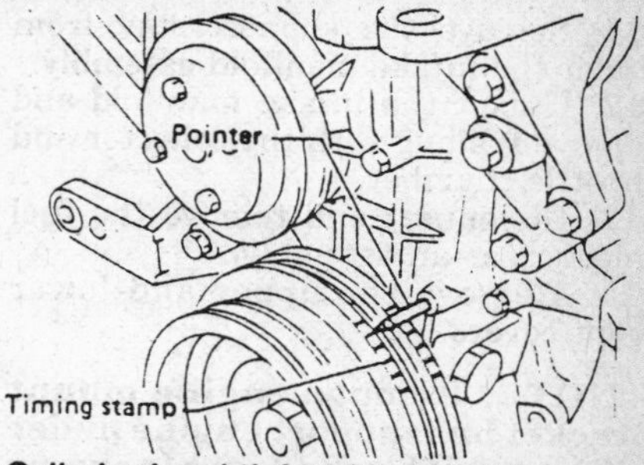


Cylinder head tightening sequence – GA16i engines. Bolt (1) is the longest bolt

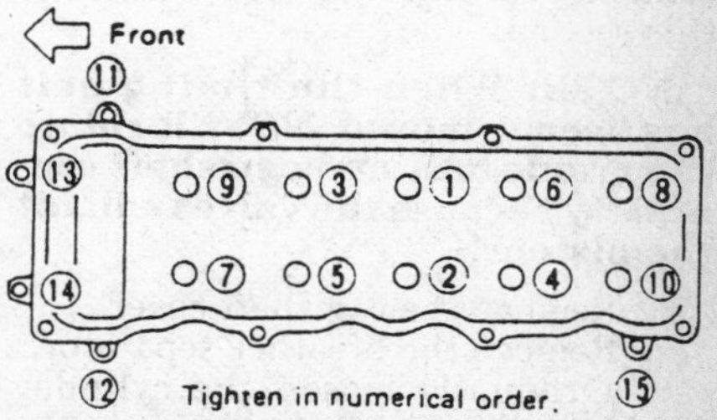


When crankshaft pulley marks are aligned as shown, the No. 1 piston is at TDC

### CA16DE and CA18DE Double Overhead Camshaft Engines

1. Crank the engine until the No. 1 piston is at Top Dead Center on its compression stroke and disconnect the negative battery cable. Drain the cooling system and remove the air cleaner assembly.
2. Loosen the alternator and remove all drive belts. Remove the alternator.
3. Disconect the air duct at the throttle chamber.
4. Tag and disconnect all lines, hoses and wires which may interfere with cylinder removal.
5. Remove the 8 screws and lift off the ornament cover.
6. Disconnect the oxygen sensor.
7. Remove the 2 exhaust heat shild covers.
8. Unbolt the exhaust manifold and wire the entire assembly out of the way.
9. Disconnect the EGR tube at the passage cover and then remove the passage cover and its gasket.
10. Disconnect and remove the crank angle sensor from the upper front cover.

**NOTE: Put aligning mark on crank angle sensor and timing belt cover.**

11. Remove the support stay from under the intake manifold assembly.
12. Unbolt the intake manifold and remove it along with the collector and throttle chamber.
13. Disconnect and remove the fuel injectors as an assembly.
14. Remove the upper and lower front covers.

**NOTE: Remove engine mount bracket but support engine under oil pan with wooden blocks or equivalent.**

15. Remove the timing belt and camshaft sprockets as detailed later in this section.

**NOTE: When the timing belt has been removed, NEVER rotate the crankshaft and camshaft separately because the valves will hit the pistons!**

16. Remove the camshaft cover.
17. Remove the breather separator.
18. Gradually loosen the cylinder head bolts in several stages, in the sequence illustrated.
19. Carefully remove the cylinder head from the block, pulling the head up evenly from both ends. If the head seems stuck, DO NOT pry it off. Tap lightly around the lower perimeter of the head with a rubber mallet to help break the joint. Label all head bolts with tape or magic marker, as they must go back in their original positions.

**To install:**

20. Thoroughly clean both the cylinder block and head mating surfaces. Avoid scratching either.
21. Installation is the reverse order of the removal procedure. When installing the bolts tighten the two center bolts temporarily to 15 ft. lbs. and install the head bolts loosely. After the timing belt and front cover have been installed, torque all the head bolts in the torque sequence provided in this section. Tighten all bolts to 22 ft. lbs. (29 Nm). Re-tighten all bolts to 76 ft. lbs. (103 Nm). Loosen all bolts completely and then re-tighten them once again to 22 ft. lbs. (29 Nm). Tighten all bolts to a final torque of 76 ft. lbs. (103 Nm). If an angle wrench is available, give all bolts a final turn to 85–90 degrees (clockwise).

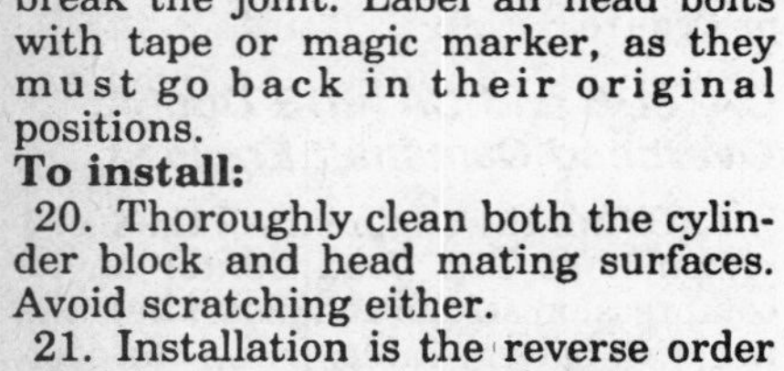

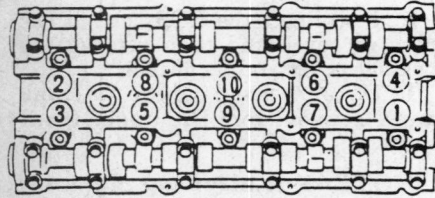


Cylinder head loosening sequence—CA16DE and CA18DE

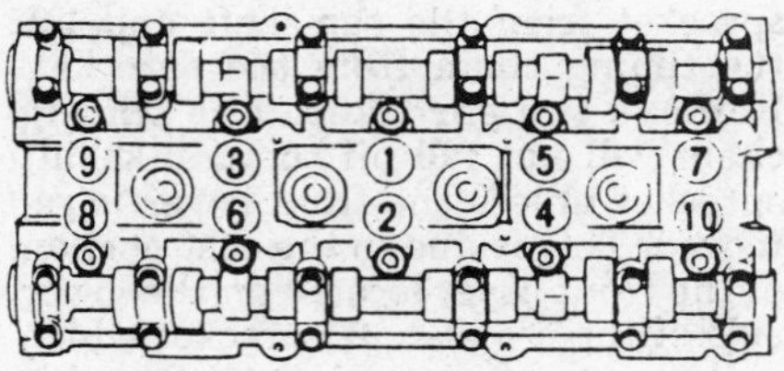


Cylinder head torque sequence—CA16DE and CA18DE

**NOTE: Newer models utilize cupped washers, always make sure that the flat side of the washer is facing downward before tightening the cylinder head bolts.**

22. Always use new gaskets on the cylinder head, manifolds and cylinder head cover (camshaft cover).

### *L24E, L28E, L28ET and LD28 Single Overhead Camshaft Engines*

1. Crank the engine until the No. 1 piston is at TDC of the compression stroke, disconnect the battery, and drain the cooling system.

**NOTE: To set the No. 1 piston at TDC of the compression stroke on the LD28 engine, remove the blind plug from the rear plate. Rotate the crankshaft until the marks on the flywheel and rear plate are in alignment. The No. 1 piston should now be at TDC.**

2. Remove the radiator hoses and the heater hoses. Unbolt the alternator mounting bracket and move the alternator to one side.
3. If the car is equipped with air conditioning or power steering, unbolt the compressor or pump and position it out of the way.

**CAUTION**

***Do not disconnect the compressor lines. Severe injury could result.***

4. Remove the fan and the fan pulley.
5. Remove the water pump. Remove the spark plug leads from the spark plugs.
6. Remove the cold start valve and the fuel pipe as an assembly. Disconnect the throttle linkage.
7. Remove all lines and hoses from the intake manifold. Mark them first so you will know where they go.
8. Unbolt the exhaust manifold from the exhaust pipe. The cylinder head can be removed with both the intake and exhaust manifolds in place.
9. Remove the camshaft cover.
10. Mark the relationship of the camshaft sprocket to the timing chain with paint. There are timing marks on the chain and the sprocket which should be visible when the No. 1 piston is at TDC, but the marks are quite small and not particularly useful.
11. Before removing the camshaft sprocket, it will be necessary to wedge the chain in place so that it will not fall down into the front cover. The factory procedure is to wedge the timing chain in place with a wooden wedge shown

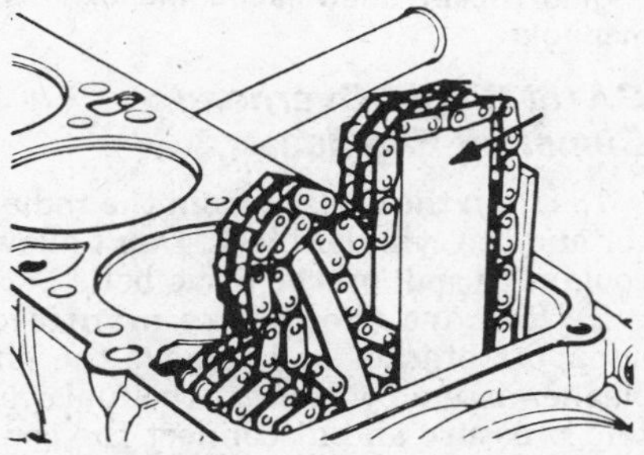

On overhead cam engines, the wedge shown by the arrow can be used to prevent the timing chain from slipping off the crankshaft sprocket.

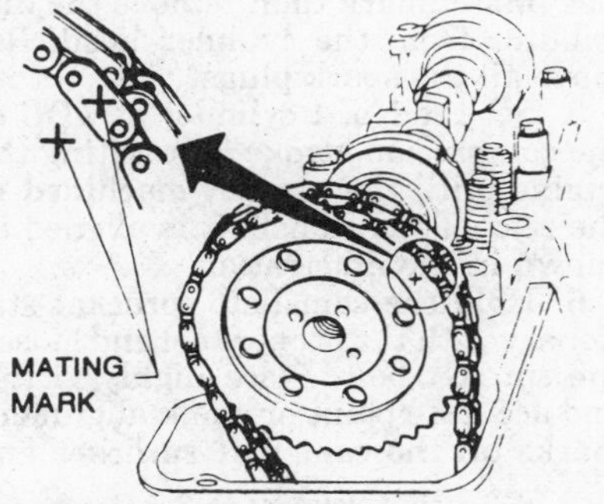


Matchmark the timing chain to the camshaft sprocket

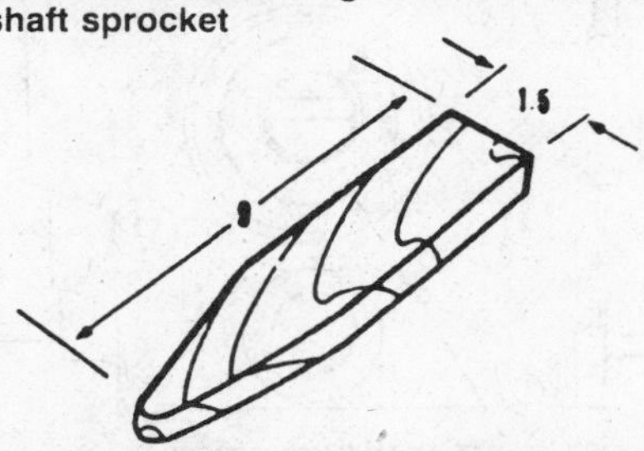

Dimensions of wooden wedge used to hold chain in place

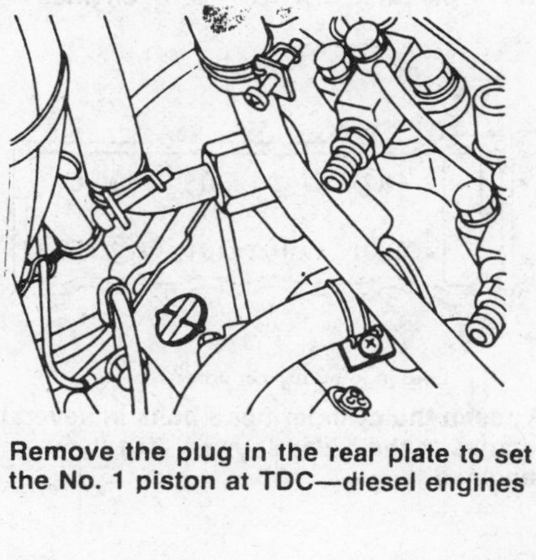

Remove the plug in the rear plate to set the No. 1 piston at TDC—diesel engines here. The problem with this procedure is that it may allow the chain tensioner to move out far enough to cock itself against the chain. If this happens, you'll find that the chain won't go back over the sprocket after you've put the sprocket back on. In this case, you'll have to remove the front cover and push the tensioner back. After you've wedged the chain, unbolt the camshaft sprocket and remove it.

12. Remove the cylinder head bolts; they require an Allen wrench type socket adapter. Keep the bolts in order as two different sizes are used.

13. Lift off the cylinder head. You may have to tap it lightly with a ruber mallet.

14. Clean the block and head mating surfaces thoroughly and check for warpage. Install a new head gasket on the block and lower the head into position.

15. Install a new head gasket and place the head in position on the block.

16. Install the head bolts in their original locations.

17. Torque the head bolts in three stages: first to 29 ft. lbs., then to 43 ft. lbs., then to 62 ft. lbs.

18. Reinstall the camshaft sprocket in its original location. The chain is installed at the same time as the sprocket. Make sure the marks made earlier line up. If the chain has slipped, or the engine has been disturbed, correct the timing.

19. Reinstall all remaining parts, coolant, etc.

20. Adjust the valves.

21. After 600 miles of driving, retorque the head bolts and readjust the valves.

### *Z22 and Z22E Single Overhead Camshaft Engines*

1. Crank the engine until the No. 1 piston is at TDC of the compression stroke, disconnect the battery, and drain the cooling system.

**NOTE: To set the No. 1 piston at TDC of the compression stroke on the LD28 engine, remove the blind plug from the rear plate. Rotate the crankshaft until the marks on the flywheel and rear plate are in alignment. The No. 1 piston should now be at TDC.**

2. Remove the radiator hoses and the heater hoses. Unbolt the alternator mounting bracket and move the alternator to one side.

3. If the car is equipped with air conditioning or power steering, unbolt the compressor or pump and position it out of the way.

**CAUTION**

***Do not disconnect the compressor lines. Severe injury could result.***

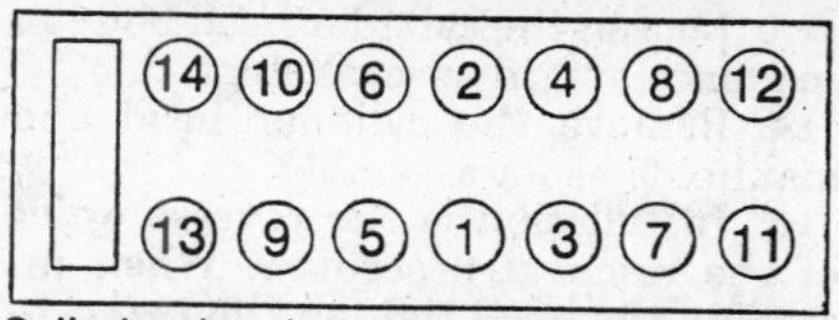


Cylinder head torque sequence—LD28 engines

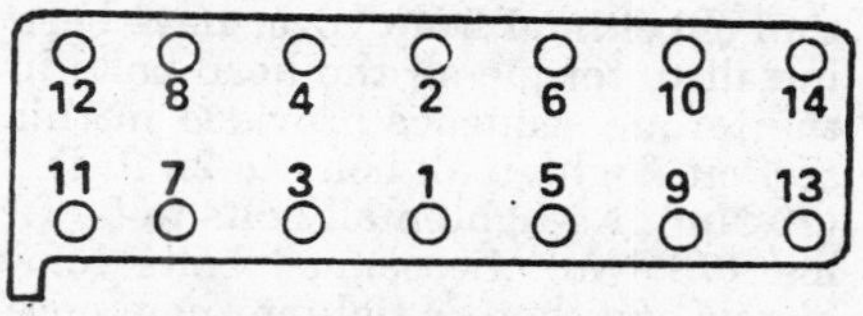


Cylinder head torque sequence—L24 and L28 engines

4. Remove the fan and the fan pulley.

5. Remove the water pump. Remove the spark plug leads from the spark plugs.

**NOTE: The spark plug leads should already be marked. However, it would be wise to mark them yourself.**

6. Disconnect the throttle linkage, the air cleaner or its intake hose assembly (fuel injection). Disconnect the fuel line, the return fuel line and any other vacuum lines or electrical leads.

**NOTE: A good rule of thumb when disconnecting the rather complex engine wiring of today's automobiles is to put a piece of masking tape on the wire or hose and on the connection from which you removed the wire or hose, then mark both pieces of tape 1, 2, 3, etc. When replacing wiring or hose, simply match the pieces of tape.**

7. Remove the EGR tube from around the rear of the engine.

8. Unbolt the exhaust manifold from the exhaust pipe.

9. Remove the PCV valve from around the rear of the engine if necessary.

10. Remove the spark plugs to protect them from damage. Remove the cylinder head (rocker) cover.

11. Mark the relationship of the camshaft sprocket to the timing chain with paint or chalk. If this is done, it will not be necessary to locate the factory timing marks. Before removing the camshaft sprocket, it will be necessary to wedge the chain in place so that it will not fall down into the front cover. The factory procedure is to wedge the timing chain in place with the wooden wedge shown here. The problem with this procedure is that it may allow the chain tensioner to move out far enough to cock itself against the chain. If this happens, you'll find that the chain won't go back over the sprocket after you've put the sprocket back on. In this case, you'll have to remove the front cover and push the tensioner back. After you've wedged the chain, unbolt the camshaft sprocket and remove it.

12. Working from both ends in, loosen the cylinder head bolts and remove them. Remove the bolts securing the cylinder head to the front cover assembly.

13. Lift the cylinder head off the engine block. It may be necessary to tap the head lightly with a rubber mallet to loosen it.

**To install the cylinder head:**

14. Thoroughly clean the cylinder block and head surfaces and check both for warpage.

15. Fit the new head gasket. Don't use sealant. Make sure that no open valves are in the way of raised pistons, and do not rotate the crankshaft or camshaft separately because of possible damage which might occur to the valves.

16. Temporarily tighten the 2 center right and left cylinder head bolts to 14 ft. lbs.

17. Install the camshaft sprocket together with the timing chain to the camshaft. Make sure the marks you made earlier line up with each other.

18. Install the cylinder head bolts and torque them to 20 ft. lbs., then 40 ft. lbs., then 58 ft. lbs. in the order shown in the illustration.

19. Assemble the rest of the components in the reverse order of disassembly. Tighten the camshaft sprocket bolt to 87–116 ft. lbs. Apply sealant to

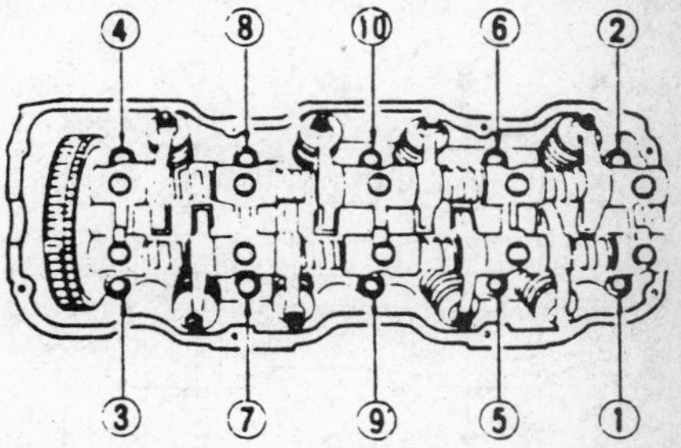


Cylinder head loosening sequence – Z-Series engines

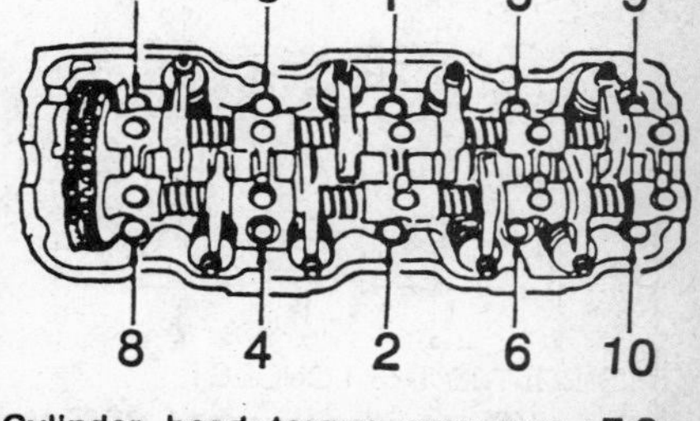


Cylinder head torque sequence – Z-Series engines

the cylinder head cut-out and then install the rubber plug. Tighten the cylinder head-to-upper front cover bolts to 2.9–7.2 ft. lbs. Adjust the valves.

**NOTE: It is always wise to drain the crankcase oil after the cylinder head has been installed to avoid coolant contamination.**

### CA18ET, CA20, CA20E and CA20S Single Overhead Camshaft Engines

1. On the CA18ET and CA20E models, remove the air intake pipe.
2. Remove the cooling fan and radiator shroud (all models).
3. Remove the alternator drive belt, power steering pump drive belt and the A/C compressor drive belt if so equipped.
4. Position the No. 1 cylinder at TDC of the compression stroke and remove the upper and lower timing belt covers.
5. Loosen the timing belt tensioner and return spring, then remove the timing belt.

**NOTE: When the timing belt has been removed, do not rotate the crankshaft and the camshaft separately, because the valves will hit the piston heads.**

6. Remove the exhaust manifold.
7. Remove the camshaft pulley.
8. Remove the water pump pulley.
9. Remove the crankshaft pulley.
10. Remove the alternator adjusting bracket.
11. Remove the water pump.
12. Remove the oil pump.

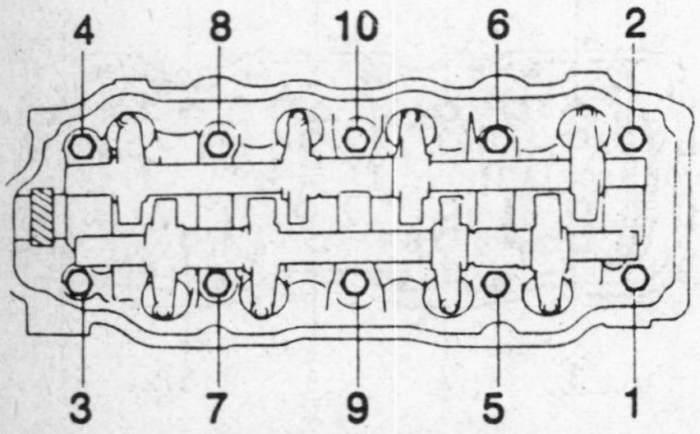


Cylinder head bolt loosening sequence—CA20 and CA 18ET engines

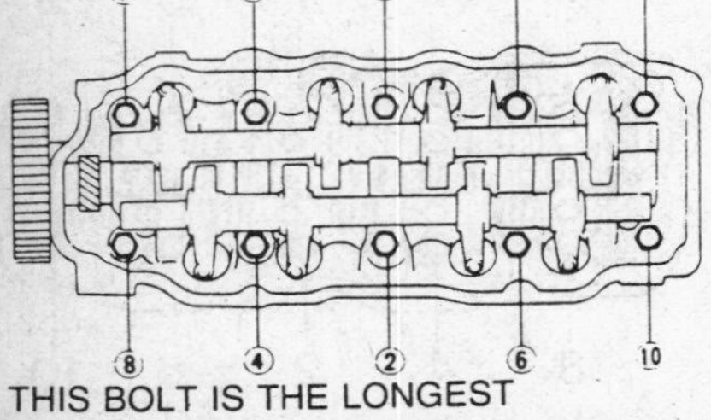


Cylinder head torque sequence—CA20 and CA18ET engines

13. Loosen the cylinder head bolts in sequence and in several steps.
14. Remove the cylinder head and manifolds as an assembly.
15. Installation is the reverse order of the removal procedure. When installing the bolts tighten the two center bolts temporarily to 15 ft. lbs. and install the head bolts loosely. After the timing belt and front cover have been installed, torque all the head bolts in the torque sequence provided in this section. Tighten all bolts to 22 ft. lbs. (29 Nm). Re-tighten all bolts to 58 ft. lbs. (78 Nm). Loosen all bolts completely and then re-tighten them once again to 22 ft. lbs. (29 Nm). Tighten all bolts to a final torque of 54–61 ft. lbs. (74–83 Nm). If an angle wrench is available, give all bolts a final turn to 90–95 degrees (clockwise). On 1986–90 models; 75–80 degrees except bolt No. 8 which is 83–88 degrees.

**NOTE: Newer models utilize cupped washers, always make sure that the flat side of the washer is facing downward before tightening the cylinder head bolts.**

**CAUTION**

***Before installing the timing belt, be certain that the crankshaft pulley key is near the top and that the camshaft knock pin or sprocket aligning mark is at the top.***

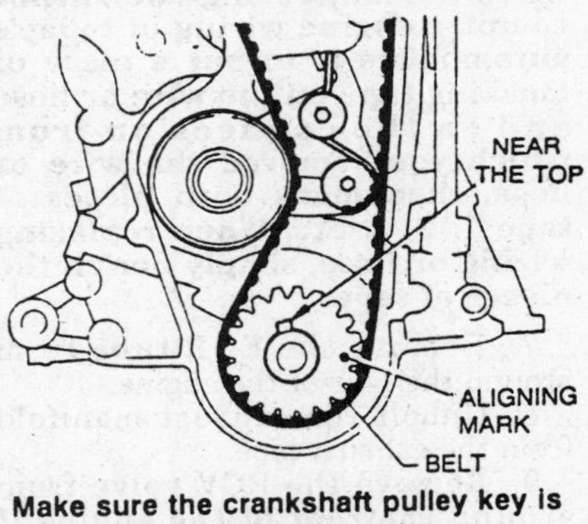


Make sure the crankshaft pulley key is near the top—C-Series engines

### KA24E Single Overhead Camshaft Engines

**NOTE: After completing this procedure, allow the rocker cover to cylinder head rubber plugs to dry for 30 minutes before starting the engine. This will allow the liquid gasket sealer to cure properly.**

1. Drain coolant from the radiator and remove drain plug from the cylinder block.
2. Remove the power steering drive belt, power steering pump, idler pulley and power steering brackets.
3. Mark and disconnect all the vacuum hoses, spark plug wires and electrical connections to gain access to cylinder head. Remove the air induction hose from the collector assembly.
4. Disconnect the accelerator bracket. If necessary mark the position and remove the accelerator cable wire end from the throttle drum.
5. Remove the bolts that attach intake manifold collector to the intake manifold. Remove and position the collector assembly to the side and out of the way.
6. Remove the bolts that attach the intake manifold to the cylinder. Remove the intake manifold. Unplug the exhaust gas sensor and remove the exhaust cover and exhaust pipe at exhaust manifold connection. Remove the exhaust manifold from the cylinder head.
7. Remove the rocker cover. If cover sticks to the cylinder head, tap it with a rubber hammer. Be careful not to strike the rocker arms when removing the rocker arm cover.

**NOTE: After removing the rocker cover matchmark the timing chain with the camshaft sprocket with paint or equivalent.**

8. Set No.1 cylinder piston at TDC. on its compression stroke. The No. 1 will be at TDC when the timing pointer is aligned with the red timing mark on the crankshaft pulley.
9. Loosen the camshaft sprocket bolt. Do not turn engine when removing the bolt.
10. Support the timing chain with a block of wood as illustrated.
11. Remove the camshaft sprocket.
12. Remove the front cover to cylinder head retaining bolts.

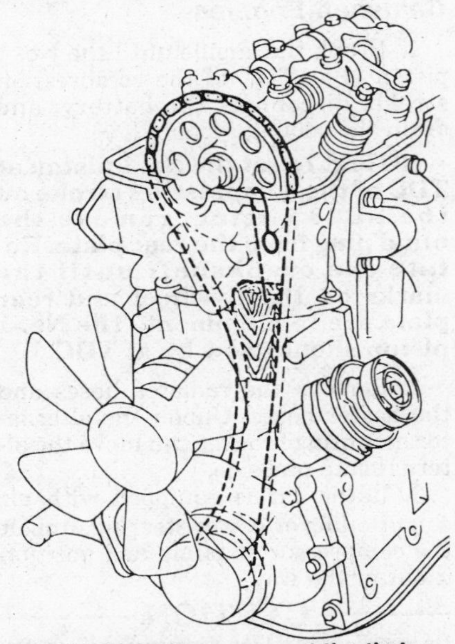

On KA24E engines, support the timing chain with a block of wood

**NOTE: The cylinder head bolts should be loosened in two or three steps in the correct order to prevent head warpage or cracking.**

13. Remove the cylinder head bolts in the correct sequence. Lift the cylinder head off the engine block. It may be necessary to tap the head lightly with a rubber mallet to loosen it.

**To install the cylinder head:**

14. Confirm that the No. 1 is at TDC. on its compression stroke as follows: Align timing mark with the red (0 degree) mark on the crankshaft pulley. Make sure the distributor rotor head is set at No. 1 on the distributor cap. Confirm that the knock pin on the camshaft is set at the top position.

15. Install the cylinder head with a new gasket and torque the head bolts in numerical order using the following 5 step procedure:

a. Torque all bolts to 22 ft. lbs.
b. Torque all bolts to 58 ft. lbs.
c. Loosen all bolts completely.
d. Torque all bolts to 22 ft. lbs.
e. Torque all bolts to 54–61 ft. lbs., or if you are using an angle wrench, turn all bolts 80–85 degrees clockwise.

**NOTE: Do not rotate crankshaft and camshaft separately, or valves will hit the piston heads.**

16. Remove the block of wood holding timing chain in the correct location. Position the timing chain on the camshaft sprocket by aligning each matchmark. Install the camshaft sprocket to the camshaft.

17. Tighten the camshaft sprocket bolt and the front cover to cylinder head retaining bolts.

18. Install the intake manifold and collector assembly with new gaskets.

19. Install the exhaust manifold with new gaskets.

20. Apply liquid gasket to the rubber plugs and install the rubber plugs in the correct location in the cylinder head. The seating surface of the rubber plugs must be clean and dry. The rubber plugs should be installed within 5 minutes of the sealant application. After the sealant is applied and the rubber plugs are in place, rock the plugs back and forth a few times to distribute the sealant evenly. Wipe the excess sealant from the cylinder head with a clean rag.

21. Install the rocker cover with new gasket.

22. Reconnect the accelerator bracket and cable if removed.

23. Connect all the vacuum hoses, and electrical connections that were removed to gain access to cylinder head. Reconnect the air induction hose to collector assembly.

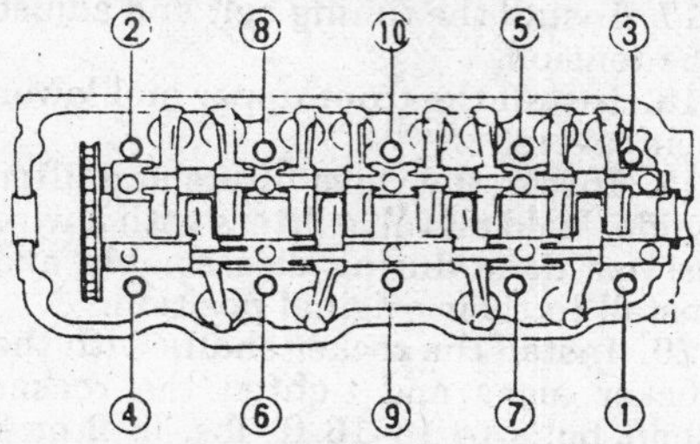

Cylinder head bolt loosening sequence —KA24E engines

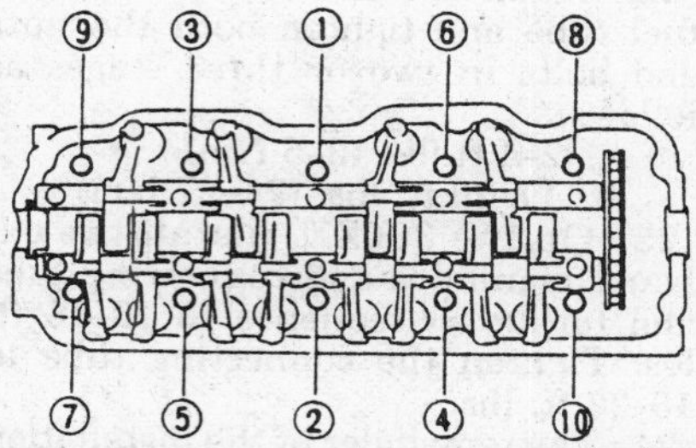

Cylinder head bolt tightening sequence —KA24E engines

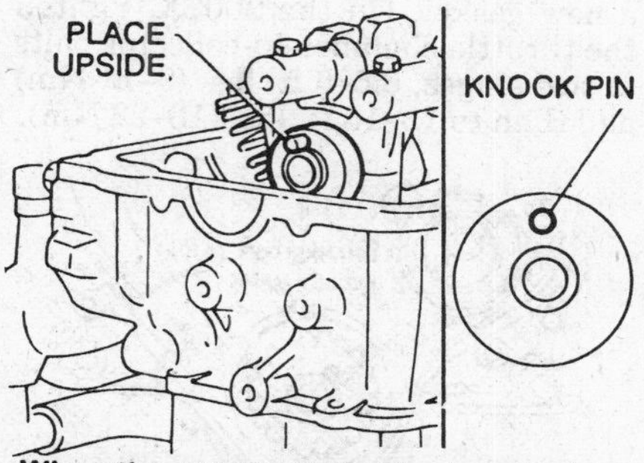

When the camshaft knock pin is at the top, No. piston is at TDC-KA24E engines

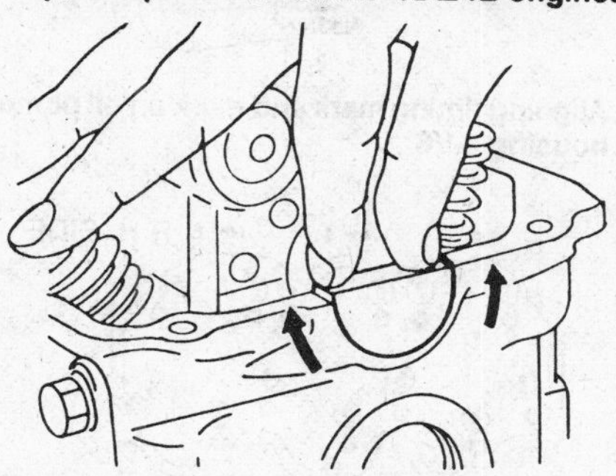
Rubber plug installation on KA24E engines

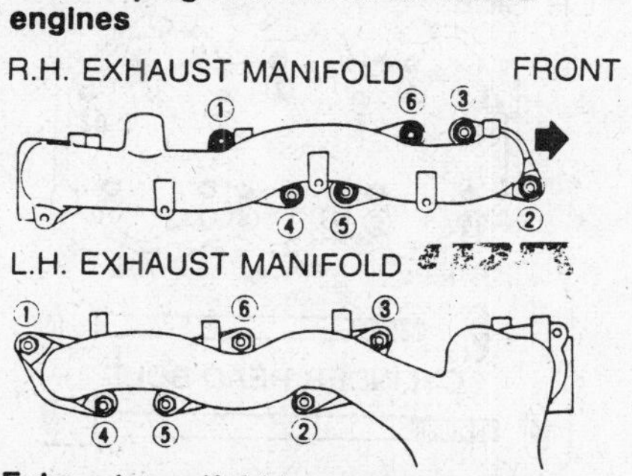

Exhaust manifold loosening sequence—VG30E (Maxima and 200SX)

24. Install the spark plugs and spark plug wires in the correct location.

25. Install the power steering brackets, idler pulley, and power steering pump. Install the drive belt and adjust the belt.

26. Install the drain plug in the cylinder block. Refill the cooling system.

### *VG30E and VG30ET V6 Engines (200SX and 300ZX)*

**NOTE: Includes camshaft, intake manifold, exhaust manifold, rocker shaft removal procedures.**

1. Remove the engine assembly. On 1984–87 300ZX, the engine must be removed from the vehicle to remove the cylinder head. On 1988–90 300ZX, the cylinder head is removed with the engine in place.

2. Remove the timing belt.

**NOTE: NEVER rotate the crankshaft and camshaft separately after the timing belt has been removed or the valves will hit the pistons!**

3. Set the No. 1 cylinder at TDC on its compression stroke.

4. Drain the coolant from the cylinder block.

5. Remove the collector cover and collector. Loosen the bolts starting from the ends and work towards the center. On the 200SX, remove the collector together with the throttle chamber, EGR valve and IAA. unit.

6. Remove the intake manifold with fuel tube assembly. Loosen the intake manifold bolts starting from the front of the engine and proceed in criss-cross pattern.

7. Remove the power steering pump bracket.

8. Remove the exhaust manifold covers.

9. Disconnect the exhaust manifold connecting tube.

10. Remove the bolts securing the camshaft pulleys and rear timing cover.

11. Remove the compressor and rocker covers.

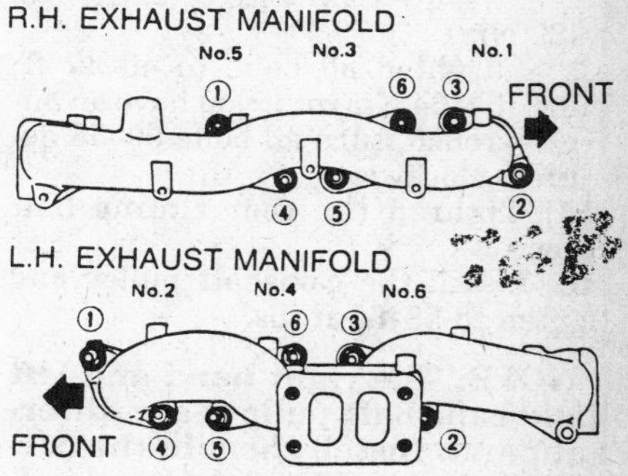

Exhaust manifold loosening sequence—VG30E and VG30ET (300ZX)

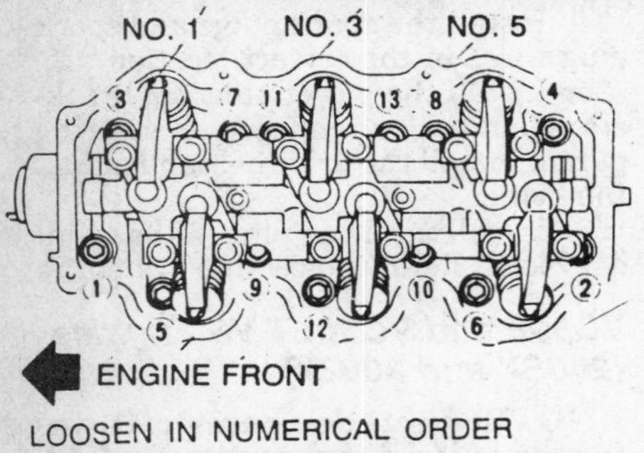


**Cylinder head loosening sequence—VG30E (200SX)**

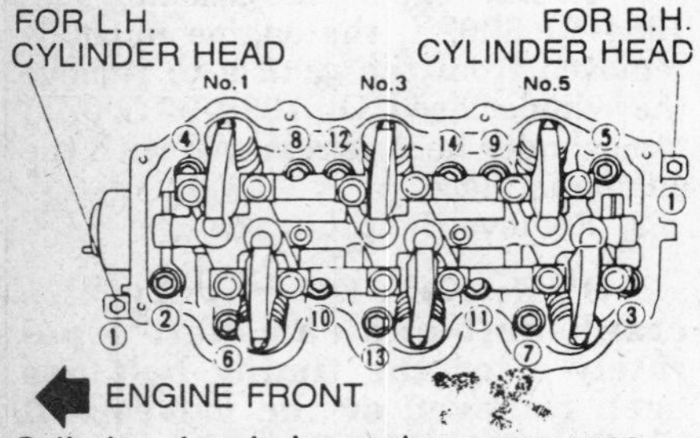


**Cylinder head loosening sequence—VG30E and VG30ET (Maxima and 300ZX)**

12. Remove the cylinder head with exhaust manifold.

**To install the cylinder head:**

13. Make sure the No. 1 cylinder is set at TDC on its compression stroke as follows:

   a. Align the crankshaft timing mark with the mark on the oil pump housing.

   b. The knock pin in the front end of the camshaft should be facing upward.

**NOTE: Do not rotate crankshaft and camshaft separately because valves will hit piston head.**

14. Position the cylinder head on the block and tighten the cylinder head bolts in 5 steps in the numerical sequence illustrated.

   a. Tighten all bolts to 22 ft. lb. (29 Nm)

   b. Tighten all bolts to 43 ft. lbs. (59 Nm)

   c. Loosen all bolts completely

   d. Tighten all bolts to 22 ft. lbs. (29 Nm)

   e. Tighten all bolts to 40–47 ft. lbs. (54–64 Nm) or if you have an angle wrench, turn all bolts 60–65 degrees clockwise.

15. Tighten the rear timing belt cover.

16. Install the camshaft pulley and tighten to 58–65 ft lbs.

**NOTE: The right hand and left hand camshaft pulleys are different parts. Install them in the correct positions. The right hand pulley has an R3 identification mark and the left hand pulley has an L3.**

17. Install the timing belt and adjust the tension.

18. Install the front upper and lower belt covers.

19. Install the valve lifters and lifter guide. Hold all valve lifters with a wire as was done during disassembly and install to their original position.

20. Install the rocker shafts with the rocker arms and tighten the rocker shaft bolts to 13–16 ft. lbs. in 2 or 3 stages.

21. Install the rocker cover.

22. Install the intake manifold and fuel tube and tighten both the nuts and bolts in two or three stages as follows:

   a. 2–4 ft.lbs. (3–5 Nm)

   b. 17–20 ft. lbs. (24–27 Nm)

23. On the 300ZX, install the exhaust manifolds and connecting tube and torque in sequence to 13–16 ft. lbs. Tighten the connecting tube to 16–20 ft. lbs.

24. The remainder of the installation is the reverse of removal. When installing the collector cover, always use a new gasket. On the 200SX, tighten the throttle chamber-to-collector bolts in two stages; 6.5–8 ft. lbs. (9–11 Nm) and then to 13–16 ft. lbs. (18–22 Nm).

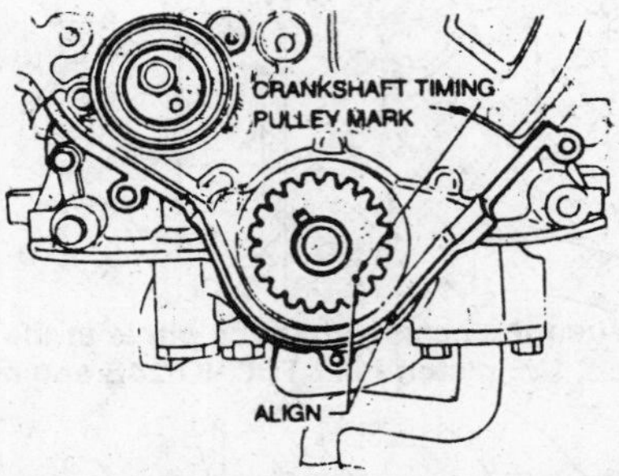


**Aligning timing mark and mark on oil pump housing—V6**

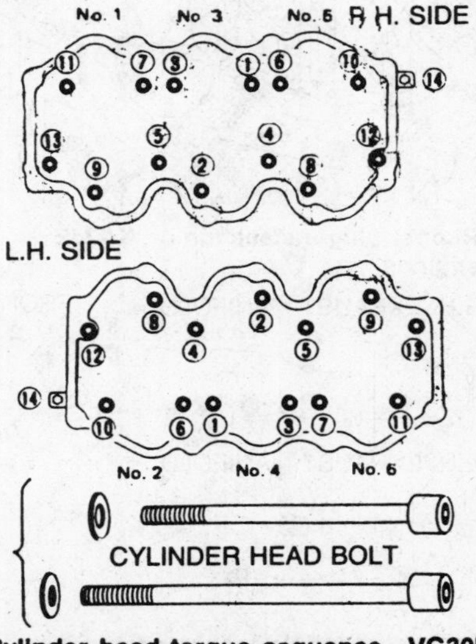


**Cylinder head torque sequence—VG30E and VG30ET (Maxima and 300ZX)**

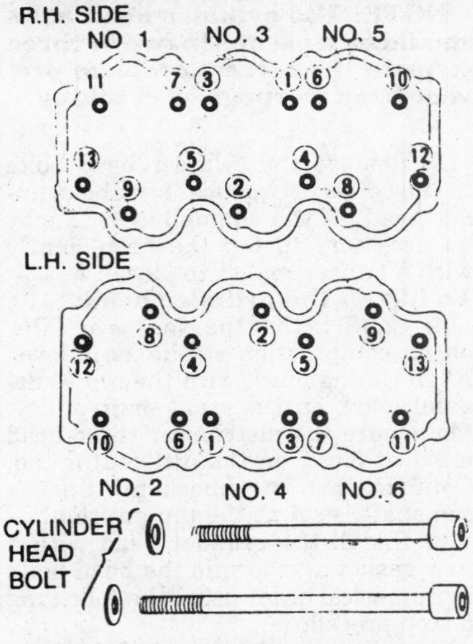


**Cylinder head torque sequence—VG30E (200SX)**

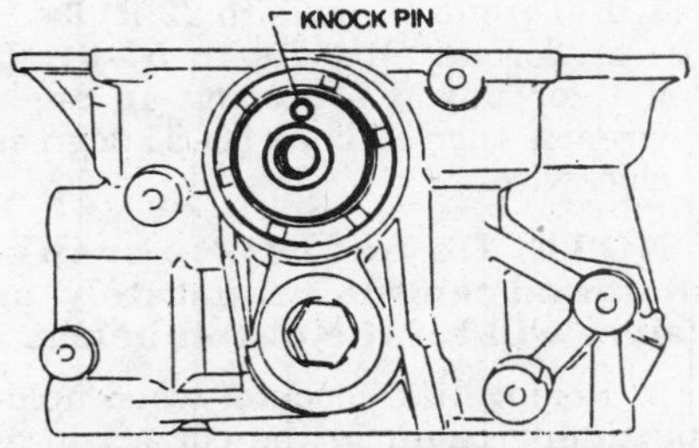


**Knock pin of camshaft facing upward—V6**

### *VG30E V6 Engines (Maxima)*

**NOTE: To remove or install the cylinder head, a special hex head wrench ST10120000 (J24239-01) or equivalent will be needed. For all torque sequences and other illustrations, refer to "VG30E V6 Engines (200SX and 300ZX)".**

1. Release the fuel pressure. Set the engine to TDC and then remove the timing belt.

**NOTE: Do not rotate either the crankshaft or camshaft from this point onward, or the valves could be bent by hitting the pistons.**

2. Drain the coolant from the engine and the cylinder block. On 1988–89 Maxima, there are 2 cylinder block drain plugs. The left side drain plug is located beside the oil level gauge and the right side drain plug is located behind the right hand drive shaft boot. Then, disconnect all the vacuum hoses and water hoses connected to the intake collector. On 1989–90 Maxima, remove the distributor and ignition wires and disconnect the accelerator control wire from the intake manifold collector.

3. Remove the collector cover and the collector from the intake manifold. On 1989–90 Maxima, there are upper and lower collector covers. Disconnect all harness connectors and vacuum lines to gain access to the cover retaining bolts on these models.
4. Remove the intake manifold and fuel tube assembly. Loosen the intake manifold bolts starting from the front of the engine and proceed in criss-cross pattern towards the center.
5. Remove the exhaust collector bracket. Remove the exhaust manifold covers. Disconnect the exhaust manifold when it connects to the exhaust pipe (3 bolts).
6. Remove the camshaft pulleys and the rear timing cover securing bolts. Remove the rocker arm covers. On 1989–90 Maxima, separate the air conditioning compressor and alternator from the their mounting brackets. Remove the mounting brackets. DO NOT disconnect the refigerant lines from the compressor or serious injury will result.
7. Remove the cylinder head bolts in the correct sequence. Lift the cylinder head off the engine block. It may be necessary to tap the head lightly with a rubber mallet to loosen it.

**To install the cylinder head:**

8. Make sure the No. 1 cylinder is set at TDC on its compression stroke as follows:
   a. Align the crankshaft timing mark with the mark on the oil pump housing.
   b. The knock pin in the front end of the camshaft should be facing upward.

**NOTE: Do not rotate crankshaft and camshaft separately because valves will hit piston head.**

9. Install the head with a new gasket. Apply clean engine oil to the threads and seats of the bolts and install the bolts with washers in the correct position. Note that bolts 4, 5, 12, and 13 are 4.95 in. (127mm) long. The other bolts are 4.13 in. (106mm) long.
10. Torque the bolts in the proper sequence as follows:
   a. Torque all bolts, in order, to 22 ft. lbs.
   b. Torque all bolts, in order, to 43 ft. lbs.
   c. Loosen all bolts completely.
   d. Torque all bolts, in order, to 22 ft. lbs.
   e. Torque all bolts, in order, to 40–47 ft. lbs. If you have a special wrench available that torques bolts to a certain angle, torque them 60-65 degrees tighter rather than going to 40–47 ft. lbs.
11. Install the rear timing cover bolts. Install the camshaft pulleys. Make sure the pulley marked **R3** goes on the right and that marked L3 goes on the left. Align the timing marks if necessary and then install the timing belt and adjust the belt tension.
12. Complete the installation of the remaining cylinder head components in reverse of the installation procedure. Refill the cooling system. Start the engine check the engine timing.

## OVERHAUL

**For all cylinder head overhaul procedures, please refer to "Engine Rebuilding" in the Unit Repair section.**

# Rocker Arms/Shaft

## REMOVAL & INSTALLATION

**NOTE: All rocker shaft removal and installation procedures are given in the "Camshaft Removal and Installation" section.**

# Intake Manifold

## REMOVAL & INSTALLATION

### *Pulsar and Sentra*

1. Remove the air cleaner assembly together with all of the attending hoses.
2. Disconnect the throttle linkage and fuel and vacuum lines from the carburetor (throttle body or throttle chamber on EFI engines).
3. The carburetor/throttle body/throttle chamber can be removed from the manifold at this point or can be removed as an assembly with the intake manifold.
4. Remove the manifold support stay on the CA16DE, CA18DE and GA16i engines.
5. Remove the EGR valve assembly, air regulator and FICD valve from the manifold on the CA16DE and CA18DE.
6. Loosen the intake manifold retaining bolts in the the proper sequence and separate the manifold from the cylinder head.

**NOTE: NEVER tighten or loosen the power valve adjusting screw on the CA16DE or CA18DE engines.**

7. Remove the intake manifold gasket and clean all the gasket contact surfaces thoroughly with a gasket scraper and suitable solvent. All traces of old gasket material must be removed to ensure proper sealing. Inpspect the intake manifold for cracks. Using a metal straightedge, check the surface of the intake manifold for warpage.

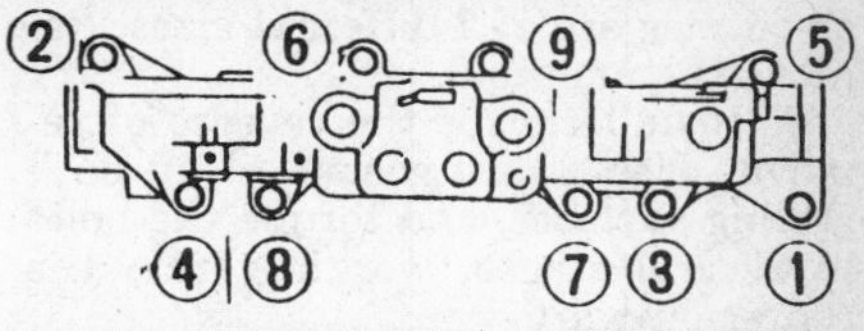


**Intake manifold nut loosening sequence – GA16i engines**

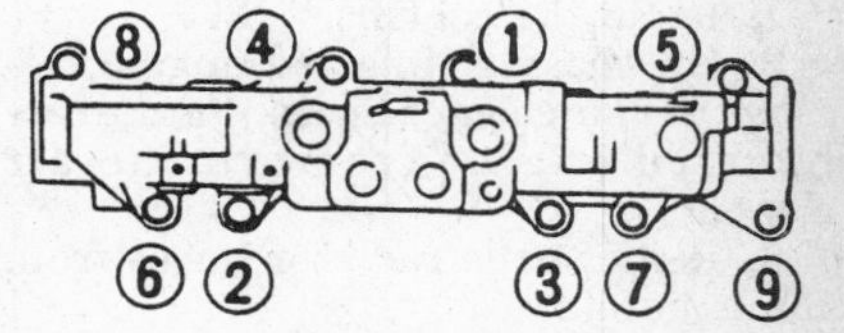


**Intake manifold nut tightening sequence – GA16i engines**

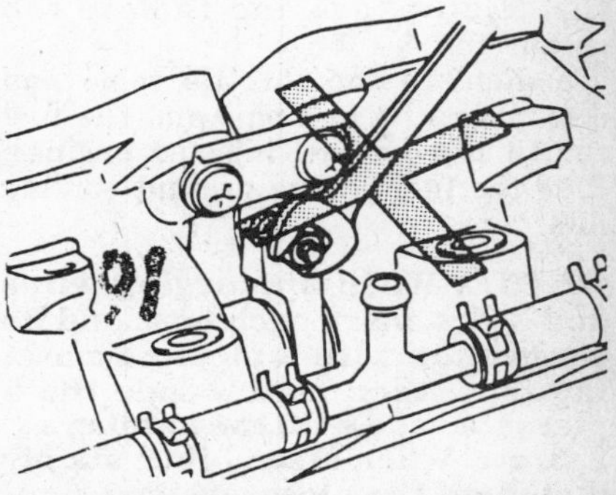

**Never touch this bolt on the CA16DE and CA18DE**

8. Place the new intake manifold gasket onto the cylinder head and position the intake manifold over the mounting studs and onto the gasket. Install the mountin nuts and torque them to specification in the proper sequence.
9. Installation of the intake manifold is in the reverse order of removal. Don't forget the support stay on the CA16DE and CA18DE engines.

### *1983–84 810 and Maxima*

**NOTE: Certain procedures may apply only to the gasoline engine.**

1. Disconnect all hoses to the air cleaner and remove the air cleaner.
2. Disconnect all air, water, vacuum and fuel hoses to the intake manifold. Remove the cold start valve and fuel pipe as an assembly. Remove the throttle linkage.
3. Remove the BPT valve control tube from the intake manifold. Remove the EGR hoses.
4. Disconnect all electrical wiring to the fuel injection unit. Note the location of the wires and mark them in some manner to facilitate reinstallation.
5. Make sure all wires, hoses, lines, etc. are removed. Unscrew the intake manifold bolts. Keep the bolts in order

since they are of 2 different sizes. Remove the manifold.

6. Installation is the reverse of removal. Use a new gasket, clean both sealing surfaces, and torque the bolts in several stages, working from the center outward.

### *200SX and Stanza*

1. Drain the coolant.
2. On the fuel injected engine, remove the air cleaner hoses. On the carbureted engine, remove the air cleaner.
3. Remove the radiator hoses from the manifold.
4. For the carbureted engine, remove the fuel, air and vacuum hoses from the carburetor. Remove the throttle linkage and remove the carburetor.
5. Remove the throttle cable and disconnect the fuel pipe and the fuel return line on fuel injected engines. Plug the fuel pipe to prevent spilling fuel.

**NOTE: When unplugging wires and hoses, mark each hose and its connection with a piece of masking tape, then match code the 2 pieces of tape with the numbers 1, 2, 3, etc. When assembling, simply match up the pieces of tape.**

6. Remove all remaining wires, tubes, the air cleaner bracket (carbureted engines) and the EGR and PCV tubes from the rear of the intake manifold. On carbureted engines, remove the air induction pipe. On fuel injected engines, remove the manifold supports.
7. Unbolt and remove the intake manifold. On fuel injected engines, remove the manifold with the fuel injectors/injection body, EGR valve, fuel pipes, etc. still attached.
8. Installation is in the reverse order of removal. Always use a new gasket. Tighten the mounting bolts from the outside, in; in two or three stages.

### *200SX (V6), 300ZX and 1985–88 Maxima*

1. Disconnect the negative battery cable and drain the cooling system.
2. Disconnect the valve cover-to-throttle chamber hose at the valve cover.
3. Disconnect the heater housing to water inlet tube at the water inlet.
4. Remove the bolt holding the water and fuel tubes to the head.
5. Relieve the fuel pressure from the fuel system, and remove the heater housing to thermostat housing tube.
6. Remove the intake collector cover and then remove the collector itself.

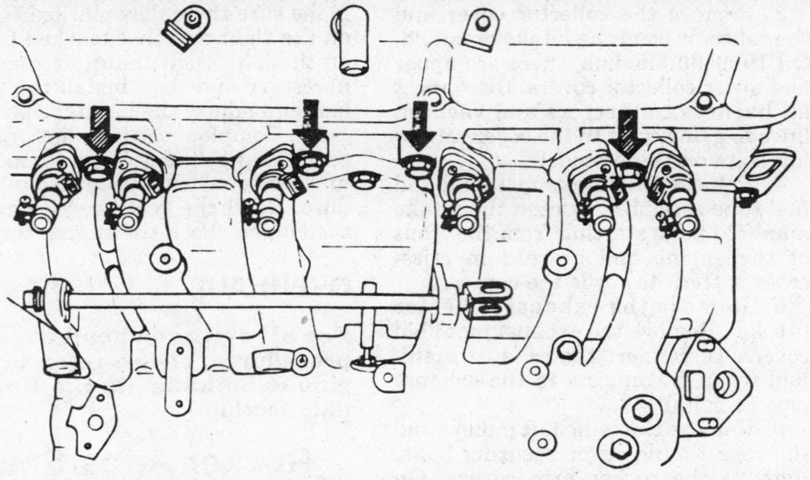

**810/Maxima intake manifold mounting bolt locations—gasoline engine**

7. Disconnect the fuel line and remove the intake manifold mount bolts. Remove the intake manifold assembly (with the fuel tube, assembly still attached) from the vehicle.

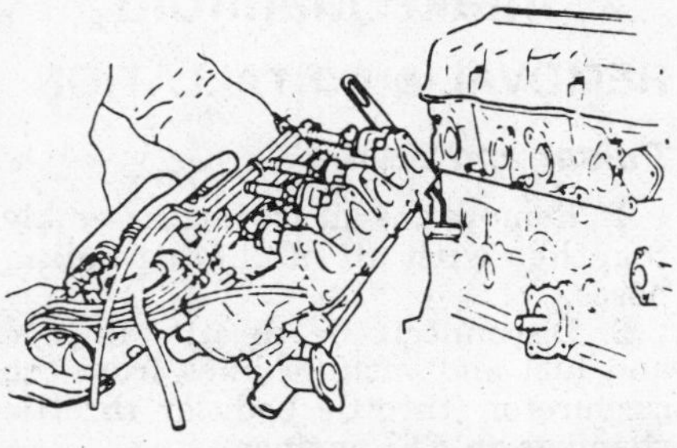

**Removing the manifold with injectors, etc., still attached—Z20E, Z22E**

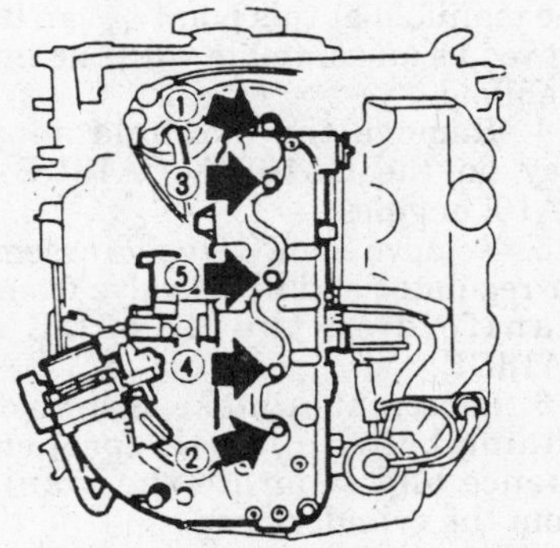

**Intake manifold collector cover bolt removal sequence—V6**

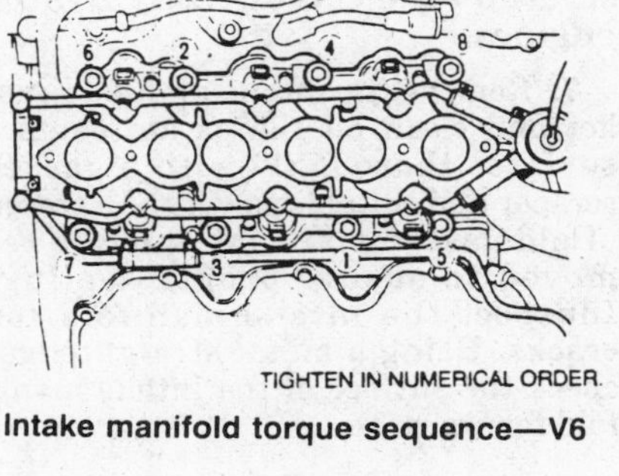
TIGHTEN IN NUMERICAL ORDER.

**Intake manifold torque sequence—V6**

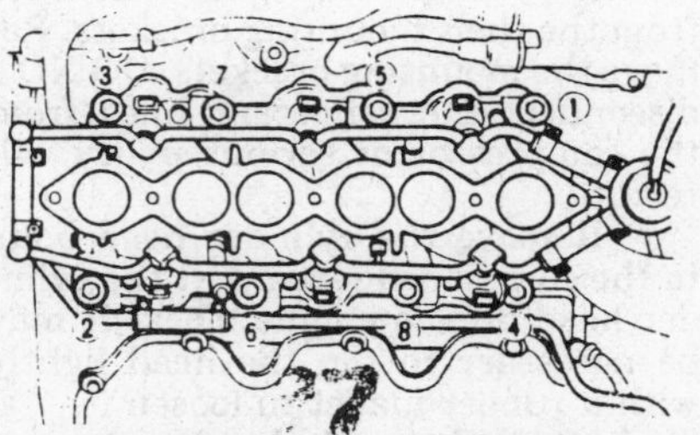

**Intake manifold bolt removal sequence—V6**

8. Installation is the reverse order of the removal procedure. Also be sure to use new gaskets when re-installing the manifold and torque the manifold bolts to 11–18 ft. lbs. in two stages, in the sequence shown.

### *1989–90 Maxima*

The 1989–90 Maxima has a slightly different collector/intake manifold assembly than used in 1985–88 models. The previous single collector is replaced by upper and lower collectors. Each collector has its own bolt removal and installation sequence.

1. Release the fuel pressure and disconnect the negative battery cable.
2. Drain coolant by removing the drain plug on the left and right sides of the cylinder block. The left side drain plug is located next to the oil level gauge and the right side drain plug is located behind the right side drive shaft boot.
3. Remove the distributor and the ignition wires. Separate the A.S.C.D. and the accelerator wires from the intake manifold collector.
4. Disconnect the harness connectors for the AAC. valve, throttle sensor and idle switch. Disconnect the air cut out valve water hose. Disconnect the PCV valve hoses. Disconnect the vacuum hoses from the vacuum gallery, swirl control valve, master brake cylin-

der, EGR. control valve and EGR. flare tube. Lable each component for assembly reference.

5. Loosen the upper collector cover bolts in proper sequence and remove the upper intake manifold collector from the engine.

6. Disconnect the engine ground harness. Loosen the lower collector bolts in sequence and remove the lower intakke manifold collector from the engine.

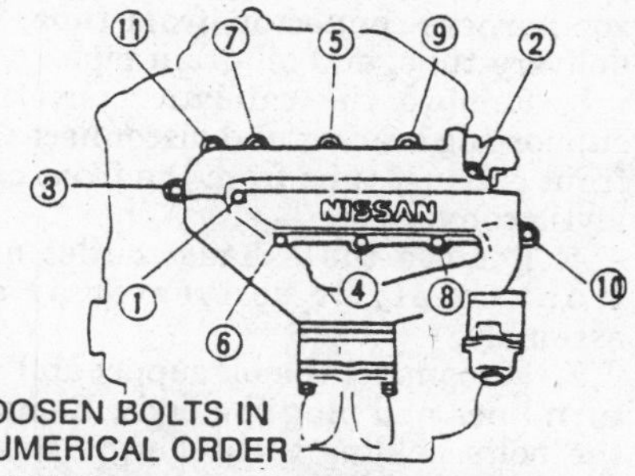


**UPPER intake manifold collector bolt loosening sequence – 1989–90 Maxima**

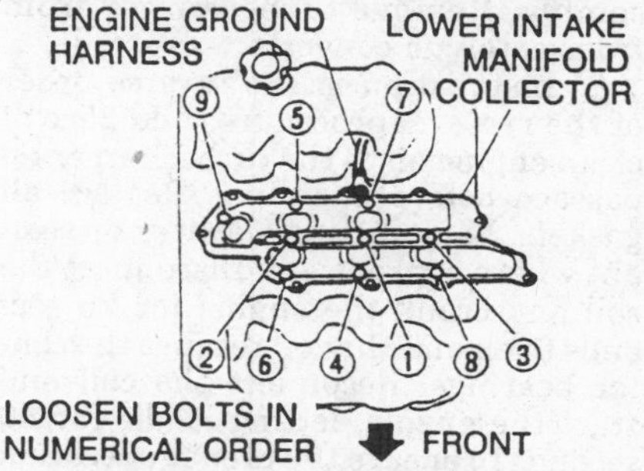


**LOWER intake manifold collector bolt loosening sequence – 1989–90 Maxima**

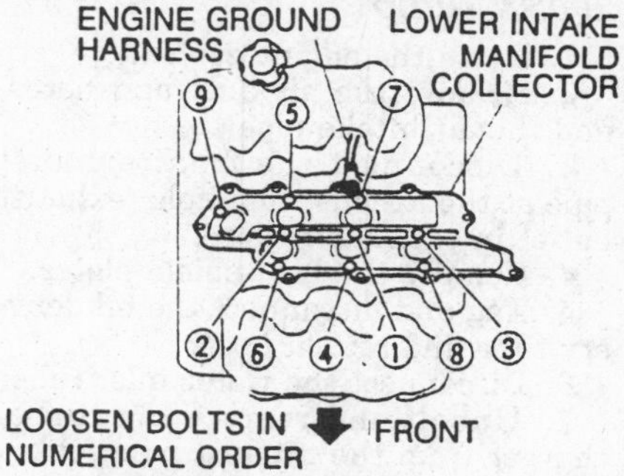


**Intake manifold bolt loosening sequence – 1989–90 Maxima**

7. Disconnect the harness connectors for all injectors, engine temperature switch and sensor, power valve control soleniod valve, EGR. control soleniod valve, EGR. temperature sensor (Calif. only). Disconnect the vacuum gallery hoses. Disconnect the pressure regulator valve vacuum hose, heater hose, fuel feed and return hose.

8. Remove the intake manifold and fuel tube assembly. Loosen intake manifold bolts in numerical order.

9. Install the intake manifold and fuel tube assembly with a new gasket to the engine. Tighten the manifold bolts and nuts in 2 or 3 stages in sequence.

10. Install the uper and lower collector and collector cover with new gaskets. Tighten collector to intake manifold bolts in 2 or 3 stages by reversing the removal sequence.

11. Connect all valves, lines, hoses, cables and or brackets to the collector cover and collector assembly.

12. Refill the cooling system and set the ignition timing.

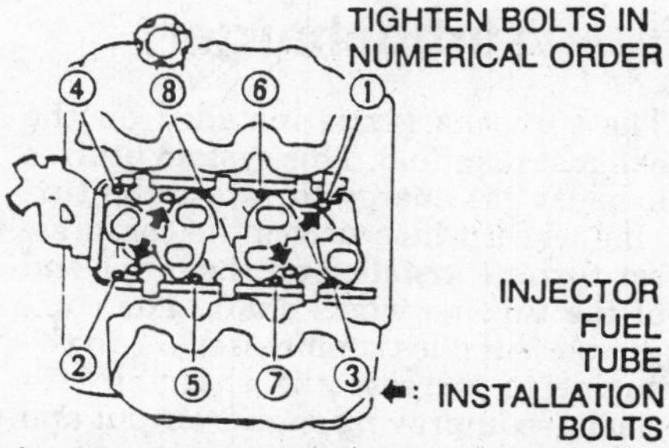


**Intake manifold bolt tightening sequence – 1989–90 Maxima**

### *240SX*

**NOTE: Release the fuel pressure before atempting to remove the intake manifold.**

1. Remove the air duct between the air flow meter and the throttle body. Disconnect the throttle linkage.

2. Disconnect the fuel line(s) from the fuel injector assembly.

3. Disconnect and label all of the electrical connectors and the vacuum hoses to the throttle, the intake manifold/collector assembly and the related components. Remove the spark plug wires.

4. Disconnect the EGR valve tube from the exhaust manifold. Remove the intake manifold mounting brackets.

5. Remove the mounting bolts and separate the intake manifold from the cylinder head.

6. Using a putty knife, clean the gasket mounting surfaces. Check the intake manifold for cracks and warpage.

7. Install the intake manifold/collector assembly and gasket on the engine. Always use a new gasket. Tighten the mounting bolts from the, center working to the end, in two or three stages. Torque the intake manifold bolts to 12–15 ft. lbs.

8. Install intake manifold mounting brackets and reconnect the EGR valve tube to the exhaust manifold.

9. Install the spark plug wires, electrical connectors and the vacuum hoses to the throttle, the intake manifold assembly and the related components.

10. Reconnect the fuel line(s) to the fuel injector assembly.

11. Install the air duct between the air flow meter and the throttle body. Connect the throttle linkage.

12. Start engine and check for leaks.

## Exhaust Manifold

### REMOVAL & INSTALLATION

**NOTE: Removing the intake manifold first on many models will provide better access to the exhaust manifold. If any fuel system components must be removed, make to relieve the fuel system pressure first.**

1. Remove the air cleaner assembly, if necessary for access. Remove the heat shield, if present.

2. Disconnect the exhaust pipe from the exhaust manifold.

3. Remove all temperature sensors, oxygen sensors, air induction pipes and other attachments from the manifold. Disconnect the EAI and EGR tubes from their fittings on the E-series manifold.

4. Loosen and remove the exhaust manifold attaching nuts and remove the manifold from the engine. Discard the exhaust manifold gaskets and replace with new.

5. Installation of the exhaust manifold is in the reverse order of removal. Tighten all bolts from the center outward in several stages.

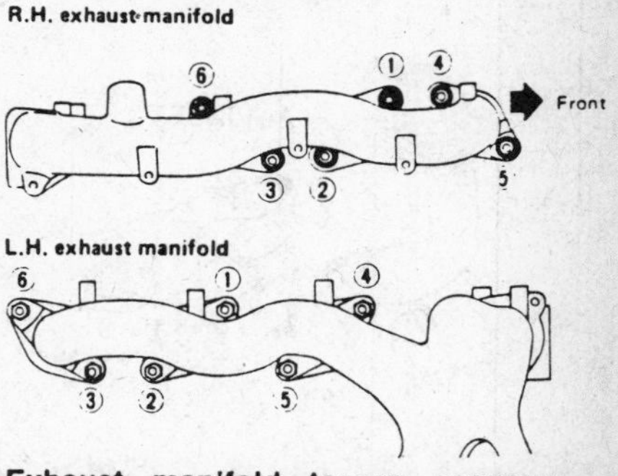


**Exhaust manifold torque sequence – VG30E (Maxima and 200SX)**

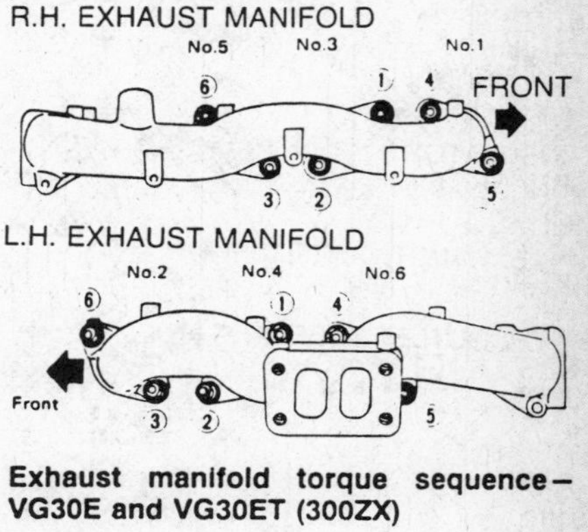


**Exhaust manifold torque sequence – VG30E and VG30ET (300ZX)**

## Combination Manifold

### REMOVAL & INSTALLATION

#### *280ZX*

**NOTE: It is important to replace the gasket whenever either manifold is removed. Because the manifolds share a common gasket, it is necessary to remove both manifolds for access to the gasket. Be sure to purchase the correct replacement gasket for the car.**

1. Disconnect the air and vacuum hoses from the air cleaner.
2. Remove the air cleaner.
3. Relieve fuel line pressure as outlined in the fuel filter replacement procedure. Disconnect the fuel injection wiring harness. Disconnect the hose from the rocker cover to the throttle chamber at the rocker cover. Drain the coolant into a clean container. Disconnect the coolant hose which runs from the heater to the coolant inlet at the inlet. Remove the bolt securing the coolant pipe/fuel pipe to the cylinder head. Remove the tube connecting the heater to the thermostat housing. Disconnect the fuel lines.
4. Disconnect the vacuum hose to the EGR valve, and the EGR tube from the exhaust manifold.
5. On models with an air pump, disconnect the air injection hose from the air injection gallery on the exhaust manifold at the check valve.
6. Disconnect the exhaust pipe from the exhaust manifold or from the exhaust outlet of the turbocharger if so equipped. Remove the exhaust manifold heat shield.
7. Remove the intake and exhaust manifold.
8. Install the manifolds in the reverse order of removal. *Always use a new gasket.* Air leaks will cause burnt valves and misfiring. Tighten the manifold bolts from the center outwards, in 2 progressive steps, to the proper torque.

## Turbocharger

The turbocharger is installed on the exhaust manifold. This system utilizes exhaust gas energy to rotate the turbine wheel which drives the compressor turbine installed on the other end of the turbine wheel shaft. The compressor supplies compressed air to the engine to increase the charging efficiency so improving engine output and torque.

Turbochargers maintain close tolerances between their rotating parts. The turbocharger unit should only be serviced internally by an engine specialist trained in turbocharger repair.

### REMOVAL & INSTALLATION

**NOTE: If the turbocharger is being replaced, always drain the crankcase and replace the oil and filter to ensure a clean oil supply. This is especially true in cases of complete turbo failure where there is the possibility of metal particles entering the engine's lubricating system and damaging the new turbocharger.**

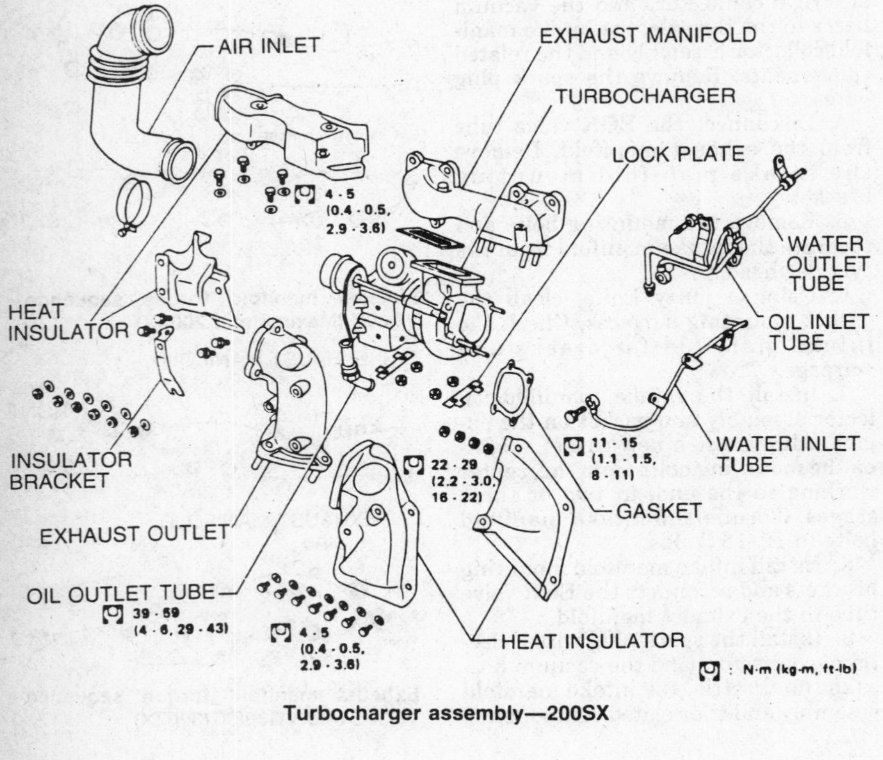

Turbocharger assembly—200SX

#### *Pulsar NX Turbo*

1. Remove the heat insulator, inlet tube, air duct hose, suction air pipe and turbocharger temperature sensor.
2. Disconnect the exhaust gas sensor harness connector, from tube, oil delivery tube, and oil drain pipe.
3. Remove the catalytic converter supporting bracket and disconnect the front exhaust tube from the front catalytic converter.
4. Remove the exhaust outlet and front catalytic converter as an assembly.
5. Disconnect the oil supply and return lines and plug the ends. Remove the bolts holding turbocharger to exhaust manifold. Remove turbocharger and front catalytic converter as an assembly. Remove turbocharger from front catalytic converter.
6. Installation is the reverse order of the removal procedure. Add 25cc of clean engine oil to the turbocharger oil passage before installing. Replace all gaskets, banjo fitting washers or sealant where appropriate. Disconnect the coil and crank the engine for 20 seconds to ensure that oil reaches the center bearings. Reconnect the coil and start the engine, letting it idle for 30 seconds to ensure the proper operation of the turbocharger.

#### *200SX Turbo*

1. Drain the engine coolant.
2. Remove the air duct and hoses, and the air intake pipe.
3. Disconnect the front exhaust pipe at the exhaust manifold (exhaust outlet in the illustration).
4. Remove the heat shield plates.
5. Tag and disconnect the oil delivery tube and return hose.
6. Disconnect the water inlet tube.
7. Unbolt and remove the turbocharger from the exhaust manifold.
8. Reverse the above procedure to install. Torque the turbocharger outlet-to-housing bolts to 16–22 ft. lbs. Add 25cc of clean engine oil to the turbocharger oil passage before installing. Replace all gaskets, banjo fitting washers or sealant where appropriate. Disconnect the coil and crank the engine for 20 seconds to ensure that oil reaches the center bearings. Reconnect the coil and start the engine, letting it idle for 30 seconds to ensure the proper operation of the turbocharger.

#### *280ZX Turbo*

1. Remove the heat insulator, inlet

tube, air duct hose and suction air pipe.

2. Disconnect the exhaust gas sensor harness connector, front tube, oil delivery tube and oil drain pipe.

3. Loosen the nuts which attach the turbocharger unit to the exhaust manifold, then remove the turbocharger.

**NOTE: The turbocharger should not be disassembled. The turbocharger is replaced as a unit if found to be defective.**

4. Installation is the reverse of the removal procedure. Add 25cc of clean engine oil to the turbocharger oil passage before installing. Replace all gaskets, banjo fitting washers or sealant where appropriate. Disconnect the coil and crank the engine for 20 seconds to ensure that oil reaches the center bearings. Reconnect the coil and start the engine, letting it idle for 30 seconds to ensure the proper operation of the turbocharger.

### *300ZX Turbo*

1. Remove the following:
a. Compressor and compressor bracket
b. Exhaust front tube
c. Center cable
d. Heat insulator for the brake master cylinder
e. Air duct and hoses
f. Exhaust manifold connecting tube and heat shield plate
g. Oil delivery tube and return hose.

2. Remove the exhaust manifold and the turbocharger as an assembly.

**NOTE: The turbocharger unit should not be disassembled.**

3. Installation is the reverse of removal. Add 25cc of clean engine oil to the turbocharger oil passage before installing. Replace all gaskets, banjo fitting washers or sealant where appropriate. Disconnect the coil and crank the engine for 20 seconds to ensure that oil reaches the center bearings. Reconnect the coil and start the engine, letting it idle for 30 seconds to ensure the proper operation of the turbocharger.

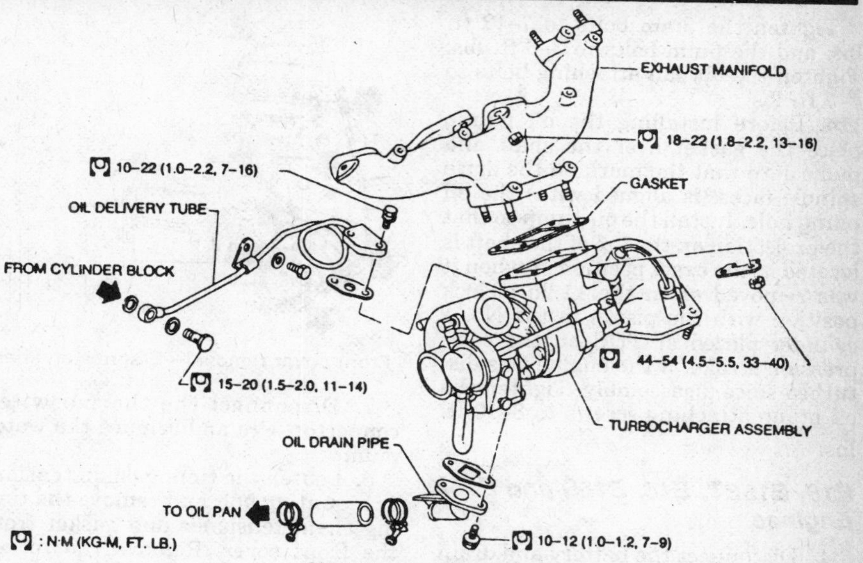


V6 turbocharger assembly

## TROUBLESHOOTING

**For more information on turbochargers, please refer to "Turbocharging" in the Unit Repair section.**

# Front Cover

## REMOVAL, INSTALLATION & OIL SEAL REPLACEMENT

### *L24E, L28E, L28ET, Z22 and Z22E Engines*

**NOTE: It may be necessary to remove the cylinder head to perform this operation if you cannot cut the front of the head gasket cleanly as described in Step 10.**

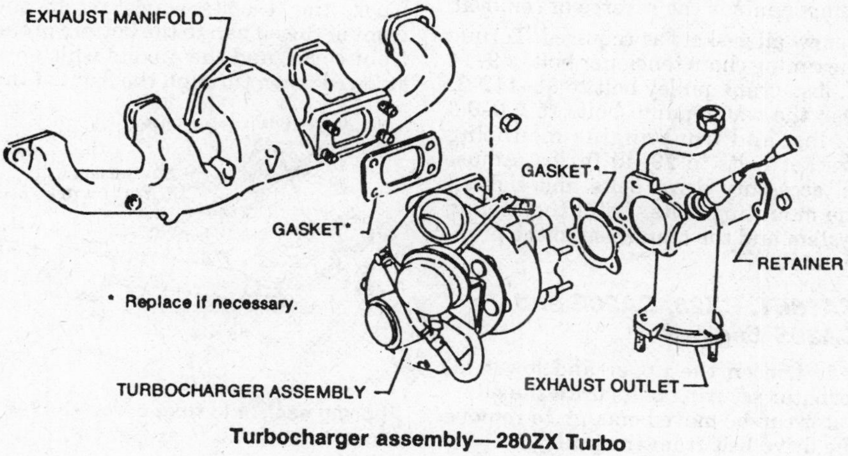


Turbocharger assembly—280ZX Turbo

1. Disconnect the negative battery cable from the battery, drain the cooling system, and remove the radiator together with the upper and lower radiator hoses.

2. Loosen the alternator drive belt adjusting screw and remove the drive belt. Remove the bolts which attach the alternator bracket to the engine and set the alternator aside out of the way.

3. Remove the distributor.

4. Remove the oil pump attaching screws, and take out the pump and its drive spindle.

5. Remove the cooling fan and the fan pulley together with the drive belt.

6. Remove the water pump.

7. Remove the crankshaft pulley bolt and remove the crankshaft pulley.

8. Remove the bolts holding the front cover to the front of the cylinder block, the 4 bolts which retain the front of the oil pan to the bottom of the front cover, and the 2 bolts which are screwed down through the front of the cylinder head and into the top of the front cover.

9. Carefully pry the front cover off the engine.

10. Cut the exposed front section of the oil pan gasket away from the oil pan. Do the same to the gasket at the top of the front cover. Remove the 2 side gaskets and clean all of the mating surfaces.

11. Cut the portions needed from a new oil pan gasket and top front cover gasket.

12. Apply sealer to all of the gaskets and position them on the engine in their proper places.

13. Apply a light coating of grease to the crankshaft oil seal and carefully mount the front cover to the front of the engine and install all of the mounting bolts.

Tighten the 8mm bolts to 7–12 ft. lbs. and the 6mm bolts to 3–6 ft. lbs. Tighten the oil pan attaching bolts to 4–7 ft. lbs.

14. Before installing the oil pump, place the gasket over the shaft and make sure that the mark on the drive spindle faces (is aligned with) the oil pump hole. Install the oil pump so that the projection on the top of the shaft is located in the exact position as when it was removed or in the 11:25 o'clock position with the piston in the No. 1 cylinder placed at TDC on the compression stroke, if the engine was disturbed since disassembly. Tighten the oil pump attaching screws to 8–10 ft. lbs.

### E15, E15ET, E16, E16S and E16i Engines

1. Disconnect the battery and drain the cooling system from the radiator and the engine block. Remove the radiator together with the upper and lower radiator hoses.
2. Loosen the air conditioning belt and remove.
3. Loosen the alternator adjusting bolt, and remove the alternator belt. Unbolt the alternator mounting bracket and remove the alternator.
4. Remove the power steering belt (if equipped) by loosening the steering pump adjusting bolt.
5. Remove the water pump pulley.
6. Remove crankshaft pulley.
7. Loosen and remove the 8 bolts securing the timing covers and remove the upper and lower covers.
8. Installation is the reverse of removal. Adjust all accessory drive belts and tighten the mounting bolts. Torque the crank pulley bolt to 83–108 ft. lbs.; the water pump pulley bolt to 2.7–3.7 ft. lbs.; and the belt cover bolts to 2.7–3.7 ft. lbs.

### GA16i Engines

1. Disconnect the negative battery cable and drain the cooling system from the radiator and the engine block. Drain the crankcase and remove the oil pan.
2. Loosen the air conditioning belt and remove.
3. Loosen the alternator adjusting bolt, and remove the alternator belt. Unbolt the alternator mounting bracket and remove the alternator.
4. Remove the power steering belt (if equipped) by loosening the steering pump adjusting bolt.
5. Remove the air cleaner.
6. Connect a chain hoist or other suitable lifting fixture to the front side lifting bracket and tension the hoist to support the engine. Remove the front engine mounting bracket.

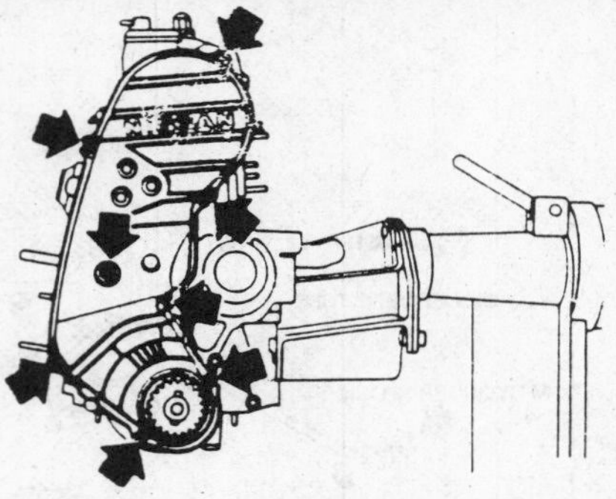

Front cover removal—E-series engines

7. Disconnect the thermoswitch connector wire and remove the water pump.
8. Loosen the timing chain tensioner mounting bolt and remove the timing chain tensioner and gasket from the front cover. Remove the rocker arm cover and cover gasket. Remove the spark plugs and set the No. 1 piston to TDC of the compression stroke. When the No. 1 piston is at TDC the crankshaft an camshaft keyways will be in the 12 o'clock position. Do not disturb the engine once in this position.
9. Remove crankshaft pulley. Be careful not to lose the Woodruff keys.
10. Loosen the retaining bolts and remove the front cover from the cylinder block. There are 6mm and 8mm size bolts. Clean all the old sealant from the surface of the front cover and the cylinder block.

**To install:**

11. Verify the No. 1 piston is at TDC. Apply a bead of high temperature liquid gasket to both sides of the front cover. Place the front cover onto the cylinder block and install the retaining bolts. Torque the 6mm bolts to 5–6 ft. lbs and the 8mm bolts to 12–15 ft. lbs.

**NOTE: When installing the front cover, be careful not to damage the cylinder head gasket.**

12. Installation of the remaining components is the reverse of removal.

Renew all gaskets as required. Torque the timing chain tensioner bolt to 9–14 ft. lbs., crank pulley bolt to 98–112 ft. lbs.; the water pump bolts to 5.0–6.0 ft. lbs. and front engine mounting bracket bolts to 29–40 ft. lbs. Adjust all accessory drive belts and tighten the mounting bolts. Refill the cooling system and the crankcase to the proper levels.

### CA18ET, CA20, CA20E and CA20S Engines

1. Loosen the upper and lower alternator securing bolts until the alternator can be moved enough to remove the drive belt from the pulley.
2. Loosen the idler pulley locknut and turn the adjusting bolt until the air conditioner compressor belt can be removed.
3. Unbolt and remove the crankshaft pulley, removing the alternator belt along with it. Remove the crankshaft damper.
4. Unbolt and remove the water pump pulley.
5. Remove the upper and lower timing belt covers and their gaskets. If the gaskets are in good condition after removal, they can be reused; if they are in way damaged or broken, replace them.
6. Reverse the above procedure for installation. Torque the front cover bolts evenly to 2.2–3.6 ft. lbs; torque the crank pulley damper bolt to 90–98 ft. lbs.; torque the crank pulley bolt to 9–10 ft. lbs.; torque the water pump pulley bolts to 4.3–7 ft. lbs. Adjust tension on all drive belts.

### KA24E Engines

1. Disconnect the negative battery cable. Drain the cooling system and remove the radiator shroud and the cooling fan.
2. Loosen the alternator drive belt adjusting screw and remove the drive belt. Remove the power steering and air conditioning drive belts.
3. Remove the spark plugs and set the No. 1 piston to TDC of the compression stroke. Mark and remove the distributor.
4. Remove the power steering pump, idler pulley and the power steering brackets.
5. Remove the air conditioning compressor idler pulley. Remove the crankshaft pullley bolt and remove the crankshaft pulley with a 2 jawed puller. Remove the oil pump attaching screws, and take out the pump and its drive spindle. Remove the rocker arm cover.
6. Remove the oil pan.
7. Remove the bolts holding the front cover to the front of the cylinder block, the 4 bolts which retain the front of the oil pan to the bottom of the front cover, and the 4 bolts which are screwed down through the front of the

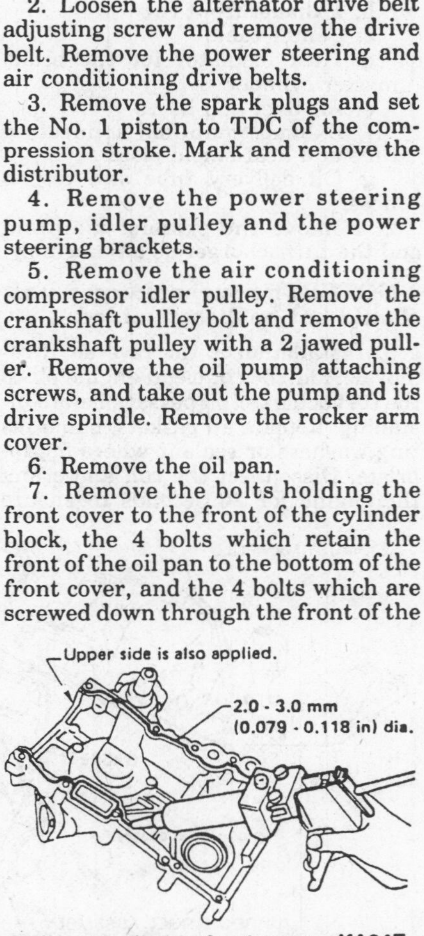


Applyng sealant to front cover—KA24E engines

cylinder head and into the top of the front cover. Carefully pry the front cover off the front of the engine. Clean all the old sealant from the surface of the front cover and the cylinder block.

**To install:**

8. Verify the No. 1 piston is at TDC. Apply a very thin bead of high temperature liquid gasket to both sides of the front cover and to where the cover mates with the cylinder head. Apply a light coating of grease to the crankshaft oil seal and carefully mount the front cover to the front of the engine and install all of the mounting bolts.

**NOTE: When installing the front cover, be careful not to damage the cylinder head gasket.**

9. Install the oil pan and rocker arm cover.
10. Before installing the oil pump, place the gasket over the shaft and make sure that the mark on the drive spindle faces (aligned) with the oil pump hole. Install the oil pump and distributor driving spindle into the front cover with a new gasket.
11. Install the crankshaft pulley and bolt. Torque the pulley bolt to 87–116 ft. lbs.
12. Install the distributor and the spark plugs.
13. Install the compressor idler pulley. Install power steering pump brackets, idler pulley and power steering pump. Install the drive belt and adjust the tension.
14. Install the radiator shroud and the cooling fan. Refill the cooling system. Reconnect the negative battery cable. Start the engine, check ignition timing and check for leaks.

## Front Cover/ Timing Belt

### ADJUSTMENT

#### *VG30E and VG30ET Engines (1988–90 Only)*

1. Confirm that No. 1 cylinder is at T.D.C. on its compression stroke. Install tensioner and tensioner spring. If stud is removed apply locking sealant to threads before installing.
2. Swing tensioner fully clockwise with hexagon wrench and temporarily tighten locknut.
3. Point the arrow on the timing belt toward the front belt cover. Align the white lines on the timing belt with the punchmarks on all three pulleys.

**NOTE: There are 133 total timing belt teeth. If timing belt is installed correctly there will be 40 teeth between lefthand and righthand camshaft sprocket timing marks. There will be 43 teeth between lefthand camshaft sprocket and crankshaft sprocket timing marks.**

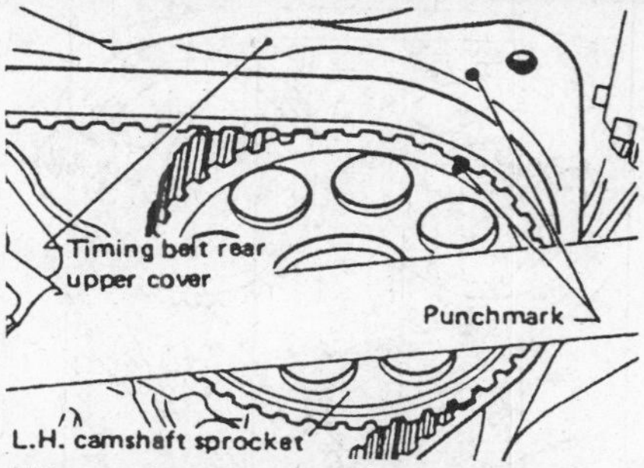

**LH camshaft sprocket timing belt alignment marks – 1988–90 VG30E and VG30ET engines**

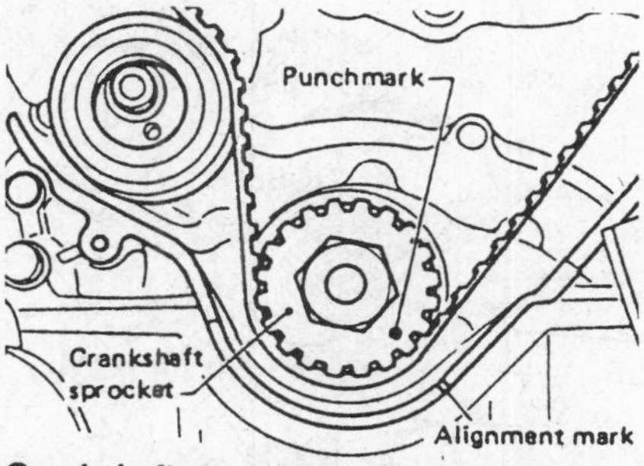

**Crankshaft sprocket timing belt alignment marks – 1988–90 VG30E and VG30ET engines**

4. Loosen tensioner locknut, keeping tensioner steady with a hexagon wrench.
5. Swing tensioner 70–80 degrees clockwise with hexagon wrench and temporarily tighten locknut.
6. Install all the spark plugs. Turn crankshaft clockwise 2 or 3 times, then slowly set No. 1 cylinder at TDC. on its compression stroke.
7. Push middle of timing belt between righthand camshaft sprocket and tensioner pulley with a force of 22 ft. lbs.
8. Loosen tensioner locknut, keeping tensioner steady with a hexagon wrench.
9. Insert a 0.138 in. (0.35mm) thick and 0.5 in. (12.7mm) wide feeler gauge between the bottom of tensioner pulley and timing belt. Turn crankshaft clockwise and position gauge completely betwwen tensioner pulley and timing belt. The timing belt will move about 2.5 teeth.
10. Tighten tensioner locknut, keeping tensioner steady with a hexagon wrench.
11. Turn crankshaft clockwise or counterclockwise and remove the gauge.
12. Rotate the engine 3 times, then set No. 1 at TDC. on its compression stroke.
13. Check timing belt deflection on 1988 models only. Timing belt deflection is 13.0-14.5mm at 22 lbs. of pressure. If it is out of specified range, readjust the timing belt by repeatng Steps 1–12.
14. Install the upper and lower timing belt covers and complete the remainder of the installation in reverse of the removal procedure.

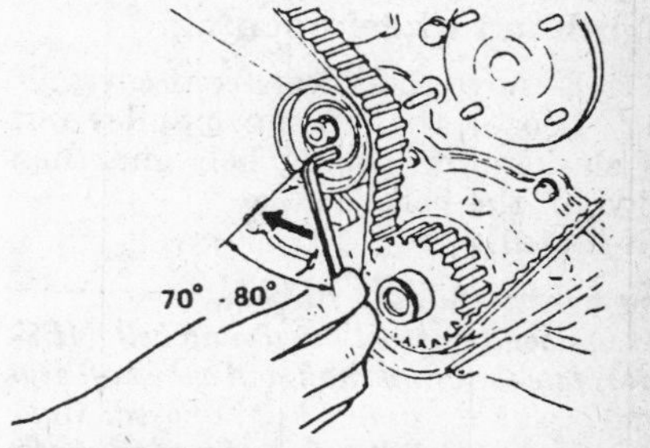

**Swing the tensioner 70–80 degrees clockwise**

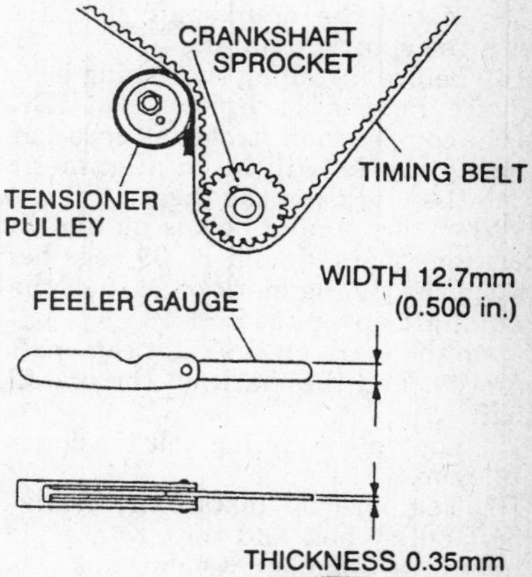

**Checking timing belt adjustment with feeler gauge – 1988–90 VG30E and VG30ET engines**

### REMOVAL & INSTALLATION

#### *CA16DE and CA18DE Engines*

1. Disconnect the negative battery cable. Drain the cooling system.
2. Disconnect the upper radiator hose at the elbow and then position it out of the way.
3. Remove the right side engine undercover.
4. Loosen the power steering pump and the A/C compressor and then remove the drive belts.
5. Remove the water pump pulley.
6. Matchmark the crank angle sensor to the upper front cover and the remove it. Carefully position it out of the way.
7. Position a floor jack under the engine and raise it just enough to support the engine.

8. Remove the upper engine mount bracket at the right side of the upper front cover.
9. Remove the upper front cover.
10. Align the timing marks on the camshaft pulley sprockets and then remove the crankshaft pulley.

**NOTE: The crankshaft pulley may be reached by removing the side cover from inside the righthand wheel opening.**

11. Remove the lower front cover.
12. Loosen the tensioner pulley nut to slacken the timing belt and then slide off the belt.

**To install:**

**CAUTION**

*Do not bend or twist the timing belt. NEVER rotate the crankshaft and camshaft separately with the timing belt removed. Make sure the timing belt is free of any oil, water or debris.*

13. Install the crankshaft sprocket with the sprocket plates.
14. Before installing the timing belt, ensure that the No. 1 piston is at TDC of the compression stroke (all sprocket timing marks will be in alignment with the marks on the case).

When the timing belt is on and in position, there should be 39 cogs between the timing mark on each of the camshaft sprocket and 48 cogs between the mark on the right camshaft sprocket and the mark on the crankshaft sprocket.

15. Loosen the timing belt tensioner pulley nut.
16. Temporarily install the crankshaft pulley bolt and then rotate the engine two complete revolutions.

**CAUTION**

*Fabricate and install a 25mm (0.98 in.) thick spacer between the end of the crankshaft and the head of the crankshaft pulley bolt to prevent bolt damage.*

17. Tighten the tensioner pulley bolt to 16–22 ft. lbs. (22–29 Nm).
18. Install the upper and lower front covers.
19. Install the crankshaft pulley with

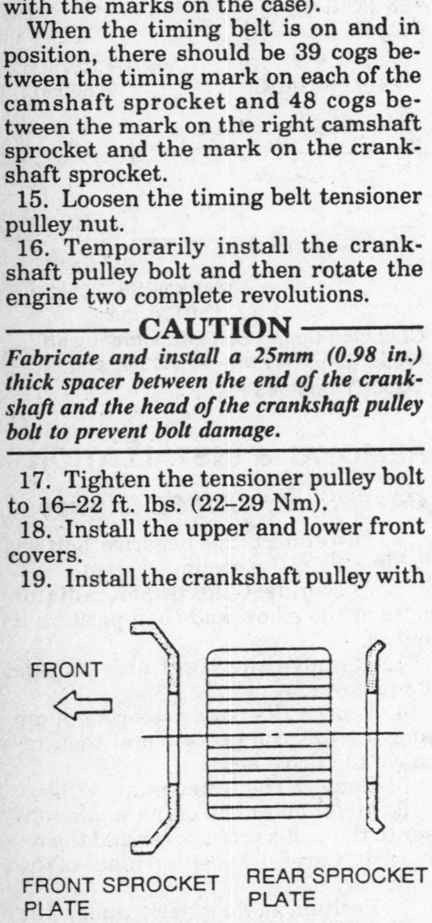

Crankshaft sprocket plate installation—CA16DE and CA18DE

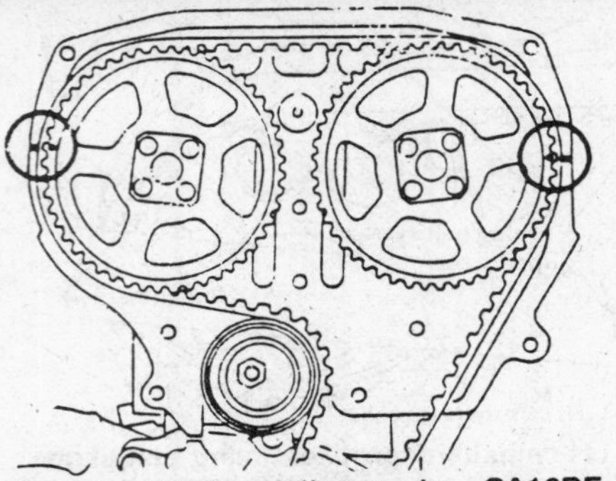
Camshaft timing pulley marks—CA16DE and CA18DE

Loosen the tensioner pulley nut—CA16DE and CA18DE

its washer and tighten it to 105–112 ft. lbs. (145–152 Nm).
20. Install the engine mount bracket.
21. Install the water pump pulley. Install the crank angle sensor so that the matchmarks made previously line up and tighten the bolts to 5.1–5.8 ft. lbs. (7–8 Nm).
22. Installation of the remaining components is in the reverse order of removal. Check the tension on all drive belts and fill the engine with coolant.

### VG30E and VG30ET Engines (300ZX)

**NOTE: On 1988–90 models, timing belt removal and installation is the same as described below with the exception that the rocker covers and rocker shafts bolts are not removed, but the spark plugs are still removed. However, these model years require that the timing belt be adjusted after installation. Timing belt adjustment is described above.**

1. Remove the engine under covers, radiator shroud, fan and pulleys.
2. Drain the coolant from the radiator and remove the water pump hose.
3. Remove the power steering, compressor and alternator drive belts.
4. Set the No. 1 cylinder at TDC on its compression stroke.
5. Remove the idler bracket of the compressor drive belt and crankshaft pulley.
6. Remove the front upper and lower belt covers.
7. Using chalk or paint, mark the relationship of the timing belt to the camshaft and the camshaft sprockets; also mark the timing belt's direction of rotation. On 1988–89 models, align the punchmark on the left hand camshaft pulley with the mark on the upper rear timing belt cover; align the punchmark on the crankshaft with the notch on the oil pump housing; temporarily install the crankshaft pulley bolt to allow for crankshaft rotation.
8. Loosen the timing belt tensioner and return spring then remove the timing belt. Check that the tensioner spring turns smoothly and check the tensioner spring for wear.

**NOTE: After Step 7, the camshaft oil seal can be replaced by removing the camshaft sprockets and lifting the oil seal off the**

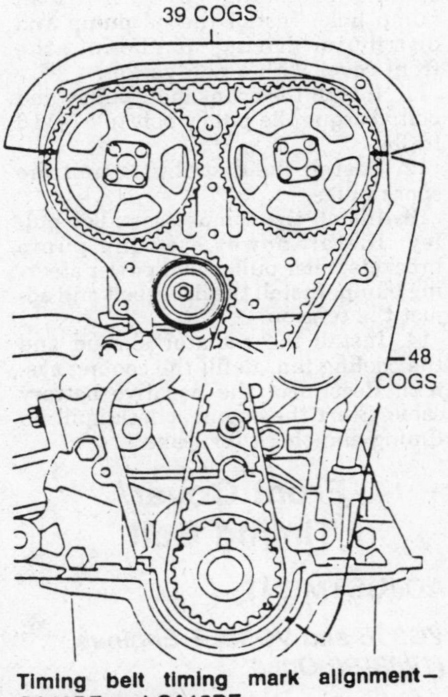

Timing belt timing mark alignment—CA16DE and CA18DE

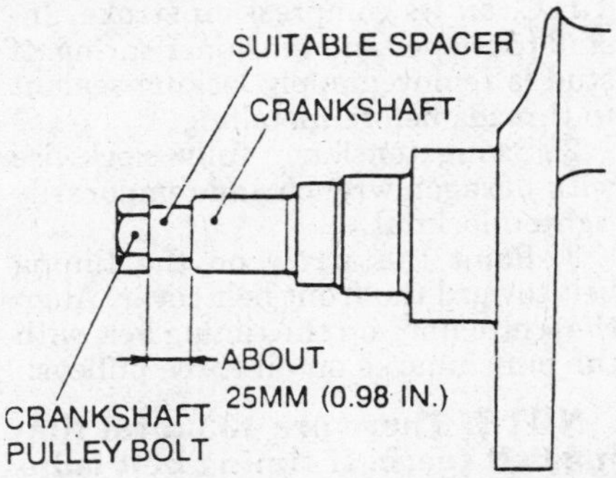

A spacer must be installed between the crankshaft and pulley bolt head before rotating the engine—CA16DE and CA18DE

**shaft. Apply clean engine oil to the new oil seal and install it on the camshaft along with the camshaft sprockets.**

9. Before installing the timing belt confirm that the No. 1 cylinder is set at TDC on its compression stroke.

10. Remove both rocker covers and loosen all rocker shaft retaining bolts (not required on 1988–90 models).

**NOTE: The rocker arm shaft bolts MUST be loosened so that the correct belt tension can be obtained.**

11. Install tensioner and return spring. Using an Allen wrench, turn the tensioner clockwise and temporarily tighten the locknut. On 1988–89 models, proceed to the "Adjustment" section to complete the remainder of the timing belt installation and adjustment procedure.

12. Make sure that the timing belt is clean and free from oil or water.

13. When installing the timing belt align the white lines on the belt with the punch mark on the camshaft pulleys and crankshaft pulley. Have the arrow on the timing belt pointing toward the front belt covers.

14. Using a Allen wrench, loosen the tensioner lock bolt, then slowly turn the tensioner clockwise and counterclockwise 2–3 times.

**NOTE: If the coarse tensioner stud has been removed, be sure to apply locking sealer to the threads before installing it.**

15. Torque the tensioner lock nut to 32–43 ft. lbs., the rocker arm shaft retaining bolts (in 2–3 stages) to 13–16 ft. lbs.

**NOTE: Before tightening, be sure to set the camshaft lobe at the position where the lobe is not lifted.**

16. Install the lower and upper belt covers.

17. The remainder of the installation is the reverse of removal.

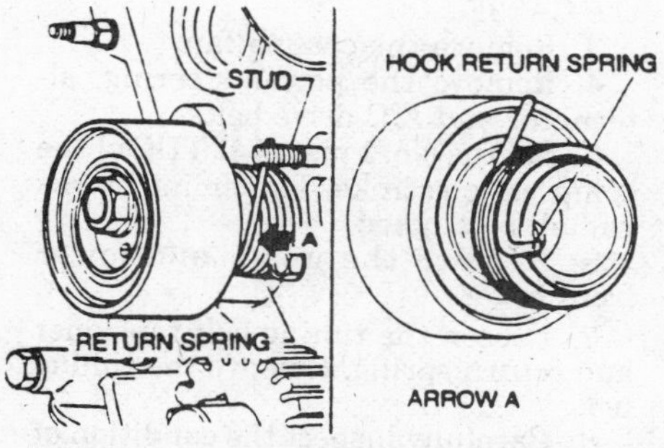


Installation of the tensioner and return spring—VG30E and VG30ET

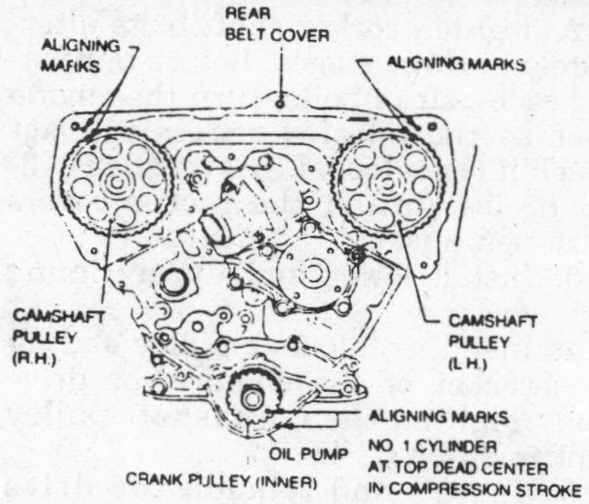


Align camshaft and crankshaft pulley marks—V6

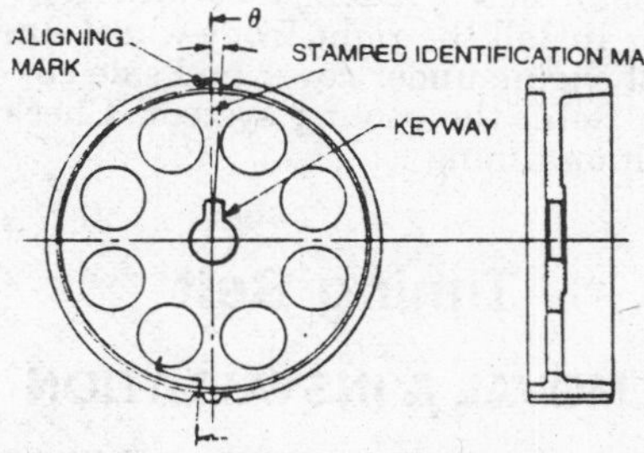


Camshaft pulley alignment marks—V6

### VG30E Engine (Maxima)

**NOTE: On 1988–90 models, timing belt removal and installation is the same as described below with the exception that the rocker covers and rocker shafts bolts are not removed, but the spark plugs are still removed. However, these model years require that the timing belt be adjusted after installation. Timing belt adjustment is described above.**

1. Raise vehicle and support safely.
2. Remove the engine under covers and drain engine coolant from the radiator.

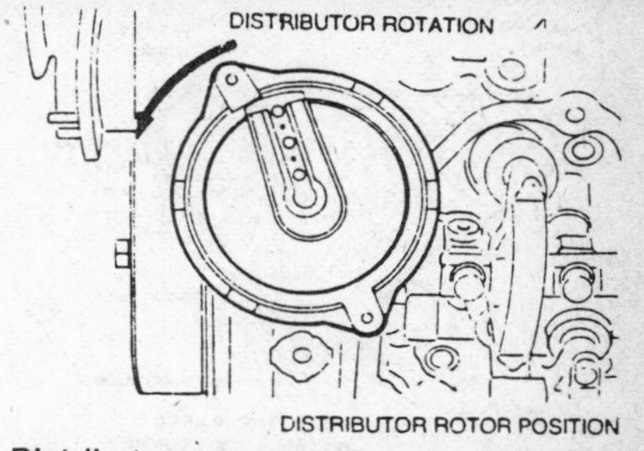


Distributor rotor position for timing belt removal—V6

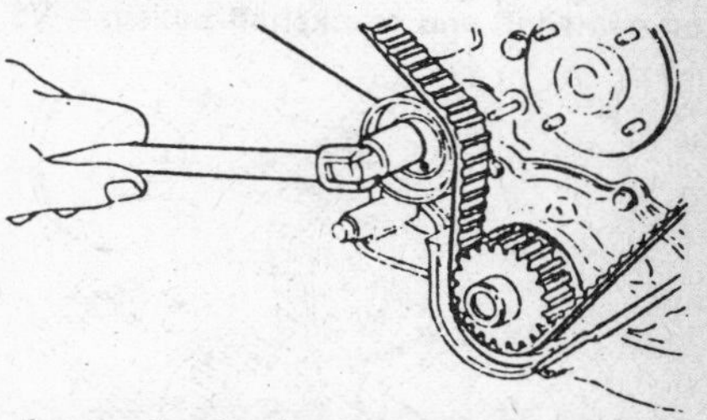

Loosening timing belt tensioner—V6

3. Remove the front right side wheel and tire assembly. Remove the engine side cover.

4. On 1985–88 models, remove the engine coolant reservoir tank and radiator hoses and the ASCD (speed control device) actuator; remove the lower coolant hose support bracket and disconnect the lower hose from the suction pipe.

5. Remove the alternator, power steering and air conditioning compresor drive belts from the engine. When removing the power steering drive belt, loosen the idler pulley from the right side wheel housing.

6. Remove the idler bracket of the compressor drive belt and crankshaft pulley. Use a 2-jawed puller to the remove the crankshaft pulley. On 1989–90 models, remove the upper radiator

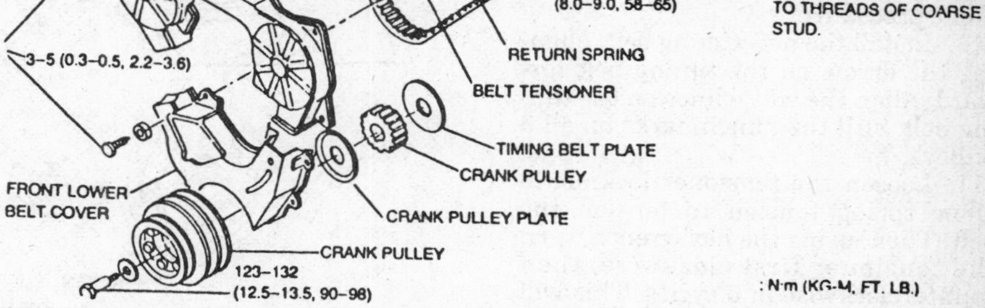

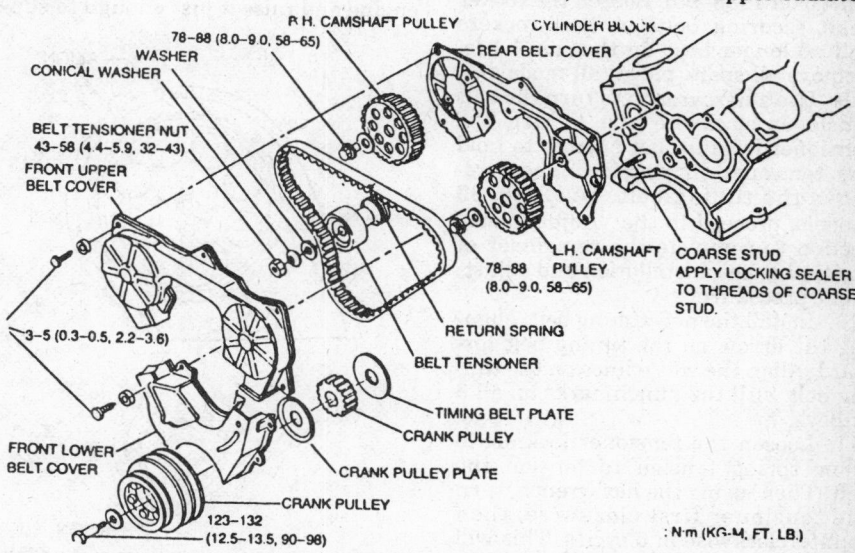


Exploded view of the V6 timing belt assembly, showing timing cover

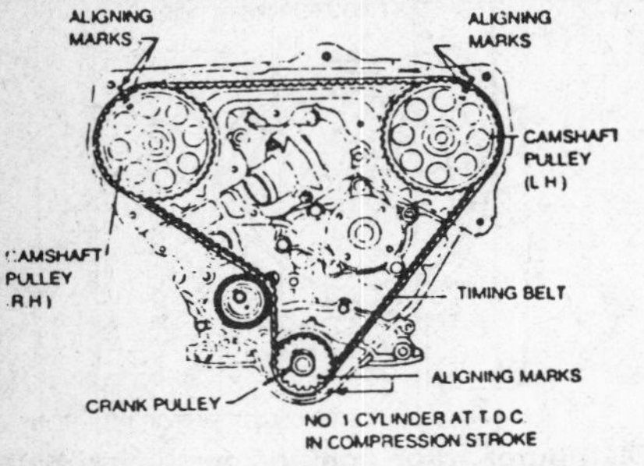


**Aligning timing belt white lines with marks on camshaft and crankshaft pulleys—V6**

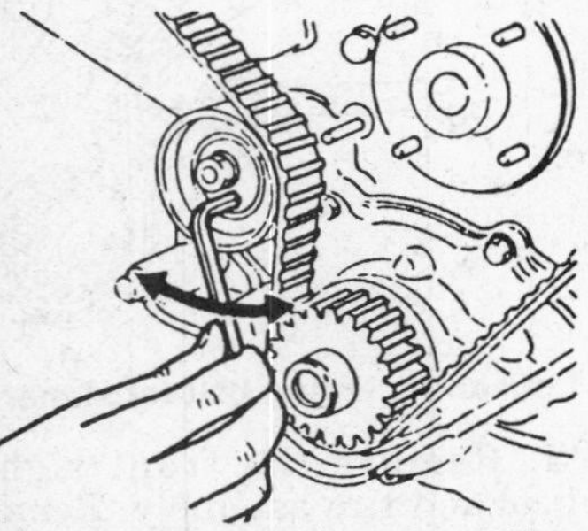

**Tightening tensioner locknut—V6**

and water inlet hoses; unbolt and remove the water pump pulley.

7. Remove the upper and lower timing belt covers. Rotate the engine with a socket wrench on the crankshaft pulley bolt to align the 2 sets of timing marks. The marks are on the camshaft pulleys and rear belt covers. On 1988–89 models, align the punchmark on the left hand camshaft pulley with the mark on the upper rear timing belt cover; align the punchmark on the crankshaft with the notch on the oil pump housing; temporarily install the crankshaft pulley bolt to allow for crankshaft rotation.

8. Remove the rocker covers (not required on 1988–90). Loosen the rocker shaft securing bolts so that rockers will no longer bear on the cam lobes. Remove all spark plugs (all models).

9. Use a hex wrench to turn the belt tensioner clockwise and tighten the tensioner locknut just enough to hold the tensioner in position. Then, remove the timing belt. On 1988–89 models, proceed to the "Adjustment" section to complete the remainder of the timing belt installation and adjustment procedure.

10. Install the new timing belt, aligning the arrow on the timing belt forward. Align the white lines on the timing belt with the punchmarks on all 3 pulleys.

11. Loosen the tensioner locknut to allow spring tension to tension the belt. Then, using the hex wrench, turn the tensioner first clockwise, then counterclockwise in 3 cycles. This will seat the belt. Now, torque the tensioner locknut to 32–43 ft. lbs.

12. Tighten rocker shaft bolts alternately in three stages. Before tightening each pair of bolts, turn the engine over so the affected rocker will not touch its cam lobe. Final torque is 13-16 ft. lbs. Install the rocker covers with new gaskets.

13. Install lower and upper timing belt covers.

14. Install crankshaft pulley and idler bracket of the compressor drive belt. Tighten the crankshaft pulley bolt to 90-98 ft. lbs.

15. Install and tension the drive belts.

16. Install the coolant reservior tank, radiator hoses, A.S.C.D. actutator.

17. Install the right front wheel. Install engine under cover and side covers. Refill the cooling system. Check ignition timing

## Timing Belt

### REMOVAL & INSTALLATION

#### *E15, E15ET, E16, E16i and E16S Engines*

1. Crank the engine until the No. 1 piston is at TDC on its compression stroke.

2. Remove the cover. Mark the relationship of the camshaft sprocket to the timing belt and the crankshaft sprocket to the timing belt with paint or a grease pencil. This will make setting everything up during reassembly much easier if the engine is disturbed during disassembly.

3. Remove the distributor.

4. Remove the thermostat housing.

5. Remove the water pump and crankshaft pulleys.

6. Position a floor jack under the engine and raise it just enough to support the engine. Remove the right side engine mounting bracket.

7. Remove the upper and lower front covers.

8. Loosen the timing belt tensioner locknut and rotate the tensioner clockwise. Retighten the locknut.

9. Mark a rotational, direction arow on the timing belt and then remove the belt.

**CAUTION**

***After removing the timing belt, NEVER rotate the crankshaft or camshaft separately or the valves will hit the pistons.***

10. Remove the belt tensioner and its return spring.

**To install:**

11. Check that the timing marks on the camshaft sprocket and upper front cover and on the crankshaft sprocket and lower front cover are in alignment. This will ensure that the No.1 piston is at TDC of its compression stroke.

12. Install the timing belt tensioner and return spring temporarily.

13. Rotate the tensioner about 70–80 degrees clockwise and then tighten the locknut.

14. Install the timing belt.

15. Loosen the tensioner locknut so that the tensioner pushes on the timing belt and then turn the camshaft sprocket about 20 degrees clockwise (2 cogs).

**CAUTION**

***All spark plugs MUST be removed before turning the camshaft sprocket.***

16. Prevent the tensioner from spinning and tighten the locknut to 12–15 ft. lbs. (16–21 Nm).

17. Installation of the remaining components is in the reverse order of removal. Adjust all drive belts and fill the engine with coolant.

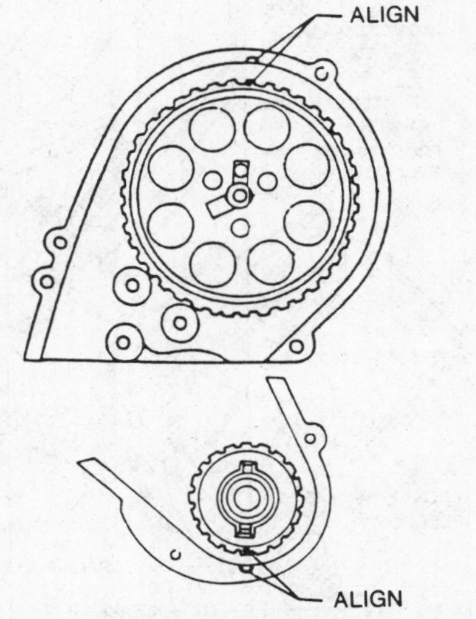


**E-series engine valve timing mark alignment**

#### *CA18ET, CA20, CA20E and CA20S Engines*

1. Disconnect the negative battery cable. Drain the coolant from the engine.

2. Remove the air intake ducts on the CA20E.

3. Remove the cooling fan.

4. Remove the power steering, alternator and A/C drive belts.

5. Set the No. 1 piston at TDC of the compression stroke. The timing marks will all be aligned.

6. Remove the upper and lower front covers.

7. Loosen the timing belt tensioner and return spring. Remove the timing belt.

8. Carefully inspect the condition of the timing belt. There should be no breaks or cracks anywhere on the belt.

Be particularly careful when checking around the bottom of the cog teeth, where they the main belt; cracks often show up here first. Evidence of any wear or damage on the belt calls for replacement.

**To install:**

9. Check to make certain that the No. 1 piston is still at TDC on the compression stroke.
10. Install the timing belt tensioner and return spring.

**NOTE: If the coarse stud has been removed, apply Loctite® or another locking thread sealer to the stud threads prior to installation.**

11. Make sure the tensioner mounting bolts are not securely tightened before installing the timing belt. The tensioner pulley should rotate smoothly.
12. Place the timing belt into position, aligning the lines on the belt with the punchmarks on the camshaft and crankshaft pulleys. The arrow on the belt should be pointing toward the front belt covers.
13. Tighten the belt tensioner and assemble the spring. Hook one end of the spring around bolt **B** and then hook the other end over the tensioner bracket pawl. Rotate the crankshaft 2

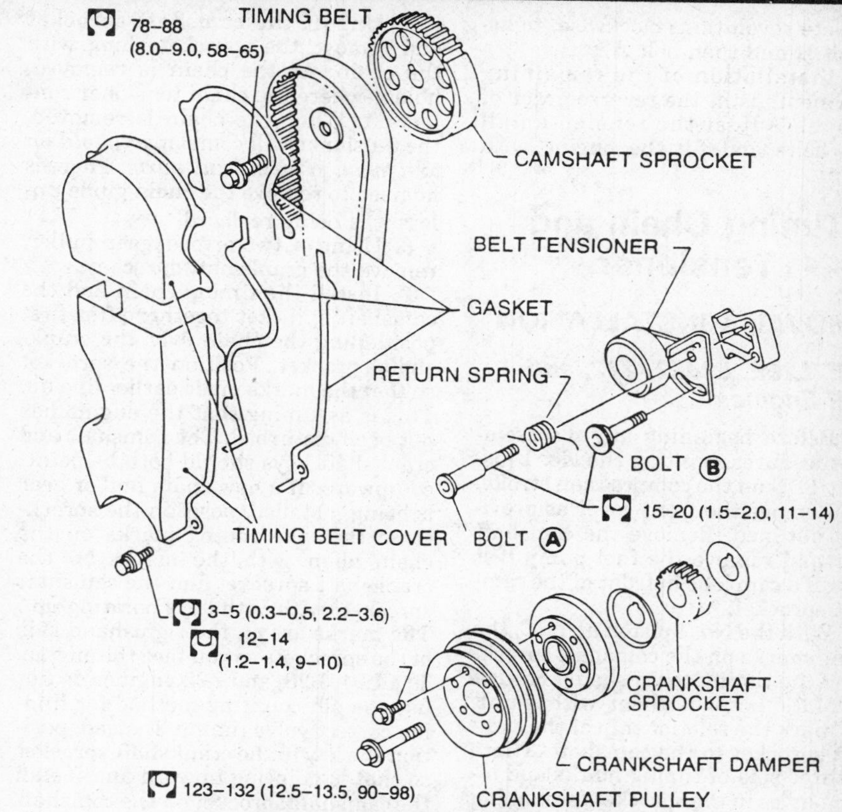


**Timing belt assembly – C-Series engines**

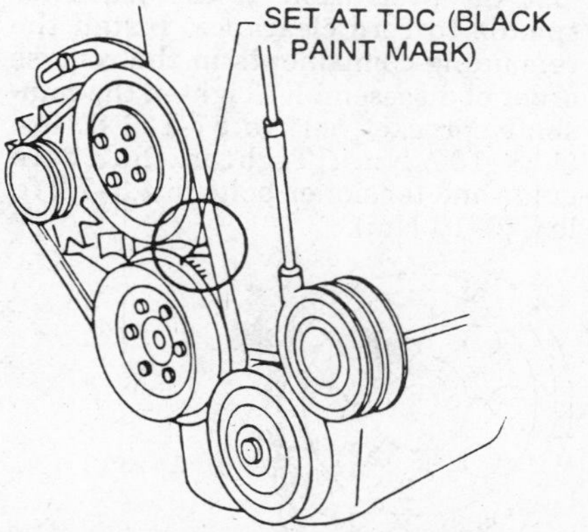


**Timing marks for finding TDC – C-Series engines**

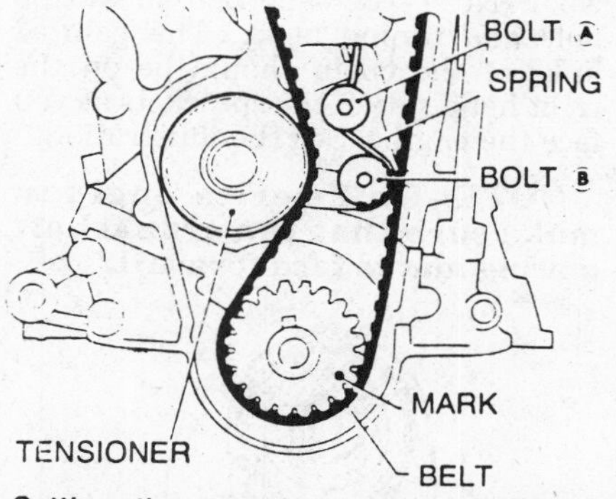


**Setting the tensioner spring – C-Series engines**

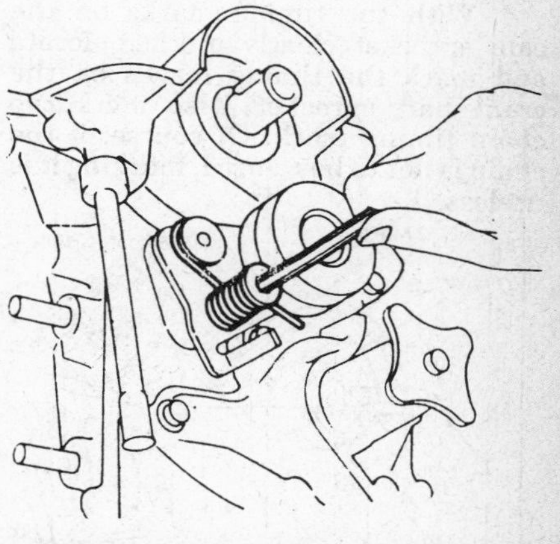

**Installing the belt tensioner and return spring – C-Series engines**

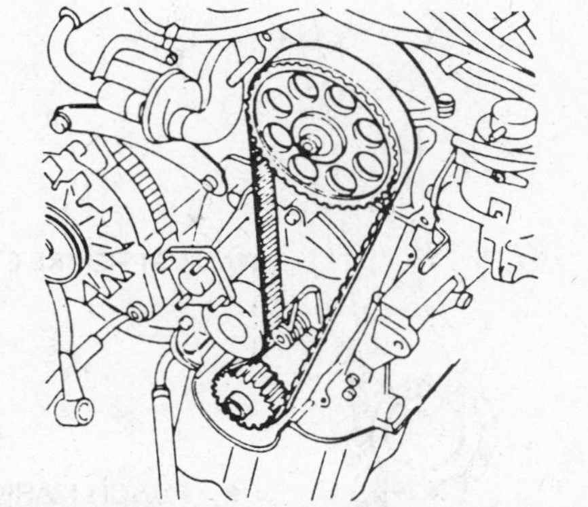

**Timing belt with covers removed – C-Series engines**

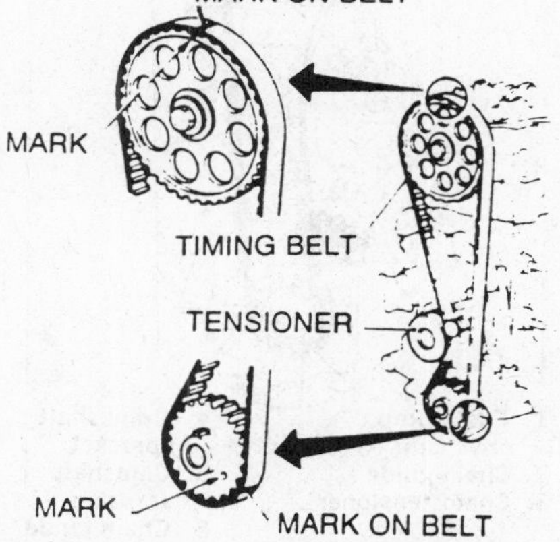


**Timing belt installation – C-Series engines**

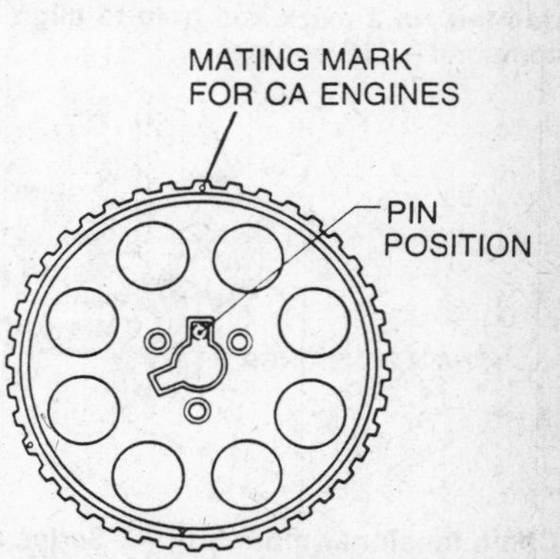


**Camshaft sprocket installation—CA20**

complete revolutions clockwise, tighten bolt **B** and then bolt **A**.

14. Installation of the remaining components is in the reverse order of removal. Adjust the tension an all drive belts and fill the engine with coolant.

## Timing Chain and Tensioner

### REMOVAL & INSTALLATION

#### *L24E, L28E, L28ET, Z22, and Z22E Engines*

1. Before beginning any disassembly procedures, position the No. 1 piston at TDC on the compression stroke.

2. Remove the front cover as previously outlined. Remove the camshaft cover and remove the fuel pump if it runs off a cam lobe in front of the camshaft sprocket.

3. With the No. 1 piston at TDC, the timing marks on the camshaft sprocket and the timing chain should be visible. Mark both of them with paint. Also mark the relationship of the camshaft sprocket to the camshaft. There are three sets of timing marks and locating holes in the sprocket for making adjustments to compensate for timing chain stretch.

4. With the timing marks on the cam sprocket clearly marked, locate and mark the timing marks on the crankshaft sprocket. Also mark the chain timing mark. Of course, if the chain is not to be re-used, marking it is useless.

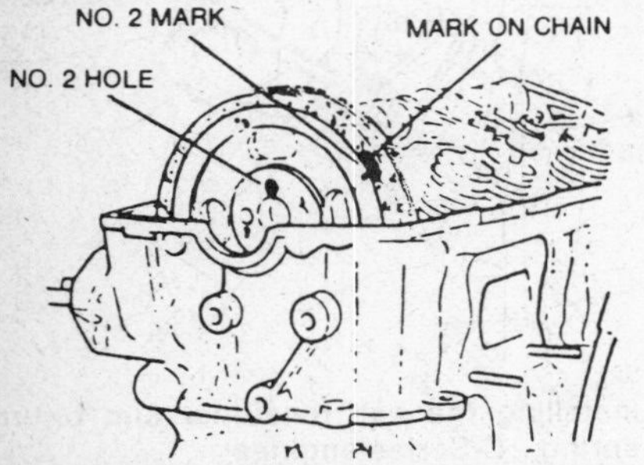


**Use the No.2 mark and hole to align the camshaft—Z22 engine**

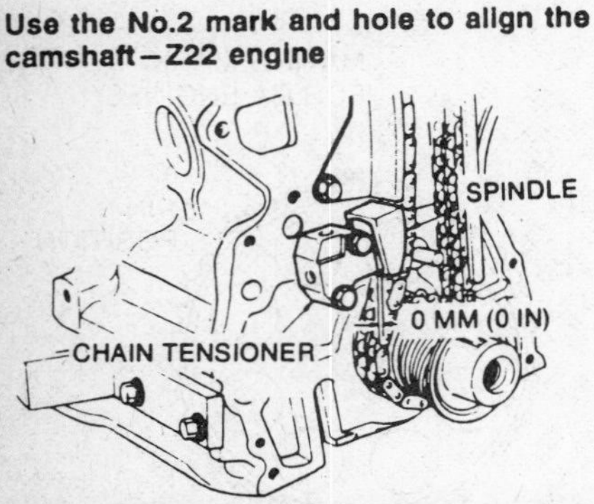


**Chain tensioner mounting—Z-Series and L28 engines**

5. Unbolt the camshaft sprocket and remove the sprocket along with the chain. As the chain is removed, hold it where the chain tensioner contacts it. When the chain is removed, the tensioner will come apart; *hold on to it to aviod losing any parts*. There is no need to remove the chain guide unless it is being replaced.

6. Using a two-armed gear puller, remove the crankshaft sprocket.

7. Install the timing chain and the camshaft sprocket together after first positioning the chain over the crankshaft sprocket. Position the sprocket so that the marks made earlier line up. This is assuming that the engine has not been disturbed. The camshaft and crankshaft keys should both be pointed upward. If a new chain and/or gear is being installed, position the sprocket so that the timing marks on the chain align with the marks on the crankshaft sprocket and the camshaft sprocket (with both keys pointing up). The marks are on the right-hand side of the sprockets as you face the engine. The L24, L28, and Z22 engines do not use the pin counting method for finding correct valve timing. Instead, position the key in the crankshaft sprocket so that is pointing upward and install the camshaft sprocket on the camshaft with its dowel pin at the top using the No. 2 (No. 1—L24 and L28) mounting hole and timing mark. The painted links of the chain should be on the right hand side of the sprockets as you face the engine. See the illustration.

**NOTE: On Z-series engines, make sure that the crankshaft mating marks face forward.**

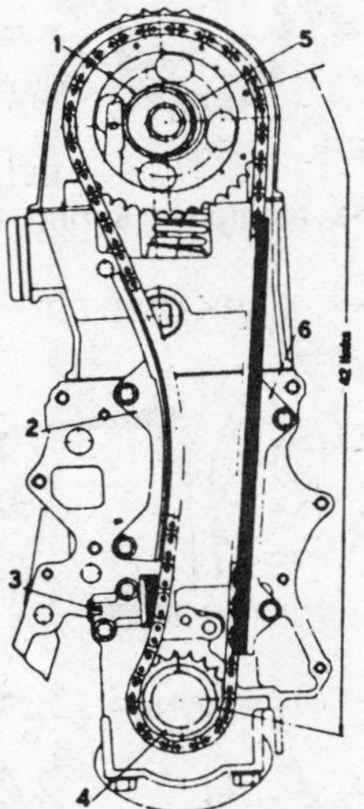


1. Fuel pump drive cam
2. Chain guide
3. Chain tensioner
4. Crankshaft sprocket
5. Camshaft sprocket
6. Chain guide

**Camshaft chain installation—all OHC except E-series**

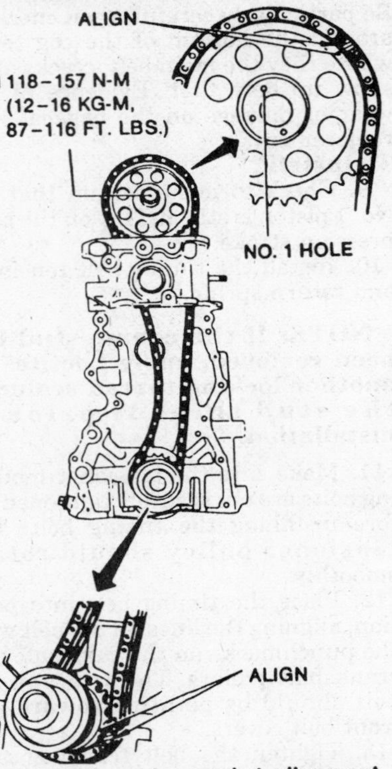


**Timing chain and sprocket alignment—L28 engines**

8. Install the chain tensioner. Adjust the protrusion of the tensioner spindle to zero clearance. Install the remaining components in the reverse order of disassembly. Tighten the camshaft sprocket bolt to 87–116 ft. lbs. (118–157 Nm). Tighten the chain guide and tensioner bolts to 4.3–7.2 ft. lbs. (6–10 Nm).

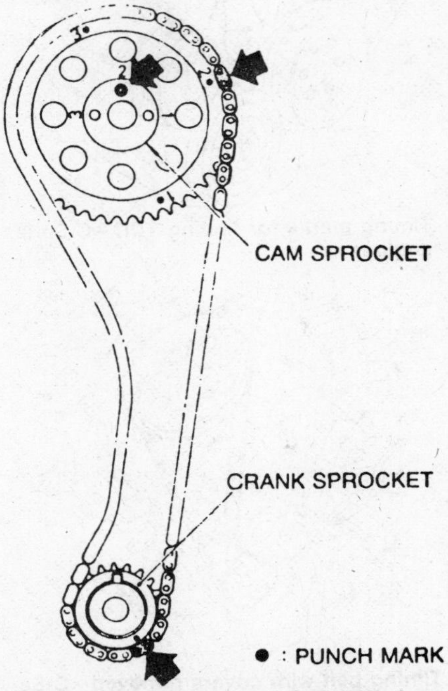


**Alignment marks on the Z-Series engines**

### *GA16i and KA24E Engines*

1. Set the No. 1 piston at TDC and remove the front cover as previously described. If necessary, define the timing matrks with chalk or paint to ensure proper alignment. Hold the camshaft sprocket stationary with a spanner wrench or similar tool and remove the camshaft sprocket bolt.

2. On GA16i engines remove the following components: chain guides, camshaft sprocket, oil pump spacer, crankshaft sprocket and timing chain. On KA24E engines remove the following components: chain tensioner, chain guides, timing chain and sprocket oil slinger, oil pump drive gear and crankshaft gear.

**To install:**

3. Verify that the No. 1 piston is at TDC.

4. On GA16i engines, perform the following (KA24E engines go to Step 5):

   a. Install the camshaft sprocket, bolt and washer. The alignment mark must face towards the front. When installing the washer, place the non-chamfered side of the washer towards the face of camshaft sprocket. Tighten the bolt just enough to hold the sprocket in place.

   b. Install the crankshaft sprocket making sure the alignment mark is facing the front.

   c. Install the timing chain by aligning the silver links at the 12 o'clock and 6 o'clock positions on the chain with the timing marks on the crankshaft and camshaft sprockets. The number of links between the 2 silver links are the same for the left and the right sides of the chain, so either side of the chain may be used to align the sprocket timing marks. Torque the camshaft sprocket bolt to 72–94 ft. lbs. once the chain is in place and aligned.

5. On KA24E engines perform the following:

   a. Install the crankshaft sprocket, oil pump drive gear and oil slinger onto the end of the crankshaft. Make sure the crankshaft sprocket timing marks face toward the front.

   b. Install the camshaft sprocket, bolt and washer. The alignment mark must face towards the front. Tighten the bolt just enough to hold the sprocket in place.

   c. Verify that the No. 1 piston is at TDC. Install the timing chain by aligning the marks on the chain with the marks on the crankshaft and camshaft sprockets (see illustration). Torque the camshaft sprocket bolt to 87–116 ft. lbs. once the timing chain is in place and aligned.

6. Install the chain guides and tenioners. On GA16i engines, when installing the chain guide, move the guide in the direction that applies tension to the chain.

7. Complete the installation of the front cover as previously described.

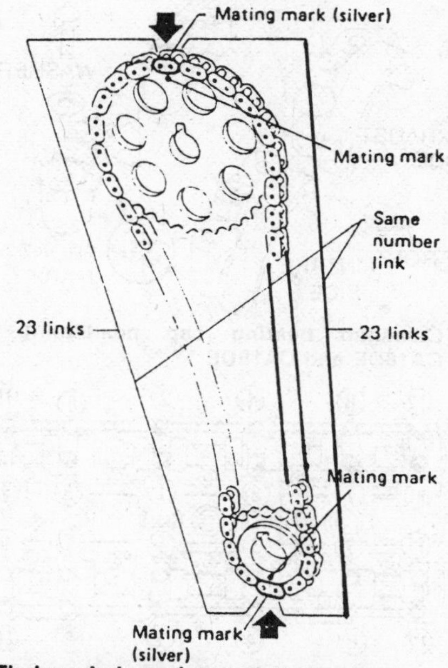


**Timing chain and sprocket alignment marks – GA16i engines**

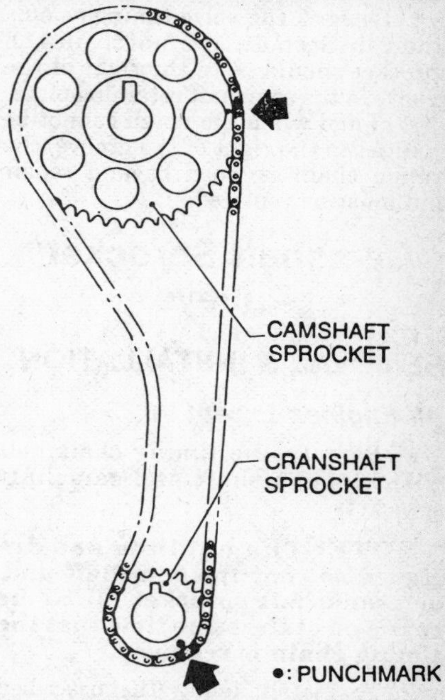


**Timing chain and sprocket alignment marks – KA24E engines**

## TIMING CHAIN ADJUSTMENT

When the timing chain stretches excessively, the valve timing will be adversely affected. There are 3 sets of holes and timing marks on the camshaft sprocket.

If the stretch of the chain roller links is excessive, adjust the camshaft sprocket location by transferring the set position of the camshaft sprocket from the factory position of No. 1 or No. 2 to one of the other positions as follows:

1. Turn the crankshaft until the No. 1 piston is at TDC on the compression stroke. Examine whether the camshaft sprocket location notch is to the left of the oblong groove on the camshaft retaining plate. If the notch in the sprocket is to the left of the groove in the retaining plate, then the chain is stretched and needs adjusting.

2. Remove the camshaft sprocket together with the chain and reinstall the sprocket and chain with the locating dowel on the camshaft inserted into either the No. 2 or 3 hole of the sprocket. The timing mark on the timing chain must be aligned with the mark on the sprocket. The amount of modification is 4 degrees of crankshaft rotation for each mark.

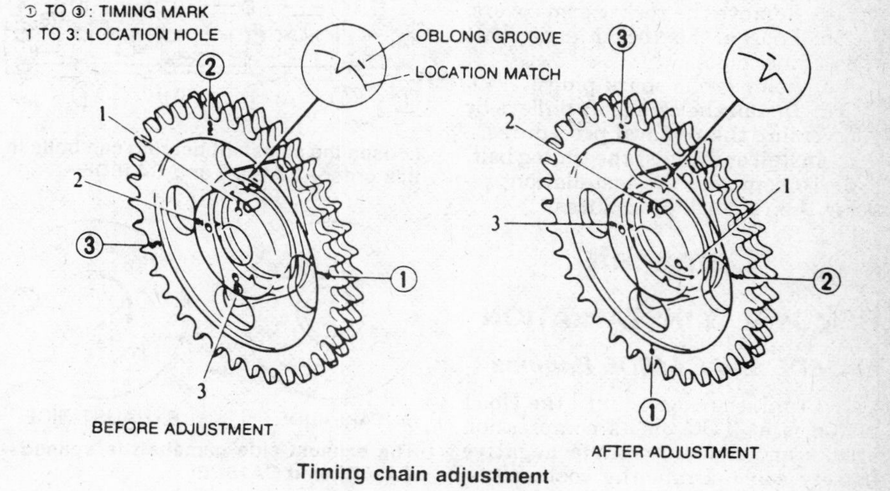


Timing chain adjustment

3. Recheck the valve timing as outlined in Step 1. The notch in the sprocket should be to the right of the groove in the camshaft retaining plate.

4. If and when the notch cannot be brought to the right of the groove, the timing chain is worn beyond repair and must be replaced.

## Camshaft Sprocket/ Pulleys

### REMOVAL & INSTALLATION

#### *All Engines Except V6*

1. Remove the timing chain/belt with the camshaft and camshaft sprockets.

**NOTE: The engines are designed so that the camshaft and/ or crankshaft sprocket MUST be removed at the same time that the timing chain is removed.**

2. To install, follow the precribed timing mark alignment procedures, use new gaskets where required and reverse the removal procedures. If necessary, adjust the timing chain.

#### *V6 Engine*

1. Remove the timing belt.
2. Using an adjustable spanner wrench (to hold the camshaft pulley) and a socket wrench, remove the camshaft pulley bolt and washer.
3. Pull the camshaft pulley(s) from the camshaft(s). Be careful not to loose the Woodruff key.

**NOTE: The right hand and left hand camshaft pulleys are different. Install them in their correct positions. The right hand pulley has an R3 identification mark and the left hand pulley has an L3.**

4. To install the camshaft pulleys, perform the following:
   a. Remove the rocker arm covers.
   b. Loosen the rocker arm shaft assembly bolts.
   c. Remove the spark plugs.
   d. Install the camshaft pulleys by reversing the removal procedures.
5. Install and adjust the timing belt.
6. To complete the installation, reverse the removal procedures.

## Camshaft

### REMOVAL & INSTALLATION

#### *CA16DE and CA18DE Engines*

1. Crank the engine until the No. 1 piston is at TDC on its compression stroke and disconnect the negative battery cable. Drain the cooling system and remove the air cleaner assembly.
2. Loosen the alternator and remove all drive belts. Remove the alternator.
3. Disconect the air duct at the throttle chamber.
4. Tag and disconnect all lines, hoses and wires which may interfere with cylinder removal.
5. Remove the eight screws and lift off the ornament cover.
6. Disconnect the oxygen sensor.
7. Remove the 2 exhaust heat shield covers.
8. Unbolt the exhaust manifold and wire the entire assembly out of the way to gain cylinder head removal clearance.
9. Disconnect the EGR tube at the passage cover and then remove the passage cover and its gasket.
10. Disconnect and remove the crank angle sensor from the upper front cover.

**NOTE: Put an aligning mark on crank angle sensor and timing belt cover.**

11. Remove the support stay from under the intake manifold assembly.
12. Unbolt the intake manifold and remove it along with the collector and throttle chamber.
13. Disconnect and remove the fuel injectors as an assembly.

**NOTE: Upper and lower front timing belt cover must be removed. Support engine under oil pan with floor jack or equivalent then remove the upper engine mount bracket at the right side of the front cover.**

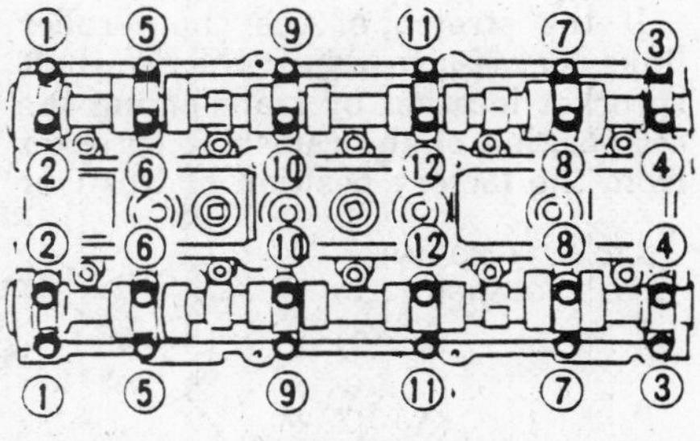


**Loosen the camshaft bearing cap bolts in this order—CA16DE and CA18DE**

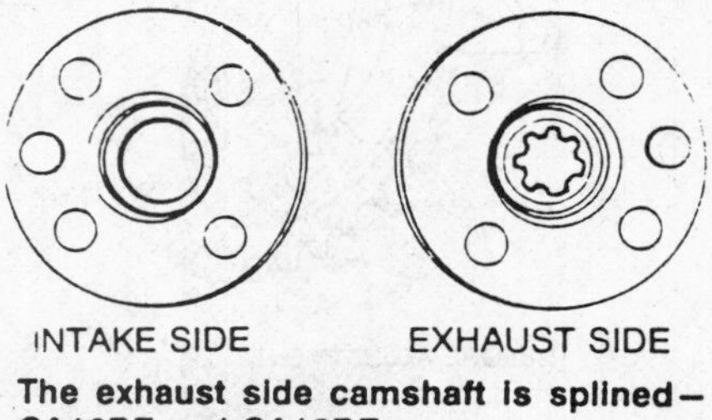


**The exhaust side camshaft is splined—CA16DE and CA18DE**

14. Remove the timing belt.
15. Remove the camshaft cover and remove the cylinder head.
16. Remove the breather separater.
17. While holding the camshaft sprockets, remove the 4 mounting bolts and then remove the sprockets themselves.
18. Remove the timing belt tensioner pulley. Remove the rear timing belt cover.
19. Loosen the camshaft bearing caps in several stages, in the order shown. Remove the bearing caps, but be sure to keep them in order.
20. Remove the front oil seals and then lift out the camshafts.
21. Check the camshaft runout, endplay, wear and journal clearance.

**To install:**

22. Position the camshafts in the cylinder head so the knockpin on each is on the outboard side.

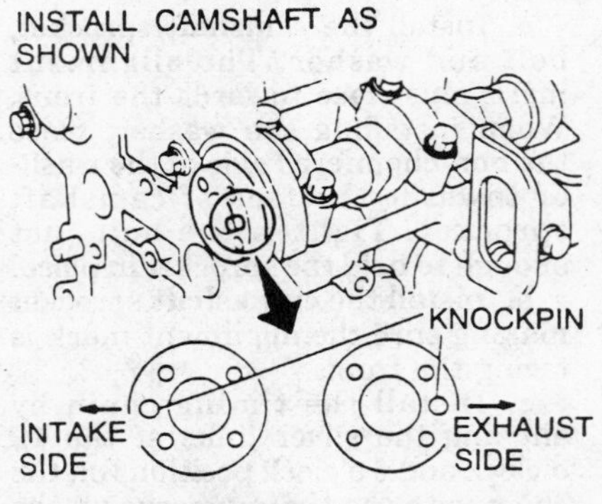


**Install the camshaft as shown—CA16DE and CA18DE**

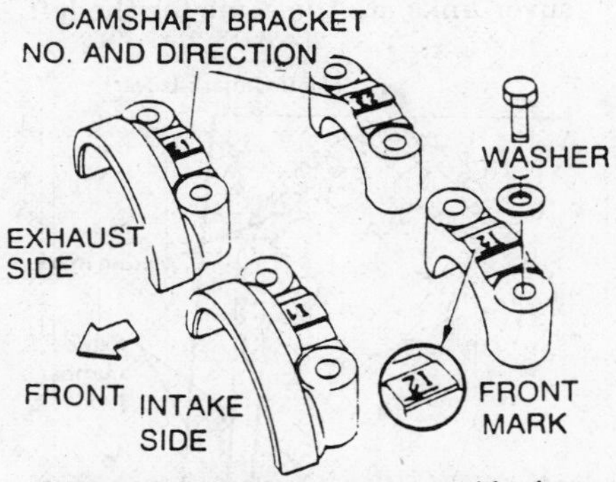


**Camshaft bearing cap positioning—CA16DE and CA18DE**

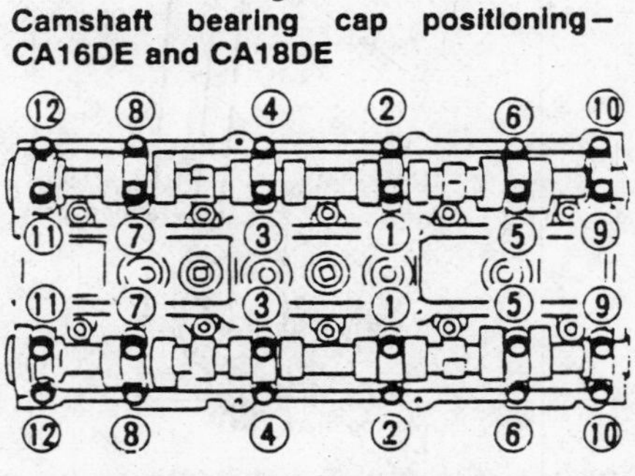


**Tighten the camshaft bearing caps in this order—CA16DE and CA18DE**

**NOTE: The exhaust side camshaft has splines to accept the crank angle sensor.**

23. Position the camshaft bearing caps and finger-tighten them. Each cap has an ID mark (E1, E2, I1, I2 etc.) and a directional arrow stamped into its top surface.
24. Coat a new oil seal with engine oil (on the lip) and install it on each camshaft end.
25. Tighten the camshaft bearing cap bolts to 7–9 ft. lbs. (9–12 Nm) in the order shown.
26. Intall the cylinder head and cover.
27. Install the rear timing cover and tighten the 4 bolts to 5–6 ft. lbs. (7–8 Nm).
28. Install the timing belt tensioner and tighten it to 16–22 ft. lbs. (22–29 Nm).
29. Install the camshaft sprockets and tighten the bolts to 10–14 ft. lbs. (14–19 Nm) while holding the camshaft in place.
30. Installation of the remaining components is in the reverse order.

### CA18ET, CA20, CA20E and CA20S Engines

1. Set the No. 1 piston to TDC of the compression stroke and then remove the timing belt.
2. Remove the valve rocker cover.
3. Fully loosen all rocker arm adjusting screws (the valve adjusting screws). Loosen the rocker shaft mounting bolts in two or three stages and then remove the rocker shafts as an assembly. Keep all components in the correct order for reassembly.
4. Hold the camshaft pulley and remove the pulley mounting bolt. Remove the pulley. Remove the camshaft thrust plate.
5. Carefully pry the camshaft oil seal out of the front of the cylinder head.
6. Slide the camshaft out the front of the cylinder head, taking extreme care not to score any of the journals.

**To install:**

7. Coat the camshaft with clean engine oil.
8. Carefully slide the camshaft into the cylinder head, coat the end with oil and install a NEW oil seal. Install the camshaft thrust plate and wedge the camshaft with a small wooden block inserted between one of the cams and the cylinder head. Torque the thrust plate bolt to 58–65 ft. lbs. Remove the wooen block.
9. Lubricate the rocker shafts lightly and install them, with the rocker arms, into the head. Both shafts have punchmarks on their leading edges, while the intake shaft is also marked with two slits on its leading edge.

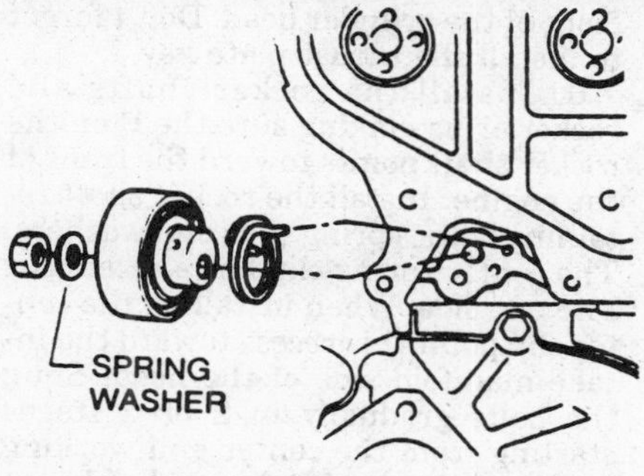


**Timing belt tensioner installation—CA16DE and CA18DE**

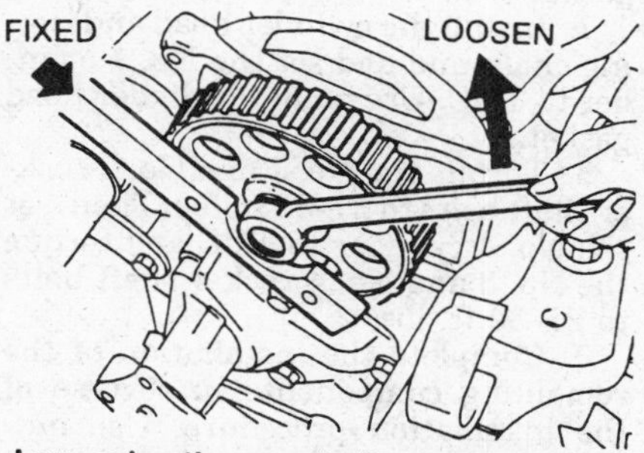


**Loosening the camshaft sprocket—C-Series engines**

**NOTE: To prevent the rocker shaft springs from slipping out of the shaft, insert the bracket bolts into the shaft prior to installation.**

10. Tighten the rocker shaft bolts gradually, in two or three stages to 13–16 ft. lbs.

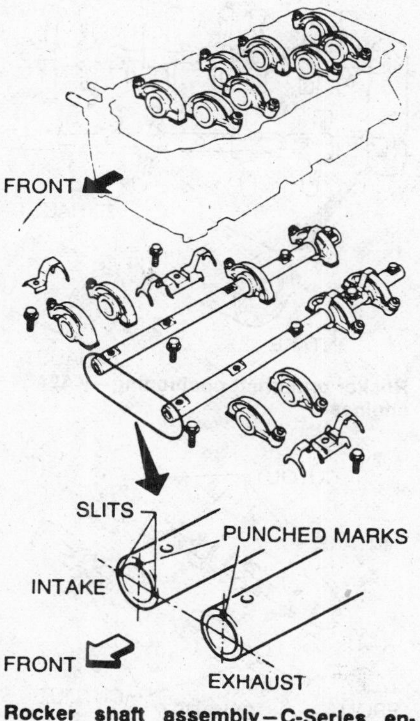


**Rocker shaft assembly—C-Series engines**

11. Install the camshaft pulley and then install the timing belt.
12. Adjust the valves as required and install the cylinder head cover.

### E15, E15ET, E16, E16S and E16i Engines

1. Remove the timing belt.
2. Remove the rocker shaft along with the rocker arms. Loosen the bolts gradually, in two or three stages.
3. Carefully slide the camshaft out the front of the cylinder head.
4. Check the camshaft runout, endplay, wear and journal clearance.
5. Slide the camshaft into the cylinder head carefully and then install a NEW oil seal.
6. Install the rear timing belt cover.
7. Set the camshaft so that the knockpin faces upward and then install the camshaft sprocket so its timing mark aligns with the one on the rear timing cover.
8. Install the timing belt.
9. Coat the rocker shaft and the interior of the rocker arm with engine

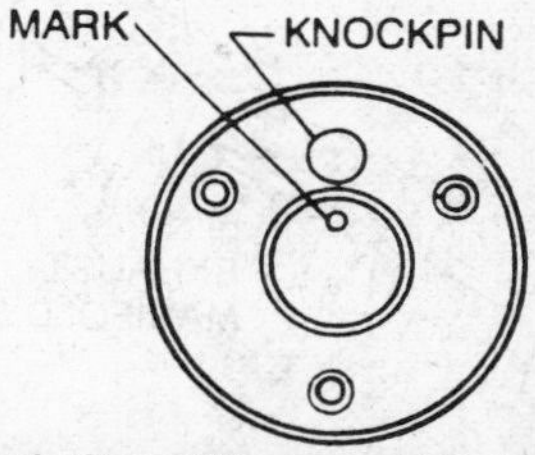


**Camshaft positioning—E-Series engines**

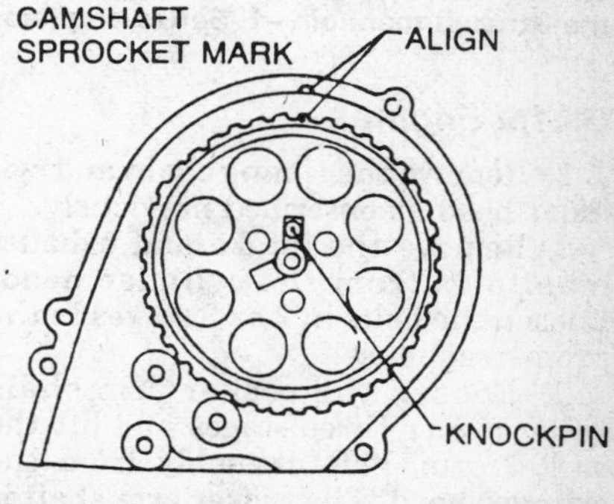


**Camshaft sprocket alignment—E-Series engines**

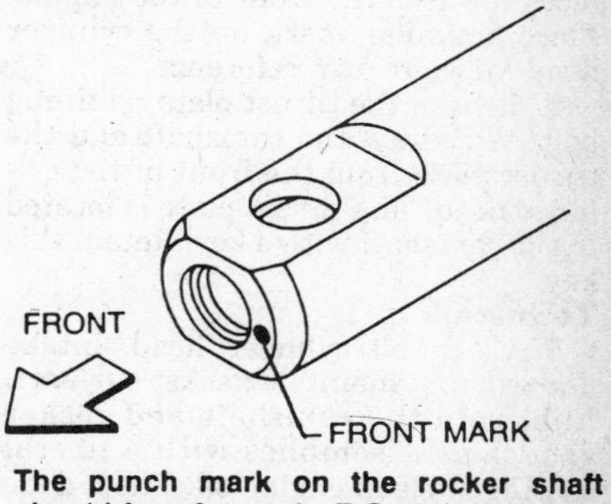


**The punch mark on the rocker shaft should face forward—E-Series engines**

oil. Install them so the punchmark on the shaft faces forward and the oil holes in the shaft face down. The cut-out in the center retainer on the shaft should face the exhaust manifold side of the engine.

10. Make sure tha valve adjusting screws are loosened and then tighten the shaft bolts to 13–15 ft. lbs. (18–21 Nm) in several stages, from the center out. The first and last mounting bolts should have a new bolt stopper installed.

11. Adjust the valves and then complete the remaining installation procedures in reverse of removal.

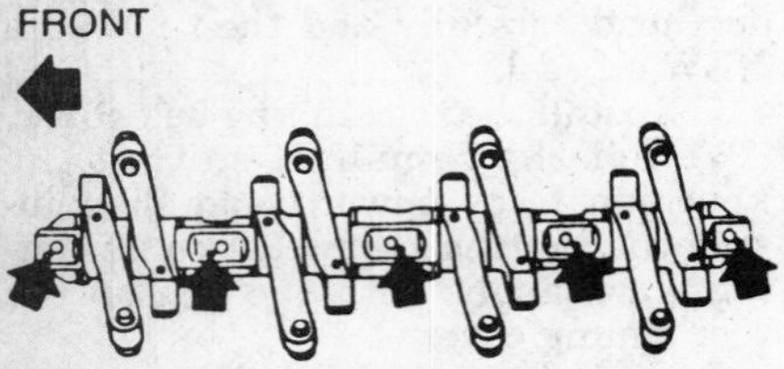


The oil holes must be facing down – E-Series engines

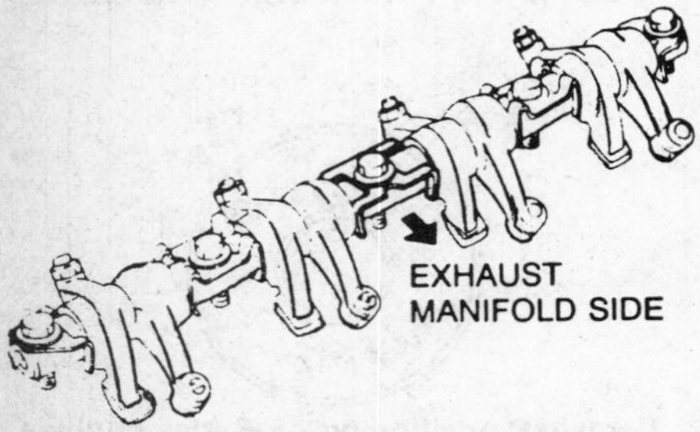


The center retainer cut-out should face the exhaust manifold – E-Series engines

### GA16i Engines

1. Remove the timing chain and cylinder head as described previously.

2. Remove the intake and exhaust manifolds from the cylinder head. Loosen the bolts in 2 or 3 stages in the proper sequence.

3. Loosen the rocker arm shaft bolts in 2 or three stages and lift the rocker arm/shaft assembly from the cylinder head. The rocker arm shaft is marked with an **F** to indicate that it faces towards the front of the engine. Place a similar mark on the cylinder head for your own reference.

4. Loosen the thrust plate retaining bolt. Withdraw the camshaft and the thrust plate from the front of the cylinder head. The thrust plate is located to the camshaft with a key. Retain this key.

**To install:**

5. Clean all cylinder head, intake and exhaust manifold gasket surfaces. Lubricate the camshaft and rocker arm/shaft assemblies with a liberal coating of clean engine oil. Then, slide the camshaft and thrust plate into the front of the cylinder head. Don't forget to install the thrust plate key.

6. Install the rocker shafts and rocker arms making sure the **F** on the rocker shaft points toward the front of the engine. Install the rocker shaft retaining bolts, spring clips and washers. The center spring clip has a recess cut into one side. When installing the center clip point this recess toward the intake manifold side of the head. Snug the bolts gradually in 2 or 3 stages starting from the center and working out. Attach the intake and exhaust manifold to the head with new gaskets.

7. Install the cylinder head and timing chain and and set the No. 1 cylinder to TDC. Use na new cylinder head gasket.

8. Torque the No. 1 and No. 2 rocker shaft bolts to 27–30 ft. lbs. Then, set the No. 4 cylinder to TDC and torque the No. 3 and No. 4 rocker shaft bolts to 27–30 ft. lbs.

9. Complete the installation of the remaining components in reverse of the installation procedure. Use new gaskets as required.

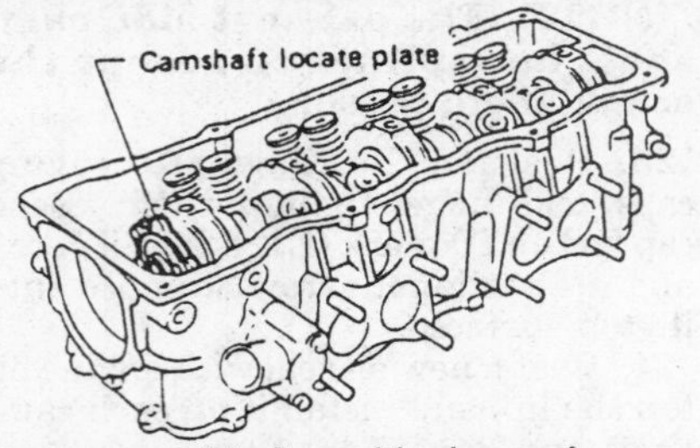


Rocker arm/shaft positioning and identification – GA16i engines

### KA24E Engines

1. Remove the timing chain and cylinder head as desribed previously. Do not remove the camshaft sprocket at this time.

2. Loosen the rocker shaft bolt evenly in proper sequence starting from the outside and working into the center.

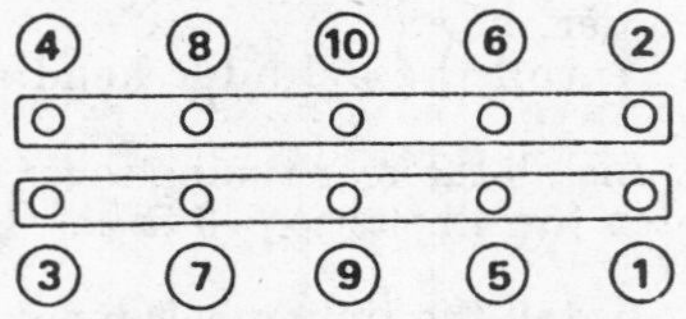


Rocker shaft bolt LOOSENING sequence – KA24E engines. Tighten in reverse of loosening sequence

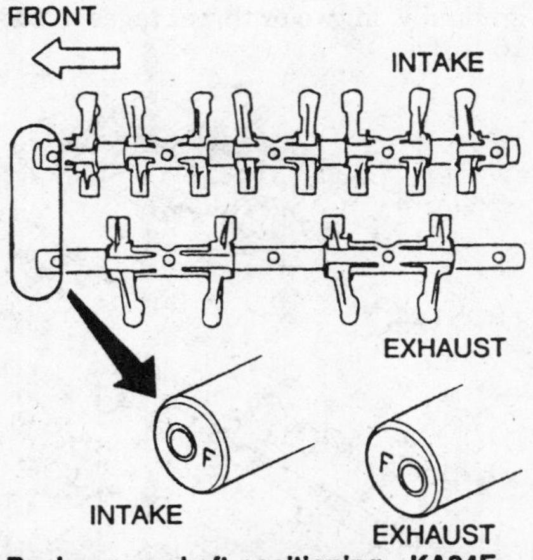


Rocker arm shaft positioning – KA24E engines

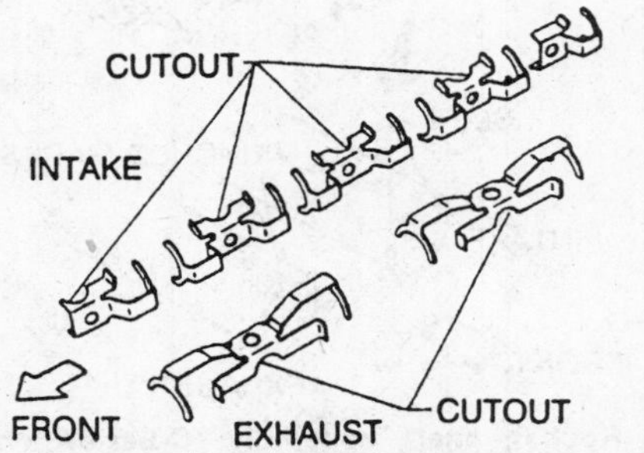


Spring clip installation – KA24E engines

3. Mount a dial indicator to the cylinder head and set the stylus of the indicator on the head of the camshaft sprocket bolt. Zero the indicator and measure the camshaft endplay by moving the camshaft back and forth. Endplay should be within 0.0028–0.0059 in.

4. Remove the camshaft brackets and lift the camshaft with sprocket from the cylinder head.

**To install:**

5. Clean all cylinder head, intake and exhaust manifold gasket surfaces. Lubricate the camshaft and rocker arm/shaft assemblies with a libral coating of clean engine oil. Lay the camshaft and sprocket into the cylinder head so the knockpin is at the front of the head at the 12 o'clock postion. Install the camshaft brackets. The camshaft bracket directional arrows must face the toward the front of the engine.

6. Install the rocker shaft and rocker arms. Both intake and exhaust rocker shafts are stamped with an **F** mark. This mark must face the front of the engine during installation. Install the rocker arm bolts and spring clips so that the cut outs are facing as shown. Torque the rocker arm bolts in the proper sequence to 27–30 ft. lbs.

7. Complete the installation of the cylinder head and timing chain in reverse of the removal procedure. Use new rubber plugs when installing the cylinder head. Use new gaskets as required.

### L24E, L28E, L28ET and LD28 Engines

1. Removal of the cylinder head

from the engine is necessary. Remove the camshaft sprocket from the camshaft together with the timing chain.

2. Loosen the valve rocker pivot locknut and remove the rocker arm by pressing down on the valve spring.

3. Remove the 2 retaining nuts on the camshaft retainer plate at the front of the cylinder head and carefully slide the camshaft out of the camshaft carrier.

4. Lightly coat the camshaft bearings with clean motor oil and carefully slide the camshaft into place in the camshaft carrier.

5. Install the camshaft retainer plate with the oblong groove in the face of the plate facing toward the front of the engine.

6. Check the valve timing as outlined under "Timing Chain Removal and Installation" and install the timing sprocket on the camshaft, tightening the bolt together with the fuel pump cam to 86–116 ft. lbs.

7. Install the rocker arms by pressing down the valve springs with a screwdriver and install the valve rocker springs.

8. Install the cylinder head, if it was removed, and assemble the rest of the engine in the reverse order of removal.

### *VG30E and VG30ET V6 Engines*

1. Remove the timing belt and drain the coolant from the cylinder block.

2. Remove the collector assembly and intake manifold.

3. Remove the cylinder head fom the engine.

4. Remove the rocker shafts with rocker arms. Bolts should be loosened in several steps in the proper sequence.

5. Remove hydraulic valve lifters and lifter guide.

6. Hold hydraulic valve lifters with wire so that they will not drop from lifter guide.

7. Using a dial gauge measure the camshaft end play. If the camshaft end play exceeds the limit (0.0012–0.0024 in.), select the thickness of a cam locate plate so that the end play is within specification. For example, if camshaft end play measures 0.08mm (0.0031 in.) with shim 2 used, then change shim 2 to shim 3 so that the camshaft end play is 0.05mm (0.0020 in.).

8. Remove the camshaft front oil seal and slide camshaft out the front of the cylinder head assembly.

9. Install camshaft, locate plate, cylinder head rear cover and front oil seal. Set camshaft knock pin at 12 o'clock position. Install cylinder head with new gasket to engine.

10. Install valve lifter guide assembly. Assemble valve lifters in their original position. After installing them in the correct location remove the wire holding them in lifter guide.

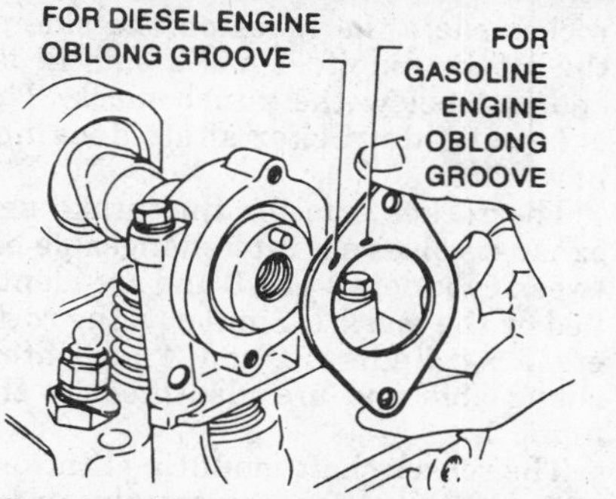

**When installing the retaining plate, make sure the oblong groove is facing the front of the engine**

11. Install rocker shafts in correct position with rocker arms. Tighten bolts in 2 or 3 stages to 13–16 ft. lbs. Before tightening, be sure to set camshaft lobe at the position where lobe is not lifted or the valve closed. You can set each cylinder 1 at a time or follow the procedure below (timing belt must be installed):

a. Set No. 1 piston at TDC. on its compression stroke and tighten rocker shaft bolts for No. 2, No. 4 and No. 6 cylinders.

b. Set No. 4 piston at TDC. on its compression stroke and tighten rocker shaft bolts for No. 1, No. 3 and No. 5 cylinders.

c. Torque specification for the rocker shaft retaining bolts is 13–16 ft. lbs.

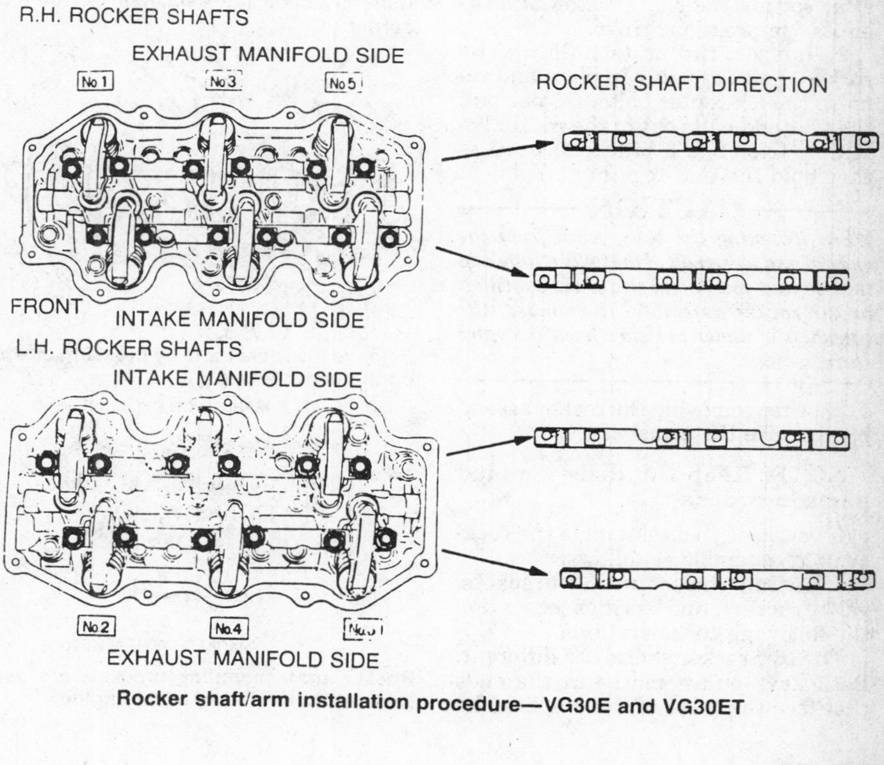

**Rocker shaft/arm installation procedure—VG30E and VG30ET**

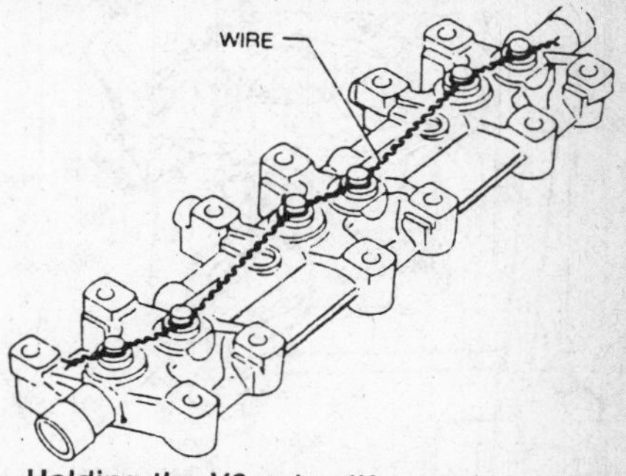

**Holding the V6 valve lifters with a wire**

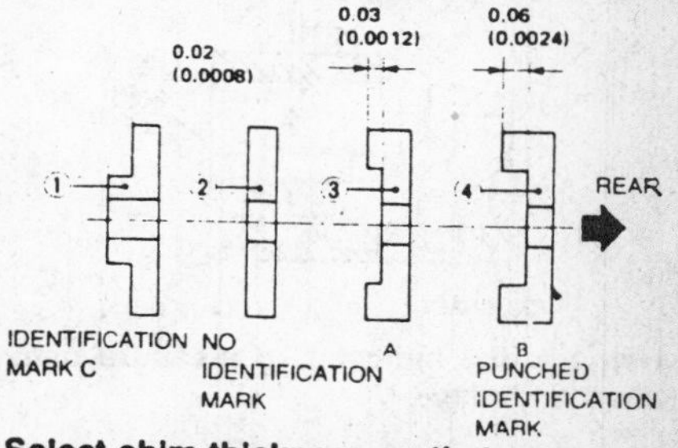

**Select shim thickness so that camshaft thickness is within specs**

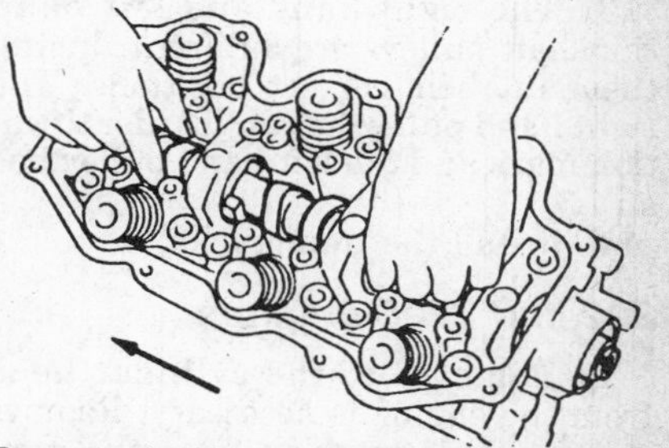
**Remove the V6 camshaft in the direction of the arrow**

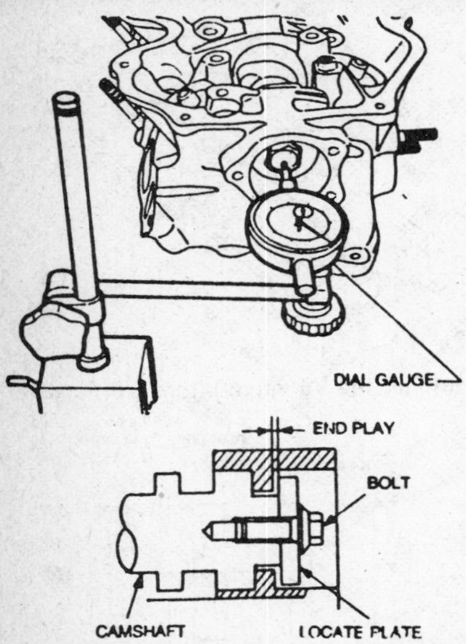


**Using a dial indicator to measure camshaft end play—V6**

12. Install the intake manifold and collector assembly with new gaskets.
13. The right hand and left hand camshaft pulleys are different. Install them in their correct positions. The right hand pulley has an R3 identification mark and the left hand pulley has an L3.
14. Install the timing belt.

### *Z22 and Z22E Engines*

1. Removal of the cylinder head from the engine is necessary. Remove the camshaft sprocket from the camshaft together with the timing chain, after setting the No. 1 piston at TDC on its compression stroke.
2. Loosen the bolts holding the rocker shaft assembly in place and remove the six center bolts. Do not pull the four end bolts out of the rocker assembly (No. 1 & 5 brackets) because they hold the unit together.

**CAUTION**

***When loosening the bolts, work from the ends in and loosen all of the bolts a little at a time so that you do not strain the camshaft or the rocker assembly. Remember, the camshaft is under pressure from the valve springs.***

3. After removing the rocker assembly, remove the camshaft.

**NOTE: Keep the disassembled parts in order.**

If you need to disassemble the rocker unit, assemble as follows:

4. Install the mounting brackets, valve rockers and springs observing the following considerations.

The two rocker shafts are different. Both have punch marks in the ends that face the front of the engine. The rocker shaft that goes on the side of the intake manifold has 2 slits in its end just below the punch mark. The exhaust side rocker shaft does not have slits.

The rocker arm for the intake and exhaust valves are interchangeable between cylinders 1 and 3 and are identified by the mark **1**. Similarly, the rockers for cylinders 2 and 4 are interchangeable and are identified by the mark **2**.

The rocker shaft mounting brackets are also coded for correct placement with either an **A** or an **Z** plus a number code.

**To install the camshaft and rocker assembly:**

5. Place the camshaft on the head with its dowel pin pointing up.
6. Fit the rocker assembly on the head, making sure you mount it on its knock pin.
7. Torque the bolts to 11–18 ft. lbs., in several stages working from the middle bolts and moving outwards on both sides and adjust valves.

**NOTE: Make sure the engine is on TDC of the compression stroke for the No. 1 piston or you may damage some valves.**

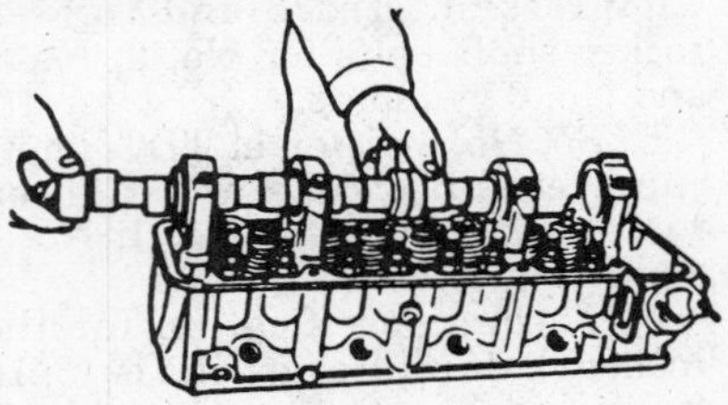

**Carefully slide the camshaft out of the carrier**

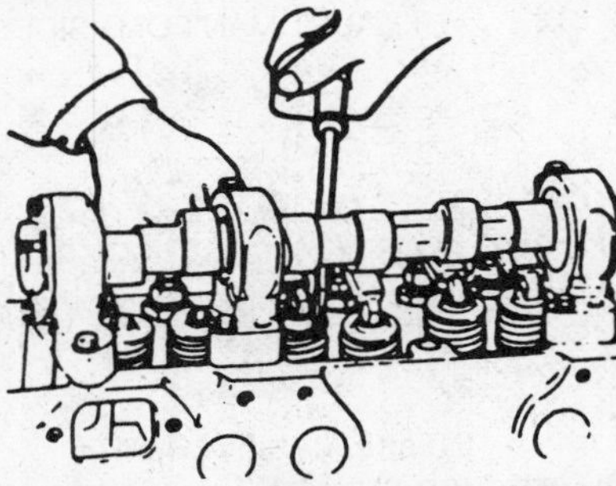

**Remove the rocker arm by pressing down on the valve spring**

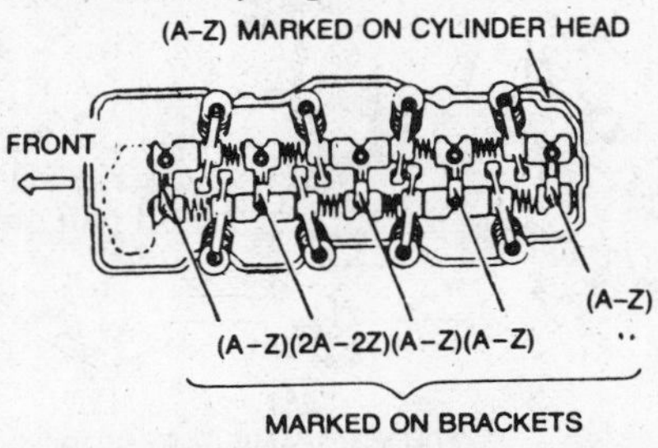


**Rocker shaft mounting brackets are assembled in this order – Z22 engine**

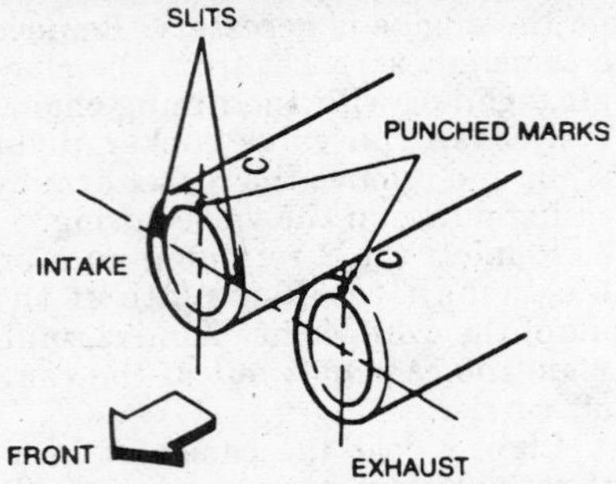


**Note the difference in rocker shafts – Z Series engines**

## Pistons and Connecting Rods

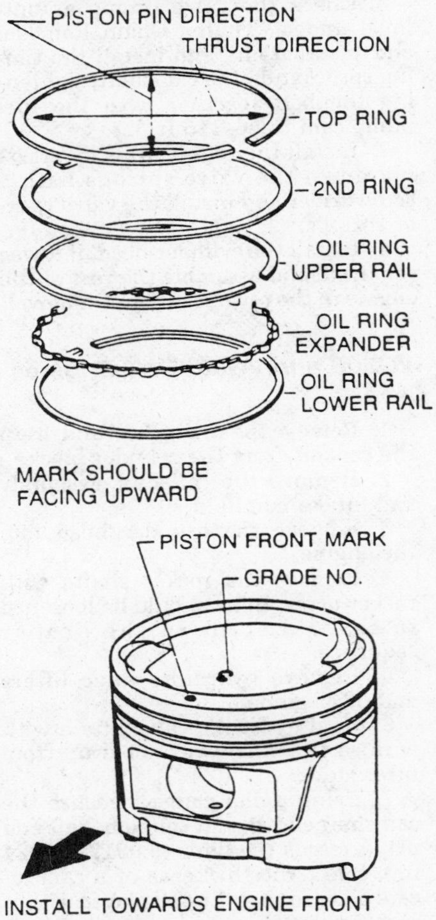


**Piston and ring identification and positioning – VG30E and VG30ET**

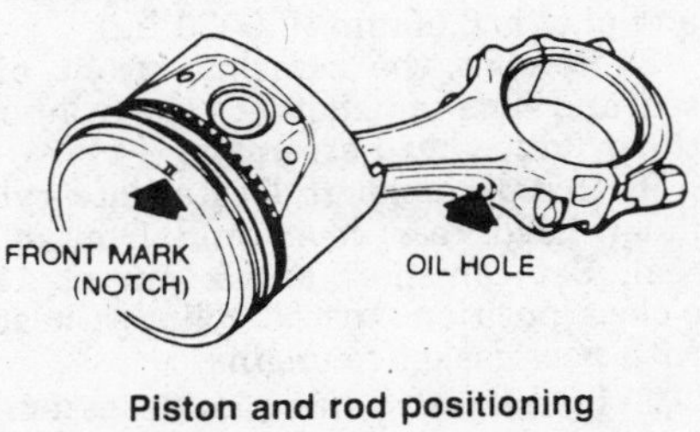


**Piston and rod positioning**

## IDENTIFICATION AND POSITIONING

The pistons are marked with a notch (or **F**) in the piston head. When installed, the notch (or **F**) markings are to be facing toward the front of the engine.

The connecting rods are installed with the oil hole facing toward the right side of the engine.

**NOTE: It is advisable to number the pistons, connecting rods, and bearing caps in some manner so that they can be reinstalled in the same cylinder, facing the same direction, from which they are removed.**

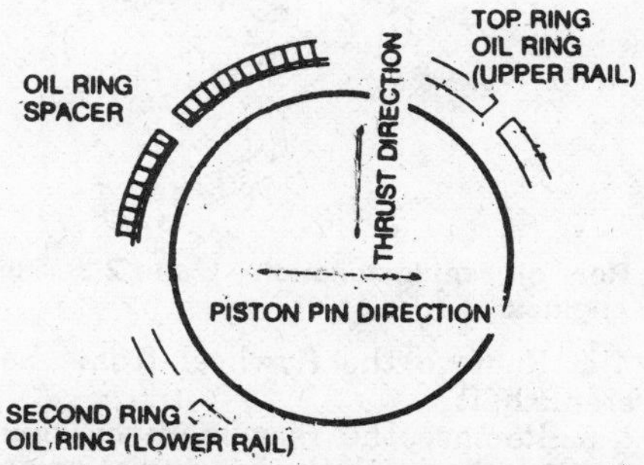


**Piston ring placement A-series and L28 engines**

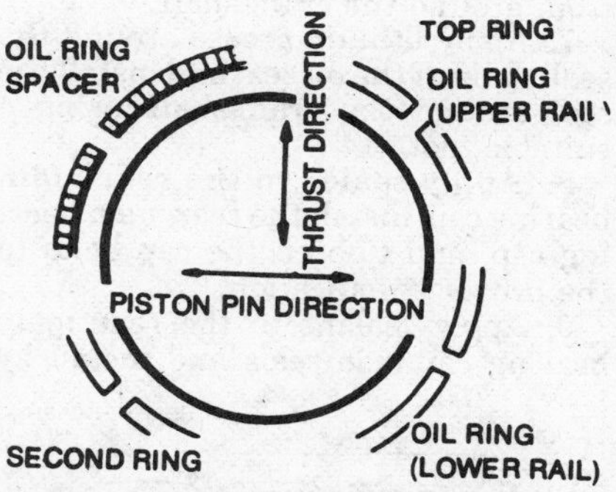


**Piston ring positioning – E, G and K series**

# ENGINE LUBRICATION

## Oil Pan

### REMOVAL & INSTALLATION

#### *All Models Except 1987–90 Pulsar and Sentra, 1985–90 Maxima, 240SX and 300ZX*

1. If the engine is in the vehicle, attach a lift, support the engine, and remove the engine mounting bolts as de-

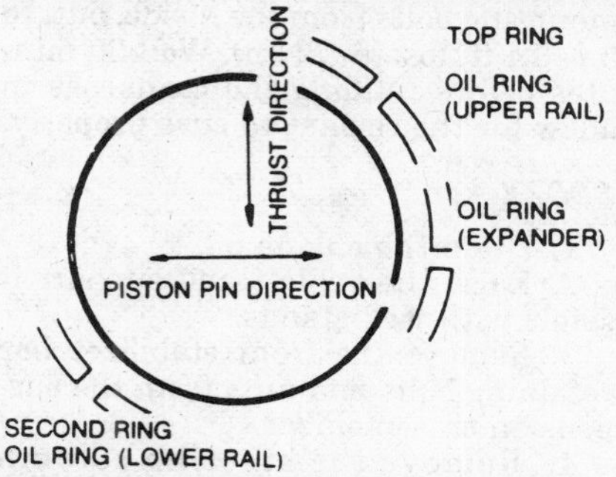


**Piston ring placement – L24E, C-Series and Z-Series engines**

scribed in "Engine Removal and Installation".

2. Raise the engine slightly, watching to make sure that no hoses or wires are damaged.
3. Drain the engine oil.
4. Remove the oil pan bolts and slide the pan out to the rear.

**To install the pan:**

5. Use a new gasket, coated on both sides with sealer.
6. Apply a thin bead of silicone seal to the engine block at the junction of the block and front cover, and the junction of the block and rear main bearing cap. Then apply a thin coat of silicone seal to the new oil pan gasket, install the gasket to the block and install the pan.
7. Tighten the pan bolts in a circular pattern from the center to the ends, to 4–7 ft. lbs. Overtightening will distort the pan lip, causing leakage.
8. Reinstall the engine mounting bolts to specified torque and maintaining support until all mounts are secure.
9. Refill the oil pan to the specified level.

#### *1987–90 Pulsar and Sentra (Gasoline Engines)*

1. Drain the engine oil.
2. Raise the vehicle and support it with safety stands.
3. Remove the right side splash cover. Remove the right side under cover.
4. Remove the center member (2WD models only).
5. Remove the forward section of the exhaust pipe.
6. Remove the front buffer rod and its bracket (1987–88 only).
7. Remove the engine gussets (1987–88).
8. Insert a seal cutter (SST KV10111100) between the oil pan and the cylinder block.

**NOTE: DO NOT use a screwdriver!**

9. Tapping the cutter with a hammer, slide it around the oil pan.
10. Remove the oil pan.

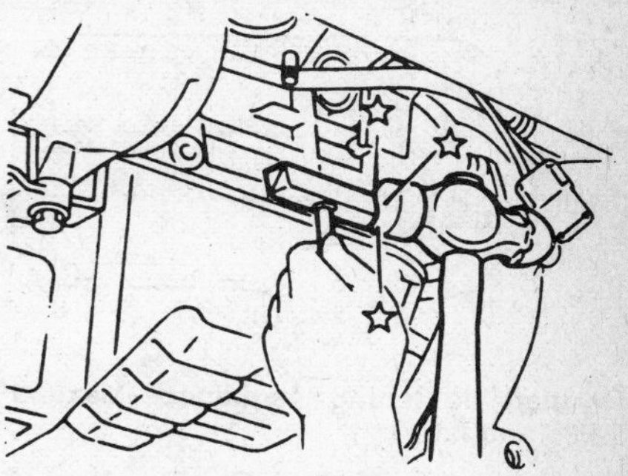

**Using a seal cutter on the oil pan**

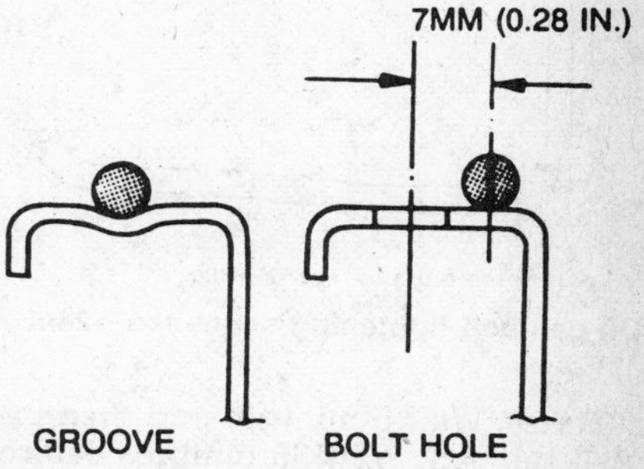


**Apply sealer on the inside of the bolt holes**

11. Remove all old liquid gasket from the pan and block mating surfaces.
12. Apply a continuous bead (3.5–4.5mm) of liquid gasket around the oil pan. Apply the sealer to the *inner* surface around the bolt holes where there is no groove.
13. Wait 5 minutes and then install the pan. Wait 30 minutes before refilling the crankcase to allow the sealant to cure properly.

#### *1985–90 Maxima*

1. Drain the engine oil.
2. Raise the vehicle and support it safely with jack stands.
3. Scribe around the hood support brackets and then remove the hood.
4. Position a block of wood between a floor jack and the engine and then raise the engine slightly in its mounts.
5. Remove the lower engine splash pans.
6. Remove the insulator bolt and nuts from the engine mounts.
7. Remove the center crossmember assembly.
8. Unbolt the front exhaust pipe and wire it out of the way.
9. Remove the oil pan.
10. To install, carefully scrape the old gasket material away from the pan and cylinder block mounting surfaces and then apply a thin continuous bead of liquid gasket around the oil pan to the four corners of the cylinder block mounting surface. Do the same to the oil pan gasket; both upper and lower

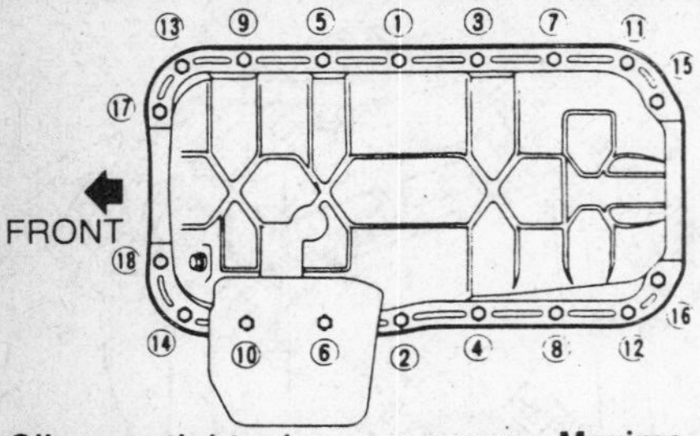


Oil pan tightening sequence—Maxima (1985 and later)

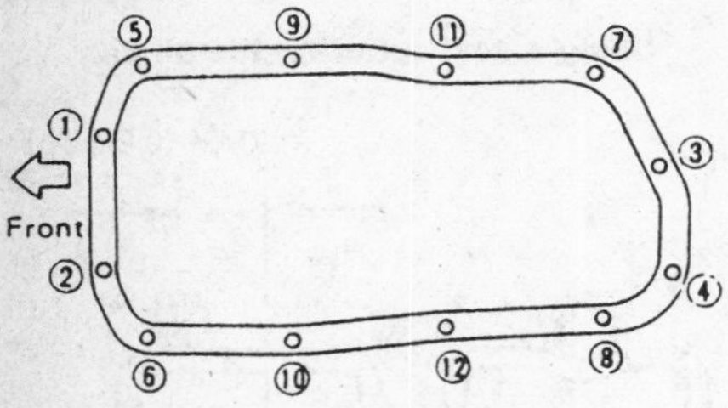


Loosen bolts in reverse order.

**Oil pan bolt tightening sequence – 240SX**

surfaces. Wait 5 minutes and then install the pan. Wait 30 minutes before refilling the crankcase to allow the sealant to cure properly.

11. Install the oil pan and tighten the mounting bolts from the inside, out, to 3.6-5.1 ft. lbs. (5–7 Nm).

### *240SX*

1. Raise the vehcile and support safely.
2. Drain the crankcase.
3. Remove the front stabilizer bar bolts and nuts and from the side member.
4. Position a block of wood between a floor jack and the engine and then raise the engine slightly in its mounts.
5. Remove the oil pan retaining bolts.
6. Insert a seal cutter (SST KV10111100) between the oil pan and the cylinder block.

**NOTE: DO NOT use a screwdriver!**

7. Tapping the cutter with a hammer, slide it around the oil pan. Do not drive the seal cutter into the oil pump or rear seal retainer portion or the aluminum mating surface will be deformed. Lower the oil pan from the cylinder block and remove it from the front side of the engine.

**To install:**

8. To install, carefully scrape the old gasket material away from the pan and cylinder block mounting surfaces and then apply a continuous bead (3.5–4.5mm) of liquid gasket around the oil pan to the four corners of the cylinder block mounting surface. Wait 5 minutes and then install the pan.
9. Install the oil pan and tighten the mounting bolts from the inside, out, to 3.6–5.1 ft. lbs. (5–7 Nm). Wait 30 minutes before refilling the crankcase to allow for the sealant to cure properly.

### *300ZX*

1. Drain the engine oil.
2. Raise the vehicle and support it safely with jack stands.
3. Remove the front stabilizer bar retaining bolts and nuts from the suspension crossmember.
4. Remove the steering column shaft from the gear housing.
5. Remove the tension rod retaining nuts from the transverse link.
6. Lift and support the engine.
7. Remove the rear plate cover from the transmission case.
8. Remove the oil pan retaining bolts.
9. Remove the suspension crossmember retaining bolts.
10. Remove the strut mounting insulator retaining nuts.
11. Remove the screws retaining the refrigerant lines and power steering tubes to the suspension crossmember.
12. Lower the suspension crossmember.
13. Remove the oil pan from the rear side.
14. Installation is the reverse of removal. Apply sealant to the surface points indicated in the illustration and wait 5 minutes and then install the pan. Torque the pan retaining bolts in numerical sequence to 3.5–5.1 ft. lbs. Wait 30 minutes before refilling the crankcase to allow for the sealant to cure properly.

**NOTE: A liquid gasket should not be used on engines originally equipped with a rubber gasket.**

## Rear Main Bearing Oil Seal

### REPLACEMENT

#### *All Engines Except CA16DE, CA18DE, CA18ET, CA20, CA20E, CA20S, GA16i and KA24E*

In order to replace the rear main oil seal, the rear main bearing cap must be removed. Removal of the rear main bearing cap requires the use of a special rear main bearing cap puller. Also, the oil seal is installed with a special crankshaft rear oil seal drift.

1. Remove the engine and transmission assembly from the vehicle.
2. Remove the transmission from the engine. Remove the oil pan.
3. Remove the clutch from the flywheel.

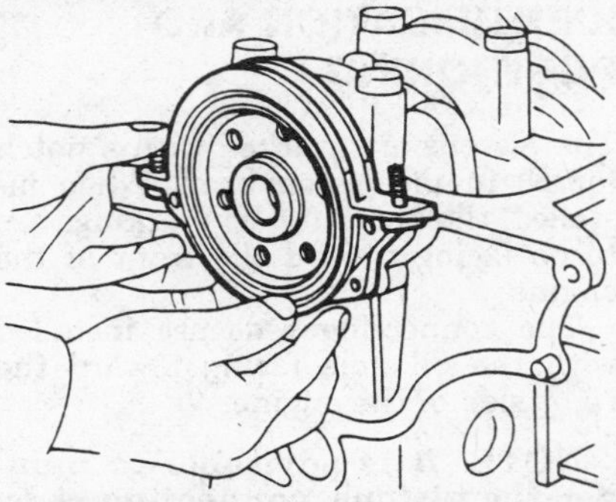

**Installing the E-series rear oil seal retainer**

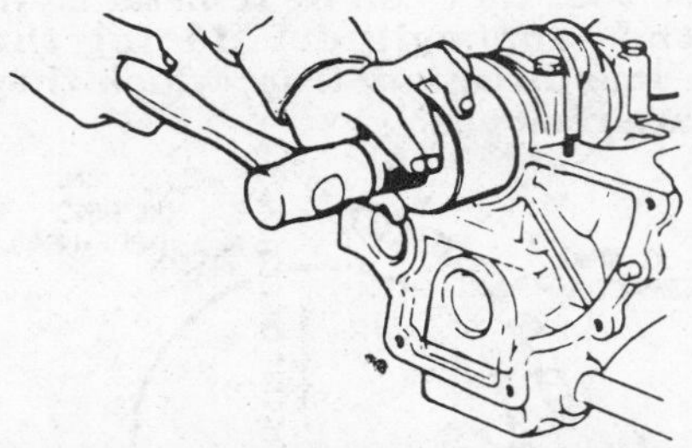

**Rear oil seal installation – L and Z series engines**

4. Remove the flywheel from the crankshaft.
5. Remove the rear main bearing cap together with the bearing cap side seals.
6. Remove the rear main oil seal from around the crankshaft.
7. Apply lithium grease around the sealing lip of the oil seal and install the seal around the crankshaft using a suitable tool.
8. Apply sealer to the rear main bearing cap, install the rear main bearing cap, and tighten the cap bolts to the proper specification.
9. Apply sealant to the rear main bearing cap side seals and install by

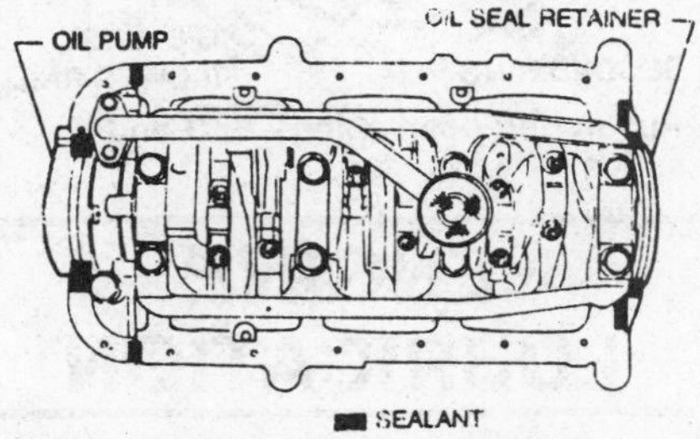


**Apply sealant to these areas before installing the oil pan gasket—V6**

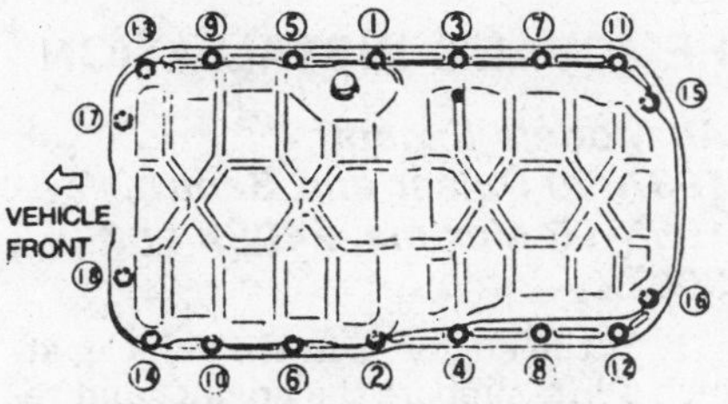


**Oil pan tightening sequence—V6**

driving the seals into place with a suitable drift.

10. Assemble the engine and install it in the vehicle in the reverse order of removal.

### CA16DE, CA18DE, CA18ET, CA20, CA20E, CA20S, GA16i and KA24E Engines

1. Remove the transmission.
2. Remove the flywheel or the drive plate.
3. Remove the rear oil seal retainer.
4. Using a pair of pliers or suitable prying tool, remove the oil seal from the retainer.
5. Thoroughly scrape the surface of the retainer to remove any traces of the existing sealant or gasket material.
6. Liberally apply clean engine oil to the new oil seal and carefully install it into the retainer using the proper tool.
7. Install the rear oil seal retainer into the engine, along with a new gasket or sealant. Torque the bolts to 2.9–4.3 ft. lbs. Install the flywheel and transmission in the reverse order of removal.

# Oil Pump

## REMOVAL & INSTALLATION

### E15, E15ET, E16, E16i and E16S Engines

1. Drain the engine oil.
2. Loosen the alternator lower bolts.
3. Remove the alternator belt and adjusting bar bolt.
4. Move the alternator out of the way and support it safely.
5. Disconnect the oil pressure gauge harness.
6. Remove the oil filter.
7. Remove the pump assembly.
8. For installation, fill the pump with clean engine oil and rotate it several times.
9. Install the pump on the engine using a new gasket. Torque the pump mounting bolts to 7–9 ft. lbs.

### CA16DE, CA18DE, CA18ET, CA20, CA20E and CA20S Engines

1. Remove all accessory drive belts and the alternator.
2. Remove the timing (cam) belt covers and remove the timing belt.
3. On 1984–88 200SX and the Stanza wagon, unbolt the engine from its mounts and lift or jack the engine up from the unibody. On the Stanza (exc. wagon) and Pulsar, remove the center member from the body.
4. Remove the oil pan.
5. Remove the oil pump assembly along with the oil strainer.
6. If installing a new or rebuilt oil pump, first pack the pump full of petroleum jelly to prevent the pump from cavitating when the engine is started. Apply RTV sealer to the front oil seal end of the pan prior to installation. Install the pump in the reverse order of removal. Torque the oil pump mounting bolts to 8–12 ft. lbs.

### GA16i Engines

The oil pump used on the GA16i engine consists of an inner and outer gear located in the front cover. Removal of the front cover is necessary to gain access to the oil pump.

1. Remove the front cover as desribed previously.
2. Loosen the oil pump cover retaining screw and mounting bolts and separate the oil pump cover from the front cover.
3. Remove the oil pump inner and outer gears.
4. Thoroughly clean the oil pump cover mating surfaces and the gear cavity.
5. Install the outer gear into the cavity.
6. Install the inner gear so that the grooved side is facing up (towards the oil pump cover). Make sure that the gears mesh properly and pack the pump cavity with petroleum jelly.
7. Install the oil pump cover. Torque the retaining screws to 2.2–3.6 ft. lbs. and the bolts to 3.6–5.1 ft. lbs.
8. Complete the installation of the front cover in reverse of the removal procedure.

### KA24E Engines

1. Drain the crankcase.
2. Turn the crankshaft so that No. 1 piston is at TDC on its compression stroke.
3. Remove the distributor cap and mark the position of the distributor rotor in relation to the distributor base with a piece of chalk.
4. Remove the splash shield.
5. Remove the oil pump body with the drive spindle assembly.
6. To install, fill the pump housing with engine oil, align the punch mark on the spindle with the hole in the pump. No. 1 piston should be at TDC on its compression stroke.
7. With a new gasket and seal placed over the drive spindle, install the oil pump and drive spindle assembly. Make sure the tip of the drive spindle fits into the distributor shaft notch securely. The distributor rotor should be pointing to the matchmark made earlier.
8. Install the splash shield.
9. Install the distributor cap.
10. Refill the engine oil. Start the engine, check ignition timing and check for oil leaks.

### L24E, L28E, L28ET, LD28, Z22 and Z22E Engines

1. Drain the crankcase.
2. Turn the crankshaft so that the No. 1 piston is at TDC on its compression stroke.
3. Remove the distributor cap and mark the position of the distributor base with a piece of chalk.
4. Remove the front stabilizer bar (if so equipped).
5. Remove the splash shield.
6. Remove the oil pump body with the drive spindle assembly.
7. Tighten the long mounting bolts to 8–11 ft. lbs. (11–15 Nm). Tighten

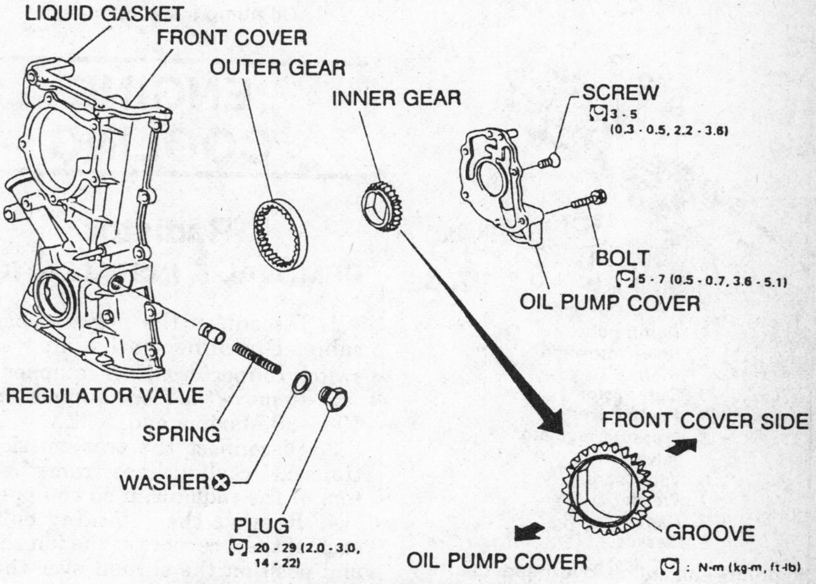


Oil pump assembly used on GA16i engines

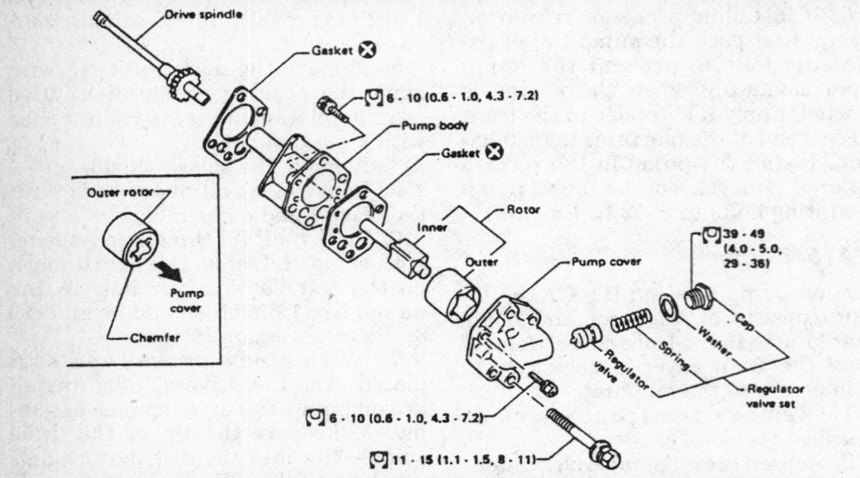


**Align the punch mark on the drive spindle with the oil hole—KA24E engines**

the short mounting bolts to 4.3–7.2 ft. lbs. (6–10 Nm).

### *VG30E and VG30ET Engines*

1. Remove the oil pan and timing belt as detailed previously in this section.
2. Remove the crankshaft timing sprocket. A pulller may be reqiured.
3. Remove the timing belt plate.
4. Remove the oil pump strainer and pick-up tube from the oil pump.
5. Remove the mounting bolts and remove the oil pump.
6. To install, use new gaskets (silicone sealant), a new oil seal and reverse the removal procedures. Refill the engine with oil.

**NOTE: Before installing the oil pump, be sure to pack the pump's cavity with petroleum jelly, then make sure the O-ring is fitted properly.**

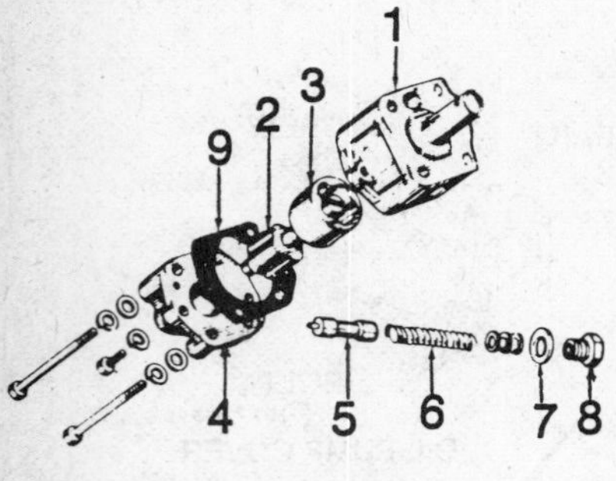


1. Pump body
2. Inner rotor and shaft
3. Outer rotor
4. Pump cover
5. Pressure regulator valve
6. Valve spring
7. Washer
8. Cap
9. Gasket

Oil pump—all inline overhead cam engines similar

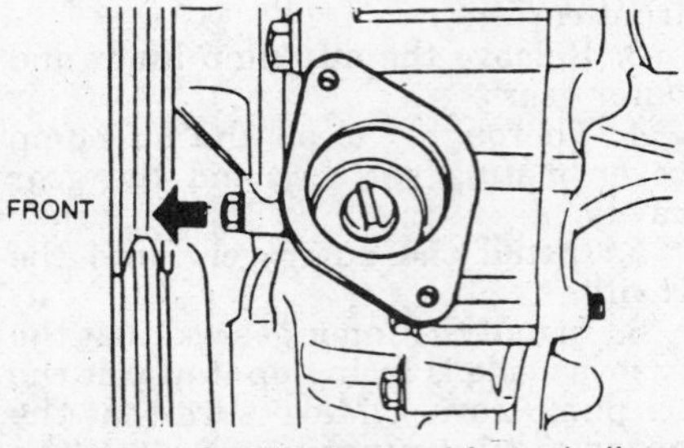


Position of the distributor drive spindle—L-series gas engines

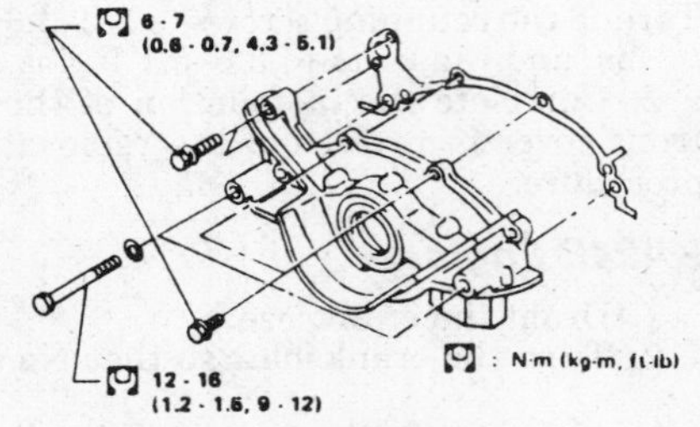


Oil pump installation—V6

# ENGINE COOLING

## Radiator

### REMOVAL & INSTALLATION

1. Disconnect the negative battery cable. Disconnect all temperature switch connectors, if so equipped.
2. Remove the front bumper on the 1985–90 Maxima and 300ZX.
3. Disconnect the transmission or transaxle cooling lines from the bottom of the radiator, if so equipped.
4. Remove the retaining bolts at each of the 4 corners of the fan shroud and position the shroud over the fan and clear of the radiator.
5. Disconnect the upper and lower hoses from the radiator.
6. Remove the radiator retaining bolts or the upper supports and lift the radiator out of the vehicle.
7. Install the radiator in the reverse order of the removal, fill the cooling system and check for leaks.

## Water Pump

### REMOVAL & INSTALLATION

#### *All Engines Except E15, E15ET, E16, E16i, E16S, GA16i, KA24E, VG30E and VG30ET*

1. Drain the engine coolant.

**NOTE: Be sure to drain the cylinder block also. Most models have a drain plug on the left side of the block.**

2. Loosen the bolts retaining the fan shroud to the radiator and remove the shroud.
3. Loosen the belt, then remove the fan and pulley from the water pump hub.
4. Remove the bolts retaining the pump and remove the pump together with the gasket from the front cover.
5. Remove all traces of gasket material and install the pump in the reverse order. Use a new gasket and sealer. Tighten the bolts uniformly.

#### *E15, E15ET, E16, E16i, E16S GA16i and KA24E Engines*

1. With the engine cold, raise the hood and open the drain cock on the radiator and drain the coolant into a suitable drain pan. Remove the radiator cap to relieve the pressure in the system.
2. Remove the power steering belt and power steering pump, do not let the power steering fluid drain out.
3. Remove the water pump drive belts, loosen the alternator mounting bolts and slide the alternator toward the engine.
4. Remove the water pump pulley and the water pump securing bolts.
5. Remove the water pump with the gasket (if installed).
6. Remove all gasket material or sealant from the water pump mating surfaces. On GA16i and KA24E engines, all sealant must be removed from the groove in the water pump surface also.
7. Installation is the reverse order of the removal procedure. On GA16i and KA24E engines, apply a bead of high temperature liquid gasket to the water pump mating surface. Be sure to check for coolant leaks after the engine has reached operating temperature.

**NOTE: Check water pump for excessive end play and rough operation. The pump cannot be disassembled and must be replaced as a unit.**

### *VG30E and VG30ET Engines*

1. Drain the coolant from the left side drain cocks on the cylinder block and radiator. On 1989–90 Maxima, there are 2 drain plugs; one on the right side of the cylinder block behind the right driveshaft boot and one on the left side of the block next to the oil level gauge.
2. Remove the radiator shroud fan and pulleys.
3. Remove the power steering, compressor and alternator drive belts.
4. Disconnect the water pump hose.
5. Remove the upper and lower timing covers.
6. On the Maxima, if the vehicle is equipped with cruise control, remove the unit from the fender well to gain better access to the water pump.
7. Remove the thermostat housing and gasket.

**NOTE: Be careful not to get coolant on the timing belt and to avoid deforming the timing cover, make sure there is enough clearance between the timing cover and the hose clamp.**

8. Remove the water pump retaining bolts (note different lengths) and remove the pump.
9. Installation is the reverse of removal. Scrape the gasket surfaces, install a new gasket and reinstall the pump. Torque the retaining bolts to 12–15 ft. lbs.

**NOTE: Check water pump for excessive end play and rough operation. The pump cannot be disassembled and must be replaced as a unit.**

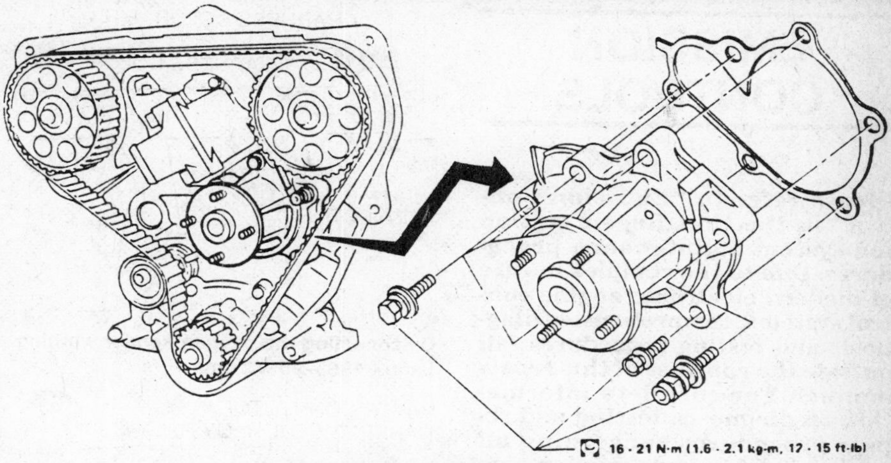


Water pump installation—V6

## Thermostat

### REMOVAL & INSTALLATION

1. Open the drain cock on the radiator and drain the coolant into a suitable drain pan. On GA16i engines, disconnect the water temperature switch connector.
2. Remove the upper radiator hose from the water outlet side and remove the bolts securing the water outlet to the cylinder head.
3. On E15 and E16 models, remove the exhaust air induction tube clamp bolts, then the water outlet bolts.
4. On 200SX (V6) and 300ZX models, remove the radiator shroud, cooling fan and water suction pipe retaining bolt. Remove the bolts securing the water outlet to the cylinder head.
5. Remove the thermostat and clean off the old gasket or sealant from the mating surfaces.
6. Installation is the reverse order of the removal procedure. When installing the thermostat, be sure to install a new gasket or sealant and be sure the air bleed hole in the thermostat is facing the left side (or upward) of the engine. The jiggle valve must always face up. Also make sure that the new thermostat to be installed is equipped with a air bleed hole.

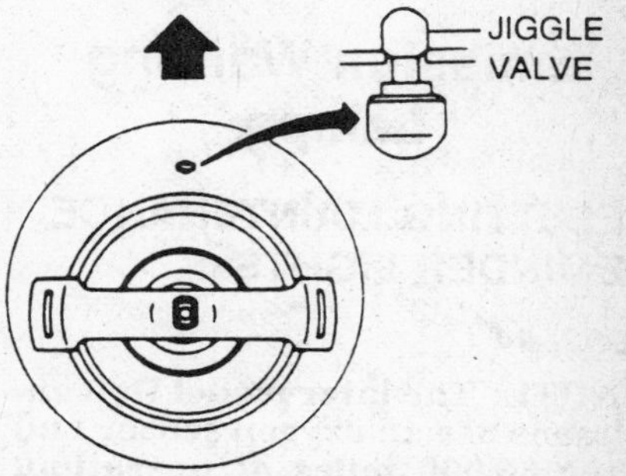


Always be sure the jiggle valve is facing upward when installing the thermostat

### COOLING SYSTEM BLEEDING

1. Fill the radiator with the proper type of coolant.
2. With the radiator cap off, start the engine and allow it to run and reach normal operating temperature.
3. Run the heater at full force and with the temperature lever in the hot position. Be sure that the heater control valve is functioning.
4. Shut the engine off and recheck the coolant level, refill as necessary.

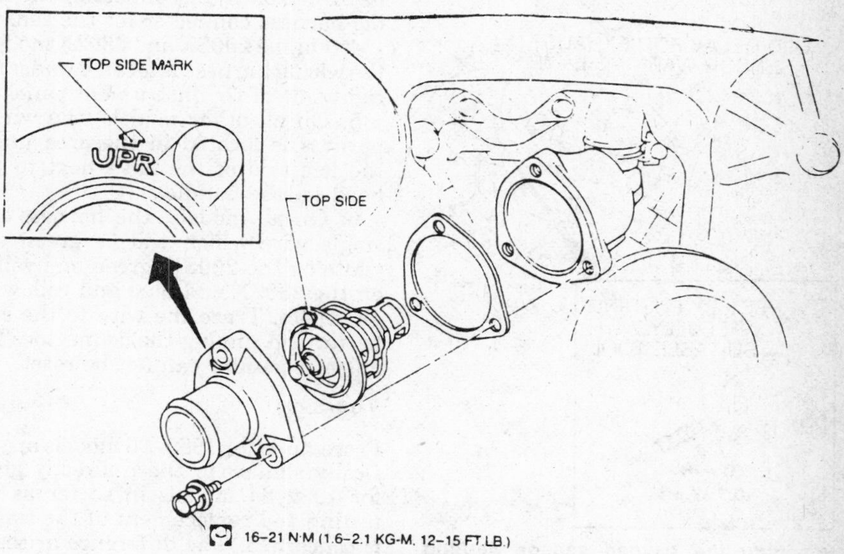


V6 thermostat installation

# EMISSION CONTROLS

**Please refer to "Emission Control" in the Unit Repair section for system maintenance procedures. Due to the complex nature of modern electronic engine control systems, comprehensive diagnosis and testing procedures fall outside the confines of this repair manual. For complete information on diagnosis, testing and repair procedures concerning all modern engine and emission control systems, please refer to "Chilton's Guide to Electronic Engine Controls".**

## Emission Warning Lamps

### RESETTING MAINTENANCE REMINDER LIGHTS

#### *1982–84*

**NOTE: The later model Datsun/Nissans use an oxygen sensor and after 30,000 miles of operation, the warning light on the dash panel will come on. When this light comes on and remains on, it is indicating that the oxygen sensor should be inspected and replaced if it is not operating properly.**

1. Disconnect the negative battery cable and remove the oxygen sensor, which is located on the exhaust manifold.

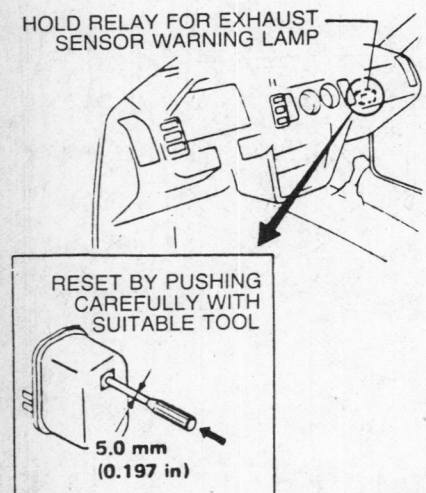

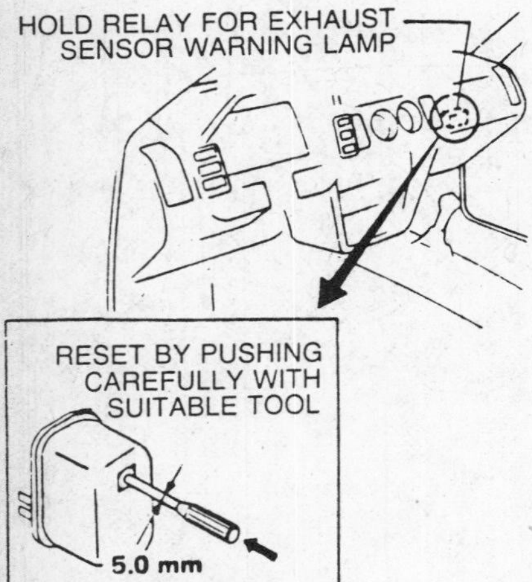


**Resetting the oxygen sensor warning lamp – 1985-86 300ZX (U.S. models)**

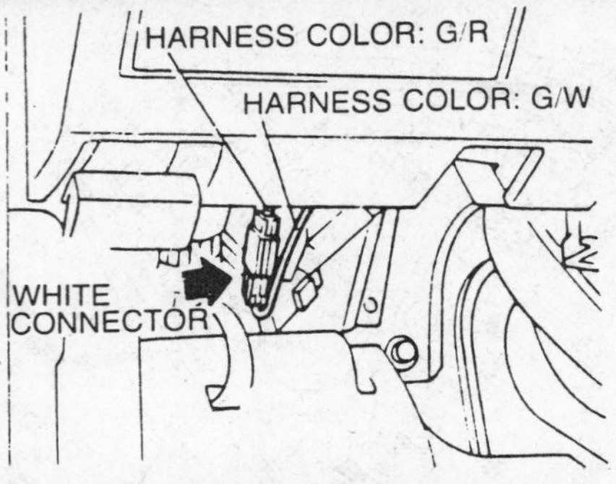


**Disconecting the oxygen sensor warning lamp – 1985–90 Maxima**

**Disconecting the oxygen sensor warning lamp – 1985–90 300ZX**

2. Coat the thread of the new sensor with a suitable anti-seize compound and reinstall it into the exhaust manifold.
3. After the new sensor has been installed or the old sensor passes inspection and has been re-installed into the exhaust manifold. The sensor light can be turned off by disconnecting the wiring harness connecter for the sensor.
4. On the 200SX and 280ZX models, the wiring harness is located under the right side of the instrument panel.
5. On all other models, the wiring harness is located in the area under the left side of the dash next to the hood release handle.
6. On all models, the harness is a single wire which will be green and white on the 200SX, green and yellow on the 280ZX and blue and yellow on all others. Trace the wire to the connector and unplug the connector. The mileage counter can not be reset.

#### *1985–90*

Procedures for 1985–90 models are basically similar to those already given for 1982–84 models in so far as the testing and replacement of the sensor is concerned. The difference arises in the resetting procedures.

U.S. models should be reset after the warning light comes on at 30,000 miles (43,000 km) and then again at 60,000 miles (96,000 km). When the warning light comes on a third time, at 90,000 miles (144,000 km), it should then be disconnected.

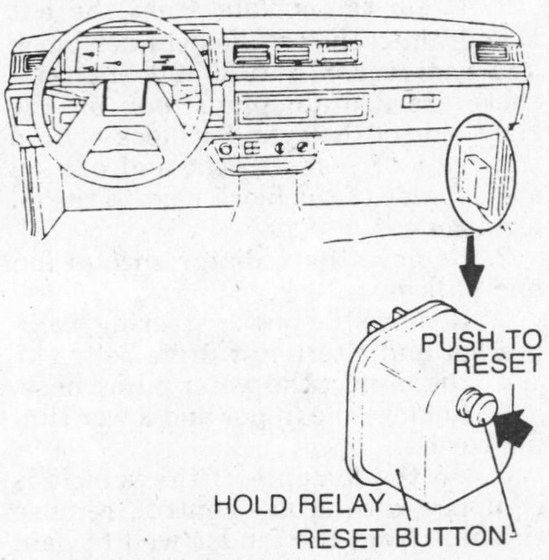


**Resetting the oxygen sensor warning lamp – 1985–90 Stanza sedan**

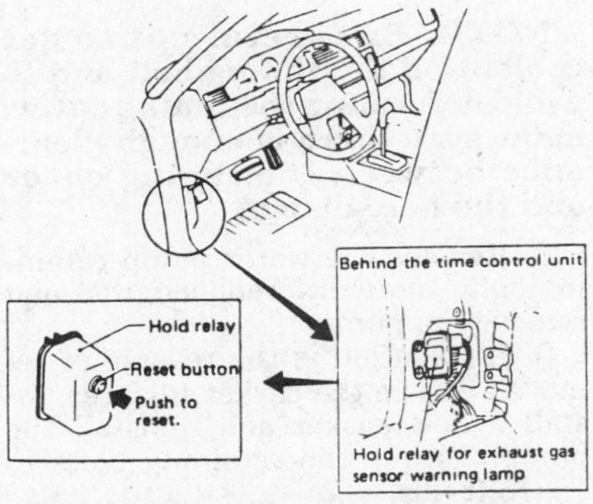


**Resetting the oxygen sensor warning lamp – 1986 Maxima**

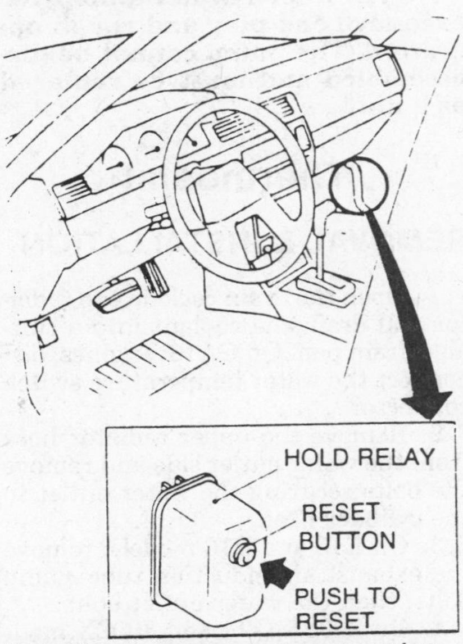


**Resetting the oxygen sensor warning lamp – 1987–90 Maxima**

On Canadian models, when the warning light comes on at 30,000 miles (43,000 km), it should be disconnected. There is no provision for resetting the warning light on models sold in Canada.

For resetting and disconnection procedures, please see the following:

**NOTE: Refer to illustrations for exact location of reset boxes and wiring harness disconnect points.**

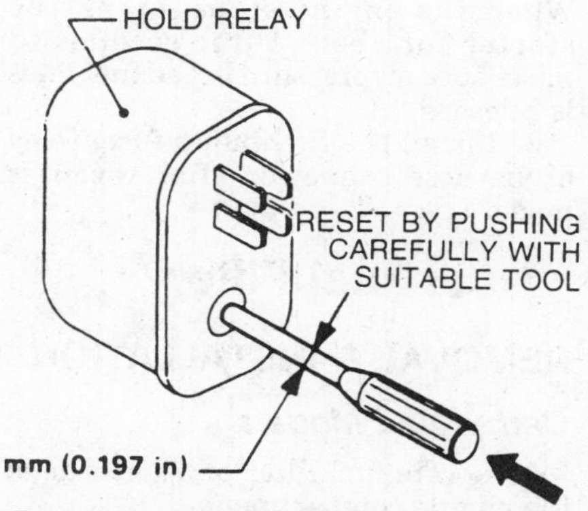


**Resetting the oxygen sensor warning lamp – 1985-86 Stanza wagon (2wd)**

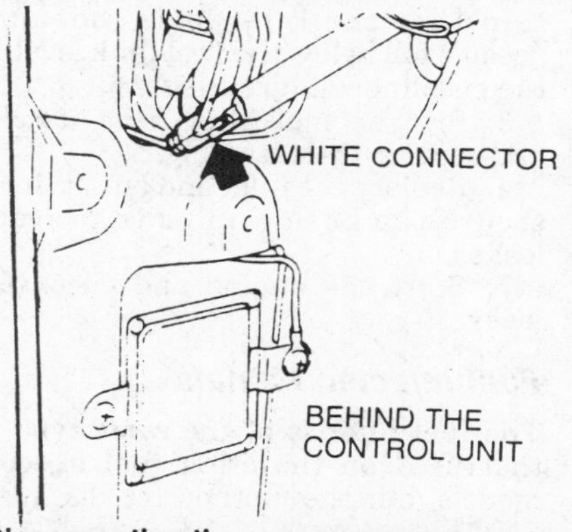


**Disconnecting the oxygen sensor warning lamp – 1985–90 Stanza (all models)**

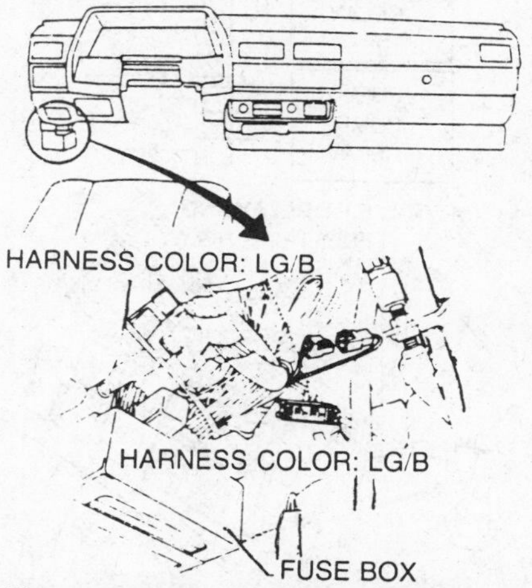


**Disconnecting the oxygen sensor warning lamp – 1985-86 Pulsar/Sentra (all models)**

1. On the Maxima, reset the warning light by pressing the reset button on the small box found under the left side of the instrument panel. To disconnect the warning, unplug the white connector behind and above the reset box. On the 1985 Maxima, unplug the

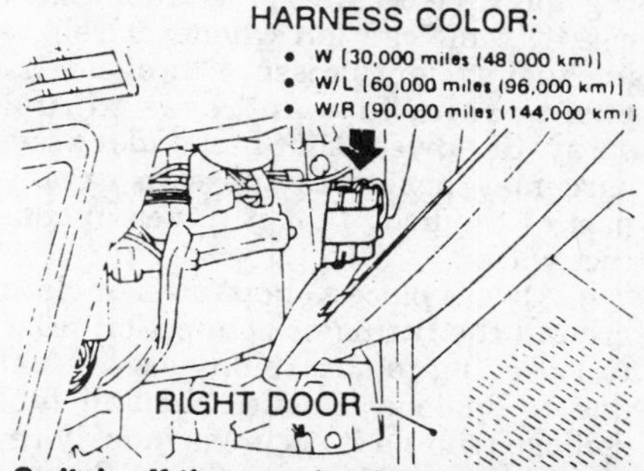


**Switch off the warning lamp after each inspection – 1987-90 300ZX with analog meter**

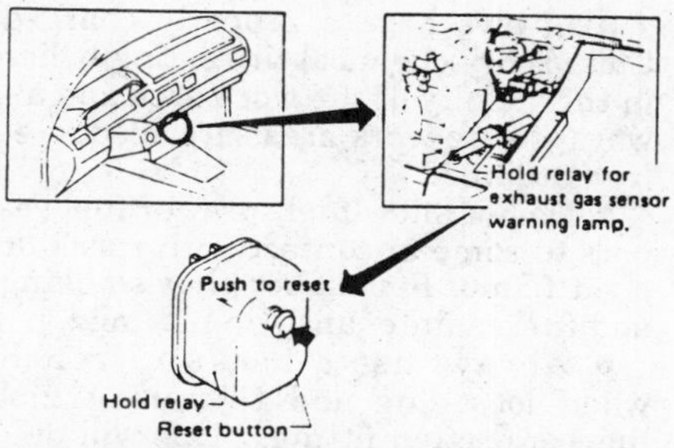


**Resetting the oxygen sensor warning lamp – 1985–89 200SX (U.S.models)**

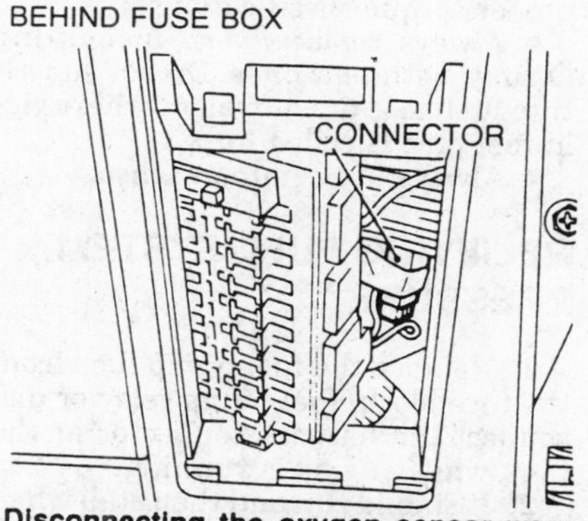


**Disconnecting the oxygen sensor warning lamp – 1985–89 200SX (U.S.models)**

connector only. On 1986 Maxima, the oxygen sensor warning lamp is located near the left side kick panel. On 1987–90 Maxima, the oxygen sensor warning lamp is located near the right side kick panel.

2. On the 300ZX, locate the reset box underneath and behind the glove compartment, insert a suitable 5mm (0.197 in.) diameter tool and push lightly one time. On 1987–90 models with an analog meter, switch off the lamp after every inspection by disconnecting one of the three connectors found behind the glove box. Disconnect the warning light by unplugging the white connector found under the left side of the instrument panel.

3. On the Stanza sedan, locate the reset box behind the right side kick panel and push the button one time.

On the 1986 Stanza wagon (2WD), the box is under the passenger seat and is reset in the same manner as the 1985–86 300ZX.

On the 1986 Stanza wagon (4WD) and all 1987–89 Stanza wagons, the reset box is also under the passenger seat, but is reset with a push button, similar to the sedan.

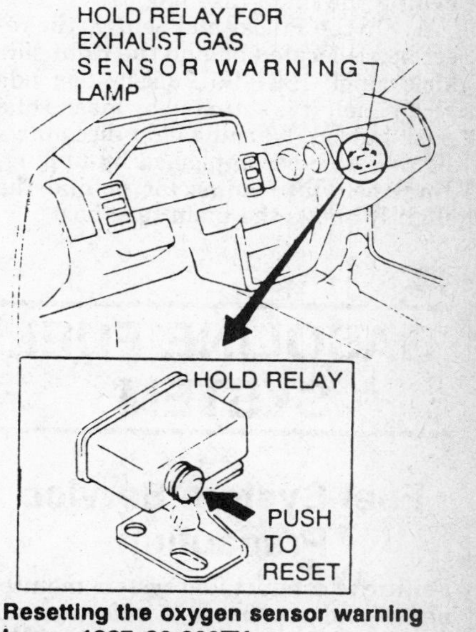


**Resetting the oxygen sensor warning lamp – 1987–90 300ZX**

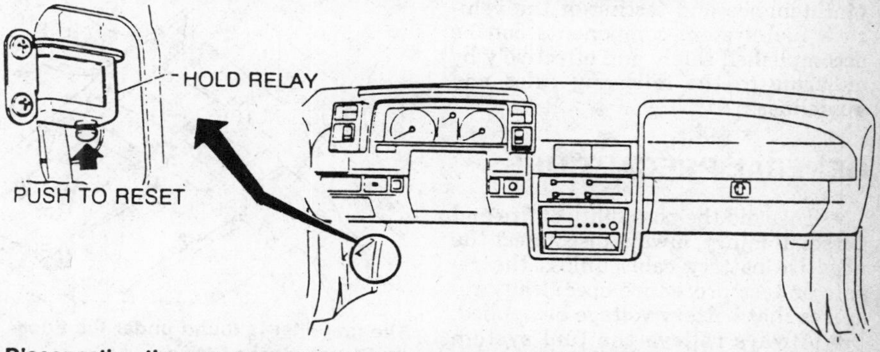


**Disconecting the oxygen sensor warning lamp – 1987–90 Pulsar/Sentra (all models)**

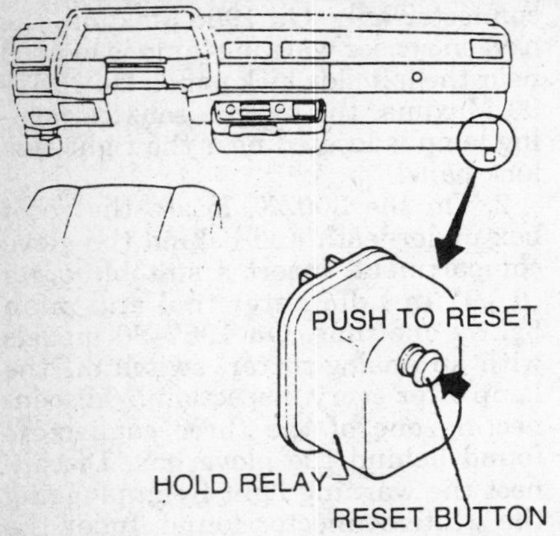


**Resetting the oxygen sensor warning lamp—1985-86 Pulsar/Sentra (U.S. models)**

On all models, the warning light is disconnected by unplugging the white connector found behind the Electronic Control Unit, underneath the left side of the instrument panel.

4. On the 200SX, the reset box may be found behind the right side of the center console. It uses a push button for resetting. To disconnect the warning light, unplug the white connector behind the main fuse box.

5. On the Pulsar and Sentra, the reset box is located behind the right side kick panel; 1987–90 Pulsar—left side kick panel. It is actuated by means of a push button. Warning light disconnection may be accomplished by unplugging the white connector behind the slightly above the main fuse box.

# GASOLINE FUEL SYSTEM

## Fuel System Service Precaution

Failure to conduct fuel system maintenance and repairs in a safe manner may result in serious personal injury. Maintenance and testing of the vehicle's fuel system components can be accomplished safely and effectively by adhering to the following rules and guidelines.

### GENERAL PRECAUTIONS

- To avoid the possibility of fire and personal injury, always disconnect the negative battery cable unless the repair or test procedure specifically requires that battery voltage be applied.
- Always relieve the fuel system pressure prior to disconnecting any fuel system component (injector, fuel rail, pressure regulator, ect...), fitting or fuel line connection. To relieve pressure wrap a shop rag around the fitting or connection being opened, a slowly open the system. Wait for pressure to relieve itself, then remove the rag and wipe up any spilled fuel. Exercise extreme caution whenever relieving fuel system pressure to avoid exposing skin, face and eyes to fuel spray. Be advised that fuel under pressure may penetrate the skin or any part of the body that it comes in contact with.
- Always place a shop towel or cloth around the fitting or connection prior to loosening to absorb any excess fuel due to spillage. Ensure that all fuel spillage (should it occur) is quickly removed from engine surfaces. Ensure that all fuel soaked cloths or towels are deposited into a suitable waste container.
- Always have a properly charged Class B dry chemical fire extinguisher in the vicinity of the work area and always ensure work areas are adequately ventilated.
- Do not allow fuel spray or fuel vapors to come in contact with spark or open flame. Remember that smoking and fuel maintenance do not mix!
- Always use a backup wrench when loosening and tightening fuel line connection fittings. This will prevent unnecessary stress and torsion to fuel line piping. Always follow the proper torque specifications.
- Always replace worn fuel fitting O-rings with new ones. Do not substitute fuel hose or equivalent where rigid fuel pipe is called for.
- Always use common sense.

### RELIEVING FUEL SYSTEM PRESSURE

1. Remove the fuel pump fuse from the fuse block, fuel pump relay or disconnect the harness connector at the tank while engine is running.

2. It should run and then stall when the fuel in the lines is exhausted.

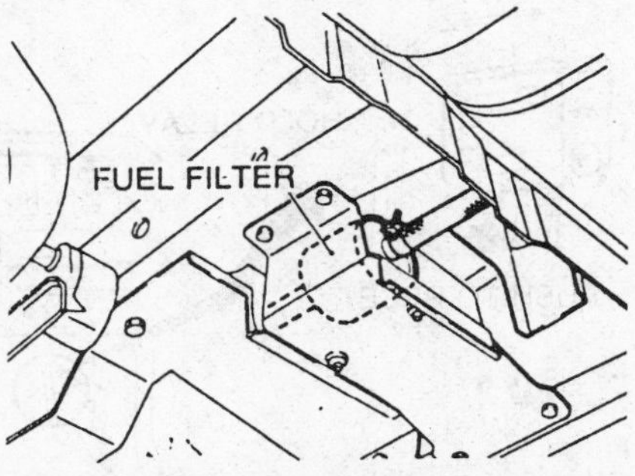


**The fuel filter is found under the floor on Stanza wagons (4wd)**

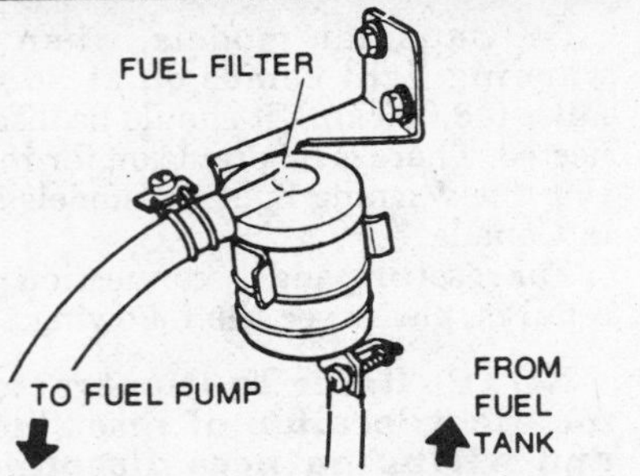


**Typical fuel filters - all models**

When the engine stops, crank the starter for about three seconds to make sure all pressure in the fuel lines is released.

3. Install the fuel pump fuse, relay or harness connector after repair is made.

## Fuel Filter

### REMOVAL & INSTALLATION

#### *Carbureted Models*

1. Locate fuel filter on right-side of the engine compartment.
2. Disconnect the inlet and outlet hoses from the fuel filter. Make certain that the inlet hose (bottom) doesn't fall below the fuel tank level or the gasoline will drain out.
3. Pry the fuel filter from its clip and replace the assembly.
4. Replace the inlet and outlet lines; secure the hose clamps to prevent leaks.
5. Start the engine and check for leaks.

#### *Fuel Injected Models*

The fuel filter is of the same type as that used on the other fuel injected models, but the method for discharg-

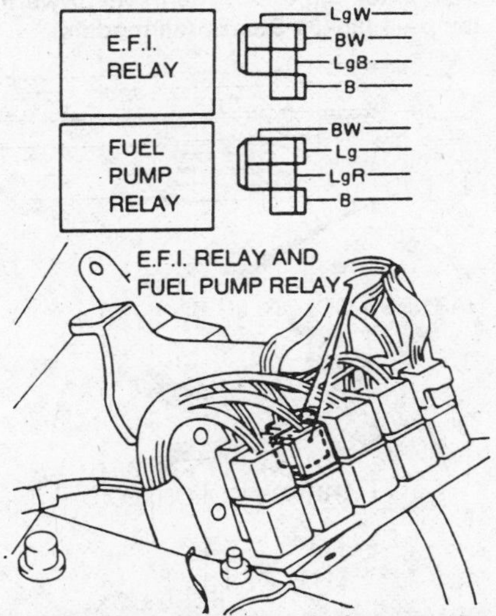


**1983-84 810 and Maxima fuel pump relay is located in the engine compartment near the battery**

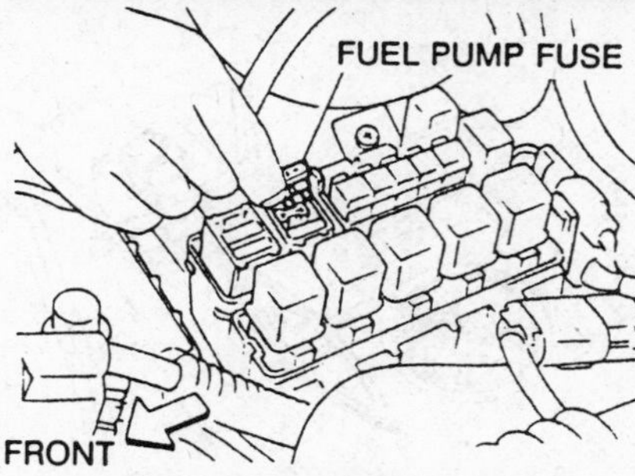

**Fuel pump fuse location – 240SX**

**The fuel pump harness connector is in the tool box on the rear right side – 1984-86 200SX**

ing the fuel injection system is different.

1. Start the engine.
2. On 1983–90 models except those noted below, disconnect the fuel pump electrical connector while the engine is running. This is usually found in-line, near the pump.

On the 1987–90 Pulsar/Sentra, 1987–90 Stanza sedans, 1986½–88 200SX, 1989–90 240SX, 1986–90 Maxima and 300ZX, remove the fuel pump fuse. On the 1986–89 Stanza wagons, pull out the fuel pump relay (first one on left, above fuse box).

3. After the engine stalls, crank the engine two or three more times.
4. Turn the ignition switch off. Reconnect connector, fuse or relay.
5. Release the clamps securing the fuel hoses to the filter. Be careful not to spill fuel on the engine. Disconnect the hoses from the filter.

**NOTE: On the Stanza 4x4 wagon, the fuel filter is found in-line, under the floor, near the fuel pump.**

6. Remove the bolt securing the filter to the bracket; remove the filter.
7. Install the new filter. Connect the fuel hoses and secure them with new clamps.
8. Replace the fuel pump hose, start the engine and check for leaks.

# Mechanical Fuel Pump

The mechanical fuel pump is driven from the camshaft on all engines. It is mounted on the side of the engine on OHV engines and on the side of the cylinder head or block on OHC engines. The pump is on the right side of all engines.

## REMOVAL & INSTALLATION

### *1983–86 Non-Turbo Pulsar, All Sentra Models, 1983 U.S. Stanza and 1983–84 Canadian Stanza*

1. Disconnect the inlet and outlet lines from the pump.
2. Remove the mounting bolts.
3. Remove the pump and discard the gasket.
4. Lubricate the pump rocker arm, rocker arm pin, and lever pin before reinstallation.
5. Bolt the pump into position, using a new gasket.
6. Connect the fuel lines.

## PRESSURE TESTING

1. Disconnect the fuel line at the carburetor.
2. Attach an adapter and tee to the fuel line and connect a pressure gauge of known calibration to the tee.
3. Run the engine at varying speeds. Pressure should remain constant, 3–4 psi. (2.8–3.8 psi on Pulsar andSentra).

# Electric Fuel Pump

## DESCRIPTION AND LOCATION

### *280ZX*

All 280ZX models are equipped with one electric fuel pump mounted near the fuel tank and the right rear wheel.

### *1983–84 810 and Maxima, 200SX, 240SX, 1984–85 Pulsar Turbo 1987–90 Pulsar and Sentra and 1984–90 Stanza*

These models use an electric fuel pump of wet type construction. A vane pump and roller are directly coupled to a motor filled with fuel. A relief valve in the pump is designed to open when the pressure in the fuel lines rises over 64 psi. The pump is automatically activated when the ignition switch is turned on to the start position. If the engine stalls for some reason, the fuel pump is cut off even though the ignition switch remains in the on position. The fuel pump on the 810/Maxima is located near the fuel tank; the 1983 200SX is located near the center of the vehicle, the 1984–88 200SX and 1989–

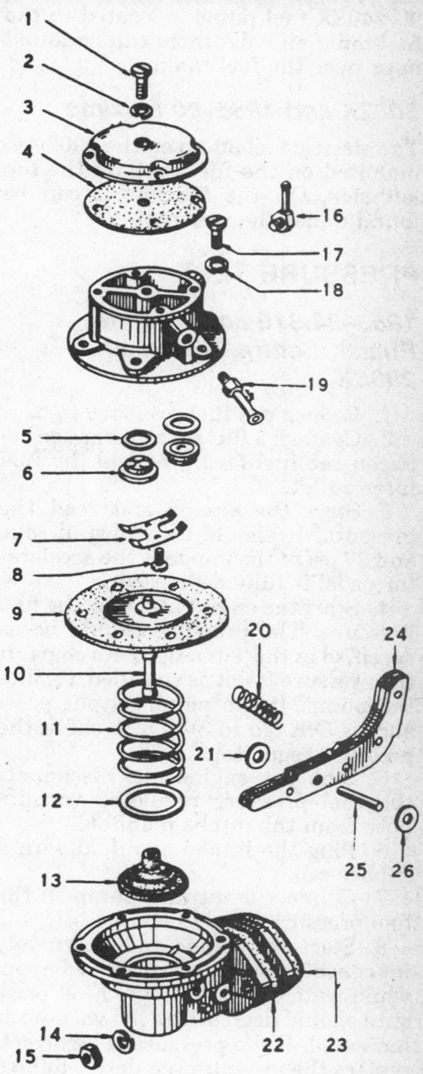

1. Screw
2. Lockwasher
3. Cover
4. Cover gasket
5. Packing
6. Valve
7. Valve retainer
8. Valve retainer screw
9. Diaphragm
10. Pull rod
11. Spring
12. Seal washer
13. Seal
14. Lockwasher
15. Nut
16. Elbow
17. Screw
18. Lockwasher
19. Connector
20. Spring
21. Rocker arm slide spacer
22. Spacer
23. Gasket
24. Rocker arm
25. Pin
26. Rocker arm slide spacer

**Typical mechanical fuel pump**

90 240SX fuel pump is located in the fuel tank; and all others can be found in or near the fuel tank.

### 300ZX and 1985–90 Maxima

The electric fuel pump on the 300ZX is mounted on the fuel tank on the top left side. On the Maxima it can be found under the rear seat.

## PRESSURE TEST

### 1983–84 810 and Maxima, Pulsar, Sentra, Stanza and 200SX

1. Reduce the fuel pressure to 0.
2. Connect a fuel pressure gauge between the fuel feed pipe and the fuel filter outlet.
3. Start the engine and read the pressure. It should be 30 psi at idle, and 37 psi at the moment the accelerator pedal is fully depressed.
4. Start the engine and read the fuel pressure. The pressure should be as specified in the Tune-up specs chart. If the pressure is not as specified, replace the pump. If the pump output pressure is O.K. go to Step 5 to check the pressure regulator.
5. Stop the engine and disconnect the fuel pressure regulator vacuum hose from the intake manifold.
6. Plug the intake manifold with a rubber cap.
7. Connect a vacuum pump to the fuel pressure regulator.
8. Start the engine and alternately increase and decrease the vacuum while watching the gauge. Fuel pressure should decrease as the vacuum is increased. If the pressure is incorrect, replace the pressure regulator, following the replacement procedure given later in this chapter. After replacement of the regulator, repeat the pressure test. If still incorrect, check the fuel lines for kinks or blockage, and replace the pump as necessary.

### 240SX, 280ZX, 300ZX and 1985–90 Maxima

1. Reduce the fuel pressure to 0.
2. Connect a fuel pressure gauge of known calibration into the fuel line in the engine compartments between the fuel pipe and the fuel filter outlet hose.
3. Start the engine and read the fuel pressure. The pressure should be as specified in the Tune-up specs chart. If the pressure is not as specified, replace the pump. If the pump output pressure is O.K. go to Step 4 to check the pressure regualtor.
4. Stop the engine and disconnect the fuel pressure regulator vacuum hose from the intake manifold.
5. Plug the intake manifold with a rubber cap.
6. Connect a vacuum pump to the fuel pressure regulator.
7. Start the engine and alternately increase and decrease the vacuum while watching the gauge. Fuel pressure should decrease as the vacuum is increased. If the pressure is incorrect, replace the pressure regulator, following the replacement procedure given later in this chapter. After replacement of the regulator, repeat the pressure test. If still incorrect, check the fuel lines for kinks or blockage, and replace the pump as necessary.

## FUNCTIONAL TEST

### 280ZX

1. Disconnect either the wire to the alternator **L** terminal, or the oil pressure switch connector.
2. Turn the ignition key to **START**. You should be able to hear the fuel pump running. If not, check the wiring circuits and fuses; if they are in order replace the fuel pump.

### 1983–84 810 and Maxima, Pulsar, Sentra, Stanza and 200SX

Fuel pressure must be reduced to 0 before tests are made.

Start the engine, disconnect the harness connector of fuel pump relay-2 while the engine is running. On 1984–88 200SXs, the fuel pump connector is inside the trunk area on the rear right-hand side of the car. After the engine stalls, crank it over 2 or 3 times to make sure all of the fuel pressure is released.

**NOTE: If the engine will not start remove the fuel pump relay-2 harness connector and crank the engine for about 5 seconds.**

## REMOVAL & INSTALLATION

### 280ZX

1. Reduce the fuel line pressure to 0. Start the engine and remove the fuel pump relay No. 2 while the engine is running. After the engine stalls, crank the engine with the starter 2 or 3 times. Turn the ignition **OFF**.
2. Disconnect the negative battery cable.
3. Remove the luggage compartment mat. Disconnect the fuel pump harness wiring at the connector at the rear of the compartment. Push the wires and the grommet through the floor.
4. Raise and support the rear of the car safely.
5. Clamp the hose between the fuel tank and the pump.
6. Loosen the fuel line clamps and disconnect the hoses from the pump.

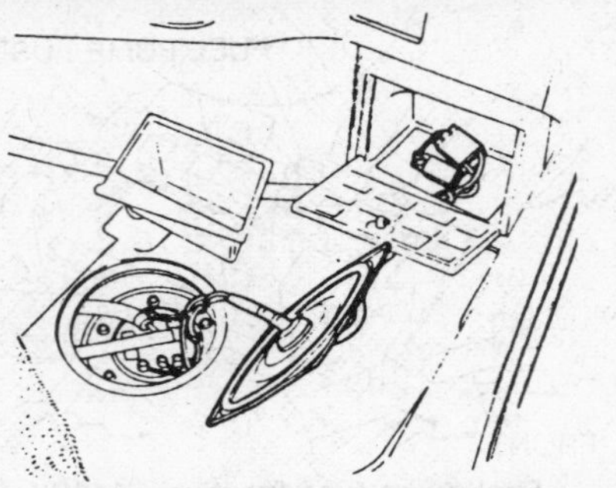

Fuel pump access plate—1987 200SX shown

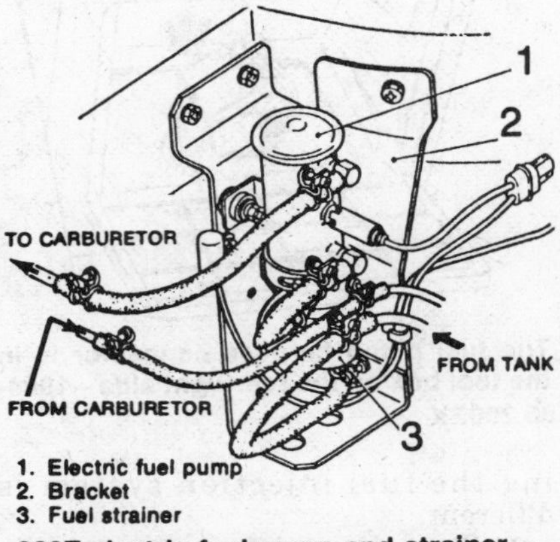


1. Electric fuel pump
2. Bracket
3. Fuel strainer

280Z electric fuel pump and strainer—typical through 1983

Have a metal container ready to catch the fuel which will spill from the lines.

7. Remove the bolts which secure the pump bracket to the body and remove the pump.
8. Installation is the reverse of the removal procedure.

### 300ZX and 1985–90 Maxima

**NOTE: Before disconnecting the fuel line, the fuel pressure must be released from the fuel line.**

1. Remove the fuel tank as described later in this section.
2. Remove the retaining bolt and remove the fuel pump.
3. Installation is the reverse of removal. Run the engine and check for leaks.

### 1983–84 810 and Maxima, 200SX, 240SX, Pulsar and Stanza

1. Relieve the pressure from the fuel system and disconnect the electrical harness connector at the pump.
2. On the 1984–89 200SX and 1989–90 240SX, open the trunk, remove the mat and flip up the fuel pump access plate in the trunk floor.
3. On models not located in the fuel tank, clamp the hose between the fuel tank and the fuel pump to prevent gas from spilling out of the tank.

4. Remove the inlet and outlet tubes at the fuel pump. Unclamp the inlet hose and allow the fuel lines to drain into a suitable container.

5. Unbolt and remove the pump and on models equipped with fuel dampers, remove the dampers at the same time as the pump.

6. Installation is the reverse order of removal procedure. Be sure to use new clamps and that all hoses are properly seated on the fuel pump body.

## Carburetor

### REMOVAL & INSTALLATION

1. Remove the air cleaner.
2. Disconnect the fuel and vacuum lines from the carburetor.
3. Remove the throttle lever.
4. Remove the 4 nuts and washers retaining the carburetor to the manifold.
5. Lift the carburetor from the manifold. Cover the manifold opening.
6. Remove and discard the gasket used between the carburetor and the manifold.
7. Install the carburetor in the reverse order of removal, using a new carburetor base gasket.

### FUEL LEVEL ADJUSTMENT

All Nihonkikaki (Nikki) and Hitachi carburetors have a glass float chamber side cover marked with a fuel level line (some have a small window in the side of the float chamber). Fuel level is adjusted by bending the float seat tab with the float cover removed and inverted, and the float fully raised.

### THROTTLE LINKAGE ADJUSTMENT

On all models, make sure the throttle is wide open when the accelerator pedal is floored. Some models have an adjustable accelerator pedal stop to prevent strain on the linkage.

### DASHPOT ADJUSTMENT

A dashpot is used on carburetors of cars with automatic transmission as

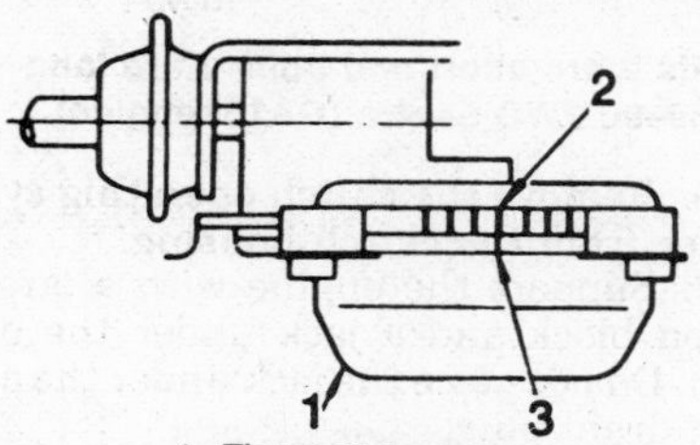


1. Thermostat cover
2. Thermostat housing
3. Groove

**Choke index setting**

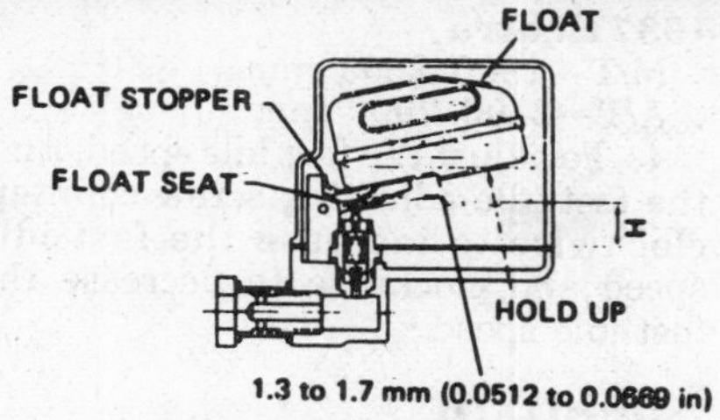


**Float level adjustment**

means of slowly closing the throttle valve to prevent stalling. It is also used in later years as an emission control device on models with either automatic or manual transmissions. The dashpot should be adjusted to contact the throttle lever on deceleration as follows:

**A-series engine**—2000–2300 rpm
**E-series engine**
1983—2300–2500 rpm
1984 and 1985–86 Canadian
M/T—2250–2450
A/T—1900–2100
1985 California
A/T—1900–2100

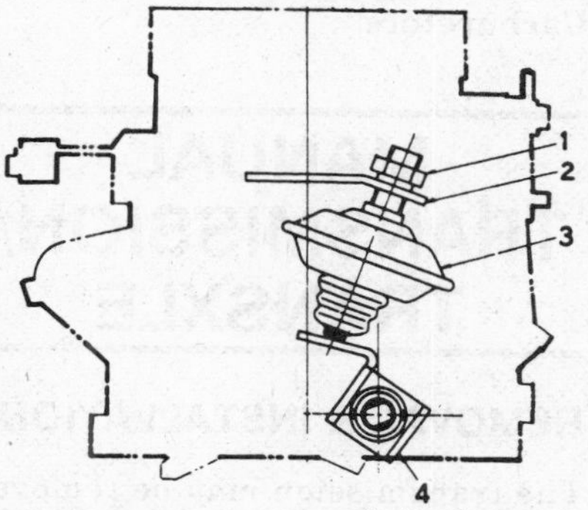


1. Locknut
2. Mounting arm
3. Dashpot
4. Throttle lever

**Typical dashpot**

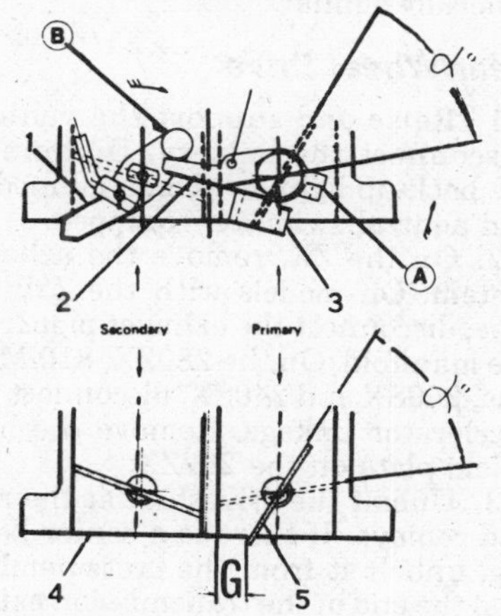


1. Connecting lever
2. Return plate
3. Adjusting plate
4. Secondary throttle chamber
5. Primary throttle valve
a. Primary throttle opening in degrees
G. Primary throttle opening in inches

**Secondary throttle adjustment**

1986—1600–2400
1987—1800–2600

**NOTE: Before attempting to adjust the dashpot, make sure the idle speed, timing and mixture adjustments are correct.**

### SECONDARY THROTTLE ADJUSTMENT

On the two stage carburetors used, the secondary throttle plate begins to open when the primary throttle plate has opened to an angle of approximately 50 degrees (from the fully closed position). This works out to a clearance measurement of approximately 0.28–0.32 in. between the throttle valve and the carburetor body. This can be measured with a drill bit of the correct diameter. If adjustment is required, bend the connecting link between the two linkage assemblies.

### AUTOMATIC CHOKE ADJUSTMENT

1. With the engine cold, make sure the choke is fully closed (press the gas pedal all the way to the floor and release).

2. Check the choke linkage for binding. The choke plate should be easily opened and closed with your finger. If the choke sticks or binds, it can usually be freed with a liberal application of a carburetor cleaner made for the purpose.

If not, the carburetor will have to be disassembled for repairs.

3. The choke is correctly adjusted when the index mark on the choke housing (notch) aligns with the center mark on the carburetor body. If the setting is incorrect, loosen the three screws clamping the choke body in place and rotate the choke cover left or right until the marks align. Tighten the screws carefully to avoid cracking the housing.

### CHOKE UNLOADER ADJUSTMENT

1. Close the choke valve completely.
2. Hold the choke valve closed by stretching a rubber band between the choke shaft lever and the carburetor.
3. Pull the throttle lever until it completely opens.
4. Adjust the gap between the choke plate and the carburetor body to:

**E-series engines:**
1983–84—0.0929 in. (E15)
1983–85—0.1165 in. (E16)
**A-series engines:**
1983–85—0.0965 in.

## FAST IDLE ADJUSTMENT

1. With the carburetor removed from the vehicle, place the upper side of the fast idle screw on the second step of the fast idle cam and measure the clearance between the throttle valve and the wall of the throttle valve chamber at the center of the throttle valve. Check it against the following specifications:

**1983–85 Stanza:**
M/T – 0.0260–0.0315
A/T – 0.0319–0.0374
**1983 Sentra (E15):**
M/T – 0.0315–0.0343 in.
A/T – 0.0421–0.0449 in.
**1983–84 Sentra, Pulsar (E16):**
**USA:**
M/T – 0.0311–0.0367 in.
A/T – 0.0425–0.0481 in.
**Canada:**
M/T – 0.0255–0.0311 in.
A/T – 0.0366–0.0422 in.
**1984–85 Sentra, Pulsar (E16):**
**USA:**
M/T – 0.0339–0.0378 in.
A/T – 0.0453–0.0492 in.
**Canada:**
M/T – 0.0283–0.0433 in.
A/T – 0.0394–0.0433 in.
**1986–87 Pulsar/Sentra:**
**Calif.:**
M/T – 0.0268–0.0039 in.
A/T – 0.0378–0.0039 in.
**Canada:**
M/T – 0.0268–0.0039 in.
A/T – 0.0378–0.0039 in.
"M/T" means manual transmission.
"A/T" means automatic transmission.

**NOTE: The first step of the fast idle adjustment procedure is not absolutely necessary.**

2. Install the carburetor on the engine.
3. Start the engine and measure the fast idle rpm with the engine at operating temperature. The cam should be at the 2nd step.

**1983 Sentra (E15):**
2400–3200 rpm
**1983–85 Sentra (E16), Pulsar:**
**Calif.:**
M/T – 2600–3400 rpm
A/T – 2900–3700 rpm
**49 states:**
M/T – 2400–3200 rpm
A/T – 2700–3500 rpm
**Canada:**
M/T – 1900–2700 rpm
A/T – 2400–3200 rpm
**1986 Pulsar/Sentra:**
**Calif.:**
M/T – 1800–2600 rpm
A/T – 2300–3100 rpm
**Canada:**
M/T – 1800–2600 rpm
A/T – 2300–3100 rpm A/T
**1987 Sentra**
M/T – 1800–2600 rpm
A/T – 2100–2900 rpm

4. To adjust the fast idle speed, turn the fast idle adjusting screw counterclockwise to increase the fast idle speed and clockwise to decrease the fast idle speed.

## OVERHAUL

**For all carburetor overhaul procedures, please refer to "Carburetor Service" in the Unit Repair Section.**

## Fuel Injection

**Due to the complex nature of modern fuel injection systems, comprehensive diagnosis and testing procedures fall outside the confines of this repair manual. For complete information on fuel injection diagnosis, testing and repair procedures please refer to "Chilton's Guide to Fuel Injection And Feedback Carburetors".**

# MANUAL TRANSMISSION/ TRANSXLE

## REMOVAL & INSTALLATION

The transmission may be removed separately from under the vehicle. Transmission removal and replacement procedure for most models is generally similar.

### *Rear Wheel Drive*

1. Raise and support the vehicle. Disconnect the battery. Disconnect the back-up light switch on all models and neutral switch, if equipped.
2. On the ZX, remove the exhaust system. On models with the Z22 engine, disconnect the exhaust pipe from the manifold. On the 280ZX, 810/Maxima, 200SX and 240SX, disconnect the accelerator linkage. Remove the heat shield plate on the 280ZX.
3. Unbolt the driveshaft at the rear and remove. If there is a center bearing, unbolt it from the crossmember. Seal the end of the transmission extension housing to prevent leakage.
4. Disconnect the speedometer drive cable from the transmission.
5. Remove the shift lever.

**NOTE: On the 300ZX, the shifter boot must not be removed from the shift lever.**

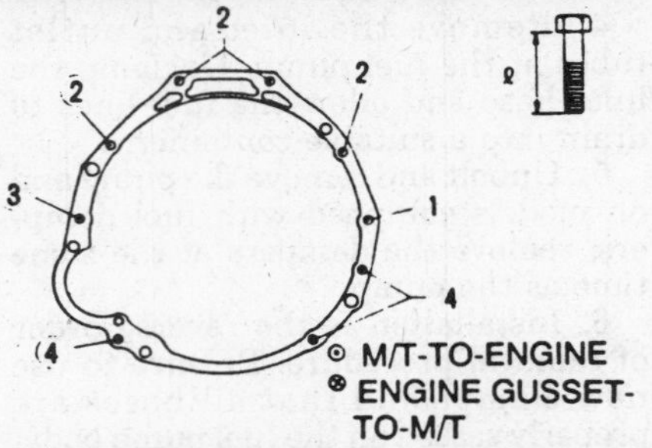


**On the 300ZX and 200SX (V6), bolts 1 & 2 are long; bolts 3 & 4 are short**

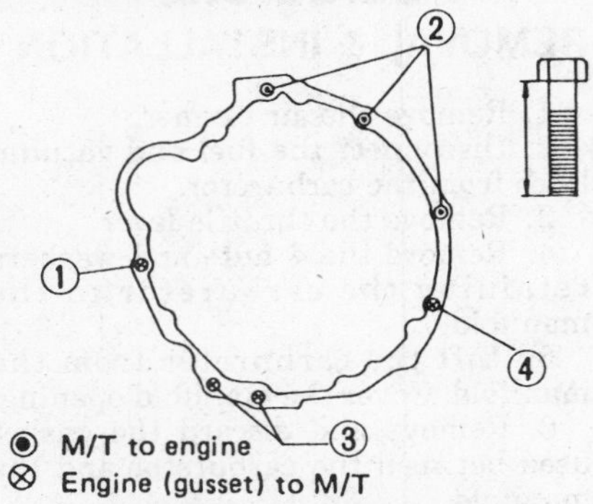


**Bolt 1: 70mm, bolt 2: 60mm, bolt 3: 30mm, bolt 4, 25mm – 240SX**

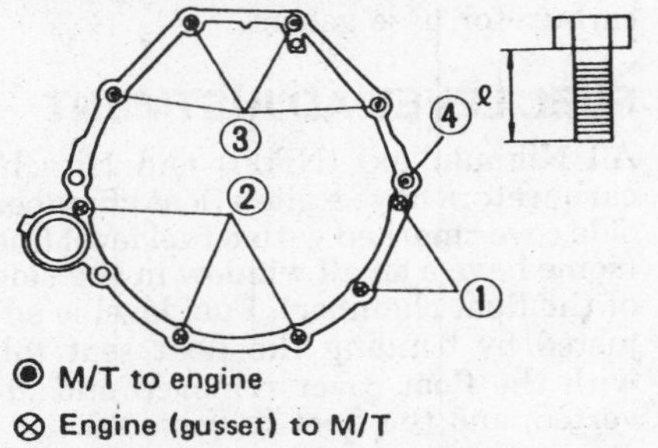


**On 1989–90 Maxima, bolts 1–3 are short; bolt 4 is long**

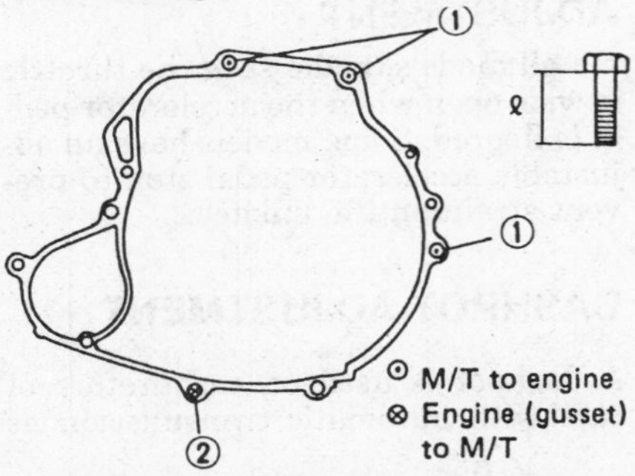


**Bolts 2 are short and bolts 1 are long – 1989–90 2WD Sentra (GA16i engine)**

6. Remove the clutch operating cylinder from the clutch housing.
7. Support the engine with a large wood block and a jack under the oil pan. Do not place the jack under the oil pan drain plug.
8. Unbolt the transmission from the crossmember. Support the transmission with a jack and remove the crossmember.

9. Lower the rear of the engine to allow clearance.
10. Remove the starter.
11. Unbolt the transmission. Lower and remove it to the rear.

**NOTE: Tagging the transmission-to-engine bolts upon removal will facilitate proper tightening during installation.**

12. Reverse the procedure for reintallation. Check the clutch linkage adjustment.
   a. On the 200SX (V6) and 300ZX, tighten the long mounting bolts (65mm & 60mm) to 29–36 ft. lbs. (39–49 Nm). Tighten the short bolts (55mm & 25mm) to 22–29 ft. lbs. (29–39 Nm).
   b. On 240SX, torque the bolts (1), (2) and (4) to 29–36 ft. lbs and bolt (3) to 22–29 ft. lbs.
   c. On the 1984–89 200SX (4 cyl.), tighten the 4 longer bolts to 29–36 ft. lbs. and the 4 shorter bolts to 22–29 ft. lbs.

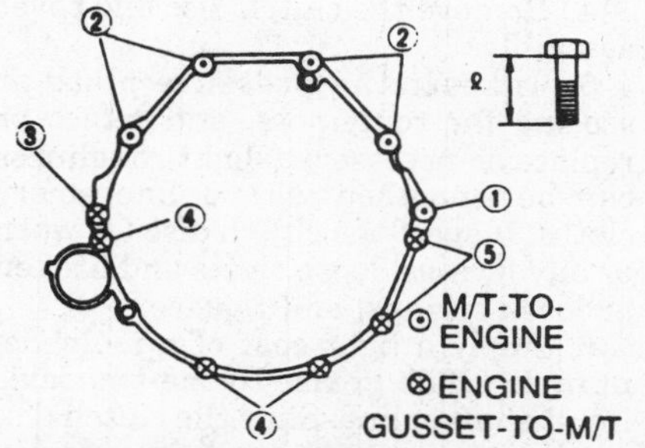


**On 1984–88 Maxima, bolts 1, 2, 3 are long; bolts 4 and 5 are short**

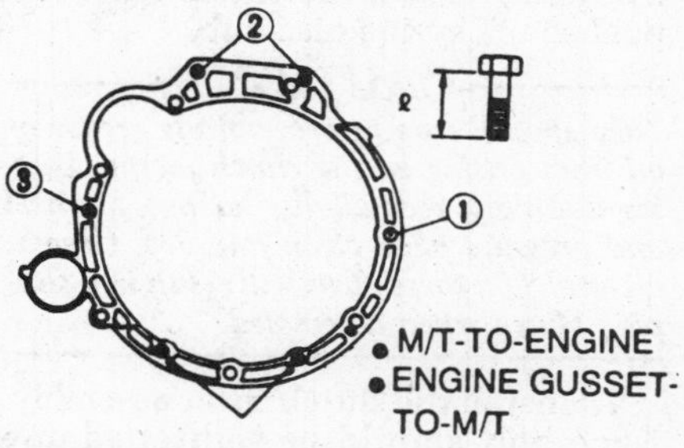


**On 1987–90 Stanza sedan, bolts 1, 2, 3 are long (No. 1 has a nut); bolts 4 are short**

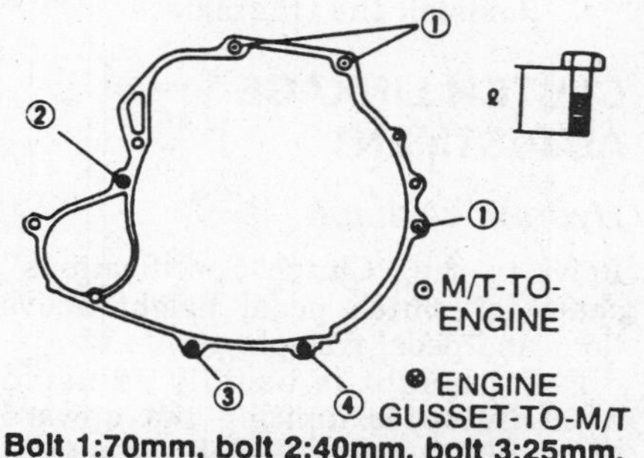


**Bolt 1:70mm, bolt 2:40mm, bolt 3:25mm, bolt 4:20mm – 1987–88 Pulsar/Sentra (E-series engines)**

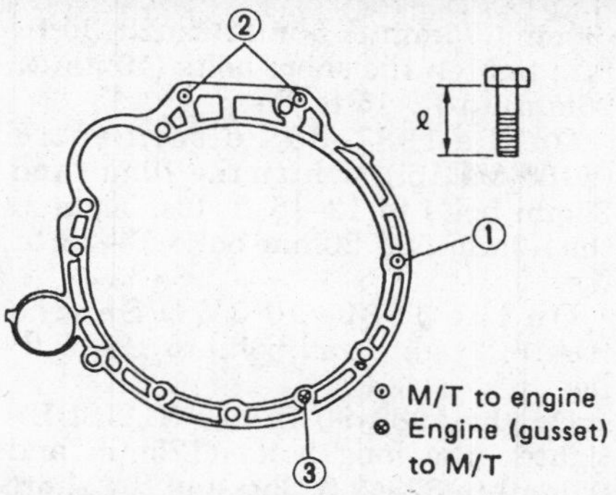


**Bolt 1 (has a nut):125mm, bolt 2:65mm, bolt 3:45mm – 1989–90 Pulsar (CA18DE engine)**

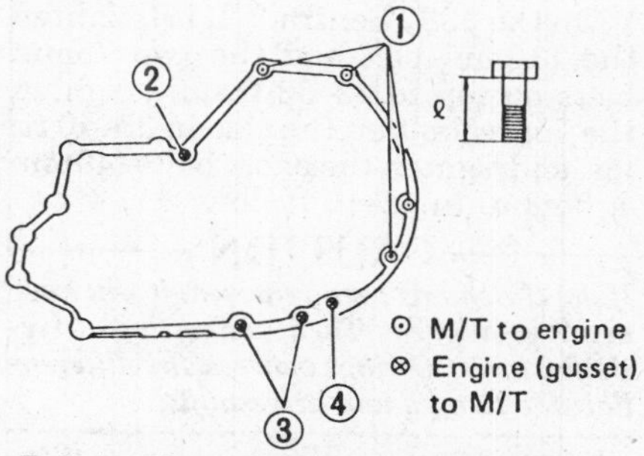


**Bolt 1 – 70mm, bolt 2 – 40mm, bolt 3 – 20mm, bolt 4 – 55mm – 1988–90 Sentra 4WD**

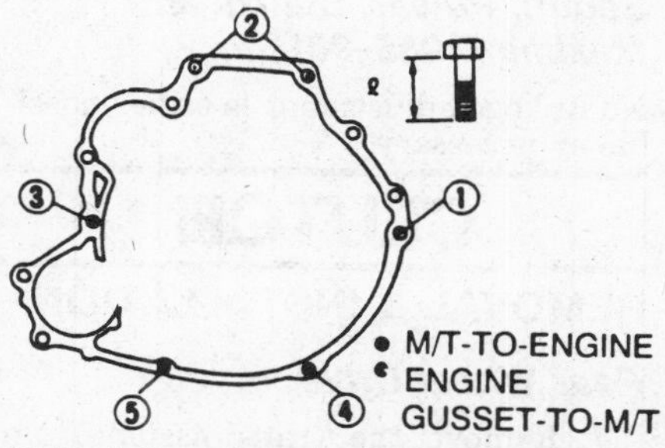


**Bolts 1–3 are long; bolts 4 & 5 are short – 1987–88 Pulsar (CA16DE and CA18DE engines)**

### *Front Wheel Drive*

#### ALL MODELS

**NOTE: You must remove the engine/transaxle as a unit.**

1. Remove the battery and battery holding plate.
2. Jack up the front of the car and safely support with jack stands.
3. Remove the radiator reservoir tank.
4. Drain the transmission gear oil.

**NOTE: Remove the transfer case on the Stanza wagon (4WD) and Sentra (4WD).**

5. Draw out the drive halfshafts from the transaxle. On 1989–90 Maxima, remove the clutch operating cylinder after removing the halfshafts from the transaxle.

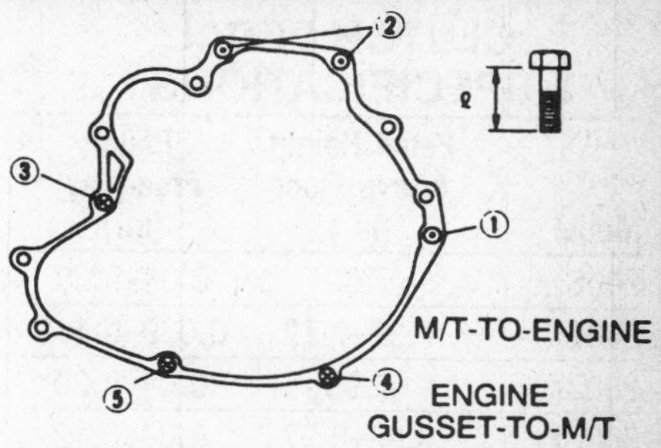


**Bolt 1: 110mm, bolt 2: 75mm, bolt 3: 75mm, bolt 4: 40mm, bolt 5: 25mm – 1987 Sentra (CD17)**

**NOTE: When removing halfshafts, use care not to damage the lip of the oil seal. After shafts are removed, insert a steel bar or wooden dowel of suitable diameter to prevent the side gears from rotating and falling into the differential case.**

6. Remove the wheel house protector.
7. Separate the control rod and support rod from the transaxle.
8. Remove the engine gusset securing bolt and the engine mounting.
9. Remove the clutch control cable from the withdrawal lever.
10. Disconnect speedometer cable from the transaxle.
11. Disconnect the wires from the reverse (back-up) and neutral switches. On 1989–90 Maxima, disconnect the speed and position switch sensors from the transaxle.
12. Support the engine by placing a jack under the oil pan, with a wooden block placed between the jack and pan for protection.
13. Support the transaxle with a hydraulic floor jack.
14. Remove the engine mounting securing bolts.
15. Remove the bolts attaching the transaxle to the engine.
16. Using the hydraulic floor jack as a carrier, carefully lower the transaxle down and away from the car.

**CAUTION**

***Be careful not to strike any adjacent parts or input shaft (the shaft protruding from the transaxle which fits into the clutch assembly) when removing the transaxle from the car.***

Installation of the transaxle is in the reverse order of removal, but pay attention to the following points:

17. Before installing, clean the mating surfaces on the engine rear plate and clutch housing. On 1988–90 Sentra 4wd, apply sealant (KP510-00150 or equivalent) to the shaded area shown in the illustration.
18. Apply a light coat of a lithium-

## CLUTCH PEDAL SPECIFICATIONS

| Model | Pedal Height Above Floor (in.) | Pedal Free-play (in.) |
|---|---|---|
| 200SX | 7.60 | 0.04–0.20 |
| 240SX | 7.32–7.72 | 0.039–0.118 |
| 280ZX | 7.99 | 0.04–0.20 |
| 300ZX | 7.68–8.07 | 0.04–0.12 |
| 1983–84 810, Maxima | 6.90 | 0.40–0.20 |
| 1985–88 Maxima | 6.73–7.13 | 0.04–0.12 |
| 1989–90 Maxima | 6.50–6.89 | 0.04–0.12 |
| 310, Pulsar 1983–84 Sentra | 8.00 | 0.43–0.83 |
| 1985 Sentra | 8.30 | 0.43–0.70 |
| 1986 Sentra | 7.90 | 0.43–0.70 |
| 1987–90 Sentra, Pulsar | 6.38–6.77 | 0.49–0.68 |
| Stanza Sedan | | |
| 1983–84 | 6.05 | 0.43–0.63 |
| 1985–86 | 6.22 | 0.47–0.67 |
| 1987–90 | 6.73 | 0.04–0.12 |
| Stanza Wagon | 9.50 | 0.04–0.12 |

based grease to the spline parts of the clutch disc and the transaxle input shaft.

19. Remove the filler plug and fill the transaxle with 4⅞ U.S. pints (4 speed) and 5¾ U.S. pints (5 speed) of a quality API GL-4 rating. Fill to the level of the plug hole (refer to "Capacities" chart at the beginning of this section).

20. Apply a thread sealant to the threads of the filler plug and install the plug in the transaxle case. Tighten the bolts securing the transaxle to the engine to 12–15 ft. lbs.

On the 1987–90 Stanza sedan, tighten the long bolts (120mm, 70mm & 65mm) to 32–43 ft. lbs. Tighten the short bolts (25mm) to 22–30 ft. lbs.

On the 1984–88 Maxima, tighten the long bolts (65mm, 60mm &55mm) to 32–43 ft. lbs. Tighten the short bolts (25mm) to 22–30 ft. lbs. (No. 4 in the illustration) or 12–15 ft. lbs. (No. 5 in the illustration). On 1989–90 Maxima tighten bolt 1 (25mm) to 12–15 ft. lbs., bolt 2 (25mm) to 22–30 ft. lbs., bolts 3 and 4 (55mm and 65mm) to 32–43 ft. lbs.

On the 1987–88 Pulsar (CA16DE and CA18DE) tighten the long bolts (90mm, 75mm & 55mm) to 22–30 ft. lbs.; tighten the short bolts (40mm & 25mm) to 12–15 ft. lbs.

On the 1987–88 Pulsar/Sentra (E16S & E16i), tighten the 70mm and 25mm bolts to 12–15 ft. lbs. Tighten the 40mm and 20mm bolts 14–22 ft. lbs.

On the 1989–90 2WD Sentra (GA16i), tighten all bolts to 12–15 ft. lbs.

On the 1989–90 Pulsar (CA18DE), tighten the long bolts (125mm and 65mm) to 32–43 ft. lbs. and the short bolt (45mm) to 22–30 ft. lbs.

On the 1988–90 Sentra 4WD, torque all the bolts to 22–30 ft. lbs.

On the 1987 Sentra (CD17), tighten the 110mm bolt and the two 75mm bolts on top to 22–30 ft. lbs.; tighten the 75mm bolt on the side to 33–40 ft. lbs. and tighten the short bolts (40mm & 25mm) to 12–16 ft. lbs.

**CAUTION**

***If the clutch has been removed, it will have to be re-aligned. Then connecting driveshafts, insert O-rings between the differential side flanges and driveshafts.***

## LINKAGE ADJUSTMENT

### *Sentra, Pulsar, Stanza and Maxima (1985–90)*

No linkage adjustment is either possible or necessary.

# CLUTCH

## REMOVAL & INSTALLATION

### *Rear Wheel Drive*

1. Remove the transmission from the engine.
2. Insert a clutch aligning bar or similar tool all the way into the clutch disc hub. This must be done so as to support the weight of the clutch disc during removal. Mark the clutch assembly-to-flywheel relationship with paint or a center punch so that the clutch assembly can be assembled in the same position from which it is removed.
3. Loosen the bolts in sequence, a turn at a time. Remove the bolts.
4. Remove the pressure plate and clutch disc.
5. Remove the release mechanism. Apply multi-purpose grease to the bearing sleeve inside groove, the contact point of the withdrawal lever and bearing sleeve, the contact surface of the lever ball pin and lever. Replace the release mechanism.
6. Inspect the pressure plate for wear, scoring, etc., and reface or replace as necessary. Inspect the release bearing and replace as necessary. Apply a small amount of grease to the transmission splines. Install the disc on the splines and slide it back and forth a few times. Remove the disc and remove any excess grease on the hub. Be sure no grease contacts the disc or pressure plate.
7. Install the disc, aligning it with a splined dummy shaft.
8. Install the pressure plate and torque the bolts to 16–22 ft. lbs.
9. Remove the dummy shaft.
10. Replace the transmission.

### *Front Wheel Drive*

1. Remove transaxle from engine.
2. Insert Nissan clutch aligning tool or a similar splined clutch tool into the clutch disc hub.
3. Loosen the bolts attaching the clutch cover to the flywheel, one turn each at a time, until the spring pressure is released.

**NOTE: Be sure to turn them out in a even crisscross pattern.**

4. Remove the clutch disc and cover assembly.
5. Inspect the pressure plate or scoring for roughness, and reface or replace as necessary (slight roughness can be smoothed with a fine emery cloth). Inspect the clutch disc for worn or oily facings, loose rivets and broken or loose springs, and replace.
6. Apply a light coat of a molybdenum-disulfide grease to the transaxle input shaft spline. Slide the clutch disc on the input shaft several times to distribute the grease. Remove the clutch disc and wipe off the excess lubricant pushed off by the disc hub.

**CAUTION**

***Take special care to prevent any grease or oil from getting on the clutch facing. During assembly, keep all disc facings, flywheel and pressure plate clean and dry. Grease, oil or dirt on these parts will result in a slipping clutch when assembled.***

7. Install the clutch cover assembly. Each bolt should be tightened one turn at a time in a criss-cross pattern. Torque the bolts to 16–22 ft. lbs.
8. Remove the clutch aligning tool.
9. Reinstall the transaxle.

## CLUTCH LINKAGE ADJUSTMENT

### *Hydraulic Clutch*

Refer to the "Clutch Specifications" chart for clutch pedal height above floor and pedal free-play.

Pedal height is usually adjusted with a stopper limiting the upward travel of the pedal. Pedal free-play is adjusted at the master cylinder pushrod. If the pushrod is non-adjustable,

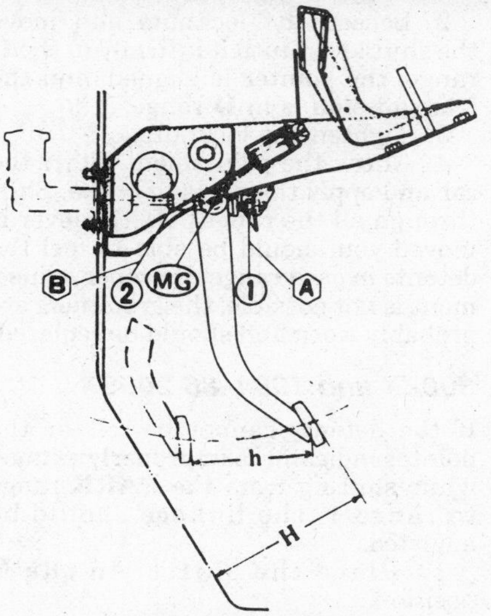


1. Adjust pedal height here
2. Adjust pedal free-play here
MG. Lubricate with multipurpose grease here
H. is pedal height
h. is free play

Clutch adjusting points

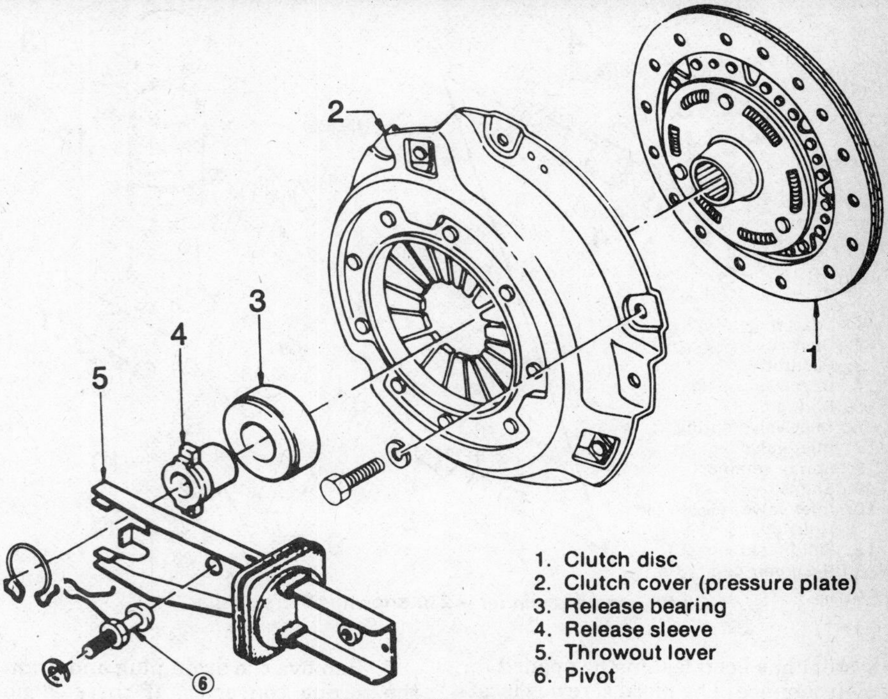


1. Clutch disc
2. Clutch cover (pressure plate)
3. Release bearing
4. Release sleeve
5. Throwout lover
6. Pivot

Typical clutch assembly

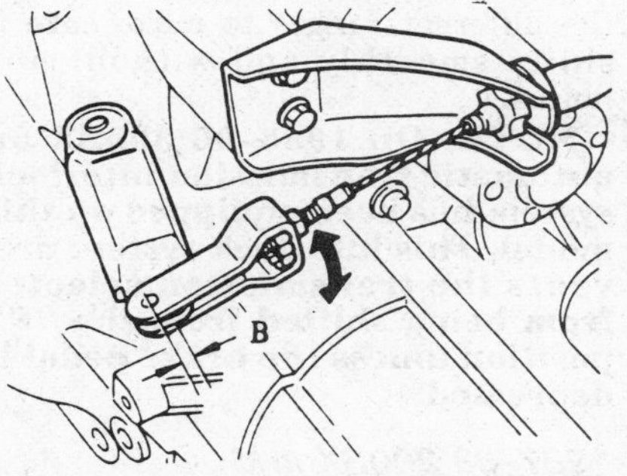


Clutch withdrawal lever adjustment—Sentra, Pulsar, Stanza; arrow shows locknut adjustment

free-play is adjusted by placing shims between the master cylinder and the firewall. On a few models, pedal free-play can also be adjusted at the operating (slave) cylinder pushrod.

## Mechanical Clutch

All 1983–90 front wheel drive models (except the Maxima, 1987–90 Stanza sedans and all Stanza wagons) use a mechanical clutch. Check pedal height and free travel, adjust if necessary. Refer to the "Clutch Specifications" chart for proper adjustment specifications.

1. Loosen the locknut and adjust the pedal height by means of the pedal stopper. Tighten the locknut.
2. Adjust withdrawal lever play at the lever tip end with the locknuts.
3. Depress and release the clutch pedal several times and then recheck the withdrawal lever play again. Readjust if necessary.
4. Measure the pedal free travel at the center of the pedal pad.

## Clutch Master Cylinder

### REMOVAL & INSTALLATION

1. Disconnect the clutch pedal arm from the pushrod.
2. Disconnect the clutch hydraulic line from the master cylinder. Plug the end of line.

**NOTE: Take precautions to keep brake fluid from coming in contact with any painted surfaces.**

3. Remove the nuts attaching the master cylinder and remove the master cylinder and pushrod toward the engine compartment side.
4. Install the master cylinder in the reverse order of removal and bleed the clutch hydraulic system.

## Clutch Slave Cylinder

### REMOVAL & INSTALLATION

1. Remove the slave cylinder attaching bolts and the pushrod from the shift fork.
2. Disconnect the flexible fluid hose from the slave cylinder and remove the unit form the vehicle. Plug the end of the hose.
3. Install the slave cylinder in the reverse order of removal and bleed the clutch hydraulic system.

### HYDRAULIC SYSTEM BLEEDING

Bleeding is required to remove air trapped in the hydraulic system. This operation is necessary whenever the

### CLUTCH PEDAL SPECIFICATIONS

| Model | Pedal Height Above Floor (in.) | Pedal Free-play (in.) |
|---|---|---|
| 200SX | 7.60 | 0.04–0.20 |
| 280ZX | 7.99 | 0.04–0.20 |
| 300ZX | 7.68–8.07 | 0.04–0.12 |
| 1983–84 810, Maxima | 6.90 | 0.40–0.20 |
| 1985–89 Maxima | 6.73–7.13 | 0.04–0.12 |
| Pulsar 1983–84 Sentra | 8.00 | 0.43–0.83 |
| 1985 Sentra | 8.30 | 0.43–0.70 |
| 1986 Sentra | 7.90 | 0.43–0.70 |
| 1987–89 Sentra | 6.38–6.77 | 0.49–0.68 |
| Stanza Sedan | | |
| 1983–84 | 6.05 | 0.43–0.63 |
| 1985–86 | 6.22 | 0.47–0.67 |
| 1987–89 | 6.93 | 0.04–0.12 |
| Stanza Wagon | 9.50 | 0.04–0.12 |

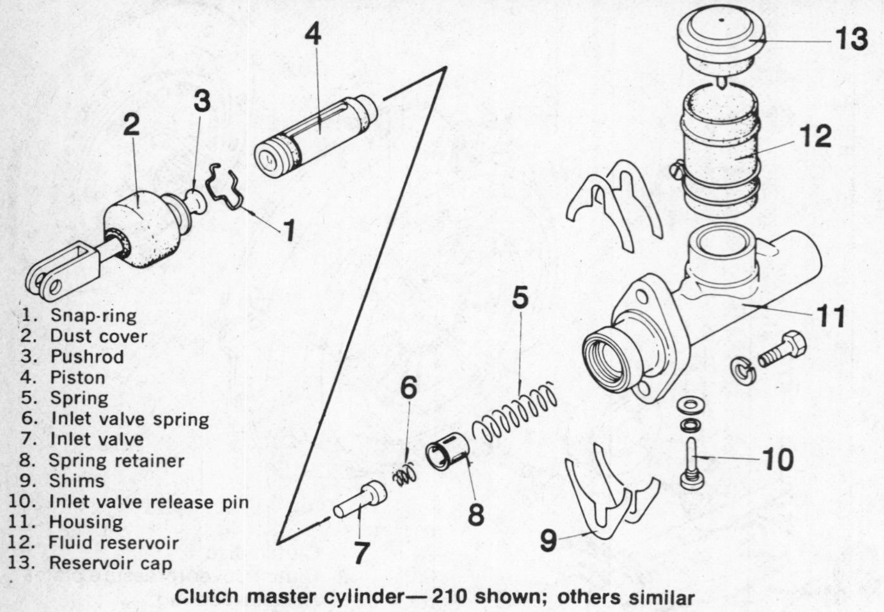


Clutch master cylinder—210 shown; others similar

system has been leaking or opened for maintenance. The bleed screw is located on the clutch operating (slave) cylinder.

1. Remove the bleed screw dust cap.
2. Attach a tube to the bleed screw, immersing the free end in a clean container of brake fluid.
3. Fill the master cylinder with fluid.
4. Open the bleed screw about ¾ turn.
5. Depress the clutch pedal quickly. Hold it down. Have an assistant tighten the bleed screw. Allow the pedal to return slowly. Bleeder screw torque is 5–6 ft. lbs.
6. Repeat Steps 2 and 5 until no more air bubbles are seen in the fluid container.
7. Remove the bleed tube. Replace the dust cap. Refill the master cylinder.

# AUTOMATIC TRANSMISSION

Only external transmission adjustments and repairs, and transmission removal and replacement, are covered in this section.

## REMOVAL & INSTALLATION

1. Disconnect the battery cable.
2. Remove the accelerator linkage.
3. Detach the shift linkage.
4. Disconnect the neutral safety switch and downshift solenoid wiring.
5. Remove the drain plug and drain the torque converter. If there is no converter drain plug, drain the transmission. If there is no transmission drain plug, remove the pan to drain. Replace the pan to keep out dirt.
6. Remove the front exhaust pipe.
7. Remove the vacuum tube and speedometer cable.
8. Disconnect the fluid cooler tubes.
9. Remove the drive shaft and starter.
10. Support the transmission with a jack under the oil pan. Support the engine also.
11. Remove the rear crossmember.
12. Mark the relationship between the torque converter and the drive plate. Remove the 4 bolts holding the converter to the drive plate through the access hole at the front, under the engine by rotating the crankshaft. Unbolt the transmission from the engine.
13. Reverse the procedure for installation. If warped, make sure the drive plate has no more than 0.020 in. runout. Torque the drive plate-to-torque converter and converter housing-to-engine bolts to 29–36 ft. lbs. Drive plate-to-crankshaft bolt torque is 101–116 ft. lbs.
14. Refill the transmission and check the fluid level.

## SHIFT LINKAGE ADJUSTMENT

### *All Models Except 240SX, 300ZX and 1984–88 200SX*

Adjustment is made at the locknuts at the base of the shifter, which control the length of the shift control rod.

1. Place the shift lever in **D**.
2. Loosen the locknuts and move the shift lever until it is firmly in the **D** range, the pointer is aligned, and the transmission is in **D** range.
3. Tighten the locknuts.
4. Check the adjustment. Start the car and apply the parking brake. Shift through all the ranges. As the lever is moved you should be able to feel the detents in each range. If proper adjustment is not possible, the grommets are probably worn and should be replaced.

### *300ZX and 1984–86 200SX*

If the detents cannot be felt or the pointer indicator is improperly aligned while shifting from the **PARK** range to range **1**, the linkage should be adjusted.

1. Place the shifter in the **N** position.
2. Loosen the locknuts.
3. Move the range selector lever at the transmission to the **N** range.
4. Tighten the locknuts when the floor control lever is in the **N** range and pushed against the **P** range side.
5. Shift the control lever through the different ranges to make sure it shifts smoothly and without any noises.

**NOTE: On 1988–90 300ZX an automatic transmission interlock system has been equipped on this model. This interlock system prevents the transmission selector from being shifted from the "P" position unless the brake pedal is depressed.**

### *1987–88 200SX and 1989–90 240SX*

If the detents cannot be felt or the pointer indicator is improperly aligned while shifting from the **P** range to range **1**, the linkage should be adjusted.

1. Place the shifter in the **P** position.
2. Loosen the locknuts.
3. Tighten the outer locknut **X** until it touches the trunnion, pulling the selector lever toward the **R** range side without pushing the button.

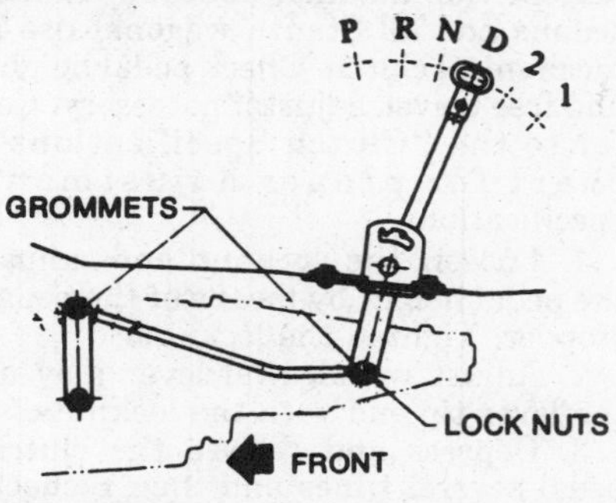


**Automatic transmission linkage adjustment**

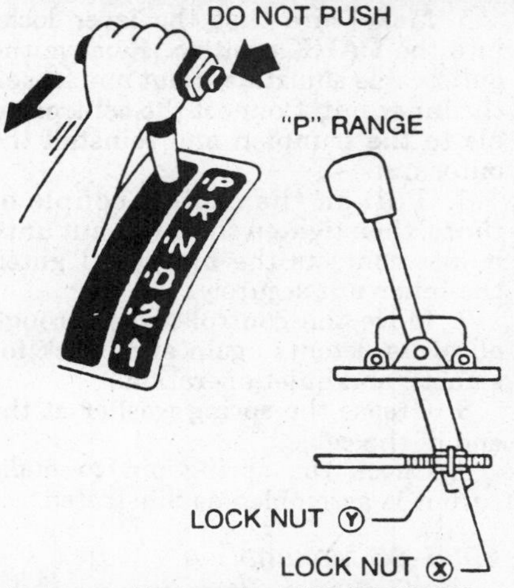


**Linkage adjustment – 1987–89 200SX, 1987–90 300ZX and 1989–90 240SX**

4. Back off the outer locknut **X** ¼–½ turns and then tighten the inner locknut **Y** to 5.8–8.0 ft. lbs. (8–11 Nm).
5. Move the selector lever from **P** to **1**. Make sure it moves smoothly.

## DOWNSHIFT SOLENOID CHECK

The solenoid is controlled by a downshift switch on the accelerator linkage inside the car. To test the switch and solenoid operation:

1. Turn the ignition on.

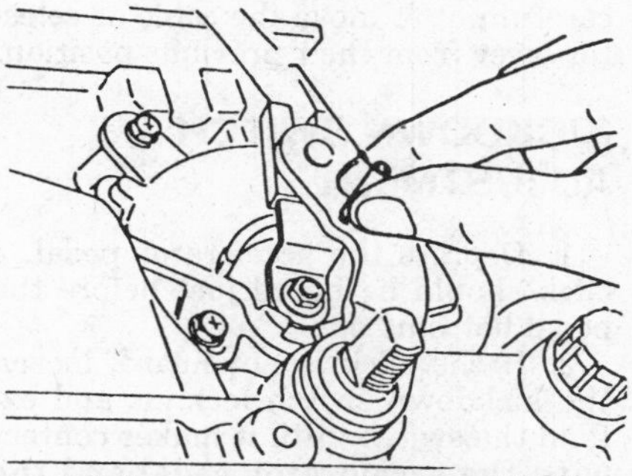

**Inhibitor switch adjustment – 240SX**

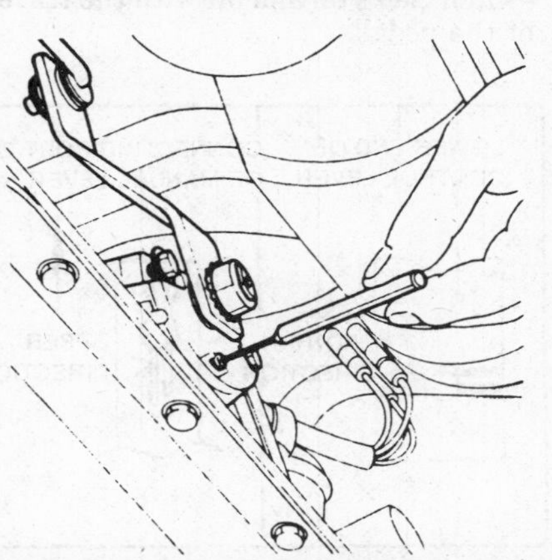

**Neutral saftey and back-up light switch adjustment – 300ZX and 1984–89 200SX**

2. Push the accelerator all the way down to actuate the switch.
3. The solenoid should click when actuated. The solenoid is screwed into the outside of the case. If there is no click, check the switch, wiring, and solenoid.
4. To remove the solenoid, first drain 2–3 pints of fluid, then unscrew the unit

## NEUTRAL SAFETY AND BACK-UP LIGHT SWITCH ADJUSTMENT

The switch unit is bolted to the left side of the transmission shift lever. The switch prevents the engine from being started in any transmission position except **PARK** or **NEUTRAL**. It also controls the back-up lights.

### *Except 240SX*

1. Remove the transmission shift lever retaining nut and the lever.
2. Remove the switch.
3. Remove the machine screw in the case under the switch.
4. Align the switch to the case by inserting a 0.059 in. (0.079 in. 300ZX and 1984–89 200SX) diameter pin through the hole in the switch into the screw hole. Mark the switch location.
5. Remove the pin, replace the machine screw, install the switch as marked, and replace the transmission shift lever and retaining nut.
6. Make sure while holding the brakes on, that the engine will start only in **P** or **NL**. Check that the back-up lights go on only in reverse.

### *240SX*

1. Disconnect the manual control linkage from the manual shaft.
2. Set the manual shaft to the **N** position.
3. Loosen the 3 inhibitor switch mounting screws enough to allow for movement of the switch.

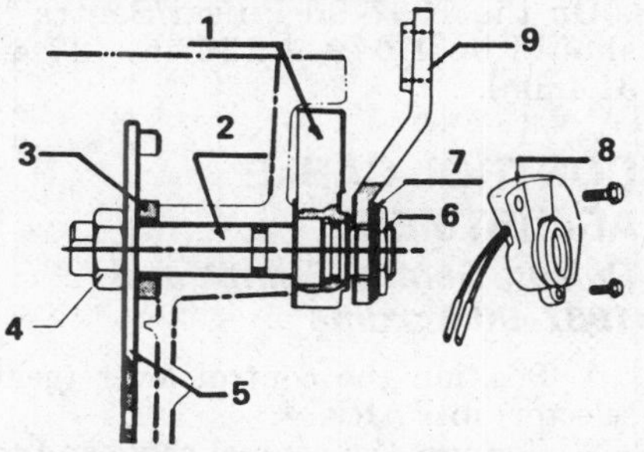


1. Neutral safety switch
2. Manual shaft
3. Washer
4. Nut
5. Manual plate
6. Nut
7. Washer
8. Neutral safety switch
9. Transmission shift lever

**Neutral safety and back-up light switch —JATCO transmission**

4. Insert a 0.157 diameter pin through the locating holes in the inhibitor switch and manual shaft and tighten the switch screws.
5. Remove the pin and reconnect the manual control linkage to the shaft. Check the switch for proper operation.

# AUTOMATIC TRANSAXLE

## REMOVAL & INSTALLATION

### *Pulsar, Sentra, Stanza and 1989–90 Maxima*

1. Disconnect the negative battery cable. Raise and support the vehicle safely.
2. Remove the left front tire and drain the transmission fluid into a suitable container.
3. Remove the left side fender protector and disconnect the halfshafts.

**NOTE: Be careful not to damage the oil seals when removing the driveshafts. After removing the halfshafts, install a suitable bar so that the side gears will not rotate and fall into the differential case.**

4. On Stanza wagon, disconnect and remove the forward exhaust pipe.
5. Disconnect the speedometer cable. Disconnect the throttle wire from the carburetor throttle lever on carbureted models.
6. Remove the control cable rear end from the unit and remove the oil level gauge tube.
7. Place a suitable transmission jack under the transaxle and engine (do not place the jack under the oil pan drain plug).
8. Disconnect the oil cooler tubes and remove the engine motor mount securing bolts.
9. Remove the starter motor and the bolts holding the transaxle to the engine.
10. Slide the rear plate to remove the bolts holding the torque converter, then install 2 or 3 bolts to secure the transaxle to the engine for safety purposes.
11. Remove the bolts securing the torque converter to the drive plate.
12. Before removing the torque converter, place chalk marks on 2 parts for alignment purposes during installation.
13. Move the jack gradually until the transaxle can be lowered and removed from the vehicle through the left side wheel house.

14. Installation is the reverse order of the removal procedure.
15. After installation be sure to add the proper amount of transmission fluid to the transaxle and road test the vehicle.

### *1985–88 Maxima*

**NOTE: The engine/transaxle unit must be removed and installed as a unit. After removal, the transaxle may be separated from the engine.**

1. Remove the transaxle/engine as an assembly.
2. Remove the transaxle-to-engine mounting bolts and then carefully draw out the rear plate.
3. Remove the bolts securing the torque converter to the drive plate.
4. Before removing the torque converter, use chalk or paint to matchmark at least two parts so that they may be replaced in their original positions during installation. Remove the torque converter.
5. Installation is in the reverse order of removal. Take note of the following:
   a. When installing the torque converter to the drive plate, be certain that the matchmarks made during removal are in alignment. Apply Loctite® or a similar sealing compound to the converter-to-drive plate bolts before installation.
   b. After the torque converter has been reinstalled, rotate the crankshaft a few times to ensure that the transaxle rotates freely, with no binding.
   c. Adjust the control cable and check the inhibitor switch as detailed later in this section.
   d. After installation of the engine/transaxle assembly into the vehicle, fill the transaxle and engine with the proper amounts of fluids and then road test the vehicle.

## THROTTLE WIRE ADJUSTMENT

The throttle wire is adjusted by means of double nuts on the carburetor or throttle side.

**NOTE: On 1989–90 Maxima, there is no throttle wire adjustment.**

1. Loosen the adjusting nuts.
2. With the throttle fully opened **($P_1$)**, turn the threaded shaft **(Q)** inward as far as it will go **(T)** and then tighten the first nut **(B)** against the bracket **(S)**.
3. Back off the first nut **(B)** 1–1½ turns on the 1983–86 Stanza; ¾–1¼ turns on the 1984–88 Maxima; and 2¾–3¼ turns on the 1987–90 Stanza

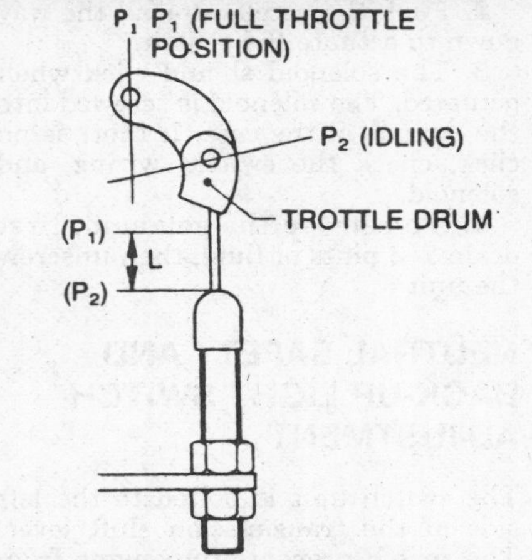

**Throttle wire stroke—Pulsar, Sentra, Stanza and 1987–90 Maxima**

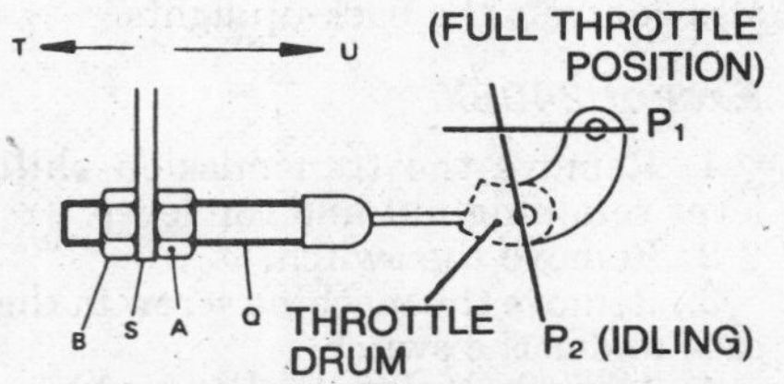

**Throttle wire adjustment—typical**

(inc. 1986 wagon) and then tighten the second nut **(A)** against the bracket. On Pulsar back off nut **B** 2¾–3¼ turns (RL4F02A transaxles) and 1–1½ turns (RL3F01A transaxles) in direction **T** and tighten nut **A**.
4. Tighten both double nuts to 5.8–7.2 ft. lbs. (8–10 Nm). The throttle drum should be held securely in the full open position.
5. On pre-1985 models, check that the throttle wire stroke between the threaded shaft and the throttle drum is 1.079–1.236 in.

On 1987–90 Stanza and and 1987–88 Maxima models, check that the throttle wire stroke **(L)** between full throttle and idling is 1.54–1.69 in. (39–43mm).

On the 1987–90 Pulsar/Sentra it should be 1.079–1.236 in. (27.4–31.4mm).

## CONTROL CABLE ADJUSTMENT

### *Pulsar, Sentra, Stanza and 1987–90 Maxima*

1. Position the control lever (gear selector) in **PARK**.
2. Connect the control cable end to the lever in the transaxle unit and tighten the cable securing bolt.
3. Move the control lever to the **1** position. Be certain that the lever works smoothly and quietly.
4. Position the lever in **PARK** once again.
5. Make sure that the lever locks into the **PARK** position. Remove the outer cable adjustment nut and loosen the inner nut. Connect the control cable to the trunnion and reinstall the outer nut.
6. Pull on the cable a couple of times, then tighten the outer nut until it just contacts the bracket. Tighten the inner nut securely.
7. Move the control lever through all of its detents again and check for smooth and quiet operation.
8. Grease the spring washer at the end of the cable.
9. Check the spring pin to make sure it is assembled as illustrated.

### *1985–86 Maxima*

1. Release the parking brake.
2. Disconnect the control cable from the gear selector lever and then pull it forward so as to place the manual lever on the transaxle in the **P** position.
3. Make certain that the halfshafts will not rotate. To do this, attempt to rotate both shafts in the same direction at the same time.
4. Loosen the 2 trunnion nuts at the forward edge of the cable.
5. Check that the selector lever moves smoothly and quietly through its range of detents, place it in the **P** position and then reconnect the control cable to the lever.
6. Tighten the 2 trunnion nuts. Be careful not to move the cable or selector lever from their previous position.

## KICKDOWN SWITCH ADJUSTMENT

1. Depress the accelerator pedal, a click should be heard just before the pedal bottoms out.
2. If the click is not heard, loosen the kickdown switch locknut and extend the switch until it makes contact with the accelerator pedal and the switch clicks on and off with the travel of the pedal.

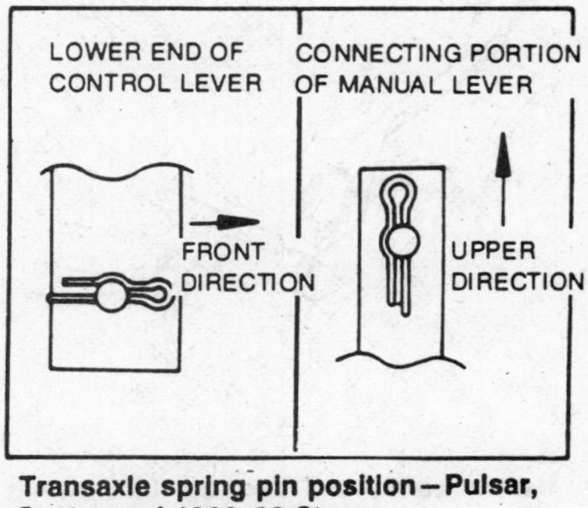

**Transaxle spring pin position—Pulsar, Sentra and 1983–86 Stanza**

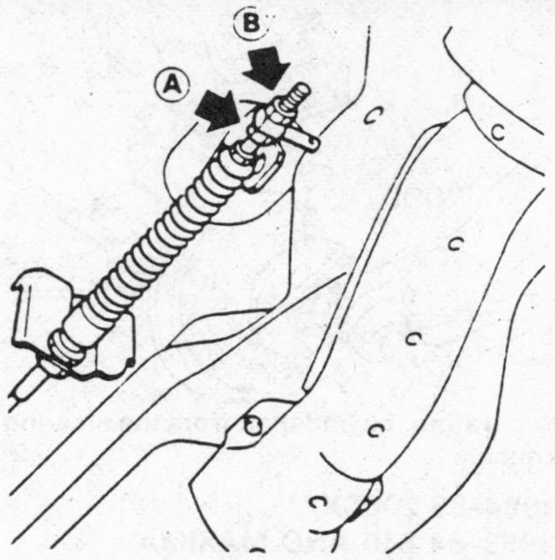


Control cable adjustment – 1985-86 Maxima

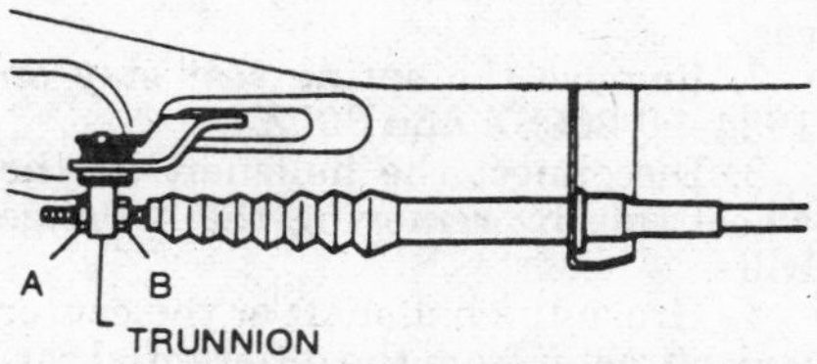


**Automatic transaxle cable adjustment— Sentra, Stanza, Pulsar**

## NEUTRAL SAFETY SWITCH ADJUSTMENT

1. Locate the neutral safety switch on the side of the transaxle and loosen (but don't remove) the mounting screws.
2. Set the manual selector shaft (NOT the gear selector lever) on the transaxle to the **N** position.
3. Insert a small pin (0.16 in – Maxima and 1987–90 Stanza including 1986 wagon); 0.098 in. – all others) through the adjustment holes of both the switch and the switch lever so that it is perpendicular to them.
4. Tighten the switch mounting screws.

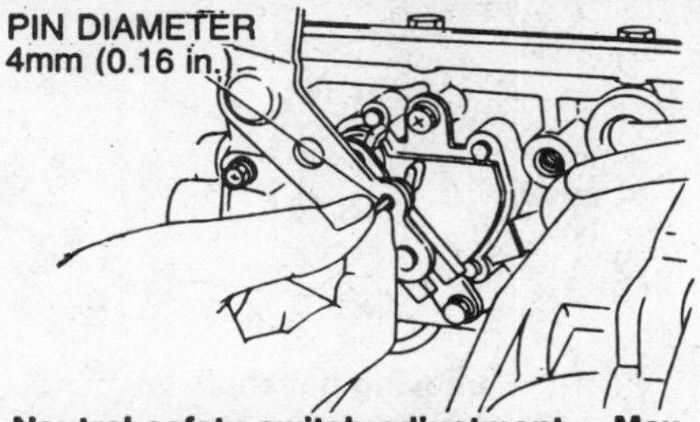


**Neutral safety switch adjustment— Maxima shown; others typical**

# TRANSFER CASE

## REMOVAL & INSTALLATION

### *Sentra (4WD) and Stanza Wagon (4WD) Only*

1. Drain the gear oil from the transaxle and the transfer case.
2. Disconnect and remove the forward exhaust pipe.
3. Using chalk or paint, matchmark the flanges on the driveshaft and then unbolt and remove the driveshaft from the transfer case as detailed later in this section.
4. Unbolt and remove the transaxle support rod from the transfer case on the Sentra.
5. Unbolt and remove the transfer control actuator from the side of the transfer case (not required on 1989–90 Sentra).
6. Disconnect and remove the right side halfshaft.
7. Unscrew and withdraw the speedometer pinion gear from the transfer case. Position it out of the way and secure it with wire.
8. Unbolt and remove the front, rear and side transfer case gussets (support members).
9. Use an hydraulic floor jack and a block of wood to support the transfer case, remove the transfer case-to-transaxle mounting bolts and then remove the case itself. Be careful when moving it while supported on the jack.
10. Installation is in the reverse order of removal. Tighten the transfer case-to-transaxle mounting bolts and the transfer case gusset mounting bolts to 22–30 ft. lbs. (30–40 Nm) on 1988 models. On 1989–90 Sentra, torque the transfer rear gusset bolts to 29–36 ft. lbs. (39–49 Nm).

Be sure to use a multi-purpose grease to lubricate all oil seal surfaces prior to reinstallation, the transfer case and the transaxle use different types and weights of lubricant.

# DRIVE AXLE

## Halfshafts

### REMOVAL & INSTALLATION

#### *Front Wheel Drive*

**ALL EXCEPT 1987–90 PULSAR AND SENTRA, STANZA WAGON, 1987–90 STANZA AND 1985–90 MAXIMA**

1. Jack up the car and support it with jack stands.
2. Remove the wheel and tire assembly.
3. Remove the brake caliper assembly.
4. Pry off the cotter pin from the castellated nut on the wheel hub.
5. Loosen, but do not remove, the wheel hub nut from the halfshaft while holding the wheel hub with a suitable tool.
6. Remove the tie rod ball joint. Remove the lower ball joint. 'Do not reuse the nut once it has been removed;' install a new nut during assembly.
7. Drain the gear oil from the transaxle.
8. Remove the bolts holding the halfshaft flange to the transaxle. Remove the halfshaft, along with the wheel hub and knuckle.
9. Insert a suitable bar, wooden dowel or similar tool into the transaxle to prevent the side gear from dropping inside.

**CAUTION**

***When removing the transaxle, be very careful not to damage the grease seal on the transaxle side.***

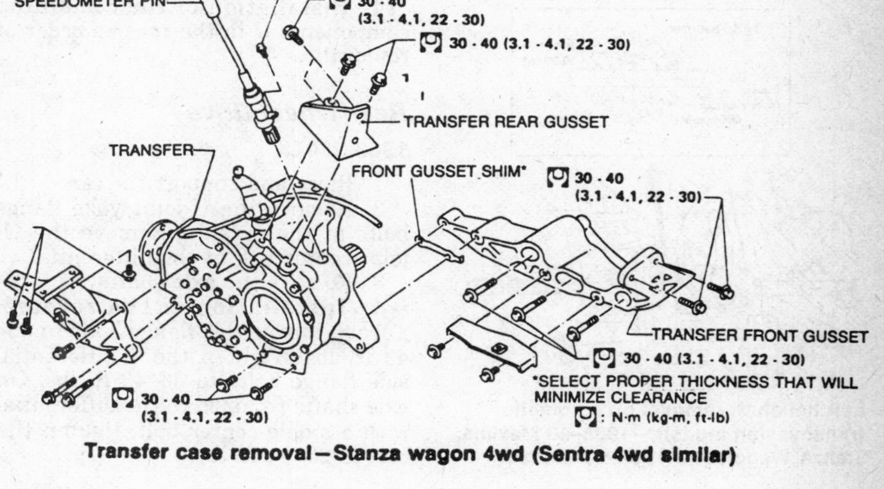


**Transfer case removal – Stanza wagon 4wd (Sentra 4wd similar)**

10. Installation is the reverse of removal. Coat the transaxle-end halfshaft spline with a molybdenum-disulfide grease before insertion. Make sure the rubber boots on both ends of the halfshaft are in good shape; it not, replace them (use new metal bands to retain the boots).

### 1987–90 PULSAR and SENTRA, STANZA WAGON, 1987–90 STANZA AND 1985–90 MAXIMA

**NOTE: Installation of the halfshafts will require a special tool for the spline alignment of the halfshaft end and the transaxle case. Do not perform this procedure without access to this tool. The Kent Moore tool Number is J-34296 and J-34297 or J-33904 for Maxima.**

1. Raise the front of the vehicle and support it with jack stands.
2. Remove the wheel and tire assembly.
3. Pull out the cotter pin from the castellated nut on the wheel hub and then remove the wheel bearing lock nut. Remove and suport the brake caliper assembly without disconnecting the brake line.
4. Separate the halfshaft from the steering knuckle by tapping it with a block of wood and a mallet.
5. Remove the tie rod ball joint. Remove the three mounting nuts for the lower ball joint and then pull it down.

**NOTE: Always use a new nut when replacing the tie rod ball joint.**

6. Using a suitable tool, reach through the engine crossmember and carefully tap the right side inner CV-joint out of the transaxle case.
7. Using a block of wood on an hydraulic floor jack, support the engine under the oil pan.

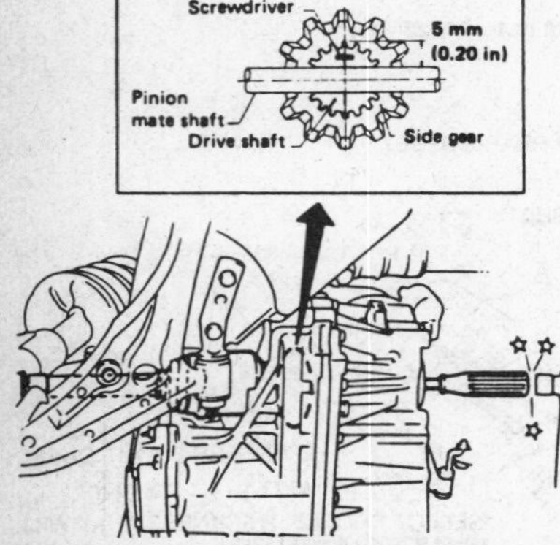


**Left halfshaft removal on automatic transmission models – 1985–90 Maxima, Stanza Wagon and 1987–90 Stanza**

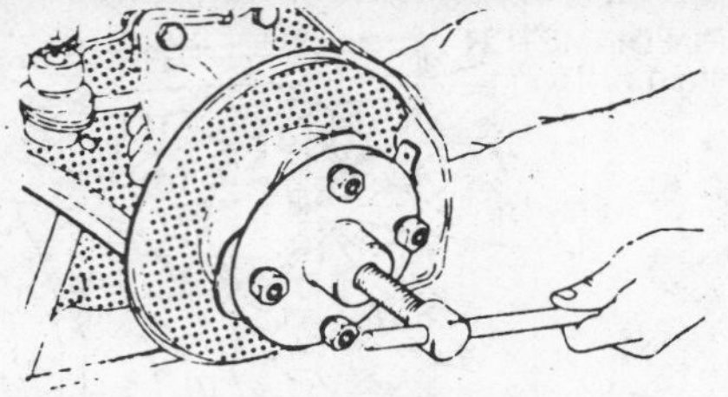

**Removing halfshaft**

8. Remove the support bearing bracket and bearing retainer bolts from the engine and then withdraw the right halfshaft (except Pulsar with E16i and GA16i and Sentra).
9. On models with manual transaxles, carefully insert a small prybar between the left CV-joint inner flange and the transaxle case mounting surface and pry the half shaft out of the case. Withdraw the shaft from the steering knuckle and remove it.
10. On models with automatic transaxles, insert a dowel through the right side halfshaft hole and use a small mallet to tap the left halfshaft out of the transaxle case. Withdraw the shaft from the steering knuckle and remove it.

**CAUTION**

***Be careful not to damage the pinion mating shaft and the side gear while tapping the left halfshaft out of the transaxle case.***

11. When installing the shafts into the transaxle, use a new oil seal and then install an alignment tool along the inner circumference of the oil seal.
12. Insert the halfshaft into the transaxle, align the serrations and then remove the alignment tool.
13. Push the halfshaft, then press-fit the circular clip on the shaft into the clip groove on the side gear.

**NOTE: After insertion, attempt to pull the flange out of the side joint to make sure that the circular clip is properly seated in the side gear and will not come out.**

14. Installation of the remaining components is in the reverse order of removal.

### *Rear Wheel Drive*

### 1983 280ZX

1. Raise and support the car.
2. Remove the U-joint yoke flange bolts at the outside. Remove the U-joint center bolt at the differential.
3. Remove the axle shaft.
4. Installation is the reverse. Torque the outside flange bolts to 36–43 ft. lbs. Tighten the 4 differential side flange bolts to 36–43 ft. lbs. On axle shafts retained to the differential with a single center bolt, tighten the bolt to 23–31 ft. lbs.

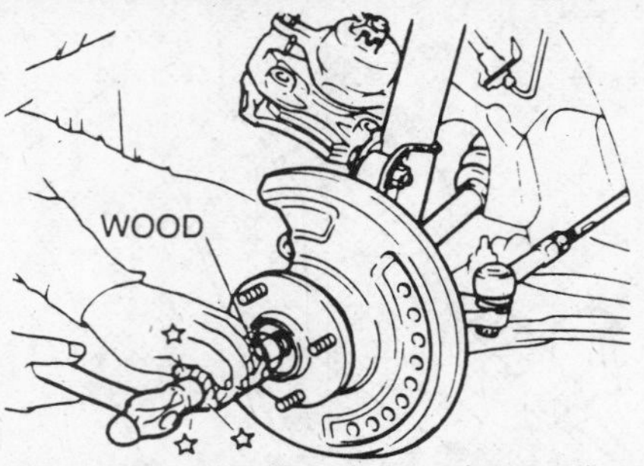


**Separating the halfshaft from the steering knuckle**

### 1984–88 200SX, 1983–84 810 AND MAXIMA, AND 1984–90 280ZX AND 300ZX

1. Raise and support the rear of the car.
2. Remove the spring seat stay on 1984–90 200SX and 300ZX.
3. Disconnect the halfshaft on the wheel side by removing the 4 flange bolts.
4. Grasp the halfshaft at the center and extract if from the differential carrier by prying it with a suitable pry bar.
5. Installation is in the reverse order of removal. Install the differential end first and then the wheel end. Tighten the 4 flange bolts to 20–27 ft. lbs.

**CAUTION**

***Take care not to damage the oil seal or either end of the halfshaft during installation.***

## CV-JOINT OVERHAUL

**For information on CV-Joints, please refer to "CV-Joint Overhaul" in the Unit Repair Section.**

# Driveshaft and U-Joints

## REMOVAL & INSTALLATION

### *200SX with Automatic Transmission, 240SX, 280ZX and 300ZX*

These driveshafts are the one piece type with a U-joint and flange at the rear. A U-joint and a splined sleeve yoke which fits into the rear of the transmission, at the front. The U-joints must be disassembled for lubrication at 24,000 mile intervals if no grease fittings are present. The splines are lubricated by transmission oil.

1. Release the handbrake.
2. The front pipe and the heat shield plate must come off on 280ZX models sold in California, and all 300ZXs.

3. Matchmark the flanges on the driveshaft and differential so that the driveshaft can be reinstalled in its original orientation; this will help maintain driveline balance.
4. Unbolt the rear flange.
5. Pull the driveshaft down and back.
6. Plug the transmission extension housing.
7. Reverse the procedure to install, oiling the splines. Flange bolt torque for 200SX – 29–33 ft. lbs., 240SX – 17–24 ft. lbs., 280ZX and 300ZX – 25–33 ft. lbs.

#### *4WD Sentra, 4WD Stanza Wagon, 200SX with Automatic Transmission and 1983–84 810 and Maxima*

These models use a driveshaft with 3 U-joints and a center support bearing. The driveshaft is balanced as an assembly. It is not recommended that it be disassembled.
1. Mark the relationship of the driveshaft flange to the differential flange.
2. Unbolt the center bearing bracket.
3. Unbolt the driveshaft flange from the differential flange.
4. Pull the driveshaft back under the rear axle. Plug the rear of the transmission to prevent oil or fluid loss.
5. On installation, align the marks made in Step 1. Torque the flange bolts to 17–24 ft. lbs. Center bearing bracket both torque is 26–35 ft. lbs.

### CENTER BEARING REPLACEMENT

The center bearing is a sealed unit which must be replaced as an assembly if defective.
1. Remove the driveshaft.
2. Paint a matchmark across where the flanges behind the center yoke are joined. This is for assembly purposes. If you don't paint or somehow mark the relationship between the 2 shafts, they may be out of balance when you put them back together.
3. Remove the bolts and separate the shafts. Make a matchmark on the front driveshaft half which lines up with the mark on the flange half.
4. Devise a way to hold the driveshaft while unbolting the companion flange from the front driveshaft. Do not place the front driveshaft tube in a vise. The best way is to grip the flange while loosening the nut with a suitable spanner wrench that is capable of mating with the 4 holes of the companion flange. It is going to require some strength to remove regardless of the method.
5. Press the companion flange off the front driveshaft and press the center bearing from its mount or use a puller.
6. The new bearing is already lubricated. Install it into the mount, making sure that the seals and so on are facing the same way as when removed.
7. Slide the companion flange onto the front driveshaft, aligning the marks made during removal. On 240SX and Sentra, position the **F** mark on the ceneter bearing towards the front of the vehicle. Install a new washer and locknut. If the washer and locknut are separate pieces, tighten them to 145-175 ft. lbs. If they are a unit, tighten it to 180–217 ft. lbs. Check that the bearing rotates freely around the driveshaft. Stake the nut.
8. Connect the companion flange to the other half of the driveshaft, aligning the marks made during removal. Tighten the bolts securely.
9. Install the driveshaft.

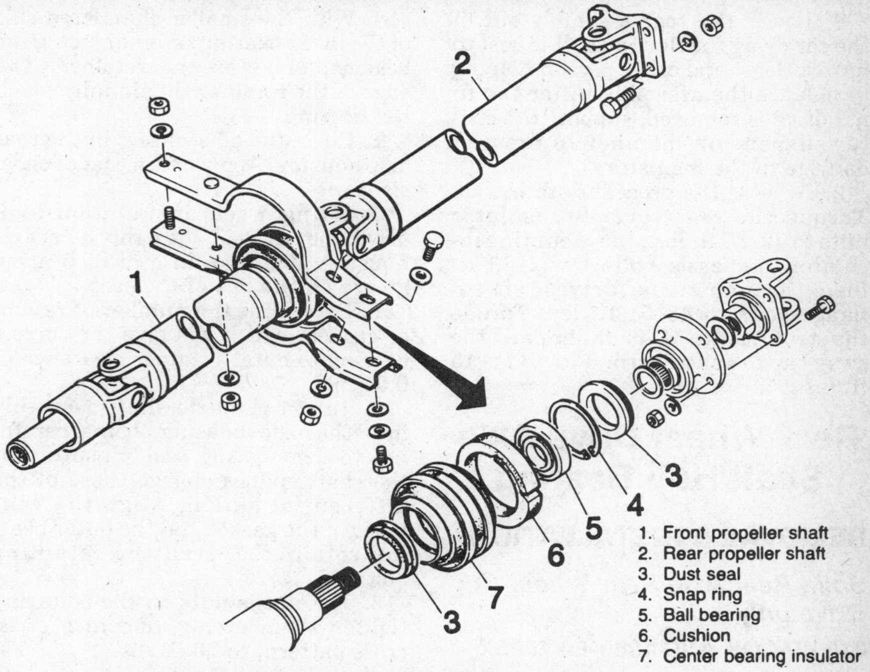


**Two piece driveshaft with center bearing and three U-joints**

## Differential Independent Rear Suspension

### REMOVAL & INSTALLATION

#### *280ZX and 1983–84 810 and Maxima Sedan*

1. Jack up the rear of the car and drain the oil from the differential.
2. Disconnect the driveshaft.
3. Disconnect the halfshafts.
4. Remove the side flange fixing bolts, and disconnect the flange yokes together with the halfshafts. Support the case with a jack.
5. Remove the 4 bolts retaining the case to the suspension carrier.
6. Pull the case backwards on the jack until clear of the car.
7. After the case is removed, support the suspension on a stand to prevent damage.
8. Installation is the reverse. Tighten the rear cover-to-insulator nuts to 65–87 ft. lbs., the case-to-suspension bolts to 43–58 ft. lbs., and the side flange and driveshaft bolts to 36–43 ft. lbs.

#### *4WD Sentra, 4WD Stanza Wagon, 240SX and 300ZX*

1. Jack up the rear of the car and drain the oil from the differential. Support with jack stands. Position the floor jack underneath the differential unit.
2. Disconnect the brake hydraulic lines and the parking brake cable. On 240SX, remove the brake caliper leaving the brake line connected.
3. Disconnect the sway bar from the control arms on either sides.
4. Remove the rear exhaust tube.
5. Disconnect the driveshaft and the rear axle shafts.
6. Remove the rear shock absorbers from the control arms.
7. Unbolt the differential unit from the chassis, at the differential mounting insulator.

8. Lower the rear assembly out of the car using the floor jack. It is best to have at least one other person helping to balance the assembly. After the final drive is removed, support the center suspension member to prevent damage to the insulators.

9. Reverse the procedure to install. Torque the rear cover-to-insulator nuts to 72–87 ft. lbs.; the mounting insulator-to-chassis bolts to 22–29 ft. lbs.; the non-turbo driveshaft-to-flange bolts to 43–51 ft. lbs. Torque the strut nuts to 51–65 ft. lbs.; and the sway bar-to-control arm nuts to 12–15 ft. lbs.

## Rear Wheel Drive Axle Shaft/Hub Bearing

### REMOVAL & INSTALLATION

#### *Solid Rear Axle/Rear Wheel Drive only*

#### 810 WAGON AND 1983–84 200SX

**NOTE: Bearings must be pressed on and off the shaft with an arbor press. Unless you have access to one, it is inadvisable to attempt any repair work on the axle shaft and bearing assemblies.**

1. Remove the hubcap or wheel cover. Loosen the lug nuts.
2. Raise the rear of the car and support it safely on stands.
3. Remove the rear wheel. Remove the 4 brake backing plate retaining nuts. Detach the parking brake linkage from the brake backing plate.
4. Attach a slide hammer to the axle shaft and remove it. Use the slide hammer and a two-pronged puller to remove the oil seal from the housing.

**NOTE: If a slide hammer is not available, the axle can sometimes be pried out using pry bars on opposing sides of the hub.**

If endplay is found to be excessive, the bearing should be replaced. Shimming the bearing is not recommended as this ignores end-play of the bearing itself and could result in improper seating of the bearing.

5. Using a chisel, carefully nick the bearing retainer in three or four places. The retainer does not have to be cut, only collapsed enough to allow the bearing retainer to be slid off the shaft.
6. Pull or press the old bearing off and install the new one by pressing it into position.
7. Install the outer bearing retainer with its raised surface facing the wheel hub, and then install the bearing an the inner bearing retainer in that order on the axle shaft.
8. With the smaller chamfered side of the inner bearing retainer facing the bearing, press on the retainer. The edge of the retainer should fully touch the bearing.
9. Clean the oil seal seat in the rear axle housing. Apply a thin coat of chassis grease.
10. Using a seal installation tool, drive the oil seal into the rear axle housing. Wipe a thin coat of bearing grease on the lips of the seal.
11. Determine the number of retainer gaskets which will give the correct bearing-to-outer retainer clearance of 0.01 in.
12. Insert the axle shaft assembly into the axle housing, being careful not to damage the seal. Ensure that the shaft splines engage those of the differential pinion. Align the vent holes of the gasket and the outer bearing retainer. Install the retaining bolts.
13. Install the nuts on the bolts and tighten them evenly, and in a criss-cross pattern, to 20 ft. lbs.

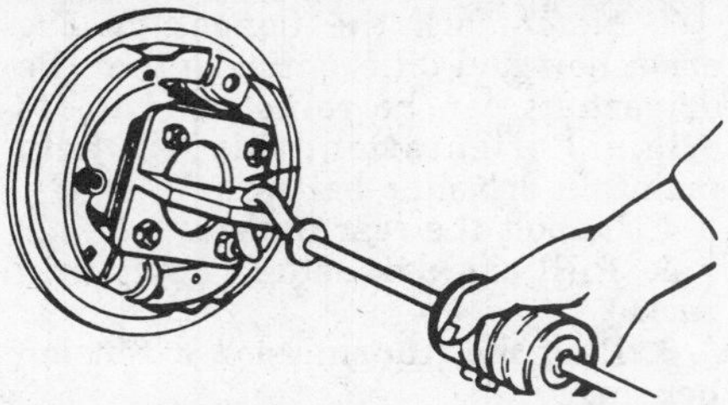

Use a slide hammer to remove the axle shaft—solid rear axle models

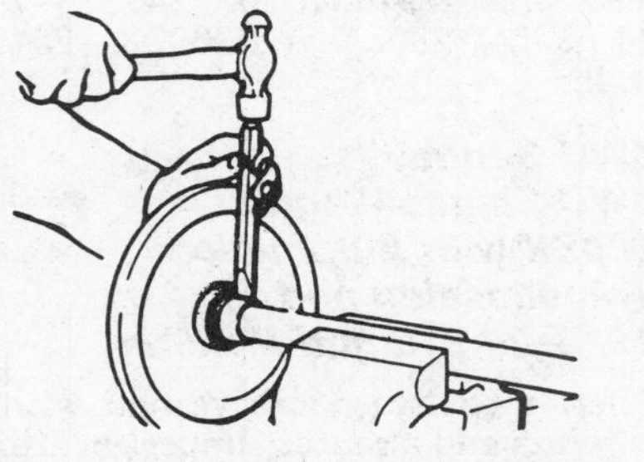

Use a chisel to collapse the bearing retainer

#### 1984–88 200SX, 1983–84 810 AND MAXIMA, 280ZX AND 300ZX

1. Block the front wheels. Loosen the wheel nuts, raise and support the car, and remove the wheel.
2. Apply the parking brake firmly. This will help hold the stub axle while you remove the axle nut. You will probably also have to hold the stub axle at the outside while removing the nut from the axle shaft side. The nut will require a good deal of force to remove, so be sure to hold the stub axle firmly.
3. On cars with rear disc brakes, unbolt the caliper and move it aside. Do not disconnect the hose from the caliper. Do not allow the caliper to hang by the hose; support the caliper with a length of wire or rest it on a suspension member.
4. Remove the brake disc on models with rear disc brakes. Remove the brake drum on cars with drum brakes.
5. Remove the stub axle with a slide hammer and an adapter. The outer wheel bearing will come off with the stub axle.
6. Remove the companion flange from the lower arm.
7. Remove and discard the grease seal and inner bearing from the lower arm using a drift made for the purpose or a length of pipe of the proper diameter.

The outer bearing can be removed from the stub axle with a puller. If the grease seal or the bearings are removed, new parts must be used on assembly.

8. Clean all the parts to be reused in solvent.
9. Sealed-type bearings are used. When the new bearings are installed, the sealed side must face out. Install the sealed side of the outer bearing facing the wheel, and the sealed side of the inner bearing facing the differential.
10. Press the outer bearing onto the stub axle.
11. The bearing housing is stamped with an **N**, **M**, or **P**. Select a spacer on the stub axle.
12. Install the stub axle into the lower arm.
13. Install the new inner bearing into the lower arm with the stub axle in place. Install a new grease seal.
14. Install the companion flange onto the stub axle.
15. Install the stub axle nut. Tighten to 181–239 ft. lbs. (217–289 ft. lbs. on 300 ZX).
16. Install the brake disc or drum, and the caliper if removed. Install the wheel and lower the car.

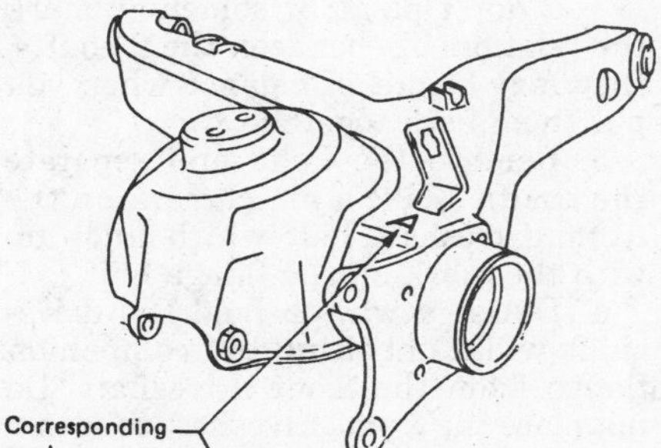


Match the bearing housing to the spacer with the proper letter

### 240SX

1. Block the front wheels. Loosen the wheel nuts, raise and support the car, and remove the wheel.

2. Apply the parking brake firmly to hold the stub axle while removing the axle nut. Hold the stub axle at the outside while removing the nut from the axle shaft side. The nut will require a good deal of force to remove, so be sure to hold the stub axle firmly.

3. Unbolt the caliper and move it aside. Do not disconnect the hose from the caliper. Do not allow the caliper to hang by the hose; support the caliper with a length of wire or rest it on a suspension member. Remove the brake disc on models with rear disc brakes.

4. Separate the driveshaft from the axle housing by lightly tapping it. Cover the driveshaft boots with a shop towel to prevent damage.

5. Unbolt and remove the axle housing from the vehicle. Remove the 4 bolts that hold the wheel bearing, flange and hug to the axle housing.

6. Press the wheel bearing from the axle hub. Mount the hub in a vise and remove the inner race using a bearing replacer/puller tool. Discard the inner race. If the grease seals are being replaced, replace them as a set.

7. Clean all parts in a suitable solvent. Check the wheel hub and axle housing for cracks, preferrably using the dye penetrant method. Check the wheel bearing seating surface for roughness, seizure or other damage that may interfere with proper bearing function. Check the ruber bushing for wear.

8. Place the hub on a block of wood and seat the inner race using a suitable drift. De careful not to damage the grease seals during installation of the inner race.

9. Press the bearing into the hub using a suitable drift. Complete the installation of the remaining components in reverse of the removal procedure. Torque the axle housing bolts to 58–72 ft. lbs. and the axle nut to 174–231 ft. lbs.

## Four Wheel Drive Rear Halfshafts

### REMOVAL & INSTALLATION

#### *4WD Sentra and 4WD Stanza Wagon*

1. Raise the rear of the vehicle and support it with jack stands.

2. Remove the wheel and tire assembly.

3. Pull out the wheel bearing cotter pin and then remove the adjusting cap and insulator.

4. Set the parking brake and then remove the wheel bearing lock nut.

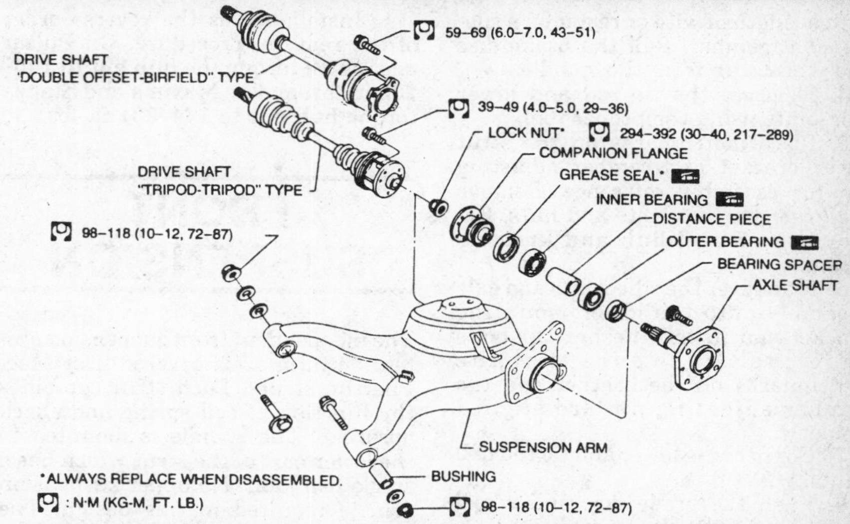


**Exploded view of the rear axle shown with either the "Double Off-Set Birfield" type driveshaft or the "Tripod-Tripod" type driveshaft—models with IRS**

5. Disconnect and plug the hydraulic brake lines. Disconnect the parking brake cable.

6. Using a block of wood and a small mallet, carefully tap the halfshaft out of the knuckle/backing plate assembly.

7. Unbolt the radius rod and the transverse link at the wheel end.

**CAUTION**

***Before removing the transverse link mounting bolt, matchmark the toe-in adjusting plate to the link.***

8. Using a suitable pry bar, carefully remove the halfshaft from the final drive.

9. On installation, position the halfshaft into the knuckle and then insert it into the final drive; makeing sure the serrations are properly aligned.

10. Push the shaft into the final drive and then press-fit the circlip on the halfshaft into the groove on the side gear.

11. After insertion, pull the halfshaft by hand to be certain that it is properly seated in the side gear and will not come out.

12. Installation of the remaining components is in the reverse order of removal.

## Front Axle Hub, Knuckle And Bearing

### REMOVAL & INSTALLATION

#### *200SX, 1983–84 810 and Maxima, 280ZX and 300ZX*

1. Raise and support the front of the vehicle safely and remove the wheels.

2. Remove the brake hose and plug the hose (if necessary).

3. Remove the caliper retaining bolts and remove the caliper from the axle.

4. Remove the bolts holding the strut to the knuckle arm.

5. Remove the knuckle arm away from the strut arm and remove the stabilizer, tension rod, and transverse link.

6. Remove the ball joint from the knuckle arm by pressing it out of the knuckle arm.

7. Installation is the reverse order of the removal procedure.

#### *240SX*

1. Block the front wheels. Loosen the wheel nuts, raise and support the car, and remove the wheel.

2. Apply the parking brake firmly and remove the wheel bearing nut. The nut will require a good deal of force to remove it.

3. Unbolt the caliper and move it aside. Do not disconnect the hose from the caliper. Do not allow the caliper to hang by the hose; support the caliper

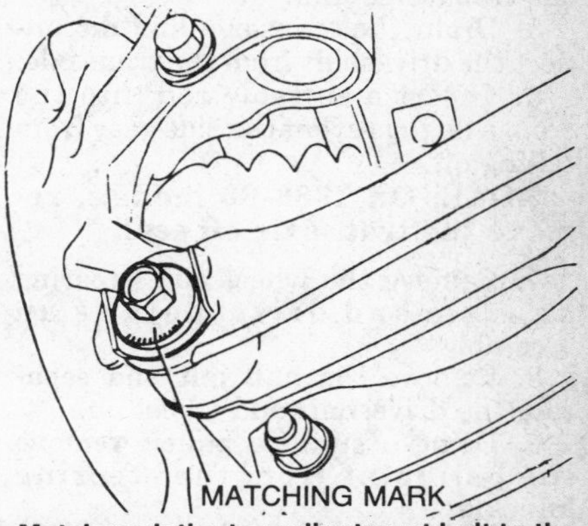


**Matchmark the toe adjustment bolt to the transverse link on the Stanza wagon (4 × 4)**

with a length of wire or rest it on a suspension member. Pull the brake disc and wheel hub from the spindle

4. Separate the tie rod and lower ball joints using the proper tool.

5. Place matchmarks on the strut lower bracket and camber adjusting pin for assembly reference. Remove the lower bracket bolts and nuts. Remove the wheel hub and knuckle assembly.

6. Manuever the wheel hub and axle assembly onto the lower mounting bracket and install the bracket bolts and nuts. Make sure that the matchmarks on the bracket and the camber adjusting pin are aligned properly.

7. Connect the lower and tie rod ball joints.

8. Push the brake disc and wheel hub onot the spindle.

9. Install the brake caliper assembly.

10. Apply the parking brake and torque the wheel bearing locknut to 108–159 ft. lbs. Mount a dial indicator so that the stylus of the dial rests on the face of the hub and check the wheel bearing axial endplay. the endplay should be 0.0012 in. or less.

11. Install the front wheels and lower the vehicle.

#### *Pulsar, Sentra, Stanza and 1985–90 Maxima*

1. Raise and support the front of the vehicle safely and remove the wheels.

2. Apply the parking brake firmly and remove the wheel bearing nut. The nut will require a good deal of force to remove it.

3. Unbolt the caliper and move it aside. Do not disconnect the hose from the caliper. Do not allow the caliper to hang by the hose; support the caliper with a length of wire or rest it on a suspension member.

4. Disconnect the side rod ball stud and remove the lower ball joint from the transverse link.

5. Drain the transaxle and disconnect the driveshaft from the transaxle.

6. Insert a suitable rod into the transaxle to prevent the side gear from falling off.

**NOTE: On 1983–90 models, remove the transaxle oil seal.**

7. Remove the wheel hub, steering knuckle and driveshaft as an assembly.

8. Remove the hub nut and separate the driveshaft and wheel hub.

9. Using a suitable puller, remove the ball joint from the steering knuckle.

10. Using a ball joint fork or equivalent, separate the wheel hub and steering knuckle.

11. Installation is the reverse order of the removal procedure. On Pulsar andSentra torque the hub nut to 145–203 ft. lbs. and on Maxima and Stanza torque hub nut to 174–231 ft. lbs.

# FRONT SUSPENSION

The independent front suspension system on all models covered uses MacPherson struts. Each strut combines the function of coil spring and shock absorber. The spindle is mounted to the lower part of the strut which has a single ball joint. No upper suspension arm is required in this design. The spindle and lower suspension transverse link (control arm) are located fore and aft by the tension rods to the front part of the chassis on most models. A cross-chassis sway bar is used on all models.

## MacPherson Strut

### REMOVAL & INSTALLATION

#### *All Models*

1. Jack up the car and support it safely. Remove the wheel.

2. Disconnect and plug the brake line.

3. Disconnect the tension rod (compression rod on the "Z" series) and stabilizer bar from the transverse link.

4. Unbolt the steering arm from the lower end of the strut..

5. Place a jack under the bottom of the strut. On 240SX, place matchmarks on the strut lower bracket and camber adjusting pin for assembly reference.

6. Open the hood and remove the nuts holding the top of the strut. On 300ZX or 1985–90 Maxima equipped with adjustable or sonar suspension shocks, disconnect the electrical lead from the actuating unit.

7. Lower the jack slowly and cautiously until the strut assembly can be removed.

8. Reverse the procedure to install. The self locking nuts holding the top of the strut must be replaced. On 240SX, make sure that the matchmarks on the bracket and the camber adjusting pin are aligned properly. On 1989–90 Maxima with sonar suspension, before installing the actuator ensure the output shaft on the inside of the actuating unit is aligned with the shock absorber control rod. If this is not done, the actuator will be damaged.

### OVERHAUL

**For all spring and shock absorber removal and installation procedures and any other strut overhaul procedures, please refer to**

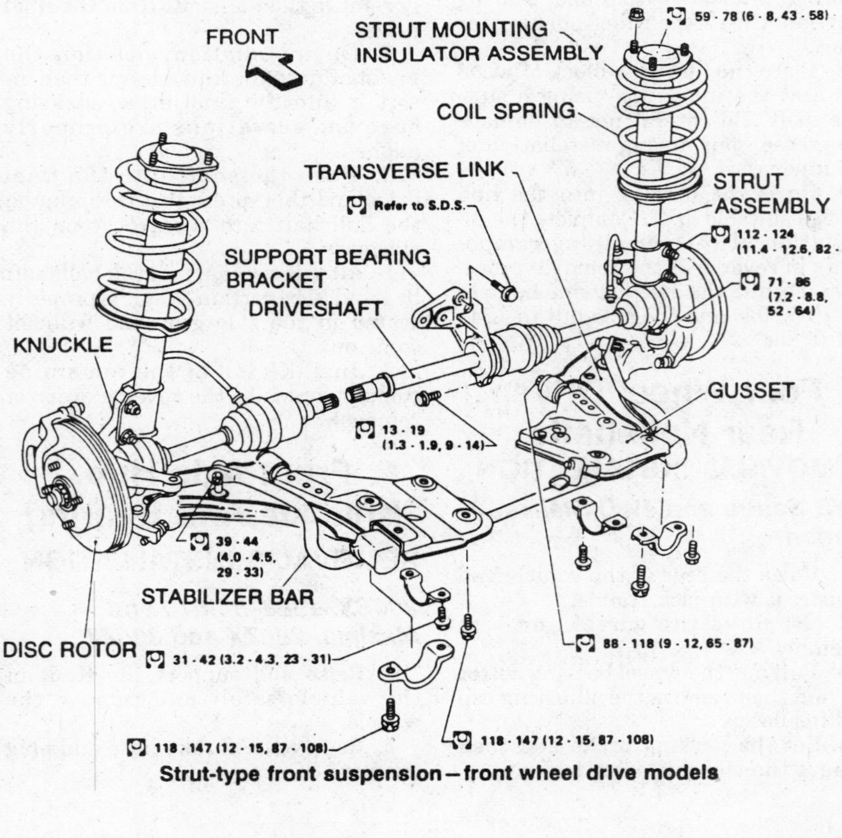

**Strut-type front suspension—front wheel drive models**

**"Strut Overhaul" in the Unit Repair Section.**

## Tension Rod And Stabilizer Bar

### REMOVAL & INSTALLATION

#### *Rear Wheel Drive*

1. Support and set the load of the vehicle.
2. Remove the tension rod-to-frame lock nuts. Remove the 2 mounting bolts at the transverse link (lower control arm) and then slide out the tension rod. On 240SX, to remove the tension rod, remove the bolt and nut that holds the rod to the tension rod bracket (through the bushing), then swing the rod upward and remove the tranverse link bolts, nuts, bushings and washers. If the bushings are worn replace them.
3. Unbolt the stabilizer bar at each transverse link or connecting rod. On 240SX, engage the flats of stabilizer bar connecting rod with a wrench to keep the rod from moving when removing the nuts.
4. Remove the 4 stabilizer bar bracket bolts, and remove the stabilizer bar.
5. Installation is in the reverse order of removal.

- Tighten the stabilizer bar-to-transverse link bolts to 12–16 ft. lbs. (16–22 Nm) and 34–38 ft. lbs. (46–52 Nm) on 240SX.
- Tighten the stabilizer bar bracket bolts to 22–29 ft. lbs. (29–39 Nm) and 29–36 ft. lbs. (39–49 Nm) on 240SX.
- Tighten the tension rod-to-transverse link nuts to 31–43 ft. lbs. (42–59 Nm). On 240SX, torque the plain nuts to 65–80 ft. lbs. (88–108 Nm) and the nuts with bushings and washers to 14–22 ft. lbs. (20–29 Nm). Make sure to hold the connecting rod stationary
- Tighten the tension rod-to-frame nut (bushing end) to 33–40 ft. lbs. (44–54 Nm). Always use a new locknut when reconnecting the tension rod to the frame
- Never tighten any bolts or nuts to their final torque unless the car is resting, unsupported, on the wheels
- Be certain the tension rod bushings are installed as shown in the illustration. Make sure the stabilzer bar ball joint socket is properly positioned.

## Stabilizer Bar

### REMOVAL & INSTALLATION

#### *Pulsar, Sentra and Stanza Wagon*

1. Disconnect the parking brake cable at the equalizer on the Stanza wagon.
2. On the Stanza wagon (4wd), remove the mounting nuts for the transaxle support rod and the transaxle control rod.
3. Disconnect the front exhaust pipe at the manifold and position it out of the way.

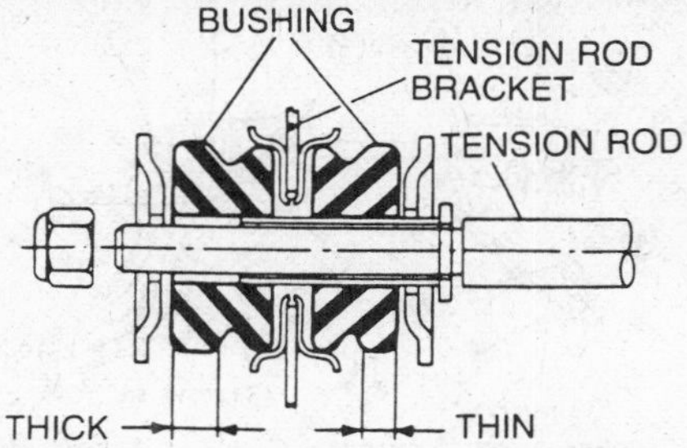

Tension rod bushing positioning—rear wheel drive models

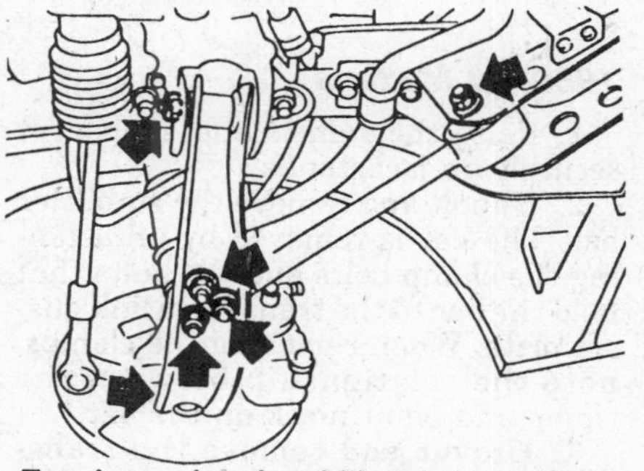
Tension rod and stabilizer bar ataching points – 240SX

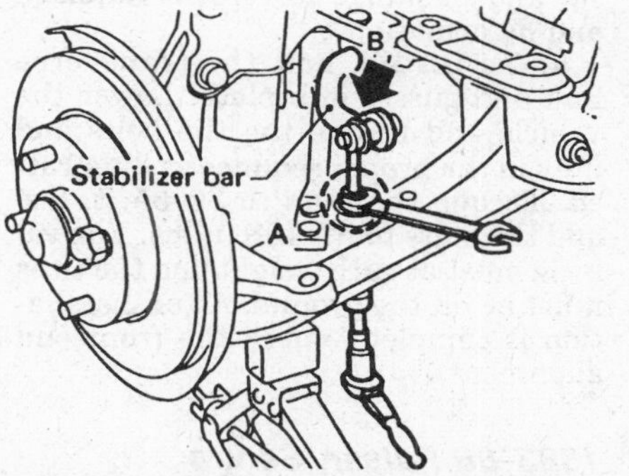

Hold the stabilizer connecting rod with a wrench when removing and installing the mounting nuts

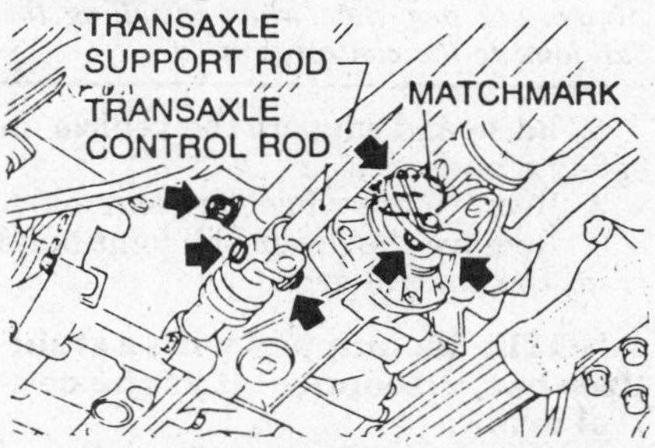

Removing the stabilizer bar on the Stanza wagon (4wd)

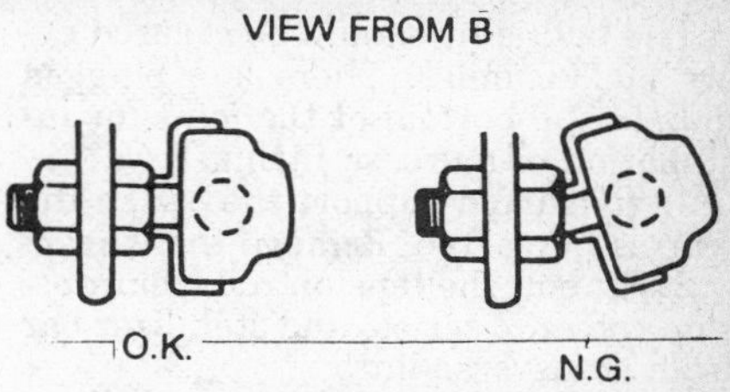

Ball joint socket positioning

4. On the Stanza wagon (4wd), matchmark the flanges and then separate the driveshaft from the transfer case.
5. Remove the stabilizer bar-to-transverse link (lower, control arm) mounting bolts. Engage the flats of stabilizer bar connecting rod with a wrench to keep the rod from moving when removing (and installing) the bolts.
6. Remove the 4 stabilizer bar bracket mounting bolts and then pull the bar out, around the link and exhaust pipe.
7. Installation is in the reverse order of removal. Never tighten the mounting bolts unless the car is resting on the ground with normal weight upon the wheels. On the 1987–90 Pulsar/Sentra, be sure the stabilzer bar ball joint socket is properly positioned.

## Ball Joint

### INSPECTION

The lower ball joint should be replaced when play becomes excessive. Nissan/Datsun does not publish specifications for this, giving instead a rotational torque figure for the ball joint. However, this requires removal for measurement. An effective way to determine play is to jack up the car until the wheel is clear of the ground. Do not place the jack under the ball joint; it must be unloaded. Place a long bar under the tire and move the wheel up and down. Keep one hand on top of the tire while doing this. If 1/4 in. or more of play exists at the top of the tire, the ball joint should be replaced. Be sure the wheel bearings are properly adjusted before making this measurement. A double check can be made; while the tire is being moved up and down, observe the ball joint. If play is seen, replace the ball joint.

### REMOVAL & INSTALLATION

#### *Lower Ball Joint*

##### REAR WHEEL DRIVE

**NOTE: On most late-model vehicles, the transverse link (lower control arm) must be removed and then the ball joint must be pressed out.**

The ball joint should be greased every 30,000 miles. There is a plugged hole in the bottom of the joint for installation of a grease fitting.

1. Raise and support the car so the wheels hang free. Remove the wheel.
2. Unbolt the tension rod (compression rod on Z series) and stabilizer bar from transverse link.
3. Unbolt the strut from the steering arm.
4. Remove the cotter pin and ball joint stud nut. Separate the ball joint and steering arm.
5. Unbolt the ball joint from the transverse link.
6. Reverse the procedure to install a new ball joint. Grease the joint after installation.

#### FRONT WHEEL DRIVE

1. Jack up the car and support it on stands. On 1989–90 Maxima, loosen but do not the strut upper nuts.
2. Remove the wheel.
3. Remove the halfshaft.
4. Separate the ball joint from the steering knuckle with a ball joint remover, being careful not to damage the ball joint dust cover if the ball joint is to be used again.
5. Remove the other ball joint from the transverse link.

Installation is the reverse of removal. Tighten the ball stud attaching nut (from ball joint-to-steering knuckle) to 22–29 ft. lbs., and the ball joint-to-transverse link bolts to 40–47 ft. lbs. (56–80 ft. lbs. – 1987–90 Stanza).

## Lower Control Arm (Transverse Link)

### REMOVAL & INSTALLATION

#### *1985–89 Maxima*

1. Raise the vehicle and support it securely on jackstands. Remove the nut fastening the link between the stabilizer bar and the control arm to the control arm.
2. Remove the 3 nuts fastening the ball joint to the lower control arm.
3. Remove the 2 bolts attaching the front and rear hinge joints of the control arm to the body.
4. Remove the control arm.
5. Installation is in the reverse order of removal. Tighten all bolts and nuts until they are snug enough to support the weight of the vehicle, but not quite fully tightened.
6. Lower the vehicle so it rests on the ground.
7. Tighten the forward bolts attaching the hinge joint to the body to 65–87 ft. lbs. Tighten the rear hinge joint bolts to 87–108 ft. lbs. and the ball joint mounting nuts to 56–80 ft. lbs.

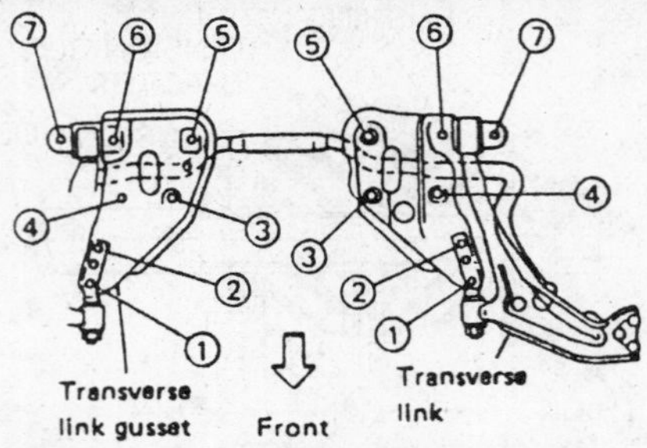


**Transverse link and gusset bolt torque sequence – 1989–90 Maxima**

#### *1989–90 Maxima*

1. Raise the vehicle and support it securely on jackstands.
2. Unbolt and remove the stabilizer bar. The bar is removed by unfastening the clamp bolts and the bolts that hold the bar to the transverse link gusset plate. When removing the clamps, note the relationship between the clamp and paint mark on the bar.
3. Unbolt and remove the transverse link and gusset.
4. Inspect the transverse link, gusset and bushings for cracks, damage and deformation.
5. To install, bolt the transverse link and gusset into place. Lower the vehicle and torque the the bolts and nuts in the proper sequnce as illustrated. Torque the nuts to 30–35 ft. lbs. and the bolts to 87–108 ft. lbs. The vehicle must at curb weight and the tires must be on the ground. After installation is complete, check the front end alignment.

#### *1983–86 Pulsar, Sentra and Stanza*

**CAUTION**

***Always use new nuts when installing the ball joint to the control arm.***

1. Raise and support the vehicle on safety stands.
2. Remove the wheel/tire assembly.
3. Remove the lower ball joint bolts from the control arm.

**NOTE: If equipped with a stabilizer bar, disconnect it at the control arm.**

4. Remove the control arm-to-body bolts.
5. Remove the gusset.
6. Remove the control arm from the vehicle.
7. Installation is in the reverse order of removal using the following torque specifications:

Gusset-to-body bolts – 65–87 ft. lbs. (1983–86 Stanza), 87–108 ft. lbs. (1987–90 Stanza) or 65–80 ft. lbs. (Pulsar and Sentra)

Control arm securing nut – 65–80 ft. lbs. (1982–86 Stanza), 87–108 ft. lbs. (1987–90 Stanza) or 72–87 ft. lbs. (Pulsar and Sentra)

Lower ball joint-to-control arm nuts – 40–51 ft. lbs. (1983–86 Stanza), 56–80 ft. lbs. (1987–90 Stanza) or 40–47 ft. lbs. (Pulsar/Sentra)

Stabilizer bar-to-control arm to 6.7–8.7 ft. lbs. (2WD Stanza and Pulsar/Sentra) or 12–16 ft. lbs. (4WD Stanza).

**NOTE: When installing the link, tighten the nut securing the link spindle to the gusset. Final tightening should be made with the weight of the vehicle on the wheels.**

## Lower Control Arm (Transverse Link) and Ball Joint

### REMOVAL & INSTALLATION

#### *Rear Wheel Drive*

1. Jack up the vehicle and support it with jack stands; remove the wheel.
2. Remove the splash board, if so equipped.
3. Remove the cotter pin and castle nut from the side rod (steering arm) ball joint and separate the ball joint from the side rod. You'll need either a fork type or puller type ball joint remover.
4. Separate the steering knuckle arm from the MacPherson strut.
5. Remove the tension rod and stabilizer bar from the lower arm.
6. Remove the nuts or bolts connecting the lower control arm (transverse link) to the suspension crossmember on all models.
7. On the 810 and Maxima, to remove the transverse link (control arm) on the steering gear side, separate the gear arm from the sector shaft and lower steering linkage; to remove the transverse link on the idler arm side, detach the idler arm assembly from the body frame and lower steering linkage.
8. Remove the lower control arm (transverse link) with the suspension ball joint and knuckle arm still attached.

Installation is the reverse of removal with the following notes:

9. When installing the control arm, temporarily tighten the nuts and/or bolts securing the control arm to the suspension crossmember. Tighten them fully only after the car is sitting on its wheels.
10. Lubricate the ball joints after assembly.

### 1987–90 Pulsar and Sentra

A ball joint removal tool will be required for this operation.

1. Raise the vehicle and support it with safety stands. Remove the wheel.
2. Remove the wheel bearing locknut.
3. Remove the tie rod ball joint with a puller.
4. Remove the lower strut-to-knuckle mounting bolts and separate the strut from the knuckle.
5. Separate the outer end of the halfshaft from the steering knuckle by carefully tapping it with a rubber mallet.

**CAUTION**

*Be sure to cover the CV-joints with a shop rag.*

6. Using a ball joint removal tool, separate the lower ball joint stud from the steering knuckle.
7. Unbolt and remove the transverse link and ball joint as an assembly.
8. Installation is in the reverse order of removal. Make sure the tab on the transverse link clamp is pointing in the proper direction. Final tightening of all bolts should take place with the weight of the vehicle on the wheels. Check wheel alignment.

## Front Axle Hub and Bearing

### ADJUSTMENT

**NOTE: For wheel bearing adjustment on front wheel drive models, please refer to "Drive Axles".**

### Rear Wheel Drive Except 240SX

1. Raise and support the vehicle safely, remove the front wheels and the brake caliper assemblies.
2. While rotating the brake disc, torque wheel bearing lock nut to 18–22 ft. lbs. on all models.
3. Loosen lock nut approximately 60 degrees on all models. Install adjusting cap and align groove of nut with hole in spindle. If alignment cannot be obtained, change position of adjusting cap. Also, if alignment cannot be obtained, loosen lock nut slightly but not more than 15 degrees.
4. Install brake shoes.

### 240SX

There is no procedure for torqueing the front wheel bearings due to the design of the bearing. Once the final torque is applied to the wheel bearing axle nut and the axial play is checked, no further adjustment is either necessary or possible.

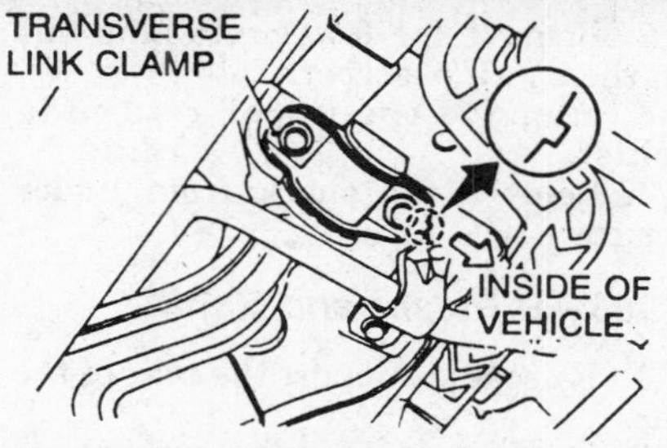


**Transverse link clamp positioning – 1987–90 Pulsar/Sentra**

Check the torque of the wheel bearing locknut. This value is 108–159 ft. lbs. Then, mount a dial indicator to the face of the hub and check the axial play. It should not exceed 0.0012 in. on all models. If the axial play is not as specified, replace the wheel bearing.

### REMOVAL & INSTALLATION

1. Raise and support the vehicle safely.
2. Remove the front wheels and the brake caliper assemblies.
3. Work off center hub cap by using thin tool. If necessary tap around it with a soft hammer while removing.
4. Pry off cotter pin and take out adjusting cap and wheel bearing lock nut.
5. Remove wheel hub with disc brake rotor from spindle with bearing installed.
6. Remove bearing from hub using long brass drift pin or equivalent.
7. To install reverse removal procedures. Adjust wheel bearings.

## Front Wheel Alignment

### ADJUSTMENT

### Caster and Camber

Caster is the forward or rearward tilt of the upper end of the kingpin, or the upper ball joint, which results in a slight tilt of the steering axis forward or backward. Rearward tilt is referred to as a positive caster, while forward tilt is referred to as a negative caster.

Camber is the inward or outward tilt from the vertical, measured in degrees, of the front wheels at the top. An outward tilt gives the wheel positive camber. Proper camber is critical to assure even tire wear.

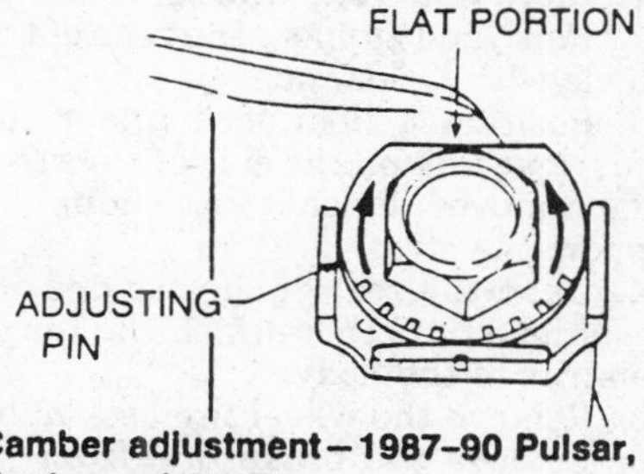


**Camber adjustment – 1987–90 Pulsar, Sentra and 240SX**

Since caster and camber are adjusted traditionally by adding or subtracting shims behind the upper control arms, and the models covered in this guide have replaced the upper control arm with the MacPherson strut, the only way to adjust caster and camber is to replace bent or worn parts of the front suspension.

**NOTE: Camber is adjustable on the 1987–90 Pulsar and Sentra and 240SX.**

### Camber

#### 1987–90 PULSAR, SENTRA AND 240SX

1. Camber is adjusted by means of a pin on the top-most lower strut mounting bolts.
2. The pin is installed with the flat side facing downward at the factory. Remove the pin and then reinstall it with the flat side facing up.
3. Turn the pin to adjust camber. Camber changes about 15' with each gradation of the adjusting pin on Pulsar and Sentra. On 240SX, camber changes about 5' with each gradation.
4. Tighten the pin to 72–87 ft. lbs. (98–118 Nm) on Pulsar and Sentra and 91–106 ft. lbs. (124–143 Nm) on 240SX.

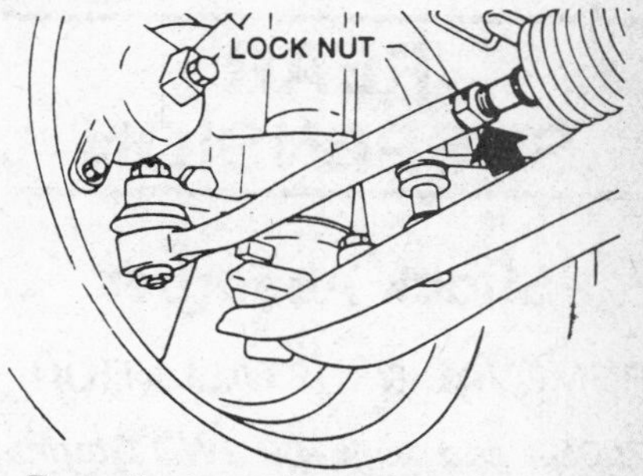


Toe adjustment is made at the tie rod

### Toe

Toe is the amount, measured in a fraction of an inch, that the wheels are closer together at one end than the other. Toe in means that the front wheels are closer together at the front than the rear, toe out means the rears are closer than the front. Most models are adjusted to have slight amount of toe in. Toe in is adjusted by turning the tie rod, which has a right-hand thread on one and a left-hand thread on the other.

The vehicle's toe can be checked without special equipment if careful measurements are made. The wheels must be straight ahead.

1. Toe in can be determined by measuring the distance between the center of the tire treads, at the front of the

tire and at the rear. If the tread pattern of your car's tires make this impossible, you can measure between the edges of the wheel rims, but make sure to move the car forward and measure in a couple of places to avoid errors caused by bent rims or wheel runout.

2. If the measurement is not within specifications, loosen the lock nuts at both ends of the tie rod (the driver's side lock nut is left-hand threaded).

3. Turn the top of the tie rod toward the front of the car to reduce toe in, or toward the rear to increase it. When the correct dimension is reached, tighten the lock nuts and check the adjustment.

**NOTE: Uneven rear tire wear on the 1984 turbo 200SX and all 1985–86 200SX models may be caused by too much negative camber of the rear wheels. New rear coil springs are available to correct this condition.**

### STEERING ANGLE ADJUSTMENT

The maximum steering angle is adjusted by stopper bolts on the steering arms. Loosen the lock nut on the stopper bold, turn the stopped bold in or out as required to obtain the proper maximum steering angle and retighten the lock nut.

# REAR SUSPENSION

## Shock Absorber

### REMOVAL & INSTALLATION

#### *200SX and 1986–89 2WD Stanza Wagon*

1. Open the trunk and remove the cover panel (if necessary) to expose the shock mounts. Pry off the mount covers, if so equipped. On leaf spring models, jack up the rear of the vehicle and support the rear axle on stands.

2. Remove the 2 nuts holding the top of the shock absorber. Unbolt the bottom of the shock absorber.

3. Remove the shock absorber.

4. Installation is the reverse of removal. Final tightening of the lower end of the shock absorber should be performed with the wheels on the ground in the unladen position.

#### *810 and Maxima Station Wagons*

1. Raise the rear of the car and support the axle on jack stands.

2. Remove the lower retaining nut on the shock absorber.

3. Remove the upper retaining bolt(s).

4. Remove the shock from under the car.

#### *1983–86 Pulsar and Sentra*

1. Raise and support the rear of the car.

2. Remove the wheels.

3. Support the rear arm with a jack at the lower end.

4. Remove the upper and lower shock mounting nuts.

5. Slowly and carefully lower the jack and remove the shock.

6. Installation is the reverse of removal.

## MacPherson Strut

### REMOVAL & INSTALLATION

#### *1987–90 Pulsar/Sentra except 4WD and 1983–86 Stanza Except Wagon*

1. Raise and support the rear of the vehicle on jackstands.

2. Remove the wheel/tire assembly.

3. Disconnect the brake tube and parking brake cable.

4. If necessary, remove the brake assembly and wheel bearing.

5. Disconnect the parallel links and radius rod from the strut or knuckle.

6. Support the strut with a jackstand.

7. Remove the strut upper end nuts and then remove the strut from the vehicle.

8. Installation is in the reverse order of removal. Tighten the strut-to-parallel link nuts to 65–87 ft. lbs., the strut-to-radius rod nuts to 54–69 ft. lbs. and the strut-to-body nuts to 23–31 ft. lbs.

On the Pulsar and Sentra, tighten the radius rod-to-knuckle nuts to 43–61 ft. lbs., the strut-to-knuckle and parallel link-to-knuckle bolts to 72–87 ft. lbs. and the strut-to-body nuts to 18–22 ft. lbs.

#### *4WD Sentra and Stanza Wagon (4wd)*

1. Block the front wheels.

2. Raise and support the rear of the vehicle with jackstands.

3. Position a floor jack under the transverse link on the side of the strut to be removed. Raise it just enough to support the strut.

4. Open the rear of the car and remove the 3 nuts that attach the top of the strut to the body.

5. Remove the wheel/tire assembly.

6. Remove the brake line from its bracket and position it out of the way.

7. Remove the 2 lower satrut-to-knuckle mounting bolts.

8. Carefully lower the floor jack and remove the strut.

9. Installation is the reverse order of removal. Final tightening of the strut mounting bolts should take place with the wheels on the ground and the vehicle unladen. Tighten the upper strut-to-body nuts to 33–40 ft. lbs. (45–60 Nm). Tighten the lower strut-to-knuckle bolts to 111–120 ft. lbs. (151–163 Nm).

#### *1983–84 810 and Maxima*

1. Raise the car and safely support the rear with jackstands and a floor jack.

2. Open the trank and remove the 3 nuts which secure the top of the strut to the body.

3. Disconnect the strut at the bottom by removing the bolt at the suspension arm.

4. Installation is in the reverse order of removal. Install the strut so that the larger hole on the lower end faces outward.

#### *1987–90 Stanza except Wagon and 1985–90 Maxima*

1. Unclip the rear brake line at the strut. Unbolt and remove the brake assembly, wheel bearings and backing plate. Position the brake caliper out of the way and suspend it so as not to stress the brake line.

2. Remove the radius rod mounting bolt, radius rod mounting bracket.

3. Remove the 2 parallel link mounting bolts.

4. Remove the rear seat and parcel shelf.

5. Position a floor jack under the strut and raise it just enought to support the strut.

6. Remove the 3 upper strut mounting nuts and then lift out the strut.

7. Installation is in the reverse order of removal. Tighten all bolts sufficiently to safely support the vehicle and then lower the car to the ground so it rests on its own weight. Tighten the upper strut mounting nuts to 23–31 ft. lbs. (31–40 ft. lbs on 1989–90 Maxima), the radius rod bracket bolts to 43–58 ft. lbs. and the parallel link mounting bolts to 65–87 ft. lbs. On 1989–90 Maxima with sonar suspension, before installing the actuator ensure the output shaft on the inside of the actuating unit is aligned with the shock absorber control rod. If this is not done, the actuator will be damaged.

#### *240SX, 280ZX and 300ZX*

1. Block the front wheels.

2. Raise and support the rear of the vehicle on jackstands.

**NOTE: The vehicle should be far enough off the ground so that the rear spring does not support any weight.**

3. Working inside the luggage compartment, turn and remove the caps above the strut mounts. Remove the 3 strut mounting nuts.
4. Remove the mounting bolt for the strut at the lower arm (transverse link) and then lift out the strut.
5. Installation is in the reverse order of removal. Install the upper end first and secure with the nuts snugged down but not fully tightened. Attach the lower end of the strut to the transverse link and the tighten the upper nuts to 22–29 ft. lbs. (30–40 Nm) and 12–14 ft. lbs. (16–19 Nm) on 240SX. Tighten the lower mounting bolt to 43–58 ft. lbs. (60–80 Nm) and 65–80 ft. lbs. (88–108 Nm) on 240SX.

### OVERHAUL

**For all spring and shock absorber removal and installation procedures, and all strut overhaul procedures, please refer to "Strut Overhaul" in the Unit Repair section.**

## Springs

### REMOVAL & INSTALLATION

#### *Coil Spring Type*

4 types of coil spring suspension are used:

Trailing Arm Type – 1983-86 Pulsar and Sentra

4/5 Bar Link Type – 810 and 1983 200SX

MacPherson Strut Type – 810 andMaxima, 240SX, 280ZX, 300ZX, 1987-90 Pulsar and Sentra, Stanza and 4WD Stanza Wagon

IRS Coil Spring Type – 1984-88 200SX with independent rear suspension

**CAUTION**

***Coil springs are under considerable tension and can exert enough force to cause bodily injury. Exercise extreme caution when working with them.***

### TRAILING ARM TYPE

1. Raise the rear of the vehicle and support it on jack stands.
2. Remove the wheels.
3. Disconnect the handbrake linkage and return spring.
4. Unbolt the axle shaft flange at the wheel end.
5. Unbolt the rubber bumper inside the bottom of the coil spring.
6. Jack up the suspension arm and unbolt the shock absorber lower mounting.
7. Lower the jack slowly and cautiously. Remove the coil spring, spring seat, and rubber bumper.
8. Reverse the procedure to install, making sure that the flat face of the spring is at the top.

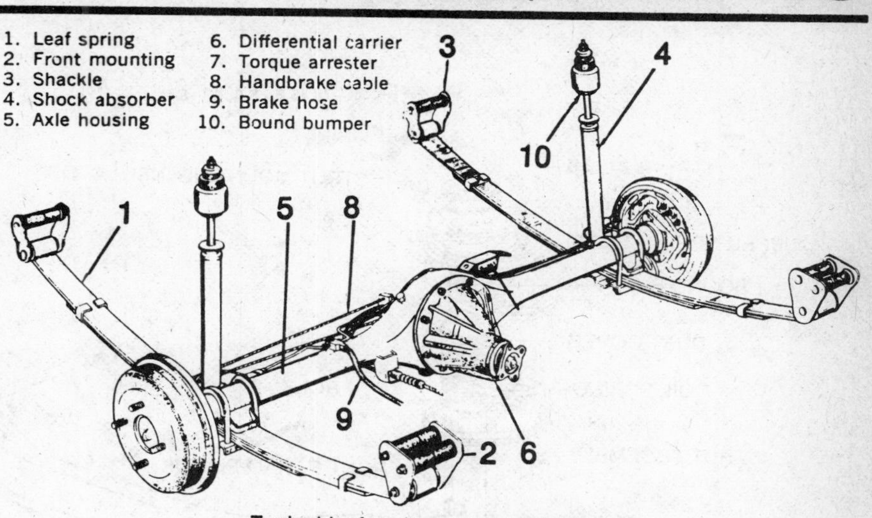


Typical leaf spring rear suspension

### 4/5 BAR LINK TYPE

1. Raise the car and support it with jack stands.
2. Support the center of the differential with a jack or other suitable tool.
3. Remove the rear wheels.
4. Remove the bolts securing the lower ends of the shock absorbers.
5. Lower the jack under the differential slowly and carefully, and remove the coil springs after they are fully extended. Remember the positioning of the upper spring seats.
6. Installation is in the reverse order of removal. Replace the upper spring seats in their correct position and tighten all bolts with the wheels on the ground.

### MACPHERSON STRUT TYPE

**NOTE: MacPherson strut removal and installation procedures are detailed previously in this section.**

### IRS COIL SPRING TYPE

This suspension is similar to the IRS MacPherson strut type, except this type utilizes separate coil springs and shock absorbers, instead of strut units.

1. Set a suitable spring compressor on the coil spring.
2. Jack up the rear end of the car.
3. Compress the coil spring until it is of sufficient length to be removed.

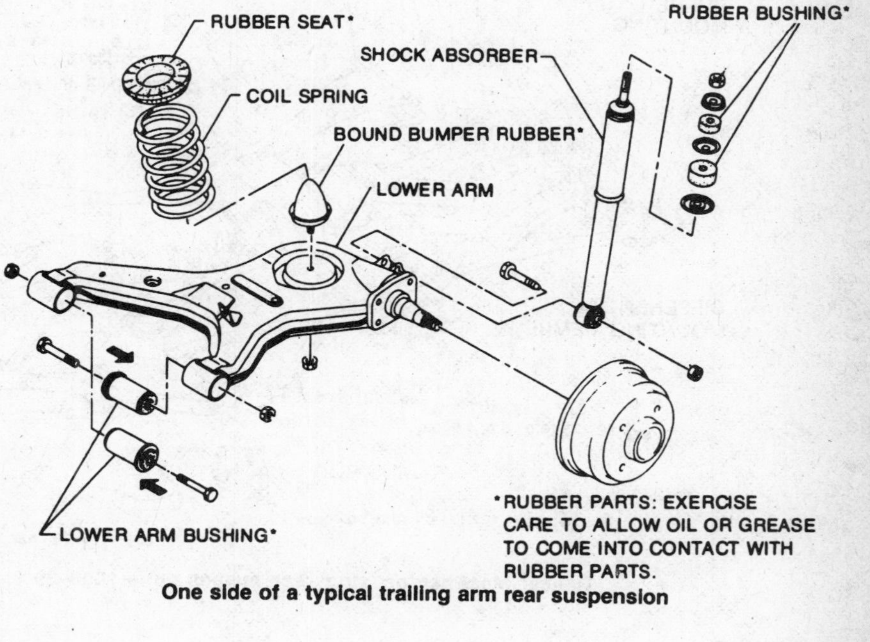


One side of a typical trailing arm rear suspension

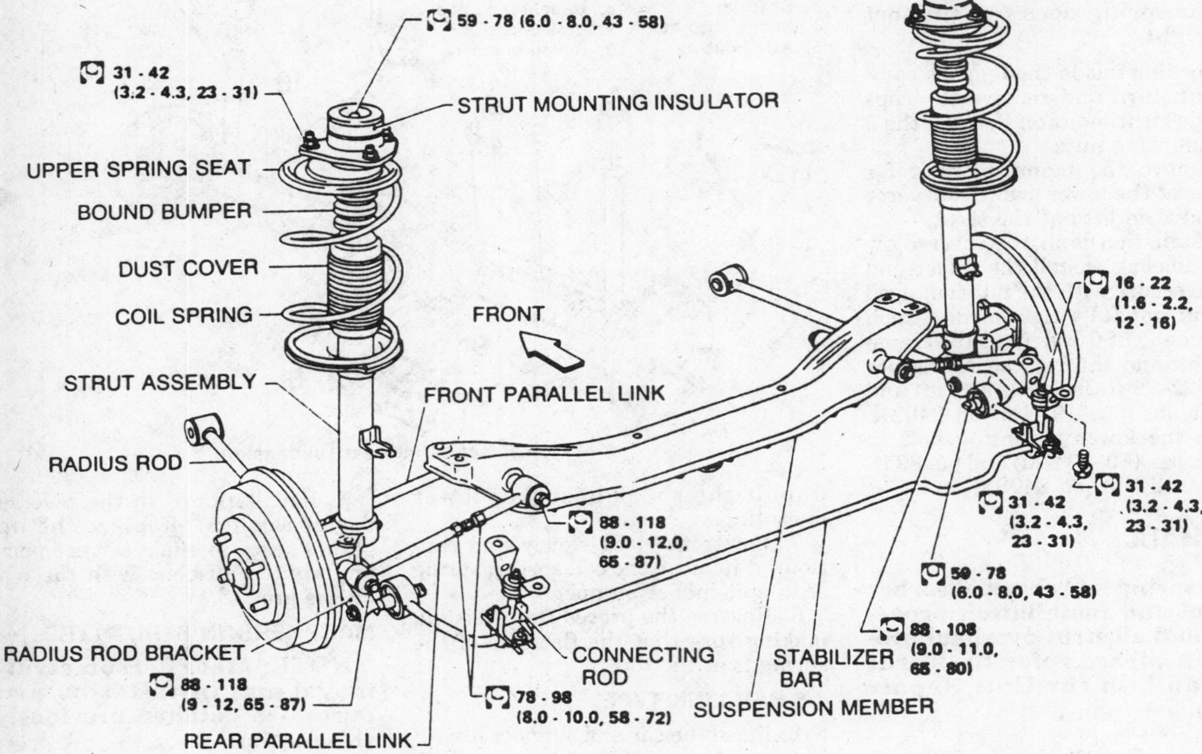


**Typical MacPherson strut-type rear suspension—front wheel drive models**

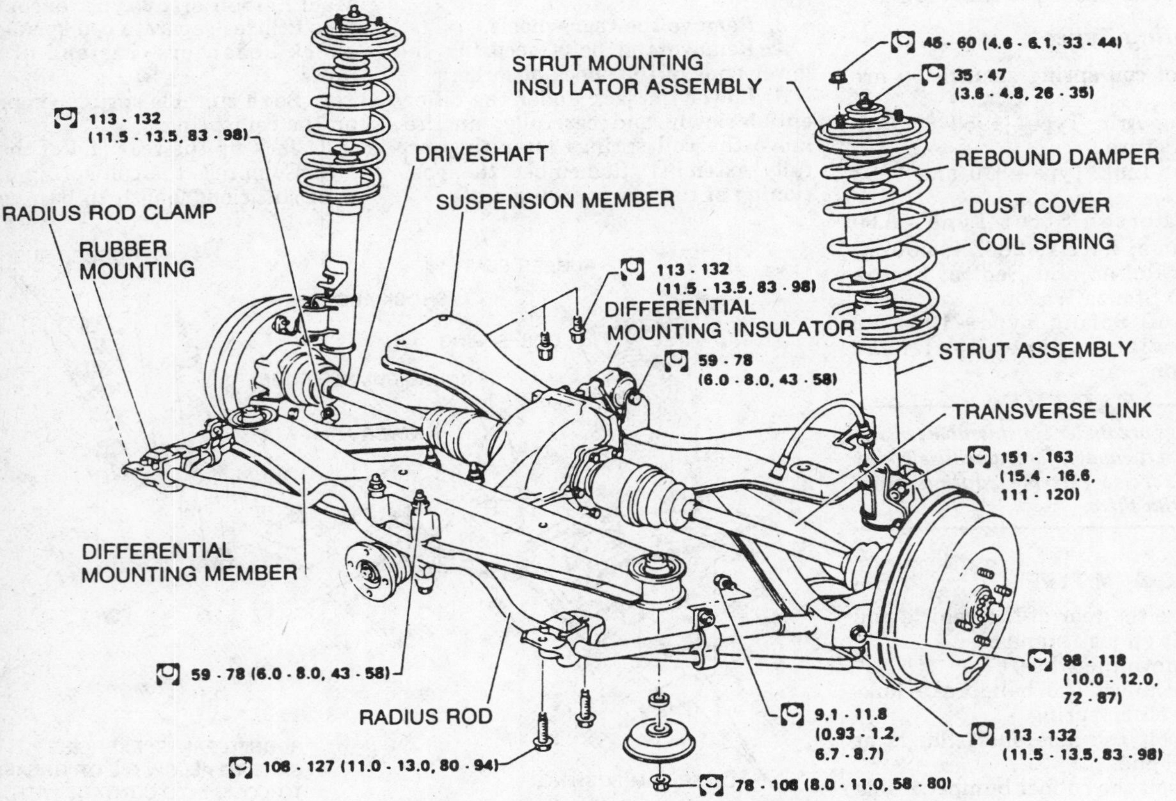


**Typical MacPherson strut rear suspension—1986–89 Stanza wagon (4wd)**

Remove the spring.

4. When installing the spring, be sure the upper and lower spring seat rubbers are not twisted and have not slipped off when installing the coil spring.

### *Torsion Bar Type*

#### 1986-88 2WD STANZA WAGON

1. Raise the rear of the vehicle and support it with jack stands.
2. Remove the wheel and tire assembly. Release the parking brake.
3. Remove the inner hub cap, the cotter pin and the wheel bearing lock nut. Remove the brake drum.
4. Disconnect and plug the hydraulic brake line. Disconnect the parking brake cable.
5. Remove the 4 brake backing plate mounting bolts and then slide the backing plate along with the inner wheel bearing off of the rear axle.
6. Disconnect the rear stabilizer bar.
7. Unbolt the anchor arm bracket and then remove the inner bushing bracket mounting bolts. Remove the torsion bar.
8. Installation is in the reverse order of removal. Tighten the inner bushing and anchor arm mounting bolts to 36–43 ft. lbs. (49–59 Nm). Tighten the stabilizer bar bolts to 65–80 ft. lbs. (88–108 Nm).

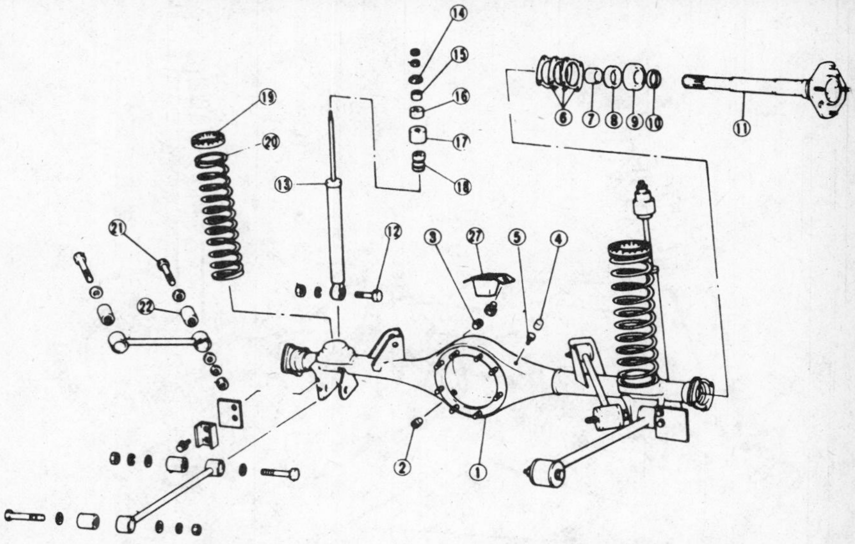

1. Rear axle case
2. Drain plug
3. Filler plug
4. Breather cap
5. Breather
6. Rear axle case end shim
7. Bearing collar
8. Oil seal
9. Rear axle bearing
10. Bearing spacer
11. Rear axle shaft
12. Shock absorber lower end bolt
13. Shock absorber assembly
14. Special washer
15. Shock absorber mounting bushing
16. Shock absorber mounting bushing
17. Bound bumper cover
18. Bound bumper rubber
19. Shock absorber mounting insulator
20. Coil spring
21. Upper link bushing bolt
22. Upper link bushing

**Four link rear suspension**

## Rear Wheel Bearings

**For wheel bearing procedures on rear wheel drive models, please refer to "Rear Axle Shaft" in the Drive Axle section.**

### ADJUSTMENT

### *Front Wheel Drive Only*

#### PULSAR AND SENTRA EXCEPT 1989–90, STANZA AND 1985–88 MAXIMA

1. Apply multi-purpose grease to the following parts:
   a. threaded portion of the wheel spindle
   b. mating surfaces of the lock washer and outer wheel bearing
   c. inner hub cap
   d. grease seal lip
2. Tighten the wheel bearing nut to 18–25 ft. lbs. (25–34 Nm).
3. Turn the wheel several times in both directions to seat the bearing correctly.
4. Loosen the wheel bearing nut until there is no preload and then tighten it to 6.5–8.7 ft. lbs. (9–12 Nm). Turn the wheel several times again and then retighten it to the same torque again.
5. Install the adjusting cap and align any of its slots with the hole in the spindle.

**NOTE: If necessary, loosen the lock nut as much as 15 degrees in order to align the spindle hole with one in the adjusting cap.**

6. Rotate the hub in both directions several times while measuring its starting torque and axial play. The axial play should be 0. The starting torque with grease seal should be 6.9 inch lbs. or less. When measured at wheel hub bolt, starting torque should be 3.1 lbs. (13.7 N).
7. Correctly measure the rotation from the starting force toward the tangential direction against the hub bolt. The above figures do not allow for any "dragging" resistance. When measuring starting torque, confirm that no

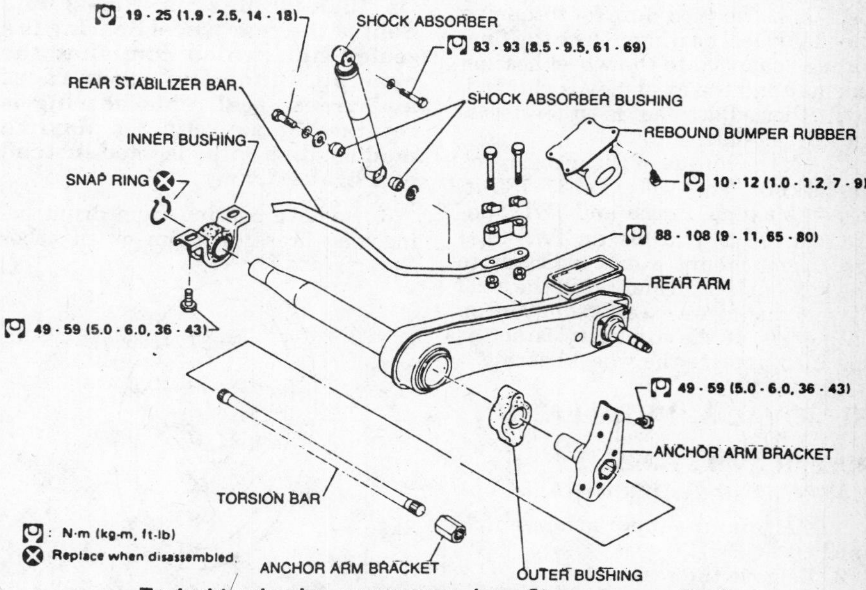


**Typical torsion bar rear suspension—Stanza wagon (2wd)**

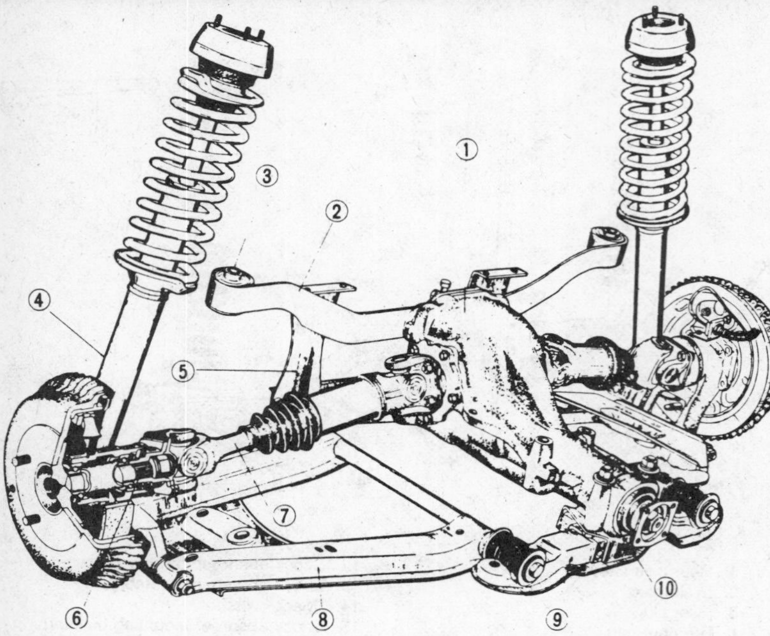


1. Differential carrier
2. Differential case mount rear member
3. Differential case mount rear insulator
4. Strut assembly
5. Link mount brace
6. Rear axle shaft
7. Drive shaft
8. Transverse link
9. Differential case mount front member
10. Differential case mount front insulator

Typical MacPherson strut-type rear suspension—rear wheel drive models

"dragging" exists. No wheel bearing axial play can exist at all.

8. Spread the cotter pin and install the inner hub cap.

9. Installation of the remaining components is in the reverse order of removal.

#### 1989–90 MAXIMA, PULSAR AND SENTRA

Due to a bearing change on these models, there is no procedure for torqueing the rear wheel bearings. Once the final torque is applied to the wheel bearing axle nut and the axial play is checked, no further adjustment is either necessary or possible.

Check the torque of the wheel bearing locknut. This value is 137–188 ft. lbs. on Maxima, Pulsar and 2WD Sentra and 174–231 ft. lbs. on 4WD Sentra. Then, mount a dial indicator to the face of the hub and check the axial play. It should not exceed 0.0020 in. on all models. If the axial play is not as specified, replace the wheel bearing.

### REMOVAL & INSTALLATION

#### PULSAR, 2WD STANZA, MAXIMA AND 2WD SENTRA

1. Raise and support the vehicle safely.
2. Remove the rear wheels.
3. Work off center hub cap by using thin tool. If necessary tap around it with a soft hammer while removing.
4. Pry off cotter pin and take out adjusting cap and wheel bearing lock nut.
5. Remove drum with bearing inside.

**NOTE: On Pulsar and 2WD Sentra models, a circular clip holds inner wheel bearing in brake hub. On 1989–90 Maxima, Pulsar and Sentra the rear wheel bearing is a sealed unit which combines the bearing, inner and outer races and grease seal. This bearing is retained by a circlip. On Maxima models, disc rotor is used instead of a brake drum.**

6. Remove bearing from drum using long brass drift pin or an arbor press (1989–90 Maxima, Pulsar and Sentra).
7. To install reverse removal procedures. On 1989–90 Maxima, Pulsar and Sentra, the bearing must be pressed into the brake drum. On these models, do not press the inner race of the bearing; do not coat the wheel bearing and outer hub mating surfaces with oil or grease and do not damage the grease seal.
8. Adjust wheel bearings as desribed above.

Use a puller to remove the steering wheel

#### 4WD SENTRA AND 4WD STANZA

1. Raise and support the vehicle safely.
2. Remove wheel bearing lock nut while depressing brake pedal.
3. Disconnect brake hydraulic line and parking brake cable.
4. Separate drive shaft from knuckle by slightly tapping it with suitable tool. Cover axle boots with waste cloth so as not to damage them when removing drive shaft.
5. Remove all knuckle retaining bolts and nuts. Make a match mark before removing adjusting pin.
6. Remove knuckle and inner and outer circular clips. Remove wheel bearings.
7. To install reverse removal procedures. Adjust wheel bearings.

# STEERING

## Steering Wheel

### REMOVAL & INSTALLATION

1. Position the wheels in the straight-ahead direction. The steering wheel should be right-side up and level.
2. Disconnect the battery ground cable.
3. Look at the back of your steering wheel. If there are countersunk screws in the back of the steering wheel spokes, remove the screws and pull off the horn pad. Some models have a horn wire running from the pad to the steering wheel. Disconnect it.

There are 3 other types of horn buttons or rings on Datsuns and Nissans. The first simply pulls off. The second, which is usually a large, semi-triangular pad, must be pushed up, then pulled off. The third must be pushed in and turned clockwise.

4. Remove the rest of the horn switching mechanism, noting the relative location of the parts. Remove the mechanism only if it hinders subsequent wheel removal procedures.

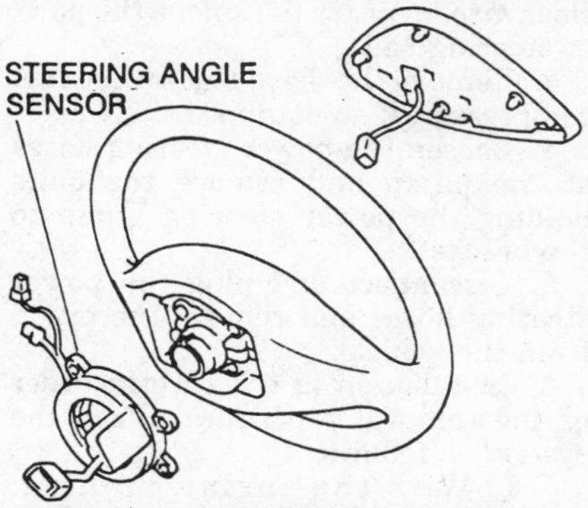


Steeing wheel on 1989–90 Maxima with sonar suspension

5. Matchmark the top of the steering column shaft and the steering wheel flange.
6. Remove the attaching nut and remove the steering wheel with a puller.

**CAUTION**

*Do not strike the shaft with a hammer; which may cause the column to collapse.*

7. Install the steering wheel in the reverse order of removal, aligning the punch marks. Do not drive or hammer the wheel into place, or you may cause the collapsible steering column to collapse. Before installing the horn pad, apply multi-purpose grease to the surface of the cancel pin and horn contact slip ring.
8. Tighten the steering wheel nuts to 28–36 ft. lbs.
9. Reinstall the horn button, pad, or ring.

## Turn Signal/ Combination Switch

### REMOVAL & INSTALLATION

On later models, the turn signal switch is part of a combination switch. The whole unit is removed together.

1. Disconnect the battery ground cable.
2. Remove the steering wheel as previously outlined. Observe the "caution" on the collapsible steering column. On 1989–90 Maxima with sonar suspension, remove the steering angle sensor from the steering column.
3. Remove the steering column covers.
4. Disconnect the electrical plugs from the switch.
5. Remove the retaining screws and remove the switch.
6. Installation is the reverse of removal. Check the switch functions for proper operation. Many models have turn signal switches that have a tab which must fit into a hole in the steering shaft in order for the system to return the switch to the neutral position after the turn has been made. Be sure to align the tab and the hole when installing.

**NOTE: On many models (all 1987–90 models), the individual stalk assemblies can be removed without removing the combination switch base assembly. Simply disconnect the electrical lead and remove the 2 stalk-to-base mounting screws.**

## Steering Lock

The steering lock/ignition switch/warning buzzer switch assembly is attached to the steering column by special screws whose heads shear off on installation. The screws must be drilled out to remove the assembly. The ignition switch is on the back of the assembly, and the warning switch on the side. The warning buzzer, which sounds when the driver's door is opened with the steering unlocked, is located behind the instrument panel.

## Manual Steering Gear

### REMOVAL & INSTALLATION

**NOTE: The 300ZX, 240SX, 1985–90 Maxima, 1987–90 Pulsar, 1987–88 200SX, 1987–90 Stanza (Sedan) and 1986–89 Stanza (Wagon) are available with power steering only.**

#### *1983–86 200SX*

1. Disconnect the exhaust pipe from the exhaust manifold, if necessary, and remove the bolt securing the exhaust pipe to the transmission mounting insulator.
2. Remove the bolt holding the worm shaft to the rubber coupling.
3. On 1984–86 models, remove the tie rod ball studs from the knuckle arms using a ball joint removal tool or the equivalent, and disconnect the steering column lower joint.
4. Remove the nut holding the pitman arm to the sector shaft and remove the pitman arm.
5. Remove the steering gear attaching bolts and then remove the steering gear from the vehicle.
6. Installation is the reverse order of the removal procedure. Check the wheel alignment after installation.

#### *280ZX and 1983–84 810 and Maxima*

1. Raise and support the front of the vehicle safely and remove the front wheels.
2. Remove the lower joint from the steering column at the rubber coupling.

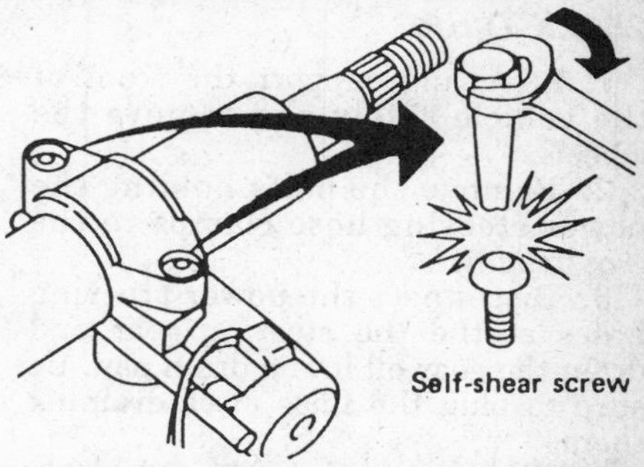


Typical steering lock self-shearing bolt

3. Remove the lower joint assembly from the pinion, and remove the splash board (280ZX only).
4. Remove the side rod studs from the steering knuckles.
5. Remove the gear housing-to-crossmember bolts and then remove the steering gear from the vehicle.
6. Installation is the reverse order of the removal procedure.

#### *Pulsar, Sentra and 1983–86 Stanza Sedan*

1. Raise and support the front of the vehicle safely and remove the wheels.
2. Disconnect the tie rod from the steering knuckle and loosen the steering gear attaching bolts.
3. Remove the bolt securing the lower joint to the steering gear pinion and remove the lower joint from the pinion.
4. Remove the bolts holding the steering gear housing to the body, and remove the steering gear and linkage assembly from the vehicle.
5. Installation is the reverse order of the removal procedure. When fitting the lower U-joint, make sure the attaching bolt is aligned perfectly with the cut out in the splined end of the steering colunm shaft.

## Power Steering Gear

### REMOVAL & INSTALLATION

#### *1983 200SX and 280ZX*

1. Remove the air cleaner and remove the bolt securing the U-joint to the worm shaft.
2. Disconnect and plug the hoses from the power steering gear.
3. Remove the pitman arm from the sector shaft, using a suitable puller.
4. Remove the steering gear securing bolts and remove the steering gear from the vehicle.
5. Installation is the reverse order of the removal procedure.

### 280ZX Turbo

1. Raise and support the front of the vehicle safely and remove the wheels.
2. Remove the bolts holding the power steering hose clamps to the crossmember.
3. Disconnect the power steering hoses at the the steering gear and drain the gear oil into a drain pan. Be sure to plug the lines after draining them.
4. Disconnect the side rod studs from the steering knuckle and remove the lower joint assembly from the pinion shaft.
5. Remove the nuts holding the engine mount insulators to the crossmember.
6. Raise the engine as previously outlined in the engine removal section, and support the crossmember with a floor jack.
7. Loosen the steering gear mounting bolts and remove the bolts holding the crossmember to the body.
8. Lower the floor jack slowly, remove the bolts holding the steering gear to the crossmember, and remove the steering gear and linkage from the vehicle.
9. Installation is the reverse order of the removal procedure.

### 1984–88 200SX

1. Remove the air cleaner and remove the bolt securing the U-joint to the worm shaft.
2. Disconnect the hoses from the power steering gear and plug the hoses to prevent leakage.
3. Remove the pitman arm from the sector shaft using a suitable tool and remove the steering gear mounting bolts.
4. Remove the exhaust pipe mounting nut.
5. Disconnect the control cable or linkage for the transmission and position it out of the way.
6. Remove the steering gear from the vehicle.
7. Installation is the reverse order of the removal procedure.

### 300ZX

1. Block the rear wheels. Raise and support the front of the vehicle on jackstands.
2. Position an oil catch pan under the power steerong gear, remove the hydraulic lines from the gear and drain the oil.
3. Loosen the steering column lower joint shaft bolt.
4. Remove the steering shaft-to-steering pinion gear. Separate the shaft from the steering gear.
5. Remove the tie rod end-to-knuckle arm cotter pins and castle nuts.
6. Separate the tie rods from the knuckle arms using a puller.
7. Remove the steering gear housing-to-suspension crossmember bolts.
8. Position a floor jack under the engine and raise it just enough to support the engine. Loosen the engine mounting bolts and raise the engine about ½ in..
9. Remove the steering gear and linkage from the vehicle.
10. Installation is in the reverse order of removal. Tighten the gear-to-crossmember bolts to 22–29 ft. lbs. and the ball joints to 40–72 ft. lbs.
11. Refill the power steering pump, start the engine and bleed the system.

### 1983–84 810 and Maxima

**NOTE: The procedure for these models, is the same as the 280ZX turbo procedures. The only difference is the engine does not have to be raised and the crossmember does not have to be removed from the body.**

### Pulsar, Sentra, Stanza, 1985–90 Maxima and 240SX

1. Raise and support the front of the vehicle safely and remove the wheels.
2. Disconnect the power steering hose from the power steering gear and plug all hoses to prevent leakage.
3. Disconnect the side rod studs from the steering knuckles.
4. On Sentra and Pulsar models, support the transaxle with a suitable transmission jack and remove the exhaust pipe and rear engine mounts.
5. On other models, remove the lower joint assembly from the steering gear pinion. Before disconnecting the lower ball joint set the steering gear assembly in neutral by making the wheels straight. Loosen the bolt and disconnect the lower joint. Matchmark the pinion shaft to the pinion housing to record the neutral gear position.
6. Remove the steering gear and linkage assembly from the vehicle.
7. Installation is the reverse order of the removal procedure. Make sure the pinion shaft and pinion housing are aligned properly.

## Power Steering Pump

### REMOVAL, INSTALLATION AND BLEEDING

### All Models

1. On all 200SX models, remove the air cleaner duct and air cleaner.
2. Loosen the idler pulley lock nut and turn the adjusting nut counterclockwise, in order to remove the power steering belt.
3. Remove the drive belt on the A/C compressor, if so equipped.
4. Loosen the power steering hoses at the pump and remove the bolts holding the power steering pump to the bracket.
5. Disconnect and plug the power steering hoses and remove the pump from the vehicle.
6. Installation is the reverse order of the removal procedure. Bleed the system as follows:
   a. With the engine running, quickly turn the steering wheel all the way to the left and all the way to the right 10 times.
   b. Stop the engine and check to see if any more fluid is required in the pump reservoir.
   c. With the steering wheel all the way to the right, open the bleeder screw and let the air flow from the pump.
   d. Tighten the bleeder screw and repeat the procedure until all the air is out of the system.

**NOTE: If all the air cannot be bled from the system, then repeat Step c with the engine running.**

### BELT TENSION ADJUSTMENT

1. Loosen the tension adjustment and mounting bolts.
2. Move the pump toward or away from the engine so that the belt deflects ¼–½ in. midway between the idler pulley and the pump pulley under moderate thumb pressure.
3. Tighten the bolts and recheck the tension adjustment.

## Tie Rod Ends (Steering Side Rods)

### REMOVAL & INSTALLATION

A ball joint remover is required for this operation.

1. Jack up the front of the vehicle and support it on jack stands.
2. Locate the faulty tie rod end. It will have a lot of play in it and the dust cover will probably be torn.
3. Remove the cotter key and nut from the tie rod stud. Note the position of the tie rod end in relation to the rest of the steering linkage.
4. Loosen the lock nut holding the tie rod to the rest of the steering linkage.
5. Free the tie rod ball joint from either the relay rod or steering knuckle by using a ball joint remover.
6. Unscrew and remove the tie rod

end, counting the number of turns it takes to completely free it.

7. Install the new tie rod end, turning it in exactly as far as you screwed out the old one. Make sure it is correctly positioned in relation to the rest of the steering linkage.

8. Fit the ball joint and nut, tighten them and install a new cotter pin. Before finally tightening the tie rod lock nut or clamp, adjust the toe of the vehicle.

# BRAKES

Front disc brakes are used on all models including station wagons with drum brakes at the rear;280ZX, 300ZX, 200SX, 240SX and later model 810 and Maxima models have rear disc brakes. All models have a vacuum booster system to lessen required pedal pressure. The parking brake operates the rear brakes through a cable system.

**For all brake system repair and service procedures not detailed below, please refer to "Brakes" in the Unit Repair Section.**

## Master Cylinder

### REMOVAL & INSTALLATION

Clean the outside of the cylinder thoroughly, particularly around the cap and fluid lines. On ZX models, remove the heatshield plate. Disconnect the fluid lines and cap them to keep dirt out. On models with a fluid level gauge, disconnect the electrical connector. Remove the clevis pin connecting the pushrod to the brake pedal arm inside the vehicle. This pin need not be removed on models with the vacuum booster. Unbolt the master cylinder from the firewall and remove along with gasket. If the pushrod is not adjustable, there will be shims between the cylinder and the firewall. These shims, or the adjustable pushrod, are used to adjust brake pedal free-play. After installation, bleed the system and check for pedal free-play. The 200SX's pushrod is not adjustable, as the rod between the brake booster and the master cylinder is secured by adhesion. After installation, bleed the system and check the pedal free-play.

### PEDAL ADJUSTMENT

**NOTE: Ordinary brake fluid will boil and cause brake failure under the high temperatures developed in disc brake systems. Special fluid meeting DOT 3 or 4 specifications for disc brake systems must be used.**

Before adjusting the pedal, make sure that the brakes are correctly adjusted.

Adjust the pedal free-play by means of an adjustable pushrod or shims between the master cylinder and the firewall. Adjust the pedal height by means of the pedal arm stop pad. Free-play should be approximately 0.04–0.12 in. on all models.

**BRAKE PEDAL SPECIFICATIONS**

| Model | Pedal Height (in.) |
|---|---|
| 1983 200SX | 7 |
| 1984–88 200SX | MT 7.28–7.68<br>AT 7.36–7.76 |
| 240SX | MT 6.97–7.36<br>AT 7.32–7.72 |
| 280ZX | 8 |
| 300ZX | MT 7.17–7.56<br>AT 7.24–7.64 |
| 1983–84 810, Maxima | 7 |
| 1985–88 810, Maxima | 7.24–7.64 |
| 1989–90 Maxima | MT 6.26–6.65<br>AT 6.65–7.05 |
| 1983–86 Pulsar | MT 7.64–8.03<br>AT 7.76–8.15 |
| 1987–88 Pulsar | MT 6.18–6.57<br>AT 6.54–6.93 |
| 1989–90 Pulsar, Sentra | MT 6.30–6.61<br>AT 6.46–6.85 |
| 1983–86 Sentra | MT 7.64–8.03<br>AT 7.76–8.15 |
| 1987–88 Sentra | MT 6.10–6.50<br>AT 6.46–6.85 |
| 1983–86 Stanza Sedan | MT 5.85–6.24<br>AT 5.93–6.32 |
| 1987–90 Stanza Sedan | 7.24–7.64 |
| 1986 2WD Stanza Wagon | MT 8.86–9.25<br>AT 8.78–9.17 |
| 1986 4WD Stanza Wagon | MT 8.46–8.86<br>AT 8.39–8.78 |

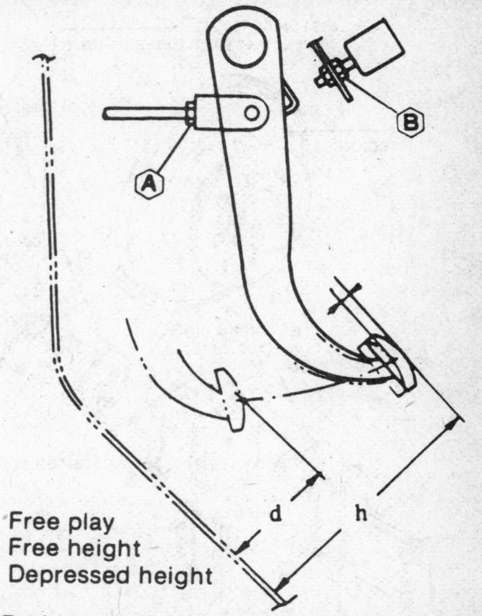


Brake pedal adjustment—all models. "B" shows locknut

## Brake Proportioning Valve

All models covered in this manual are equipped with brake proportioning valves of several different types. The valves all do the same job, which is to separate the front and rear brake lines, allowing them to function independently, and preventing the rear brakes from locking before the front brakes. Damage, such as brake line leakage, in either the front or rear brake system will not affect the normal operation of the unaffected system. If, in the event of a panic stop, the rear brakes lock up before the front brakes, it could mean the proportioning valve is defective. In that case, replace the entire proportioning valve.

### REMOVAL & INSTALLATION

**NOTE: On many models, the proportioning valve is incorporated into the master cylinder. Consequently, removal and installation procedures are limited to replacement of the master cylinder unit as a whole.**

1. Disconnect and plug the brake lines at the valve.
2. Unscrew the mounting bolt(s) and remove the valve.

**NOTE: Do not disassemble the valve**

3. Installation is in the reverse order of removal. Bleed the system.

## Power Brake Booster

### REMOVAL & INSTALLATION

1. Remove the master cylinder.
2. Remove the vacuum hose at the power brake booster.
3. Remove the pushrod from the brake pedal.
4. From under the instrument panel, remove the cowl-to-booster nuts. Remove the brake booster.
5. Installation is in the reverse order of removal.

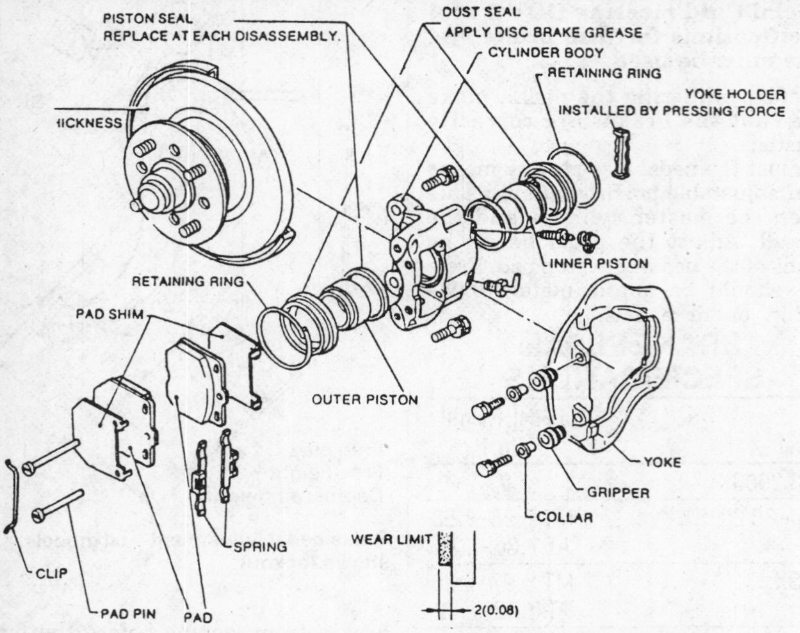


**N22 front disc brake assembly—N20, N22A, N32, N34L similar**

# Front Disc Brake Pads

## REMOVAL & INSTALLATION

### *Maxima, 200SX and 240SX*

#### TYPES N20, N22, N22A, N32, N34L

1. Raise and support the front of the car safely. Remove the front wheels.
2. Remove the retaining clip from the outboard pad.
3. Remove the pad pins retaining the anti-squeal springs.
4. Remove the pads.
5. To install, open the bleeder screw slightly and push the outer piston into the cylinder until the dust seal groove aligns with the end of the seal retaining ring, then close the bleed screw. Install the inner pad.
6. Pull the yoke out to push the inner piston into place. Install the outer pad.
7. Lightly coat the areas where the pins touch the pads, and where the pads touch the caliper (at the top) with grease.
8. Install the anti-squeal springs and pad pins. Install the clip.
9. Apply the brakes a few times to seat the pads. Check the master cylinder level. Add fluid if necessary. Bleed the brakes as required.

#### TYPE CL22V

1. Raise the front of the car and support it safely.
2. Unscrew and remove the lower pin bolt (sub pin).
3. Swing the cylinder body upward and then remove the pad retainer, the inner and outer shims and the pads themselves.

**NOTE: Do not depress the brake pedal when the cylinder body is in the raised position or the piston will pop out.**

4. Clean the piston end of the cylinder body and the pin bolt holes.
5. Pull the cylinder body to the outer side and install the inner pad.
6. Install the outer pad, the shim and the pad retainer.
7. Reposition the cylinder body and then tighten the pin bolt to 12–15 ft. lbs. (16–21 Nm).

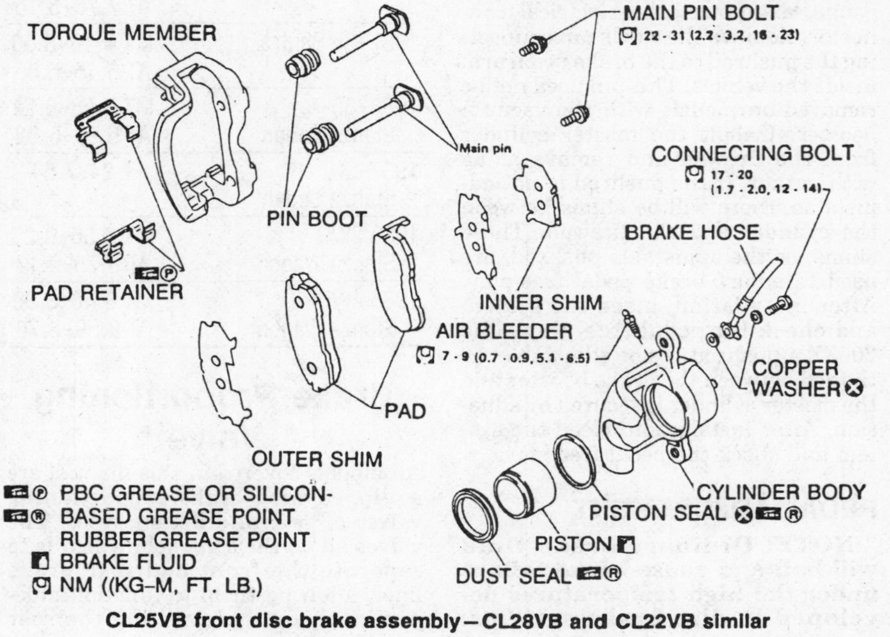


**CL25VB front disc brake assembly—CL28VB and CL22VB similar**

8. Apply the brakes a few times to seat the new pads. Check the fluid level and bleed the brakes as required.

#### TYPE AD22V

1. Raise the front of the vehicle and support safely. Remove the front wheels.
2. Remove the lower caliper guide pin.
3. Rotate the brake caliper body upward.
4. Remove the brake pad retainer and the inner and outer pad shims.
5. Remove the brake pads.

**NOTE: Do not depress the brake pedal when the caliper body is raised. The brake piston will be forced out of the caliper.**

6. Clean the piston end of the caliper body and the pin bolt holes. Be careful not to get oil on the brake rotor.
7. Pull the caliper body to the outer side and install the inner brake pad.
8. Install the outer pad, shim and pad retainer.
9. Reposition the caliper body and then tighten the guide pin bolt to 23–30 ft. lbs.
10. Apply the brakes a few times to seat the pads before driving out on the road.

#### TYPES CL28VB, CL22VB AND CL25VB

1. Raise the vehicle and support it safely. Remove the front wheels. Remove the pin (lower) bolt from the caliper.
2. Swing the caliper body upward on the upper bolt. Remove the pad retainers and inner and outer shims.

**NOTE: Do not depress the brake pedal when the cylinder body is in the raised position or the piston will pop out of the cylinder.**

3. Check the level of fluid in the master cylinder. If the fluid is near the maximum level, use a clean syringe to remove fluid until the level is down well below the lip of the reservoir. Then, use a large C-clamp or piston expansion tool to press the caliper piston back into the caliper, to allow room for the installation of the thicker new pads.
4. Install the new pads, utilizing new shims, in reverse order. Torque the lower retaining bolt to 16–23 ft. lbs.

### *280ZX and 300ZX*

#### TYPES CL28V, CL28VA, CL28VB AND CL28VE

1. Raise and support the front of the vehicle on jackstands. Remove the wheels.
2. Remove the lower pin bolt which retains the caliper to the torque member.
3. Rotate the caliper up and out of the way, exposing the pads. Do not try to move the caliper sideways.
4. Remove the pad retainers, the inner and outer shims, then the pads.
5. To install, clean the piston end and pin bolts.
6. Install a new inner pad. Rotate the caliper back down into place, slightly open the bleeder screw, then using a long bar, lever the caliper to the outside to press the piston into place. Rotate the caliper back up and out of the way.
7. Lightly coat the sliding surfaces of the torque member with grease. Install a new outer pad with the inner and outer shims. Install the pad retainers; be careful not to install them upside down.
8. Rotate the caliper down and install the pin bolt. Tighten to 16-23 ft. lbs. (22-31 Nm).
9. Apply the brakes a few times to seat the pads. Check the master cylinder level and add fluid if necessary. Bleed the brakes if necessary.

### *Pulsar, Sentra and Stanza*

1. Raise and support the front of the vehicle on jackstands, then remove the wheels.
2. Remove the bottom guide pin (Stanza and Sentra) or the lock pin (Pulsar) from the caliper and swing the caliper cylinder body upward.
3. Remove the brake pad retainers and the pads.
4. Install the brake pads and caliper assembly.

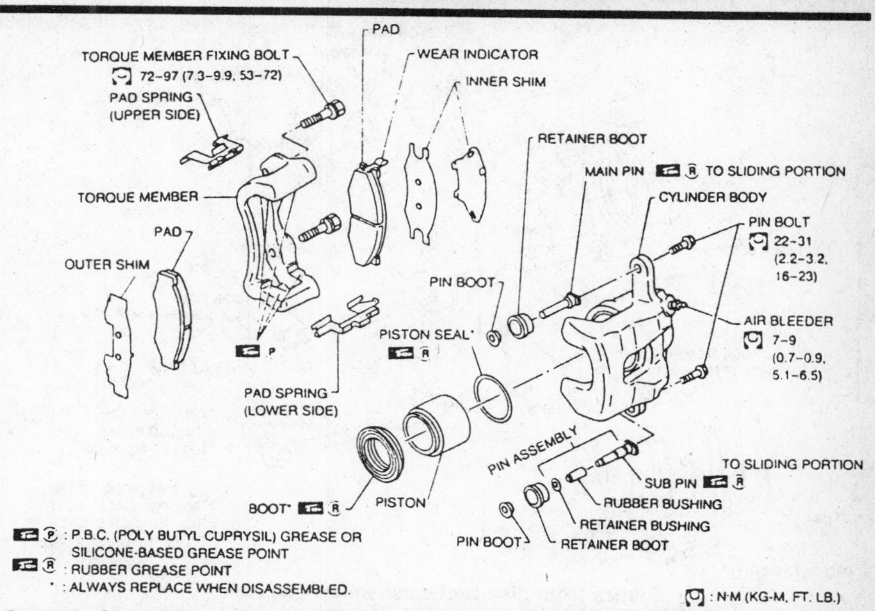


**CL28VA, CL28VB front disc brake assembly—1984–90 280ZX, 300ZX (except 1987–90 turbo)**

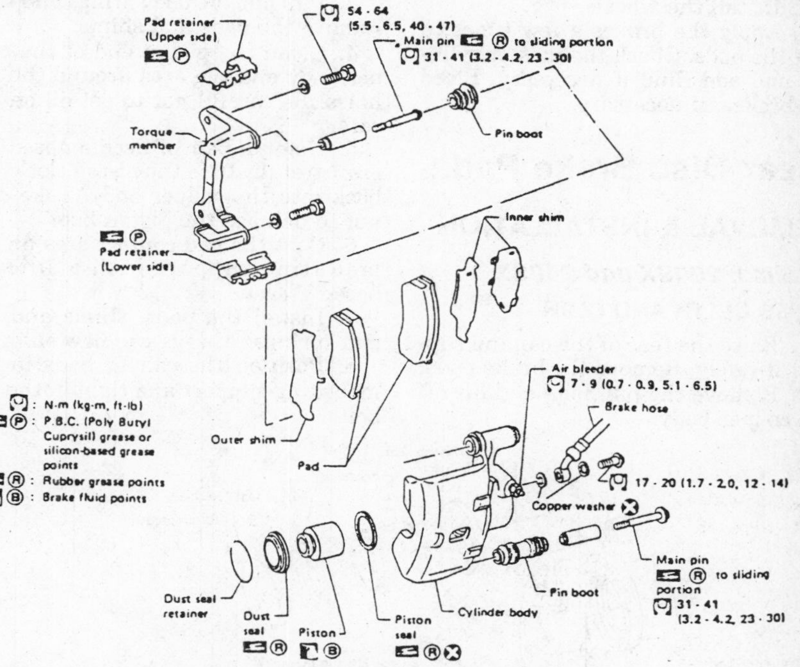


**Pulsar front disc brake assembly—typical**

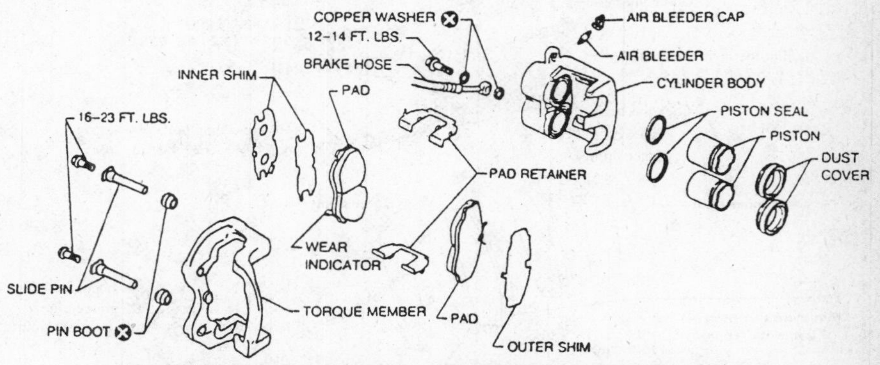


**CL28VE front disc brake assembly—1987–90 300ZX with turbo**

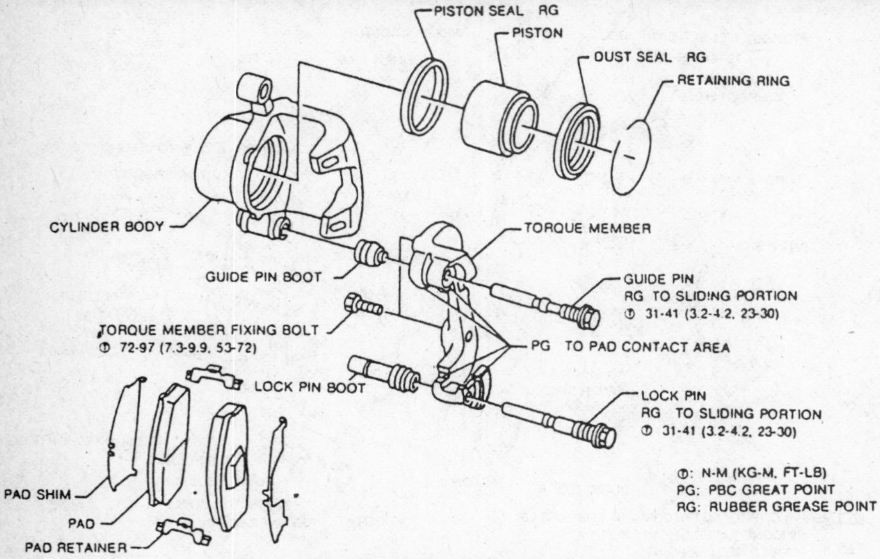


**Stanza front disc brake assembly—typical**

5. Install the wheels.
6. Apply the brakes a few times to seat the pads. Check the master cylinder and add fluid if necessary. Bleed the brakes, if necessary.

## Rear Disc Brake Pads

### REMOVAL & INSTALLATION

#### *Maxima, 200SX and 240SX*

**TYPES CL11H AND CL9H**

1. Raise the rear of the car and support it safely. Remove the brake pads.
2. Remove the pin bolts and lift off the caliper body.
3. Pull out the pad springs and then remove the pads and shims.
4. Clean the piston end of the caliper body and the area around the pin holes. Be careful not to get oil on the rotor.
5. Using a pair of needle nosed pliers, carefully turn the piston clockwise back into the caliper body. Take care not to damage the piston boot.
6. Coat the pad contact area on the mounting support with a silicone based grease.
7. Install the pads, shims and the pad springs. Always use new shims.
8. Position the caliper body in the mounting support and tighten the pin bolts.

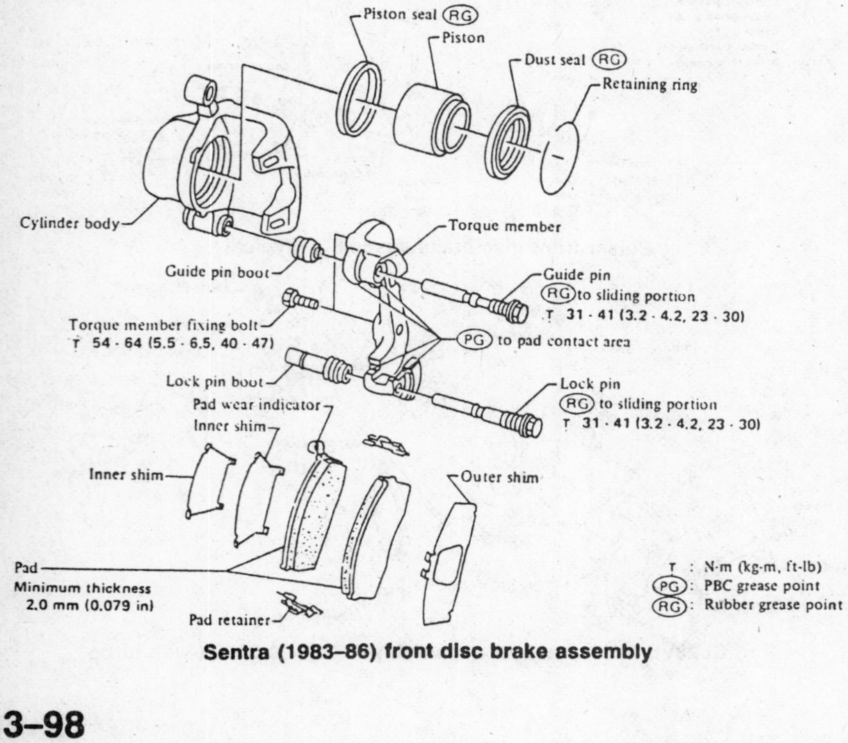


**Sentra (1983–86) front disc brake assembly**

9. Replace the wheel, lower the car and bleed the system.

**TYPES CL11HB AND CL14B**

1. Raise the vehicle and support it safely. Remove the rear wheel.
2. Remove the 2 pin bolts and the lock spring. Remove the caliper and suspending it above the disc so as to avoid putting any strain on the hose.
3. Remove the pad retainers, pads, and shims.

**NOTE: Do not depress the brake pedal when the cylinder body is in the raised position or the piston will pop out. Avoid damaging the piston seal when removing/installing the pads and retainers.**

4. Check the level of fluid in the master cylinder. If the fluid is near the maximum level, use a clean syringe to remove fluid until the level is down well below the lip of the reservoir. Then, press the caliper piston back into the caliper by turning it clockwise (it has a helical groove on the outer diameter). This will allow room for the installation of the thicker new pads.
5. Install the new pads using new shims in reverse order of the removal procedure.

#### *280ZX and 300ZX*

1. Raise and support the rear of the vehicle and support safely. Remove the wheels.
2. Disconnect the parking brake cable.
3. Remove the clip at the outside of the pad pins.
4. Remove the pad pins. Hold the anti-squeal springs in place by hand.
5. Remove the pads.
6. Clean the end of the piston with clean brake fluid. Lightly coat the caliper-to-pad, the yoke-to-pad, the retaining pin-to-pad and the retaining pin-to-bracket surfaces with grease.
7. Push in on the piston while at the same time turning it clockwise into the bore. Then, with a lever between the rotor and yoke, push the yoke over until there is clearance to install the pads, equally.
8. Install the shims, the pads, the anti-squeal springs and the pins. Install the clip. Note that the inner pad has a tab which must fit into the piston notch. Make sure the piston notch is centered to allow for proper pad installation.
9. Apply the brakes a few times to center the pads. Check the master cylinder fluid level and add fluid, if necessary.

## Brake Shoes

### REMOVAL & INSTALLATION

#### *Maxima and 200SX*

1. Raise the vehicle and remove the wheels.
2. Release the parking brake. Disconnect the cross rod from the brake cylinder lever. Remove the brake drum. Place a heavy rubber band around the cylinder to prevent the piston from popping out.
3. Remove the return springs and shoes.
4. Hook the return springs into the new shoes. Connect the springs between the shoes and the backing plate. The longer return spring must be next to the wheel cylinder. Apply a thin film of grease to the pivot points at the ends of the brake shoes. Grease the shoe locating buttons on the backing plate, also. Keep the grease away fromt the linings or drums.
5. Place one shoe in the adjuster and piston slots, and pry the other shoe into position.
6. Replace the drums and wheels. Adjust the brakes. Bleed the the air from the system if the brake lines were disconnected.
7. Reconnect the handbrake, making sure that it does not cause the shoes to drag when it is released.

#### *280ZX and 300ZX*

1. Raise the rear of the evhicle and support safely. Remove the rear wheels and the drums.
2. Remove the anti-rattle springs.
3. Remove both brake shoes together.
4. Apply multi-purpose grease to the adjusting wheel, the threaded and the sliding portions of the adjust screw.
5. Apply multi-purpose grease to the backing plate, the anchor block and sliding portions of the wheel cylinder. Avoid getting grease onto the lining surfaces.
6. Install the shoes, the anti-rattle springs and the return spring.
7. Install the drum and adjust the adjuster mechanism.

#### *Pulsar, Sentra and Stanza*

1. Raise the rear of the vehicle and support safely. Remove the rear wheels and the drums.
2. Release the parking brake lever, then remove the anti-rattle spring and the pin from the brake shoes. To remove the anti-rattle spring and pin, push the spring/pin assembly into the brake shoe, turn it 90 degrees and release it; the retainer cap, spring, washer and pin will separate.

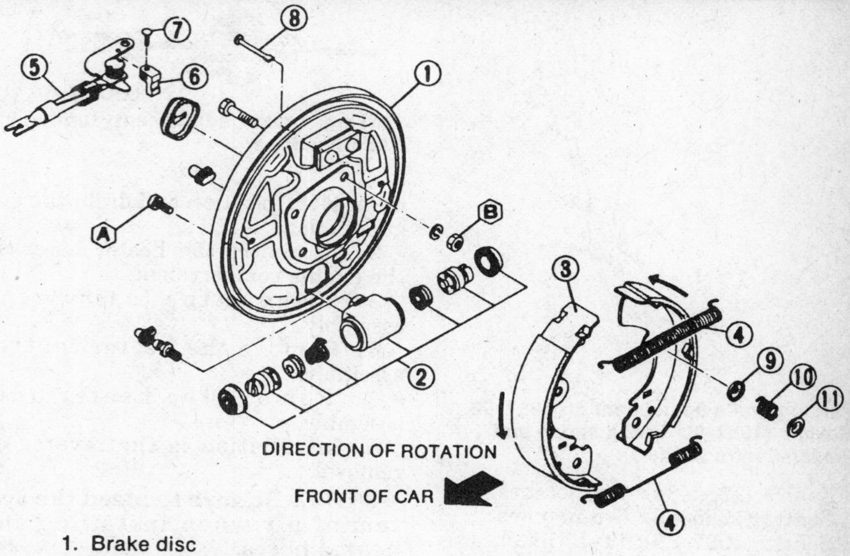


1. Brake disc
2. Wheel cylinder assembly
3. Brake shoe assembly
4. Return spring
5. Adjuster assembly
6. Stopper
7. Stopper pin
8. Anti-rattle pin
9. Spring seat
10. Anti-rattle spring
11. Retainer

**200SX rear brake drum assembly**

3. Support the brake shoe assembly and remove the return springs and brake shoes.

**NOTE: If the brake shoes are difficult to remove, loosen the brake adjusters. Place a heavy rubber band around the cylinder to prevent the piston from popping out.**

4. Clean the backing plate and check the wheel cylinder for leaks.
5. Lubricate the backing plate pads and the screw adjusters with lithium base grease. Install the brake shoes and springs.
6. Install the drum assembly.
7. Adjust brakes and bleed the system if necessary.

## Wheel Cylinder

### REMOVAL & INSTALLATION

**NOTE: Nissan/Datsun obtains parts from two manufacturers; Nabco and Tokico. Parts are not interchangeable! The manufacturer's name can be found on the wheel cylinder.**

1. Disconnect the hydraulic line and remove the wheel cylinder from the brake backing plate.
2. Remove the dust boot and take out the piston. Disacard the piston cup. The dust boot can be reused although it is best to replace it.
3. Wash all of the components in clean brake fluid.
4. Inspect the piston and piston bore. Replace any components that are severely corroded, scored or worn. The piston and piston bore may be polished lightly with crocus cloth; move the cloth around the piston bore, not in and out.
5. Wash the wheel cylinder and piston in clean brake fluid.
6. Coat all new components to be installed with clean brake fluid.
7. Assemble the cylinder and install it on the backing plate. Connect the hydraulic line.
8. Bleed the brake system.

## Parking Brake Cable

### ADJUSTMENT

Handbrake adjustments are generally not needed, unless the cables have stretched or replaced.

#### *All Models*

1. Pull up the handbrake lever, counting the number of notches for full engagement. Full engagement should be:

810: 5–6 notches
200SX: 7–8 notches
240SX: 6–8 notches
280ZX: 4–6 notches
300ZX: 8–10 notches
Maxima (1984): 5–6 notches
Maxima (1985–86): 7–8 notches
Maxima (1987–88): 11–13 notches
Maxima (1989–90): 9–11 notches
Pulsar (1983–84): 6–7 notches
Pulsar (1985–86): 6–8 notches
Pulsar (1987–90): 7–11 notches

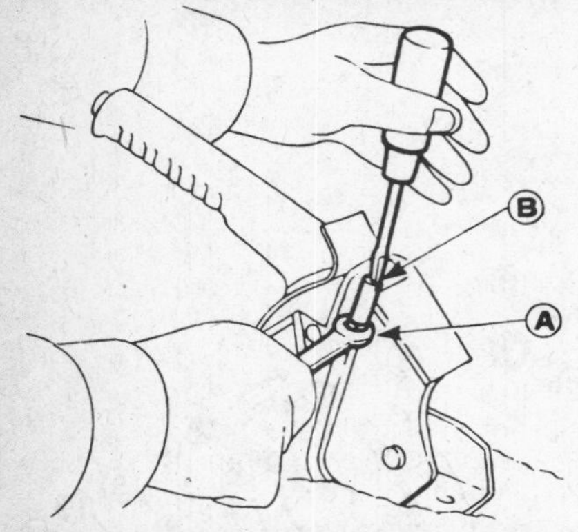


**Parking brake adjustment on 1987–90 Maxima (1987–90 Stanza sedan and Pulsar/Sentra similar)**

Sentra (1982–84): 6–7 notches
Sentra (1985–86): 6–8 notches
Sentra (1987–88): 11–13 notches
Sentra (1989–90): 7–11 notches
Stanza sedan (1982–86): 7–8 notches
Stanza sedan (1987–88): 11–13 notches
Stanza sedan (1989–90): 11–13 notches
Stanza wagon (2wd): 11–17 notches
Stanza wagon (4wd): 8–9 notches

2. Release the parking brake.
3. Adjust the lever stroke at the cable equalizer under the car; loosen the lock nut and tighten the adjusting nut to reduce the number of notches necessary for engagement. Tighten the lock nut. On the 1989–90 240SX, 1987–90 Maxima, 1987–90 Stanza sedan and the 1987–90 Pulsar/Sentra, the locknut and adjuster can be found inside the handbrake assembly, in the passenger compartment.
4. Check the adjustment and repeat as necessary.
5. After adjustment, check to see that the rear brake levers (at the calipers) return to their full off positions when the lever is released, and that the rear cables are not slack when the lever is released.
6. To adjust the warning lamp, bend the warning lamp switch plate down so that the light comes on when the lever is engaged 1–2 notches.

# CHASSIS ELECTRICAL

## Heater Unit

### REMOVAL & INSTALLATION

#### *Pulsar and Sentra*

1. Set the **TEMP** lever to the maximum **HOT** position and drain the engine coolant.
2. Disconnect the heater hoses at the engine compartment.
3. Remove the instrument assembly.
4. Remove the heater control assembly.
5. Remove the heater unit assembly.
6. Installation is the reverse of removal.

**NOTE: Be sure to bleed the system of air when installing the heater hoses.**

**Parking brake adjustment turnbuckle, underneath car**

#### *Stanza*

1. Remove the instrument panel.
2. Disconnect the heater hoses and vacuum tube in the engine compartment.
3. Remove the heater control assembly.
4. Unbolt and remove the heater unit.
5. Installation is the reverse of removal.

**NOTE: Be sure to bleed the system of air when installing the heater hoses.**

#### *200SX and 240SX*

**NOTE: You may be able to delete several of the above steps if only certain components of the heater unit need service. In some cases where removal of ducting is called for, it may just simply be disconnected from its attachment point.**

1. Set the **TEMP** lever to the **HOT** position and drain the coolant.
2. Disconnect the heater hoses from the driver's side of the heater unit.
3. At this point for the 200SX the manufacturer suggests removing the front seats. To do this, remove the plastic covers over the ends of the seat runners, both front and back, to expose the seat mounting bolts. Remove the bolts and remove the seats.
4. Remove the console box and the floor carpets.
5. Remove the instrument panel lower covers from both the driver's and passenger's sides of the car. Remove the lower cluster lids.
6. Remove the left side ventilator duct. On 240SX, detach the defroster duct from the upper center heater unit opening.
7. Remove the radio, sound balancer and stereo cassette deck as required.
8. Remove the instrument panel-to-transmission tunnel stay.
9. Remove the rear heater duct from the floor of the vehicle.
10. Remove the center ventilator duct.
11. Remove the left and right hand side ventilator ducts from the lower heater outlets.
12. Disconnect the wiring harness connections.
13. Remove the 2 screws at the bottom sides of the heater unit and the 1 screw at the top of the unit and remove the unit together with the heater control assembly.
14. Installation is the reverse of removal.

#### *280ZX without Air Conditioning*

1. Disconnect the negative battery cable.
2. Remove the lower instrument panel cover and the glove box.
3. Remove the floor nozzle, defroster duct, and the side defroster duct on the right side.
4. Remove the heater duct.
5. Disconnect the blower motor wiring harness.
6. Disconnect the control cable at the blower assembly by removing the clip.
7. Remove the bolts securing the blower assembly to the firewall and remove the blower assembly.
8. The motor and fan can be removed by removing the 3 motor retaining screws. The fan simply bolts onto the motor shaft.
9. Installation is in the reverse order of removal.

The motor and fan can also be removed without removing the entire blower housing assembly as follows:

a. Disconnect the negative battery cable
b. Remove the lower instrument panel cover and the floor nozzle on the right side
c. Disconnect the blower motor wiring harness
d. Remove the 3 motor attaching screws and remove the motor and fan as a unit from the blower housing
e. Installation is the reverse of the removal procedure.

#### *280ZX with Air Conditioning*

1. Disconnect the negative battery cable.
2. Remove the instrument panel lower cover on the right side. Remove the glove box.
3. Remove the floor nozzle, the defroster duct, and the side defroster duct on the passenger's side.

4. Disconnect the blower motor electrical harness.
5. Disconnect and label the 2 vacuum hoses.
6. Remove the 3 blower assembly mounting bolts and remove the assembly.
7. Installation is the reverse order of removal.

The motor can be removed without removing the blower assembly as follws:

a. Disconnect the negative batter cable
b. Remove the instrument panel lower cover and the floor nozzle on the right side
c. Disconnect the blower motor electrical harness
d. Remove the 3 blower motor attaching screws and remove the motor and fan as an assembly from the blower housing
e. Installation is the reverse of the removal procedure.

#### 300ZX, 810 and Maxima

**NOTE: Several of the following steps may be deleted if only certain components of the heater assembly need service.**

1. Set the **TEMP** lever to the **HOT** position and drain the coolant.
2. Disconnect the heater hoses from the driver's side of the heater unit.
3. At this point the manufacturer suggests removing the front seats (810 and Maxima only). To do this, remove the plastic covers over the ends of the seat runners, front and back, to expose the seat mounting bolts. Remove the bolts and lift out the seats.
4. Remove the front carpets.
5. Remove the instrument panel lower covers from both the driver's and passenger's sides of the car.
6. Remove the left side ventilator duct.
7. Remove the instrument panel assembly as detailed later in this section.
8. Remove the rear heater duct from the floor of the car (810/Maxima only).
9. Tag and disconnect the wiring harness connectors.
10. Remove the 2 screws at the bottom sides of the heater unit and the 1 screw from the top of the unit. Lift out the heater together with the heater control assembly.
11. Installation is the reverse of removal.

## Heater Core

### REMOVAL & INSTALLATION

#### Pulsar and Sentra

1. Remove the heater unit.
2. Disconnect the inlet and outlet hoses.
3. Remove the case clips and split the case. Remove the core.
4. Installation is the reverse of removal. Always check the operation of the air mix door when re-attaching the heater case halves.

#### 200SX and 240SX

1. Remove the heater unit as described earlier.
2. Remove the hoses from the heater core and then slide the core from the case.
3. Installation is the reverse of removal.

#### 280ZX

1. Remove the heater unit.
2. Remove the water cock.
3. Remove the case clips and split the heater case. Remove the core.

#### 300ZX, 810 and Maxima

1. Remove the heater unit.
2. Remove the center vent cover and heater control assembly, loosening the clips and screws.
3. Remove the screws securing the door shafts.
4. Remove the clips from the case and split the case. Remove the core.
5. Installation is the reverse of removal.

#### Stanza

1. Remove pedal bracket mounting bolts, steering column mounting bolts, brake and clutch pedal cotter pins.
2. Move the pedal bracket and steering column to the left.
3. Disconnect the air mix door control cable and heater valve control elver, then remove the control lever.
4. Remove the core cover.
5. Disconnect the hoses at the core.
6. Installation is the reverse of removal. Be sure to bleed the system.

## Windshield Wiper Motor

### REMOVAL & INSTALLATION

#### Pulsar and Sentra

The wiper motor is on the firewall under the hood The operating linkage is on the firewall inside the car.

1. Detach the motor wiring plug.
2. Inside the car, remove the nut connecting the linkage to the wiper shaft.
3. Unbolt and remove the wiper motor from the firewall.
4. Reverse the procedure for installation.

#### 200SX, 240SX, 280ZX and Stanza

1. Disconnect the battery ground cable.
2. Disconnect the electrical connector at the motor. Remove the cowl cover as required.
3. Remove the motor attaching bolts. The motor is under the hood, on the firewall.
4. Remove the nut securing the arm to the motor shaft. Remove the motor.
5. Installation is the reverse of removal.

#### 300ZX, 810 and Maxima

The wiper motor and operating linkage is on the firewall under the hood.

1. Lift the wiper arms. Remove the securing nuts and detach the arms.
2. Remove the nuts holding the wiper pivots to the body. Remove the air intake grille for access.
3. Open the hood and unscrew the motor from the firewall.
4. Disconnect the wiring connector and remove the wiper motor with the linkage.
5. Reverse the procedure for installation.

**NOTE: If the wipers do not park correctly, adjust the position of the automatic stop cover on the wiper motor.**

## Windshield Wiper Switch

### REMOVAL & INSTALLATION

#### Front

The windshield wiper switch is part of the combination switch which is mounted on the steering column. Refer to the "Combination Switch, Removal and Installation" procedures, and replace the windshield wiper switch.

#### Rear

##### 280ZX

The rear window wiper switch is located on the left-side of the instrument panel.

1. Pull the rear window wiper switch knob from the switch.
2. Using a spanner wrench tool or equivalent, remove the retaining nut and the washer from the switch.
3. Remove the switch from the back of the instrument panel and disconnect the electrical connector.
4. To install, reverse the removal procedures.

##### 300ZX, STANZA AND SENTRA

The rear window wiper switch is located on the right side of the instrument panel.

1. Remove the instrument cluster.
2. Remove the nut retaining the instrument combination switch to the dash.

**NOTE: The instrument combination switches are secured at hooks and basements.**

3. Disconnect the electrical connectors from the rear of the switch, then remove it.
4. To install, reverse the removal procedures.

**NOTE: On Stanza wagon the rear window wiper/washer is located left-side of the instrument panel. On Sentra wagon the rear window wiper/washer is located right-side of the instrument panel. Removal of the rear wiper/washer switch on these models is similar to the above procedures.**

## Instrument Cluster

### REMOVAL & INSTALLATION

#### *810 and Maxima*

1. Disconnect the negative battery cable.
2. Remove the instrument panel lower cover.
3. Remove the steering wheel.
4. Disconnect the speedometer cable.
5. Remove the 6 mounting screws and lift out the cluster lid.
6. Unscrew the mounting bolts and lift off the left side instrument pad (this is the hooded part of the dashboard that the instrument cluster sits in).
7. Loosen the instrument cluster mounting screws, pull it out slightly and disconnect all wiring. Remove the cluster.
8. Installation is in the reverse order of removal.

#### *280ZX*

1. Disconnect the negative battery cable.
2. Remove the steering wheel.
3. Remove the steering column cover.
4. Remove the instrument panel lower cover on the left side.
5. Disconnect the speedometer cable at the intermediate connection.
6. Remove the combination switch.
7. Remove the cluster retaining screws, pull out slightly and disconnect the electrical connectors. Remove the instrument cluster.

#### *200SX and 240SX*

1. Disconnect the battery ground terminal.
2. It may be necessary to remove the steering wheel and covers to remove the instrument cluster.
3. Remove the screws holding the cluster lid in place and remove the lid.
4. Remove the 5 bolts (200SX) or 3 screws (240SX) holding the cluster in place and pull the cluster out, then remove all connections from its back. Make sure you mark the wiring to avoid confusion during reassembly.

#### *Pulsar, Sentra and Stanza*

1. Disconnect the battery terminals.
2. Remove the steering wheel and the steering column covers.
3. Remove the instrument cluster lid by removing its screws.
4. Remove the instrument cluster screws, pull the unit out and disconnect all wiring and cables from its rear. Mark the wires to avoid confusion during assembly. Be careful not to damage the printed circuit.
5. Remove the cluster.
6. Installation is the reverse of removal.

## Headlight Switch

### REMOVAL & INSTALLATION

Since the headlight switch is part of the combination switch, please refer to "Combination Switch" in this section.

## Stoplight Switch

### REMOVAL & INSTALLATION

1. Remove the floor mats.
2. Disconnect the multi-connector from the switch.
3. Note and record the amount of threads exposed on the switch.
4. Loosen the locknut and adjusting nuts and remove the switch from the mounting bracket.
5. Place the new switch in the mounting bracket.
6. Install and tighten the adjusting and lock nuts so that the same amount of threads is exposed as recorded in Step 3.
7. Connect the multi-connector and check that the brake lights illuminate when the brake pedal is depressed.
8. Replace the floor mats.

## Fuses, Relays and Circuit Breakers

### LOCATION

| Model | Fuse Box Location | Fusible Link Location |
|---|---|---|
| 810 | Under dash at extreme right | Right rear of engine compartment ① |
| 200SX | Underneath glovebox at extreme left | Off of battery (+) cable ② |
| 240SX | Underneath dash at extreme left | Off of battery (+) cable ② |
| 280ZX | Under dash at extreme right | Right rear of engine compartment ① |
| 300ZX | Under dash at extreme left | Off of battery (+) cable |
| Maxima | Under dash at extreme left | Off of battery (+) cable |
| Pulsar | Under dash at extreme left | Off of battery (+) cable |
| Sentra | Under dash at extreme left | Off of battery (+) cable |
| 1983–86 Stanza | Under dash at extreme right | Off of battery (+) cable |
| 1987–90 Stanza | Under dash at extreme left | Off of battery (+) cable |

① A fusible link for the fuel injection system is at the (+) battery cable
② In relay/fuse box to rear of battery

# Porsche 14

911, 924, 928, 944—All Models

# SERIAL NUMBER IDENTIFICATION

## Vehicle Identification Plate

The chassis number on all vehicles is located on the left (driver) side windshield post and is visible from the outside of the vehicle. On the 911 and 911 Turbo, the chassis number is also found in the luggage compartment under the rug and on the identification plate near the front hood lock catch. On all other vehicles, the VIN plate is in the engine compartment near the battery.

## Engine Number

On all vehicles except the 911 and 911 Turbo, the engine serial number is stamped on the left of the crankcase near the clutch housing. On the 911 and 911 Turbo, the engine number is located on the right side of the crankcase adjacent to the blower.

## Transaxle Number

The manual transaxle number is usually stamped in a cross reinforcement rib in the rear area of the transaxle case. The automatic transaxle number is usually stamped in an intermediate plate between the transaxle case and final drive case. Either way, the numbers should be visible from underneath the vehicle.

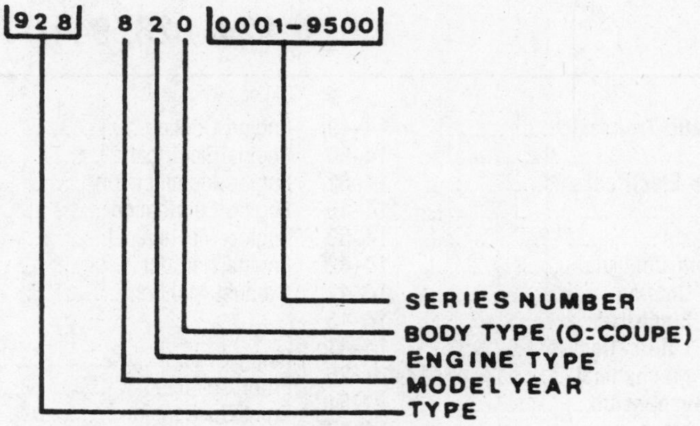


928 VIN Identification

CHASSIS NUMBER

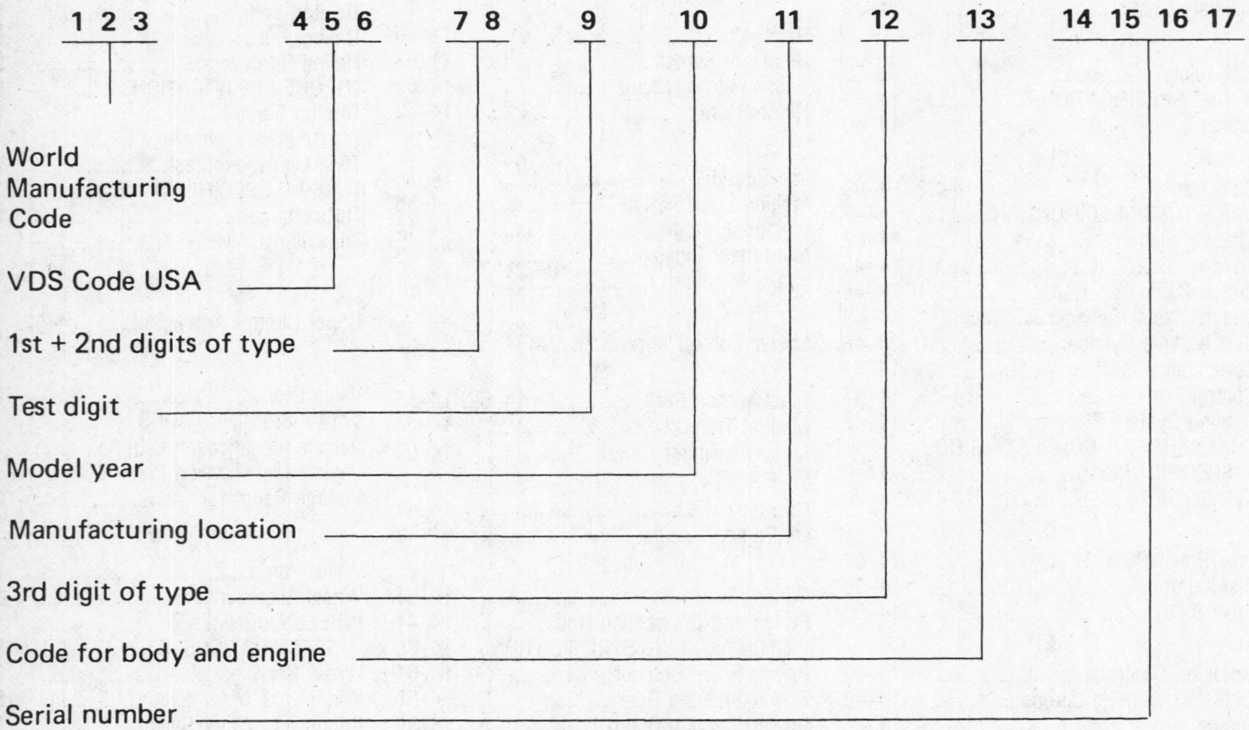


911 VIN Identification

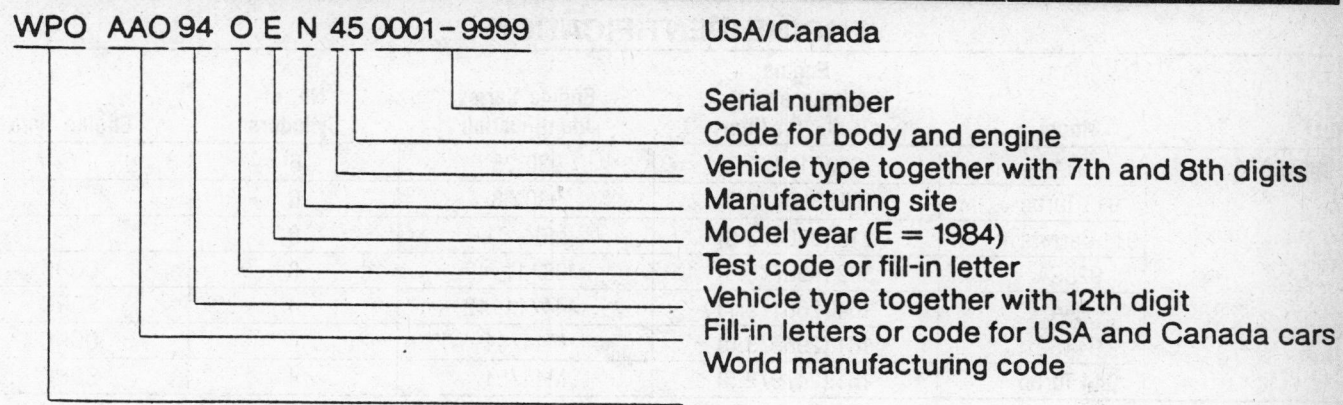

WPO AAO 94 O E N 45 0001-9999 USA/Canada

- Serial number
- Code for body and engine
- Vehicle type together with 7th and 8th digits
- Manufacturing site
- Model year (E = 1984)
- Test code or fill-in letter
- Vehicle type together with 12th digit
- Fill-in letters or code for USA and Canada cars
- World manufacturing code

**944 VIN Identification**

## ENGINE IDENTIFICATION

| Year | Model | Engine Displacement cu. in. (cc/liter) | Engine Series Identification | No. of Cylinders | Engine Type |
|---|---|---|---|---|---|
| 1983 | 911 | 183 (2994/3.0) | 930.16 | 6 | ① |
| | 928 | 284 (4664/4.7) | M28/19② | 8 | SOHC |
| | 944 | 151 (2479/2.5) | M44/02③ | 4 | SOHC |
| 1984 | 911 | 193 (3164/3.2) | 930.21 | 6 | ① |
| | 928 | 284 (4664/4.7) | M28/19② | 8 | SOHC |
| | 944 | 151 (2479/2.5) | M44/02③ | 4 | SOHC |
| 1985 | 911 | 193 (3164/3.2) | 930.21 | 6 | ① |
| | 928 | 302 (4957/5.0) | M28/43④ | 8 | DOHC |
| | 944 | 151 (2479/2.5) | M44/07⑤ | 4 | SOHC |
| 1986 | 911 | 193 (3164/3.2) | 930.21 | 6 | ① |
| | 911 Turbo | 201 (3299/3.3) | 930.68 | 6 | ① |
| | 928 | 302 (4957/5.0) | M28/43④ | 8 | DOHC |
| | 944 | 151 (2479/2.5) | M44/07⑤ | 4 | SOHC |
| | 944 Turbo | 151 (2479/2.5) | M44/51 | 4 | SOHC |
| 1987 | 911 | 193 (3164/3.2) | 930.21 | 6 | ① |
| | 911 Turbo | 201 (3299/3.3) | 930.68 | 6 | ① |
| | 924S | 151 (2479/2.5) | M44/07⑤ | 4 | SOHC |
| | 928S4 | 302 (4957/5.0) | M28/43④ | 8 | DOHC |
| | 944 | 151 (2479/2.5) | M44/07⑤ | 4 | SOHC |
| | 944S | 151 (2479/2.5) | M44/40⑥ | 4 | DOHC |
| | 944 Turbo | 151 (2479/2.5) | M44/51 | 4 | SOHC |
| 1988 | 911 | 193 (3164/3.2) | 930.21 | 6 | ① |
| | 911 Turbo | 201 (3299/3.3) | 930.68 | 6 | ① |
| | 924S | 151 (2479/2.5) | M44/07⑤ | 4 | SOHC |
| | 928S4 | 302 (4957/5.0) | M28/43④ | 8 | DOHC |
| | 944 | 151 (2479/2.5) | M44/07⑤ | 4 | SOHC |
| | 944S | 151 (2479/2.5) | M44/40⑥ | 4 | DOHC |
| | 944 Turbo | 151 (2479/2.5) | M44/51 | 4 | SOHC |

## ENGINE IDENTIFICATION

| Year | Model | Engine Displacement cu. in. (cc/liter) | Engine Series Identification | No. of Cylinders | Engine Type |
|---|---|---|---|---|---|
| 1989-90 | 911 | 193 (3164/3.2) | 930.25 | 6 | ① |
| | 911 Turbo | 201 (3299/3.3) | 930.68 | 6 | ① |
| | 911 Carrera 4 | 219 (3600/3.6) | M64/01 | 6 | ① |
| | 928S4 | 302 (4957/5.0) | M28/41, 42 | 8 | DOHC |
| | 944 | 164 (2681/2.7) | M44/11, 12 | 4 | SOHC |
| | 944S2 | 181 (2969/3.0) | M44/41 | 4 | DOHC |
| | 944 Turbo | 151 (2479/2.5) | M44/51 | 4 | SOHC |

DOHC Dual Overhead Camshaft
SOHC Single Overhead Camshaft
① Air cooled, 6 cylinder, horizontally opposed, rear-mounted
② M28/20 with automatic transaxle
③ M44/04 with automatic transaxle
④ M28/44 with automatic transaxle
⑤ M44/08 with automatic transaxle
⑥ 16 valve engine

## GENERAL ENGINE SPECIFICATIONS

| Year | Model | Engine Displacement cu. in. (cc) | Fuel System Type | Net Horsepower @ rpm | Net Torque @ rpm (ft. lbs.) | Bore × Stroke (in.) | Com-pression Ratio | Oil Pressure @ rpm |
|---|---|---|---|---|---|---|---|---|
| 1983 | 911 | 183 (2994) | CIS | 172 @ 5500 | 175 @ 4200 | 3.74 × 2.77 | 9.3:1 | 50 @ 5000 |
| | 928 | 284 (4664) | AFC | 234 @ 5250 | 263 @ 5250 | 3.82 × 3.11 | 9.3:1 | 70 @ 5500 |
| | 944 | 151 (2479) | DME | 143 @ 5500 | 137 @ 3000 | 3.94 × 3.11 | 9.5:1 | 50–70 @ 5500 |
| 1984 | 911 | 193 (3164) | DME | 200 @ 5900 | 185 @ 4800 | 3.74 × 2.93 | 9.5:1 | 50 @ 5000 |
| | 928 | 284 (4664) | AFC | 234 @ 5250 | 263 @ 4000 | 3.82 × 3.11 | 9.3:1 | 70 @ 5500 |
| | 944 | 151 (2479) | DME | 143 @ 5500 | 137 @ 3000 | 3.94 × 3.11 | 9.5:1 | 50–70 @ 5500 |
| 1985 | 911 | 193 (3164) | DME | 200 @ 5900 | 185 @ 4800 | 3.74 × 2.93 | 9.5:1 | 50 @ 5000 |
| | 928S | 302 (4957) | LH | 288 @ 5750 | 302 @ 2700 | 3.94 × 3.11 | 10.0:1 | 70 @ 5500 |
| | 944 | 151 (2479) | DME | 143 @ 5500 | 137 @ 3000 | 3.94 × 3.11 | 9.5:1 | 50–70 @ 5500 |
| 1986 | 911 | 193 (3164) | KE | 200 @ 5900 | 185 @ 4800 | 3.74 × 2.93 | 9.5:1 | 50 @ 5000 |
| | 911 Turbo | 201 (3299) | KE | 282 @ 5500 | 278 @ 4000 | 3.82 × 2.93 | 7.0:1 | 60 @ 5500 |
| | 928S | 302 (4957) | LH | 288 @ 5750 | 302 @ 2700 | 3.94 × 3.11 | 10.0:1 | 70 @ 5500 |
| | 944 | 151 (2479) | DME | 147 @ 5800 | 144 @ 3000 | 3.94 × 3.11 | 9.7:1 | 50–70 @ 5500 |
| | 944 Turbo | 151 (2479) | DME | 220 @ 5800 | 243 @ 3500 | 3.94 × 3.11 | 8.0:1 | 70 @ 5500 |
| 1987 | 911 | 193 (3164) | DME | 214 @ 5900 | 195 @ 4800 | 3.74 × 2.93 | 9.5:1 | 50 @ 5000 |
| | 911 Turbo | 201 (3299) | KE | 282 @ 5500 | 278 @ 4000 | 3.82 × 2.93 | 7.0:1 | 60 @ 5500 |
| | 924S | 151 (2479) | DME | 147 @ 5800 | 140 @ 3000 | 3.94 × 3.11 | 9.7:1 | 50–70 @ 5500 |
| | 928S4 | 302 (4957) | LH | 316 @ 6000 | 317 @ 3000 | 3.94 × 3.11 | 10.0:1 | 70 @ 5500 |
| | 944 | 151 (2479) | DME | 147 @ 5800 | 144 @ 3000 | 3.94 × 3.11 | 9.7:1 | 50–70 @ 5500 |
| | 944S | 151 (2479) | DME | 188 @ 6000 | 170 @ 4300 | 3.94 × 3.11 | 10.9:1 | 50–70 @ 5500 |
| | 944 Turbo | 151 (2479) | DME | 220 @ 5800 | 243 @ 3500 | 3.94 × 3.11 | 8.0:1 | 50–70 @ 5500 |
| 1988 | 911 | 193 (2164) | DME | 214 @ 5900 | 195 @ 4800 | 3.74 × 2.93 | 9.5:1 | 50 @ 5000 |
| | 911 Turbo | 201 (3299) | KE | 282 @ 5500 | 278 @ 4000 | 3.82 × 2.93 | 7.0:1 | 60 @ 5500 |
| | 924S | 219 (3600) | DME | 147 @ 5800 | 140 @ 3000 | 3.94 × 3.11 | 9.7:1 | 50–70 @ 5500 |
| | 928S4 | 302 (4957) | LH | 316 @ 6000 | 317 @ 3000 | 3.94 × 3.11 | 10.0:1 | 70 @ 5500 |
| | 944 | 164 (2681) | DME | 147 @ 5800 | 144 @ 3000 | 3.94 × 3.11 | 9.7:1 | 50–70 @ 5500 |
| | 944S | 181 (2969) | DME | 188 @ 6000 | 170 @ 4300 | 3.94 × 3.11 | 10.9:1 | 50–70 @ 5500 |
| | 944 Turbo | 151 (2479) | DME | 220 @ 5800 | 243 @ 3500 | 3.94 × 3.11 | 8.0:1 | 50–70 @ 5500 |

## GENERAL ENGINE SPECIFICATIONS

| Year | Model | Engine Displacement cu. in. (cc) | Fuel System Type | Net Horsepower @ rpm | Net Torque @ rpm (ft. lbs.) | Bore × Stroke (in.) | Com-pression Ratio | Oil Pressure @ rpm |
|---|---|---|---|---|---|---|---|---|
| 1989-90 | 911 | 193 (2164) | DME | 214 @ 5900 | 195 @ 4500 | 3.74 × 2.93 | 9.5:1 | 66 @ 5000 |
| | 911 Turbo | 201 (3299) | KE | 282 @ 5500 | 288 @ 4000 | 3.82 × 2.93 | 7.0:1 | 66 @ 5500 |
| | 911 Carrera 4 | 219 (3600) | DME | 247 @ 6100 | 247 @ 4800 | 3.94 × 3.01 | 11.3:1 | 74 @ 5000 |
| | 928S4 | 302 (4957) | LH | 316 @ 6000 | 317 @ 3000 | 3.94 × 3.11 | 10.0:1 | 74 @ 4000 |
| | 944 | 164 (2681) | DME | 162 @ 5800 | 166 @ 4200 | 4.09 × 3.11 | 10.9:1 | 52 @ 6000 |
| | 944S2 | 181 (2969) | DME | 208 @ 5800 | 207 @ 4100 | 4.09 × 3.11 | 10.9:1 | 52 @ 6000 |
| | 944 Turbo | 151 (2479) | DME | 247 @ 6000 | 258 @ 4000 | 3.94 × 3.11 | 8.0:1 | 52 @ 6000 |

AFC Air Flow Controlled Fuel Injection
CIS Bosch Constant Injection System
DME Digital Motor Electronic Fuel Injection
KE Bosch Electronic CIS Fuel Injection
LH Bosch Air Flow Controlled Fuel Injection

## TUNE-UP SPECIFICATIONS

| Year | Model | Engine Displacement cu. in. (cc) | Spark Plugs Type | Spark Plugs Gap (in.) | Ignition Timing (deg @ rpm) | Com-pression Pressure (psi) | Fuel Pump (psi) | Idle Speed (rpm) | Valve Clearance In. | Valve Clearance Ex. |
|---|---|---|---|---|---|---|---|---|---|---|
| 1983 | 911 | 183 (2994) | W225T30 | .030 | 25B @ 4000 | ① | 66-76 | 850-1000 | 0.004 | 0.016 |
| | 928 | 284 (4664) | WR8DS | .030 | 26B @ 3000 | ① | 76-85 | 700-800 | Hyd. | Hyd. |
| | 944 | 151 (2479) | WR8DS | .030 | 10B @ 850 | ① | 34-40 | 800-850 | Hyd. | Hyd. |
| 1984 | 911 | 193 (3164) | WR7DC | .028 | 25B @ 3800 | ① | 34-40 | 760-840 | 0.004 | 0.004 |
| | 928 | 284 (4664) | WR8DS | .030 | 26B @ 3000 | ① | 76-85 | 700-800 | Hyd. | Hyd. |
| | 944 | 151 (2479) | WR8DS | .030 | 10B @ 850 | ① | 34-40 | 800-850 | Hyd. | Hyd. |
| 1985 | 911 | 193 (3164) | WR7DC | .028 | 26B @ 4000 | ① | 34-40 | 780-820 | 0.004 | 0.004 |
| | 928S | 302 (4957) | WR7DC | .028 | 10B @ 680 | ① | 34-40 | 700-750 | Hyd. | Hyd. |
| | 944 | 151 (2479) | WR7DC | .028 | 10B @ 850 | ① | 34-40 | 800-850 | Hyd. | Hyd. |
| 1986 | 911 | 193 (3164) | WR7DC | .028 | 26B @ 4000 | ① | 34-40 | 780-820 | 0.004 | 0.004 |
| | 911 Turbo | 201 (3299) | W3DP | .028 | 26B @ 4000 | ① | 34-40 | 850-950 | 0.004 | 0.004 |
| | 928S | 302 (4957) | WR7DC | .028 | 10B @ 680 | ① | 28-37 | 660-700 | Hyd. | Hyd. |
| | 944 | 151 (2479) | WR7DC | .028 | 10B @ 850 | ① | 34-40 | 800-880 | Hyd. | Hyd. |
| | 944 Turbo | 151 (2479) | WR6DC | .028 | 5B @ 840 | ① | 34-40 | 800-880 | Hyd. | Hyd. |
| 1987 | 911 | 193 (3164) | WR7DC | .028 | 26B @ 4000 | ① | 34-40 | 780-820 | 0.004 | 0.004 |
| | 911 Turbo | 201 (3299) | W3DP | .028 | 26B @ 4000 | ① | 34-40 | 850-950 | 0.004 | 0.004 |
| | 924S | 151 (2479) | WR7DC | .028 | 5B @ 840 | ① | 34-40 | 800-880 | Hyd. | Hyd. |
| | 928S4 | 302 (4957) | WR7DC | .028 | NA | ① | NA | 800-880 | Hyd. | Hyd. |
| | 944 | 151 (2479) | WR7DC | .028 | 10B @ 850 | ① | 34-40 | 800-880 | Hyd. | Hyd. |
| | 944S | 151 (2479) | WR7DC | .028 | NA | ① | 34-40 | 800-880 | Hyd. | Hyd. |
| | 944 Turbo | 151 (2479) | WR6DC | .028 | 5B @ 840 | ① | 34-40 | 800-880 | Hyd. | Hyd. |
| 1988 | 911 | 193 (2164) | WR7DC | .028 | 26B @ 4000 | ① | 34-40 | 780-820 | 0.004 | 0.004 |
| | 911 Turbo | 201 (3299) | W3DP | .028 | 26B @ 4000 | ① | 34-40 | 850-950 | 0.004 | 0.004 |
| | 924S | 219 (3600) | WR7DC | .028 | 5B @ 840 | ① | 34-40 | 800-880 | Hyd. | Hyd. |
| | 928S4 | 302 (4957) | WR7DC | .028 | 10° ± 2 BTDC② | ① | NA | 800-880 | Hyd. | Hyd. |
| | 944 | 164 (2681) | WR7DC | .028 | 10B @ 850 | ① | 34-40 | 800-880 | Hyd. | Hyd. |
| | 944S | 181 (2969) | WR7DC | .028 | 10° ± 3 BTDC③ | ① | NA | 800-880 | Hyd. | Hyd. |
| | 944 Turbo | 151 (2479) | WR6DS | .028 | 5B @ 840 | ① | 34-40 | 800-880 | Hyd. | Hyd. |

## TUNE-UP SPECIFICATIONS

| Year | Model | Engine Displacement cu. in. (cc) | Spark Plugs Type | Spark Plugs Gap (in.) | Ignition Timing (deg @ rpm) | Compression Pressure (psi) | Fuel Pump (psi) | Idle Speed (rpm) | Valve Clearance In. | Valve Clearance Ex. |
|---|---|---|---|---|---|---|---|---|---|---|
| 1989 | 911 | 193 (2164) | WR7DC | .028 | 0° ± 3 BTDC② | ① | 34–40 | 880 ± 20 | 0.004 | 0.004 |
| | 911 Turbo | 201 (3299) | W3DP0 | .028 | 26B @ 4000 | ① | NA | 900 ± 50 | 0.004 | 0.004 |
| | 911 Carrera 4 | 219 (3600) | FR5DTC | .031 | 0° ± 3 | ① | 53–59 | 880 ± 40 | 0.004 | 0.004 |
| | 928S4 | 302 (4957) | WR7DC | .028 | 10° ± 2 BTDC② | ① | 56 | 675 ± 25 | Hyd. | Hyd. |
| | 944 | 164 (2681) | WR7DC | .028 | 5° ± 3 BTDC② | ① | 53–59 | 840 ± 40 | Hyd. | Hyd. |
| | 944S2 | 181 (2969) | WR5DC | .028 | 10° ± 3 | ① | NA | 840 ± 40 | Hyd. | Hyd. |
| | 944 Turbo | 151 (2479) | WR7DC | .028 | 5° ± 3 BTDC② | ① | 34–40 | 840 ± 40③ | Hyd. | Hyd. |
| 1990 | SEE UNDERHOOD SPECIFICATIONS STICKER | | | | | | | | | |

**NOTE:** The Underhood Specifications sticker often reflects tune-up specifications changes made in production. Sticker Figures must be used if they disagree with those in this chart

B Before Top Dead Center
BTDC Before Top Dead Center
NA Not available at time of publication
① All cylinders should be within 22 psi of the highest reading
② Checking only, not adjustable
③ With idle stabilization system disconnected

## FIRING ORDERS

**NOTE: To avoid confusion, always replace spark plug wires one at a time.**

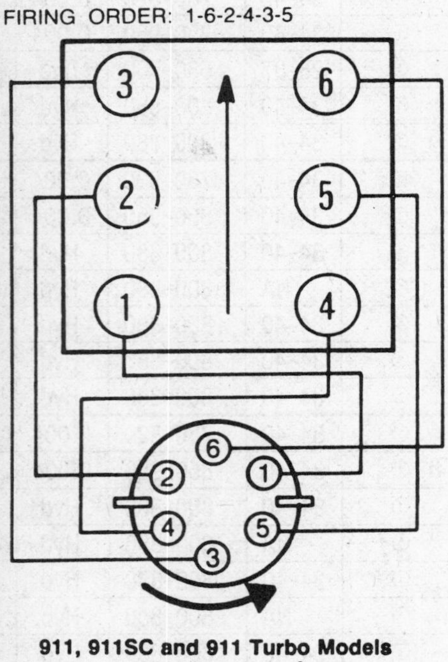


911, 911SC and 911 Turbo Models

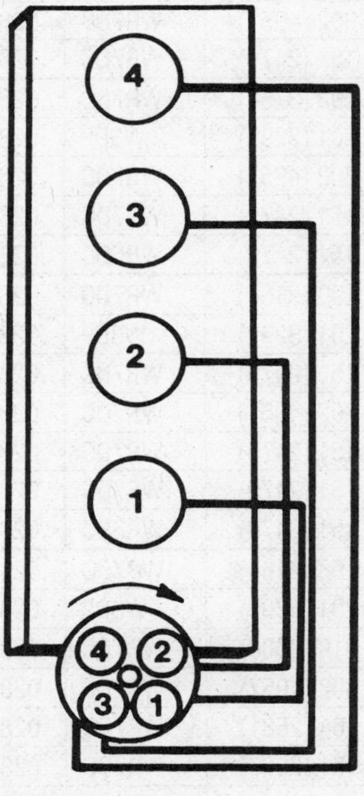

924S and 944 Models

## FIRING ORDERS

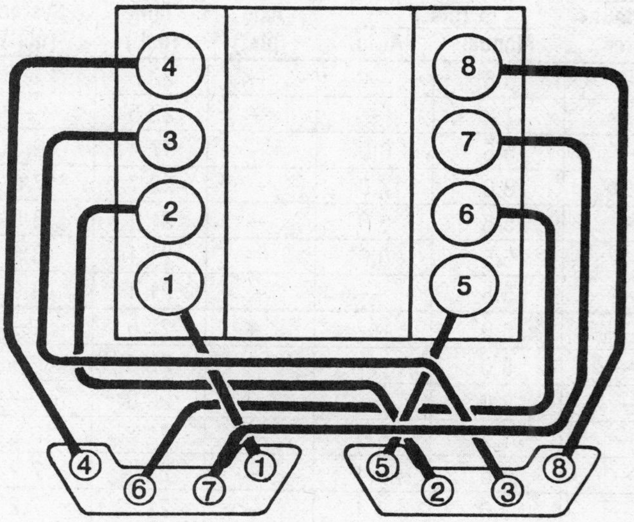


Firing order: 1–3–7–2–6–5–4–8
928S4

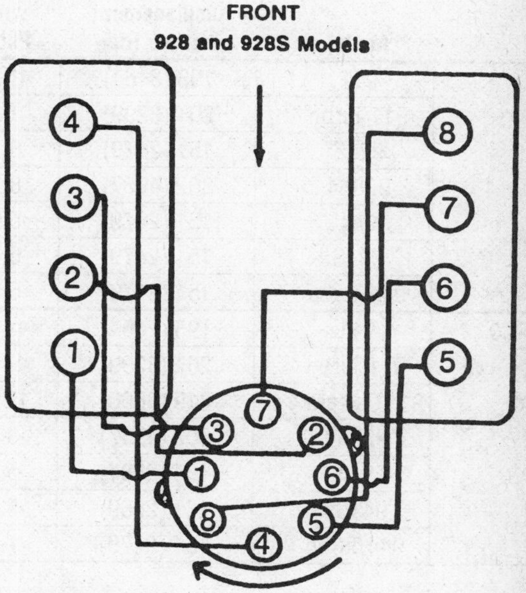


Firing order: 1–3–7–2–6–5–4–8
928 AND 928S

## CAPACITIES

| Year | Model | Engine Displacement cu. in. (cc) | Engine Crankcase with Filter | Engine Crankcase without Filter | Transaxle (pts.) Manual | Transaxle (pts.) Auto. | Drive Axle (pts.) | Fuel Tank (gal.) | Cooling System (qts.) |
|---|---|---|---|---|---|---|---|---|---|
| 1983 | 911 | 183 (2994) | 10.6 | — | 6.4 | — | — | 21 | — |
| | 928 | 284 (4664) | 8.5 | 8.0 | 8.0 | 12.0 | — | 23 | 17.0 |
| | 944 | 151 (2479) | 6.4 | — | 5.5 | 6.0 | — | 17.4 | 8.5 |
| 1984 | 911 | 193 (3164) | 10.6 | — | 6.6 | — | — | 22.5 | — |
| | 928 | 284 (4664) | 8.5 | 8.0 | 8.0 | 12.0 | — | 23 | 17.0 |
| | 944 | 151 (2479) | 6.4 | — | 5.5 | 6.0 | — | 17.4 | 8.5 |
| 1985 | 911 | 193 (3164) | 10.6 | — | 6.6 | — | — | 22.5 | — |
| | 928 | 302 (4957) | 8.5 | 8.0 | 8.0 | 17.0 | — | 22.7 | 17.0 |
| | 944 | 151 (2479) | 6.4 | — | 5.5 | 6.0 | — | 21.1 | 8.5 |
| 1986 | 911 | 193 (3164) | 10.6 | — | 6.6 | — | — | 22.5 | — |
| | 911 Turbo | 201 (3299) | 10.6 | — | 7.8 | — | — | 22.5 | — |
| | 928 | 302 (4957) | 8.5 | 8.0 | 8.0 | 17.0 | — | 22.7 | 17.0 |
| | 944 | 151 (2479) | 6.4 | — | 5.5 | 6.0 | — | 21.1 | 8.5 |
| | 944 Turbo | 151 (2479) | 6.9 | — | 5.5 | — | — | 21.1 | 9.0 |
| 1987 | 911 | 193 (3164) | 10.6 | — | 6.6 | — | — | 22.5 | — |
| | 911 Turbo | 201 (3299) | 10.6 | — | 7.8 | — | — | 22.5 | — |
| | 924S | 151 (2479) | 6.4 | — | 5.5 | 6.0 | — | 17.4 | 9.0 |
| | 928S4 | 302 (4957) | 8.5 | 8.0 | 8.0 | 17.0 | — | 22.7 | 17.0 |
| | 944 | 151 (2479) | 6.4 | — | 5.5 | 6.0 | — | 21.1 | 8.5 |
| | 944S | 151 (2479) | 6.4 | — | 5.5 | 6.0 | — | 21.1 | 8.5 |
| | 944 Turbo | 151 (2479) | 6.9 | — | 5.5 | — | — | 21.1 | 9.0 |

## CAPACITIES

| Year | Model | Engine Displacement cu. in. (cc) | Engine Crankcase with Filter | Engine Crankcase without Filter | Transaxle (pts.) Manual | Transaxle (pts.) Auto. | Drive Axle (pts.) | Fuel Tank (gal.) | Cooling System (qts.) |
|---|---|---|---|---|---|---|---|---|---|
| 1988 | 911 | 193 (3164) | 10.6 | — | 6.6 | — | — | 22.5 | — |
| | 911 Turbo | 201 (3299) | 10.6 | — | 7.8 | — | — | 22.5 | — |
| | 924S | 151 (2479) | 6.4 | — | 5.5 | 6.0 | — | 17.4 | 9.0 |
| | 928S4 | 302 (4957) | 8.5 | 8.0 | 8.0 | 17.0 | — | 22.7 | 17.0 |
| | 944 | 151 (2479) | 6.4 | — | 5.5 | 6.0 | — | 21.1 | 8.5 |
| | 944S | 151 (2479) | 6.4 | — | 5.5 | 6.0 | — | 21.1 | 8.5 |
| | 944 Turbo | 151 (2479) | 6.9 | — | 5.5 | — | — | 21.1 | 9.0 |
| 1989-90 | 911 | 193 (2164) | 14.0 | — | 6.0 | — | — | 22.5 | — |
| | 911 Turbo | 201 (3299) | 14.0 | — | 8.0 | — | — | 22.5 | — |
| | 911 Carrera 4 | 219 (3600) | 12.0 | — | 8.0① | — | — | 20.3 | — |
| | 928S4 | 302 (4957) | 8.0 | — | 8.2 | 16.0 | — | 22.7 | 16.5 |
| | 944 | 164 (2681) | 5.8 | — | 3.6 | 8.4 | — | 21.1 | 7.2 |
| | 944S2 | 181 (2969) | 5.8 | — | 3.6 | 8.4 | — | 21.1 | 7.2 |
| | 944 Turbo | 151 (2479) | 7.2 | — | 4.1 | — | — | 21.1 | 9.0 |

## CRANKSHAFT AND CONNECTING ROD SPECIFICATIONS

| Year | Engine Displacement cu. in. (cc) | Crankshaft Main Brg. Journal Dia. | Crankshaft Main Brg. Oil Clearance | Crankshaft Shaft End-play | Thrust on No. | Connecting Rod Journal Diameter | Connecting Rod Oil Clearance | Connecting Rod Side Clearance |
|---|---|---|---|---|---|---|---|---|
| 1983 | 151 (2479) | 2.8000 | 0.0008–0.0039 | 0.0044–0.0124 | 3 | 2.0800 | 0.0008–0.0028 | — |
| | 183 (2994) | 2.2429–2.2437 | 0.0004–0.0028 | 0.0004–0.0077 | 1 | 2.0461–2.0468 | 0.0012–0.0035 | 0.0079–0.0158 |
| | 284 (4664) | 2.8000 | 0.0008–0.0039 | 0.0044–0.0124 | 3 | 2.0800 | 0.0008–0.0028 | — |
| 1984 | 151 (2479) | 2.8000 | 0.0008–0.0039 | 0.0044–0.0124 | 3 | 2.0800 | 0.0008–0.0028 | — |
| | 193 (3164) | 2.2429–2.2437 | 0.0004–0.0028 | 0.0004–0.0077 | 1 | 2.0461–2.0468 | 0.0012–0.0035 | 0.0079–0.0158 |
| | 284 (4664) | 2.8000 | 0.0008–0.0039 | 0.0044–0.0124 | 3 | 2.0800 | 0.0008–0.0028 | — |
| 1985 | 151 (2479) | 2.8000 | 0.0008–0.0039 | 0.0044–0.0124 | 3 | 2.0800 | 0.0008–0.0028 | — |
| | 193 (3164) | 2.2429–2.2437 | 0.0004–0.0028 | 0.0004–0.0077 | 1 | 2.0461–2.0468 | 0.0012–0.0035 | 0.0079–0.0158 |
| | 302 (4957) | 2.8000 | 0.0008–0.0039 | 0.0044–0.0124 | 3 | 2.0800 | 0.0008–0.0028 | — |
| 1986 | 151 (2479) | 2.8000 | 0.0004–0.0028 | 0.0044–0.0124 | 3 | 2.0800 | 0.0008–0.0028 | — |
| | 193 (3164) | 2.2429–2.2437 | 0.0004–0.0028 | 0.0004–0.0077 | 1 | 2.0461–2.0468 | 0.0012–0.0035 | 0.0079–0.0158 |
| | 201 (3299) | 2.2429–2.2437 | 0.0004–0.0028 | 0.0004–0.0077 | 1 | 2.0461–2.0468 | 0.0012–0.0035 | 0.0079–0.0158 |
| | 302 (4957) | 2.8000 | 0.0008–0.0039 | 0.0044–0.0124 | 3 | 2.0800 | 0.0008–0.0028 | — |

## CRANKSHAFT AND CONNECTING ROD SPECIFICATIONS

All measurements are given in inches

| Year | Engine Displacement cu. in. (cc) | Crankshaft Main Brg. Journal Dia. | Crankshaft Main Brg. Oil Clearance | Crankshaft Shaft End-play | Crankshaft Thrust on No. | Connecting Rod Journal Diameter | Connecting Rod Oil Clearance | Connecting Rod Side Clearance |
|---|---|---|---|---|---|---|---|---|
| 1987 | 151 (2479) | 2.8000 | 0.0004–0.0028 | 0.0044–0.0124 | 3 | 2.0800 | 0.0008–0.0028 | — |
| | 193 (3164) | 2.2429–2.2437 | 0.0004–0.0028 | 0.0004–0.0077 | 1 | 2.0461–2.0468 | 0.0012–0.0035 | 0.0079–0.0158 |
| | 201 (3299) | 2.2429–2.2437 | 0.0004–0.0028 | 0.0004–0.0077 | 1 | 2.0461–2.0468 | 0.0012–0.0035 | 0.0079–0.0158 |
| | 302 (4957) | 2.8000 | 0.0008–0.0039 | 0.0044–0.0124 | 3 | 2.0800 | 0.0008–0.0028 | — |
| 1988 | 151 (2479) | 2.8000 | 0.0004–0.0028 | 0.0044–0.0124 | 3 | 2.0800 | 0.0008–0.0028 | — |
| | 193 (3164) | 2.2429–2.2437 | 0.0004–0.0028 | 0.0004–0.0077 | 1 | 2.0461–2.0468 | 0.0012–0.0035 | 0.0079–0.0158 |
| | 201 (3299) | 2.2429–2.2437 | 0.0004–0.0028 | 0.0004–0.0077 | 1 | 2.0461–2.0468 | 0.0012–0.0035 | 0.0079–0.0158 |
| | 302 (4957) | 2.8000 | 0.0008–0.0039 | 0.0044–0.0124 | 3 | 2.0800 | 0.0008–0.0028 | — |
| 1989–90 | 151 (2479) | 2.8000 | 0.0004–0.0028 | 0.0044–0.0124 | 3 | 2.0800 | 0.0008–0.0028 | — |
| | 193 (3164) | 2.2429–2.2437 | 0.0004–0.0028 | 0.0004–0.0077 | 1 | 2.0461–2.0468 | 0.0012–0.0035 | 0.0079–0.0158 |
| | 201 (3299) | 2.2429–2.2437 | 0.0004–0.0028 | 0.0004–0.0077 | 1 | 2.0461–2.0468 | 0.0012–0.0035 | 0.0079–0.0158 |
| | 302 (4957) | 2.8000 | 0.0008–0.0039 | 0.0044–0.0124 | 3 | 2.0800 | 0.0008–0.0028 | — |

## VALVE SPECIFICATIONS

| Year | Engine Displacement cu. in. (cc) | Seat Angle (deg.) | Face Angle (deg.) | Spring Test Pressure (lbs.) | Spring Installed Height (in.) | Stem-to-Guide Clearance (in.) Intake | Stem-to-Guide Clearance (in.) Exhaust | Stem Diameter (in.) Intake | Stem Diameter (in.) Exhaust |
|---|---|---|---|---|---|---|---|---|---|
| 1983 | 183 (2994) | 45 | 45 | 176.4 @ 1.21 ① | 1.3779 ② | 0.030–0.057 | 0.050–0.077 | 0.353 | 0.352 |
| | 284 (4664) | 45 | 45 | — | — | 0.020 | 0.020 | 0.352 | 0.352 |
| | 151 (2479) | 45 | 45 | — | — | 0.032 | 0.032 | 0.352 | 0.352 |
| 1984 | 193 (3164) | 45 | 45 | 176.4 @ 1.21 ① | 1.3779 ② | 0.030–0.057 | 0.050–0.077 | 0.353 | 0.352 |
| | 284 (4664) | 45 | 45 | — | — | 0.020 | 0.020 | 0.352 | 0.352 |
| | 151 (2479) | 45 | 45 | — | — | 0.032 | 0.032 | 0.352 | 0.352 |
| 1985 | 193 (3164) | 45 | 45 | 176.4 @ 1.21 ① | 1.3779 ② | 0.030–0.057 | 0.050–0.077 | 0.353 | 0.352 |
| | 302 (4957) | 45 | 45 | — | — | 0.020 | 0.020 | 0.352 | 0.352 |
| | 151 (2479) | 45 | 45 | — | — | 0.032 | 0.032 | 0.352 | 0.352 |
| 1986 | 193 (3164) | 45 | 45 | 176.4 @ 1.21 ① | 1.3779 ② | 0.030–0.057 | 0.050–0.077 | 0.353 | 0.352 |
| | 201 (3299) | 45 | 45 | 176.4 @ 1.21 ① | 1.3779 ② | 0.030–0.057 | 0.050–0.077 | 0.353 | 0.352 |
| | 302 (4957) | 45 | 45 | — | — | 0.020 | 0.020 | 0.352 | 0.352 |
| | 151 (2479) | 45 | 45 | — | — | 0.032 | 0.032 | 0.352 | 0.352 |

## VALVE SPECIFICATIONS

| Year | Engine Displacement cu. in. (cc) | Seat Angle (deg.) | Face Angle (deg.) | Spring Test Pressure (lbs.) | Spring Installed Height (in.) | Stem-to-Guide Clearance (in.) | | Stem Diameter (in.) | |
|---|---|---|---|---|---|---|---|---|---|
| | | | | | | Intake | Exhaust | Intake | Exhaust |
| 1987 | 193 (3164) | 45 | 45 | 176.4 @ 1.21 ① | 1.3779 ② | 0.030–0.057 | 0.050–0.077 | 0.353 | 0.352 |
| | 201 (3299) | 45 | 45 | 176.4 @ 1.21 ① | 1.3779 ② | 0.030–0.057 | 0.050–0.077 | 0.353 | 0.352 |
| | 302 (4957) | 45 | 45 | — | — | 0.020 | 0.020 | 0.352 | 0.352 |
| | 151 (2479) | 45 | 45 | — | — | 0.032 | 0.032 | 0.352 | 0.352 |
| 1988 | 193 (3164) | 45 | 45 | 176.4 @ 1.21 ① | 1.3779 ② | 0.030–0.057 | 0.050–0.077 | 0.353 | 0.352 |
| | 201 (3299) | 45 | 45 | 176.4 @ 1.21 ① | 1.3779 ② | 0.030–0.057 | 0.050–0.077 | 0.353 | 0.352 |
| | 302 (4957) | 45 | 45 | — | — | 0.020 | 0.020 | 0.352 | 0.352 |
| | 151 (2479) | 45 | 45 | — | — | 0.032 | 0.032 | 0.352 | 0.352 |
| 1989-90 | 193 (3164) | 45 | 45 | 176.4 @ 1.21 ① | 1.3779 ② | 0.030–0.057 | 0.050–0.077 | 0.353 | 0.352 |
| | 201 (3299) | 45 | 45 | 176.4 @ 1.21 ① | 1.3779 ② | 0.030–0.057 | 0.050–0.077 | 0.353 | 0.352 |
| | 302 (4957) | 45 | 45 | — | — | 0.020 | 0.020 | 0.352 | 0.352 |
| | 151 (2479) | 45 | 45 | — | — | 0.032 | 0.032 | 0.352 | 0.352 |

① 165.3 @ 1.25 for exhaust valve
② 1.3976 in. for exhaust

## PISTON AND RING SPECIFICATIONS

All measurements are given in inches

| Year | Engine Displacement cu. in. (cc) | Piston Clearance | Ring Gap | | | Ring Side Clearance | | |
|---|---|---|---|---|---|---|---|---|
| | | | Top Compression | Bottom Compression | Oil Control | Top Compression | Bottom Compression | Oil Control |
| 1983 | 183 (2994) | 0.0060 | 0.004–0.008 | 0.004–0.008 | 0.006–0.012 | 0.003–0.004 | 0.002–0.003 | 0.001–0.002 |
| | 284 (4664) | 0.0031 | 0.008–0.018 | 0.008–0.018 | 0.008–0.055 | 0.002–0.003 | 0.002–0.003 | 0.001–0.005 |
| | 151 (2479) | 0.0031 | 0.008–0.018 | 0.008–0.018 | 0.015–0.055 | 0.002–0.003 | 0.002–0.003 | 0.001–0.005 |
| 1984 | 193 (3164) | 0.0060 | 0.004–0.008 | 0.004–0.008 | 0.006–0.012 | 0.003–0.004 | 0.002–0.003 | 0.001–0.002 |
| | 284 (4664) | 0.0031 | 0.008–0.018 | 0.008–0.018 | 0.008–0.055 | 0.002–0.003 | 0.002–0.003 | 0.001–0.005 |
| | 151 (2479) | 0.0031 | 0.008–0.018 | 0.008–0.018 | 0.015–0.055 | 0.002–0.003 | 0.002–0.003 | 0.001–0.005 |
| 1985 | 193 (3164) | 0.0060 | 0.004–0.008 | 0.004–0.008 | 0.006–0.012 | 0.003–0.004 | 0.002–0.003 | 0.001–0.002 |
| | 302 (4957) | 0.0031 | 0.008–0.018 | 0.008–0.018 | 0.016–0.055 | 0.002–0.003 | 0.002–0.003 | 0.001–0.005 |
| | 151 (2479) | 0.0031 | 0.008–0.018 | 0.008–0.018 | 0.015–0.055 | 0.002–0.003 | 0.002–0.003 | 0.001–0.005 |

## PISTON AND RING SPECIFICATIONS

All measurements are given in inches

| Year | Engine Displacement cu. in. (cc) | Piston Clearance | Ring Gap | | | Ring Side Clearance | | |
|---|---|---|---|---|---|---|---|---|
| | | | Top Compression | Bottom Compression | Oil Control | Top Compression | Bottom Compression | Oil Control |
| 1986 | 193 (3164) | 0.0060 | 0.004–0.008 | 0.004–0.008 | 0.006–0.012 | 0.003–0.004 | 0.002–0.003 | 0.001–0.002 |
| | 201 (3299) | 0.0060 | 0.004–0.008 | 0.004–0.008 | 0.006–0.012 | 0.003–0.004 | 0.002–0.003 | 0.001–0.002 |
| | 302 (4957) | 0.0031 | 0.008–0.018 | 0.008–0.018 | 0.015–0.055 | 0.002–0.003 | 0.002–0.003 | 0.001–0.005 |
| | 151 (2479) | 0.0031 | 0.008–0.018 | 0.008–0.018 | 0.005–0.055 | 0.002–0.003 | 0.002–0.003 | 0.001–0.005 |
| 1987 | 193 (3164) | 0.0060 | 0.004–0.008 | 0.004–0.008 | 0.006–0.012 | 0.003–0.004 | 0.002–0.003 | 0.001–0.002 |
| | 201 (3299) | 0.0060 | 0.004–0.008 | 0.004–0.008 | 0.006–0.012 | 0.003–0.004 | 0.002–0.003 | 0.001–0.002 |
| | 302 (4957) | 0.0031 | 0.008–0.018 | 0.008–0.018 | 0.015–0.055 | 0.002–0.003 | 0.002–0.003 | 0.001–0.005 |
| | 151 (2479) | 0.0031 | 0.008–0.018 | 0.008–0.018 | 0.015–0.055 | 0.002–0.003 | 0.002–0.003 | 0.001–0.005 |
| 1988 | 193 (3164) | 0.0060 | 0.004–0.008 | 0.004–0.008 | 0.006–0.012 | 0.003–0.004 | 0.002–0.003 | 0.001–0.002 |
| | 201 (3299) | 0.0060 | 0.004–0.008 | 0.004–0.008 | 0.006–0.012 | 0.003–0.004 | 0.002–0.003 | 0.001–0.002 |
| | 302 (4957) | 0.0031 | 0.008–0.018 | 0.008–0.018 | 0.015–0.055 | 0.002–0.003 | 0.002–0.003 | 0.001–0.005 |
| | 151 (2479) | 0.0031 | 0.008–0.018 | 0.008–0.018 | 0.015–0.055 | 0.002–0.003 | 0.002–0.003 | 0.001–0.005 |
| 1989 | 193 (3164) | 0.0060 | 0.004–0.008 | 0.004–0.008 | 0.006–0.012 | 0.003–0.004 | 0.002–0.003 | 0.001–0.002 |
| | 201 (3299) | 0.0060 | 0.004–0.008 | 0.004–0.008 | 0.006–0.012 | 0.003–0.004 | 0.002–0.003 | 0.001–0.002 |
| | 302 (4957) | 0.0031 | 0.008–0.018 | 0.008–0.018 | 0.015–0.055 | 0.002–0.003 | 0.002–0.003 | 0.001–0.005 |
| | 151 (2479) | 0.0031 | 0.008–0.018 | 0.008–0.018 | 0.015–0.055 | 0.002–0.003 | 0.002–0.003 | 0.001–0.005 |
| 1990 | 193 (3164) | 0.0060 | 0.004–0.008 | 0.004–0.008 | 0.006–0.012 | 0.003–0.004 | 0.002–0.003 | 0.001–0.002 |
| | 201 (3299) | 0.0060 | 0.004–0.008 | 0.004–0.008 | 0.006–0.012 | 0.003–0.004 | 0.002–0.003 | 0.001–0.002 |
| | 302 (4957) | 0.0031 | 0.008–0.018 | 0.008–0.018 | 0.015–0.055 | 0.002–0.003 | 0.002–0.003 | 0.001–0.005 |
| | 151 (2479) | 0.0031 | 0.008–0.018 | 0.008–0.018 | 0.015–0.055 | 0.002–0.003 | 0.002–0.003 | 0.001–0.005 |

## TORQUE SPECIFICATIONS

All readings in ft. lbs.

| Year | Engine Displacement cu. in. (cc) | Cylinder Head Bolts | Main Bearing Bolts | Rod Bearing Bolts | Crankshaft Pulley Bolts | Flywheel Bolts | Manifold Intake | Manifold Exhaust | Spark Plugs |
|---|---|---|---|---|---|---|---|---|---|
| 1983 | 151 (2479) | ⑦ | ⑧ | 55.3 | 155⑪ | 65 | 15 | 15 | 18–22 |
| | 183 (2994) | 24 | 25 | 36 | 58 | 65 | 18 | 14–17 | 18–22 |
| | 284 (4664) | ⑦ | ⑧ | 44.5 | 181 | 69 | 17 | 15 | 18–22 |
| 1984 | 151 (2479) | ⑦ | ⑧ | 55.3 | 155⑪ | 65 | 15 | 15 | 18–22 |
| | 193 (3164) | 24 | 25 | 36 | 58 | 65 | 18 | 14–17 | 18–22 |
| | 284 (4664) | ⑦ | ⑧ | 44.5 | 181 | 69 | 17 | 15 | 18–22 |
| 1985 | 151 (2479) | ⑦ | ⑧ | 55.3 | 155⑪ | 65 | 15 | 15 | 18–22 |
| | 193 (3164) | 24 | 25 | 36 | 58 | 65 | 18 | 14–17 | 18–22 |
| | 302 (4957) | ⑨ | ⑩ | 54 | 213 | 65 | 17 | 15 | 18–22 |
| 1986 | 151 (2479) | ⑦ | ⑧ | 55.3 | 155⑪ | 65 | 15 | 15 | 18–22 |
| | 193 (3164) | 24 | 25 | 36 | 58 | 65 | 18 | 14–17 | 18–22 |
| | 201 (3299) | 24 | 25 | 36 | 58 | 65 | 18 | 14–17 | 18–22 |
| | 302 (4957) | ⑨ | ⑩ | 54 | 213 | 65 | 17 | 15 | 18–22 |
| 1987 | 151 (2479) | ⑦ | ⑧ | 55.3 | 155⑪ | 65 | 15 | 15 | 18–22 |
| | 193 (3164) | 24 | 25 | 36 | 58 | 65 | 18 | 14–17 | 18–22 |
| | 201 (3299) | 24 | 25 | 36 | 58 | 65 | 18 | 14–17 | 18–22 |
| | 302 (4957) | ⑨ | ⑩ | 54 | 213 | 65 | 17 | 15 | 18–22 |
| 1988 | 151 (2479) | ⑦⑥ | ⑤ | 55.3 | 155⑪ | 65 | 15 | 15 | 18–22 |
| | 193 (3164) | ③④ | 25 | ① | 58② | 65 | 18 | 14–17 | 18–22 |
| | 201 (3299) | ③④ | 25 | ① | 58② | 65 | 18 | 14–17 | 18–22 |
| | 302 (4957) | ⑨ | ⑩ | 54 | 213 | 65 | 17 | 15 | 18–22 |
| 1989-90 | 151 (2479) | ⑦⑥ | ⑤ | 55.3 | 155⑪ | 65 | 15 | 15 | 18–22 |
| | 193 (3164) | ③④ | 25 | ① | 58② | 65 | 18 | 14–17 | 18–22 |
| | 201 (3299) | ③④ | 25 | ① | 58② | 65 | 18 | 14–17 | 18–22 |
| | 302 (4957) | ⑨ | ⑩ | 54 | 213 | 65 | 17 | 15 | 18–22 |

① Step 1—14 ft. lbs.
Step 2—Turn additional 90° ± 2°

② If equipped with air conditioning—123

③ Step 1—11 ft. lbs.
Step 2—Turn additional 90° ± 2°

④ Apply a thin coat of Optimoly HT

⑤ M12 bolts
Step 1—14
Step 2—29
Step 3—54
M10 bolts
Step 1—14
Step 2—36
M6 bolts
Step 1—6
M8 bolts
Step 1—14

⑥ Dip studs in engine oil

⑦ Tighten in 3 steps (in order each time)
1st—14 ft. lbs.;
2nd—36 ft. lbs.;
3rd—65 ft. lbs.
30 minutes later, loosen each bolt 1/4 turn then repeat the tightening sequence.

⑧ M10 bolts
Step 1—14.5 ft. lbs.
Step 2—33.5 ft. lbs.
M12 bolts
Step 1—14.5 ft. lbs.
Step 2—30.0 ft. lbs.
Step 3—48 ft. lbs.

⑨ Step 1—14 ft. lbs.
Step 2—turn additional 90°
Step 3—turn additional 90°

⑩ M12 bolts
Step 1—14 ft. lbs.
Step 2—29 ft. lbs.
Step 3—54 + 3.6 ft. lbs.
M10 bolts
Step 1—14 ft. lbs.
Step 2—36 + 3.6 ft. lbs.

⑪ Gear wheel to crankshaft

## BRAKE SPECIFICATIONS

All measurements in inches unless noted

| Year | Model | Lug Nut Torque (ft. lbs.) | Master Cylinder Bore | Brake Disc Minimum Thickness | Brake Disc Maximum Runout | Maximum Brake Drum Diameter | Maximum Lining Thickness Front | Maximum Lining Thickness Rear |
|---|---|---|---|---|---|---|---|---|
| 1983 | 911 | 94 | 0.813 | ① | 0.004 | — | 0.080 | 0.080 |
| | 928 | 94 | 0.950 | 1.228 | 0.004 | — | 0.080 | 0.080 |
| | 944 | 94 | 0.940 | 0.728③ | 0.004 | — | 0.080 | 0.080 |
| 1984 | 911 | 94 | 0.813 | 0.890 | 0.004 | — | 0.080 | 0.080 |
| | 911 Turbo | 94 | 0.937 | ⑥ | 0.004 | — | 0.080 | 0.080 |
| | 928 | 94 | 0.950 | 1.228 | 0.004 | — | 0.080 | 0.080 |
| | 944 | 94 | 0.940 | 0.807⑦ | 0.004 | — | 0.080 | 0.080 |
| 1985 | 911 | 94 | 0.813 | 0.890 | 0.004 | — | 0.080 | 0.080 |
| | 911 Turbo | 94 | 0.937 | ⑥ | 0.004 | — | 0.080 | 0.080 |
| | 928 | 94 | 0.950 | 1.228 | 0.004 | — | 0.080 | 0.080 |
| | 944 | 94 | 0.940 | 0.807⑦ | 0.004 | — | 0.080 | 0.080 |
| 1986 | 911 | 94 | 0.813 | 0.890 | 0.004 | — | 0.080 | 0.080 |
| | 911 Turbo | 94 | 0.937 | ⑥ | 0.004 | — | 0.080 | 0.080 |
| | 928 | 94 | 0.950 | 1.228 | 0.004 | — | 0.080 | 0.080 |
| | 944 | 94 | 0.940 | 0.807⑦ | 0.004 | — | 0.080 | 0.080 |
| 1987 | 911 | 94 | 0.813 | 0.890 | 0.004 | — | 0.080 | 0.080 |
| | 911 Turbo | 94 | 0.937 | ⑥ | 0.004 | — | 0.080 | 0.080 |
| | 924S | 94 | 0.940 | 0.807⑦ | 0.004 | — | 0.080 | 0.080 |
| | 928S4 | 94 | 0.950 | 1.228 | 0.004 | — | 0.080 | 0.080 |
| | 944 | 94 | 0.940 | 0.807⑦ | 0.004 | — | 0.080 | 0.080 |
| 1988 | 911 | 94 | 0.813 | 0.890 | 0.004 | — | 0.080 | 0.080 |
| | 911 Turbo | 94 | 0.937 | ⑥ | 0.004 | — | 0.080 | 0.080 |
| | 924S | 94 | 0.940 | 0.807⑦ | 0.004 | — | 0.080 | 0.080 |
| | 928S4 | 94 | 0.950 | 1.228 | 0.004 | — | 0.080 | 0.080 |
| | 944 | 94 | 0.940 | 0.807⑦ | 0.004 | — | 0.080 | 0.080 |
| | 944S | 94 | 0.940 | 0.807⑦ | 0.004 | — | 0.080 | 0.080 |
| | 944 Turbo | 94 | 0.940 | 0.807⑦ | 0.004 | — | 0.080 | 0.080 |
| 1989-90 | 911 | 94 | 0.810 | 0.940 | 0.004 | — | 0.080 | 0.080 |
| | 911 Turbo | 94 | 0.940 | 1.260② | 0.004 | — | 0.080 | 0.080 |
| | 911 Carrera 4 | 94 | 0.940 | 1.100④ | 0.004 | — | 0.080 | 0.080 |
| | 928S4 | 94 | 0.940 | 1.260⑤ | 0.004 | — | 0.080 | 0.080 |
| | 944 | 94 | 0.940 | 0.810⑥ | 0.004 | — | 0.080 | 0.080 |
| | 944S2 | 94 | 0.940 | 0.810⑥ | 0.004 | — | 0.080 | 0.080 |
| | 944 Turbo | 94 | 0.940 | 1.260⑤ | 0.004 | — | 0.080 | 0.080 |

① Front—0.752
Rear—0.732
② Rear—1.100
③ Rear—0.732
④ Rear—0.950
⑤ Rear—0.940
⑥ Front—1.205
Rear—0.790
⑦ Rear—0.788

## WHEEL ALIGNMENT

| | | Caster | | Camber | | | Steering |
|---|---|---|---|---|---|---|---|
| Year | Model | Range (deg.) | Preferred Setting (deg.) | Range (deg.) | Preferred Setting (deg.) | Toe-in (in.) | Axis Inclination (deg.) |
| 1983 | 911 | 6 3/16P–6 5/16P | 6 1/16P | 5/16P–11/16P | 1/2P | 0 | — |
| | 928 | 3 1/4P–3 3/4P | 3 1/2P | 11/16N–5/16N | 1/2N | 3/32–5/32 | — |
| | 944 | 2 1/4P–3P | 2 1/2P | 1/16N–9/16N | 5/16P | 1/16–1/8 | — |
| 1984 | 911 | 6 3/16P–6 5/16P | 6 1/16P | 5/16P–11/16P | 1/2P ① | 0 | — |
| | 928 | 3 1/4P–3 3/4P | 3 1/2P | 11/16N–5/16N | 1/2N | 3/32–5/32 | — |
| | 944 | 2 1/4P–3P | 2 1/2P | 1/16N–9/16N | 5/16P | 1/16–1/8 | — |
| 1985 | 911 | 5 11/16P–6 5/16P | 6 1/16P | 3/16P–5/16P | 1/4P ① | 1/4 | — |
| | 928 | 3P–4P | 3 1/2P | 11/16N–5/16N | 1/2N | 3/32–5/32 | — |
| | 944 | 2 1/4P–3P | 2 1/2P | 1/16N–9/16N | 5/16P | 1/16–1/8 | — |
| 1986 | 911 | 5 11/16P–6 5/16P | 6 1/16P | 3/16P–5/16P | 1/4P ① | 1/4 | — |
| | 928 | 3P–4P | 3 1/2P | 11/16N–5/16N | 1/2N | 3/32–5/32 | — |
| | 944 | 2 1/4P–3P | 2 1/2P | 1/16N–9/16N | 5/16P | 1/16–1/8 | — |
| 1987 | 911 | 5 11/16P–6 5/16P | 6 1/16P | 3/16P–5/16P | 1/4P ① | 1/4 | — |
| | 924S | 2 1/4P–3P | 2 1/2P | 1/16N–9/16N | 5/16P | 1/16–1/8 | — |
| | 928 | 3P–4P | 3 1/2P | 11/16N–5/16N | 1/2N | 3/32–5/32 | — |
| | 944 | 2 1/4P–3P | 2 1/2P | 1/16N–9/16N | 5/16P | 1/16–1/8 | — |
| 1988 | 911 | 5 13/16P–6 5/16P | 6 1/16P | 3/16P | 0 | 1/8 | — |
| | 911 Turbo | 5 13/16P–6 5/16P | 6 1/16P | 3/16P | 0 | 1/8 | — |
| | 924S | 2 1/4P–3P | 2 1/2P | 9/16N–1/16N | 5/16N | 5/64 | — |
| | 928S4 | 3P–4P | 3 1/2P | 11/16N–5/16N | 1/2N | 5/32 | — |
| | 944 | 2 1/4P–3P | 2 1/2P | 9/16N–1/16N | 5/16N | 5/64 | — |
| | 944S | 2 1/4P–3P | 2 1/2P | 9/16N–1/16N | 5/16N | 5/64 | — |
| | 944 Turbo | 2 1/4P–3P | 2 1/2P | 9/16N–1/16N | 5/16N | 5/64 | — |
| 1989–90 | 911 | 5 13/16P–6 5/16P | 6 1/16P | 3/16P | 0 | 1/8 | — |
| | 911 Turbo | 5 13/16P–6 5/16P | 6 1/16P | 3/16P | 0 | 1/8 | — |
| | 928S4 | 3P–4P | 3 1/2P | 11/16N–5/16N | 1/2N | 5/32 | — |
| | 944 | 2 1/4P–3P | 2 1/2P | 9/16N–1/16N | 5/16N | 5/64 | — |
| | 944S2 | 2 1/4P–3P | 2 1/2P | 9/16N–1/16N | 5/16N | 5/64 | — |
| | 944 Turbo | 2 1/4P–3P | 2 1/2P | 9/16N–1/16N | 5/16N | 5/64 | — |

① 911 Turbo—1/2P

# TUNE-UP PROCEDURES

## Ignition Timing

### ADJUSTMENT

*1983 911 and 911 Turbo*

1. Start the engine and allow it to warm up to normal operating temperature, approximately 194°F (90°C).
2. Turn the ignition switch **OFF** and connect an inductive timing light according to the manufacturers instructions. Connect an inductive tester/tachometer.
3. Remove the red and blue distributor vacuum hoses. Adjust the engine idle speed to 950 rpm.
4. When the timing light flashes, the 5 degrees BTDC mark on the

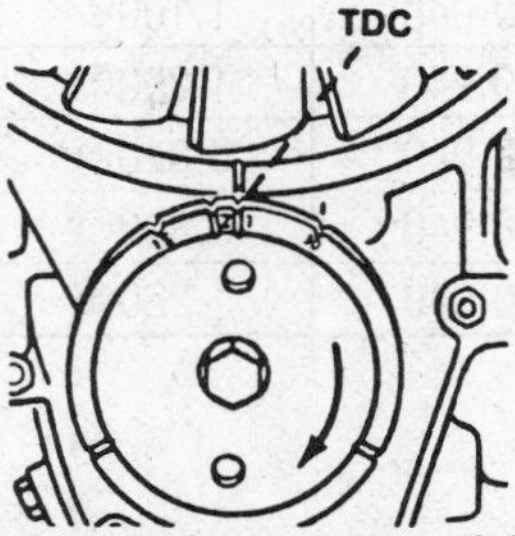


Timing marks on 911 models

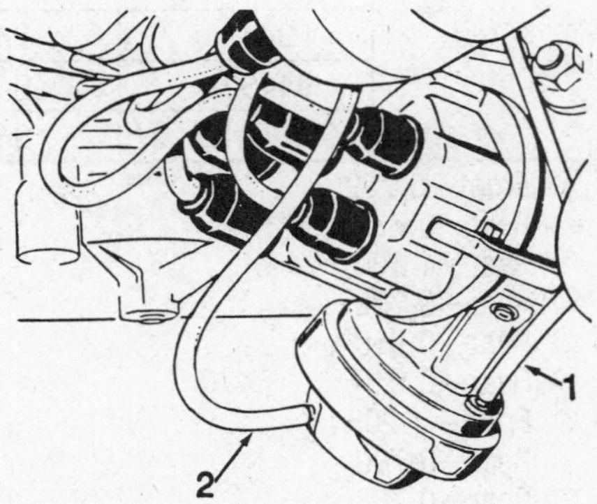


Distributor vacuum hoses—1983 911

crankshaft pulley should be aligned with the reference notch on the fan (blower) housing at 950 rpm. If the notches do not align, loosen the retaining nut at the bottom of the distributor mounting flange and slowly rotate the distributor as necessary until the notch and pulley mark are aligned.

5. Ignition timing is now correct at idle. Reconnect the vacuum hoses and recheck idle speed. Adjust if necessary.

6. To check the centrifugal advance mechanism, make sure the ignition timing is properly adjusted for the idle rpm. Disconnect the distributor vacuum hoses. Check the timing it should be 15–20 degrees BTDC at 3000 rpm, and 19–25 degrees BTDC at 6000 rpm.

7. To check the vacuum retard, run the engine at idle speed. Connect the blue (retard) hose at connection 1 of the double vacuum box on the distributor and disconnect the red (advance) hose at connection 2. Check the ignition timing with the timing light; it should be 3–7 degrees ATDC.

8. To check the vacuum advance, connect the blue (retard) hose on connection 2. Adjust engine speed to 950 rpm. Ignition timing should be 8–12 degrees BTDC. Connect all vacuum hoses and check that the engine idle speed is 950 rpm. Adjust if necessary.

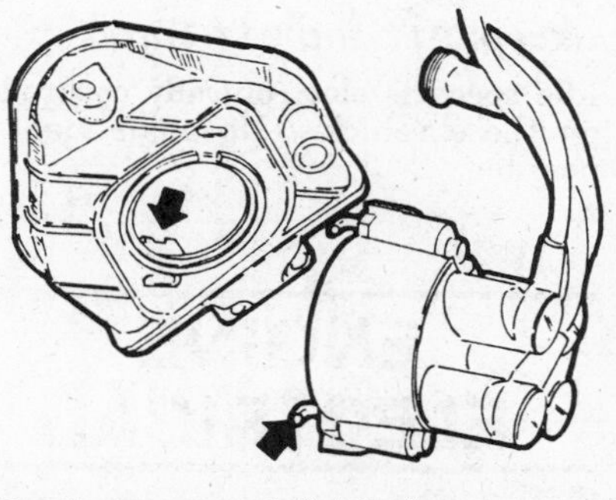

**Distributor cap and distributor cap mount of the 944. Note how the distributor cap screw clips are to engage (arrows)**

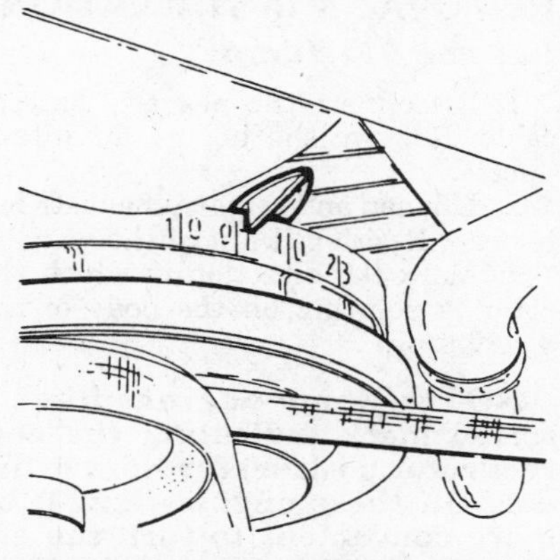

**Timing marks on the 928 and 928S are located on the vibration damper at the front of the engine.**

### *1984–90 911 and 911 Turbo*

To check the idle speed, a Porsche special tool (VAG 1367 tester) is required. Terminals **B** and **C** of the test jack, which is located next to the coil must be bridged with a jumper wire in order to bypass the idle regulator. Timing is then checked in the normal manner. At 800 rpm, ignition timing should be 3 degrees ATDC.

Full throttle ignition timing is again checked with the VAG 1367 tester, or with a stroboscopic timing light directed at the 25 degrees timing mark on the crankshaft pulley. Make sure the engine is at normal operating temperature, approximately 194°F (90°C), and that all electrical accessories are **OFF**. Make sure that the distributor rotor is correctly installed in relation to the mark on the distributor housing.

Bridge terminals **B** and **C** of the test jack; this stimulates full throttle on the control unit and stops operation of the idle regulator. Full throttle timing should be 25 degrees BTDC at 3800 rpm.

### *944 and 924S*

The Digital Motor Electronic (DME) ignition system is self-adjusting. No periodic ignition timing adjustments are necessary or possible.

### *1983–84 928*

1. Start the engine and allow it to reach normal operating temperature, then turn the ignition switch **OFF**.

2. Connect a timing light to the engine. A positive (+) terminal for connecting the timing light is located in the engine compartment. Connect a tachometer according to the manufacturers instructions.

**NOTE: Make sure the ignition switch is OFF when connecting test equipment to the ignition system.**

3. With the timing light connected to the ignition cable for No. 1 cylinder, detach both vacuum hoses at the distributor and start the engine.

4. The timing marks are located on the crankshaft pulley and are colored for identification. With the engine at 3000 rpm, focus the timing light on the timing marks.

5. To adjust the timing, loosen the distributor holddown bolt and turn the distributor as necessary. Tighten the holddown bolt when the timing is correct.

6. Once all adjustments are complete, turn the ignition **OFF** and disconnect all test equipment.

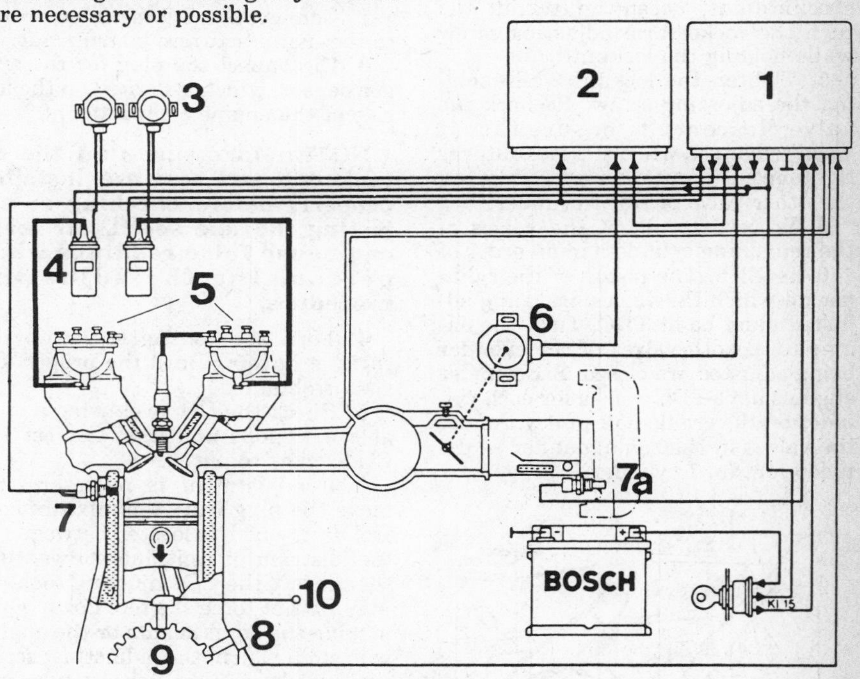


1 – EZF control unit
2 – LH injection control unit
3 – Ignition final stages
4 – Ignition coils
5 – Distributor (2 x 4)
6 – Throttle switchs
7 – Temperature sensor II
7a – Temperature sensor I
8 – Ignition timing sensor
9 – Pulse gear ring
10 – TDC sensor

**Schematic of EZF ignition system used on 928S models**

*928S and 928S4*

The EZF ignition system used on 928S is self-adjusting. The EZK ignition system on 928S4 uses knock sensors to allow the control unit to constantly adjust the ignition timing according to engine operating conditions. In either case, ignition timing is computer-controlled and not adjustable.

## Valve Lash

### ADJUSTMENT

*911 and 911 Turbo*

1. The engine must be cold when adjusting the valves. Remove the rocker arm covers.
2. The valves of each cylinder are adjusted with that piston at the top of its compression stroke. Both the intake and exhaust valves will be closed at this point. Turn the engine to align the TDC mark **Z1** with the reference mark.
3. Using the appropriate size feeler gauge, check the clearance between the valve stem and the rocker arm. The feeler gauge should just slip through; if it has to be forced, the clearance will be incorrect.
4. If the clearance is not within specifications, loosen the locknut and turn the rocker arm adjusting screw while holding the locknut.
5. Tighten the locknut while holding the adjusting screw. Recheck the valve clearance to ensure that it wasn't changed when the locknut was tightened. Repeat this procedure on the other valve of No. 1 cylinder.
6. Proceed to adjust the valves of the remaining cylinders in an order of 1–6–2–4–3–5. The piston of the cylinder on which the valves are being adjusted must be at TDC. Turn the engine until both valves of the cylinder being adjusted are closed. Six cylinder engines have TDC marks for each cylinder on the crankshaft pulley. Adjust the valves in the same manner as detailed for No. 1 cylinder.

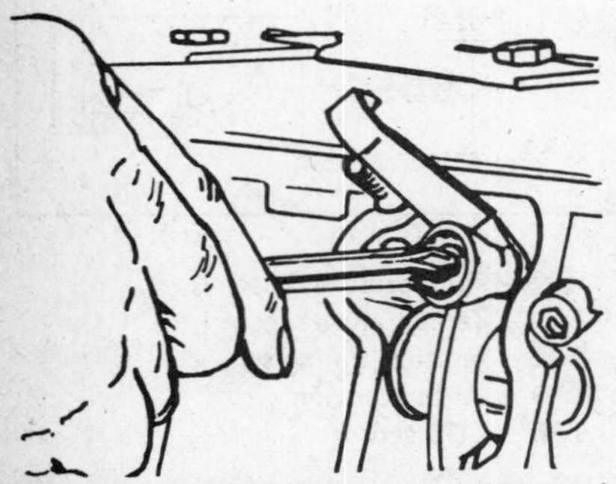

**Valve clearance adjustment on 911 models**

**Valve Adjusting Screw ID No. 2**

| Color | mm | Replaced by |
|---|---|---|
| White | 6.6 | "no notch" |
| Blue | 6.9 | "one notch" |
| Red | 7.2 | "two notch" |
| No color | new | "three notch" |
| Yellow | 7.5 | "four notch" |

7. Install the rocker arm or camshaft housing covers with the new gaskets. Start the engine and check for leaks.

*Except 911 and 911 Turbo*

The overhead camshafts operate bucket-type hydraulic valve lifters, located directly over the valve stems. No periodic valve adjustment is necessary.

## Idle Speed

### IDLE SPEED ADJUSTMENT

*1983 911 and 1986–90 911 Turbo (CIS fuel injection system)*

1. Install the exhaust pickup line on to the test connection of the catalytic converter.
2. Connect the CO tester according to the manufacturers instructions.
3. Disconnect the plug for the oxygen sensor, which is located on the left side of the engine compartment.

**NOTE: Make sure that the oil tank cap and seal are installed properly before checking or adjusting the idle speed. Air leaks can cause false readings when performing the adjusting procedure.**

4. Turn the control screw on the throttle housing until the proper idle rpm is obtained.
5. Check the CO level using a suitable emissions analyzer. Correct the CO level as required.
6. If adjustment is necessary, remove the plug from the mixture control unit, which is located between the fuel distributor unit and the venturi, then insert the CO adjusting tool.
7. Do not force the tool down while making the adjustments or the engine will stall. Turn the adjusting screw very slowly, as the slightest turn will change the CO reading radically.
8. Remove the adjusting tool. Accelerate the engine. Allow the engine to return to idle and recheck both the idle speed and the CO level.
9. Once all adjustments are complete, disconnect the test equipment and plug all connections as required.

*1984–90 911*

**NOTE: Idle adjustment on these vehicles can only be performed using a CO analyzer. For accurate adjustments, the procedure must be closely followed.**

1. Run the engine up to normal operating temperature. Engine oil temperature must be approximately 194°F (90°C). Intake air temperature must be between 59–95°F.
2. Disconnect the oxygen sensor.
3. Connect the CO analyzer in front of the catalytic converter. Check the CO content percentage at idle. Content in the exhaust gas should be 0.6–1.0%.
4. Reconnect the oxygen sensor.
5. Bridge terminals **B** and **C** on the test connection jack located to the rear of the coil on the driver's side enne compartment wall to bypass the idle stabilizer.
6. Check the idle speed (rpm) and adjust if necessary. Idle speed should be 800 rpm. Adjustments are made with the throttle housing adjustment screw.
7. Remove the bridge from the test jack. Recheck thgie CO% content and idle rpm. Remove the CO analyzer probe and close the catalytic converter connection.

*Except 911 and 911 Turbo*

Idle speed is electronically controlled on these vehicles. No adjustment is possible.

# ENGINE ELECTRICAL

## Distributor

### REMOVAL & INSTALLATION

*911 and 911 Turbo*

1. Disconnect the negative battery cable. Remove the heated air intake duct.
2. Unsnap and remove the distributor cap. Position it out of the way.
3. Mark the direction in which the rotor is pointing on the body of the distributor.

**NOTE: Some engines have a scribe mark indicating the correct rotor position for No. 1 cylinder. On these engines it will be more convenient to turn the engine so that the rotor points to this mark before removing the distributor.**

1. Rotor
2. Stator

**Exploded view of 911 distributor**

4. Detach the distributor leads. Remove the vacuum line.
5. Loosen and remove the retaining nut from the base of the distributor. Pull the distributor straight out of the engine. Check and, if necessary, replace the sealing ring on the distributor housing.
6. Insert the distributor into the engine. Swivel the rotor back and forth to engage the distributor and crankshaft gears. If the engine has been turned while the distributor was out, bring the No. 1 cylinder to TDC before installing the distributor.
7. Check and adjust the ignition timing as necessary.

### *1983–84 928*

1. Disconnect the negative battery cable.
2. Unsnap the 2 retaining clips and remove the distributor cap.
3. Set the No. 1 cylinder at top dead center (TDC). The No. 1 cylinder is at top dead center when the TDC mark on the flywheel or crank pulley aligns with the timing pointer and the distributor cap tower for the No. 1 cylinder spark plug wire. Turn the engine over by hand until these signs are evident.
4. Disconnect the vacuum hose(s) from the distributor, then disconnect the electrical connections at the distributor.
5. Loosen and remove the distributor holddown bolt and clamp, then remove the distributor.
6. If the engine has not been turned over since the distributor was removed, align the rotor on the distributor with the No. 1 cylinder distributor cap tower. There is a notch in the distributor body which the rotor will point to when in this position. Install the distributor.
7. If the engine was turned while the distributor was removed, it will be necessary to relocate No. 1 cylinder to TDC on the compression stroke. Remove No. 1 cylinder spark plug, then turn the engine over in the normal direction of rotation while checking for compression with your thumb over the No. 1 cylinder spark plug hole. When this happens, continue turning the engine until the timing mark for TDC on the flywheel or crank pulley aligns with the timing pointer. Install the distributor.
8. Install the vacuum hoses, electrical connections and distributor cap. Check and adjust the ignition timing.

### *944, 924S and 928S*

The distributor is not removable. Only the cap is removable. Noise appearing to originate in the vicinity of the distributor of the distributor on the 944 is usually due to a worn Woodruff key on the camshaft sprocket.

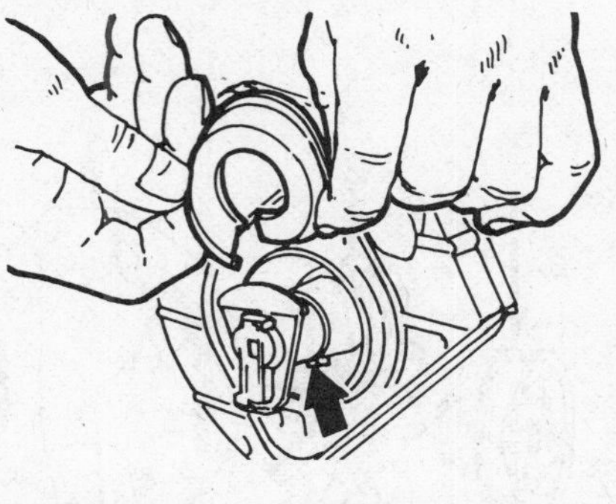

On the 944, the distributor rotor is held to the shaft by a screw (arrow).

**NOTE: The distributor rotor is retained by 1 or 3 screws accessible after removing the dust cover. If the rotor is removed, new retaining screws must be installed, or the old ones coated with nonhardening sealant.**

### *928S4*

All 32-valve engines use 2 distributors, each driven by the exhaust camshaft for the cylinder bank it controls and mounted on the front of the engine. The distributor caps are retained by 3 screws, as is the rotor. The rotor can only be installed 1 way.

# Alternator

## PRECAUTIONS

To prevent possibly serious damage to the alternator, regulator and any onboard microprocessor control computers, the following precautions should be taken whenever working with the electrical system.

- Never reverse the battery connections.
- Booster batteries for starting must be connected properly: positive-to-positive and negative-to-negative with the ignition **OFF**.
- Disconnect the battery cables before using a fast charger; the charger has a tendency to force current through the diodes in the opposite directions for which they were designed. This burns out the diodes.
- Never use a fast charger as a booster for starting the vehicle.
- Never disconnect the voltage regulator while the engine is running.
- Avoid long soldering times when replacing diodes or transistors. Prolonged heat is damaging to AC generators.
- Do not use test lamps of more than 12 volts for checking diode continuity.
- Do not short across or ground any of the terminal on the AC generator.
- The polarity of the battery, generator, and regulator must be matched and considered before making any electrical connections within the system.
- Never operate the alternator on an open circuit and make sure that all connections within the circuit are clean and tight.
- Disconnect the battery terminals when performing any service on the electrical system. This will eliminate the possibility of accidental reversal of polarity.
- Disconnect the battery ground cable if arc welding is to be done on any part of the vehicle.

## REMOVAL & INSTALLATION

### *911 and 911 Turbo*

The alternator is located in the blower housing.

1. Disconnect the negative battery cable.
2. Remove the air cleaner assembly.
3. Remove the upper shroud retaining bolts.
4. Hold the alternator pulley and remove the pulley nut.
5. Remove the drive belt.
6. Remove the blower housing strap retaining bolts.
7. Pull the assembly towards the rear until there is enough clearance to disconnect the wiring.
8. Remove the alternator.
9. Install the alternator in the reverse order of removal. Be sure that the blower housing is seated on the dowel in the crankcase.
10. Tighten the pulley nut to 29 ft. lbs. (39 Nm).

Alternator pulley nut removal

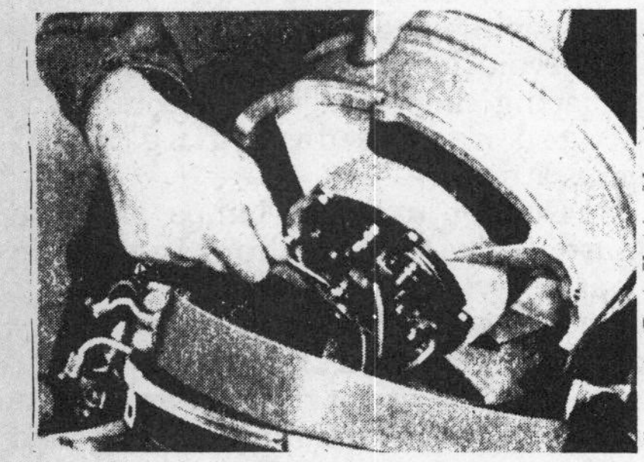

Alternator removal

Fan belt pulley adjustment spacers

## BELT TENSION ADJUSTMENT

### *911 and 911 Turbo*

A correctly tensioned belt can be deflected ½–¾ in. by light hand pressure. If the tension is not within specifications, follow the steps below to adjust or replace the belt.

1. Disconnect the negative battery cable. Remove the pulley nut.
2. Remove the outside half of the pulley.
3. Remove the adjustment spacers to increase belt tension. Add spacers to decrease belt tension.
4. When the correct spacer grouping is achieved, install the belt, pulley half, spacers, and nut.
5. Tighten the nut to 29 ft. lbs. (39 Nm).

**NOTE: If you have removed spacers, install the extra spacers on the outside of the pulley so they won't become lost or misplaced.**

6. Recheck the belt tension after about 60 miles of driving.

### *Except 911 and 911 Turbo*

1. Disconnect the negative battery cable.
2. Raise the vehicle and support it safely.
3. Remove the engine splash shield and the alternator cooling vent cover and tube.
4. Loosen the belt tension lock bolt, move the alternator inward and remove the belt from the pulley.

**NOTE: On the 924S and 944, first loosen the end bolts of the tensioner, then loosen the locknuts of the tensioner and rotate the tensioner tube as necessary.**

5. Remove the wire connections from the rear of the alternator.
6. Remove the alternator pivot bolt and remove the alternator from the engine.
7. Installation is the reverse of removal.

## Voltage Regulator

## REMOVAL & INSTALLATION

### *911 and 911 Turbo*

1. Disconnect the battery ground cable.
2. Disconnect the wiring from the regulator.
3. Remove the mounting screws and remove the regulator.
4. Install the regulator. Do not overtighten the screws.

### *Except 911 and 911 Turbo*

The voltage regulator is bolted to the rear of the alternator. Remove the alternator before attempting to remove the voltage regulator.

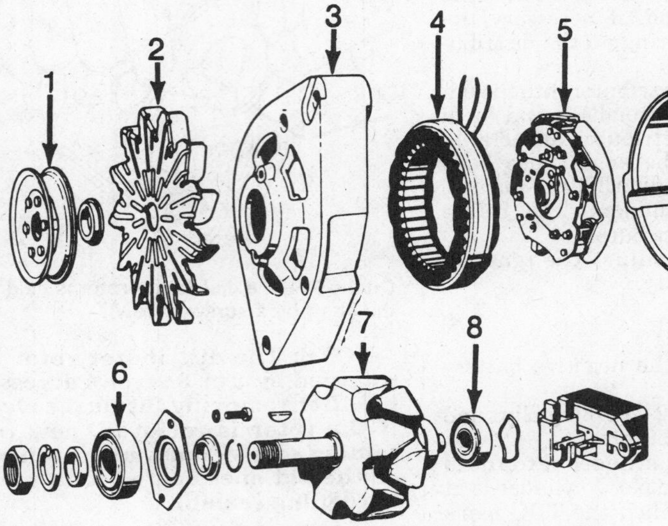

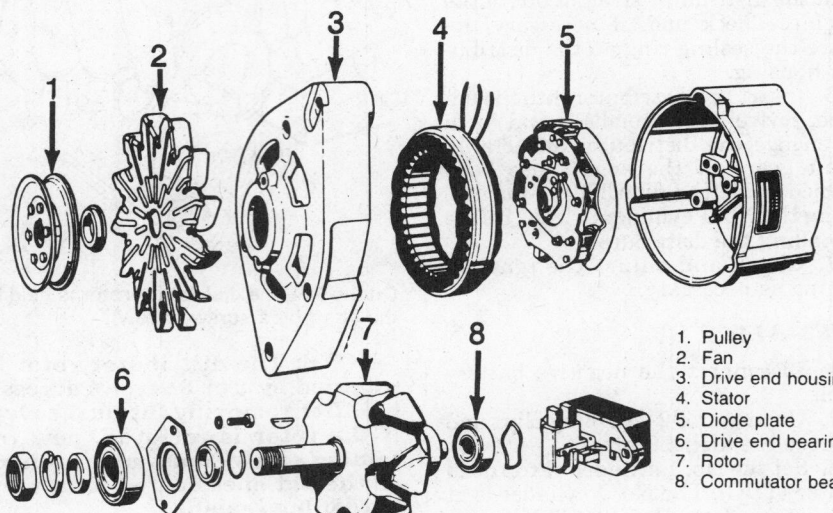

1. Pulley
2. Fan
3. Drive end housing
4. Stator
5. Diode plate
6. Drive end bearing
7. Rotor
8. Commutator bearing

Exploded view of a typical alternator

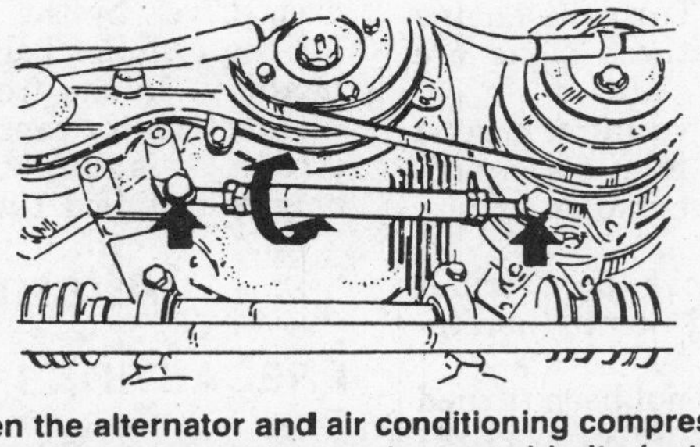

To loosen the alternator and air conditioning compressor drive belt of the 944: Loosen the tensioner end bolts (outer arrow); loosen the locknuts; then turn the tensioner tube (circular arrow) as required. When tightening the belt, the end bolts are to be tightened last

# Starter

## REMOVAL & INSTALLATION

### *911 and 911 Turbo*

1. Disconnect the negative battery cable.
2. Raise and support the vehicle safely.
3. Tag and then remove the starter electrical connections.
4. Loosen the retaining bolts while supporting the starter, then remove the bolts and pull out the starter.
5. Install the starter in the reverse order of the removal procedure. Make sure that the terminal connections are correctly installed, clean and tight.
6. Lower the vehicle. Connect the battery ground strap.

### *Except 911 and 911 Turbo*

1. Disconnect the negative battery cable.
2. Raise and support the vehicle safely.
3. Disconnect the 2 small wires form the starter solenoid. One wire connects to the ignition coil and the second to the ignition switch through the wiring harness.
4. Disconnect the large cable, which is the positive battery cable, from the solenoid.
5. Remove the 2 starter retaining bolts.
6. Pull the starter straight out and to the front, then lower it out of the vehicle.
7. Installation is the reverse of removal.

## STARTER DRIVE REPLACEMENT

### *911 and 911 Turbo*

1. Disconnect the negative battery cable. Raise and support the vehicle safely.
2. Remove the starter. Press clutch operating shaft by turning slighty.
3. Pull both off the shaft by turning slightly.
4. Hold the armature in a vise and push the pinion and sleeve onto the shaft until the detent locks.

### *Except 911 and 911 Turbo*

1. Disconnect the negative battery cable. Raise and support the vehicle safely.
2. Remove the starter. Remove the solenoid. Remove the end bearing cap.
3. Loosen both of the long housing screws.
4. Remove the lockwasher and spacer washer.
5. Remove the long housing screws and remove the end cover.
6. Pull the 2 field coil brushes out of the brush housing.
7. Remove the brush housing assembly.
8. Loosen the nut on the solenoid housing, remove the sealing disc, and remove the solenoid operating lever.
9. Loosen the large screws on the side of the starter body and remove the field coil along with the brushes.

**NOTE: If the brushes require replacement, the field coil and brushes and/or the brush housing and its brushes must be replaced as a unit. The armature should be turned on a lathe if it is out-of-round, scored or grooved.**

10. If the starter drive is being replaced, push the lock ring down and remove the circlip on the end of the shaft. Remove the lock ring and remove the drive.
11. Assembly is the reverse of disassembly. Use a gear puller to install the lock ring in its groove. Use a new circlip on the shaft.

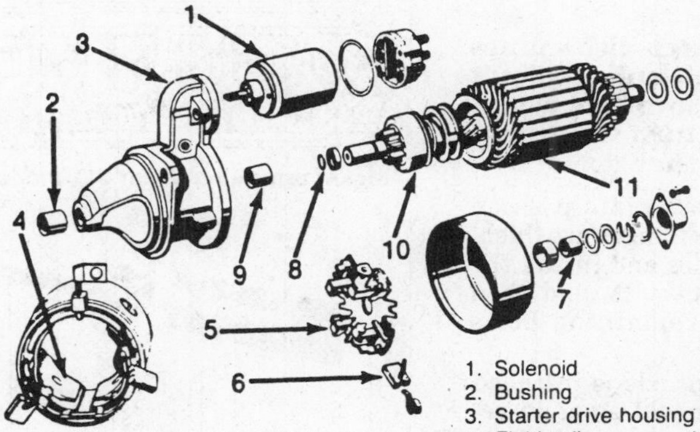

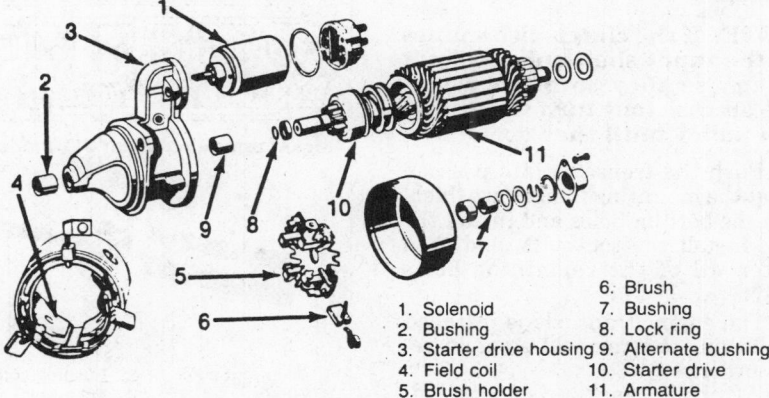

1. Solenoid
2. Bushing
3. Starter drive housing
4. Field coil
5. Brush holder
6. Brush
7. Bushing
8. Lock ring
9. Alternate bushing
10. Starter drive
11. Armature

**Exploded view of the starter**

## STARTER SOLENOID REPLACEMENT

1. Disconnect the negative battery cable. Raise and support the vehicle safely. Remove the starter.
2. Remove the nut which secures the connector strip on the end of the solenoid.
3. Take out the 2 retaining screws on the mounting bracket and withdraw the solenoid after it has been unhooked from the operating lever.
4. Installation is the reverse of removal. In order to facilitate engagement of the lever, the pinion should be pulled as far as possible when inserting the solenoid.

# ENGINE MECHANICAL 911 AND 911 TURBO

## Engine

### REMOVAL & INSTALLATION

All 911 engines are removed and installed from below the vehicle, with the transaxle attached. The recommended method for removal is to raise the rear of the vehicle high enough for working clearance and then support it safely.

1. Disconnect the negative battery cable.
2. Open the engine compartment lid and detach the hot air ducts from the air gates and exhaust manifold heat exchangers.
3. Detach the 2 heater control cables. Disconnect the brake booster vacuum line.
4. Remove the hot air ducts from the T-union between the air cleaners and then remove the Tee union from the blower housing.
5. Remove the tops of the air cleaners. If equipped with air conditioning, remove the compressor and position it to the side.
6. Tag for identification and then remove the electrical cables from the generator and blower housing.
7. Tag for identification and then remove the wires from the ignition coil. Remove the connections from the oil temperature and pressure sending units.
8. Carefully relieve the fuel system pressure, then remove the fuel line

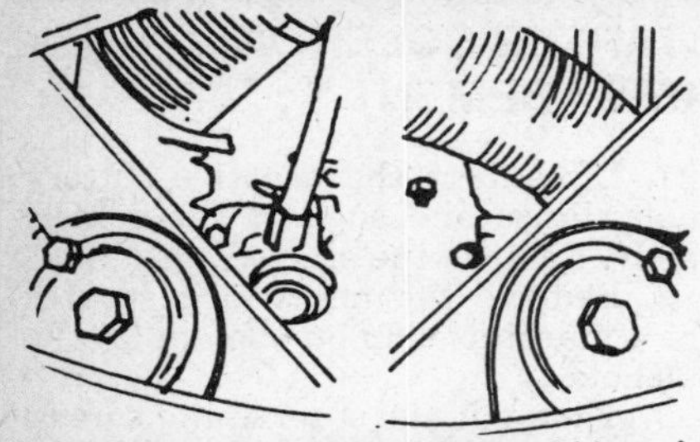

Rear engine-to-body mounts on 911 models

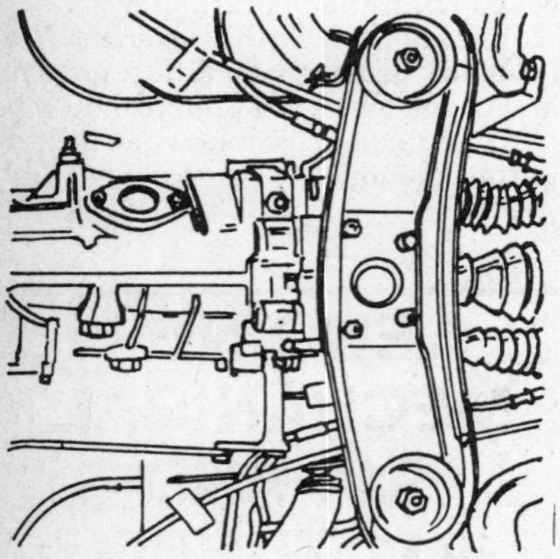

Transaxle crossmember mounting on 911 models

from the fuel pump and detach its clip from the engine shield.

9. Raise and support the vehicle safely. Drain the engine oil. drain the transaxle fluid.

10. Remove the Allen bolts retaining the axle shaft flange to the transaxle. Free the axle shafts from the transaxle and drop them out of the way.

**NOTE: On later models, be sure to properly suspend the left axle shaft to avoid damage to the transaxle cooling line coil**

11. On 1987–90 911 Turbo, unbolt the clutch release cylinder. Move the assembly to the side with the lines connected. Do not depress the clutch pedal with the release cylinder unbolted.

12. Remove the starter electrical leads. Disconnect the clutch cable from the control lever, if equipped. Remove the ground strap. Detach the back-up light lead.

13. Remove the rear stabilizer, if equipped. Disconnect the electronic speedometer sensor and rubber plug, as required.

14. Disconnect the throttle linkage from the crossshaft at the transaxle. Remove the cover in the center of the rear floor.

15. Detach the rubber shift lever cover from the flange on the body and pull it forward on the control lever.

16. Remove the safety wire from the square-headed joint. Loosen the screw and slide the shift rod off its base.

17. Position the jack, including the flat support plate, under the engine/transaxle. The jack should be under the point of balance of the powertrain.

18. Raise the jack a slight amount. Remove the body mounting bolts on either side of the engine compartment.

19. Remove the body mounting bolts from the short transaxle crossmember. The engine is removed with this crossmember attached.

20. Very carefully lower the engine while your assistants help balance it.

21. Roll the engine/transaxle out from under the vehicle. Remove the starter. Release the throw-out fork tension by disconnecting the return spring if used. After releasing throw-out bearing tension, it is necessary to slide the throw-out fork past the bearing. To do this, insert a suitable tool in the opening in the transaxle and turn the bearing 90 degrees. Slide the fork past the bearing. The transaxle may now be separated from the engine.

22. Remove the engine-to-transaxle bolts and nuts. Carefully pull the transaxle away from the engine. Be sure that the full weight of the transaxle is supported, so as not to damage the pilot bushing, throwout bearing, clutch disc, or pressure plate.

23. Whichever component you are repairing, rebuilding, or replacing may now be moved to a suitable workbench, dolly or engine stand.

24. Before reinstalling the transaxle, fill the pilot bushing in the gland nut with a small amount of graphite grease (no more than 3cc, or $\frac{1}{10}$ oz.).

25. Lightly grease the transaxle input shaft splines, starter shaft bushing, and the starter and flywheel gear teeth.

26. Carefully attach the transaxle to the engine. Remember the transaxle input shaft will be passing through the throw-out bearing, pressure plate, clutch disc, and pilot bushing, so give ample support during the attachment procedure.

**NOTE: If the clutch disc splines and the input shaft splines don't line up, as they so often won't, have an assistant turn the crankshaft pulley until they do.**

27. Push the transaxle into position so that the mounting flanges are flush. Align the bottom holes and install the bolts. Install the top bolts, and then tighten all of the remaining bolts evenly.

28. The engine/transaxle is installed by following the removal steps in reverse order.

29. After the engine is installed, check the clutch adjustment. Refill the engine and transaxle with the correct

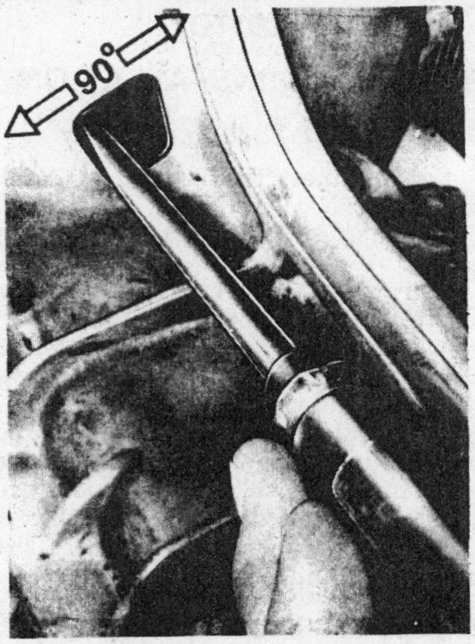


Sliding the fork past the throwout bearing on 911 models

Releasing throwout bearing tension on 911 models

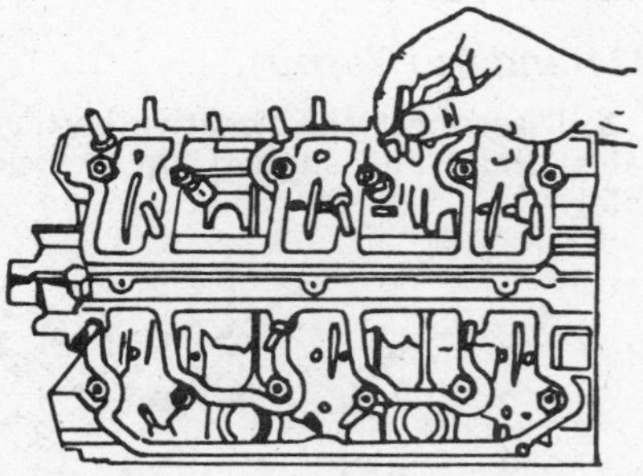

Rocker arm removal on 911 models

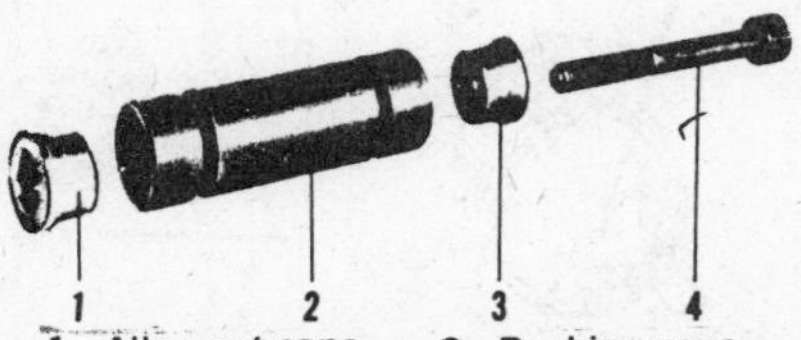


1. Allen nut cone
2. Shaft
3. Bushing cone
4. Allen bolt

Typical 911 rocker arm shaft assembly

lubricant. Lower the vehicle.

30. Start the engine and check for leaks.

# Rocker Shafts

## REMOVAL & INSTALLATION

Each rocker arm has an individual shaft on this single overhead camshaft engine. One or all of the shafts and rocker arms may be removed with the engine in the chassis.

1. Disconnect the negative battery cable. Remove the hot air ducts between the fan and the heat exchanger assembly.
2. Remove the camshaft housing cover nuts and spring washers. Remove the covers. Scribe the rocker arms being removed so that they can be returned to the same position.
3. Unscrew the Allen bolt in the rocker shaft. Push the shaft out of its bore and remove it along with the rocker arm.

**NOTE: If the rocker arm is under pressure, you won't be able to push the shaft out. Turn the crankshaft until the rocker rests on the heel of the cam lobe.**

4. Check the rocker arm and shaft for excessive wear or damage. Replace any suspect part.

**NOTE: End rockers are installed with the Allen screw heads facing towards cylinders No. 2 and No. 5 respectively.**

5. Place the rocker arm on its shaft.
6. The rocker arm shaft should be centered in its bore so that each groove is recessed 0.059 in. (1.15mm).
   a. Insert a 0.06 in. feeler gauge in the groove on a side of the shaft. Push the shaft in until the feeler gauge is held tight against the edge.
   b. Carefully remove the gauge and push the shaft in approximately 0.06 in. more, using the feeler gauge to judge the distance.
7. Tighten the Allen bolt to 13 ft. lbs. (17.5 Nm).
8. Install the camshaft cover.

# Exhaust Manifold Heat Exchanger

## REMOVAL & INSTALLATION

1. Disconnect the negative battery cable. Raise and support the vehicle safely.
2. Remove the muffler. Detach and remove the connecting hose from the heat exchanger to the heater valve chamber.
3. Detach the heater hose from the heat exchanger. Remove the 3 sunken bolts from the bottom of the heat exchanger.
4. Remove the 6 cylinder head-to-heat exchanger nuts Remove the heat exchanger.
5. Examine the heat exchanger for damaged flanges or cracks. Replace it, if necessary.
6. Install the heat exchanger in the reverse order of removal. Use new flange gaskets and tighten the retaining nuts and bolts alternately.

# Engine

## DISASSEMBLY AND ASSEMBLY

**NOTE: Further component removal and installation requires engine removal and disassembly. Follow steps of engine disassembly and then assembly for the part being replaced.**

1. Remove the engine/transaxle from the vehicle. Separate the 2 assemblies and position the engine in a suitable holding fixture.
2. Remove the muffler and heat exchanger.
3. Remove the rear engine cover plate.

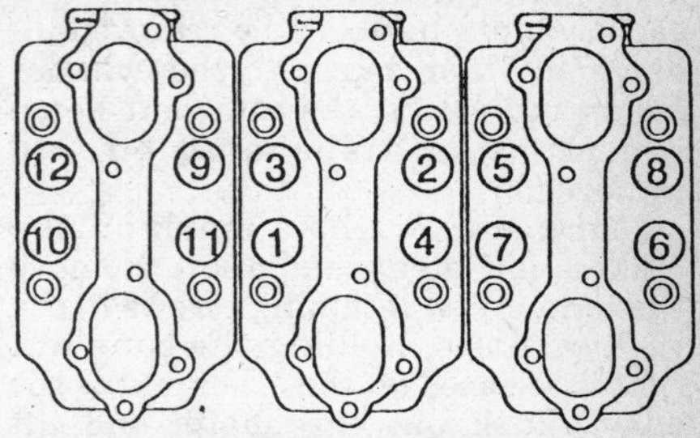


**Cylinder head torque sequence—911**

4. Remove the intake distributor and intake pipe with the injection valves.
5. Remove the distributor and the front engine cover plate.
6. Remove the cooling blower impeller, then remove the cooling blower housing with the alternator attached.
7. Remove the engine mount.
8. Remove the front and rear cylinder jackets with the warm air guides.
9. Remove the oil cooler, oil filter, and oil pump.
10. Remove the cylinder head covers. Remove the rocker arm shafts with the protective tubes, pushrods and lifters.
11. Removal of the cylinder heads involves removing the overhead camshafts. All 3 cylinder heads on each bank can be removed as a unit complete with the camshaft and rockers or

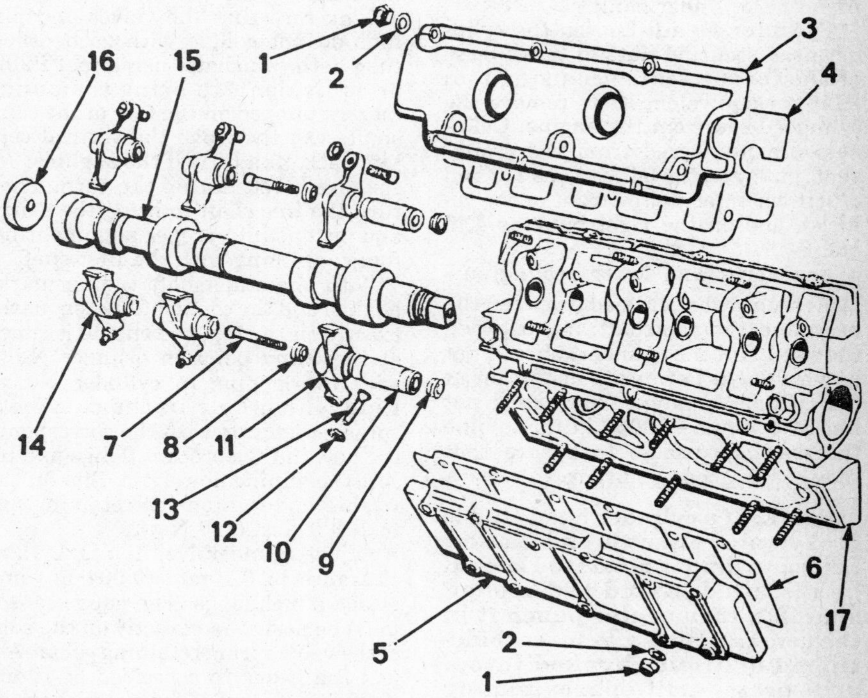


1. Nut
2. Aluminum washer
3. Cover
4. Gasket
5. Cover
6. Gasket
7. Bolt
8. Bushing
9. Nut
10. Rocker arm shaft
11. Rocker arm
12. Nut
13. Adjusting screw
14. Rocker arm assembly
15. Camshaft
16. Cover
17. Housing

**Exploded view of 911 camshaft housing assembly**

each cylinder head can be removed individually. For access to the cylinder heads and valves, the camshaft housing must be disassembled and removed.

**Rockers:** Scribe a mark on the rockers for later installation. Remove the 5mm Allen retaining screws in the rocker shafts, holding the cone-nut that is released on the other end of the shaft. Push out the shafts and lift away the rockers. Position the camshaft so that the cam lobe does not press against the rocker being removed.

**Camshaft:** Remove the timing chain cover at each camshaft. Unbolt the chain tensioner and the intermediate wheel, using tools P202 and P203, or equivalent. Withdraw the dowel pin from the camshaft wheel with tool P212, or equivalent. Remove the sliding wedges and withdraw the wheel and flange. Take the key from the camshaft, then unscrew the 3 sealing ring screws and remove the sealing ring together with the O-ring and the gasket. Withdraw the camshaft toward the rear. Note that both camshafts turn in the same direction and therefore require that the cam lobes be positioned differently.

**Cam Housing:** Unscrew the hex nuts and the 3 Allen screws to lift off the camshaft housing. Each housing fits either cylinder bank.

**Cylinder Head:** Loosen the cylinder head securing nuts in the reverse of the torque sequence using tool P119, or equivalent, then remove the cylinder head from the engine. Cylinders are numbered from the crankshaft pulley on the left bank as 1, 2 and 3 (left when facing the front of the vehicle), and on the right bank as 4, 5 and 6.

The upper and lower sealing surfaces of the cylinder head (between the head and the camshaft and between the head and the cylinder) should not be machined. Permitted distortion at the cylinder sealing surface must not exceed 0.15mm (0.0059 in.). Examine the mating surfaces to ensure that they are in good condition.

**NOTE: If a cylinder head stud is broken above the threads, a new Dilavar cylinder head stud should be installed. Grind the broken stud flat, then center punch it in the center. Using a $\frac{1}{4}$ in. carbide-tipped drill bit chucked into a drill press, drill approximately 15mm into the stud. Drive a No. 3 screw extractor approximately 10mm into the bore. Heat the case evenly in an oven or with a torch to 392°F (200°C) to loosen the grip of the Loctite. Turn out the broken stud, retap the threads in the crankcase and install a new Dilavar stud (part number 928 101 921 00).**

When installing the cylinder heads, use new cylinder head gaskets with the perforations set towards the cylinder. Carefully position each head, insert the washers and tighten the hex nuts lightly.

The camshaft housing is sealed to the cylinder heads only with sealing compound. Assemble the camshaft housing and oil return pipes on the cylinder heads, but only hand-tighten.

Porsche suggests that at this point in reassembly, the cylinder head be torqued down first and then the camshaft housing. Some mechanics prefer to torque the camshaft housing first for more accurate tensioning. Either way, the camshaft must be checked frequently for free turning. If tightening 1 side binds the crankshaft, tightening the opposite side must free it again. If not, the housing must be loosened, and tightening steps must be made in a different sequence.

Tighten the cylinder head to specification. Tighten the camshaft housing to 15–18 ft. lbs. (20–24 Nm).

**Valve Timing Adjustment 1983–86:** Turn the crankshaft until the mark **Z1** on the crankshaft pulley lines up exactly with the crankcase joint. Taking care that the valves and pistons do not collide with each other, turn both camshafts using tool P202, or equivalent, to bring the punch marks stamped on the face of the camshafts exactly above the vertical center. Back off a little if the slightest resistance is felt during the turn. Then turn the free shaft to bring the valves and pistons into proper alignment before continuing with the first shaft.

With the crankshaft timing marks aligned and the camshaft punch marks exactly on the top, the engine is timed at the firing point in cylinder No. 1 with overlapping in cylinder No. 4. Find which hole in the camshaft sprocket lines up with the corresponding hole in the sprocket flange and insert the alining dowel pin. Slip on the washer and tighten the retaining nut to 101 ft. lbs. (137 Nm).

Adjust cylinder No. 1 intake valve clearance to 0.10mm (0.004 in.) and attach a dial gauge. The gauge sensor must be positioned exactly on the edge of the valve spring retaining collar. Adjust the gauge to a preload of 10mm (0.39 in.) to provide for a sensor travel when the cam lobe depresses the valve. Depress the chain tensioner, using a suitable tool in order to tighten the chain (on the side to be measured) and turn the crankshaft a complete turn until the timing marks are aligned again. The dial gauge should read between 4.2 and 4.6mm (0.165–0.181 in.) A preferred range is 4.25–4.45mm.

If the gauge shows a lower or higher reading, the camshaft has to be readjusted as follows:

1. Remove the sprocket retaining nut, spring washer and aligning dowel pin.
2. Make sure that the crankshaft pulley mark is still aligned with the crankcase joint.
3. Depress the tensioner to tighten the chain and turn the camshaft until the dial gauge indicates 4.4–4.45mm (0.173–0.175 in.)
4. Find the hole in the camshaft sprocket which lines up with the sprocket flange and insert the dowel pin. Replace the spring washer and nut and tighten.
5. Turn the crankshaft 2 complete turns to the right and read the dial gauge. If the specified value is still not obtained, repeat the Steps above.

When the valves overlap in cylinder No. 1, cylinder No. 4 is at firing point (TDC). Repeat the procedure for cylinder No. 4 valve timing adjustment.

**Valve Timing Adjustment 1987–90:** Turn the crankshaft until the **Z1** mark on the pulley is aligned accurately with the joint of the crankcase or the stripe on the blower housing. Position both camshafts with punch marks or code **903** facing upward. The basic engine setting for No. 1 cylinder at TDC and No. 4 cylinder is given by aligning the **Z1** mark on the pulley to the joint and punch marks on the camshafts face up.

In the above mentioned position a bore in the sprocket will be aligned with a bore in the sprocket flange. Insert the dowel pin in the bores. Screw the bolts for the sprockets, finger tight. In case one of the camshafts has been moved, take a dowel pin out of the camshaft in the basic setting position so that it cannot turn.

To fine adjust the components, Check and adjust the valve clearance. Cylinders No. 1 and No. 4 must be adjusted properly to obtain the proper timing.

To perform the left camshaft adjustment, install a dial indicator gauge on the stud of the camshaft case. Set the gauge to zero with an approximate preload of 10mm on the spring retainer of the closed intake valve on the No. 1 cylinder. Turn the crankshaft a complete turn in the clockwise direction from **Z1** while observing the dial gauge. The proper reading should be 1.1–1.4mm. Unscrew and remove the mounting bolt on the left chain sprocket. Using a puller tool remove the dowel pin. Rotate the crankshaft untilthe **Z1** mark in properly outlined. Install the dowel pin and screw the bolt in finger tight. Rotate the crankshaft 2 complete revolutions clockwise and recheck the adjustment. Tighten the bolt on the left camshaft to a final torque of 87 ft. lbs (120Nm).

To perform the right camshaft adjustment, install a dial indicator gauge on the stud of the camshaft case. Set the gauge to zero with an approximate preload of 10mm on the spring retainer of the closed intake valve on the No. 4 cylinder. Turn the crankshaft a complete turn in the clockwise direction from **Z1** while observing the dial gauge. The proper reading should be 1.1–1.4mm. Unscrew and remove the mounting bolt on the left chain sprocket. Using a puller tool remove the dowel pin. Rotate the crankshaft untilthe **Z1** mark in properly outlined. Install the dowel pin and screw the bolt in finger tight. Rotate the crankshaft 2 complete revolutions clockwise and recheck the adjustment. Tighten the bolt on the left camshaft to a final torque of 87 ft. lbs (120Nm).

**Lower Assembly:** Remove the cylinder heads, cylinders and pistons. Remove the clutch and flywheel. Disassemble the crankcase, being careful not to score any of the mating surfaces by trying to pry the halves apart. Remove the camshaft and crankshaft with the connecting rods.

Assembly is the reverse of disassembly, noting the following procedures:

1. Check the riveting of the camshaft gear and the camshaft. Check the camshaft for out-of-true using V-blocks. The maximum allowable wear is 0.0016 in. Check the endplay of the guide bearing which should be 0.0016–0.0051 in.
2. The oil holes in the crankshaft bearing journals and bearings should have no sharp edges. Carefully remove any metallic, foreign substances before installing the crankshaft and connecting rods.
3. Install the camshaft and gear so that the tooth marked with **0** is located between the 2 teeth of the crankshaft gear which are identified with a punch mark. Coat the mating surfaces of the housing halves with a thin coat of sealing compound. Be sure that no sealing compound enters the oil ducts.
4. Assemble the crankcase halves and lightly tighten the screw for the oil intake pipe. Screw on the sealing nuts with the sealing ring on the outside and tighten to the specified torque. Rotate the crankshaft to ensure free rotation.
5. Grease the needle bearing in the flywheel with a small amount of multipurpose grease. Moisten the felt ring with engine oil, wiping off any excess.
6. Install the flywheel and adjust the axial play of the crankshaft. Measure the axial play by installing the flywheel with 2 spacing washers but without the sealing rings. Using a dial gauge, measure the play by rotating the flywheel. The thickness of the third spacer can be computed by subtracting 0.0039 in. from the measured result. Remove the flywheel and install the sealing ring, felt ring and 3 spacers. Three spacers must always be installed for the required thickness. Spacers are available in the following sizes: 0.0094, 0.0118, 0.0126, 0.0134, 0.0142, and 0.0150 in. Each spacer is marked for proper identification. The axial play of the crankshaft, measured with the engine assembled and the flywheel screwed on, should be 0.0028–0.0051 in.
7. Clean the contact surface of the clutch disc and flywheel. Check the splining of the input shaft and coat lightly with molybdenum disulphide powder, applied with a brush. The clutch disc should slide easily.
8. Check the clutch throwout bearing. Do not wash in solvent, but wipe it clean. Replace bearings which are contaminated or noisy. Grease the guide bushing lightly with molybdenum disulphide paste.
9. Center the clutch disc and clutch flywheel using an input shaft. When a new clutch is installed, the balancing marks should be 180 degrees apart. A white paint stripe on the outside edge of the flywheel indicates the heavy end, and a white paint stripe indicates the heavy end of the clutch. Tighten the bolts to 14.5 ft. lbs. (20 Nm).
10. Clean all pistons and check for wear. Check the marking of the pistons according to the following designations:
    a. The letter head next to the arrow is the index of the spare parts number.
    b. The punched-in arrow indicates that the piston must be installed with the arrow facing the flywheel.
    c. The color dot (blue, pink or green) indicates the paired size of the piston.
    d. A statement of weight class (+ or –) is punched in or printed. The weight class is indicated by a color dot (brown equals (–) weight and grey equals (+) weight).
    e. Number indicates the piston size in mm.
11. Fit the compression and oil scraper rings. The designation **TOP** should face up.
12. Insert the locking rings of pistons 1 and 2 on the side facing the flywheel. The locking rings of pistons 3 and 4 should be fitted on the impeller side.
13. Install the piston pin. The piston pin may slide in easily by hand, which is normal. Should the pin not fit easily, heat the piston to approximately 176°F and slide in the piston pin without bottoming the pin on the locking ring. Seat the second locking ring. Lubricate the piston and piston pin.
14. Compress the piston rings using a suitable tool, then lubricate the cylinder bore and fit the cylinder bore to the crankcase with the sealing ring. The studs of the crankcase may not touch the cooling fins of the cylinder.
15. Check the cylinder head for cracks and the spark plug threads for damage. Replace the sealing ring and the cylinder head. Pre-tighten the cylinder head nuts slightly, then tighten in sequence to the specified torque.
16. Replace the baffle plate. Coat the lifters with clean engine oil and install them. Slide the protective tubes with the new sealing rings up to the stop, taking care not to damage the sealing rings. Slide the bearing pieces on the rocker arm shafts so that the slots face downward and the broken edges outward when settling on the studs. The clip which secures the protective tubes should enter the slots of the bearing pieces and rest against the bottom edges of the protective tubes.
17. Lubricate the gear wheel and driveshaft and insert into the oil pump housing. Install the oil pump cover with the lubricated rubber sealing ring. Check the gear wheels for proper running. Install the oil pump, with a new seal, into the crankcase. The journal of the driveshaft should be in alignment with the slot in the camshaft gear. Center the oil pump by rotating the crankshaft two revolutions and then tightening the nuts.
18. Clean the sealing surface on the flange for the oil filter. Lubricate the rubber seal slightly and screw the filter in until the filter is seated. Tighten the oil filter.
19. Install the oil cooler after checking for leaks and tightening all welded seats.
20. Install the front and rear cylinder jackets and warm air guides. Replace the engine mount.
21. Install the cooling blower housing with the alternator and adjust the V-belt tension. Replace the cooling blower impeller and the front engine cover plate.
22. Install the ignition distributor. Bring cylinder No. 1 to TDC on the compression stroke. The black notch should be in alignment with the reference mark. The center offset slot in the head of the ignition distributor driveshaft should be at an angle of approximately 12 degrees in relation to the longitudinal axis of the engine. Turn the distributor rotor to the mark for cylinder No. 1 on the distributor housing. Insert the ignition distributor.
23. Replace the oil filler neck with

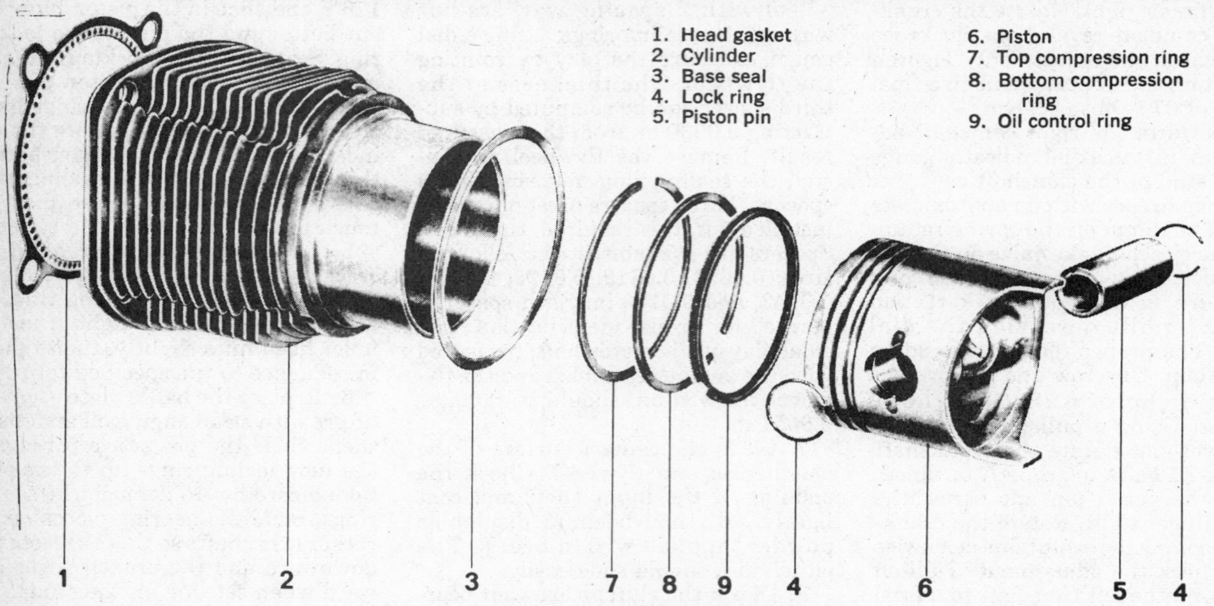


911 cylinder and piston assembly

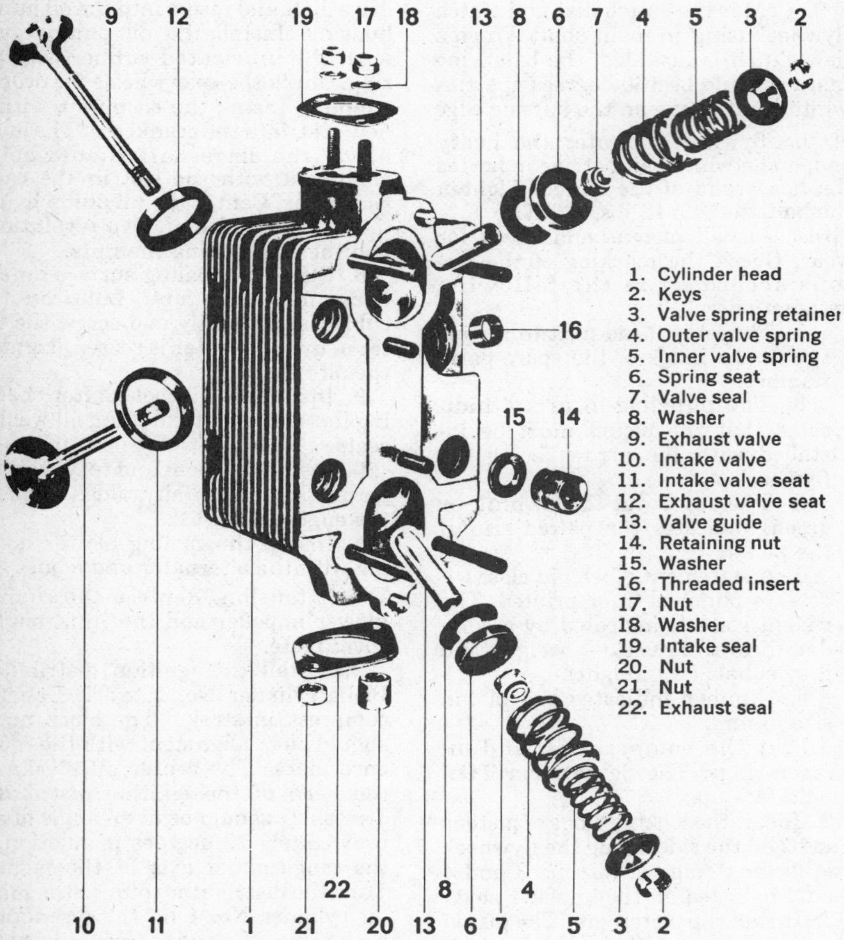


911 cylinder head components

Remove the 911 camshaft housing and cylinder heads as a unit

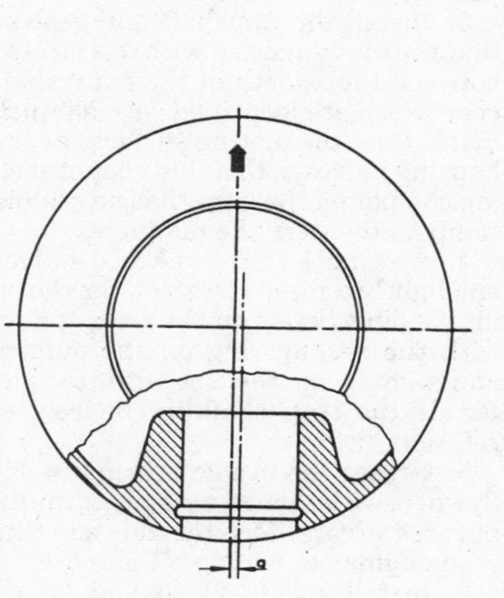


911 piston positioning

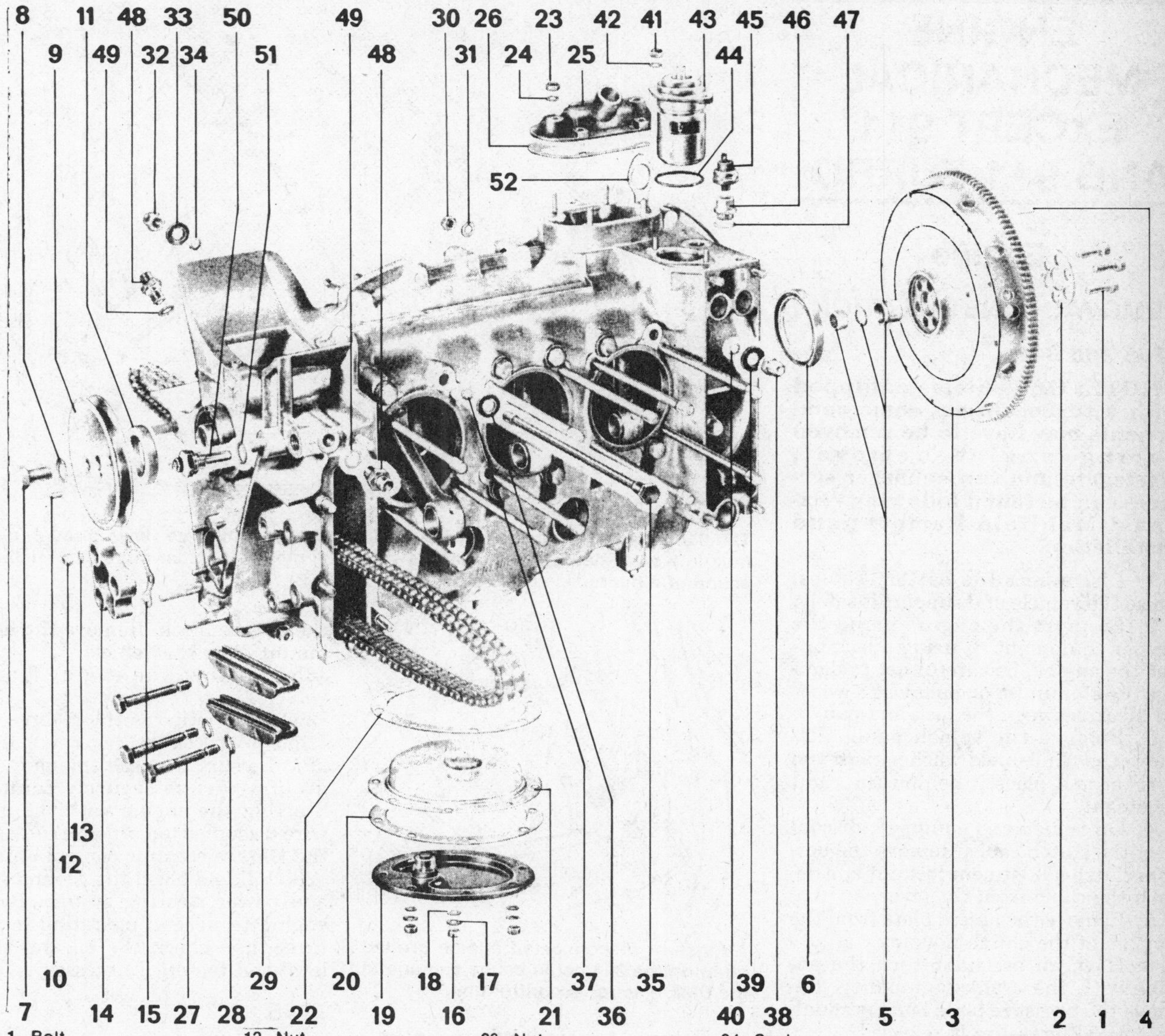


1. Bolt
2. Washer
3. Flywheel
4. Pin
5. Bushing
6. Seal
7. Bolt
8. Spring washer
9. Pulley
10. Pin
11. Seal
12. Nut
13. Washer
14. Cover
15. Seal
16. Nut
17. Spring washer
18. Washer
19. Cover
20. Seal
21. Oil strainer
22. Seal
23. Nut
24. Washer
25. Breather cover
26. Seal
27. Slide rail bolt
28. Seal
29. Slide rail
30. Nut
31. Washer
32. Nut
33. Washer
34. Seal
35. Crankcase bolt
36. Washer
37. Seal
38. Nut
39. Washer
40. Seal
41. Nut
42. Spring washer
43. Thermostat
44. Seal
45. Oil pressure switch
46. Nut
47. Washer
48. Plug
49. Washer
50. Oil temperature switch
51. Washer
52. Hook

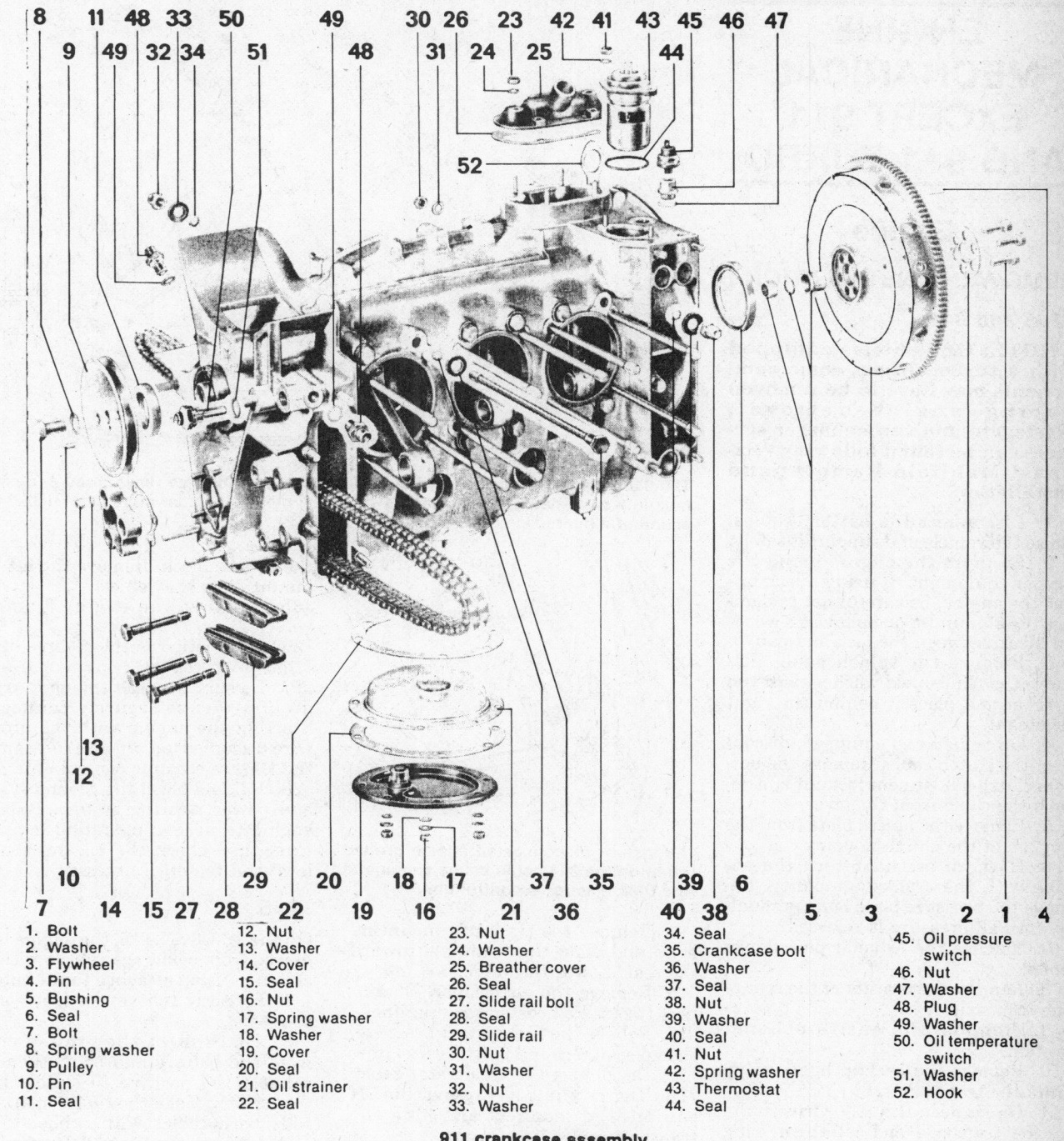

**911 crankcase assembly**

the oil vent.

24. Replace the intake distributor with the intake pipes and injection valves.

25. Mount the rear engine cover plate, then replace the exhaust muffler and heat exchanger.

26. Mate the engine to the transaxle. Install the assembly in the vehicle.

27. Fill the engine with oil.

# ENGINE MECHANICAL EXCEPT 911 AND 911 TURBO

## Engine

### REMOVAL & INSTALLATION

#### *924S and 944*

**NOTE: On vehicles equipped with a turbocahrger, some components may have to be removed during engine removal. Wastegate and turbocharger services can be found following "Exhaust Manifold Removal and Installation."**

1. Disconnect the battery cables. Raise the vehicle and support it safely.
2. Support the engine using the proper equipment. If using a jack under the engine, be careful not to damage the aluminum oil pan. Use a wooden block between the jack and pan.
3. Remove the splash panel. Remove the windshield washer tank and bracket and place it behind the right headlight.
4. On vehicles so equipped, disconnect the clutch cable. Remove the bottom clutch adjustment locknut and detach the cable from the lever.
5. Remove the access plate from the bottom of the clutch housing.
6. Have an assistant turn the engine with the crankshaft pulley. Remove the pressure plate bolts gradually until all pressure is released.
7. Remove the exhaust pipe flange bolts.
8. Remove the bracket at the rear of the transaxle.
9. Remove the entire exhaust system.
10. Remove the backup light switch from the transaxle.
11. Disconnect the axle driveshafts at the transaxle and let them hang down out of the way.

**NOTE: If the vehicle is going to be moved around with the engine out of the vehicle, wire the driveshafts up so that they don't become damaged.**

12. Remove the clutch housing-to-engine bolts. If equipped with a clutch slave cylinder, remove it from its mounting and position it to the side.
13. Place a wooden block under the front tunnel reinforcement to support the transaxle tube.

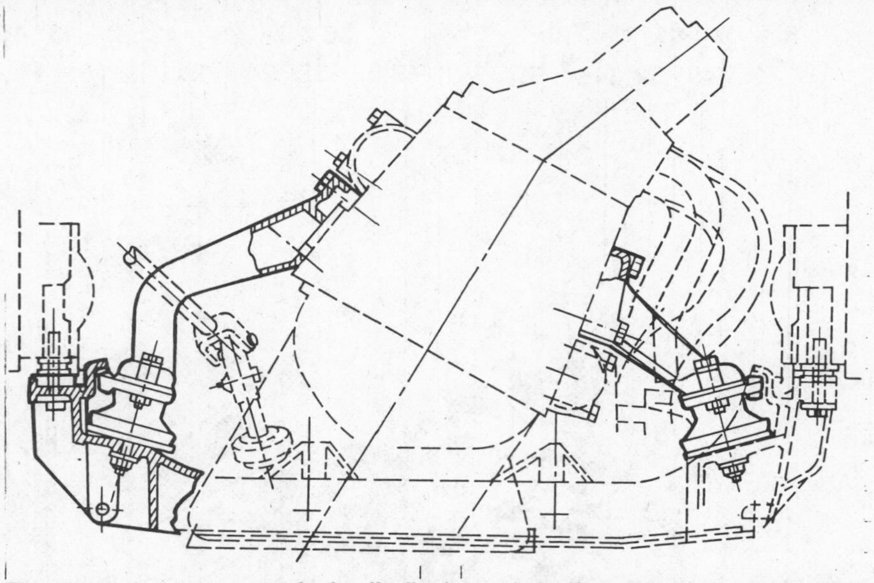

The 944 engine mounts are hydraulically damped. Antifreeze flows through a small hole in a plate between 2 chambers when the mount is under stress, not unlike the action of a hydraulic shock absorber.

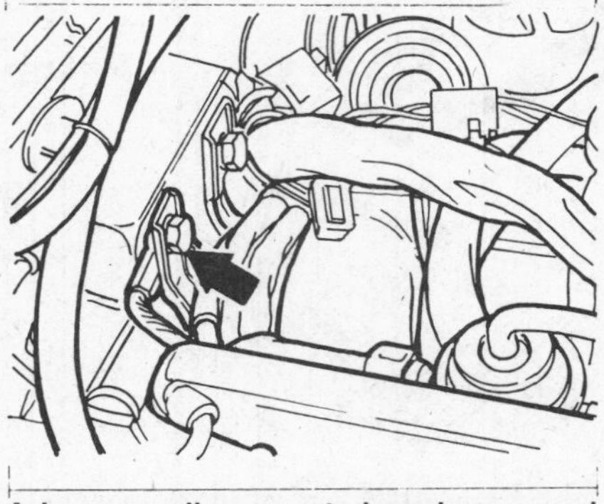

A loose or disconnected engine ground strap on the 944 could cause damage to the DME electronic control unit.

14. Remove the transaxle mounting bolts and slide the transaxle toward the rear. Lower the vehicle.
15. Remove the air cleaner. Disconnect the brake booster vacuum line.
16. Relieve the fuel system pressure, then disconnect and plug the fuel line.
17. Disconnect the accelerator cable.
18. Drain the cooling system. If equipped, disconnect and plug the transaxle cooler lines.
19. Disconnect the radiator hoses. Remove the electric cooling fan.
20. Remove the hood. Detach the air conditioning compressor and place it out of the way. Do not disconnect the refrigerant lines.
21. Remove the radiator and expansion tank. Disconnect the heater hoses from the engine.
22. Disconnect the starter wiring.
23. Attach the engine lift chains to the engine. Disconnect the steering at the rack universal joint.
24. Disconnect the 2 side mounts on the engine block. Remove the lift side mount from the vehicle.
25. Remove the engine from the vehicle.
26. Installation is the reverse of the removal procedure.
27. Be sure that the engine-to-frame ground wire is securely connected. Starting the engine with the ground wire disconnected or loose can damage the DME electronic control unit.
28. Fill and bleed the cooling system and power steering system. Run the engine to normal operating temperature, then check the oil and coolant level and top off if necessary.

#### *944S*

On the 16 valve 944S, the engine is removed from below the vehicle with the clutch housing attached to the engine.

1. Properly relieve the fuel system pressure.
2. Disconnect the ground cable from the battery and body, then disconnect the positive (+) cable from the battery. Take the cables apart and slide both cables with rubber grommets through the firewall. Remove the cable retainers.
3. Raise the vehicle and support it safely. Remove the front wheels.
4. Remove the cover plate in the footwell on the right (passenger) side. Unscrew the carrier for the DME control unit and disconnect the control unit plugs.
5. Loosen the fuel return hose clamp and pull off the hose. Disconnect the fuel feed hose using a backup wrench to hold the fitting while loosening the connection.

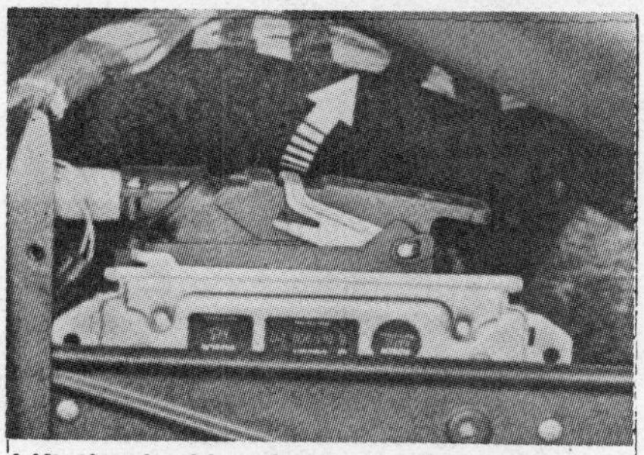

Lift the locking lever to disconnect the DME connector from the computer in the footwell of the passenger side

Disconnect the fuel feed and return lines, cruise control cable and plug connector – 1987–90 944S

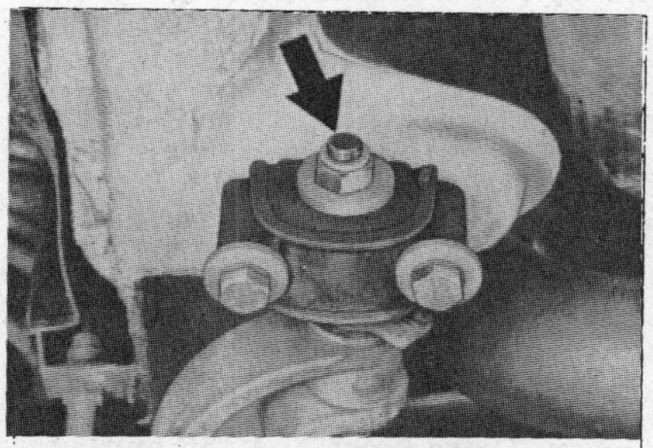

Loosen the through bolt when removing the control arms on 1987–90 944S. Do not remove the bushing bracket bolts

6. Disconnect the cable on the cruise control servo motor and disconnect the electrical connectors at the fuel injectors.

7. Loosen the ventilation hose for the toothed belt cover on the air filter lower section at the rear. Loosen and remove the complete filter system. Remove the air flow sensor.

8. Loosen the distributor cap and rotor and remove them. Mark the position of the rotor for installation reference.

9. Remove the oil filter and automatic transaxle fluid supply tank.

10. Remove the throttle operating cable with deflection roller and bracket assembly. Disconnect the oxygen sensor plug connector, then loosen and remove the hose clamps on the intake distributor and brake booster.

11. Loosen the cable retainers from the bulkhead, then disconnect the electrical connectors after tagging them for installation. Remove the vacuum hose from the tank ventilation valve.

12. Remove the engine splash guard.

13. Drain the cooling system and disconnect the venting hose for the alternator.

14. Disconnect and remove the coolant hose on the radiator at the bottom right.

15. Disconnect the electrical connections to the fan motors. Disconnect the fan motor brackets from the radiator and remove from below.

16. Disconnect and remove the coolant and vent hose on the radiator at the top left. Disconnect the harness connector at the temperature switch on the radiator. Disconnect and remove the coolant hose from the expansion tank.

17. Loosen the radiator mounting and remove the radiator from below.

18. Suspend the engine by its front transporting bracket using special tool 10-222-A, or equivalent, to hold the engine in its installed position. Make sure the suspension tool is correctly seated and supporting the engine securely.

19. Loosen the A/C compressor drive belt tensioner and remove the belt. Disconnect the compressor mounting bolts and wire it out of the way with the refrigerant lines connected. Do not let the compressor hang by the refrigerant lines.

20. Disconnect and remove the stabilizer with holders on the body and control arms. Disconnect the right and left tie rods.

21. Disconnect the hose between the transaxle cooler and steering.

22. Disconnect the power steering pump, remove the spacer sleeve from the front and wire the pump to the steering gear. Do not let the pump hang by the power steering lines.

23. Disconnect the left and right control arms on the front axle crossmember and rear mount, then remove from the front.

24. Disconnect the universal joint on the steering gear and upper hydraulic engine mounts on the engine supports. Remove the front axle crossmember with steering gear and power steering pump from below.

25. Tag and disconnect the starter wire connectors and remove the starter.

26. Remove the clutch slave cylinder from the clutch housing with the line connected. Loosen and remove the holder for the fluid line on the clutch housisng upper section.

27. Loosen the exhaust assembly at the flange of the exhaust manifold and at the exhaust test line. Disconnect the oxygen sensor.

28. Disconnect the flange behind the catalytic converter and suspension and remove the assembly.

29. Remove the upper transaxle/clutch housing mounting bolts.

30. Disconnect the coolant hoses for the heater above the exhaust manifold and on the cylinder head.

31. Attach a lifting device to the engine and tighten it to support the full weight. This is where it gets a little tricky, because the engine is removed from below. That means you have to use some sort of hoist that is tall enough to allow the body to be raised, and will allow the engine to be lowered onto a dolly. A chain hoist positioned directly over the engine compartment works best. Although not mentioned in the manufacturers service manual, it seems likely that this operation is more easily performed with the hood removed. Mark the hinge locations for assembly reference.

**CAUTION**

***Make sure the engine is securely supported by the lifting device before proceeding. Serious injury and damage could result.***

32. Remove the lower transaxle/clutch housing mounting bolts.

33. Pull the engine forward and press the rubber sleeve out of the firewall and into the engine compartment. Remove the wire harness carefully from the front passenger footwell.

**NOTE: Remember that the connector end of the wire harness plugs into a computer which is very sensitive to damage or contamination on the connections. Keep the plug clean and handle it carefully during service.**

34. Disconnect the engine from the central tube or shaft and carefully lower the engine onto a dolly. Lower slowly while watching for snags or obstructions and make sure it is securely supported on the dolly before disconnecting the hoist. Roll the engine from beneath the vehicle and continue service as required.

35. Installation is the reverse of removal. When installing the engine, note the following:

a. Guide the DME wire harness connector through the firewall carefully and connect it securely. Make sure the connectors are free from grease, dirt or damage before installing the connector onto the computer in the front passenger footwell.

b. Install, but don't tighten the transaxle/clutch housing bolts. Tighten the mounting bolts to final torque only after the installation of the hydraulic engine mounts on the front axle crossmember. Torque the mounting bolts to 31 ft. lbs. (42 Nm).

c. When installing control arms, pressing down slightly on the sleeves in the rubber/metal mounts makes installation easier.

d. A steel washer 4mm thick is laid at each of the bolted connections between the right (passenger) side engine support and the hydraulic mount. Make sure they are installed properly.

e. Make sure the radiator fits correctly into its rubber mounts.

36. Torque all bolts to specifications as follows:

a. Stabilizer to aluminum control arm – 18 ft. lbs. (25 Nm)

b. Tie rod to steering knuckle – 15–22 ft. lbs. (20–30 Nm)

c. Steering universal joint – 22 ft. lbs. (30 Nm)

d. Control arm to crossmember – 48 ft. lbs. (65 Nm)

e. Crossmember to body – 63 ft. lbs. (85 Nm)

37. Fill and bleed the cooling system and power steering system. Run the engine to normal operating temperature, then check the oil and coolant level and top off if necessary.

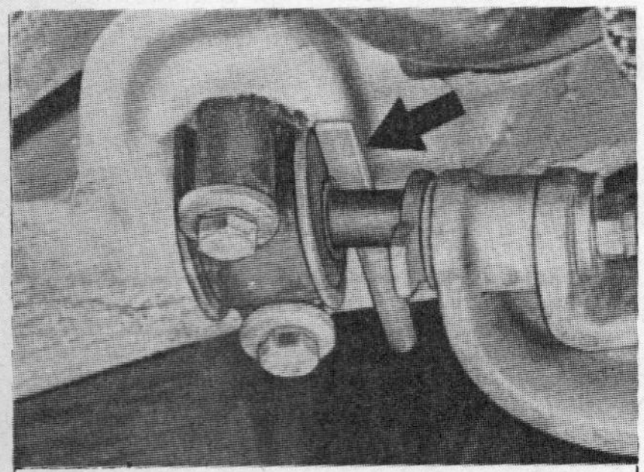

**Use a small prybar (arrow) to press down slightly on the sleeves in the control arm bushing mounts to make installation easier**

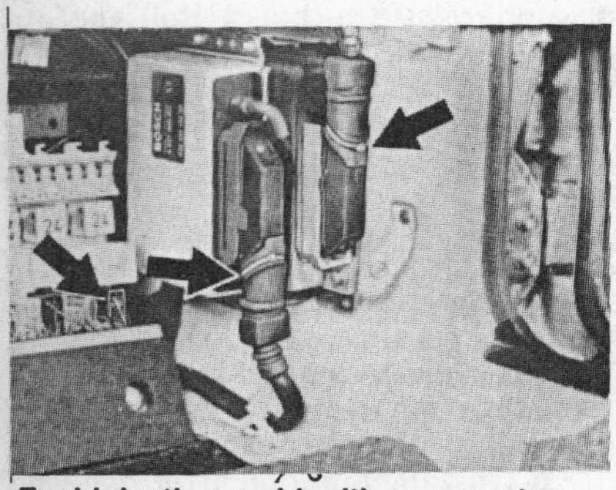

**Fuel injection and ignition computers – 1987–90 928S**

### *928, 928S and 928S4*

1. Disconnect the battery ground cable. 1985–90 vehicles are equipped with an engine control computer located on the right (passenger side) kick panel. When removing the engine, carefully disconnect the main harness connector from the computer and feed the wire through the firewall and into the engine compartment. Use care when handling the connector end of the harness to protect it from contamination or damage during service.

2. Properly relieve the fuel system pressure. Remove the engine compartment cross brace.

**NOTE: The vehicle must be on its wheels when the cross brace is removed or replaced.**

3. Disconnect wiring and hoses to the under side of the hood, loosen hood bolts and supports, and remove the hood.

4. Remove the air intake hoses and the air cleaner assembly.

5. Raise and support the vehicle.

6. Remove the bottom splash pan and drain the coolant from the radiator.

7. Drain the engine block of coolant by removing the drain plugs on the right and left sides of the crankcase.

8. Drain the engine oil.

9. Remove the lower body brace.

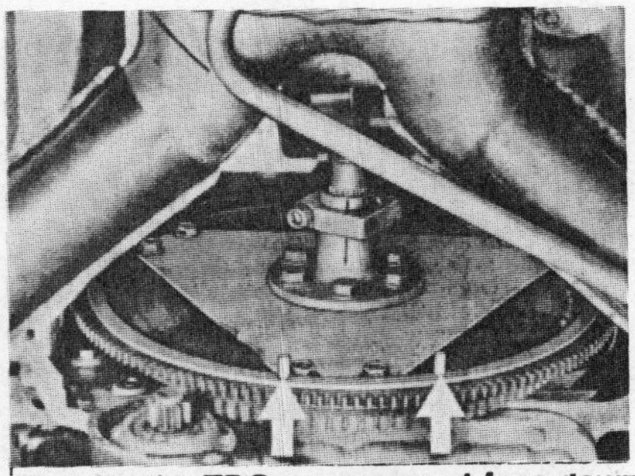

**Pins for the TDC sensor must face down as shown when removing the engine on 928 models**

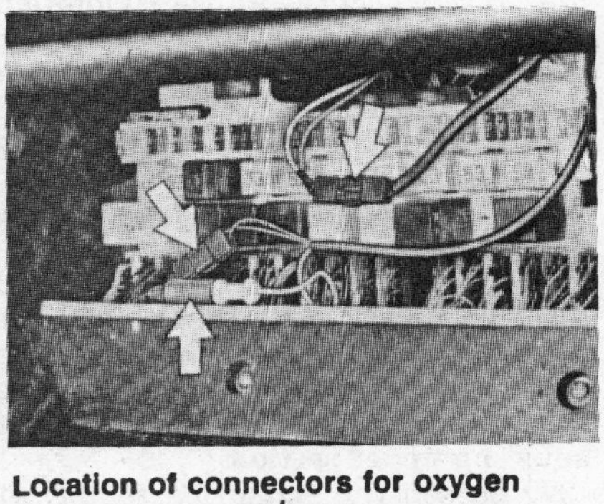

**Location of connectors for oxygen sensor, sensor heating and ignition control unit – 1987–90 928S**

10. Disconnect the exhaust pipe flanges at the exhaust manifolds and the right and left side heat shields. Disconnect the secondary air injection lines.

11. Disconnect the body ground cable from the engine.

12. Remove the clutch slave cylinder at the clutch housing. Do not disconnect the hydraulic line.

13. Tag and disconnect the starter wires, then remove the starter along with the clutch housing cover. Remove the starter wires from the clamps on the steering crossmember.

14. Disconnect the clutch release lever at the ball pin by depressing the release lever in the direction of the clutch.

15. On automatic transaxle equipped vehicles, remove both transaxle mount bolts. Remove the vacuum hose for the automatic transaxle at the cylinder head, along with its clamp.

16. Remove the bolts from the clamping sleeve on the driveshaft and slide the sleeve rearward on the central shaft.

**NOTE: On the 928S, the TDC sensor pins on the flywheel must be at the bottom (facing toward the ground) to prevent damage during engine removal.**

17. Unscrew the throwout bearing sleeve mounting bolts and push the sleeve toward the clutch.

18. Disconnect the left and right engine shock absorber at the control arms and remove with the right and left upper shock mounts.

19. On vehicles with air conditioning:

a. Disconnect the temperature switch wires on the radiator.

b. Disconnect the power lead to the compressor.

c. Loosen the compressor, remove the compressor from the mounting brackets. Do not remove the hoses.

d. Suspend the compressor from the frame with a wire.

20. Remove the air pump filter housing and disconnect the alternator cooling hose.

21. Remove the lower fan shroud from the radiator, remove the cooling hoses and the oil cooler line from the radiator bottom.

22. By lifting the engine a side at a time, remove the engine mounts and carefully set the engine on the front crossmember.

23. On manual transaxle equipped vehicles, remove the clutch housing to engine bolts and lower the vehicle to the ground.

24. Remove the upper coolant hose and the vent from the radiator and

thermostat housing.

25. Remove the upper oil cooler line form the upper part of the radiator.

26. Loosen the top mounting of the radiator and remove the assembly carefully.

27. Remove the heater hoses and electrical connections from the engine. Tag all electrical connections for identification before removal.

28. On 1983–84 vehicles, remove the electronic control unit and loosen the ignition coil and set aside. On 1985–90 vehicles, pull off the ignition leads on the left and right sides of the distributor cap. Disconnect both ignition coils and lay them aside. Disconnect the ground wire in front of the right ignition coil on the body.

29. Relieve the fuel system pressure, then disconnect the fuel feed and return lines. Use a backup wrench on the fuel fittings to avoid twisting the line connections.

**CAUTION**

***Fuel pressure must be relieved before attempting to disconnect any fuel lines. Take precautions to avoid the risk of fire.***

30. On 1983–84 vehicles, disconnect the hydraulic lines at the power steering pump, then cap them to prevent contamination by dirt or grease. On 1985–90 vehicles, disconnect the oil hoses on the power steering supply tank, drain the oil, then remove the tank.

31. On 1983–84 vehicles, disconnect the vacuum line to the power brake cylinder at the manifold. On 1985–90 vehicles, disconnect the vacuum hoses to the EZF control unit and brake booster. Remove the hose from the fuel vapor canister to the charging valve.

32. Disconnect the throttle, cruise control and automatic transaxle cables by either removing the holder and clamp, or at the ball connectors on the linkage bracket. Tag each cable ball to identify its position for assembly.

**NOTE: On air conditioned vehicles, cover the condenser with a wood board to prevent damage during engine removal.**

33. On 1985–90 vehicles, remove the central fuse/relay cover and disconnect the plugs for the oxygen sensor, sensor heating and ignition control unit. Disconnect the multipin connectors from the fuel injection and ignition computers at the right kick panel in the passenger compartment. Push the grommet and wire harness through into the engine compartment and carefully remove the connectors.

**NOTE: Remember that each multipin connector end of the wire harness plugs into a computer which is very sensitive to damage or contamination on the connections. Keep the plugs clean and handle them carefully during service.**

34. Attach a lifting cable to the lifting device and to the engine. Raise the assembly slightly and remove the engine block-to-clutch housing upper mounting bolts. Disconnect the left and right engine mount bolts at the bottom.

35. Pull the engine forward and remove the short driveshaft with the guide tube.

36. Lift the engine carefully while tilting forward and slowly remove it from the engine compartment. As soon as clearance permits, disconnect and remove the pressure hose from the power steering pump after marking its installed position for installation reference. Remove the engine slowly and watch for snagged wires, linkage, etc. during removal.

37. Installation is the reverse of removal. Refill all fluids, then start the engine and allow it to reach normal operating temperature while checking for leaks.

## Cylinder Head

### REMOVAL & INSTALLATION

#### *928, 928S and 928S4*

**NOTE: The cylinder heads can be removed with the engine in the vehicle. 1985–90 928S and 928S4 engines are equipped with dual distributors driven off the exhaust camshafts. The cylinder head and camshaft case are a component and the cylinder heads are identical for right and left sides, but the head gaskets are not. The following is a general procedure for both early and late engines.**

1. Disconnect the negative battery

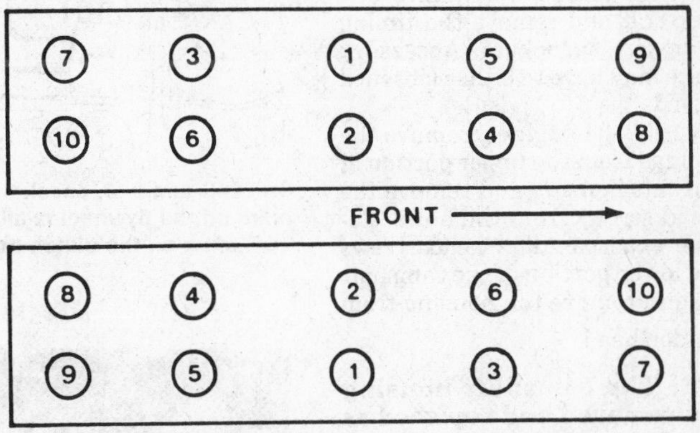


Cylinder head torque sequence – 1983–86 928

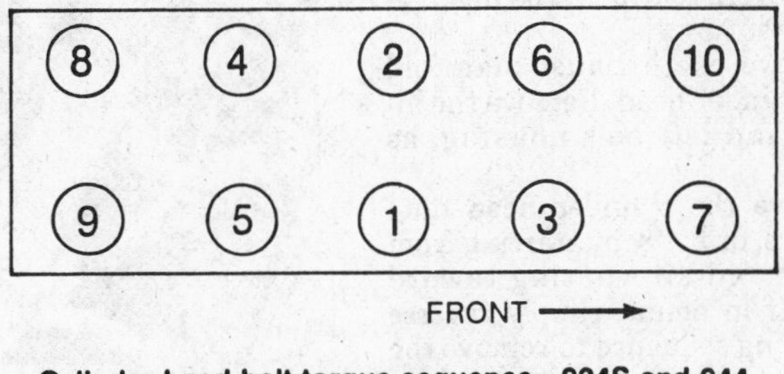


Cylinder head bolt torque sequence – 924S and 944

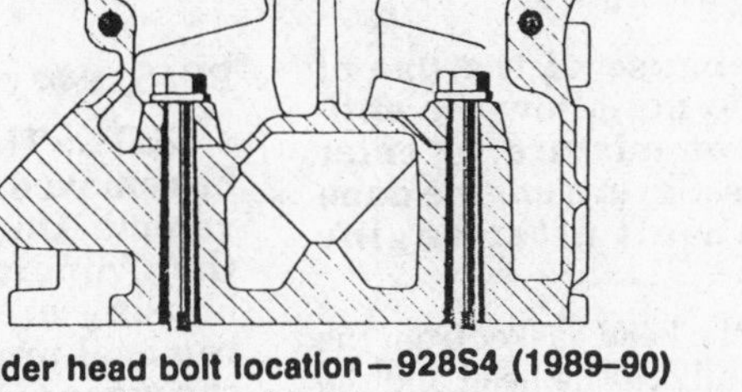

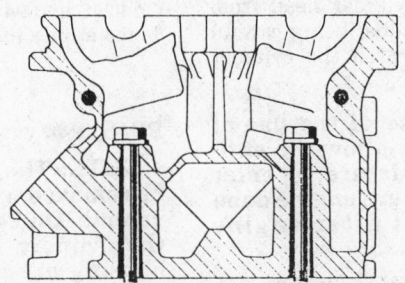

Cylinder head bolt location – 928S4 (1989–90)

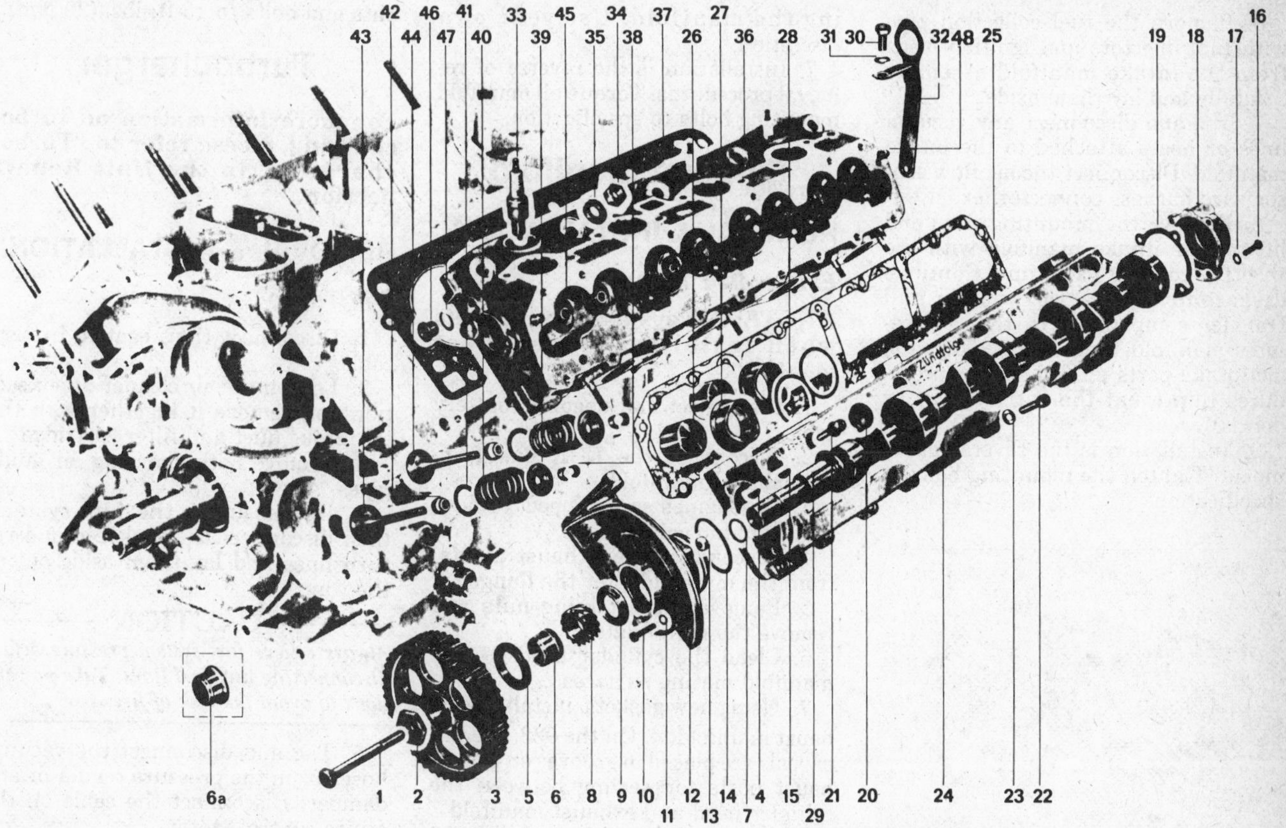


1. Bolt
2. Washer
3. Camshaft sprocket
4. Woodruff key
5. Camshaft oil seal
6. Spacer
6a. Spacer
7. O-ring
8. Distributor drive gear
9. Spacer
10. Bolt
11. Washer
12. Bearing carrier
13. Seal
14. O-ring
15. Woodruff key
16. Bolt
17. Washer
18. End cover
19. Gasket
20. Plug
21. Bolt with washers
22. Bolt
23. Washer
24. Camshaft housing
25. Gasket
26. Hydraulic valve liner
27. Lifter sleeve
28. Gasket
29. Left camshaft
30. Bolt
31. Washer
32. Lifting eye
33. Spark plug
34. Nut
35. Washer
36. Cylinder head
37. Left gasket
38. Valve keeper
39. Spring retainer
40. Valve spring
41. Shim
42. Valve stem sea
43. Intake valve
44. Exhaust valve
45. Valve guide
46. Plug
47. Seal
48. Dowel pin

**Cylinder head and related components—928S**

Turbo has a partially recessed silicone bead on both sides and the word **TURBO** stamped in the top surface for identification.

20. Installation is the reverse of the removal procedure. After installing the head, tighten the mounting bolts in sequence to the correct torque specifications. Torque the camshaft housing mounting bolts to 14 ft. lbs. (19 Nm) and the aluminum plugs to 29 ft. lbs. (39 Nm). Install and adjust the camshaft drive (timing) belt. Adjust the power steering pump, alternator and air conditioning compressor drive belt tension.

### OVERHAUL

**For all cylinder head overhaul procedures, please refer to "Engine Rebuilding" in the Unit Repair section.**

## Intake Manifold

### REMOVAL & INSTALLATION

#### *924S and 944*

The intake manifold consists of a cast aluminum assembly with equal length air intake tubes that bolt directly to the cylinder head. The throttle valve assembly bolts to a single flange.

1. Disconnect the negative battery cable.
2. Remove the air cleaner assembly, air intake ducts and filter. On the 944 turbo, remove both charging air guide pipes.
3. Depressurize the fuel system, then disconnect the fuel feed and return lines. Disconnect the vacuum hoses on the pressure regulator and damper.
4. Disconnect the cable to the cruise

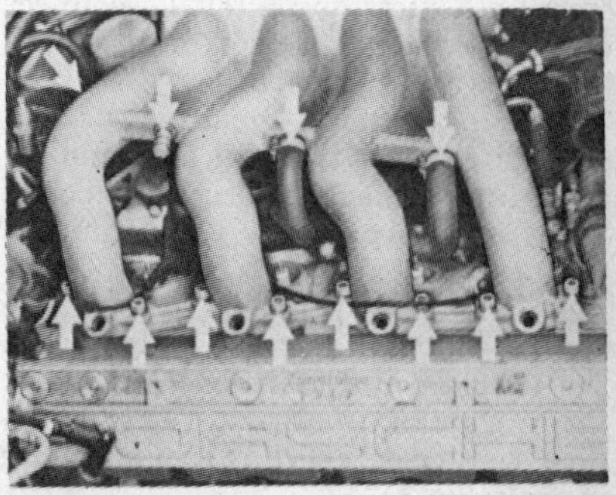

**Typical intake manifold mounting on 924S and 944 models (944 Turbo shown)**

control motor, if equipped, along with the throttle and transaxle linkage.

5. Disconnect the spark plug wires and remove the distributor cap. Disconnect the fuel collection pipe with the fuel injectors and ignition leads on the intake manifold and camshaft housing.

6. Remove the fuel collection pipe with fuel injectors and ignition leads from the intake manifold assembly carefully and lay them aside.
7. Tag and disconnect any vacuum lines or hoses attached to the intake manifold. Disconnect the air flow sensor wire harness connector.
8. Remove the mounting nuts and lift off the intake manifold with the throttle housing as a unit. Continue disassembly on a workbench and transfer components to the replacement manifold, if necessary. Cover the air intake ports during service procedures to prevent the entry of dirt or debris.
9. Installation is the reverse of removal. Tighten the mounting bolts to specification.

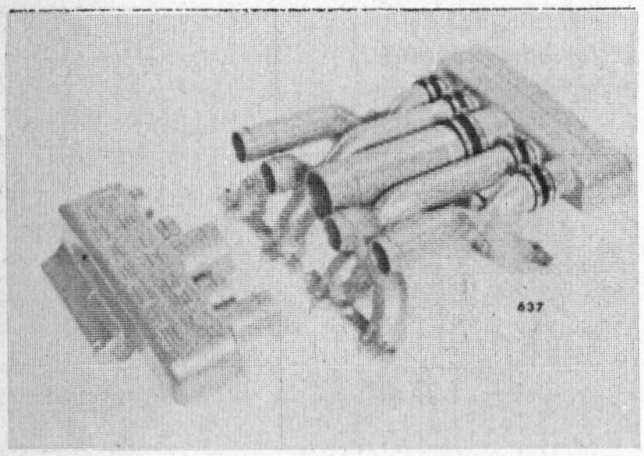

Typical intake manifold assembly on 928 models

### *928, 928S and 928S4*

The intake manifold assembly consists of a series of equal length pipes, attached by hose clamps and short rubber sleeves to the air cleaner plenum and bolted to the cylinder head.
1. Disconnect the negative battery cable.
2. Remove the air cleaner assembly, air intake ducts and filter. Disconnect the mass air flow sensor, if necessary to gain working clearance.
3. Depressurize the fuel system, then disconnect the fuel feed and return lines. Disconnect the vacuum hoses on the pressure regulator and damper.
4. Disconnect the cable to the cruise control motor, if equipped, along with the throttle and transaxle linkage at the bracket, if necessary. Tag the linkage for identification during installation.
5. Tag and disconnect all vacuum lines and wire connectors as necessary to allow removal of the manifold assembly.
6. Remove the mounting bolts from the intake manifold tubes at the cylinder head and remove the manifold with the fuel injectors attached. It may be easier of the early engines to remove the injectors before disconnecting the manifold. Use your own discretion.
7. Installation is the reverse of removal procedures. Torque all manifold mounting bolts to specification.

## Exhaust Manifold

### REMOVAL & INSTALLATION

#### *Except 944 Turbo*

**NOTE: Always use new gaskets when installing the exhaust manifold.**

1. Disconnect the negative battery cable.
2. Disconnect the EGR line from the exhaust manifold.
3. On engines so equipped, remove the air pump connections.
4. Disconnect the exhaust pipe(s) from the manifold(s) at the flange.
5. Remove the retaining nuts and remove the manifold(s).
6. Clean the cylinder heads(s) and manifold mating surfaces.
7. Using new gaskets, install the exhaust manifold(s). On the 928, the filler seals are placed in grooves on the exhaust ports for sealing between the cylinder head and exhaust manifold.
8. Tighten the nuts to 15 ft. lbs. (20 Nm). Work from the inside out.
9. Install the remaining components in the reverse order of remove. Use a new manifold flange gasket, as required.

#### *944 Turbo*

1. Disconnect the negative battery cable.
2. Depressurize the fuel system, then disconnect the fuel hoses from the pressure regulator and the pressure chamber. Tie the fuel hoses back out of the way.
3. Release the pressure from the coolant tank by loosening the radiator cap. Loosen and remove the coolant hoses on the connecting pipe near the water pump. Cap all hoses with a suitable plug to prevent coolant loss during service.
4. Remove the coolant connecting pipe bolts and position the pipe over the cam housing.
5. To remove the exhaust manifolds, it is necessary to remove some of the mounting studs. Both manifolds must be removed together. Remove both exhaust manifold studs from cylinders 1 and 3, and the front stud from cylinders 2 and 4.
6. Working from above, remove the 2–3 manifold first, then remove the 1–4 manifold.
7. Installation is the reverse of removal procedure. Torque all manifold nuts and bolts to 15 ft. lbs. (20 Nm).

## Turbocharger

**For more information on turbocharging, please refer to "Turbocharging" in the Unit Repair Section.**

### REMOVAL & INSTALLATION

#### *944 Turbo*

1. Disconnect the negative battery cable.
2. Loosen the air cleaner upper section and remove it together with the air intake duct and filter cartridge.
3. Remove both charging air guide pipes.
4. Depressurize the fuel system, then disconnect the fuel feed and return lines and lay them aside out of the way.

**CAUTION**

***Always relieve fuel system pressure before disconnecting any fuel lines. Take precautions to avoid the risk of fire.***

5. Tag and disconnect the vacuum hoses from the pressure regulator and damper. Disconnect the cable on the cruise control motor.
6. Disconnect the spark plug cables and remove the distributor cap.
7. Disconnect the fuel collection pipe with the fuel injectors and ignition leads on the intake manifold and camshaft housing.
8. Remove the fuel collection pipe with the fuel injectors attached from the intake manifold carefully and place the assembly aside. Do not allow grease or dirt to contaminate the ends of the injectors during service.
9. Disconnect the throttle cable, then tag and disconnect any remaining vacuum hoses on the intake manifold. Remove the intake manifold assembly with the throttle housing and cover the intake ports on the cylinder head to prevent the entry of dirt or debris during service.
10. Disconnect and remove the guide tube with the oil dipstick and the deflection plate for the master cylinder.
11. Remove the engine splash guard. Drain the cooling system, then loosen and pull off the air hose alternator venting.
12. Disconnect the flange between the turbocharger and the exhaust assembly.
13. Disconnect the exhaust flange on the turbine housing. Disconnect the coolant lines and oil pressure line on the turbocharger.
14. Loosen and remove the intake air cowl between the air flow sensor and turbocharger compressor housing.

Disconnect the pressure hose to the charging air cooler (intercooler) and remove the turbocharger assembly from the vehicle.

15. Installation is the reverse of removal. Note the following:

a. Always use new seals.

b. Make sure the seal fits correctly on the left engine port.

c. Insert the seals for the exhaust flanges after coating them with grease to prevent their falling out when installing the turbocharger assembly.

d. Replace the locknuts for the exhaust flanges and tighten the M8 bolt of the exhaust flange only after installation of all bolts for the exhaust flanges and turbocharger.

## Timing Belt Cover

### REMOVAL & INSTALLATION

#### *928, 928S and 928S4*

The timing cover consists of an outer right upper, and outer left upper and an outer bottom cover. Left and right inner belt guide covers are also used. The outer upper covers can be removed without the removal of the drive belts on 1983–84 engines. On 1985–90 engines with dual distributors, the distributor caps and rotors must be removed to remove the upper front covers. The alternator, power steering and air conditioner compressor belts must be removed if the entire timing belt cover is being removed. Disconnect the intake air ducts and air flow sensor, if necessary to gain working clearance.

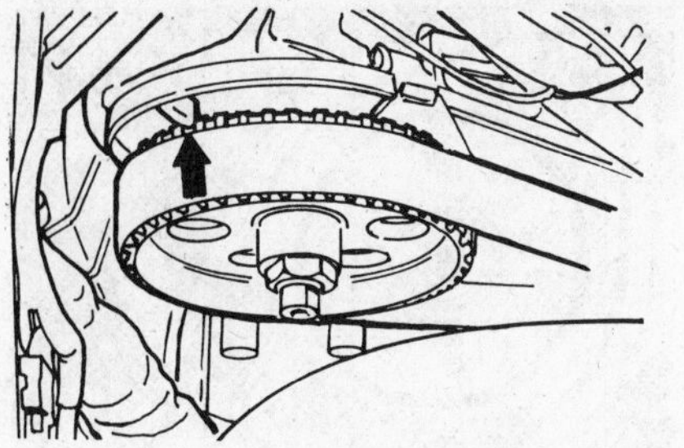

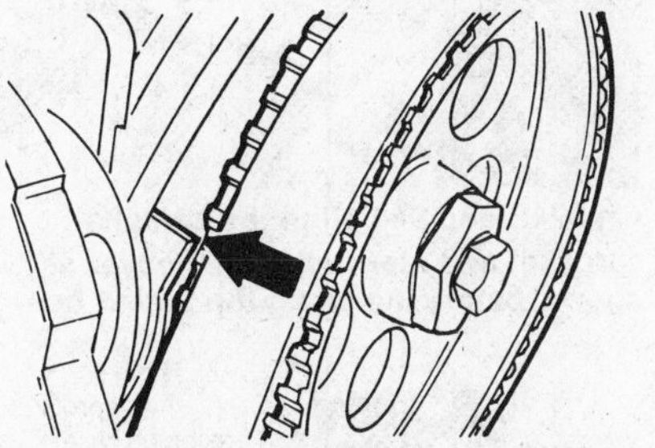

When the 928, 928S engine is at TDC on No. 1 cylinder, the camshaft sprocket marks (arrow) will align with the marks on the housing.

#### *924S and 944*

**NOTE: On the 944 Turbo, the intercooler assembly and air charge pipes will have to be removed to gain working clearance when removing the timing belt cover.**

1. Disconnect the negative battery cable.

2. Loosen the alternator and compressor drive belt tensioner and remove the belt. Remove the power steering drive belt, if equipped.

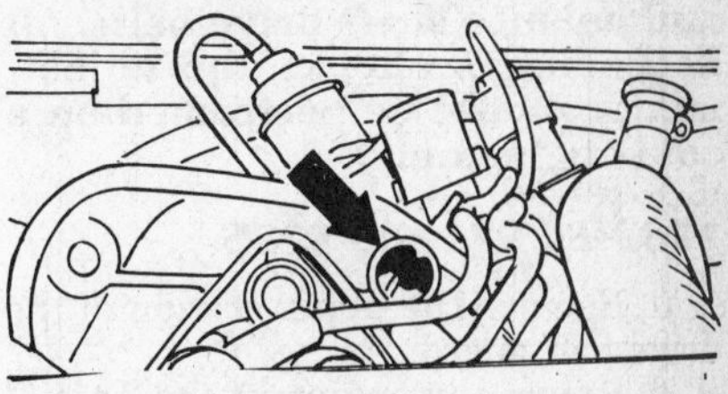

On 924S and 944 the TDC mark on the camshaft sprocket will align with the cast mark as shown

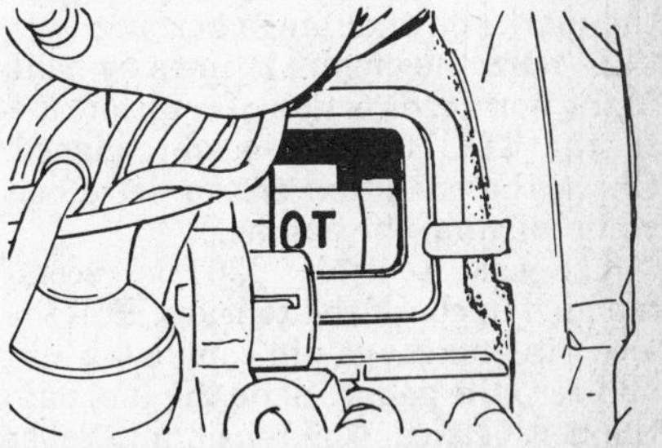


On 924S and 944 check that the scribe mark on the flywheel is aligned with the TDC mark on the clutch housing

3. Remove the distributor cap and rotor.

4. Remove the cover retaining bolts and lift off the timing belt cover.

5. Installation is the reverse of the removal procedure.

## Timing Belts

### CHECKING TENSION

**NOTE: A special tension gauge tool (No. 9201) is recommended to check the tension of the camshaft**

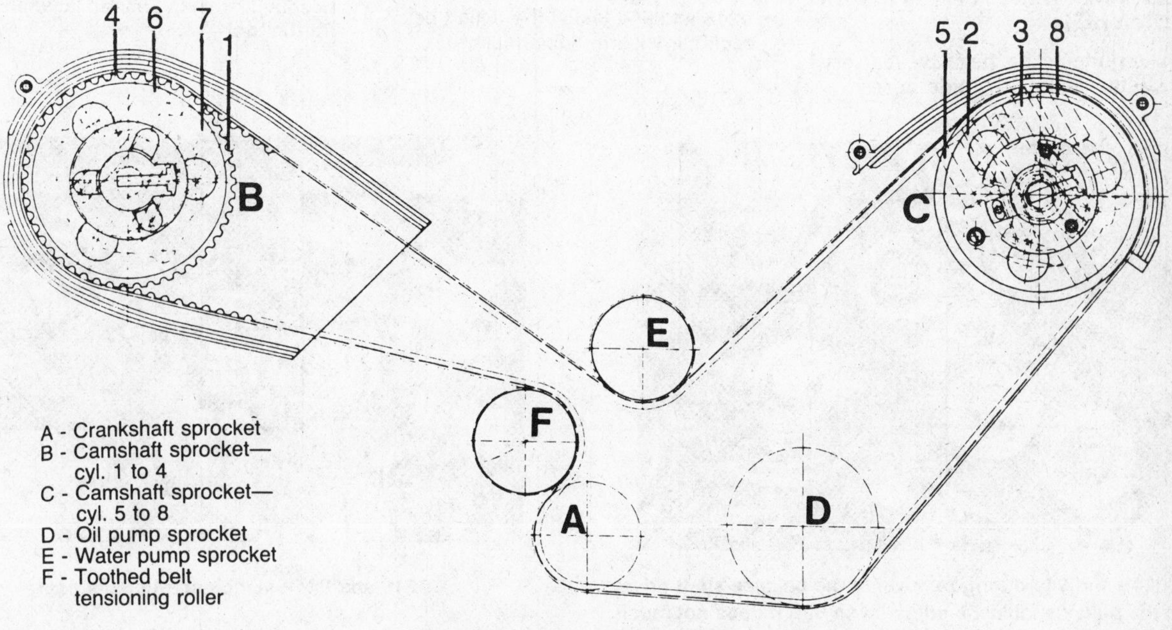


Camshaft drive belt routing on 928 models

**and balance shaft drive belts. All belt tension checks and adjustments should be performed on a cold engine only.**

### *1983–84 928 and 928S*

1. Remove the upper section of the drive belt guard.
2. Rotate the engine in the normal direction of rotation and set the engine to TDC on the compression stroke of No. 1 cylinder. The marks of the camshaft sprockets should be aligned with the marks on the flange bearing.
3. Turn the engine 2 times by hand in the normal direction of rotation, until the TDC mark is again aligned. Check the condition of the drive belt while turning the engine.
4. Special tool No. 9201 is recommended to check the tension. Pull the lock pin and gauge pin completely out and zero the gauge. Slide the tool onto the belt between the tensioning roller and the lower camshaft sprocket. The measuring pin must rest in the groove of the belt. Push the tester down slowly until the gauge needle engages the belt. Keep the tester horizontal and out of contact with the surrounding objects. Read the value on the gauge. Repeat the process to be sure of an accurate reading.
5. Properly apply tension the drive belt. The gauge should read 9.2 on the scale for a new belt or 7.6–9.0 for a used belt.

### *1985–90 928S and 928S4*

**NOTE: These vehicles incorporate a cambelt tension warning light in the instrument cluster. The warning light will illuminate when the belt tension is insufficient.**

1. Disconnect the negative battery cable. Remove the air guide hoses.

On 924S and 944 align the camshaft sprocket and rear timing belt cover as shown before installing the timing belt

On 924S and 944 to adjust the timing belt tensioner turn the large hex nut as required to loosen or tighten the belt

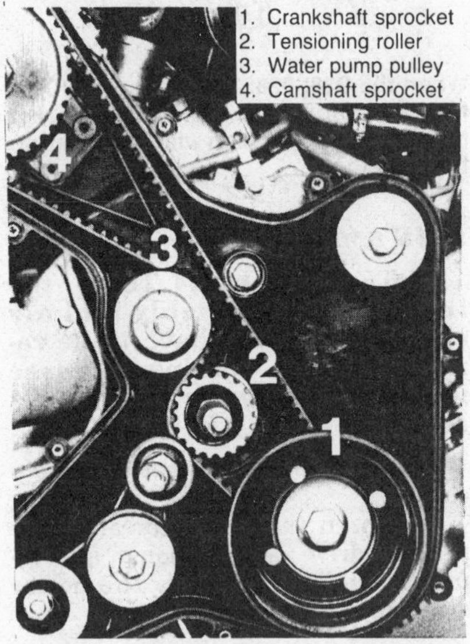


On 924S and 944 install the timing belt on each sprocket in numerical order

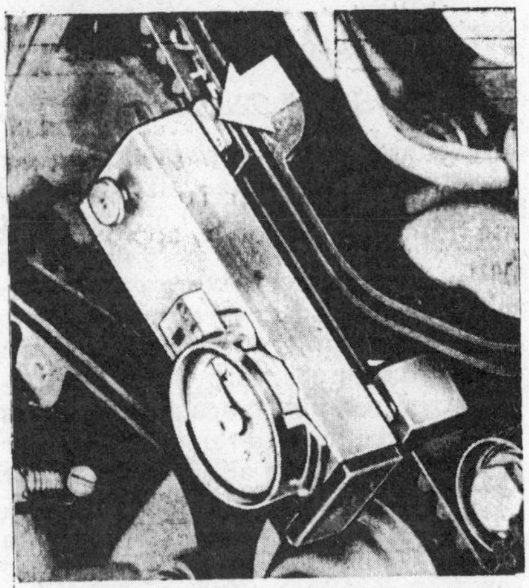

Special timing belt tension tool shown installed on the 944 timing belt. Note that the tool is installed in the same manner on the balance shaft drive belt. Measuring needle (arrow) is pushed in when setting up the tool

On 924S and 944 during removal of the balance shaft drive belt the pulley should be adjusted so that it does not touch the belt

924S and 944 balance shaft adjustment

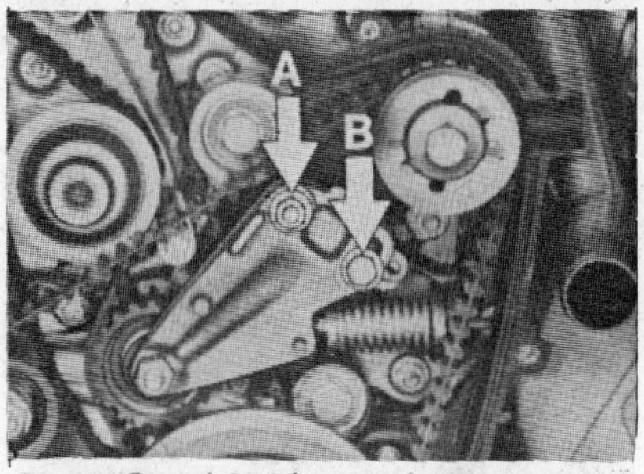


On 924S and 944 loosen bolts A and B to adjust the timing belt tension

Hydraulic chain tensioner used on 928, 928S4 and 944

2. Remove the air guide retaining screws and the air guide from the top of the radiator.

3. Remove the distributor caps and the toothed belt cover upper section on the right hand side. Unscrew and push the toothed belt cover on the left hand side forward.

4. Turn the engine in the normal direction of rotation until No. 1 cylinder is at TDC on the compression stroke. Never turn the engine counterclockwise. Marks on the camshaft and flange bearing must be aligned in this position.

5. Turn the engine 2 more turns until the TDC mark is reached again. Check the bolt, while turning the engine, for wear and damage.

6. Pull the lock pin on tool No. 9201 out and move the test pin opposite the lock pin to the starting position. Place the drag needle the gauge needle.

7. Slide the tool on a released section of the toothed belt. The sliding shoe of the tool on a smooth belt surface and the rolled fitted in a tooth gap.

8. Slowly press down on the tester housing until the gauge tip engages. Read the test gauge without tension, the tester must be kept horizontal to the toothed belt. The tester must not rest on the plastic cover. The sliding shoes must have their entire surface on the belt. The tool must not be turned or moved on the belt during the testing procedure.

9. The drag needle must always be placed on the gauge needle after the lock pin had engaged. Pull out the lock pin to have the gauge tip disengage.

10. Repeat tension test several times with the engine at TDC. The gauge should read 5.0 ± 0.3. Adjust the belt if necessary.

11. The belt adjusting screw is located on the bottom right side of the engine.

12. Loosen the locknut, tighten the screw to tighten the belt or loosen the screw to loosen the belt. Tighten the locknut.

13. Turn the engine 2 complete turns and recheck belt tension.

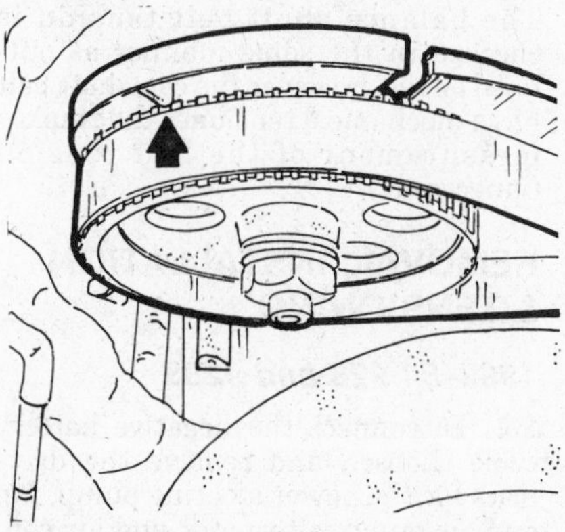

Right-hand camshaft alignment on 928 and 928S

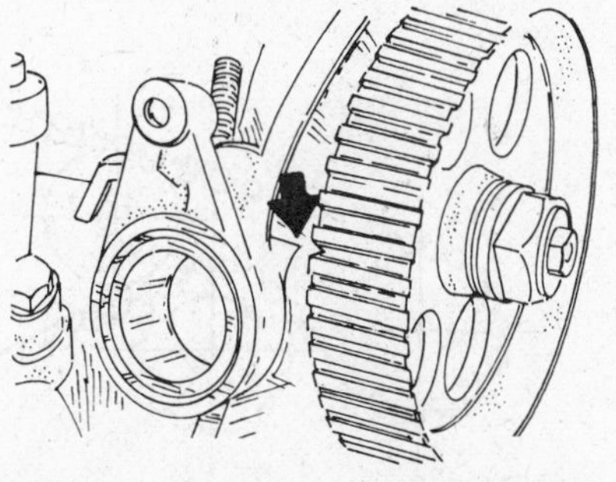

Left hand camshaft alignment of the 928

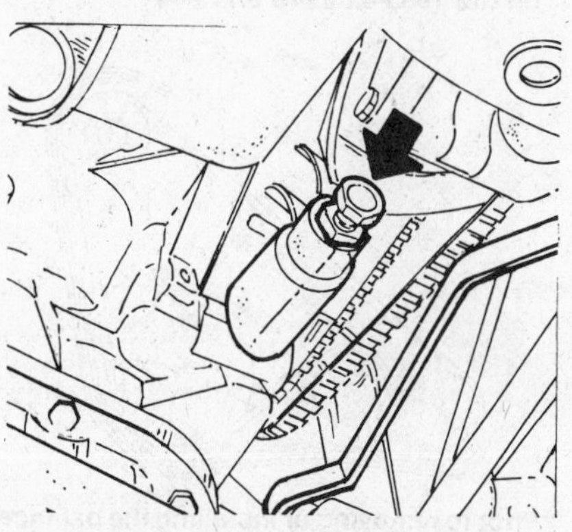

Timing belt tensioner on the 928 and 928S viewed from beneath the car.

### *944S*

1. Be sure that the engine is cold. Disconnect the negative battery cable.

2. Remove the complete air filter housing. Remove the air hose from the top of the cam belt housing.

3. Remove the cable holder from the top of the cam belt housing.

4. Remove the top camshaft drive belt housing retaining bolts. Remove the housing assembly.

5. Remove the high tension wire on the distributor cap, comming from the coil.

6. Remove the top metal drive belt cover together with the installed distributor cap and position it to the rear.

7. Position the engine at TDC on the compression stroke. Check the condition of the belt while slowly turning the crankshaft clockwise until the TDC mark on No. 1 cylinder on the camshaft drive sprocket is aligned with the mark on the rear toothed belt cover.

8. Raise and support the vehicle safely. Check the TDC marking on the flywheel bell housing. Lower the vehicle.

9. To adjust the camshaft belt, loosen the tensioner nut and the tensioner bolt. Press the belt twice with your thumb against the bell housing between the camshaft sprocket and the water pump pulley.

10. Torque the nut and bolt to 14 ft. lbs. (20Nm). Reinstall the removed components.

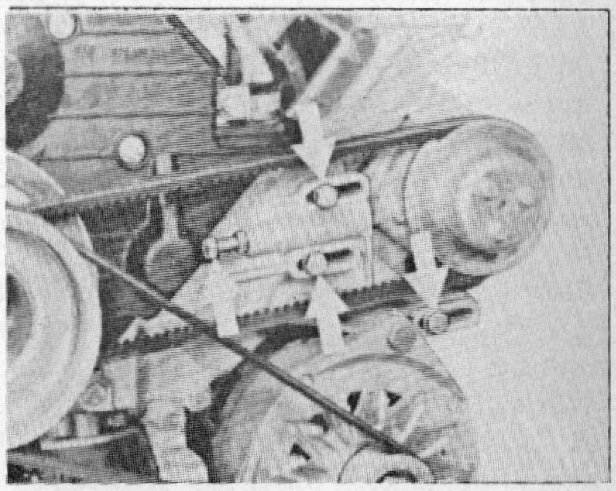

On 928S and 928S4 loosen the bolts (arrows) to remove the drive belts

On 928S and 928S4 mount the special tool as shown to hold the crankshaft in position

### 924S, 944 and 944 Turbo

#### BALANCE SHAFTS DRIVE BELT

1. Remove the splash guard under the engine.
2. Remove the alternator and the compresser belt.
3. Remove the upper and lower belt covers.
4. Release the tension from the belt. There are 2 methods to release the tension. On older engines equipped with guide rollers without a slot, turn the eccentric to release the tension from the belt. On newer engines equipped with a locking nut on the guide roller (with slot), loosen the locknut and slide the roller away from the belt.
5. Remove the plug from the distributor cap mount.
6. Turn the crankshaft in the direction of normal rotation until the TDC mark on the camshaft sprocket aligns with the cast mark.
7. Check to be sure the scribe mark on the flywheel is visible through the clutch housing and opposite the TDC mark.
8. Check that the balance shaft marks are aligned with the marks on the rear belt cover.
9. Special No. 9201 is recommended to check the belt tension. Pull out the lockpin and let the gauge slide drop. Zero the gauge and slide it onto the belt. Push up on the measuring slide until you can hear the lockpin engage. Pull out the lockpin and let the gauge slide drop. Zero the gauge and slide it onto the belt. Push up on the measuring slide until you can hear the lockpin engage. Pull out the lockpin and remove the gauge. Read the measured value. If the guide rollers have no slot, the gauge should read 4.0–4.6 for a new belt, or 3.7–4.3 for a used belt. If the guide roller has a slot, the gauge should read 2.4–3.0 for new and used belts. If necessary, adjust the tension.

#### CAMSHAFT BELT

1. Remove the splash guard, belt covers and alternator compressor belt.
2. Turn the crankshaft in the direction of normal rotation and check the condition of the drive belt. If damaged or worn, it should be replaced.
3. Remove the plug from the distributor cap mount.
4. Turn the crankshaft in the direction of normal rotation until the TDC mark on the camshaft sprocket is aligned with the cast mark on the mounting for the distributor cap.
5. Be sure the TDC mark on the flywheel and clutch housing are aligned.
6. Turn the crankshaft counterclockwise approximately 10 degrees (1½ teeth on the camshaft sprocket). This step is mandatory. If it is not performed, the tension measurement may be incorrect and engine damage could result.
7. Prepare the gauge to take the reading. Pull the lockpin from Tool No. 9201 and listen for the gauge slide to drop. Zero the gauge and slide it onto the belt. Push up on the measuring slide until you can hear the lockpin engage. Pull the lockpin out and read the gauge. It should read 2.4–3.0 for used belts, or 3.7–4.3 for new belts.
8. As required, adjust the belt tension.

### 924S, 944, 944 Turbo and 944S

The balance shaft belt tension is checked in the same manner as outlined above, however the camshaft belt has a mechanical tensioner that makes measurement of the belt tension unnecessary.

## REMOVAL, INSTALLATION & TENSIONING

### 1983–84 928 and 928S

1. Disconnect the negative battery cable. Loosen and remove the drive belts for the power steering pump, fan and air pump, alternator and air conditioning compressor.
2. Remove the fan assembly and bracket for clearance.

**NOTE: Do not lay the fan assembly flat. The silicone oil filler will leak out and the fan will become inoperative.**

3. Tag and disconnect any hoses or lines that may interfere with the cover or belt removal.
4. Remove the upper right, upper left and the bottom cover from the front of the engine.
5. Rotate the engine to TDC with the No. 1 piston on the compression stroke and the distributor rotor pointing to the No. 1 cylinder spark plug wire terminal of distributor cap.
6. Loosen the belt tensioner bolt and remove the belt from the sprockets.
7. Align the camshaft notches with the marks on the cam housings and install a new toothed belt, being sure the crankshaft marks remain aligned at TDC.

**NOTE: The water pump pulley is turned by the back of the toothed belt.**

8. The drive belt adjusting screw is located on the bottom of the engine at the right front.
On 1983–84 vehicles, loosen the lock-

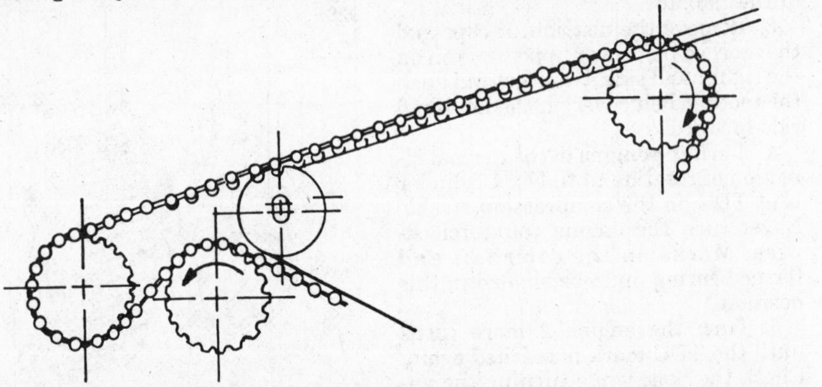

Maintain 0.002-0.004 in. clearance between the guide roller and the lower balance shaft on the 1983-88 924S and 944

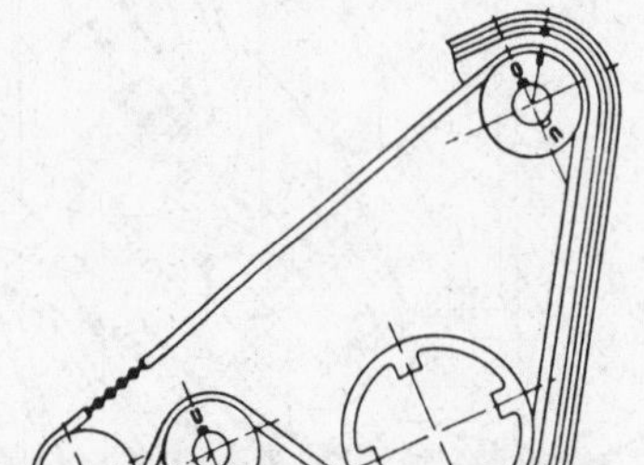

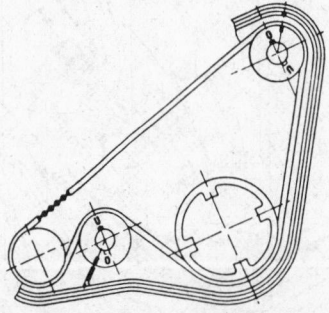

Prior to removing or installing the balance shaft drive belt, the balance shaft sprocket marks should be aligned with the marks on the rear cover as shown

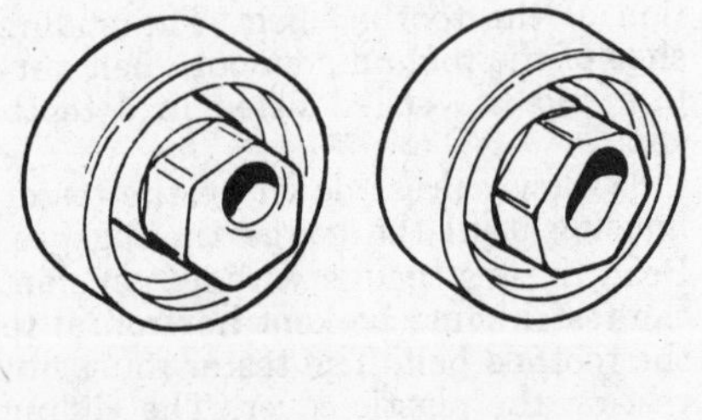

Old style eccentric tensioner (without slot) is on the left; newer style eccentric tensioner (with slot) is on the right

nut on the adjusting screw and turn it until the correct tension is achieved. Tighten the locknut and turn the engine 2 additional turns, then recheck the tension. Turn the engine in the normal direction of rotation; rotating the engine backwards could damage the belt.

9. Install the covers, hoses or lines, fan and bracket assembly, and the drive belts. Adjust the drive belts to have a deflection of ½ in. between pulleys.

10. Check and adjust the ignition timing as necessary.

### *1985–90 928S and 928S4*

1. Disconnect the negative battery cable. Remove the air cleaner intake hoses.
2. Remove the air guide from the top of the radiator.
3. Loosen and remove all drive belts. Tag and disconnect the cables from the throttle, cruise control and automatic transaxle.
4. Remove the fan assembly from the engine after disconnecting all wires and cables. If equipped with a viscous fan coupling, do not lay the fan flat or the fluid will leak out. Once the fluid is gone, so is the fan.
5. Remove the distributor caps and wires. Remove the distributor rotors. Disconnect the wiring connectors for the A/C compressor and belt tension indicator.
6. Remove the mounting screws for the upper belt cover on both sides and remove the upper right side cover.
7. Remove and position the power steering pump out of the way with the hoses attached. Wire the power steering pump, if necessary; do not allow it to hang by the fluid hoses.
8. Remove the clutch slave cylinder with the fluid line attached. Take off the clamp on the clutch hose holder and remove the pushrod. Allow the cylinder to hang out of the way. Do not operate the clutch pedal with the slave cylinder disconnected.
9. Align the 45 degrees before TDC mark on the vibration damper with the red needle by turning the crankshaft clockwise. Make sure No. 1 cylinder is on the compression stroke when aligning the 45 BTDC mark. Camshafts may now be turned without damaging the valves after aligning the 45 degree mark.
10. Mount special crankshaft holding tool No. 9161/1 in position. Remove the 27mm crankshaft bolt and remove the pulley, vibration damper and collar.
11. Remove the guide tube for the engine oil dipstick. Remove the alternator and mounting brackets.
12. Remove the center belt cover and left upper cover.
13. Loosen the toothed belt tension with the adjuster screw.
14. Remove the tension roller assembly.
15. Remove the belt from the right side (cylinders No. 1 and No. 4) camshaft sprocket and water pump sprocket, then from the left side (cylinders No. 5 and No. 8) camshaft sprocket, oil pump sprocket and crankshaft sprocket.
16. Install in the reverse order of removal. Turn the engine in the normal direction of rotation carefully to align No. 1 piston at TDC, then rotate the camshafts to the timing marks. Hold the camshafts firmly in this position and install and tension the drivebelt by turning the adjusting screw located on the bottom of the engine on the right front side. A belt tension gauge tool (No. 9201, or equivalent) is necessary for adjustment. Set the belt tension to 4.7–5.3 on the gauge scale.

### *1983–86 924S, 944 and 944 Turbo*

1. Disconnect the negative battery cable.
2. Remove the engine splash guard.
3. Remove the drive belt for the alternator and air conditioning compressor from the front of the engine.
4. Remove the upper and lower timing belt cover.
5. Rotate the engine as necessary to position the No. 1 piston on TDC-compression. Align the marks on both the camshaft pulley and the flywheel.
6. Remove the distributor cap. Unscrew the distributor arm and remove the plastic cap.
7. Remove the distributor cap mount.
8. Release the tension of the camshaft drive (timing) belt and carefully remove the belt from the sprocket. Do not rotate any of the sprockets while the belt is removed.
9. After making sure that all timing marks are still properly aligned, the new belt may be installed in the following manner:
    a. Install the belt on the crankshaft sprocket first, then to the tensioning roller, water pump pulley, and the camshaft sprocket. Preload the belt slightly by hand each time it is routed around the components, so that it can be pushed onto the camshaft sprocket.
    b. Again, make sure all timing marks have remained aligned.
    c. Carefully turn the crankshaft about 10 crankshaft degrees counterclockwise, which is equal to 1½ teeth from the mark on the camshaft sprocket.

**NOTE: A belt tension gauge tool number 9201 is needed to complete the remainder of this procedure.**

    d. Pull the lockpin out of the special tool. Completely push out the gauge pin which is opposite the lock pin.
    e. Zero the telltale needle of the special tool onto the belt. The slides of the special tool must rest flat with the full surface of the belt. Do not turn or move the belt while testing the belt tension.
    f. Push the measuring needle of the tool inward slowly until you hear the lockpin engage. Read the value on the dial gauge of the special tool. The value should read as follows:
    New belt – 3.7–4.3
    Old belt – 2.4–3.0
    g. If necessary, adjust the belt tensions according to the above specifications by turning the tensioning roller clockwise to loosen, or counterclockwise to tighten. Once the correct belt tension is set, tighten the roller mounting nut to 61 ft. lbs. (45 Nm).
    h. Remove the special tool from the belt and install the remaining components in the reverse of Steps 1–8.

### *1987–90 924S, 944 and 944 Turbo*

1. Disconnect the negative battery cable.
2. Remove the engine splash guard.
3. Remove the drive belt for the power steering pump (if equipped), alternator and air conditioning compressor from the front of the engine.
4. Remove the distributor cap. Unscrew the distributor arm and remove the plastic cap.
5. Rotate the engine as necessary to position the No. 1 piston on TDC-compression. Align the marks on both the camshaft pulley and the flywheel.
6. Remove the upper and lower timing belt cover.
7. Remove the distributor cap mount.
8. Release the tension of the camshaft drive (timing) belt by loosening the mechanical adjuster bolts and prying gently with a suitable small prybar. Remove the tensioner assembly from the crankcase upper section and carefully remove the camshaft belt from the sprockets.
9. Install the new belt in reverse sequence. Install the mechanical tensioner and allow it to tension the drive belt by spring tension alone. Do not attempt to increase the belt tension by prying on the mechanical adjuster.

Tighten the tensioner bolts to 15 ft. lbs. (20 Nm). Rotate the engine 2 times in the normal direction of rotation and check the timing mark alignment before completing the installation procedure.

Correct alignment of early version camshaft marks. The marks should face the exhaust side of the cylinder head as shown

Correct alignment of late version camshaft marks with the bright links on the camshaft chain

Installing camshaft timing equipment on 928, 928S4 and 944

### *944S*

1. Be sure that the engine is cold. Disconnect the negative battery cable.
2. Remove the complete air filter housing. Remove the air hose from the top of the cam belt housing.
3. Remove the cable holder from the top of the cam belt housing.
4. Remove the top camshaft drive belt housing retaining bolts. Remove the housing assembly.
5. Remove the high tension wire on the distributor cap, comming from the coil.
6. Remove the top metal drive belt cover together with the installed distributor cap and position it to the rear.
7. Raise and support the vehicle safely. Remove the lower engine protection cover. Loosen the adjusting rod for the servo pump and remove the belt.
8. Loosen the adjusting rod for the alternator and air conditioning compressor. Remove the drive belt.
9. Remove the bottom belt cover. Do not loosen or remove the pulley pack on the crankshaft. Position the engine at TDC on the compression stroke.
10. Loosen the nut on the balance shaft tensioning wheel about 1 turn. To counterhold the component use tool 9200. Matchmark the belt for reinstallation.
11. Remove the balance shaft belt. Lower the vehicle.
12. Loosen the camshaft drive belt. Slide the belt from the camshaft gear.
13. Remove the idle roller on the oil pump bolt. Remove both nuts on the belt guide rail. Pull off the guide rail. Remove the nuts on the tensioner. Remove the complete unit.

**NOTE: For easier belt removal, bring the tensioner into the center of the adjusting area of the tensioner assembly.**

14. Remove the camshaft drive belt. Raise and support the vehicle safely, as the belt must be reinstalled from under the vehicle.
15. To install the new belt, slip it over the pulley pack by starting at the bottom right side. Push the belt over the balance shaft drive gear. As required, push the cam cover back to gain clearance.
16. Once installed, check the crankshaft TDC on the flywheel housing. If necessary, bring the engine to TDC by turning the crankshaft slightly to the right or left. Do not rotate the engine more than 20 degrees either way.
17. Lower the vehicle. Reinstall the belt tensioner and torque the retaining bolts to 14 ft. lbs.
18. Move the tensioner to the fully off position. Slip the new cam belt onto the camshaft drive gear. Do not move the camshaft.
19. Reinstall the idler roller onto the oil pump. Torque the retaining bolt to 33 ft. lbs.
20. Reinstall the belt rail. Be sure to use new nuts and torque them to 8 ft. lbs. Raise and support the vehicle safely.
21. Rotate the engine 2 revolutions and bring it back to TDC on the compression stroke. Lower the vehicle.
22. Check to be sure that the crank and the camshaft are in proper alignment. Readjust the cam belt, by loosening the bolt and nut on the tensioner. Torque them to 20 ft. lbs.

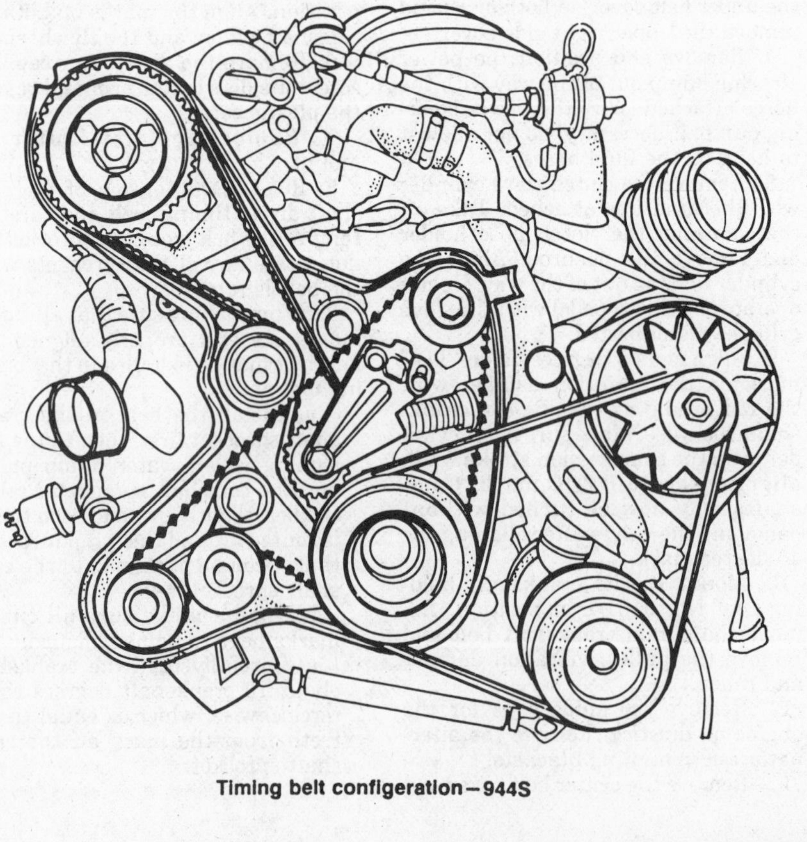

Timing belt configeration—944S

23. Raise and support the vehicle safely. Reinstall the balance shaft drive belt and assure correct position of the balance shaft. Loosen the idler pulley. Adjust the idler pulley using special tool 9207 to a preload of 1mm. Torque the bolt to 33 ft. lbs.

24. Reinstall the lower balance shaft drive gear bolt and washers. Torque the rtaining bolt to 33 ft. lbs.

25. Continue the installation in the reverse order of the removal procedure.

## Camshaft Coupler And Chain Tensioner

### REMOVAL & INSTALLATION

#### *1985–90 928S, 928S4 and 944S*

**NOTE: The intake camshaft is chain-driven off of the exhaust camshaft. This chain is tightened by a hydraulic chain tensioner which maintains the proper chain tension automatically. No adjustment is necessary, but note that the tensioners are different for right and left sides on the 928S and 928S4.**

1. With the vehicle on the ground and full weight on the wheels, remove the cross strut.
2. Remove the air intake hoses and complete air cleaner assembly.
3. Loosen the hose clamps on the intake air distributor and vacuum line. Pull off and lay the suction pump aside. Remove the intake air distributor.
4. Remove the lifting bracket from the left rear of the engine.
5. Twist and pull the spark plug wires from the plug. Remove the plug wires form the valve cover clips and remove the valve cover(s).

**NOTE: Take note when removing valve cover retaining bolts, some are equipped with a seal. These bolts must be returned to their original positions.**

6. Remove the hollow union bolt and check valve from the cylinder head. A seal is used under the bolt head. Remove the chain tensioner.
7. The chain tensioner piston is under spring pressure. Compress the tensioner piston when removing and secure with suitable binding wire.
8. Install tensioner in reverse order. To apply tensioner to chain on Nos. 1–4 cylinders push tensioner chain up. Nos. 5–8 cylinders, push tensioner chain down. Tighten the chain tensioner bolts to 6 ft. lbs. (8 Nm) after installation. No further adjustment is necessary.

## Balance Shaft Drive Belt

### REMOVAL & INSTALLATION

#### *924S, 944, 944 Turbo and 944S*

1. Disconnect the negative battery cable.
2. Remove the engine splash guard.
3. Remove the alternator and air conditioning drive belt.
4. Remove the camshaft drive (timing) belt cover.
5. Loosen the balance shaft idler pulley so that the pulley does not touch the balance shaft drive belt.
6. Rotate the crankshaft clockwise as necessary to position the No. 1 cylinder at TDC on the compression stroke.

**NOTE: At this point, the marks on the balance shaft sprockets should be aligned with the marks on the rear belt cover.**

7. Turn the tensioner nut counterclockwise to loosen the balance shaft drive belt. Carefully remove the old belt from the sprocket.

**NOTE: There are 2 types of tensioners used. The older type (without a slot) is an eccentric that is turned to adjust tension. The newer type (with a slot) is held in place by a locknut and slides away from the belt to release tension. Do not move any sprocket while the belt is removed, or while installing the new belt.**

8. Carefully route the new belt around the sprocket, making sure that the color coded tooth of the belt faces away from the sprockets.
9. Adjust the belt tension in the same manner as the camshaft drive (timing) belt. Turn the tensioner nut (same as used during Step 7) to tighten the belt to the proper value (2.4–3.0 dial reading).

On guide rollers with no slot, loosen the locknut and turn the eccentric clockwise to tighten or counterclockwise to loosen. Tighten the locknut to 33 ft. lbs. (44 Nm).

10. On rollers with a slot, adjust the idler pulley so that there is 0.5mm clearance between the pulley and the portion of the belt below the pulley. Tighten the pulley nut in this position. The remaining components are installed in the reverse order of removal.

**NOTE: If the correct clearance cannot be obtained, rotate the pulley 180 degrees and repeat Step 10. A special clearance gauge (tool No. 9207) is available to aid in the adjustment.**

## Timing Sprockets

### REMOVAL & INSTALLATION

On all vehicles, the camshaft and crankshaft sprockets are located by keys on their respective shafts and each is retained by a single bolt. To remove either or both of the sprockets, first remove the timing belt cover and belt and then use the following general procedure.

**NOTE: If equipped, don't remove the 4 bolts which retain the outer belt pulley to the timing belt sprocket.**

1. Remove the center bolt.
2. Gently pry the sprocket off the shaft. If the sprocket is stubborn, use a gear puller. Don't hammer on the sprocket.
3. Remove the sprocket and the key.
4. Install the sprocket in the reverse order of removal.
5. Tighten the center bolt on the crankshaft sprocket to 58 ft. lbs. (79 Nm); tighten the camshaft sprocket retaining bolt to 33 ft. lbs. (45 Nm).

**NOTE: The 944 is equipped with polygon head bolts instead of the Allen head bolts should be torqued to 48 ft. lbs. (65 Nm).**

6. Install the timing belt. Check valve timing and belt tension, then install the cover.

## Camshaft

### REMOVAL & INSTALLATION

#### *1983–84 928, 924S, 944 and 944 Turbo*

Refer to the "Cylinder Head Removal and Installation" section for the removal of the cam housing as a unit.

1. Remove the hydraulic lifters, lifter sleeves and gaskets from the cam housing.
2. Remove the rear housing end plate and gasket.
3. On the 928, remove the camshaft sprocket, the front bearing carrier on the right head an the distributor and bearing carrier on the left cam housing. On the 944, remove the camshaft sprocket and the bearing carriers.
4. Pull the camshaft to the rear and out of the cam housing.
5. The distributor gear and spacer can be removed from the camshaft at this time.
6. Installation is the reverse of removal.

**NOTE: The front camshaft seals can be replaced while the front bearing carriers are off the cam housing or when the timing sprocket is removed from the camshaft.**

### *1985–90 928S, 928S4 and 944S*

The camshaft housing and cylinder head are a complete unit on these vehicles. Refer to the "Cylinder Head Removal and Installation" procedures and remove the camshaft housing covers, timing belt and camshaft sprocket. Remove the hydraulic chain tensioner, then remove the camshaft bearing caps and lift out both camshafts together with the timing chain.

Camshaft bearing caps are numbered from 1–8. Check that the bearing cap positions and cylinder head numbers are correct when installing. Bearing caps are installed so that the numbers are on the outside. The camshafts themselves have identification numbers located on the face of the camshaft and the timing chain sprockets have marks to help when adjusting the timing. The drive chain has 2 copper-plated links which are used for the basic adjustment of the exhaust camshaft to the intake camshaft.

## CAMSHAFT TIMING ADJUSTMENT

### *1985–90 928S and 928S4*

1. Set the No. 1 cylinder at TDC on the compression stroke and make sure the camshaft drive belt tension is adjusted properly.
2. Check that the marks on the camshaft sprockets and flange bearings are aligned properly.
3. Check that the marks (early version) or cast tabs (late version) on the camshafts are aligned properly. The marks should face the exhaust side of the cylinder head, while the cast tabs should align with the bright links on the camshaft chain.
4. Install a dial gauge holder (such as VW 387) with a dial gauge on the cylinder head. Set the dial gauge with a 5mm preload to Zero on the hydraulic lifter of No. 6 cylinder intake valve. The dial gauge must be perpendicular to the intake valve.
5. Slowy move the crankshaft in the normal direction of rotation (clockwise) past TDC while observing the reading on the dial gauge. Continue turning until the dial indicates 2.0 ± 0.1mm lift. The 20 degrees ATDC mark should now be lined up with the pointer on the drive belt cover. If it is, then the valve timing is correct and no adjustment is necessary.

**NOTE: Make all measurements using metric specifications when checking or adjusting valve timing, and make all steps and adjustments as smoothly and accurately as possible. If the engine is rotated a little past 2mm lift when setting up the measurement, continue around in the normal direction of rotation and begin at Step 1 again. Never rotate the engine counterclockwise to align any timing marks; always rotate the engine clockwise. All timing degree specifications and timing mark alignments are on the No. 1 cylinder compression stroke, either approaching or leaving TDC.**

6. If the alignment of the pointer and the 20 degrees ATDC mark is not correct, remove the ignition rotor and install 3 additional M5 × 15 bolts into the camshaft sprocket to prevent the camshaft and sprocket from turning while loosening the sprocket bolts.
7. Turn the crankshaft clockwise until the dial gauge reads 2.0 ± .01mm, then loosen the sprocket bolts.
8. Turn the crankshaft to 20 degrees ATDC (on cylinder No. 1 compression stroke), then retorque the camshaft mounting bolt to 47 ft. lbs. (65 Nm). Hold the sprocket securely with the bolts as before.
9. Remove the M5 × 15 bolts from the sprocket and recheck the camshaft timing on cylinder bank 1–4 by rotating the engine clockwise to TDC on cylinder No. 6 (not No. 1).
10. Install the dial gauge on the hydraulic lifter for the intake valve of No. 1 cylinder. The dial gauge must be perpendicular to the intake valve.
11. Slowly rotate the crankshaft clockwise away from TDC/No. 6 and observe the reading on the dial gauge. Continue turning until the dial indicates 1.6 ± 0.1mm lift. The 20 degrees ATDC mark should now be aligned with the pointer on the drive belt cover.
12. If the alignment of the pointer and the 20 degrees ATDC mark is not correct, repeat the timing procedure from Step 1.
13. When installing the cylinder head cover, additional sealing is required. Apply a small bead of silicone Silastic 730 RTV sealer (or equivalent) in the area whereend camshaft bearing caps meet the head cover mating surface. Avoid using excessive amounts of the sealer and torque the head cover bolts to 7 ft. lbs. (10 Nm). On 928S4 engines, 12 spacers are used between the guide washers and the mounting bolt heads. These spacers should only be added to the 4 mounting bolts along the bottom (exhaust side) of the cover and the 2 mounting bolts, 1 centered at each end of the cover.

### *1987–90 944S*

1. Rotate the engine in the normal direction of rotation to set No. 1 cylinder at TDC/compression. Check the cambelt tension adjustment.
2. Remove the distributor cap and make sure the rotor is pointing straight up. Check that the cam lobes for No. 1 cylinder are leaning in toward each another with the noses at approximately 10 and 2 o'clock. The notch on the flywheel should also be aligned with the TDC notch in the bellhousing, visible from beneath the vehicle. If the engine is out of the vehicle, align the **OT** marks on the crankshaft pulley with the mark on the engine case, just under the magnetic timing probe bracket.
3. Install a dial gauge holder and indicator on the piston crown of No. 1 cylinder and preload to 3mm. Install a second dial indicator to the hydraulic tappet of No. 1 intake valve and again preload to 3mm. The second dial indicator must be perpendicular to the intake valve.
4. Remove the rotor and install three M5 × 15 bolts to secure the camshaft sprocket while loosening the sprocket center bolt. Loosen the center bolt while counterholding to prevent engine rotation, then loosen the M5 x 15 bolts.
5. Turn the engine against its normal direction of rotation slowly, until the camshaft gear comes up against the stop withing the feather key groove. Tighten the M5 × 15 bolts to 4 ft. lbs. (6 Nm) and the sprocket center bolt to 29 ft. lbs. (40 Nm).
6. Rotate the engine in the normal direction of rotation slowly, until the highest piston stroke position is indicated by the dial gauge.

**NOTE: Do not rotate the engine against the normal direction of rotation in an attempt to correct for overshoot. If you pass the indicated timing mark positions, keep rotating the engine around and start all over again.**

7. Set the dial indicator on the hydraulic tappet of No. 1 intake valve to 0, then slowly rotate past TDC (No. 1/compression) while observing the dial indicator reading. Rotate until the dial gauge indicates 1.4 ± 0.1mm.
8. Loosen the central and auxiliary bolts, while making sure the dial gauge reading doesn't change, then rotate the engine slowly until the highest piston stroke is indicated on the gauge. In this position, No. 4 cylinder is at TDC/compression.

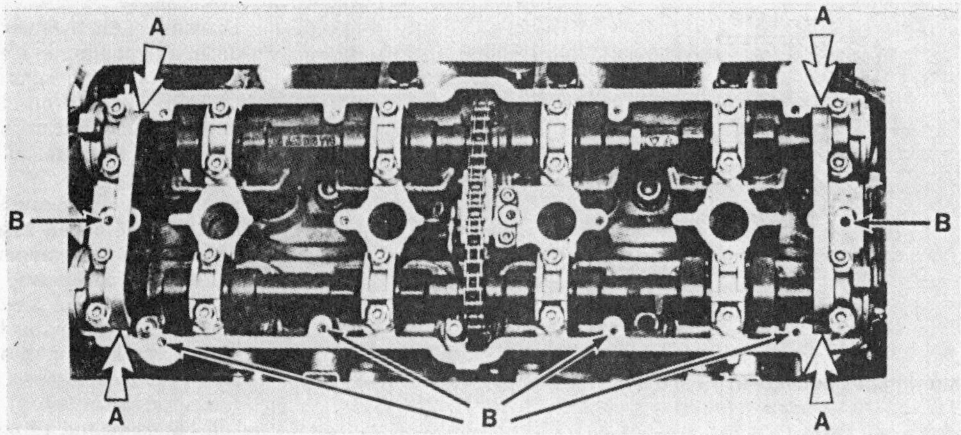


On 928S4 models, apply silicone sealer at the arrows (A) and the spacers at the cover bolt holes indicated (B)

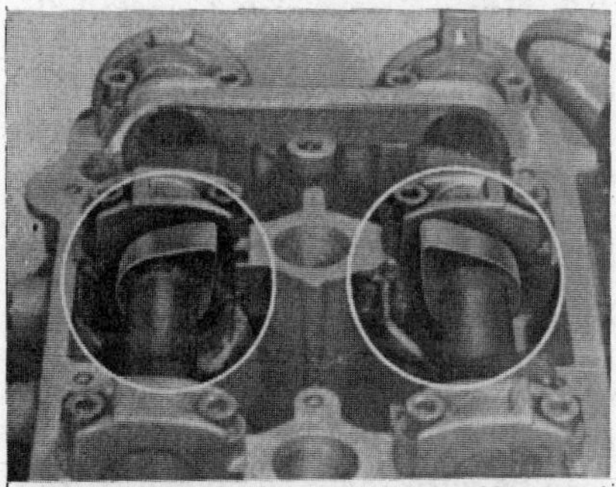

Correct cam lobe alignment for No. 1 cylinder at TDC/compression on 944S models

Install dial gauges as shown to set camshaft timing on 944S models

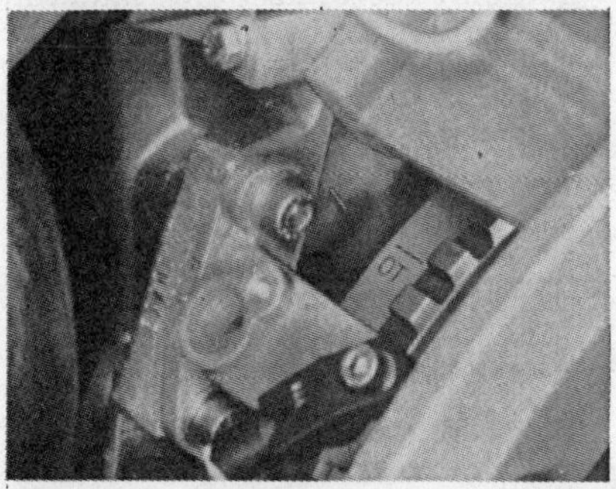

TDC mark alignment on the crankshaft pulley for 944S models.

Install three M5 x 15 bolts as shown to hold the sprocket in place

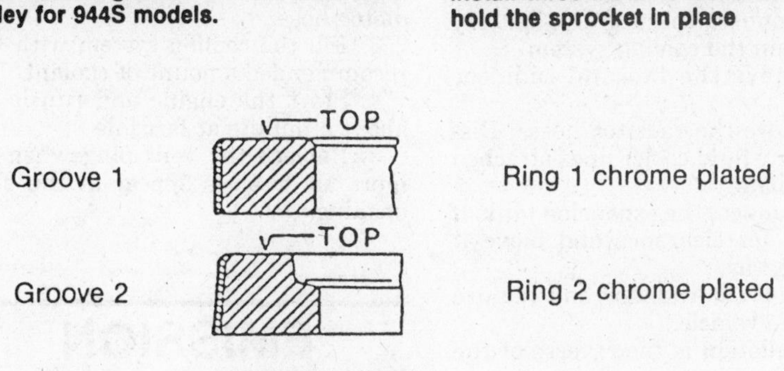


Piston ring positioning—924S and 944 (1983–87)

9. Tighten the auxiliary bolts and the sprocket center bolt. Torque the center bolt to 48–52 ft. lbs. (65–70 Nm). Rotate the crankshaft 2 more times in the normal direction of rotation, then recheck the adjustment. If correct, remove the M5 × 15 bolts from the sprocket and install the rotor and distributor cap.

## Piston and Connecting Rod

### POSITIONING

#### *Except 911 and 911 Turbo*

The pistons and connecting rods may be removed after the cylinder head and the pan have been removed. The connecting rod ends are offset. Make sure that the narrow side with the small chamfer faces the neighboring connecting rod, while the wide side with the large chamfer faces the crankshaft web. The pistons must be installed with the valve pockets facing toward the exhaust manifold. The wrist pin is pressed out of the piston after the snaprings are removed.

# ENGINE LUBRICATION

## Oil Pan

### REMOVAL & INSTALLATION

#### *911 and 911 Turbo*

For all lubrication service procedures, see "Engine Disassembly" in the 911 Engine Mechanical section.

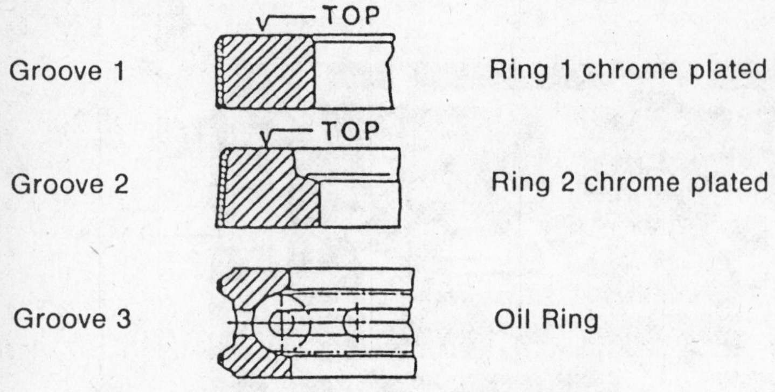


**Piston ring positioning—924S and 944 (1988–90)**

#### *Except 911 and 911 Turbo*

1. Raise and support the vehicle safely.
2. Remove the bottom protective engine plate.
3. Drain the engine oil and unscrew the oil fill pipe from the pan. Disconnect the oil level indicator wire.
4. Remove the oil pan retaining bolts and maneuver the oil pan downward so that the oil pump suction tube is not twisted or damaged.
5. Clean all gasket mating surfaces carefully. Using a new gasket, install the oil pan in the reverse order of removal.

## Rear Main Bearing Oil Seal

### REPLACEMENT

#### *911 and 911 Turbo*

For all lubrication service procedures, see "Engine Disassembly" in the 911 Engine Mechanical section.

#### *Except 911 and 911 Turbo*

The rear main oil seal can be replaced by separating the clutch housing from the engine and removing the flywheel. Remove the seal from the engine block with a sharp edged tool, being careful not to mark the crankshaft surface. Using a special centering tool, install the seal into the engine block with the lubricated lip towards the crankshaft. Reassemble in the reverse order of disassembly.

## Oil Pump

### REMOVAL & INSTALLATION

#### *911 and 911 Turbo*

For all lubrication service procedures, see "Engine Disassembly" in the 911 Engine Mechanical section.

#### *Except 911 and 911 Turbo*

The oil pump is located on the front of the engine block and is driven by the toothed timing belt.

1. Remove the timing belt.
2. Remove the oil pump sprocket and the oil pump retaining bolts.
3. Remove the oil pump from the engine block.
4. Installation is the reverse of removal. Install a new O-ring seal on the pump body.

**NOTE: An oil pump shaft seal is used and can be replaced after removal of the sprocket and woodruff key.**

# ENGINE COOLING

## Radiator

### REMOVAL & INSTALLATION

1. Disconnect the negative battery cable. Drain the cooling system.
2. Remove the fan and radiator shroud.
3. Remove the radiator hoses. Disconnect any fluid cooler lines attached to the radiator.
4. Disconnect the expansion tank, if necessary for clearance and move it out of the way.
5. Unbolt the radiator and remove it from the vehicle.
6. Installation is the reverse of the removal procedure.

## Water Pump

### REMOVAL & INSTALLATION

1. Be sure that the engine is cold. Disconnect the negative battery cable. drain the cooling system.
2. Rotate the engine to TDC, with the No. 1 piston on the firing stroke and the distributor rotor pointing to the No. 1 terminal of the distributor cap.
3. On the 924S and 944, remove the timing belt cover assembly. On the 928, remove the upper right and left timing belt covers and remove the fan and bracket.
4. When removing the cooling fan, be sure to keep it in an upright position if it is a viscus coupling cooling fan.
5. Loosen and remove the toothed drive belt from the water pump pulley.
6. Remove the bolts and water pump from the engine block.
7. Using a new gasket, install the water pump in the reverse order of removal.

## Thermostat

### REMOVAL & INSTALLATION

The thermostat is located in the upper radiator hose neck on the engine. What follows is a general procedure for all engines.

1. Be sure that the engine is cold. Disconnect the negative battery cable. drain the cooling system.
2. Don't disconnect the radiator hose, just unbolt the neck and lift out the thermostat.
3. Clean the mating surfaces and install the new thermostat (spring down) using a new gasket.
4. Refill the cooling system.

### COOLING SYSTEM BLEEDING

1. Set the heater to the full hot position
2. Remove the vent plug on the radiator hose
3. Fill the cooling system with the recommended amount of coolant
4. Start the engine and run it for about a minute at fast idle
5. Replace the vent plug when no more air bubbles appear at the plug opening.

# EMISSION CONTROLS

**Please refer to "Emission Control" in the Unit Repair section for system maintenance procedures. Due to the complex nature**

**of modern electronic engine control systems, comprehensive diagnosis and testing procedures fall outside the confines of this repair manual. For complete information on diagnosis, testing and repair procedures concerning all modern engine and emission control systems, please refer to "Chilton's Guide To Electronic Engine Controls."**

## Emission Warning Lamps

### RESETTING

All vehicles are equipped with an oxygen sensor. The **OXS** light will come on at 30,000 miles on all vehicles except the 928S with LH Jetronic fuel injection and the 944. When this light comes on it is time to replace the sensor. The 928S and the 944 do not have a reminder light but it is recommended that the sensor be replaced after 60,000 miles.

#### *911 and 911 Turbo*

1. Disconnect the negative battery cable. The sensor plug is located on the left side of the engine compartment, just below the ignition coil.
2. Disconnect the electrical wire at the plug and push the grommet and plug through the grommet hole.
3. Raise and support the vehicle safely. Remove the left rear tire and wheel assembly.
4. Remove the exhaust shield. Pull the safety plug from the sensor. Remove the sensor from its mounting.
5. Installation is the reverse of the removal procedure. Be sure to coat the sensor with the proper anti-seize compound. Use care not to get any of the anti-seize compound in the sensor slot.

#### *928, 928S and 928S4*

1. Disconnect the negative battery cable. The sensor wire connector is located inside the vehicle behind the lower section of the foot support on the passenger side.
2. Disconnect the electrical wire at the plug and push the grommet and plug through the grommet hole.
3. Raise and support the vehicle safely.
4. Remove the sensor from its mounting.
5. Installation is the reverse of the removal procedure. Be sure to coat the sensor with the proper anti-seize compound. Use care not to get any of the anti-seize compound in the sensor slot.

#### *944, 944 Turbo and 944S2*

1. Disconnect the negative battery cable. Raise and support the vehicle safely.
2. Locate the sensor in the exhaust pipe. Disconnect the electrical connector. Pull the plug from the sensor.
3. Remove the sensor from its mounting.
4. Installation is the reverse of the removal procedure. Be sure to coat the sensor with the proper anti-seize compound. Use care not to get any of the anti-seize compound in the sensor slot.

# FUEL SYSTEM

## Fuel System Service Precaution

### RELIEVING FUEL SYSTEM PRESSURE

1. Be sure that the engine is cold.
2. Disconnect the electrical lead from the fuel pump. Remove the fuel pump fuse from its mounting.
3. Run the engine until it stalls. Crank the engine several times.
4. Install the fuel pump fuse. Connect the fuel pump electrical connector.
5. Disconnect the negative battery cable.
6. Carefully crack the fuel line, using the proper tools. If any fuel is remaining in the system, do not allow it to spray all over.

## Fuel Filter

### REMOVAL & INSTALLATION

#### *911 and 911 Turbo*

The fuel filter is located in the fuel line, mounted near the tank. Replacement involves depressurizing the fuel system and disconnecting the line fittings from the filter canister. Install a new fuel filter and tighten the fittings using a backup wrench on the nuts to avoid twisting the fuel line.

#### *924S, 944, 944S and 944 Turbo*

On the 924S and 944, the fuel filter is located at the right rear of the vehicle above the axle halfshaft.

1. Properly relieve the fuel system pressure. Disconnect the negative battery cable. Raise and support the vehicle safely.
2. Place a shop rag under the filter. Using a line wrench, unscrew both line connections from the filter.
3. Loosen the filter clamp and remove the filter.
4. Install the replacement filter in the line and tighten both fittings. Tighten the filter clamp, if so equipped.

#### *928, 928S and 928S4*

The fuel filter and fuel accumulator on the 928 is located behind a cover, in front of the right rear wheel well. On the 928S and 928S4, remove the shield underneath the gas tank. Disconnect the fuel lines, remove the filter and install in reverse order.

## Fuel Pump

### PRESSURE TESTING

No adjustments may be made to the fuel pump. If the pump is not functioning properly, it must be discarded and replaced. To check the function of the fuel pump, the pump should be connected to a pressure gauge. Be careful not to switch the electrical leads. If the pump fails to pump its normal capacity, or it cannot pump that capacity at its specified rate of current consumption, it must be replaced.

A pressure tester such as P 378, or equivalent is necessary to check the fuel pressure on all vehicles. The pres-

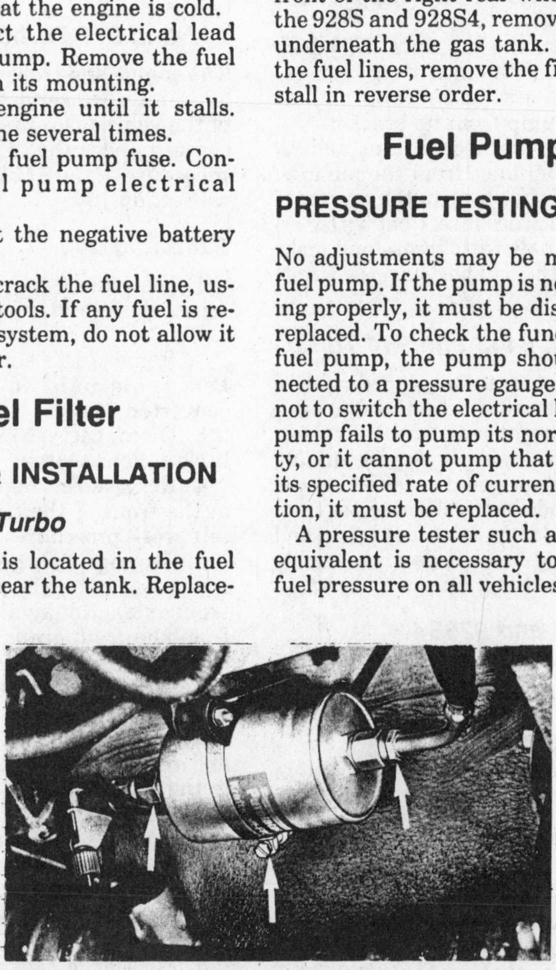

Fuel filter on the 944. Loosen the line fittings first (outer arrows) then the filter mounting clamp (inner arrow) to remove the filter

sure gauge is attached the fuel distributor test connection after first relieving the fuel system pressure. Make sure the sealing ball does not fall out when taking off the capped nut. Start the engine and measure the fuel pressure at idle. The fuel pressure should be approximately 28 psi (2 bar) at idle.

**CAUTION**

***Relieve fuel system pressure before attempting to disconnect any fuel lines. Take precautions to avoid the risk of fire while working on the fuel system and cap all line openings to prevent contamination of the fuel system by dirt.***

### REMOVAL & INSTALLATION

#### 911 and 911 Turbo

The 911 Turbo is equipped with 2 electric pumps. One is mounted at the front crossmember, near the fuel tank; the second at the rear, near the engine. The fuel pumps are located at the front near the tank.

1. Properly relieve the fuel system pressure. Disconnect the negative battery cable. Raise and support the vehicle.
2. Remove the cap nuts. Withdraw the pump with its mounting bracket.
3. Loosen the hose clamp and remove the pump from its bracket.
4. Loosen the hose clamps and remove the fuel lines from the pump.
5. Install the pump in the reverse of the removal procedure. Coat both electrical terminals with grease and make sure that the rubber boot is firmly seated.

#### 924S, 944, 944S and 944 Turbo

These vehicles are equipped with a fuel pump located near the fuel tank behind the right rear wheel. Replacement involves simply depressurizing the fuel system and disconnecting the fuel lines and electrical connector from the pump. Remove the fuel pump and its mounting bracket as an assembly and separate the 2 on a workbench.

#### 928, 928S and 928S4

A single fuel pump is located with the fuel filter on a mutual mounting bracket, underneath a plastic hood on top of the fuel tank.

1. Properly relieve the fuel system pressure. Disconnect the negative battery cable.
2. Raise and support the vehicle safely. Expose the fuel pump.
3. Pinch shut the hose running from the fuel tank to the fuel pump with a suitable clamp.
4. Disconnect the pump wiring, disconnect both fittings from the pump, loosen its retaining strap and remove the pump. Some fuel will be present in the lines. Have a container ready to catch it.
5. Install a new pump in the reverse order of pump removal.

## Fuel Injection

**Due to the complex nature of modern fuel injection systems, comprehensive diagnosis and testing procedures fall outside the confines of this repair manual. For complete information on fuel injection diagnosis, testing and repair procedures, please refer to "Chilton's Guide To Fuel Injection And Feedback Carburetors".**

# MANUAL TRANSAXLE

### REMOVAL & INSTALLATION

#### 911 and 911 Turbo

The engine and transaxle are removed as a unit, then serviced separately out of the vehicle. Transaxle separation is covered under the "Engine Removal" procedure in the 911 Engine Mechanical section.

#### 924S and 944

1. Disconnect the negative battery cable. Raise and support the vehicle safely.
2. Remove the entire exhaust system from behind the catalytic converter.
3. Disconnect the wires from the backup light switch.
4. Remove the reinforcement strut at the front of the transaxle to facilitate work procedures.
5. Engage 4th gear (four speed transaxle) or 5th gear (five speed transaxle). Remove the rubber cap from the front transaxle cover. Position the socket head screw for removal by turning a rear wheel (hold the other wheel). Unscrew the screw from the coupling using a long reach extension and a 6 mm socket. Keep the transaxle in the proper gear.
6. Detach the axle halfshafts from the transaxle and suspend them on wire to prevent damage.
7. Remove the self-locking nuts from the transaxle mounts (the rubber/metal mounts).
8. Position a jack underneath the transaxle and secure the transaxle to it using a strap.
9. Unscrew the bolts from the rubber/metal mounts, lift the transaxle slightly with he jack and remove the mounts. Do not lift the unit too far, as the brake line for the left rear wheel may be damaged.
10. Disconnect the shift linkage.
11. Remove the bolts between the drive shaft tube and the transaxle. Remove or disconnect any other interfering components, then carefully remove the transaxle unit, moving rearward and down.
12. Installation is the reverse of removal.

#### 928, 928S and 928S4

1. Remove the nuts from the spring strut bolts extending into the trunk compartment.
2. Remove the battery and loosen the rear wheel lugnuts.
3. Place the transaxle in 5th gear.
4. Raise the vehicle and remove the rubber plug from underneath the front of the transaxle. Looking into the hole, position the coupling bolt head between the drive and input shafts, so that it can be removed.

**NOTE: During removal of the bolt, do not allow the shaft to turn and jam the socket or bolt in the transaxle housing.**

5. Place the transaxle in **N**, remove the rear wheels and remove the brake calipers. Wire the calipers to the frame; do not allow them to hang from their brake hoses.
6. Remove the exhaust system from the catalytic converter rearward.
7. Remove the exhaust heat shield and the battery box.
8. Disconnect the backup light switch wires and loosen the pulse transmitter for the speedometer. Remove the wires form the clip.
9. Move the dust cover from the shift rod coupling and remove the locking set screw. Remove the shift rod from the main rod.
10. Disconnect the axle shafts at the transaxle end. Suspend the axles from the crossmember.
11. Disconnect the stabilizer bar at the lower control arm.
12. Support the transaxle assembly from the stabilizer bar with the use of a strap, chain or heavy wire.
13. Remove the transaxle to rear axle crossmember bolts and the bolts between the rear axle crossmember and frame.
14. Mark the position of the rear axle crossmember and place a jack under member. Remove the bolts and tilt the rear axle so that the spring struts and control arms do not twist. Support the rear axle in the tilted position to keep the weight off the lower control arm

link pins.

15. Place under the transaxle assembly and remove the bolts between the drive shaft tube and the transaxle. Remove the holding strap, pull the unit rearward and lower.

16. Installation is the reverse of removal.

## LINKAGE ADJUSTMENT

Linkage adjustments are not normally required and should be attempted only if familiar with direct-distant shift mechanisms.

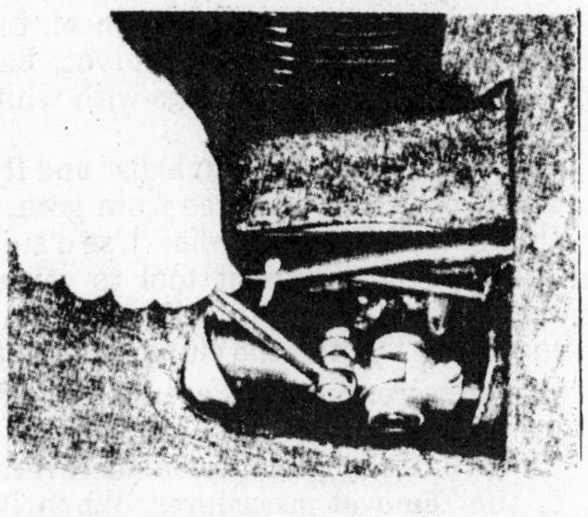

Shift linkage adjustment on 911 models

### 911 and 911 Turbo

1. Position the shift lever in the **N** detent. Remove the rear tunnel cover in front of the rear seat.
2. Pull the rubber dust cover forward on the shift rod.
3. Loosen the clamp bolt on the shift rod.
4. Move the transaxle selector shaft all the way to its left stop, keeping it in **N**.
5. With the transaxle still in **N**, move the gearshift rod to the right to its stop.
6. Tighten the clamp bolt to 18 ft. lbs. (24 Nm).
7. Test the shift lever. Play should be the same in all gears in all directions.

# CLUTCH

## REMOVAL & INSTALLATION

### 911 and 911 Turbo

1. Remove the engine and transaxle as a unit from the vehicle. Separate the engine/transaxle assembly.
2. Gradually loosen the pressure plate bolts 1 or 2 turns at a time in a crisscross pattern to prevent distortion.

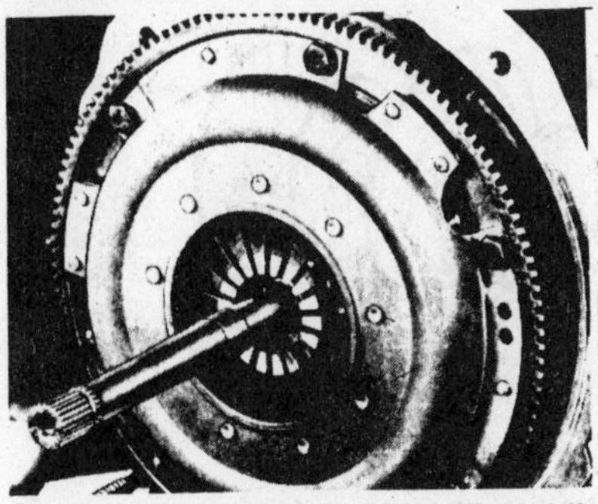

Centering the clutch disc with a pilot shaft

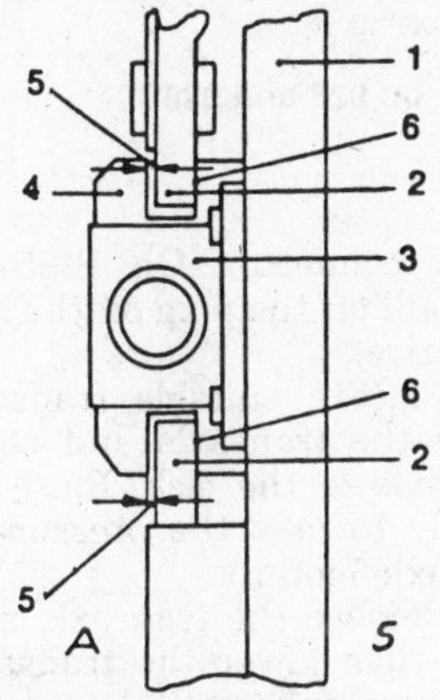


1. Intermediate ring
2. Intermediate plate
3. Stop bracket
4. Stop
5. Distance 0.7 to 1.0 mm
6. Position of intermediate plate
A. Release bearing side
S. Flywheel side

To prevent clutch drag on the 928, move the three clutch stop brackets toward the pressure plate until the correct gap (5) exists

3. Remove the pressure plate and clutch disc.
4. Check the clutch disc for uneven or excessive lining wear. Examine the pressure plate for cracking, scorching, or scoring. Replace any questionable components.
5. Check the clutch release bearing for wear, and replace if necessary. Measure the clutch disc for wear; new thickness is 8.1mm, and the maximum wear limit is 6.3mm. Clutch disc runout (maximum) is 0.6mm.
6. Fill the pilot bearing with about 2cc of grease.
7. Install the clutch disc and pressure plate. Use a pilot shaft or an old transaxle input shaft to keep the disc centered.
8. Gradually tighten the pressure plate-to-flywheel bolts in a criss-cross pattern. Torque the bolts to 18 ft. lbs. (24 Nm).
9. Install the throwout bearing.
10. Install the transaxle on the engine and install the engine/transaxle assembly.

### 924S and 944

**NOTE: The flywheel sensing components used in these vehicles for the digital ignition system are very delicate and easily damaged. Exercise care when handling, removing and installing these components.**

1. Disconnect the negative battery cable and the ground wire from the body to the clutch housing. Raise and support the vehicle safely.
2. Remove the socket head bolts and remove the reference mark sensor and speed sensor from the bracket.

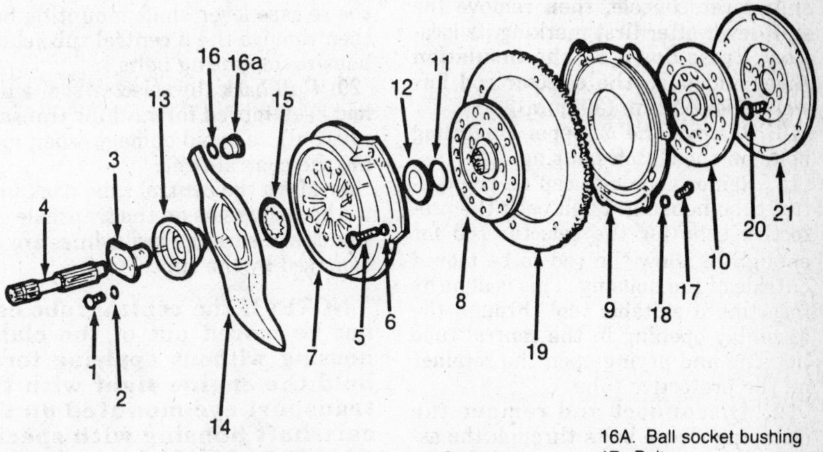


1. Bolt
2. Washer
3. Guide sleeve
4. Driveshaft
5. Bolt
6. Washer
7. Pressure plate
8. Clutch disc (spring loaded)
9. Intermediate plate
10. Clutch disc (not spring loaded)
11. Snap-ring
12. Thrust washer
13. Release bearing
14. Release lever
15. Preload washer
16. Snap-ring
16A. Ball socket bushing
17. Bolt
18. Washer
19. Starter ring
20. Bolt
21. Flywheel with centering collar

Diameter centered clutch assembly on 928 and 928S

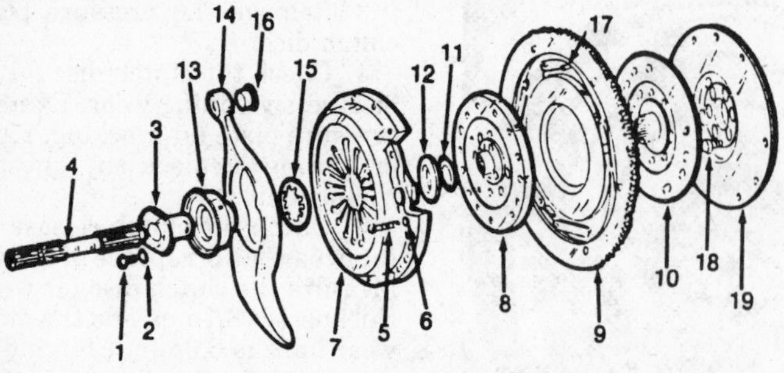


1. Bolt
2. Washer
3. Guide sleeve
4. Driveshaft
5. Bolt
6. Washer
7. Pressure plate
8. Clutch disc (spring loaded)
9. Starter ring
10. Clutch disc (not spring loaded)
11. Snap-ring
12. Thrust washer
13. Release bearing
14. Release lever
15. Preload washer
16. Ball socket bushing
17. Intermediate plate

**Dowel pin centered clutch assembly on 928 and 928S**

3. Disconnect the wire harness for the starter at the upper mounting point. It may be necessary to remove the air cleaner to gain access.

4. Disconnect the oxygen sensor wire and remove the exhaust assembly at the manifold.

5. Remove the heat shield above the catalytic converter and the splash shield. Remove the rear exhaust pipe bracket together with the bracket bolted on the central tube.

6. Pull back the dust cover, then remove the lockwire on the clamp bolt of the selector linkage and remove the bolt.

7. Lift and fold down the dust cover and sleeve on the shift lever. Remove the shift lever boot retainer and remove the shift knob.

8. Remove the circlip on the shift lever, then pull off the selector rod and washer on the bolt of the shift lever.

9. Remove the insulator above the shift lever console, then remove the shift lever after first marking its location. Press down on the insulation sheet and push the selector rod forward about 12 in. (300mm).

10. Remove the 2 upper mounting bolts on the clutch housing.

11. Remove the end cap on the central tube housing. Push back the protective tube for the selector rod far enough to allow the rod to be moved outside of the housing. This is done by inserting a suitable tool through the assembly opening in the central tube housing and prying open the retainer on the protective tube.

12. Disconnect and remove the clamping sleeve bolts through the assembly openings, then push the clamping sleeve toward the transaxle.

13. Disconnect the halfshafts from the transaxle and wire them in a horizontal position. Do not let the shafts hang down.

14. Disconnect the backup light switch connector. On 1985–90 vehicles, pull off the plug on the speedometer drive.

15. Place a suitable transaxle jack under the transaxle and secure the transaxle to the jack. Raise the jack slightly to take the pressure off the transaxle mounts.

16. Remove the transaxle mounting bolts, then lower the transaxle with the central tube until the tube rests on the crossmember. Remove the transaxle/central tube flange bolts, then remove the transaxle from the rear.

17. Remove the starter, then unscrew the clutch line mounting clamps.

18. Detach the clutch slave cylinder from the clutch housing, but do not disconnect the hydraulic line from the cylinder.

19. Disconnect the starter wire harness from the clutch housing. Pull out the release lever shaft mounting bolt, then remove the 4 central tube/clutch housing mounting bolts.

20. Pull back the selector rod (which had been moved forward for transaxle removal), to avoid damage when moving the central tube.

21. Move the central tube back until the housing rests on the transaxle carrier. Make sure the brake lines are not damaged by the tube.

**NOTE: If the central tube cannot be moved out of the clutch housing without applying force, hold the engine tight with the transport eye mounted on the camshaft housing with special tool VW 10–222. If this is the case, the engine has excessive inclination at the rear. Check the engine mounts.**

22. Remove the guard on the clutch housing and the right support.

23. Remove the 2 lower mounting bolts on the clutch housing after removing the engine mount nuts and pushing the engine to the right. Move out the guard and clutch housing with the release lever as an assembly.

24. Disconnect the clutch assembly from the flywheel and remove it.

25. Check the flywheel, starter ring gear, pilot bearing in the flywheel, crankshaft seal, release bearing, guide sleeve, release lever, pressure plate and clutch disc for wear or damage. Replace parts as necessary.

26. Coat the guide sleeve with multipurpose grease, then apply a light coat to the spline of the drive shaft and the area of the pilot bearing/flywheel. Lubricate the release lever pivot, ball socket and needle bearings with white grease.

27. Make sure the clutch disc and flywheel are clean and free from grease, then install the clutch disc. Use a suitable clutch alignment tool to center the clutch disc and install the mounting bolts. Tighten the clutch disc bolts in a crisscross pattern evenly to 18 ft. lbs. (25 Nm).

28. Continue installation in reverse of the removal procedures. When installing the clutch housing assembly, make sure the flywheel reference bolts are facing down to avoid damage during installation. Tighten the central tube mounting bolts after the engine and transaxle mounting bolts have been tightened. Torque the clutch housing to engine bolts to 54 ft. lbs (75 Nm), the central tube flange to clutch housing bolts to 30 ft. lbs. (42 Nm), and the driveshaft to transaxle input shaft clamp bolt to 58 ft. lbs. (80 Nm).

**Checking clutch wear on 924S and 944**

### *928, 928S and 928S4*

1. Disconnect the negative battery cable.

2. Raise and support the vehicle safely.

3. Remove the lower body brace.

4. Remove the clutch slave cylinder and keep hydraulic lines attached.

5. Remove the starter and clutch housing cover as a unit and attach to the stabilizer bar with a wire. Remove the catalytic converter.

6. Remove the coupling screws and push the coupler rearward on the driveshaft.
7. Remove the release bearing sleeve bolts and move the sleeve towards the flywheel.
8. Matchmark the clutch components and loosen all pressure plate mounting bolts evenly until all the pressure is removed from the plate.
9. Remove the mounting bolts and press down on the release lever (towards the flywheel) and disconnect the release lever at the ball stud.
10. Push the complete clutch assembly rearward and move the assembly downward and out of the clutch housing.

**NOTE: The clutch assembly consists of the pressure plate, front and rear clutch discs, release lever, release bearing sleeve and short driveshaft.**

11. Installation is the reverse of removal. When installing, note that the clutch discs are different:
   a. The clutch disc with the rigid center is installed between the flywheel and the intermediate plate.
   b. The clutch disc with the spring center is installed between the intermediate plate and the pressure plate.

**NOTE: To prevent clutch drag, move the 3 stop brackets towards the pressure plate until a gap of 0.0275–0.0394 in. exists between the intermediate plate and the stop bracket.**

## FREE-PLAY ADJUSTMENT

### *1983–84 911 and 911 Turbo*

These vehicles are equipped with an auxiliary spring to reduce pedal effort. Free-play is no longer checked at the pedal. Play is checked by measuring the distance between the adjusting belt and the positioning lever. The distance should be 0.04 in. (1mm).

1. Release the cable.
2. Adjust clutch play to 0.047 in. (1.2mm).
3. Tighten the cable at the holder until play is reduced to 1mm. (0.04 in.).
4. Adjust the stop on the pedal floor plate so that the release travel is 25mm (0.984 in.) for the 911S or 27mm (1.063 in.) when the clutch pedal is depressed.

### *1985–90 911 and 911 Turbo*

A self-adjusting hydraulic clutch is installed on these vehicles. No adjustment is necessary.

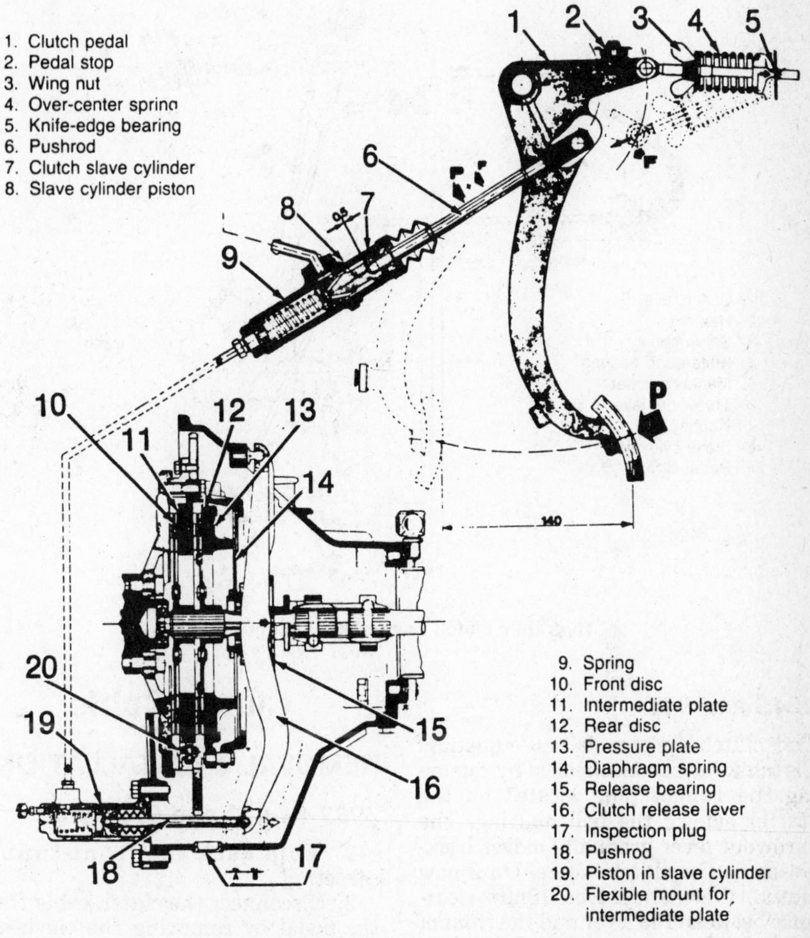


**Hydraulic clutch actuation system on the 928 and 928S. Clutch wear can be checked after removing the rubber plug (17).**

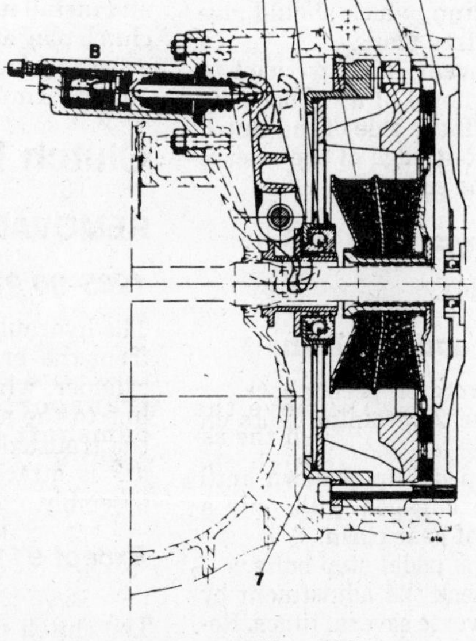


1. **Clutch lever**
2. **Release bearing**
3. **Rubber damper**
4. **Contact plate**
5. **Drive plate**
6. **Flywheel**
B. **Slave cylinder**

**Hydraulic clutch assembly—911**

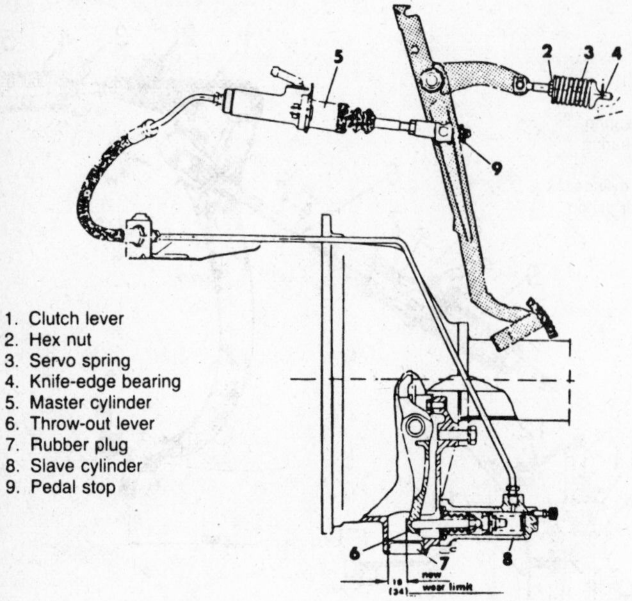


Hydraulic clutch assembly – except 911

### *924S and 944*

The clutch linkage is self-adjusting. Clutch wear can be checked by removing the rubber plug located on the starter side of the bell housing. The throwout lever gradually moves backwards as the clutch wears. On a new clutch, there should be 18mm clearance between the lever and the front of the hole. On a worn clutch the replace distance is 34mm.

### *1983–86 928 and 928S*

Clutch adjustment is not necessary because of the automatic adjustment of the slave cylinder. The only clearance check should be $^3/_{32}$ in. free play between the pushrod and the clutch master cylinder piston, which should give a $^3/_{16}$ in. pedal free play.

The clutch wear limit is reached when, upon removal of a rubber plug on the slave cylinder side of the clutch housing, the front edge of the release lever can just be seen.

## PEDAL TRAVEL ADJUSTMENT

### *1983–84 911 and 911 Turbo*

1. Pull the front carpeting back.
2. Loosen the 2 retaining bolts on the pedal stop.
3. Move the pedal up or down until reverse can be engaged with only a slight amount of gear clash.
4. Tighten the pedal stop bolts.
5. Double check the adjustment by shifting into reverse several times. Reinstall the floor carpeting.

# Clutch Cable

## REMOVAL & INSTALLATION

### *1983–84 911 and 911 Turbo*

1. Fold back the front tunnel carpeting.
2. Disconnect the clutch cable from the pedal by removing the clevis retaining pin.
3. Pull up the clutch cable and remove the clevis and locknut from the threaded portion of the clutch cable.
4. Remove the cable from the clutch release lever at the transaxle.
5. Pull the clutch cable out of the vehicle to the rear.
6. Lubricate the new clutch cable and install it from the rear. Check the clutch play at the adjustment bolt with a feeler gauge. If necessary, adjust to $1.0 \pm 0.1$mm with the adjusting bolt.

# Clutch Master Cylinder

## REMOVAL & INSTALLATION

### *1985–90 911 and 911 Turbo*

The hydraulic clutch receives its fluid from the brake fluid tank to master cylinder, where it passes through the line to the slave cylinder mounted on the transaxle case. The master cylinder is attached to the pedal bracket assembly.

### *Except 911 and 911 Turbo*

The clutch master cylinder is located beside the brake master cylinder in the engine compartment and shares the brake master cylinder's fluid reservoir. Access is limited and, depending on the year and options, several other components may have to be relocated before the clutch master cylinder can be removed.

1. Drain the clutch section of the fluid reservoir. Remove and plug the line leading to the clutch master cylinder from the brake master cylinder fluid reservoir.

**NOTE: Be very careful not to let any brake fluid drip onto painted surfaces, as it will permanently discolor them.**

2. From inside the vehicle, disconnect the clutch master cylinder pushrod.
3. Disconnect the fluid tube which runs to the clutch slave cylinder from the master cylinder and plug it. Before loosening the tube's fitting, wrap a rag around it so that brake fluid is not spilled.
4. Disconnect and remove the master cylinder from the vehicle.
5. Installation is the reverse of removal. Bleed the system at the slave cylinder.

# Clutch Slave Cylinder

## REMOVAL & INSTALLATION

### *1985–90 911 and 911 Turbo*

The slave cylinder is removed by disconnecting the fluid line and removing the mounting bolts, then pulling the slave cylinder out with the pushrod. When installing, lubricate the pushrod and make sure the end engages the clutch lever. Bleed the cylinder by loosening the bleeder screw above the hydraulic line connection, as described below.

### *Except 911 and 911 Turbo*

1. Drain the clutch section of the brake fluid reservoir.
2. Raise and support the vehicle safely. Locate the slave cylinder – it is at the bottom of the bell housing.
3. Disconnect the clutch fluid line form the slave cylinder.
4. Remove the retaining bolts and remove the slave cylinder.
5. Installation is the reverse of removal. Prime the cylinder with clean brake fluid before installing.

## BLEEDING THE HYDRAULIC CLUTCH SYSTEM

When the slave cylinder is installed, the system must be bled. To bleed the system, fill the clutch portion of the fluid reservoir with clean brake fluid, then attach a hose to the bleed nipple on the slave cylinder and position the other end of the hose so that it is submerged in a partially filled container of brake fluid. Have an assistant pump up the clutch pedal several times, then open the bleed nipple with a wrench. Air bubbles will appear at the side of the hose submerged in the brake fluid. When the bubbles stop (with your assistant's foot still pressing on the clutch pedal), close the bleed nipple. Have your assistant pump up the pedal again and repeat the process until no bubbles appear in the container, then close the bleed nipple and test the pedal. If the pedal feels spongy, there is probably still some air in the system. Repeat the bleeding procedure. During the bleeding process, make sure the fluid in the clutch section of the reservoir does not completely disappear or air will enter the system.

# AUTOMATIC TRANSAXLE

## REMOVAL & INSTALLATION

1. Disconnect the negative battery cable.
2. Disconnect the battery ground strap from the body.
3. Disconnect the multi-plugs in the spare tire well and pull the wires out from below.
4. Remove the upper and lower air cleaner housings. Remove the upper air guide section.
5. Disconnect the control cable on the throttle housing. Disconnect the oxyqen sensor wire on the fuse panel and pull it out from below.
6. Remove the engine air guide. Raise and safely support the vehicle.
7. Remove the complete exhaust system with all of the heat shields.
8. emove the starter and suspend it out of the way.
9. Place a suitable drain pan under the transaxle and drain the fluid. Remove the fluid reservoir.
10. Disconnect the halfshafts from the rear of the transaxle and suspend them on a piece of wire.
11. Remove the transaxle crossmember suspension mounting bolts. Support the transaxle on the stabilizer bar, using support tool 9164 or equivalent.
12. Mark the position of the toe eccentric and the rear axle crossmember for reinstallation purposes. Remove the rear axle crossmember. Remove the clamp bolt from the central tube.
13. Disconnect the selector lever cable on the transaxle lever, unscrew the cable holder and sleeve.
14. Remove the fluid cooler and return lines. Plug the bores.
15. Pull off the vacuum modulator hose. Disconnect the pressure cable on the transaxle and pull the guide out carefully.
16. Place a universal transaxle jack or equivalent under the transaxle and tighten the retaining strap.
17. Remove the front and rear transaxle reinforcement plates. Lift the transaxle sligtly and remove the support tool from the stabilizer.
18. Lower transaxle far enough to so that central tube mounting bolts and control cable bolt can be removed.
19. After removing the central tube-to-transaxle bolts, reposition the central tube in the installed position and loosely install the mounting plate. Place a block of wood under the central tube to keep it in position.
20. Slowly lower the transaxle assembly, pulling back on it as it comes out. Remove the transaxle from under the vehicle.
21. Before installation, coat the splines of the central shaft with and appropriate lubricant.
22. With the transaxle on a suitable lifting device, slowly raise it into an installed position under the vehicle. While raising it slide it onto the central shaft.
23. Install and lightly tighten the central shaft bolts. Lift the transaxle slightly and remove the block of wood and the support from the central shaft.
24. Lower the transaxle slightly nd install the remaining central shaft bolts. Tighten all central shaft bolts to 87 ft. lbs. (120 Nm).
25. Mount the guide tube for the control cable on the converter housing. Tighten it to 6 ft. lbs.
26. Push the wiring harness up through the spare tire well.
27. Lift the transaxle up slightly and install the holding tool 9164 or equivalent, to the stabilizer bar.
28. Install the rear axle mount and tighten all bolts. Lift the transaxle and remove the holding tool.
29. Install the transaxle crossmember and bolts, tighten all bolts to 85 ft. lbs.
30. Adjust the transaxle suspension using the following procedure:
    a. Install the transaxle crossmember mounting bolts loosely.
    b. Lift the transaxle in the middle of the case far enough so that there is a gap between both transaxle mounts and the crossmember. Measure this gap on both sides and take up the difference with shims.
    c. Lower the transaxle and tighten the bolts to 85 ft. lbs.
    d. Check the clearance on the transaxle stops after tightening the bolts, there should be at least 1mm clearance between the case stop and the transaxle.
31. Check the selector lever adjustment and the throttle cable adjustment.
32. Reconnect the halfshafts and lower the vehicle.
33. Road test the vehicle and check all gearshift operations.

**Replace the transmission filter by removing the mounting screws at the arrows**

## PAN REMOVAL

The vehicle must be on a level surface when draining or refilling the transaxle. Operate the vehicle until the transaxle reaches normal operating temperature before servicing the pan and filter. Be careful, the fluid will be hot.

1. Raise and support the vehicle safely. Remove the oil drain plug in the transaxle oil pan and let the fluid drain into a suitable container.
2. Turn the crankshaft until the torque converter drain plug can be seen and removed from below, then remove the plug and drain the torque converter.
3. Remove the transaxle oil pan bolts and lower the oil pan.
4. Remove the mounting screws and lower the transaxle filter. Install the new filter.
5. Install the transaxle oil pan with a new gasket and tighten the mounting bolts to 6 ft. lbs. (8 Nm).
6. Refill the transaxle with fluid after installing the drain plugs with new seals in the pan and torque converter and tightening them to 10 ft. lbs. (14 Nm). Add approximately 6 qts. of fluid, then start the engine and allow it to idle with the shift selector in **P**. Apply the brakes and shift the transaxle through all the gears, stopping momentarily at each gear selector position. Recheck the fluid level and top off if necessary.

### SHIFT LINKAGE ADJUSTMENT

1. Raise and support the vehicle safely.
2. Move the selector lever into the **P** position.
3. Loosen the clamping bolt at the transaxle lever.
4. Pull the transaxle lever against the stop.
5. Tighten the clamping bolt with the lever in this position.

**NOTE: When tightening the clamping bolt, make sure that the cable does not twist and that the transaxle lever does not bend. The in-vehicle selector lever must not touch the selector gate in either the P or the 1 positions.**

6. Apply the brakes while running the engine at idle and move the selector lever form **P** to **R**, then from **N** to **D**. In each case the gear should engage within a second after the selector is moved. The clearance between the selector and the front of the selector gate in **P** should be the same as the clearance between the selector and the back of the gate in 1st gear.

### NEUTRAL SAFETY SWITCH ADJUSTMENT

The neutral safety switch prevents the engine from being started in any position except **P** and **N**. To test it, set the parking brake firmly and apply the brakes, then position the gear selector lever in every position of its quadrant and attempt to start the engine. If the engine starts in any position besides **P** or **N**, the neutral safety switch is out of adjustment. To adjust it, remove the selector gate for the selector lever, loosen the neutral safety switch mounting bolts and adjust its position, then retighten the bolts and repeat the test.

On the 928, the neutral safety switch is mounted on the side of the transaxle. To adjust it, first loosen the switch mounting bolts, then insert a locating pin made from 4mm diameter welding wire, or similar 4mm bar stock, through the lug and into the locating bore in the switch housing. Tighten the mounting bolts to 7 ft. lbs. (10 Nm) and remove the locating pin.

### THROTTLE CABLE AND TRANSAXLE CABLE ADJUSTMENTS

1. Screw in the cable sleeve mounting nut on the transaxle bracket completely and tighten.
2. Loosen the bolts on the roller holder bracket, push the roller holder in its slot forward (as seen from the driving direction) as far as possible and tighten the bolts.
3. Completely loosen the short cable at the firewall and the long cable on the roller holder.
4. Turn the roller so that the operating lever faces forward at an angle of 29 degrees; in this position the opening for the cable locator will face the reinforcement rib of the holder.
5. Hold the roller in this position and mount the throttle valve pushrod without tension on the rod.
6. Place the cable around the roller in the correct position and adjust the long cable sleeve until the cable locator just rests in the opening without tension.
7. Adjust the cable going to the accelerator pedal so that it does not have tension at the adjuster.

When the cable has been adjusted correctly, the accelerator peal will be in its neutral position (11 degrees 30 minutes inclination from the pedal stop), the throttle valve will be closed and the lever on the transaxle will be on its bottom stop.

8. To check the full throttle position adjustment, depress the accelerator pedal to the first noticable pressure point and check whether the throttle valve is fully open.
9. To check the kickdown adjustment, depress the pedal past the full throttle pressure point until it comes against its stop and check to make sure the roller has lifted off the operating lever by about ¼ in. In this position the lever on the transaxle should be resting on the final stop or at most about 1 degree away.

# DRIVE AXLE

## Halfshaft

### REMOVAL & INSTALLATION

#### *911 and 911 Turbo*

1. Raise the vehicle and support it safely.
2. Remove the wheels. Remove the brake caliper and disc.
3. Raise the trailing arm with a hydraulic jack.
4. Remove the lower shock absorber mounting.
5. Install a fixture similar to Porsche tool P36b to hold the hub.
6. Remove the cotter pin and, using a long ratchet handle extension, remove the hub nut.

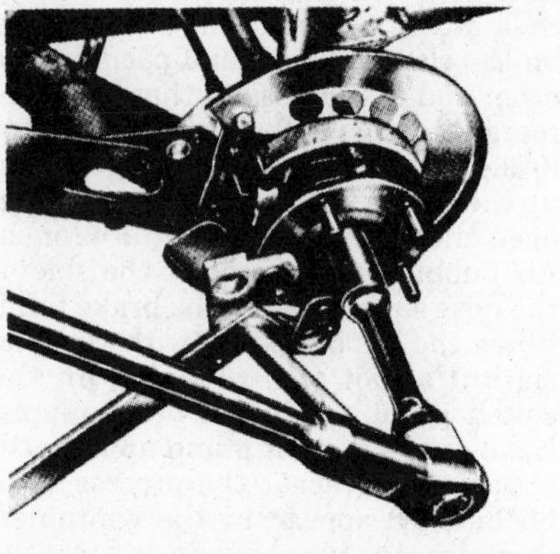

Hub nut removal (Porsche tool P36b shown)

7. Remove the Allen bolts at the axle driveshaft/transaxle flange.
8. Use a flat chisel to pry the flanges apart. Don't damage the flanges when separating them.
9. Check the axle driveshaft joints for excessive play and replace them if necessary.
10. Use a new gasket on the transaxle flange. Ensure that the flanges are clean and free from burrs.
11. Pack the joints with a moly type grease.
12. Install the axle driveshaft using a reverse of the removal procedure.
13. Tighten the flange bolts to 60 ft. lbs. (81.5 Nm). The hollow side of the lock washer should face the spacer slot.
14. Using a long extension handle wrench, tighten the castellated nut to 217–253 ft. lbs. (295–344 Nm) and install a new cotter pin.
15. Tighten the shock absorber bolt to 54 ft. lbs. (73 Nm).
16. Install the brake caliper and disc.
17. Install the wheels and lower the vehicle.

#### *Except 911 and 911 Turbo*

1. Raise the vehicle and support it safely.
2. Remove the 6 star bolts on the inside joint at the transaxle.
3. Remove the 6 bolts at the stub axle. Use a wide, flat bladed prybar to pry the flanges apart.
4. Drop the axle driveshaft down and out on the 924 and 944. On the 928, remove the axle from the upper left side of the hub assembly.
5. Pack the constant velocity joints with grease before installation.
6. Installation is the reverse of removal. Tighten the bolts to 30 ft. lbs. (41 Nm).

## CV-JOINT OVERHAUL

**For all CV-joint overhaul procedures, please refer to "CV-Joint Overhaul" in the Unit Repair section.**

# FRONT SUSPENSION

## Shock Absorbers

### REMOVAL & INSTALLATION

***911 and 911 Turbo***

1. Raise the vehicle and support it safely. Remove the wheels.
2. Remove the brake line from the clip on the suspension strut. A small amount of brake fluid will run out of the line, plug it so that dirt cannot enter the system.
3. Unscrew the retaining bolts and remove the caliper.
4. Using a soft mallet, tap the hub cap to loosen it.
5. Pry the hubcap off with a small prybar.
6. Loosen the Allen screw in the wheel bearing clamp. Unscrew the clamp nut and remove the nut and washer.
7. Remove the wheel hub along with the brake disc and wheel bearing.
8. Remove the backing plate retaining bolts and remove the plate.
9. Withdraw the cotter pin from the castellated nut on the tie rod end and remove the nut. Using a suitable puller, remove the tie rod joint from the strut.
10. Remove the control arm-to-strut ball joint retaining bolt and pull the ball joint out of the strut by pulling down on the lower control arm.

**NOTE: The torsion bar adjusting screw will have to be loosened and the adjusting arm removed.**

11. Remove the keeper for the nut on the top of the strut. Unscrew the nut and remove it, the keeper plate, and washer.
12. Remove the strut from the bottom. It will be necessary to loosen and pull the side of the luggage compartment out for clearance.
13. Check the shock absorber strut for excessive free travel and leaking. Replace the shock absorber if it is at all suspect.
14. Install the strut in a reverse order of the removal.
15. Tighten the top nut to 58 ft. lbs.

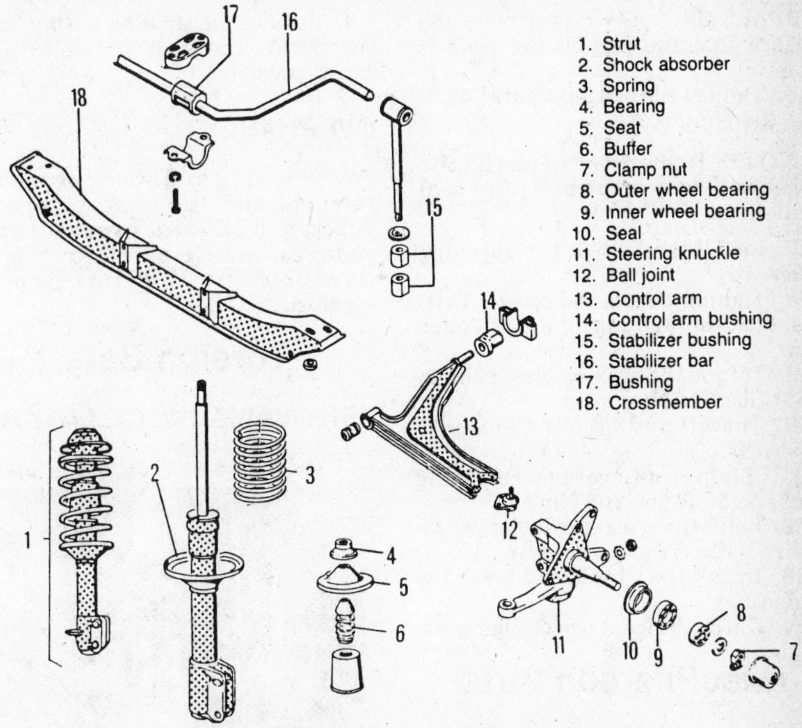

1. Strut
2. Shock absorber
3. Spring
4. Bearing
5. Seat
6. Buffer
7. Clamp nut
8. Outer wheel bearing
9. Inner wheel bearing
10. Seal
11. Steering knuckle
12. Ball joint
13. Control arm
14. Control arm bushing
15. Stabilizer bushing
16. Stabilizer bar
17. Bushing
18. Crossmember

**Typical front suspension and related components**

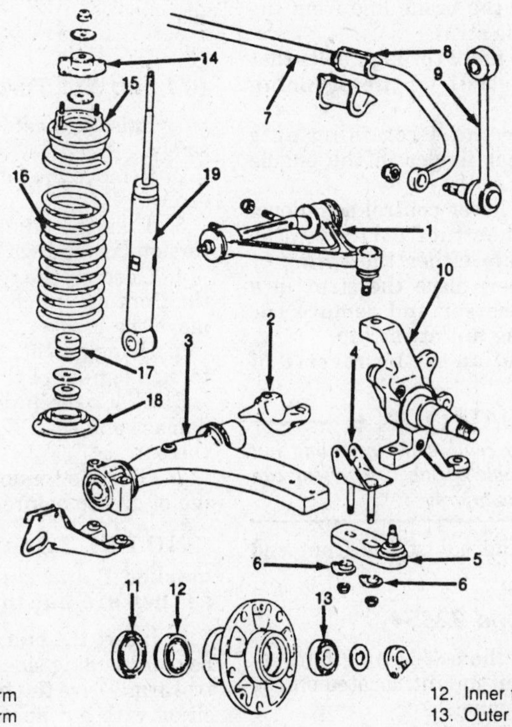

1. Upper control arm
2. Lower control arm support
3. Lower control arm
4. Lower shock mount
5. Lower ball joint
6. Caster eccentric (outer), camber eccentric (inner)
7. Stabilizer bar
8. Bushing
9. Link
10. Steering knuckle
11. Inner front wheel seal
12. Inner front wheel bearing
13. Outer front wheel bearing
14. Upper shock mount
15. Upper spring seat
16. Spring
17. Suspension stop
18. Lower spring seat
19. Shock absorber

**Exploded view of the 928 and 928S front suspension**

(79 Nm). Use a new keeper plate and ensure that the peg on the plate is pointing up.

16. Tighten the ball joint nut to 47 ft. lbs. (64 Nm).

**NOTE: Remember to install the washer between the ball joint seal and strut.**

17. Install the torsion bar adjusting lever.
18. Tighten the tie rod nut to 33 ft. lbs. (45 Nm) and install a new cotter pin.
19. Torque the backing plate bolts to 18 ft. lbs. (24 Nm).
20. Install and adjust the wheel bearings.
21. Tighten the caliper retaining bolts to 50 ft. lbs. (68 Nm).
22. Refill the master cylinder, as required. Bleed the brakes.
23. Install the wheels and lower the vehicle.
24. Check the front wheel alignment.

## MacPherson Strut

### REMOVAL & INSTALLATION

#### *924, 924S and 944*

1. Raise the vehicle and support it safely.
2. Remove the brake line from the bracket on the strut.
3. Remove the 2 through bolts that retain the strut to the steering knuckle.
4. Remove the 4 retaining nuts from the inner fender in the engine compartment.
5. Pry the lower control arm down and remove the strut from the vehicle.
6. To replace either the spring or shock absorber, place the strut in a spring compressor and remove the large retaining nut at the top.
7. Installation is the reverse of removal.

**CAUTION**

***Any attempt to remove the retaining nut without a suitable spring compressor can result in serious injury.***

8. Check and adjust the front end alignment.

#### *928, 928S and 928S4*

1. Remove the self-locking nuts on the upper strut mount, located on the inner fender panel.
2. Raise and support the vehicle safely. Remove the front wheel. Remove the flange locknut and press the upper ball joint from the spindle carrier.
3. Remove the inner pivot shaft nuts from the upper control arm.
4. Remove the strut mounting bolts and remove the strut and upper arm as an assembly.

### OVERHAUL

**For all spring and shock absorber removal and installation procedures, and all strut overhaul procedures, please refer to "Strut Overhaul" in the Unit Repair section.**

## Torsion Bars

### REMOVAL & INSTALLATION

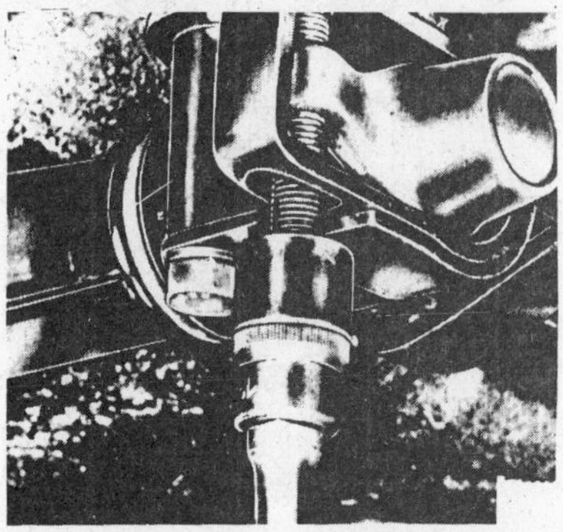

**Torsion bar adjusting screw on 911 models**

#### *911 and 911 Turbo*

1. Raise the vehicle and support it safely.
2. Remove the torsion bar adjusting screw.
3. Take the adjusting lever off the torsion bar and withdraw the seal.
4. Unscrew the retaining bolts from the front mount cover bracket and remove the bracket.
5. Using a drift, carefully drive the torsion bar out of the front of the arm.
6. Check the torsion bar for spline damage and rust. If necessary, replace the bar.
7. Give the torsion bar a light coating of grease before installing it.

**NOTE: Torsion bars are marked L and R to identify them as they are not interchangeable.**

8. Insert the end cap of the torsion bar, protruding side out, into the control arm. Drive the torsion bar into position with a drift. Carefully.
9. Tighten the retaining bolts on the front mount to 34 ft. lbs. (46 Nm).
10. Slide the seal onto the torsion bar from the open side of the crossmember.
11. Using a tire iron, or other suitable lever, pry the control arm down as far as possible. While holding the control arm, slide the adjusting lever onto the splines of the torsion bar. There should only be a slight amount of clearance at the lever adjusting point.
12. Grease the adjusting screw threads with a moly grease and hand tighten the screw.
13. Check that the end cap is properly seated in the control arm.
14. Install the rubber mount cover bracket. Tighten the retaining bolts to 34 ft. lbs. (46 Nm).
15. Lower the vehicle.
16. Check the front wheel alignment.

## Stabilizer Bar

### REMOVAL & INSTALLATION

#### *911 and 911 Turbo*

1. Raise and support the vehicle safely.
2. Loosen the stabilizer clamp bolts and pry the lever ends off their mounts.
3. Remove the stabilizer bar along with the levers.
4. Check the rubber bushings for deterioration and, if necessary, replace them. Lubricate the bushings with glycerine or some other rubber preservative. Do not use oil or grease for lubrication.
5. Install the stabilizer bar in a reverse order of the removal.
6. The square end of the stabilizer should protrude slightly above the clamp. Tighten the clamp nuts to 18 ft. lbs. (24 Nm).

## Ball Joint

### INSPECTION

With the front wheels in the straight-ahead position, insert a suitable prybar between the control arm and wheel rim. Insert a vernier caliper between the upper edge of the control arm and lower edge of the steering knuckle mounting bolt and measure the distance. Press down on the prybar to lever out the play, then check the distance again with the caliper. The wear limit is 1.5mm.

### REMOVAL & INSTALLATION

#### *911 and 911 Turbo*

1. Raise the vehicle and support it safely. Remove the wheels.
2. Remove the brake line from the clip on the suspension strut. A small amount of brake fluid will run out of the line, plug it so that dirt cannot enter the system.
3. Unscrew the retaining bolts and

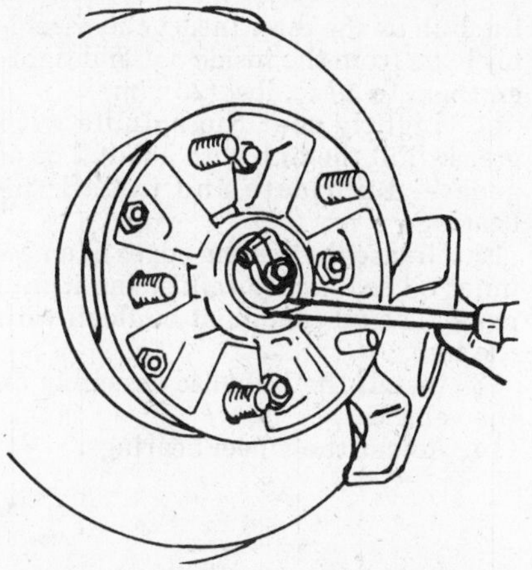

Checking wheel bearing play on 911 models

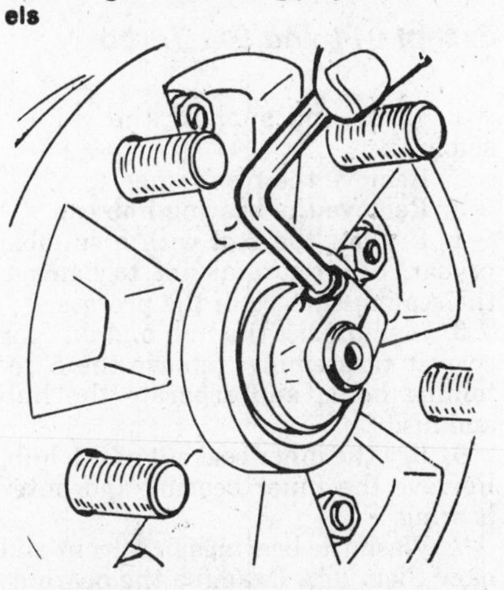

Final tightening of the wheel clamp nut on 911 models. Check the play again before installing the hub cap

remove the caliper.

4. Using a soft mallet, tap the hub cap to loosen it.
5. Pry the hubcap off with a small prybar.
6. Loosen the Allen screw in the wheel bearing clamp. Unscrew the clamp nut and remove the nut and washer.
7. Remove the wheel hub along with the brake disc and wheel bearing.
8. Remove the backing plate retaining bolts and remove the plate.
9. Withdraw the cotter pin from the castellated nut on the tie rod end and remove the nut. Using a suitable puller, remove the tie rod joint from the strut.
10. Remove the control arm-to-strut ball joint retaining bolt and pull the ball joint out of the strut by pulling down on the lower control arm.

**NOTE: The torsion bar adjusting screw will have to be loosened and the adjusting arm removed.**

11. Installation is the reverse of the removal procedure.

### *924S and 944*

1. Raise and support the vehicle safely. Remove the lower control arm.
2. Drill out the the rivets retaining the ball joint to the control arm.
3. Install the replacement ball joint using the bolts and nuts supplied in the kit.
4. Reinstall the control arm and align the front wheels.

### *928, 928S and 928S4*

**NOTE: The front wheels must be realigned after the suspension work is done.**

The upper ball joint is replaced as a unit with the upper arm assembly. Refer to the "Strut Removal and Installation" procedure. The lower ball joint may be replaced by removing the nut from the ball joint stud and pressing the stud from the spindle. The alignment eccentric bolts are removable and the ball joint can be removed from the lower arm assembly.

# Upper Control Arms

## REMOVAL & INSTALLATION

### *928, 928S and 928S4*

The upper control arm can be removed after first removing the MacPherson Strut assembly and disconnecting the ball joint from the steering knuckle. See the "MacPherson Strut Removal & Installation" procedures. When installing, tighten the upper control arm-to-body nuts to 101 ft. lbs. (140 Nm) and the upper control arm-to-steering knuckle nut to 47 ft. lbs. (65 Nm).

# Lower Control Arm

## REMOVAL & INSTALLATION

### *924S and 944*

1. Raise the vehicle and support it safely.
2. Remove the bolts at the front that retain the control arm to the suspension crossmember.
3. Detach the stabilizer bar from the control arm.
4. Remove the 2 bolts that retain the control arm bracket at the rear.
5. Remove the ball joint pinch bolt at the steering knuckle.
6. Pry the control arm down and remove it from the vehicle.
7. Installation is the reverse of removal. Caster must be reset after the control arm has been removed.

### *928, 928S and 928S4*

**NOTE: The front wheels must be aligned upon completion of the installation.**

1. Raise and support the vehicle safely, then remove the wheel.
2. Mark the alignment eccentrics on the lower arm for approximate installation location, if the ball joint is to be removed.
3. Remove the strut bottom link bracket and stabilizer link bolt.
4. Remove the lower ball joint stud nut and press the stud from the spindle. Move the spindle and upper arm upward and block it to gain working clearance.
5. Remove the bolts from the tie-down bracket and control arm bracket. Lower the control arm from the vehicle.
6. The lower ball joint can be replaced, if necessary, while the lower arm is out of the vehicle.
7. Installation is the reverse of removal.

# Front Wheel Bearings

## ADJUSTMENT

### *911 and 911 Turbo*

Check and adjust the front wheel bearings after the vehicle has not been run for a few hours. The bearings will be cold then. The front wheel bearings are correctly adjusted when the thrust washer can be moved slightly sideways under light pressure from a small prybar, but no bearing play is evident when the wheel hub is shaken axially.

1. Raise the vehicle and support it safely. Remove the wheels. Turn the hub several times to seat the bearings.
2. Pry the hub cap off and perform the above check Don't press the prybar against the hub. Hold it lightly in your hand so you get a better feel.
3. If the bearings require an adjustment, loosen the Allen screw and turn the clamp nut in or out as necessary.
4. Tighten the clamp nut Allen screw to 11 ft. lbs. (15 Nm) without altering the adjusted position of the clamp nut.
5. Double check the adjustment and readjust, if necessary.
6. Give the clamp nut and thrust washer a light coating of lithium grease. Tap the hub cap into place with a plastic or rubber mallet.
7. Install the wheels and lower the vehicle.

### *Except 911 and 911 Turbo*

The front wheel bearings are correctly adjusted when the thrust washer can be moved slightly sideways under light

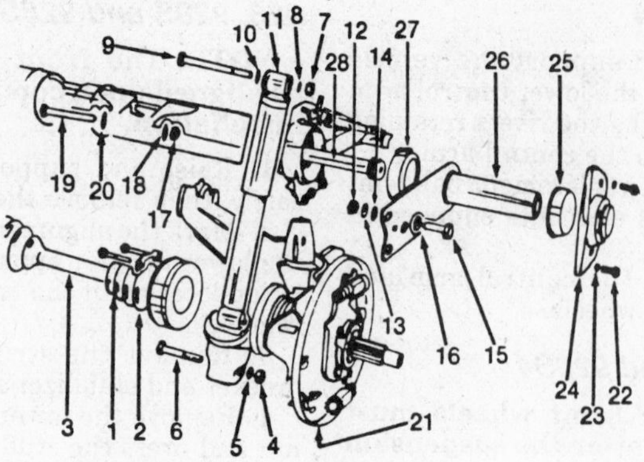


1. Allen head bolt
2. Plate
3. Axle shaft
4. Nut
5. Lockwasher
6. Bolt
7. Nut
8. Lockwasher
9. Bolt
10. Washer
11. Shock absorber
12. Nut
13. Washer
14. Plain washer
15. Bolt
16. Plain washer
17. Nut, self-locking
18. Plain washer
19. Bolt
20. Plain washer
21. Trailing arm
22. Bolt
23. Lockwasher
24. Cover
25. Rubber mount, outer
26. Torsion plate
27. Rubber mount, inner
28. Torsion bar

**Typical rear suspension and related components**

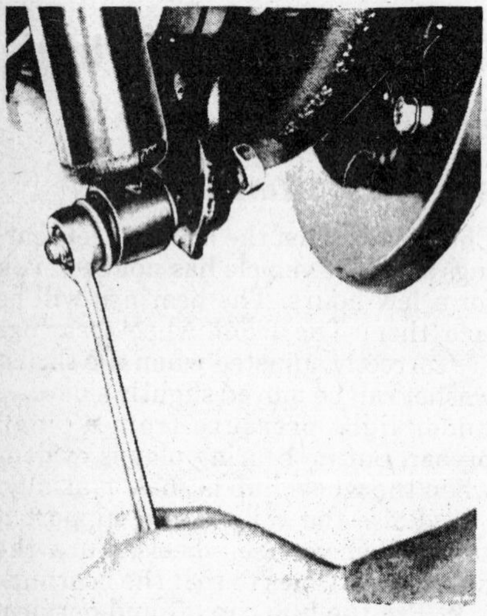

**Bottom rear shock absorber mount on 911 models**

pressure, but no bearing play is evident when the wheel hub is shaken axially.

1. Raise the vehicle and support it safely. Remove the tire and wheel assemblies.
2. Pry the hub cap off and perform the above check. Don't press against the hub.
3. If the bearings require an adjustment, loosen the Allen screw and turn the clamp nut. Proper adjustment is achieved when the flat washer can just be moved by finger pressure on a suitable tool.
4. Tighten the clamp nut Allen screw to 11 ft. lbs. (15 Nm) without altering the adjusted position of the clamp nut.

## REMOVAL & INSTALLATION

### *911 and 911 Turbo*

**NOTE: The inner bearing, seal, and outer bearing may be removed and lubricated once the hub/disc assembly is removed from the vehicle. If after cleaning, the bearings are noticeably worn or damaged they should be replaced along with their races. If the bearings are satisfactory, skip the race removal steps.**

1. Remove the brake disc/hub assembly.
2. Matchmark the hub and disc for correct reassembly, remove the 5 retaining bolts, and separate the hub and disc.
3. Pry the inner seal out of the hub. Remove the inner bearing and outer bearing.
4. Wash the bearings in solvent and blow them dry. Examine the bearings for pitting, scoring, or other damage. Replace the bearing and race as a unit if there is any question as to their condition.
5. Heat the wheel hub to 250–300°F.
6. Press the inner bearing race out of the hub on a press table, using suitable spacers to prevent damaging the hub.
7. Press out the outer bearing race, using suitable spacers and a support the assembly.
8. Press a new inner bearing race into the hub and then press in a new outer bearing race.
9. Pack the bearings with a lithium multipurpose grease.
10. Align the matchmarks and install the hub in the disc. Insert the assembly bolts from the inside out and tighten them to 17 ft. lbs. (23 Nm).
11. Lightly coat the spindle with grease. Fill the hub with about 2 oz of grease. Lubricate and install the bearings.
12. Grease the sealing edges of a new inner oil seal and carefully tap it into place. The oil seal must be flush with the hub.
13. Install the hub/disc assembly on the vehicle.
14. Adjust the wheel bearings.

### *Except 911 and 911 Turbo*

1. Raise and support the vehicle safely.
2. Remove the front wheels.
3. Remove the bearing hub cap.
4. Pry out the seal with a suitable prybar, being careful not to damage the sealing surface in the process.
5. Matchmark the hub and disc for correct reassembly, remove the 5 retaining bolts, and separate the hub and disc.
6. Pry the inner seal out of the hub. Remove the inner bearing and outer bearing.
7. Wash the bearings in solvent and blow them dry. Examine the bearings for pitting, scoring, or other damage. Replace the bearing and race as a unit if there is any question as to their condition.
8. Heat the wheel hub to 250–300°F.
9. Press the inner bearing race out of the hub on a press table, using suitable spacers to prevent damaging the hub.
10. Press out the outer bearing race, using suitable spacers and a support.
11. Press a new inner bearing race into the hub and then press in a new outer bearing race.
12. Pack the bearings with a lithium multipurpose grease.
13. Align the matchmarks and install the hub in the disc. Insert the assembly bolts from the inside out and tighten them to 7 ft. lbs. (10 Nm).
14. Lightly coat the spindle with grease. Fill the hub with about 2 oz of grease. Lubricate and install the bearings.
15. Grease the sealing edges of a new inner oil seal and carefully tap it into place. The oil seal must be flush with the hub.
16. Install the hub/disc assembly on the vehicle.
17. Adjust the wheel bearings.

## Front Wheel Alignment

### CAMBER ADJUSTMENT

#### *911 and 911 Turbo*

Camber is adjusted at the top of the strut. Pull back the luggage compartment rug to expose the 3 mounting bolts. Scrape the undercoating from the bolts and plates. Scribe the positions of the 2 plates under the bolts. Loosen the bolts and move the strut in or out as necessary to correct the camber angle.

#### *924S and 944*

Camber is adjusted at the upper strut-to steering knuckle retaining bolt.

#### *928, 928S and 928S4*

Camber is adjusted by turning the cam bolts on the inner arm bushings.

### CASTER ADJUSTMENT

#### *911 and 911 Turbo*

Caster is adjusted in the same manner as camber, except that the strut is moved forward or backward to change the caster angle.

#### *Except 911 and 911 Turbo*

Caster is adjusted by loosening the 2 control arm-to-crossmember bolts and moving the control arm laterally. 1983–88 928 vehicles have the slots for adjusting the caster eccentrics sealed with an elastic sealing compound. This compound must be removed to make camber adjustment, then replace after adjustment to prevent the entry of dirt which could make adjusting difficult.

### TOE-IN ADJUSTMENT

#### *911 and 911 Turbo*

Toe-in is set with the front wheels straight ahead. Tie rod length is adjusted by loosening the tie rod clamps and moving them an equal amount in or out to obtain the correct toe-in.

#### *924S and 944*

Toe-in is set by loosening the locknuts on the tie rod ends and turning them in or out as necessary.

#### *928 and 928S*

Toe-in adjustments are made by turning cam bolts, located at the rear of the front control arms.

**Caster and camber adjustment locations on 911 models**

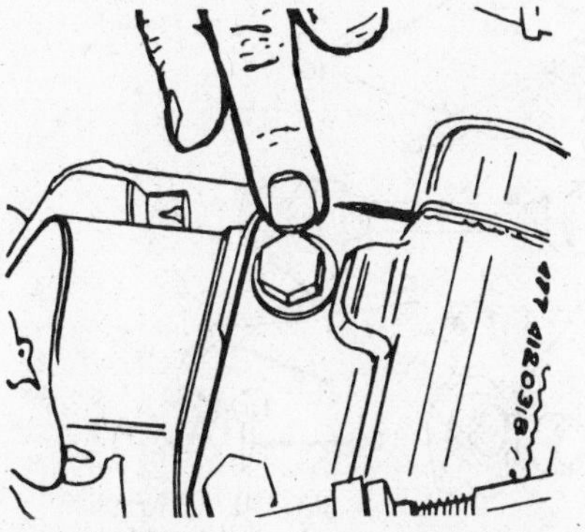

**On 944 camber is adjusted at the upper strut eccentric**

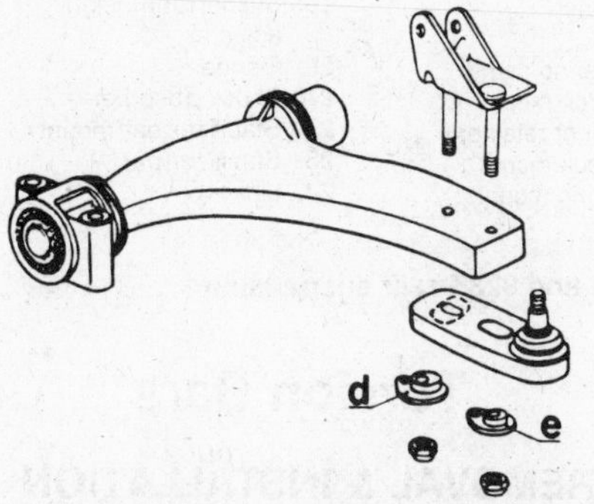


**Front suspension caster (e) and camber (d) adjustment eccentrics on the 928 and 928S**

**On 944 caster is adjusted at the lower control arm mounting**

# REAR SUSPENSION

## Shock Absorbers

### REMOVAL & INSTALLATION

#### *911 and 911 Turbo*

1. Open the engine compartment lid and remove the rubber cover from the top of the shock absorber.
2. Raise and support the vehicle safely.
3. Hold the shock absorber shaft and remove the nut.
4. On the bottom, remove the retaining nut and bolt.
5. Remove the shock absorber.
6. If the shock exhibits excessive free travel or is leaking, replace it.
7. Install the shock up through the body and screw the nut on hand-tight.
8. Align the shock absorber eye with the hole in the trailing arm and install the nut and bolt.
9. Tighten the top nut and install the rubber cover.
10. Tighten the bottom retaining bolt to 54 ft. lbs. (73 Nm).

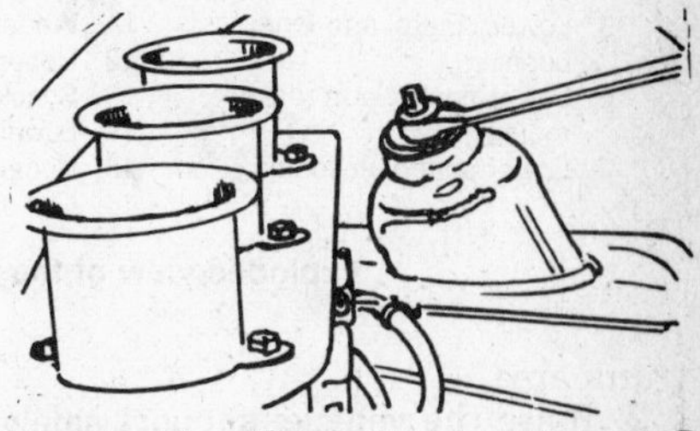

**Top rear shock absorber mount on 911 models**

#### *924S and 944*

1. This procedure is performed with the weight of the vehicle resting on the rear wheels. Raise and support the vehicle safely.
2. Remove the bottom shock retaining bolt and nut.
3. Remove the top bolt.
4. Remove the shock absorber.
5. Install the replacement shock in the reverse order of removal. Tighten the retaining bolts to 50 ft. lbs. (68 Nm).

## MacPherson Struts

### REMOVAL & INSTALLATION

#### *928, 928S and 928S4*

1. Remove the locking nuts form the spring strut, located within the

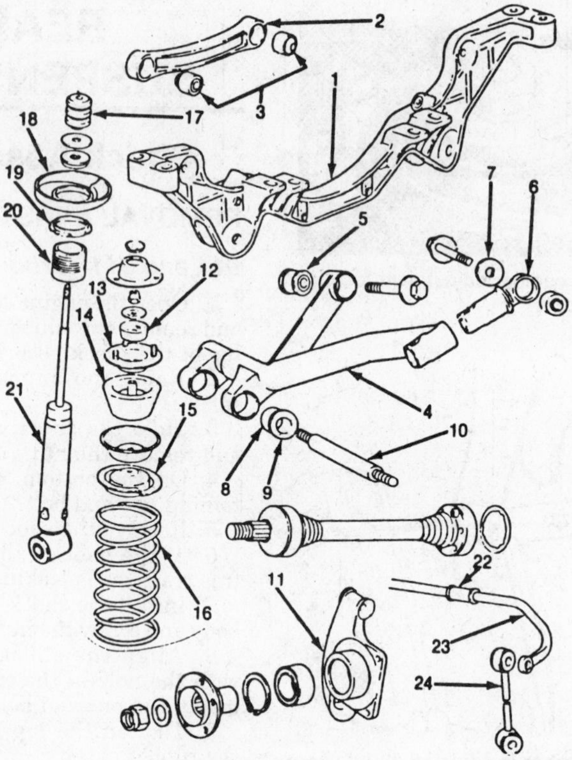


1. Rear axle crossmember
2. Upper strut
3. Upper strut bushings
4. Lower control arm
5. Lower control arm inner bushing
6. Lower control arm rocker mount
7. Lower control eccentric
8. Lower control arm outer bushing
9. Cone washer
10. Pivot pin
11. Wheel bearing carrier
12. Upper shock mount
13. Shock mount retainer
14. Lower shock mount
15. Upper spring mount
16. Coil spring
17. Shock bumper
18. Lower spring seat
19. Suspension height adjuster
20. Flange
21. Shock absorber
22. Stabilizer bar mount
23. Stabilizer bar
24. Link

**Exploded view of the 928 and 928S rear suspension**

trunk area.

2. Raise the vehicle, support safely and remove the wheel.
3. Remove the front nut on the outer pivot pin rod and remove the pivot rod from the rubber bushings.
4. Disconnect the stabilizer bar link from the lower control arm.
5. Remove the spring strut form the vehicle.
6. Installation is the reverse of removal.

**NOTE: The spring can be removed from the shock unit with the use of a spring clamping tool. An adjusting nut and sleeve is used to control the vehicle rear height.**

## OVERHAUL

**For all spring and shock absorber removal and installation procedures, and all strut overhaul procedures, please refer to "Strut Overhaul" in the Unit Repair section.**

# Torsion Bars

## REMOVAL & INSTALLATION

### *911 and 911 Turbo*

1. Raise and support the vehicle safely.
2. Remove the wheel on the side where the torsion bar is being removed.
3. Fabricate a holding fixture or obtain porsche tool P 289. The fixture is necessary to hold the trailing arm while it is raised and lowered. The special Porsche tool for this purpose is P 289.
4. Using a hydraulic jack under the holding fixture, raise the trailing arm.
5. Remove the lower shock absorber bolt.
6. Remove the trailing arm retaining bolts. Remove the toe and chamber adjusting bolts.
7. Remove the 4 retaining bolts from the trailing arm cover. Withdraw the spacer.
8. Using 2 small prybars, pry off the trailing arm cover.
9. Remove the holding fixture.
10. Knock out the round body plug and remove the trailing arm.
11. Paint a reference mark on the torsion bar support, matching the location of the Left or Right side identification letter, so that the torsion bar may be installed in the same position.

**NOTE: The torsion bars are splined to allow adjustment of the rear riding height.**

12. Remove the torsion bar. Do not scratch the protective paint on the torsion bar, or it will corrode and possible develop fatigue cracks.

**NOTE: If you are removing a broken torsion bar, the inner end can be knocked from its seat by removing the opposite torsion bar and tapping through with a steel rod. Torsion bars are not interchangeable from side-to-side and are marked Left and Right for identification.**

13. Check the torsion bar splines for damage and replace if necessary. If any corrosion is present on the bar, replace it.
14. Coat the torsion bar lightly with a multipurpose grease. Carefully grease the splines.
15. Apply glycerine or another rubber preservative to the torsion bar support.
16. Install the torsion bar, matching the Left or Right with the paint mark you made before removal.
17. Install the trailing arm cover into position and start the 3 accessible bolts.
18. Raise the trailing arm into place with the holding fixture (or special tool P 289) until the spacer and the fourth bolt can be installed.
19. Assemble the remaining components in a reverse order of their removal.
20. Tighten the trailing arm cover bolts to 34 ft. lbs. (46 Nm). Tighten the trailing arm retaining bolts to 65 ft. lbs. (88 Nm).
21. Tighten the camber adjusting bolt to 43 ft. lbs. (58 Nm) and the toe-in adjusting bolt to 36 ft. lbs. (49 Nm). Tighten the shock absorber bolt to 45 ft. lbs. (61 Nm).
22. Adjust the rear wheel camber and toe-in.

### *924S and 944*

**NOTE: This procedure requires that the rear wheel camber and toe-in be checked and adjusted as the final step.**

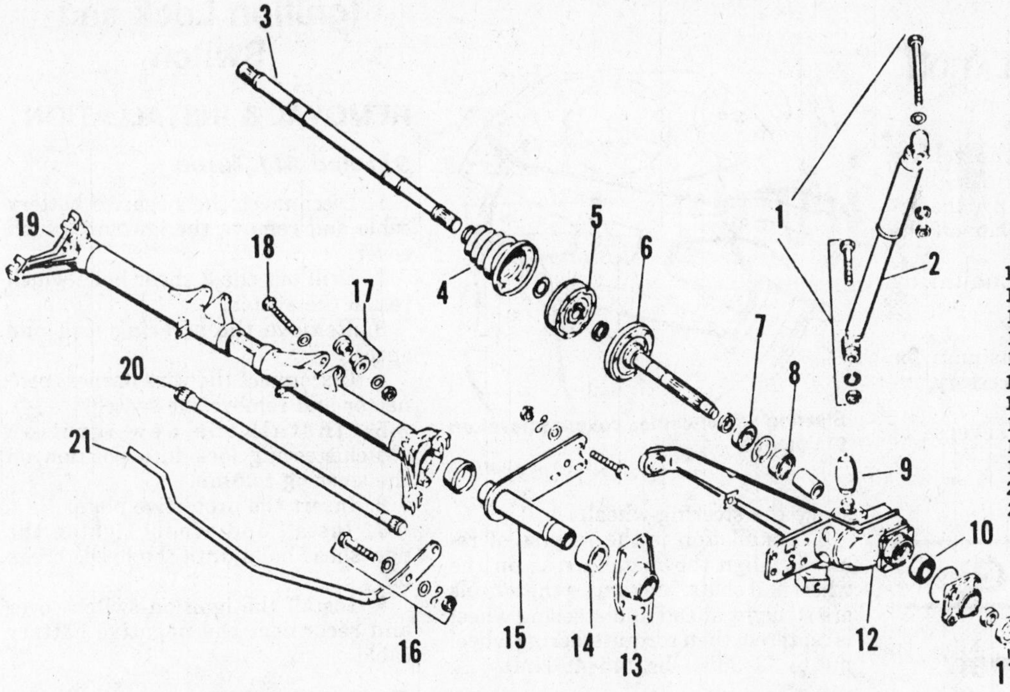


Typical rear control arm and related components

1. Raise and support the vehicle safely.
2. Remove the wheel on the side where the torsion bar is being removed.
3. Using a hydraulic jack and a block of wood with a slot cut in it, raise the trailing arm.
4. Remove the lower strut bolt.
5. Remove the trailing arm retaining bolts, then remove the toe and camber adjusting bolts.
6. Remove the 4 retaining bolts from the trailing arm cover.
7. Pry off the trailing arm cover.
8. Lower the jack.
9. Remove the round body plug and remove the trailing arm.
10. Paint a reference mark on the torsion bar support, matching the location of the Left or Right side identification letter, so that the torsion bar may be installed in the same position.

**NOTE: The torsion bars are splined to allow adjustment of the rear riding height.**

11. Remove the torsion bar. Do not scratch the protective paint on the torsion bar, or it will corrode and possibly develop fatigue cracks.

**NOTE: If you are removing a broken torsion bar, the inner end can be knocked from its seat by removing the opposite torsion bar and tapping it through with a steel bar. Torsion bars are not interchangeable from side to side and are marked Left and Right for identification.**

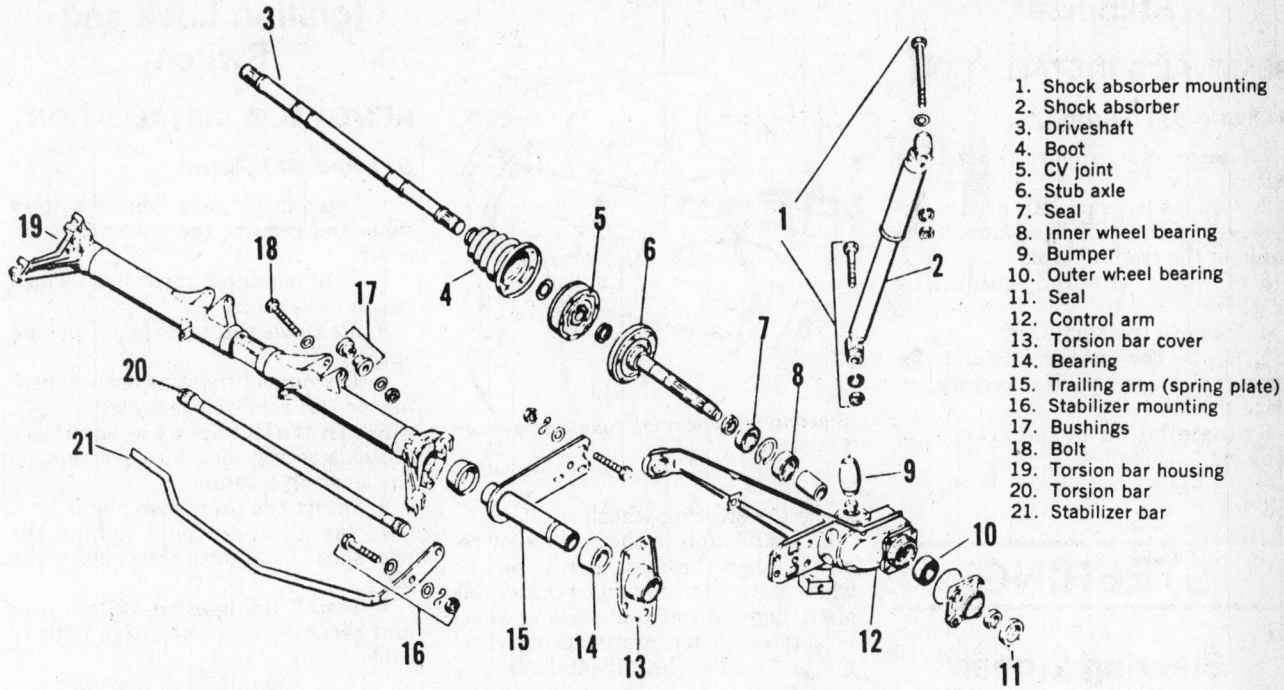

12. Check the torsion bar splines for damage and replace the bar if necessary. If there is any corrosion on the bar, replace it.
13. Coat the torsion bar lightly with grease. Carefully grease the splines.
14. apply glycerine or another rubber preservative to the torsion bar support.
15. Install the torsion bar, matching the L or R with the paint mark you made before removal.
16. Install the trailing arm cover into position and start the 3 accessible bolts.
17. Raise the trailing arm into place with a jack and wooden block until the spacer and the fourth bolt can be installed.
18. Assemble the remaining components in the reverse order of their removal.
19. tighten the trailing arm cover bolts to 25 ft. lbs. (34 Nm). Tighten the shock absorber bolt to 50 ft. lbs. (68 Nm).
20. Adjust rear wheel camber and toe in.

## Upper Control Arm

### REMOVAL & INSTALLATION

#### *928, 928S and 928S4*

1. Raise and support the vehicle safely. Remove the rear wheels and support the lower arm assembly with a jack.
2. Loosen and remove the inner and outer bolts from the upper arm ends.
3. Remove the upper arm from the rear crossmember and from the rear flexible mount. The bushings are replaceable.
4. Installation is the reverse of removal.

## Lower Control Arm

### REMOVAL & INSTALLATION

**NOTE: For rear trailing arm removal and installation procedures on the 924S and 944, refer to the "Torsion Bar Removal & Installation" procedure.**

#### *928, 928S and 928S4*

1. Raise and support the vehicle safely. Remove the rear wheels.
2. Support the hub assembly and the spring strut with a hydraulic jack.
3. Remove the outer pivot pins nuts and washers. Disconnect the stabilizer bar link.
4. Remove the inner pivot bolts from the hub assembly and the spring strut. The bushings are replaceable.
5. Installation is the reverse of removal.

## Stabilizer

### REMOVAL & INSTALLATION

#### *911 and 911 Turbo*

1. Raise and support the vehicle safely.
2. Using a large prybar, pry the upper eyes of the stabilizer bar off the studs in the trailing arm.
3. Remove the body mounting brackets.
4. Remove the stabilizer.
5. Check the rubber bushings for wear or damage and, if necessary, replace them.
6. Installation is the reverse of removal.

# STEERING

## Steering Wheel

### REMOVAL & INSTALLATION

#### *911 and 911 Turbo*

1. Disconnect the negative battery cable. Place the wheels in a straight ahead position.
2. Twist the center cover to the left and remove it.
3. Remove the horn contact pin.
4. Remove the steering wheel nut.
5. Mark the steering wheel and the shaft so that it can be reinstalled in the same position.
6. Remove the steering wheel, using the proper tool. Catch the bearing support ring and spring.
7. Install the spring and bearing support ring on the wheel hub.
8. Lightly grease the horn contact ring.
9. Install the wheel. Make sure that you align the match marks before removal.
10. Tighten the steering wheel nut to 58 ft. lbs. (79 Nm).
11. Twist the center cover back on to the right to snap it into place.

#### *Except 911 and 911 Turbo*

1. Disconnect the negative battery cable.
2. Remove horn pad and straighten the front wheels.
3. If necessary, disconnect the horn wiring. Matchmark the steering wheel to the steering shaft.
4. Remove retaining nut and washer.
5. Use a suitable steering wheel puller to remove the wheel. Do not

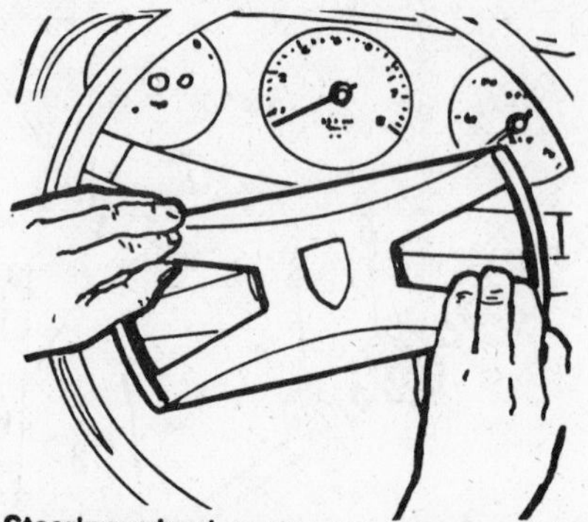

**Steering wheel center cover removal on 911 models**

strike the steering wheel.

6. Installation is the reverse of removal. Align the matchmarks on the wheel and shaft. Make sure the wheels are straight ahead and steering wheel is centered, then torque steering wheel nut to 33–36 ft. lbs. (45–49 Nm).

## Turn Signal Switch

### REMOVAL & INSTALLATION

#### *911 and 911 Turbo*

The combination turn signal, headlight dimmer, and flasher switch is located in the steering column housing. The wiper/washer switch removal and installation procedure is identical.

1. Disconnect the negative battery cable. Remove the steering wheel.
2. Reach under the instrument panel and disconnect all wiring to the switch.
3. Remove the 2 horn contact ring screws, disconnect the wire, and remove the ring.
4. Remove the 2 upper housing retaining nuts. Pull the entire assembly off the column, leading the switch wires through the hole in the housing.
5. Remove the 3 retaining screws and remove the switch.
6. Reverse the removal steps to reinstall the switch.

#### *Except 911 and 911 Turbo*

1. Disconnect the negative battery cable.
2. Remove the steering wheel.
3. Disconnect the wire harness connector at the switch.
4. Remove the 4 screws holding the switch to the steering column and remove the switch.
5. Install in reverse of the removal procedure. Do not overtighten the mounting screws.

## Ignition Lock and Switch

### REMOVAL & INSTALLATION

#### *911 and 911 Turbo*

1. Disconnect the negative battery cable and remove the ignition switch cover.
2. Drill out the 2 shear bolts which retain the switch.
3. Remove the steering lock and spacer.
4. Disconnect the wire harness connector and remove the switch.
5. Install the new ignition switch/steering lock into position on the steering column.
6. Insert the protective plate.
7. Install and evenly tighten the new shear bolts until the heads break off.
8. Install the ignition switch cover and reconnect the negative battery cable.

#### *Except 911 and 911 Turbo*

1. Disconnect the negative battery cable.
2. Remove steering wheel as previously described.
3. Drill out the casing tube shear bolts, then disconnect the wire harness connectors and pull the column and casing out of the vehicle.
4. Remove the pinch bolt holding the switch housing to the column.
5. Remove the retaining screw and pull the ignition switch from the rear of the casing.
6. Depress the lock cylinder retainer using a suitable tool and remove the lock cylinder.
7. Installation is the reverse of removal. Make sure the wheels are straight ahead and steering wheel is centered when installing. Tighten the shear bolts until the heads break off.

## Steering Gear

### REMOVAL & INSTALLATION

#### *911 and 911 Turbo*

1. Remove the front luggage compartment carpeting. Raise and support the vehicle safely.
2. Remove the auxiliary heater duct from the steering post and position it to the side.
3. Open the access door and the intermediate steering shaft cover by prying the spring clips off with a small prybar.
4. As necessary, remove the 3 heater/fuel pump retaining bolts and position the pump to the side.

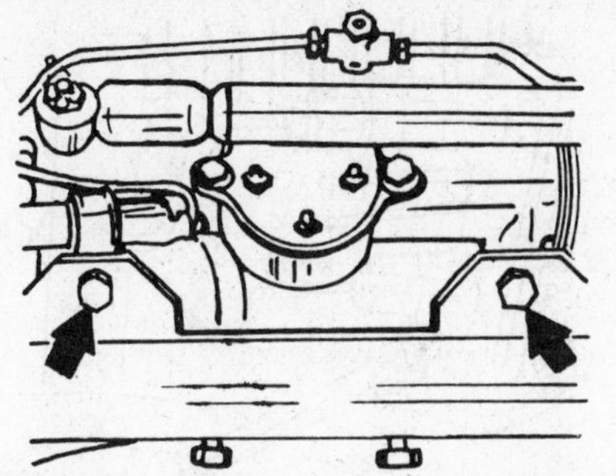

Rack and pinion retaining bolts on 911 models

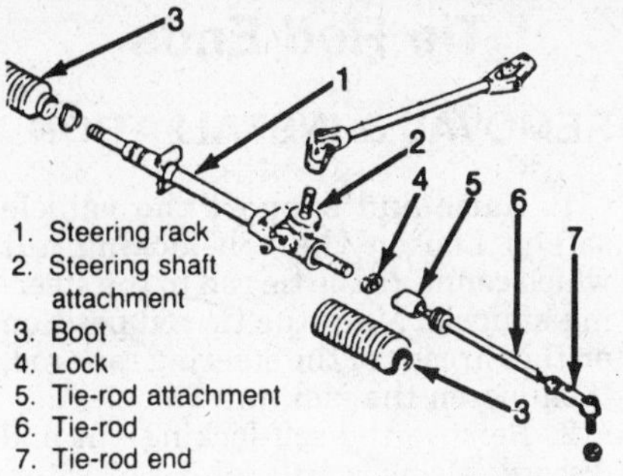


Steering rack of the 924, 924 Turbo, and 944

5. Remove the cotter pin from the lower universal joint bolt and loosen the castellated nut. Pull the universal joint off the steering shaft.
6. Remove the Allen bolts from the steering shaft bushing bracket. Remove the bracket and pull the bushing and dust cover.
7. Loosen and remove the steering coupling bolts.
8. Remove the retaining bolts and remove the bottom shield.
9. Remove the cotter pins and nuts, and then pull the tie rod ends out of the suspension struts with a suitable puller.
10. Remove the 2 rack and pinion housing retaining bolts.
11. Remove the right side crossmember brace.
12. Pull the steering assembly out the right side of the vehicle.
13. Remove the retaining bolts from the tie rod yokes.
14. Installation is the reverse of the removal procedure.
15. Tighten the yoke bolts to 34 ft. lbs. (46 Nm).
16. Make sure that the crossmember brace mounts without binding. Tighten the nuts to 47 ft. lbs. (64 Nm) and the bolts to 34 ft. lbs. (46 Nm).
17. Install the steering housing bolts with new lockwashers and tighten to 34 ft. lbs. (46 Nm).
18. Tighten the tie rod end nuts to 33 ft. lbs. (45 Nm) and install new cotter pins.
19. Tighten the steering bushing bracket Allen bolts to 18 ft. lbs. (24 Nm).
20. Install new washers on the steering coupling bolts and tighten them to 18 ft. lbs. (24 Nm).
21. Lower the vehicle.

#### *Except 911 and 911 Turbo*

1. Raise the vehicle and support it safely. Remove the front wheels and splash shield.
2. Remove the stabilizer by disconnecting the stabilizer mounts on the control arms and stabilizer suspension

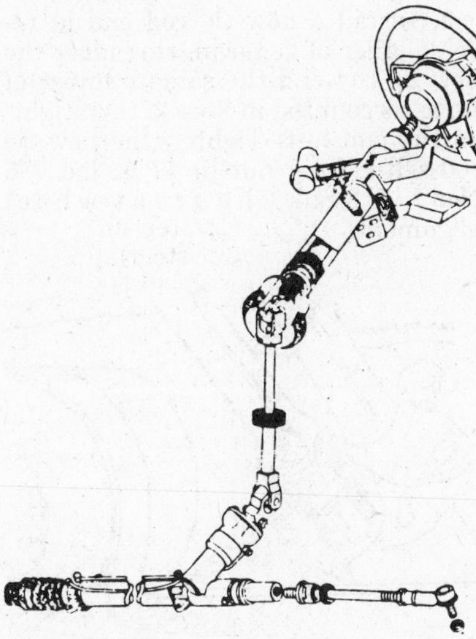

Steering column and gear used on the 928 and 928S

on the side members.
3. Disconnect the ground wire on the front axle crossmember. Remove the bolt connecting gear box to steering column driveshaft.
4. Disconnect and press out the tie rod ends from the steering knuckles. Disconnect the power steering fluid lines at the pump, if equipped, and cap the ends to prevent contamination by dirt during service.
5. Remove the 4 mounting bolts and remove the steering gear and tie rods from the vehicle.
6. Remove the tie rods from the steering gear on a workbench, if necessary.
7. To install, reverse the above. Center steering gear with Porsche special tool 9116 or equivalent. Be sure that both tie rod lengths are equal (68–68.5mm). Tighten tie rod counter nuts to 29 ft. lbs. (39 Nm) and gear box to driveshaft bolt to 23 ft. lbs. (31 Nm). If equipped with power steering, tighten the fluid line connections to 14 ft. lbs. (20 Nm) and bleed the system.

### ADJUSTMENT

Tighten adjusting screw (on front of gear box) until it just touches the washer. Hold adjusting screw tightly and tighten locknut.

## Power Steering Pump

### REMOVAL & INSTALLATION

#### *944*

1. Disconnect the negative battery cable. Remove the lower engine splash shield.
2. Disconnect the fluid lines on the power steering pump. Catch the escaping fluid in a suitable container and discard. Do not reuse power steering fluid.
3. Unscrew the connecting rod on the power steering pump and nut, then turn the connecting rod down.
4. Remove the mounting bolts from the pump housing and remove the drive belt.
5. Raise the power steering pump in its bracket and remove the spacer from below.
6. Lower the power steering pump from the vehicle.
7. Installation is the reverse of removal. Tighten the power steering pressure hose fitting at the pump to 22 ft. lbs. (30 Nm). Adjust the pump drive belt tension and bleed the power steering system.

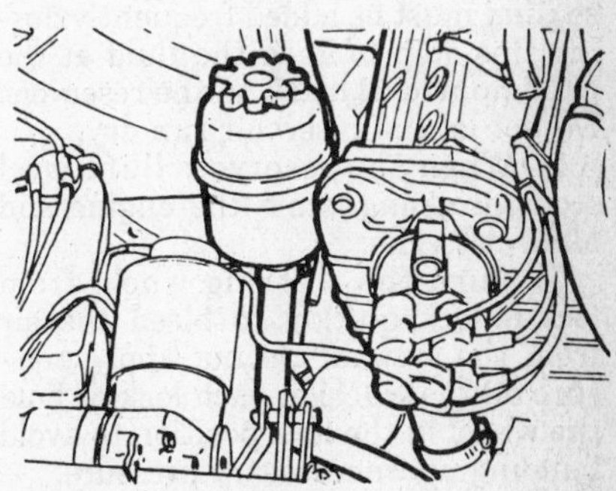

The 944 power steering reservoir is located on the inner wheel well under the hood.

#### *928 and 928S*

1. Disconnect the intake hose to the air cleaner on the left side, then drain the hydraulic fluid from the reservoir into a suitable container and discard. Do not reuse power steering fluid.
2. Remove the engine splash shield.
3. Loosen the front mounting bolts on the power steering pump slightly, then remove the rear bolt from the pump.

4. Remove the drive belt from the power steering pump pulley.

5. Remove the left upper section of the drive belt cover to facilitate removal procedures.

6. Disconnect the pressure and suction hoses from the pump. Cap the hose ends to prevent contamination by dirt during service procedure.

7. Remove the front mounting bolts and lower the power steering pump from the vehicle.

8. Installation is the reverse of removal. Make sure the power steering hoses are not routed close to the exhaust manifold, or hose failure will occur. Tighten the pump hose connections to 43 ft. lbs. (60 Nm). Adjust the drive belt tension and bleed the power steering system.

### BELT ADJUSTMENT

The power steering pump drive belt is properly adjusted if the belt can be moved about 10mm at a point midway between the pulleys.

### SYSTEM BLEEDING

1. Fill the power steering reservoir with fluid, then start and immediately stop the engine several times to allow the system to fill with fluid. The level in the reservoir will drop very quickly, so fluid must be added frequently during this step to keep the fluid at the maximum level mark on the reservoir. Do not let the reservoir run dry.

2. When the reservoir fluid level stops dropping, start the engine and allow it to idle.

3. Turn the steering wheel from lock-to-lock quickly to bleed the air from the system. Do not apply pressure on the wheel at each lock or hold the wheel in the lock position to avoid building up unnecessary pressure.

4. Watch the oil level during this procedure and keep adding oil until the level stops dropping. The fluid level should remain constant at the full mark on the reservoir tank and no air bubbles should rise in the hydraulic fluid while turning the steering wheel.

5. Stop the engine and observe the fluid level in the reservoir. It should not rise more than 10mm. If the fluid level between a running and stopped engine deviates more than 10mm, there is still air trapped in the hydraulic system. Repeat the procedure. After all air is bled from the system, recheck the fluid level in the reservoir and top off as necessary.

## Tie Rod Ends

### REMOVAL & INSTALLATION

1. Raise and support the vehicle safely. Loosen the self-locking nut which connects the tie rod to the steering knuckle. Mark the tie rod position on the threads of the steering rack rod, then loosen the jam nut.

2. Remove the self-locking nut and discard. Using a ball joint separator, remove the tie rod end from the steering knuckle. Unscrew the tie rod end from the steering rack, counting how many complete turns it takes to remove it.

3. Install a new tie rod end in reverse order of removal, threading the new tie rod end the same number of turns as counted in Step 2, then tighten the jam nut. Tighten the new tie rod self-locking nut to 47 ft. lbs. (65 Nm). Check the front wheel alignment.

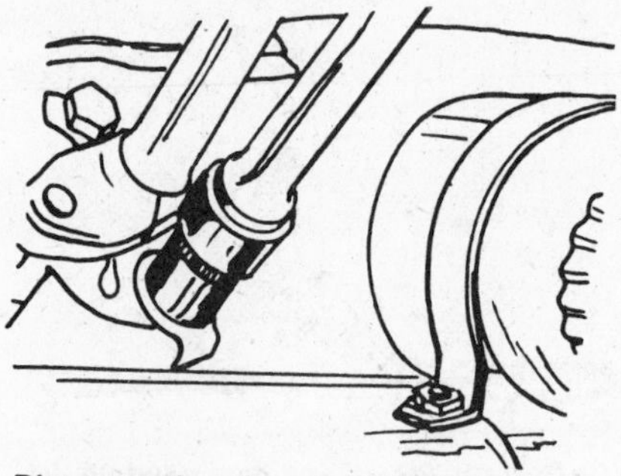

**Disconnecting the steering coupling on 911 models**

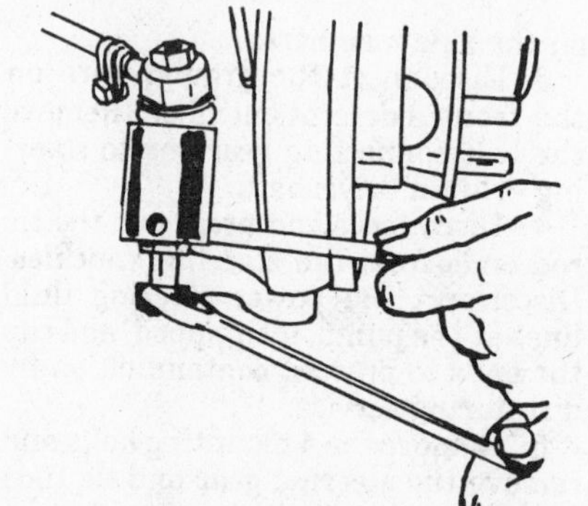

**Removing the tie-rod ends on 911 models**

## BRAKES

**For all brake system repair and service procedures not detailed below, please refer to "Brakes" in the Unit Repair section.**

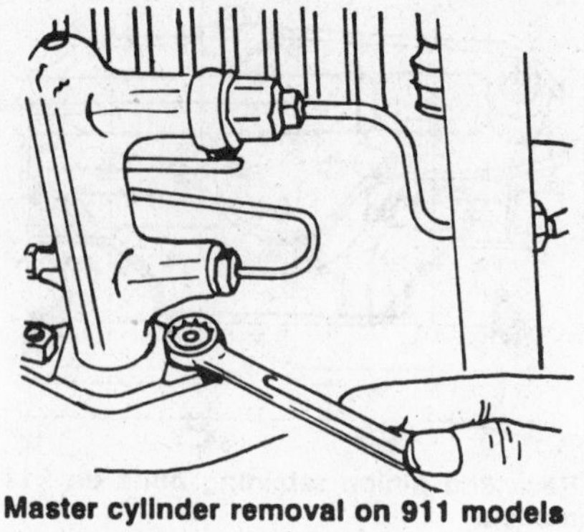

**Master cylinder removal on 911 models**

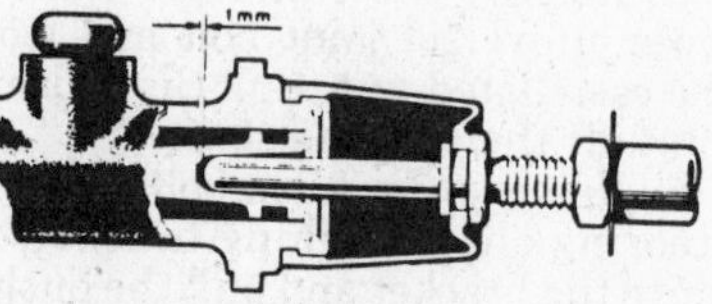

**Correct piston pushrod clearance on 911 models**

## Master Cylinder

### REMOVAL & INSTALLATION

#### *911 and 911 Turbo*

1. Disconnect the negative battery cable. Pull the accelerator back and out of its pushrod. Pull back the driver's side carpeting.

2. Unscrew the floorboard retainer(s) under the brake and clutch pedals.

3. Remove the master cylinder dust cover.

4. Raise the vehicle and support it safely.

5. Siphon and discard the brake fluid from the reservoir.

6. Unbolt the front splash shield.

7. Remove the brake lines from the master cylinder. Disconnect the brake failure warning light sending unit wire.

8. Remove the 2 master cylinder mounting nuts.

9. Disconnect the reservoir lines and remove the master cylinder.

10. Before installing the master cylinder, apply body sealer around the mounting flange.

11. Install the cylinder, making sure that the piston pushrod is correctly positioned. Torque the mounting nuts to 18 ft. lbs. (24 Nm).

12. The piston pushrod should have 0.04 in. (1mm) clearance between it and the piston. Loosen the piston rod nut and turn the rod to adjust the clearance.

13. Refill the system with new brake fluid. Bleed the brakes.

14. Tighten the splash shield large bolts to 34 ft. lbs. (46 Nm) and the smaller bolts to 18 ft. lbs. (24 Nm).
15. Test the brake failure warning light for proper operation as follows:
   a. Switch on the ignition. The handbrake warning light will go on. If it doesn't, replace the bulb.
   b. Start the engine. While you depress the brake pedal, have an assistant open a bleeder valve on 1 of the wheels to simulate a brake failure. The light should go on.
   c. When your assistant closes the valve, the light should go out.
   d. Repeat the test on the other brake circuit.

If the light fails to light during 1 of the tests, check the circuit failure sender which screws into the master cylinder.

### *Except 911 and 911 Turbo*

1. Disconnect the negative battery cable. To prevent brake fluid from spilling out and damaging the paint, place a protective cover over the fender.
2. Disconnect and plug the brake lines.
3. Disconnect the electrical plug from the sending unit for the brake failure switch.
4. Remove the 2 master cylinder mounting nuts.
5. Lift the master cylinder and reservoir out of the engine compartment being careful not to spill any fluid on the fender. Discard the brake fluid. Do not depress the brake pedal while the master cylinder is removed.
6. Position the master cylinder and reservoir assembly onto the studs for the booster and tighten the nuts to 10 ft. lbs. (13 Nm).
7. Remove the plugs and connect the brake lines.
8. Bleed the brake system.

# Power Brake Booster

## REMOVAL & INSTALLATION

### *911 and 911 Turbo*

1. Disconnect the negative battery cable. Remove the lock pin for the master cylinder operating rod.
2. Remove the mounting bolts for the brake master cylinder, located inside on the luggage compartment floor plate.
3. Siphon the fluid from the brake reservoir, being careful not to spill any brake fluid on painted surfaces. Discard the fluid.
4. Disconnect the stop light switch, vacuum hose and remove the brake fluid lines.
5. Remove the upper bolt for the brace and the nuts for the booster base.
6. Remove the brake booster and master cylinder as an assembly. The brace and operating rod do not have to be disconnected at the pedal assembly to remove the brake booster.
7. Installation is the reverse of removal. Torque the booster base nuts and master cylinder bolt to 18 ft. lbs. (25 Nm). Torque the support rod bolt to 25 ft. lbs. (35 Nm). Bleed the brake system.

### *924S and 944*

1. Disconnect the negative battery cable. Pull the brake fluid reservoir out of the master cylinder and drain the brake fluid into a suitable container. Discard the fluid and do not allow it to spill on any painted surfaces.
2. Disconnect the brake lines from the master cylinder, then remove the master cylinder.
3. Disconnect the vacuum hose to the check valve on the booster and remove the oil dipstick.
4. Carefully pry off the fuel line holding clip on the mounting bolt.
5. Remove the lockpin for the pushrod on the brake pedal.
6. Remove the mounting nuts for the brake booster/adapter assembly. The mounting nuts are accessible after disconnecting the throttle cable and pulling down the insulation sheet in the footwell.
7. Remove the brake booster from above in the engine compartment.
8. Installation is the reverse of removal. Tighten the booster and master cylinder mounting nuts to 15 ft. lbs (21 Nm). Bleed the brake system.

### *928, 928S and 928S4*

1. Remove the brake master cylinder as previously described.
2. On 1983 vehicles, remove the pressure regulator on the wheel housing.
3. Depress the brake pedal and secure the pushrod for the master cylinder with a suitable hose clamp.
4. Adjust the connector to limit the amount of protrusion of the pushrod from the booster, then depress the brake pedal again and adjust the position of the hose clamp. Remove the connector.
5. Remove the cover, then remove the brake booster mounting nuts. If applicable, remove the right front brake line from the holder and push it toward the engine carefully.
6. Route the hose for the clutch master cylinder and the wire harness connectors so they will not interfere with removal.
7. Remove the brake booster. The air cleaner lower section may have to be removed to allow clearance for the booster assembly.
8. Installation is the reverse of removal. Replace the gasket between the booster and firewall. Tighten the booster and master cylinder mounting nuts to 17 ft. lbs. (23 Nm). Bleed the brake system.

# Disc Brake Pads

## REMOVAL & INSTALLATION

1. Disconnect the negative battery cable. Raise and support the vehicle safely.
2. Remove the tire and wheel assembly.
3. Remove the caliper retaining bolts or clips. Remove the disc brake linings from their mountings.
4. Properly position the caliper to the side, do not let it hang for any extended period of time.
5. Installation is the reverse of the removal procedure.
6. On vehicles so equipped, after replacing the brake pads with power brakes the brake warning light will come on. To reset the light, disconnect the negative battery cable for 1 minute.
7. On the 944 Turbo, the silencers for the 4 piston front calipers must be replaced when new disc pads are installed.

# Parking Brake Cable

## ADJUSTMENT

### *911 and 911 Turbo*

1. Raise the vehicle and support it safely. Remove the wheels.
2. Release the handbrake lever.
3. Push the brake pads away from the disc so that it can be turned by hand.
4. Loosen the cable adjusting nuts to release tension.
5. Insert a suitable tool into the disc access hole and rotate the handbrake star wheel until the disc can no longer be turned by hand.
6. Repeat this operation on the other side.
7. Readjust the cable nuts to take up the slack.
8. Pull up the center tunnel cover and handbrake lever boot at the rear. By looking through the 2 inspection holes, see if the cable equalizer is exactly perpendicular to the vehicles centerline.
9. If the equalizer positioning is off, correct it by loosening or tightening the cable adjusting nuts. Tighten the

locknuts after the adjustment is correct.

10. Back off each brake star wheel by 4 or 5 teeth until the disc can be turned by hand.

11. Check the handbrake lever clearance. There should be a slight clearance at the lever. The handbrake should be set when the lever is pulled up.

12. After completing the handbrake adjustment, depress the brake pedal several times to reposition the rear caliper pistons. Check the fluid level in the reservoir and top it up, if necessary.

#### *Except 911 and 911 Turbo*

1. Raise the vehicle and remove the rear wheels.
2. Release the parking brake lever and move the disc brake pads so that the rotor can be easily moved.
3. Loosen the cable adjusting nuts so that no tension exists on the cable.
4. Insert a suitable tool through the hole in the brake rotor and turn the brake adjuster until the rotor cannot be moved.
5. Turn the adjuster in the opposite direction just until the rotor is free to rotate.
6. Pull the brake lever up 2 notches and adjust the cable so that the rotors can just be turned.

**NOTE: At 4 notches of the lever, the rotors should be tight and unable to turn.**

7. Release the handbrake and make sure the rotors turn freely. Install the wheels and lower the vehicle.

### REMOVAL & INSTALLATION

#### *911 and 911 Turbo*

1. Raise the vehicle and support it safely. Remove the wheels.
2. Remove the center tunnel cover and handbrake lever boot.
3. Remove the heater control knob.
4. Remove the handbrake support housing bolts.
5. Unscrew the heater control lever nut. Remove the cup spring, discs, and the lever.
6. Slightly raise the handbrake support housing. Snap off the retaining clip and pull out the cable equalizing stud.
7. Disconnect the handbrake light switch wire.
8. Remove the handbrake support housing.
9. Detach the cables from the cable equalizer.
10. Remove the rear brake calipers.
11. Remove the rear brake discs and spacer rings.
12. Remove the cotter pin, castellated nut and disc from each cable. Pull the cable toward the center of the vehicle.
13. Pull the cables out from the center tunnel in the passenger compartment.
14. Lubricate the replacement cables with multipurpose grease and then feed them into the tube.
15. Place a washer between the spacer sleeve and the brake expander. Place another washer under the castellated nut.
16. Tighten the nut until a new cotter pin can be inserted. Make sure that the brake expander is correctly seated.
17. Install the brake disc and calipers.
18. Connect the handbrake light wire to the switch.
19. Insert the heater control lever into the handbrake support housing.
20. Install and clip the equalizer stud. Ensure that the handbrake cables are correctly seated.
21. Torque the handbrake support housing bolts to 18 ft. lbs. (24 Nm).
22. Install a friction disc, the heater control lever, another friction disc, pressure disc, cup spring, and the nut.
23. Tighten the nut so that the lever doesn't slip back when the heater is on full, and yet isn't too tight to operate.
24. Bleed the brakes.
25. Check the handbrake adjustment.
26. Install the wheels and lower the vehicle.

#### *Except 911 and 911 Turbo*

The parking brake cable is attached to the handbrake lever by 2 nuts, 1 of which serves as a locknut for the adjusting nut. To remove the cable, remove both the locknut and adjusting nut and feed the cable rearward. Disconnect the parking brake cable at the rear wheels, then install the new cable and feed it back forward to the handbrake lever. Adjust the parking brake cable as previously described.

# CHASSIS ELECTRICAL

## Heater Core and Blower Assembly

### REMOVAL & INSTALLATION

#### *911 and 911 Turbo*

1. Disconnect the battery cable. Drain the cooling system.
2. Remove the front luggage compartment carpeting.
3. Open the blower compartment lid. Remove the steering shaft cover.
4. Disconnect the electrical wiring.
5. Loosen the hose clamps and disconnect the hoses from the blower.
6. Pull the blower off the air intake stack and remove it from the vehicle.
7. Install the blower on the intake stack. Make sure that the sealing ring is correctly seated.
8. Fasten the hoses on the blower and tighten the hose clamps.
9. Connect the electrical wiring.
10. Install the steering shaft cover and close the blower compartment lid.
11. Cement the carpeting to the right front side panel.
12. Connect the battery cable.

#### *Except 911 and 911 Turbo*

The heater core and blower are contained in the heater assembly which is removed and disassembled to service either component. The heater assembly is located under the center of the instrument panel. What follows is a general procedure.

1. Disconnect the battery ground cable.
2. Drain the cooling system.
3. Disconnect the 2 hoses from the heater core connections at the firewall.
4. Unplug the heater electrical connector.
5. Detach the center console and the right side of the instrument panel.
6. Remove the heater control knobs from the instrument pane.
7. Remove the 2 retaining screws and remove the controls from the instrument panel.
8. Disconnect the heater control cables.
9. Using a suitable tool, pry the retaining clip off the heater housing. Detach the left and right hoses.
10. Remove the heater-to-instrument panel mounting screws and lower the heater.
11. Pull out the 2 pins and remove the heater top cover. Pry the retaining clips off and separate the 2 heater halves.
12. Remove the heater core and/or blower.
13. Installation is the reverse of removal. Refill the cooling system.

## Radio

### REMOVAL & INSTALLATION

1. Disconnect the negative battery cable.

2. Remove the radio knobs.
3. Release the radio bezel by pressing the springs in the shaft openings outward to their stops.
4. Remove the bezel.
5. Remove the nuts on the shafts.
6. Loosen the brackets and pull the radio out.
7. Disconnect the fuse, ground, speakers, and antenna wires. Remove the radio.
8. Installation is the reverse of the removal procedure.

## Windshield Wiper Switch

### REMOVAL & INSTALLATION

#### *911 and 911 Turbo*

The combination turn signal, headlight dimmer, and flasher switch is located in the steering column housing. The wiper/washer switch removal and installation procedure is identical.

1. Disconnect the negative battery cable. Remove the steering wheel.
2. Reach under the instrument panel and disconnect all wiring to the switch.
3. Remove the 2 horn contact ring screws, disconnect the wire, and remove the ring.
4. Remove the 2 upper housing retaining nuts. Pull the entire assembly off the column, leading the switch wires through the hole in the housing.
5. Remove the 3 retaining screws and remove the switch.
6. Reverse the removal steps to reinstall the switch.

#### *Except 911 and 911 Turbo*

1. Disconnect the negative battery cable.
2. Remove the steering wheel.
3. Disconnect the wire harness connector at the switch.
4. Remove the 4 screws holding the switch to the steering column and remove the switch.
5. Install in reverse of the removal procedure. Do not overtighten the mounting screws.

## Windshield Wiper Motor

### REMOVAL & INSTALLATION

#### *911 and 911 Turbo*

The windshield wiper motor and linkage are located in front of the instrument panel.

1. Pull back the front luggage compartment carpeting. Disconnect the battery cable.
2. Remove the retaining clip and air duct. Remove the fresh air box.
3. Disconnect the blower motor wires.
4. Remove the wiper arms. Remove the rubber bushings under the arms and unscrew the shaft retaining nuts.
5. Pull the motor and linkage down as a unit. Separate the motor and linkage.
6. Installation is the reverse of the removal procedure.

#### *Except 911 and 911 Turbo*

The windsheild wiper motor is located on the driver's side of the cowl under a plastic cover.

1. Remove the cover.
2. Disconnect the negative battery cable.
3. Unscrew the wiper linkage, disconnect the electrical plugs, unscrew the motor, remove the mounting screw on the frame, lift frame slightly, and remove motor.
4. Installation is the reverse of removal. Note the following during installation:
   a. Connect the plug and turn on the ignition before fastening the linkage.
   b. Move the wiper arms to the off position and mount the linkage.

## Instrument Cluster

### REMOVAL & INSTALLATION

#### *911 and 911 Turbo*

The gauges are mounted in individual rubber rings.

1. Disconnect the negative battery cable. Pry the gauge out until you can grip it firmly, and then pull it out of the instrument panel.
2. Disconnect the wiring and/or cable and remove the gauge.
3. Connect the wiring or cable and position the gauge in its opening.
4. Align the gauge and then push it into place.

#### *Except 911 and 911 Turbo*

1. Disconnect the negative battery cable.
2. Remove the steering wheel.
3. Remove the steering column switch, if necessary for working clearance.
4. Remove the instrument cover mounting screws.
5. Remove the rear window wiper and defogger switch, if necessary for clearance.
6. Pull the instrument cluster forward, then disconnect the multipin connector(s) at the rear of the instrument cluster.
7. Lift the instrument cluster carefully and tilt it to the rear. Unscrew the mounting bolt and remove the instrument cluster.

## Headlight Switch

### REMOVAL & INSTALLATION

#### *911 and 911 Turbo*

The combination turn signal, headlight dimmer, and flasher switch is located in the steering column housing. The headlight switch removal and installation procedure is identical.

1. Disconnect the negative battery cable. Remove the steering wheel.
2. Reach under the instrument panel and disconnect all wiring to the switch.
3. Remove the 2 horn contact ring screws, disconnect the wire, and remove the ring.
4. Remove the 2 upper housing retaining nuts. Pull the entire assembly off the column, leading the switch wires through the hole in the housing.
5. Remove the 3 retaining screws and remove the switch.
6. Reverse the removal steps to reinstall the switch.

#### *Except 911 and 911 Turbo*

1. Disconnect the negative battery cable.
2. Remove the steering wheel.
3. Disconnect the wire harness connector at the switch.
4. Remove the 4 screws holding the switch to the steering column and remove the switch.
5. Install in reverse of the removal procedure. Do not overtighten the mounting screws.

## Stoplight Switch

### REMOVAL & INSTALLATION

1. Disconnect the negative battery cable. Remove the underdash trim panel, if equipped.
2. Disconnect the electrical connector from the switch assembly.
3. Remove the switch from the vehicle.
4. Installation is the reverse of the removal procedure.

## Fuse and Circuit Breakers

### LOCATION

On the 911 and 911 Turbo, the fuse box is located in the left front of the luggage compartment.

The fuse panel on the 924S and 944 is located underneath the dashboard on the driver's side of the vehicle. The relays are arranged above the fuses. On some vehicles, an additional line of fuses is located above the main fuse/relay panel.

The fuse panel on the 928, 928S and 928S4 is located beneath a hinged wooden panel at the front of the passenger's floor area. Pull back the carpet to expose the cover. The relays are arranged below the fuse line.

On all vehicles, fuse amperage ratings and applications are given in the owner's manual.

# 15

# Saab

## 900, 9000—All Models

# SERIAL NUMBER IDENTIFICATION

## Vehicle Identification Plate

### 900 Series

The vehicle serial number is located in 2 places on all vehicles. The serial number is stamped on a plate at the lower left hand corner of the windshield, and the serial number is punched in the vehicle body under the left side of the rear seat cushion.

The vehicle serial number is located on the right side of the rear cross beam in the luggage compartment.

### 9000 Series

These vehicles have the chassis number plate located on the inner right fender panel and the left fire wall area of the engine compartment. The chassis number is also punched in the vehicle body, left of the right rear light, behind the panel in the luggage compartment.

## Engine Number

The engine identification number is stamped on a plate which is secured to the upper portion of the engine directly forward of the fuel injection unit.

## Transmission Number

The engine identification number is stamped on a plate which is secured to the transmission case.

## ENGINE IDENTIFICATION

| Year | Model | Engine Displacement cu. in. (cc/liter) | Engine Series Identification | No. of Cylinders | Engine Type |
|---|---|---|---|---|---|
| 1983 | 900 | 121 (1985/2.0) | B201 | 4 | SOHC 8-Valve |
| | 900 | 121 (1985/2.0) | B201 (Turbo) | 4 | SOHC 8-Valve |
| 1984 | 900 | 121 (1985/2.0) | B201 | 4 | SOHC 8-Valve |
| | 900 | 121 (1985/2.0) | B201 (Turbo) | 4 | SOHC 8-Valve |
| 1985 | 900 | 121 (1985/2.0) | B201 | 4 | SOHC 8-Valve |
| | 900 | 121 (1985/2.0) | B202 (Turbo) | 4 | DOHC 16-Valve |
| | 9000 | 121 (1985/2.0) | B202 (Turbo) | 4 | DOHC 16-Valve |
| 1986 | 900 | 121 (1985/2.0) | B201 | 4 | SOHC 8-Valve |
| | 900 | 121 (1985/2.0) | B202 (Turbo) | 4 | DOHC 16-Valve |
| | 900 | 121 (1985/2.0) | B202 | 4 | DOHC 16-Valve |
| | 9000 | 121 (1985/2.0) | B202 (Turbo) | 4 | DOHC 16-Valve |
| 1987 | 900 | 121 (1985/2.0) | B201 | 4 | SOHC 8-Valve |
| | 900 | 121 (1985/2.0) | B202 (Turbo) | 4 | DOHC 16-Valve |
| | 900 | 121 (1985/2.0) | B202 | 4 | DOHC 16-Valve |
| | 9000 | 121 (1985/2.0) | B202 (Turbo) | 4 | DOHC 16-Valve |
| 1988 | 900 | 121 (1985/2.0) | B201 | 4 | SOHC 8-Valve |
| | 900 | 121 (1985/2.0) | B202 (Turbo) | 4 | DOHC 16-Valve |
| | 900 | 121 (1985/2.0) | B202 | 4 | DOHC 16-Valve |
| | 9000 | 121 (1985/2.0) | B202 (Turbo) | 4 | DOHC 16-Valve |
| 1989-90 | 900 | 121 (1985/2.0) | B201 | 4 | SOHC 8-Valve |
| | 900 | 121 (1985/2.0) | B202 (Turbo) | 4 | DOHC 16-Valve |
| | 900 | 121 (1985/2.0) | B202 | 4 | DOHC 16-Valve |
| | 9000 | 121 (1985/2.0) | B202 (Turbo) | 4 | DOHC 16-Valve |

SOHC Single Overhead Camshaft
DOHC Double Overhead Camshaft

## GENERAL ENGINE SPECIFICATIONS

| Year | Model | Engine Displacement cu. in. (cc) | Fuel System Type | Net Horsepower @ rpm | Net Torque @ rpm (ft. lbs.) | Bore × Stroke (in.) | Com-pression Ratio | Oil Pressure @ rpm |
|---|---|---|---|---|---|---|---|---|
| 1983 | 900 | 121 (1985) | Fuel Injection | 110 @ 5500 ② | 119 @ 3500 ③ | 3.543 × 3.071 | 9.25:1 | 64–71 ④ |
| | 900 Turbo | 121 (1985) | Fuel Injection | 135 @ 4800 | 160 @ 3500 | 3.543 × 3.071 | 8.5:1 | 64–71 ④ |
| 1984 | 900 | 121 (1985) | Fuel Injection | 110 @ 5500 ② | 119 @ 3500 ③ | 3.543 × 3.071 | 9.25:1 | 64–71 ④ |
| | 900 Turbo | 121 (1985) | Fuel Injection | 135 @ 4800 | 160 @ 3500 | 3.543 × 3.071 | 8.5:1 | 64–71 ④ |
| 1985 | 900 | 121 (1985) | Fuel Injection | 110 @ 5500 ② | 119 @ 3500 ③ | 3.543 × 3.071 | 9.25:1 | 64–71 ④ |
| | 900 Turbo | 121 (1985) | Fuel Injection | 160 @ 5500 | 188 @ 3000 | 3.543 × 3.071 | 9.0:1 | 64–71 ④ |
| | 9000 | 121 (1985) | Fuel Injection | 175 @ 5300 | 201 @ 3000 | 3.543 × 3.071 | 9.0:1 | 64–71 ④ |
| 1986 | 900 | 121 (1985) | Fuel Injection | 110 @ 5500 ② | 119 @ 3500 ③ | 3.543 × 3.071 | 9.25:1 | 64–71 ④ |
| | 900 Turbo | 121 (1985) | Fuel Injection | 160 @ 5500 | 188 @ 3000 | 3.543 × 3.071 | 9.0:1 | 64–71 ④ |
| | 900 ① | 121 (1985) | Fuel Injection | 160 @ 5500 | 188 @ 3000 | 3.543 × 3.071 | 9.0:1 | 51–74 ④ |
| | 9000 | 121 (1985) | Fuel Injection | 175 @ 5300 | 201 @ 3000 | 3.543 × 3.071 | 9.0:1 | 51–74 ④ |
| 1987 | 900 | 121 (1985) | Fuel Injection | 110 @ 5250 | 119 @ 3500 | 3.543 × 3.071 | 9.25:1 | 64–71 ④ |
| | 900S ① | 121 (1985) | Fuel Injection | 125 @ 5500 | 123 @ 3000 | 3.543 × 3.071 | 10.1:1 | 51–74 ④ |
| | 900 Turbo | 121 (1985) | Fuel Injection | 160 @ 5500 ⑤ | 188 @ 3000 ⑥ | 3.543 × 3.071 | 9.0:1 | 64–71 ④ |
| | 9000 | 121 (1985) | Fuel Injection | 160 @ 5500 | 188 @ 3000 | 3.543 × 3.071 | 9.0:1 | 64–71 ④ |
| | 9000S | 121 (1985) | Fuel Injection | 125 @ 5500 | 125 @ 3000 | 3.543 × 3.071 | 10.0:1 | 51–74 ④ |
| 1988 | 900 | 121 (1985) | Fuel Injection | 110 @ 5250 | 119 @ 3500 | 3.543 × 3.071 | 9.25:1 | 64–71 ④ |
| | 900S ① | 121 (1985) | Fuel Injection | 125 @ 5500 | 123 @ 3000 | 3.543 × 3.071 | 10.1:1 | 51–74 ④ |
| | 900 Turbo | 121 (1985) | Fuel Injection | 160 @ 5500 ⑤ | 188 @ 3000 ⑥ | 3.543 × 3.071 | 9.0:1 | 64–71 ④ |
| | 9000 | 121 (1985) | Fuel Injection | 160 @ 5500 | 188 @ 3000 | 3.543 × 3.071 | 9.0:1 | 64–71 ④ |
| | 9000S | 121 (1985) | Fuel Injection | 125 @ 5500 | 125 @ 3000 | 3.543 × 3.071 | 10.0:1 | 51–74 ④ |
| 1989-90 | 900 | 121 (1985) | Fuel Injection | 110 @ 5250 | 119 @ 3500 | 3.543 × 3.071 | 9.25:1 | 64–71 ④ |
| | 900S ① | 121 (1985) | Fuel Injection | 125 @ 5500 | 123 @ 3000 | 3.543 × 3.071 | 10.1:1 | 51–74 ④ |
| | 900 Turbo | 121 (1985) | Fuel Injection | 160 @ 5500 ⑤ | 188 @ 3000 ⑥ | 3.543 × 3.071 | 9.0:1 | 64–71 ④ |

## GENERAL ENGINE SPECIFICATIONS

| Year | Model | Engine Displacement cu. in. (cc) | Fuel System Type | Net Horsepower @ rpm | Net Torque @ rpm (ft. lbs.) | Bore × Stroke (in.) | Com-pression Ratio | Oil Pressure @ rpm |
|---|---|---|---|---|---|---|---|---|
| 1989-90 | 9000 | 121 (1985) | Fuel Injection | 160 @ 5500 | 188 @ 3000 | 3.543 × 3.071 | 9.0:1 | 64–71 ④ |
| | 9000S | 121 (1985) | Fuel Injection | 125 @ 5500 | 125 @ 3000 | 3.543 × 3.071 | 10.0:1 | 51–74 ④ |

① DOHC Double Overhead Camshaft
② 115 @ 5500 without catalytic converter
118 @ 4800 Canada
③ 123 @ 3500 without Catalytic Converter or Canada
④ at 2000 rpm
⑤ SPG option—165 @ 5500
⑥ SPG option—195 @ 3000

## ENGINE TUNE-UP SPECIFICATIONS

| Year | Model | Engine Displacement cu. in. (cc) | Spark Plugs Type | Spark Plugs Gap (in.) | Ignition Timing (deg.) MT | Ignition Timing (deg.) AT | Com-pression Pressure (psi) | Fuel Pump (psi) | Idle Speed (rpm) MT | Idle Speed (rpm) AT | Valve Clearance In. | Valve Clearance Ex. |
|---|---|---|---|---|---|---|---|---|---|---|---|---|
| 1983 | 900 | 121 (1985) | ① | 0.024–0.028 | ⑤ | ⑤ | NA | ⑧ | 875 | 875 | .008–.010 | .016–.018 |
| | 900 Turbo | 121 (1985) | ② | 0.024–0.028 | ⑤ | ⑤ | NA | ⑧ | 875 | 875 | .008–.010 | .018–.020 |
| 1984 | 900 | 121 (1985) | ① | 0.024–0.028 | ⑤ | ⑤ | NA | ⑧ | 875 | 875 | .008–.010 | .016–.018 |
| | 900 Turbo | 121 (1985) | ② | 0.024–0.028 | ⑤ | ⑤ | NA | ⑧ | 875 | 875 | .008–.010 | .018–.020 |
| 1985 | 900 | 121 (1985) | ① | 0.024–0.028 | ⑤ | ⑤ | NA | ⑧ | 875 | 875 | .008–.010 | .016–.018 |
| | 900 Turbo | 121 (1985) | ③ | 0.024–0.028 | ⑥ | ⑥ | NA | ⑧ | 875 | 875 | Hyd. | Hyd. |
| | 9000 | 121 (1985) | ③ | 0.024–0.028 | ⑥ | ⑥ | NA | ⑧ | 875 | 875 | Hyd. | Hyd. |
| 1986 | 900 | 121 (1985) | ① | 0.024–0.028 | ⑤ | ⑤ | NA | ⑧ | 875 | 875 | .008–.010 | .016–.018 |
| | 900 ⑨ | 121 (1985) | ④ | 0.024–0.028 | ⑦ | ⑦ | NA | ⑧ | 875 | 875 | Hyd. | Hyd. |
| | 900 Turbo | 121 (1985) | ③ | 0.024–0.028 | ⑥ | ⑥ | NA | ⑧ | 875 | 875 | Hyd. | Hyd. |
| | 9000 | 121 (1985) | ③ | 0.024–0.028 | ⑥ | ⑥ | NA | ⑧ | 875 | 875 | Hyd. | Hyd. |
| 1987 | 900 | 121 (1985) | ① | 0.024–0.028 | ⑤ | ⑤ | NA | ⑧ | 875 | 875 | .008–.010 | .016–.018 |
| | 900 ⑨ | 121 (1985) | ④ | 0.024–0.028 | ⑦ | ⑦ | NA | ⑧ | 875 | 875 | Hyd. | Hyd. |
| | 900 Turbo | 121 (1985) | ③ | 0.024–0.028 | ⑥ | ⑥ | NA | ⑧ | 875 | 875 | Hyd. | Hyd. |
| | 9000 | 121 (1985) | ③ | 0.024–0.028 | ⑥ | ⑥ | NA | ⑧ | 875 | 875 | Hyd. | Hyd. |

## ENGINE TUNE-UP SPECIFICATIONS

| Year | Model | Engine Displacement cu. in. (cc) | Spark Plugs Type | Spark Plugs Gap (in.) | Ignition Timing (deg.) MT | Ignition Timing (deg.) AT | Com-pression Pressure (psi) | Fuel Pump (psi) | Idle Speed (rpm) MT | Idle Speed (rpm) AT | Valve Clearance In. | Valve Clearance Ex. |
|---|---|---|---|---|---|---|---|---|---|---|---|---|
| 1988 | 900 | 121 (1985) | ① | 0.024–0.028 | ⑤ | ⑤ | NA | ⑧ | 875 | 875 | .008–.010 | .016–.018 |
| | 900 ⑨ | 121 (1985) | ④ | 0.024–0.028 | ⑦ | ⑦ | NA | ⑧ | 875 | 875 | Hyd. | Hyd. |
| | 900 Turbo | 121 (1985) | ③ | 0.024–0.028 | ⑥ | ⑥ | NA | ⑧ | 875 | 875 | Hyd. | Hyd. |
| | 9000 | 121 (1985) | ③ | 0.024–0.028 | ⑥ | ⑥ | NA | ⑧ | 875 | 875 | Hyd. | Hyd. |
| 1989 | 900 | 121 (1985) | ⑩ | 0.024–0.028 | ⑤ | ⑤ | NA | ⑧ | 875 | 875 | .008–.010 | .016–.018 |
| | 900 ⑨ | 121 (1985) | ⑩ | 0.024–0.028 | ⑦ | ⑦ | NA | ⑧ | 875 | 875 | Hyd. | Hyd. |
| | 900 Turbo | 121 (1985) | ③ | 0.024–0.028 | ⑥ | ⑥ | NA | ⑧ | 875 | 875 | Hyd. | Hyd. |
| | 9000 | 121 (1985) | ③ | 0.024–0.028 | ⑥ | ⑥ | NA | ⑧ | 875 | 875 | Hyd. | Hyd. |
| 1990 | SEE UNDERHOOD SPECIFICATION STICKER | | | | | | | | | | | |

DOHC—Double Overhead Camshaft
① BP6ES, W7DC, N9Y, N9YC
② BP6ES, W7DC, N9YC, BP7ES
③ BCP7EV
④ BCP6ES, C9YC, F7DC
⑤ 20° @ 2000 rpm
18° @ 2000 rpm Canada with manual transmission
23° @ 2000 rpm Canada with automatic transmission
⑥ 16° BTDC @ 850 rpm
⑦ 14° @ 850 rpm
⑧ Fuel injected engines—Fuel line pressure before the control pressure regulator is 66.9–69.7 (setting valve), and 48.5–54.0 psi (warm engine) after the control pressure regulator (located in fuel distributor).
⑨ DOHC—Double Overhead Camshaft
⑩ BCP5ES

## FIRING ORDERS

**NOTE:** To avoid confusion, always replace spark plug wires one at a time.

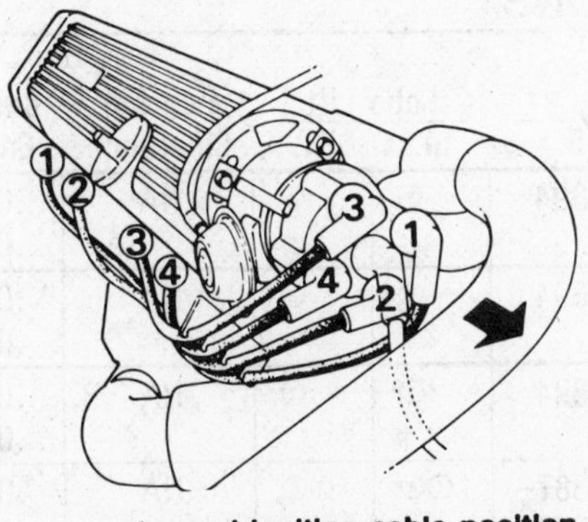

**Firing order and ignition cable positioning eight valve engine**

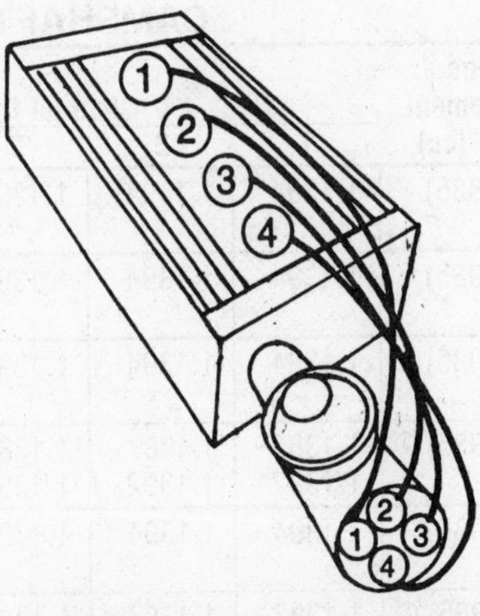

**Firing order and ignition cable positioning sixteen valve engine**

## CAPACITIES

| Year | Model | Engine Displacement cu. in. (cc) | Engine Crankcase with Filter | Engine Crankcase without Filter | Transmission (pts.) 4-Spd | Transmission (pts.) 5-Spd | Transmission (pts.) Auto. | Drive Axle (pts.) | Fuel Tank (gal.) | Cooling System (qts.) |
|---|---|---|---|---|---|---|---|---|---|---|
| 1983 | 900 | 121 (1985) | 4.0 | 3.5 | 5.2 | 6.4 | 17 | 2.6 ② | 16.5 | 10.5 |
| | 900 Turbo | 121 (1985) | 4.5 | 4.0 | 5.2 | 6.4 | 17 | 2.6 ② | 16.5 | 10.5 |
| 1984 | 900 | 121 (1985) | 4.0 | 3.5 | 5.2 | 6.4 | 17 | 2.6 ② | 16.5 | 10.5 |
| | 900 Turbo | 121 (1985) | 4.5 | 4.0 | 5.2 | 6.4 | 17 | 2.6 ② | 16.5 | 10.5 |
| 1985 | 900 | 121 (1985) | 4.0 | 3.5 | 5.2 | 6.4 | 17 | 2.6 ② | 16.5 | 10.5 |
| | 900 Turbo | 121 (1985) | 4.5 | 4.0 | 5.2 | 6.4 | 17 | 2.6 ② | 16.5 | 10.5 |
| | 9000 | 121 (1985) | 4.5 | 4.0 | 5.2 | 6.4 | 17 | 2.6 ② | 16.5 | 10.5 |
| 1986 | 900 | 121 (1985) | 4.0 | 3.5 | 5.2 | 6.4 | 17 | 2.6 ② | 18.0 | 10.5 |
| | 900 Turbo | 121 (1985) | 4.5 | 4.0 | 5.2 | 6.4 | 17 | 2.6 ② | 18.0 | 10.5 |
| | 900 ① | 121 (1985) | 4.0 | 3.5 | 5.2 | 6.4 | 17 | 2.6 ② | 18.0 | 10.5 |
| | 9000 | 121 (1985) | 4.5 | 4.0 | 5.2 | 6.4 | 17 | 2.6 ② | 18.0 | 10.5 |
| 1987 | 900 | 121 (1985) | 4.0 | 3.5 | 5.2 | 6.4 | 17 | 2.6 ② | 18.0 | 10.5 |
| | 900 Turbo | 121 (1985) | 4.5 | 4.0 | 5.2 | 6.4 | 17 | 2.6 ② | 18.0 | 10.5 |
| | 900 ① | 121 (1985) | 4.0 | 3.5 | 5.2 | 6.4 | 17 | 2.6 ② | 18.0 | 10.5 |
| | 9000 | 121 (1985) | 4.5 | 4.0 | 5.2 | 6.4 | 17 | 2.6 ② | 18.0 | 10.5 |
| 1988 | 900 | 121 (1985) | 4.0 | 3.5 | 5.2 | 6.4 | 17 | 2.6 ② | 18.0 | 10.5 |
| | 900 Turbo | 121 (1985) | 4.5 | 4.0 | 5.2 | 6.4 | 17 | 2.6 ② | 18.0 | 10.5 |
| | 900 ① | 121 (1985) | 4.0 | 3.5 | 5.2 | 6.4 | 17 | 2.6 ② | 18.0 | 10.5 |
| | 9000 | 121 (1985) | 4.5 | 4.0 | 5.2 | 6.4 | 17 | 2.6 ② | 18.0 | 10.5 |
| 1989-90 | 900 | 121 (1985) | 4.0 | 3.5 | 5.2 | 6.4 | 17 | 2.6 ② | 18.0 | 10.5 |
| | 900 Turbo | 121 (1985) | 4.5 | 4.0 | 5.2 | 6.4 | 17 | 2.6 ② | 18.0 | 10.5 |
| | 900 ① | 121 (1985) | 4.0 | 3.5 | 5.2 | 6.4 | 17 | 2.6 ② | 18.0 | 10.5 |
| | 9000 | 121 (1985) | 4.5 | 4.0 | 5.2 | 6.4 | 17 | 2.6 ② | 18.0 | 10.5 |

① DOHC—Double Overhead Camshaft
② 3.0 for Borg Warner Type 37

## CAMSHAFT SPECIFICATIONS

| Year | Engine Displacement cu. in. (cc) | Journal Diameter 1 | Journal Diameter 2 | Journal Diameter 3 | Journal Diameter 4 | Journal Diameter 5 | Lobe Lift In. | Lobe Lift Ex. | Bearing Clearance | Camshaft End Play |
|---|---|---|---|---|---|---|---|---|---|---|
| 1983 | 121 (1985) | 1.1394 | 1.1394 | 1.1394 | 1.1394 | 1.1394 | ① | ② | NA | .0031-.0098 |
| 1984 | 121 (1985) | 1.1394 | 1.1394 | 1.1394 | 1.1394 | 1.1394 | ① | ② | NA | .0031-.0098 |
| 1985 | 121 (1985) | 1.1394 | 1.1394 | 1.1394 | 1.1394 | 1.1394 | ① | ② | NA | .0031-.0098 |
| | 121 (1985) ③ | 1.1387-1.1392 | 1.1387-1.1392 | 1.1387-1.1392 | 1.1387-1.1392 | 1.1387-1.1392 | ①④ | ②⑤ | NA | .0031-.0138 |
| 1986 | 121 (1985) | 1.1394 | 1.1394 | 1.1394 | 1.1394 | 1.1394 | ① | ② | NA | .0031-.0098 |
| | 121 (1985) ③ | 1.1387-1.1392 | 1.1387-1.1392 | 1.1387-1.1392 | 1.1387-1.1392 | 1.1387-1.1392 | ①④ | ②⑤ | NA | .0031-.0138 |

## CAMSHAFT SPECIFICATIONS

| Year | Engine Displacement cu. in. (cc) | Journal Diameter 1 | 2 | 3 | 4 | 5 | Lobe Lift In. | Lobe Lift Ex. | Bearing Clearance | Camshaft End Play |
|---|---|---|---|---|---|---|---|---|---|---|
| 1987 | 121 (1985) | 1.1394 | 1.1394 | 1.1394 | 1.1394 | 1.1394 | ① | ② | NA | .0031–.0098 |
| | 121 (1985) ③ | 1.1387–1.1392 | 1.1387–1.1392 | 1.1387–1.1392 | 1.1387–1.1392 | 1.1387–1.1392 | ①④ | ②⑤ | NA | .0031–.0138 |
| 1988 | 121 (1985) | 1.1394 | 1.1394 | 1.1394 | 1.1394 | 1.1394 | ① | ② | NA | .0031–.0098 |
| | 121 (1985) ③ | 1.1387–1.1392 | 1.1387–1.1392 | 1.1387–1.1392 | 1.1387–1.1392 | 1.1387–1.1392 | ①④ | ②⑤ | NA | .0031–.0138 |
| 1989-90 | 121 (1985) | 1.1394 | 1.1394 | 1.1394 | 1.1394 | 1.1394 | ① | ② | NA | .0031–.0098 |
| | 121 (1985) ③ | 1.1387–1.1392 | 1.1387–1.1392 | 1.1387–1.1392 | 1.1387–1.1392 | 1.1387–1.1392 | ①④ | ②⑤ | NA | .0031–.0138 |

① Injection Engine 0.425 in.
Turbo, not APC 0.358 in.
Turbo with APC 0.425 in.

② Injectino Engine 0.433 in.
Turbo, not APC 0.413 in.
Turbo with APC 0.433 in.

APC = Automatic Performance Control

③ DOHC—Double Overhead Camshaft
④ .3406–.2618 9000 Series Vehicle
⑤ .3406 9000 Series Vehicle

## CRANKSHAFT AND CONNECTING ROD SPECIFICATIONS

All measurements are given in inches.

| Year | Engine Displacement cu. in. (cc) | Crankshaft Main Brg. Journal Dia. | Main Brg. Oil Clearance | Shaft End-play | Thrust on No. | Connecting Rod Journal Diameter | Oil Clearance | Side Clearance |
|---|---|---|---|---|---|---|---|---|
| 1983 | 121 (1985) | 2.283–2.284 | 0.0008–0.0024 | 0.003–0.011 | 3 | 2.2047–2.2054 | .0010–.0024 | NA |
| 1984 | 121 (1985) | 2.283–2.284 | 0.0008–0.0024 | 0.003–0.011 | 3 | 2.2047–2.2054 | .0010–.0024 | NA |
| 1985 | 121 (1985) | 2.283–2.284 | 0.0008–0.0024 | 0.003–0.011 | 3 | 2.2047–2.2054 | .0010–.0024 | NA |
| 1986 | 121 (1985) | 2.283–2.284 | 0.0008–0.0024 | 0.003–0.011 | 3 | 2.2047–2.2054 | .0010–.0024 | NA |
| 1987 | 121 (1985) | 2.283–2.284 | 0.0008–0.0024 | 0.003–0.011 | 3 | 2.2047–2.2054 | .0010–.0024 | NA |
| 1988 | 121 (1985) | 2.283–2.284 | 0.0008–0.0024 | 0.003–0.011 | 3 | 2.2047–2.2054 | .0010–.0024 | NA |
| 1989-90 | 121 (1985) | 2.283–2.284 | 0.0008–0.0024 | 0.003–0.011 | 3 | 2.2047–2.2054 | .0010–.0024 | NA |

NA Not available at time of publication

## VALVE SPECIFICATIONS

| Year | Engine Displacement cu. in. (cc) | Seat Angle (deg.) | Face Angle (deg.) | Spring Test Pressure (lbs.) | Spring Installed Height (in.) | Stem-to-Guide Clearance (in.) Intake | Stem-to-Guide Clearance (in.) Exhaust | Stem Diameter (in.) Intake | Stem Diameter (in.) Exhaust |
|---|---|---|---|---|---|---|---|---|---|
| 1983 | 121 (1985) | 45 | 44.5 | 178–198 @ 1.16 | 1.56 | 0.020 | 0.020 | 0.3134–0.3139 | 0.3132–0.3142 |

## VALVE SPECIFICATIONS

| Year | Engine Displacement cu. in. (cc) | Seat Angle (deg.) | Face Angle (deg.) | Spring Test Pressure (lbs.) | Spring Installed Height (in.) | Stem-to-Guide Clearance (in.) | | Stem Diameter (in.) | |
|---|---|---|---|---|---|---|---|---|---|
| | | | | | | Intake | Exhaust | Intake | Exhaust |
| 1984 | 121 (1985) | 45 | 44.5 | 178–198 @ 1.16 | 1.56 | 0.020 | 0.020 | 0.3134–0.3139 | 0.3132–0.3142 |
| 1985 | 121 (1985) | 45 | 44.5 | 178–198 @ 1.16 | 1.56 | 0.020 | 0.020 | 0.3134–0.3139 | 0.3132–0.3142 |
| | 121 (1985) ① | 45 | 44.5 | 133–145 @ 1.18 | 1.45 | 0.020 | 0.020 | 0.2740–0.2746 | 0.2738–0.2748 |
| 1986 | 121 (1985) | 45 | 44.5 | 178–198 @ 1.16 | 1.56 | 0.020 | 0.020 | 0.3134–0.3139 | 0.3132–0.3142 |
| | 121 (1985) ① | 45 | 44.5 | 133–145 @ 1.18 | 1.45 | 0.020 | 0.020 | 0.2740–0.2746 | 0.2738–0.2748 |
| 1987 | 121 (1985) | 45 | 44.5 | 178–198 @ 1.16 | 1.56 | 0.020 | 0.020 | 0.3134–0.3139 | 0.3132–0.3142 |
| | 121 (1985) ① | 45 | 44.5 | 133–145 @ 1.18 | 1.45 | 0.020 | 0.020 | 0.2740–0.2746 | 0.2738–0.2748 |
| 1988 | 121 (1985) | 45 | 44.5 | 178–198 @ 1.16 | 1.56 | 0.020 | 0.020 | 0.3134–0.3139 | 0.3132–0.3142 |
| | 121 (1985) ① | 45 | 44.5 | 133–145 @ 1.18 | 1.45 | 0.020 | 0.020 | 0.2740–0.2746 | 0.2738–0.2748 |
| 1989–90 | 121 (1985) | 45 | 44.5 | 178–198 @ 1.16 | 1.56 | 0.020 | 0.020 | 0.3134–0.3139 | 0.3132–0.3142 |
| | 121 (1985) ① | 45 | 44.5 | 133–145 @ 1.18 | 1.45 | 0.020 | 0.020 | 0.2740–0.2746 | 0.2738–0.2748 |

① DOHC Double Overhead Camshaft

## PISTON AND RING SPECIFICATIONS

All measurements are given in inches.

| Year | Engine Displacement cu. in. (cc) | Piston Clearance | Ring Gap | | | Ring Side Clearance | | |
|---|---|---|---|---|---|---|---|---|
| | | | Top Compression | Bottom Compression | Oil Control | Top Compression | Bottom Compression | Oil Control |
| 1983 | 121 (1985) | .0009–.0020 | 0.014–0.022 | 0.012–0.018 | 0.015–0.055 | 0.002–0.003 | 0.002–0.003 | NA |
| 1984 | 121 (1985) | .0009–.0020 | 0.014–0.022 | 0.012–0.018 | 0.015–0.055 | 0.002–0.003 | 0.002–0.003 | NA |
| 1985 | 121 (1985) | .0009–.0020 | 0.014–0.022 | 0.012–0.018 | 0.015–0.055 | 0.002–0.003 | 0.002–0.003 | NA |
| | 121 (1985) ① | .0009–.0020 | 0.013–0.021 | 0.011–0.017 | 0.014–0.055 | 0.002–0.003 | 0.002–0.003 | NA |
| 1986 | 121 (1985) | .0009–.0020 | 0.014–0.022 | 0.012–0.018 | 0.015–0.055 | 0.002–0.003 | 0.002–0.003 | NA |
| | 121 (1985) ① | .0009–.0020 | 0.013–0.021 | 0.011–0.017 | 0.014–0.055 | 0.002–0.003 | 0.002–0.003 | NA |
| 1987 | 121 (1985) | .0009–.0020 | 0.014–0.022 | 0.012–0.018 | 0.015–0.055 | 0.002–0.003 | 0.002–0.003 | NA |
| | 121 (1985) ① | .0009–.0020 | 0.013–0.021 | 0.011–0.017 | 0.014–0.055 | 0.002–0.003 | 0.002–0.003 | NA |

## PISTON AND RING SPECIFICATIONS

All measurements are given in inches.

| Year | Engine Displacement cu. in. (cc) | Piston Clearance | Ring Gap Top Compression | Ring Gap Bottom Compression | Ring Gap Oil Control | Ring Side Clearance Top Compression | Ring Side Clearance Bottom Compression | Ring Side Clearance Oil Control |
|---|---|---|---|---|---|---|---|---|
| 1988 | 121 (1985) | .0009–.0020 | 0.014–0.022 | 0.012–0.018 | 0.015–0.055 | 0.002–0.003 | 0.002–0.003 | NA |
| | 121 (1985) ① | .0009–.0020 | 0.013–0.021 | 0.011–0.017 | 0.014–0.055 | 0.002–0.003 | 0.002–0.003 | NA |
| 1989-90 | 121 (1985) | .0009–.0020 | 0.014–0.022 | 0.012–0.018 | 0.015–0.055 | 0.002–0.003 | 0.002–0.003 | NA |
| | 121 (1985) ① | .0009–.0020 | 0.013–0.021 | 0.011–0.017 | 0.014–0.055 | 0.002–0.003 | 0.002–0.003 | NA |

① DOHC Double Overhead Camshaft
NA Not available at time of publication

## TORQUE SPECIFICATIONS

All readings in ft. lbs.

| Year | Engine Displacement cu. in. (cc) | Cylinder Head Bolts | Main Bearing Bolts | Rod Bearing Bolts | Crankshaft Pulley Bolts | Flywheel Bolts | Manifold Intake | Manifold Exhaust | Spark Plugs |
|---|---|---|---|---|---|---|---|---|---|
| 1983 | 121 (1985) | ① | 40 | 80 | 140 | 43 | 13 | 18 | 18–21 |
| 1984 | 121 (1985) | ① | 40 | 80 | 140 | 43 | 13 | 18 | 18–21 |
| 1985 | 121 (1985) | ①② | 40 | 80 | 140 | 43 | 13 | 18 | 18–21 |
| 1986 | 121 (1985) | ①② | 40 | 80 | 140 | 43 | 13 | 18 | 18–21 |
| 1987 | 121 (1985) | ①② | 40 | 80 | 140 | 43 | 13 | 18 | 18–21 |
| 1988 | 121 (1985) | ①② | 40 | 80 | 140 | 43 | 13 | 18 | 18–21 |
| 1989-90 | 121 (1985) | ①② | 40 | 80 | 140 | 43 | 13 | 18 | 18–21 |

① 1983–89
1st stage—43 ft. lbs.
2nd stage—72 ft. lbs.—run engine to warm. Allow 30 minutes cool time—Retighten to 72 ft. lbs.
1984–90: Tighten each bolt another 1³/₄ (90 degrees) of a turn.

② Turbo 16-Valve
1st stage—45 ft. lbs.
2nd stage—67 ft. lbs. Engine to normal operating temp. Allow to cool for 30 minutes.
3rd stage—Tighten another 90 degrees turn (¼ turn). Retorque after 1200 miles or after engine reaches normal operating temperature.

## BRAKE SPECIFICATIONS

All measurements in inches unless noted.

| Year | Model | Lug Nut Torque (ft. lbs.) | Master Cylinder Bore | Brake Disc Minimum Thickness | Brake Disc Maximum Runout | Standard Brake Drum Diameter | Minimum Lining Thickness Front | Minimum Lining Thickness Rear |
|---|---|---|---|---|---|---|---|---|
| 1983 | 900 | 65–80 | NA | 0.461 ① | — | — | 0.040 | 0.040 |
| 1984 | 900 | 65–80 | NA | 0.461 ① | — | — | 0.040 | 0.040 |
| 1985 | 900 | 65–80 | NA | 0.461 ① | — | — | 0.040 | 0.040 |
| | 9000 | 76–90 | NA | 0.787 ② | .768 ③ | — | 0.039 | 0.039 |

## BRAKE SPECIFICATIONS

All measurements in inches unless noted.

| Year | Model | Lug Nut Torque (ft. lbs.) | Master Cylinder Bore | Brake Disc Minimum Thickness | Brake Disc Maximum Runout | Standard Brake Drum Diameter | Minimum Lining Thickness Front | Minimum Lining Thickness Rear |
|---|---|---|---|---|---|---|---|---|
| 1986 | 900 | 65–80 | NA | 0.461 ① | — | — | — | — |
| | 9000 | 76–90 | NA | 0.787 ② | .768 ③ | — | 0.039 | 0.039 |
| 1987 | 900 | 65–80 | NA | 0.461 ① | — | — | — | — |
| | 9000 | 76–90 | NA | 0.787 ② | 0.768 ③ | — | 0.039 | 0.039 |
| 1988 | 900 | 65–80 | NA | 0.461 ① | — | — | — | — |
| | 9000 | 76–90 | NA | 0.787 ② | .768 ③ | — | 0.039 | 0.039 |
| 1989-90 | 900 | 65–80 | NA | 0.461 ① | — | — | — | — |
| | 9000 | 76–90 | NA | 0.787 ② | .768 ③ | — | 0.039 | 0.039 |

NA—Not available at time of publication
① .374 Rear
② .295 Rear
③ .276 Rear

## WHEEL ALIGNMENT

| Year | Model | Caster Range (deg.) | Caster Preferred Setting (deg.) | Camber Range (deg.) | Camber Preferred Setting (deg.) | Toe-in (in.) | Steering Axis Inclination (deg.) |
|---|---|---|---|---|---|---|---|
| 1983 | 900 | 1 1/2–2 1/2 ① | 2 ① | 0–1 | 1/2 | 5/64 | NA |
| 1984 | 900 | 1 1/2–2 1/2 ① | 2 ① | 0–1 | 1/2 | 5/64 | NA |
| 1985 | 900 | 1 1/2–2 1/2 ① | 2 ① | 0–1 | 1/2 | 5/64 | NA |
| | 9000 | 1 1/8–2 1/8 | 1 5/8 | 1 1/8N–1/8N | 5/8N | 1/16 | NA |
| 1986 | 900 | 1 1/2–2 1/2 ① | 2 ① | 0–1 | 1/2 | 5/64 | NA |
| | 9000 | 1 1/8–2 1/8 | 1 5/8 | 1 1/8N–1/8N | 5/8N | 1/16 | NA |
| 1987 | 900 | 1 1/2–2 1/2 ① | 2 ① | 0–1 | 1/2 | 5/64 | NA |
| | 9000 | 1 1/8–2 1/8 | 1 5/8 | 1 1/8N–1/8N | 5/8N | 1/16 | NA |
| 1988 | 900 | 1 1/2–2 1/2 ① | 2 ① | 0–1 | 1/2 | 5/64 | NA |
| | 9000 | 1 1/8–2 1/8 | 1 5/8 | 1 1/8N–1/8N | 5/8N | 1/16 | NA |
| 1989-90 | 900 | 1 1/2–2 1/2 ① | 2 ① | 0–1 | 1/2 | 5/64 | NA |
| | 9000 | 1 1/8–2 1/8 | 1 5/8 | 1 1/8N–1/8N | 5/8N | 1/16 | NA |

NA—Not available at time of publication
① Manual Steering 1/2–1 1/2
N Negative

# TUNE UP PROCEDURES

## Ignition Timing

### ADJUSTMENT

Ignition timing is set in the conventional manner, using the marks that are located on the flywheel. However, the engine is also equipped for checking the timing using an ignition service (ISI) instrument.

The equipment in the vehicle comprises a pin in the engine flywheel and a service socket in the clutch cover. The ignition service instrument is connected to the clutch cover by means of a special connector and t the plug lead No. 1 cylinder by means of a terminal. The ignition service instrument is also connected to the ignition service socket at the fuse box and by means of an impulse transmitter at the plug lead for No. 1 cylinder.

The Saab ignition service instrument consists of a tachometer, cam angle meter, stroboscope lamp and switch for operating the starter.

## Valve Lash

### ADJUSTMENT

All 1985–90 vehicles equipped with a turbocharged engine require no normal valve adjustment as they are equipped with hydraulic tappets.

1. Remove the valve cover. The pistons of cylinders numbers 1 and 4 must be at TDC before distributor and valve cover can be removed.
2. Using an special tool Saab No. 8392185 or equivalent, rotate the crankshaft as necessary to position the high point of the camshaft lobe 180 degrees away from the valve depressor face, base circle of the cam lobe must contact the valve depressor, on the valve which the clearance is to be checked.

**NOTE: The special crankshaft turning wrench fits the center screw of the crankshaft belt pulley at the dash panel.**

3. Check the maximum and minimum clearances using a feeler gauge. The minimum feeler gauge should slip in, but the maximum feeler gauge should not.
4. Measure and record the clearance of all the valves in the same manner. Adjust the clearance of any valves that are not within specification.
5. To adjust the valves, remove the camshaft, tappets and adjusting pallets (shims) of any valves that need to be adjusted.
6. Using a micrometer, measure and record the thickness of the pallet (shim). This thickness plus the valve clearance adds up to the total distance between the valve and the cam.
7. The choice of the adjusting pallet (shim) is determined by the measured total distance between the valve depressor (tappet) and the cam, less the specified valve clearance for an intake or exhaust valve as the case may be.
8. Insert the new adjusting pallet (shim) an the valve depressor (tappet) and reinstall the camshaft.
9. Repeat the measurement procedure to insure that the clearances are correct.
10. Install the valve cover using a new valve cover gasket.

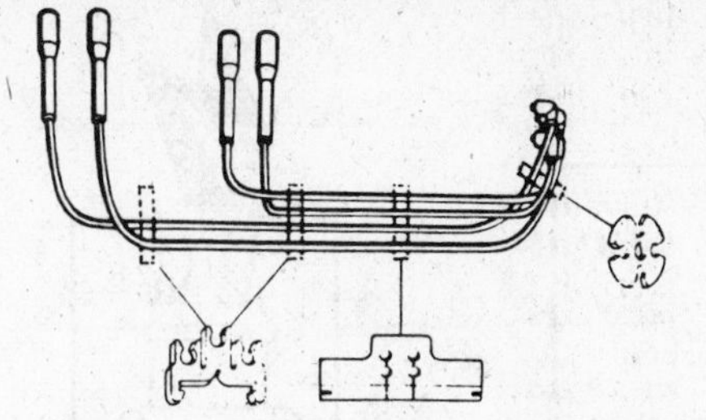

Secondary wiring routing—eight valve engine

## Idle Speed and Mixture

### ADJUSTMENT

#### *8 Valve Engine*

1. Run the engine until it reaches operating temperature.
2. Adjust the idle speed to 875±50 rpm.
3. If the vehicle is not equipped with a catalytic converter, remove the pulse/air hose and plug the air intake to the non-return valves. Connect the CO meter sensor to the exhaust pipe.

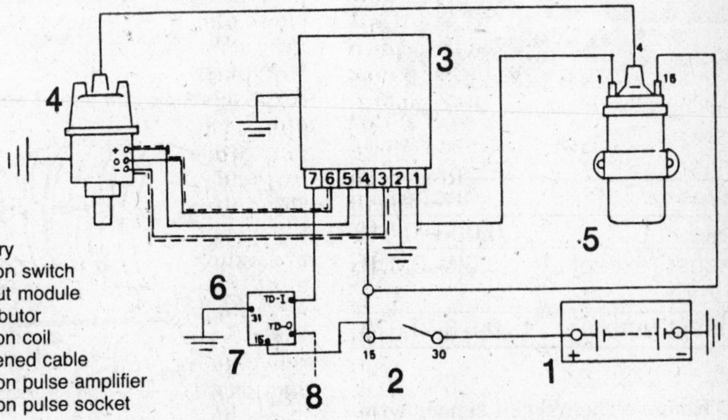


1 Battery
2 Ignition switch
3 Output module
4 Distributor
5 Ignition coil
6 Screened cable
7 Ignition pulse amplifier
8 Ignition pulse socket

Electronic ignition system components—9000 Series

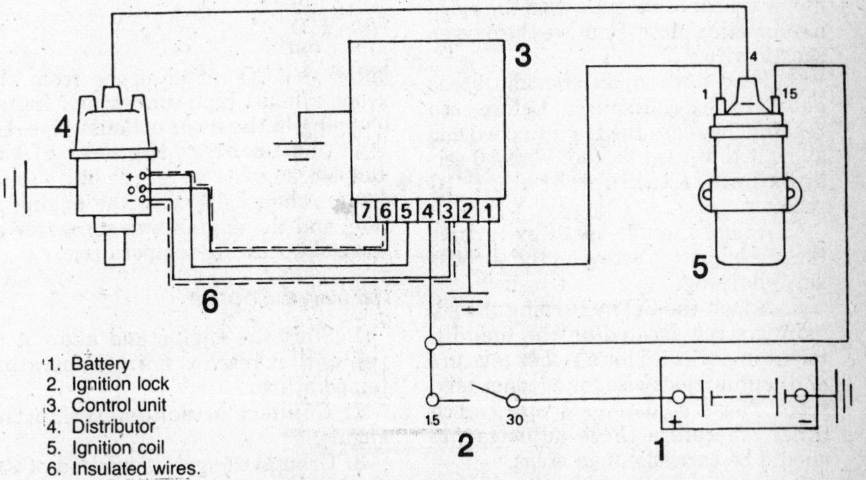


1. Battery
2. Ignition lock
3. Control unit
4. Distributor
5. Ignition coil
6. Insulated wires.

Electronic ignition system schematic—eight valve engine

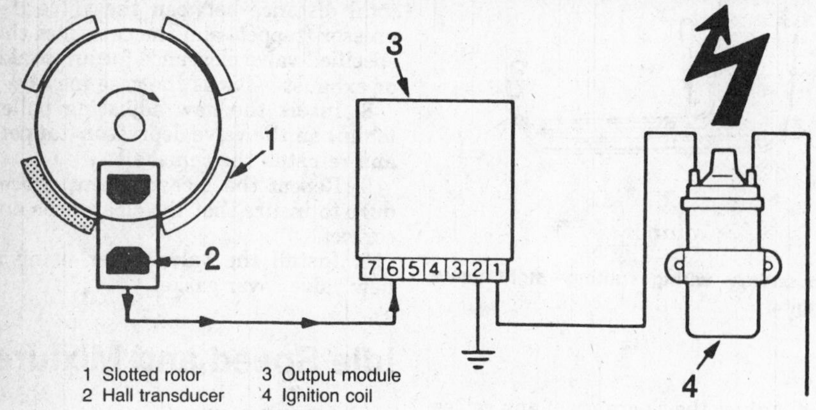


1 Slotted rotor 3 Output module
2 Hall transducer 4 Ignition coil

**Output module – sixteen valve engine**

**Checking valve clearance with feeler gauge**

| Valves | inches |
|---|---|
| Intake | 0.008–0.010 |
| Exhaust (except turbo) | 0.016–0.018 |
| Exhaust (turbo) | 0.018–0.020 |

4. Remove the oxygen sensor wire.
5. On vehicles equipped with a catalytic converter, remove and plug the front exhaust pipe and connect the CO meter sensor to the pipe with the aid of a connecting piece. Remove the oxygen sensor wire.
6. Read and adjust the idle speed and CO valve as required. Before each reading, increase the engine speed and allow it to return to idle. Wait 30 seconds before taking the next CO reading.
7. Adjust the idle speed by turning the idle adjusting screw on the throttle valve housing.
8. Adjust the CO by turning the adjusting screw located on the fuel distributor clockwise for a richer mixture and counterclockwise for a leaner mixture. These adjustments affect each other, therefore these adjustments should be carried out in steps.
9. On catalyst equipped vehicles, connect the oxygen sensor wire and remove the CO meter probe from the front exhaust pipe connection. Install the plug in the front exhaust pipe. Insert the probe at the rear of the tailpipe. The CO meter reading should be less than 0.3% with the engine at idle, and the engine and converter at normal operating temperature.

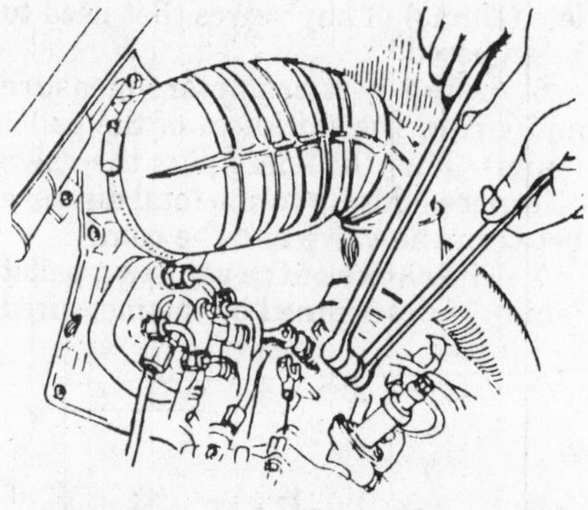

**CIS injection idle speed adjustment**

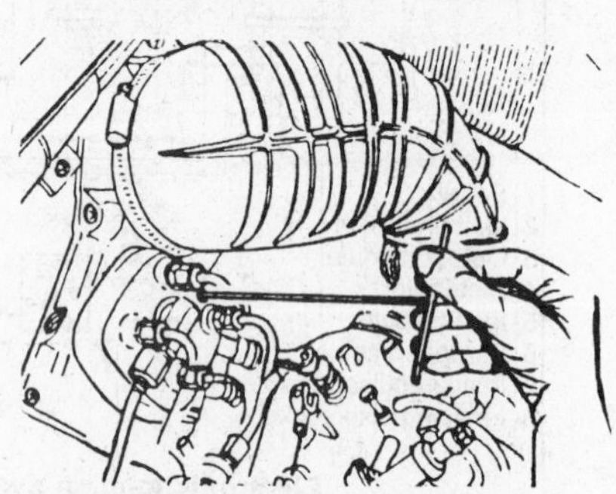

**CIS injection Co value adjustment**

### *16 Valve Engine*

1. Start the engine and allow it to run until it reaches normal operating temperature.
2. Connect a tachometer to the engine.
3. Ground the green/red lead of the single pole test socket on the right hand wheel housing to close the idling control valve. Use a jumper lead to do the grounding.
4. Set the idling speed to 800±25 rpm.
5. Disconnect the jumper lead from the test socket. Check that the engine speed changes and then settles down at 850±75 rpm.
6. CO value at simulated full load conditions should be 4.0–6.0%. Refer to underhood specifications label.

**NOTE: Be careful not to confuse the connector for the throttle switch with that of the idling control valve, as this will destroy the electronic control unit!**

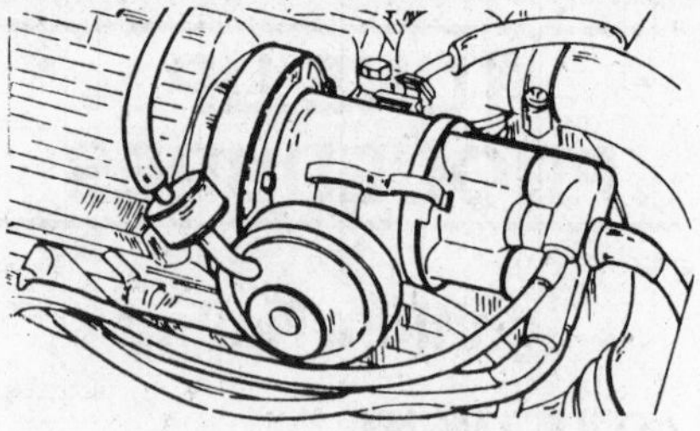

**Distributor assemvly location**

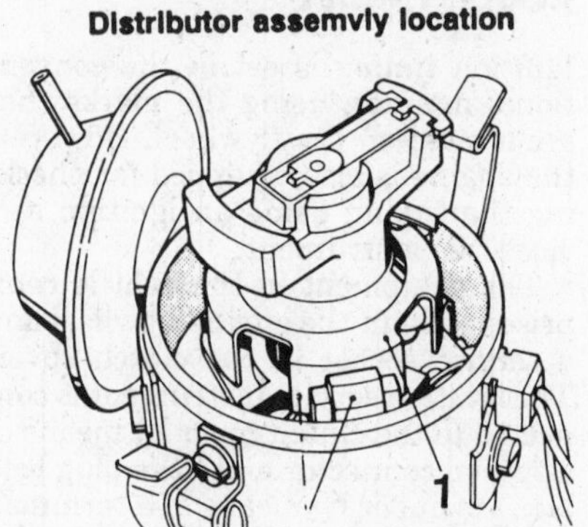


1. Slotted rotor
2. Hall transmitter

**Distributor assembly with Hall effect pick up**

# ENGINE ELECTRICAL

## Distributor

### REMOVAL & INSTALLATION

1. Disconnect the negative battery cable. Remove the distributor cap after marking the location of the No. 1 spark plug wire on the distributor housing. No. 1 cylinder is at the rear of the engine.
2. Disconnect the primary wire and Hall transducer connector from the distributor and hose from the vacuum advance unit.

3. Crank the engine until the flywheel marking is at TDC (0 degrees) and the distributor rotor is pointing to the indicating or reference mark on the distributor housing for the number 1 cylinder.

4. Matchmark the distributor housing to the valve cover housing. Remove the distributor retaining bolts and pull the distributor forward from the end of the valve cover housing. Note the position of the distributor drive lugs. Do not rotate the engine crankshaft when the distributor is removed from the engine.

5. Installation is the reverse of the removal procedure. Be sure to align the distributor rotor to the number 1 spark plug wire reference mark on the distributor housing, while aligning the match marks on the valve cover housing and distributor housing.

## Alternator

### PRECAUTIONS

Several precautions must be observed with alternator equipped vehicles to avoid damage to the unit.

- If the battery is removed for any reason, make sure it is reconnected with the correct polarity. Reversing the battery connections may result in damage to the one-way rectifiers.
- When utilizing a booster battery as a starting aid, always connect the positive to positive terminals, and the negative terminal from the booster battery to a good engine ground on the car being started.
- Never use a fast charger as a booster to start vehicles with alternating-current (AC) circuits.
- Disconnect the battery cables when charging the battery with a fast charger.
- Never attempt to polarize an alternator.
- Avoid long soldering times when making alternator repairs. Prolonged head will damage the alternator.
- Do not use test lamps of more than 12 volts when checking diode continuity.
- Do not short across or ground any of the alternator terminals.
- The polarity of the battery, alternator and regulator must be matched and considered before making any electrical connections within the system.
- Never separate the alternator on an open circuit. Make sure all connections within the circuit are clean and tight.
- Disconnect the battery ground terminal when performing any service on electrical components.
- Disconnect the battery if arc welding is to be done on the vehicle.

### BELT TENSION ADJUSTMENT

Adjust the alternator belt tension so that the belt can be depressed about ½ in. at the midpoint of its longest straight run.

### REMOVAL & INSTALLATION

#### 1983–84

1. Disconnect the negative battery cable.
2. Remove the alternator wiring connections, retaining screw and the adjusting screw.

**NOTE: A new alternator mounting using a thru-bolt and nut, was introduced during the 1983 model year. The thru-bolt and nut cannot be removed with the alternator mounted in the vehicle. The alternator mounting must be unbolted from the engine before the alternator can be separated from the mounting. Use the same precautions concerning the battery cable and alternator wiring as exercised with the earlier unit.**

3. Remove the alternator belt.
4. Remove the alternator from the vehicle.
5. Installation is the reverse of removal.

#### 1985–90

1. Disconnect the negative battery cable.
2. Raise and support the vehicle safely.
3. Remove the right front wheel assembly.

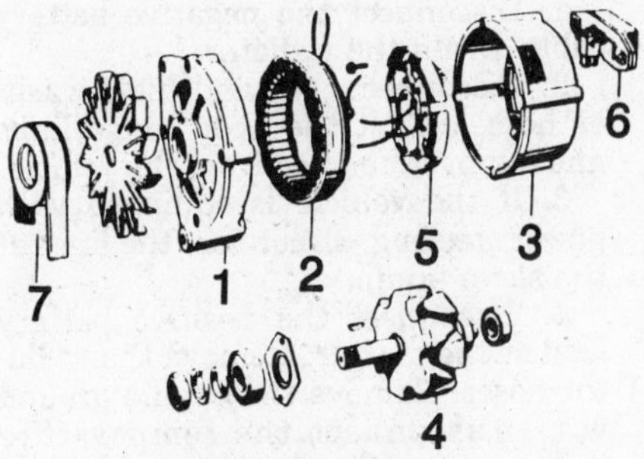


1 Drive end bracket
2 Stator
3 Slip-ring end bracket
4 Rotor
5 Rectifier unit
6 Voltage regulator and brush holder
7 Pulley

**Exploded view of Bosch 80A alternator**

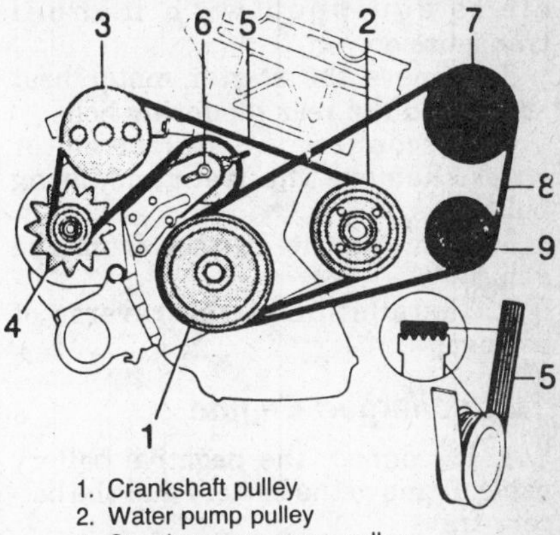


1. Crankshaft pulley
2. Water pump pulley
3. Steering servo pump pulley
4. Alternator pulley
5. Multi-groove belt
6. Belt tensioner
7. Compressor
8. Compressor belt
9. Adjusting device

**Serpentine drive belt routing**

4. Remove the inner fender panel from the right fender.
5. Loosen the alternator belt and remove it from the alternator pulley.
6. Remove the alternator wire connections from the rear of the alternator.
7. Loosen the 2 securing bolts for the alternator.
8. Using a pry bar, push the alternator to the left, pull the alternator forward and remove it from the vehicle.
9. Installation is the reverse of the removal procedure.

## Voltage Regulator

### REMOVAL & INSTALLATION

**NOTE: The voltage regulator is incorporated into the back of the alternator.**

1. Disconnect the negative battery cable.
2. Remove the voltage regulator connecting wires.
3. Remove the holddown screws and remove the unit from the vehicle.
4. Installation is the reverse of removal.

## Starter

### REMOVAL & INSTALLATION

#### Except Turbocharged Engine

1. Disconnect the negative battery cable.
2. Remove the flywheel cover. Remove the gearbox dipstick if the vehi-

cle is equipped with manual transmission.

3. Remove the starter motor heat shield and the rear mounting bolts.

4. Disconnect the starter motor wires. Remove the front mounting bolts.

5. Remove the starter from the vehicle.

6. Installation is the reverse of removal.

***Turbocharged Engine***

1. Disconnect the negative battery cable. Remove the battery and the battery tray.

2. Remove the turbocharger suction pipe, preheater hose and the flywheel cover.

3. Remove the gearbox dipstick if equipped with manual transmission. Remove the bracket and bolts between the turbocharger and the gearbox.

4. Disconnect the starter motor wires.

5. Loosen the oil return pipe on the turbocharger enough to allow it to be bent slightly.

6. Remove the starter motor heat shield and the rear mounting bolts.

7. Remove the front starter mounting bolts.

8. Remove the starter from the vehicle. The starter will have to be tilted downward and then lifted out forward.

9. Installation is the reverse the removal procedure. Be sure to use a new gasket on the oil return pipe connecting flange on the turbocharger.

### STARTER DRIVE REPLACEMENT

1. Have the starter armature out of the starter case and locked in a vise with the starter drive unit upward.

2. Remove the circlip on the end of the armature shaft, limiting the movement of the drive unit.

3. Remove the washer and the drive gear assembly from the armature shaft. A planetary gear set is located between the starter drive gear and the armature coils.

4. Install the drive gear, the limiting washer, and the circlip. Complete the starter assembly.

### STARTER SOLENOID REPLACEMENT

1. Disconnect the negative battery cable.

2. Remove the starter assembly from the vehicle.

3. Separate the solenoid assembly from the starter assembly.

4. Installation is the reverse of the removal procedure.

1 Drive end bush
2 Pinion bracket assembly
3 Circlip
4 Stop ring
5 Pinion-end bush
6 Starter pinion
7 Pinion-engaging lever
8 Bearing bracket
9 Seal
10 Epicyclic gear set
11 Armature
12 Solenoid
13 Casing
14 Brush-holder assembly
15 Seal
16 Seal
17 Bracket, commutator end
18 Bush, commutator end
19 Seal
20 Shim
21 Spring washer
22 End cover

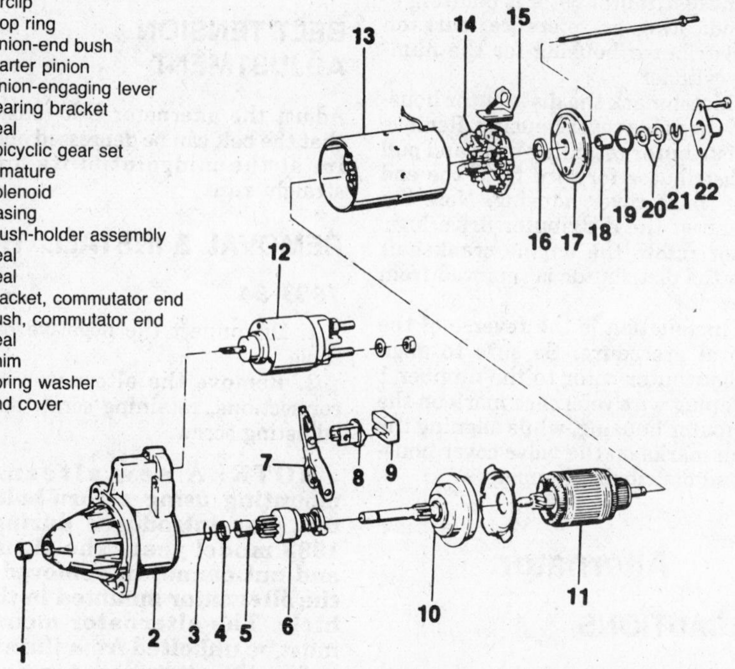


Exploded view of starter assembly—typical

# ENGINE MECHANICAL

## Engine

### REMOVAL & INSTALLATION

***900 Series***

#### 8 VALVE ENGINE

**NOTE: The engine and transmission should be removed as a unit.**

1. Disconnect the negative battery cable. Drain the radiator.

2. Disconnect the windshield washer hose, unbolt the hood hinge links and remove the hood from the vehicle.

3. If the vehicle is equipped with power steering, disconnect the lines at the servo pump.

4. Disconnect the positive battery lead at the starter. Remove the radiator hoses. Remove the engine ground wire. Disconnect the temperature transmitter cable. Remove the coil.

5. Disconnect the cable harness from the clutch cover. If the vehicle is equipped with manual transmission, disconnect the hydraulic line from the clutch slave cylinder and plug the lines.

6. Disconnect the CI system electrical connections from the warm up regulator, thermo-time switch cold start valve and the auxiliary air valve. On catalytic converter equipped vehicles, also disconnect the oxygen sensor and the throttle switch cables.

7. Disconnect the oil pressure transmitter cable. Loosen the fuel line connections at the fuel distributor. Remove the air filter along with the mixture control unit.

8. Disconnect the throttle cable. Disconnect the hose at the expansion tank. Disconnect the heater hoses at the heater. Disconnect the brake vacuum hose.

9. Remove the clips and remove the bellows from the inner drivers.

10. Place the spacer (Saab tool No. 83-93-209) or equivalent between the upper control arm underside and the vehicle body.

**NOTE: Insert the tool from the engine compartment side. The spacer makes the front suspension unloaded when the vehicle is raised.**

11. Lift the front end of the vehicle and support it safely.

12. Remove the lower end piece from the control arm. Pull out the steering knuckle assembly and support the end piece against the control arm outer end.

13. If the vehicle is equipped with manual transmission put the gear lever in neutral. Remove the nut and tap

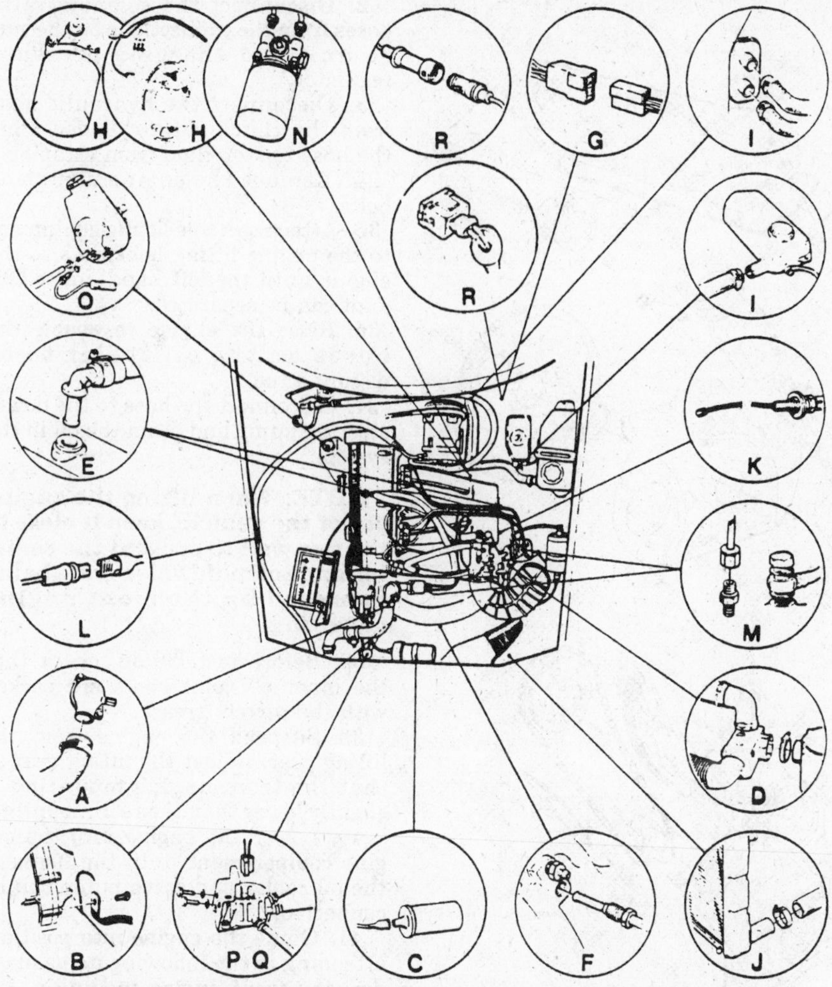


Disconnect these points before removing the engine—8 valve engines

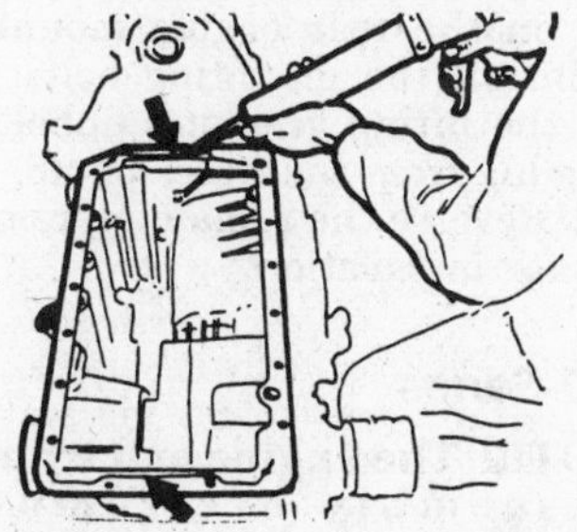

Sealer should only be applied to the grooves at each end of the steel engine-to-transaxle gasket on 1984 and later models

out the taper pin in the gear shift rod joint. Separate the joint from the gear shift rod.

14. If the vehicle is equipped with automatic transmission, remove the retaining screw from the gear selector cable at the transmission. Withdraw the cable with the gear selector rod in its extreme forward position **P**. Slide back the spring loaded sleeve on the gear shift rod and unhook the end of the cable.

15. Separate the exhaust pipe from the exhaust manifold. Disconnect the speedometer cable from the transmission.

16. Remove the rear engine mounting bolts. Slacken the front engine mounting nut so that the mounting can be lifted out of the bracket.

17. Attach the hoist to the 2 lugs on the engine and raise the assembly slightly. Move the assembly to one side and free the 2 U-joints.

18. Carefully remove the unit from the vehicle.

19. Installation is the reverse of removal. Upon installation properly seal the transaxle to engine assembly.

### 16 VALVE ENGINE

**NOTE: The engine and transaxle assembly are removed together.**

1. Remove the hood, after scribing lines around the mounting bolt positions to aid later refitting.

2. Install Saab special tool No 83-93-209 under the upper control arm on the right hand side.

3. Disconnect and remove the battery.

4. Drain the engine coolant.

5. Slacken the wheel nuts on the right hand front wheel.

6. Raise the front of the vehicle and place jack stands underneath the front jacking points.

7. Put the transmission selector into **R**.

8. Underneath the vehicle, remove the taper pin from the gearshift rod joint.

9. Disconnect the speedometer cable.

10. Remove the bolt securing the exhaust pipe to the clamp bracket on the transaxle.

11. Loosen the clips around the rubber boots on the CV-joints and slide the boots clear (this operation can also be done from above).

12. On the right hand side of the vehicle, remove the front wheel.

13. Separate the end piece from the lower control arm.

14. Separate the universal joint and position the knuckle in front of the driver. Support the end piece against the outer end of the control arm.

15. Disconnect the positive lead from the battery and free it from the clips holding it to the body. Disconnect the ground cable from the transaxle.

16. Disconnect the starter motor leads.

17. Unbolt the exhaust pipe from the exhaust manifold.

18. Disconnect the pressure pipe from the steering servo pump and have a plug handy to prevent oil escaping from the pipe. Take care not to drip oil onto the engine mounting and control arm rubbers.

19. From the left hand side of the vehicle, disconnect the cooling system hoses at the following connections, the heat exchanger valve, the expansion tank, the bottom of the radiator and the thermostat housing.

20. Disconnect the left hand fuel injection system cable harness as follows, at the air mass meter sensor, at the throttle switch, at the A.I.C. actuator, at the injectors, at the the NTC resistor (thermostatic switch) and at the ground points on the front lifting lug. Use the proper tool to release the tension in the springs on the terminal blocks.

21. Disconnect the block and plug connector (ground lead). Disconnect the lead at the alternator and the green/white cable to the positive terminal on the regulator. Disconnect the ground (black) cable. Disconnect the black cable from the oil pressure switch. Disconnect the cable for the A.I.C. actuator. Disconnect the yellow/

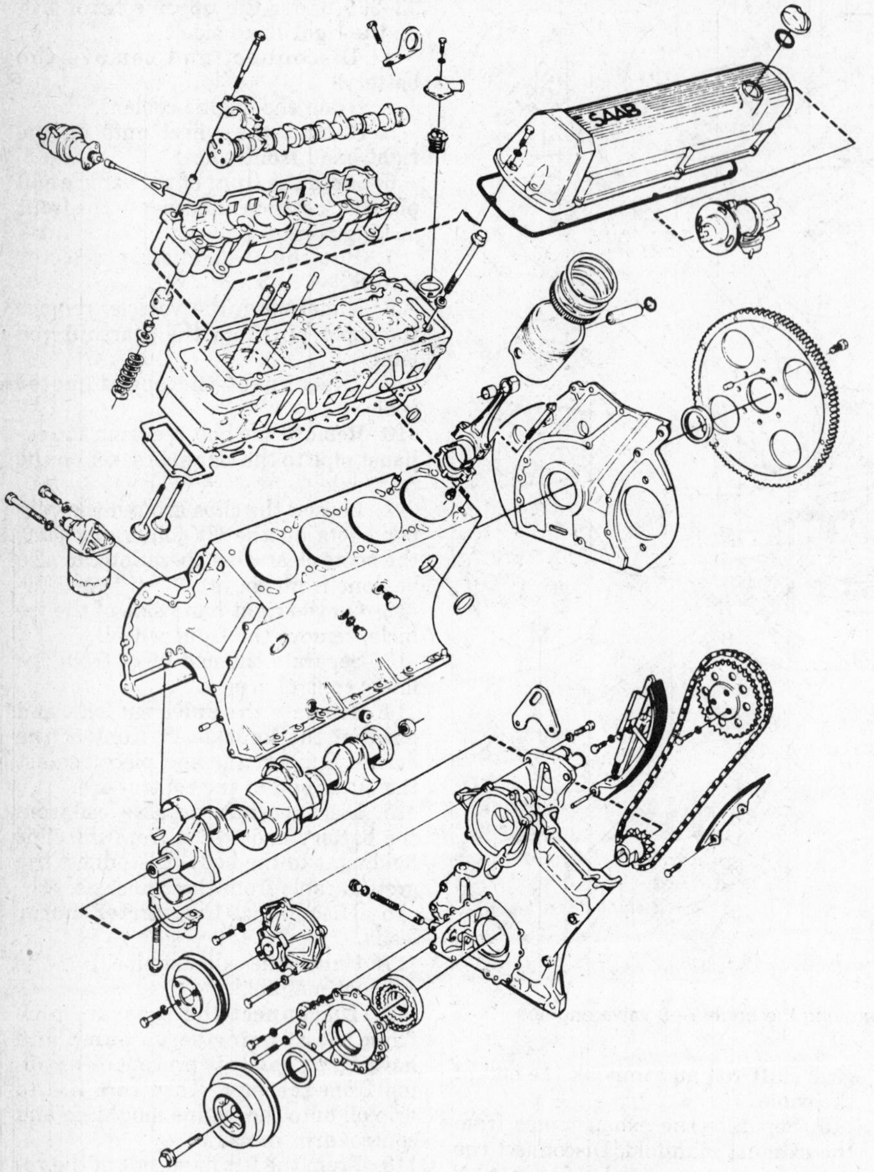


Eight valve engine and related components

white cable from the temperature transmitter. Disconnect the gray cable from the knock detector. Release the cable harness from the clip on the fuel injection manifold, from the rear of the engine and from the coolant hose between the engine and the expansion tank.

22. Withdraw the loose cables and guide the harness unit out of the engine compartment. Place it on top of the power distribution unit.

23. Remove the adjusting bolt in the alternator bracket, remove the drive belts and lift off the alternator.

24. Disconnect the brake servo hose from the intake manifold. Disconnect the throttle cable and sheath.

25. Remove the air conditioner compressor and bracket from the block. Place them on the filter housing for the heater system. Secure the alternator so it will not drop or become damaged.

26. Disconnect the fuel lines at their connections at the front of the fuel injection manifold and on the fuel pressure regulator.

27. Remove the coil.

28. Disconnect the turbo pressure line from the turbo compressor and the intercooler/throttle housing.

29. Remove the auxiliary fan.

30. Remove the air mass meter together with the suction pipe for the turbo unit. Disconnect the hoses at the solenoid valve and the crankcase ventilation at the suction pipe.

31. Disconnect the cables from the Hall transmitter and coil in the distributor. Free the Hall transmitter cable from the clips on the clutch cover.

32. Disconnect the solenoid valve hoses from the connections on the turbo unit and charging pressure regulator.

33. Disconnect the hydraulic hose from the clutch slave cylinder. Plug the hose to stop fluid from escaping.

34. Remove the engine mounting bolts.

35. Attach suitable lifting equipment to the engine lifting hooks. Raise the engine until the left hand, inner CV-joint can be separated.

36. Raise the engine to enable the hoses on the oil cooler to be disconnected.

37. Disconnect the hose to the power steering pump and drain the oil in the system.

**NOTE: When lifting the engine out of the vehicle, keep it close to the fire wall to prevent the radiator and solenoid valve from being damaged by the front engine mounting.**

38. Before installation, check that the inner CV-joint boots are packed with the correct grease.

39. Suspend the engine from the lifting gear. Adjust the lifting gear so that the front engine mounting is slightly lower than the rear mounting.

40. Lower the engine into the engine compartment until the hoses to the oil cooler and servo pump can be connected.

41. Guide the engine into position, attending to the following items in order, the front engine mounting, left hand inner CV-joint and right hand inner CV-joint. Lower the engine until it rests on the rear engine mountings and install the mounting bolts. Unhook the lifting gear and unbolt the lifting lug from the water pump.

42. Reverse the remaining removal steps for installation.

### *9000 Series*

**NOTE: The engine and transaxle assembly are removed together.**

1. Raise the vehicle and support it safely.

2. Drain the cooling system. Remove the battery.

3. Remove the thru-bolt for the expansion tank, disconnect the tank from the suction and remove the overflow hoses from the radiator.

4. Disconnect the upper radiator hose.

5. Loosen the drive belt for the compressor by loosening the lock nut, and loosening the adjusting nut under the lock nut.

6. Disconnect the upper connection on the oil cooler, loosen the pipe clip on

the radiator and slide the pipe down behind the radiator.

7. Unplug the connector to the electromagnetic clutch on the compressor and loosen the compressor mounting complete with the belt tensioner.

8. Place a protective cloth over the radiator member and rest the compressor on the radiator member. Secure the compressor to the radiator member.

9. Remove the turbo pressure pipe, situated between the turbo unit and the intercooler.

10. Disconnect the Lambda probe connector leads and disconnect them from the clips.

11. From the engine compartment, unbolt the flange joint between the exhaust pipe and the exhaust manifold. Push the exhaust pipe to one side and unhook the rubber hangers from the exhaust system. Disconnect the bottom coolant hose from the water pump.

12. From underneath the vehicle, remove the bottom retaining bolt for the radiator fan.

13. Disconnect the speedometer drive from the gearbox.

14. Select the 4th gear and separate the rubber joint in the gear selector linkage.

15. Remove the clips on the rubber gaiters over the inboard universal joints and slide the gaiters off the drive axles.

16. Disconnect the electrical leads from the alternator and the starter motor. Unplug the connector for the oil pressure switch.

17. Remove the clips and remove the top radiator hose.

18. Disconnect the top radiator at the cylinder head.

19. Unscrew the junction block from the battery shelf. Remove the clamp for the fuel filter.

20. Remove the battery shelf from the compartment.

21. Disconnect the high tension lead from the ignition coil at the distributor cap.

22. Remove the solenoid valve from the bracket on the radiator and unplug the electrical connections.

23. Remove the bolts from the top of the radiator fan. Disconnect the wiring loam and lift out the fan.

24. Pull the connector off the air mass meter. Disconnect the air mass meter from the air intake duct socket connector and the air cleaner. Leave the rubber socket connector attached to the turbo unit.

25. Remove the air intake duct by pulling it out of the aperture in the wing and twisting the ends inwards.

26. Remove the air cleaner top section first, then the remaining section.

27. Disconnect the relief valve hose from the turbo pressure pipe and remove the pipe.

28. Disconnect the Hall Effect transducer, the earth lead from the gear box and the electrical connector for the back-up lights.

29. Disconnect the end of the throttle cable and disconnect the throttle linkage.

30. Install a clamp to the hydraulic line to the slave cylinder and pinch the line tightly. With proper wrenches, open the line to the clutch slave cylinder.

31. Remove the front wheels.

32. From both sides of the vehicle, slacken the lower bolts retaining the steering swivel member to the strut assembly. Remove the 2 upper bolts.

33. Pivot the steering swivel member outwards to pull the inboard universal joint out of the drive shaft. Position dust covers over the exposed drive shaft cups.

34. Remove the engine stay bolt.

35. Remove the steering reservoir for the servo and position it within the engine compartment. Drain the fluid from the container.

36. Disconnect the large bore hose and the delivery hose from the steering servo pump and plug the open ends.

37. Disconnect the fuel return lie from the pressure regulator.

38. Remove the nut from the rear engine mounting and back off the front mount bolts a few turns.

39. Attach the lifting sling (Saab No. 83–92–409) to the rear lifting lug.

40. Lift the engine sufficiently to provide access for the removal of the components located between the engine and the fire wall.

41. Disconnect the vacuum hoses from the inlet manifold.

42. Remove the coolant hoses running between the heat exchanger and the water pump pipe.

43. Separate the coupling between the fuel pipe and the fuel injection manifold. Do not allow the fuel to spill or collect.

44. Cut the clips securing the wiring looms to the oil pipe, water pipe, inlet manifold steady bar and the oil supply pipe.

45. Unclip the wiring loom to the fuel injection manifold.

46. Disconnect the grounding connections and the electrical connectors from the wiring harness.

47. Unbolt the air cooled oil cooler and place it on top of the engine. The 2 lower bolts need only be loosened.

48. Carefully remove the engine from the vehicle, taking care not to damage the radiator.

49. Installation is the reverse of the removal procedure. Fill the engine with coolant, oil and power steering fluid. Test engine operation.

## Cylinder Head

### REMOVAL & INSTALLATION

#### *900 Series*

**8 VALVE ENGINE**

1. Disconnect the negative battery cable. Drain the radiator.

2. Remove the rubber bellows from between the air flow sensor and the throttle valve housing and disconnect the throttle cable from the throttle valve housing.

3. Disconnect the cable from the temperature transmitter. Remove the vacuum hose of the power brake booster from the intake manifold.

4. Disconnect the fuel lines from the fuel distributor to the injection valves. Tape the ends of the lines to prevent dirt from entering the system. Remove the bracket from the throttle valve housing mounting.

5. Remove the hose clamps at the connections to the thermostat housing, water pump and intake manifold.

6. Unbolt the exhaust pipe from the exhaust manifold.

7. Remove the distributor cap and ignition wires. Rotate the engine until cylinders No. 1 and No. 4 are at TDC. This must be done due to the design of the distributor driving dog which only allows the valve cover/distributor assembly to be removed with the engine in this position. Remove the valve cover.

8. Remove the camshaft sprocket bolts. Keep the chain on the sprocket and place sprocket/chain assembly between chain guide and tensioner. A center bolt is not used on the sprocket.

9. Remove the 2 bolts from the timing cover under the front of the head.

10. Remove the cylinder head bolts.

11. Raise the vehicle and support it safely. Place a support under the rear end of the engine. Remove the engine mounting bolt in the cylinder head.

12. Remove the screws in the transmission cover. Remove the cylinder head from the vehicle.

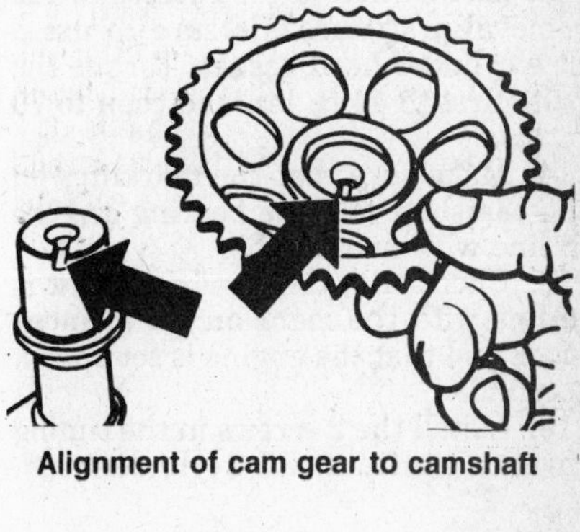

Alignment of cam gear to camshaft

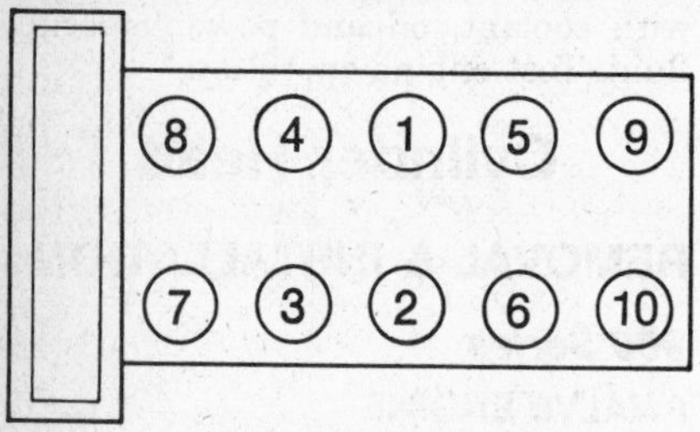

Cylinder head bolt torque sequence

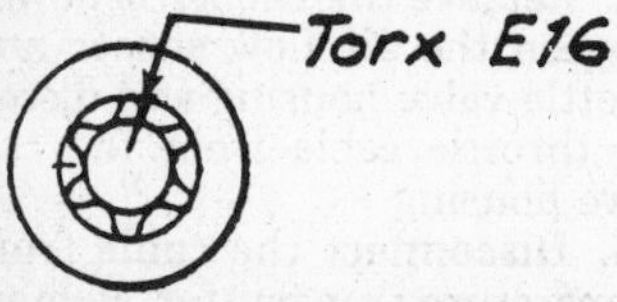

Top view of Torx head cylinder head bolts

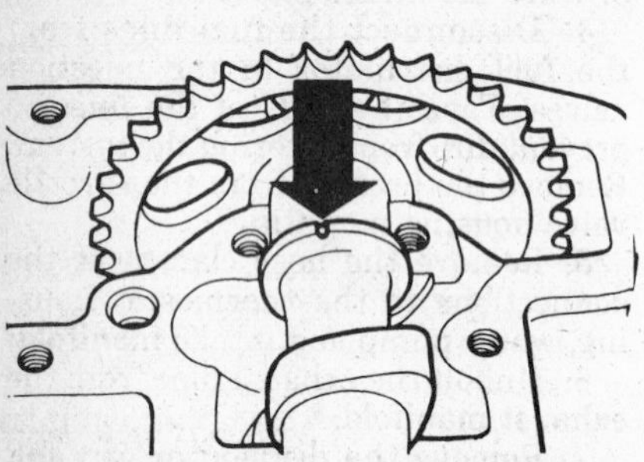
Alignment of marks on camshaft bearing caps

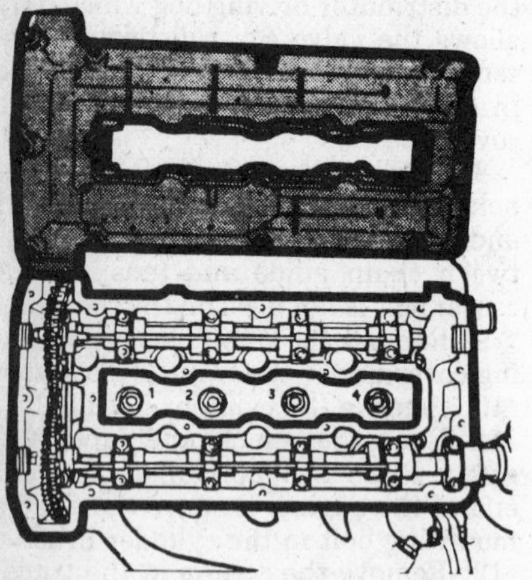
Top view of 16 valve cylinder head

13. Installation is the reverse of the removal procedure. Be sure to use a new cylinder head gasket. Torque the bolts first to 44 ft. lbs. and then to 70 ft. lbs.

14. Make sure that the markings on the camshaft and the bearing cap are in line with one another.

15. Check that the flywheel mark is in line with the mark on the cylinder block and that the engine is set on No. 1 cylinder.

16. Install the 2 screws in the timing cover on the front of the cylinder head.

Install the timing chain and sprocket as follows. Remove the tension from the chain tensioner with special tool No. 83-93-357 or equivalent. Hook the tool into the catch of the tensioner and pull upwards. Place the timing sprocket on the camshaft so that the mark on the sprocket and the screw holes coincide. If necessary, move the chain to position. Install the 3 retaining bolts in the sprocket and camshaft. If the distributor is mounted to the valve cover, the rotor should be facing the line on the edge of the distributor housing.

**16 VALVE ENGINE**

1. Remove the hood after scribing reference marks next to the mounting bolts, to aid later installation.
2. Remove the battery.
3. Drain the coolant from the radiator and cylinder block.
4. Remove the exhaust manifold and turbo unit.
5. Remove the tensioning pulley and drive belt for the air conditioner compressor.
6. Slacken the securing bolts for the steering pump bracket, remove the drive belt and push the pump out of the way.
7. Undo the wiring harness clips on the cylinder head.
8. Remove the 2 bolts in the timing cover, which are screwed into the cylinder head from underneath.
9. Remove the bolts in the right-hand engine mounting which are screwed into the cylinder head, together with the spacer sleeves.
10. Disconnect the hose between the thermostat housing and the radiator at the thermostat housing.
11. Remove the fuel pressure regulator and disconnect the ground leads for the fuel injection system.
12. Remove the AIC actuator. Remove the bracket for the A/C compressor from the cylinder head.
13. Remove the intake manifold complete with injectors and injection manifold.
14. Disconnect the lead from the temperature transmitter.
15. Remove the lid on the valve cover and the ignition cables together with the distributor cap.
16. Remove the valve cover. Disconnect the crankcase ventilation hose and remove the semi-circular rubber plug halves from the cylinder head.
17. Remove the A/C compressor and put it on the air intake for the heating system.
18. Line up the timing marks on the crankshaft and camshafts. To do this, remove the cover on the transaxle bell housing which reveals the timing marks on the flywheel. Turn the engine so that the **0** mark on the flywheel is lined up with the mark on the housing, or the end plate if the clutch cover has been removed. This makes certain that the pistons for No. 1 and 4 cylinders are at TDC.

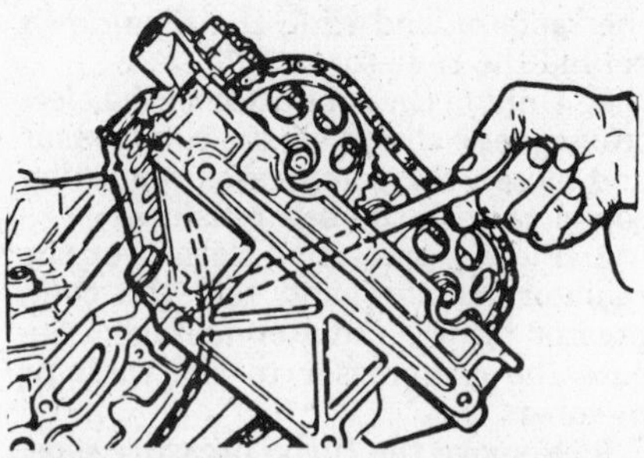
Releasing chain tensioner—sixteen valve engine

19. Remove the cam chain tensioner.
20. Block up the engine to lift the cylinder head off the block. Remove the cylinder head bolts and siphon off the oil from the cylinder head.
21. Install a guide pin in one of the bolt holes and lift off the cylinder head, making sure the pivoting guide for the cam chain is not damaged.
22. To install, align the **0** mark on the flywheel with the timing mark on the housing. Line up the marks on the camshafts with their respective timing marks.
23. Install the cylinder head gasket, making sure that it is held in position by the guide sleeves in the cylinder head flange.
24. Install the guide pin (Saab special tool No. 83-92-128 or equivalent) and position the timing chain and pivoting guide.
25. Carefully install the cylinder head. Use the guide pin as a pivot for the head, which must be turned slightly to enable it to pass the pivoting guide. Thereafter, alignment will be determined by the guide sleeves.
26. Install the cylinder head bolts and tighten them in 3 stages. Stage 1, torque to 45 ft. lbs. evenly. Stage 2, torque to 63 ft. lbs. evenly. Stage 3, another 90 degrees (¼ turn). Retighten the bolts after the engine has reached normal operating temperature. Remember to install the 2 M8 sized bolts in the underside of the cylinder head.
27. Install the camshaft sprockets, fitting the sprocket for the exhaust cam first. Make sure that the chain between the crankshaft sprocket and the camshaft sprocket is kept tight. Next install the intake cam sprocket. Keep the chain tight between the sprockets.
28. Lightly tighten the center bolts securing the camshaft sprockets. Adjust the chain tensioner and install it under tension. Tighten the bolt.
29. Release the tensioner by pressing

the pivoting guide firmly against it. Thereafter, press the pivoting guide against the chain to put a basic tension on the chain.

30. Depress the pivoting guide to check that the tensioner is working. Rotate the crankshaft 2 complete turns clockwise, viewed from the transmission end. Check that the earlier settings of the crankshaft and camshaft timings have not changed. Tighten the cam sprocket bolts to 49 ft. lbs.

31. Continue the installation in the reverse order of the removal procedure.

### 9000 Series

1. Disconnect the negative battery cable. Raise and support the vehicle safely.
2. Remove the right front wheel assembly and the inner fender panel.
3. Drain the coolant. Remove the radiator expansion tank. Disconnect the steering servo reservoir and set aside. Leave the hoses attached.
4. Loosen the compressor drive belt and remove the belt.
5. Disconnect the electrical leads from the air compressor.
6. Unbolt the compressor from its mounting bracket. Disconnect the top pipe connecting on the air cooled oil cooler and push the pipe to one side. Rest the compressor on the radiator crossmember. Unbolt the compressor mounting bracket and remove it.
7. Unbolt the front exhaust pipe flange and unhook the rubber hangers.
8. Remove the steady bar for the turbo unit and the oil return pipe.
9. Disconnect the hose from the intercooler at the turbo unit. Disconnect the oil supply pipe from the turbo.
10. Disconnect the hose between the air mass meter and the turbo unit. Disconnect the coolant hose from the thermostat housing and the hose from the cylinder head.
11. Disconnect the oil supply hose or pipe so as not to obstruct the removal of the exhaust manifold. If necessary, remove the clip holding the pipe to the cylinder head and slave cylinder.
12. Unbolt and lift off the exhaust manifold complete with the turbo unit, pushing the oil supply pipe out of the way at the same time.
13. Disconnect the lead to the temperature transducer.
14. Remove the engine stay bracket from its attachment point on the wing.
15. Remove and remove the bolt securing the engine stay bracket to the cylinder head. Remove the intake manifold from the cylinder head.
16. Disconnect the breather hose for the crankcase ventilation from the camshaft cover.
17. Disconnect the vacuum hose and the Hall Effect transducer lead from the distributor and remove the distributor cap complete with the high tension leads.
18. Unscrew and remove the spark plug inspection plate and the clips for the high tension leads.
19. Remove the camshaft cover.
20. Line up the crankshaft with the **0** timing mark and check that the camshaft timing marks also coincide. Remove the camshaft sprockets.
21. Remove the camshaft tensioner. Remove the 2 cylinder head bolts adjacent to the timing cover, which is accessible from below.
22. Disconnect the starter motor lead from the clip on the thermostat housing.
23. Remove the Torx® type cylinder head bolts.
24. Install a guide pin in the drilled hole in the right hand top corner of the cylinder head. Make sure that the timing chain is positioned such that the pivoting chain guide will not obstruct the cylinder head and carefully lift the cylinder head from the engine block.
25. Before installation, clean both the cylinder head and the engine block surfaces. Install a new gasket. Be sure the crankshaft is lined up in the **0** position and that the camshafts are in line with their respective timing marks.

**NOTE: When the pistons of the No. 1 and No. 4 cylinders are at top dead center, the crankshaft 0 mark on the flywheel must be in line with the mark on the clutch cover or the end plate, if the clutch cover has been removed. The marks on the camshafts must be in line with those on the cam bearing caps. This indicates the exhaust valves for No. 1and No. 4 cylinders are closed.**

26. Install a guide pin in the drilled hole in the top of the right hand corner of the cylinder head and lower the cylinder head carefully into position on the engine block. Locate the cylinder head on the guide sleeves.
27. Install the cylinder head bolts, tightening them in the correct sequence to the specified torque.

Stage 1–Torque to 44 ft. lbs.

Stage 2–Torque to 67 ft. lbs.

Stage 3–Run the engine to normal operating temperature and allow the engine to cool for 30 minutes.

Stage 4–Slacken the bolts and retighten each bolt to 66 ft. lbs.

Stage 5–Tighten by turning the bolts through a further 90 degrees (¼ turn).

28. Position the inlet valve camshaft sprocket, followed by the exhaust valve camshaft sprocket. Be sure that the chain is correctly positioned between the guides. Tighten the sprocket center bolts to 48 ft. lbs.
29. Install the timing chain tensioner. Advance the tensioner before installing it. Release the tensioner and rotate the crankshaft 2 revolutions. Make sure the camshaft and flywheel timing marks are correctly aligned.
30. Install the both halves of the split seal and the camshaft cover. Install the bolt at the distributor end and the middle bolt at the other end first. Tighten the bolts to 16 ft. lbs.
31. Check that the timing marks for the distributor rotor are lined up, Install the distributor cap and connect the lead for the Hall Effect transducer. Connect all vacuum hoses.
32. Connect the high tension leads to the spark plugs. Secure the leads in the clips. Install the inspection plate and tighten the retaining screws.
33. Install the clip securing the starter motor lead to the thermostat housing.
34. Install a new gasket on the inlet manifold and install the manifold in place. Install the top securing bolts first and then install the lower bolts, using an extension bar.
35. Install the bolt for the engine stay bracket to the cylinder head and position the stay bracket in place. Install a new gasket onto the exhaust manifold and position the exhaust manifold to the cylinder head.
36. Install the oil supply pipe. Install the clip and the slave cylinder bolt. Install the oil return line and the steady bar for the turbo unit.
37. Connect the hose between the turbo unit and the intercooler. Connect the cooler hose to the thermostat housing and the hose to the cylinder head.
38. Install the air mass meter socket connector into the turbo unit and tighten the clip. Connect the hose between the intercooler and the turbo unit.
39. Install and tighten the nuts securing the front section of the exhaust pipe to the turbo compressor. Bolt the A/C compressor mounting bracket onto the cylinder head and engine block.
40. Install the A/C compressor. Leave the coolant hose in the bracket when installing the compressor.
41. Connect the electrical leads and make sure the lead is clear of the compressor pulley. Install the steering servo reservoir. Install the coolant expansion tank and tighten the hose clip.
42. Connect the top pipe to the air cooled oil cooler and secure the cooler

to the radiator. Install the overflow line between the expansion tank and the radiator.

43. Install the compressor belt, adjust the tension and tighten the belt tensioner bolt. Install the inner right wheel arch, and install the wheel.

44. Lower the vehicle and tighten the wheel. Connect the negative battery cable and fill the cooling system with coolant. Start the engine and test the engine operation.

## OVERHAUL

**For all cylinder head overhaul procedures, please refer to the "Engine Rebuilding" in the Unit Repair section.**

# Intake Manifold

## REMOVAL & INSTALLATION

### *8 Valve Engine*

1. Disconnect the negative battey cable. Disconnect all hoses, wires and connectors that would inhibit the intake manifold from being removed.
2. It may be necessary to remove the distributor cap and the ignition wires to gain clearance. Remove the throttle valve housing.
3. Remove the intake manifold retaining bolts. Remove the intake manifold from the engine.
4. Installation is the reverse of the removal procedure. Be sure the proper gasket is used. A coolant leakage could occur if the wrong one is used.

### *16 Valve Engine*

1. Disconnect the negative battery cable. Disconnect all hoses, wires and connectors that would inhibit the intake manifold being removed.
2. Remove the turbo pressure pipe, the lubricating oil pressure pipe and the return oil pipe.
3. Remove the intake manifold retaining bolts. Remove the intake manifold along with the injection manifold, injectors and the AIC regulator.
4. Installation is the reverse of the removal procedure. Be sure the proper gasket is used. A coolant leak could occur if the wrong one is used.

# Exhaust Manifold

## REMOVAL & INSTALLATION

1. Disconnect the negative battery cable. Disconnect all necessary hoses, wires, and connectors that would inhibit the exhaust manifold from being removed.
2. Unbolt the exhaust pipe at the connecting flange.
3. If the vehicle is equipped with a heat shield, remove it.
4. Remove the exhaust manifold bolts. Remove the exhaust manifold from the vehicle.
5. Installation is the reverse of removal.

# Turbocharger

## REMOVAL & INSTALLATION

### *900 Series*

1. Disconnect the negative battery cable. Remove the charge pressure regulator and block off the exhaust pipe. Remove the battery as required. Remove the tension on compressor belt.
2. Disconnect the hose between the compressor and the throttle housing.
3. Disconnect the oil supply line and the oil return line at the turbo unit.
4. Remove the retaining bolts securing the turbo to the exhaust manifold. Remove the turbo unit from the vehicle. Plug the holes in the turbo unit to prevent dirt from entering.
5. Installation is the reverse of the removal procedure.
6. Fill the lubricating inflow of the turbo unit with engine oil before connecting the oil return line at the turbo.
7. Crank the engine for about 30 seconds with terminal 15 on the ignition coil disconnected. This will fill the lubricating system of the turbo before the engine is started.

### *9000 Series*

1. Disconnect the negative battery cable. Release the tension on the compressor belt by slackening the belt tensioner.
2. Disconnect the top pipe coupling on the air cooled oil cooler and disconnect the clips securing the pipe to the radiator.
3. Remove the compressor mounting bolts. Insert a sheet of metal to protect the oil cooler and lift the compressor towards the expansion tank.
4. Remove the solenoid valve from its mounting on the radiator and disconnect the electrical leads.
5. Disconnect the electrical leads at the radiator fan. Unbolt and remove the fan.
6. Unplug the electrical connectors for the air mass meter. Disconnect the toggle fasteners securing the air mass meter to the air cleaner cover and pull the rubber socket connector off the turbo unit.
7. Disconnect the turbo pressure pipe from the compressor.

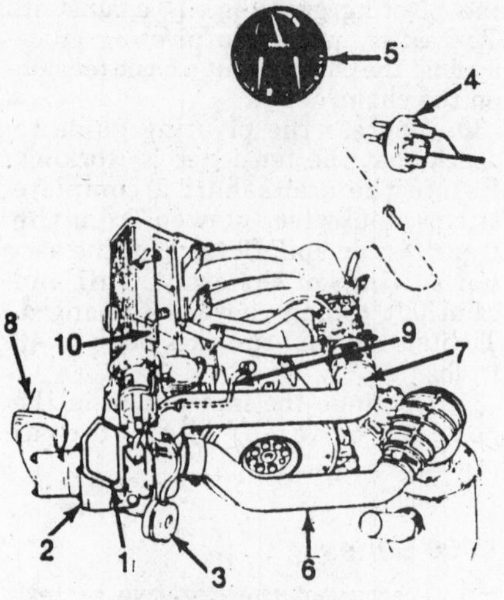


1. Turbocharger
2. Wastegate boost control
3. Diaphragm capsule
4. Over-pressure guard
5. Turbo gauge
6. Hose, air cleaner to turbocharger
7. Hose, turbocharger to inlet manifold
8. Exhaust outlet pipe
9. Oil supply line
10. Oil return line

**Eight valve engine turbocharger assembly**

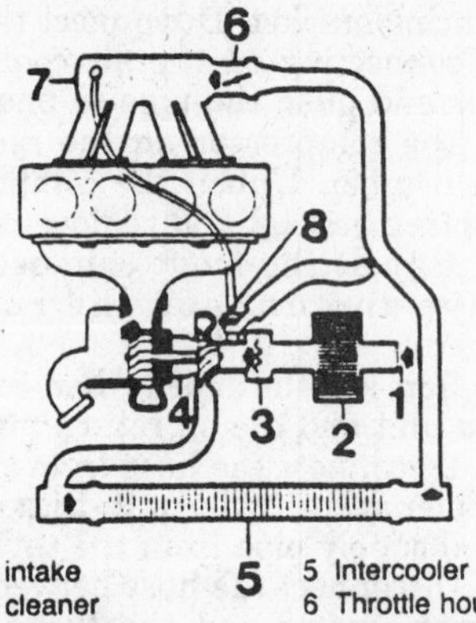


1 Air intake
2 Air cleaner
3 Air massmeter
4 Turbo unit
5 Intercooler
6 Throttle housing
7 Inlet manifold
8 Relief valve

**Sixteen valve engine turbocharger assembly**

8. Remove the oil pipe to the turbo unit. Unbolt the clutch slave cylinder and remove the clip securing the oil pipe to the cylinder head. Disconnect the oil pipe banjo coupling from the block and undo the clip on the inlet manifold.
9. Disconnect the exhaust pipe from the turbo compressor.
10. Disconnect the front rubber hangers for the exhaust pipe.
11. Remove the steady bar bracket between the sump and the compressor. Remove the securing bolts and loosen the oil return lines. Cap the aperture to prevent washers or nuts

from the exhaust manifold dropping inside during the removal.

12. Remove the nuts securing the exhaust manifold to the cylinder head.

13. Lift the exhaust manifold from the cylinder head, along with the turbo unit.

14. Should further disassembly be necessary, complete as required.

15. To install, position the turbo unit to the exhaust manifold and tighten the retaining nuts. Install the new lock nuts with the locking flange turned inwards.

16. Install a new gasket over the studs for the exhaust manifold and install the manifold/turbo unit to the cylinder head assembly. Tighten the nuts to 30 ft. lbs.

17. Install the clip holding the turbo oil supply pipe to the inlet manifold. Connect and tighten the banjo coupling to the engine block. Make sure that the copper washers are in good condition. Secure the pipe to the turbo unit.

18. Install the return oil pipe and the steady bar bracket between the turbo unit and the crankcase. Connect the rubber hangers for the front exhaust hanger.

19. Bolt the exhaust pipe to the turbo compressor. Use new locking nuts with the locking flanges turned outward. Tighten to 19 ft. lbs.

20. Install the turbo pressure pipe to the compressor and assemble the air mass meter and rubber socket connector between the air cleaner body and the inlet side of the turbo compressor.

21. Assemble the fan and solenoid valve, securing the electrical leads into their clips. Connect the return hose to the solenoid valve. Insert a piece of metal to protect the oil cooler and install the A/C compressor.

22. Reconnect the oil pipe to the oil cooler and secure the pipe clip to the radiator. Install the compressor belt and tighten it to specification.

### TROUBLESHOOTING

**For more information on turbocharging, please refer to "Turbocharging" in the Unit Repair section.**

## Front Cover

### REMOVAL & INSTALLATION

1. Disconnect the negative battery cable.

2. Drain the engine oil and the coolant.

3. Remove the camshaft cover retaining bolts and lift off the cover.

4. Remove the bracket for the steering servo pump, complete with the pump and alternator.

5. Remove the chain tensioner.

6. Secure the flywheel and loosen the crankshaft pulley nut and remove the pulley.

7. Remove the belt tensioner and the water pump pipe.

8. Remove the oil pipes and the water pump pulley.

9. Remove the oil pump.

10. Remove the bolts and lift off the timing cover.

11. Install in the reverse order of removal.

### OIL SEAL REPLACEMENT

#### 8 Valve Engine

1. Disconnect the negative battery cable. Remove the alternator belt. If the vehicle is equipped with power steering or air conditioning, remove the required belts.

2. Remove the clutch cover (torque converter cover) and lock the crankshaft using Saab tool No. 83-92-987 or equivalent by locking the tool to the ring gear.

3. From under the vehicle, remove the pulley retaining bolt using Saab tool No. 83-92-961 or equivalent. Remove the pulley from the vehicle.

4. Pull off the old seal ring using a suitable tool.

5. Installation is the reverse of removal. Torque the retaining bolt to 137 ft. lbs.

#### 16 Valve Engine

1. Disconnect the negative battery cable. Raise and support the vehicle safely.

2. Remove the right front wheeland tire assembly. remove the inner front fender panel.

3. Loosen and remove the drive belts.

4. Remove the retaining bolt for the crankshaft pulley.

5. Remove the crankshaft pulley.

6. Using a pry bar, carefully remove the oil seal without marring the crankshaft stub end.

7. Install a new, oiled seal, using an appropriate seal installer.

8. Install the pulley and tighten the retaining bolt to 134 ft. lbs. (180 Nm).

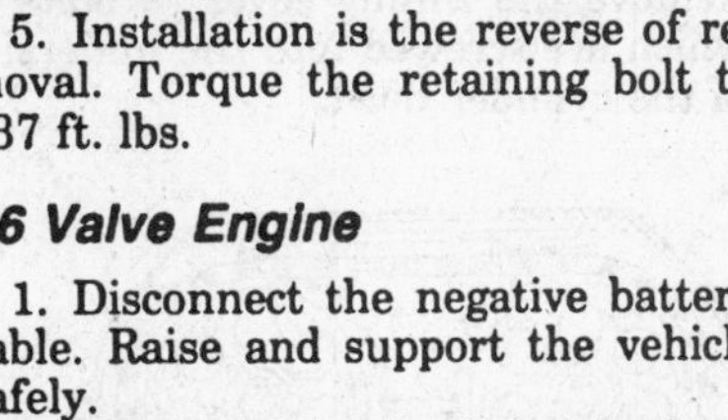

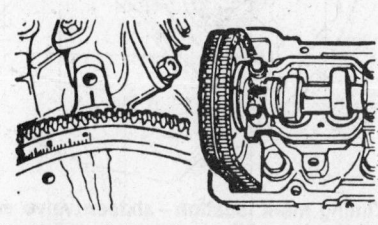

Timing mark location – eight valve engine

9. Tighten the drive belts, using a belt tension gauge. (New belt – 180 lbs.; Used belt – 120 lbs.)

10. Install the forward section of the inner fender panel.

11. Replace the front wheel and lower the vehicle.

## Timing Chain and Sprockets

### REMOVAL & INSTALLATION

#### 8 Valve Engine

1. Disconnect the negative battery cable. Remove the engine from the vehicle.

2. Remove the distributor cap and ignition wires. Rotate the engine until cylinders No. 1 and No. 4 are at TDC. This must be done due to the design of the distributor driving dog which only allows the valve cover/distributor assembly to be removed with the engine in this position.

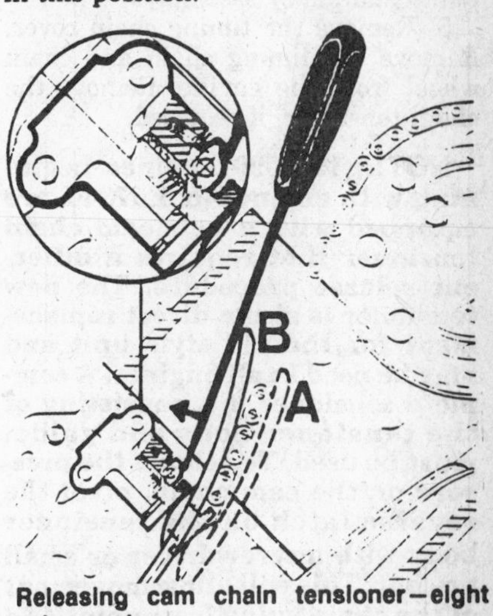


Releasing cam chain tensioner – eight valve engine

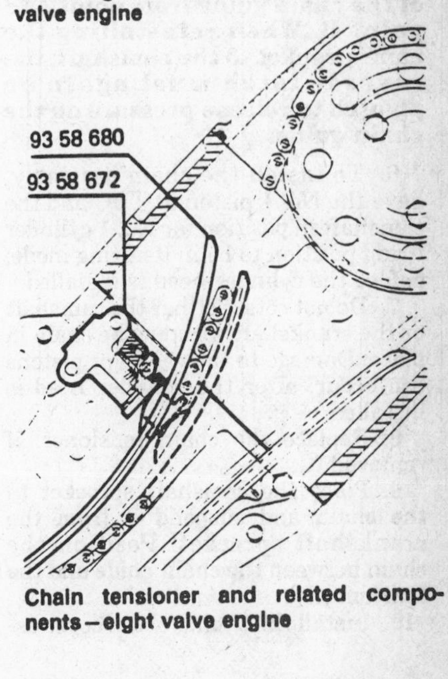


Chain tensioner and related components – eight valve engine

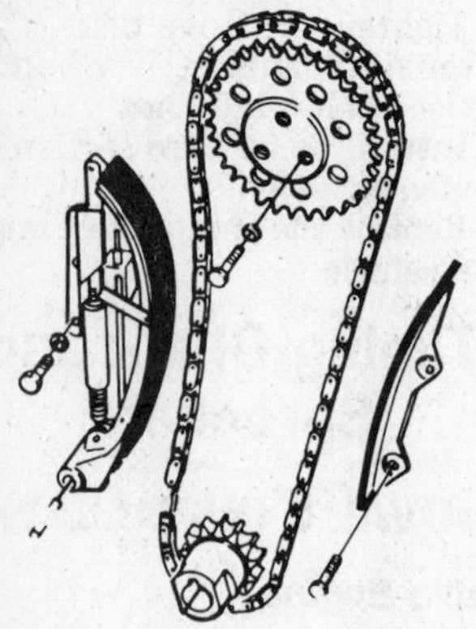

Timing chain assembly—eight valve engine

3. Remove the valve cover assembly. Remove the sprocket from the camshaft and rest it on the chain tensioner and the chain guide.

4. Remove the cylinder head. Remove the crankshaft pulley and oil pump assembly. Remove the water pump and pulley assembly.

5. Remove the timing chain cover. Remove the timing chain and chain wheel from the engine. Remove the chain tensioner, if required.

**NOTE: 1984–90 engines beginning with engine No. E57340, are equipped with a new cam chain tensioner that requires a different release procedure. The new tensioner is also a direct replacement for the old style unit and may be used in all engines. A complete tensioner kit, consisting of the tensioner body and guide, must be used. To release the pressure on the cam chain, pivot the reverse latch on the tensioner body with a screwdriver or small pry bar. This will allow movement of the chain guide from point A to point B. When reinstalling the cam sprocket to the camshaft, the reverse latch must again be pivoted to release pressure on the chain guide.**

6. To install the chain assembly, have the No. 1 piston at TDC and the camshaft in position for No. 1 cylinder firing position to be in its firing mode, before the cylinder head is installed.

7. Do not rotate either the camshaft or the crankshaft without the chain in place. Damage to the valves or pistons can occur, after the cylinder head is installed.

8. Replace the chain tensioner, if removed.

9. Place the camshaft sprocket to the chain and suspend it from the crankshaft sprocket. Position the chain between the chain guide and the tensioner.

10. Install the timing chain cover assembly while pulling up the chain to avoid being caught under the cover.

11. Install the water pump assembly and install the cylinder head. Torque the head bolts to specification.

12. Using the tensioner release tool, disengage the tensioner and install the cam sprocket and chain to the camshaft. Align the marks on the sprocket and the camshaft bearing.

13. Install the sprocket retaining bolts. Release the tensioner assembly. Install the oil pump assembly, seal and pulley.

14. Continue the installation as required. Do not use an early type inlet manifold gasket as coolant leakage could occur within the engine.

### *16 Valve Engine*

1. Disconnect the negative battery cable. Remove the engine from the vehicle.

2. Remove the lid on the valve cover and remove the ignition wires. Remove the valve cover.

3. Position the crankshaft for TDC, with the **0** mark on the flywheel in line with the timing mark on the transaxle end plate. These marks must be aligned before the timing chain is removed.

4. Remove the crankshaft pulley using a puller. Remove the water pump, located behind the crankshaft pulley. Remove the timing cover, 2 bolts of which are screwed into the underside of the cylinder head.

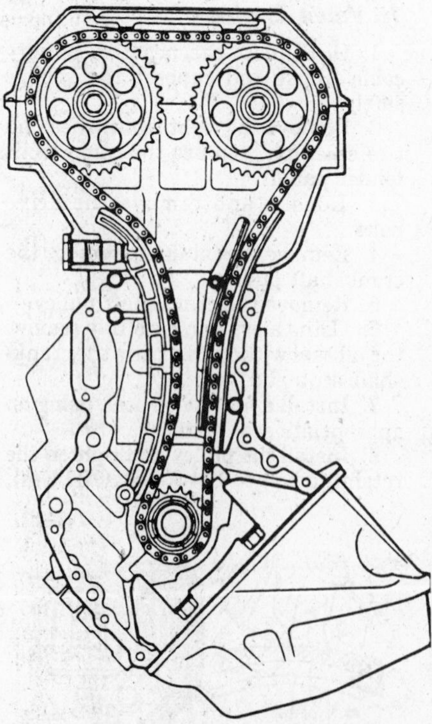

Timing mark location—sixteen valve engine

5. The cam chain and crankshaft timing sprocket should now both be visible. From above, release the timing chain tensioner by pressing the pivoting guide firmly against it. Remove the chain tensioner.

6. Using a special tool to hold the camshafts, remove the center bolts securing the camshaft sprockets. Throughout this procedure, keep the camshafts in their basic correct setting. If they are rotated out of position at any stage, especially without their sprockets and chain, the valves can be damaged.

7. Disconnect the timing chain from the sprockets and remove the chain, clearing it from the crankshaft sprockets.

8. To install the timing chain, place the chain around the crankshaft sprocket. Run the chain up through

Crankshaft locking procedure

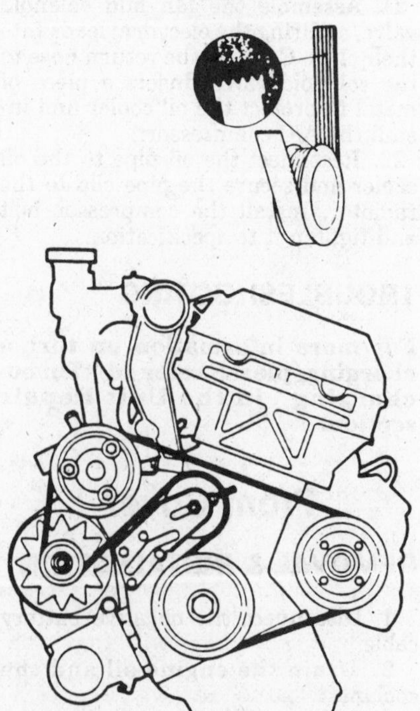

Serpentine drive belt adjustment

the opening in the cylinder head if not already done. Install the chain and sprocket on the exhaust cam first. Make sure the chain is taut between the crankshaft and camshaft sprockets. Install the bolts but do not tighten.

9. Install the chain and sprocket to the intake cam. Keep the chain taut between the cam sprockets while it is being installed. Install the bolts but do not tighten. Make sure the chain is seated in the guide tensioner grooves.

10. Tension the chain tensioner by fully depressing the piston and then rotating it to the locked position.

11. Install the chain tensioner with the piston under tension. Make sure that the copper gasket is in good condition and that the sealing surface is clean and free from burrs.

12. Trigger the chain tensioner by pressing the pivoting chain guide against it, thereafter, press the pivoting guide against the chain to give the chain its basic tension. Check that the chain tensioner maintains tension on the chain when the pressure on the chain guide is released and that the basic setting stop for the tensioner holds the chain guide tight against the chain. A limited amount of play will be present until the hydraulic pressure takes over once the engine is running.

13. Check the setting by rotating the crankshaft 2 complete turns in its normal direction of rotation around to the timing mark. The basic setting of the cams should remain unaltered.

14. Lock the exhaust cam by using a wrench on the cast hex bolt and torque the sprocket bolt to 48 ft. lbs. Repeat this on the intake cam.

15. Complete the procedure on the intake cam sprocket. When loosening or torquing the sprocket center bolts, hold the cam still using a wrench installed over the flats on the camshaft. The accuracy of the timing chain adjustment will depend on the condition of the chain.

## Camshaft

### REMOVAL & INSTALLATION

#### *8 Valve Engine*

1. Disconnect the negative battery cable. Remove the distributor cap and ignition wires. Rotate the engine until cylinders No. 1 and No. 4 are at TDC. This must be done due to the design of the distributor driving dog which only allows the valve cover/distributor assembly to be removed with the engine in this position.

2. Remove the valve cover assembly.

3. Be sure both the crankshaft and camshaft are at the No. 1 cylinder firing mode and the indexing lines still are aligned.

4. Remove the camshaft sprocket, keeping the chain on the sprocket. Place the sprocket between the chain guide and tensioner.

5. Remove the camshaft bearing caps and lift the camshaft from the bearing assembly housing. The bearing assembly housing can then be removed, if necessary.

6. Installation is the reverse of the removal procedure. Be sure that the timing marks are properly aligned.

#### *16 Valve Engine*

1. Disconnect the negative battery cable. Remove the engine from the vehicle.

2. Remove the lid on the valve cover. Disconnect the spark plug wires and vacuum hose from the distributor and remove the distributor cap.

3. Remove the valve cover and position the crankshaft for TDC. The 0 mark on the flywheel should be in line with the timing mark on the bell housing end plate.

4. Remove the distributor. Remove the oil pipe.

5. Remove the center bolts securing the camshaft sprockets. Use a proper holding tool to hold the camshafts from rotating. Always keep the camshafts in their correct basic setting. If the setting of the crankshaft or camshafts is altered at this stage the valves can be damaged.

6. Remove the camshaft timing chain tensioner. Remove the camshaft sprockets.

7. Remove the camshaft bearing caps. Keep them in correct order for later reassembly. Lift out the camshafts.

8. Installation is the reverse the removal procedure. When installing, the bearing caps marked 1–5 belong to the intake cam, while those marked 6–10 go with the exhaust cam. Torque the bearing cap bolts to 11 ft. lbs.

## Piston and Connecting Rod

### POSITIONING

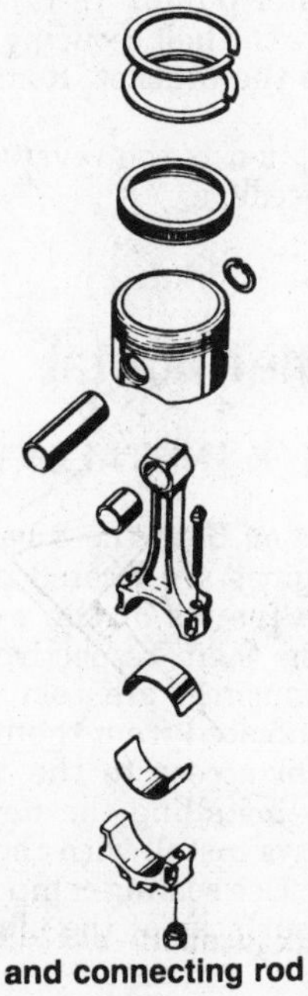

Piston and connecting rod assembly

# ENGINE LUBRICATION

## Rear Main Bearing Oil Seal

### REMOVAL & INSTALLATION

This seal is otherwise known as the crankshaft seal at the flywheel end. The seal can be changed with the engine in the vehicle, but the clutch and flywheel must first be removed.

1. Remove the clutch and the flywheel from the vehicle.

2. Remove the old seal ring using the proper tool.

3. Install the new seal with the spring ring turned inwards toward the crankshaft using the proper seal installation tool.

4. Continue the installation in the reverse order of the removal.

## Oil Pump

### REMOVAL & INSTALLATION

#### *8 Valve Engine*

The oil pump is a gear type pump and is driven by the crankshaft. It is positioned between the timing cover and crankshaft pulley. The pump assembly can be removed with the engine in the vehicle.

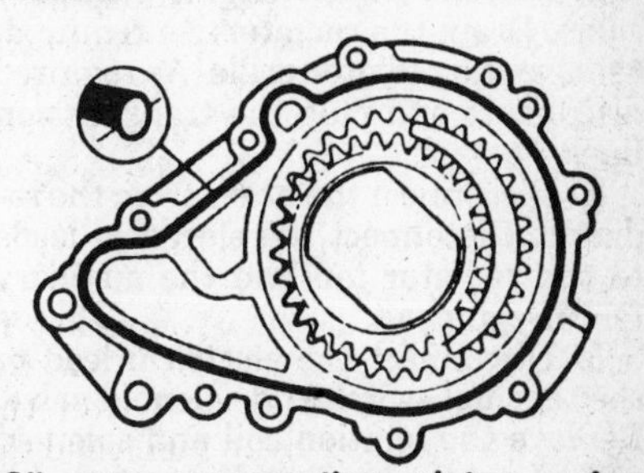

Oil pump crosssection – sixteen valve engine

1. Disconnect the negative battery cable. Remove the crankshaft pulley.
2. Lock the crankshaft in place by using a flywheel locking bracket.
3. Remove the oil pump retaining bolts. Remove the oil pump from the timing cover.
4. Before installation, prime the pump assembly and be sure the mark on the outer gear is visible.
5. Install a new gasket and install the pump and the timing cover. Complete the assembly as required.
6. Before starting the engine, remove the oil filter base and fill the passageway on the pressure side with oil. Replace the filter base.

### *16 Valve Engine*

1. Raise the vehicle and support it safely.
2. Remove the right front wheel and the front inner fender panel section.
3. Loosen and remove the multigroove belt. Loosen the compressor drive belt.
4. Remove the crankshaft pulley. It may be necessary to hold the crankshaft while removing the pulley bolt.
5. Remove the oil pump cover retaining bolts. Remove the oil pump.
6. Before installing the pump, install a new O-ring seal.
7. Install the pump to the engine and install the retaining bolts.
8. Install the pulley and drive belts. Tighten the pulley bolt to 140 ft. lbs. torque. Tighten the new drive belt to 180 lbs. strand tension or a used belt to 120 lbs. strand tension.
9. Install the inner fender panel and the right front wheel. Lower the vehicle and check oil pump operation.

# ENGINE COOLING

## Radiator

### REMOVAL & INSTALLATION

1. Disconnect the negative battery cable. Drain the radiator. As required, remove the radiator grille. As required disconnect and plug the transmission lines.
2. Disconnect the hoses from the radiator. Disconnect the electrical leads to the radiator fan and the auxiliary fan, if equipped.
3. Disconnect the electrical lead to the thermal switch and solenoid valve. Remove the ignition coil and solenoid valve from the bracket. Remove the oil cooler.
4. Remove the 2 bolts from the upper radiator support Lift the radiator out of the vehicle by pulling the top of the radiator slightly backwards.
5. Installation is the reverse of the removal procedure.

## Water Pump

### REMOVAL & INSTALLATION

### *8 Valve Engine*

1. Disconnect the negative battery cable. Drain the cooling system.
2. Remove the necessary components in order to gain access to the water pump assembly.
3. Remove the drive belts. Remove the water pump pulley.
4. Remove the water pump retaining bolts. Remove the water pump from the engine.
5. Installation is the reverse of the removal procedure.

### *16 Valve Engine*

1. Disconnect the negative battery cable. Raise and support the vehicle safely.
2. Remove the right front wheel assembly. Remove the front section of the inner fender panel.
3. Drain the engine coolant. Loosen the drive belts. Remove the water pump pulley and the belt tensioning pulley.
4. Remove the clips holding the oil lines at the oil cooler. Remove the clips securing the water pipe to the engine block. Disconnect the coolant hoses from the water pump.
5. Remove the bolt securing the water pump to the bracket. Remove the water pump.
6. Installation is the reverse of the removal procedure.

## Thermostat

### REMOVAL & INSTALLATION

Thermostats on both the 8 valve and 16 valve engines are located in housings on the fronts of the cylinder heads, facing their respective radiators. The housings are cast elbows, which are unbolted from the heads in order to gain access to the thermostats. When installing the new thermostat, always install with the spring facing down. Use sealing compound on the joining surfaces of the elbow and head.

# EMISSION CONTROLS

**Please refer to "Emission Control" in the Unit Repair section for system maintenance procedures. Due to the complex nature of modern electronic engine control systems, comprehensive diagnosis and testing procedures fall outside the confines of this repair manual. For complete information on diagnosis, testing and repair procedures concerning all modern engine and emission control systems, please refer to "Chilton's Guide to Electronic Engine Controls".**

## Emission Warning Lamps

### RESETTING

On all models except the Turbo, the **EXH** maintenance light on the dash comes on every 30,000 miles. The oxygen sensor should be changed at this time. On the Turbo models, the **EXH** maintenance light is not used and the oxygen sensor is replaced every 60,000 miles.

To reset the milage counter for the **EXH** light, press the reset button on the counter unit. The unit is located at the flasher relay under the instrument panel.

# FUEL SYSTEM

## Fuel System Service Precautions

Read the following precautions before starting any work on the fuel injection system.

- Always make sure that the battery is properly connected to the electrical system of the car before attempting to start the engine.
- Under no circumstances must any attempt be made to start the engine using an external power source, such as batteries connected or a rapid charger with the battery connected to the electrical system of the car.
- If a rapid charger is used, make sure that both battery leads are disconnected.

- Never disconnect the battery while the engine is running.
- Make sure that all electrical connections are making contact.
- Never unplug or plug in the connector for the electronic control unit with the ignition switched on.
- Before conducting a compression test, disconnect the distributor, remove the fuse for the fuel pump and unplug the electronic control unit.
- Never subject the car to temperatures exceeding 176 degrees unless the electronic control unit has beenremoved from the car.
- Always remove the electronic control unit from the car before carrying out any electric welding.
- Take care never to reverse the polarity of the fuel pump.

### RELIEVING FUEL SYSTEM PRESSURE

1. Remove the luggage compartment floor and the panel over the fuel pump and unplug the connector for the leads to the pump.
2. Disconnect the delivery line from the fuel pump.
3. Open the glove compartment and the hinged cover for the fuse panel.
4. Remove fuses 14 and 22 and connect ajumper lead between the terminals and across switch No. 8393886 to provide power to the pump. Make sure the switch is **OFF**.
5. Start the pump by moving the switch to **ON**.
6. The pressure is released through the discharge outlet on the pump.

## Fuel Filter

### REMOVAL & INSTALLATION

1. Disconnect the electrical connectors at the fuel pump. Remove the fuel pump fuse.
2. Crank the engine until fuel is exhausted from the system. Disconnect the negative battery cable.
3. Carefully remove the fuel filter fittings, using the proper wrench and covering it with a shop towel.
4. Remove the fuel filter assembly from the vehicle.
5. Installation is the reverse of the removal procedure. The filter is installed with arrows pointing in direction of flow.

## Fuel Pump

### PRESSURE TESTING

#### *Voltage Check*

1. Remove the round cover plate from the top of the fuel pump.
2. Measure the voltage between the positive and negative terminals when the fuel pump is operating.
3. The lowest permissible voltage is 11.5 volts.

#### *Capacity Check*

**NOTE: Be sure that the fuel filter is not clogged and that the battery is fully charged.**

1. Disconnect the return fuel pipe from the fuel distributor.
2. Connect the test pipe to the fuel distributor and place the other end in a suitable container.
3. On vehicles with the safety switch on the air flow sensor, remove the switch connector from the air flow sensor.
4. On vehicles with the fuel pump relay and the pulse sensor, remove the pump relay. Connect a jumper lead between terminals 30 and 87 on 900 series vehicles.
5. Switch on the ignition and allow the pump to run for 30 seconds. Measure the quantity of fuel. The proper specification should be 900cc/30 seconds. This should be measured in the return line.

### REMOVAL & INSTALLATION

**NOTE: All vehicles are equipped with a plastic gas tank. Care should be exercised when removing the fuel pump from the plastic gas tank.**

1. Disconnect the electrical connectors at the fuel pump. Remove the fuel pump fuse.
2. Crank the engine until fuel is exhausted from the system. Disconnect the negative battery cable.
3. Remove the rear floor panel in the luggage compartment. Remove the valve cover from above the fuel pump.
4. Disconnect the electrical connections from the fuel pump.
5. Carefully disconnect the fuel lines from the fuel pump. Be sure to use the proper wrench and cover it with a shop towel while removing the connections.
6. Remove the fuel pump mounting clamp. Lift the fuel pump from the tank assembly.
7. Installation is the reverse of the removal.

## Fuel Injection

**Due to complex nature of modern fuel injection systems, comprehensive diagnosis and testing procedures fall outside the confines of this repair manual. For complete information on fuel injection diagnosis, testing and repair procedures please refer to "Chilton's Guide to Fuel Injection And Feedback Carburetors".**

# MANUAL TRANSAXLE

### REMOVAL & INSTALLATION

#### *900 Series*

1. Remove the engine and transaxle from the vehicle as an assembly.
2. Position the engine and transaxle assembly in a suitable holding fixture. Drain the engine oil.
3. Remove the clutch shaft using a slide hammer and special tool 87–90–529.
4. Remove the slave cylinder retaining bolts. Remove the bolts retaining the transaxle assembly to the engine.
5. Carefully separate the engine from the transaxle.

#### *9000 Series*

1. Disconnect the negative battery cable. Remove the battery. Raise and support the vehicle safely.
2. Remove the air intake duct for the air cleaner from the fender. Remove the washer fluid reservoir and disconnect the positive lead from the washer terminal block.
3. Remove the fuel filter, the terminal block and the battery tray.
4. Remove the electrical connector from the air mass meter and remove the air mass meter carefully.
5. Remove the intake dust cover for the air cleaner.
6. Disconnect the Hall transmitter lead at the distributor.
7. Remove the cover and the filter element from the air cleaner.
8. Remove the air cleaner body.
9. Remove the turbo pressure pipe.
10. Disconnect the battery ground cable and the back-up light switch leads from the gear box assembly.
11. Install a clamp onto the hose in the slave cylinder line and pinch the hose together. Separate the pressure line between the pipe and the hose.
12. Remove the left engine mount and attach the engine to an engine lifting beam, or its equivalent.
13. Be sure the lifting beam or its equivalent is properly secured and seated.
14. Remove the left front wheel assembly and the inner fender panel.
15. Separate the suspension arm from the ball joint on the left side.

16. Disconnect the speedometer cable. Do not allow the drive gear to fall into the gear box.
17. Separate the 2 halves of the selector rod joint and remove the clip from the dust cover on the intermediate drive shaft.
18. Unbolt the support bar from the inlet manifold. Unbolt the starter motor from the gear box and push the support bar out of the way. Allow the starter motor to hang, but support it to prevent undue strain on the electrical wires.
19. Leave 1 of the bolts in position in the top of the flange between the engine and the gear box. Remove the other bolts and install the locating dowels, if available.
20. Loosen the 2 subframe pivot mountings and remove the 4 securing bolts.
21. Unbolt the front attachment point for the subframe. Unbolt the 4 subframe mounting bolts.
22. Remove the bolts securing the lower attaching point for the wheel arch bracket and let the subframe hang from the antiroll bar.
23. Remove the clip securing the rubber boot on the inboard universal joint. Withdraw the driveshaft and install protective covers to the open ends of the boot and drive cup.
24. Attach a lifting sling to the transaxle and remove the remaining bolt. Carefully remove the transaxle assembly from the vehicle.
25. Installation is the reverse of the removal procedure.

# CLUTCH

## REMOVAL & INSTALLATION

### 900 Series

1. Disconnect the negative battery cable. Remove the clutch housing cover.
2. Install the spacer (Saab part No. 83-90-023) between the clutch fork and the diaphragm spring. Keep the clutch pedal depressed when the ring is being installed.
3. Unhook the spring clip and remove the cover located in front of the clutch shaft. Remove the clutch shaft plastic propeller.
4. Remove the clutch shaft by means of an M8 bolt installed in the shaft end and Saab tool No. 83-93-175. Withdraw the shaft as far as possible.
5. Remove the clutch slave cylinder retaining bolts.
6. Remove the clutch retaining bolts and remove the clutch, clutch disc and the slave cylinder complete with the clutch release bearing. Be sure that the slave cylinder sleeve is not damaged by the clutch during the removal procedure.
7. Installation is the reverse of the removal procedure.

### 9000 Series

1. Disconnect the negative battery cable. Remove the transaxle assembly.
2. Install a flywheel locking tool, if available and remove the clutch assembly from the flywheel.
3 To install the clutch assembly, use a centering arbor type tool or an appropriate input shaft to center the clutch plate to the flywheel.
4. Tighten the pressure plate bolts to 10.4–19.4 ft. lbs. Remove the flywheel lock, if used.
5. Slide the transaxle assembly over the locating dowels, engaging the transaxle input shaft into the clutch plate splines.
6. Secure the transaxle to the engine with the necessary attaching bolts. Remove the lifting sling from the transaxle.
7. Continue the installation in the reverse order of the removal procedure.

## CLUTCH HEIGHT/FREE-PLAY ADJUSTMENT

1. Remove the inspection hole cover and look through the inspection hole.
2. When the distance between the plastic sleeve front edge and the front edge of the turned surface is less than 2.0mm the clutch disc must be replaced.

## Clutch Master Cylinder

## REMOVAL & INSTALLATION

1. Disconnect the negative battery cable. Remove the clamp holding the pipe from the cylinder at the body and remove the pipe at the cylinder.
2. Remove the left hand screen under the instrument panel.
3. Remove the pin holding the push rod to the clutch pedal.
4. Remove the bolts inside the dash panel. Remove the clutch cylinder from inside the engine compartment.
5. Remove the hose from the fluid container and hang it out of the way so that the fluid does not come out.
6. Installation is the reverse of the removal procedure.

Pressure plate and related components

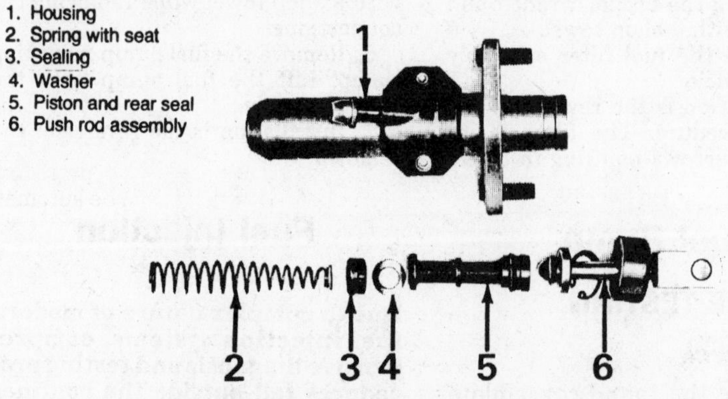

Exploded view of clutch master cylinder

## Clutch Slave Cylinder

## REMOVAL & INSTALLATION

### 900 Series

1. Disconnect the negative battery cable.
2. Remove the clutch assembly.
3. Remove the clutch release bearing together with the clutch slave cylinder.
4. Installation is the reverse of the removal procedure.

### 9000 Series

1. Disconnect the negative battery cable.

2. Remove the transaxle from the vehicle.
3. Remove the clutch release bearing. Disconnect the pressure pipe. Remove the bleed nipple.
4. Remove the retaining bolts that hold the slave cylinder in place.
5. Remove the clutch slave cylinder.
6. Installation is the reverse of the removal procedure.

### BLEEDING THE HYDRAULIC CLUTCH SYSTEM

1. Connect a hose to the slave cylinder bleeder valve. Place the other end of the hose in a suitable jar partially filled with brake fluid.
2. Fill the master cylinder with brake fluid.
3. Open the bleeder valve on the slave cylinder a half turn.
4. Place a cooling system tester gauge over the opening of the master cylinder.
5. Pump the tester until all air has been expelled from the system.
6. Close the slave cylinder bleeder valve.
7. Check that all air has been removed from the system by depressing the clutch pedal.

# AUTOMATIC TRANSAXLE

## Transaxle

### REMOVAL & INSTALLATION

#### *900*

**NOTE: The engine and transaxle must be removed as an assembly. Removal of the engine by itself is not recommended.**

1. Disconnect both battery cables. Drain the engine coolant.
2. Disconnect the windshield washer hose. Mark the engine hood hinges. Remove engine hood retaining bolts then hood assembly.
3. Disconnect and remove the following items:
   a. Disconnect all electrical connections from the starter motor.
   b. Disconnect the upper radiator hose.
   c. Disconnect all ground leads.
   d. Disconnect the temperature sending unit electrical connection.
   e. Remove the ignition coil.
   f. Disconnect the lower radiator hose.
   g. Remove the air cleaner, air intake, preheater hose, crank case ventilation hose and intake hose.
   h. Disconnect and plug the end of the fuel lines.
   i. Disconnect the choke cable and the throttle cable.
   j. Disconnect the hoses to the expansion tank.
   k. Disconnect the oil pressure sending unit electrical connection.
   l. Disconnect the alternator wiring harness.
   m. Disconnect the heater hoses and the brake servo vacuum hoses.

4. On fuel injected vehicles disconnect the electric wiring and fuel connections to the fuel injection system. Disconnect the flow meter and air cleaner with electrical connections.
5. On vehicles equipped with the APC system disconnect the wiring to the solenoid valve. Remove the solenoid valve and the electrical connector to the knock sensor.
6. Remove the boot clips and rubber boots from the inner axle shafts.
7. Place special spacer tool 8393209 or equivalent between the underside of the upper frame and the vehicle body from the wheel housing side. The spacer tool relives the front suspension of load when the vehicle is raised.
8. Remove the lower end piece from the frame. Remove the steering knuckle package and support the end piece against the outer end of the frame.
9. Remove the gear selector cable retaining screw at the gearbox. Pull out the cable with the gear selector rod to its outer or P position. Move back the spring loaded sleeve on the gear selector rod and unhook the cable end piece.
10. Remove the exhaust pipe from the exhaust manifold.
11. Disconnect the speedometer cable from the transaxle.
12. Remove the rear engine mounting bolts.
13. Using a suitable lifting tool slightly raise the engine transaxle assembly. Move the unit slightly to the side and remove the 2 universal joints.
14. Lift the engine transaxle assembly out of the vehicle. If vehicle is equipped with power assisted steering disconnect and plug the 2 hydraulic lines at the servo pump.
15. At this point of the procedure separate the engine from the automatic transaxle.
16. Clean the outside of the engine and automatic transaxle and drain the oil out of the engine.
17. Remove the cover over the flywheel ring gear. On turbocharged vehicles remove the turbocharger support.
18. Remove the starter motor if necessary.
19. Disconnect the throttle cable at the throttle housing.
20. Remove all retaining bolts between the engine and transaxle and disconnect the hydraulic hoses from the oil cooler.
21. Remove the retaining bolts securing the ring gear to the torque converter.
22. Turn the flexplate, so that the plate angles will be horizontal. Lift the engine carefully off the transaxle.
23. Install the torque converter support special tool 8790255 or equivalent.
24. Position the transaxle assembly on suitable workstand or holding fixture.

**To install:**

25. Before installing the transaxle to the engine make sure that the mating surfaces are thoroughly clean.
26. Check that there are no cracks in the flexplate, of the engine particularly on a turbocharged engine.
27. Remove the torque converter support. Apply anti-corrosion grease to the center pin of the torque converter and the center of the flexplate. Make sure that the 2 guide sleeves are installed into the gearcase.
28. Install a new sheet metal gasket to the joint face of the gearcase. Apply Bostik silicone compound part number 2680 or equivalent into the grooves in the gasket. Install the transaxle to the engine.
29. Position the flexplate so that the sheet metal angles are horizontal.
30. Take care not to damage the torque converter when lowering the engine onto the transaxle.
31. Apply thread sealing compound and tighten all retaining bolts.
32. Align the torque converter with the flexplate then gradually tighten the retaining bolts to 25–30 ft. lbs. (33–39 Nm).
33. Install the starter motor. Connect the throttle cable to the throttle housing.
34. On turbocharged vehicles install the support for the turbocharger. Install the cover over the ring gear.
35. Refill the engine with the correct amount of engine oil.
36. Pack the inner universal joins and rubber boots with a suitable grease.
37. Install new gaskets to the exhaust manifold flanges. Install new clamps on the inner axle shafts.
38. Position the engine transaxle assembly so that the front mounting will engage in its bracket slightly before the rear mountings.
39. Lower the engine transaxle assembly into the vehicle. Guide the front mounting into the bracket and

lower the rear of the engine transaxle assembly to approximately 2 inches (50–60mm) above the mountings.

40. Position the engine to the side, guide the left hand universal joint into position and then move the engine to the left.

41. Carefully lower the engine transaxle assembly and guide it onto the engine mountings, at the same time aligning the right hand universal joint with its axle shaft.

42. Line up the exhaust system flanges. Check that the gaskets are correctly installed.

43. Install the right hand end piece to the frame. Check that the right hand universal joint is lined up with the axle shaft.

44. Install the bolts into the rear engine mountings and tighten all of the engine mountings and bolt together the exhaust flanges.

45. Reconnect the speedometer cable.

46. Reconnect the cable to the gear selector rod and bolt the cable end piece to the transaxle casing. Make sure gear selector operates properly.

47. Install the boot clamps to the inner universal joints. Remove the special spacer tool number 8393209.

48. Connect and install the following items:

a. Connect all electrical connections to the starter motor.

b. Connect the upper radiator hose.

c. Connect all ground leads.

d. Connect the temperature sending unit electrical connection.

e. Install the ignition coil.

f. Connect the lower radiator hose.

g. Install the air cleaner, air intake, preheater hose, crank case ventilation hose and intake hose.

h. Connect the fuel lines.

i. Connect the choke cable and the throttle cable.

j. Connect the hoses to the expansion tank.

k. Connect the oil pressure sending unit electrical connection.

l. Connect the alternator wiring harness.

m. Connect the heater hoses and the brake servo vacuum hoses.

49. On fuel injected vehicles connect the electric wiring and fuel connections to the fuel injection system. Reconnect the flow meter and air cleaner electrical connections.

**NOTE: On fuel injected engines make sure that there is at least ½ in. (10mm) of clearance at the bottom of the throttle control assembly.**

50. On vehicles equipped with the APC system reconnect the wiring to the solenoid valve. Install the solenoid valve and the electrical connector to the knocking sensor.

51. Refill the coolant and bleed the cooling system through the bleeder nipple on the thermostat housing. If the the vehicle is equipped with power assisted steering connect the hydraulic lines to the servo pump.

52. Reconnect both battery cables. Refill the transaxle assembly with the correct amount of specified fluid.

53. Install the engine hood in the marked position and connect the windshield washer hose.

54. Road test the vehicle in all driving ranges for proper operation.

### 9000 Series

1. Disconnect the battery cables and remove the battery.

2. Remove the windshield washer fluid reservoir. Plug the outlet to keep the fluid from running out.

3. Open the terminal box and disconnect the cables.

**NOTE: When removing the fuel filter, wrap a rag around the line to prevent fuel from spraying out. Use proper caution when working with the fuel system.**

4. Release the fuel filter clamp and remove the filter. Remove the battery cable.

5. Disconnect the wiring from the air mass meter and remove the meter.

6. Disconnect the hose from the transaxle and the bypass hose from the turbocharger delivery pipe. Remove the delivery pipe.

7. Disconnect the throttle cable form the throttle housing.

8. Disconnect the gear selector lever cable from the selector lever. Do not separate the ball joint on the cable.

9. Disconnect the inlet hose from the oil cooler on top of the transaxle. Disconnect the selector lever from the transaxle.

10. Remove the return line from the oil cooler. Place a drain pan under the transaxle to collect the oil.

11. Remove the clamp retaining the turbocharger oil supply line to the transaxle, if equipped.

12. Disconnect the speedometer cable from the transaxle. Remove the top retaining bolt for the starter motor.

13. Disconnect the starter motor stay from the intake manifold. Disconnect the top end of the starter stay from the wheel housing.

14. Place engine support yoke 83–93–977 or equivalent, in position on the wheel housing to support the engine when the transaxle has been removed.

15. Raise and safely support the vehicle. Remove the left front wheel and remove the inner fender liner.

16. Remove the starter motor and suspend it out of the way. Remove the bolts retaining the torque converter to the drive plate.

17. Remove the bolts retaining the ball joint to the suspension arm. Remove the anti-roll bar mounting nut from the suspension arm. Remove the 2 bolts retaining the anti-roll bar bearing.

18. Remove the front engine mount bolt.

19. Split the sub-frame at the front and slightly open the joint. Remove the 2 bolts at the rear of the sub-frame, 1 of the bolts retains the steering gear.

20. Remove the bolts for the rear sub-frame joint and remove the 2 bolts in the front corner. Lower the sub-frame from the vehicle.

21. Remove the clamps from both the left and right CV-joints, separate the joints. Allow the driveshafts to hang down.

22. Position a suitable lifting device under the transaxle and lower it from the vehicle.

**To install:**

23. Install a suitable converter holding device to prevent the converter from falling out during installation. With the transaxle on a suitable lifting device, raise it into position under the vehicle.

24. Guide the transaxle into position aligning the converter pin as a guide. Install 1 bolt to retain the assembly.

25. Reattach the driveshafts and install the clamps over the CV-boots.

26. Install the transaxle mounting bolt through the engine mount.

27. Raise the sub-frame assembly into position. Make sure the engine mount is in position.

28. Install all sub-frame bolts and the engine mount bolt.

29. Install the anti-roll bar and bearing into the suspension arm. Install all of the suspension arm bolts.

30. Install the torque converter-to-driveplate bolts. Use Loctite® 242 on the bolts.

31. Install the starter and stay. Lower the vehicle.

32. Remove the engine support tool. Install the upper starter mount bolts. Connect the speedometer cable.

33. Install the turbocharger oil pipe to the engine block.

34. Reconnect the selector lever cable. The selector should be in the **N** detent. Adjust the selector as needed.

35. Reconnect the oil cooler hose to the transaxle oil cooler.

36. Reconnect the turbocharger delivery pipe. Install the air mass meter.

37. Install the battery tray. Install the fuel filter.

38. Attach the battery cable to the battery tray. Reconnect the cables to the terminal box.
39. Install the winshield washer fluid bottle and connect the electrical leads.
40. Install the battery and reconnect the cables.
41. Raise and safely support the vehicle.
42. Install the inner fender cover. Install the wheel and tire assembly.
43. Lower the vehicle, refill the fluid in the transaxle.
44. Road test the vehicle and check the operation of the transaxle. Adjust the throttle linkage as needed. Check the fluid level.

## PAN REMOVAL

1. Disconnect the negative battery cable. Raise and support the vehicle safely.
2. Properly support the transaxle assembly. Remove the transaxle crossmember.
3. Drain the automatic transaxle fluid. Remove the pan retaining bolts. Remove the transaxle pan from the vehicle.
4. Installation is the reverse of the removal procedure.

## FILTER SERVICE

1. Disconnect the negative battery cable. Remove the transaxle fluid pan.
2. Remove the fluid lines for the front servo brake band that are connected to the drain valve. Remove the level lines. Note the position of the O-ring.
3. Remove the filter assembly.
4. Installation is the reverse of the removal procedure.

## LINKAGE ADJUSTMENT

1. Remove the gear selector lever cover.
2. Slack off the gear selector lever housing nuts with tool No. 83-91-23 or equivalent.
3. Lift the gear selector lever housing and turn it so that the adjustment nuts of the cable will be reachable.
4. Adjust the cable longer or shorter to bring the **N** and **D** clearance to specification.
5. Assemble the gear selector housing and check the clearance in **N** and **D**.
6. The proper setting of the selector cable can be accomplished by adding or removing shims at the transmission case end of the cable. A maximum of 3 shims may be used.

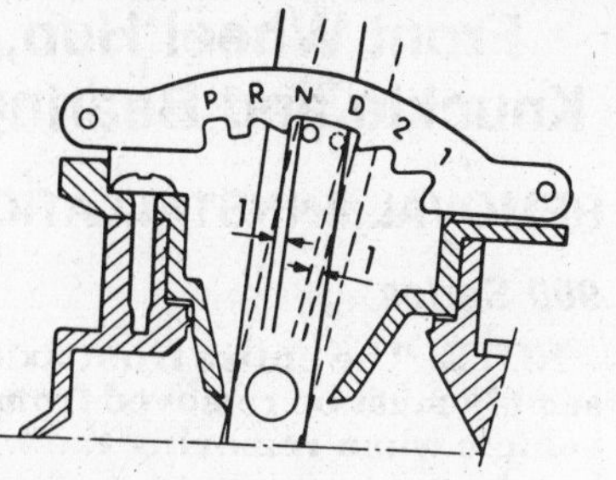


Manual linkage clearance, equal in "N" and "D"

## NEUTRAL SAFETY SWITCH ADJUSTMENT

1. Disconnect the wires from the switch. The wide terminals are for back-up lights and the narrow ones are for the starter motor.
2. Loosen the lock nut and unscrew the switch 2 turns.
3. With the selector in **D**, connect a test light between the narrow terminals. The light should light up.
4. Screw in the switch until the light goes out. Mark that position on both the transmission and the switch.
5. Move the test light, the wide terminals and screw switch in until the light goes out again. Count the number between the lights going out.
6. Turn the switch to a point halfway between the 2 lights-out points.
7. Secure the locknut to 4–6 ft. lbs. torque. If the safety switch is locked too tight, it may be damaged.

## BAND ADJUSTMENT

### *Type 35 Transmission*

#### FRONT BAND (INSIDE TRANSMISSION)

1. Place tool No. 87-90-73 or equivalent, ¼ in. thickness gauge between the adjusting screw and the boss on the piston.
2. Loosen the lock nut.
3. Tighten the adjusting screw to 2 inch lbs. of torque and tighten the lock nut. On transmissions with self adjusting mechanism, check the gap between the self adjusting spring and the lever. It should be 1.5–2.0 thread flights.

#### REAR BAND

The rear band adjusting screw is located outside the transmission case on the drivers side of the vehicle.
1. Loosen the lock nut a few turns.
2. Tighten the adjusting screw to 20 ft. lbs. and then back off ¾ turn.
3. Hold the adjusting screw and torque the lock nut to 30–40 ft. lbs.

### *Type 37 Transmission*

#### FRONT BAND (INSIDE TRANSMISSION)

#### Type 001 to 007 A/T

Up to serial numbers 001–1700, 002–2800
1. Loosen the lock nut and position tool number 87-90-073 or equivalent ¼ in. thick, between the adjusting screw and the piston pin.
2. Tighten the adjusting screw to 9 ft. lbs. and then loosen 1 turn.
3. Hold the adjusting screw and tighten the lock nut to 24–28 ft. lbs.

#### After serial numbers 001–1710, 002–2801

1. Loosen the lock nut and position tool number 87-90-030 or equivalent, $^{11}/_{32}$ in. thick, between the screw and the piston pin.
2. Tighten the adjusting screw to 9 ft. lbs. DO NOT loosen the adjusting screw.
3. Hold the adjusting screw and tighten the lock nut to 24–28 ft. lbs.

#### Type 008, 009 A/T.

1. Adjustment of the front band is accomplished after the removal of the rear oil pan.
2. Loosen the lock nut and place a spacer tool number 87-91-329, which measures 0.310 in., between the adjusting screw and the piston rod.
3. Tighten the adjusting screw to a torque of 11 inch lbs. The adjusting screw must not be moved following the adjustment.
4. Hold the adjusting screw in this position and tighten the lock nut to 15–20 ft. lbs.

#### REAR BAND

The rear band adjusting screw is located on the outside of the transmission on the left side.
1. Loosen the lock nut a few turns.
2. Tighten the adjusting screw to 10 ft. lbs. with tool number 87-90-115 or equivalent. Back off the adjusting screw ¾ turn.
3. Hold the adjusting screw and tighten the lock nut to 24–28 ft. lbs.

# DRIVE AXLE

## Halfshaft

### REMOVAL & INSTALLATION

#### *900 Series*

**NOTE: The entire front axle assembly must be removed in order**

**to remove the halfshaft from the vehicle.**

1. Disconnect the negative battery cable. Remove the upper shock absorber bolt.
2. Raise the vehicle and support it safely. Remove the wheel and tire assembly.
3. Remove the brake housing and position it on the wheel housing to avoid damage to the brake hose. Remove the brake disc and parking brake assembly along with the cable.
4. Remove the large clamp from the rubber bellows on the inner universal joint. To separate the inner universal joint, install the cover (Saab part No. 7323736) in the rubber bellows to stop the needle bearings from falling out and to keep dirt from entering. Install the protective cap (Saab part No. 7838469) on the inner driver.
5. Disconnect the tie rod from the steering arm using the proper tool. Remove the nut on the upper ball joint. Remove the bolts from the lower control arm bracket.
6. Remove the halfshaft through the wheel housing and remove the entire front axle assembly.
7. If the differential bearing cap is to be removed, remove the retaining bolts and remove the cap and the inner drive using the proper removal tools.
8. Installation is the reverse of the removal procedure.

#### 9000 Series

1. Disconnect the negative battery cable. Remove the hubcap and loosen the center axle nut. Raise and support the vehicle safely.
2. Remove the inner fender panel for working access.
3. Unbolt the MacPherson strut from the steering swivel member and detach the flexible brake hose from the clip on the strut.
4. Loosen the clip on the rubber boot on the inboard universal joint.
5. Separate the 2 halves of the joint. Install protective covers over the rubber boot and the drive axle.
6. Remove the hub center nut and withdraw the driveshaft from the steering swivel member.
7. Installation is the reverse of the removal procedure.
8. Torque the bolts securing the strut to the steering swivel to 56–75 ft. lbs.
9. Tighten the hub center nut to 195–208 ft. lbs.

### CV-JOINT OVERHAUL

**For all CV-Joint overhaul procedures, please refer to "CV-Joint Overhaul" in the Unit Repair section.**

## Front Wheel Hub, Knuckle and Bearings

### REMOVAL & INSTALLATION

#### 900 Series

**NOTE: The entire front axle assembly must be removed from the vehicle when removing the wheel bearings.**

1. Disconnect the negative battery cable. Remove the upper bolt of the shock absorber.
2. Raise the vehicle and support it safely. Remove the tire and wheel assembly.
3. Remove the brake housing and position it by the wheel housing to avoid damage to the brake hose. Remove the brake disc and parking brake assembly with the cable.
4. Remove the large clamp from the rubber bellows on the inner universal joint. To separate the inner universal joint, install the cover (SAAB part No. 7323736) in the rubber bellows to stop the needle bearing from falling out and to keep dirt from entering. Install the protective cap (SAAB part No. 7838469) on the inner drive.
5. Disconnect the tie rod from the steering arm using the proper tool. Remove the nut on the upper ball joint. Remove the bolts from the lower control arm bracket.
6. Remove the drive shaft through the wheel housing and remove the entire front axle assembly.
7. Place the steering knuckle housing in a press and press out the drive shaft.
8. Remove the lockring and press out the bearing using a suitable drift.
9. Installation is the reverse of the removal procedure.

#### 9000 Series

The front wheel bearing are double row angular contact bearings which are permanently lubricated and maintenance free. The bearings cannot be replaced individually. To remove the hub proceed as follows.

1. Loosen the hub center nut and the wheel bolts.
2. Raise the vehicle and support it safely.
3. Remove the tire and wheel assembly. Remove the hub center nut and thrust washer.
4. Remove the flexible brake hose from its support clip.
5. Unbolt the caliper and rest it upon the suspension arm.
6. Unscrew the locating stud for the disc and remove it from the hub.
7. Push in on the driveshaft. Remove the 4 bolts securing the hub to the steering swivel member.
8. Lift the hub and disc back plate from the suspension assembly. Renew the bearings or replace the hub.
9. The installation of the hub is in the reverse of the removal procedure.
10. Tighten the hub securing bolts to 40–43 ft. lbs., and the center hub nut to 195–208 ft. lbs.

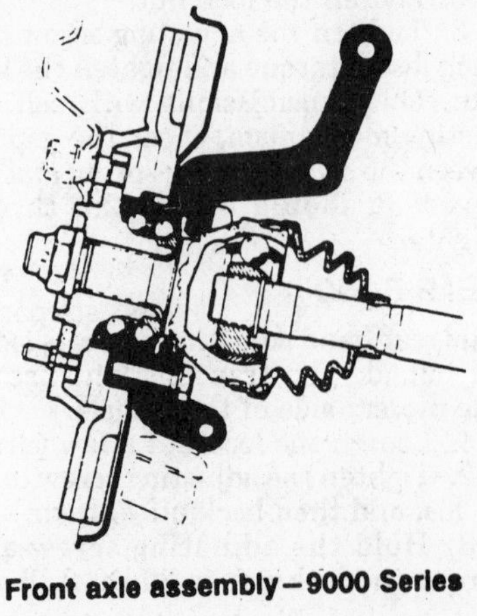

Front axle assembly—9000 Series

# FRONT SUSPENSION

## Shock Absorbers

### REMOVAL & INSTALLATION

#### 900 Series

1. Disconnect the negative battery cable. Remove the upper shock absorber nut.
2. Raise the vehicle and support it safely. Remove the tire and wheel assembl.
3. Remove the shock absorber retaining bolts. Remove the shock from the vehicle. Save all washers and rubber parts.
4. Installation is the reverse of removal.

## MacPherson Struts

### REMOVAL & INSTALLATION

#### 9000 Series

1. Disconnect the negative battery cable. Raise and support the vehicle safely. Remove the front tire and wheel assembly.
2. Remove the front brake hose from the retaining clip on the strut assembly.
3. Unbolt the strut from the steering swivel arm.

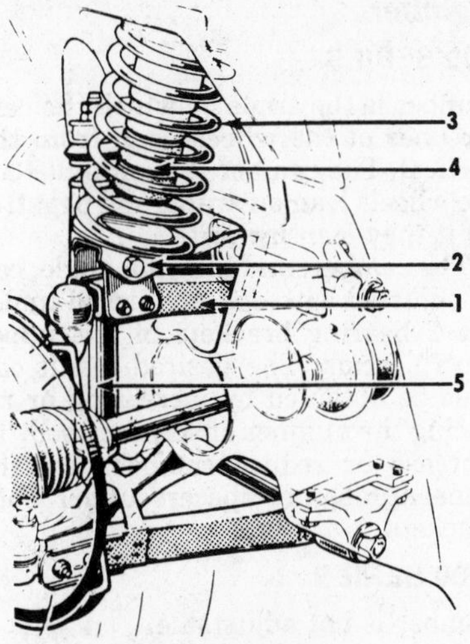


1. Upper control arm
2. Lower spring support
3. Coil spring
4. Rubber buffer
5. Shock absorber

Front suspension assembly

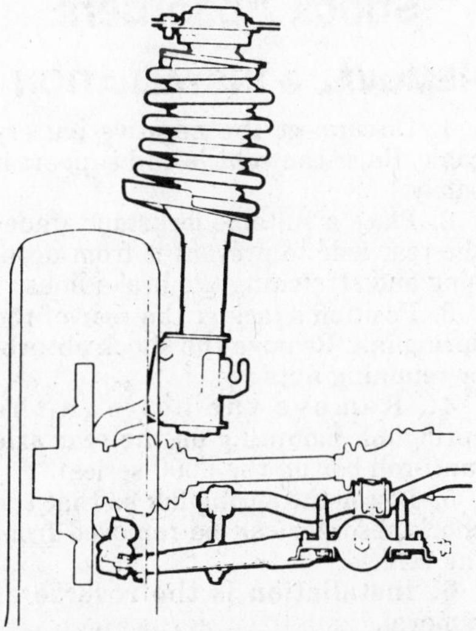

Front suspension assembly – 9000 Series

4. Remove the 3 retaining bolts from the top of the strut.

5. Remove the strut from the vehicle..

6. Installation is the reverse of the removal procedure.

### OVERHAUL

**For all spring and shock absorber removal and installation procedures, and all strut overhaul procedures, please refer to "Strut Overhaul" in the Unit Repair Section.**

## Springs

### REMOVAL & INSTALLATION

#### *900 Series*

1. Disconnect the negative battery cable. Remove the upper shock absorber retaining nuts.

2. Raise and support the vehicle safely. Remove the tire and wheel assembly.

3. Install a spring compression tool or equivalent, engaging the upper shanks directly in the spring at the second free turn from the top of the lower shanks around the spring caps. These alignment shanks are located on the last turn of the spring with the color coded cup right beside the end of the coil.

4. Compress the spring at the top end, approximately 1½ in. If the upper spring attachment of the steel cone is left behind in the wheel housing, remove it.

5. Remove the spring and the steel cone from the vehicle.

6. Installation is the reverse of removal.

## Ball Joints

### REMOVAL & INSTALLATION

1. Disconnect the negative battery cable. Raise and support the vehicle safely. Remove the tire and wheel assembly.

2. Remove the brake housing and position it out of the way so that the brake hose will not be damaged.

3. Remove the nut that holds the ball joint ball bolt to the steering knuckle housing. Remove the bolt using the proper removal tool.

4. Remove the ball joint from the control arm assembly.

5. Installation is the reverse of removal.

## Upper Control Arm

### REMOVAL & INSTALLATION

#### *900 Series*

**NOTE: To remove the left upper control arm, the engine must first be removed from the vehicle.**

1. Raise the vehicle and support it safely.

2. Remove the tire and wheel assembly. Remove the shock absorber. Compress the coil spring, using a spring compression tool.

3. Remove the 2 bolts attaching the upper ball joint and lower spring seat to the upper control arm.

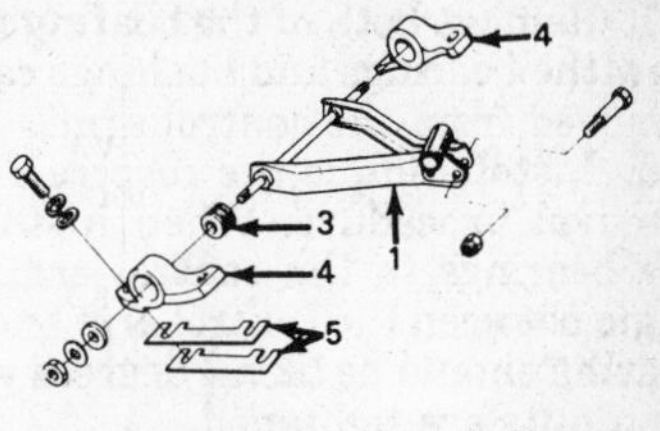


1. Upper control arm
3. Rubber bushing
4. Bearing
5. Spacers

Upper control arm assembly

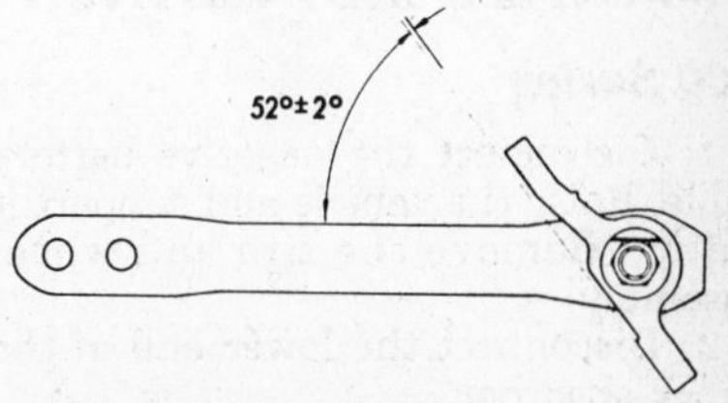


Checking the angle between the upper control arm and bearing

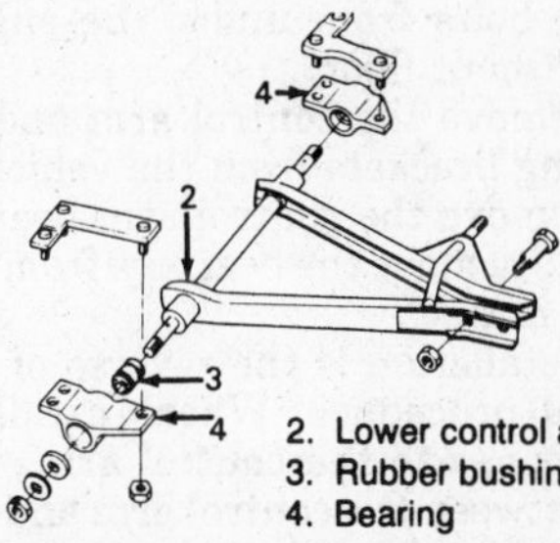


2. Lower control arm
3. Rubber bushing
4. Bearing

Lower control arm bushings – 900 Series

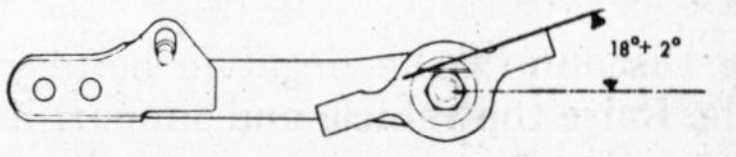


Checking the angle between the lower control arm and bearing

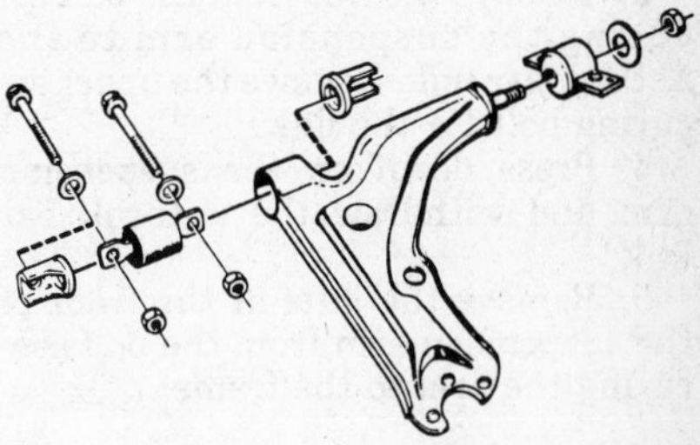

Lower control arm bushings – 9000 Series

4. Remove the bolts from both upper control arm bearing brackets.

5. Remove the coil spring from the vehicle.

6. Remove the control arm and bearings from the vehicle. Save the spacers under the bearings and record the number of spacers used under each bearing.

7. Remove both of the bearing nuts. Now the bearings and bushings can be removed from the control arm.

8. Installation is the reverse of the removal procedure. When installing the bearings to the control arm, the angle between the control arm and the bearing should be 52±2 degrees when both nuts are tightened.

## Lower Control Arm

### REMOVAL & INSTALLATION

#### *900 Series*

1. Disconnect the negative battery cable. Raise the vehicle and support it safely. Remove the tire and wheel assembly.
2. Disconnect the lower end of the shock absorber.
3. Remove the 2 bolts that attach the ball joint to the control arm.
4. Remove the lower control arm attaching bolts from under the engine compartment floor.
5. Remove the control arm and its attaching brackets from the vehicle.
6. Remove the control arm bearing nuts and remove the bearings from the control arm.
7. Installation is the reverse of the removal procedure. When installing the bearings to the control arm., the angle between the control arm and the bearing should be 18±2 degrees when both nuts are tightened.

#### *9000 Series*

1. Disconnect the negative battery cable. Raise the vehicle and support it safely. Remove the tire and wheel assembly.
2. Remove the bolts securing the suspension arm to the ball joint.
3. Remove the nut from the bolt securing the suspension arm to the antiroll bar link. Remove the upper securing bolt for the link.
4. Press down on the suspension arm and withdraw the anti-roll bar link.
5. Remove the nuts at the front of the suspension arm from the bolts securing the arm to the frame.

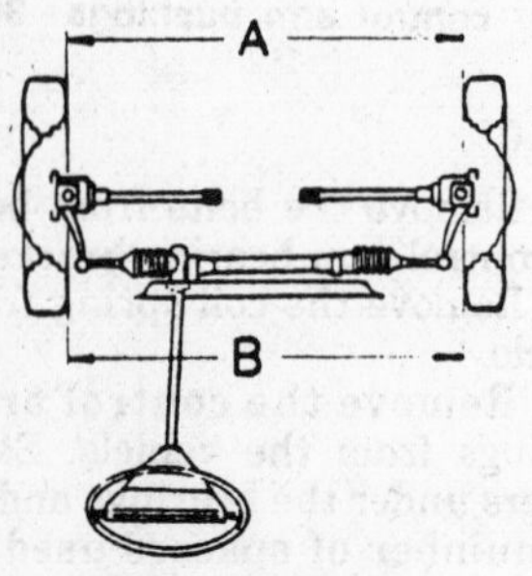


**Toe-in adjustment**

6. Remove the rear bolts securing the reinforcement member to the frame.
7. Remove the bolts securing the control arm rear pivot to the frame. Remove the control arm.
8. To install the arm, reverse the removal procedure, leaving the nuts for the bushings in the suspension arm rear pivot loose.
9. After the arm is installed and the remaining bolts in place, tighten the rear pivot bolts.
10. Check the wheel alignment and adjust as required, after the vehicle has been allowed to settle by bouncing or driving.

## Front Wheel Alignment

### ADJUSTMENT

#### *Toe-In*

1. Roll the vehicle straight forward on a level floor and stop it without using brakes. It must not be moved backward after this.
2. Take a reading of measurement A with the toe-in gauge between the front wheel rims level with the axles. Mark the measurement points with chalk. Roll the vehicle forward until the chalk marks are level with but behind the axles, and take a reading of B. Any necessary adjustment is made by altering the length of the tie rod.
3. Remove the nut on the outer end of the tie rod and the outer clip on the steering gear rubber bellow.
4. Using the proper tool rotate the tie rod right or left and adjust it until the toe-in is within specification. Hold the bellows during the twisting.
5. Lock the locking nut when adjustment is complete.

#### *Caster*

**900 SERIES**

The caster is the angle by which the steering knuckle axis departs from the vertical when viewed from the side and the measurement is generally expressed in degrees. If the caster needs adjusting, spacers are inserted under the bearing brackets of the upper control arms.

To increase the caster, transfer spacers from the front bracket to the rear bracket. To reduce the caster, transfer spacers from the rear bracket to the front bracket. In either case, the total spacer thickness removed from one bracket must be added to the other one.

**9000 SERIES**

Caster is not adjustable.

#### *Camber*

**900 SERIES**

Camber is the angle by which the center lines of the wheels lean from the vertical. The camber is position (+) if the wheels lean outward, and negative (–) if they lean inward.

The camber, and king pin angle, can be adjusted with spacers placed under the 2 bearing brackets of the upper control arms. The desired result can thus be obtained by increasing or reducing the number of spacers used. To increase or reduce camber, use the same number of spacers under both brackets.

**9000 SERIES**

Camber is not adjustable.

# REAR SUSPENSION

## Shock Absorbers

### REMOVAL & INSTALLATION

1. Disconnect the negative battery cable. Raise the vehicle and support it safely.
2. Place a suitable jackstand under the rear axle to prevent it from dropping and stretching the brake lines.
3. Position a jack at the rear of the springlink. Remove the shock absorber retaining nuts.
4. Remove the bolts in the springlink mounting on the rear axle (anti-roll bar on the 9000 series).
5. Lower the springlink so that the shock absorber can be removed from the vehicle.
6. Installation is the reverse of removal.

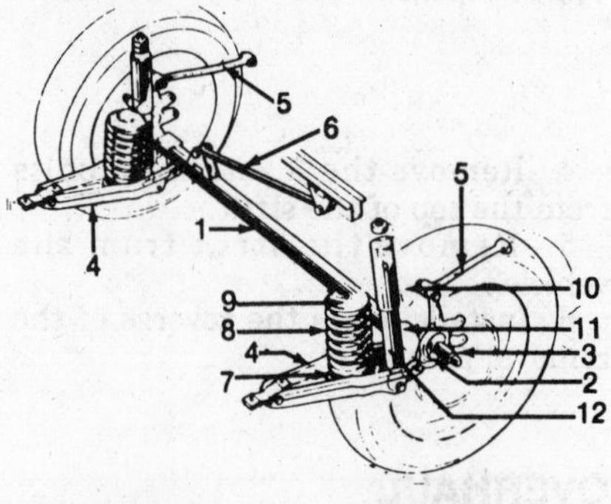


1. Rear axle
2. End piece
3. Stub axle
4. Spring links
5. Rear links
6. Cross bar
7. Spring seat
8. Coil spring
9. Spring insulator
10. Rubber buffer
11. Stop
12. Shock absorber

**Rear suspension assembly**

## Springs

### REMOVAL & INSTALLATION

1. Disconnect the negative battery cable. Raise and support the vehicle safely.
2. Remove the tire and wheel assembly. Position a jack under the springlink and disconnect the lower end of the shock absorber.
3. From underneath of the vehicle, remove the 2 lock nuts that secure the front springlink bearing to the body of the vehicle.
4. Position a jackstand under the rear axle to prevent the brake lines from being damaged by the weight of the rear axle.
5. Lower the springlink so that the spring can be removed from the vehicle together with the upper spring support and the rubber spacer at the lower spring seating which is retained by the spring tension.
6. Installation is the reverse of the removal procedure.

## Rear Wheel Bearings

### REMOVAL & INSTALLATION

#### *900 Series*

#### UP TO AND INCLUDING CHASSIS NOS. AC1021263, AC2007508, AC3006827 AND AC6001805

**NOTE: Each rear wheel hub has 2 tapered roller bearings. The inner bearing as a larger diameter than the outer bearing.**

1. Raise the vehicle and support it safely.
2. Remove the tire and wheel assembly. Remove the brake housing and the brake disc. Support the brake housing to avoid damage to the brake pipe.
3. Remove the dust cap. Remove the locknut and the washer. Pull off the hub, if necessary, use a suitable puller.
4. Remove the seal ring using a suitable tool. Remove the inner rings of both bearings.
5. Place a suitable drift in the milled recesses of the hub and drive out the outer bearing rings. It is advisable to place wooden board under the hub to avoid deforming the end faces.
6. Installation is the reverse of the removal procedure. Torque the lock nut to 36 ft. lbs., than slacken the nut completely and torque it to 2.9 ft. lbs.

#### INSTALLATION FROM CHASSIS NOS. AC1021264, AC2007509, AC3006828 AND AC6001806

1. Slide the hub onto the stub axle and install the washer lock nut.
2. Tighten the lock nut to a torque of 210 ft. lbs. (300 Nm). If the part of the nut collar that had previously been staked comes in line with the locking groove, install a new nut.
3. Stake the nut collar into the locking groove.
4. Complete the assembly by installing the dust cap and install the brake disc, brake housing, wheel and wheel nuts.

#### *9000 Series*

The wheel bearings are not press fitted on the outboard drive shaft or stub axle, but are incorporated in the hub. The wheel bearings are double row, angular contact bearings which are permanently lubricated and maintenance free. The bearings cannot be replaced individually.

1. Disconnect the negative battery cable. Raise the vehicle and support it safely.
2. Remove the tire and wheel assembly.
3. Remove the brake caliper and disc back plate. Support the disc caliper on the rear axle. Remove the brake disc.
4. Remove the dust cap from the hub center nut. Remove the center nut and thrust washer. Pull the hub from the axle.
5. Upon installation of the hub, install the thrust washer and the nut.
6. Tighten the center nut to a torque of 195–208 ft. lbs..
7. Lock the nut by using drift to punch the flange of the nut in the stub axle thread. Install the dust cap, the disc brake components, the wheel, and then lower the vehicle.

# STEERING

## Steering Wheel

### REMOVAL & INSTALLATION

1. Disconnect the negative battery cable.
2. On some vehicles it will be necessary to remove the bottom cover of the steering wheel bearing.
3. Remove the steering wheel safety pad. Remove the steering wheel emblem. Remove the horn contact. Remove the steering wheel holding nut and washer.
4. Remove the steering wheel using the proper steering wheel removal tool.
5. Installation is the reverse of removal.

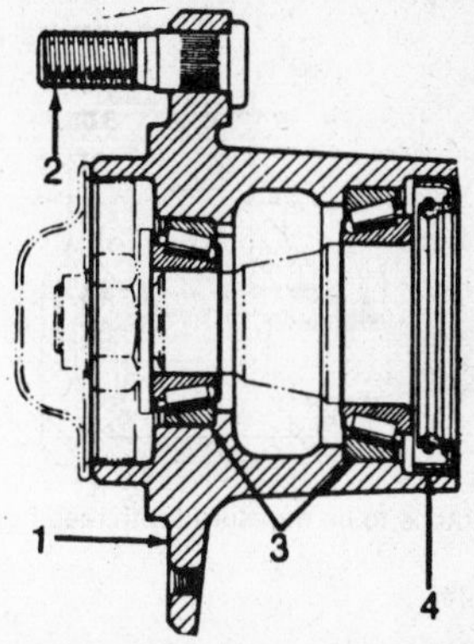

Rear wheel hub and bearings—typical

## Combination Switch

### REMOVAL & INSTALLATION

1. Disconnect the negative battery cable.
2. Remove the steering wheel.
3. Remove the cover beneath the bearing support.
4. Remove the combination switch retaining bolts and electrical connections.
5. Remove the switch from the vehicle.
6. Installation is the reverse of the removal procedure.

## Manual Steering Gear

### REMOVAL & INSTALLATION

#### *900 Series*

1. Disconnect the negative battery cable. Remove the left screen under the instrument panel and loosen the rubber bellows at the body lead through for the steering gear intermediate shaft, if required.
2. Raise and support the vehicle safely. Remove the bolt holding the joint to the steering gear pinion or intermediate shaft.
3. Loosen the steering column tube from the body and separate the steering column joint from the pinion. Position the steering column so that the wiring harness is not damaged.
4. Remove both tire and wheel assemblies. Remove the tie rod ends at the steering arms with the proper removal tool. Remove the 2 steering gear clamps.
5. Move the rack to the right as far as possible. Lift the steering gear to the right so that the tie rod can be bent down in the opening of the engine compartment floor.
6. Pull the rack to the left and lift the steering gear down through the opening in the engine compartment floor.

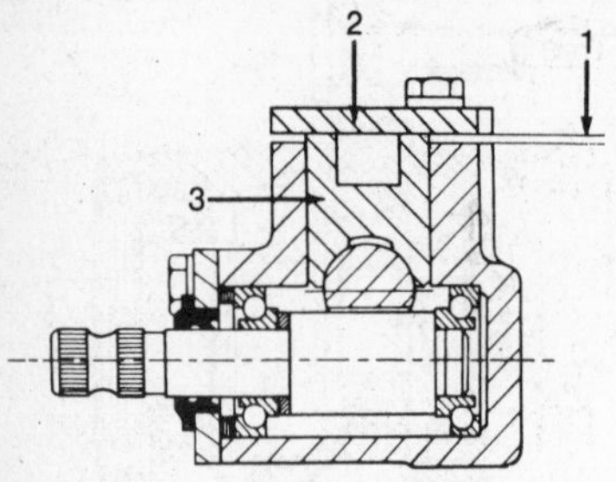


1. Clearance to be measured with feeler gauge
2. Cap
3. Plunger

**Radial-play adjustment**

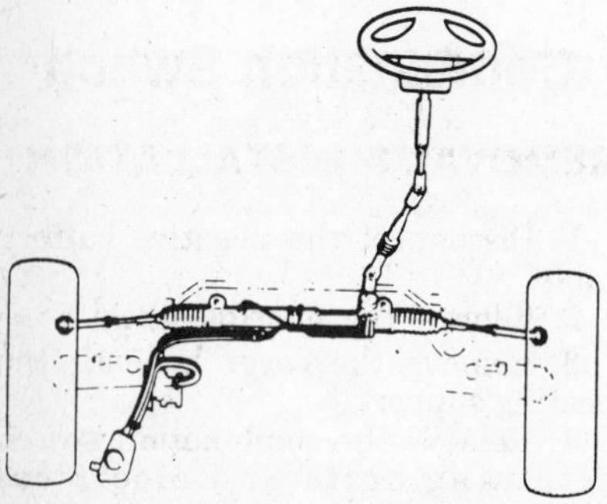

**Power steering assembly—9000 Series**

7. Installation is the reverse of the removal procedure.

## ADJUSTMENT

### *Radial Play*

1. Install the plunger without the spring and screw on the cap without the gasket by hand until it butts against the plunger. Do not use a wrench, as you will damage the cap.
2. Measure the clearance between the cap and the housing with a feeler gauge.
3. Add 0.002–0.006 in. to the measured clearance to allow for the play to be left between the plunger and cap after assembly. Measure the thickness of the gasket and shims with a micrometer. Shims are available in thickness of 0.005 in., 0.0075 in., 0.010 in., 0.015 in. and 0.020 in.

# Power Steering Gear

## REMOVAL & INSTALLATION

### *900 Series*

1. Disconnect the negative battery cable. Remove the left screen under the instrument panel and loosen the rubber bellows at the body lead through for the steering gear intermediate shaft, if required. Disconnect and plug the power steering fluid lines.
2. Raise and support the vehicle safely. Remove the bolt holding the joint to the steering gear pinion or intermediate shaft.
3. Loosen the steering column tube from the body and separate the steering column joint from the pinion. Position the steering column so that the wiring harness is not damaged.
4. Remove both tire and wheel assemblies. Remove the tie rod ends at the steering arms with the proper removal tool. Remove the 2 steering gear clamps.
5. Move the rack to the right as far as possible. Lift the steering gear to the right so that the tie rod can be bent down in the opening of the engine compartment floor.
6. Pull the rack to the left and lift the steering gear down through the opening in the engine compartment floor.
7. Installation is the reverse of the removal procedure.

### *9000 Series*

1. Disconnect the negative battery cable. Remove the padding from under the instrument panel and the trim on the left hand side of the center tunnel, as required. Fold back the carpet where the steering column passes through the fire wall. Remove the rubber boot from the intermediate shaft.
2. Remove the pinch bolt in the lower clamp, loosen the bolt in the upper clamp and remove the intermediate shaft.
3. Remove the cover panel from the fire wall. Take care not to damage the gasket, seal and plastic bushing.
4. Raise and support the vehicle safely. Remove both tire and wheel assemblies.
5. Remove the rear section of the inner fender panel under the left fender.
6. Separate the left and right tie rod ends from the steering arms.
7. Drain the power steering fluid from the pump reservoir.
8. Disconnect the hoses from the pump and reservoir. Plug the openings to prevent fluid from leaking out and dirt from entering.
9. Remove the retaining bolts from the rack and pinion assembly.
10. Remove the vertical brace between the engine subframe and the body.
11. Lift out the rack and pinion unit through the left fender inner panel opening. Do not damage the rubber boots or brake hose.
12. Installation is the reverse of the removal procedure. Fill the reservoir and bleed the system by allowing the engine to run at idle.

## ADJUSTMENT

### *Radial Play*

#### 900 SERIES

1. Screw in the adjusting screw all the way until the resistance of the twisting steering gear is felt.
2. Back off the adjusting screw ½ turn.
3. Check that the steering gear can be turned from lock to lock in both directions without jamming.
4. Tighten the lock nut with a torque of 50–60 ft. lbs.

#### 9000 SERIES

1. Turn the adjusting screw completely in.
2. Back off the adjusting screw approximately 40–60 ft. lbs.
3. Tighten the lock nut to 47–54 ft. lbs. (65–75 Nm).

# Power Steering Pump

## REMOVAL & INSTALLATION

### *900 Series*

1. Disconnect the negative battery cable. Drain the fluid from the power steering pump.
2. Drain the coolant from the drain cock on the engine block and disconnect the hose from between the expansion tank and the water pump.
3. Disconnect the power steering pump hoses. Grip the hexagonal nipple on the pump when removing the delivery line.
4. Unbolt the pump unit from the bracket and the engine mounting. Remove the power steering belt. Remove the pump complete with its mounting.
5. Installation is the reverse of the removal procedure.

### *9000 Series*

1. Disconnect the negative battery cable. Remove the fluid from the pump reservoir.
2. Raise and support the vehicle safely. Remove the right front wheel and the right inner fender panel.
3. Remove the drive belt. Remove the bracket for the engine oil filler pipe. Remove the engine stay bracket. Disconnect the hoses from the pump. Plug the openings.
4. Remove the pump retaining bolts. Remove the pump. Note that 1 bolt is located behind the pump pulley and is accessible only through the aperature in the pulley.
5. Installation is the reverse of the removal procedure.

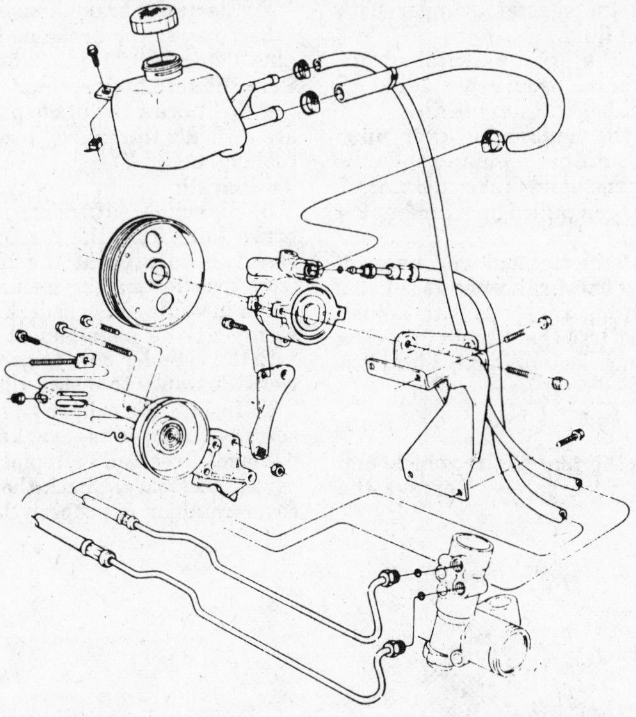

Power steering system and related components – 9000 Series

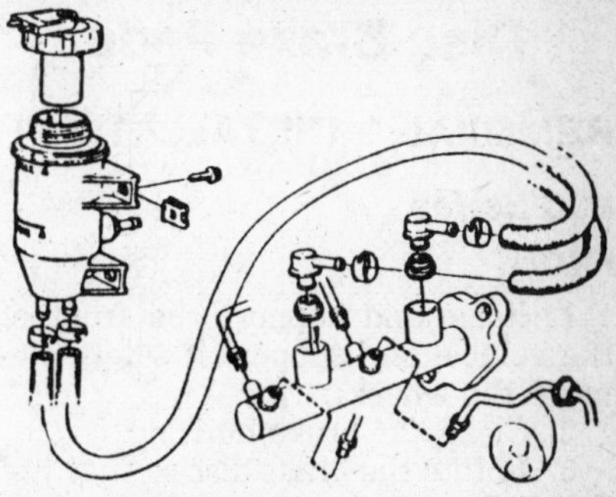

Brake master cylinder and related components – 9000 Series

## BELT ADJUSTMENT

### *900 Series*

Tighten the belt so that when pressure is applied to the belt at a given point the distance between both belt pulleys is 5–10mm.

### *9000 Series*

1. After the belt has been installed, a strand tension gauge must be used to tighten the belt properly.
2. A new belt must be tightened to 185 ± 15 lbs. or 800 ± 65 N.
3. A used belt must be tightened to 120 ± 10 lbs. or 535 ± 45 N.

## SYSTEM BLEEDING

1. Fill the power steering pump with the proper fluid.
2. Start the engine and top off the level of fluid to 0.4 in. above the bottom of the filter.
3. Turn the steering wheel from left to right several times to expel air from the system.
4. Refill the pump as needed.
5. Allow the engine to operate at idle.

## Tie Rod Ends

### REMOVAL & INSTALLATION

1. Disconnect the negative battery cable. Raise and support the vehicle safely.
2. Remove the tire and wheel assembly. Remove the nut.
3. Disconnect the ball joint bolt from the steering arm using the proper removal tool. Do not knock the ball joint bolt out, as this could cause damage to the ball joint and other related parts.
4. Back off the nut that locks the end assembly to the tie rod.
5. Unscrew the end assembly from the tie rod.
6. Installation is the reverse of the removal procedure. Check and adjust the toe-in as required.

# BRAKES

**For all service and adjustment procedures not detailed below, please refer to "Brakes" in the Unit Repair Section.**

## Master Cylinder

### REMOVAL & INSTALLATION

1. Disconnect the negative battery cable. Disconnect the electrical connection to the brake warning switch.
2. Disconnect the hose from the clutch master cylinder to the fluid reservoir. Insert a plastic stopper in the nipple of the reservoir.
3. Disconnect the brake lines to the master cylinder.
4. Remove the nuts that hold the master cylinder to the power brake booster. Remove the master cylinder from the vehicle.
5. Installation is the reverse of removal. Bleed the system as required.

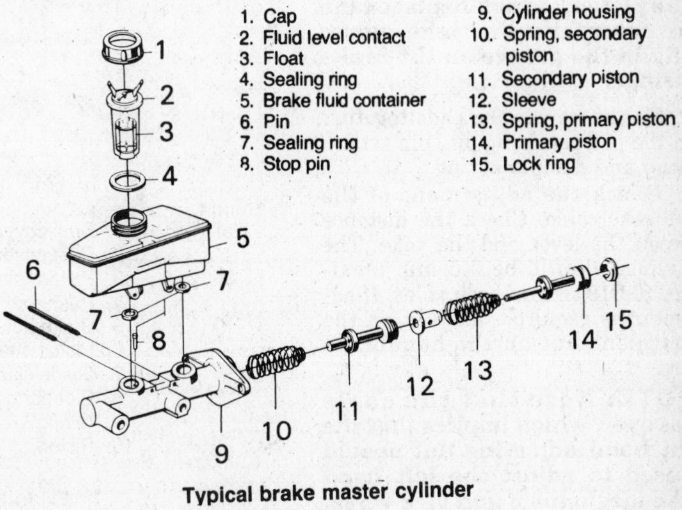


Typical brake master cylinder

## Disc Brake Pads

### REMOVAL & INSTALLATION

#### *900 Series*

#### FRONT

1. Raise and support the front of the vehicle and support it safely. Remove the wheel.
2. Clean the brake housing.
3. Rotate the brake disc so that 1 of the recesses in the edge of the disc is in line with the brake pads.
4. Remove the damper spring, pin retaining clip and pad retaining pin. If the pad retaining pin is dificult to remove, use a tapping-out tool No. 83 90 270 and removal tool 89 96 175.
5. Withdraw the brake pads, if the pads are seating firmly, use pad extractor No. 89 95 771.

**To install:**

6. Siphon a sufficient quantity of brake fluid from the master cylinder reservoir to prevent the brake fluid from overflowing the master cylinder when installing new pads. This is necessary as the piston must be forced into the cylinder bore to provide sufficient clearance to install the pads.
7. Inspect the caliper and piston assembly for breaks, cracks or other damage. Overhaul or replace the caliper as necessary.
8. Push the piston next to the rotor back into the cylinder bore until the end of the piston is flush with the boot retaining ring. Rotate the piston using tool No. 89 96 043, while simultaneously pushing the piston back into the cylinder. The automatic handbrake is reset this way.

**CAUTION**

***If the piston is pushed further than this, the seal will be damaged and the caliper assembly will have to be overhauled.***

**NOTE: Check that the position of the piston has not displaced the dust cover and the yoke moves easily in the groove on the brake housing.**

9. Fit the new brake pads together with the pad retaining pin, pin retaining clip and damper spring.
10. Check the adjustment of the handbrake cable. Check the distance between the lever and the yoke. The clearance should be 0.5 mm maximum, (0.019 in.) on both sides. If adjustment is required, make it on the adjustment nut on the handbrake lever.

**NOTE: Note that the cable cross over, which implies that the right hand adjusting nut should be used to adjust the left hand brake mechanism and vice-versa.**

11. Refill the master cylinder with fresh brake fluid.
12. With the engine switched off, pump the brake pedal repeatedly intil the foot brake starts to operate.
13. Pull the handbrake lever up 5 notches. Continue to pump the brake pedal until the hand brake operates after having been pulled up a further 2-4 notches.
14. Install the tire and wheel assembly. Pump the brake pedal several times to bring the pads into adjustment. Road test the vehicle. If a firm pedal cannot be obtained, bleed the brakes.

#### REAR

1. Raise the rear of the vehicle and support it with safely. Remove the wheel.
2. Clean the brake housing.
3. Tap out the brake pad retaining pins using a 0.11 in. (2.5mm) drift. Save the retaining spring.
4. Withdraw the brake pads. If they are difficult to remove, use extractor tool No. 89 95 771.

**To install:**

5. Siphon a sufficient quantity of brake fluid from the master cylinder reservoir to prevent the brake fluid from overflowing the master cylinder when installing new pads. This is necessary as the piston must be forced into the cylinder bore to provide sufficient clearance to install the pads.
6. Inspect the caliper and piston assembly for breaks, cracks or other damage. Overhaul or replace the caliper as necessary. Check that the dust cover retainer is properly in position

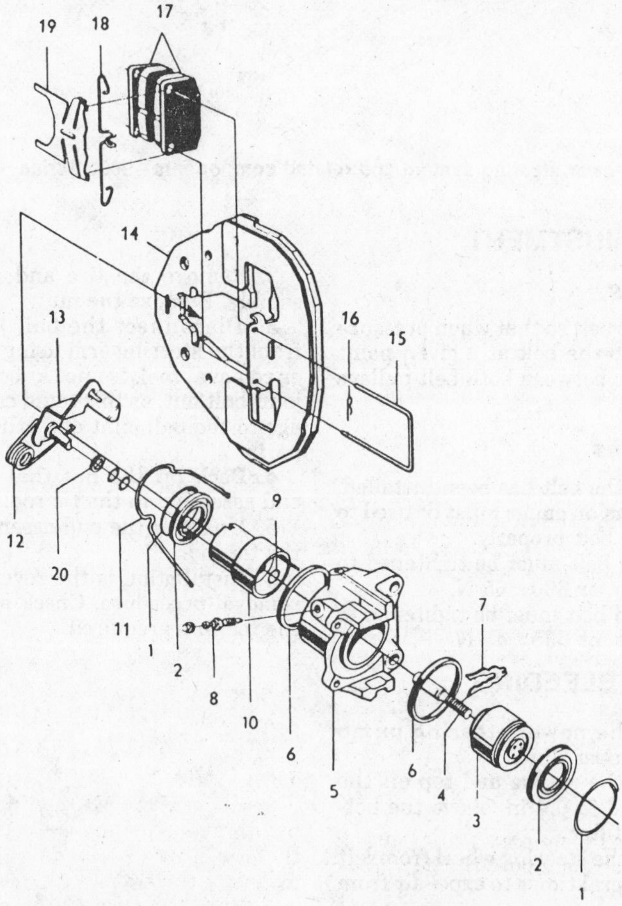


1. Dust cover holder
2. Dust cover
3. Piston (direct)
4. Push rod
5. Brake housing
6. Piston seal
7. Guide clip
8. Bleeder nipple
9. O-ring
10. Piston
11. Yoke spring
12. Spring (handbrake lever)
13. Handbrake lever
14. Yoke
15. Pad retaining pin
16. Lock clip
17. Brake pad
18. Spring
19. Damper spring
20. Retainer (two O-rings)

**Exploded view of the front brake caliper**

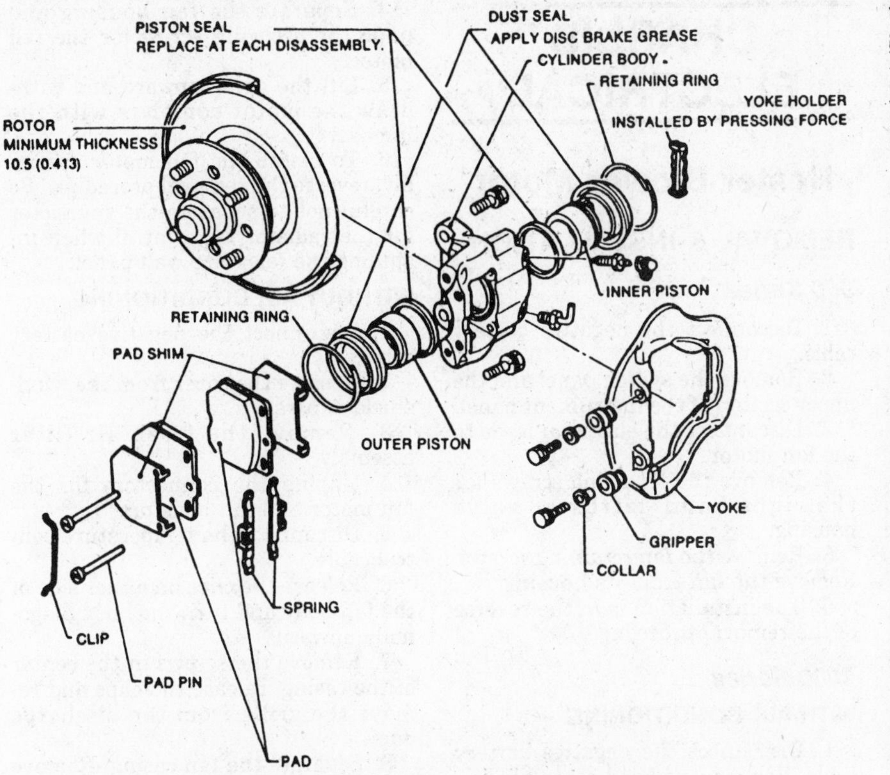


**Exploded view of the brake caliper (sliding type)**

and that the cover is in good condition.

7. Push the piston back into the cylinder bore just enough to allow clearance for installation of the new pads.

8. Fit the pad retaining pins and the pin retaining clip.

9. Refill the master cylinder to the correct level with the proper brake fluid.

10. Replace the wheel and lower the vehicle. Pump the brake pedal several times to bring the pads into correct adjustment. Road test the vehicle.

**NOTE: If a firm pedal cannot be obtained, the system will require bleeding.**

### *9000 Series*

#### FRONT

1. Raise and support the front of the vehicle and support it safely. Remove the wheel.

2. Remove the lower guide pin bolt.

3. Pivot the caliper upwards and remove the pads.

4. Check that the guide pins slide freely and that the dust covers are in good condition.

5. Clean the abutment surfaces between the pads and the carrier.

**To install:**

6. Fit the new pads and pivot the hydraulic body back to its normal position.

7. Refit and tighten the bolt in the lower guide pin.

8. Install the wheel and lower the car.

9. Pump the brake pedal to move the pads to their operating positions.

#### REAR

1. Raise the rear of the vehicle and support it with safely. Remove the wheel.

2. Release the handbrake and remove the retaining spring.

3. Slide the handbrake cable out of the slot of the lever.

4. Remove the dust caps and then use a 7mm allen key (hexagon bit adapter) to remove the guide pins.

5. Lift off the hydraulic body and remove the pads.

**To install:**

6. Remove the screw plug from the handbrake adjusting screw and screw the piston into the hydraulic body by means of the adjusting screw.

7. Place the new pads into position.

8. Replace the hydraulic body and install the guide pins complete with dust caps.

9. Install the retaining spring for the handbrake lever.

10. Screw the adjusting screw fully home and then back it off approximately ¼-½ turn. Check that the brake disc is running freely and refit the plug.

11. Install the handbrake cable to the lever and check with a feeler gauge, that the clearance between the lever and the stop is 1 + 0.5mm (0.04 + 0.020 in.) Adjust as necessary by means of the adjusting screw at the handbrake lever inside the car.

12. Replace the wheel and lower the car.

## Power Brake Booster

### REMOVAL & INSTALLATION

1. Disconnect the negative battery cable. Remove the steering column bearing cover, ash tray and safety padding screw. Remove the upper circlip on the brake pedal push rod, if equipped.

2. Remove the 2 electrical connections on the brake light switch. Remove the safety padding screws in the engine compartment.

3. Remove the vacuum hose from the non-return valve which is located on the vacuum booster.

4. Disconnect the brake lines and the electrical connections for the brake warning switch from the master cylinder. Disconnect the line to the clutch master cylinder from the fluid reservoir. Insert stoppers in the lines to prevent loss of the brake fluid.

5. Remove the cotter pin from the servo unit push rod at the brake pedal.

6. Remove the vacuum booster together with the master cylinder and the bracket.

**NOTE: The bracket is mounted on the dash panel with 4 bolts and nuts. Three of these bolts are accessible from underneath in the passenger compartment after removal of the screen section and parts of the dash panel insulation felt below the instrument panel. The 4th nut is accessible from the engine compartment by the bracket.**

7. Separate the master cylinder and the bracket from the vacuum booster.

8. Installation is the reverse of removal. Bleed the system as required.

## Parking Brake Cable

### ADJUSTMENT

#### *900 Series*

Check the adjustment of the handbrake cable. Check the distance between the handbrake lever and the yoke: the clearance should be a maximum 0.019 in. and should be equal on both sides. Adjust as necessary using the adjustment nut on the handbrake lever.

Note that the cables cross over therefore, the right hand adjustment nut should be used to adjust the left hand brake mechanism and vice versa. The parking brake is self adjusting on the rear calipers, however if necessary, check with a feeler gauge, that the clearance between the lever and the stop is 1 + 0.5mm (0.04 + 0.020 in.) Adjust as necessary by means of the adjusting screw at the handbrake lever inside the car.

### REMOVAL & INSTALLATION

#### 900 Series

1. Disconnect the negative battery cable.
2. Remove the drivers seat. Remove the carpet to provide access to the heater ducts.
3. Remove the gear lever cover. Be sure not to damage the ignition switch light.
4. Remove the air ducts and cover plates. Disconnect the cable from the adjustment nut on the handbrake lever. Remove the clip holding the 2 cables to the floor.
5. Remove the rubber bushing in the side of the wheel housing. Disconnect the cable from the handbrake lever at the brake cylinder housing.
6. Remove the cable from underneath inside the engine compartment.
7. Installation is the reverse of the removal procedure.

#### 9000 Series

1. Disconnect the negative battery cable. Remove the passenger seat.
2. Slide the bush seal off the handbrake lever from inside the vehicle. Lift the plastic locking plate off the adjusting nuts.
3. Remove the rear section of the console assembly. Remove the bezel and slide the rubber boot off of the gear lever.
4. Remove the floor trim and fold back the carpet. Remove the screws retaining the cable cover. Remove the adjusting nuts from the ends of the cable at the handbrake.
5. Unhook the cable from the slot in the handbrake lever which is located on the caliper. Remove the boot and withdraw the cable.
6. Unscrew the cable lead through the bracket and the spring link.
7. Remove the cable from the vehicle.
8. Installation is the reverse of th removal procedure.

# CHASSIS ELECTRICAL

## Heater Blower Motor

### REMOVAL & INSTALLATION

#### 900 Series

1. Disconnect the negative battery cable.
2. Remove the switch panel and the upper section of the instrument panel.
3. Disconnect the electrical leads to the fan motor.
4. Remove the retaining screws for the right hand defroster valve housing.
5. Remove the fan retaining screws. Remove the fan from its housing.
6. The installation is in the reverse of the removal procedure.

#### 9000 Series

##### WITH AIR CONDITIONING

1. Disconnect the negative battery cable. Remove the hood assembly.
2. Disconnect the wiper arms. Remove the covers on the evaporator and wiper motor. Unplug the connector for the fan control unit on vehicles with automatic climate control.
3. Remove the false fire wall panel.
4. Remove the plastic drainage tube moulding below the windshield moulding.
5. Remove the securing bolts the electronic ignition control unit and position it out of the way.
6. Remove the clip and unplug the connectors. Remove the complete wiper assembly.
7. Remove the rubber lead through panel for the coolant hoses. Drain cooling system. Disconnect the quick release couplings for the coolant hoses at the heat exchanger.
8. Remove the throttle dash pot assembly.
9. Remove the vacuum pump retaining screws. Position the pump out of the way.
10. Remove the evaporator body retaining screws and the clips for the refrigerant hoses.
11. Remove the lock washer and disconnect the cable for the temperature valve.
12. Carefully lift the evaporator and remove the clips on either side of the fan. Remove the complete fan assembly by twisting the fan diagonally upwards.
13. Remove the screw in the center of the casing. Release the clips and the grille at the discharge duct.
14. Separate the fan housing and undo the securing screw for the fan motor.
15. Lift the cover upward and withdraw the motor complete with the impeller.
16. To install the fan motor assembly, reverse the removal procedure. Be careful not to separate the connector for the radiator fan control when installing the false fire wall panel.

##### WITHOUT AIR CONDITIONING

1. Disconnect the negative battery cable.
2. Remove the cover from the windshield wipers.
3. Remove the fresh air filter assembly.
4. Unplug the connectors for the fan motor and fan resistors.
5. Disconnect the temperature control cable.
6. Release the clips on either side of the fan body and turn the body diagonally upwards.
7. Remove the screws in the center of the casing, release the clips and remove the grille from the discharge duct.
8. Separate the fan casing. Remove the screw securing the fan motor.
9. Lift the cover for the lead and withdraw the motor complete with impeller.
10. Installation is the reverse of the removal procedure.

## Heater Core

### REMOVAL & INSTALLATION

#### 900 Series

1. Disconnect the negative battery cable. Remove the dash panel under the switches on the steering column and the lower section of the instrument panel.
2. Remove the air diffuser and retaining screws.
3. Remove the left defroster and speaker grill.
4. Remove the control rod from between the coolant shut off valve and the control rod by sliding the rod as far forward as it will go to free it from the knob, then pull it rearward to free it from the shut off valve.

**NOTE: The plastic joint at the control knob is accessible from underneath once the switches below the heater controls have been moved backward.**

5. Remove the lower section of the heater housing.
6. Drain the coolant and disconnect the hoses. Plug the ends of the hoses to prevent coolant from leaking into the compartment.

7. Separate the heater core from the housing and guide it backward and downward. It will be necessary to disconnect the brake pedal return spring and depress the brake pedal slightly.
8. The water valve and the heater core can be separated after their removal. Do not kink or break the capillary tube.
9. Installation is the reverse of the removal procedure.

### 9000 Series

1. Disconnect the negative battery cable. Remove the hood assembly.
2. Disconnect the wiper arms. Remove the covers on the evaporator and wiper motor. Unplug the connector for the fan control unit on vehicles with automatic climate control.
3. Remove the false fire wall panel. Drain the radiator.
4. Remove the plastic drainage tube moulding below the windshield moulding.
5. Remove the securing bolts the electronic ignition control unit and position it out of the way.
6. Remove the clip and unplug the connectors. Remove the complete wiper assembly.
7. Remove the rubber lead through panel for the coolant hoses. Drain cooling system. Disconnect the quick release couplings for the coolant hoses at the heat exchanger.
8. Remove the throttle dash pot assembly.
9. Remove the vacuum pump retaining screws. Position the pump out of the way.
10. Remove the evaporator body retaining screws and the clips for the refrigerant hoses.
11. Remove the lock washer and disconnect the cable for the temperature valve.
12. Carefully lift the evaporator and remove the clips on either side of the fan. Remove the complete fan assembly by twisting the fan diagonally upwards.
13. Remove the screw in the center of the casing. Release the clips and the grille at the discharge duct.
14. Separate the fan housing and undo the securing screw for the fan motor.
15. Lift the cover upward and withdraw the motor complete with the impeller.
16. Release the retaining clips and disconnect the hoses from the heater core.
17. Pull the heater core from the engine side of the fire wall.
18. To install, position new O-rings and connect the heater hoses. Complete the assembly in the reverse order of the removal procedure.

# Radio

Most radios used in Saab vehicles are dealer installed or aftermarket units. It is therefore impossible to give specific procedures for removal and installation of these units. Care should be exercised when servicing a vehicle that has a radio problem. Late model vehicles, with factory installed radios, are equipped with a theft proof mechanism that renders the radio non functionable unless the owner knows the 6 digit combination.

# Windshield Wiper Switch

## REMOVAL & INSTALLATION

1. Disconnect the negative battery cable.
2. Pull the steering wheel as far forward as it will go. Remove the cover from under the steering column assembly.
3. Disconnect the electrical connector from the switch assembly.
4. Remove the switch retaining screws. Remove the switch from the vehcile.
5. Installation is the reverse of the removal procedure.

# Windshield Wiper Motor

## REMOVAL & INSTALLATION

### 900 Series

1. Disconnect the negative battery cable. Remove the wiper arms from the vehicle. Remove the rubber grommets.

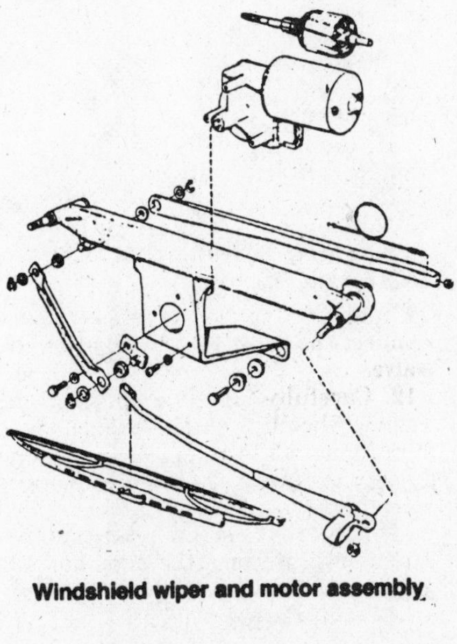

Windshield wiper and motor assembly

2. Remove the 4 mounting screws. Disconnect the electrical lead. Remove the wiper unit from the vehicle.
3. Separate the wiper motor from the wiper assembly.
4. Installation is the reverse of the removal procedure.

### 9000 Series

1. Disconnect the negative battery cable.
2. Raise the covers on the wiper arms, remove the retaining nuts and lift the arms off.
3. Remove the rubber grommets from the spindles and remove the 4 bulkhead panel bolts.
4. Lift the bulkhead panel from the vehicle.
5. Disconnect the electrical connector from the wiper motor.
6. Remove the spindle nuts and remove the 4 retaining bolts for the wiper motor bracket.
7. Push downward and pull forward on the push rod for the left hand wiper.
8. Lift out the wiper motor assembly complete with the bracket and the push rod linkage.
9. Installation is the reverse of the removal procedure.

# Instrument Cluster

## REMOVAL & INSTALLATION

### 900 Series

1. Disconnect the negative battery cable. Remove the steering wheel.
2. Remove the 4 screws in the switch panel and tilt the panel back.
3. Remove the left speaker/defroster grille. Pull apart the instrument panel connectors. Disconnect the speedometer cable.
4. Remove the instrument panel retaining screws. Carefully remove the unit from the vehicle.
5. Installation is the reverse of the removal procedure.

### 9000 Series

1. Disconnect the negative battery cable.
2. Remove the speaker grilles on either side of the panel.
3. Unscrew the top section of the instrument panel, which is retained by 7 screws including 1 in the glove box.
4. Lift off the top instrument panel section.
5. Remove the air duct from the opening in the top.
6. Disconnect the speedometer cable, the vacuum hoses to the turbo pressure gauge and unplug all connectors to the display panel.

7. Remove the 2 screws of the instrument display panel.
8. Withdraw the instrument cluster through the top of the instrument panel.
9. Installation is the reverse of the removal procedure. Be sure the air duct fitting is tight when reassembling the duct tubing.

## Ignition Switch

### REMOVAL & INSTALLATION

#### 900 Series

1. Disconnect the negative battery cable.
2. Remove the center console.
3. Disconnect the electrical connections from the switch.
4. Remove the assembly from the vehicle.
5. Installation is the reverse of removal.

#### 9000 Series

1. Disconnect the negative battery cable.
2. Remove the steering wheel assembly.
3. Remove the cover panels from the wiper/washer and direction indicator switches.
4. Remove the upper section of the instrument panel. Remove the instrument cluster assembly.
5. Remove the clip securing the wiring loom and flexible ducts to the steering column.
6. Unplug the connector for the wipers, direction signals and leads for the horn switch and ignition switch.
7. Remove the pinch bolt in the upper joint, loosen the other bolts and withdraw the universal joint from the splines on the steering column shaft.
8. Remove the steering column wheel adjustment assembly by tapping out the roll pin and removing the nut and washer. Withdraw the shaft from the clamp and lift the upper section of the steering wheel adjustment assembly. Remove the 3 socket headed bolts and lift off the holder for the directional indicator unit.
9. Remove the upper section of the steering column, removing the rubber bushing completely from the housing.
10. Remove the shake-proof washer. Remove the column bearing.
11. With the switch support out remove the socket headed screws and remove the ignition switch.
12. To remove the cylinder, turn the ignition key to position 1, press in on the locking tab and withdraw the cylinder.
13. Installation is the reverse of the removal procedure.

## Headlight Switch

### REMOVAL & INSTALLATION

1. Disconnect the negative battery cable.
2. Pull the switch from its mounting on the instrument panel assembly.
3. Disconnect the electrical connectors from the switch.
4. Remove the switch from the vehicle.
5. Installation is the reverse of the removal procedure.

## Stoplight Switch

### REMOVAL & INSTALLATION

1. Disconnect the negative battery cable.
2. Remove the necessary trim and padding to gain access to the switch assembly.
3. Disconnect the electrical connections from the switch assembly.
4. Remove the switch from its mounting.
5. Installation is the reverse of the removal procedure.

## Fuses and Circuit Breakers

### LOCATION

The fuse panel is located under the hood of the vehicle. It is on the left hand side for the 900 series vehicles. The fuse panel for the 9000 series vehicles is located and accessed through an access panel in the glove compartment.

# Subaru 16

## 1600, 1800, Legacy, Justy, XT Coupe – All Models

# SERIAL NUMBER IDENTIFICATION

## Vehicle Identification Plate

The vehicle identification plate is located on the bulkhead in the engine compartment.

## Engine Number

The engine serial number is stamped on the front right side of the crankcase, on all engines except the 1200cc engine. On the 1200cc engine, the serial number is stamped at the right rear side of the engine below the cylinder head.

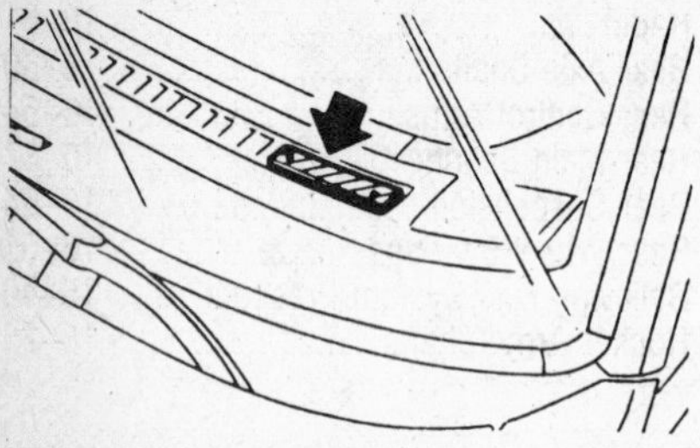

**Vehicle Identification Number is located on the left-side of the dash**

## Vehicle Identification Number

The Vehicle Identification Number (VIN) is stamped on a plate located on the top of the dashboard on the drivers side, and is visible through the windshield.

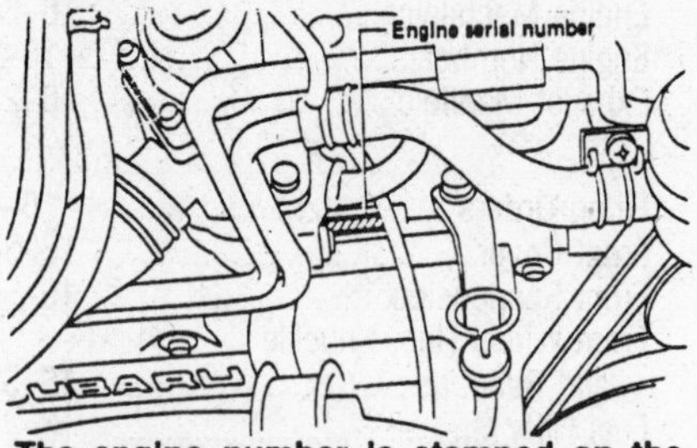


**The engine number is stamped on the front right-side of the crankcase – except 1200 (OHC) engines**

**Vehicle Identification Plate is located on a plate attached to the bulkhead panel in the engine compartment**

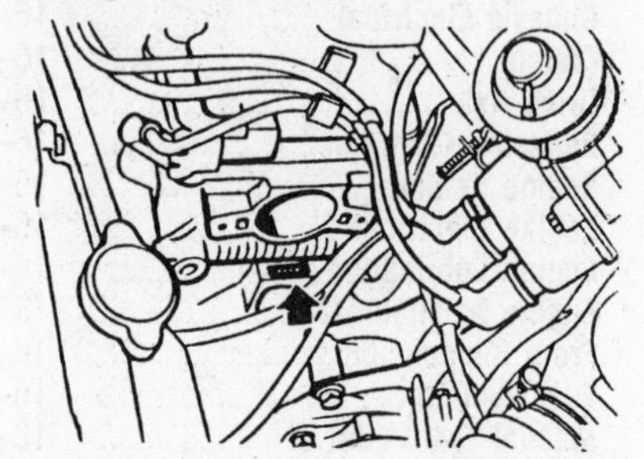

**The engine number is stamped on the rear-side of the engine, below the cylinder head – 1200 (OHC) engines**

## ENGINE IDENTIFICATION

| Year | Model | Engine Displacement cu. in. (cc/liter) | Engine Series Identification | No. of Cylinders | Engine Type |
|---|---|---|---|---|---|
| 1983 | STD | 96 (1600/1.6) | 2 | 4 | OHV |
| | STD 4WD | 96 (1600/1.6) | 3 | 4 | OHV |
| | STD | 109 (1800/1.8) | 4 | 4 | OHV |
| | STD 4WD | 109 (1800/1.8) | 5 | 4 | OHV |
| 1984 | STD | 96 (1600/1-6) | 2 | 4 | OHV |
| | STD 4WD | 96 (1600/1.6) | 3 | 4 | OHV |
| | STD | 109 (1800/1.8) | 4 | 4 | OHV |
| | STD 4WD | 109 (1800/1.8) | 5 | 4 | OHV |
| 1985 | STD | 96 (1600/1.6) | 2 | 4 | OHV |
| | STD 4WD | 96 (1600/1.6) | 3 | 4 | OHV |
| | STD | 109 (1800/1.8) | 4 | 4 | OHC |
| | STD 4WD | 109 (1800/1.8) | 5① | 4 | OHC |
| | XT Coupe | 109 (1800/1.8) | 4 | 4 | OHC |
| | XT Coupe | 109 (1800/1.8) | 7 | 4 | OHC |
| 1986 | STD | 96 (1600/1.6) | 2 | 4 | OHV |
| | STD 4WD | 96 (1600/1.6) | 3 | 4 | OHV |
| | STD | 109 (1800/1.8) | 4 | 4 | OHC |
| | STD 4WD | 109 (1800/1.8) | 5① | 4 | OHC |
| | XT Coupe | 109 (1800/1.8) | 4 | 4 | OHC |
| | XT Coupe 4WD | 109 (1800/1.8) | 7 | 4 | OHC |

## ENGINE IDENTIFICATION

| Year | Model | Engine Displacement cu. in. (cc/liter) | Engine Series Identification | No. of Cylinders | Engine Type |
|---|---|---|---|---|---|
| 1987 | Justy | 73 (1200/1.2) | 7 | 3 | OHC |
| | Justy 4WD | 73 (1200/1.2) | 8 | 3 | OHC |
| | STD | 109 (1800/1.8) | 4 | 4 | OHC |
| | STD 4WD | 109 (1800/1.8) | 5① | 4 | OHC |
| | XT Coupe | 109 (1800/1.8) | 4 | 4 | OHC |
| | XT Coupe 4WD | 109 (1800/1.8) | 7 | 4 | OHC |
| 1988 | Justy | 73 (1200/1.2) | 7 | 3 | OHC |
| | Justy 4WD | 73 (1200/1.2) | 8 | 3 | OHC |
| | STD | 109 (1800/1.8) | 4 | 4 | OHC |
| | STD 4WD | 109 (1800/1.8) | 5① | 4 | OHC |
| | XT Coupe | 109 (1800/1.8) | 4 | 4 | OHC |
| | XT Coupe 4WD | 109 (1800/1.8) | 7 | 4 | OHC |
| | XT Coupe | 160 (2700/2.7) | 8 | 6 | OHC |
| | XT Coupe 4WD | 160 (2700/2.7) | 9 | 6 | OHC |
| 1989-90 | Justy | 73 (1200/1.2) | 7 | 3 | OHC |
| | Justy 4WD | 73 (1200/1.2) | 8 | 3 | OHC |
| | STD | 109 (1800/1.8) | 4 | 4 | OHC |
| | STD 4WD | 109 (1800/1.8) | 5① | 4 | OHC |
| | XT Coupe | 109 (1800/1.8) | 4 | 4 | OHC |
| | XT Coupe 4WD | 109 (1800/1.8) | 7 | 4 | OHC |
| | XT Coupe | 160 (2700/2.7) | 8 | 6 | OHC |
| | XT Coupe 4WD | 160 (2700/2.7) | 9 | 6 | OHC |
| | Legacy | 135 (2200/2.2) | 6 | 4 | OHC |

① Air Suspension

**NOTE:** STD designates—4 door sedan
Station wagon
Touring wagon
3 door wagon

## GENERAL ENGINE SPECIFICATIONS

| Year | Model | Engine Displacement cu. in. (cc) | Fuel System Type | Net Horsepower @ rpm | Net Torque @ rpm (ft. lbs.) | Bore × Stroke (in.) | Com-pression Ratio | Oil Pressure @ 2000 rpm |
|---|---|---|---|---|---|---|---|---|
| 1983 | 4 cyl (OHV) | 97 (1600) | Carb. | 67 @ 5200 | 81 @ 2400 | 3.62 × 2.36 | 9.0:1 | 36–57 |
| | 4 cyl (OHV) | 109 (1800) | Carb. | 72 @ 4800 | 92 @ 2400 | 3.62 × 2.64 | 8.7:1 | 50–57 |
| | 4 cyl (OHV) | 109 (1800) | FI Turbo | 111 @ 4800 | 123 @ 2000 | 3.62 × 2.64 | 7.7:1 | 57–64 |
| 1984 | 4 cyl (OHV) | 97 (1600) | Carb. | 67 @ 5200 | 81 @ 2400 | 3.62 × 2.36 | 9.0:1 | 36–57 |
| | 4 cyl (OHV) | 109 (1800) | Carb. | 72 @ 4800 | 92 @ 2400 | 3.62 × 2.64 | 8.7:1 | 50–57 |
| | 4 cyl (OHV) | 109 (1800) | FI Turbo | 111 @ 4800 | 123 @ 2000 | 3.62 × 2.64 | 7.7:1 | 57–64 |
| 1985 | 4 cyl (OHV) | 97 (1600) | Carb. | 67 @ 5200 | 81 @ 2400 | 3.62 × 2.36 | 8.5:1 | 57-64 |
| | 4 cyl (OHC) | 109 (1800) | Carb. | 82 @ 4800 | 101 @ 2800 | 3.62 × 2.64 | 9.0:1 | 57–64 |
| | 4 cyl (OHC) | 109 (1800) | MFI | 94 @ 5200 | 101 @ 2800 | 3.62 × 2.64 | 9.0:1 | 57–64 |
| | 4 cyl (OHC) | 109 (1800) | MFI Turbo | 111 @ 4800 | 134 @ 2800 | 3.62 × 2.64 | 7.7:1 | 57–64 |

## GENERAL ENGINE SPECIFICATIONS

| Year | Model | Engine Displacement cu. in. (cc) | Fuel System Type | Net Horsepower @ rpm | Net Torque @ rpm (ft. lbs.) | Bore × Stroke (in.) | Com-pression Ratio | Oil Pressure @ 2000 rpm |
|---|---|---|---|---|---|---|---|---|
| 1986 | 4 cyl (OHV) | 97 (1600) | Carb. | 67 @ 5200 | 81 @ 2400 | 3.62 × 2.36 | 8.5:1 | 57–64 |
| | 4 cyl (OHC) | 109 (1800) | Carb. | 82 @ 4800 | 101 @ 2800 | 3.62 × 2.64 | 9.0:1 | 57–64 |
| | 4 cyl (OHC) | 109 (1800) | SPFI | 90 @ 5600 | 101 @ 2800 | 3.62 × 2.64 | 9.5:1 | 57–64 |
| | 4 cyl (OHC) | 109 (1800) | MFI Turbo | 110 @ 4800 | 134 @ 2800 | 3.62 × 2.64 | 7.7:1 | 57–64 |
| 1987 | 3 cyl (OHC) | 73 (1200) | EFC Carb. | 66 @ 5200 | 70 @ 3200 | 3.07 × 3.27 | 9.0:1 | 35–40 |
| | 4 cyl (OHC) | 109 (1800) | Carb. | 82 @ 4800 | 92 @ 2400 | 3.62 × 2.64 | 9.0:1 | 57–64 |
| | 4 cyl (OHC) | 109 (1800) | SPFI | 90 @ 5600 | 101 @ 2800 | 3.62 × 2.64 | 9.5:1 | 57–64 |
| | 4 cyl (OHC) | 109 (1800) | MPFI | 94 @ 5200 | 101 @ 2800 | 3.62 × 2.64 | 9.0:1 | 57–64 |
| | 4 cyl (OHC) | 109 (1800) | MPFI Turbo | 110 @ 4800 | 134 @ 2400 | 3.62 × 2.64 | 7.7:1 | 57–64 |
| 1988 | 3 cyl (OHC) | 73 (1200) | EFC Carb. | 66 @ 5200 | 70 @ 3200 | 3.07 × 3.27 | 9.0:1 | 35–40 |
| | 4 cyl (OHC) | 109 (1800) | SPFI | 84 @ 5200 | 137 @ 2800 | 3.62 × 2.64 | 9.5:1 | 57–64 |
| | 4 cyl (OHC) | 109 (1800) | MPFI Turbo | 115 @ 5200 | 181 @ 2800 | 3.62 × 2.64 | 7.7:1 | 57–64 |
| | 6 cyl (OHC) | 160 (2700) | MPFI | NA | NA | 3.62 × 2.64 | 9.5:1 | 57–64 |
| 1989-90 | 3 cyl (OHC) | 73 (1200) | EFC Carb. | 66 @ 5200 | 70 @ 3600 | 3.07 × 3.27 | 9.1:1 | 35–40 |
| | 4 cyl (OHC) | 109 (1800) | EEM-SPFI | 90 @ 5200 | 101 @ 2800 | 3.62 × 2.64 | 9.5:1 | 57–64 |
| | 4 cyl (OHC) | 109 (1800) | EEM-MPFI Turbo | 115 @ 5200 | 134 @ 2800 | 3.62 × 2.64 | 7.7:1 | 57–64 |
| | 4 cyl (OHC) | 109 (1800) | EFC Carb. ① | 73 @ 4400 | 94 @ 2400 | 3.62 × 2.64 | 8.7:1 | 57–64 |
| | 4 cyl (OHC) | 109 (1800) | EEM MPFI ② | 97 @ 5200 | 103 @ 3200 | 3.62 × 2.64 | 9.5:1 | 57–64 |
| | 4 cyl (OHC) | 135 (2200) | EEM-MPFI | 130 @ 5400 | 137 @ 4400 | 3.82 × 2.95 | 9.5:1 | ③ |
| | 6 cyl (OHC) | 160 (2700) | EEM-MPFI | 145 @ 5200 | 156 @ 4000 | 3.62 × 2.64 | 9.5:1 | 57–64 |

EEM Electronic Engine Management
EFC Electronic Fuel Control
MFI Multi-point Fuel Injection
MPFI Multi-point Fuel Injection
SPFI Single Point Fuel Injection
FI Fuel Injection

① 1989–90 GL Hatchback
② 1989–90 XT
③ 14 psi @ 600 rpm
43 psi @ 5000 rpm

## ENGINE TUNE-UP SPECIFICATIONS

| Year | Model | Engine Displacement cu. in. (cc) | Spark Plugs Type | Spark Plugs Gap (in.) | Ignition Timing (deg.) MT | Ignition Timing (deg.) AT | Com-pression Pressure (psi) | Fuel Pump (psi) | Idle Speed (rpm) MT | Idle Speed (rpm) AT | Valve Clearance In. | Valve Clearance Ex. |
|---|---|---|---|---|---|---|---|---|---|---|---|---|
| 1983 | STD | 96 (1600) | BPR6ES-11 | 0.040 | 8B | — | 175 | 1.3–2.0 | 700 | 800 | 0.010 | 0.014 |
| | STD | 109 (1800) | BPR6ES-11 | 0.040 | 8B② | 8B | 175 | 1.3–2.0 ⑤ | 700③ | 800 | 0.010 ④ | 0.014 ④ |
| 1984 | STD | 96 (1600) | BPR6ES-11 | 0.040 | 8B | — | 175 | 1.3–2.0 | 700 | — | 0.010 | 0.014 |
| | STD | 109 (1800) | BPR6ES-11 | 0.040 | 8B② | 8B | 175 | 1.3–2.0 ⑤ | 700③ | 800 | 0.010 ④ | 0.014 ④ |

## ENGINE TUNE-UP SPECIFICATIONS

| Year | Model | Engine Displacement cu. in. (cc) | Spark Plugs Type | Spark Plugs Gap (in.) | Ignition Timing (deg.) MT | Ignition Timing (deg.) AT | Compression Pressure (psi) | Fuel Pump (psi) | Idle Speed (rpm) MT | Idle Speed (rpm) AT | Valve Clearance In. | Valve Clearance Ex. |
|---|---|---|---|---|---|---|---|---|---|---|---|---|
| 1985 | STD | 96 (1600) | BPR6ES-11 | 0.040 | 8B | — | 168 | 1.3–2.0 | 700 | — | Hyd. | Hyd. |
| | STD | 109 (1800) | BPR6ES-11 | 0.040 | 8B⑧ | 8B⑨ | 168⑦ | 2.6–3.3 ⑩ | 650⑪ | 800 | Hyd. | Hyd. |
| | XT Coupe | 109 (1800) | BPR6ES-11 | 0.040 | 6B⑥ | 6B | 161⑦ | 61–71 | 700 | 800 | Hyd. | Hyd. |
| 1986 | STD | 96 (1600) | BPR6ES-11 | 0.040 | 8B | — | 168 | 1.3–2.0 | 700 | — | Hyd. | Hyd. |
| | STD | 109 (1800) | BPR6ES-11 | 0.040 | 8B⑧ | 8B⑨ | 168⑦ | 2.6–3.3 ⑩ | 650⑪ | 800 | Hyd. | Hyd. |
| | XT Coupe | 109 (1800) | BPR6ES-11 | 0.040 | 6B⑥ | 6B | 161⑦ | 61–71 | 700 | 800 | Hyd. | Hyd. |
| 1987 | Justy | 73 (1200) | BPR6ES-11 | 0.040 | 5B | — | 160 | 1.3–2.0 | 750–850 | — | .0051–.0067 | .0091–.0100 |
| | STD | 109 (1800) | BPR6ES-11 | 0.040 | 20B | 20B | 168 | ① | 600–800 | 700–900 | Hyd. | Hyd. |
| | XT Coupe | 109 (1800) | BPR6ES-11 | 0.040 | 20 | 20 | 168 | 61–71 | 600–800 | 700–900 | Hyd. | Hyd. |
| 1988 | Justy | 73 (1200) | BPR6ES-11 | 0.040 | 5B | — | 160 | 1.3–2.0 | 750–850 | — | .0051–.0067 | .0091–.0106 |
| | STD | 109 (1800) | BPR6ES-11 | 0.040 | 20B | 20B | 168 | 61–71 ⑯ | 600–800 | 700–900 | Hyd. | Hyd. |
| | XT Coupe | 109 (1800) | BPR6ES-11 | 0.040 | 20B | 20B | 168 | 61–71 | 600–800 | 700–900 | Hyd. | Hyd. |
| | XT-6 Coupe | 160 (2700) | BPR6ES-11 | 0.040 | 20 | 20B | 168 | 61–71 | 650–850 | 650–850 | Hyd. | Hyd. |
| 1989 | Justy | 73 (1200) | BPR6ES-11 | 0.040 | 5B | 5B ⑮ | 160 | 1.3–2.0 | 750–850 ⑫ | 800–900 ⑬ | .0057–.0067 | .0091–.0106 |
| | STD | 109 (1800) | BPR6ES-11 | 0.040 | 20B⑭ | 20B | 168 | 61–71 ⑯ | 600–800 | 700–900 | Hyd. | Hyd. |
| | XT Coupe | 109 (1800) | BPR6ES-11 | 0.040 | 20B | 20B | 168 | 61–71 | 600–800 | 700–900 | Hyd. | Hyd. |
| | XT-6 Coupe | 160 (2700) | BPR6ES-11 | 0.040 | 20B | 20B | 168 | 61–71 | 600–800 | 700–900 | Hyd. | Hyd. |
| | Legacy | 135 (2200) | SEE UNDERHOOD SPECIFICATIONS STICKER | | | | | | | | Hyd. | Hyd. |
| 1990 | SEE UNDERHOOD SPECIFICATIONS STICKER | | | | | | | | | | | |

B BTDC

① Carb.—2.6–3.3
MPFI—61–71
SPFI—36–50

② Turbocharged engine—15B

③ Turbocharged engine—800

④ If equipped with hydraulic lifters no adjustment is required

⑤ Turbocharged engine—43

⑥ Turbocharged engine M/T—25 @ 700
Turbocharged engine P/T—25 @ 800

⑦ Turbocharged engine—145

⑧ MPFI engine—6B
Turbocharged engine—20B

⑨ MPFI engine—6B
Turbocharged engine—20B

⑩ 61–71 except carbureted engine

⑪ 700 except carbureted engine

⑫ Idle-up system on—850–950

⑬ Idle-up system on—900–1000

⑭ MPFI-Turbo with automatic transaxle—20B

⑮ With ECVT

⑯ SPFI—36–50

## FIRING ORDERS

**NOTE: To avoid confusion, always replace spark plug wires one at a time.**

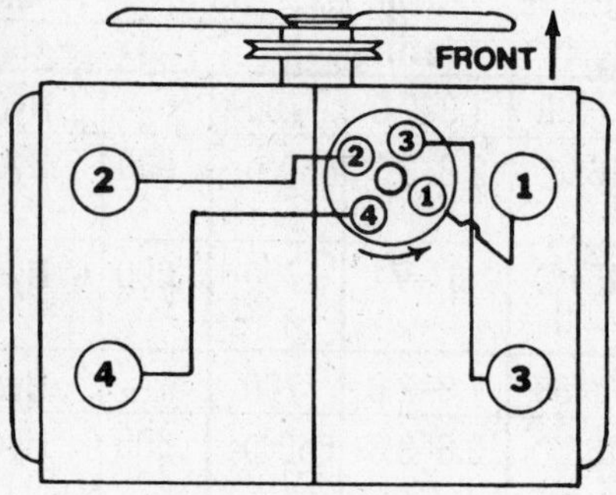


**1600 and 1800cc Engines**
**Firing order: 1–3–2–4**

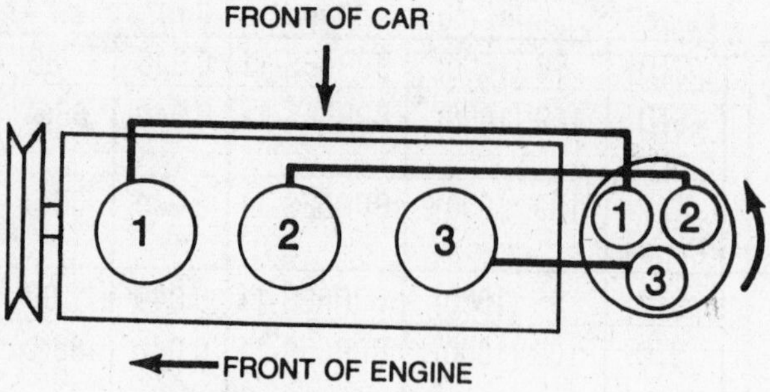


**1200cc Engine**
**Firing order: 1–3–2**

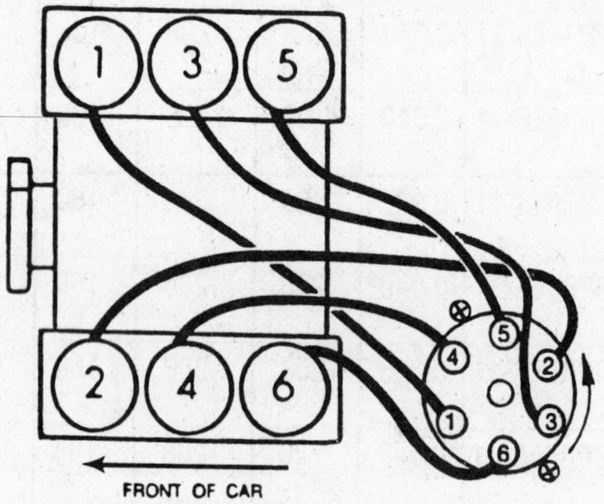


**2700cc Engine**
**Firing order: 1–6–3–2–5–4**

## CAPACITIES

| Year | Model | Engine Displacement cu. in. (cc) | Engine Crankcase with Filter | Engine Crankcase without Filter | Transmission (pts.) 4-Spd | Transmission (pts.) 5-Spd | Transmission (pts.) Auto. | Drive Axle (pts.) | Fuel Tank (gal.) | Cooling System (qts.) |
|---|---|---|---|---|---|---|---|---|---|---|
| 1983 | STD | 96 (1600) | 4.2 | 3.2 | 5.8 | 5.8 | 10–13② | 1.6 | 15.9④ | 5.6 |
| | STD | 109 (1800) | 4.2 | 3.2 | 5.8 | 5.8 | 10–13② | 1.6 | 15.9④ | 5.8 |
| 1984 | STD | 96 (1600) | 4.2 | 3.2 | 5.8 | 5.8 | 10–13② | 1.6 | 15.9④ | 5.6 |
| | STD | 109 (1800) | 4.2 | 3.2 | 5.8 | 5.8 | 10–13② | 1.6 | 15.9④ | 5.8 |
| 1985 | STD | 96 (1600) | 4.2 | 3.2 | 5.8 | 5.8 | 10–13② | 1.6 | 15.9 | 5.6 |
| | STD | 109 (1800) | 4.2 | 3.2 | 5.8 | 5.8 | 10–13 | 1.6 | 15.9 | 5.8 |
| | XT Coupe | 109 (1800) | 4.2 | 3.2 | — | 5.4 | 12–14③ | 1.6 | 15.9 | 6.1 |
| 1986 | STD | 96 (1600) | 4.2 | 3.2 | — | 5.4 | 12–14③ | 1.6 | 15.9 | 5.6 |
| | STD | 109 (1800) | 4.2 | 3.2 | — | 5.4 | 12–14③ | 1.6 | 15.9 | 5.8 |
| | XT Coupe | 109 (1800) | 4.2 | 3.2 | — | 5.4 | 12–14④ | 1.6 | 15.9 | 6.1 |

## CAPACITIES

| Year | Model | Engine Displacement cu. in. (cc) | Engine Crankcase with Filter | Engine Crankcase without Filter | Transmission (pts.) 4-Spd | Transmission (pts.) 5-Spd | Transmission (pts.) Auto. | Drive Axle (pts.) | Fuel Tank (gal.) | Cooling System (qts.) |
|---|---|---|---|---|---|---|---|---|---|---|
| 1987 | Justy | 73 (1200) | 3.0 | 2.0 | – | 4.8⑦ | – | 1.6 | 9.2 | 4.5 |
| | STD | 109 (1800) | 4.2 | 3.2 | – | 6.0 | 10–13③ | 1.6 | 15.9 | 5.8 |
| | XT Coupe | 109 (1800) | 4.2 | 3.2 | – | 5.4① | 18 | 1.6 | 15.9 | 5.8 |
| 1988 | Justy | 73 (1200) | 3.0 | 2.0 | – | 4.8⑦ | – | 0.8 | 9.2 | 4.5 |
| | STD | 109 (1800) | 4.2 | 3.2 | – | 6.0 | 10–13③ | 1.6 | 15.9 | 5.8 |
| | XT Coupe | 109 (1800) | 4.2 | 3.2 | – | 5.4⑦ | 20 | 1.6 | 15.9 | 5.8 |
| | XT Coupe | 160 (2700) | 4.2 | 3.2 | – | 5.4⑦ | 20 | 1.6 | 15.9 | 7.4 |
| 1989-90 | Justy | 73 (1200) | 3.0 | 2.0 | – | 4.8⑦ | 6.6–7.2 | 0.8 | 9.2 | 4.5 |
| | STD | 109 (1800) | 4.2 | 3.2 | – | 6.0⑦ | 14 | 1.6 | 15.9 | 5.8 |
| | XT Coupe | 109 (1800) | 4.2 | 3.2 | – | 7.0⑤ | 19.6 | 3.0 | 15.9 | 5.8 |
| | XT-6 Coupe | 160 (2700) | 5.3 | 4.2 | – | 7.4⑤ | 19.6⑥ | 3.0 | 15.9 | 7.4 |
| | Legacy | 135 (2200) | 4.8 | 4.3 | – | 7.0⑧ | 18.2 | 1.6 | 15.9 | 6.3 |

① 4WD – 11.9
② 4WD – 12–14
③ Differential – 2.6
④ 4WD – 14–15 gals.
STD Hatchback – 13.2
⑤ 4WD – 1.6 pts.
⑥ 4WD – 20 pts.
⑦ 4WD – 1.68 pts.
⑧ 4WD – 7.4 pts.

## CAMSHAFT SPECIFICATIONS

All measurements given in inches.

| Year | Engine Displacement cu. in. (cc) | Journal Diameter 1 | Journal Diameter 2 | Journal Diameter 3 | Journal Diameter 4 | Journal Diameter 5 | Lobe Lift In. | Lobe Lift Ex. | Bearing Clearance | Camshaft End Play |
|---|---|---|---|---|---|---|---|---|---|---|
| 1983 | 97 (1600) | 1.0220–1.0226 | 1.0220–1.0226 | 1.4157–1.4163 | – | – | 0.2093–0.2132 | 0.2093–0.2132 | 0.0010–0.0023 | 0.0008–0.0035 |
| | 109 (1800) | 1.2582–1.2589 | 1.2582–1.2589 | 1.4157–1.4163 | – | – | 0.2093–0.2132 ① | 0.2093–0.2132 ① | 0.0010–0.0023 | 0.0008–0.0035 |
| 1984 | 97 (1600) | 1.0220–1.0226 | 1.0220–1.0226 | 1.4157–1.4136 | – | – | 0.2093–0.2132 | 0.2093–0.2132 | 0.0010–0.0023 | 0.0008–0.0035 |
| | 109 (1800) | 1.2582–1.2589 | 1.2582–1.2589 | 1.4157–1.4163 | – | – | 0.2093–0.2132 ① | 0.2093–0.2132 ① | 0.0010–0.0023 | 0.0008–0.0035 |
| 1985 | 97 (1600) | 1.0220–1.0226 | 1.0220–1.0226 | 1.4157–1.4163 | – | – | 0.2093–0.2132 | 0.2093–0.2132 | 0.0010–0.0023 | 0.0008–0.0035 |
| | 109 (1800) | 1.4946–1.4953 | 1.9080–1.9087 | 1.9671–1.9677 | ③ | – | ② | ② | 0.0008–0.0021 | 0.0012–0.0102 |
| 1986 | 97 (1600) | 1.0220–1.0226 | 1.0220–1.0226 | 1.4157–1.4163 | – | – | 0.2093–0.2132 | 0.2093–0.2132 | 0.0010–0.0023 | 0.0008–0.0035 |
| | 109 (1800) | 1.4946–1.4953 | 1.9080–1.9087 | 1.9671–1.9677 | ③ | – | ②④ | ②④ | 0.0008–0.0021 | 0.0012–0.0102 |

## CAMSHAFT SPECIFICATIONS

All measurements given in inches.

| Year | Engine Displacement cu. in. (cc) | Journal Diameter 1 | 2 | 3 | 4 | 5 | Lobe Lift In. | Ex. | Bearing Clearance | Camshaft End Play |
|---|---|---|---|---|---|---|---|---|---|---|
| 1987 | 73 (1200) | — | — | — | — | — | 1.4520–1.4528 | 1.4520–1.4528 | — | 0.0012–0.0150 |
| | 109 (1800) | 1.4946–1.4953 | 1.9080–1.9087 | 1.8883–1.8890 | ③ | — | 1.5650–1.5689 | 1.5650–1.5689 | 0.0008–0.0021 | 0.0012–0.0102 |
| 1988 | 73 (1200) | — | — | — | — | — | 1.4520–1.4528 | 1.4520–1.4528 | — | 0.0012–0.0150 |
| | 109 (1800) | 1.4946–1.4953 | 1.9080–1.9087 | 1.8883–1.8890 | ③ | — | 1.5650–1.5689 | 1.5650–1.5689 | 0.0008–0.0021 | 0.0012–0.0102 |
| | 160 (2700) | 1.4946–1.4953 | 1.9080–1.9087 | 1.8883–1.8890 | 1.8687–1.8693 | ③ | 1.5606–1.5646 | 1.5606–1.5646 | 0.0008–0.0021 | 0.0012–0.0102 |
| 1989-90 | 73 (1200) | — | — | — | — | — | 1.4520–1.4528 | 1.4520–1.4528 | — | 0.0012–0.0150 |
| | 109 (1800) | 1.4946–1.4953 | 1.9080–1.9087 | 1.8883–1.8890 | ③ | — | 1.5650–1.5689 | 1.5650–1.5689 | 0.0028 | 0.0006–0.0050 |
| | 135 (2200) | ⑤ | ⑥ | ⑦ | — | — | 1.2752–1.2791 | 1.2752–1.2791 | 0.0022–0.0035 | 0.0012–0.0102 |
| | 160 (2700) | 1.4946–1.4953 | 1.9080–1.9087 | 1.8883–1.8890 | 1.8687–1.8693 | ③ | 1.5606–1.5646 | 1.5606–1.5646 | 0.0028 | 0.0012–0.0102 |

① If equipped with Hydraulic lifters – 0.1934–0.1973 in.
② Cam Lobe Height
Carburetor (standard) – 1.5394–1.5433 in.
Carburetor (undersize) – 1.5606–1.5646 in.
MPFI (non-turbo) – 1.5650–1.5689 in.
MPFI (turbo) – 1.5606–1.5646 in.
③ Camshaft distributor LH journal: 1.5340–1.5346 in.
④ Cam Lobe Height
SPFI 1.5650–1.5689 in.
⑤ RH front and LH rear – 1.2573–1.2579 in.
⑥ RH and LH center – 1.4738–1.4744 in.
⑦ RH rear and LH front – 1.4935–1.4941 in.

## CRANKSHAFT AND CONNECTING ROD SPECIFICATIONS

All measurements are given in inches.

| Year | Engine Displacement cu. in. (cc) | Crankshaft Main Brg. Journal Dia. | Crankshaft Main Brg. Oil Clearance | Crankshaft Shaft End-play | Crankshaft Thrust on No. | Connecting Rod Journal Diameter | Connecting Rod Oil Clearance | Connecting Rod Side Clearance |
|---|---|---|---|---|---|---|---|---|
| 1983 | 97 (1600) | 1.9968–1.9673 ① | 0.0004–0.0016 ② | 0.0004–0.0037 | 2 | 1.7715–1.7720 | 0.0008–0.0028 | 0.0028–0.0130 |
| | 109 (1800) | 2.1636–2.1642 | 0.0004–0.0012 ② | 0.0004 0.0037 | 2 | 1.7715 1.7720 | 0.0008–0.0028 | 0.0028–0.0130 |
| 1984 | 97 (1600) | 1.9668–1.9673 ① | 0.0004–0.0014 ⑤ | 0.0004–0.0037 | 2 | 1.7715–1.7720 | 0.0008–0.0028 | 0.0028–0.0130 |
| | 109 (1800) | 2.1636–2.1642 | 0.0004–0.0012 ② | 0.0004–0.0037 | 2 | 1.7715–1.7720 | 0.0008–0.0028 | 0.0028–0.0130 |
| 1985 | 97 (1600) | 1.9668–1.9673 ① | 0.0004–0.0014 ⑤ | 0.0004–0.0037 | 2 | 1.7715–1.7720 | 0.0008–0.0028 | 0.0028–0.0130 |
| | 109 (1800) | ③ | ④ | 0.0004–0.0037 | 2 | 1.7715–1.7720 | 0.0004–0.0021 | 0.0028–0.0130 |

## CRANKSHAFT AND CONNECTING ROD SPECIFICATIONS

All measurements are given in inches.

| Year | Engine Displacement cu. in. (cc) | Crankshaft Main Brg. Journal Dia. | Crankshaft Main Brg. Oil Clearance | Crankshaft Shaft End-play | Crankshaft Thrust on No. | Connecting Rod Journal Diameter | Connecting Rod Oil Clearance | Connecting Rod Side Clearance |
|---|---|---|---|---|---|---|---|---|
| 1986 | 97 (1600) | 1.9668–1.9673 ① | 0.0004–0.0014 ⑤ | 0.0004–0.0037 | 2 | 1.7715–1.7720 | 0.0004–0.0028 | 0.0028–0.0130 |
| | 109 (1800) | ③ | ④ | 0.0004–0.0037 | 2 | 1.7715–1.7720 | 0.0004–0.0021 | 0.0028–0.0130 |
| 1987 | 73 (1200) | 1.6525–1.6529 | 0.0006–0.0018 | 0.0031–0.0070 | 4 | 1.6531–1.6535 | 0.0008–0.0021 | 0.0028–0.0118 |
| | 109 (1800) | ③ | ④ | 0.0004–0.0037 | 2 | 1.7715–1.7720 | 0.0004–0.0021 | 0.0028–0.0130 |
| 1988 | 73 (1200) | 1.6525–1.6529 | 0.0006–0.0018 | 0.0031–0.0070 | 4 | 1.6531–1.6535 | 0.0008–0.0021 | 0.0028–0.0118 |
| | 109 (1800) | ③ | ④ | 0.0004–0.0037 | 2 | 1.7715–1.7720 | 0.0004–0.0021 | 0.0028–0.0130 |
| | 160 (2700) | ⑤ | ⑥ | 0.0004–0.0037 | 2 | 1.7715–1.7720 | 0.0004–0.0028 | 0.0028–0.0130 |
| 1989-90 | 73 (1200) | 1.6525–1.6529 | 0.0006–0.0018 | 0.0031–0.0070 | 4 | 1.6531–1.6535 | 0.0008–0.0021 | 0.0028–0.0118 |
| | 109 (1800) | ③ | ④ | 0.0004–0.0037 | 2 | 1.7715–1.7720 | 0.0004–0.0021 | 0.0028–0.0130 |
| | 135 (2200) | 2.3616–2.3622 | 0.0004–0.0012 | 0.0012–0.0045 | 3 | 2.0466–2.0477 | 0.0005–0.0015 | 0.0028–0.0130 |
| | 160 (2700) | ⑤ | ⑥ | 0.0004–0.0037 | 2 | 1.7715–1.7720 | 0.0004–0.0028 | 0.0028–0.0130 |

OHV Overhead Valve
OHC Overhead Cam
① Center – 1.9673–1.9633
② Center – 0.0004–0.0010
③ Front – 2.1637–2.1642
Center – 2.1635–2.1642
Rear – 2.1636–2.1642
④ Front and Rear – 0.0001–0.0014
Center – 0.0003–0.0011
⑤ Center – 0.0004–0.0012
⑤ Front – 2.1637–2.1642
Center Both – 2.1635–2.1642
Rear – 2.1636–2.1642
⑥ Front and Rear – 0.0001–0.0014
Center Both – 0.0004–0.0012

## VALVE SPECIFICATIONS

| Year | Engine Displacement cu. in. (cc) | Seat Angle (deg.) | Face Angle (deg.) | Spring Test Pressure (lbs.)③ | Spring Installed Height (in.)③ | Stem-to-Guide Clearance (in.) Intake | Stem-to-Guide Clearance (in.) Exhaust | Stem Diameter (in.) Intake | Stem Diameter (in.) Exhaust |
|---|---|---|---|---|---|---|---|---|---|
| 1983 | 97 (1600)① | 45 | 45–45.5 | 41.7–48.3 @ 1.122④ | 1.48⑩ | 0.0014–0.0026 | 0.0016–0.0028 | 0.3130–0.3136 | 0.3128–0.3134 |
| | 109 (1800)① | 45 | 45–45.5 | 41.7–48.3 @ 1.122④ | 1.48⑩ | 0.0014–0.0026 | 0.0016–0.0028 | 0.3130–0.3136 | 0.3128–0.3134 |
| | 109 (1800)② | 45 | 45–45.5 | 45.2–51.8 @ 1.181④ | 1.48⑩ | 0.0014–0.0026 | 0.0016–0.0028 | 0.3130–0.3136 | 0.3128–0.3134 |

## VALVE SPECIFICATIONS

| Year | Engine Displacement cu. in. (cc) | Seat Angle (deg.) | Face Angle (deg.) | Spring Test Pressure (lbs.)③ | Spring Installed Height (in.)③ | Stem-to-Guide Clearance (in.) | | Stem Diameter (in.) | |
|---|---|---|---|---|---|---|---|---|---|
| | | | | | | Intake | Exhaust | Intake | Exhaust |
| 1984 | 97 (1600)① | 45 | 45–45.5 | 41.7–48.3 @ 1.122④ | 1.48⑩ | 0.0014–0.0026 | 0.0016–0.0028 | 0.3130–0.3136 | 0.3128–0.3134 |
| | 109 (1800)① | 45 | 45–45.5 | 41.7–48.3 @ 1.122④ | 1.48⑩ | 0.0014–0.0026 | 0.0016–0.0028 | 0.3130–0.3136 | 0.3128–0.3134 |
| | 109 (1800)② | 45 | 45–45.5 | 45.2–51.8 @ 1.181④ | 1.48⑩ | 0.0014–0.0026 | 0.0016–0.0028 | 0.3130–0.3136 | 0.3128–0.3134 |
| 1985 | 97 (1600) | 45 | 45–45.5 | 41.7–48.3 @ 1.122④ | 1.48⑩ | 0.0014–0.0026 | 0.0016–0.0028 | 0.3130–0.3136 | 0.3128–0.3134 |
| | 109 (1800) | 45 | 45 | 45.2–51.8 @ 1.121④ | 1.12⑪ | 0.0014–0.0026 | 0.0016–0.0028 | 0.2736–0.2742 | 0.2734–0.2740 |
| 1986 | 97 (1600) | 45 | 45–45.5 | 41.7–48.3 @ 1.122④ | 1.48⑩ | 0.0014–0.0026 | 0.0016–0.0028 | 0.3130–0.3136 | 0.3128–0.3134 |
| | 109 (1800) | 45 | 45 | 45.2–51.8 @ 1.121④ | 1.12⑪ | 0.0014–0.0026 | 0.0016–0.0028 | 0.2736–0.2742 | 0.2734–0.2740 |
| 1987 | 73 (1200) | 45 | 45 | ⑧ | 125 | 0.0008–0.0020 | 0.0016–0.0028 | 0.2742–0.2748 | 0.2734–0.2740 |
| | 109 (1800) | 45 | 45 | 45.2–51.8 @ 1.121④ | 1.12⑪ | 0.0014–0.0026 | 0.0016–0.0028 | 0.2736–0.2742 | 0.2734–0.2740 |
| 1988 | 73 (1200) | 45 | 45 | ⑧ | 1.25 | 0.0008–0.0020 | 0.0016–0.0028 | 0.2742–0.2748 | 0.2734–0.2740 |
| | 109 (1800) | 45 | 45 | 45.6–53.6 @113–130⑫ | 1.98⑬ | 0.0014–0.0026 | 0.0016–0.0028 | 0.2736–0.2742 | 0.2734–0.2740 |
| | 160 (2700) | 45 | 45 | 39.9–45.9 @113–130⑮ | ⑭ | 0.0014–0.0026 | 0.0016–0.0028 | 0.2736–0.2742 | 0.2734–0.2740 |
| 1989-90 | 73 (1200) | 45 | 45 | ⑧ | 1.25 | 0.0008–0.0020 | 0.0016–0.0028 | 0.2742–0.2748 | 0.2734–0.2740 |
| | 109 (1800) | 45 | 45 | 45.6–53.6 @113–130⑫ | 1.98⑬ | 0.0014–0.0026 | 0.0016–0.0028 | 0.2736–0.2742 | 0.2734–0.2740 |
| | 135 (2200) | 45 | 45 | ⑯ | — | 0.0014–0.0024 | 0.0016–0.0026 | 0.2343–0.2348 | 0.2341–0.2346 |
| | 160 (2700) | 45 | 45 | 39.9–45.9 @113–130⑮ | ⑭ | 0.0014–0.0026 | 0.0016–0.0028 | 0.2736–0.2742 | 0.2734–0.2740 |

OHV Overhead Valve
OHC Overhead Cam
① With manual trans.
② With auto. trans.
③ All values are for inner spring
④ Outer spring—112–127 @ 1.201
⑤ Outer spring—116.6–134.7 @ 1.260
⑥ Outer spring—100.5–115.5 @ 1.240
⑦ Outer spring—112.9–129.7 @ 1.240
⑧ Spring— 112.8–129.8 @ 1.248
⑨ Outer spring—1.20
⑩ Outer spring—1.56
⑪ Outer spring—1.24
⑫ Inner spring—19.8–22.7 @ 45.2–51.8
⑬ Outer spring—.087
⑭ Outer spring—.091
⑮ Inner spring—19.8–22.7 @ 45.2–51.8
⑯ 1.457 in. @ 34.0–39.0 lbs.
1.154 in. @ 92.2–106.1 lbs.

## PISTON AND RING SPECIFICATIONS

All measurments are given in inches.

| Year | Engine Displacement cu. in. (cc) | Piston Clearance | Ring Gap Top Compression | Ring Gap Bottom Compression | Ring Gap Oil Control | Ring Side Clearance Top Compression | Ring Side Clearance Bottom Compression | Ring Side Clearance Oil Control |
|---|---|---|---|---|---|---|---|---|
| 1983 | 97 (1600) | 0.0004–0.0016 | 0.0079–0.0138 | 0.0079–0.0138 | 0.0079–0.0354 ① | 0.0016–0.0031 | 0.0012–0.0028 | Snug |
| | 109 (1800) | 0.0004–0.0016 | 0.0079–0.0138 | 0.0079–0.0138 | 0.0079–0.0354 ① | 0.0016–0.0031 | 0.0012–0.0028 | Snug |
| 1984 | 97 (1600) | 0.0004–0.0016 | 0.0079–0.0138 | 0.0079–0.0138 | 0.0079–0.0354 ① | 0.0016–0.0031 | 0.0012–0.0028 | Snug |
| | 109 (1800) | 0.0004–0.0016 | 0.0079–0.0138 | 0.0079–0.0138 | 0.0079–0.0354 ① | 0.0016–0.0031 | 0.0012–0.0028 | Snug |
| 1985 | 97 (1600) | 0.0004–0.0016 | 0.0079–0.0138 | 0.0079–0.0138 | 0.0079–0.0354 ① | 0.0016–0.0031 | 0.0012–0.0028 | Snug |
| | 109 (1800) | 0.0004–0.0016 | 0.0079–0.0138 | 0.0079–0.0138 | 0.0120–0.0350 ① | 0.0016–0.0031 | 0.0012–0.0028 | Snug |
| 1986 | 97 (1600) | 0.0004–0.0016 | 0.0079–0.0138 | 0.0079–0.0138 | 0.0790–0.0354 ① | 0.0016–0.0031 | 0.0012–0.0028 | Snug |
| | 109 (1800) | 0.0004–0.0016 | 0.0079–0.0138 | 0.0079–0.0138 | 0.0120–0.0350 ① | 0.0016–0.0031 | 0.0012–0.0028 | Snug |
| 1987 | 73 (1200) | 0.0015–0.0024 | 0.0079–0.0138 | 0.0079–0.0138 | 0.0120–0.0350 ① | 0.0014–0.0030 | 0.0010–0.0026 | Snug |
| | 109 (1800) | 0.0004–0.0016 | 0.0079–0.0138 | 0.0079–0.0138 | 0.0120–0.0350 ① | 0.0016–0.0031 | 0.0012–0.0028 | Snug |
| 1988 | 73 (1200) | 0.0015–0.0024 | 0.0079–0.0138 | 0.0079–0.0138 | 0.0120–0.0350 ① | 0.0014–0.0030 | 0.0010–0.0026 | Snug |
| | 109 (1800) | 0.0004–0.0016 | 0.0079–0.0138 | 0.0079–0.0138 | 0.0120–0.0350 ① | 0.0016–0.0031 | 0.0012–0.0028 | Snug |
| | 160 (2700) | 0.0004–0.0016 | 0.0079–0.0138 | 0.0079–0.0138 | 0.0120–0.0350 ① | 0.0016–0.0031 | 0.0012–0.0028 | Snug |
| 1989-90 | 73 (1200) | 0.0015–0.0014 | 0.0079–0.0138 | 0.0079–0.0138 | 0.0120–0.0350 ① | 0.0014–0.0030 | 0.0010–0.0026 | Snug |

## PISTON AND RING SPECIFICATIONS

All measurments are given in inches.

| Year | Engine Displacement cu. in. (cc) | Piston Clearance | Ring Gap Top Compression | Ring Gap Bottom Compression | Ring Gap Oil Control | Ring Side Clearance Top Compression | Ring Side Clearance Bottom Compression | Ring Side Clearance Oil Control |
|---|---|---|---|---|---|---|---|---|
| 1989-90 | 109 (1800) | 0.0004–0.0016 | 0.0079–0.0138 | 0.0079–0.0138 | 0.0120–0.0350 ① | 0.0016–0.0031 | 0.0012–0.0028 | Snug |
| | 132 (2200) | 0.0004–0.0016 | 0.0079–0.0138 | 0.0079–0.0138 | 0.0076–0.0276 ① | 0.0016–0.0031 | 0.0012–0.0028 | Snug |
| | 160 (2700) | 0.0004–0.0016 | 0.0079–0.0138 | 0.0079–0.0138 | 0.0120–0.0350 ① | 0.0016–0.0031 | 0.0012–0.0028 | Snug |

OHV Overhead Valve
OHC Overhead Cam
① For rails only

## TORQUE SPECIFICATIONS

All readings in ft. lbs.

| Year | Engine Displacement cu. in. (cc) | Cylinder Head Bolts | Main Bearing Bolts | Rod Bearing Bolts | Crankshaft Pulley Bolts | Flywheel Bolts | Manifold Intake | Manifold Exhaust | Spark Plugs |
|---|---|---|---|---|---|---|---|---|---|
| 1983 | 97 (1600) | 37–43① | 29–31 | ④ | 47–54 | 30–33③ | 13–16 | 19–22 | 14–22 |
| | 109 (1800) | 47② | 29–31 | ④ | 47–54 | 30–33③ | 13–16 | 19–22 | 14–22 |
| 1984 | 97 (1600) | 37–43① | 29–31 | ④ | 47–54 | 30–33③ | 13–16 | 19–22 | 14–22 |
| | 109 (1800) | 47② | 29–31 | ④ | 47–54 | 30–33③ | 13–16 | 19–22 | 14–22 |
| 1985 | 97 (1600) | 37–43① | 29–31 | ④ | 47–54 | 30–33③ | 13–16 | 19–22 | 14–22 |
| | 109 (1800) | 44–50 | 29–31 | ⑤ | 66–79 | 51–55 | 13–16 | 19–22 | 14–22 |
| 1986 | 97 (1600) | 37–43① | 29–31 | ④ | 47–54 | 30–33③ | 13–16 | 19–22 | 14–22 |
| | 109 (1800) | 44–50 | 29–31 | ⑤ | 66–79 | 51–55 | 13–16 | 19–22 | 14–22 |
| 1987 | 73 (1200) | 51–56⑥ | 30–35 | 29–33 | 47–54 | 65–71 | 14–22 | 14–22 | 13–15 |
| | 109 (1800) | 44–50 | 30–35 | 29–31 | 66–79 | 51–55 | 13–16 | 19–22 | 13–15 |
| 1988 | 73 (1200) | 51–57⑥ | 30–35⑥ | 29–33 | 47–54 | 65–71 | 14–22 | 14–22 | 13–17 |
| | 109 (1800) | 44–50 | 30–35 | 29–31 | 66–79 | 51–55 | 13–16 | 19–22 | 13–17 |
| | 160 (2700) | 44–50 | 30–35 | 29–31 | 66–79 | 51–55 | 13–16 | 19–22 | 13–17 |
| 1989-90 | 73 (1200) | 51–57⑥ | 30–35 | 29–33 | 58–72 | 65–71⑧ | 14–22 | 14–22 | 13–17 |
| | 109 (1800) | 47② | 29–35 | 29–31 | 66–79 | 51–55 | 13–16 | 19–22 | 13–17 |
| | 132 (2200) | ⑨ | ⑩ | 32–34 | 66–79 | 58–62 | NA | NA | 14–22 |
| | 160 (2700) | 47② | 29–35 | 29–31 | 66–79 | 51–55 | 13–16 | 19–22 | 13–17 |

NA Not available
OHV Overhead Valve
OHC Overhead Cam
① 1st step—22 ft. lbs.
② 1st step—22 ft. lbs.
2nd step—43 ft. lbs.
3rd step—47 ft. lbs.
③ Driveplate (A/T)—36–39 ft. lbs.
④ 10mm bolts—29–35 ft. lbs.
8mm bolts—17–19 ft. lbs.
6mm bolts—3–4 ft. lbs.
⑤ 10mm bolts—29-35 ft. lbs.
8mm bolts—17–20 ft. lbs.
⑥ 1st step—29 ft. lbs.
2nd step—54 ft. lbs.
3rd step—back off 90 degrees or more in reverse of tightening sequence
4th step—54 ft. lbs.
⑦ With oil on treads
⑧ ECVT—54–61 ft. lbs.
⑨ 1st step—51 ft. lbs.
2nd step—back off bolts by 180 degrees
3rd step—25 ft. lbs. (bolts 1 & 2)
4th step—14 ft. lbs. (bolts 3–6)
5th step—Tighten all bolts 80–90 degrees in sequence
6th step—Retighten all bolts 80–90 degrees in sequence; not to exceed 180 degrees in 5th or 6th step
⑩ See text

## BRAKE SPECIFICATIONS

All measurements in inches unless noted

| Year | Model | Lug Nut Torque (ft. lbs.) | Master Cylinder Bore | Brake Disc Minimum Thickness | Brake Disc Maximum Runout | Standard Brake Drum Diameter | Minimum Lining Thickness Front | Minimum Lining Thickness Rear |
|---|---|---|---|---|---|---|---|---|
| 1983 | STD | 58–72 | 0.8125 | 0.394 | 0.0039 | 7.09 | 0.295① | 0.259 |
| 1984 | STD | 58–72 | 0.8125 | 0.394 | 0.0039 | 7.09 | 0.295① | 0.259 |
| 1985 | STD | 58–72 | 0.8125 | 0.610 | 0.0039 | 7.09 | 0.295① | 0.259② |
| | XT Coupe | 58–72 | 0.8125 | 0.630③ | 0.0039 | 7.09 | 0.295① | 0.259② |
| 1986 | STD | 58–72 | 0.8125 | 0.630③ | 0.0039 | 7.09 | 0.295① | 0.259② |
| | XT Coupe | 58–72 | 0.8125 | 0.630③ | 0.0039 | 7.09 | 0.295① | 0.259② |
| 1987 | Justy | 58–72 | ⑤ | ⑧ | 0.0060 | 7.09⑩ | 0.295① | 0.067⑦ |
| | STD | 58–72 | 0.8125 | 0.630③ | 0.0040 | 7.09⑩ | 0.295① | 0.259② |
| | XT Coupe | 58–72 | 0.8125 | 0.630③ | 0.0040 | 7.09⑩ | 0.295① | 0.259② |
| 1988 | Justy | 58–72 | ⑤ | ⑧ | 0.0060 | 7.09⑩ | 0.295① | 0.067⑦ |
| | STD | 58–72 | 0.8125 | 0.630 | 0.0040 | 7.09⑩ | 0.295① | 0.259B |
| | XT Coupe | 58–72 | 0.8125 | 0.787③ | 0.0040 | 7.09⑩ | 0.295① | 0.259④ |
| 1989-90 | Justy | 58–72 | ⑤ | 0.610⑧ | 0.0060 | 7.09⑩ | 0.295① | 0.067⑦ |
| | STD | 58–72 | ⑨ | 0.630③ | 0.0040 | 7.09⑩ | 0.295 | 0.059② |
| | XT Coupe | 58–72 | ⑨ | 0.630⑪ | 0.0040 | 7.09⑩ | 0.295 | 0.059②④ |
| | Legacy | 58–72 | ⑬ | 0.870⑫ | 0.0039⑭ | 0.390⑮ | 0.295 | 0.256 |

① Justy GL—0.315 in (includes metal backing

② Rear disc brake including metal backing

③ Rear disc brake—0.335 in. service limit
0.390 in standard

④ XT Coupe with 2700cc engine. Rear disc brake including metal backing—0.315

⑤ Small diameter—⅞ in.
Large diameter—1 in.

⑥ Standard—7.09 in. rear drum

⑦ Standard—0.173 in.

⑧ Standard—0.709 in.

⑨ Small diameter—$^{13}/_{16}$ in.
Large diameter—1 in.

⑩ Service limit—7.17 in.

⑪ XT-6—0.787 in.

⑫ Standard thickness—0.940

⑬ L, LS models—1 in.
LX modles—1$^{1}_{16}$ in.

## WHEEL ALIGNMENT

| Year | Model | Caster Range (deg.) | Caster Preferred Setting (deg.) | Camber Range (deg.) | Camber Preferred Setting (deg.) | Toe-in (in.) | Steering Axis Inclination (deg.) |
|---|---|---|---|---|---|---|---|
| 1983 | 2WD except SW | 1¼N-¼P | ½N | $1\frac{7}{16}$P-$2\frac{15}{16}$P | $2\frac{3}{16}$P | ¼-$\frac{5}{32}$ | NA |
| | 2WD SW | $\frac{13}{16}$N-$\frac{11}{16}$P | $\frac{1}{16}$N | 1P-2½P | 1¾P | 0-$\frac{5}{64}$ | NA |
| | 4WD except SW | 1¼N-¼P | ½N | $1\frac{11}{16}$P-$3\frac{3}{16}$P | $2\frac{7}{16}$P | $\frac{15}{64}$-$\frac{5}{32}$① | NA |
| | 4WD SW | $1\frac{7}{16}$N-$\frac{1}{16}$P | $\frac{11}{16}$N | $1\frac{11}{16}$P-$3\frac{3}{16}$P | $2\frac{7}{16}$P | $\frac{15}{64}$-$\frac{5}{32}$ | NA |
| 1984 | 2WD except SW | 1¼N-¼P | ½N | $1\frac{7}{16}$P-$2\frac{15}{16}$P | $2\frac{3}{16}$P | ¼-$\frac{5}{32}$ | NA |
| | 2WD SW | $\frac{13}{16}$N-$\frac{11}{16}$P | $\frac{1}{16}$N | 1P-2½P | 1¾P | 0-$\frac{5}{64}$ | NA |
| | 4WD except SW | 1¼N-¼P | ½N | $1\frac{11}{16}$P-$3\frac{3}{16}$P | $2\frac{7}{16}$P | $\frac{15}{64}$-$\frac{5}{32}$① | NA |
| | 4WD SW | $1\frac{7}{16}$N-$\frac{1}{16}$P | $\frac{11}{16}$N | $1\frac{11}{16}$P-$3\frac{3}{16}$P | $2\frac{7}{16}$P | $\frac{15}{64}$-$\frac{5}{32}$① | NA |
| 1985 | 2WD XT Coupe | $3\frac{5}{16}$P-$4\frac{13}{16}$P | $4\frac{1}{16}$P | ¾N-¾P | 0 | ⅛-⅛ | NA |
| | 4WD XT Coupe | 2⅝P-4⅛P | 3⅜P | $\frac{1}{16}$N-1⅜P | ⅝P | $\frac{3}{64}$-⅛ | NA |
| | 2WD Sedan | 1¾P-3¼P | 2½P | 0-1½P | ¾P | $\frac{13}{64}$-$\frac{3}{64}$ | NA |

## WHEEL ALIGNMENT

| Year | Model | Caster Range (deg.) | Caster Preferred Setting (deg.) | Camber Range (deg.) | Camber Preferred Setting (deg.) | Toe-in (in.) | Steering Axis Inclination (deg.) |
|---|---|---|---|---|---|---|---|
| 1985 | 4WD Sedan with Air Sup. | 1 7/16P-2 15/16P | 2 3/16P | 7/16P-1 15/16P | 1 13/16P | 13/64-3/64A | NA |
| | 4WD Sedan without Air Sup. | 1 1/16P-2 9/16P | 1 13/16P | 15/16P-2 7/16P | 1 11/16P | 13/64-3/64① | NA |
| | 2WD SW | 1 5/16P-2 13/16P | 2 1/16P | 1/4P-1 3/4P | 1P | 13/64-3/64① | NA |
| | 4WD SW with Air Sup. | 1 7/16P-2 15/16P<br>1 7/16P-2 15/16P | 2 3/16P<br>2 3/16P | 7/16P-1 15/16P<br>7/16P-1 15/16P | 1 13/16P<br>1 13/16P | 13/64-3/64① | NA |
| | 4WD SW without Air Sup. | 13/16P-2 5/16P | 1 9/16P | 15/16P-2 7/16P | 1 3/4P | 13/64-3/64① | NA |
| | 2WD Hatchback | 1 1/4N-1/4P | 1/2N | 1 7/16P-2 15/16P | 2 3/16P | 1/4-5/32 | NA |
| 1986 | 2WD XT Coupe | 3 5/16P-4 13/16P | 4 1/16P | 3/4N-3/4P | 0 | 1/8-1/8 | NA |
| | 4WD XT Coupe | 2 5/8P-4 1/8P | 3 3/8P | 1/16N-1 3/8P | 5/8P | 3/64-1/8 | NA |
| | 2WD Sedan | 1 3/4P-3 1/4P | 2 1/2P | 0-1 1/2P | 3/4P | 13/64-3/64① | NA |
| | 4WD Sedan with Air Sup. | 1 7/16P-2 15/16P | 2 3/16P | 7/16P-1 15/16P | 1 13/16P | 13/64-3/64① | NA |
| | 4WD Sedan without Air Sup. | 1 1/16P-2 9/16P<br>1 1/16P-2 9/16P | 1 13/16P<br>1 13/16P | 15/16P-2 7/16P<br>15/16P-2 7/16P | 1 11/16P<br>1 11/16P | 13/64-3/64①<br>NA | |
| | 2WD SW | 1 5/16P-2 13/16P | 2 1/16P | 1/4P-1 3/4P | 1P | 13/64-3/64① | NA |
| | 4WD SW with Air Sup. | 1 7/16P-2 15/16P | 2 3/16P | 7/16P-1 15/16P | 1 13/16P | 13/64-3/64① | NA |
| | 4WD SW without Air Sup. | 13/16P-2 5/16P | 1 9/16P | 15/16P-2 7/16P | 1 3/4P | 13/64-3/64① | NA |
| | 2WD Hatchback | 1 1/4N-1/4P | 1/2N | 1 7/16P-2 15/16P | 2 3/16P | 1/4-5/32 | NA |
| 1987 | 2WD XT Coupe | 3 5/16P-4 13/16P | 4 1/16P | 3/4N-3/4P | 0 | 1/8-1/8 | NA |
| | 4WD XT Coupe | 2 5/8P-4 1/8P | 3 3/8P | 1/16N-1 3/8P | 5/8P | 3/64-1/8 | NA |
| | 2WD Sedan | 1 3/4P-3 1/4P | 2 1/2P | 0-1 1/2P | 3/4P | 13/64-3/64① | NA |
| | 4WD Sedan with Air Sup. | 1 7/16P-2 15/16P | 2 3/16P | 7/16P-1 15/16P | 1 13/16P | 5/64-5/16① | NA |
| | 4WD Sedan without Air Sup. | 1 1/16P-2 9/16P | 1 13/16P | 15/16P-2 7/16P | 1 11/16P | 5/64-5/16① | NA |
| | 2WD SW | 1 5/16P-2 13/16P | 2 1/16P | 1/4P-1 3/4P | 1⑯ | 13/64-3/64① | NA |
| | 4WD SW with Air Sup. | 1 7/16P-2 15/16P | 2 3/16P | 7/16P-1 15/16P | 1 13/16P | 5/64-5/15① | NA |
| | 4WD SW without Air Sup. | 13/16P-2 5/16P | 1 9/16P | 15/16P-2 7/16P | 1 3/4P | 5/64-5/16① | NA |
| | Justy | 1 1/2P-3 1/2P | 2 1/2P | 5/16N-1 11/16P | 11/16P | 3/32-1/2① | NA |
| 1988 | 2WD XT Coupe | 3 15/16P-4 13/16P | 4 1/16P | 3/4N-3/4P | 0 | 1/8-1/8 | NA |
| | 4WD XT Coupe (4 cylinder) | 2 5/8P-4 1/8P | 3 3/8P | 1/16N-1 3/8P | 5/8P | 3/64-1/8 | NA |
| | 4WD XT Coupe (6 cylinder) | 2 3/4P-4 1/4P | 3 1/2P | 1/16P-1 9/16P | 13/16P | 3/64-13/64 | NA |
| | 2WD Sedan | 1 3/4P-3 1/4P | 2 1/2P | 0-1 1/2P | 3/4P | 13/64-3/64① | NA |

## WHEEL ALIGNMENT

| Year | Model | Caster Range (deg.) | Caster Preferred Setting (deg.) | Camber Range (deg.) | Camber Preferred Setting (deg.) | Toe-in (in.) | Steering Axis Inclination (deg.) |
|---|---|---|---|---|---|---|---|
| 1988 | 4WD Sedan with Air Sup. | 1 7/16P–2 15/16P | 2 3/16P | 7/16P–1 15/16P | 1 13/16P | 5/64–5/16① | NA |
| | 4WD Sedan without Air Sup. | 1 1/16P–2 9/16P | 1 13/16P | 15/16P–2 7/16P | 1 11/16P | 5/64–5/16① | NA |
| | 2WD SW | 1 5/16P–2 13/16P | 2 1/16P | 1/4P–1 3/4P | 1P | 13/64–3/64 | NA |
| | 4WD SW with Air Sup. | 1 7/16P–2 15/16P | 2 3/16P | 7/16P–1 15/16P | 1 13/16P | 5/64–5/16① | NA |
| | 4WD SW | 13/16P–2 5/16P | 1 9/16P | 15/16P–2 7/16P | 1 3/4P | 5/64–5/16 | NA |
| | Justy | 1 1/2P–3 1/2P | 2 1/2P | 5/16N–1 11/16P | 11/16P | 3/32–1/2① | NA |
| 1989-90 | 2WD XT Coupe | 3 15/16P–4 13/16P | 4 1/16P | 3/4N–3/4P | 0 | 1/8–1/8 | NA |
| | 4WD XT Coupe (4 cylinder) | 2 5/8P–4 1/8P | 3 3/8P | 1/16N–1 3/8P | 5/8P | 3/64–1/8 | NA |
| | 4WD XT Coupe (6 cylinder) | 2 3/4P–4 1/4P | 3 1/2P | 1/16P–1 9/16P | 13/16P | 3/64–13/64 | NA |
| | 2WD Sedan | 1 3/4P–3 1/4P | 2 1/2P | 0–1 1/2P | 3/4P | 13/64–3/64① | NA |
| | 4WD Sedan with Air Sup. | 1 7/16P–2 15/16P | 2 3/16P | 7/16P–1 15/16P | 1 13/16P | 5/64–5/16① | NA |
| | 4WD Sedan without Air Sup. | 1 1/16P–2 9/16P | 1 13/16P | 15/16P–2 7/16P | 1 11/16P | 5/64–5/16① | NA |
| | 2WD SW | 1 5/16P–2 13/16P | 2 1/16P | 1/4P–1 3/4P | 1P | 13/64–3/64 | NA |
| | 4WD SW with Air Sup. | 1 7/16P–2 15/16P | 2 3/16P | 7/16P–1 15/16P | 1 13/16P | 5/64–5/16① | NA |
| | 4WD SW | 13/16P–2 5/16P | 1 9/16P | 15/16P–2 7/16P | 1 3/4P | 5/64–5/16 | NA |
| | Justy | 1 1/2P–3 1/2P | 2 1/2P | 5/16N–1 11/16P | 11/16P | 3/32–1/2① | NA |
| | Legacy FWD Sedan | – | 3 1/6P | – | 1/4P | 0 | NA |
| | Legacy FWD Wagon | – | 2 5/6P | – | 1/4P | 0 | NA |
| | Legacy 4WD Sedan | – | 3P | – | 0 | 0 | NA |
| | Legacy With Air Sup. | – | 3P | – | 0 | 0 | NA |

Air Sup. Air suspension
SW Station Wagon
P Positive
N Negative
① Toe out

# TUNE UP PROCEDURES

## Ignition Timing

### ADJUSTMENT

#### *Justy*

1. Connect test mode connectors (2 pin type, Green in color), located beneath the left side of the instrument panel.
2. Allow the engine to reach operating temperature. Adjust the idle speed to specification. Connect a timing light, according to manufacturers instructions.
3. Start the engine and check the ignition timing. If timing is not within specification, loosen the distributor holddown bolt.
4. Rotate the distributor until the correct timing specification is reached. Tighten the distributor holddown bolt.
5. Disconnect the test mode connector.

#### *XT Coupe*

**1983–86**

1. Allow the engine to reach operating temperature. Adjust the idle speed to specification. Connect a timing light, according to manufacturers instructions.
2. If equipped, disconnect and plug the vacuum advance hose at the distributor.
3. If equipped with a turbocharger, disconnect the black eight pole connec-

tor between the distributor and the knock control unit.

4. Start the engine and check the ignition timing. If timing is not within specification, loosen the distributor holddown bolt.

5. Rotate the distributor until the correct timing specification is reached. Tighten the distributor holddown bolt. Connect the distributor vacuum line, as required.

6. If equipped with a turbocharger, connect the eight pole black connector.

#### 1987–90

1. Allow the engine to reach operating temperature. Adjust the idle speed to specification. Connect a timing light, according to manufacturers instructions.

2. Be sure that the idle contact of the throttle sensor is in the engaged position. Connect the test mode connectors together, located in the trunk area for both the 1800cc and 2700cc engines, using the MPFI system. The connectors will be found a longside of each other.

**NOTE: The check engine warning light will come on. This does not indicate that there is a problem. The ignition timing must not be adjusted and cannot be checked while the idle switch is disengaged or the test mode connectors disconnected.**

3. If timing is not within specification, loosen the distributor holddown bolt.

4. Rotate the distributor until the correct timing specification is reached. Tighten the distributor holddown bolt.

### *Except Justy, XT Coupe and Legacy*

#### 1983–86

1. Allow the engine to reach operating temperature. Adjust the idle speed to specification. Connect a timing light, according to manufacturers instructions.

2. If equipped, disconnect and plug the vacuum advance hose at the distributor.

3. If equipped with a turbocharger, disconnect the black 8 pole connector between the distributor and the knock control unit.

4. Start the engine and check the ignition timing. If timing is not within specification, loosen the distributor holddown bolt.

5. Rotate the distributor until the correct timing specification is reached. Tighten the distributor holddown bolt. Connect the distributor vacuum line, as required.

6. If equipped with a turbocharger, connect the 8 pole black connector.

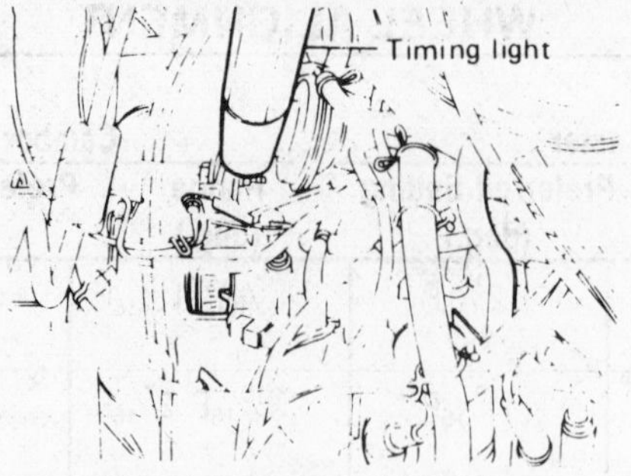


**Timing mark location except XT Coupe**

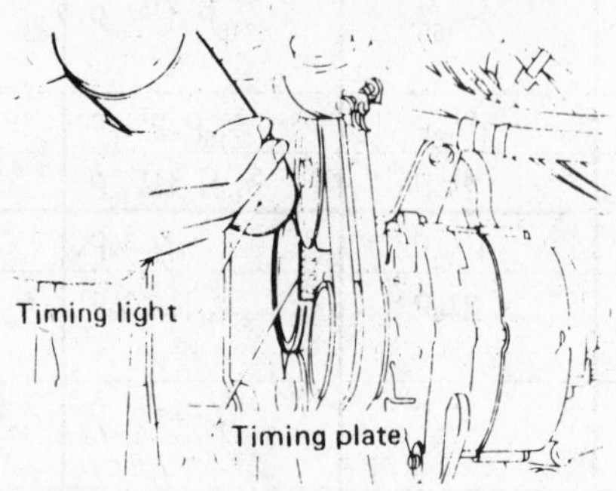


**Timing mark location 1800cc (OHC) engine except XT Coupe**

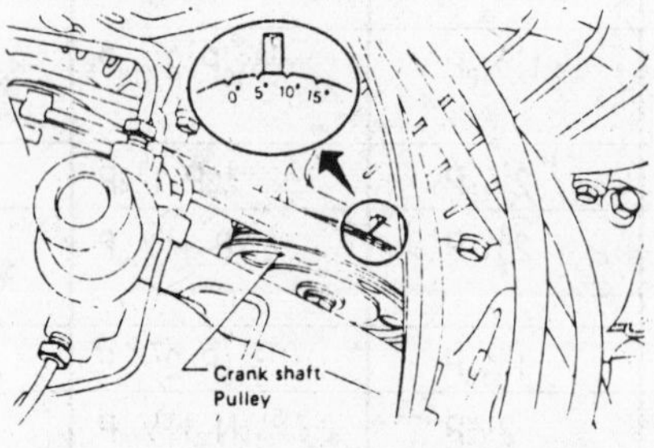


**Timing mark location 1200cc engine**

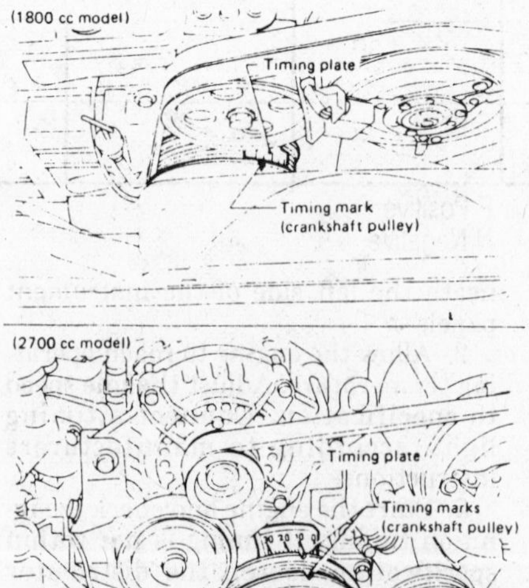


**Timing mark locations for XT coupe equipped 1800cc and 2700cc engines**

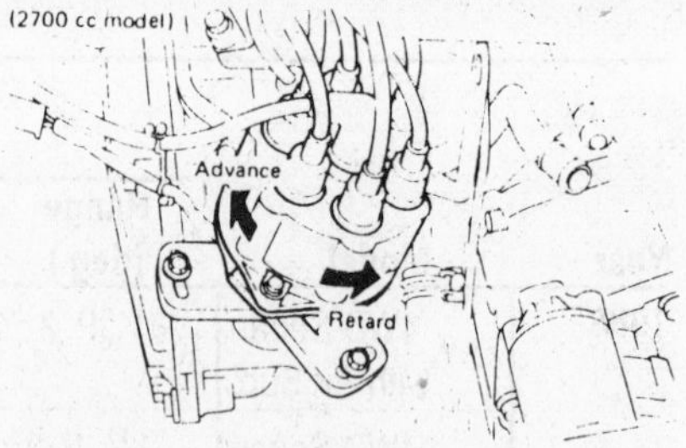


**Distributor movement to change basic timing – 2700cc engine**

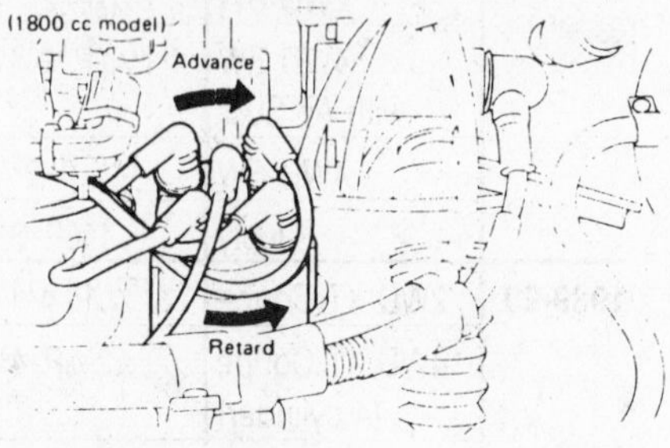


**Distributor movement to change basic timing – 1800cc engine**

#### 1987–90

1. Allow the engine to reach operating temperature. Adjust the idle speed to specification. Connect a timing light, according to manufacturers instructions.

2. If the engine is equipped with a carburetor, disconnect and plug the distributor vacuum line.

3. Be sure that the idle switch is in the engaged position. Connect the test mode connectors, located under the left side of the dash on vehicles using the MPFI system and on the left side of the engine compartment on vehicles using the SPFI system. The connectors will be located side by side.

**NOTE: The check engine warning light will come on. This does not indicate that there is a problem. The ignition timing must not be adjusted and cannot be checked while the idle switch is inoperative or the test mode connectors disconnected.**

4. If timing is not within specification, loosen the distributor holddown bolt.

5. Rotate the distributor until the correct timing specification is reached. Tighten the distributor holddown bolt.

**NOTE: There is no timing procedures available for the 1990 2200cc (2.2L), SOHC, 4 valve engine, since the ignition system is distributorless and is operated from crankshaft and camshaft sensors, using the "waste type" spark system**

## Valve Lash

### ADJUSTMENT

#### *Except 1200cc Engine*

**1983–84**

**NOTE: The 1985–90 1800cc, 2200cc and 2700cc engines use hydraulic lifters. No periodic adjustment is necessary.**

1. Disconnect the negative battery cable. Before adjusting the valves, make sure the cylinder head bolts are torqued to specification. To torque the head and intake manifold bolts, use the following procedure.
   a. Make sure the engine is cold.
   b. Remove the valve covers.
   c. On the right side of the engine, loosen the 3 intake manifold to cylinder head bolts no more than 60 degrees. Do not loosen the left side intake manifold to cylinder head bolts.
   d. Torque the bolts to specification. It is important to follow the proper tightening sequence when checking the head bolts. Warpage of the cylinder or water leaks could occur if the proper tightening pattern is not followed.
   e. Loosen the center cylinder head bolt no more than 60 degrees. If the bolts are loosened to 90 degrees, coolant leaks may occur.
   f. Lubricate the bolt with engine oil, torque and loosen the bolts 4–5 times. Retighten the bolt to the specified torque.
   g. Move on to the next bolt and perform the same Steps as before, proceed until all of the bolts have been tightened.
   h. Go back to No. 1 bolt and recheck the torque, tighten if necessary. Recheck the rest of the bolts following the specified order.
   i. After rechecking all the head bolts tighten the intake manifold bolts on the right side, cylinder head.
   j. Rotate the engine so that the No. 1 piston is at top dead center (TDC) of its compression stroke. To determine the TDC, remove the distributor cap and the plastic flywheel housing dust cover, if equipped. The No. 1 piston is at TDC when the distributor rotor is pointing to the No. 1 spark plug lead terminal and the **0** degree mark on the flywheel or the crankshaft pulley is opposite the pointer on the housing or front cover.
2. Using a feeler gauge between the valve stem and the rocker arm, check the clearance of both the intake and exhaust valves of the No. 1 cylinder.
3. If the clearance is not within specification, loosen the rocker arm locknut and turn the adjusting stud until the valve clearance is correct. The stud should just touch the gauge, don't clamp the gauge tightly between the stud and head of the valve.
4. Tighten the locknut and recheck the valve stem to rocker clearance.
5. The other valves are adjusted in the same way, position each piston to TDC of its compression stroke, then check and adjust the valves for that cylinder. The proper valve adjustment sequence is 1–3–2–4, which is the firing order.
6. To bring the No. 3 piston to TDC of its compression stroke, rotate the crankshaft 180 degrees and make sure that the distributor rotor is pointing to the No. 3 spark plug terminal. Rotate the crankshaft 180 degrees after each valve adjustment before going on to the next adjustment.
7. Using the valve clearance adjusting tool 498767000 or equivalent, and a feeler gauge, adjust the valve clearance of the cylinder which on TDC.
8. After adjusting the valve clearance, torque the rocker arm locknuts to 10–13 ft. lbs. Rotate the crankshaft several times, then recheck the valve clearance.
9. When the valve adjustment is complete, install the distributor cap, the valve covers and the dust cover, if equipped on the flywheel housing port.

#### *1200cc Engine*

**1987–90**

**NOTE: The valve clearance should be checked every 15 months or 15,000 miles, whichever occurs first.**

1. Disconnect the negative batter cable. With the engine cold, remove the valve cover. Before adjusting the valve clearance, check the cylinder head bolt torque.
2. Rotate the crankshaft to position the cylinder being adjusted on the TDC of it's compression stroke. Make sure that the 0 degree mark on the crankshaft pulley is aligned with the timing pointer at the front of the engine.
3. Loosen the rocker arm locknuts of the cylinder being adjusted.
4. Using the valve clearance adjusting tool 498767000 or equivalent, and a feeler gauge, adjust the valve clearance of the cylinder which on TDC.
5. After adjusting the valve clearance, torque the rocker arm locknuts to 12–17 ft. lbs. Rotate the crankshaft several times, then recheck the valve clearance.

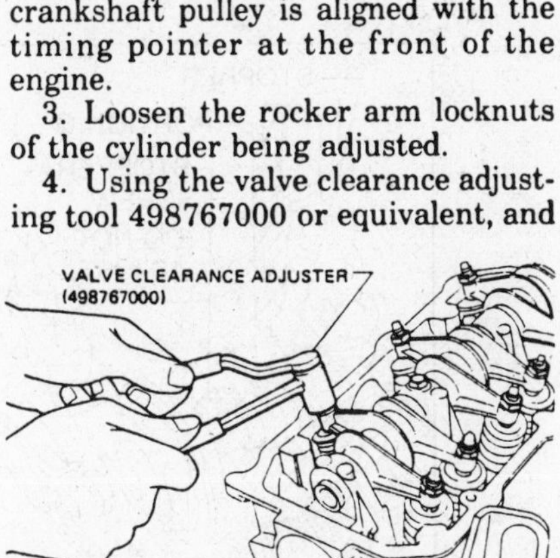


**Adjusting the valve clearance – 1200 (OHC) engine**

## Idle Speed

### ADJUSTMENT

#### *Justy*

1. Run the engine until normal operating temperature is reached.
2. Check and adjust the ignition timing, as required. Position the gear selector lever in the neutral detent.
3. Install a tachometer to the engine according to manufacturers instructions.
4. Be sure that all electrical accessories are turned off. Be sure that the idle up system is in the disengaged position.
5. If the vehicle is not equipped with air conditioning, adjust the idle speed with the idle up system off and using the throttle adjusting screw. Adjust the idle speed with the idle up system on using the idle up adjusting screw. Be sure that the headlights are on.
6. If equipped with air conditioning, adjust the idle speed with the idle up system off and the FICD for the air conditioning system off using the throttle adjusting screw. Adjust the idle speed using the air conditioning idle up adjusting screw with the air conditioning on. Adjust the idle speed with the idle up system on and the air conditioning on using the idle up adjusting screw. Be sure that the headlights are on.

#### *XT Coupe*

1. Run the engine until normal operating temperature is reached.
2. Check and adjust the ignition timing, as required. Position the gear selector lever in the neutral detent for manual transaxle and in park for automatic transaxle.
3. Install a tachometer to the engine according to manufacturer's instructions.
4. Be sure that the auxiliary air valve is completely closed.
5. Adjust the idle speed to specification by using the idle adjusting screw, which is located on the throttle body assembly.

#### *Except Justy and XT Coupe*

**CARBURETED ENGINE**

1. Operate the engine and allow it to reach normal operating temperature.

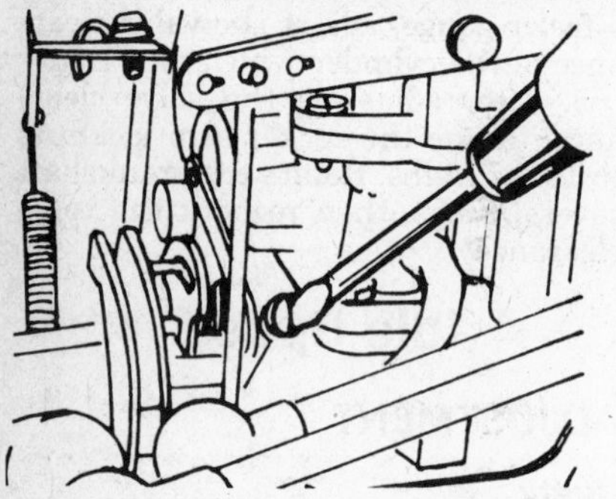

Idle speed adjustment

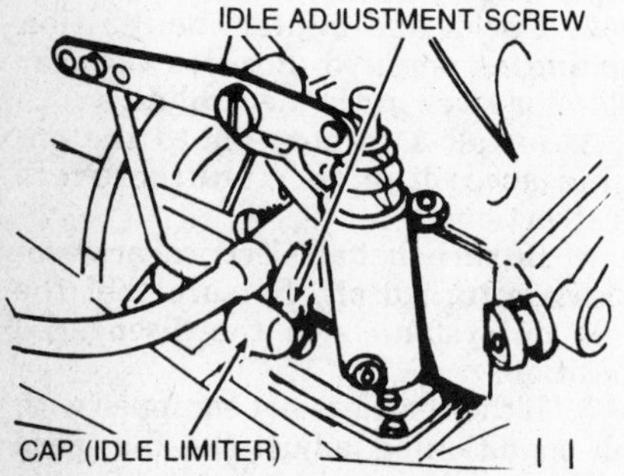


Idle mixture adjustment

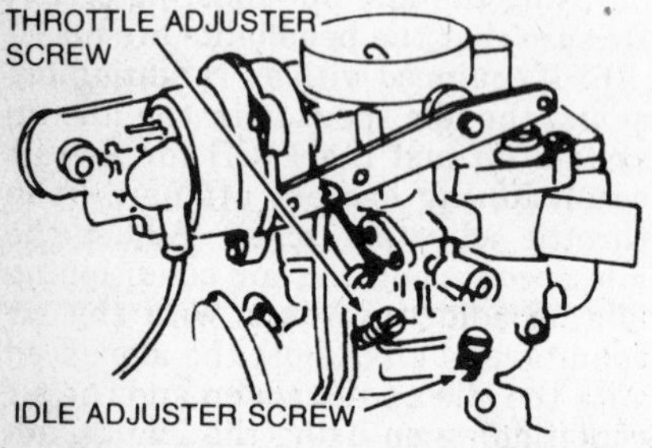


Throttle adjuster and idle adjuster screw locations

2. Stop the engine and connect a tachometer in accordance with the manufacturers instructions.

3. Perform the following as necessary.

a. If equipped with air injection system, disconnect the air hoses from the air distribution manifolds, plug the hoses and the manifold openings.

b. If equipped with a distributor vacuum retard unit, disconnect and plug the hose that runs to the distributor.

c. If equipped with a secondary air cleaner or purge valve hose, disconnect and plug the hose to the engine.

4. Remove the air cleaner assembly.

5. Check and adjust the idle speed to specification by turning the throttle adjusting screw.

#### FUEL INJECTED ENGINE

1. Run the engine until normal operating temperature is reached.

2. Check and adjust the ignition timing, as required. Position the gear selector lever in the neutral detent for manual transaxle and in park for automatic transaxle.

3. Install a tachometer to the engine according to manufacturer's instructions.

4. Be sure that the auxiliary air valve is completely closed.

5. Adjust the idle speed to specification by using the idle adjusting screw, which is located on the throttle body assembly.

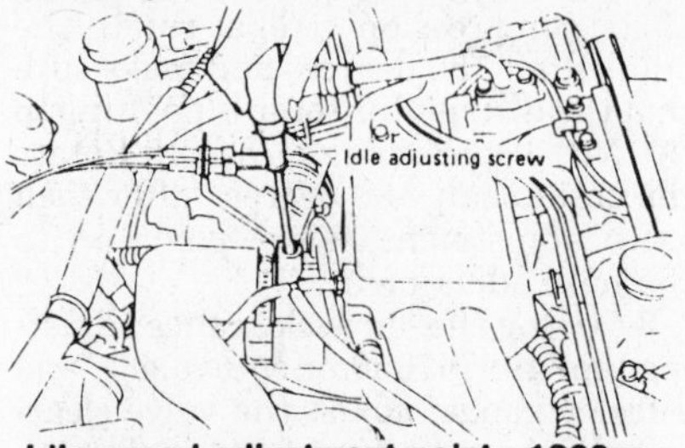


Idle speed adjustment point – 1800cc engine with FI

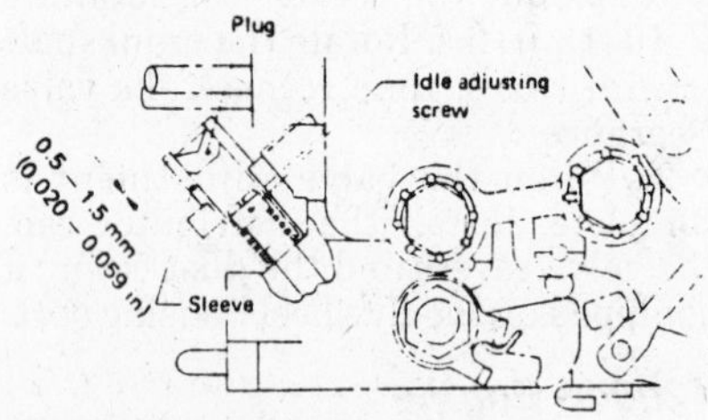


View of the idle mixture screw and plug – carburetor models

## Idle Mixture

### ADJUSTMENT

#### *Carbureted Engine*

1. Remove the carburetor from the engine and position it in a suitable holding fixture. Using a drill, make a hole through the idle mixture screw plug, then pry the plug from the carburetor.

2. Reinstall the carburetor on the engine. Start the engine and allow it to reach normal operating temperature.

3. Disconnect and plug the air suction valve to air cleaner hose.

4. Disconnect and plug the idle compensator to intake manifold hose, plug both openings.

5. Without the secondary air, inspect the idle speed and the CO%. Using the throttle adjusting screw and the idle mixture adjusting screw, adjust the idle speed to specification. Adjust the CO%, specification should be 1.0–2.0% (without secondary air) or 0–0.4% (with secondary air).

#### *Fuel Injected Engine*

Idle mixture adjustment cannot be accomplished on vehicles equipped with SPFI or MPFI fuel injection systems.

# ENGINE ELECTRICAL

**NOTE: The 1800cc and 2700cc engines with both the SPFI and MPFI systems use a LED and photodiode pulse pick-up in the distributor for cylinder and crankshaft location determination, for use in the electronic ignition system. The ignition circuits operates in the same basic manner as the standard electronic distributors used on the remaining engines.**

## Distributor

### REMOVAL & INSTALLATION

#### *Undisturbed Engine*

1. Disconnect the negative battery cable. Remove the air cleaner assem-

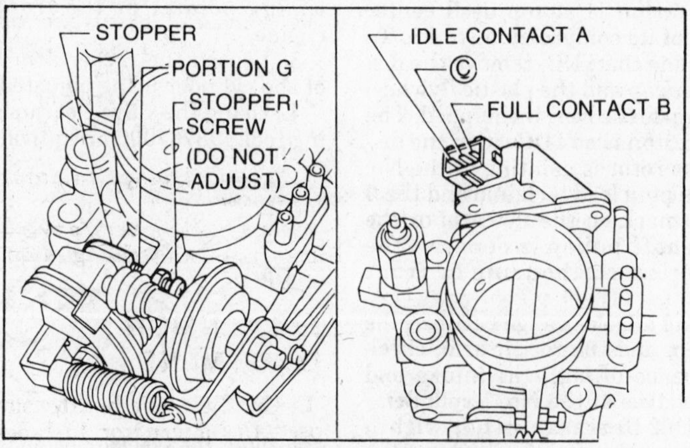


Fuel injection adjustment terminals

bly. If equipped, label and disconnect the hose from the distributor.

2. Disconnect the primary wire from the coil. On vehicles equipped with a breakerless ignition, disconnect the distributor electrical wiring connector from the vehicle wiring harness.

3. Disconnect the distributor cap retaining clamps or remove the screws and the cap from the distributor. Position the cap and ignition wires aside.

**NOTE: If necessary to remove the ignition wires from the cap to provide room to remove the distributor, be sure to label the wires and the cap terminals for easy and accurate reinstallation.**

4. Position the engine at TDC with No. 1 cylinder on the compression stroke or using chalk, mark the distributor rotor to distributor housing and the distributor housing to engine relationships.

5. Remove the distributor to engine holddown bolt.

6. Remove the distributor from the engine, taking care not to damage or lose the O-ring.

**NOTE: Do not disturb the engine while the distributor is removed. If the engine cranked or rotated while the distributor is removed, the engine will have to be retimed.**

7. If the engine was not disturbed while the distributor was removed, position the distributor in the block (make sure the O-ring is in place), align the distributor rotor to housing marks and the distributor housing to engine marks.

**NOTE: If equipped with an octane selector, install and tighten the holddown bolt finger tight.**

8. To complete the installation, reverse the removal procedures. Recheck the ignition timing.

### *Disturbed Engine*

If the engine has been cranked, disassembled or the timing otherwise lost, proceed as follows.

1. If equipped, remove the plastic dust cover from the timing port on the flywheel housing.

2. Remove the No. 1 spark plug. Use a wrench on the crankshaft pulley bolt and place the transmission in the **N** position and slowly rotate the engine until the TDC **0** degree mark on the flywheel aligns with the pointer.

3. If Step 2 is impractical for any reason, the following method can be used to get the No. 1 piston on TDC. Remove the 2 bolts that hold the right valve cover and remove the cover to expose the valves on No. 1 cylinder. Rotate the engine so that the valves in No. 1 cylinder are closed and the TDC **0** degree mark on the flywheel lines up with the pointer.

4. Align the small depression on the distributor drive pinion with the mark on the distributor housing; this will align the rotor with the No. 1 spark plug terminal on the distributor cap.

**NOTE: If equipped with an octane selector, set the pointer midway between the A and R. Make sure the O-ring is located in the proper position.**

5. Align the distributor housing to engine matchmarks and install the distributor into the engine. Make sure the drive is engaged. Install the holddown bolt fingertight. Using a timing light, perform the ignition timing procedures.

6. To complete the installation, remove the timing light and reverse the removal procedures.

# Alternator

## PRECAUTIONS

Observing these precautions will ensure safe handling of the electrical system components and will avoid damage to the vehicle's electrical system.

- Be absolutely sure of the polarity of a booster battery before making connections. Connect the cables positive to positive and negative to negative. If jump starting, connect the positive cables first and the last connection to a ground on the body of the booster vehicle, so that arcing cannot ignite the hydrogen gas that may have accumulated near the battery. Even a momentary connection of a booster battery with polarity reserved may damage the alternator diodes.
- Disconnect both vehicle battery cables before attempting to charge the battery.
- Never ground the alternator output or battery terminal. Be cautious when using metal tools around a battery to avoid creating a short circuit between the terminals.
- Never run an alternator without a load unless the field circuit is disconnected.
- Never attempt to polarize an alternator.
- Never disconnect any electrical components with the ignition switch turned On.

## BELT TENSION ADJUSTMENT

1. To adjust the belt tension, first loosen the alternator to bracket adjusting bolt.

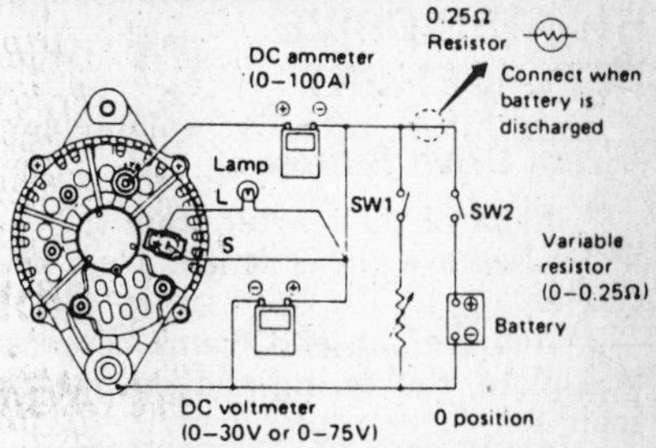

**Test procedure for alternator**

2. Lift up on the alternator to increase the tension on the belt. When it takes moderate thumb pressure to move the longest span of belt ½ in., the tension adjustment is correct.

3. Tighten the adjusting bolt so that the alternator will not move in the adjusting bracket.

## REMOVAL & INSTALLATION

1. Disconnect the negative battery cable.

2. Label and disconnect the wiring from the alternator. Remove the necessary components in order to gain access to the alternator retaining bolts.

3. Remove the alternator retaining bolts.

4. Remove the drive belt. Remove the alternator from the vehicle.

5. Installation is the reverse of the removal procedure.

# Voltage Regulator

**NOTE: The alternators have a solid state regulator as part of the assembly. This regulator is nonadjustable and is serviced, when necessary, by replacement.**

## REMOVAL & INSTALLATION

The alternator must be removed from the engine and disassembled to replace the voltage regulator.

# Starter

## REMOVAL & INSTALLATION

1. Remove the spare tire from the engine compartment, as required.

2. Disconnect the negative battery cable. As required, raise and support the vehicle safely.

3. Disconnect the wiring harness from the starter.

4. Remove the starter retaining bolts. Remove the starter from its mounting.

5. Installation is the reverse of the removal procedure.

## STARTER DRIVE REPLACEMENT

### Direct Drive Starter

1. Remove the starter from the vehicle. Remove the solenoid from the starter.
2. Remove the end frame cap, the lock plate, the spring and the rubber seal.
3. Remove the through bolts, then pull the end frame rearward and remove it. Remove the brushes from their holders by first pushing the holder spring aside.
4. Remove the brush holder plate and pull the yoke from the main housing, which surrounds the stator coils. Remove the plate and seal from the rear of the yoke.
5. Unscrew and remove the solenoid lever set bolt. Pull the armature, the overrunning clutch and the lever from the yoke.
6. Using a length of pipe the same diameter as the armature shaft, tap the pinion stop collar toward the starter drive to expose the snapring. Using a pair of snapring pliers, remove the snapring from the armature shaft, then slide off the pinion stop collar.
7. Remove the starter drive from the threaded spline. Be careful not to damage the spline.
8. To install the starter drive, slip the starter drive onto the armature shaft and drive the pinion stop collar past the snapring groove. Gently push the snapring over the end of the armature shaft. Work it down until it slips in to the snapring groove.
9. Supporting the stop collar, the armature must hang below unsupported, press the end of the armature shaft downward until the collar rests against the ring and the ring is in the groove of the collar.
10. To complete the reassembly, reverse the disassembly procedure.

### Reduction Gear Starter

1. Remove the starter from the vehicle. Disconnect the solenoid to starter body lead wire nut and separate the wire from the starter body. Never loosen the terminal bolt.
2. Remove the through bolts and the solenoid to housing screws.
3. If equipped with rear frame to starter screws, remove the screws and the rear frame.
4. Separate the housing and the solenoid.
5. Remove the starter drive unit. Take care not to lose the spring or the ball.
6. Remove the field brushes from the brush holder, then remove the holder. Be careful not to scratch the armature.
7. Remove the idler gear and starter drive from the solenoid. Be careful not to lose the rollers.
8. Inspect the component parts for wear. If the solenoid is faulty, replace it as a unit. Check the gears for chips or worn teeth. If the brushes are worn, replace the assembly.
9. Take care when soldering in the field brushes, do not get excessive solder or dirt on the field coils.
10. To ressemble the starter motor, reverse the disassembly procedures. Using high temperature grease, grease the ball, rollers and gears. If you have removed the armature, be sure to reinstall the felt washer.
11. Install the starter.

## STARTER SOLENOID REPLACEMENT

### Direct Drive Starter

1. Remove the starter from the vehicle. Remove the nut from underneath the solenoid terminal and disconnect the wires.
2. Remove the solenoid to starter screws.
3. Lift the solenoid and pull it rearward to separate it from the starter.
4. To install, reverse the removal procedures. Be sure to engage the hook on the end of the solenoid with the starter drive lever before installing the solenoid to starter screws.

### Reduction Gear Starter

1. Remove the starter from the vehicle. Disconnect the solenoid to starter body lead wire nut and separate the wire from the starter body. Never loosen the terminal bolt.
2. Remove the 2 through bolts and the solenoid to housing screws.
3. If equipped with rear frame to starter screws, remove the screws and the rear frame.
4. Separate the housing and the solenoid.
5. Installation is the reverse of the removal procedure.

# ENGINE MECHANICAL

## Engine

### REMOVAL & INSTALLATION

#### Legacy

**2200cc ENGINE**

**NOTE: There have been no firm 2200cc engine removal and installation or disassembly and assembly procedures authorized by the manufacturer at time of this publication. Where service information has been collected and verified, procedures are included.**

#### Justy

**NOTE: The engine and transaxle are removed as an assembly.**

1. Disconnect the negative battery cable. Matchmark and remove the hood.
2. Drain the cooling system. Drain the engine oil. Drain the transaxle fluid.
3. Remove the front bumper and grille assembly.
4. Disconnect the radiator hoses. Remove the radiator retaining bolts. Remove the radiator from the vehicle.
5. Remove the air cleaner assembly. Disconnect the accelerator linkage. Disconnect the clutch cable, if equipped with manual transaxle.
6. Disconnect the heater hoses from the heater unit. Disconnect the brake booster hose. Disconnect the speedometer cable from the transaxle.
7. If equipped with 4WD disconnect the hoses for the assembly. Disconnect any other required hoses and vacuum lines necessary to remove the engine.
8. Raise and support the vehicle safely. Disconnect the exhaust pipes from the their mounting. Disconnect the gearshift rod from the transaxle.
9. Matchmark and remove the driveshaft. Properly support the engine and transaxle assembly. Remove the center member and crossmember assembly.
10. Remove the engine mount retaining bolts. Lower the vehicle.
11. Using the proper lifting equipment, carefully remove the engine and transaxle assembly from the vehicle.
12. Installation is the reverse of the removal procedure.

#### XT Coupe

**1800cc ENGINE**

1. Properly relieve the fuel pump pressure. Disconnect the negative battery cable.
2. Matchmark and remove the hood. Drain the cooling system. Drain the engine oil. Properly discharge the air conditioning system, if equipped.
3. Remove the spare tire assembly. Remove the spare tire support. Remove the battery cable clamp assembly. Remove the air cleaner assembly.
4. Disconnect and plug the fuel line hoses. Disconnect the canister hoses and the brake booster hose.
5. If equipped with automatic transaxle, remove the diaphragm vacuum hose.
6. If equipped with a turbocharger, remove the vacuum switch hose at the heater vacuum tank. Remove the wastegate valve hoses.

7. If equipped with 4WD, remove the selective drive vacuum line and the differential lock vacuum hose.
8. Disconnect the electrical wiring harness connectors, the oxygen sensor electrical connector, the ignition coil wire and the distributor connector at the crank sensor.
9. Disconnect the alternator electrical connector, the air conditioning compressor connector, the pulse coil connector, the radiator fan motor connector and the thermoswitch connector.
10. Disconnect the accelerator cable. If equipped with manual transaxle, disconnect the hill holder cable connection on the clutch release fork.
11. If the vehicle is not equipped with a turbocharger, raise and support the vehicle safely. Remove the exhaust system. Lower the vehicle.
12. If equipped with a turbocharger, remove the accelerator cable cover and the the top turbocharge cover assembly.
13. To remove the lower turbocharger cover assembly, raise and support the vehicle safely, loosen the front exhaust pipe connection. Lower the vehicle and remove the lower turbocharger cover from the center exhaust pipe.
14. Disconnect the center exhaust pipe to turbocharger connection. Raise and support the vehicle safely. Disconnect the center exhaust pipe to rear exhaust pipe connection. Remove the hanger bolt and disconnect the center exhaust pipe at the transaxle. Remove the center exhaust pipe.
15. Lower the vehicle. Remove the radiator. Disconnect and plug the heater hoses.
16. Disconnect and plug the air conditioning hoses at the compressor, if equipped. Remove the power steering pump assembly, if equipped.
17. Remove the engine pitching stopper rod. Remove the timing cover plate. Remove the retaining bolts that hold the torque converter to the drive plate, if the vehicle is equipped with automatic transaxle.
18. Properly support the engine and the transaxle assemblies, using the proper equipment.
19. Remove the bolts which hold the engine mount to the front crossmember. Remove the bolts which hold the lower side of the engine to the transaxle.
20. Properly install the proper engine lifting equipment to the engine. Remove the bolts that retain the upper side of the engine to the transaxle.
21. Carefully remove the engine from the vehicle. If the vehicle is equipped with manual transaxle, move the engine horizontally until the mainshaft is withdrawn from the clutch cover.
22. Installation is the reverse of the removal procedure.

### 2700cc ENGINE

1. Properly relieve the fuel system pressure. Disconnect the negative battery cable. Matchmark and remove the hood.
2. Properly discharge the air conditioning system, if equipped. Drain the engine oil. Drain the cooling system.
3. Disconnect the canister hose and the hose bracket. Disconnect and plug the fuel lines.
4. Disconnect the power brake vacuum line booster. If equipped with manual transaxle and 4WD, disconnect the differential lock vacuum hose.
5. Disconnect the engine wiring harness connectors, the oxygen sensor connector, the bypass air valve control connector, the ignition coil and the distributor connector to the crank sensor.
6. Disconnect the alternator connector, the air condition compressor connector, the engine ground connector, the radiator fan motor connector and the thermoswitch electrical connector.
7. Disconnect the accelerator cable. Disconnect the cruise control cable, if equipped. Disconnect and plug the heater hoses.
8. Disconnect the hill holder cable on the clutch release fork side of the assembly, if the vehicle is equipped with manual transaxle.
9. Raise and support the vehicle safely. Disconnect the front exhaust pipe from the engine.
10. Disconnect the front to rear exhaust pipe connection. Disconnect the front exhaust pipe at the transaxle and hanger locations.
11. Lower the vehicle. Disconnect and plug the air conditioning compressor hoses.
12. Remove the radiator fan shroud assembly. If equipped with automatic transaxle, disconnect and plug the fluid lines. Remove the radiator.
13. Remove the timing hole plug. Remove the bolts that retain the torque converter to the drive plate, if the vehicle is equipped with automatic transaxle.
14. Remove the buffer rod mounting bolts. Remove the bolts that support the engine mount to the front crossmember. Remove the bolts that hold the lower side of the engine to the transaxle assembly.
15. Install the proper engine lifting equipment. Properly support the transaxle assembly.
16. Remove the bolts that retain the upper side of the engine to the transaxle
17. Carefully remove the engine from the vehicle. If equipped with manual transaxle, move the engine in the axial direction until the mainshaft is withdrawn from the clutch cover.
18. Installation is the reverse of the removal procedure.

## *Except Justy, XT Coupe and Legacy*

### 1600cc OHV ENGINE

1. Matchmark and remove the hood. Disconnect the negative battery terminal.
2. Remove the ground cable to intake manifold bolt and disconnect the cable.
3. Remove the spare tire from the engine compartment. Remove the air cleaner assembly.
4. Disconnect and plug the fuel lines. Drain the engine oil. Drain the cooling system.
5. Disconnect the radiator hoses. Disconnect the heater hoses. If equipped with an automatic transaxle, disconnect the oil cooler lines from the radiator.
6. Disconnect the following electrical wiring connectors:
   a. Alternator electrical connector
   b. Oil pressure sender connector
   c. Engine cooling fan connectors
   d. Temperature sender connector
   e. Primary distributor lead
   f. Secondary ignition leads (ignition side)
   g. Starter wiring harness
   h. Anti dieseling solenoid lead
   i. Automatic choke lead
   j. EGR vacuum solenoid
   k. EGR coolant temperature switch
   l. If equipped with an automatic transaxle, disconnect the neutral safety switch harness and downshift solenoid harness.
7. Remove the radiator mounting bolts. Remove the radiator. If equipped with 4WD, remove the engine fan from the pulley.
8. Remove the crankshaft damper, using the proper removal tools.
9. Remove the starter electrical connections. Remove the starter.
10. Disconnect the following cables, hoses and linkages.
   a. Loosen the screw on the carburetor throttle lever. Remove the outer end of the accelerator cable and withdraw it.
   b. Remove the vacuum hose and the purge hose from the vapor canister.
   c. If equipped with a manual transaxle, remove the clutch return spring from the release lever/intake manifold and the clutch cable from the lever.
   d. If equipped with an automatic transaxle, disconnect the vacuum hose from the transaxle.
   e. Disconnect the vacuum hose

from the power brake unit, if equipped.

11. On 4WD vehicles, remove the skid plate to chassis bolts and the plate.

12. To remove the exhaust pipe, perform the following.

a. Remove the exhaust pipe to cylinder head nuts.

b. Remove the exhaust pipe to pre muffler bolts.

c. While supporting the exhaust pipe by hand, remove the exhaust pipe to transaxle bracket bolts, then lower the exhaust pipe.

13. If equipped with an automatic transaxle, remove the timing hole cover from the torque converter housing. Remove the torque converter to drive plate bolts.

14. Connect a chain hoist and a cable to the engine, with hooks at the front and rear engine hangers. Adjust the hoist so that the weight of the engine is supported but do not raise the engine.

15. Using a floor jack, position it under the transaxle.

16. Remove the engine to transaxle nuts. Remove the front engine mount to crossmember nuts.

17. Using the hoist, raise the engine slightly. Keeping it level, move the engine forward, off the transaxle input shaft. Remove the engine from the vehicle.

**NOTE: Do not raise the engine more than 1.0 in. prior to removing it from the input shaft or damage may occur to the driveshaft double offset joints. If equipped with a manual transaxle, be sure that the input shaft does not interfere with the clutch spring assembly. If equipped with an automatic transaxle, leave the torque converter on the transaxle input shaft.**

18. Installation is the reverse of the removal procedure.

### 1800cc OHV AND OHC ENGINE

1. If equipped with fuel injection, properly relieve the fuel pump pressure. Disconnect the negative battery cable.

2. Matchmark and remove the hood. Drain the cooling system. Drain the engine oil. Properly discharge the air conditioning system, if equipped.

3. Remove the spare tire assembly. Remove the spare tire support. Remove the battery cable clamp assembly. Remove the air cleaner assembly.

4. Disconnect and plug the fuel line hoses. Disconnect the canister hoses and the brake booster hose.

5. If equipped with automatic transaxle, remove the diaphragm vacuum hose.

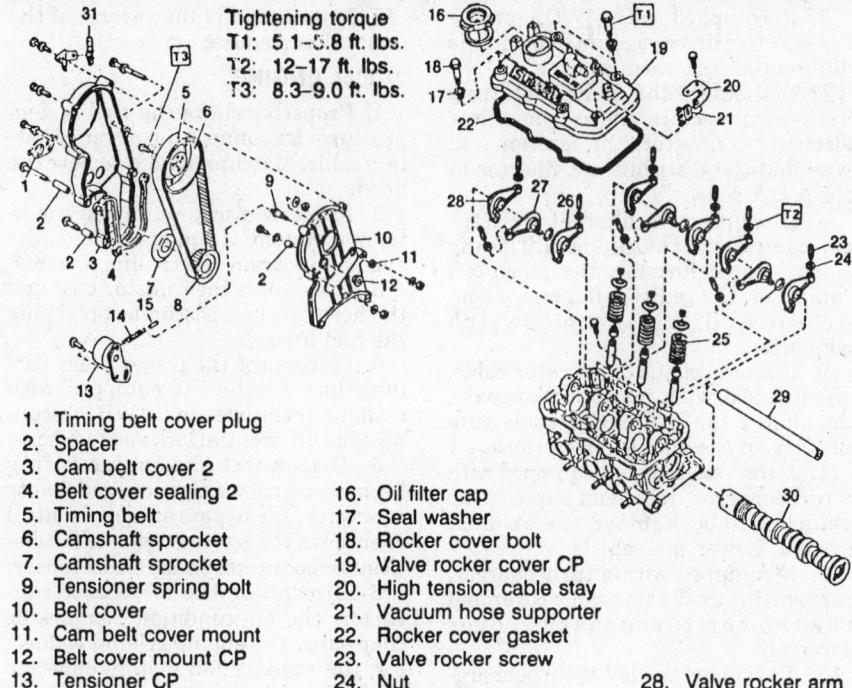

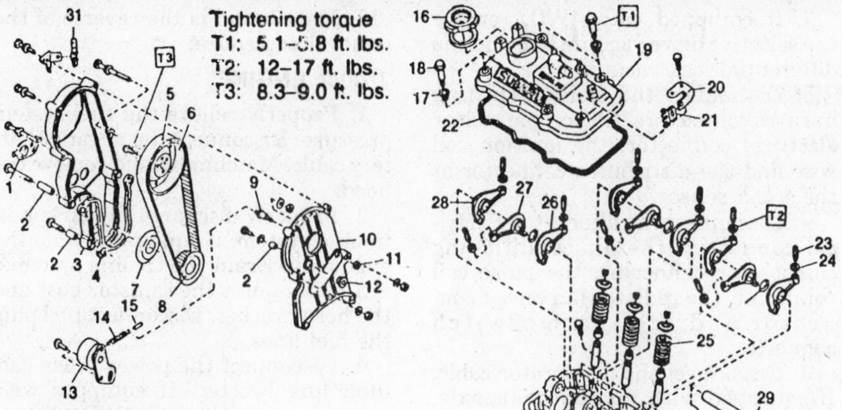


1. Timing belt cover plug
2. Spacer
3. Cam belt cover 2
4. Belt cover sealing 2
5. Timing belt
6. Camshaft sprocket
7. Camshaft sprocket
9. Tensioner spring bolt
10. Belt cover
11. Cam belt cover mount
12. Belt cover mount CP
13. Tensioner CP
14. Cam belt tensioner spring
15. Tensioner spring amper
16. Oil filter cap
17. Seal washer
18. Rocker cover bolt
19. Valve rocker cover CP
20. High tension cable stay
21. Vacuum hose supporter
22. Rocker cover gasket
23. Valve rocker screw
24. Nut
25. Valve Spring
26. Valve rocker arm No. 2
27. Valve rocker arm No. 3
28. Valve rocker arm
29. Valve rocker shaft
30. Camshaft
31. Stay

**Cylinder head and related components 1200cc engine**

6. If equipped with a turbocharger, remove the vacuum switch hose at the heater vacuum tank. Remove the wastegate valve hoses.

7. If equipped with 4WD, remove the selective drive vacuum line and the differential lock vacuum hose.

8. Disconnect the electrical wiring harness connectors, the oxygen sensor electrical connector, the ignition coil wire and the distributor connector at the crank sensor.

9. Disconnect the alternator electrical connector, the air conditioning compressor connector, the pulse coil connector, the radiator fan motor connector and the thermoswitch connector.

10. Disconnect the accelerator cable. If equipped with manual transaxle, disconnect the hill holder cable connection on the clutch release fork.

11. If the vehicle is not equipped with a turbocharger, raise and support the vehicle safely. Remove the exhaust system. Lower the vehicle.

12. If equipped with a turbocharger, remove the accelerator cable cover and the the top turbocharge cover assembly.

13. To remove the lower turbocharger cover assembly, raise and support the vehicle safely, loosen the front exhaust pipe connection. Lower the vehicle and remove the lower turbocharger cover from the center exhaust pipe.

14. Disconnect the center exhaust pipe to turbocharger connection. Raise and support the vehicle safely. Disconnect the center exhaust pipe to rear exhaust pipe connection. Remove the hanger bolt and disconnect the center exhaust pipe at the transaxle. Remove the center exhaust pipe.

15. Lower the vehicle. Remove the radiator. Disconnect and plug the heater hoses.

16. Disconnect and plug the air conditioning hoses at the compressor, if equipped. Remove the power steering pump assembly, if equipped.

17. Remove the pitching stopper rod. Remove the timing cover plate. Remove the retaining bolts that hold the torque converter to the drive plate, if the vehicle is equipped with automatic transaxle.

18. Properly support the engine and the transaxle assemblies, using the proper equipment.

19. Remove the bolts which hold the engine mount to the front crossmember. Remove the bolts which hold the lower side of the engine to the transaxle.

20. Properly install the proper engine lifting equipment to the engine. Remove the bolts that retain the upper side of the engine to the transaxle.

21. Carefully remove the engine from the vehicle. If the vehicle is equipped with manual transaxle, move the engine horizontally until the mainshaft is withdrawn from the clutch cover.

22. Installation is the reverse of the removal procedure.

# Cylinder Head

## REMOVAL & INSTALLATION

### *Justy*

1. Disconnect the negative battery cable. Drain the cooling system.
2. Remove the air cleaner assembly. Remove the drive belts. Remove the spark plug wires.
3. Position the engine at TDC with No. 1 cylinder on the compression stroke. Matchmark and remove the distributor assembly.
4. Remove the crankshaft pulley, using pulley removal tool 499205500 or equivalent. Remove the outer front timing belt cover.

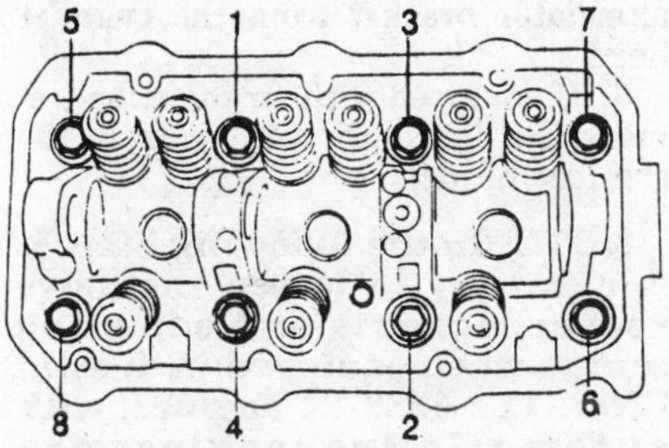


**Cylinder head bolt torque sequence 1200cc engine**

5. Loosen the tensioner bolt and position it in the direction that loosens the belt. Tighten the tensioner polt in that position.
6. Remove the camshaft drive plate. Mark the timing belt, in the direction of rotation, for reinstallation and than remove it from the engine.
7. Remove the tensioner and spring. Remove the camshaft pulley, using pulley removal tool 499205500 or equivalent. Remove the inner belt cover and cover mount.
8. Remove the PCV hose from the rocker arm cover. Remove the rocker arm cover retaining bolts. Remove the rocker arm cover from the engine. Remove the rocker arm assembly.
9. Remove the exhaust manifold retaining bolts. Remove the exhaust manifold from the engine. Discard the gasket.
10. Disconnect all required electrical wiring and vacuum lines. Remove the air suction valve and pipe, if equipped.
11. Disconnect the accelerator linkage. Remove the intake manifold retaining bolts. Remove the intake manifold along with the carburetor. Discard the gasket.
12. Be sure that the engine is cold before removing the cylinder head bolts. Loosen, than remove the cylinder head bolts. Carefully remove the cylinder head from the engine.

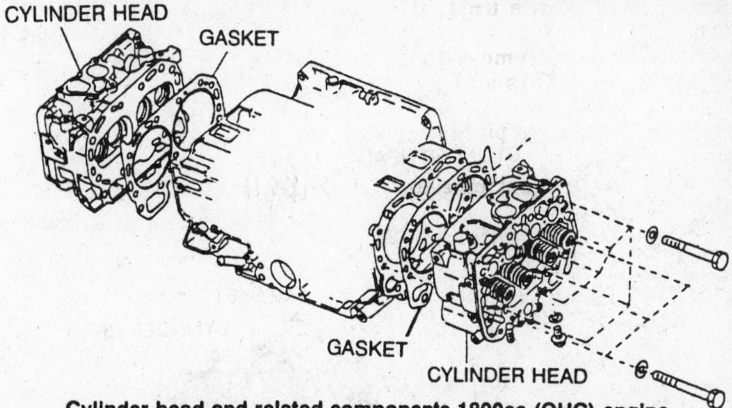


**Cylinder head and related components 1800cc (OHC) engine**

13. Installation is the reverse of the removal procedure. Be sure to use new gaskets or RTV sealant, as required.
14. Be sure to torque the cylinder head retaining bolts in the proper order and to the proper specification. Adjust the valves to specification, as required.

### *XT Coupe*

#### 1800cc ENGINE

1. Disconnect the negative battery cable. Drain the cooling system. Properly discharge the air conditioning system, if equipped.
2. Remove the timing belt assemblies. Remove the camshaft assemblies.
3. On non air conditioning equipped vehicles, remove the bolt attaching the alternator bracket to the cylinder head and the bolt retaining the adjusting bar to the cylinder head.
4. Be sure that the engine is cold before removing the intake manifold retaining bolts. Loosen, than remove the intake manifold bolts. Carefully remove the manifold from the engine.
5. Remove the water bypass line at the cylinder head. Remove the spark plugs.
6. Be sure that the engine is cold before removing the cylinder head bolts. Loosen, than remove the cylinder head bolts. Carefully remove the cylinder head from the engine.
7. Installation is the reverse of the removal procedure. Be sure to use new gaskets or RTV sealant, as required.

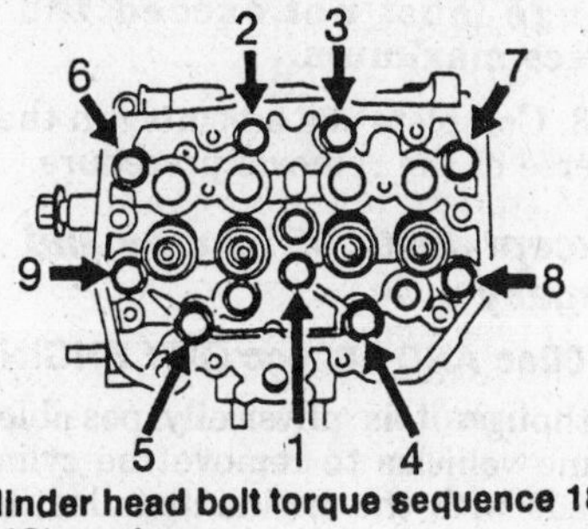


**Cylinder head bolt torque sequence 1800 (OHC) engine**

8. Be sure to torque the cylinder head retaining bolts in the proper order and to the proper specification. Adjust the valves to specification, as required.

#### 2700cc ENGINE

1. Disconnect the negative battery cable. Drain the cooling system. Properly discharge the air conditioning system, if equipped.
2. Remove the timing belt assemblies. Remove the camshaft assemblies.
3. Remove the alternator. Remove the air conditioning compressor.
4. Be sure that the engine is cold before removing the intake manifold retaining bolts. Loosen, than remove the intake manifold bolts. Carefully remove the manifold from the engine.
5. Remove the water bypass line at the cylinder head. Remove the alternator bracket at the cylinder head. Remove the spark plugs.
6. Be sure that the engine is cold before removing the cylinder head bolts. Loosen, than remove the cylinder head bolts. Carefully remove the cylinder head from the engine.
7. Installation is the reverse of the removal procedure. Be sure to use new gaskets or RTV sealant, as required.
8. Be sure to torque the cylinder head retaining bolts in the proper order and to the proper specification. Adjust the valves to specification, as required.

### *Legacy*

#### 2200cc ENGINE

1. Remove the negative battery cable. Remove the V-belt.
2. Remove the power steering pump assembly.
3. Remove the alternator and its bracket.
4. Remove the intake manifold cover and disconnect the PCV hose.
5. Disconnect the spark plug wire connectors and remove the connector from the bracket attching bolt.
6. Remove the crankshaft and cam

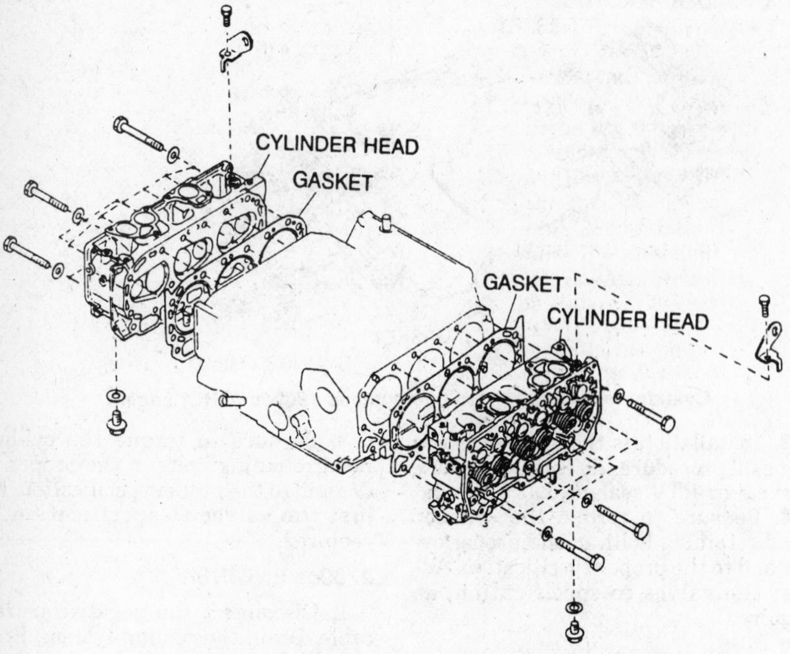


**Cylinder head and related components 2700cc engine**

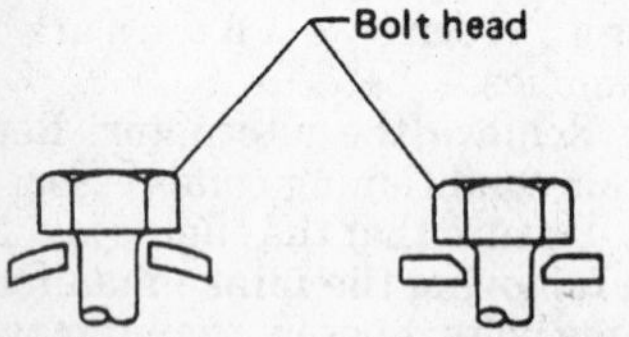


| Bolt position | Color | Bolt length |
|---|---|---|
| ①, ②, ⑨, ⑬ | Silver | 118.5 mm (4.665 in) |
| Others | Yellow | 132.5 mm (5.217 in) |

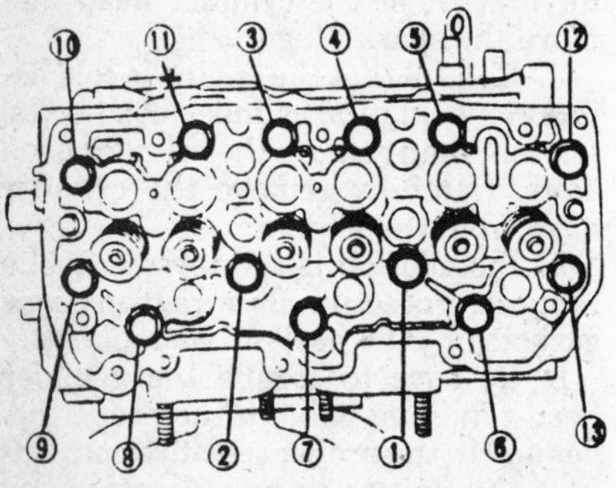


**Cylinder head bolt torque sequence 2700cc engine**

angle sensors. Remove the oil pressure switch conector.

7. Remove the knock sensor and the PCV blowby hose.

8. Remove the intake manifold and gasket. Remove the water pipe.

9. Remove the timing belt, camshaft sprocket and related components.

10. Remove the left hand dipstick tube attaching bolt.

11. Remove the cylinder head bolts in sequence, leaving 2 top (1 and 3) loosely in block to keep cylinder head from falling.

12. If necessary, tap cylinder head with a plastic hammer to loosen from cylinder block.

13. Remove the retaining bolts and separate the cylinder head from the engine block.

14. Remove the cylinder head gasket.

**To install:**

15. Using new cylinder head gaskets, install the head and gasket on the engine block.

16. Apply a coating of engine oil to the cylinder head bolts and washers.

17. Tighten alal cylinder head bolts to 51 ft. lbs. (69 Nm) torque in sequence.

18. Back off all bolts 180 degrees.

19. Retighten No.1 and No.2 bolts in sequence to 25 ft. lbs. (34 Nm).

20. Retighten bolts Nos. 3, 4, 5 and 6 to 14 ft. lbs. (20 Nm).

21. Tighten all bolts an additional 80–90 degrees in sequence. Do not tighten over 90 degrees .

22. Further tighten all bolts an additional 80–90 degrees in sequence.

**NOTE: The total retightening range must not exceed 180 degrees maximum.**

23. Complete the assembly in the reverse of the removal procedure.

### *Except Justy, XT Coupe and Legacy*

#### 1600cc AND 1800cc OHV ENGINES

Although it is physically possible on some vehicles to remove the cylinder heads with the engine installed, head gasket failure will result upon installation, due to misalignment of the cylinder head. The cylinder heads should be removed with the engine cold to prevent warpage.

1. Remove the engine from the vehicle. position it ina suitable holding fixture.

2. Remove the EGR pipe from the intake manifold and cylinder head. On the 1983–84 vehicles, remove the thermostatic water valve, the hose and the oil filter pipe bracket.

3. On the turbocharged vehicles, remove the turbocharger and exhaust manifold, then disconnect the fuel injection lines.

4. Remove the spark plugs. Disconnect the crankcase ventilation hose. Remove the valve covers.

5. Loosen the alternator adjusting bolts, remove the alternator and the alternator bracket from the cylinder head.

6. If equipped with air injection, remove the distribution tubes from the cylinder heads.

**NOTE: In the following Step, it is necessary to loosen the valve rocker locknuts and adjusting screws when equipped with solid lifter. The 1983–84 engines, with automatic transaxles, are equipped with hydraulic lifters, the adjustment of the lifter screws and locknuts must not be disturbed.**

7. If equipped with an 1800cc engine and a turbocharger, remove the knock sensor using the proper removal socket. Remove the fuel injectors.

8. If equipped with solid lifters, loosen the valve rocker locknuts and adjusting screws. Loosen the rocker shaft mounting nuts, then remove the rocker arm assembly and pushrods.

**NOTE: If the pushrods are to be reused, keep them in order so that they are installed in the original positions. The pushrods for all engines are identified by knurling, or the absence of knurling. If replacing the pushrods, make sure the knurled patterns are similar or that the unmarked pushrods are replaced by unmarked pushrods as the markings vary from year to year.**

9. Loosen the cylinder head nuts in sequence and remove the cylinder heads and gaskets.

10. Using an appropraite tool, clean the gasket mounting surfaces.

11. To install, use new gaskets, sealant (on both sides of the new cylinder head gasket) and reverse the removal procedures. Torque the cylinder head to engine bolts in sequence. After the cylinder head is torqued to specification, remove the rocker arm shaft

bolts/nuts and the spacers, then install the rocker arm shafts. On later vehicles, torque the cylinder head with the rocker arm shaft in place, in the proper sequence. Recheck the torque of the No. 1 bolt after torque is correct on the others. On vehicles which use studs and nuts, lightly oil the threads before install the nuts.

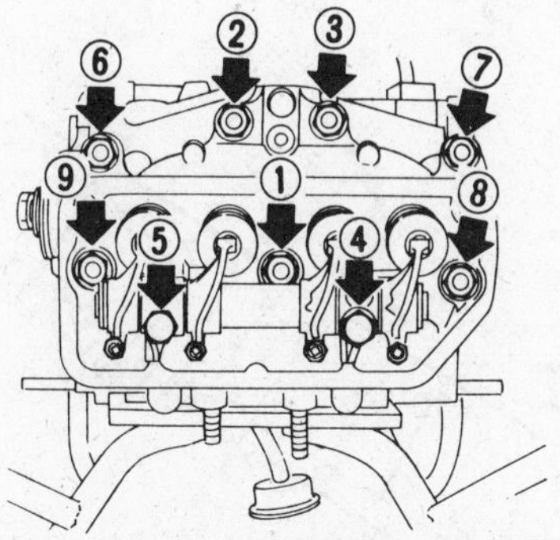

Cylinder head bolt torque sequence 1600cc and 1800cc (OHV) engines

**NOTE: The cylinder heads must be installed with the cylinders in the vertical position to avoid misalignment and to permit the head gasket to settle evenly around the cylinder.**

### 1800cc OHC ENGINE

1. Disconnect the negative battery cable. Drain the cooling system. Properly discharge the air conditioning system, if equipped.
2. Remove the timing belt assemblies. Remove the camshaft assemblies.
3. On non air conditioning equipped vehicles, remove the bolt attaching the alternator bracket to the cylinder head and the bolt retaining the adjusting bar to the cylinder head.
4. Be sure that the engine is cold before removing the intake manifold retaining bolts. Loosen, than remove the intake manifold bolts. Carefully remove the manifold from the engine.
5. Remove the water bypass line at the cylinder head. Remove the spark plugs.
6. Be sure that the engine is cold before removing the cylinder head bolts. Loosen, than remove the cylinder head bolts. Carefully remove the cylinder head from the engine.
7. Installation is the reverse of the removal procedure. Be sure to use new gaskets or RTV sealant, as required.
8. Be sure to torque the cylinder head retaining bolts in the proper order and to the proper specification. Adjust the valves to specification, as required.

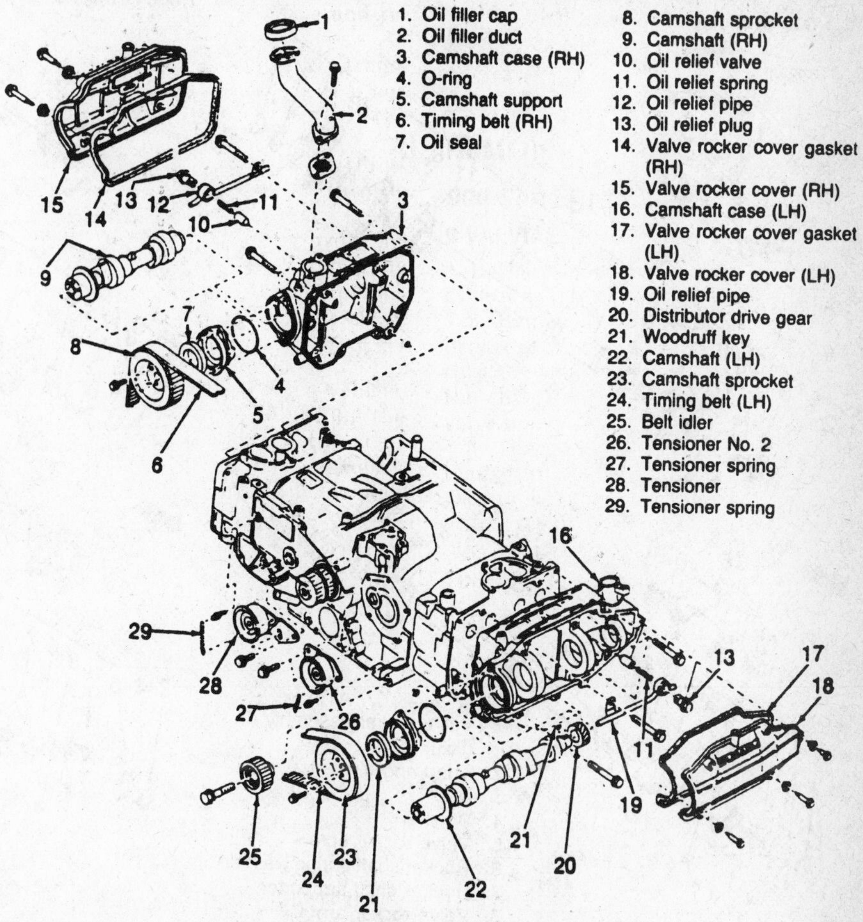

Cylinder head assembly 1800cc (OHC) engine

## OVERHAUL

**For all cylinder head overhaul procedures, please refer to the "Engine Rebuilding" in the Unit Repair section.**

# Rocker Shafts

## REMOVAL & INSTALLATION

### *Justy*

1. Disconnect the negative battery cable. Remove the air cleaner assembly.
2. Remove the valve cover retaining bolts. Remove the valve cover from the engine.
3. Using the valve clearance adjuster tool 498767000 or equivalent, loosen the valve rocker nut and screw.
4. Remove the bolt from the valve rocker shaft journal. Pull the rocker shaft out from the cylinder head. Remove the spring washer and the valve rocker arms.
5. Installation is the reverse of the removal procedure. Be sure to use a new gasket or RTV sealant, as required. Adjust the valves to specification, as required.

### *XT Coupe*

#### 1800cc AND 2700cc ENGINE

Neither engine uses a rocker arm shaft, the valve rocker simply floats between the valve stem and the hydraulic lifter, the center of the valve rocker rides against the camshaft.

### *Except Justy and XT Coupe*

#### 1600cc AND 1800cc OHV ENGINES

1. Remove the engine from the vehicle. Position the assembly in a suitable holding fixture.
2. Remove the valve cover to cylinder head bolts and the valve covers, discard the gaskets.
3. Remove the rocker arm assemblies to cylinder heads bolts and the rocker arm assemblies from the engine.
4. As required, withdraw the pushrods from their bores, being sure to keep them in the same order in which they were removed.
5. Installation is the reverse of the removal procedure. Be sure to use new

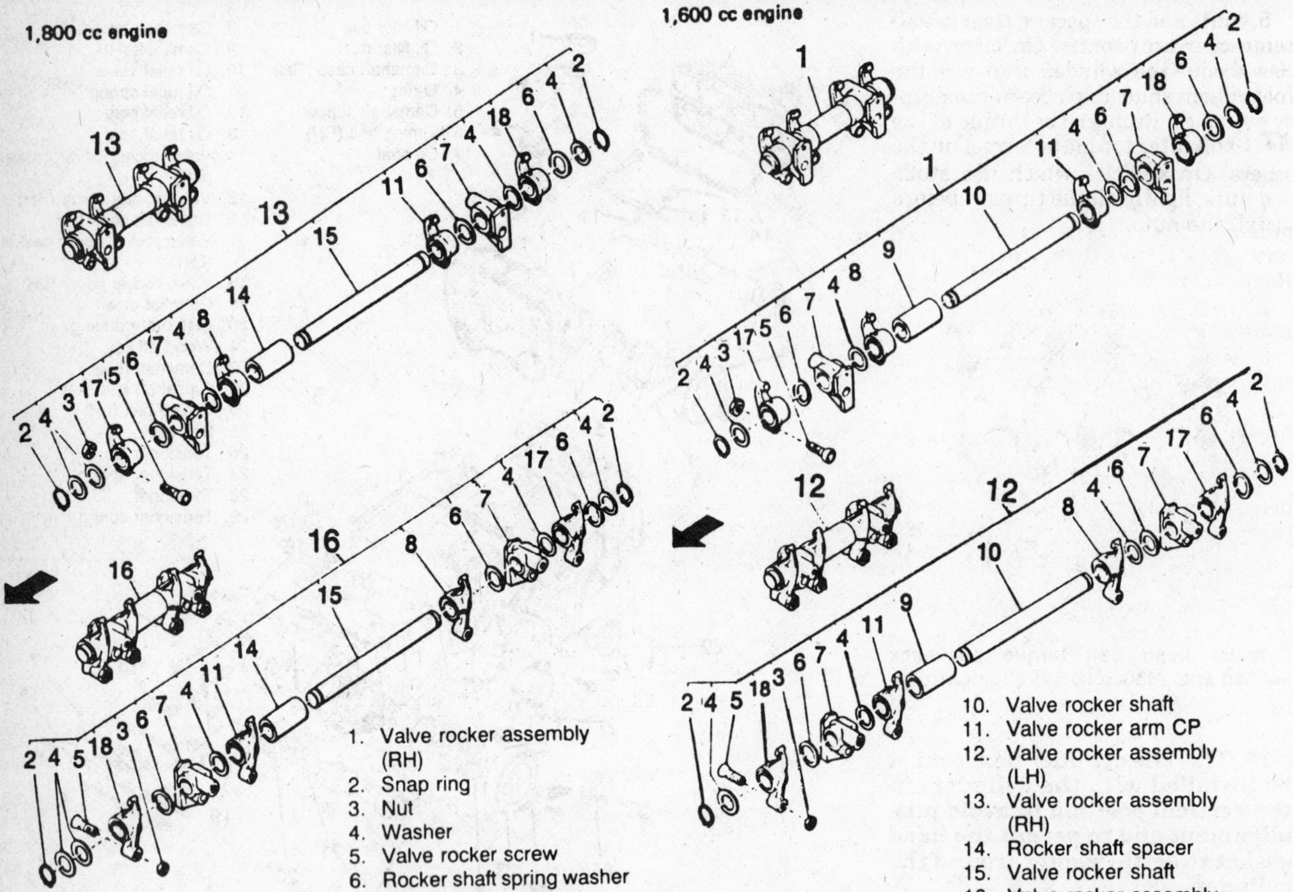


**Rocker arm assemblies 1600cc and 1800cc (OHV) engines**

gaskets or RTV sealant, as required. Adjust the valves, as required.

### 1800cc OHC ENGINE

This engine does not use a rocker arm shaft, the valve rocker simply floats between the valve stem and the hydraulic lifter, the center of the valve rocker rides against the camshaft.

## Intake Manifold

### REMOVAL & INSTALLATION

*Justy*

1. Disconnect the negative battery cable. Drain the cooling system. Remove the air cleaner assembly.
2. Disconnect the accelerator cable. Disconnect the required vacuum lines. Remove the upper radiator hose.
3. Remove the necessary components in order to gain access to the intake manifold retaining bolts.
4. Remove the intake manifold retaining bolts. Remove the intake manifold along with the carburetor assembly. Discard the gasket.

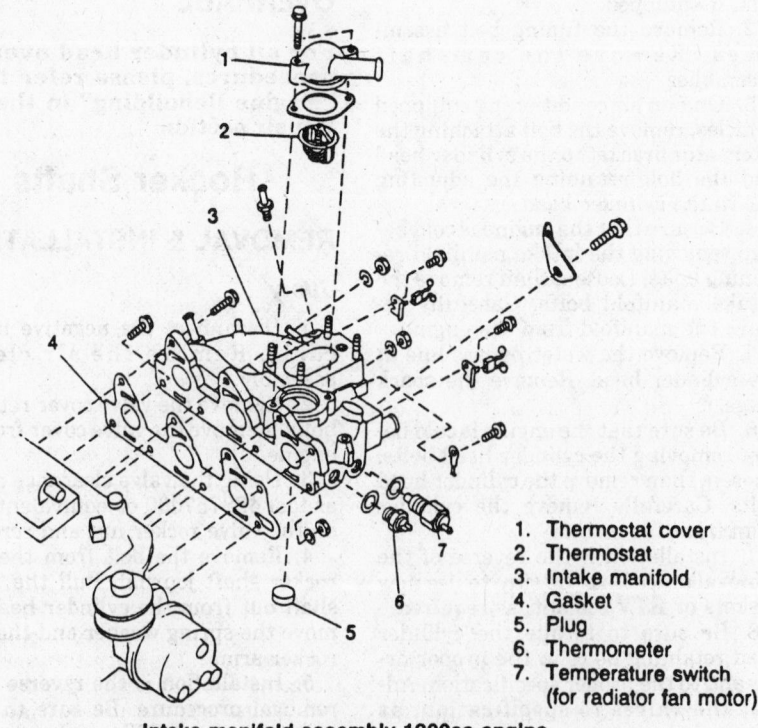

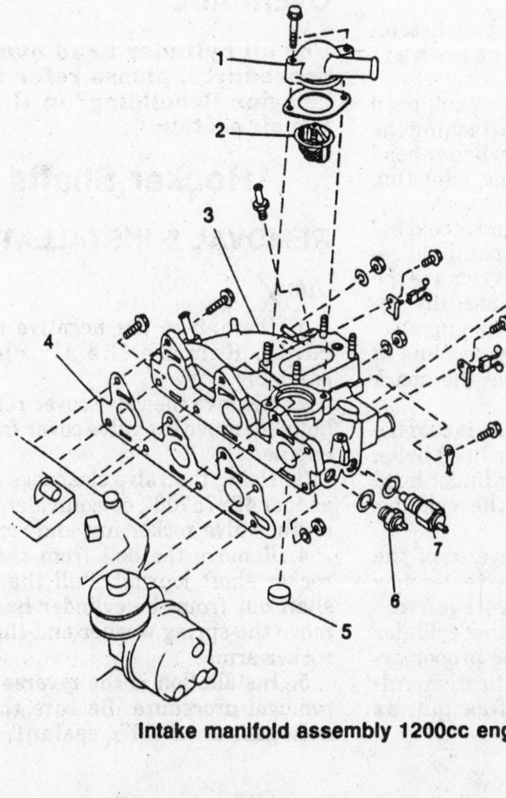


**Intake manifold assembly 1200cc engine**

5. Installation is the reverse of the removal procedure. Be sure to use a new gasket. Torque the intake manifold retaining bolts to specification.

### *XT Coupe*

**1800cc ENGINE**

1. Properly relieve the fuel system pressure. Disconnect the negative battery cable. Drain the cooling system. Remove the air cleaner assembly.
2. Remove the fuel pipe covers. Remove the fuel pipe assemblies.
3. Disconnect the required electrical connectors and vacuum hoses.
4. Remove the purge control solenoid valve. Remove the water pipe assembly.
5. Remove the necessary components in order to gain access to the intake manifold collector retaining bolts.
6. Remove the intake manifold collector retaining bolts. Remove the intake manifold collector from the engine. Discard the gaskets.
7. As required, remove the fuel injectors from their bores. Remove the intake manifold retaining bolts. Remove the intake manifold from the engine. Discard the gaskets.
8. Installation is the reverse of the removal procedure. Be sure to torque the retaining bolts to specification.

**2700cc ENGINE**

1. Properly relieve the fuel system pressure. Disconnect the negative battery cable. Drain the cooling system. Remove the air cleaner assembly.
2. Remove the fuel pipe covers. Remove the fuel pipe assemblies.
3. Disconnect the required electrical connectors and vacuum hoses.
4. Remove the purge control solenoid valve. Remove the water pipe assembly.
5. Remove the necessary components in order to gain access to the intake manifold collector retaining bolts.
6. Remove the intake manifold collector retaining bolts. Remove the intake manifold collector from the engine. Discard the gaskets.
7. As required, remove the fuel injectors from their bores. Remove the intake manifold retaining bolts. Remove the intake manifold from the engine. Discard the gaskets.
8. Installation is the reverse of the removal procedure. Be sure to torque the retaining bolts to specification.

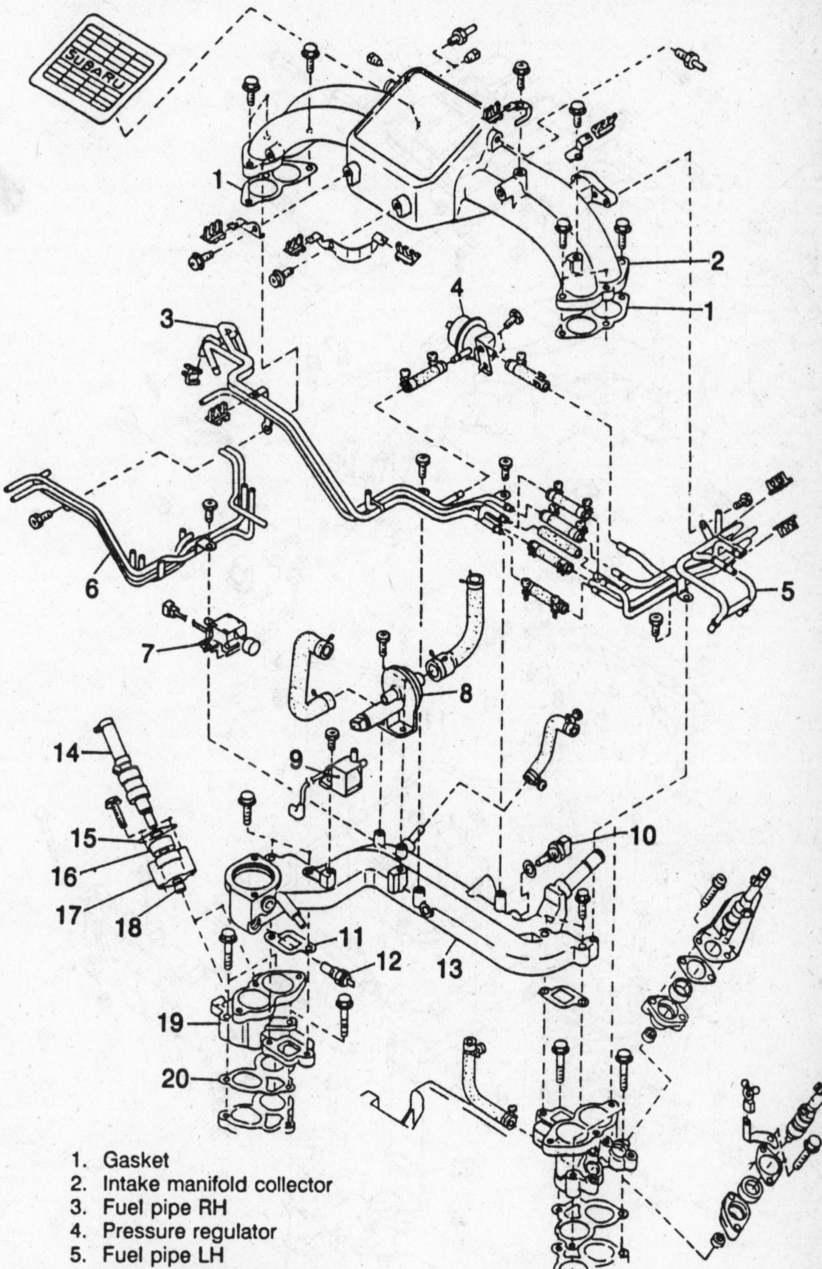

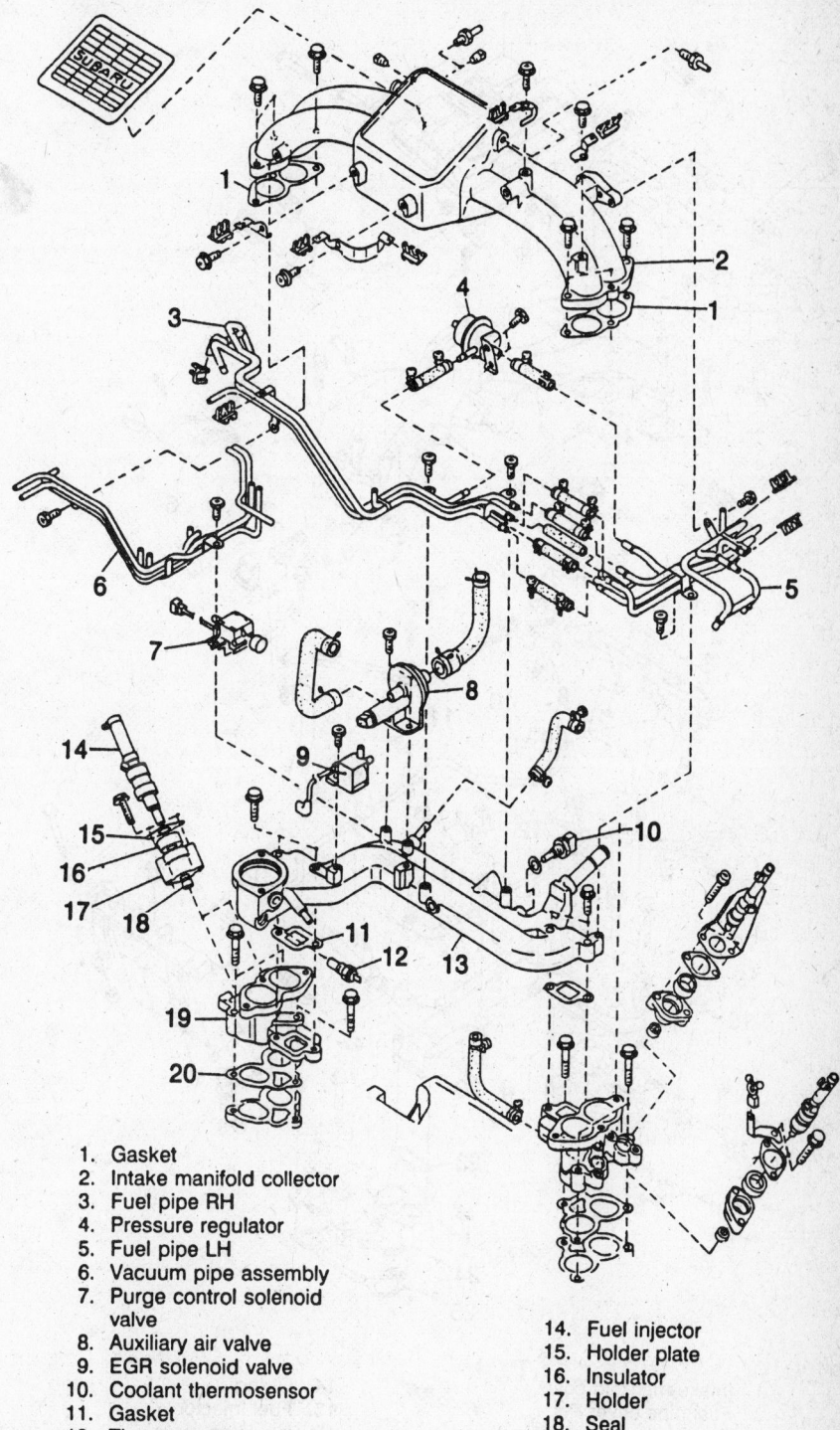

1. Gasket
2. Intake manifold collector
3. Fuel pipe RH
4. Pressure regulator
5. Fuel pipe LH
6. Vacuum pipe assembly
7. Purge control solenoid valve
8. Auxiliary air valve
9. EGR solenoid valve
10. Coolant thermosensor
11. Gasket
12. Thermometer
13. Water pipe
14. Fuel injector
15. Holder plate
16. Insulator
17. Holder
18. Seal
19. Intake manifold
20. Gasket

**Intake manifold assembly 1800cc (OHC) engine with MPFI**

### *Legacy*

**2200cc ENGINE**

1. Remove the negative battery cable. Remove the V-belt.
2. Remove the power steering pump assembly.
3. Remove the alternator and its bracket.
4. Remove the intake manifold cover and disconnect the PCV hose.
5. Disconnect the spark plug wire connectors and remove the connector from the bracket attching bolt.
6. Remove the crankshaft and cam angle sensors. Remove the oil pressure switch conector.
7. Remove the knock sensor and the PCV blowby hose.
8. Remove the intake manifold and gasket. Remove the water pipe.
9. To install, reverse the removal procedure, using new gasket.

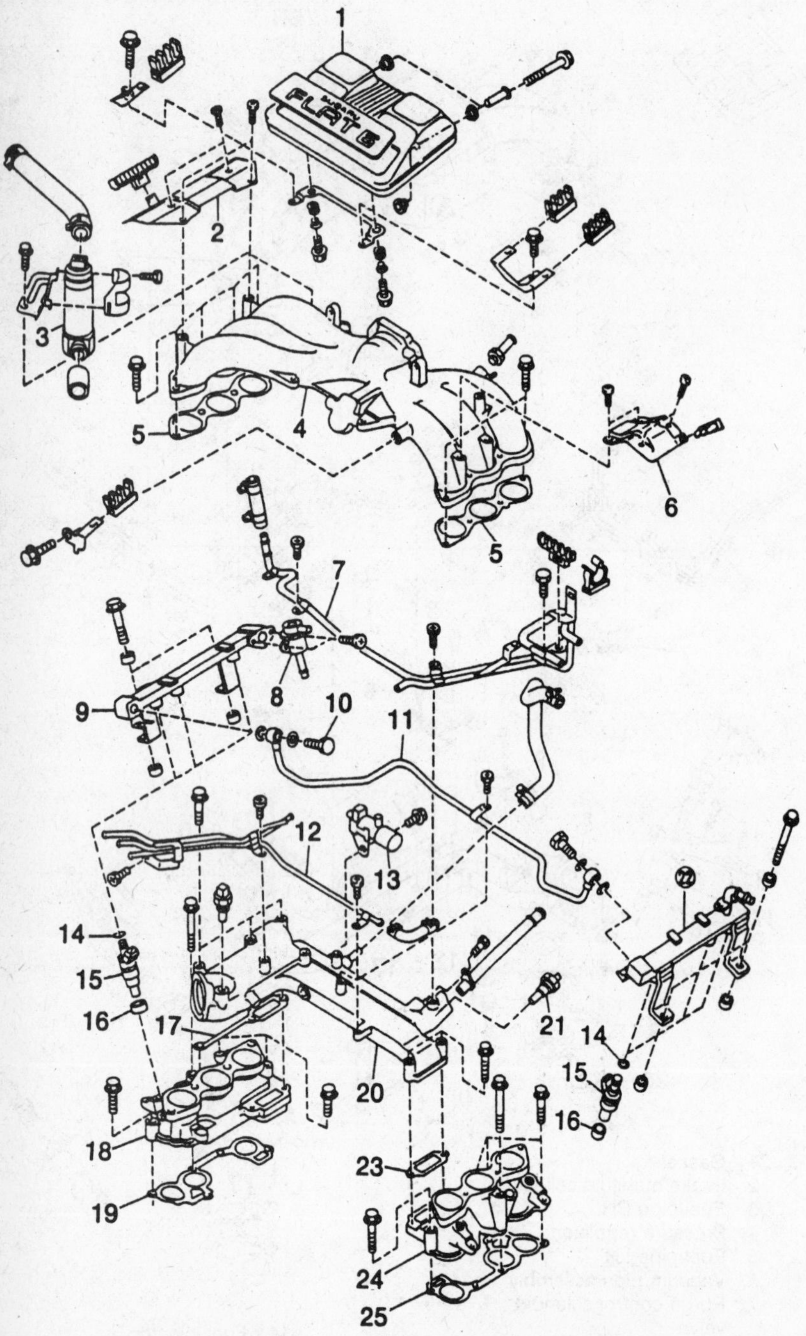


1. Intake manifold cover
2. Fuel pipe cover RH
3. Bypass air control valve
4. Intake manifold collector
5. Gasket
6. Fuel pipe cover LH
7. Fuel pipe assembly
8. Pressure regulator
9. Fuel pipe RH
10. Union bolt
11. Fuel Pipe
12. Fuel Pipe assembly
13. Purge control solenoid vavle
14. O-ring
15. Fuel injector
16. Insulator
17. Gasket
18. Intake manifold RH
19. Gasket
20. Water pipe
21. Coolant thermostat
22. Fuel pipe LH
23. Gasket
24. Intake manifold LH
25. Gasket

**Intake manifold assembly 2700cc engine**

### *Except Justy, XT Coupe and Legacy*

#### 1600cc AND 1800cc ENGINES

1. If equipped with fuel injection, properly relieve the fuel system pressure. Disconnect the negative battery cable. Remove the spare tire from the engine compartment.
2. Disconnect the emission control system hoses, remove the mounting bracket screws and withdraw the air cleaner assembly.
3. If equipped with a turbocharger or a fuel injection system, loosen the hose clamps and remove the air intake duct.
4. Drain the cooling system. Remove the water hoses from the thermostat housing. Disconnect the thermoswitch connector.
5. If equipped with a distributor vacuum control valve, disconnect the hoses and electrical leads from it.
6. Disconnect the automatic choke to voltage regulator wire at the connector, the EGR solenoid wiring, if equipped and the EGR pipe.
7. Disconnect the throttle cable from it's bracket. If equipped with a carburetor, disconnect the fuel line.
8. If equipped with a turbocharger or fuel injection system, disconnect the hose clamps, pull off hoses and remove the fuel pressure regulator assembly.
9. If equipped with and MPFI system, remove the fuel injectors from the intake manifold.
10. Remove the intake manifold to cylinder head bolts. Remove the intake manifold assembly from the engine. The air cleaner brackets will come off as the unit is unbolted. Make sure to note locations of these brackets and remove them.
11. Installation is the reverse of the removal procedure. Be sure to use new gaskets or RTV sealant, as required.

## Exhaust Manifold

### REMOVAL & INSTALLATION

#### *Justy*

1. Disconnect the negative battery cable. Remove the air cleaner assembly.
2. Raise and support the vehicle safely. Disconnect the exhaust manifold from the exhaust pipe. Lower the vehicle.
3. Disconnect the oxygen sensor electrical connector. Remove the exhaust manifold cover plate assembly.
4. Remove the exhaust manifold retaining bolts. Remove the exhaust manifold from the engine. Discard the gasket.

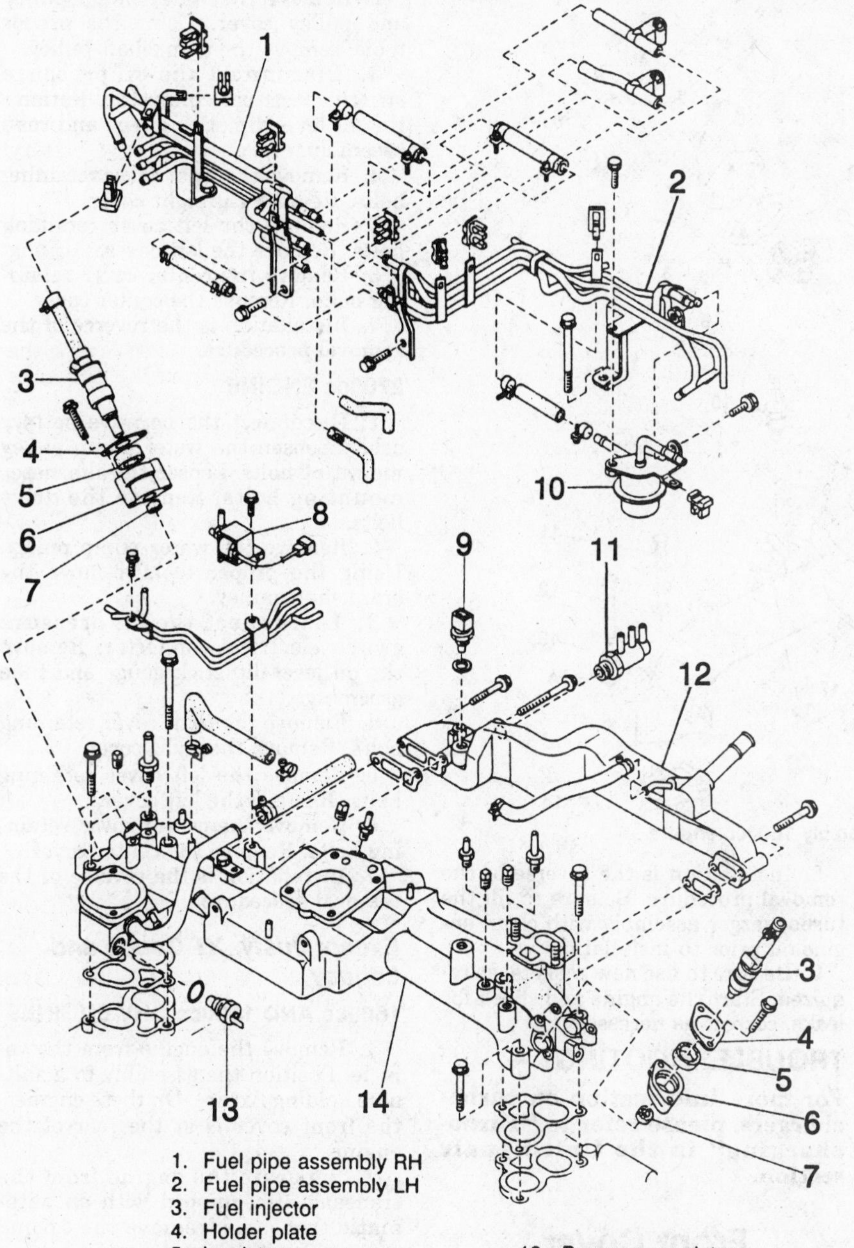


1. Fuel pipe assembly RH
2. Fuel pipe assembly LH
3. Fuel injector
4. Holder plate
5. Insulator
6. Holder
7. Seal
8. EGR solenoid valve
9. Coolant therosensor
10. Pressure regulator
11. Thermo valve
12. Water pipe
13. Thermometer
14. Intake manifold

**Intake manifold assembly 1800cc engine with TBI**

5. Installation is the reverse of the removal procedure. Be sure to use a new gasket. Torque the exhaust manifold retaining bolts to specification.

### *XT Coupe*

#### 1800cc ENGINE

1. Disconnect the negative battery cable. Raise and support the vehicle safely.
2. Disconnect the oxygen sensor electrical connector.
3. Remove the exhaust manifold assembly to cylinder head retaining bolts.
4. Remove the exhaust manifold assembly to exhaust pipe retaining bolts.
5. If equipped with a turbocharger, remove the exhaust pipe to turbocharger assembly. Remove the turbocharger plate and gasket.
6. Remove the exhaust manifold assembly from the vehicle.
7. Installation is the reverse of the removal procedure. Be sure to use new gaskets, as required.

#### 2700cc ENGINE

1. Disconnect the negative battery cable. Raise and support the vehicle safely.
2. Disconnect the oxygen sensor electrical connector.
3. Remove the exhaust manifold assembly to cylinder head retaining bolts.
4. Remove the exhaust manifold assembly to exhaust pipe retaining bolts.
5. Remove the exhaust manifold assembly from the vehicle.
6. Installation is the reverse of the removal procedure. Be sure to use new gaskets, as required.

### *Except Justy, XT Coupe and Legacy*

#### EXCEPT TURBOCHARGED ENGINE

1. Disconnect the negative battery cable. Raise and support the vehicle safely.
2. Disconnect the electrical connector from the oxygen sensor.
3. From the upper shell cover, remove the air duct.
4. Loosen the front exhaust pipe to cylinder head nuts.
5. Remove the front exhaust pipe to rear exhaust pipe nuts, then separate the pipes, discard the gasket.
6. Remove the front exhaust pipe to bracket bolt. While supporting the front exhaust pipe, remove the pipe to cylinder head nuts and front exhaust pipe from the vehicle; discard the gaskets.
7. Installation is the reverse of the removal procedure. Be sure to use new gaskets, as required.

#### TURBOCHARGED ENGINE

1. Disconnect the negative battery cable. Raise and support the vehicle safely.
2. If equipped, remove the both sheetmetal covers from the turbocharger. Remove the turbocharger to exhaust pipe bolts and separate the turbocharger from the pipe.
3. Remove the turbo bracket to front exhaust pipe nuts and the right side splash pan.
4. If equipped with 4WD, remove the skid plate to chassis bolts and the plate from the vehicle.
5. Loosen the engine to mount bracket bolts and the engine to pitching stopper bolts. Using the proper equipment, raise the engine slightly until the bolts protrude above the surface of the crossmember.
6. Disconnect the front exhaust pipe to cylinder head bolts and separate the exhaust pipe from its mounting. If equipped with a power steering, be careful not to damage the power steering hoses.

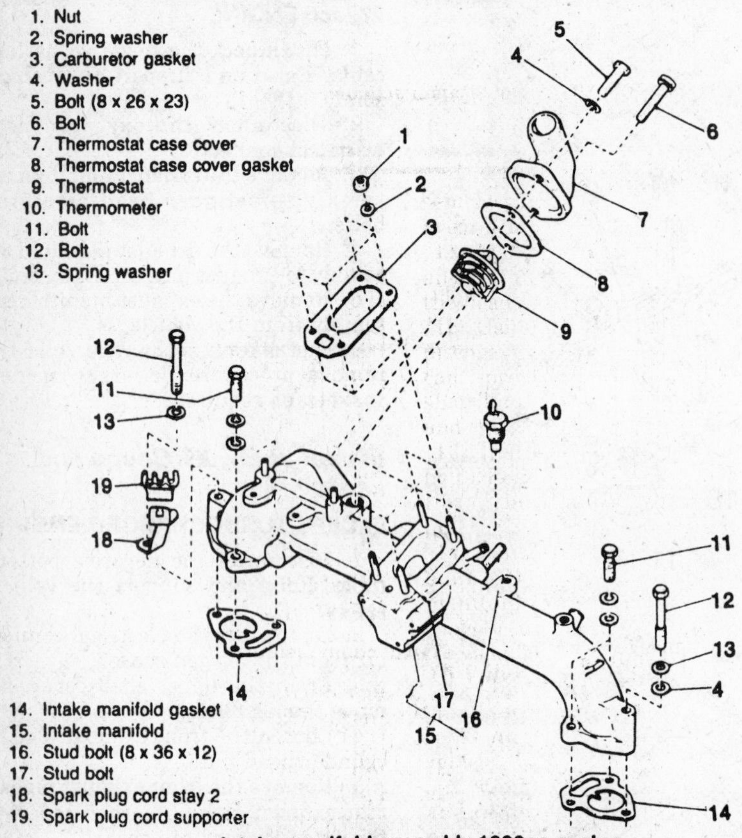


**Intake manifold assembly 1600cc engine**

7. Installation is the reverse of the removal procedure. Be sure to use new gaskets, as required.

## Turbocharger

### REMOVAL & INSTALLATION

#### *1800cc Engine*

1. Disconnect the negative battery cable. Drain the cooling system. Remove the air cleaner.
2. Disconnect the airflow meter to turbocharger inlet clamp, then remove the air intake duct. Cover the airflow meter and turbocharger openings.
3. Loosen the turbocharger to air outlet hose clamp and the throttle body inlet to air inlet hose clamp. Remove the turbocharger to throttle body hose. Plug all of the openings.
4. Remove the turbocharger to center exhaust pipe nuts and the front exhaust pipe to turbocharger nuts.
5. Disconnect and plug the coolant lines.
6. Remove the oil feed line to turbocharger bolt and disconnect the turbocharger to oil return hose clamp and the return hose.
7. Remove the turbocharger from the exhaust manifold.

**NOTE: When removing the turbocharger from the vehicle, disconnect the oil return hose.**

8. Installation is the reverse of the removal procedure. Be sure to fill the turbocharger assembly with clean engine oil prior to installation.
9. Be sure to use new gaskets, as required. Start the engine and check for leaks, correct as necessary.

### TROUBLESHOOTING

**For more information on turbochargers, please refer to "Turbocharging" in the Unit Repair section.**

## Front Cover

### REMOVAL & INSTALLATION

#### *Justy*

1. Disconnect the negative battery cable. Remove the drive belts.
2. Remove the outer front cover retaining bolts. Remove the outer front belt cover.
3. Installation is the reverse of the removal procedure.

#### *XT Coupe*

#### 1800cc ENGINE

1. Disconnect the negative battery cable. Loosen the water pump pulley mounting bolts. On vehicles not equipped with air conditioning, loosen the alternator mounting bolts and remove the drive belt.
2. Remove the water pump pulley and pulley cover. Using the proper tools, remove the crankshaft pulley.
3. Disconnect the oil pressure switch electrical connector. Remove the oil level dip stick gauge and tube assembly.
4. Remove the right cover retaining bolts. Remove the right cover.
5. Remove the left cover retaining bolts. Remove the left cover.
6. Remove the center cover retaining bolts. Remove the center cover.
7. Installation is the reverse of the removal procedure.

#### 2700cc ENGINE

1. Disconnect the negative battery cable. Loosen the water pump pulley mounting bolts. Loosen the alternator mounting bolts. Remove the drive belts.
2. Remove the water pump pulley. Using the proper tools, remove the crankshaft pulley.
3. Disconnect the oil pressure switch electrical connector. Remove the oil level dip stick gauge and tube assembly.
4. Remove the right cover retaining bolts. Remove the right cover.
5. Remove the left cover retaining bolts. Remove the left cover.
6. Remove the center cover retaining bolts. Remove the center cover.
7. Installation is the reverse of the removal procedure.

#### *Except Justy, XT Coupe and Legacy*

#### 1600cc AND 1800cc OHV ENGINES

1. Remove the engine from the vehicle. Position the assembly in a suitable holding fixture. On these engines, the front cover is at the rear of the engine.
2. Separate the engine from the transaxle. If equipped with an automatic transaxle, remove the torque converter with the transaxle.
3. If equipped with a manual transaxle, remove the clutch assembly from the flywheel. Remove the flywheel or the converter drive plate from the crankshaft.
4. Remove the flywheel housing to engine bolts and work the housing from the 2 aligning dowels.
5. Using an appropraite tool, clean the gasket mounting surfaces.
6. To install, use a new gasket and reverse the removal procedure.

#### 1800cc OHC ENGINE

1. Disconnect the negative battery cable. Loosen the water pump pulley mounting bolts. On vehicles not equipped with air conditioning, loosen the alternator mounting bolts and remove the drive belt.

2. Remove the water pump pulley and pulley cover. Using the proper tools, remove the crankshaft pulley.
3. Disconnect the oil pressure switch electrical connector. Remove the oil level dip stick gauge and tube assembly.
4. Remove the right cover retaining bolts. Remove the right cover.
5. Remove the left cover retaining bolts. Remove the left cover.
6. Remove the center cover retaining bolts. Remove the center cover.
7. Installation is the reverse of the removal procedure.

### FRONT OIL SEAL REPLACEMENT

#### *Except 1600cc and 1800cc OHV Engines*

1. Remove the timing belt cover assembly.
2. On the 1800cc engine, slide both the No. 1 and No. 2 crankshaft sprockets from the crankshaft. On the 1200cc engine, slide crankshaft sprocket from the crankshaft. When removing the crankshaft sprockets, be sure to remove the Woodruff key from the crankshaft.
3. Using a small pry bar, pry the front oil seal from the crankcase.
4. To install, use a new oil seal lubricated with engine oil and drive it into the crankcase until it seats. When installing the new oil seal, be careful not to cut the sealing lips.
5. To complete the installation, reverse the removal procedures.

#### *1600cc and 1800cc OHV Engines*

1. Raise and support the vehicle safely.
2. Disconnect the negative battery terminal from the battery.
3. If equipped, remove the splash pan.
4. Loosen the alternator mounting bolts, slacken the drive belt tension and remove the drive belt. If equipped with air conditioning, loosen the compressor and remove the drive belt. If equipped with power steering, remove the mounting bolts and the drive belt.
5. Remove the crankshaft pulley to crankshaft bolt and the pulley from the crankshaft.
6. Using a small pry bar, pry the oil seal from the crankcase, be careful not to damage the crankshaft or the crankcase.
7. Using a new oil seal, lubricate it with engine oil and drive it into the crankcase, be careful not to cut the oil seal lips or distort the seal housing.
8. To complete the installation, reverse the removal procedure.

## Timing Chain and Sprockets

### REMOVAL & INSTALLATION

#### *Except Justy and XT Coupe*

#### 1600cc AND 1800cc OHV ENGINES

1. Remove the engine from the vehicle. Position the assembly in a suitable holding fixture.
2. Remove the front cover assembly, which on this engine is at the rear of the engine assembly.
3. Remove the camshaft sprocket from its mounting.
4. Installation is the reverse of the removal procedure. Be sure to properly align the camshaft sprocket and the crankshaft sprocket.

## Timing Belt and Tensioner

### REMOVAL & INSTALLATION

#### *Justy*

1. Disconnect the negative battery cable. Remove the alternator drive belt. Loosen the crankshaft pulley bolts, but do not remove.

**Note: An access hole is provided in the wheelhouse panel to loosen and then remove the crankshaft pulley bolts.**

2. Position the crankshaft with No. 3 cylinder at TDC.
3. Remove the crankshaft bolts and pulley, using pulley removal tool 499205500 or equivalent. Remove the outer front timing belt cover.
4. Loosen the tensioner bolt and position it in the direction that loosens the belt. Tighten the tensioner bolt in that position.
5. Remove the camshaft drive pulley plate. Mark the timing belt, if to be used again, in the direction of rotation for reinstallation. Remove the belt from the sprockets.

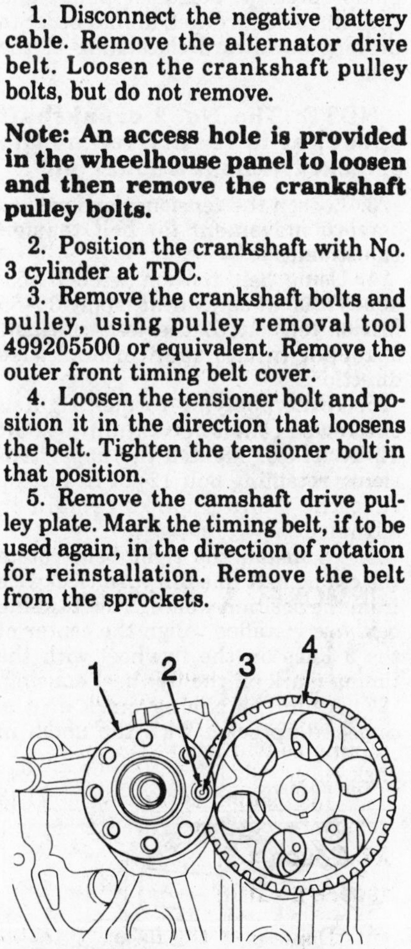


1 Crankshaft gear  3 Punch
2 Large chamfer  4 Camshaft gear

**Timing gear alignment 1600cc and 1800cc (OHV) engines**

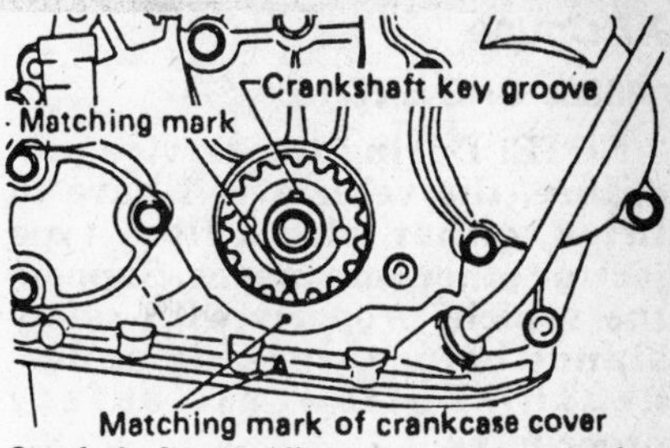


**Crankshaft gear alignment 1200cc engine**

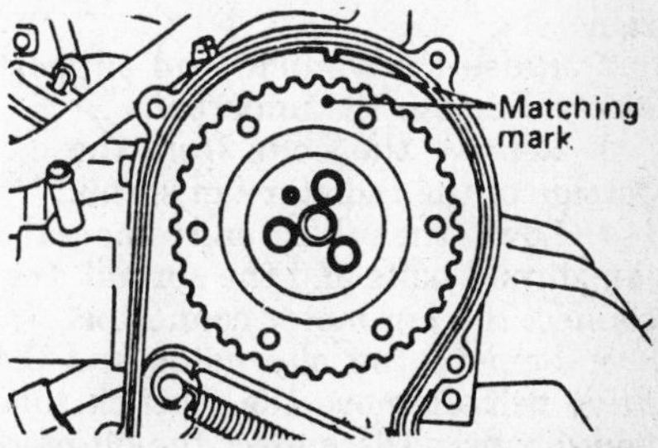


**Camshaft gear alignment 1200cc engine**

6. If necessary, remove the tensioner and spring. Remove the camshaft pulley, using pulley removal tool 499205500 or equivalent. Remove the inner belt cover and cover mount only as required.

**To install:**

7. When installing the timing belt, rotate and align the matching mark of the camshaft driven pulley 0.120 in. diameter hole with the matching mark of the cambelt side cover.
8. Align the matching mark of the crankshaft drive pulley with the matching mark of the crankshaft cover. Install the camshaft drive belt.
9. Loosen the tensioner bolt ½ turn.
10. Tighten the tensioner bolt below the adjusting wheel first. Tighten the other bolt. Check to be sure that all sprocket and housing matching marks are in agreement.
11. Install the camshaft drive pulley plate.
12. Install the cam belt cover.
13. Install the crankshaft pulley and bolts.
14. Tighten the crankshaft bolts to 58–72 ft. lbs. and complete any remaining assembly procedures as required.

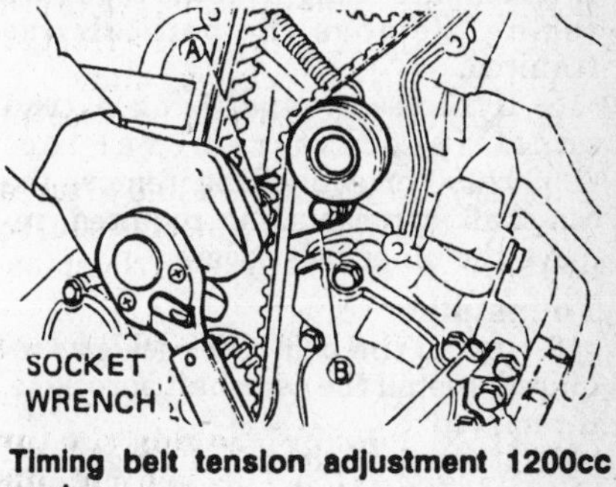


**Timing belt tension adjustment 1200cc engine**

*XT Coupe*

**1800cc OHC ENGINE**

**NOTE: During the service procedure, the vehicle will have to lifted, either with a floor type jack or other safe means. Support the vehicle properly with safety stands before working underneath. Follow all safety procedures.**

1. Disconnect the negative battery cable.
2. Raise the vehicle and support safely. Remove the underpans
3. Remove the bolts from the underside of the radiator fan shroud
4. Lower the vehicle and remove the fan shroud bolts and the shroud. Disconnect the fan motor connector.
5. Remove the alternator and the drive belt. Remove the dipstick tube and dipstick. Disconnect the oil pressure gauge harness.
6. Remove the water pump pulley and the air intake boot.
7. Attach a stopper tool to the flywheel or torque converter to prevent it from turning. With the crankshaft stationary, remove the crank pulley.
8. Remove the front left hand, right hand and center belt covers, in that order..
9. To remove the right belt, loosen tensioner No. 1 (right) mounting bolts on the No. 1 cylinder side. With the tensioner in the fully slackened position, tighten the mounting bolts.
10. Mark the belt in the direction of rotation and front and rear indicator, if it is to be reused. Remove the right timing belt.
11. Loosen tensioner No. 2 (left) mounting bolts on the No. 2 cylinder side. With the tensioner in the fully slackened position, tighten the mounting bolts.
12. Remove the right crankshaft sprocket (front). Mark the direction of rotation and front and rear indicator on the belt, if it is to be reused and remove the left timing belt.
13. If necessary, remove the left crankshaft sprocket (rear without dowel pin).
14. If necessary, remove the tensioner assemblies along with the tensioner spring. Remove the belt idler as required.
15. If necessary and using a camshaft sprocket removal tool 499207000 or equivalent, remove the camshaft sprockets. As required, remove the inner belt covers.

**To install:**

16. Install the belt cover seals as required. Install the camshaft sprockets, if removed.
17. If removed, install the right tensioner and attach the tensioner spring to the tensioner and position it to the right side cylinder block. Hand tighten the bolts. Attach the spring to the assembly and tighten the top bolt. Loosen it ½ turn. Push down on the tensioner until it stops, hand tighten the lower bolt.
18. To install the left tensioner, if removed, attach the tensioner spring to the tensioner and position it to the left side cylinder block. Hand tighten the bolts. Attach the spring to the assembly and tighten the top bolt. Loosen it ½ turn. Raise the tensioner until it stops, hand tighten the lower bolt.
19. Install the belt idler to the cylinder block. Install the crankshaft sprockets. Temporarily install the crankshaft pulley.
20. To install the left timing belt, align the center of the 3 lines on the flywheel with the timing mark on the flywheel housing.
21. Align the timing mark on the camshaft sprocket with the notch in the belt cover.
22. Install the timing belt to the crankshaft sprocket (No. 2), the oil pump sprocket, belt idler pulley and the camshaft sprocket, in that order to prevent downward slackening of the belt.

**NOTE: The No. 2 crankshaft sprocket is identified as the sprocket without a dowel pin.**

23. Loosen the tensioner and ensure smooth movement for belt tension adjustment.
24. Using belt tension wrench tool 499437000 of equivalent, apply 33–55 lbs. of tension to the left camshaft sprocket in the counterclockwise direction.
25. While applying torque, tighten the lower tensioner retaining bolt 12–14 ft. lbs. Tighten the upper tensioner retaining bolt 12–14 ft. lbs. Be sure the timing marks remain in alignment.
26. To install the right belt, rotate the crankshaft one full turn clockwise from the position where the left timing belt was installed. Align the center of the 3 lines on the flywheel with the timing mark on the flywheel housing.
27. Align the timing mark on the camshaft sprocket with the notch in the belt cover. Install the right timing belt over the crankshaft sprocket (with dowel pin) and camshaft sprocket.

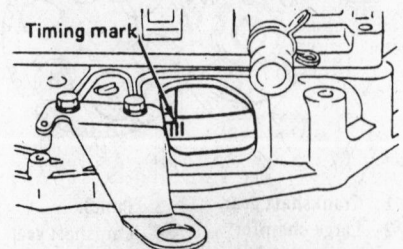


Flywheel timing mark alignment 1800cc (OHC) engine

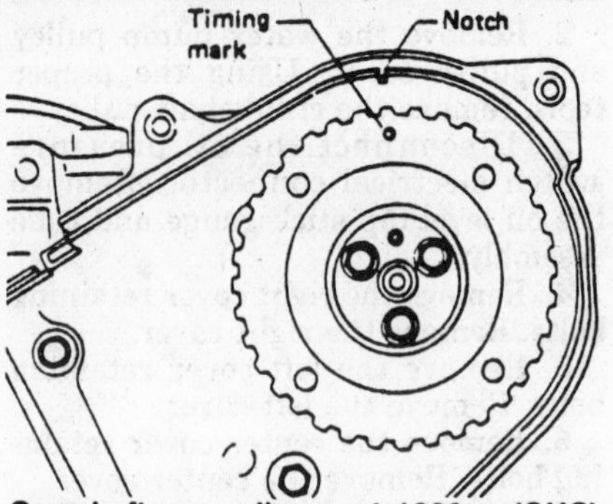


Camshaft gear alignment 1800cc (OHC) engine

28. Using belt tension wrench tool 499437000or equivalent, apply 33–55 lbs. of tension to the right camshaft sprocket in the counterclockwise direction. While applying torque, tighten the lower tensioner retaining bolt 12–14 ft. lbs. Tighten the upper tensioner retaining bolt 12–14 ft. lbs. Be certain the timing marks remain in alignment.
29. Remove the crankshaft pulley and install the necessary seals, if not in place and install the front center cover to the engine block.
30. Install the left and right hand belt covers.
31. Install the crankshaft pulley and while holding the crankshaft stationary, tighten the bolt to 66–79 ft. lbs.
32. Complete the assembly of the water pump pulley, the oil dipstick tube, the alternator drive belt and the radiator shroud. Complete any other Step that is needed to complete this procedure.

**2700cc ENGINE**

1. Disconnect the negative battery cable. Loosen the V-belt tensioner locknut fully counterclockwise.
2. Loosen 2 alternator mounting bolts. Loosen water pump pulley mounting bolts. Remove the water pump pulley.
3. Lock the crankshaft and remove the cranskshaft pulley.
4. Remove the belt covers, right, left and center. To remove the right belt, loosen the tensioner mounting bolts on the No. 1 cylinder. With the tensioner in the fully slackened position, tighten the mounting bolts.
5. Mark the belt in the direction of rotation. Remove the right timing belt.
6. If necessary, remove the right tensioner assembly. Remove the crankshaft sprocket.
7. To remove the left belt, remove the idler pulley. Remove the rubber plug. Remove the plug screw from the belt tension adjuster lowerside.

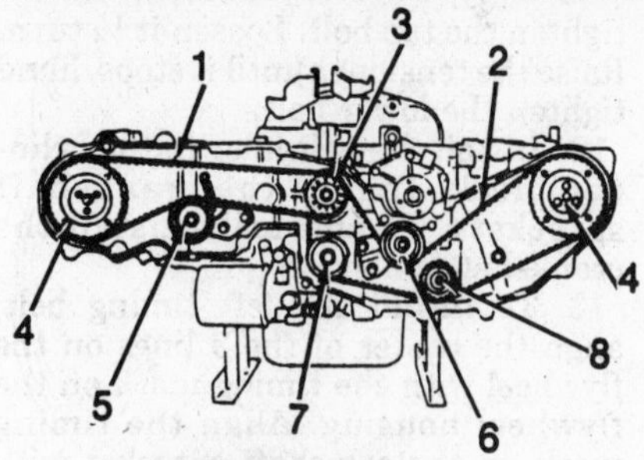


1. Timing belt RH
2. Timing belt LH
3. Crankshaft sprocket
4. Camshaft sprocket
5. Tensioner RH
6. Tensioner LH
7. Oil pump sprocket
8. Idler

**Timing belt configuration 1800cc (OHC) and 2700cc engines**

8. Position a screwdriver type tool into the hole in the bottom of the belt tension adjuster. Turn the screw clockwise to loosen the belt tension.

9. Install belt adjuster stopper tool 13082AA000. Remove the left belt tensioner assembly.

10. Mark the belt in the direction of rotation. Remove the left timing belt.

11. If necessary, remove the crankshaft sprocket and the idler pulley. Remove the belt tensioner assembly. Reinstall the plug screw in its mounting.

12. As required, remove the inner belt covers. As required, check the belt tensioners and replace as necessary.

**To install:**

13. Align the center of the 3 lines on the flywheel with the timing mark on the flywheel housing. Install the camshaft sprockets, if removed and align the timing mark on the camshaft sprocket with the notch in the belt cover.

14. Install the hydraulic belt tensioner assembly. Remove the plug screw from the tensioner lower side. Install a screwdriver into the hole in the bottom of the tensioner and turn the screw clockwise to compress the rubber boot. Install the belt adjuster stopper tool.

**NOTE: The clip furnished as a spare part can be used in place of the belt adjuster stopper tool.**

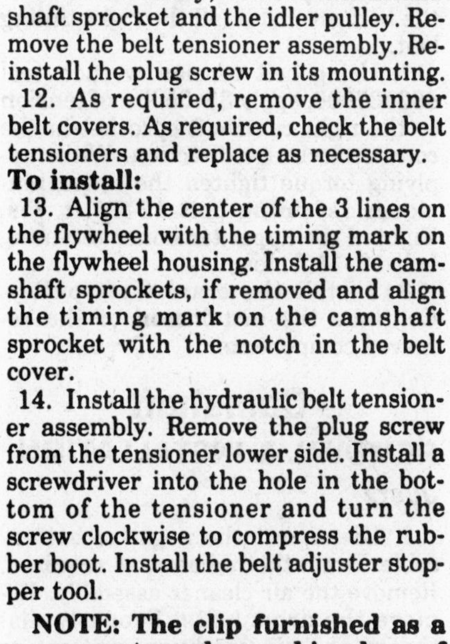

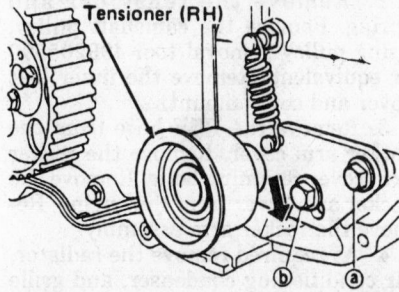


**Timing belt tension adjustment 2700cc engine**

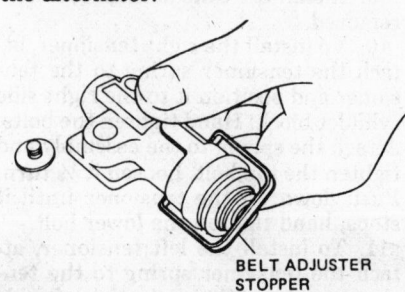

15. Using a syringe type tool, add oil through the air vent hole on top of the rubber boot of the belt tensioner. Install the belt tensioner (17–20 ft. lbs.) and install the rubber plug. Install the idler pulley (29–35 ft. lbs.).

16. Install the crankshaft sprocket No. 2, which is identified by the absence of a dowel pin, onto the crankshaft. Be sure all marks are in alignment and install the timing belt from the crankshaft side. Be careful not to loosen the belt.

17. Install the left tensioner and be sure its movement is correct. Tighten to 29–35 ft. lbs.

18. Check for proper operation. Remove the belt adjuster stopper tool. Be sure that the end of the left tensioner arm contacts the top of the belt tensioner adjuster.

19. To install the right belt, rotate the crankshaft 1 turn clockwise from the position where the left timing belt was installed. Align the center of the 3 lines on the flywheel with the timing mark on the flywheel housing.

20. Align the timing mark on the camshaft sprocket with the notch in the belt cover. Temporarily tighten the tensioner bolts while moving the right tensioner downward. Slightly loosen the higher bolt.

21. Install the crankshaft sprocket to the crankshaft. Install the timing belt from the crankshaft side.

22. Loosen the lower right tensioner assembly retaining bolt and apply tension to the belt.

23. Using belt tension wrench tool 499437100 or equivalent, apply 33–55 lbs. of tension to the right camshaft sprocket in the counterclockwise direction. While applying torque tighten the lower tensioner retaining bolt 17–20 ft. lbs. Tighten the upper tensioner retaining bolt 17–20 ft. lbs.

24. Using a belt tension wrench, apply 33–55 lbs of torque to the belt and tighten the idler pulley.

25. Install the crankshaft pulley and tighten to 66–79 ft. lbs. Install the oil dipstick, if removed.

26. Install the water pipe, the water pump pulley, the center, right and left covers, the A/C compressor and install the alternator.

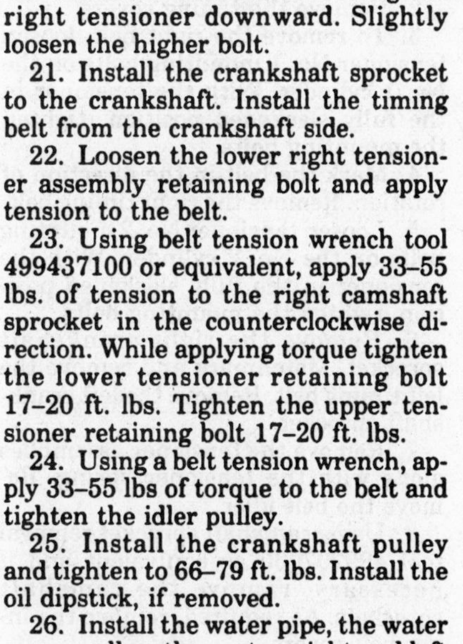


**Installation of belt adjuster stopper clip—2700cc engine**

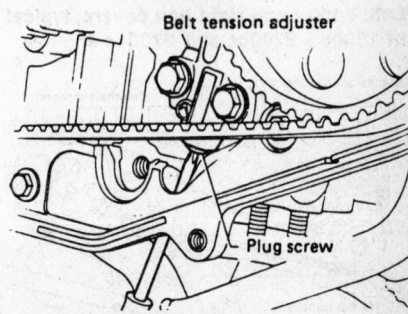

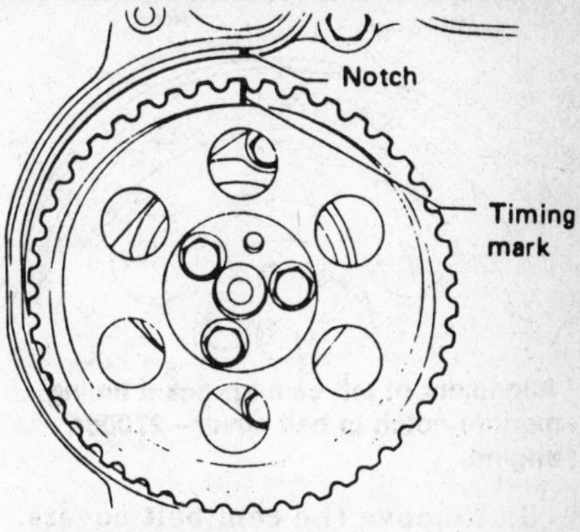


**Camshaft gear alignment 2700cc engine**

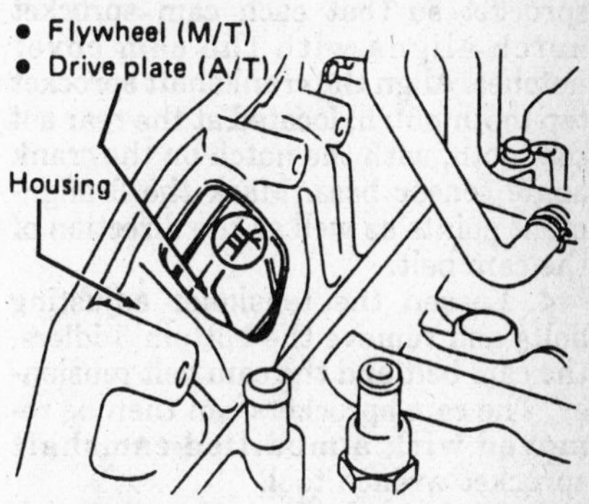


**Flywheel timing mark alignment 2700cc engine**

27. Install the V belt and adjust tension to 143–166 lbs. for a new belt and 99–143 lbs. for a used belt. Lock adjuster bolt by turning counterclockwise. Complete any further installation.

### *Legacy*

#### 2200cc ENGINE

The 2200cc OHC engine uses a single cam belt drive system with a serpentine type belt. The left side of the engine uses a hydraulic cam belt tensioner which is continuously self adjusting.

1. Remove the accessories, alternator and brackets, the power steering pump and the A/C compressor.

2. Remove the crankshaft pulley bolt by using a special crankshaft holding tool.Remove the pulley.

**Removing the plug screw from the belt tension adjuster—2700cc engine**

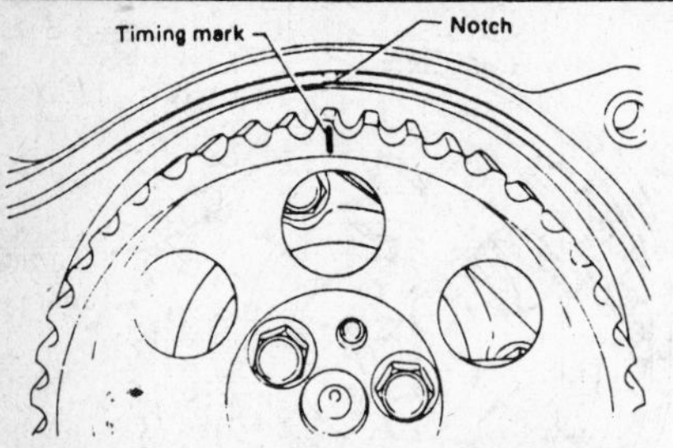


**Alignment of left cam sprocket timing mark to notch in belt cover—2700cc engine**

3. Remove the cam belt covers. Align the crankshaft and camshaft sprocket so that each cam sprocket notch aligns with the cam cover notches. Align the crankshaft sprocket top tooth notch, located at the rear aof the tooth, with the notch on the crank angle sensor boss. Mark the 3 alignment points as well as the direction of the cam belt.

4. Loosen the tensioner adjusting bolts and remove the bottom 3 idlers, the cam belt and the cam belt tensioner. The cam sprockets can then be removed with a modified camshaft sprocket wrench tool.

5. If the sprockets are removed, note the reference sensor at the rear of the left cam sprocket.

**To install:**

6. Install the crankshaft sprocket and all of the idlers except for the lower right. Compress the hydraulic tensioner in a vise slowly and temporarily secure the plunger with a pin. Install the tensioner and the pully.

7. After the cam belt components are installed, align the crankshaft sprocket notch on the rear sprocket tooth with the crank angle sensor boss. This places the sprocket notch in the 12 o'clock position.

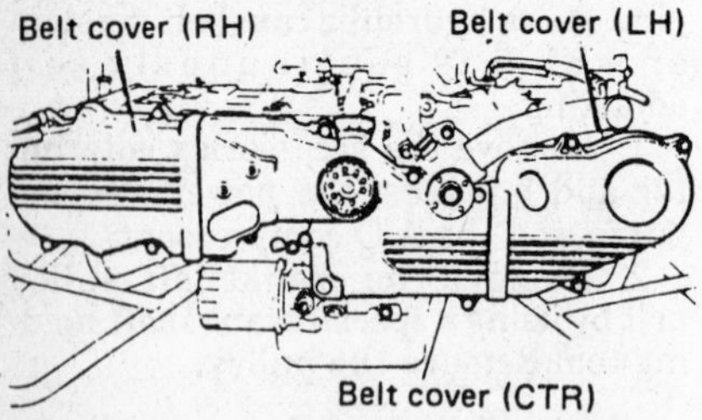


**Left, center and right belt covers, typical of 1800cc, 2200cc and 2700cc engines**

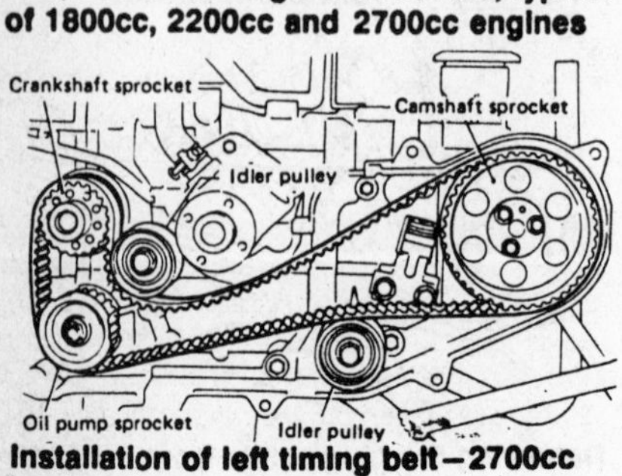


**Installation of left timing belt—2700cc engine**

8. Align the camshaft sprockets with the notches in the cam belt cover. As the directional marked belt is installed, align the marks on the belt with the crankshaft sprocket and the left camshaft sprocket. Install the lower right idler.

9. Load the tensioner by pushing it towards the crankshaft with a prybar and tighten the bolts. Remove the tensioner retention pin and the belt tension is automatically set. Rock the crankshaft back and forth 1 time to distribute the belt tension.

10. Verify the correctness of the timing by noting that the notches on the 2 cam pulleys and the notch on the crankshaft pulley all point to the 12 o'clock position when the belt is properly installed.

11. Complete the engine component assembly by installing the cam belt covers, the crankshaft pulley bolt and pulley and the remaining components.

### *Except Justy, XT Coupe and Legacy*

#### 1800cc OHC ENGINE

1. Disconnect the negative battery cable.

2. Remove the timing covers.

3. To remove the right belt, loosen tensioner No. 1 mounting bolts on the No. 1 cylinder. With the tensioner in the fully slackened position, tighten the mounting bolts.

4. Mark the belt in the direction of rotation. Remove the right timing belt.

5. Loosen tensioner No. 2 mounting bolts on the No. 2 cylinder. With the tensioner in the fully slackened position, tighten the mounting bolts.

6. Remove the right crankshaft sprocket. Matchmark and remove the left timing belt. Remove the left crankshaft sprocket.

7. Remove the tensioner assemblies along with the tensioner spring. Remove the belt idler.

8. Using camshaft sprocket removal tool 499207000 or equivalent and if necessary, remove the camshaft sprockets. As required, remove the inner belt covers.

**To install:**

9. Install the camshaft sprockets, if removed.

10. To install the right tensioner, attach the tensioner spring to the tensioner and position it to the right side cylinder block. Hand tighten the bolts. Attach the spring to the assembly and tighten the top bolt. Loosen it ½ turn. Push down on the tensioner until it stops, hand tighten the lower bolt.

11. To install the left tensioner, attach the tensioner spring to the tensioner and position it to the left side cylinder block. Hand tighten the bolts. Attach the spring to the assembly and tighten the top bolt. Loosen it ½ turn. Raise the tensioner until it stops, hand tighten the lower bolt.

12. Install the belt idler to the cylinder block. Install the crankshaft sprockets. Temporarily install the crankshaft pulley.

13. To install the left timing belt, align the center of the 3 lines on the flywheel with the timing mark on the flywheel housing. Align the timing mark on the camshaft sprocket with the notch in the belt cover. Install the timing belt to the No. 2 crankshaft gear (without dowel pin), oil pump gear and the belt idler, in that order.

14. Using belt tension wrench tool 499437000 or equivalent, apply 33–55 lbs. of tension to the left camshaft sprocket in the counterclockwise direction. While applying torque, tighten the lower tensioner retaining bolt 12–14 ft. lbs. Tighten the upper tensioner retaining bolt 12–14 ft. lbs.

15. To install the right belt, rotate the crankshaft 1 turn clockwise from the position where the left timing belt was installed. Align the center of the 3 lines on the flywheel with the timing mark on the flywheel housing.

16. Align the timing mark on the camshaft sprocket with the notch in the belt cover. Install the right timing belt.

17. Using belt tension wrench tool 499437000, apply 33–55 lbs. of tension to the right camshaft sprocket in the counterclockwise direction. While applying torque tighten the lower tensioner retaining bolt 12–14 ft. lbs. Tighten the upper tensioner retaining bolt 12–14 ft. lbs.

18. Install the crankshaft pulley. Continue the installation of the removed components.

## Camshaft

### REMOVAL & INSTALLATION

#### *Justy*

1. Disconnect the negative battery cable. Drain the radiator, as required. Remove the air cleaner assembly. Remove the drive belts. Properly discharge the air condition system, as required.

2. Remove the tensioner and spring. Remove the camshaft pulley, using pulley removal tool 499205500 or equivalent. Remove the inner belt cover and cover mount.

3. Remove the PCV hose from the rocker arm cover. Remove the rocker arm cover retaining bolts. Remove the rocker arm cover from the engine. Remove the rocker arm assembly.

4. As required remove the radiator, air conditioning condenser, and grille work in order to remove the camshaft from the cylinder head.

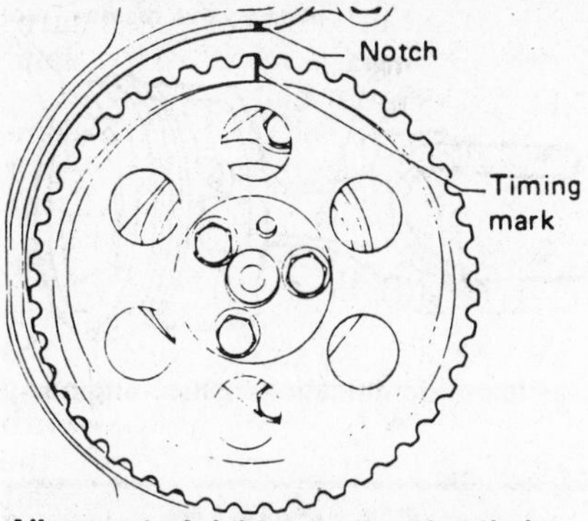


Alignment of right cam sprocket timing mark to notch in belt cover—2700cc engine

5. Carefully withdraw the camshaft from the cylinder head.
6. Installation is the reverse of the removal procedure. Before installing the camshaft be sure to coat it with clean engine oil.
7. Be sure to use new gaskets or RTV sealant, as required. Adjust the valves to specification, as required.

### *XT Coupe*

#### 1800cc ENGINE

1. Disconnect the negative battery cable. Drain the cooling system.
2. Remove the timing covers. Matchmark and remove the timing belt.
3. Remove the distributor. Remove the water pipe assembly.
4. Remove the valve cover retaining bolts. Remove the valve covers.
5. Remove the camshaft case, camshaft support and camshaft assembly as a complete unit. When removing the camshaft case, the valve rockers may come off their mounting.
6. As required, remove the lash adjusters from the cylinder head. Be sure to keep the adjusters and the rockers in the proper order for reinstallation.
7. Remove the camshaft support from the camshaft case. Carefully remove the camshaft from its mounting.
8. Installation is the reverse of the removal procedure. Be sure to coat the camshaft assembly with clean engine oil prior to installation.
9. When installing the camshaft case to the cylinder head, use sealing compound 1207B or equivalent. Torque the retaining bolts 17–20 ft. lbs.
10. Adjust the valves, as required. Be sure to use new gaskets or RTV sealant, as required.

#### 2700cc ENGINE

1. Disconnect the negative battery cable. Drain the cooling system.
2. Remove the timing covers. Matchmark and remove the timing belt.
3. Remove the distributor. Remove the water pipe assembly.
4. Remove the valve cover retaining bolts. Remove the valve covers.
5. Remove the camshaft case, camshaft support and camshaft assembly as a complete unit. When removing the camshaft case the valve rockers may come off their mounting.
6. As required, remove the lash adjusters from the cylinder head. Be sure to keep the adjusters and the rockers in the proper order for reinstallation.
7. Remove the camshaft support from the camshaft case. Carefully remove the camshaft from its mounting.
8. Installation is the reverse of the removal procedure. Be sure to coat the camshaft assembly with clean engine oil prior to installation.

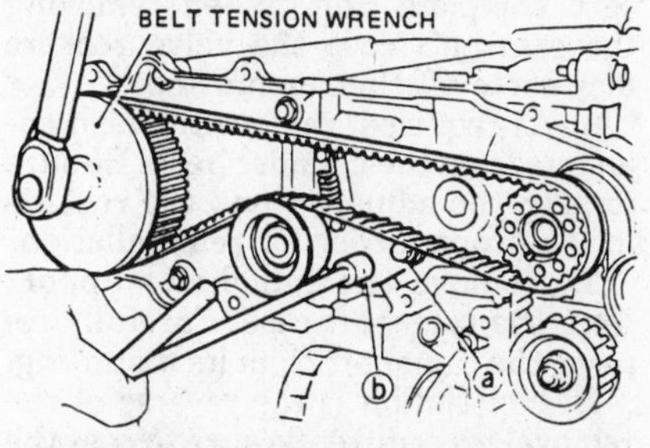


Adjustment of right timing belt tension with belt tension wrench—2700cc engine

9. When installing the camshaft case to the cylinder head using sealing compound 1207B or equivalent. Torque the retaining bolts 17–20 ft. lbs.
10. Adjust the valves, as required. Be sure to use new gaskets or RTV sealant, as required.

### *Legacy*

#### 2200cc ENGINE

**NOTE: It is assumed that engine has been removed from the vehicle.**

1. Remove the timing belt covers, the timing belt, camshaft sprockets

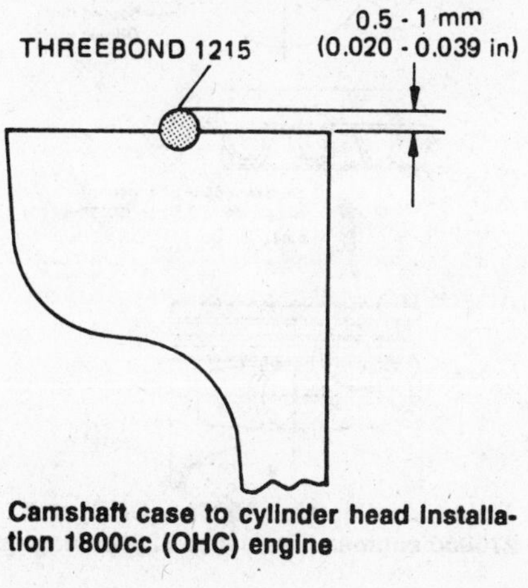


Camshaft case to cylinder head installation 1800cc (OHC) engine

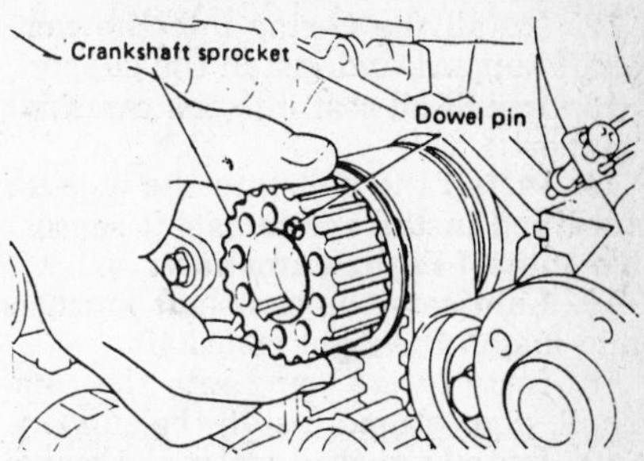


Installation of No. 1 (outer) crankshaft sprocket with dowel pin—2700cc engine

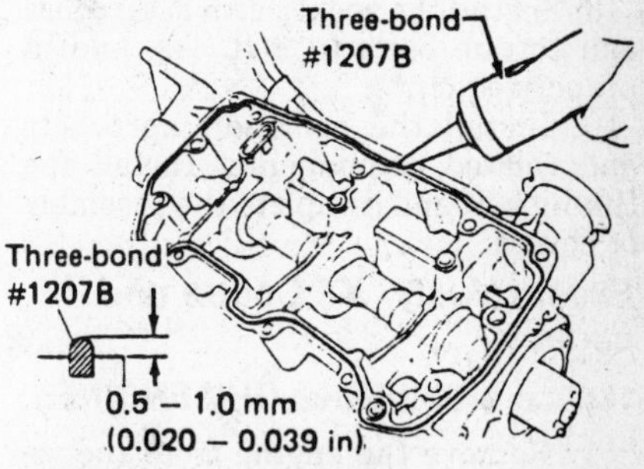


Camshaft case to cylinder head installation 2700cc engine

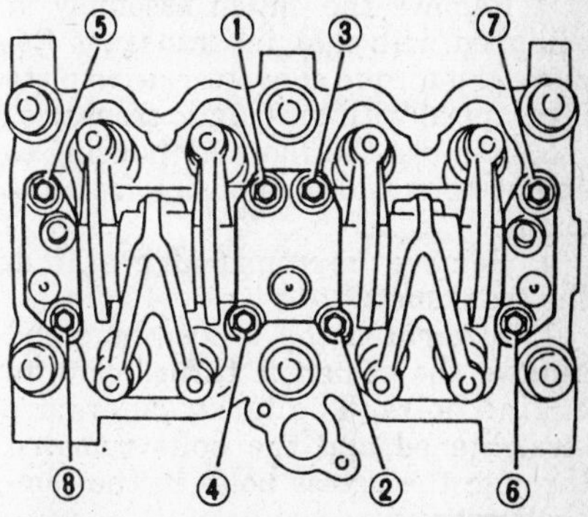


Rocker arm assembly bolt REMOVAL sequence—2200cc engine

and other components necessary to expose the camshaft.
2. Remove the valve covers. Remove the rocker arm assembly bolts in sequence.

**Left Camshaft:**

3. Remove the cam angle sensor.
4. Remove the oil dipstick tube attaching bolt.
5. Remove the camshaft support on the left side.
6. Remove the O-ring.
7. Remove the camshaft and seal(rear) from the left side.

**Right Camshaft:**

8. Remove the camshaft support on the right side.
9. Remove the O-ring.
10. Remove the camshaft and seal(rear) from the right side. Remove the oil seal from the camshaft support.

**To install left camshaft:**

11. Lubricate the camshaft journals, install the oil seal (rear) and install the camshaft into the cylinder head.

12. Install the O-ring into the camshaft support and install the support.
13. Install oil seal into the camshaft support.
14. Install the bolt into the dipstick tube and install the camshaft sensor.

**To install right camshaft:**

15. Lubricate the camshaft journals and install the right camshaft.
16. Install the O-ring into the camshaft support and install the support.
17. Install a new oil seal in the rear of the cylinder head.

**To complete assembly:**

18. Install the rocker arm assemblies and torque bolts to 9 ft. lbs. and in proper sequence.
19. Install the camshaft sprockets and related components. Install the timing belt and complete the assembly of covers.

### *Except Justy, XT Coupe and Legacy*

#### 1600cc AND 1800cc OHV ENGINES

1. Remove the engine from the vehicle. Position the assembly in a suitable holding fixture.
2. Remove the clutch assembly, if equipped with manual transaxle. Remove the torque converter drive plate if equipped with automatic transaxle.
3. Remove the flywheel housing to engine bolts and the housing from the engine.
4. Remove the crankshaft gear from the crankshaft.
5. Straighten the lockwashers and remove the camshaft thrust plate to engine bolts. The lockwashers are straightened and the bolts removed through the access holes in the camshaft gear.
6. Remove the rocker arm to cylinder head covers, the rocker arm to cylinder head assemblies, the push rods and valve lifters. When removing these components, be sure to keep them in order for reassembly.
7. Pull the camshaft toward the rear of the engine and remove it from the engine. Be careful not to damage the bearing journals or the camshaft lobes.

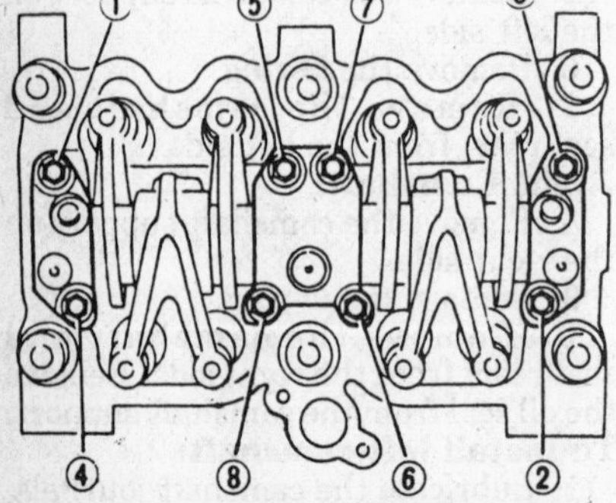


**Rocker arm assembly bolt INSTALLATION and torque sequence—2200cc engine**

8. Remove the oil seal and replace it with a new seal. Inspect the camshaft for wear and damage, if necessary replace it.
9. Installation is the reverse of the removal procedure. Be sure to use new gaskets or RTV sealant, as required.

#### 1800cc OHC ENGINE

1. Disconnect the negative battery cable. Drain the cooling system.
2. Remove the timing covers. Matchmark and remove the timing belt.
3. Remove the distributor. Remove the water pipe assembly.
4. Remove the valve cover retaining bolts. Remove the valve covers.
5. Remove the camshaft case, camshaft support and camshaft assembly as a complete unit. When removing the camshaft case the valve rockers may come off their mounting.
6. As required, remove the lash adjusters from the cylinder head. Be sure to keep the adjusters and the rockers in the proper order for reinstallation.
7. Remove the camshaft support from the camshaft case. Carefully remove the camshaft from its mounting.
8. Installation is the reverse of the removal procedure. Be sure to coat the camshaft assembly with clean engine oil prior to installation.
9. When installing the camshaft case to the cylinder head using sealing compound 1207B or equivalent. Torque the retaining bolts 17–20 ft. lbs.
10. Adjust the valves, as required. Be sure to use new gaskets or RTV sealant, as required.

## Piston and Connecting Rod

### POSITIONING

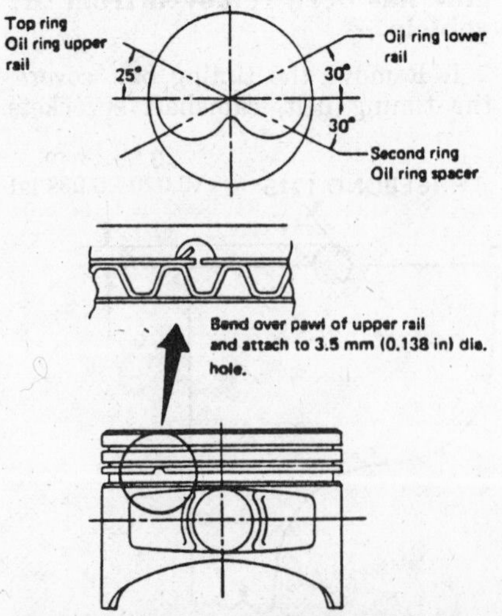


**Piston identification 1800cc (OHC) and 2700cc engines. Typical of 2200cc engine**

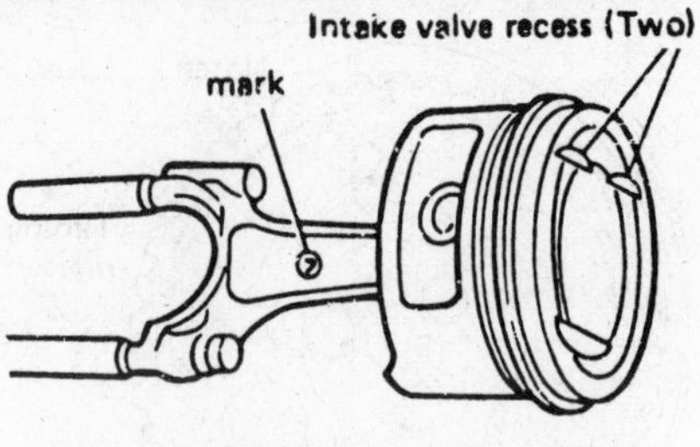


**Piston identification 1200cc engine**

# ENGINE LUBRICATION

## Oil Pan

### REMOVAL & INSTALLATION

### *Justy*

#### 1200cc ENGINE

1. Disconnect the negative battery cable. Drain the engine oil.
2. Raise and support the vehicle safely.
3. Remove the required components in order to gain access to the oil pan retaining bolts. Remove the flywheel housing assembly.
4. Remove the oil pan retaining bolts. Remove the oil pan from the engine. It may be necessary to position the engine so that the crankshaft lobes do not interfere with oil pan removal.
5. Installation is the reverse of the removal procedure. Be sure to use new gaskets or RTV sealant, as required.

### *XT Coupe*

#### 1800cc AND 2700cc ENGINES

1. Disconnect the negative battery cable. Drain the engine oil.
2. Raise and support the vehicle safely.
3. Remove the required components in order to gain access to the oil pan retaining bolts.
4. Remove the oil pan retaining bolts. Remove the oil pan from the engine.
5. Installation is the reverse of the removal procedure. Be sure to use new gaskets or RTV sealant, as required.

### *Except Justy and XT Coupe*

#### 1600cc AND 1800cc OHV ENGINES

1. Disconnect the negative battery cable. Drain the engine oil.
2. Raise and support the vehicle safely.
3. Remove the required components in order to gain access to the oil pan retaining bolts.
4. Remove the oil pan retaining bolts. Remove the oil pan from the engine.

5. Installation is the reverse of the removal procedure. Be sure to use new gaskets or RTV sealant, as required.

### 1800cc AND 2200cc OHC ENGINES

1. Disconnect the negative battery cable. Drain the engine oil.
2. Raise and support the vehicle safely.
3. Remove the required components in order to gain access to the oil pan retaining bolts.
4. Remove the oil pan retaining bolts. Remove the oil pan from the engine.
5. Installation is the reverse of the removal procedure. Be sure to use new gaskets or RTV sealant, as required.

## Rear Main Bearing Oil Seal

### REMOVAL & INSTALLATION

#### *Justy*

#### 1200cc ENGINE

1. Remove the engine from the vehicle and position it in a suitable holding fixture.
2. Remove the clutch assembly and the flywheel from the crankshaft.
3. Using a small pry bar, pry the rear oil seal from the crankcase. Be careful not to damage the crankshaft or the crankcase housing.
4. To install, use a new oil seal, lubricate the seal with engine oil.
5. Using the crankshaft rear oil seal guide tool 498725600 or equivalent, and the rear oil seal press tool 498725500 or equivalent, drive the new oil seal into the housing until it seats.
6. To complete the installation, reverse the removal procedures.

#### *XT Coupe*

#### 1800cc AND 2700cc ENGINES

1. Remove the engine from the vehicle. Position the engine in a suitable holding fixture.
2. Using clutch disc guide tool 499747000 or equivalent, remove the clutch assembly on manual transaxle equipped vehicles.
3. If equipped with automatic transaxle, remove the torque converter drive plate from the crankshaft.
4. Using a small pry bar, pry the oil seal from the crankcase. Be careful not to damage the crankshaft or the crankcase housing.
5. Using a new rear oil seal, coat the seal lips with grease and the housing with engine oil.
6. Using rear oil seal installation tool 499587000 or equivalent, drive the new oil seal into the crankcase until it seats.
7. To complete the installation, reverse the removal procecdures

#### *Except Justy and XT Coupe*

#### 1600cc AND 1800cc OHV ENGINES

The rear main oil seal is located in the flywheel housing (timing gear cover). The flywheel housing covers the timing gears and acts as the timing gear cover. In order to remove it, the engine must be removed from the vehicle. The oil seal is pressed into the housing.

1. Remove the engine from the vehicle. Position it in a suitable holding fixture. Separate the engine from the transaxle assembly.
2. Using the clutch disc guide tool 499747000 or equivalent, remove the clutch assembly, if equipped with manual transaxle. If equipped with automatic transaxle, remove the torque converter drive plate from the crankshaft.
3. Remove the flywheel housing from the engine. Using a small pry bar, pry the oil seal from the housing.
4. To install, use a new oil seal and press it into the flywheel housing. When installing the oil seal onto the crankshaft, be careful that it doesn't become torn.
5. Continue the installation in the reverse order of the removal procedure.

#### 1800cc AND 2200cc OHC ENGINES

1. Remove the engine/transmission from the vehicle. Position the engine in a suitable holding fixture.
2. Using clutch disc guide tool 499747000 or equivalent, remove the clutch assembly on manual transaxle equipped vehicles.
3. If equipped with automatic transaxle, remove the torque converter drive plate from the crankshaft.
4. Using a small pry bar, pry the oil seal from the crankcase. Be careful not to damage the crankshaft or the crankcase housing.
5. Using a new rear oil seal, coat the seal lips with grease and the housing with engine oil.
6. Using rear oil seal installation tool 499587000 or equivalent, drive the new oil seal into the crankcase until it seats.
7. To complete the installation, reverse the removal proceedures

## Oil Pump

### REMOVAL & INSTALLATION

#### *Justy*

#### 1200cc ENGINE

1. Disconnect the negative battery cable. Drain the engine oil. Drain the cooling system.

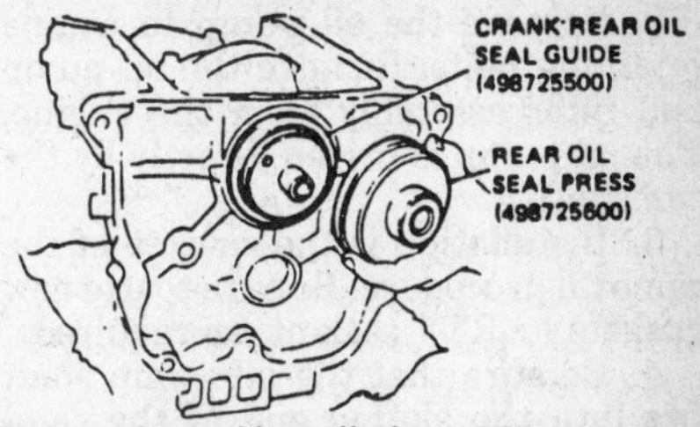

**Rear main seal installation 1200cc engine**

2. Remove the oil dipstick, dipstick giude and guide sealing.
3. Remove the alternator. Remove the timing belt.
4. Raise and support the vehicle safely. Remove the oil pan. Lower the vehicle.
5. Remove the water pump cover. Remove the water pump impeller. When removing the impeller, lock the balance shaft using the proper tool.
6. Remove the crankcase cover retaining bolts. Remove the crankcase cover along with the oil pump assembly.
7. Installation is the reverse of the removal procedure. Be sure to use new gaskets or RTV sealant, as required.

#### *XT Coupe*

#### 1800cc AND 2700cc ENGINES

1. Disconnect the negative battery cable. Drain the engine oil.
2. Remove the timing belts. Before removing the camshaft drive belts, loosen the oil pump pulley mounting nut.
3. Remove the oil pump retaining bolts. Remove the oil pump along with the oil filter.
4. Remove the oil pump outer rotor from the cylinder block. Remove the oil filter from the oil pump.
5. Installation is the reverse of the removal procedure.

#### *Except Justy and XT Coupe*

#### 1600cc AND 1800cc OHV ENGINES WITHOUT TURBOCHARGER

1. Disconnect the negative battery cable. Drain the engine oil.

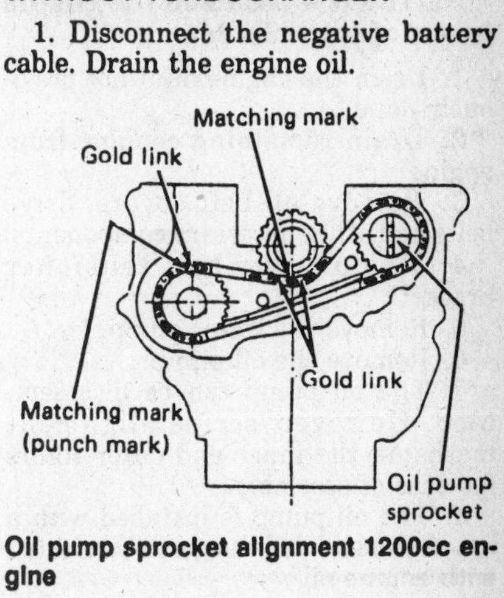

**Oil pump sprocket alignment 1200cc engine**

2. Remove the oil pump to engine retaining bolts. Remove the oil pump and filter assembly from the engine. The oil pump is driven directly by the camshaft.

3. Installation is the reverse of the removal procedure. Be sure to use new gaskets or RTV sealant, as required.

4. Be sure that the oil pump shaft fits into the slotted end of the camshaft and that the mating surfaces are flush.

#### 1800cc OHV ENGINE WITH TURBOCHARGER

1. Disconnect the negative battery cable. Drain the engine oil. Remove the oil filter from its mounting.

2. Remove the 3 bolts which fasten the 2 oil cooler lines and the turbocharger supply line of the attachment. Remove the oil cooler pipes brace to engine bolt.

3. Using 1 hand to support the attachment, unscrew the connector which retains it to the other. Gently pull the attachment free of the O-rings which seal it.

4. Remove the oil pump to engine bolts and the pump from the vehicle.

5. Installation is the reverse of the removal procedure. Be sure to use new gaskets or RTV sealant, as required.

#### 1800cc OHC ENGINE

1. Disconnect the negative battery cable. Drain the engine oil.

2. Remove the timing belts. Before removing the camshaft drive belts, loosen the oil pump pulley mounting nut.

3. Remove the oil pump retaining bolts. Remove the oil pump along with the oil filter.

4. Remove the oil pump outer rotor from the cylinder block. Remove the oil filter from the oil pump.

5. Installation is the reverse of the removal procedure.

#### 2200cc ENGINE

**NOTE: It is assumed the engine is out of the vehicle.**

1. Drain the engine oil if not previously done.

2. Drain remaining coolant from engine.

3. Remove all belt covers, drive belts and other necessary components.

4. Remove the belt tensioner bracket.

5. Remove the water pump.

6. Remove the oil pump.

7. The oil pump can be disassembled. However, scribe alignment marks on the inner and outer rotors for ease of assembly.

8. The oil pump is installed with a new front seal and the gears lubricated with engine oil.

9. Use new O-ring and gaskets where necessary. Complete the assembly.

# ENGINE COOLING

## Radiator

### REMOVAL & INSTALLATION

#### *Justy*

1. Disconnect the negative battery cable. Drain the cooling system.

2. Disconnect the radiator fan electrical connection. Remove the upper and lower radiator hoses.

3. Remove the radiator mounting bolts. Remove the radiator from the vehicle.

4. Installation is the reverse of the removal procedure.

#### *XT Coupe*

#### 1800cc AND 2700cc ENGINE

1. Disconnect the negative battery cable. Drain the cooling system.

2. Remove the radiator hoses. Disconnect and plug the automatic transaxle lines, if equipped.

3. Disconnect the main wire harness at the thermoswitch. Disconnect the fan electrical connection.

4. Disconnect the electrical wire from the secondary fan motor. Remove the upper and lower bolts retaining the shrouds to the radiator assembly.

5. Remove the shroud assembly along with the fan motor.

6. Remove the radiator mounting bolts. Remove the radiator from the vehicle.

7. Installation is the reverse of the removal procedure.

#### *Legacy*

#### 2200cc ENGINE

1. Disconnect the battery cables and remove the battery from the vehicle.

2. Drain the engine coolant and disconnect the radiator hoses at the engine.

3. Remove the V-belt cover.

4. Remove the reservoir overflow tank and hose.

5. Disconnect the radiator and A/C fan electrical wiring connectors.

6. Remove the radiator brackets at the top radiator support panel. Move the radiator sightly to the left.

7. Disconnect the AT cosoler lines from the radiator. Allow the fluid to drain into a container.

8. Lift ther radiator/fan assemblies up and out of the vehicle.

**To install:**

9. Attach radiator mounting cushions to the pins on the lower side of the radiator.

10. Fit the cushions on the lower side of the radiator, into holes on the body side and install the radiator with inlet and outlet hoses attached.

11. Install the radiator brackets and tighten the attaching bolts.

12. Connect the electrical wiring, the inlet and outlet hoses, install the reservoirtank and overflow hose.

13. Install the V-belt and tighten. Install the bvattery and connect the cables.

14. Remove the air vent plug on the radiator. Install the coolant into the radiator.

15. Operate the engine and correct the coolant level as required. Open the air vent plug as required to remove air from system.

**CAUTION**

***Allow engine/coolant to cool before opening pressure cap or removing air vent plug. Excessive coolant temperature can cause personal injury should coolant blow-off occur.***

#### *Except Justy, XT Coupe and Legacy*

#### 1600cc AND 1800cc OHV ENGINES

1. Disconnect the negative battery cable. Drain the cooling system.

2. Remove the radiator hoses. Disconnect and plug the automatic transaxle lines, if equipped.

3. Disconnect the main wire harness at the thermoswitch. Disconnect the fan electrical connection.

4. Disconnect the electrical wire from the secondary fan motor. Remove the upper and lower bolts retaining the shrouds to the radiator assembly.

5. Remove the shroud assembly along with the fan motor.

6. Remove the radiator mounting bolts. Remove the radiator from the vehicle.

7. Installation is the reverse of the removal procedure.

#### 1800cc OHC ENGINE

1. Disconnect the negative battery cable. Drain the cooling system.

2. Remove the radiator hoses. Disconnect and plug the automatic transaxle lines, if equipped.

3. Disconnect the main wire harness at the thermoswitch. Disconnect the fan electrical connection.

4. Disconnect the electrical wire from the secondary fan motor. Remove the upper and lower bolts retaining the shrouds to the radiator assembly.

5. Remove the shroud assembly along with the fan motor.
6. Remove the radiator mounting bolts. Remove the radiator from the vehicle.
7. Installation is the reverse of the removal procedure.

## Water Pump

### REMOVAL & INSTALLATION

#### *Justy*

1. Disconnect the negative battery cable. Drain the engine oil. Drain the cooling system.
2. Remove the oil dipstick, dipstick giude and guide sealing.
3. Remove the alternator. Remove the timing belt.
4. Raise and support the vehicle safely. Remove the oil pan. Lower the vehicle.
5. Remove the water pump cover. Remove the water pump impeller. When removing the impeller, lock the balance shaft using the proper tool.
6. Remove the crankcase cover retaining bolts. Remove the crankcase cover along with the remaining water pump assembly.
7. Installation is the reverse of the removal procedure. Be sure to use new gaskets or RTV sealant, as required.

#### *XT Coupe*

##### 1800cc ENGINE

1. Disconnect the negative battery cable. Drain the cooling system.
2. Disconnect the radiator hose and bypass hose from the water pump.
3. Loosen the pulley nuts. Loosen the alternator mounting bolts. Remove the drive belt.
4. Remove the timing belt cover. Remove the water pump retaining bolts. Remove the water pump from the engine.
5. Installation is the reverse of the removal procedure. Be sure to use a new gasket or RTV sealant, as required.

##### 2700cc ENGINE

1. Disconnect the negative battery cable. Drain the cooling system.
2. Disconnect the radiator hose, bypass hose and air vent hose from the water pump.
3. Loosen the pulley nuts. Loosen the belt tensioner pulley locking nut. Remove the drive belt.
4. Remove the timing belt cover. Remove the water pump retaining bolts. Remove the water pump from the engine.
5. Installation is the reverse of the removal procedure. Be sure to use a new gasket or RTV sealant, as required.

#### *Legacy*

##### 2200cc ENGINE

1. Disconnect the negative cable from the battery.
2. Drain the cooling system.
3. Disconnect the lower radiator hose.
4. Disconnect the electrical connectors and remove the radiator fan motor assembly.
5. Remove the V-belts as necessary.
6. Remove the timing belt covers and the timing belt.
7. Remove the tensioner adjuster and the cam angle sensor.
8. Remove the left camshaft pulley.
9. Remove the left rear timing belt cover.
10. Remove the tensioner bracket.
11. Disconnect the radiator and heater hoses from the water pump assembly.
12. Remove the water pump assembly.
13. Inspect the water pump and replace as required.
14. After the water pump is in place, complete the assembly of the components in the reverse of their removal.
15. Fill the cooling system and correct the level as required, during and after the warm-up.

**CAUTION**

***Allow engine/coolant to cool before opening pressure cap or removing air vent plug. Excessive coolant temperature can cause personal injury should coolant blow-off occur.***

#### *Except Justy, XT Coupe and Legacy*

##### 1600cc AND 1800cc OHV ENGINES

1. Disconnect the negative battery cable. Drain the cooling system.
2. Loosen the alternator bracket to engine bolts and remove the drive belt. Some vehicles equipped with air conditioning, will have a mechanical fan connected to the water pump.
3. Remove the hoses clamps and the hoses from the water pump.
4. Remove the water pump to engine bolts and remove the pump assembly from the engine.

**NOTE: On the 1800cc engine equipped with a turbocharger, the timing scale plate will come off along with the top left bolts. Note the location of the scale and then remove it with the 2 bolts.**

5. Installation is the reverse of the removal procedure. Be sure to use new gaskets or RTV sealant, as required.

##### 1800cc OHC ENGINE

1. Disconnect the negative battery cable. Drain the cooling system.
2. Disconnect the radiator hose and bypass hose from the water pump.
3. Loosen the pulley nuts. Loosen the alternator mounting bolts. Remove the drive belt.
4. Remove the timing belt cover. Remove the water pump retaining bolts. Remove the water pump from the engine.
5. Installation is the reverse of the removal procedure. Be sure to use a new gasket or RTV sealant, as required.

## Thermostat

### REMOVAL & INSTALLATION

#### *Justy*

1. Disconnect the negative battery cable. Drain the cooling system.
2. Remove the thermostat housing retaining bolts. Remove the thermostat housing and cover assembly.
3. Remove the thermostat from the intake manifold.
4. Installation is the reverse of the removal procedure. Be sure to use a new gasket or RTV sealant, as required.

#### *XT Coupe*

##### 1800cc AND 2700cc ENGINES

1. Disconnect the negative battery cable. Drain the cooling system.
2. Remove the thermostat housing retaining bolts. Remove the thermostat housing and cover assembly.
3. Remove the thermostat from the intake manifold.
4. Installation is the reverse of the removal procedure. Be sure to use a new gasket or RTV sealant, as required.

#### *Legacy*

##### 2200cc ENGINE

**NOTE: The thermostat housing is bolted to the lower front of the water pump assembly. The manufacturer has not published a procedure for thermostat replacement. The thermostat may have to be replace from under the vehicle or the removal of necessary components in order to remove it from the top of the vehicle.**

#### *Except Justy, XT Coupe and Legacy*

##### 1600cc AND 1800cc ENGINES

1. Disconnect the negative battery cable. Drain the cooling system.
2. Remove the thermostat housing retaining bolts. Remove the thermostat housing and cover assembly.
3. Remove the thermostat from the intake manifold.
4. Installation is the reverse of the removal procedure. Be sure to use a new gasket or RTV sealant, as required.

# EMISSION CONTROLS

**Please refer to "Emission Control" in the Unit Repair section for system maintenance procedures. Due to the complex nature of modern electronic engine control systems, comprehensive diagnosis and testing procedures fall outside the confines of this repair manual. For complete information on diagnosis, testing and repair procedures concerning all modern engine and emission control systems, please refer to "Chilton's Guide to Electronic Engine Controls".**

### RESETTING EMISSION MAINTENANCE LAMP

Some 1985–87 vehicles are equipped with an EGR lamp that illuminates when the vehicle attains 60,000 miles (96,000 km). In order to reset the lamp for an other 60,000 mile increment, the following procedure must be done.

1. Remove the lower instrument panel cover, exposing the fuse panel.
2. Directly behind or along side of the fuse panel, a blue two piece connector will be noted. Disconnect the two blue connectors.
3. Along side the blue connectors will be a green connector that is not connected to any other wire.
4. Connect the green connector into the matching blue connector, thus resetting the emission lamp and recycling the system for another 60,000 mile increment.
5. Be sure the indicator lamp is out and re-install the lower instrument panel cover.

# FUEL SYSTEM

## Fuel System Service Precaution

### RELIEVING FUEL SYSTEM PRESSURE

#### *Fuel Injected Vehicles*

1. Disconnect the electrical wiring connector from the fuel pump.
2. Start the engine. Once the engine has stopped, crank the engine for more than 5 seconds. If the engine starts, let the engine run until it stops.
3. Turn the ignition switch **OFF**.
4. Reconnect the electrical wiring connector of the fuel pump.

## Fuel Filter

### REMOVAL & INSTALLATION

#### *Justy*

1. Carefully relieve the fuel pump pressure. As required, raise and support the vehicle safely.
2. Remove the flange bolts and remove the lower fuel pump bracket assembly.
3. Disconnect and plug the fuel lines at the fuel filter.
4. Remove the fuel filter retaining bolts. Remove the fuel filter assembly from its mounting.
5. Installation is the reverse of the removal procedure.

#### *XT Coupe*

1. Properly relieve the fuel system pressure.
2. The fuel filter is located inside the engine compartment on the left fender assembly.
3. Disconnect the fuel lines from the fuel filter.
4. Pull the fuel filter from the bracket and remove it from the vehicle.
5. Installation is the reverse of the removal procedure. Start the engine and check for leaks.

#### *Except Justy, XT Coupe and Legacy*

##### CARBURETED ENGINE

1. Disconnect the negative battery cable.
2. Raise and support the vehicle safely.
3. Disconnect the fuel hoses from the fuel filter.
4. Pull the fuel filter from the bracket and remove it from the vehicle.
5. Installation is the reverse of the removal procedure.

##### FUEL INJECTED ENGINE

1. Properly relieve the fuel system pressure.
2. The fuel filter is located inside the engine compartment on the left fender assembly.
3. Disconnect the fuel lines from the fuel filter.
4. Pull the fuel filter from the bracket and remove it from the vehicle.
5. Installation is the reverse of the removal procedure. Start the engine and check for leaks.

## Electric Fuel Pump

### PRESSURE TESTING

1. Raise and support the vehicle safely.
2. Using a fuel pressure gauge, connect into the fuel line.
3. Turn the ignition switch to the **ON** position. Observe the fuel pressure, it should be:

   2.6–3.3 psi for carburetor equipped vehicles.

   61–71 psi for MPFI equipped vehicles.

   36–50 psi for SPFI equipped vehicles.
4. If the fuel pump does not meet specification, replace it.
5. After testing, disconnect the pressure gauge and reconnect the fuel line.

### REMOVAL & INSTALLATION

#### *Justy*

1. Carefully relieve the fuel pump pressure. As required, raise and support the vehicle safely.
2. Remove the flange bolts and remove the lower fuel pump bracket assembly.
3. Disconnect and plug the fuel lines at the fuel pump assembly. Disconnect the fuel pump electrical connector.
4. Remove the fuel pump assembly retaining bolts. Remove the fuel pump assembly from its mounting.
5. Installation is the reverse of the removal procedure.

#### *XT Coupe*

1. Properly relieve the fuel system pressure.
2. Raise and support the the vehicle safely. Devise a clamp for the thicker hose leading to the pump and clamp it off a few inches from the nipple on the pump. This will prevent the fuel from running out of the tank while the pump is disconnected.
3. Being careful not to bend the hose sharply, loosen the hose clamp and disconnect the large hose leading into the pump. Do the same with the outlet from the damper.
4. Remove the pump bracket to chassis retaining bolts. Remove the fuel pump and pump damper assembly.
5. Installation is the reverse of the removal procedure.

#### *Except Justy, XT Coupe and Legacy*

##### CARBURETED ENGINE

1. Carefully relieve the fuel pump

pressure. As required, raise and support the vehicle safely.

2. Remove the flange bolts and remove the lower fuel pump bracket assembly.

3. Disconnect and plug the fuel lines at the fuel pump assembly. Disconnect the fuel pump electrical connector.

4. Remove the fuel pump assembly retaining bolts. Remove the fuel pump assembly from its mounting.

5. Installation is the reverse of the removal procedure.

### FUEL INJECTED ENGINE

1. Properly relieve the fuel system pressure.

2. Raise and support the the vehicle safely. Devise a clamp for the thicker hose leading to the pump and clamp it off a few inches from the nipple on the pump. This will prevent the fuel from running out of the tank while the pump is disconnected.

3. Being careful not to bend the hose sharply, loosen the hose clamp and disconnect the large hose leading into the pump. Do the same with the outlet from the damper.

4. Remove the pump bracket to chassis retaining bolts. Remove the fuel pump and pump damper assembly.

5. Installation is the reverse of the removal procedure.

## Carburetor

### REMOVAL & INSTALLATION

#### *Justy*

1. Disconnect the negative battery cable. Remove the air cleaner assembly.

2. Disconnect the fuel line. Disconnect the return and vent line hoses.

3. Disconnect the main diaphragm, distributor vacuum line and canister vent hose.

4. Disconnect the idle solenoid valve wires and hoses. Disconnect the harness electrical connector.

5. Disconnect the primary and secondary air bleed hoses. Disconnect the accelerator cable from the throttle lever.

6. Remove the carburetor retaining bolts. remove the carburetor from its mounting. Discard the gasket.

7. Installation is the reverse of the removal procedure. Be sure to use a new base gasket.

#### *Except Justy and XT Coupe*

1. Disconnect the negative battery cable. Remove the air cleaner assembly.

2. Disconnect the fuel line. Disconnect the return and vent line hoses.

3. Disconnect the carburetor vent hose for the ECC system. Disconnect the remaining required vacuum hoses.

4. Disconnect the EGR tube, if equipped. Disconnect the distributor vacccum hose.

5. If equipped with an Hitachi carburetor, disconnect the ignition retard, if applicable. Disconnect the vacuum hoses from the solenoid valves, the main diaphragm on high altitude carburetors and the secondary main air bleed. Disconnect the duty solenoid valve connector, if equipped.

6. Disconnect the electrical harness connectors and the accelerator cable from the throttle lever.

7. Drain the radiator, to a level below the water heated throttle bore.

8. Remove the carburetor to intake manifold nuts. Remove the carburetor from the vehicle.

9. If the vehicle is equipped with a Carter Weber carburetor, disconnect the vent hose and remove the connector with the spacer and gasket.

10. Installation is the reverse of the removal procedure.

### PRIMARY/SECONDARY THROTTLE LINKAGE ADJUSTMENT

#### *Hitachi Carburetor*

1. With the carburetor removed from the engine, operate the linkage so that the connecting rod contacts the groove on the end of the secondary actuating lever.

2. Measure the clearance between the lower end of the primary throttle valve and it's bore. It should be:

1983-84 – 0.24 in..
1985-90 except Justy – 0.27 in.
1987-90 Justy – 0.26 in.

3. Adjust the clearance by bending the connecting rod.

4. Check that the linkage operates smoothly.

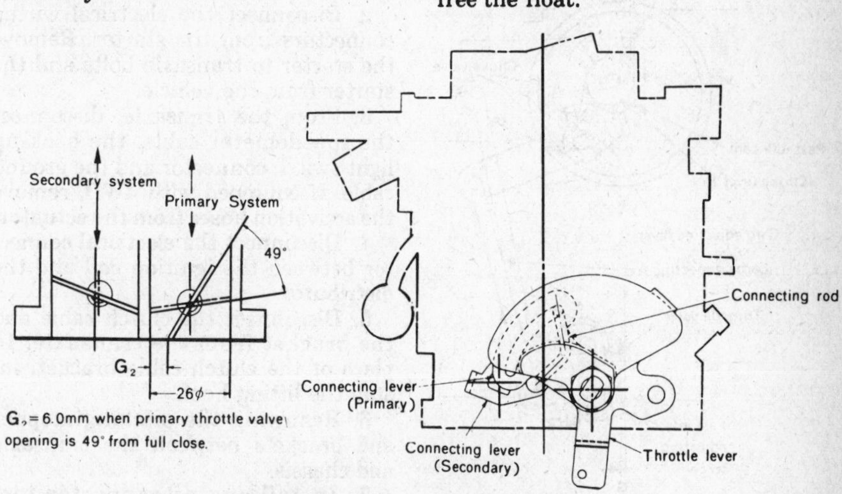


Throttle linkage adjustment—Hitachi

### FLOAT AND FUEL LEVEL ADJUSTMENT

#### *Hitachi Carburetor*

On vehicles with a sight glass on the carburetor float bowl, the fuel should be within 1/16 in. with the dot on the glass when the engine is running. The float level may be adjusted with the carburetor installed on the engine:

1. Disconnect the accelerator pump actuating rod from the pump lever.

2. Remove the throttle return spring.

3. Disconnect the choke cable from the choke lever, and remove it from the spring hanger.

4. Remove the spring hanger, the choke bellcrank and the remaining air horn retaining screws.

5. Lift the air horn slightly, disconnect the choke connecting rod and remove the air horn.

6. Invert the air horn, and measure the distance between the surface of the air horn and the float.

7. Bend the float arm until the clearance is approximately:

1983 – 0.41 in.
1984 – 0.433–0.453 in.
1985 – 0.709–0.724 in.
1986-90 except Justy – 0.453–0.492 in.
1987-90 Justy – 0.437 in.

8. Invert the air horn to it's installed position and measure the distance between the float arm and the needle valve stem. This dimension should be:

1982-85 – 0.050–0.065 in.
1986-900.059–0.075 in.

9. The dimension is adjusted by bending the float stops.

#### *Carter Weber Carburetor*

1. Remove the air horn gasket, then position the float at the air horn.

2. Turn the air horn upside down to free the float.

3. Measure the distance between the surface of the air horn and the float. Bend portion (A) to adjust.

4. Turn the air horn right side up to lower the float. Measure the distance from the lower surface of the air horn to the tip end of the float and make sure it is not less than 1.50 in. Bend portion (B) to adjust. The needle must be free while adjusting the distance.

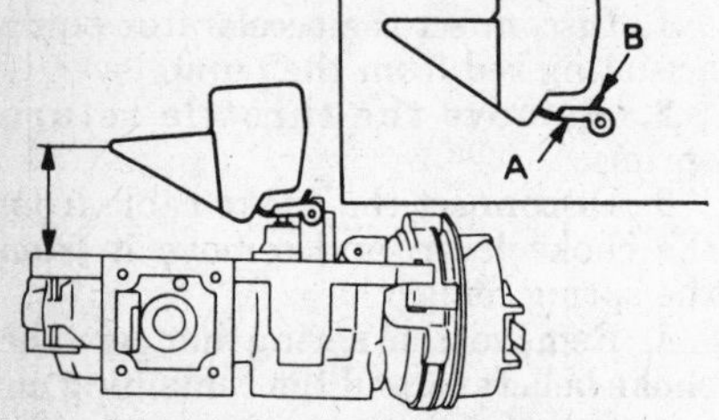


Float setting—Carter/Weber

## FAST IDLE ADJUSTMENT

### *Hitachi Carburetor*

1. Remove the carburetor from the intake manifold.

2. With the choke plate fully closed, operate the fast idle cam and the linkage to position the primary throttle valve at that it's slightly open position.

**NOTE: In this position, the top of the cam adjusting lever rests on the highest (first) step of the fast idle cam; this angle is called the fast idle opening angle (suitable for cold weather starting).**

3. Using a carburetor plug gauge set or drill bit, measure the G1 clearance (the clearance between the lower edge of the primary throttle valve and its bore). To adjust the valve opening, adjust the fast idle screw.

4. To install, reverse the removal procedures. Start the engine and check the carburetor performance.

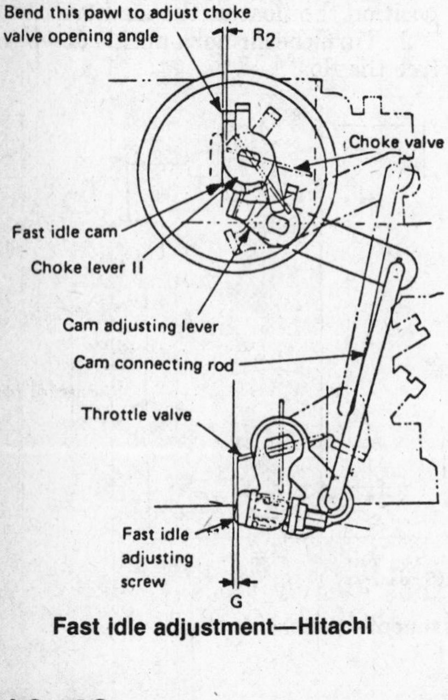


Fast idle adjustment—Hitachi

### *Carter Weber Carburetor*

**NOTE: Before adjusting the fast idle, make sure the idle speed and mixture have been adjusted properly.**

1 With engine at ooperating temperature and the choke fully open, place the fast idle lever on the 3rd step of the cam.

2. Turn the fast idle adjusting screw until the speed is 2000 rpm.

## OVERHAUL

**For all carburetor overhaul procedures, please refer to "Carburetors Overhaul" in the Unit Repair section.**

# Fuel Injection

**Due to the complex nature of mofern fuel injection systems, comprehensive diagnosis and testing procedure fall outside the confines of this repair manual. For complete diagnosis, testing and repair procedures, please refer to "Chilton's Guide to Fuel Injection and Feedback Carburetors."**

# MANUAL TRANSAXLE

## REMOVAL & INSTALLATION

### *Justy*

1. Disconnect the negative battery cable. Remove the air cleaner assembly. Raise and support the vehicle safely.

2. Disconnect the electrical wiring connectors from the starter. Remove the starter to transaxle bolts and the starter from the vehicle.

3. From the transaxle, disconnect the speedometer cable, the back-up light switch connector and the ground cable. If equipped with 4WD, remove the activation hoses from the actuator.

4. Disconnect the electrical connector between the ignition coil and the distributor.

5. Disconnect the clutch cable and the bracket from the transaxle. In place of the clutch cable bracket, install the lifting hook.

6. Removing the pitching stopper and brackets between the transaxle and chassis.

7. Install engine supporter tool 921540000 or equivalent.

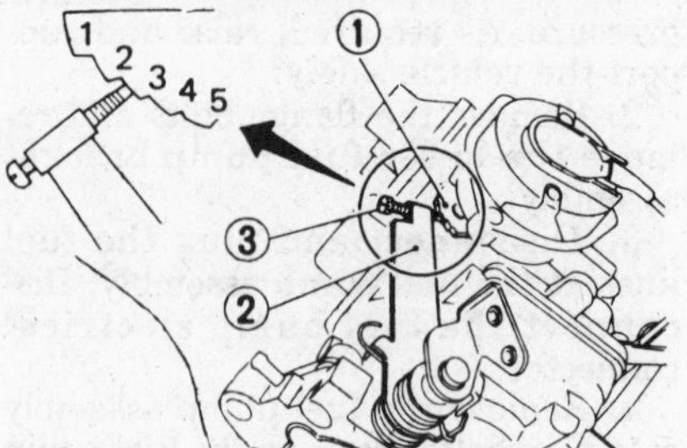


1. Cam
2. Fast idle lever
3. Fast idle adjusting screw

Fast idle adjustment—Carter/Weber

8. Install the vertical hoist to the transaxle lifting hook and raise the transaxle slightly.

9. From under the vehicle, remove the under covers.

10. Disconnect the rear exhaust pipe from the front exhaust pipe and the vehicle.

11. Remove the center crossmember to engine/transaxle assembly bolts.

12. Using a pin punch and a hammer, drive out the axle shaft to driveshaft spring pin. Discard the spring pin and separate the axle shaft.

13. Remove the transaxle mounting bracket.

14. Disconnect the gearshift rod and stay from the transaxle.

15. Properly support the engine assembly. Remove the transaxle to engine bolts.

16. Using the vertical hoist, lift the transaxle from the vehicle.

17. Installation is the reverse of the removal procedure. Be sure to use new spring pins.

### *XT Coupe*

#### 1800cc ENGINE

1. Disconnect the negative battery cable. Remove the air cleaner assembly.

2. If equipped with a turbocharger, refer to the turbocharger removal procedure and remove the center exhaust pipe from its mounting on the transaxle.

3. Raise and support the vehicle safely. Disconnect the front exhaust pipe from the engine.

4. If equipped with 4WD, discon-

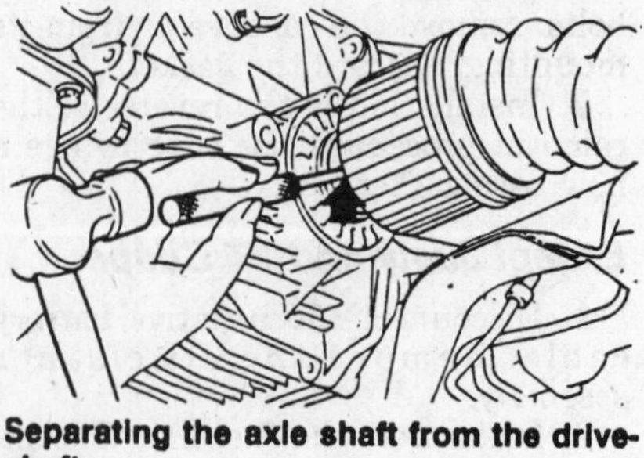

Separating the axle shaft from the driveshaft

nect the rear exhaust pipe from the muffler.

5. Remove the clutch cable and the hill holder cable, if equipped.

6. Disconnect the speedometer cable from the transaxle.

7. Disconnect the electrical harness connectors from the neutral start switch and the back-up light switch.

8. If equipped with 4WD disconnect the transaxle electrical harness. This harness consists of the back-up light switch and the indicator light or switch for the 4WD mechanism.

9. If equipped with 4WD, disconnect the vacuum hose and the differential lock vacuum hose, as necessary.

10. Remove the starter to transaxle bolts. Remove the starter from the transaxle. Lower the vehicle.

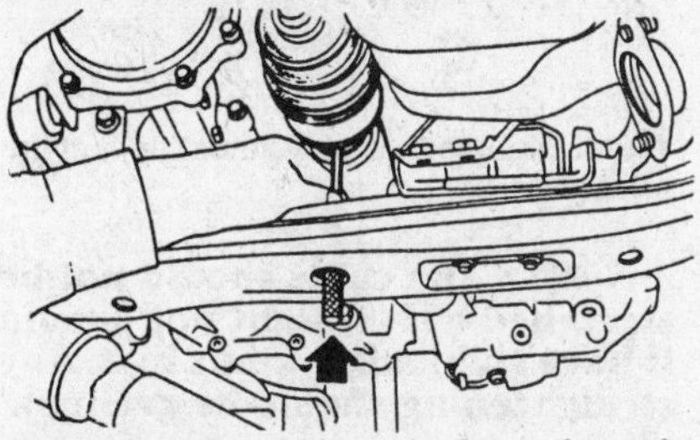

Removing the spring pin from the axle shaft – Justy

11. Remove the pitching stopper rod to engine bracket bolt, the rod and the engine bracket from the engine. Using the engine support bracket tool 927010000 or equivalent, install it to the engine hanger. Using the engine support assembly tool No. 927000000 or equivalent, install it to the support bracket.

12. On the right side of the vehicle that secures the transverse link to the stabilizer. Remove the lower bolt and separate the link from the stabilizer.

13. Remove the right hand brake cable bracket from the transverse link. Remove the bolt retaining the link to the crossmember on each side.

14. Lower the transverse link. Using tool 398791700 or equivalent, remove the spring pin and separate the axle shaft from the driveshaft on each side of the assembly by pushing the rear of the tire outward.

15. Remove the engine to transaxle mounting bolts. Position the proper transaxle jack under the transaxle assembly.

16. Remove the rear cushion rubber mounting bolts. Remove the rear crossmember assembly.

17. Turn the engine support tool adjuster counterclockwise in order to slightly raise the engine.

18. Move the transaxle jack toward the rear of the vehicle until the mainshaft is withdrawn from the clutch cover.

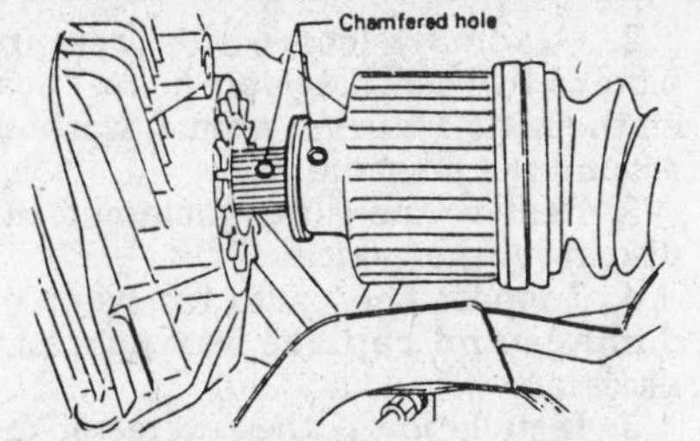


Aligning the chamfered holes of the axle shaft with the driveshaft

19. Carefully remove the transaxle assembly from the vehicle.

20. Installation is the reverse of the removal procedure.

### 2700cc ENGINE

1. Disconnect the negative battery cable. Remove the air cleaner assembly.

2. Remove the clutch cable and the hill holder cable. Remove the speedometer cable.

3. Remove the oxygen sensor electrical connector and the neutral switch connector.

4. If equipped with 4WD, remove the disconnect the electrical connections at the back up light and differential lock indicator switch assembly. Disconnect the differential lock vacuum hose.

5. Disconnect the starter electrical connections. Remove the starter retaining bolts. Remove the starter from the transaxle case.

6. Remove the air intake boot. Disconnect the pitching stopper rod from its mounting bracket. Remove the right side engine to transmission mounting bolt.

7. Install engine support bracket 927160000 and engine support tool 927150000 or their equivalents. Remove the buffer rod from the engine and body side bracket.

**NOTE: Before attaching the special engine support tools, connect the adjuster to the buffer rod assembly on the right side of the engine.**

8. Raise and support the vehicle safely.

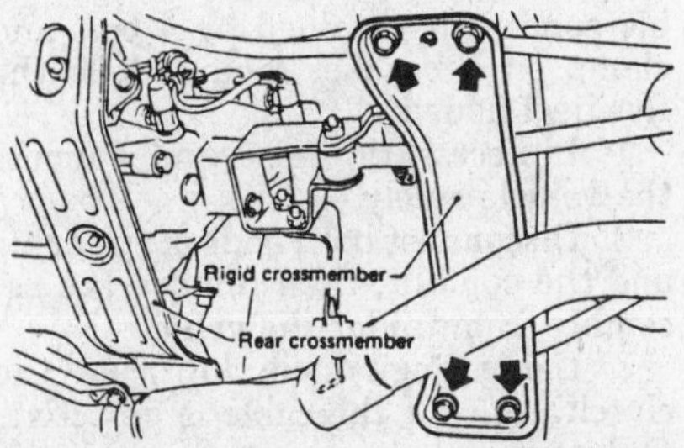


View of the rigid and rear crossmembers – XT Coupe

9. Disconnect the exhaust pipes at the exhaust manifold flange. Remove the exhaust system up to the rear exhaust pipe assembly.

10. If equipped with 4WD, matchmark and remove the driveshaft. Remove the complete gear shift assembly.

11. Loosen the upper bolt and nut from the plate that secures the transverse link to the stabilizer. Remove the lower bolt and separate the link from the stabilizer.

12. Remove the right hand brake cable bracket from the transverse link. Remove the bolt retaining the link to the crossmember on each side.

13. Lower the transverse link. Using tool 398791700 or equivalent, remove the spring pin and separate the axle shaft from the driveshaft on each side of the assembly by pushing the rear of the tire outward.

14. Remove the engine to transaxle mounting bolts. Position the proper transaxle jack under the transaxle assembly.

15. Remove the rear cushion rubber mounting bolts. Remove the rear crossmember assembly.

16. Turn the engine support tool adjuster counterclockwise in order to slightly raise the engine.

17. Move the transaxle jack toward the rear of the vehicle until the mainshaft is withdrawn from the clutch cover.

18. Carefully remove the transaxle assembly from the vehicle.

19. Installation is the reverse of the removal procedure.

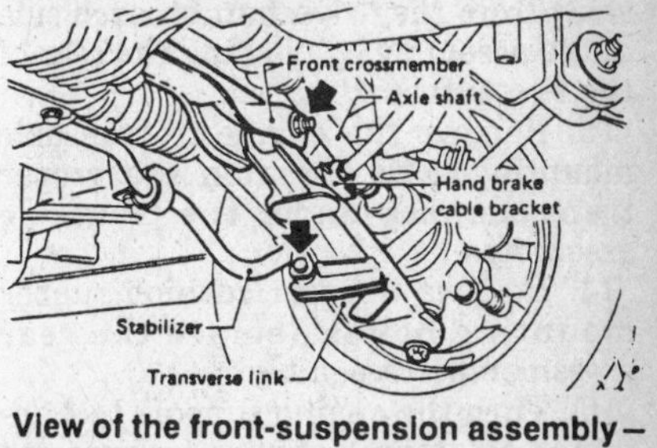


View of the front-suspension assembly – XT Coupe

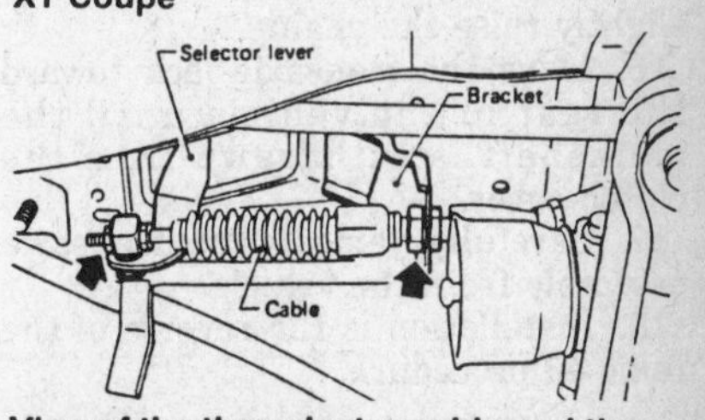


View of the the selector cable and the selector cable bracket – XT Coupe.

### *Except Justy, XT Coupe and Legacy*

1. Disconnect the negative battery cable. Remove the engine/transaxle ground strap and starter.

2. Remove the starter retaining bolts. Disconnect the starter electrical connectors.
3. Remove the starter from the vehicle.
4. If equipped with a turbocharger, refer to the turbocharger removal procedure and remove the center pipe assembly.
5. From the right side, remove the transaxle assembly to chassis support bolt and loosen the lower nuts.
6. Raise and support the vehicle safely.
7. On vehicles not equipped with a turbocharger, remove the exhaust pipe to cylinder head nuts, the exhaust pipe to rear pipe bolts, the exhaust pipe to hanger bracket and the front exhaust pipe from the vehicle.
8. If equipped with 4WD, disconnect the rear exhaust pipe from the muffler. Disconnect the driveshaft from the rear of the transaxle.
9. Remove the retaining spring, the CP rod and stay from the transaxle. Loosen the stabilizer to transverse link nuts and bolts, on the lower side of the plate.
10. Loosen the upper bolt and nut from the plate that secures the transverse link to the stabilizer. Remove the lower bolt and separate the link from the stabilizer.
11. Remove the right hand brake cable bracket from the transverse link. Remove the bolt retaining the link to the crossmember on each side.
12. Lower the transverse link. Using tool 398791700 or equivalent, remove the spring pin and separate the axle shaft from the driveshaft on each side of the assembly by pushing the rear of the tire outward.
13. Remove the engine to transaxle mounting bolts. Position the proper transaxle jack under the transaxle assembly.
14. Remove the rear cushion rubber mounting bolts. Remove the rear crossmember assembly.
15. Turn the engine support tool adjuster counterclockwise in order to slightly raise the engine.
16. Move the transaxle jack toward the rear of the vehicle until the mainshaft is withdrawn from the clutch cover.
17. Carefully remove the transaxle assembly from the vehicle.
18. Installation is the reverse of the removal procedure.

# CLUTCH

### REMOVAL & INSTALLATION

1. Remove the transaxle from the vehicle.
2. Gradually loosen the pressure plate to flywheel assembly bolts. Loosen the bolts 1 turn at a time, working around the pressure plate.
3. Remove the clutch plate and the disc. from the vehicle.
4. Inspect the parts for wear or damage and replace any parts as necessary.
5. Installation is the reverse of the removal procedure.
6. Use clutch disc guide tool 499747000 or equivalent, to align the clutch on the non-turbocharged 1600cc, 1800cc and 2700cc engines. Use tool 499747100 or equivalent, to align the clutch on the turbocharged 1800cc engine. Use tool 499745500 or equivalent, to align the clutch on the 1200cc engine.
7. When installing the clutch pressure plate assembly, make sure that the marks on the flywheel and the clutch pressure plate assembly are at least 120 degrees apart. This is for purposes of balance. Also, make sure that the clutch disc is installed properly, noting the **FRONT** and **REAR** markings.

### FREE PLAY ADJUSTMENT

1. Remove the clutch release fork return spring.
2. Loosen the cable locknut, then adjust the spherical nut so that there is the following play between the spherical nut and the release fork seat.
   1983–84 – 0.08–0.12 in.
   1985–90 (1600cc, 1800cc and 2700cc engines, 2WD except turbocharger) – 0.08–0.12 in.
   1985–90 (2WD/4WD turbocharged, 1800cc engine and the 4WD 2700cc engine) – 0.12–0.16 in.
   1987–90 (1200cc engine) – 0.08–0.16 in.
3. Tighten the locknut and reconnect the release spring.

## Clutch Cable

### REMOVAL & INSTALLATION

The clutch cable is connected to the clutch pedal at 1 end and to the clutch release lever at the other end. The cable conduit is retained by a bolt and clamp on a bracket mounted on the flywheel housing.

1. If necessary, raise and support the vehicle safely.
2. Disconnect both ends of the cable and the conduit, then remove the assembly from under the vehicle.
3. Using engine oil, lubricate the clutch cable. If the cable is defective, replace it.
4. Installation is the reverse the removal procedure.

### CABLE ADJUSTMENT

The clutch cable can be adjusted at the cable bracket where the cable is attached to the side of the transaxle housing.

1. Remove the circlip and clamp.
2. Slide the cable end in the direction desired and then replace the circlip and clamp into the nearest gutters on the cable end.

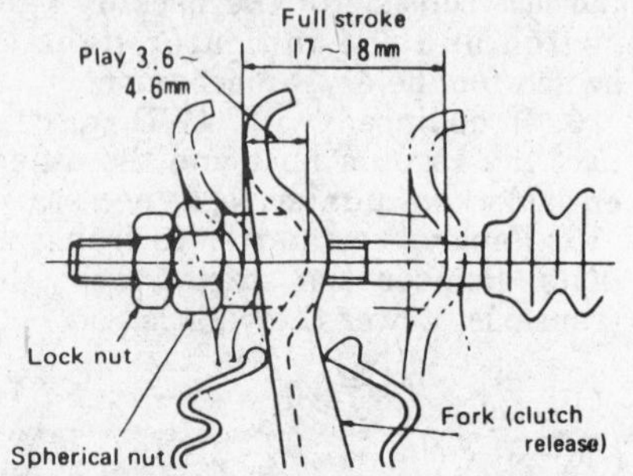

Clutch linkage free-play adjustment at the release fork

**NOTE: The cable should not be stretched out straight nor should it have right angle kinks in it. Any straightening should be gradual.**

3. Check the clutch for proper operation.

# AUTOMATIC TRANSAXLE

## Transaxle

### REMOVAL & INSTALLATION

*Justy*

#### WITH ECVT TRANSAXLE

**NOTE: When removing and installing ECVT transaxle, always remove and install the engine and transaxle as an assembly.**

1. Disconnect the negative battery cable. Drain the coolant by removing drain plug from radiator.
2. Remove the grille. Disconnect hoses and electric wiring from radiator and remove the radiator.
3. Remove front hood release cable and remove radiator upper support member. Disconnect horn and remove the air cleaner assembly.
4. Disconnect the following hoses and cables:
   a. Hoses from carburetor
   b. Hoses from the heater unit
   c. Hose for brake booster
   d. Clutch cable
   e. Accelerator cable
   f. Choke cable from carburetor (if so equipped)

g. Speedometer cable
h. Distributor wiring

5. Disconnect selector cable. Set selector lever at **N** position. Remove clip and detach selector cable from bracket. Remove snap pin, clevis pin and separate selector cable from transaxle.

6. Remove the pitching stopper from the bracket.

7. Disconnect the starter cable, engine wiring harness connectors, ground lead terminals and brush holder harness connector.

8. Remove the hanger from the rear of transaxle.

9. Remove under covers and remove the exhaust system.

10. Remove the driveshaft from transaxle.

11. Remove transverse link.

12. Remove the spring pin retaining the axle shaft by using a sutiable tool and separate front axle shaft from the transaxle.

13. Remove engine and transmission mounting brackets.

14. Raise the engine and remove center member and crossmember.

15. Lift up the engine/transaxle assembly carefully and remove it from the vehicle.

**To install:**

16. Position the engine/transaxle assembly in the vehicle. Install engine and transmission mounting brackets.

17. Install center member and crossmember.

18. Install the axle shaft to transaxle with new spring pin.

19. Install gearshift rod and stay to transaxle.

20. Install the exhaust sustem. Connect driveshaft to transaxle.

21. Install transverse link and under covers to the vehicle.

22. Reconnect the pitching stopper to bracket.

23. Reconnect the following hoses and cables:

a. Hoses to carburetor
b. Hoses to the heater unit
c. Hose to brake booster
d. Clutch cable to transaxle
e. Accelerator cable
f. Choke cable from carburetor (if so equipped)
g. Speedometer cable
h. Distributor wiring

24. Reconnect the starter cable, engine wiring harness connectors, ground lead terminals and brush holder harness connector. Install the air cleaner assembly.

25. Install radiator upper member and connect hood release cable to lock assembly. Reconnect the horn.

26. Install the radiator and connect hoses and electric wiring. Attach grille to the vehicle.

27. Refill the coolant. Reconnect the battery cable.

28. Check all fluid levels. Road test vehicles for proper operation in all driving ranges.

## *XT Coupe*

### 1800cc ENGINE

1. Disconnect the negative battery cable. Remove the air cleaner assembly.

2. If equipped with a turbocharger, refer to the turbocharger removal procedure and remove the center exhaust pipe from its mounting on the transaxle.

3. Raise and support the vehicle safely. Disconnect the front exhaust pipe from the engine.

4. Disconnect the oxygen sensor electrical harness. If equipped with 4WD, disconnect the rear exhaust pipe from the muffler.

5. Disconnect the speedometer cable from the transaxle. Disconnect the electrical harness connectors from the neutral start switch and the back-up light switch.

6. If equipped with 4WD, disconnect the transaxle electrical harness.

7. This harness consists of the back-up light switch and the indicator light or switch for the 4WD mechanism.

8. If equipped with 4WD, disconnect the vacuum hose.

9. Remove the air breather to pitching stopper clip band.

10. Remove the starter to transaxle bolts. Remove the starter from the transaxle. Lower the vehicle.

11. Remove the timing hole plug. Remove the torque converter retaining bolts.

12. Remove the pitching stopper rod to engine bracket bolt, the rod and the engine bracket from the engine. Using the engine support bracket tool 927010000 or equivalent, install it to the engine hanger. Using the engine support assembly tool No. 927000000 or equivalent, install it to the support bracket.

13. On the right side of the vehicle, remove the engine to transaxle bolt.

14. Raise and support the vehicle safely. Disconnect and plug the transaxle fluid lines.

15. If equipped with 4WD, remove the rear driveshaft center bearing assembly to chassis bolts and the driveshaft to rear differential flange bolts, then remove the driveshaft from the vehicle.

16. Remove the CP stay to transaxle bolt, the spring and the CP rod to transaxle bolt. Remove the selector lever assembly.

17. Loosen the upper bolt and nut from the plate that secures the transverse link to the stabilizer. Remove the lower bolt and separate the link from the stabilizer.

18. Remove the right hand brake cable bracket from the transverse link. Remove the bolt retaining the link to the crossmember on each side.

19. Lower the transverse link. Using tool 398791700 or equivalent, remove the spring pin and separate the axle shaft from the driveshaft on each side of the assembly by pushing the rear of the tire outward.

20. Remove the engine to transaxle mounting bolts. Position the proper transaxle jack under the transaxle assembly.

21. Remove the rear cushion rubber mounting bolts. Remove the rear crossmember assembly.

22. Turn the engine support tool adjuster counterclockwise in order to slightly raise the engine.

23. Move the torque converter and transaxle unit aaway from the engine. Carefully remove the transaxle assembly from the vehicle.

24. The installation of the assembly is the reverse of the removal procedure.

### 2700cc ENGINE

1. Disconnect the negative battery cable. Remove the air cleaner assembly.

2. Remove the speedometer cable. If equipped with 4WD, remove the speed sensor connector.

3. Remove the oxygen sensor electrical connector and the neutral switch connector. Remove the transmission electrical harness connector.

4. Disconnect the starter electrical connections. Remove the starter retaining bolts. Remove the starter from the transaxle case.

5. Remove the air intake boot. Remove the timing hole plug. Remove the torque converter retaining bolts.

6. Disconnect the pitching stopper rod from its mounting bracket. Remove the right side engine to transmission mounting bolt.

7. Install engine support bracket 927160000 and engine support tool 927150000, or their equivalents. Remove the buffer rod from the engine and body side bracket.

**NOTE: Before attaching the special engine support tools, connect the adjuster to the buffer rod assembly on the right side of the engine.**

8. Raise and support the vehicle safely. Disconnect and plug the transaxle fluid lines.

9. Disconnect the exhaust pipes at the exhaust manifold flange. Remove the exhaust system up to the rear exhaust pipe assembly.

10. If equipped with 4WD, matchmark and remove the driveshaft. Remove the complete gear shift assembly.

11. Loosen the upper bolt and nut from the plate that secures the transverse link to the stabilizer. Remove the lower bolt and separate the link from the stabilizer.
12. Remove the right hand brake cable bracket from the transverse link. Remove the bolt retaining the link to the crossmember on each side.
13. Lower the transverse link. Using tool 398791700 or equivalent, remove the spring pin and separate the axle shaft from the driveshaft on each side of the assembly by pushing the rear of the tire outward.
14. Remove the engine to transaxle mounting bolts. Position the proper transaxle jack under the transaxle assembly.
15. Remove the rear cushion rubber mounting bolts. Remove the rear crossmember assembly.
16. Turn the engine support tool adjuster counterclockwise in order to slightly raise the engine.
17. Move the torque converter and transaxle unit away from the engine. Carefully remove the transaxle assembly from the vehicle.
18. Installation is the reverse of the removal procedure.

### *1600 and 1800 Sedan/Station Wagon, XT Coupe*

#### 2WD AND 4WD NON-ELECTRONIC 3 AND 4 SPEED TRANSAXLES

1. Disconnect the negative battery cable.
2. Remove clamp from spare tire supporter and remove the spare tire.

**NOTE: Use care when removing spare tire assembly from the vehicle.**

3. Remove spare tire supporter and battery clamp.
4. Remove speedometer cable and retaining clip. Before disconnecting speedometer cable, remove front exhaust pipe on 4 speed automatic transaxle.
5. Disconnect the following electrical harness connections on the 3 speed automatic transaxle:
   a. Oxygen sensor connector
   b. ATF temperature switch connector
   c. Kickdown solenoid valve connector
   d. 4WD solenoid valve connector on 4WD equipped vehicles
6. Disconnect the following electrical harness connections on the 4 speed automatic transaxle:
   a. Oxygen sensor connector
   b. Transaxle harness connector
   c. Inhibitor switch connector
   d. Revolution sensor connector on 4WD equipped vehicles
7. Disconnect the diaphragm vacuum hose on 3 speed automatic transaxle and 4WD vacuum hose on 4WD equipped vehicles.
8. Remove clip band which secures air breather hose to pitching stopper.
9. Remove the pitching stopper rod. Remove the starter.
10. Remove timing hole inspection plug and remove the 4 bolts which hold torque converter to drive plate.
11. Support the engine assembly with special engine support tool No.926610000 or equivalent.
12. Remove engine to transaxle mounting nut and bolt on the right side.
13. Remove the exhaust system.

**NOTE: Apply a penetrating oil or equivalent to all exhaust retaining nuts in advance to facilitate removal.**

14. On turbocharged vehicles, remove accelerator cable cover and upper and lower turbocharger covers. Remove the center exhaust pipe at turbocharger location and at rear exhaust pipe. Remove any exhaust brackets or hangers that attach to the transaxle as necessary.
15. On non-turbocharged vehicles, disconnect front exhaust pipe from the engine and from the rear exhaust pipe. Remove any exhaust brackets or hangers that attach to the transaxle as necessary.
16. Drain all transaxle fluid from the oil pan into a suitable drain pan.
17. Remove the driveshaft on 4WD vehicles. Plug the opening at the rear of extension housing to prevent oil from flowing out.
18. Disconnect the linkage rod (3 speed) or cable (4 speed) from the select lever.
19. Remove stabilizer from transverse link by loosening (not removing) nut and bolt on the lower side of plate.
20. Remove hand brake cable bracket from transverse link and bolt holding transverse link to crossmember on each side. Lower the transverse link.
21. Remove spring pin and separate axle shaft from transaxle on each side.

**NOTE: Use a suitable tool to remove spring pin. Discard old spring pin and always install a new pin.**

22. Disconnect the axle shaft from transaxle on each side. Be sure to remove axle shaft from transaxle by pushing the rear of tire outward.
23. Remove engine to transaxle mounting nuts.
24. Disconnect oil cooler hoses and oil supply pipe. Be careful not to damage the oil supply pipe O-ring.
25. Place transmission jack or equivalent under transaxle. Always support transaxle case with a transmission jack.

**NOTE: Do not place jack under oil pan otherwise oil pan may be damaged.**

26. Remove rear cushion rubber mounting nuts and rear crossmember. Move torque converter and transaxle as a unit away from the engine. Remove the transaxle.

**To install:**

27. Install transaxle to engine and temporarily tighten engine to transaxle mounting nuts.
28. Install rear crossmember to rear cushion rubber mounts. Align rear cushion guide with rear crossmember guide hole and tighten nuts.
29. Install rear crossmember to car body. Be careful not to damage threads. Torque rear crossmember bolts to 39–49 ft. lbs.
30. Tighten engine to transaxle nuts on the lower side to 34–40 ft. lbs. Remove transmission jack from the vehicle.
31. Install axle shaft to transaxle and install spring pin into place.

**NOTE: Always use new spring pin. Be sure to align the axle shaft and shaft from the transaxle at chamfered holes and engage shaft splines correctly.**

32. Install transverse link temporarily to front crossmember by using bolt and self-locking nut. Do not complete final torque at this point.
33. Install stabilizer temporarily to transverse link. Install hand brake cable bracket to transverse link.
34. Connect the linkage rod (3 speed) or cable (4 speed) to the select lever. Make sure that the lever operates smoothly all across the operating range.
35. Install propeller shaft on 4WD vehicles. Torque propeller shaft to rear differential retaining bolts to 13–20 ft. lbs. and center bearing location retaining bolts to 25–33 ft. lbs.
36. Connect oil cooler hoses and oil supply pipe. Lower car to floor.
37. Tighten transvere link to front crossmember mounting bolts and tranverse link to stabilizer mounting bolts with the tires placed on the ground when the vehicle is not loaded. Tightening torque for transverse link to front crossmember (self-locking nuts) 43–51 ft. lbs. and transverse link to stabilizer 14–22 ft. lbs.
38. Tighten engine to transaxle nuts on the upper side to 34–40 ft. lbs.
39. Raise car and safely support. Install exhaust system.

**NOTE: Before installing exhaust system, connect speedometer cable on 4 speed vehicles.**

40. On turbocharged vehicles, install the center exhaust pipe at turbocharger location and at rear exhaust pipe. Install any exhaust brackets or hangers that attach to the transaxle as necessary. Install upper and lower turbocharger covers and accelerator cable cover.

41. On non-turbocharged vehicles, connect front exhaust pipe to the engine and rear exhaust pipe. Install any exhaust brackets or hangers that attach to the transaxle as necessary.

42. Remove the special engine support tool. Install and tighten torque converter to drive plate mounting bolts to 17–20 ft. lbs.

43. Install timing hole inspection plug.

44. Install starter.

45. Install pitching stopper. Be sure to tighten the bolt for the body side first, and then the 1 for engine or transaxle side. Tightening torque for car body side is 27–49 ft. lbs. and for engine or transmission side is 33–40 ft. lbs.

46. Reconnect the following electrical harness connections on the 3 speed automatic transaxle:

a. Oxygen sensor connector
b. ATF temperature switch connector
c. Kickdown solenoid valve connector
d. 4WD solenoid valve connector on 4WD equipped vehicles

47. Reconnect the following electrical harness connections on the 4 speed automatic transaxle:

a. Oxygen sensor connector
b. Transaxle harness connector
c. Inhibitor switch connector
d. Revolution sensor connector on 4WD equipped vehicles

48. Reconnect the diaphragm vacuum hose on 3 speed automatic transaxle and 4WD vacuum hose on 4WD equipped vehicles.

49. Secure air breather hose to pitching stopper with a clip band.

50. Reconnect the speedometer cable. Manually tighten cable nut all the way and then turn it approximately 30 degrees more with a tool.

51. Connect the battery ground cable. Refill and check transaxle oil level.

52. Install spare tire supporter and battery clamp. Install spare tire.

53. Road test vehicle for proper operation across all operating ranges.

### *1987–90 XT Coupe and 1990 Legacy*

#### 4 SPEED ELECTRONIC TRANSAXLE

1. Disconnect the negative battery cable.

2. Remove speedometer cable or electronic wiring connector from speed sensor.

3. Disconnect the following electrical harness connections on the automatic transaxle:

a. Oxygen sensor connector
b. Transaxle harness connector
c. Inhibitor switch connector
d. Revolution sensor connector on 4WD equipped vehicles
e. Crankshaft and camshaft angle sensor connector on Legacy vehicles
f. Knock sensor connectors and transaxle ground terminal on Legacy vehicles

4. Remove clip band which secures air breather hose to pitching stopper.

5. Remove the starter and air intake boot.

6. Remove timing hole inspection plug and remove the 4 bolts which hold torque converter to drive plate.

7. Disconnect pitching stopper rod from bracket.

8. Remove engine to transaxle mounting nut and bolt on the right side.

9. Remove the buffer rod from the vehicle. Support the engine assembly with special engine support tool or equivalent.

10. Remove the exhaust system. Remove exhaust brackets or hangers that attach to the transaxle as necessary.

11. Matchmark and remove the driveshaft on 4WD vehicles. Plug the opening at the rear of extension housing to prevent oil from flowing out.

12. Disconnect the gear shift cable from the transaxle select lever.

13. Remove stabilizer from transverse link.

14. Remove hand brake cable bracket from transverse link and bolt holding transverse link to crossmember on each side. Lower the transverse link.

15. Remove spring pin and separate axle shaft from transaxle on each side.

**NOTE: Use a suitable tool to remove spring pin. Discard old spring pin and always install a new pin.**

16. Disconnect the axle shaft from transaxle on each side. Be sure to remove axle shaft from transaxle by pushing the rear of tire outward.

17. Remove engine to transaxle mounting nuts.

18. Disconnect oil cooler hoses.

19. Place transmission jack or equivalent under transaxle. Always support transaxle case with a transmission jack.

**NOTE: Do not place jack under oil pan otherwise oil pan may be damaged.**

20. Remove rear cushion rubber mounting nuts and rear crossmember.

21. Move torque converter and transaxle as a unit away from the engine. Remove the transaxle.

**To Install:**

22. Install transaxle to engine and temporarily tighten engine to transaxle mounting nuts.

23. Install rear crossmember to rear cushion rubber mounts. Align rear cushion guide with rear crossmember guide hole and tighten nuts.

24. Install rear crossmember to car body. Be careful not to damage threads. Torque rear crossmember bolts to 39–49 ft. lbs.

25. Tighten engine to transaxle retaining nuts to 34–40 ft. lbs. Remove transmission jack from the vehicle.

26. Remove the engine support tool and install buffer rod.

27. Install axle shaft to transaxle and install spring pin into place.

**NOTE: Always use new spring pin. Be sure to align the axle shaft and shaft from the transaxle at chamfered holes and install shaft splines correctly.**

28. Install transverse link temporarily to front crossmember by using bolt and self locking nut. Do not complete final torque at this point.

29. Install stabilizer temporarily to transverse link. Install hand brake cable bracket to transverse link.

30. Lower car to floor. Tighten transvere link to front crossmember mounting bolts and tranverse link to stabilizer mounting bolts with the tires placed on the ground when the vehicle is not loaded. Tightening torque for transverse link to front crossmember (self locking nuts) 43–51 ft. lbs. and transverse link to stabilizer 14–22 ft. lbs.

31. Raise and safely support the vehicle. Reconnect the gear shift cable to the select lever. Make sure that the lever operates smoothly all across the operating range.

32. Install propeller shaft on 4WD vehicles. Torque propeller shaft to rear differential retaining bolts to 17–24 ft. lbs. and center bearing location retaining bolts to 25–33 ft. lbs.

33. Connect oil cooler hoses.

34. Tighten engine to transaxle bolts to 34–40 ft. lbs.

35. Install starter.

36. Install pitching stopper. Be sure to tighten the bolt for the body side first and then the 1 for engine or transaxle side. Tightening torque for car body side is 27–49 ft. lbs. and for engine or transaxle side is 33–40 ft. lbs.

37. Install and tighten torque converter to drive plate mounting bolts to 17–20 ft. lbs.

38. Install timing hole inspection

plug, air intake boot and air breather hose to pitching stopper.

39. Reconnect the following electrical harness connections on the automatic transaxle:

a. Oxygen sensor connector

b. Transaxle harness connector

c. Inhibitor switch connector

d. Revolution sensor connector on 4WD equipped vehicles

e. Crankshaft and camshaft angle sensor connector on Legacy vehicles

f. Knock sensor connectors and transaxle ground terminal on Legacy vehicles

40. Reconnect the speedometer cable. Manually tighten cable nut all the way and then turn it approximately 30 degrees more with a tool.

41. Install exhaust system and exhaust brackets or hangers that attach to the transaxle as necessary.

42. Connect the battery ground cable. Refill and check transaxle oil level.

43. Road test vehicle for proper operation across all operating ranges.

## PAN REMOVAL

1. Raise and support the vehicle safely.
2. Position a drain pan under the transaxle, remove the drain plug and drain the transaxle.
3. Remove the oil pan to transaxle bolts and lower the oil pan from the transaxle.
4. Installation is the reverse of the removal procedure. Be sure to use a new gasket or RTV sealant, as required.

## FILTER SERVICE

1. Remove the transaxle oil pan.
2. Remove the oil stainer to transaxle bolt and the oil strainer from the transaxle.
3. Installation is the reverse of the removal procedure. Be sure to use a new gasket or RTV sealant, as required.

## SHIFT LINKAGE ADJUSTMENT

1. Loosen the clamp nuts on the shifting rod at the bottom of the shift lever on the transaxle.
2. Place the selector lever in **N** and hold it forward against the detent.
3. Check that the transaxle shift lever is in the **N** position by pulling it all the way back into **P** and then pushing it forward 2 positions.
4. Tighten the clamp nuts.

## KICKDOWN SOLENOID ADJUSTMENT

If used, an audible click should be heard from the solenoid on the right side of the transaxle, when the accelerator pedal is pushed down all the way with the engine off and the ignition switch in the **ON** position. The switch is operated by the upper part of the accelerator lever inside the vehicle. The position of the switch can be varied to give quicker or slower kickdown response.

## NEUTRAL SAFETY SWITCH ADJUSTMENT

This switch is mounted on the transaxle shift lever shaft, bolted to the transaxle. It also operates the back-up lights.

1. Remove the shift lever shaft nut.
2. Remove the shift lever from the shaft.
3. Make sure that the slot in the shaft is vertical, **N** position.
4. Remove the switch mounting bolts but leave the switch in place.
5. Remove the setscrew from the lower face of the switch.
6. Insert a 0.059 in. drill bit through the set screw hole. Turn the switch slightly so that the bit passes through into the back part of the switch.
7. Bolt the switch down.
8. Remove the drill bit and replace the set screw.
9. Install the lever and tighten the shaft nut.
10. Make sure that the engine can start only in **P** or **N** and that the back-up lights turn functioning in Reverse. Adjust the shift linkage, if necessary.

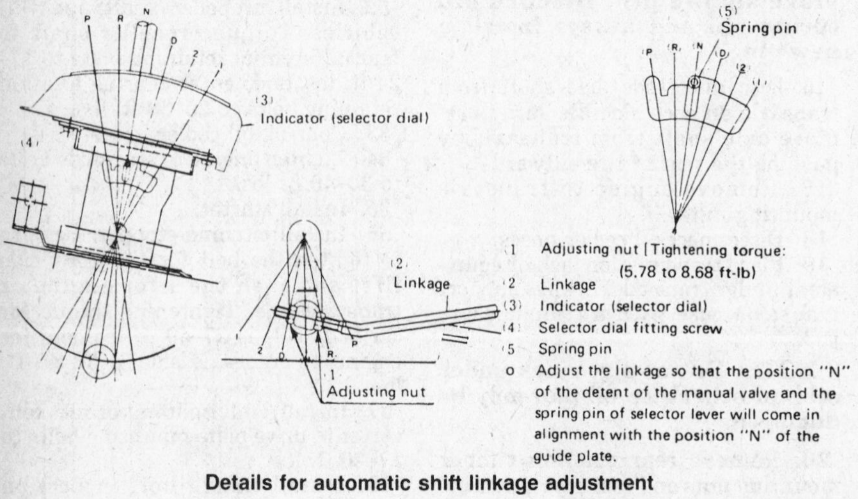


**Details for automatic shift linkage adjustment**

## BRAKE BAND ADJUSTMENT

### *Except 1988–90 Vehicles*

1. Raise and support the vehicle safely.
2. Locate the adjusting screw above the pan on the left side of the transaxle.
3. Loosen the locknut.
4. Torque the adjusting screw to 6.5 ft. lbs., then turn it back exactly 2 full turns.
5. Tighten the lock nut.

**NOTE: Following the above procedure will adjust the transaxle brake band to the factory specified setting.**

6. If any of the following conditions are detected, the adjusting screw can be moved 1/4 turn in either direction after Step 4. Turn the adjusting screw 1/4 turn clockwise if the transaxle jolts when shifting from 1st to 2nd, engine speed abruptly rises from 2nd to 3rd, or shift delays in kickdown from 3rd to 2nd.
7. Turn the adjusting screw 1/4 turn counterclockwise if the transaxle slips between 1st and 2nd speeds or t here is a braking action between the 2nd and 3rd shift.

### 1988–90 VEHICLES

If both 2nd and 4th gears are possible, but the engine rpm increases considerably when shifting up from 2nd to 3rd, it is attributed to excessive clearance between the reverse clutch drum and the brake band. Tighten the adjusting screw by turning it clockwise to correct this condition.

If both 2nd and 4th gear is possible but a shift delay is present at kickdown from 3rd to 2nd, it is attributed to excessive clearance between the reverse clutch drum and the brake band. Tighten the adjusting screw by turning it clockwise to correct this condition.

# TRANSFER CASE

## REMOVAL & INSTALLATION

1. Disconnect the negative battery cable.

2. Raise and support the vehicle safely.
3. Remove the transaxle assembly from the vehicle.
4. Position the assembly in a suitable holding fixture.
5. Disassemble the transfer case from the transxle.
6. Installation is the reverse of the removal procedure.

# DRIVE AXLE

## Halfshaft

### REMOVAL & INSTALLATION

*Justy*

1. Raise and support the vehicle safely. Remove the tire and wheel assembly.
2. Remove the disc brake assembly. Remove the dust cover, cotter pin, castle nut, conical spring. Remove the center piece, using the proper tools.
3. Pull the hub and disc assembly from the halfshaft. Remove the disc cover from the housing.
4. Drive out the spring pin connecting the halfshaft to the differential, using the proper tool.
5. Remove the cotter pin and the castle nut from the tie rod end ball joint.
6. Remove the tie rod end ball joint from the knuckle arm, using the proper puller.
7. Remove the bolt that retains the housing to the strut. Carefully push down the housing in order to remove it from the strut.
8. Remove the ball joint of the transverse link from the housing. Remove the housing and the halfshaft assembly as a complete unit.
9. Separate the housing from the halfshaft, using removal tools 922493000 and 921122000 or their equivalents.
10. Installation is the reverse of the removal procedure.

*Except Justy*

1. Release the parking brake. Raise and support the vehicle safely. Remove the tire and wheel assembly.
2. Pull out the parking brake cable outer clip from the caliper. Disconnect the parking brake cable end from the caliper lever.
3. Drive out the double offset joint spring pin, using the proper tools.
4. Loosen the 2 retaining bolts and remove the disc brake assembly from the housing. Remove the 2 bolts that connect the housing and the damper strut.

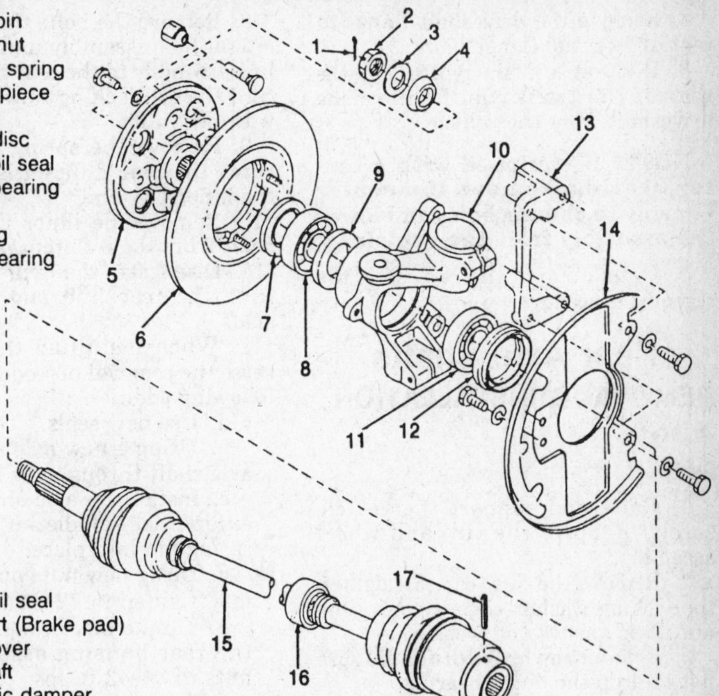

1. Cotter pin
2. Castle nut
3. Concial spring
4. Center piece
5. Hub
6. Brake disc
7. Outer oil seal
8. Outer bearing
9. Spacer
10. Housing
11. Inner bearing
12. Inner oil seal
13. Support (Brake pad)
14. Disc cover
15. Halfshaft
16. Dynamic damper
17. Spring pin

**Front halfshaft assembly and related components Justy**

5. Remove the dust cover, cotter pin. Disconnect the tie rod end ball joint from the housing knuckle arm, using the proper puller tool.
6. Remove the halfshaft from the differential spindle along with the housing assembly.
7. Remove the housing from the halfshaft, using tool No. 926470000 or equivalent.
8. Installation is the reverse of the removal procedure.

### CV-JOINT OVERHAUL

**For all overhaul procedures, please refer to "CV-Joint Overhaul" in the Unit Repair section.**

## Driveshaft

### REMOVAL & INSTALLATION

*4WD Vehicles*

1. Raise and support the vehicle safely.

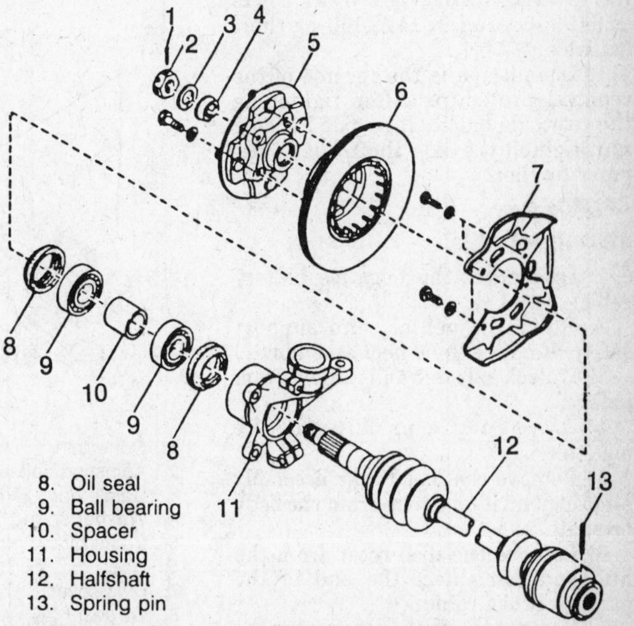

1. Cotter pin
2. Castle nut
3. Washer spring
4. Center piece
5. Hub
6. Brake disc
7. Disc cover
8. Oil seal
9. Ball bearing
10. Spacer
11. Housing
12. Halfshaft
13. Spring pin

**Front halfshaft assembly and related components except Justy and XT Coupe with 2700cc engine**

2. Remove the driveshaft flange to rear differential flange bolts.

3. Position a drain pan under the rear of the transaxle. Remove the driveshaft from the vehicle.

**NOTE: If equipped with a center bearing, remove the center bearing to chassis bolts and lower the assembly from the vehicle.**

4. Installation is the reverse of the removal procedure.

## Rear Axle Shafts

### REMOVAL & INSTALLATION

#### *Justy*

#### 2WD

1. Raise and support the vehicle safely. Remove the tire and wheel assembly.
2. Remove the dust cap. Straighten the locking washer edge. Remove the nut, lock washer and washer.
3. Remove the brake drum. Be sure not to drop the outer bearing.
4. Remove the brake line bracket from the spindle housing.
5. Loosen the bolts and remove the brake assembly. Suspend the assembly out of the way with wire.
6. Remove the bracket assembly.
7. Remove the brake assembly. Suspend the assembly out of the way with wire.
8. Using the proper tools, drive out the spring pin connecting the halfshaft assembly to the differential.
9. Remove the strut, lower link and trailing link. Pull the housing along with the halfshaft from its mounting.
10. Separate the housing from the halfshaft, using removal tools 922493000 and 921122000 or their equivalent.
11. Installation is the reverse of the removal procedure. After tightening the rear axle halfshaft to axle housing nut, tighten the axle shaft nut 30 degrees further.

#### *Legacy*

#### 4WD REAR AXLE

1. Disconnect the negative battery cable.
2. Raise the vehicle and support safely. Remove the wheel assemblies.
3. Unlock axle nut and remove from axle.
4. Loosen the parking brake adjuster.
5. Remove the disc brake assembly and suspend it on a wire from the body or strut.
6. Remove the disc rotor from the hub and disconnect the end of the parking brake cable.
7. Remove the speed senor from the backing plate, if equipped with automatic brake system (ABS).
8. Remove the bolts that secure the lateral link assembly and the trailing link assembly to the rear housing. Discard the self-locking nuts and replace with new nuts.
9. Remove the spring pin that secures the rear differential spindle to the inner CV joint.
10. Remove the inner CV joint and shaft from the differential spindle.
11. Disengage the rear drive shaft from the rear hub and remove the shaft.
12. When installing the shaft, reverse the removal procedures with the following additions:
    a. Use new seals.
    b. Using a new axle nut, pull the axle shaft through the hub splines.
    c. Install the axle shaft onto the differential spindle and install the spring pin into place.
    d. Using new nuts on the trailing link, tighten to 72–94 ft. lbs.
    e. Torque disc brake assembly to the rear housing assembly bolts/nuts to 34–43 ft. lbs.
    f. Torque the axle nut to 123–152 ft. lbs.
    g. Wheel nut torque to 58–72 ft. lbs.

#### 2WD REAR AXLE

1. Disconnect the negative battery cable.
2. Raise the vehicle and support safely.
3. Remove the wheels and unlock the axle nut. Remove the axle nut.
4. Loosen the parking brake adjuster. Remove the disc brake assembly from the backing plate and suspend it with a wire from the strut.
5. Remove the disc brake rotor from the hub and disconnect the end of the parking brake cable.
6. Remove the bolts that retain the lateral link, trailing link and the strut to the rear spindle.
7. Remove the rear spidle, backing plate and hub as a unit.
8. The installation is the reverse of the removal procedure. Use the following torque values during installation.
    a. Rear spindle to strut assembly – 98–119 ft. lbs.
    b. Rear spindle assembly to trailing link – 72–94 ft. lbs.
    c. Rear spindle to lateral link – 87–116 ft. lbs.
    d. Disc brake assembly to backing plate – 34–43 ft. lbs.
    e. Axle nut – 123–152 ft. lbs.
    f. Wheel nuts – 58–72 ft. lbs.

#### *Except Justy and Legacy*

#### 2WD

1. Raise and support the vehicle safely. Remove the tire and wheel assembly.
2. Remove the dust cap. Starighten the lock washer. Remove the nut, lock washer and washer.
3. Remove the brake drum. Be sure not to drop the outer bearing.
4. Remove the brake line bracket from the spindle housing.
5. Loosen the bolts and remove the brake assembly. Suspend the assembly out of the way with wire.
6. Remove the damper strut, lower link and trailing link.

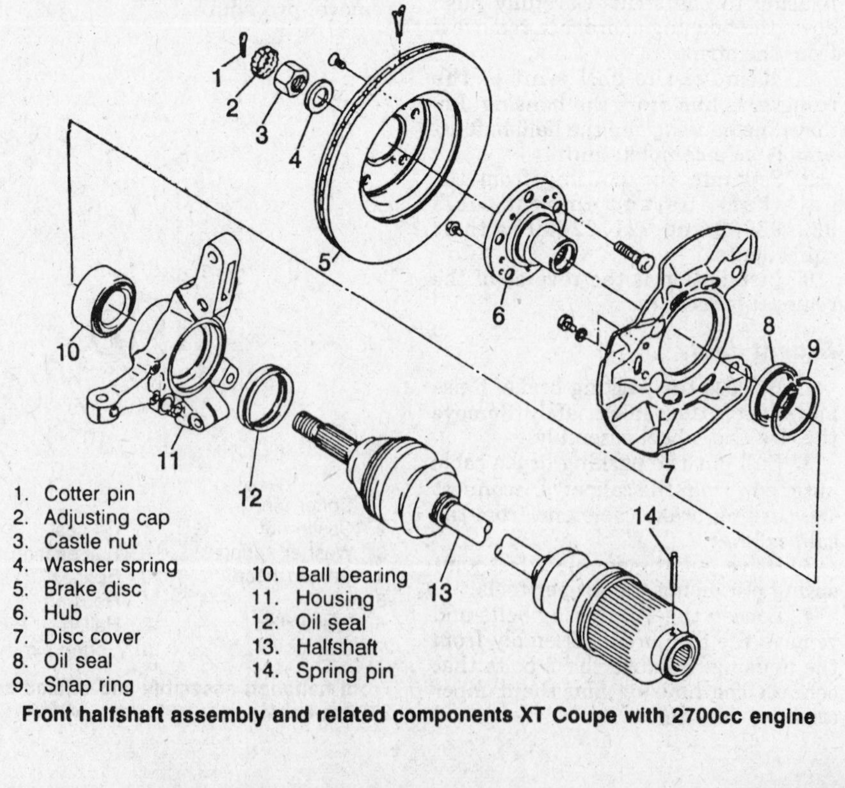


Front halfshaft assembly and related components XT Coupe with 2700cc engine

7. Remove the spindle assembly retaining bolts. Remove the spindle from its mounting.
8. Installation is the reverse of the removal procedure.

**4WD**

1. Firmly apply the parking brake.
2. Remove the rear wheel cap and the cotter pin, then loosen the castle nut.
3. Disconnect the shock absorber from the inner arm.
4. Loosen the crossmember outer bushing lock bolts. Remove the inner trailing arm to chassis bolt and the inner arm.
5. Raise and support the vehicle safely. Remove the rear wheel assemblies.
6. Using a 0.24 in. (6mm) diameter steel rod or a pin punch, drive the inner/outer spring pins from the double offset joints
7. With the trailing arm fully lowered, remove the ball joint from the trailing arm spindle and the inner double offset joint and the differential spindle.
8. Remove the castle nut and the brake drum or rear wheei caliper If equipped, remove the brake caliper and properly position it out of the way. Do not disconnect the brake hose from the caliper.
9. Disconnect and plug the brake hose from the inner arm bracket.
10. If equipped with rear brake drums, remove the brake assembly from the trailing arm.
11. Disconnect the inner arm from the outer arm and remove the inner arm from the vehicle.
12. Secure the inner arm in a vise, then using a hammer and a punch, straighten the staked portion of the ring nut or remove the cotter pin from the castled nut. Using the wrench tool No. 925550000 or equivalent, remove the ring nut.
13. Using a plastic hammer on the outside of the spindle, drive it inward to remove it.
14. Clean, inspect and replace the necessary parts.
15. Using an abor press and a piece of 1.38 in. dia. (35mm) pipe, insert the spindle from the inside and press the outer bearing's inner race from outside.
16. Using the wrench tool No. 925550000 or equivalent, torque the axle shaft ring nut to 127–163 ft. lbs. Using a punch and a hammer, stake the ring nut, facing the ring nut groove or install a new cotter pin in the castled nut.
17. To complete the installation, use new spring pins and reverse the removal procedures. Torque the backing plate to axle housing bolts to 34–43 ft.

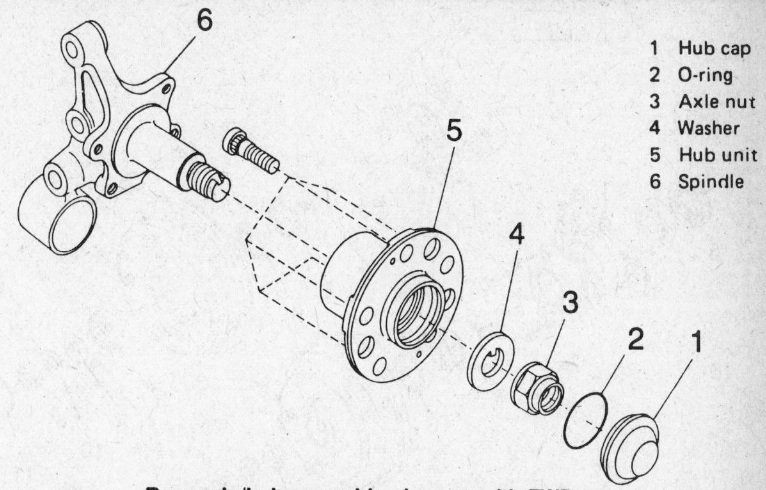


**Rear axle/hub assembly – Legacy with FWD**

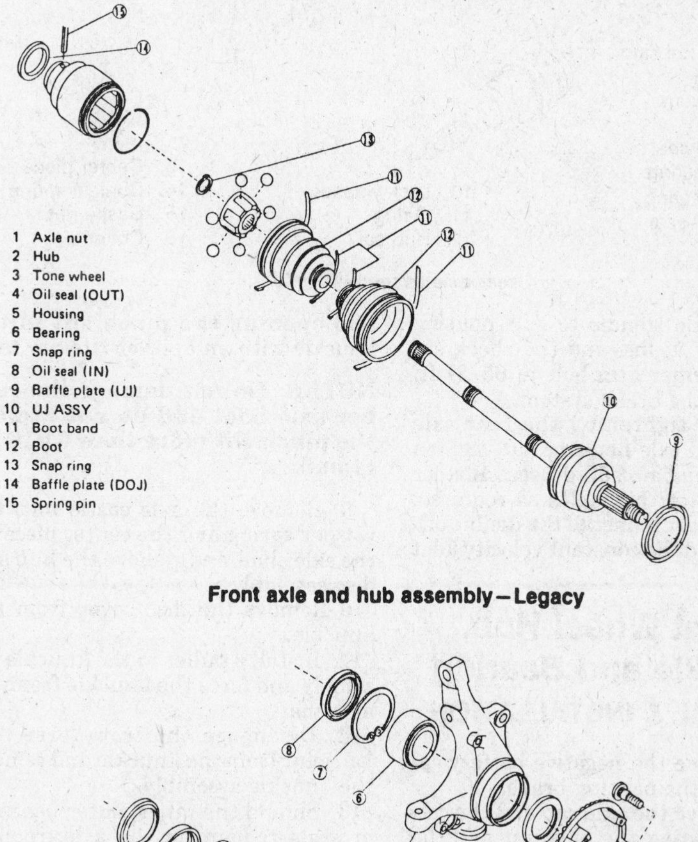


**Front axle and hub assembly – Legacy**

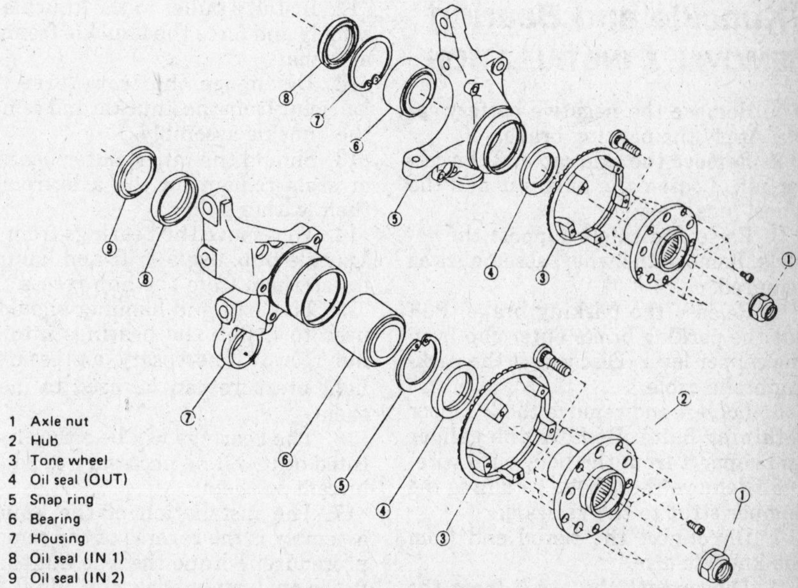


**Rear hub assembly – Legacy with 4WD**

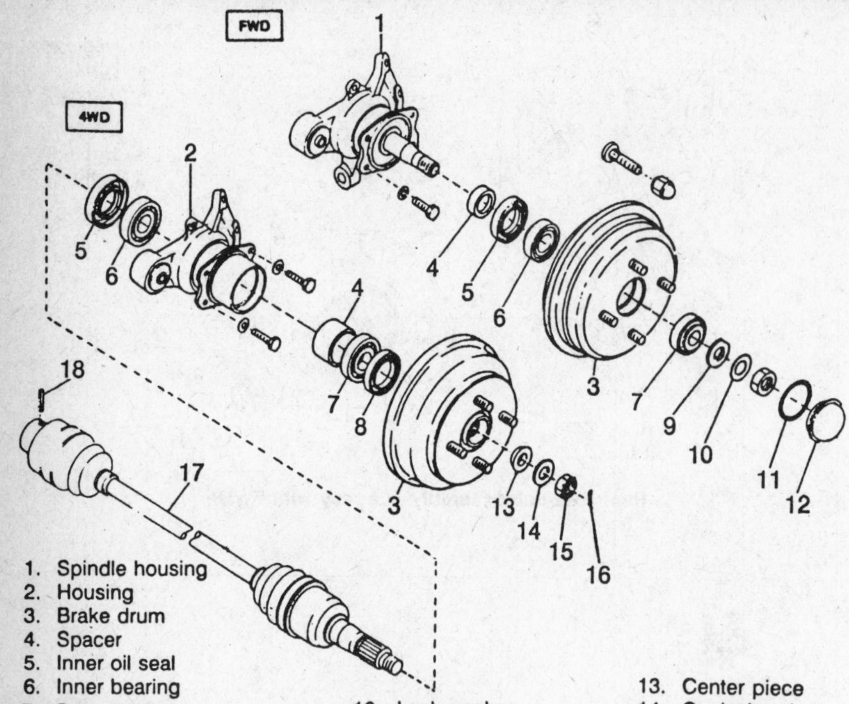

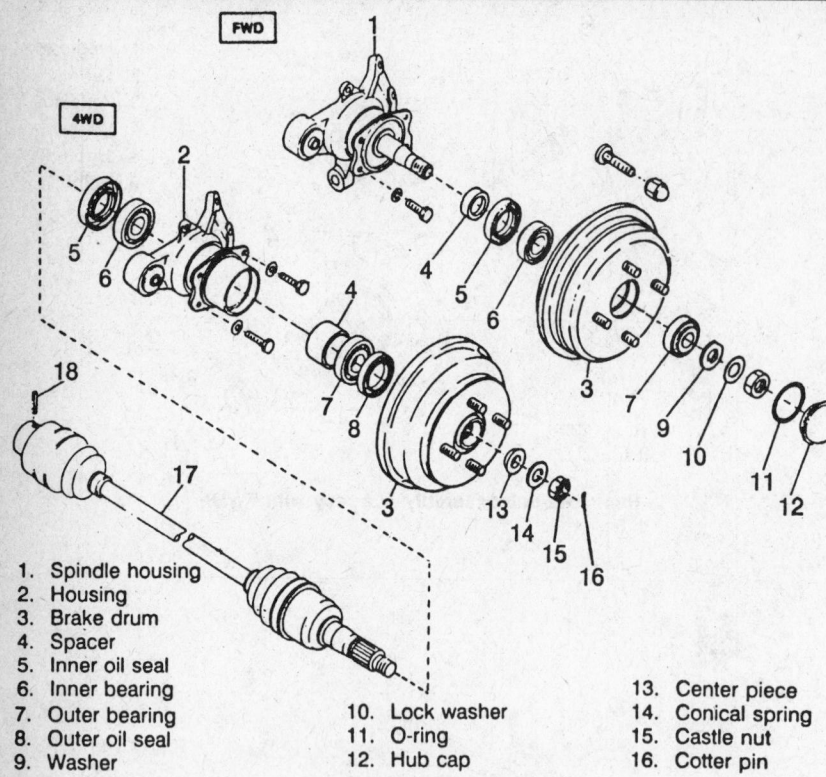

1. Spindle housing
2. Housing
3. Brake drum
4. Spacer
5. Inner oil seal
6. Inner bearing
7. Outer bearing
8. Outer oil seal
9. Washer
10. Lock washer
11. O-ring
12. Hub cap
13. Center piece
14. Conical spring
15. Castle nut
16. Cotter pin

**Rear axle assembly Justy**

lbs., the axle spindle to axle housing nut to 145 ft. lbs. and the shock absorber to inner arm bolt to 65–87 ft. lbs. Bleed the brake system.

18. After tightening the rear axle halfshaft to axle housing nut, tighten the axle shaft nut 30 degrees further to align cotter pin holes as required. Be careful not to install the double offset joint and the constant velocity joint oppositely.

## Front Wheel Hub, Kunckle and Bearing

### REMOVAL & INSTALLATION

1. Remove the negative battery cable. Apply the parking brake.
2. Remove the axle cap and the cotter pin. Loosen the axle nut and the wheel lugs.
3. Raise and safely support the vehicle. Remove the wheel assemblies as required.
4. Release the parking brake. Pull out the parking brake outer clip from the caliper lever. Disconnect the parking brake cable.
5. Loosen and remove the 2 caliper retaining bolts. Remove the caliper and support from the body with wire.
6. Remove the 2 bolts retaining the damper strut to the knuckle.
7. Disconnect the tierod end from the knuckle arm.
8. Disconnect the strut from the knuckle by removing the pinch bolt and opening the pinch slit in the knuckle with an appropriate pry tool.

**NOTER: Do not damage the rubber axle boot and do not expand the pinch slit more than 0.016 in. (4mm).**

9. Remove the axle castle nut, the washer spring and the center piece on the axle shaft and remove the hub and disc assembly.
10 Remove the disc cover from the knuckle.
11. Install a puller to the knuckle assembly and force the knuckle from the axle shaft.
12. Disengage the transverse link ball joint from the knuckle and remove the knuckle assembly.
13. Should the inner, outer bearings or seals remain on the axle, remove them with a puller.
14. To remove the bearings from the knuckle hub, use a drift and hammer to tap them from the hub recess.
15. The drift and hammer should be used to install the bearings into the hub recess. If necessary, a press using light pressure can be used to install them.
16. The bearings will be either lubricated or it will be necessary to add lubricant to them.
17. The installation of the knuckle assembly is the reverse of the removal procedure. Torque the axle nut to 130 ft. lbs on Justy models and 145 ft. lbs. on all other models.

# FRONT SUSPENSION

## MacPherson Strut

### REMOVAL & INSTALLATION

#### *Justy*

1. Disconnect the negative battery cable. Remove the bolts that retain the strut assembly to the body.
2. Raise and support the vehicle safely. Remove the tire and wheel assembly.
3. Remove the brake hose from the brake hose bracket on the strut assembly. Remove the retaining bolt that retains the brake hose bracket to the strut.
4. Properly support the hub and disc assembly. Remove the retaining bolt from the strut to the housing.
5. Fit the proper tool into the housing slit and pull the strut assembly from the housing.
6. Remove the strut from the vehicle.
7. Installation is the reverse of the removal procedure.

#### *Except Justy*

1. Disconnect the negative battery cable. If equipped with air suspension, remove the cover and the air line assembly.
2. Remove the bolts that retain the strut assembly to the body.
3. Raise and support the vehicle safely. Remove the tire and wheel assembly.
4. Disconnect the brake hose from the caliper body. Pull the brake hose retaining clip and remove the brake hose from the damper strut bracket.
5. Remove the bolt that retains the damper strut to the housing. Remove the bolt that retains the damper strut bracket to the housing.
6. Pull the strut assembly out of the housing gradually and carefully, with the housing assembly in the downward position.
7. Remove the strut assembly from the vehicle.
8. Installation is the reverse of the removal procedure. As required, bleed the brake system.

### OVERHAUL

**For all spring and shock absorber removal and installation procedures, and all strut overhaul procedures, please refer to "Strut Overhaul" in the Unit Repair Section.**

## Ball Joints

### INSPECTION

1. Raise and support the vehicle safely.
2. Using a pry bar, position it under the wheel, then pry upward on the wheel several times. If more than 0.012 in. (3mm) of movement is noticed at the ball joint it should be replaced.
3. Inspect the dust seal, if damaged it should be replaced.

### REMOVAL & INSTALLATION

1. Raise and support the vehicle safely. Remove the tire and wheel assembly.
2. Properly support the lower control arm assembly. Remove the cotter pin and castle nut from the ball joint.
3. Disconnect the ball joint from the lower control arm assembly.
4. Remove the bolt retaining the ball joint to the housing. Remove the ball joint from the houising.
5. Installation is the reverse of the removal procedure.

## Lower Control Arm

### REMOVAL & INSTALLATION

#### *Justy*

1. Raise and support the vehicle safely. Remove the tire and wheel assembly.
2. Properly support the lower control arm. Remove the bolt that retains the lower control arm to the crossmember.
3. Remove the bolt coupling housing to ball joint retaining bolt. Using the proper tool, insert it into the slit and pull the ball joint from the housing.
4. Remove the lower control arm from the vehicle.
5. Installation is the reverse of the removal procedure.

#### *Except Justy*

1. Raise and support the vehicle safely. Remove the tire and wheel assembly.
2. As required, remove the parking brake cable from the lower control arm assembly.
3. Remove the bolt that retains the stabilizer assembly to the lower control arm.
4. Remove the front exhaust pipe, as necessary to gain working clearance.
5. Properly support the lower control arm assembly. Remove the ball joint from its mounting.

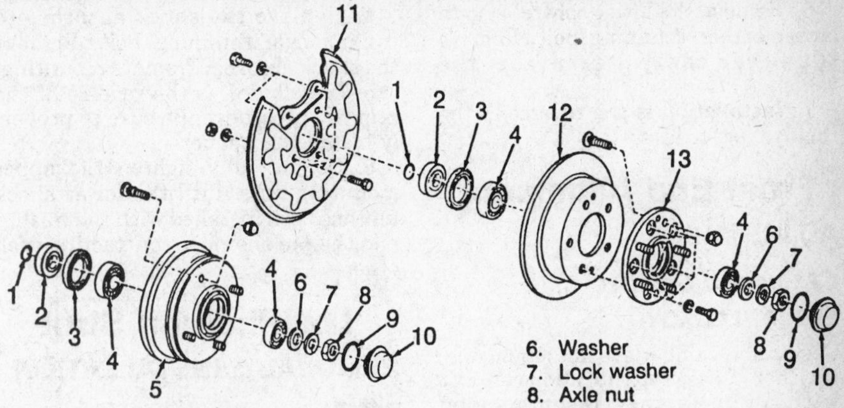

1. O-ring
2. Spacer
3. Oil seal
4. Taper roller bearing
5. Brake drum
6. Washer
7. Lock washer
8. Axle nut
9. O-ring
10. Drum cap
11. Disc cover
12. Disc rotor
13. Hub

**Rear axle assembly XT Coupe with 2700cc engine and 2WD**

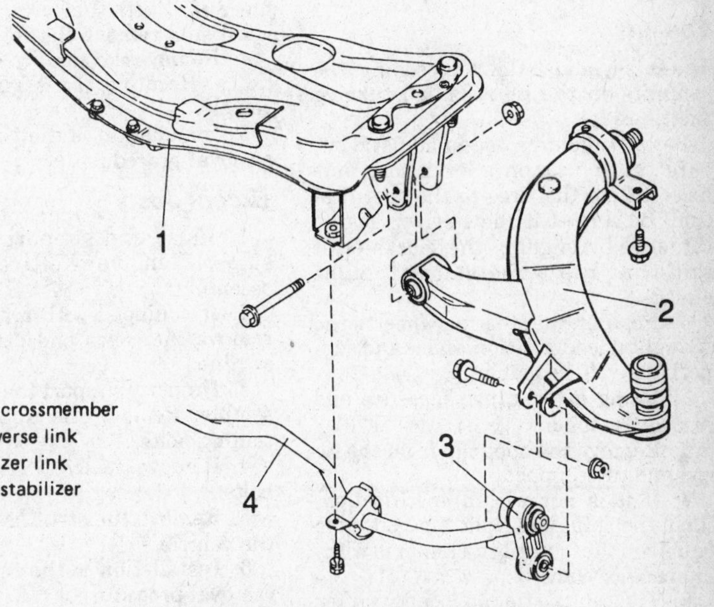

1 Front crossmember
2 Transverse link
3 Stabilizer link
4 Front stabilizer

**Front lower control arm—Legacy models**

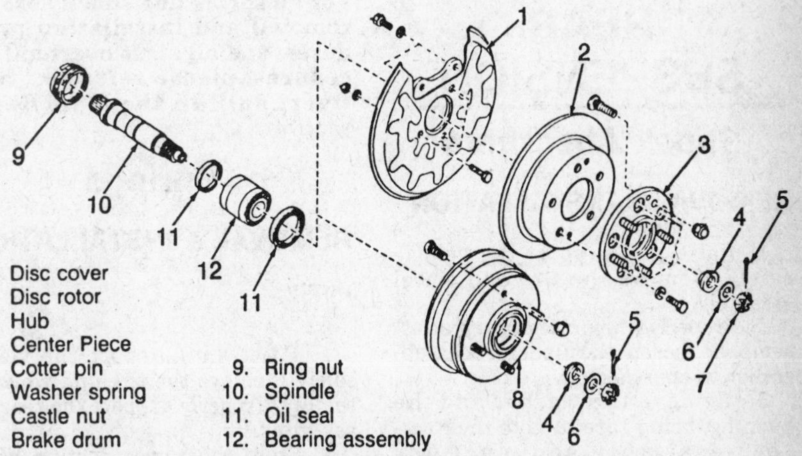

1. Disc cover
2. Disc rotor
3. Hub
4. Center Piece
5. Cotter pin
6. Washer spring
7. Castle nut
8. Brake drum
9. Ring nut
10. Spindle
11. Oil seal
12. Bearing assembly

**Rear axle assembly XT Coupe with 2700cc engine and 4WD**

6. Remove the lower control arm to crossmember retaining bolt. Remove the lower control arm from the vehicle.

7. Installation is the reverse of the removal procedure.

## Front End Alignment

### ADJUSTMENT

#### *Caster and Camber*

**EXCEPT LEGACY**

Caster and camber are not adjustable. If either of these specifications are not within the factory recommended range, this would indicate bent or damaged parts that must be replaced.

**LEGACY**

Caster is none adjustable, but camber cam be manually adjusted. Eccentric bolts are located in the joint at the strut and housing.

#### *Toe-In*

Toe-in is adjusted by loosening the locknuts on the tie rods and turning the tie rods.

Before adjusting toe-in adjustment, park the vehicle on a level, solid surface, inflate the tires to the specification. Be sure that the steering gear is centered by aligning the marks on it and that the wheels are straight ahead.

1. Position the steering wheel in the straight ahead position. Raise and support the vehicle safely.
2. Using a toe gauge measure and record the toe-in.
3. Remove the boot clip from the tie rod end, if equipped.
4. If it is not within specification, turn the left and right tie rod ends equal amounts until the toe-in is within specification.
5. Tighten the tie rod locknuts after the toe-in adjustment is completed.

# REAR SUSPENSION

## Shock Absorbers

### REMOVAL & INSTALLATION

1. Raise and support the vehicle safely. Remove the tire and wheel assembly.
2. Properly support the rear axle assembly. Loosen the upper shock absorber to chassis nuts.
3. Remove the washer and the bushing, being sure to note their correct assembly sequence for installation.
4. Remove the shock absorber to trailing arm retaining bolt. Remove the shock absorber from its mounting.
5. Installation is the reverse of the removal procedure. Be sure to properly install the washers.
6. Do not fully tighten the upper mounting nuts until the lower shock nut has been installed with the washer and the pin shoulder contracting each other.

## MacPherson Strut

### REMOVAL & INSTALLATION

#### *Justy*

1. Raise and support the vehicle safely. Remove the tire and wheel assembly. Properly support the rear axle assembly.
2. From the upper portion of the strut mount, remove the trim cover.
3. Remove the strut to body retaining nut. Push the lower arm downward, and remove the coil spring.
4. Remove the strut to axle housing bolts. Remove the strut from the vehicle.
5. Installation is the reverse of the removal procedure.

#### *Except Justy*

1. Raise and support the vehicle safely. Remove the tire and wheel assembly.
2. If equipped with air suspension, remove the cover and disconnect the air line.
3. Properly support the rear axle assembly. Remove the upper strut retaining bolts.
4. Remove the lower strut retaining bolts.
5. Remove the strut assembly from the vehicle.
6. Installation is the reverse of the removal procedure.

### OVERHAUL

**For all spring and shock absorber removal and installation procedures, and all strut overhaul procedures, please refer to "Strut Overhaul" in the Unit Repair section.**

## Springs

### REMOVAL & INSTALLATION

#### *Justy*

1. Raise and support the vehicle safely. Remove the tire and wheel assembly. Properly support the rear axle assembly.
2. From the upper portion of the strut mount, remove the trim cover.
3. Remove the strut to body retaining nut. Push the lower arm downward, and remove the coil spring.
4. Installation is the reverse of the removal procedure.

## Torsion Bar

### REMOVAL & INSTALLATION

#### *1983–84 Vehicles*

1. Raise and support the vehicle safely. Remove the tire and wheel assembly.
2. Support the rear axles in a position eliminating load from the torsion bar.
3. Remove the lockbolt for the outer bushing and the outer arm to inner arm bolts. Pull the outer arm and torsion bar out of the crossmember. The torsion bar may not be removed from the outer arm.

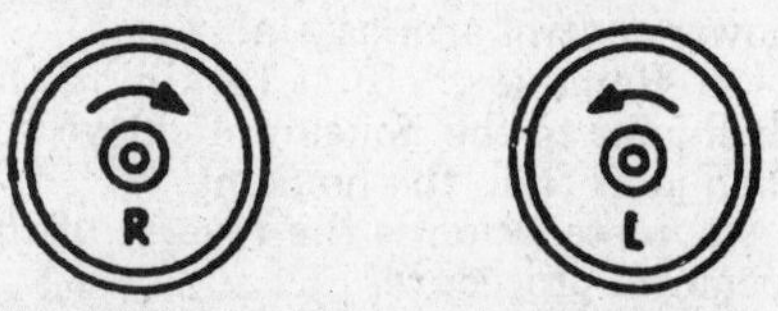


**View of torsion bar directional markings-rear suspension system 1982–84 vehicles**

**NOTE: If equipped with 4WD, remove the center arm after the torsion bars are removed from both sides.**

4. Inspect the center arm and torsion bars for damage and replace if necesary.
5. Installation is the reverse of the removal procedure.
6. The torsion bar splines must be aligned with those in the outer arm and the crossmember so that the outer arm align with the inner arm, as it did during removal, or the ride height will be effected.
7. If removing both torsion bars, make sure the markings **R** or **L** correspond with the side of the vehicle the bar is being installed.

## Rear Control Arms

### REMOVAL & INSTALLATION

#### *Justy*

1. Raise and support the vehicle safely. Remove the tire and wheel assembly.
2. Properly support the rear axle assembly. Remove the coil spring assembly.
3. Remove the control arm to crossmember bolt. Separate the control arm from the crossmember.
4. Remove the control arm to axle

housing bolt Separate the control arm from the axle housing.

5. Remove the assembly from the vehicle.

6. Installation is the reverse of the removal procedure.

### *Legacy*

#### TRAILING LINK

1. Loosen the rear wheel lugs, raise and safely support the vehicle and remove the wheel assemblies.
2. Remove the rear parking brake clamps and the ABS sensors, as required.
3. Remove the bolts retaining the trailing link to the body.
4. Remove the bolts retaining the trailing link to the rear housing.
5. Remove the trailing link from the vehicle.
6. To install the trailing link, place in position and install the bolts at each end.
7. Torque the bolts to 72–94 ft. lbs.
8. Complete the assembly.

#### LATERAL LINK

1. Remove the stabilizer from the lateral link.
2. Remove the parking brake cable and the ABS sensor clamp from the trailing link, as required.
3. Loosen the bolts that secure the trailing link to the bracket and remove the bolts that retain the trailing link to the rear housing.
4. If equipped with 4WD, remove the Double Offset Joint (DOJ) pin and axle shaft to provide working space.
5. Remove the front lateral link from the rear cross member.
6. Temporarily install front lateral link to the rear crossmember and remove the rear lateral link from the crossmember.
7. To install the link, reverse the removal proceedure. Torque the bolts to the following specifications:
   a. 4WD–61–83 ft. lbs.
   b. FWD–87–116 ft. lbs.

### *Except Justy and Legacy*

1. Raise and support the vehicle safely. Remove the tire and wheel assembly.
2. Properly support the rear axle assembly.
3. Remove the strut to lower control arm bolt and separate the strut from the lower control arm.
4. If equipped with 4WD, use a 0.24 in. (6mm) pin punch and drive the spring pins from the halfshaft to axle shaft and the halfshaft to differential assembly. While pushing downward on the inner arm, separate the halfshaft from the axle shaft. Pull the halfshaft from the differential and position it out of the way.

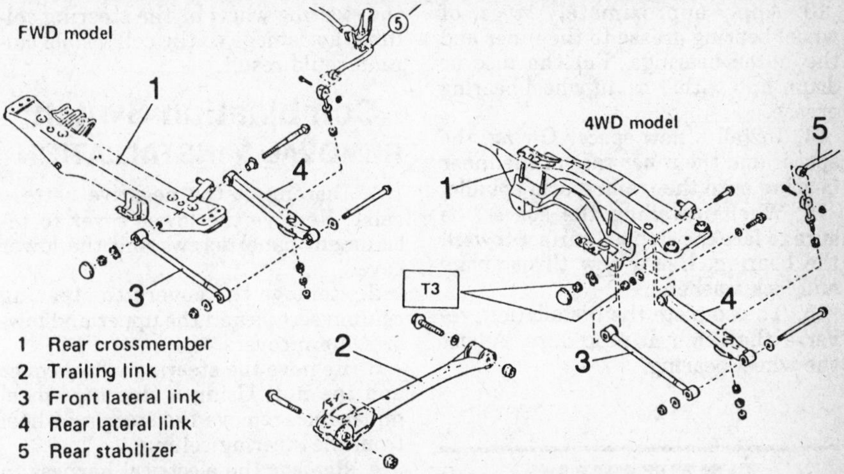


**Rear trailing link assembly for both FWD and 4WD Legacy models**

5. Disconnect and plug the brake hose from the brake line at the lower control arm.
6. Remove the outer arm to lower control arm bolts, then separate the lower control arm from the outer arm. Properly support the inner arm.
7. Remove the inner arm to crossmember bolt. Remove the lower control arm from the vehicle.
8. Installation is the reverse of the removal procedure.
9. If equipped with 4WD, use new spring pins. As required, bleed the brake system.

## Rear Wheel Bearings

### ADJUSTMENT

#### *2WD*

1. Raise and support the vehicle safely. Remove the rear wheel assembly.
2. Temporarily tighten the axle nut to 36 ft. lbs. on all vehicles except Justy. Tighten the nut to 29 ft. lbs. for Justy.
3. Turn the drum or disc back and forth several times to ensure that bearings are properly seated.
4. Turn the nut backwards $\frac{1}{8}$–$\frac{1}{10}$ turn in order to obtain the correct starting force.
5. Using a spring gauge at 90 degrees to the wheel lug, check the rotating force. Specifications should be 1.9–3.2 lbs. for all vehicles except Justy. The specifications for Justy are 3.1–4.4 lbs.
6. After the adjsutment is completed, bend the lock washer. After installing a new O-ring to the grease cap, install the cap.

### REMOVAL & INSTALLATION

1. Raise and support the vehicle safely. Remove the rear tire and wheel assembly.
2. If equipped with rear disc brakes, remove the caliper and properly support it.
3. Using a small prybar, remove the rear wheel grease cap.
4. Using a hammer and a punch, flatten the lock washer and loosen the axle nut. Remove the lock washer and the thrust plate. When removing the drum or disc, be careful not to drop the inner race from the outer bearing.

**NOTE: If the brake drum on the Justy is difficult to remove, use wheel puller tool 9224930000 or equivalent, to remove the brake drum.**

5. Using a gear puller, remove the spacer and the inner race of the inner bearing.
6. Using a brass drift and a hammer, drive the outer race of the inner bearing from the drum or disc.
7. Using a brass drift and a hammer, drive the outer race of the outer bearing from the drum or disc.
8. Clean and inspect the parts for damage, replace defective parts, if necessary.
9. Using bearing installation tool 925220000 or equivalent for all vehicles except Justy, or tool 922111000 or equivalent for Justy, press the outer race of the inner bearing into the drum or disc until it seats against the shoulder.
10. When pressing the bearing, be sure not to exceed the load to the bearing, so as not to damage it.
11. Apply a small amount of grease to the oil seal lips, then install the oil seal until it is flush with the drum or disc.
12. Using bearing installation tool 921130000 or equivalent for all vehicles except Justy, or tool 922111000 or equivalent for Justy, press the outer race of the outer bearing into the drum or disc until it seats against the shoulder.

13. Apply approximately 1/8 oz. of wheel bearing grease to the inner and the outer bearings. Fill the disc or drum hub with 1 oz. of wheel bearing grease.
14. Install a new spacer O-ring, the spacer and the inner race of the inner bearing onto the trailing arm spindle.
15. When installing the spacer, be sure to face the stepped surface toward the bearing. Use a new thrust plate and lock washer.
16. To complete the installation, reverse the removal procedure. Adjust the wheel bearing.

# STEERING

## Steering Wheel

### REMOVAL & INSTALLATION

1. Disconnect the negative battery cable.
2. Disconnect the horn lead from the wiring harness, located beneath the instrument panel. On the XT Coupe, remove the horn pad.

**NOTE: If equipped with telescopic steering wheel, remove the telescopic lever assembly.**

3. Working behind the steering wheel, remove the steering wheel cover to steering wheel screws. It may be necessary to lower the column from the dash by removing the screws.
4. Lift the crash pad assembly from the front of the wheel.
5. Matchmark the steering wheel and the column for installation.
6. Remove the steering wheel retaining nut. Using a steering wheel puller tool, remove the steering wheel from the column.
7. Installation is the reverse of the removal procedure. Do not hammer on the steering wheel or the steering column, as damage to the collapsible column could result.

## Combination Switch

### REMOVAL & INSTALLATION

1. Disconnect the negative battery cable. Remove the lower cover to instrument panel screws and the lower cover.
2. Remove the covers to steering column screws and the upper and lower column covers.
3. Remove the steering wheel cover and the nut. Using a steering wheel puller tool, remove the steering wheel from the steering column.
4. Remove the electrical harness to steering column clip and band fitting, then disconnect the electrical connectors.
5. Remove the combination switch to control wing bracket screws. Remove the switch assembly from its mounting.
6. Installation is the reverse of the removal procedure.

## Ignition Switch

### REMOVAL & INSTALLATION

**NOTE: The ignition switch is mounted to the steering column using shear bolts. These bolts are constructed so that the heads shear off when the bolt is torqued.**

1. Disconnect the negative battery cable. Remove the steering wheel.
2. Remove the upper and lower steering column covers from the steering column.
3. Remove the hazard knob.
4. Drill a pilot hole into the shear bolts, then using a screw extractor, remove the screws from the steering column.
5. Remove the ignition switch from the steering column.

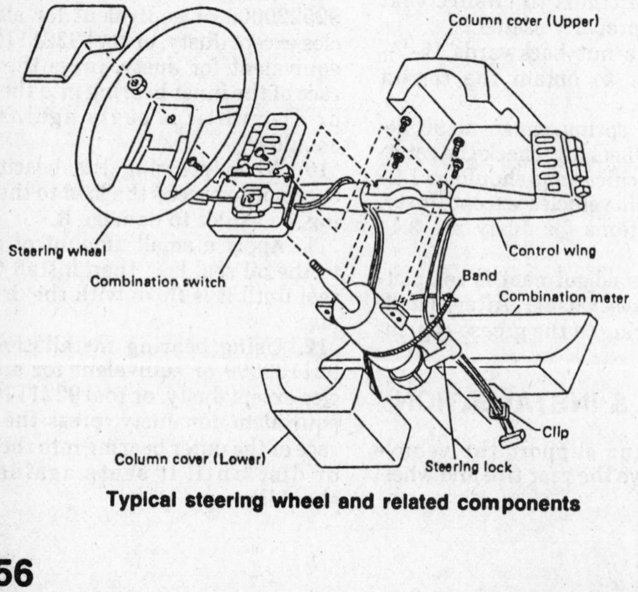

**Typical steering wheel and related components**

6. Installation is the reverse of the removal procedure. Be sure to use new shear bolts to install the ignition switch.

## Manual Steering Gear

### REMOVAL & INSTALLATION

#### *Justy*

1. Disconnect the negative battery cable. Raise and support the vehicle safely. Remove the front tire and wheel assemblies.
2. Disconnect the universal joint coupling bolts. Remove the dust seal.
3. Using the proper tools, disconnect the tie rod ends from the knuckle arms.
4. Remove the steering gear retaining bolts. Lower the assembly and pull the pinion out of the dust seal toward the engine compartment.
5. Remove the steering gear from the vehicle.
6. Installation is the reverse of the removal procedure.

#### *XT Coupe*

1. Be sure that the parking brake lever is in the released position. Disconnect the negative battery cable.
2. Raise and support the vehicle safely. Remove the front tire and wheel assemblies.
3. Remove the outer tie rod end cotter pin. Remove the castle nut. Using the proper tool, remove the tie rod end from the steering knuckle.
4. Remove the pinch bolt from the torque rod universal joint.

**NOTE: Do not attempt to remove the steering gear assembly or crossmember with the pinch bolt installed to the torque rod universal joint.**

5. Loosen the exhaust manifold retaining bolts. Lower the exhaust pipe.
6. Remove the steering gear retaining bolts.
7. Move the assembly toward the pinion. As the pinion shafts comes off the torque rod, rotate the steering gear rearward and remove it from the vehicle, toward the pinion.
8. Installation is the reverse of the removal procedure.

#### *Except Justy and XT Coupe*

1. Disconnect the negative battery cable.
2. Raise and support the vehicle safely. Remove the front tire and wheel assemblies.
3. Remove the tie rod end cotter pin and loosen the castle nut. Using a ball joint puller tool, separate the tie rod ends from the housing knuckle arm.
4. If necessary, disconnect the handbrake cable hanger from the tie rod.

5. On 1983–84 vehicles, remove the rubber coupling bolts. On 1985–90 vehicles, remove the pinch bolt from the torque rod universal joint. Disconnect the pinion with the gearbox from the steering column.

6. If equipped with an hot air pipe, disconnect it.

7. Disconnect the exhaust manifold to engine bolts, pull downward on the exhaust manifold.

8. Remove the boot from the steering gear.

9. Remove the steering gear to crossmember bolts, pull downward on the steering gear to disconnect the pinion flange. Turn the gearbox rearward and remove it toward the left side.

10. When removing the gearbox, be careful not to damage the gearbox boot. Inspect the removed parts for wear or damage and if necessary, replace the parts.

11. To install, reverse the removal procedures. Torque the steering gearbox to crossmember bolts to:

1983–84 – 33–40 ft. lbs.
1985–90 – 35–52 ft. lbs.

12. Torque the pinch bolt to universal joint to 15–20 ft. lbs.

13. Torque the exhaust manifold to engine bolts to 19–22 ft. lbs.

14. Torque the rubber coupling to steering gear bolts to 10–14.5 ft. lbs.

15. Torque the tie rod end to steering knuckle nut to 18–22 ft. lbs.

16. Adjust the toe-in and the turning angles to specifications.

17. When torquing the tie rod end to steering knuckle nuts, torque the nut 60 degrees turn (except Justy) or 45 degrees turn (Justy) further, after torquing to specification.

## ADJUSTMENT

1. Tighten the backlash adjuster until it bottoms, back off the screw 15 degrees for all 1983–84 vehicles and Justy and 25 degrees for all 1985–90 vehicles except Justy.

2. Torque the locknut to 22–36 ft. lbs. for all 1983–84 vehicles, XT Coupe and Justy and 36–47 ft. lbs. for all 1985–90 vehicles, except XT Coupe and Justy.

3. A clearance of 0.0025 in. is provided between the screw tip and the sleeve plate for all 1983–84 vehicles and Justy.

4. A clearance of 0.004 in. for all 1985–90 vehicles except Justy, is provided between the screw tip and the sleeve plate.

# Power Steering Gear

## REMOVAL & INSTALLATION

1. Disconnect the negative battery cable. Remove the spare tire. If equipped with a turbocharger, remove the spare tire support.

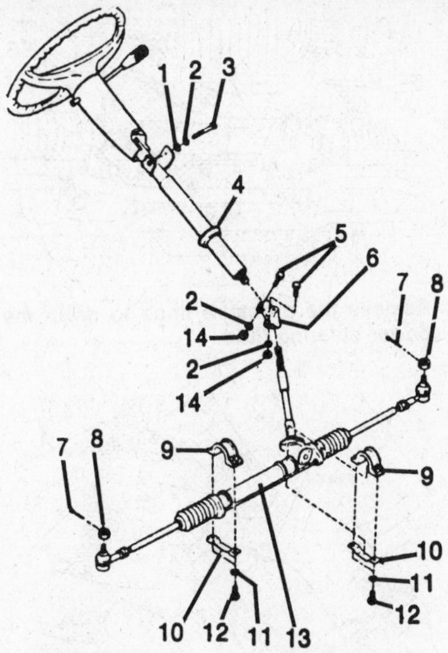


1. Washer
2. Spring washer
3. Bolt
4. Bushing
5. Bolt
6. Universal joint
7. Cotter pin
8. Castle nut
9. Gearbox bracket
10. Lock plate
11. Washer
12. Bolt
13. Steering gearbox
14. Nut

Typical steering system

2. If necessary, disconnect the thermo sensor connector.

3. Raise and support the vehicle safely. Remove the front tire and wheel assemblies.

4. Disconnect the electrical connector from the oxygen sensor. Remove the front exhaust pipe assembly. If equipped with an air stove, remove it.

5. Remove the tie rod end cotter pin and loosen the castle nut. Using a ball joint puller tool, separate the tie rod ends from the steering knuckle arm.

6. As required, remove the jack up plate and the clamp.

7. From the power steering gear, remove the center pressure pipe, connect a vinyl hose to the pipe and joint, then turn the steering wheel to discharge the fluid into a container.

**NOTE: When discharging the power steering fluid, turn the steering wheel fully, left and right. Be sure to disconnect the other pipe and drain the fluid in the same manner.**

8. Make alignment marks on the steering shaft universal joint assembly to power steering unit and the steering shaft to universal joint assembly. Remove the lower and upper universal joint to shaft bolts. Lift the universal joint assembly upward and secure it out of the way.

9. From the control valve of the gearbox assembly, remove the power steering **C** and **D** pressure pipes. Remove pipe **D** first and pipe **C** second.

10. From the control valve of the gearbox assembly, remove the power steering **A** and **B** pressure pipes. Remove pipe **A** first and pipe **B** second.

11. Remove the power steering gearbox to crossmember assembly bolts. Remove the gearbox assembly from the vehicle.

12. Installation is the reverse of the removal procedure. When installing the universal joint assembly, be sure to align the matchmarks.

13. Torque the power steering gearbox to crossmember bolts to 33–40 ft. lbs. for all 1983–84 vehicles and 35–52 ft. lbs. for all 1985–90 vehicles.

14. Torque the power steering pressure pipes 7–12 ft. lbs., the universal joint assembly to power steering gearbox bolts 16–19 ft. lbs. and the universal joint assembly to steering shaft bolts 16–19 ft. lbs.

15. Torque the tie rod end to steering knuckle nut 18–22 ft. lbs. After torquing this nut, turn it 60 degrees further.

16. Torque the wheel lug nuts to specification. Refill and bleed the power steering system. Check and adjust the toe-in and the steering angle.

## ADJUSTMENT

Tighten the backlash adjuster until it bottoms, back off the screw 30 degrees and torque the locknut to 22–36 ft. lbs., 0.0049 in. should be provided between the screw tip and the sleeve plate.

# Power Steering Pump

## REMOVAL & INSTALLATION

### *1983–84 Except Turbocharged Engine*

1. Disconnect the negative battery cable.

2. Remove the spare tire from the engine compartment. If equipped with a carburetor, remove the carburetor shield.

3. Raise and support the vehicle safely. Remove the jack up plate.

4. Position a drain pan under the power steering gear box. Remove the fluid line flare nuts from the center of the power steering gearbox, then turn the steering wheel from left to right to drain the gearbox.

5. Loosen the idler pulley adjustment bolts and remove the drive belt. It may be necessary to hit the idler pulley with a plastic hammer, to loosen it.

6. Disconnect the electrical connectors and remove the air cleaner hoses. Remove the air cleaner assembly, the engine oil dipstick and any other items that will prevent the pump removal.

7. Disconnect the fluid hoses from the back of the pump.

8. Remove the power steering pump

to vehicle bolts. Remove the pump from the vehicle.

9. Installation is the reverse of the removal procedure. Torque the power steering pump bracket to engine bolts to 18–25 ft. lbs., power steering pump to engine bracket bolts to 33–44 ft. lbs. and the belt tensioner to engine bolt to 14–22 ft. lbs.

10. Adjust the drive belt tension. Refill and bleed the power steering system.

### *1983–84 Turbocharged Engine*

1. Disconnect the negative battery cable. If necessary, remove the spare tire from the engine compartment.

2. Drain the power steering fluid from the oil reservoir located on the pump.

3. Loosen, but do not remove the power steering pump pulley nut.

4. Loosen the idler pulley to engine bolts, move the idler pulley toward the power steering pump and remove the drive belts.

5. Remove the power steering pump pulley nut and the pulley.

6. Using 2 wrenchs, disconnect the power steering pump line at the pipe. Loosen the oil line clamp and disconnect it from the reservoir.

7. Remove the power steering pump to bracket bolts. Remove the pump from the engine.

8. Installation is the reverse of the removal procedure. Torque the power steering pump bracket to engine bolts to 13–16 ft. lbs., the power steering pump to bracket bolts to 22–36 ft. lbs.

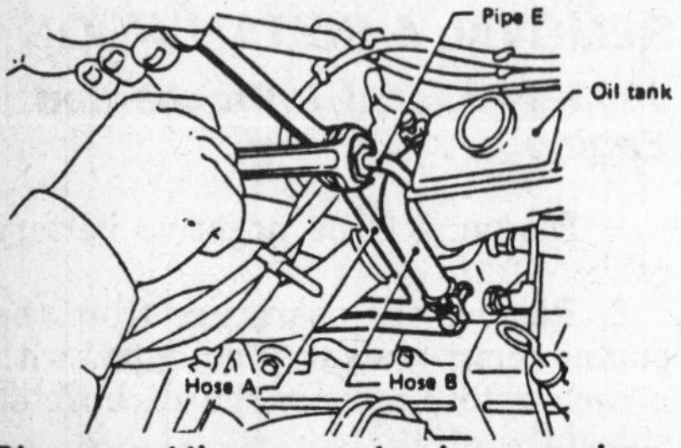


**Disconnect the power steering pump hoses from the pressure lines 1985–89 vehicles**

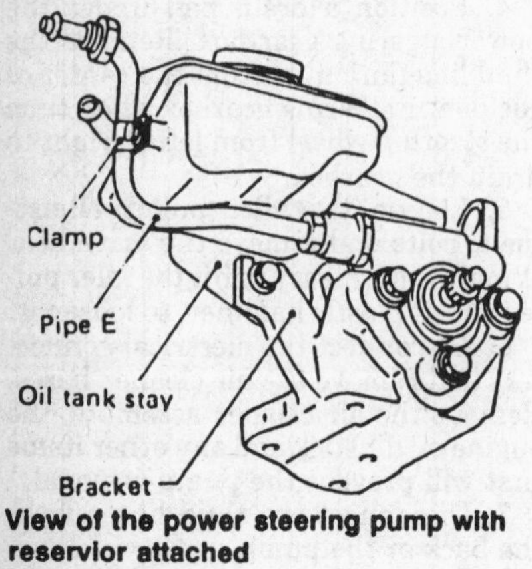


**View of the power steering pump with reservior attached**

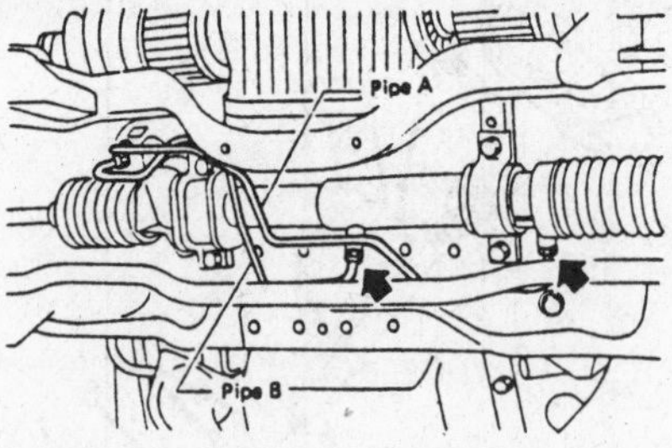


**Remove the pressure lines to drain the power steering fluid**

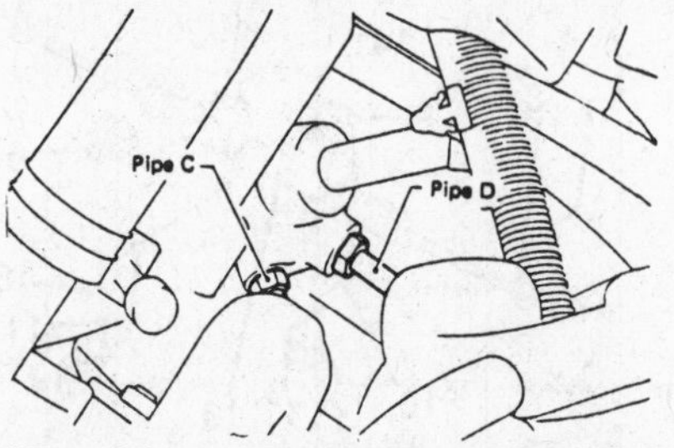


**View of the power steering gear pressure lines**

and the power steering pump pulley nut to 31–46 ft. lbs.

9. Refill the power steering pump reservoir. Adjust the drive belt tension. Bleed the power steering system.

### *1985–90 Models*

1. Disconnect the negative battery cable.

2. Using a siphon, drain the power steering fluid from the reservoir.

3. Loosen, but do not remove the power steering pump pulley nut. Loosen the pulley drive belts.

4. Remove the power steering pump pulley nut and the pulley.

5. Disconnect and plug the **A** pressure hose from the **E** pipe. Disconnect the **B** pressure hose from the oil tank.

6. When disconnecting the **A** hose, use wrenches to prevent the **E** pipe from twisting.

7. Remove the **E** hose to reservoir clamp. Loosen the reservoir to bracket bolt, then remove the **A** and **B** bolts on the upper part of the reservoir, this will allow the fluid to run out.

**NOTE: To minimize the fluid loss from the reservoir, remove both bolts while the reservoir is pressed against the oil pump, then quickly remove the reservoir. It is a good idea to remove the pump and the reservoir as a unit, then separate the reservoir from the pump on a bench.**

8. Remove the power steering pump to bracket bolts. Remove the pump from the vehicle.

9. Installation is the reverse of the removal procedure. be sure to use new O-rings.

10. Torque the power steering pump to bracket bolts to 22–36 ft. lbs.

11. Torque the reservoir stay to bracket bolts to 14–17 ft. lbs.

12. Torque the reservoir to pump bolts to 14–22 ft. lbs.

13. Torque the pulley nut to pump nut to 31–46 ft. lbs.

14. Refill the power steering reservoir. Bleed the power steering system.

### DRIVE BELT ADJUSTMENT

1. Using a pair of adjustable jawed pliers (with a piece of rag between the jaws), remove the idler cover cap by turning and pulling.

2. Turn the adjusting bolt until the correct belt tension is obtained. If removing the belt, loosen the adjusting bolt until the drive belt can be removed.

3. After a new belt is installed and the correct tension obtained, replace the idler cap cover by pushing in and turning.

### SYSTEM BLEEDING

1. Be sure that the power steering reservoir is filled with fluid. Raise and support the vehicle safely.

2. With the engine running, turn the steering wheel back and forth, from lock to lock, until the air is removed from the fluid.

3. Lower the vehicle, recheck the reservoir fluid level and correct as required.

## Tie Rod Ends

### REMOVAL & INSTALLATION

1. Raise and support the vehicle safely.

2. Remove the front tire and wheel assemblies.

3. Remove the cotter pin and castle nut from the tie rod end stud.

4. Using a ball joint puller tool, separate the tie rod end from the steering knuckle.

5. Installation is the reverse of the removal procedure. Torque the castle nut to 18–22 ft. lbs.

# BRAKES

**For all brake system repair and service procedures not detailed below, please refer to "Brakes" in the Unit Repair section.**

## Master Cylinder

### REMOVAL & INSTALLATION

1. Disconnect the negative battery cable. Disconnect and plug the brake lines at the master cylinder.

2. It is advised to throughly drain the fluid from the master cylinder before performing any removal procedures.
3. If equipped with fluid level indicator, disconnect the electrical harness connector from the master cylinder.
4. Remove the master cylinder to power brake booster retaining nuts. Remove the master cylinder from its mounting.
5. Installation is the reverse of the removal procedure. As required, bleed the brake system.

## Proportioning Valve

The proportioning valve is attached to a bracket and is located directly under the master cylinder. It's purpose is to provide even braking pressure to all of the wheels.

### REMOVAL & INSTALLATION

1. Disconnect the negative battery cable. Disconnect and plug the brake tubes from the proportioning valve. If equipped with an electrical connector, disconnect it.
2. Remove the proportioning valve to bracket bolts. Remove the valve from the vehicle.
3. Installation is the reverse of the removal procedure. As required, bleed the brake system.

## Power Brake Booster

### REMOVAL & INSTALLATON

1. Disconnect the negative battery cable. Disconnect the vacuum hose from the power brake booster. If equipped, disconnect the connector for the brake fluid level indicator.
2. Remove the master cylinder from the brake booster. Depending upon the vehicle it may not be necessary to completely remove the master cylinder. It may be possible to remove the retaining bolts and position the assembly to the side.
3. Remove the brake pedal push rod to power booster spring pin and clevis pin, then disconnect the push rod from the brake pedal.
4. From under the dash, remove the power booster to firewall bolts.
5. Remove the brake booster assembly from the vehicle.
6. Installation is the reverse of the removal procedure. Bleed the brake system, as required.

## Disc Brake Pads

### REMOVAL & INSTALLATION

#### *Front*

1. Raise and support the vehicle safely. Remove the wheel assemblies.
2. Release the parking brake and disconnect the cable from the caliper lever.
3. Remove the lock pin bolts from the lower front of the caliper.
4. Rotate the caliper on the support, swinging it upward and out of the way.
5. Remove the brake disc pads, noting the position of the shim pads and pad clips.

**To install:**

6. Inspect the brake rotor, calipers and retaining components. Correct as necessary.
7. Remove a small portion of brake flyuid from the master cylinder reservior. With an appropraite tool, turn the caliper piston clockwise into the cylinder bore and align the notches. Be sure the boot is not twisted or pinched.

**NOTE: Do not force the piston straight into the caliper bore. The piston is mounted on a threaded spindle which will bend under pressure.**

8. Install the new pads into the calipers, being sure all shims and clips are in their original positions.
9. Swing the calipers down into position and install the lock pin bolts.
10. Re-connect the parking brake cable and fill the master cylinder reservior.
11. Install the wheel assembly. Bleed the brakes as required and lower the vehicle. Road test the vehicle.

#### *Rear*

1. Raise and safely support the vehicle. Remove the wheel assemblies.
2. Disconnect the brake pad lining wear indicator, if equipped. Remove any anti-rattle springs or clips, if equipped.
3. Pull the caliper away from the center of the vehicle to push piston into caliper bore. Remove the caliper guide pins and remove the caliper from the rotor. Hang the caliper from the body with a support wire.
4. Slide the disc pads from the caliper, noting any shims or shields behind the pad.

**NOTE: If equipped with parking brake, use a suitable tool to rotate the piston back into the caliper bore. If not equipped with parking brake, the piston can be pushed straight back into the bore.**

5. Push the piston into the caliper bore. To install the pads, position any shims or shields in place and reverse the removal procedure.

## Brake Shoes

### REMOVAL & INSTALLATION

1. Raise and safely support the vehicle. Remove the rear wheels.
2. Remove the brake drums.
3. Remove the adjusting wedge spring and the upper and lower return springs.
4. Remove the hold-down springs.
5. Lift the brake shoes from the backing plate and disconnect the parking brake, if equipped.
6. Disconnect the rear shoe from the push bar.
7. Clamp the push bar in a vise and remove the tension spring and adjusting wedge.
8. The installation is the reverse of the removal procedure.
9. Center the brake shoes on the backing plate, making sure the adjusting wedge is fully released before installing the drum.
10. Install the drums and the wheel assemblies.
11. Apply the brakes serveral times to automatically adjust the shoes. If necessary, bleed the brake system to obtain proper brake operation.
12. Road test the vehicle as required.

## Wheel Cylinder

### REMOVAL & INSTALLATION

1. Raise and support the vehicle safely. Remove the wheel and tire assembly.
2. Remove the brake drum and the brake shoes from the backing plate.
3. Disconnect and plug the brake line at the back of the wheel cylinder.
4. Remove the wheel cylinder to backing plate bolts. Remove the wheel cylinder from the backing plate.
5. Installation is the reverse of the removal procedure. Be sure to bleed the brake system, as required.

## Parking Brake Cable

### ADJUSTMENT

1. Pull the parking brake lever up forcefully. Release it and repeat several times.
2. It should take the specified number of notches to apply the parking brake.
   1983–90 except Justy – 3–5 notches
   1987–90 Justy – 6 notches
3. Loosen the locknut on the turnbuckle and adjust the length of the cable, so that the parking brake is applied within specification.
4. Tighten the locknut and recheck operation of the parking brake lever.

### REMOVAL & INSTALLATION

#### *Justy*

1. Set the parking brake lever.
2. Remove the hub cap, the cotter pin, the castle nut and the wheel lug nuts.
3. Raise and support the vehicle safely. Release the brake lever.
4. Remove the wheel assemblies and the brake drums.
5. Disassemble the equalizer joint to separate the parking brake cable from the rod.
6. Remove the exhaust cover to vehicle bolts and the cover.
7. Remove the cable clamps and the hangers.
8. Disconnect the parking brake cable from the parking brake lever.
9. Disconnect the parking brake cable from the backing plate of the rear brake assemblies.
10. Installation is the reverse of the removal procedure. Torque the mounting clamps and hanger bolts to 9–17 ft. lbs. and the exhaust cover to body bolts to4–7 ft. lbs. Adjust the parking brakes.

#### *Except Justy*

1. Raise and support the vehicle safely. Remove the front wheels.
2. Remove the parking brake cover and loosen the locknut. Loosen the parking brake adjuster until the tension is almost released, then, disconnect the inner cable ends from the equalizer.
3. Remove the clips that fasten the cable grommets in place where the cable passes through the body.
4. Pull the parking brake cable clamp from the caliper and disconnect the end of the cable.
5. Remove the cable to transverse link bracket bolts and the bracket.
6. Remove the cable to crossmember bracket bolt and the bracket.
7. Detach the cable rear crossmember guide and pull the cable from the passenger compartment.
8. Installation is the reverse of the removal procedure. Make sure the cable passes through the guide inside the driveshaft tunnel. Adjust the parking brakes.

# CHASSIS ELECTRICAL

## Blower Motor

### REMOVAL & INSTALLATION

#### *Justy*

1. Disconnect the negative battery cable.
2. Remove the coupler that connects the instrument panel harness to the blower motor.
3. Remove the coupler that connects the resistor to the instrument panel harness.
4. Detach the blower assembly. Remove the screws retaining the blower motor to the blower assembly.
5. Remove the motor assembly. Remove the nut retaining the fan to the motor assembly.
6. Installation is the reverse of the removal procedure.

#### *XT Coupe*

**NOTE: Depending upon working clearance the air conditioning system may have to be discharged in order to service the blower motor. If this is the case, be sure to observe all the required saftey precautions when discharging and recharging the air conditioning system.**

1. Disconnect the negative battery cable.
2. Remove the lower instrument panel cover on the passenger side of the vehicle.
3. Remove the glove box assembly, as required for working clearance.
4. Remove the heater duct, if the vehicle is not equipped with air conditioning.
5. If the vehicle is equipped with air conditioning, separate the evaporator from the blower assembly.
6. Disconnect the blower motor harness and the resistor electrical harness connector.
7. Remove the blower motor retaining bolts. Remove the blower motor assembly from its mounting.
8. Installation is the reverse of the removal procedure.

#### *Except Justy, XT Coupe and Legacy*

**NOTE: Depending upon working clearance the air conditioning system may have to be discharged in order to service the blower motor. If this is the case, be sure to observe all the required saftey precautions when discharging and recharging the air conditioning system.**

1. Disconnect the negative battery cable.
2. Remove the lower instrument panel cover on the passenger side of the vehicle. Remove the glove box assembly, as required for working clearance.
3. If the assembly is equipped with a vacuum actuator, set the control lever to the **CIRC** position and disconnect the vacuum hose from the assembly. Remove the actuator from its mounting.
4. Remove the heater duct, if the vehicle is not equipped with air conditioning.
5. If the vehicle is equipped with air conditioning, separate the evaporator from the blower assembly.
6. Disconnect the blower motor harness and the resistor electrical harness connector.
7. Remove the blower motor retaining bolts. Remove the blower motor assembly from its mounting. As required, separate the fan from the blower motor.
8. Installation is the reverse of the removal procedure.

## Heater Core

### REMOVAL & INSTALLATION

#### *Justy*

1. Disconnect the negative battery cable. Drain the cooling system.
2. Disconnect the heater hoses from the heater core assembly.
3. Pull off the right and left defroster ducts from the defroster nozzles. Pull the ducts from the heater unit.
4. Disconnect the electrical wires from the fan switch and the blower motor.
5. Disconnect the air mix cable from the heater unit. Disconnect the mode cable from the heater unit.
6. Remove the bolts that retain the heater unit to the instrument panel.
7. As required, for working clearance remove the glove box door assembly.
8. Disconnect the inside/outside air control cable from the blower assembly.
9. Remove the instrument panel assembly.
10. Remove the heater unit retaining bolts. Remove the heater unit from the vehicle.
11. Remove the heater core cushion. Loosen the heater core holder and than remove it. Pull the heater core from its mounting and remove it from the heater case.
12. Installation is the reverse of the removal procedure.

#### *XT Coupe*

**NOTE: Depending upon working clearance the air conditioning system may have to be discharged in order to service the blower motor. If this is the case, be sure to**

**observe all the required saftey precautions when discharging and recharging the air conditioning system.**

1. Disconnect the negative battery cable. Drain the cooling system.
2. disconnect the heater hoses from the heater core assembly.
3. Remove the instrument panel assembly.
4. Disconnect the electrical harness connector from the blower motor assembly. Disconnect the temperature control cable.
5. Remove the heater unit retaining bolts. Remove the heater unit from the vehicle.
6. Remove the heater core retaining connectors. Remove the heater core from its mounting.
7. Installation is the reverse of the removal procedure.

#### Except Justy, XT Coupe and Legacy

##### 1983–1984

1. Disconnect the negative battery cable. Drain the cooling system.
2. Disconnect the heater hoses from the heater unit.
3. Remove the rubber grommet the heater hoses run through on the kick panel inside the vehicle. The location is slightly above and to the right of the accelerator pedal.
4. Remove the radio box or console and the instrument panel.
5. If equipped with a luggage shelf, remove it.
6. Disconnect the heater control cables and the fan motor electrical harness.
7. Disconnect the heater unit to blower assembly duct. Remove the ducts from the right and left defroster nozzles.
8. Remove the heater unit to chassis bolts, lift the unit and remove it from the vehicle.
9. Remove the water valve cover and disconnect the water valve. Disconnect the control rod from the defroster doors.
10. Separate the heater case by removing the twelve retaining springs.
11 Disconnect the air intake shutter return spring. Remove the heater core.
12. Installation is the reverse of the removal procedure.

##### 1985–90

**NOTE: Depending upon working clearance the air conditioning system may have to be discharged in order to service the blower motor. If this is the case, be sure to observe all the required safety precautions when discharging and recharging the air conditioning system.**

1. Disconnect the negative battery cable. Drain the cooling system.
2. disconnect the heater hoses from the heater core assembly.
3. Remove the instrument panel assembly. Remove the console assembly.
4. Disconnect the electrical harness connector from the blower motor assembly. Disconnect the temperature control cable.
5. Remove the heater unit retaining bolts. Remove the heater unit from the vehicle.
6. Remove the heater core retaining connectors. Remove the heater core from its mounting.
7. Installation is the reverse of the removal procedure.

## Radio

### REMOVAL & INSTALLATION

#### Justy

1. Disconnect the negatiove battery cable. Remove the front radio panel.
2. Remove the center panel. Remove the radio retaining screws.
3. Pull the radio forward. Disconnect the antenna lead in wire. Disconnect the radio electrical connectors.
4. Remove the radio from the vehicle.
5. Installation is the reverse of the removal procedure.

#### Except Justy

1. Disconnect the negative battery cable.
2. On the XT Coupe, remove the drivers side floor mat. Remove and disconnect the electrical connectors from the left side center under portion of the instrument panel. If equipped, remove the clock assembly.
3. On all vehicles except XT Coupe, remove the center panel assembly.
4. Remove the radio retaining screws. Pull the radio assembly forward.
5. Disconnect the required electrical connectors from the back side of the radio.
6. Remove the radio along with the antenna lead in wire and bracket.
7. Remove the screws and separate the bracket from the radio. Remove the radio from the vehicle.
8. Installation is the reverse of the removal procedure.

## Windshield Wiper Switch

### REMOVAL & INSTALLATION

1. Disconnect the negative battery terminal from the battery.
2. Remove the necessary dash to chassis screws in order to gain access to the wiper switch retaining screws.
3. Remove the windshield wiper switch to dash screws.
4. Remove the wiper switch.
5. Installation is the reverse of the removal procedure.

## Windshield Wiper Motor

### REMOVAL & INSTALLATION

#### Justy

1. Disconnect the negative battery cable.
2. At the wiper motor, disconnect the electrical connector.
3. Remove the wiper motor to cowl bolts.
4. Separate the wiper link from the motor.
5. Remove the wiper motor to cowl panel screws and the wiper motor to link bolts, then separate the motor from the panel.
6. If necessary, replace the wiper motor.
7. To install, reverse the removal procedures. Check the wiper operation.

#### Except Justy and Legacy

1. Disconnect the negative battery cable.
2. Remove the wiper blades from the wiper arms by pulling the retaining lever up and sliding the blade away from the arm.
3. Slide the covering boot up the wiper arm.
4. Remove the wiper arms to linkage nuts and the arms.
5. Disconnect the electrical wiring connectors from the wiper motor.
6. Remove the cowl to body screws and the cowl from the vehicle.
7. Find or fabricate a ring which has the same diameter as the outer diameter of the plastic joint that retains the linkage to the wiper motor. Force the ring down over the joint to force the 4 plastic retaining jaws inward, then disconnect and remove the linkage.
8. Remove the wiper motor to firewall bolts and the motor.
9. To install, reverse the removal procedures. Install the wiper arms after the ignition switch has been **ON** for a few seconds to put the linkage in **Park** position.

## Instrument Cluster

### REMOVAL & INSTALLATION

#### *Justy*

1. Disconnect the negative battery cable. Remove the steering wheel.
2. Remove the defroster duct assembly.
3. Disconnect the heater control cable from the inside/outside air selector rod at the heater unit.
4. Disconnect the speedometer cable. Disconnect the electrical harness connectors.
5. Remove the covers for the instrument cluster retaining bolts.
6. Remove the instrument cluster retaining bolts. Remove the instrumnet cluster from its mounting.
7. Installation is the reverse of the removal procedure.

#### *XT Coupe*

1. Disconnect the negative battery cable. Remove the lower cover on the driver's side. Remove the side ventilation duct.
2. Open the fuse box lid. Remove the fuse box to instrument panel screws and the fuse box.
3. Remove the lower cover on the passengers side. Using a medium prybar, pry the upper cover, at 3 points, from the instrument panel.
4. Remove the console. Remove the steering column assembly, the combination meter and the control wing as a unit.
5. Disconnect the electrical harness connectors from the radio and other necessary components.
6. Remove the instrument panel to chassis bolts and the instrument panel from the vehicle.
7. Installation is the reverse of the removal procedure.

#### *Except Justy, XT Coupe and Legacy*

1. Disconnect the negative battery cable.
2. Remove the bolts securing the steering column and pull it down.
3. Disconnect the electrical wiring connectors, then remove the cluster visor screws and the visor, except on GL and GLF.
4. On the GL and GLF, remove the center ventilator control lever by pulling it. Remove the 3 screws accessible through the ventilator grill to the right of the cluster and the 1 screw accessible through the grill on the left. Remove the visor.
5. On the station wagon 4WD GL, remove the turn signal lamp switch.
6. Remove the cluster retaining screws, then pull the cluster out far enough to disconnect the speedometer cable and electrical connectors from behind, then remove the cluster assembly from the vehicle.
7. Installation is the reverse of the removal procedure.

## Headlight Switch

### REMOVAL & INSTALLATION

#### *1983–84*

The switch is located at the left side of the instrument panel and is combined with the illumination intensity control switch.

1. Disconnect the negative battery cable.
2. Remove the steering column to dash screws and pull downward on the steering column.
3. Remove the instrument cluster visor to dash screws and the visor from the instrument cluster.
4. Disconnect the electrical harness connector from the headlight switch assembly.
5. Pull the headlight knob out, then remove the headlight switch to visor nut and the switch from the visor.
6. Installation is the reverse of the removal procedure.

#### *1985–89*

##### EXCEPT JUSTY

The headlight switch is a part of a lighting switch assembly, installed on a control wing at the left side of the steering wheel.

1. Disconnect the negative battery cable.
2. Remove the lower steering column upper and lower cover screws. Remove the upper and lower covers from the column.
3. Remove the steering wheel center cover, the steering wheel to shaft nut and the steering wheel from the steering column.
4. Disconnect the electrical harness to steering column clip and band.
5. Remove the combination switch to steering column screws and the switch assembly from the steering wheel.
6. Remove the left control wing to steering column bolts and the left control wing from the steering column.
7. Remove the control wing case screws and separate the cases from each other. This will provide access to the headlight switch.
8. To replace the headlight switch knob, perform the following procedure.
   a. Using a pin rod, lightly push the pawl (inside the switch knob) inward and pull the knob outward. When removing the switch knob, be careful not to damage the switch brush.
   b. To install the knob onto the switch, place the knob on the switch, place your finger on the back side of the switch and squeeze the knob onto the switch.
9. If necessary, replace the headlight switch.
10. Installation is the reverse of the removal procedure. When reassembling the control wing cases, be careful not to get the electrical harness caught between the cases.

##### JUSTY

The headlight switch is a part of a gang switch located on the left side of the instrument panel

1. Disconnect the negative battery cable.
2. Remove the lower instrument panel cover and disconnect the electrical connectors.
3. Remove the upper instrument cluster glass screw and pull outward on the glass.
4. From the rear of the instrument panel cover, remove the lighting switch to panel screw and the lighting switch assembly from the cover.
5. Installation is the reverse of the removal procedure.

## Stoplight Switch

### REMOVAL & INSTALLATION

The stoplamp switch is located on the brake pedal bracket, under the instrument panel. The switch is held in place by two locknuts which allow the proper adjustment to be accomplished. To replace the switch, the wiring is disconnected, the locknuts are loosened and the switch removed.
After installation, the travel to operate the switch plunger is 0.071 – 0.130 in.

## Fuse Box

### LOCATION

The fuse box is located under the left side of the instrument panel. The amperage for each fuse is stamped on the fuse box cover.
If equipped with 4WD, a fuse holder is located near the ignition coil. For servicing purposes, to change 4WD to FWD, insert a 15A fuse into the FWD fuse holder. The FWD pilot lamp (on the instrument panel) will turn illuminate to indicate the the vehicle is set in the FWD mode.

On the Justy, a main fuse is located in the engine compartment, next to the brake master cylinder. All current, except for the starter, will flow through this fuse. When replacing the main fuse, be aware of the amperage rating, a 30A (pink) or a 60A (yellow).

# Toyota 17

## Camry, Celica, Corolla, Cressida, FX, MR2, Starlet, Supra, Tercel

# SERIAL NUMBER IDENTIFICATION

## Vehicle Identification Plate

All models have the vehicle identification number (VIN) stamped on a plate which is attached to the left side of the instrument panel. This plate is visible through the windshield.

The serial number consists of a series identification number followed by a six digit production number.

## Engine Number

Basically, 1983-90 Toyota vehicles have used seven types of engines:

- A-series
  - 3A, 3A-C
  - 4A-C, 4A-CL
  - 4A-F, 4A-FE
  - 4A-GE, 4A-GEC, 4A-GELC
  - 4A-GZE
- E-series
  - 3E
- K-series
  - 4K-E
- M-series
  - 5M-GE, 7M-GE, 7M-GTE
- R-series
  - 22R, 22R-E
- S-series
  - 2S-E
  - 3S-FE, 3S-GE, 3S-GTE
- Z-series
  - 2VZ-FE.

Engines within each series are similar, as the cylinder block designs are the same. Variances within each series may be due to ignition types (point or electronic), displacements (bore x stroke), cylinder head design (single or double overhead camshafts and fuel injection). Refer to the accompanying engine I.D. chart.

When ordering engine parts, it may be necessary to obtain the engine serial number. Serial numbers of the engines may be found on the following locations:

A-series engines – stamped vertically on the left side rear of the engine block.

E-series engines – stamped on the left side rear of the engine block.

K-series engines – stamped on the right side of the engine, below the spark plugs.

M-series engines – stamped horizontally on the passenger side of the engine block, behind the alternator.

R-series engines – stamped horizontally on the driver's side of the engine, behind the alternator.

S-series engines – on the 2S-E, stamped horizontally on the right side of the block. On the 3S-E, 3S-GE and 3S-GTE, it can be found on the left side of the block, under the thermostat housing.

Z-series engines – stamped on the front, right (passenger) side of the cylinder block.

## ENGINE IDENTIFICATION

| Year | Model | Engine Displacement cu. in. (cc/liter) | Engine Series Identification | No. of Cylinders | Engine Type |
|---|---|---|---|---|---|
| 1983 | Tercel | 88.6 (1452/1.4) | 3A, 3A-C | 4 | SOHC |
| | Corolla | 97.0 (1587/1.6) | 4A-C, 4A-LC | 4 | SOHC |
| | Starlet | 78.7 (1290/1.3) | 4K-E | 4 | OHV |
| | Camry | 121.7 (1995/2.0) | 2S-E | 4 | SOHC |
| | Celica | 144.4 (2367/2.4) | 22R, 22R-E | 4 | SOHC |
| | Supra | 168.4 (2759/2.8) | 5M-GE | 6 | DOHC |
| | Cressida | 168.4 (2759/2.8) | 5M-GE | 6 | DOHC |
| 1984 | Tercel | 88.6 (1452/1.4) | 3A, 3A-C | 4 | SOHC |
| | Corolla | 97.0 (1587/1.6) | 4A-C, 4A-LC | 4 | SOHC |
| | Starlet | 78.7 (1290/1.3) | 4K-E | 4 | OHV |
| | Camry | 121.7 (1995/2.0) | 2S-E | 4 | SOHC |
| | Celica | 144.4 (2367/2.4) | 22R, 22R-E | 4 | SOHC |
| | Supra | 168.4 (2759/2.8) | 5M-GE | 6 | DOHC |
| | Cressida | 168.4 (2759/2.8) | 5M-GE | 6 | DOHC |
| 1985 | Tercel | 88.6 (1452/1.4) | 3A, 3A-C | 4 | SOHC |
| | Corolla | 97.0 (1587/1.6) | 4A-C, 4A-LC | 4 | SOHC |
| | | 97.0 (1587/1.6) | 4A-GE | 4 | DOHC |
| | Camry | 121.7 (1995/2.0) | 2S-E | 4 | SOHC |
| | Celica | 144.4 (2367/2.4) | 22R, 22R-E | 4 | SOHC |
| | Supra | 168.4 (2759/2.8) | 5M-GE | 6 | DOHC |

## ENGINE IDENTIFICATION

| Year | Model | Engine Displacement cu. in. (liter) | Engine Series Identification (VIN) | No. of Cylinders | Engine Type |
|---|---|---|---|---|---|
| 1985 | MR2 | 97.0 (1587/1.6) | 4A-GE | 4 | DOHC |
| | Cressida | 168.4 (2759/2.8) | 5M-GE | 6 | DOHC |
| 1986 | Tercel | 88.6 (1452/1.4) | 3A, 3A-C | 4 | SOHC |
| | Corolla | 97.0 (1587/1.6) | 4A-C, 4A-LC | 4 | SOHC |
| | | 97.0 (1587/1.6) | 4A-GE | 4 | DOHC |
| | Camry | 121.7 (1995/2.0) | 2S-E | 4 | SOHC |
| | Celica | 121.7 (1995/2.0) | 2S-E | 4 | SOHC |
| | | 121.9 (1998/2.0) | 3S-GE | 4 | DOHC |
| | Supra | 168.4 (2759/2.8) | 5M-GE | 6 | DOHC |
| | | 180.3 (2954/3.0) | 7M-GE | 6 | DOHC |
| | MR2 | 97.0 (1587/1.6) | 4A-GE | 4 | DOHC |
| | Cressida | 168.4 (2759/2.8) | 5M-GE | 6 | DOHC |
| 1987 | Tercel | 88.6 (1452/1.4) | 3A-C | 4 | SOHC |
| | | 88.9 (1456/1.5) | 3E | 4 | SOHC |
| | Corolla | 97.0 (1587/1.6) | 4A-LC | 4 | SOHC |
| | | 97.0 (1587/1.6) | 4A-GEC, 4A-GELC | 4 | DOHC |
| | Camry | 121.9 (1998/2.0) | 3S-FE | 4 | DOHC |
| | Celica | 121.9 (1998/2.0) | 3S-FE, 3S-GE | 4 | DOHC |
| | Supra | 180.3 (2954/3.0) | 7M-GE | 6 | DOHC |
| | | 180.3 (2954/3.0) | 7M-GTE | 6 | DOHC, TURBO |
| | MR2 | 97.0 (1587/1.6) | 4A-GELC | 4 | DOHC |
| | Cressida | 168.4 (2759/2.8) | 5M-GE | 6 | DOHC |
| 1988 | Tercel | 88.6 (1452/1.4) | 3A-C | 4 | SOHC |
| | | 88.9 (1456/1.5) | 3E | 4 | SOHC |
| | Corolla | 97.0 (1587/1.6) | 4A-LC | 4 | SOHC |
| | | 97.0 (1587/1.6) | 4A-GEC, 4A-GELC | 4 | DOHC |
| | | 97.0 (1587/1.6) | 4A-F | 4 | DOHC |
| | Camry | 121.9 (1998/2.0) | 3S-FE | 4 | DOHC |
| | Celica | 121.9 (1998/2.0) | 3S-FE, 3S-GE | 4 | DOHC |
| | | 121.9 (1998/2.0) | 3S-GTE | 4 | DOHC, TURBO |
| | Supra | 180.3 (2954/3.0) | 7M-GE | 6 | DOHC |
| | | 180.3 (2954/3.0) | 7M-GTE | 6 | DOHC, TURBO |
| | MR2 | 97.0 (1587/1.6) | 4A-GELC | 4 | DOHC |
| | | 97.0 (1587/1.6) | 4A-GZE | 4 | DOHC, SUPER |
| | Cressida | 168.4 (2759/2.8) | 5M-GE | 6 | DOHC |
| 1989-90 | Tercel | 88.9 (1456/1.5) | 3E | 4 | SOHC |
| | Corolla | 97.0 (1587/1.6) | 4A-GEC, 4A-GELC | 4 | DOHC |
| | | 97.0 (1587/1.6) | 4A-F, 4A-FE | 4 | DOHC |
| | Camry | 121.9 (1998/2.0) | 3S-FE | 4 | DOHC |
| | | 153.0 (2507/2.5) | 2VZ-FE | 6 | DOHC |
| | Celica | 121.9 (1998/2.0) | 3S-FE, 3S-GE | 4 | DOHC |

## ENGINE IDENTIFICATION

| Year | Model | Engine Displacement cu. in. (cc/liter) | Engine Series Identification | No. of Cylinders | Engine Type |
|---|---|---|---|---|---|
| 1989-90 | | 121.9 (1998/2.0) | 3S-GTE | 4 | DOHC, TURBO |
| | Supra | 180.3 (2954/3.0) | 7M-GE | 6 | DOHC |
| | | 180.3 (2954/3.0) | 7M-GTE | 6 | DOHC, TURBO |
| | MR2 | 97.0 (1587/1.6) | 4A-GELC | 4 | DOHC |
| | | 97.0 (1587/1.6) | 4A-GZE | 4 | DOHC, SUPER |
| | Cressida | 180.3 (2954/3.0) | 7M-GE | 6 | DOHC |

OHV Overhead Valves
SOHC Single Overhead Camshaft
DOHC Double Overhead Camshaft
TURBO Turbocharged
SUPER Supercharged

## GENERAL ENGINE SPECIFICATIONS

| Year | Model | Engine Displacement cu. in. (cc) | Fuel System Type | Net Horsepower @ rpm | Net Torque @ rpm (ft. lbs.) | Bore × Stroke (in.) | Com-pression Ratio | Oil Pressure ③ |
|---|---|---|---|---|---|---|---|---|
| 1983 | Tercel | 88.6 (1452) | 2 bbl | 62 @ 5200 | 75 @ 2800 | 3.05 × 3.03 | 9.0:1 | 4.3 |
| | Corolla | 97.0 (1587) | 2 bbl | 70 @ 4800 | 85 @ 2800 | 3.19 × 3.03 | 9.0:1 | 4.3 |
| | Starlet | 78.7 (1290) | EFI | 58 @ 4200 | 74 @ 3400 | 2.95 × 2.87 | 9.5:1 | 4.3 |
| | Camry | 121.7 (1995) | EFI | 93 @ 4200 | 113 @ 2400 | 3.31 × 3.54 | 8.7:1 | 4.3 |
| | Celica | 144.4 (2367) | 2 bbl | 96 @ 4800 | 129 @ 2800 | 3.62 × 3.50 | 9.0:1 | 4.3 |
| | | 144.4 (2367) | EFI | 105 @ 4800 | 137 @ 2800 | 3.62 × 3.50 | 9.0:1 | 4.3 |
| | Supra | 168.4 (2759) | EFI | 150 @ 5200 | 159 @ 4400 | 3.27 × 3.35 | 8.8:1 | 4.3 |
| | Cressida | 168.4 (2759) | EFI | 143 @ 5200 | 154 @ 4400 | 3.27 × 3.35 | 8.8:1 | 4.3 |
| 1984 | Tercel | 88.6 (1452) | 2 bbl | 62 @ 5200 | 75 @ 2800 | 3.05 × 3.03 | 9.0:1 | 4.3 |
| | Corolla | 97.0 (1587) | 2 bbl | 70 @ 4800 | 85 @ 2800 | 3.19 × 3.03 | 9.0:1 | 4.3 |
| | Starlet | 78.7 (1290) | EFI | 58 @ 4200 | 74 @ 3400 | 2.95 × 2.87 | 9.5:1 | 4.3 |
| | Camry | 121.7 (1995) | EFI | 93 @ 4200 | 113 @ 2400 | 3.31 × 3.54 | 8.7:1 | 4.3 |
| | Celica | 144.4 (2367) | 2 bbl | 96 @ 4800 | 129 @ 2800 | 3.62 × 3.50 | 9.0:1 | 4.3 |
| | | 144.4 (2367) | EFI | 105 @ 4800 | 137 @ 2800 | 3.62 × 3.50 | 9.0:1 | 4.3 |
| | Supra | 168.4 (2759) | EFI | 150 @ 5200 | 159 @ 4400 | 3.27 × 3.35 | 8.8:1 | 4.3 |
| | Cressida | 168.4 (2759) | EFI | 143 @ 5200 | 154 @ 4400 | 3.27 × 3.35 | 8.8:1 | 4.3 |
| 1985 | Tercel | 88.6 (1452) | 2 bbl | 62 @ 4800 | 76 @ 2800 | 3.05 × 3.03 | 9.0:1 | 4.3 |
| | Corolla | 97.0 (1587) | 2 bbl | 70 @ 4800 | 85 @ 2800 | 3.19 × 3.03 | 9.0:1 | 4.3 |
| | | 97.0 (1587) | EFI | 112 @ 6600 | 97 @ 4800 | 3.19 × 3.03 | 9.4:1 | 4.3 |
| | Camry | 121.7 (1995) | EFI | 93 @ 4200 | 113 @ 2400 | 3.31 × 3.54 | 8.7:1 | 4.3 |
| | Celica | 144.4 (2367) | 2 bbl | 96 @ 4800 | 129 @ 2800 | 3.62 × 3.50 | 9.0:1 | 4.3 |
| | | 144.4 (2367) | EFI | 116 @ 4800 | 140 @ 2800 | 3.62 × 3.50 | 9.0:1 | 4.3 |
| | Supra | 168.4 (2759) | EFI | 161 @ 5600 | 169 @ 4400 | 3.27 × 3.35 | 8.8:1 | 4.3 |
| | MR2 | 97.0 (1587) | EFI | 112 @ 6600 | 97 @ 4800 | 3.19 × 3.03 | 9.4:1 | 4.3 |
| | Cressida | 168.4 (2759) | EFI | 156 @ 5200 | 165 @ 4400 | 3.27 × 3.35 | 8.8:1 | 4.3 |

## GENERAL ENGINE SPECIFICATIONS

| Year | Model | Engine Displacement cu. in. (cc) | Fuel System Type | Net Horsepower @ rpm | Net Torque @ rpm (ft. lbs.) | Bore × Stroke (in.) | Compression Ratio | Oil Pressure ③ |
|---|---|---|---|---|---|---|---|---|
| 1986 | Tercel | 88.6 (1452) | 2 bbl | 62 @ 4800 | 76 @ 2800 | 3.05 × 3.03 | 9.0:1 | 4.3 |
| | Corolla | 97.0 (1587) | 2 bbl | 74 @ 5200 | 85 @ 2800 | 3.19 × 3.03 | 9.0:1 | 4.3 |
| | | 97.0 (1587) | EFI | 112 @ 6600 | 97 @ 4800 | 3.19 × 3.03 | 9.4:1 | 4.3 |
| | Camry | 121.7 (1995) | EFI | 95 @ 4400 | 116 @ 4000 | 3.31 × 3.54 | 8.7:1 | 4.3 |
| | Celica | 121.7 (1995) | EFI | 97 @ 4400 | 118 @ 4000 | 3.31 × 3.54 | 8.7:1 | 4.3 |
| | | 121.9 (1998) | EFI | 135 @ 6000 | 125 @ 4800 | 3.39 × 3.39 | 9.2:1 | 4.3 |
| | Supra | 168.4 (2759) | EFI | 161 @ 5600 | 169 @ 4400 | 3.27 × 3.35 | 9.2:1 | 4.3 |
| | | 180.3 (2954) | EFI | 200 @ 6000 | 185 @ 4800 | 3.27 × 3.58 | 9.2:1 | 4.3 |
| | MR2 | 97.0 (1587) | EFI | 112 @ 6600 | 97 @ 4800 | 3.19 × 3.03 | 9.4:1 | 4.3 |
| | Cressida | 168.4 (2759) | EFI | 156 @ 5200 | 165 @ 4400 | 3.27 × 3.35 | 9.2:1 | 4.3 |
| 1987 | Tercel | 88.6 (1452) | 2 bbl | 62 @ 4800 | 76 @ 2800 | 3.05 × 3.03 | 9.0:1 | 4.3 |
| | | 88.9 (1456) | 2 bbl | 78 @ 6000 | 87 @ 4000 | 2.87 × 3.43 | 9.3:1 | 4.3 |
| | Corolla | 97.0 (1587) | 2 bbl | 74 @ 5200 | 86 @ 2800 | 3.19 × 3.03 | 9.0:1 | 4.3 |
| | | 97.0 (1587) | EFI | 112 @ 6600② | 97 @ 4800 | 3.19 × 3.03 | 9.4:1 | 4.3 |
| | Camry | 121.9 (1998) | EFI | 115 @ 5200 | 124 @ 4400 | 3.39 × 3.39 | 9.3:1 | 4.3 |
| | Celica | 3S-FE 121.9 (1998) | EFI | 115 @ 5200 | 124 @ 4400 | 3.39 × 3.39 | 9.3:1 | 4.3 |
| | | 3S-GE 121.9 (1998) | EFI | 135 @ 6000 | 125 @ 4800 | 3.39 × 3.39 | 9.2:1 | 4.3 |
| | Supra | 7M-GE 180.3 (2954) | EFI | 200 @ 6000 | 185 @ 4800 | 3.27 × 3.58 | 9.2:1 | 4.3 |
| | | 7M-GTE 180.3 (2954) | EFI | 230 @ 5600 | 246 @ 4000 | 3.27 × 3.58 | 8.4:1 | 4.3 |
| | MR2 | 97.0 (1587) | EFI | 112 @ 6600 | 97 @ 4800 | 3.19 × 3.03 | 9.4:1 | 4.3 |
| | Cressida | 168.4 (2759) | EFI | 156 @ 5200 | 165 @ 4400 | 3.27 × 3.35 | 9.2:1 | 4.3 |
| 1988 | Tercel | 88.6 (1452) | 2 bbl | 62 @ 4800 | 76 @ 2800 | 3.05 × 3.03 | 9.0:1 | 4.3 |
| | | 88.9 (1456) | 2 bbl | 78 @ 6000 | 87 @ 4000 | 2.87 × 3.43 | 9.3:1 | 4.3 |
| | Corolla | 4A-LC 97.0 (1587) | 2 bbl | 74 @ 5200 | 86 @ 2800 | 3.19 × 3.03 | 9.0:1 | 4.3 |
| | | 4A-F 97.0 (1587) | 2 bbl | 90 @ 6000 | 95 @ 3600 | 3.19 × 3.03 | 9.5:1 | 4.3 |
| | | 97.0 (1587) | EFI | 116 @ 6600④ | 110 @ 4800⑤ | 3.19 × 3.03 | 9.4:1 | 4.3 |
| | Camry | 121.9 (1998) | EFI | 115 @ 5200 | 124 @ 4400 | 3.39 × 3.39 | 9.3:1 | 4.3 |
| | Celica | 3S-FE 121.9 (1998) | EFI | 115 @ 5200 | 124 @ 4400 | 3.39 × 3.39 | 9.3:1 | 4.3 |
| | | 3S-GE 121.9 (1998) | EFI | 135 @ 6000 | 125 @ 4800 | 3.39 × 3.39 | 9.2:1 | 4.3 |
| | | 3S-GTE 121.9 (1998) | EFI | 190 @ 6000 | 190 @ 3200 | 3.39 × 3.39 | 8.5:1 | 4.3 |
| | Supra | 7M-GE 180.3 (2954) | EFI | 200 @ 6000 | 185 @ 4800 | 3.27 × 3.58 | 9.2:1 | 4.3 |
| | | 7M-GTE 180.3 (2954) | EFI | 230 @ 5600 | 246 @ 4000 | 3.27 × 3.58 | 8.4:1 | 4.3 |

## GENERAL ENGINE SPECIFICATIONS

| Year | Model | Engine Displacement cu. in. (cc) | Fuel System Type | Net Horsepower @ rpm | Net Torque @ rpm (ft. lbs.) | Bore × Stroke (in.) | Compression Ratio | Oil Pressure ③ |
|---|---|---|---|---|---|---|---|---|
| 1988 | MR2 | 4A-GELC 97.0 (1587) | EFI | 112 @ 6600 | 100 @ 4800 | 3.19 × 3.03 | 9.4:1 | 4.3 |
| | | 4A-GZE 97.0 (1587) | EFI | 145 @ 6400 | 140 @ 4000 | 3.19 × 3.03 | 8.0:1 | 4.3 |
| | Cressida | 168.4 (2759) | EFI | 156 @ 5200 | 165 @ 4400 | 3.27 × 3.35 | 9.2:1 | 4.3 |
| 1989-90 | Tercel | 88.9 (1456) | 2 bbl | 78 @ 6000 | 87 @ 4000 | 2.87 × 3.43 | 9.3:1 | 4.3 |
| | Corolla | 4A-FE 97.0 (1587) | EFI | 100 @ 5600 | 101 @ 4400 | 3.19 × 3.03 | 9.5:1 | 4.3 |
| | | 4A-F 97.0 (1587) | 2 bbl | 90 @ 6000 | 95 @ 3600 | 3.20 × 3.00 | 9.5:1 | 4.3 |
| | | 97.0 (1587) | EFI | 116 @ 6600 | 100 @ 4800 | 3.19 × 3.03 | 9.4:1 | 4.3 |
| | Camry | 121.9 (1998) | EFI | 115 @ 5200 | 124 @ 4400 | 3.39 × 3.39 | 9.3:1 | 4.3 |
| | | 153.0 (2507) | EFI | 153 @ 5600 | 155 @ 4400 | 3.44 × 2.74 | 9.0:1 | 4.3 |
| | Celica | 3S-FE 121.9 (1998) | EFI | 115 @ 5200 | 124 @ 4400 | 3.39 × 3.39 | 9.3:1 | 4.3 |
| | | 3S-GE 121.9 (1998) | EFI | 135 @ 6000 | 125 @ 4800 | 3.39 × 3.39 | 9.2:1 | 4.3 |
| | | 3S-GTE 121.9 (1998) | EFI | 190 @ 6000 | 190 @ 3200 | 3.39 × 3.39 | 8.5:1 | 4.3 |
| | Supra | 7M-GE 180.3 (2954) | EFI | 200 @ 6000 | 188 @ 3600 | 3.27 × 3.58 | 9.2:1 | 4.3 |
| | | 7M-GTE 180.3 (2954) | EFI | 232 @ 5600 | 254 @ 3200 | 3.27 × 3.58 | 8.4:1 | 4.3 |
| | MR2 | 4A-GELC 97.0 (1587) | EFI | 115 @ 6600 | 100 @ 4800 | 3.19 × 3.03 | 9.4:1 | 4.3 |
| | | 4A-GZE 97.0 (1587) | EFI | 145 @ 6400 | 140 @ 4000 | 3.19 × 3.03 | 8.0:1 | 4.3 |
| | Cressida | 180.3 (2954) | EFI | 190 @ 5600 | 185 @ 4400 | 3.27 × 3.58 | 9.2:1 | 4.3 |

EFI Electronic Fuel Injection
① 1A-C
② FX-16: 108 @ 6600
③ At idle
④ FX-16: 110 @ 6600
⑤ FX-16: 98 @ 4800

## GASOLINE ENGINE TUNE-UP SPECIFICATIONS

| Year | Model | Engine Displacement cu. in. (cc) | Spark Plugs Type | Spark Plugs Gap (in.) | Ignition Timing (deg.) MT | Ignition Timing (deg.) AT | Compression Pressure (psi) | Fuel Pump (psi) | Idle Speed (rpm) MT | Idle Speed (rpm) AT | Valve Clearance In. | Valve Clearance Ex. |
|---|---|---|---|---|---|---|---|---|---|---|---|---|
| 1983 | Tercel | 3A 88.6 (1452) | BPR5EA-L | 0.031 | 5B | 5B | 178 | 2.6–3.5 | ⑥ | ⑥ | 0.008 | 0.012 |
| | | 3A-C 88.6 (1452) | BPR5EA-11 | 0.043 | 5B | 5B | 178 | 2.6–3.5 | ⑦ | ⑦ | 0.008 | 0.012 |
| | Corolla | 97.0 (1587) | BPR5EA-L11 ② | 0.043 | 5B | 5B | 178 | 2.5–3.5 | ⑧ | ⑧ | 0.008 | 0.012 |

## GASOLINE ENGINE TUNE-UP SPECIFICATIONS

| Year | Model | Engine Displacement cu. in. (cc) | Spark Plugs Type | Spark Plugs Gap (in.) | Ignition Timing (deg.) MT | Ignition Timing (deg.) AT | Compression Pressure (psi) | Fuel Pump (psi) | Idle Speed (rpm) MT | Idle Speed (rpm) AT | Valve Clearance In. | Valve Clearance Ex. |
|---|---|---|---|---|---|---|---|---|---|---|---|---|
| 1983 | Starlet | 78.7 (1290) | BPR5EP-11 | 0.043 | 5B | — | 185 | 36–38 | 700 | — | Hyd. | Hyd. |
| | Camry | 121.7 (1995) | BPR5EA-L11 | 0.043 | 5B | 5B | 171 | 28–36 | 700 | 700 | Hyd. | Hyd. |
| | Celica | 22R 144.4 (2367) | BPR5EY | 0.031 | 8B | 8B | 171 | 2.5–3.8 | 700 | 700 | 0.008 | 0.012 |
| | | 22R-E 144.4 (2367) | BPR5EY | 0.031 | 5B | 5B | 171 | 35–38 | 750 | 750 | 0.008 | 0.012 |
| | Supra | 168.4 (2759) | BPR5EP-11 | 0.043 | 10B | 10B | 164 | 35–38 | 650 | 650 | Hyd. | Hyd. |
| | Cressida | 168.4 (2759) | BPR5EP-11 | 0.043 | — | 10B | 164 | 35–38 | — | 650 | Hyd. | Hyd. |
| 1984 | Tercel | 3A 88.6 (1452) | BPR5EA-L | 0.031 | 5B | 5B | 178 | 2.6–3.5 | ⑥ | ⑥ | 0.008 | 0.012 |
| | | 3A-C 88.6 (1452) | BPR5EA-11 ⑨ | 0.043 | 5B | 5B | 178 | 2.6–3.5 | ⑦ | ⑦ | 0.008 | 0.012 |
| | Corolla | 97.0 (1587) | BPR5EL-L11 ⑩ | 0.043 | 5B | 5B | 178 | 2.5–3.5 | ⑪ | ⑪ | 0.008 | 0.012 |
| | Starlet | 78.7 (1290) | BPR5EP-11 | 0.043 | 5B | — | 185 | 36–38 | 700 | — | Hyd. | Hyd. |
| | Camry | 121.7 (1995) | BPR5EA-L11 | 0.043 | 5B | 5B | 171 | 28–36 | 700 | 750 | Hyd. | Hyd. |
| | Celica | 22R 144.4 (2367) | BPR5EY | 0.031 | 8B | 8B | 171 | 2.5–3.8 | 700 | 700 | 0.008 | 0.012 |
| | | 22R-E 144.4 (2367) | BPR5EY | 0.031 | 5B | 5B | 171 | 35–38 | 750 | 750 | 0.008 | 0.012 |
| | Supra | 168.4 (2759) | BPR5EP-11 | 0.043 | 10B | 10B | 164 | 35–38 | 650 | 650 | Hyd. | Hyd. |
| | Cressida | 168.4 (2759) | BPR5EP-11 | 0.043 | — | 10B | 164 | 35–38 | — | 650 | Hyd. | Hyd. |
| 1985 | Tercel | 3A 88.6 (1452) | BPR5EY | 0.031 | 5B | 5B | 178 | 2.6–3.5 | ⑥ | ⑥ | 0.008 | 0.012 |
| | | 3A-C 88.6 (1452) | BPR5EY-11 ⑫ | 0.043 | 5B | 5B | 178 | 2.6–3.5 | ⑦ | ⑦ | 0.008 | 0.012 |
| | Corolla | 4A-C, 4A-LC 97.0 (1587) | BPR5EY-11 ⑬ | 0.043 | 5B | 5B | 178 | 2.5–3.5 | ⑪ | ⑪ | 0.008 | 0.012 |
| | | 4A-GE 97.0 (1587) | BCPR5EP-11 | 0.043 | 10B | — | 179 | 33–39 | 800 | — | 0.008 | 0.012 |
| | Camry | 121.7 (1995) | BPR5EA-L11 | 0.043 | 5B | 5B | 171 | 28–36 | 700 | 750 | Hyd. | Hyd. |
| | Celica | 22R 144.4 (2367) | BPR5EY | 0.031 | 8B | 8B | 171 | 2.5–3.8 | 700 | 700 | 0.008 | 0.012 |
| | | 22R-E 144.4 (2367) | BPR5EY | 0.031 | 5B | 5B | 171 | 35–38 | 750 | 750 | 0.008 | 0.012 |
| | Supra | 168.4 (2759) | BPR5EP-11 | 0.043 | 10B | 10B | 164 | 35–38 | 650 | 650 | Hyd. | Hyd. |
| | MR2 | 97.0 (1587) | BCPR5EP-11 | 0.043 | 10B | 10B | 179 | 33–39 | 800 | 800 | 0.008 | 0.012 |
| | Cressida | 168.4 (2759) | BPR5EP-11 | 0.043 | — | 10B | 164 | 35–38 | — | 650 | Hyd. | Hyd. |
| 1986 | Tercel | 3A 88.6 (1452) | BPR5EY | 0.031 | 5B | 5B | 178 | 2.6–3.5 | ⑥ | ⑥ | 0.008 | 0.012 |
| | | 3A-C 88.6 (1452) | BPR5EY-11 ⑫ | 0.043 | 5B | 5B | 178 | 2.6–3.5 | ⑦ | ⑦ | 0.008 | 0.012 |

## GASOLINE ENGINE TUNE-UP SPECIFICATIONS

| Year | Model | Engine Displacement cu. in. (cc) | Spark Plugs Type | Spark Plugs Gap (in.) | Ignition Timing (deg.) MT | Ignition Timing (deg.) AT | Compression Pressure (psi) | Fuel Pump (psi) | Idle Speed (rpm) MT | Idle Speed (rpm) AT | Valve Clearance In. | Valve Clearance Ex. |
|---|---|---|---|---|---|---|---|---|---|---|---|---|
| 1986 | Corolla | 4A-C, 4A-LC 97.0 (1587) | BPR5EY-11 | 0.043 | 5B | 5B | 178 | 2.5–3.5 | ⑪ | ⑪ | 0.008 | 0.012 |
| | | 4A-GE 97.0 (1587) | BCPR5EP-11 | 0.043 | 10B | 10B | 179 | 33–38 | 800 | 800 | 0.008 | 0.012 |
| | Camry | 121.7 (1995) | BPR5EY-11 | 0.043 | 10B | 10B | 171 | 28–36 | 700 | 700 | Hyd. | Hyd. |
| | Celica | 121.7 (1995) | BPR5EY-11 | 0.043 | 10B | 10B | 171 | 35–38 | 700 | 700 | Hyd. | Hyd. |
| | | 121.9 (1998) | BCPR5EP-11 | 0.043 | 10B | 10B | 171 | 35–38 | 750 | 750 | 0.008 | 0.012 |
| | Supra | 168.4 (2759) | BPR5EP-11 | 0.043 | 10B | 10B | 164 | 35–38 | 650 | 650 | Hyd. | Hyd. |
| | | 180.3 (2954) | BCPR5EP-11 | 0.043 | 10B | 10B | 156 | 33–40 | 700 | 700 | 0.008 | 0.010 |
| | MR2 | 97.0 (1587) | BCPR5EP-11 | 0.043 | 10B | 10B | 179 | 33–38 | 800 | 800 | 0.008 | 0.012 |
| | Cressida | 168.4 (2759) | BPR5EP-11 | 0.043 | — | 10B | 164 | 35–38 | — | 650 | Hyd. | Hyd. |
| 1987 | Tercel | 88.6 (1452) | BPR5EY-11 ⑫ | 0.043 | 5B | 5B | 178 | 2.6–3.5 | 650 | 900 | 0.008 | 0.012 |
| | | 88.9 (1456) | BPR5EY-11 | 0.043 | 3B | 3B | 184 | 2.6–3.5 | 650 | 900 | 0.008 | 0.008 |
| | Corolla | 4A-LC 97.0 (1587) | BPR5EY-11 | 0.043 | 5B | 5B | 178 | 2.5–3.5 | 700 | 850 | 0.008 | 0.012 |
| | | 4A-GE 97.0 (1587) | BCPR5EP-11 | 0.043 | 10B | 10B | 179 | 33–38 | 800 | 800 | 0.008 | 0.010 |
| | Camry | 121.9 (1998) | BCPR5EY-11 | 0.043 | 10B | 10B | 178 | 38–44 | 700 | 750 | 0.009 | 0.013 |
| | Celica | 3S-FE 121.9 (1998) | BCPR5EY-11 | 0.043 | 10B | 10B | 178 | 38–44 | 700 | 700 | 0.009 | 0.013 |
| | | 3S-GE 121.9 (1998) | BCPR5EP-11 | 0.043 | 10B | 10B | 178 | 33–38 | 750 | 750 | 0.008 | 0.010 |
| | Supra | 7M-GE 180.3 (2954) | BCPR5EP-11 | 0.043 | 10B | 10B | 156 | 33–40 | 700 | 700 | 0.008 | 0.010 |
| | | 7M-GTE 180.3 (2954) | BCPR6EP-N8 | 0.031 | 10B | 10B | 142 | 33–40 | 650 | 650 | 0.008 | 0.010 |
| | MR2 | 97.0 (1587) | BCPR5EP-11 | 0.043 | 10B | 10B | 179 | 33–38 | 800 | — | 0.008 | 0.010 |
| | Cressida | 168.4 (2759) | BPR5EP-11 | 0.043 | — | 10B | 164 | 35–38 | — | 650 | Hyd. | Hyd. |
| 1988 | Tercel | 88.6 (1452) | BPR5EY-11 ⑫ | 0.043 | 5B | 5B | 178 | 2.6–3.5 | 650 | 900 | 0.008 | 0.012 |
| | | 88.9 (1456) | BPR5EY-11 | 0.043 | 3B | 3B | 184 | 2.6–3.5 | 650 | 900 | 0.008 | 0.008 |
| | Corolla | 4A-LC 97.0 (1587) | BPR5EY-11 | 0.043 | 5B | 5B | 163 | 2.5–3.5 | 650 | 750 | 0.008 | 0.012 |
| | | 4A-F 97.0 (1587) | BPR5EY-11 | 0.043 | 5B | 5B | 191 | 2.5–3.5 | 650 | 750 | 0.008 | 0.010 |
| | | 4A-GE 97.0 (1587) | BCPR5EP-N8 | 0.043 | 10B | 10B | 179 | 33–38 | 800 | 800 | 0.008 | 0.010 |
| | Camry | 121.9 (1998) | BCPR5EY-11 | 0.043 | 10B | 10B | 178 | 38–44 | 700 | 750 | 0.009 | 0.013 |
| | Celica | 3S-FE 121.9 (1998) | BCPR5EY-11 | 0.043 | 10B | 10B | 178 | 38–44 | 650 | 650 | 0.009 | 0.013 |

## GASOLINE ENGINE TUNE-UP SPECIFICATIONS

| Year | Model | Engine Displacement cu. in. (cc) | Spark Plugs Type | Spark Plugs Gap (in.) | Ignition Timing (deg.) MT | Ignition Timing (deg.) AT | Compression Pressure (psi) | Fuel Pump (psi) | Idle Speed (rpm) MT | Idle Speed (rpm) AT | Valve Clearance In. | Valve Clearance Ex. |
|---|---|---|---|---|---|---|---|---|---|---|---|---|
| 1988 | Celica | 3S-GE 121.9 (1998) | BCPR5EP-11 | 0.043 | 10B | 10B | 178 | 33–38 | 750 | 750 | 0.008 | 0.010 |
| | | 3S-GTE 121.9 (1998) | BCPR5EP-8 | 0.031 | 10B | — | 178 | 33–38 | 750 | — | 0.008 | 0.010 |
| | Supra | 7M-GE 180.3 (2954) | BCPR5EP-11 | 0.043 | 10B | 10B | 156 | 33–40 | 700 | 700 | 0.008 | 0.010 |
| | | 7M-GTE 180.3 (2954) | BCPR6EP-N8 | 0.031 | 10B | 10B | 142 | 33–40 | 650 | 650 | 0.008 | 0.010 |
| | MR2 | 4A-GE 97.0 (1587) | BCPR5EP-11 | 0.043 | 10B | 10B | 179 | 38–44 | 800 | 800 | 0.008 | 0.010 |
| | | 4A-GZE 97.0 (1587) | BCPR6EP-11 | 0.043 | 10B | 10B | 156 | 33–38 | 800 | 800 | 0.008 | 0.010 |
| | Cressida | 168.4 (2759) | BPR5EP-11 | 0.043 | — | 10B | 164 | 35–38 | — | 650 | Hyd. | Hyd. |
| 1989 | Tercel | 88.9 (1456) | BPR5EY-11 | 0.043 | 3B | 3B | 184 | 2.6–3.5 | 700 | 900 | 0.008 | 0.008 |
| | Corolla | 4A-FE 97.0 (1587) | BCPR5EY | 0.031 | 10B | 10B | 191 | 38–44 | 800 | 800 | 0.008 | 0.010 |
| | | 4A-F 97.0 (1587) | BCPR5EY-11 | 0.043 | 5B | 5B | 191 | 2.5–3.5 | 650 | 750 | 0.008 | 0.010 |
| | | 4A-GE 97.0 (1587) | BCPR5EP-11 | 0.043 | 10B | 10B | 179 | 38–44 | 800 | 800 | 0.008 | 0.010 |
| | Camry | 121.9 (1998) | BCPR5EY-11 | 0.043 | 10B | 10B | 178 | 38–44 | 700 | 700 | 0.009 | 0.013 |
| | | 153.0 (2507) | BCPR6E-11 | 0.043 | 10B | 10B | 142 | 38–44 | 700 | 700 | 0.007 | 0.013 |
| | Celica | 3S-FE 121.9 (1998) | BCPR5EY-11 | 0.043 | 10B | 10B | 178 | 38–44 | 700 | 700 | 0.009 | 0.013 |
| | | 3S-GE 121.9 (1998) | BCPR5EP-11 | 0.043 | 10B | 10B | 178 | 33–38 | 750 | 750 | 0.008 | 0.010 |
| | | 3S-GTE 121.9 (1998) | BCPR5EP-8 | 0.031 | 10B | — | 178 | 33–38 | 750 | — | 0.008 | 0.010 |
| | Supra | 7M-GE 180.3 (2954) | BCPR5EP-11 | 0.043 | 10B | 10B | 156 | 38–44 | 700 | 700 | 0.008 | 0.010 |
| | | 7M-GTE 180.3 (2954) | BCPR6EP-N8 | 0.031 | 10B | 10B | 142 | 33–40 | 650 | 650 | 0.008 | 0.010 |
| | MR2 | 4A-GE 97.0 (1587) | BCPR5EP-11 | 0.043 | 10B | 10B | 179 | 38–44 | 800 | 800 | 0.008 | 0.010 |
| | | 4A-GZE 97.0 (1587) | BCPR6EP-11 | 0.043 | 10B | 10B | 156 | 33–38 | 800 | 800 | 0.008 | 0.010 |
| | Cressida | 180.3 (2954) | BCPR5EP-11 | 0.043 | — | 10B | 156 | 38–44 | — | 700 | 0.008 | 0.010 |
| 1990 | SEE UNDERHOOD SPECIFICATIONS STICKER | | | | | | | | | | | |

**NOTE:** The Underhood Specifications sticker often reflects tune-up specification changes made in production. Sticker figures must be used if they disagree with those in this chart.

MT Manual transmission
AT Automatic transmission
NA Not adjustable
A After Top Dead Center
B Before Top Dead Center

Hyd. Hydraulic valve lash adjusters
① 1A-C
② Calif.: BPR5EA-L; 0.031 in.
③ Canada: BPR5ES; 0.031 in.

④ Without power steering:
U.S MT—650 rpm
U.S. AT—750 rpm
Can. MT—700 rpm
Can. AT—750 rpm
With power steering: 850 rpm

## GASOLINE ENGINE TUNE-UP SPECIFICATIONS

| Year | Model | Engine Displacement cu. in. (cc) | Spark Plugs Type | Spark Plugs Gap (in.) | Ignition Timing (deg.) MT | Ignition Timing (deg.) AT | Compression Pressure (psi) | Fuel Pump (psi) | Idle Speed (rpm) MT | Idle Speed (rpm) AT | Valve Clearance In. | Valve Clearance Ex. |
|---|---|---|---|---|---|---|---|---|---|---|---|---|

⑤ Canada: 850 rpm
⑥ W/PS: MT—800 rpm
AT—900 rpm
W/O PS: MT—650 rpm
AT—800 rpm
⑦ W/PS: MT—800 rpm
AT: 900 rpm
W/O PS: 4 spd—550 rpm
5 spd—650 rpm
AT—800 rpm
⑧ W/PS: MT—650 rpm
AT—800 rpm
W/O PS: MT—800 rpm
AT—900 rpm
⑨ Calif.: BPR5EA-L11
Can. wagon w/3A-C: BPR5EA-L
⑩ Canada: BPR5EA-L; 0.031 in.
⑪ W/PS: MT—800 rpm (1986—750 rpm)
AT—900 rpm (1986—850 rpm)
W/O PS: MT—700 rpm
AT—800 rpm
⑫ Can. wagon w/MT: BPR5EY; 0.031 in.
⑬ Canada: BPR5EY; 0.031 in.

## FIRING ORDERS

**NOTE: To avoid confusion, always replace spark plug wires one at a time.**

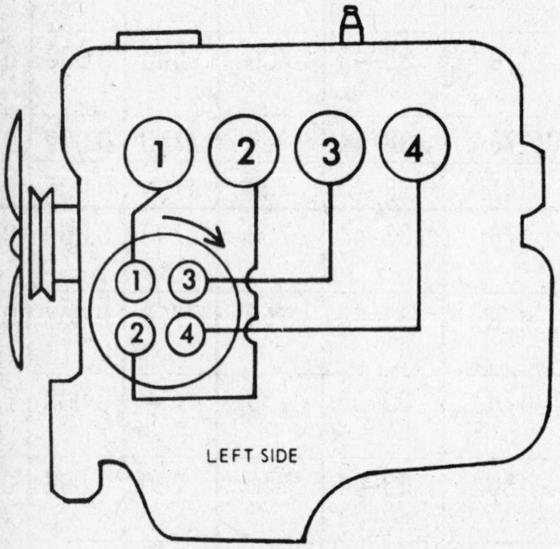


22R and 22R-E engines

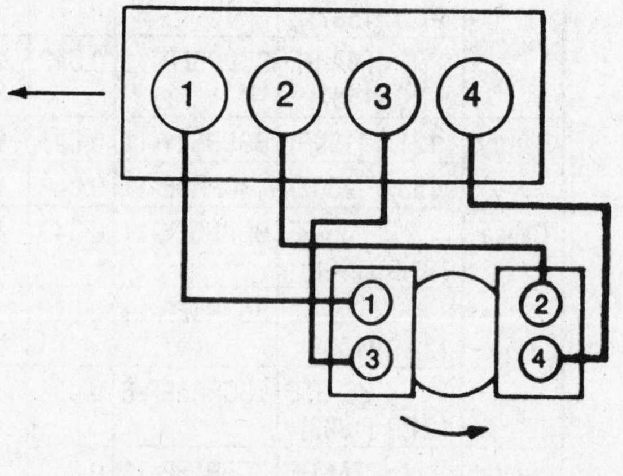

3A, 3A-C, 4A-F, 4A-C, 4A-GE (all) and 4A-GZE engines

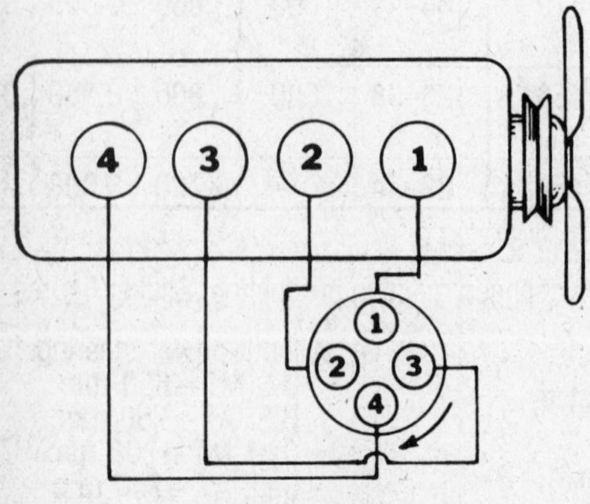

4K-E engines

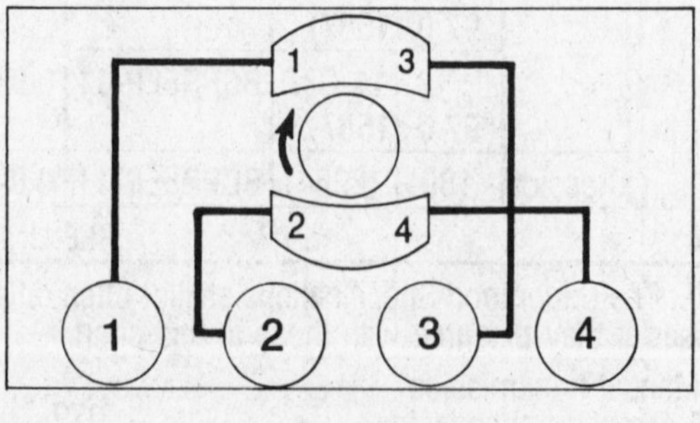

2S-E engines

## FIRING ORDERS

NOTE: To avoid confusion, always replace spark plug wires one at a time.

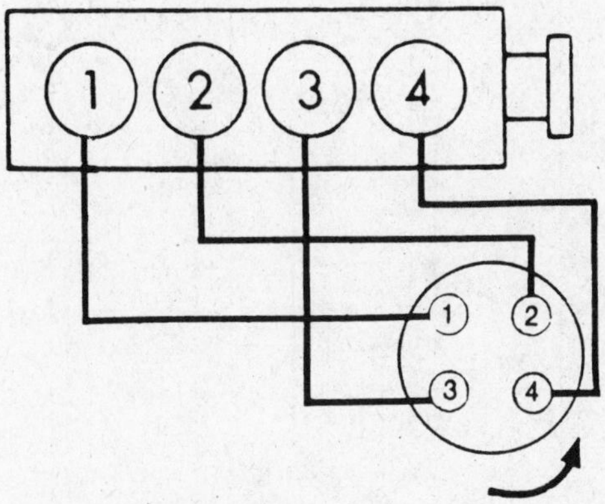

3E engines

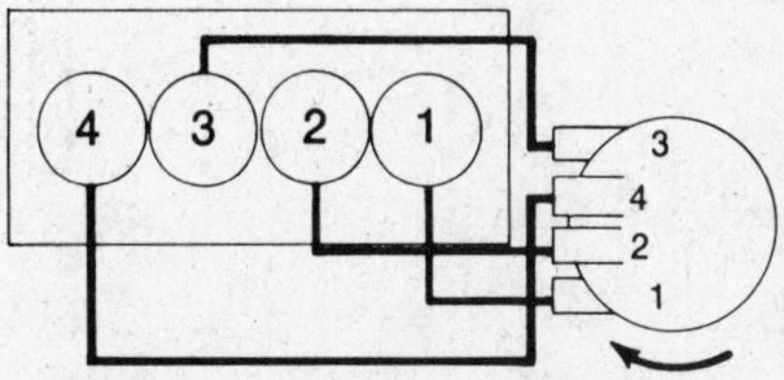

3S-FE, 3S-GE and 3S-GTE engines

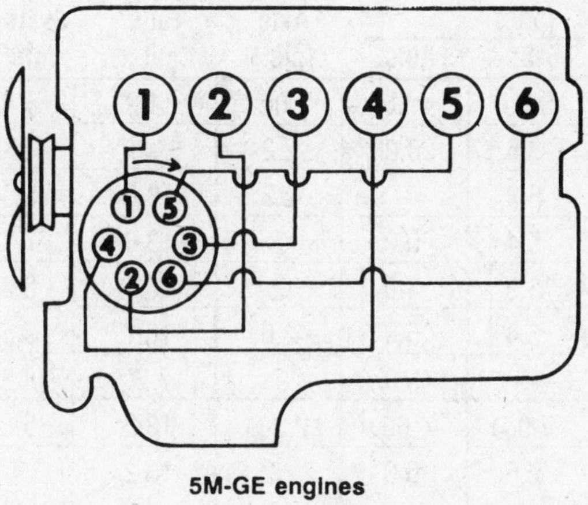

5M-GE engines

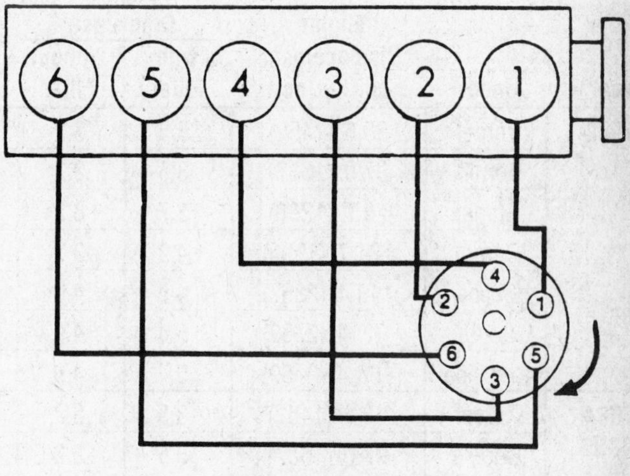

7M-GE engines

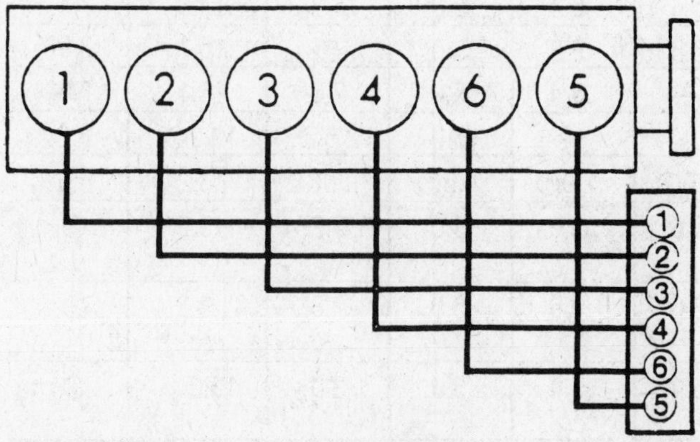

7M-GTE engines

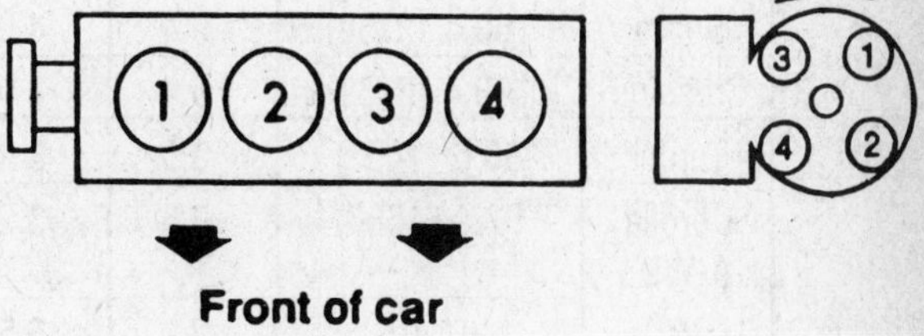


4A-F and 4A-FE engines

## FIRING ORDERS

**NOTE: To avoid confusion, always replace spark plug wires one at a time.**

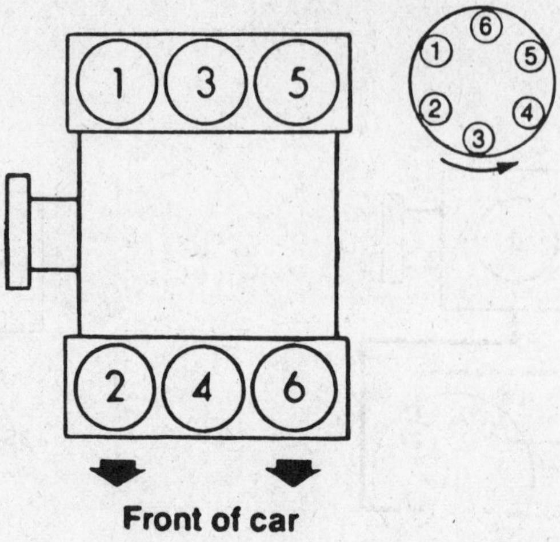


2VZ-FE engines

## CAPACITIES

| Year | Model | Engine Displacement cu. in. (cc) | Engine Crankcase with Filter | Engine Crankcase without Filter | Transmission (pts.) 4-Spd | Transmission (pts.) 5-Spd | Transmission (pts.) Auto. | Drive Axle (pts.) | Fuel Tank (gal.) | Cooling System (qts.) |
|---|---|---|---|---|---|---|---|---|---|---|
| 1983 | Tercel | 88.6 (1452) | 3.5 | 3.2 | 6.8④ | 6.8④ | 4.6⑤ | 2.0⑥ | 11.9 | 5.4 |
| | Corolla | 97.0 (1587) | 3.5 | 3.2 | 3.6 | 3.6 | 5.0 | 2.2 | 13.2⑦ | ⑧ |
| | Starlet | 78.7 (1290) | 3.7 | 3.2 | 5.2 | 5.2 | — | 2.2 | 10.6 | 5.5 |
| | Camry | 121.7 (1995) | 4.2 | 3.7 | 5.4 | 5.4 | 5.0 | ⑨ | 13.8 | 7.4 |
| | Celica | 144.4 (2367) | 4.9 | 4.0 | 5.8 | 5.8 | 5.0 | ① | 16.1 | 8.9 |
| | Supra | 168.4 (2759) | 5.4 | 4.9 | — | 5.4 | 5.0 | 2.6 | 16.1 | 9.5 |
| | Cressida | 168.4 (2759) | 5.4 | 4.9 | — | — | 5.0 | ② | 17.2③ | 8.8 |
| 1984 | Tercel | 88.6 (1452) | 3.5 | 3.2 | 7.0④ | 7.0④ | 4.6⑤ | 2.0⑥ | 13.2 | 5.6 |
| | Corolla (RWD) | 97.0 (1587) | 3.5 | 3.2 | 3.6 | 3.6 | 5.0 | 2.2 | 13.2 | ⑧ |
| | (FWD) | 97.0 (1587) | 3.5 | 3.2 | 5.4 | 5.4 | 5.0 | 3.0 | 13.2⑦ | ⑧ |
| | Starlet | 78.7 (1290) | 3.7 | 3.2 | 5.2 | 5.2 | — | 2.2 | 10.6 | 5.5 |
| | Camry | 121.7 (1995) | 4.2 | 3.8 | 5.4 | 5.4 | 5.0 | 4.2 | 14.5 | 7.4 |
| | Celica | 144.4 (2367) | 4.9 | 4.0 | 5.8 | 5.8 | 5.0 | ⑪ | 16.1 | 8.9 |
| | Supra | 168.4 (2759) | 5.4 | 4.9 | — | 5.4 | 5.0 | 2.6 | 16.1 | 7.8 |
| | Cressida | 168.4 (2759) | 5.4 | 4.9 | — | — | 5.0 | 2.6⑫ | 18.2③ | 9.2 |
| 1985 | Tercel | 88.6 (1452) | 3.5 | 3.2 | 7.0④ | 7.0④ | 4.6⑤ | 2.0⑥ | 13.2 | 5.6 |
| | Corolla (RWD) | 97.0 (1587) | 3.5 | 3.2 | 3.6 | 3.6 | 5.0 | 2.2 | 13.2 | ⑧ |
| | (FWD) | 4A-GE 97.0 (1587) | 3.9 | 3.5 | 3.6 | 3.6 | 5.0 | 2.8 | 13.2 | ⑧ |
| | (FWD) | 4A-C 97.0 (1587) | 3.5 | 3.2 | 5.4 | 5.4 | 5.0 | 3.0 | 13.2⑦ | ⑧ |

## CAPACITIES

| Year | Model | Engine Displacement cu. in. (cc) | Engine Crankcase with Filter | Engine Crankcase without Filter | Transmission (pts.) 4-Spd | Transmission (pts.) 5-Spd | Transmission (pts.) Auto. | Drive Axle (pts.) | Fuel Tank (gal.) | Cooling System (qts.) |
|---|---|---|---|---|---|---|---|---|---|---|
| 1985 | Camry | 121.7 (1995) | 4.2 | 3.8 | 5.4 | 5.4 | 5.0 | 4.2 | 14.5 | 7.4 |
| | Celica | 144.4 (2367) | 4.9 | 4.0 | 5.8 | 5.8 | 5.0 | (11) | 16.1 | 8.9 |
| | Supra | 168.4 (2759) | 5.4 | 4.9 | — | 5.4 | 5.0 | 2.6 | 16.1 | 7.8 |
| | MR2 | 97.0 (1587) | 3.9 | 3.5 | — | 4.8 | — | — | 10.8 | 13.6 |
| | Cressida | 168.4 (2759) | 5.4 | 4.9 | — | — | 5.0 | 2.6⑫ | 18.2③ | 9.2 |
| 1986 | Tercel | 88.6 (1452) | 3.5 | 3.2 | 7.0④ | 7.0④ | 4.6⑤ | 2.0⑥ | 13.2 | 5.6 |
| | Corolla (RWD) | 97.0 (1587) | 3.5 | 3.2 | 3.6 | 3.6 | 5.0 | 2.2 | 13.2 | ⑧ |
| | (RWD) | 4A-GE 97.0 (1587) | 3.9 | 3.5 | 3.6 | 3.6 | 5.0 | 2.8 | 13.2 | ⑧ |
| | (FWD) | 97.0 (1587) | 3.5 | 3.2 | 5.4 | 5.4 | 5.0 | 3.0 | 13.2⑦ | ⑧ |
| | Camry | 121.7 (1995) | 4.2 | 3.8 | 5.4 | 5.4 | 5.0 | 4.2 | 14.5 | 7.4 |
| | Celica | 121.7 (1995) | 4.2 | 3.8 | 5.4 | 5.4 | 5.0 | 4.2 | 15.9 | 7.4 |
| | | 121.9 (1998) | 4.1 | 3.8 | 5.4 | 5.4 | 5.0 | 4.2 | 15.9 | 7.4 |
| | Supra | 168.4 (2759) | 5.4 | 4.9 | — | 5.4 | 5.0 | 2.6 | 16.1 | 7.8 |
| | | 180.3 (2954) | 4.7 | 3.9 | — | 5.0 | 3.4 | 2.8 | 18.5 | 8.6 |
| | MR2 | 97.0 (1587) | 3.9 | 3.5 | — | 4.8 | — | — | 10.8 | 13.6 |
| | Cressida | 168.4 (2759) | 5.4 | 4.9 | — | — | 5.0 | 2.6⑫ | 18.2③ | 9.2 |
| 1987 | Tercel | 88.6 (1452) | 3.5 | 3.2 | 7.2④ | 7.2④ | 4.6⑤ | 2.0 | 13.2 | 5.6 |
| | | 88.9 (1456) | 3.4 | 3.1 | 5.0 | 5.0 | 5.2 | 3.0 | 11.9 | 4.9 |
| | Corolla (RWD) | 97.0 (1587) | 3.5 | 3.2 | 3.6 | 3.6 | 5.0 | 2.2 | 13.2 | ⑧ |
| | (RWD) | 4A-GE 97.0 (1587) | 3.9 | 3.5 | 3.6 | 3.6 | 5.0 | 2.8 | 13.2 | ⑧ |
| | (FWD) | 97.0 (1587) | 3.5 | 3.2 | 5.4 | 5.4 | 5.0 | 3.0 | 13.2⑦ | 6.3 |
| | Camry | 121.9 (1998) | 4.1 | 3.9 | 5.4 | 5.4 | 5.2 | 3.4 | 15.9 | 6.8 |
| | Celica | 3S-FE 121.9 (1998) | 4.1 | 3.9 | 5.4 | 5.4 | 4.2 | 3.4 | 15.9 | 6.8 |
| | | 3S-GE 121.9 (1998) | 4.1 | 3.9 | 5.4 | 5.4 | 5.0 | 3.4 | 15.9 | 7.4 |
| | Supra | 7M-GE 180.3 (2954) | 4.7 | 3.9 | — | 5.0 | 3.4 | 2.8 | 18.5 | 8.6 |
| | | 7M-GTE 180.3 (2954) | 4.7 | 3.9 | — | 6.4 | 3.4 | 2.8 | 18.5 | 8.7 |
| | MR2 | 97.0 (1587) | 3.9 | 3.5 | — | 4.8 | — | — | 10.8 | 13.6 |
| | Cressida | 168.4 (2759) | 5.4 | 4.9 | — | — | 3.4 | 2.6⑫ | 18.5 | 8.7 |
| 1988 | Tercel | 88.6 (1452) | 3.5 | 3.2 | 8.2 | 8.2 | 8.8 | 2.2 | 13.2 | 5.6 |
| | | 88.9 (1456) | 3.4 | 3.1 | 5.0 | 5.0 | 4.6 | 3.0 | 11.9 | 5.3 |
| | Corolla | 4A-LC 97.0 (1587) | 3.5 | 3.2 | 5.4 | 5.4 | ⑬ | 3.0 | 13.2⑦ | 6.4 |

## CAPACITIES

| Year | Model | Engine Displacement cu. in. (cc) | Engine Crankcase with Filter | Engine Crankcase without Filter | Transmission (pts.) 4-Spd | Transmission (pts.) 5-Spd | Transmission (pts.) Auto. | Drive Axle (pts.) | Fuel Tank (gal.) | Cooling System (qts.) |
|---|---|---|---|---|---|---|---|---|---|---|
| 1988 | Corolla | 4A-F 97.0 (1587) | 3.3 | 3.2 | 5.4 | 5.4 | ⑬ | 3.0 | 13.2 | 6.3 |
| | | 4A-GE 97.0 (1587) | 3.9 | 3.5 | 5.4 | 5.4 | ⑬ | 3.0 | 13.2 | 6.3 |
| | Camry | 121.9 (1998) | 4.1 | 3.9 | 5.4 | 5.4 | 5.2 | 3.4⑭ | 15.9 | 6.8 |
| | Celica | 3S-FE 121.9 (1998) | 4.1 | 3.9 | 5.4 | 5.4 | 5.2 | 3.4 | 15.9 | 6.8 |
| | | 3S-GE 121.9 (1998) | 4.1 | 3.9 | 5.4 | 5.4 | 5.2 | 3.4 | 15.9 | 7.4 |
| | | 3S-GTE 121.9 (1998) | 3.8 | 3.6 | – | 10.2 | – | – | 15.9 | 8.5 |
| | Supra | 7M-GE 180.3 (2954) | 4.4 | 4.1 | – | 5.0 | 3.4 | 2.8 | 18.5 | 8.6 |
| | | 7M-GTE 180.3 (2954) | 4.4 | 4.1 | – | 6.4 | 3.4 | 2.8 | 18.5 | 8.7 |
| | MR2 | 97.0 (1587) | 3.5 | 3.2 | – | ⑮ | 6.6 | – | 10.8 | ⑯ |
| | Cressida | 168.4 (2759) | 5.2 | 4.9 | – | – | 3.4 | 2.6 | 18.5 | 8.7 |
| 1989-90 | Tercel | 88.9 (1456) | 3.4 | 3.1 | 5.0 | 5.0 | 4.6 | 3.0 | 11.9 | 5.5 |
| | Corolla | 4A-F, 4A-FE 97.0 (1587) | 3.4 | 3.2 | 5.4 | 5.4 | ⑬ | 3.0 | 13.2 | 5.9 |
| | | 4A-GE 97.0 (1587) | 3.9 | 3.6 | 5.4 | 5.4 | ⑬ | 3.0 | 13.2 | 6.3 |
| | Camry | 121.9 (1998) | 4.1 | 3.9 | – | 5.4⑰ | 5.2 | 3.4⑭ | 15.9 | 6.8 |
| | | 153.0 (2507) | 4.1 | 3.9 | – | – | 5.2 | 2.2 | 15.9 | 9.0 |
| | Celica | 3S-FE 121.9 (1998) | 4.1 | 3.9 | – | 5.4 | 5.2 | 3.4 | 15.9 | 6.6 |
| | | 3S-GE 121.9 (1998) | 4.1 | 3.8 | – | 5.4 | 5.2 | 3.4 | 15.9 | 6.4 |
| | | 3S-GTE 121.9 (1998) | 3.8 | 3.5 | – | 10.2 | – | 2.4 | 15.9 | 6.8 |
| | Supra | 7M-GE 180.3 (2954) | 4.7 | 4.3 | – | 5.0 | 3.4 | 2.8 | 18.5 | 8.6 |
| | | 7M-GTE 180.3 (2954) | 4.9 | 4.5 | – | 6.4 | 3.4 | 2.8 | 18.5 | 8.7 |
| | MR2 | 97.0 (1587) | 3.5 | 3.2 | – | ⑮ | 6.6 | – | 10.8 | 13.6 |
| | Cressida | 180.3 (2954) | 4.7 | 4.3 | – | – | 3.4 | 2.6 | 18.5 | 8.8 |

① Unitized:2.6
Banjo: 2.8

② 7.5 in.:1.3
8.0 in.:1.9

③ Station wagon:16.2

④ 4wd: 8.2

⑤ 4wd: 8.8

⑥ 4wd: 2.2

⑦ Station wagon: 12.4

⑧ 1983-84: MT–5.7, AT–6.6
1985-87: FWD–6.3; RWD MT–5.9, AT–5.8

⑨ MT: 5.4
AT: 4.2

⑩ FWD: 5.4

⑪ IRS W/MT: 2.6; W/AT: 2.2

⑫ Station wagon: 3.0

⑬ A240E, A241H: 6.6
A131L: 5.2

⑭ 4wd rear diff.: 2.4

⑮ C52: 5.4; E51: 8.8

⑯ MT: 12.9
AT: 13.6

⑰ 4wd:10.4

## CAMSHAFT SPECIFICATIONS

All measurements given in inches.

| Year | Engine Displacement cu. In. (cc) | Journal Diameter 1 | 2 | 3 | 4 | 5 | 6 | 7 | Bearing Clearance | Camshaft End Play |
|---|---|---|---|---|---|---|---|---|---|---|
| 1983 | 3A, 3A-C 88.6 (1452) | 1.1015–1.1022 | 1.1015–1.1022 | 1.1015–1.1022 | 1.1015–1.1022 | — | — | — | 0.0015–0.0029 | 0.0031–0.0071 |
| | 4A-C, 4A-LC 97.0 (1587) | 1.1015–1.1022 | 1.1015–1.1022 | 1.1015–1.1022 | 1.1015–1.1022 | — | — | — | 0.0015–0.0029 | 0.0031–0.0071 |
| | 4K-E 78.7 (1290) | 1.7011–1.7018 | 1.6911–1.6917 | 1.6813–1.6819 | 1.6716–1.6722 | — | — | — | ② | 0.0030–0.0060 |
| | 2S-E 121.7 (1995) | 1.8291–1.8297 | 1.8192–1.8199 | 1.8094–1.8100 | 1.7996–1.8002 | 1.7897–1.7904 | 1.7799–1.7805 | — | 0.0010–0.0026 | 0.0031–0.0091 |
| | 22R, 22RE 144.4 (2367) | 1.2984–1.2992 | 1.2984–1.2992 | 1.2984–1.2992 | 1.2984–1.2992 | — | — | — | 0.0004–0.0020 | 0.0031–0.0071 |
| | 5M-GE 168.4 (2759) | 1.4944–1.4951 | 1.6913–1.6919 | 1.7110–1.7116 | 1.7307–1.7313 | 1.7504–1.7510 | 1.7700–1.7707 | 1.7897–1.7904 | 0.0010–0.0026 | 0.0028–0.0098 |
| 1984 | 3A, 3A-C 88.6 (1452) | 1.1015–1.1022 | 1.1015–1.1022 | 1.1015–1.1022 | 1.1015–1.1022 | — | — | — | 0.0015–0.0029 | 0.0031–0.0071 |
| | 4A-C, 4A-LC 97.0 (1587) | 1.1015–1.1022 | 1.1015–1.1022 | 1.1015–1.1022 | 1.1015–1.1022 | — | — | — | 0.0015–0.0029 | 0.0031–0.0071 |
| | 4K-E 78.7 (1290) | 1.7011–1.7018 | 1.6911–1.6917 | 1.6813–1.6819 | 1.6716–1.6722 | — | — | — | ② | 0.0030–0.0060 |
| | 2S-E 121.7 (1995) | 1.8291–1.8297 | 1.8192–1.8199 | 1.8094–1.8100 | 1.7996–1.8002 | 1.7897–1.7904 | 1.7799–1.7805 | — | 0.0010–0.0026 | 0.0031–0.0091 |
| | 22R, 22RE 144.4 (2367) | 1.2984–1.2992 | 1.2984–1.2992 | 1.2984–1.2992 | 1.2984–1.2992 | — | — | — | 0.0004–0.0020 | 0.0031–0.0071 |
| | 5M-GE 168.4 (2759) | 1.4944–1.4951 | 1.6913–1.6919 | 1.7110–1.7116 | 1.7307–1.7313 | 1.7504–1.7510 | 1.7700–1.7707 | 1.7897–1.7904 | 0.0010–0.0026 | 0.0028–0.0098 |
| 1985 | 3A, 3A-C 88.6 (1452) | 1.1015–1.1022 | 1.1015–1.1022 | 1.1015–1.1022 | 1.1015–1.1022 | — | — | — | 0.0015–0.0029 | 0.0031–0.0071 |
| | 4A-C, 4A-LC 97.0 (1587) | 1.1015–1.1022 | 1.1015–1.1022 | 1.1015–1.1022 | 1.1015–1.1022 | — | — | — | 0.0015–0.0029 | 0.0031–0.0071 |
| | 4A-GE 97.0 (1587) | 1.3768–1.3791 | 1.3768–1.3791 | 1.3768–1.3791 | 1.3768–1.3791 | — | — | — | 0.0014–0.0028 | 0.0031–0.0075 |
| | 2S-E 121.7 (1995) | 1.8291–1.8297 | 1.8192–1.8199 | 1.8094–1.8100 | 1.7996–1.8002 | 1.7897–1.7904 | 1.7799–1.7805 | — | 0.0010–0.0026 | 0.0031–0.0091 |
| | 22R, 22RE 144.4 (2367) | 1.2984–1.2992 | 1.2984–1.2992 | 1.2984–1.2992 | 1.2984–1.2992 | — | — | — | 0.0004–0.0020 | 0.0031–0.0071 |
| | 5M-GE 168.4 (2759) | 1.4944–1.4951 | 1.6913–1.6919 | 1.7110–1.7116 | 1.7307–1.7313 | 1.7504–1.7510 | 1.7700–1.7707 | 1.7897–1.7904 | 0.0010–0.0026 | 0.0028–0.0098 |
| 1986 | 3A, 3A-C 88.6 (1452) | 1.1015–1.1022 | 1.1015–1.1022 | 1.1015–1.1022 | 1.1015–1.1022 | — | — | — | 0.0015–0.0029 | 0.0031–0.0071 |
| | 4A-C, 4A-LC 97.0 (1587) | 1.1015–1.1022 | 1.1015–1.1022 | 1.1015–1.1022 | 1.1015–1.1022 | — | — | — | 0.0015–0.0029 | 0.0031–0.0071 |
| | 4A-GE 97.0 (1587) | 1.0610–1.0616 | 1.0610–1.0616 | 1.0610–1.0616 | 1.0610–1.0616 | — | — | — | 0.0014–0.0028 | 0.0031–0.0075 |
| | 2S-E 121.7 (1995) | 1.8291–1.8297 | 1.8192–1.8199 | 1.8094–1.8100 | 1.7996–1.8002 | 1.7897–1.7904 | 1.7799–1.7805 | — | 0.0010–0.0026 | 0.0031–0.0091 |

## CAMSHAFT SPECIFICATIONS

All measurements given in inches.

| Year | Engine Displacement cu. in. (cc) | Journal Diameter 1 | 2 | 3 | 4 | 5 | 6 | 7 | Bearing Clearance | Camshaft End Play |
|---|---|---|---|---|---|---|---|---|---|---|
| 1986 | 3S-GE 121.9 (1998) | 1.0614–1.0620 | 1.0614–1.0620 | 1.0614–1.0620 | 1.0614–1.0620 | — | — | — | 0.0010–0.0024 | 0.0039–0.0094 |
| | 5M-GE 168.4 (2759) | 1.4944–1.4951 | 1.6913–1.6919 | 1.7110–1.7116 | 1.7307–1.7313 | 1.7504–1.7510 | 1.7700–1.7707 | 1.7897–1.7904 | 0.0010–0.0026 | 0.0028–0.0098 |
| | 7M-GE 180.3 (2954) | 1.0610–1.0616 | 1.0586–1.0620 | 1.0586–1.0620 | 1.0586–1.0620 | 1.0586–1.0620 | 1.0586–1.0620 | 1.0586–1.0620 | 0.0010–0.0037③ | 0.0031–0.0075 |
| 1987 | 3A-C 88.6 (1452) | 1.1015–1.1022 | 1.1015–1.1022 | 1.1015–1.1022 | 1.1015–1.1022 | — | — | — | 0.0015–0.0029 | 0.0031–0.0071 |
| | 3E 88.9 (1456) | 1.0622–1.0628 | 1.0622–1.0628 | 1.0622–1.0628 | 1.0622–1.0628 | — | — | — | 0.0015–0.0029 | 0.0031–0.0071 |
| | 4A-LC 97.0 (1587) | 1.1015–1.1022 | 1.1015–1.1022 | 1.1015–1.1022 | 1.1015–1.1022 | — | — | — | 0.0015–0.0029 | 0.0031–0.0071 |
| | 4A-GEC, 4A-GELC 97.0 (1587) | 1.0610–1.0616 | 1.0610–1.0616 | 1.0610–1.0616 | 1.0610–1.0616 | — | — | — | 0.0014–0.0028 | 0.0031–0.0075 |
| | 3S-FE 121.9 (1998) | 1.0614–1.0620 | 1.0614–1.0620 | 1.0614–1.0620 | 1.0614–1.0620 | — | — | — | 0.0010–0.0024 | 0.0018–0.0039 |
| | 3S-GE 121.9 (1998) | 1.0614–1.0620 | 1.0614–1.0620 | 1.0614–1.0620 | 1.0614–1.0620 | — | — | — | 0.0010–0.0024 | 0.0047–0.0079 |
| | 5M-GE 168.4 (2759) | 1.4944–1.4951 | 1.6913–1.6919 | 1.7110–1.7116 | 1.7307–1.7313 | 1.7504–1.7510 | 1.7700–1.7707 | 1.7897–1.7904 | 0.0010–0.0026 | 0.0028–0.0098 |
| | 7M-GE, 7M-GTE 180.3 (2954) | 1.0610–1.0616 | 1.0586–1.0620 | 1.0586–1.0620 | 1.0586–1.0620 | 1.0586–1.0620 | 1.0586–1.0620 | 1.0586–1.0620 | 0.0010–0.0037③ | 0.0031–0.0075 |
| 1988 | 3A-C 88.6 (1452) | 1.1015–1.1022 | 1.1015–1.1022 | 1.1015–1.1022 | 1.1015–1.1022 | — | — | — | 0.0015–0.0029 | 0.0031–0.0071 |
| | 3E 88.9 (1456) | 1.0622–1.0628 | 1.0622–1.0628 | 1.0622–1.0628 | 1.0622–1.0628 | — | — | — | 0.0015–0.0029 | 0.0031–0.0071 |
| | 4A-F 97.0 (1587) | 0.9035–0.9041⑤ | 0.9035–0.9041 | 0.9035–0.9041 | 0.9035–0.9041 | — | — | — | 0.0015–0.0028 | ⑥ |
| | 4A-LC 97.0 (1587) | 1.1015–1.1022 | 1.1015–1.1022 | 1.1015–1.1022 | 1.1015–1.1022 | — | — | — | 0.0015–0.0029 | 0.0031–0.0071 |
| | 4A-GZE, 4A-GEC, 4A-GELC 97.0 (1587) | 1.0610–1.0616 | 1.0610–1.0616 | 1.0610–1.0616 | 1.0610–1.0616 | — | — | — | 0.0014–0.0028 | 0.0031–0.0075 |
| | 3S-FE 121.9 (1998) | 1.0614–1.0620 | 1.0614–1.0620 | 1.0614–1.0620 | 1.0614–1.0620 | — | — | — | 0.0010–0.0024 | 0.0018–0.0039 |
| | 3S-GE, 3S-GTE 121.9 (1998) | 1.0614–1.0620 | 1.0614–1.0620 | 1.0614–1.0620 | 1.0614–1.0620 | — | — | — | 0.0010–0.0024 | 0.0047–0.0079④ |
| | 5M-GE 168.4 (2759) | 1.4944–1.4951 | 1.6913–1.6919 | 1.7110–1.7116 | 1.7307–1.7313 | 1.7504–1.7510 | 1.7700–1.7707 | 1.7897–1.7904 | 0.0010–0.0026 | 0.0028–0.0098 |
| | 7M-GE, 7M-GTE 180.3 (2954) | 1.0610–1.0616 | 1.0586–1.0620 | 1.0586–1.0620 | 1.0586–1.0620 | 1.0586–1.0620 | 1.0586–1.0620 | 1.0586–1.0620 | 0.0010–0.0037③ | 0.0031–0.0075 |
| 1989-90 | 3E 88.9 (1456) | 1.0622–1.0628 | 1.0622–1.0628 | 1.0622–1.0628 | 1.0622–1.0628 | — | — | — | 0.0015–0.0029 | 0.0031–0.0071 |

## CAMSHAFT SPECIFICATIONS

All measurements given in inches.

| Year | Engine Displacement cu. in. (cc) | Journal Diameter 1 | 2 | 3 | 4 | 5 | 6 | 7 | Bearing Clearance | Camshaft End Play |
|---|---|---|---|---|---|---|---|---|---|---|
| 1989–90 | 4A-F, 4A-FE 97.0 (1587) | 0.9035–0.9041⑤ | 0.9035–0.9041 | 0.9035–0.9041 | 0.9035–0.9041 | — | — | — | 0.0015–0.0028 | ⑥ |
| | 4A-GZE, 4A-GEC, 4A-GELC 97.0 (1587) | 1.0610–1.0616 | 1.0610–1.0616 | 1.0610–1.0616 | 1.0610–1.0616 | — | — | — | 0.0014–0.0028 | 0.0031–0.0075 |
| | 3S-FE 121.9 (1998) | 1.0614–1.0620 | 1.0614–1.0620 | 1.0614–1.0620 | 1.0614–1.0620 | — | — | — | 0.0010–0.0024 | 0.0018–0.0039 |
| | 3S-GE, 3S-GTE 121.9 (1998) | 1.0614–1.0620 | 1.0614–1.0620 | 1.0614–1.0620 | 1.0614–1.0620 | — | — | — | 0.0010–0.0024 | 0.0047–0.0114 |
| | 2VZ-FE 153.0 (2507) | 1.0610–1.0616 | 1.0610–1.0616 | 1.0610–1.0616 | 1.0610–1.0616 | 1.0610–1.0616 | — | — | 0.0014–0.0028 | 0.0012–0.0031 |
| | 7M-GE, 7M-GTE 180.3 (2954) | 1.0610–1.0616 | 1.0586–1.0620 | 1.0586–1.0620 | 1.0586–1.0620 | 1.0586–1.0620 | 1.0586–1.0620 | 1.0586–1.0620 | 0.0010–0.0037③ | 0.0031–0.0075 |

① Nos. 1 & 4: 0.0010–0.0026
Nos. 2 & 3: 0.0014–0.0028

② Nos. 1 & 4: 0.0010–0.0026
Nos. 2 & 3: 0.0016–0.0030

③ No. 1: 0.0014–0.0028

④ 3S-GTE: 0.0039–0.0094

⑤ Exhaust No. 1: 0.9822–0.9829

⑥ Intake: 0.0012–0.0033
Exhaust: 0.0014–0.0035

## CRANKSHAFT AND CONNECTING ROD SPECIFICATIONS

All measurements are given in inches.

| Year | Engine Displacement cu. in. (cc) | Crankshaft: Main Brg. Journal Dia. | Crankshaft: Main Brg. Oil Clearance | Crankshaft: Shaft End-play | Crankshaft: Thrust on No. | Connecting Rod: Journal Diameter | Connecting Rod: Oil Clearance | Connecting Rod: Side Clearance |
|---|---|---|---|---|---|---|---|---|
| 1983 | 3A, 3A-C 88.6 (1452) | 1.8892–1.8898 | 0.0012–0.0026 | 0.0008–0.0073 | 3 | 1.5742–1.5748 | 0.0008–0.0020 | 0.0059–0.0098 |
| | 4A-C, 4A-LC 97.0 (1587) | 1.8892–1.8898 | 0.0005–0.0019 | 0.0008–0.0073 | 3 | 1.5742–1.5748 | 0.0008–0.0020 | 0.0059–0.0098 |
| | 4K-E 78.7 (1290) | 1.9676–1.9685 | 0.0006–0.0016 | 0.0016–0.0095 | 3 | 1.6526–1.6535 | 0.0006–0.0016 | 0.0079–0.0150 |
| | 2S-E 121.7 (1995) | 2.1648–2.1654 | 0.0008–0.0019① | 0.0008–0.0087 | 3 | 1.8892–1.8898 | 0.0009–0.0022 | 0.0063–0.0083 |
| | 22R, 22R-E 144.4 (2367) | 2.3614–2.3622 | 0.0006–0.0020 | 0.0008–0.0087 | 3 | 2.0862–2.0866 | 0.0010–0.0022 | 0.0063–0.0102 |
| | 5M-GE 168.4 (2759) | 2.3617–2.3627 | 0.0013–0.0023 | 0.0020–0.0098 | 4 | 2.0463–2.0472 | 0.0008–0.0021 | 0.0063–0.0117 |
| 1984 | 3A, 3A-C 88.6 (1452) | 1.8892–1.8898 | 0.0012–0.0026 | 0.0008–0.0073 | 3 | 1.5742–1.5748 | 0.0008–0.0020 | 0.0059–0.0098 |
| | 4A-C, 4A-LC 97.0 (1587) | 1.8892–1.8898 | 0.0005–0.0019 | 0.0008–0.0073 | 3 | 1.5742–1.5748 | 0.0008–0.0020 | 0.0059–0.0098 |
| | 4K-E 78.7 (1290) | 1.9676–1.9685 | 0.0006–0.0016 | 0.0016–0.0095 | 3 | 1.6526–1.6535 | 0.0006–0.0016 | 0.0079–0.0150 |
| | 2S-E 121.7 (1995) | 2.1648–2.1654 | 0.0008–0.0019① | 0.0008–0.0087 | 3 | 1.8892–1.8898 | 0.0009–0.0022 | 0.0063–0.0083 |

## CRANKSHAFT AND CONNECTING ROD SPECIFICATIONS

All measurements are given in inches.

| Year | Engine Displacement cu. in. (cc) | Crankshaft: Main Brg. Journal Dia. | Crankshaft: Main Brg. Oil Clearance | Crankshaft: Shaft End-play | Crankshaft: Thrust on No. | Connecting Rod: Journal Diameter | Connecting Rod: Oil Clearance | Connecting Rod: Side Clearance |
|---|---|---|---|---|---|---|---|---|
| 1984 | 22R, 22R-E 144.4 (2367) | 2.3614–2.3622 | 0.0010–0.0022 | 0.0008–0.0087 | 3 | 2.0862–2.0866 | 0.0010–0.0022 | 0.0063–0.0102 |
| | 5M-GE 168.4 (2759) | 2.3617–2.3627 | 0.0013–0.0023 | 0.0020–0.0098 | 4 | 2.0463–2.0472 | 0.0008–0.0021 | 0.0063–0.0117 |
| 1985 | 3A, 3A-C 88.6 (1452) | 1.8892–1.8898 | 0.0012–0.0026 | 0.0008–0.0073 | 3 | 1.5742–1.5748 | 0.0008–0.0020 | 0.0059–0.0098 |
| | 4A-C, 4A-LC 97.0 (1587) | 1.8892–1.8898 | 0.0005–0.0019 | 0.0008–0.0073 | 3 | 1.5742–1.5748 | 0.0008–0.0020 | 0.0059–0.0098 |
| | 4A-GE 97.0 (1587) | 1.8892–1.8898 | 0.0005–0.0019 | 0.0008–0.0087 | 3 | 1.5742–1.5748 | 0.0008–0.0020 | 0.0059–0.0098 |
| | 2S-E 121.7 (1995) | 2.1648–2.1654 | 0.0008–0.0019① | 0.0008–0.0087 | 3 | 1.8892–1.8898 | 0.0009–0.0022 | 0.0063–0.0083 |
| | 22R, 22R-E 144.4 (2367) | 2.3614–2.3622 | 0.0010–0.0022 | 0.0008–0.0087 | 3 | 2.0862–2.0866 | 0.0010–0.0022 | 0.0063–0.0102 |
| | 5M-GE 168.4 (2759) | 2.3617–2.3627 | 0.0013–0.0023 | 0.0020–0.0098 | 4 | 2.0463–2.0472 | 0.0008–0.0021 | 0.0063–0.0117 |
| 1986 | 3A, 3A-C 88.6 (1452) | 1.8892–1.8898 | 0.0005–0.0015 | 0.0008–0.0073 | 3 | 1.5742–1.5748 | 0.0008–0.0020 | 0.0059–0.0098 |
| | 4A-C, 4A-LC 97.0 (1587) | 1.8892–1.8898 | 0.0005–0.0015 | 0.0008–0.0073 | 3 | 1.5742–1.5748 | 0.0008–0.0020 | 0.0059–0.0098 |
| | 4A-GE 97.0 (1587) | 1.8892–1.8898 | 0.0005–0.0015 | 0.0008–0.0087 | 3 | 1.5742–1.5748 | 0.0008–0.0020 | 0.0059–0.0098 |
| | 2S-E 121.7 (1995) | 2.1648–2.1654 | 0.0008–0.0019① | 0.0008–0.0087 | 3 | 1.8892–1.8898 | 0.0009–0.0022 | 0.0063–0.0083 |
| | 3S-GE 121.9 (1998) | 2.1648–2.1654 | 0.0008–0.0019① | 0.0008–0.0087 | 3 | 1.8892–1.8898 | 0.0009–0.0022 | 0.0063–0.0124 |
| | 5M-GE 168.4 (2759) | 2.3617–2.3627 | 0.0013–0.0023 | 0.0020–0.0098 | 4 | 2.0463–2.0472 | 0.0008–0.0021 | 0.0063–0.0117 |
| | 7M-GE 180.3 (2954) | 2.3625–2.3627 | 0.0012–0.0022 | 0.0020–0.0098 | 4 | 2.1659–2.1663 | 0.0012–0.0019 | 0.0063–0.0117 |
| 1987 | 3A-C 88.6 (1452) | 1.8891–1.8898 | 0.0006–0.0013 | 0.0008–0.0087 | 3 | 1.5742–1.5748 | 0.0008–0.0020 | 0.0059–0.0098 |
| | 3E 88.9 (1456) | 1.9683–1.9685 | 0.0006–0.0014 | 0.0008–0.0087 | 3 | 1.8110–1.8113 | 0.0006–0.0019 | 0.0059–0.0138 |
| | 3S-FE, 3S-GE 121.9 (1998) | 2.1648–2.1653 | 0.0007–0.0015① | 0.0008–0.0087 | 3 | 1.8892–1.8898 | 0.0009–0.0022 | 0.0063–0.0123 |
| | 4A-LC 97.0 (1587) | 1.8891–1.8898 | 0.0006–0.0013 | 0.0008–0.0087 | 3 | 1.5742–1.5748 | 0.0008–0.0020 | 0.0059–0.0098 |
| | 4A-GEC,4A-GELC 97.0 (1587) | 1.8891–1.8898 | 0.0005–0.0015 | 0.0008–0.0087 | 3 | 1.5742–1.5748 | 0.0008–0.0020 | 0.0059–0.0098 |
| | 5M-GE 168.4 (2759) | 2.3625–2.3627 | 0.0012–0.0048 | 0.0020–0.0098 | 4 | 2.1659–2.1663 | 0.0008–0.0021 | 0.0063–0.0117 |
| | 7M-GE, 7M-GTE 180.3 (2954) | 2.3625–2.3627 | 0.0012–0.0022 | 0.0020–0.0098 | 4 | 2.1659–2.1663 | 0.0012–0.0019 | 0.0063–0.0117 |

## CRANKSHAFT AND CONNECTING ROD SPECIFICATIONS

All measurements are given in inches.

| Year | Engine Displacement cu. in. (cc) | Crankshaft Main Brg. Journal Dia. | Crankshaft Main Brg. Oil Clearance | Crankshaft Shaft End-play | Crankshaft Thrust on No. | Connecting Rod Journal Diameter | Connecting Rod Oil Clearance | Connecting Rod Side Clearance |
|---|---|---|---|---|---|---|---|---|
| 1988 | 3A-C 88.6 (1452) | 1.8891–1.8898 | 0.0006–0.0013 | 0.0008–0.0087 | 3 | 1.5742–1.5748 | 0.0008–0.0020 | 0.0059–0.0098 |
| | 3E 88.9 (1456) | 1.9683–1.9685 | 0.0006–0.0014 | 0.0008–0.0087 | 3 | 1.8110–1.8113 | 0.0006–0.0019 | 0.0059–0.0138 |
| | 3S-FE, 3S-GE, 3S-GTE 121.9 (1998) | 2.1648–2.1653 | 0.0007–0.0015① | 0.0008–0.0087 | 3 | 1.8892–1.8898 | 0.0009–0.0022 | 0.0063–0.0123 |
| | 4A-F, 4A-LC 97.0 (1587) | 1.8891–1.8898 | 0.0006–0.0013 | 0.0008–0.0087 | 3 | 1.5742–1.5748 | 0.0008–0.0020 | 0.0059–0.0098 |
| | 4A-GEC,4A-GELC 97.0 (1587) | 1.8891–1.8898 | 0.0005–0.0015 | 0.0008–0.0087 | 3 | 1.5742–1.5748 | 0.0008–0.0020 | 0.0059–0.0098 |
| | 4A-GZE 97.0 (1587) | 1.8891–1.8898 | 0.0006–0.0013 | 0.0008–0.0087 | 3 | 1.6529–1.6535 | 0.0008–0.0020 | 0.0059–0.0098 |
| | 5M-GE 168.4 (2759) | 2.3625–2.3627 | 0.0012–0.0048 | 0.0020–0.0098 | 4 | 2.1659–2.1663 | 0.0008–0.0021 | 0.0063–0.0117 |
| | 7M-GE, 7M-GTE 180.3 (2954) | 2.3625–2.3627 | 0.0012–0.0048 | 0.0020–0.0098 | 4 | 2.1659–2.1663 | 0.0008–0.0021 | 0.0063–0.0117 |
| 1989-90 | 3E 88.9 (1456) | 1.9683–1.9685 | 0.0006–0.0014 | 0.0008–0.0087 | 3 | 1.8110–1.8113 | 0.0006–0.0019 | 0.0059–0.0138 |
| | 3S-FE, 3S-GE, 3S-GTE 121.9 (1998) | 2.1649–2.1655 | 0.0006–0.0013① | 0.0008–0.0087 | 3 | 1.8892–1.8898 | 0.0009–0.0022 | 0.0063–0.0123 |
| | 4A-F, 4A-FE 97.0 (1587) | 1.8891–1.8898 | 0.0006–0.0013 | 0.0008–0.0087 | 3 | 1.5742–1.5748 | 0.0008–0.0020 | 0.0059–0.0098 |
| | 4A-GEC,4A-GELC 97.0 (1587) | 1.8891–1.8898 | 0.0006–0.0013 | 0.0008–0.0087 | 3 | 1.6529–1.6535 | 0.0008–0.0020 | 0.0059–0.0098 |
| | 4A-GZE 97.0 (1587) | 1.8891–1.8898 | 0.0006–0.0013 | 0.0008–0.0087 | 3 | 1.6529–1.6535 | 0.0008–0.0020 | 0.0059–0.0098 |
| | 2VZ-FE 153.0 (2507) | 2.5191–2.5197 | 0.0011–0.0022 | 0.0008–0.0087 | 3 | 1.8892–1.8898 | 0.0011–0.0026 | 0.0059–0.0130 |
| | 7M-GE, 7M-GTE 180.3 (2954) | 2.3625–2.3627 | 0.0012–0.0019 | 0.0020–0.0098 | 4 | 2.1659–2.1663 | 0.0008–0.0021 | 0.0063–0.0117 |

① No. 3: 0.0012–0.0022 (1987)
No. 3: 0.0011–0.0019 (1988)
No. 3: 0.0010–0.0017 (1989-90)

## VALVE SPECIFICATIONS

| Year | Engine Displacement cu. in. (cc) | Seat Angle (deg.) | Face Angle (deg.) | Spring Test Pressure (lbs.) | Spring Installed Height (in.) | Stem-to-Guide Clearance (in.) Intake | Stem-to-Guide Clearance (in.) Exhaust | Stem Diameter (in.) Intake | Stem Diameter (in.) Exhaust |
|---|---|---|---|---|---|---|---|---|---|
| 1983 | 3A, 3A-C 88.6 (1452) | 45 | 44.5 | 52.0 | 1.520 | 0.0010–0.0024 | 0.0012–0.0026 | 0.2744–0.2750 | 0.2742–0.2748 |

## VALVE SPECIFICATIONS

| Year | Engine Displacement cu. in. (cc) | Seat Angle (deg.) | Face Angle (deg.) | Spring Test Pressure (lbs.) | Spring Installed Height (in.) | Stem-to-Guide Clearance (in.) | | Stem Diameter (in.) | |
|---|---|---|---|---|---|---|---|---|---|
| | | | | | | Intake | Exhaust | Intake | Exhaust |
| 1983 | 4A-C, 4A-LC 97.0 (1587) | 45 | 44.5 | 52.0 | 1.520 | 0.0010–0.0024 | 0.0012–0.0026 | 0.2744–0.2750 | 0.2742–0.2748 |
| | 4K-E 78.7 (1290) | 45 | 44.5 | 77.2 | 1.512 | 0.0012–0.0026 | 0.0014–0.0028 | 0.3136–0.3142 | 0.3134–0.3140 |
| | 2S-E 121.7 (1995) | 45.5 | 45.5 | 68.0 | 1.555 | 0.0010–0.0024 | 0.0012–0.0026 | 0.3138–0.3144 | 0.3136–0.3142 |
| | 22R, 22-RE 144.4 (2367) | 45 | 44.5 | 55.1 | 1.594 | 0.0008–0.0024 | 0.0012–0.0028 | 0.3138–0.3145 | 0.3136–0.3142 |
| | 5M-GE 168.4 (2759) | 45 | 44.5 | ① | ② | 0.0010–0.0024 | 0.0012–0.0026 | 0.3138–0.3144 | 0.3134–0.3140 |
| 1984 | 3A, 3A-C 88.6 (1452) | 45 | 44.5 | 52.0 | 1.520 | 0.0010–0.0024 | 0.0012–0.0026 | 0.2744–0.2750 | 0.2742–0.2748 |
| | 4A-C, 4A-LC 97.0 (1587) | 45 | 44.5 | 52.0 | 1.520 | 0.0010–0.0024 | 0.0012–0.0026 | 0.2744–0.2750 | 0.2742–0.2748 |
| | 4K-E 78.7 (1290) | 45 | 44.5 | 77.2 | 1.512 | 0.0012–0.0026 | 0.0014–0.0028 | 0.3136–0.3142 | 0.3134–0.3140 |
| | 2S-E 121.7 (1995) | 45.5 | 45.5 | 68.0 | 1.555 | 0.0010–0.0024 | 0.0012–0.0026 | 0.3138–0.3144 | 0.3136–0.3142 |
| | 22R, 22-RE 144.4 (2367) | 45 | 44.5 | 55.1 | 1.594 | 0.0008–0.0024 | 0.0012–0.0028 | 0.3138–0.3145 | 0.3136–0.3142 |
| | 5M-GE 168.4 (2759) | 45 | 44.5 | ① | ② | 0.0010–0.0024 | 0.0012–0.0026 | 0.3138–0.3144 | 0.3134–0.3140 |
| 1985 | 3A, 3A-C 88.6 (1452) | 45 | 44.5 | 52.0 | 1.520 | 0.0010–0.0024 | 0.0012–0.0026 | 0.2744–0.2750 | 0.2742–0.2748 |
| | 4A-C, 4A-LC 97.0 (1587) | 45 | 44.5 | 52.0 | 1.520 | 0.0010–0.0024 | 0.0012–0.0026 | 0.2744–0.2750 | 0.2742–0.2748 |
| | 4A-GE 97.0 (1587) | 45 | 44.5 | 34.8 | 1.366 | 0.0010–0.0024 | 0.0012–0.0026 | 0.2350–0.2356 | 0.2348–0.2354 |
| | 2S-E 121.7 (1995) | 45.5 | 45.5 | 71.4 | 1.555 | 0.0010–0.0024 | 0.0012–0.0026 | 0.3138–0.3144 | 0.3136–0.3142 |
| | 22R, 22-RE 144.4 (2367) | 45 | 44.5 | 55.1 | 1.594 | 0.0008–0.0024 | 0.0012–0.0028 | 0.3138–0.3145 | 0.3136–0.3142 |
| | 5M-GE 168.4 (2759) | 45 | 44.5 | ① | ② | 0.0010–0.0024 | 0.0015–0.0027 | 0.3138–0.3144 | 0.3134–0.3140 |
| 1986 | 3A, 3A-C 88.6 (1452) | 45 | 44.5 | 52.0 | 1.520 | 0.0010–0.0024 | 0.0012–0.0026 | 0.2744–0.2750 | 0.2742–0.2748 |
| | 4A-C, 4A-LC 97.0 (1587) | 45 | 44.5 | 52.0 | 1.520 | 0.0010–0.0024 | 0.0012–0.0026 | 0.2744–0.2750 | 0.2742–0.2748 |
| | 4A-GE 97.0 (1587) | 45 | 44.5 | 34.8 | 1.366 | 0.0010–0.0024 | 0.0012–0.0026 | 0.2350–0.2356 | 0.2348–0.2354 |
| | 2S-E 121.7 (1995) | 45.5 | 45.5 | 71.4 | 1.555 | 0.0010–0.0024 | 0.0012–0.0026 | 0.3138–0.3144 | 0.3136–0.3142 |
| | 3S-GE 121.9 (1998) | 45.5 | 44.5 | 38.6 | 1.366 | 0.0010–0.0023 | 0.0012–0.0025 | 0.2346–0.2352 | 0.2344–0.2350 |

## VALVE SPECIFICATIONS

| Year | Engine Displacement cu. in. (cc) | Seat Angle (deg.) | Face Angle (deg.) | Spring Test Pressure (lbs.) | Spring Installed Height (in.) | Stem-to-Guide Clearance (in.) | | Stem Diameter (in.) | |
|---|---|---|---|---|---|---|---|---|---|
| | | | | | | Intake | Exhaust | Intake | Exhaust |
| 1986 | 5M-GE 168.4 (2759) | 45 | 44.5 | ① | ② | 0.0010–0.0024 | 0.0015–0.0027 | 0.3138–0.3144 | 0.3134–0.3140 |
| | 7M-GE 180.3 (2954) | 45 | 44.5 | 35.0 | 1.378 | 0.0010–0.0024 | 0.0012–0.0026 | 0.2350–0.2356 | 0.2348–0.2354 |
| 1987 | 3A-C 88.6 (1452) | 45 | 44.5 | 52.0 | 1.520 | 0.0010–0.0024 | 0.0012–0.0026 | 0.2744–0.2750 | 0.2742–0.2748 |
| | 3E 88.9 (1456) | 45 | 44.5 | 35.1 | 1.384 | 0.0010–0.0024 | 0.0012–0.0026 | 0.2350–0.2356 | 0.2348–0.2354 |
| | 3S-FE 121.9 (1998) | 45.5 | 44.5 | 39.6 | 1.366 | 0.0010–0.0024 | 0.0012–0.0026 | 0.2350–0.2356 | 0.2348–0.2354 |
| | 3S-GE 121.9 (1998) | 45.5 | 44.5 | 38.6 | 1.366 | 0.0010–0.0023 | 0.0012–0.0025 | 0.2346–0.2352 | 0.2344–0.2350 |
| | 4A-LC 97.0 (1587) | 45 | 44.5 | 52.0 | 1.520 | 0.0010–0.0024 | 0.0012–0.0026 | 0.2744–0.2750 | 0.2742–0.2748 |
| | 4A-GEC,4A-GELC 97.0 (1587) | 45 | 44.5 | 35.9 | 1.366 | 0.0010–0.0024 | 0.0012–0.0026 | 0.2350–0.2356 | 0.2348–0.2354 |
| | 5M-GE 168.4 (2759) | 45 | 44.5 | ① | ② | 0.0010–0.0024 | 0.0012–0.0026 | 0.3138–0.3144 | 0.3136–0.3142 |
| | 7M-GE,7M-GTE 180.3 (2954) | 45 | 44.5 | 35.0 | 1.378 | 0.0010–0.0024 | 0.0012–0.0026 | 0.2350–0.2356 | 0.2348–0.2354 |
| 1988 | 3A-C 88.6 (1452) | 45 | 44.5 | 52.0 | 1.520 | 0.0010–0.0024 | 0.0012–0.0026 | 0.2744–0.2750 | 0.2742–0.2748 |
| | 3E 88.9 (1456) | 45 | 44.5 | 35.1 | 1.384 | 0.0010–0.0024 | 0.0012–0.0026 | 0.2350–0.2356 | 0.2348–0.2354 |
| | 3S-FE 121.9 (1998) | 45.5 | 44.5 | 39.6 | 1.366 | 0.0010–0.0024 | 0.0012–0.0026 | 0.2350–0.2356 | 0.2348–0.2354 |
| | 3S-GE,3S-GTE 121.9 (1998) | 45.5 | 44.5 | 38.6 ③ | 1.366 | 0.0010–0.0023 | 0.0012–0.0025 | 0.2346–0.2352 | 0.2344–0.2350 |
| | 4A-F 97.0 (1587) | 45 | 44.5 | 34.8 | 1.366 | 0.0010–0.0024 | 0.0012–0.0026 | 0.2350–0.2356 | 0.2348–0.2354 |
| | 4A-LC 97.0 (1587) | 45 | 44.5 | 52.0 | 1.520 | 0.0010–0.0024 | 0.0012–0.0026 | 0.2744–0.2750 | 0.2742–0.2748 |
| | 4A-GEC, 4A-GELC 4A-GZE 97.0 (1587) | 45 | 44.5 | 35.9 | 1.366 | 0.0010–0.0024 | 0.0012–0.0026 | 0.2350–0.2356 | 0.2348–0.2354 |
| | 5M-GE 168.4 (2759) | 45 | 44.5 | ① | ② | 0.0010–0.0024 | 0.0012–0.0026 | 0.3138–0.3144 | 0.3136–0.3142 |
| | 7M-GE,7M-GTE 180.3 (2954) | 45 | 44.5 | 35.0 | 1.378 | 0.0010–0.0024 | 0.0012–0.0026 | 0.2350–0.2356 | 0.2348–0.2354 |
| 1989-90 | 3E 88.9 (1456) | 45 | 44.5 | 35.1 | 1.384 | 0.0010–0.0024 | 0.0012–0.0026 | 0.2350–0.2356 | 0.2348–0.2354 |
| | 3S-FE 121.9 (1998) | 45.5 | 44.5 | 39.6 | 1.366 | 0.0010–0.0024 | 0.0012–0.0026 | 0.2350–0.2356 | 0.2348–0.2354 |

## VALVE SPECIFICATIONS

| Year | Engine Displacement cu. in. (cc) | Seat Angle (deg.) | Face Angle (deg.) | Spring Test Pressure (lbs.) | Spring Installed Height (in.) | Stem-to-Guide Clearance (in.) Intake | Stem-to-Guide Clearance (in.) Exhaust | Stem Diameter (in.) Intake | Stem Diameter (in.) Exhaust |
|---|---|---|---|---|---|---|---|---|---|
| 1989-90 | 3S-GE, 3S-GTE 121.9 (1998) | 45.5 | 44.5 | 38.6 ③ | 1.366 | 0.0010–0.0023 | 0.0012–0.0025 | 0.2346–0.2352 | 0.2344–0.2350 |
| | 4A-F, 4A-FE 97.0 (1587) | 45 | 44.5 | 34.8 | 1.366 | 0.0010–0.0024 | 0.0012–0.0026 | 0.2350–0.2356 | 0.2348–0.2354 |
| | 4A-GEC, 4A-GZE 97.0 (1587) | 45 | 44.5 | 34.7 | 1.366 | 0.0010–0.0024 | 0.0012–0.0026 | 0.2350–0.2356 | 0.2348–0.2354 |
| | 2VZ-FE 153.0 (2507) | 45 | 44.5 | 41.0–47.2 | 1.331 | 0.0010–0.0024 | 0.0012–0.0026 | 0.2350–0.2356 | 0.2348–0.2354 |
| | 7M-GE, 7M-GTE 180.3 (2954) | 45 | 44.5 | 35.0 | 1.378 | 0.0010–0.0024 | 0.0012–0.0026 | 0.2350–0.2356 | 0.2348–0.2354 |

① Intake: 76.5–84.4; Exhaust: 73.4–80.9
② Intake: 1.575; Exhaust: 1.693
③ 3S-GTE: 44.1

## PISTON AND RING SPECIFICATIONS

All measurments are given in inches.

| Year | Engine Displacement cu. in. (cc) | Piston Clearance | Ring Gap Top Compression | Ring Gap Bottom Compression | Ring Gap Oil Control | Ring Side Clearance Top Compression | Ring Side Clearance Bottom Compression | Ring Side Clearance Oil Control |
|---|---|---|---|---|---|---|---|---|
| 1983 | 3A, 3A-C 88.6 (1452) | 0.0039–0.0047 | 0.0079–0.0157 | 0.0059–0.0138 | 0.0039–0.0236 | 0.0016–0.0031 | 0.0012–0.0028 | Snug |
| | 4A-C, 4A-LC 97.0 (1587) | 0.0039–0.0047 | ① | ② | ③ | 0.0016–0.0031 | 0.0012–0.0028 | Snug |
| | 4K-E 78.7 (1290) | 0.0012–0.0020 | 0.0063–0.0118 | 0.0059–0.0118 | ④ | 0.0012–0.0028 | 0.0008–0.0024 | Snug |
| | 2S-E 121.7 (1995) | 0.0006–0.0014 | 0.0110–0.0197 | 0.0079–0.0177 | 0.0079–0.0311 | 0.0012–0.0028 | 0.0012–0.0028 | Snug |
| | 22R, 22R-E 144.4 (2367) | 0.0020–0.0028 | 0.0094–0.0142 | 0.0071–0.0154 | Snug | 0.0080 max. | 0.0080 max. | Snug |
| | 5M-GE 168.4 (2759) | 0.0020–0.0028 | 0.0083–0.0146 | 0.0067–0.0209 | 0.0079–0.0276 | 0.0012–0.0028 | 0.0008–0.0024 | Snug |
| 1984 | 3A, 3A-C 88.6 (1452) | 0.0039–0.0047 | 0.0079–0.0157 | 0.0059–0.0138 | 0.0039–0.0236 | 0.0016–0.0031 | 0.0012–0.0028 | Snug |
| | 4A-C, 4A-LC 97.0 (1587) | 0.0039–0.0047 | ① | ② | ③ | 0.0016–0.0031 | 0.0012–0.0028 | Snug |
| | 4K-E 78.7 (1290) | 0.0012–0.0020 | 0.0063–0.0118 | 0.0059–0.0118 | ④ | 0.0012–0.0028 | 0.0008–0.0024 | Snug |
| | 2S-E 121.7 (1995) | 0.0006–0.0014 | 0.0110–0.0197 | 0.0079–0.0177 | 0.0079–0.0311 | 0.0012–0.0028 | 0.0012–0.0028 | Snug |
| | 22R, 22R-E 144.4 (2367) | 0.0020–0.0028 | 0.0094–0.0142 | 0.0071–0.0154 | Snug | 0.0080 max. | 0.0080 max. | Snug |

## PISTON AND RING SPECIFICATIONS

All measurments are given in inches.

| Year | Engine Displacement cu. in. (cc) | Piston Clearance | Ring Gap Top Compression | Ring Gap Bottom Compression | Ring Gap Oil Control | Ring Side Clearance Top Compression | Ring Side Clearance Bottom Compression | Ring Side Clearance Oil Control |
|---|---|---|---|---|---|---|---|---|
| 1984 | 5M-GE 168.4 (2759) | 0.0020–0.0028 | 0.0083–0.0146 | 0.0067–0.0209 | 0.0079–0.0276 | 0.0012–0.0028 | 0.0008–0.0024 | Snug |
| 1985 | 3A, 3A-C 88.6 (1452) | 0.0039–0.0047 | 0.0079–0.0157 | 0.0059–0.0138 | 0.0039–0.0236 | 0.0016–0.0031 | 0.0012–0.0028 | Snug |
| | 4A-C, 4A-LC 97.0 (1587) | 0.0039–0.0047 | 0.0098–0.0185 | 0.0059–0.0165 | 0.0118–0.0401 | 0.0016–0.0031 | 0.0012–0.0028 | Snug |
| | 4A-GE 97.0 (1587) | 0.0039–0.0047 | 0.0098–0.0185 | 0.0059–0.0165 | 0.0118–0.0401 | 0.0012–0.0028 | 0.0008–0.0024 | Snug |
| | 2S-E 121.7 (1995) | 0.0006–0.0014 | 0.0110–0.0209 | 0.0083–0.0189 | 0.0079–0.0323 | 0.0012–0.0028 | 0.0008–0.0024 | Snug |
| | 22R, 22R-E 144.4 (2367) | 0.0012–0.0020 | 0.0094–0.0142 | 0.0071–0.0154 | Snug | 0.0080 max. | 0.0080 max. | Snug |
| | 5M-GE 168.4 (2759) | 0.0020–0.0028 | 0.0091–0.0161 | 0.0098–0.0217 | 0.0067–0.0335 | 0.0012–0.0028 | 0.0008–0.0024 | Snug |
| 1986 | 2S-E 121.7 (1995) | 0.0006–0.0014 | 0.0110–0.0209 | 0.0083–0.0189 | 0.0079–0.0323 | 0.0012–0.0028 | 0.0008–0.0024 | Snug |
| | 3A, 3A-C 88.6 (1452) | 0.0039–0.0047 | 0.0079–0.0185 | 0.0059–0.0204 | 0.0118–0.0402 | 0.0016–0.0031 | 0.0012–0.0028 | Snug |
| | 3S-GE 121.9 (1998) | 0.0012–0.0020 | 0.0130–0.0213 | 0.0079–0.0173 | 0.0079–0.0354 | 0.0008–0.0024 | 0.0006–0.0022 | Snug |
| | 4A-C, 4A-LC 97.0 (1587) | 0.0035–0.0043 | 0.0098–0.0185 | 0.0059–0.0165 | 0.0118–0.0401 | 0.0016–0.0031 | 0.0012–0.0028 | Snug |
| | 4A-GE 97.0 (1587) | 0.0039–0.0047 | 0.0098–0.0185 | 0.0078–0.0165 | 0.0118–0.0401 | 0.0012–0.0028 | 0.0008–0.0024 | Snug |
| | 5M-GE 168.4 (2759) | 0.0024–0.0031 | 0.0114–0.0185 | 0.0098–0.0217 | 0.0067–0.0335 | 0.0012–0.0028 | 0.0008–0.0024 | Snug |
| | 7M-GE 180.3 (2954) | 0.0024–0.0031 | 0.0091–0.0150 | 0.0098–0.0209 | 0.0039–0.0201 | 0.0012–0.0028 | 0.0008–0.0024 | Snug |
| 1987 | 3A-C 88.6 (1452) | 0.0039–0.0047 | 0.0079–0.0185 | 0.0079–0.0204 | 0.0118–0.0402 | 0.0016–0.0031 | 0.0012–0.0028 | Snug |
| | 3E 88.9 (1456) | 0.0028–0.0035 | 0.0102–0.0142 | 0.0118–0.0177 | 0.0059–0.0157 | 0.0016–0.0031 | 0.0012–0.0028 | Snug |
| | 3S-FE 121.9 (1998) | 0.0018–0.0026 | 0.0106–0.0193 | 0.0106–0.0197 | 0.0079–0.0323 | 0.0012–0.0028 | 0.0012–0.0028 | Snug |
| | 3S-GE 121.9 (1998) | 0.0012–0.0020 | 0.0130–0.0213 | 0.0079–0.0173 | 0.0079–0.0350 | 0.0012–0.0028 | 0.0008–0.0024 | Snug |
| | 4A-LC 97.0 (1587) | 0.0035–0.0043 | 0.0098–0.0138 | 0.0059–0.0165 | 0.0078–0.0276 | 0.0016–0.0031 | 0.0012–0.0028 | Snug |
| | 4A-GEC, 4A-GELC 97.0 (1587) | 0.0039–0.0047 | 0.0098–0.0138 | 0.0078–0.0118 | 0.0078–0.0276 | 0.0016–0.0031 | 0.0012–0.0028 | Snug |
| | 5M-GE 168.4 (2759) | 0.0024–0.0031 | 0.0091–0.0150 | 0.0098–0.0209 | 0.0040–0.0201 | 0.0012–0.0028 | 0.0008–0.0024 | Snug |
| | 7M-GE 180.3 (2954) | 0.0024–0.0031 | 0.0091–0.0150 | 0.0098–0.0209 | 0.0039–0.0201 | 0.0012–0.0028 | 0.0008–0.0024 | Snug |

## PISTON AND RING SPECIFICATIONS

All measurments are given in inches.

| Year | Engine Displacement cu. in. (cc) | Piston Clearance | Ring Gap Top Compression | Ring Gap Bottom Compression | Ring Gap Oil Control | Ring Side Clearance Top Compression | Ring Side Clearance Bottom Compression | Ring Side Clearance Oil Control |
|---|---|---|---|---|---|---|---|---|
| 1987 | 7M-GTE 180.3 (2954) | 0.0028–0.0035 | 0.0114–0.0173 | 0.0098–0.0209 | 0.0039–0.0220 | 0.0012–0.0028 | 0.0008–0.0024 | Snug |
| 1988 | 3A-C 88.6 (1452) | 0.0039–0.0047 | 0.0079–0.0185 | 0.0079–0.0204 | 0.0118–0.0402 | 0.0016–0.0031 | 0.0012–0.0028 | Snug |
| | 3E 88.9 (1456) | 0.0028–0.0035 | 0.0102–0.0142 | 0.0118–0.0177 | 0.0059–0.0157 | 0.0016–0.0031 | 0.0012–0.0028 | Snug |
| | 3S-FE 121.9 (1998) | 0.0018–0.0026 | 0.0106–0.0205 | 0.0106–0.0209 | 0.0079–0.0323 | 0.0018–0.0028 | 0.0018–0.0028 | Snug |
| | 3S-GE 121.9 (1998) | 0.0012–0.0020 | 0.0130–0.0264 | 0.0177–0.0323 | 0.0079–0.0283 | 0.0012–0.0028 | 0.0008–0.0024 | Snug |
| | 3S-GTE 121.9 (1998) | 0.0012–0.0020 | 0.0130–0.0224 | 0.0177–0.0272 | 0.0079–0.0244 | 0.0015–0.0031 | 0.0012–0.0028 | Snug |
| | 4A-F 97.0 (1587) | 0.0024–0.0031 | 0.0098–0.0138 | 0.0059–0.0118 | 0.0039–0.0236 | 0.0016–0.0031 | 0.0012–0.0028 | Snug |
| | 4A-LC 97.0 (1587) | 0.0035–0.0043 | 0.0098–0.0138 | 0.0059–0.0165 | 0.0078–0.0276 | 0.0016–0.0031 | 0.0012–0.0028 | Snug |
| | 4A-GEC, 4A-GELC, 4A-GZE 97.0 (1587) | 0.0039–0.0047 ⑤ | 0.0098–0.0185 | 0.0078–0.0118 | ⑥ | 0.0016–0.0031 | 0.0012–0.0028 | Snug |
| | 5M-GE 168.4 (2759) | 0.0024–0.0031 | 0.0091–0.0150 | 0.0098–0.0209 | 0.0040–0.0201 | 0.0012–0.0028 | 0.0008–0.0024 | Snug |
| | 7M-GE 180.3 (2954) | 0.0020–0.0028 | 0.0091–0.0150 | 0.0098–0.0209 | 0.0039–0.0157 | 0.0012–0.0028 | 0.0008–0.0024 | Snug |
| | 7M-GTE 180.3 (2954) | 0.0028–0.0035 | 0.0114–0.0173 | 0.0098–0.0209 | 0.0039–0.0173 | 0.0012–0.0028 | 0.0008–0.0024 | Snug |
| 1989-90 | 3E 88.9 (1456) | 0.0028–0.0035 | 0.0102–0.0142 | 0.0118–0.0177 | 0.0059–0.0157 | 0.0016–0.0031 | 0.0012–0.0028 | Snug |
| | 3S-FE 121.9 (1998) | 0.0018–0.0026 | 0.0106–0.0197 | 0.0106–0.0201 | 0.0079–0.0217 | 0.0012–0.0028 | 0.0012–0.0028 | Snug |
| | 3S-GE 121.9 (1998) | 0.0012–0.0020 | 0.0130–0.0217 | 0.0177–0.0276 | 0.0079–0.0236 | 0.0012–0.0028 | 0.0008–0.0024 | Snug |
| | 3S-GTE 121.9 (1998) | 0.0012–0.0020 | 0.0130–0.0217 | 0.0177–0.0264 | 0.0079–0.0236 | 0.0015–0.0031 | 0.0012–0.0028 | Snug |
| | 4A-F 97.0 (1587) | 0.0024–0.0031 | 0.0098–0.0138 | 0.0059–0.0118 | 0.0039–0.0236 | 0.0016–0.0031 | 0.0012–0.0028 | Snug |
| | 4A-FE 97.0 (1587) | 0.0024–0.0031 | 0.0098–0.0138 | 0.0059–0.0118 | 0.0039–0.0236 | 0.0020–0.0031 | 0.0012–0.0028 | Snug |
| | 4A-GEC, 4A-GELC, 4A-GZE 97.0 (1587) | 0.0039–0.0047 ⑤ | 0.0098–0.0185 | 0.0079–0.0165 | ⑥ | 0.0016–0.0031 | 0.0012–0.0028 | Snug |
| | 2VZ-FE 153.0 (2507) | 0.0018–0.0026 | 0.0118–0.0205 | 0.0138–0.0236 | 0.0079–0.0217 | 0.0004–0.0031 | 0.0012–0.0028 | Snug |
| | 7M-GE 180.3 (2954) | 0.0020–0.0028 ⑦ | 0.0091–0.0150 | 0.0098–0.0209 | 0.0039–0.0157 | 0.0012–0.0028 | 0.0008–0.0024 | Snug |

## PISTON AND RING SPECIFICATIONS

All measurments are given in inches.

| Year | Engine Displacement cu. in. (cc) | Piston Clearance | Ring Gap Top Compression | Ring Gap Bottom Compression | Ring Gap Oil Control | Ring Side Clearance Top Compression | Ring Side Clearance Bottom Compression | Ring Side Clearance Oil Control |
|---|---|---|---|---|---|---|---|---|
| 1989-90 | 7M-GTE 180.3 (2954) | 0.0028–0.0035 | 0.0114–0.0173 | 0.0098–0.0209 | 0.0039–0.0173 | 0.0012–0.0028 | 0.0008–0.0024 | Snug |

① 4A-C: TP – 0.0098–0.0138
Riken – 0.0079–0.0138

② 4A-C: 0.0059–0.0118

③ 4A-C: TP – 0.0079–0.0276
Riken – 0.0118–0.0354

④ 4K-E: Code T – 0.0080–0.0280
Code R – 0.0120–0.0350

⑤ 4A-GZE: 0.0047–0.0055

⑥ Code T: 0.0059–0.0205
Code R: 0.0118–0.0402

⑦ 1990 Supra: 0.0031–0.0039

## TORQUE SPECIFICATIONS

All readings in ft. lbs.

| Year | Engine Displacement cu. in. (cc) | Cylinder Head Bolts | Main Bearing Bolts | Rod Bearing Bolts | Crankshaft Pulley Bolts | Flywheel Bolts | Manifold Intake | Manifold Exhaust | Spark Plugs |
|---|---|---|---|---|---|---|---|---|---|
| 1983 | 3A, 3A-C 88.6 (1452) | 40–47 | 40–47 | 26–32 | 80–94 | 55–61 | 15–21 | 15–21 | 11–15 |
| | 22R, 22R-E 144.4 (2367) | 53–63 | 69–83 | 40–47 | 102–130 | 73–86 | 13–19 | 29–36 | 11–15 |
| | 2S-E 121.7 (1995) | 45–50 | 40–45 | 33–38 | 78–82 | 70–75 | 30–33 | 30–33 | 11–15 |
| | 4A-C, 4A-LC 97.0 (1587) | 40–47 | 40–47 | 26–32 | 80–94 | 55–61 | 15–21 | 15–21 | 11–15 |
| | 4K-E 78.7 (1290) | 40–47 | 40–47 | 29–37 | 55–75 | 40–47 | 15–21 ① | 15–21 ① | 11–15 |
| | 5M-GE 168.4 (2759) | 55–61 | 72–78 | 31–34 | 98–119 | 51–57 | 15–17 | 26–32 | 11–15 |
| 1984 | 22R, 22R-E 144.4 (2367) | 53–63 | 69–83 | 40–47 | 102–130 | 73–86 | 13–19 | 29–36 | 11–15 |
| | 2S-E 121.7 (1995) | 45–50 | 40–45 | 33–38 | 78–82 | 70–75 | 30–33 | 30–33 | 11–15 |
| | 3A, 3A-C 88.6 (1452) | 40–47 | 40–47 | 34–39 | 80–94 | 55–61 | 15–21 | 15–21 | 11–15 |
| | 4A-C, 4A-LC 97.0 (1587) | 40–47 | 40–47 | 26–32 | 80–94 | 55–61 | 15–21 | 15–21 | 11–15 |
| | 4K-E 78.7 (1290) | 40–47 | 40–47 | 29–37 | 55–75 | 40–47 | 15–21 ① | 15–21 ① | 11–15 |
| | 5M-GE 168.4 (2759) | 55–61 | 72–78 | 31–34 | 98–119 | 51–57 | 15–17 | 26–32 | 11–15 |
| 1985 | 22R, 22R-E 144.4 (2367) | 53–63 | 69–83 | 40–47 | 102–130 | 73–86 | 13–19 | 29–36 | 11–15 |

## TORQUE SPECIFICATIONS

All readings in ft. lbs.

| Year | Engine Displacement cu. in. (cc) | Cylinder Head Bolts | Main Bearing Bolts | Rod Bearing Bolts | Crankshaft Pulley Bolts | Flywheel Bolts | Manifold Intake | Manifold Exhaust | Spark Plugs |
|---|---|---|---|---|---|---|---|---|---|
| 1985 | 2S-E 121.7 (1995) | 45–50 | 40–45 | 33–38 | 78–82 | 70–75 | 30–33 | 30–33 | 11–15 |
| | 3A, 3A-C 88.6 (1452) | 40–47 | 40–47 | 34–39 | 80–94 | 55–61 | 15–21 | 15–21 | 11–15 |
| | 4A-C, 4A-LC 97.0 (1587) | 40–47 | 40–47 | 26–32 | 80–94 | 55–61 | 15–21 | 15–21 | 11–15 |
| | 4A-GE 97.0 (1587) | 40–47 | 40–47 | 26–32 | 80–94 | 55–61 | 15–21 | 15–21 | 11–15 |
| | 5M-GE 168.4 (2759) | 55–61 | 72–78 | 31–34 | 155–163 | 51–57 | 15–17 | 26–32 | 11–15 |
| 1986 | 2S-E 121.7 (1995) | 45–50 | 40–45 | 33–38 | 78–82 | 70–75 | 30–33 | 30–33 | 11–15 |
| | 3A, 3A-C 88.6 (1452) | 40–47 | 40–47 | 34–39 | 80–94 | 55–61 | 15–21 | 15–21 | 11–15 |
| | 3S-GE 121.9 (1998) | 38–42 | 40–45 | 40–45 | 78–82 | ③ | 12–16 | 30–34 | 11–15 |
| | 4A-C, 4A-LC 97.0 (1587) | 40–47 | 40–47 | 26–32 | 80–94 | 55–61 | 15–21 | 15–21 | 11–15 |
| | 4A-GE 97.0 (1587) | 40–47 | 40–47 | 26–32 | 80–94 | 55–61 | 15–21 | 15–21 | 11–15 |
| | 5M-GE 168.4 (2759) | 55–61 | 72–78 | 31–34 | 155–163 | 51–57 | 15–17 | 26–32 | 11–15 |
| | 7M-GE 180.2 (2954) | 55–61 | 72–78 | 45–49 | 185–205 | 51–57 | 11–15 | 26–32 | 11–15 |
| 1987 | 3A-C 88.6 (1452) | 40–47 | 40–47 | 34–39 | 80–94 | 55–61 | 15–21 | 15–21 | 16–20 |
| | 3E 88.9 (1456) | ④ | 40–47 | 27–31 | 105–117 | 60–70 | 11–17 | 33–42 | 11–15 |
| | 3S-FE 121.9 (1998) | 45–50 | 40–45 | 33–38 | 78–82 | 70–75 | 11–17 | 27–33 | 11–15 |
| | 3S-GE 121.9 (1998) | 38–42 | 40–45 | 44–50 | 78–82 | ③ | 12–16 | 30–34 | 11–15 |
| | 4A-LC 97.0 (1587) | 40–47 | 40–47 | 32–40 | 80–94 | 55–61 | 15–21 | 15–21 | 16–20 |
| | 4A-GEC, 4A-GELC 97.0 (1587) | 40–47 | 40–47 | 32–40 | 100–110 | 50–58 | 15–21 | 15–21 | 11–15 |
| | 5M-GE 168.4 (2759) | 55–61 | 72–78 | 31–34 | 185–205 | 51–57 | 11–15 | 26–32 | 11–15 |
| | 7M-GE, 7M-GTE 180.2 (2954) | 55–61 | 72–78 | 45–49 | 185–205 | 51–57 | 11–15 | 26–32 | 11–15 |
| 1988 | 3A-C 88.6 (1452) | 40–47 | 40–47 | 34–39 | 80–94 | 55–61 | 15–21 | 15–21 | 16–20 |
| | 3E 88.9 (1456) | ④ | 40–47 | 27–31 | 105–117 | 60–70 | 11–17 | 33–42 | 11–15 |

## TORQUE SPECIFICATIONS

All readings in ft. lbs.

| Year | Engine Displacement cu. in. (cc) | Cylinder Head Bolts | Main Bearing Bolts | Rod Bearing Bolts | Crankshaft Pulley Bolts | Flywheel Bolts | Manifold Intake | Manifold Exhaust | Spark Plugs |
|---|---|---|---|---|---|---|---|---|---|
| 1988 | 3S-FE 121.9 (1998) | 45–50 | 40–45 | 33–38 | 78–82 | 70–75 | 11–17 | 27–33 | 11–15 |
| | 3S-GE, 3S-GTE 121.9 (1998) | 38–42 | 40–45 | 44–50 | 78–82 | ③ | 12–16 | 30–34 ⑤ | 11–15 |
| | 4A-F 97.0 (1587) | 40–47 | 40–47 | 32–40 | 80–94 | 55–61 | 11–17 | 15–21 | 11–15 |
| | 4A-LC 97.0 (1587) | 40–47 | 40–47 | 32–40 | 80–94 | 55–61 | 15–21 | 15–21 | 16–20 |
| | 4A-GEC, 4A-GELC, 4A-GZE 97.0 (1587) | ④ | 40–47 | 32–40 | 100–110 | 50–58 | 15–21 | 27–31 | 11–15 |
| | 5M-GE 168.4 (2759) | 55–61 | 72–78 | 31–34 | 185–205 | 51–57 | 11–15 | 26–32 | 11–15 |
| | 7M-GE, 7M-GTE 180.2 (2954) | 55–61 | 72–78 | 45–49 | 185–205 | 51–57 | 11–15 | 26–32 | 11–15 |
| 1989-90 | 3E 88.9 (1456) | ④ | 40–47 | 27–31 | 105–117 | 60–70 | 11–17 | 33–42 | 11–15 |
| | 3S-FE 121.9 (1998) | 45–50 | 40–45 | 33–38 | 78–82 | 70–75 | 11–17 | 27–33 | 11–15 |
| | 3S-GE, 3S-GTE 121.9 (1998) | 38–42 | 40–45 | 44–50 | 78–82 | ③ | 12–16 | 30–34 | 11–15 |
| | 4A-F, 4A-FE 97.0 (1587) | 40–47 | 40–47 | 32–40 | 80–94 | 55–61 | 11–17 | 15–21 | 11–15 |
| | 4A-GEC, 4A-GELC 4A-GZE 97.0 (1587) | ④ | 40–47 | ⑥ | 95–105 | 50–58 | 18–22 | 27–31 | 11–15 |
| | 2VZ-FE 153.0 (2507) | ④ | 43–47 | 16–20 | 176–186 | 58–64 | 11–15 | 26–32 | 11–15 |
| | 7M-GE, 7M-GTE 180.2 (2954) | 55–61 | 72–78 | 45–49 | 185–205 | 51–57 | 11–15 | 26–32 | 11–15 |

① Intake and exhaust manifolds combined
② 12mm bolt: 12–16; 14mm bolt: 63–68
③ New: 65; Used: 63
④ See text
⑤ 3S-GTE: 38
⑥ 29 ft. lbs. and an additional 90° turn

## BRAKE SPECIFICATIONS

All measurements in inches unless noted

| Year | Model | Lug Nut Torque (ft. lbs.) | Master Cylinder Bore | Brake Disc Minimum Thickness | Brake Disc Maximum Runout | Standard Brake Drum Diameter | Minimum Lining Thickness Front | Minimum Lining Thickness Rear |
|---|---|---|---|---|---|---|---|---|
| 1983 | Tercel | 65–86 | ① | 0.394 | 0.006 | 7.126② | 0.040 | 0.040 |
| | Corolla | 65–86 | ① | 0.453 | 0.006 | 9.079 | 0.040 | 0.040 |

## BRAKE SPECIFICATIONS

All measurements in inches unless noted

| Year | Model | Lug Nut Torque (ft. lbs.) | Master Cylinder Bore | Brake Disc Minimum Thickness | Brake Disc Maximum Runout | Standard Brake Drum Diameter | Minimum Lining Thickness Front | Minimum Lining Thickness Rear |
|---|---|---|---|---|---|---|---|---|
| 1983 | Starlet | 65–86 | 0.813 | 0.350 | 0.006 | 7.950 | 0.040 | 0.040 |
| | Camry | 65–86 | ① | 0.827 | 0.006 | 7.913 | 0.040 | 0.040 |
| | Celica | 65–86 | ① | 0.750 | 0.006 | 9.079 | 0.118 | 0.040 |
| | Supra | 65–86 | ① | 0.750④ | 0.006 | – | 0.118 | 0.040 |
| | Cressida | 65–86 | ① | 0.669 | 0.006 | 9.079 | 0.040 | 0.040 |
| 1984 | Tercel | 65–86 | ① | 0.394 | 0.006 | 7.126② | 0.040 | 0.040 |
| | Corolla | 65–86 | ① | 0.453 | 0.006 | 9.079⑤ | 0.040 | 0.040 |
| | Starlet | 65–86 | 0.813 | 0.350 | 0.006 | 7.950 | 0.040 | 0.040 |
| | Camry | 65–86 | ① | 0.827 | 0.006 | 7.913 | 0.040 | 0.040 |
| | Celica | 65–86 | ① | 0.750 | 0.006 | 9.079 | 0.118 | 0.040 |
| | Supra | 65–86 | ① | 0.750④ | 0.006 | – | 0.118 | 0.040 |
| | Cressida | 65–86 | ① | 0.669 | 0.006 | 9.079 | 0.040 | 0.040 |
| 1985 | Tercel | 65–86 | ① | 0.394 | 0.006 | 7.126② | 0.040 | 0.040 |
| | Corolla | 65–86 | ① | ⑥ | 0.006 | 9.079⑤ | 0.040 | 0.040 |
| | Camry | 65–86 | ① | 0.827 | 0.006 | 7.913 | 0.040 | 0.040 |
| | Celica | 65–86 | ① | 0.750 | 0.006 | 9.079 | 0.118 | 0.040 |
| | Supra | 65–86 | ① | 0.750④ | 0.006 | – | 0.118 | 0.040 |
| | MR2 | 65–86 | ① | 0.669③ | 0.006 | – | 0.040 | 0.040 |
| | Cressida | 65–86 | ① | 0.827⑦ | 0.006 | 9.079 | 0.040 | 0.040 |
| 1986 | Tercel | 65–86 | ① | 0.394 | 0.006 | 7.126② | 0.040 | 0.040 |
| | Corolla | 65–86 | ① | ⑥ | 0.006 | 9.079⑤ | 0.040 | 0.040 |
| | Camry | 65–86 | ① | 0.827 | 0.006 | 7.913 | 0.040 | 0.040 |
| | Celica | 65–86 | ① | 0.827⑧ | 0.006 | 7.913 | 0.040 | 0.040 |
| | Supra | 65–86 | ① | 0.750④ | 0.006 | – | 0.118 | 0.040 |
| | MR2 | 65–86 | ① | 0.669③ | 0.006 | – | 0.040 | 0.040 |
| | Cressida | 65–86 | ① | 0.827⑦ | 0.006 | 9.079 | 0.040 | 0.040 |
| 1987 | Tercel | 65–86 | ① | 0.394 | 0.006 | 7.126② | 0.040 | 0.040 |
| | Corolla | 65–86 | ① | ⑥ | 0.006 | 9.079⑤ | 0.040 | 0.040 |
| | Camry | 65–86 | ① | 0.827 | 0.006 | 9.079 | 0.040 | 0.040 |
| | Celica | 65–86 | ① | 0.827⑧ | 0.006 | 7.913 | 0.040 | 0.040 |
| | Supra | 65–86 | ① | 0.827④ | 0.006 | – | 0.040 | 0.040 |
| | MR2 | 65–86 | ① | 0.827③ | 0.006 | – | 0.040 | 0.040 |
| | Cressida | 65–86 | ① | 0.827⑦ | 0.006 | 9.079 | 0.040 | 0.040 |
| 1988 | Tercel | 65–86 | ① | 0.394 | 0.006 | 7.126② | 0.040 | 0.040 |
| | Corolla | 65–86 | ① | ⑥ | 0.006 | 7.874 | 0.040 | 0.040 |
| | Camry | 65–86 | ① | 0.945⑨ | 0.003 | 9.079 | 0.040 | 0.040 |
| | Celica | 65–86 | ① | 0.827⑧ | 0.006 | 7.913 | 0.040 | 0.040 |
| | Supra | 65–86 | ① | 0.827④ | 0.005 | – | 0.040 | 0.040 |
| | MR2 | 65–86 | ① | 0.827③ | 0.006 | – | 0.040 | 0.040 |
| | Cressida | 65–86 | ① | 0.827④ | 0.006 | – | 0.040 | 0.040 |

## BRAKE SPECIFICATIONS

All measurements in inches unless noted

| Year | Model | Lug Nut Torque (ft. lbs.) | Master Cylinder Bore | Brake Disc Minimum Thickness | Brake Disc Maximum Runout | Standard Brake Drum Diameter | Minimum Lining Thickness Front | Minimum Lining Thickness Rear |
|---|---|---|---|---|---|---|---|---|
| 1989-90 | Tercel | 65–86 | ① | 0.394 | 0.006 | 7.087② | 0.040 | 0.040 |
| | Corolla | 65–86 | ① | ⑥ | 0.004 | 7.874 | 0.040 | 0.040 |
| | Camry | 65–86 | ① | 0.945⑨ | 0.003⑩ | 7.874 | 0.040 | 0.040 |
| | Celica | 65–86 | ① | 0.827⑧ | 0.003 | 7.874 | 0.040 | 0.040 |
| | Supra | 65–86 | ① | 0.827④ | 0.005 | – | 0.040 | 0.040 |
| | MR2 | 65–86 | ① | 0.827③ | 0.006 | – | 0.040 | 0.040 |
| | Cressida | 65–86 | ① | 0.827④ | 0.003⑩ | – | 0.040 | 0.040 |

① Not specified by the manufacturer
② Wagon & 4wd: 7.913
③ Rear disc: 0.354
④ Rear disc: 0.669
⑤ FWD: 7.874
⑥ 1984-87 FWD (exc. FX16): 0.492
1988-90 FWD & FX16: 0.669
1982-87 RWD: 0.669
1982-87 Rear disc: 0.315
1988-90 Rear disc: 0.354
⑦ Rear disc: 1985-87 – 0.354
⑧ ABS or 4wd: 0.945
Rear disc: 0.354
⑨ 4wd rear disc: 0.354
⑩ Rear disc: 0.006

## WHEEL ALIGNMENT

| Year | Model | Caster Range (deg.) | Caster Preferred Setting (deg.) | Camber Range (deg.) | Camber Preferred Setting (deg.) | Toe-in (in.) | Steering Axis Inclination (deg.) |
|---|---|---|---|---|---|---|---|
| 1983 | Tercel (2wd) | ③ | ④ | $\frac{1}{6}$N–$\frac{5}{6}$P | $\frac{1}{3}$P | 0.06 out–0.04 in | 12$\frac{1}{2}$ |
| | (4wd) | 1$\frac{5}{6}$P–2$\frac{5}{6}$P | 2$\frac{1}{2}$P | $\frac{1}{3}$P–1$\frac{1}{3}$P | $\frac{5}{6}$P | 0 | 11$\frac{2}{3}$ |
| | Corolla (Sedan) | $\frac{3}{4}$P–2$\frac{1}{4}$P | 1$\frac{3}{4}$P | $\frac{1}{2}$P–1$\frac{1}{2}$P | 1P | 0.04–0.16 | 8$\frac{1}{2}$P |
| | (Wagon) | 1$\frac{1}{16}$P–2$\frac{1}{4}$P | 1$\frac{17}{32}$P | $\frac{1}{2}$P–1$\frac{1}{2}$P | 1P | 0.04–0.16 | 8$\frac{1}{3}$ |
| | Starlet | 1$\frac{1}{3}$P–2$\frac{1}{3}$P | 1$\frac{5}{6}$P | $\frac{1}{6}$P–1$\frac{1}{6}$P | $\frac{2}{3}$P | 0.04–0.12 | 9$\frac{3}{4}$ |
| | Camry | ⑤ | ⑥ | 0–1P | $\frac{1}{2}$P | ⑦ | 12$\frac{1}{2}$ |
| | Celica | 2$\frac{5}{6}$P–3$\frac{5}{6}$P | 3$\frac{1}{3}$P | $\frac{1}{2}$P–1$\frac{1}{2}$P | 1P | ② | 9$\frac{1}{3}$ |
| | Supra | 3$\frac{2}{3}$P–4$\frac{2}{3}$P | 4$\frac{1}{6}$P | $\frac{1}{3}$P–1$\frac{1}{3}$P | $\frac{5}{6}$P | 0.08–0.16 in | 10$\frac{1}{2}$ |
| | Cressida | 1P–2P | 1$\frac{1}{2}$P | $\frac{1}{3}$P–1$\frac{1}{3}$P | $\frac{5}{6}$P | 0.08–0.16 out | 9 |
| 1984 | Tercel (Sedan) | ③ | ④ | $\frac{1}{6}$N–$\frac{5}{6}$P | $\frac{1}{3}$P | 0.06 out–0.04 in | 12$\frac{1}{2}$ |
| | (Wagon) | ⑧ | ⑨ | $\frac{1}{4}$N–$\frac{3}{4}$P | $\frac{1}{4}$P | 0.04 out–0.04 in | 13 |
| | (4wd) | 2P–3P | 2$\frac{1}{2}$P | $\frac{1}{3}$P–2$\frac{1}{3}$P | 1$\frac{1}{3}$P | 0.04 out–0.04 in | 11$\frac{2}{3}$ |
| | Corolla (exc. SR5) | $\frac{1}{3}$P–1$\frac{1}{3}$P | $\frac{5}{6}$P | 1N–0 | $\frac{1}{2}$N | 0–0.04 | – |
| | (SR5) | ⑩ | ⑪ | $\frac{1}{4}$N–$\frac{3}{4}$P | $\frac{1}{4}$P | 0–0.08 | – |
| | Starlet | 1$\frac{1}{3}$P–2$\frac{1}{3}$P | 1$\frac{5}{6}$P | $\frac{1}{6}$P–1$\frac{1}{6}$P | $\frac{2}{3}$P | 0.04–0.12 | 9$\frac{3}{4}$ |
| | Camry | ⑤ | ⑥ | 0–1P | $\frac{1}{2}$P | ⑦ | 12$\frac{1}{2}$ |
| | Celica | 2$\frac{5}{6}$P–3$\frac{5}{6}$P | 3$\frac{1}{3}$P | $\frac{1}{2}$P–1$\frac{1}{2}$P | 1P | ② | 9$\frac{1}{3}$ |

## WHEEL ALIGNMENT

| Year | Model | Caster Range (deg.) | Caster Preferred Setting (deg.) | Camber Range (deg.) | Camber Preferred Setting (deg.) | Toe-in (in.) | Steering Axis Inclination (deg.) |
|---|---|---|---|---|---|---|---|
| 1984 | Supra | 3 2/3P–4 2/3P | 4 1/6P | 1/3P–1 1/3P | 5/6P | 0.08–0.16 in | 10 1/2 |
| | Cressida (Sedan) | 2P–3P | 2 1/2P | 1/4P–1 1/4P | 3/4P | 0.08–0.16 | 9 |
| | (Wagon) | 1 2/3P–2 2/3P | 2 1/6P | 2/3P–1 1/3P | 5/6P | 0.08–0.16 | 9 |
| 1985 | Tercel (Sedan) | ③ | ④ | 1/6N–5/6P | 1/3P | 0.06 out–0.04 in | 12 1/2 |
| | (Wagon) | ⑧ | ⑨ | 1/4N–3/4P | 1/4P | 0.04 out–0.04 in | 13 |
| | (4wd) | 2P–3P | 2 1/2P | 1/3P–2 1/3P | 1 1/3P | 0.04 out–0.04 in | 11 2/3 |
| | Corolla (exc. SR5) | 1/3P–1 1/3P | 5/6P | 1N–0 | 1/2N | 0–0.04 | – |
| | (SR5) | ⑩ | ⑪ | 1/4N–3/4P | 1/4P | 0–0.08 | – |
| | Camry | ⑤ | ⑥ | 0–1P | 1/2P | ⑦ | 12 1/2 |
| | Celica | 2 5/6P–3 5/6P | 3 1/3P | 1/2P–1 1/2P | 1P | ② | 9 1/3 |
| | Supra | 3 2/3P–4 2/3P | 4 1/6P | 1/3P–1 1/3P | 5/6P | 0.08–0.16 in | 10 1/2 |
| | MR2 | 4 3/4P–5 3/4P | 5 1/4P | 1/4N–3/4P | 1/4P | 0–0.08 | 12P |
| | Cressida (Sedan) | 2P–3P | 2 1/2P | 1/4P–1 1/4P | 3/4P | 0.08–0.16 | 9 |
| | (Wagon) | 1 2/3P–2 2/3P | 2 1/6P | 2/3P–1 1/3P | 5/6P | 0.08–0.16 | 9 |
| 1986 | Tercel (Sedan) | ③ | ④ | 1/6N–5/6P | 1/3P | 0.06 out–0.04 in | 12 1/2 |
| | (Wagon) | ⑧ | ⑨ | 1/4N–3/4P | 1/4P | 0.04 out–0.04 in | 13 |
| | (4wd) | 1 15/16P–2 15/16P | 2 7/16P | 1/16P–1 1/16P | 9/16P | 0.08 out–0 | 11 13/16 |
| | Corolla (RWD) | ⑫ | ⑬ | 1/2N–1P | 1/4P | 0.04 out–0.12 in | 9 |
| | (FWD) | 3/16P–1 11/16P | 15/16P | 1N–1/2P | 1/4N | 0.04 out–0.12 in | 12 1/2 |
| | Camry | 7/16P–1 3/4P | 1P | 3/16N–1 1/4P | 9/16P | 0–0.16 | 12 1/2 |
| | Celica | 7/16P–1 15/16P | 1 3/16P | 15/16N–9/16P | 3/16N | 0.08 out–0.08 in | 13 1/2 |
| | Supra | 3 7/16P–4 15/16P | 4 3/16P | 1/16P–1 9/16P | 13/16P | 0.04–0.20 | 10 1/4 |
| | MR2 | 4 3/4P–5 3/4P | 5 1/4P | 1/4N–3/4P | 1/4P | 0–0.08 | 12 |
| | Cressida (Sedan) | 4 1/16P–5 9/16P | 4 13/16P | 5/16N–1 3/16P | 7/16P | 0–0.16 | 10 1/2 |
| | (Wagon) | 3 1/2P–5P | 4 1/4P | 5/16N–1 3/16P | 7/16P | 0–0.16 | 10 1/2 |
| 1987 | Tercel (Sedan) | ⑭ | ⑮ | 3/4N–3/4P | 0 | 0.08 out–0.08 in | 12 1/2 |
| | (Wagon) | ⑧ | ⑨ | 3/4N–3/4P | 0P | 0.12 out–0.04 in | 12 1/2 |
| | (4wd) | 1 11/16P–3 3/16P | 2 1/4P | 3/16N–1 5/16P | 9/16P | 0.12 out–0.04 in | 12 |
| | Corolla (RWD) | ⑫ | ⑬ | 1/2N–1P | 1/4P | 0.04 out–0.12 in | 9 |
| | (FWD) | 1/8P–1 5/8P | 7/8P | 1N–1/2P | 1/4N | 0.04 out–0.12 in | 12 1/2 |
| | Camry (Sedan) | 15/16P–2 7/16P | 1 11/16P | 3/16N–1 5/16P | 9/16P | 0.04 out–0.12 in | 12 3/4 |
| | (Wagon) | 1/4P–1 3/4P | 1P | 1/4N–1 1/4P | 1/2P | 0.04 out–0.12 in | 13 |

## WHEEL ALIGNMENT

| Year | Model | Caster Range (deg.) | Caster Preferred Setting (deg.) | Camber Range (deg.) | Camber Preferred Setting (deg.) | Toe-in (in.) | Steering Axis Inclination (deg.) |
|---|---|---|---|---|---|---|---|
| 1987 | Celica | 7/16P–1 15/16P | 1 3/16P | 15/16N–9/16P | 3/16N | 0.08 out–0.08 in | 13 1/2 |
| | Supra | 6 3/4P–8 1/4P | 7 1/2P | 13/16N–11/16P | 1/16N | 0.08 out–0.08 in | 11 |
| | MR2 | 4 5/16P–5 13/16P | 5 1/16P | 1/2N–1P | 1/4P | 0–0.08 | 12 |
| | Cressida (Sedan) | 4 1/16P–5 9/16P | 4 13/16P | 5/16N–1 3/16P | 7/16P | 0–0.16 | 10 1/2 |
| | (Wagon) | 3 1/2P–5P | 4 1/4P | 5/16N–1 3/16P | 7/16P | 0–0.16 | 10 1/2 |
| 1988 | Tercel (Sedan) | ⑭ | ⑮ | 3/4N–3/4P | 0 | 0.08 out–0.08 in | 11 1/2 |
| | (Wagon) | 1 11/16P–3 3/16P | 2 1/4P | 3/16N–1 5/16P | 9/16P | 0.12 out–0.04 in | 12 |
| | Corolla (FX/FX16) | 1/8P–1 5/8P | 7/8P | 1N–1/2P | 1/4N | 0.04 out–0.12 in | 12 1/2 |
| | (4A-F) | ⑯ | ⑰ | 15/16N–9/16P | 3/16N | 0–0.08 | 12 11/16 |
| | (4A-GE) | 9/16P–2 1/16P | 1 5/16P | 1N–1/2P | 1/4N | 0–0.08 | 12 13/16 |
| | Camry (Sedan) | 15/16P–2 7/16P | 1 11/16P | 3/16N–1 5/16P | 9/16P | 0.04 out–0.12 in | 12 3/4 |
| | (Wagon) | 1/4P–1 3/4P | 1P | 1/4N–1 1/4P | 1/2P | 0.04 out–0.12 in | 13 |
| | Celica | 7/16P–1 15/16P | 1 3/16P | 15/16N–9/16P | 3/16N | 0.08 out–0.08 in | 13 1/2 |
| | Supra | 6 3/4P–8 1/4P | 7 1/2P | 13/16N–11/16P | 1/16N | 0.08 out–0.08 in | 11 |
| | MR2 | 4 5/16P–5 13/16P | 5 1/16P | 1/2N–1P | 1/4P | 0–0.08 | 12 |
| | Cressida | 4 1/16P–5 9/16P | 4 13/16P | 5/16N–1 3/16P | 7/16P | 0–0.16 | 10 1/2 |
| 1989-90 | Tercel | ⑭ | ⑮ | 3/4N–3/4P | 0 | 0.08 out–0.08 in | 11 1/2 |
| | Corolla | 1/8P–1 5/8P | 7/8P | 1N–1/2P | 1/4N | 0.04 out–0.12 in | 12 1/2 |
| | (4A-F,4A-FE) | ⑯ | ⑰ | 15/16N–9/16P | 3/16N | 0–0.08 | 12 11/16 |
| | (4A-GE) | 9/16P–2 1/16P | 1 5/16P | 1N–1/2P | 1/4N | 0–0.08 | 12 13/16 |
| | Camry (Sedan) | 15/16P–2 7/16P | 1 11/16P | 3/16N–1 5/16P | 9/16P | 0.04 out–0.12 in | 12 3/4 |
| | (Wagon) | 1/4P–1 3/4P | 1P | 1/4N–1 1/4P | 1/2P | 0.04 out–0.12 in | 13 |
| | Celica | 7/16P–1 15/16P | 1 3/16P | 15/16N–9/16P | 3/16N | 0.08 out–0.08 in | 13 1/2 |
| | Supra | 6 3/4P–8 1/4P | 7 1/2P | 13/16N–11/16P | 1/16N | 0.08 out–0.08 in | 11 |
| | MR2 | 4 5/16P–5 13/16P | 5 1/16P | 1/2N–1P | 1/4P | 0–0.08 | 12 1/16 |
| | Cressida | 4 1/16P–5 9/16P | 4 13/16P | 5/16N–1 3/16P | 7/16P | 0–0.16 | 10 1/2 |

① Man. Str.: 0–0.08
Pwr. Str.: 0.12–0.20

② Man. Str.: 0.12–0.20
Pwr. Str.: 0.16–0.24

③ Man. Str.: 2/3P–1 2/3P
Pwr. Str.: 2 1/6P–3 1/6P

④ Man. Str.: 1 1/6P
Pwr. Str.: 2 2/3P

⑤ Man. Str.: 1/2P–1 1/2P
Pwr. Str.: 2P–3P

⑥ Man. Str.: 1P
Pwr. Str.: 2 1/2P

⑦ Man. Str.: 0
Pwr. Str.: 0.08

⑧ Man. Str.: 1/6N–1 1/3P
Pwr. Str.: 1 1/4P–3P

⑨ Man. Str.: 2/3P
Pwr. Str.: 2 1/4P

⑩ Man. Str.: 2 1/4P–3 1/4P
Pwr. Str.: 3 1/6P–4 1/6P

⑪ Man. Str.: 2 3/4P
Pwr. Str.: 3 2/3P

⑫ Man. Str.: 2P–3 1/2P
Pwr. Str.: 3P–3 1/2P

⑬ Man. Str.: 2 3/4P
Pwr. Str.: 3 3/4P

⑭ Man. Str.: 1/4P–1 3/4P
Pwr. Str.: 1 3/4P–3 1/4P

⑮ Man. Str.: 1P
Pwr. Str.: 2 1/2P

⑯ Exc. Coupe: 9/16P–2 1/16P
Coupe: 3/4P–2 1/4P

⑰ Exc. Coupe: 1 5/16P
Coupe: 1 1/2P

# TUNE-UP PROCEDURES

## Ignition Timing

### ADJUSTMENT

***4K-E Engines***
***1983-85 2S-E Engines***
***3A, 3A-C, 4A-C & 4A-F Engines***
***22R and 1983-84 22R-E Engines***

1. Warm up the engine and set the parking brake. Connect a tachometer and check the engine speed to see that it is within specifications. Adjust as required.
2. On vehicles with electronic ignition, hook the dwell meter or tachometer to the negative (-) side of the coil, not to the distributor primary lead, damage to the ignition control until will result.
3. A-series engines and all other 1984-90 engines require a special type of tachometer which hooks up to the service connector wire coming out of the distributor. As many tachometers are not compatible with this hookup, we recommend that you consult with the manufacturer before purchasing a certain type.
4. Connect a timing light to the engine, as outlined in the instructions supplied by the manufacturer of the light.
5. Disconnect the vacuum line from the distributor vacuum unit and plug the line. If a vacuum advance/retard distributor is used, disconnect and plug both vacuum lines from the distributor.
6. Allow the engine to run at the specified idle speed with the gear shift in **N** for vehicles with manual transmissions, and in **D** for vehicles with automatic transmissions. Be sure that the parking brake is firmly set and that the wheels are chocked.
7. Point the timing light at the timing marks. With the engine at idle, timing should be at the specification. If it is not, loosen the pinch bolt at the base and rotate the distributor to advance or retard the timing, as required.
8. Stop the engine and tighten the pinch bolt. Start the engine and recheck the timing. Stop the engine and disconnect the timing light and the tachometer. Connect the vacuum line(s) to the vacuum and advance unit.

***2VZ-FE Engines***
***1986 2S-E Engines***
***1985 22R-E Engines***
***3S-FE, 3S-GE and 3S-GTE Engines***
***4A-FE, 4A-GE, 4A-GEC, 4A-GELC and 4A-GZE Engines***
***5M-GE, 7M-GE and 7M-GTE Engines***

1. Connect a timing light to the engine following the manufacturer's instructions.
2. These engines require a special type of tachometer which hooks up to the service connector wire coming out of the distributor. As many tachometers are not compatible with this hookup, we recommend that you consult with the manufacturer before purchasing a certain type.
3. Start the engine and run it at idle. Remove the rubber cap from the check connector (or open the lid) and short the connector at terminals **T** and **$E_1$** (1988 Calif. vehicles and all 1989-90 models with the 3S-FE, 2VZ-FE and 7M-GE: **$TE_1$** and **$E_1$**).
4. Loosen the distributor pinch bolt just enough so that the distributor can be turned. Aim the timing light at the marks on the crankshaft pulley and slowly turn the distributor until the timing mark is aligned. Tighten the distributor pinch bolt. Unshort the connector.

**NOTE: The 7M-GTE utilizes a cam position sensor in place of a distributor. Turn this as you would a distributor.**

***3E Engines***

1. Remove the cap. Using the proper tachometer, connect the test probe of the tachometer to the service probe connector at the integrated ignition assembly (IIA).
2. Disconnect the vacuum hose from the IIA sub diaphragm and plug it.
3. With the engine idling and the electric fan off, check the timing.
4. Loosen the holddown bolt. Adjust the timing as required.
5. Retighten the holddown bolt. Recheck the ignition timing.

## CHECK CONNECTOR LOCATIONS

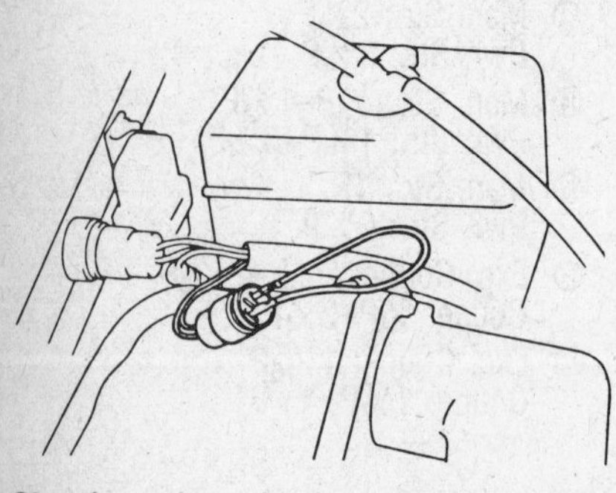

Shorting the check connector—1985 22R-E

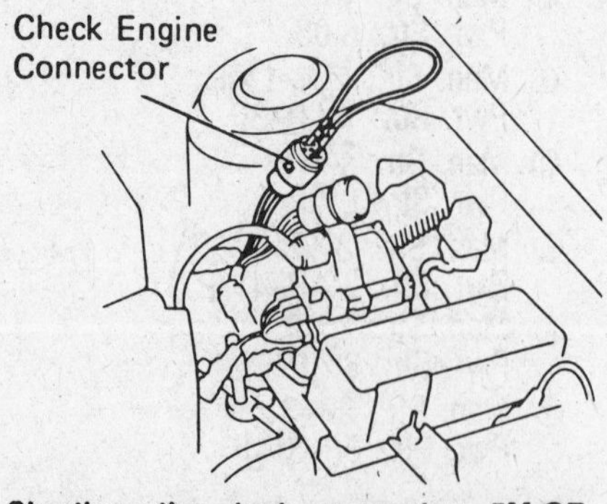


Shorting the test connector–5M-GE (Supra) engines

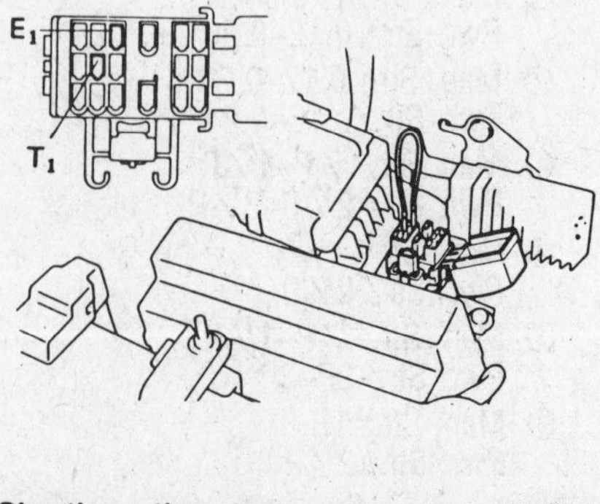


Shorting the test connector–5M-GE (Cressida) engines

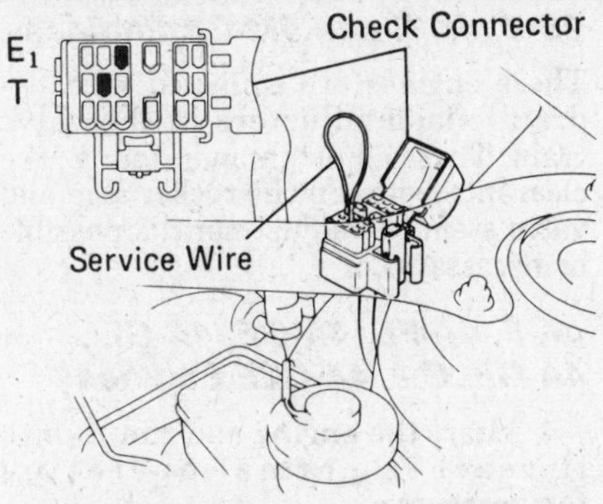


**Shorting the test connector – 1986 2S-E, 3S-FE, 3S-GE, 3S-GTE and 2VZ-FE engines**

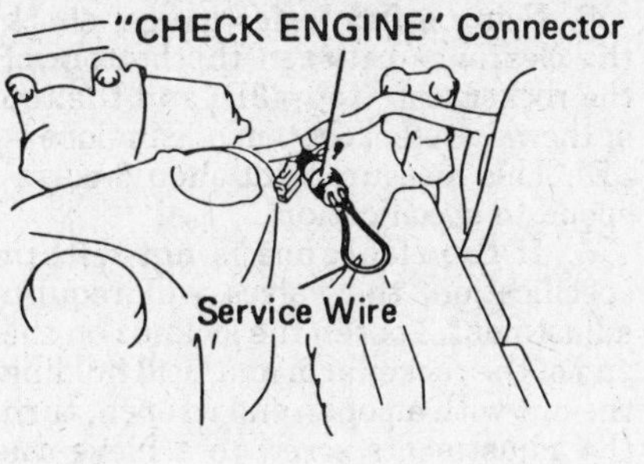


**Shorting the test connector – 1983-8 4A-GE (Corolla) engines**

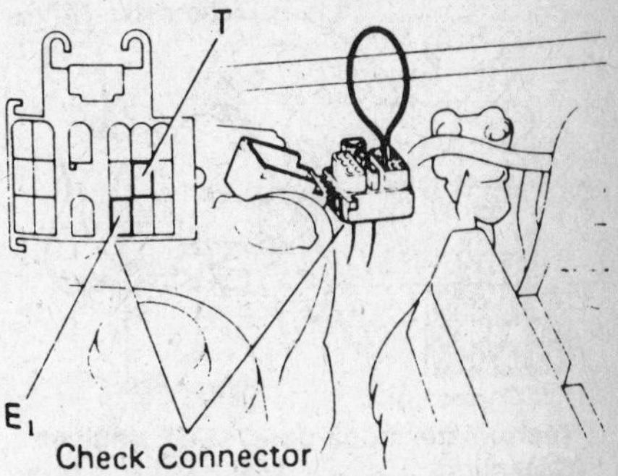


**Shorting the test connector – 4A-GEC, 4A-GELC and 4A-GZE engines**

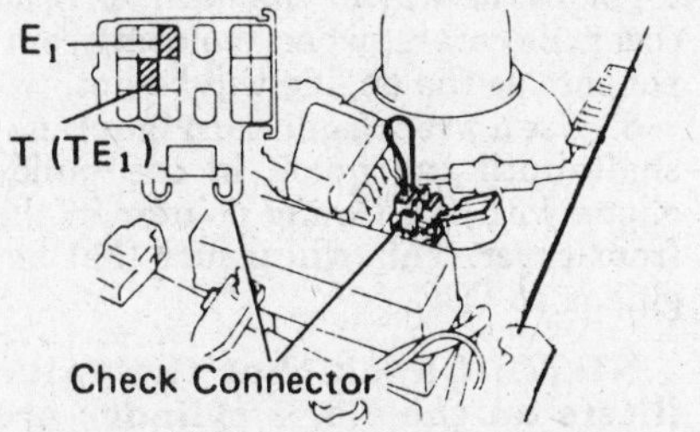


**Shorting the test connector – 7M-GE (Supra) engines**

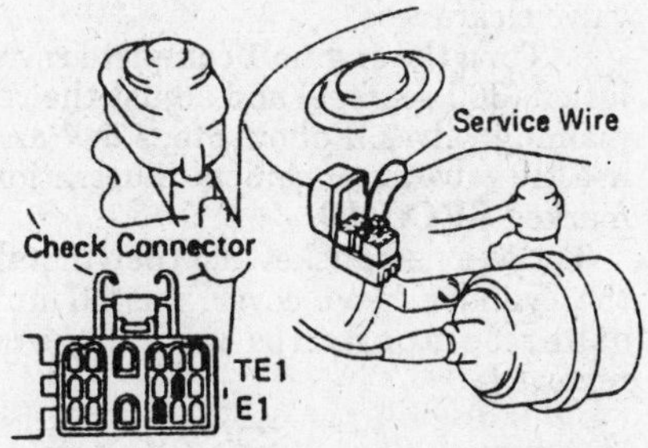


**Shorting the test connector – 7M-GE engines (Cressida)**

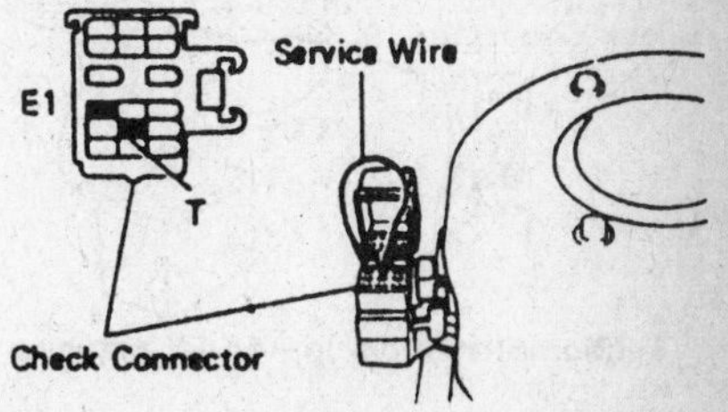


**Shorting the test connector – 4A-FE engines**

# TACHOMETER HOOK-UP

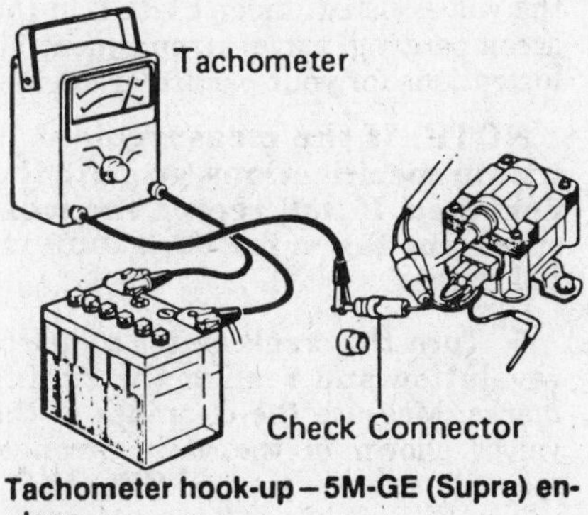


**Tachometer hook-up – 5M-GE (Supra) engines**

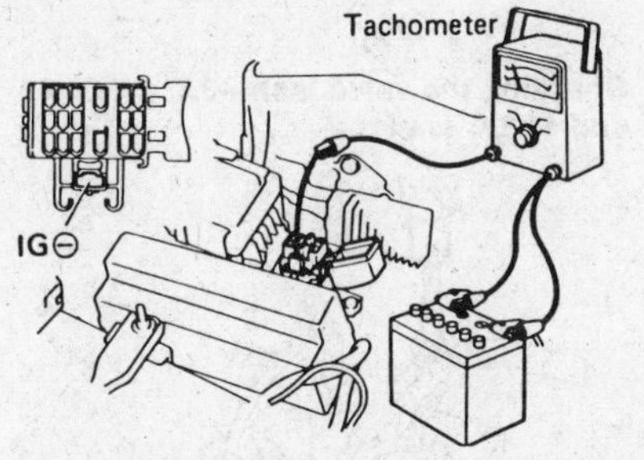


**Tachometer hook-up – 5M-GE (Cressida) 1983-85 2S-E, 7M-GE (Supra) and 7M-GTE engines**

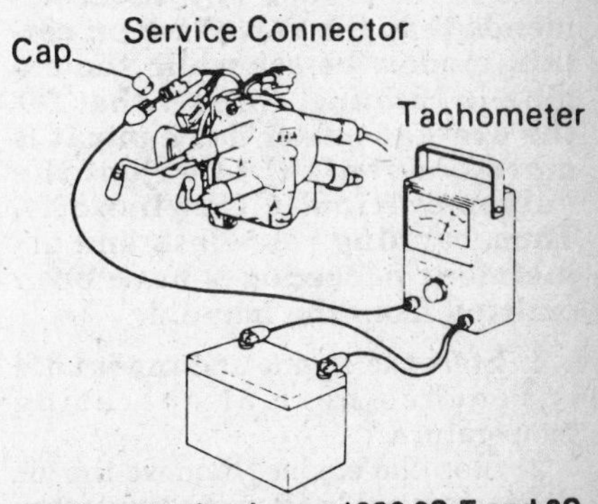


**Tachometer hook-up – 1986 2S-E and 3S-FE engines**

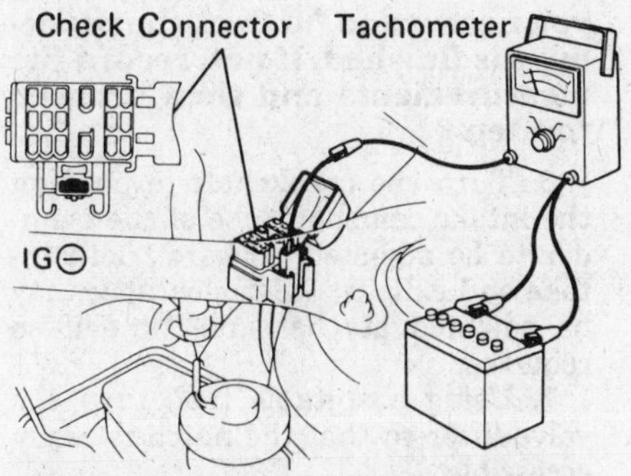


**Tachometer hook-up – 2VZ-FE, 3S-GE, 3S-GTE and 1989-90 4A-GE (Corolla) engines**

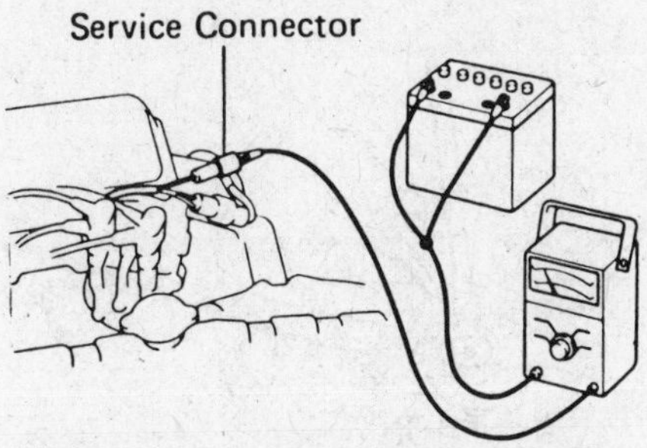


**Tachometer hook-up – 3E, 4A-C, 4A-F, 4A-LC engines (1983-89 3A-C similar)**

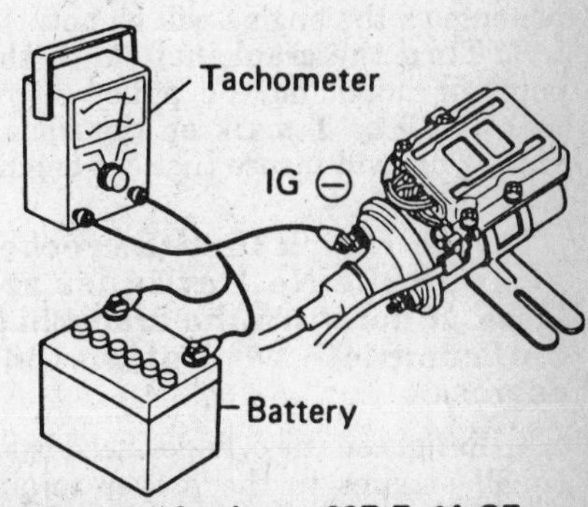


**Tachometer hook-up – 22R-E, 4A-GE (all exc. 1989-90 Corolla) and 4A-GZE engines**

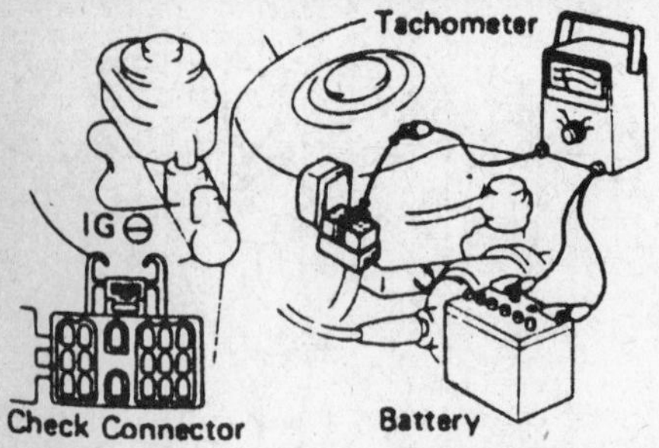


Tachometer hook-up—7M-GE engines (Cressida)

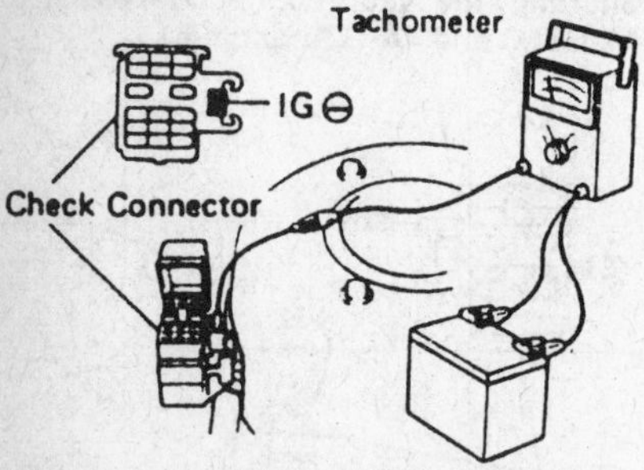


Tachometer hook-up—4A-FE engines

## Valve Lash

### ADJUSTMENT

#### *3E Engines*
#### *22R and 22R-E Engines*
#### *3A, 3A-C and 4A-C Engines*

**NOTE: Although Toyota recommends that the valve lash on certain models be set while the engine is running, we feel that for the average owner/mechanic it is more convenient to adjust the valves statically (engine off). Thus, running valve lash and adjustment procedures have been omitted from the manual.**

1. Start the engine and run it until it reaches normal operating temperature.
2. Stop the engine. Remove the air cleaner assembly. Remove any other hoses, cables, etc. which are attached to, or in the way of the cylinder head cover. Be careful when removing components as the engine will be hot.
3. Turn the crankshaft until the point or notch on the pulley aligns with the **0** or **T** mark on the timing scale. This will insure that the engine is at TDC.

**NOTE: Check that the rocker arms on the No.1 cylinder are loose. If not, turn the crankshaft one complete revolution (360 degrees).**

4. Retighten the cylinder head bolts on all engines to the proper torque specifications. Also, retighten the valve rocker support bolts to the proper specifications.
5. Using a flat feeler gauge, check the clearance between the bottom of the rocker arm (top—3E) and the top of the valve stem (botom of cam lobe—3E). This measurement should correspond to specification.
6. If the clearance is not within specification, the valves will require adjustment. Loosen the locknut on the end of the rocker arm and, still holding the nut with an open end wrench, turn the adjustments screw to achieve the correct clearance.
7. Once the correct valve clearance is achieved, keep the adjustment screw from turning with a suitable tool and then tighten the locknut. Recheck the valve clearances.
8. Turn the engine 1 complete revolution (360 degrees) and adjust the remaining valves. Follow Steps 5–7 and use the valve arrangement illustration marked **SECOND.**
9. Use a new gasket and then install the cylinder head cover. Install any other components which were removed.

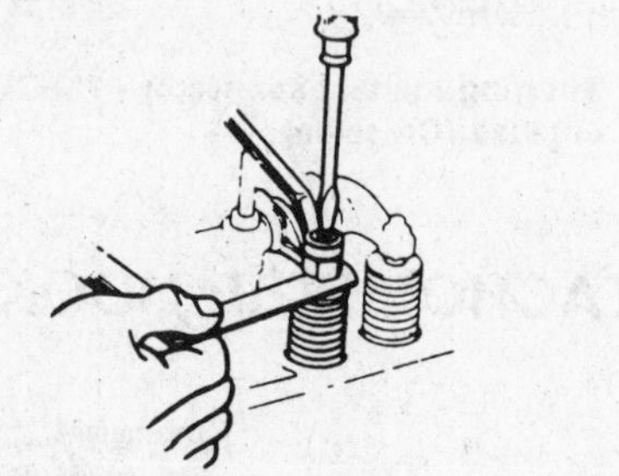

Checking the valve lash—3A, 3A-C, 4A-C and 4A-LC engines

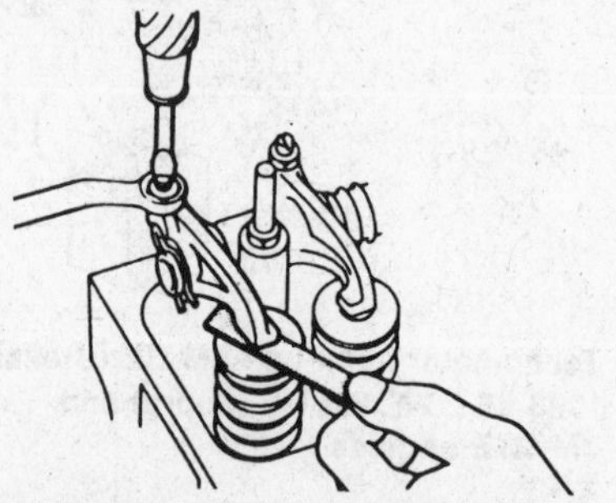

Checking the valve lash—22R and 22R-E engines

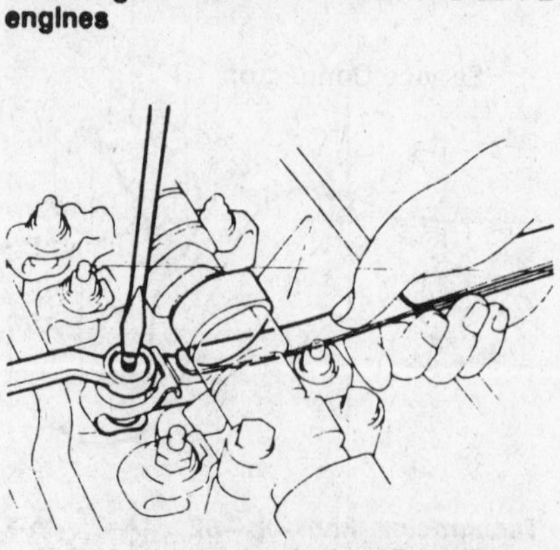

Checking the valve lash—3E engines

#### *2S-E, 4K-E and 5M-GE Engines*

These engines are equipped with hydraulic lash adjusters in the valve train. These adjusters maintain a zero clearance between the rocker arm and valve stem, no adjustment is possible or necessary.

#### *4A-F, 4A-FE, 4A-GE, 4A-GEC, 4A-GELC & 4A-GZE Engines*

1. Start the engine and run it until it reaches normal operating temperature.
2. Stop the engine. Remove the air cleaner assembly. Remove any other hoses, cables, etc. which are attached to, or in the way of the cylinder head cover. Be careful when removing components as the engine will be hot.
3. Use a wrench and turn the crankshaft until the notch in the pulley aligns with the timing pointer in the front cover. This will insure that engine is at TDC.

**NOTE: Check that the valve lifters on the No. 1 cylinder are loose and those on No. 4 cylinder are tight. If not, turn the crankshaft one complete revolution (360 degrees) and then realign the marks.**

4. Using a flat feeler gauge measure the clearance between the camshaft lobe and the valve lifter. Check only the valves listed under **FIRST** in the accompanying valve arrangement illustrations for your particular engine.

**NOTE: If the measurement is within specifications, go on to the next step. If not, record the measurement taken for each individual valve.**

5. Turn the crankshaft 1 complete revolution and realign the timing marks. Measure the clearance of the valves shown in the valve arrangement illustration marked **SECOND.**

**NOTE: If the measurement for this set of valves (and also the previous one) is within specification, you need go no further, the procedure is finished. If not, record the measurements and then proceed to Step 6.**

6. Turn the crankshaft to position the intake camshaft lobe of the cylinder to be adjusted, upward. Both intake and exhaust valve clearance may be adjusted at the same time if so required.
7. Using a suitable tool, turn the valve lifter so that the notch is easily accessible.
8. Install SST No. 09248-70011 (4A-GE) or 09248-55010 (4A-F, 4A-FE, 4A-GEC, 4A-GELC, 4A-GZE) be-

tween the 2 camshafts lobes and then turn the handle so that the tool presses down both (intake and exhaust) valve lifters evenly. On the 4A-GE, the tool will work on only one valve lifter at a time.

**NOTE: On the 4A-FE, 4A-GEC, 4A-GELC and 4A-GZE, position the notch toward the spark plug before pressing down the valve lifter.**

9. Using a suitable tool and a magnet, remove the valve shims.
10. Measure the thickness of the old shim with a micrometer. Using this measurement and the clearance ones made earlier, determine what size replacement shim will be required in order to bring the valve clearance into specification.
11. Install the new shim, remove the special tool and then recheck the valve clearance. Installation of the remaining components is in the reverse order of removal.

### *2VZ-FE Engines*

1. Remove the air intake chamber and the cylinder head covers.
2. Use a wrench and turn the crankshaft until the notch in the pulley aligns with the timing mark **0** of the No. 1 timing belt cover. This will insure that engine is at TDC.

**NOTE: Check that the valve lifters on the No. 1 (intake) cylinder are loose and those on No. 1 cylinder (exhaust)are tight. If not, turn the crankshaft 1 complete revolution (360 degrees) and then realign the marks.**

3. Using a flat feeler gauge measure the clearance between the camshaft lobe and the valve lifter. This measurement should correspond to specification. Check only the valves listed under **FIRST** in the accompanying valve arrangement illustrations for your particular engine.

**NOTE: If the measurement is within specifications, go on to the next step. If not, record the measurement taken for each individual valve.**

4. Turn the crankshaft ⅔ revolution (240 degrees).
5. Measure the clearance of the valves shown in the valve arrangement illustration marked **SECOND**.

**NOTE: If the measurement is within specifications, go on to the next step. If not, record the measurement taken for each individual valve.**

6. Turn the crankshaft ⅔ revolution (240 degrees).
7. Measure the clearance of the valves shown in the valve arrangement illustration marked **THIRD**.

**NOTE: If the measurement for this set of valves (and also the previous ones) is within specifications, you need go no further, the procedure is finished. If not, record the measurements and then proceed to Step 8.**

8. Turn the crankshaft to position the intake camshaft lobe of the cylinder to be adjusted, upward.
9. Using a suitable tool, turn the valve lifter so that the notch is easily accessible (it should be toward the spark plug).
10. Install SST No. 09248–55010 between the 2 camshafts lobes and then turn the handle so that the tool presses down the valve lifter evenly.
11. Using a suitable tool and a magnet, remove the valve shims.
12. Measure the thickness of the old shim with a micrometer. Using this measurement and the clearance ones made earlier (from Step 3, 5 or 7), determine what size replacement shim will be required in order to bring the valve clearance into specification.

**NOTE: Replacement shims are available in 17 sizes, in increments of 0.05mm (0.0020 in.), from 2.50mm (0.0984 in.) to 3.300mm (0.1299 in.)**

13. Install the new shim, remove the special tool and then recheck the valve clearance.
14. Installation of the remaining components is in the reverse order of removal.

### *3S-FE, 3S-GE and 3S-GTE Engines*

1. Remove the cylinder head covers.
2. Use a wrench and turn the crankshaft until the notch in the pulley aligns with the timing mark **0** of the No. 1 timing belt cover. This will insure that engine is at TDC.

**NOTE: Check that the valve lifters on the No. 1 cylinder are loose and those on No. 4 cylinder are tight. If not, turn the crankshaft 1 complete revolution (360 degrees) and then realign the marks.**

3. Using a flat feeler gauge measure the clearance between the camshaft lobe and the valve lifter. This measurement should correspond to specification. Check only the valves listed under **FIRST** in the accompanying valve arrangement illustrations for your particular engine.

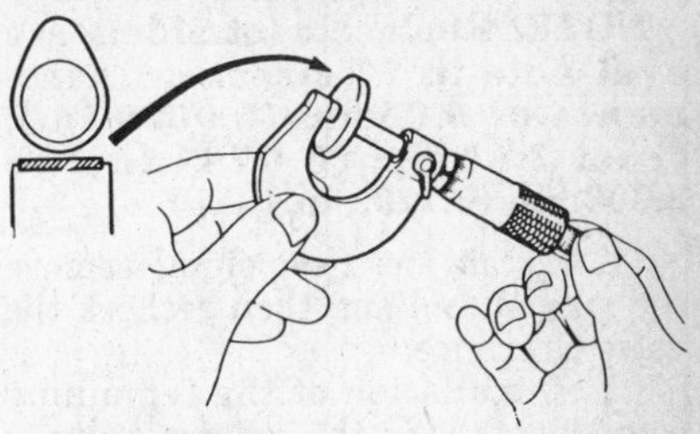

**Measuring the shim size (thickness)**

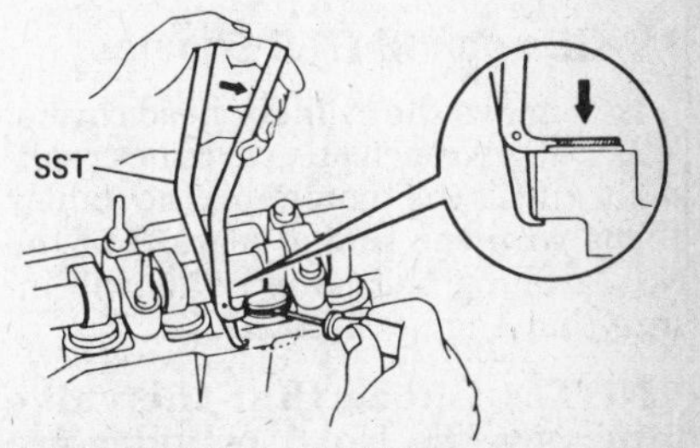


**Depressing the valve lifter to remove the shim—3S-GE and 4A-GE engines**

**NOTE: If the measurement is within specifications, go on to the next step. If not, record the measurement taken for each individual valve.**

4. Turn the crankshaft 1 complete revolution and realign the timing marks as previously described.
5. Measure the clearance of the valves shown in the valve arrangement illustration marked **SECOND**.

**NOTE: If the measurement for this set of valves (and also the previous one) is within specifications, you need go no further, the procedure is finished. If not, record the measurements and then proceed to Step 6.**

6. Turn the crankshaft to position the intake camshaft lobe of the cylinder to be adjusted, upward.

**NOTE: Both intake and exhaust valve clearance may be adjusted at the same time if so required.**

7. Using a suitable tool, turn the valve lifter so that the notch is easily accessible.
8. Install SST No. 09248–70012 (3S-GE), No. 09248–55010 (3S-FE) between the 2 camshaft lobes and then turn the handle so that the tool presses down both (intake and exhaust) valve lifters evenly.
9. Using a suitable tool and a magnet, remove the valve shims.
10. Measure the thickness of the old shim with a micrometer. Using this measurement and the clearance ones made earlier (from Step 3 or 5), determine what size replacement shim will be required in order to bring the valve clearance into specification.

**NOTE: Replacement shims are available in 27 sizes, in increments of 0.05mm (0.0020 in.), from 2.00mm (0.0787 in.) to 3.300mm (0.1299 in.)**

11. Install the new shim, remove the special tool and then recheck the valve clearance.

12. Installation of the remaining components is in the reverse order of removal.

### *7M-GE and 7M-GTE Engines*

1. Remove the cylinder head covers.

2. Use a wrench and turn the crankshaft until the notch in the pulley aligns with the timing mark **0** of the No. 1 timing belt cover. This will insure that engine is at TDC.

**NOTE: Check that the valve lifters on the No. 1 cylinder are loose and those on No. 6 cylinder are tight. If not, turn the crankshaft 1 complete revolution (360 degrees) and then realign the marks.**

3. Using a flat feeler gauge measure the clearance between the camshaft lobe and the valve lifter. This measurement should correspond to specification. Check only the valves listed under **FIRST** in the accompanying valve arrangement illustrations for your particular engine.

**NOTE: If the measurement is within specifications, go on to the next step. If not, record the measurement taken for each individual valve.**

4. Turn the crankshaft ⅔ revolution (240 degrees).

5. Measure the clearance of the valves shown in the valve arrangement illustration marked **SECOND**.

**NOTE: If the measurement is within specifications, go on to the next step. If not, record the measurement taken for each individual valve.**

6. Turn the crankshaft ⅔ revolution (240 degrees).

7. Measure the clearance of the valves shown in the valve arrangement illustration marked **THIRD**.

**NOTE: If the measurement for this set of valves (and also the previous ones) is within specifications, you need go no further, the procedure is finished. If not, record the measurements and then proceed to Step 8.**

8. Turn the crankshaft to position the intake camshaft lobe of the cylinder to be adjusted, upward.

**NOTE: Both intake and exhaust valve clearance may be adjusted at the same time if so required.**

9. Using a suitable tool, turn the valve lifter so that the notch is easily accessible.

10. Install SST No. 09248-55010 between the 2 camshafts lobes and then turn the handle so that the tool presses down both (intake and exhaust) valve lifters evenly.

11. Using a suitable tool and a magnet, remove the valve shims.

12. Measure the thickness of the old shim with a micrometer. Using this measurement and the clearance ones made earlier (from Step 3, 5 or 7), determine what size replacement shim will be required in order to bring the valve clearance into specification.

**NOTE: Replacement shims are available in 17 sizes, in increments of 0.05mm (0.0020 in.), from 2.00mm (0.0787 in.) to 3.300mm (0.1299 in.)**

13. Install the new shim, remove the special tool and then recheck the valve clearance.

14. Installation of the remaining components is in the reverse order of removal.

## VALVE ADJUSTMENT

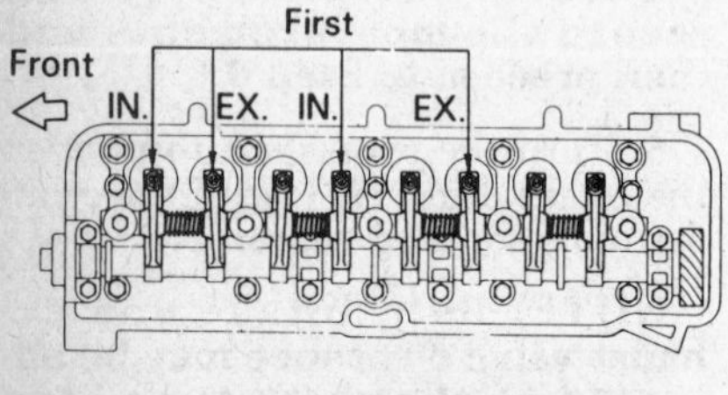


**Adjust these valves FIRST—3A, 3A-C, 4A-C and 4A-LC engines**

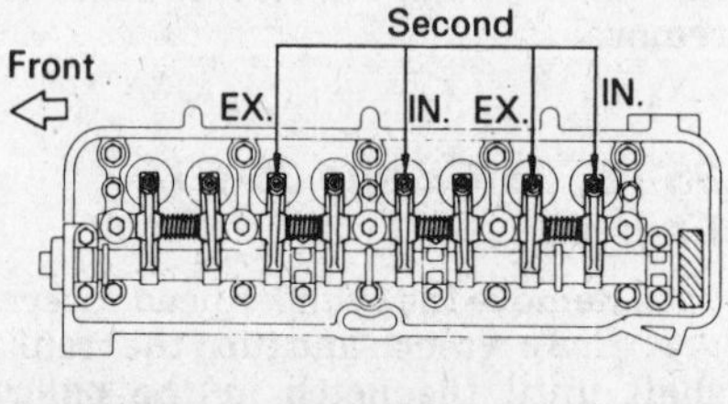


**Adjust these valves SECOND—3A, 3A-C, 4A-C and 4A-LC engines**

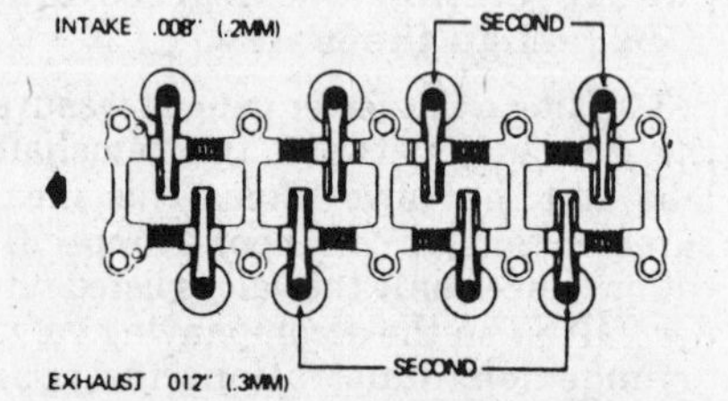


**Adjust these valves SECOND—22R and 22R-E engines**

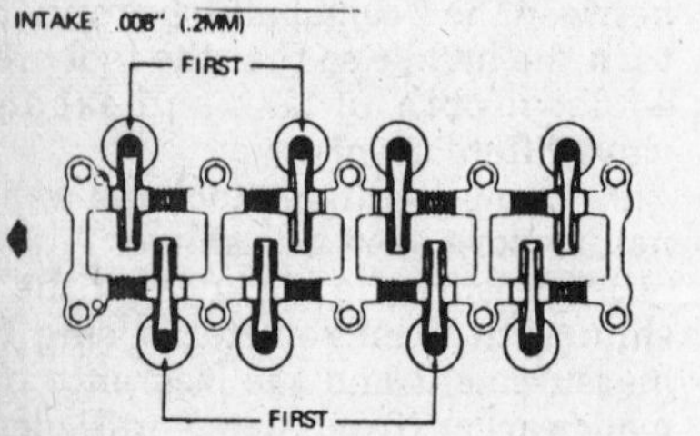


**Adjust these valves FIRST—22R and 22R-E engines**

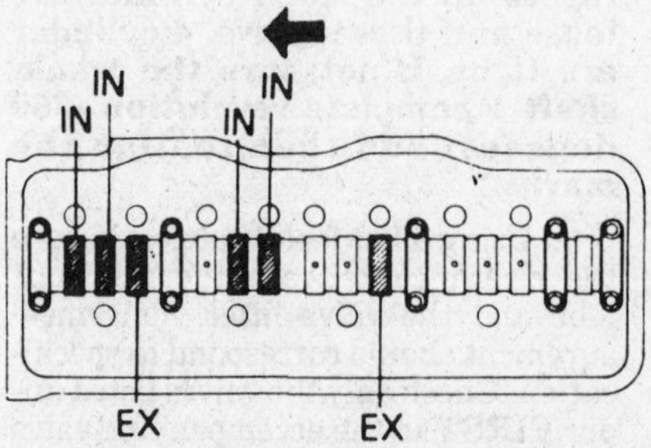


**Adjust these valves FIRST—3E engines**

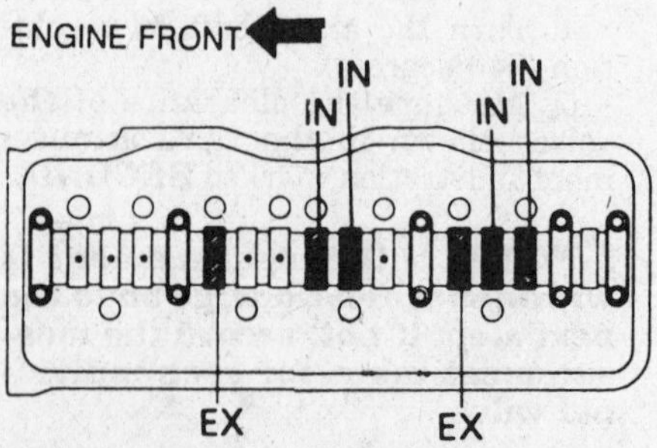


**Adjust these valves SECOND—3E engines**

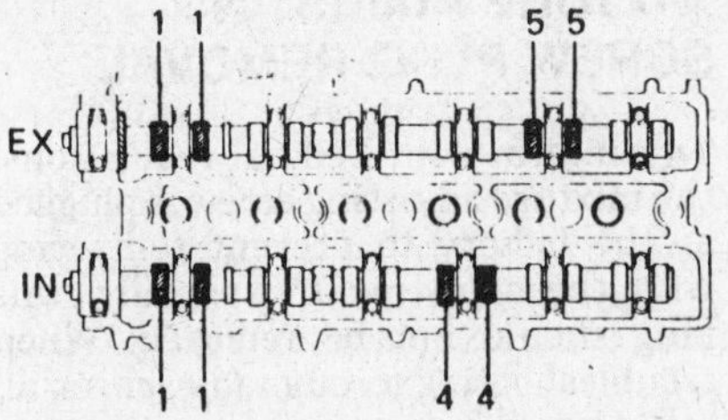


**Adjust these valves FIRST–7M-GE and 7M-GTE engines**

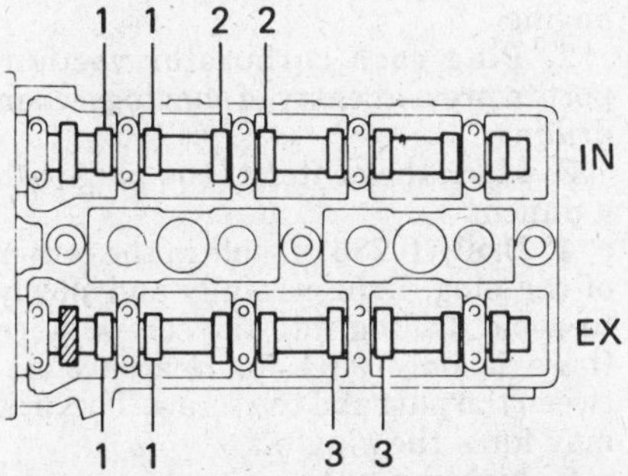


**Adjust these valves FIRST–3S-GE, 4A-GE, 4A-GEC and 4A-GELC (Corolla) engines**

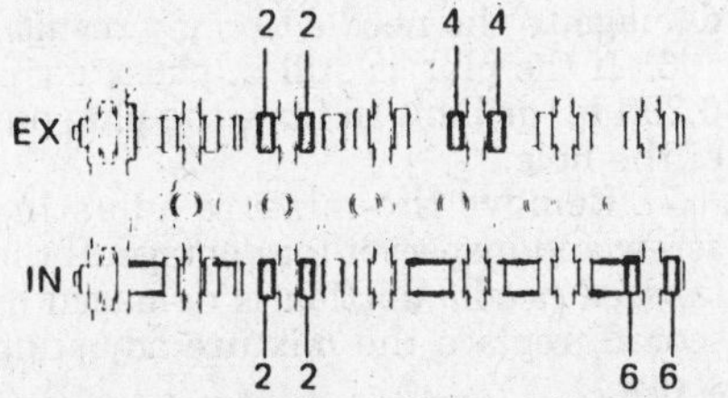


**Adjust these valves THIRD–7M-GE and 7M-GTE engines**

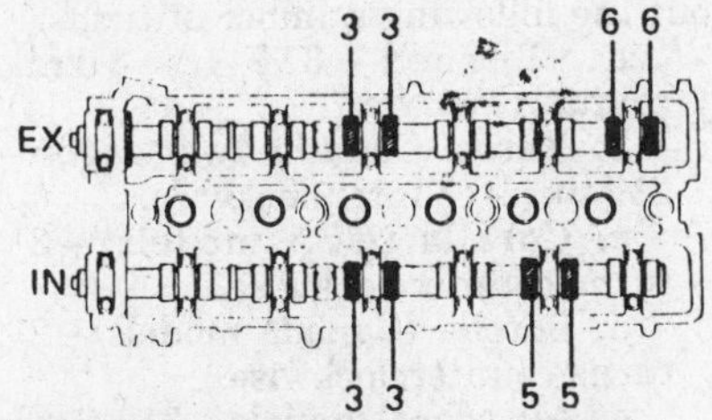


**Adjust these valves FIRST–3S-GE, 3S-GTE, 4A-GE, 4A-GEC and 4A-GELC (Corolla) engines**

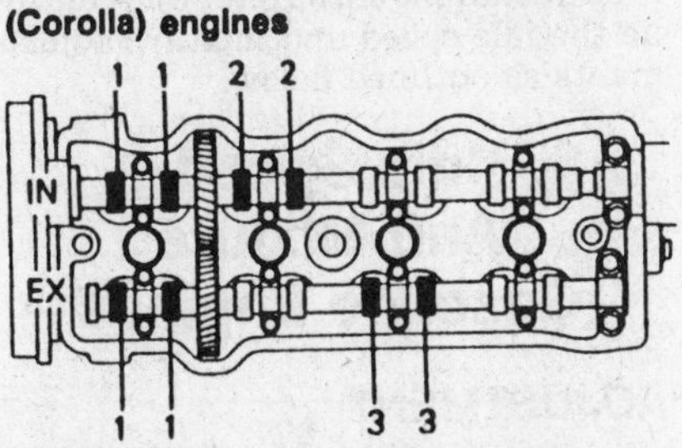


**Adjust these valves FIRST–3S-FE engines**

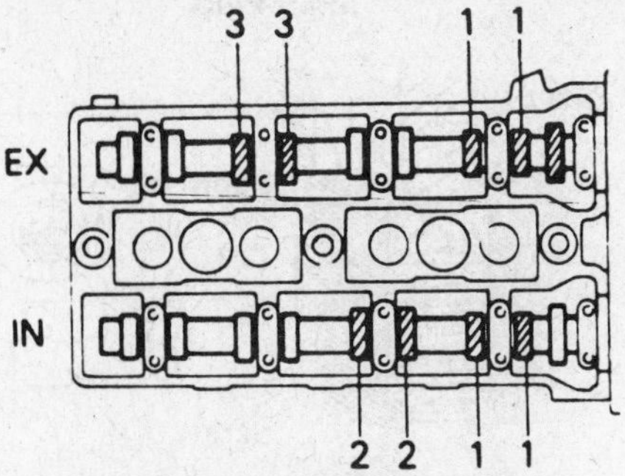


**Adjust these valves FIRST–4A-GE, 4A-GELC and 4A-GZE (MR2) engines**

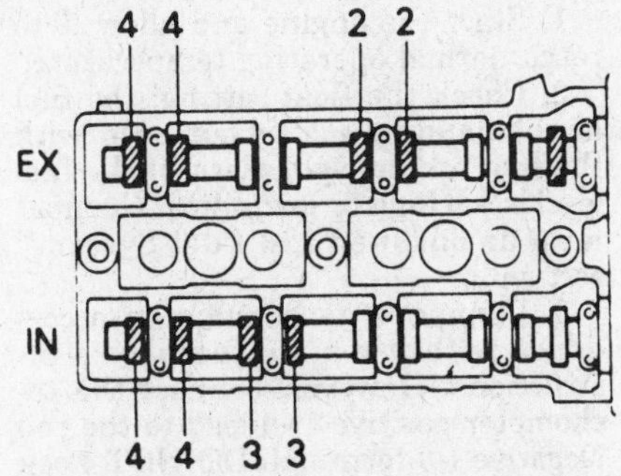


**Adjust these valves SECOND–4A-GE, 4A-GELC and 4A-GZE (MR2) engines**

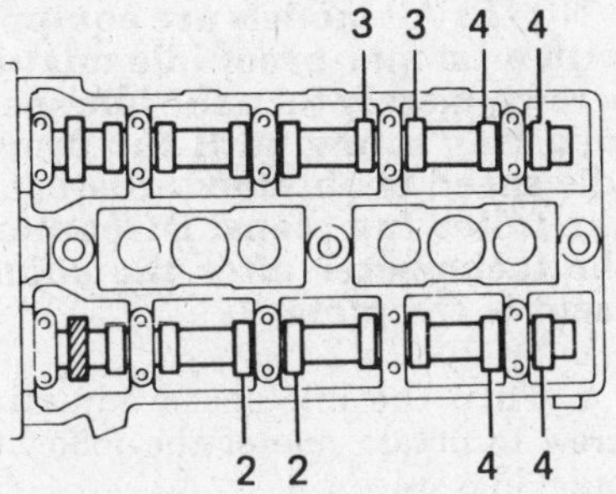


**Adjust these valves SECOND–3S-GE, 3S-GTE, 4A-GE, 4A-GEC and 4A-GELC (Corolla) engines**

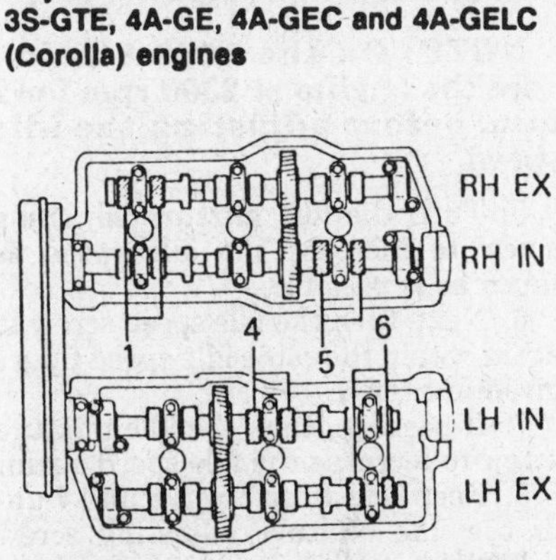


**Adjust these valves THIRD–2VZ-FE engines**

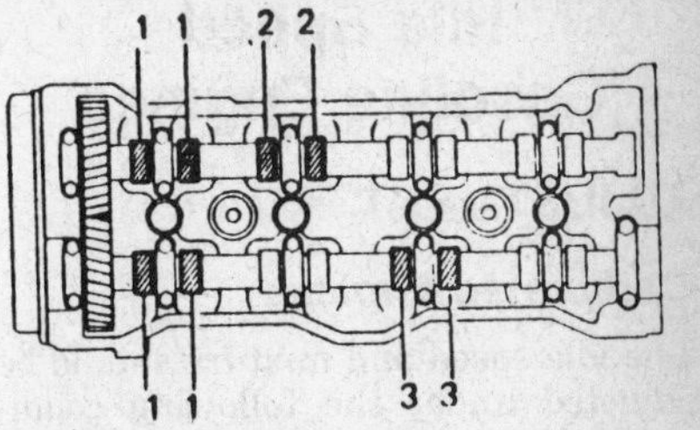


**Adjust these valves FIRST–4A-F and 4A-FE engines**

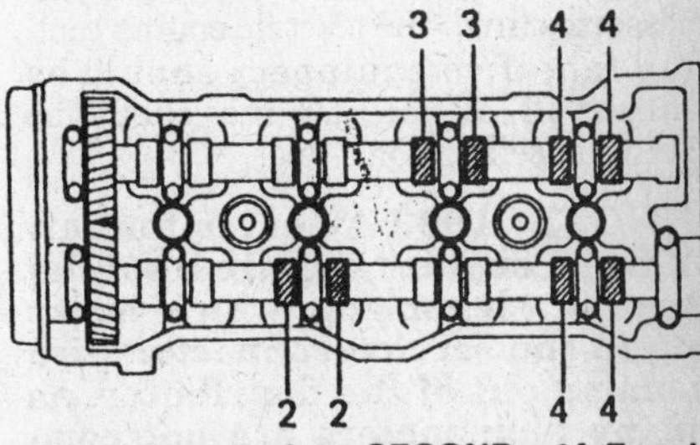


**Adjust these valves SECOND–4A-F and 4A-FE engines**

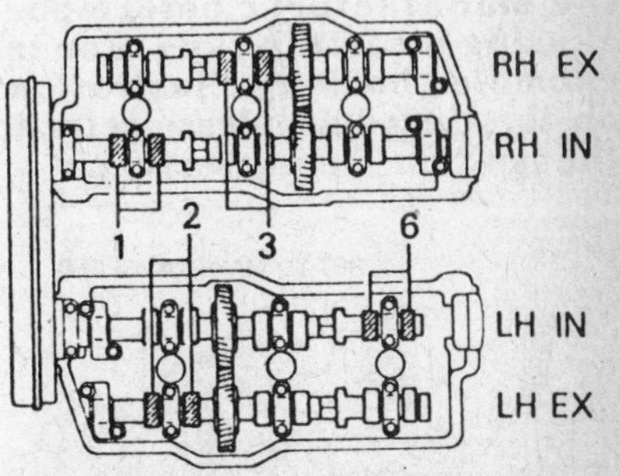


**Adjust these valves FIRST–2VZ-FE engines**

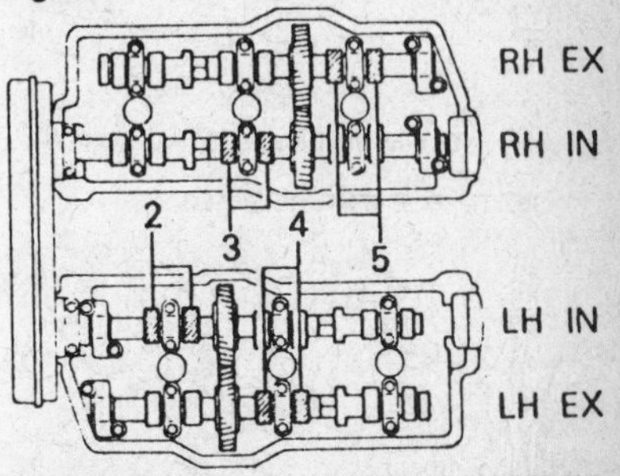


**Adjust these valves SECOND–2VZ-FE engines**

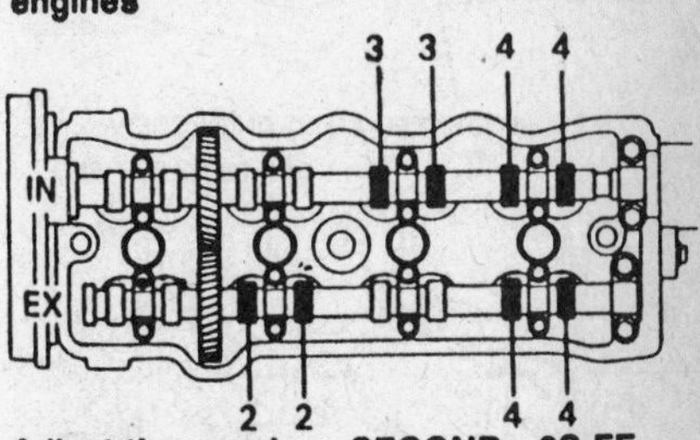


**Adjust these valves SECOND–3S-FE engines**

# Idle Speed Gasoline Engines

## ADJUSTMENT

### *Carbureted Engines*

The idle speed and mixture should be adjusted under the following conditions: the air cleaner must be installed, the choke fully opened, the transmission should be in Neutral (**N**), all accessories (incl. the electric engine cooling fan, if so equipped) should be turned off, all vacuum lines should be set to specification.

**NOTE: 1983 A-series and all 1984-90 engines require a special type of tachometer which hooks up to the service connector wire coming out of the distributor. As many tachometers are not compatible with this hook-up, we recommend that you consult with the manufacturer before purchasing a certain type. For tachometer hook-up illustrations on these models, please refer to the Ignition Timing section.**

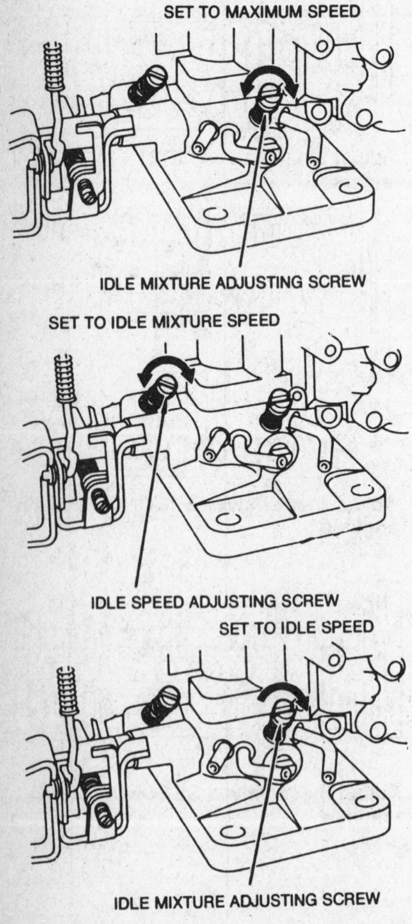


Carburetor adjustment points for the "A' series engines—typical

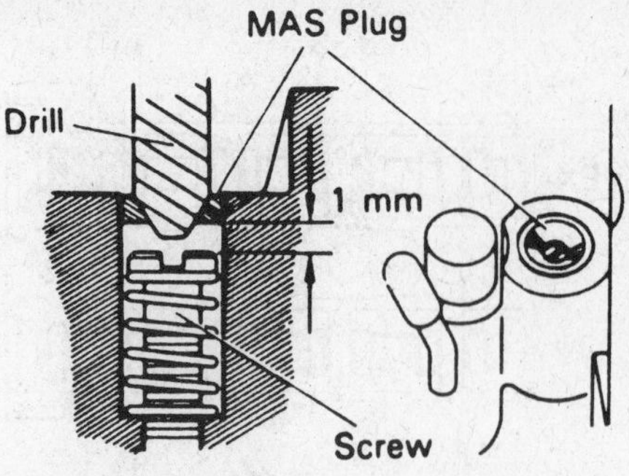


Drilling out the mixture adjustment plug

1. Start the engine and allow it to reach normal operating temperature.
2. Check the float setting; the fuel level should be just about even with the spot on the sight glass. If the fuel level is too high or low, adjust the float level as outlined in "Fuel System" section.
3. Connect a tachometer in accordance with it's manufacturer's instructions. However, connect the tachometer positive (+) lead to the coil Negative (–) terminal. DO NOT hook it up to the distributor side; damage to transistorized ignition could result.

**NOTE: All models are equipped with a tamper-proof idle mixture screws, merely turn the idle speed adjusting screw until the proper idle speed is obtained. Disregard the following steps. Disconnect the tachometer after the adjustment is complete.**

4. Turn the idle speed adjusting screw to obtain one of the following initial idle speeds:
   2A-3A – 750 rpm

**NOTE: On the 1983 Starlet, race the engine at 2500 rpm for 2 min. before adjusting the idle speed.**

5. Turn the idle mixture adjusting screw to increase the idle speed as much as is possible.
6. Next, turn the idle speed screw to again obtain the same idle speed figure given in Step 4.
7. If possible, turn the idle mixture screw to increase the idle speed again.
8. Keep repeating Steps 6 and 7 until the idle mixture adjusting screw will no longer increase the idle speed above the figure specified in Step 4.
9. Slowly turn the idle mixture screw clockwise, until the idle speed specified in the "Tune-Up Specifications" chart is reached (this makes the mixture leaner).
10. Disconnect the tachometer.

## MIXTURE ADJUSTING SCREW PLUG REMOVAL

To conform with Federal regulations, the mixture adjusting screw is plugged at the factory to prevent tampering with the adjustment. Normally, this plug should not be removed. When troubleshooting a rough idle, check all other possible causes before removing the plug and adjusting the idle mixture.

1. Remove the carburetor from the engine.
2. Plug each carburetor vacuum port to prevent entry of shavings when drilling.
3. Mark the center of the plug with a punch.
4. Drill a 0.256 in. hole in the center of the plug. Drill carefully and slowly to avoid drilling into the screw, since there is only 0.04 in. clearance between the plug and the screw. The drill may force the plug off.
5. Lightly seat the mixture screw by inserting a screwdriver into the drilled hole and turning the screw clockwise. Be careful not to tighten the screw or damage to the needle tip may result.
6. If the plug is still in place, use a 0.295 in. drill bit to force the plug out of the hole.
7. Remove the mixture adjusting screw and inspect it for damage. If the tapered needle portion is damaged or scored, replace the mixture adjusting screw.
8. Fully seat the mixture adjusting screw lightly once again, then back it out the following number of turns:
   a. Tercel – 3½ turns counterclockwise.
   b. Tercel Canada 4wd wagon – 2½ turns counterclockwise.
   c. Corolla (USA models) – 3¼ turns counterclockwise.
   d. Corolla (Canada models) – 2½ turns counterclockwise.
   e. All other models – 3½ turns counterclockwise.
9. Install the carburetor and continue the idle speed and mixture adjustments as outlined below.

# Idle Speed And Mixture Gasoline Engines

## ADJUSTMENT

### *Carbureted Engines*

1. All adjustments should be made with the engine at normal operating temperature under the following conditions:
   a. Air cleaner installed.
   b. Choke fully open.

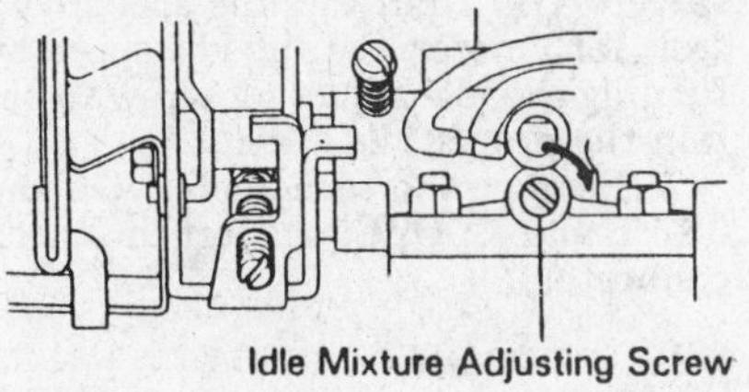


**Location of the idle mixture adjusting screw–carbureted engines**

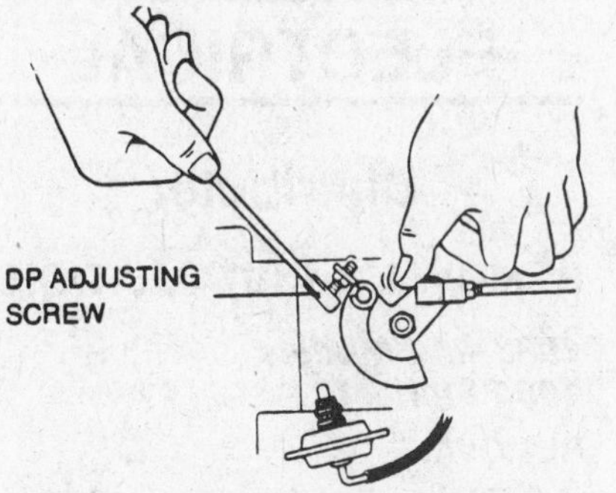


**Loosen the locknut and turn the adjusting screw to set the dashpot**

c. All accessories switched off.
d. All vacuum lines connected.
e. Ignition timing set to specifications.
f. Transmission in Neutral.

2. Start the engine and allow it to reach normal operating temperature.

3. Turn the idle mixture screw to obtain the maximum idle speed, then use the idle speed screw to adjust the idle to 700 rpm. Continue going back and forth until the idle speed doesn't rise when the mixture screw is adjusted.

**NOTE: The cooling fan should be off for all adjustments.**

4. Adjust the idle speed down to 650 rpm by turning in the idle mixture screw (lean drop method of adjustment).

5. Adjust the idle speed to specifications by turning the idle speed adjusting screw.

6. Once the idle speed is adjusted, install a new tamper-proof plug over the mixture adjusting screw.

### *Fuel Injected Engines*

#### 5M-GE, 7M-GE AND 7M-GTE Engines

**NOTE: This procedure will require a voltmeter and a EFI idle adjusting wire harness (Special Service Tool No. 09842-14010), available at your Toyota dealer.**

1. Behind the battery on the left front fender apron is a service connector. Remove the rubber caps from the connector and connect the EFI idle adjusting wire harness.

2. Connect the positive lead of the voltmeter to red wire of the wiring harness and then connect the negative lead to the black wire.

**NOTE: On later models, short the $O_2$ sensor by connecting a jumper wire between terminals T ($TE_1$) and $E_1$ on the service connector. Then connect the (+) lead of the voltmeter to terminal VF ($VF_1$) and the (-) lead to $E_1$.**

3. Hook up a tachometer as per manufacturer's instructions.

**NOTE: Please refer to "Ignition Timing" for tachometer hook-up illustrations.**

4. Warm up to the oxygen sensor by running the engine at 2500 rpm for about 2 minutes. The needle of the voltmeter should be fluctuating at this time, if not, turn the idle mixture adjusting screw until it does.

5. Set the idle speed to specifications (see "Tune-Up Specifications" chart) by turning the idle speed adjusting screw.

**NOTE: The idle speed should be set immediately after warm-up while the needle of the voltmeter is fluctuating.**

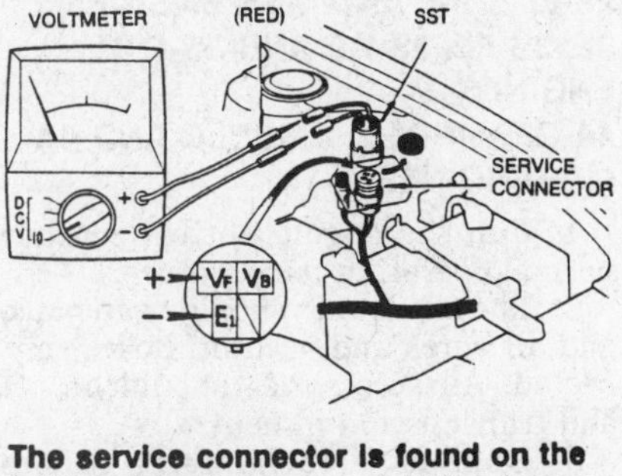


**The service connector is found on the left front fender apron; right front apron on the 1983 Supra**

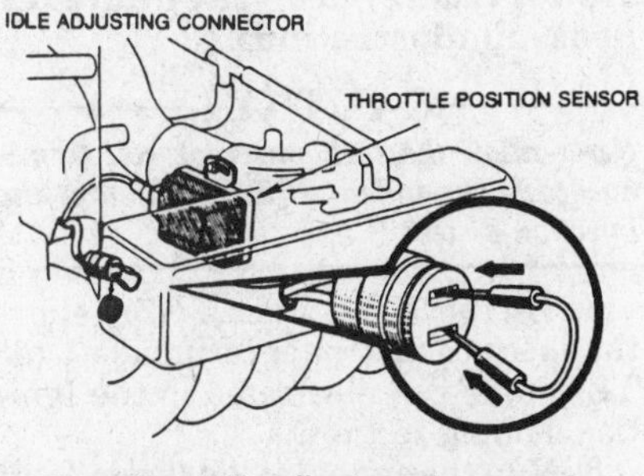


**Short the idle adjustment connector**

**Idle adjusting harness Special Service Tool**

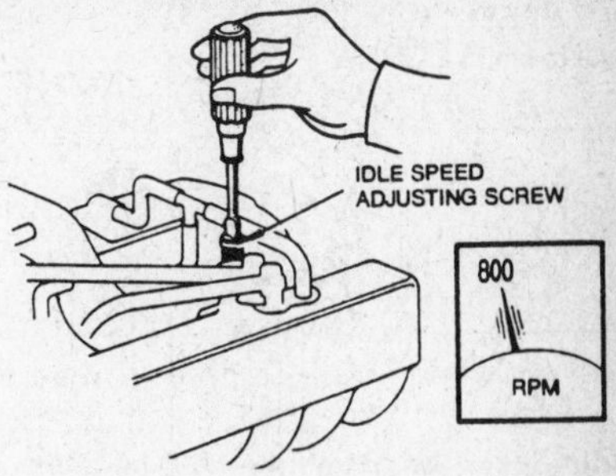


**Idle speed adjustment–22R-E engines**

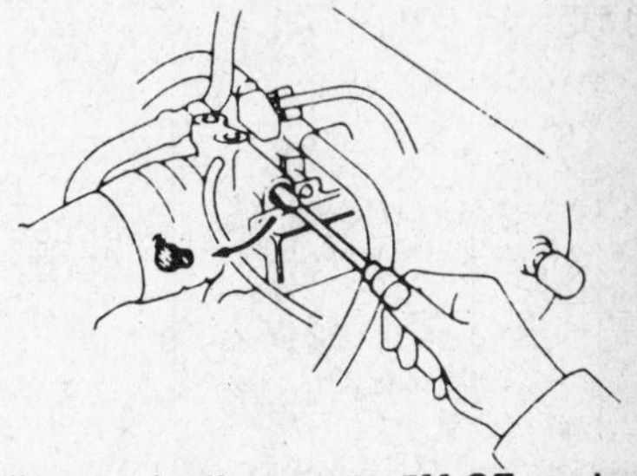

**Idle speed adjustment–5M-GE engines**

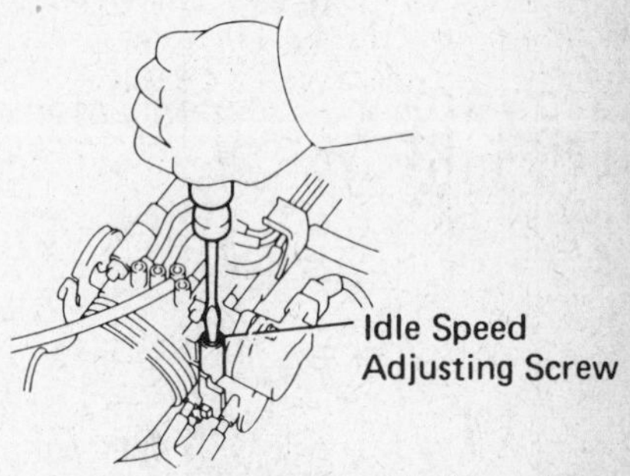


**Idle speed adjustment–4A-GE engines**

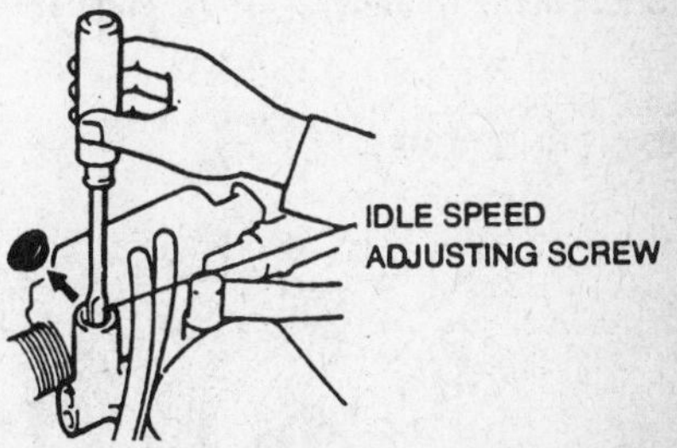


**Idle speed adjustment on the 4K-E engines**

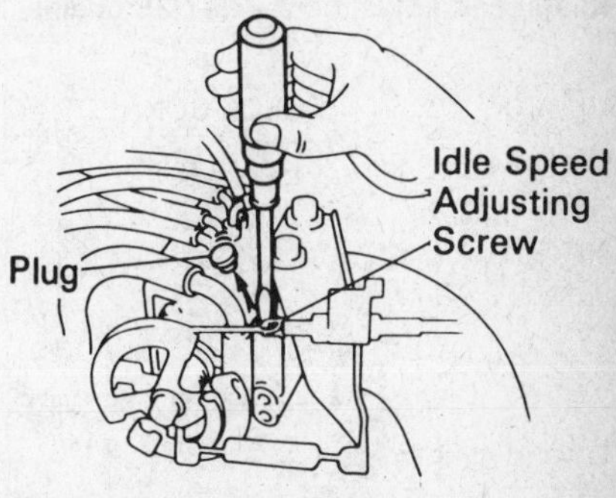


**Idle speed adjustment–2S-E engines**

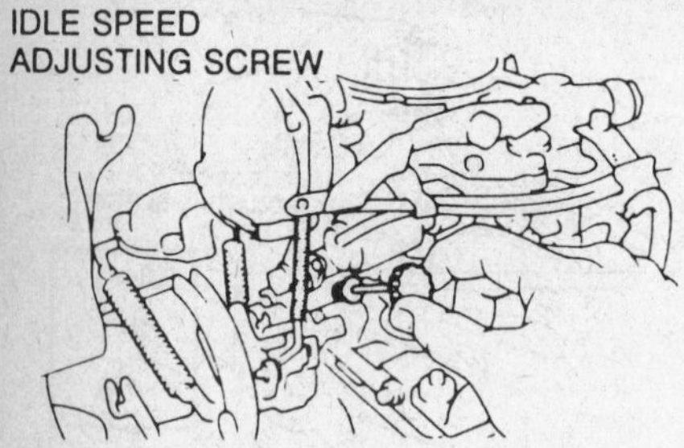

**Idle speed adjustment – 4A-F engines**

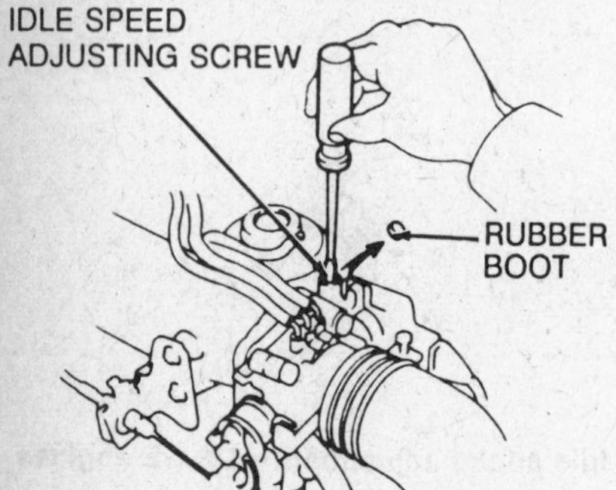

**Idle speed adjustment – 3S-FE engines**

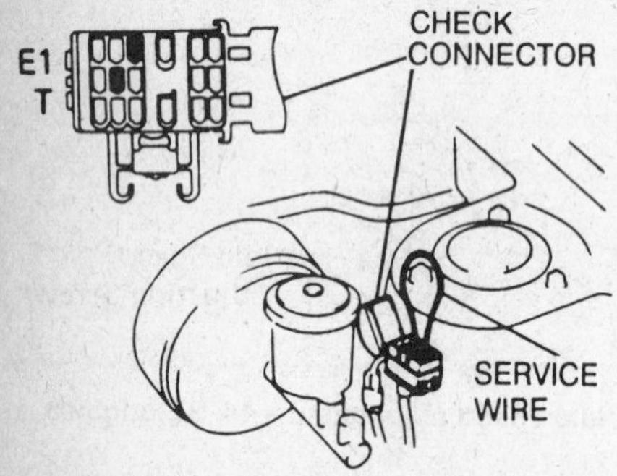

**Short these terminals – 3S-FE engines**

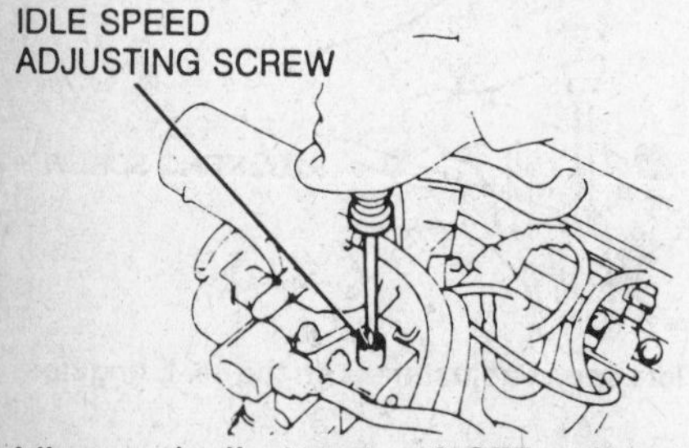

**Idle speed adjustment – 4A-GZE engines**

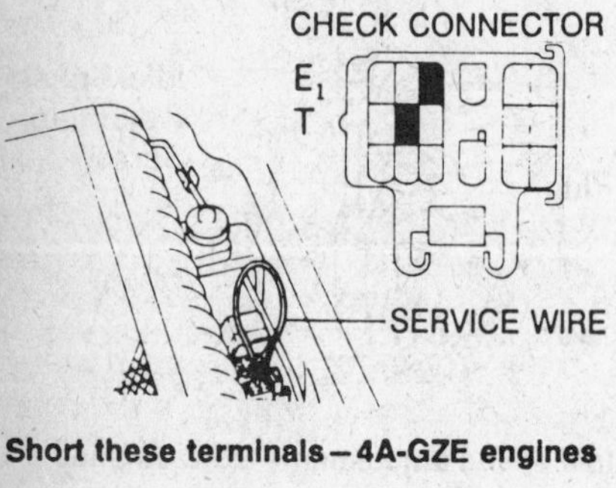

**Short these terminals – 4A-GZE engines**

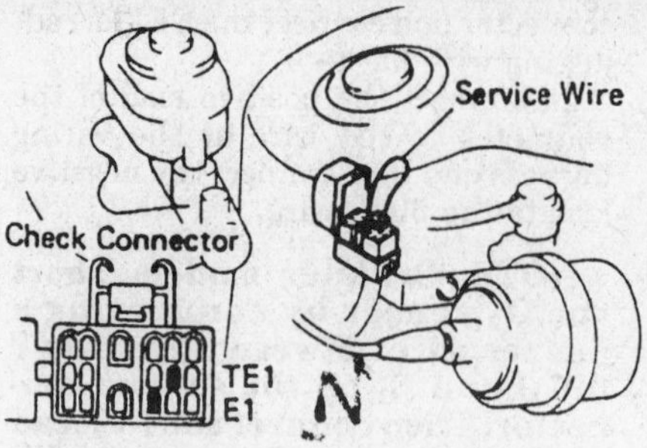

**Short these terminals – 7M-GE and 7M-GTE engines**

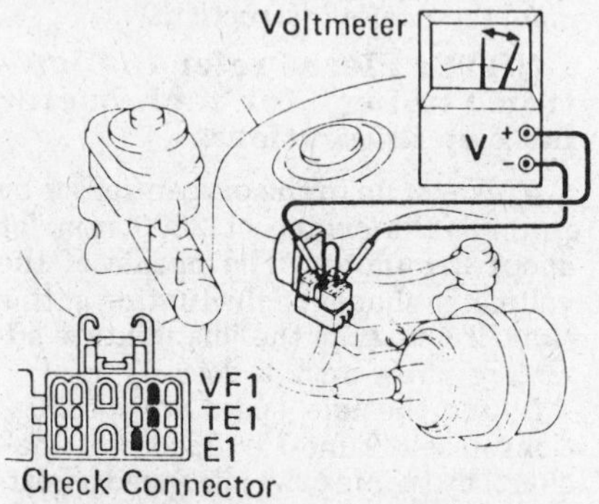

**Checking the $O_2$ sensor – 7M-GE and 7M-GTE engines**

6. The idle adjustment procedure for 5M-GE, 7M-GE and 7M-GTE engines is now complete.

#### 2S-E, 22R-E AND 4K-E ENGINES 3E, 3S-FE, 3S-GE AND 3S-GTE ENGINES 4A-GE, 4A-GEC, 4A-GELC AND 4A-GZE ENGINES

1. Run the engine until it reaches normal operating temperature.
2. The air cleaner should be in place and all wires and vacuum hoses connected. All accessories should be off and transmission in neutral.
3. Connect a tachometer to the engine.

**NOTE: Please refer to "Ignition Timing" for tachometer hook-up illustrations.**

**CAUTION**

*Never allow the tachometer or coil terminals to be grounded. This will damage the injection system.*

4. On the 3S-FE and 4A-GZE, short the check connector at terminals T (or $TE_1$)and $E_1$ as illustrated in the Ignition Timing section.
5. Run the engine at 2500 rpm for 2 minutes. On the 3S-FE and 4A-GZE, run the engine at 1000–3000 rpm for 5 seconds.
6. Let the engine return to idle. Pinch the No. 1 air intake chamber vacuum hose on the 3S-GE. On the 2S-E, disconnect the vacuum switching valve (VCV) from the idle speed control (ISC) motor. Set the idle speed by turning the idle adjusting screw to obtain the proper idle speed.
7. Remove the tachometer. On the 3S-FE and 4A-GZE, unshort the check connector.

# ENGINE ELECTRICAL

## Distributor

### REMOVAL & INSTALLATION

#### *1983 – All Models*
#### *1984 Starlet*

#### REMOVAL

1. Disconnect the negative battery cable. Unfasten the cables from the spark plugs, after marking the wiring order. Remove the high tension cable from the coil.
2. Remove the primary wire and the vacuum line from the distributor. Remove the distributor cap.
3. Matchmark the distributor housing and the engine block. Mark the rotor position in the distributor as well. This will aid in correct positioning of the distributor during installation.
4. Remove the clamp from the distributor. Withdraw the distributor from the block.

#### INSTALLATION – TIMING NOT DISTURBED

1. Insert the distributor in the block and align the matchmarks made during removal.
2. Engage the distributor drive with the oil pump driveshaft.

**NOTE: Before installing the distributor on A-series engines, there is one further step. On 1983 vehicles: Align the protrusion on the housing center of the flange with that of the bolt hole on the cylinder head.**

3. Install the distributor clamp, cap, high tension wire, primary wire, and vacuum line.
4. Install the wires on the spark plugs.
5. Start the engine. Check the timing and adjust the octane selector, if so equipped.

#### INSTALLATION – TIMING DISTURBED

#### Except 5M-GE Engines

1. Determine top dead center (TDC)

of the No. 1 cylinder's compression stroke by removing the spark plug from the No. 1 cylinder and placing a finger or a compression gauge over the spark plug hole. Crank the engine until compression pressure starts to build up. Continue cranking the engine until the timing marks indicate TDC (or 0 degrees).

2. Align the timing marks. Temporarily install the rotor in the distributor shaft so that the rotor is pointing toward the No. 1 terminal in the distributor cap. The points should be about to open.

3. Use a suitable tool to align the slot on the distributor drive (oil pump drive shaft) with the key on the bottom of the distributor shaft.

4. Install the distributor in the block by rotating it slightly (no more than one gear tooth in either direction) until the driven gear meshes with the drive. Oil the distributor spiral gear and the oil pump driveshaft end before distributor installation.

5. Rotate the distributor, once it is installed, so that the points are just about to open. Temporarily tighten the pinch bolt.

6. Remove the rotor and install the dust cover. Replace the rotor and the distributor cap. Install the primary wire and the vacuum line.

7. Install the No. 1 cylinder spark plug. Connect the cables to the spark plugs in the proper order by using the marks made during removal. Install the high tension wire on the coil.

8. Start the engine. Adjust the ignition timing and the octane selector, if so equipped.

**5M-GE Engines**

1. Determine top dead center (TDC) of the No. 1 cylinder's compression stroke by removing the spark plug from the No. 1 cylinder and placing a finger or a compression gauge over the spark plug hole. Crank the engine until compression pressure starts to build up. Continue cranking the engine until the timing marks indicate TDC (or 0 degrees).

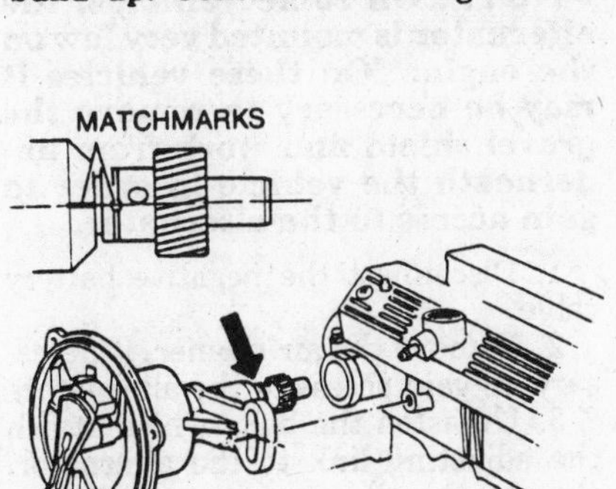

Align the matchmarks on the distributor gear and housing—5M-GE

2. Remove the oil filler cap. Looking into the camshaft housing with the aid of a flashlight, check to make sure that the match hole on the second (No. 2) journal of the camshaft housing is aligned with the hole in the No. 2 journal of the camshaft. If the holes are not aligned, rotate the camshaft one full turn.

3. Install a new O-ring on the distributor cap shaft. Make sure the distributor cap is still removed at this time. Align the matchmark on the distributor spiral gear with that of the distributor housing.

4. Insert the distributor into the camshaft housing, aligning the center of the mounting flange with that of the bolt hole in the side of the housing.

5. Align the rotor tooth in the distributor with the pickup coil. Temporarily install the distributor pinch bolt. Install the distributor cap, and install the oil filler cap.

6. Install the No. 1 cylinder spark plug. Connect the cables to the spark plugs in the proper order by using the marks made during removal. Install the high tension wire on the coil.

7. Start the engine. Adjust the ignition timing and the octane selector, if so equipped.

### *1984-90—All Models Except Starlet*

**NOTE: Proc‹ ›res for the 5M-GE are the sam‹ › as those in the "1983" procedures.**

### *Removal and Installation*

1. Disconnect the battery ground, disconnect the electrical leads, vacuum hoses, and spark plug wires from the distributor.

2. On the Supra (w/7M-GE), remove the oil filler cap and turn the crankshaft clockwise until the nose of the camshaft is visable through the hole. Turn the crankshaft counterclockwise 120 degrees. Now turn it clockwise 10–40 degrees until the TDC marks on the front cover and the crankshaft pulley are aligned.

3. Remove the intercooler on the 3S-GTE.

4. Remove the hold down bolts, and pull the distributor from the engine.

5. Set the engine at TDC of the No. 1 cylinder's firing stroke. This can be accomplished by removing the No. 1 spark plug and turning the engine by hand with your thumb over the spark plug hole. As No. 1 is coming up on its firing stroke, you'll feel pressure against your thumb. Make sure the timing marks are set at 0.

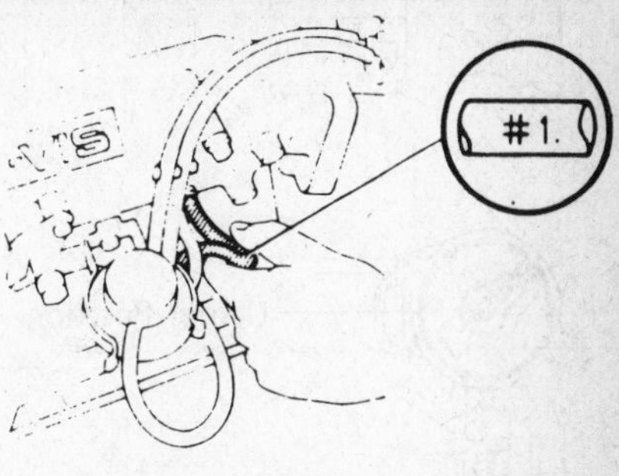

Pinch the No. 1 vacuum hose—3S-GE

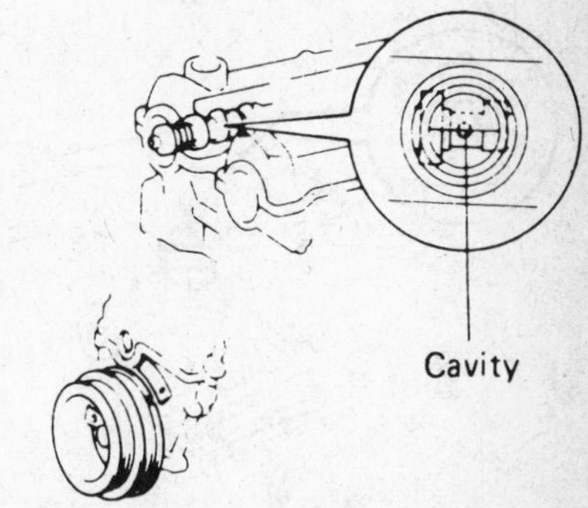

Setting the No. 1 cylinder to TDC of the compression stroke—4A-GE

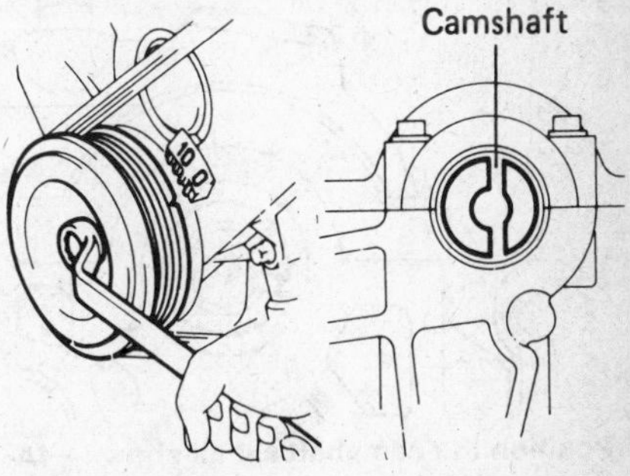

Positioning the No. 1 camshaft—3S-FE, 3S-GE and 3S-GTE engines

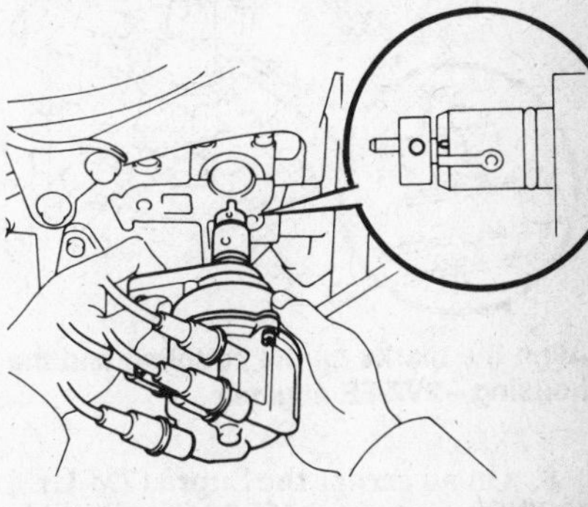
Distributor alignment—3S-FE and 3S-GE engines

**NOTE: On the 4A-GE, 4A-GEC, 4A-GELC and 4A-GZE, align the groove on the crankshaft pulley with the "0" mark on the No. 1 timing cover. Remove the oil filler cap and check that you can see the cavity in the camshaft.**

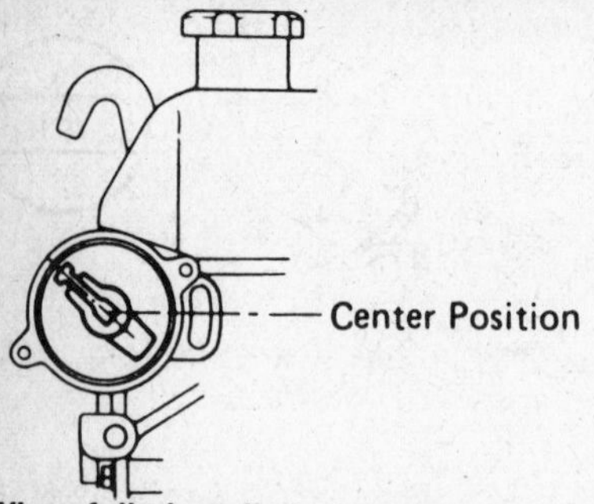


When fully installed, the rotor will rotate to the position shown—22R-E

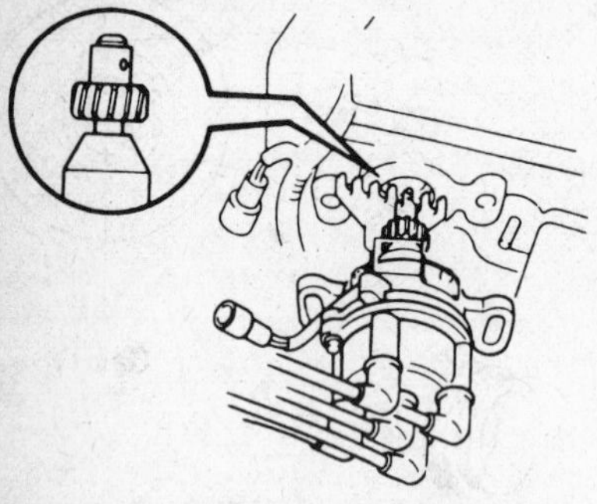

Align the drilled mark on the drive gear with the cavity of the housing—4A-GE

Position the camshaft slit as shown—4A-F engines

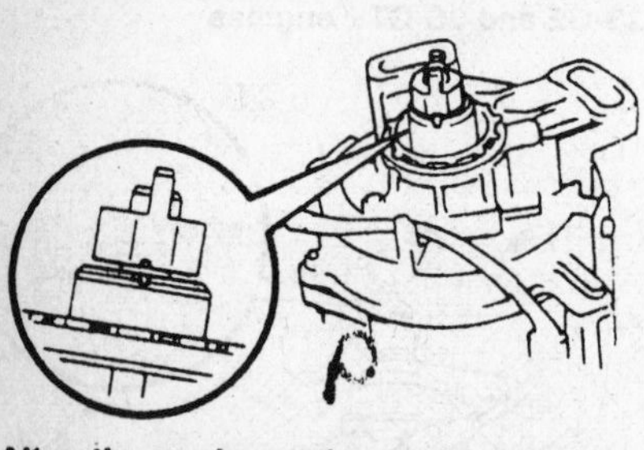

Align the marks on the coupling and the housing—2VZ-FE engines

6. On all except the Supra (7M-GE), 1989-90 Cressida, MR2, Corolla (4A-GE) and Camry, coat the spiral gear and governor shaft tip with clean engine oil. Align the protrusion on the distributor housing with the pin on the spiral gear drill mark side. Insert the distributor, aligning the center of the flange with the bolt hole on the cylinder head. Tighten the bolts.

7. On the Supra (7M-GE) and 1989-90 Cressida, align the drilled mark on

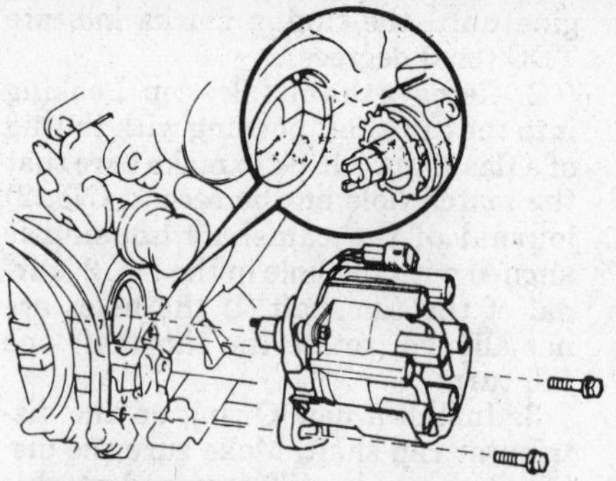

Distributor Installation—2VZ-FE engines

the driven gear with the groove on the distributor housing. Insert the distributor, aligning the stationary flange center with bolt hole in the head. Tighten the bolts.

8. On the 1983-86 Camry, remove the right front wheel and fender apron seal, remove the hole plug of the No. 2 timing belt cover, and, using a mirror, align the mark on the oil seal retainer with the center of the small hole on the camshaft pulley clockwise. Install the plug, fender apron and seal, and the wheel. Coat the spiral gear with clean engine oil, align the protrusion on the housing with the mark on the spiral gear and insert the distributor, aligning the center of the flange with the bolt hole on the head. Tighten the bolts.

9. On the 1984-85 Celica, rotate the crankshaft until the timing mark is aligned with the 5° BTDC mark; make sure the rocker arms on the No. 1 cylinder are loose. Install the rotor and then begin to install the distributor with the rotor pointing upward and the distributor mounting hole at about center position on the bolt hole; When fully installed, the rotor will rotate to the position shown. Remove the rotor and align the signal rotor tooth with the pickup coil projection. Tighten the mounting bolts.

10. On the 1986 Celica with the 2S-E engine, refer to Step 4 and the 1983-86 Camry procedures.

11. On the 1986 Celica GTS and all 1987-90 Celicas and Camrys, turn the crankshaft clockwise until the slot in the forward end of the No. 1 camshaft (front of car) is positioned in the vertical position. Lightly coat a new O-ring with the engine oil and then slide it into position. Align the drilled mark (or cutout) on the coupling with the notch of the shaft housing. Insert the distributor into the cylinder head so that the center of the flange is aligned with that of the bolt hole on the cylinder head.

12. On the MR2 and the Corolla GTS (4A-GE), install a new O-ring. Align the drilled mark on the distributor driven gear with the cavity of the housing. Insert the distributor, aligning the center of the flange with that of the bolt hole on the cylinder head. Tighten the holddown bolts.

13. On the Corolla (4A-F, 4A-FE), install a new O-ring. Align the protrusion on the distributor housing with the groove of the coupling side. On the 4A-FE, aligning the center of the flange with that of the bolt hole on the cylinder head. Tighten the hold-down bolts.

14. On the Camry with the 2VZ-FE, align the cut-out marks of the coupling and the housing and then insert the distributor so that the line on the housing and the cut-out on the distributor attachment cap are aligned. Tighten the hold-down bolts.

15. On all vehicles, connect the spark plug wires and then check the ignition timing.

## Alternator

### PRECAUTIONS

- Always observe proper polarity of the battery connections; be especially careful when jump starting the car.
- Never ground or short out any alternator or regulator terminals.
- Never operate the alternator with any of its or the battery's leads disconnected.
- Always remove the battery or disconnect its output lead while charging it.
- Always disconnect the ground cable when replacing any electrical components.
- Never subject the alternator to excessive heat or dampness if the engine is being steam cleaned.
- Never use arc welding equipment with the alternator connected.

### REMOVAL & INSTALLATION

**NOTE: On some vehicles, the alternator is mounted very low on the engine. On these vehicles it may be necessary to remove the gravel shield and work from underneath the vehicle in order to gain access to the alternator.**

1. Disconnect the negative battery cable.
2. Remove the air cleaner, if necessary, to gain access to the alternator.
3. Unfasten the bolts which attach the adjusting link to the alternator. Remove the alternator drive belt.

**NOTE: On the 2VZ-FE, remove the No. 2 right side mounting stay.**

4. Unfasten and tag the alternator

attaching bolt and then withdraw the alternator from its bracket.

5. Installation is the reverse of the removal procedure. After installing the alternator, adjust the belt tension.

## BELT TENSION ADJUSTMENT

Inspection and adjustment to the alternator drive belt should be performed every 3000 miles or if the alternator has been removed.

1. Inspect the drive belt to see that it is not cracked or worn. Be sure that its surfaces are free of grease or oil.
2. Push down on the belt halfway between the fan and the alternator pulleys (or crankshaft pulley) with thumb pressure. Belt deflection should be 3/8–1/2 in.
3. If the belt tension requires adjustment, loosen the adjusting link bolt and move the alternator until the proper belt tension is obtained.
4. Do not over-tighten the belt, as damage to the alternator bearings could result. Tighten the adjusting link bolt.

# Voltage Regulator

## REMOVAL & INSTALLATION

### External Regulator Only

1. Disconnect the negative battery cable.
2. Disconnect the wiring harness connector from the regulator.
3. Remove the regulator securing bolts. Remove the regulator, complete with its condenser.
4. Installation is the reverse of the removal procedure.

## VOLTAGE ADJUSTMENT

### External Regulator Only

1. Connect a voltmeter to the battery terminals.
2. Start the engine and gradually increase its speed to about 1500 rpm.
3. At this speed, voltage reading should fall within specification.
4. If the voltage does not fall within the specifications, remove the cover

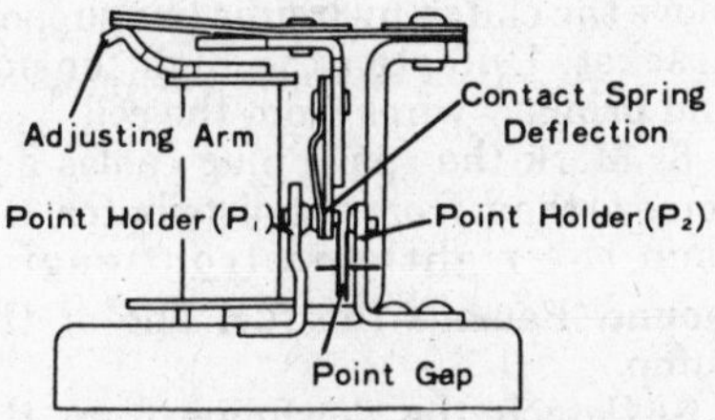


Field relay components

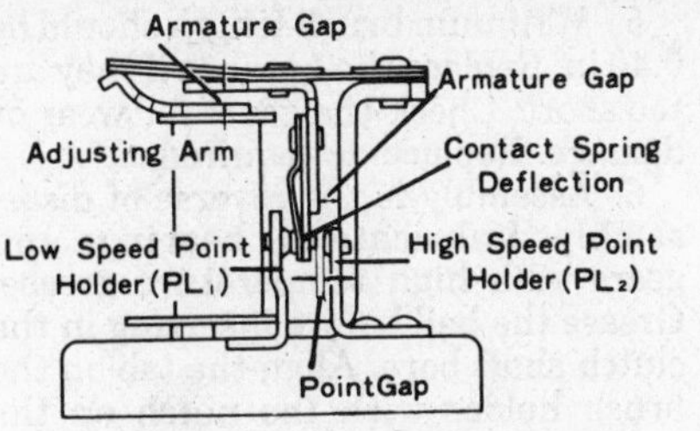


Voltage regulator components

from the regulator and adjust it by bending the adjusting arm.

5. Repeat Steps 2 and 3. If the voltage cannot be brought to specifications, proceed with the mechanical adjustments.

## MECHANICAL ADJUSTMENTS

### External Regulator Only

**NOTE: Perform the proceeding voltage adjustment before beginning the mechanical adjustments.**

### FIELD RELAY

1. Remove the cover from the regulator assembly.
2. Use a feeler gauge to check the amount that the contact spring is deflected while the armature is being depressed.
3. If the measurement is not within specifications, adjust the regulator by bending point holder **P**.
4. Check the point gap with a feeler gauge against specifications.
5. Adjust the point gap, as required, by bending the point holder $P_1$.
6. Clean off the points with emery cloth if they are dirty and wash them with solvent.

### VOLTAGE REGULATOR

1. Use a feeler gauge to measure the air (armature) gap. If it is not within the specifications, adjust it by bending the low speed point holder.
2. Check the point gap with a feeler gauge. If it is not within specifications, adjust it by bending the high speed point holder. Clean the points with emery cloth and wash them off with solvent.
3. Check the amount of contact spring deflection while depressing the armature. The specification should be the same as that for the contact spring on the field relay. If the amount of deflection is not within specification, replace, do not adjust, the voltage regulator.

If the voltage cannot be brought within specifications after regulator replacement, the alternator is probably defective and should be replaced.

**NOTE: On all vehicles with the IC-type regulator there are no adjustments necessary. If found to be defective, it must be replaced.**

# Internal (IC) Regulator

The IC regulator is mounted on the alternator housing, is transistorized, and is nonadjustable.

## REMOVAL & INSTALLATION

1. Disconnect the negative battery cable.
2. Remove the end cover of the regulator.
3. Remove the 3 screws that go through the terminals.
4. Remove the (2) top mounting screws that mount the regulator to the alternator. Remove the regulator.
5. To install the new IC regulator. Place the regulator in position on the alternator. Install and secure the (2) top mounting screws. Install the (3) terminal screws. Install the end cover.
6. Reconnect the battery ground cable.

# Starter

## REMOVAL & INSTALLATION

1. Disconnect the negative battery cable. Disconnect the cable which runs from the starter to the battery, at the battery end.
2. Remove the air cleaner assembly, if necessary, to gain access to the starter.
3. On some vehicles with automatic transmissions, it may be necessary to disconnect the throttle linkage connecting rod or the transmission oil filler tube.
4. On the 3S-GE, disconnect the exhaust pipe at the manifold. On the 2VZ-FE, remove the ignitor bracket.
5. Disconnect all of the wiring at the starter. Remove the starter retaining bolts. Remove the starter from the vehicle..
6. Installation is the reverse of the removal procedure.

## STARTER DRIVE REPLACEMENT

### Direct Drive Starter

1. Remove the starter from the engine.
2. Remove the solenoid from the starter.
3. Remove the thru-bolts and take off the end plate.
4. Slide the armature shaft far enough out to disengage the clutch forks.

5. Remove the retaining clip and washer from the shaft.
6. Slide the starter drive assembly from the shaft.
7. Install in reverse of removal. Always use a new retaining clip.

#### Reduction Gear Starter

1. Remove the starter from the vehicle. Disconnect the solenoid lead.
2. Loosen the two bolts on the starter housing and separate the field frame from the solenoid. Remove the O-ring and felt dust seal.
3. Remove the two screws and separate the starter drive from the solenoid. Withdraw the clutch and gears. Remove the ball from the clutch shaft bore or solenoid.
4. Using the proper tool, separate the brush and brush spring and remove the brush from the brush holder.

### STARTER SOLENOID & BRUSH REPLACEMENT

#### Direct Drive Starter

1. Remove the starter from the vehicle. Remove the field coil lead from the solenoid terminal.
2. Unfasten the solenoid retaining screws. Remove the solenoid by tilting it upward and withdrawing it.
3. Remove the end frame bearing cover screws and remove the cover. Remove the thru-bolts. Remove the commutator endframe.
4. Withdraw the brushes from their holder if they are to be replaced. Minimum brush length should be 0.40 in. Replace the brushes with new ones if required.
5. Dress the new brushes with emery cloth so that they will make proper contact.
6. Use a spring scale to check the brush spring tension. Replace the springs if they do not meet specifications.
7. Assembly is the reverse of disassembly. Pack the end bearing cover with multipurpose grease before installing it.

#### Reduction Gear Starter

1. Remove the starter from the vehicle. Disconnect the solenoid lead.
2. Loosen the two bolts on the starter housing and separate the field frame from the solenoid. Remove the O-ring and felt dust seal.
3. Remove the two screws and separate the starter drive from the solenoid. Withdraw the clutch and gears. Remove the ball from the clutch shaft bore or solenoid.
4. Using the proper tool, separate the brush and brush spring and remove the brush from the brush holder.
5. Minimum brush length should be 0.40 in. Replace the brushes if they are too short. Check the gears for wear or damage. Replace as required.
6. Assembly is the reverse of disassembly. Lubricate all bearings and gears with high temperature grease. Grease the ball before inserting in the clutch shaft bore. Align the tab on the brush holder with the notch on the field frame. Check the positive (+) brush leads to see that they are not grounded. Align the mark on the solenoid with the bolt anchors on the field frame.

# ENGINE MECHANICAL

## Engine

### REMOVAL & INSTALLATION

#### 1983 22R Engines

1. Disconnect the battery cables. Matchmark and remove the hood. Drain the coolant. Remove the air cleaner assembly.
2. Disconnect the accelerator linkage from the carburetor. Disconnect the transmission cable from the carburetor if equipped with automatic transmission.
3. Mark and disconnect all wiring and hoses from the engine. Label each item so that it may be reattached correctly during assembly.
4. Remove the radiator grille. Remove the hood lock brace, radiator upper baffle, and the hood lock. Remove the radiator and the fan shroud.
5. If the vehicle is equipped with air conditioning, properly discharge the refrigerant. Remove the air conditioning condenser from the vehicle.
6. Loosen the air conditioning compressor mounting bolts, remove the drive belt, remove the mounting bolt, and lay the compressor aside.
7. If the vehicle is equipped with power steering, loosen the idler pulley bolts. Remove the power steering pump drive belt. Remove the power steering pump mounting bolts. Move the pump out of the way. It is not necessary to disconnect the hydraulic lines from the pump.
8. Disconnect the upper side of the engine shock absorber from the left engine mount. Remove the engine mount bolts from each side of the engine.
9. Remove the console to gain access to the shift lever on vehicles with manual transmissions. Remove the shift lever.
10. Raise and support the vehicle safely. Remove the engine undercover. Drain the engine oil.
11. Remove the exhaust pipe clamp from the transmission housing, disconnect the exhaust pipe from the manifold.
12. On vehicles equipped with manual transmission, remove the clutch release cylinder. Disconnect the speedometer cable from the transmission.
13. On vehicles equipped with automatic transmission, disconnect the shift linkage from the shift lever.
14. Disconnect the wiring from the back-up light switch, neutral start switch, overdrive solenoid, oil pressure sending unit and starter assembly.
15. Place a jack under the transmission, with a block of wood between the jack and the transmission. Raise the jack just enough to support the transmission. Remove the transmission crossmember. Remove the driveshaft.
16. Attach the engine lifting equipment to the engine. Carefully lift the engine and the transmission assembly out of the vehicle.
17. Installation is the reverse of the removal procedure.

#### 1984-85 22R Engines

1. Drain the cooling system, transmission, and engine oil.
2. Disconnect the battery-to-starter cable at the positive battery terminal.
3. Scribe marks on the hood and its hinges. Remove the hood supports from the body. Remove the hood. Do not remove the supports from the hood.
4. Unfasten the headlight bezel retaining screws and remove the bezels. Remove the radiator grille attachment screws and remove the grille.
5. Remove the fan shroud, the hood lock base and the base support. Remove the wiring from the coolant temperature and oil pressure sending units. Remove the air cleaner assembly.
6. Unfasten the accelerator torque rod from the carburetor. On vehicles equipped with automatic transmissions, remove the transmission linkage.
7. Remove the emission control system hoses and wiring as necessary. Remove the clutch hydraulic line support bracket. Unfasten the high tension and primary wires from the coil.
8. Mark the spark plug cables and remove them from the distributor. Detach the righthand front engine mount. Remove the fuel line at the pump.
9. Detach the downpipe from the exhaust manifold. Detach the left

hand front engine mount. Disconnect all of the wiring harness multiconnectors.

10. If the vehicle is equipped with manual transmission remove the center console if so equipped. Remove the shift lever boot.

11. Unfasten the 4 shift lever cap retaining screws. Remove the cap and withdraw the shift lever assembly.

12. If equipped with automatic transmission, remove the transmission selector linkages. On vehicles equipped with a floor mounted selector, disconnect the control rod from the transmission. On vehicles equipped with column mounted gear selector, remove the shifter rod.

13. Disconnect the neutral safety switch wiring connector. Raise and support the vehicle safely.

14. Remove the retaining screws and remove the parking brake equalizer support bracket. Disconnect the cable which runs between the lever and the equalizer.

15. Remove the speedometer cable from the transmission. Disconnect the back-up light wiring. Remove the driveshaft.

16. Detach the clutch release cylinder assembly, complete with hydraulic lines. Do not disconnect the lines. Unbolt the rear support member mounting insulators.

17. Support the transmission and detach the rear support member retaining bolts. Remove the support member.

18. Install lifting hooks on the engine lifting brackets. Attach a suitable hoist to the engine. Remove the jack from under the transmission.

19. Raise the engine and move it toward the front of the vehicle. Use care to avoid damaging the components which remain on the vehicle.

20. Installation is the reverse of the removal procedure.

### 1983-85 22R-E Engines

1. Disconnect the battery cables. Matckmark and remove the hood. Drain the coolant. Remove the air cleaner assembly.

2. Mark and disconnect all wiring and hoses from the engine. Label each item so that it may be reattached correctly during assembly.

3. Remove the radiator grille. Remove the hood lock brace, radiator upper baffle, and the hood lock. Remove the radiator and the fan shroud.

4. Disconnect the automatic transmission actuator cable, accelerator cable and throttle cable from the bracket on the side of the EFI intake chamber.

5. Tag and disconnect the PCV hoses, the brake booster hose, the cruise control actuator hose, the air control valve hose and the air control valve. Remove the EGR vacuum modulator and bracket.

6. Tag and disconnect the remaining emission control hoses as necessary, including the air valve hoses from the intake chamber and throttle body, the water bypass hoses from the throttle body, the air control valve hose to the actuator and the pressure regulator hose from the intake chamber.

7. Tag and disconnect the cold start injector pipe and the cold start injector, the throttle position sensor wire and the air valve wire.

8. Remove the bolt holding the EGR valve to the intake chamber. Disconnect the chamber from the stay, then remove the chamber from the intake manifold with the throttle body attached.

9. Tag and disconnect the water temperature sender, overdrive thermoswitch, start injection time, temperature sensor and injection wires.

10. Remove the 2 bolts from the top and bottom of the steering universal, and remove the sliding yoke.

11. Disconnect the tie rod ends. Disconnect the pressure line mounting bolts from the front crossmember.

12. Without disconnecting the oil pipe, remove the mounting bolts to the rack and pinion assembly and carefully suspend it from the front crossmember without stretching the fluid hoses.

13. If the vehicle is equipped with power steering, loosen the idler pulley bolts. Remove the power steering pump drive belt. Remove the power steering pump mounting bolts. Move the pump out of the way. It is not necessary to disconnect the hydraulic lines from the pump.

14. Disconnect the upper side of the engine shock absorber from the left engine mount. Remove the engine mount bolts from each side of the engine.

15. Remove the console to gain access to the shift lever. Remove the shift lever.

16. Raise and support the vehicle safely. Remove the engine undercover. Drain the engine oil.

17. Remove the exhaust pipe clamp from the transmission housing, disconnect the exhaust pipe from the manifold, and allow the pipe to hang downward.

18. On vehicles equipped with manual transmission, remove the clutch release cylinder. Disconnect the speedometer cable from the transmission.

19. On vehicles equipped with automatic transmission, disconnect the shift linkage from the shift lever.

20. Disconnect the wiring from the back-up light switch, neutral start switch, overdrive solenoid, oil pressure sending unit and starter assembly.

21. Place a jack under the transmission, with a block of wood between the jack and the transmission. Raise the jack just enough to support the transmission. Remove the transmission crossmember. Remove the driveshaft.

22. Attach the engine lifting equipment to the engine. Carefully lift the engine and the transmission assembly out of the vehicle.

23. Installation is the reverse of the removal procedure.

### 1983-86 2S-E Engines

1. Disconnect and remove the battery. Drain the coolant system. Remove the hood.

2. Disconnect and tag all cables, electrical wires and vacuum lines attached to various engine parts.

3. Remove the cruise control actuator and bracket. Disconnect the radiator and heater hoses. Disconnect the automatic transmission cooler lines. Remove the radiator.

4. Remove the air cleaner assembly and air flow meter. Disconnect all wiring and linkage at the transmission.

5. Pull out the fuel injection system wiring harness. Secure the assembly to the right side of fender apron.

6. Disconnect and plug the fuel lines at the fuel filter and return pipes. Unbolt the air conditioning compressor and position it out of the way.

7. Disconnect the speedometer cable at the transmission. Remove the clutch release cylinder without disconnecting the fluid line.

8. Raise and support the vehicle safely. Drain the engine oil. Drain the transaxle fluid. Unbolt both halfshafts.

9. Unbolt the power steering pump and position it out of the way. Disconnect the exhaust pipe from the manifold. Disconnect the front and rear engine mounts at the frame member.

10. Attach an engine crane at the lifting eyes. Take up the engine weight with the crane and remove the right and left side engine mounts.

11. Carefully, remove the engine and transaxle assembly from the vehicle.

12. Installation is the reverse of the removal procedure.

### 2VZ-FE Engines

1. Disconnect the negative battery cable and remove the battery. Drain the coolant and remove the hood. Its always a good idea to scribe matchmarks around the hood hinges prior to removal.

2. Remove the ignition coil, ignitor and bracket assembly.

3. Remove the radiator. Remove the radiator reservoir tank.

4. On models with automatic transmissions, disconnect the throttle cable from the throttle body.
5. Remove the cruise control actuator and vacuum pump.
6. Remove the air cleaner assembly.
7. On models with manual transmissions, remove the clutch release cylinder and position it out of the way with the hydraulic line still attached.
8. Disconnect the speedometer and transaxle control cables.
9. Remove the alternator and the belt adjusting bar.
10. Remove the A/C compressor and position it out of the way without disconnecting the refrigerant lines.
11. Disconnect the 2 water by-pass hoses and fuel lines. Tag and disconnect the brake booster, A/C control valve and charcoal canister vacuum hoses.
12. Tag and dsiconnect any additional wires and lines which may interfere with engine removal.
13. Raise the front of the vehicle and support it with safety stands. Remove the engine undercovers and drain the oil.
14. Remove the lower suspension crossmember and remove the halfshafts.
15. Remove the power steering pump and position it out of the way without disconnecting the hydraulic lines.
16. Remove the front exhaust pipe.
17. Remove the engine mounting center member (8 bolts and 2 nuts). Remove the front, center and rear engine mount insulator and bracket assemblies.
18. Lower the vehicle. Remove the glove box and then tag and disconnect the 3 TCCS ECU connectors, the circuit opening, cowl wire and instrument wire connectors. Pull the main engine harness out through the fire wall.
19. Remove the power steering reservoir tank and position it out of the way without disconnecting the hydraulic lines.
20. Remove the 2 right side engine mounting stays. Remove the left side engine mounting stay.
21. Attach an engine hoist chain to the 2 engine hangers. On models with ABS, remove the clamp bolts for the power steering oil cooler pipes. Remove the right and left engine mount insulators and their brackets. Slowly remove the engine/transaxle assembly as a unit.
22. Installation is in the reverse order of removal.

### 1983-86 3A and 3A-C Engines

1. Disconnect the negative battery cable. Remove the hood. Remove the air cleaner asssembly. Drain the radiator.
2. Cover both halfshaft boots with a shop towel. Remove the solenoid valve connector, water temperature switch connector, and the electric fan connector.
3. Remove the exhaust support plate bolts, and the exhaust pipe.
4. Remove the top radiator support. Remove the top and bottom radiator hoses. Disconnect and plug the transmission fluid lines, as required. Remove the radiator with the fan assembly.
5. Remove the windshield washer tank. Remove the heater hoses. Remove and plug the lines to the fuel pump.
6. Remove the accelerator cable, choke cable, and the ground strap. Remove the brake booster vacuum line. Remove the coil wire and unplug the alternator.
7. Remove the clutch release cable. Remove the wires on the starter. Remove the temperature sending and oil pressure switch connectors. Remove the battery ground strap from the block.
8. Raise and support the vehicle safely. Remove the engine mounting bolts. Remove the engine shock absorbers. As required, remove the starter assembly.
9. Support the differential assembly with a jack. Remove the transaxle mounting bolts.
10. On vehicles equipped with automatic transmission it will be necessary to remove the torque converter retaining bolts.
11. The grille may be removed if necessary to give better leverage when removing the engine.
12. Using the proper engine lifting equipment carefully remove the engine from the vehicle. If equipped with automatic transaxle, while the engine is suspended from the hoist, pull it forward about 2 in. Insert a pry bar in this opening and gently separate the torque converter from the engine.
13. Tie the transaxle housing to the cowl to keep support on the transaxle.
14. Installation is the reverse of the removal procedure.

### 1987-88 3A-C Engines

1. Disconnect and remove the battery. Remove the battery carrier. Remove the hood.
2. Drain the coolant. Disconnect and plug the transaxle fluid lines, if equipped. Remove the radiator. Remove the washer tank. Disconnect the heater hoses. If equipped with air condition remove the condenser fan assembly.
3. Remove the power steering pump and position it to the side. Remove the air conditioning compressor and position it to the side.
4. Disconnect the engine ground strap, the oxygen sensor wire, the distributor connector, the ground strap from the dash panel, the oil pressure switch wire, the coolant fan wire, the water temperature gauge wire, the back up light switch and neutral safety switch wires.
5. Disconnect the accelerator cable. If the vehicle is equipped with automatic transaxle disconnect the accelerator cable.
6. Disconnect and plug the fuel line hoses. Disconnect the vacuum hose for the VSV idle-up. Disconnect the brake booster hose.
7. Disconnect the air suction filter from the cylinder block. Remove the transaxle upper mount bolts.
8. Raise and support the vehicle safely. Remove the front exhaust pipe. Remove the oil cooler lines, if equipped.
9. If equipped, disconnect the clutch release cable. Remove the stiffner plates. Disconnect the engine mounting absorber.
10. Remove the engine mount bolts. Remove the torque converter cover. Remove the torque converter bolts.
11. Properly position a lifting device under the transaxle assembly. Remove the lower transaxle retaining bolts. As required, remove the starter.
12. Properly support the engine/transaxle assembly. Attach the engine chain hoist to the engine lifting hooks. Carefully remove the engine from the vehicle.
13. Installation is the reverse of the removal procedure.

### 1987-90 3E Engines

1. Disconnect and remove the battery. Remove the hood. Remove the engine under covers.
2. Drain the coolant. Disconnect and plug the transaxle fluid lines, if equipped. Remove the radiator. Remove the washer tank. Disconnect the heater hoses.
3. If the vehicle is equipped with cruise control, disconnect and remove the actuator assembly. Disconnect the accelerator cable. If the vehicle is equipped with automatic transaxle disconnect the accelerator cable.
4. Disconnect and plug the fuel line hoses. Remove the charcoal canister assembly. Disconnect the brake booster hose.
5. Disconnect the speedometer cable from the transaxle. Disconnect the transaxle control cables from their mounting.
6. Remove the clutch release cylinder. Remove the selecting bell crank.
7. Disconnect the engine ground

strap, the oxygen sensor wire, the oil pressure switch wire, the coolant fan wire, the water temperature gauge wire, the back up light switch and neutral safety switch wires.

8. Disconnect the wiring harness from the intake manifold. Remove the intake manifold ground strap. Disconnect the CMH connector, the alternator electrical connector and the starter electrical wires. Remove the VSV.

9. Remove the power steering pump and position it to the side. Remove the air conditioning compressor and position it to the side.

10. Disconnect the exhaust pipe at the manifold. Remove the halfshafts.

11. Properly support the engine/transaxle assembly. Attach the engine chain hoist to the engine lifting hooks.

12. Remove the rear mounting thru-bolt. Remove the rear mounting assembly. Remove the front mounting thru-bolt. Remove the front mounting assembly.

13. Remove the right and left side mounting bolts and brackets. Carefully lift the engine assembly out of the vehicle.

14. Installation is the reverse of the removal procedure.

### *1987-90 3S-FE Engines*

#### CAMRY – 2WD

1. Disconnect the negative battery cable. Remove the hood. Drain the engine coolant. Tag and disconnect all vacuum hoses, electrical wires and cables that are necessary to remove the engine.

2. Remove the radiator. If the vehicle is equipped with automatic transaxle, disconnect the throttle cable and bracket from the throttle body.

3. Disconnect the accelerator cable from the throttle body. Remove the cruise control actuator and bracket, if equipped.

4. Disconnect the ground wire from the alternator upper bracket. Remove the air cleaner assembly, air flow meter and air cleaner hose.

5. Remove the igniter. Remove the heater hoses. Disconnect and plug the fuel lines. Disconnect the speedometer cable.

6. If equipped with manual transaxle, remove the clutch release cylinder and tube bracket. Do not disconnect the tube from the bracket. Disconnect the transaxle control cable.

7. Remove the air conditioning compressor and position it to the side. Do not disconnect the lines. Remove the power steering pump and position it to the side. Do not disconnect the lines.

8. Raise and support the vehicle safely. Drain the engine oil. Remove the engine under covers.

9. Remove the suspension lower crossmember. Remove the halfshafts.

10. Disconnect the exhaust pipe from the catalytic converter. Disconnect the engine mounting center crossmember member.

11. Lower the vehicle. Disconnect the TCCS and the ECU electrical connectors.

12. Properly attach the lifting device to the engine. Raise the engine slightly and remove the engine retaining brackets and bolts.

13. Carefully remove the engine/transaxle assembly from the vehicle. Be carefull not to hit the power steering gear housing or the neutral safety switch.

14. Installation is the reverse of the removal procedure.

#### CAMRY ALL-TRAC – 4WD

1. Disconnect the negative battery cable and drain the engine coolant. Remove the hood.

2. Disconnect the accelerator cable from the throttle body. Remove the radiator.

3. Disconnect the heater hoses.

4. Disconnect the inlet hose at the fuel filter. Disconnect the return hose at the fuel return pipe.

5. Disconnect and remove the cruise control actuator.

6. Remove the air cleaner assembly.

7. Remove the clutch slave cylinder and hose bracket without disconnecting the hydraulic line. Position the assembly out of the way. Disconnect the speedometer cable and the transaxle control cables.

8. Disconnect and remove the A/C compressor with the refrigerant lines still attached; position it out of the way.

9. Tag and disconnect all wires, connecters and vacuum lines in the way of engine removal.

10. Raise the front of the vehicle and support it with safety stands. Drain the engine oil and remove the engine undercovers.

11. Remove the lower suspension crossmember and the halfshafts. Disconnect and remove the driveshaft.

12. Remove the power steering pump with the hydraulic lines still attached and position it out of the way. Remove the front exhaust pipe.

13. Remove the engine mounting center member and the stabilizer bar. Lower the car.

14. Disconnect the TCCS ECU connectors and pull them out through the firewall. Remove the power steering pump reservoir tank.

15. Attach an engine lifting device to the eyelets on the engine. Remove the right side engine mount stay and then remove the insulator and bracket. Remove the left side engine mount insulator and bracket. Remove the engine and transaxle as an assembly. Be carefull not to hit the power steering gear housing or the neutral safety switch.

16. Installation is the reverse of the removal procedure. Please observe the following torques on installation:

a. Right and left engine mount bracket bolts and nuts – 38 ft. lbs. (52 Nm)

b. Right side engine mount stay bolt and nut – 54 ft. lbs. (73 Nm)

c. Engine mounting center member: member-to-body bolts – 29 ft. lbs. (39 Nm); member-to-other bolts – 38 ft. lbs. (52 Nm)

d. Lower crossmember bolts: outer – 153 ft. lbs. (206 Nm); inner – 29 ft. lbs. (39 Nm).

#### CELICA

1. Disconnect the battery cables. Remove the battery. Remove the hood. Drain the engine coolant. Tag and disconnect all vacuum hoses, electrical wires and cables that are necessary to remove the engine.

2. Disconnect the ignition coil connector and high tension wire from the coil. Remove the suspension upper brace.

3. Remove the radiator. Remove the reservoir tank. If the vehicle is equipped with automatic transaxle, disconnect the throttle cable and bracket from the throttle body.

4. Disconnect the accelerator cable from the throttle body. Remove the cruise control actuator and bracket, if equipped. Remove the oxygen sensor.

5. Remove the air cleaner assembly, air flow meter and air cleaner hose. Remove the air cleaner bracket.

6. Remove the igniter. Remove the heater hoses. Disconnect and plug the fuel lines. Disconnect the speedometer cable.

7. If equipped with manual transaxle, remove the clutch release cylinder and tube bracket. Do not disconnect the tube from the bracket. Disconnect the transaxle control cable.

8. Remove the air conditioning compressor and position it to the side. Do not disconnect the lines.

9. Raise and support the vehicle safely. Drain the engine oil. Drain the transaxle fluid. Remove the right under cover.

10. Remove the power steering pump and position it to the side. Do not disconnect the lines.Remove the suspension lower crossmember. Remove the halfshafts.

11. Disconnect the exhaust pipe from the catalytic converter. Remove the engine rear mounting bolt. Lower the vehicle. Disconnect the TCCS and the ECU electrical connectors. Remove

the power steering pump reservoir mounting bolts.

12. Properly attach the lifting device to the engine. Raise the engine slightly and remove the engine retaining brackets and bolts.

13. Carefully remove the engine/transaxle assembly from the vehicle. Be carefull not to hit the power steering gear housing or the neutral safety switch.

14. Installation is the reverse of the removal procedure.

### 1986-90 3S-GE Engines

1. Disconnect and remove the battery. Matchmark and remove the hood. Drain the cooling system.

2. Tag and disconnect the connector high tension lead at the ignition coil. Remove the 4 bolts and 2 nuts securing the upper suspension brace. Remove the brace.

3. On vehicles equipped with automatic transmission, disconnect the throttle cable and its bracket at the throttle body.

4. Disconnect the throttle cable from the throttle body on vehicles equipped with manual transmission.

5. Remove the overflow tank. Remove the cruise control actuator and its bracket. Remove the oxygen sensor.

6. Tag and disconnect the cooling fan leads at the radiator. Disconnect the heater hoses. Disconnect the automatic transmission fluid cooler lines, if equipped. Remove the radiator and the 2 supports.

7. Remove the air cleaner assembly and bracket. Remove the igniter.

8. Tag, disconnect and plug the fuel hoses at the filter and fuel return pipe. Disconnect the speedometer cable.

9. Disconnect the transaxle control cable at the shift and selector levers on vehicles equipped with manual transaxle and then remove it from the bracket. On vehicles equipped with automatic transaxle, disconnect the cable at the swivel and at the bracket and then remove it.

10. Unbolt the air conditioning compressor and position it out of the way with the refrigerant lines still attached.

11. Tag and disconnect any remaining wires or electrical leads. Tag and disconnect any remaining vacuum hoses.

12. Raise and support the vehicle safely. Drain the engine oil.

13. Remove the right side engine under cover. Remove the lower suspension crossmember. Remove both halfshaft assemblies.

14. Unbolt the power steering pump. Disconnect the 2 vacuum hoses and remove the drive belt. Position the pump out of the way with the hydraulic lines still connected to it.

15. Disconnect the exhaust pipe at the manifold. Remove the rear engine mount bolt. Lower the vehicle and then remove the front engine mount bolts. Remove the power steering pump reservoir and position it out of the way.

16. Attach an engine hoist to the lifting hooks. Take up the engine's weight with the hoist and remove the right and left engine mounts.

17. Slowly and carefully, remove the engine and transaxle assembly. Be careful not to hit the power steering gear housing or the neutral safety switch.

18. Installation is the reverse of the removal procedure.

### 1988-90 3S-GTE Engines

1. Disconnect the negative battery cable and remove the battery. Drain all coolant from the engine and turbocharger intercooler.

2. Scribe matchmarks around the hinges and remove the hood.

3. Disconnect the accelerator cable at the throttle body. Remove the radiator. Disconnect the heater and intercooler hoses.

4. Disconnect the fuel inlet line at the fuel filter and the return line at the return pipe.

5. Remove the cruise control actuator and bracket. Remove the air cleaner assembly.

6. Remove the clutch release cylinder and bracket without disconnecting the hydraulic line. Wire it out of the way.

7. Disconnect the speedometer and transaxle control cables. Remove the alternator.

8. Remove the A/C compressor without disconnecting the refrigerant lines and position it out of the way.

9. Tag and disconnect any wires, connectors and vacuum lines which might interfere with engine removal.

10. Raise the vehicle and support it with safety stands. Drain the engine oil and remove the undercovers.

11. Remove the lower suspension crossmember. Remove the front halfshafts and the driveshaft.

12. Remove the power steering pump and bracket without disconnecting the hydraulic lines and position it out of the way.

13. Disconnect the front exhaust pipe at the manifold and tailpipe and remove it.

14. Remove the engine mounting center member and lower the vehicle.

15. Unplug the 3 TCCS ECU connectors, remove the 2 screws and pull the connectors out through the firewall. Remove the power steering pump reservoir tank.

16. Attach an engine hoist chain to the lifting brackets on the engine. Remove the 2 bolts holding the right engine mount insulator to the mounting bracket. Remove the 4 bolts holding the left engine mount insulator to the mounting bracket and then lower the engine out of the vehicle.

17. Installation is in the reverse order of removal. Please note the following:

a. Tighten the right and left engine mount bracket bolts to 38 ft. lbs. (52 Nm).

b. When installing the engine mounting center member, tighten the outer bolts to 29 ft. lbs. (39 Nm), tighten the inner bolts to 38 ft. lbs. (52 Nm).

c. Tighten the front exhaust pipe bolts to 46 ft. lbs. (62 Nm).

d. When installing the lower suspension crossmember, tighten the outer bolts to 154 ft. lbs. (208 Nm), tighten the inner bolts to 29 ft. lbs. (39 Nm).

### 1983-86 4A-C Engines
### 1983-87 4A-LC Engines

1. Drain the cooling system, transmission, and engine oil.

2. Disconnect the battery-to-starter cable at the positive battery terminal.

3. Scribe marks on the hood and its hinges. Remove the hood supports from the body. Remove the hood. Do not remove the supports from the hood.

4. Unfasten the headlight bezel retaining screws and remove the bezels. Remove the 5 radiator grille attachment screws and remove the grille.

5. Remove the hood lock assembly after detaching the release cable. Unfasten the nuts from the horn retainers and disconnect the wiring. Remove the horn assembly.

6. Detach both the upper and lower hoses from the radiator. On vehicles equipped with automatic transmission, disconnect the lines from the oil cooler. Remove the radiator.

7. Unfasten the clamps and remove the heater and bypass hoses from the engine. Remove the heater control cable from the water valve.

8. Remove the wiring from the coolant temperature and oil pressure sending units. Remove the air cleaner assembly.

9. Unfasten the accelerator torque rod from the carburetor. On vehicles equipped with automatic transmissions remove the transmission linkage.

10. Remove the emission control system hoses and wiring, as necessary. Remove the clutch hydraulic line support bracket. Unfasten the high tension and primary wires from the coil.

11. Mark the spark plug cables and remove them from the distributor. De-

tach the righthand front engine mount. Remove the fuel line at the pump.

12. Detach the downpipe from the exhaust manifold. Detach the left hand front engine mount. Disconnect all of the wiring harness multiconnectors.

13. On vehicles equipped with manual transmission, remove the shift lever boot and the shift lever cap boot.

14. Unfasten the 4 gear selector cap retaining screws and remove the gasket and withdraw the gear selector lever assembly from the top of the transmission. On 5 speed transmission, the floor console must be removed first.

15. Raise and support the vehicle safely. On vehicles equipped with automatic transmission, disconnect the gear selector control rod.

16. Detach the exhaust pipe support bracket. Disconnect the driveshaft from the rear of the transmission.

17. Unfasten the speedometer cable from the transmission. Disconnect the wiring from the back-up light switch and the neutral safety switch, if equipped.

18. Detach the clutch release cylinder assembly, complete with hydraulic lines. Do not disconnect the lines. Unbolt the rear support member mounting insulators.

19. Support the transmission and detach the rear support member retaining bolts. Remove the support member.

20. Install lifting hooks on the engine lifting brackets. Attach a suitable hoist to the engine. Remove the jack from under the transmission.

21. Raise the engine and move it toward the front of the vehicle. Use care to avoid damaging the components which remain on the vehicle.

22. Installation is the reverse of the removal procedure.

### 1988 4A-LC Engines

1. Remove the battery and hood. Drain the coolant and the oil.

2. Remove the air cleaner hose and air cleaner. Remove the coolant reservoir tank. Remove the radiator and shroud.

3. Disconnect the actuator, accelerator and throttle cables at the carburetor. Disconnect all wires, hoses and lines which might interfere with engine removal.

4. Disconnect the fuel lines at the fuel pump. Disconnect the heater hoses.

5. Remove the power steering pump and A/C compressor and position them out of the way. Do not disconnect the hydraulic or refrigerant lines.

6. Disconnect the speedometer cable at the transaxle. Remove the clutch release cylinder without disconnecting the hydraulic line and position it out of the way.

7. Disconnect the shift control cable and then raise the vehicle and support it with safety stands.

8. Disconnect the exhaust pipe at the manifold. Disconnect the front and rear engine mounts at the center member. Remove the center member.

9. Disconnect the halfshafts at the transaxle and lower the vehicle.

10. Attach an engine hoist chain to the lift brackets on the engine. Remove the right engine mount thru-bolt. Remove the left engine mount and bracket. Lift the engine out of the vehicle.

11. Lower the engine into the vehicle. Align the right engine mount with the bracket and install the thru-bolt. Install the left engine mount bracket to the transaxle and then install the engine mount into the bracket. Align the mount with the bracket on the body and install the thru-bolt.

12. Installation is in the reverse order of removal. Please note the following:

a. Tighten the engine mount center member to 29 ft. lbs. (39 Nm).

b. Tighten the front and rear engine mounts to 29 ft. lbs. (39 Nm).

c. Tighten the exhaust pipe-to-manifold bolts to 46 ft. lbs. (62 Nm).

d. Refill the engine and transaxle with coolant and lubricant and road test the vehicle.

### 1988-90 4A-F Engines

1. Remove the battery. Scribe matchmarks around the hood hinges and then remove the hood. Remove the engine undercovers.

2. Drain the engine coolant and oil. Drain the gear oil from the transaxle.

3. Remove the air cleaner along with its hose.

4. Remove the coolant reservoir tank. Remove the radiator and cooling fan.

5. Disconnect the accelerator and throttle cables at the carburetor on models with automatic transmissions.

6. Disconnect the No. 2 junction block, the ground strap connector and the ground strap. Disconnect the vacuum hoses at the brake booster, power steering pump, A/C compressor and EBCV.

7. Disconnect the fuel lines at the fuel pump. Disconnect the heater hoses at the water inlet housing.

8. Disconnect the power steering pump and lay it aside with the hydraulic lines still attached. Do the same with the A/C compressor.

9. Disconnect the speedometer cable. On models with a manual transmission, remove the clutch release cylinder and position it out of the way with the hydraulic lines still attached.

10. Disconnect the shift control cables and then raise the front of the vehicle. Support it with safety stands.

11. Remove the 2 nuts from the flange and then disconnect the exhaust pipe at the manifold. Disconnect the halfshafts at the transaxle.

12. Remove the 2 hole covers and then remove the front, center and rear engine mounts from the center member. Remove the 5 bolts and insulators and remove the center member.

13. Attach an engine hoist chain to the lifting brackets on the engine and then remove the 3 bolts and mounting stay. Remove the bolt, 2 nuts and the thru-bolt and pull out the right side engine mount. Remove the 2 bolts and the left mounting stay. Remove the 3 bolts and disconnect the left engine mount bracket from the transaxle. Lift the engine/transaxle assembly out of the vehicle.

14. Installation is in the reverse order of removal. Please note the following:

a. Tighten the right engine mount insulator bolt to 47 ft. lbs. (64 Nm); tighten the nut to 38 ft. lbs. (52 Nm). Align the insulator with the bracket on the body and tighten the bolt to 64 ft. lbs. (87 Nm).

b. Align the left engine mount insulator bracket with the transaxle bracket and tighten the bolt to 35 ft. lbs. (48 Nm).

c. Install the right mounting stay and tighten the 3 bolts to 31 ft. lbs. (42 Nm). Install the left stay and tighten the 2 bolts to 15 ft. lbs. (21 Nm).

d. Install the engine center member and tighten the 5 bolts to 45 ft. lbs. (61 Nm).

e. Install the front and rear engine mounts and bolts. Align the bolts holes in the brackets with the center member and tighten the front mount bolts to 35 ft. lbs. (48 Nm); tighten the center and rear mounts to 38 ft. lbs. (52 Nm). Install the 2 hole covers and tighten the rear mounting bolt to 58 ft. lbs. (78 Nm).

### 1989-90 4A-FE Engines

1. Remove the battery. Scribe matchmarks around the hood hinges and then remove the hood. Remove the engine undercovers.

2. Drain the engine coolant and oil. Drain the gear oil from the transaxle.

3. Remove the air cleaner along with its hose.

4. Remove the coolant reservoir tank. Remove the radiator and cooling fan.

5. Disconnect the accelerator and throttle cables at the bracket on models with automatic transmissions.
6. Remove the cruise control actuator.
7. Disconnect the No. 2 junction block, the ground strap connector and the ground strap.
8. Disconnect the check, vacuum sensor and $O_2$ sensor connectors. Disconnect the A/C wire.
9. Disconnect the vacuum hoses at the brake booster, power steering pump, A/C compressor, vacuum sensor, charcoal canister and vacuum switch.
10. Disconnect the fuel lines at the fuel pump. Disconnect the heater hoses at the water inlet housing.
11. Disconnect the power steering pump and lay it aside with the hydraulic lines still attached. Do the same with the A/C compressor.
12. Disconnect the speedometer cable. On models with a manual transmission, remove the clutch release cylinder and position it out of the way with the hydraulic lines still attached.
13. Disconnect the shift control cables and then raise the front of the vehicle. Support it with safety stands.
14. Disconnect the oil cooler lines and the exhaust pipe (at the manifold).
15. Disconnect the halfshafts and the driveshaft at the transaxle.
16. Attach an engine hoist chain to the lifting brackets on the engine and raise it just enough to relieve pressure on the mounts.
17. Pull out the hole covers and remove the 5 bolts on the front and rear engine mounts. Remove the mounts from the center crossmember. Remove the 4 center crossmember bolts and the 8 bolts from the sub-frame. remove the front and rear mounting bolts and then remove the member.
18. Remove the engine mount stay. and then remove the mount. Remove the air cleaner bracket. Disconnect the left side mounting bracket from the transaxle bracket and then lift out the engine/transaxle assembly slowly and carefully.
19. Installation is in the reverse order of removal. Please note the following:

a. Tighten the right engine mount insulator bolt and nuts to 38 ft. lbs. (52 Nm). Align the insulator with the bracket on the body and tighten the bolt to 64 ft. lbs. (87 Nm).
b. Align the left engine mount insulator bracket with the transaxle bracket and tighten the bolt to 35 ft. lbs. (48 Nm).
c. Install the left stay and tighten the 2 bolts to 15 ft. lbs. (21 Nm).
d. Install the engine center member and tighten the 5 bolts to 45 ft. lbs. (61 Nm).
e. Install the front and rear engine mounts and bolts. Align the bolts holes in the brackets with the center member and tighten the front mount bolts to 35 ft. lbs. (48 Nm); tighten the center and rear mounts to 42 ft. lbs. (57 Nm). Install the 8 sub-frame bolts and tighten the lower arm bolt to 152 ft. lbs. (206 Nm) and the rear bolt to 94 ft. lbs. (127 Nm).

### *1984-86 4A-GE Engines*

#### COROLLA

1. Disconnect the battery cables. Remove the battery. Remove the hood and the engine cover.
2. Remove the No. 2 air cleaner hose. Disconnect the actuator and accelerator cables from their bracket on the cylinder head.
3. Remove the center console, lift up the shift boot and then remove the shifter.
4. Remove the air cleaner assembly. Drain the engine oil. Drain the transmission fluid.
5. Drain the radiator. Remove the radiator hoses. Remove the radiator and shroud.
6. Remove the power steering pump along with its bracket. Loosen the water pump pulley retaining nuts, remove the drive belt adjusting bolt. Remove the drive belt.
7. Remove the retaining nuts and then remove the fluid coupling with the fan and the water pump pulley.
8. Remove the air conditioning compressor and bracket. Position the assembly out of the way. Do not disconnect the 2 air conditioning hoses.
9. Remove the distributor assembly. Tag and disconnect the electrical wires at the starter assembly.
10. Remove the exhaust pipe bracket from the pipe and the clutch housing. Disconnect the exhaust manifold from the exhaust pipe. Disconnect the oxygen sensor, remove the heat insulator from the manifold. Remove the manifold.
11. Remove the pulsation damper at the fuel delivery pipe. Disconnect the fuel hose with the 2 washers and then disconnect the fuel return hose from the pressure regulator.
12. Remove the cold start injector pipe. Remove the PCV hose at the intake manifold. Tag and disconnect all related vacuum hoses.
13. Remove the wiring harness and the vacuum pipe from the No. 3 timing cover. Tag and disconnect all related wires and then position the harness out of the way.
14. Raise the vehicle and support it safely. Remove the engine mounting bolts on either side of the engine.
15. Unbolt the clutch release cylinder without disconnecting the hydraulic line and then position it out of the way.
16. Disconnect the halfshaft. Tag and disconnect the speedometer cable and the back-up switch connector. Remove the O-ring.
17. Disconnect the bond cables from the clutch and extension housings. Lower the vehicle.
18. Attach an engine hoist to the lift bracket on the engine. Support the rear engine mounting with a jack to prevent damage. Remove the rear engine mounting bolts. Remove the engine from the vehicle.
19. Remove the starter, the 2 stiffener plates and then separate the transmission from the engine.
20. Installation is in the reverse of the removal procedure.

#### MR2

1. Disconnect and remove the battery. Remove the air cleaner assembly. Drain the coolant. Drain the engine oil.
2. Remove the fuel tank protectors and the engine undercover.
3. Disconnect the accelerator cable. Disconnect the cruise control at the cable actuator, if equipped. On vehicles with automatic transmission, disconnect the throttle cable.
4. Disconnect the heater hoses at the water inlet housing on the rear of the cylinder head cover. Disconnect the radiator hose and the air bleeder hose at the water inlet housing.
5. Disconnect and plug the fuel line at the fuel filter. Disconnect the fuel return hose. Tag and disconnect the vacuum hose at the charcoal canister.
6. Tag and disconnect the engine ground strap and the main wiring harness connector at the engine. Disconnect the back-up light switch connector as required.
7. Disconnect the speedometer cable. Remove the transaxle gravel shield. Remove the ground strap from the water inlet housing.
8. Remove the radiator overflow tank. Remove the air conditioning drive belt. Remove the alternator drive belt. Remove the alternator. Disconnect the radiator hose at the water outlet housing.
9. Tag and disconnect the 2 connectors at the igniter, the noise filter connector, the cooling fan electrical connector, the cylinder head ground strap, the air condition compressor connector and the high tension leads at the ignition coil.
10. Remove the rear luggage compartment trim. Tag and disconnect the circuit opening relay connector, the

ball connections at the electronic control unit and the electrical lead for the cooling fan computer.

11. Pull the main wiring harness out and through the engine compartment.

12. Remove the mounting bolts and remove the air conditioning compressor. Position it out of the way without disconnecting the refrigerant lines.

13. On vehicles equipped with a manual transmission, disconnect the control cables from the outer shift lever and gear shift selector lever. On vehicles equipped with automatic transmission, disconnect the control cable at the gear shift lever.

14. On vehicles equipped with a manual transmission, remove the control cable bracket on the transaxle. Remove the clutch release cylinder.

15. Disconnect the engine oil cooler lines, if equipped. Disconnect the automatic transmission fluid lines if equipped.

16. Remove the exhaust pipe assembly. Remove the oxygen sensor at the exhaust manifold.

17. On vehicles equipped with automatic transmsssion, remove the mounting bolts and remove the stiffener plate at the transaxle. Remove the flywheel shield.

18. Remove the right halfshaft. Disconnect the left halfshaft from the side gear shaft and position it out of the way.

19. Remove the front and rear engine mount bolts. Place a block of wood on an hydraulic floor jack and carefully position the jack under the engine. Raise the jack just enough to ease the engine's weight on the mounts. Remove the right and left engine mounts.

20. Make sure there are no remaining wires or hoses connected to the engine and then slowly and carefully raise the vehicle while lowering the jack supporting the engine/transaxle assembly.

21. Installation is the reverse of the removal procedure.

### 1987-90 4A-GEC and 4A-GELC Engines

1. Disconnect and remove the battery. Remove the air cleaner assembly. Drain the coolant. Drain the engine oil.

2. Remove the fuel tank protectors and the engine undercover.

3. Disconnect the accelerator cable. Disconnect the cruise control at the cable actuator, if equipped. On vehicles with automatic transmission, disconnect the throttle cable.

4. Disconnect the heater hoses at the water inlet housing on the rear of the cylinder head cover. Disconnect the radiator hose and the air bleeder hose at the water inlet housing.

5. Disconnect and plug the fuel line at the fuel filter. Disconnect the fuel return hose. Tag and disconnect the vacuum hose at the charcoal canister.

6. Tag and disconnect the engine ground strap and the main wiring harness connector at the engine. Disconnect the back-up light switch connector as required.

7. Disconnect the speedometer cable. Remove the transaxle gravel shield. Remove the ground strap from the water inlet housing.

8. Remove the radiator overflow tank. Remove the air conditioner drive belt. Remove the alternator drive belt. Remove the alternator. Disconnect the radiator hose at the water outlet housing.

9. Tag and disconnect the 2 connectors at the igniter, the noise filter connector, the cooling fan electrical connector, the cylinder head ground strap, the air condition compressor connector and the high tension leads at the ignition coil.

10. Remove the rear luggage compartment trim. Tag and disconnect the circuit opening relay connector, the ball connections at the electronic control unit and the electrical lead for the cooling fan computer.

11. Pull the main wiring harness out and through the engine compartment.

12. Remove the mounting bolts and remove the air conditioning compressor. Position it out of the way without disconnecting the refrigerant lines.

13. On vehicles equipped with a manual transmission, disconnect the control cables from the outer shift lever and gear shift selector lever. On vehicles equipped with automatic transmission, disconnect the control cable at the gear shift lever.

14. On vehicles equipped with a manual transmission, remove the control cable bracket on the transaxle. Remove the clutch release cylinder.

15. Disconnect the engine oil cooler lines, if equipped. Disconnect the automatic transmission fluid lines if equipped.

16. Remove the exhaust pipe assembly. Remove the oxygen sensor at the exhaust manifold.

17. On vehicles equipped with automatic transmsssion, remove the mounting bolts and remove the stiffener plate at the transaxle. Remove the flywheel shield.

18. Remove the right halfshaft. Disconnect the left halfshaft from the side gear shaft and position it out of the way.

19. Remove the front and rear engine mount bolts. Place a block of wood on an hydraulic floor jack and carefully position the jack under the engine. Raise the jack just enough to ease the engine's weight on the mounts. Remove the right and left engine mounts.

20. Make sure there are no remaining wires or hoses connected to the engine and then slowly and carefully raise the vehicle while lowering the jack supporting the engine/transaxle assembly.

21. Installation is the reverse of the removal procedure. Please not the following:

a. Tighten the right engine mount insulator bolt and nuts to 38 ft. lbs. (52 Nm). Align the insulator with the bracket on the body and tighten the bolt to 64 ft. lbs. (87 Nm).

b. Align the left engine mount insulator bracket with the transaxle bracket and tighten the bolt to 35 ft. lbs. (48 Nm).

c. Install the left stay and tighten the 2 bolts to 15 ft. lbs. (21 Nm).

d. Install the engine center member and tighten the 5 bolts to 45 ft. lbs. (61 Nm).

e. Install the front, center and rear engine mounts and bolts. Align the bolts holes in the brackets with the center member and tighten the front mount bolts to 35 ft. lbs. (48 Nm); tighten the center mounts to 38 ft. lbs. (52 Nm); and the rear mount bolts to 42 ft. lbs. (57 Nm).

f. Bounce the engine several times to unload the front and rear mounts (A/T only) and then tighten the rear bolt to 64 ft. lbs. (87 Nm). Install the front bolt and tighten it to 64 ft. lbs. (87 Nm).

### 1988-90 4A-GZE Engines

1. Disconnect the negative battery cable. Remove the fuel tank protectors and the engine undercover.

2. Drain the engine oil and the coolant. Remove the supercharger intercooler and battery.

3. Disconnect the A/C idle-up, charcoal canister and cruise control vacuum hoses. Disconnect the air bleeder hose at the water inlet housing.

4. Disconnect the throttle cable on models with automatic transmissions.

5. Disconnect the cruise control cable, the heater hoses and the No. 6 radiator hose.

6. Disconnect the fuel inlet and return lines. Disconnect the speedometer cable and the brake booster vacuum line.

7. Remove the radiator reservoir tank. Disconnect the No. 1 radiator hose at the water outlet housing.

8. Tag and disconnect any remaining hoses, wires or lines which may interfere with engine removal.

9. Remove the 5 clip fasteners and pull out the rear luggage compartment trim. Disconnect the connectors and

pull the wiring harness into the engine compartment.

10. Remove the A/C drive belt. Remove the A/C compressor and position it out of the way with the refrigerant lines still connected.

11. Disconnect the shifter control cables. Remove the clutch release cylinder and bracket and position it out of the way with the hydraulic lines still attached.

12. Disconnect the coolant lines at the engine and transmission oil coolers.

13. Remove the front exhaust pipe. Remove the rear halfshafts.

14. Remove the front and rear engine mount insulators. Lower the engine slightly and then remove the right and left engine mounts. Carefully support the engine and raise the vehicle up, over the engine.

15. Installation is in the reverse order of removal. Please note the following:

a. When installing the rear engine mount insulator, tighten the 10mm bolts to 38 ft. lbs. (52 Nm); tighten the 12mm bolts to 58 ft. lbs. (78 Nm).

b. Install the front engine mount insulator to the body and tighten the inner bolt to 38 ft. lbs. (52 Nm), tighten the outer bolts to 54 ft. lbs. (73 Nm). Connect the mounting bracket to the insulator and install the thru-bolt. Bounce the engine several times and tighten the thru-bolt to 58 ft. lbs. (78 Nm).

c. Replenish all fluids and raod test the vehicle.

### *1983-84 4K-E Engines*

1. Drain the cooling system. Unfasten the cable which runs from the battery to the starter at the battery terminal. Scribe marks on the hood and hinges. Remove the hood.

2. Unfasten the headlight bezel retaining screws and remove the bezels. Remove the 5 radiator grille attachment screws and remove the grille.

3. Remove the hood lock assembly after detaching the release cable. Unfasten the nuts from the horn retainers and disconnect the wiring. Remove the horn assembly.

4. Remove the air cleaner from its bracket. Remove the windshield washer tank from its bracket. Remove both the upper and lower radiator hoses from the engine. On vehicles with automatic transmission, disconnect the oil lines from the oil cooler. Remove the radiator mounting bolts and remove the radiator.

5. Remove the accelerator cable from its support on the valve cover.

6. Detach the water hose retainer from the cylinder head. Disconnect the bypass and heater hoses at the water pump. Disconnect the other end of the heater hose from the water valve. Remove the heater control cable from the water valve.

7. Disconnect the wiring harness multi connectors. Detach the downpipe from the exhaust manifold. Detach the wires from the water temperature and oil pressure sending units.

8. Remove the nut from the front lefthand engine mount. Remove the fuel line from the fuel pump. Remove the battery ground cable from the cylinder block.

9. Remove the nut from the front righthand engine mount. Remove the clip and detach the cable from the clutch release lever. Remove the primary and high tension wires from the coil.

10. Detach the back-up light switch wire at its connector on the right side of the extension housing. Remove the carpet from the transmission tunnel. Remove the boots from the shift lever.

11. Remove the snapring from the gearshift selector lever base. Withdraw the selector lever assembly.

12. Raise and support the vehicle safely. Disconnect the driveshaft from the transmission. Drain the oil from the manual transmission. Detach the exhaust pipe support bracket from the extension housing.

13. Remove the insulator bolt from the rear engine mount. Place a jack under the transmission and remove the 4 bolts from the rear crossmember.

14. Install lifting hooks on the engine lifting brackets. Attach a suitable hoist. Lift the engine slightly then move it toward the front of the vehicle. Bring the engine the rest of the way out at an angle.

15. Installation is the reverse of the removal procedure.

### *1983-88 5M-GE Engines*

1. Disconnect the battery cables and remove the battery. Match mark the hood and remove it. Remove the air cleaner assembly.

2. Remove the fan shroud. Drain the cooling system. Disconnect both the upper and lower radiator hoses. Disconnect and plug the oil lines from the oil cooler on vehicles equipped with automatic transmission.

3. Detach the hose which runs to the thermal expansion tank and remove the expansion tank from its mounting bracket. Remove the radiator.

4. On vehicles equipped with automatic transmission, remove the throttle cable bracket from the cylinder head. Remove the accelerator and actuator cable bracket from the cylinder head.

5. Tag and disconnect the cylinder head ground cable, the oxygen sensor wire, the oil pressure sending unit, alternator wires, the high tension coil wire, the water temperature sending, the thermo switch wires, the starter wires, the ECT connectors, the solenoid resistor wire connector and the knock sensor wire.

6. Tag and disconnect the brake booster vacuum hose from the air intake chamber, along with the EGR valve vacuum hose. Disconmnect the actuator vacuum hose from the air intake chamber, if equipped with cruise control. Disconnect the heater bypass hoses from the engine.

7. Remove the glove box, and remove the ECU computer module. Disconnect the 3 connectors, and pull out the EFI wiring harness from the engine compartment side of the firewall.

8. Remove the 4 shroud and 4 fluid coupling screws, and the shroud and coupling as a unit. Remove the engine undercover protector.

9. Disconnect the coolant reservoir hose. Remove the radiator. Remove the coolant expansion tank.

10. Remove the air conditioning compressor drive belt, and remove the compressor mounting bolts. Without disconnecting the refrigerant hoses, lay the compressor to one side and secure it.

**NOTE: The air conditioning system is charged with the refrigerant R-12, which is dangerous when released. Do not disconnect the hoses when removing the engine, unless absolutely necessary.**

11. Disconnect the power steering pump drive belt and remove the pump stay. Unbolt the pump and lay it aside without disconnecting the fluid hoses.

12. Remove the engine mounting bolts from each side of the engine. Remove the engine ground cable.

13. On vehicles equipped with manual transmission, remove the shift lever from the inside of the vehicle.

14. Raise and support the vehicle safely. Drain the engine oil.

15. Disconnect the exhaust pipe from the exhaust manifold. Remove the exhaust pipe clamp from the transmission housing.

16. On vehicles equipped with manual transmission, remove the clutch slave cylinder. Disconnect the speedometer cable at the transmission.

17. On vehicles equipped with automatic transmission, disconnect the shift linkage from the shift lever. On vehicles equipped with manual transmission, disconnect the wire from the

back-up light switch. Remove the stiffener plate from the ground cable.

18. Disconnect and plug the fuel line from the fuel filter and the return hose from the fuel hose support.

19. Remove the 2 bolts from the top and bottom of the steering universal, and remove the sliding yoke.

20. Disconnect the tie rod ends. Disconnect the pressure line mounting bolts from the front crossmember.

21. Remove the intermediate shaft from the driveshaft.

22. Position a jack under the transmission, with a wooden block between the two to prevent damage to the transmission case. Place a wooden block between the cowl panel and the cylinder head rear end to prevent damage to the heater hoses.

23. Unbolt the engine rear support member from the frame, along with the ground cable.

24. Make sure all wiring is disconnected, all hoses disconnected, and everything clear of the engine and transmission. Attach an engine lift hoist chain to the lift brackets on the engine, and carefully lift the engine and transmission up and out of the vehicle.

25. Installation is the rverse of the removal procedure.

### *1986 7M-GE Engines*

1. Disconnect the battery cables and remove the battery. Drain the cooling system. Remove the hood.

2. Remove the washer tank. Remove the air cleaner assembly. If equipped with automatic transmission remove the throttle cable bracket from the valve cover.

3. Remove the accelerator cable and the cruise control actuator bracket from the valve cover.

4. Tag and disconnect the engine ground strap, the oxygen sensor wire, the oil pressure switch wire, the alternator wires, the high tension wire from the distributor, the distributor electrical connector, the water temperature sender switch electrical connector, the ECT wires, the starter wires, the solenoid resistor wire connector and the knock sensor electical connector.

5. Disconnect the brake booster hose, the actuator vacuum hose, if equipped with cruise control. Disconnect the EGR vacuum hose. Disconnect the heater hoses.

6. Remove the glove box. Remove the computer. Disconnect the 3 electrical wires and pull out the EFI wire harness from the cowl panel.

7. Remove the radiator fan shroud and fan assembly. Remove the radiator. Remove the coolant reserve tank.

8. If equipped with air conditioning, remove the air compressor assembly and position it to the side. If equipped with power steering, remove the power steering pump and position it to the side.

9. Remove the engine mounting bolts. From inside the vehicle remove the shift lever, if equipped with manual transmission.

10. Raise and support the vehicle safely. Drain the engine oil.

11. Disconnect the exhaust pipe from the exhaust manifold. Remove the exhaust pipe clamp from the transmission housing.

12. If equipped with manual transmission remove the clutch master cylinder.

13. Remove the speedometer cable. If equipped with automatic transmission disconnect the shift linkage from the shift lever.

14. Disconnect the electrical wire from the back-up light switch. Remove the stiffener plate along with the ground strap.

15. Disconnect and plug the fuel line at the pump. Remove the power steering gear housing.

16. Remove the intermediate shaft from the driveshaft. Properly support the engine and transmission. Remove the engine mounts. Remove the transmission mount and crossmember.

17. Position a piece of wood between the engine firewall and the rear of the cylinder head to prevent damage to the heater hose.

18. Make sure there are no remaining wires or hoses connected to the engine and then slowly and carefully remove the engine and transmission from the vehicle.

19. Installation is the reverse of the removal procedure.

### *1987-90 7M-GE and 7M-GTE Engines*

#### SUPRA

1. Disconnect the negative battery cable. Remove the hood. Remove the engine under cover.

2. Drain the cooling system. Remove the radiator. Drain the engine oil. On 7M-GE, remove the air cleaner assembly. On 7M-GTE, remove the No. 4 air cleaner pipe along with the No. 1 and 2 air cleaner hose.

3. Remove the No. 7 air cleaner hose with the air flow meter and air cleaner cap. Remove the radiator.

4. Remove the air conditioning belt. Remove the alternator drive belt, water pump pulley and fan assembly. Remove the power steering belt.

5. Disconnect the brake booster hose, the heater valve hose, the cruise control hose and the charcoal canister hose. Remove the heater hoses.

6. Disconnect:

a. the engine ground strap

b. the noise filter connector

c. the theft deterrent horn connector

d. the check connector

e. the solenoid resistor connector

f. if equipped, the ignition coil connector on the 7M-GE

g. the igniter connectors on the 7M-GTE

h. the main relay connector

i. the alternator electrical connectors

j. the oxygen sensor connector on the 7M-GE

k. the heater valve connector

l. the ECU connector and the ECT connector.

7. Disconnect the cruise control cable, if equipped. Disconnect the accelerator cable. Disconnect the throttle cable, if equipped with automatic transmission.

8. Remove the air conditioning compressor. It may be possible to position the unit to the side without completely removing it from the vehicle.

9. On the 7M-GTE, remove the No. 6 air cleaner hose and the upper radiator outlet hose.

10. Remove the power steering pump. It may be possible to position the unit to the side without completely removing it from the vehicle.

11. If equipped with manual transmission remove the shift lever. Disconnect the ground strap from the fuel hose clamp. On the 7M-GTE, remove the engine mounting absorber.

12. Disconnect and plug the fuel lines.

13. Raise and support the vehicle safely. Remove the exhaust pipe. Remove the driveshaft.

14. Disconnect the speedometer cable. If equipped with automatic transmission, remove the shift linkage. If equipped with manual transmission, remove the clutch release cylinder.

15. Properly support the engine and transmission assembly. Remove the No. 1 front crossmember. Remove the engine retaining mounts.

16. Position a piece of wood between the engine firewall and the rear of the cylinder head to prevent damage to the heater hose.

17. Make sure there are no remaining wires or hoses connected to the engine and then slowly and carefully remove the engine and transmission from the vehicle.

18. Installation is the reverse of the removal procedure.

#### CRESSIDA

1. Disconnect the negative battery cable. Drain the engine coolant and remove the hood.

2. Remove the battery and tray.

3. Tag and disconnect the accelerator, throttle and cruise control cables.

4. Remove the air cleaner assembly complete with the air flow meter, hoses and connector pipe.

5. Tag and disconnect the following:

a. connector at the fuse and relay block

b. alternator lead

c. A/C connector

d. check and igniter connectors

e. high tension lead at the coil

f. noise filter

g. brake booster, charcoal canister and cruise control vacuum lines.

6. Remove the radiator.

7. Remove the drive belt and unbolt the A/C compressor. Position it out of the way and suspend it with wire. Do not disconnect the refrigerant lines!

8. Remove the drive belt and unbolt the power steering pump. Position it out of the way and suspend it with wire. Do not disconnect the hydraulic lines!

9. Remove the windshield washer fluid reservoir.

10. Remove the glove box and disconnect the 6 connectors and then pull the main wiring harness through the firewall and into the engine compartment.

11. Disconnect the heater hoses.

12. Raise the vehicle and support it with safety stands. Remove the engine under cover and drain the oil.

13. Disconnect the exhaust pipe at the manifold.

14. Disconnect the driveshaft at the transmission flange and position it out of the way.

15. Disconnect the speedometer cable and the transmission linkage.

16. Disconnect the starter lead and the ground lines at the stiffener plate and left side engine mount.

17. Disconnect the fuel lines.

18. Remove the front wheels and then disconnect the power steering rack. Leave the hydraulic lines attached and lay the rack aside.

19. Loosen the 8 bolts and the ground strap and then remove the rear engine support.

20. Lower the vehicle and remove the 4 engine mount-to-suspension bolts. Attach an engine hoist to the 2 engine hangers and then slowly *and carefully* lift the engine out of the vehicle.

21. Installation is in the reverse order of removal.

# Cylinder Head

**NOTE: Do not perform this operation on a warm engine. Remove the head bolts in sequence and in several steps. Loosen the head bolts evenly. Keep the pushrods in their original order. Do not attempt to slide the cylinder head off the block, as it is located with dowel pins. Lift the head straight up and off the block.**

## REMOVAL & INSTALLATION

### 22R Engines

1. Disconnect the negative battery cable.

2. Remove the 3 exhaust pipe flange nuts and separate the pipe from the manifold.

3. Drain the engine oil. Drain the cooling system both radiator and block. Remove the air cleaner assembly.

4. Mark all vacuum hoses to aid installation, and disconnect them. Remove all linkages, fuel lines, etc., from the carburetor, cylinder head, and manifolds. Remove the wire supports.

5. Mark the spark plug leads and disconnect them from the plugs.

6. If equipped, disconnect and move the air injection system hoses. Mark the hose locations so that they may be properly reinstalled.

7. If equipped with air conditioning, remove the upper compressor mounting bracket.

8. If equipped with power steering, remove the power steering pump and position it out of the way without disconnecting the hydraulic lines.

9. Matchmark the distributor housing and block. Remove the distributor. Remove the valve cover.

10. Using a wrench on the crankshaft pulley, rotate the crankshaft until the No. 1 cylinder is at TDC on its compression stroke (both valves of the No. 1 cylinder closed).

11. Place matchmarks on both the camshaft sprocket and the timing chain to indicate the relationship between these items.

12. Remove the rubber camshaft seals. Use a 19mm wrench to remove the cam sprocket bolt. Slide the distributor drive gear off of the cam and wire the cam sprocket in place.

13. Remove the timing chain cover 14mm bolt at the front end of the head. This must be done before the head bolts are removed.

14. Remove the cylinder head bolts in the proper order. Improper removal could cause head damage.

15. Using pry bars applied evenly at the front and the rear of the valve rocker assembly, pry the assembly off of its mounting dowels.

16. Lift the head off of its dowels. Do not pry it off. Support the head on a workbench.

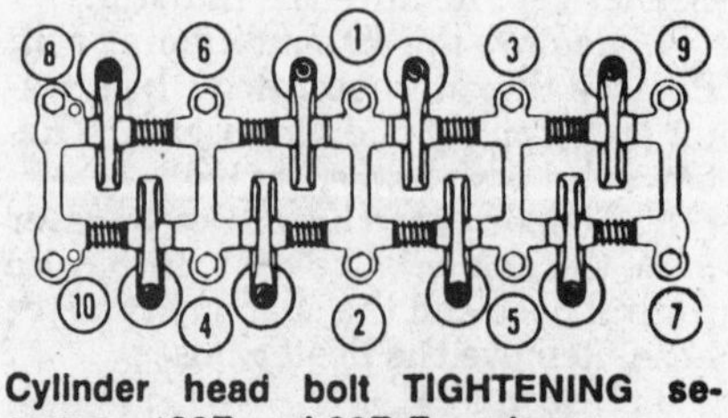


Cylinder head bolt TIGHTENING sequence—22R and 22R-E engines

17. Installation is the reverse of the removal procedure. Torque the cylinder head to specification and in proper sequence.

### 22R-E Engines

1. Disconnect the negative battery cable. Drain the engine coolant. Drain the engine oil. Remove the air cleaner assembly.

2. Disconnect the oxygen sensor wire and then disconnect the exhaust pipe from the manifold. Disconnect the upper radiator hose from the heater hose.

3. Disconnect the actuator, accelerator and throttle cables from the bracket on the side of the cylinder head.

4. Tag and disconnect all hoses from the head. Remove the EGR vacuum modulator and its bracket.

5. Tag and disconnect the throttle position sensor wire, the cold start injector pipe and wire.

6. Remove the EGR valve. Disconnect the air intake chamber and its mounting, unscrew the mounting bolts and remove the chamber along with the throttle body.

7. Tag and disconnect all remaining wires. Remove the fuel line, the pulsation damper and the air valve.

8. Remove the spark plugs. Remove the power steering pump, if equipped and position it to one side with the hoses still attached.

9. Remove the cylinder head cover. After removing the cylinder head cover, cover the oil return hole in the head with a rag to prevent objects from falling in.

10. Matchmark the distributor housing and block. Remove the distributor. Remove the valve cover.

11. Using a wrench on the crankshaft pulley, rotate the crankshaft until the No. 1 cylinder is at TDC on its compression stroke (both valves of the No. 1 cylinder closed).

12. Place matchmarks on both the camshaft sprocket and the timing chain to indicate the relationship between these items.

13. Remove the rubber camshaft seals. Use a 19mm wrench to remove the cam sprocket bolt. Slide the distributor drive gear off of the cam and wire the cam sprocket in place.

14. Remove the timing chain cover 14mm bolt at the front end of the head. This must be done before the head bolts are removed.

15. Remove the cylinder head bolts in the proper order. Improper removal could cause head damage.

16. Using pry bars applied evenly at the front and the rear of the valve

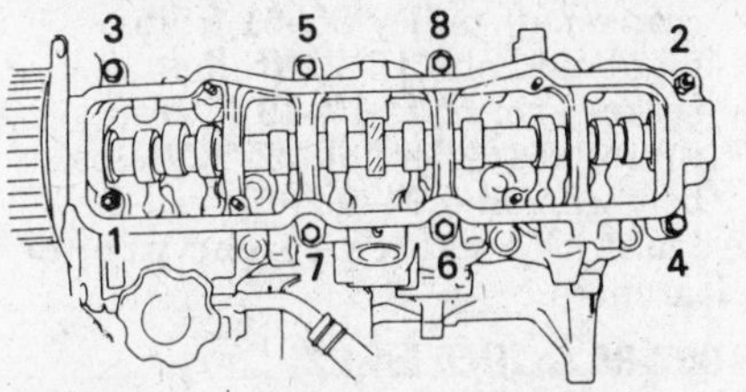

Camshaft housing bolt LOOSENING sequence – 2S-E engines

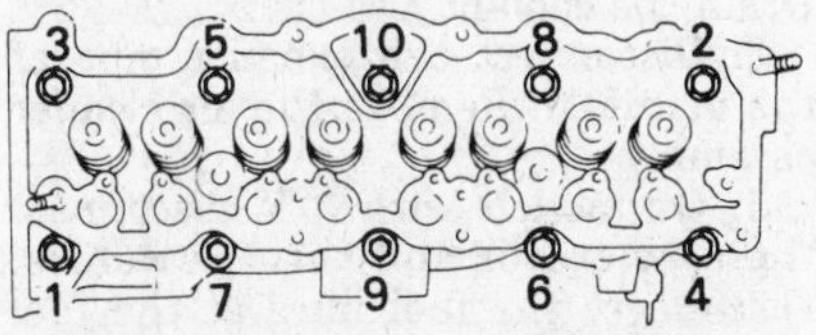

Cylinder head bolt LOOSENING sequence – 2S-E engines

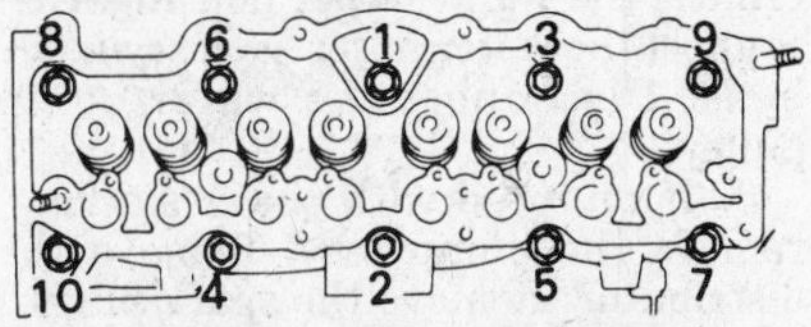

Cylinder head bolt TIGHTENING sequence – 2S-E engines

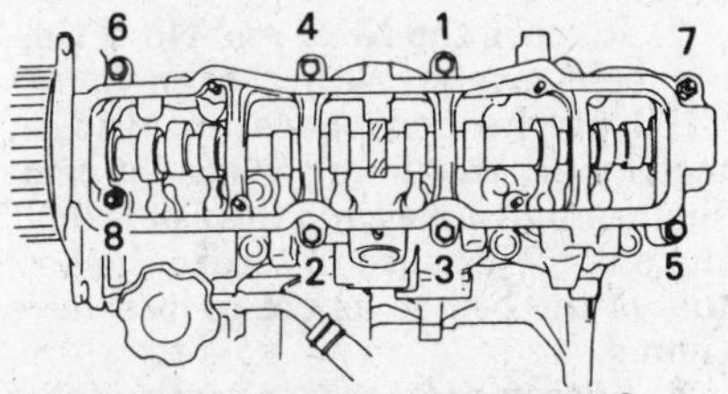

Camshaft housing TIGHTENING sequence – 2S-E engines

rocker assembly, pry the assembly off of its mounting dowels.

17. Lift the head off of its dowels. Do not pry it off. Support the head on a workbench.

18. Installation is the reverse of the removal procedure. Torque the cylinder head to specification and in proper sequence.

### 2S-E Engines

1. Disconnect the negative battery cable. Drain the coolant. Disconnect the throttle cable.

2. Remove the air cleaner assembly. Disconnect and tag all wires connected to or running across the head. Disconnect and tag all vacuum hoses connected to or running across the head.

3. Remove the vacuum pipe from the valve cover cover. Disconnect and tag any remaining cables. Remove the alternator. Remove the distributor.

4. Remove the upper radiator hose and bypass hose. Unbolt and remove the water outlet housing. Disconnect the heater hoses.

5. Disconnect the 2 air hoses from the fuel injection air valve. Unbolt and remove the rear end housing. Remove the heater pipe.

6. Disconnect the fuel line at the filter and the fuel return line at the return pipe.

7. Raise and support the vehicle safely. Drain the oil.

8. Disconnect the exhaust pipe at the manifold. Disconnect the power steering pump hoses.

9. Remove the intake manifold stay. Lower the vehicle.

10. Remove the timing belt. Remove the No. 1 idler pulley and tension spring.

11. Remove the throttle body. Remove the valve cover.

12. Unbolt and remove the camshaft housing. Loosen the bolts gradually in the proper order. Remove the rocker arms and the lash adjusters.

13. Loosen and remove the head bolts, in 3 passes and in the reverse of the installation torque sequence. Remove the cylinder head from the vehicle. Place it on wood blocks in a clean work area.

14. Installation is the reverse of the removal procedure.

15. Always use a new head gasket. Tighten the head bolts, in 3 passes, according to specification.

16. When installing the camshaft housing, note that RTV silicone gasket compound is used in place of a gasket. Run a 2mm bead of compound around the sealing surface of the housing. Torque the housing bolts, in 3 passes, according to specification, to 11 ft. lbs.

### 2VZ-FE Engines

1. Disconnect the negative battery cable and drain the engine coolant.

2. Disconnect the throttle cable at the throttle body. If equipped, remove the cruise control actuator and vacuum pump.

3. Remove the air cleaner hose.

4. Raise the front of the vehicle and remove the engine undercovers.

5. Remove the lower suspension crossmember and the front exhaust pipe.

6. Remove the alternator. Remove the ISC valve.

7. Remove the throttle body. Remove the EGR pipe, valve and vacuum modulator.

8. Remove the vacuum pipe and the distributor.

9. Remove the exhaust crossover pipe. Disconnect the cold start injector and then remove the injector tube.

10. Tag and disconnect all hoses leading to the air intake chamber and then remove the chamber.

11. Remove the fuel delivery pipes and the injectors.

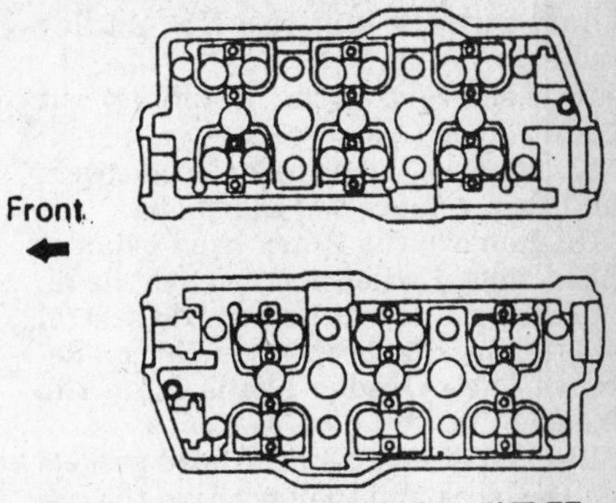

Remove the 2 hex head bolts – 2VZ-FE engines

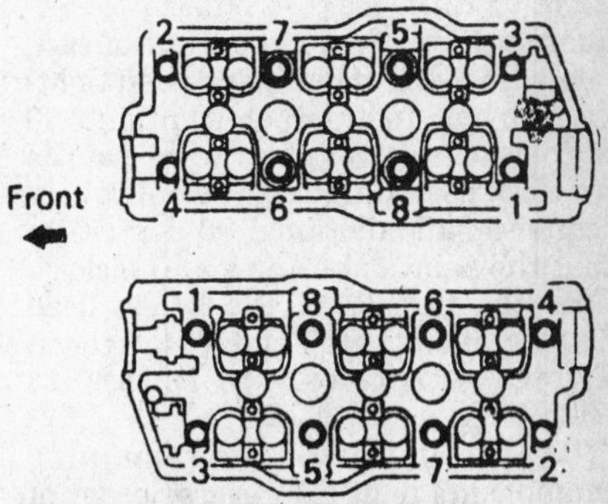

Cylinder head bolt LOOSENING sequence – 2VZ-FE engines

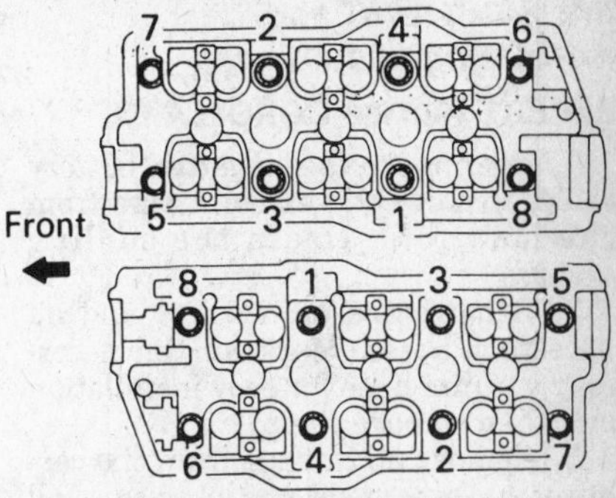

Cylinder head bolt TIGHTENING sequence – 2VZ-FE engines

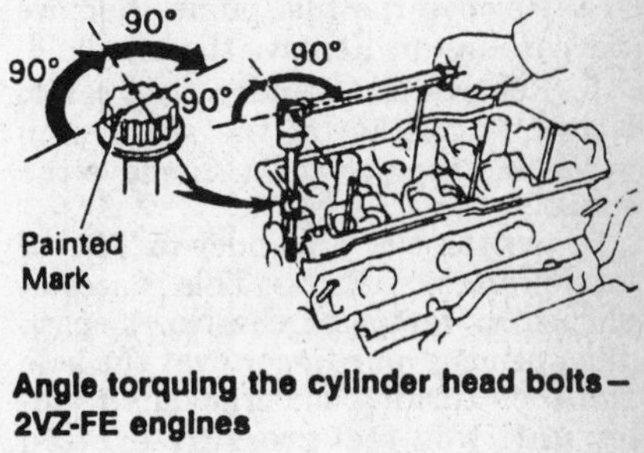

Angle torquing the cylinder head bolts – 2VZ-FE engines

12. Disconnect the water temperature sensor and remove the upper radiator hose. Remove the water outlet. Remove the water by-pass outlet.

13. Loosen the 2 bolts and remove the cylinder head rear plate.

14. Remove the intake manifold. Remove the exhaust manifolds.

15. Remove the timing belt, cam-

shaft pulleys and the No. 2 idler pulley.

16. Remove the No. 3 timing belt cover.

17. Remove the cylinder head covers and then remove the camshafts.

18. Remove the 2 hex head cylinder head bolts. Loosen and remove the remaining cylinder head bolts, in several stages, in the proper sequence. Remove the cylinder heads from the block.

19. Install new cylinder head gaskets on the block and then position the cylinder heads. Install the regular (12-sided) cylinder head bolts and tighten them to 25 ft. lbs. (34 Nm) in the sequence shown. Mark the front of each bolt with a dab of paint and then tighten each bolt, in order, an additional 90 degrees (the dab of paint will be at the 3 o'clock position. Retighten all bolt, in sequence, an additional 90 degrees so that the paint dab is now at 6 o'clock. Coat the threads of the 2 hex head bolts with engine oil and install them. Tighten each bolt to 13 ft. lbs. (18 Nm).

20. Installation of the remaining components is in the reverse order of removal.

### *3A, 3A-C, 4A-C and 4A-LC Engines*

#### EXCEPT 1987-88 COROLLA FX

1. Disconnect the negative battery cable. Remove the exhaust pipe from the manifold. Drain the cooling system.

2. Remove the air cleaner and all necessary hoses. Mark all the necessary vacuum lines for easy installation and then remove them.

3. Remove all linkage from the carburetor. Disconnect and plug the fuel lines at the cylinder head and manifold.

4. Remove the fuel pump. Remove the carburetor. Remove the manifold.

5. Remove the cylinder head cover. Note the position of the spark plug wires and remove them. Remove the spark plugs.

6. Set the No. 1 cylinder to TDC of its compression stroke. This is accomplished by removing the No. 1 spark plug, placing your finger over the hole and then turning the crankshaft pulley until you feel pressure exerted against your finger.

7. Remove the crankshaft pulley with the proper tool. Remove the water pump pulley. Remove the top and bottom timing cover.

8. Matchmark the camshaft pulley and timing belt for reassembly. Loosen the belt tensioner. Remove the water pump.

9. Remove the timing belt. Do not bend, twist, or turn the belt inside out.

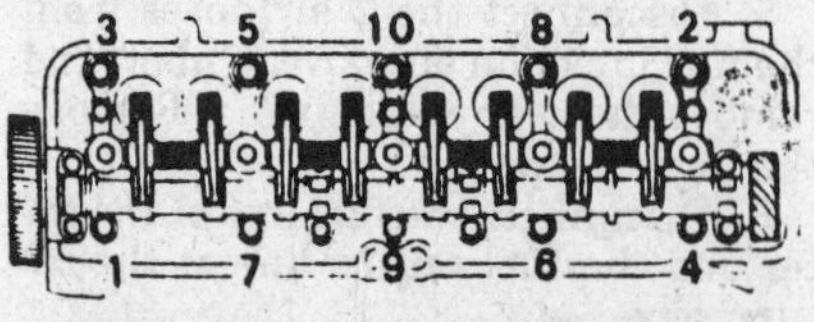

**Cylinder head bolt LOOSENING sequence —3A, 3A-C, 4A-C and 4A-LC engines**

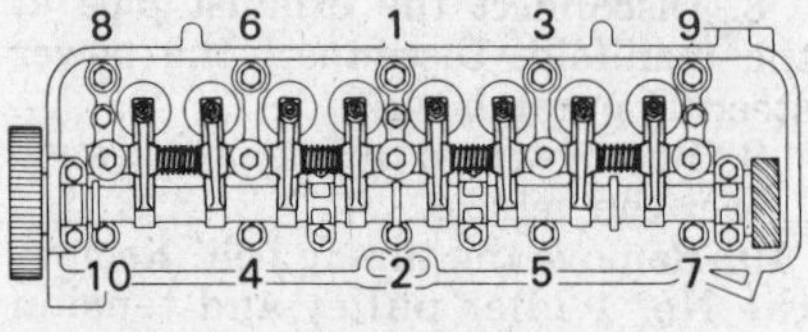

**Cylinder head bolt TIGHTENING sequence —3A, 3A-C, 4A-C and 4A-LC engines**

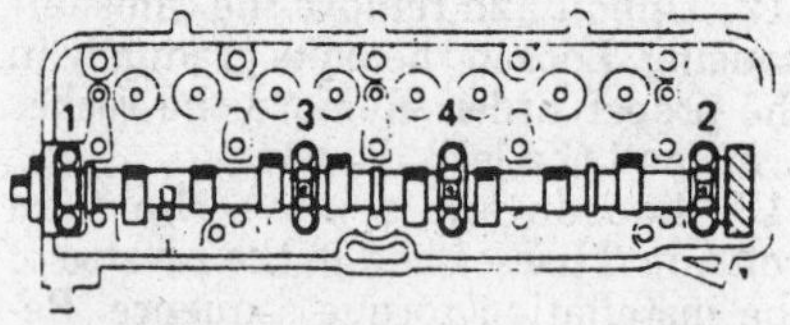

**Camshaft bearing cap bolt LOOSENING sequence—3A, 3A-C, 4A-C and 4A-LC engines**

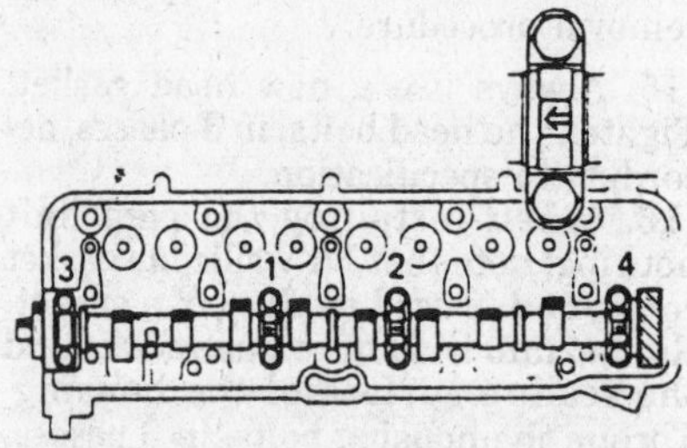

**Camshaft bearing cap bolt TIGHTENING sequence—3A, 3A-C, 4A-C and 4A-LC engines**

10. Remove the rocker arm bolts and remove the rocker arms. Remove the camshaft pulley by holding the camshaft with a suitable tool and removing the belt in the pulley end of the shaft. Do not hold the cam on the lobes, as damage will result.

11. Remove the camshaft seal. Remove the camshaft bearing caps and set them down in the order they appear on the engine. Remove the camshaft.

12. Loosen the head bolts in the reverse order of the torque sequence. Lift the head directly up. Do not attempt to slide it off.

13. Installation is the reverse of the removal procedure

14. When replacing the head always use a new gasket. Also replace the camshaft seal, making sure to grease the lip before installation.

15. The following torques are needed for installation:
- cam bearing caps 8–10 ft. lbs.
- cam sprocket 29–39 ft. lbs.
- crankshaft pulley 55–61 ft. lbs.
- manifold bolts 15–21 ft. lbs.
- rocker arm bolts 17–19 ft. lbs.
- timing gear idler bolt 22–32 ft. lbs.
- belt tension 0.24–0.28 in.

Adjust the valves to the proper clearances.

#### 1987-88 COROLLA FX

1. Disconnect the negative battery cable. Remove the engine undercover. Drain the coolant and oil.

2. Disconnect the exhaust pipe at the manifold. Remove the air cleaner assembly.

3. On models with A/T, disconnect the accelerator and throttle cables. Disconnect the fuel lines at the fuel pump.

4. Disconnect the water hose and remove the water outlet housing. Disconnect the water hoses at the cylinder head. Disconnect the water pump pulley.

5. If equipped with power steering, remove the pump stay. Remove the distributor. Remove the spark plugs.

6. Remove the cylinder head cover and gasket. Lift out the half circle plug.

7. Remove the No. 1 and No. 2 timing belt covers. With the engine at TDC of the compression stroke, matchmark the timing belt to the camshaft timing pulley and then slide it off the pulley—be sure to secure the bottom of the belt so as not to lose valve timing.

8. Loosen each rocker arm support bolt a little at a time and in the order shown. Remove the rocker arms.

9. Secure the camshaft (an adjustable wrench works well for this) and remove the camshaft timing pulley. Measure the camshaft thrust clearance. With the camshaft still secure, loosen the distributor drive gear bolt. Loosen the camshaft bearing cap bolts gradually and in the order shown. Remove the camshaft.

10. Loosen and remove the cylinder head bolts gradually, in several stages. Remove the cylinder head.

**To install:**

11. Position the cylinder head on the block with a new gasket and tighten the head bolts in several stages, in the order shown, to a final torque of 43 ft. lbs. (59 Nm).

12. Install the distributor drive gear and plate washer to the camshaft, coat the bearing journals with clean engine oil and position the caminto the head. Position the bearing caps over each journal with the arrow pointing forward. Install a new oil seal and then tighten the cap bolts to 9 ft. lbs. (13 Nm) in the correct order.

13. Install the camshaft timing pul-

ley and tighten the bolt to 34 ft. lbs. (47 Nm).

14. Install and tighten the rocker arm support bolts gradually in 3 passes and in the proper sequence. Tighten to 18 ft. lbs. (25 Nm).

**NOTE: It is a good idea to loosen the rocker arm adjusting screw before installation.**

15. Align the mark on the No. 1 camshaft bearing cap with the small hole in the timing pulley and install the timing belt so the marks made earlier are in alignment.

16. Installation of the remaining components is in the reverse order of removal.

### 3E Engines

1. Disconnect the negative battery cable. Drain the coolant. remove the engine under cover.

2. If equipped with power steering, remove the power steering pump and bracket. If equipped with air conditioning and without power steering remove the idler pulley bracket.

3. Disconnect the radiator hoses. Disconnect the accelerator cable. If equipped with automatic transmission, disconnect the throttle cable from the bracket.

4. Remove the timing belt and the camshaft timing pulley. Disconnect the heater inlet hose. Disconnect and plug the fuel lines.

5. Remove the air suction hose and valve assembly. Disconnect the brake booster hose from the intake manifold.

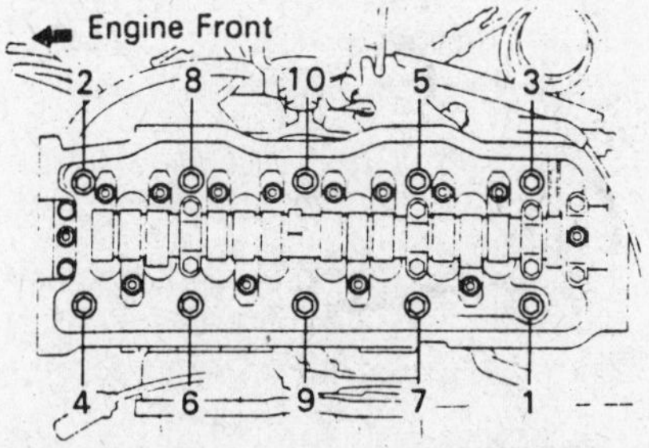


**Cylinder head bolt LOOSENING sequence – 3E engines**

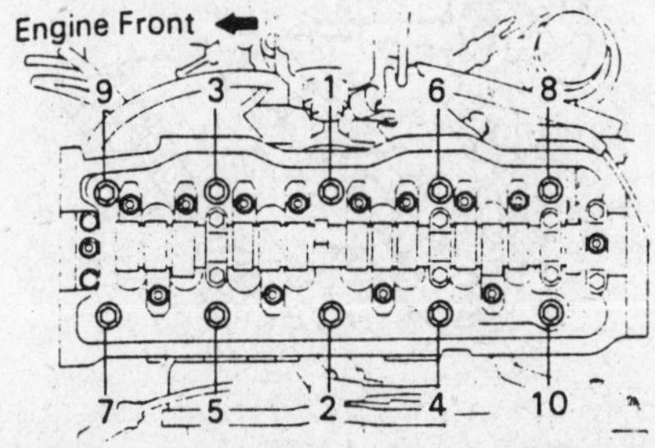


**Cylinder head bolt TIGHTENING sequence – 3E engines**

Disconnect the water inlet hose. Disconnect the intake manifold water hose from the intake manifold.

6. Tag and disconnect all electrical wires, vacuum lines and cables that will interfere with cylinder head removal.

7. Remove the EVAP, VSV and the No. 2 cold enrichment breaker valve. Disconnect the water bypass hoses from the carburetor. Remove the valve cover.

8. Disconnect the exhaust pipe. Remove the intake manifold stay and ground strap. Remove the wire harness clamp bolt from the intake manifold.

9. Measure the cylinder head camshaft thrust clearance using a dial indicator gauge. Standard clearance should be 0.0031–0.071 in. Maximum clearance should be 0.0098 in. If not within specification replace defective parts as required.

10. Loosen then remove the cylinder head bolts in 3 phases and in the proper sequence. Remove the cylinder head from the engine.

11. Installation is the reverse of the removal procedure.

12. Be sure to use a new head gasket. Tighten the cylinder head to 22 ft. lbs. (29 Nm); tighten it again to 36 ft. lbs. (49 Nm) and then retighten each bolt an additional 90 degree turn each..

### 3S-FE Engines

1. Disconnect the negative battery cable. Drain the coolant.

2. If equipped with automatic transmission, disconnect the throttle cable and bracket from the throttle body.

3. Disconnect the accelerator cable and bracket from the throttle body and intake chamber.

4. If equipped with cruise control, remove the actuator and bracket. Remove the air cleaner hose. Remove the alternator.

5. Remove the oil pressure gauge, engine hangers and alternator upper bracket.

6. Raise and support the vehicle safely. Remove the right tire and wheel assembly.

7. Remove the right under cover. Remove the suspension lower crossmember. Disconnect the exhaust pipe from the catalytic converter. Separate the exhaust pipe from the catalytic converter.

8. Disconnect the water temperature sender gauge connector, water temperature sensor connector, cold start injector time switch connector, upper radiator hose, water hoses, and the emission control vacuum hoses.

9. Remove the water outlet and gaskets. Remove the distributor. Remove the water bypass pipe. Remove the EGR valve and modulator.

10. Remove the throttle body assembly. Remove the cold start injector pipe. Remove the air intake chamber air hose, the throttle body air hose, and the power steering pump hoses, if equipped. Remove the air tube.

11. Remove the intake manifold retaining bolts. Remove the intake manifold. Remove the fuel delivery pipe and the injectors. Remove the spark plugs.

12. Remove the camshaft timing pulley. Remove the No. 1 idler pulley and tension spring. Remove the No. 3 timing belt cover. Properly support the timing belt so that meshing of the crankshaft timing pulley does not occur and the timing belt does not shift.

13. Remove the cylinder head cover. Arrange the grommets in order so that they can be reinstalled in the correct order.

14. Remove the camshafts.

15. Loosen, then remove the cylinder head bolts in 3 phases and in the proper sequence. Remove the cylinder head from the engine.

16. Installation is the reverse of the removal procedure.

17. Be sure to use a new cylinder head gasket. Apply a light coat of clean engine oil to the threads of the head bolts prior to installation. Torque the cylinder head to specification and in 3 phases to 47 ft. lbs. (64 Nm).

### 3S-GE Engines

1. Disconnect the negative battery cable. Drain the coolant.

2. Tag and disconnect the ignition coil connector and the spark plug wire at the ignition coil. Remove the 4 nuts and 2 bolts and lift out the upper suspension brace.

3. On vehicles equipped with automatic transmission, disconnect the throttle cable with its bracket from the

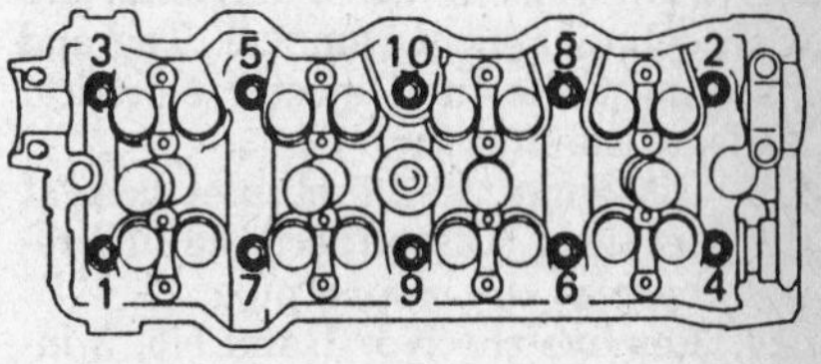


**Cylinder head bolt LOOSENING sequence – 3S-FE engines**

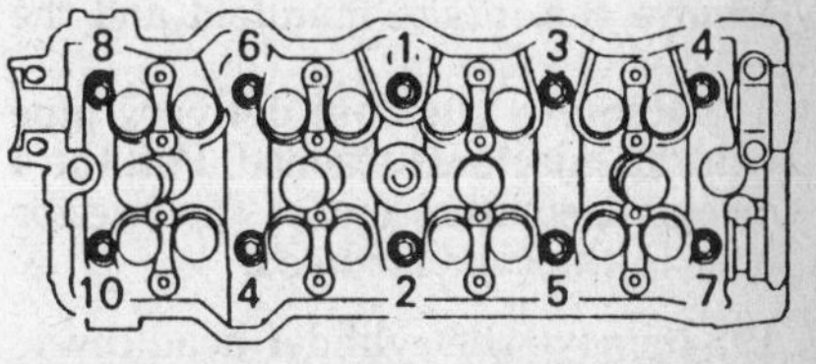


**Cylinder head bolt TIGHTENING sequence – 3S-FE engines**

throttle body. Disconnect the accelerator cable from the throttle body. Remove the radiator overflow tank.

4. If equipped, remove the cruise control actuator and its bracket.

5. Disconnect the air flow meter connector. Remove the air cleaner cap clips. Loosen the hose clamp and remove the air cleaner hose and the air flow meter along with the air cleaner top. Lift out the filter element and then remove the air cleaner case.

6. Tag and disconnect the oxygen sensor lead. Remove the 4 mounting bolts and remove the exhaust manifold heat insulator. Remove the alternator and its main bracket.

7. Raise and support the vehicle safely. Remove the right front wheel.

8. Remove the right side engine under cover and remove the lower suspension crossmember.

9. Disconnect the exhaust pipe at the manifold. Remove the exhaust manifold stay and the EGR pipe. Unbolt the manifold and remove it along with the lower heat insulator.

10. Remove the distributor. Tag and disconnect the oil pressure switch connector.

11. Tag and disconnect all electrical leads and vacuum hoses at the water outlet. Remove the upper radiator hoses, the heater outlet hose and the water bypass hose. Remove the water outlet.

12. Disconnect the heater inlet hose and the water bypass hose and then remove the water bypass pipe.

13. Disconnect the throttle position sensor lead, the ventilation hose, the air valve hose and any emission control vacuum hoses at the throttle body. Remove the 4 bolts and lift out the throttle body.

14. Remove the forward engine hanger and the No. 2 intake manifold stay. Remove the EGR vacuum modulator.

15. Tag and disconnect any remaining vacuum hoses which may interfere with cylinder head removal. Tag and disconnect the fuel injector electrical leads at the injector.

16. Disconnect the fuel inlet hose at the fuel filter. Disconnect the fuel return hose at the return pipe.

17. Remove the No. 1 and No. 3 intake manifold stays. Tag and disconnect the 2 VSV connectors. Disconnect the 2 power steering vacuum hoses. Remove the intake manifold and the air control valve.

18. Remove the fuel delivery pipe with the injectors attached. Pull the 4 injector insulators out of the injector holes in the cylinder head.

19. Remove the cylinder head cover. Remove the spark plugs. Remove the No. 1 engine hanger.

20. Remove the power steering reservoir and position it out of the way with the hydraulic lines still attached.

21. Remove the camshaft timing pulleys. Remove the No. 1 idler pulley and tension spring.

22. Remove the bolt holding the No. 2 and No. 3 timing covers. Remove the 4 mounting bolts and remove the No. 3 timing cover.

23. Loosen and remove the camshaft bearing caps, in several stages, and in the proper sequence. Lift out the camshafts and the oil seal. When removing the camshaft bearing caps, keep them in the proper order.

24. Loosen and remove the cylinder head bolts, in several stages, and in the proper sequence. Remove the cylinder head.

**To install:**

25. Position the cylinder head onto the cylinder block with a new gasket. Lightly coat the cylinder head bolts with engine oil, install them into the head and tighten them in several passes, in the proper sequence, to 40 ft. lbs. (53 Nm).

26. Position the camshafts into the cylinder head so that the No. 1 cam lobes are facing outward.

27. Apply silicone sealant to the outer edge of the mating surface on the No. 1 bearing cap only. Position the bearing caps over each journal with the arrows pointing forward and in numerical order from the front to the rear.

28. Lightly coat the cap bolt threads with engine oil. Tighten them in several stages, and in the proper sequence, to 14 ft. lbs. (19 Nm).

29. Check the camshaft thrust clearance. Coat the inside of a new oil seal with grease and carefully tap it onto the camshaft with a drift (SST No. 09223-50010). Install the No. 3 timing belt cover.

30. Connect the idler pulley tension spring to the pulley and the pin on the cylinder head. Install the idler pulley onto the pivot pin, force it to the left as far as it will go and tighten it. Make sure that the tension spring is not out of the groove in the pin. Install the camshaft timing pulleys and the timing belt.

31. Installation of the remaining components is in the reverse order of removal. Tighten the lower suspension crossmember end bolts to 154 ft. lbs. and the center bolt to 29 ft. lbs. Tighten the upper suspension brace bolts to 15 ft. lbs. and the nuts to 47 ft. lbs. Refill the engine with coolant. Check the idle speed and ignition timing.

### 3S-GTE Engines

1. Disconnect the negative battery

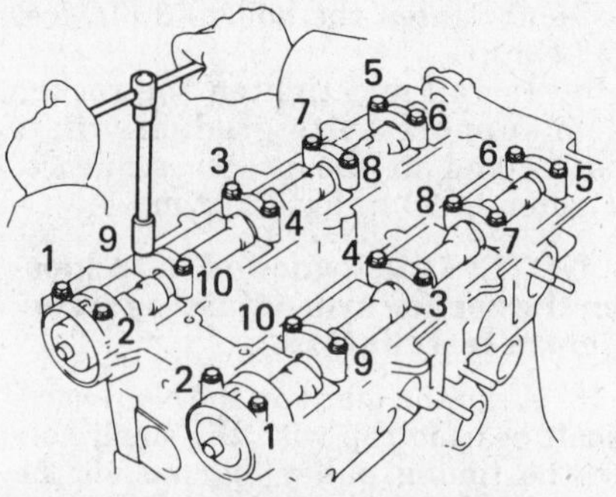

**Remove the camshaft bearing caps in this order – 3S-GE and 3S-GTE engines**

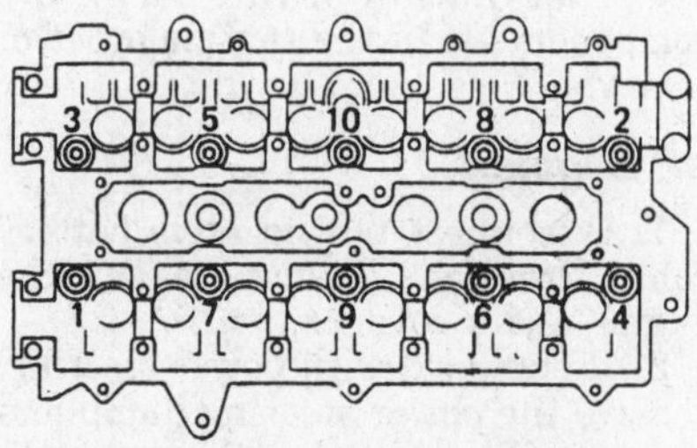

**Cylinder head bolt LOOSENING sequence – 3S-GE and 3S-GTE engines**

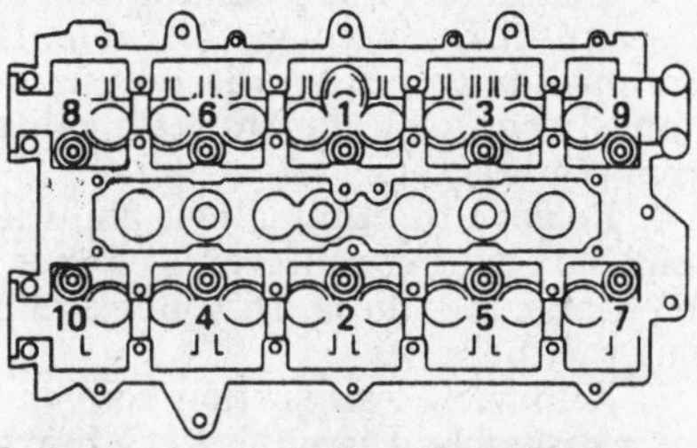

**Cylinder head bolt TIGHTENING sequence – 3S-GE and 3S-GTE engines**

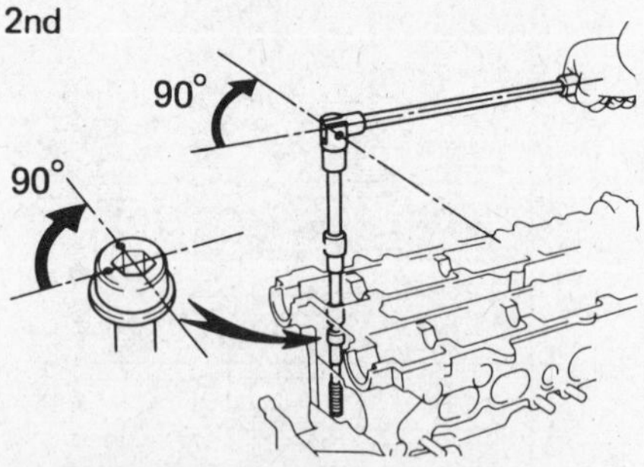


**Mark the head bolts prior to angle-torquing – 3S-GE and 3S-GTE engines**

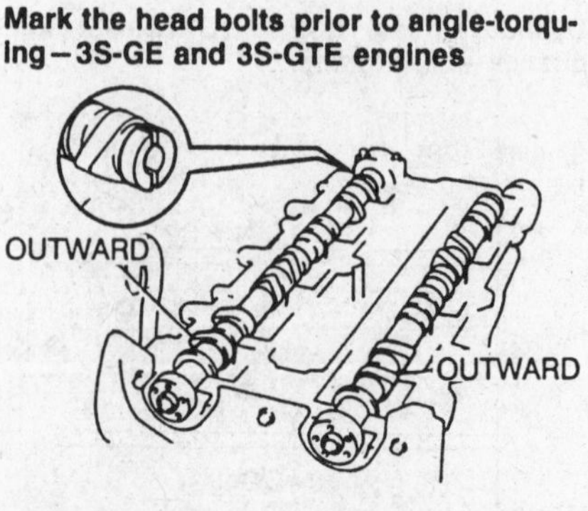


**Camshaft positioning – 3S-GE and 3S-GTE engines**

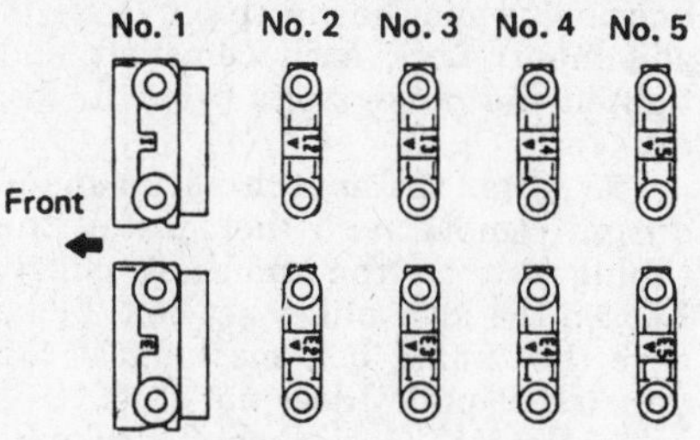


Camshaft bearing cap positioning – 3S-GE and 3S-GTE engines

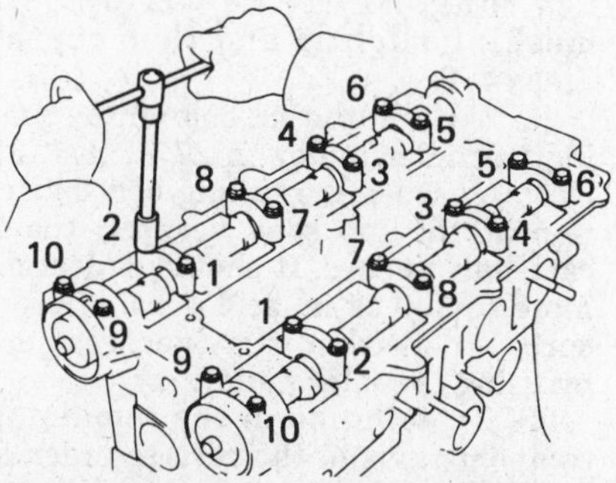

Tighten the bearing cap bolts in this order – 3S-GE and 3S-GTE engines

terminal. Drain the coolant from the engine and intercooler.

2. Remove the upper suspension brace that runs between the strut towers. Disconnect the accelerator cable at the throttle body. Remove the radiator reservoir tank.

3. Remove the air cleaner assembly. Remove the alternator. Raise the vehicle and support it on safety stands.

4. Remove the right wheel. Remove the engine undercovers.

5. Remove the front exhaust pipe and the catalytic converter. Remove the alternator brackets.

6. Remove the turbocharger. Remove the exhaust manifold. Remove the distributor.

7. Disconnect the air hose and remove the No. 2 air pipe.

8. Remove the left engine hanger along with the reservoir tank. Remove the oil pressure switch.

9. Remove the water outlet housing and the water bypass pipe.

10. Remove the throttle body and disconnect the cold start injector lead.

11. Remove the EGR valve, vacuum modulator and EGR control VSV. Remove the delivery pipe and all injectors. Remove the vacuum pipe.

12. Remove the intake manifold stays and then remove the No. 1 air pipe.

13. Disconnect the vacuum hose and remove the fuel pressure VSV. Remove the T-VIS VSV, the vacuum tank and the turbo pressure VSV.

14. Remove the intake manifold along with the air control valve. Remove the power steering reservoir tank without disconnecting the hydraulic hoses. Position it out of the way.

15. Remove the spark plugs and the No. 2 front cover. Remove the timing belt and the PCV pipe.

16. Remove the cylinder head cover. Remove the camshaft timing pulleys and the No. 1 idler pulley. Remove the No. 3 timing belt cover.

17. Gradually loosen and remove the camshaft bearing cap bolts in several passes, in the proper sequence. Remove the bearing caps, oil seals and lift out the camshafts.

18. Remove the right rear engine hanger. Remove the cylinder head bolts in several stages, in the sequence illustrated and lift off the cylinder head.

**To install:**

19. Position the cylinder head and a new gasket on the block. Coat the head bolts with engine oil and tighten them in several passes, in the sequence shown to 40 ft. lbs. (54 Nm). Mark the front of each bolt with a dab of paint and then retighten the bolts a further 90 degrees turn. The paint dabs should now all be at a 90 degree angle to the front of the head.

20. Install the right rear engine hanger and tighten it to 14 ft. lbs. (19 Nm).

21. Position the camshafts in the cylinder head with the No. 1 lobes facing outward. Coat the No. 1 bearing cap with seal packing and then install all the caps over the bearing journals. Coat the bearing cap bolts with engine oil and then tighten them to 14 ft. lbs. (19 Nm) in several stages, in the order shown. Grease 2 new oil seals and install them into the camshafts.

22. Install the No. 3 timing belt cover and the No. 1 idler pulley. Install the camshaft timing pulleys.

23. Install the cylinder head cover and the timing belt.

24. Installation of the remaining components is in the reverse order of removal.

### 4A-F Engines

1. Disconnect the negative battery cable at the battery. Drain the engine coolant.

2. Remove the engine undercover and then disconnect the exhaust pipe at the manifold.

3. Remove the air cleaner and hoses. Disconnect the accelerator and throttle cables at the bracket on models with an automatic transmission.

4. Tag and disconnect all wires, lines and hoses that may interfere with cylinder head removal.

5. Disconnect the fuel lines at the fuel pump. Disconnect the heater hoses at the engine.

6. Disconnect the water hose and the by-pass hose at the rear of the cylinder head. Remove the 2 bolts and pull off the water outlet pipe.

7. Remove the 2 mounting bolts and lift out the exhaust manifold stay. Remove the upper manifold insulator and then remove the exhaust manifold.

8. Remove the distributor.

9. Disconnect the 2 water hoses at the water inlet (front of head) and then remove the inlet housing.

10. Remove the fuel pump.

11. Disconnect the PCV and water hoses at the intake manifold. Remove the manifold stay and then remove the intake manifold (don't forget the wire clamp!).

12. Remove the drive belts and the power steering pump support.

13. Remove the spark plugs and the cylinder head cover.

14. Remove the No. 3 and No. 2 front covers. Turn the crankshaft pulley and align its groove with the **0** mark on the No. 1 front cover. Check that the camshaft pulley hole aligns with the mark on the No. 1 camshaft bearing cap (exhaust side).

15. Remove the plug from the No. 1 front cover and matchmark the timing belt to the camshaft pulley. Loosen the idler pulley mounting bolt and push the pulley to the left as far as it will go; tighten the bolt. Slide the timing belt off the camshaft pulley and support it so it won't fall into the case.

16. Remove the camshaft pulley and check the camshaft thrust clearance. Remove the camshafts.

17. Gradually loosen the cylinder head mounting bolts in several passes, in the sequence illustrated. Remove the cylinder head.

**To install:**

18. Position the cylinder head on the block with a new gasket. Lightly coat the cylinder head bolts with engine oil and then install them. Tighten the bolts in 3 stages, in the proper sequence. On the final pass, torque the bolt to 44 ft. lbs. (60 Nm).

19. Position the camshafts into the cylinder head. Position the bearing caps over each journal with the arrows pointing forward.

20. Tighten each bearing cap a little at a time and in the reverse of the removal sequence. Tighten to 9 ft. lbs. (13 Nm) Recheck the camshaft end play.

21. Install the camshaft timing pulleys making sure that the camshaft knock pins and the matchmarks are in alignment. Lock each camshaft and tighten the pulley bolts to 43 ft. lbs. (59 Nm).

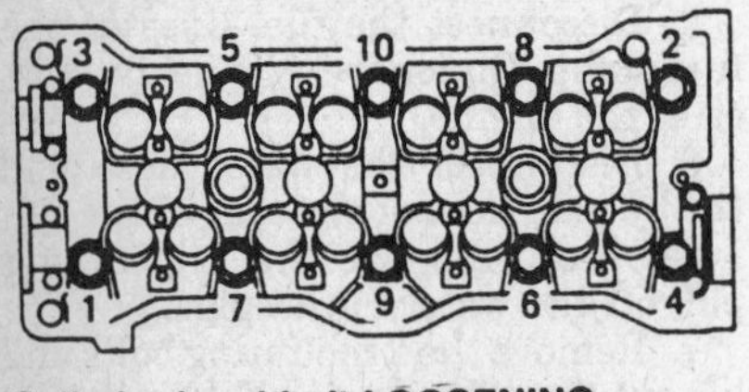


Cylinder head bolt LOOSENING sequence – 4A-F and 4A-FE engines

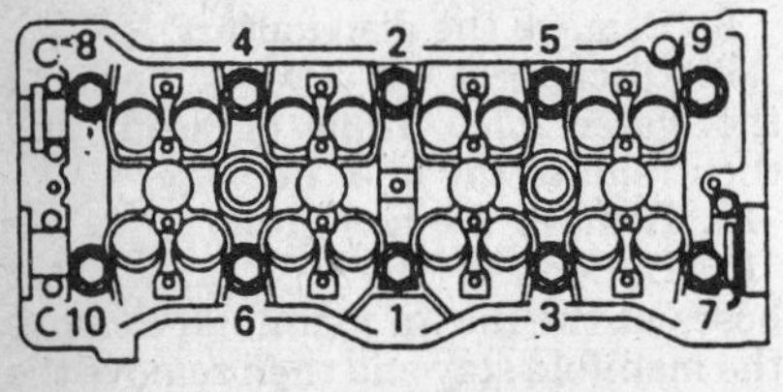


Cylinder head bolt TIGHTENING sequence – 4A-F and 4A-FE engines

22. Align the matchmarks made during removal and then install the timing belt on the camshaft pulley. Loosen the idler pulley set bolt. Make sure the timing belt meshing at the crankshaft pulley does not shift.

23. Rotate the crankshaft clockwise 2 revolutions from TDC to TDC. Make sure that each pulley aligns with the marks made previously. If the marks are not in alignment, the valve timing is wrong. Shift the timing belt meshing slightly and then repeat Steps 21–23.

24. Tighten the set bolt on the timing belt idler pulley to 27 ft. lbs. (37 Nm). Measure the timing belt deflection at the top span between the 2 camshaft pulleys. It should deflect no more than 0.16 in. at 4.4 lbs. of pressure. If deflection is greater, readjust by using the idler pulley.

25. Installation of the remaining components is in the reverse order of removal.

### 4A-FE Engines

1. Disconnect the negative battery cable at the battery. Drain the engine coolant.

2. Remove the engine undercover and then disconnect the exhaust pipe at the manifold.

3. Remove the air cleaner and hoses; disconnect the intake air temperature sensor. Disconnect the accelerator and throttle cables at the bracket on models with an automatic transmission.

4. Remove the cruise control actuator cable.

5. Tag and disconnect all wires, lines and hoses that may interfere with cylinder head removal.

6. Disconnect the fuel lines at the fuel pump. Disconnect the heater hoses at the engine.

7. Disconnect the water hose and the by-pass hose at the rear of the cylinder head. Remove the 2 bolts and pull off the water outlet pipe.

8. Remove the 2 mounting bolts and lift out the exhaust manifold stay. Remove the upper manifold insulator and then remove the exhaust manifold.

9. Remove the distributor.

10. Disconnect the 2 water hoses at the water inlet (front of head) and then remove the inlet housing.

11. Disconnect the PCV, fuel return and vacuum sensing hoses.

12. Remove the fuel inlet pipe and the cold start injector pipe. Disconnect the 4 vacuum hoses and then remove the EGR vacuum modulator.

13. Remove the fuel delivery pipe along with the injectors, spacers and insulators.

14. Unbolt the engine wire cover at the intake manifold and then disconnect the wire at the cylinder head.

15. Remove the intake manifold.

16. Remove the drive belts and then remove the water pump.

17. Remove the spark plugs and the cylinder head cover.

18. Remove the No. 3 and No. 2 front covers. Turn the crankshaft pulley and align its groove with the **0** mark on the No. 1 front cover. Check that the camshaft pulley hole aligns with the mark on the No. 1 camshaft bearing cap (exhaust side).

19. Remove the plug from the No. 1 front cover and matchmark the timing belt to the camshaft pulley. Loosen the idler pulley mounting bolt and push the pulley to the left as far as it will go; tighten the bolt. Slide the timing belt off the camshaft pulley and support it so it won't fall into the case.

20. Remove the camshaft pulley and check the camshaft thrust clearance. Remove the camshafts.

21. Gradually loosen the cylinder head mounting bolts in several passes, in the sequence illustrated. Remove the cylinder head.

**To install:**

22. Position the cylinder head on the block with a new gasket. Lightly coat the cylinder head bolts with engine oil and then install them. Tighten the bolts in 3 stages, in the proper sequence. On the final pass, torque the bolt to 44 ft. lbs. (60 Nm).

23. Position the camshafts into the cylinder head. Position the bearing caps over each journal with the arrows pointing forward.

24. Tighten each bearing cap a little at a time and in the reverse of the removal sequence. Tighten to 9 ft. lbs. (13 Nm) Recheck the camshaft end play.

25. Install the camshaft timing pulleys making sure that the camshaft knock pins and the matchmarks are in alignment. Lock each camshaft and tighten the pulley bolts to 43 ft. lbs. (59 Nm).

26. Align the matchmarks made during removal and then install the timing belt on the camshaft pulley. Loosen the idler pulley set bolt. Make sure the timing belt meshing at the crankshaft pulley does not shift.

27. Rotate the crankshaft clockwise 2 revolutions from TDC to TDC. Make sure that each pulley aligns with the marks made previously. If the marks are not in alignment, the valve timing is wrong. Shift the timing belt meshing slightly and then repeat Steps 4–6.

28. Tighten the set bolt on the timing belt idler pulley to 27 ft. lbs. (37 Nm). Measure the timing belt deflection at the top span between the 2 camshaft pulleys. It should deflect no more than 0.24 in. at 4.4 lbs. of pressure. If deflection is greater, readjust by using the idler pulley.

29. Installation of the remaining components is in the reverse order of removal.

### 4A-GE, 4A-GEC and 4A-GELC Engines

1. Disconnect the negative battery cable. Remove the engine undercover. Drain the coolant. Drain the engine oil.

2. Loosen the clamp and then disconnect the No. 1 air cleaner hose from the throttle body. Disconnect the actuator and accelerator cables from the bracket on the throttle body.

3. If equipped with power steering, Remove the power steering pump and its bracket. Position the pump to one side.

4. Loosen the water pump pulley set nuts. Remove the drive belt adjusting bolt and then remove the belt. Remove the set nuts and then remove the fluid coupling along with the fan and the water pump pulley.

5. Disconnect the upper radiator hose at the water outlet on the cylinder head. Disconnect the 2 heater hoses at the water bypass pipe and the cylinder head rear plate.

6. Remove the distributor. Remove the cold start injector pipe and the PCV hose from the cylinder head.

7. Remove the pulsation damper from the delivery pipe. Disconnect the fuel return hose from the pressure regulator.

8. Tag and disconnect all vacuum hoses which may interfere with cylinder head remvoval. Remove the wiring harness and the vacuum pipe from the No. 3 timing cover. Tag and disconnect all wires which might interfere with

cylinder head removal Position the wiring harness to one side.

9. Disconnect the exhaust bracket from the exhaust pipe. Disconnect the exhaust manifold from the exhaust pipe.

10. Remove the vacuum tank and the VCV valve. Remove the exhaust manifold.

11. Remove the 2 mounting bolts and remove the water outlet housing from the cylinder head with the No. 1 bypass pipe and gasket. Pull the No. 1 bypass pipe out of the housing.

12. Remove the fuel delivery pipe along with the fuel injectors. When removing the delivery pipe, be very careful not to drop or bump the fuel injector nozzles. Do not remove the injector cover.

13. Unscrew the 2 mounting bolts and remove the intake manifold stay. Remove the intake manifold along with the air control valve.

14. Remove the cylinder head covers and their gaskets. Remove the spark plugs. Check the valve clearance. Remove the No. 1 and No. 2 timing belt covers and their gaskets.

15. Rotate the crankshaft pulley until its groove is in alignment with the 0 mark on the No. 1 timing belt cover. Check that the valve lifters on the No. 1 cylinder are loose. If not, rotate the crankshaft 1 complete revolution (360 degrees).

16. Place matchmarks on the timing belt and 2 timing pulleys. Loosen the idler pulley bolts and move the pulley to the left as far as it will go and then retighten the bolt.

17. Remove the timing belt from the camshaft pulleys. When removing the timing belt, support the belt so that the meshing of the crankshaft timing pulley and the timing belt does not shift. Never drop anything inside the timing case cover. Be sure that the timing belt does not come in contact with dust or oil.

18. Lock the camshafts and remove the timing pulleys. Remove the No. 4 timing belt cover.

19. Using a dial indicator, measure the end play of each camshaft. If not within specification, replace the thrust bearing.

20. Loosen each camshaft bearing cap bolt a little at a time and in the sequence shown. Remove the bearing caps, camshaft and oil seal.

21. Using SST No. 09205-16010, loosen the cylinder head bolts gradually in 3 stages, and in the proper order.

22. Remove the cylinder head from the vehicle.

**To install:**

23. Position the cylinder head on the block with a new gasket. Lightly coat the cylinder head bolts with engine oil and then install the short head bolts on the intake side and the long ones on the exhaust side. Tighten the bolts in 3 stages, in the proper sequence. On the final pass, torque the bolt to 43 ft. lbs.

On 1988-89 engines, coat the head bolts with engine oil and tighten them in several passes, in the sequence shown to 22 ft. lbs. (29 Nm). Mark the front of each bolt with a dab of paint and then retighten the bolts a further 90 degree turn. The paint dabs should now all be at a 90 degree angle to the front of the head. Retighten the bolts one more time a further 90 degree turn. The paint dabs should now all be pointing toward the rear of the head.

24. Position the camshafts into the cylinder head. Position the bearing caps over each journal with the arrows pointing forward.

25. Tighten each bearing cap a little at a time and in the reverse of the removal sequence. Tighten to 9 ft. lbs. (13 Nm) Recheck the camshaft end play.

26. Using SST No. 09223-50010, drive the camshaft oil seals onto the end of the camshafts. Be careful not to install the oil seals crooked. Install the No. 4 timing belt cover.

27. Install the camshaft timing pulleys making sure that the camshaft knock pins and the matchmarks are in alignment. Lock each camshaft and tighten the pulley bolts to 34 ft. lbs. (47 Nm).

28. Align the matchmarks made during removal and then install the timing belt on the camshaft pulley. Loosen the idler pulley set bolt. Make sure the timing belt meshing at the crankshaft pulley does not shift.

29. Rotate the crankshaft clockwise 2 revolutions from TDC to TDC. Make sure that each pulley aligns with the marks made previously. If the marks are not in alignment, the valve timing is wrong. Shift the timing belt meshing slightly and then repeat Steps 27–29.

30. Tighten the set bolt on the timing belt idler pulley to 27 ft. lbs. (37 Nm). Measure the timing belt deflection at

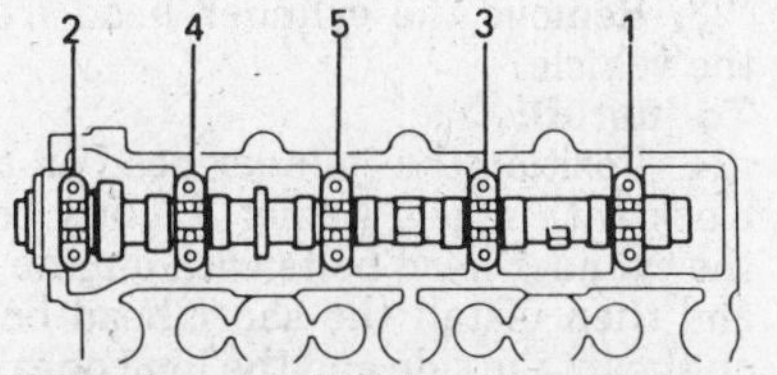


**Loosen the camshaft bearing cap bolts in this order – 4A-GE (all) and 4A-GZE engines**

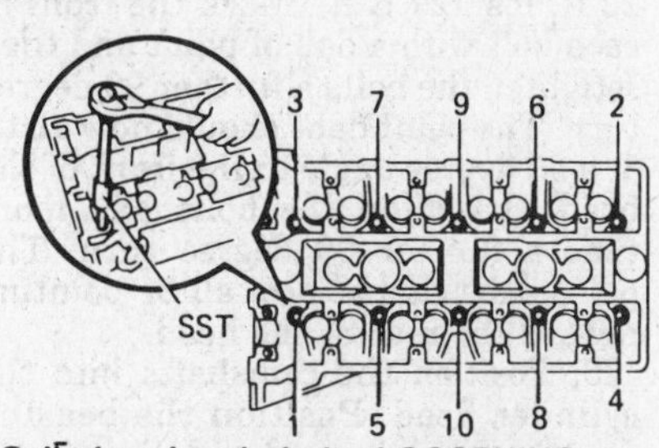


**Cylinder head bolt LOOSENING sequence – 4A-GE (all) and 4A-GZE engines**

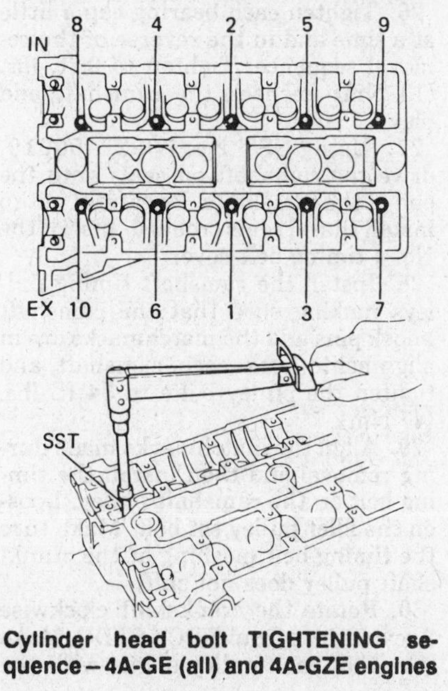


**Cylinder head bolt TIGHTENING sequence – 4A-GE (all) and 4A-GZE engines**

**Position the camshafts into the cylinder head as shown – 4A-GE (all) and 4A-GZE engines**

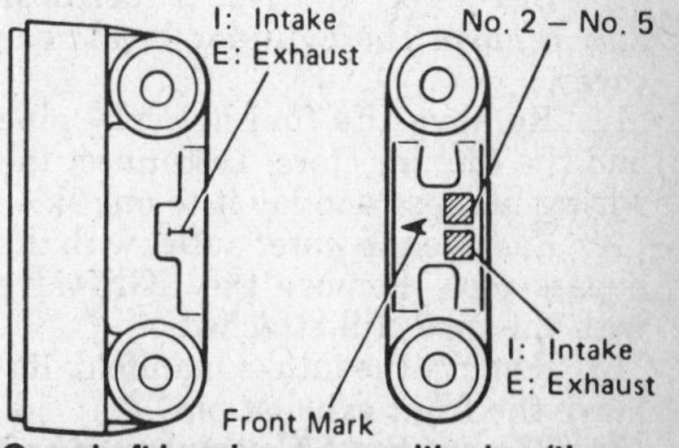


**Camshaft bearing cap positioning (the arrows must always point forward) – 4A-GE (all) and 4A-GZE engines**

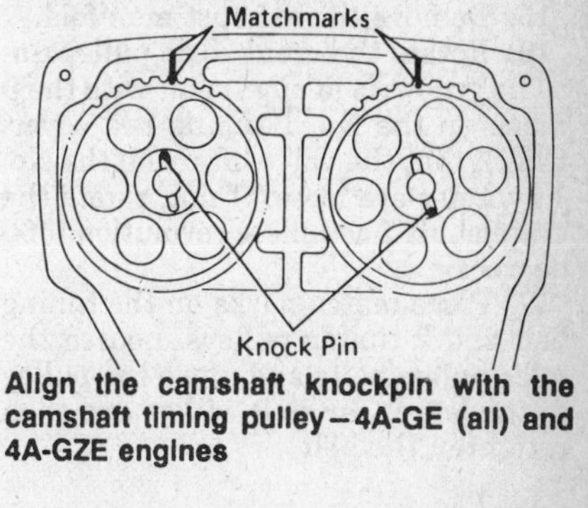


**Align the camshaft knockpin with the camshaft timing pulley – 4A-GE (all) and 4A-GZE engines**

the top span between the 2 camshaft pulleys. It should deflect no more than 0.16 in. at 4.4 lbs. of pressure. If deflection is greater, readjust by using the idler pulley.

31. Installation of the remaining components is in the reverse order of removal.

### 4A-GZE Engines

1. Disconnect the negative battery cable. Scribe matchmarks around the hinges and remove the hood. Remove the engine undercovers.
2. Drain the engine coolant and remove the intercooler. Remove the battery.
3. Disconnect the air bleeder hose at the water inlet housing. Disconnect the cruise control vacuum hose and the A/T throttle cable.
4. Remove the air flow meter with the No. 3 air cleaner hose. Disconnect the accelerator cable.
5. Remove the accelerator link and disconnect the A/C idle-up vacuum hoses.
6. Disconnect the heater hose at the rear of the cylinder head. Disconnect the brake booster vacuum hose and remove the radiator reservoir tank. Disconnect the No. 1 radiator hose at the water outlet housing.
7. Tag and disconnect any remaining hoses, wires or connections which may interfere with cylinder head removal.
8. Remove all drive belts and then remove the water pump pulley. Remove the supercharger.
9. Remove the No. 2 air outlet duct and the No. 3 fuel pipe. Remove the No. 1 vacuum transmitting pipe.
10. Disconnect the No. 2 fuel hose and remove the cylinder head rear cover.
11. Remove the fuel delivery pipe and the fuel injectors. Disconnect the wiring harness and lay it to one side.
12. Remove the water outlet with the bypass pipe. Remove the EGR valve with the pipe still attached.
13. Remove the intake manifold. Remove the front exhaust pipe.
14. Remove the A/C compressor and bracket. Remove the distributor and alternator with its bracket.
15. Remove the exhaust manifold.
16. Rotate the crankshaft pulley until its groove is in alignment with the **0** mark on the No. 1 timing belt cover. Check that the valve lifters on the No. 1 cylinder are loose. If not, rotate the crankshaft 1 complete revolution (360 degrees).
17. Place matchmarks on the timing belt and 2 timing pulleys. Loosen the idler pulley bolts and move the pulley to the left as far as it will go and then retighten the bolt.
18. Remove the timing belt from the camshaft pulleys. When removing the timing belt, support the belt so that the meshing of the crankshaft timing pulley and the timing belt does not shift. Never drop anything inside the timing case cover. Be sure that the timing belt does not come in contact with dust or oil.
19. Lock the camshafts and remove the timing pulleys. Remove the No. 4 timing belt cover.
20. Using a dial indicator, measure the end play of each camshaft. If not within specification, replace the thrust bearing.
21. Loosen each camshaft bearing cap bolt a little at a time and in the sequence shown. Remove the bearing caps, camshaft and oil seal.
22. Using SST No. 09205-16010, loosen the cylinder head bolts gradually in 3 stages, and in the proper order.
23. Remove the cylinder head from the vehicle.

**To install:**

24. Position the cylinder head on the block with a new gasket. Lightly coat the cylinder head bolts with engine oil and then install the short head bolts on the intake side and the long ones on the exhaust side. Tighten them in several passes, in the sequence shown to 22 ft. lbs. (29 Nm). Mark the front of each bolt with a dab of paint and then retighten the bolts a further 90 degree turn. The paint dabs should now all be at a 90 degree angle to the front of the head. Retighten the bolts one more time a further 90 degree turn. The paint dabs should now all be pointing toward the rear of the head.
25. Position the camshafts into the cylinder head. Position the bearing caps over each journal with the arrows pointing forward.
26. Tighten each bearing cap a little at a time and in the reverse of the removal sequence. Tighten to 9 ft. lbs. (13 Nm) Recheck the camshaft end play.
27. Using SST No. 09223-50010, drive the camshaft oil seals onto the end of the camshafts. Be careful not to install the oil seals crooked. Install the No. 4 timing belt cover.
28. Install the camshaft timing pulleys making sure that the camshaft knock pins and the matchmarks are in alignment. Lock each camshaft and tighten the pulley bolts to 34 ft. lbs. (47 Nm).
29. Align the matchmarks made during removal and then install the timing belt on the camshaft pulley. Loosen the idler pulley set bolt. Make sure the timing belt meshing at the crankshaft pulley does not shift.
30. Rotate the crankshaft clockwise 2 revolutions from TDC to TDC. Make sure that each pulley aligns with the marks made previously. If the marks are not in alignment, the valve timing is wrong. Shift the timing belt meshing slightly and then repeat Steps 28–30.
31. Tighten the set bolt on the timing belt idler pulley to 27 ft. lbs. (37 Nm). Measure the timing belt deflection at the top span between the 2 camshaft pulleys. It should deflect no more than 0.16 in. at 4.4 lbs. of pressure. If deflection is greater, readjust by using the idler pulley.
32. Installation of the remaining components is in the reverse order of removal.

### 4K-E Engines

1. Disconnect the negative battery cable. Drain the engine coolant. Loosen the two hose clamps and remove the air cleaner hose.
2. Disconnect the throttle cable from the two places it attaches to the air intake chamber and the throttle body.
3. Tag and disconnect the four vacuum hoses connected to the air intake chamber. Do the same for the spark plug wires, the temperature detect switch wire and the water temperature sender gauge wire.
4. Tag and disconnect all remaining wires, hoses and leads attached to the cylinder head or which might interfere with its removal. Remove the spark plugs and tube. Remove the intake and exhaust manifold.
5. Remove the cylinder head cover. Remove the rocker shaft assembly. Remove the pushrods. Make sure that the pushrods remain in the correct order.
6. Loosen the cylinder head bolts in the proper sequence. Cylinder head

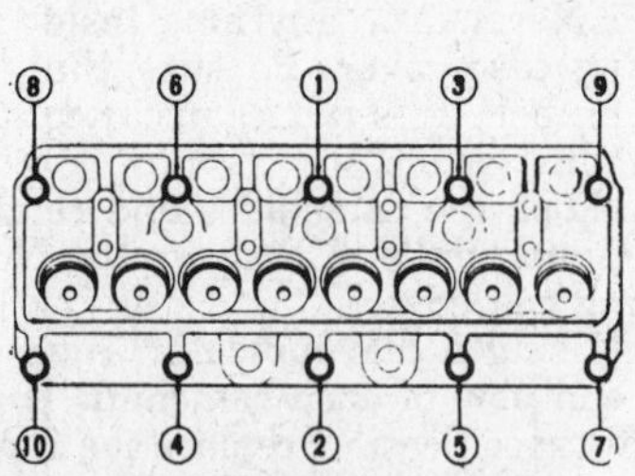


**Cylinder head bolt TIGHTENING sequence—4K-E engines**

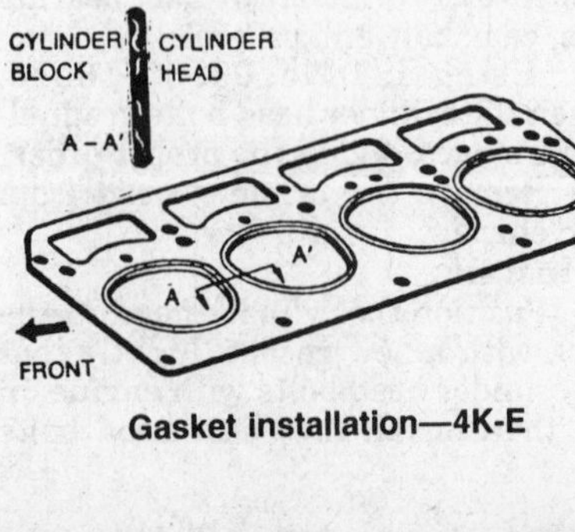


**Gasket installation—4K-E**

warpage or cracking could result from removing the bolts in the wrong order.

7. Lift the cylinder head from the dowels on the block and place it on wooden blocks. If the head is difficult to remove, carefully pry with a small prybar between the head and the block. Be very careful not to damage the cylinder head and/or block surfaces.

8. Installation is the reverse of the removal procedure. Clean the cylinder head and block gasket mounting surfaces. Be sure to properly install the head gasket. The cylinder head bolts should be torqued in the proper sequence and to the proper specification. Adjust the valves.

### 5M-GE Engines

1. Disconnect the battery cables. Drain the cooling system.

2. Disconnect the exhaust pipe from the exhaust manifold.

3. Remove the throttle cable bracket from the cylinder head if equipped with automatic transmission, and remove the accelerator and actuator cable bracket.

4. Tag and disconnect the ground cable, oxygen sensor wire, high tension coil wire, distributor connector, solenoid resistor wire connector and thermo- switch wire, if equipped with automatic transmission.

5. Tag and disconnect the brake booster vacuum hose, EGR valve vacuum hose, fuel hose from the intake manifold and actuator vacuum hose, if equipped with cruise control.

6. Disconnect the upper radiator hose from the thermostat housing, and disconnect the 2 heater hoses.

7. Disconnect the No. 1 air hose from the air intake connector. Remove the 2 clamp bolts, loosen the throttle body hose clamp and remove the air intake connector and the connector pipe.

8. Tag and disconnect all emission control hoses from the throttle body and air intake chamber, the 2 PCV hoses from the cam cover and the fuel hose from the fuel hose support.

9. Remove the air intake chamber stay and the vacuum pipe and ground cable. Remove the bolt that attaches the spark plug wire clip, leaving the wires attached to the clip. Remove the distributor from the cylinder head with the cap and wires attached, by removing the distributor holding bolt.

10. Tag and disconnect the cold start injector wire and disconnect the cold start injector fuel hose from the delivery pipe.

11. Loosen the nut of the EGR pipe, remove the 5 bolts and 2 nuts and remove the air intake chamber and gasket.

12. Remove the glove box and remove the ECU module. Disconnect the 3 connectors and pull the EFI (fuel injection) wire harness out through the engine side of the firewall.

13. Remove the pulsation damper and the No. 1 fuel pipe. Remove the water outlet housing by first loosening the clamp and disconnecting the water by pass hose.

14. Remove the intake manifold.

15. Disconnect the power steering pump drive belt and remove the power steering pump without disconnecting the fluid hoses. Position the pump out of the way.

16. Disconnect the oxygen sensor connector and remove the exhaust manifold.

17. Remove the timing belt and camshaft timing gears. Remove the timing belt cover stay, and remove the oil pressure regulator and gasket. Remove the No. 2 timing belt cover and gasket.

18. Tag and disconnect any other wires, linkage and/or hoses still attached to the cylinder head.

19. Carefully remove the 14 head bolts gradually in two or three passes and in numerical order. Head warpage or cracking could result from removing the head bolts in incorrect order.

20. Carefully lift the cylinder head from the dowels on the cylinder block, resting the mating surface on wooden blocks on the work bench. If the head is difficult to remove, tap around the mating surface gently with a rubber hammer. Keep in mind the head is aluminum and is easily damaged.

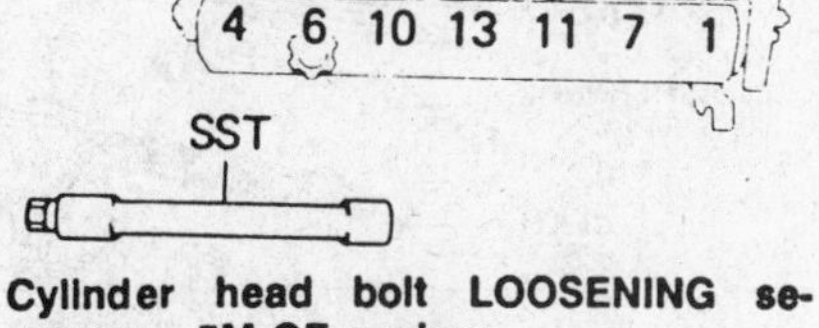


Cylinder head bolt LOOSENING sequence – 5M-GE engines

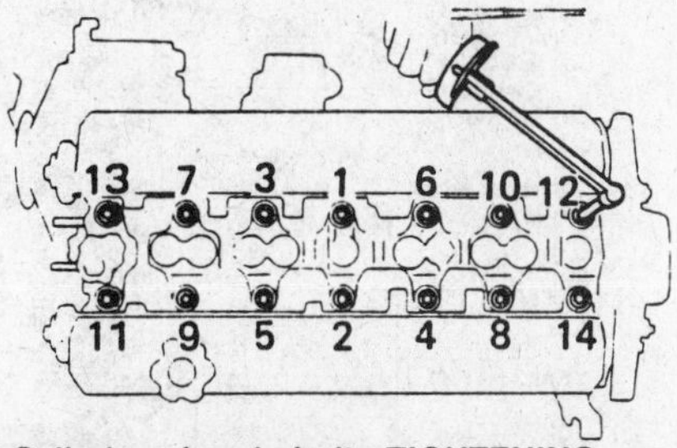


Cylinder head bolt TIGHTENING sequence – 5M-GE engines

21. Installation is the reverse of the removal procedure.

22. Prior to installation, thoroughly clean the cylinder block and head mating surfaces.

23. Be sure to torque the cylinder head to specification and in the proper sequence.

24. Adjust the valves to specification, as required.

### 7M-GE and 7M-GTE Engines

1. Disconnect the negative battery cable. Drain the coolant.

2. Disconnect the exhaust pipe from the exhaust manifold. Disconnect the cruise control cable, if equipped.

3. Disconnect the accelerator cable. Disconnect the throttle cable, if equipped with automatic transmission. Disconnect the engine ground strap.

4. On the 7M-GE, remove the No. 1 air cleaner hose along with the intake air pipe assembly. On the 7M-GTE, remove the No. 4 air cleaner pipe along with the No. 1 and No. 2 air cleaner hose.

5. Disconnect the cruise control vacuum hose, the charcoal canister hose and the brake booster hose.

6. Remove the radiator inlet hose. Disconnect the heater inlet hose. Remove the alternator assembly.

7. On the 7M-GTE, remove the power steering reservoir tank. On the 7M-GTE, remove the cam position sensor.

8. Remove the air intake chamber with the connector. Remove the PCV pipe. Disconnect and tag all required hoses and vacuum connections that are required to remove the cylinder head from the vehicle.

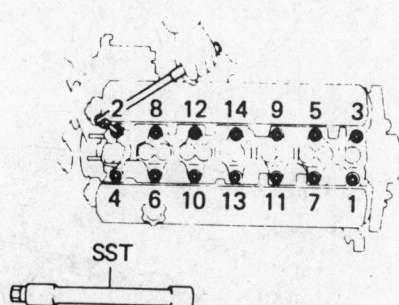

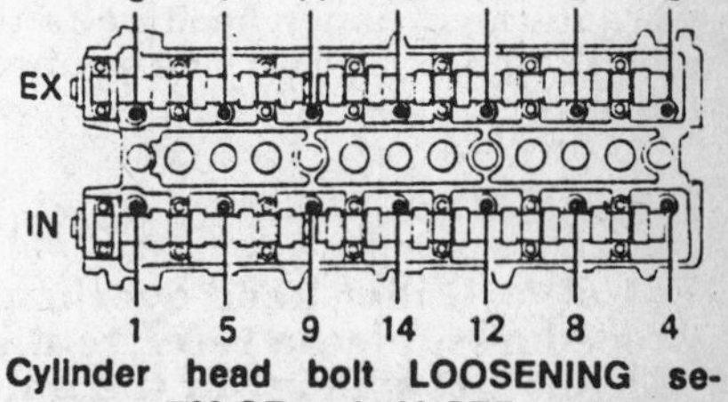


Cylinder head bolt LOOSENING sequence – 7M-GE and 7M-GTE engines

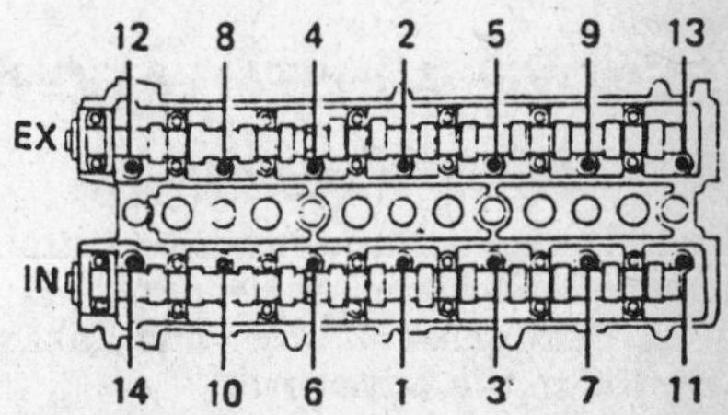


Cylinder head bolt TIGHTENING sequence – 7M-GE and 7M-GTE engines

9. Remove the EGR pipe mounting bolts. Remove the manifold stay retaining bolts. On the 7M-GE, remove the throttle body bracket. On the 7M-GTE, remove the ISC pipe.
10. Remove the air intake connector mounting bolt (7M-GTE). On the 7M-GE, remove the cold start injector tube. On the 7M-GTE, disconnect the cold start injector. Disconnect the EGR vacuum modulator from the bracket.
11. Disconnect the engine wire from the clamps of the intake chamber. Remove the nuts and bolts, vacuum pipes and intake chamber with the connector and gasket.
12. On the 7M-GTE, remove the ignition coil and bracket. Disconnect all electrical connections that are required to remove the cylinder head from the engine.
13. Remove the pulsation damper, the VSV and the No. 1 fuel pipe. Remove the No. 2 and No. 3 fuel pipes. On the 7M-GTE, remove the auxiliary air pipe.
14. On the 7M-GE, remove the high tension wires and the distributor. Remove the oil dipstick. On the 7M-GTE, remove the turbocharger assembly.
15. Remove the exhaust manifold. Remove the water outlet housing. Remove the cylinder head covers. Remove the spark plugs.
16. Remove the timing belt and the camshaft timing pulleys. Remove the cylinder head retaining bolts gradually and in the proper sequence. Carefully remove the cylinder head from the engine. As the cylinder head is lifted, separate the No. 5 water bypass line from its union.
17. Installation is the reverse of the removal procedure.
18. Be sure to use a new gasket and install it in the proper direction. Torque the cylinder head bolts to specification and in the proper sequence.

## OVERHAUL

**For all cylinder head overhaul procedures, please refer to the "Engine Rebuilding" in the Unit Repair section.**

## Rocker Arm Shafts

### REMOVAL & INSTALLATION

#### *22R and 22R-E Engines*

1. Disconnect the negative battery cable. Remove the air cleaner.
2. Disconnect all hoses and linkage clipped to the valve cover.
3. Remove the spark plug wires. Remove the carburetor. Remove the valve cover.

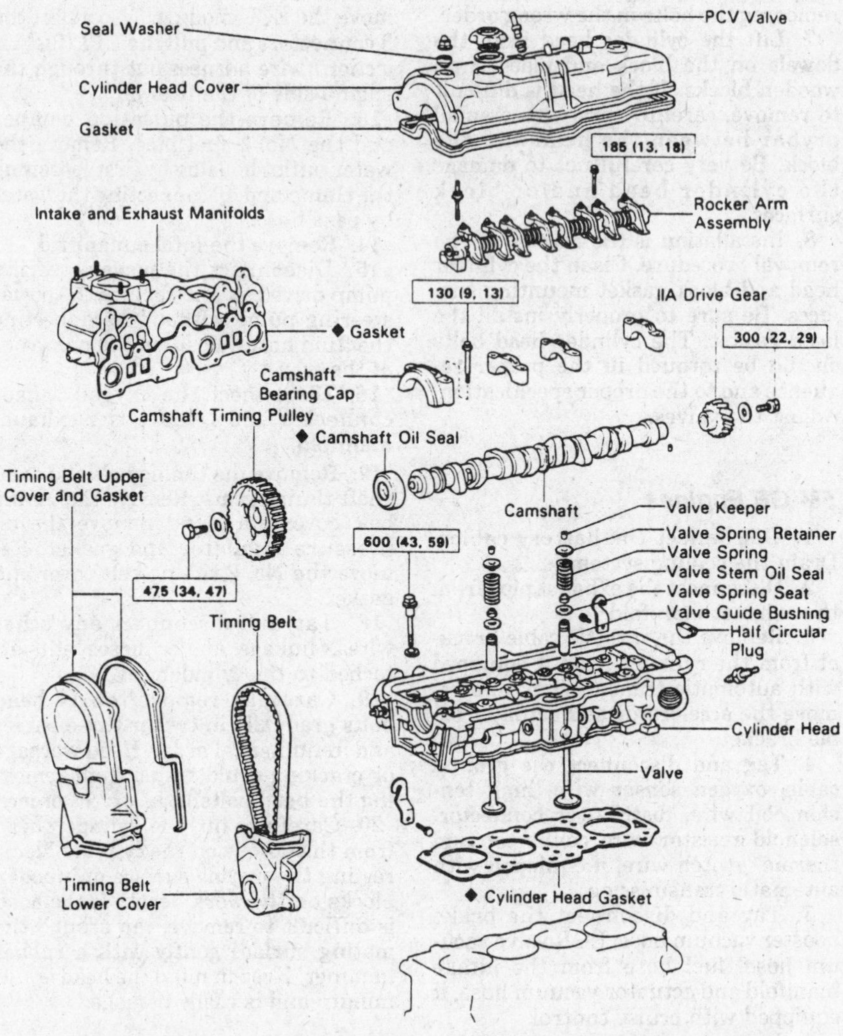

**Exploded view of the cylinder head – 3A, 3A-C, 4A-C and 4A-LC engines**

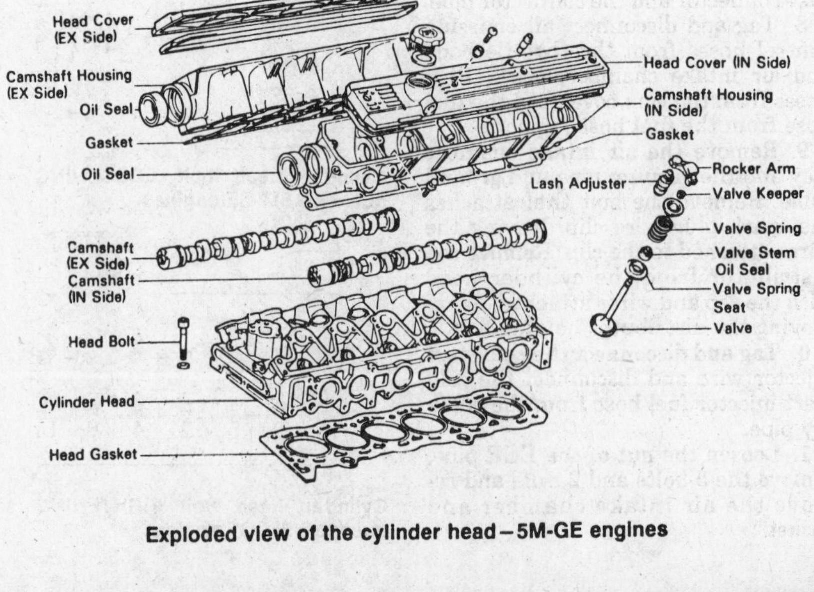

**Exploded view of the cylinder head – 5M-GE engines**

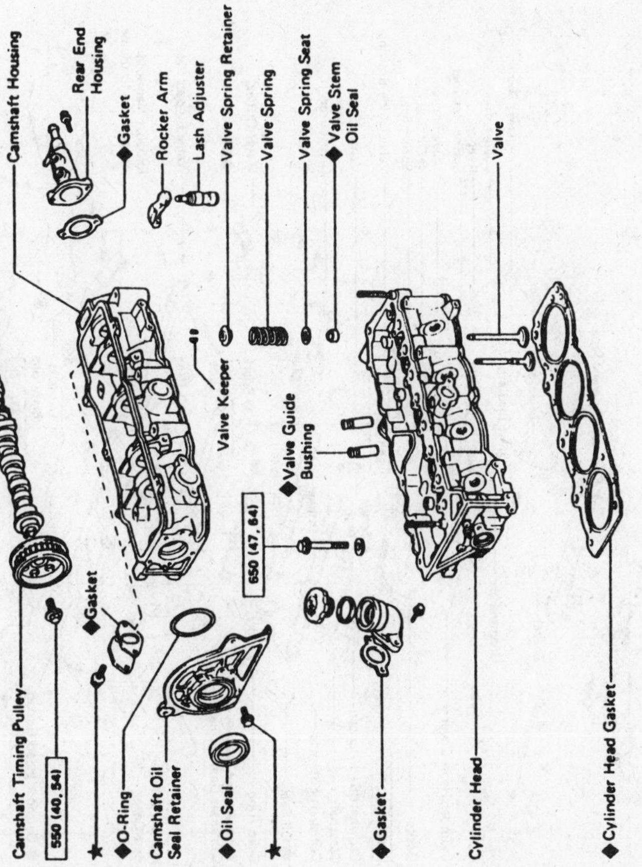
Camshaft Timing Pulley
550 (40, 54)
Gasket
O-Ring
Camshaft Oil Seal Retainer
Oil Seal
Gasket
Cylinder Head
Cylinder Head Gasket
650 (47, 84)
Valve Guide Bushing
Valve Keeper
Cylinder Head Cover
Gasket
150 (11, 15)
Camshaft
Camshaft Housing
Rear End Housing
Gasket
Rocker Arm
Lash Adjuster
Valve Spring Retainer
Valve Spring
Valve Spring Seat
Valve Stem Oil Seal
Valve

Exploded view of the cylinder head – 2S-E engines

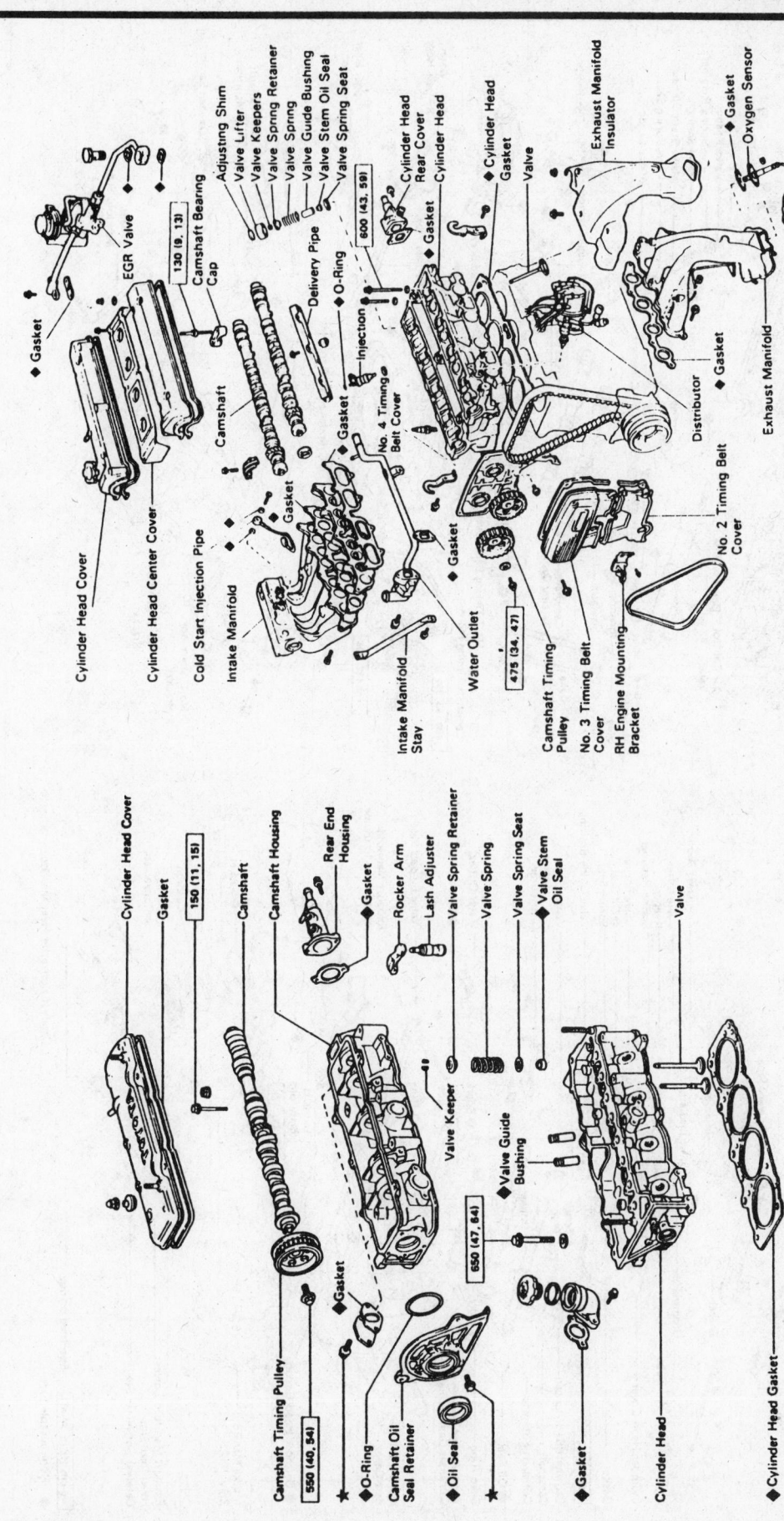

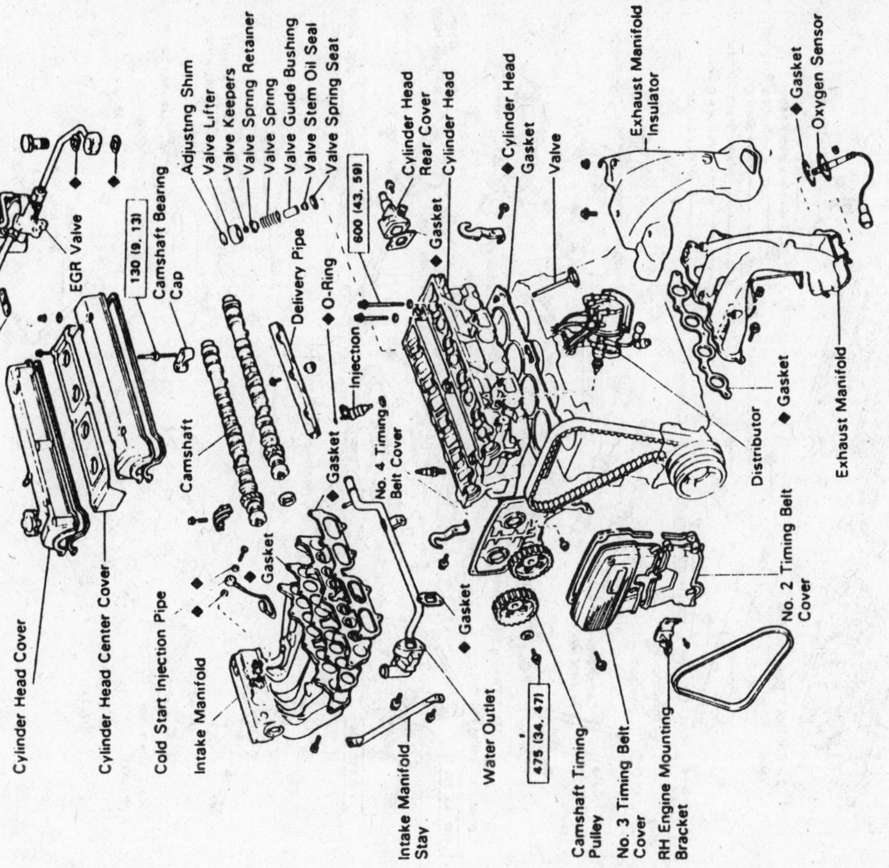
Cylinder Head Cover
Cylinder Head Center Cover
Cold Start Injection Pipe
Intake Manifold
Intake Manifold Stay
Water Outlet
475 (34, 47)
Camshaft Timing Pulley
No. 3 Timing Belt Cover
RH Engine Mounting Bracket
Gasket
EGR Valve
130 (9, 13)
Camshaft Bearing Cap
Adjusting Shim
Valve Lifter
Valve Keepers
Valve Spring Retainer
Valve Spring
Valve Guide Bushing
Valve Stem Oil Seal
Valve Spring Seat
Camshaft
Gasket
Delivery Pipe
O-Ring
Injection
Gasket
No. 4 Timing Belt Cover
600 (43, 59)
Cylinder Head Rear Cover
Cylinder Head
Gasket
Cylinder Head Gasket
Valve
Gasket
Timing Belt
No. 2 Timing Belt Cover
Distributor
Gasket
Exhaust Manifold
Exhaust Manifold Insulator
Gasket
Oxygen Sensor

Exploded view of the cylinder head – 4A-GE (all) engines; 4A-GZE similar

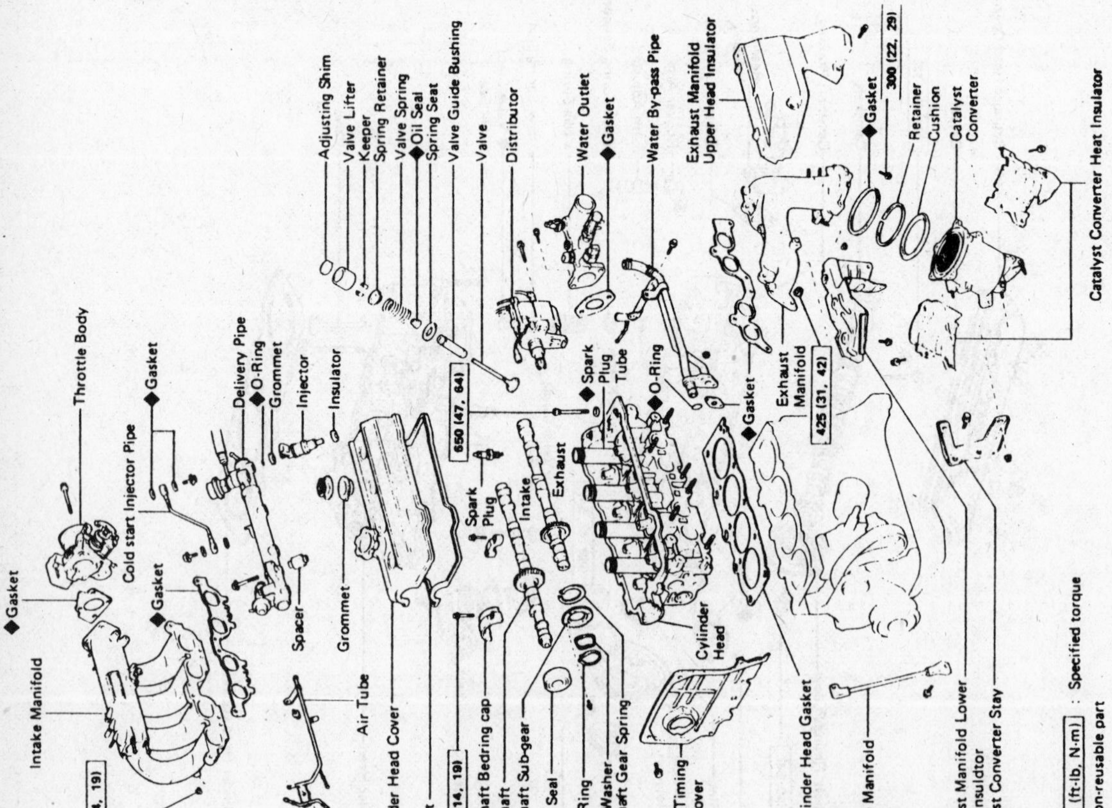

195 (14, 19)
Intake Manifold
◆Gasket
Throttle Body
Cold start Injector Pipe
◆Gasket
◆Gasket
Delivery Pipe
◆O-Ring
Grommet
Injector
Insulator
Spacer
Grommet
Air Tube
Adjusting Shim
Valve Lifter
Keeper
Spring Retainer
Valve Spring
◆Oil Seal
Spring Seat
Valve Guide Bushing
Valve
Distributor
Water Outlet
◆Gasket
Water By-pass Pipe
Exhaust Manifold Upper Head Insulator
◆Gasket
300 (22, 29)
Retainer
Cushion
Catalyst Converter
Catalyst Converter Heat Insulator
Cylinder Head Cover
Gasket
190 (14, 19)
Camshaft Bearing cap
Camshaft
Camshaft Sub-gear
◆Oil Seal
Snap Ring
Wave Washer
Camshaft Gear Spring
650 (47, 64)
Spark Plug
Intake
Exhaust
◆Spark Plug Tube
◆O-Ring
◆Gasket
Exhaust Manifold
425 (31, 42)
Cylinder Head
No. 3 Timing Belt Cover
◆Cylinder Head Gasket
Intake Manifold Stay
Exhaust Manifold Lower Head Insuldtor
Catalyst Converter Stay
kg-cm (ft-lb, N·m) : Specified torque
◆ Non-reusable part

**Exploded view of the cylinder head—3S-FE engines**

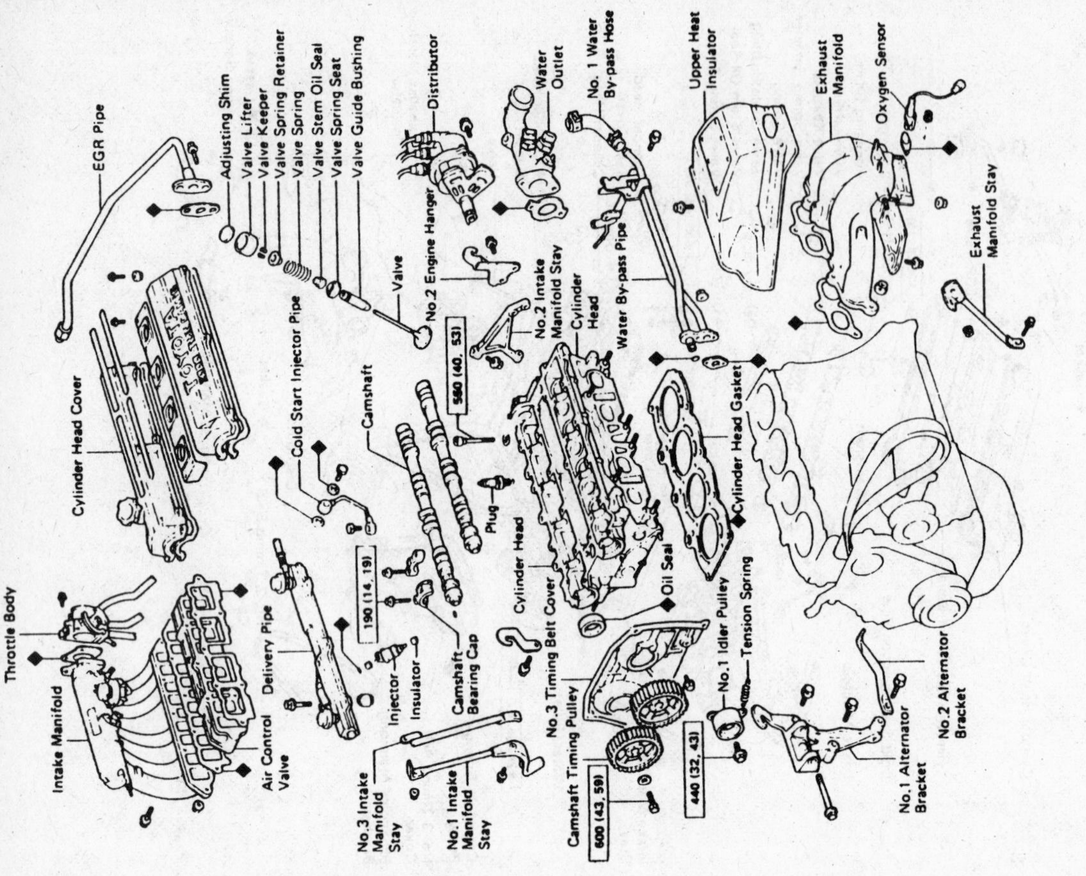

Intake Manifold
Throttle Body
Air Control Valve
Delivery Pipe
Cylinder Head Cover
EGR Pipe
Adjusting Shim
Valve Lifter
Valve Keeper
Valve Spring Retainer
Valve Spring
Valve Stem Oil Seal
Valve Spring Seat
Valve Guide Bushing
Distributor
Water Outlet
No. 1 Water By-pass Hose
Upper Heat Insulator
Exhaust Manifold
Oxygen Sensor
Exhaust Manifold Stay
Cold Start Injector Pipe
Camshaft
Valve
No.2 Engine Hanger
560 (40, 53)
No.2 Intake Manifold Stay
Cylinder Head
Water By-pass Pipe
Plug
Cylinder Head
Cylinder Head Gasket
190 (14, 19)
Camshaft Bearing Cap
Injector
Insulator
No.3 Intake Manifold Stay
No.1 Intake Manifold Stay
No.3 Timing Belt Cover
Oil Seal
Camshaft Timing Pulley
600 (43, 59)
No.1 Idler Pulley
Tension Spring
440 (32, 43)
No.2 Alternator Bracket
No.1 Alternator Bracket

**Exploded view of the cylinder head—3S-GE engines**

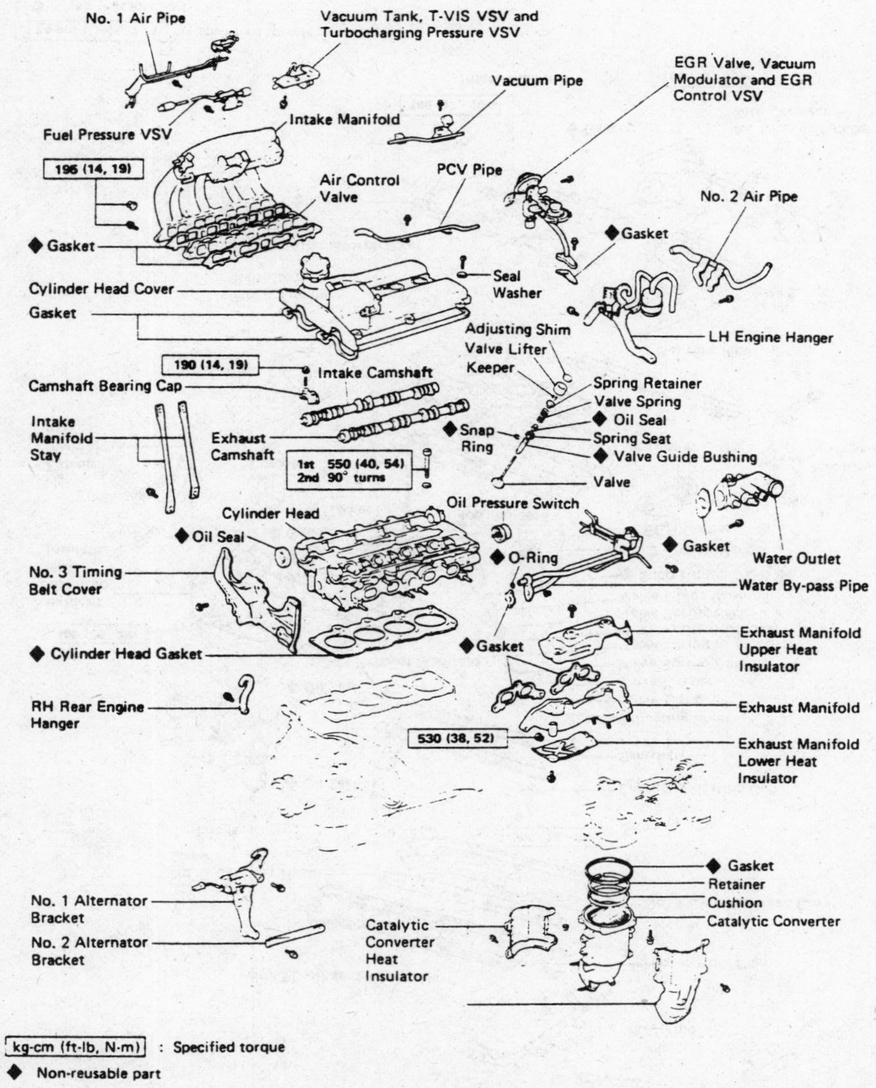

No. 1 Air Pipe
Vacuum Tank, T-VIS VSV and Turbocharging Pressure VSV
EGR Valve, Vacuum Modulator and EGR Control VSV
Vacuum Pipe
Intake Manifold
Fuel Pressure VSV
196 (14, 19)
Air Control Valve
PCV Pipe
No. 2 Air Pipe
◆ Gasket
◆ Gasket
Cylinder Head Cover
Gasket
Seal Washer
Adjusting Shim
Valve Lifter
Keeper
LH Engine Hanger
190 (14, 19)
Intake Camshaft
Camshaft Bearing Cap
Spring Retainer
Valve Spring
◆ Oil Seal
Spring Seat
◆ Valve Guide Bushing
Intake Manifold Stay
Exhaust Camshaft
◆ Snap Ring
1st 550 (40, 54) 2nd 90° turns
Valve
Oil Pressure Switch
Cylinder Head
◆ Oil Seal
◆ Gasket
◆ O-Ring
Water Outlet
No. 3 Timing Belt Cover
Water By-pass Pipe
◆ Gasket
Exhaust Manifold Upper Heat Insulator
◆ Cylinder Head Gasket
RH Rear Engine Hanger
Exhaust Manifold
530 (38, 52)
Exhaust Manifold Lower Heat Insulator
◆ Gasket
Retainer
Cushion
Catalytic Converter
No. 1 Alternator Bracket
No. 2 Alternator Bracket
Catalytic Converter Heat Insulator
kg-cm (ft-lb, N·m) : Specified torque
◆ Non-reusable part

Exploded view of the cylinder head—3S-GTE engines

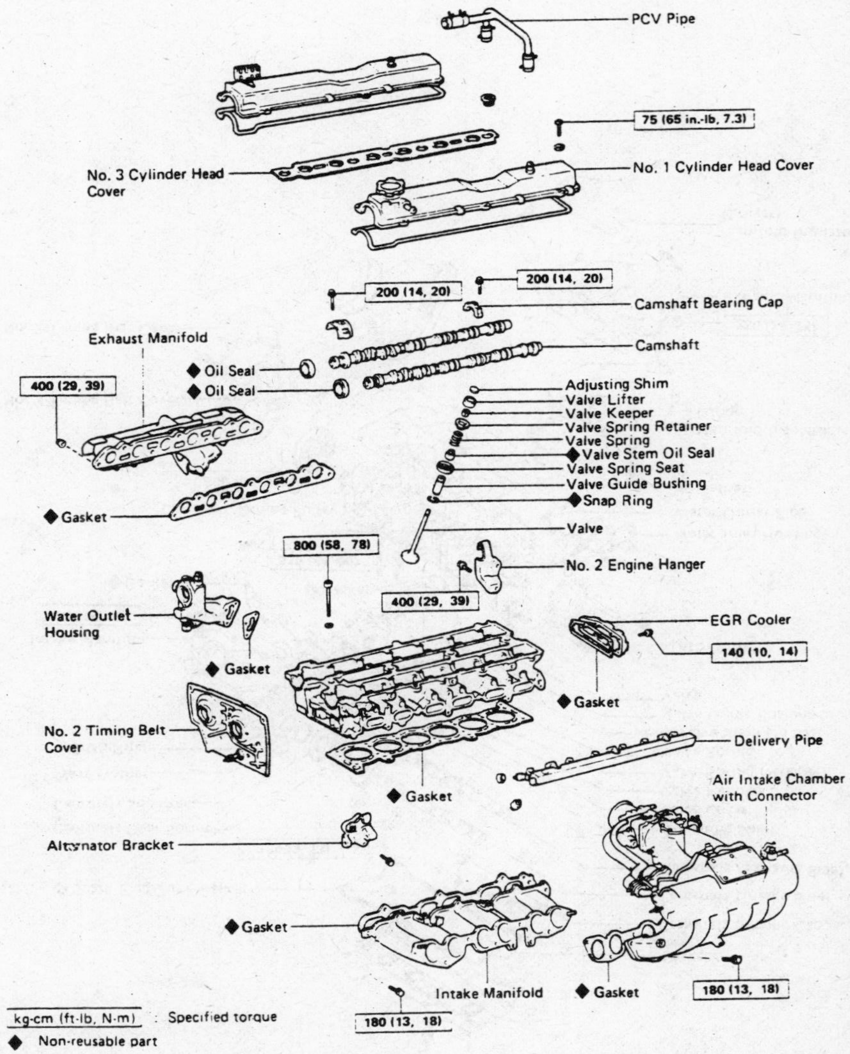

PCV Pipe
75 (65 in.-lb, 7.3)
No. 3 Cylinder Head Cover
No. 1 Cylinder Head Cover
200 (14, 20)
200 (14, 20)
Camshaft Bearing Cap
Exhaust Manifold
Camshaft
◆ Oil Seal
◆ Oil Seal
400 (29, 39)
Adjusting Shim
Valve Lifter
Valve Keeper
Valve Spring Retainer
Valve Spring
◆ Valve Stem Oil Seal
Valve Spring Seat
Valve Guide Bushing
◆ Snap Ring
◆ Gasket
Valve
800 (58, 78)
No. 2 Engine Hanger
400 (29, 39)
Water Outlet Housing
EGR Cooler
140 (10, 14)
◆ Gasket
◆ Gasket
No. 2 Timing Belt Cover
Delivery Pipe
Air Intake Chamber with Connector
◆ Gasket
Alternator Bracket
◆ Gasket
Intake Manifold
◆ Gasket
180 (13, 18)
180 (13, 18)
kg-cm (ft-lb, N·m) : Specified torque
◆ Non-reusable part

Exploded view of the cylinder head—7M-GE engines

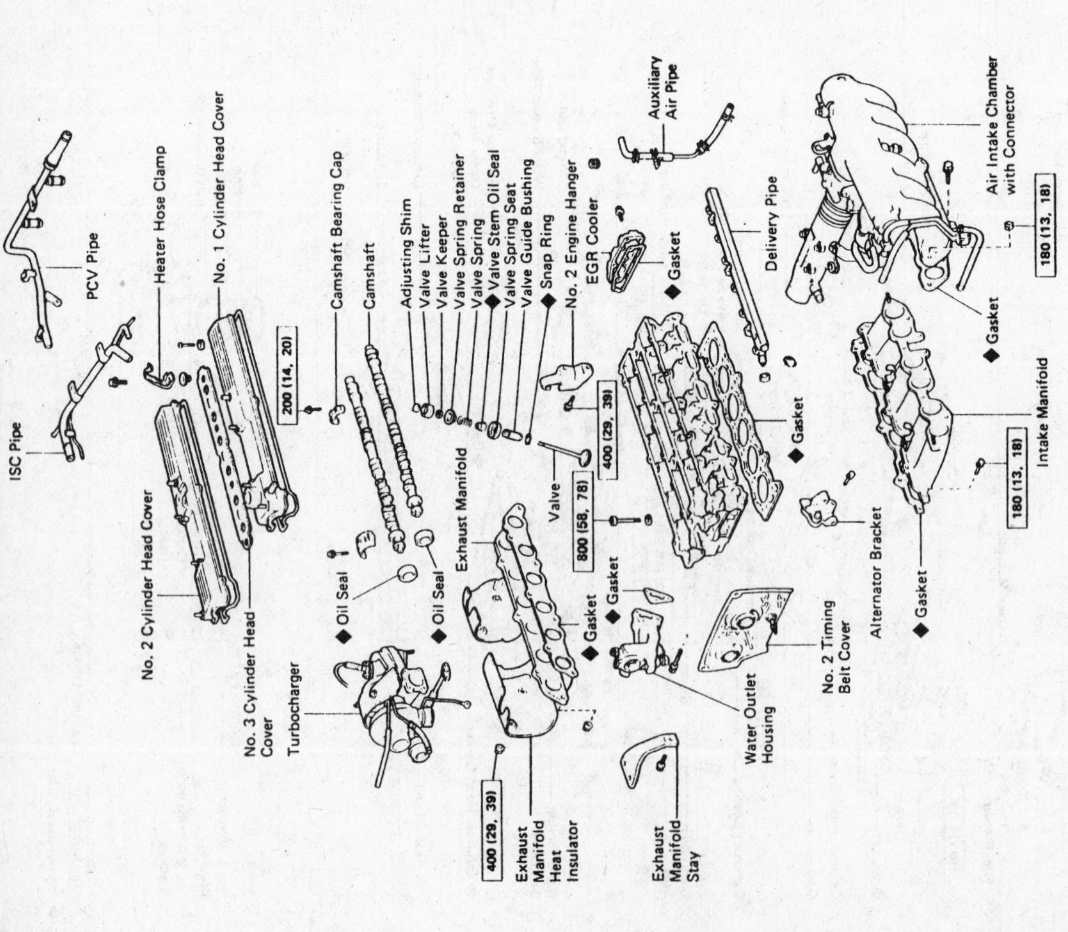


kg-cm (ft-lb, N-m) : Specified torque
◆ Non-reusable part

**Exploded view of the cylinder head—7M-GTE engines**

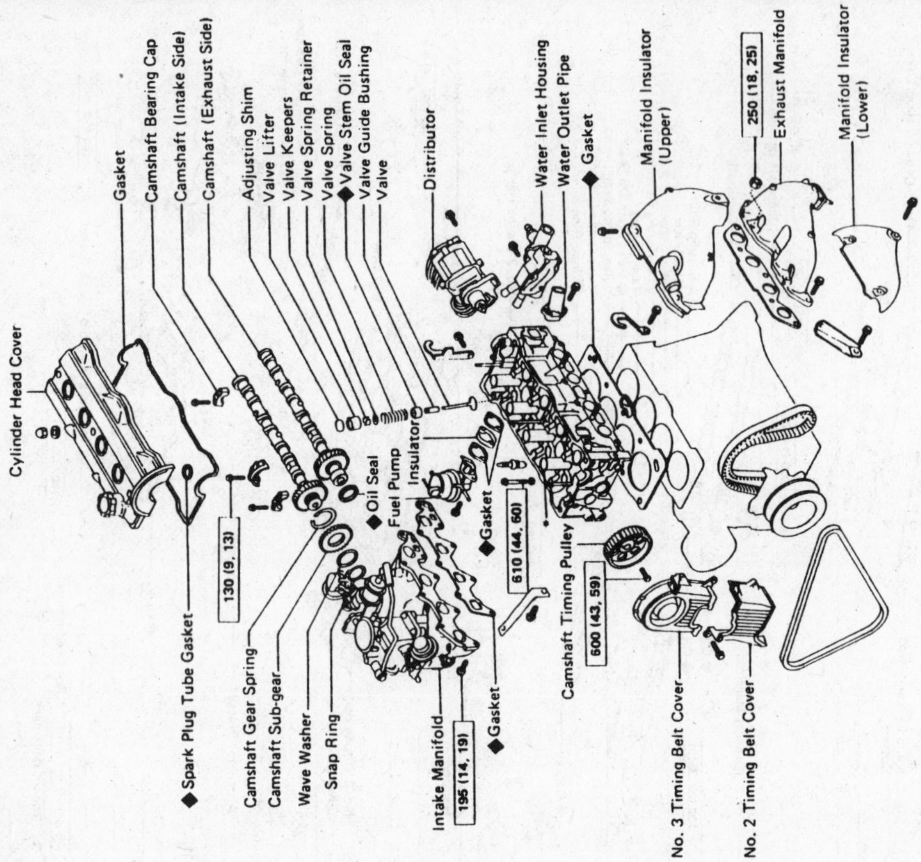


**Exploded view of the cylinder head—4A-F engines**

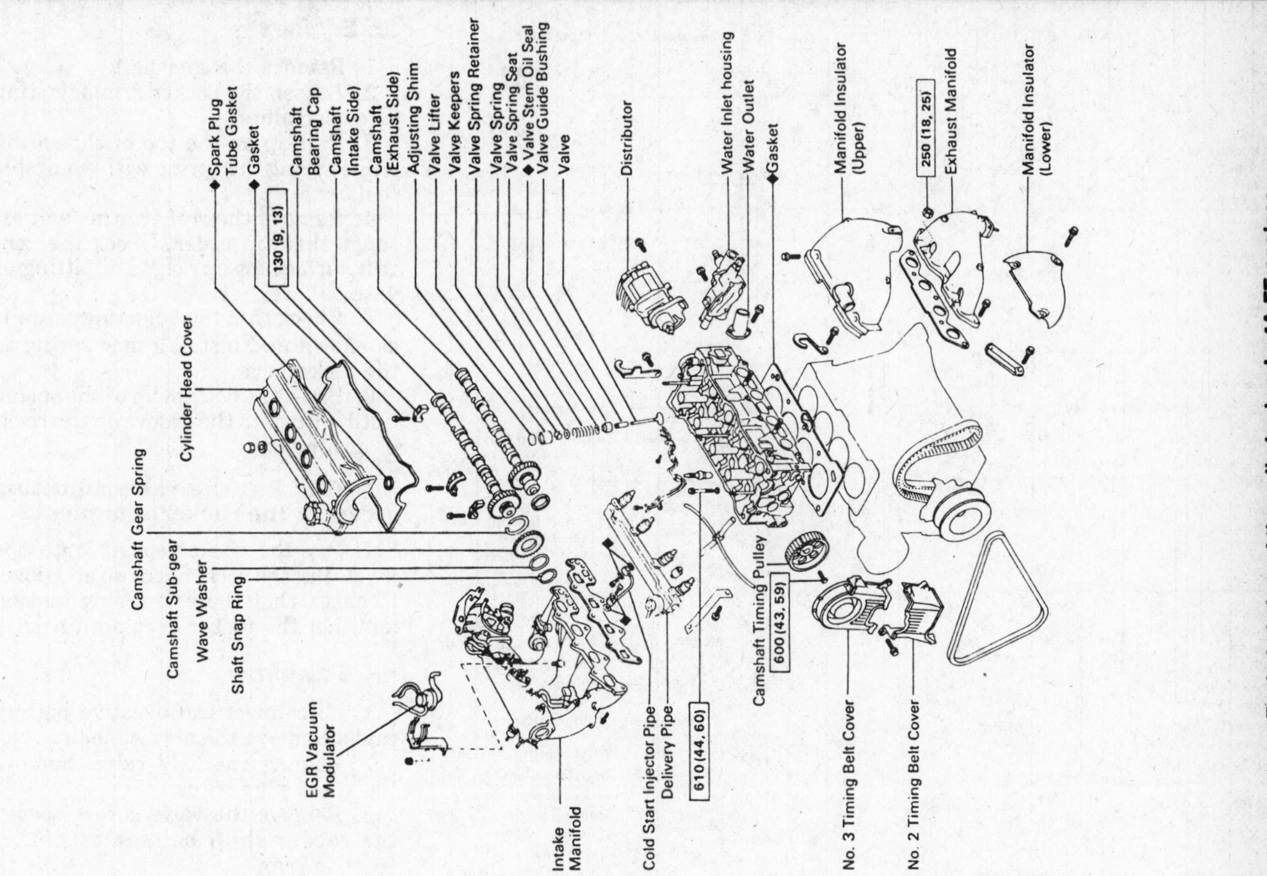
Spark Plug Tube Gasket
Gasket
130 (9, 13)
Camshaft Bearing Cap
Camshaft (Intake Side)
Camshaft (Exhaust Side)
Adjusting Shim
Valve Lifter
Valve Keepers
Valve Spring Retainer
Valve Spring
Valve Spring Seat
Valve Stem Oil Seal
Valve Guide Bushing
Valve
Distributor
Water Inlet housing
Water Outlet
Gasket
Manifold Insulator (Upper)
250 (18, 25)
Exhaust Manifold
Manifold Insulator (Lower)
Cylinder Head Cover
Camshaft Gear Spring
Camshaft Sub-gear
Wave Washer
Shaft Snap Ring
EGR Vacuum Modulator
Intake Manifold
Cold Start Injector Pipe
Delivery Pipe
610 (44, 60)
Camshaft Timing Pulley
600 (43, 59)
No. 3 Timing Belt Cover
No. 2 Timing Belt Cover

Exploded view of the cylinder head—4A-FE engines

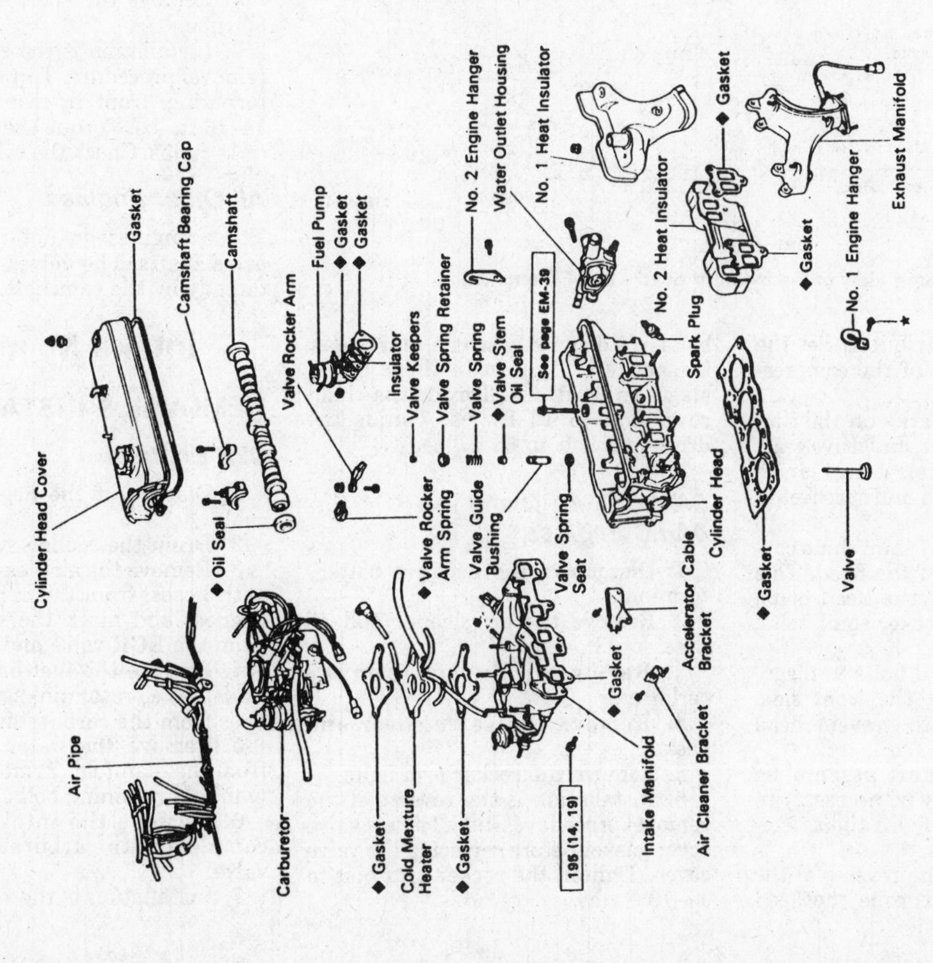
Air Pipe
Cylinder Head Cover
Gasket
Camshaft Bearing Cap
Camshaft
Oil Seal
Valve Rocker Arm
Fuel Pump
Gasket
Gasket
Insulator
Valve Keepers
Valve Spring Retainer
Valve Spring
Valve Stem Oil Seal
See page EM-39
No. 2 Engine Hanger
Water Outlet Housing
No. 1 Heat Insulator
Gasket
Carburetor
Gasket
Cold Mexture Heater
Gasket
Valve Rocker Arm Spring
Valve Guide Bushing
Valve Spring Seat
Cylinder Head
Spark Plug
No. 2 Heat Insulator
Gasket
No. 1 Engine Hanger
Exhaust Manifold
195 (14, 19)
Intake Manifold
Gasket
Air Cleaner Bracket
Accelerator Cable Bracket
Gasket
Valve

Exploded view of the cylinder head—3E engines

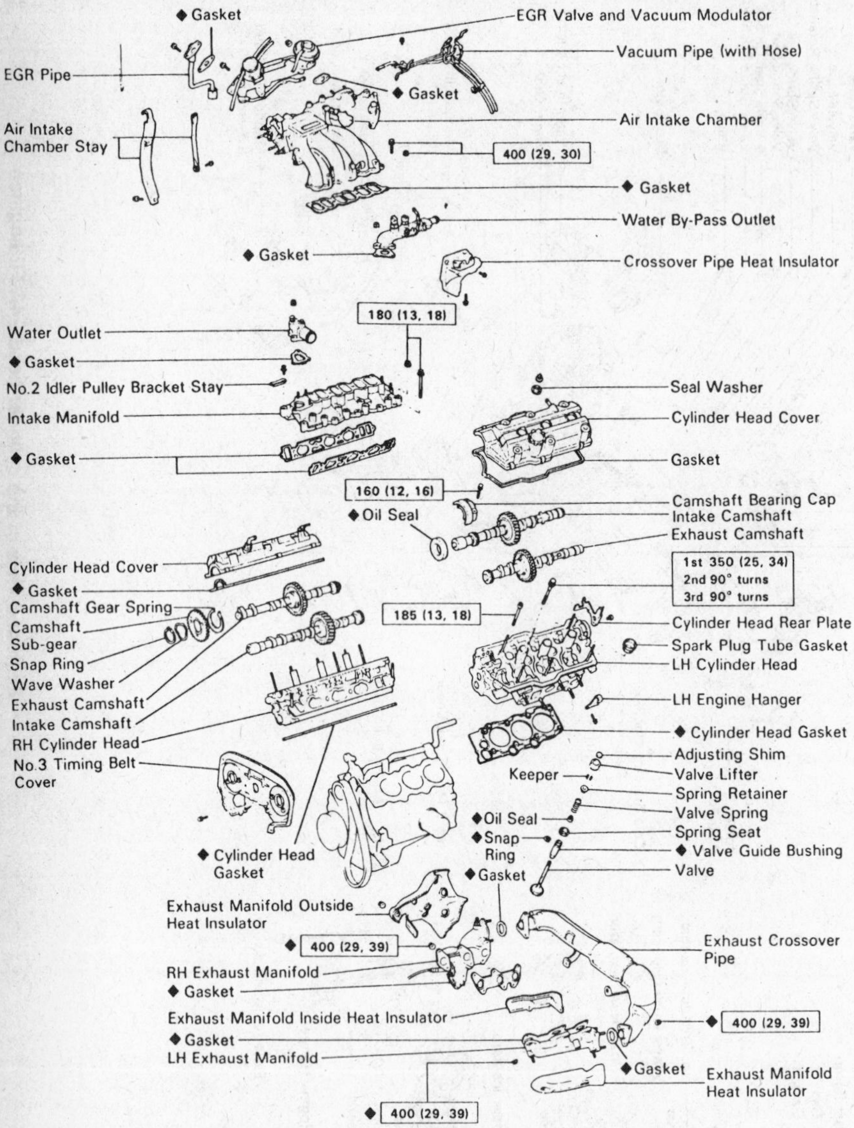


**Exploded view of the cylinder head—2VZ-FE engines**

4. Remove the distributor. Set the No. 1 piston at TDC of the compression stroke.
5. Paint mating marks on the timing chain and sprocket, and drive gear.
6. Remove the distributor drive gear, leaving the chain and sprocket in position.
7. Remove the one 14mm chain cover bolt in the front of the head. This must be done before the head bolts, which also serve as rocker shaft bolts, are removed.
8. Remove the head bolts in diagonal pattern. Start at the front side. This must be done to prevent head warpage.
9. Remove the shaft assemblies from the head. It may be necessary to use a pry bar to evenly lift the assemblies from the dowels.
10. Installation is the reverse of the removal procedure. Torque the head bolts in a diagonal pattern, starting at the center. Tighten in three equal stages to 64 ft. lbs. Torque the chain cover bolt to 12 ft. lbs. Torque the drive gear bolt to 65 ft. lbs.

### *3A, 3A-C, 4A-C and 4A-LC Engines*

1. Disconnect the negative battery terminal.
2. Remove the air cleaner and all necessary hoses.
3. Remove all linkage from the carburetor.
4. Remove the valve cover and gasket.
5. Remove the rocker arm bolts.
6. Installation is the reverse of the removal procedure. Install a new valve cover gasket before replacing the valve cover. Tighten the rocker arm bolt to 17–19 ft. lbs.

### *3E Engines*

1. Remove the camshaft.
2. Loosen the rocker arm adjusting screw locknuts.
3. Pull up on the top of the spring while prying the spring with a suitable tool.
4. Remove the rocker arms and arrange them in order. Check the contact surface for any signs of pitting or wear.
5. Check that the adjusting screw is as shown and install a new spring to the rocker arm.
6. Press the bottom lip of the spring until it fits into the groove on the rocker arm pivot.

**NOTE: Put the valve adjusting screw in the rocker arm pivot.**

7. Pry the rocker spring onto the pivot. Pul the rocker arm up and down to check that there is spring tension and that the rocker does not rattle.

### *4K-E Engines*

1. Disconnect the negative battery cable. Remove the air cleaner.
2. Remove the PCV valve. Remove the spark plug wires.
3. Remove the valve cover. Loosen the rocker shaft bolts, alternating front to rear.
4. Remove the shaft assembly and oil tube.
5. Installation is the reverse of the removal procedure. Torque bolts in alternating, front to rear sequence, to 14–16 ft. lbs. Torque the oil pipe bolts to 14 ft. lbs. Check the valve clearance.

### *All Other Engines*

These engines do not utilize rocker arms shafts. The valves are activated directly by the camshaft.

# Intake Manifold

## REMOVAL & INSTALLATION

### *22R Engines*

1. Disconnect the negative battery cable.
2. Drain the cooling system.
3. Remove the air cleaner, complete with hoses, from the carburetor. Disconnect and mark the vacuum lines from the EGR valve and carburetor.
4. Remove the fuel lines, electrical leads, accelerator linkage, and water hose from the carburetor.
5. Remove the water bypass hose from the manifold. Remove the intake manifold retaining bolts.
6. Remove the intake manifold, complete with carburetor and EGR valve.
7. Installation is the reverse of the

removal procedure. Be sure to use a new gasket, as required. Tighten the bolts in several stages working from the inside bolts outward.

### 22R-E Engines

1. Disconnect the negative battery cable. Drain the cooling system.
2. Disconnect the air intake hose from both the air cleaner assembly on one end and the air intake chamber on the other.
3. Tag and disconnect all vacuum lines attached to the intake chamber and manifold.
4. Tag and disconnect the wires to the cold start injector, throttle position sensor, and the water hoses from the throttle body. Remove the EGR valve from the intake chamber.
5. Tag and disconnect the actuator cable, accelerator cable and automatic transmission throttle cable, if equipped from the cable bracket on the intake chamber.
6. Unbolt the air intake chamber from the intake manifold and remove the chamber with the throttle body attached. Disconnect the fuel hose from the delivery pipe.
7. Tag and disconnect the air valve hose from the intake manifold. Make sure all hoses, lines and wires are tagged for later installation and disconnected from the intake manifold.
8. Remove the intake manifold retaining bolts. Remove the manifold from the cylinder head, removing the delivery pipe and injection nozzle in unit with the manifold.
9. Installation is the reverse of the removal procedure. Use new gaskets, as required.

### 2S-E Engines

1. Disconnect the negative battery cable. Drain the coolant.
2. Disconnect and tag any wires, hoses or cable in the way of manifold removal. Remove the throttle body assembly.
3. Remove the intake manifold retaining bolts. Remove the intake manifold from the vehicle.manifold.
4. Installation is the reverse of the removal procedure. Use new gaskets, as required.

### 2VZ-FE Engines

1. Disconnect the negative battery cable and drain the engine coolant.
2. Disconnect the throttle cable at the throttle body. If equipped, remove the cruise control actuator and vacuum pump.
3. Remove the air cleaner hose.
4. Raise the front of the vehicle and remove the engine undercovers.
5. Remove the lower suspension crossmember and the front exhaust pipe.
6. Remove the alternator. Remove the ISC valve.
7. Remove the throttle body. Remove the EGR pipe, valve and vacuum modulator.
8. Remove the vacuum pipe and the distributor.
9. Remove the exhaust crossover pipe. Disconnect the cold start injector and then remove the injector tube.
10. Tag and disconnect all hoses leading to the air intake chamber and then remove the chamber.
11. Remove the fuel delivery pipes and the injectors.
12. Disconnect the water temperature sensor and remove the upper radiator hose. Remove the water outlet. Remove the water by-pass outlet.
13. Loosen the 2 bolts and remove the cylinder head rear plate.
14. Remove the No. 2 idler pulley bracket stay.
15. Remove the 8 bolts and 4 nuts and lift out the intake manifold with its 2 gaskets.
16. Use 2 new gaskets when installing the manifold and tighten the bolts, from the center outward, to 13 ft. lbs. (18 Nm).
17. Installation of the remaining components is in the reverse order of removal.

### 3E Engines

1. Disconnect the negative battery cable. Drain the coolant. Remove the air cleaner assembly.
2. Disconnect and tag wires, hoses or cables in the way of manifold removal.
3. Remove the necessary components in order to gain access to the intake manifold retaining bolts.
4. Remove the carburetor assembly. Remove the intake manifold water hose.
5. Remove the intake manifold retaining bolts. Remove the intake manifold from the vehicle.
6. Installation is the reverse of the removal procedure. Use new gaskets, as required. Tighten to 14 ft. lbs. (19 Nm).

### 3S-FE Engines

1. Disconnect the negative battery cable. Drain the coolant. Remove the air cleaner assembly.
2. Disconnect and tag wires, hoses or cables in the way of manifold removal.
3. Remove the necessary components in order to gain access to the intake manifold retaining bolts.
4. Remove the throttle body assembly. Remove the cold start injector pipe.
5. Remove the air tube assembly. If equipped with power steering remove the hoses before removing the air tube assembly.
6. Remove the intake manifold retaining bolts. Remove the intake manifold from the vehicle.
7. Installation is the reverse of the removal procedure. Use new gaskets, as required. Tighten the intake manifold mounting bolts to 14 ft. lbs. (19 Nm). Tighten the 12mm manifold stay bolt to 14 ft. lbs. (19 Nm); tighten the 14mm bolts to 31 ft. lbs. (42 Nm).

### 3S-GE and 3S-GTE Engines

1. Disconnect the negative battery cable. Drain the coolant. Remove the air cleaner assembly.
2. Disconnect and tag wires, hoses or cables in the way of manifold removal.
3. Remove the necessary components in order to gain access to the intake manifold retaining bolts.
4. Remove the intake manifold retaining bolts. Remove the intake manifold from the vehicle.
5. Installation is in the reverse of the removal procedure. Use new gaskets, as required.

### 4A-F, 4A-FE, 4A-GE, 4A-GEC, 4A-GELC & 4A-GZE Engines

1. Disconnect the negative battery cable. Drain the coolant. Remove the air cleaner assembly.
2. Disconnect and tag wires, hoses or cables in the way of manifold removal.
3. Remove the necessary components in order to gain access to the intake manifold retaining bolts.
4. Remove the intake manifold retaining bolts. Remove the intake manifold from the vehicle.
5. Installation is the reverse of the removal procedure. Use new gaskets, as required.

### 5M-GE Engines

1. Disconnect the negative battery cable. Drain the engine coolant.
2. Disconnect and tag wires, hoses or cables in the way of manifold removal.
3. Remove the air intake chamber. Disconnect and move the wiring away from the fuel delivery and injector pipe. Remove the fuel injector and delivery pipe.
4. Remove the fuel pressure regulator, which is mounted on the center of the intake manifold.
5. Remove the EGR valve from the rear of the manifold. Mark and disconnect the radiator hoses, heater hoses, and vacuum lines from the intake manifold.

6. Remove the distributor cap and position it out of the way.

7. Remove the intake manifold retaining bolts. Remove the intake manifold and gasket from the engine.

8. Installation is the reverse of the removal procedure. Use new gaskets, as required. Torque the manifold fasteners to 10–15 ft. lbs.

### 7M-GE and 7M-GTE Engines

1. Disconnect the negative battery cable. Drain the coolant. Remove the air cleaner assembly.

2. Disconnect and tag wires, hoses or cables in the way of manifold removal.

3. Remove the necessary components in order to gain access to the intake manifold retaining bolts.

4. Remove the air intake connector along with the air intake chamber assembly.

5. Remove the fuel delivery pipe with the injectors still attached.

**NOTE: Be careful that the injectors do not fall out of the delivery pipe.**

6. Remove the intake manifold retaining bolts. Remove the intake manifold from the vehicle.

7. Installation is the reverse of the removal procedure. Use new gaskets, as required. Tighten the bolts from the inside to the outside, to 13 ft. lbs. (18 Nm).

# Exhaust Manifold

## REMOVAL & INSTALLATION

### 22R and 22R-E Engines

1. Disconnect the negative battery cable. Remove the 3 exhaust pipe flange bolts and disconnect the exhaust pipe from the manifold.

2. Disconnect the spark plug leads. Matchmark the distributor rotor, housing and the engine block. Remove the distributor.

3. Remove the air cleaner tube from the heat stove. Remove the outer part of the heat stove.

4. Remove the manifold complete with air injection tubes and the inner portion of the heat stove. Separate the inner portion of the heat stove from the manifold.

5. Installation is the reverse of the removal procedure. Tighten the retaining nuts to 29–36 ft. lbs. working from the inside out. Install the distributor and set the timing. Tighten the exhaust pipe flange nuts to 25–32 ft. lbs.

### 2S-E Engines

1. Disconnect the negative battery cable. Raise the vehicle and support it safely. Remove the right hand gravel shield from beneath the engine.

2. Remove the downpipe support bracket. Unfasten the bolts from the flange and detach the downpipe from the manifold.

3. Remove the automatic choke and air cleaner stove hoses from the exhaust manifold, if so equipped. Remove the EGR valve, if so equipped.

4. Remove, or move aside, any of the air injection system components which may be in the way when removing the manifold.

5. Remove the exhaust manifold retaining bolts, in two or three stages, starting from the inside, working out. Remove the exhaust manifold from the vehicle.

6. Installation is the reverse of the removal procedure. Use a new gasket, as required. Tighten the retaining bolts to specifications.

### 2VZ-FE Engines

1. Disconnect the negative battery cable and drain the engine coolant.

2. Disconnect the throttle cable at the throttle body. If equipped, remove the cruise control actuator and vacuum pump.

3. Remove the air cleaner hose.

4. Raise the front of the vehicle and remove the engine undercovers.

5. Remove the lower suspension crossmember and the front exhaust pipe.

6. Remove the alternator. Remove the ISC valve.

7. Remove the throttle body. Remove the EGR pipe, valve and vacuum modulator.

8. Remove the vacuum pipe and the distributor.

9. Remove the exhaust crossover pipe. Disconnect the cold start injector and then remove the injector tube.

10. Tag and disconnect all hoses leading to the air intake chamber and then remove the chamber.

11. Remove the fuel delivery pipes and the injectors.

12. Disconnect the water temperature sensor and remove the upper radiator hose. Remove the water outlet. Remove the water by-pass outlet.

13. Loosen the 2 bolts and remove the cylinder head rear plate.

14. Remove the intake manifold.

15. Disconnect the $0_2$ sensor and then remove the outside heat insulator for the righ manifold. Remove the manifold and gasket and then remove the inner heat shield.

16. Remove the left side heat shield and then remove the manifold.

17. Install the manifolds with new gaskets and tighten the bolts to 29 ft. lbs. (39 Nm).

18. Installation of the remaining components is in the reverse order of removal.

### 3E Engines

1. Disconnect the negative battery cable. Remove the exhaust manifold heat insulator shield assembly.

2. Remove the necessary components in order to gain access to the exhaust manifold retaining bolts.

3. Disconnect the exhaust manifold bolts at the exhaust pipe. Disconnect the oxygen sensor electrical wire. It may be necessary to raise and support the vehicle safely before removing these bolts.

4. Remove the exhaust manifold retaining bolts. Remove the exhaust manifold from the vehicle.

5. Installation is the reverse of theremoval procedure. Be sure to use new gaskets, as required. The **E** mark on the gasket must face outward. Tighten to 38 ft. lbs. (51 Nm).

### 3S-FE Engines

1. Disconnect the negative battery cable. Remove the exhaust manifold heat insulator shield assembly.

2. Remove the necessary components in order to gain access to the exhaust manifold retaining bolts.

3. Disconnect the exhaust manifold bolts at the exhaust pipe. It may be necessary to raise and support the vehicle safely before removing these bolts.

4. Remove the exhaust manifold retaining bolts. Remove the exhaust manifold from the vehicle.

5. Installation is the reverse of theremoval procedure. Be sure to use new gaskets, as required. The **R** mark should be toward the rear. Tighten the bolts to 31 ft. lbs. (41 Nm).

### 5M-GE Engines
### 3S-GE and 3S-GTE Engines
### 4A-F, 4A-FE, 4A-GE, 4A-GEC, 4A-GELC & 4A-GZE Engines

1. Disconnect the negative battery cable. Raise and support the vehicle safely. Remove the right hand gravel shield from underneath the car.

2. Remove the exhaust pipe support stay. Unbolt the exhaust pipe from the exhaust manifold flange.

3. Disconnect the oxygen sensor connector. On the 3S-GE and 4A-F, remove the upper heat insulator.

4. Remove the manifold retaining bolts. Remove the exhaust manifold from the vehicle.

5. Installation is the reverse of the removal procedure. Use a new gasket, as required. Torque all nuts evenly to the specified torque.

### 7M-GE and 7M-GTE Engines

1. Disconnect the negative battery cable. Remove the exhaust manifold heat insulator shield assembly, if equipped.
2. Remove the necessary components in order to gain access to the exhaust manifold retaining bolts.
3. Disconnect the exhaust manifold bolts at the exhaust pipe. It may be necessary to raise and support the vehicle safely before removing these bolts.
4. If equipped with turbocharger, remove it.
5. Remove the exhaust manifold retaining bolts. Remove the exhaust manifold from the vehicle.
6. Installation is the reverse of theremoval procedure. Be sure to use new gaskets, as required. Tighten the bolts from the inside to the outside, to 13 ft. lbs. (18 Nm).

# Combination Manifold

## REMOVAL & INSTALLATION

### 3A, 3A-C, 4A-C and 4A-LC Engines

1. Disconnect the negative battery cable.
2. Remove the air cleaner and all necessary hoses.
3. Remove all the carburetor linkages.
4. Remove the carburetor.
5. Remove the intake/exhaust manifold pipe.
6. Remove the intake/exhaust manifold.
7. Installation is the reverse of the removal procedure. Tighten the manifold bolts to 15–21 ft. lbs.

### 4K-E Engines

1. Disconnect the negative battery cable. Loosen the 2 hose clamps and remove the air cleaner hose.
2. Disconnect the throttle cable from its 2 attachment points on the air intake chamber and the throttle body. Position the cable out of the way.
3. Tag and disconnect all vacuum hoses leading from the air intake chamber.
4. Tag and disconnect the 3 electrical leads attached to the air intake chamber.
5. Unscrew and remove the 2 air intake chamber support brackets. Remove the air intake pipe-to-manifold retaining bolts and lift off the air intake chamber and pipes as an assembly. The air intake assembly must be supported while removing the pipe retaining bolts.
6. Tag and disconnect the 4 injector wires. Remove the 2 wire harness clamps and then remove the EFI solenoid wiring harness from the delivery pipe.
7. Disconnect the heater outlet hoses. Disconnect the exhaust pipe from the exhaust manifold. Remove the 6 mounting bolts and then remove the combination manifold.
8. Installation is the reverse of the removal procedure. Use new gaskets, as required.

# Turbocharger

## REMOVAL & INSTALLATION

### 3S-GTE Engines

1. Disconnect the negative battery cable. Drain the coolant from the engine and intercooler.
2. Remove the air cleaner assembly. Remove the catalytic converter and the $O_2$ sensor.
3. Disconnect the 2 intercooler water lines and the reservoir tank line. Loosen the clamps, disconnect the air hose and remove the intercooler.
4. Remove the alternator duct and the No. 2 alternator bracket.
5. Remove the turbo heat insulator and the turbo outlet elbow. Remove the turbo stay.
6. Remove the turbocharger.
7. Installation is in the reverse order of removal. Pour about 20cc of new oil into the turbocharger oil inlet and then spin the impeller to lubricate the bearing. Tighten the turbo-to-manifold bolts to 47 ft. lbs. (64 Nm).

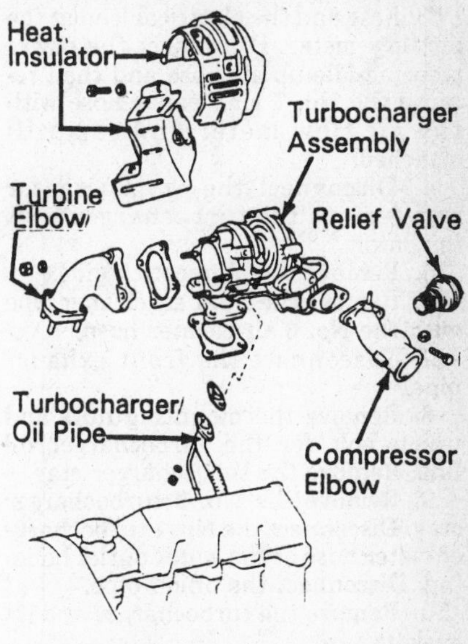


Typical turbocharger assembly

### 7M-GTE Engines

1. Disconnect the negative battery cable and drain the coolant.
2. Remove the No. 4 air cleaner pipe with the No. 1 and No. 2 air cleaner hoses still attached.
3. Disconnect the 3 air hoses, the

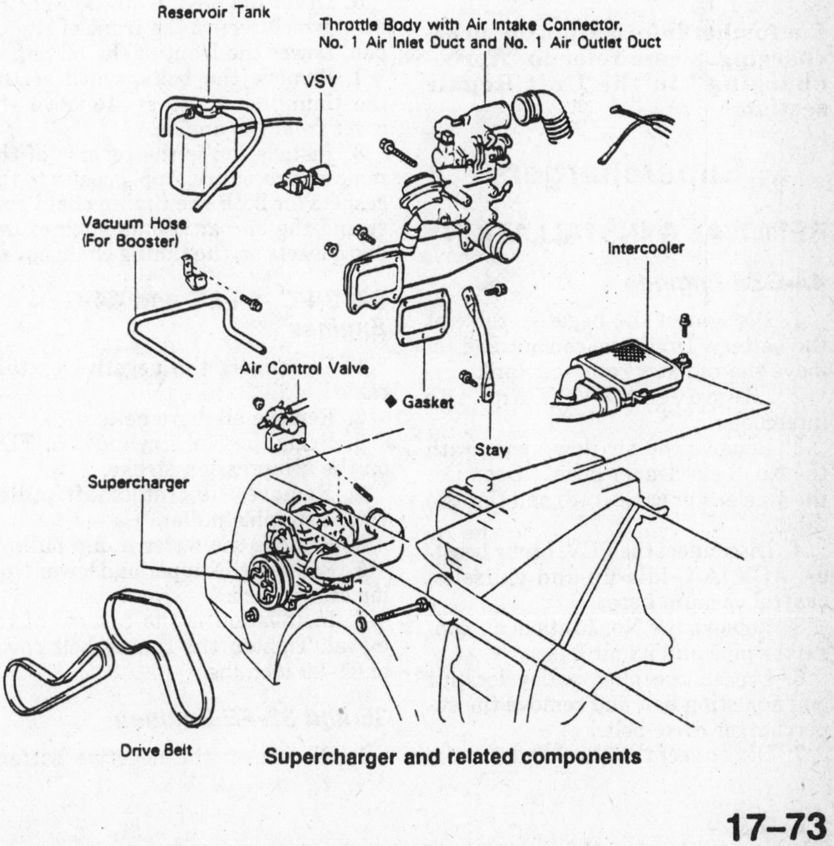


Supercharger and related components

PCV hose and the electrical lead at the air flow meter. Disconnect the power steering idle-up air hose and then remove the No. 7 air cleaner hose with the air flow meter and cap still attached.

4. Disconnect the oxygen sensor and remove the turbocharger heat insulator.
5. Remove the oil dipstick gide.
6. Remove the No. 1 air cleaner pipe with the No. 6 air cleaner hose.
7. Disconnect the front exhaust pipe.
8. Remove the mounting nuts and union bolt for the turbocharger oil line. Remove the turbocharger stay.
9. Remove the No. 2 turbocharger stay. Disconnect the No. 1 turbocharger water hose at the water outlet housing. Disconnect the union pipe.
10. Remove the turbocharger and its gasket.
11. Prior to installing the turbocharger, pour approximately 20cc (1.2 cu. in.) of new oil into the oil inlet and then turn the impeller wheel by hand a few times inorder to lubricate the bearing.
12. Position a new gasket with the protrusion pointing toward the rear and then install the turbocharger unit. Tighten the mounting bolts to 33 ft. lbs. (44 Nm). Tighten the union bolt to 25 ft. lbs. (34 Nm) and the nut to 9 ft. lbs. (13 Nm). The remainder of the installation is in the reverse order of removal.

### TROUBLESHOOTING

**For further information on turbocharging, please refer to "Turbocharging" in the Unit Repair section.**

## Supercharger

### REMOVAL & INSTALLATION

#### *4A-GZE Engines*

1. Disconnect the negative cable at the battery. Drain the coolant and remove the radiator reservoir tank.
2. Remove the VSV and the intercooler.
3. Remove the air flow meter with the No. 3 air cleaner hose. Disconnect the accelerator cable (rod) and throttle cable.
4. Disconnect the PCV, brake booster, ACV, A/C idle-up and emission control vacuum hoses.
5. Remove the No. 1 intake air connector pipe and its air hose.
6. Loosen the idler pulley locknut and adjusting bolt and remove the supercharger drive belt.
7. Disconnect the No. 2 and 3 water bypass hoses. Loosen the air hose clamp.
8. Remove the air inlet duct stay. Remove the throttle body.
9. Disconnect the ACV and supercharger connectors and the 2 ACV hoses. Remove the 2 nuts and the ACV. Remove the pivot bolt and nut, remove the 2 stud bolts and then rotate the assembly so the hub is facing upward; remove the supercharger.
10. Installation is in the reverse order of removal. Tighten the 2 stud bolts to 25 ft. lbs. (34 Nm).

## Front Cover

### REMOVAL & INSTALLATION

#### *22R and 22R-E Engines*

1. Disconnect the negative battery cable. Remove the cylinder head from the engine.
2. Remove the radiator. Remove the alternator.
3. If equipped with an air pump, remove the pump and bracket from the engine. If equipped with power steering, remove the pump.
4. Remove the fan and water pump as a complete assembly. To prevent the fluid from running out from the fan coupling, do not tip the assembly over on its side.
5. Unfasten the crankshaft pulley securing bolts and remove the pulley with a gear puller. Do not remove the 10mm bolt from its hole, if installed, as it is used for balancing.
6. Drain the engine oil. Loosen the bolts which secure the front of the oil pan. Lower the front of the oil pan.
7. Remove the bolts which secure the timing chain cover. Remove the cover from the engine.
8. Installation is the reverse of the removal procedure. Apply sealer to the gaskets for both the timing chain cover and the oil pan. Some engines use two gaskets on the timing chain cover.

#### *3A, 3A-C, 4A-LC and 4A-C Engines*

1. Disconnect the negative battery cable.
2. Remove all drive belts.
3. Bring the No. 1 cylinder to TDC on the compression stroke.
4. Remove the crankshaft pulley with a suitable puller.
5. Remove the water pump pulley.
6. Remove the upper and lower timing case covers.
7. Installation is the reverse of removal. Tighten the timing belt cover to 61–99 inch lbs.

#### *3E and 3S-FE Engines*

1. Disconnect the negative battery cable. On 3E engine, remove the air cleaner assembly. Remove all drive belts.
2. On the 3S-FE engine remove the alternator and bracket. If equipped with cruise control remove the actuator and bracket assembly.
3. Raise and support the vehicle safely. Remove the right tire and wheel asssembly. Remove the right side engine under cover. Remove the right side engine mount insulator.
4. On the 3E engine, remove the cylinder head cover.
5. Remove the crankshaft pulley. Remove the engine front cover retaining bolts. Remove both front covers from the engine.
6. Installation is the reverse of the removal procedure.

#### *4K-E Engines*

1. Disconnect the negative battery cable. Drain the cooling system. Drain the oil.
2. Remove the air cleaner assembly, complete with hoses, from its bracket.
3. Remove the hood latch as well as its brace and support.
4. Remove the headlight bezels. Remove the grille assembly.
5. Remove the hoses from the engine. If equipped, remove the radiator shroud. Remove the radiator retaining bolts. Remove the radiator from the vehicle.
6. Loosen the drive belt adjusting link. Remove the drive belt. Remove the alternator retaining bolts. Remove the alternator from the vehicle.
7. If equipped, disconnect the hoses from the air pump and remove it.
8. Remove the fan and water pump as an assembly.
9. Unfasten the crankshaft pulley retaining bolt. Remove the crankshaft pulley with a gear puller. Remove the gravel shield from underneath the engine.
10. Remove the nuts and washers from both the right and left front engine mounts. Detach the exhaust pipe flange from the exhaust manifold. Slightly raise the front of the engine.
11. Remove the front oil pan bolts, to gain access to the bottom of the timing chain cover. It may be necessary to insert a thin suitable tool between the pan and the gasket in order to break the pan loose. Use care not to damage the gasket.
12. Remove the cover from the engine.
13. Installation is the reverse of the removal procedure.

#### *7M-GE and 7M-GTE Engines*

1. Disconnect the negative battery cable. Drain the cooling system. Re-

move the radiator. Remove the water outlet.

2. Remove the spark plugs. Remove the drive belts and then remove the alternator. Remove the No. 3 timing belt cover.

3. Position the engine at TDC on the compression stroke. Remove the timing belt from the camshaft sprockets. If reusing the belt, matchmark the belt and the sprockets in the direction of engine rotation.

4. Remove the camshaft pulleys. Remove the crankshaft pulley using the proper removal tools. Remove the power steering air pipe, if equipped.

5. If equipped with air conditioning remove the compressor and position it out of the way. Do not disconnect the refrigerant lines.

6. Remove the No. 1 timing belt cover. Remove the timing belt. Remove the idler pulley and the tension spring. Remove the oil pump drive pulley.

7. Installation is the reverse of the removal procedure. Refer to Timing Belt for further details.

### *All Other Engines*

For front cover removal procedures on these engines, please refer to the "Timing Belt Removal and Installation" procedure later in this section.

## OIL SEAL REPLACEMENT

1. Remove the front cover.
2. Inspect the oil seal for signs of wear, leakage, or damage.
3. If worn, pry the old seal out. Remove it toward the front of the cover. Once the seal has been removed, it must be replaced.
4. Use a socket, pipe, or block of wood and a hammer to drive the oil seal into place. Work from the front of the cover. Be extremely careful not to damage the seal.
5. Install the front cover.

# Timing Chain And Sprockets

## REMOVAL & INSTALLATION

### *22R and 22R-E Engines*

1. Remove the cylinder head. Remove the front cover.
2. Seperate the chain from the damper. Remove the chain along with the camshaft sprocket.
3. Remove the crankshaft sprocket and the oil pump drive with a puller. Inspect the chain for wear or damage. Replace it, if necessary.
4. Inspect the chain tensioner for wear. If it measures less than 0.43 in., replace it.

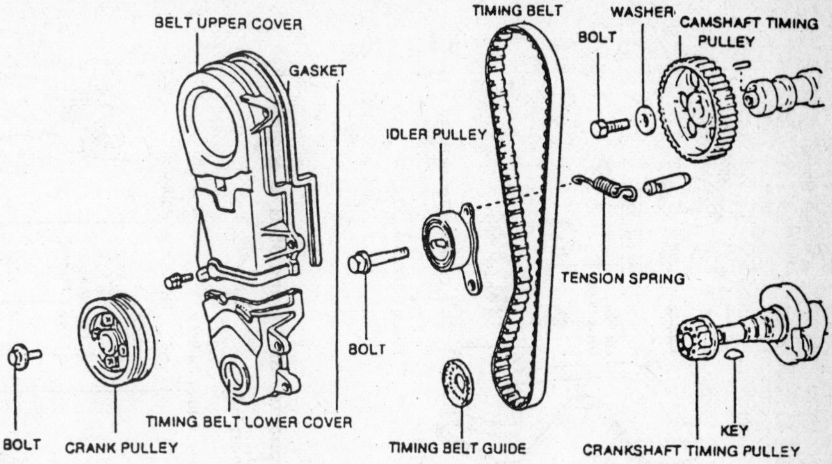


**Front cover and related components—3A and 3A-C engines**

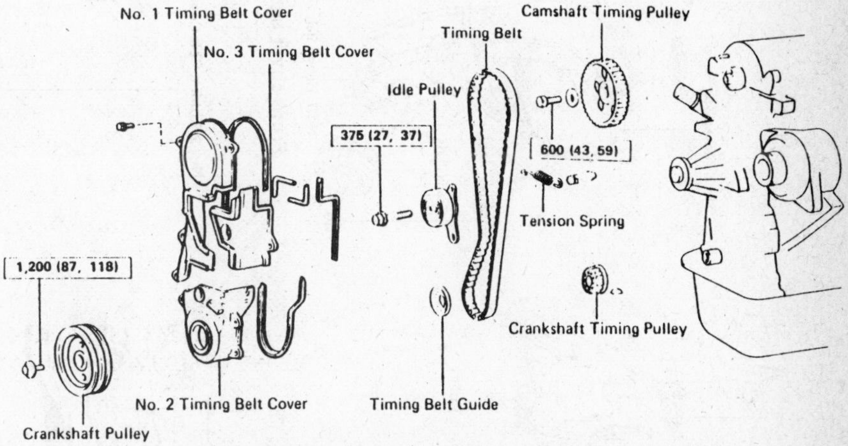


**Front cover and related components—4A-C and 4A-LC engines**

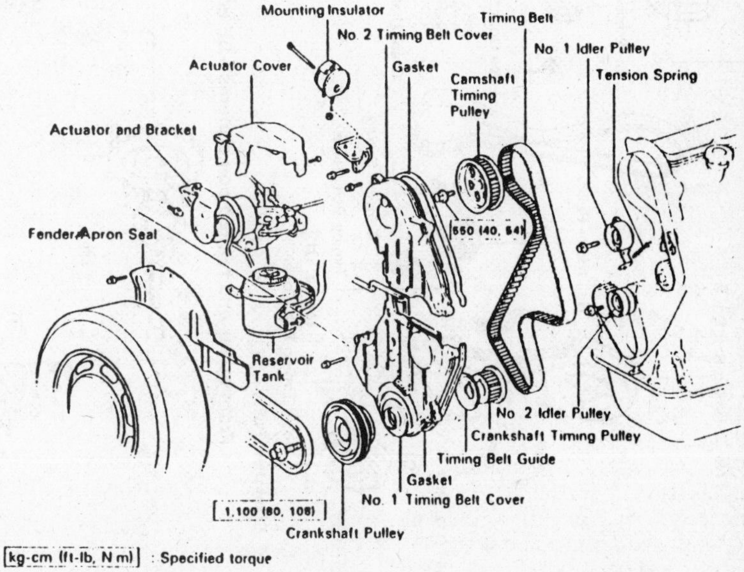


**Front cover and related components—2S-E engines**

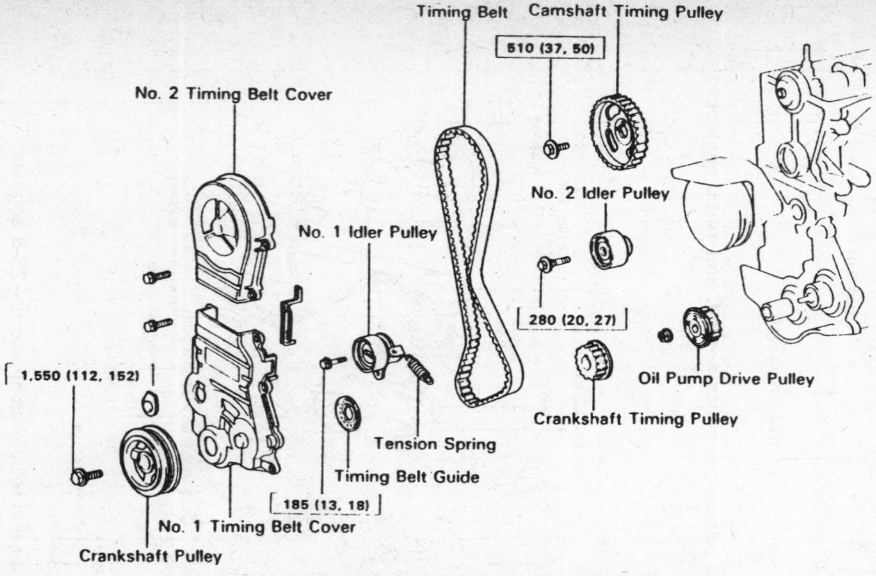


**Front cover and related components—3E engines**

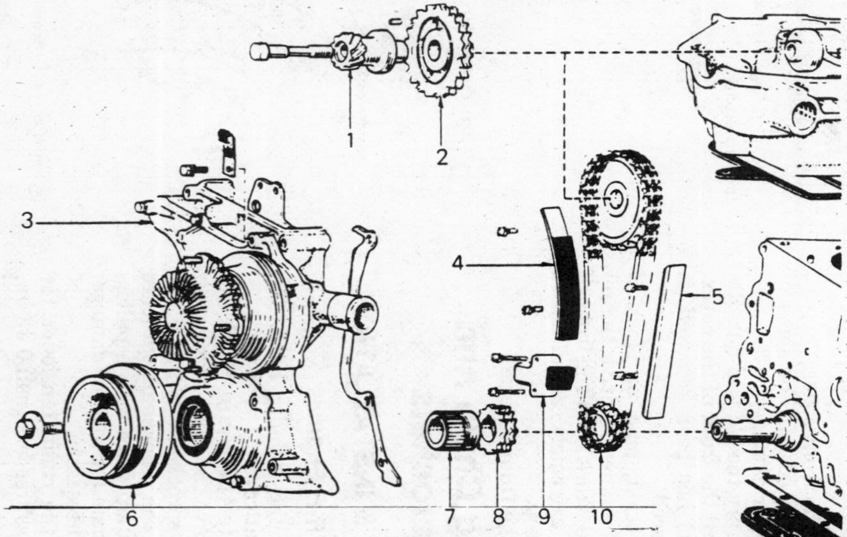


1. Distributor drive gear
2. Camshaft sprocket
3. Chain cover
4. Chain damper No. 2
5. Chain damper No. 1
6. Crankshaft pulley
7. Pump drive spline
8. Crankshaft sprocket
9. Chain tensioner
10. Chain

**Front cover and related components—22R and 22R-E engines**

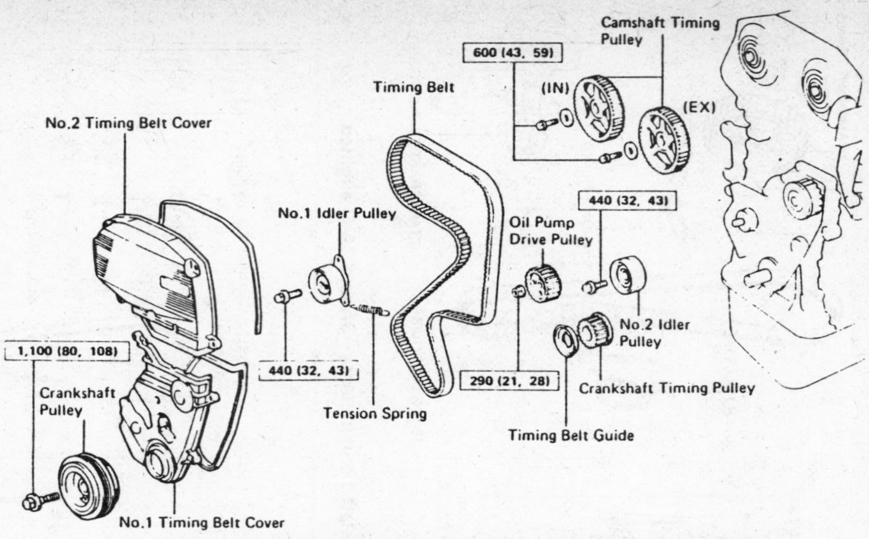


**Front cover and related components—3S-GE and 3S-GTE engines**

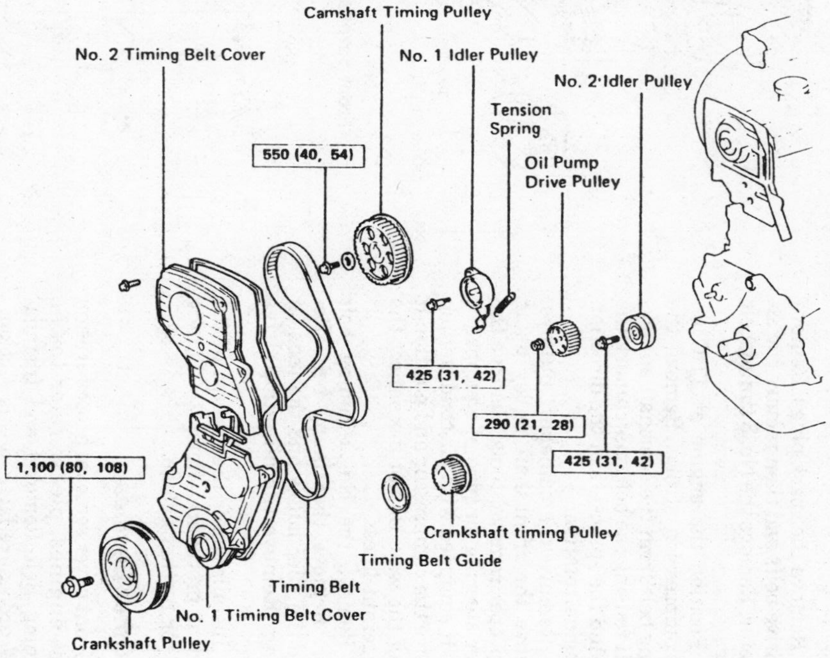

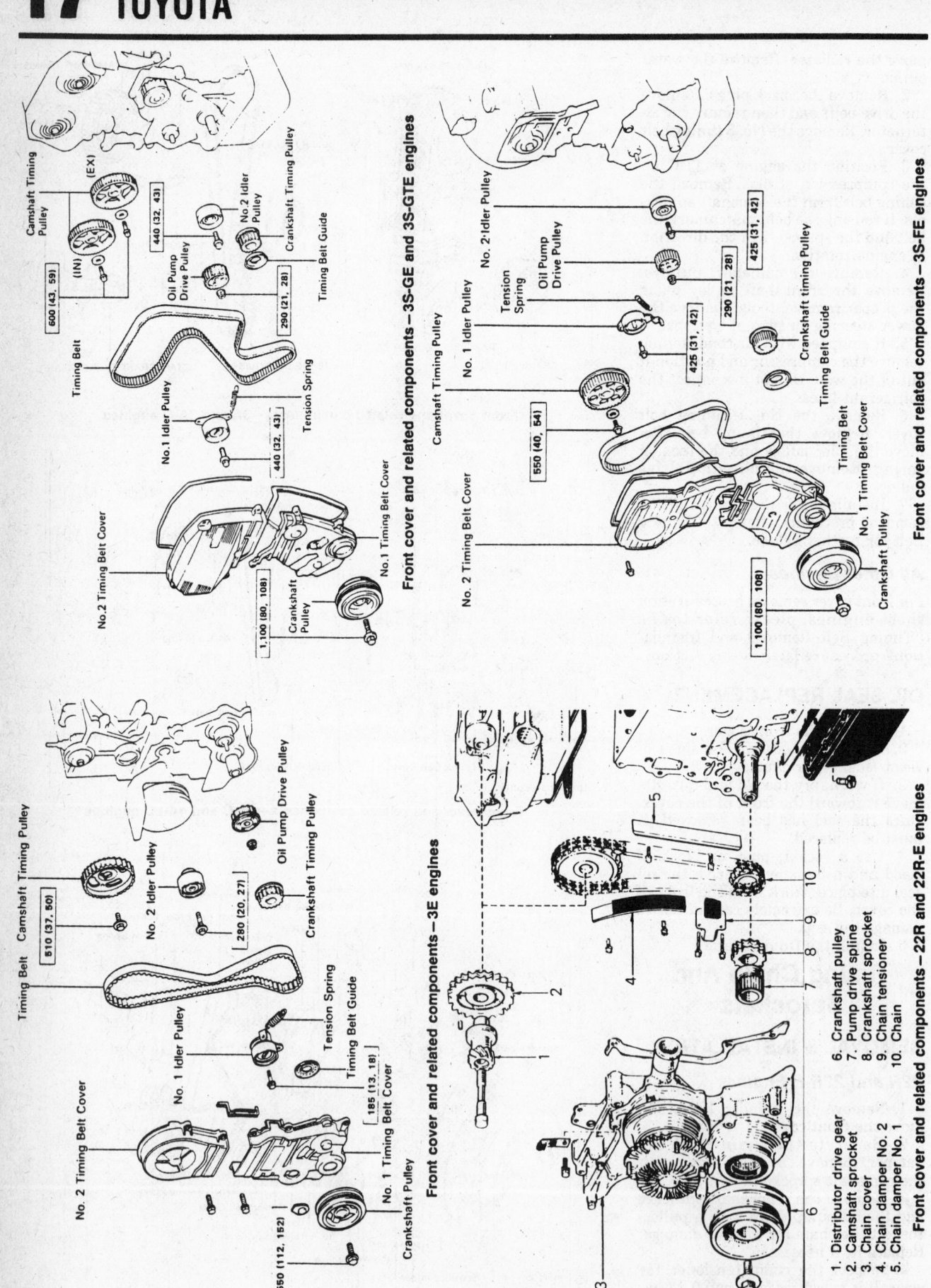

**Front cover and related components—3S-FE engines**

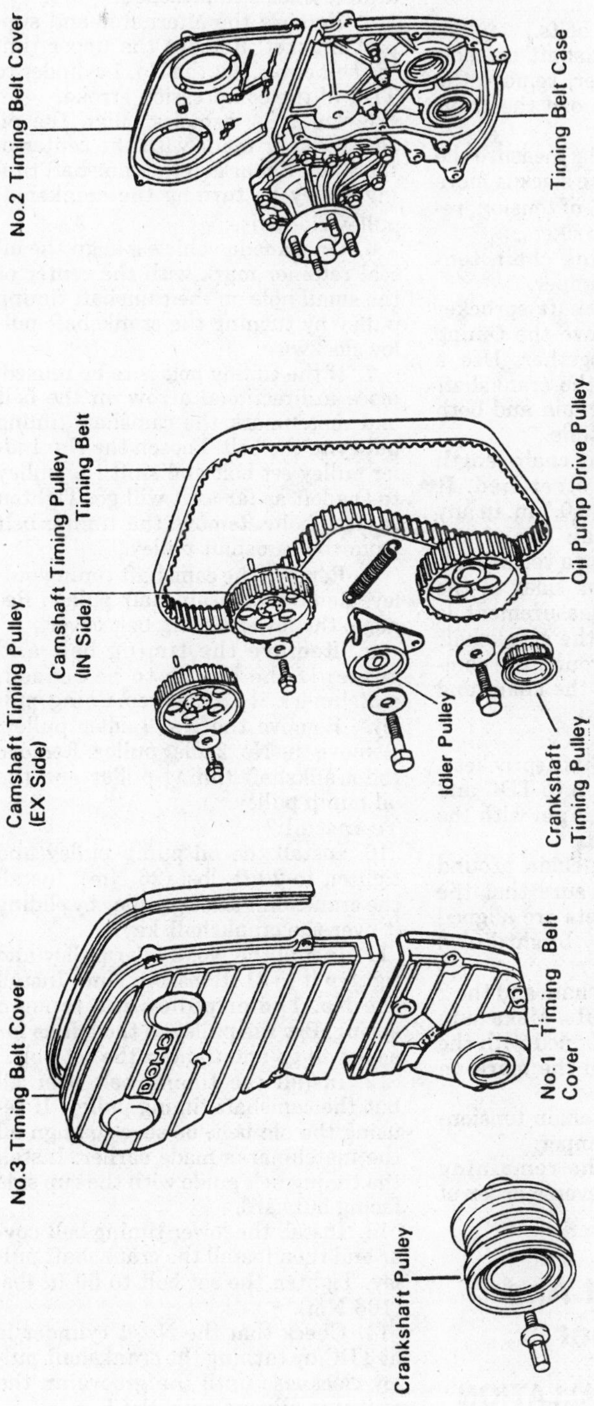

Front cover and related components—5M-GE, 7M-GE and 7M-GTE engines

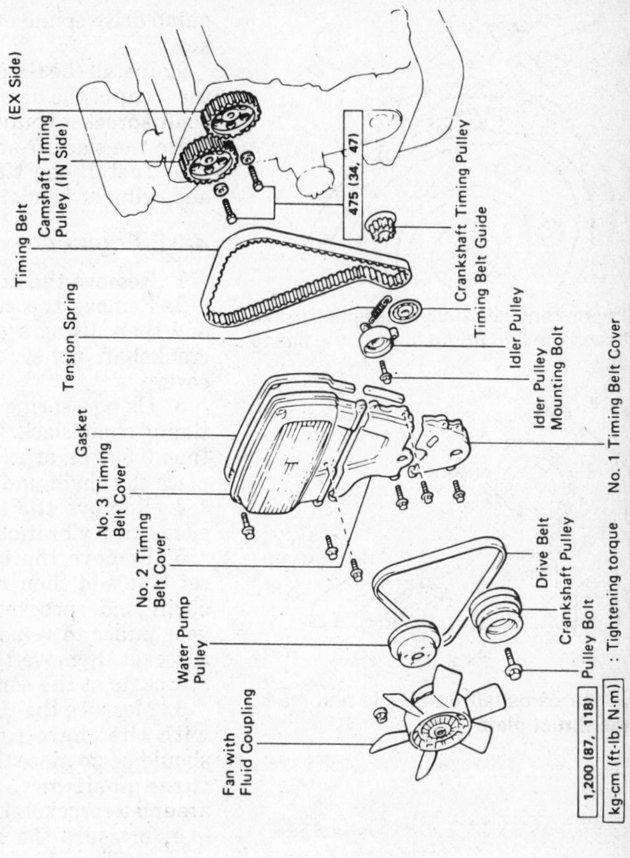

Front cover and related components—4A-GE (all) and 4A-GZE engines

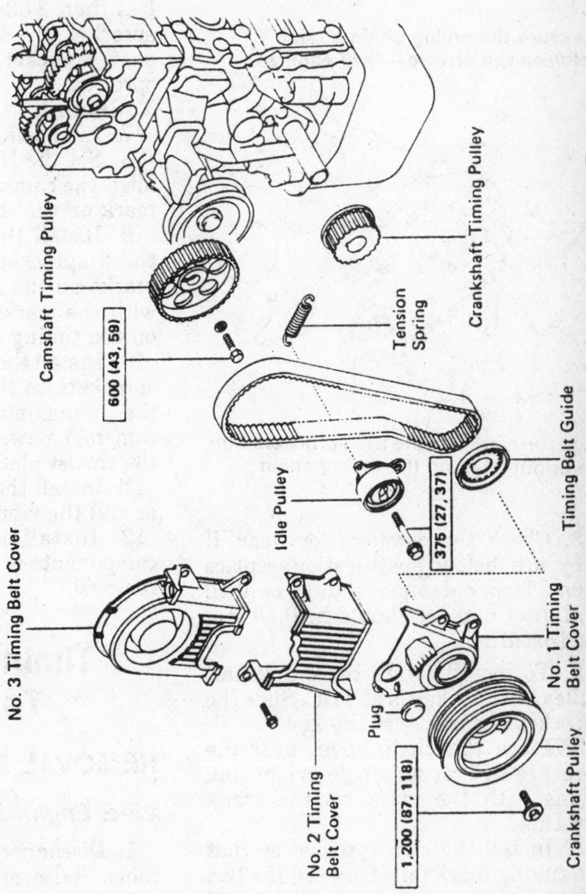

Front cover and related components—4A-F and 4A-FE engines

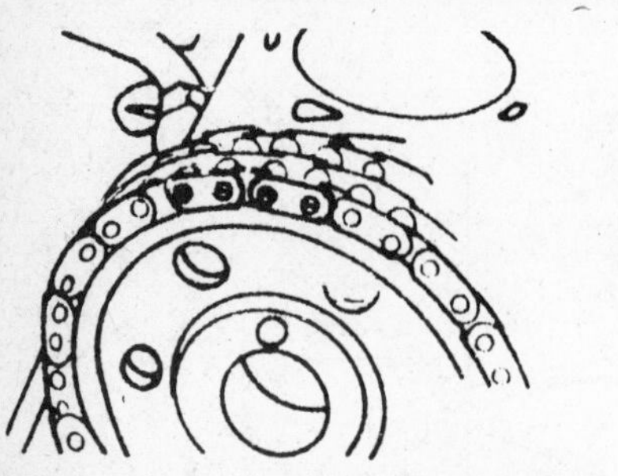

"R" series engines—align the timing marks between the two bright links of the timing chain

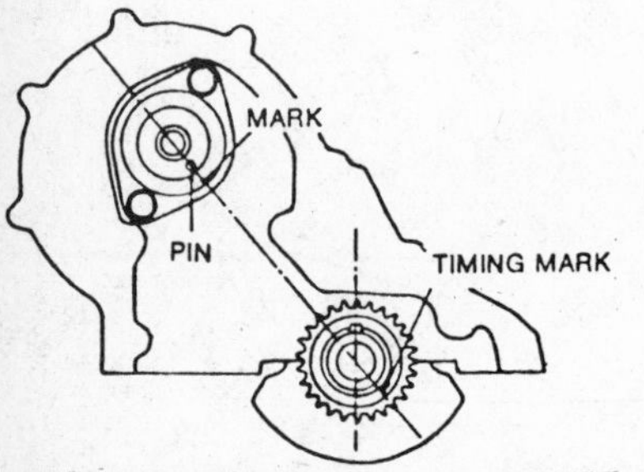


Align the camshaft dowel pin and mark on the thrust plate

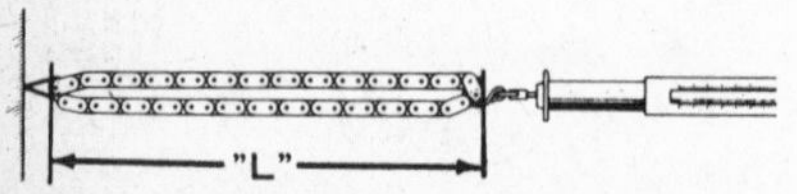


Measure the timing chain stretch between the arrows—4K-E engines

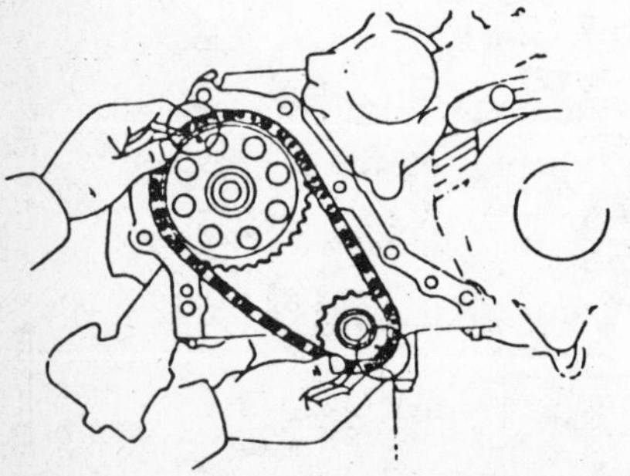

Align the marks on the two sprockets with the bright links on the timing chain

5. Check the dampers for wear. If they are below specification replace them. Upper damper should be 0.20 in. Lower damper should be 0.18 in.

**To install:**

6. To install rotate the crankshaft pulley until its key is at TDC. Slide the sprocket in place over the key.

7. Place the chain cover over the sprocket so that its single bright link aligns with the mark on the crank sprocket.

8. Install the cam sprocket so that the timing mark falls between the two bright links on the chain. Fit the oil pump drive spline over the crankshaft key.

9. Install the timing cover gasket on the front of the block. Rotate the camshaft sprocket counterclockwise to remove the slack from the chain.

10. Install the timing chain cover and cylinder head.

### *4K-E Engines*

1. Remove the drive belts.

2. Remove the crankshaft set bolt and then, using a puller, remove the crankshaft pulley. Remove the front cover.

3. Using a spring scale, measure the timing chain slack. If the slack is more than 0.531 in. at 22 lbs. of tension, replace the chain and sprockets.

4. Remove the timing chain tensioner and vibration damper.

5. Remove the camshaft sprocket set bolt and then remove the timing chain and sprocket together. Use a gear puller to remove the crankshaft sprocket. Remove the chain and both sprockets at the same time.

6. Measure the timing chain length with the chain fully stretched. It should be no more than 10.7 in. in any three positions. Wrap the chain around a sprocket. Using a vernier caliper, measure the outer sides of the chain rollers. If the measurement is less than 2.339 in. on the crankshaft sprocket or 4.480 in. around the camshaft sprocket, replace the chain and sprocket.

**To install:**

7. Install the crankshaft sprocket.

8. Set the No. 1 piston to TDC and align the camshaft dowel pin with the mark on the thrust plate.

9. Install the timing chain around the 2 sprockets, make sure that the marks on the 2 sprockets are aligned with the marks (usually bright links) on the timing chain.

10. Install the timing chain and the 2 sprockets on to the shafts. Make sure the timing marks are aligned with the camshaft dowel pin and the mark on the thrust plate.

11. Install the timing chain tensioner and the vibration damper.

12. Installation of the remaining components is in the reverse order of removal.

# Timing Belt And Tensioner

## REMOVAL & INSTALLATION

### *2S-E Engines*

1. Disconnect the negative battery cable. Raise and support the vehicle safely. Remove the right front tire and wheel assembly. Remove the right side fender liner.

2. Remove the windshield washer and radiator reservoir tanks. Remove the cruise control actuator, if equipped.

3. Remove the power steering belt. Remove the power steering pump and position it out of the way with the hydraulic lines still attached.

4. Remove the alternator and support bracket. Remove the upper timing belt cover. Set the No. 1 cylinder to TDC of the compression stroke.

5. On USA vehicles, align the oil seal retainer mark with the center of the small **E** mark on the camshaft timing pulley by turning the crankshaft pulley clockwise.

6. On Canada vehicles, align the oil seal retainer mark with the center of the small hole on the camshaft timing pulley by turning the crankshaft pulley clockwise.

7. If the timing belt is to be reused, place a directional arrow on the belt and matchmark the camshaft timing pulley to the belt. Loosen the No. 1 idler pulley set bolt and shift the pulley to the left as far as it will go. Tighten the set bolt. Remove the timing belt from the camshaft pulley.

8. Remove the camshaft timing pulley. Remove the camshaft pulley. Remove the lower timing belt cover.

9. Remove the timing belt and guide. If the belt is to be reused, matchmark it to the remaining pulleys. Remove the No. 1 idler pulley. Remove the No. 2 idler pulley. Remove the crankshaft timing pulley and the oil pump pulley.

**To install:**

10. Install the oil pump pulley and tighten to 20 ft. lbs. (26 Nm). Install the crankshaft timing pulley by sliding it over the crankshaft key.

11. Install the No. 2 idler pulley and tighten it to 31 ft. lbs. (42 Nm). Install the No. 1 idler pulley and tension spring. Pry the pulley to the left as far as it will go and tighten the set bolt.

12. Install the timing belt over all but the camshaft timing pulley. If reusing the old belt, be sure to align all the matchmarks made earlier. Install the timing belt guide with the cup side facing outward.

13. Install the lower timing belt cover and then install the crankshaft pulley. Tighten the set bolt to 80 ft. lbs. (108 Nm).

14. Check that the No. 1 cylinder is at TDC by turning the crankshaft pulley clockwise until the groove on the pulley is aligned with the **0** mark on the timing cover.

15. When installing the camshaft timing pulley, align the camshaft knock pin with the matchmark on the camshaft oil seal retainer. On USA ve-

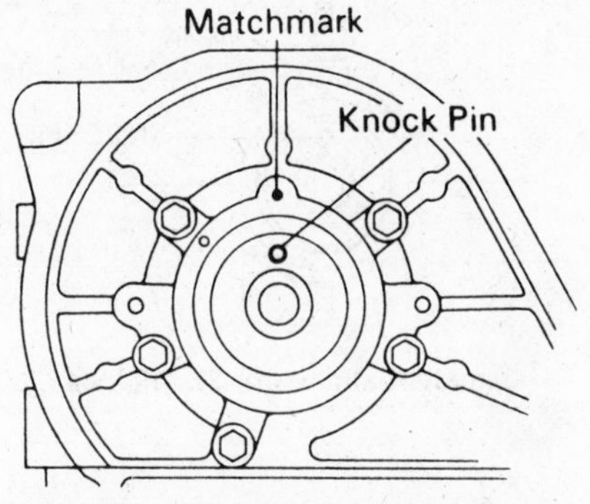

Align the camshaft knock pin with the matchmark on the camshaft oil seal retainer—2S-E

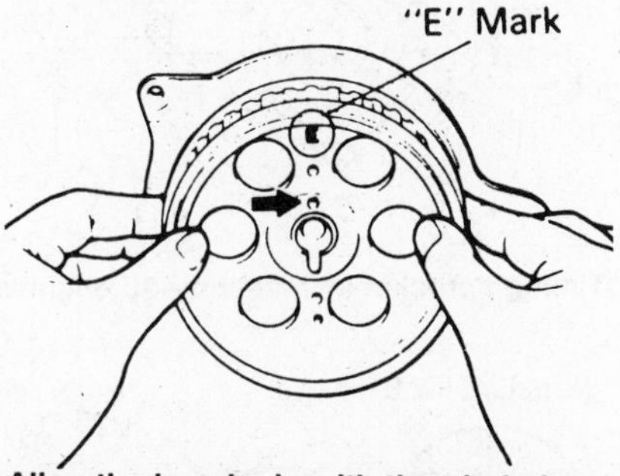

Align the knock pin with the pin hole on the timing pulley "E" mark slide—U.S. 2S-E

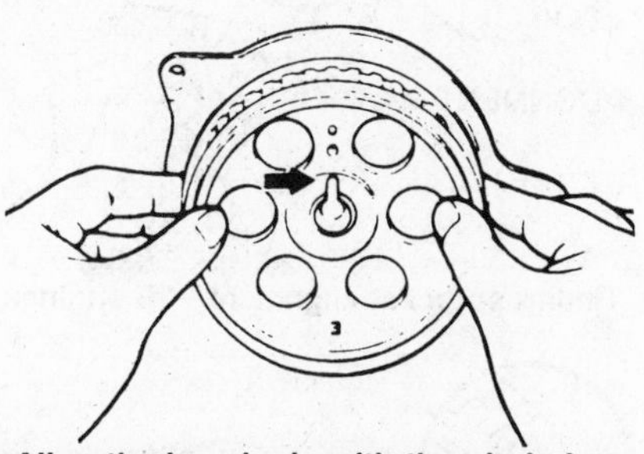
Align the knock pin with the pin hole on the timing pulley—Canada 2S-E

hicles, align the knock pin with the pin hole on the timing pulley **E** mark side. On Canada vehicles, align the knock pin with the pin hole on the timing pulley.

16. Check that the matchmark on the oil seal retainer and the center of the small hole on the camshaft timing pulley are in alignment. Tighten the pulley set bolt to 40 ft. lbs.

17. Install the timing belt around the camshaft pulley. Loosen the idler pulley set bolt ½ turn. Turn the crankshaft pulley 2 complete revolutions clockwise and then tighten the No. 1 idler pulley set bolt to 31 ft. lbs. (42 Nm).

18. Installation of the remaining components is in the reverse order of removal. Tighten the right engine mount to 38 ft. lbs. (52 Nm).

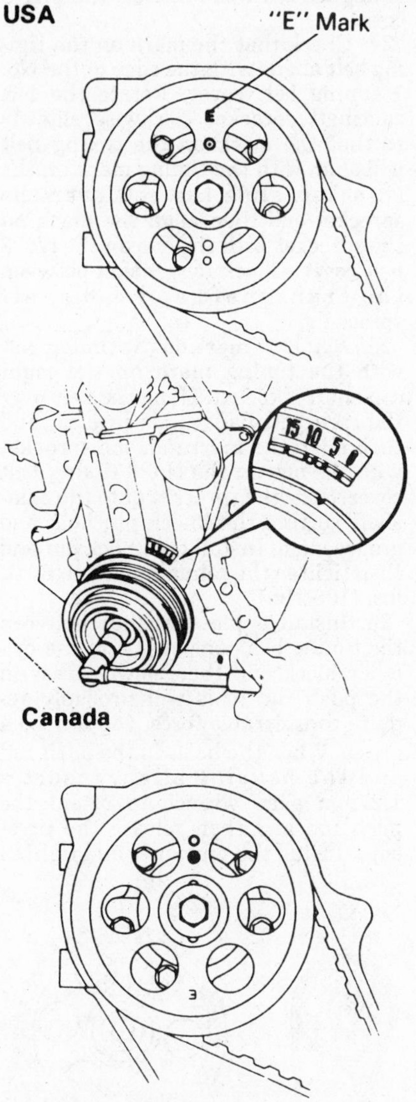

Setting the No. 1 cylinder to TDC of the compression stroke—2S-E

### 2VZ-FE Engines

1. Disconnect the negative battery cable. If equipped, remove the cruise control actuator and vacuum pump.

2. Remove the power steering oil reservoir tank and position it out of the way without disconnecting the hydraulic lines.

3. Raise the front of the vehicle and support it with safety stands. Remove the right side wheel.

4. Remove the alternator and power steering pump drive belts.

5. Remove the right side fender apron seal.

6. Remove the right side engine mounting stays, position a floor jack under the engine and raise it just enough to release the pressure on the mount and then remove it. On models with ABS, first remove the clamp bolts for the power steering oil cooler lines.

7. Remove the spark plugs.

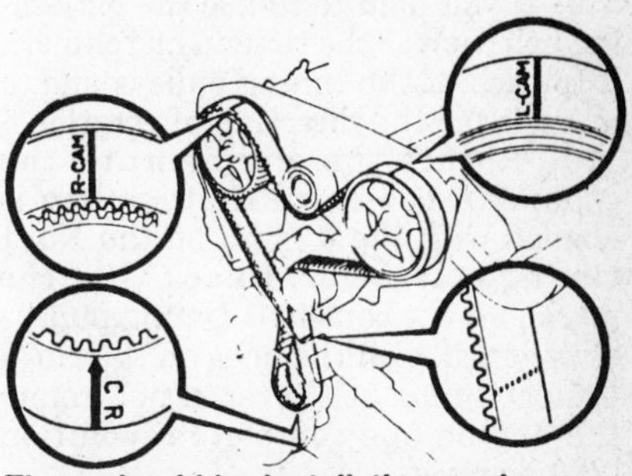

There should be installation marks on the timing belt—2VZ-FE engines

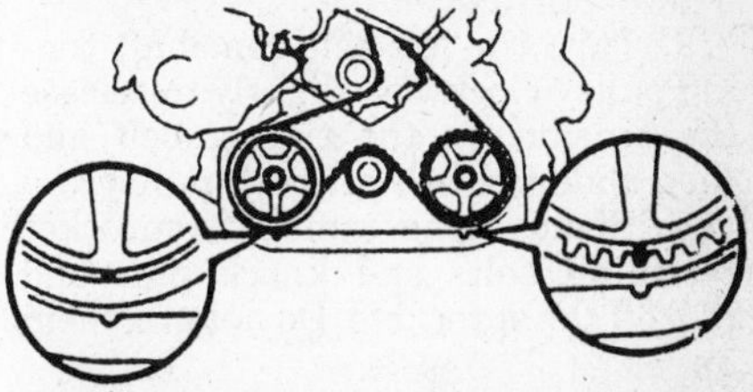
Check that the marks on the sprockets and the No. 3 cover are aligned—2VZ-FE engines

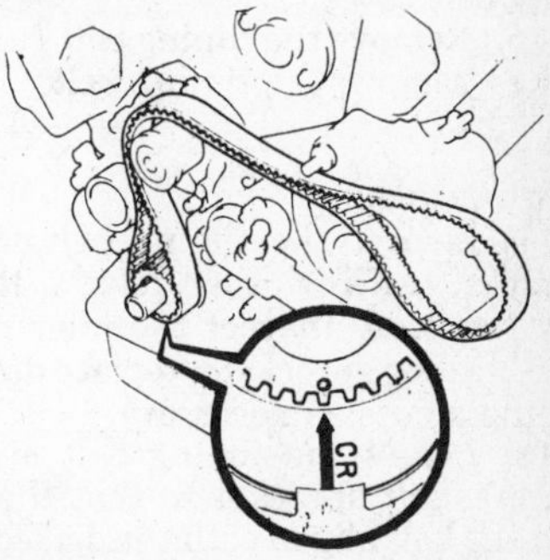

Installing the belt on the crankshaft—2VZ-FE engines

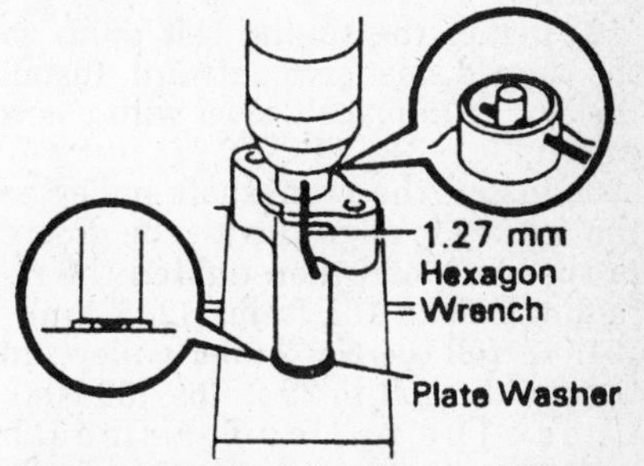

Set the timing belt tensioner—2VZ-FE engines

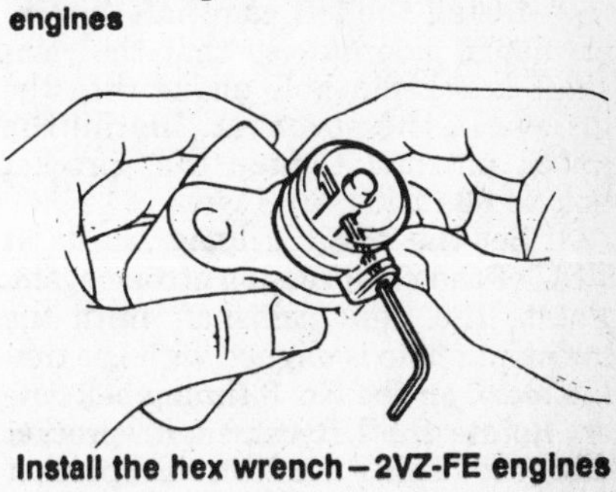
Install the hex wrench—2VZ-FE engines

8. Remove the No. 2 (upper) timing belt cover and then remove the right side engine mounting bracket.
9. If you plan to re-use the old timing belt, now is the time to matchmark it to each of the timing pulleys and to mark it for the direction of rotation.
10. Rotate the engine until the groove in the crankshaft pulley is aligned with the **0** mark on the No. 1 timing belt cover. Check that the marks on the camshaft timing pulleys are aligned with the ones on the No. 3 (inner) timing belt cover; if not, rotate the engine one complete revolution (360 degrees).
11. Remove the timing belt tensioner and its dust cover.
12. Turn the left side camshaft timing pulley clockwise slightly to release the tension on the timing belt and then slide the belt off both pulleys.
13. Remove the camshaft sprocket retaining bolts and knock pins and pull off the sprockets. Do not mix them up.
14. Remove the No. 2 idler pulley.
15. Remove the crankshaft pulley and then remove the No. 1 (lower) timing belt cover.
16. Remove the timing belt guide and then remove the timing belt.

**To install:**

17. Inspect the timing belt for any cracks, tears or other defects. Replace as required. Inspect the idler pulleys and timing sprockets; replace defective components as necessary.
18. Install the timing belt over the crankshaft sprocket so that the mark on the belt aligns with the drilled mark on the sprocket. Install the belt over the No. 1 idler and water pump pulleys.
19. Install the timing belt guide so the cupped side faces outward. Install the No. 1 timing belt cover with a new gasket.
20. Install the crankshaft pulley so the set key is aligned with the groove in the shaft and then tighten the retaining bolt to 181 ft. lbs. (245 Nm).
21. Install the No. 2 idler pulley and tighten the bolt to 29 ft. lbs. (39 Nm). Check the pulley for smooth operation.
22. Install the left camshaft sprocket, flange side out, so that the camshaft knock pin hole aligns with the groove in the sprocket. Install the knock pin and tighten the sprocket bolt to 80 ft. lbs. (108 Nm).
23. Set the No. 1 cylinder so its at TDC of the compression stroke again. Rotate the right camshaft until the knock pin hole is aligned with the timing mark on the No. 3 timing belt cover. Rotate the left camshaft sprocket until the timing mark on the sprocket is aligned with the one on the No. 3 cover.
24. Check that the mark on the timing belt aligns with the edge of the No. 1 timing belt cover. Rotate the left camshaft sprocket clockwise slightly so that the mark on the timing belt will align with the timing mark on the sprocket, slide the belt over the sprocket and then align the mark on the sprocket with the one on the No. 3 belt cover. Check for tension between the crankshaft and camshaft sprockets.
25. Align the mark on the timing belt with the timing mark on the right camshaft sprocket. Hang the belt over the sprocket, flange side inward, and then align the marks on the sprocket with the one on the No. 3 timing belt cover. Slide the sprocket onto the camshaft so that the knock pin hole and groove align. Install the knock pin and then tighten the retaining bolt to 80 ft. lbs. (108 Nm).
26. Install a plate washer between the timing belt tensioner and the cylinder block and then slowly press in the push rod (this will probably require considerable force, you'll need a press). When the holes in the push rod and the housing align, insert a 1.27mm allen wrench to retain the push rod and then release the pressure. Install the tensioner and tighten the mounting bolts to 20 ft. lbs. (26 Nm); remove the allen wrench.
27. Rotate the crankshaft pulley two complete revolutions clockwise and check that each pulley is still aligned with the timing marks. If not, remove the belt and start over again.
28. Installation of the remaining components is in the reverse order of removal.

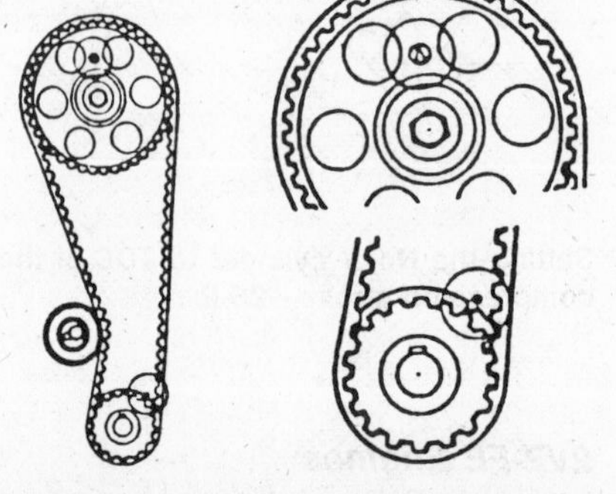

When checking the valve timing, turn the crankshaft two (2) complete revolutions clockwise from TDC to TDC and make sure that each pulley aligns with the marks shown

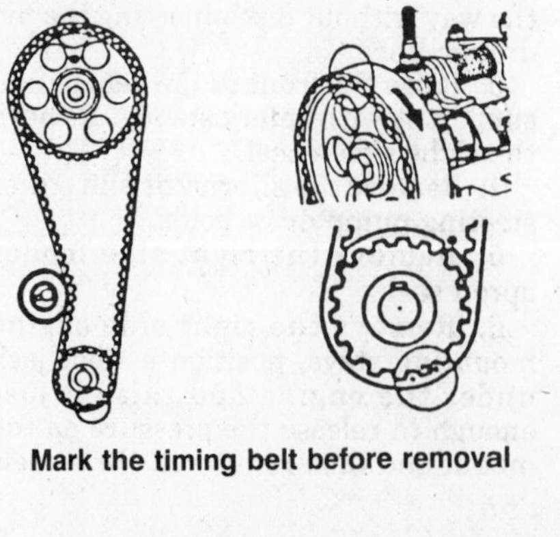

Mark the timing belt before removal

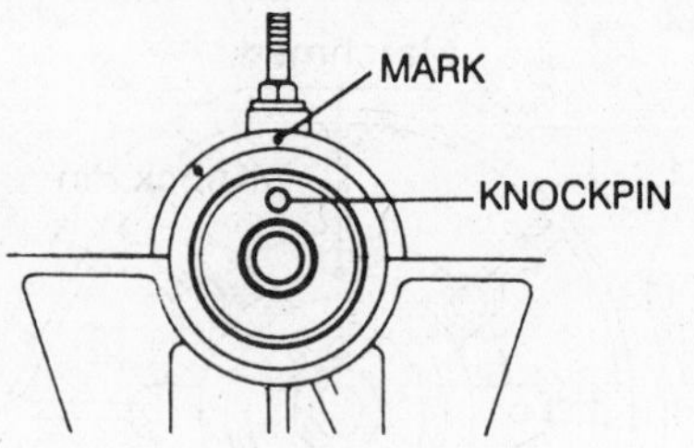


Camshaft aligment – 3E engines

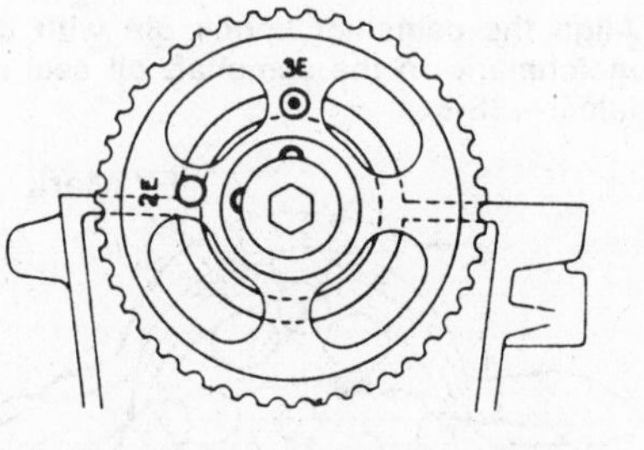


Timing sprocket installation – 3E engines

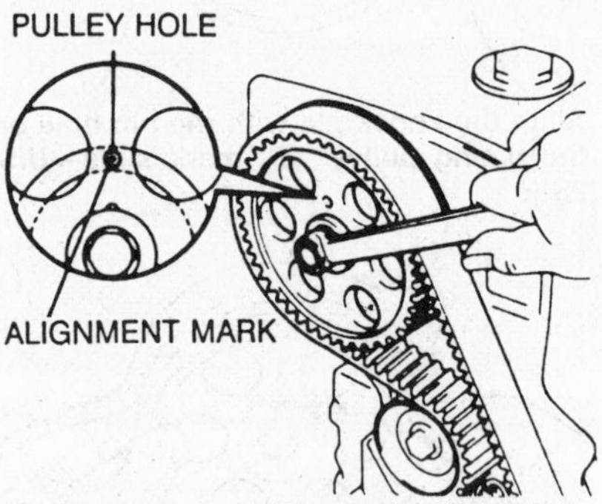


Timing sprocket alignment – 3E engines

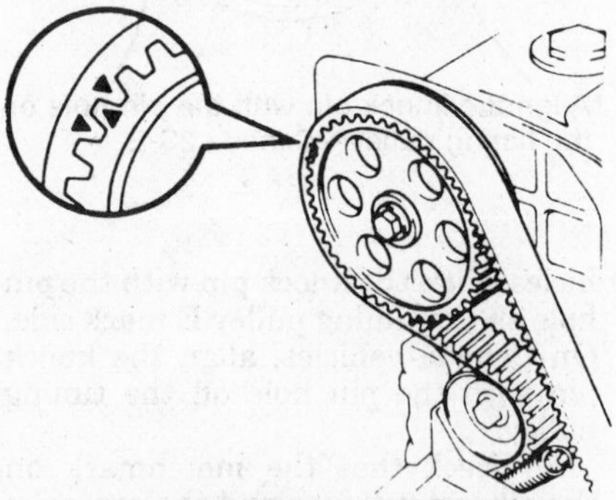

Timing belt alignment – 3E engines

### 3A, 3A-C, 4A-C and 4A-LC Engines

1. Remove the timing belt upper and lower covers.
2. If the timing belt is to be reused, mark an arrow in the direction of engine revolution on its surface. Matchmark the belt to the pulleys as shown in the illustration.
3. Loosen the idler pulley bolt, push it to the left as far as it will go and then temporarily tighten it.
4. Remove the timing belt, idler pulley bolt, idler pulley and the return spring Do not bend, twist, or turn the belt inside out. Do not allow grease or water to come in contact with it.
5. Inspect the timing belt for cracks, missing teeth or overall wear. Replace as necessary. Install the return spring and idler pulley.
6. Install the timing belt. Align the marks made earlier if reusing the old belt.
7. Adjust the idler pulley so that the belt deflection is 0.24–0.28 in. at 4.5 lbs. Check the valve timing.
8. Installation of the remaining components is in the reverse order of removal.

### 3E Engines

1. Disconnect the negative battery cable. Remove the right side engine under cover.
2. Remove the drive belts. Remove the alternator and alternator bracket. Remove the air cleaner assembly. Remove the spark plugs.
3. Raise the engine and remove the right side engine mounting insulator assembly.
4. Remove the cylinder head cover. Set the engine to TDC on the compression stroke. Remove the crankshaft pulley using the proper removal tool.
5. Remove both timing belt covers. Remove the timing belt guide. Remove the timing belt and the No. 1 idler pulley. If using the old belt matchmark it in the direction of engine rotation. Matchmark the pulleys.
6. Remove the tension spring. Remove the No. 2 idler pulley. Remove the crankshaft pulley. Remove the camshaft pulley. Remove the oil pump pulley.

**To install:**

7. Inspect the belt for defects. Replace as required. Inspect the idler pulleys and springs. Replace defective components as required.
8. Align and install the oil pump pulley. Torque the retaining bolt to 20 ft. lbs. (26 Nm).
9. To install the camshaft timing pulley, align the camshaft knock pin with the No. 1 bearing cap mark. Align the knock pin hole on the 3E mark side with the camshaft knock pin hole. Torque the retaining bolt to 37 ft. lbs. (50 Nm).
10. Install the crankshaft timing pulley and align the TDC marks on the oil pump body and the crankshaft timing pulley. Install the No. 1 idler pulley. Pry the idler pulley toward the left as far as it will go and tempororarily tighten the retaining bolt.
11. Install the No. 2 idler pulley and torque the retaining bolt to 20 ft. lbs. (27 Nm). Install the timing belt. If reusing the old belt align it with the marks made during the removal procedure.
12. Inspect the valve timing and the belt tension by loosening the No. 1 idler pulley set bolt. Temporarily install the crankshaft pulley bolt and turn the crankshaft 2 complete revolutions in the clockwise direction.
13. Check that each pulley aligns with the proper markings. Torque the No. 1 idler pulley bolt to 13 ft. lbs. (18 Nm). Check for proper belt tension. Install the belt guide.
14. Install the timing belt covers. Align and install the crankshaft pulley. Torque the retaining bolt to 112 ft. lbs. (152 Nm).
15. Continue the installation in the reverse order of the removal procedure.

### 3S-FE Engines

1. Disconnect the negative battery cable. Raise and support the vehicle safely. Remove the right tire and wheel assembly.
2. If equipped remove the cruise control actuator and bracket. Remove the drive belts.
3. Remove the alternator and alternator bracket. Raise the engine enough to remove the right side engine mounting insulator and brackets.
4. Remove the spark plugs. Remove the No. 2 (upper) timing cover. Position the No. 1 cylinder to TDC on the compression stroke so the groove in the crankshaft pulley is aligned with the **0** mark in the No. 1 front cover. If the hole in the camshaft pulley is not aligned with the mark on the bearing cap, turn the crankshaft 1 complete revolution (360 degrees).
5. If reusing the belt place matchmarks on the timing belt and the camshaft pulley. Loosen the mount bolt of the No. 1 idler pulley and position the pulley toward the left as far as it will go. Tighten the bolt. Remove the belt from the camshaft pulley.
6. Remove the camshaft pulley. Remove the crankshaft pulley using the proper removal tool. Remove the No. 1 (lower) timing cover.
7. Remove the timing belt and the belt guide. If reusing the belt mark the belt and the crankshaft pulley in the direction of engine rotation.
8. Remove the No. 1 idler pulley and the tension spring. Remove the No. 2 idler pulley. Remove the crankshaft timing pulley. Remove the oil pump pulley.

**To install:**

9. Inspect the belt for defects. Replace as required. Inspect the idler pulleys and springs. Replace defective components as required.
10. Align the cuttouts of the oil pump pulley and shaft. Install the oil pump pulley and torque the retaining nut to 21 ft. lbs. (28 Nm).
11. To install the crankshaft pulley, align the pulley set key with the key groove of the pulley and slide it in position. Install the No. 2 idler pulley and torque the bolt to 31 ft. lbs. (42 Nm). Be sure that the pulley moves freely.
12. Temporarily install the No. 1 idler pulley and tension spring. Pry the pulley toward the left as far as it will go. Tighten the bolt.
13. Temporarily install the timing belt. If reusing the old belt align the marks made during removal. Install the timing belt guide.
14. Install the No. 1 timing belt cover. Install the crankshaft pulley and tighten the bolt to 80 ft. lbs. (108 Nm).
15. Install the camshaft pulley by aligning the camshaft knock pin with the knock pin groove in the pulley. Install the washer and torque the retaining bolt to 40 ft. lbs. (54 Nm).
16. With the engine set at TDC on the compression stroke install the timing belt. If reusing the belt align with the marks made during the removal procedure.
17. Once the belt is installed be sure that there is tension between the crankshaft pulley, water pump pulley and camshaft pulley. Loosen the No. 1 idler pulley mount bolt ½ turn. Turn the crankshaft pulley 2 revolutions from TDC to TDC, in the clockwise direction. Torque the No. 1 idler pulley mount bolt to 31 ft. lbs. (42 Nm).
18. Continue the installation in the reverse order of the removal procedure.

### 3S-GE and 3S-GTE Engines

1. Disconnect the negative battery cable. Raise and support the vehicle safely. Remove the right front tire and wheel assembly. Remove the right side fender liner.
2. Remove the windshield washer and radiator reservoir tanks. Remove the cruise control actuator, if equipped.
3. Remove the power steering belt. Remove the power steering pump and position it out of the way with the hydraulic lines still attached.

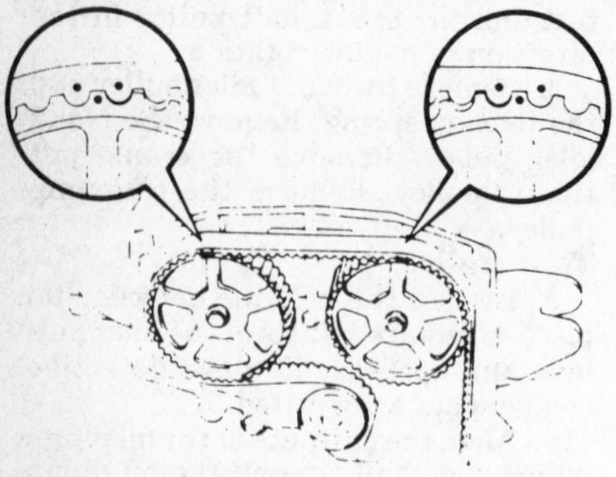

If the timing belt is to be reused on the 3S-GE, place matchmarks on the belt and pulleys

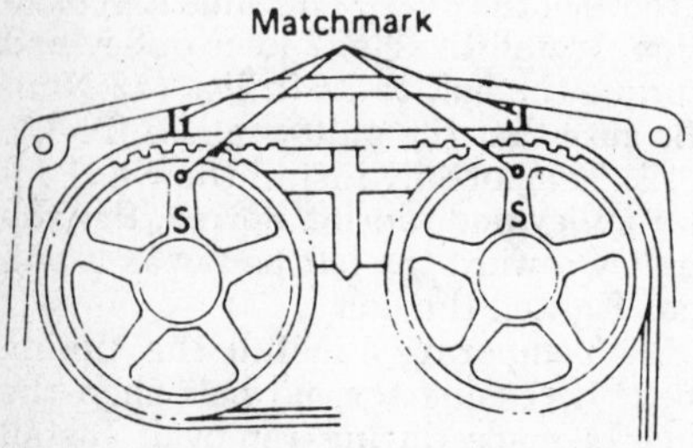


Align the matchmarks on the camshaft timing pulleys with those on the rear timing belt cover—3S-GE

**Hold the camshaft with an adjustable wrench when removing the camshaft timing pulleys – 3S-GE engines**

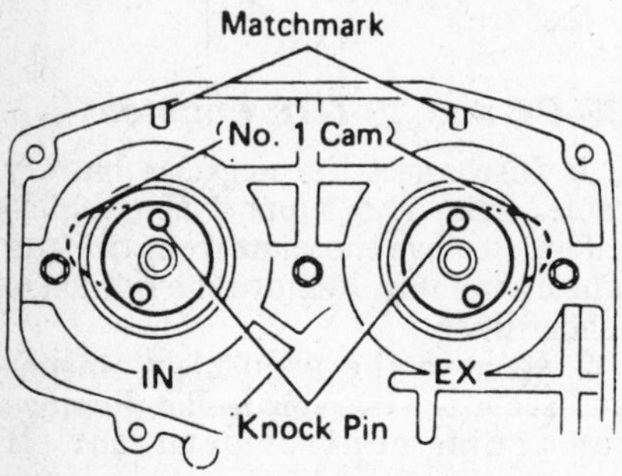


Turn the camshafts so that the knock pins align with the matchmark on the rear timing cover and the No. 1 lobes are facing outward—3S-GE (two hole type)

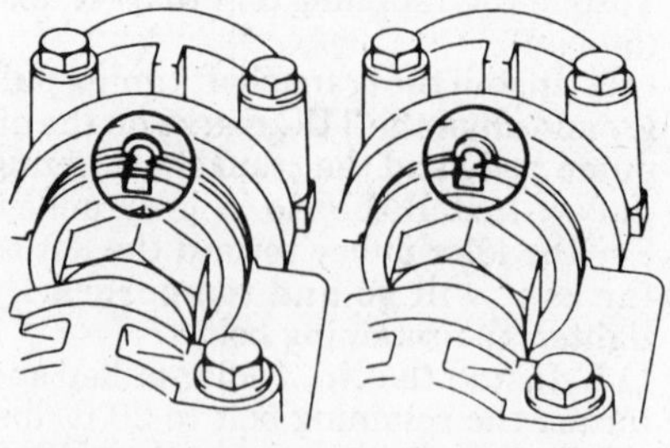

Align the knock pin and the No. 1 bearing cap mark—3S-GE (five hole type)

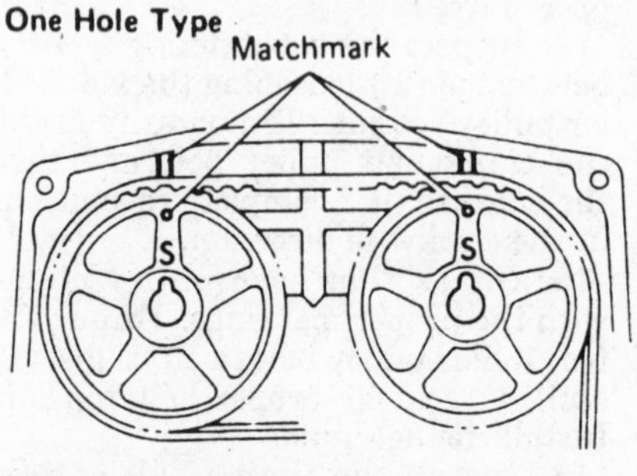


Align the camshaft knock pin with the hole in the camshaft timing pulley—3S-GE (one hole type pulley only)

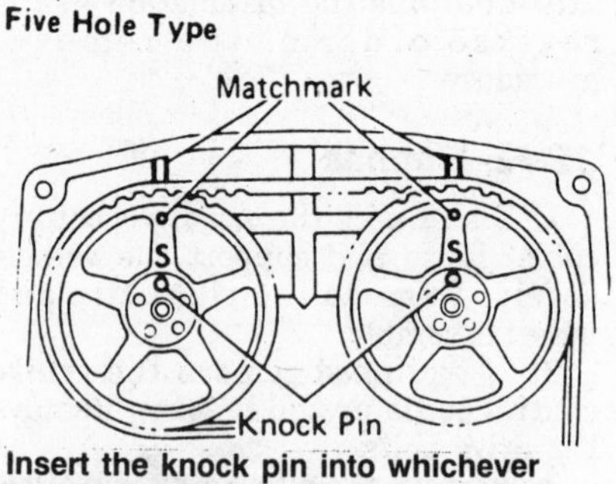


Insert the knock pin into whichever camshaft timing pulley and camshaft holes are aligned—3S-GE (five hole type pulley only)

4. Remove the alternator and support bracket. Remove the upper timing belt cover.

5. Set the No. 1 cylinder to TDC of the compression stroke by aligning the groove on the crankshaft pulley with the **0** mark on the lower timing belt cover. Check that the matchmarks on the 2 camshaft timing pulleys and the rear timing belt cover are aligned, if not, turn the crankshaft 1 complete revolution clockwise (360 degrees).

6. If the timing belt is to be reused, draw a directional arrow on it and matchmark the belt to the 2 camshaft pulleys. Loosen the No. 1 idler pulley bolt and shift the pulley as far left as possible; tighten the set bolt. Remove the timing belt from the 2 camshaft pulleys. Support the belt so that the meshing of the belt with the remaining pulleys does not shift.

7. Carefully hold the camshafts with an adjustable wrench and remove the camshaft pulley set bolts. Remove the pulleys and their set pins.

8. Remove the crankshaft pulley. Remove the lower timing belt.

9. Remove the timing belt guide and then remove the timing belt from the remaining pulleys. Be sure to matchmark the belt to the pulleys if it is to be reused.

10. Remove the No. 1 idler pulley and the tension spring. Remove the No. 2 idler pulley, the crankshaft timing pulley and the oil pump pulley.

**To install:**

11. Install the oil pump pulley and tighten it to 21 ft. lbs. (28 Nm). Install the crankshaft timing pulley by sliding it onto the crankshaft over the Woodruff key. Install the No. 2 idler pulley and tighten it to 32 ft. lbs. (43 Nm).

12. Install the No. 1 idler pulley and the tension spring. Move the pulley as far to the left as it will go and then tighten it.

13. Install the timing belt on all pulleys except the 2 camshaft pulleys. Make sure the matchmarks made earlier are in alignment.

14. Install the timing belt guide with the cup side out. Install the lower timing belt cover and then install the crankshaft pulley. Tighten it to 80 ft. lbs. (108 Nm).

15. Check that the No. 1 cylinder is at TDC of the compression stroke for the crankshaft. The crankshaft pulley groove should be aligned with the **0** mark on the lower timing belt cover.

16. Check that the No. 1 cylinder is at TDC of the compression stroke for the camshaft.

**NOTE: There are 2 types of camshafts, one with 2 holes on the timing pulley contact surface and one with 5 holes on the timing pulley contact surface. All replacement camshaft have 5 holes.**

2 Hole: Using a wrench, turn the camshafts so that the camshaft knock pin aligns with the matchmark on the rear timing belt cover. And the No. 1 cam lobe is pointing outward as shown.

5 Hole: Using a wrench, turn the camshaft so that the knock pin aligns with the notch in the No. 1 camshaft bearing cap.

17. Hang the timing belt on the 2 camshaft timing pulleys. Align all matchmarks made during removal. The **S** mark on the pulley should face outward.

**NOTE: There are 2 types of camshaft pulleys. One has 5 holes on the camshaft contact surface and one has 1 hole on the contact surface. All replacement pulleys have, you guessed it, 5 holes.**

Align the timing pulley matchmark with the rear timing belt cover matchmark and install the pulleys with the belt.

**NOTE: On 1 hole pulleys, match the camshaft knock pin with the camshaft pulley hole. On 5 hole pulleys, insert the knock pin into whichever pulley and camshaft holes are aligned.**

Hold the camshaft with an adjustable wrench and tighten the pulley set bolt to 43 ft. lbs. (59 Nm).

18. Loosen the No. 1 idler pulley set bolt just enough to move the pulley so it tensions the timing belt. Turn the crankshaft 2 complete revolutions clockwise and then tighten the idler pulley set bolt to 32 ft. lbs. (43 Nm). Check for proper timing belt tension.

19. Installation of the remaining components is in the reverse order of removal. Tighten the engine mount bracket bolts to 38 ft. lbs. (52 Nm). Tighten the engine mount bolts to 58 ft. lbs. (78 Nm) and the nuts to 38 ft. lbs. (52 Nm).

### 4A-F and 4A-FE Engines

1. Raise the front of the vehicle and support it with safety stands. Remove the right wheel and undercover. Remove the air cleaner.
2. Remove the drive belts. Remove the power steering pump and the A/C compressor (and their brackets!) and position them out of the way. Leave the hydraulic and refrigerant lines connected.
3. Remove the spark plugs and the cylinder head cover. Be sure to scrape off any left-over gasket material. Rotate the crankshaft pulley so that the **0** mark is in alignment with the groove in the No. 1 front cover. Check that the lifters on the No. 1 cylinder are loose; if not, turn the crankshaft 1 complete revolution (360 degrees).
4. Position a floor jack under the engine and remove the right side engine mounting insulator.
5. Remove the water pump and crankshaft pulleys. The crankshaft pulley will require a two-armed puller.
6. Loosen the 9 bolts and remove the Nos. 1, 2 and 3 front covers. Remove the timing belt guide.
7. Loosen the bolt on the idler pulley, push it to the left as far as it will go and then retighten it. If reusing the timing belt, draw an arrow on it in the direction of engine revolution (clockwise) and then matchmark the belt to the pulleys as indicated.
8. Remove the timing belt. Remove the idler pulley bolt, the pulley and the tension spring.
9. Remove the crankshaft timing pulley.
10. Lock the camshaft and remove the camshaft timing pulleys.

**To install:**

11. Install the camshaft timing pulley so it aligns with the knockpin on the exhaust camshaft. Tighten the pulley to 34 ft. lbs. (47 Nm) – 1988; 43 ft. lbs. (59 Nm) – 1989-90. Align the mark on the No. 1 camshaft bearing cap with the center of the small hole in the pulley.
12. Install the crankshaft timing pulley so that the marks on the pulley and the oil pump body are in alignment.
13. Install the idler pulley and its tension spring, move it to the left as far as it will go and tighten it temporarily.

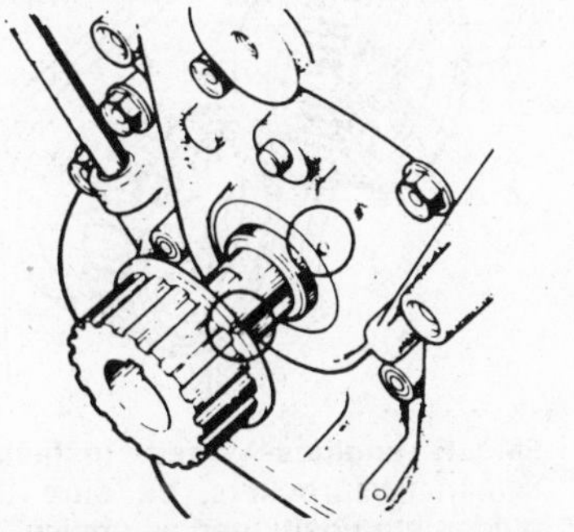

**When installing the crankshaft pulley, make sure the TDC marks on the oil pump body and the pulley are in alignment—4A-GE**

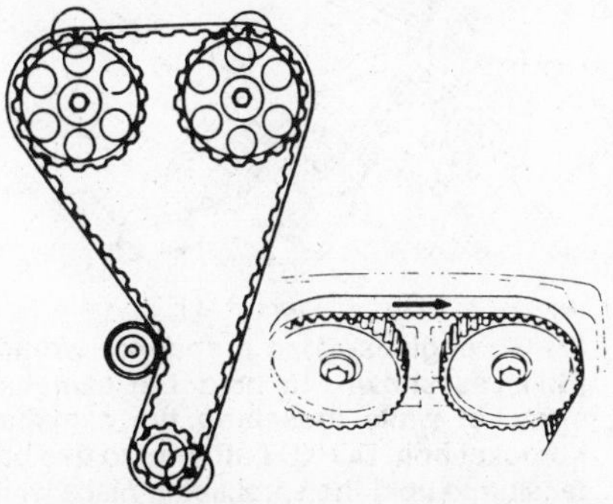

**If the timing belt is to be reused, draw a directional arrow and matchmark the belt to the pulleys as shown—4A-GE**

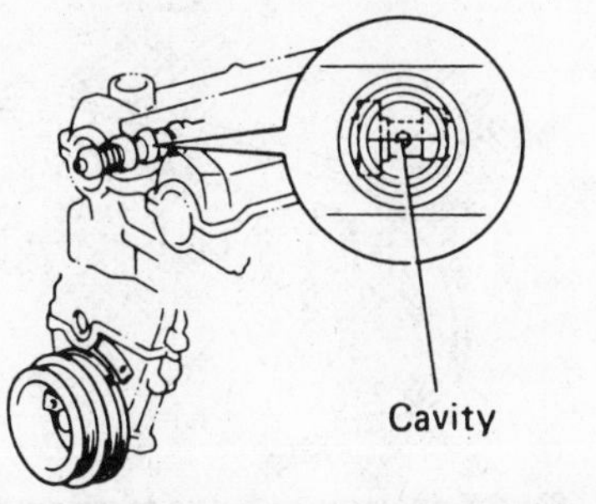


**When setting the No. 1 cylinder at TDC on the 4A-GE, remove the oil filler cap and check that the cavity in the camshaft is visible**

14. Align the matchmarks made during removal and then install the timing belt on the camshaft pulley. Loosen the idler pulley set bolt. Make sure the timing belt meshing at the crankshaft pulley does not shift.
15. Rotate the crankshaft clockwise 2 revolutions from TDC to TDC. Make sure that each pulley aligns with the marks made previously. If the marks are not in alignment, the valve timing is wrong. Shift the timing belt meshing slightly and then repeat Steps 14–15.
16. Tighten the set bolt on the timing belt idler pulley to 27 ft. lbs. (37 Nm). Measure the timing belt deflection at the top span between the 2 camshaft pulleys. It should deflect no more than 0.16 in. at 4.4 lbs. of pressure – 1988; 0.24 in. at 4.4 lbs. of pressure – 1989-90. If deflection is greater, readjust by using the idler pulley.
17. Installation of the remaining components is in the reverse order of removal.

### 4A-GE, 4A-GEC, 4A-GELC and 4A-GZE Engines

1. Disconnect the negative battery cable. Disconnect the No. 2 air cleaner hose from the air cleaner.
2. If equipped with power steering, remove the power steering pump and position it out of the way. Do not disconnect the pump hydraulic lines.
3. Loosen the water pump pulley set nuts, remove the drive belt adjusting bolt and then remove the drive belt. Remove the set nuts and then remove the fluid coupling along with the fan and the water pump pulley.
4. Remove the spark plugs. Rotate the crankshaft pulley so that the groove on it is in alignment with the **0** mark on the No. 1 timing belt cover. Remove the oil filler cap and check that the cavity in the camshaft is visible. If not, turn the camshaft 1 complete revolution (360 degrees).
5. On the MR2 and 1988-90 Corolla, remove the right side engine mount insulator.
6. Lock the crankshaft pulley and remove the pulley bolt. Using a gear puller, remove the crankshaft pulley. Remove the three timing belt covers and their gaskets. Remove the timing belt guide.
7. Loosen the bolt on the idler pulley, push it to the left as far as it will go and then retighten it. If reusing the timing belt, draw an arrow on it in the direction of engine revolution (clockwise) and then matchmark the belt to the pulleys as indicated.
8. Remove the timing belt. Remove the idler pulley bolt, the pulley and the tension spring.
9. Remove the cylinder head covers,

lock the camshaft and remove the camshaft timing pulleys.

**To install:**

10. Install the camshaft timing pulleys and cylinder head covers. Tighten the pulley to 34 ft. lbs. (47 Nm).

11. Install the crankshaft timing pulley so that the marks on the pulley and the oil pump body are in alignment.

12. Install the idler pulley and its tension spring, move it to the left as far as it will go and tighten it temporarily.

13. Install the timing belt. If the old one is being used, align all the marks made during removal.

14. Installation of the remaining components is in the reverse order of removal.

### *5M-GE Engines*

1. Disconnect the negative battery cable.

2. Loosen the mounting bolts of each of the crankshaft-driven components at the front of the engine and remove the drive belts.

3. Rotate the crankshaft in order to set the No. 1 cylinder to TDC of its compression stroke (both valves of the No. 1 cylinder closed, and TDC marks aligned).

4. Remove the upper, front (No. 3) timing belt cover and gasket (5 bolts).

5. Loosen the idler pulley bolt and lever the idler pulley toward the alternator side of the engine in order to relieve the tension on the timing belt. Handtighten the idler pulley bolt.

6. Remove the timing belt from the camshaft pulleys.

7. Remove the camshaft timing pulleys as follows. Hold the pulleys stationary with a spanner wrench. Remove the center pulley bolt. Do not attempt to use timing belt tension as a tool to remove the center pulley bolts, as the belt could become damaged.

**NOTE: Do not interchange the intake and exhaust timing pulleys, as they differ for use with each camshaft.**

8. Remove the center crankshaft pulley bolt. Using a puller, remove the crankshaft pulley.

9. Using chalk or crayon, mark the timing belt to indicate its direction of rotation. This mark must face the same direction during installation of the belt.

10. Remove the lower timing belt cover, then the belt.

11. If damaged, the crankshaft pulley can be removed using a puller; the oil pump drive shaft pulley can be removed in the same manner as the camshaft pulleys.

12. Inspect the timing belt for damage, such as cuts, cracks, missing teeth, abrasions, nicks, etc. If the belt teeth are damaged, check that the camshafts rotate freely and correct as necessary.

13. Should damage be evident on the belt face, check the idler pulley belt surface for damage. If damage is present on one side of the belt only, check the belt guide and the alignment of each pulley. If the belt teeth are excessively worn, check the timing belt cover gasket for damage and/or proper installation.

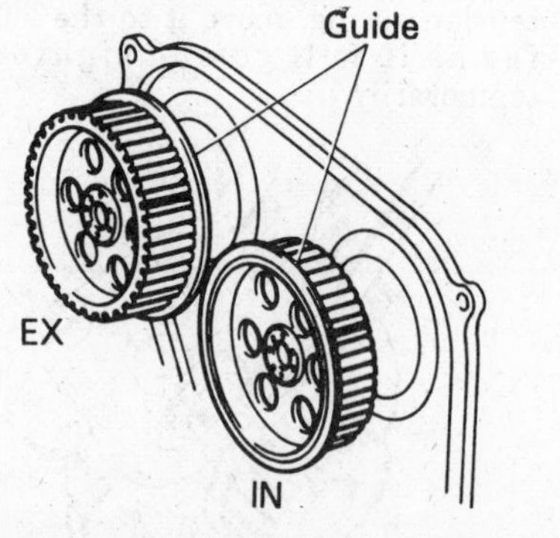


5M-GE engines—When installing the camshaft sprockets, be sure that the guides are positioned as shown. (IN—intake camshaft sprocket; EX—exhaust camshaft sprocket)

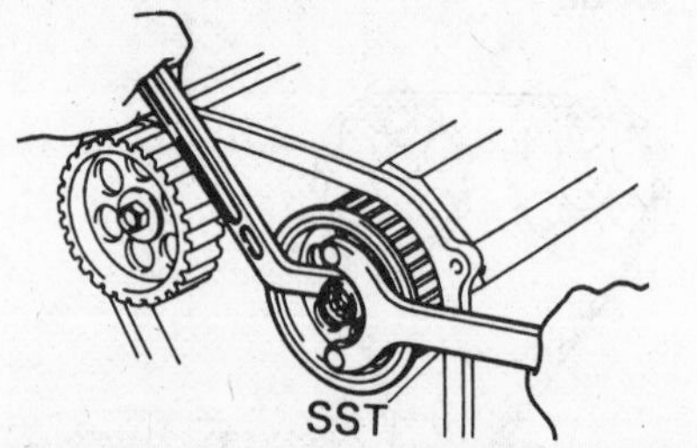


5M-GE engines—Use a spanner wrench (SST) as shown, to hold the camshaft sprocket while loosening the camshaft sprocket bolt. DO NOT attempt to use belt tension to hold the sprocket in place while removing the camshaft sprocket bolt

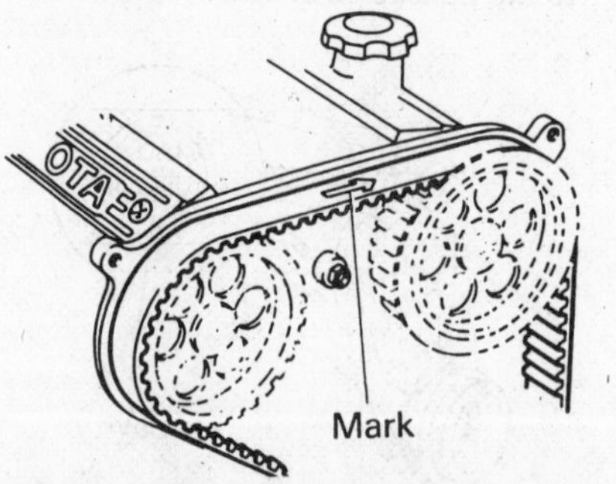


5M-GE engines—Paint a mark on the timing belt prior to belt removal to indicate the belts direction of normal rotation. Point the mark in the same direction if the belt is to be reinstalled

14. Check the idler pulley for damage and smoothness of rotation. Also check the free length of the tension spring, which should be 2.776 in., measured between the inside of each

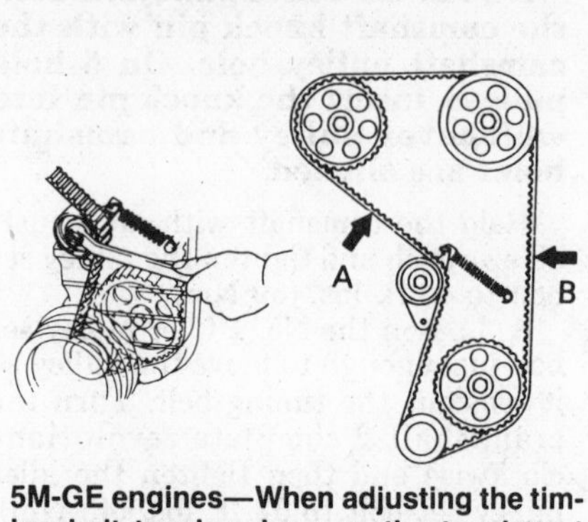


5M-GE engines—When adjusting the timing belt tension, be sure the tension at "A" is the same as that at "B"

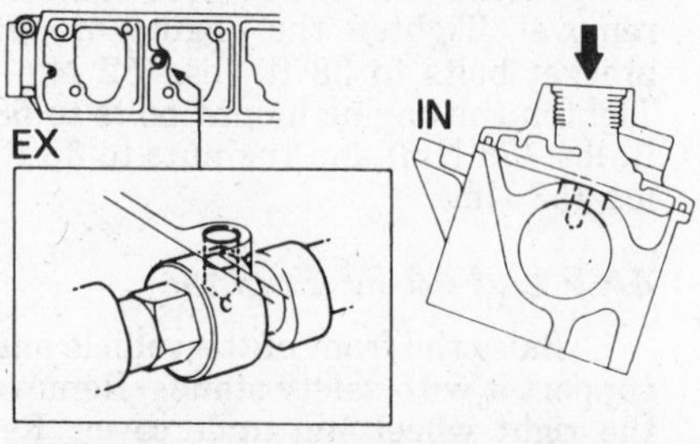


5M-GE engines—Proper alignment of the camshaft matchmarks with the match holes of the camshaft housings (IN—intake; EX—exhaust)

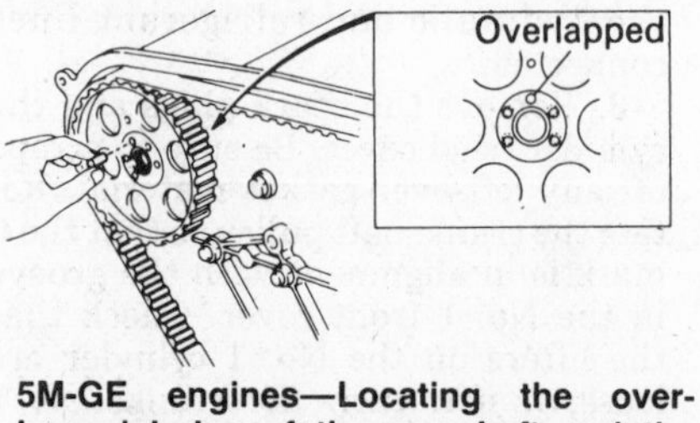


5M-GE engines—Locating the overlapped holes of the camshaft and the camshaft sprocket. Install the match pin into the aligned set of holes (typical of either the intake or exhaust camshaft)

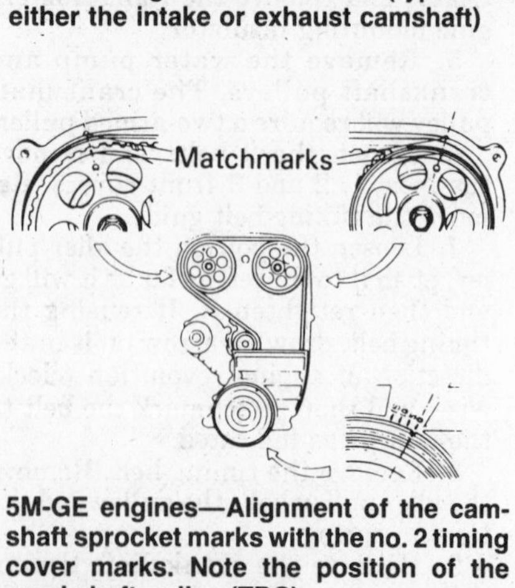


5M-GE engines—Alignment of the camshaft sprocket marks with the no. 2 timing cover marks. Note the position of the crankshaft pulley (TDC)

end "clip". Replace the spring if the length exceeds this limit.

**To install:**

15. Install the timing belt as follows. Install the crankshaft and oil pump drive shaft if these items were removed previously. Torque the oil pump drive shaft center pulley bolt to 16 ft. lbs. (22 Nm). The crankshaft pulley must be evenly driven into place.
16. Install the idler pulley and the tension spring. Lever the pulley towards the alternator side of the engine and tighten the bolt.
17. Check the mark made during Step 9 of removal and temporarily install the timing belt on the crankshaft pulley. The mark must face in the same direction as it did originally.
18. Install the lower timing belt cover. Install the crankshaft pulley and torque the center pulley bolt to 98–119 ft. lbs. (1983-87); 195 ft. lbs. (1988).
19. Remove the oil filter cap of the intake camshaft cover, and the complete camshaft cover on the exhaust side.
20. Check that the match holes of both No. 2 camshaft journals are visible through the camshaft housing match holes. If necessary, temporarily install the camshaft pulley and guide pin, and rotate the camshaft(s) until the holes are aligned.
21. Install the timing pulleys. Note that the belt guide of the exhaust camshaft pulley should be positioned towards the engine; the belt guide of the intake camshaft pulley should be positioned away from the engine. Do not yet install the pulley retaining bolts.
22. Align the following marks. Each camshaft pulley mark must be aligned with its respective mark on the rear, upper (No. 2) timing belt cover. Align the crankshaft pulley notch with the TDC (0) mark of the timing tab.

**NOTE: The No. 1 cylinder MUST be positioned at TDC on its compression stroke.**

23. Install the timing belt.
24. Loosen the idler pulley bolt and tension the timing belt. The timing belt tension must be the same between the exhaust camshaft pulley and the crankshaft pulley, as it is between the intake camshaft pulley and the oil pump drive shaft pulley.
25. There are five pin holes on each camshaft and each timing pulley. On the exhaust side: Install the match pin into the one hole of the pulley which is aligned with one of the camshaft pin holes. Repeat this on the intake side. Only one of the holes of each side should be aligned to allow insertion of the match pins.
26. Using a spanner wrench to hold the camshaft pulleys, install and tighten the camshaft pulley bolts. These bolts should be torqued to 51 ft. lbs. (69 Nm).
27. Install the exhaust camshaft cover, using a new gasket. Install the oil filler cap. Install the timing belt cover and gasket.
28. Install and adjust the drive belts at the front of the engine. Reconnect the battery cable.

### 7M-GE and 7M-GTE Engines

1. Disconnect the negative battery cable. Drain the cooling system. Remove the radiator. Remove the water outlet.
2. Remove the spark plugs. Remove the drive belts. Remove the No. 3 timing belt cover.
3. Position the engine at TDC on the compression stroke. Remove the timing belt from the camshaft sprockets. If reusing the belt, matchmark the belt and the sprockets in the direction of engine rotation.
4. Remove the camshaft pulleys. Remove the crankshaft pulley using the proper removal tools. Remove the power steering air pipe, if equipped.
5. If equipped with air condition remove the compressor and position it out of the way. Do not disconnect the refrigerant lines.
6. Remove the No. 1 timing belt cover. Remove the timing belt. Remove the idler pulley and the tension spring. Remove the oil pump drive pulley.
7. Inspect the belt for defects. Replace as required. Inspect the idler pulleys and springs. Replace defective components as required.
8. Install the oil pump drive pulley and retaining bolt. Tighten the bolt to 16 ft. lbs. (22 Nm).
9. Install the crankshaft timing pulley. Temporarily install the idler pulley and tension spring. Tighten the assembly to 36 ft. lbs. (49 Nm). Pry the idler pulley toward the left as far as it will go and temporarily tighten the bolt.
10. Temporarily install the timing belt. If reusing the old belt install it using the marks made during the removal procedure. Install the No. 1 timing belt cover.
11. If equipped with air conditioning, install the compressor assembly. If equipped, install the power steering air pipe.
12. Align the set key with the key groove and install the crankshaft pulley and torque the retaining bolt to 195 ft. lbs. (265 Nm).
13. Install the camshaft timing pulleys. Torque the retaining bolts to 36 ft. lbs. (49 Nm).
14. Loosen the idler pulley bolt. Install the timing belt to the INTAKE side and the EXHAUST side. Tighten the idler pulley bolt to 36 ft. lbs. (49 Nm).
15. Make sure that the timing belt tension **A** is equal to the timing belt tension **B**. If not adjust the idler pulley. Turn the engine 2 complete revolutions in the clockwise direction and check to see that everything is aligned properly.
16. Turn both the intake and exhaust camshaft pulleys inward at the same time to slaken the timing belt between the two sprockets. Belt defelection should be 4.4–6.6 lbs. If not adjust the idler pulley.
17. Installation of the remaining components is in the reverse order of removal.

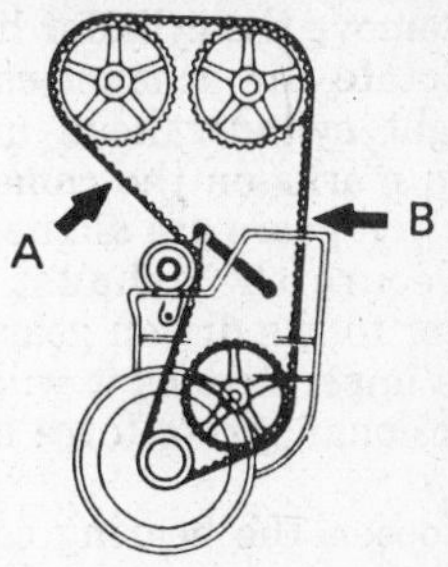

**7M-GE and 7M-GTE timing belt tension check**

## Timing Sprockets

### REMOVAL & INSTALLATION

Timing sprocket/pulley removal and installation procedures are detailed within the individual Timing Chain or Timing Belt sections.

## Camshaft

### REMOVAL & INSTALLATION

#### 2S-E Engines

1. Remove the timing belt. Remove the cylinder head cover.
2. Remove the camshaft pulley. Remove the camshaft bearing caps.
3. Turning the camshaft slowly, slide it from the housing.
4. Installation is the reverse of the removal procedure. Always use new oil seals.

#### 2VZ-FE Engines

**NOTE: Due to a nominal thrust clearance, the camshafts must be held absolutely level during removal. If not, the section of the cylinder head recieving the thrust may crack or be damaged, thus causing the camshaft to break. Be very careful!**

1. Remove the cylinder head.
2. Rotate the exhaust camshaft in the right cylinder head until the 2 pointed marks on the camshaft drive and driven gears are aligned.
3. Secure the exhaust camshaft sub-gear to the driven gear with bolt. This is imperative as it will eliminate the torsional spring force of the sub-gear.
4. Loosen the bearing cap bolts in the proper sequence and then remove the 4 bearing caps and the right side exhaust camshaft.
5. Loosen the bearing cap bolts in the proper sequence and then remove the 5 bearing caps and the right side intake camshaft.

**NOTE: Be sure to arrange all the bearing caps in their proper order.**

6. Rotate the exhaust camshaft in the left cylinder head until the pointed mark on the camshaft drive and driven gears are aligned.
7. Secure the exhaust camshaft sub-gear to the driven gear with bolt. This is imperative as it will eliminate the torsional spring force of the sub-gear.
8. Loosen the bearing cap bolts in the proper sequence and then remove the 4 bearing caps and the left side exhaust camshaft.
9. Loosen the bearing cap bolts in the proper sequence and then remove the 5 bearing caps and the left side intake camshaft.

**NOTE: Be sure to arrange all the bearing caps in their proper order.**

**To install:**

10. Coat the thrust portion of the right side intake camshaft with grease and then position the camshaft into the head so that the 2 timing marks are at a 90 degree angle to the head.
11. Coat the edges of the No. 1 bearing cap with sealant and then install all 5 caps in their proper locations. Coat the bolts with engine oil and then tighten them, in sequence, in several stages, to 12 ft. lbs. (16 Nm).
12. Coat the thrust portion of the right side exhaust camshaft with grease and then position the camshaft into the head so that the 2 timing marks align with those on the intake shaft.
13. Install all 4 bearing caps in their proper locations. Coat the bolts with engine oil and then tighten them, in sequence, in several stages, to 12 ft. lbs. (16 Nm).
14. Remove the service bolt.
15. Coat the thrust portion of the left side intake camshaft with grease and then position the camshaft into the

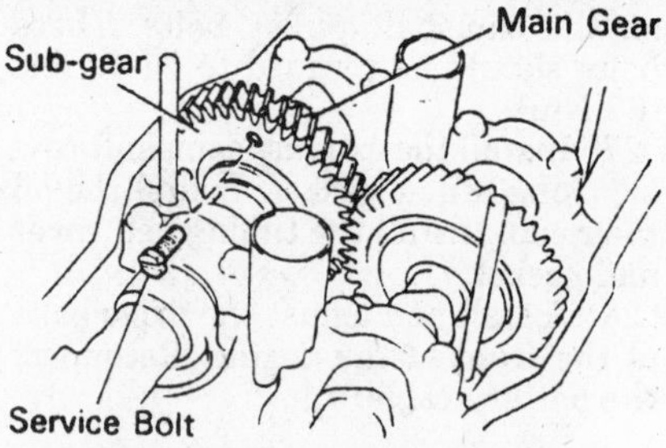

**Install a service bolt in the exhaust camshaft sub-gear (right)—2VZ-FE engines**

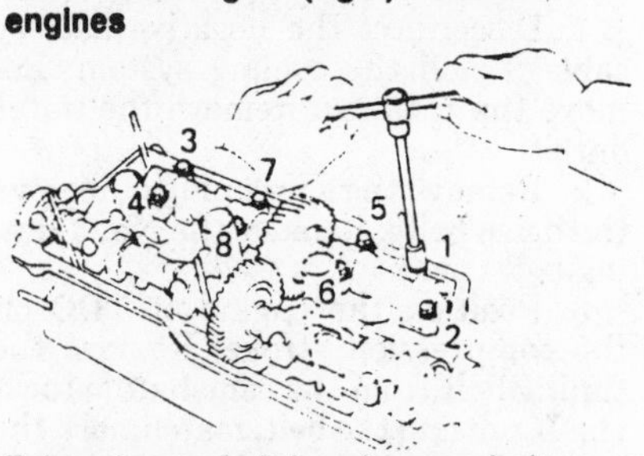
**Exhaust camshaft bearing cap bolt LOOSENING sequence (right)—2VZ-FE engines**

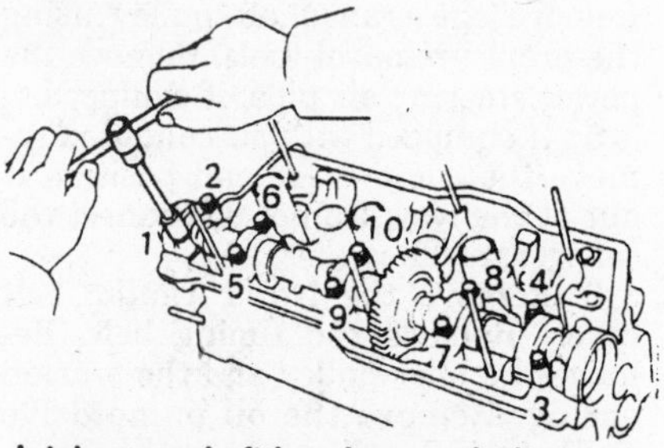
**Intake camshaft bearing cap bolt LOOSENING sequence (right)—2VZ-FE engines**

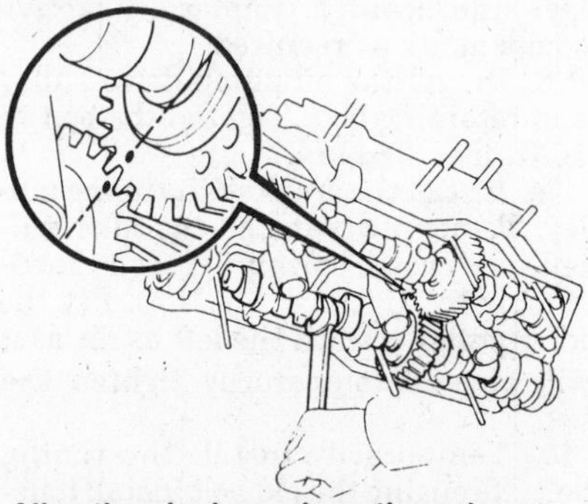
**Align the single mark on the exhaust camshaft (left)—2VZ-FE engines**

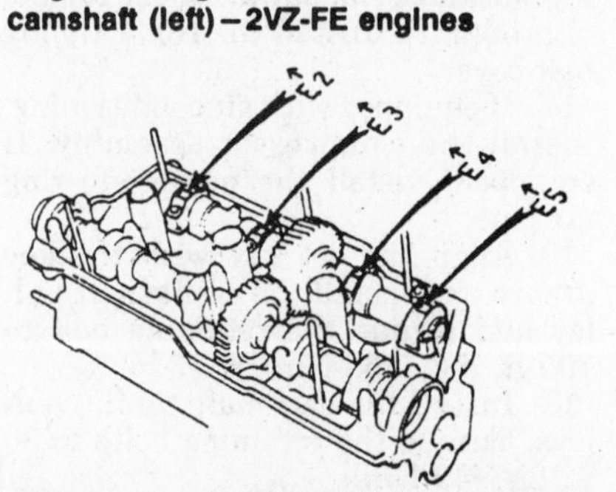
**Exhaust camshaft bearing cap installation (right)—2VZ-FE engines**

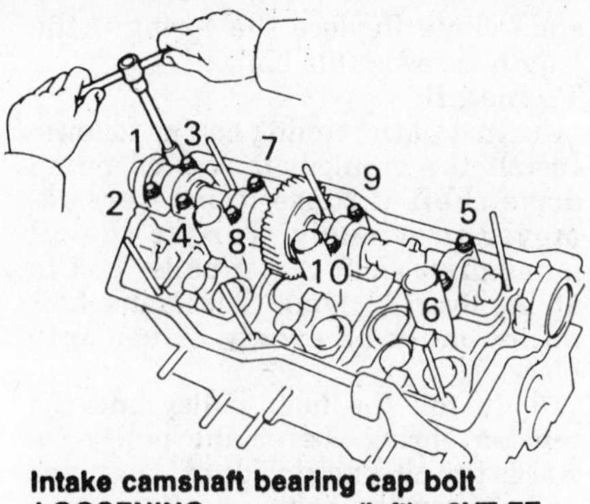
**Intake camshaft bearing cap bolt LOOSENING sequence (left)—2VZ-FE engines**

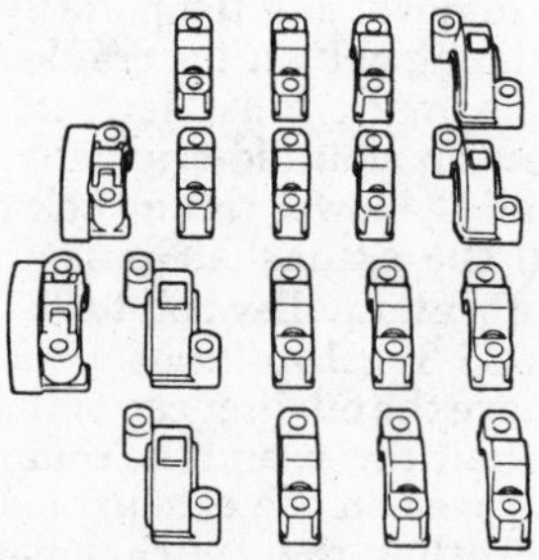

**Camshaft bearing cap identification—2VZ-FE engines**

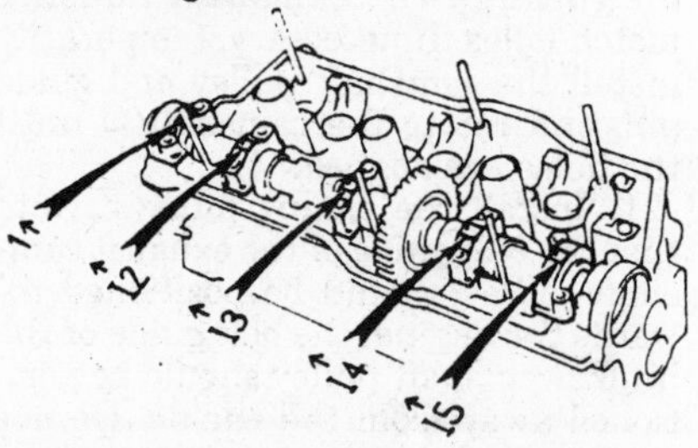
**Intake camshaft bearing cap installation (right)—2VZ-FE engines**

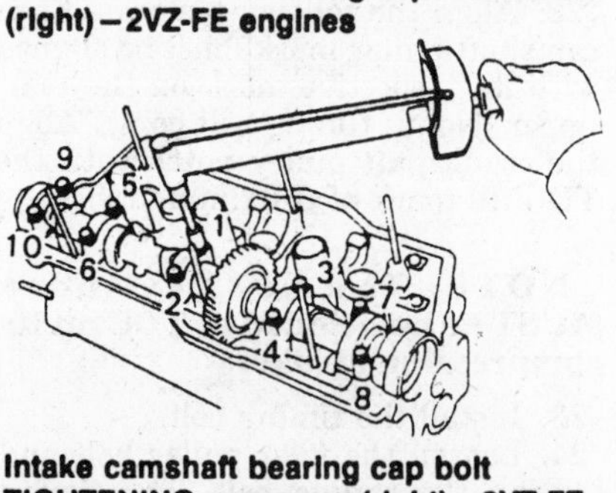
**Intake camshaft bearing cap bolt TIGHTENING sequence (right)—2VZ-FE engines**

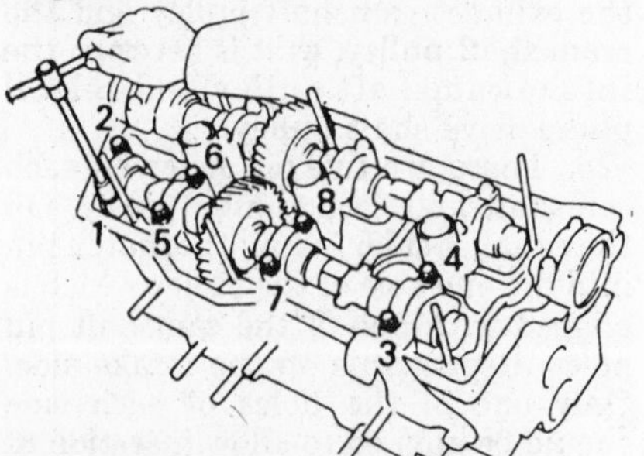
**Exhaust camshaft bearing cap bolt LOOSENING sequence (left)—2VZ-FE engines**

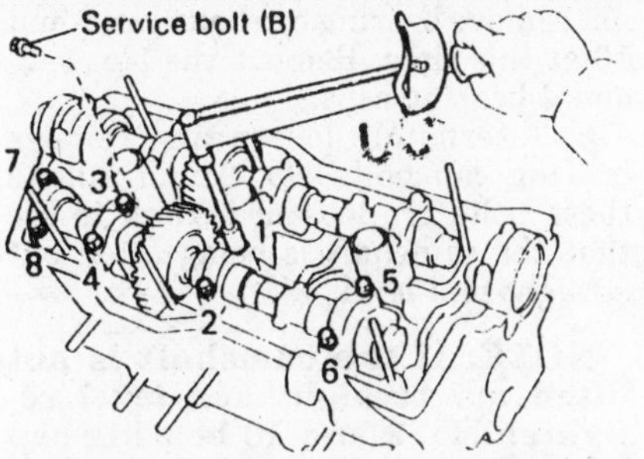


Exhaust camshaft bearing cap bolt TIGHTENING sequence (right)–2VZ-FE engines

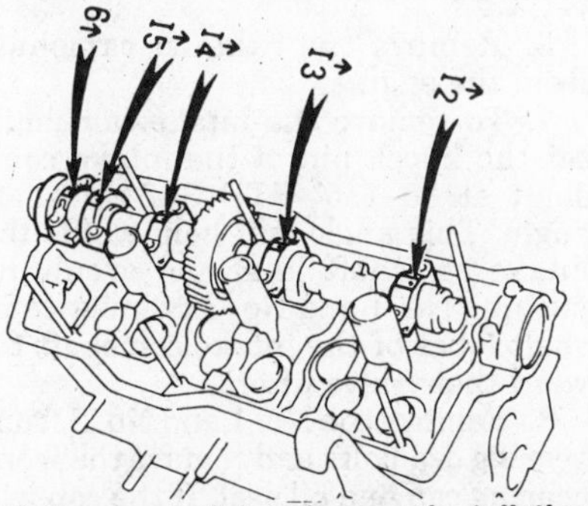


Intake camshaft bearing cap installation (left)–2VZ-FE engines

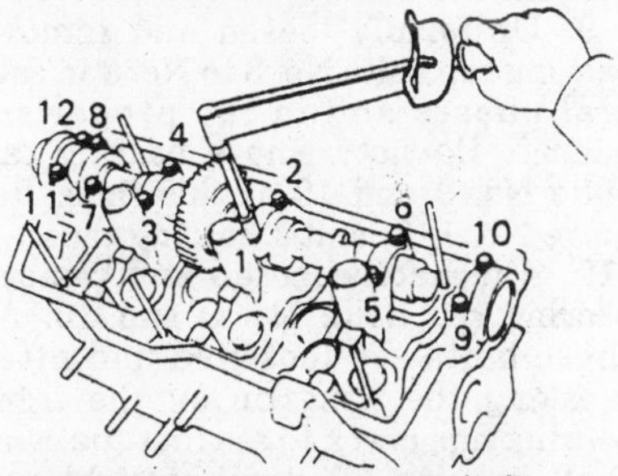


Intake camshaft bearing cap bolt TIGHTENING sequence (left)–2VZ-FE engines

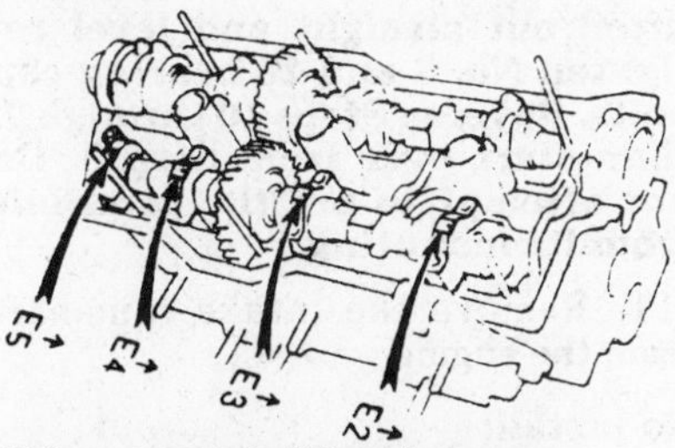


Exhaust camshaft bearing cap installation (left)–2VZ-FE engines

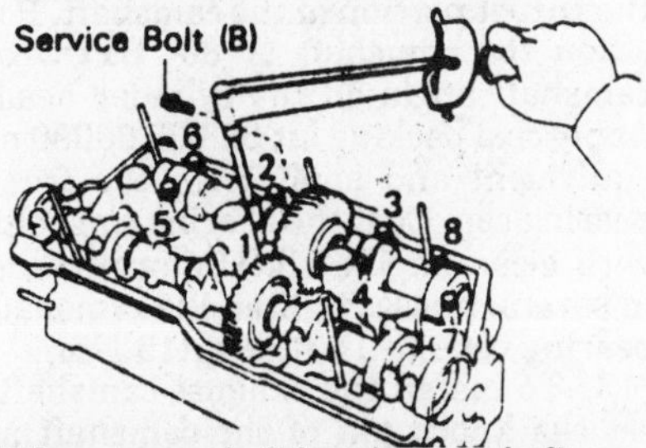


Exhaust camshaft bearing cap bolt TIGHTENING sequence (left)–2VZ-FE engines

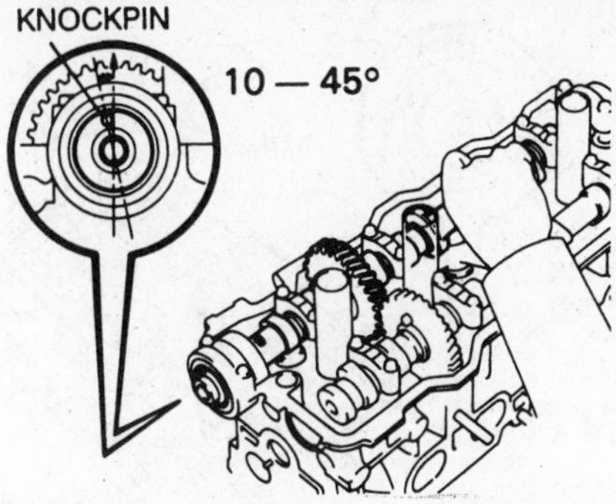


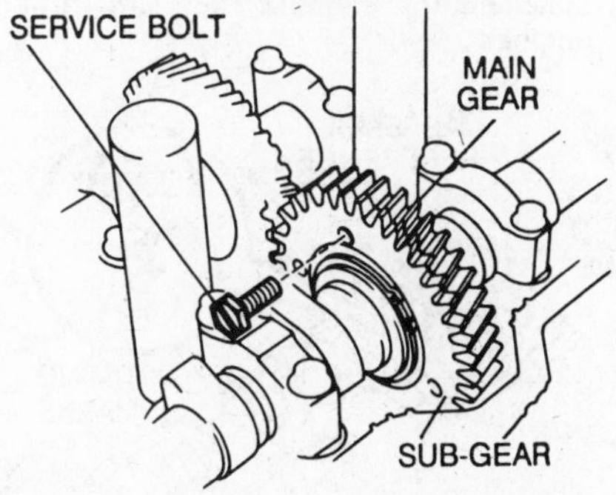


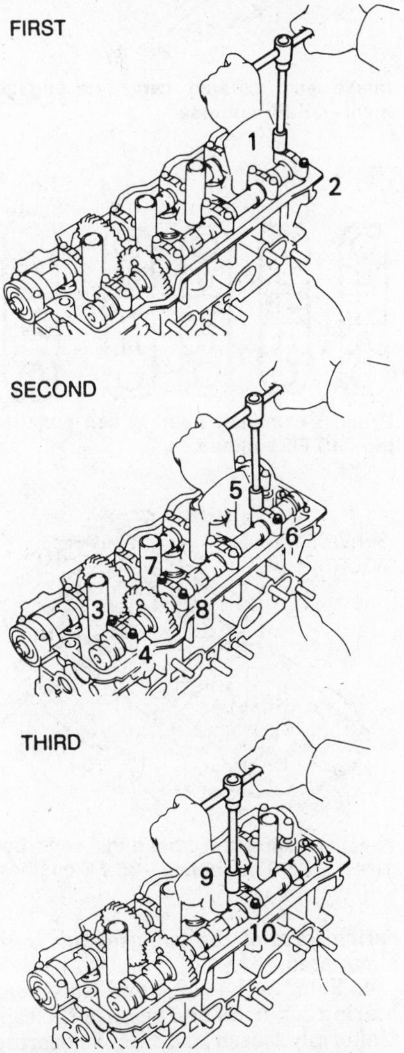


Exhaust camshaft removal procedure–3S-FE engines

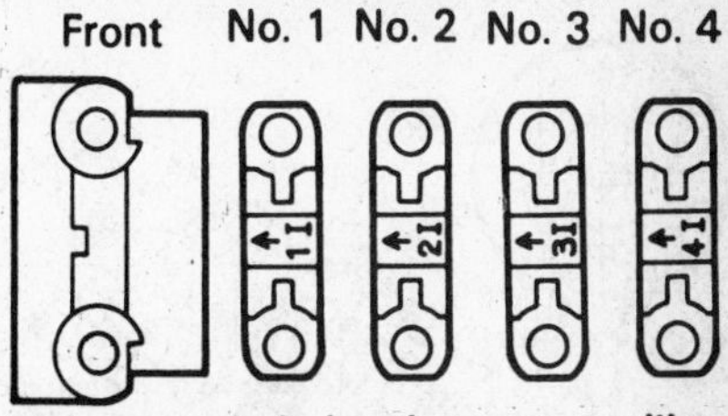


Intake camshaft bearing cap positioning–3S-FE engines

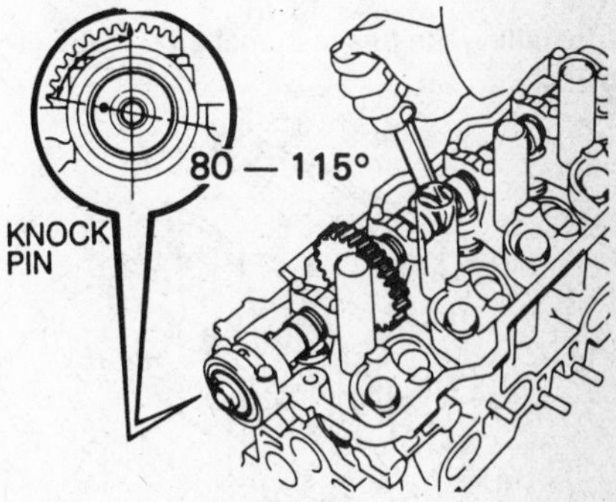


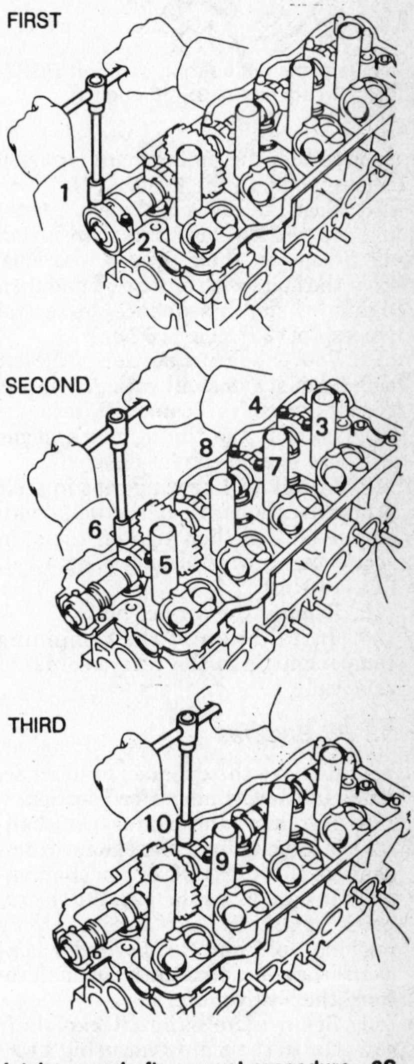


Intake camshaft removal procedure–3S-FE engines

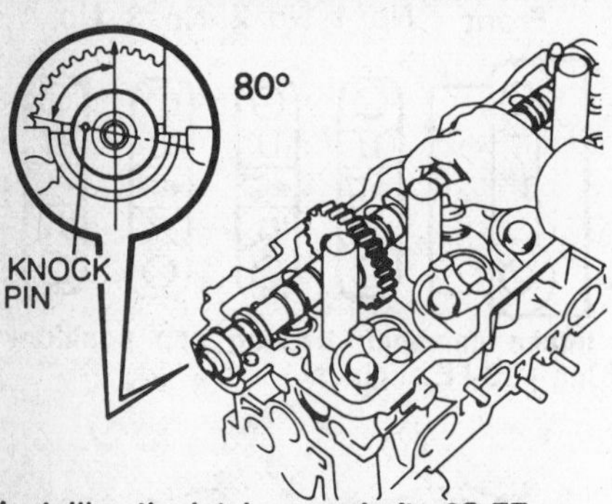

Installing the intake camshaft—3S-FE engines

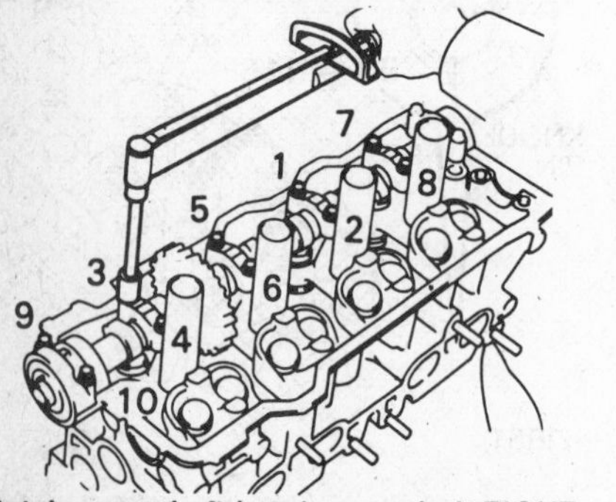

Intake camshaft bearing cap bolt TIGHTENING sequence—3S-FE engines

head so that the timing mark is at a 90 degree angle to the head.

16. Coat the edges of the No. 1 bearing cap with sealant and then install all 5 caps in their proper locations. Coat the bolts with engine oil and then tighten them, in sequence, in several stages, to 12 ft. lbs. (16 Nm).

17. Coat the thrust portion of the left side exhaust camshaft with grease and then position the camshaft into the head so that the timing mark aligns with the one on the intake shaft.

18. Install all 4 bearing caps in their proper locations. Coat the bolts with engine oil and then tighten them, in sequence, in several stages, to 12 ft. lbs. (16 Nm).

19. Remove the service bolt.

20. Installation of the remaining components is in the reverse order of removal.

### 3S-FE Engines

1. Remove the cylinder head as detailed in the Cylinder Head section.

2. To remove the exhaust camshaft, set the knock pin of the exhaust camshaft at 10–45° BTDC of camshaft angle. This angle will help to lift the exhaust camshaft level and evenly by pushing No. 2 and No. 4 cylinder camshaft lobes of the exhaust camshaft toward their valve lifters.

3. Secure the exhaust camshaft sub-gear to the main gear using a service bolt. When removing the exhaust camshaft be sure that the torsional

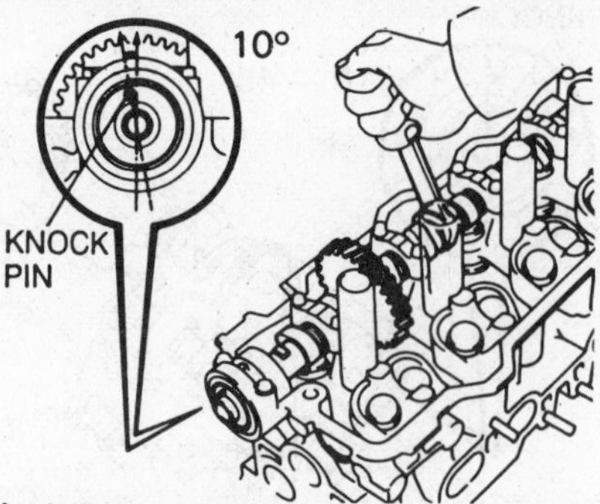

Installing the exhaust camshaft—3S-FE engines

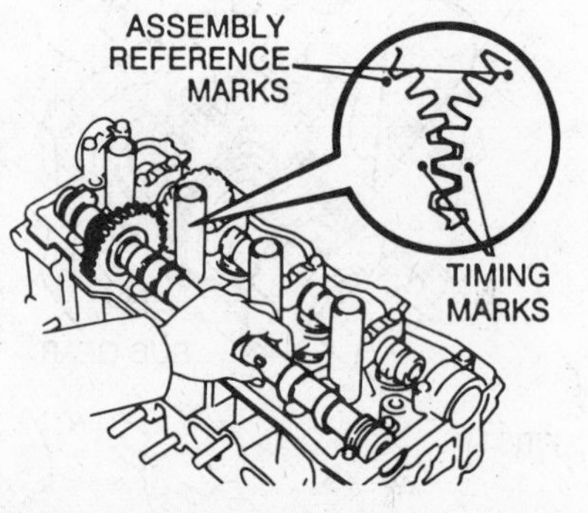

Intake and exhaust camshaft engagement—3S-FE engines

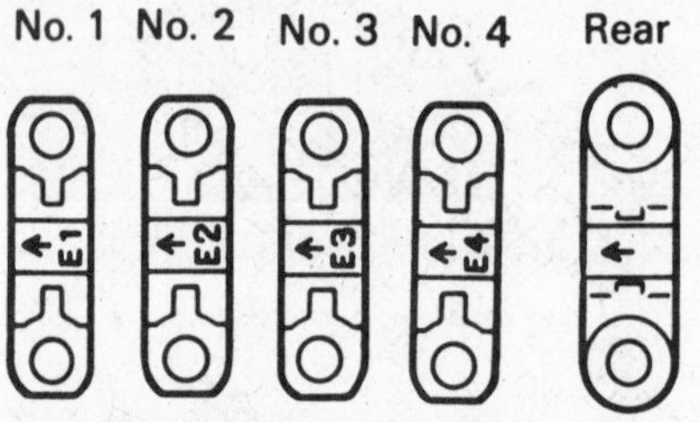

Exhaust camshaft bearing cap positioning—3S-FE engines

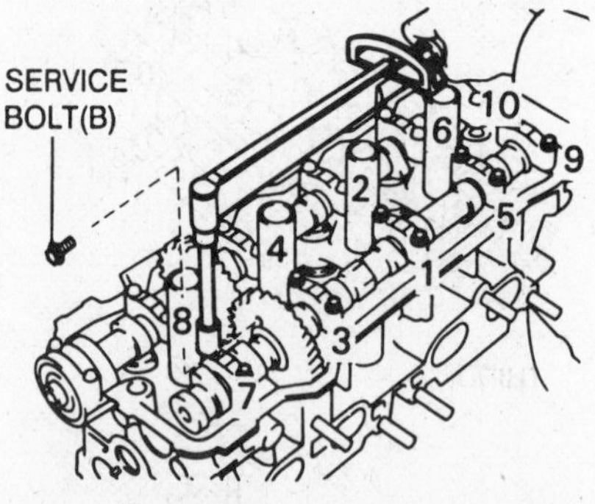

Exhaust camshaft bearing cap bolt TIGHTENING sequence—3S-FE engines

spring force of the sub-gear has been eliminated.

4. Remove the No. 1 and No. 2 rear bearing cap bolts and remove the cap. Uniformly loosen and remove bearing cap bolts No. 3 to No. 8 in several passes and in the proper sequence. Do not remove bearing cap bolts No. 9 and 10 at this time. Remove the No. 1, 2, and 4 bearing caps.

5. Alternately loosen and remove bearing cap bolts No. 9 and 10. As these bolts are loosened check to see that the camshaft is being lifted out straight and level.

**NOTE: If the camshaft is not lifted out straight and level retighten No. 9 and 10 bearing cap bolts. Reverse Steps 4 through 1, than start over from Step 3. Do not attempt to pry the camshaft from its mounting.**

6. Remove the exhaust camshaft from the engine.

7. To remove the intake camshaft, set the knock pin of the intake camshaft at 80–115° BTDC of camshaft angle. This angle will help to lift the intake camshaft level and evenly by pushing No. 1 and No. 3 cylinder camshaft lobes of the intake camshaft toward their valve lifters.

8. Remove the No. 1 and No. 2 front bearing cap bolts and remove the front bearing cap and oil seal. If the cap will not come apart easily, leave it in place without the bolts.

9. Uniformly loosen and remove bearing cap bolts No. 3 to No. 8 in several phases and in the proper sequence. Do not remove bearing cap bolts No. 9 and 10 at this time. Remove No. 1, 3, and 4 bearing caps.

10. Alternately loosen and remove bearing cap bolts No. 9 and 10. As these bolts are loosened and after breaking the adhesion on the front bearing cap, check to see that the camshaft is being lifted out straight and level.

**NOTE: If the camshaft is not lifted out straight and level retighten No. 9 and 10 bearing cap bolts. Reverse Steps 10 through 7, than start over from Step 8. Do not attempt to pry the camshaft from its mounting.**

11. Remove the intake camshaft from the engine.

**To install:**

12. Before installing the intake camshaft, apply multi purpose grease to the thrust portion of the camshaft. Position the camshaft at 80° BTDC of camshaft angle on the cylinder head. Apply seal packing kit 08826-00080 or equivalent and apply it to the front bearing cap. Coat the bearing cap bolts with clean engine oil. Uniformly and in several phases tighten the camshaft bearing caps to 14 ft. lbs. (19 Nm).

13. To install the exhaust camshaft, set the knock pin of the camshaft at 10° BTDC of camshaft angle. Apply multipurpose grease to the thrust por-

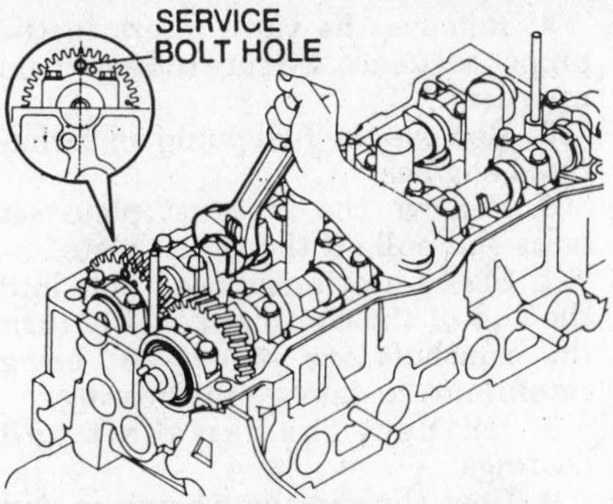


Service bolt hole positioning (intake camshaft) – 4A-F and 4A-FE engines

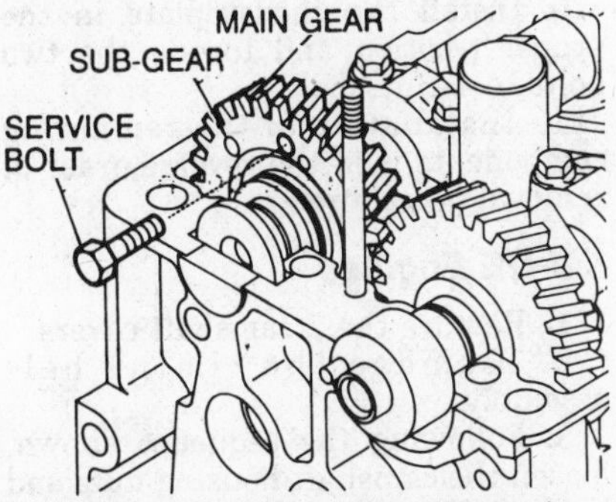


Installing the service bolt in the intake camshaft – 4A-F and 4A-FE engines

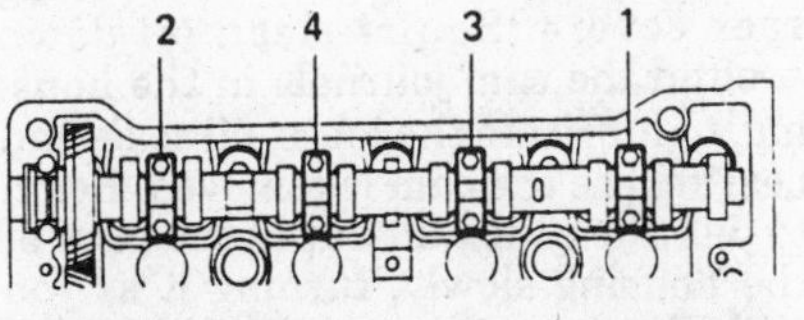


Camshaft bearing cap bolt LOOSENING sequence – 4A-F and 4A-FE engines

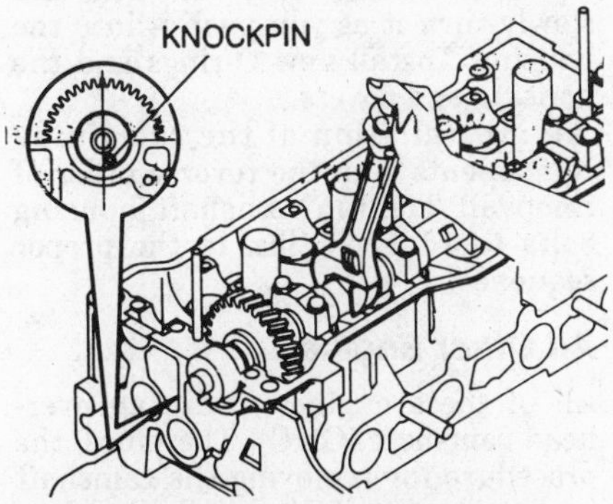


Knockpin positioning on the exhaust camshaft – 4A-F and 4A-FE engines

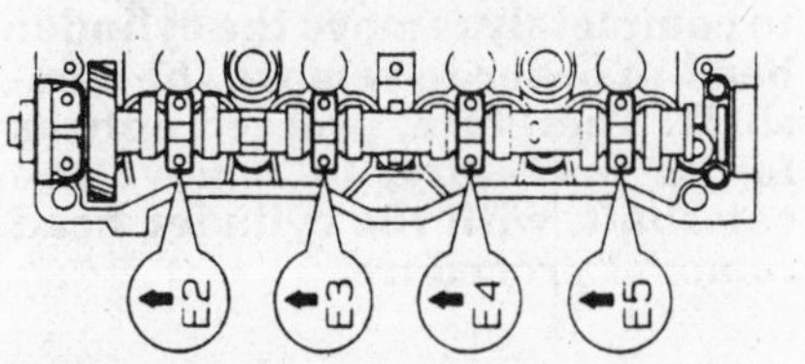


Exhaust camshaft bearing cap positioning – 4A-F and 4A-FE engines

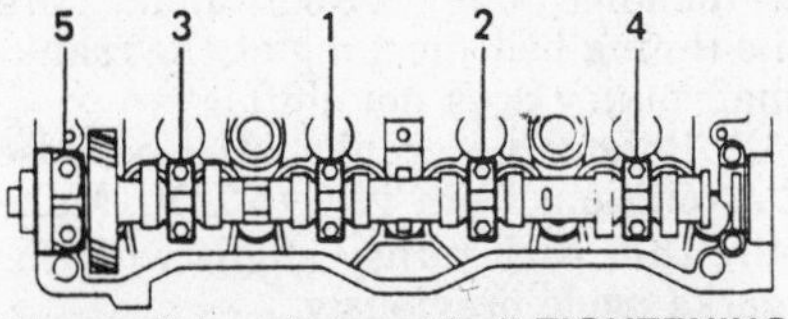


Camshaft bearing cap bolt TIGHTENING sequence – 4A-F and 4A-FE engines

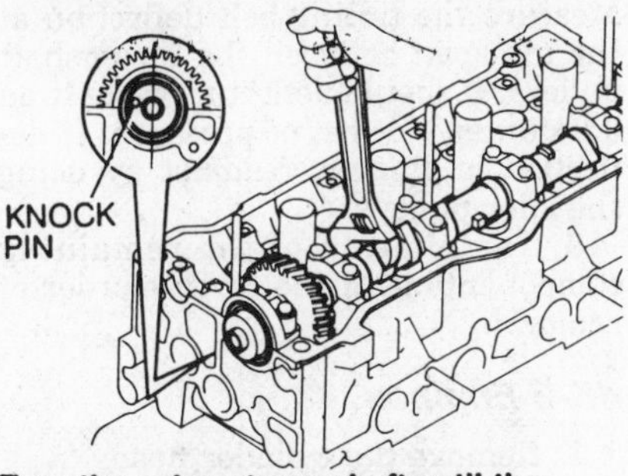


Turn the exhaust camshaft until the knockpin is here – 4A-F and 4A-FE engines

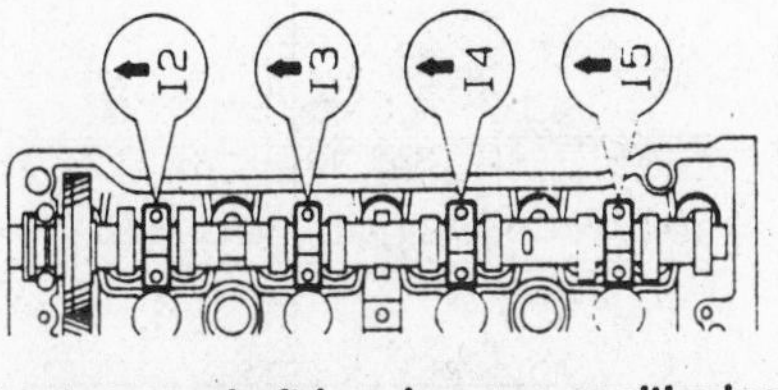


Intake camshaft bearing cap positioning – 4A-F and 4A-FE engines

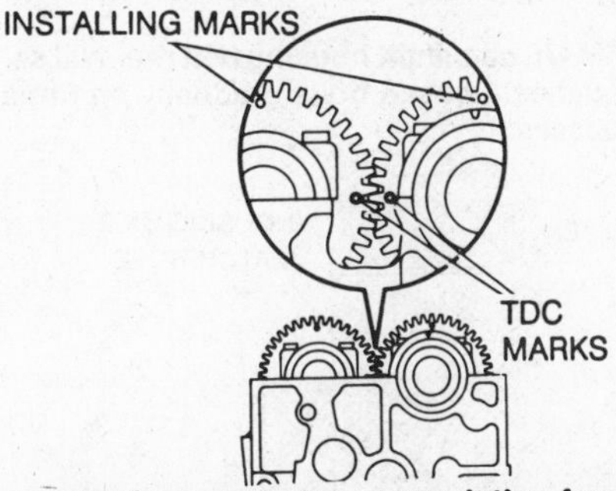


Rotate the camshaft one revolution from TDC to TDC and check that the marks are lined up – 4A-F and 4A-FE engines

tion of the camshaft. Position the exhaust camshaft gear with the intake camshaft gear so that the timing marks are in alignment with one another. Be sure to use the proper alignment marks on the gears. Do not use the assembly reference marks.

14. Turn the intake camshaft clockwise or counterclockwise little by little until the exhaust camshaft sits in the bearing journals evenly without rocking the camshaft on the bearing journals.

15. Coat the bearing cap bolts with clean engine oil. Uniformly and in several phases tighten the camshaft bearing caps to 14 ft. lbs. (19 Nm). Remove the service bolt from the assembly.

16. Installation of the remaining components is in the reverse order of removal.

### 4A-F and 4A-FE Engines

1. Disconnect the negative battery cable at the battery. Drain the engine coolant.
2. Remove the spark plugs and the cylinder head cover.
3. Remove the No. 3 and No. 2 front covers. Turn the crankshaft pulley and align its groove with the **0** mark on the No. 1 front cover. Check that the camshaft pulley hole aligns with the mark on the No. 1 camshaft bearing cap (exhaust side).
4. Remove the plug from the No. 1 front cover and matchmark the timing belt to the camshaft pulley. Loosen the idler pulley mounting bolt and push the pulley to the left as far as it will go; tighten the bolt. Slide the timing belt off the camshaft pulley and support it so it won't fall into the case.
5. Remove the camshaft pulley and check the camshaft thrust clearance. Remove the camshafts.

**NOTE: Due to the relatively small amount of camshaft thrust clearance, the camshaft must be held level during removal. If the camshaft is not level on removal, the portion of the head receiving the thrust may crack or be damaged.**

6. Set the service bolt hole on the intake camshaft gear (the one NOT attached to the timing pulley!) at the 12 o'clock position so that the Nos. 1 and 3 cylinder camshaft lobed can push their lifters evenly. Loosen the No. 1 bearing caps on each camshaft a little at a time and remove them.
7. Secure the intake camshaft subgear to the main gear with a service bolt to eliminate any torsional spring force. Loosen the remaining bearing caps a little at a time, in the proper sequence and remove the intake camshaft. If the camshaft cannot be lifted out straight and level, retighten the bolts in the No. 3 bearing cap and loosen them a little at a time with the gear pulled up.
8. Turn the exhaust camshaft approximately 105 degrees so the knock pin is about 5 minutes before the 6:30 o'clock position. Loosen the remaining bearing caps a little at a time, in the proper sequence and remove the exhaust camshaft. If the camshaft cannot be lifted out straight and level, retighten the bolts in the No. 3 bearing cap and loosen them a little at a time with the gear pulled up.

**To install:**

9. Position the exhaust camshaft into the cylinder head as it was re-

moved. Position the bearing caps over each journal so that the arrows point forward and then tighten the bolts gradually, in the proper sequence to 9 ft. lbs. (13 Nm).

10. Coat the lip of a new oil seal with MP grease and drive it into the camshaft.

11. Set the knock pin on the exhaust camshaft so it is just above the edge of the cylinder head and engage the intake camshaft gear to the exhaust gear so that the mark on each gear is in alignment. Roll the intake camshaft down onto the bearing journals while engaging the gears with each other.

12. Position the bearing caps over each journal on the intake camshaft so that the arrows point forward and then tighten the bolts gradually, in the proper sequence to 9 ft. lbs. (13 Nm).

13. Remove the service bolt and install the No. 1 intake bearing cap. If it does not fit properly, pry the camshaft gear backwards until it does. Tighten the bolts to 9 ft. lbs. (13 Nm).

14. Rotate the camshafts 1 revolution (360 degrees) from TDC to TDC and check that the marks on the 2 gears are still aligned.

15. Install the camshaft timing pulley making sure that the camshaft knock pins and the matchmarks are in alignment. Lock each camshaft and tighten the pulley bolts to 43 ft. lbs. (59 Nm).

16. Align the matchmarks made during removal and then install the timing belt on the camshaft pulley. Loosen the idler pulley set bolt. Make sure the timing belt meshing at the crankshaft pulley does not shift.

17. Rotate the crankshaft clockwise 2 revolutions from TDC to TDC. Make sure that each pulley aligns with the marks made previously.

18. Tighten the set bolt on the timing belt idler pulley to 27 ft. lbs. (37 Nm). Measure the timing belt deflection at the top span between the 2 camshaft pulleys. It should deflect no more than 0.24 in. at 4.4 lbs. of pressure. If deflection is greater, readjust by using the idler pulley.

19. Installation of the remaining components is in the reverse order of removal.

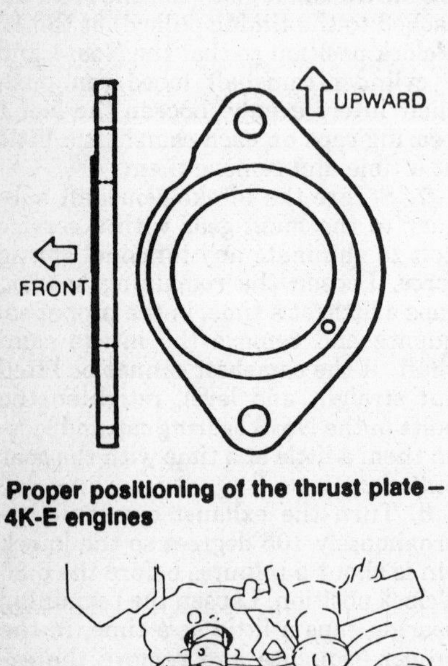


**Proper positioning of the thrust plate – 4K-E engines**

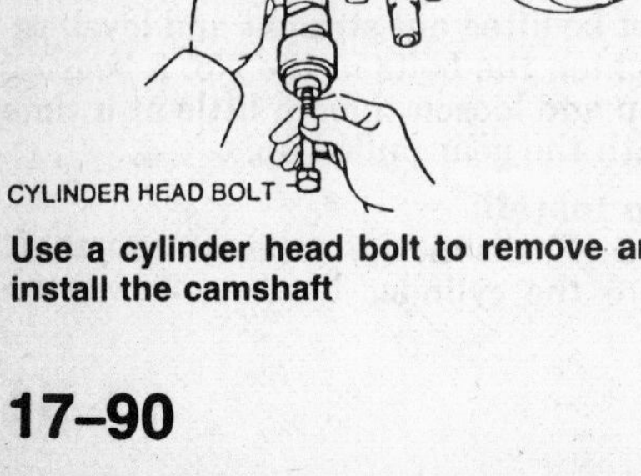


**Use a cylinder head bolt to remove and install the camshaft**

### 4K-E Engines

1. Remove the cylinder head.
2. Remove the distributor. Remove the radiator.
3. Remove the timing chain.

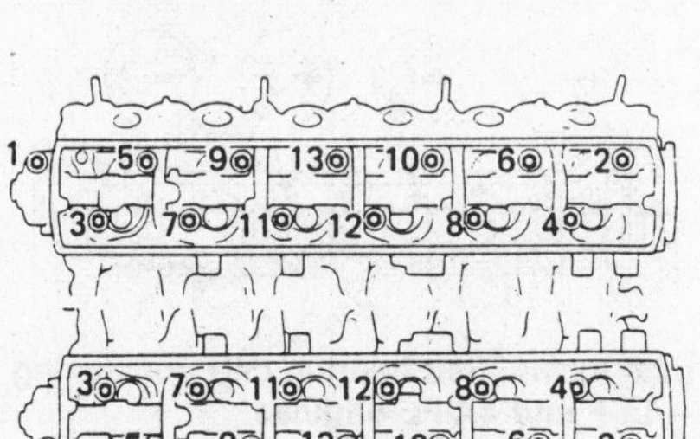


**5M-GE camshaft housing bolt removal sequence. Loosen bolts gradually on three passes**

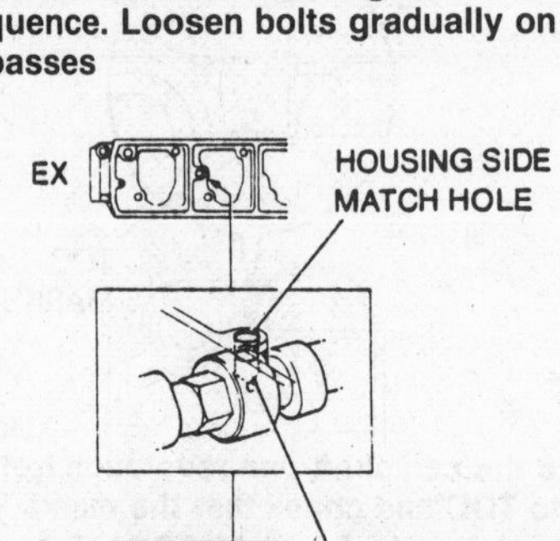


**5M-GE camshaft housing torque sequence**

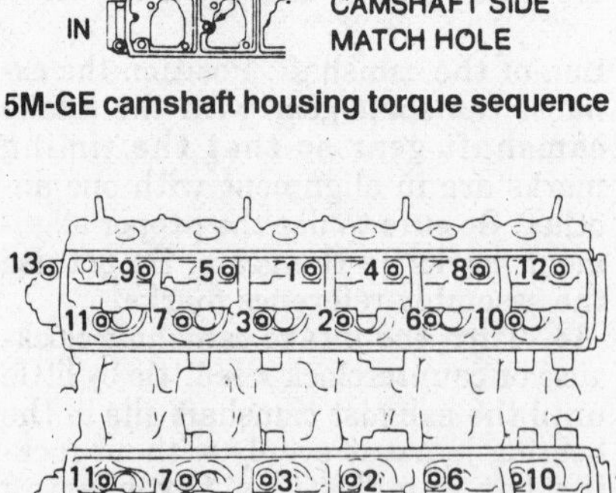


**Before installing the camshaft housings, align the match hole on each No. 2 cam journal with the hole in the housing**

4. Remove the valve lifters in the proper sequence. Be sure to keep them in order.

5. Remove the fuel pump on carbureted engines.

6. Remove the 2 thrust plate set bolts and pull off the thrust plate.

7. Screw a cylinder head bolt into the end of the camshaft. Slowly turn the camshaft and pull it out being careful not to damage the bearing.

8. Inspect the camshaft and bearings.

9. Coat the camshaft bearings and journals lightly with oil and then carefully install it into the cylinder block.

10. Install the thrust plate in the proper position and torque the two bolts to 4–6 ft. lbs.

11. Installation of the remaining components is in the reverse order of removal procedure.

### 5M-GE Engines

1. Remove the 2 camshaft covers.

2. Remove the timing belt assembly.

3. Following the sequence shown, loosen the camshaft housing nuts and bolts in three passes. Remove the housings (with camshafts) from the cylinder head.

4. Remove the camshaft housing rear covers. Squirt clean oil down around the cam journals in the housing, to lubricate the lobes, oil seals and bearings as the cam is removed. Begin to pull the camshaft out of the back of the housing slowly, turning it as you pull. Remove the cam completely.

5. To install, lubricate the entire camshaft with clean oil. Insert the cam into the housing from the back, and slowly turn it as you push it into the housing. Install new O-rings and the housing end covers.

6. Installation of the remaining components is in the reverse order of removal. Tighten camshaft housing bolts to 15–17 ft. lbs. in the proper sequence.

### All Other Engines

All of these engines utilize an overhead camshaft (OHC). Therefore, the procedure for removing the camshaft is given as part of the cylinder head removal procedure.

**NOTE: It will not be necessary to completely remove the cylinder head in order to remove the camshaft. Therefore, proceed only as far as necessary, to remove the camshaft, with the cylinder head removal procedure.**

## Piston and Connecting Rod

### POSITIONING

**For all piston and connecting rod overhaul procedures, please refer to "Engine Rebuilding" in the Unit Repair section.**

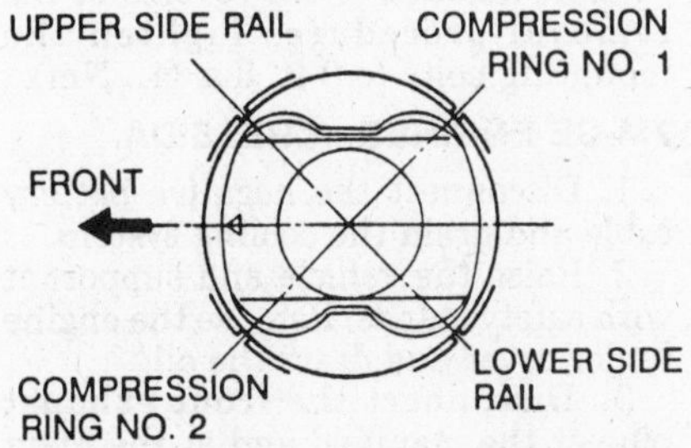


**Piston ring gap positioning – 7M-GE and 7M-GTE engines**

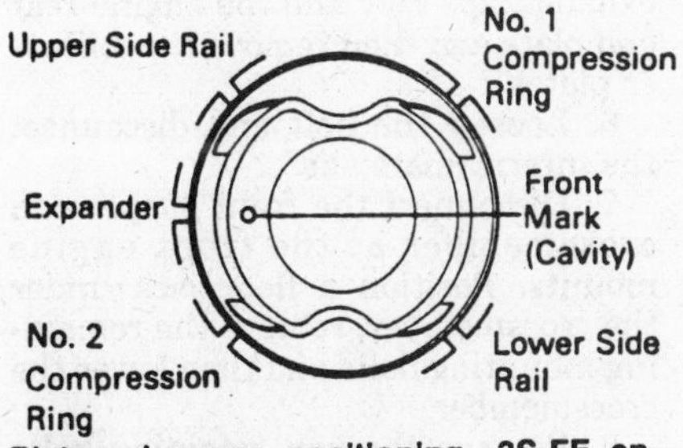


**Piston ring gap positioning – 3S-FE engines**

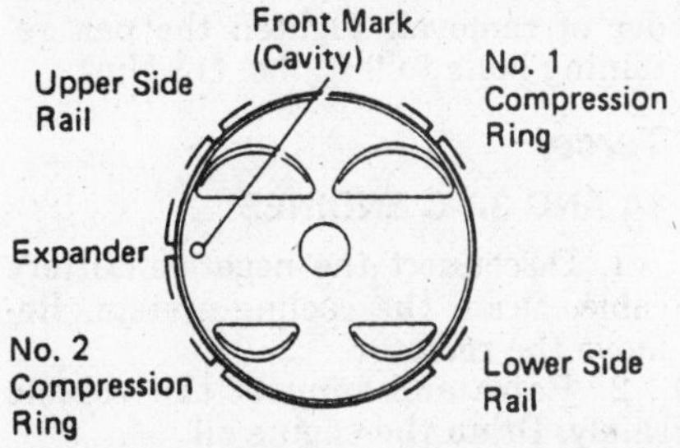


**Piston ring gap positioning – 3S-GE and 3S-GTE engines**

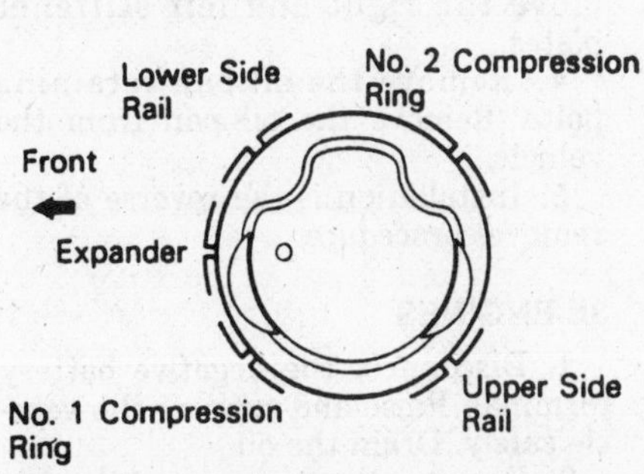


**Piston ring gap positioning – 3E engines**

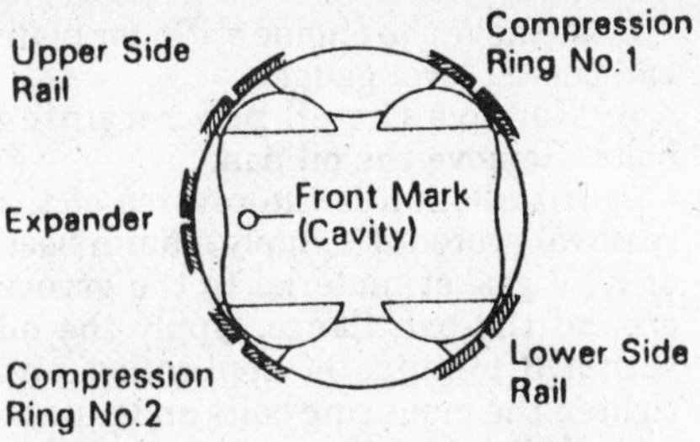


**Piston ring gap positioning – 2VZ-FE engines**

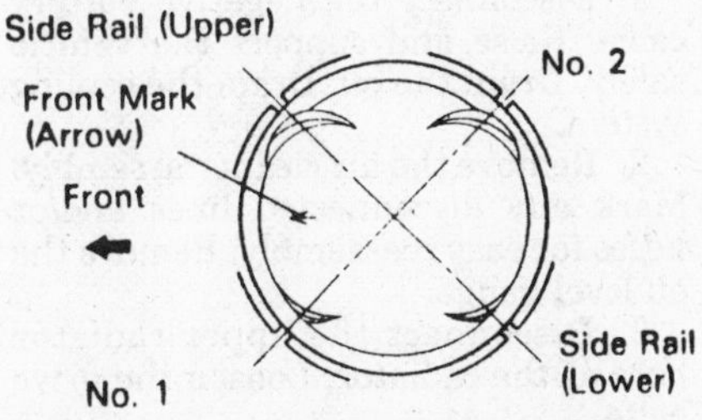


**Piston ring gap positioning – 4A-GZE engines**

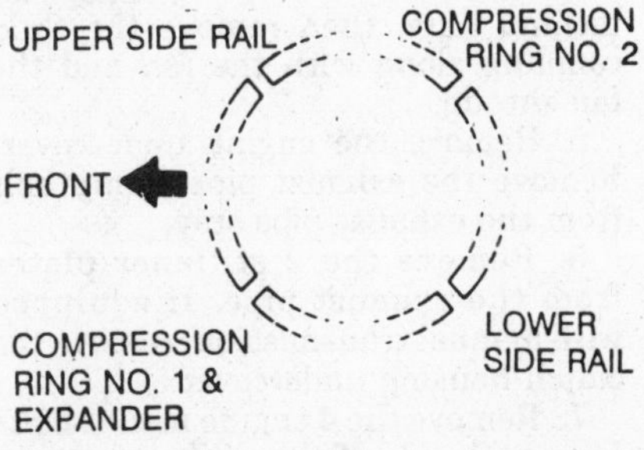


**Piston ring gap positioning – 5M-GE engines**

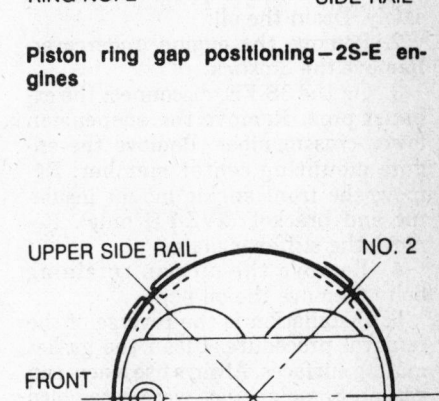

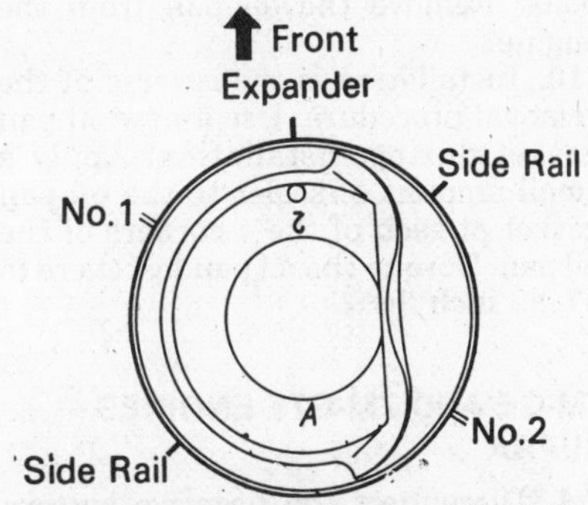


**Piston ring gap positioning – 3A, 3A-C, 4A-C and 4A-LC engines**

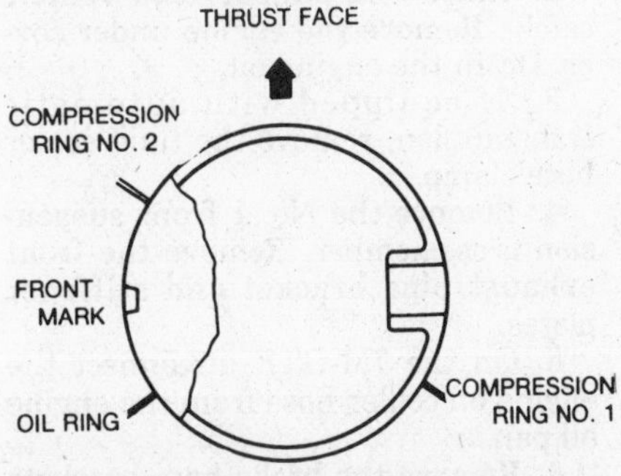


**Piston ring gap positioning – 22R and 22R-E engines**

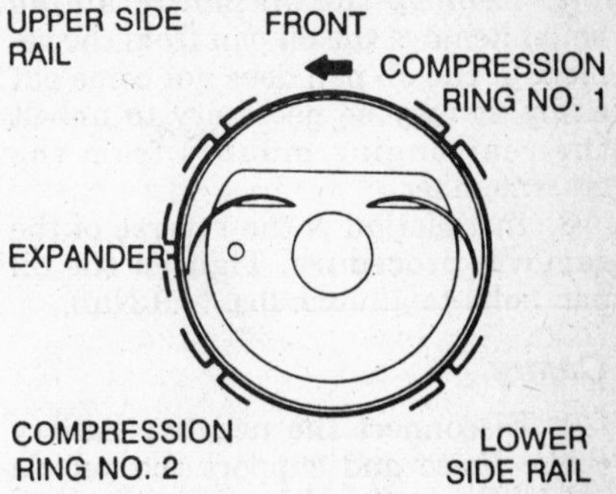


**Piston ring gap positioning – 2S-E engines**

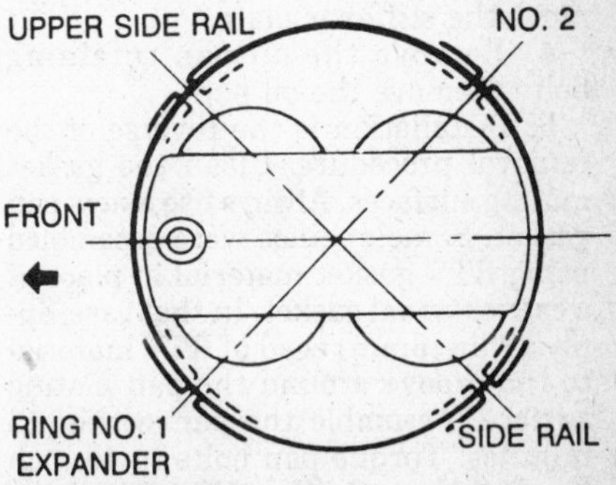


**Piston ring gap positioning – 4A-F, 4A-FE and 4A-GE (all) engines**

# ENGINE LUBRICATION

## Oil Pan

### REMOVAL & INSTALLATION

#### *Corolla and Starlet*

1. Disconnect the negative battery cable. Raise and support the vehicle safely. Drain the oil.
2. Remove the splash shield from underneath the engine.
3. Place a jack under the transmission to support it.
4. Remove the bolts which secure the engine rear supporting crossmember to the chassis. On the 4A-GE (1987-90), remove the center mounting and stiffener plate.
5. Raise the jack under the transmission, slightly.
6. Remove the front exhaust pipe (1987-90).

7. Remove the oil pan retaining bolts. Remove the oil pan from the vehicle. If the oil pan does not come out easily, it may be necessary to unbolt the rear engine mounts from the crossmember.

8. Installation is the reverse of the removal procedure. Tighten the oil pan bolts to 43 inch lbs. (4.9 Nm).

### Camry

1. Disconnect the negative battery cable. Raise and support the vehicle safely. Drain the oil.

2. Remove the engine undercover. Remove the dipstick.

3. On the 3S-FE, disconnect the exhaust pipe. Remove the suspension lower crossmember. Remove the engine mounting center member. Remove the front engine mount insulator and bracket (2VZ-FE only). Remove the stiffener plate.

4. Remove the oil pan retaining bolts. Remove the oil pan.

5. Installation is the reverse of the removal procedure. Clean the gasket mating surfaces. Always use a new pan gasket. Some engines were assembled using RTV gasket material in place of a conventional gasket. In that case, apply a thin (5mm) bead of RTV material to the groove around the pan mating surface. Assemble the pan within 15 minutes. Torque pan bolts to 48 inch lbs. (5.4 Nm). On the 2VZ-FE, tighten the pan bolts to 52 inch lbs. (5.9 Nm).

### Cressida, Celica and Supra

#### 22R AND 22R-E ENGINES

1. Disconnect the negative battery cable. Raise and support the vehicle safely.

2. Remove the engine undercover. Drain the engine oil.

3. Remove the engine shock absorber. Remove the motor mount bolts.

4. Place a jack under the transmission and raise the engine slightly.

5. Remove the oil pan retaining bolts. Remove the oil pan from the vehicle.

6. Installation is the reverse of the removal procedure. Use a new oil pan gasket during installation. Tighten the oil pan fasteners to 35–69 inch lbs.

#### 2S-E, 3S-FE, 3S-GE and 3S-GTE ENGINES

1. Disconnect the negative battery cable. Raise the vehicle and support it safely. Drain the engine oil.

2. Remove the engine undercovers.

3. On the 3S-GE, disconnect the exhaust pipe from the exhaust manifold.

4. Remove the lower suspension crossmember. Remove the center engine mount.

5. Remove the engine stiffener plate and the oil level gauge.

6. Remove the oil pan retaining bolts. Remove the oil pan.

7. Installation is the reverse of the removal procedure. Apply a 5mm bead of RTV gasket material to the groove around the pan flange. Apply the oil within 3 minutes of application and tighten the mounting bolts and nuts to 48 inch lbs. (5.4 Nm).

#### 5M-GE ENGINES

1. Disconnect the negative battery cable. Raise and support the vehicle safely. Drain the oil. Drain the cooling system.

2. Remove the air cleaner assembly. Mark any disconnected lines and/or hoses for easy reassembly. Remove the oil level gauge.

3. Disconnect the upper radiator hose at the radiator. Loosen the drive belts.

4. Remove the fan shroud bolts. Remove the 4 fluid coupling flange attaching nuts, then remove the fluid coupling along with the fan and the fan shroud.

5. Remove the engine undercover. Remove the exhaust pipe clamp bolt from the exhaust pipe stay.

6. Remove the 2 stiffener plates from the exhaust pipe. If equipped with manual transmission, remove the clutch housing undercover.

7. Remove the 4 engine mount bolts from each side of the engine.

8. Place a jack under the transmission and raise the engine about 1¾ in.

9. Remove the oil pan retaining bolts. Remove the oil pan from the engine.

10. Installation is the reverse of the removal procedure. Use a new oil pan gasket during installation. Apply a small amount of sealer to the oil pan gasket at each of the 4 corners of the oil pan. Torque the oil pan fasteners to 57–82 inch lbs.

#### 7M-GE AND 7M-GTE ENGINES – SUPRA

1. Disconnect the negative battery cable. Remove the hood.

2. Raise and support the vehicle safely. Remove the engine under cover. Drain the engine oil.

3. If equipped with automatic transmission, remove the fluid cooler hose clamp.

4. Remove the No. 1 front suspension crossmember. Remove the front exhaust pipe bracket and stiffener plates.

5. On the 7M-GTE disconnect the engine oil cooler hose from the engine oil pan.

6. Remove the brake hose brackets and clips. Disconnect the intermediate shaft. Disconnect the stabilizer bar links from the lower control arms.

7. Properly support the engine assembly. Remove the engine mounting bolts. Remove the TEMS actuator assembly.

8. Remove the shock absorbers from the body. Disconnect the front suspension member.

9. Remove the oil pan retaining bolts. Remove the oil pan from the engine.

10. Installation is the reverse of the removal procedure. Tighten the mounting bolts to 9 ft. lbs. (13 Nm).

#### 7M-GE ENGINES – CRESSIDA

1. Disconnect the negative battery cable and drain the cooling system.

2. Raise the vehicle and support it with safety stands. Remove the engine under cover and drain the oil.

3. Disconnect the front exhaust pipe at the manifold and at the main tube and remove it.

4. Disconnect the automatic transmission oil cooler pipe.

5. Remove the 9 bolts, gound strap, exhaust pipe stay and the engine rear end plate and then remove the stiffener plates.

6. Loosen the bolt and disconnect the intermediate shaft.

7. Disconnect the front suspension crossmember at the front engine mounts. Position a floor jack under the crossmember, remove the remaining mounting bolts and then lower the crossmember.

8. Remove the pan retaining bolts and then carefully pry the pan from the cylinder block.

9. Installation is in the reverse order of removal. Tighten the pan retaining bolts to 9 ft. lbs. (13 Nm).

### Tercel

#### 3A AND 3A-C ENGINES

1. Disconnect the negative battery cable. Drain the cooling system. Remove the radiator.

2. Raise and support the vehicle safely. Drain the engine oil.

3. Remove the engine under cover. Remove the stabilizer bracket bolts and lower the stabilizer assembly. Remove the right and left stiffener plates.

4. Remove the oil pan retaining bolts. Remove the oil pan from the vehicle.

5. Installation is the reverse of the removal procedure.

#### 3E ENGINES

1. Disconnect the negative battery terminal. Raise and support the vehicle safely. Drain the oil.

2. Remove the right hand engine under cover. Remove the sway bar and

any other necessary steering linkage parts.

3. Disconnect the exhaust pipe from the manifold. Raise the engine enough to take the weight off of it.

4. Remove the timing belt.

5. Continue to raise the engine enough to remove the oil pan. Remove the oil pan retaining bolts. Remove the oil pan.

6. Installation is the reverse of the removal procedure.

### *MR2*

1. Disconnect the negative battery cable. Raise and support the vehicle safely. Drain the engine oil.

2. Remove the exhaust manifold pipe. Remove the timing belt. Remove the crankshaft timing pulley.

3. Support the weight of the engine with a floor jack and then remove the right side engine mount.

4. Remove the oil pan retaining bolts. Remove the oil pan..

5. Installation is in the reverse order of removal. Apply a 5mm bead of RTV gasket material to the groove around the pan flange. Apply the oil pan within 3 minutes of application and tighten the mounting bolts and nuts to 43 inch lbs.

## Rear Main Oil Seal

### REMOVAL & INSTALLATION

**NOTE: The 3A and 3A-C engines must be removed from the vehicle before this procedure can be attempted.**

1. Remove the transmission.

2. Remove the clutch cover assembly and flywheel.

3. Remove the oil seal retaining plate, complete with the oil seal.

4. Using a suitable tool pry the old seal from the retaining plate. Be careful not to damage the plate.

5. Install the new seal, carefully, by using a block of wood to drift it into place. Do not damage the seal as a leak will result.

6. Lubricate the lips of the seal with multipurpose grease. Installation is the reverse of removal.

## Oil Pump

### REMOVAL & INSTALLATION

### *2S-E, 3A, 3A-C, 3S-GE, 3S-GTE, 4A-C, 4A-F and 4A-GE Engines*

1. Remove the fan shroud. Raise and support the vehicle safely.

2. Drain the oil. On the Tercel, drain the coolant and remove the radiator.

3. Remove the oil pan and the oil strainer. Remove the oil pan baffle plate on the 4A-GE. Remove the crankshaft pulley and the timing belt. Remove the oil dipstick guide and then the dipstick.

4. Remove the mounting bolts and then use a rubber mallet to carefully tap the oil pump body from the cylinder block.

5. To install, position a new gasket on the cylinder block.

6. Position the oil pump on the block so that the teeth on the pump drive gear are engaged with the teeth of the crankshaft gear.

7. Installation of the remaining components is in the reverse order of removal.

### *22R and 22R-E Engines*

1. Remove the oil pan.

2. Remove the 3 bolts which secure the oil strainer.

3. Remove the drive belts, the pulley bolt, and the crankshaft pulley.

4. Unfasten the bolts which secure the oil pump housing and remove the pump assembly.

5. Remove the oil pump drive spline and the rubber O-ring.

6. Installation is the reverse of removal. Apply a sealer to the top oil pump housing bolts. Use a new oil strainer gasket.

### *2VZ-FE, 3E and 3S-FE Engines*

1. Remove the oil pan. Remove the oil strainer. On the 3E, remove the dipstick.

2. Raise the engine using a chain hoist. Remove the timing belt and pulleys.

3. On the 2VZ-FE, remove the alternator and the A/C compressor and bracket. Do not disconnect the refrigerant lines.

4. Remove the oil pump from the engine.

5. Installation is the reverse of the removal procedure.

### *4A-C (FWD) Engines*

1. Disconnect the negative battery cable. Remove the hood.

2. Raise and support the vehicle safely. Remove the engine cover under. Drain the oil.

3. Disconnect the center engine mount. Remove the oil pan and oil strainer.

4. Attach an engine hoist to the two engine lifting brackets and suspend the engine.

5. Remove the drive belts. Remove the water pump pulley, air condition idler pulley and the crankshaft pulley.

6. Remove the timing belt. Remove the oil lever gauge guide and then the gauge.

7. Remove the mounting bolts and then use a rubber mallet to carefully tap the oil pump body from the cylinder block.

8. To install, position a new gasket on the cylinder block.

9. Position the oil pump on the block so that the teeth on the pump drive gear are engaged with the teeth of the crankshaft gear.

10. Installation of the remaining components is in the reverse order of removal.

### *All Others*

1. Remove the oil pan.

2. Unbolt the oil pump retaining bolts. Remove the oil pump from the engine.

3. Installation is the reverse of the removal procedure.

# ENGINE COOLING

## Radiator

### REMOVAL & INSTALLATION

1. Disconnect the negative battery cable. Drain the cooling system.

2. Remove the radiator hoses. If equipped with an automatic transmission, disconnect and plug the oil cooler lines.

3. Remove the ignition coil, ignitor and bracket assembly on the 2VZ-FE.

4. Remove the hood lock from the radiator upper support, as required. It may be necessary to remove the grille in order to gain access to the hood lock/radiator support assembly.

5. Remove the fan shroud, as required. If equipped with an electric fan (2 on the MR2), disconnect the wiring harness and thermoswitch connector.

6. Disconnect the hose from the thermal expansion tank and remove the tank from its bracket.

7. Unbolt and remove the radiator upper support.

8. Remove the radiator retaining bolts. Remove the radiator from the vehicle.

9. Installation is the reverse of the removal procedure.

## Water Pump

### REMOVAL & INSTALLATION

1. Disconnect the negative battery cable. Drain the cooling system.

2. Remove the fan shroud retaining bolts and remove the fan shroud, if equipped. Loosen and remove all drive belts.

3. Remove all necessary components in order to gain access to the water pump retaining bolts.

4. On some vehicles it will be necessary to remove the timing covers. On the 1987-90 Camry, remove the timing belt and pulleys.

5. As required remove the complete air cleaner assembly.

6. Remove all hoses from the water pump assembly.

7. Remove the water pump retaining bolts. Remove the water pump and fan assembly.

**NOTE: If the fan is equipped with a fluid coupling, do not tip the fan/pump assembly on its side, as the fluid will run out.**

8. Installation is the reverse of the removal procedure. Always use a new gasket between the pump body and its mounting. Check for leaks after installation is completed.

## Thermostat

### REMOVAL & INSTALLATION

1. Disconnect the negative battery cable. Drain the cooling system.

2. Remove the upper radiator hose from the thermostat housing.

3. Remove the thermostat housing retaining bolts. Remove the thermostat housing from the engine.

4. Remove the thermostat.

5. Installation is the reverse of the removal procedure. Be sure to use a new thermostat gasket. Be sure that the thermostat is installed with the spring pointing down and the jiggle valve up. On the 3S-FE, align the jiggle valve with the protrusion on the thermostat housing. On the 2VZ-FE, align the jiggle valve with the upper stud bolt in the housing.

### COOLING SYSTEM BLEEDING

1. Fill the radiator with the proper type of coolant.

2. With the radiator cap off, start the engine and allow it to run and reach normal operating temperature.

3. Run the heater at full force and with the temperature lever in the hot position. Be sure that the heater control valve is functioning.

4. Shut the engine off and recheck the coolant level, refill as necessary.

# EMISSION CONTROLS

**Please refer to "Emission Control" in the Unit Repair section for system maintenance procedures. Due to the complex nature of modern electronic engine control systems, comprehensive diagnosis and testing procedures fall outside the confines of this repair manual. For complete information on diagnosis, testing and repair procedures concerning all modern engine and emission control systems, please refer to "Chilton's Guide to Electronic Engine Controls".**

### MAINTENANCE REMINDER SYSTEM

**NOTE: The warning light comes on while the engine is being cranked, to test its operation, just like any of the other warning lights.**

1. If the warning light comes on and stays on, check the components of the air injection system. If these are not defective, check the ignition system for faulty leads, plugs, points, or control box.

2. If no problems can be found, check the wiring for the light for shorts or opened circuits.

3. If nothing else can be found wrong, check the operation of the emission control system computer.

### OXYGEN SENSOR WARNING LIGHT

Many vehicles are equipped with an oxygen sensor warning light on the instrument panel. The light may go on when the vehicle is started, then it should go out. If the light stays on, check your odometer. The light is hooked up to an elapsed mileage counter which goes off every 30,000 miles. This is your signal that it is time to replace the oxygen sensor and have the entire system checked out. After replacement of the sensor, the elapsed mileage counter must be reset.

# FUEL SYSTEM

## Fuel Filter

### REPLACEMENT

*Carbureted Engines*

All engines employ a disposable, in line filter; when dirty, or at recommended intervals, remove from line and replace.

*Fuel Injected Engines*

IN-LINE FILTERS

1. Unbolt the retaining screws and remove the protective shield for the fuel filter.

2. Place a pan under the delivery pipe (large connection) to catch the dripping fuel and SLOWLY loosen the union bolt to bleed off the fuel pressure.

3. Remove the union bolt and drain the remaining fuel.

4. Disconnect and plug the inlet line.

5. Unbolt and remove the fuel filter.

**NOTE: When tightening the fuel line bolts to the fuel filter, you must use a torque wrench. The tightening torque is very important, as under or over tightening may cause fuel leakage. Insure that there is no fuel line interference and that there is sufficient clearance between it and any other parts.**

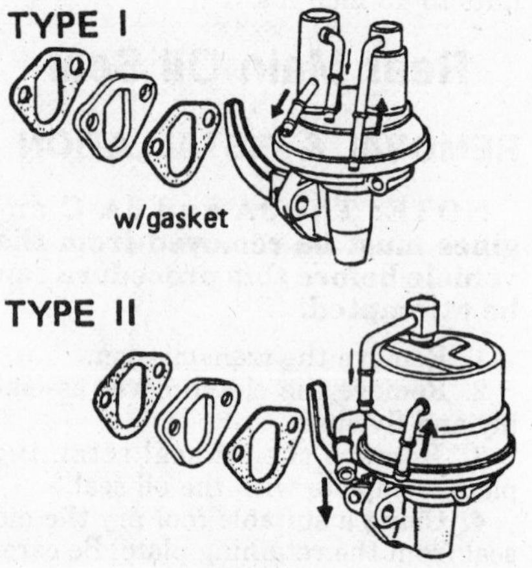

Typical mechanical fuel pump styles

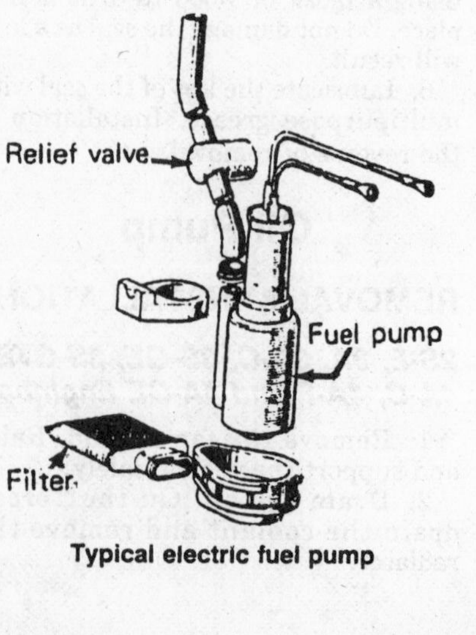

Typical electric fuel pump

6. Coat the flare nut, union nut and bolt threads with engine oil.
7. Hand tighten the inlet line to the fuel filter.
8. Install the fuel filter and then tighten the inlet bolt to 23–33 ft. lbs.
9. Reconnect the delivery pipe using new gaskets and then tighten the union bolt to 18–25 ft. lbs.
10. Run the engine for a few minutes and check for any fuel leaks.
11. Install the protective shield.

#### IN-TANK FILTERS

1. Disconnect the negative battery cable. Drain the gasoline from the fuel tank.
2. Remove the fuel tank.
3. Remove the fuel pump bracket retaining bolts and remove the fuel pump bracket.
4. Remove the retaining clip from the fuel filter hose and remove the fuel filter.
5. Install a new fuel filter and reverse the removal procedure to complete the installation procedure.

## Mechanical Fuel Pump

All 3A, 3E, 3A-C, 4A-C and 4A-F engines use a mechanical type fuel pump. It is located on the right rear of the cylinder head. 22R engines also use a mechanical type fuel pump. It is located on the right front of the cylinder head.

### PRESSURE TESTING

1. Remove the line which runs from the fuel pump to the carburetor.
2. Attach a pressure gauge to the outlet side of the pump.
3. Run the engine and check the pressure.
4. Check the pressure against the specifications.
5. If the pressure is below the specifications replace the pump.
6. Reconnect the carburetor line.

### REMOVAL & INSTALLATION

1. Disconnect and plug the fuel lines to the pump.
2. Remove the bolts which hold the pump to the cylinder head.
3. Remove the pump assembly.
4. Installation is the reverse of removal. Always use a new gasket when installing a fuel pump.

## Electric Fuel Pump

All models (except those mentioned previously) use an electric fuel pump.

On models with carbureted engines, and all late model engines with fuel injection, the electric fuel pump is located inside of the fuel tank. On certain early fuel injected engines, the fuel pump is mounted at the rear of the vehicle, outside of the fuel tank.

Either type of fuel pump cannot be repaired if defective – it must be replaced.

### PRESSURE TESTING

**CAUTION**

***Do not operate the fuel pump unless it is immersed in gasoline and connected to its resistor.***

#### *Carbureted Engines*

1. Disconnect the lead from the oil pressure warning light sender.
2. Unfasten the line from the outlet side of the fuel filter.
3. Connect a pressure gauge to the filter outlet with a length of rubber hose.
4. Turn the ignition switch to the **ON** position, but do not start the engine.
5. Check the pressure gauge reading against the figure given in the "Tune-Up Specifications" chart.
6. Check for a clogged filter or pinched lines if the pressure is not up to specification.
7. If there is nothing wrong with the filter or lines, replace the fuel pump.
8. Turn the ignition off and reconnect the fuel line to the filter. Connect the lead to the oil pressure sender.

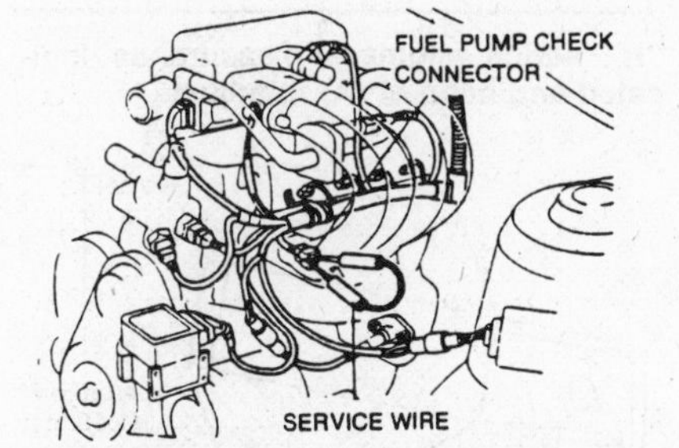


**Shorting the fuel pump check connector – typical**

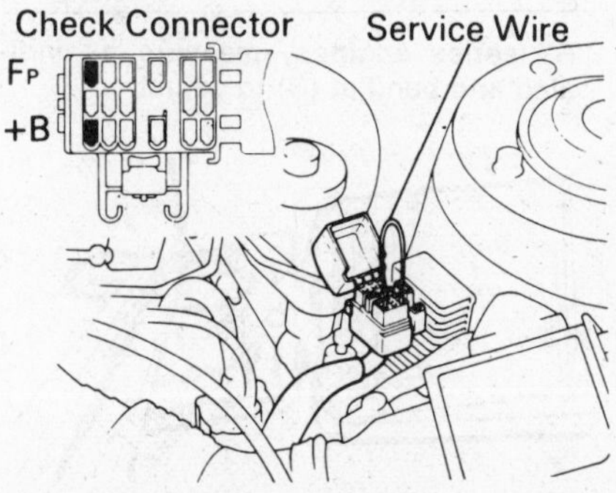


**Shorting the fuel pump check connector—box-type (3S-GE shown)**

#### *Fuel Injected Engines*

1. Turn the ignition switch to the **ON** position, but don't start the engine.
2. Remove the rubber cap from the fuel pump check connector and short both terminals.

**NOTE: The check connector on the 2S-E, 2VZ-FE, 3S-FE, 3S-GE, 3S-GTE, 4A-FE, 4A-GE, 4A-GZE, 5M-GE, 7M-GE and 7M-GTE is actually a small plastic box with a flip-up lid; it is found near the strut tower or battery. Terminals Fp and +B must be shorted.**

3. Check that there is pressure in the hose to the cold start injector (pressure regulator fuel return hose – 4A-FE and 4A-GE; hose from the fuel filter – 2VZ-FE, 3S-FE, 3S-GE and 3S-GTE).

**NOTE: At this time you should be able to hear the fuel return noise from the pressure regulator.**

4. If no pressure can be felt in the line, check the fuses and all other related electrical connections. If everything is alright, the fuel pump will probably require replacement.
5. Remove the service wire, reinstall the rubber cap and turn off the ignition switch.

### REMOVAL & INSTALLATION

#### *In-Tank Models*

1. Disconnect the negative (–) cable from the battery.

**NOTE: On most models, removal of the fuel tank is necessary.**

2. On sedans and hardtops, remove the trim panel from inside the trunk.
3. On station wagons, raise the rear of the vehicle, in order to gain access to the pump.
4. Remove the screws which secure the pump access plate to the tank. Withdraw the plate, gasket, and pump assembly.
5. Disconnect the leads and hoses from the pump.
6. Installation is performed in the reverse order of removal. Use a new gasket on the pump access plate.

#### *In-Line Models*

The pump used on these models is removed by simply disconnecting the fuel lines and electrical connector from the pump and dismounting the pump.

## Carburetors

The carburetors used on Toyota models are conventional 2 barrel, downdraft types similar to domestic carburetors.

## REMOVAL & INSTALLATION

**NOTE: During carburetor removal, be sure to mark all hoses, lines and electrical connectors, etc., so that these items may be properly reconnected during installation.**

1. Remove the air cleaner housing, disconnect all air hoses from the air cleaner base, and disconnect the battery ground cable.

**NOTE: On 22R engines, drain the coolant to prevent it from running into the intake manifold when the carburetor is removed.**

2. Disconnect the fuel line, choke pipe, and distributor vacuum line. On 22R engines disconnect the choke coolant hose.
3. Remove the accelerator linkage. (With an automatic transmission, also remove the throttle rod to the transmission.)
4. Disconnect any remaining hoses, etc., from the carburetor.
5. Remove the 4 nuts that secure the carburetor to the manifold and lift off the carburetor and gasket.
6. Cover the open manifold with a clean rag to prevent small objects from dropping into the engine.
7. Installation is performed in the reverse order of removal. After the engine is started, check for fuel leaks and float level settings.

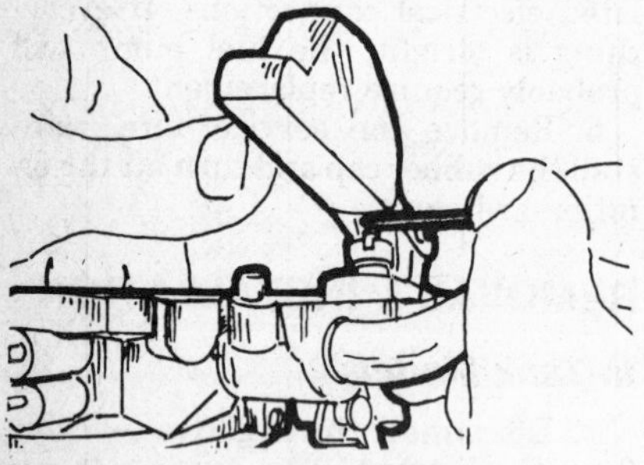

Measure the lowered float level—A-series engines

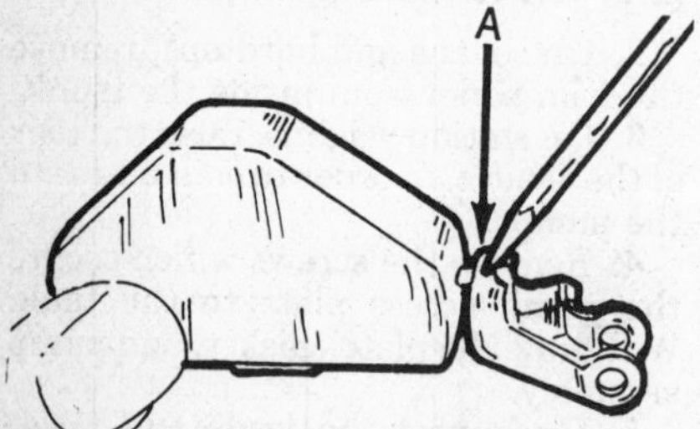


Adjust the raised float level at (A)—A-series engines

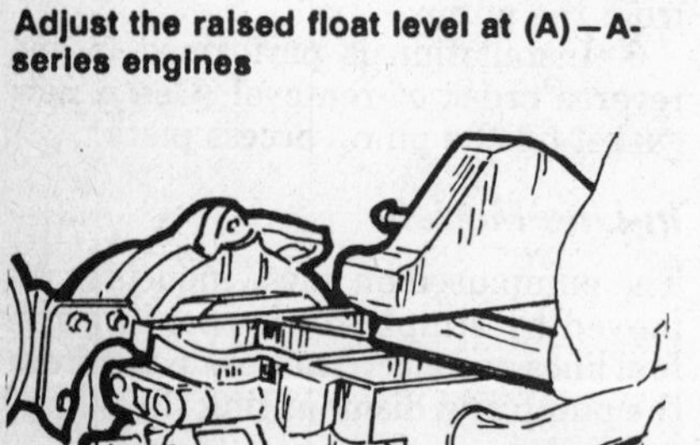

Measure the raised float level as shown—A-series engines

## OVERHAUL

**For all carburetor overhaul procedures, please refer to "Carburetor Service" in the Unit Repair section.**

## FLOAT LEVEL ADJUSTMENT

Float level adjustments are unnecessary on models equipped with a carburetor sight glass, if the fuel level falls within the lines or aligns with the dot when the engine is running.

There are 2 float level adjustments which may be made on Toyota carburetors. One is with the air horn inverted, so that the float is in a fully raised position; the other is with the air horn in an upright position, so that the float falls to the bottom of its travel.

The float level is either measured with a special carburetor float level gauge, which comes with a rebuilding kit, or with a standard wire gauge.

**NOTE: Gap specifications are also given so that a float level gauge may be fabricated.**

Adjust the float level by bending the tabs on the float levers, either upper or lower, as required.

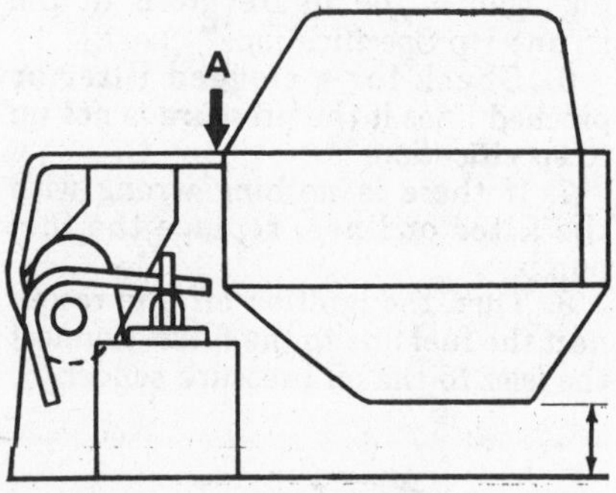


"R" series engines—measure as indicated and bend at (A) to adjust

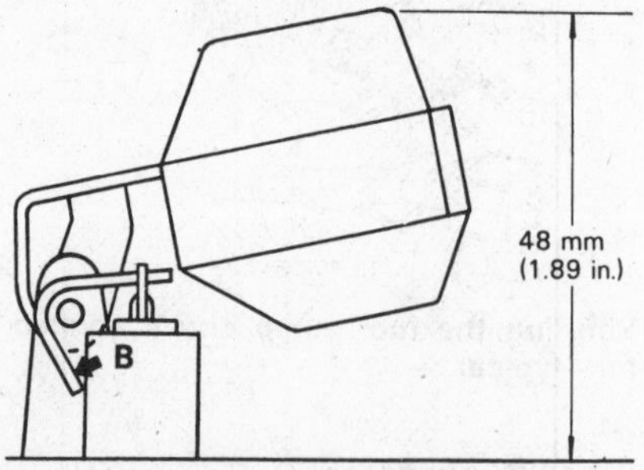


"R" series engines—measure as indicated and bend at (B) to adjust

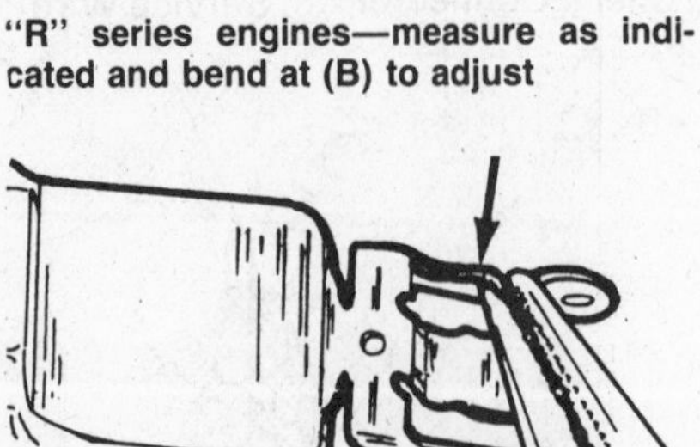

Adjust the lowered float level at (B)—A-series engines

## FAST IDLE ADJUSTMENT

### *Off Vehicle*

The fast idle adjustment is performed with the choke valve fully closed.

Adjust the gap between the throttle valve edge and bore to the specifications, where given, in the "Fast Idle Specifications" chart. Use a wire gauge to determine the gap.

The chart below also gives the proper primary throttle valve opening angle, where necessary, and the proper means of fast idle adjustment.

**NOTE: The throttle valve opening angle is measured with a gauge supplied in the carburetor rebuilding kit. It is also possible to make one out of cardboard by using a protractor to obtain the correct angle.**

### *On Vehicle*

**NOTE: Disconnect the EGR valve vacuum line on 22R engines.**

1. Apply the emergency brake and block the wheels. Start the engine and let it run until it reaches normal operating temperature. Connect a suitable tachometer to the engine and check the idle speed and adjust as necessary.
2. Stop the engine and remove the air cleaner. Plug the air suction hose (on California and Canada models) to

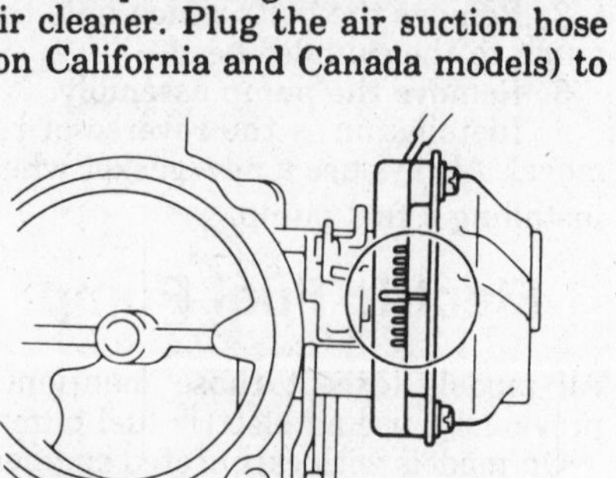

Align the marks on the choke housing

prevent leakage of the exhaust gas and plug the air suction valve hose (California models) and plug the hot idle compensator hose to prevent rough idling.

3. Disconnect the hose from the Thermostatic Vacuum Switching Valve (TVSV) **M** port (second from the top) and plug the **M** port. This will shut off the choke opener and the EGR system.

4. Set the fast idle cam, by holding the throttle slightly open and pushing the choke valve closed as you release the throttle valve.

5. Start the engine, but do not depress the accelerator pedal. set the fast idle speed by turning the fast idle adjustment screw. The fast idle speed should be 3000 rpm (3E w/AT: 2800).

6. After setting the fast idle speed check the curb idle speed and throttle position speed and adjust as necessary.

## AUTOMATIC CHOKE ADJUSTMENT

**NOTE: The automatic choke should be adjusted with the carburetor installed and the engine running. On 22R engines, do not loosen the center bolt; the coolant will leak out.**

1. Check to see that the choke valve will close from fully opened when the coil housing is turned counterclockwise.

2. Align the mark on the coil housing with the center line on the thermostat case. In this position, the choke valve should be fully closed when the ambient temperature is 77°F.

3. If necessary, adjust the mixture by turning the coil housing. If the mixture is too rich, rotate the housing clockwise; of too lean, rotate the housing counterclockwise.

**NOTE: Each graduation on the thermostat case is equivalent to 9°F.**

## MANUAL CHOKE ADJUSTMENT

1. Close the choke by turning the choke shaft lever.

2. Check the 1st throttle valve opening angle with the tool supplied in the rebuild kit.

3. Adjust by turning the fast idle adjusting screw.

## CHOKE BREAK ADJUSTMENT

### *22R and 4A-F Engines*

1. Push the rod which comes out of the upper (choke break) diaphragm so that the choke valve opens.

2. Measure the choke valve opening angle. It should be 38 degrees.

3. Adjust the angle, if necessary, by bending the relief lever link.

## INITIAL IDLE MIXTURE SCREW ADJUSTMENT

When assembling the carburetor, turn the idle mixture screw the number of turns specified below. After the carburetor is installed, perform the appropriate idle/speed mixture adjustment as outlined above.

3A, 3A-C, 4A-C – 2¾ turns from seating (1983); 3¼ turns from seating (1984-88, U.S.); 2½ turns from seating (1984-87, Canada)

4A-F – 3¼ turns from seating

22R – 1¾ turns from seating

**CAUTION**

***Seat the idle mixture screw lightly; overtightening will damage its tips.***

## UNLOADER ADJUSTMENT

Make the unloader adjustment with the primary valve fully opened. The total angle of choke valve opening, in the chart, is measured with either a special gauge, supplied in the carburetor rebuilding kit, or a gauge of the proper angle fabricated from cardboard.

## CHOKE UNLOADER ADJUSTMENT

| | Choke Valve Angle (deg.) | | | |
|---|---|---|---|---|
| Engine | Throttle Valve Fully Closed (deg.) | From Closed to Fully Open (deg.) | Throttle Valve Open (Total) (deg.) | Bend to Adjust |
| 22R | – | 50① | 90 | Fast idle lever, follower or choke shaft tab |
| 3T-C, 1A, 3A 3A-C, 4A-C, 4A-F | 20 | – | 47② | Fast idle lever |

– Not applicable

① 45° for 22R engines

② 1983–86
U.S. – 41°
Canada – 47°
1987–89
Except Canada Tercel w/MT – 41°
Canada Tercel w/MT – 47°

## FLOAT LEVEL ADJUSTMENT

| Engine | Float Raised: Gauge Type | Float Raised: Measure Distance Between | Float Raised: Gap (in.) | Float Lowered: Gauge Type | Float Lowered: Measure Distance Between | Float Lowered: Gap (in.) |
|---|---|---|---|---|---|---|
| 3T-C | Block | Float tip and air horn | 0.138 | Wire | Needle valve bushing pin and float lip | 0.047 |
| 1A-C, 3A, 3A-C 4A-C, 4AF | Special | Float tip and air horn | 0.158① | Special | Needle valve plunger and float tab | 0.047② |
| 4K-C | Special | Float tip and air horn | 0.030 | Special | Needle valve plunger and float tip | 0.02 |
| 3E | Special | Float tip and air horn | 0.169 | Special | Neddle valve plunger and float lip | 0.039 |
| 1982–83 22R | Special | Float top and air horn | 0.386 | Special | Needle valve plunger and float lip | 1.890 |

① 1983 and later—0.283
② 1983 and later—0.0657–0.0783

## FAST IDLE ADJUSTMENT

| Engine | Throttle Valve to Bore Clearance (in.) | Primary Throttle Angle (deg.) | To Adjust Fast Idle |
|---|---|---|---|
| 4K-C | 0.040① | 9② | Bend the fast idle lever |
| 3T-C | 0.032 | 7 | Turn the fast idle adjusting screw |
| 22R | 0.047 | 24 | Turn the fast idle screw |
| 1A-C | — | 22 | Turn the fast idle screw |
| 3A-C, 4A-C, 4A-F | — | ③ | Turn the fast idle screw |
| 3E | — | ④ | Turn the No. 1 fast idle screw |

— Not applicable
① 0.037 in 1982–83
② 20° open
③ 1982—22°
1983–89 except Canada 4A-C and Canada wagon w/4×4—20°
1983–89 Canada 4A-C and Canada wagon w/4×4)—21°
4A-F—21°
④ MT—18.7°
AT—19.0°

## Fuel Injection

**Due to the complex nature of modern fuel injection systems, comprehensive diagnosis and testing procedures fall outside the confined of this repair manual. For complete information on fuel injection diagnosis, testing and repair procedures please refer to Chilton's Guide To Fuel Injection and Feedback Carburetors.**

# MANUAL TRANSMISSION

### REMOVAL & INSTALLATION

#### *Starlet*

1. Disconnect the negative battery cable. Drain the radiator and remove the upper radiator hose. Remove the shift lever.
2. Raise and support the vehicle safely. Remove the driveshaft. Disconnect the exhaust system at the catalytic converter.
3. Disconnect the speedometer cable. Disconnect the clutch release cable at the clutch fork. Disconnect the back-up light switch electrical connector.
4. Support the engine and the transmission using the proper equipment. Unbolt the engine rear mounts. Remove the rear crossmember.
5. Remove the exhaust pipe bracket. Remove the starter assembly.
6. Remove the transmission-to-engine retaining bolts. Carefully remove the transmission from the vehicle.
7. Installation is the reverse of the removal procedure.

#### *Corolla (RWD)*

**1983**

1. Disconnect the negative battery cable. Drain the radiator and remove the upper radiator hose. Remove the shift lever.
2. Raise and support the vehicle safely. Drain the transmission fluid. Remove the driveshaft.
3. Disconnect the speedometer cable. Disconnect the back-up light switch electrical connectors.
4. Disconnect the exhaust pipe clamp. Remove the clutch release cylinder. Remove the starter.
5. Support the engine and transmission using the proper equipment. Remove the rear crossmember assembly.
6. Remove the transmission-to-engine retaining bolts. Remove the transmission from the vehicle.
7. Installation is the reverse of thremoval procedure.

**1984-87**

1. Disconnect the negative battery cable. Turn the distributor to gain working clearance.
2. Remove the console. Remove the shift lever.

3. Raise and support the vehicle safely. Drain the transmission fluid. Remove the front exhaust pipe.

4. Disconnect the driveshaft flange from the flange on the differential. Remove the center support bearing and the heat insulator assembly. Remove the driveshaft.

5. Disconnect the speedometer cable. Disconnect the back-up light switch electrical connector.

6. Remove the clutch release cylinder. Remove the starter.

7. Support the engine and the transmission using the proper equipment. Remove the rear crossmember.

8. Remove the stiffener plate. Remove the transmission to engine retaining bolts. Carefully remove the transmission from the vehicle.

9. Installation is the reverse of the removal procedure.

### Cressida

**NOTE: Manual transmissions are not available in 1988-90 Cressidas.**

1. Disconnect the negative battery cable. Drain the radiator and remove the upper radiator hose.

2. Remove the console. Remove the shift lever assembly.

3. Raise and support the vehicle safely. Drain the transmission fluid.

4. If the vehicle is equipped with power steering, remove the steering gear housing. It may be possible to remove the gear and properly suspend it out of the way without disconnecting the fluid lines.

5. Remove the driveshaft. Disconnect the exhaust pipe from the tailpipe. Remove the clamp from the transmission case.

6. Disconnect the speedometer cable. Disconnect the back-up light switch electrical connector.

7. Remove the clutch release cylinder. Remove the starter.

8. Support the engine and the transmission using the proper equipment. remove the rear crossmember assembly.

9. Remove the transmission-to-engine retaining bolts. Carefully lower the transmission to the floor.

10. Installation is the reverse of the removal procedure.

### Supra

#### 1983-86

1. Disconnect the negative battery cable. Drain the radiator and remove the upper radiator hose.

2. Remove the console and the shift lever.

3. Raise the vehicle and support it safely. Drain the transmission fluid. Matchmark and remove the driveshaft from the vehicle.

4. If the vehicle is equipped with power steering, remove the steering gear housing. It may be possible to remove the gear and properly suspend it out of the way without disconnecting the fluid lines.

5. Remove the bolt from the exhaust pipe stiffener plate. Disconnect the speedometer cable and the back-up light switch connector from the transmission.

6. Unbolt the clutch release cylinder. It may not be necessary to disconnect the hydraulic line from the clutch cylinder. Remove the starter assembly.

7. Support the engine and the transmission using the proper equippment. Remove the transmission support crossmember.

8. Remove the transmission mounting bolts. Carefully, move the transmission rearward, down, and out of the vehicle.

9. Installation is the reverse of the removal procedure.

#### 1987-90

1. Disconnect the negative battery cable. Remove the center console trim panel. Remove the shift lever.

2. Raise and support the vehicle safely. Drain the transmission fluid. Remove the driveshaft.

3. Disconnect the front exhaust pipe from the tailpipe. On some vehicles it will be necessary to remove the front exhaust pipe.

4. Disconnect the speedometer cable. Disconnect the back-up light switch electrical connector. If the vehicle is equipped with ABS, disconnect the rear speed sensor electrical connector.

5. Remove the clutch release cylinder. Remove the starter assembly.

6. Support the engine and the transmission using the proper equippment. Remove the transmission support crossmember.

7. Remove the transmission mounting bolts. Remove the flywheel housing bolts. Carefully, move the transmission rearward, down, and out of the vehicle.

**NOTE: On some vehicles it will be necessary to remove the transmission with the clutch cover and disc. To do this pull the release fork through the left clutch housing hole and then remove the assembly.**

8. Installation is the reverse of the removal procedure. Tighten the mounting bolts to 29 ft. lbs. (39 Nm).

### Celica (RWD)

#### 1983-85

1. Disconnect the negative battery cable. Drain the radiator and remove the upper radiator hose. Remove the console and the shift lever.

2. Raise the vehicle and support it safely. Drain the transmission fluid.

3. Matchmark and remove the driveshaft from the vehicle. Remove the bolt from the exhaust pipe stiffener plate.

4. If the vehicle is equipped with power steering, remove the steering gear housing. It may be possible to remove the gear and properly suspend it out of the way without disconnecting the fluid lines.

5. Disconnect the speedometer cable and the back-up light switch connector from the transmission. Remove the exhaust pipe clamp bolt.

6. Unbolt the clutch release cylinder. It may not be necessary to disconnect the hydraulic line from the clutch cylinder. Remove the starter assembly.

7. Support the engine and the transmission using the proper equippment. Remove the transmission support crossmember.

8. Remove the transmission mounting bolts. Carefully, move the transmission rearward, down, and out of the vehicle.

9. Installation is the reverse of the removal procedure.

## LINKAGE ADJUSTMENT

Linkage adjustment on these models is not possible.

# MANUAL TRANSAXLE

## REMOVAL & INSTALLATION

### Tercel

#### 1983-84

1. Disconnect the negative battery cable. Drain the radiator and remove the top radiator hose.

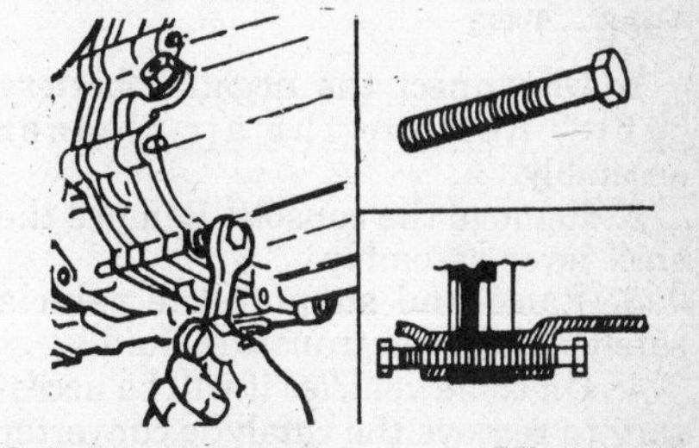

Split the transmission from the transaxle like this on the Tercel

2. Remove the air cleaner assembly. Disconnect the clutch cable. Remove the upper transaxle-to-engine bolts. Remove both halfshafts.

3. Raise and support the vehicle safely. Drain the transaxle fluid. Remove the front exhaust pipe.

4. Remove the right side stiffener plate bolts. Remove the No. 1 gear shift rod. Remove the lever housing rod.

5. Disconnect the back-up light switch electrical connector. Disconnect the speedometer cable. Disconnect the ground strap.

6. Support the engine and the transaxle using the proper equipment. Remove the remaining transaxle-to-engine retaining bolts. Remove the rear crossmember assembly.

7. Carefully remove the transaxle from the vehicle.

8. Installation is the reverse of the removal procedure.

### 1985-86 – 2WD

1. Disconnect the negative battery cable. Remove the air cleaner assembly.

2. Raise and support the vehicle safely. Drain the transaxle fluid.

3. On some vehicles it will be necessary to remove the catalytic converter air inlet pipe. Remove the front exhaust pipe.

4. Disconnect the gear shift rod. Disconnect the shift lever housing rod. Disconnect the back-up light switch electrical connector. Disconnect the speedometer cable.

5. Support the engine and the transaxle using the proper equipment. Remove the transaxle-to-engine retaining bolts. Remove the rear crossmember assembly.

6. Remove the 10 retaining bolts and 2 nuts from the assembly. From the transaxle side of the assembly install 4 bolts of equal length and equally spaced into the assembly. Seperate the transaxle from the transaxle case by turning these bolts a little at a time. Carefully remove the transaxle from the vehicle.

7. Installation is the reverse of the removal procedure.

### 1986 – 4WD

1. Disconnect the negative battery cable. Remove the air cleaner assembly.

2. Remove the console. Remove the shift lever assembly.

3. Raise and support the vehicle safely. Drain the transaxle fluid.

4. On some vehicles it will be necessary to remove the catalytic converter air inlet pipe. Remove the front exhaust pipe.

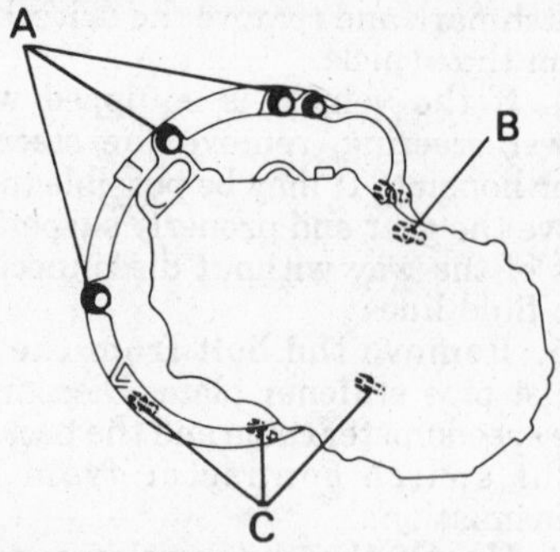


**Mounting bolt installation – 1987-89 Tercel (2wd)**

5. Disconnect the selector rod from the rear drive shift link lever. Disconnect the speedometer cable.

6. Disconnect the back-up light switch electrical connector. Disconnect the 4WD and the low gear indicator switch electrical connectors.

7. Support the engine and the transaxle using the proper equipment. Remove the transaxle-to-engine retaining bolts. Remove the rear crossmember assembly.

8. Remove the 10 retaining bolts and 2 nuts from the assembly. From the transaxle side of the assembly install 4 bolts of equal length and equally spaced into the assembly. Seperate the transaxle from the transaxle case by turning these bolts a little at a time. Carefully remove the transaxle from the vehicle.

9. Installation is the reverse of the removal procedure.

### 1987-90 SEDAN – 2WD

1. Disconnect the negative battery cable. If the vehicle is equipped with cruise control remove the battery. Remove the cruise control actuator and retaining bracket.

2. Remove the clutch release cylinder and tube clamp. Disconnect the back-up light switch electrical connector.

3. Disconnect the transaxle shift control cables. Remove the selecting bellcrank along with the bracket from the transaxle case. Remove the upper transaxle-to-engine retaining bolts.

4. Raise and support the vehicle safely. Remove the under covers. Drain the transaxle fluid. Disconnect the speedometer cable.

5. Disconnect both halfshafts. Remove the engine rear mounting brackets. Remove the starter assembly.

6. Support the engine and transaxle assembly using the proper equipment. Disconnect the left engine mounting.

7. Remove the remaining engine-to-transaxle retaining bolts. Carefully remove the transaxle assembly from the vehicle.

8. Installation is the reverse of the removal procedure. Tighten the transaxle-to-engine bolts to 47 ft. lbs. (64 Nm) – **A**; 34 ft. lbs. (46 Nm) – **B**; and 65 inch lbs. (7.4 Nm) – **C**. Tighten the front engine mount bracket bolts to 43 ft. lbs. (58 Nm). Tighten the rear engine mount bracket bolts to 21 ft. lbs. (28 Nm). Tighten the left engine mount bolts to 35 ft. lbs. (48 Nm) and the front and rear mount bolts to 47 ft. lbs. (64 Nm).

### 1987 WAGON – 2WD

1. Disconnect the negative battery cable. Remove the air cleaner assembly. Remove the upper transaxle-to-engine retaining bolts.

2. Remove both halfshaft assemblies.

3. Raise and support the vehicle safely. Drain the transaxle fluid. Disconnect the clutch cable.

4. On some vehicles it will be necessary to remove the catalytic converter air inlet pipe. Remove the front exhaust pipe.

5. Disconnect the selector rod. Disconnect the shift lever housing rod. Disconnect the speedometer cable.

6. Disconnect the back-up light switch electrical connector. Remove the right side stiffener plate.

7. Support the engine and transaxle assembly using the proper equipment. Remove the rear crossmember. Remove the remaining engine-to-transaxle retaining bolts.

8. Carefully remove the transaxle from the vehicle.

9. Installation is the reverse of the removal procedure. Tighten the 14mm transaxle-to-engine bolts to 29 ft. lbs. (39 Nm) and the 17mm bolts to 43 ft. lbs. (59 Nm). Tighten the rear support member bolts to 70 ft.lbs. (95 Nm) and the right stiffener plate bolts to 29 ft. lbs. (39 Nm).

### 1987-88 WAGON – 4WD

1. Disconnect the negative battery cable. Remove the air cleaner assembly.

2. Remove the console. Remove the shift lever assembly. Remove the upper engine-to-transaxle retaining bolts.

3. Raise and support the vehicle safely. Drain the transaxle fluid. Remove both halfshafts.

4. On some vehicles it will be necessary to remove the catalytic converter air inlet pipe. Remove the front exhaust pipe.

5. Disconnect the selector rod from the rear drive shift link lever. Disconnect the speedometer cable. Remove the right stiffener plate.

6. Disconnect the back-up light switch electrical connector. Disconnect the 4WD and the low gear indicator switch electrical connectors.

7. Support the engine and the transaxle using the proper equipment. Remove the remaining transaxle-to-engine retaining bolts. Remove the rear crossmember assembly.

**NOTE: Properly position a piece of wood between the engine and the firewall so that the assembly will not make contact with the power brake booster when it is removed.**

8. Carefully remove the transaxle assembly from the vehicle.
9. Installation is the reverse of the removal procedure. Tighten the 14mm transaxle-to-engine bolts to 29 ft. lbs. (39 Nm) and the 17mm bolts to 43 ft. lbs. (59 Nm). Tighten the rear support member bolts to 70 ft.lbs. (95 Nm) and the right stiffener plate bolts to 29 ft. lbs. (39 Nm).

## *Corolla (FWD)*

### 1984-85

1. Disconnect the negative battery cable. Drain the radiator.
2. Remove the air cleaner. Disconnect the back-up light switch.
3. Remove the speedometer cable. Disconnect the control cable at the transaxle.
4. Unbolt the coolant inlet line from the transaxle. Remove the clutch release cylinder.
5. Raise and support the vehicle safely. Remove the undercover.
6. Remove the front and rear support members. Remove the engine center support member.
7. Unbolt the right halfshaft from the transaxle. Disconnect the steering knuckle from the lower arm.
8. Pull the steering knuckle outward and remove the left halfshaft.
9. Remove the starter. Remove the flywheel cover plate.
10. Properly support the engine and disconnect the left engine mount.
11. Properly support the transaxle assembly. Remove the transaxle-to-engine attaching bolts. Lower the left side of the engine and pull the transaxle free.
12. Installation is the reverse of the removal procedure. Coat the input shaft splines with chassis lube prior to installation.

### 1986-90 2WD – EXCEPT C52 TRANSAXLE

1. Disconnect the negative battery cable. Remove the air cleaner assembly.
2. Disconnect the back-up light switch electrical connector. Remove the speedometer cable. Disconnect the transmission control cables.
3. Raise and support the vehicle safely. Remove the water inlet from the transaxle. Remove the clutch release cylinder.
4. Remove the under cover. Remove the front and rear mounting. Remove the engine mounting center member.
5. Disconnect the halfshaft from the transaxle. Disconnect the steering knuckle from the lower control arm. Pull the steering knuckle outward and remove the left halfshaft.
6. Remove the starter. Disconnect the ground strap. Remove the No. 2 engine rear plate.
7. Support the engine and the transaxle using the proper equipment. Remove the left engine mounting.
8. Remove the engine-to-transaxle retaining bolts. Carefully remove the transaxle assembly from the vehicle.
9. Installation is the reverse of the removal procedure. Tighten the 12mm engine-to-transaxle bolts to 47 ft. lbs. (64 Nm) and the 10mm bolts to 34 ft. lbs. (46 Nm). Tighten the left engine mount bolts to 38 ft. lbs. (52 Nm). Tighten the front and rear engine mount bolts and the engine mounting center member bolts to 29 ft. lbs. (39 Nm).

### 1987-90 2WD – C52 TRANSAXLE

1. Disconnect the negative battery cable. Drain the radiator. Remove the air cleaner assembly. Remove the engine cooling fan assembly.
2. Disconnect the oxygen sensor electrical connector and the back-up light switch connector.
3. Remove the clutch release cylinder. It may be possible to leave the fluid lines attached to the cylinder.
4. Disconnect the water inlet from the transaxle. Disconnect the transaxle control cables. Disconnect the speedometer cable. Disconnect the ground cable.
5. Remove the starter. Remove the engine under covers. Remove the front exhaust pipe.
6. Disconnect the front and rear enginemountings. Remove the engine mounting center member.
7. Remove the left front wheel. Loosen the 6 nuts while depressing the brake pedal. Disconnect the halfshaft from the side gear shaft. Disconnect the lower ball joint from the lower control arm. Pull the shock absorber outward. Remove the halfshaft.
8. Support the engine and the transaxle assembly using the proper equipment. Remove the No. 2 engine rear plate. Remove the left hand engine mounting.
9. Remove the transaxle retaining bolts. Carefully remove the transaxle assembly from the vehicle.
10. Installation is the reverse of the removal procedure. Tighten the 12mm engine-to-transaxle bolts to 47 ft. lbs. (64 Nm) and the 10mm bolts to 34 ft. lbs. (46 Nm). Tighten the left engine mount bolts to 38 ft. lbs. (52 Nm). Tighten the front and rear engine mount bolts and the engine mounting center member bolts to 29 ft. lbs. (39 Nm).

### 1989-90 4WD

1. Remove the engine and transaxle as an assembly.
2. Remove the rear end plate.
3. Disconnect the vacuum lines and then remove the transfer case vacuum actuator.
4. Remove the right and center transfer case stiffener plates.
5. Pull the transaxle out slowly until there is approximately 2.36–3.15 in. (60–80mm) clearance between the transaxle and the engine.
6. Turn the output shaft in a clockwise direction and then remove the transaxle.
7. Install the transaxle assembly to the engine and tighten the 10mm bolts to 34 ft. lbs. (46 Nm). Tighten the 12mm bolts to 47 ft. lbs. (64 Nm).
8. Tighten the 8mm stiffener plate bolts to 14 ft. lbs. (20 Nm) and the 10mm bolts to 27 ft. lbs. (37 Nm).
9. Tighten the rear end plate mounting bolts to 17 ft. lbs. (23 Nm).
10. Install the engine/transaxle assembly.

## *Camry*

### 1983-86

1. Disconnect the negative battery cable. Remove the engine and the transaxle as an assembly from the vehicle.
2. Position the assembly in a suitable holding fixture.
3. Seperate the engine from the transaxle.
4. Installation is the reverse of the removal procedure.

### 1987-90 – 2WD

1. Disconnect the negative battery cable. Remove the clutch release cylinder and tube clamp. Remove the clutch tube bracket.
2. Disconnect the control cables. Disconnect the back-up light switch electrical connector. Remove the ground strap.
3. Remove the starter assembly. Remove the transaxle upper mounting bolts.
4. Raise and support the vehicle safely. Remove the under covers. Drain the transaxle fluid. Disconnect the speedometer cable.
5. Remove the suspension lower crossmember. Remove the engine mounting center member.
6. Disconnect both driveshafts. Remove the center driveshaft. Disconnect the left steering knuckle from the

lower control arm. Remove the stabilizer bar.

7. Properly support the engine and remove the left engine mount.

8. Properly support the transaxle assembly. Remove the engine-to-transaxle bolts, lower the left side of the engine and carefully ease the transaxle out of the engine compartment.

9. Installation is the reverse of the removal procedure. Please note the following:

a. Tighten the 12mm mounting bolts to 47 ft. lbs. (64 Nm) and the 10mm bolts to 34 ft. lbs. (46 Nm).

b. Tighten the left engine mount to 38 ft. lbs. (52 Nm).

c. Tighten the 4 center engine mount bolts to 29 ft. lbs. (39 Nm).

d. Tighten the front and rear engine mount bolts to 32 ft. lbs. (43 Nm).

e. Tighten the lower crossmember bolts to 153 ft. lbs. (207 Nm)—4 outer bolts; and, 29 ft. lbs. (39 Nm)—2 inner bolts.

#### 1988-90 ALL-TRAC—4WD

1. Remove the engine/transaxle assembly as previously detailed.

2. Remove the transfer case stiffener plate and the exhaust pipe front brake.

3. Remove the left stiffener plate and the front engine mount.

4. Remove the left engine mount bracket and then separate the transaxle from the engine.

5. Installation is in the reverse order of removal. Tighten the 12mm transaxle-to-engine mounting bolts to 47 ft. lbs. (64 Nm) and the 10mm bolts to 34 ft. lbs. (46 Nm).

### MR2

1. Disconnect the negative battery cable. Drain the radiator. Raise and suport the vehicle safely. Drain the transaxle fluid.

2. Disconnect the back-up light switch and the speedometer cable at the transaxle. On models with the 4A-GZE, remove the intercooler.

3. Loosen the mounting bolts and remove the water inlet from the transaxle.

4. Remove the engine undercover. Remove the fuel tank protector.

5. Disconnect the transaxle control cables at the transaxle and position them out of the way.

6. Remove the water hose clamp from the control cable bracket and then remove the No. 2 control cable bracket.

7. Remove the main control cable bracket and the clutch release cylinder. Position these components out of the way.

8. Disconnect the exhaust pipe from the manifold, remove the pipe bracket from the chassis and then remove the exhaust pipe assembly from the bracket.

9. Remove the transaxle protector. Disconnect the halfshaft from the side gear shaft. Remove the starter assembly.

10. Remove the No. 2 engine rear plate. Remove the front and rear engine mounts from the body.

11. Properly support the engine and remove the left engine mount.

12. Properly support the transaxle assembly. Remove the engine-to-transaxle bolts, lower the left side of the engine and carefully ease the transaxle out of the engine compartment.

13. Remove the side gear shaft from the transaxle.

14. Installation is the reverse of the removal procedure. Tighten the 12mm engine-to-transaxle bolts to 47 ft. lbs. (64 Nm) and the 10mm bolts to 34 ft. lbs. (46 Nm). Tighten the left and rear engine mounts to 38 ft. lbs. (52 Nm).

### Celica (FWD)

#### 1986-90—2WD

1. Disconnect the negative battery cable. On some 1987-90 vehicles it may be necessary to remove the battery. Remove the air cleaner assembly.

2. On 1987-90 vehicles remove the clutch tube bracket. Disconnect the back-up light switch at the transaxle. Disconnect the speedometer and the engine ground strap.

3. Disconnect the transaxle control cable and position them out of the way.

4. Unbolt the clutch release cylinder. It may be possible to position it out of the way with the hydraulic line still attached.

5. Remove the upper transaxle retaining bolts. Raise and support the vehicle safely. Remove the engine undercover. Drain the transaxle fluid.

6. Disconnect the exhaust pipe from the manifold. Remove the lower suspension crossmember. Remove the starter assembly.

7. Properly support the engine and transaxle assembly. Remove the front and rear transaxle mounts. Remove the center engine mount.

8. Disconnect both halfshafts at the transaxle. Unbolt the steering knuckle from the suspension arm and pull it outward. Remove the left halfshaft.

9. On some vehicles, remove the No. 2 rear engine plate. With the engine properly supported remove the left engine mount.

10. Remove the engine-to-transaxle bolts, lower the left side of the engine and carefully ease the transaxle out of the engine compartment.

11. Installation is the reverse of the removal procedure. Tighten the 12mm engine-to-transaxle bolts to 47 ft. lbs. (64 Nm) and the 10mm bolts to 34 ft. lbs. (46 Nm). Tighten the left engine mount bolts to 38 ft. lbs. (52 Nm) Tighten the center member bolts and the front and rear engine mount bolts to 29 ft. lbs. (39 Nm).

#### 1988-90 ALL-TRAC—4WD

1. Remove the engine and transaxle assembly.

2. Separate the transaxle from the engine.

3. Installation is in the reverse order of removal. Tighten the 12mm engine-to-transaxle bolts to 47 ft. lbs. (64 Nm) and the 10mm bolts to 34 ft. lbs. (46 Nm). Tighten the left engine mount bolts to 38 ft. lbs. (52 Nm) Tighten the center member bolts and the front and rear engine mount bolts to 29 ft. lbs. (39 Nm).

## LINKAGE ADJUSTMENT

### Camry

#### 1983-86

1. Disconnect the negative battery cable. Remove the console.

2. Insert a guide pin (0.020 in. rod) into the shift lever hole. Turn the buckle to align the shift lever hole and the shift support hole.

3. If adjustment is required loosen the locknut, make the adjustment and retighten the locknut.

# CLUTCH

## REMOVAL & INSTALLATION

1. Disconnect the negative battery

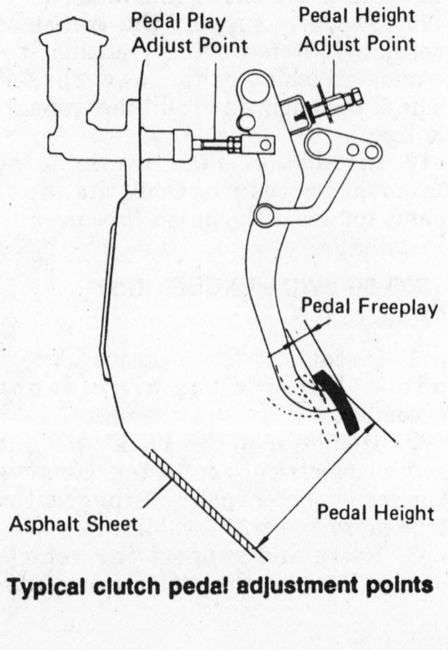


**Typical clutch pedal adjustment points**

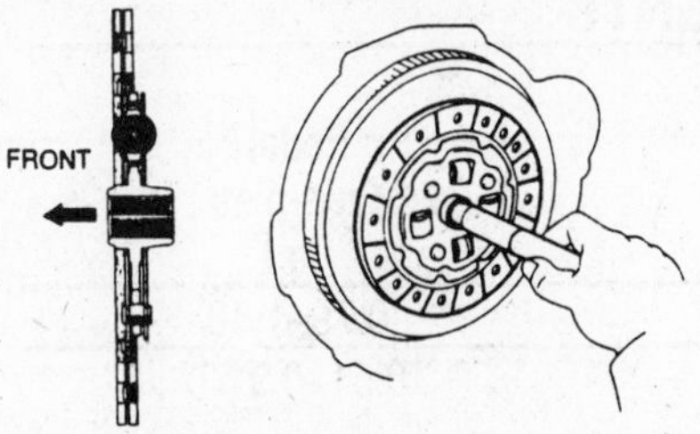


Use a clutch pilot tool to center the clutch disc on the flywheel

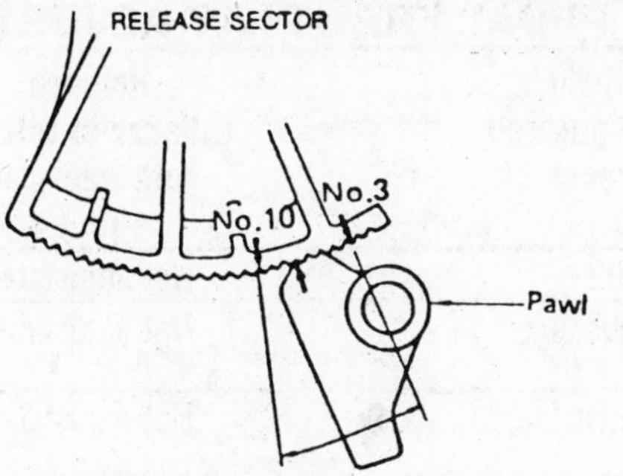


Pawl and sector position for a new clutch – 1983-86 Tercel

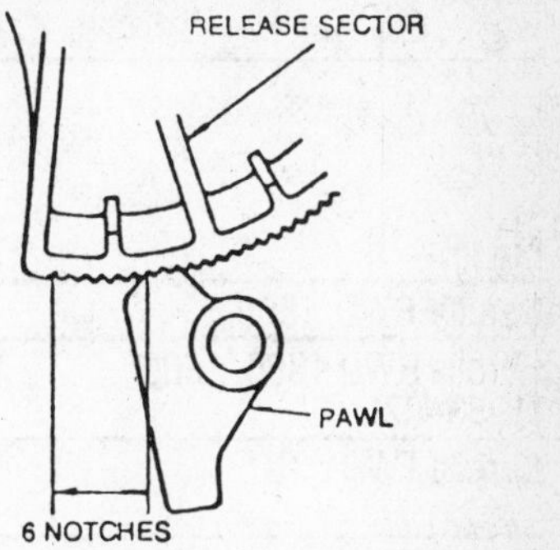


Minimum pawl and sector position for a used clutch – Starlet and 1983-86 Tercel

cable. Remove the transmission assembly from the vehicle.

**NOTE: On some 1987-90 Supra's, the clutch assembly is removed along with the transmission. On the 1983-86 Camry, the 1989-90 Corolla (4wd) and the 1988-90 Camry/Celica All-Trac 4WD, the engine and transaxle are removed from the vehicle as an assembly.**

2. Remove the clutch pressure plate retaining bolts. Remove the pressure plate assembly.
3. Remove the clutch disc.
4. Installation is the reverse of the removal procedure.

### FREE-PLAY ADJUSTMENT

#### *All Except 1983-86 Tercel Sedan, 1983-88 Tercel Wagon and Starlet*

1. Adjust the clearance between the master cylinder piston and the pushrod to specification by loosening the pushrod locknut and rotating the pushrod while depressing the clutch pedal lightly.
2. Tighten the locknut when finished the adjustment.
3. Adjust the release cylinder freeplay by loosening the release cylinder pushrod locknut and rotating the pushrod until proper specification is obtained.
4. Measure the clutch pedal freeplay after performing the adjustments. If it fails to fall within specification, repeat the procedure.

#### *1983-86 Tercel Sedan, 1983-88 Tercel Wagon and Starlet*

1. Depress the clutch pedal several times.
2. Depress the clutch pedal until resistance is felt. Freeplay should be within specification.
3. Check the clutch release sector pawl. Six notches should remain between the pawl and the end of the sector. If less than 6 notches, replace the clutch disc. If the clutch disc has been replaced, the pawl should be between 3 and 10 notches.
4. To obtain either the used or new position on the Starlet, change the position of the E-ring.

## Clutch Cable

### REMOVAL & INSTALLATION

#### *Starlet*

1. Disconnect the negative battery cable.
2. Remove and record the E-ring position on the clutch pedal.
3. Disconnect the sector tension spring from the clutch pedal.
4. Disconnect the clutch release cable from the release fork lever.
5. Disconnect the clutch release cable from the release sector.
6. Remove the glove box door. Remove the clips and the cable from the groove of the pulley. Remove the release cable.
7. Installation is the reverse of the removal procedure.

#### *Tercel*

##### 1983-86 SEDAN & 1983-88 WAGON

1. Disconnect the negative battery cable.
2. Disconnect the sector tension spring from the clutch pedal.
3. Disconnect the clutch release cable from the release fork lever.
4. Turn the release sector toward the front side and disconnect the release cable from the release sector. Remove the release cable.
5. Installation is the reverse of the removal procedure.

## Clutch Master Cylinder

### REMOVAL & INSTALLATION

#### *Rear Wheel Drive Vehicles*

1. Disconnect the negative battery cable. Remove the pushrod clevis pin and clip.
2. On the MR-2, remove the spare tire gaurd and luggage compartment trim cover.

**NOTE: On some vehicles it will be necessary to remove the under dash panel in order to gain access to the pushrod clevis pin.**

3. Disconnect the fluid line. Remove the clutch master cylinder retaining bolts. Remove the component from the vehicle.
4. Installation is the reverse of the removal procedure. Bleed the system as required.

#### *Front Wheel Drive Vehicles*

1. Disconnect the negative battery cable. On the Tercel, remove the reservoir tank from the clutch master clyinder.
2. Remove the ABS control relay on models so equipped.
3. Remove the pushrod clevis pin and clip.

**NOTE: On some vehicles it will be necessary to remove the under dash panel in order to gain access to the pushrod clevis pin.**

4. On the 1988-90 Corolla (4A-GE) remove the brake booster.
5. Disconnect the fluid line. Remove the clutch master cylinder retaining bolts. Remove the component from the vehicle.
6. Installation is the reverse of the removal procedure. Bleed the system as required.

## Clutch Slave Cylinder

### REMOVAL & INSTALLATION

1. Disconnect the negative battery cable. Raise and support the vehicle safely.
2. Remove the gravel shield, if equipped. Disconnect the fluid line from the assembly.
3. Remove the slave cylinder retaining bolts. Remove the clutch slave cylinder from the vehicle.
4. Installation is the reverse of the removal procedure. Bleed the system as required.

## CLUTCH PEDAL FREE-PLAY ADJUSTMENTS

| Model | Master Cylinder piston-to-pushrod Clearance (in.) | Release cylinder-to-release fork free-play (in.) | Pedal Free-play (in.) |
|---|---|---|---|
| Corolla RWD 1600 | 0.02 | Not adjustable | 0.79–1.58 |
| Corolla RWD 1800, 1600 (1983–87) | Not adjustable | Not adjustable | 0.51–0.91④ |
| Corolla FWD | Not adjustable | Not adjustable | 0.51–0.91 (gas)⑤ 0.20–0.59 (diesel)⑤ |
| Celica | Not adjustable | Not adjustable | 0.51–0.91① |
| Supra | Not adjustable | Not adjustable | 0.20–0.59 |
| Starlet | Not adjustable | Not adjustable | 0.08–1.18② |
| Tercel | Not adjustable | Not adjustable | 0.08–1.10③ |
| Camry | Not adjustable | Not adjustable | 0.20–0.59 |
| Cressida | Not adjustable | Not adjustable | 0.20–0.59 |
| MR2 | Not adjustable | Not adjustable | 0.197–0.59 |

FWD Front Wheel Drive
RWD Rear Wheel Drive
① FWD – 0.20–0.59
② 1983–84 – 0.08–1.38
③ 1986–87 – 0.08–0.98
1988–90 Sedan – 0.20–0.59
④ 1986–87 4A-GE – 0.20–0.59
⑤ 1986–87 – 0.28–0.67
1988–90–0.20–0.59

## BLEEDING THE CLUTCH HYDRAULIC SYSTEM

1. Check and fill the clutch fluid reservoir to the specified level as necessary. During the bleeding process, continue to check and replenish the reservoir to prevent the fluid level from getting lower than ½ the specified level.
2. Remove the dust cap from the bleeder screw on the clutch slave cylinder and connect a tube to the bleeder screw and insert the other end of the tube into a clean glass or metal container.

**NOTE: Take precautionary measures to prevent the brake fluid from getting on any painted surfaces.**

3. Pump the clutch pedal several times, hold it down and loosen the bleeder screw slowly.
4. Tighten the bleeder screw and release the clutch pedal gradually. Repeat this operation until air bubbles disappear from the brake fluid being expelled out through the bleeder screw.
5. Repeat until all evidence of air bubbles completely disappears from the fluid being pumped out of the tube.
6. When the air is completely removed tighten the bleeder screw and replace the dust cap.
7. Check and refill the master cylinder reservoir as necessary.
8. Depress the clutch pedal several times to check the operation of the clutch and check for leaks.

# AUTOMATIC TRANSMISSION

## REMOVAL & INSTALLATION

### *Corolla (RWD)*

1. Disconnect the negative battery cable. On 1983 vehicles, drain the radiator and remove the upper radiator hose.
2. Remove the air cleaner assembly. Disconnect the transmission throttle cable. Disconnect the starter assembly electrical connections.
3. Raise and support the vehicle safely. Drain the transmission fluid. Remove the driveshaft.
4. Remove the exhaust pipe clamp. Disconnect the exhaust pipe from the exhaust manifold.
5. Disconnect the manual shift linkage. Disconnect the oil cooler lines. Remove the starter.
6. Support the engine and transmission using the proper equipment. Remove the rear crossmember.
7. Disconnect the speedometer cable. Disconnect all necessary electrical wiring from the transmission.
8. Remove the torque converter cover. Remove the torque converter-to-engine retaining bolts.
9. Remove the bolts retaining the transmission to the engine. Carefully remove the transmission from the vehicle.
10. Installation is the reverse of the removal procedure.

### *Cressida*

1. Disconnect the negative battery cable. Drain the radiator and remove the upper radiator hose. Remove the air cleaner assembly. Disconnect the transmission throttle cable.
2. Raise and support the vehicle safely. Drain the transmission fluid. Remove the driveshaft along with the center bearing.
3. Remove the exhaust pipe together with the catalytic converter. Disconnect the manual shift linkage. Remove the speedometer cable.
4. Disconnect the oil cooler lines. As necessary, remove the transmission oil filler tube. As required, remove the starter assembly. Remove the speedometer cable.
5. Remove both stiffener plates and the catalytic converter cover from the transmission housing and cylinder block.
6. Support the engine and trans-

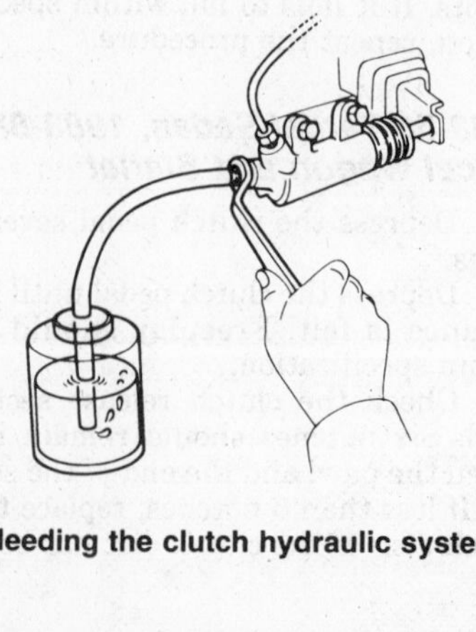

Bleeding the clutch hydraulic system

## PEDAL HEIGHT SPECIFICATIONS

| Model/ Year | Height (in.) | Measure Between |
|---|---|---|
| Tercel | | Pedal pad and floor mat |
| 1983 | 6.65 | |
| 1984–85 | 6.97–7.36 | |
| 1986–87 | 7.15–7.44 | |
| 1988–88 Wagon | 6.96–7.24 | |
| 1988–90 | 6.14–6.54 | |
| 1989–90 | 6.38–6.77 | Dash panel and pedal |
| Corolla 1800 | 6.89–7.28 | Pedal pad and floor mat |
| Corolla 1600 RWD | | Pedal pad and floor mat |
| 1983–85 | 6.34–6.72 | |
| 1986–87 | 6.44–6.83 | |
| Corolla FWD | | Pedal pad and floor mat |
| 1983–85 | 5.650–6.043 | |
| 1986–87 | 5.827–6.220 | |
| 1988 | 5.827–6.220 | |
| FX/FX16 | | |
| 1988-90 Sedan | 5.71–6.10 | |
| Celica | | Pedal pad and floor mat |
| 1983–85 | 6.06–6.46 | |
| 1986–90 | 6.02–6.42 | |
| Supra | | Pedal pad and floor mat |
| 1983–86 | 6.06–6.46 | |
| 1987–90 | 6.18–6.57 | |
| Cressida | 6.10–6.50 | From floor mat |
| Cressida SW | 9.6 | Pedal pad and firewall |
| Starlet | 6.93 | Pedal pad and floor mat |
| Camry | | Ped pad and kick panel |
| 1983–85 | 7.539–7.933 | |
| 1986 | 7.99–8.39 | |
| 1987–90 | 7.52–7.91 | |
| MR2 | | Ped pad and floor mat |
| 1985–87 | 6.03–6.41 | |
| 1988–90 | 6.18–6.57 | |

SW Station Wagon

mission using the proper equipment. Remove the rear crossmember.

7. Remove the torque converter cover. Remove the torque converter-to-engine retaining bolts.

8. Remove the bolts retaining the transmission to the engine. Carefully remove the transmission from the vehicle.

9. Installation is the reverse of the removal procedure. Tighten the transmission housing bolts to 47 ft. lbs. (64 Nm). Tighten the torque converter bolts to 20 ft. lbs. (27 Nm).

### *Supra*

1. Disconnect the negative battery cable. On 1983-86 vehicles drain the radiator and remove the upper radiator hose. Remove the air cleaner assembly. Disconnect the transmission throttle cable.

2. Raise and support the vehicle safely. Drain the transmission fluid. Disconnect the electrical connectors for the neutral safety switch and back-up lights.

3. Remove the intermediate driveshaft along with the center bearing. Disconnect the exhaust pipe from the tail pipe.

4. Disconnect the transmission oil cooler lines. Disconnect the manual shift linkage. Disconnect the speedometer cable.

5. Remove the exhaust pipe bracket and torque converter cover. Remove both stiffener brackets.

6. On 1983-86 vehicles remove the power steering gear housing from the crossmember. Be sure to plug the fluid lines, as required.

7. Support the engine and transmission using the proper equipment. Remove the rear crossmember.

8. Remove the engine under cover. Remove the torque converter-to-engine retaining bolts. Remove the starter.

9. Remove the bolts retaining the transmission to the engine. Carefully remove the transmission from the vehicle.

10. Installation is the reverse of the removal procedure. Adjust the throttle cable and fill the transmission with Dexron®II.

### *Celica (RWD)*

1. Disconnect the negative battery cable. Drain the radiator and remove the upper radiator hose. Remove the air cleaner assembly. Disconnect the transmission throttle cable.

2. Raise and support the vehicle safely. Drain the transmission fluid. Remove the driveshaft along with the center bearing. Disconnect the necessary electical connectors in order to remove the transmission.

3. Disconnect the manual shift linkage. Remove the speedometer cable. Remove the sliding yoke from the gear housing and shift mechanism.

4. Disconnect the oil cooler lines. Remove the front exhaust pipe.

5. Remove the power steering gear housing from the crossmember. Be sure to plug the fluid lines, as required.

6. Support the engine and transmission using the proper equipment. Remove the rear crossmember.

7. Remove the engine under cover. Remove the torque converter cover. Remove the torque converter-to-en-

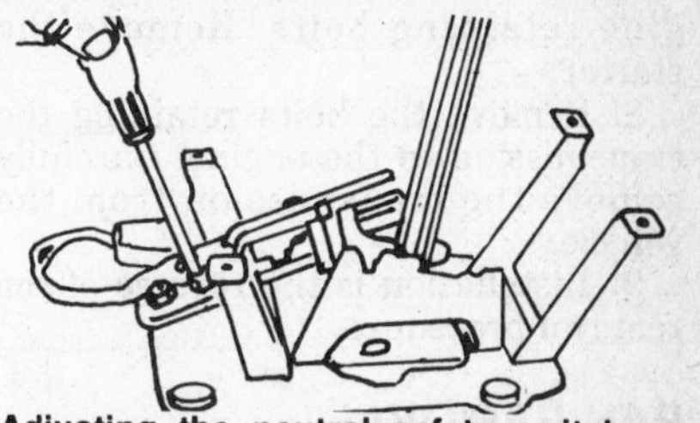

Adjusting the neutral safety switch on models with the three speed Toyoglide and floor mounted shift

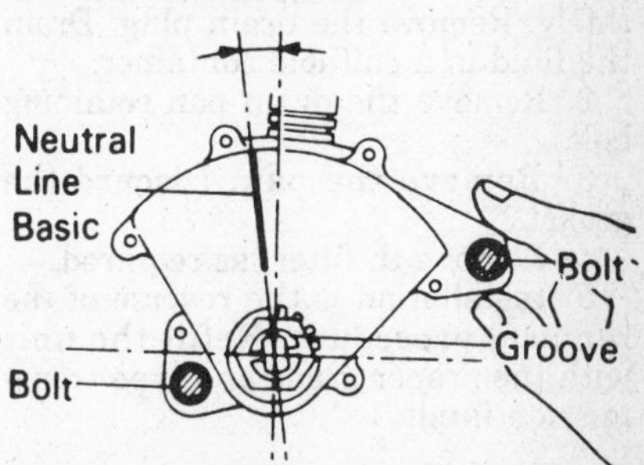


Neutral safety switch adjustment—most late models similar

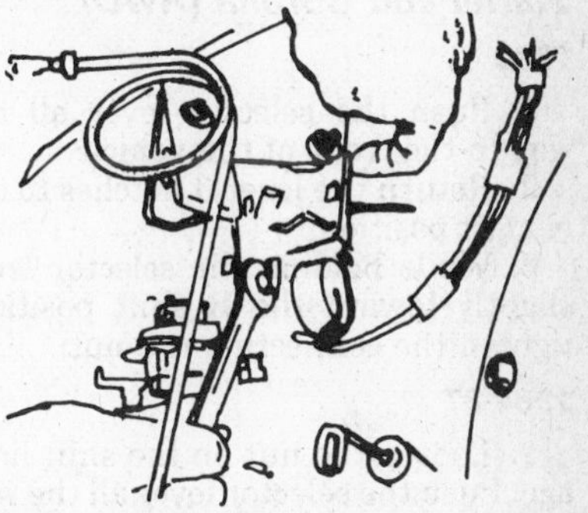

Adjusting the neutral safety switch on models with the three speed Toyoglide and a column-mounted shift

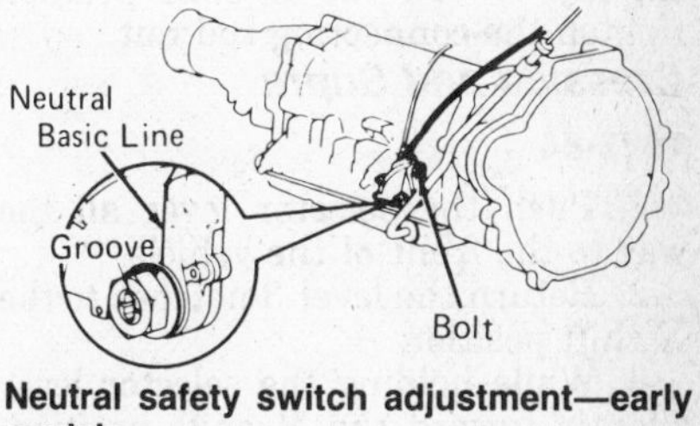


Neutral safety switch adjustment—early models

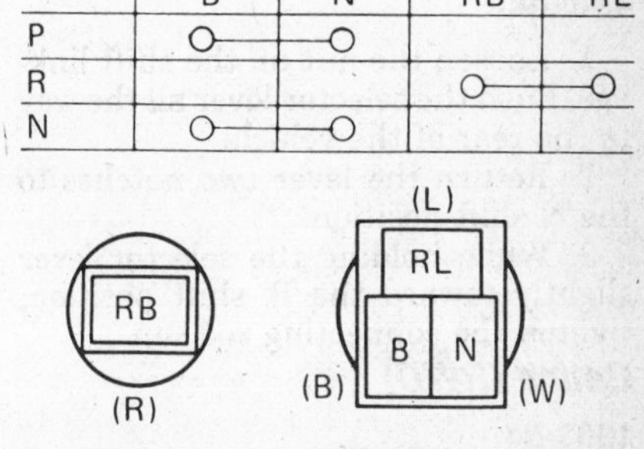


Checking the neutral safety switch for continuity between the connectors

gine retaining bolts. Remove the starter.

8. Remove the bolts retaining the transmission to the engine. Carefully remove the transmission from the vehicle.

9. Installation is the reverse of the removal procedure.

## PAN REMOVAL

1. Raise and support the vehicle safely. Remove the drain plug. Drain the fluid in a suitable container.
2. Remove the drain pan retaining bolts.
3. Remove the pan. Discard the gasket.
4. Remove th filter, as required.
5. Installation is the reverse of the removal procedure. Refill the unit with the proper grade and type transmission fluid.

## LINKAGE ADJUSTMENT

### *Starlet and Corolla (RWD)*

#### 1983

1. Push the selector lever all the way to the front of the vehicle.
2. Return the lever 3 notches to the **N** shift position.
3. While holding the selector lever slightly toward the **R** shift position, tighten the connecting rod nut.

#### 1984-87

1. Loosen the nut on the shift linkage. Push the selector lever all the way to the rear of the vehicle.
2. Return the lever 2 notches to the **N** shift position.
3. While holding the selector lever slightly toward the **R** shift position tighten the connecting rod nut.

### *Cressida and Supra*

#### 1983-84

1. Push the selector lever all the way to the front of the vehicle.
2. Return the lever 3 notches to the **N** shift position.
3. While holding the selector lever slightly toward the **R** shift position, tighten the connecting rod nut.

#### 1985-90

1. Loosen the nut on the shift linkage. Push the selector lever all the way to the rear of the vehicle.
2. Return the lever two notches to the **N** shift position.
3. While holding the selector lever slightly toward the **R** shift position, tighten the connecting rod nut.

### *Celica (RWD)*

#### 1983-84

1. Push the selector lever all the way to the front of the vehicle.
2. Return the lever 3 notches to the **N** shift position.
3. While holding the selector lever slightly toward the **R** shift position, tighten the connecting rod nut.

#### 1985

1. Loosen the nut on the shift linkage. Push the selector lever all the way to the rear of the vehicle.
2. Return the lever 2 notches to the **N** shift position.
3. While holding the selector lever slightly toward the **R** shift position tighten the connecting rod nut.

## NEUTRAL SAFETY SWITCH

### *Starlet and Corolla (RWD)*

#### 1983

1. Loosen the neutral start switch bolt. Position the selector in the **N** position.
2. Align the switch shaft groove with the neutral base line which is located on the switch.
3. Tighten the bolt.

#### 1984-87

1. Loosen the neutral start switch retaining bolts. Disconnect the switch electrical connector.
2. Position the selector lever in the **N** position.
3. Connect an ohmmeter between the terminals.
4. Adjust the switch to the point where there is continunity between terminals **N** and **B**.
5. Connect the switch electrical connector.

### *Cressida and Supra*

#### 1983-84 AND 1987-90

1. Loosen the neutral start switch bolt. Position the selector in the **N** position.
2. Align the switch shaft groove with the neutral base line which is located on the switch.

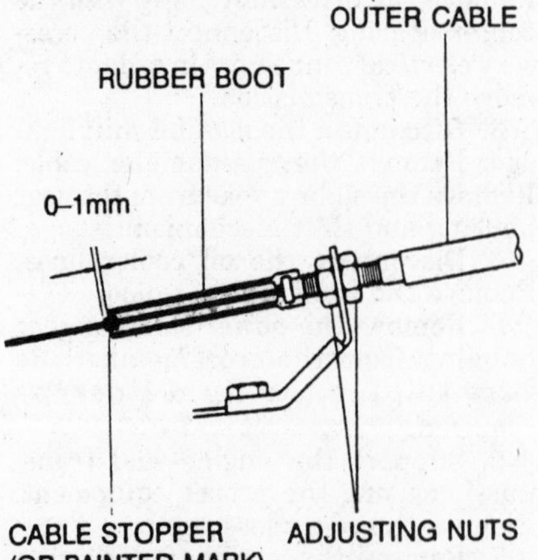


**Throttle cable adjustment**

3. Tighten the bolt to 9 ft. lbs. (13 Nm).

#### 1985-86

1. Loosen the neutral start switch retaining bolts. Disconnect the switch electrical connector.
2. Position the selector lever in the **N** position.
3. Connect an ohmmeter between the terminals.
4. Adjust the switch to the point where there is continunity between terminals **N** and **B**.
5. Connect the switch electrical connector.

### *Celica (RWD)*

#### 1983

1. Loosen the neutral start switch bolt. Position the selector in the **N** position.
2. Align the switch shaft groove with the neutral base line which is located on the switch.
3. Tighten the bolt.

#### 1984-85

1. Loosen the neutral start switch retaining bolts. Disconnect the switch electrical connector.
2. Position the selector lever in the **N** position.
3. Connect an ohmmeter between the terminals.
4. Adjust the switch to the point where there is continunity between terminals **N** and **B**.
5. Connect the switch electrical connector.

## THROTTLE CABLE

1. Remove the air cleaner.
2. Confirm that the accelerator linkage opens the throttle fully. Adjust the linkage as necessary.
3. Peel the rubber dust boot back from the throttle cable.
4. Loosen the adjustment nuts on the throttle cable bracket (cylinder head cover) just enough to allow cable housing movement.
5. Have an assistant depress the accelerator pedal fully.
6. Adjust the cable housing so that the distance between its end and the cable stop collar is 0.04 in.
7. Tighten the adjustment nuts. Make sure that the adjustment hasn't changed. Install the dust boot and the air cleaner.

# AUTOMATIC TRANSAXLE

## REMOVAL & INSTALLATION

### *Tercel*

1. Disconnect the negative battery

cable. On some vehicles it will be necessary to drain the radiator and remove the upper radiator hose. Remove the air cleaner assembly.

2. Raise and support the vehicle safely. Remove both halfshafts. Drain the fluid from the transaxle. On some vehicles it may be necessary to drain the differential fluid.

3. Remove the torque converter cover. Remove the bolts that retain the torque converter to the crankshaft. Remove the exhaust pipe. Remove the shift lever rod.

4. Remove the speedometer cable andback-up light connector. If equipped with 4wd, remove the electrical solenoid connector. Disconnect and remove all throttle linkage.

5. Remove the fluid lines from the transaxle. On some vehicles it may be necessary to remove the starter assembly. On 4wd vehicles, remove the rear driveshaft.

6. Support the engine and transaxle using a suitable jack. Remove the rear crossmember.

7. Remove the transaxle-to-engine retaining bolts. Seperate the transaxle from the engine and carefully remove it from the vehicle.

8. Installation is the reverse of the removal procedure. Tighten the transmission-to-engine bolts to 47 ft. lbs. (64 Nm). Tighten the left engine mount bracket bolts to 32 ft. lbs. (43 Nm). Tighten the rear engine mount bracket bolts to 43 ft. lbs. (58 Nm). Tighten the torque converter mounting bolts to 13 ft. lbs. (18 Nm).

### *Corolla (FWD)*

1. Disconnect the negative battery cable. Remove the air cleaner.

2. Disconnect the neutral start switch. Disconnect the speedometer cable.

3. Remove the shift control cable. Disconnect the throttle linkage.

4. Disconnect the oil cooler hose.

5. Drain the radiator. Remove the water inlet pipe.

6. Raise and support the vehicle safely. Drain the transaxle fluid. As required remove the exhaust front pipe.

7. Remove the engine undercover. Remove the front and rear transaxle mounts.

8. Support the engine and transaxle using the proper equipment. Remove the engine center support member.

9. Remove the halfshafts. Remove the starter assembly. As required remove the steering knuckles.

10. Remove the flywheel cover plate. Remove the torque converter bolts.

11. Remove the left engine mount. Remove the transaxle-to-engine bolts. Slowly and carefully back the transaxle away from the engine. Lower the assembly to the floor.

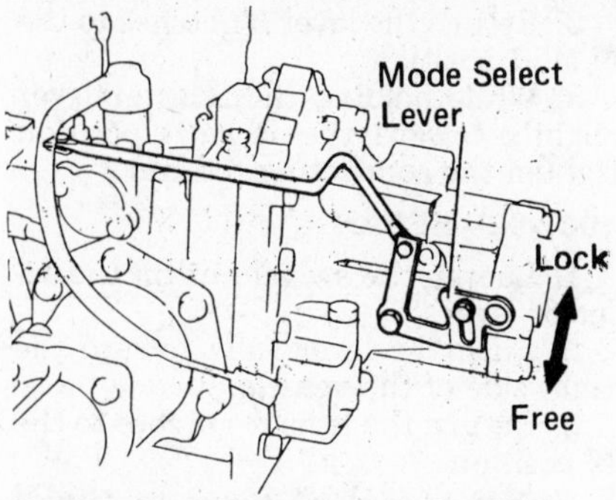


**Setting the mode selector—Corolla w/A241H**

12. Installation is the reverse of the removal procedure. When installing the A241H on 4wd models, be sure that the mode selector lever is positioned in the **FREE** mode and attach the lock bolt.

### *Camry*

#### 1983-86

1. Disconnect the negative battery cable.

2. Remove the engine and transaxle assembly from the vehicle as one component.

3. Position the engine/transaxle assembly in a suitable holding fixture. Seperate the engine from the transaxle assembly.

4. Installation is the reverse of the removal procedure.

#### 1987-90

1. Disconnect the negative battery cable. Remove the air flow meter and the air cleaner assembly.

2. Disconnect the transaxle wire connector. Disconnect the neutral safety switch electrical connector.

3. Disconnect the transaxle ground strap. Disconnect the throttle cable from the throttle linkage.

4. Remove the transaxle case protector. Disconnect the speedometer cable. Disconnect the control cable.

5. Disconnect the oil cooler hoses. Remove the upper starter retaining bolts, as required remove the starter assembly. Remove the upper transaxle housing bolts. Remove the engine rear mount insulator bracket set bolt.

6. Raise and support the vehicle safely. Drain the transaxle fluid.

7. Remove the left front fender apron seal. Disconnect both driveshafts.

8. Remove the suspension lower crossmember assembly. Remove the center driveshaft.

9. Remove the engine mounting center crossmember. Remove the stabilizer bar. Remove the left steering knuckle from the lower control arm.

10. Remove the torque converter cover. Remove the torque converter retaining bolts.

11. Properly support the engine and transaxle assembly. Remove the rear engine mounting bolts. Remove the remaining transaxle to engine retaining bolts.

12. Carefully remove the transaxle assembly from the vehicle.

13. Installation is the reverse of the removal procedure. Tighten the 12mm transaxle housing bolts to 47 ft. lbs. (64 Nm); tighten the 10mm bolts to 34 ft. lbs. (46 Nm). Tighten the rear engine mount set bolts to 38 ft. lbs. (52 Nm). Tighten the torque converter mounting bolts to 20 ft. lbs. (27 Nm).

### *MR2*

1. Disconnect the negative battery cable. Remove the air flow meter and the air cleaner hose.

2. Remove the intercooler on the 4A-GZE.

3. Remove the water inlet set bolts. Disconnect the ground strap. Remove the transaxle mounting set bolt.

4. Disconnect the speedometer cable at the transaxle. Disconnect the throttle cable from the throttle linkage and the bracket.

5. Raise and support the vehicle safely. Drain the transaxle fluid. Remove the left tire.

6. Remove the transaxle gravel shield. Disconnect the speedometer cable at the transaxle assembly.

7. Disconnect the oil cooler lines at the transaxle. Remove the transaxle control cable clip and retainer and then disconnect the cable from the bracket. Remove the bracket.

8. Remove the starter assembly. Disconnect the exhaust pipe at the manifold. Remove the pipe.

9. Remove the stiffner plate. Remove the rear engine end plate. Remove the torque converter cover. Remove the torque converter retaining bolts.

10. Disconnect both the right and left halfshafts from their side gear shafts. Depress and hold the brake pedal while removing the halfshaft retaining nuts. Properly position the halfshaft out of the way.

11. Disconnect the suspension arm from the rear axle carrier, using the proper tools. Disconnect the rear axle carrier from the lower control arm.

12. Disconnect the halfshaft from the side gear shaft. Properly position the driveshaft out of the way.

13. Support the engine and transaxle assembly, using the proper equipment. Remove the transaxle-to-engine retaining bolts. Disconnect the front and rear transmission mount bolts.

14. Carefully lower the transaxle assembly to the floor.

15. Installation is the reverse of the removal procedure. Tighten the transmission-to-engine bolts to 47 ft. lbs. (64 Nm).

### *Celica (FWD)*

1. Disconnect the negative battery cable. Remove the air flow meter and the air cleaner hose.
2. Disconnect the speedometer cable. Remove the starter assembly electrical connections. Disconnect the throttle cable from the throttle linkage and bracket.
3. Disconnect the ground strap. Remove the starter retaining bolts and as required remove the starter assembly.
4. Remove the upper transaxle housing retaining bolts. Remove the engine rear mount insulator bracket retaining bolt.
5. Raise and support the vehicle safely. Drain the transaxle fluid. Remove the engine under covers.
6. Remove the lower suspension crossmember. Disconnect the front and rear mounting. Remove the engine mounting center member.
7. Remove the left halfshaft. Disconnect the right halfshaft.
8. Disconnect the exhaust pipe from the manifold. Remove the stiffner plate. Disconnect the control cable.
9. Disconnect the oil cooler hoses. Remove the torque converter cover. Remove the torque converter retaining bolts.
10. Support the engine and transaxle assembly, using the proper equipment. Remove the transaxle-to-engine retaining bolts. Disconnect the front and rear transmission mount bolts.
11. Carefully lower the transaxle assembly to the floor.
12. Installation is the reverse of the removal procedure. Tighten the 12mm engine-to-transaxle bolts to 47 ft. lbs. (64 Nm) and the 10mm bolts to 34 ft. lbs. (46 Nm). Tighten the torque converter bolts to 20 ft. lbs. (27 Nm).

## PAN REMOVAL

1. Raise and support the vehicle safely. Remove the drain plug. Drain the fluid in a suitable container.
2. Remove the drain pan retaining bolts.
3. Remove the pan. Discard the gasket.
4. Remove th filter, as required.
5. Installation is the reverse of the removal procedure. Refill the unit with the proper grade and type transmission fluid.

## LINKAGE ADJUSTMENT

### *Tercel*

#### 1983-86 – SEDAN

1. Push the selector lever all the way to the front of the vehicle.
2. Return the lever 3 notches to the **N** shift position.
3. While holding the selector lever slightly toward the **R** shift position tighten the connecting rod nut.

#### 1987-90 – SEDAN

1. Loosen the swivel nut on the selector lever.
2. Push the lever fully toward the right side of the vehicle.
3. Return the lever 2 notches to the **N** position.
4. Set the shift lever in the **N** position.
5. While holding the selector lever slightly toward the **R** shift position tighten the swivel nut to 48 inch lbs. (5.4 Nm).

#### WAGON

1. Push the selector lever all the way to the rear of the vehicle.
2. Return the lever 2 notches to the **N** shift position.
3. Set the selector lever in the **N** position.
4. While holding the selector lever slightly toward the **R** shift position tighten the connecting rod nut.

### *Corolla (FWD), Camry, MR2 and Celica (FWD)*

1. Loosen the swivel nut on the selector lever.
2. Push the lever fully toward the right side of the vehicle.
3. Return the lever 2 notches to the **N** position.
4. Set the selector lever in the **N** position.
5. While holding the selector lever slightly toward the **R** shift position tighten the swivel nut to 48 inch lbs. (5.4 Nm).

## NEUTRAL SAFETY SWITCH

### *Tercel, MR2 and Celica (FWD)*

1. Loosen the neutral start switch bolt. Position the selector in the **N** position.
2. Align the switch shaft groove with the neutral base line which is located on the switch.
3. Tighten the bolt to 48 inch lbs. (5.4 Nm). On the Tercel wagon, tighten to 9 ft. lbs. (13 Nm).

### *Corolla (FWD)*

#### 1984-85

1. Loosen the neutral start switch retaining bolts.
2. Connect an ohmmeter between the terminals.
3. Adjust the switch to the point where there is continuity between the terminals.

#### 1986-90

1. Loosen the neutral start switch bolt. Position the selector in the **N** position.
2. As required disconnect the switch electrical connector. Align the switch shaft groove with the neutral base line which is located on the switch.
3. Tighten the bolt to 48 inch lbs. (5.4 Nm).

### *Camry*

#### 1983-85

1. Loosen the neutral start switch retaining bolts.
2. Connect an ohmmeter between the terminals.
3. Adjust the switch to the point where there is continuity between the terminals.

#### 1986-90

1. Loosen the neutral start switch bolt. Position the selector in the **N** position.
2. Align the switch shaft groove with the neutral basic line which is located on the switch.
3. Tighten the bolt to 48 inch lbs. (5.4 Nm).

## THROTTLE CABLE

1. Remove the air cleaner.
2. Confirm that the accelerator linkage opens the throttle fully. Adjust the linkage as necessary.
3. Peel the rubber dust boot back from the throttle cable.
4. Loosen the adjustment nuts on the throttle cable bracket (cylinder head cover) just enough to allow cable housing movement.
5. Have an assistant depress the accelerator pedal fully.
6. Adjust the cable housing so that the distance between its end and the cable stop collar is 0.04 in.
7. Tighten the adjustment nuts. Make sure that the adjustment hasn't changed. Install the dust boot and the air cleaner.

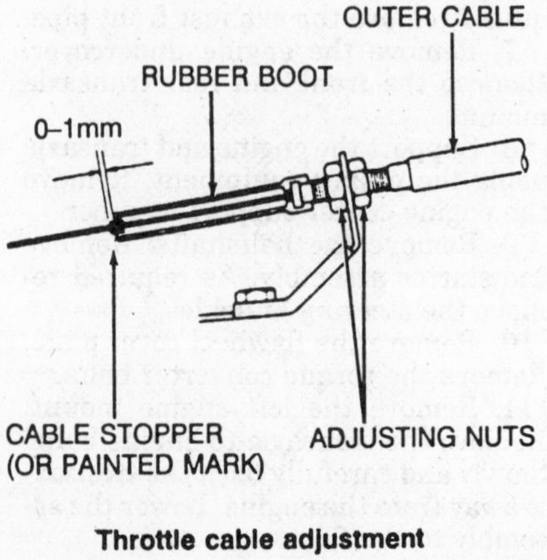


**Throttle cable adjustment**

# TRANSFER CASE

## REMOVAL & INSTALLATION

### 1988-90 Camry/Celica All-Trac

1. Remove the engine/transaxle assembly.
2. Separate the transaxle from the engine.
3. Remove the 3 bolts and 5 nuts and separate the transfer case from the transaxle. You may need a rubber mallet to get the two separated.
4. Installation is in the reverse order of removal. Remove any packng material from the transfer case mating surface. Be careful not to get any oil on it. Tighten the mounting bolts and nuts to 51 ft. lbs. (69 Nm).

# DRIVE AXLE

## Halfshafts

## REMOVAL & INSTALLATION

### Tercel

1. Raise the front of the vehicle and support it with jacks stands.
2. Remove the cotter pin and locknut cap.
3. Have an assistant step on the brake pedal and at the same time, loosen the bearing locknut.
4. Remove the brake caliper and then position it out of the way. Remove the brake disc.
5. Remove the cotter pin and nut from the tie rod end and then, using a tie rod end puller, disconnect the tie rod end from the steering knuckle.
6. Matchmark the lower strut mounting bracket where it attaches to the steering knuckle, remove the mounting bolts and then disconnect the steering knuckle from the strut bracket.
7. Using SST 09950-20017 puller or equivalent, pull the axle hub off of the outer halfshaft end.
8. Remove the stiffener plate from the left side of the transaxle assembly.
9. Using a special tool available from Toyota, tap the halfshaft out of the transaxle casing.

**NOTE: Be sure to cover the halfshaft input hole.**

10. Installation is in the reverse order of removal. Please note the following:
    a. Coat the oil seal in the transaxle input hole with MP grease before inserting the halfshaft.
    b. Tighten the steering knuckle-to-strut bolts to 105 ft. lbs. (1988-90: 166 ft. lbs.)
    c. Tighten the tie rod end nut to 36 ft. lbs. (49 Nm).
    d. Tighten the bearing locknut to 137 ft. lbs. (186 Nm).
    e. Tighten the stiffner plate bolts to 29 ft. lbs. (39 Nm).
    f. Check the front wheel alignment.

### 1985-88 Corolla (4A-GE)
### 1983-87 Corolla FX/FX16
### 1983-87 Corolla FWD (4A-C)

1. Raise and support the front end on jackstands.
2. Remove the cotter pin, locknut cap and locknut from the hub.
3. Remove the engine under cover. Remove the 6 nuts attaching the halfshaft (front drive shaft) to the transaxle (differential side gear).
4. Remove the brake caliper from the steering knuckle and support it out of the way with a wire. Remove the rotor disc.
5. Disconnect the steering knuckle from the lower arm by removing the bolt and two nuts, then disconnect the lower arm from the steering knuckle.
6. Using SST 09950-20017 puller or equivalent, pull the axle hub from the halfshaft. Be sure to cover the dust boot with a shop rag to prevent damage to the bolt.
7. Installation is the reverse of removal. Torque the steering knuckle to 47 ft. lbs. (64 Nm) – 1983-86 sedan/wagon and 1986-89 FX; 105 ft. lbs. (142 Nm) – 1987-89 sedan/wagon; the caliper bolts to 65 ft. lbs. (88 Nm); the bearing nut to 137 ft. lbs. (186 Nm) and the halfshaft nuts to 27 ft. lbs. (36 Nm).

### 1988-90 Corolla (FWD) – Except 1988 4A-GE

1. Raise the front of the vehicle and support it with jacks stands.
2. Remove the cotter pin and locknut cap.
3. Have an assistant step on the brake pedal and at the same time, loosen the bearing locknut.
4. Remove the engine undercovers and then drain the gear oil or fluid.
5. Remove the cotter pin and nut from the tie rod end and then, using a tie rod end puller, disconnect the tie rod end from the steering knuckle.
6. Remove the mounting bolts and then disconnect the steering knuckle from the lower control arm.
7. Use a plastic hammer and drive the outer end of the shaft out of the axle hub.
8. Using a special tool available from Toyota (prybar, drift ans hammer), tap or pry the halfshaft out of the transaxle casing.

**NOTE: Be sure to cover the halfshaft input hole.**

9. Installation is in the reverse order of removal. Please note the following:
    a. Coat the oil seal in the transaxle input hole with MP grease before inserting the halfshaft.
    b. Tighten the steering knuckle-to-lower arm bolts to 105 ft. lbs. (142 Nm).
    c. Tighten the tie rod end nut to 36 ft. lbs. (49 Nm).
    d. Tighten the bearing locknut to 137 ft. lbs. (186 Nm).
    e. Check that there is 0.08–0.12 in. (2–3mm) axial play on each shaft.
    f. Check the front wheel alignment.

### 1986-90 Celica (FWD) – 2wd

1. Raise and support the front of the vehicle on jackstands.
2. Remove the wheels.
3. Remove the cotter pin, cap and locknut from the hub.
4. Remove the engine under covers.
5. Drain the transmission fluid or the differential fluid on the GTS.
6. Remove the transaxle gravel shield on the GTS.
7. Loosen the six nuts attaching the inner end of the halfshaft to transaxle (all except Celica GTS). It's a good idea to have a friend sit in the car and depress the brake pedal while removing the nuts.

**NOTE: Wrap the exposed end of the halfshaft in an old shop cloth to prevent damage to it.**

Remove the cotter pin from the tie end rod and then press the tie rod out of the steering knuckle.

8. Remove the bolt and 2 nuts and disconnect the steering knuckle from the lower arm control.
9. On all but the GTS, use a two-armed gear puller or the like and press the halfshaft out of the steering knuckle.
10. On the GTS, mark a spot somewhere on the left halfshaft and measure the distance between the spot and the transaxle case. Using SST 09520-32060, pull the halfshaft out of the transaxle.
11. On the GTS, use a two-armed puller and press the outer end of the right halfshaft out of the steering knuckle. Use a pair of pliers to remove the snap ring at the inner end and pull the halfshaft out of the center driveshaft.
12. On all but the GT-S, remove the snap ring on the center shaft with a

pair of pliers and then pull the center shaft out of the transaxle case.

13. When installing the center driveshaft on ST and GT models, coat the transaxle oil seal with grease, insert the halfshaft through the bearing bracket and secure it with a new snap ring.

14. Repeat Step 13 when installing the inner end of the right halfshaft on the GTS.

15. On the right halfshaft of the GTS, use a new snap ring, coat the transaxle oil seal with grease and then press the inner end of the shaft into the differential housing. Check that the measurement made in Step 10 is the same. Check that there is 0.08–0.11 in. (2–3mm) of axial play. Check also that the halfshaft will not come out by trying to pull it with your hand.

16. Press the outer end of each halfshaft into the steering knuckle on the GTS.

17. On the ST and GT, press the outer end of the halfshafts into the steering knuckle and then fingertighten the nuts on the inner end.

18. Connect the steering knuckle to the lower control arm and tighten the bolts to 94 ft. lbs. (127 Nm).

19. Connect the tie rod end to the steering knuckle and tighten the nut to 36 ft. lbs. (49 Nm). Install a new cotter pin.

20. Tighten the hub locknut to 137 ft. lbs. (186 Nm) while depressing the brake pedal. Install the cap and use a new cotter pin.

21. On the ST and GT, tighten the 6 nuts on the inner halfshaft ends to 27 ft. lbs. (36 Nm) while depressing the brake pedal.

22. Install the transaxle gravel shield on the GTS.

23. Fill the transaxle with gear oil or fluid.

24 Install the engine under cover.

### *1988-90 Celica All-Trac – 4wd*

#### FRONT

1. Raise and support the front of the vehicle on jackstands.

2. Remove the wheels.

3. Remove the cotter pin, cap and locknut from the hub.

4. Remove the transaxle gravel shield on models with w/MT. Remove the engine under cover and front fender apron seal.

5. Remove the cotter pin and nut from the tie rod end and then disconnect it from the steering knuckle.

6. Remove the bolt and 2 nuts and disconnect the steering knuckle from the lower control arm.

7. Loosen the 6 nuts attaching the inner end of the halfshaft to the transaxle side gear shaft. It's a good idea to have a friend sit in the car and depress the brake pedal while removing the nuts.

8. Grasp the halfshaft and push the axle carrier outward until the shaft can be removed from the side gear shaft.

**NOTE: Wrap the exposed end of the halfshaft in an old shop cloth to prevent damage to it.**

9. Use a rubber mallet and tap the outer end of the shaft from the axle hub.

**To install:**

10. Press the outer end of the halfshaft into the axle hub, position the inner end and install the 6 nuts fingertight.

11. Connect the tie rod end to the steering knuckle and tighten the nut to 36 ft. lbs. (49 Nm). Install a new cotter pin. If the cotter pin holes do not line up, tighten the nut until they align. Never loosen it.

12. Connect the steering knuckle to the lower control arm and tighten to 94 ft. lbs. (127 Nm).

13. Tighten the 6 inner shaft mounting nuts to 48 ft. lbs. (65 Nm). Measure the distance between the right and left side shafts; it must be less then 27.75 in. (704.7mm).

14. With the brake pedal depressed, install the bearing locknut and tighten it to 137 ft. lbs. (186 Nm). Install the cap and a new cotter pin.

15. Install the wheels and lower the car.

#### REAR

1. Raise the rear of the car and support it with safety stands. Remove the wheels.

2. Remove the cotter pin and locknut cap. Have a friend depress the brake pedal and then remove the bearing nit.

3. Scribe matchmarks on the inner joint tulip and the side gear shaft flange. Loosen and remove the 4 nuts.

4. Disconnect the inner end of the shaft by puching it upward and then pull the outer end from the axle carrier. Remove the halfshaft.

5. Position the halfshaft into the axle carrier and pull the inner end down until the matchmarks are aligned.

6. Connect the halfshaft to the side gear shaft and tighten the nuts to 51 ft. lbs. (69 Nm).

7. Install the bearing nut and tighten it to 137 ft. lbs. (186 Nm) with the brake pedal depressed. Install the cap and a new cotter pin.

8. Install the wheels and lower the car.

### *1983-88 Camry – 2wd*

1. Raise and support the front of the vehicle on jackstands.

2. Remove the wheels.

3. Remove the cotter pin, cap and locknut from the hub.

4. Remove the transaxle gravel shield on models with w/MT. Remove the engine under cover and front fender apron seal.

5. Loosen the 6 nuts attaching the inner end of the halfshaft to the transaxle or center shaft. It's a good idea to have a friend sit in the car and depress the brake pedal while removing the nuts.

**NOTE: Wrap the exposed end of the halfshaft in an old shop cloth to prevent damage to it.**

6. Remove the brake caliper with the hydraulic line still attached, position it out of the way and suspend it with a wire. Remove the rotor.

7. On the left side of 1983-86 models w/AT and on all 1987-88 models, remove the two bolts attaching the ball joint to the steering knuckle. Pull the lower control arm down while pulling the strut outward; this will disconnect the inner end of the halfshaft from the transaxle.

8. Using a two-armed puller, or the like, press the outer end of the halfshaft from the steering knuckle and then remove the halfshaft.

9. On gasoline engined models, it is also possible to remove the right side center shaft. Drain the transaxle fluid, remove the snap ring with pliers and pull the shaft out of the transaxle case.

**To install:**

10. When installing the center driveshaft, coat the transaxle oil seal with grease, insert the driveshaft through the bearing bracket and secure it with a new snap ring.

11. Press the outer end of the halfshaft into the steering knuckle, position the inner end and install the 6 nuts fingertight.

12. Reconnect the ball joint to the steering knuckle on models that it was disconnected and tighten the bolts to 83 ft. lbs. (113 Nm) – 1983-86; 94 ft. lbs. (127 Nm) – 1987-88.

13. Install the rotor and brake caliper. Tighten the caliper-to-knuckle bolts to 65 ft. lbs. (88 Nm).

14. Tighten the wheel bearing locknut to 137 ft. lbs. (186 Nm) while depressing the brake pedal. Install the locknut cap and use a new cotter pin.

15. Tighten the 6 inner end nuts to 27 ft. lbs. (36 Nm) while depressing the brake pedal.

16. Install the transaxle gravel shield on models so equipped.

17. Fill the transaxle with fluid (ATF DEXRON® II on models with a gasoline engine).

### *1989-90 Camry – 2wd*

1. Raise and support the front of the vehicle on jackstands.
2. Remove the wheels.
3. Remove the cotter pin, cap and locknut from the hub.
4. Remove the engine under covers.
5. Drain the transmission fluid or the differential fluid on the wagon.
6. Remove the transaxle gravel shield on the wagon.
7. Loosen the six nuts attaching the inner end of the halfshaft to transaxle (all except wagon). It's a good idea to have a friend sit in the car and depress the brake pedal while removing the nuts.

**NOTE: Wrap the exposed end of the halfshaft in an old shop cloth to prevent damage to it.**

Remove the cotter pin from the tie end rod and then press the tie rod out of the steering knuckle.

8. Remove the bolt and 2 nuts and disconnect the steering knuckle from the lower arm control.
9. On all but the wagon (4 cyl), use a two-armed gear puller or the like and press the halfshaft out of the steering knuckle.
10. On the wagon (4 cyl), mark a spot somewhere on the left halfshaft and measure the distance between the spot and the transaxle case. Using SST 09520-32012, pull the halfshaft out of the transaxle.
11. On the wagon (4 cyl), use a two-armed puller and press the outer end of the right halfshaft out of the steering knuckle. Use a pair of pliers to remove the snap ring at the inner end and pull the halfshaft out of the center driveshaft.
12. On all but the wagon (4 cyl), remove the snap ring on the center shaft with a pair of pliers and then pull the center shaft out of the transaxle case.
13. When installing the center driveshaft on sedan and V6 models, coat the transaxle oil seal with grease, insert the halfshaft through the bearing bracket and secure it with a new snap ring.
14. Repeat Step 13 when installing the inner end of the right halfshaft on the wagon (4 cyl).
15. On the right halfshaft of the wagon (4 cyl), use a new snap ring, coat the transaxle oil seal with grease and then press the inner end of the shaft into the differential housing. Check that the measurement made in Step 10 is the same. Check that there is 0.08–0.12 in. (2–3mm) of axial play. Check also that the halfshaft will not come out by trying to pull it with your hand.
16. Press the outer end of each halfshaft into the steering knuckle on the wagon (4 cyl).
17. On all except the wagon (4 cyl), press the outer end of the halfshafts into the steering knuckle and then fingertighten the nuts on the inner end.
18. Connect the steering knuckle to the lower control arm and tighten the bolts to 83 ft. lbs. (113 Nm).
19. Connect the tie rod end to the steering knuckle and tighten the nut to 36 ft. lbs. (49 Nm). Install a new cotter pin.
20. Tighten the hub locknut to 137 ft. lbs. (186 Nm) while depressing the brake pedal. Install the cap and use a new cotter pin.
21. On all except the wagon (4 cyl), tighten the 6 nuts on the inner halfshaft ends to 27 ft. lbs. (36 Nm) while depressing the brake pedal.
22. Install the transaxle gravel shield on the wagon.
23. Fill the transaxle with gear oil or fluid.
24 Install the engine under cover.

### *Camry All-Trac – 4wd*

#### FRONT – 1988

1. Raise and support the front of the vehicle on jackstands.
2. Remove the wheels.
3. Remove the cotter pin, cap and locknut from the hub.
4. Remove the transaxle gravel shield on models with w/MT. Remove the engine under cover and front fender apron seal.
5. Remove the cotter pin and nut from the tie rod end and then disconnect it from the steering knuckle.
6. Remove the bolt and 2 nuts and disconnect the steering knuckle from the lower control arm.
7. Loosen the 6 nuts attaching the inner end of the halfshaft to the transaxle side gear shaft. It's a good idea to have a friend sit in the car and depress the brake pedal while removing the nuts.
8. Grasp the halfshaft and push the axle carrier outward until the shaft can be removed from the side gear shaft.

**NOTE: Wrap the exposed end of the halfshaft in an old shop cloth to prevent damage to it.**

9. Use a rubber mallet and tap the outer end of the shaft from the axle hub.

**To install:**

10. Press the outer end of the halfshaft into the axle hub, position the inner end and install the 6 nuts fingertight.
11. Connect the tie rod end to the steering knuckle and tighten the nut to 36 ft. lbs. (49 Nm). Install a new cotter pin. If the cotter pin holes do not line up, tighten the nut until they align. Never loosen it.
12. Connect the steering knuckle to the lower control arm and tighten to 94 ft. lbs. (127 Nm).
13. Tighten the 6 inner shaft mounting nuts to 48 ft. lbs. (65 Nm). Measure the distance between the right and left side shafts; it must be less then 27.75 in. (704.7mm).
14. With the brake pedal depressed, install the bearing locknut and tighten it to 137 ft. lbs. (186 Nm). Install the cap and a new cotter pin.
15. Install the wheels and lower the car.

#### FRONT – 1989-90

1. Raise and support the front of the vehicle on jackstands.
2. Remove the wheels.
3. Remove the cotter pin, cap and locknut from the hub.
4. Remove the engine undercovers.
5. Disconnect the tie rod end from the steering knuckle.
6. Disconnect the lower control arm at the steering knuckle and pull it down and out of the way.
7. Use a plastic hammer and carefully tap the outer end of the halfshaft until it frees itself from the axle hub.
8. Cover the outer boot with a rag and then remove the inner end of the halfshaft from the transaxle. On the left shaft, use a small prybar or a tire iron. On the right shaft, use a hammer and a drift.

**To install:**

9. Coat the lip of the oil seal with grease and then carefully drive the inner end of the shaft into the transaxle until it makes contact with the pinion shaft.

**NOTE: Be careful not to damage the boots when installing the halfshafts; also, position the boot snapring so that the opening is facing downward.**

10. Maneuever the outer end of each shaft into the axle hub, being careful not to damage the boots.
11. Check that there is 0.08–0.12 in. (2–3mm) of axial play. Check also that the halfshaft will not come out by trying to remove it with your hand.
12. Connect the lower control arm to the steering arm and tighten the bolt to 83 ft. lbs. (113 Nm).
13. Connect the tie rod to the steering knuckle and tighten the nut to 36 ft. lbs. (49 Nm). Use a new cotter pin to secure it.
14. Install the axle bearing locknut and tighten it to 137 ft. lbs. (186 Nm) while stepping on the brake pedal. Install the locknut cap and then a new cotter pin.
15. Fill the transaxle with gear oil or fluid, install the undercovers and wheels. Lower the car and check the front end alignment.

**REAR—1988-90**

1. Raise the rear of the car and support it with safety stands. Remove the wheels.
2. Remove the cotter pin and locknut cap. Have a friend depress the brake pedal and then remove the bearing nit.
3. Scribe matchmarks on the inner joint tulip and the side gear shaft flange. Loosen and remove the 4 nuts.
4. Disconnect the inner end of the shaft by puching it upward and then pull the outer end from the axle carrier. Remove the halfshaft.
5. Position the halfshaft into the axle carrier and pull the inner end down until the matchmarks are aligned.
6. Connect the halfshaft to the side gear shaft and tighten the nuts to 51 ft. lbs. (69 Nm).
7. Install the bearing nut and tighten it to 137 ft. lbs. (186 Nm) with the brake pedal depressed. Install the cap and a new cotter pin.
8. Install the wheels and lower the car.

***MR2***

1. Raise and support the front of the vehicle on jackstands.
2. Remove the wheels.
3. Remove the cotter pin, cap and locknut from the hub.
4. Remove the transaxle gravel shield.
5. Loosen the 6 nuts attaching the inner end of the halfshaft to transaxle. It's a good idea to have a friend sit in the car and depress the brake pedal while removing the nuts.

**NOTE: Wrap the exposed end of the halfshaft in an old shop cloth to prevent damage to it.**

6. On models equipped with a automatic transaxle, remove the 2 bolts holding the ball joint to the rear axle carrier and disconnect the lower arm from the rear axle carrier.
7. Also on models equipped with a automatic transaxle, remove the cotter pin and nut and using SST 09610-20012 or equivalent, disconnect the suspension arm from the rear axle carrier.
8. While holding the halfshaft, use a plastic mallet and carefully knock the outer end of the wheel hub assembly. Remove the halfshaft.

**To install:**

9. Press the outer end of the halfshaft into the wheel hub assembly.
10. Position the inner end of the halfshaft and install the 6 nuts fingertight.
11. Install the transaxle gravel shield.
12. Tighten the wheel bearing locknut to 137 ft. lbs. (186 Nm) while depressing the brake pedal. Install the locknut cap and use a new cotter pin.
13. Tighten the 6 inner end nuts to 27 ft. lbs. (36 Nm) while depressing the brake pedal. Torque the suspension arm nut to 36 ft. lbs. (49 Nm) and the lower arm to rear axle carrier to 83 ft. lbs. (113 Nm).
14. Fill the transaxle with fluid.

***1983-86 Supra***
***1983-88 Cressida***
***1983-85 Celica GTS (RWD)***

1. Raise and support the rear of the vehicle on jackstands.
2. Place matchmarks on the halfshaft and flanges.
3. Remove the 4 nuts retaining the halfshaft to the differential and disconnect the halfshaft from the differential.
4. Remove the 4 nuts retaining the halfshaft to the axle shaft and disconnect the halfshaft from the axleshaft. Remove the halfshaft from the under the vehicle.
5. Installation is the reverse order of the removal procedure. Be sure to line up the matchmarks on the halfshaft and torque the retaining nuts to 51 ft. lbs.

***1987-89 Supra***
***1989-90 Cressida***

1. Raise and support the rear of the vehicle safely. Remove the rear wheels.
2. Using a suitable jack, raise the No. 2 suspension arm until it is horizontal. Place matchmarks to the rear halfshaft and side gear shaft flange.
3. Remove the 6 retaining nuts (while and assistant is depressing the brake pedal) and disconnect the rear halfshaft from the differential.
4. Remove the cotter pin and lock nut cap. Loosen and remove the bearing lock nut.
5. Using a suitable plastic hammer, tap out the rear halfshaft.
6. Installation is the reverse order of the removal procedure. Tighten the bearing lock nut to 203 ft. lbs. (275 Nm) and the 6 halfshaft retaining bolts to 51 ft. lbs. (69 Nm).

## CV-JOINT OVERHAUL

**For all CV-joint overhaul procedures, please refer to "CV-Joint Overhaul" in the Unit Repair section.**

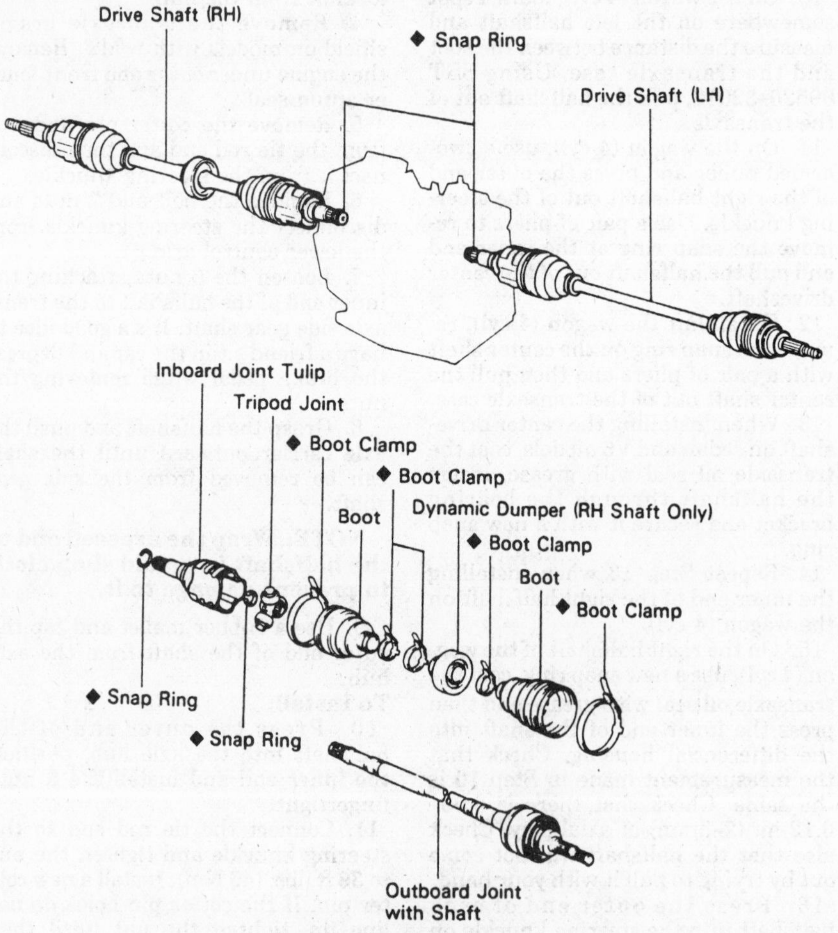


Front halfshaft—Tercel

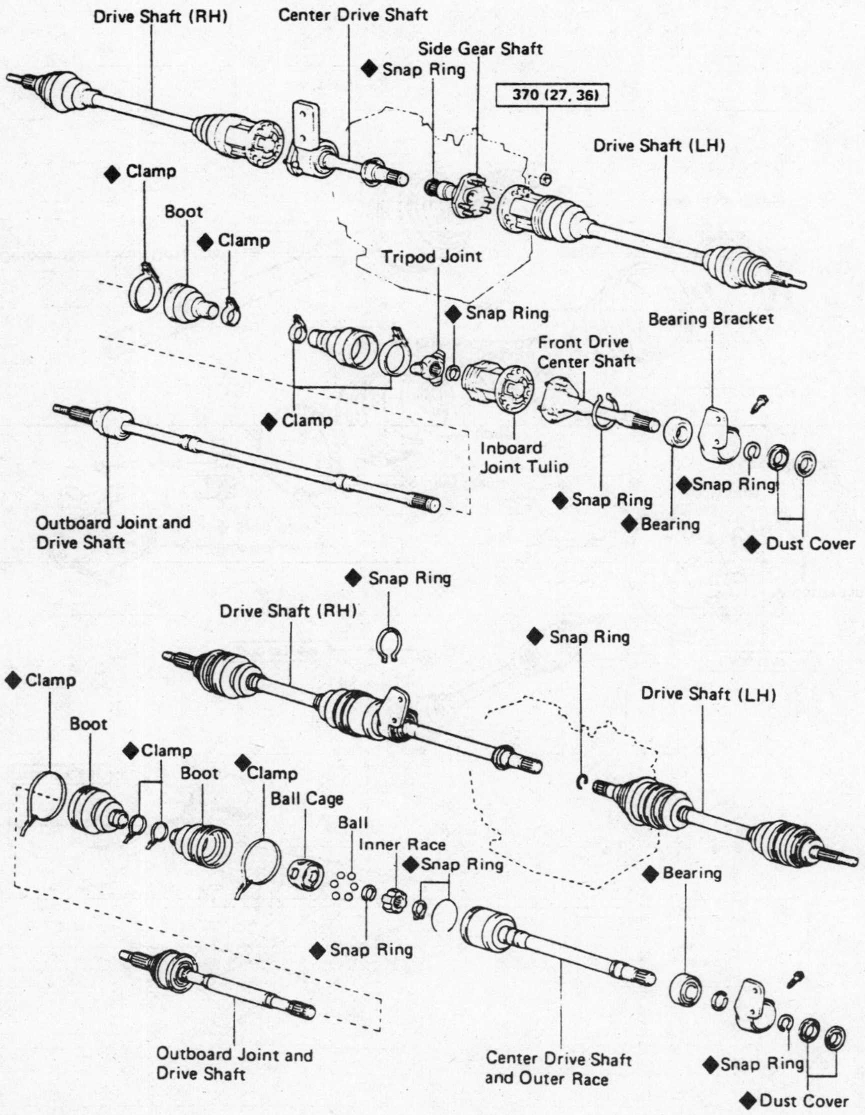


Front halfshaft – MR2 (4A-GZE)

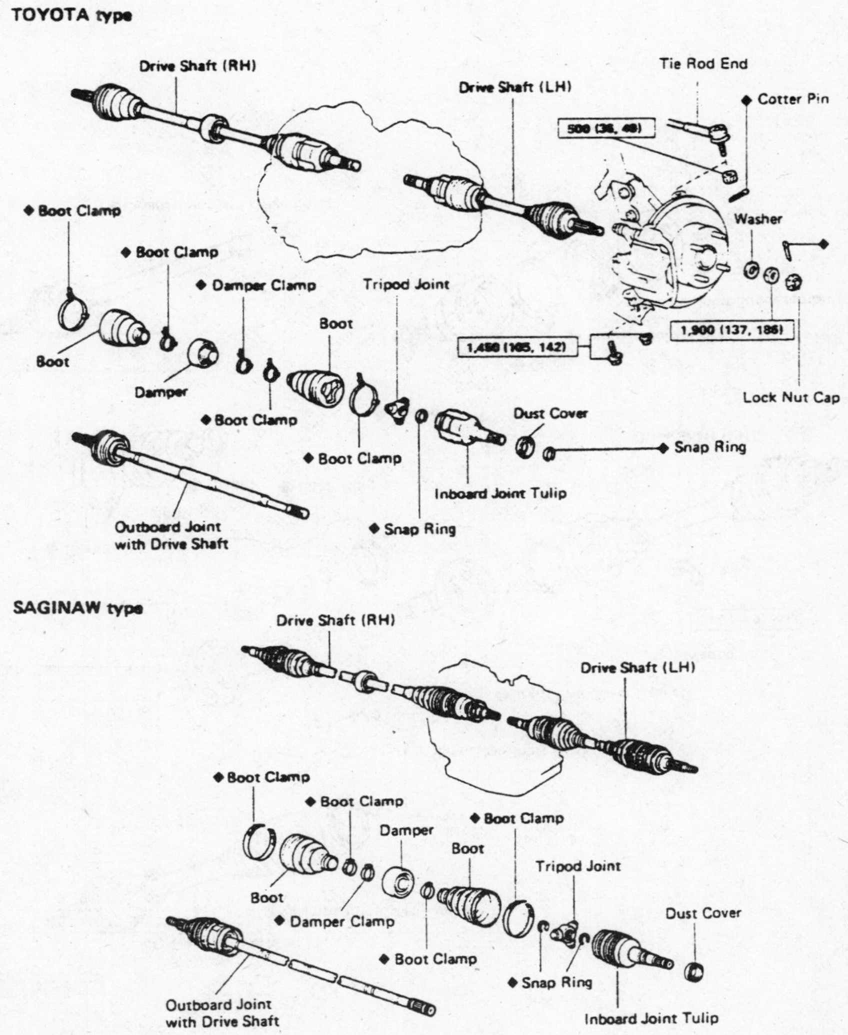


Front halfshafts – Corolla (exc. FX) 2wd

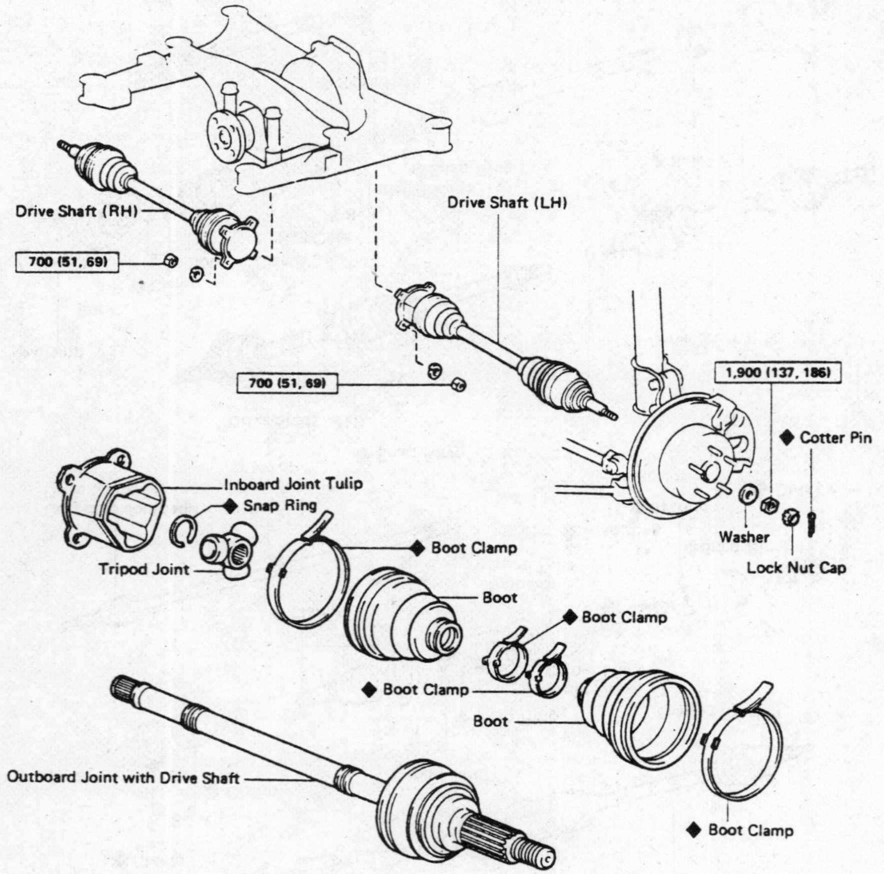


Rear halfshaft – 1983-88 Cressida

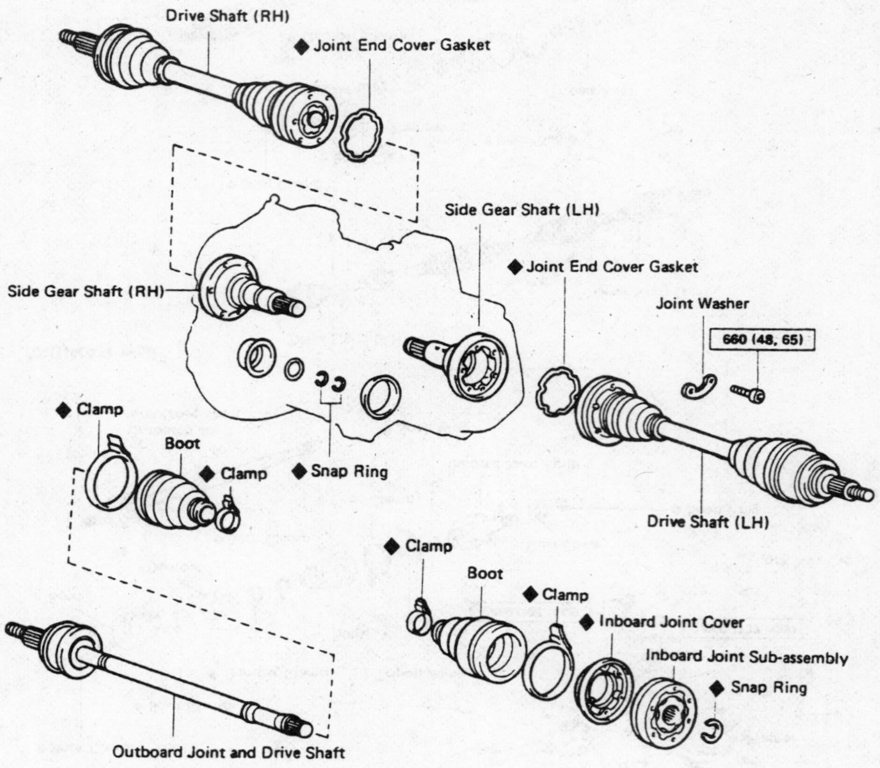


Front halfshaft – Celica All-Trac (4wd) and 1988 Camry All-Trac (4wd)

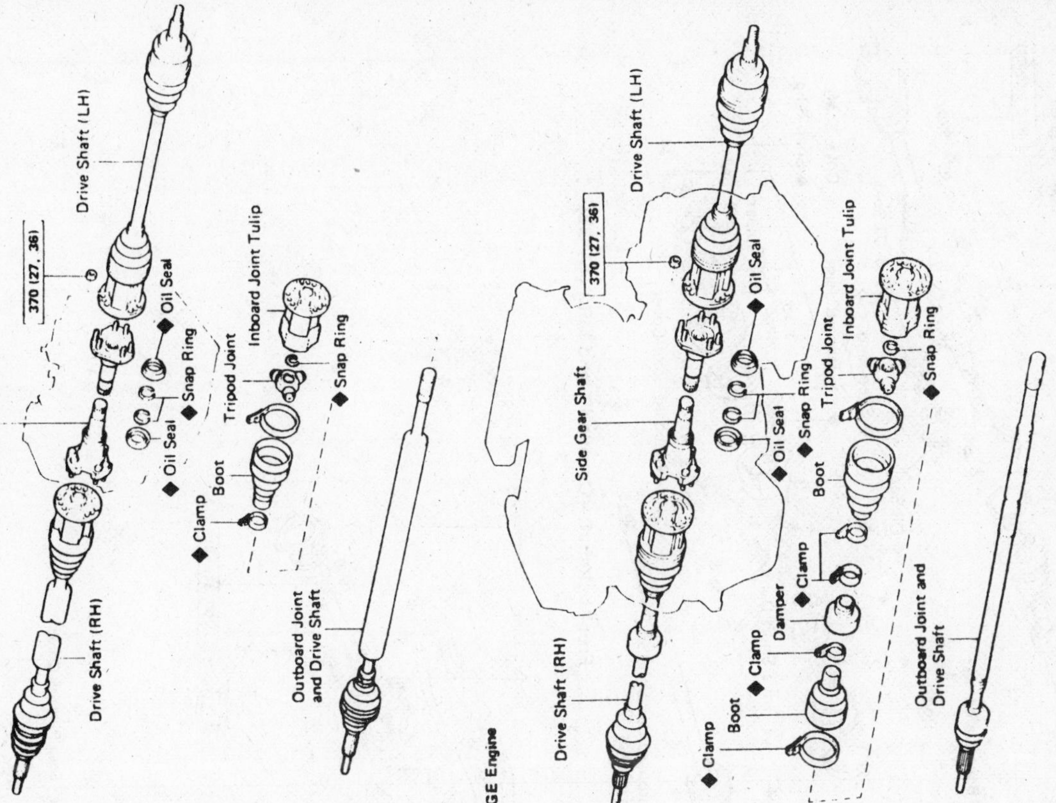


Front halfshafts—Corolla FX

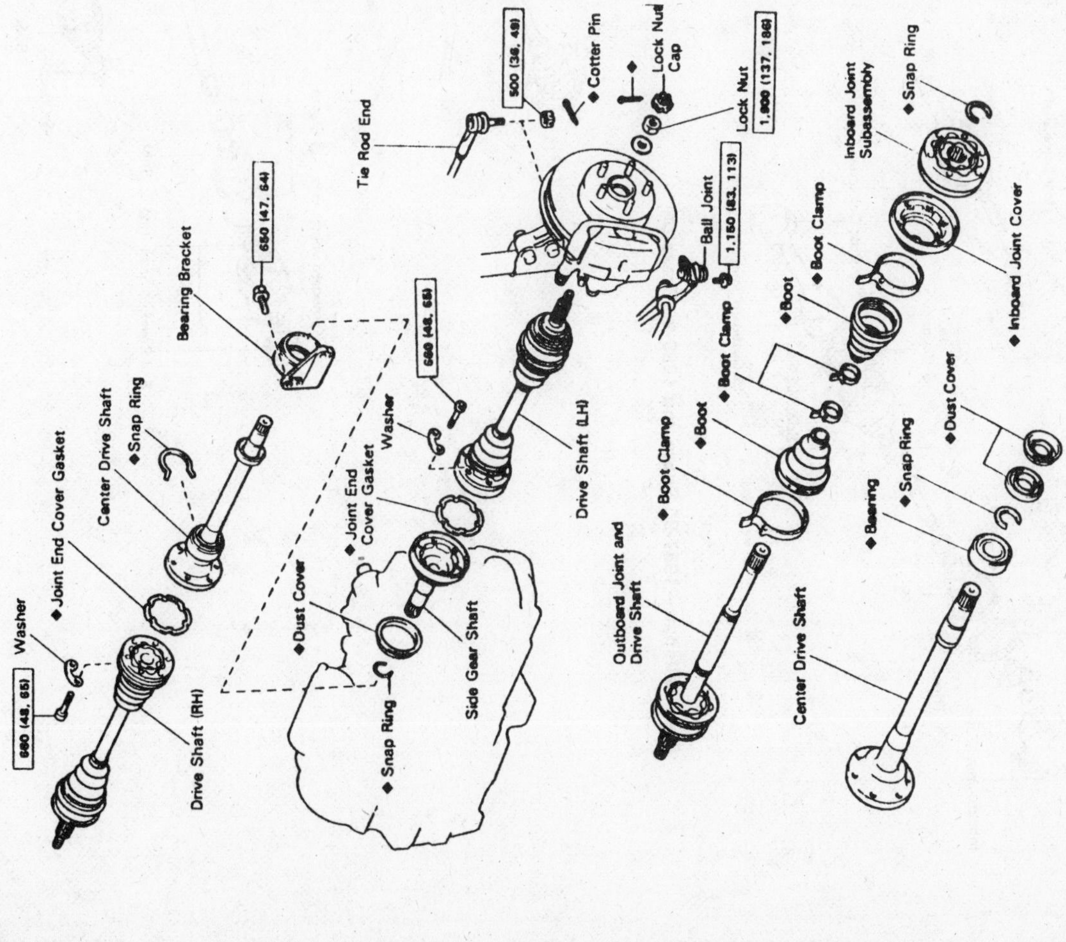


Front halfshafts—Camry 2wd (2VZ-FE)

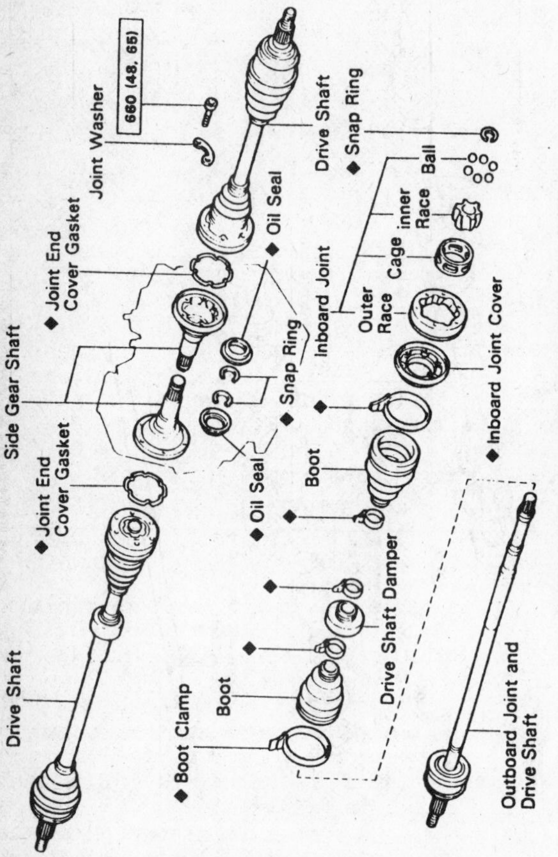


Front halfshaft – Corolla FX and MR2 (4A-GE)

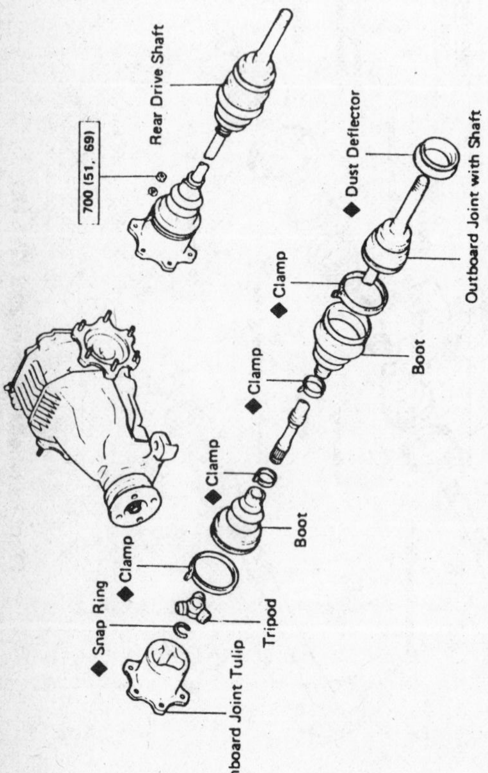


Rear halfshaft – 1987-90 Supra and 1989-90 Cressida

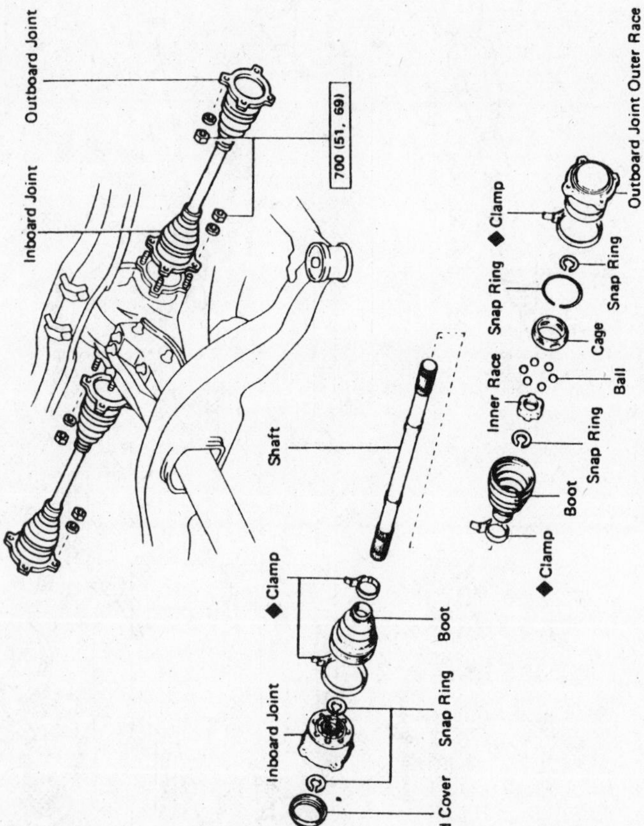


Rear halfshaft – Cressida

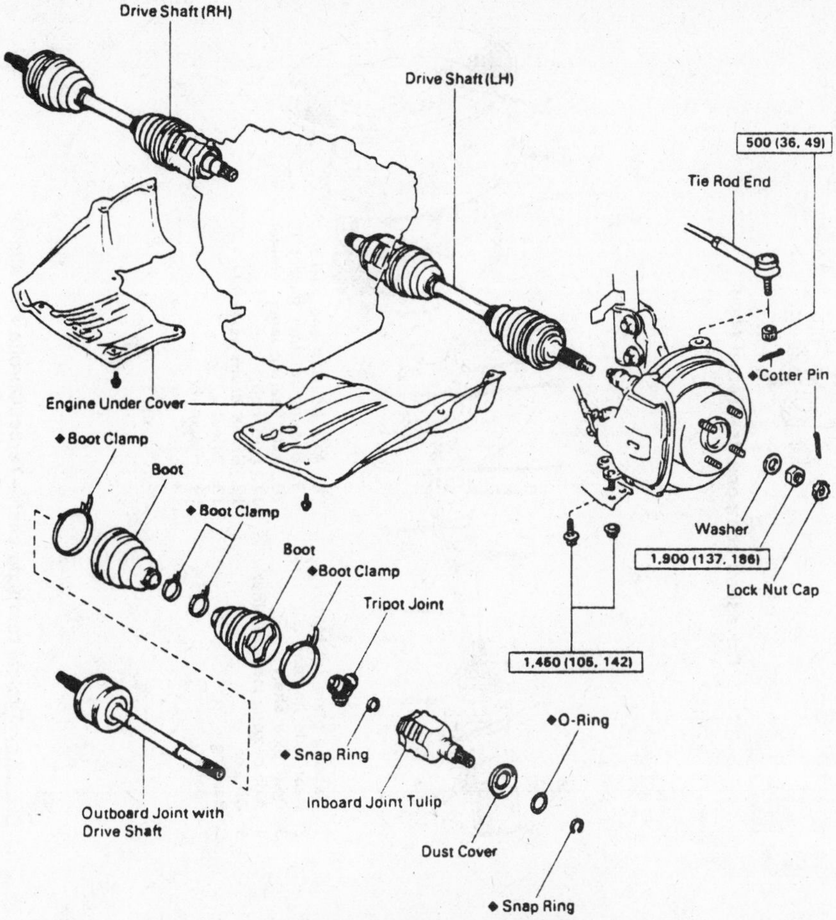

**Front halfshafts – Corolla 4wd**

# Driveshaft and U-Joints

## REMOVAL & INSTALLATION

### *Rear Wheel Drive Only*

1. Raise the rear of the car and support the rear axle housing with jackstands.
2. Matchmark the driveshaft and companion flange. Unfasten the bolts which attach the driveshaft universal joint yoke flange to the mounting flange on the differential drive pinion.
3. On models equipped with three universal joints, perform the following:
   a. Remove the driveshaft sub-assembly from the U-joint sleeve yoke.
   b. Remove the center support bearing from its bracket.
4. Remove the driveshaft end from the transmission.
5. Install an old U-joint yoke in the transmission or, if none is available, use a plastic bag secured with a rubber band over the hole to keep the transmission oil from running out.

**NOTE: On 1983-87 Supra models, the exhaust pipe assembly must be removed in order to remove the driveshaft assembly.**

6. Remove the driveshaft from beneath the vehicle.

**To install:**

7. Apply multipurpose grease on the section of the U-joint sleeve which is to be inserted into the transmission.
8. Insert the driveshaft sleeve into the transmission.

**CAUTION**

***Be careful not to damage any of the seals.***

9. For models equipped with three U-joints and center bearings, perform the following:
   a. Adjust the center bearing clearance with no load placed on the driveline components; the top of the rubber center cushion should be 0.04 in. behind the center of the elongated bolt hole.
   b. Install the center bearing assembly.

**NOTE: Use the same number of washers on the center bearing brackets as were removed.**

   c. Matchmark the arrow marks on the driveshaft and grease fittings.

10. Align the matchmarks. Secure the U-joint flange to the differential pinion flange with the mounting bolts.

**CAUTION**

***Be sure that the bolts are of the same type as those removed and that they are tightened securely.***

11. Remove the jack stands and lower the vehicle.
12. Tighten the center bearing-to-bracket bolts to 30 ft. lbs. (40 Nm)–1983-88 Cressida, 27 ft. lbs. (37 Nm)–1989-90 Cressida; and, 36 ft. lbs. (49 Nm)–Supra. Tighten the flange bolts to 31 ft. lbs. (42 Nm)–1983-88 Cressida; and, 54 ft. lbs. (74 Nm)–Supra and 1989-90 Cressida.

### *1989-90 Corolla–4wd*
### *1983-88 Tercel Wagon–4wd*
### *1988-90 Camry All-Trac–4wd*
### *1988-90 Celica All-Trac–4wd*

1. Matchmark the front driveshaft flange and the front center bearing flange. Remove the 4 bolts, washers and nuts and disconnect the rear end of the front driveshaft from the front center bearing flange. Pull the shaft out of the transfer case and remove it. Plug the transfer case to prevent leakage.
2. With an assistant depressing the brake pedal, loosen the cross groove set bolts ½ turn. These bolts are at the front edge of the rear driveshaft (rear edge of the rear center bearing.
3. Matchmark the rear flange of the rear driveshaft to the differential pinion flange and then disconnect them.
4. Remove the 2 mounting bolts from the front and rear center bearings and then remove the 2 center bearings, intermediate shaft and rear driveshaft as an assembly.
5. Matchmark the univeral joint and the rear center bearing flange, remove the bolts and separate the rear driveshaft from the rear center bearing.
6. Pull the front and rear center bearings from the intermediate shaft.

**To install:**

7. Install the 2 center bearings onto the intermediate shaft ends and then temporarily install the assembly.
8. Align the matchmarks and connect the rear driveshaft to the differential. Tighten the bolts to 54 ft. lbs. (74 Nm); 27 ft. lbs. (37 Nm) on the Corolla.
9. Press the front driveshaft yoke into the transfer case, align the matchmarks at the rear of the shaft with those on the front center bearing flange and tighten the bolts to 54 ft. lbs. (74 Nm); 27 ft. lbs. (37 Nm) on the Corolla.
10. With the front edge of the rear

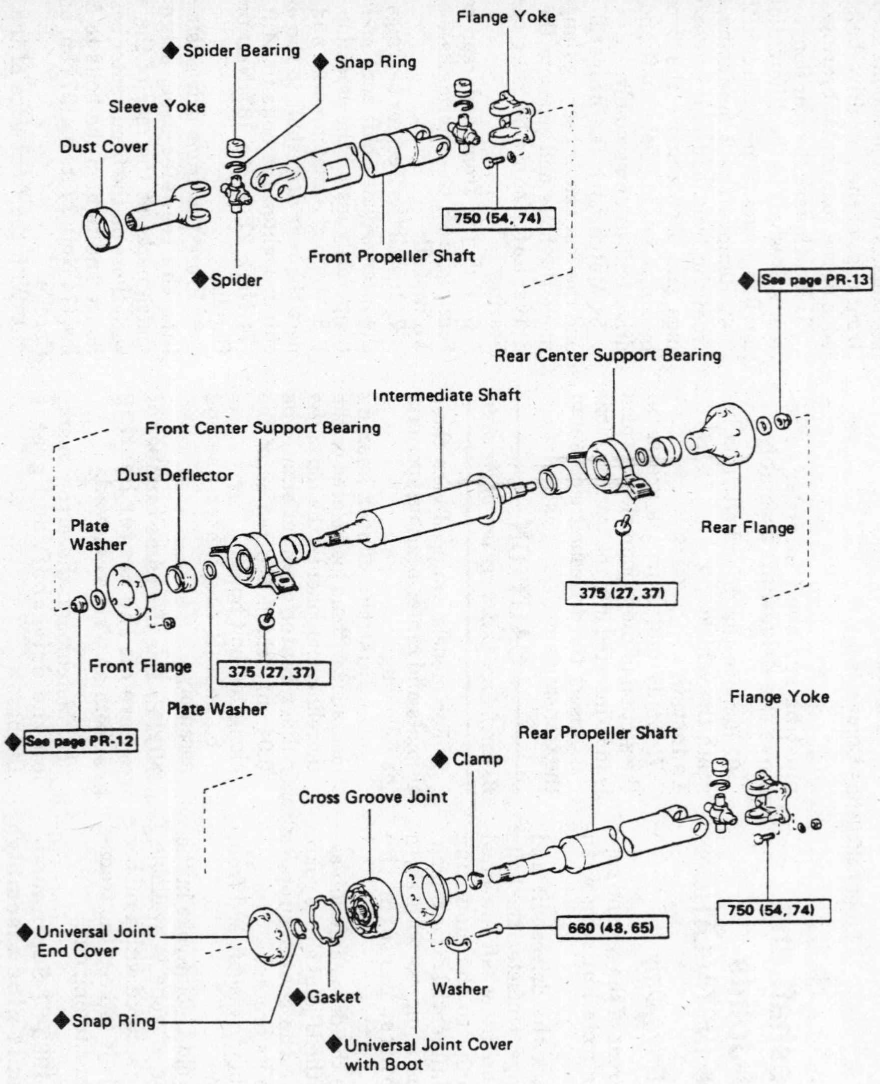


Driveshaft components—Camry/Celica All-Trac (4wd) and Corolla (4wd)

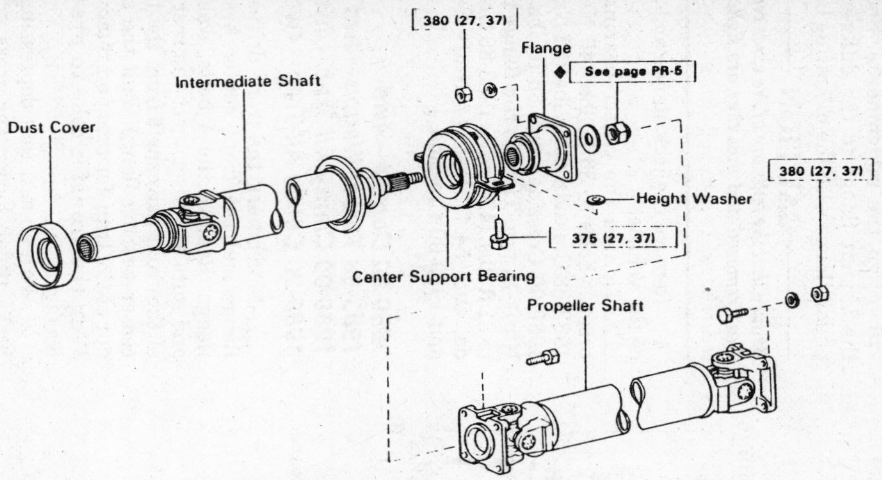

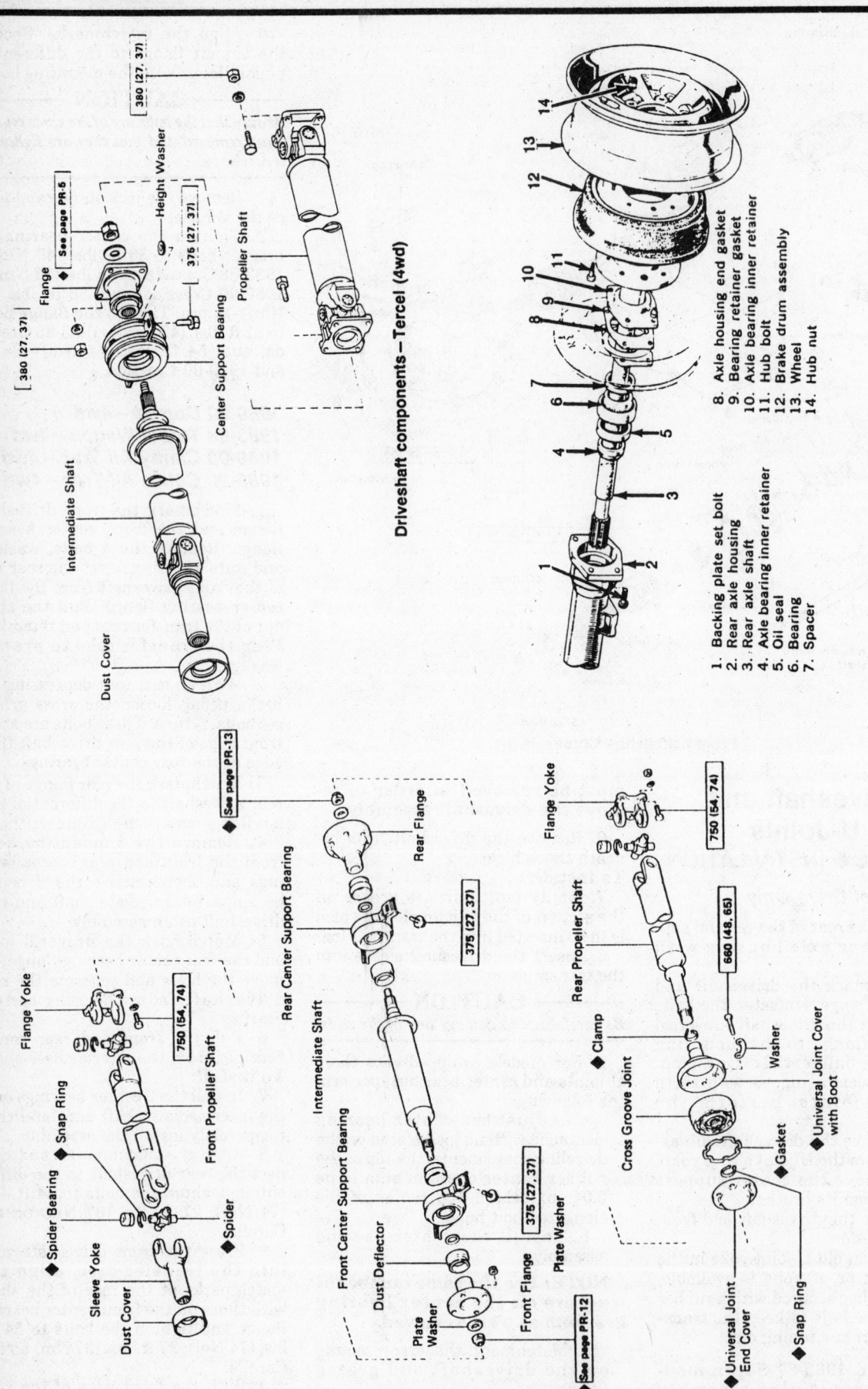

Driveshaft components—Tercel (4wd)

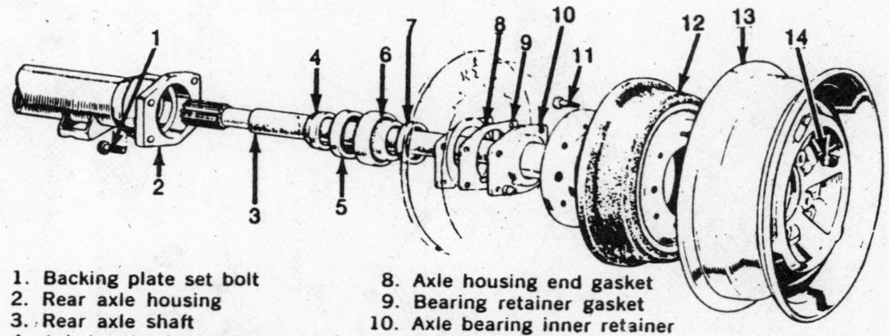


1. Backing plate set bolt
2. Rear axle housing
3. Rear axle shaft
4. Axle bearing inner retainer
5. Oil seal
6. Bearing
7. Spacer
8. Axle housing end gasket
9. Bearing retainer gasket
10. Axle bearing inner retainer
11. Hub bolt
12. Brake drum assembly
13. Wheel
14. Hub nut

Typical rear axle shaft—Tercel/Corolla 4wd similar

drivehshaft in position, depress the brake pedal and tighten the cross groove joint set bolts to 20 ft. lbs. (27 Nm). 1989-90 Celica–48 ft. lbs. (65 Nm).

11. With the car in an unladen condition, adjust the distance between the rear edge of the boot cover and the rear driveshaft to 2.58–2.78 in. (65.5–70.5mm). 1989-90 Celica–2.85–3.05 in. (72.5–77.5mm).

12. With the car in an unladen condition, adjust the distance between the rear side of the center bearing housing and the rear side of the cushion to 0.45–0.53 in. (11.5–13.5mm).

13. Tighten the center bearing mounting bolts to 27 ft. lbs. (37 Nm). Make sure that the center line of the bracket is at right angles to the shaft axial direction.

### U-JOINT OVERHAUL

**NOTE: As the U-joints on many late model vehicles are non-serviceable, the entire driveshaft must be replaced in the event of U-joint problems.**

## Rear Axle Shafts, Bearings And Seals

**NOTE: For rear axle shaft removal on front wheel drive models (except 4wd), please refer to "Rear Axle Hub, Carrier and Bearing" in the Rear Suspension section.**

### REMOVAL & INSTALLATION

#### *Rear Wheel Drive and 4wd Models Only*

**COROLLA–4WD**
**TERCEL WAGON–4WD**
**1983-85 CELICA (EXC. GTS)**

1. Raise the rear of the car and support it securely by using jack stands.
2. Drain the oil from the axle housing.
3. Remove the wheel disc, unfasten the lug nuts, and remove the wheel.
4. Punch matchmarks on the brake drum and the axle shaft to maintain rotational balance.
5. Remove the brake drum and related components.
6. Remove the rear bearing retaining nut.
7. Remove the backing plate attachment nuts through the access holes in the rear axle shaft flange.
8. Use a slide hammer with a suitable adapter to withdraw the axle shaft from its housing.

**CAUTION**

***Use care not to damage the oil seal when removing the axle shaft.***

9. Repeat the procedure for the axle shaft on the opposite side.

**CAUTION**

***Be careful not to mix the components of the two sides.***

10. Installation is performed in the reverse order of removal. Coat the lips of the rear housing oil seal with multipurpose grease prior to installation of the rear axle shaft. Torque the bearing retaining nut to specifications.

**NOTE: Always use new nuts, as they are the self-locking type.**

**1983-86 SUPRA**
**1983-88 CRESSIDA**
**1983-85 CELICA GTS**

1. Raise the rear of the vehicle and support it safely with jackstands.
2. Disconnect the axle driveshaft from the axle flange and lower the axle drive shaft out of the way.
3. Apply the parking brake completely (pulled up as far as possible).
4. Remove the axle flange nut.

**NOTE: The axle flange nut is staked in place. It will be necessary to loosen the staked part of the nut with a hammer and chisel, prior to loosening the nut.**

5. Using Toyota special service tool No. SST 09557-22022 (or its equivalent), disconnect the axle flange from the axle shaft. Be careful not to lose the plate washer from the bearing side of the flange.
6. Remove the parking brake shoes.
7. Using Toyota special service tool No. SST 09520-00031 (or its equivalent), pull out the rear axle shaft, along with the oil seal and outer bearing.

**Inspect the components:**

8. Clean and inspect the bearings, races, and seal. If these parts are in good condition, repack the bearings with MP grease No. 2 and proceed to Step 15 to install the axle shaft.

**To replace the bearings and seals:**

9. Using a hammer and chisel, increase the clearance between the axle shaft hub and the outer bearing.
10. Using a puller installed with the jaws in the gap made in Step 9, pull the outer bearing from the axle shaft and remove the oil seal.
11. Drive the outer bearing race out of the hub with a brass drift and a hammer.

**NOTE: Bearing and races must be replaced in matched sets. NEVER use a new bearing with an old race, or vice-versa.**

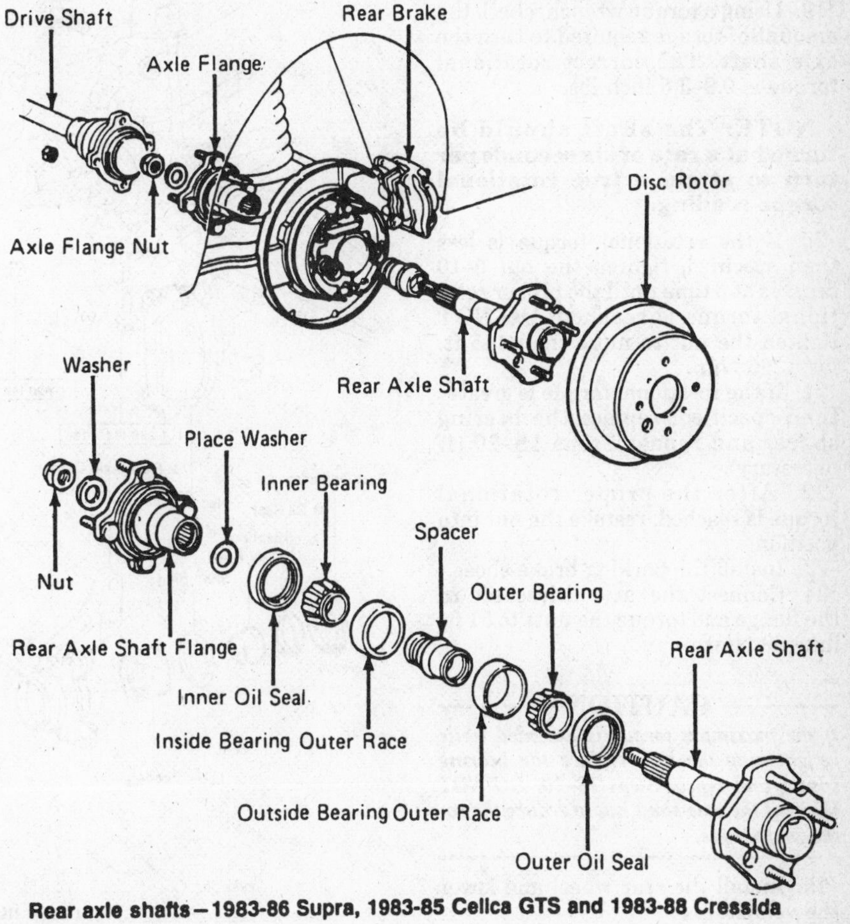


**Rear axle shafts–1983-86 Supra, 1983-85 Celica GTS and 1983-88 Cressida**

12. Drive the new outer bearing race into the axle shaft hub until it is completely seated.

**NOTE: The inner bearing race is replaced in the same manner as Steps 11 and 12.**

13. Repack and install both bearings into the hub, being careful not to mis the bearings.

**NOTE: The bearings should be packed with No.2 multipurpose grease.**

14. Drive the seals into place. The inner seal should be driven to a depth of 1.22 in.; the outer to 0.217 in.

**To install the rear axle shaft:**

15. Apply a thin coat of grease to the axle shaft flange. Install the rear axle shaft into the housing and install the flange with the plate washer.

16. Using Toyota special service tool No. SST 09557-22022 (or its equivalent), draw the axle shaft into the flange.

17. Remove the special service tool and install a new axle shaft flange nut. Torque the nut to 22–36 ft. lbs. There should be no horizontal play evident at the axle shaft.

18. Turn the axle shaft back and forth and retorque the nut to 58 ft. lbs. (78 Nm).

19. Using a torque wrench, check the amount of torque required to turn the axle shaft. The correct rotational torque is 0.9–3.5 inch lbs.

**NOTE: The shaft should be turned at a rate of six seconds per turn to attain a true rotational torque reading.**

20. If the rotational torque is less than specified, tighten the nut 5–10 degrees at a time until the proper rotational torque is reached. DO NOT tighten the nut to more than 145 ft. lbs. (196 Nm).

21. If the rotational torque is greater than specified, replace the bearing spacer and repeat Steps 18–20 (if necessary).

22. After the proper rotational torque is reached, restake the nut into position.

23. Install the parking brake shoes.

24. Connect the axle driveshaft to the flange and torque the nuts to 51 ft. lbs. (69 Nm).

**CAUTION**

***If the maximum torque is exceeded while retightening the nut, replace the bearing spacer and repeat Steps 18–20. DO NOT back off the axle shaft nut to reduce the rotational torque.***

25. Install the rear wheel and lower the vehicle.

**ALL OTHER MODELS**

Please refer to Rear Axle Hub, Carrier and Bearing in this section.

## Rear Axle Hub, Carrier And Bearing

### REMOVAL & INSTALLATION

#### *MR2*

1. Raise the rear of the vehicle and support it with jackstands.

2. Remove the rear wheel and tire assembly. Remove the cotter pin, bearing lock nut cap and bearing lock nut.

3. Disconnect the parking brake cable. Remove the disc brake caliper from the rear axle carrier and suspend it with wire. Remove the rotor disc (check the bearing play in axial direction – 0.0020 in. or less.

4. Disconnect the rear axle carrier from the lower arm. Remove the cotter pin and nut from the suspension arm.

5. Using a suitable tool separate the suspension arm from the rear axle carrier.

6. Place matchmarks on the strut lower bracket and camber adjusting cam.

7. Remove the 2 axle carrier set nuts and 2 bolts with the camber adjusting cam. Remove the rear axle carrier and axle hub.

8. Remove the dust deflector from the axle hub. Using a suitable puller remove the inner oil seal. Remove the hole snap ring.

9. Remove the 3 bolts holding the disc brake dust cover to the rear axle carrier. Using a suitable puller remove the axle hub from the rear axle carrier.

10. Remove the bearing inner (inside) race. Using a suitable puller remove the bearing inner race (outside) from the rear axle hub.

11. Using a suitable puller remove the outer oil seal.

12. Remove the hub bearing by first placing the removed inner race (oustide) in the bearing and using a suitable press, press out the bearing. Be sure to always replace the bearing as an assembly.

13. Installation is the reverse order of the removal procedure. Observe the following torques:

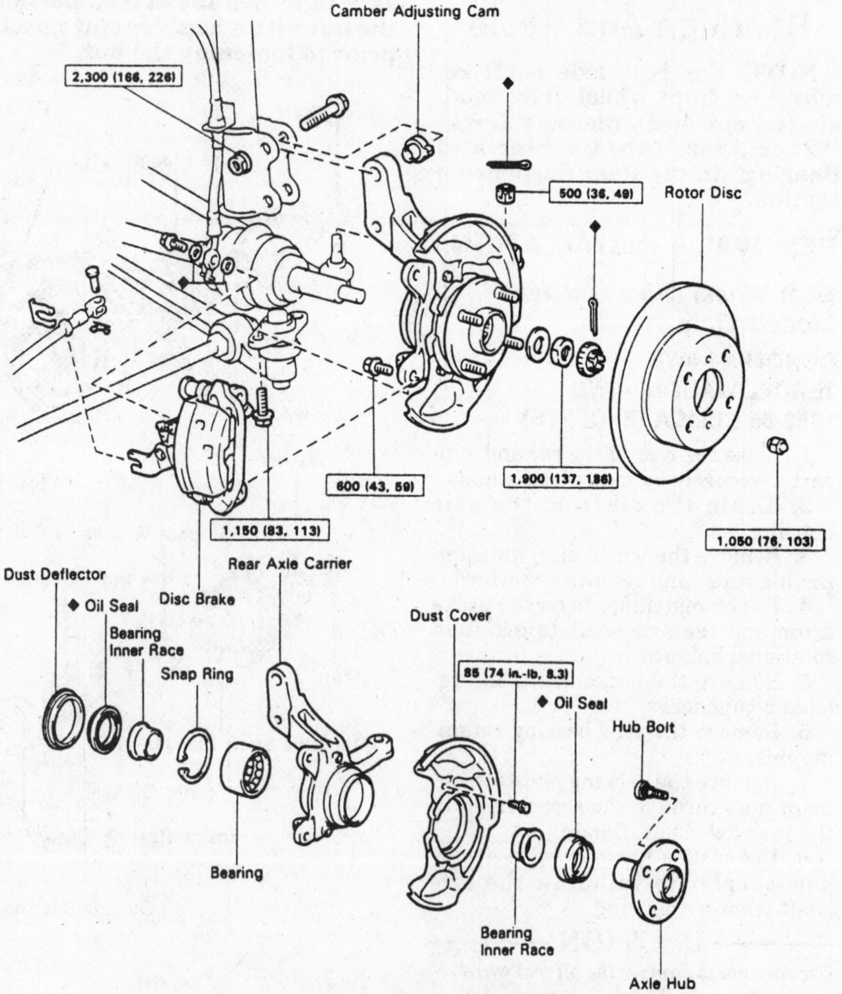


**Rear axle hub and carrier – MR2**

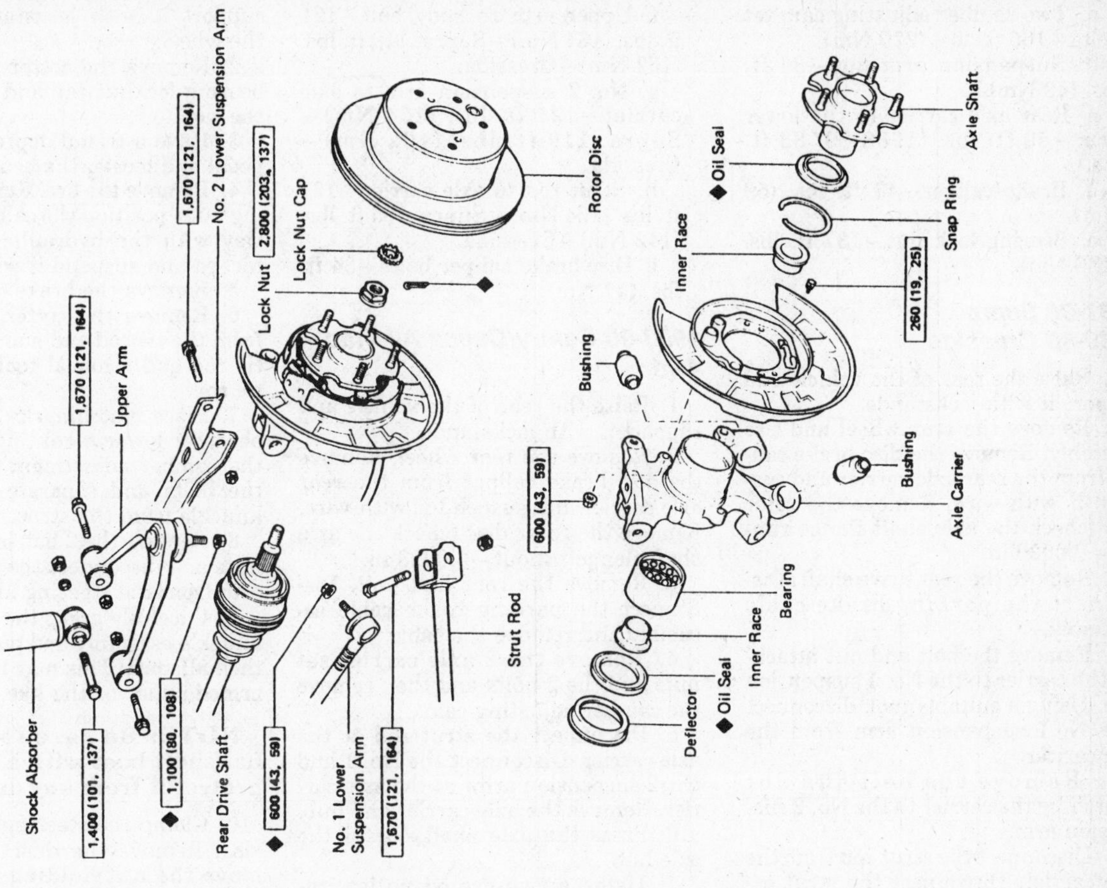


Rear axle hub and carrier—1987-90 Supra

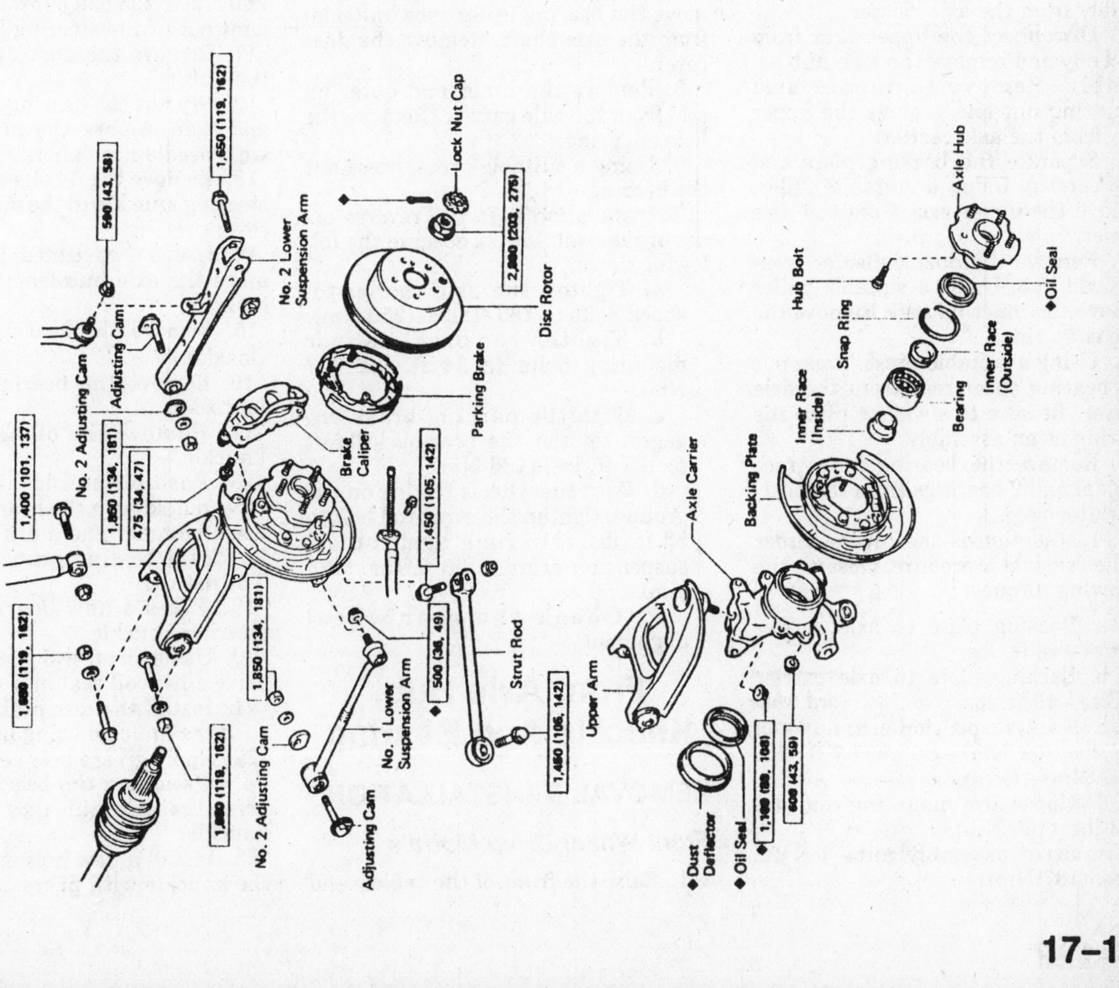


Rear axle, hub and bearing—1989-90 Cressida

a. Two camber adjusting cam set bolts – 166 ft. lbs. (226 Nm).

b. Suspension arm nut – 36 ft. lbs. (49 Nm).

c. Rear axle carrier to the lower arm – 59 ft. lbs. (1988-89: 83 ft. lbs.).

d. Brake caliper – 43 ft. lbs. (59 Nm).

e. Bearing lock nut – 137 ft. lbs. (186 Nm).

### 1987-90 Supra 1989-90 Cressida

1. Raise the rear of the vehicle and support it with jackstands.
2. Remove the rear wheel and tire assembly. Remove the disc brake caliper from the rear axle carrier and suspend it with wire. Remove the rotor disc (check the axle shaft flange runout – 0.0020 in.
3. Remove the rear drive shaft. Disconnect the parking brake cable assembly.
4. Remove the bolt and nut attaching the carrier to the No. 1 suspension arm. Using a suitable tool, disconnect gthe No.1 suspension arm from the axle carrier.
5. Remove the bolt and nut attaching the carrier to the No. 2 suspension arm.
6. Disconnect the strut rod from the axle carrier. Disconnect the strut assembly from the axle carrier.
7. Disconnect the upper arm from the body and remove the axle hub assembly. Remove the upper arm mounting nut and remove the upper arm from the axle carrier.
8. Separate the backing plate and axle carrier. Using a suitable puller, remove the upper arm from the axle carrier.
9. Remove the dust deflector from the axle hub. Using a suitable puller remove the inner oil seal. Remove the hole snap ring.
10. Using a suitable press, press out the bearing outer race from the axle carrier. Be sure to always replace the bearing as an assembly.
11. Remove the bearing inner race (inside) and 2 bearings from the bearing outer race.
12. Installation is the reverse order of the removal procedure. Observe the following torques:

a. Backing plate to axle carrier nuts – 43 ft. lbs.

b. Backing plate to axle carrier bolts – 19 ft. lbs.

c. No. 1 suspension arm nut – 43 ft. lbs. (59 Nm) – Supra. 36 ft. lbs. (49 Nm) – Cressida.

d. Upper arm mounting nut – 80 ft. lbs. (108 Nm).

e. Strut assembly nut – 101 ft. lbs. (137 Nm).

f. Upper arm to body bolt – 121 ft. lbs. (164 Nm) – Supra. 119 ft. lbs. (162 Nm) – Cressida.

g. No. 2 suspension arm to axle carrier – 121 ft. lbs. (164 Nm) – Supra. 119 ft. lbs. (162 Nm) – Cressida.

h. Strut rod to axle carrier – 121 ft. lbs. (164 Nm) – Supra. 105 ft. lbs. (142 Nm) – Cressida.

i. Disc brake caliper bolts – 34 ft. lbs. (47 Nm).

### 1988-90 Camry/Celica All-Trac – 4wd

1. Raise the rear of the vehicle and support it with jackstands.
2. Remove the rear wheel. Remove the disc brake caliper from the rear axle carrier and suspend it with wire. Remove the rotor disc (check the axle shaft flange runout – 0.0028 in.
3. Remove the rear halfshaft. Disconnect the parking brake cable assembly and remove the cable.
4. Remove the 2 axle carrier set nuts and the 2 bolts and then remove the camber adjusting cam.
5. Disconnect the strut rod at the axle carrier. Disconnect the No. 1 and No. 2 suspension arms at the axle carrier. Remove the axle carrier and hub.
6. Press the axle shaft out of the axle hub.
7. Using a two-armed puller, remove the bearing inner race (outside) from the axle shaft. Remove the dust cover.
8. Remove the inner and outer oil seal from the axle carrier. Remove the hole snapring.
9. Using a suitable press, press out the bearing.
10. Installation is in the reverse order of removal. Please observe the following notes:

a. Tighten the axle carrier-to-shock bolts to 188 ft. lbs. (255 Nm).

b. Tighten the brake caliper mounting bolts to 34 ft. lbs. (47 Nm).

c. With the parking brake engaged, tighten the bearing locknut to 137 ft. lbs. (186 Nm).

d. With the wheels resting on the ground, tighten the strut rod bolt to 83 ft. lbs. (113 Nm); tighten the 2 suspension arms to 90 ft. lbs. (123 Nm).

e. Check the rear wheel alignment.

# Front Axle Hub, Knuckle And Bearing

## REMOVAL & INSTALLATION

### Front Wheel Drive Models

1. Raise the front of the vehicle and support it with jackstands. Remove the wheel.
2. Remove the cotter pin from the bearing locknut cap and then remove the cap.
3. Have a friend depress the brake pedal and loosen the bearing locknut.
4. Remove the brake caliper mounting nuts, position the caliper out of the way with the hydraulic line still attached and suspend it with a wire.
5. Remove the brake disc.
6. Remove the cotter pin and nut from the tie rod end and then, using a tie rod end removal tool, remove the tie rod.
7. Place matchmarks on the shock absorber lower mounting bracket and the camber adjustment cam, remove the bolts and separate the steering knuckle from the strut.
8. Remove the 2 ball joint attaching nuts and disconnect the lower control arm from the steering knuckle.
9. Carefully grasp the axle hub and knuckle assembly and pull it out from the halfshaft. This may require a two-armed puller or the like.

**NOTE: Be sure to cover the halfshaft boot with a shop rag to protect it from any damage.**

10. Clamp the steering knuckle in a vise. Remove the dust deflector. remove the nut holding the steering knuckle to the ball joint. Press the ball joint out of the steering knuckle.
11. Remove the dust deflector from the hub.
12. Pry out the bearing inner oil seal and then remove the hole snap ring with needle-nose pliers.
13. Remove the 3 bolts attaching the steering knuckle to the disc brake dust cover.
14. Use a two-armed puller to remove the axle hub from the steering knuckle.
15. Remove the bearing inner race (inside).
16. Remove the bearing inner race (outside).
17. Remove the oil seal from the knuckle.
18. Position an old bearing inner race (outside) on the bearing and then use a hammer and a drift to carefully knock the bearing out of the knuckle.

**To install:**

19. Press a new bearing into the steering knuckle.
20. Using an oil seal installation tool, drive a new oil seal into the knuckle.
21. Install the disc brake dust cover onto the knuckle using liquid sealant.
22. Apply grease between the oil seal lip, oil seal and the bearing and then press the axle hub into the steering knuckle.
23. Install a new hole snap ring into the knuckle with pliers.

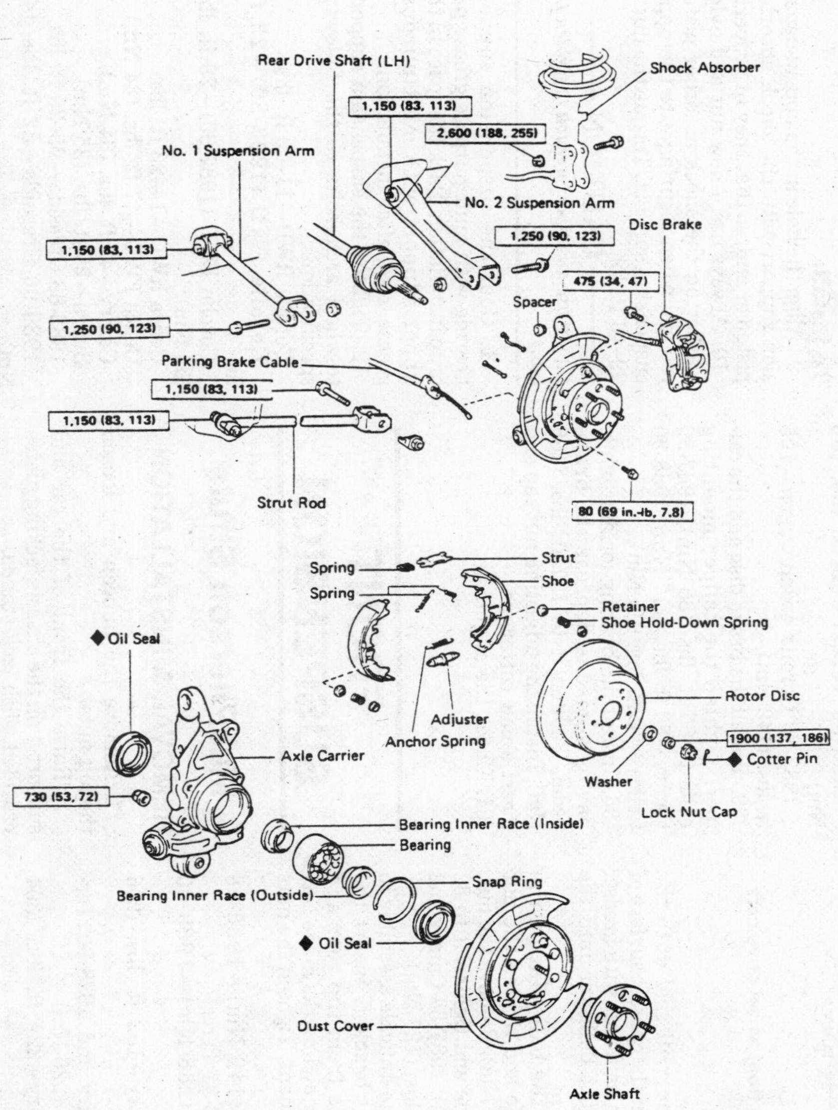


Rear axle hub and carrier—Camry/Celica All-Trac (4wd)

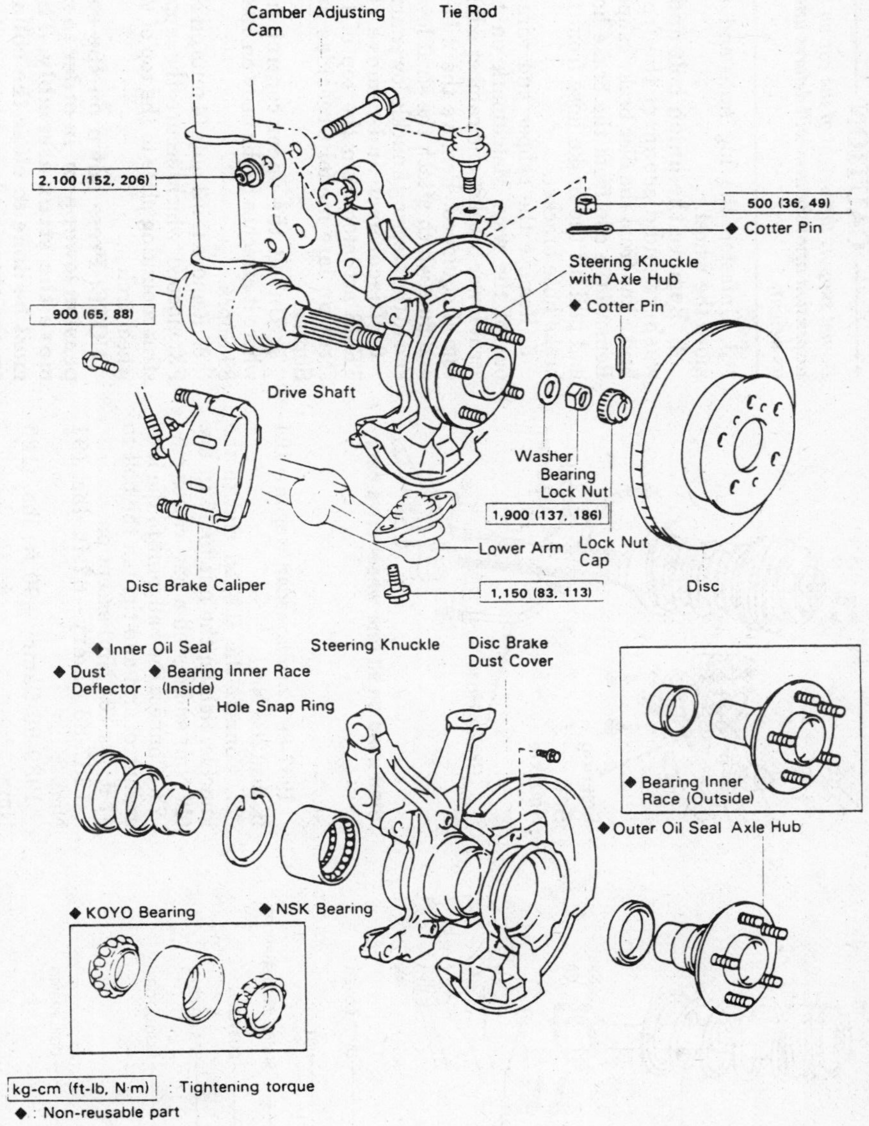


Front axle hub and steering knuckle assembly—front wheel drive models

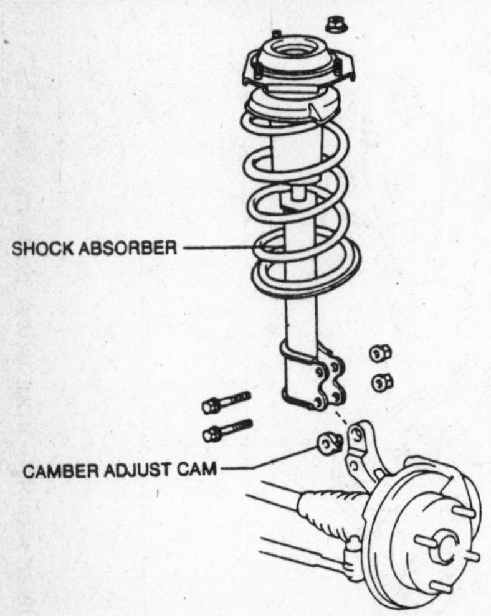


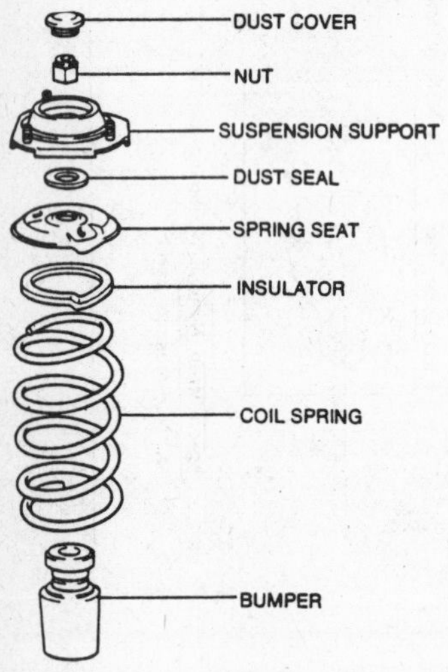


**Strut used on all front wheel drive cars**

24. Press a new oil seal onto the knuckle and coat the contact surface of the seal and the halfshaft with grease. Press a new dust deflector into the knuckle.

25. Position the ball joint on the steering knuckle and tighten the nut to 14 ft. lbs. (20 Nm). Remove the nut, install a new one and tighten it to 82 ft. lbs. (111 Nm). 1987-88 Camry and Corolla – 94 ft. lbs. (127 Nm).

26. Connect the knuckle assembly to the lower strut bracket. Insert the mounting bolts from the rear and make sure the matchmarks made earlier are in alignment. Tighten the nuts to:

105 ft. lbs. (142 Nm) – 1986-88 Celica and 1983-87 Tercel

188 ft. lbs. (255 Nm) – 1989-90 Celica

1983-86 Camry – 152 ft. lbs. (206 Nm)

1987-88 Camry and 1988-90 Tercel – 166 ft. lbs. (226 Nm)

1989-90 Camry – 224 ft. lbs. (304 Nm)

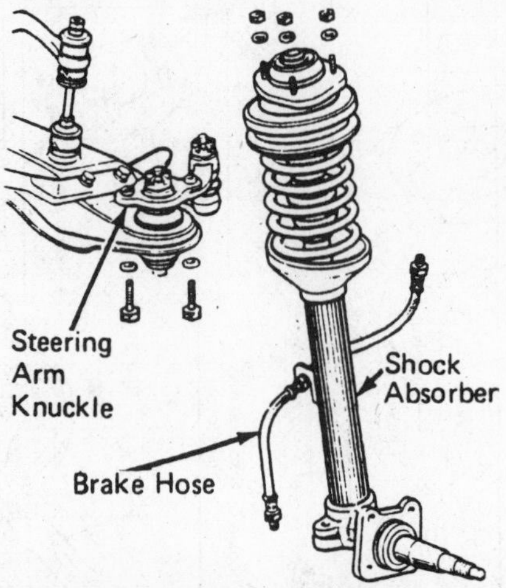


**Strut used on all rear wheel drive cars**

1987-89 Corolla sedan/wagon – 194 ft. lbs (263 Nm).

27. Connect the tie rod end to the knuckle, tighten the nut to 36 ft. lbs. (49 Nm) and install a new cotter pin.

28. Connect the ball joint to the lower control arm and tighten the bolt to 47 ft. lbs. (64 Nm) except on:

1987-88 Camry – 67 ft. lbs. (91 Nm)

1989-90 Camry – 90 ft. lbs. (123 Nm)

1988-90 Celica – 94 ft. lbs. (122 Nm)

1988-90 Tercel – 59 ft. lbs. (80 Nm)

1987-89 Corolla sedan/wagon – 105 ft. lbs. (142 Nm).

29. Install the brake disc and the caliper. Tighten the caliper mounting bolts to 65 ft. lbs. (88 Nm). 1987-90 Camry – 86 ft. lbs. (117 Nm). 1988-90 Celica – 70 ft. lbs. (95 Nm).

30. Install the bearing locknut while having someone depress the brake pedal. Tighten it to 137 ft. lbs. (186 Nm). Install the adjusting nut cap and insert a new cotter pin.

31. Check the alignment.

# FRONT SUSPENSION

## MacPherson Struts

### REMOVAL & INSTALLATION

1. Remove the hubcap and loosen the lug nuts.

2. Raise the front of the car and support it on the chassis jacking plates provided, with jack stands.

**CAUTION**

***Do not support the weight of the car on the suspension arm; the arm will deform under its weight.***

3. Unfasten the lug nuts and remove the wheel.

4. Remove the union bolt and 2 washers and disconnect the front brake line from the disc brake caliper. Remove the clip from the brake hose and pull off the brake hose from the brake hose bracket.

5. Remove the caliper and wire it out of the way. Matchmark on the strut lower bracket and camber adjust cam if equipped. Remove the 2 bolts and nuts which attach the strut lower end to the steering knuckle lower arm.

6. Disconnect and remove the TEMS actuator from the top of the strut on late model Cressidas and Supras.

7. Unbolt the upper control arm where it attaches to the body on 1987-89 Supra.

8. Remove the 3 nuts (4 nuts on the FX models) which secure the upper strut mounting plate to the top of the wheel arch.

**NOTE: Press down on the suspension lower arm, in order to remove the strut assembly. This must be done to clear the collars on the steering knuckle arm bolt holes when removing the shock/spring assembly.**

**To install:**

9. Align the hole in the upper suspension support with the shock absorber piston or end, so that they fit properly.

10. Always use a new nut and nylon washer on the shock absorber piston rod end when securing it to the upper suspension support. Torque the nut to 29–40 ft. lbs.

**CAUTION**

***Do not use an impact wrench to tighten the nut.***

11. Coat the suspension support bearing with multipurpose grease prior to installation. Pack the space in the upper support with multipurpose grease, also, after installation.

12. Tighten the suspension support-to-wheel arch bolts to the following specifications:

Corolla RWD – 11-16 ft. lbs.

Corolla FWD (1983-86) – 23 ft. lbs.

Corolla FWD (1987-90) – 29 ft. lbs. (39 Nm).

Celica RWD – 14–23 ft. lbs.

Celica FWD – 47 ft. lbs. (64 Nm).

Camry – 47 ft. lbs. (64 Nm).

Supra – 26 ft. lbs. (35 Nm).

1983-88 Cressida – 25–29 ft. lbs.

1989-90 Cressida – 32 ft. lbs. (43 Nm).

1983-87 Tercel – 11–15 ft. lbs.
1988-90 Tercel – 20–25 ft. lbs.
MR2 – 21–25 ft. lbs.

13. Tighten the shock absorber-to-steering knuckle arm bolts to the following specifications:

Corolla (RWD) – 50–65 ft. lbs.
Corolla (FWD) – Gas 105 ft. lbs.; Diesel 152 ft. lbs.; 1988-90 sedan/wagon 194 ft. lbs. (263 Nm).
1983-87 Tercel – 105 ft. lbs.
1988-90 Tercel Sedan – 166 ft. lbs.
1985-88 MR2 – 105 ft. lbs.
1989-90 MR2 – 119 ft. lbs.
1983-86 Supra – 72 ft. lbs.
1987-90 Supra – 106 ft. lbs.
Celica RWD – 72 ft. lbs.
1986-88 Celica FWD – 152 ft. lbs.
1989-90 Celica FWD – 188 ft. lbs.
Cressida – 80 ft. lbs.
1987-88 Camry – 166 ft. lbs.
1989-90 Camry – 224 ft. lbs. (304 Nm).
All others – 65 ft. lbs.

14. Adjust the front wheel bearing preload.

15. Bleed the brake system.

### OVERHAUL

**For all spring and shock absorber removal and installation procedures, and all strut overhaul procedures, please refer to "Strut Overhaul" in the Unit Repair section.**

## Lower Control Arm/ Ball Joints

### INSPECTION

#### *Corolla (RWD), Cressida and Starlet*

Raise the front end and position a piece of wood under the wheel and lower the car until there is an ½ load on the strut. Check the front wheel play. Replace the lower ball joint if the play at the wheel rim exceeds 0.1 in. vertical motion or 0.25 in. horizontal motion. be sure that the dust covers are not torn and that they are securely glued to the ball joints.

**CAUTION**

***Do not jack up the control arm on Corolla or Cressida models; damage to the arm will result.***

#### *Tercel, Camry, Corolla (FWD) and Celica/Supra*

1. Jack up the vehicle and place wooden blocks under the front wheels. The block height should be 7.09–7.87 inches.

2. Use jack stands for additional safety.

3. Make sure the front wheels are in a straight forward position.

4. Check the wheels.

5. Lower the jack until there is approximately half a load on the front springs.

6. Move the lower control arm up and down to check that there is no ball joint play.

### REMOVAL & INSTALLATION

**NOTE: On models equipped with both upper and lower ball joints – if both ball joints are to be removed, always remove the lower and then the upper ball joint.**

#### *Corolla (RWD) and Starlet*

The ball joint and control arm cannot be separated from each other. If one fails, then both must be replaced as an assembly, in the following manner:

1. Peform Steps 1–7 of the first "Front Spring Removal and Installation" procedure. Skip Step 6.

2. Remove the stabilizer bar securing bolts.

3. Unfasten the torque strut mounting bolts.

4. Remove the control arm mounting bolt and detach the arm from the front suspension member.

5. Remove the steering knuckle arm from the control arm with a ball joint puller.

Inspect the suspension components, which were removed for wear or damage. Replace any parts, as required. **Installation is the reverse of removal. Note the following, however:**

6. When installing the control arm on the suspension member, tighten the bolts partially at first.

7. Complete the assembly procedure and lower the car to the ground.

8. Bounce the front of the car several times. Allow the suspension to settle, then tighten the lower control arm bolts to 51–65 ft. lbs.

**CAUTION**

***Use only the bolt which was designed to fit the lower control arm. If a replacement is necessary, see an authorized dealer for the proper part.***

9. Remember to lubricate the ball joint. Check the front end alignment.

#### *1983-85 Celica (RWD)*

1. Raise the car and support it with jack stands.

**CAUTION**

***Do not jack up your car on the lower control arms.***

2. Remove the front wheels.

3. Remove the tie rod end.

4. Remove the stabilizer bar end.

5. Remove the strut bar end.

6. Place a jack under the lower control arm for support.

7. Remove the bolt from the bottom of the steering knuckle.

8. Remove the bolt from the lower control arm.

9. Remove the control arm.

**NOTE: The lower ball joint cannot be separated from the lower control arm. It must be replaced as a complete unit.**

10. The following torques are required:

Bottom steering knuckle nut 40–52 ft. lbs.; stabilizer bar 11–15 ft. lbs.; tie rod end 37–50 ft. lbs.; strut bar 29–39 ft. lbs.; lower control arm 51–65 ft. lbs.

#### *1986-90 Celica (FWD)*

1. Raise the front of the vehicle and support it with jack stands. Remove the wheel.

2. Remove the bolt and 2 nuts and disconnect the lower control arm from the steering knuckle.

3. Remove the nut and disconnect the stabilizer bar from the control arm.

4. On all but the left-side control arm on models with automatic transmissions, remove the control arm front set nut and washer. Remove the rear bracket bolts and then remove the arm.

5. On the left arm on models with automatic transmissions, remove the control arm front set nut and washer. Remove the 4 bolts and 2 nuts that attach the lower suspension crossmember to the frame and remove the crossmember. Remove the bolt and nut and lift out the lower arm with the lower arm shaft.

**To install:**

6. On all but the left-side control arm on models with automatic transmissions, install the lower control arm shaft washer with the tapered side toward the body. Install the lower arm with the bracket and then temporarily install the washer and nut to the lower arm shaft and bracket bolts.

7. On the left-side arm on models with automatic transmissions, position the washer on the lower arm shaft and then install them to the lower arm. Temporarily install the washer and nut to the shaft with the tapered side toward the body. Install the lower arm with the shaft to the body and temporarily install the rear brackets. Install the bolt and nut to the lower arm shaft and tighten them to 154 ft. lbs. (208 Nm). Install the crossmember to the body and tighten the 4 bolts to 154 ft. lbs. (208 Nm). Tighten the 2 nuts to 29 ft. lbs. (39 Nm).

8. Connect the lower arm to the steering knuckle and tighten the bolt and two nuts to 94 ft. lbs. (127 Nm).
9. Connect the stabilizer bar to the control arm and tighten the nut to 26 ft. lbs. (35 Nm).
10. Install the wheel, lower the vehicle and bounce it several times to set the suspension.
11. Tighten the front set nut to 156 ft. lbs. (212 Nm). Tighten the rear bracket bolts to 72 ft. lbs. (98 Nm).

### MR2

1. Raise the front of the vehicle and support it with jackstands. Remove the wheel.
2. Remove the cotter pin and castle nut and then press the lower arm out of the ball joint.
3. Press the ball joint out of the steering knuckle.
4. Remove the 2 nuts and disconnect the strut bar from the control arm.
5. Remove the lower control arm-to-body bolt and remove the arm.
6. When installing the lower arm, position it in the strut bar and tighten the nuts fingertight. Do the same thing with the arm-to-body bolt.
7. Connect the control arm to the ball joint and tighten the castle nut to 58 ft. lbs. (78 Nm). Install a new cotter pin.
8. Tighten the strut bar-to-arm bolts to 83 ft. lbs. (113 Nm).
9. Install the tires, lower the car and bounce it several times to set the suspension.
10. Tighten the control arm-to-body bolt to 94 ft. lbs. (127 Nm) and check the wheel alignment.

### 1983-86 Supra
### 1983-90 Cressida

1. Raise the front of the vehicle and support it on jackstands. Remove the wheel.
2. Remove the 2 knuckle arm-to-strut bolts, pull down on the control arm and disconnect it and the knuckle arm from the strut.
3. Remove the cotter pin and nut and press the tie rod off the knuckle arm.
4. Remove the nut attaching the stabilizer bar to the control arm and disconnect the bar.
5. Remove the 2 nuts and then disconnect the strut bar from the control arm.
6. Disconnect the control arm from the crossmember and remove it and the rack boot protector as an assembly.
7. Remove the cotter pin and nut and then press the knuckle arm off the control arm.

**To install:**

8. Press the knuckle arm into the control arm and then install the assembly into the crossmember.
9. Connect the stabilizer bar to the control arm and tighten the nut to 13 ft. lbs. (18 Nm).
10. Connect the strut bar to the control arm and tighten the nuts to 48 ft. lbs. (60 Nm)–1983-87; 54 ft. lbs. (73 Nm)–1988; 76 ft. lbs. (103 Nm)–1989-90.
11. Connect the knuckle arm to the strut housing and tighten the bolts to 72 ft. lbs. (98 Nm)–1983-87; 80 ft. lbs. (108 Nm)–1988-90.
12. Install the wheel and lower the vehicle. Bounce the car several times to set the suspension and then tighten the control arm-to-body bolt to 80 ft. lbs. (108 Nm)–1983-88; 121 ft. lbs. (164 Nm)–1989-90.
13. Check the front wheel alignment.

### 1987-90 Supra

**NOTE: This procedure is for ball joint removal only. To remove the lower control arm, please refer to the Lower Control Arm procedure.**

1. Raise the front of the vehicle and support it with safety stands.
2. Remove the wheel.
3. Remove the steering knuckle and then remove the upper control arm.
4. Remove the lower ball joint mounting nuts and the bolt. Remove the attachment plate.
5. Remove the lower ball joint.
6. Installation is in the reverse order of removal. Tighten the ball joint mounting bolt and nuts to 94 ft. lbs. (127 Nm).

### 1983-90 Tercel
### 1983-86 Camry
### 1983-86 Corolla (FWD)

1. Raise the front of the vehicle and support it with jackstands. Remove the wheel.
2. Remove the 2 bolts attaching the ball joint to the steering knuckle.
3. Remove the stabilizer bar nut, retainer and cushion.
4. Jack up the opposite wheel until the body of the car just lifts off the jackstand.
5. Loosen the lower control arm mounting bolt, wiggle the arm back and forth and then remove the bolt. Disconnect the lower control arm from the stabilizer bar.

**NOTE: When removing the lower control arm (on the Tercel), be careful not to lose the caster adjustment spacer.**

6. On the Tercel and Camry, carefully mount the lower control arm in a vise and then, using a ball joint removal tool, disconnect the ball joint from the arm.

**To install:**

7. Tighten the ball joint-to-control arm nut to 51–65 ft. lbs. and use a new cotter pin (Tercel) and 67 ft. lbs. (Camry).
8. Tighten the steering knuckle-to-control arm bolts to 59 ft. lbs. on the Tercel; 47 ft. lbs. on the Corolla and 83 ft. lbs. on the Camry.
9. Tighten the stabilizer bar bolt to 13 ft. lbs. on the Corolla.
10. Before tightening the stabilizer bar nuts, on the Tercel and Camry, or the control arm bracket bolts on the Corolla, mount the wheels and lower the car. Bounce the car several times to settle the suspension and then tighten the stabilizer bolts on the Tercel and Camry to 66–90 ft. lbs.
11. Tighten the arm-to-body bolts on the Tercel and Camry to 83 ft. lbs. On the Corolla, tighten the front arm bolts to 83 ft. lbs. and the rear bolts to 64 ft. lbs.
12. Check the front end alignment.

### 1987-90 Corolla (FWD)

1. On all models except the left side on those with AT:
   a. Remove the bolt and 2 nuts attaching the ball joint to the lower arm and disconnect the lower arm from the steering knuckle.
   b. On models with the 4A-F or 4A-FE, remove the nut holding the stabilizer bar to the lower arm and disconnect the bar from the arm.
   c. On models with the 4A-GE, remove the lower nut on the stabilizer bar link and disconnect the link from the arm.
   d. Remove the rear bracket bolts and nut. Remove the lower arm front mounting bolt.
   e. Remove the rear bracket and the stabilizer bar bracket and lift out the lower control arm.
2. To remove the left control arm on models with AT:
   a. Disconnect the arm at the steering knuckle.
   b. Disconnect the stabilizer bar at the lower arm.
   c. Remove the lower arm rear brackets. Move the stabilizer bar toward the rear and remove the bracket.
   d. Remove the 6 bolts and 2 nuts and remove the suspension crossmember with the lower arm.
   e. Remove the lower arm from the crossmember.
3. To install the left control arm on models with AT, install the lower arm on the crossmember and install the assembly to the body.
4. On all others, install the lower

arm to the body, move the stabilizer bar into position and install the front mounting bolt. Install the stabilizer bar and rear brackets.

5. Connetc the lower arm to the steering knuckle and tighten the bolts to 105 ft. lbs. (142 Nm).

6. On models with the 4A-F, connect the stabilizer bar to the lower arm and tighten the nut to 13 ft. lbs. (18 Nm).

7. On models with the 4A-GE, connect the stabilizer bar link to the lower arm and tighten the nut to 26 ft. lbs. (35 Nm).

8. Lower the vehicle and bounce it several times to stabilize the suspension. Tighten the lower arm front bolt to 174 ft. lbs. (235 Nm)—1987-88; 152 ft. lbs. (206 Nm)—1989-90. Tighten the rear bracket bolts to 94 ft. lbs. (127 Nm) on the lower arm side; 37 ft. lbs. (50 Nm) on the stabilizer bar side; tighten the small bolt and nut to 14 ft. lbs. (19 Nm).

9. Check the front end alignment.

### *1987-90 Camry*

1. Raise the front of the vehicle and support it with jackstands. Remove the wheel.

2. Remove the 2 bolts attaching the ball joint to the steering knuckle.

3. Remove the stabilizer bar nut, retainer and cushion.

4. Remove the nut attaching the lower arm shaft to the lower arm.

5. Remove the lower suspension crossmember (2 bolts and 4 nuts).

6. Remove the lower control arm and lower arm shaft as an assembly.

7. Grip the lower arm assembly in a vise and remove the ball joint cotter pin and retaining nut. With a ball joint removal tool, pull the ball joint out of the control arm.

**To install:**

8. Position the ball joint in the lower arm and tighten the nut to 67 ft. lbs. (91 Nm)—1987-88; 90 ft. lbs. (123 Nm)—1989-90. Install a new cotter pin.

9. Install the lower arm to the stabilizer bar and then install the lower arm shaft to the body. Install the lower arm nut and retainer. Screw on a new stabilizer bar end nut and retainer.

10. Conect the ball joint to the steering knuckle and tighten the bolts to 94 ft. lbs. (127 Nm)—1987-88; 83 ft. lbs. (113 Nm)—1989-90.

11. Install the suspension lower crossmember. Tighten the inner bolts to 32 ft. lbs. (43 Nm) and the outer ones to 153 ft. lbs. (207 Nm).

12. Install the wheels and lower the car. Bounce it several times to set the suspension.

13. Tighte the stabilizer bar end nut and the lower arm shaft-to-lower arm bolt to 156 ft. lbs. (212 Nm).

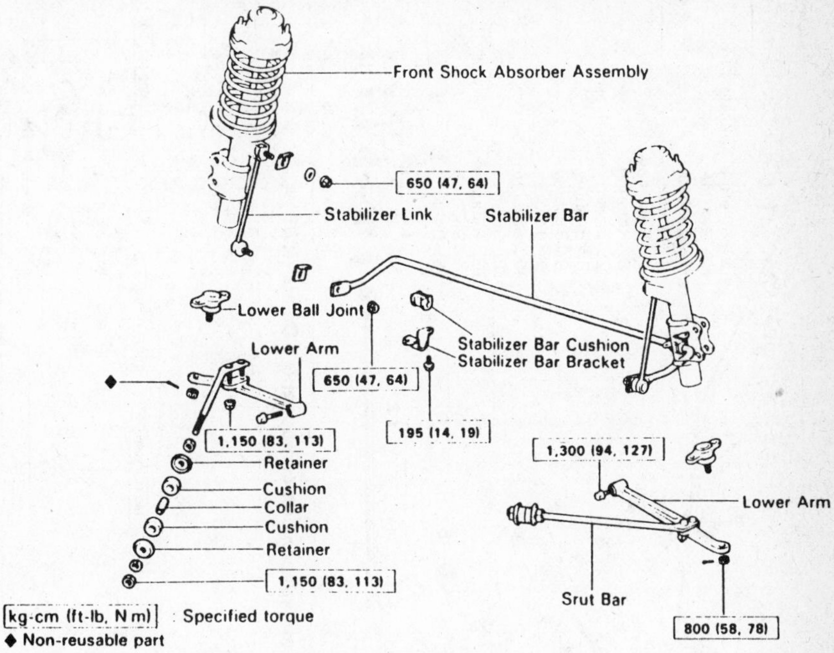


Front suspension components—MR2

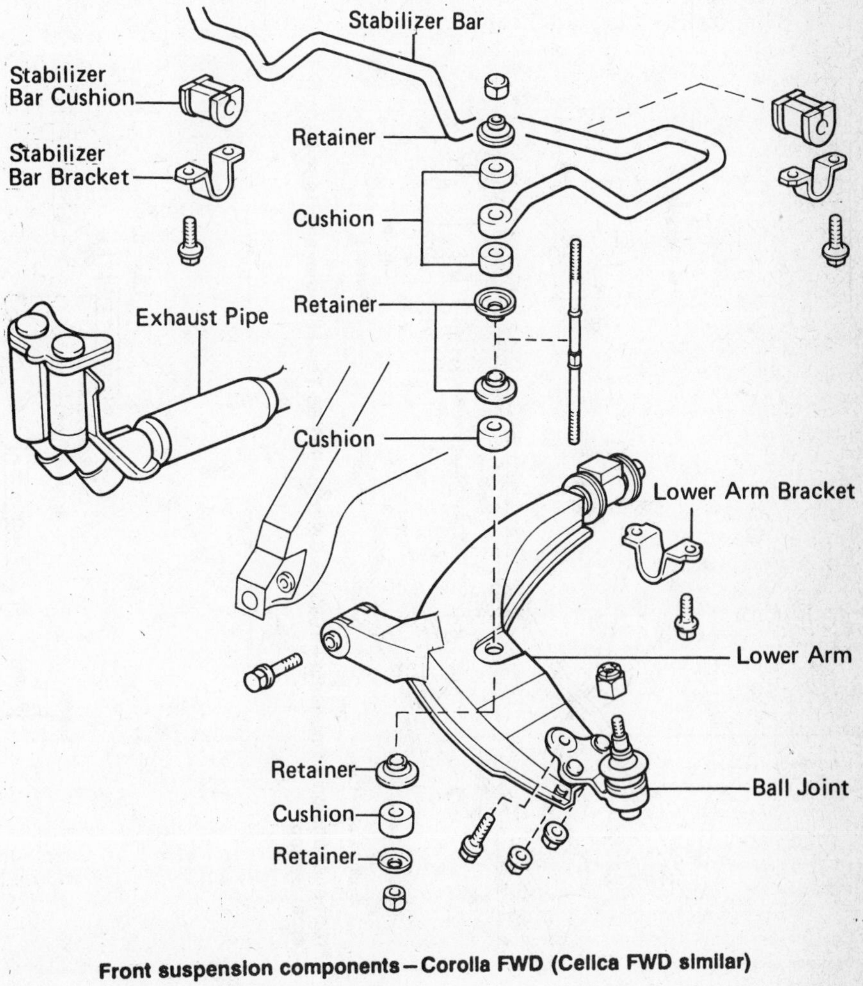


Front suspension components—Corolla FWD (Celica FWD similar)

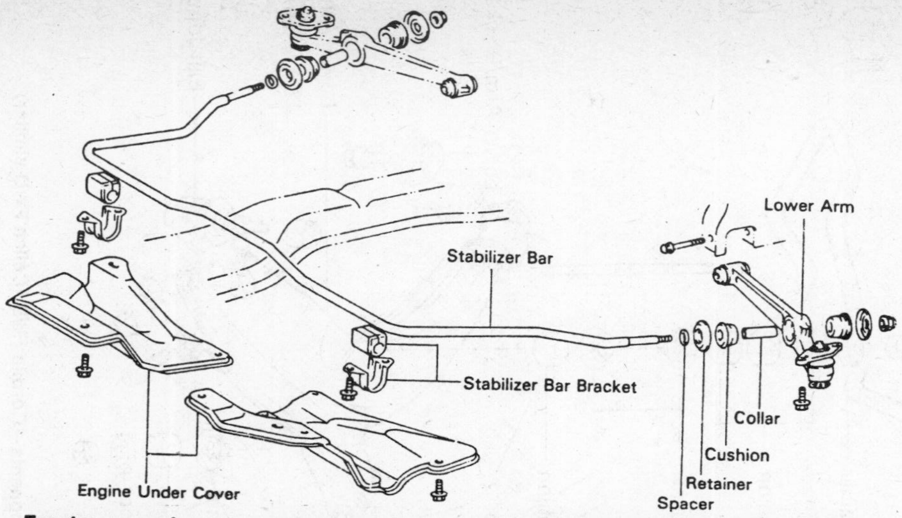


**Front suspension comonents—1983-86 Camry, 1983-86 Tercel sedan and 1986-88 Tercel wagon**

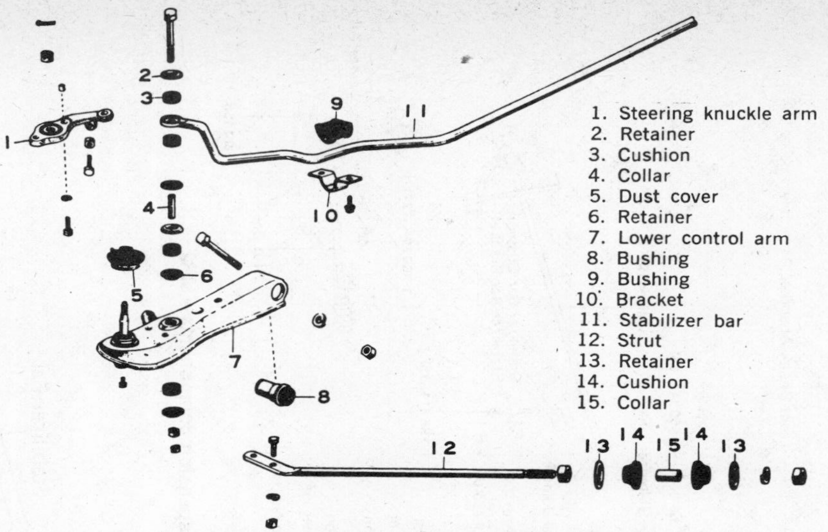


**Front suspension components—Celica (RWD)**

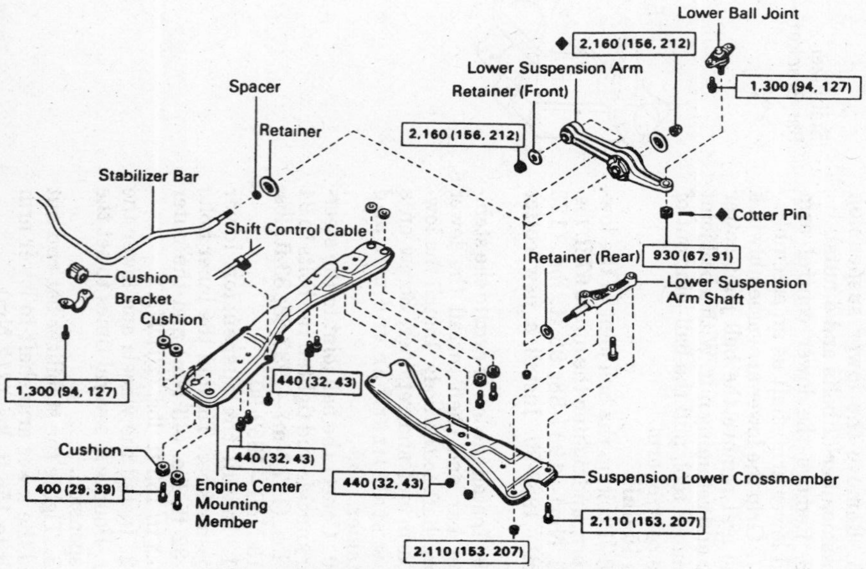


**Front suspension components—1987-90 Camry**

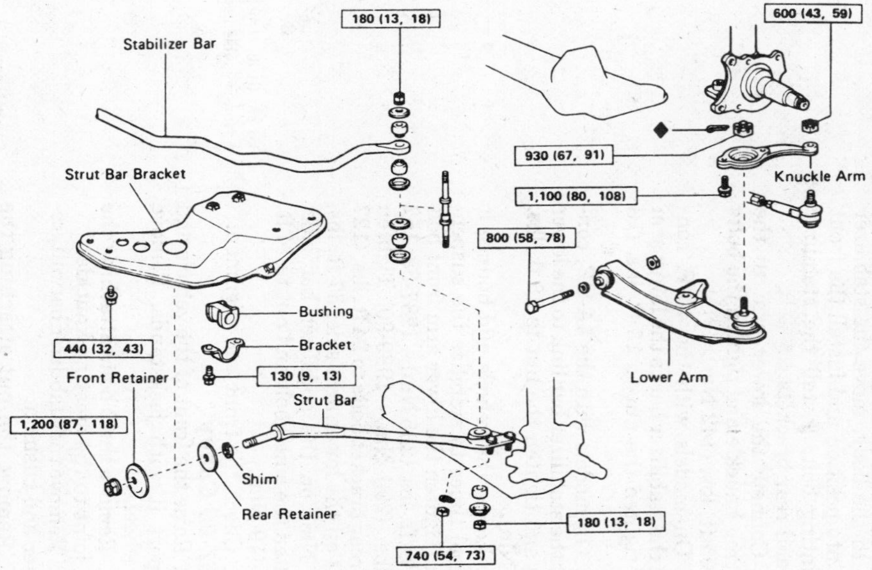


**Front suspension components—1983-88 Cressida**

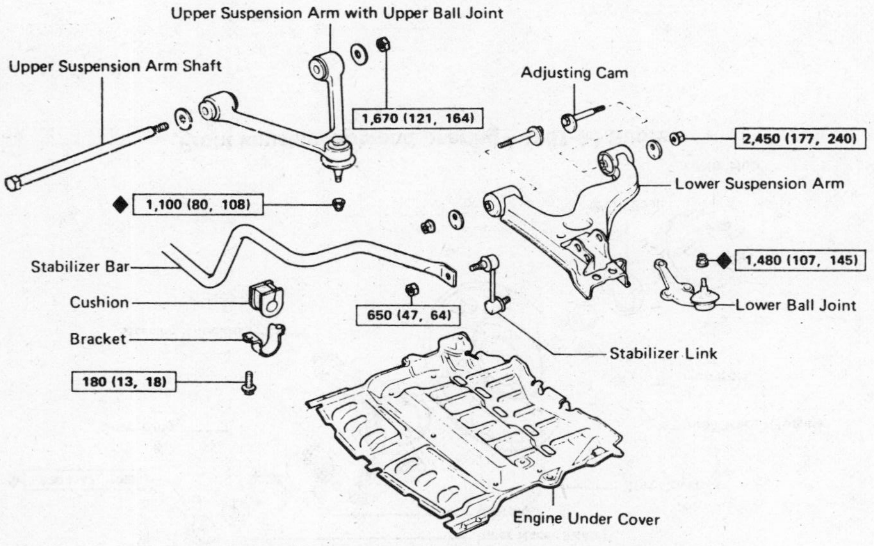


Front suspension components – 1987-90 Supra

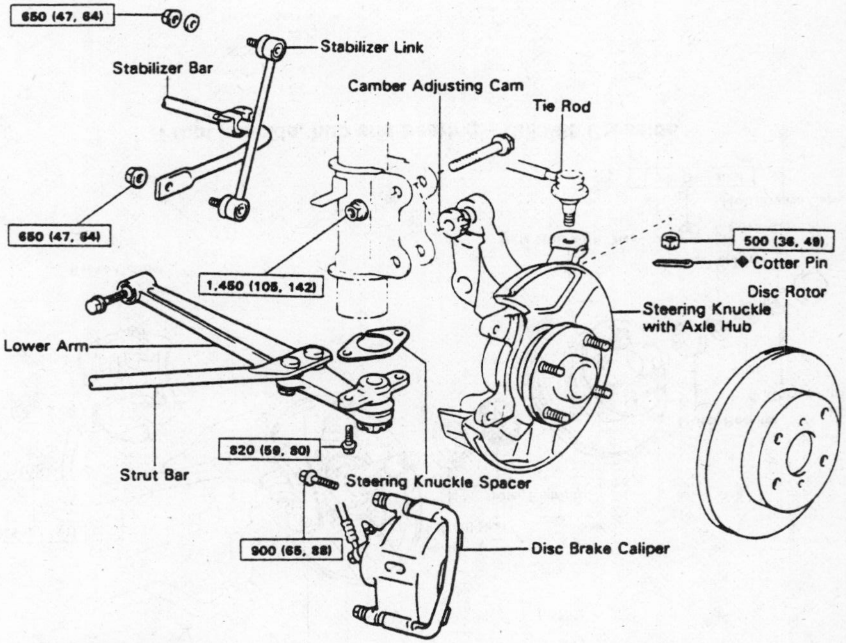


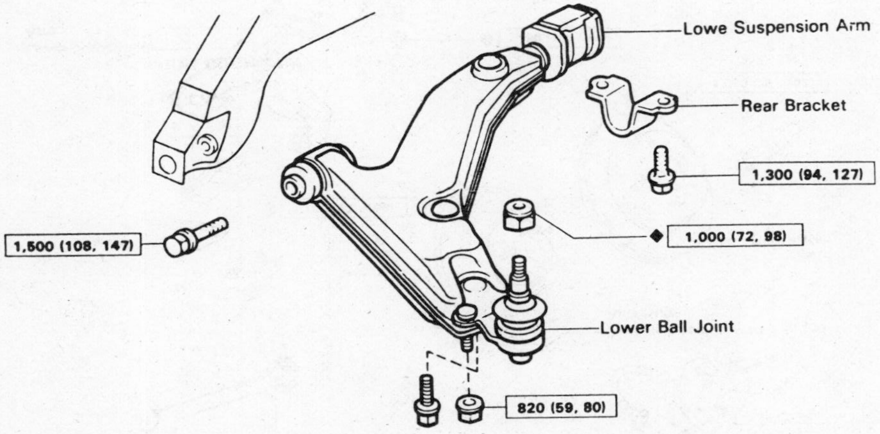


Front suspension components – 1987-90 Tercel sedan

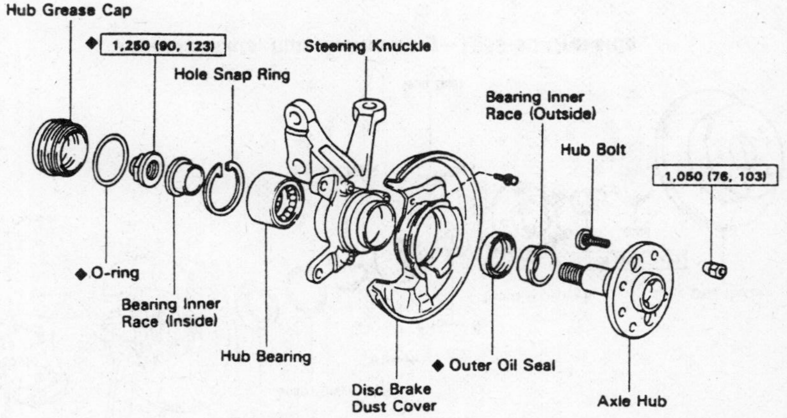


Front knuckle, hub and bearing – MR2

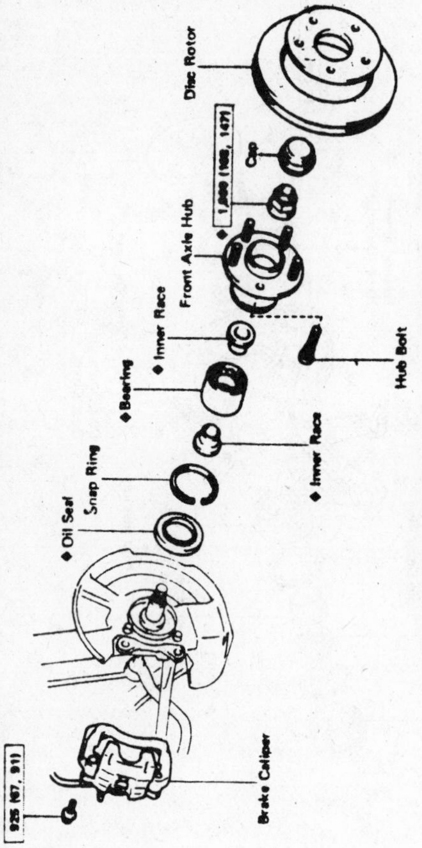


Front knuckle, hub and bearing – 1989-90 Cressida

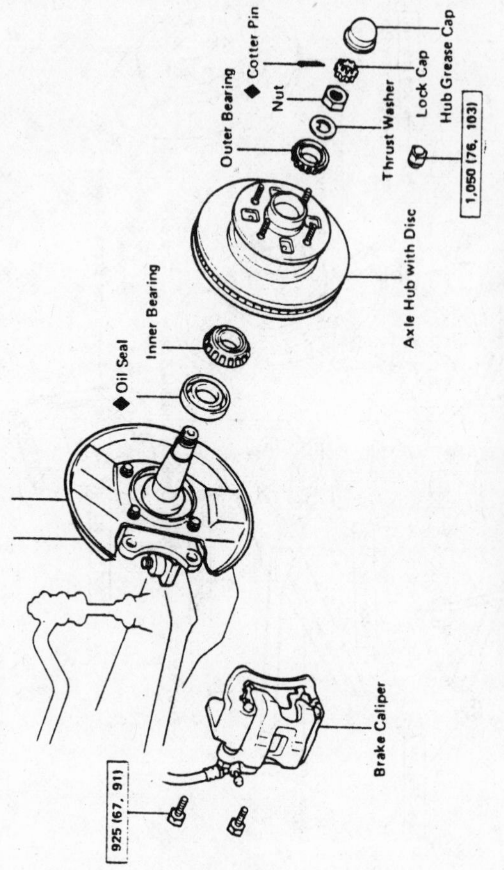


Front knuckle, hub and bearing – 1983-88 Cressida

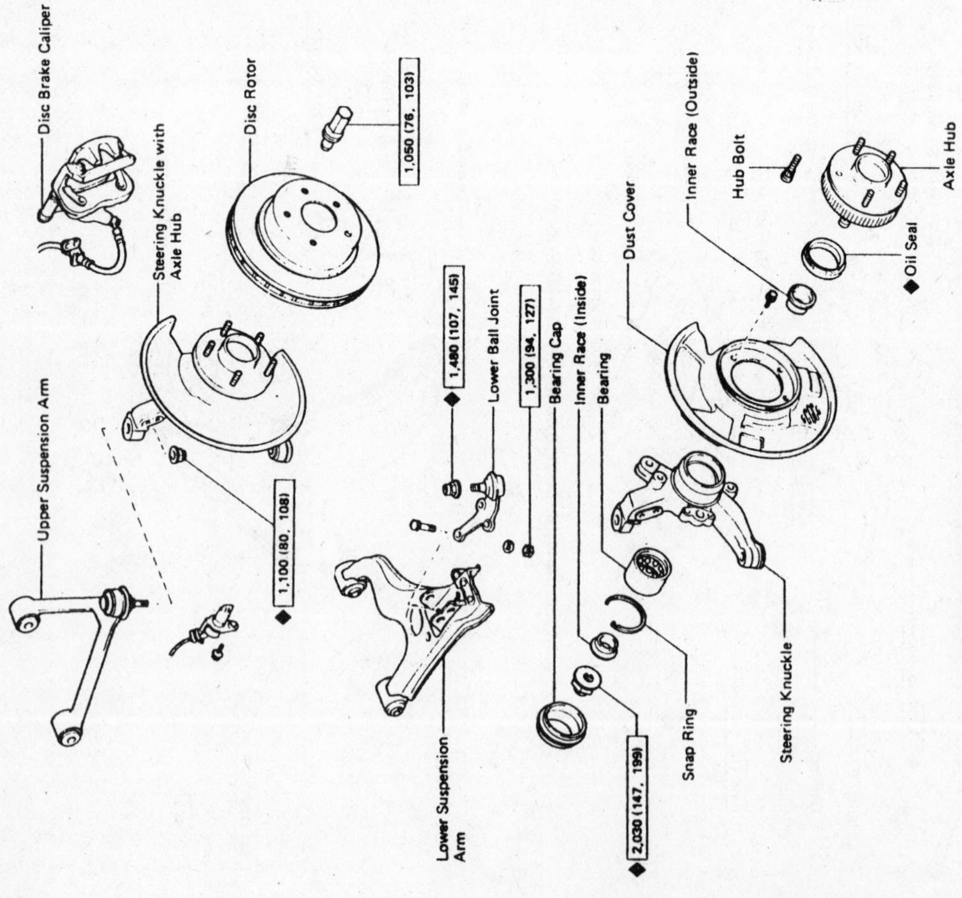


Front knuckle, hub and bearing – 1987-90 Supra

## Upper Ball Joint

### INSPECTION

Disconnect the ball joint from the steering knuckle and check free-play by hand. Replace the ball joint, if it is noticeably loose.

### REMOVAL & INSTALLATION

**NOTE: On models equipped with both upper and lower ball joints—if both are to be removed, always remove the lower one first.**

#### *1987-90 Supra*

On these models, the ball joint is an integral component of the upper control arm. Ball joint replacement requires that the entire arm assembly be replaced. Please refer to Upper Control Arm.

## Lower Control Arm

### REMOVAL & INSTALLATION

#### *Corolla (RWD) and Starlet*

1. Raise and support the front end.
2. Remove the wheel.
3. Disconnect the steering knuckle from the control arm.
4. Disconnect the tie rod, stabilizer bar and strut bar from the control arm.
5. Remove the control arm mounting bolts, and remove the arm.
6. Install in reverse of above. Tighten, but do not torque fasteners until car is on the ground.
7. Lower car to ground, rock it from side-to-side several times and torque control arm mounting bolts to 51–65 ft. lbs., stabilizer bar to 16 ft. lbs., strut bar to 40 ft. lbs., and shock absorber to 65 ft. lbs.

#### *1987-90 Supra*

1. Raise the front of the vehicle and support it with safety stands. Remove the wheels.
2. Disconnect the stabilizer bar link from the lower control arm. Remove the locknut and press the ball joint out of the steering knuckle.
3. Disconnect the lower control arm at the strut. Matchmark the front and rear adjusting cams to the body. Remove the nuts and cams and then remove the lower arm.
4. Unbolt the ball joint from the control arm.

**To install:**

5. Install the ball joint to the arm and tighten the nuts to 94 ft. lbs. (127 Nm).
6. Position the lower control arm and install the adjusting cams and nuts (fingertight).
7. Connect the ball joint to the steering knuckle and tighten a conventional nut to 14 ft. lbs. (20 Nm). Install a locknut on top of the other and tighten it to 107 ft. lbs. (145 Nm).
8. Tighten the arm-to-strut bolt to 106 ft. lbs. (143 Nm). Tighten the stabilizer bar link nut to 47 ft. lbs. (64 Nm).
9. Install the wheels and lower the vehicle. Bounce the car several times to set the suspension. Align the matchmarks on the adjusting cams and the body and tighten them to 177 ft. lbs. (240 Nm). Check the front alignment.

#### *All Others*

Please refer to "Lower Control Arm/Ball Joints."

## Upper Control Arm

### REMOVAL & INSTALLATION

#### *1987-90 Supra*

1. Riase the front of the vehicle and support it with safety stands. Remove the wheels.
2. Unclip the brake hose bracket at the steering knuckle, remove the retaining nut and press the upper arm out of the knuckle.
3. Remove the upper mounting bolt and nut and lift out the upper control arm.
4. Connect the upper arm to the body. Connect the arm to the steering knuckle.
5. Install the wheels and lower the car. Bounce it several times to set the suspension and then tighten the arm-to-knuckle nut to 80 ft. lbs. (108 Nm). Tighten the arm-to-body bolt to 121 ft. lbs. (164 Nm).

## Front Knuckle, Hub And Bearing

### REMOVAL & INSTALLATION

#### *Rear Wheel Drive*

1. Remove the disc/hub assembly.
2. If either the disc or the entire hub assembly is to be replaced, unbolt the hub from the disc.

**NOTE: If only the bearings are to be replaced, do not separate the disc and hub.**

3. Using a brass rod as a drift, tap the inner bearings cone out. Remove the oil seal and the inner bearings.

**NOTE: Throw the old oil seal away.**

### PRELOAD SPECIFICATIONS

| Model/Year | Initial Torque Setting (ft. lbs.) | Preload (oz.) |
|---|---|---|
| Tercel '80–'83 | 22 | 13–30 |
| Corolla① | 19–23 | 11–25 |
| Celica | 19–26 | 11–25 |
| Corona | 19–26 | 12–31 |
| Supra① | 19–23 | 11–24 |
| Cressida① | 22 | 37–56 |
| Starlet | | |
| '81–'82 | 22 | 1–1.5 |
| '83–'84 | 22 | 0.8–1.9 |

①Except models w/IRS

4. Drive out the inner bearing cup.
5. Drive out the outer bearing cup.

Inspect the bearings and the hub for signs of wear or damage. Replace components, as necessary.

**To install:**

6. Install the inner bearing cup an then the outer bearing cup, by driving them into place.

**CAUTION**

***Use care not to cock the bearing cups in the hub.***

7. Pack the bearings, hub inner well and grease cap with multipurpose grease.
8. Install the inner bearing into the hub.
9. Carefully install a new oil seal with a soft drift.
10. Install the hub on the spindle. Be sure to install all of the washers and nuts which were removed.
11. Adjust the bearing preload.
12. Install the caliper assembly and the wheel.

#### *Front Wheel Drive Models*

**Please refer to Front Axle, Hub and Bearing in the Drive Axle section.**

### PRELOAD ADJUSTMENT

1. With the front hub/disc assembly installed, tighten the castellated nut to the torque figure specified.
2. Rotate the disc back and forth, two or three times, to allow the bearing to seat properly.
3. Loosen the castellated nut until it is only fingertight.
4. Tighten the nut firmly, using a box wrench.
5. Measure the bearing preload with a spring scale attached to a wheel mounting stud. Check it against the specifications.

6. Install the cotter pin.

**NOTE: If the hole does not align with the nut (or cap) holes, tighten the nut slightly until it does.**

7. Finish installing the brake components and the wheel.

## Front Wheel Alignment

### ADJUSTMENT

Front end alignment measurements require the use of special equipment. Before measuring alignment or attempting to adjust it, always check the following points:

1. Be sure that the tires are properly inflated.
2. See that the wheels are properly balanced.
3. Check the ball joints to determine if they are worn or loose.
4. Check front wheel bearing adjustment.
5. Be sure that the car is on a level surface.
6. Check all suspension parts for tightness.

#### *Caster*

**1983-84 CRESSIDA**
**1983-85 CELICA (RWD)**
**COROLLA (RWD) AND SUPRA**

Caster is the tilt of the front steering axis either forward or backward away from the front of the vehicle.

If the caster is found to be out of tolerance with the specifications, it may be adjusted by turning the nuts on the rear end of the strut bar (where it attaches to the body) on all models. The caster is decreased by lengthening the strut bar and increased by shortening it. One turn of the adjusting nut is equal to 8' (minute) of tilt on the Corolla (RWD) and 9' on the Celica/Supra and Cressida, 1' is $^1/_{60}$ of a degree.

**NOTE: If the caster still cannot be adjusted within the limits, inspect or replace any damaged or worn suspension parts.**

**STARLET, 1983-87 TERCEL SEDAN AND 1983-88 TERCEL WAGON**

Caster on the Starlet and Tercel is adjusted by changing the number of spacers on the stabilizer bar. One spacer will change the caster 24' on the Starlet and 13' on the Tercel. One minute (1') is equal to $^1/_{60}$ of a degree.

**NOTE: If the caster still canot be adjusted within the limits, inspect or replace any damaged or worn suspension parts.**

**CAMRY AND 1985-90 CRESSIDA**

Increase or decrease the number of spacers on the stabilizer bar (strut bar – 1989-90 Cressida). Each spacer changes caster by 30' (20' – 1989-90 Cressida). Never install more than 2 spacers.

**1984-90 COROLLA (FWD)**
**1986-90 CELICA (FWD)**
**1988-90 TERCEL SEDAN**

Caster is not adjustable.

**MR2**

Caster is changed by turning the adjusting nut on the strut bar. Each revolution of the nut changes the caster by 18'.

#### *Camber*

**1983-86 SUPRA**
**1983-85 CELICA (RWD)**
**STARLET, COROLLA (RWD) AND CRESSIDA**

Camber is the slope of the front wheels from the vertical when viewed from the front of the vehicle. When the wheels tilt outward at the top, the camber is positive (+). When the wheels tilt inward at the top, the camber is negative (–). The amount of positive and negative camber is measured in degrees from the vertical and the measurement is called camber angle. Camber is preset at the factory, therefore, it is not adjustable. If the camber angle is out of tolerance, inspect or replace worn or damaged suspension parts.

**MR2**
**1983-88 CAMRY**
**1987-89 COROLLA FX**
**1986-90 CELICA (FWD)**
**1984-86 COROLLA FWD (SEDAN/WAGON)**
**1983-87 TERCEL SEDAN**
**1983-88 TERCEL WAGON**

Camber on these models is adjustable by means of a camber adjustment bolt on the lower strut mounting bracket. Loosen the shock absorber set nut and then turn the adjusting bolt until the camber is within specifications. Camber will change about 20' (MR2: 18') for each graduation on the cam. One minute (1') is equal to $^1/_{60}$ of a degree.

**1989-90 CAMRY**
**1988-90 TERCEL SEDAN**
**1987-90 COROLLA SEDAN/WAGON**

Camber is not adjustable

#### *Caster and Camber*

**1987-90 SUPRA**

Caster and camber are adjustable by means of a front and rear adjusting cam on the lower control arm. Due to the complexity of computing adjustment measurements, we recommend that only a qualified service technician undertake these adjustments.

#### *Toe*

Toe is the amount, measured in a fraction of an inch, that the front wheels are closer together at one end than the other. Toe-in means that the front wheels are closer together at the front of the tire than at the rear; toe-out means that the rear of the tires are closer together than the front.

The wheels must be dead straight ahead. The car must have a full tank of gas, all fluids must be at their proper levels, all other suspension and steering adjustments must be correct and the tires must be properly inflated to their cold specifications.

1. Toe can be determined by measuring the distance between the centers of the tire treads, at the front of the tire and the rear. If the tread pattern of your car's tires makes this impossible, you can measure between the edges of the wheel rims, but be sure to move the car and measure in a few places to avoid errors caused by bent rims or wheel run-out.
2. If the measurement is not within specifications, loosen the 4 retaining clamp locknuts on the adjustable tie rods.
3. Turn the left and right tie rods EQUAL amounts until the measurements are within specifications.
4. Tighten the lock bolts and then recheck the measurements. Check to see that the steering wheel is still in the proper position. If not, remove it and reposition it.

# REAR SUSPENSION

## Shock Absorbers

### REMOVAL & INSTALLATION

***Starlet***
***Corolla (RWD)***
***Celica (RWD) – exc. GTS***
***1989-90 Corolla (FWD) – 4wd***

1. Raise the rear of the car and support it with jackstands. Position an hydraulic jack under the rear axle.
2. Unfasten the upper shock absorber retaining nuts. It may be necessary to hold the shock absorber shaft with a suitable tool while removing the top retaining nut.

**NOTE: Always remove and install the shock absorbers one at a time. Do not allow the rear axle to hang in place as this may cause undue damage.**

3. Remove the lower shock retaining nut where it attaches to the rear axle housing.
4. Remove the shock absorber.
5. Inspect the shock for wear, leaks or other signs of damage.
6. Installation is in the reverse order of removal. Please note the following:

tighten the upper retaining nuts to 18 ft. lbs. (25 Nm).

tighten the lower retaining nuts to 27 ft. lbs. (37 Nm).

### 1983-86 Supra
### 1983-88 Cressida
### 1983-85 Celica GTS (RWD)

1. Jack up the rear end of the car, keeping the pad of the hydraulic floor jack underneath the differential housing. Support the suspension control arms with safety stands.
2. Remove the brake hose clips. Disconnect the stabilizer bar end.
3. Disconnect the halfshaft at the CV-joint on the wheel side.
4. With a jackstand underneath the suspension control arm, unbolt the shock absorber at its lower end. Using a screwdriver to keep the shaft from turning, remove the nut holding the shock absorber to its upper mounting. On models w/TEMS, disconnect the actuator and remove it. Remove the shock.
5. Installation is in the reverse order of removal. Torque the halfshaft nuts to 44–57 ft. lbs.; torque the upper shock mounting nut to 14–22 ft. lbs., and the lower shock mounting nut to 22–32 ft. lbs.

# MacPherson Struts

## REMOVAL & INSTALLATION

### Tercel

1. Working inside the car, remove the shock absorber cover and package tray bracket.
2. Raise the rear of the vehicle and support it with jackstands. Remove the wheel.
3. Disconnect the brake line from the wheel cylinder (if necessary). Disconnect the brake line from the flexible hose at the mounting bracket on the strut tube. Disconnect the flexible hose from the strut.
4. Loosen the nut holding the suspension support to the shock absorber.

**CAUTION**

*Do not remove the nut.*

5. Remove the bolts and nuts mounting on the strut on the axle carrier and then disconnect the strut.
6. Remove the 3 upper strut mounting nuts and carefully remove the strut assembly.
7. Installation is in the reverse order of removal. Please note the following:
   a. Tighten the upper strut retaining nuts to 17 ft. lbs – 1983-87; 23 ft. lbs. (31 Nm) – 1988-90.
   b. Tighten the lower strut-to-axle carrier bolts to 105 ft. lbs. – 1983-87
   c. Tighten the nut holding the suspension support to the shock absorber to 36 ft. lbs. – 1983-87
   d. Tighten the strut-to-axle beam nut to 47 ft. lbs. (64 Nm) – 1988-90.
   e. Bleed the brakes.

### Camry
### Corolla (FWD) – 2wd

1. On the 4-door sedan, remove the package tray and vent duct.
2. On the hatchback, remove the speaker grilles.
3. Disconnect the brake line from the wheel cylinder.
4. Remove the brake line from the brake hose.
5. Disconnect the brake hose from its bracket on the strut.
6. Remove the strut suspension support cover. Loosen, but do not remove, the nut holding the suspension support to the strut.
7. Unbolt the strut from the rear arm and or axle carrier.
8. Unbolt the strut from the body.
9. Installation is the reverse of removal. Tighten the strut-to-body bolts to 17 ft. lbs. (1983-86 Camry), 23 ft. lbs. (1987-88 Camry), 29 ft. lbs. (1987-89 Corolla sedan/wagon and 1989-90 Camry); the strut-to-axle carrier bolts to 119 ft. lbs., 166 ft. lbs. (1987-90 Camry); 105 ft. lbs. (Corolla) and the suspension support-to-strut nut to 36 ft. lbs.
10. Refill and bleed the brake system.

### 1986-90 Celica (FWD)

1. Raise the rear of the vehicle and support it with jackstands. Position an hydraulic jack underneath the rear hub assembly; raise it just enough to support the assembly.
2. On the liftback, remove the rear speaker grilles.
3. On the coupe, remove the suspension service hole cover.
4. On the ST and GT models, disconnect and plug the brake line at the backing plate. Remove the clip and E-ring and then disconnect the brake hose and tube from the strut housing.
5. On the GTS, remove the union bolts and gaskets and disconnect the brake line from the brake cylinder. Remove the clip and E-ring from the strut and then disconnect the brake hose from the strut housing.
6. Loosen, but do not remove, the nut attaching the suspension support to the strut.
7. Disconnect the stabilizer bar at the lower end of the strut housing.
8. Disconnect the strut at the axle carrier.
9. Remove the 3 strut-to-body bolts and then remove the strut.

**To install:**

10. Tighten the upper strut-to-body nuts to 23 ft. lbs. (31 Nm).
11. Tighten the lower strut-to-carrier bolts to 119 ft. lbs. (162 Nm).
12. Connect the stabilizer bar to the strut and tighten the bolts to 26 ft. lbs. (35 Nm).
13. Tighten the strut holding nut to 36 ft. lbs. (49 Nm). Install the dust cover onto the suspension support.
14. Reconnect the brake line and hose. Bleed the system, lower the car and check the rear wheel alignment.

### MR2

1. Raise the rear of the vehicle and support it with jackstands. Position an hydraulic floor jack underneath the rear hub assembly; raise it just enough to support the assembly.
2. Remove the union bolts and gaskets and disconnect the brake line from the brake cylinder. Remove the clip and E-ring from the strut and then disconnect the brake hose from the strut housing.
3. Matchmark the lower strut bracket and the camber adjusting cam, remove the 2 axle carrier bolts and the adjusting cam and disconnect the strut from the carrier.
4. Remove the engine hood side panel.
5. Remove the 3 upper strut-to-body nuts and then remove the strut.

**To install:**

6. Position the strut and tighten the upper mounting nuts to 23 ft. lbs. (31 Nm).
7. Install the engine hood side panel.
8. Connect the axle carrier to the lower strut bracket. Insert the mounting bolts from the rear and align the matchmarks made in Step 3. Tighten the nuts to 105 ft. lbs. (142 Nm) – 1985-88; 166 ft. lbs. (226 Nm) – 1989-90.
9. Connect the brake line, bleed the system and check rear wheel alignment.

### 1987-90 Supra
### 1989-90 Cressida

1. Raise and support the rear of the

vehicle safely. Remove the wheel assemblies.

2. Remove the speaker grill and interior quarter panel trim (if equipped with TEMS).

3. Disconnect the strut from the axle carrier.

4. Remove the strut cap. Remove the TEMS (Toyota electronic modulated suspension) actuator.

5. Remove the 3 strut mounting nuts from the body and remove the strut assembly.

6. Mount the strut assembly in a suitable vise. Using a suitable spring compressor, compress the coil spring.

7. Remove the strut suspension support nut. Remove the strut suspension support, remove the coil spring and bumper.

**To install:**

8. Mount the strut in a suitable vise. Using a suitable spring compressor, compress the coil spring.

9. Install the bumper to the strut, align the coil spring end with the lower seat hollow and install the coil spring.

10. Align the strut suspension support hole and piston rod and install it. Align the suspension support with the strut lower bushing.

11. Install the strut suspension support nut and torque it to 20 ft. lbs. (27 Nm).Connect the strut assembly with the 3 retaining nuts and torque them to 10 ft. lbs. (14 Nm).

12. Connect the strut assembly to the axle carrier and torque it to 101 ft. lbs. (137 Nm).

13. Install the TEMS actuator and strut cap. Install the quarter panel trim panel and speaker grille.

### OVERHAUL

**For all spring and shock absorber removal and installtion procedures, and all strut overhaul procedure, please refer to "Strut Overhaul" in the Unit Repair section.**

## Springs

### REMOVAL & INSTALLATION

#### *Leaf Springs*

1. Loosen the rear wheel lub nuts.

2. Raise the rear of the vehicle. Support the frame and rear axle housing with stands.

3. Remove the lug nuts and the wheel.

4. Remove the cotter pin, nut, and washer from the lower end of the shock absorber.

5. Detach the shock absorber from the spring seat pivot pin.

6. Remove the parking brake cable clamp.

**NOTE: Remove the parking brake equalizer, if necessary.**

7. Unfasten the U-bolt nuts and remove the spring seat assemblies.

8. Adjust the height of the rear axle housing so that the weight of the rear axle is removed from the rear springs.

9. Unfasten the spring shackle retaining nuts. Withdraw the spring shackle inner plate. Carefully pry out the spring shackle with a bar.

10. Remove the spring bracket pin from the front end of the spring hanger and remove the rubber bushings.

11. Remove the spring.

**CAUTION**

***Use care not to damage the hydraulic brake line or the parking brake cable.***

**To install:**

12. Install the rubber bushings in the eye of the spring.

13. Align the eye of the spring with the spring hanger bracket and drive the pin through the bracket holes and rubber bushings.

**NOTE: Use soapy water as lubricant, if necessary, to aid pin installation. Never use oil or grease.**

14. Fingertighten the spring hanger nuts and/or bolts.

15. Install the rubber bushings in the spring eye at the opposite end of the spring.

16. Raise the free end of the spring. Install the spring shackle through the bushings and the bracket.

17. Install the shackle inner plate and fingertighten the retaining nuts.

18. Center the bolt head in the hole which is provided in the spring seat on the axle housing.

19. Fit the U-bolts over the axle housing. Install the lower spring seat.

20. Tighten the U-bolt nuts.

**NOTE: Some models have 2 sets of nuts, while others have a nut and lockwasher.**

21. Install the parking brake cable clamp. Install the equalizer, if it was removed.

22. On passenger cars:

a. Install the shock absorber end at the spring seat. Tighten the nuts.

b. Install the wheel and lug nuts. Lower the car to the ground.

c. Bounce the car several times.

d. Tighten the spring bracket pins and shackles.

#### *Coil Springs*

1. Loosen the rear wheel lug nuts.

2. Jack up the rear axle housing and support the frame with jack stands. Leave the jack in place under the rear axle housing.

3. Remove the lug nuts and wheel.

4. If so equipped, disconnect the rear stabilizer bar from the axle housing (or suspension arm, on 1983-89 Supra, 1983-85 Celica GTS and 1983-88 Cressida). Remove the bolt holding the stabilizer bar bushing to the rear axle housing.

5. Unfasten the lower shock absorber end. On the Corolla RWD, Corolla FWD (4wd) and Tercel 4wd, disconnect the lateral control rod from the axle.

**NOTE: On Supra, 1983-88 Cressida and Celica GTS (1983-85) models with IRS suspension, remove the rear halfshafts.**

6. Slowly lower the jack under the rear axle housing until the axle is at the bottom of its travel.

7. Withdraw the coil spring, complete with its insulator.

8. Inspect the coil spring and insulator for wear, cracks, or weakness; replace either or both, as necessary.

9. Installation is performed in the reverse order of removal.

## Lower Control Arms

### REMOVAL & INSTALLATION

#### *MR2*

1. Raise the rear of the vehicle and suupport it with safety stands. Remove the wheel.

2. Remove the cotter pin and retaining nut from the bottom of the ball joint stem. Using a ball joint removal tool, press the ball joint out of the control arm.

3. Remove the strut rod nut and retainer from the lower control arm.

4. Remove the bolt holding the lower control arm to the body. Remove the cushion and then disconnect the lower arm from the strut rod. Remove the lower control arm.

5. Connect the lower arm to the strut rod. Install the strut rod nut, cushion and retainer.

6. Connect the lower arm to the body and install the retaining nut fingertight.

7. Connect the lower control arm to the ball joint and tighten the retaining nut to 67 ft. lbs. (91 Nm). Install a new cotter pin.

**NOTE: If the holes do not line up when installing the new cotter pin, tighten the nut until they are aligned. Do not loosen the nut!**

8. Install the wheel and lower the vehicle. Tighten the strut rod nut to 86 ft. lbs. (117 Nm) and the arm-to-body bolt to 94 ft. lbs. (127 Nm).

#### *1987-90 Supra*
#### *1989-90 Cressida*

1. Raise the rear of the vehicle and

support it with safety stands. Remove the wheels.

2. Remove the halfshaft.

3. Remove the nut and disconnect the No. 1 lower arm from the axle carrier. Matchmark the adjusting cam to the body, remove the cam and bolt and then lift out the No. 1 arm.

4. Remove the bolt and nut and disconnect the No. 2 lower arm from the axle carrier. Matchmark the adjusting cam to the body, remove the cam and bolt and then lift out the No. 2 arm.

**To install:**

5. Position the No. 2 arm and install the adjusting cam and bolt so the matchmarks are in alignment. Connect the arm to the axle carrier.

6. Position the No. 1 arm and install the adjusting cam and bolt so the matchmarks are in alignment. Connect the arm to the axle carrier. Use a new nut and tighten it to 43 ft. lbs. (59 Nm).

7. Install the halfshaft.

8. Install the wheels and lower the vehicle. Bounce it several times to set the suspension and then tighten the body-to-arm bolts and nuts to 136 ft. lbs. (184 Nm)–Supra; 134 ft. lbs. (181 Nm)–Cressida. Tighten the No. 2 arm-to-carrier bolt to 121 ft. lbs. (164 Nm)–Supra; 119 ft. lbs. (162 Nm)–Cressida. Tighten the No. 1 arm-to-carrier nut to 36 ft. lbs. (49 Nm).

9. Check the rear wheel alignment.

## Upper Control Arm

### REMOVAL & INSTALLATION

#### *1987-90 Supra*
#### *1989-90 Cressida*

1. Raise the rear of the vehicle and support it with safety stands. Remove the wheels.

2. Unbolt the brake caliper and suspend it with wire so it is out of the way. Remove the halfshaft.

3. Disconnect the parking brake cable at the equalizer. Remove the 2 cable brackets from the body and then pull the cable through the suspension member.

4. Disconnect the 2 lower arms and the strut rod at the axle carrier. Disconnect the lower strut mount.

5. Disconnect the upper arm at the body and remove the axle hub assembly.

6. Remove the upper arm mounting nut. Remove the backing plate mounting nuts and separate the plate from the carrier. Press the upper arm out of the axle carrier.

**To install:**

7. Connect the upper arm to the body.

8. Connect the axle hub assembly to the arm with a new nut.

9. Connect the No. 1 lower control arm with a new nut and tighten it to 43 ft. lbs. (59 Nm)–Supra; 36 ft. lbs. (49 Nm)–Cressida. Connect the No. 2 lower arm and the strut rod.

10. Tighten the upper arm mounting nut to 80 ft. lbs. (108 Nm). Tighten the strut to 101 ft. lbs. (137 Nm).

11. Reconnect the parking brake cable and install the halfshaft. Install the brake caliper and tighten the bolts to 34 ft. lbs. (47 Nm).

12. Install the wheels and lower the car. Bounce it several times to set the suspension and then tighten the upper arm-to-body bolt, the No. 2 lower arm-to-carrier and the strut rod to 121 ft. lbs. (164 Nm)–Supra; 119 ft. lbs. (162 Nm)–Cressida.

## Upper And Lower Control Arms

### REMOVAL & INSTALLATION

#### *Tercel Wagon–4wd*
#### *1989-90 Corolla–4wd*

1. Raise the rear of the vehicle and support it with safety stands. Remove the wheels and support the rear axle with a floor jack.

2. Remove the upper control arm-to-body bolt. Remove the upper arm-to-axle bolt and lift out the upper control arm.

3. Remove the lower control arm-to-body bolt. Remove the lower arm-to-axle bolt and lift out the lower control arm.

4. Install the upper control arm with the nuts and bolts just snugged down.

5. Install the lower control arm with the nuts and bolts just snugged down.

6. Install the wheels, remove the safety stands and floor jack and then lower the vehicle.

7. Bounce the vehicle several times to stabilize the suspension and then raise the axle housing until the body is free.

8. Tighten all bolts to 83 ft. lbs. (113 Nm) on the Tercel; 72 ft. lbs. (98 Nm) on the Corolla.

## Rear Axle Hub, Carrier and Bearing

**For information on all rear wheel drive models and all 4wd models, please refer to Rear Axle Shaft in the Drive Axle section.**

### REMOVAL & INSTALLATION

#### *Front Wheel Drive Only*

#### 1983-86 TERCEL SEDAN

1. Raise the rear of the vehicle and support it with jackstands.

2. Remove the rear wheel and tire assembly.

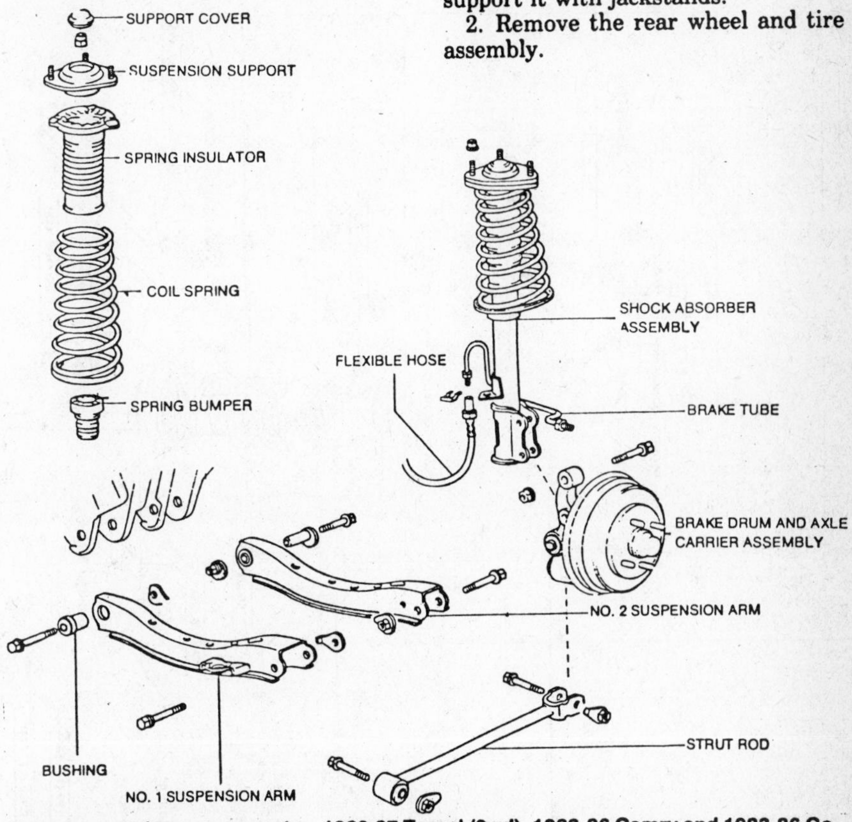


**Rear suspension components–1983-87 Tercel (2wd), 1983-86 Camry and 1983-86 Corolla FWD (exc. FX)**

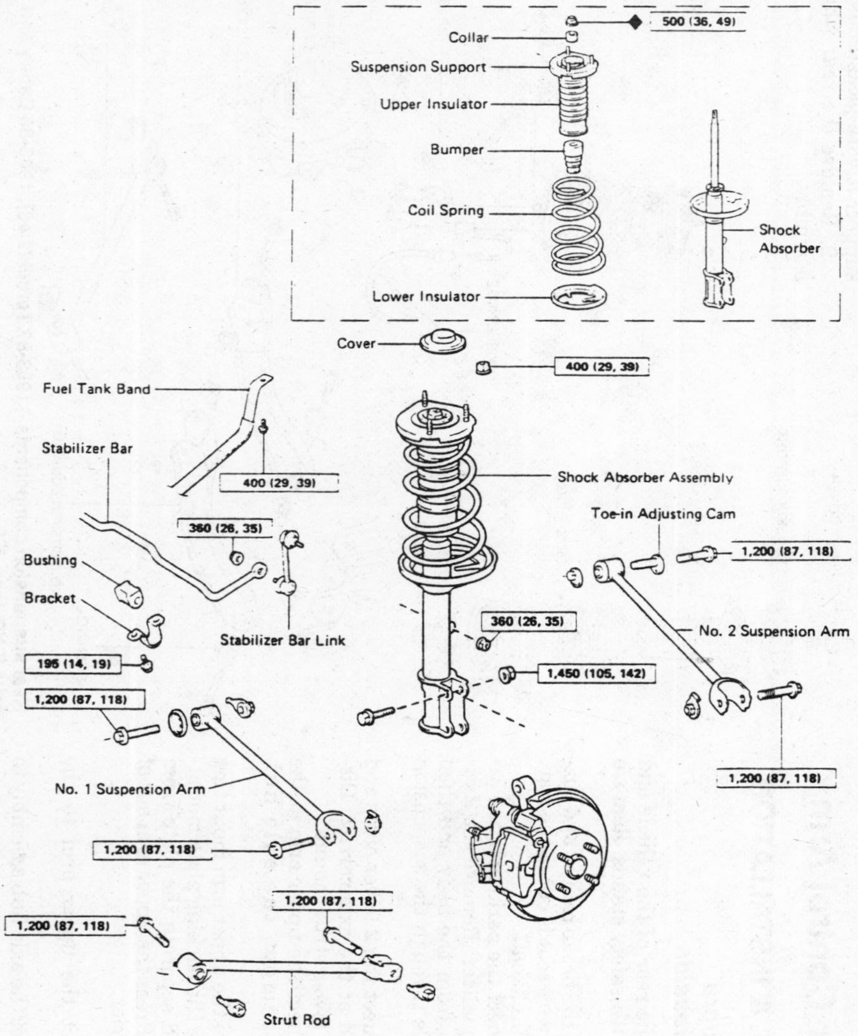


**Rear suspension components – 1987-90 Corolla (exc. FX)**

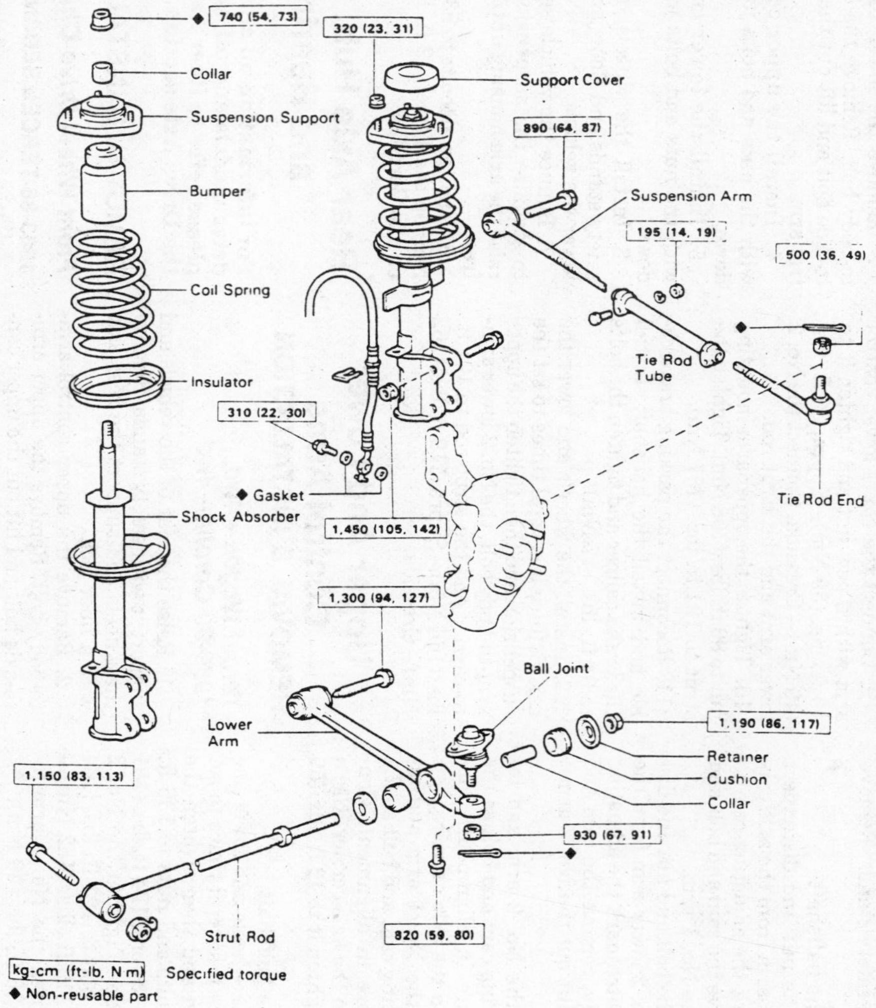


**Rear suspension components – MR2**

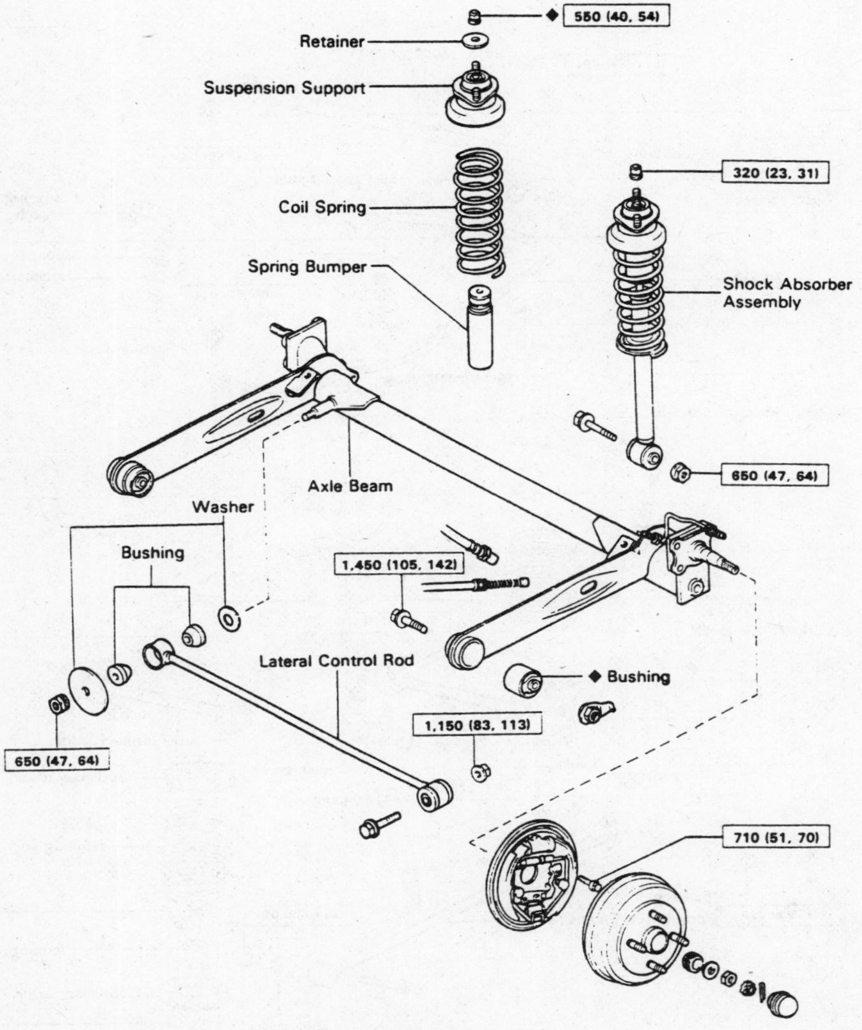


Rear suspension components – 1987-90 Tercel sedan (2wd)

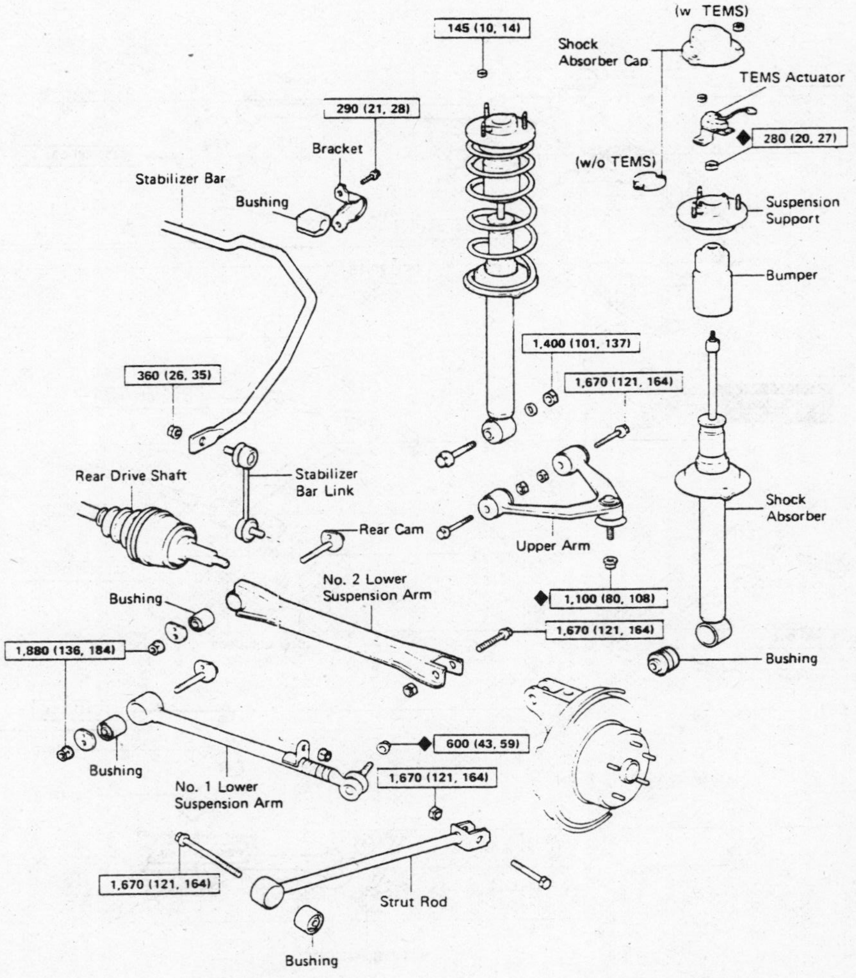


Rear suspension components – 1987-90 Supra

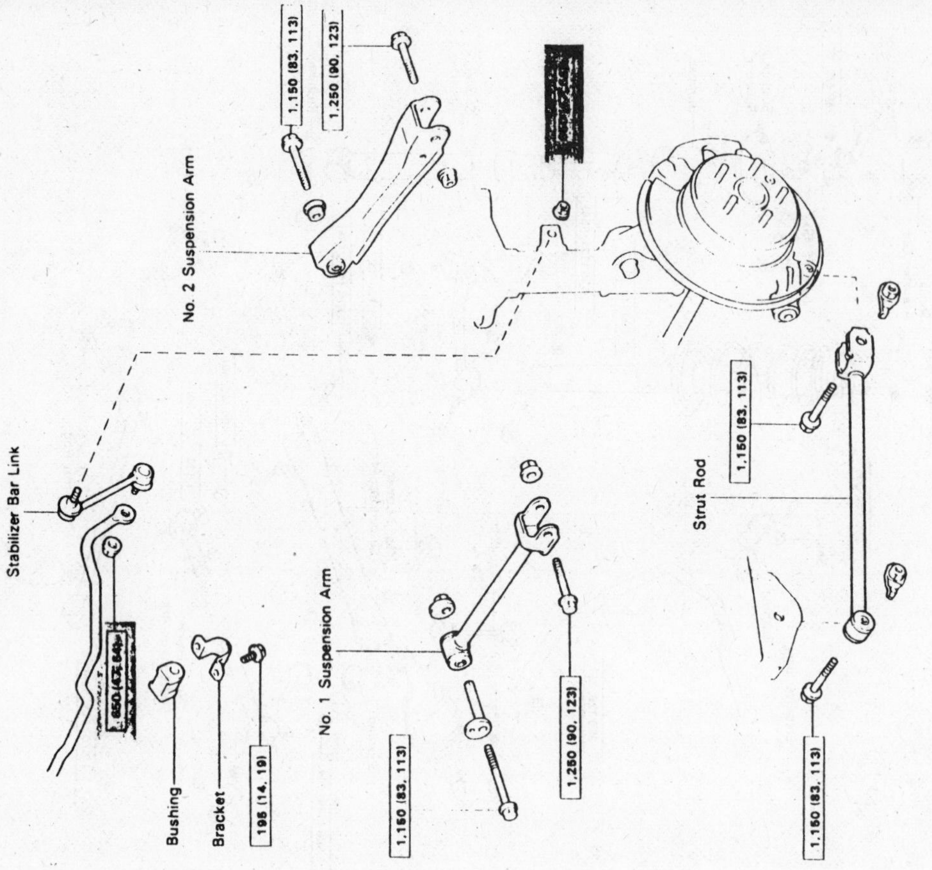


Rear suspension components – 1988-90 Camry/Celica All-Trac (4wd)

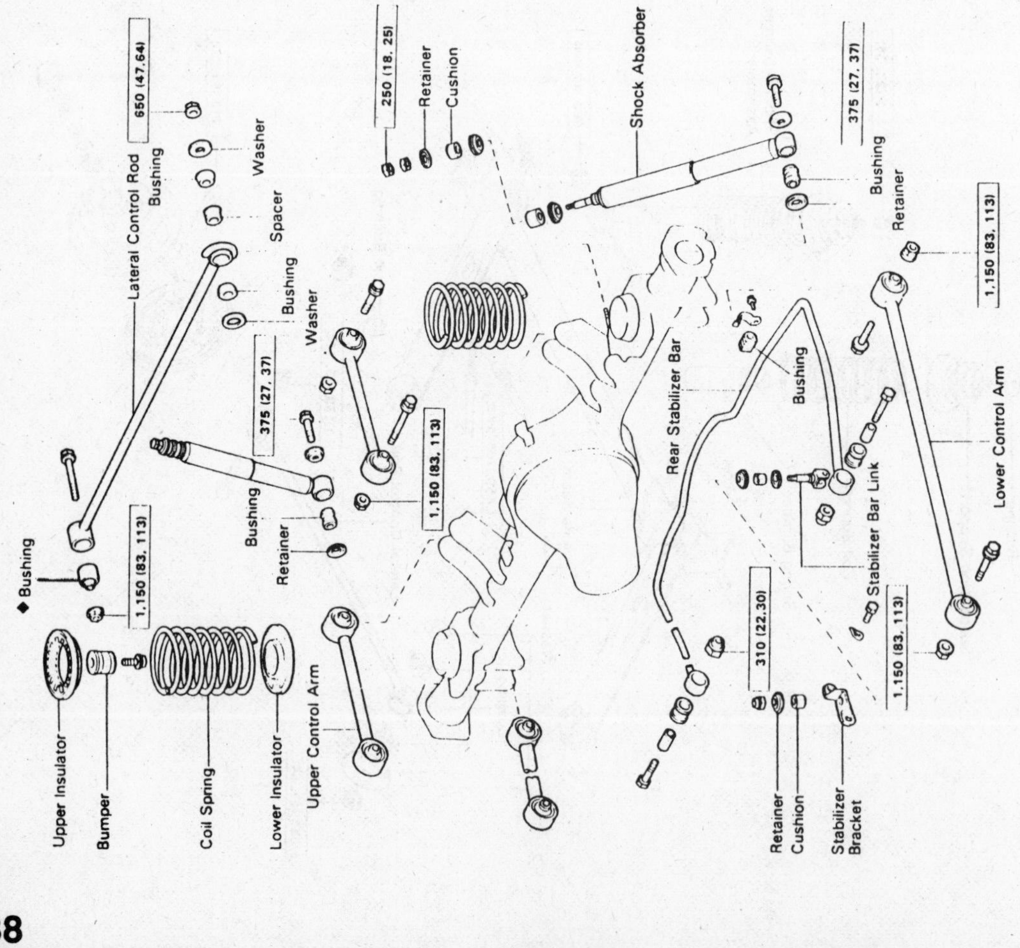


Rear suspension components – Tercel (4wd)

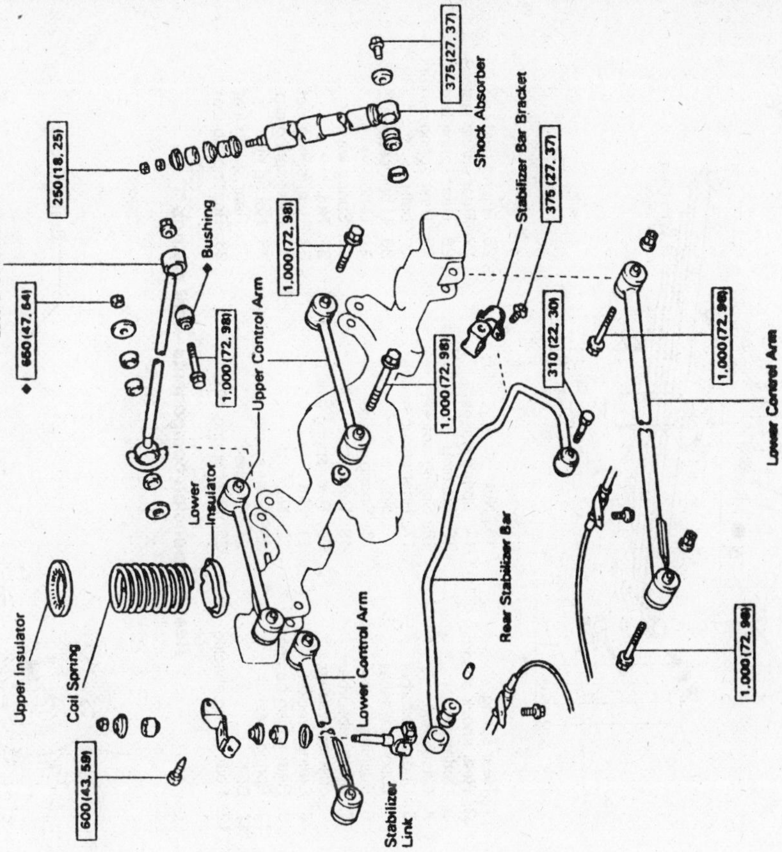


Rear suspension components – Corolla 4wd

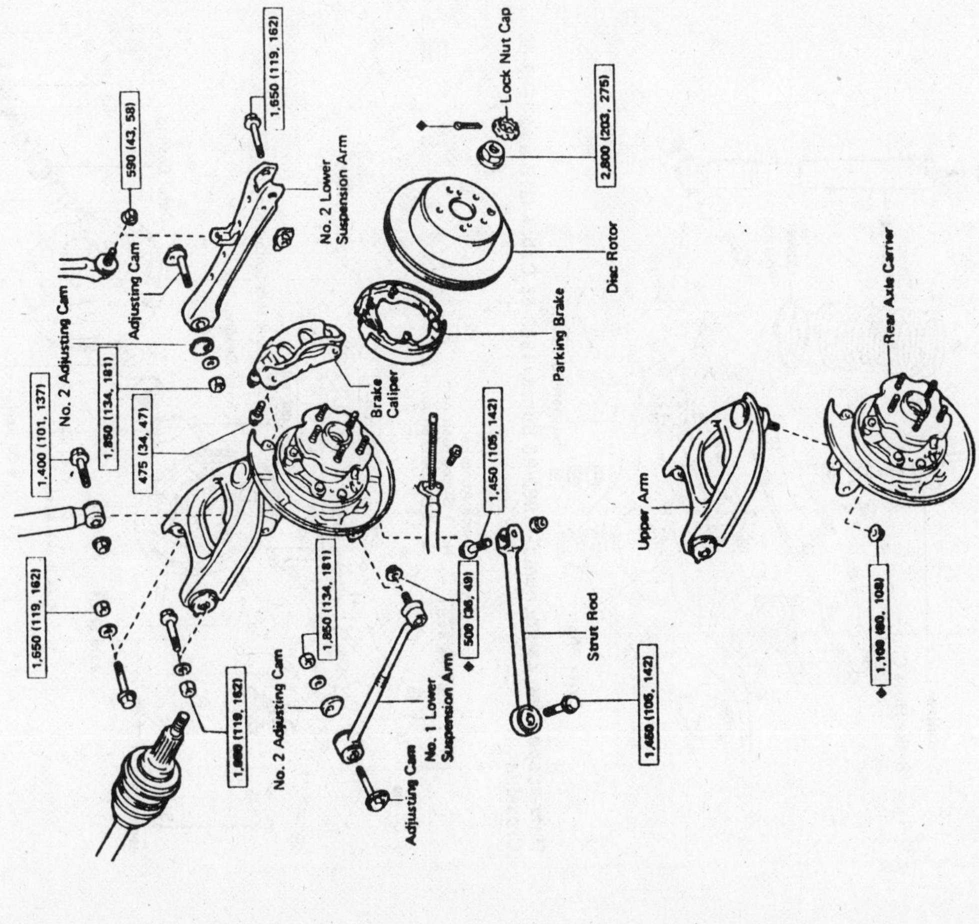


Rear suspension components – 1989-90 Cressida

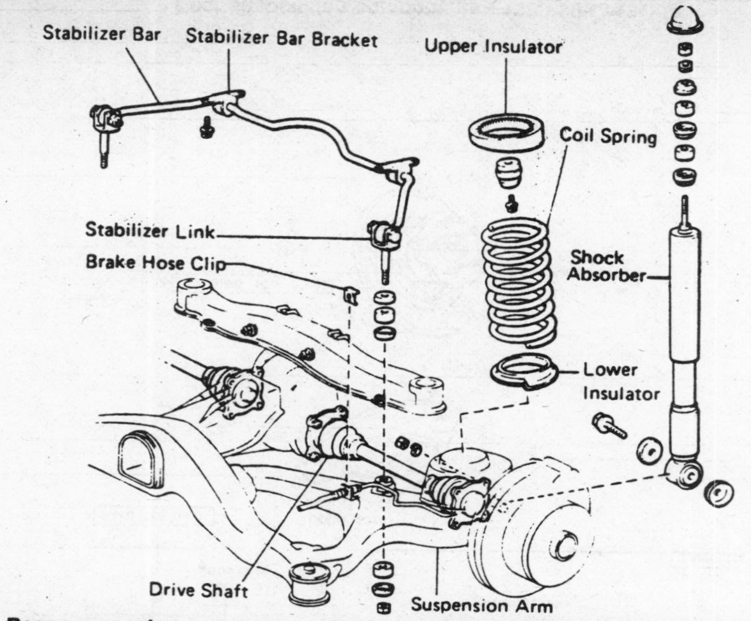


**Rear suspension components—1983-86 Supra, 1983-85 Celica GTS and 1983-88 Cressida**

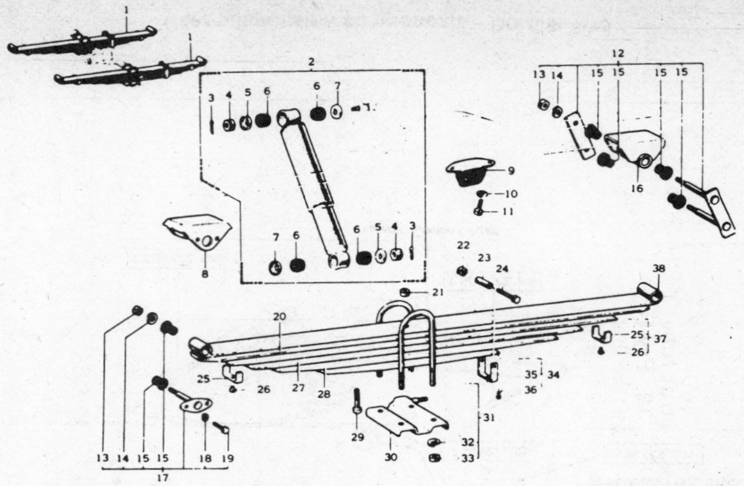

1. Rear spring
2. Rear shock absorber
3. Cotter pin
4. Castle nut
5. Shock absorber cushion washer
6. Bushing
7. Shock absorber cushion washer
8. Spring bracket
9. Rear spring bumper
10. Spring washer
11. Bolt
12. Rear spring shackle
13. Nut
14. Spring washer
15. Bushing
16. Spring bracket
17. Rear spring hanger pin
18. Spring washer
19. Bolt
20. Rear spring leaf
21. Nut
22. Nut
23. Rear spring clip bolt
24. Clip bolt
25. Rear spring clip
26. Round rivet
27. Rear spring leaf
28. Rear spring leaf
29. Rear spring center bolt
30. U-bolt seat
31. U-bolt
32. Spring washer
33. Nut
34. Rear spring leaf
35. Rear spring clip
36. Round rivet
37. Rear spring leaf
38. Rear spring leaf

**Rear suspension components—leaf springs**

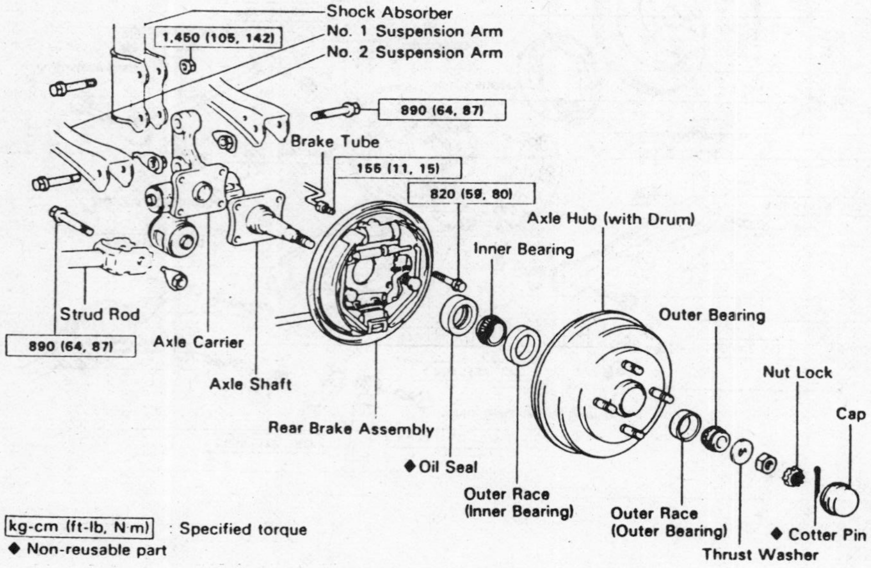


**Rear axle hub and carrier—1983-86 Tercel sedan**

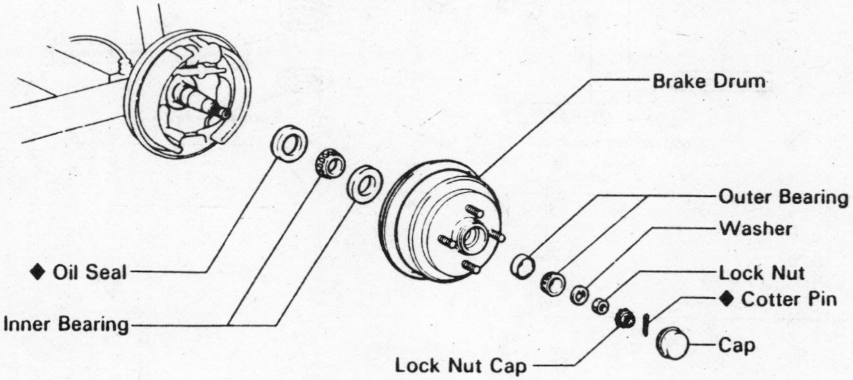


**Rear axle hub and bearing—1987-90 Tercel sedan**

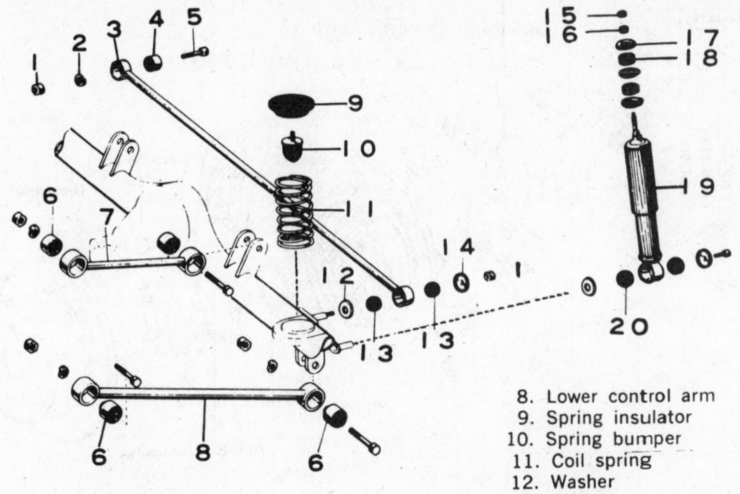

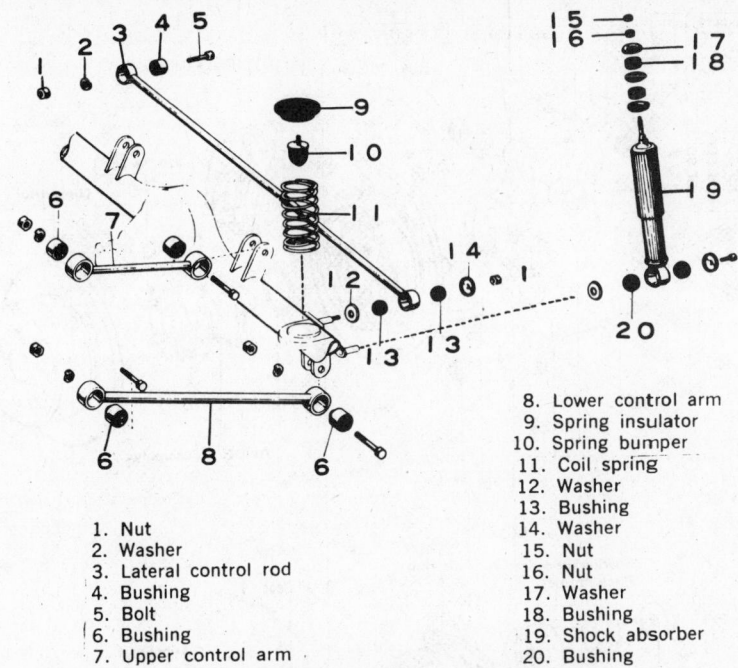

1. Nut
2. Washer
3. Lateral control rod
4. Bushing
5. Bolt
6. Bushing
7. Upper control arm
8. Lower control arm
9. Spring insulator
10. Spring bumper
11. Coil spring
12. Washer
13. Bushing
14. Washer
15. Nut
16. Nut
17. Washer
18. Bushing
19. Shock absorber
20. Bushing

**Rear suspension components – Celica (RWD)**

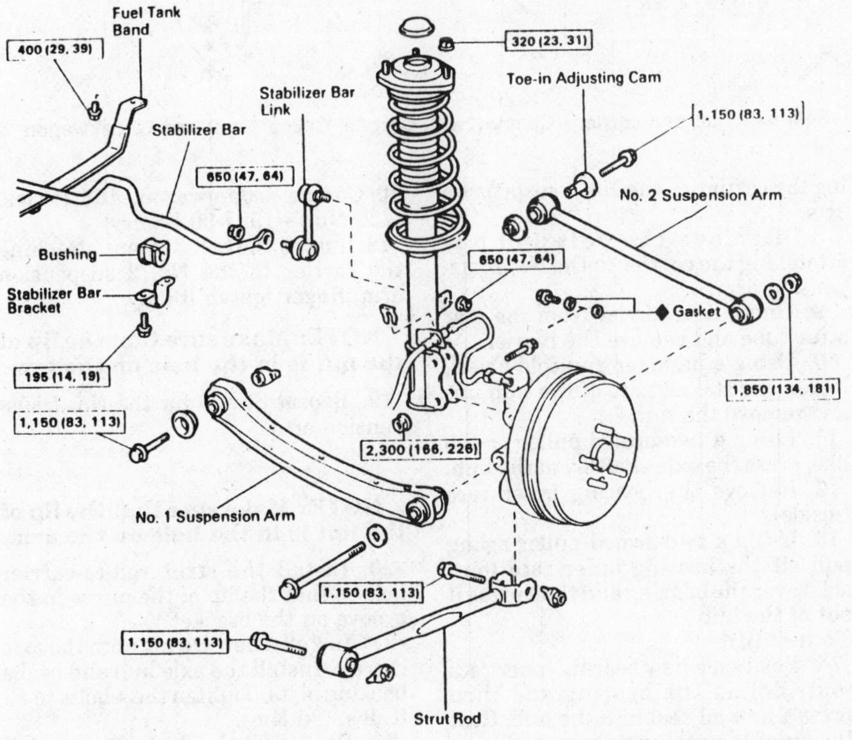


**Rear suspension components – 1987-90 Camry (2wd) and 1986=90 Celica (2wd)**

3. Remove the brake drum.
4. Remove the locknut cap and cotter pin. Pry off the locknut and then remove the locknut itself.
5. Pull off the axle hub along with the outer wheel bearing and thrust washer.
6. Disconnect and plug the brake line where it connects to the brake backing plate.
7. Unbolt the rear axle shaft from the carrier and remove it along with the brake backing plate.
8. Remove the bolt and nut attaching the carrier to the strut rod.
9. Remove the bolt and nut attaching the carrier to the No. 1 suspension arm.
10. Remove the bolt and nut attaching the carrier to the No. 2 suspension arm.
11. Unbolt the carrier from the rear strut tube and remove the carrier.
12. Pry the inner bearing oil seal out of the brake drum and then remove the inner bearing.
13. Using a brass drift and hammer, drive out the bearing races.

**To install:**

14. Press new outer bearing races into the axle hub and fill it and the bearing cap with grease.
15. Coat your palm with grease and press the bearing into your palm until the grease oozes out the other side.
16. Position the inner bearing into the hub and then drive in a new oil seal. Coat the seal with grease.
17. Position the axle carrier onto the strut tube and tighten the bolts to 105 ft. lbs. (142 Nm).
18. Install the bolt and nut attaching the carrier to the No. 2 suspension arm; fingertighten it only.

**NOTE: Make sure that the lip of the nut is on the flange of the arm, not over it.**

19. Repeat Step 18 for the No. 1 suspension arm.

**NOTE: Make sure that the lip of the nut is in the hole on the arm.**

20. Install the strut rod-to-carrier bolt so that the lip of the nut is in the groove on the bracket.
21. Install the axle shaft and brake backing plate. Tighten the 4 bolts to 59 ft. lbs. (80 Nm).
22. Reconnect the brake line and then slide the axle hub/brake drum onto the axle shaft. Install the outer bearing, fill the hole with grease and position the thrust washer. Install the bearing locknut and tighten it to 22 ft. lbs. (29 Nm).
23. Spin the axle hub several times to snug down the bearing and then loosen the bearing locknut until it can be turned by hand.

**NOTE: There must be absolutely NO brake drag at this time.**

24. Retighten the bearing locknut until there is a bearing preload of 0.9–2.2 lbs.(3.2–9.8 N) while turning the wheel.
25. Install the locknut lock, a new cotter pin and the cap. If the cotter pin hole does not line up properly, align the holes by tightening the nut.
26. Bleed the brakes.
27. Lower the vehicle and bounce it a few times to set the rear suspension.
28. Tighten the suspension arm bolts and the strut rod bolt to 64 ft. lbs. (87 Nm).

### 1987-90 TERCEL SEDAN

1. Raise the rear of the vehicle and support it with jackstands.
2. Remove the rear wheel.
3. Remove the brake drum.
4. Remove the locknut cap and cotter pin. Pry off the locknut and then remove the locknut itself.
5. Pull off the axle hub along with the outer wheel bearing and thrust washer.
6. Pry the inner bearing oil seal out of the brake drum and then remove the inner bearing.
7. Using a brass drift and hammer, drive out the bearing races.

**To install:**

8. Press new outer bearing races into the axle hub and fill it and the bearing cap with grease.
9. Coat your palm with grease and press the bearing into your palm until the grease oozes out the other side.
10. Position the inner bearing into the hub and then drive in a new oil seal. Coat the seal with grease.
11. Position the axle hub/brake drum onto the axle shaft. Install the outer bearing, fill the hole with grease and position the thrust washer. Install the bearing locknut and tighten it to 22 ft. lbs. (29 Nm).
12. Spin the axle hub several times to snug down the bearing and then loosen the bearing locknut until it can be turned by hand.

**NOTE: There must be absolutely NO brake drag at this time.**

13. Retighten the bearing locknut until there is a bearing preload of 0.9–2.2 lbs.(3.2–9.8 N) while turning the wheel.
14. Install the locknut lock, a new cotter pin and the cap. If the cotter pin hole does not line up properly, align the holes by tightening the nut.
15. Lower the vehicle.

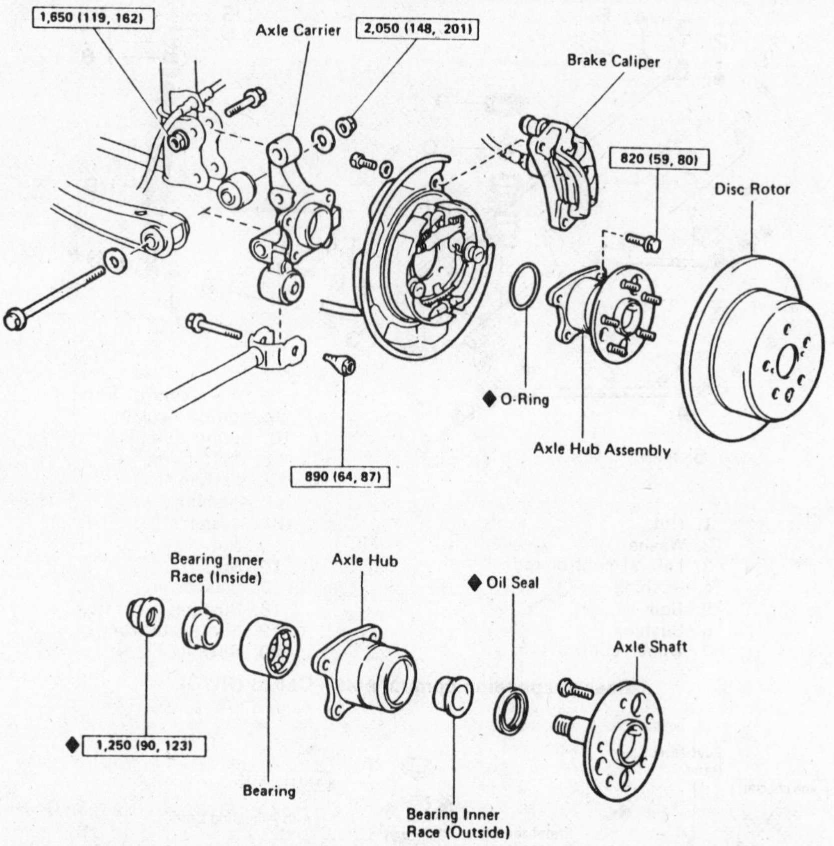


Rear axle hub and carrier—Camry (2wd), Corolla, Celica (2wd) and Tercel wagon

### CAMRY (2WD)
### TERCEL WAGON (2WD)
### 1986-90 CELICA FWD (2WD)
### 1984-90 COROLLA FWD (2WD)

1. Raise the rear of the vehicle and support it with jackstands.
2. Remove the rear wheel and tire assembly.
3. Remove the brake drum. On the Corolla FX, remove the disc brake caliper from the axle carrier and suspend it with a wire.
4. Disconnect and plug the brake line at the backing plate.
5. Remove the 4 axle hub-to-carrier bolts and slide off the hub and brake assembly. Remove the O-ring from the backing plate.
6. Remove the bolt and nut attaching the carrier to the strut rod.
7. Remove the bolt and nut attaching the carrier to the No. 1 suspension arm.
8. Remove the bolt and nut attaching the carrier to the No. 2 suspension arm.
9. Unbolt the carrier from the rear strut tube and remove the carrier.
10. Using a hammer and cold chisel, loosen the staked part of the hub nut and remove the nut.
11. Using a two-armed puller or the like, press the axle shaft from the hub.
12. Remove the bearing inner race (inside).
13. Using a two-armed puller again, pull off the bearing inner race (outside) over the bearing and then press it out of the hub.

**To install:**

14. Position a new bearing inner race (outside) on the bearing and then press a new oil seal into the hub. Coat the lip of the seal with grease.
15. Position a new bearing inner race (inside) on the bearing and then press the inner race with the hub onto the axle shaft.
16. Install the nut and tighten it to 90 ft. lbs. (123 Nm). Stake the nut with a brass drift.
17. Position the axle carrier on the strut tube and tighten the nuts to 119 ft. lbs. (162 Nm), 105 ft. lbs. (142 Nm)—1987-90 Corolla FX and 1987-90 Corolla sedan/wagon; 166 ft. lbs. (226 Nm)—1987-90 Camry.
18. Install the bolt and nut attaching the carrier to the No. 2 suspension arm; fingertighten it only.

**NOTE: Make sure that the lip of the nut is in the hole on the arm.**

19. Repeat Step 5 for the No. 1 suspension arm.

**NOTE: Make sure that the lip of the nut is in the hole on the arm.**

20. Install the strut rod-to-carrier bolt so that the lip of the nut is in the groove on the bracket.
21. Install a new O-ring onto the axle carrier. Install the axle hub and brake backing plate. Tighten the 4 bolts to 59 ft. lbs. (80 Nm).
22. Reconnect the brake line, install the brake drum and then bleed the brakes.
23. Lower the vehicle and bounce it a few times to set the rear suspension.
24. Tighten the suspension arm bolts and the strut rod bolt to 64 ft. lbs. (87 Nm). On the 1987-90 Camry and Celica, tighten the strut rod mounting bolts to 83 ft. lbs. (113 Nm) and the suspension arm bolts to 134 ft. lbs. (181 Nm).

# STEERING

## Steering Wheel

### REMOVAL & INSTALLATION

#### *Three Spoke*

**CAUTION**

***Do not attempt to remove or install the steering wheel by hammering on it. Damage to the energy-absorbing steering column could result.***

1. Unfasten the horn and turn signal multi-connector(s) at the base of the steering column shroud.
2. Loosen the trim pad retaining screws from the back side of the steering wheel.
3. Lift the trim pad and horn button assembly(ies) from the wheel.
4. Remove the steering wheel hub retaining nut.
5. Scratch matchmarks on the hub and shaft to aid in correct installation.
6. Use a steering wheel puller to remove the steering wheel.

Installation is the reverse of removal. Tighten the wheel retaining nut to 25 ft. lbs.

#### *Two Spoke*

The two spoke steering wheel is removed on the same manner as the three spoke, except that the trim pad should be pried off with a small prybar. Remove the pad by lifting it toward the top of the wheel.

#### *Four Spoke*

**CAUTION**

***Do not attempt to remove or install the steering wheel by hammering on it. Damage to the energy absorbing steering column could result.***

1. Unfasten the horn and turn signal connectors at the base of the steering column shroud, underneath the instrument panel.
2. Gently pry the center emblem off of the steering wheel.
3. Insert a wrench through the hole and remove the steering wheel retaining nut.
4. Scratch matchmarks on the hub and shaft to aid installation.
5. Use a steering wheel puller to remove the steering wheel.

Installation is the reverse of removal. Tighten the steering wheel retaining nut to 15–22 ft. lbs., except on the Celica/Supra which is tightened to 22–28 ft. lbs.

## Combination Switch

### REMOVAL & INSTALLATION

1. Disconnect the negative battery cable.
2. Unscrew the 2 retaining bolts and remove the steering column garnish.
3. Remove the upper and lower steering column covers.
4. Remove the steering wheel as detailed previously.
5. Trace the switch wiring harness to the multi-connector. Push in the lock levers and pull apart the connectors.
6. On models equipped with electronic modulated suspension (TEMS), remove the steering sensor. Unscrew the 4 mounting screws and remove the switch.
7. Installation is in the reverse order of removal.

## Ignition Lock/Switch

### REMOVAL & INSTALLATION

1. Disconnect the negative (–) battery cable.
2. Unfasten the ignition switch connector underneath the instrument panel.
3. Remove the screws which secure the upper and lower halves of the steering column cover. Remove the lower instrument panel garnish on Corona models first.
4. Turn the lock cylinder to the ACC position with the ignition key.
5. Push the lock cylinder stop in with a small, round object (cotter pin, punch, etc.).

**NOTE: On some models it may be necessary to remove the steering wheel and combination switch first.**

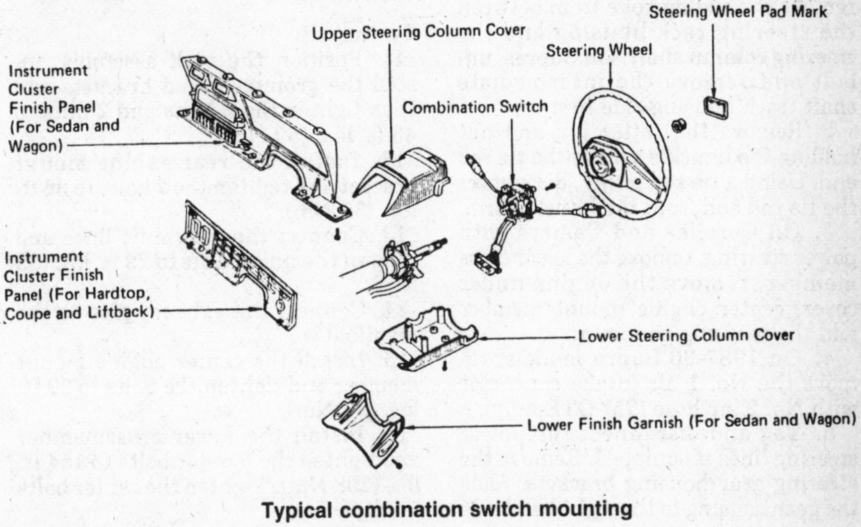

Typical combination switch mounting

6. Withdraw the lock cylinder from the lock housing while depressing the stop tab.
7. To remove the ignition switch, unfasten its securing screws and withdraw the switch from the lock housing.

**To install:**

8. Align the locking cam with the hole in the ignition switch and insert the switch into the lock housing.
9. Secure the switch with its screw(s).
10. Make sure that both the lock cylinder and column lock are in the ACC position. Slide the cylinder into the lock housing until the stop tab engages the hole in the lock.
11. The remainder of the installation in the reverse order of removal.

## Steering Gear

### REMOVAL & INSTALLATION

#### *Corolla (RWD)*

1. Raise and support the vehicle safely. Remove the front wheels. Remove the bolt attaching the coupling yoke (U-joint) to the steering worm.
2. Disconnect the relay rod from the pitman arm. Disconnect the cotter pin and nut holding the knuckle arm to the tie rod.

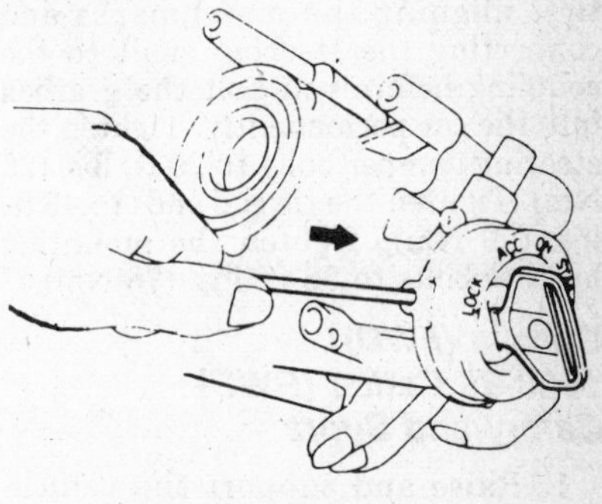
Ignition lock/switch removal

3. On 1983-87 Corollas with power steering, remove the front exhaust pipe, disconnect and plug the hydraulic lines and then wire them out of the way.

4. Remove the gear housing bracket set bolts and remove the steering gear housing down and to the left.

5. Install in reverse of removal. Torque the housing-to-frame bolts to 25–36 ft. lbs.; the coupling yoke bolt to 15–20 ft. lbs. (26 ft. lbs.–1983-87); the relay rod to 36–50 ft. lbs.

### *Cressida*

1. Raise and support the vehicle safely and remove the front wheels. Open the hood, and find the steering gearbox. Place matchmarks on the coupling and steering column shaft. Disconnect the solenoid connectors.

2. Disconnect the Pitman arm from the relay rod using a tie rod puller on the Pitman arm set nut. Disconnect the tie rod ends from the steering knuckles.

3. Remove the steering damper on models so equipped.

4. Disconnect the steering gearbox at the coupling. Unbolt the gearbox from the chassis and remove. Remove the grommets from the gear housing.

5. Installation is in the reverse order of removal, with the exception of first aligning the matchmarks and connecting the steering shaft to the coupling before you bolt the gearbox into the car permanently. Tighten the steering damper bolts to 20 ft. lbs. (26 Nm). Tighten the tie rod ends to 43 ft. lbs. (59 Nm). Tighten the mounting bracket bolts to 56 ft. lbs. (76 Nm).

### *Corolla (FWD)*
### *1983-85 Celica (RWD)*
### *Camry and Supra*

1. Raise and support the vehicle safely. Remove the front wheels. Open the hood. Remove the 2 set bolts, and remove the sliding yoke from between the steering rack housing and the steering column shaft. On Supras, unbolt and remove the intermediate shaft (rack housing side first).

2. Remove the cotter pin and nut holding the knuckle arm to the tie rod end. Using a tie rod puller, disconnect the tie rod end from the knuckle arm.

3. On Corollas and Camrys with power steering, remove the lower cross member, remove the engine under cover, center engine mount member and the rear engine mount.

4. On 1987-90 Supra models, remove the No. 1 air intake connector with No. 2 air hose (7M-GTE only).

5. Tag and disconnect the power steering lines if equipped. Remove the steering gear housing brackets. Slide the gear housing to the right hand side and then to the left hand side to remove the housing.

6. Installation is the reverse of removal. Torque the rack housing mounting bolts to 29–39 ft. lbs., on the Celica and Supra; 43 ft. lbs. on the Corolla and Camry, and the tie rod set nuts to 37–50 ft. lbs. on the Celica and Supra; 36 ft. lbs. on the the Corolla and Camry. Use a new cotter pin. On Supras, install the intermediate shaft column side first, then rack side. On Corollas w/power steering, tighten the rear engine mount bolts to 29 ft. lbs. (38 ft. lbs. on Camry). Tighten the center mounting member to 29 ft. lbs. On power steering-equipped cars, bleed the power steering system and check for fluid leaks. Adjust toe-in on all models.

### *1986-90 Celica (FWD)*

1. Raise and support the vehicle safely. Remove the front wheels.

2. Remove the both engine under covers.

3. Remove the 2 bolts that connect the steering column U-joint to the rack and then disconnect the column from the rack.

4. Remove the cotter pin and nut and then using a tie rod end removal tool, disconnect the tie rod end from the steering knuckle.

5. Remove the lower suspension crossmember.

6. Remove the mounting bolts and remove the center engine mount member.

7. Disconnect the exhaust pipe from the manifold. Position it out of the way.

8. Tag and disconnect the 2 hydraulic lines. Position them out of the way and suspend them with a wire.

9. Remove the rear engine mount bracket.

10. Remove the mounting bolts and brackets and lower steering rack from the vehicle.

**To install:**

11. Position the rack assembly, install the grommets and brackets and then tighten the 2 bolts and 2 nuts to 43 ft. lbs. (59 Nm).

12. Install the rear engine mount bracket and tighten the 2 bolts to 38 ft. lbs. (52 Nm).

13. Connect the hydraulic lines and tighten the union nuts to 29 ft. lbs. (39 Nm).

14. Connect the exhaust pipe to the manifold.

15. Install the center engine mount member and tighten the bolts to 29 ft. lbs. (39 Nm).

16. Install the lower crossmember and tighten the 5 outer bolts to 154 ft. lbs. (208 Nm). Tighten the center bolts to 29 ft. lbs.

17. Installation of the remaining components is in the reverse order of removal. Tighten the tie rod end nuts to 36 ft. lbs. (49 Nm) and use a new cotter pin. Tighten the steering column U-joint bolts to 26 ft. lbs. (35 Nm). Fill the power steering pump with DEXRON® II, bleed the system and check the wheel alignment.

### *MR2, Tercel and Starlet*

1. Jack up the vehicle and support it with jack stands.

2. Remove both front wheels.

3. Place matchmark on the main shaft, joint yoke and pinion shaft. Remove the intermediate shaft from the worm gear shaft.

4. Remove both tie rod ends.

5. Remove the lower suspension crossmember. Remove the center floor crossmember.

6. Remove the rack housing bracket mounting bolts and brackets.

**NOTE: Be careful not to damage the rubber boots.**

7. Remove the steering linkage.

8. Installation is the reverse of removal.

## ADJUSTMENTS

Adjustments to the steering gear are not necessary during normal service. Adjustments are performed only as part of overhaul.

# Power Steering Pump

## REMOVAL & INSTALLATION

### *All Except 1987-90 Supra and 1989-90 Cressida*

1. Raise and support the front of the vehicle safely. Remove the fan shroud.

2. On Camry and Celica (FWD), remove the right front wheel and the engine under cover. Remove the lower suspension crossmember.

3. Unfasten the nut from the center of the pump pulley. Disconnect the vacuum hose from the air control valve, if so equipped.

**NOTE: Use the drive belt as a brake to keep the pulley from rotating.**

4. Withdraw the drive belt. On some models it may be necessary to remove the pulley in order to remove the drive belt.

5. On models equipped with an idler pulley and on the Corolla FX, push on the drive belt to hold the pulley in place and remove the pulley set nut. Loosen the idler pulley set nut and ad-

justing bolt. Remove the drive belt and loosen the drive pulley to remove the Woodruff key.

6. Remove the pulley and the Woodruff key from the pump shaft.

7. Detach and plug the intake and outlet hoses from the pump reservoir.

**NOTE: Tie the hose ends up high so the fluid cannot flow out of them. Drain or plug the pump to prevent fluid leakage.**

8. Remove the bolt from the rear mounting brace.

9. Remove the front bracket bolts and withdraw the pump.

**To install:**

10. Tighten the pump pulley mounting bolt to 25–39 ft. lbs.

11. Tighten the 5 outer mounting bolts on the lower crossmember to 154 ft. lbs. Tighten the center bolt to 29 ft. lbs. (Celica FWD).

12. Adjust the pump drive belt tension. The belt should deflect 0.13–0.93 in. under thumb pressure applied midway between the air pump and the power steering pump.

13. Fill the reservoir with DEXRON®II automatic transmission fluid. Bleed the air from the system.

### *1987-90 Supra*
### *1989-90 Cressida*

#### 7M-GE

1. Raise and support the vehicle safely. Drain the fluid from the reservoir tank.

2. Disconnect the air hose from the air control tank. Disconnect the return hose from the reservoir tank.

3. Remove the engine under cover. Disconnect and plug the pressure hose from the power steering pump.

4. Holding the power steering pump pulley, remove the pulley set nut. Remove the drive belt adjusting nut.

5. Remove the power steering pump set bolt. Remove the drive belt, pulley and woodruff key.

6. Disconnect the oil cooler hose bracket from the power steering pump. Remove the drive belt adjust bolt and remove the power steering set bolt and power steering pump.

7. Installation is the reverse order of the removal procedure. Be sure to bleed the system upon completion of the installation procedure.

#### 7M-GTE

1. Raise and support the vehicle safely. Drain the fluid from the reservoir tank.

2. Remove the No. 1 and No. 2 air hoses with the No. 4 air cleaner pipe.

3. Disconnect the connector from the air flow meter. Remove the air flow meter installation bolt. Loosen the 5 clamps and disconnect the air hoses, release the 3 clips on the air cleaner case. Loosen the No. 7 air hose clamp and remove the No. 7 air cleaner hose with the air flow meter.

4. Remove the oil reservoir tank with bracket. Disconnect the 2 air hoses from the air control valve on the power steering pump.

5. Remove the adjusting strut. Remove the engine under cover.

6. Holding the power steering pump pulley, remove the pulley set nut. Remove the drive belt adjusting nut.

7. Remove the power steering pump set bolt. Remove the drive belt, pulley and woodruff key.

8. Disconnect and plug the pressure hose from the power steering pump.

9. Remove the power steering set bolt and power steering pump.

10. Installation is the reverse order of the removal procedure. Be sure to bleed the system upon completion of the installation procedure.

## BLEEDING

1. Raise the front of the car and support it securely with jack stands.

2. Fill the pump reservoir with DEXRON®II automatic transmission fluid.

3. Rotate the steering wheel from lock-to-lock several times. Add fluid if necessary.

4. With the steering wheel turned fully to one lock, crank the starter while watching the fluid level in the reservoir.

**NOTE: Do not start the engine. Operate the starter with a remote starter switch or have an assistant do it from inside the car. Do not run the starter for prolonged periods.**

5. Repeat Step 4 with the steering wheel turned to the opposite lock.

6. Start the engine. With the engine idling, turn the steering wheel from lock-to-lock several times.

7. Lower the front of the car and repeat Step 6.

8. Center the wheel at the midpoint of its travel. Stop the engine.

9. The fluid level should not have risen more than 0.2 in. If it does, repeat Step 7.

10. Check for fluid leakage.

# Tie Rod Ends

## REMOVAL & INSTALLATION

1. Scribe alignment marks on the tie rod and rack end (rack and pinion cars only).

2. Working at the steering knuckle arm, pull out the cotter pin and then remove the castellated nut.

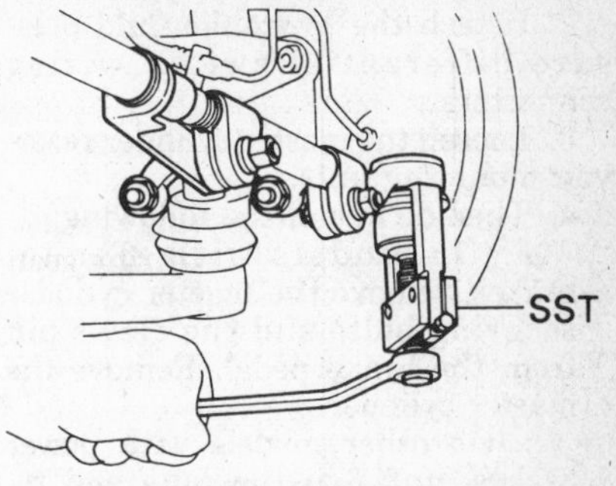

Typical tie rod end removal

3. Using a tie rod end puller, disconnect the tie rod from the steering knuckle arm.

4. Repeat the first 2 steps on the other end of the tie rod (where it attaches to the relay rod or steering rack).

**To install:**

**(non-rack and pinion cars):**

5. Turn the tie rods in their adjusting tubes until they are of equal lengths.

6. Turn the tie rod so that they cross at 90 degrees. Tighten the adjusting tube clamps so that they lock the ends in position.

7. Connect the tie rods and tighten the nuts to 37–50 ft. lbs.

8. Check the toe. Adjust if necessary.

**Rack and pinion cars:**

9. Align the alignment marks on the tie rod and rack end.

10. Install the tie rod end.

11. Tighten the nuts to 11–14 ft. lbs. on 1983 models; 19 ft. lbs. on 1984-90 models.

# BRAKES

**For all brake system repair and service procedures not detailed below, please refer to "Brakes" in the Unit Repair section.**

# Master Cylinder

## REMOVAL & INSTALLATION

**CAUTION**

***Be careful not to spill brake fluid on the painted surfaces of the vehicle; it will damage the paint.***

1. Disconnect the level warning switch connector. Remove the fluid in the master cylinder with a suitable syringe or the like. Unfasten the hydraulic lines from the master cylinder.

**NOTE: On the MR2, remove the luggage compartment trim cover first.**

2. Detach the hydraulic fluid pressure differential switch wiring connectors.
3. Loosen the master cylinder reservoir mounting nuts.
4. Then do one of the following:
a. On models with manual brakes, remove the master cylinder securing bolts and the clevis pin from the brake pedal. Remove the master cylinder.
b. On other models with power brakes, unfasten the nuts and remove the master cylinder assembly from the power brake unit.
5. Before tightening the master cylinder mounting nuts or bolts, screw the hydraulic line into the cylinder body a few turns.
6. After installation is completed, bleed the master cylinder and the brake system.

## Proportioning Valve

A proportioning valve is used on all models to reduce the hydraulic pressure to the rear brakes because of weight transfer during high speed stops. This helps to keep the rear brakes from locking up by improving front to rear brake balance.

### REMOVAL & INSTALLATION

1. Disconnect the brake lines from the valve unions.
2. Remove the valve mounting bolt, if used, and remove the valve.

**NOTE: If the proportioning valve is defective, it must be replaced as an assembly; it cannot be rebuilt.**

3. Installation is the reverse of removal. Bleed the brake system after it is completed.

## Power Brake Booster

### REMOVAL & INSTALLATION

1. Remove the master cyclinder. Disconnect the vacuum hose from the brake booster.
2. Remove the instrument lower finish panel (not necessary on all models). On the MR2, remove the wheel guard, instrument lower finish panel and air duct.
3. Remove the brake pedal return spring. Remove clip and clevis pin.
4. Remove the 4 brake booster nuts and clevis pin. Pull out the brake booster and gasket.
5. Installation is the reverse order of the removal procedure. Bleed the brake system after it is completed.

## Disc Brake Pads

### REMOVAL & INSTALLATION

**NOTE: If a squealing noise can be heard from the brakes while driving, check the pad wear indicator. If the indicator is contacting the brake disc, the pads should be replaced immediately.**

***1983-85 Celica 2wd–Front***
***1984-85 Celica 2wd–Rear***
***1988-90 Celica 4wd–Front***
***1984-87 Corolla (RWD)–Front***
***1985-87 Corolla (RWD)–Rear***
***1983-90 Cressida–Front***
***1985-90 Cressida–Rear***
***1985-90 MR2–Rear***
***1983-86 Supra–Front***
***1983-86 Supra–Rear***

1. Raise the vehicle and support it with safety stands. Remove the wheel. Siphon a sufficient quantity of brake fluid from the master cylinder reservoir to prevent any brake fluid from overflowing the master cylinder when removing or installing new pads. This is necessary as the piston must be forced into the caliper bore to provide sufficient clearance when installing the pads.
2. Grasp the caliper from behind and carefully pull it toward you to seat the piston in its bore.
3. On the 1985-87 Corolla RWD with rear discs, remove the parking brake cable clip, cotter pin and hole pin and then disconnect the cable from the parking brake cable bracket.
4. Loosen and remove the lower caliper slide pin (mounting bolt).
5. Swivel the caliper upward and out of the way, exposing the brake pads. Do not disconnect the brake line.
6. Slide out the old brake pads along with any anti-squeal shims, anti-rattle springs, pad wear indicators, pad guide plates and pad support plates. Take great care to note the position of all assorted pad hardware for the pupose of installation later on!
7. Check the brake disc (rotor) for thickness and runnout. Inspect the caliper and piston assembly for breaks, cracks, fluid seepage or other damage. Overhaul or replace as necessary.
8. Install the pad support plates, anti-rattle springs or guide plates into the torque plate.
9. Install the pad wear indicators onto the pad.
10. Install the anti-squeal shims on the outside of each pad and then install the pad assemblies into the torque plate.
11. Swivel the caliper back down over the pads. If it won't fit, use a C-clamp or hammer handle and carefully force the piston into its bore.

On the MR2 rear disc, turn the piston clockwise while pushing it in until it locks in place. Fit the protrusion on the inner pad into the groove in the piston stopper and then install the caliper. Be careful not to pinch the boot.
12. Install the lower slide pin or mounting bolt and tighten it to:
a. 1985-87 Corolla RWD–rear: 14 ft. lbs. (20 Nm)
b. 1984-87 Corolla RWD–front: 14 ft. lbs. (20 Nm)
c. 1983-86 Supra–front: 14 ft. lbs. (20 Nm)
d. 1983-86 Supra–rear: 14 ft. lbs. (20 Nm)
e. 1985-90 MR2–rear: 14 ft. lbs. (20 Nm)
f. 1983-85 Celica 2wd–front: 14 ft. lbs. (20 Nm)
g. 1983-85 Celica 2wd–rear: 14 ft. lbs. (20 Nm)
h. 1988-90 Celica 4wd–front: 27 ft. lbs. (36 Nm)
i. All others: 65 ft. lbs. (88 Nm).
13. Install the parking brake cable on the Corolla with rear discs and then adjust the automatic adjuster by pulling and releasing the parking brake lever several times.
14. Install the wheel and lower the vehicle. Check the brake fluid level. Adjust the parking brake on rear disc brake models.

***1983-90 Camry–Front***
***1989-90 Camry–Rear***
***1986-90 Celica 2wd–Front***
***1986-90 Celica 2wd–Rear***
***1988-90 Celica 4wd–Rear***
***1984-90 Corolla (FWD)–Front***
***1987-90 Corolla (FWD)–Rear***
***1985-90 MR2–Front***
***1983-84 Starlet–Front***
***1987-90 Supra–Front***
***1987-90 Supra–Rear***
***1983-90 Tercel–Front***

1. Raise the vehicle and support it with safety stands. Remove the wheel. Siphon a sufficient quantity of brake fluid from the master cylinder reservoir to prevent any brake fluid from overflowing the master cylinder when removing or installing new pads. This is necessary as the piston must be forced into the caliper bore to provide sufficient clearance when installing the pads.
2. Grasp the caliper from behind and carefully pull it toward you to seat the piston in its bore.
3. Loosen and remove the 2 caliper mounting pins (bolts) and then remove the caliper assembly. Position it out of the way. Do not disconnect the brake line.

4. Slide out the old brake pads along with any anti-squeal shims, springs, pad wear indicators and pad support plates. Take great care to note the position of all assorted pad hardware for the pupose of installation later on!

5. Check the brake disc (rotor) for thickness and runnout. Inspect the caliper and piston assembly for breaks, cracks, fluid seepage or other damage. Overhaul or replace as necessary.

6. Install the pad support plates into the torque plate.

7. Install the pad wear indicators onto the pads. Be sure that the arrow on the indicator plate is pointing in the direction of rotation.

8. Install the anti-squeal shims on the outside of each pad and then install the pad assemblies into the torque plate.

9. Position the caliper back down over the pads. If it won't fit, use a C-clamp or hammer handle and carefully force the piston into its bore.

10. Install the caliper mounting bolts and tighten to:

a. 1987-90 Corolla FWD–rear: 14 ft. lbs. (20 Nm)

b. 1983-84 Starlet–front: 14 ft. lbs. (20 Nm)

c. 1986-90 Celica–rear: 14 ft. lbs. (20 Nm)

d. 1989-90 Camry–rear: 14 ft. lbs. (20 Nm)

e. 1987-90 Supra–rear: 14 ft. lbs. (20 Nm)

f. 1987-90 Supra–front: 27 ft. lbs. (36 Nm)

g. 1987-90 Camry–front: 29 ft. lbs. (39 Nm).

h. All others: 18 ft. lbs. (25 Nm).

11. Install the wheel and lower the vehicle. Check the brake fluid level.

### *1983 Corolla–Front*
### *1983-84 Cressida–Rear*

1. Raise the vehicle and support it with safety stands. Remove the wheel. Siphon a sufficient quantity of brake fluid from the master cylinder reservoir to prevent any brake fluid from overflowing the master cylinder when removing or installing new pads. This is necessary as the piston must be forced into the caliper bore to provide sufficient clearance when installing the pads.

2. Remove the pad protector.

3. Remove the No. 2 (outer) anti-rattle spring. Hold the No. 1 (inner) anti-rattle spring and remove the lower hole pin. Remove the No. 1 spring and then remove the other hole pin.

4. Pull the pads and anti-squeal shims out of the caliper.

5. Check the brake disc (rotor) for thickness and run-out. Inspect the caliper and piston assembly for breaks, cracks, fluid seepage or other damage. Overhaul or replace as necessary.

6. Position a hammer handle between the brake disc and the caliper piston and lever the piston back into the bore.

7. Install the anti-squeal shims to the pads and then insert the pads into the caliper.

8. Install the upper hole pin. Install the No. 1 anti-rattle spring and hold its lower end down. Install the other hole pin and then install the No. 2 spring.

9. Install the pad protector.

10. Install the wheel and lower the vehicle. Check the brake fluid level.

# Brake Shoes

## REMOVAL & INSTALLATION

### *1983-85 Celica*
### *1983-87 Corolla (RWD)*
### *1983-88 Cressida*
### *1983-90 Tercel sedan*

1. Raise the vehicle and support it with safety stands. Remove the wheel.

2. Remove the brake drum. Tap the drum lightly with a rubber mallet in order to free it. If the brake drum cannot be removed easily, insert a small prybar through the hole in the backing plate and hold the automatic adjuster lever away from the adjusting bolt. Using another prybar, relieve the brake shoe tension by rotating the adjusting bolt (star wheel) in a clockwise direction. If the drum still will not come off, use a puller; but, first make sure that the parking brake is released.

**CAUTION**

***Do not depress the brake pedal once the brake drum has been removed!***

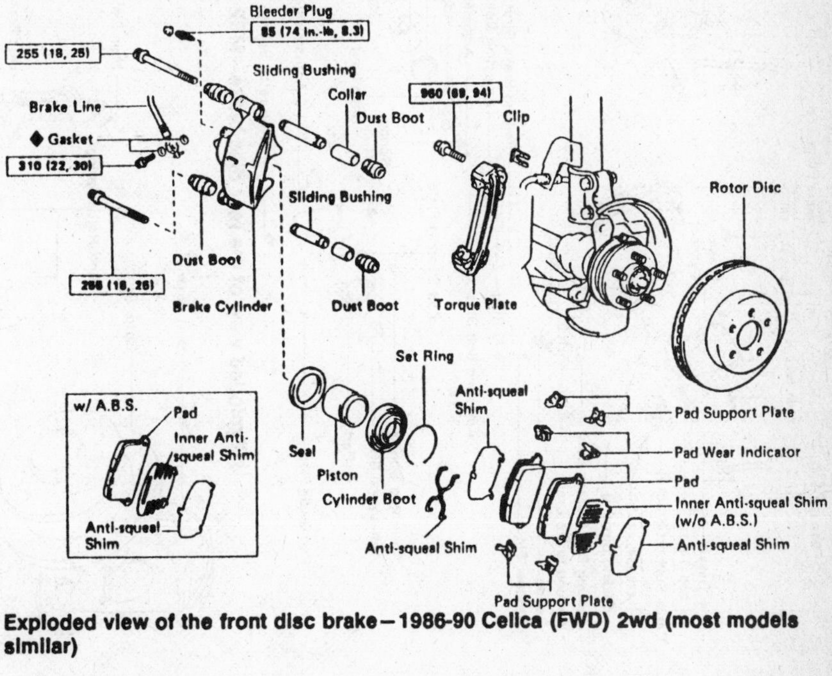


**Exploded view of the front disc brake–1986-90 Celica (FWD) 2wd (most models similar)**

3. Carefully unhook the tension spring from the leading (front) brake shoe. On the Tercel, its a return spring; you must also remove the clamp. Press the hold-down spring retainer in and turn the pin. Remove the hold-down spring, retainers and the pin. Pull out the brake shoe and unhook the anchor spring from the lower edge.

4. Remove the hold-down spring from the trailing (rear) shoe as previously detailed. Pull the shoe out with the adjuster strut, automatic adjuster assembly and springs attached and disconnect the parking brake cable. Remove the tension/return and anchor springs from the rear shoe. Take note of where they attach for later on!

5. Remove the adjusting strut. Unhook the adjusting lever spring from the rear shoe and then remove the automatic adjuster assembly by popping out the C-clip.

6. Inspect the shoes for signs of unusual wear or scoring.

7. Check the wheel cylinder for any sign of fluid seepage or frozen pistons.

8. Clean and inspect the brake backing plate and all other components. Check that the brake drum inner diameter is within specified limits. Lubricate the backing plate bosses and the anchor plate.

9. Mount the automatic adjuster assembly onto a new rear brake shoe. Make sure that the C-clip fits properly. Connect the adjusting strut and install the spring.

10. Connect the parking brake cable to the rear shoe and then position the shoe so that the lower end rides in the anchor plate and the upper end is against the boot in the wheel cylinder. Install the pin and the hold-down

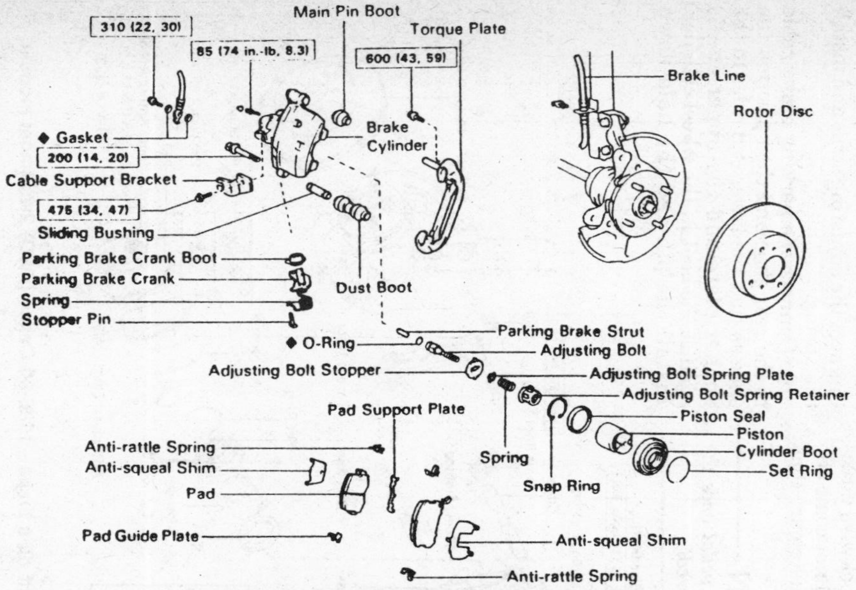

Exploded view of the rear disc brake—MR2

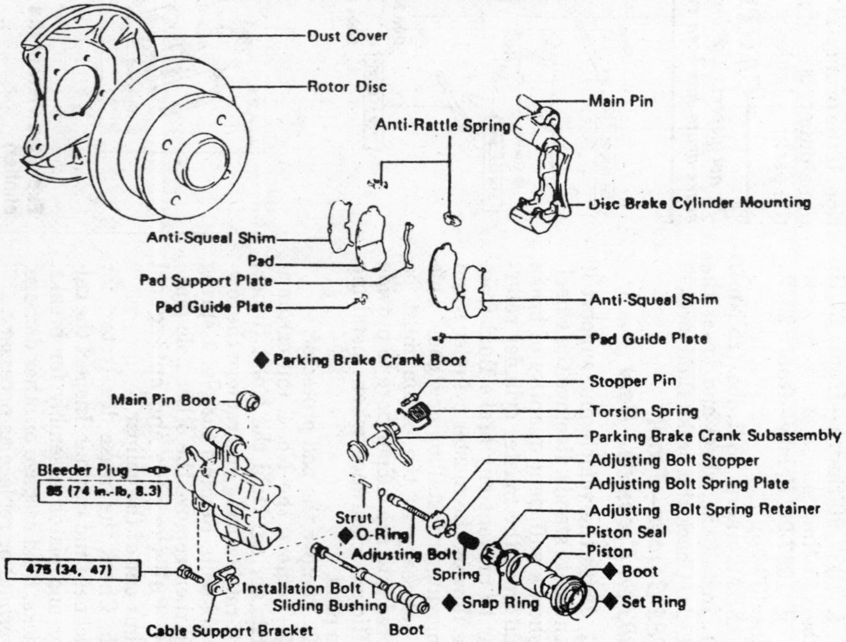

Exploded view of the rear disc brake—1985-87 Corolla (RWD)

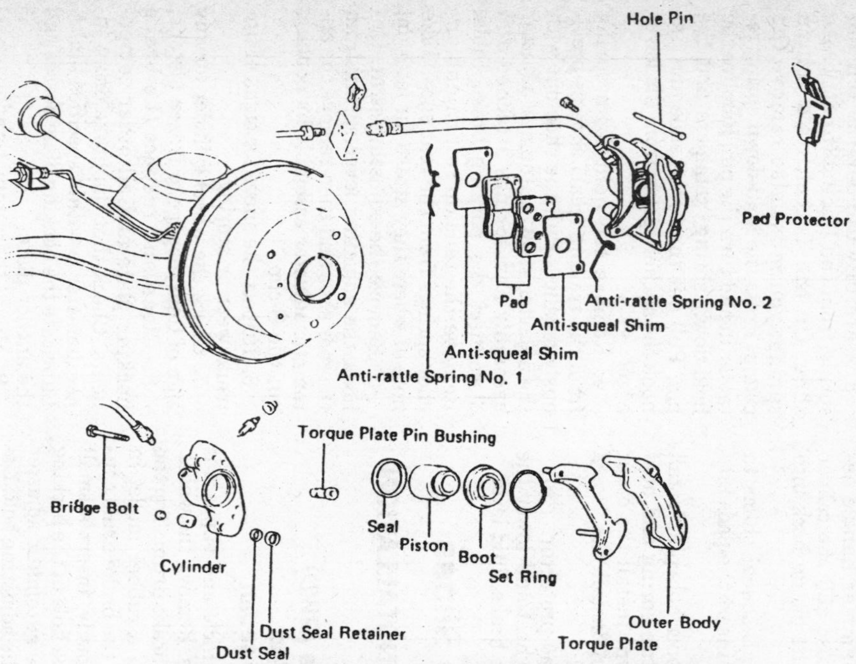

Exploded view of the rear disc brake—1983-84 Cressida

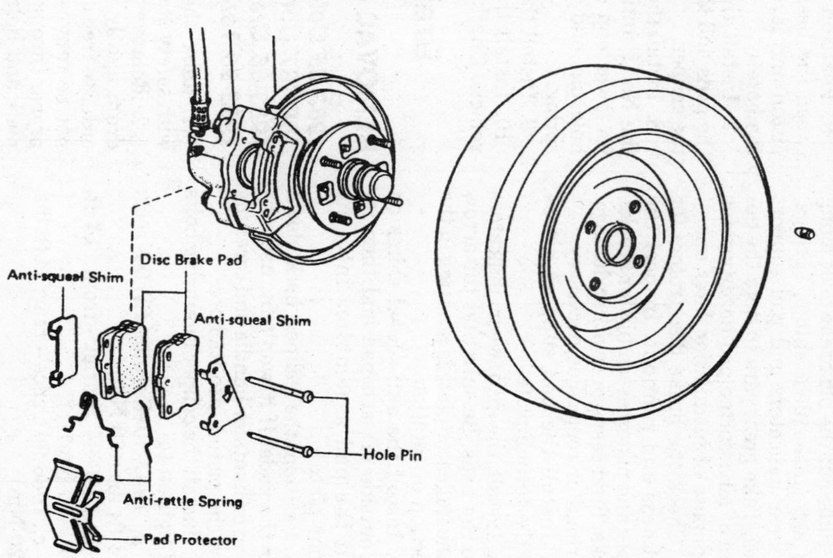

Exploded view of the front disc brake—1983 Corolla

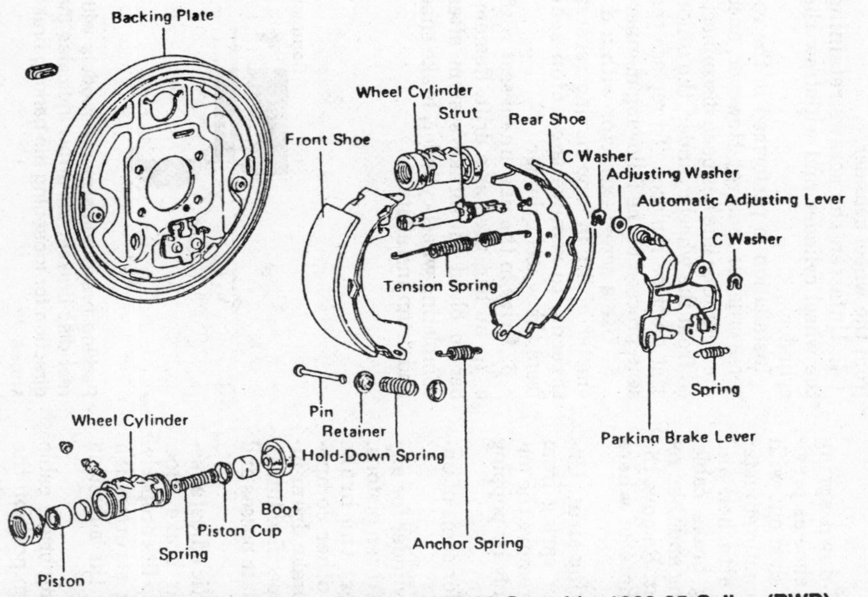


Exploded view of the rear drum brake—1983-88 Cressida, 1983-85 Celica (RWD) and 1984-87 Corolla (RWD)

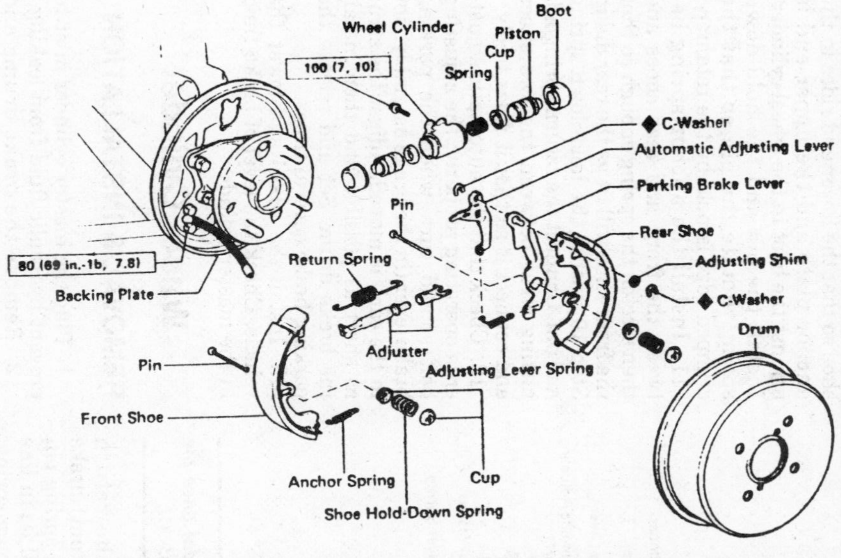


Exploded view of the rear drum brake—1986-90 Celica (FWD), 1985-87 Tercel Wagon 2wd and 1985-90 Corolla (FWD) 2wd

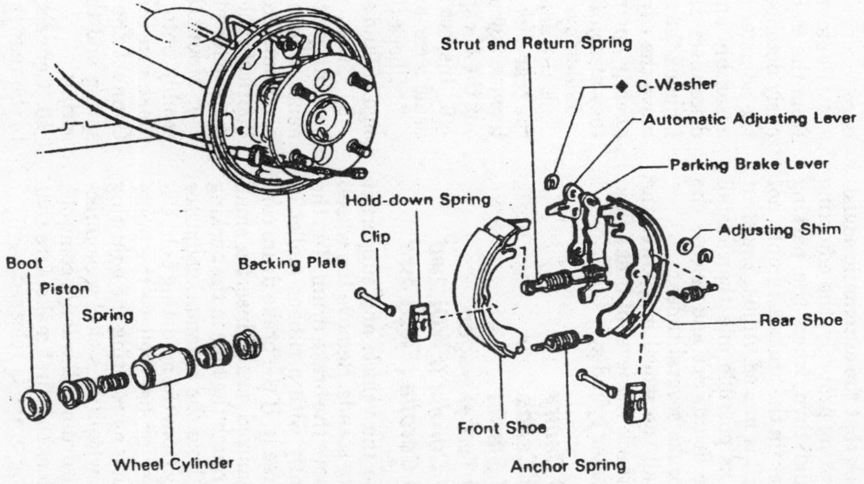


Exploded view of the rear drum brake—Starlet, 1983-87 Tercel Wagon 4wd, 1988 Tercel Wagon 2wd and 1989-90 Corolla 4wd

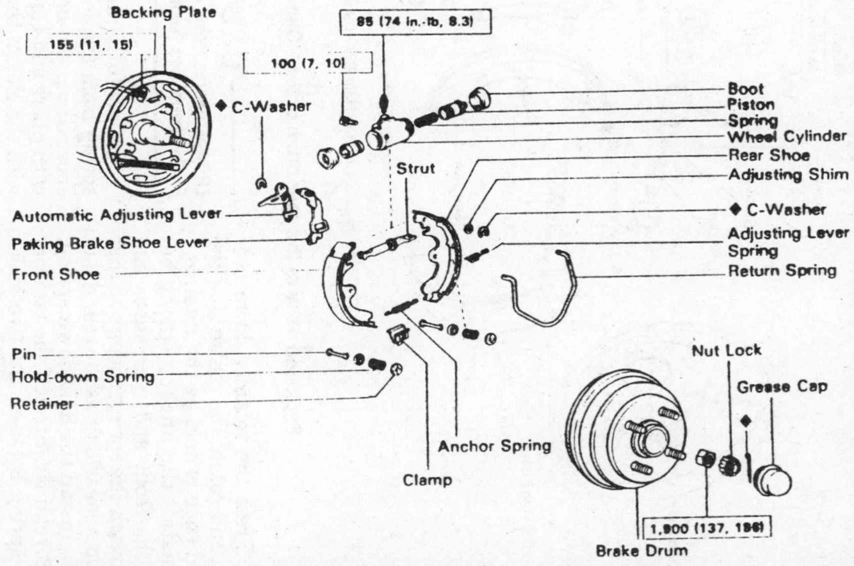


Exploded view of the rear drum brake—Tercel sedan

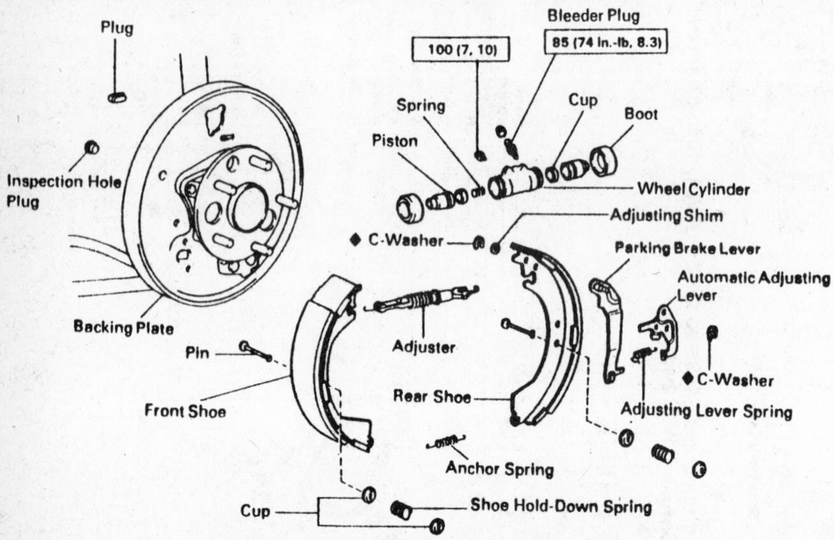


**Exploded view of the rear drum brake—Camry**

spring. Press the retainer down over the pin and rotate the pin so that the crimped edge is held by the retainer.

11. Install the anchor spring between the front and rear shoes and then stretch the spring enough so that the front shoe will fit as the rear did in Step 10. Install the hold-down spring, pin and retainer. Stretch the tension/return spring between the two shoes and connect it so that it rides freely. Don't forget the return spring clamp on the Tercel.

12. Check that the automatic adjuster is operating properly; the adjusting bolt should turn when the parking brake lever (in the brake assembly, not in the car!) is moved. Adjust the strut as short as possible and then install the brake drum. Set and release the parking brake several times.

13. Install the wheel and lower the vehicle. Check the level of brake fluid in the master cylinder.

### *1983-90 Camry*
### *1986-90 Celica*
### *1983-84 Starlet*
### *1983-89 Tercel wagon*
### *1985-90 Corolla (FWD) 2wd*
### *1989-90 Corolla (FWD) 4wd*

1. Raise the vehicle and support it with safety stands. Remove the wheel.

2. Remove the brake drum. Tap the drum lightly with a rubber mallet in order to free it. If the brake drum cannot be removed easily, insert a small prybar through the hole in the backing plate and hold the automatic adjuster lever away from the adjusting bolt. Using another prybar, relieve the brake shoe tension by rotating the adjusting bolt (star wheel) in a clockwise direction. If the drum still will not come off, use a puller; but, first make sure that the parking brake is released.

**CAUTION**

***Do not depress the brake pedal once the brake drum has been removed!***

3. Carefully unhook the return spring from the leading (front) brake shoe. Grasp the hold-down spring pin with pliers and turn it until its in line with the slot in the hold-down spring. Remove the hold-down spring and the pin. Pull out the brake shoe and unhook the anchor spring from the lower edge.

4. Remove the hold-down spring from the trailing (rear) shoe as previously detailed. Pull the shoe out with the adjuster strut, automatic adjuster assembly and springs attached and disconnect the parking brake cable. Unhook the return spring and then remove the adjusting strut. Remove the anchor spring. Take note of where they attach for later on!

5. Remove the adjusting strut. Unhook the adjusting lever spring from the rear shoe and then remove the automatic adjuster assembly by popping out the C-clip.

6. Inspect the shoes for signs of unusual wear or scoring.

7. Check the wheel cylinder for any sign of fluid seepage or frozen pistons.

8. Clean and inspect the brake backing plate and all other components. Check that the brake drum inner diameter is within specified limits. Lubricate the backing plate bosses and the anchor plate.

9. Mount the automatic adjuster assembly onto a new rear brake shoe. Make sure that the C-clip fits properly. Connect the adjusting strut/return spring and then install the adjusting spring.

10. Connect the parking brake cable to the rear shoe and then position the shoe so that the lower end rides in the anchor plate and the upper end is against the boot in the wheel cylinder. Install the pin and the hold-down spring. Rotate the pin so that the crimped edge is held by the retainer.

11. Install the anchor spring between the front and rear shoes and then stretch the spring enough so that the front shoe will fit as the rear did in Step 10. Install the hold-down spring and pin. Connect the return spring/adjusting strut between the two shoes and connect it so that it rides freely.

12. Check that the automatic adjuster is operating properly; the adjusting bolt should turn when the parking brake lever (in the brake assembly, not in the car!) is moved. Adjust the strut as short as possible and then install the brake drum. Set and release the parking brake several times.

13. Install the wheel and lower the vehicle. Check the level of brake fluid in the master cylinder.

## Wheel Cylinder

### REMOVAL & INSTALLATION

1. Plug the master cylinder inlet to prevent hydraulic fluid from leaking.

2. Remove the brake drums and shoes.

3. Working from behind the backing plate, disconnect the hydraulic line from the wheel cylinder.

4. Unfasten the screws retaining the wheel cylinder and withdraw the cylinder.

Installation is performed in the reverse order of removal. However, once the hydraulic line has been disconnected from the wheel cylinder, the union seat must be replaced. To replace the seat, proceed in the following manner:

5. Use a screw extractor with a diameter of 0.1 in. and having reverse threads, to remove the union seat from the wheel cylinder.

6. Drive in the new union seat with a $^{5}/_{16}$ in. bar, used as a drift. Remember to bleed the brake system after completing wheel cylinder, brake shoe and drum installation.

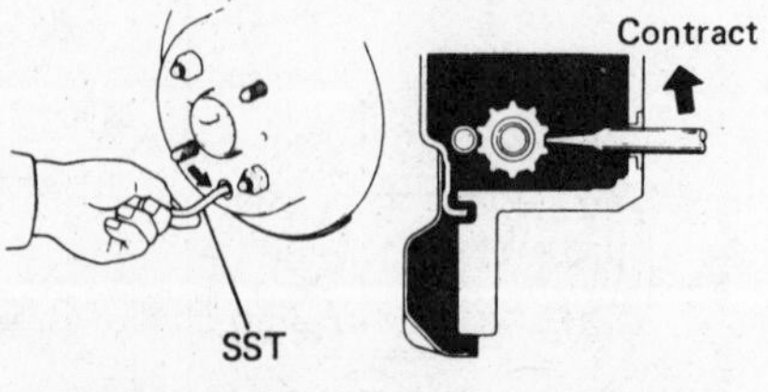


**Parking brake adjustment—models with rear disc brakes; the arrow indicates the direction for loosening the parking brake shoes**

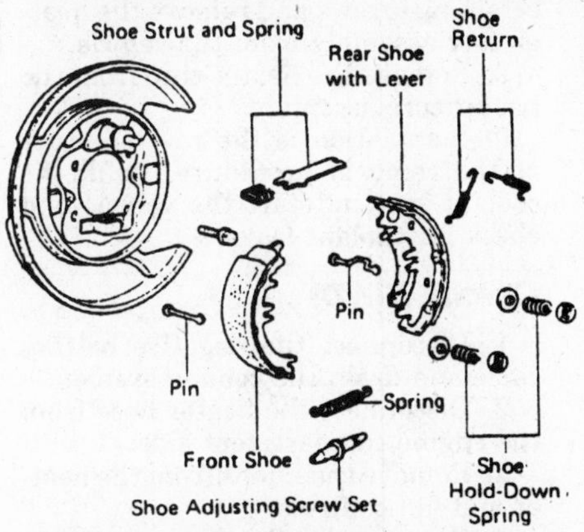


**Exploded view of the parking brake on models with rear disc brakes**

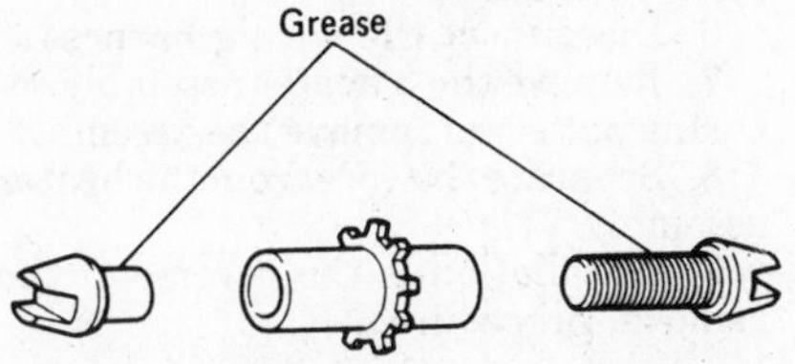


**Before assembly, lubricate the adjuster parts as indicated—models with rear disc brakes**

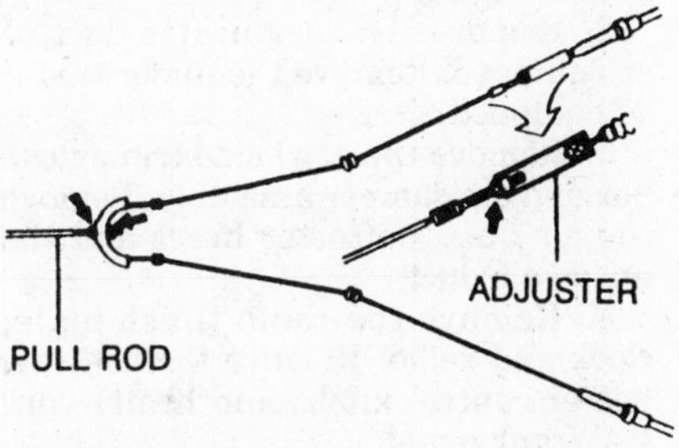


**Parking brake adjustment – Cressida**

## Parking Brake Cable

### ADJUSTMENT

**NOTE: The rear brake components should be in good condition and properly adjusted before performing this adjustment.**

1. Slowly pull the parking brake lever upward, without depressing the button on the end of it, while counting the number of notches required until the parking brake is applied.

**NOTE: Two "clicks" are equal to one notch.**

2. Check the number of notches against specifications.
3. If the brake system requires adjustment, loosen the cable adjusting nut cap which is located at the rear of the parking brake lever.

**NOTE: On some models, the adjustment and lock nuts are located under the vehicle, beneath the lever assembly.**

4. Take up the slack in the parking brake cable by rotating the adjusting nut with another open end wrench.
   a. If the number of notches is less than specified, turn the nut counterclockwise.
   b. If the number of notches is more than specified, turn the nut clockwise.
5. Tighten the adjusting cap, using care not to disturb the setting of the adjusting nut.
6. Check the rotation of the rear wheels to be sure that the brakes are not dragging.
7. The following is a list of parking brake adjustment specifications:
   a. 1983-87 Tercel 2wd – 5-8 clicks.
   b. 1988-90 Tercel 2wd – 7-9 clicks.
   c. 1983-88 Tercel 4wd – 6-8 clicks.
   d. 1983-87 Celica – 5-8 clicks.
   e. 1988-90 Celica – 4-7 clicks.
   f. 1984-87 Corolla RWD (rear drum brakes) – 5-8 clicks.
   g. 1984-87 Corolla RWD (rear disc brakes) – 6-9 clicks.
   h. 1984-90 Corolla FWD – 4-7 clicks (FX16 and models w/rear disc – 5-8).
   i. 1986-90 MR2 – 5-8 clicks.
   j. 1983-90 Cressida – 5-8 clicks.
   k. 1983-90 Camry (2wd) – 5-8 clicks.
   l. 1983 Supra – 4-7 clicks.
   m. 1984-90 Supra – 5-8 clicks.
   n. 1983-84 Starlet – 4-7 clicks.

# CHASSIS ELECTRICAL

## Heater Blower Motor

**NOTE: On most of the later Toyota models, the air conditioner assembly is integral with the heater assembly (including the blower motor) and therefore the blower motor removal may differ from the procedures detailed below. In some case it may be necessary to remove the A/C-Heater housing and assembly to remove the blower motor.**

### REMOVAL & INSTALLATION

#### *Celica and Supra*

1. Disconnect the negative battery cable. Working from under the instrument panel, unfasten the defroster hoses from the heater box.
2. Unplug the multi-connector. Loosen the mounting screws and withdraw the blower assembly.
3. Installation is the reverse order of the removal procedure.

#### *Cressida*

1. Disconnect the negative battery cable. Remove the instrument panel undercover and cowl side trim panel.
2. Remove the air duct and the glove box. Disconnect the heater control cable from the blower motor and remove the blower duct.
3. Disconnect the heater relay from the heater relay electrical connector.
4. Remove the retaining screws from the blower motor assembly. Remove the assembly from the vehicle.
5. Remove the blower motor from the blower motor assembly.
6. Installation is the reverse order of the removal procedure.

#### *Corolla (RWD) and Starlet*

1. Disconnect the negative battery cable and disconnect the blower motor wiring harness.
2. Remove the right hand defroster hose.
3. Remove the 3 retaining screws which secure the blower motor and lift out the blower motor. Separate the fan from the motor.
4. Installation is the reverse order of the removal procedure.

#### *Corolla (FWD) and Tercel*

1. Disconnect the negative battery cable. Remove the under tray, if so equipped.
2. Remove the blower duct and air duct. Before removing the air duct, remember to remove the 2 attaching clamps.
3. Remove the glove box and the heater control cable.
4. Disconnect the electrical connector on the blower motor.
5. Remove the blower motor retaining bolts and remove the blower motor.
6. Installation is the reverse order of the removal procedure.

**NOTE: Due to the lack of information available at the time of this publication, a general blower motor removal and installation procedure is outlined for the later Toyota models. The removal steps can be altered as required.**

#### *All Other Models*

1. Disconnect the negative battery

cable. Remove the 3 screws attaching the retainer.

2. Remove the glove box. Remove the duct between the blower motor assembly and the heater assembly.

3. Disconnect the blower motor wire connector at the blower motor case.

4. Disconnect the air source selector control cable at the blower motor assembly.

5. Loosen the nuts and bolts attaching the blower motor to the blower case, remove the blower motor from the vehicle.

6. Installation is the reverse order of the removal procedure.

## Heater Core

**NOTE: On some of the later Toyota models, the air conditioner assembly is integral with the heater assembly (including the heater core) and therefore the heater core removal may differ from the procedures detailed below. In some case it may be necessary to remove the A/C-Heater housing and assembly to remove the heater core.**

### REMOVAL & INSTALLATION

#### *Celica, Supra and Camry*

1. Drain the cooling system.
2. Remove the console, if so equipped, by removing the shift knob (manual), wiring connector, and console attaching screws.
3. Remove the carpeting from the tunnel.
4. If necessary, remove the cigarette lighter and ash tray.
5. Remove the package tray, if it makes access to the heater core difficult.
6. Remove the securing screws and remove the center air outlet on the Mark II.
7. Remove the bottom cover/intake assembly screws and withdraw the assembly.
8. Remove the cover from the water valve.
9. Remove the water valve.
10. Remove the hose clamps and remove the hoses from the core.
11. Remove the core.
12. Installation is the reverse of the removal procedure.

#### *Cressida*

1. Disconnect the negative battery cable. Drain the coolant system into a suitable drain pan. Remove the hood release and the fuel lid release levers.
2. Remove the left hand instrument panel undercover and lower center pad. Remove the finish plate, then remove the radio assembly.
3. Remove the heater control knobs, heater control panel and ashtray.
4. Remove the right side instrument panel undercover, glove box door and glove box.
5. Remove the front pillar garnish, cluster finish panel and instrument cluster gauge assembly.
6. Remove the safety pad and side defroster hose. Remove the heater assembly air ducts.
7. Remove the lower pad reinforcement and remove the front seats. Remove the center console assembly and the cowl side trim panel.
8. Remove the scuff plate, then position the floor carpeting aside. Remove the rear heater duct, if so equipped and heater control assembly.
9. Disconnect the heater hoses from the heater core assembly, remove the heater core grommet.
10. Remove the blower motor duct, center duct and instrument panel brace. Remove the heater core assembly from the vehicle.
11. Remove the nuts securing the heater core to the heater core assembly and remove the heater core.
12. Installation is the reverse order of the removal procedure. Refill the coolant system, start the vehicle and check for coolant leaks.

#### *Corolla (FWD)*

1. Disconnect the negative battery cable. Drain the coolant system into a suitable drain pan.
2. Remove the center console, scarf plate and front seats.
3. Position the floor carpet out of the way and remove the heater duct, if so equipped.
4. Remove the under tray, glove box and blower duct.
5. On the Corolla station wagon and sedan models, remove the following components:
   a. Remove the heater control knobs and lens. Remove the cluster lower center panel finish, ashtray and heater control assembly.
   b. Remove the instrument cluster finish panel, radio and air ducts.
6. On the Corolla coupe and liftback models, remove the following components:
   a. The instrument cluster finish panel, instrument cluster, radio trim panel and radio.
   b. Ashtray, heater control knobs, heater control panel, heater control assembly and air duct.
7. Disconnect the heater hoses from the heater core assembly and remove the heater hose grommet.
8. Remove the heater core assembly retaining screws and remove the heater core assembly from the vehicle.
9. Remove the heater core from the heater core assembly.
10. Installation is the reverse order of the removal procedure. Refill the coolant system, start the vehicle and check for coolant leaks.

#### *Corolla (RWD)*

1. Disconnect the negative battery cable and drain the cooling system.
2. Disconnect the heater hose from the engine compartment side.
3. Remove the knobs from the heater and fan controls.
4. Remove the 2 securing screws, and take the heater control panel off.
5. Remove the heater control, complete with cables.
6. Disconnect the wiring harness.
7. Remove the 3 heater assembly securing bolts and remove the assembly.
8. Separate the core from the heater assembly.
9. Installation is the reverse of the removal procedure.

#### *Starlet*

1. Disconnect the negative battery cable. Drain the coolant system into a suitable drain pan.
2. Remove the rear heater duct, if so equipped. Remove the under tray if so equipped.
3. Remove the cowl side trim, glove box and air damper assembly. Remove the air duct, defroster hoses and the inside air duct.
4. Remove the radio finish plate, clock and radio. Remove the ashtray, heater control knobs and heater control front panel.
5. Remove the heater blower switch and heater control assembly. Remove the ignition coil, then disconnect the heater hoses from the heater core assembly.
6. Remove the heater hose grommet. Remove the screws securing the heater core assembly and remove the heater core assembly from the vehicle.
7. Remove the heater core from the heater core assembly.
8. Installation is the reverse order of the removal procedure. Refill the coolant system, start the vehicle and check for coolant leaks.

#### *Tercel*

1. Disconnect the negative battery terminal.
2. Drain the radiator.
3. Remove the ash tray and retainer.
4. Remove the rear heater duct (optional).
5. Remove the left and right side defroster ducts.

6. Remove the under tray (optional).
7. Remove the glove box.
8. Remove the main air duct.
9. Disconnect the radio and remove it.
10. Disconnect the heater control cables and remove them.
11. Disconnect the heater hoses.
12. Remove the front and rear air ducts.
13. Remove the electrical connector.
14. Remove the heater bolts and remove the heater.

**NOTE: Slide the heater to the right side of car to remove it.**

15. Remove the heater core.
16. Installation is the reverse of removal.

**NOTE: Due to the lack of information available at the time of this publication, a general heater core removal and installation procedure is outlined for the later Toyota models. The removal steps can be altered as required by the technician.**

#### *All Other Models*

1. Disconnect the negative battery cable. Drain the coolant system into a suitable drain pan. Disconnect the heater hose at the engine compartment.
2. Remove the 6 clips retaining the lower part of the heater unit case, then remove the lower part of the case.
3. Using a suitable tool, carefully pry open the lower part of the heater unit case.
4. Remove the heater core assembly from the heater unit case.
5. Installation is the reverse order of the removal procedure. Reconnect the heater hose and refill the coolant system. Start the engine and check for coolant leaks.

## Radio

### REMOVAL & INSTALLATION

#### *Celica, Supra, Camry and Cressida*

1. Remove the knobs from the radio.
2. Remove the nuts from the radio control shafts.
3. Detach the antenna lead from the jack on the radio case.
4. Remove the cowl air intake duct.
5. Detach the power and speaker leads.
6. Remove the radio support nuts and bolts.
7. Remove the radio from beneath the dashboard.
8. Remove the nuts which secure the speaker through the service hole in the top of the glove box.
9. Remove remainder of the speaker securing nuts from above the radio mounting location.
10. Remove the speaker.
11. Installation is the reverse of removal.

#### *Corolla, Tercel and Starlet*

1. Remove the 2 screws from the top of the dashboard center trim panel.
2. Lift the center panel out far enough to gain access to the cigarette lighter wiring and disconnect the wiring. Remove the trim panel.
3. Unfasten the screws which secure the radio to the instrument panel braces.
4. Lift out the radio and disconnect the leads from it. Remove the radio.
5. Installation is the reverse of removal.

## Windshield Wiper Switch

### REMOVAL & INSTALLATION

The windshield wiper switch is incorporated with the cobination switch, therefore it is necessary to refer to the comination switch removal procedure in order to remove the windshield wiper switch. Once the combination switch is removed, simply unscrew the wiper switch from the combination switch assembly.

## Front Windshield Wiper Motor

### REMOVAL & INSTALLATION

#### *Tercel and Corolla (FWD)*

1. Disconnect the negative battery terminal.
2. Insert a small prybar between the linkage and the motor.
3. Pry up to separate the linkage from the motor.
4. Disconnect the electrical connector from the motor.
5. Remove the mounting bolts and remove the motor.
6. Installation is the reverse of removal.

#### *Corolla (RWD) and Starlet*

1. Disconnect the wiper motor connector.
2. Remove the service cover and loosen the wiper motor bolts.
3. Use a small prybar to separate the wiper link-to-motor connection.

**CAUTION**
***Be careful not to bend the linkage.***

4. Withdraw the wiper motor assembly.
5. Installation is in the reverse order of removal.

#### *Celica, Supra, Camry and Cressida*

1. Remove the access hole cover.
2. Separate the wiper and motor by prying gently with a small prybar.
3. Remove the left and right cowl ventilators.
4. Remove the wiper arms and the linkage mounting nuts. Push the linkage pivot ports into the ventilators.
5. Loosen the wiper link connectors at their ends and with the linkage from the cowl ventilator.
6. Start the wiper motor and turn the ignition key off when the crank is at the position illustrated.

**NOTE: The wiper motor is difficult to remove when it is in the parked position. If the motor is turned off at the wiper switch, it will automatically return to this position.**

7. Unplug the connector.
8. Loosen the motor mounting bolts and withdraw the motor.
9. Installation is the reverse of removal. Be sure to install the wiper motor with it in the park position by connecting the multi-connector and operating the wiper control switch. Assemble the crank.

#### *MR2*

1. With the wiper arms in the **UP** position and the wiper switch on **LOW**, turn the ignition switch **OFF**.
2. Disconnect the negative battery cable. Disconnect the wiper motor electrical connector, then remove the light retractor relay from the wiper bracket.
3. Remove the wiper motor set bolts. Manually lower the wiper arms, then hook the wiper link hook to the dash panel service hole.
4. Disconnect the wiper motor link. Remove the wiper motor attaching bolts then remove the wiper motor.
5. Installation is the reverse order of the removal procedure.

## Rear Wiper Motor

### REMOVAL & INSTALLATION

#### *All Models*

1. Disconnect the negative battery terminal.
2. Remove the wiper arm and rear

door trim cover. Disconnect the wiper motor wire connector.

3. Remove the wiper motor bracket attaching bolts and the wiper motor along with the bracket.

4. Installation is the reverse order of the removal procedure.

## Instrument Cluster

### REMOVAL & INSTALLATION

#### *Corolla (RWD) and Starlet*

1. Disconnect the negative battery cable.
2. Remove the instrument cluster surround.
3. Remove the center trim panel. Disconnect the cigarette lighter wiring before completely removing the panel.
4. Remove the speedometer cable and disconnect it.
5. Pull the instrument cluster out just far enough so that its wiring harness may be disconnected.
6. Remove the cluster.
7. Installation is the reverse of removal.

#### *Cressida*

1. Disconnect the battery.
2. Detach the heater control cables at the heater box.
3. Loosen the steering column clamping nuts and lower the column.

**CAUTION**

***Be careful when handling the column; it is the collapsible type. Cover the column shroud with a cloth to protect it.***

4. Loosen the instrument cluster retainingscrews and tilt the panel forward.
5. Detach the speedometer cable and wiring connectors. Remove the entire cluster assembly.
6. Remove the instruments from the panel as required.
7. Installation is the reverse of removal.

#### *Tercel and Corolla (FWD)*

1. Disconnect the negative battery terminal.
2. Remove the steering column cover.

**NOTE: Be careful not to damage the collapsible steering column mechanism.**

3. Remove the screws from the instrument panel.
4. Gently pull the panel out approximately half way.
5. Disconnect the speedometer and any other electrical connections that are necessary.
6. Remove the panel at this time.
7. Installation is the reverse of removal.

#### *Camry, Celica and Supra*

1. Disconnect the negative battery cable at the battery.
2. Remove the fuse box cover from under the left side of the instrument panel.
3. Remove the heater control knobs.
4. Using a screwdriver, carefully pry off the heater control panel.
5. Unscrew the cluster finish panel retaining screws and pull out the bottom of the panel.
6. Unplug the 2 electrical connectors and unhook the speedometer cable.
7. Remove the instrument cluster.
8. Installation is performed in the reverse of the previous steps.

## Headlight Switch

### REMOVAL & INSTALLATION

1. Disconnect the negative battery cable. Scribe alignment lines on the steering wheel and steering shaft.
2. Using a steering wheel puller, remove the steering wheel.
3. Remove the headlight and dimmer switch assembly.
4. Installation is the reverse order of the removal procedure.

## Stoplight Switch

### REMOVAL & INSTALLATION

1. Disconnect the negative battery cable. Remove the brake pedal tension spring.
2. Disconnect the stoplight switch connector.
3. Remove the switch mounting nut, then slide the switch from the mounting bracket on the pedal.
4. Installation is the reverse order of the removal procedure.

## Fuses and Fusible Links

All models have one fusible link and it is usually located in the main battery feed wire need the battery. This link will protect all the circuits except for the starter motor.

### FUSE BLOCK LOCATION

#### *All Except MR2 and Starlet*

There are 3 fuse blocks, one is located in the engine compartment on the driver's side wheel well. One on the right side kick panel under the instrument panel and the other on the left side kick panel under the instrument panel. The main fuse block being the one located on the left (driver's) side kick panel. Some of the earlier models have only one fuse block which is usually located on the left kick panel.

#### *MR2*

The fuse block is located on the left (driver's) side kick panel.

#### *Starlet*

The fuse block is located behind a flip-down door on the cowl of the instrument panel on the left hand side.

# Volkswagen 18

Cabriolet, Fox, Golf, Jetta, Rabbit, Quantum, Scirocco

# SERIAL NUMBER IDENTIFICATION

## Vehicle Identification Plate

All models also have an identification plate bearing the chassis number on the top of the instrument panel at the driver's side. This plate is easily visible through the windshield and aids in rapid identification.

On the 1983–90 models, the eighth position of the VIN code indicates engine and the tenth position, the year. The year code will be a letter. "J"–1988; "K"–1989; etc.

## Engine Number

The diesel engine number is stamped on the block between the injection pump and the vacuum pump. On all models, except the Fox, the engine number is stamped on the engine block between the fuel pump and the distributor. The Fox's engine number is located on the left side of the engine block just below the cylinder head and on the vehicle data plate.

Chassis number

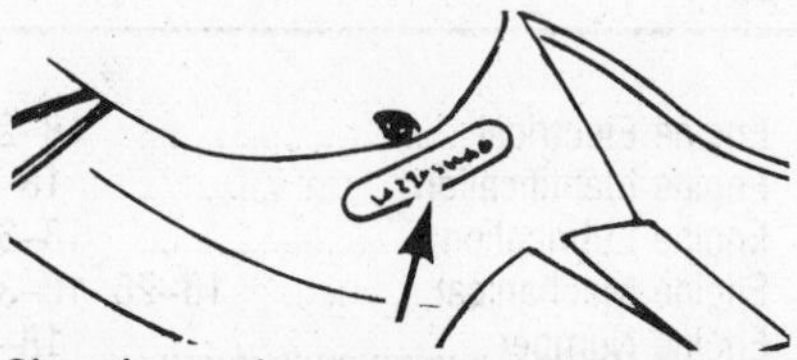

Chassis number location under rear seat

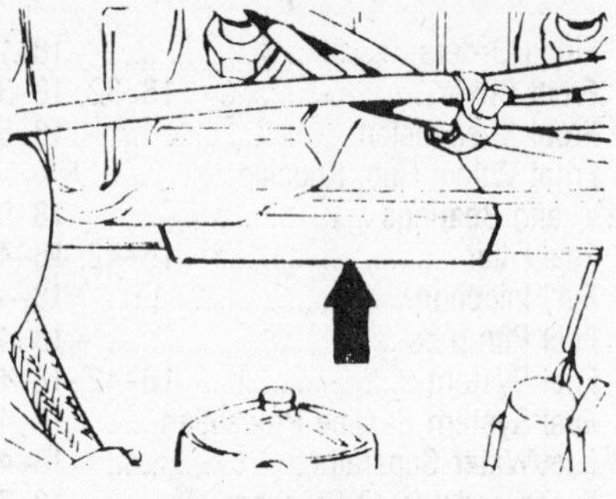

Engine number location

## Vehicle Identification Label

This label is located in the luggage compartment beside the spare wheel on the Rabbit, Golf and GTI, at the rear panel on the Jetta, Fox and Scirocco/Cabriolet, under the floor covering on the Quantum, on the left side of the cross panel behind the rear bench seat on the Rabbit Convertible (Cabriolet).

The label is marked with the Vehicle Identification Number, Vehicle Code, Engine and Transmission Code, Paint and Interior code (needed for matching paint colors) and Option codes.

## Transmission Numbers

The transmission numbers on both the manual and automatic transaxles are stamped on the clutch or converter housing where it bolts up to the engine. The number consists of 4 segments the first being the 2-letter transmissions code, the 2nd is the day of production, the 3rd is the month of production, and the 4th is the year.

### ENGINE IDENTIFICATION

| Year | Model | Engine Displacement cu. in. (cc/liter) | Engine Series Identification | No. of Cylinders | Engine Type |
|---|---|---|---|---|---|
| 1983 | Jetta (Diesel) | 97.0 (1588/1.6) | JK, CY | 4 | Water cooled in-line Diesel |
| | Jetta (Turbo Diesel) | 97.0 (1588/1.6) | JK, CY | 4 | Water cooled in-line Diesel |
| | Jetta | 105.0 (1715/1.7) | WT, EN | 4 | SOHC |
| | Quantum (Turbo Diesel) | 97.0 (1588/1.6) | JR, MF | 4 | SOHC |
| | Quantum | 130.8 (2144/2.2) | WE, KX, KM | 5 | SOHC |
| | Quantum | 105.0 (1715/1.7) | EN, JF, WT | 4 | SOHC |
| | Quantum | 109.0 (1780/1.8) | JH | 4 | SOHC |
| | Rabbit (Diesel) | 97.0 (1588/1.6) | JK, CY | 4 | Water cooled in-line Diesel |
| | Rabbit | 105.0 (1715/1.7) | WT, EN | 4 | SOHC |
| | Rabbit (Conv.) | 109.0 (1780/1.8) | JH | 4 | SOHC |
| | Rabbit (GTI) | 109.0 (1780/1.8) | JH | 4 | SOHC |
| | Scirocco | 109.0 (1780/1.8) | JH | 4 | SOHC |
| | GTI | 109.0 (1780/1.8) | JH | 4 | SOHC |
| | GLI | 109.0 (1780/1.8) | JH | 4 | SOHC |

## ENGINE IDENTIFICATION

| Year | Model | Engine Displacement cu. in. (cc/liter) | Engine Series Identification | No. of Cylinders | Engine Type |
|---|---|---|---|---|---|
| 1984 | Jetta | 105.0 (1715/1.7) | EN, JF, WT | 4 | SOHC |
| | Jetta (Diesel) | 97.0 (1588/1.6) | JP, ME | 4 | SOHC |
| | Jetta (Turbo Diesel) | 97.0 (1588/1.6) | JR, MF | 4 | Water cooled in-line Diesel |
| | Quantum | 109.0 (1780/1.8) | UM | 4 | SOHC |
| | Quantum | 130.8 (2144/2.2) | WE, KX, KM | 5 | SOHC |
| | Quantum (Turbo Diesel) | 97.0 (1588/1.62) | JR, MF | 4 | Water cooled in-line Diesel |
| | Rabbit | 105.0 (1715/1.7) | EN, JF, WT | 4 | SOHC |
| | Rabbit (Conv.) | 109.0 (1780/1.8) | GX | 4 | SOHC |
| | Rabbit (GTI) | 109.0 (1780/1.8) | HT | 4 | SOHC |
| | Rabbit (Diesel) | 97.0 (1588/1.6) | JP, ME | 4 | Water cooled in-line Diesel |
| | Scirocco | 109.0 (1780/1.8) | GX | 4 | SOHC |
| | GTI | 109.0 (1780/1.8) | HT | 4 | SOHC |
| | GLI | 109.0 (1780/1.8) | — | 4 | SOHC |
| 1985 | Jetta | 109.0 (1780/1.8) | GX | 4 | SOHC |
| | Jetta (Diesel) | 97.0 (1588/1.6) | ME | 4 | Water cooled in-line Diesel |
| | Jetta (Turbo Diesel) | 97.0 (1588/1.6) | MF | 4 | Water cooled in-line Diesel |
| | Quantum | 109.0 (1780/1.8) | GX | 4 | SOHC |
| | Quantum (Turbo Diesel) | 97.0 (1588/1.6) | MF | 4 | Water cooled in-line Diesel |
| | Quantum GL5 | 136.0 (2226/2.2) | WE, KX, KM | 5 | SOHC |
| | Scirocco | 109.0 (1780/1.8) | GX | 4 | SOHC |
| | Cabriolet | 109.0 (1780/1.8) | GX | 4 | SOHC |
| | GTI | 109.0 (1780/1.8) | HT | 4 | SOHC |
| | GLI | 109.0 (1780/1.8) | HT | 4 | SOHC |
| | Golf | 109.0 (1780/1.8) | GX | 4 | SOHC |
| | Golf (Diesel) | 97.0 (1588/1.6) | ME | 4 | Water cooled in-line Diesel |
| 1986 | Jetta | 109.0 (1780/1.8) | GX | 4 | SOHC |
| | Jetta (Diesel) | 97.0 (1588/1.6) | ME | 4 | Water cooled in-line Diesel |
| | Jetta (Turbo Diesel) | 97.0 (1588/1.6) | MF | 4 | Water cooled in-line Diesel |
| | Quantum GL5 | 136.0 (2226/2.2) | WE, KX | 5 | SOHC |
| | Quantum (Turbo Diesel) | 97.0 (1588/1.6) | MF | 4 | Water cooled in-line Diesel |
| | Quantum (Syncro) | 136.0 (2226/2.2) | JT | 5 | SOHC |
| | Cabriolet | 109.0 (1780/1.8) | GX | 4 | SOHC |
| | Scirocco | 109.0 (1780/1.8) | GX | 4 | SOHC |
| | GTI | 109.0 (1780/1.8) | RD | 4 | SOHC |
| | GLI | 109.0 (1780/1.8) | RD | 4 | SOHC |
| | Golf | 109.0 (1780/1.8) | GX | 4 | SOHC |
| | Golf (Diesel) | 97.0 (1588/1.6) | ME | 4 | Water cooled in-line Diesel |

## ENGINE IDENTIFICATION

| Year | Model | Engine Displacement cu. in. (cc/liter) | Engine Series Identification | No. of Cylinders | Engine Type |
|---|---|---|---|---|---|
| 1987 | Jetta | 109 (1780/1.8) | RV | 4 | SOHC |
| | Jetta GL | 109 (1780/1.8) | PF | 4 | SOHC |
| | Jetta GLI 16V | 109 (1780/1.8) | PL | 4 | DOHC |
| | Quantum GL5 | 136 (2226/2.2) | KX | 5 | SOHC |
| | Quantum Syncro | 136 (2226/2.2) | JT | 5 | SOHC |
| | Scirocco-16V | 109 (1780/1.8) | PL | 4 | DOHC |
| | Cabriolet | 109 (1780/1.8) | JH | 4 | SOHC |
| | Golf/GL | 109 (1780/1.8) | RV | 4 | SOHC |
| | Golf/GT | 109 (1780/1.8) | PF | 4 | SOHC |
| | Golf GTI 16V | 109 (1780/1.8) | PL | 4 | DOHC |
| | Fox/GL | 109 (1780/1.8) | UM | 4 | SOHC |
| 1988 | Jetta | 109 (1780/1.8) | RV | 4 | SOHC |
| | Jetta GL | 109 (1780/1.8) | PF | 4 | SOHC |
| | Jetta GLI 16V | 109 (1780/1.8) | PL | 4 | DOHC |
| | Jetta Carat | 109 (1780/1.8) | PF | 4 | SOHC |
| | Quantum GL5 | 136 (2226/2.2) | KX | 5 | SOHC |
| | Quantum Syncro | 136 (2226/2.2) | JT | 5 | SOHC |
| | Scirocco-16V | 109 (1780/1.8) | PL | 4 | DOHC |
| | Cabriolet | 109 (1780/1.8) | JH | 4 | SOHC |
| | Golf/GL | 109 (1780/1.8) | RV | 4 | SOHC |
| | Golf/GT | 109 (1780/1.8) | PF | 4 | SOHC |
| | Golf GTI 16V | 109 (1780/1.8) | PL | 4 | DOHC |
| | Fox/GL | 109 (1780/1.8) | UM | 4 | SOHC |
| 1989-90 | Jetta | 109 (1780/1.8) | RV | 4 | SOHC |
| | Jetta (Diesel) | 97.0 (1588/1.6) | ME | 4 | Water cooled in-line Diesel |
| | Jetta GL | 109 (1780/1.8) | PF | 4 | SOHC |
| | Jetta GLI 16V | 109 (1780/1.8) | PL | 4 | DOHC |
| | Jetta Carat | 109 (1780/1.8) | PF | 4 | SOHC |
| | Quantum GL5 | 136 (2226/2.2) | KX | 5 | SOHC |
| | Quantum Syncro | 136 (2226/2.2) | JT | 5 | SOHC |
| | Scirocco-16V | 109 (1780/1.8) | PL | 4 | DOHC |
| | Cabriolet | 109 (1780/1.8) | JH | 4 | SOHC |
| | Golf/GL | 109 (1780/1.8) | RV | 4 | SOHC |
| | Golf/GT | 109 (1780/1.8) | PF | 4 | SOHC |
| | Golf GTI 16V | 109 (1780/1.8) | PL | 4 | DOHC |
| | Fox/GL | 109 (1780/1.8) | UM | 4 | SOHC |

## GENERAL ENGINE SPECIFICATIONS

| Year | Model | Engine Displacement cu. in. (cc) | Fuel System Type | Net Horsepower @ rpm | Net Torque @ rpm (ft. lbs.) | Bore × Stroke (in.) | Com-pression Ratio | Oil Pressure @ rpm |
|---|---|---|---|---|---|---|---|---|
| 1983 | Jetta | 105.0 (1715) | CIS Fuel Inj. | 74 @ 5000① | 90 @ 3000 | 3.13×3.40 | 8.2:1 | 28 @ 2000 |
| | Jetta (Diesel) | 97.0 (1588) | Fuel Inj. | 52 @ 4800 | 72 @ 2000 | 3.01×3.40 | 23.0:1 | 28 @ 2000 |
| | Jetta (Turbo Diesel) | 97.0 (1588) | Fuel Inj. | 68 @ 4500 | 98 @ 2800 | 3.01×3.40 | 23.0:1 | 74 @ 5000 |
| | Quantum | 105.0 (1715) | CIS Fuel Inj. | 74 @ 5000① | 90 @ 3000 | 3.13×3.40 | 8.2:1 | 28 @ 2000 |
| | Quantum | 109.0 (1780) | CIS Fuel Inj. | 88 @ 5500 | 96 @ 3250 | 3.19×3.40 | 9.0:1 | 28 @ 2000 |
| | Quantum | 130.8 (2144) | CIS Fuel Inj. | 100 @ 5100 | 112 @ 3000 | 3.12×3.40 | 8.2:1 | 28 @ 2000 |
| | Quantum (Turbo Diesel) | 97.0 (1588) | Fuel Inj. | 68 @ 4500 | 98 @ 2800 | 3.01×3.40 | 23.0:1 | 74 @ 5000 |
| | Rabbit | 105.0 (1715) | CIS Fuel Inj. | 74 @ 5000① | 90 @ 3000 | 3.13×3.40 | 8.2:1 | 28 @ 2000 |
| | Rabbit | 105.0 (1715) | 1 bbl. | 65 @ 5000 | 88 @ 2800 | 3.13×3.40 | 8.2:1 | 28 @ 2000 |
| | Rabbit (Conv.) | 109.0 (1780) | CIS Fuel Inj. | 74 @ 5000 | 90 @ 3000 | 3.13×3.40 | 8.2:1 | 28 @ 2000 |
| | Rabbit (GTI) | 109.0 (1780) | CIS Fuel Inj. | 90 @ 5500 | 100 @ 3000 | 3.19×3.40 | 8.5:1 | 28 @ 2000 |
| | Rabbit (Diesel) | 97.0 (1588) | Fuel Inj. | 52 @ 4800 | 97 @ 2800 | 3.01×3.40 | 23.0:1 | 74 @ 5000 |
| | Scirocco | 105.0 (1715) | CIS Fuel Inj. | 74 @ 5000① | 90 @ 3000 | 3.13×3.40 | 8.2:1 | 28 @ 2000 |
| | Scirocco | 109.0 (1780) | CIS Fuel Inj. | 90 @ 5500 | 100 @ 3000 | 3.19×3.40 | 8.5:1 | 28 @ 2000 |
| | GTI | 109.0 (1780) | CIS Fuel Inj. | 90 @ 5500 | 100 @ 3000 | 3.19×3.40 | 8.5:1 | 28 @ 2000 |
| | GLI | 109.0 (1780) | CIS Fuel Inj. | 90 @ 5500 | 100 @ 3000 | 3.19×3.40 | 8.5:1 | 28 @ 2000 |
| | GTI (Diesel) | 97.0 (1588) | Fuel Inj. | 52 @ 4800 | 72 @ 3000 | 3.01×3.40 | 23.0:1 | 74 @ 5000 |
| 1984 | Jetta | 105.0 (1715) | CIS Fuel Inj. | 74 @ 5000 | 90 @ 3000 | 3.13×3.40 | 8.2:1 | 28 @ 2000 |
| | Jetta (Diesel) | 97.0 (1588) | Fuel Inj. | 52 @ 4800 | 72 @ 2000 | 3.01×3.40 | 23.0:1 | 28 @ 2000 |
| | Jetta (Turbo Diesel) | 97.0 (1588) | Fuel Inj. | 68 @ 4500 | 98 @ 2800 | 3.01×3.40 | 23.0:1 | 74 @ 5000 |
| | Quantum | 109.0 (1780) | CIS Fuel Inj. | 88 @ 5500 | 96 @ 3250 | 3.19×3.40 | 9.0:1 | 28 @ 2000 |
| | Quantum | 130.0 (2144) | CIS Fuel Inj. | 100 @ 3000 | 112 @ 3000 | 3.12×3.40 | 8.2:1 | 28 @ 2000 |
| | Quantum (Turbo Diesel) | 97.0 (1588) | Fuel Inj. | 68 @ 4500 | 98 @ 2800 | 3.01×3.40 | 23.0:1 | 74 @ 5000 |
| | Rabbit | 105.0 (1715) | 1 bbl. | 65 @ 5000 | 88 @ 2800 | 3.13×3.40 | 8.2:1 | 28 @ 2000 |
| | Rabbit (Conv.) | 109.0 (1780) | CIS Fuel Inj. | 90 @ 5500 | 100 @ 3000 | 3.19×3.40 | 8.5:1 | 28 @ 2000 |
| | Rabbit (GTI) | 109.0 (1780) | CIS Fuel Inj. | 90 @ 5500 | 100 @ 3000 | 3.19×3.40 | 8.5:1 | 28 @ 2000 |
| | Rabbit (Diesel) | 97.0 (1588) | Fuel Inj. | 52 @ 4800 | 97 @ 2800 | 3.01×3.40 | 23.0:1 | 74 @ 5000 |
| | Rabbit | 105.0 (1715) | CIS Fuel Inj. | 74 @ 5000 | 90 @ 3000 | 3.13×3.40 | 8.2:1 | 28 @ 2000 |
| | Scirocco | 109.0 (1780) | CIS Fuel Inj. | 90 @ 5500 | 100 @ 3000 | 3.19×3.40 | 8.5:1 | 28 @ 2000 |
| | GTI (Diesel) | 97.0 (1588) | Fuel Inj. | 52 @ 4800 | 72 @ 3000 | 3.01×3.40 | 23.0:1 | 74 @ 5000 |
| | GTI | 109.0 (1780) | CIS Fuel Inj. | 90 @ 5500 | 100 @ 3000 | 3.19×3.40 | 8.5:1 | 28 @ 2000 |
| | GLI | 109.0 (1780) | CIS Fuel Inj. | 90 @ 5500 | 100 @ 3000 | 3.19×3.40 | 8.5:1 | 28 @ 2000 |
| 1985 | Jetta | 109.0 (1780) | CIS Fuel Inj. | 85 @ 5250 | 98 @ 3000 | 3.19×3.40 | 8.5:1 | 28 @ 2000 |
| | Jetta (Diesel) | 97.0 (1588) | Fuel Inj. | 52 @ 4800 | 72 @ 2000 | 3.01×3.40 | 23.0:1 | 28 @ 2000 |
| | Jetta (Turbo Diesel) | 97.0 (1588) | Fuel Inj. | 68 @ 4500 | 48 @ 2800 | 3.01×3.40 | 23.0:1 | 74 @ 5000 |
| | Quantum | 109.0 (1780) | CIS Fuel Inj. | 88 @ 5500 | 96 @ 3250 | 3.19×3.40 | 9.0:1 | 28 @ 2000 |
| | Quantum (Turbo Diesel) | 97.0 (1588) | Fuel Inj. | 68 @ 4500 | 98 @ 2800 | 3.01×3.40 | 23.0:1 | 74 @ 5000 |
| | Quantum | 136.0 (2226) | Fuel Inj. | 110 @ 5500 | 122 @ 2500 | 3.19×3.40 | 8.5:1 | 28 @ 2000 |
| | Cabriolet | 109.0 (1780) | CIS Fuel Inj. | 90 @ 5500 | 100 @ 3000 | 3.19×3.40 | 8.5:1 | 28 @ 2000 |
| | Scirocco | 109.0 (1780) | CIS Fuel Inj. | 90 @ 5500 | 100 @ 3000 | 3.19×3.40 | 8.5:1 | 28 @ 2000 |
| | GTI | 109.0 (1780) | CIS Fuel Inj. | 100 @ 5500 | 107 @ 3000 | 3.20×3.40 | 10.0:1 | 28 @ 2000 |
| | GLI | 109.0 (1780) | CIS Fuel Inj. | 100 @ 5500 | 107 @ 3000 | 3.20×3.40 | 10.0:1 | 28 @ 2000 |
| | Golf | 109.0 (1780) | CIS Fuel Inj. | 85 @ 5250 | 98 @ 3000 | 3.19×3.40 | 8.5:1 | 28 @ 2000 |
| | Golf (Diesel) | 97.0 (1588) | Fuel Inj. | 52 @ 4800 | 70 @ 2000 | 3.01×3.40 | 23.0:1 | 74 @ 5000 |

## GENERAL ENGINE SPECIFICATIONS

| Year | Model | Engine Displacement cu. in. (cc) | Fuel System Type | Net Horsepower @ rpm | Net Torque @ rpm (ft. lbs.) | Bore × Stroke (in.) | Com-pression Ratio | Oil Pressure @ rpm |
|---|---|---|---|---|---|---|---|---|
| 1986 | Jetta | 109.0 (1780) | CIS Fuel Inj. | 88 @ 5500 | 110 @ 3250 | 3.19×3.40 | 9.0:1 | 28 @ 2000 |
| | Jetta (Diesel) | 97.0 (1588) | Fuel Inj. | 52 @ 4800 | 72 @ 2000 | 3.01×3.40 | 23.0:1 | 28 @ 2000 |
| | Jetta (Turbo Diesel) | 97.0 (1588) | Fuel Inj. | 68 @ 4500 | 98 @ 2800 | 3.01×3.40 | 23.0:1 | 74 @ 5000 |
| | Quantum | 109.0 (1780) | CIS Fuel Inj. | 88 @ 5500 | 96 @ 3250 | 3.19×3.40 | 9.0:1 | 28 @ 2000 |
| | Quantum (Turbo Diesel) | 97.0 (1588) | Fuel Inj. | 68 @ 4500 | 98 @ 2800 | 3.01×3.40 | 23.0:1 | 74 @ 5000 |
| | Quantum | 136.0 (2226) | Fuel Inj. | 110 @ 5500 | 122 @ 2500 | 3.19×3.40 | 8.5:1 | 28 @ 2000 |
| | Cabriolet | 109.0 (1780) | CIS Fuel Inj. | 90 @ 5500 | 100 @ 3000 | 3.19×3.40 | 8.5:1 | 28 @ 2000 |
| | Scirocco | 109.0 (1780) | CIS Fuel Inj. | 90 @ 5500 | 100 @ 3000 | 3.19×3.40 | 8.5:1 | 28 @ 2000 |
| | GTI | 109.0 (1780) | CIS Fuel Inj. | 100 @ 5500 | 110 @ 3250 | 3.20×3.40 | 10.0:1 | 28 @ 2000 |
| | GLI | 109.0 (1780) | CIS Fuel Inj. | 100 @ 5500 | 110 @ 3250 | 3.20×3.40 | 10.0:1 | 28 @ 2000 |
| | Golf | 109.0 (1780) | CIS Fuel Inj. | 85 @ 5250 | 98 @ 3000 | 3.19×3.40 | 9.0:1 | 28 @ 2000 |
| | Golf (Diesel) | 97.0 (1588) | Fuel Inj. | 52 @ 4800 | 70 @ 2000 | 3.01×3.40 | 23.0:1 | 74 @ 5000 |
| 1987 | Jetta | 109 (1780) | Digifant II | 100 @ 5400 | 107 @ 3400 | 3.19×3.40 | 10.0:1 | 28 @ 2000 |
| | Jetta GL | 109 (1780) | Digifant II | 105 @ 5400 | 110 @ 3400 | 3.19×3.40 | 10.0:1 | 28 @ 2000 |
| | Jetta GLI 16V | 109 (1780) | CIS-E Fuel Inj. | 123 @ 5800 | 120 @ 4250 | 3.19×3.40 | 10.0:1 | 28 @ 2000 |
| | Quantum GL5 | 136 (2226) | CIS-E Fuel Inj. | 110 @ 5500 | 122 @ 2400 | 3.19×3.40 | 8.5:1 | 28 @ 2000 |
| | Quantum Syncro | 136 (2226) | CIS-E Fuel Inj. | 115 @ 5500 | 126 @ 3000 | 3.19×3.40 | 8.5:1 | 28 @ 2000 |
| | Scirocco 16V | 109 (1780) | CIS-E Fuel Inj. | 123 @ 5800 | 120 @ 4250 | 3.19×3.40 | 10.0:1 | 28 @ 2000 |
| | Cabriolet | 109 (1780) | CIS-E Fuel Inj. | 90 @ 5500 | 100 @ 3000 | 3.19×3.40 | 9.0:1 | 28 @ 2000 |
| | Golf GL | 109 (1780) | Digifant II | 100 @ 5400 | 107 @ 3400 | 3.19×3.40 | 10.0:1 | 28 @ 2000 |
| | Golf GT | 109 (1780) | Digifant II | 105 @ 5400 | 110 @ 3400 | 3.19×3.40 | 10.0:1 | 28 @ 2000 |
| | Golf GTI 16V | 109 (1780) | CIS-E Fuel Inj. | 123 @ 5800 | 120 @ 4250 | 3.19×3.40 | 10.0:1 | 28 @ 2000 |
| | Fox/GL | 109 (1780) | CIS-E Fuel Inj. | 81 @ 5500 | 93 @ 3250 | 3.19×3.40 | 9.0:1 | 28 @ 2000 |
| 1988 | Jetta | 109 (1780) | Digifant II | 100 @ 5400 | 107 @ 3400 | 3.19×3.40 | 10.0:1 | 28 @ 2000 |
| | Jetta GL | 109 (1780) | Digifant II | 105 @ 5400 | 110 @ 3400 | 3.19×3.40 | 10.0:1 | 28 @ 2000 |
| | Jetta GLI 16V | 109 (1780) | CIS-E Fuel Inj. | 123 @ 5800 | 120 @ 4250 | 3.19×3.40 | 10.0:1 | 28 @ 2000 |
| | Jetta Carat | 109 (1780) | Digifant II | 105 @ 5400 | 110 @ 3400 | 3.19×3.40 | 10.0:1 | 28 @ 2000 |
| | Quantum GL5 | 136 (2226) | CIS-E Fuel Inj. | 110 @ 5500 | 122 @ 2400 | 3.19×3.40 | 8.5:1 | 28 @ 2000 |
| | Quantum Syncro | 136 (2226) | CIS-E Fuel Inj. | 115 @ 5500 | 126 @ 3000 | 3.19×3.40 | 8.5:1 | 28 @ 2000 |
| | Scirocco 16V | 109 (1780) | CIS-E Fuel Inj. | 123 @ 5800 | 120 @ 4250 | 3.19×3.40 | 10.0:1 | 28 @ 2000 |
| | Cabriolet | 109 (1780) | CIS-E Fuel Inj. | 90 @ 5500 | 100 @ 3000 | 3.19×3.40 | 9.0:1 | 28 @ 2000 |
| | Golf GL | 109 (1780) | Digifant II | 100 @ 5400 | 107 @ 3400 | 3.19×3.40 | 10.0:1 | 28 @ 2000 |
| | Golf GT | 109 (1780) | Digifant II | 105 @ 5400 | 110 @ 3400 | 3.19×3.40 | 10.0:1 | 28 @ 2000 |
| | Golf GTI 16V | 109 (1780) | CIS-E Fuel Inj. | 123 @ 5800 | 120 @ 4250 | 3.19×3.40 | 10.0:1 | 28 @ 2000 |
| | Fox/GL | 109 (1780) | CIS-E Fuel Inj. | 81 @ 5500 | 93 @ 3250 | 3.19×3.40 | 9.0:1 | 28 @ 2000 |
| 1989-90 | Jetta | 109 (1780) | Digifant II | 100 @ 5400 | 107 @ 3400 | 3.19×3.40 | 10.0:1 | 28 @ 2000 |
| | Jetta (Diesel) | 97.0 (1588) | Fuel Inj. | 52 @ 4800 | 72 @ 2000 | 3.01×3.40 | 23.0:1 | 28 @ 2000 |
| | Jetta GL | 109 (1780) | Digifant II | 105 @ 5400 | 110 @ 3400 | 3.19×3.40 | 10.0:1 | 28 @ 2000 |
| | Jetta GLI 16V | 109 (1780) | CIS-E Fuel Inj. | 123 @ 5800 | 120 @ 4250 | 3.19×3.40 | 10.0:1 | 28 @ 2000 |
| | Jetta Carat | 109 (1780) | Digifant II | 105 @ 5400 | 110 @ 3400 | 3.19×3.40 | 10.0:1 | 28 @ 2000 |
| | Quantum GL5 | 136 (2226) | CIS-E Fuel Inj. | 110 @ 5500 | 122 @ 2400 | 3.19×3.40 | 8.5:1 | 28 @ 2000 |
| | Quantum Syncro | 136 (2226) | CIS-E Fuel Inj. | 115 @ 5500 | 126 @ 3000 | 3.19×3.40 | 8.5:1 | 28 @ 2000 |
| | Scirocco 16V | 109 (1780) | CIS-E Fuel Inj. | 123 @ 5800 | 120 @ 4250 | 3.19×3.40 | 10.0:1 | 28 @ 2000 |
| | Cabriolet | 109 (1780) | CIS-E Fuel Inj. | 90 @ 5500 | 100 @ 3000 | 3.19×3.40 | 9.0:1 | 28 @ 2000 |

## GENERAL ENGINE SPECIFICATIONS

| Year | Model | Engine Displacement cu. in. (cc) | Fuel System Type | Net Horsepower @ rpm | Net Torque @ rpm (ft. lbs.) | Bore × Stroke (in.) | Com-pression Ratio | Oil Pressure @ rpm |
|---|---|---|---|---|---|---|---|---|
| 1989-90 | Golf GL | 109 (1780) | Digifant II | 100 @ 5400 | 107 @ 3400 | 3.19×3.40 | 10.0:1 | 28 @ 2000 |
| | Golf GT | 109 (1780) | Digifant II | 105 @ 5400 | 110 @ 3400 | 3.19×3.40 | 10.0:1 | 28 @ 2000 |
| | Golf GTI 16V | 109 (1780) | CIS-E Fuel Inj. | 123 @ 5800 | 120 @ 4250 | 3.19×3.40 | 10.0:1 | 28 @ 2000 |
| | Fox/GL | 109 (1780) | CIS-E Fuel Inj. | 81 @ 5500 | 93 @ 3250 | 3.19×3.40 | 9.0:1 | 28 @ 2000 |

## GASOLINE ENGINE TUNE-UP SPECIFICATIONS

| Year | Model | Engine Displacement cu. in. (cc) | Spark Plugs Type | Spark Plugs Gap (in.) | Ignition Timing (deg.) MT | Ignition Timing (deg.) AT | Com-pression Pressure (psi) | Fuel Pump (psi) | Idle Speed (rpm) MT | Idle Speed (rpm) AT | Valve Clearance In. ② | Valve Clearance Ex. ② |
|---|---|---|---|---|---|---|---|---|---|---|---|---|
| 1983 | Jetta | 105.0 (1715) | W175T30 N8Y | 0.024–0.032 | 3 ATDC @ Idle | 3 ATDC @ Idle | 131–174 | NA | 850–1000 | 850–1000 ① | 0.008–0.012 | 0.016–0.020 |
| | Quantum | 105.0 (1715) | W175T30 N8Y | 0.024–0.032 | 3 ATDC @ Idle | 3 ATDC @ Idle | 131–174 | NA | 850–1000 | 850–1000 ① | 0.008–0.012 | 0.016–0.020 |
| | Quantum | 130.8 (2144) | W7D N8Y | 0.024–0.028 | 6 BTDC @ Idle | 3 ATDC @ Idle | 131–174 | NA | 850–1000 | 850–1000 | 0.008–0.012 | 0.016–0.020 |
| | Rabbit | 105.0 (1715) | W175T30 N8Y | 0.024–0.032 | 3 ATDC @ Idle | 3 ATDC @ Idle | 131–174 | NA | 850–1000 | 850–1000 ① | 0.008–0.012 | 0.016–0.020 |
| | Scirocco | 105.0 (1715) | W175T30 N8Y | 0.024–0.032 | 3 ATDC @ Idle | 3 ATDC @ Idle | 131–174 | NA | 850–1000 | 850–1000 ① | 0.008–0.012 | 0.016–0.020 |
| | Scirocco | 109.0 (1780) | WR7DS N8YGY | 0.024–0.028 | 6 BTDC @ Idle | 6 BTDC @ Idle | 131–174 | NA | 880–1000 | 880–1000 | 0.008–0.012 | 0.016–0.020 |
| | Cabriolet | 109.0 (1780) | WR7DS N8YGY | 0.024–0.028 | 6 BTDC @ Idle | 6 BTDC @ Idle | 131–174 | NA | 880–1000 | 880–1000 | 0.008–0.012 | 0.016–0.020 |
| | GTI | 109.0 (1780) | WR7DS N8YGY | 0.024–0.028 | 6 BTDC @ Idle | 6 BTDC @ Idle | 131–174 | NA | 880–1000 | 880–1000 | 0.008–0.012 | 0.016–0.020 |
| | GLI | 109.0 (1780) | WR7DS N8YGY | 0.024–0.028 | 6 BTDC @ Idle | 6 BTDC @ Idle | 131–174 | NA | 880–1000 | 880–1000 | 0.008–0.012 | 0.016–0.020 |
| 1984 | Jetta | 105.0 (1715) | W175T30 N8Y | 0.024–0.032 | 3 ATDC @ Idle | 3 ATDC @ Idle | 131–174 | NA | 850–1000 | 850–1000 ① | 0.008–0.012 | 0.016–0.020 |
| | Quantum | 105.0 (1715) | W175T30 N8Y | 0.024–0.032 | 3 ATDC @ Idle | 3 ATDC @ Idle | 131–174 | NA | 850–1000 | 850–1000 ① | 0.008–0.012 | 0.016–0.020 |
| | Quantum | 130.8 (2144) | W7D N8Y | 0.024–0.028 | 6 BTDC @ Idle | 3 ATDC @ Idle | 142–184 | NA | 850–1000 | 850–1000 | 0.008–0.012 | 0.016–0.020 |
| | Rabbit | 105.0 (1715) | W175T30 N8Y | 0.024–0.032 | 3 ATDC @ Idle | 3 ATDC @ Idle | 131–174 | NA | 850–1000 | 850–1000 ① | 0.008–0.012 | 0.016–0.020 |
| | Cabriolet | 109.0 (1780) | WR7DS N8YGY | 0.024–0.028 | 6 BTDC @ Idle | 6 BTDC @ Idle | 131–174 | NA | 880–1000 | 880–1000 | 0.008–0.012 | 0.016–0.020 |
| | Scirocco | 105.0 (1715) | W175T30 N8Y | 0.024–0.032 | 3 ATDC @ Idle | 3 ATDC @ Idle | 131–174 | NA | 850–1000 | 850–1000 ① | 0.008–0.012 | 0.016–0.020 |
| | Scirocco | 109.0 (1780) | W175T30 N8YGY | 0.024–0.028 | 6 BTDC @ Idle | 6 BTDC @ Idle | 131–174 | NA | 880–1000 | 880–1000 | 0.008–0.012 | 0.016–0.020 |
| | GTI | 109.0 (1780) | WR7DS N8YGY | 0.024–0.028 | 6 BTDC @ Idle | 6 BTDC @ Idle | 131–174 | NA | 880–1000 | 880–1000 | 0.008–0.012 | 0.016–0.020 |
| | GLI | 109.0 (1780) | WR7DS N8YGY | 0.024–0.028 | 6 BTDC @ Idle | 6 BTDC @ Idle | 131–174 | NA | 880–1000 | 880–1000 | 0.008–0.012 | 0.016–0.020 |

## GASOLINE ENGINE TUNE-UP SPECIFICATIONS

| Year | Model | Engine Displacement cu. in. (cc) | Spark Plugs Type | Spark Plugs Gap (in.) | Ignition Timing (deg.) MT | Ignition Timing (deg.) AT | Com-pression Pressure (psi) | Fuel Pump (psi) | Idle Speed (rpm) MT | Idle Speed (rpm) AT | Valve Clearance In. ② | Valve Clearance Ex. ② |
|---|---|---|---|---|---|---|---|---|---|---|---|---|
| 1985 | Jetta | 109.0 (1780) | WR7DS N8GY | 0.024–0.032 | 6 BTDC @ Idle | 6 BTDC @ Idle | 123–174 | NA | 850–1000 | 850–1000 | Hyd. | Hyd. |
| | Quantum | 109.0 (1780) | WR7DS N8GY | 0.028–0.032 | 6 BTDC @ Idle | 6 BTDC @ Idle | 123–174 | NA | 850–1000 | 850–1000 | Hyd. | Hyd. |
| | Quantum | 136.0 (2226) | WR7DS N8GY | 0.028–0.032 | 6 BTDC @ Idle | 3 ATDC @ Idle | 123–174 | NA | 850–1000 | 850–1000 | 0.008–0.012 | 0.016–0.020 |
| | Cabriolet | 109.0 (1780) | WR7DS N8GY | 0.024–0.032 | 6 BTDC @ Idle | 6 BTDC @ Idle | 123–174 | NA | 850–1000 | 850–1000 | Hyd. | Hyd. |
| | Scirocco | 109.0 (1780) | WR7DS N8GY | 0.024–0.032 | 6 BTDC @ Idle | 6 BTDC @ Idle | 123–174 | NA | 850–1000 | 850–1000 | Hyd. | Hyd. |
| | GTI | 109.0 (1780) | WR7DS N8GY | 0.024–0.032 | 6 BTDC @ Idle | 6 BTDC @ Idle | 123–174 | NA | 850–1000 | 850–1000 | Hyd. | Hyd. |
| | GLI | 109.0 (1780) | WR7DS N8GY | 0.024–0.032 | 6 BTDC @ Idle | 6 BTDC @ Idle | 123–174 | NA | 850–1000 | 850–1000 | Hyd. | Hyd. |
| | Golf | 109.0 (1780) | WR7DS N8GY | 0.024–0.032 | 6 BTDC @ Idle | 6 BTDC @ Idle | 123–174 | NA | 850–1000 | 850–1000 | Hyd. | Hyd. |
| 1986 | Jetta | 109.0 (1780) | W7DTC N8GY | 0.028–0.032 | 6 BTDC @ Idle | 6 BTDC @ Idle | 123–174 | NA | 800–900 | 800–900 | Hyd. | Hyd. |
| | Quantum | 109.0 (1780) | W7DTC | 0.028–0.035 | 6 BTDC @ Idle | 6 BTDC @ Idle | 123–174 | NA | 800–900 | 800–900 | Hyd. | Hyd. |
| | Quantum | 136.0 (2226) | W7DTC | 0.024–0.031 | 6 BTDC @ Idle | 3 ATDC @ Idle | 123–174 | NA | 800–900 | 800–900 | Hyd. | Hyd. |
| | Cabriolet | 109.0 (1780) | WR7DS N8GY | 0.024–0.032 | 6 BTDC @ Idle | 6 BTDC @ Idle | 123–174 | NA | 850–1000 | 850–1000 | Hyd. | Hyd. |
| | Scirocco | 109.8 (1799) | F6DTC | 0.027–0.035 | 6 BTDC @ Idle | 6 BTDC @ Idle | 123–174 | NA | 800–900 | 800–900 | Hyd. | Hyd. |
| | GTI | 109.0 (1780) | W7DTC N8GY | 0.028–0.032 | 6 BTDC @ Idle | 6 BTDC @ Idle | 123–174 | NA | 800–900 | 800–900 | Hyd. | Hyd. |
| | GLI | 109.0 (1780) | W7DTC N8GY | 0.028–0.032 | 6 BTDC @ Idle | 6 BTDC @ Idle | 123–174 | NA | 800–900 | 800–900 | Hyd. | Hyd. |
| | Golf | 109.0 (1780) | WR7DS N8GY | 0.028–0.032 | 6 BTDC @ Idle | 6 BTDC @ Idle | 123–174 | NA | 800–900 | 800–900 | Hyd. | Hyd. |
| 1987 | Jetta | 109 (1780) | WR7DS | 0.024–0.032 | 6 BTDC @ Idle | 6 BTDC @ Idle | 131–174 ① | NA | 800–900 | 800–900 | Hyd. | Hyd. |
| | Jetta GL | 109 (1780) | W7DTC | 0.027–0.035 | 6 BTDC @ Idle | 6 BTDC @ Idle | 131–174 | NA | 800–900 | 800–900 | Hyd. | Hyd. |
| | Jetta GLI 16V | 109 (1780) | F6DTC | 0.027–0.035 | 6 BTDC @ Idle | 6 BTDC @ Idle | 145–189 | NA | 800–900 | 800–900 | Hyd. | Hyd. |
| | Quantum GL5 | 136 (2226) | WR7DS | 0.027–0.035 | 6 BTDC @ Idle | 6 BTDC @ Idle | 131–174 | NA | 750–850 | 750–850 | Hyd. | Hyd. |
| | Quantum Syncro | 136 (2226) | WR7DS | 0.027–0.035 | 6 BTDC @ Idle | 6 BTDC @ Idle | 131–174 | NA | 750–850 | 750–850 | Hyd. | Hyd. |
| | Scirocco 16V | 109 (1780) | F6DTC | 0.027–0.035 | 6 BTDC @ Idle | 6 BTDC @ Idle | 145–189 | NA | 800–900 | 800–900 | Hyd. | Hyd. |
| | Cabriolet | 109 (1780) | W7DTC | 0.027–0.035 | 6 BTDC @ Idle | 6 BTDC @ Idle | 131–174 | NA | 850–1000 | 850–1000 | Hyd. | Hyd. |
| | Golf GL | 109 (1780) | WR7DS | 0.024–0.032 | 6 BTDC @ Idle | 6 BTDC @ Idle | 131–174 | NA | 800–900 | 800–900 | Hyd. | Hyd. |

## GASOLINE ENGINE TUNE-UP SPECIFICATIONS

| Year | Model | Engine Displacement cu. in. (cc) | Spark Plugs Type | Spark Plugs Gap (in.) | Ignition Timing (deg.) MT | Ignition Timing (deg.) AT | Compression Pressure (psi) | Fuel Pump (psi) | Idle Speed (rpm) MT | Idle Speed (rpm) AT | Valve Clearance In. ② | Valve Clearance Ex. ② |
|---|---|---|---|---|---|---|---|---|---|---|---|---|
| 1987 | Golf GT | 109 (1780) | W7DTC | 0.027–0.035 | 6 BTDC @ Idle | 6 BTDC @ Idle | 131–174 | NA | 800–900 | 800–900 | Hyd. | Hyd. |
| | Golf GTI 16V | 109 (1780) | F6DTC | 0.027–0.035 | 6 BTDC @ Idle | 6 BTDC @ Idle | 145–189 | NA | 800–900 | 800–900 | Hyd. | Hyd. |
| | Fox/GL | 109 (1780) | W7DTC | 0.027–0.035 | 6 BTDC @ Idle | 6 BTDC @ Idle | 131–174 | NA | 800–1000 | 800–1000 | Hyd. | Hyd. |
| 1988 | Jetta | 109 (1780) | WR7DS | 0.024–0.032 | 6 BTDC @ Idle | 6 BTDC @ Idle | 131–174 ① | NA | 800–900 | 800–900 | Hyd. | Hyd. |
| | Jetta GL | 109 (1780) | W7DTC | 0.027–0.035 | 6 BTDC @ Idle | 6 BTDC @ Idle | 131–174 | NA | 800–900 | 800–900 | Hyd. | Hyd. |
| | Jetta GLI 16V | 109 (1780) | F6DTC | 0.027–0.035 | 6 BTDC @ Idle | 6 BTDC @ Idle | 145–189 | NA | 800–900 | 800–900 | Hyd. | Hyd. |
| | Jetta Carat | 109 (1780) | W7DTC | 0.027–0.035 | 6 BTDC @ Idle | 6 BTDC @ Idle | 131–174 | NA | 800–900 | 800–900 | Hyd. | Hyd. |
| | Quantum GL5 | 136 (2226) | WR7DS | 0.027–0.035 | 6 BTDC @ Idle | 6 BTDC @ Idle | 131–174 | NA | 750–850 | 750–850 | Hyd. | Hyd. |
| | Quantum Syncro | 136 (2226) | WR7DS | 0.027–0.035 | 6 BTDC @ Idle | 6 BTDC @ Idle | 131–174 | NA | 750–850 | 750–850 | Hyd. | Hyd. |
| | Scirocco 16V | 109 (1780) | F6DTC | 0.027–0.035 | 6 BTDC @ Idle | 6 BTDC @ Idle | 145–189 | NA | 800–900 | 800–900 | Hyd. | Hyd. |
| | Cabriolet | 109 (1780) | W7DTC | 0.027–0.035 | 6 BTDC @ Idle | 6 BTDC @ Idle | 131–174 | NA | 850–1000 | 850–1000 | Hyd. | Hyd. |
| | Golf GL | 109 (1780) | WR7DS | 0.024–0.032 | 6 BTDC @ Idle | 6 BTDC @ Idle | 131–174 | NA | 800–900 | 800–900 | Hyd. | Hyd. |
| | Golf GT | 109 (1780) | W7DTC | 0.027–0.035 | 6 BTDC @ Idle | 6 BTDC @ Idle | 131–174 | NA | 800–900 | 800–900 | Hyd. | Hyd. |
| | Golf GTI 16V | 109 (1780) | F6DTC | 0.027–0.035 | 6 BTDC @ Idle | 6 BTDC @ Idle | 145–189 | NA | 800–900 | 800–900 | Hyd. | Hyd. |
| | Fox/GL | 109 (1780) | W7DTC | 0.027–0.035 | 6 BTDC @ Idle | 6 BTDC @ Idle | 131–174 | NA | 800–1000 | 800–1000 | Hyd. | Hyd. |
| 1989 | Jetta | 109 (1780) | WR7DS | 0.024–0.032 | 6 BTDC @ Idle | 6 BTDC @ Idle | 131–174 ① | NA | 800–900 | 800–900 | Hyd. | Hyd. |
| | Jetta GL | 109 (1780) | W7DTC | 0.027–0.035 | 6 BTDC @ Idle | 6 BTDC @ Idle | 131–174 | NA | 800–900 | 800–900 | Hyd. | Hyd. |
| | Jetta GLI 16V | 109 (1780) | F6DTC | 0.027–0.035 | 6 BTDC @ Idle | 6 BTDC @ Idle | 145–189 | NA | 800–900 | 800–900 | Hyd. | Hyd. |
| | Jetta Carat | 109 (1780) | W7DTC | 0.027–0.035 | 6 BTDC @ Idle | 6 BTDC @ Idle | 131–174 | NA | 800–900 | 800–900 | Hyd. | Hyd. |
| | Quantum GL5 | 136 (2226) | WR7DS | 0.027–0.035 | 6 BTDC @ Idle | 6 BTDC @ Idle | 131–174 | NA | 750–850 | 750–850 | Hyd. | Hyd. |
| | Quantum Syncro | 136 (2226) | WR7DS | 0.027–0.035 | 6 BTDC @ Idle | 6 BTDC @ Idle | 131–174 | NA | 750–850 | 750–850 | Hyd. | Hyd. |
| | Scirocco 16V | 109 (1780) | F6DTC | 0.027–0.035 | 6 BTDC @ Idle | 6 BTDC @ Idle | 145–189 | NA | 800–900 | 800–900 | Hyd. | Hyd. |
| | Cabriolet | 109 (1780) | W7DTC | 0.027–0.035 | 6 BTDC @ Idle | 6 BTDC @ Idle | 131–174 | NA | 850–1000 | 850–1000 | Hyd. | Hyd. |
| | Golf GL | 109 (1780) | WR7DS | 0.024–0.032 | 6 BTDC @ Idle | 6 BTDC @ Idle | 131–174 | NA | 800–900 | 800–900 | Hyd. | Hyd. |

## GASOLINE ENGINE TUNE-UP SPECIFICATIONS

| Year | Model | Engine Displacement cu. in. (cc) | Spark Plugs Type | Spark Plugs Gap (in.) | Ignition Timing (deg.) MT | Ignition Timing (deg.) AT | Compression Pressure (psi) | Fuel Pump (psi) | Idle Speed (rpm) MT | Idle Speed (rpm) AT | Valve Clearance In. ② | Valve Clearance Ex. ② |
|---|---|---|---|---|---|---|---|---|---|---|---|---|
| 1989 | Golf GT | 109 (1780) | W7DTC | 0.027–0.035 | 6 BTDC @ Idle | 6 BTDC @ Idle | 131–174 | NA | 800–900 | 800–900 | Hyd. | Hyd. |
| | Golf GTI 16V | 109 (1780) | F6DTC | 0.027–0.035 | 6 BTDC @ Idle | 6 BTDC @ Idle | 145–189 | NA | 800–900 | 800–900 | Hyd. | Hyd. |
| | Fox/GL | 109 (1780) | W7DTC | 0.027–0.035 | 6 BTDC @ Idle | 6 BTDC @ Idle | 131–174 | NA | 800–1000 | 800–1000 | Hyd. | Hyd. |
| 1990 | All | SEE UNDERHOOD SPECIFICATION STICKER | | | | | | | | | | |

**NOTE:** The underhood specifications sticker often reflects tune-up specification changes made in production. Sticker figures must be used if they disagree with those in this chart.

① Without idle stabilizer
② Valve clearance need not be adjusted unless it varies more than 0.002 in. from specifications

## FIRING ORDERS

**NOTE: To avoid confusion, always replace spark plug wires 1 at a time.**

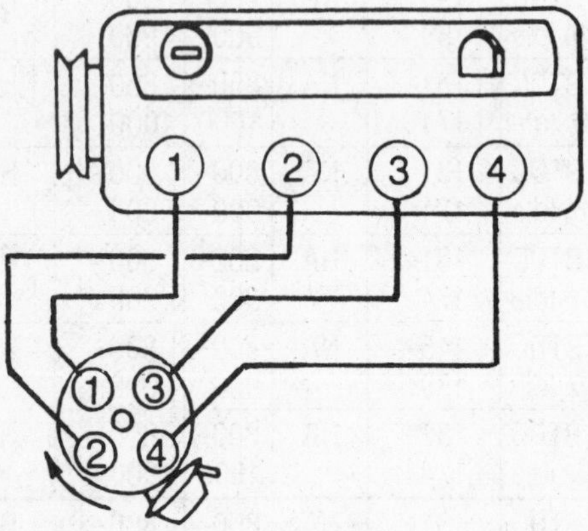

Firing order: 4 cylinder engines; 1–3–4–2

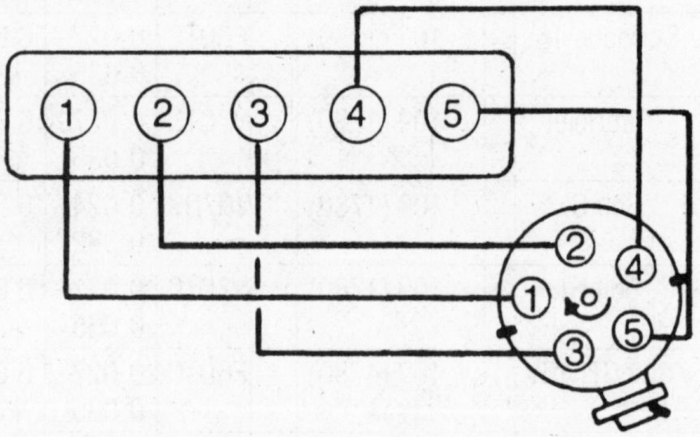

Firing order: 5 cylinder engine: 1–2–4–5

## DIESEL ENGINE TUNE-UP SPECIFICATIONS

| Year | Engine Displacement cu. in. (cc) | Valve Clearance ① Intake (in.) | Valve Clearance ① Exhaust (in.) | Intake Valve Opens (deg.) | Injection Pump Setting (deg.) | Injection Nozzle Pressure (psi) New | Injection Nozzle Pressure (psi) Used | Idle Speed (rpm) | Cranking Compression Pressure (psi) |
|---|---|---|---|---|---|---|---|---|---|
| 1983 | 97.0 (1588) | 0.008–0.012 ① | 0.016–0.020 ① | N.A. | Align Marks | 1885③ | 1706③ | 800–850②④ | 406 minimum |
| 1984 | 97.0 (1588) | 0.008–0.012 ① | 0.016–0.020 ① | N.A. | Align Marks | 1885③ | 1706③ | 800–850②④ | 406 minimum |
| 1985 | 97.0 (1588) | 0.008–0.012 ① | 0.016–0.020 ① | N.A. | Align Marks | 1885③ | 1706③ | 800–850②④ | 406 minimum |

## DIESEL ENGINE TUNE-UP SPECIFICATIONS

| Year | Engine Displacement cu. in. (cc) | Valve Clearance ① Intake (in.) | Valve Clearance ① Exhaust (in.) | Intake Valve Opens (deg.) | Injection Pump Setting (deg.) | Injection Nozzle Pressure (psi) New | Injection Nozzle Pressure (psi) Used | Idle Speed (rpm) | Cranking Compression Pressure (psi) |
|---|---|---|---|---|---|---|---|---|---|
| 1986 | 97.0 (1588) | 0.008–① 0.012 | 0.016–① 0.020 | N.A. | Align Marks | 1885③ | 1706③ | 800–850②④ | 406 minimum |
| 1989 | 97.0 (1588) | 0.008–① 0.012 | 0.016–① 0.020 | N.A. | Align Marks | 1885③ | 1706③ | 800–850②④ | 406 minimum |

N.A. Not Available
① Warm clearance given.
Cold clearance:
Intake—0.006-0.010
Exhaust—0.014-0.018
② Volkswagen has lowered the idle speed on early models to this specification.
Valve clearance need not be adjusted unless it varies more than 0.002 in. from specification.
③ Turbo diesel—
New—2306
Used—2139
④ Turbo diesel—900-1000

## CAPACITIES

| Year | Model | Engine Displacement cu. in. (cc) | Engine Crankcase with Filter | Engine Crankcase without Filter | Transmission (pts.) 4-Spd | Transmission (pts.) 5-Spd | Transmission (pts.) Auto. | Drive Axle (pts.) | Fuel Tank (gal.) | Cooling System (qts.) |
|---|---|---|---|---|---|---|---|---|---|---|
| 1983 | Jetta | 105.0 (1715) | 4.3 | 3.7 | — | 4.2 | 6.4 | 1.6 | 10.5 | 5.1 |
| | Jetta (Diesel) | 97.0 (1588) | 4.8 | 4.3 | — | 4.2 | 6.4 | 1.6 | 10.5 | 6.9 |
| | Jetta (Turbo-Diesel) | 97.0 (1588) | 4.8 | 4.3 | — | 4.2 | 6.4 | 1.6 | 10.5 | 6.9 |
| | Quantum (4 cyl.) | 105.0 (1715) | 3.6 | 3.2 | — | 4.2 | 6.4 | 1.6 | 16.0 | 5.5 |
| | Quantum (5 cyl.) | 109.0 (1780) | 4.0 | 3.5 | — | 4.2 | 6.4 | 1.6 | 16.0 | 5.5 |
| | Quantum (Diesel) | 130.8 (2144) | 4.0 | 3.5 | — | 4.2 | 6.4 | 1.6 | 16.0 | 6.5 |
| | Quantum (Turbo-Diesel) | 97.0 (1588) | 4.8 | 4.3 | — | 4.2 | 6.4 | 1.6 | 16.0 | 6.5 |
| | Rabbit | 105.0 (1715) | 4.3 | 3.7 | 3.2 | 4.2 | 6.4 | 1.6 | 10.0 | 6.9 |
| | Rabbit | 109.0 (1780) | 4.3 | 3.7 | 3.2 | 4.2 | 6.4 | 1.6 | 10.0 | 7.3 |
| | Rabbit (Conv.) | 109.0 (1780) | 4.3 | 3.7 | — | 4.2 | 6.2 | 1.6 | 10.5 | 7.3 |
| | Rabbit (Diesel) | 97.0 (1588) | 4.8 | 4.3 | 3.2 | 4.2 | 6.4 | 1.6 | 10.0 | 6.9 |
| | Scirocco | 105.0 (1715) | 4.3 | 3.7 | NA | 4.2 | 6.4 | 1.6 | 10.5 | 5.1 |
| | Scirocco | 109.0 (1780) | 4.3 | 3.7 | NA | 4.2 | 6.4 | 1.6 | 10.5 | 6.5 |
| | GTI | 109.0 (1780) | 4.3 | 3.7 | 3.2 | 4.2 | 6.4 | 1.6 | 10.0 | 7.3 |
| | GTI (Diesel) | 97.0 (1588) | 4.8 | 4.3 | 3.2 | 4.2 | 6.4 | 1.6 | 11.0 | 6.5 |
| | GLI | 109.0 (1780) | 4.3 | 3.7 | 3.2 | 4.2 | — | 1.6 | 14.5 | 6.5 |
| 1984 | Jetta | 105.0 (1715) | 4.3 | 3.7 | — | 4.2 | 6.4 | 1.6 | 10.5 | 5.1 |
| | Jetta (Diesel) | 97.0 (1588) | 4.8 | 4.3 | — | 4.2 | 6.4 | 1.6 | 10.5 | 6.9 |
| | Quantum (4 cyl.) | 109.0 (1780) | 3.6 | 3.2 | — | 4.2 | 6.4 | 1.6 | 16.0 | 5.5 |
| | Quantum (5 cyl.) | 130.0 (2144) | 4.0 | 3.5 | — | 4.2 | 6.4 | 1.6 | 16.0 | 5.5 |
| | Quantum (Diesel) | 97.0 (1588) | 4.0 | 3.5 | — | 4.2 | 6.4 | 1.6 | 16.0 | 6.5 |
| | Rabbit | 105.0 (1715) | 4.3 | 3.7 | 3.2 | 4.2 | 6.4 | 1.6 | 10.0 | 6.9 |
| | Rabbit (Conv.) | 109.0 (1780) | 4.3 | 3.7 | — | 4.2 | 6.2 | 1.6 | 10.5 | 7.3 |
| | Rabbit (Diesel) | 97.0 (1588) | 4.8 | 4.3 | 3.2 | 4.2 | 6.4 | 1.6 | 10.0 | 6.9 |

## CAPACITIES

| Year | Model | Engine Displacement cu. in. (cc) | Engine Crankcase with Filter | Engine Crankcase without Filter | Transmission (pts.) 4-Spd | 5-Spd | Auto. | Drive Axle (pts.) | Fuel Tank (gal.) | Cooling System (qts.) |
|---|---|---|---|---|---|---|---|---|---|---|
| 1984 | Scirocco | 109.0 (1780) | 4.3 | 3.7 | — | 4.2 | 6.4 | 1.6 | 10.5 | 6.5 |
| | GTI | 109.0 (1780) | 4.3 | 3.7 | 3.2 | 4.2 | 6.4 | 1.6 | 10.0 | 7.3 |
| | GTI (Diesel) | 97.0 (1588) | 4.8 | 4.3 | 3.2 | 4.2 | 6.4 | 1.6 | 11.0 | 6.5 |
| | GLI | 109.0 (1780) | 4.3 | 3.7 | 3.2 | 4.2 | — | 1.6 | 14.5 | 6.5 |
| 1985 | Jetta | 105.0 (1715) | 4.3 | 3.7 | — | 4.2 | 6.4 | 1.6 | 13.7 | 7.3 |
| | Jetta (Diesel) | 97.0 (1588) | 4.8 | 4.3 | — | 4.2 | 6.4 | 1.6 | 13.7 | 7.3 |
| | Jetta (Turbo-Diesel) | 97.0 (1588) | 4.8 | 4.3 | — | 4.2 | 6.4 | 1.6 | 13.7 | 7.3 |
| | Quantum (4 cyl.) | 109.0 (1780) | 3.6 | 3.2 | — | 4.2 | 6.4 | 1.6 | 16.0 | 5.5 |
| | Quantum (5 cyl.) | 136.0 (2226) | 4.0 | 3.5 | — | 4.2 | 6.4 | 1.6 | 16.0 | 6.5 |
| | Quantum (Diesel) | 97.0 (1588) | 4.0 | 3.5 | — | 4.2 | 6.4 | 1.6 | 16.0 | 6.9 |
| | Cabriolet | 109.0 (1780) | 4.3 | 3.7 | — | 4.2 | 6.4 | 1.6 | 13.7 | 7.3 |
| | Scirocco | 109.0 (1780) | 4.3 | 3.7 | — | 4.2 | 6.4 | 1.6 | 13.7 | 6.5 |
| | GTI | 109.0 (1780) | 4.3 | 3.7 | — | 4.2 | — | 1.6 | 14.5 | 7.3 |
| | GLI | 109.0 (1780) | 4.3 | 3.7 | — | 4.2 | — | 1.6 | 14.5 | 7.3 |
| | Golf | 109.0 (1780) | 4.3 | 3.7 | — | 4.2 | 6.4 | 1.6 | 14.5 | 7.3 |
| | Golf (Diesel) | 97.0 (1588) | 4.8 | 4.3 | — | 4.2 | 6.4 | 1.6 | 14.5 | 7.3 |
| 1986 | Jetta | 109.0 (1780) | 4.3 | 3.7 | — | 4.2 | 6.4 | 1.6 | 13.7 | 7.3 |
| | Jetta (Diesel) | 97.0 (1588) | 4.8 | 4.3 | — | 4.2 | 6.4 | 1.6 | 13.7 | 7.3 |
| | Jetta (Turbo-Diesel) | 97.0 (1588) | 4.8 | 4.3 | — | 4.2 | 6.4 | 1.6 | 13.7 | 7.3 |
| | Quantum (4 cyl.) | 109.0 (1780) | 3.6 | 3.2 | — | 4.2 | 6.4 | 1.6 | 16.0 | 5.5 |
| | Quantum (5 cyl.) | 136.0 (2226) | 4.0 | 3.5 | — | 4.2 | 6.4 | 1.6 | 16.0 | 6.5 |
| | Quantum (Diesel) | 97.0 (1588) | 4.0 | 3.5 | — | 4.2 | 6.4 | 1.6 | 16.0 | 6.9 |
| | Cabriolet | 109.0 (1780) | 4.3 | 3.7 | — | 4.2 | 6.4 | 1.6 | 13.7 | 7.3 |
| | Scirocco | 109.0 (1780) | 4.3 | 3.7 | — | 4.2 | 6.4 | 1.6 | 13.7 | 6.5 |
| | GTI | 109.0 (1780) | 4.3 | 3.7 | — | 4.2 | — | 1.6 | 14.5 | 7.3 |
| | GLI | 109.0 (1780) | 4.3 | 3.7 | — | 4.2 | — | 1.6 | 14.5 | 7.3 |
| | Golf | 109.0 (1780) | 4.3 | 3.7 | — | 4.2 | 6.4 | 1.6 | 14.5 | 7.3 |
| | Golf (Diesel) | 97.0 (1588) | 4.8 | 4.3 | — | 4.2 | 6.4 | 1.6 | 14.5 | 7.3 |
| 1987 | Jetta | 109 (1780) | 4.3 | 3.8 | — | 4.2 | 6.4 | — | 14.5 | 7.3 |
| | Jetta GL | 109 (1780) | 4.3 | 3.8 | — | 4.2 | 6.4 | — | 14.5 | 7.3 |
| | Jetta GLI 16V | 109 (1780) | 4.3 | 3.8 | — | 4.2 | 6.4 | — | 14.5 | 7.3 |
| | Quantum GL5 | 136 (2226) | 4.0 | 3.8 | — | 4.2 | 6.4 | — | 15.8 | 8.5 |
| | Quantum Syncro | 136 (2226) | 4.0 | 3.5 | — | 5.0 | 6.4 | 1.2 | 18.5 | 8.5 |
| | Scirocco 16V | 109 (1780) | 4.3 | 3.8 | — | 4.2 | 6.4 | — | 13.8 | 5.1 |
| | Cabriolet | 109 (1780) | 4.3 | 3.8 | — | 4.2 | 6.4 | — | 13.8 | 5.1 |
| | Golf GL | 109 (1780) | 4.3 | 3.8 | — | 4.2 | 6.4 | — | 14.5 | 7.3 |
| | Golf GT | 109 (1780) | 4.3 | 3.8 | — | 4.2 | 6.4 | — | 14.5 | 7.3 |
| | Golf GTI 16V | 109 (1780) | 4.3 | 3.8 | — | 4.2 | 6.4 | — | 14.5 | 7.3 |
| | Fox/GL | 109 (1780) | 3.7 | 3.2 | 3.6 | — | — | — | 12.4 | 6.9 |
| 1988 | Jetta | 109 (1780) | 4.3 | 3.8 | — | 4.2 | 6.4 | — | 14.5 | 7.3 |
| | Jetta GL | 109 (1780) | 4.3 | 3.8 | — | 4.2 | 6.4 | — | 14.5 | 7.3 |
| | Jetta GLI 16V | 109 (1780) | 4.3 | 3.8 | — | 4.2 | 6.4 | — | 14.5 | 7.3 |
| | Jetta Carat | 109 (1780) | 4.3 | 3.8 | — | 4.2 | 6.4 | — | 14.5 | 7.3 |

## CAPACITIES

| Year | Model | Engine Displacement cu. in. (cc) | Engine Crankcase with Filter | Engine Crankcase without Filter | Transmission (pts.) 4-Spd | Transmission (pts.) 5-Spd | Transmission (pts.) Auto. | Drive Axle (pts.) | Fuel Tank (gal.) | Cooling System (qts.) |
|---|---|---|---|---|---|---|---|---|---|---|
| 1988 | Quantum GL5 | 136 (2226) | 4.0 | 3.8 | — | 4.2 | 6.4 | — | 15.8 | 8.5 |
| | Quantum Syncro | 136 (2226) | 4.0 | 3.5 | — | 5.0 | 6.4 | 1.2 | 18.5 | 8.5 |
| | Scirocco 16V | 109 (1780) | 4.3 | 3.8 | — | 4.2 | 6.4 | — | 13.8 | 5.1 |
| | Cabriolet | 109 (1780) | 4.3 | 3.8 | — | 4.2 | 6.4 | — | 13.8 | 5.1 |
| | Golf GL | 109 (1780) | 4.3 | 3.8 | — | 4.2 | 6.4 | — | 14.5 | 7.3 |
| | Golf GT | 109 (1780) | 4.3 | 3.8 | — | 4.2 | 6.4 | — | 14.5 | 7.3 |
| | Golf GTI 16V | 109 (1780) | 4.3 | 3.8 | — | 4.2 | 6.4 | — | 14.5 | 7.3 |
| | Fox/GL | 109 (1780) | 3.7 | 3.2 | 3.6 | — | — | — | 12.4 | 6.9 |
| 1989–90 | Jetta | 109 (1780) | 4.3 | 3.8 | — | 4.2 | 6.4 | — | 14.5 | 7.3 |
| | Jetta (Diesel) | 97.0 (1588) | 4.8 | 4.3 | — | 4.2 | 6.4 | — | 13.7 | 7.3 |
| | Jetta GL | 109 (1780) | 4.3 | 3.8 | — | 4.2 | 6.4 | — | 14.5 | 7.3 |
| | Jetta GLI 16V | 109 (1780) | 4.3 | 3.8 | — | 4.2 | 6.4 | — | 14.5 | 7.3 |
| | Jetta Carat | 109 (1780) | 4.3 | 3.8 | — | 4.2 | 6.4 | — | 14.5 | 7.3 |
| | Quantum GL5 | 136 (2226) | 4.0 | 3.8 | — | 4.2 | 6.4 | — | 15.8 | 8.5 |
| | Quantum Syncro | 136 (2226) | 4.0 | 3.5 | — | 5.0 | 6.4 | 1.2 | 18.5 | 8.5 |
| | Scirocco 16V | 109 (1780) | 4.3 | 3.8 | — | 4.2 | 6.4 | — | 13.8 | 5.1 |
| | Cabriolet | 109 (1780) | 4.3 | 3.8 | — | 4.2 | 6.4 | — | 13.8 | 5.1 |
| | Golf GL | 109 (1780) | 4.3 | 3.8 | — | 4.2 | 6.4 | — | 14.5 | 7.3 |
| | Golf GT | 109 (1780) | 4.3 | 3.8 | — | 4.2 | 6.4 | — | 14.5 | 7.3 |
| | Golf GTI 16V | 109 (1780) | 4.3 | 3.8 | — | 4.2 | 6.4 | — | 14.5 | 7.3 |
| | Fox/GL | 109 (1780) | 3.7 | 3.2 | 3.6 | 4.2 | — | — | 12.4 | 6.9 |

## CRANKSHAFT AND CONNECTING ROD SPECIFICATIONS

All measurements are given in inches.

| Year | Engine Displacement cu. in. (cc) | Crankshaft Main Brg. Journal Dia. | Crankshaft Main Brg. Oil Clearance | Crankshaft Shaft End-play | Crankshaft Thrust on No. | Connecting Rod Journal Diameter | Connecting Rod Oil Clearance | Connecting Rod Side Clearance |
|---|---|---|---|---|---|---|---|---|
| 1983 | 97.0 (1588) | 2.126 | 0.001–0.003 | 0.003–0.007 | 3 | 1.811 | 0.0049 ① | 0.015 ① |
| | 105.0 (1715) | 2.126 | 0.001–0.003 | 0.003–0.007 | 3 | 1.811 | 0.0049 ① | 0.015 ① |
| | 109.0 (1780) | 2.126 | 0.001–0.003 | 0.003–0.007 | 3 | 1.881 | 0.001–0.003 | 0.015 ① |
| | 120.0 (1970) | 2.3609–2.3617 | 0.002–0.004 | 0.0027–0.005 | 1 at flywheel | 2.1644–2.1653 | 0.0008–0.0027 | 0.004–0.016 |
| | 130.8 (2144) | 2.2822 | 0.0006–0.003 | 0.003–0.007 | 4 | 1.811 | 0.0006–0.002 | 0.016 ① |
| 1984 | 97.0 (1588) | 2.126 | 0.001–0.003 | 0.003–0.007 | 3 | 1.811 | 0.0049 ① | 0.015 ① |
| | 105.0 (1715) | 2.126 | 0.001–0.003 | 0.003–0.007 | 3 | 1.811 | 0.0049 ① | 0.015 ① |
| | 109.0 (1780) | 2.126 | 0.001–0.003 | 0.003–0.007 | 3 | 1.881 | 0.001–0.003 | 0.015 ① |
| | 130.8 (2144) | 2.2822 | 0.0006–0.003 | 0.003–0.007 | 4 | 1.811 | 0.0006–0.002 | 0.016 ① |

## CRANKSHAFT AND CONNECTING ROD SPECIFICATIONS

All measurements are given in inches.

| Year | Engine Displacement cu. in. (cc) | Crankshaft | | | | Connecting Rod | | |
|---|---|---|---|---|---|---|---|---|
| | | Main Brg. Journal Dia. | Main Brg. Oil Clearance | Shaft End-play | Thrust on No. | Journal Diameter | Oil Clearance | Side Clearance |
| 1985 | 97.0 (1588) | 2.126 | 0.001–0.003 | 0.003–0.007 | 3 | 1.811 | 0.0049 ① | 0.015 ① |
| | 109.0 (1780) | 2.126 | 0.001–0.003 | 0.003–0.007 | 3 | 1.881 | 0.0049 ① | 0.015 |
| | 115.9 (1915) | 2.3992–2.3996 ② | NA | 0.003–0.005 | 1 at flywheel | 2.1993 2.1998 | NA | 0.028 |
| | 136.0 (2226) | 2.126 | 0.001–0.003 | 0.003–0.007 | 3 | 1.811 | 0.001–0.003 | 0.015 ① |
| 1986 | 97.0 (1588) | 2.126 | 0.001–0.003 | 0.003–0.007 | 3 | 1.881 | 0.0049 ① | 0.015 ① |
| | 109.0 (1780) | 2.126 | 0.001–0.003 | 0.003–0.007 | 3 | 1.881 | 0.0049 ① | 0.015 ① |
| | 128.1 (2100) | 2.126 | 0.001–0.003 | 0.003–0.007 | 3 | 1.881 | 0.0049 ① | 0.015 ① |
| | 136.0 (2226) | 2.282 | 0.001–0.003 | 0.003–0.007 | 3 | 1.881 | 0.0006–0.002 | 0.015 ① |
| 1987 | 109.0 (1780) | 2.126 | 0.001–0.003 | 0.003–0.007 | 3 | 1.881 | 0.0049 ① | 0.015 ① |
| | 136.0 (2226) | 2.282 | 0.001–0.003 | 0.003–0.007 | 3 | 1.881 | 0.0006–0.002 | 0.015 ① |
| 1988 | 109.0 (1780) | 2.126 | 0.001–0.003 | 0.003–0.007 | 3 | 1.881 | 0.0049 ① | 0.015 ① |
| | 136.0 (2226) | 2.282 | 0.001–0.003 | 0.003–0.007 | 3 | 1.881 | 0.0006–0.002 | 0.015 ① |
| 1989-90 | 97.0 (1588) | 2.126 | 0.001–0.003 | 0.003–0.007 | 3 | 1.881 | 0.0049 ① | 0.015 ① |
| | 109.0 (1780) | 2.126 | 0.001–0.003 | 0.003–0.007 | 3 | 1.881 | 0.0049 ① | 0.015 ① |
| | 136.0 (2226) | 2.282 | 0.001–0.003 | 0.003–0.007 | 3 | 1.881 | 0.0006–0.002 | 0.015 ① |

**NOTE:** Main and connecting rod bearings are available in 3 undersizes.
① Wear Limit
② Bearings marked with blue dot. Bearing marked with red dot—2.3988-2.3991.

## VALVE SPECIFICATIONS

| Year | Engine Displacement cu. in. (cc) | Seat Angle (deg.) | Face Angle (deg.) | Spring Test Pressure (lbs.) | Spring Installed Height (in.) | Stem-to-Guide Clearance (in.) Intake | Stem-to-Guide Clearance (in.) Exhaust | Stem Diameter (in.) Intake | Stem Diameter (in.) Exhaust |
|---|---|---|---|---|---|---|---|---|---|
| 1983 | 97.0 (1588) | 45 | 45 | NA | NA | 0.039 max | 0.051 max | 0.3140 | 0.3130 |
| | 97.0 Diesel (1588) | 45 | 45 | 96–106 @ 0.92 | NA | 0.051 max | 0.051 max | 0.3140 | 0.3130 |
| | 105.0 (1715) | 45 | 45 | NA | NA | 0.039 max | 0.051 max | 0.3140 | 0.3130 |
| | 109.0 (1780) | 45 | 45 | NA | NA | 0.039 max | 0.051 max | 0.3140 | 0.3130 |
| | 130.8 (2144) | 45 | 45 | NA | NA | 0.039 max | 0.051 max | 0.3140 | 0.3130 |
| 1984 | 97.0 Diesel (1588) | 45 | 45 | 96–106 @ 0.92 | NA | 0.051 max | 0.051 max | 0.3140 | 0.3130 |
| | 105.9 (1715) | 45 | 45 | NA | NA | 0.039 max | 0.051 max | 0.3140 | 0.3130 |
| | 109.0 (1780) | 45 | 45 | NA | NA | 0.039 max | 0.051 max | 0.3140 | 0.3130 |
| | 130.8 (2144) | 45 | 45 | NA | NA | 0.039 max | 0.051 max | 0.3140 | 0.3130 |
| 1985 | 97.0 Diesel (1588) | 45 | 45 | 96–106 @ 0.92 | NA | 0.051 max | 0.051 max | 0.3140 | 0.3130 |
| | 109.0 (1780) | 45 | 45 | NA | NA | 0.039 max | 0.051 max | 0.3140 | 0.3130 |
| | 136.0 (2226) | 45 | 45 | NA | NA | 0.039 max | 0.051 max | 0.3140 | 0.3130 |
| 1986 | 97.0 Diesel (1588) | 45 | 45 | 96–106 @ 0.92 | NA | 0.051 max | 0.051 max | 0.3140 | 0.3130 |
| | 109.0 (1780) | 45 | 45 | NA | NA | 0.039 max | 0.051 max | 0.3140 | 0.3130 |
| | 136.0 (2226) | 45 | 45 | NA | NA | 0.039 max | 0.051 max | 0.3140 | 0.3130 |
| 1987 | 109.0 (1780) | 45 | 45 | NA | NA | 0.039 max | 0.051 max | 0.3140 | 0.3130 |
| | 136.0 (2226) | 45 | 45 | NA | NA | 0.039 max | 0.051 max | 0.3140 | 0.3130 |
| 1988 | 109.0 (1780) | 45 | 45 | NA | NA | 0.039 max | 0.051 max | 0.3140 | 0.3130 |
| | 136.0 (2226) | 45 | 45 | NA | NA | 0.039 max | 0.051 max | 0.3140 | 0.3130 |
| 1989–90 | 97.0 Diesel (1588) | 45 | 45 | 96–106 @ 0.92 | NA | 0.051 max | 0.051 max | 0.3140 | 0.3130 |
| | 109.0 (1780) | 45 | 45 | NA | NA | 0.039 max | 0.051 max | 0.3140 | 0.3130 |
| | 136.0 (2226) | 45 | 45 | NA | NA | 0.039 max | 0.051 max | 0.3140 | 0.3130 |

**NOTE:** Exhaust valves must be ground by hand
NA Not Available

## PISTON AND RING SPECIFICATIONS

All measurements are given in inches.

| Year | Engine Displacement cu. in. (cc) | Piston Clearance | Ring Gap | | | Ring Side Clearance | | |
|---|---|---|---|---|---|---|---|---|
| | | | Top Compression | Bottom Compression | Oil Control | Top Compression | Bottom Compression | Oil Control |
| 1983 | 97.0 (1588) | 0.001–0.003 | 0.0120–0.0180 | 0.0120–0.0180 | 0.0120–0.0180 | 0.0008–0.0020 | 0.0008–0.0020 | 0.0008–0.0020 |
| | 97.0 (1588) Diesel | 0.001–0.003 | 0.0120–0.0200 | 0.0120–0.0200 | 0.0100–0.0160 | 0.0020–0.0040 | 0.0020–0.0030 | 0.0010–0.0020 |
| | 105.0 (1715) | 0.001–0.003 | 0.0120–0.0180 | 0.0120–0.0180 | 0.0120–0.0180 | 0.0008–0.0020 | 0.0008–0.0020 | 0.0008–0.0020 |
| | 109.0 (1780) | 0.001–0.003 | 0.0120–0.0180 | 0.0120–0.0180 | 0.0120–0.0180 | 0.0008–0.0020 | 0.0008–0.0020 | 0.0008–0.0020 |
| | 120.0 (1970) | 0.0016–0.0023 | 0.0160–0.0210 | 0.0160–0.0210 | 0.0100–0.0160 | 0.0020–0.0030 | 0.0020–0.0030 | 0.0010–0.0020 |
| | 130.8 (2144) | 0.0011 | 0.0100–0.0200 | 0.0100–0.0200 | 0.0100–0.0200 | 0.0008–0.0030 | 0.0008–0.0030 | 0.0008–0.0030 |
| 1984 | 97.0 (1588) Diesel | 0.001–0.003 | 0.0120–0.0200 | 0.0120–0.0200 | 0.0100–0.0160 | 0.0020–0.0040 | 0.0020–0.0030 | 0.0010–0.0020 |
| | 105.9 (1715) | 0.001–0.003 | 0.0120–0.0180 | 0.0120–0.0180 | 0.0120–0.0180 | 0.0008–0.0020 | 0.0008–0.0020 | 0.0008–0.0020 |
| | 109.0 (1780) | 0.001–0.003 | 0.0120–0.0180 | 0.0120–0.0180 | 0.0120–0.0180 | 0.0008–0.0020 | 0.0008–0.0020 | 0.0008–0.0020 |
| | 115.9 (1915) | 0.001–0.008 | 0.0120–0.0180 | 0.0120–0.0200 | 0.0100–0.0160 | 0.0020–0.0030 | 0.0020–0.0030 | 0.0010–0.0020 |
| | 120.0 (1970) | 0.0016–0.0023 | 0.0160–0.0210 | 0.0160–0.0210 | 0.0100–0.0160 | 0.0020–0.0030 | 0.0020–0.0030 | 0.0010–0.0020 |
| 1985 | 97.0 (1588) Diesel | 0.001–0.003 | 0.0120–0.0200 | 0.0120–0.0200 | 0.0100–0.0180 | 0.0020–0.0040 | 0.0020–0.0030 | 0.0010–0.0020 |
| | 109.0 (1780) | 0.001–0.003 | 0.0120–0.0180 | 0.0120–0.0180 | 0.0120–0.0180 | 0.0008–0.0020 | 0.0008–0.0020 | 0.0008–0.0020 |
| | 115.9 (1915) | 0.001–0.008 | 0.0120–0.0180 | 0.0120–0.0200 | 0.0100–0.0160 | 0.0020–0.0030 | 0.0020–0.0030 | 0.0010–0.0020 |
| | 120.0 (1970) | 0.0016–0.0023 | 0.0160–0.0210 | 0.0160–0.0210 | 0.0100–0.0160 | 0.0020–0.0030 | 0.0020–0.0030 | 0.0010–0.0020 |
| | 130.8 (2144) | 0.0011 | 0.0100–0.0200 | 0.0100–0.0200 | 0.0100–0.0200 | 0.0008–0.0030 | 0.0008–0.0030 | 0.0008–0.0030 |
| 1986 | 97.0 (1588) Diesel | 0.001–0.003 | 0.0120–0.0200 | 0.0120–0.0200 | 0.0100–0.0180 | 0.0020–0.0040 | 0.0020–0.0030 | 0.0010–0.0020 |
| | 109.0 (1780) | 0.001–0.003 | 0.0120–0.0180 | 0.0120–0.0180 | 0.0120–0.0180 | 0.0008–0.0020 | 0.0008–0.0020 | 0.0008–0.0020 |
| | 128.1 (2109) | 0.001–0.008 | 0.0120–0.0180 | 0.0120–0.0200 | 0.0100–0.0160 | 0.0020–0.0030 | 0.0020–0.0030 | 0.0010–0.0020 |
| | 136.0 (2226) | 0.0011 | 0.0100–0.0200 | 0.0100–0.0200 | 0.0100–0.0200 | 0.0008–0.0030 | 0.0008–0.0030 | 0.0008–0.0030 |
| 1987 | 109.0 (1780) | 0.001–0.003 | 0.0120–0.0180 | 0.0120–0.0180 | 0.0120–0.0180 | 0.0008–0.0020 | 0.0008–0.0020 | 0.0008–0.0020 |
| | 136.0 (2226) | 0.0011 | 0.0100–0.0200 | 0.0100–0.0200 | 0.0100–0.0200 | 0.0008–0.0030 | 0.0008–0.0030 | 0.0008–0.0030 |
| 1988 | 109.0 (1780) | 0.0010–0.0030 | 0.0120–0.0180 | 0.0120–0.0180 | 0.0120–0.0180 | 0.0008–0.0020 | 0.0008–0.0020 | 0.0008–0.0020 |
| | 136.0 (2226) | 0.0011 | 0.0100–0.0200 | 0.0100–0.0200 | 0.0100–0.0200 | 0.0008–0.0030 | 0.0008–0.0030 | 0.0008–0.0030 |

## PISTON AND RING SPECIFICATIONS

All measurements are given in inches.

| Year | Engine Displacement cu. in. (cc) | Piston Clearance | Ring Gap Top Compression | Ring Gap Bottom Compression | Ring Gap Oil Control | Ring Side Clearance Top Compression | Ring Side Clearance Bottom Compression | Ring Side Clearance Oil Control |
|---|---|---|---|---|---|---|---|---|
| 1989-90 | 97.0 (1588) Diesel | 0.001–0.003 | 0.0120–0.0200 | 0.0120–0.0200 | 0.0100–0.0180 | 0.0020–0.0040 | 0.0020–0.0030 | 0.0010–0.0020 |
| | 109.0 (1780) | 0.0010–0.0030 | 0.0120–0.0180 | 0.0120–0.0180 | 0.0120–0.0180 | 0.0008–0.0020 | 0.0008–0.0020 | 0.0008–0.0020 |
| | 136.0 (2226) | 0.0011 | 0.0100–0.0200 | 0.0100–0.0200 | 0.0100–0.0200 | 0.0008–0.0030 | 0.0008–0.0030 | 0.0008–0.0030 |

## TORQUE SPECIFICATIONS

All readings in ft. lbs.

| Year | Engine Displacement cu. in. (cc) | Cylinder Head Bolts | Main Bearing Bolts | Rod Bearing Bolts ① | Crankshaft Pulley Bolts | Flywheel Bolts | Manifold Intake | Manifold Exhaust | Spark Plugs |
|---|---|---|---|---|---|---|---|---|---|
| 1983 | 97.0 Diesel (1588) | ② | 47 | 33 ③ | 56 | 54 | 18 | 18 | 22 |
| | 105.0 (1715) | ② | 47 | 33 ③ | 58 | 54 | 18 | 18 | 22 |
| | 109.0 (1780) | ② | 47 | 33 ③ | 58 | 54 | 18 | 18 | 22 |
| | 130.8 (2144) | ② | 47 | 36 ③ | 58 | 54 | 18 | 18 | 22 |
| 1984 | 97.0 Diesel (1588) | ② | 47 | 33 ③ | 56 | 54 | 18 | 18 | 14 |
| | 105.9 (1715) | ② | 47 | 33 ③ | 58 | 54 | 18 | 18 | 14 |
| | 109.0 (1780) | ② | 47 | 33 ③ | 58 | 54 | 18 | 18 | 14 |
| | 120.0 (1970) | ② | 47 | 33 ③ | 58 | 54 | 18 | 18 | 14 |
| 1985 | 97.0 Diesel (1588) | ② | 47 | 33 ③ | 130 | 54 | 18 | 18 | 14 |
| | 109.0 (1780) | ② | 47 | 33 ③ | 145 | 54 | 18 | 18 | 14 |
| | 120.0 (1970) | ② | 47 | 33 ③ | 145 | 54 | 18 | 18 | 14 |
| | 130.8 (2144) | ② | 47 | 33 ③ | 145 | 54 | 18 | 18 | 14 |
| 1986 | 97.0 Diesel (1588) | ② | 47 | 33 ③ | 130 | 54 | 18 | 18 | 14 |
| | 109.0 (1780) | ② | 47 | 33 ③ | 145 | 54 | 18 | 18 | 14 |
| | 136.0 (2226) | ② | 47 | 33 ③ | 253 | 54 | 18 | 18 | 14 |
| 1987 | 109.0 (1780) | ② | 47 | 33 ③ | 145 ④ | 54 | 18 | 18 | 14 |
| | 136.0 (2226) | ② | 47 | 33 ③ | 253 | 54 | 18 | 18 | 14 |
| 1988 | 109.0 (1780) | ② | 47 | 33 ③ | 145 ④ | 54 | 18 | 18 | 14 |
| | 136.0 (2226) | ② | 47 | 33 ③ | 253 | 54 | 18 | 18 | 14 |
| 1989-90 | 97.0 Diesel (1588) | ② | 47 | 33 ③ | 130 | 54 | 18 | 18 | 14 |
| | 109.0 (1780) | ② | 47 | 33 ③ | 145 ④ | 54 | 18 | 18 | 14 |
| | 136.0 (2226) | ② | 47 | 33 ③ | 253 | 54 | 18 | 18 | 14 |

① Always use new bolts.
② With 12 points (polygon) head bolts
Torque in 4 steps:
1st step—29 ft/lbs.
2nd step—43 ft/lbs.
3rd step—additional ½ turn (180 degrees) further in one movement (two 90 degree turns are permissible)
Note tightening sequence
Do not retorque at 1000 miles

With 6 point (hex) head bolts
Torque in steps to 54 ft. lbs. with engine cold, when engine is warmed up, torque to 61 ft. lbs. Head bolts must be retorqued after 1000 miles.

③ Stretch bolts: 22 ft. lbs. plus ¼ (90 degree) turn.

④ Engine UM up to JN707651
133 ft. lbs.
From Engine JN707652
66 ft. lbs. plus ½ turn (180°)

## BRAKE SPECIFICATIONS

All measurements in inches unless noted

| Year | Model | Lug Nut Torque (ft. lbs.) | Master Cylinder Bore | Brake Disc Minimum Thickness | Brake Disc Maximum Runout | Maximim Brake Drum Diameter | Minimum Lining Thickness Front | Minimum Lining Thickness Rear |
|---|---|---|---|---|---|---|---|---|
| 1983 | Jetta | 80 | 0.820 | 0.410 ① | 0.002 | 7.080 | 0.250 | 0.098 |
| | Quantum | 80 | 0.820 | 0.410 ① | 0.002 | 7.080 | 0.250 | 0.098 |
| | Rabbit | 80 | 0.820 | 0.410 ① | 0.002 | 7.080 | 0.250 | 0.098 |
| | Scirocco | 80 | 0.820 | 0.410 ① | 0.002 | 7.080 | 0.250 | 0.098 |
| 1984 | Jetta | 80 | 0.820 | 0.410 ① | 0.002 | 7.080 | 0.250 | 0.098 |
| | Quantum | 80 | 0.820 | 0.410 ① | 0.002 | 7.080 | 0.250 | 0.098 |
| | Rabbit | 80 | 0.820 | 0.410 ① | 0.002 | 7.080 | 0.250 | 0.098 |
| | Scirocco | 80 | 0.820 | 0.410 ① | 0.002 | 7.080 | 0.250 | 0.098 |
| 1985 | Jetta | 80 | 0.820 | 0.393 ②④ | 0.002 | 7.087 | 0.276 | 0.098 ③ |
| | Quantum | 80 | 0.820 | 0.410 ① | 0.002 | 7.080 | 0.250 | 0.098 |
| | Rabbit | 80 | 0.820 | 0.410 ① | 0.002 | 7.080 | 0.250 | 0.098 |
| | Scirocco | 80 | 0.820 | 0.410 ① | 0.002 | 7.080 | 0.250 | 0.098 |
| | GTI | 80 | 0.820 | 0.393 ②④ | 0.002 | 7.087 | 0.276 | 0.098 ③ |
| | GLI | 80 | 0.820 | 0.393 ②④ | 0.002 | 7.087 | 0.276 | 0.098 ③ |
| | Golf | 80 | 0.820 | 0.393 ②④ | 0.002 | 7.087 | 0.276 | 0.098 ③ |
| 1986 | Jetta | 80 | 0.820 | 0.393 ②④ | 0.002 | 7.087 | 0.276 | 0.098 ③ |
| | Quantum | 80 | 0.820 | 0.410 ① | 0.002 | 7.080 | 0.250 | 0.098 |
| | Scirocco | 80 | 0.820 | 0.410 ① | 0.002 | 7.080 | 0.250 | 0.098 |
| | GTI | 80 | 0.820 | 0.393 ②④ | 0.002 | 7.087 | 0.276 | 0.098 ③ |
| | GLI | 80 | 0.820 | 0.393 ②④ | 0.002 | 7.087 | 0.276 | 0.098 ③ |
| | Golf | 80 | 0.820 | 0.393 ②④ | 0.002 | 7.087 | 0.276 | 0.098 ③ |
| 1987 | Jetta | 81 | 0.820 | 0.393 ②④ | 0.002 | 7.087 | 0.276 | 0.098 ③ |
| | Quantum | 81 | 0.820 | 0.410 ① | 0.002 | 7.080 | 0.250 | 0.098 |
| | Scirocco | 81 | 0.820 | 0.410 ① | 0.002 | 7.080 | 0.250 | 0.098 |
| | GTI | 81 | 0.820 | 0.393 ②④ | 0.002 | 7.087 | 0.276 | 0.098 ③ |
| | GLI | 81 | 0.820 | 0.393 ②④ | 0.002 | 7.087 | 0.276 | 0.098 ③ |
| | Golf | 81 | 0.820 | 0.393 ②④ | 0.002 | 7.087 | 0.276 | 0.098 ③ |
| | Fox/GL | 81 | 0.820 | 0.393 | 0.002 | 7.087 | 0.276 | 0.098 ③ |
| 1988 | Jetta | 81 | 0.820 | 0.393 ②④ | 0.002 | 7.100 | 0.276 | 0.098 ③ |
| | Quantum | 81 | 0.820 | 0.410 ②④ | 0.002 | 7.900 | 0.276 | 0.098 ③ |
| | Scirocco | 81 | 0.820 | 0.410 ②④ | 0.002 | — | 0.276 | ③ |
| | Cabriolet | 81 | 0.820 | 0.393 ②④ | 0.002 | 7.100 | 0.276 | 0.098 |
| | Golf | 81 | 0.820 | 0.393 ②④ | 0.002 | 7.100 | 0.276 | 0.098 ③ |
| | Fox/GL | 81 | 0.820 | 0.393 | 0.002 | 7.100 | 0.276 | 0.098 |
| 1989-90 | Jetta | 81 | 0.820 | 0.393 ②④ | 0.002 | 7.100 | 0.276 | 0.098 ③ |
| | Quantum | 81 | 0.820 | 0.410 ②④ | 0.002 | 7.900 | 0.276 | 0.098 ③ |
| | Scirocco | 81 | 0.820 | 0.410 ②④ | 0.002 | — | 0.276 | ③ |
| | Cabriolet | 81 | 0.820 | 0.393 ②④ | 0.002 | 7.100 | 0.276 | 0.098 |
| | Golf | 81 | 0.820 | 0.393 ②④ | 0.002 | 7.100 | 0.276 | 0.098 ③ |
| | Fox/GL | 81 | 0.820 | 0.393 | 0.002 | 7.100 | 0.276 | 0.098 |

**NOTE:** Minimum lining thickness is as recommended by manufacturer. Due to variations in state inspection regulations, the minimum thickness may be different than that recommended by the manufacturer.

① Vented discs: 0.728
② Vented discs; 0.708
③ Disc brake: 0.276
④ Rear disc brake: 0.315

## FRONT WHEEL ALIGNMENT

| Year | Model | ①Caster Range (deg.) | ①Caster Preferred Setting (deg.) | ①Camber Range (deg.) | ①Camber Preferred Setting (deg.) | Toe-in (in.) | Steering Axis Inclination (deg.) |
|---|---|---|---|---|---|---|---|
| 1983 | Rabbit | 1 5/16P–2 5/16P | 1 13/16P | 3/16N–13/16P | 5/16P | 5/16 | 10 1/2P |
| | Jetta | 1 5/16P–2 5/16P | 1 13/16P | 3/16N–13/16P | 5/16P | 5/16 | 10 1/2P |
| | Scirocco | 1 5/16P–2 5/16P | 1 13/16P | 3/16N–13/16P | 5/16P | 5/16 | 10 1/2P |
| | Quantum | 0–1P | 1/2P | 1 5/32N–5/32N | 21/32N | 5/32 | NA |
| 1984 | Rabbit | 1 5/16P–2 5/16P | 1 13/16P | 3/16N–13/16P | 5/16P | 5/16 | 10 1/2P |
| | Jetta | 1 5/16P–2 5/16P | 1 13/16P | 3/16N–13/16P | 5/16P | 5/16 | 10 1/2P |
| | Scirocco | 1 5/16P–2 5/16P | 1 13/16P | 3/16N–13/16P | 5/16P | 5/16 | 10 1/2P |
| | Quantum | 0–1P | 1/2P | 1 5/32N–5/32N | 21/32N | 5/32 | NA |
| 1985 | Rabbit | 1 5/16P–2 5/16P | 1 13/16P | 3/16N–13/16P | 5/16P | 5/16 | 10 1/2P |
| | Jetta | 1P–2P | 1P | 13/16N–5/32N | 1/2N | 0 | NA |
| | Scirocco | 1 5/16P–2 5/16P | 1 13/16P | 3/16N–13/16P | 5/16P | 5/16 | 10 1/2P |
| | Quantum | 0–1P | 1/2P | 1 5/32N–5/32N | 21/32N | 5/32 | NA |
| | Golf | 1P–2P | 1P | 3/4N–1/16N | 3/8N | 0 | NA |
| | GTI | 1 1/16P–2 1/16P | 1 9/16P | 15/16N–1/4N | 9/16N | 0 | NA |
| | GLI | 1 1/16P–2 1/16P | 1 9/16P | 15/16N–1/4N | 9/16N | 0 | NA |
| 1986 | Scirocco | 1 5/16P–2 5/16P | 1 13/16P | 3/16N–13/16P | 5/16P | 5/16 | 10 1/2P |
| | Quantum | 0–1P | 1/2P | 1 5/32N–5/32N | 21/32N | 5/32 | NA |
| | Golf | 1P–2P | 1P | 3/4N–1/16N | 3/8N | 0 | NA |
| | GTI | 1 1/16P–2 1/16P | 1 9/16P | 15/16N–1/4N | 9/16N | 0 | NA |
| | Jetta | 1P–2P | 1P | 13/16N–5/32N | 1/2N | 0 | NA |
| | GLI | 1 1/16P–2 1/16P | 1 9/16P | 15/16N–1/4N | 9/16N | 0 | NA |
| 1987 | Jetta | 1P–2P | 1 1/2P | 13/16N–3/16N | 1/2N | 0 | NA |
| | GLI | 1 1/16P–2 1/16P | 1 9/16P | 15/16N–1/4N | 9/16N | 0 | NA |
| | Quantum | 0–1P | 1/2P | 27/32N–5/32P | 11/32N | 0 | NA |
| | Quantum Syncro | 11/16P–1 5/16P | 1P | 27/32N–5/32P | 11/32N | 13/64P | NA |
| | Scirocco 16V | 1 15/16P–2 5/16P | 1 13/16P | 3/16N–13/16P | 5/16P | 1/8P | NA |
| | Cabriolet | 1 5/16P–2 5/16P | 1 13/16P | 3/16N–13/16P | 5/16P | 1/8P | NA |
| | Golf | 1P–2P | 1 1/2P | 13/16N–3/16N | 1/2N | 0 | NA |
| | GTI | 1 1/16P–2 1/16P | 1 9/16P | 15/16N–1/4N | 9/16N | 0 | NA |
| | Fox/GL | 1 11/16P–2 5/16P | 2P | 13/16N–3/16N | 1/2N | 0 | NA |
| 1988 | Jetta | 1P–2P | 1 1/2P | 13/16N–3/16N | 1/2N | 0 | NA |
| | GLI | 1 1/16P–2 1/16P | 1 9/16P | 15/16N–1/4N | 9/16N | 0 | NA |
| | Quantum | 0–1P | 1/2P | 27/32N–5/32P | 11/32N | 0 | NA |
| | Quantum Syncro | 11/16P–1 5/16P | 1P | 27/32N–5/32P | 11/32N | 13/64P | NA |
| | Scirocco 16V | 1 15/16P–2 5/16P | 1 13/16P | 3/16N–13/16P | 5/16P | 1/8P | NA |
| | Cabriolet | 1 5/16P–2 5/16P | 1 13/16P | 3/16N–13/16P | 5/16P | 1/8P | NA |
| | Golf | 1P–2P | 1 1/2P | 13/16N–3/16N | 1/2N | 0 | NA |
| | GTI | 1 1/16P–2 1/16P | 1 9/16P | 15/16N–1/4N | 9/16N | 0 | NA |
| | Fox/GL | 1 11/16P–2 5/16P | 2P | 13/16N–3/16N | 1/2N | 0 | NA |

## FRONT WHEEL ALIGNMENT

| Year | Model | Caster ① Range (deg.) | Caster ① Preferred Setting (deg.) | Camber ① Range (deg.) | Camber ① Preferred Setting (deg.) | Toe-in (in.) | Steering Axis Inclination (deg.) |
|---|---|---|---|---|---|---|---|
| 1989-90 | Jetta | 1P-2P | 1 1/2P | 13/16N-3/16N | 1/2N | 0 | NA |
| | GLI | 1 1/16P-2 1/16P | 1 9/16P | 15/16N-1/4N | 9/16N | 0 | NA |
| | Quantum | 0-1P | 1/2P | 27/32N-5/32P | 11/32N | 0 | NA |
| | Quantum Syncro | 11/16P-1 5/16P | 1P | 27/32N-5/32P | 11/32N | 13/64P | NA |
| | Scirocco 16V | 1 15/16P-2 5/16P | 1 13/16P | 3/16N-13/16P | 5/16P | 1/8P | NA |
| | Cabriolet | 1 5/16P-2 5/16P | 1 13/16P | 3/16N-13/16P | 5/16P | 1/8P | NA |
| | Golf | 1P-2P | 1 1/2P | 13/16N-3/16N | 1/2N | 0 | NA |
| | GTI | 1 1/16P-2 1/16P | 1 9/16P | 15/16N-1/4N | 9/16N | 0 | NA |
| | Fox/GL | 1 11/16P-2 5/16P | 2P | 13/16N-3/16N | 1/2N | 0 | NA |

N Negative
P Positive
① Not Adjustable

# TUNE-UP PROCEDURES

## Ignition Timing

### ADJUSTMENT

1. Run the engine to normal operating temperature. Connect a tachometer.
2. Disconnect the plugs on the idle stabilizer at the control unit and plug them together. On the carbureted Rabbit except models with the Carter TYF feedback model, disconnect the vacuum retard hose and plug it. Disconnect and plug both vacuum lines on models with the Carter TYF carburetor.
3. Check the idle speed. It should be between 800–1000 rpm.
4. With a timing light attached according to manufacturer's instructions, shine the light on the timing hole. The pointer in the hole must line up with the notch in the flywheel. To adjust the timing, loosen the distribution at its base and turn it until the timing marks line up. For checking purposes the timing should be at 6 degrees BTDC.
5. On the carbureted Rabbit, reinstall the vacuum hoses. Idle speed should drop to 600–750 rpm.
6. Stop the engine and reconnect the plugs at the control unit. On the carbureted Rabbit, start the engine and rev it a few times to activate the idle stabilizer. On the carbureted Rabbit, the idle speed should now be 850–950 rpm.

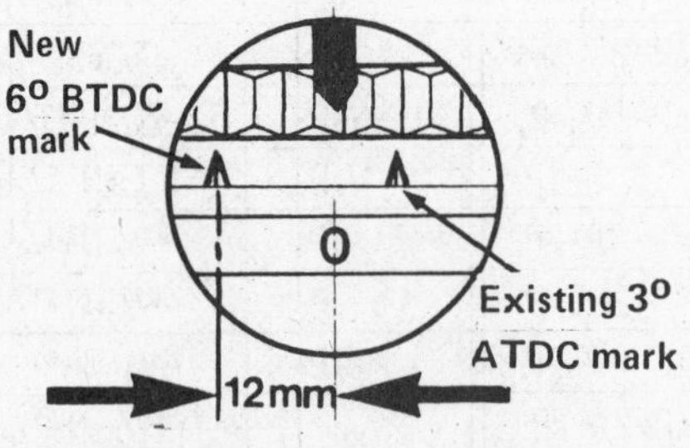


Timing mark conversion—1.7 liter Rabbit with 5-speed transmission and fuel injection

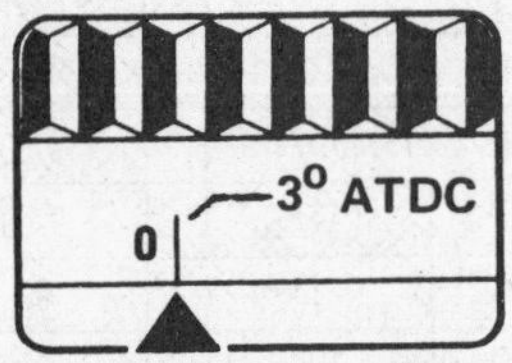


Timing mark–Quantum with automatic transmission

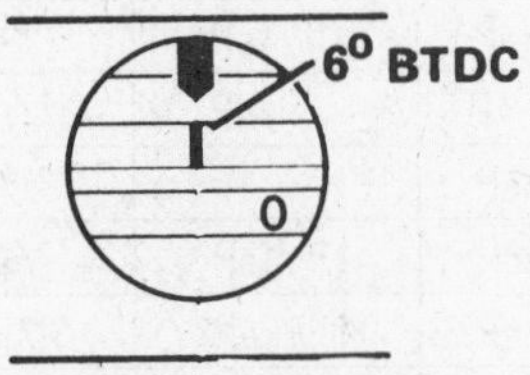


1.8L timing mark

## Valve Lash

### ADJUSTMENT

#### *Gasoline Engines*

**NOTE: 1985–90 models with gas engines come equipped with hydraulic lifters. No adjustment is necessary. 1986 and 1989–90 models with diesel engines (Jetta and Golf), except for early production Golfs, are equipped with hydrau-**

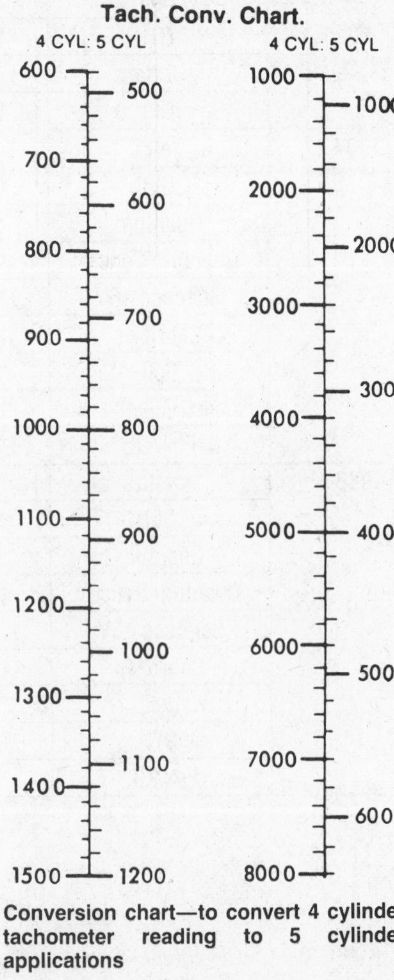


Conversion chart—to convert 4 cylinder tachometer reading to 5 cylinder applications

**lic valve lifters; as with the gasoline engines. No adjustment is required. A label on the valve cover will identify the type lifter (mechanical or hydraulic) the engine has installed.**

The overhead cam acts directly on the valves through bucket-type cam followers which fit over the springs and valves. Adjustment is made with an adjusting disc (shim) which fits into the cam follower. Different thickness discs result in changes in valve clearance.

**NOTE: VW recommends that 2 special tools (VM 546 and the special pliers (VW 208), be used to remove and install the adjustment discs. One is a pry bar to compress the valve springs and the other a pair of special pliers to remove the disc. If the purchase of these tools is not possible, a flat metal plate can be used to compress the valve springs. Care must be taken not to gouge the camshaft lobes. The cam follower has 2 slots which permit the disc to be lifted out.**

Valve clearance is checked with the engine moderately warm (coolant temperature should be about 95°F (35°C).

1. Remove the accelerator linkage, the upper drive belt cover. Remove the air cleaner and any hoses or lines needed.

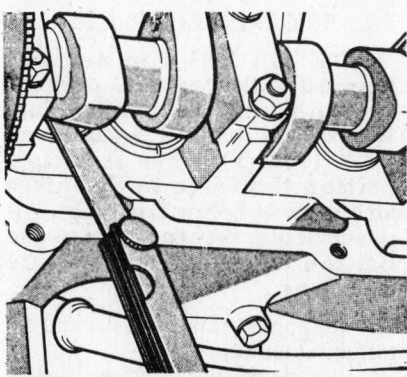

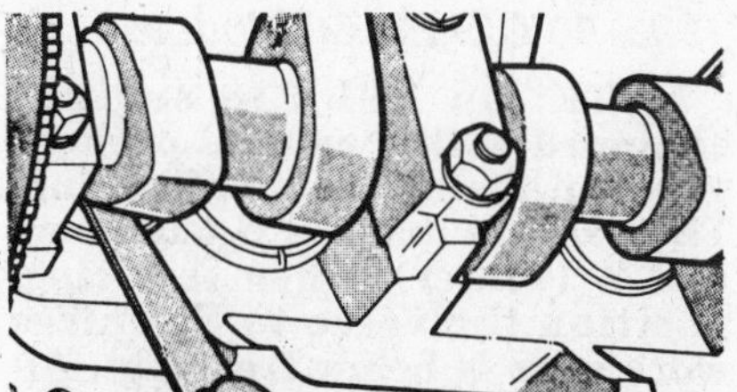

Check the valve clearance with a feeler gauge. The camshaft lobe should not be putting pressure on the valve shim.

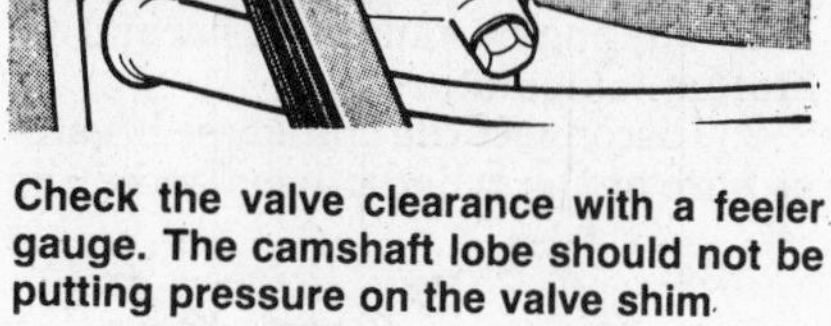

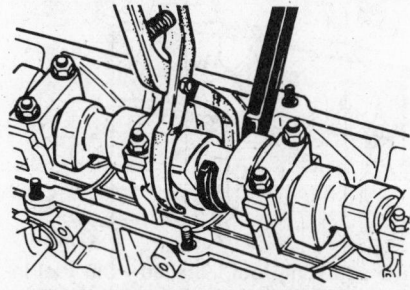

Tools used for valve adjustment

2. Remove the cylinder head cover. Valve clearance is checked in the firing order 1-3-4-2 for the 4 cylinder and 1-2-4-5-3 for the 5 cylinder engines, with the piston of the cylinder being checked at TDC of the compression stroke. Both valves will be closed at this position and the cam lobes will be pointing straight up.
3. Turn the crankshaft pulley bolt with a socket wrench to position the camshaft for checking.

**CAUTION**

***Do not turn the camshaft by the camshaft mounting bolt, this will stretch the drive belt. When turning the crankshaft pulley bolt, turn it CLOCKWISE ONLY.***

4. With the No. 1 piston at TDC of the compression stroke, determine the clearance with a feeler gauge. Intake clearance should be 0.008–0.012 in; exhaust clearance should be 0.016–0.020 in.
5. Check the other cylinders in the firing order, turning the crankshaft to bring each particular piston to the top of the compression stroke. Record the individual clearances.
6. If measured clearance is within tolerance levels (0.002 in.), it is not necessary to replace the adjusting discs.
7. If adjustment is necessary, the discs will have to be removed and replaced with thicker or thinner ones which will yield the correct clearance. Discs are available in 0.002 in. increments from 0.12 in. to 0.17 in.

**NOTE: The thickness of the adjusting discs are etched on 1 side. When installing, the marks must face the cam followers. Discs can be reused if they are not worn or damaged.**

8. To remove the discs, turn the cam followers so that the grooves are accessible when the pry bar is depressed.
9. Press the cam follower down with the pry bar and remove the adjusting discs with the proper tool.
10. Replace the adjustment discs as necessary to bring the clearance within the 0.002 in. tolerance level. If the measured clearance is larger than the given tolerance, remove the existing disc and insert a thicker one to bring the clearance up to specification. If it is smaller, insert a thinner one.
11. Recheck all valve clearances after adjustment.
12. Install the valve cover. Connect the accelerator linkage and hoses.

### Diesel Engines

Check the valve clearance every 20,000 miles. The valves must be checked in the same order as the firing order, with the engine at normal operating temperature.

1. Remove the camshaft cover.
2. Set the engine at TDC on No. 1 cylinder by aligning the **0** degree Timing mark on the flywheel with the pointer.

**NOTE: When adjusting clearances on a diesel, the pistons must not be at TDC. Turn the crankshaft ¼ turn past TDC, so that the valves do not contact the pistons when the tappets are depressed.**

3. The valve clearances of cylinder No. 1 should be checked when the valves of No. 4 cylinder overlap, i.e., when both No. 4 cylinder valves move in opposite directions simultaneously. It may be necessary to turn the crankshaft slightly to find this position. When this happens, the exhaust valve is closing and the intake opening. Check and note the clearance of both the intake and exhaust valves for No. 1 cylinder.
4. Turn the crankshaft 180 degrees in the normal direction of rotation. Check and note the valve clearances of cylinder No. 3 at the overlap position of cylinder No. 2.
5. Turn the crankshaft 180 degrees. Check and note the valve clearances of cylinder No. 1.
6. Turn the crankshaft 180 degrees. Check and note the valve clearances of cylinder No. 2 at the overlap position of cylinder No. 3.
7. Compare the noted clearances with those listed in the "Tune-Up Specifications" chart. Adjustment is made by replacing the tappet clearance shim in the top of each tappet. These are available in 26 sizes ranging from 3.0mm (0.119 in.) to 4.25mm (0.166 in.) in increments of 0.05mm (0.002 in.). The thickness of each shim is marked on the bottom (these shims are available from VW dealers).

**NOTE: If a valve clearance deviates 0.002 in. or less from the specified clearance, it need not be adjusted.**

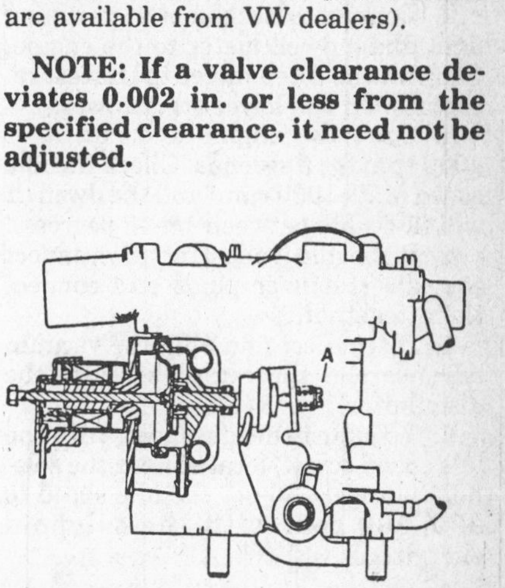


Idle speed adjustment screw (A)—Carter TYF carburetor

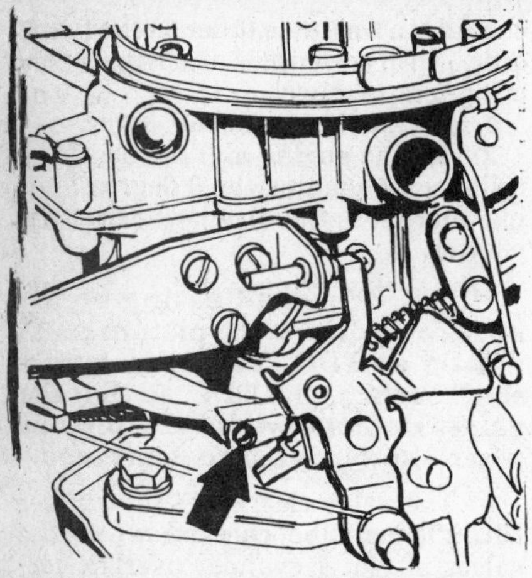

Idle mixture adjustment 1983-85 Rabbit

8. To remove a tappet clearance shim turn the cylinder to TDC and press down the tappet so that the shim can be lifted out. A special tool is available from VW for this operation. Once the shim is removed, check its size and determine what size will be needed to produce the required adjustment.

9. Install the required shim. When all the clearances have been corrected, recheck valve clearances.

## Idle Speed and Mixture Carbureted Gasoline Engines

### IDLE SPEED ADJUSTMENT

#### *1983–84 Rabbit*

1. Run the engine to normal operating temperatures. Make sure that the choke is fully **OPEN** and not sticking. Remove the PCV valve from the valve cover. Turn **OFF** all of the electrical equipment.
2. Connect a tachometer, a timing light and a dwell meter to the engine. Connect the dwell meter to the test receptacle on the lower strut tower.
3. Start the engine and run it at 2000 rpm for 5 seconds. Check the idle speed (850–1000 rpm) and the dwell (it will fluctuate between 18–45 degrees).
4. If the idle is incorrect, disconnect the idle stabilizer plugs and connect them together.
5. Disconnect and plug the vacuum advance and the retard hoses at the distributor.
6. To adjust the idle speed, turn the idle speed screw, located near the solenoid plunger. Adjust the idle speed to 820–900 rpm with the solenoid energized.

**NOTE: On vehicles equipped with A/C, turn the A/C ON, set the control to COLD, the fan to FAST, disengage the A/C compressor clutch and adjust the idle speed to 820–900 rpm.**

7. When the idle speed is adjusted, remove the test equipment and reinstall the hoses and electrical connectors.

### IDLE MIXTURE ADJUSTMENT

This adjustment is to be performed with a CO meter unless an oxygen sensor is present in the system, then adjust the mixture with a dwell meter tool VW 1367.

#### *1983–84 Rabbit*

1. Remove the air cleaner and the fuel lines. Disconnect the throttle linkage and the electrical connectors. Remove the carburetor from the engine.
2. Remove the tamper-proof plug from the idle mixture screw.
3. Reinstall the carburetor, then check and/or adjust the idle speed and the timing.
4. Adjust the idle mixture screw to obtain a dwell reading of 28–50 degrees.
5. Install a new tamper-proof plug to cover the idle speed screw. Install the fuel lines and the linkages

#### *1984–85 Rabbit*

1. Run the engine until it reaches normal operating temperatures.
2. Check the timing and the idle speed.
3. Place the CO sensor in the exhaust pipe.
4. Turn the idle mixture screw to reach the correct CO level (0.30–1.10%).

### FAST IDLE SPEED ADJUSTMENT

#### *Rabbit Only*

1. Run the engine to normal operating temperatures.
2. Check and/or adjust the idle speed and the timing.

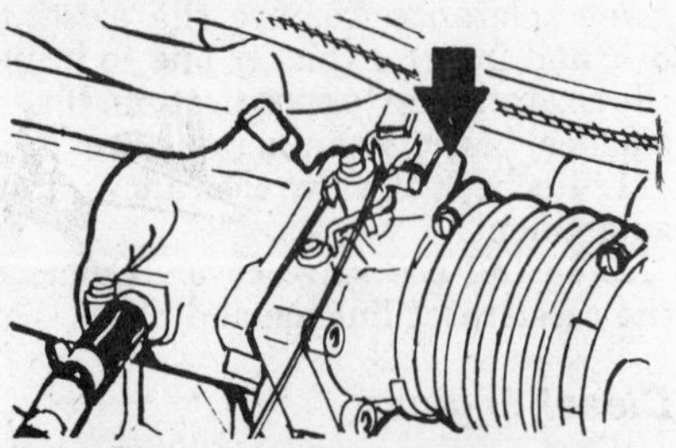

Idle speed adjustment screw—fuel injected Rabbit, Jetta, Scirocco

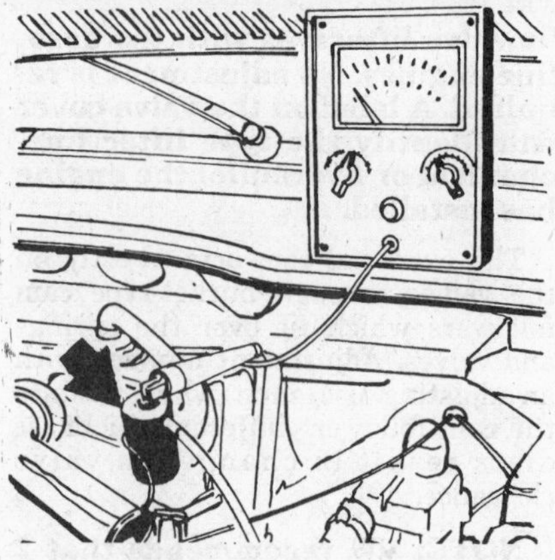

Special adapter VW 1324 is necessary to use an external tachometer on diesel engines

3. Set the fast idle screw on the 2nd step of the fast idle cam.
4. Disconnect the purge valve electrical connector.
5. Disconnect and plug the vacuum hose at the EGR valve.
6. Adjust the fast idle screw to 2600–3000 rpm.
7. After adjustment, reinstall the hoses and wiring connector.

## Idle Speed and Mixture Fuel Injected Gasoline Engines

### IDLE AND CO ADJUSTMENT

#### *1983–90 CIS-E—All Models*

**NOTE: On 1.8L CIS engines equipped with a manual preheat valve on the air cleaner housing. The valve is marked S (summer) and W (winter). When servicing, position the valve to S (unless work area is below freezing). After servicing, return valve to the position that matches climate conditions.**

1. The engine must be at normal operating temperature.
2. Disconnect the crankcase breather hose at the cylinder head cover and

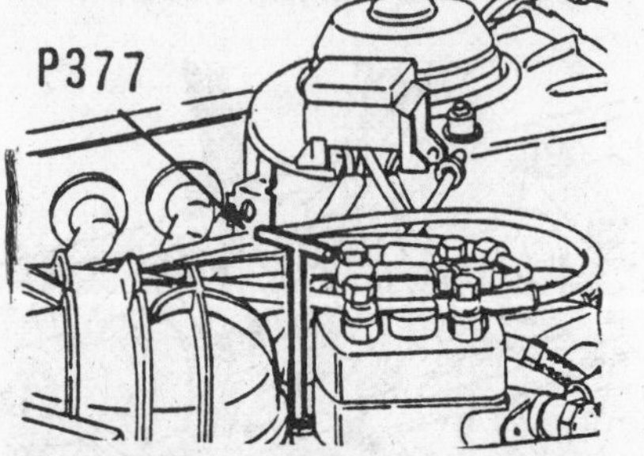


CO adjusting tool installed—CIS fuel injection (Rabbit, Jetta, Scirocco shown)

on 5 cylinder models and plug the hose.

3. Disconnect the 2 plugs on the idle stabilizer at the control unit and plug them together.

4. Turn **OFF** all of the electrical accessories.

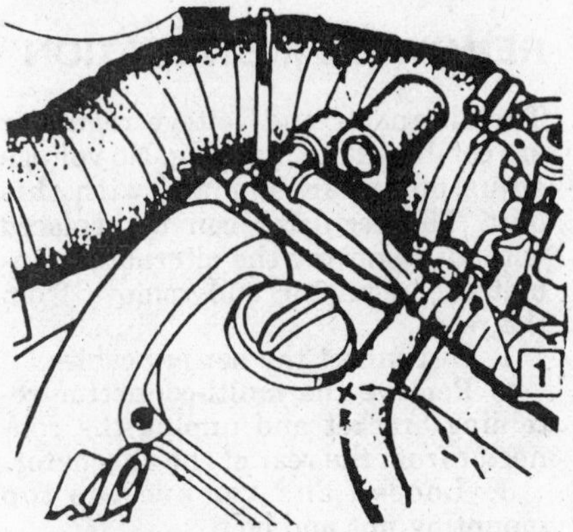


Adjusting the idle speed – Digifant II

**NOTE: On the Quantum, remove the cap from the T-piece in the charcoal canister vent hose near the right fender. On all others, remove the charcoal canister vent hose at the elbow below the intake boot.**

5. Connect a tachometer and timing light. Check the timing. Adjust if necessary.

6. Using adapter hose US–4492, connect a CO meter to the CO test point on the engine.

7. Start the engine, accelerate briefly, check and/or adjust the idle speed and the timing.

8. Remove the air sensor housing plug, insert adjusting tool P377 and adjust the dwell to 38–52 degrees, by turning the mixture adjust screw.

9. Check the CO reading. If it is too high, check for leaks in the intake or exhaust systems and malfunctions in the fuel system.

10. Check the idle speed against the specifications. Adjust the idle at the idle adjustment screw on the throttle chamber (850–1000 rpm).

11. When adjustment is completed, reinstall the vacuum lines at the canister.

12. Reconnect the crankcase breather hose and remove the test equipment.

#### *1985–87 CIS and Emission Controls*

1. The following must be checked prior to adjustment: engine oil temperature at normal operating 176° F, radiator fan and A/C **OFF**, no exhaust system leaks and oxygen regulation operating.

2. Clamp the idle speed boost hose tightly to prevent flow.

3. Pull the breather hoses from the cylinder head to allow fresh air circulation – hose at intake manifold, hose from air cleaner.

4. Remove the T-connector from the carbon canister at the intake air boot. Turn the T-connector 90 degrees and insert blank side with 0.059 in. restrictor into the hole in the intake boot.

5. Connect a suitable duty meter to measure ignition timing and rpm.

6. Start and run engine at idle. Check timing (4–8 BTDC) and idle rpm (under 1000).

7. Adjust as necessary. Timing 6 degrees BTDC. Idle 900 rpm.

8. Stop engine and remove the test equipment. Connect all hoses removed. Unplug and connect the T-fitting at the carbon canister.

#### *Digifant II*

1. Start engine and run until it reaches normal operating temperature.

2. Turn **OFF** all accessories. Connect exhaust probe EPA 105 or equivalent to the CO receptacle.

3. Disconnect the crankcase breather hose (PCV) and plug the open end.

4. Start the engine and let it idle. Disconnnect the coolant temperature sensor.

5. Advance the engine rpm over 2100 rpm at least 3 times and then let it idle.

6. Check the idle speed and CO content and adjust if necessary. The correct idle speed should be 750–850 rpm. The CO content should be 0.30–1.10%.

7. To adjust the CO to specification:
   a. remove the tamper proof plug from the CO adjusting screw.
   b. using a 5mm hex wrench, rotate the adjusting to obtain the correct reading.
   c. when adjustment is correct, install a new tamper proof plug over the adjusting screw.

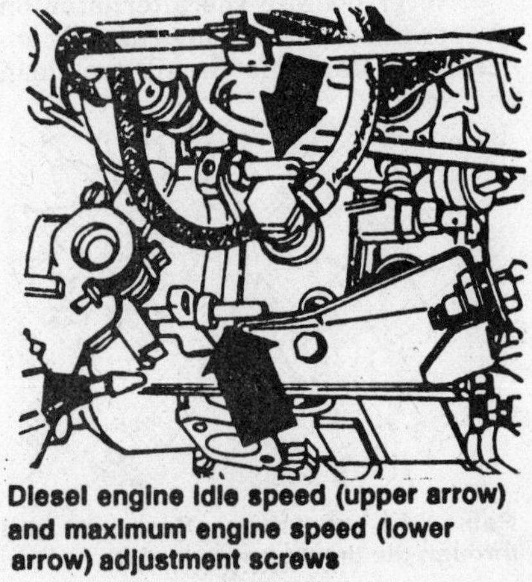

Diesel engine idle speed (upper arrow) and maximum engine speed (lower arrow) adjustment screws

8. To adjust the idle speed to specification, turn the idle adjusting screw (clockwise to decrease rpm and counter-clockwise to increase).

9. When all adjustments are complete, reconnect the coolant temperature sensor and the crankcase breather hose.

10. Check readings again and if they are still within the correct range, remove all test equipment.

## Idle Speed Diesel Engine

### IDLE SPEED/MAXIMUM SPEED ADJUSTMENTS

Volkswagen diesel engines have both an idle speed and a maximum speed adjustment. The maximum engine speed adjustment prevents the engine from over-revving and self-destructing. The adjusters are located side by side on top of the injection pump. The screw closest to the engine is the idle speed adjuster, while the outer screw is the maximum speed adjuster.

1. The idle and maximum speed must be adjusted with the engine warm (normal operating temperature).

2. Adjust all engines to the specified idle speed.

3. When adjustment is correct, lock the locknut on the screw and apply non-hardening thread sealer (Loctite or similar) to prevent the screw from vibrating loose.

4. The maximum speed for all engines is between 5300–5400 rpm or 5050–5150 (turbo). If it is not in this range, loosen the screw and correct the speed (turning the screw clockwise decreases rpm).

5. Lock the nut on the adjusting screw and apply a dab of thread sealer.

# ENGINE ELECTRICAL

## Distributor

### REMOVAL & INSTALLATION

#### *Timing Undisturbed*

1. Take off the vacuum hose(s) at the distributor. Disconnect the coil high tension wire.

2. Detach the primary wire. Late models use a connector plug retained by a spring clip. Unfasten the clip and disconnect the plug. Remove the dis-

tributor cap and shield (if equipped).

3. Tag and disconnect any additional wires leading from the distributor. Bring the No. 1 cylinder to top dead center (TDC) on the compression stroke by rotating the engine so that the rotor points to the No. 1 spark plug wire tower on the distributor cap and the timing marks are aligned at 0 degree. Mark the rotor to distributor relationship. Also, matchmark the distributor housing to crankcase relationship.

4. Remove the bolt and lift off the retaining flange. Lift the distributor straight out of the engine.

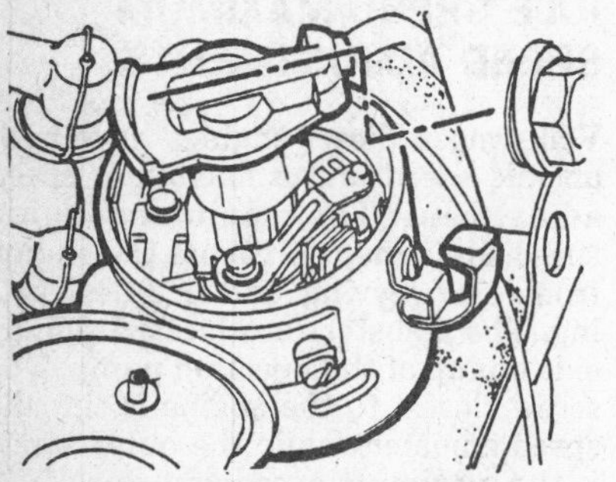

Rotor alignment with the notch for No. 1 cylinder

**NOTE: If the engine has not been disturbed while the distributor was out i.e., the crankshaft was not turned, then reinstall the distributor in the reverse order of removal. Carefully align the marks.**

### *Timing Disturbed*

1. Bring the No. 1 cylinder to TDC on the compression stroke and align the timing marks on 0 degree. Align the matchmarks and insert the distributor into the crankcase. If the matchmarks are gone, have the rotor pointing to the No. 1 spark plug wire tower upon insertion.

2. If the oil pump drive doesn't engage, remove the distributor and using a long screwdriver, turn the pump shaft so that it is parallel to the centerline.

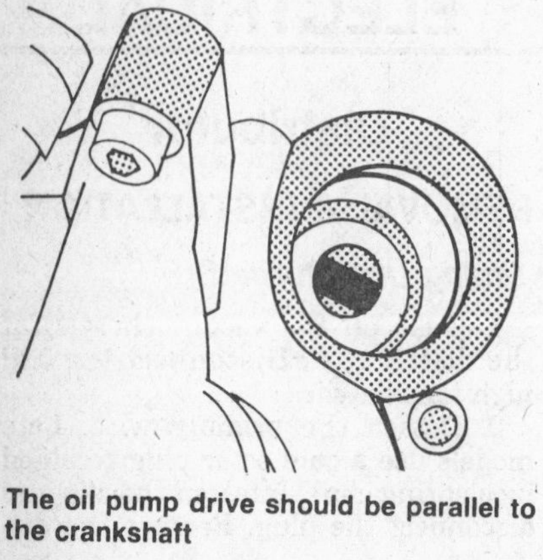

The oil pump drive should be parallel to the crankshaft

3. Install the distributor, aligning the marks and reconnect the condenser and coil wires. Reinstall the distributor cap and tighten the retaining nut.

4. Install the cap. Check and adjust the engine timing.

## Alternator

### PRECAUTIONS

An alternating current (AC) generator (alternator) is used. Unlike the direct current (DC) generators used in many older cars, there are several precautions which must be strictly observed in order to avoid damaging the unit.

- Battery polarity should be checked before any connection, such as jumper cables or battery charge leads, are made. Reversing the battery connections will result in damage to the diodes.
- The battery must never be disconnected while the alternator is running.
- Booster batteries should be connected positive to positive and negative to the booster battery and a good ground on the disabled vehicle's engine.
- Never use a fast charger as a booster to start cars with AC circuits; use a "trickle charger."
- When servicing the battery with a charger, always disconnect the car battery cables.
- Never attempt to polarize an AC generator.
- Avoid long soldering times when replacing diodes or transistors. Prolonged heat is damaging to alternators.
- Do not use test lamps of more than 12 volts (V) for checking diode continuity.
- Do not short across or ground any of the terminals on the alternator.
- The polarity of the battery, alternator and regulator must be matched and considered before making any electrical connections within the system.
- Never operate the alternator on an open circuit. Make sure that all connections within the circuit are clean and tight.

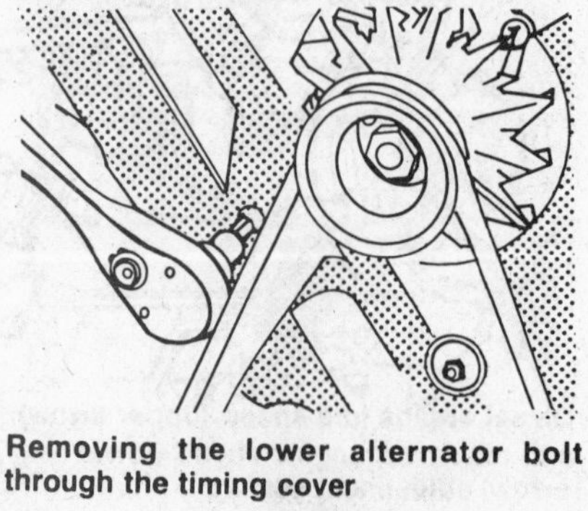

Removing the lower alternator bolt through the timing cover

- Disconnect the battery terminals when performing any service on the electrical system. This will eliminate the possibility of accidental reversal of polarity.
- Disconnect the battery ground cable if arc welding is to be done on any part of the car.

### REMOVAL & INSTALLATION

The alternator and voltage regulator are combined in 1 housing. No voltage adjustment can be made with this unit. The regulator can be replaced without removing the alternator. Unbolt the regulator and remove from the rear.

1. Disconnect the battery cables.
2. Remove the multi-connector retaining bracket and unplug the connector from the rear of the alternator.
3. Loosen and remove the top mounting nut and bolt.
4. Using a socket inserted through the timing belt cover (it is not necessary to remove the cover), loosen the lower mounting bolt.
5. Swing the alternator over and remove the alternator belt.
6. Remove the lower nut and bolt.
7. Remove the alternator.
8. Install the alternator with the lower bolt. Do not tighten it at this point.
9. Install the alternator belt over the pulleys.
10. Loosely install the top mounting bolt and pivot the alternator until the belt is correctly tensioned.
11. Tighten the top and bottom bolts to 14 ft. lbs.
12. Connect the alternator and battery wires.

### BELT REPLACEMENT AND TENSIONING

1. Loosen the top alternator mounting bolt.
2. Using a socket inserted through the timing belt cover and loosen the lower mounting bolt.
3. Lever the alternator over and remove the belt.
4. Slip the new belt over the pulleys.
5. Pull the alternator over until the belt deflection midway between the crankshaft pulley and the alternator pulley is $^3/_8$–$^9/_{16}$ in.
6. Securely tighten the mounting bolts.

**NOTE: Models equipped with a 1.8L engine from April 1985 have a toothed bracket and tensioning gear for belt tension adjustment. Loosen the bracket mounting, pivot and cradle bolts. Rotate the adjuster tension gear bolt with a**

**torque wrench and crossfoot until 6-7 ft. lbs. of tension is on the belt adjuster. Tighten the center bolt while maintaining the proper torque. Tighten the bracket and cradle mounting bolts. On Fox models equipped with A/C, the A/C belt tension can only be adjusted by removing the compressor pulley. The pulley splits in 2 halves and uses shims in the center of the halves to adjust the tension. Add shims to decrease the belt tension and remove shims to increase the tension. On all other models equipped with A/C, the belt tension is adjusted in the traditional manner.**

## Voltage Regulator

### REMOVAL & INSTALLATION

**NOTE: The voltage regulator is attached to the rear of the alternator. Since no adjustment can be performed on the regulator, it is serviced by replacement ONLY.**

1. Remove the 2 mounting screws.
2. Disconnect the electrical connectors and remove the regulator.
3. To install, reverse the removal procedures. Care must be taken to install the electrical connectors in their proper location.

## Starter

### REMOVAL & INSTALLATION

#### *Bosch Starters*

1. Disconnect the battery ground cable.
2. Raise the front of the vehicle.

**NOTE: If equipped with a diesel engine, it may be necessary to install an engine support and remove the right engine mount.**

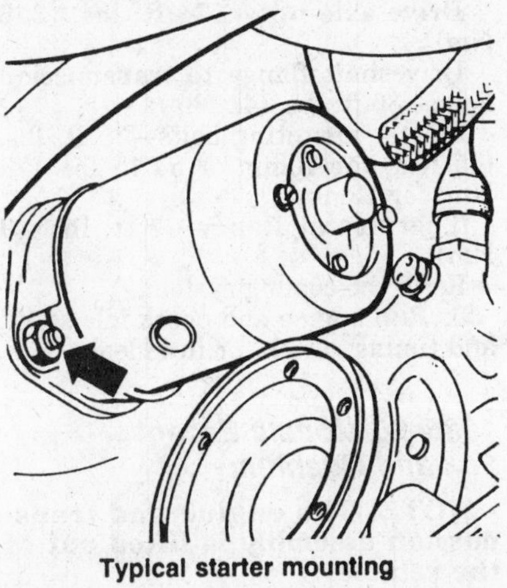

Typical starter mounting

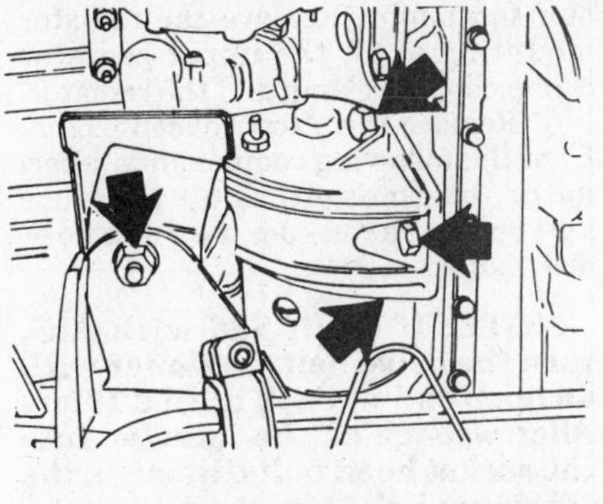

Quantum starter mounting bolt locations

3. Tag and disconnect the wires from the starter solenoid.
4. Disconnect the large cable.
5. Remove the starter retaining nuts.
6. Unscrew the bolt. Remove the starter.
7. To install, reverse the removal procedures.

#### *Mitsubishi Starters*

1. Disconnect the battery ground cable.
2. Support the weight of the engine with either Volkswagen special tool 10–222 or use a jack with a block of wood under the oil pan. Don't jack the engine too high, just take the weight off the motor mounts. Be careful not to bend the oil pan.
3. Remove the engine/transmission cover plate.
4. Unbolt and remove the starter side motor mount and carrier.
5. Disconnect and mark the starter wiring.
6. Remove starter mounting bolts and remove the starter.
7. To install, reverse the removal procedures. Torque the starter bolts and nuts to 14 ft. lbs.

### OVERHAUL

Use the following procedure to replace brushes or starter drive.

1. Remove the solenoid.
2. Remove the end bearing cap.
3. Loosen both of the long housing screws.
4. Remove the lockwasher and spacer washers.
5. Remove the long housing screws and remove the end cover.
6. Pull the 2 field coil brushes out of the brush housing.
7. Remove the brush housing assembly.
8. Loosen the nut on the solenoid housing, remove the sealing disc and remove the solenoid operating lever.
9. Loosen the large screws on the side of the starter body and remove the field coil along with the brushes.

**NOTE: If the bushes require replacement, the field coil and brushes and/or the brush housing and its brushes must be replaced as a unit.**

10. If the starter drive is being replaced, push the stop-ring down and remove the circlip on the end of the shaft. Remove the stop-ring and remove the drive.
11. Assembly of the starter is carried out in the reverse order of disassembly. Use a gear puller to install the stop-ring in its groove (on models so equipped). Use a new circlip on the shaft.

### SOLENOID REPLACEMENT

1. Remove the starter.
2. Remove the nut which secures the connector strip at the end of the solenoid.
3. Take out the 2 retaining screws on the mounting bracket and withdraw the solenoid after it has been unhooked from its actuating lever.
4. When replacing a defective solenoid with a new one, care should be taken to see that the distance is 19mm when the magnet is drawn inside the solenoid.
5. Installation is the reverse of removal. In order to facilitate engagement of the actuating rod, the pinion should be pulled out as far as possible when inserting the solenoid.

## Diesel Glow Plugs

### GLOW PLUG SYSTEM CHECK

**NOTE: The 1983–86 diesels, except turbocharged models, have a new type quick-glow system. Nominal glow time is 7 seconds. Although the wiring for this system is the same as the earlier system, the glow plugs and relay cannot be paired or interchanged with earlier parts or vice versa.**

1. Connect a test light between, No. 4 cylinder glow plug and ground. The glow plugs are connected by a flat, coated busbar (located near the bottom of the cylinder head).
2. Turn the ignition key to the heating (pre-glow) position. The test light should light.
3. If not, possible problems include the glow plug relay, the ignition switch and the fuse box relay plate and the glow plug fuse or a break in the wire to the relay terminal.

### INDIVIDUAL GLOW PLUG TEST

1. Remove the wire and busbar from the glow plugs.
2. Connect a test light to the battery positive terminal.
3. Touch the test light probe to each glow plug in turn. If the test light lights, the plug is good. If the light does not light, replace the glow plug(s).

# GASOLINE ENGINE MECHANICAL

## Engine

### REMOVAL & INSTALLATION

#### *1983–84 Models Except Quantum*

The engine and transmission assembly is to be lowered from the vehicle. If the vehicle is carbureted, simply remove any hoses or wiring from the carburetor, which will interfere with the engine removal procedures; ignore any procedures relating to the fuel injection system.

**NOTE: If equipped with A/C, turn ON the ignition and the A/C control (engine not running), remove the compressor clutch bolt, press the clutch from the A/C compressor shaft (using a ⅝ in. × 18 UNF bolt), turn OFF the ignition and the A/C. Disconnect the compressor clutch wire.**

1. Disconnect the negative battery cable.
2. Remove the fuel tank cap to relieve the pressure on the fuel system.

**NOTE: If equipped with an automatic transmission, place the selector lever in the PARK position and disconnect the positive battery cable.**

3. Remove the air intake duct between the fuel distributor and the throttle housing.
4. Remove the radiator cap. Turn the heater temperature control valve to fully OPEN. Place a container under the thermostat housing, remove the thermostat flange and drain the coolant.
5. Remove the upper radiator and heater hoses from the engine. Remove the electrical connector from the radiator fan motor. Remove the radiator mounting nuts, the upper radiator clamp clip, the clamp and the radiator.
6. Remove the electrical connectors from the following components: alternator, thermoswitch, oil pressure switch, warm-up regulator, distributor.

**NOTE: If equipped with A/C, turn the drive belt tensioner with an open end wrench until a 10mm Allen wrench can be inserted into the socket head bolts. Remove the tensioner bolts and the tensioner. Remove the alternator, the timing belt cover and the compressor mounting bracket bolts (under the timing cover). Disconnect the pre-heat hose. Remove the diagonal braces, the support brace and the compressor bracket. Move the compressor aside; DO NOT disconnect the refrigerant hoses.**

7. Remove the pre-heat tube from the rear of the engine.
8. Remove the distributor vacuum hoses and the EGR temperature valve.
9. Remove the coil and the coolant temperature sensor wires.

**CAUTION**

***Use care when disconnecting the fuel lines. Fuel under pressure may still be in the lines and if sprayed, may cause fire or personal injury.***

10. Place a suitable container (to catch the fuel) under the cold start valve, then remove the fuel line and the warm-up regulator.
11. Remove the electrical connectors from the cold start valve and the auxiliary air regulator.
12. At the throttle body, remove the vacuum lines of the brake booster and the vacuum amplifier (if equipped).
13. Remove the PCV hose from the cylinder head cover.
14. At the throttle body. pull back the accelerator cable clip and disconnect the cable from the ball. Loosen the accelerator cable locknut and remove the cable from the cylinder head cover.
15. Remove the fuel injectors, then position the entire assembly aside.
16. Disconnect the electrical connectors from the starter, the back-up light switch and the ground cable from the transmission.
17. If equipped with a manual transmission, at the clutch cable, loosen the locknut, remove the clip from under the clutch lever and the cable. If equipped with an automatic transmission, disconnect the selector cable from the transmission and the bracket.
18. Remove the speedometer cable clamp and the cable.
19. Remove the upper starter bolts and the starter.
20. Remove the nuts from the exhaust flex-pipe and the relay shaft. Disconnect the lever from the relay shaft.
21. Remove the driveshafts from the mounting flanges.
22. Remove the horn (move aside), the front mount cup bolts, the cup and the front mount.
23. At both front wheels, remove the axle nuts.
24. At both steering knuckles, remove the ball joint lock bolts. Using a large pry bar, pry the ball joints from the bearing housings.
25. Swing the wheel and strut assembly away from the vehicle. Remove the drive axles from the wheel hubs.

**NOTE: With the driveshafts removed, reconnect the ball joints and lock bolts so that the vehicle may be lowered on its wheels.**

26. Remove the transmission mounting nuts and the right front wheel and tire assembly.
27. Attach an engine sling tool US–1105 or equivalent to the engine and using an overhead crane, lift the engine slightly.
28. Remove the clip from the gearshift lever rod. Remove the rod from the selector shaft lever and the relay shaft with the gearshift lever rod attached. Open the clip on the front of the selector rod and remove the rod from the relay lever.
29. Remove the right and left side engine mount to body bolts.
30. Carefully Lower the engine and transmission assembly onto a dolly.
31. Raise the vehicle and slide the engine and transmission assembly clear of the vehicle.
32. To install, reverse the removal procedures.

Torque the following components:

Ball joint to steering knuckle – 36 ft. lbs. (49 Nm)

Drive axle nut – 174 ft. lbs. (236 Nm)

Driveshaft flange to transmission bolts – 30 ft. lbs. (41 Nm)

Starter mounting bolts – 33 ft. lbs. (45 Nm) for 10mm or 54 ft. lbs. (73 Nm) for 12mm

Thermostat flange – 7 ft. lbs. (9 Nm).

Refill the cooling system.

33. Run engine and check idle speed and timing, check for fluid leaks.

#### *1985–90 Models Except Fox and Quantum*

**NOTE: The engine and transmission assembly is lifted out of the vehicle.**

Front engine mount location on Golf, Jetta and Scirocco

1. Disconnect the battery cables and remove the battery.
2. Relieve the fuel system pressure.

**NOTE: If equipped with an automatic transmission, place the selector lever in the PARK position.**

3. Remove the air intake duct between the fuel distributor and the throttle housing.
4. Remove the radiator cap. Turn the heater temperature control valve to fully **OPEN**. Place a container under the thermostat housing, remove the thermostat flange and drain the coolant.
5. Remove the upper radiator and heater hoses from the engine. Remove the electrical connector from the radiator fan motor. Remove the radiator mounting nuts, the upper radiator clamp clip and the clamp. Remove the radiator shroud and the radiator.
6. At the front of the vehicle, remove the apron, the trim and the grille. Disconnect the headlight electrical connectors and the hood release cable from the hood latch assembly.

**NOTE: If equipped with power steering, remove the drive belt and the pump mounting bolts. Remove the power steering pump and move it aside. DO NOT disconnect the power steering pressure lines.**

7. Remove the electrical connectors from the following components: the alternator, the thermoswitch, the oil pressure switch, the warm-up regulator and the distributor.

**NOTE: If equipped with A/C, remove the trim panel and the lower apron. Remove the condenser and duct work from the crossmember and radiator. Remove the idle boost valve vacuum hose and the air filter assembly. Disconnect the air flow assembly and the compressor, then move it aside.**

8. Remove the pre-heat tube from the rear of the engine.
9. Remove the distributor vacuum hoses and the EGR temperature valve.
10. Remove the coil and the coolant temperature sensor, the Lambda sensor and the knock sensor wires.

**CAUTION**

***Use care when disconnecting the fuel lines. Fuel under pressure may still be in the lines and if sprayed, may cause fire or personal injury.***

11. Place a container under the cold start valve, then remove the fuel line and the warm-up regulator.
12. Remove the electrical connectors from the cold start valve and the auxiliary air regulator.
13. At the throttle body, remove the vacuum lines of the brake booster, the vacuum amplifier and the vacuum amplifier (if equipped).
14. Remove the PCV hose from the cylinder head cover.
15. At the throttle body, pull back the accelerator cable clip and disconnect the cable from the ball. Loosen the accelerator cable locknut and remove the cable from the cylinder head cover.
16. Remove the fuel injectors, then position the entire assembly aside.
17. Disconnect the electrical connectors from the starter, the back-up light switch and the ground cable from the transmission.
18. If equipped with a manual transmission, at the clutch cable, loosen the locknut, remove the clip from under the clutch lever and remove the cable. If equipped with an automatic transmission, disconnect the selector cable from the transmission and the bracket.
19. Remove the speedometer cable clamp and the cable. Remove the upper starter bolts and the starter.
20. If equipped with a manual transmission, remove the transmission and upshift indicator vacuum switches. If equipped with an automatic transmission, remove the CIS-E wiring harness.

**NOTE: On the GTI/GLI models, remove the idle stabilizer control valve, the throttle plate switch and the knock sensor.**

21. Remove the nuts from the exhaust flex-pipe and the relay shaft. Disconnect the lever from the relay shaft.
22. Remove the driveshafts from the mounting flanges.

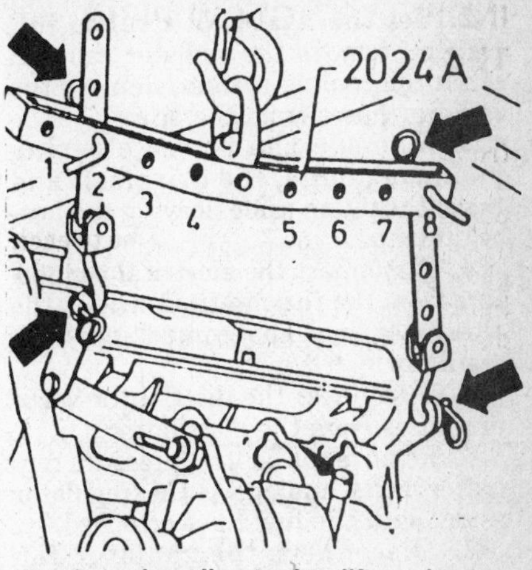


Using engine sling tool to lift engine from vehicle

23. Remove the horn (move aside) and the front mount cup bolts. Remove the cup and the front mount.
24. Remove the rear engine mounting nuts.

**NOTE: On vehicles equipped with the 16 valve engine, the intake manifold will have to be removed in order to remove the engine.**

25. Attach an engine sling tool VW-2024A or equivalent to the engine. Using an overhead crane, lift the engine slightly.
26. Remove the clip from the gearshift lever rod, the rod from the selector shaft lever and the relay shaft with the gearshift lever rod. Open the clip on the front of the selector rod and remove the rod from the relay lever.
27. Remove the right and left side engine mount to body bolts.
28. Slightly lower and tilt the engine and transmission. Lift the engine/transmission assembly, turning it slightly, out of the car.
29. To install, reverse the removal procedures.

Torque the following components:

Ball joint to steering knuckle – 36 ft. lbs. (49 Nm)

Drive axle nut – 174 ft. lbs. (236 Nm)

Driveshaft flange to transmission bolts – 30 ft. lbs. (41 Nm)

Starter bolts – 33 ft. lbs. (45 Nm)

Transmission to body mount – 33 ft. lbs. (41 Nm) for 10mm bolts or 54 ft. lbs. (73 Nm) for 12mm bolts

Power steering bolts – 14 ft. lbs. (19 Nm)

Thermostat flange bolts – 7 ft. lbs. (9 Nm)

Refill the cooling system.

### *4 Cylinder Quantum*

1. Disconnect the negative battery cable.

2. Set the heater control to full **OPEN**, remove the radiator cap and drain the cooling system. Remove the radiator hoses from the engine.
3. Remove the power steering mounting bolts, the drive belt and move the pump aside, leaving the hoses attached.
4. Disconnect the electrical connectors from the thermo-time switch, the alternator and the control pressure regulator.
5. Disconnect the distributor vacuum hoses from the distributor.
6. Remove the control pressure regulator bolts and move the regulator aside, with the fuel lines attached.
7. Disconnect the radiator fan wires. Remove the radiator bolts and the radiator assembly with the air duct.
8. Remove the clip on the clutch cable and disconnect the cable.
9. Remove the left engine mount nut.
10. Disconnect the coolant temperature sender wire from the engine, oxygen sensor thermo-switch, the Hall sending unit wire and the coil wire from the distributor.
11. Disconnect the electrical connectors from the auxiliary air regulator, the cold start and the frequency valves.
12. Remove the emissions canister hose from the air duct.
13. Remove the preheater hose and the cold start valve (leave the fuel line attached).
14. Disconnect the distributor vacuum hose from the intake manifold. Remove the accelerator cable, the crankcase breather hose and the brake booster hose.

**CAUTION**

***Use care when disconnecting the fuel lines. Fuel under pressure may still be in the lines and if sprayed, may cause fire or personal injury.***

15. Remove the fuel injectors (protect them with caps), the fuel distributor (leave the lines attached) and move them aside.

**NOTE: If equipped with A/C, remove the following components: the throttle body housing, the auxiliary air regulator, the horn bracket, the crankcase pulley nuts, the drive belt, the compressor bracket bolts, the compressor and the condenser. Place and tie the compressor and the condenser aside.**

16. Remove the right engine mount nuts.
17. Remove the exhaust pipe at the manifold.

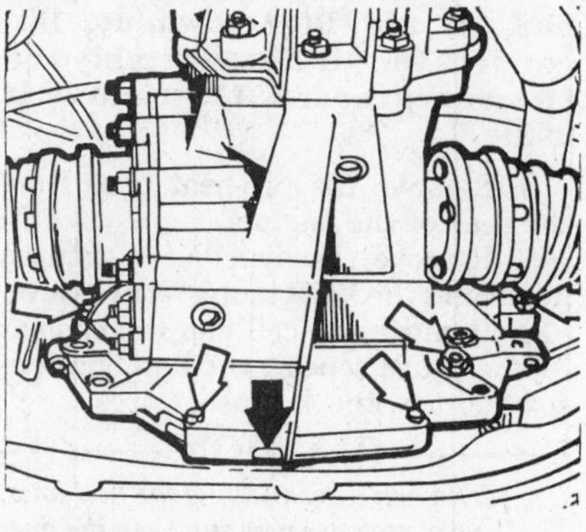

Remove the lower engine/transmission bolts and flywheel cover (arrows)

18. Remove the starter wiring and the starter. Remove the lower engine to transmission bolts and the flywheel cover plate.
19. If equipped with an automatic transmission, remove the torque converter to flywheel bolts. Attach the engine support tool VW 785/1B or equivalent to the transmission and support it.
20. Loosen the nuts on the outer half of the damper pulley and remove the drive belt.
21. Remove the A/C compressor bracket mounting bolts and move the compressor aside (with the lines attached).
22. Attach the engine sling US-1105 or equivalent to the engine, support it with a vertical hoist and lift the engine slightly, then remove the right engine mount.
23. Remove the upper engine to transmission bolts, separate the engine from the transmission. Lift and turn the engine to remove it from the vehicle.

**NOTE: If equipped with an automatic transmission, secure the torque converter to the transmission to keep it from falling out.**

24. To install, reverse the removal procedures.

Torque the following components:

Transmission to engine bolts – 40 ft. lbs. (54 Nm)

Engine mount bolts – 25 ft. lbs. (34 Nm)

Exhaust pipe to exhaust manifold to 18 ft. lbs. (24 Nm)

Starter bolts – 14 ft. lbs. (19 Nm)

Torque converter to drive plate bolts – 22 ft. lbs. (30 Nm)

Support bolts – 18 ft. lbs. (24 Nm)

Power steering pump bolts – 14 ft. lbs. (19 Nm)

A/C compressor lower bolts – 18 ft. lbs. (24 Nm) and the upper bolts – 22 ft. lbs. (30 Nm)

Adjust the belt tension to ³⁄₈ in. deflection and refill the cooling system.

### *5 Cylinder Quantum*

1. Disconnect the negative battery cable.
2. Move the heater control valve to fully **OPEN** and remove the radiator cap.
3. At the power steering pump, remove the drive belt cover, the drive belt, the mounting bolts and the pump. Move the pump aside with the hoses connected.
4. Remove the grille and the radiator cover.
5. Remove the lower radiator hose and drain the coolant.
6. Remove the front bumper with the energy absorber.
7. Remove the vacuum hoses from the intake manifold, the upper radiator hose, the radiator hose from the thermostat housing and the heater hose (drain the remaining coolant).
8. Disconnect the electrical connectors from the oil pressure switch, the control pressure regulator and the thermo-time switches.
9. Remove the cylinder head cover ground wire.
10. Remove the control pressure regulator (leave the lines attached) and the ball joint circlip (disconnect it at the push rod).
11. Remove the alternator drive belt, the bracket bolts and the alternator assembly, move aside.
12. Remove the air duct and the front engine stop.
13. Disconnect the electrical connectors from the cold start valve, the frequency valve and the throttle switch. Disconnect the electrical leads at the idle stabilizer valve, the Hall sender at the distributor and the oxygen sensor.
14. Remove the accelerator cable circlip and disconnect the cable rod from the throttle body.
15. Remove the distributor cap, the cold start valve and the vacuum hose from the thermo valve.
16. Remove the fuel injection cooling hose.

Front bumper and energy absorber removal

17. Remove the fuel injectors from the intake manifold; leave the fuel lines connected.

**NOTE: When removing the fuel injectors and the cold start valve, place caps on the ends to protect them from damage.**

18. Remove the air filter housing bolts and the filter.

**NOTE: If equipped with an automatic transmission, disconnect the oil cooler hoses.**

19. Remove the heater hoses. Remove the exhaust pipe bracket from the engine and transmission assembly.

**NOTE: If equipped with A/C, remove the drive belt, the electrical connector at the compressor, the compressor bracket to engine bolts and the compressor assembly. Move it aside and support it. DO NOT support the compressor with the pressure hoses.**

20. Attach the supporting tool 2084 to the crankshaft pulley and remove the crankshaft bolt.
21. Of the 4 crankshaft pulley bolts, remove 2 and loosen 2. To loosen the pulley, tap lightly on the remaining bolts. Remove the bolts and the pulley

**NOTE: When removing the pulley from the crankshaft, leave the drive belt sprocket attached to the crankshaft.**

22. Remove the front engine mount and the subframe to body bolts. Remove the exhaust pipe from the exhaust manifold and the support bracket.
23. Disconnect the starter cables and the starter.
24. Remove the torque converter to flywheel bolts, the bolts can be removed through the starter hole. Remove the lower engine-to-transmission bolts. Unhook the shift rod clip and disconnect the rod.
25. Remove the rubber plugs from the left side frame member. Using the support tool VW 785/1, connect it to the transmission and to the frame member, then adjust to make contact with the transmission.
26. Remove both engine mount nuts and the upper engine to transmission bolts (leave 1 bolt in place).
27. Attach the engine support tool US 1105 and the lift tool 9019 to the engine.

**NOTE: If equipped with an auto. trans., secure the torque converter before removing the engine from the transmission.**

28. Remove the last engine to transmisssion bolt and lift the engine, while prying the engine apart from the transmission. Remove the engine from the vehicle.
29. To install, reverse the removal procedures.

Torque the following components:

Transmission to engine bolts—22 ft. lbs. (30 Nm) for 8mm bolts, 32 ft. lbs. (43 Nm) for 10mm bolts or 43 ft. lbs. (58 Nm) for 12mm bolts

Engine mount bolts—32 ft. lbs. (43 Nm)

Exhaust pipe to manifold bolts—22 ft. lbs. (30 Nm)

Subframe to body bolts 51 ft. lbs. (69 Nm)

Torque converter to flywheel bolts—22 ft. lbs. (30 Nm)

Front engine stop bolts—32 ft. lbs. (43 Nm)

Damper pulley center bolt—253 ft. lbs. (343 Nm)

Crankshaft pulley bolts—14 ft. lbs. (19 Nm)

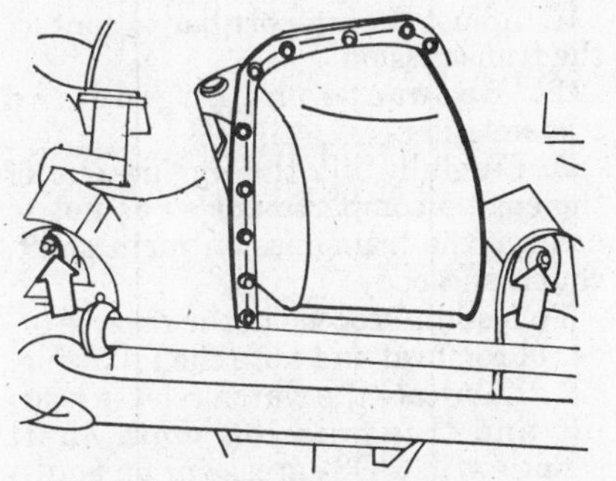

Quantum—engine side mounts

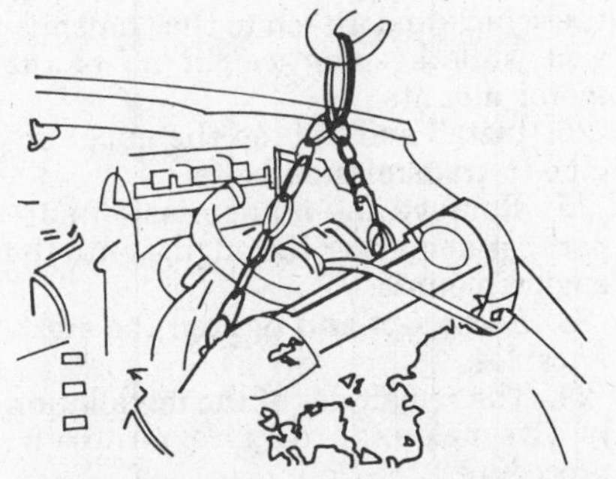

Lifting the engine from the Quantum—the engine must be tilted to remove

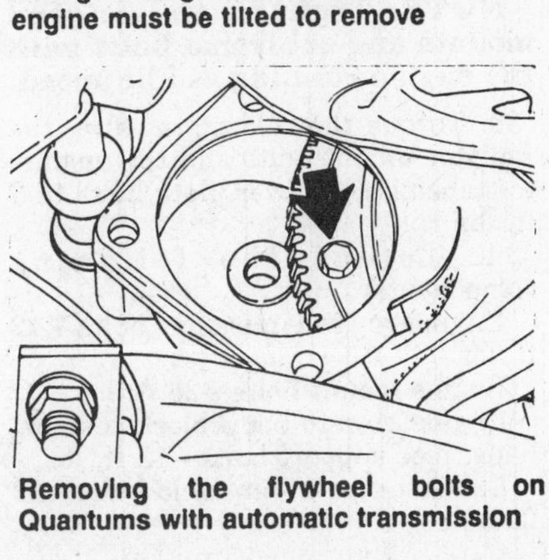

Removing the flywheel bolts on Quantums with automatic transmission

Power steering pump bolts—14 ft. lbs. (19 Nm)

Adjust the belt tension and refill the cooling system.

**NOTE: When installing the crankshaft pulley, align the match mark on the sprocket with the mark on the pulley. When installing the crankshaft bolt, lubricate the threads with Loctite® 573 or equivalent. When installing the engine, shake the engine into position (this will allow the engine to seat properly).**

### *Fox*

**NOTE: The engine is lifted out of the vehicle after separation from the transmission.**

1. Disconnect the battery ground cable and remove the battery.
2. Open the heating valve and the cap on the coolant expansion tank. Drain the coolant by removing the hoses. Disconnect the electrical connector from the radiator cooling fan.

**CAUTION**

***Do not disconnect or loosen any refrigerant hose connections during engine removal on cars equipped with air conditioning.***

3. On cars equipped with air conditioning:
   a. Loosen the compressor support bolts and remove the compressor.
   b. Remove the radiator cooling fan, air ducts and radiator.
   c. Remove the condenser.
   d. Place the air conditioning compressor and condenser out of the way without disconnecting any refrigerant lines.
4. Disconnect the radiator thermo switch and remove the radiator cover. Remove the radiator with the air ducts and fan.
5. Detach and label all the electrical wires connecting the engine to the body.
6. Disconnect and plug the fuel line at the fuel pump. Detach the coolant hoses at the left end of the engine. Disconnect the accelerator cable and remove the air cleaner.
7. Disconnect the speedometer cable from the transmission. Detach the clutch cable.
8. Remove the vacuum hoses. Remove the wire from the ignition coil, the vacuum unit hose and the plug for the Hall system from the distributor.
9. Remove the fuel injectors and install protective caps and plugs.
10. Remove the cold start valve leaving the fuel line connected.
11. Loosen the charcoal filter clamp and move the filter to the rear of the engine compartment.

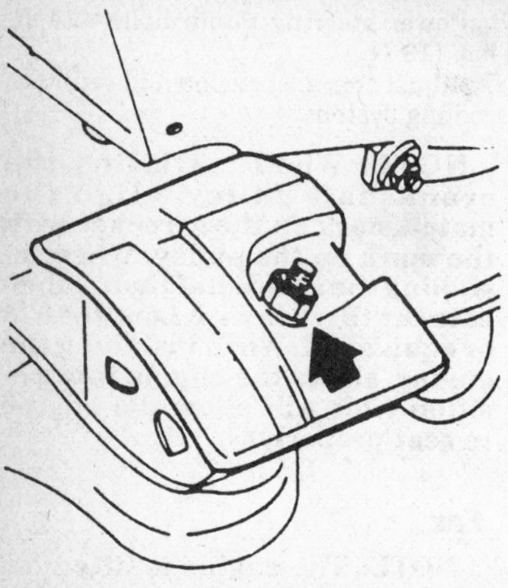

Engine mount attachment

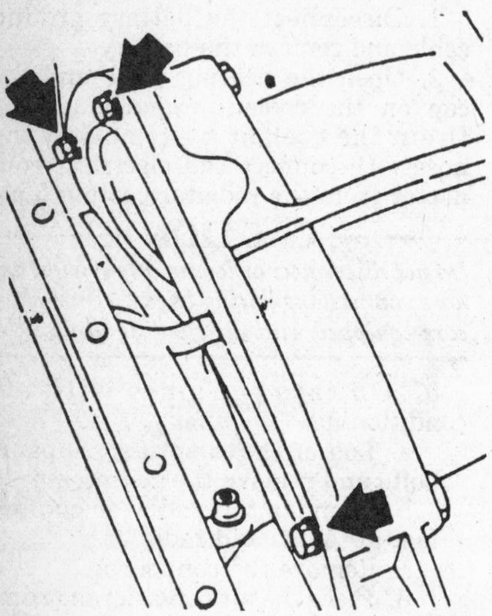

Converter cover plate removal

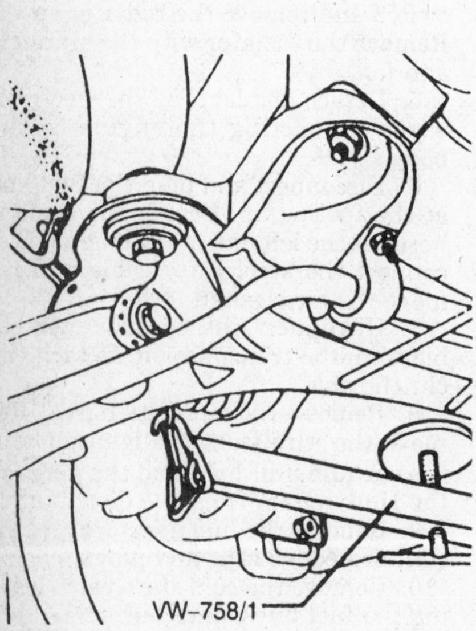


Transmission support tool VW-758/1 installation

12. Remove the upper engine to transmission bolts.
13. Remove the left and right engine mounting nuts.
14. Remove the engine stop and the air duct from the intake manifold.
15. Disconnect and label the starter cables. Then remove the starter mounting bolts and the starter.
16. Remove the 2 lower engine to transmission bolts. Then remove the cover plate bolts and the cover plate.
17. Disconnect the exhaust pipe from the manifold at the flange. Then remove the bolt from the exhaust pipe support and remove the exhaust pipe from the manifold.
18. Install transmission support bar VW-758/1 or equivalent with slight preload.
19. Install chain US-1105 or equivalent on the engine lifting eyes, located on the left side of the cylinder head.
20. Lift the engine until its weight is taken off the engine mounts.
21. Adjust the support bar to contact the transmission.
22. Separate the engine and transmission.
23. Carefully lift the engine out of the engine compartment so as not to damage the transmission main shaft, clutch and body.

To install: Proceed in the reverse order of removal and note the following.

24. Lubricate the clutch release bearing and transmission main shaft splines with $MOS_2$ grease or an equivalent. Do Not lubricate the guide sleeve or the clutch release bearing.
25. Carefully guide the engine into the vehicle and attach to the transmission while keeping weight off of the motor mounts.
26. Install and tighten the upper engine-to-transmission bolts.
27. Remove the transmission support bar and lower the engine onto the engine mounts.
28. Reconnect and tighten the starter cables.
29. The remainder of the installation is the reverse of the removal procedure.

**NOTE: Tighten the engine mounts and subframe bolts with the engine running at idle speed.**

30. Torque the cold start valve, the radiator mount bolts and the engine-to-transmission cover plate bolts to 7 ft. lbs.
31. Torque the following components:

Engine-to-transmission bolts – 42 ft. lbs.

Engine mount bolts – 26 ft. lbs.

Engine stop-to-body block and exhaust pipe support bolts – 18 ft. lbs.

Exhaust pipe-to-manifold bolts – 22 ft. lbs.

Starter bolts – 15 ft. lbs.

## Cylinder Head

### REMOVAL & INSTALLATION

**NOTE: The engine should be cold before the cylinder head can be removed. The 4 cylinder engine head is retained by 10 head bolts and the 5 cylinder engine uses 12 head bolts.**

**CAUTION**

*Do not disconnect or loosen any refrigerant hose connections during cylinder head removal.*

#### *Carbureted Engines*

1. Disconnect the battery ground cable.
2. Drain the cooling system.
3. Remove the air cleaner. Disconnect the fuel line.
4. Disconnect the radiator, heater and choke hoses.
5. Disconnect all electrical wires. Remove the spark plug wires.
6. Separate the exhaust manifold from the exhaust pipe.
7. Disconnect the EGR line from the exhaust manifold. Remove the EGR valve and filter from the intake manifold.
8. Remove the carburetor.
9. Disconnect the air pump fittings.
10. Remove the timing belt cover and belt.
11. Loosen the cylinder head bolts in the reverse of the tightening sequence.
12. Remove the bolts and lift the head straight off.
13. Install the new cylinder head gasket with the word **TOP** or **OBEN** up.
14. Install bolts No. 10 and 8 first;

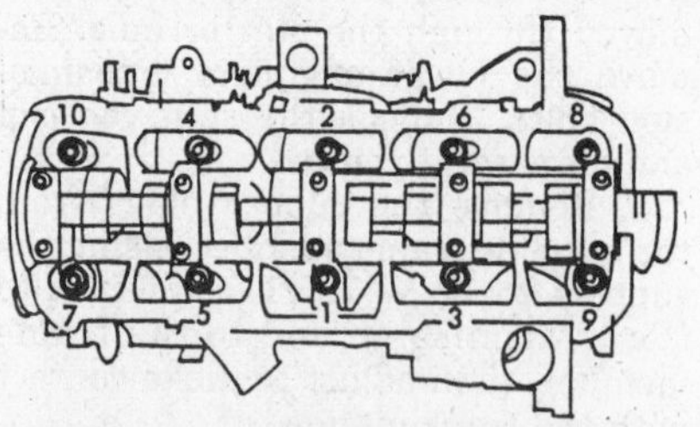


Cylinder head tightening sequence – 4 cylinder carbureted engines

Cylinder head gaskets for the 1.8 liter engine have two breather holes and larger bore dimension

these holes are smaller and will properly locate the gasket and cylinder head.

15. Install the remaining bolts. Torque the cylinder head bolts in sequence and to specification.

16. To complete the installation, reverse the removal procedures.

### *Fuel Injected Engines*

1. Disconnect the battery ground cable.
2. Drain the cooling system.
3. Disconnect the air duct from the throttle valve assembly.
4. Disconnect the throttle valve assembly.
5. Remove the injectors and disconnect the line from the cold start valve.
6. Disconnect the radiator and heater hoses.
7. Disconnect the vacuum and PCV lines (label lines for installation).
8. Remove the auxiliary air regulator from the intake manifold.
9. Disconnect all electrical lines and remove the spark plugs (label all lines and wires for installation).
10. Separate the exhaust manifold from the exhaust pipe.
11. Remove the EGR line from the exhaust manifold.
12. Remove the intake manifold.
13. Remove the timing belt cover and belt.
14. Loosen the cylinder head bolts in the reverse of the tightening sequence.
15. Remove the bolts and lift the head straight off.

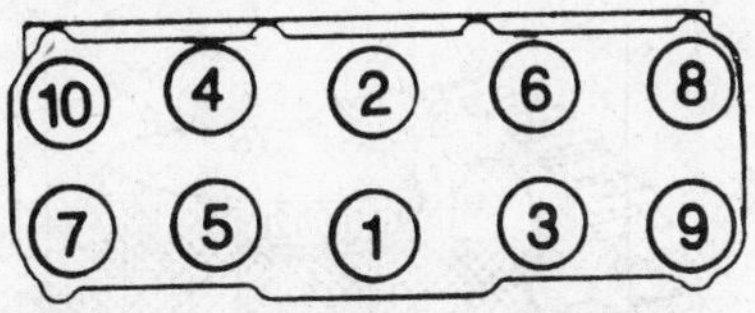


**Cylinder head tightening sequence—4 cylinder 8 valve engines**

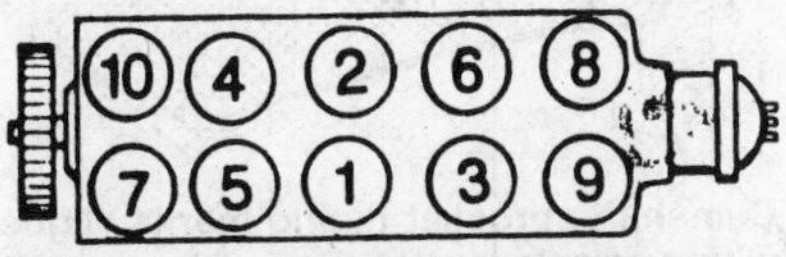


**Cylinder head tightening sequence—4 cylinder 16 valve engines**

16. Check the flatness of the cylinder block in both width and length, then diagonally from each corner.

17. Install the new cylinder head gasket with the word **TOP** or **OBEN** facing upward.

18. Install bolts No. 10 and 8 first. These holes are smaller and will properly locate the gasket and cylinder head.

19. Install the remaining bolts. Torque the bolts in sequence in 3 steps: 29 ft. lbs., (39 Nm) 44 ft. lbs. (60 Nm) and an additional ½ turn.

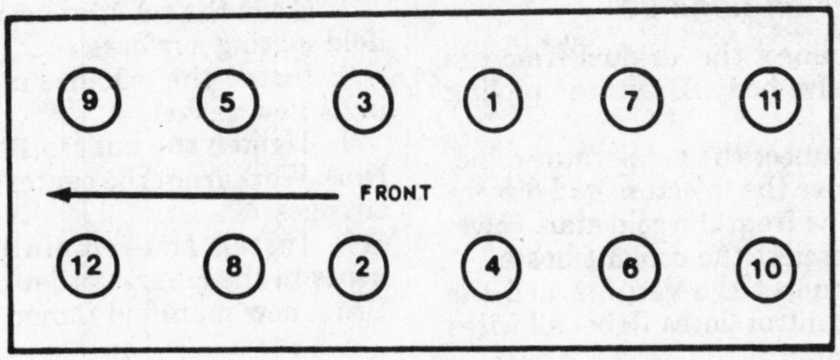


Cylinder head tightening sequence—5 cylinder engines

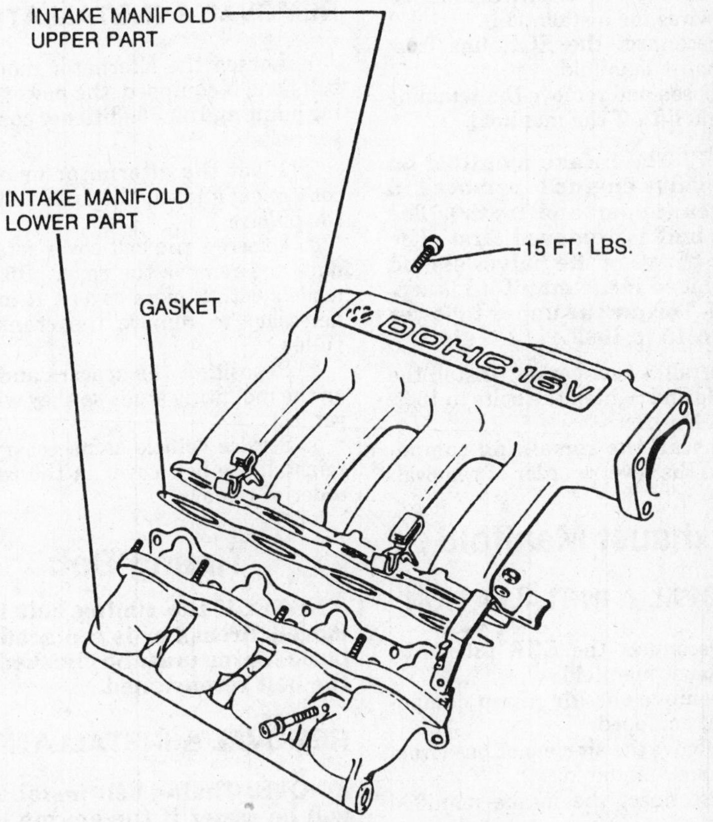


Intake manifold 16 valve engines

**NOTE: Polygon (12 point) head bolts are torqued cold. Torque in sequence to 54 ft. lbs. (73 Nm) and an additional ¼ turn.**

20. To complete the installation, reverse the removal procedures.

## OVERHAUL

**For all cylinder head overhaul procedures, refer to "Engine Rebuilding" in the Unit Repair section.**

# Intake Manifold

## REMOVAL & INSTALLATION

### *Carbureted Engines*

1. Remove the air cleaner. Drain the cooling system.
2. Disconnect the accelerator cable.
3. Disconnect the EGR valve connections.
4. Detach all electrical leads.
5. Disconnect the coolant hoses.
6. Disconnect the fuel line from the carburetor.
7. Remove the vacuum hoses from the carburetor.
8. Loosen and remove the retaining bolts and lift off the manifold.
9. Install a new gasket. Install the manifold and tighten the bolts in sequence from the center bolts to the outside bolts. Tightening torque is 18 ft. lbs. (24 Nm).
10. Install the remaining components in the reverse order of removal. Refill the cooling system. run the engine and check for leaks.

***Fuel Injected Engines***

1. Disconnect the air duct from the throttle valve body. Drain the cooling system.
2. Disconnect the accelerator cable.
3. Remove the injectors and disconnect the line from the cold start valve.
4. Disconnect the coolant hoses.
5. Disconnect the vacuum and the emission control hoses (label all wires for installation).
6. Remove the auxiliary air regulator.
7. Disconnect all electrical lines (label all wires for installation).
8. Disconnect the EGR line from the exhaust manifold.
9. Loosen and remove the retaining bolts and lift off the manifold.

**NOTE: The intake manifold on the 16 valve engine is removed in 2 halves (upper and lower). The upper half is removed first. The gasket between the halves should be replaced if the manifold is separated. Torque the upper to lower bolts to 15 ft. lbs.**

10. Install a new gasket. Install the manifold and tighten the bolts to 18 ft. lbs. (24 Nm).
11. Install the remaining components in the reverse order of removal.

## Exhaust Manifold

### REMOVAL & INSTALLATION

1. Disconnect the EGR tube from the exhaust manifold.
2. Remove the air pump components, if equipped.
3. Remove the air cleaner hose from the exhaust manifold.
4. Disconnect the intake manifold support.
5. Separate the exhaust pipe from the manifold or turbocharger.
6. Remove the turbocharger (if equipped). Remove the retaining nuts and remove the manifold.

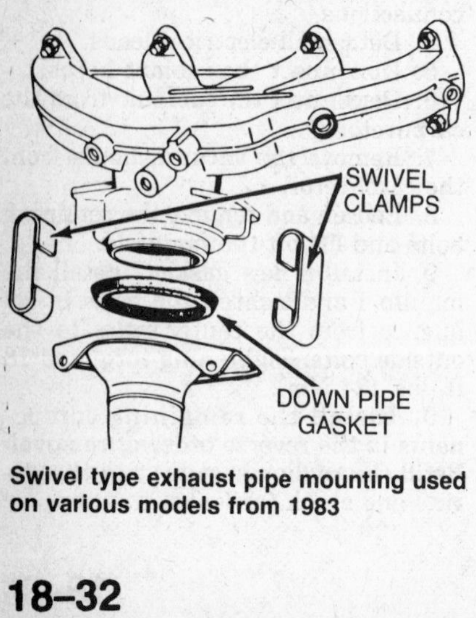


Swivel type exhaust pipe mounting used on various models from 1983

7. Clean the cylinder head and manifold mating surfaces.
8. Install the exhaust manifold using a new gasket.
9. Tighten the nuts to 18 ft. lbs. (24 Nm). Work from the center to the outer edges.
10. Install the remaining components in the reverse order of removal. Use a new manifold flange gasket.

## Front Cover

### REMOVAL & INSTALLATION

1. Loosen the alternator mounting bolts and if equipped, the power steering pump and air conditioner compressor bolts.
2. Pivot the alternator or driven component and slip the drive belt from the pulleys.
3. Unscrew the belt cover retaining nuts and remove the cover. On some models with 2 piece covers, it may be necessary to remove the crankshaft pulley.
4. Reposition the spacers and nuts on the mounting studs so they will not get lost.
5. Service vehicle as necessary and reinstall the belt cover in the reverse order of removal.

## Timing Belt

**NOTE: If the timing belt is removed, breaks or is replaced, the basic timing must be checked and the belt retensioned.**

### REMOVAL & INSTALLATION

**NOTE: Timing belt installation will be easier if the engine is set for No. 1 cylinder at TDC (top dead center) prior to belt removal or replacement.**

1. Remove the timing belt cover(s).
2. Turn the engine until the **0** degree mark on the flywheel is aligned with the stationary pointer on the bell housing. Turn the camshaft or make sure the camshaft sprocket is turned until the mark on the rear of the sprocket is aligned (4 cylinder engines) with the upper edge of the rear drive belt cover (or cylinder head cover edge, depending on year) on the left side (spark plug side) of the engine or (5 cylinder engines) the left side edge of the camshaft housing. The notch on the crankshaft pulley should align with the dot on the intermediate shaft sprocket and the distributor rotor (remove distributor cap) should be pointing toward the mark on the rim of the distributor housing.
3. Remove the crankshaft drive pulley(s).
4. On 4 cylinder engines, hold the large nut on the tensioner pulley and loosen the smaller pulley lock nut. Turn the tensioner counterclockwise to relieve the tension on the timing belt.
5. On 5 cylinder engines, loosen the water pump bolts and turn the pump clockwise to relieve timing belt tension.
6. Slide the timing belt from the pulleys.
7. Install the timing belt and re-tension with pulley or water pump. Reinstall the crankshaft pulley(s). Recheck alignment of timing marks.

**CAUTION**

***If the timing marks are not correctly aligned with the No. 1 piston at TDC of the compression stroke and the belt is installed,***

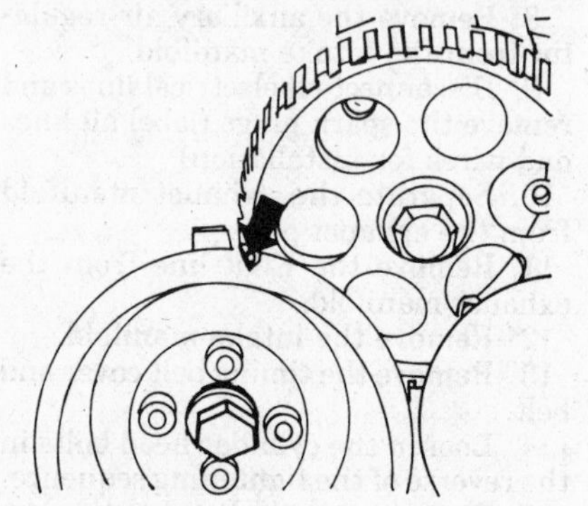

Crankshaft pulley and intermediate shaft sprocket alignment

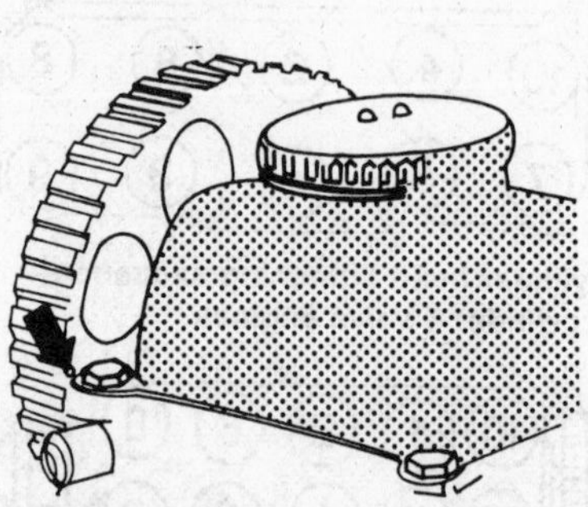

Camshaft sprocket timing marks aligned with cover flange (shown) or inner-upper timing cover bracket

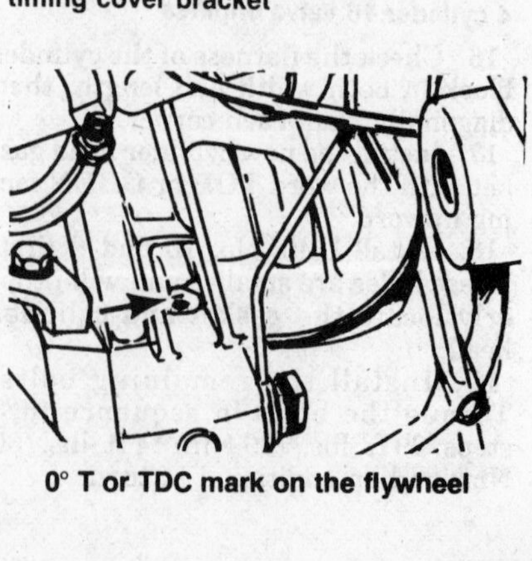

0° T or TDC mark on the flywheel

***valve timing will be incorrect. Poor performance and possible engine damage can result from improper valve timing.***

8. Check the timing belt tension. The tension is correct when the belt can be twisted 90 degrees with the thumb and the index finger along the straight run between the camshaft sprocket and the water pump.

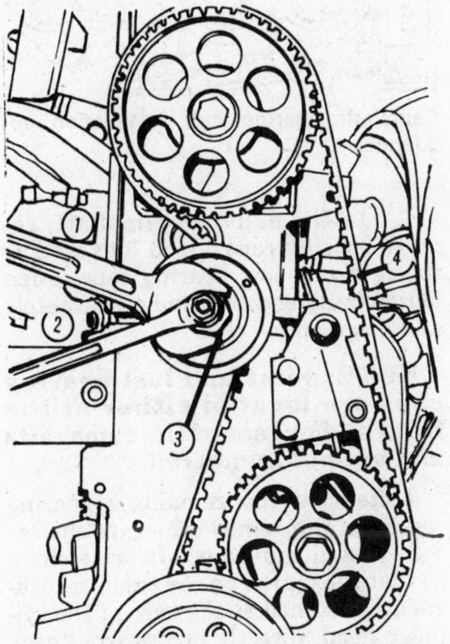

**Turn the tensioner (3) toward (1) to tighten belt and toward (2) to loosen. Check tension at (4)**

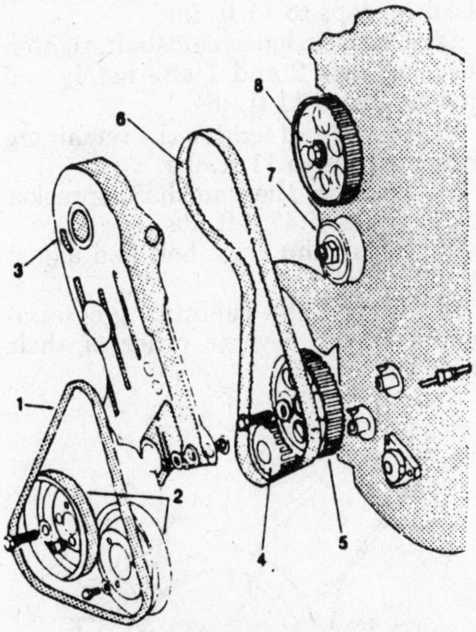

1. Alternator belt
2. Belt pulleys
3. Timing gear cover
4. Crankshaft sprocket
5. Intermediate sprocket
6. Drive belt
7. Tensioner
8. Camshaft sprocket

**Exploded view of camshaft drive arrangement**

9. Turn the engine 2 complete revolutions (clockwise rotation) and align the flywheel mark at TDC. Recheck belt tension and timing marks. Readjust as required.

10. Reinstall the timing belt cover and drive belts in the reverse order of removal.

# Timing Sprockets

## REMOVAL & INSTALLATION

### *All Engines*

1. Remove all accessory drive belts. Remove the timing belt cover.
2. Remove the timing belt from the sprockets. Remove the retaining bolt from the sprocket and gently pry the sprocket off the shaft.
3. If the sprocket will not easily slide off the shaft, use a gear puller. Do not hammer on the sprocket damage to the sprocket could occur.
4. Install the sprocket in the reverse order of removal.
5. Tighten the center bolt to 58 ft. lbs. (78 Nm). Models having a crankshaft sprocket with a self-contained index lug require 145 ft. lbs. (196 Nm) of torque on the center bolt.
6. Install the timing belt and check the belt tension. Install the front cover and accessory drive belts. Check the drive belt tension and the engine timing.

## OIL SEAL REPLACEMENT

### *4 Cylinder Engines*

1. Remove the timing belt.
2. Remove the crankshaft sprocket bolt and sprocket.
3. Use the front cover oil seal removal tool VW-10-219 or equivalent to pull the seal from the carrier.

**NOTE: When removing the oil seal, BE CAREFUL not to damage the carrier. Any damage caused to the seal carrier could result in an oil leak.**

4. To install, use installation tool VW-10-203 or equivalent to press the seal flush with the carrier. Remove the Installation tool and install the aluminum installation ring adapter to the tool and reinstall the tool to the seal. Press the seal 0.08 in. (2.0mm) into the carrier.
5. To complete the installation, reverse the removal procedures. Torque the crankshaft pulley bolt to 58 ft. lbs. (80 Nm) for 12mm or 145 ft. lbs. (200 Nm) for 14mm. Check and/or adjust the timing.

### *5 Cylinder Engines*

1. Remove the front cover and remove the timing belt.
2. Remove the damper pulley to crankshaft bolt and the damper pulley and sprocket assembly.
3. Using the seal removal tool VW-2086 or equivalent, pull the oil seal from the seal carrier.
4. To install, attach guide sleeve tool VW-2080A or equivalent to the crankshaft, lubricate the oil seal lips and slide it over the guide tool. Slide the outer sleeve over the guide sleeve. Using the sprocket bolt, press the seal in the oil pump housing until the seal is seated. Remove the installation tools.
5. To complete the installation, reverse the removal procedures. Torque the damper pulley-to-crankshaft bolt to 252 ft. lbs. (350 Nm). Check and/or adjust the timing.

# Camshaft

## REMOVAL & INSTALLATION

### *All Engines Except 16 Valve*

1. Remove the timing belt cover(s), the timing belt, camshaft sprocket and camshaft (valve) cover.

**NOTE: Number the bearing caps from front to back. Scribe an arrow facing front. The caps are offset and must be installed correctly. Factory numbers on the caps are not always on the same side.**

2. Remove the front and rear bearing caps. Loosen the remaining bearing cap nuts diagonally in several steps, starting from the outside caps near the ends of the head and working toward the center.
3. Remove the bearing caps and the camshaft.
4. Install a new oil seal and end plug in the cylinder head. Lightly coat the camshaft bearing journals and lobes with a film of assembly lube or heavy engine oil. Install the bearing caps in the reverse order of removal. Tighten the cap nuts diagonally and in several steps until they are torqued to 14 ft. lbs.
5. Install the drive sprocket and timing belt. Check valve clearance and adjust if necessary. Install remaining parts in reverse order of removal.

### *16 Valve Engine*

1. Remove the timing belt cover.
2. Remove the bolts from the upper intake manifold and remove the manifold and gasket.

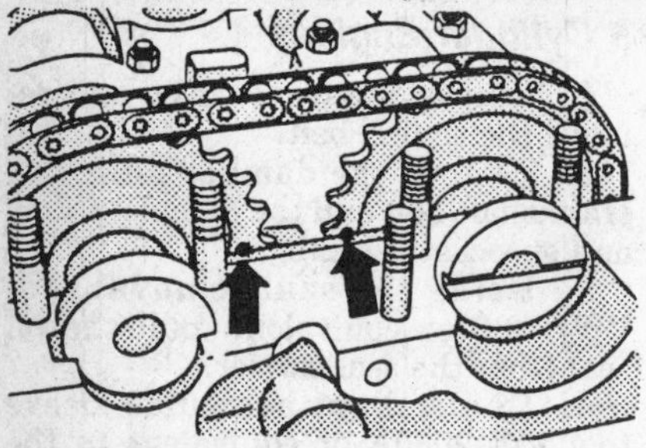

Camshaft sprocket timing marks at TDC

3. Remove the bolts from the cylinder head cover and remove the cover and gaskets.
4. Turn the engine to TDC on cylinder No. 1, then slacken and remove the timing belt.
5. Remove the camshaft sprocket.
6. On the intake camshaft, remove bearing caps 5 and 7 as well as the last bearing caps. Then loosen bearing caps 6 and 8 alternately and diagonally.

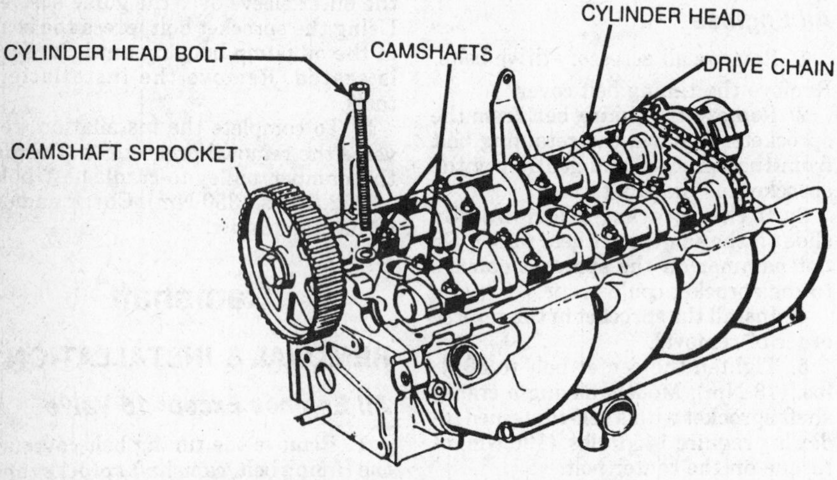


Cylinder head assembly 16 valve engines

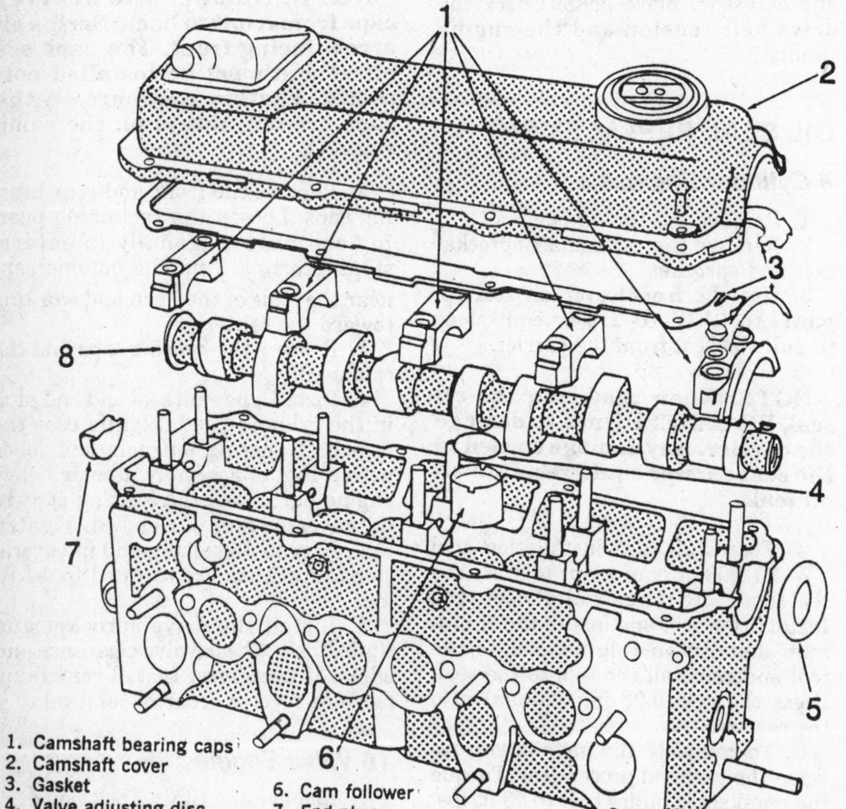


1. Camshaft bearing caps
2. Camshaft cover
3. Gasket
4. Valve adjusting disc
5. Oil seal
6. Cam follower
7. End plug
8. Camshaft

Exploded view of the camshaft assembly—gasoline engines (diesel similar)

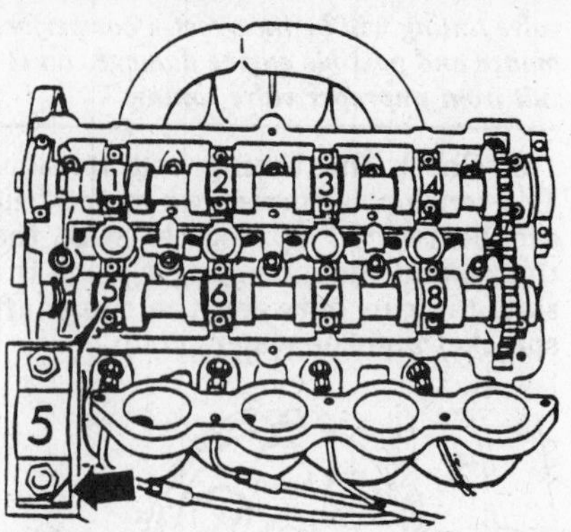


Camshaft bearing cap installation sequence

7. On the exhaust camshaft, remove bearing caps 1 and 3 as well as the first and last bearing caps. Then loosen bearing caps 2 and 4 alternately and diagonally.

**NOTE: First and last bearing caps are located either at the front and/or rear of the camshafts and are not numbered.**

8. Remove the remaining bearing cap bolts and remove the cam shafts.
9. Install the camshaft drive chain so that the marks on the chain sprockets are matched at the base of the cylinder head, directly across from each other.
10. On the intake camshaft, install and tighten bearing caps 6 and 8 alternately and diagonally to 11 ft. lbs.
11. Install and tighten the remaining bearing caps to 11 ft. lbs.
12. On the exhaust camshaft, tighten bearing caps 2 and 4 alternately and diagonally to 11 ft. lbs.
13. Install and tighten the remaining bearing caps to 11 ft. lbs.
14. Position the camshaft sprocket and torque to 47.9 ft. lbs.
15. Install the drive belt and adjust the timing.
16. Install the remaining components in the reverse order of their removal.

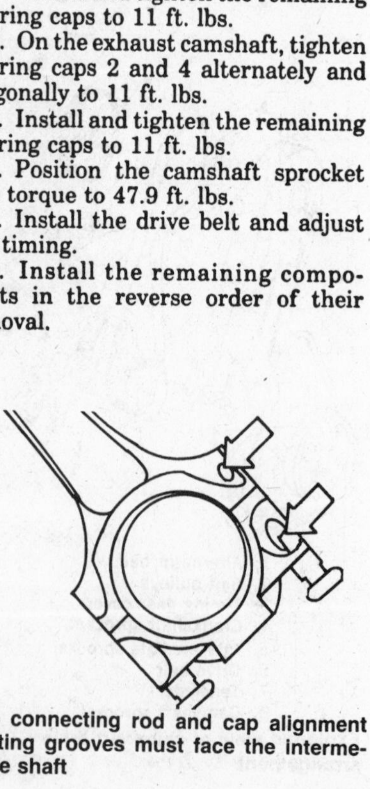

The connecting rod and cap alignment casting grooves must face the intermediate shaft

## Piston and Connecting Rod

**NOTE: 1.8L engines using rod bolts with a smooth surface between threads and short knurled shank and having a round head containing 6 notches are stretch type bolts and cannot be reused. Always use new bolts when servicing.**

### POSITIONING

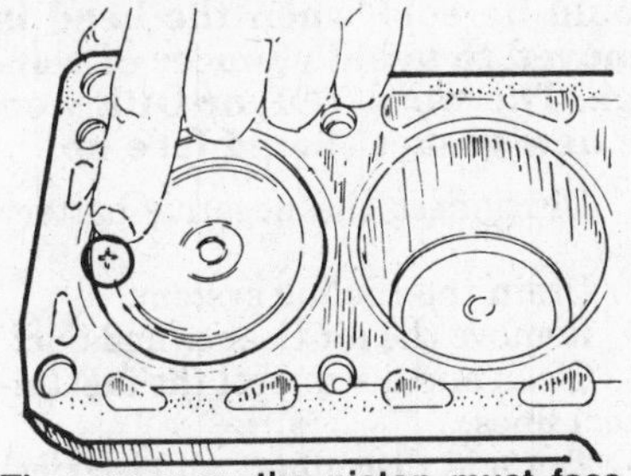

The arrow on the piston must face the camshaft drive belt

# DIESEL ENGINE MECHANICAL

## Engine

### REMOVAL & INSTALLATION

#### *All Models Except Quantum*

1. Disconnect the negative battery cable.
2. Turn the heater control to fully OPEN. Remove the radiator cap, the radiator hose at the thermostat housing and drain the cooling system.
3. Remove the radiator fan, the alternator and the fuel fitter.
4. Disconnect the electrical connectors at the fuel shut-off solenoid, the glow plugs, the oil pressure switch and the coolant temperature sensor.

**NOTE: If equipped with power steering, remove the drive belt, the bracket bolts (leave the lines attached) and move the assembly aside.**

5. Remove the heater and the radiator hoses.
6. At the injection pump, disconnect the accelerator cable with the bracket and remove the fuel supply and the return hoses.
7. Disconnect the cold start cable.

**NOTE: If equipped with A/C, remove the drive belt, the electrical connector at the compressor, the compressor bracket to engine bolts and the compressor assembly, then move it aside and support it on a wire. DO NOT support the compressor with the hoses under tension.**

8. Disconnect the electrical connectors from the starter, the back-up switch and the transmission mount ground wire.

**NOTE: If equipped with a manual transmission, disconnect the clutch cable and remove the relay shaft lever.**

9. Remove the exhaust pipe nuts or spring clips.

**NOTE: If equipped with a turbocharger, disconnect the turbocharger to exhaust manifold bolts, the turbocharger to transmission bracket, the air intake ducts and the oil line. Remove the turbocharger from the engine.**

10. Disconnect the halfshafts from the drive flanges. Lower the vehicle to the ground, then remove the axle hub nuts and disconnect the lower ball joints from the steering knuckles.
11. Raise the vehicle, swing the strut assemblies away from the vehicle and pull out the drive shafts.
12. Remove the starter, the horn, the oil filter and the front engine mount.
13. Reconnect the ball joints so that the vehicle may be lowered to the ground.
14. Remove the rear engine mount and the right front wheel.
15. Attack the engine support tool US 1105 and a vertical lift to the engine, then lift it slightly.

**NOTE: If equipped with a manual transmission, remove the relay shaft and the gearshift lever rods.**

16. Remove both side engine mount to body bolts.
17. Lower the engine and transmission assembly onto a dolly. Raise the vehicle and slide the dolly from under the vehicle.
18. To install, reverse the removal procedures.

Torque the following components:

Transmission-to-engine bolts – 33 ft. lbs. (45 Nm) for 10mm or 54 ft. lbs. (73 Nm) for 12mm

Engine mount bolts – 25 ft. lbs. (34 Nm)

Turbocharger-to-exhaust manifold bolts – 18 ft. lbs. (24 Nm)

Starter bolts – 14 ft. lbs. (19 Nm)

Torque converter-to-drive plate bolts – 22 ft. lbs. (30 Nm)

Front engine stop bolts – 18 ft. lbs. (24 Nm)

Power steering pump bolts – 14 ft. lbs. (19 Nm)

A/C compressor bolts – 18 ft. lbs. (24 Nm) for 8mm or 58 ft. lbs. (78 Nm) for 12mm

Adjust the belt tension and refill the cooling system.

#### *1983 Quantum*

**CAUTION**

***Do not disconnect the refrigerant lines on cars equipped with air conditioning.***

1. Remove the negative battery cable.
2. Set the heat control to hot. Remove the lower radiator hose and remove the thermostat to drain the coolant. Remove the thermoswitch electrical connector and the radiator brace at the bottom of the radiator, remove the top radiator shroud, upper hose, radiator mounting bolts and remove the radiator and fan.
3. Remove the supply and return lines from the injection pump. Disconnect the throttle cable from the pump and remove the cable mounting bracket. Disconnect the cold start cable at the pin and remove the electrical connector from the fuel shut-off solenoid.
4. Disconnect the electrical connectors from the oil pressure switch, coolant temperature sensor and glow plugs. Remove the radiator hose from the head and the vacuum hose from the vacuum pump.
5. Loosen the adjusting nuts and unhook the clutch cable from the lever.
6. Remove the hose from the water pump.
7. Unbolt the rear of the turbocharger (if equipped) from the exhaust system.
8. Loosen the right engine mount.
9. Remove the alternator after tagging the wires for installation.
10. Remove the front engine mounts.
11. Disconnect the exhaust pipe from the manifold and the pump bracket from the transmission.
12. Loosen the left engine mount.
13. Remove the starter.
14. Remove the engine to transmission bolts and the flywheel cover bolts.
15. Attach a lifting chain to the engine and raise the engine until the transmission touches the steering rack. Remove the left engine mount.
16. Support the transmission with a jack. Raise and turn the engine at the same time to remove.
17. Installation is the reverse. Tighten the engine-to-transmission bolts to 40 ft. lbs. (54 Nm) and the engine mount bolts to 29 ft. lbs. (39 Nm). After installation adjust the throttle and cold starting cables.

### 1984–86 Quantum

1. Disconnect the negative battery cable.
2. Remove the horn and the cover plates of the engine and the transmission.
3. Move the heater control valve to fully **OPEN** and remove the radiator cap.
4. Remove the 2 lower hoses of the thermostat housing and drain the coolant.
5. Disconnect the electrical connections from the fan, the thermoswitch and the series resistor near the alternator.
6. Remove the radiator to engine coolant hose, the radiator bolts, the right fan connector and the radiator.
7. Remove the fuel supply and the return lines from the fuel injector.
8. Remove the accelerator cable from the fuel injection pump and from the support bracket.
9. Disconnect the cold start cable at the electrical connector and the mounting washer from the support.
10. Disconnect the electrical connector at the fuel shut-off solenoid and the gear shift indicator switch with the wiring from the bracket.
11. Remove the air filter-to-turbocharger air filter hose.
12. Disconnect the electrical connector from the oil pressure switch, the coolant temperature sensors and the glow plugs.
13. Remove the power steering bracket bolts (leave the lines attached) and move the assembly aside.
14. Disconnect the hose from the vacuum pump.
15. Remove the clutch cable lock plate and unhook the cable.
16. Remove the 2 nuts from both engine mounts and the engine torque support bolts at the front of the engine.
17. Remove the alternator and the front engine stop.

**NOTE: If equipped with A/C, remove the pulley nuts from the compressor, the drive belt, the compressor bracket bolts and the compressor. Place and tie the compressor aside so that the hoses are not under pressure.**

18. Remove the turbocharger from the exhaust manifold and the turbocharger to transmission bracket.
19. Disconnect the electrical connectors and remove the starter. Place the starter on the engine subframe.
20. Remove the 2 bottom engine to transmission bolts and the flywheel cover plate bolts.

**NOTE: If equipped with an automatic transmission, remove the cover plate and the torque converter mounting bolts.**

21. Install the engine support bar VW 785/1B or equivalent under the front of the transmission and support it.
22. Attach the engine lifting tool US 1105 or equivalent and a vertical lift to the engine and lift the engine and transmission assembly free of the engine mounts.
23. Adjust the support bar under the transmission.
24. Remove the 3 upper transmission-to-engine bolts and pry the engine from the transmission.

**NOTE: If equipped with an automatic transmission, secure the torque converter-to-the transmission to keep it from falling out.**

25. Lift the engine from the engine compartment.
26. To install, reverse the removal procedures.

Torque the following components:

Transmission to engine bolts – 40 ft. lbs. (54 Nm)

Engine mount bolts – 25 ft. lbs. (34 Nm)

Turbocharger to exhaust manifold bolts – 18 ft. lbs. (24 Nm)

Starter bolts – 14 ft. lbs. (19 Nm)

Torque converter-to-drive plate bolts – 22 ft. lbs. (30 Nm)

Front engine stop bolts – 18 ft. lbs. (24 Nm)

Power steering pump bolts – 14 ft. lbs. (19 Nm)

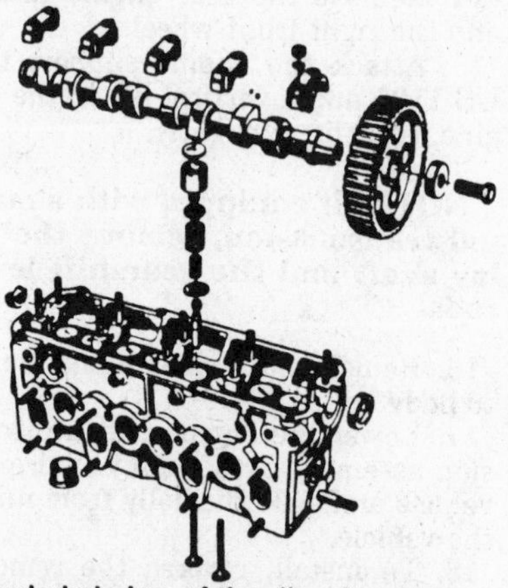

Exploded view of the diesel engine cylinder head

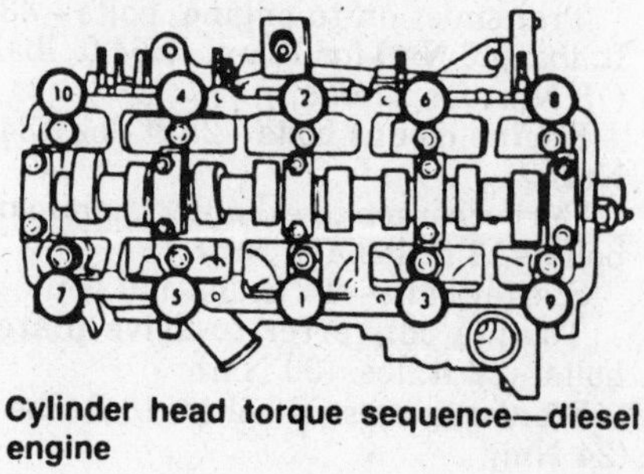


Cylinder head torque sequence—diesel engine

A/C compressor bolts – 18 ft. lbs. (24 Nm) for 8mm or 58 ft. lbs. (78 Nm) for 12mm

Adjust the belt tension and refill the cooling system.

## Cylinder Head

### REMOVAL & INSTALLATION

#### Diesel and Turbo Diesel

**NOTE: The cylinder head is retained by Allen bolts. The engine should be cold when the head is removed to avoid chances of warpage. The word TOP or OBEN on the new gasket should face up.**

1. Disconnect the negative battery cable.
2. Drain the cooling system.
3. Remove the air cleaner and duct.
4. Clean and disconnect the fuel (injector) lines.
5. Tag and disconnect all electrical wires and leads.
6. If equipped, disconnect and plug all lines coming from the brake booster vacuum pump and remove the pump.
7. Disconnect the air supply tubes (turbo diesels only) and then unbolt and remove the intake manifold.
8. Disconnect and plug all lines coming from the power steering pump and remove the pump and V-belt (if equipped).
9. Disconnect and remove the oil supply and return lines from the turbocharger (if equipped).
10. Remove the exhaust manifold heat shields (if equipped). Remove the glow plugs and the fuel injectors.
11. Separate the exhaust pipe from the exhaust manifold or turbocharger and then remove the manifold.

**NOTE: On turbo diesels, the exhaust manifold is removed with the turbocharger and wastegate still attached.**

12. Disconnect all radiator and heater hoses where they are attached to the cylinder head and position them out of the way.
13. Remove the drive belt cover and the drive belt.
14. Remove the PCV hose.
15. Remove the cylinder head cover.
16. Loosen the cylinder head bolts in the reverse order of the tightening sequence.
17. Remove the bolts and lift the cylinder head straight off.

**NOTE: If the head sticks, loosen it by compression or rap it upward with a soft rubber mallet. Do not force anything between the head and the engine block to**

**pry it upward; this may result in serious damage.**

18. Clean the cylinder head and engine block mating surfaces thoroughly and then install the new gasket without any sealing compound. Make sure the words **TOP** or **OBEN** are facing up when the gasket is installed.

**NOTE: Depending upon the piston height above the top surface of the engine block, there are 3 gaskets of different thicknesses which can be used. Be sure that the new gasket has the same identifying number as the gasket being replaced.**

19. Place the cylinder head on the engine block and install bolts No. 8 and 10 first. These holes are smaller and will properly locate the head on the engine block.
20. Install the remaining bolts.

Torque the bolts in sequence using 3 steps:

**(6 points)**—35 ft. lbs. (47 Nm), 50 ft. lbs. (60 Nm), 65 ft. lbs. (88 Nm) and retorque to 65 ft. lbs. (88 Nm), after warming the engine

**(12 point)**—29 ft. lbs. (39 Nm), 43 ft. lbs. (58 Nm), an additional ½ turn and retorque an additional ¼ turn, after warming the engine.

21. Installation of all other components is in the reverse order of removal.
22. After about 1000 miles, remove the cylinder head cover and retighten the cylinder head bolts, turning the bolts in sequence ¼ turn (90 degrees) WITHOUT loosening them first. This is done 1 bolt at a time, in the proper sequence, without interruption.

### OVERHAUL

**For all cylinder head overhaul procedures, please refer to "Engine Rebuilding" in the Unit Repair section.**

## Intake Manifold

### REMOVAL & INSTALLATION

#### *Diesel and Turbo Diesel*

1. Disconnect the negative battery cable.
2. Disconnect the air duct from the throttle valve body. Drain the cooling system.
3. Disconnect the accelerator cable. Disconnect the hose that runs between the air duct and the turbocharger (turbo diesel only).
4. Remove the air cleaner. Remove the injectors and disconnect the line from the cold start valve.
5. Disconnect all coolant valves. Disconnect and plug all lines coming from the brake booster vacuum pump and remove the pump.
6. Disconnect all vacuum and emission control hoses (label all hoses for installation). Disconnect the PCV line.
7. Disconnect the EGR line from the exhaust manifold. Disconnect and remove the blow-off valve and then disconnect the hose which runs from the intake manifold to the turbocharger (turbo diesel only).
8. Loosen and remove the retaining bolts and lift off the manifold.
9. Install a new gasket. Install the manifold and tighten the bolts to 18 ft. lbs.
10. Install the remaining components in the reverse order of removal. Run the engine and check for leaks.

## Exhaust Manifold

### REMOVAL & INSTALLATION

1. Disconnect the EGR tube from the exhaust manifold.
2. Remove the interfering air pump components if so equipped.
3. Remove the air cleaner hose from the exhaust manifold.
4. Disconnect the intake manifold support.
5. Separate the exhaust pipe from the manifold.
6. Remove the retaining nuts and remove the manifold.
7. Clean the cylinder head and manifold mating surfaces.
8. Install the exhaust manifold using a new gasket.
9. Tighten the nuts to 18 ft. lbs. Work from the inside out.
10. Install the remaining components in the reverse order of removal. Use a new manifold flange gasket.

## Turbocharger

### REMOVAL & INSTALLATION

1. Disconnect the negative battery cable.
2. Remove the engine and transmission cover shield to gain access to the turbocharger.
3. Loosen the stabilizer bar clamps on both sides of the stabilizer and push the bar down out of the way.
4. Loosen the oil return connector bolt at the bottom of the turbocharger. Remove the side support bolt. Have a container ready to catch the oil when disconnecting the bottom adapter.
5. Remove the turbocharger heat shield mounting nuts and the oil return line.
6. Remove both hoses, turbocharger to intake manifold and air cleaner. Loosen and remove the oil supply line to the turbocharger.
7. Remove the exhaust pipe to turbocharger mounting bolts and the turbocharger mounting bolts and the turbocharger to exhaust manifold bolts. Remove the turbocharger.

**To install:**

8. Position the turbocharger on the exhaust manifold and hand tighten the mounting bolts. Install the lower vertical oil return connector mounting bolt and the lower side support bolt, tighten hand tight. Torque the mounting bolts in the following sequence: Manifold-to-turbocharger; 50 ft. lbs. (68 Nm). Lower oil connection; 18 ft. lbs. (24 Nm). Lower side mount; 18 ft. lbs. (24 Nm).
9. Fill the upper oil supply connection on the turbocharger with oil. Install the remaining turbocharger with oil. Install the remaining turbocharger connections, shields, etc. in the reverse order of removal.
10. When installation is complete, start the engine and allow to idle for several minutes. Do not increase engine speed above idle until the turbocharger oil supply system has had a chance to fill.

### TROUBLESHOOTING

**For more information on Turbocharging, please refer to "Turbocharging" in the Unit Repair section.**

## Front Cover

### REMOVAL & INSTALLATION

1. Loosen the alternator mounting bolts.
2. Pivot the alternator and slip the drive belt off the sprockets.
3. Unscrew the cover retaining nuts (4) and remove the cover.
4. To install, reposition the spacers on the studs and then install the washers and nuts.
5. Install the alternator belt and adjust its tension.

## Timing Belt

**NOTE: If the timing belt is removed or replaced, the basic valve timing must be checked and the belt retensioned.**

### REMOVAL & INSTALLATION

**NOTE: This procedure will require a number of special tools.**

1. Remove the timing belt cover. Remove the cylinder head cover.

2. Turn the engine so that the No. 1 cylinder is at TDC and fix the camshaft in position with tool 2065A. Align the tool as follows:

a. Turn the camshaft until 1 end of the tool touches the cylinder head.

b. Measure the gap at the other end of the tool with a feeler gauge.

c. Take half of the measurement and insert a feeler gauge of this thickness between the tool and the cylinder head; turn the camshaft so that the tool rests on the feeler gauge.

d. Insert a second feeler gauge of the same thickness between the other end of the tool and the cylinder head.

3. Lock the injection pump sprocket in position with pin VW–2064.

4. Check that the marks on the sprocket, bracket and pump body are in alignment (engine at TDC).

5. Loosen the timing belt tensioner. Remove the V-belt from the crankshaft.

6. Remove the timing belt.

**To install:**

7. Check that the TDC mark on the flywheel is aligned with the reference marks.

8. Loosen the camshaft sprocket bolt ½ turn and then loosen the gear from the camshaft end by tapping it with a rubber mallet.

9. Install the timing belt and remove pin 2064 from the injection pump sprocket.

10. Tension the belt by turning the tensioner to the right. Check the belt tension as detailed later, in the section.

11. Tighten the camshaft sprocket bolt to 33 ft. lbs.

12. Remove the tool from the camshaft.

13. Turn the crankshaft 2 turns in the direction of engine rotation (clockwise) and then strike the belt once with a rubber mallet between the camshaft sprocket and the injection pump sprocket.

14. Check the belt tension again. Check the injection pump timing.

## VALVE TIMING INSPECTION

1. Remove the timing belt covers. Remove the Valve cover.

**NOTE: The drive belt must be checked for proper tension and must be centered in the sprockets before checking the timing.**

2. Turn the engine so that the No. 1 cylinder is at TDC. The No. 1 cylinder camshaft lobes should be pointing upward and the TDC mark on the flywheel should be aligned with the bellhousing mark.

3. Fix the camshaft in position with tool VW 2065/2065A or equivalent. Align the tool as follows:

a. Turn the crankshaft until 1 end of the tool touches the cylinder head.

b. Measure the gap at the other end of the tool with a feeler gauge.

c. Take half of the measurement and insert a feeler gauge of that thickness between the tool and the cylinder head; turn the camshaft so the tool rests on the feeler gauge.

d. Insert a second feeler gauge of the same thickness on the other side, between the tool and the cylinder head.

4. Lock the injector pump sprocket in position with pin VW–2064 or equivalent.

5. Check that the marks on the sprocket, pump and mounting plate are aligned. Check that the TDC mark on the flywheel is aligned with the bellhousing mark.

## ADJUSTMENT

1. After the camshaft is set in position and the timing is at TDC, loosen the camshaft sprocket mounting bolt ½ turn.

2. Tap the back of sprocket with a rubber hammer to loosen. Hand tighten the bolt to remove endplay.

3. Loosen the belt tensioner and remove the belt from the injector pump sprocket.

4. Turn the injector pump sprocket until the marks on the sprocket, pump and mounting bracket align. Insert pin 2064 through the hole in the sprocket and mounting bracket to lock in position.

5. Reinstall the camshaft drive belt. Tighten the camshaft mounting bolt to 33 ft. lbs. Remove the camshaft setting bar and the lock pin from the injector pump sprocket. Install VW tool VW210 (Belt tension gauge).

6. Adjust tension by turning the tensioner clockwise, reading on the tension gauge should be 12–13. Lock tensioner in position.

7. Turn the crankshaft 2 complete turns (clockwise rotation) and recheck belt tension. Strike the drive belt once with a rubber hammer between the camshaft and injector pump sprockets to eliminate play.

8. Recheck the timing and re-adjust if necessary.

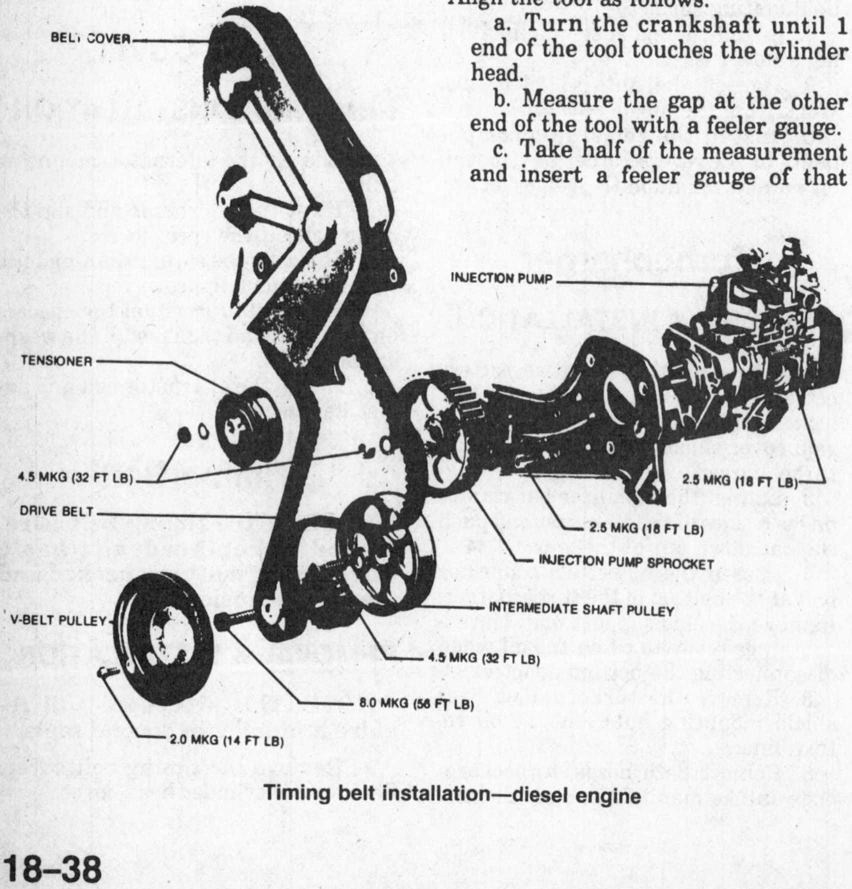


Timing belt installation—diesel engine

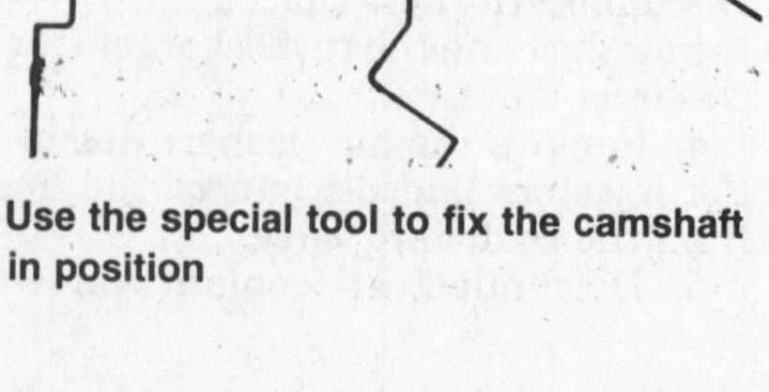

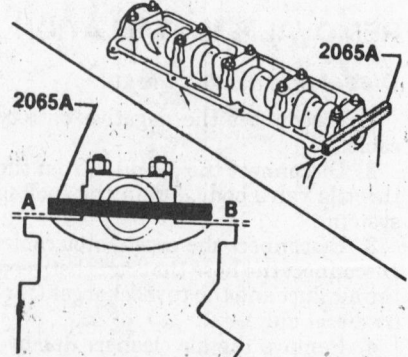


Use the special tool to fix the camshaft in position

## Timing Sprockets

### REMOVAL & INSTALLATION

The intermediate shaft and crankshaft sprockets are located by keys on their respective shafts and each is retained by a bolt. The camshaft sprocket is taper-fit and has no key. To remove any or all of the pulleys, first remove the timing belt cover and belt.

**NOTE: When removing the crankshaft pulley, don't remove the 4 Allen head bolts which hold the outer belt pulley to the timing belt sprocket.**

1. Remove the center bolt or nut.
2. Gently pry the sprocket off the shaft.
3. Remove the sprocket and key (if used).
4. Install in the reverse order of removal.
5. Coat the center bolt with Loctite® or a similar locking compound and tighten to 33 ft. lbs. on the top sprockets and 108 ft. lbs. on the crankshaft sprocket.
6. Install the timing belt, check the valve timing and the belt tension. Install the timing belt cover.

### OIL SEAL REPLACEMENT

#### *Except Quantum*

1. Remove the timing belt cover and the timing belt.
2. Remove the crankshaft sprocket.
3. Using a small pry bar, pry the seal from the carrier or use the seal extractor tool VW-10-219 or equivalent to pull out the seal.

**NOTE: When removing the seal, be careful not to damage the carrier.**

4. To install, lubricate the new seal lips, use the seal installation tool VW-10-203 or equivalent to press the new seal into the carrier and reverse the removal procedures. Torque the crankshaft pulley bolt to 58 ft. lbs. (80 Nm) for 12mm or 145 ft. lbs. (200 Nm) for 14mm. Check and/or adjust the timing.

#### *Quantum*

1. Remove the timing belt cover and remove the timing belt.
2. Remove the crankshaft sprocket.
3. Install the hex head bolt of the seal removal tool VW-3083 or equivalent into the seal extractor guide VW-2085.
4. Attach the tools to the oil seal and pull the seal from the carrier.
5. To install, slide the sleeve of the installation tool VW-3083 onto the crankshaft journal, lubricate the seal and slide it over the sleeve. Install the thrust sleeve against the oil seal and press it in until seated.
6. To complete the installation procedures, reverse the removal procedures. Torque the crankshaft pulley bolt to 58 ft. lbs. (80 Nm) for 12mm or 145 ft. lbs. (200 Nm) for 14mm. Check and/or adjust the timing.

## Camshaft

### REMOVAL & INSTALLATION

1. Remove the timing belt.
2. Remove the camshaft sprocket.
3. Remove the air cleaner.
4. Remove the camshaft cover.
5. Unscrew and remove the No. 1, 3 and 5 bearing caps (No. 1 is at the front).
6. Unscrew the No. 2 and 4 bearing caps, diagonally and in increments.
7. Lift the camshaft out of the cylinder head.
8. Lubricate the camshaft journals and lobes with assembly lube or gear oil before installing it in the cylinder head.
9. Replace the camshaft oil seal with a new seal whenever the cam is removed.
10. Install the No. 1, 3 and 5 bearing caps and tighten the nuts to 14 ft. lbs. Note that the bores are offset and the numbers are not always on the same side.
11. Install the No. 2 and 4 bearing caps and diagonally tighten the nuts to 14 ft. lbs.

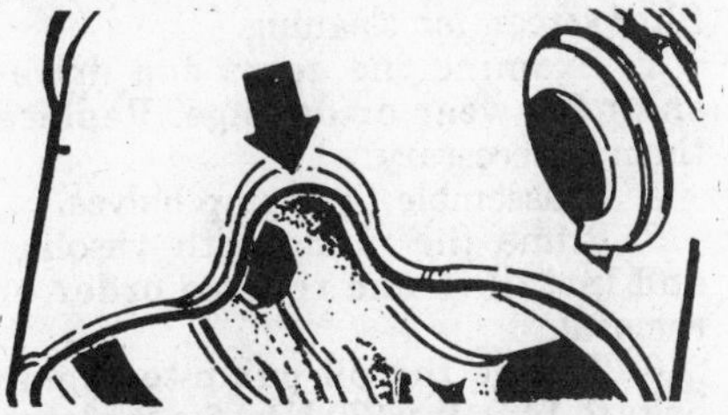

Turbo diesel pistons are equipped with a cut-out to provide clearance for a block mounted oil spray valve

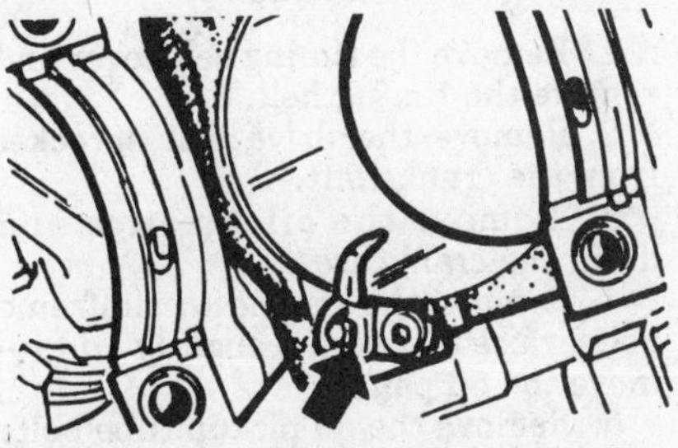

Oil jet used in turbo diesel engine to provide a spray of oil to the piston which helps cooling and lubrication

**NOTE: If checking endplay, install a dial indicator so that the feeler touches the camshaft snout. End-play should be no more than 0.006 in. (0.15mm).**

## Piston and Connecting Rods

### POSITIONING

**For all piston and connecting rod overhaul procedures, please refer to "Engine Rebuilding" in the unit repair section.**

# ENGINE LUBRICATION

## Oil Pan

### REMOVAL & INSTALLATION

#### *Gasoline Engines*

#### ALL MODELS EXCEPT QUANTUM

1. Drain the engine oil.
2. Loosen and remove the bolts retaining the oil pan.
3. Lower the pan from the car.
4. Install the pan using a new oil pan gasket.
5. Tighten the retaining bolts in a criss-cross pattern. Tighten hex head bolts to 14 ft. lbs. (20 Nm).
6. Refill the engine with oil. Start the engine and examine the pan for leaks.

#### QUANTUM

1. Drain the oil pan.
2. Support and slightly raise the engine with an overhead hoist.
3. Gradually loosen the engine crossmember mounting bolts. Remove the left and right side engine mounts.
4. Lower the crossmember very carefully.
5. Loosen and remove the oil pan retaining bolts.
6. Lower the pan from the vehicle.
7. Install the pan using a new gasket and sealer.
8. Tighten the retaining bolts in a crosswise pattern. Tighten 4 cylinder pan bolts to 14 ft. lbs. (20 Nm), or 5 cylinder pan bolts to 7 ft. lbs. (10 Nm).
9. Raise the crossmember. Tighten the crossmember bolts to 42 ft. lbs. (57 Nm) and the engine mounting bolts to 32 ft. lbs. (43 Nm).
10. Refill the engine with oil. Start the engine and check for leaks.

*Diesel Engines*

1. Drain the oil pan.
2. Support and slightly raise the engine with an overhead hoist.
3. Gradually loosen the engine crossmember mounting bolts. Remove the front and rear side engine mounts.
4. Lower the crossmember very carefully.
5. Loosen and remove the oil pan retaining bolts.
6. Lower the pan from the car.
7. Install the pan using a new gasket and sealer.
8. Tighten the retaining bolts in a crosswise pattern. Tighten hex head bolts to 14 ft. lbs., or Allen head bolts to 7 ft. lbs.
9. Raise the crossmember. Tighten the crossmember bolts to 42 ft. lbs. and the engine mounting bolts to 32 ft. lbs.
10. Refill the engine with oil. Start the engine and check for leaks.

## Rear Main Oil Seal

### REPLACEMENT

The rear main oil seal is located in a housing on the rear of the cylinder block. To replace the seal on all models it is necessary to remove the transmission and flywheel.

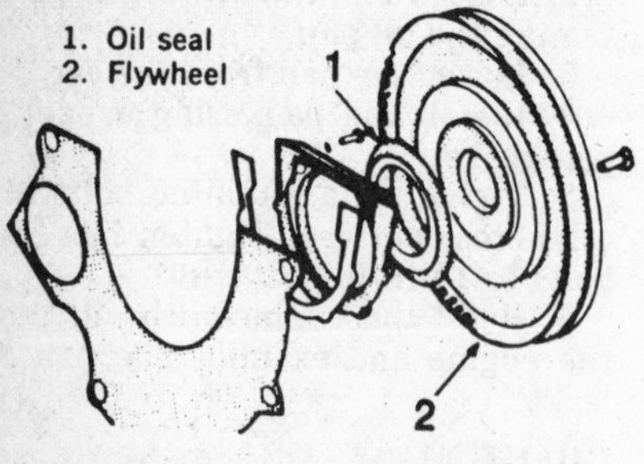


Rear main oil seal assembly

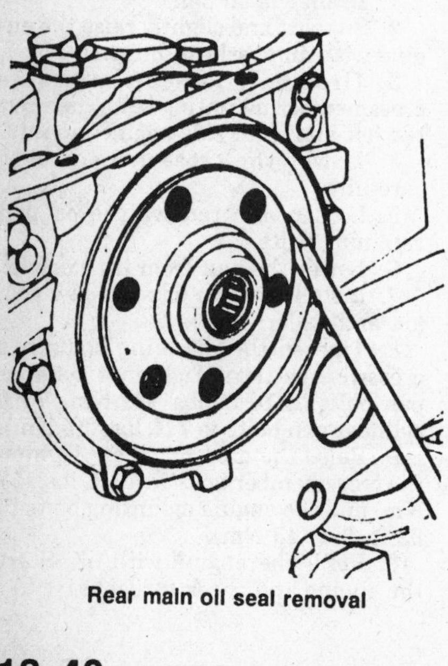

Rear main oil seal removal

1. Remove the transmission and flywheel.
2. Using a small pry bar tool VW-2086 (5 cyl.), VW-10-221 (4 cyl.) or equivalent, pry the old seal out of the support ring.
3. Remove the seal.
4. To install, lightly oil the new seal and press it into place using tool VW-2003/2A or equivalent, to start the seal and tool VW-2003/1 or equivalent, to seat the seal. Be careful not to damage the seal or score the crankshaft.
5. Install the flywheel and transmission.

Torque the following components:

Pressure plate-to-crankshaft bolts – 54 ft. lbs. (73 Nm) for 1982 models, or 72 ft. lbs. (100 Nm) for 1983–90 models

Flywheel-to-pressure plate – 14 ft. lbs. (20 Nm)

Flywheel-to-engine bolts, on all diesel engines – 36 ft. lbs.

## Oil Pump

### REMOVAL & INSTALLATION

*Gasoline Engines*

**4 CYLINDER ENGINES**

1. Remove the oil pan.
2. Remove the 2 mounting bolts.
3. Pull the oil pump down and out of the engine.
4. Unscrew the mounting bolts and separate the pump halves.
5. Remove the driveshaft and gear from the upper body.
6. Clean the bottom half in solvent. Pry up the metal edges to remove the filter screen for cleaning.
7. Examine the gears and driveshaft for wear or damage. Replace them if necessary.
8. Reassemble the pump halves.
9. Prime the pump with vasoline and install in the reverse order of removal.
10. Torque the oil pump-to-engine bolts to 14 ft. lbs. (20 Nm) for the large bolt and 7 ft. lbs. (10 Nm) for the small bolt.

**5 CYLINDER ENGINES**

1. Remove the timing belt cover and remove the timing belt.
2. Remove the drive belt sprocket from the crankshaft.
3. Remove the oil dip stick and drain the crankcase.
4. Remove the engine to subframe bolts, raise the engine slightly and remove the oil pan.
5. Remove the oil pickup tube bolts and the tube.
6. Remove the oil pump to engine bolts and the oil pump.
7. Remove the gasket and clean the gasket mounting surfaces.
8. At the rear of the oil pump, remove the end cover bolts and the cover.
9. Check the pump for wear and/or damage, replace the parts if necessary.
10. Pack the pump with petroleum jelly and reassemble the pump.
11. To install, reverse the removal procedures. Torque the pump-to-engine bolts to 14 ft. lbs. (20 Nm). Refill the engine with oil. Start the engine and check for leaks.

*Diesel Engines*

1. Remove the oil pan.
2. Remove the 2 mounting bolts.
3. Pull the oil pump down and out of the engine.
4. Unscrew the two bolts holding the pump together and separate the pump halves.
5. Remove the driveshaft and gear from the upper body.
6. Clean the bottom half in solvent. Pry up the metal edges to remove the filter screen for cleaning.
7. Examine the gear and driveshaft for wear or damage. Replace them if necessary.
8. Reassemble the pump halves.
9. Prime the pump with oil and install in the reverse order of removal.

# ENGINE COOLING

**NOTE: When replacing coolant/antifreeze in all models, only a phosphate-free product must be used to help prevent damage to the water jacket sealing surfaces of the cylinder head. Other types of coolant may cause corrosion of the cooling system thus leading to engine overheating and damage.**

## Radiator

### REMOVAL & INSTALLATION

*Gasoline Engines*

**4 CYLINDER ENGINES**

1. Drain the cooling system.

**NOTE: Various late models have the radiator retained by locating tabs at the bottom and 2 mounting brackets at the top.**

2. Remove the inner shroud mounting bolts.

3. Disconnect the lower radiator hose.
4. Disconnect the thermostatic switch lead.

**NOTE: The 1984–86 diesel Quantum may have 2 cooling fans on the radiator.**

5. Remove the lower radiator shroud.
6. Remove the lower radiator mounting brackets.
7. Disconnect the upper radiator hose.
8. Detach the upper radiator shroud.
9. Remove the side mounting bolts and top clip and lift the radiator and fan out as an assembly.
10. To install, reverse the removal procedures. Torque the mounting bolts to 7 ft. lbs. (10 Nm).

#### 5 CYLINDER ENGINE

1. Drain the cooling system.
2. Remove the 3 pieces of the radiator cowl and the fan motor assembly. Take care in removing the fan motor connectors to avoid bending them.
3. Remove the upper and lower radiator hoses and the coolant tank supply hose.
4. Disconnect the coolant temperature switch located on the lower right side of the radiator.
5. Remove the radiator mounting bolts and lift out the radiator.
6. Installation is the reverse of removal. Torque radiator mounting bolts to 7 ft. lbs. (10 Nm).

### *Diesel Engine*

1. Drain the cooling system.
2. Remove the inner shroud mounting bolts.
3. Disconnect the lower radiator hose.
4. Disconnect the thermostatic switch lead, if equipped.
5. Remove the lower radiator shroud.
6. Remove the lower radiator mounting units.

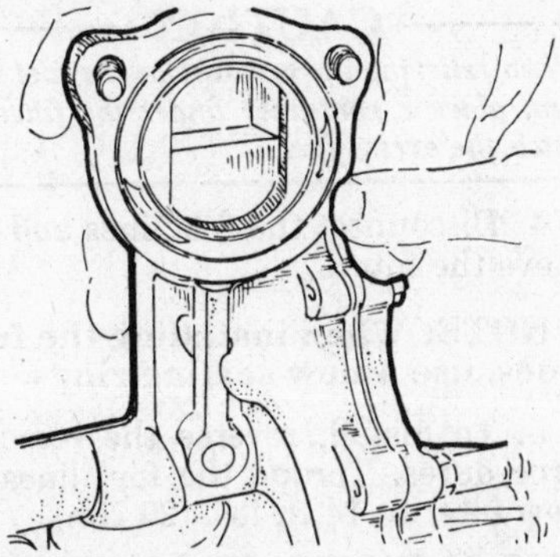

Check the condition of the O-ring before installing the water pump

7. Disconnect the upper radiator hose.
8. Detach the upper radiator shroud.
9. Remove the side mounting bolts and lift the radiator and fan out as an assembly.
10. Installation is the reverse of removal.

# Water Pump

## REMOVAL & INSTALLATION

### *Gasoline Engines*

#### 4 CYLINDER ENGINES

1. Drain the cooling system.
2. Remove the alternator and drive belt. Remove the air injection pump belt, if equipped.
3. Disconnect the lower radiator hose, engine hose and heater hose from the water pump. Remove the timing belt cover to water pump bolt.
4. Remove the 4 pump retaining bolts. Notice where the different length bolts are located.
5. Turn the pump slightly and lift it out of the engine block.
6. Installation is the reverse of removal. Use a new seal on the mating surface of the engine. Torque the pump-to-engine bolts to 15 ft. lbs. (20 Nm).

**NOTE: On 1985–90 Golf models install the water pump pulley with the word "Klima" facing outward.**

#### 5 CYLINDER ENGINE

1. Drain the cooling system.
2. Remove the timing belt cover.
3. Turn the crankshaft to place the engine on TDC; align the flywheel with the mark on the clutch housing.
4. Loosen the water pump to relieve the tension on the timing belt.
5. Remove the timing belt.
6. Remove the water pump mounting bolts and the pump.
7. Clean the water pump mounting surfaces.
8. To install, use a new O-ring and reverse the removal procedures. Torque the water pump-to-engine bolts to 14 ft. lbs. (20 Nm).

### *Diesel Engine*

1. Drain the cooling system.
2. Remove the alternator and drive belt.
3. Remove the timing belt cover.
4. Disconnect the lower radiator hoses, engine hose and heater hose from the water pump.
5. Remove the pump retaining bolts. Notice where the different length bolts are located, for installation.
6. Turn the pump slightly and lift it out of the engine block.
7. Installation is the reverse of removal. Use a new seal on the mating surface with the engine. Check O-ring condition and replace if necessary.

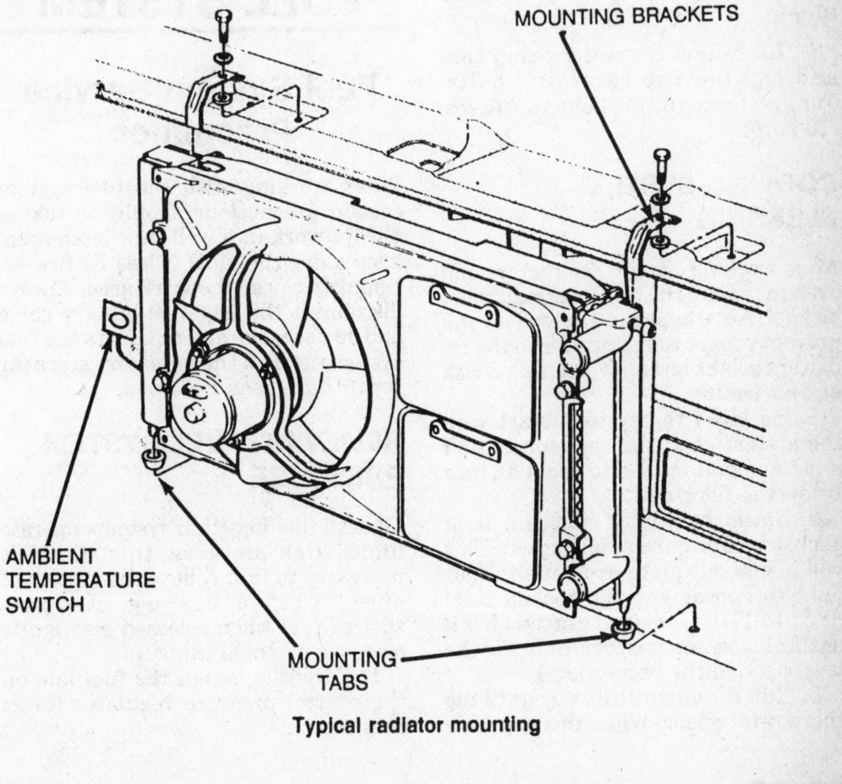


Typical radiator mounting

## Thermostat

### REMOVAL & INSTALLATION

*4 Cylinder Engines*

1. Drain the cooling system.
2. Remove the 2 retaining bolts from the lower water pump neck.

**NOTE: It's not necessary to disconnect the hose.**

3. Move the neck, with the hoses attached, out of the way.
4. Remove the thermostat.
5. Install a new seal on the water pump neck.
6. Install the thermostat with the spring end up.
7. Replace the water pump neck and tighten the 2 retaining bolts. Torque the bolts to 7 ft. lbs. (10 Nm).

*5 Cylinder Engine*

The thermostat is located on the lower radiator hose neck, on the left side of the engine block, behind the water pump housing.

1. Drain the cooling system.
2. Remove the 2 retaining bolts from the lower waterpump neck.
3. Move the water pump neck, with the hoses attached, out of the way.
4. Carefully pry the thermostat out of the engine block.
5. Install a new O-ring on the water pump neck.
6. Install the thermostat.

**NOTE: When installing the thermostat, the spring end should be pointing toward the engine block.**

7. Reposition the water pump neck and tighten the retaining bolts. Torque the mounting bolts to 7 ft. lbs. (10 Nm).

### COOLING SYSTEM BLEEDING

After working on the cooling system, even to replace the thermostat, it must be bled. Air trapped in the system will prevent proper filling and leave the radiator coolant level low, causing a risk of overheating.

1. To bleed the system, start with the system cool, the radiator cap off and the radiator filled to about an inch below the filler neck.
2. Start the engine and run it at slightly above normal idle speed. This will insure adequate circulation. If air bubbles appear and the coolant level drops, fill the system with an antifreeze/water mixture to bring the level back to the proper level.
3. Run the engine this way until the thermostat opens. When this happens, coolant will move abruptly across the top of the radiator and the temperature of the radiator will suddenly rise.
4. At this point, air is often expelled and the level may drop quite a bit. Keep refilling the system until the level is near the top of the radiator and remains constant.
5. If the vehicle has an overflow tank, fill the radiator right up to the filler neck. Replace the radiator filler cap.

# EMISSION CONTROLS

**Please refer to "Emission Control" in the Unit Repair section for system maintenance procedures. Due to the complex nature of the modern electronic engine control systems, comprehensive diagnosis and testing procedures fall outside the confines of this repair manual. For complete information on diagnosis, testing and repair procedures concerning all modern engine and emission control systems, please refer to "Chilton's Guide to Electronic Engine Controls".**

# GASOLINE FUEL SYSTEM

## Fuel System Service Precaution

When working with the fuel system certain precautions should be taken; always work in a well ventilated area, keep a dry chemical (Class B) fire extinguisher near the work area. Always disconnect the negative battery cable and do not make any repairs to the fuel system until all the necessary steps for repair have been reviewed.

### RELIEVING FUEL SYSTEM PRESSURE

Modern fuel injection systems operate under high pressure, this makes it necessary to first relieve the system of pressure before servicing. The pressurized fuel when released may ignite or cause personal injury.

1. Carefully loosen the fuel line on the control pressure regulator (large connector).

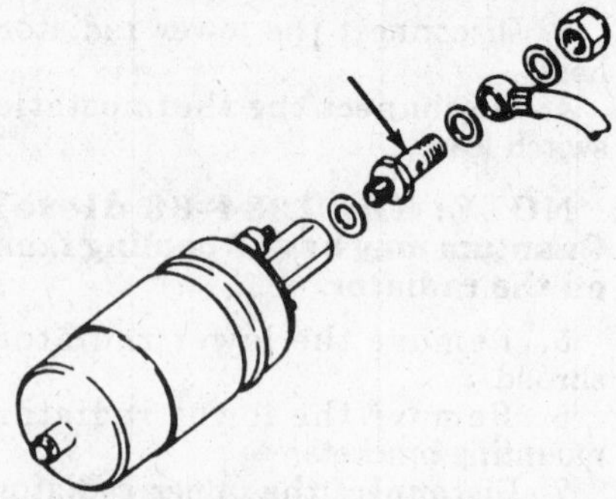

Fuel pressure regulator on the fuel pump

2. Wrap a clean rag around the connection while loosening to catch any fuel.

## Fuel Filter

### REMOVAL & INSTALLATION

*Carburetor*

**NOTE: The fuel filter is installed between the fuel pump and the carburetor.**

1. Wrap a towel around the filter and remove the fuel lines.
2. Remove the filter from the mounting bracket.

**NOTE: When installing a new fuel filter, place it with the 2 tubes facing UP.**

3. To install, reverse the removal procedures.

*Fuel Injection*

**ALL EXCEPT 1985–90 CABRIOLET, GOLF, GTI AND JETTA**

**NOTE: The filter is located in the engine compartment.**

1. Disconnect the negative battery cable.
2. Remove the fuel filter mounting nuts and lift the filter from the mount.
3. Loosen the filter cap and the fuel lines to relieve the pressure in the system.

**CAUTION**

***When relieving the pressure in the fuel system, place a container under the filter to catch the excess fuel.***

4. Disconnect the fuel lines and remove the filter.

**NOTE: When installing the fuel lines, use 4 new sealing rings.**

5. To install, reverse the removal procedures. Torque the fuel lines to new filter to 14 ft. lbs. (20 Nm).

**1985–90 CABRIOLET, GOLF, GTI AND JETTA**

**NOTE: The fuel filter is located in the fuel pump assembly, mounted under the vehicle, in front of the fuel tank.**

1. Disconnect the negative battery cable.
2. Raise and safely support the rear of the vehicle.
3. Relieve the fuel system pressure.

**CAUTION**

***When relieving the pressure in the fuel system, place a container under the filter to catch the excess fuel.***

4. Remove the fuel lines, the mounting bracket nut and the filter.

**NOTE: When installing the fuel lines, use 4 new sealing rings.**

5. To install, reverse the removal procedures. Torque the fuel lines to new filter to 14 ft. lbs. (20 Nm).

## Mechanical Fuel Pump

**NOTE: The mechanical fuel pump found on carbureted Rabbits is mounted on the side of the engine block.**

### CLEANING

The filter screen can be removed from the pump and cleaned.

1. Remove the center cover screw.
2. Remove the screen and gasket. Clean the screen in solvent.
3. Replace the screen.
4. Install a new gasket and replace the cover.

**NOTE: Make sure the depression in the pump cover engages the projection on the body of the pump.**

### REMOVAL & INSTALLATION

The pump cannot be repaired and must be replaced when defective.

1. Disconnect and plug both fuel lines.
2. Remove the 2 Allen head retaining bolts.
3. Remove the fuel pump and its plastic flange.
4. Replace the pump in the reverse order of removal. Use a new flange seal.

## Electric Fuel Pump

### TESTING

#### *Electrical*

**NOTE: Volkswagen uses a continuous injection system (CIS) in its fuel injected gasoline engines. The system includes an electric fuel pump mounted in front of the right rear axle on Fox, Rabbit and Scirocco/Cabriolet models. The Jetta, Golf and GTI fuel pump is on the passenger's side in front of the rear wheel (accessible through a cover plate). The Quantum fuel pump is mounted inside the top of the car's plastic fuel tank (accessible through the rear cargo area, underneath the carpet).**

1. Have an assistant operate the starter. Listen at the rear wheel on all models to determine if the pump is running.
2. If the pump is not running, check the fuse on the front of the fuel pump relay.
3. If the fuse is good, replace the fuel pump relay.

**1985 and later gas engine fuel pump assembly**

4. If the fuel pump still does not operate, the fuel pump is faulty and must be replaced.

#### *Fuel Pump Delivery*

1. Check the condition of the fuel filter, make sure it is clean.
2. Connect a jumper wire between the No. 1 terminal on the ignition coil and ground.
3. Disconnect the return fuel line and hold it in a measuring container with a capacity of 1 quart or 1000cc.
4. Have an assistant run the starter for 30 seconds while watching the quantity of fuel delivered. The minimum allowable flow is 760cc ($^9/_{10}$ of a quart) in 30 seconds.

**NOTE: Before testing the fuel pump pressure, the battery must be fully charged and the fuel tank at least ½ full.**

5. If the flow is below specification, check for a dirty fuel filter, blocked lines or blocked fuel tank strainer (if so equipped). If all of these are in good condition, replace the pump.

### REMOVAL & INSTALLATION

#### *All Except 1985–90 Cabriolet, Golf, GTI, Jetta And Quantum*

**NOTE: The fuel pump is located under the vehicle in front of the rear axle on the right side.**

1. Disconnect the negative battery cable.
2. Raise and support the rear of the vehicle on jackstands.
3. Disconnect the electrical connector.
4. Relieve the fuel system pressure.

**CAUTION**

***When relieving the pressure in the fuel system, place a container under the fuel pump to catch the excess fuel.***

5. Remove the mounting bolts and the fuel pump.

**NOTE: When installing the fuel lines, use 4 new sealing rings.**

6. To install, reverse the removal procedures.

#### *1985–90 Cabriolet, Golf, GTI, Jetta and Quantum*

**NOTE: The fuel pump assembly is located under the vehicle in front of the fuel tank.**

1. Disconnect the negative battery cable.
2. Raise and support the vehicle on jackstands.
3. Disconnect the electrical connector.
4. Loosen the fuel lines to relieve the pressure in the system.

**CAUTION**

***When relieving the pressure in the fuel system, place a container under the filter to catch the excess fuel.***

5. Remove the adapter and the mounting ring from the fuel pump, then pull the pump from the assembly

**CAUTION**

***Use care when removing the fuel pump, excess fuel may drain from the reservoir.***

6. To install, use a new O-ring and reverse the removal procedures.

## Transfer Pump

**NOTE: The transfer is a new feature on the 1985–90 models, it is located in the fuel tank and attached to the end of the sending unit.**

### REMOVAL & INSTALLATION

1. Disconnect the negative cable.
2. Open the rear of the vehicle, pull

back the carpet and remove the access plate from the floor (3 screws).
3. Disconnect the electrical connector from the sending unit.
4. Remove the fuel hoses from the sending unit.
5. Unscrew the plastic cap and lift the sending unit from the fuel tank.
6. Remove the transfer pump from the sending unit.
7. To install, reverse the removal procedures. Use an new o-ring at the sending unit.

## Carburetor

### REMOVAL & INSTALLATION

1. Remove the air cleaner.
2. Disconnect the fuel line.
3. Drain some of the coolant and then disconnect the choke hoses.
4. Disconnect the distributor and EGR valve vacuum lines.
5. Disconnect the electrical lead for the idle cut-off valve. For 1983–84 models, also disconnect the feedback solenoid, anti-diesel connector and the bowl vent connector.
6. Remove the clip which secures the throttle linkage to the carburetor. Detach the linkage, being careful not to lose any washers or bushings.
7. Unbolt the carburetor from the manifold and remove it.
8. Use a new gasket when replacing the carburetor. Don't overtighten the nuts, tighten in an criss-cross pattern.

### AUTOMATIC CHOKE ADJUSTMENT

The standard adjustment on all versions of the automatic choke is with the 2 notches aligned with the notch on the housing. To adjust, loosen the 3 clamping screws and move the outer part of the choke unit.

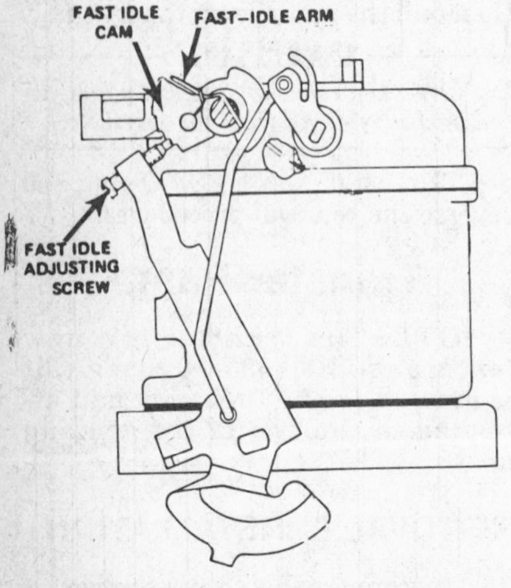


**Adjusting the fast idle—1983–84 Rabbit**

### THROTTLE GAP ADJUSTMENT

#### *1983–84 Rabbit*

Throttle gap is set at the factory and should not be tampered with.

### FAST IDLE ADJUSTMENT

#### *1983–84 Rabbit*

1. Run the engine until it reaches normal operating temperature. Make sure that the timing and idle speed are set to specifications.
2. Run the engine at idle and set the fast idle adjustment screw to the second step of the fast idle cam.
3. Disconnect the purge valve. Disconnect and plug the vacuum hose at the EGR valve.
4. Connect a tachometer as per the manufacturer's instructions and check that the engine speed is 2800–3200 rpm. If not, turn the fast idle screw until it is.
5. Reconnect the purge valve and the vacuum hose at the EGR valve.

### CHOKE GAP ADJUSTMENT

#### *1983–84 Rabbit*

1. Set the cold idle speed adjuster screw in its upper notch.
2. Connect a manually operated vacuum pump to the connection on the pulldown unit and build up vacuum.
3. Close the choke valve by hand with the lever and check the choke valve gap with a drill. The gap should be 3.3–3.7mm.
4. Adjust the gap using the adjusting screw in the end of the vacuum unit at the side of the choke unit. After adjusting, lock the screw with sealant.

### THROTTLE LINKAGE ADJUSTMENT

Throttle linkage adjustments are not normally required. However, it is a good idea to make sure that the throttle valve(s) in the carburetor open all the way when the accelerator pedal is held on the wide-open position. Only the primary (first stage) throttle valve will open when the pedal is pushed with the engine off: the secondary throttle on Volkswagen 2-barrel carburetors is vacuum-operated.

### OVERHAUL

**For all carburetor overhaul procedures, please refer to "Carburetor Service" in the Unit Repair section.**

## Fuel Injection

**Due to the complex nature of modern fuel injection systems, comprehensive diagnosis and testing procedures fall outside the confines of this repair manual. For complete information on fuel injection diagnosis, testing and repair procedures please refer to "Chilton's Guide To Fuel Injection And Feedback Carburetors".**

# DIESEL FUEL SYSTEM

## Fuel Filter

### REMOVAL & INSTALLATION

**NOTE: The fuel filter is located in the engine compartment near the fuel injection pump.**

#### *All Except 1985–86 and 1989–90 Golf and Jetta*

1. Disconnect the negative battery cable.
2. Using tool US-4462, loosen the fuel filter clamp.
3. Remove the top 2 filter assembly nuts.
4. Lift the filter assembly straight up and remove the old filter.

**NOTE: When installing a new filter, coat the outside and partly fill it with diesel fuel.**

5. To install, reverse the removal procedures. Torque the filter assembly to mount nuts to 18 ft. lbs. (25 Nm). Start the engine, accelerate it a few times (to clear the air bubbles) and check for fuel leaks.

#### *1985–86 and 1989–90 Golf and Jetta*

1. Using clamps, pinch off the fuel lines at the fuel filter.
2. Remove the fuel lines from the filter.
3. Loosen the mounting clamp or screws and lift the filter assembly straight up. Remove the old filter.

**NOTE: When installing a new filter, coat the outside and partly fill it with diesel fuel.**

4. To install, reverse the removal procedures. Torque the filter assembly to mount nuts to 18 ft. lbs. (25 Nm).

Start the engine, accelerate it a few times (to clear the air bubbles) and check for fuel leaks.

### DRAINING WATER

1. Disconnect the negative battery cable.
2. Remove the fuel return line from the injection pump to provide room to open the vent screw on the fuel filter flange.
3. Remove the 2 filter assembly mounting nuts and lift the filter from the mount.

**NOTE: When draining the water from the fuel filter, place a container under the filter to catch the water and the excess fuel.**

4. Loosen the drain plug on the bottom of the filter and drain the fuel into a container, until it runs free of water.
5. Tighten the drain plug.
6. To install, reverse the removal procedures. Torque the filter assembly mounting nuts to 18 ft. lbs. (25 Nm). Start the engine, accelerate it a few times (to clear the air bubbles) and check for leaks.

## Water Separator

### *1985–86 and 1989–90 Models*

**NOTE: The water separator is located in front of the fuel tank under the right side of the vehicle; it's purpose is to filter the water from the fuel. When the water level in the separator reaches a certain point, a sensor turns on the glow plug indicator light, causing it to blink continuously.**

### REMOVAL & INSTALLATION

1. Disconnect the negative battery cable.
2. Raise and support the vehicle on jackstands.
3. At the separator, disconnect the electrical connector and clamp both fuel hoses.

**CAUTION**

***Place a fuel catch pan under the separator to catch the excess fuel.***

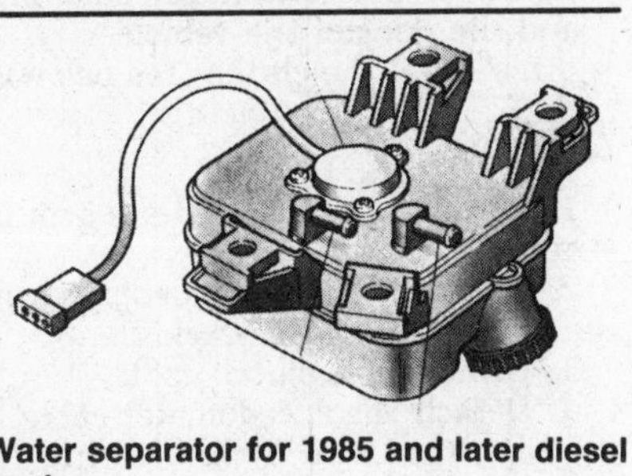

Water separator for 1985 and later diesel engine

4. Remove the fuel hoses from the separator and drain the excess fuel into the catch pan.
5. Remove the 3 mounting bolts and lower the separator from the vehicle.
6. To install, reverse the removal procedures.

### DRAINING WATER

1. Raise and support the vehicle on jackstands.
2. At the separator, connect a hose from the separator drain to a catch pan.

**CAUTION**

***Place a fuel catch pan under the separator to catch the excess fuel.***

3. Open the drain valve (3 turns) and remove the water until a steady stream of fuel flows from the separator, then close the valve.

## Diesel Injection Pump

### REMOVAL & INSTALLATION

1. Remove the timing belt cover(s).
2. Remove the cylinder head cover and the plug cover on top of the bell housing.
3. Turn the crankshaft to place the No. 1 cyl on TDC of the compression stroke (the TDC mark on the flywheel must align with the pointer).
4. Loosen the camshaft nut and tap the back of the camshaft sprocket with a rubber mallet until it is loose, then remove the sprocket.
5. Fasten the setting bar tool VW-2065A or equivalent to the end of the camshaft. Turn the camshaft until 1 end of the bar touches the cylinder head. Using a feeler gauge, measure the clearance at the other end. Using 2 feeler gauges of half of the acquired measurement, insert them between each end of the bar and the cylinder head.
6. Loosen the tensioner pulley and remove the timing belt from the engine.
7. Loosen the shaft nut from the injection pump sprocket.
8. Install the sprocket puller tool VW-3032 or equivalent and apply tension to the injection pump sprocket.
9. Using a light hammer, strike the puller spindle head with a few light blows to loosen the sprocket from the tapered shaft.
10. Remove the injection pump shaft nut and the sprocket.
11. Using a box wrench tool VW-3035 or equivalent, disconnect the fuel lines from the injection pump and cover the openings with a clean cloth.

**CAUTION**

***To avoid damaging the injection pump plunger, DO NOT loosen the bolts on the fuel distributor head.***

12. Disconnect the fuel cut-off valve, the accelerator and the cold start cables from the injection pump.
13. Remove the injection pump to mounting bracket bolts and the injection pump from the engine.
14. To install, set the injection timing (align the mark on top of the injection pump with the mark on the mounting plate) and reverse the removal procedures. Torque the injection pump mounting bolts to 18 ft. lbs. (25 Nm), the injection pump sprocket nut to 33 ft. lbs. (45 Nm) and the fuel injection lines to pump to 18 ft. lbs. (25 Nm).

**NOTE: When installing the fuel supply and the return pipe union screws, DO NOT interchange them; the return pipe union screw is marked with OUT on the head.**

### INJECTION TIMING

1. Remove the timing belt.
2. Turn the crankshaft to place the No. 1 cyl on TDC of the compression stroke (the TDC mark on the flywheel must align with the pointer).

**NOTE: The cold start cable MUST NOT be pulled in (the actuation lever on the injection pump must be in NEUTRAL).**

3. Turn the injection pump sprocket so that the mark on the sprocket is aligned with the mark on the mounting plate.
4. Using the pin tool 2064, insert it through the sprocket hole, locking the sprocket to the injection pump.
5. Loosen the camshaft nut and tap the back of the camshaft sprocket with a rubber mallet until it is loose, then remove the sprocket.
6. Fasten the setting bar tool VW-2065A or equivalent to the end of the camshaft. Turn the camshaft until the end of the bar touches the cylinder

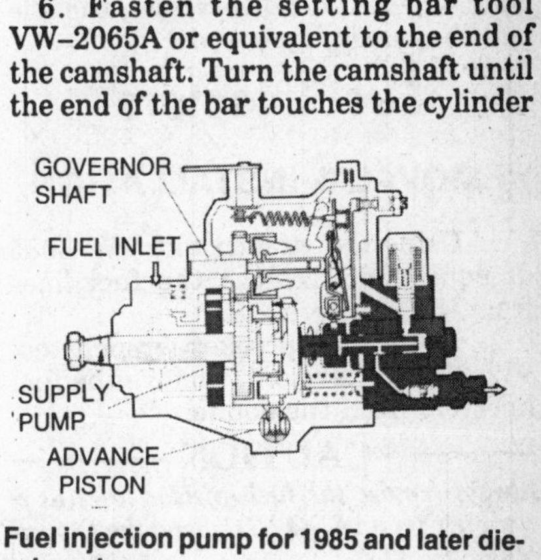


Fuel injection pump for 1985 and later diesel engine

head. Using a feeler gauge, measure the clearance at the other end. Using 2 feeler gauges of half of the acquired measurement, insert them between each end of the bar and the cylinder head.

7. Install the camshaft sprocket, torque the sprocket nut to 33 ft. lbs. (45 Nm) and remove the setting bar tool.

8. Install the timing belt and remove the lock pin tool from the injection pump sprocket.

9. Tension the drive belt by turning the tensioner pulley clockwise until belt flex of ½ in. (13mm) is established between the camshaft and the pump sprockets.

10. Turn the crankshaft 2 complete revolutions and check the belt tension.

**NOTE: It may be necessary to strike the timing belt between the camshaft and the pump sprockets with a rubber mallet to eliminate the play in the drive belt.**

11. Remove the sealing plug on the injection pump head, then install the adapter tool VW-2066 or equivalent and a dial micrometer (preload the micrometer to 2.5mm).

12. Slowly turn the engine counterclockwise until the dial gauge stops moving, then zero the micrometer.

13. Turn the engine clockwise until the TDC mark on the flywheel aligns with the pointer on the bell housing.

**NOTE: The adjusting value is 0.036–0.038 in. (0.93–0.97mm) for the diesel engine or 0.038–0.040 in. (0.98–1.02mm) for the turbo diesel.**

14. If adjustment of the pump is necessary, loosen the 2 upper mounting bolts, the rear support bolt and the lower front bolt through the sprocket, then turn the pump until the correct value is reached.

15. To complete the installation, reverse the removal procedures. Torque the pump cover plug to 11 ft. lbs. (15 Nm). Check the delivery rate, the idle and the maximum speeds.

## Fuel Injectors

### REMOVAL & INSTALLATION

1. Using the wrench tool VW-3035 or equivalent, remove the fuel lines from the injectors.

2. Using the sprocket wrench tool VW-27 or equivalent, remove the fuel injectors from the engine.

**CAUTION**

***Always remove the fuel injector lines as a complete set and DO NOT bend the formed pipes.***

**NOTE: When installing the injectors, always use new heat shields. Install them with the wide sides facing up.**

3. To install, reverse the removal procedures. Torque the fuel injectors to 51 ft. lbs. (70 Nm) and the fuel lines to injectors to 18 ft. lbs. (25 Nm).

# MANUAL TRANSAXLE

### REMOVAL & INSTALLATION

#### *All Except Fox and Quantum*

1. Disconnect the negative battery cable.

2. Disconnect the back-up light switch connector and the speedometer cable from the transaxle (plug the speedometer cable hole).

3. Connect the engine sling tool VW-10-222A to the engine and support slightly.

4. Remove the upper transaxle-to-engine bolts.

5. At the transaxle housing, disconnect the clutch cable from the clutch release lever.

6. Remove the 3 mounting bolts from the right engine support.

7. At the gear selector lever shaft, disconnect the short rod and the connecting rod from the lever. Remove the long selector rod from the relay lever.

8. Remove the mounting bolt and the 2 upper bolts from the left transaxle housing-to-mount.

9. Remove the left wheel housing liner.

10. Detach the halfshaft from the transaxle and support on a wire.

11. Remove the large and the small cover plates from behind the right drive flange.

**NOTE: On 1983–84 models, DO NOT remove the large cover plate.**

12. Remove the starter and the front mount assembly.

13. Remove the 3rd mounting bolt from the left transaxale mount.

14. Lower the transaxle slightly and remove the left transaxle mounting bolts.

15. Push the engine and transaxle assembly to the right as far as possible ⅛ in. (4mm).

16. Place a transaxle support jack under the transaxle, remove the lower transaxle-to-engine bolts and lower the transaxle from the vehicle.

17. To install, coat the input shaft lightly with Moly lube and reverse the removal procedures.

Torque the following components:

Engine-to-transaxle bolts – 55 ft. lbs. (75 Nm)

Starter bolts – 44 ft. lbs. (60 Nm)

Halfshaft-to-flange – 33 ft. lbs. (45 Nm)

Transaxle-to-housing mount – 44 ft. lbs. (60 Nm)

Adjust the clutch free play.

#### *Fox*

1. Disconnect the battery ground cable.

2. Disconnect the exhaust pipe from the manifold and its bracket on the transaxle.

3. Remove the square-headed bolt on the shift linkage. Later models have a hex head bolt.

4. Press the shift linkage coupling off.

5. Disconnect the clutch cable.

6. Disconnect the speedometer cable.

7. Detach the halfshafts from the transaxle.

8. Remove the starter.

9. Remove the inspection plate.

10. Remove the engine-to-transaxle bolts.

11. Remove the transaxle crossmember.

12. Support the transaxle with a jack.

13. Pry the transaxle out from the engine.

14. Lift the transaxle out of the car with an assistant.

15. Installation is the reverse of removal. Observe the following when installing the transaxle.

a. When installing the transaxle crossmember, do not fully tighten the bolts until the transaxle is aligned and fully installed in the vehicle.

b. Tighten the engine-to-transaxle bolts to 40 ft. lbs.

c. Tighten the halfshaft bolts to 33 ft. lbs. (45 Nm).

d. On models with the rubber core rear transaxle mount, the rubber core must be centered in its housing.

e. Make sure there is a ⅜ in. clearance between the header pipe and the floor of the vehicle.

f. Adjust the clutch (see below).

#### *Quantum*

1. Disconnect the battery ground strap.

2. Disconnect the exhaust pipe from the manifold and its bracket.

3. Unhook the clutch cable.

4. Detach the speedometer cable.

5. Remove the upper engine-to-transaxle bolts.

6. Remove the engine support bolts on both sides of the engine block (front).
7. Remove the front muffler and exhaust pipe.
8. Unbolt both halfshaft at the transaxale.

**NOTE: On Quantum Syncro models the driveshaft to the rear axle assembly will also have to be removed in order to remove the transaxle.**

9. Disconnect the back-up light wiring.
10. Remove the inspection plate on the bottom of transaxle case.
11. Remove the starter bolt.
12. Remove the shift rod coupling bolt; pry off the shift rod coupling ball with a prybar.
13. Pull off the shift rod coupling from the shift rod.
14. Place a jack under the transaxle and lift slightly.
15. Remove the transaxle support bolts and transaxle rubber mounts.
16. Remove the front transaxle support bolts and the lower transaxle-to-engine support bolts.
17. Slowly pry the transaxle from the engine.
18. Lower the transaxle out of the car.

**NOTE: Lubricate the main shaft splines with molybdenum-disulfide grease.**

19. To install, reverse the removal procedures and finger tighten the bolts. When the mounting bolts are aligned and free of tension, tighten them.

Torque the following components:
Transaxle-to-engine bolts – 40 ft. lbs. (54 Nm)
Axleshaft-to-drive flange bolts – 33 ft. lbs. (45 Nm)
Transaxle-to-mount bolts – 18 ft. lbs. (24 Nm)
Transaxle mount-to-body bolts – 80 ft. lbs. (108 Nm).

## SHIFT LINKAGE ADJUSTMENT

### *Quantum*

An adjusting tool, VW-3057 must be used on this model.
1. Place the lever in Neutral.
2. Working under the car, loosen the clamp nut.
3. Inside the car, remove the gear lever knob and the shift boot. It is not necessary to remove the console. Align the centering holes of the lever housing and the lever bearing housing.
4. Install the tool with the locating pin toward the front. Push the lever to the left side of the tool cut-out. Tighten the lower knurled knob to secure the tool.
5. Move the top slide of the tool to the left stop and tighten the upper knurled knob.

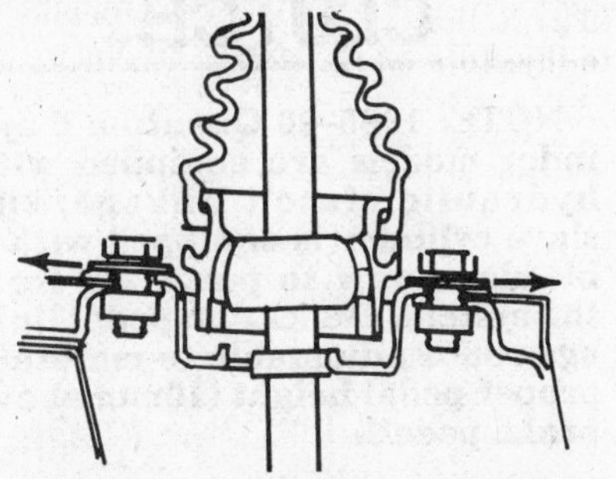

Quantum second gear shift lever adjustment

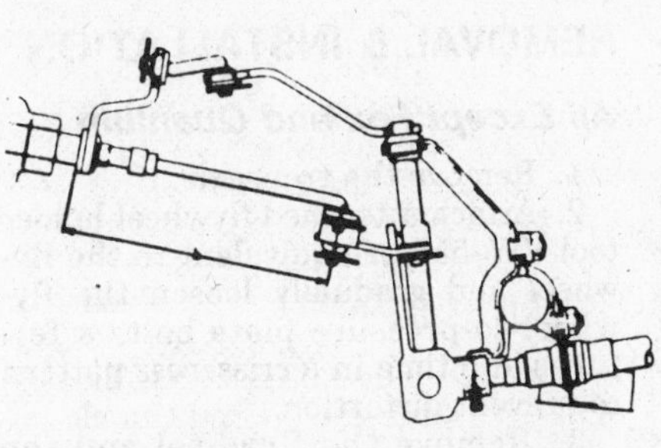

The long rod on the Rabbit and Scirocco shift linkage is to be adjusted to a length (b) of 6.42-6.50 in.

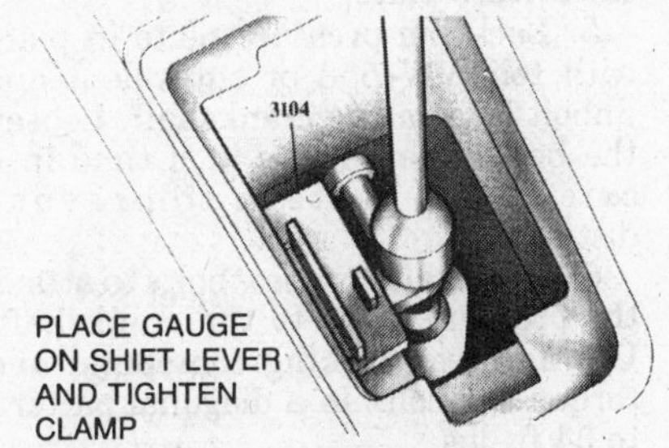


Adjusting the shift linkage on the 1985 and later manual transaxle

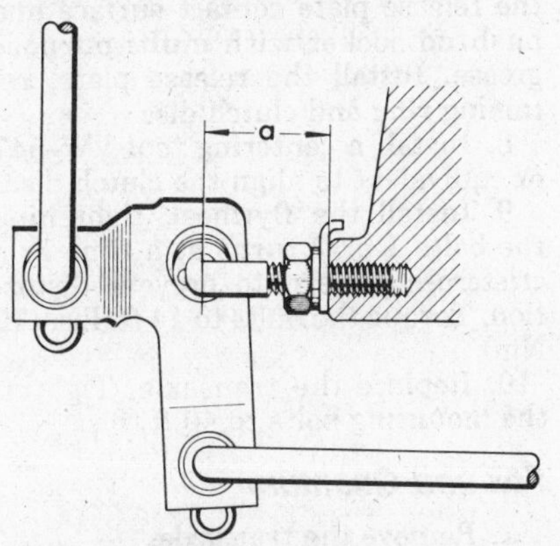


The short angled rod on the Rabbit and Scirocco shift linkage is to be adjusted to a length (a) of 1.18—1.25 in.

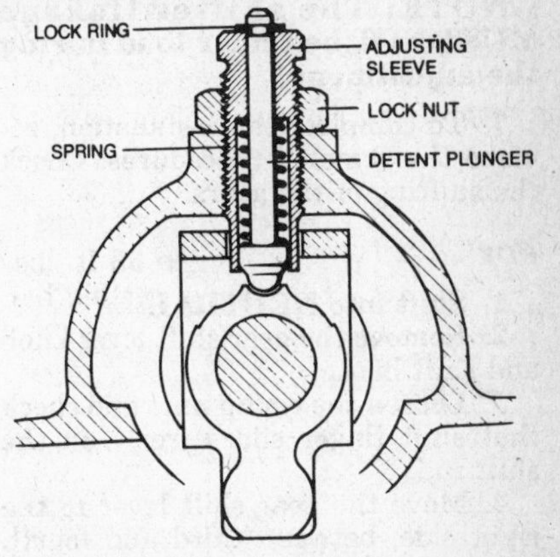


On Rabbit, Jetta and Scirocco, loosen the locknut and turn the adjusting sleeve

6. Push the shift lever to the right side of the cutout. Align the shift rod and shift finger under the car and tighten the clamp nut. Remove the tool.
7. Place the lever in first. Press the lever to the left side against the stop. Release the lever; it should spring back ¼–½ in. If not, move the lever housing slightly sideways to correct. Check that all gears can be engaged easily, particularly reverse.

### *Rabbit, Scirocco, Cabriolet and 1983–84 Jetta*

1. Align the holes of the lever housing plate with the holes of the lever bearing plate.
2. Loosen the shift rod clamp. Pull the boot off the lever housing and push it out of the way. It may be necessary to loosen the screws in the cover plate to free the boot.
3. Check that the shift finger is in the center of the stopping plate.
4. Adjust the shift rod end so that it is ¾ in. ($^{9}/_{32}$ in. for 5 speed transmissions) from the right side of the lever housing. Tighten the shift rod clamp and check the shifter operation.

### *1985–90 Golf and Jetta*

1. Place the shifter lever into the NEUTRAL position.
2. Under the vehicle, loosen the clamp on the shifter rod.

**NOTE: The shifter lever MUST move freely on the shifter rod.**

3. Remove the shifter knob and the boot.
4. Position the gauge alignment tool VW-3104 on the shifting mechanism (lock it in place).
5. Place the transaxle selector lever in the **NEUTRAL** position.
6. Align the shift rod with the selector lever and torque the clamp to 19 ft. lbs. (26 Nm).

**NOTE: The shifter linkage MUST NOT be under load during the adjustment.**

7. To complete the installation, reverse the removal procedures. Check the shifting of the gears.

### *Fox*

1. Shift into **NEUTRAL.**
2. Remove the gear shift lever knob and shift boot.
3. Loosen the clamp nuts and check that shift finger slides freely on the shift rod.
4. Move the gear shift lever to the right side, between third and fourth gear position. The gear shift lever should remain perpendicular to the ball housing.
5. With the inner shift lever in neutral and the gear shift lever between second and third gear, tighten the clamp nut.
6. Check the engagement of all gears, including reverse and make sure that the gear shift lever moves freely.

## SELECTOR SHAFT LOCKBOLT ADJUSTMENT

### *1983–84 Models*

Make this adjustment on Rabbit, Jetta, Scirocco and Cabriolet models after linkage adjustment, if the linkage still feels spongy or jams.

1. Disconnect the shift linkage and put the transmission in Neutral.
2. Loosen the locknut and turn the adjusting sleeve in until the lockring lifts off the sleeve.
3. Turn the adjusting sleeve back until the lockring just contacts the sleeve. Tighten the locknut.
4. Turn the shaft slightly. The lockring should lift as soon as the shaft is turned.
5. Reconnect the linkage.

## FIFTH GEAR LOCKBOLT ADJUSTMENT

### *Golf, Rabbit, Scirocco, Cabriolet and Jetta*

This adjustment is made with the transmission in neutral. The fifth gear lockbolt is located on top of the transmission next to the selector shaft lockbolt. It has a large protective cap over it.

1. Remove the protective cap.
2. Loosen the locknut and tighten the adjusting sleeve until the detent plunger in the center of the sleeve just begins to move up.
3. Loosen the adjusting sleeve ⅓–½ of a turn and tighten the locknut. Make sure the transmission shifts in and out of fifth gear easily. Replace the protective cap.

# CLUTCH

**NOTE: 1985–90 Quantum 5 cylinder models are equipped with hydraulic clutch linkage, the slave cylinder is equipped with a bleeder screw to purge air from the system. The clutch pedal linkage rod is adjustable to maintain proper pedal height (10mm above brake pedal).**

## Clutch Assembly

### REMOVAL & INSTALLATION

#### *All Except Fox and Quantum*

1. Remove the transaxle.
2. Attach a toothed flywheel holder tool VW–558 or equivalent to the flywheel and gradually loosen the flywheel-to-pressure plate bolts a few turns at a time in a crisscross pattern to prevent distortion.
3. Remove the flywheel and the clutch disc.
4. Use a small prybar to remove the release plate retaining ring. Remove the release plate.
5. Lock the pressure plate in place with tool VW–558 or equivalent and unbolt it from the crankshaft. Loosen the bolts a few turns at a time in a crisscross pattern to prevent distortion.
6. To install, use new bolts to attach the pressure plate to the crankshaft. Use a thread locking compound and torque the bolts in a diagonal pattern to 54 ft. lbs.
7. Lubricate the clutch disc splines with multi-purpose grease. Lubricate the release plate contact surface and pushrod socket with multi-purpose grease. Install the release plate, retaining ring and clutch disc.
8. Install a centering tool VW–547 or equivalent to align the clutch disc.
9. Install the flywheel, tightening the bolts 1 or 2 turns at a time in a crisscross pattern to prevent distortion. Torque the bolts to 14 ft. lbs. (19 Nm).
10. Replace the transaxle. Tighten the mounting bolts to 40 ft. lbs.

#### *Fox and Quantum*

1. Remove the transaxle.
2. Matchmark the flywheel and pressure plate if the pressure plate is going to be reused.
3. Gradually loosen the pressure plate bolts 1 or 2 turns at a time in a crisscross pattern to prevent distortion.
4. Remove the pressure plate and disc.
5. Check the clutch disc for uneven or excessive lining wear. Examine the pressure plate for cracking, scorching or scoring. Replace any questionable components.

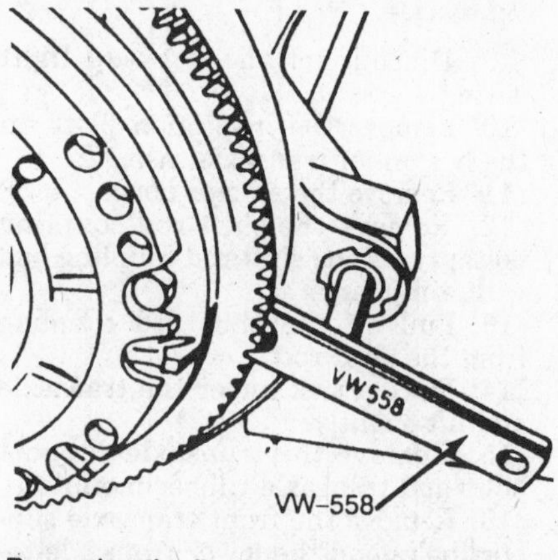

Removing the flywheel using holding tool VW–558

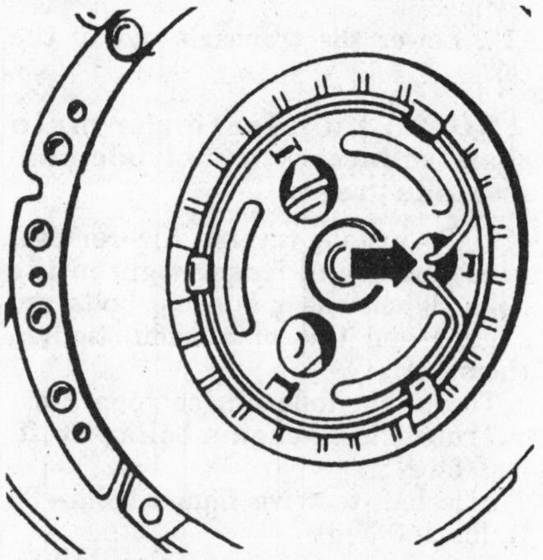
Removing the clutch retaining ring

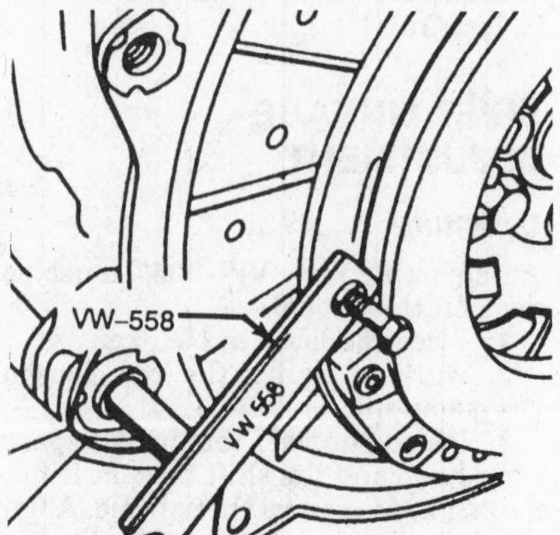

Removing the clutch pressure plate using tool VW–558

6. Install the clutch disc and pressure plate. Use alignment tool VW-547 or equivalent to keep the clutch disc centered.
7. Gradually tighten the pressure plate-to-flywheel bolts in a crisscross pattern. Tighten the bolts to 18 ft. lbs.
8. Install the throwout bearing.
9. Install the transaxle. Tighten the transaxle to engine bolts to 40 ft. lbs.
10. Check the operation of the clutch.

## PEDAL HEIGHT/FREE-PLAY ADJUSTMENT

Clutch pedal free-play should be $^{27}/_{32}$–1 in. free-play.

1. Adjust the clutch pedal free-play by loosening or tightening the 2 nuts (or locknut and threaded sleeve) on the end of the clutch cable. The cable adjuster is near the oil filter on the Fox and Quantum. On the Golf, Rabbit, Jetta, Scirocco and Cabriolet, the adjuster is on the drivers front side of the transaxle.

**NOTE: Clutch pedal free-play cannot be measured if the floor covering interferes with the pedal movement. Check the upper pedal area with the clutch fully depressed for any interference.**

2. Loosen the locknut and loosen or tighten the adjusting nut or sleeve until desired play is present. Depress the clutch pedal several times and recheck free-play. Readjust if necessary. Tighten the locknut.
3. On late model vehicles, Volkswagen recommends that a special tool (US5043) be used to determine proper adjustment. The procedure for adjustment follows; depress the clutch pedal several times. Loosen the locknut and insert the tool. Adjust the sleeve until zero clearance between the sleeve and tool is reached. Tighten the locknut.

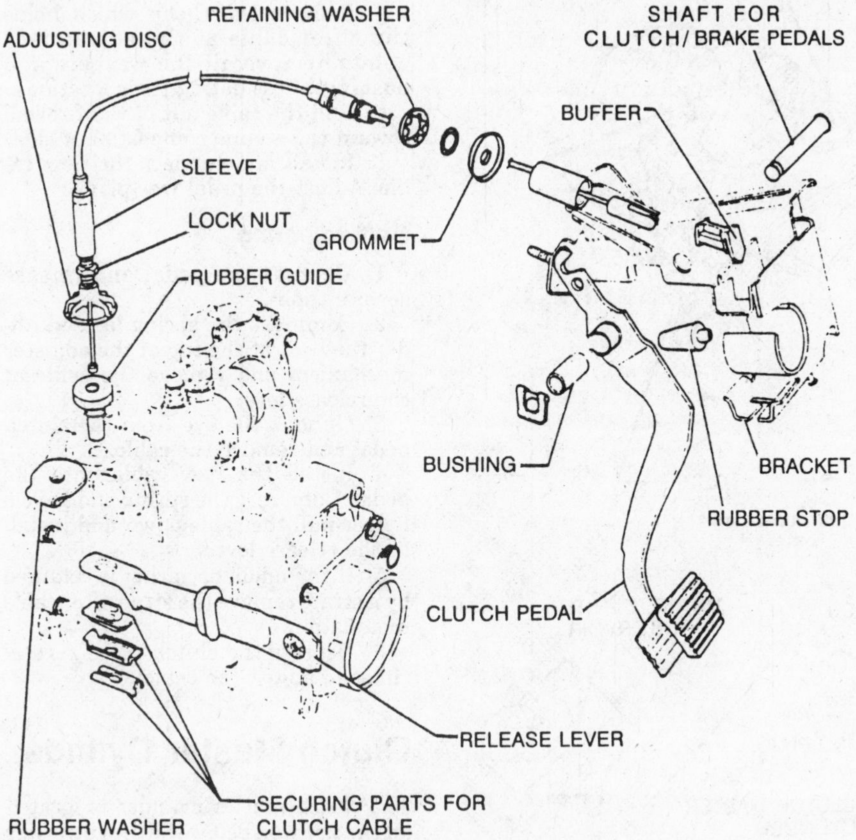


Clutch pedal and cable assembly

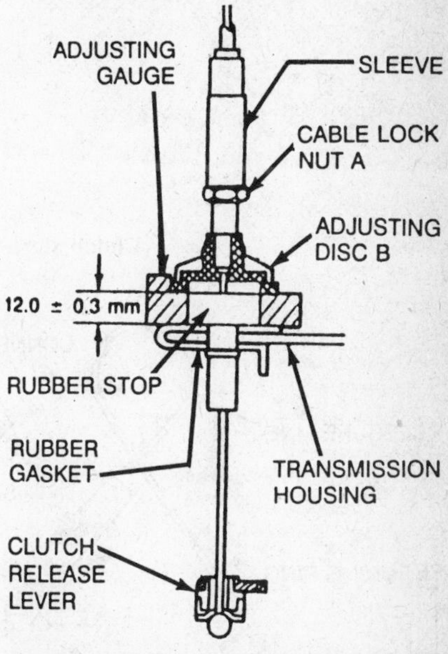


Clutch pedal freeplay checking and adjusting

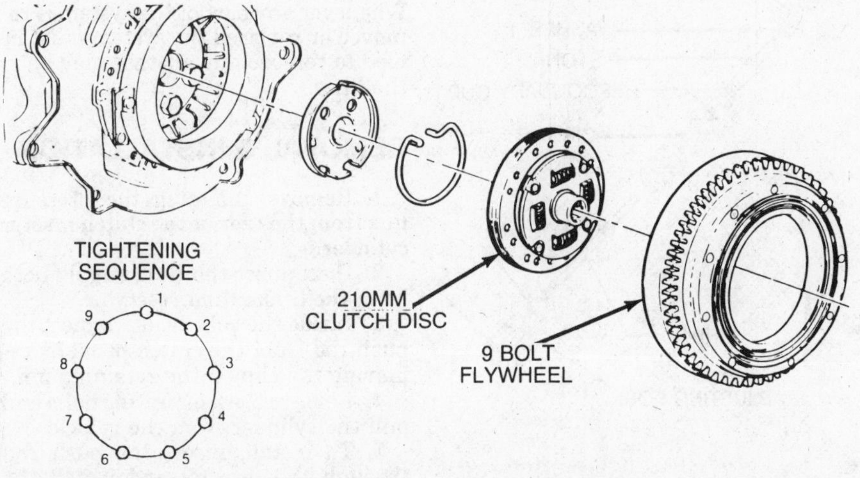


Clutch assembly on transverse mounted engines. 210mm late model shown

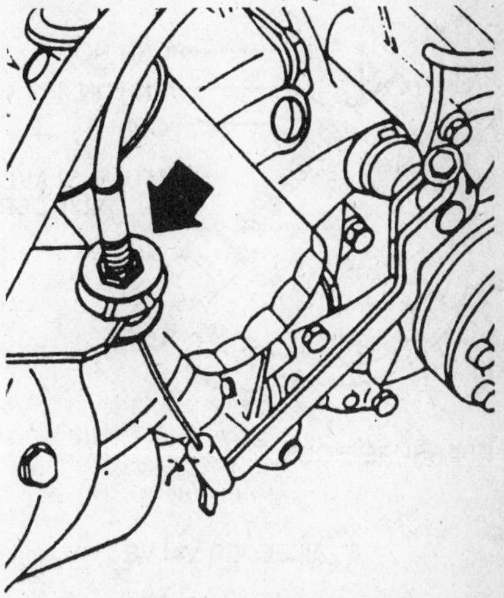

Clutch pedal freeplay adjuster

Remove tool and depress the clutch pedal at least 5 times. Check the free-play at the clutch pedal, readjust if necessary.

**NOTE: 1986–90 5 speed models (gas engine) are equipped with a self-adjusting clutch cable. The cable incorporates an adjustment mechanism on the transmission side of the cable which automatically adjusts to compensate for normal clutch disc wear.**

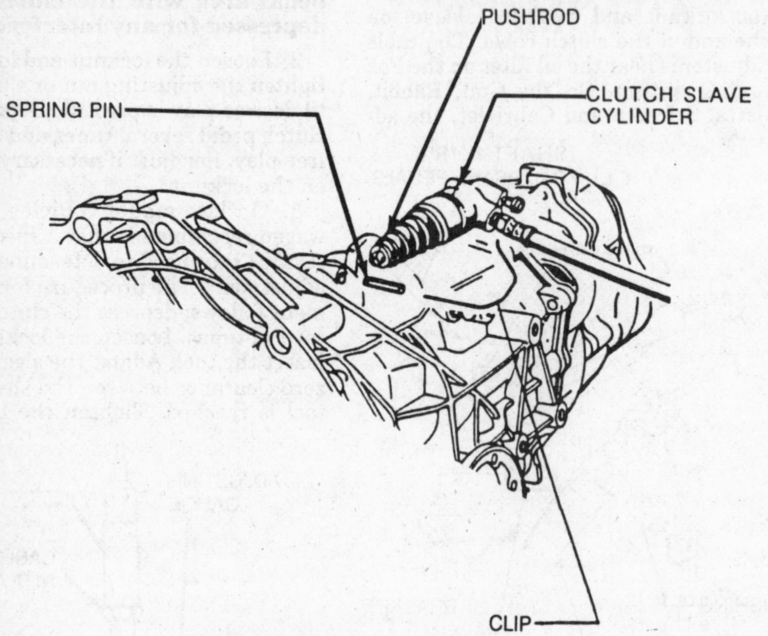


Clutch slave cylinder mounting

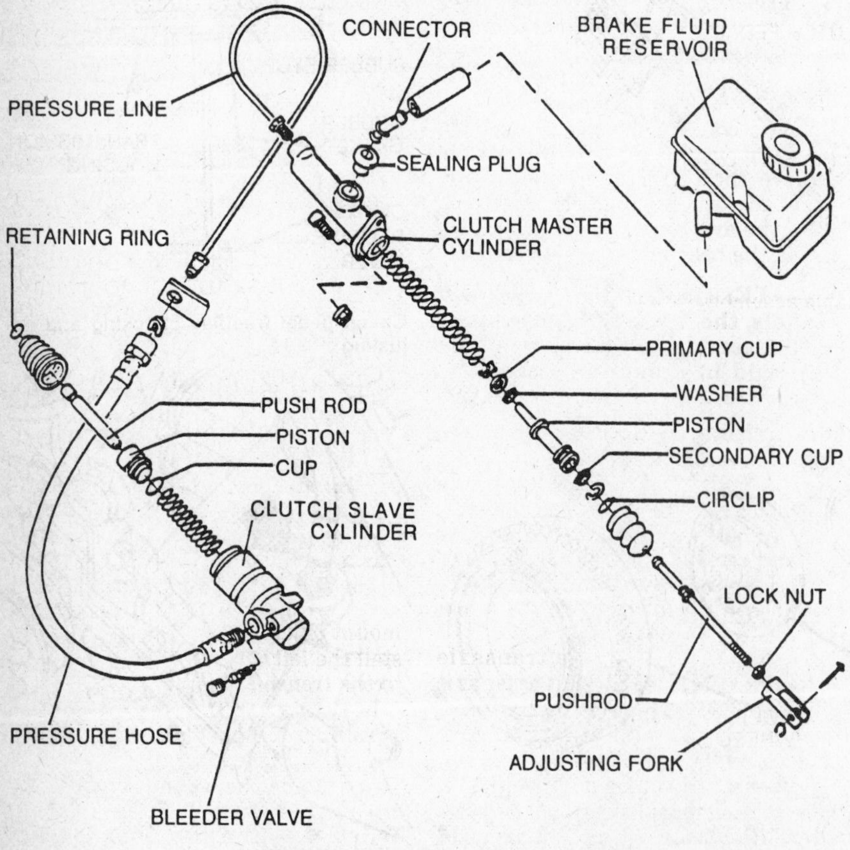


Hydraulic clutch system components

## Clutch Cable

### REMOVAL & INSTALLATION

#### *Except Self-Adjusting*

1. Loosen the adjustment.
2. Disengage the cable from the clutch arm.
3. Unhook the cable from the pedal. Remove the threaded eye from the end of the cable. Remove the adjustment nut(s).
4. Remove the C-clip which holds the outer cable at the adjustment point. Remove all the washers and bushings, first noting their locations.
5. Pull the cable out of the firewall toward the engine compartment side.
6. Install and connect the new cable. Adjust the pedal free-play.

#### *Self-adjusting*

1. Depress the pedal and release several times.
2. Compress the spring located under the boot at the top of the adjuster mechanism and remove the cable at the release lever.
3. Unhook the eye from the clutch pedal and remove the cable.
4. Install the new cable onto the pedal. Compress the spring and have a helper pull the cable down and install to the release lever.
5. If the adjuster spring is retained by a strap, remove the strap after cable installation.
6. Depress the clutch pedal several times to adjust the cable.

## Clutch Master Cylinder

The clutch master cylinder is located on the fire wall below the brake master cylinder. The clutch slave cylinder is located on top of the transmission. The clutch master cylinder is supplied fluid from the brake fluid reservoir. Whenever any part of the system is removed or replaced the system must be bled to remove any air that may be in the lines.

### REMOVAL & INSTALLATION

1. Remove and plug the pressure line from the rear of the clutch master cylinder.
2. Disconnect the fluid supply hose from the brake fluid reservoir.
3. Inside the vehicle, disconnect the push rod from the clutch pedal by removing the clip on the retaining pin.
4. Remove the 2 mounting bolts and pull the cylinder from the vehicle.
5. To install, insert the push rod through the firewall and install the cylinder mounting bolts. Torque the

clutch master cylinder mounting bolts to 14 ft. lbs.

6. Install the supply line to the brake master cylinder and install the pressure line to the rear of the clutch master cylinder.

7. Fill the brake reservoir and bleed the clutch system.

## Clutch Slave Cylinder

1. Raise and safely support the vehicle.

2. Disconnect and plug the pressure line to the slave cylinder.

3. Remove the slave cylinder by removing the spring pin and clip from the transmission.

4. To install, align the slave cylinder on the transmission housing and insert the spring pin and clip.

5. Connect the pressure line and lower the vehicle.

6. Fill the brake reservoir and bleed the system.

### BLEEDING THE HYDRAULIC CLUTCH

1. Clean all dirt and grease from the cap to make sure that no foreign subtances enter the system.

2. Remove the cap and diaphragm and fill the reservoir to the top with the approved DOT 3 brake fluid. Fully loosen the bleed screw which is in the slave cylinder body next to the inlet connection.

3. At this point bubbles of air will appear at the bleed screw outlet. When the slave cylinder is full and a steady stream of fluid comes out of the slave cylinder bleeder, tighten the bleed screw.

4. Assemble the diaphragm and cap to the reservoir, fluid in the reservoir should be level with the step. Exert a light load of about 20 lbs. to the slave cylinder piston by pushing the release lever towards the cylinder and loosen the bleed screw. Maintain a constant light load, fluid and any air that is left will be expelled through the bleed port. Tighten the bleed screw when a steady flow of fluid and no air is being expelled.

5. Fill the reservoir fluid level back to normal capacity and if necessary repeat Step 4.

6. Exert a light load to the release lever, but do not open the bleeder screw as the piston in the slave cylinder will move slowly down the bore. Repeat this operation 2–3 times, the fluid movement will force any air left in the system into the reservoir. The hydraulic system should now be fully bled.

7. Check the the operation of the clutch hydraulic system and repeat this procedure if necessary. Check the push rod travel at the slave cylinder to insure the minimum travel 0.57 in.

# AUTOMATIC TRANSAXLE

### REMOVAL & INSTALLATION

1. Disconnect the negative battery cable.

2. Raise and safely support the front of the vehicle.

3. Disconnect the speedometer cable.

4. Remove the accelerator cable from the throttle valve housing.

5. Remove 2 of the upper engine/transaxle bolts. Support the engine with either special tool VW-10-222 or equivalent.

6. Disconnect the exhaust pipe.

7. Remove the torque converter cover plate.

8. Remove the circlip holding the selector lever cable to the lever and remove the cable.

9. Remove the starter.

10. The torque converter is mounted to the flywheel by 3 bolts. The bolts are accessible through the starter hole, turn the engine by hand in order to remove all 3.

11. Remove the halfshaft-to-transaxle bolts.

12. Matchmark the position of the ball joint on the left control arm and remove the ball joint from the arm. Hold the wheel assembly out away from the arm to provide clearance between the halfshaft and the transaxle.

**NOTE: On Quantum Syncro models, the driveshaft to the rear axle assembly will also have to be removed in order to remove the transaxle.**

13. Remove the exhaust pipe from the transaxle bracket.

14. Disconnect the remaining transaxle controls.

15. Unbolt the transaxle crossmember and remove it from the transaxle.

16. Support the transaxle on a jack and loosen the lower engine-to-transaxle bolts.

17. Remove all engine/transaxle bolts. Pull the left wheel out as far as it will go and slowly lower the transmission, making sure the torque converter does not fall off.

18. Loosen the union nut on the ATF filler pipe so that the pipe can be swivelled. Remove the engine/transaxle bolts and lower the unit.

19. Installation is the reverse of removal with the following notes.

a. The torque converter nipple must be about $^{13}/_{16}$ in. from the bell housing face surface. If it sticks out further than this, the oil pump shaft has pulled out. To correct this realign the converter and shaft.

b. Tighten the engine/transaxle bolts to 40 ft. lbs. (30 Nm) and the torque converter bolts to 20–23 ft. lbs. (27–31 Nm). New torque converter bolts should be used. Torque the axleshaft bolts to 33 ft. lbs. (45 Nm) and the ball joint-to-control arm bolts to 45 ft. lbs. (61 Nm). Check the shift linkage adjustment.

#### *1983–84 Rabbit, Scirocco and Jetta*

1. Disconnect both battery cables.

2. Disconnect the speedometer cable at the transmission.

3. Support the left end of the engine at the lifting eye. Attach a hoist to the transaxle.

4. Unbolt the rear transmission carrier from the body then from the transaxle. Unbolt the left side carrier from the body.

5. Unbolt the halfshafts and support securely.

6. Remove the starter.

7. Remove the 3 converter-to-drive plate bolts.

8. Shift the transaxle into **P** and disconnect the floorshift linkage at the transmission.

9. Remove the accelerator and carburetor cable bracket at the transmission.

10. Unbolt the left side transmission carrier from the transmission.

11. Unbolt the front transmission mount from the transmission.

12. Unbolt the bottom of the engine from the transmission. Lift the transaxle slightly, remove the rest of the bolts, pull the transmission off the mounting dowels and lower the transaxle out of the car. Secure the converter.

13. To install, be sure the torque converter is fully seated on the clutch support. Push the transmission onto the mounting dowels and install 2 bolts. Lift the unit until the left driveshaft can be installed and install the rest of the bolts. Torque to 39 ft. lbs. (53 Nm).

14. Tighten the front transmission mount bolts to 39 ft. lbs. (53 Nm). Install the left side transmission carrier to the transmission.

15. Connect the accelerator and carburetor cable bracket. Connect the floorshift linkage.

16. Tighten the torque converter-to-drive plate bolts to 22 ft. lbs. (30 Nm). Torque the driveshaft bolts to 32 ft. lbs. (43 Nm).

17. Install the rear transmission carrier and make sure that the left side carrier is aligned in the center of the body mount. Bolt the left side carrier to the body.

18. Connect the speedometer cable and the battery cables.

### *1985–90 Golf, Jetta and Scirocco/Cabriolet*

1. Disconnect the negative battery cable.

2. Remove the speedometer cable from the transaxle and the upper starter mounting bolts.

3. Connect the engine support tool VW-10-222A or equivalent to the engine and lift it slightly.

4. Remove the 3 bolts from the right engine mount. Remove the left transaxle mount complete with the support.

5. Push the engine to the rear and remove the front engine mount.

6. Remove the left halfshaft, the lower starter bolts and the starter.

7. Remove the transaxle oil pan protective plate.

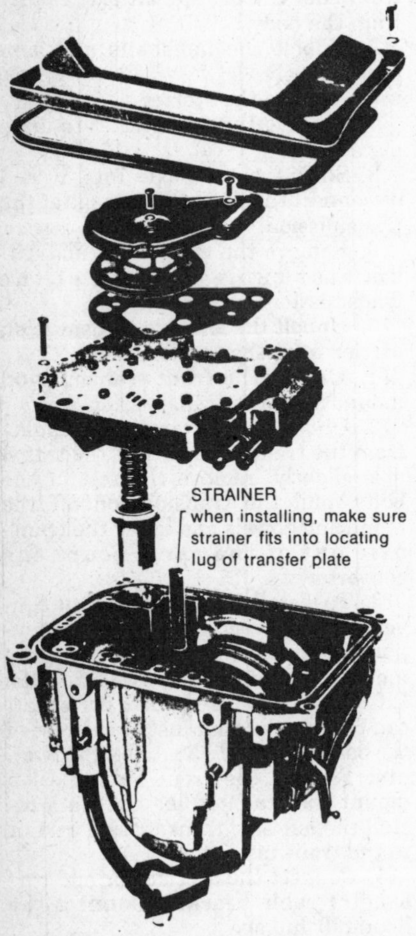
STRAINER
when installing, make sure strainer fits into locating lug of transfer plate

Beginning with transaxle 13 03 8, an additional strainer is used beneath the valve body. It cannot be installed on earlier models

8. Place the shift selector lever in the **PARK** position, remove the selector cable and bracket from the transaxle.

9. Remove the accelerator cable and the accelerator pedal cable.

**NOTE: When removing the accelerator cable, BE CAREFUL not to change the adjustment.**

10. Remove the 3 torque converter bolts from the drive plate.

11. Remove the right ball joint from the control arm and the right halfshaft from the transaxle.

**NOTE: When removing the ball joint from the control arm, be careful not to damage the boot.**

12. Push the engine to the right as far as possible, remove the left halfshaft and securely support it aside.

13. Place a transmission jack under the transaxle and support it.

14. Remove the lower transaxle-to-engine bolts and push the transaxle from the centering pins.

15. Pull the transaxle back and lower it from the vehicle, being careful not to let the torque converter fall from the transaxle.

16. To install, reverse the removal procedures. Torque the transaxle-to-engine bolts to 55 ft. lbs. (75 Nm), the torque converter-to-drive plate to 26 ft. lbs. (35 Nm) and the halfshaft-to-flange to 33 ft. lbs. (45 Nm). Adjust the accelerator cable and the shift selector lever.

## PAN REMOVAL AND FILTER SERVICE

### *Quantum*

VW recommends that the automatic transmission fluid be replace every 30,000 miles or 20,000 miles if used for trailer towing, mountain driving, or other severe service.

1. Raise and safely support the vehicle.

2. Slide a drain pan under the transmission. Remove the drain plug and allow all the fluid to drain.

**NOTE: Some models are not equipped with pan drain plugs. In this case, empty the pan by loosening the pan bolts and allowing the fluid to drain out.**

3. Remove the pan retaining bolts and lower the pan.

4. Discard the old gasket and clean the pan with solvent.

5. Unscrew and clean the circular strainer. If it is dirty, it should be replaced.

6. Install the strainer and torque to 4 ft. lbs. (5 Nm).

7. Refill the transmission with about 2¾ qts of fluid. Check the level with the dipstick.

8. Run the engine to normal operating temperature and recheck the fluid level.

### *Golf, Rabbit, Scirocco, Cabriolet, GTI, GLI and Jetta*

**NOTE: As of transmission No. 09096 a new, cleanable oil filter is used which requires a deeper oil pan. Also beginning with transmission number EQ-15 106, the drain plug was no longer installed in the oil pan.**

1. Raise and safely support the vehicle. Remove the drain plug and let the fluid drain into a pan. If the pan has no drain plug, loosen the pan bolts until a corner of the pan can be lowered to drain the fluid.

2. Remove the pan bolts and take off the pan.

3. Discard the old gasket and clean the pan.

4. To install, install the strainer into the transaxle. The specified torque for the strainer screws is 2 ft. lbs. (3 Nm).

**NOTE: Beginning with transmission number 13 03 8, there is an additional strainer under the valve body. When installing it, be sure if fits into the locating lug of the transfer plate.**

5. Replace the pan with a new gasket and tighten the bolts, in a crisscross pattern, to 14 ft. lbs.

6. Using a long-necked funnel, pour in 2½ qts. of Dexron® automatic transmission fluid through the dipstick tube. Start the engine and shift through all the transmission ranges with the car stationary. Check the level on the dipstick with the lever in **NEUTRAL**. The fluid level should be at the lower end of the dipstick. Run the vehicle to normal operating temperature and recheck the fluid level.

## TRANSMISSION CABLE ADJUSTMENT

**NOTE: Make sure the throttle is closed and the choke and fast idle cam are off (carbureted models).**

1. Detach the cable end at the transmission.

2. Press the lever at the transmission into its closed throttle position.

3. Attach the cable end onto the transmission lever without moving the lever.

4. Adjust the cable length to the correct setting.

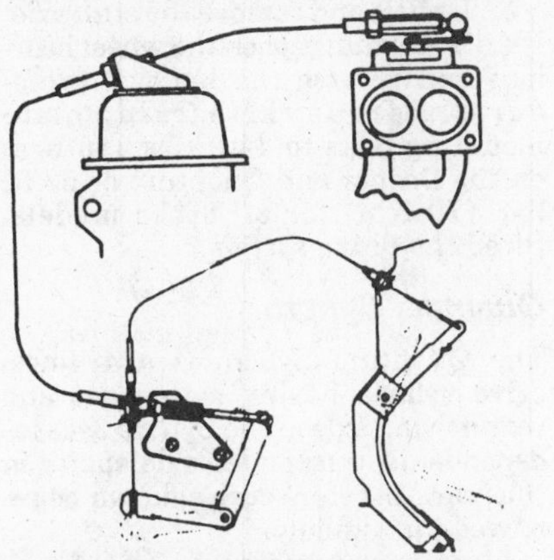

Rabbit, Jetta, Scirocco automatic transmission cable arrangement—fuel injected

## NEUTRAL START/BACK-UP LIGHT SWITCH

The combination neutral start and back-up light switch is mounted inside the shifter housing. The starter should operate in PARK or NEUTRAL only. Adjust the switch by moving it on its mounts. The back-up lights should only come on when the switch selector is in the REVERSE position.

## SECOND GEAR (REAR) BAND ADJUSTMENT

**NOTE: The transmission must be horizontal when band adjustments are performed.**

1. Loosen the locknut on the adjusting screw, which is located on the front of the Rabbit and Scirocco transmission.
2. Tighten the adjusting screw to 7 ft. lbs. (10 Nm).
3. Loosen the screw and tighten it again to 4 ft. lbs. (5 Nm).
4. Turn the screw out exactly 2½ turns and then tighten the locknut.

# DRIVE AXLE

## Halfshaft

### REMOVAL & INSTALLATION

#### *Fox and Quantum*

**NOTE: When removing the right side halfshaft, detach the exhaust pipe from the manifold and the transaxle bracket.**

1. With the car on the ground, remove the front axle nut.
2. Raise and safely support the front of the vehicle.
3. Remove the socket head bolts retaining the halfshaft to the transaxle flange.

**NOTE: When removing the left side halfshaft on automatic transmission models, matchmark the ball joint (left side) mounting position in relation to the lower control arm. Remove the 2 ball joint retaining nuts and separate the ball joint from the control arm to create room to remove the halfshaft.**

4. Pull the transaxle side of the halfshaft out and up, place it on top of the transaxle.
5. Pull the halfshaft from the steering knuckle.
6. Installation is the reverse of removal. Tighten the transaxle bolts to 25–33 ft. lbs. (34–45 Nm). The axle nut should be tightened to 145 ft. lbs. (196 Nm) (M 18 nut), or 175 ft. lbs. (237 Nm) (M 20 nut).

**NOTE: Be aware that the halfshafts are 2 different lengths on automatic transmission models, with the left side shaft being slightly longer than the right. The halfshafts can not be interchanged.**

#### *Golf, Rabbit, Scirocco, Cabriolet, GTI, GLI and Jetta*

1. With the car on the ground, remove the front axle nut.
2. Raise and safely support the front of the vehicle.
3. Remove the socket head bolts retaining the halfshaft to the transaxle flange.
4. Remove the bolt holding the ball joint to the steering knuckle and separate the knuckle from the ball joint.
5. Remove the halfshaft by pulling it out of the steering knuckle.
6. Installation is the reverse of removal. Tighten the halfshaft-to-transaxle bolts to 33 ft. lbs. (44 Nm), the ball joint bolt to 21 ft. lbs. (28 Nm) and the axle nut to 173 ft. lbs. (234 Nm).
7. Check the front end alignment.

### CV-JOINT OVERHAUL

The constant velocity joints (CV) can be disassembled. However, VW states that the components are machined to a matched tolerance and that the entire CV-joint must be replaced as an assembly.

**For all CV-joint overhaul procedures, refer to "CV-Joint Overhaul" in the Unit Repair section.**

## Rear Axle Shafts/Stub Axles

### REMOVAL & INSTALLATION

#### *All Except Quantum Syncro*

1. Raise the rear of the vehicle and support it safely. Remove the grease cap, cotter pin, locknut, adjusting nut, spacer, wheel bearing and brake drum.
2. Disconnect and plug the brake line. Remove the brake backing plate with the brakes attached.

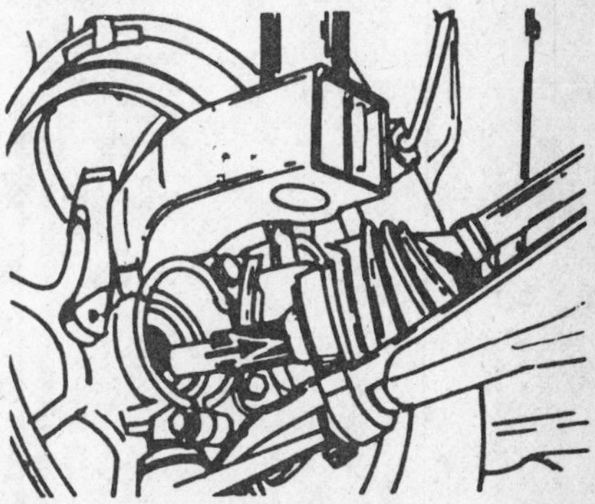

Removing the axle shaft from the steering knuckle on Fox and Quantum models

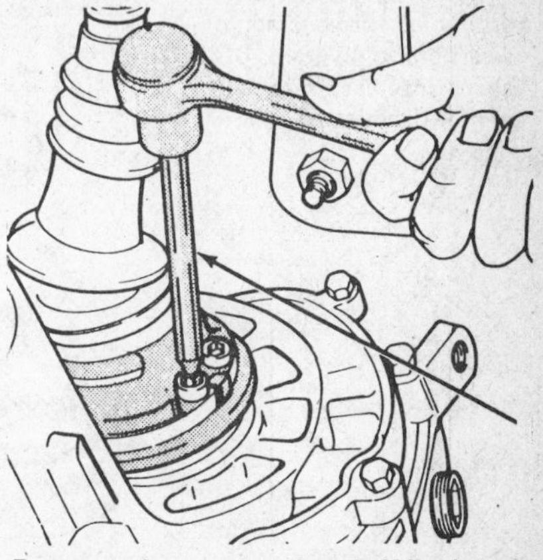

Remove the socket head (Allen) bolts holding the axle shaft to the transaxle

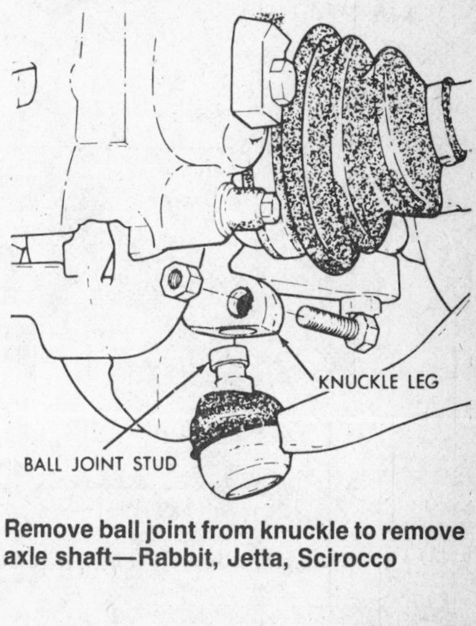


Remove ball joint from knuckle to remove axle shaft—Rabbit, Jetta, Scirocco

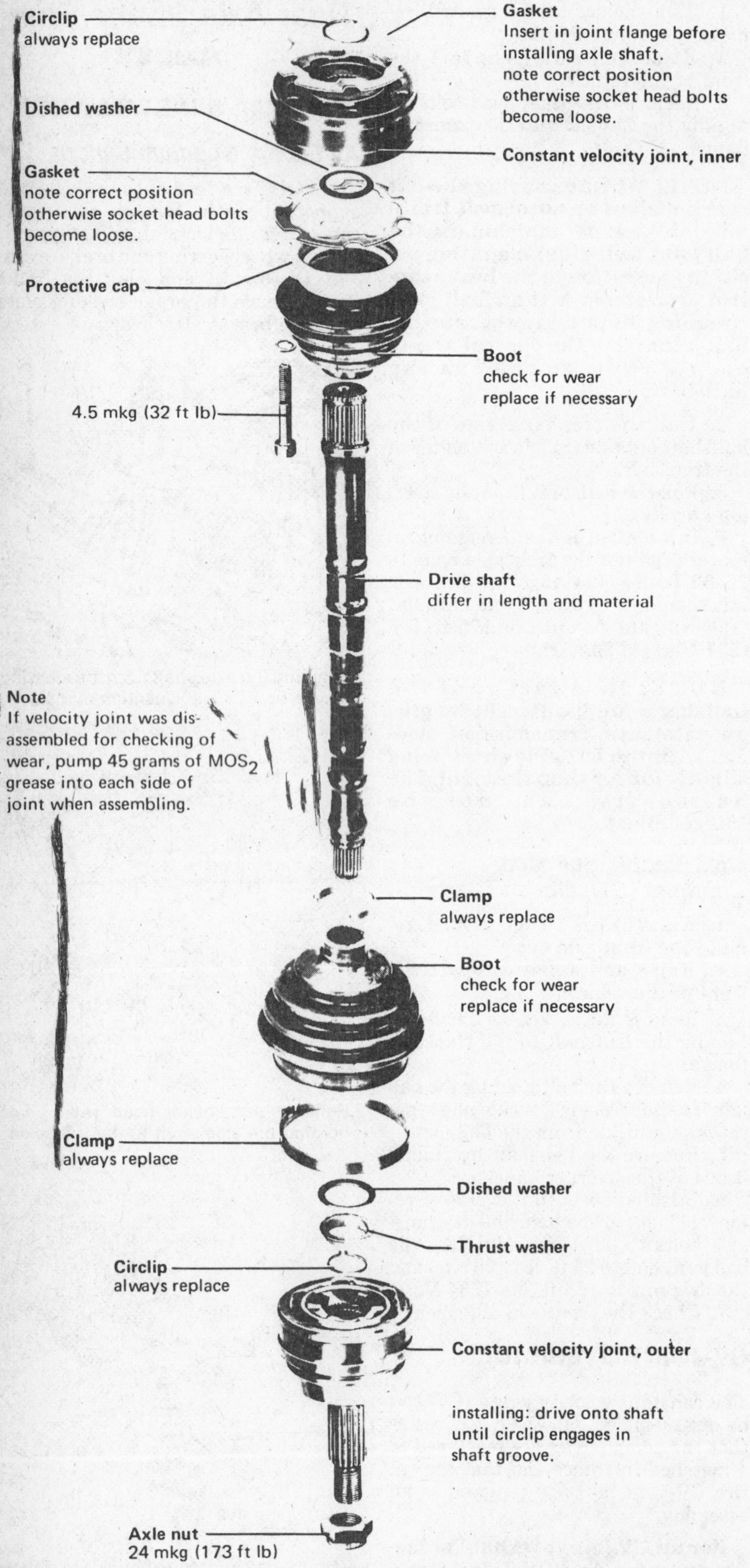
Circlip
always replace
Gasket
Insert in joint flange before installing axle shaft.
note correct position otherwise socket head bolts become loose.
Dished washer
Constant velocity joint, inner
Gasket
note correct position otherwise socket head bolts become loose.
Protective cap
Boot
check for wear
replace if necessary
4.5 mkg (32 ft lb)
Drive shaft
differ in length and material
Note
If velocity joint was disassembled for checking of wear, pump 45 grams of $MOS_2$ grease into each side of joint when assembling.
Clamp
always replace
Boot
check for wear
replace if necessary
Clamp
always replace
Dished washer
Thrust washer
Circlip
always replace
Constant velocity joint, outer
installing: drive onto shaft until circlip engages in shaft groove.
Axle nut
24 mkg (173 ft lb)

Exploded view of the Rabbit, Jetta and Scirocco halfshaft

3. Unbolt and remove the stub axle.

4. To install, repack the wheel bearings and reverse the removal procedures. Torque the backing plate mounting bolts to 44 ft. lbs. (60 Nm) on the Dasher and Quantum or 52 ft. lbs. (70 Nm) for all other models. Bleed the brake system.

### *Quantum Syncro*

The Quantum Syncro is a 4 wheel drive vehicle having both front and rear driving axles. The Syncro uses independently suspended axle shafts in the rear, therefore each side can be removed individually.

1. Raise and safely support the rear of the vehicle.
2. Remove the wheel and tire assembly.
3. Remove the bolts retaining the axle shaft to the axle housing, support the axle shaft to keep it from falling and damaging the CV-joint.
4. Remove the disc brake caliper and support out of the way, do not hang it by the brake lines.
5. Remove the outer axle retaining nut and remove the brake disc.
6. Slide the axle shaft out of the vehicle.
7. To install, slide the axle shaft into the hub assembly. Install the outer axle nut and torque to 170 ft. lbs. Install the brake disc and caliper assembly, tighten the caliper retaining bolt to 48 ft. lbs.
8. Install the axle shaft-to-axle housing retaining bolts, to 33 ft. lbs.
9. Install the wheel and tire.

## Front Wheel Hub, Knuckle and Bearings

The front wheel bearings are non-adjustable on all models and are sealed, so they should be maintenance-free.

**NOTE: Replacement wheel bearings for Quantum models with an enlarged outside diame-**

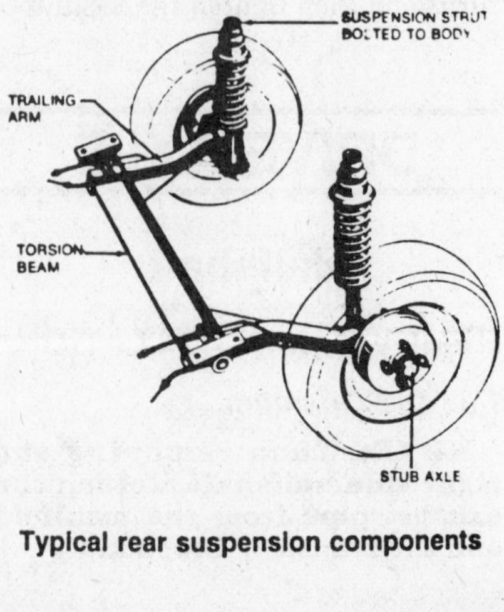
SUSPENSION STRUT BOLTED TO BODY
TRAILING ARM
TORSION BEAM
STUB AXLE

Typical rear suspension components

ter require NO moly paste lubrication (Bearing number 321 498 625D).

## REMOVAL & INSTALLATION

### *Fox and Quantum*

1. Remove the grease cup from the wheel spindle.
2. Remove the wheel spindle.
3. Raise and safely support the front of the vehicle, allowing the front wheels to hang. Remove the wheel assembly.
4. Remove the brake caliper from the steering knuckle and suspend on a wire, DO NOT remove the brake hose.
5. Remove the brake disc from the hub assembly.
6. Loosen the ball joint-to-steering knuckle bolt and separate the ball joint from the steering knuckle by prying down on it with a large pry bar.
7. Remove the tie rod end-to-steering knuckle nut and use a ball joint puller to separate the tie rod from the steering knuckle.
8. While supporting the halfshaft, pull the steering knuckle and hub assembly out from the vehicle. After separating the halfshaft from the steering knuckle assembly, support it with a wire.

**NOTE: If the Quantum is equipped with a 5 cylinder engine, connect a wheel puller to the hub flange, then push the halfshaft from the steering knuckle and strut assembly.**

9. Remove the strut assembly from the vehicle.
10. Place a set of parallel rail blocks on an arbor press to support the steering knuckle and strut assembly. Place the steering knuckle and hub assembly on top of the tools with the hub facing down.
11. Stack tools VW-295A, VW-420 and VW-412 or equivalents in order on top of the hub shaft. Press the hub from the steering knuckle and strut assembly.
12. Secure the hub in a vise. Using tools VW-295A and US-1078 or equivalent, pull the inner race from the hub shaft.
13. Remove the internal snaprings from the steering knuckle.
14. With the steering knuckle assembly in the same pressing position, stack tools VW-519, VW-432 and VW-409 or equivalent in order on the bearing. Press the bearing from the steering knuckle and strut assembly.
15. Thoroughly clean all of the parts. Inspect all parts and replace worn or damaged parts.

1. Cotter pin
2. Tie rod
3. Axle driveshaft
4. Circlip
5. Retainer nut
6. Brake caliper
7. Wheel bearing
8. Hub
9. Brake disc
10. Axle nut

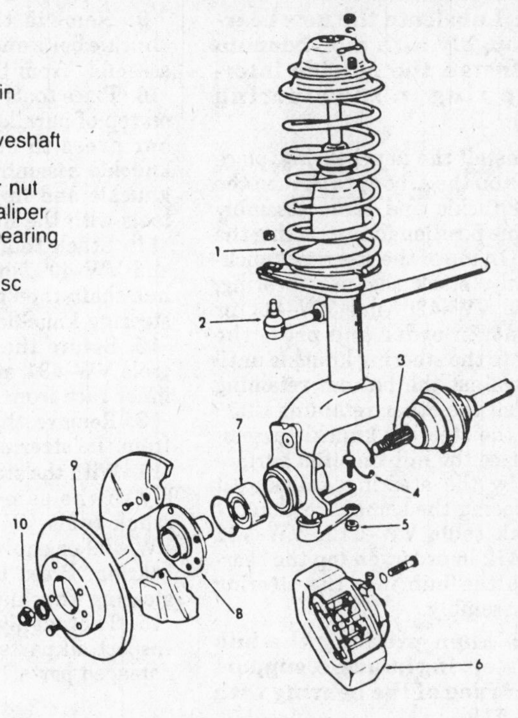


Typical front suspension components

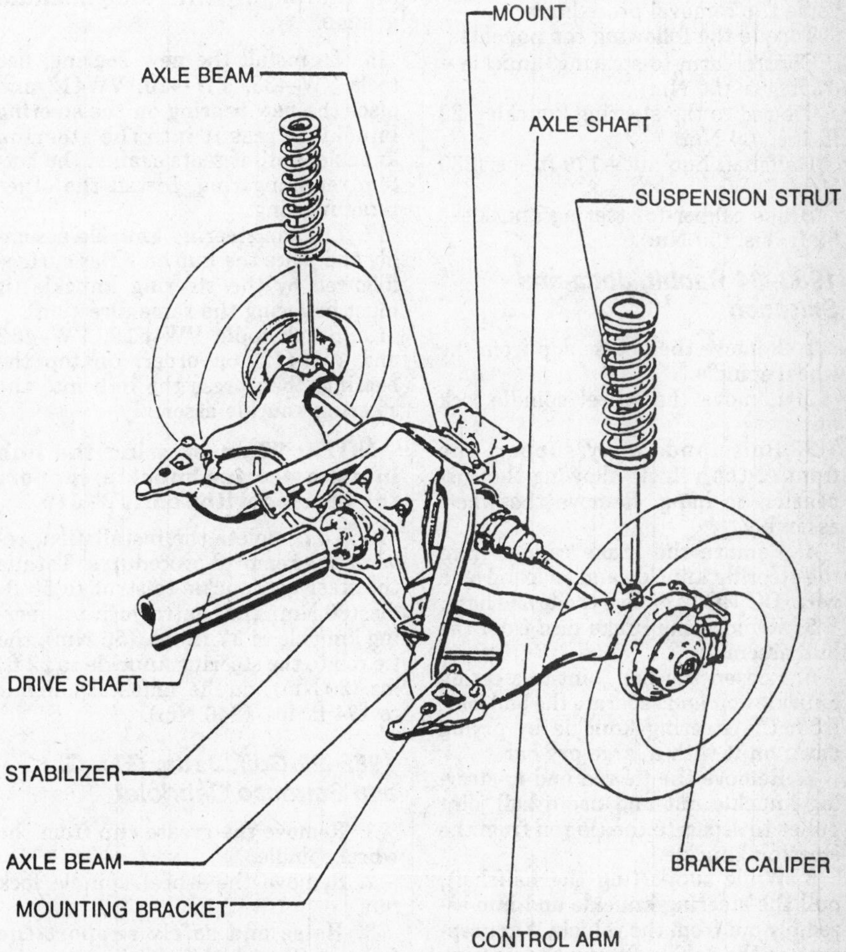


Rear axle and suspension—Quantum Syncro

**NOTE: Lubricate the new bearing thoroughly with molybdenum grease. Install the outside internal snap ring in the steering knuckle.**

16. To install the new bearing, place a flat plate on the arbor press, then the steering knuckle and strut assembly (in the same position for extracting the bearing). On top of the steering knuckle assembly, stack the new bearing, then tools VW–420 and VW–411 or equivalent, in order and press the bearing into the steering knuckle until it seats against the bottom retaining ring. Install the other retaining ring.
17. Lift the steering knuckle assembly and place the hub on a flat surface followed by the steering knuckle (it must be facing the same direction).
18. Stack tools VW–519, VW–432 and VW–412 in order, on top the bearing. Press the hub into the steering knuckle assembly.

**NOTE: When pressing the hub into the steering knuckle, support the inner race of the bearing with tool VW–519.**

19. To complete the installation, reverse the removal procedures.

Torque the following components:

Control arm-to-steering knuckle – 37 ft. lbs. (50 Nm)

Tie rod to the steering knuckle – 22 ft. lbs. (30 Nm)

Halfshaft hub nut – 170 ft. lbs. (230 Nm)

Brake caliper-to-steering knuckle – 52 ft. lbs. (50 Nm).

### *1983–84 Rabbit, Jetta and Scirocco*

1. Remove the grease cup from the wheel spindle.
2. Remove the wheel spindle lock nut.
3. Raise and safely support the front of the vehicle allowing the suspension to hang. Remove the wheel assembly.
4. Remove the brake caliper from the steering knuckle and suspend on a wire, DO NOT remove the brake hose.
5. Remove the brake disc from the hub assembly.
6. Loosen the ball joint-to-steering knuckle bolt and separate the ball joint from the steering knuckle by prying down on it with a large pry bar.
7. Remove the tie rod end-to-steering knuckle nut and use a ball joint puller to separate the tie rod from the steering knuckle.
8. While supporting the halfshaft, pull the steering knuckle and hub assembly out from the vehicle. After separating the halfshaft from the steering knuckle assembly, support it with a wire.
9. Remove the strut-to-steering knuckle bolts and the steering knuckle assembly from the vehicle.
10. Place tools VW–401 and VW–402 on top of parallel rail blocks on an arbor press to support the steering knuckle assembly. Place the steering knuckle and hub assembly on top of tools with the hub facing down.
11. Stack tool VW–418A, VW–421 and VW–409, in order, on top of the hub shaft, then press the hub from the steering knuckle.
12. Secure the hub in a vise. Using tools VW–431 and US–1078, pull the inner race from the hub shaft.
13. Remove the internal snap rings from the steering knuckle.
14. With the steering knuckle assembly in the same pressing position, stack tools VW–519, VW–432 and VW–409 or equivalent in order on the bearing. Press the bearing from the steering knuckle and strut assembly.
15. Thoroughly clean all of the parts. Inspect all parts and replace worn or damaged parts.

**NOTE: Lubricate the new bearing thoroughly with molybdenum grease.**

16. To install the new bearing, use tools VW–433, VW–420, VW412 and place the new bearing on the steering knuckle. Press it into the steering knuckle, until it seats against the bottom retaining ring. Install the other retaining ring.
17. Lift the steering knuckle assembly and place the hub on a flat surface followed by the steering knuckle (it must be facing the same direction).
18. Stack tools VW–519, VW–432 and VW–412, on order, on top the bearing, then press the hub into the steering knuckle assembly.

**NOTE: When pressing the hub into the steering knuckle, support the bearing with tool VW–519.**

19. To complete the installation, reverse the removal procedures. Torque the steering knuckle-to-strut to 59 ft. lbs. (80 Nm), the control arm-to-steering knuckle to 37 ft. lbs. (50 Nm), the tie rod to the steering knuckle to 22 ft. lbs. (30 Nm) and the halfshaft hub nut to 174 ft. lbs. (240 Nm).

### *1985–90 Golf, Jetta, GTI, GLI and Scirocco/Cabriolet*

1. Remove the grease cup from the wheel spindle.
2. Remove the wheel spindle lock nut.
3. Raise and safely support the front of the vehicle allowing the suspension to hang. Remove the wheel assembly.
4. Remove the brake caliper from the steering knuckle and suspend on a wire, DO NOT remove the brake hose.
5. Remove the brake disc and the backing plate from the hub assembly.
6. Loosen the ball joint-to-steering knuckle bolt and separate the ball joint from the steering knuckle by prying down on it with a large pry bar.
7. Remove the tie rod end-to-steering knuckle nut and use a ball joint puller to separate the tie rod from the steering knuckle.
8. While supporting the halfshaft, pull the steering knuckle and hub assembly out from the vehicle. After separating the halfshaft from the steering knuckle assembly, support it with a wire.
9. Remove the strut-to-steering knuckle bolts and the steering knuckle from the vehicle.
10. Place tools VW–401 and 3110 on an arbor press. Place the steering knuckle and hub assembly on top of tool 3110 with the hub facing down inside of the tool.
11. Place tools VW–295 and VW–408A on top of the hub shaft, then press the hub from the steering knuckle.
12. Secure the hub in a vise. Using tool 30–11, pull the inner race from the hub shaft.
13. Remove the internal snap ring from the steering knuckle.
14. With the steering knuckle in the same position on tool 3110, place tools VW–433 and VW–407 on the bearing and press the bearing from the steering knuckle.
15. Thoroughly clean all of the parts. If worn or damaged parts are present, replace them with new ones.

**NOTE: Lubricate the new bearing thoroughly with molybdenum grease.**

16. To install the new bearing, place tools VW–401, VW–402 and VW–459/2 on the arbor press. Place the steering knuckle on tool VW–459/2 with large opening facing upward.
17. Place the new bearing on the steering knuckle and tools VW–472/1 and VW–412 on top of the bearing, then press the bearing into the steering knuckle until it seats. Install the internal locking ring and the inner race.
18. Replace tool VW–459/2 with tool VW–519, place the hub on top of bearing and press the hub into the steering knuckle.

**NOTE: When pressing the hub into the steering knuckle, support the bearing.**

19. To complete the installation, reverse the removal procedures. Torque

the steering knuckle-to-strut to 59 ft. lbs. (80 Nm), the control arm-to-steering knuckle to 37 ft. lbs. (50 Nm), the tie rod to the steering knuckle to 26 ft. lbs. (35 Nm) and the halfshaft hub nut to 170 ft. lbs. (230 Nm).

# FRONT SUSPENSION

## MacPherson Strut

### REMOVAL & INSTALLATION

#### *Fox and Quantum*

1. With the car on the ground, remove the front axle nut. Loosen the wheel bolts.
2. Raise and support the front of the car. Remove the wheels.
3. Remove the brake caliper from the strut and hang it with wire. Detach the brake line clips from the strut.
4. At the tie rod end, remove the cotter pin, back off the castellated nut and pull the end off the strut with a puller.
5. Loosen the stabilizer bar bushings and detach the end from the strut being removed.
6. Remove the ball joint from the strut.
7. Pull the halfshaft from the strut.
8. Remove the upper strut-to-fender retaining nuts.
9. Pull the strut assembly down and out of the car.
10. Installation is the reverse of removal.

Torque the following components:

Axle nut—145 ft. lbs. (196 Nm) (M 18 nut) or 175 ft. lbs. (237 Nm) (M 20 nut)

Ball joint-to-strut nut to 25 ft. lbs. (34 Nm) (M8 nut) or 36 ft. lbs. (49 Nm) (M10 nut)

Caliper-to-strut bolts—44 ft. lbs. (60 Nm)

Stabilizer-to-control arm bolts—7 ft. lbs. (9 Nm)

#### *1983–84 Rabbit, Jetta and Scirocco*

1. Remove the brake hose from the strut clip.
2. Mark the position of the camber adjustment bolts before removing them from the hub (wheel bearing housing). These bolts also serve as the lower strut mounting bolts.
3. Remove the upper mounting nuts and remove the strut from the car.
4. Installation is the reverse of removal. The upper nuts are tightened to 14 ft. lbs. (19 Nm) and the adjusting bolt (upper) to hub to 58 ft. lbs. ( 80 Nm). Tighten the lower adjusting bolt-to-hub to 43 ft. lbs. (58 Nm). Use new washers on the lower bolts. If the shock absorber was replaced, camber will have to be adjusted.

#### *1985–90 Golf, Jetta, GTI, GLI, Scirocco and Cabriolet*

1. Raise and support the front of the vehicle. Remove the wheel if necessary.
2. Mark the position of the lower strut bolts before removing them from the steering knuckle.
3. Remove the upper mounting nut and the strut from the vehicle.

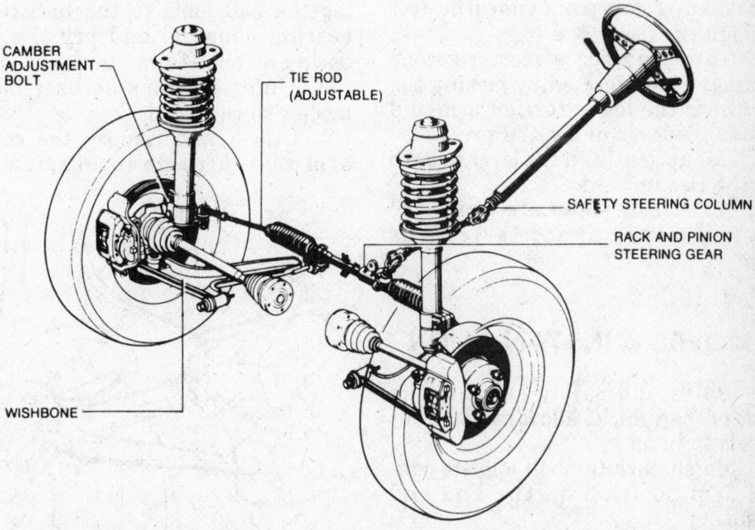


Typical Rabbit, Jetta, Scirocco steering and front suspension components

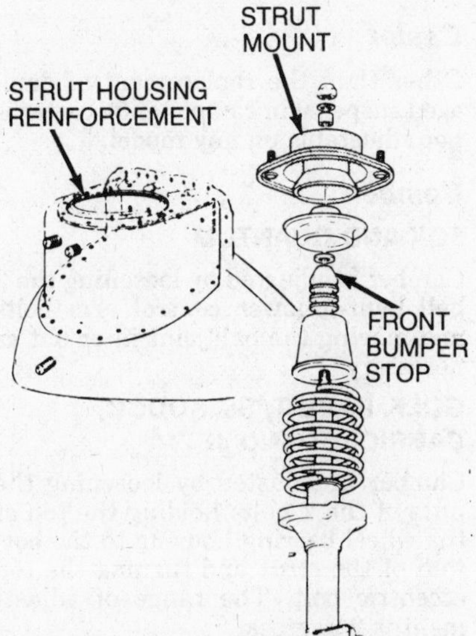


Front strut and mounting—GTI

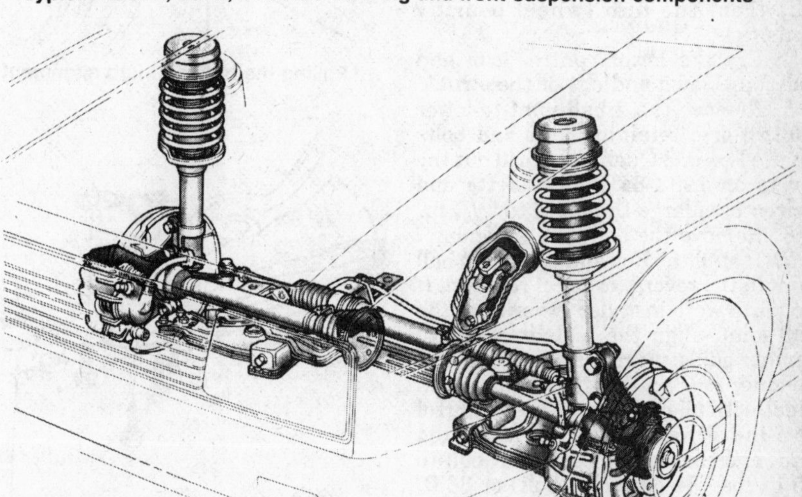

View of the front suspension system for 1985 and later models—except Quantum

4. To install, reverse the removal procedures. Torque the strut-to-body nut to 44 ft. lbs. (60 Nm) and the strut-to-steering knuckle bolts to 59 ft. lbs. (80 Nm).

### OVERHAUL

**For all spring and shock absorber removal and installation procedures and all overhaul procedures, please refer to "Strut Overhaul" in the Unit Repair section.**

## Ball Joints

### INSPECTION

1. A quick initial inspection can be made with the vehicle on the ground.
2. If the ball joints are excessively worn, there will be an audible tap as the ball moves around in its socket. Excess play can sometimes be felt through the tire.
3. On all models, a more rigorous test may be performed by jacking the car under the lower torsion arm and inserting a lever under the tire.
4. Lift up gently on the lever so as to pry the tire upward.
5. If the ball joints are worn, the tire will move upward ⅛–¼ in. or more.

### REMOVAL & INSTALLATION

1. Raise and safely support the front of the vehicle, allowing the front wheels to hang.
2. Matchmark the ball joint-to-control arm position on the Fox and Quantum.
3. Remove the retaining bolt and nut from the hub (wheel bearing housing).
4. Pry the lower control arm and ball joint down and out of the strut.
5. Remove the 2 ball joint-to-lower control arm retaining nuts and bolts on the Fox and Quantum. Drill out the rivets on 1983–84 Rabbit, Jetta and Scirocco; enlarge the holes to $^{21}/_{64}$ in.
6. Remove the ball joint assembly.
7. Install the Fox and Quantum ball joint in the reverse order of removal. If no parts were installed other than the ball joint, align the matchmarks. No camber adjustment is necessary if this is done. Pull the ball joint into alignment with pliers. Tighten the 2 control arm-to-ball joint bolts to 47 ft. lbs. (64 Nm) and the strut-to-ball joint bolt to 25 ft. lbs. (34 Nm) (M8 bolt) or 36 ft. lbs. (49 Nm) (M10 bolt).
8. On all other models bolt the new ball joint in place. Torque the bolts to 18 ft. lbs. (25 Nm). Tighten the retaining bolt for the ball joint stud to 37 ft. lbs. (50 Nm).

## Lower Control Arm

### REMOVAL & INSTALLATION

#### *All Models Except 1985–90 Golf, Jetta, Scirocco and Cabriolet*

**NOTE: When removing the left side (driver's side) control arm on 1983–84 Rabbit, Jetta and Scirocco models equipped with an automatic transmission, remove the front left engine mounting nut, remove the nut for the rear mounting, remove the engine mounting support and raise the engine to expose the front control arm bolt.**

1. Raise and safely support the vehicle. Remove the wheel.
2. Remove the nut and bolt attaching the ball joint to the hub (wheel bearing housing) and pry the joint down and out of the hub.
3. Unfasten the stabilizer bar on models so equipped.
4. Unbolt and remove the control arm-to-subframe (crossmember) mounting bolts on the Fox or Quantum. On the 1983–84 Rabbit, Jetta and Scirocco, remove the control arm mounting bolts from the frame.
5. Remove the control arm.
6. Installation is the reverse of removal.

Torque the following components:

Fox or Quantum control arm-to-subframe bolts – 44 ft. lbs. (60 Nm)

1983–84 Rabbit, Jetta and Scirocco control arm-to-frame front bolt – 50 ft. lbs. (68 Nm)

Bushing clamp bolts – 32 ft. lbs. (43 Nm)

Ball joint-to-hub bolt – 21 ft. lbs. (28 Nm) on the Rabbit, Jetta and Scirocco and to 25 ft. lbs. (34 Nm) (M 8 nut) or 36 ft. lbs. (48 Nm) (M 10 nut).

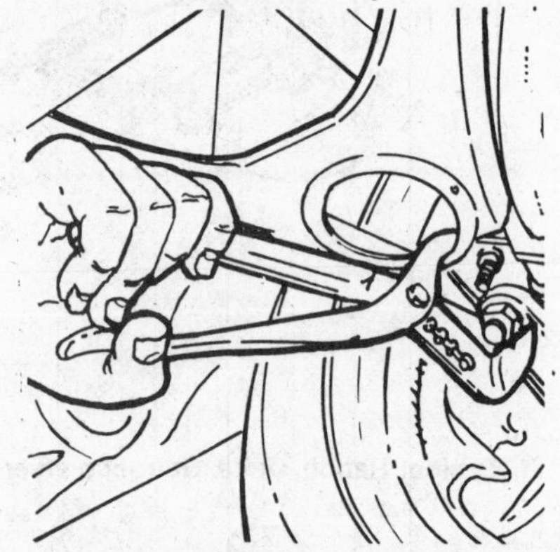

Pulling the ball joint into alignment

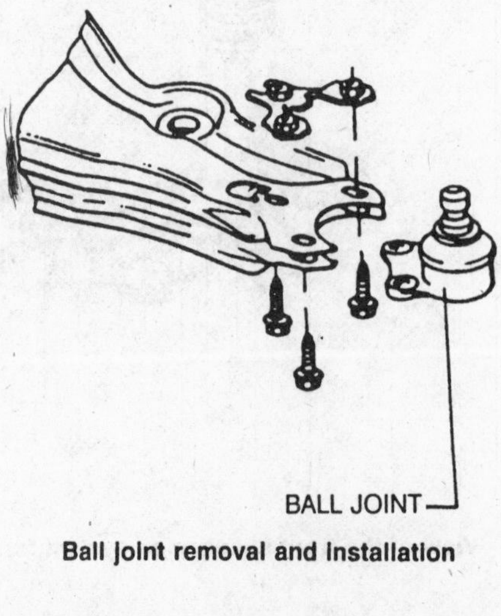


Ball joint removal and installation

#### *1985–90 Golf, Jetta and Scirocco/Cabriolet*

1. Separate the ball joint from the steering knuckle.

**NOTE: If replacing the lower control arm, separate the ball joint from the control arm.**

2. If equipped, remove the stabilizer bar from the control arm.
3. Remove the control arm-to-subframe bolts and the control arm from the vehicle.
4. To install, reverse the removal procedures. Torque the control arm-to-subframe to 96 ft. lbs. (130 Nm), the stabilizer-to-control arm to 18 ft. lbs. (25 Nm) or the ball joint-to-steering knuckle to 37 ft. lbs. (50 Nm).

## Front Wheel Alignment

### ADJUSTMENT

#### *Caster*

Other than the replacement of damaged suspension components, caster is not adjustable on any model.

#### *Camber*

##### FOX AND QUANTUM

Camber is adjusted by loosening the 2 ball joint-to-lower control arm bolts and moving the ball joint in or out as necessary.

##### GOLF, RABBIT, SCIROCCO, CABRIOLET AND JETTA

Camber is adjusted by loosening the nuts of the 2 bolts holding the top of the wheel bearing housing to the bottom of the strut and turning the top eccentric bolt. The range of adjustment is 2 degrees.

On models from 1985 the original top bolt can be replaced with a long shank bolt (N903334.01) and adjusted after the new bolt is installed – if more adjustment is necessary the lower bolt can also be replaced with a new one.

### *Toe-In*

#### QUANTUM

Toe-in is checked with the wheels straight ahead. The left tie rod is adjustable. Loosen the nuts and clamps and adjust the length of the tie rod for correct toe-out. If the steering wheel is crooked, remove and align it.

#### FOX

**NOTE: Steering gear tool 3075 must be used to adjust toe on vehicles with 2 adjustable tie rods.**

1. Turn the steering gear to the center position.
2. Remove the front bolt from the steering gear cover.
3. Attach centering tool VW-3075 or equivalent with the bracket over the mounting nut on the left tie rod.
4. Remove the bolt from the spacer on the chain of the centering tool.
5. Put the spacer under the hole marked with an **L** and insert a bolt through this hole and the hole in the spacer, then tighten to the steering gear.
6. Measure and divide the total toe in half.
7. Loosen the clamps and outer lock nut on both sides.
8. Turn both tie rods until the specified setting for Toe is reached.
9. Tighten the clamps and lock nuts on the tie rods.
10. Check and reposition steering wheel in center position if necessary.
11. Remove the centering tool and tighten the front bolt to 15 ft. lbs. (20 Nm).
12. If the steering wheel is crooked after the toe adjustment has been made, remove, straighten and reinstall the wheel.

#### GOLF, RABBIT, SCIROCCO, CABRIOLET AND JETTA

Toe-in is checked with the wheels straight ahead. Only the right tie rod is adjustable, but replacement left tie rods are adjustable. Replacement left tie rods should be set to the same length as the original. Toe-in should be adjusted only with the right tie rod. If the steering wheel is crooked, remove and align it.

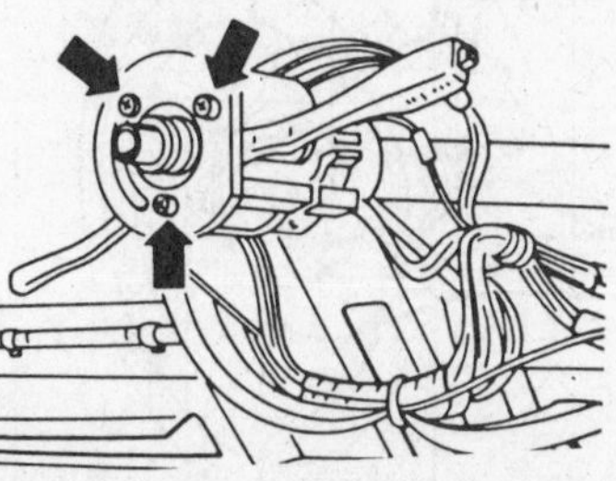

**Removing the steering column switches on the 1985 and later Quantum**

# REAR SUSPENSION

## MacPherson Strut

### REMOVAL & INSTALLATION

#### *Golf, Fox, Rabbit, Jetta, GTI, Scirocco and Cabriolet*

1. Raise and support the rear of the vehicle.
2. Support the axle, but do not put any load on the springs.
3. Remove the rubber guard from inside the car.
4. Remove the nut, washer and mounting disc.
5. Unbolt the strut assembly from the rear axle and remove it.
6. To install reverse the removal procedures. Torque the strut-to-body nut to 44 ft. lbs. (60 Nm) and strut-to-axle bolt to 59 ft. lbs. (80 Nm).

#### *Quantum*

1. Remove the shock strut cover inside car.
2. Unscrew the strut from the body.
3. Slowly lift the vehicle until the wheels are slightly off the ground.
4. Unscrew the strut from the axle.
5. Take the strut out of the lower mounting. Press the wheel down slightly when removing the strut.

**CAUTION**

***Do not remove both suspension struts at the same time as this will overload the axle beam bushings.***

6. Guide the strut out carefully between the wheel and the wheel housing. Do not damage the paint on the spring and wheel housing.

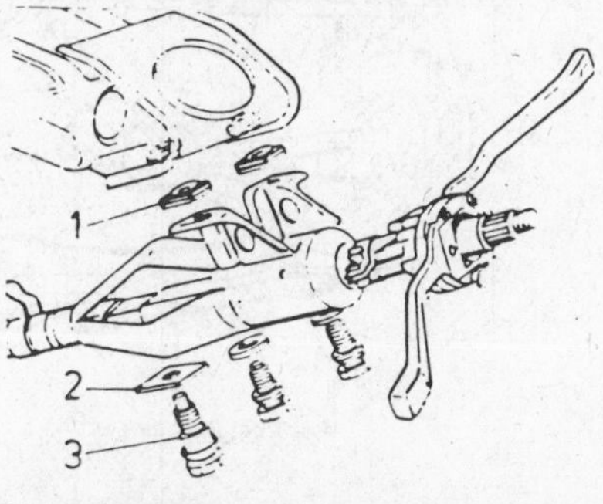


**Removing the steering column mounting parts for 1985 and later Jetta**

7. To install reverse the removal procedures. Torque the strut-to-body to 26 ft. lbs. (35 Nm) and the strut-to-axle to 52 ft. lbs. (70 Nm).

### OVERHAUL

**For all spring and shock absorber removal and installation procedures and all overhaul procedures, please refer to "Strut Overhaul" in the Unit Repair section.**

## Rear Wheel Bearings

### ADJUSTMENT

1. Remove the grease cap from the rear wheel hub.
2. Remove the cotter pin from the spindle and the spindle nut.
3. While turning the wheel, by hand, in the forward direction, tighten the spindle nut to 12 ft. lbs.

**NOTE: The tightening procedure will remove any grease or burrs which could cause excessive wheel bearing play.**

4. Back-off the nut to the "just loose" position.
5. Hand tighten the spindle nut and loosen it until 1 of the spindle holes aligns with a slot in the nut.
6. Install a new cotter pin and bend the ends around the nut.
7. The wheel should move freely without binding.

# STEERING

## Steering Wheel

### REMOVAL & INSTALLATION

1. Disconnect the negative battery cable.
2. The center cover pad may be pulled from the wheel on most models (cover varies depending on model), or is attached by screws from the back of the steering wheel.
3. Disconnect the horn wire.
4. Loosen and remove the steering shaft nut.

**NOTE: Mark the steering shaft and steering wheel so that the wheel may be installed in the same position on the shaft.**

5. Using a steering wheel puller, remove the wheel from the splined steering shaft. Do not strike the end of the steering shaft.

6. Replace the wheel in the reverse order of removal. Make sure to align the matchmarks made on the steering wheel and steering shaft.

7. On the Golf, Rabbit, Jetta, GTI, GLI, Scirocco and Cabriolet, install the steering wheel with the road wheels straight ahead and the canceling lug pointing to the left. On the Fox and Quantum, with the road wheels straight ahead, the canceling lug on the steering wheel must point to the right and the turn signal lever must be in the neutral position.

8. The gap between the turn signal switch housing and the back of the wheel is 0.08–0.159 in. Install the switch with the lever in the neutral position. Tighten the steering shaft nut to 30 ft. lbs. (40 Nm) for 1985–90, Golf, Jetta, Scirocco and Cabriolet or 36 ft. lbs. (49 Nm) for all other models.

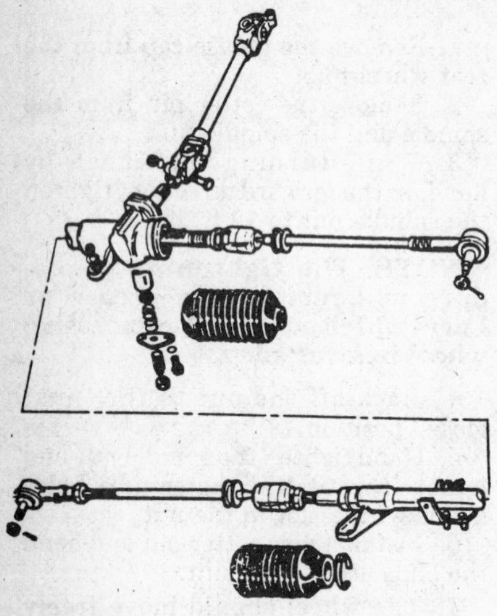

Rabbit, Jetta, Scirocco steering gear

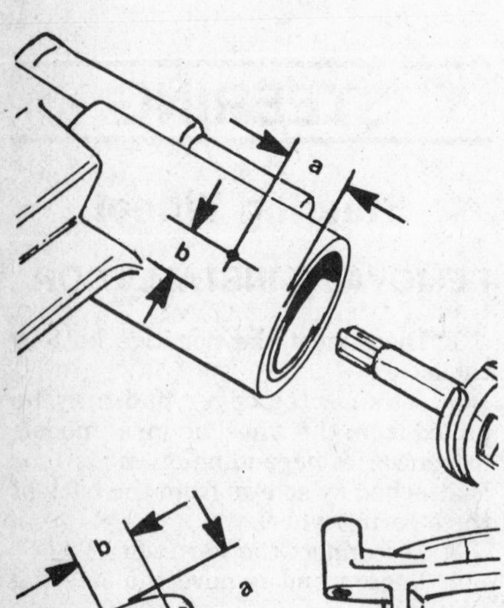

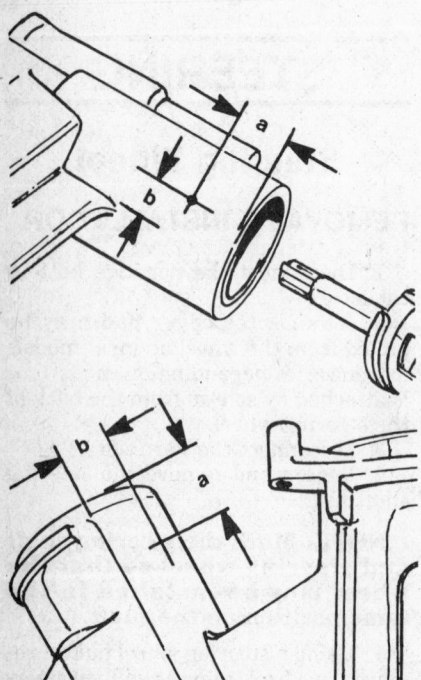


Dimensions for drilling ignition lock cylinder hole (if not equipped)

## Combination Switch

### REMOVAL & INSTALLATION

1. Disconnect the negative battery cable.
2. Remove the steering wheel.
3. Remove the 4 turn signal switch securing screws.
4. Disconnect the turn signal switch wiring plug under the steering column.
5. Pull the switch and wiring guide rail up and out of the steering column.
6. To install, slide the switch and wiring into position. Connect the turn signal connector under the steering column. Install the retaining screws. Make sure the spacers located behind the switch, if installed originally, are in position. The distance between the steering wheel and the steering column housing is 0.08–0.159. Install the switch with the lever on the central position.

## Ignition Switch

### REMOVAL & INSTALLATION

1. Disconnect the negative battery terminal.
2. Remove the steering wheel.
3. Loosen the mounting screws and then remove the upper and lower steering column trim.
4. Unscrew the 4 retaining bolts and then pull off the steering column switch.
5. Loosen the steering lock housing clamp bolt and pull the assembly up and out slightly.
6. Disconnect the wiring and remove the steering lock housing.
7. Unscrew the ignition switch screw and pull out the switch.
8. Installation is in the reverse order of removal.
9. Check the operation of the switch.

## Ignition Lock Cylinder

### REMOVAL & INSTALLATION

On some models, the hole in the lock body for removing the steering lock cylinder was not drilled by Volkswagen. To make the hole, use the following measurements. Drill the hole where **A** and **B** intersect on the lock body. The hole should be drilled ⅛ in. deep.

a – 12mm (0.472 in.)
b – 10mm (0.393 in.)

Remove the lock cylinder by pushing a small drill bit or piece of wire into the hole and pulling the cylinder out.

## Ignition Lock Body

### REMOVAL & INSTALLATION

1. Remove the steering wheel and turn signal switch. Remove the steering column shaft covers.

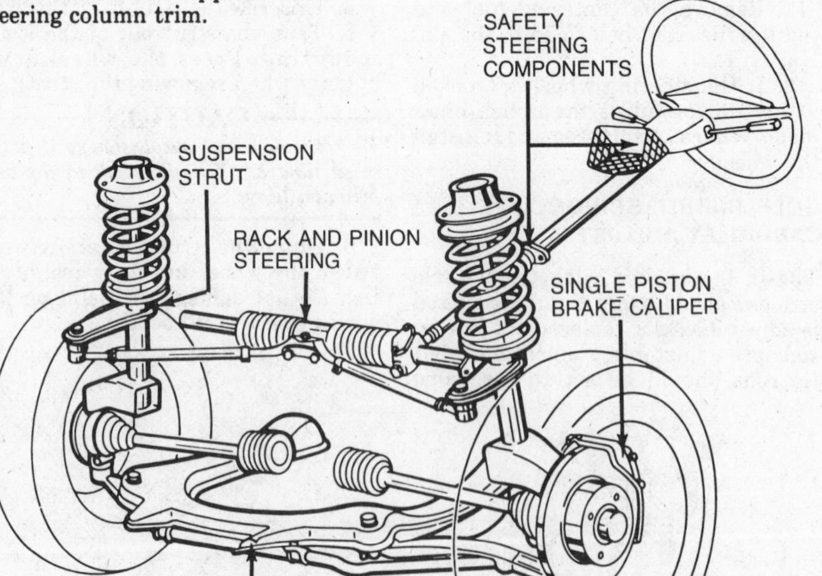


Fox front suspension and steering components – Quantum similar

2. The lock is clamped to the steering column with special bolts whose heads shear off on installation. These must be drilled out in order to remove the switch.

3. To install, attach the lock body to the column using breakaway screws. Install the turn signal switch and steering wheel, make sure that the lock tang is aligned with the slot in the steering column.

## Manual Steering Gear

### REMOVAL & INSTALLATION

#### Fox and Quantum

1. Pry off the lock plate and remove both tie rod mounting bolts from the steering rack, inside the engine compartment. Pry the tie rods out of the mounting pivot.
2. Remove the lower instrument panel trim.
3. Remove the shaft clamp bolt, pry off the clip and drive the shaft toward the inside of the car with a brass drift.
4. Remove the steering gear mounting bolts.
5. Turn the wheels all the way to the right and remove the steering gear through the opening in the right wheelhousing.
6. For installation, temporarily install the tie rod mounting pivot to the rack with both mounting bolts. Remove 1 bolt, install the tie rod and replace the bolt. Do the same on the other tie rod. Make sure to install a new lockplate. Torque the tie rod bolts to 39 ft. lbs. (53 Nm), the mounting pivot bolt to 15 ft. lbs. (20 Nm) and the steering gear-to-body mounting bolts to 15 ft. lbs.

#### 1983–84 Rabbit, Jetta and Scirocco

1. Disconnect the steering shaft universal joint and wire up out of the way.
2. Disconnect the tie rods at the steering rack and wire up and out of the way.
3. Remove the steering rack and drive.
4. Install the steering rack and drive and torque the attaching hardware to 14 ft. lbs. (19 Nm).
5. Set the steering rack with equal distances between the housing on the right side and left side.
6. Install the tie rods and screw both sides to the measurements shown in the illustration.
7. Tighten the steering gear adjusting screw until it touches the thrust washer. Tighten the locknut.
8. Install the steering shaft.
9. Check the front end alignment.

#### 1985–90 Golf, Jetta, GTI, GLI, Scirocco and Cabriolet

1. Raise and support the front of the vehicle on jackstands.
2. At the steering gear, pull back the tie rod boot from the steering gear, remove the lock ring and separate the tie rod from the steering gear.

**NOTE: After the tie rod has been removed from the steering gear, support it on a piece of wire.**

3. At the steering rod-to-steering gear junction, pull back the boot and remove the steering rod-to-steering gear retaining bolt, then separate the steering rod from the steering gear.
4. Remove the 4 steering gear-to-subframe clamp nuts, the clamps and the steering gear from the vehicle.
5. To install, reverse the removal procedures. Torque the steering gear clamp nuts and the steering rod-to-steering gear retaining bolt to 22 ft. lbs. (30 Nm).

### ADJUSTMENT

1. Raise and support the vehicle on jackstands, then turn the wheels to the straight ahead position.
2. On the side of the steering gear, turn the adjusting nut 20 degrees clockwise.
3. Road test to see if the steering is binding.

**NOTE: If the steering is binding, turn the bolt counterclockwise; if the steering is not binding increase the clockwise rotation of the bolt.**

4. The correct adjustment is achieved when the steering is free and not binding.

## Power Steering Gear

### REMOVAL & INSTALLATION

#### Fox and Quantum

1. Pry off the lock plate and remove both tie rod mounting bolts from the steering rack, inside the engine compartment. Pry the tie rods out of the mounting pivot.
2. Remove the lower instrument panel trim.
3. Remove the shaft clamp bolt, pry off the clip and drive the shaft toward the inside of the car with a brass drift.
4. Disconnect the power steering lines. Remove the steering gear mounting bolts.
5. Turn the wheels all the way to the right and remove the steering gear through the opening in the right wheelhousing.
6. To install, temporarily install the tie rod mounting pivot to the rack with both mounting bolts. Remove 1 bolt, install the tie rod and replace the bolt. Do the same on the other tie rod. Make sure to install a new lockplate. Torque the tie rod bolts to 39 ft. lbs. (53 Nm), the mounting pivot bolt to 15 ft. lbs. (20 Nm) and the steering gear-to-body mounting bolts to 15 ft. lbs.

#### 1985–90 Golf, Jetta, GTI, GLI, Scirocco and Cabriolet

1. Raise and safely support the vehicle on.
2. Remove the suction hose at the power steering pump and the pressure lines from the steering gear.

**NOTE: Place a catch pan under the power steering pump suction hose to catch the fluid when removing the power steering lines, then discard the fluid.**

3. At the tie rod ends, loosen the tie rod lock nuts, mark the position of the tie rod to the tie rod end. Unscrew the tie rod from the tie rod ends, count and record the number of turns necessary to remove the rods (for installation purposes).
4. At the steering rod-to-steering gear junction, pull back the boot and remove the clamping bolts, then separate the steering rod from the steering gear.
5. Remove the steering gear-to-subframe clamp nuts, the clamps and the steering gear assembly from the vehicle.

**NOTE: If it is necessary to remove the tie rods from the steering gear, place the assembly in a vise, pull back the boot and separate the tie rod from the steering gear.**

6. Connect the engine support tool VW-10-222A or equivalent, to the engine and transaxle assembly, remove the engine and transaxle mount bolts, raise the engine-to-transaxale assembly to remove the steering gear assembly.

**NOTE: To remove the steering gear assembly, the left wheel may have to be removed.**

7. To install, use new O-rings at the pressure hose connections and reverse the removal procedures. Torque the pressure hose-to-steering gear fittings to 15 ft. lbs. (20 Nm), the steering gear clamp nuts and the steering rod-to-steering gear retaining bolt to 22 ft. lbs. (30 Nm). Fill the reservoir with approved power steering fluid and bleed the system.

### ADJUSTMENTS

1. Remove the power steering gear.
2. Loosen the crown nut at the adjusting bolt on the side of the steering gear.
3. Using tool VW-524 or equivalent, turn the adjusting nut until the rack can be moved by hand without binding.
4. Hold the adjusting nut securely and tighten the crown nut.
5. To install, use new O-rings at the pressure hose connections and reverse the removal procedures. Torque the pressure hose-to-steering gear fittings to 15 ft. lbs. (20 Nm), the steering gear clamp nuts and the steering rod-to-steering gear retaining bolt to 22 ft. lbs. (30 Nm). Fill the reservoir with approved power fluid and bleed the system.

## Power Steering Pump

### REMOVAL & INSTALLATION

1. Place a catch pan under the power steering pump to catch the fluid.
2. Remove the suction hose and the pressure line from the pump, drain the fluid into the catch pan (discard the fluid).
3. Loosen the tensioning bolt at the front of the tensioning bracket and remove the drive belt from the pump's drive pulley.
4. Remove the pump's mounting bolts and lift the pump from the vehicle.
5. To install, reverse the removal procedures. Torque the mounting bolts to 15 ft. lbs. (20 Nm). Tension the drive belt. Fill the reservoir with approved power steering fluid and bleed the system.

### BELT ADJUSTMENT

**NOTE: To tension the drive belt, adjust the tensioner bolt, so that the belt will flex ½ in. under light thumb pressure.**

### SYSTEM BLEEDING

1. With the wheels turned all the way to the left, add power steering fluid to the **COLD** mark on the fluid level indicator.
2. Start the engine and run at fast idle momentarily, shut engine **OFF** and recheck fluid level. If necessary add fluid to to bring level to the **COLD** mark.
3. Start the engine and bleed the system by turning the wheels from side to side without hitting the stops.

**NOTE: Fluid with air in it has a light tan or red appearance.**

4. Return the wheels to the center position and keep the engine running for 2 or 3 minutes.
5. Road test the car and recheck the fluid level making sure it is at the **HOT** mark.

## Tie Rod Ends

### REMOVAL & INSTALLATION

#### *Fox and Quantum*

1. Raise the car and remove the front wheels.
2. Disconnect the outer end of the steering tie rod from the steering knuckle by removing the cotter pin and nut and pressing out the tie rod end. A small puller or press is required to free the tie rod end.
3. Under the hood, pry off the lockplate and remove the mounting bolts from both tie rod inner ends. Pry the tie rod out of the mounting pivot.
4. First install the mounting pivot to the rack with both mounting bolts. Remove 1 bolt, install the tie rod and replace the bolt. Do the same on the other tie rod. Be sure to install a new lockplate. The inner tie rod end bolts should be torqued to 40 ft. lbs. (54 Nm).
5. If replacing, both tie rods on the Fox, or the adjustable left tie rod on the Quantum, adjust it to the same length as the old one(s). Check the toe in.
6. Use new cotter pins when installing the outer tie rod ends. Torque the nut to 22 ft. lbs. (30 Nm).

#### *1983–84 Rabbit, Jetta and Scirocco*

1. Center the steering rack.
2. Remove the cotter pin and nut from the tie rod end.
3. Disconnect the tie rod from the steering rack.
4. If the left side tie rod is being replaced , adjust it to 14.92 in. (379mm).
5. Adjust the steering rack and tie rods.
6. Tighten the tie rod end retaining nut to 21 ft. lbs. (28 Nm) and install a new cotter pin.

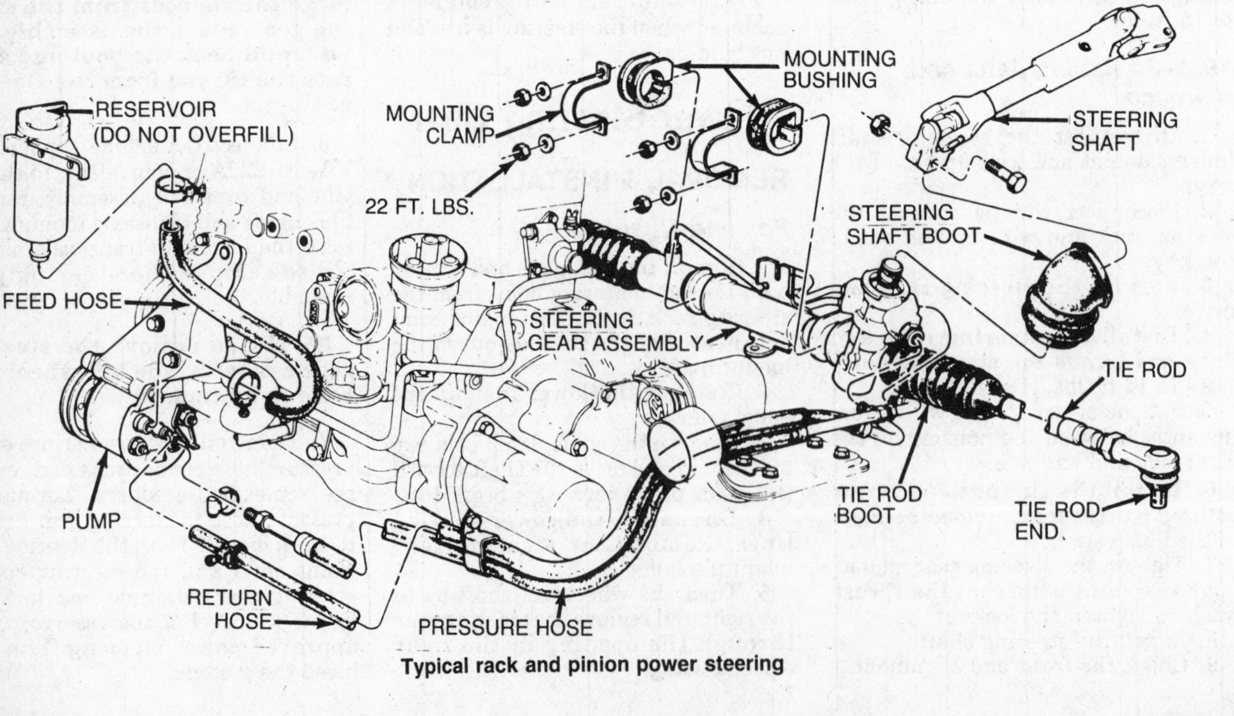

Typical rack and pinion power steering

### *1985–90 Golf, Jetta, GTI, GLI and Scirocco/Cabriolet*

1. Raise and safely support the vehicle.

**NOTE: If equipped with manual steering, the left tie rod is nonadjustable and must be removed from the steering knuckle. To separate the ball joint from the steering knuckle, remove the locking nut, use a ball joint puller to pull the ball joint from the steering knuckle.**

2. At the tie rod ends, loosen the tie rod lock nuts, mark the position of the tie rod to the tie rod end. Unscrew the tie rod from the tie rod ends, count and record the number of turns necessary to remove the rods (for installation purposes).
3. At the steering rod-to-steering gear junction, pull back the boot and remove the clamping bolts, then separate the steering rod from the steering gear.
4. To install, reverse the removal procedures. Torque the ball joint-to-steering knuckle to 26 ft. lbs. (35 Nm).

# BRAKES

**For all brake system repair and service procedures not detailed below, please refer to "Brakes" in the Unit Repair section.**

## Master Cylinder

### REMOVAL & INSTALLATION

1. Disconnect and plug the brake lines.
2. Disconnect the electrical plug from the sending unit for the brake failure switch.
3. Remove the 2 master cylinder mounting nuts.
4. Lift the master cylinder and reservoir out of the engine compartment.

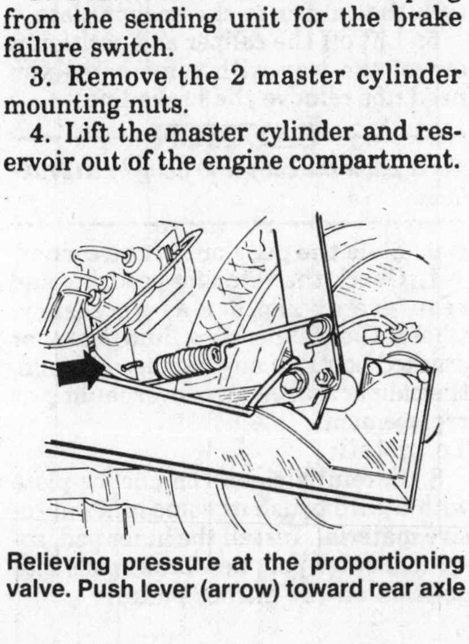

**Relieving pressure at the proportioning valve. Push lever (arrow) toward rear axle**

**CAUTION**

***Do not depress the brake pedal while the master cylinder, front brake discs or drum brake shoes are removed.***

5. Position the master cylinder and reservoir assembly onto the mounting studs on the booster and install the washers and nuts. Tighten the nuts to 15 ft. lbs. (20 Nm).
6. Remove the plugs and connect the brake lines.
7. Bleed the entire brake system.

## Proportioning Valve

### REMOVAL & INSTALLATION

1. Raise the rear of the vehicle and support it safely.
2. Using a brake line wrench, loosen the lines to the proportioning valve.
3. Remove the retaining nuts that secure the proportioning valve to the frame.
4. Installation is the reverse of removal.
5. Bleed the brake system.

## Power Brake Booster

### REMOVAL & INSTALLATION

1. Remove the master cylinder from in front of the booster.
2. In the driver's compartment, remove the clevis pin on the end of the booster pushrod by unclipping it and pulling it out of the clevis.
3. On the gasoline engine models, remove the vacuum line running from the booster to intake manifold. On diesel engines, the line connects to a vacuum pump located where the distributor on a gasoline engine would be. Remove the line.
4. On the Rabbit, Jetta, Scirocco and Cabriolet, unbolt the booster bracket where it connects to the firewall. On the Fox and Quantum remove the 2 nuts from inside the driver's compartment, or the 4 nuts holding the booster to its bracket. Remove the booster.
5. The brake booster cannot be repaired and must be replaced as a unit.
6. Installation is the reverse of removal.
7. Install the master cylinder and bleed the system.

## Vacuum Pump

### REMOVAL & INSTALLATION

#### *Diesel Engines*

One line of the vacuum pump runs to the power brake booster and the other line runs to the engine. Unclamp and remove both lines. Unbolt and remove the pump. The diaphragm inside the pump is replaceable. Remove the screws holding the vacuum hose inlet cover to the pump body and remove the cover. Unscrew the retaining nut and remove the diaphragm. Install the new diaphragm with the molded center toward the top. Don't overtighten the retaining nut.

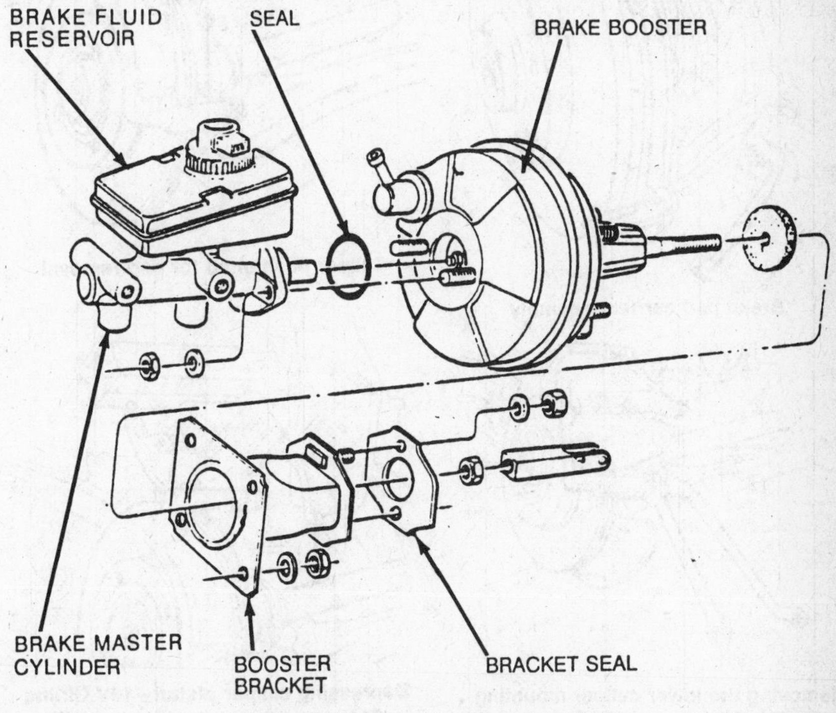


**Master cylinder and booster assembly**

## Disc Brake Pads

### REMOVAL & INSTALLATION

#### *Front Disc Brakes*

**ALL EXCEPT 1989–90 16V MODELS AND FOX**

1. Raise and support the front of the vehicle safely. Remove the wheels.
2. Siphon a sufficient quantity of brake fluid from the master cylinder reservoir to prevent the brake fluid from overflowing the master cylinder when removing or installing new pads. This is necessary as the piston must be forced into the cylinder bore to provide sufficient clearance to remove the pads.
3. Remove the caliper mounting bolts. Push the caliper up and swing it out from the bottom. Position the caliper out of the way and support it with wire so that it doesn't hang by the brake line.
4. Remove the pads from the pad carrier. Remove any shims or shields behind the pads and note their positions.

**To install:**

5. Install the anti-rattle hardware and then the pads (in their proper positions!).
6. Using a suitable tool, push the caliper piston into the bore.
7. Install any pad shims.
8. Reposition the caliper and tighten the caliper mounting bolts.
9. Refill the master cylinder with fresh brake fluid.
10. Install the wheels and then pump the brake pedal several times to bring the pads into adjustment. Road test the vehicle.

**NOTE: If a firm pedal cannot be obtained, bleed the system.**

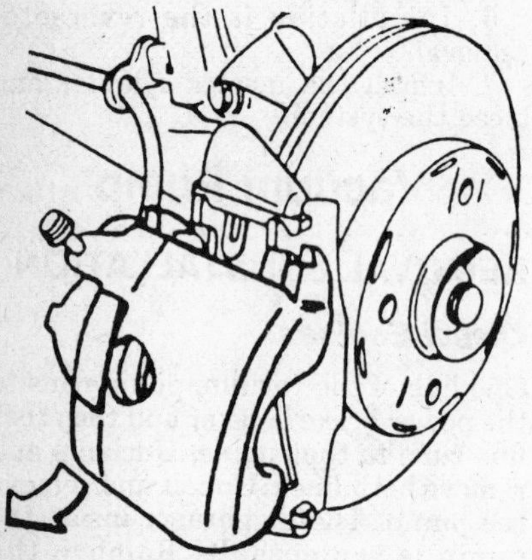

Removing/installing the caliper assembly.

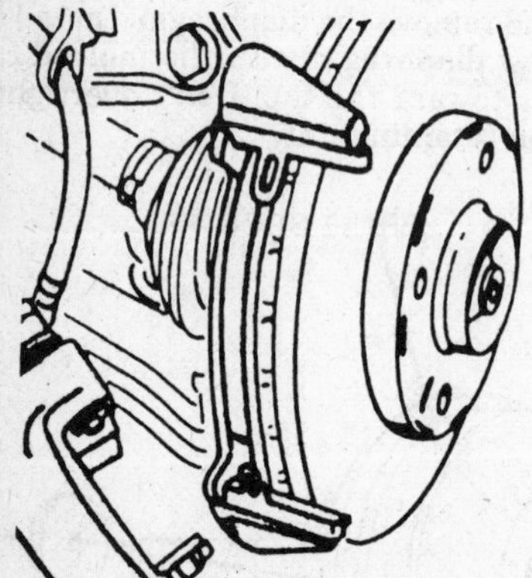

Brake pad carrier assembly

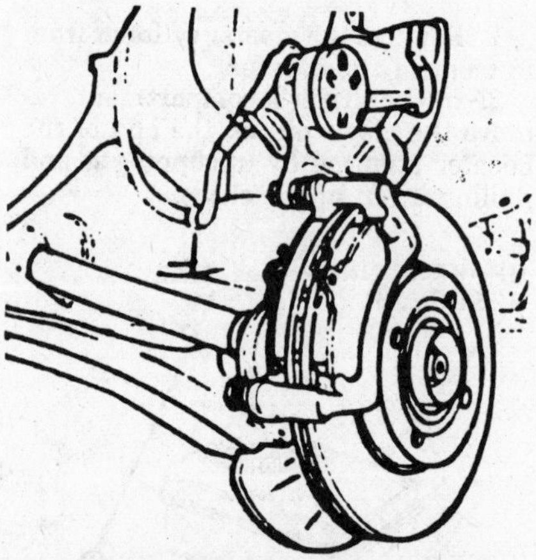

Caliper positioned for pad removal

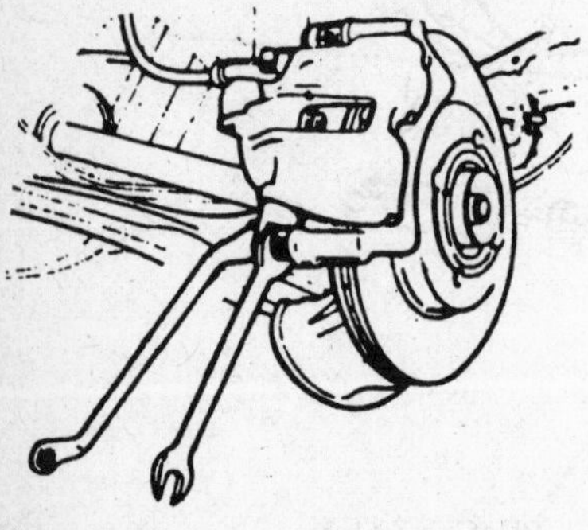

Removing the lower caliper mounting bolt—16V Girling caliper

Depressing caliper piston—16V Girling caliper

**1989–90 16V MODELS**

1. Raise and support the front of the vehicle safely. Remove the wheels.
2. Siphon a sufficient quantity of brake fluid from the master cylinder reservoir to prevent the brake fluid from overflowing the master cylinder when removing or installing new pads. This is necessary as the piston must be forced into the cylinder bore to provide sufficient clearance to remove the pads.
3. Remove the lower caliper mounting bolt while holding the guide pin. Push the caliper up and swing it out from the bottom.
4. Remove the pads from the pad carrier. Remove any shims or shields behind the pads and note their positions.

**To install:**

5. Install the anti-rattle hardware and then the pads (in their proper positions!).
6. Using a suitable tool, push the caliper piston into the bore.
7. Install any pad shims and insert the pads onto the pad carrier.
8. Swing the caliper down and tighten the caliper mounting bolts to 26 ft. lbs.
9. Refill the master cylinder with fresh brake fluid.
10. Install the wheels and then pump the brake pedal several times to bring the pads into adjustment. Road test the vehicle.

**FOX**

1. Raise the front of the vehicle and support it with jackstands. Remove the wheels.
2. Siphon some brake fluid from the master cylinder reservoir to prevent its overflowing when the piston is retracted into the cylinder bore.
3. Unhook the retaining spring at the top and bottom.
4. Remove the guide pins that attach the caliper to the anchor plate.
5. Lift off the caliper and position it out of the way with some wire—you need not remove the brake lines.

**CAUTION**

*Never allow the caliper to hang by its brake lines.*

6. Slide the pads out of the carrier.
7. Check the rotor for scouring and resuface or replace as necessary. Check the caliper for fluid leaks or cracked boots. If any damage is found, the caliper will require overhauling or replacement.

**To install:**

8. Carefully clean the anchor plate with a wire brush or some other abrasive material. Install the inner pad, rotor and outer pad, new brake pads into position on the anchor plate.

**NOTE: When replacing brake pads, always replace both pads on both sides of the vehicle. Mixed pads will cause uneven braking.**

9. Slowly and carefully push the piston into its bore until it's bottomed and then position the caliper onto the anchor plate. Install the guide pins by pushing them carefully into the bushings and threading them into the adapter. Tighten the guide pins to 30 ft. lbs.
10. Fill the reservoir with brake fluid and pump the brake pedal several times to set the piston. It should not be necessary to bleed the system; however, if a firm pedal cannot be obtained, the system must be bled.
11. Install the wheels and lower the vehicle.

### *Rear Disc Brakes*

1. Raise the rear of the vehicle and support it with jackstands. Remove the wheels.
2. Siphon some brake fluid from the master cylinder reservoir to prevent its overflowing when the piston is retracted into the cylinder bore.
3. Remove the parking brake cable clip from the caliper. Remove the parking brake cable.
4. Remove the upper mounting bolt from the brake caliper.
5. Swing the housing downward and remove the brake pads.
6. Check the rotor for scouring and resuface or replace as necessary. Check the caliper for fluid leaks or cracked boots. If any damage is found, the caliper will require overhauling or replacement.

**To install:**

**NOTE: When replacing brake pads, always replace both pads on both sides of the vehicle. Mixed pads will cause uneven braking.**

7. Retract the piston into the housing by rotating the piston clockwise using a 12mm Allen wrench.
8. Carefully clean the anchor plate with a wire brush or some other abrasive material. Install the new brake pads into position on the brake pad carrier.
9. Install the caliper to pad carrier using a new self locking bolt and torque to 26 ft. lbs.
10. Fasten the hand brake cable to the caliper.
11. Fill the reservoir with brake fluid and pump the brake pedal several times to set the piston. It should not be necessary to bleed the system; however, if a firm pedal cannot be obtained, the system must be bled.

**NOTE: After installing new pads on models where caliper is mounted as a rear disc brake depress the pedal firmly (about 40 times—engine off) to set proper adjustment. Check the parking brake operation, adjust the cable if necessary.**

12. Install the wheels and lower the vehicle.

## Brake Shoes

### REMOVAL & INSTALLATION

1. Raise the rear of the vehicle and support it with jackstands. Remove the wheel and tire assembly.
2. Remove the brake drum.

**NOTE: If it is necessary to retract the shoes in order to remove a worn drum, remove 1 of the wheel bolts and insert a small prybar through the bolt hole. Push the adjusting wedge upward with the prybar.**

3. Remove the adjusting wedge spring.
4. Remove the upper and lower return springs.
5. Remove the hold-down springs.
6. Lift the shoes from the backing plate and disconnect the parking brake lever from the cable.
7. Disconnect the rear shoe from the push bar.
8. Clamp the push bar in a vise and remove the tensioning spring and adjusting wedge.

**To install:**

9. Check the wheel cylinder for frozen pistons or leaks. If any defects are found replace the wheel cylinder.
10. Inspect the springs. If the springs are damaged or show signs of overheating they should be replaced. Indications of overheated springs are paint discoloration and distortion.

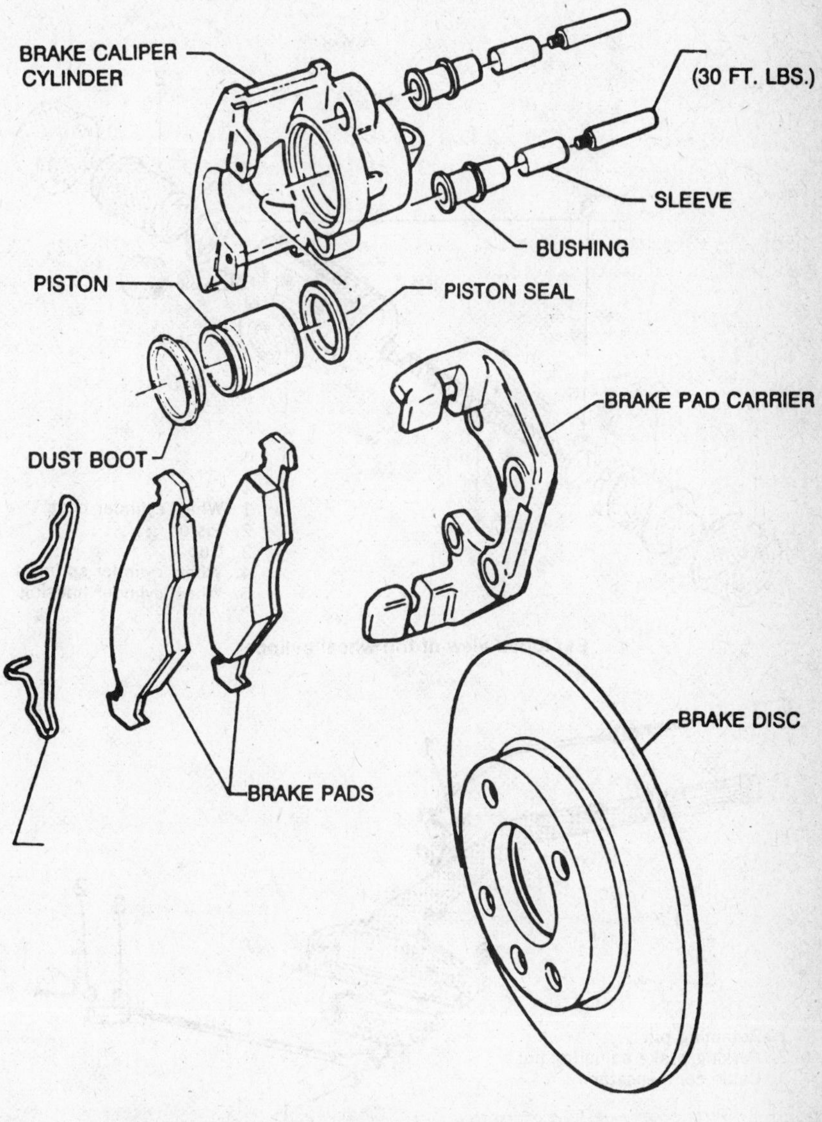


Exploded view of the callper and brake pad assembly—Fox

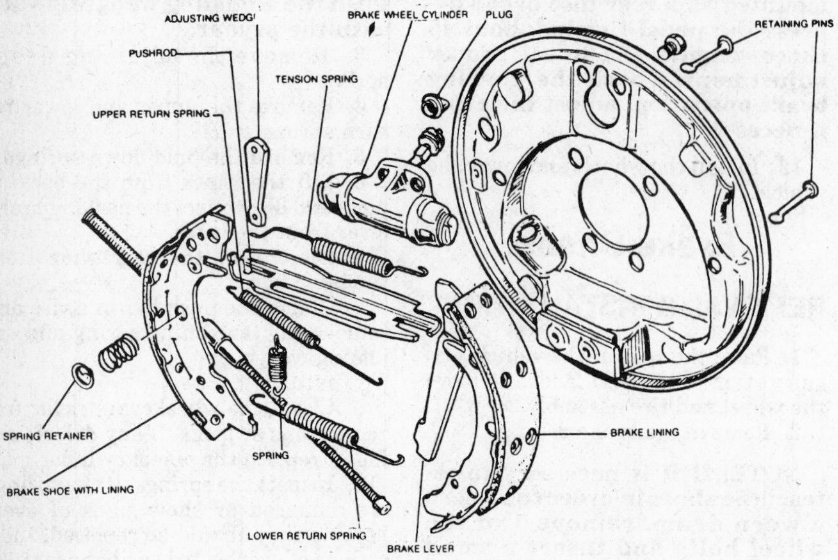


**Exploded view of the rear brake assembly—all models with rear drum brakes**

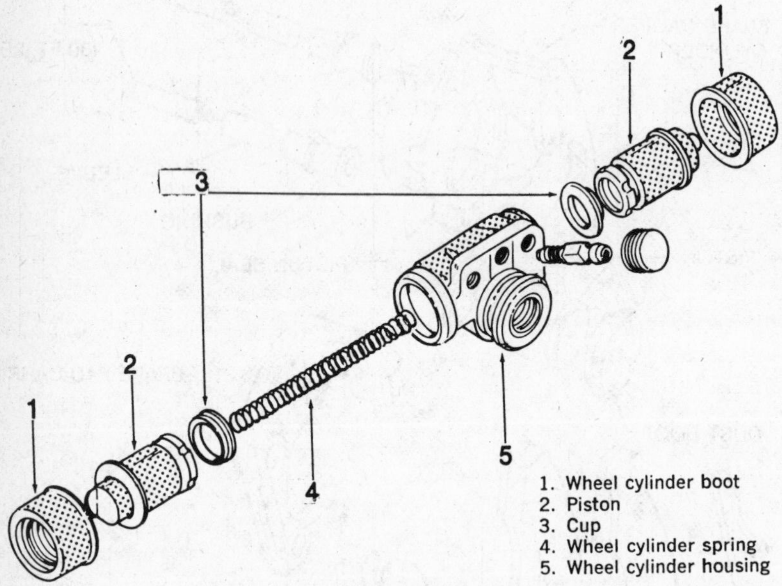


1. Wheel cylinder boot
2. Piston
3. Cup
4. Wheel cylinder spring
5. Wheel cylinder housing

**Exploded view of the wheel cylinder**

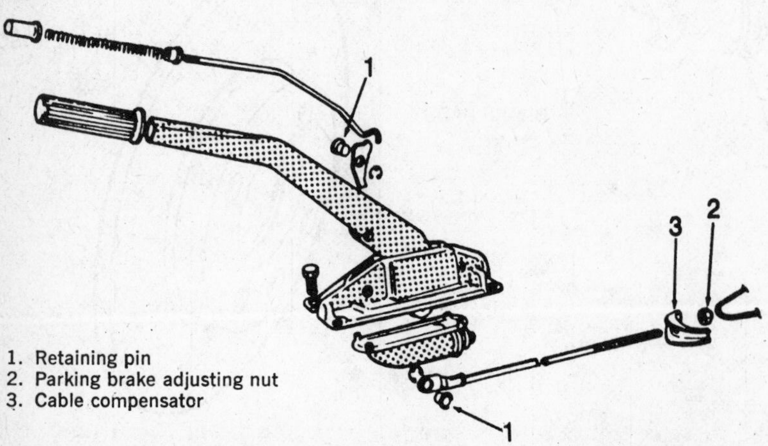


1. Retaining pin
2. Parking brake adjusting nut
3. Cable compensator

**Dasher parking brake linkage and adjusting point (Quantum similar)**

11. Inspect the brake drum and recondition or replace as necessary.
12. Clean and lubricate all contact points on the backing plate with a suitable brake lubricant.
13. Attach the push bar and tensioning spring to the new front shoe.
14. Insert the adjusting wedge so that its lug is pointing toward the backing plate.
15. Remove the parking brake lever from the old shoe and attach it onto the new rear brake shoe.
16. Install the bush bar onto the rear brake shoe and parking brake lever assembly.
17. Connect the parking brake cable to the lever and place the whole assembly onto the backing plate.
18. Install the hold-down springs.
19. Install the upper and lower return springs.
20. Install the adjusting wedge spring.
21. Center the brake shoes on the backing plate making sure that the adjusting wedge is fully released before installing the drum.
22. Install the drum and wheel assembly and adjust the rear wheel bearings.
23. Apply the brake pedal a few times to bring the brake shoe into adjustment.
24. Bleed the system and road test the vehicle.

## Wheel Cylinder

### REMOVAL & INSTALLATION

1. Remove the brake shoes.
2. Loosen the brake line on the rear of the cylinder, but do not pull the line away from the cylinder or it may bend.
3. Remove the bolts and lockwashers that attach the wheel cylinder to the backing plate and remove the cylinder.
4. Position the new wheel cylinder on the backing plate and install the cylinder attaching bolts and lockwashers.
5. Attach the brake line.
6. Install the brakes and bleed the system.

## Parking Brake Cable

### ADJUSTMENT

Fox and Quantum parking brake adjustment is made at the cable compensator, which is attached to the lever pushrod underneath the car. On all other models, the position of the cable end nuts are below the front of the hand brake lever. Adjustment is performed at the cable end nuts.

### Rear Drum Brakes

1. Block the front wheels. Raise and safely support the rear of the vehicle.
2. Apply the parking brake so that the lever is on the second notch.
3. The Fox and Quantum adjustment is made directly under the passenger compartment.
4. Tighten the compensator nut or adjusting nuts until both rear wheels can just be turned by hand. On models with self-adjusting rear brakes, the wheels will not turn by hand.
5. Release the parking brake lever and check that both wheels can be easily turned.
6. Lubricate the Fox and Quantum compensator with chassis grease.

### Rear Disc Brakes

**CAUTION**

***After installing new rear brake pads, push the brake pedal FIRMLY several times to permit the pistons and the brake pads to adjust to the brake disc. ALWAYS adjust the rear disc brakes before adjusting the parking brake.***

1. Block the front wheels, then raise and support the rear of the vehicle.
2. Disengage the parking brake.
3. Tighten the adjusting nuts of the parking brake cables until the parking brake levers (on top of each rear wheel caliper) rise off the stops.

**NOTE: The maximum distance the lever can rise off the stop is 0.039 in. (1mm).**

4. Reconnect the parking brake cable.

## REMOVAL & INSTALLATION

### Rear Drum Brakes

#### ALL MODELS EXCEPT FOX AND QUANTUM

1. Raise and safely support the rear of the vehicle.
2. Block the front wheels and release the handbrake.
3. Remove the rear brake shoes.
4. Remove the cable adjusting nut(s) and detach the cable guides from the floor pan.
5. Replace the cable and brake shoes. Check the parking brake adjustment.

#### FOX AND QUANTUM

1. Raise and safely support the rear of the vehicle. Release the parking brake.
2. Remove the rear brake drums.
3. Disconnect the cable from the shoe assembly by pushing the spring forward and removing the cable from the adjusting arm.
4. Remove the cable compensating spring.
5. Back off the equalizer nut and guide the cable through the trailing arms and supports.
6. Installation is the reverse of removal.
7. Adjust if necessary.

### Rear Disc Brakes

1. Raise and safely support the rear of the vehicle.
2. Release the parking brake.

**NOTE: It may be necessary to unscrew the adjusting nuts to provide slack in the brake cable.**

3. At each rear wheel brake caliper, remove the spring clip retaining the parking brake cable to the caliper.
4. Lift the cable from the caliper mount and disengage it from the parking brake lever.
5. To install, reverse the removal procedures and adjust the parking brake cables.

# CHASSIS ELECTRICAL

## Heater Core

The heater core and blower on all models are contained in the heater box (fresh air housing located in the center of the passenger compartment under the dashboard). On air conditioned Fox, Rabbit, Jetta, Scirocco and Cabriolet, the evaporator is located in the heater box. On air conditioned Quantums, the evaporator is located under the hood separate from the heater box.

## REMOVAL & INSTALLATION

### All Except Fox

1. Disconnect the negative battery cable.
2. Drain the cooling system.
3. Remove the 2 heater inlet hoses at the firewall.
4. Inside the car, remove the center console side panels, if equipped. Locate the heater core cover located on the side of the case. Press down on the retaining tabs and remove the cover.
5. The heater core can now be slid from the case.
6. To install, insert the heater core into the case. Install the heater core cover, making sure that the gasket on the cover is properly fitted.
7. Connect the heater hoses at the fire wall. Fill the cooling system.

### Fox

1. Disconnect the negative battery cable.
2. Drain the engine coolant.
3. Disconnect the heater inlet hoses at the firewall.
4. Inside the vehicle, remove the center console side panels. Disconnect the temperature control cables at the heater case.
5. Remove the left and right air distribution ducts.
6. In the engine compartment, remove the cowl cover and remove the air distribution housing cover.
7. Inside the vehicle, remove the lower housing retaining clips and remove the housing.

**NOTE: On vehicles equipped with A/C the heater box also contains the A/C system evaporator mounted in the lower housing cover. When removing the lower cover on these models lay the cover and evaporated aside WITHOUT removing the refrigerant lines.**

8. Remove the bolts retaining the heater case and remove the case.
9. Remove the clips holding the case together and split the case, the heater core can now be removed.
10. To install, insert the heater core into the case and reassemble the case.
11. Install the case into the vehicle. Attach the lower heater case cover to the heater case. Install the air distribution ducts and the control cables.
12. Install the center console side panels. Reconnect the heater inlet hoses. Install the air distribution housing cover and the cowl.

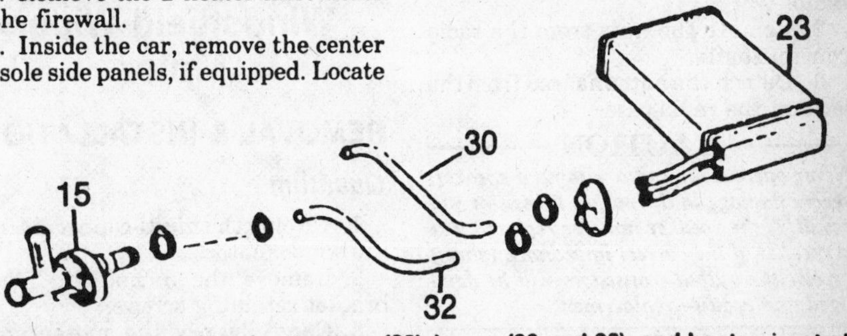


**Rabbit, Scirocco and Jetta heater core (23), hoses (30 and 32), and heater control valve (15)**

13. Fill the cooling system.

## Heater Blower Motor

### REMOVAL & INSTALLATION

#### *All Except 1985–90 Golf and Jetta*

1. Disconnect the negative battery cable.
2. Remove and tag the electrical connections from the blower motor.
3. Remove the clamp or screws holding the motor in place and remove the motor.
4. Installation is the reverse of removal, make sure that the seal around the motor is installed properly.

#### *1985–90 Golf and Jetta*

**NOTE: The blower motor is located behind the glove box and it may be necessary to remove the glove box to gain access to the motor.**

##### WITHOUT AIR CONDITIONING

1. Disconnect the wires at the blower motor.
2. At the blower motor flange near the cowl, disengage the retaining lug (pull down on the lug).
3. Turn the motor in the clockwise direction, to release it from it's mount, then lower it from the plenum.
4. To install, reverse the removal procedures.

##### WITH AIR CONDITIONING

1. Disconnect the wires from the blower motor.
2. Remove the 3 mounting screws and pull the motor from the plenum.
3. To install, reverse the removal procedures.

## Radio

### REMOVAL & INSTALLATION

#### *Except 1987–90 Models With Heidleberg 5–Electronic Tuned*

1. Remove the knobs from the radio.
2. Remove the nuts from the radio control shafts.
3. Detach the antenna lead from the jack on the radio case.

**CAUTION**

***Never operate the radio without a speaker; severe damage to the output transistor will result. If the speaker must be replaced, use a speaker of the correct impedance (ohms) or else the output transistors will be damaged and require replacement.***

4. Detach the power and speaker leads.
5. Remove the radio support nuts and bolts.
6. Withdraw the radio from beneath the dashboard.
7. Installation is performed in the reverse order of removal.

#### *Heidleberg 5*

The Heidleberg 5 radio is equipped with an electronic locking circuit to deter radio theft. Whenever the radio is removed or the battery is disconnected, the locking circuit code must be entered in order for the radio to operate. There are 2 codes that can be entered, the first is the original factory code. The second is the programed personal code entered by the vehicle owner. If the codes are not entered the radio will not operate. If the correct code is not entered in 6 tries the radio becomes electronically locked-up and must be replaced.

The Heidleberg 5 radio is retained in the instrument panel by means of lock clips at the sides of the radio body. To remove the radio from its mounting position, 2 special tools are required. Insert the tools, into the holes, in the side of the radio face plate. The tools will "click" into position. With the tools installed the radio can be pulled from the instrument panel. Disconnect the electrical leads to complete the removal. When installing the radio, be sure to connect the electrical leads in their proper position.

## Windshield Wiper/ Washer Switch

### REMOVAL & INSTALLATION

1. Remove the steering wheel.
2. Remove the 3 retaining screws and remove the combination turn signal, headlight switch.
3. Remove the windshield wiper/washer switch.
4. To install, place the wiper switch into position and install the retaining screws.

## Windshield Wiper Motor

### REMOVAL & INSTALLATION

#### *Quantum*

1. Unplug the multi-connector from the wiper motor.
2. Remove the 3 motor-to-linkage bracket retaining screws.
3. Carefully pry the motor crank out of the 2 linkage arms.
4. Remove the motor from the car.
5. Install the motor in the reverse order of removal. The crank arm should be at a right angle to the motor.

#### *1983–84 Rabbit, Scirocco and Jetta*

When removing the wiper motor, leave the mounting frame in place. On all models with 2 front wiper arms, do not remove the wiper drive crank from the motor shaft.

On Sciroccos with 1 front wiper arm, matchmark the drive crank and motor arm and then remove the arm.

1. Disconnect the battery ground cable.
2. Detach the connecting rods from the wiper motor crank arm.
3. Disconnect the electrical connector.
4. Remove the 4 wiper motor mounting bolts.
5. Remove the motor. Reverse the procedure for installation.

#### *1985–90 Golf, Fox, Rabbit, GTI, Jetta, Scirocco and Cabriolet*

1. Disconnect the electrical connector to the wiper motor.
2. Disconnect the crank arm from the wiper arm assembly.
3. Remove the retaining nut and the crank arm from the wiper motor shaft.
4. Remove the motor mounting bolts and the motor from the vehicle.
5. To install, run the motor and turn it off (it will stop in the **PARK** position).
6. Install the motor.
7. To install the crank arm, raise it 4 degrees from horizontal on the right side and connect it to the motor shaft.
8. To complete the installation, connect the crank arm to the wiper assembly and reverse the removal procedures.

## Instrument Cluster

### REMOVAL & INSTALLATION

#### *1983–84 Rabbit and Jetta*

1. Disconnect the battery ground cable.
2. Remove the air temperature control trim plate.
3. Remove the radio.
4. Unscrew the speedometer drive cable from the back of the speedometer. Detach the electrical plug.
5. Remove the attaching screw inside the radio/glove box opening.
6. Remove the instrument cluster. Reverse the procedure for installation.
7. When installing the cluster be sure to install all wiring correctly.

### *1983–84 Scirocco*

1. Disconnect battery ground cable.
2. Remove the 2 Phillips head screws on the inner top surface of the instrument compartment.
3. Start to pull down on the instrument cluster and remove the screws in the top of the cluster.
4. Tip out the top of the instrument cluster.
5. Remove the speedometer cable by twisting the tabs of the plastic fixture around the end of the cable.
6. Disconnect the multi-point connector and remove instrument cluster.
7. To install, reverse the removal procedures.

### *1983–90 Quantum*

1. Disconnect battery ground strap.
2. Carefully pry off switch trim below instruments.
3. Pull heater control knobs off and press out heater control trim.
4. Remove 2 Phillips head screws holding heater control trim to panel.

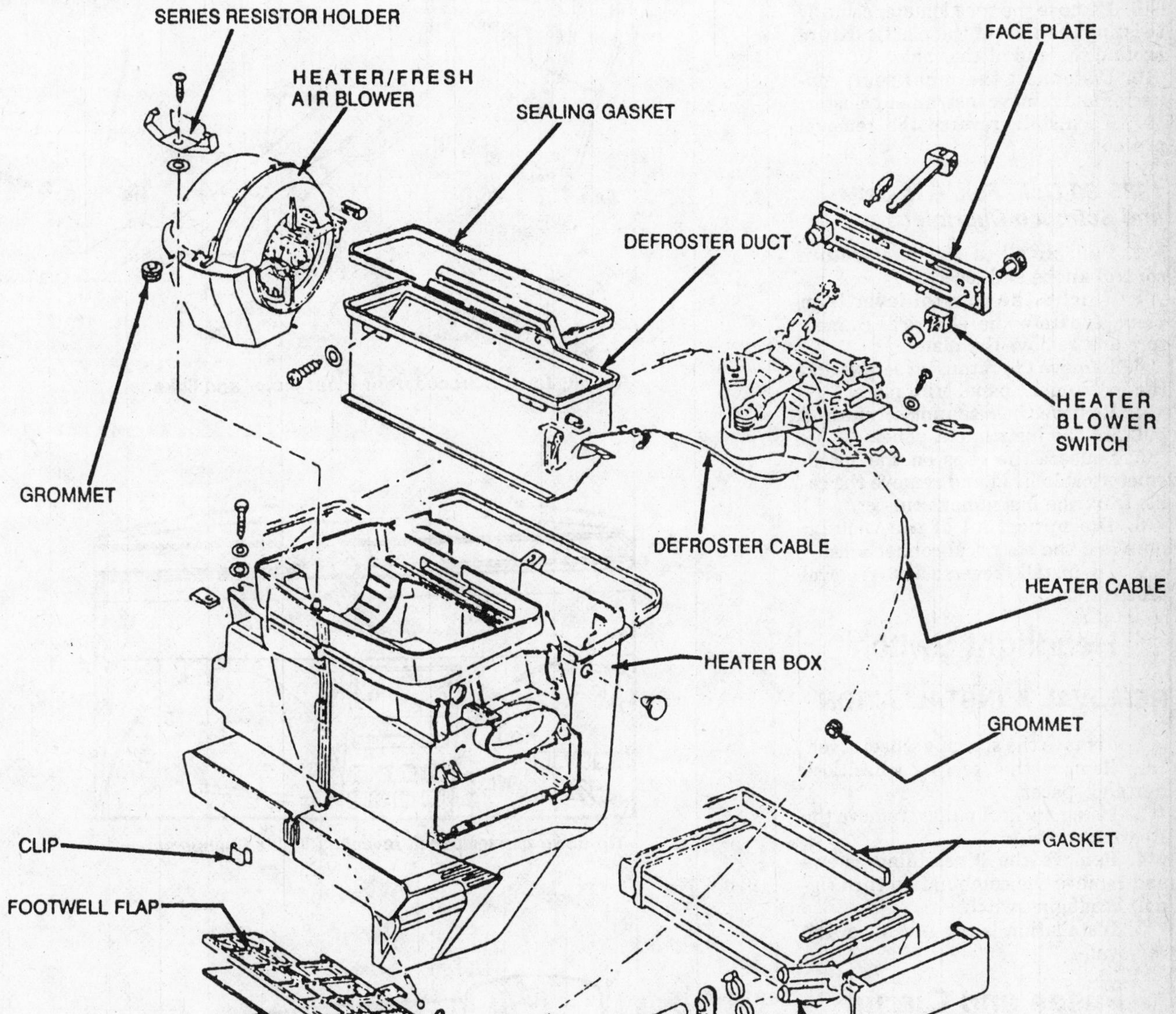

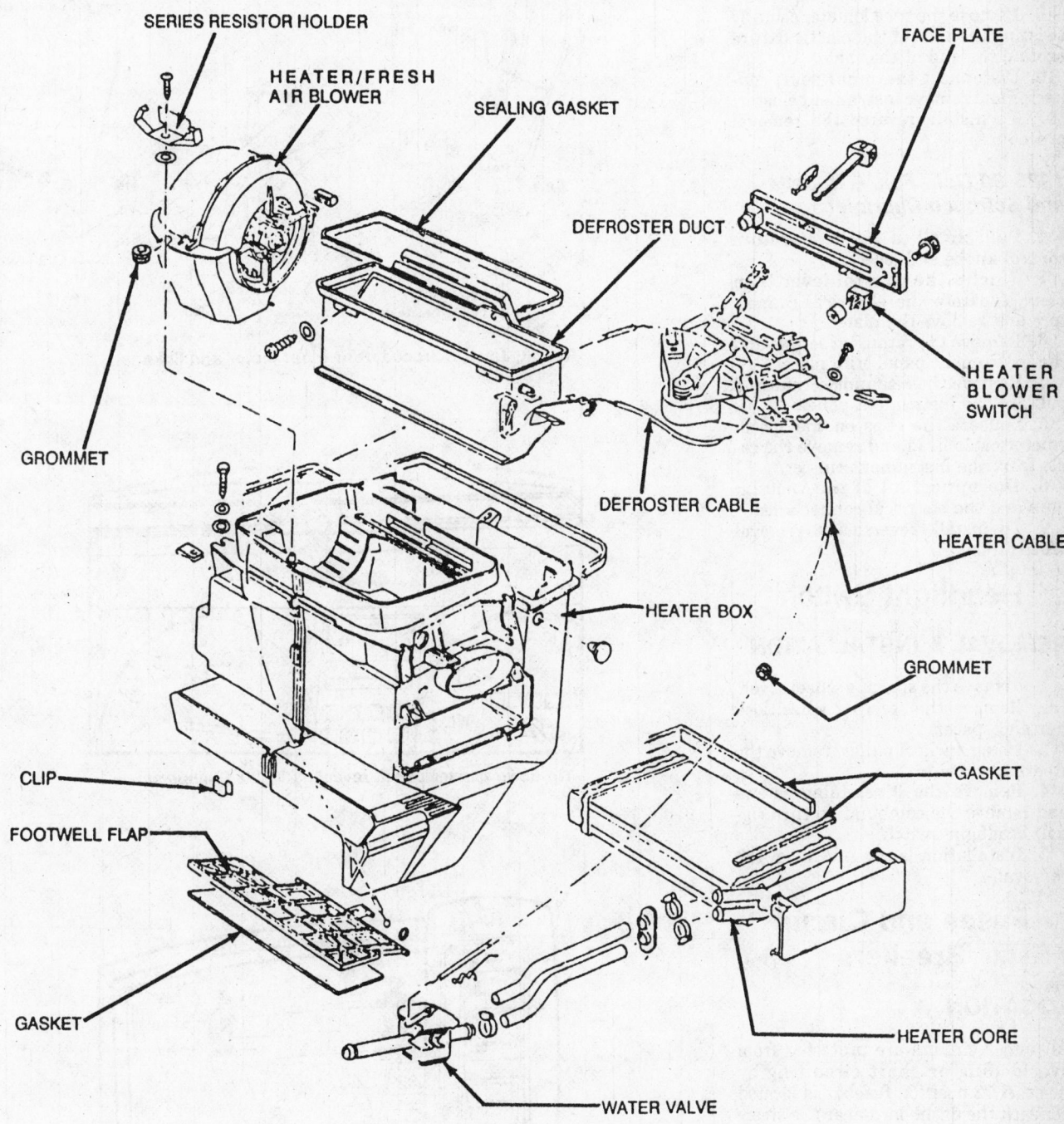


**Scirocco and Cabriolet heater box assembly**

5. Remove the 7 Phillips screws around perimeter of instrument cluster.
6. Disconnect all wiring to switches and warning lamps. Remove all trim panels.
7. Start to pull down on the instrument cluster and remove the screws in the top of the cluster.
8. Tip out the top of the instrument cluster.
9. Remove the speedometer cable by twisting the tabs of the plastic fixture around the end of the cable.
10. Disconnect the multi-point connector and remove instrument cluster.
11. To install, reverse the removal procedures.

#### *1985–90 Golf, Fox, GTI, Jetta and Scirocco/Cabriolet*

1. Pull off all of the temperature control knobs and levers.
2. Unclip the control lever trim plate, separate the electrical connectors and remove the plate.
3. Remove the retaining screws and the instrument panel trim plate.
4. Remove the retaining screws and pull out the instrument panel.
5. Squeeze the clips on the speedometer cable head and remove the cable from the instrument cluster.
6. Disconnect all of the vacuum hose and the electrical connections.
7. To install, reverse the removal procedures.

## Headlight Switch

### REMOVAL & INSTALLATION

1. Remove the steering wheel cover.
2. Remove the steering wheel lock nut and spacer.
3. Using a wheel puller, remove the steering wheel.
4. Remove the 3 retaining screws and remove the combination turn signal, headlight switch.
5. Installation is the reverse of the removal.

## Fuses and Circuit Breakers

### LOCATION

All major circuits are protected from overloading or short circuiting by fuses. A 12 position fusebox is located beneath the dashboard near the steering column, or located in the luggage compartment on some air conditioned models.

When a fuse blows, the cause should be investigated. Never install a fuse of a larger capacity than specified.

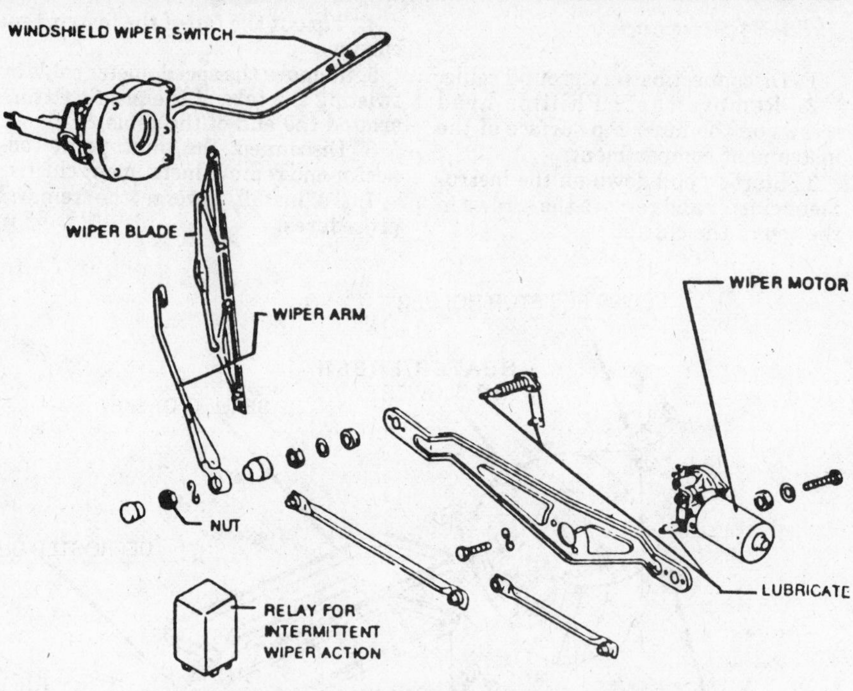


Rabbit, Jetta, Scirocco front wiper motor and linkage

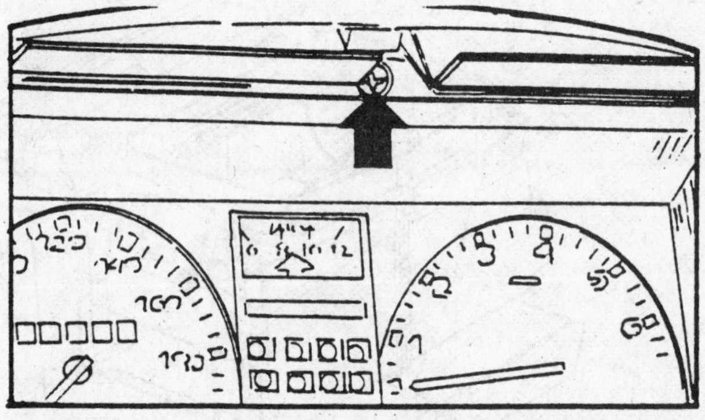

Tip down cluster panel, revealing inside Phillips screw

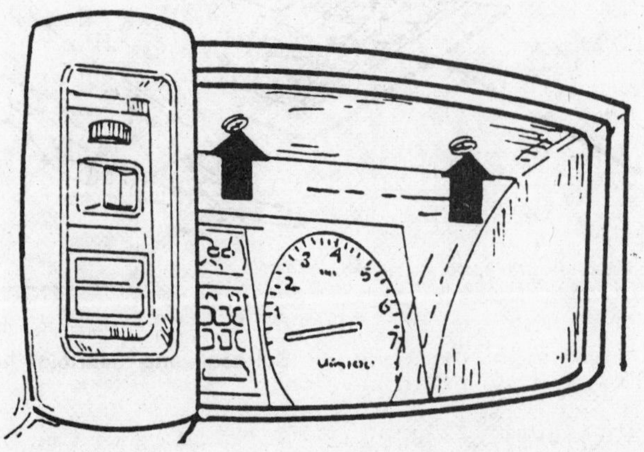

Instrument cluster removal—Scirocco (Quantum similar)

# Volvo 19

## 240, 740, 760, 780 Series—All Models

# SERIAL NUMBER IDENTIFICATION

## Vehicle Identification Plate

The VIN plate on these cars is located on the top left surface of the dash, and is also stamped on the right hand door pillar. Emission control information is on a label located on the left hand shock tower under the hood. There is also a model plate on the right hand shock tower that includes the VIN number, engine type, emission equipment, vehicle weights and color codes.

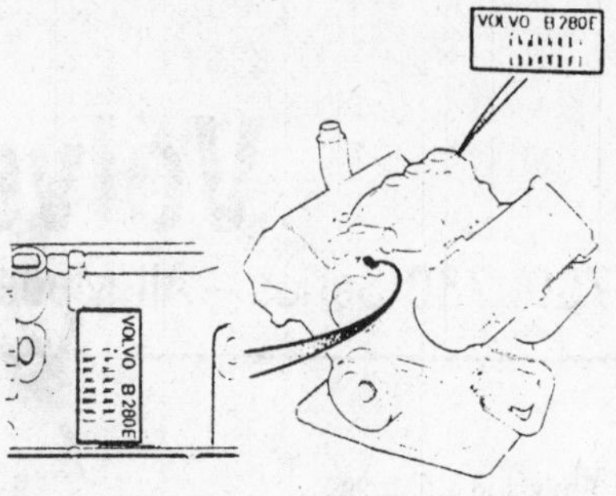
VOLVO B280F
VOLVO B280F

B280F engine identification location

499858
B234F NR: 305
B234F 499858

B234F engine identification location

## Engine Number

The engine type designation, part number, and serial number are given on the left side of the block. The last figures of the part number are stamped on a tab and are followed by the serial number stamped on the block.

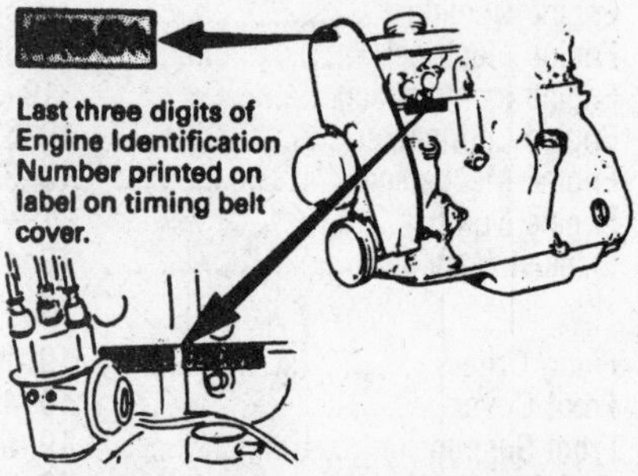
Last three digits of Engine Identification Number printed on label on timing belt cover.

B21 series engine number locations

D24 and D24T engine number location

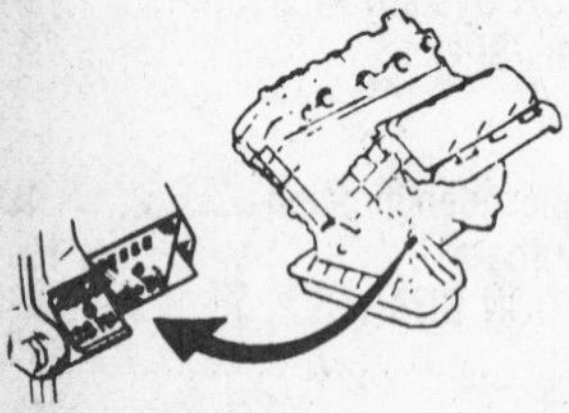

B28F engine number locations

## Transmission Number

The transmission type designation, serial number, and part number appear on a metal plate riveted to the underside of the transmission. The final drive reduction ratio, part number, and serial number are found on a metal plate riveted to the left-hand side of the differential.

### ENGINE IDENTIFICATION

| Year | Model | Engine Displacement cu. in. (cc/liter) | Engine Series Identification | No. of Cylinders | Engine Type |
|---|---|---|---|---|---|
| 1983 | 240 DL | 140 (2320/2.3) | B23F | 4 | OHC |
| | DL | 130 (2127/2.2) | B21F-Turbo | 4 | OHC |
| | DL | 145 (2383/2.4) | D24 | 6 | OHC |
| | DL① | 130 (2127/2.2) | B21A | 4 | OHC |
| | GL | 140 (2320/2.3) | B23F | 4 | OHC |
| | GL | 145 (2383/2.4) | D24 | 6 | OHC |
| | GL① | 140 (2320/2.3) | B23E | 4 | OHC |
| | GLT① | 140 (2320/2.3) | B23E | 4 | OHC |
| | Turbo | 130 (2127/2.2) | B21F-Turbo | 4 | OHC |
| | 760 GLE | 174 (2849/2.9) | B28F | 6 | OHC |
| | GLE | 145 (2383/2.4) | D24-Turbo | 6 | OHC |
| | Turbo | 140 (2320/2.3) | B23F-Turbo | 4 | OHC |
| 1984 | 240 Diesel | 145 (2383/2.4) | D24 | 6 | OHC |
| | DL | 140 (2320/2.3) | B23F | 4 | OHC |
| | DL① | 130 (2127/2.2) | B21A | 4 | OHC |
| | GL | 140 (2320/2.3) | B23F | 4 | OHC |
| | GLE① | 140 (2320/2.3) | B23F | 4 | OHC |
| | Turbo | 130 (2127/2.2) | B21F-Turbo | 4 | OHC |

## ENGINE IDENTIFICATION

| Year | Model | Engine Displacement cu. in. (cc/liter) | Engine Series Identification | No. of Cylinders | Engine Type |
|---|---|---|---|---|---|
| 1984 | 760 GLE | 174 (2849/2.9) | B28F | 6 | OHC |
| | GLE | 145 (2383/2.4) | D24-Turbo | 6 | OHC |
| | Turbo | 140 (2320/2.3) | B23F-Turbo | 4 | OHC |
| 1985 | 240 Diesel | 145 (2383/2.4) | D24 | 6 | OHC |
| | DL | 140 (2320/2.3) | B230F | 4 | OHC |
| | GL | 140 (2320/2.3) | B230F | 4 | OHC |
| | Turbo | 130 (2127/2.2) | B21F-Turbo | 4 | OHC |
| | 740 GLE | 140 (2320/2.3) | B230F | 4 | OHC |
| | TD② | 145 (2383/2.4) | D24-Turbo | 6 | OHC |
| | Turbo | 140 (2320/2.3) | B230F-Turbo | 4 | OHC |
| | 760 GLE | 174 (2849/2.9) | B28F | 6 | OHC |
| | GLE TD | 145 (2383/2.4) | D24-Turbo | 6 | OHC |
| | Turbo | 140 (2320/2.3) | B230F-Turbo | 4 | OHC |
| 1986 | 240 DL | 140 (2320/2.3) | B230F | 4 | OHC |
| | GL | 140 (2320/2.3) | B230F | 4 | OHC |
| | 740 GL | 140 (2320/2.3) | B230F | 4 | OHC |
| | GLE | 140 (2320/2.3) | B230F | 4 | OHC |
| | GLE TD | 145 (2383/2.4) | D24-Turbo | 6 | OHC |
| | Turbo | 140 (2320/2.3) | B230F-Turbo | 4 | OHC |
| | 760 GLE | 174 (2849/2.9) | B28F | 6 | OHC |
| | Turbo | 140 (2320/2.3) | B230F-Turbo | 4 | OHC |
| 1987 | 240 DL | 140 (2320/2.3) | B230F | 4 | OHC |
| | GL | 140 (2320/2.3) | B230F | 4 | OHC |
| | 740 GL | 140 (2320/2.3) | B230F | 4 | OHC |
| | GLE | 140 (2320/2.3) | B230F | 4 | OHC |
| | Turbo | 140 (2320/2.3) | B230F-Turbo | 4 | OHC |
| | 760 GLE | 174 (2849/2.9) | B280F | 6 | OHC |
| | Turbo | 140 (2320/2.3) | B230F-Turbo | 4 | OHC |
| | 780 | 174 (2849/2.9) | B280F | 6 | OHC |
| 1988 | 240 DL | 140 (2320/2.3) | B230F | 4 | OHC |
| | GL | 140 (2320/2.3) | B230F | 4 | OHC |
| | 740 GL | 140 (2320/2.3) | B230F | 4 | OHC |
| | GLE | 140 (2320/2.3) | B230F | 4 | OHC |
| | Turbo | 140 (2320/2.3) | B230F-Turbo | 4 | OHC |
| | 760 GLE | 174 (2849/2.9) | B280F | 6 | OHC |
| | Turbo | 140 (2320/2.3) | B230F-Turbo | 4 | OHC |
| | 780 | 174 (2849/2.9) | B280F | 6 | OHC |
| 1989-90 | 240 DL | 140 (2320/2.3) | B230F | 4 | OHC |
| | GL | 140 (2320/2.3) | B230F | 4 | OHC |
| | 740 GL | 140 (2320/2.3) | B230F | 4 | OHC |
| | GLE | 140 (2320/2.3) | B234F | 4 | DOHC |
| | Turbo | 140 (2320/2.3) | B230F-Turbo | 4 | OHC |
| | 760 GLE | 174 (2849/2.9) | B280F | 6 | OHC |
| | Turbo | 140 (2320/2.3) | B230F-Turbo | 4 | OHC |
| | 780 | 174 (2849/2.9) | B280F | 6 | OHC |

① Canada only ② Station Wagon

## GENERAL ENGINE SPECIFICATIONS

| Year | Model | Engine Displacement cu. in. (cc) | Fuel System Type | Net Horsepower @ rpm | Net Torque @ rpm (ft. lbs.) | Bore × Stroke (in.) | Com-pression Ratio | Oil Pressure @ rpm |
|---|---|---|---|---|---|---|---|---|
| 1983 | 240 DL | 140 (2320) B23F | LH | 107 @ 5400 | 127 @ 3500 | 3.78 × 3.15 | 10.3:1 | 35–85 @ 2000 |
| | DL | 130 (2127) B21F-Turbo | CIS | 127 @ 5400 | 150 @ 3750 | 3.62 × 3.15 | 7.5:1 | 35–85 @ 2000 |
| | DL | 145 (2383) D24 | DFI | 78 @ 4800 | 102 @ 3000 | 3.01 × 3.40 | 23.5:1 | 28 @ 2000 |
| | DL① | 130 (2127) B21A | 1 bbl Zenith | 100 @ 5250 | 122 @ 2500 | 3.62 × 3.15 | 9.3:1 | 35–85 @ 2000 |
| | GL | 140 (2320) B23F | LH | 107 @ 5400 | 127 @ 3500 | 3.78 × 3.15 | 10.3:1 | 35–85 @ 2000 |
| | GL | 145 (2383) D24 | DFI | 78 @ 4800 | 102 @ 3000 | 3.01 × 3.40 | 23.5:1 | 28 @ 2000 |
| | GL① | 140 (2320) B23E | CIS | 115 @ 5000 | 133 @ 3000 | 3.62 × 3.15 | 10.3:1 | 35–85 @ 2000 |
| | GLT① | 140 (2320) B23E | CIS | 115 @ 5000 | 133 @ 3000 | 3.62 × 3.15 | 10.3:1 | 35–85 @ 2000 |
| | Turbo | 130 (2127) B21F-Turbo | CIS | 127 @ 5400 | 150 @ 3750 | 3.62 × 3.15 | 7.5:1 | 35–85 @ 2000 |
| | 760 GLE | 174 (2849) B28F | CIS | 134 @ 5500 | 159 @ 2700 | 3.58 × 2.86 | 8.8:1 | 60 @ 3000 |
| | GLE | 145 (2383) D24-Turbo | DFI | 106 @ 4800 | 140 @ 2400 | 3.01 × 3.40 | 23.0:1 | 28 @ 2000 |
| | Turbo | 140 (2320) B23F-Turbo | LH | 157 @ 5300 | 184 @ 2900 | 3.78 × 3.15 | 8.7:1 | 35–85 @ 2000 |
| 1984 | 240 Diesel | 145 (2383) D24 | DFI | 78 @ 4800 | 102 @ 3000 | 3.01 × 3.40 | 23.5:1 | 28 @ 2000 |
| | DL | 140 (2320) B23F④ | LH | 113 @ 5400 | 136 @ 2750 | 3.78 × 3.15 | 9.5:1 | 35–85 @ 2000 |
| | DL | 140 (2320) B23F⑤ | LH | 114 @ 5400 | 133 @ 3500 | 3.78 × 3.15 | 10.3:1 | 35–85 @ 2000 |
| | DL① | 130 (2127) B21A | 1 bbl Zenith | 100 @ 5250 | 122 @ 2500 | 3.62 × 3.15 | 9.3:1 | 35–85 @ 2000 |
| | GL | 140 (2320) B23F④ | LH | 113 @ 5400 | 136 @ 2750 | 3.78 × 3.15 | 9.5:1 | 35–85 @ 2000 |
| | GL | 140 (2320) B23F⑤ | LH | 114 @ 5400 | 133 @ 3500 | 3.78 × 3.15 | 10.3:1 | 35–85 @ 2000 |
| | GLE① | 140 (2320) B23F④ | LH | 113 @ 5400 | 136 @ 2750 | 3.78 × 3.15 | 9.5:1 | 35–85 @ 2000 |
| | GLE① | 140 (2320) B23F⑤ | LH | 114 @ 5400 | 133 @ 3500 | 3.78 × 3.15 | 10.3:1 | 35–85 @ 2000 |
| | Turbo | 130 (2127) B21F-Turbo | CIS | 131 @ 5400 | 155 @ 3750 | 3.62 × 3.15 | 7.5:1 | 35–85 @ 2000 |
| | 760 GLE | 174 (2849) B28F | CIS | 134 @ 5500 | 159 @ 2700 | 3.58 × 2.86 | 8.8:1 | 60 @ 3000 |
| | GLE | 145 (2383) D24-Turbo | DFI | 106 @ 4800 | 140 @ 2400 | 3.01 × 3.40 | 23.0:1 | 28 @ 2000 |
| | Turbo | 140 (2320) B23F-Turbo | LH | 157 @ 5300 | 184 @ 2900 | 3.78 × 3.15 | 8.7:1 | 35–85 @ 2000 |
| 1985 | 240 Diesel | 145 (2383) D24 | DFI | 80 @ 4800 | 103 @ 2800 | 3.01 × 3.40 | 23.0:1 | 28 @ 2000 |

## GENERAL ENGINE SPECIFICATIONS

| Year | Model | Engine Displacement cu. in. (cc) | Fuel System Type | Net Horsepower @ rpm | Net Torque @ rpm (ft. lbs.) | Bore × Stroke (in.) | Com-pression Ratio | Oil Pressure @ rpm |
|---|---|---|---|---|---|---|---|---|
| 1985 | DL | 140 (2320) B230F | LH | 114 @ 5400 | 136 @ 2750 | 3.78 × 3.15 | 9.8:1 | 35–85 @ 2000 |
| | GL | 140 (2320) B230F | LH | 114 @ 5400 | 136 @ 2750 | 3.78 × 3.15 | 9.8:1 | 35–85 @ 2000 |
| | Turbo | 130 (2127) B21F-Turbo | CIS | 162 @ 5100 | 181 @ 3900 | 3.62 × 3.15 | 7.5:1 | 35–85 @ 2000 |
| | 740 GLE | 140 (2320) B230F | LH | 114 @ 5400 | 136 @ 2750 | 3.78 × 3.15 | 9.8:1 | 35–85 @ 2000 |
| | TD | 145 (2383) D24-Turbo | DFI | 106 @ 4800 | 140 @ 2400 | 3.01 × 3.40 | 23.0:1 | 28 @ 2000 |
| | Turbo | 140 (2320) B230F-Turbo | LH | 160 @ 5300 | 187 @ 2900 | 3.78 × 3.15 | 8.7:1 | 35–85 @ 2000 |
| | 760 GLE | 174 (2849) B28F | CIS | 134 @ 5500 | 159 @ 2700 | 3.58 × 2.86 | 8.8:1 | 60 @ 3000 |
| | GLE TD | 145 (2383) D24-Turbo | DFI | 106 @ 4800 | 140 @ 2400 | 3.01 × 3.40 | 23.0:1 | 28 @ 2000 |
| | Turbo | 140 (2320) B230F-Turbo | LH | 160 @ 5300 | 187 @ 2900 | 3.78 × 3.15 | 8.7:1 | 35–85 @ 2000 |
| 1986 | 240 DL | 140 (2320) B230F | LH | 114 @ 5400 | 136 @ 2750 | 3.78 × 3.15 | 9.8:1 | 35–85 @ 2000 |
| | GL | 140 (2320) B230F | LH | 114 @ 5400 | 136 @ 2750 | 3.78 × 3.15 | 9.8:1 | 35–85 @ 2000 |
| | 740 GL | 140 (2320) B230F | LH | 114 @ 5400 | 136 @ 2750 | 3.78 × 3.15 | 9.8:1 | 35–85 @ 2000 |
| | GLE | 140 (2320) B230F | LH | 114 @ 5400 | 136 @ 2750 | 3.78 × 3.15 | 9.8:1 | 35–85 @ 2000 |
| | GLE TD | 145 (2383) D24-Turbo | DFI | 106 @ 4800 | 140 @ 2400 | 3.01 × 3.40 | 23.0:1 | 28 @ 2000 |
| | Turbo | 140 (2320) B230F-Turbo | LH | 160 @ 5300 | 187 @ 2900 | 3.78 × 3.15 | 8.7:1 | 35–85 @ 2000 |
| | 760 GLE | 174 (2849) B28F | CIS | 136 @ 5500 | 159 @ 2700 | 3.58 × 2.86 | 8.8:1 | 60 @ 3000 |
| | Turbo | 140 (2320) B230F-Turbo | LH | 160 @ 5300 | 187 @ 2900 | 3.78 × 3.15 | 8.7:1 | 35–85 @ 2000 |
| 1987 | 240 DL | 140 (2320) B230F | LH | 114 @ 5400 | 136 @ 2750 | 3.78 × 3.15 | 9.8:1 | 35–85 @ 2000 |
| | GL | 140 (2320) B230F | LH | 114 @ 5400 | 136 @ 2750 | 3.78 × 3.15 | 9.8:1 | 35–85 @ 2000 |
| | 740 GL | 140 (2320) B230F | LH | 114 @ 5400 | 136 @ 2750 | 3.78 × 3.15 | 9.8:1 | 35–85 @ 2000 |
| | GLE | 140 (2320) B230F | LH | 114 @ 5400 | 136 @ 2750 | 3.78 × 3.15 | 9.8:1 | 35–85 @ 2000 |
| | Turbo | 140 (2320) B230F-Turbo | LH | 160 @ 5300 | 187 @ 2900 | 3.78 × 3.15 | 8.7:1 | 35–85 @ 2000 |
| | 760 GLE | 174 (2849) B280F | LH | 146 @ 5100 | 173 @ 3750 | 3.58 × 2.86 | 9.5:1 | 57 @ 3000 |
| | Turbo | 140 (2320) B230F-Turbo | LH | 160 @ 5300 | 187 @ 2900 | 3.78 × 3.15 | 8.7:1 | 35–85 @ 2000 |
| | 780 | 174 (2849) B280F | LH | 146 @ 5100 | 173 @ 3750 | 3.58 × 2.86 | 9.5:1 | 57 @ 3000 |

## GENERAL ENGINE SPECIFICATIONS

| Year | Model | Engine Displacement cu. in. (cc) | Fuel System Type | Net Horsepower @ rpm | Net Torque @ rpm (ft. lbs.) | Bore × Stroke (in.) | Com-pression Ratio | Oil Pressure @ rpm |
|---|---|---|---|---|---|---|---|---|
| 1988 | 240 DL | 140 (2320) B230F | LH | 114 @ 5400 | 136 @ 2750 | 3.78 × 3.15 | 9.8:1 | 35–85 @ 2000 |
| | GL | 140 (2320) B230F | LH | 114 @ 5400 | 136 @ 2750 | 3.78 × 3.15 | 9.8:1 | 35–85 @ 2000 |
| | 740 GL | 140 (2320) B230F | LH | 114 @ 5400 | 136 @ 2750 | 3.78 × 3.15 | 9.8:1 | 35–85 @ 2000 |
| | GLE | 140 (2320) B230F | LH | 114 @ 5400 | 136 @ 2750 | 3.78 × 3.15 | 9.8:1 | 35–85 @ 2000 |
| | Turbo | 140 (2320) B230F-Turbo | LH | 160 @ 5300 | 187 @ 2900 | 3.78 × 3.15 | 8.7:1 | 35–85 @ 2000 |
| | 760 GLE | 174 (2849) B280F | LH | 146 @ 5100 | 173 @ 3750 | 3.58 × 2.86 | 9.5:1 | 57 @ 3000 |
| | Turbo | 140 (2320) B230F-Turbo | LH | 160 @ 5300 | 187 @ 2900 | 3.78 × 3.15 | 8.7:1 | 35–85 @ 2000 |
| | 780 | 174 (2849) B280F | LH | 146 @ 5100 | 173 @ 3750 | 3.58 × 2.86 | 9.5:1 | 57 @ 3000 |
| 1989–90 | 240 DL | 140 (2320) B230F | LH | 114 @ 5400 | 136 @ 2750 | 3.78 × 3.15 | 9.8:1 | 35–85 @ 2000 |
| | GL | 140 (2320) B230F | LH | 114 @ 5400 | 136 @ 2750 | 3.78 × 3.15 | 9.8:1 | 35–85 @ 2000 |
| | 740 GL | 140 (2320) B230F | LH | 114 @ 5400 | 136 @ 2750 | 3.78 × 3.15 | 9.8:1 | 35–85 @ 2000 |
| | GLE | 140 (2320) B234F | LH | 153 @ 5700 | 150 @ 4450 | 3.78 × 3.15 | 10.0:1 | 73 @ 3000 |
| | Turbo | 140 (2320) B230F-Turbo | LH | 160 @ 5300 | 187 @ 2900 | 3.78 × 3.15 | 8.7:1 | 35–85 @ 2000 |
| | 760 GLE | 174 (2849) B280F | LH | 146 @ 5100 | 173 @ 3750 | 3.58 × 2.86 | 9.5:1 | 57 @ 3000 |
| | Turbo | 140 (2320) B230F-Turbo | LH | 160 @ 5300 | 187 @ 2900 | 3.78 × 3.15 | 8.7:1 | 35–85 @ 2000 |
| | 780 | 174 (2849) B280F | LH | 146 @ 5100 | 173 @ 3750 | 3.58 × 2.86 | 9.5:1 | 57 @ 3000 |
| | Turbo | 140 (2320) B230F-Turbo | LH | 175 @ 5300 | 187 @ 2900 | 3.78 × 3.15 | 8.7:1 | 35–85 @ 2000 |

CIS Continuous Injection System
DFI Diesel Fuel Injection
LH LH-Jetronic Injection

① Canada only
② Station Wagon
③ California only
④ With manual transmission
⑤ With automatic transmission

## GASOLINE ENGINE TUNE-UP SPECIFICATIONS

| Year | Model | Engine Displacement cu. in. (cc) | Spark Plugs Type | Spark Plugs Gap (in.) | Ignition Timing③ (deg.) MT | Ignition Timing③ (deg.) AT | Com-pression Pressure (psi) | Fuel Pump (psi) | Idle Speed (rpm) MT | Idle Speed (rpm) AT | Valve Clearance In. | Valve Clearance Ex. |
|---|---|---|---|---|---|---|---|---|---|---|---|---|
| 1983 | 240 DL | 140 (2320) B23F | WR7DS | 0.030 | 12B ④ | 12B ④ | NA | 64–75 | 750 | 750 | 0.014–0.016 | 0.014–0.016 |
| | DL | 130 (2127) B21F-Turbo | WR7DS | 0.030 | 12B | 12B | NA | 64–75 | 900 | 900 | 0.014–0.016 | 0.014–0.016 |
| | DL | 130 (2127) B21A① | W7DC | 0.030 | 7B ④ | 7B ④ | NA | 64–75 | 900 | 900 | 0.014–0.016 | 0.014–0.016 |

## GASOLINE ENGINE TUNE-UP SPECIFICATIONS

| Year | Model | Engine Displacement cu. in. (cc) | Spark Plugs Type | Spark Plugs Gap (in.) | Ignition Timing③ (deg.) MT | Ignition Timing③ (deg.) AT | Compression Pressure (psi) | Fuel Pump (psi) | Idle Speed (rpm) MT | Idle Speed (rpm) AT | Valve Clearance In. | Valve Clearance Ex. |
|---|---|---|---|---|---|---|---|---|---|---|---|---|
| 1983 | GL | 140 (2320) B23F | WR7DS | 0.030 | 12B ④ | 12B ④ | NA | 64–75 | 750 | 750 | 0.014–0.016 | 0.014–0.016 |
| | GL | 140 (2320) B23E① | W6DC | 0.030 | 10B ④ | 10B ④ | NA | 64–75 | 900 | 900 | 0.014–0.016 | 0.014–0.016 |
| | GLT | 140 (2320) B23E① | W6DC | 0.030 | 10B ④ | 10B ④ | NA | 64–75 | 900 | 900 | 0.014–0.016 | 0.014–0.016 |
| | Turbo | 130 (2127) B21F-Turbo | WR7DS | 0.030 | 12B ④ | 12B ④ | NA | 64–75 | 900 | 900 | 0.014–0.016 | 0.014–0.016 |
| | 760 GLE | 174 (2849) B28F | WR6DS | 0.026 | 23B ⑦ | 23B ⑦ | NA | 64–75 | 750 | 750 | 0.004–0.006 | 0.010–0.012 |
| | Turbo | 140 (2320) B23F-Turbo | WR7DC | 0.026 | 12B ④ | 12B ④ | NA | 64–75 | 750 | 750 | 0.014–0.016 | 0.014–0.016 |
| 1984 | 240 DL | 140 (2320) B23F | WR7DS | 0.030 | 12B ④ | 12B ④ | NA | 64–75 | 750 | 750 | 0.014–0.016 | 0.014–0.016 |
| | DL | 130 (2127) B21A① | W7DC | 0.030 | 12B ④ | 12B ④ | NA | 64–75 | 900 | 900 | 0.014–0.016 | 0.014–0.016 |
| | GL | 140 (2320) B23F | WR7DS | 0.030 | 12B ④ | 12B ④ | NA | 64–75 | 750 | 750 | 0.014–0.016 | 0.014–0.016 |
| | GLE | 140 (2320) B23F① | WR7DS | 0.030 | 12B ④ | 12B ④ | NA | 64–75 | 750 | 750 | 0.014–0.016 | 0.014–0.016 |
| | Turbo | 130 (2127) B21F-Turbo | WR7DS | 0.030 | 12B ⑤ | 12B ⑤ | NA | 64–75 | 900 | 900 | 0.014–0.016 | 0.014–0.016 |
| | 760 GLE | 174 (2849) B28F | WR6DS | 0.026 | 23B ⑦ | 23B ⑦ | NA | 64–75 | 750 | 750 | 0.004–0.006 | 0.010–0.012 |
| | Turbo | 140 (2320) B23F-Turbo | WR7DC | 0.026 | 12B ④ | 12B ④ | NA | 64–75 | 750 | 750 | 0.014–0.016 | 0.014–0.016 |
| 1985 | 240 DL | 140 (2320) B230F | WR7DC | 0.030 | 12B ④ | 12B ④ | NA | 36 | 750 | 750 | 0.014–0.016 | 0.014–0.016 |
| | GL | 140 (2320) B230F | WR7DC | 0.030 | 12B ④ | 12B ④ | NA | 36 | 750 | 750 | 0.014–0.016 | 0.014–0.016 |
| | Turbo | 130 (2127) B21F-Turbo | WR7DS | 0.030 | 12B ④ | 12B ④ | NA | 64–75 | 900 | 900 | 0.014–0.016 | 0.014–0.016 |
| | 740 GLE | 140 (2320) B230F | WR7DC | 0.030 | 12B ④ | 12B ④ | NA | 36 | 750 | 750 | 0.014–0.016 | 0.014–0.016 |
| | Turbo | 140 (2320) B230F-Turbo | WR7DC | 0.026 | 12B ④ | 12B ④ | NA | 43 | 750 | 750 | 0.014–0.016 | 0.014–0.016 |
| | 760 GLE | 174 (2849) B28F | HR6DC | 0.026 | 23B ⑦ | 23B ⑦ | NA | 64–75 | 750 | 750 | 0.004–0.006 | 0.010–0.012 |
| | Turbo | 140 (2320) B230F-Turbo | WR7DC | 0.026 | 12B ④ | 12B ④ | NA | 43 | 750 | 750 | 0.014–0.016 | 0.014–0.016 |
| 1986 | 240 DL | 140 (2320) B230F | WR7DC | 0.030 | 12B ④ | 12B ④ | NA | 36 | 750 | 750 | 0.014–0.016 | 0.014–0.016 |
| | GL | 140 (2320) B230F | WR7DC | 0.030 | 12B ④ | 12B ④ | NA | 36 | 750 | 750 | 0.014–0.016 | 0.014–0.016 |
| | 740 GL | 140 (2320) B230F | WR7DC | 0.030 | 12B ④ | 12B ④ | NA | 36 | 750 | 750 | 0.014–0.016 | 0.014–0.016 |
| | GLE | 140 (2320) B230F | WR7DC | 0.030 | 12B ④ | 12B ④ | NA | 36 | 750 | 750 | 0.014–0.016 | 0.014–0.016 |

## GASOLINE ENGINE TUNE-UP SPECIFICATIONS

| Year | Model | Engine Displacement cu. in. (cc) | Spark Plugs Type | Spark Plugs Gap (in.) | Ignition Timing③ (deg.) MT | Ignition Timing③ (deg.) AT | Compression Pressure (psi) | Fuel Pump (psi) | Idle Speed (rpm) MT | Idle Speed (rpm) AT | Valve Clearance In. | Valve Clearance Ex. |
|---|---|---|---|---|---|---|---|---|---|---|---|---|
| 1986 | Turbo | 140 (2320) B230F-Turbo | WR7DC | 0.026 | 12B ④ | 12B ④ | NA | 43 | 750 | 750 | 0.014–0.016 | 0.014–0.016 |
| | 760 GLE | 174 (2849) B28F | HR6DC | 0.026 | 23B ⑦ | 23B ⑦ | NA | 64–75 | 750 | 750 | 0.004–0.006 | 0.010–0.012 |
| | Turbo | 140 (2320) B230F-Turbo | WR7DC | 0.026 | 12B ④ | 12B ④ | NA | 43 | 750 | 750 | 0.014–0.016 | 0.014–0.016 |
| 1987 | 240 DL | 140 (2320) B230F | WR7DC | 0.030 | 12B ④ | 12B ④ | NA | 36 | 750 | 750 | 0.014–0.016 | 0.014–0.016 |
| | GL | 140 (2320) B230F | WR7DC | 0.030 | 12B ④ | 12B ④ | NA | 36 | 750 | 750 | 0.014–0.016 | 0.014–0.016 |
| | 740 GL | 140 (2320) B230F | WR7DC | 0.030 | 12B ④ | 12B ④ | NA | 36 | 750 | 750 | 0.014–0.016 | 0.014–0.016 |
| | GLE | 140 (2320) B230F | WR7DC | 0.030 | 12B ④ | 12B ④ | NA | 36 | 750 | 750 | 0.014–0.016 | 0.014–0.016 |
| | Turbo | 140 (2320) B230F-Turbo | WR7DC | 0.026 | 12B ④ | 12B ④ | NA | 43 | 750 | 750 | 0.014–0.016 | 0.014–0.016 |
| | 760 GLE | 174 (2849) B280F | HR6DC | 0.026 | 16B ④ | 16B ④ | NA | 35 | 750 | 750 | 0.004–0.006 | 0.010–0.012 |
| | Turbo | 140 (2320) B230F-Turbo | WR7DC | 0.026 | 12B ④ | 12B ④ | NA | 43 | 750 | 750 | 0.014–0.016 | 0.014–0.016 |
| | 780 | 174 (2849) B280F | HR6DC | 0.026 | 16B ④ | 16B ④ | NA | 35 | 750 | 750 | 0.004–0.006 | 0.010–0.012 |
| 1988 | 240 DL | 140 (2320) B230F | WR7DC | 0.030 | 12B ④ | 12B ④ | NA | 36 | 750 | 750 | 0.014–0.016 | 0.014–0.016 |
| | GL | 140 (2320) B230F | WR7DC | 0.030 | 12B ④ | 12B ④ | NA | 36 | 750 | 750 | 0.014–0.016 | 0.014–0.016 |
| | 740 GL | 140 (2320) B230F | WR7DC | 0.030 | 12B ④ | 12B ④ | NA | 36 | 750 | 750 | 0.014–0.016 | 0.014–0.016 |
| | GLE | 140 (2320) B230F | WR7DC | 0.030 | 12B ④ | 12B ④ | NA | 36 | 750 | 750 | 0.014–0.016 | 0.014–0.016 |
| | Turbo | 140 (2320) B230F-Turbo | WR7DC | 0.026 | 12B ④ | 12B ④ | NA | 43 | 750 | 750 | 0.014–0.016 | 0.014–0.016 |
| | 760 GLE | 174 (2849) B280F | HR6DC | 0.026 | 16B ④ | 16B ④ | NA | 35 | 750 | 750 | 0.004–0.006 | 0.010–0.012 |
| | Turbo | 140 (2320) B230F-Turbo | WR7DC | 0.026 | 12B ④ | 12B ④ | NA | 43 | 750 | 750 | 0.014–0.016 | 0.014–0.016 |
| | 780 | 174 (2849) B280F | HR6DC | 0.026 | 16B ④ | 16B ④ | NA | 35 | 750 | 750 | 0.004–0.006 | 0.010–0.012 |
| 1989 | 240 DL | 140 (2320) B230F | WR7DC | 0.030 | 12B ④ | 12B ④ | NA | 36 | 750 | 750 | 0.014–0.016 | 0.014–0.016 |
| | GL | 140 (2320) B230F | WR7DC | 0.030 | 12B ④ | 12B ④ | NA | 36 | 750 | 750 | 0.014–0.016 | 0.014–0.016 |
| | 740 GL | 140 (2320) B230F | WR7DC | 0.030 | 12B ④ | 12B ④ | NA | 36 | 750 | 750 | 0.014–0.016 | 0.014–0.016 |
| | GLE | 140 (2320) B234F | WR7DC | 0.030 | 15B ⑧ | 15B ⑧ | NA | 36 | 850 | 850 | Hyd. | Hyd. |
| | Turbo | 140 (2320) B230F-Turbo | WR7DC | 0.026 | 12B ④ | 12B ④ | NA | 43 | 750 | 750 | 0.014–0.016 | 0.014–0.016 |

## GASOLINE ENGINE TUNE-UP SPECIFICATIONS

| Year | Model | Engine Displacement cu. in. (cc) | Spark Plugs Type | Spark Plugs Gap (in.) | Ignition Timing③ (deg.) MT | Ignition Timing③ (deg.) AT | Com-pression Pressure (psi) | Fuel Pump (psi) | Idle Speed (rpm) MT | Idle Speed (rpm) AT | Valve Clearance In. | Valve Clearance Ex. |
|---|---|---|---|---|---|---|---|---|---|---|---|---|
| 1989 | 760 GLE | 174 (2849) B280F | HR6DC | 0.026 | 16B ④ | 16B ④ | NA | 35 | 750 | 750 | 0.004–0.006 | 0.010–0.012 |
| | Turbo | 140 (2320) B230F-Turbo | WR7DC | 0.026 | 12B ④ | 12B ④ | NA | 43 | 750 | 750 | 0.014–0.016 | 0.014–0.016 |
| | 780 | 174 (2849) B280F | HR6DC | 0.026 | 16B ④ | 16B ④ | NA | 35 | 750 | 750 | 0.004–0.006 | 0.010–0.012 |
| | Turbo | 140 (2320) B230F-Turbo | WR7DC | 0.026 | 12B ④ | 12B ④ | NA | 43 | 750 | 750 | 0.014–0.016 | 0.014–0.016 |
| 1990 | ALL | SEE UNDERHOOD SPECIFICATIONS STICKER | | | | | | | | | | |

**NOTE:** Some models are equipped with the Constant Idle Speed system (CIS) and cannot be adjusted.
Hyd. Hydraulic
① Canada only
② Station Wagon
③ Vacuum advance disconnected, A/C turned off
④ @ 750 rpm
⑤ @ 900 rpm
⑥ @ 800 rpm
⑦ @ 2500 rpm
⑧ @ 850 rpm

## DIESEL ENGINE TUNE-UP SPECIFICATIONS

| Year | Model | Engine Displacement cu. in. (cc) | Valve Clearance① Intake (in.) | Valve Clearance① Exhaust (in.) | Intake Valve Opens (deg.) | Injection Pump Setting⑧ (deg.) | Injection Nozzle Pressure (psi) New Used | Idle Speed (rpm) | Cranking Compression Pressure (psi)⑤ |
|---|---|---|---|---|---|---|---|---|---|
| 1983 | 240 DL | 145 (2383) D24 | 0.006–0.010 | 0.014–0.018 | NA | 0.0265–0.0295 ② | 1845–1700 ③ | 720–880 ④ | 340– |
| | GL | 145 (2383) D24 | 0.006–0.010 | 0.014–0.018 | NA | 0.0265–0.0295 ② | 1845–1700 ③ | 720–880 ④ | 340–455 |
| | 760 GLE | 145 (2383) D24-Turbo⑥ | 0.006–0.010 | 0.014–0.018 | NA | 0.0283–0.0315 | 2318-2062 ⑦ | 750 | 313–455 |
| 1984 | 240 Diesel | 145 (2383) D24 | 0.006–0.010 | 0.014–0.018 | NA | 0.0265–0.0295 ② | 1845–1700 ③ | 720–880 ④ | 340–455 |
| | 760 GLE | 145 (2383) D24-Turbo | 0.006–0.010 | 0.014–0.018 | NA | 0.0283–0.0315 | 2318-2062 ⑦ | 750 | 313–455 |
| 1985 | 240 Diesel | 145 (2383) D24 | 0.006–0.010 | 0.014–0.018 | NA | 0.0265–0.0295 ② | 1845–1700 ③ | 720–880 ④ | 340–455 |
| | 740 TD (S) | 145 (2383) D24-Turbo⑥ | 0.006–0.010 | 0.014–0.018 | NA | 0.0283–0.0315 | 2318–2062 ⑦ | 830 | 313 455 |
| | 760 GLE TD | 145 (2383) D24-Turbo⑥ | 0.006–0.010 | 0.014–0.018 | NA | 0.0283–0.0315 | 2318–2062 ⑦ | 830 | 313–455 |
| 1986 | 740 GLE TD | 145 (2383) D24-Turbo⑥ | 0.006–0.010 | 0.014–0.018 | NA | 0.0283–0.0315 | 2318–2062 ⑦ | 830 | 313–455 |

NOTE: When setting injection timing, distributor plunger stroke must be at top dead center
① Cold
② See text. Acceptable range when checking 0.0287–0.0315 in.
③ Acceptable range. When servicing set to 1775–1920 psi
④ Maximum safe speed—5100-5200 rpm (high idle)
⑤ Maximum difference between cylinders 115 lbs. psi
⑥ Turbo-Diesel
⑦ Acceptable range. When servicing set to 2205-2318 psi.
⑧ Plunger stroke

## FIRING ORDER

**NOTE: To avoid confusion, always replace spark plug wires one at a time.**

FIRING ORDER
1-6-3-5-2-4

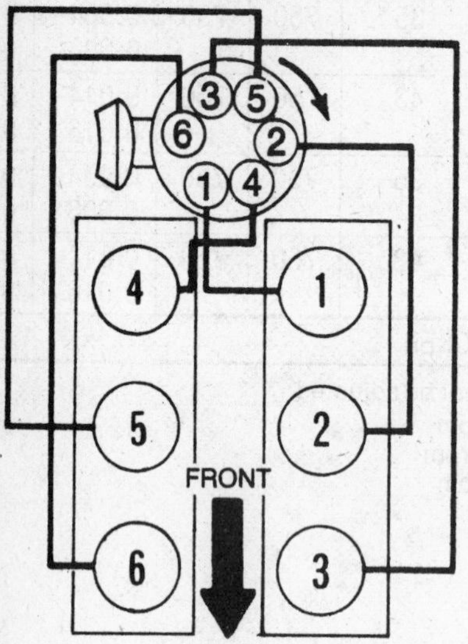


B27F, B28

FIRING ORDER
1-3-4-2

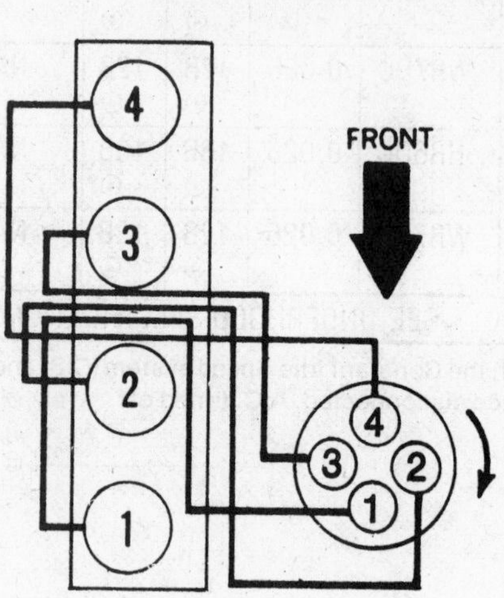


B23, B230 and B234 series

FIRING ORDER
1-5-3-6-4-2

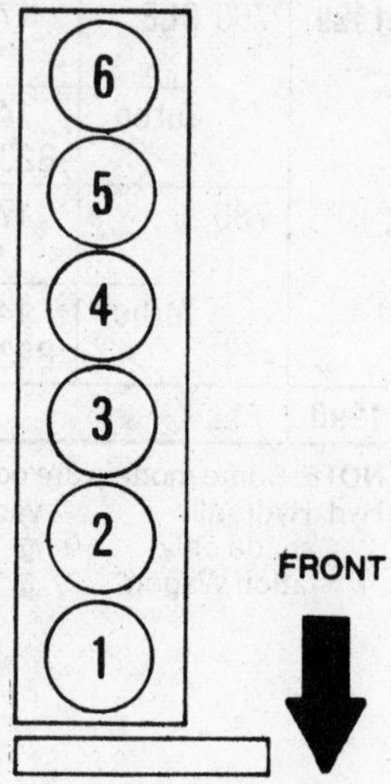


D24 Diesel

## CAPACITIES

| Year | Model | Engine Displacement cu. in. (cc) | Engine Crankcase③ with Filter | Engine Crankcase③ without Filter | Transmission (pts) 4-Spd | Transmission (pts) 5-Spd | Transmission (pts) Auto. | Drive Axle (pts.) | Fuel Tank (gal.) | Cooling System (qts.) |
|---|---|---|---|---|---|---|---|---|---|---|
| 1983 | 240 DL | 140 (2320) B23F | 4.0 | 3.5 | 4.8 | — | 15.6 | ④ | 15.8 | 10.0 |
| | DL | 130 (2127) B21F-Turbo | 4.0 | 3.5 | 4.8 | — | 15.6 | ④ | 15.8 | 10.0 |
| | DL | 145 (2383) D24 | 7.4 | 6.6 | 4.8 | — | 15.6 | ④ | 15.8 | 10.0 |
| | DL | 130 (2127) B21A① | 4.0 | 3.5 | 4.8 | — | 15.6 | ④ | 15.8 | 10.0 |
| | GL | 140 (2320) B23F | 4.0 | 3.5 | 4.8 | — | 15.6 | ④ | 15.8 | 10.0 |
| | GL | 145 (2383) D24 | 7.4 | 6.6 | 4.8 | — | 15.6 | ④ | 15.8 | 10.0 |
| | GL | 140 (2320) B23E① | 4.0 | 3.5 | 4.8 | — | 15.6 | ④ | 15.8 | 10.0 |
| | GLT | 140 (2320) B23E① | 4.0 | 3.5 | 4.8 | — | 15.6 | ④ | 15.8 | 10.0 |
| | Turbo | 130 (2127) B21F-Turbo | 4.0 | 3.5 | 4.8 | — | 15.6 | ④ | 15.8 | 10.0 |
| | 760 GLE | 174 (2849) B28F | 6.9 | 6.3 | 4.8 | — | 15.6 | ④ | 15.8 | 10.5 |
| | GLE | 145 (2383) D24-Turbo | 6.3 | 5.2 | 4.8 | — | 15.6 | ④ | 15.8 | 11.5 |
| | Turbo | 140 (2320) B23F-Turbo | 4.1 | 3.6 | 4.8 | — | 15.6 | ④ | 15.8 | 10.0 |

## CAPACITIES

| Year | Model | Engine Displacement cu. in. (cc) | Engine Crankcase③ with Filter | Engine Crankcase③ without Filter | Transmission (pts) 4-Spd | Transmission (pts) 5-Spd | Transmission (pts) Auto. | Drive Axle (pts.) | Fuel Tank (gal.) | Cooling System (qts.) |
|---|---|---|---|---|---|---|---|---|---|---|
| 1984 | 240 Diesel | 145 (2383) D24 | 7.4 | 6.6 | 4.8 | — | 15.6 | ④ | 15.8 | 10.0 |
| | DL | 140 (2320) B23F | 4.0 | 3.5 | 4.8 | — | 15.6 | ④ | 15.8 | 10.0 |
| | DL | 130 (2127) B21A① | 4.0 | 3.5 | 4.8 | — | 15.6 | ④ | 15.8 | 10.0 |
| | GL | 140 (2320) B23F | 4.0 | 3.5 | 4.8 | — | 15.6 | ④ | 15.8 | 10.0 |
| | GLE | 140 (2320) B23F① | 4.0 | 3.5 | 4.8 | — | 15.6 | ④ | 15.8 | 10.0 |
| | Turbo | 130 (2127) B21F-Turbo | 4.0 | 3.5 | 4.8 | — | 15.6 | ④ | 15.8 | 10.0 |
| | 760 GLE | 174 (2849) B28F | 6.9 | 6.3 | 4.8 | — | 15.6 | ④ | 15.8 | 10.5 |
| | GLE | 145 (2383) D24-Turbo | 6.3 | 5.2 | 4.8 | — | 15.6 | ④ | 15.8 | 11.5 |
| | Turbo | 140 (2320) B23F-Turbo | 4.1 | 3.6 | 4.8 | — | 15.6 | ④ | 15.8 | 10.0 |
| 1985 | 240 Diesel | 145 (2383) D24 | 7.4 | 6.6 | 4.8 | — | 15.6 | ④ | 15.8 | 10.0 |
| | DL | 140 (2320) B230F | 4.0 | 3.5 | 4.8 | — | 15.6 | ④ | 15.8 | 10.0 |
| | GL | 140 (2320) B230F | 4.0 | 3.5 | 4.8 | — | 15.6 | ④ | 15.8 | 10.0 |
| | Turbo | 130 (2127) B21F-Turbo | 4.0 | 3.5 | 4.8 | — | 15.6 | ④ | 15.8 | 10.0 |
| | 740 GLE | 140 (2320) B230F | 4.1 | 3.6 | 4.8 | — | 15.6 | ④ | 15.8 | 10.0 |
| | TD② | 145 (2383) D24-Turbo | 6.3 | 5.2 | 4.8 | — | 15.6 | ④ | 15.8 | 11.5 |
| | Turbo | 140 (2320) B230F-Turbo | 4.1 ③ | 3.6 ③ | 4.8 | — | 15.6 | ④ | 15.8 | 10.0 |
| | 760 GLE | 174 (2849) B28F | 6.9 | 6.3 | 4.8 | — | 15.6 | ④ | 15.8 | 10.5 |
| | GLE TD | 145 (2383) D24-Turbo | 6.3 | 5.2 | 4.8 | — | 15.6 | ④ | 15.8 | 11.5 |
| | Turbo | 140 (2320) B230F-Turbo | 4.1 ③ | 3.6 ③ | 4.8 | — | 15.6 | ④ | 15.8 | 10.0 |
| 1986 | 240 DL | 140 (2320) B230F | 4.0 | 3.5 | 4.8 | — | 15.6 | ④ | 15.8 | 10.0 |
| | GL | 140 (2320) B230F | 4.0 | 3.5 | 4.8 | — | 15.6 | ④ | 15.8 | 10.0 |
| | 740 GL | 140 (2320) B230F | 4.1 | 3.6 | 4.8 | — | 15.6 | ④ | 15.8 | 10.0 |
| | GLE | 140 (2320) B230F | 4.1 | 3.6 | 4.8 | — | 15.6 | ④ | 15.8 | 10.0 |
| | GLE TD | 145 (2383) D24-Turbo | 6.3 | 5.2 | 4.8 | — | 15.6 | ④ | 15.8 | 11.5 |

## CAPACITIES

| Year | Model | | Engine Displacement cu. in. (cc) | Engine Crankcase with Filter | Engine Crankcase without Filter | Transmission (pts) 4-Spd | Transmission (pts) 5-Spd | Transmission (pts) Auto. | Drive Axle (pts.) | Fuel Tank (gal.) | Cooling System (qts.) |
|---|---|---|---|---|---|---|---|---|---|---|---|
| 1986 | | Turbo | 140 (2320) B230F-Turbo | 4.1 ③ | 3.6 ③ | 4.8 | — | 15.6 | ④ | 15.8 | 10.0 |
| | 760 GLE | | 174 (2849) B28F | 6.9 | 6.3 | 4.8 | — | 15.6 | ④ | 15.8 | 10.5 |
| | | Turbo | 140 (2320) B230F-Turbo | 4.1 ③ | 3.6 ③ | 4.8 | — | 15.6 | ④ | 15.8 | 10.0 |
| 1987 | 240 DL | | 140 (2320) B230F | 4.0 | 3.5 | — | 2.8 | 15.6 | ④ | 15.8 | 10.0 |
| | | GL | 140 (2320) B230F | 4.0 | 3.5 | — | 2.8 | 15.6 | ④ | 15.8 | 10.0 |
| | 740 GL | | 140 (2320) B230F | 4.1 | 3.6 | 4.8 | — | 15.6 | ④ | 15.8 | 10.0 |
| | | GLE | 140 (2320) B230F | 4.1 | 3.6 | 4.8 | — | 15.6 | ④ | 15.8 | 10.0 |
| | | Turbo | 140 (2320) B230F-Turbo | 4.1 ③ | 3.6 ③ | 4.8 | — | 15.6 | ④ | 15.8 | 10.0 |
| | 760 GLE | | 174 (2849) B280F | 6.3 | 5.8 | 4.8 | — | 15.8 | ④ | 15.8 | 10.5 |
| | | Turbo | 140 (2320) B230F-Turbo | 4.1 ③ | 3.6 ③ | 4.8 | — | 15.8 | ④ | 15.8 | 10.0 |
| | 780 | | 174 (2849) B280F | 6.3 | 5.8 | 4.8 | — | 15.8 | ④ | 15.8 | 10.5 |
| 1988 | 240 DL | | 140 (2320) B230F | 4.0 | 3.5 | — | 3.2 | 15.8 | ④ | 15.8 | 10.0 |
| | | GL | 140 (2320) B230F | 4.0 | 3.5 | — | 3.2 | 15.8 | ④ | 15.8 | 10.0 |
| | 740 GL | | 140 (2320) B230F | 4.1 | 3.6 | — | 3.2 | 15.8 | ④ | 15.8 | 10.0 |
| | | GLE | 140 (2320) B230F | 4.1 | 3.6 | — | 3.2 | 15.8 | ④ | 15.8 | 10.0 |
| | | Turbo | 140 (2320) B230F-Turbo | 4.1 ③ | 3.6 ③ | — | 4.8 | 15.8 | ④ | 15.8 | 10.0 |
| | 760 GLE | | 174 (2849) B280F | 6.3 | 5.8 | — | — | 15.8 | ④ | 21.1 | 10.5 |
| | | Turbo | 140 (2320) B230F-Turbo | 4.1 ③ | 3.6 ③ | — | — | 15.8 | ④ | 21.1 | 10.0 |
| | 780 | | 174 (2849) B280F | 6.3 | 5.8 | — | — | 15.8 | ④ | 21.1 | 10.5 |
| 1989-90 | 240 DL | | 140 (2320) B230F | 4.0 | 3.5 | — | 3.2 | 15.8 | ④ | 15.8 | 10.0 |
| | | GL | 140 (2320) B230F | 4.0 | 3.5 | — | 3.2 | 15.8 | ④ | 15.8 | 10.0 |
| | 740 GL | | 140 (2320) B230F | 4.1 | 3.6 | — | 3.2 | 15.8 | ④ | 15.8 | 10.0 |
| | | GLE | 140 (2320) B234F | 4.2 | 3.7 | — | 4.8 | 15.8 | ④ | 15.8 | 10.0 |
| | | Turbo | 140 (2320) B230F-Turbo | 4.1 ③ | 3.6 ③ | — | 4.8 | 15.8 | ④ | 15.8 | 10.0 |

## CAPACITIES

| Year | Model | Engine Displacement cu. in. (cc) | Engine Crankcase③ with Filter | Engine Crankcase③ without Filter | Transmission (pts) 4-Spd | Transmission (pts) 5-Spd | Transmission (pts) Auto. | Drive Axle (pts.) | Fuel Tank (gal.) | Cooling System (qts.) |
|---|---|---|---|---|---|---|---|---|---|---|
| 1989-90 | 760 GLE | 174 (2849) B280F | 6.3 | 5.8 | — | — | 15.8 | ④ | 21.1 | 10.5 |
| | Turbo | 140 (2320) B230F-Turbo | 4.1 ③ | 3.6 ③ | — | — | 15.8 | ④ | 21.1 | 10.0 |
| | 780 | 174 (2849) B280F | 6.3 | 5.8 | — | — | 15.8 | ④ | 21.1 | 10.5 |
| | Turbo | 140 (2320) B230F-Turbo | 4.1 ③ | 3.6 ③ | — | — | 15.8 | ④ | 21.1 | 10.5 |

① Canada only
② Station wagon
③ Models with turbo—add 0.6 qt. if oil cooler has been drained
④ 1030 axle—2.8 pts.
1031 axle—3.4 pts.

## CRANKSHAFT AND CONNECTING ROD SPECIFICATIONS

All measurements are given in inches.

| Year | Engine Displacement cu. in. (cc) | Crankshaft Main Brg. Journal Dia. | Crankshaft Main Brg. Oil Clearance | Crankshaft Shaft End-play | Crankshaft Thrust on No. | Connecting Rod Journal Diameter | Connecting Rod Oil Clearance | Connecting Rod Side Clearance |
|---|---|---|---|---|---|---|---|---|
| 1983 | 130 (2127) B21A① | 2.4981–2.4986 | 0.0011–0.0033 | 0.0015–0.0058 | 5 | 2.1255–2.1260 | 0.0009–0.0028 | 0.006–0.014 |
| | 130 (2127) B21F-Turbo | 2.4981–2.4986 | 0.0011–0.0033 | 0.0015–0.0058 | 5 | 2.1255–2.1260 | 0.0009–0.0028 | 0.006–0.014 |
| | 140 (2320) B23F | 2.4981–2.4986 | 0.0011–0.0033 | 0.0015–0.0058 | 5 | 2.1255–2.1260 | 0.0009–0.0028 | 0.006–0.014 |
| | 140 (2320) B23E① | 2.4981–2.4986 | 0.0011–0.0033 | 0.0015–0.0058 | 5 | 2.1255–2.1260 | 0.0009–0.0028 | 0.006–0.014 |
| | 140 (2320) B23F-Turbo | 2.4981–2.4986 | 0.0011–0.0033 | 0.0015–0.0058 | 5 | 2.1255–2.1260 | 0.0009–0.0028 | 0.006–0.014 |
| | 145 (2383) D24 | 2.2833–2.2825 | 0.0006–0.0030 | 0.0028–0.0071 | 4 | 1.8802–1.8810 | 0.0047 ② | 0.0158 |
| | 145 (2383) D24-Turbo | 2.2833–2.2825 | 0.0006–0.0030 | 0.0028–0.0071 | 4 | 1.8802–1.8810 | 0.0047 ② | 0.0158 |
| | 174 (2849) B28F | 2.7583 | 0.0035 | 0.0106 | 4 | 2.0585 | 0.0031 | 0.015 |
| 1984 | 130 (2127) B21A① | 2.4981–2.4986 | 0.0011–0.0033 | 0.0015–0.0058 | 5 | 2.1255–2.1260 | 0.0009–0.0028 | 0.006–0.014 |
| | 130 (2127) B23F | 2.4981–2.4986 | 0.0011–0.0033 | 0.0015–0.0058 | 5 | 2.1255–2.1260 | 0.0009–0.0028 | 0.006–0.014 |
| | 140 (2320) B23F-Turbo | 2.4981–2.4986 | 0.0011–0.0033 | 0.0015–0.0058 | 5 | 2.1255–2.1260 | 0.0009–0.0028 | 0.006–0.014 |
| | 140 (2320) B23F-Turbo | 2.4981–2.4986 | 0.0011–0.0033 | 0.0015–0.0058 | 5 | 2.1255–2.1260 | 0.0009–0.0028 | 0.006–0.014 |
| | 145 (2383) D24 | 2.2833–2.2825 | 0.0006–0.0030 | 0.0028–0.0071 | 4 | 1.8802–1.8810 | 0.0047 ② | 0.0158 |
| | 145 (2383) D24-Turbo | 2.2833–2.2825 | 0.0006–0.0030 | 0.0028–0.0071 | 4 | 1.8802–1.8810 | 0.0047 ② | 0.0158 |
| | 174 (2849) B28F | 2.7583 | 0.0035 | 0.0106 | 4 | 2.0585 | 0.0031 | 0.015 |

## CRANKSHAFT AND CONNECTING ROD SPECIFICATIONS

All measurements are given in inches.

| Year | Engine Displacement cu. in. (cc) | Crankshaft Main Brg. Journal Dia. | Crankshaft Main Brg. Oil Clearance | Crankshaft Shaft End-play | Crankshaft Thrust on No. | Connecting Rod Journal Diameter | Connecting Rod Oil Clearance | Connecting Rod Side Clearance |
|---|---|---|---|---|---|---|---|---|
| 1985 | 130 (2127) B21F-Turbo | 2.4981–2.4986 | 0.0011–0.0033 | 0.0015–0.0058 | 5 | 2.1255–2.1260 | 0.0009–0.0028 | 0.006–0.014 |
| | 140 (2320) B230F | 2.4981–2.4986 | 0.0011–0.0033 | 0.0015–0.0058 | 5 | 2.1255–2.1260 | 0.0009–0.0028 | 0.006–0.014 |
| | 140 (2320) B230F-Turbo | 2.4981–2.4986 | 0.0011–0.0033 | 0.0015–0.0058 | 5 | 2.1255–2.1260 | 0.0009–0.0028 | 0.006–0.014 |
| | 145 (2383) D24 | 2.2833–2.2825 | 0.0006–0.0030 | 0.0028–0.0071 | 4 | 1.8802–1.8810 | 0.0047 ② | 0.0158 |
| | 145 (2383) D24-Turbo | 2.2833–2.2825 | 0.0006–0.0030 | 0.0028–0.0071 | 4 | 1.8802–1.8810 | 0.0047 ② | 0.0158 |
| | 174 (2849) B28F | 2.7583 | 0.0035 | 0.0106 | 4 | 2.0585 | 0.0031 | 0.015 |
| 1986 | 140 (2320) B230F | 2.4981–2.4986 | 0.0011–0.0033 | 0.0015–0.0058 | 5 | 2.1255–2.1260 | 0.0009–0.0028 | 0.006–0.014 |
| | 140 (2320) B230F-Turbo | 2.4981–2.4986 | 0.0011–0.0033 | 0.0015–0.0058 | 5 | 2.1255–2.1260 | 0.0009–0.0028 | 0.006–0.014 |
| | 145 (2383) D24-Turbo | 2.2833–2.2825 | 0.0006–0.0030 | 0.0028–0.0071 | 4 | 1.8802–1.8810 | 0.0047 ② | 0.0158 |
| | 174 (2849) B28F | 2.7583 | 0.0035 | 0.0106 | 4 | 2.0585 | 0.0031 | 0.015 |
| 1987 | 140 (2320) B230F | 2.4981–2.4986 | 0.0011–0.0033 | 0.0015–0.0058 | 5 | 2.1255–2.1260 | 0.0009–0.0028 | 0.006–0.014 |
| | 140 (2320) B230F-Turbo | 2.4981–2.4986 | 0.0011–0.0033 | 0.0015–0.0058 | 5 | 2.1255–2.1260 | 0.0009–0.0028 | 0.006–0.014 |
| | 174 (2849) B280F | 2.7583 | 0.0035 | 0.0106 | 4 | 2.0585 | 0.0031 | 0.015 |
| 1988 | 140 (2320) B230F | 2.4981–2.4986 | 0.0011–0.0033 | 0.0015–0.0058 | 5 | 2.1255–2.1260 | 0.0009–0.0028 | 0.006–0.014 |
| | 140 (2320) B230F-Turbo | 2.4981–2.4986 | 0.0011–0.0033 | 0.0015–0.0058 | 5 | 2.1255–2.1260 | 0.0009–0.0028 | 0.006–0.014 |
| | 174 (2849) B280F | 2.7583 | 0.0035 | 0.0106 | 4 | 2.0585 | 0.0031 | 0.015 |
| 1989-90 | 140 (2320) B230F | 2.4981–2.4986 | 0.0011–0.0033 | 0.0015–0.0058 | 5 | 2.1255–2.1260 | 0.0009–0.0028 | 0.006–0.014 |
| | 140 (2320) B230F-Turbo | 2.4981–2.4986 | 0.0011–0.0033 | 0.0015–0.0058 | 5 | 2.1255–2.1260 | 0.0009–0.0028 | 0.006–0.014 |
| | 140 (2320) B234F | 1.9640–1.9648 | 0.0011–0.0033 | 0.0015–0.0058 | 5 | 2.0472–2.0476 | 0.0009–0.0028 | 0.006–0.018 |
| | 174 (2849) B280F | 2.7583 | 0.0035 | 0.0106 | 4 | 2.0585 | 0.0031 | 0.015 |

① Canada only

② New clearance—0.0005–0.0024 in.

## VALVE SPECIFICATIONS

| Year | Engine Displacement cu. in. (cc) | Seat Angle (deg.) | Face Angle (deg.) | Spring Test Pressure (lbs. @ in.) | Spring Installed Height (in.) | Stem-to-Guide Clearance (in.) | | Stem Diameter (in.) | |
|---|---|---|---|---|---|---|---|---|---|
| | | | | | | Intake | Exhaust | Intake | Exhaust |
| 1983 | 130 (2127) B21A① | 44.75 | 45.5 | 170 @ 1.06 | 1.77 | 0.0012–0.0024 | 0.0024–0.0035 | 0.3132–0.3135 | 0.3128–0.3126 |
| | 130 (2127) B21F-Turbo | 44.75 | 45.5 | 170 @ 1.06 | 1.77 | 0.0012–0.0024 | 0.0024–0.0035 | 0.3132–0.3135 | 0.3128–0.3126 |
| | 140 (2320) B23F | 45 | 44.5 | 165 @ 1.06 | 1.77 | 0.0012–0.0024 | 0.0024–0.0035 | 0.3132–0.3138 | 0.3128–0.3124 |
| | 140 (2320) B23E① | 45 | 44.5 | 165 @ 1.06 | 1.77 | 0.0012–0.0024 | 0.0024–0.0035 | 0.3132–0.3138 | 0.3128–0.3124 |
| | 140 (2320) B23F-Turbo | 45 | 44.5 | 165 @ 1.06 | 1.77 | 0.0012–0.0024 | 0.0024–0.0035 | 0.3132–0.3138 | 0.3128–0.3124 |
| | 145 (2383) D24 | 45 | ⑤ | ⑥ | ⑦ | ⑧ | ⑧ | 0.3140 | 0.3130 |
| | 145 (2383) D24-Turbo | 45 | ⑤ | ⑥ | ⑦ | ⑧ | ⑧ | 0.3140 | 0.3130 |
| | 174 (2849) B28F | ② | ② | 143 @ 1.18 | 1.85 | ③ | ③ | ④ | ④ |
| 1984 | 130 (2127) B21A① | 44.75 | 45.5 | 170 @ 1.06 | 1.77 | 0.0012–0.0024 | 0.0024–0.0035 | 0.3132–0.3135 | 0.3128–0.3126 |
| | 130 (2127) B21F-Turbo | 44.75 | 45.5 | 170 @ 1.06 | 1.77 | 0.0012–0.0024 | 0.0024–0.0035 | 0.3132–0.3135 | 0.3128–0.3126 |
| | 140 (2320) B23F | 45 | 44.5 | 165 @ 1.06 | 1.77 | 0.0012–0.0024 | 0.0024–0.0035 | 0.3132–0.3138 | 0.3128–0.3124 |
| | 140 (2320) B23F-Turbo | 45 | 44.5 | 165 @ 1.06 | 1.77 | 0.0012–0.0024 | 0.0024–0.0035 | 0.3132–0.3138 | 0.3128–0.3124 |
| | 145 (2383) D24 | 45 | ⑤ | ⑥ | ⑦ | ⑧ | ⑧ | 0.3140 | 0.3130 |
| | 145 (2383) D24-Turbo | 45 | ⑤ | ⑥ | ⑦ | ⑧ | ⑧ | 0.3140 | 0.3130 |
| | 174 (2849) B28F | ② | ② | 143 @ 1.18 | 1.85 | ③ | ③ | ④ | ④ |
| 1985 | 130 (2127) B21F-Turbo | 44.75 | 45.5 | 170 @ 1.06 | 1.77 | 0.0012–0.0024 | 0.0024–0.0035 | 0.3132–0.3135 | 0.3128–0.3126 |
| | 140 (2320) B230F | 45 | 44.5 | 170 @ 1.06 | 1.79 | 0.0012–0.0024 | 0.0024–0.0036 | 0.3132–0.3138 | 0.3128–0.3134 |
| | 140 (2320) B230F-Turbo | 45 | 44.5 | 170 @ 1.06 | 1.79 | 0.0012–0.0024 | 0.0024–0.0036 | 0.3132–0.3138 | 0.3128–0.3134 |
| | 145 (2383) D24 | 45 | ⑤ | ⑥ | ⑦ | ⑧ | ⑧ | 0.3140 | 0.3130 |
| | 145 (2383) D24-Turbo | 45 | ⑤ | ⑥ | ⑦ | ⑧ | ⑧ | 0.3140 | 0.3130 |
| | 174 (2849) B28F | ② | ② | 143 @ 1.18 | 1.85 | ③ | ③ | ④ | ④ |

## VALVE SPECIFICATIONS

| Year | Engine Displacement cu. in. (cc) | Seat Angle (deg.) | Face Angle (deg.) | Spring Test Pressure (lbs. @ in.) | Spring Installed Height (in.) | Stem-to-Guide Clearance (in.) | | Stem Diameter (in.) | |
|---|---|---|---|---|---|---|---|---|---|
| | | | | | | Intake | Exhaust | Intake | Exhaust |
| 1986 | 140 (2320) B230F | 45 | 44.5 | 158 @ 1.08 | 1.79 | 0.0012–0.0024 | 0.0024–0.0036 | 0.3132–0.3138 | 0.3128–0.3134 |
| | 140 (2320) B230F-Turbo | 45 | 44.5 | 158 @ 1.08 | 1.79 | 0.0012–0.0024 | 0.0024–0.0036 | 0.3132–0.3138 | 0.3128–0.3134 |
| | 145 (2383) D24-Turbo | 45 | ⑤ | ⑥ | ⑦ | ⑧ | ⑧ | 0.3140 | 0.3130 |
| | 174 (2849) B28F | ② | ② | 143 @ 1.18 | 1.85 | ③ | ③ | ④ | ④ |
| 1987 | 140 (2320) B230F | 45 | 44.5 | 158 @ 1.08 | 1.79 | 0.0012–0.0024 | 0.0024–0.0036 | 0.3132–0.3138 | 0.3128–0.3134 |
| | 140 (2320) B230F-Turbo | 45 | 44.5 | 158 @ 1.08 | 1.79 | 0.0012–0.0024 | 0.0024–0.0036 | 0.3132–0.3138 | 0.3128–0.3134 |
| | 174 (2849) B280F | 45 | 44.5 | 143 @ 1.18 | 1.85 | ③ | ③ | ④ | ④ |
| 1988 | 140 (2320) B230F | 45 | 44.5 | 158 @ 1.08 | 1.79 | 0.0012–0.0024 | 0.0024–0.0036 | 0.3132–0.3138 | 0.3128–0.3134 |
| | 140 (2320) B230F-Turbo | 45 | 44.5 | 158 @ 1.08 | 1.79 | 0.0012–0.0024 | 0.0024–0.0036 | 0.3132–0.3138 | 0.3128–0.3134 |
| | 174 (2849) B280F | 45 | 44.5 | 143 @ 1.18 | 1.85 | ③ | ③ | ④ | ④ |
| 1989-90 | 140 (2320) B230F | 45 | 44.5 | 158 @ 1.08 | 1.79 | 0.0012–0.0024 | 0.0024–0.0036 | 0.3132–0.3138 | 0.3128–0.3134 |
| | 140 (2320) B234F | 45 | 44.5 | 144 @ 1.04 | 1.69 | 0.0012–0.0024 | 0.0016–0.0028 | NA NA | NA NA |
| | 140 (2320) B230F-Turbo | 45 | 44.5 | 158 @ 1.08 | 1.79 | 0.0012–0.0024 | 0.0024–0.0036 | 0.3132–0.3138 | 0.3128–0.3134 |
| | 174 (2849) B280F | 45 | 44.5 | 143 @ 1.18 | 1.85 | ③ | ③ | ④ | ④ |

NOTE: Exhaust valves for turbo engines (including turbo diesel) are stellite coated and must not be machined. They may be ground against the valve seat.

NA Not available
① Canada only
② Intake—29.5 degrees
Exhaust—30 degrees
③ Tapered valve guide ID—0.3150-0.3158
④ Tapered valve stem
Intake
Base—0.3135-0.3141
Top—3139-0.3145
Exhaust
Base—0.3127-0.3133
Top—3136-0.3141
⑤ Intake—44.5 degrees
Exhaust—45 degrees
⑥ Two springs per valve
Inner spring—49 lbs. @ 0.72 in.;
Oouter spring—100 lbs. @ 0.878 in.
⑦ Inner 1.335 in.; outer 1.583 in.
⑧ Clearance measured with new valve guide and with valve stem edge to edge with valve guide upper end. Max. clearance 0.051 in.; new clearance 0.012 in.

## PISTON AND RING SPECIFICATIONS

All measurements are given in inches.

| Year | Engine Displacement cu. in. (cc) | Piston Clearance | Ring Gap Top Compression | Ring Gap Bottom Compression | Ring Gap Oil Control | Ring Side Clearance Top Compression | Ring Side Clearance Bottom Compression | Ring Side Clearance Oil Control |
|---|---|---|---|---|---|---|---|---|
| 1983 | 130 (2127) B21A① | 0.0004–0.0016 | 0.0140–0.0260 | 0.0140–0.0220 | 0.010–0.024 | 0.0016–0.0028 | 0.0016–0.0028 | 0.0012–0.0024 |
| | 130 (2127) B21F-Turbo | 0.0008–0.0016 | 0.0140–0.0260 | 0.0140–0.0220 | 0.010–0.024 | 0.0016–0.0028 | 0.0016–0.0028 | 0.0012–0.0024 |
| | 140 (2320) B23F | 0.0020–0.0028 ② | 0.0014–0.0026 | 0.0014–0.0022 | 0.010–0.024 | 0.0015–0.0028 | 0.0015–0.0028 | 0.0012–0.0024 |
| | 140 (2320) B23E① | 0.0020–0.0028 ② | 0.0014–0.0026 | 0.0014–0.0022 | 0.010–0.024 | 0.0015–0.0028 | 0.0015–0.0028 | 0.0012–0.0024 |
| | 140 (2320) B23F-Turbo | 0.0020–0.0028 ② | 0.0014–0.0026 | 0.0014–0.0022 | 0.010–0.024 | 0.0015–0.0028 | 0.0015–0.0028 | 0.0012–0.0024 |
| | 145 (2383) D24 | 0.0012–0.0020 | 0.0012–0.0020 | 0.0012–0.0020 | 0.010–0.019 | 0.0043–0.0055 | 0.0028–0.0039 | 0.0012–0.0028 |
| | 145 (2383) D24-Turbo | 0.0012–0.0020 | 0.0012–0.0020 | 0.0012–0.0020 | 0.010–0.019 | 0.0043–0.0055 | 0.0028–0.0039 | 0.0012–0.0028 |
| | 174 (2849) B28F | 0.0007–0.0015 | 0.0157–0.0236 | 0.0157–0.0236 | 0.0157–0.0570 | 0.0017–0.0029 | 0.0009–0.0212 | 0.0003–0.0091 |
| 1984 | 130 (2127) B21A① | 0.0004–0.0016 | 0.0140–0.0260 | 0.0140–0.0220 | 0.010–0.024 | 0.0016–0.0028 | 0.0016–0.0028 | 0.0012–0.0024 |
| | 130 (2127) B21F-Turbo | 0.0008–0.0016 | 0.0140–0.0260 | 0.0140–0.0220 | 0.010–0.024 | 0.0016–0.0028 | 0.0016–0.0028 | 0.0012–0.0024 |
| | 140 (2320) B23F | 0.0020–0.0028 ② | 0.0014–0.0026 | 0.0014–0.0022 | 0.010–0.024 | 0.0015–0.0028 | 0.0015–0.0028 | 0.0012–0.0024 |
| | 140 (2320) B23F-Turbo | 0.0020–0.0028 ② | 0.0014–0.0026 | 0.0014–0.0022 | 0.010–0.024 | 0.0015–0.0028 | 0.0015–0.0028 | 0.0012–0.0024 |
| | 145 (2383) D24 | 0.0012–0.0020 | 0.0012–0.0020 | 0.0012–0.0020 | 0.010–0.019 | 0.0043–0.0055 | 0.0028–0.0039 | 0.0012–0.0028 |
| | 145 (2383) D24-Turbo | 0.0012–0.0020 | 0.0012–0.0020 | 0.0012–0.0020 | 0.010–0.019 | 0.0043–0.0055 | 0.0028–0.0039 | 0.0012–0.0028 |
| | 174 (2849) B28F | 0.0007–0.0015 | 0.0157–0.0236 | 0.0157–0.0236 | 0.0157–0.0570 | 0.0017–0.0029 | 0.0009–0.0212 | 0.0003–0.0091 |
| 1985 | 130 (2127) B21F-Turbo | 0.0008–0.0016 | 0.0140–0.0260 | 0.0140–0.0220 | 0.010–0.024 | 0.0016–0.0028 | 0.0016–0.0028 | 0.0012–0.0024 |
| | 140 (2320) B230F | 0.0004–0.0012 | 0.0118–0.0217 | 0.0118–0.0217 | 0.0118–0.0236 | 0.0024–0.0036 | 0.0016–0.0028 | 0.0012–0.0026 |
| | 140 (2320) B230F-Turbo | 0.0004–0.0012 | 0.0118–0.0217 | 0.0118–0.0217 | 0.0118–0.0236 | 0.0024–0.0036 | 0.0016–0.0028 | 0.0012–0.0026 |
| | 145 (2383) D24 | 0.0012–0.0020 | 0.0012–0.0020 | 0.0012–0.0020 | 0.010–0.019 | 0.0043–0.0055 | 0.0028–0.0039 | 0.0012–0.0028 |
| | 145 (2383) D24-Turbo | 0.0012–0.0020 | 0.0012–0.0020 | 0.0012–0.0020 | 0.010–0.019 | 0.0043–0.0055 | 0.0028–0.0039 | 0.0012–0.0028 |
| | 174 (2849) B28F | 0.0007–0.0015 | 0.0157–0.0236 | 0.0157–0.0236 | 0.0157–0.0570 | 0.0017–0.0029 | 0.0009–0.0212 | 0.0003–0.0091 |

## PISTON AND RING SPECIFICATIONS

All measurements are given in inches.

| Year | Engine Displacement cu. in. (cc) | Piston Clearance | Ring Gap Top Compression | Ring Gap Bottom Compression | Ring Gap Oil Control | Ring Side Clearance Top Compression | Ring Side Clearance Bottom Compression | Ring Side Clearance Oil Control |
|---|---|---|---|---|---|---|---|---|
| 1986 | 140 (2320) B230F | 0.0004–0.0012 | 0.0118–0.0217 | 0.0118–0.0217 | 0.0118–0.0236 | 0.0024–0.0036 | 0.0016–0.0028 | 0.0012–0.0026 |
| | 140 (2320) B230F-Turbo | 0.0004–0.0012 | 0.0118–0.0217 | 0.0118–0.0217 | 0.0118–0.0236 | 0.0024–0.0036 | 0.0016–0.0028 | 0.0012–0.0026 |
| | 145 (2383) D24-Turbo | 0.0012–0.0020 | 0.0012–0.0020 | 0.0012–0.0020 | 0.010–0.019 | 0.0043–0.0055 | 0.0028–0.0039 | 0.0012–0.0028 |
| | 174 (2849) B28F | 0.0007–0.0015 | 0.0157–0.0236 | 0.0157–0.0236 | 0.0157–0.0570 | 0.0017–0.0029 | 0.0009–0.0212 | 0.0003–0.0091 |
| 1987 | 140 (2320) B230F | 0.0004–0.0012 | 0.0118–0.0217 | 0.0118–0.0217 | 0.0118–0.0236 | 0.0024–0.0036 | 0.0016–0.0028 | 0.0012–0.0026 |
| | 140 (2320) B230F-Turbo | 0.0004–0.0012 | 0.0118–0.0217 | 0.0118–0.0217 | 0.0118–0.0236 | 0.0024–0.0036 | 0.0016–0.0028 | 0.0012–0.0026 |
| | 174 (2849) B280F | 0.0007–0.0015 | 0.0157–0.0236 | 0.0157–0.0236 | 0.0157–0.0570 | 0.0017–0.0029 | 0.0009–0.0212 | 0.0003–0.0091 |
| 1988 | 140 (2320) B230F | 0.0004–0.0012 | 0.0118–0.0217 | 0.0118–0.0217 | 0.0118–0.0236 | 0.0024–0.0036 | 0.0016–0.0028 | 0.0012–0.0026 |
| | 140 (2320) B230F-Turbo | 0.0004–0.0012 | 0.0118–0.0217 | 0.0118–0.0217 | 0.0118–0.0236 | 0.0024–0.0036 | 0.0016–0.0028 | 0.0012–0.0026 |
| | 174 (2849) B280F | 0.0007–0.0015 | 0.0157–0.0236 | 0.0157–0.0236 | 0.0157–0.0570 | 0.0017–0.0029 | 0.0009–0.0212 | 0.0003–0.0091 |
| 1989-90 | 140 (2320) B230F | 0.0004–0.0012 | 0.0118–0.0217 | 0.0118–0.0217 | 0.0118–0.0236 | 0.0024–0.0036 | 0.0016–0.0028 | 0.0012–0.0026 |
| | 140 (2320) B234F | 0.0004–0.0012 | 0.0120–0.0220 | 0.0120–0.0220 | 0.0120–0.0240 | 0.0024–0.0036 | 0.0016–0.0028 | 0.0012–0.0026 |
| | 140 (2320) B230F-Turbo | 0.0004–0.0012 | 0.0118–0.0217 | 0.0118–0.0217 | 0.0118–0.0236 | 0.0024–0.0036 | 0.0016–0.0028 | 0.0012–0.0026 |
| | 174 (2849) B280F | 0.0007–0.0015 | 0.0157–0.0236 | 0.0157–0.0236 | 0.0157–0.0570 | 0.0017–0.0029 | 0.0009–0.0212 | 0.0003–0.0091 |

① Canada only

② Pistons with two different heights have been fitted to B23E engines. Piston clearance on version 1 (3.1654 in piston height) listed above; clearance on version 2 pistons (3.0079 in.) is 0.004–0.0016 in.

## TORQUE SPECIFICATIONS

All readings in ft. lbs.

| Year | Engine Displacement cu. in. (cc) | Cylinder Head Bolts | Main Bearing Bolts | Rod Bearing Bolts | Crankshaft Pulley Bolts | Flywheel Bolts | Manifold Intake | Manifold Exhaust | Spark Plugs |
|---|---|---|---|---|---|---|---|---|---|
| 1983 | 130 (2127) B21A① | ⑧ | 85–91 | 43–48 | 107–128 | 47–54 | 15 | 15 | 15–18 |
| | 130 (2127) B21F-Turbo | ⑧ | 85–91 | 43–48 | 107–128 | 47–54 | 15 | 15 | 15–18 |
| | 140 (2320) B23F | ⑧ | 85–91 | 43–48 | 107–128 | 47–54 | 15 | 15 | 15–18 |
| | 140 (2320) B23E① | ⑧ | 85–91 | 43–48 | 107–128 | 47–54 | 15 | 15 | 15–18 |
| | 140 (2320) B23F-Turbo | ⑧ | 85–91 | 43–48 | 107–128 | 47–54 | 15 | 15 | 15–18 |
| | 145 (2383) D24 | ⑤ | 48 | 33 | 332⑥ | 55 | 18 | 18 | ⑦ |
| | 145 (2383) D24-Turbo | ⑤ | 48 | 33 | 332⑥ | 55 | 18 | 18 | ⑦ |
| | 174 (2849) B28F | ③ | ④ | 33–37 | 177–206 | 33–37 | 7–11 | 7–11 | 8–11 |
| 1984 | 130 (2127) B21A① | ⑧ | 85–91 | 43–48 | 107–128 | 47–54 | 15 | 15 | 15–18 |
| | 130 (2127) B21F-Turbo | ⑧ | 85–91 | 43–48 | 107–128 | 47–54 | 15 | 15 | 15–18 |
| | 140 (2320) B21F | ⑧ | 85–91 | 43–48 | 107–128 | 47–54 | 15 | 15 | 15–18 |
| | 140 (2320) B23F-Turbo | ⑧ | 85–91 | 43–48 | 107–128 | 47–54 | 15 | 15 | 15–18 |
| | 145 (2383) D24 | ⑤ | 48 | 33 | 332⑥ | 55 | 18 | 18 | ⑦ |
| | 145 (2383) D24-Turbo | ⑤ | 48 | 33 | 332⑥ | 55 | 18 | 18 | ⑦ |
| | 174 (2849) B28F | ③ | ④ | 33–37 | 177–206 | 33–37 | 7–11 | 7–11 | 8–11 |
| 1985 | 130 (2127) B21F-Turbo | ⑧ | 85–91 | 43–48 | 107–128 | 47–54 | 15 | 15 | 15–18 |
| | 140 (2320) B230F | ⑧ | 80 | 14 ⑨ | 43 ⑩ | 47–54 | 12 | 12 | 18 |
| | 140 (2320) B230F-Turbo | ⑧ | 80 | 14 ⑨ | 43 ⑩ | 47–54 | 12 | 12 | 18 |
| | 145 (2383) D24 | ⑤ | 48 | 33 | 332⑥ | 55 | 18 | 18 | ⑦ |
| | 145 (2383) D24-Turbo | ⑤ | 48 | 33 | 332⑥ | 55 | 18 | 18 | ⑦ |
| | 174 (2849) B28F | ③ | ④ | 33–37 | 177–206 | 33–37 | 7–11 | 7–11 | 8–11 |

## TORQUE SPECIFICATIONS

All readings in ft. lbs.

| Year | Engine Displacement cu. in. (cc) | Cylinder Head Bolts | Main Bearing Bolts | Rod Bearing Bolts | Crankshaft Pulley Bolts | Flywheel Bolts | Manifold Intake | Manifold Exhaust | Spark Plugs |
|---|---|---|---|---|---|---|---|---|---|
| 1986 | 140 (2320) B230F | ⑧ | 80 | 14 ⑨ | 43 ⑩ | 47-54 | 12 | 12 | 18 |
| | 140 (2320) B230F-Turbo | ⑧ | 80 | 14 ⑨ | 43 ⑩ | 47-54 | 12 | 12 | 18 |
| | 145 (2383) D24-Turbo | ⑤ | 48 | 33 | 332⑥ | 55 | 18 | 18 | ⑦ |
| | 174 (2849) B28F | ③ | ④ | 33-37 | 177-206 | 33-37 | 7-11 | 7-11 | 8-11 |
| 1987 | 140 (2320) B230F | ⑧ | 80 | 14 ⑨ | 43 ⑩ | 47-54 | 12 | 12 | 18 |
| | 140 (2320) B230F-Turbo | ⑧ | 80 | 14 ⑨ | 43 ⑩ | 47-54 | 12 | 12 | 18 |
| | 174 (2849) B280F | ⑪ | ④ | 33-37 | 177-206 | 33-37 | 7-11 | 7-11 | 8-11 |
| 1988 | 140 (2320) B230F | ⑧ | 80 | 14 ⑨ | 43 ⑩ | 47-54 | 12 | 12 | 18 |
| | 140 (2320) B230F-Turbo | ⑧ | 80 | 14 ⑨ | 43 ⑩ | 47-54 | 12 | 12 | 18 |
| | 174 (2849) B280F | ⑪ | ④ | 33-37 | 177-206 | 33-37 | 7-11 | 7-11 | 8-11 |
| 1989-90 | 140 (2320) B230F | ⑧ | 80 | 14 ⑨ | 43 ⑩ | 47-54 | 12 | 12 | 18 |
| | 140 (2320) B234F | ⑫ | 80 | 15 ⑨ | 44 ⑩ | 47-54 | 12 | 12 | 14-22 |
| | 140 (2320) B230F-Turbo | ⑧ | 80 | 14 ⑨ | 43 ⑩ | 47-54 | 12 | 12 | 18 |
| | 174 (2849) B280F | ⑪ | ④ | 33-37 | 177-206 | 33-37 | 7-11 | 7-11 | 8-11 |

① Canada only

② Torque head bolts in two stages; first, tighten in sequence to 43 ft. lbs., then to 76-83 ft. lbs.

③ Torque head bolts in sequence to 7 ft. lbs., then 22 ft. lbs., then 44 ft. lbs. Wait 10-15 minutes and slacken the bolts 1/2 turn. Then torque to 11-14 ft. lbs. and then protractor torque to 116-120° (1/3 of a turn). Finally run to operating temperature, shut off and allow to cool for 30 min. Following the sequence, slacken, torque to 11-14 ft. lbs., and protractor torque to 113-117° each bolt.

④ Torque main bearing nuts to 22 ft. lbs., in sequence. Then slacken 1st nut 1/2 turn, tighten to 22-26 ft. lbs., and protractor torque to 73-77°. Repeat for remaining nuts following the sequence.

⑤ Torquing these bolts is a 6-step procedure:
A. Torque to 30 ft. lbs.
B. Torque to 44 ft. lbs.
C. Torque to 55 ft. lbs.
D. Tighten 180°, in one movement, without stopping.
E. Run engine until oil temperature is minimum 50°C-120°F.
F. Tighten 90°, in one movement, without stopping. After driving 600-1,000 miles., retorque bolts w/engine cold. DO NOT slacken first.

⑥ Using regular torque wrench. If Volvo tool 5188 is used, torque to 255 ft. lbs.

⑦ Injector: 50 ft. lbs.

⑧ Torque head bolts in three stages; first, tighten in sequence to 15 ft. lbs., then to 44 ft. lbs. Protractor (angle) tighten 90°more in one movement.

⑨ Angle—tighten 90°

⑩ Angle—tighten 60°

⑪ Torque all head bolts in sequence to 44 ft. lbs. (60 Nm), then loosen bolt No. 1 and retorque it to 15 ft. lbs. (20Nm), then tighten it to 106°; repeat for all bolts following number sequence. Loosen and tighten one bolt at a time. Run engine to operating temperature. Then let cool for 2 hours. Finally, tighten each bolt in sequence an additional 45°.

⑫ Torque head bolts in 3 stages; first tighten in sequence to 15 ft. lbs., then to 30 ft. lbs. Protractor (angle) tighten 115° more in one movement.

## BRAKE SPECIFICATIONS

All measurements in inches unless noted.

| Year | Model | Lug Nut Torque (ft. lbs.) | Master Cylinder Bore | Brake Disc | | Standard Brake Drum Diameter | Minimum Lining Thickness | |
|---|---|---|---|---|---|---|---|---|
| | | | | Minimum Thickness | Maximum Runout | | Front | Rear |
| 1983 | 240 DL | 88 | 0.878 | ② (F)<br>0.330 (R) | 0.004 (F)<br>0.004 (R) | — | 0.060 | 0.060 |
| | GL | 88 | 0.878 | ② (F)<br>0.330 (R) | 0.004 (F)<br>0.004 (R) | — | 0.060 | 0.060 |
| | GLT | 88 | 0.878 | ② (F)<br>0.330 (R) | 0.004 (F)<br>0.004 (R) | — | 0.060 | 0.060 |
| | Turbo | 88 | 0.878 | ② (F)<br>0.330 (R) | 0.004 (F)<br>0.004 (R) | — | 0.060 | 0.060 |
| | 760 GLE | 63 | ③ | ④ (F)<br>0.330 (R) | 0.004 (F)<br>0.004 (R) | — | 0.118 | 0.078 |
| | Turbo | 63 | ③ | ④ (F)<br>0.330 (R) | 0.004 (F)<br>0.004 (R) | — | 0.118 | 0.078 |
| 1984 | 240 Diesel | 88 | 0.878 | ② (F)<br>0.330 (R) | 0.004 (F)<br>0.004 (R) | — | 0.060 | 0.060 |
| | DL | 88 | 0.878 | ② (F)<br>0.330 (R) | 0.004 (F)<br>0.004 (R) | — | 0.060 | 0.060 |
| | GL | 88 | 0.878 | ② (F)<br>0.330 (R) | 0.004 (F)<br>0.004 (R) | — | 0.060 | 0.060 |
| | GLE | 88 | 0.878 | ② (F)<br>0.330 (R) | 0.004 (F)<br>0.004 (R) | — | 0.060 | 0.060 |
| | Turbo | 88 | 0.878 | ② (F)<br>0.330 (R) | 0.004 (F)<br>0.004 (R) | — | 0.060 | 0.060 |
| | 760 GLE | 63 | ③ | ④ (F)<br>0.330 (R) | 0.003 (F)<br>0.004 (R) | — | 0.118 | 0.078 |
| | Turbo | 63 | ③ | ④ (F)<br>0.330 (R) | 0.003 (F)<br>0.004 (R) | — | 0.118 | 0.078 |
| 1985 | 240 Diesel | 88 | 0.878 | ② (F)<br>0.330 (R) | 0.004 (F)<br>0.004 (R) | — | 0.060 | 0.060 |
| | DL | 88 | 0.878 | ② (F)<br>0.330 (R) | 0.004 (F)<br>0.004 (R) | — | 0.060 | 0.060 |
| | GL | 88 | 0.878 | ② (F)<br>0.330 (R) | 0.004 (F)<br>0.004 (R) | — | 0.060 | 0.060 |
| | Turbo | 88 | 0.878 | ② (F)<br>0.330 (R) | 0.004 (F)<br>0.004 (R) | — | 0.060 | 0.060 |
| | 740 GLE | 63 | ③ | ④ (F)<br>0.330 (R) | 0.003 (F)<br>0.004 (R) | — | 0.118 | 0.078 |
| | TD① | 63 | ③ | ④ (F)<br>0.330 (R) | 0.003 (F)<br>0.004 (R) | — | 0.118 | 0.078 |
| | Turbo | 63 | ③ | ④ (F)<br>0.330 (R) | 0.003 (F)<br>0.004 (R) | — | 0.118 | 0.078 |
| | 760 GLE | 63 | ③ | ④ (F)<br>0.330 (R) | 0.003 (F)<br>0.004 (R) | — | 0.118 | 0.078 |
| | GLE TD | 63 | ③ | ④ (F)<br>0.330 (R) | 0.003 (F)<br>0.004 (R) | — | 0.118 | 0.078 |
| | Turbo | 63 | ③ | ④ (F)<br>0.330 (R) | 0.003 (F)<br>0.004 (R) | — | 0.118 | 0.078 |

## BRAKE SPECIFICATIONS

All measurements in inches unless noted.

| Year | Model | Lug Nut Torque (ft. lbs.) | Master Cylinder Bore | Brake Disc Minimum Thickness | Brake Disc Maximum Runout | Standard Brake Drum Diameter | Minimum Lining Thickness Front | Minimum Lining Thickness Rear |
|---|---|---|---|---|---|---|---|---|
| 1986 | 240 DL | 88 | 0.878 | ② (F)<br>0.330 (R) | 0.004 (F)<br>0.004 (R) | — | 0.060 | 0.060 |
| | GL | 88 | 0.878 | ② (F)<br>0.330 (R) | 0.004 (F)<br>0.004 (R) | — | 0.060 | 0.060 |
| | 740 GL | 63 | ③ | ④ (F)<br>0.330 (R) | 0.003 (F)<br>0.004 (R) | — | 0.118 | 0.078 |
| | GLE | 63 | ③ | ④ (F)<br>0.330 (R) | 0.003 (F)<br>0.004 (R) | — | 0.118 | 0.078 |
| | GLE TD | 63 | ③ | ④ (F)<br>0.330 (R) | 0.003 (F)<br>0.004 (R) | — | 0.118 | 0.078 |
| | Turbo | 63 | ③ | ④ (F)<br>0.330 (R) | 0.003 (F)<br>0.004 (R) | — | 0.118 | 0.078 |
| | 760 GLE | 63 | ③ | ④ (F)<br>0.330 (R) | 0.003 (F)<br>0.004 (R) | — | 0.118 | 0.078 |
| | Turbo | 63 | ③ | ④ (F)<br>0.330 (R) | 0.003 (F)<br>0.004 (R) | — | 0.118 | 0.078 |
| 1987 | 240 DL | 88 | 0.878 | ② (F)<br>0.330 (R) | 0.004 (F)<br>0.004 (R) | — | 0.060 | 0.060 |
| | GL | 88 | 0.878 | ② (F)<br>0.330 (R) | 0.003 (F)<br>0.004 (R) | — | 0.060 | 0.060 |
| | 740 GL | 63 | ③ | ④ (F)<br>0.330 (R) | 0.003 (F)<br>0.004 (R) | — | 0.118 | 0.078 |
| | GLE | 63 | ③ | ④ (F)<br>0.330 (R) | 0.003 (F)<br>0.004 (R) | — | 0.118 | 0.078 |
| | Turbo | 63 | ③ | ④ (F)<br>0.330 (R) | 0.003 (F)<br>0.004 (R) | — | 0.118 | 0.078 |
| | 760 GLE | 63 | ③ | ④ (F)<br>0.330 (R) | 0.003 (F)<br>0.004 (R) | — | 0.118 | 0.078 |
| | Turbo | 63 | ③ | ④ (F)<br>0.330 (R) | 0.003 (F)<br>0.004 (R) | — | 0.118 | 0.078 |
| | 780 | 63 | ③ | ④ (F)<br>0.330 (R) | 0.003 (F)<br>0.004 (R) | — | 0.118 | 0.078 |
| 1988 | 240 DL | 88 | 0.878 | ② (F)<br>0.330 (R) | 0.004 (F)<br>0.004 (R) | — | 0.060 | 0.060 |
| | GL | 88 | 0.878 | ② (F)<br>0.330 (R) | 0.003 (F)<br>0.004 (R) | — | 0.060 | 0.060 |
| | 740 GL | 63 | ③ | ④ (F)<br>0.330 (R) | 0.003 (F)<br>0.004 (R) | — | 0.118 | 0.078 |
| | GLE | 63 | ③ | ④ (F)<br>0.330 (R) | 0.003 (F)<br>0.004 (R) | — | 0.118 | 0.078 |
| | Turbo | 63 | ③ | ④ (F)<br>0.330 (R) | 0.003 (F)<br>0.004 (R) | — | 0.118 | 0.078 |
| | 760 GLE | 63 | ③ | ④ (F)<br>0.330 (R) | 0.003 (F)<br>0.004 (R) | — | 0.118 | 0.078 |
| | Turbo | 63 | ③ | ④ (F)<br>0.330 (R) | 0.003 (F)<br>0.004 (R) | — | 0.118 | 0.078 |
| | 780 | 63 | ③ | ④ (F)<br>0.330 (R) | 0.003 (F)<br>0.004 (R) | — | 0.118 | 0.078 |

## BRAKE SPECIFICATIONS

All measurements in inches unless noted

| Year | Model | Lug Nut Torque (ft. lbs.) | Master Cylinder Bore | Brake Disc Minimum Thickness | Brake Disc Maximum Runout | Standard Brake Drum Diameter | Minimum Lining Thickness Front | Minimum Lining Thickness Rear |
|---|---|---|---|---|---|---|---|---|
| 1989–90 | 240 DL | 88 | 0.878 | ② (F)<br>0.330 (R) | 0.004 (F)<br>0.004 (R) | — | 0.060 | 0.060 |
| | GL | 88 | 0.878 | ② (F)<br>0.330 (R) | 0.003 (F)<br>0.004 (R) | — | 0.060 | 0.060 |
| | 740 GL | 63 | ③ | ④ (F)<br>0.330 (R) | 0.003 (F)<br>0.004 (R) | — | 0.118 | 0.078 |
| | GLE | 63 | ③ | ④ (F)<br>0.330 (R) | 0.003 (F)<br>0.004 (R) | — | 0.118 | 0.078 |
| | Turbo | 63 | ③ | ④ (F)<br>0.330 (R) | 0.003 (F)<br>0.004 (R) | — | 0.118 | 0.078 |
| | 760 GLE | 63 | ③ | ④ (F)<br>0.330 (R) | 0.003 (F)<br>0.004 (R) | — | 0.118 | 0.078 |
| | Turbo | 63 | ③ | ④ (F)<br>0.330 (R) | 0.003 (F)<br>0.004 (R) | — | 0.118 | 0.078 |
| | 780 | 63 | ③ | ④ (F)<br>0.330 (R) | 0.003 (F)<br>0.004 (R) | — | 0.118 | 0.078 |

① Station wagon
② Ventilated—0.820
Non-ventilated—0.536
③ Early type—0.878
Late type—0.938
④ Ventilated—0.788
Non-ventilated—0.433

## WHEEL ALIGNMENT

| Year | Model | Caster Range (deg.) | Caster Preferred Setting (deg.) | Camber Range (deg.) | Camber Preferred Setting (deg.) | Toe-in (in.) | Steering Axis Inclination (deg.) |
|---|---|---|---|---|---|---|---|
| 1983 | 240 DL | 3P–4P② | — | 1P–1 1/2P | — | 1/8③ | 12 |
| | GL | 3P–4P② | — | 1P–1 1/2P | — | 1/8③ | 12 |
| | GLT | 3P–4P② | — | 1/4P–3/4P | — | 1/8③ | 12 |
| | Turbo | 3P–4P② | — | 1P–1 1/2P | — | 1/8③ | 12 |
| | 760 GLE | 4 1/2P–5 1/2P | — | 3/16N–13/16P | — | 9/64 | NA |
| | Turbo | 4 1/2P–5 1/2P | — | 3/16N–13/16P | — | 9/64 | NA |
| 1984 | 240 Diesel | 3P–4P② | — | 1P–1 1/2P | — | 1/8③ | 12 |
| | DL | 3P–4P② | — | 1P–1 1/2P | — | 1/8③ | 12 |
| | GL | 3P–4P② | — | 1P–1 1/2P | — | 1/8③ | 12 |
| | GLE | 3P–4P② | — | 1/4P–3/4P | — | 1/8③ | 12 |
| | Turbo | 3P–4P② | — | 1P–1 1/2P | — | 1/8③ | 12 |
| | 760 GLE | 4 1/2P–5 1/2P | — | 3/16N–13/16P | — | 9/64 | NA |
| | Turbo | 4 1/2P–5 1/2P | — | 3/16N–13/16P | — | 9/64 | NA |

## WHEEL ALIGNMENT

| Year | Model | Caster Range (deg.) | Caster Preferred Setting (deg.) | Camber Range (deg.) | Camber Preferred Setting (deg.) | Toe-in (in.) | Steering Axis Inclination (deg.) |
|---|---|---|---|---|---|---|---|
| 1985 | 240 Diesel | 3P–4P | — | 1/4P–3/4P | 1/2P | 1/8 | 12 |
| | DL | 3P–4P | — | 1/4P–3/4P | 1/2P | 1/8 | 12 |
| | GL | 3P–4P | — | 1/4P–3/4P | 1/2P | 1/8 | 12 |
| | Turbo | 3P–4P | — | 1/4P–3/4P | 1/2P | 1/8 | 12 |
| | 740 GLE | 4 1/2P–5 1/2P | — | 3/16N–13/16P | — | 9/64 | NA |
| | TD① | 4 1/2P–5 1/2P | — | 3/16N–13/16P | — | 9/64 | NA |
| | Turbo | 4 1/2P–5 1/2P | — | 3/16N–13/16P | — | 9/64 | NA |
| | 760 GLE | 4 1/2P–5 1/2P | — | 3/16N–13/16P | — | 9/64 | NA |
| | GLE TD | 4 1/2P–5 1/2P | — | 3/16N–13/16P | — | 9/64 | NA |
| | Turbo | 4 1/2P–5 1/2P | — | 3/16N–13/16P | — | 9/64 | NA |
| 1986 | 240 DL | 3P–4P | — | 1/4P–3/4P | 1/2P | 1/8 | 12 |
| | GL | 3P–4P | — | 1/4P–3/4P | 1/2P | 1/8 | 12 |
| | 740 GL | 4 1/2P–5 1/2P | — | 3/16N–13/16P | — | 9/64 | NA |
| | GLE | 4 1/2P–5 1/2P | — | 3/16N–13/16P | — | 9/64 | NA |
| | GLE TD | 4 1/2P–5 1/2P | — | 3/16N–13/16P | — | 9/64 | NA |
| | Turbo | 4 1/2P–5 1/2P | — | 3/16N–13/16P | — | 9/64 | NA |
| | 760 GLE | 4 1/2P–5 1/2P | — | 3/16N–13/16P | — | 9/64 | NA |
| | Turbo | 4 1/2P–5 1/2P | — | 3/16N–13/16P | — | 9/64 | NA |
| 1987 | 240 DL | 3P–4P | — | 1/4P–3/4P | 1/2P | 1/8 | 12 |
| | GL | 3P–4P | — | 1/4P–3/4P | 1/2P | 1/8 | 12 |
| | 740 GL | 4 1/2P–5 1/2P | — | 3/16N–13/16P | — | 9/64 | NA |
| | GLE | 4 1/2P–5 1/2P | — | 3/16N–13/16P | — | 9/64 | NA |
| | Turbo | 4 1/2P–5 1/2P | — | 3/16N–13/16P | — | 9/64 | NA |
| | 760 GLE | 4 1/2P–5 1/2P | — | 3/16N–13/16P | — | 9/64 | NA |
| | Turbo | 4 1/2P–5 1/2P | — | 3/16N–13/16P | — | 9/64 | NA |
| | 780 | 4 1/2P–5 1/2P | — | 3/16N–13/16P | — | 9/64 | NA |
| 1988 | 240 DL | 3P–4P | — | 1/4P–3/4P | 1/2P | 1/8 | 12 |
| | GL | 3P–4P | — | 1/4P–3/4P | 1/2P | 1/8 | 12 |
| | 740 GL | 4 1/2P–5 1/2P | — | 3/16N–13/16P | — | 9/64 | NA |
| | GLE | 4 1/2P–5 1/2P | — | 3/16N–13/16P | — | 9/64 | NA |
| | Turbo | 4 1/2P–5 1/2P | — | 3/16N–13/16P | — | 9/64 | NA |
| | 760 GLE | 4 1/2P–5 1/2P | — | 3/16N–13/16P | — | 9/64 | NA |
| | Turbo | 4 1/2P–5 1/2P | — | 3/16N–13/16P | — | 9/64 | NA |
| | 780 | 4 1/2P–5 1/2P | — | 3/16N–13/16P | — | 9/64 | NA |
| 1989-90 | 240 DL | 3P–4P | — | 1/4P–3/4P | 1/2P | 1/8 | 12 |
| | GL | 3P–4P | — | 1/4P–3/4P | 1/2P | 1/8 | 12 |
| | 740 GL | 4 1/2P–5 1/2P | — | 3/16N–13/16P | — | 9/64 | NA |
| | GLE | 4 1/2P–5 1/2P | — | 3/16N–13/16P | — | 9/64 | NA |
| | Turbo | 4 1/2P–5 1/2P | — | 3/16N–13/16P | — | 9/64 | NA |
| | 760 GLE | 4 1/2P–5 1/2P | — | 3/16N–13/16P | — | 9/64 | NA |
| | Turbo | 4 1/2P–5 1/2P | — | 3/16N–13/16P | — | 9/64 | NA |
| | 780 | 4 1/2P–5 1/2P | — | 3/16N–13/16P | — | 9/64 | NA |

N – Negative
P – Positive

① Station Wagon
② Manual steering: 2P–3P
③ Manual steering: 13/64

# TUNE-UP PROCEDURES

## Breaker Points

### ADJUSTMENT

#### *With a Dwell Meter*

Adjusting the B21A breaker points with a dwell meter (if available) is a more precise method of adjustment than the feeler gauge method. Calibrate the dwell meter to the 4-cylinder position, and connect it between the distributor primary terminal and a ground. Remove the distributor cap and rotor. Loosen the breaker point set screw about 1/8 of a turn. Observing the dwell meter, reset the screw of the stationary contact to obtain the proper (62 degrees) dwell angle. Tighten the set screw and recheck the dwell. Install the rotor and cap, start the engine, and make a final dwell check.

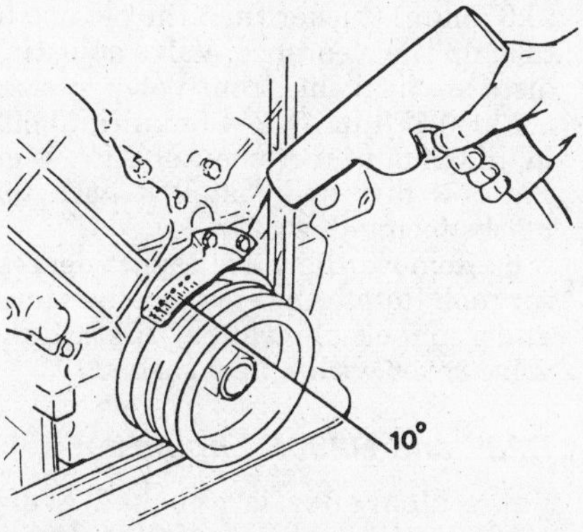

Engine timing marks—B27F and B28F engines

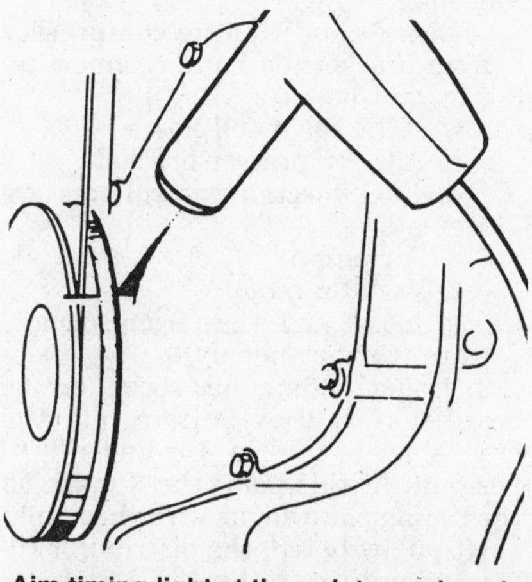
Aim timing light at the pointer and marks on the damper

#### *With a Feeler Gauge*

The Canadian B21A models (carburetor-equipped) are also equipped with a conventional breaker points type ignition system.

To replace and adjust a new set of points, remove the distributor cap and rotor. Disconnect the wire leads from both points and condenser. Remove the points holddown screw, condenser attaching screw, and remove the points assembly and condenser. Lightly grease the distributor cam lobe on the surface that makes contact with the points set. Install the new points assembly and condenser, attach the wire leads of both and tighten the condenser attaching screw. Do not fully tighten the points holddown screw.

Turn the crankshaft bottom pulley (by placing a socket on the pulley bolt) until the cam lobe on the distributor shaft has fully raised the breaker arm. The points should now be up on the peak of the shaft eccentric, and should be at their most wide open point. Insert a 0.017 in. (0.432mm) feeler gauge in between both contacts, and loosen the breaker plate holddown screw. There will be a slight drag on the feeler gauge when the gap is properly set. Tighten the holddown screw when you are satisfied, rotate the engine once and recheck the gap. Make sure all leads are securely attached, replace the rotor and distributor cap.

## Ignition Timing

### ADJUSTMENT

#### *All Except Diesel*

1. Clean the crankshaft damper and pointer on the water pump housing with a solvent-soaked rag so that the marks can be seen.
2. Connect a timing light according to the manufacturer's instructions.
3. Scribe a mark on the crankshaft damper and on the marker with chalk or luminescent (day-glo) paint to highlight the correct timing setting.
4. Disconnect and plug the distributor vacuum line (if equipped) and also disconnect the hose between the air cleaner and the inlet duct (if equipped) at the duct.
5. Disconnect and plug the vacuum hose at the EGR valve (if equipped).
6. Attach a tachometer to the engine and set the idle speed to specifications.
7. With the engine running, aim the timing light at the pointer and the marks on the damper.
8. If the marks do not coincide, stop the engine, loosen the distributor pinch bolt, and start the engine again. While observing the timing light flashes on the markers, grasp the distributor vacuum regulator and rotate the distributor until the marks do coincide.
9. Stop the engine and tighten the distributor pinch bolt, taking care not to disturb the setting.
10. Reconnect all disconnected hoses and remove the timing light and tachometer from the engine.

#### *Diesel*

1. Remove the rear timing gear cover and disconnect the cold-start device. Loosen the forward screw on the cold-start device control lever, press the lever back toward the stop.

**NOTE: Do not loosen the screw closest to the timing belt.**

2. Rotate the engine to align the mark on the injection gear with the mark on the pump bracket. The **0** mark on the flywheel should be centered at the timing mark window and

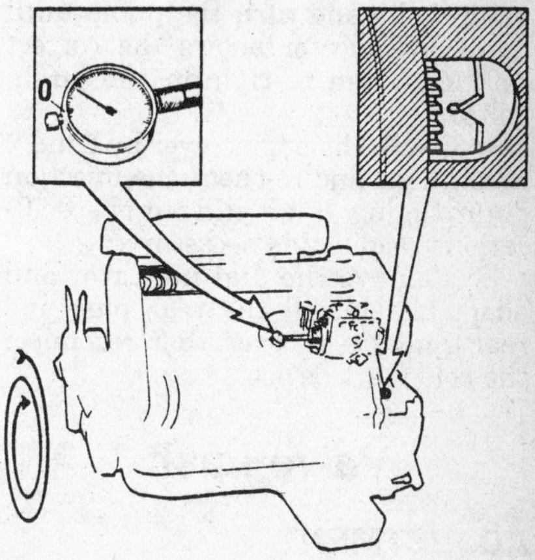

D24 and D24T injection pump timing check

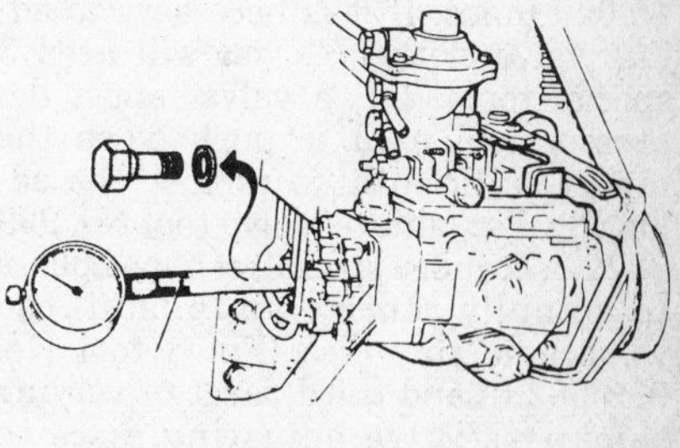
Installing the dial indicator

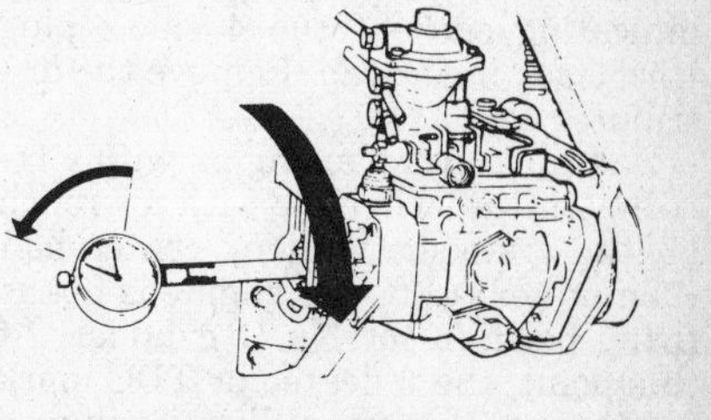
Setting the injection pump

with No.1 cylinder at top dead center.

3. Remove the plug from the rear of the pump and install the Volvo dial indicator adapter No. 5194 or equivalent, with a measuring range of 0–0.1 in. (0–3mm). Set the indicator gauge at approximately 0.08 in. (2mm).

4. Rotate the engine slowly counterclockwise until the lowest reading on the dial indicator is observed, then reset the dial indicator to zero.

5. Rotate the engine slowly in the clockwise direction until the **0** mark on the flywheel is centered at the timing mark window. The dial indicator should read within the specified range.

**NOTE: When the engine is turned past the timing mark, turn the engine back a ¼ of a turn. Rotate the engine in the clockwise direction until the 0 mark on the flywheel is centered in the timing mark window.**

6. If the dial indicator setting is outside the specified range, loosen the pump bolts and turn the pump until the dial indicator shows the correct setting. Then re-tighten the pump bolts.

7. Crank the engine over by hand 2 revolutions and re-check the injection pump timing. If it is still out of specifications readjust as necessary.

8. Remove the dial indicator and adapter, reinstall the rear plug and rear timing gear cover, then reconnect the cold start device.

## Valve Lash

### ADJUSTMENT

#### *B21, B23 and B230 Engines*

Valve clearance is checked every 15,000 miles. If it is necessary to adjust valve clearance, you will need 3 special tools: 1st, a valve tappet depressor tool used to push down the tappet sufficiently to remove the adjusting disc (shim) (Volvo tool No. 999 5022); second, a specially shaped pliers to actually remove and install the valve adjusting disc (Volvo tool No. 999 5026); and third, a set of varying thickness valve adjusting discs to make the necessary adjustments.

1. Remove the valve cover. Scribe chalk marks on the distributor body indicating each of the 4 spark plug wire leads in the cap. Remove the distributor cap.

2. Crank over the engine with a remote starter switch, or with a wrench on the crankshaft pulley center bolt (22mm hex) until the engine is in the firing position for No. 1 cylinder. At this point, the **0** degree or TDC mark on the crankshaft pulley is aligned with the timing pointer, the rotor is pointing at the No. 1 spark plug wire cap position, and the camshaft lobes for No. 1 cylinder are pointing at the 10 o'clock and 2 o'clock positions. At this point, the clearance between the cam lobe and valve depressor (tappet) may be checked for the intake and exhaust valve of cylinder No. 1, using a feeler gauge. When checking clearance, the wear limit is 0.012–0.018 in. (0.3–0.4mm) for a cold engine, and 0.012–0.020 in. (0.3–0.5mm) for a hot one (176°F/80°C).

3. Repeat Step 2 for cylinders No. 3, 4, and 2 (in that order). Each time, rotate the crankshaft pulley 180 degrees

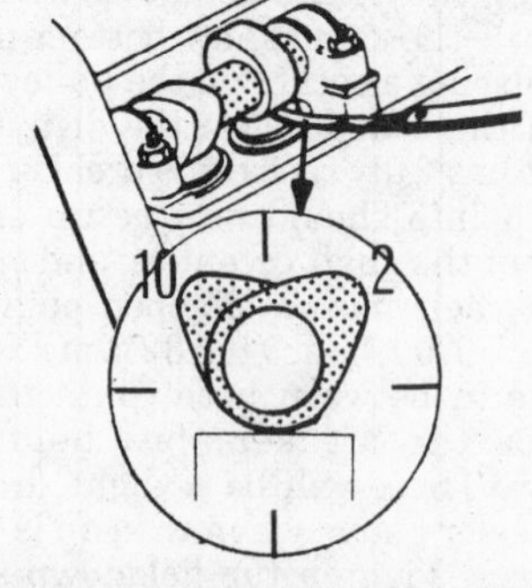


**B21, B23, and B230 series camshaft lobes at "10 and 2 O'clock" positions, indicating that subject cylinder is in the firing position and the valves can be adjusted**

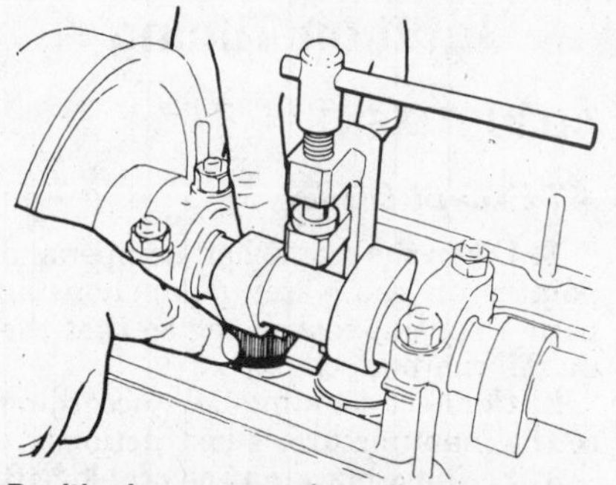

**Positioning a new valve adjustment shim in the head. Shim must be oiled**

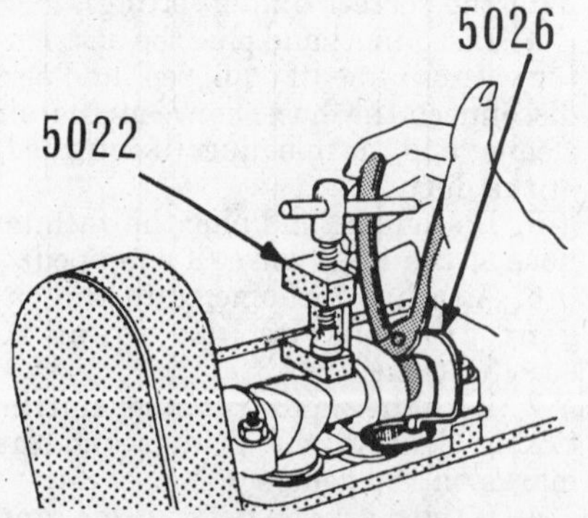


**B21, B23, and B230 series valve adjustment tools—tappet depressor is on left, shim pliers on right**

so that the rotor is pointing to the spark plug wire cap position for that cylinder, and the cam lobes are pointing at the 10 and 2 o'clock positions for the valves of that cylinder.

4. If any of the valve clearance measurements are outside the wear limit, you will have to remove the old valve adjusting disc and install a new one to bring the clearance within specifications. First, rotate the valve depressors (tappets) until their notches are at a right angle to the engine center line. Attach valve depressor tool No. 999 5022 or equivalent to the camshaft and screw down the tool spindle until the depressor (tappet) groove is just above the edge of its bore and still accessible with the special pliers (tool No. 999 5026).

5. Remove the valve adjusting disc and measure with a micrometer. The valve clearance should be set to these tolerances: 0.014–0.016 in. (0.35–0.40mm) for a cold engine, and 0.016–0.018 in. (0.40–0.45mm) for a hot one. So, if the measured clearance had been 0.019 in. (0.48mm) and the desired clearance 0.016 in. (0.40mm) (for a net difference of 0.003 in. [0.076mm]), then the new valve adjusting disc should be 0.003 in. (0.076mm) thicker than the old one to take up the clearance. Valve adjusting discs are available from Volvo in sizes 0.130–0.180 in. (3.3–4.6mm)(in 0.002 in. [0.050mm] increments). Always oil the new disc and install it with the marks facing down.

6. Remove the valve tappet depressor tool. Rotate the engine a few times and recheck clearance. Install the valve cover with a new gasket.

#### *B28F and B280F Engines*

Valve clearance is checked every 15,000 miles. No special tools are required.

1. In order to gain access to the valve covers, disconnect or remove the following:

a. Air conditioning compressor from bracket (do not disconnect refrigerant hoses)
b. EGR valve and hoses
c. A/C compressor bracket
d. Fuel injection control pressure regulator
e. Air pump
f. Vacuum pump
g. Hoses and wires from solenoid valve (California only)

2. Using a 36mm hex socket on the crankshaft pulley bolt, rotate the crankshaft to the No. 1 cylinder TDC position. At this point the **0** mark on the timing plate aligns with the crankshaft pulley notch, the distributor rotor is pointing to the No. 1 cylinder spark plug wire cap position, and both

valves for No. 1 cylinder have clearance. At this position, adjust the intake valves of cylinders No. 1, 2 and 4, and the exhaust valves of cylinders No. 1, 3, and 6. Insert a feeler gauge between the rocker arm and valve stem.

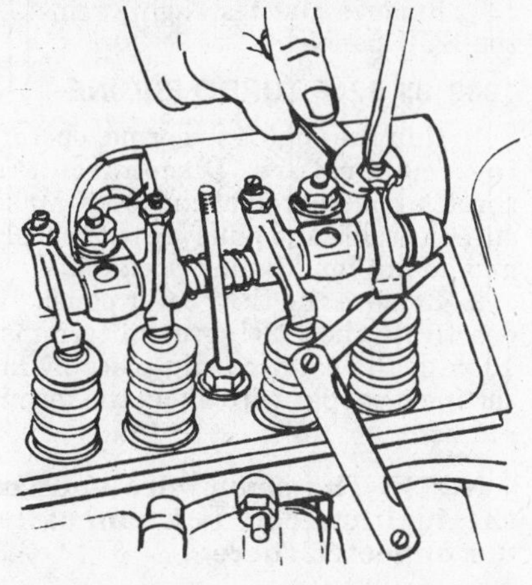

Adjusting valve clearance on the B27 and B28 V6

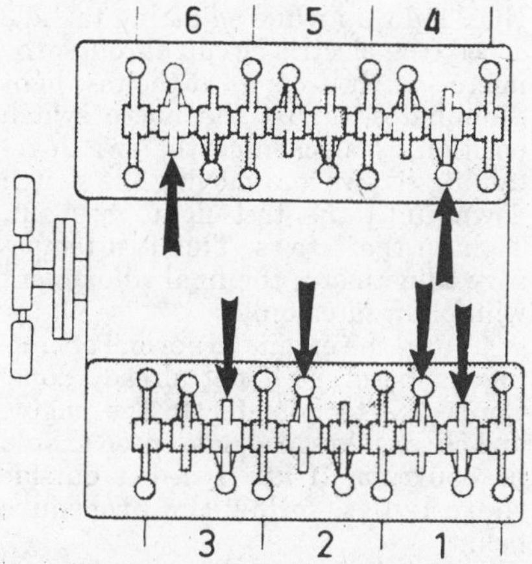


On B27 and 28 with no. 1 cylinder at TDC, adjust these valves (arrows)

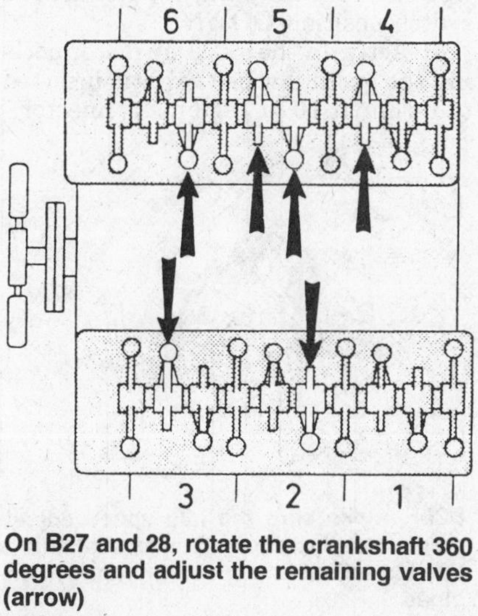


On B27 and 28, rotate the crankshaft 360 degrees and adjust the remaining valves (arrow)

Loosen the locknut and turn the adjusting screw in the required direction. Tighten the locknut and recheck clearance.

Clearance for B280F should be:
Cold engine
Intake – 0.004–0.006 in. (0.10–0.15mm)
Exhaust – 0.010–0.012 in. (0.25–0.30mm)
Hot engine
Intake – 0.006–0.008 in. (0.15–0.20mm)
Exhaust – 0.012–0.014 in. (0.30–0.35mm)

Clearance for B28 should be:
Cold engine
Intake – 0.008–0.010 in. (0.20–0.25mm)
Exhaust – 0.012–0.014 in. (0.30–0.35mm).

3. Rotate the crankshaft pulley 1 full 360 degrees turn to adjust the remaining valves. At this point, the **0** mark will again align with the pulley notch, the rotor is pointing 180 degrees opposite its former position, and the No. 1 cylinder rockers contact the ramps of the camshaft. At this position (see illustration), adjust the intake valves of cylinders No. 3, 5, and 6, and the exhaust valves of cylinders No. 2, 4, and 5.

4. Install the valve covers with new gaskets. Connect all disconnected equipment.

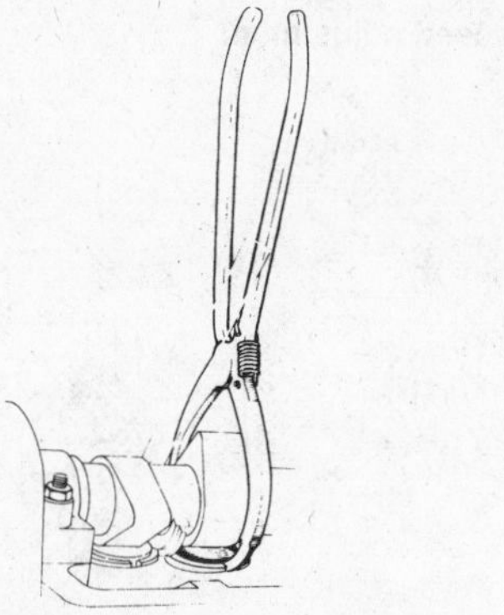

Removing valve adjusting disc (shim)—D24 engines

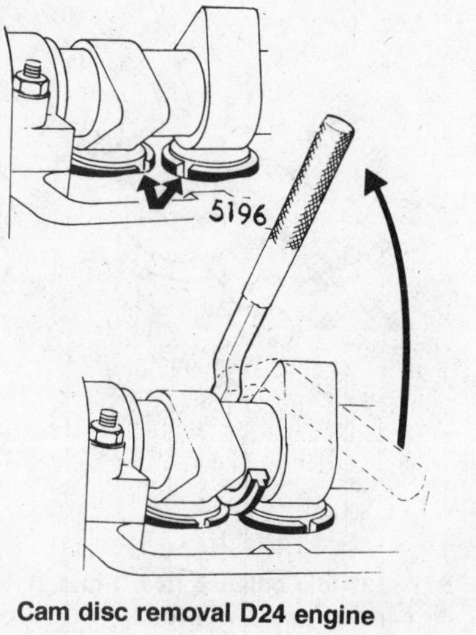


Cam disc removal D24 engine

### *D24 and D24T Diesel Engines*

**NOTE: Always check valve clearances with the cylinder at TDC; turn the engine ¼ turn past TDC to set valves.**

1. Remove the valve cover.
2. Use a 17mm socket on the crankshaft pulley. Turn the pulley until the engine is ready to fire on the No. 1 cylinder. The flywheel timing mark should be at zero.

**NOTE: The piston should be at ¼ turn past top dead center when setting the valve clearance.**

3. Line up the valve depressors.
4. Turn them so that the notches point slightly upward.

**NOTE: Use tool No. 5196 or equivalent to depress the valve depressors, This tool is available from your Volvo dealer.**

5. The depressor grooves must be above the face so that the disc can be gripped with pliers. These pliers are available from your Volvo dealer under part number 5195.
6. Remove the disc.
7. Calculate the disc thickness, using a micrometer. The discs are available in thicknesses of 0.1299–0.1673 in. (3.3–4.25mm) with increments of 0.002 in. (0.05mm).
8. Clearance should be:
Cold engine
Intake – 0.008 in. (0.2mm)
Exhaust – 0.0016 in. (0.04mm)
Warm engine
Intake – 0.0010 in. (0.025mm)
Exhaust – 0.0018 in. (0.046mm)

**NOTE: Always use new discs when performing this procedure.**

9. Oil the new disc and install it with the marked side down.
10. Check the remaining valve clearances.
11. Use the following sequence 1, 5, 3, 6, 2, 4.
12. Recheck the valve clearance for all cylinders.
13. Rotate the engine several times, and recheck the clearance.
14. Install the valve cover with a new gasket.

## Idle Speed and Mixture Gasoline Engines

### ADJUSTMENT

Adjustment of idle mixture on both of these systems requires the use of a CO meter. However, the idle speed adjustment may be set using a tachometer (follow the manufacturer's instructions for hook-up).

#### *Mechanical Injection (K-Jetronic) CIS*

**1983 B23E ENGINES**

1. Run the engine to normal operating temperature. Disconnect the throttle control rod at the lever. Make sure the cable and pulley run smoothly and do not bind in any position.

2. Remove the ECU cover panel. To deactivate the ECU, ground terminal 10 with the connector in place by inserting a copper wire along the terminal wire.

**NOTE: The same wire ends at the ignition coil but cannot be disconnected there.**

3. Connect a tachometer to the engine according to the manufacturer's instructions. Connect a test light across the battery positive terminal and the terminal on the throttle micro switch with the yellow wire connected. Start the engine. The test light must NOT light up. If it does, adjust the micro switch position by slackening the switch retaining screws. Move the switch down until the light goes out, then retighten the screws. This adjustment is temporary; final adjustment will follow later on.

4. Idle speed should be 700 rpm. If outside these limits, adjust idle speed by proceeding to Step 5. If idle speed is within these limits, continue to Step 6.

5. If the idle speed is outside the stated limits, use the throttle position adjustment screw to adjust the speed to 700 rpm. The test light must NOT light up; if it does, readjust the micro switch position. Remove the ground from terminal 10 to reactivate the ECU. The idle speed should have changed to 750 rpm (700–800 rpm is permitted). Stop the engine.

6. Reconnect the throttle control rod at the lever, making sure the cable pulley is completely retracted. If the control rod length must be adjusted, disconnect the throttle cable and automatic transmission kickdown cable (if equipped). Loosen the locknuts on either end of the rod and adjust the rod as necessary by turning it, then tighten the locknuts. Attach the throttle cable and adjust it if necessary by turning the nut on the end of the cable as shown. Automatic transmission kickdown cable length should be checked at closed and open throttle with the engine **OFF**. Open throttle cable measurement should be checked with the throttle pedal in the car depressed, NOT by actuating the linkage by hand. The cable should be pulled out 1.9 in. (50mm).

7. Adjust the micro switch by moving the switch **UP**, with the engine not running and the throttle closed. Slacken the switch retaining screws, and move the switch **UP** until the test light lights up. Set the switch position by moving the switch **DOWN** 0.08–0.10 in. (2–5.5mm). The test light must not light up, or the adjustment will have to be preformed again.

8. Remove the test light, reinstall the ECU panel.

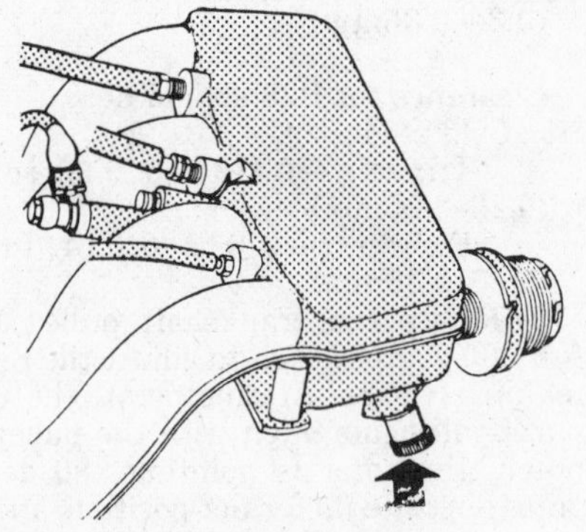

**Mechanical (K-Jetronic) injection idle speed adjustment**

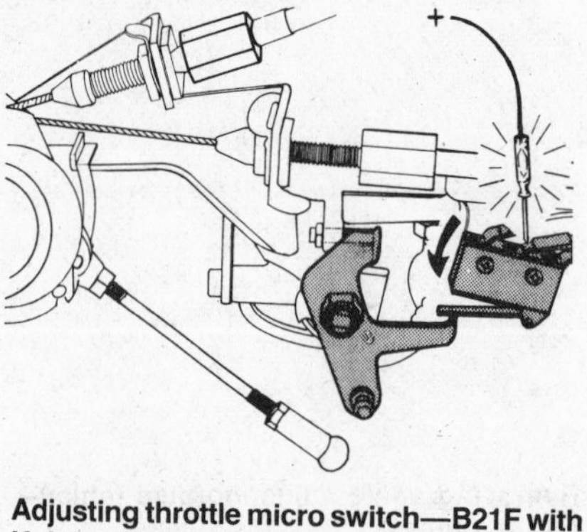


**Adjusting throttle micro switch—B21F with K-Jetronic injection. Adjust idle if test light lights up at idle speed**

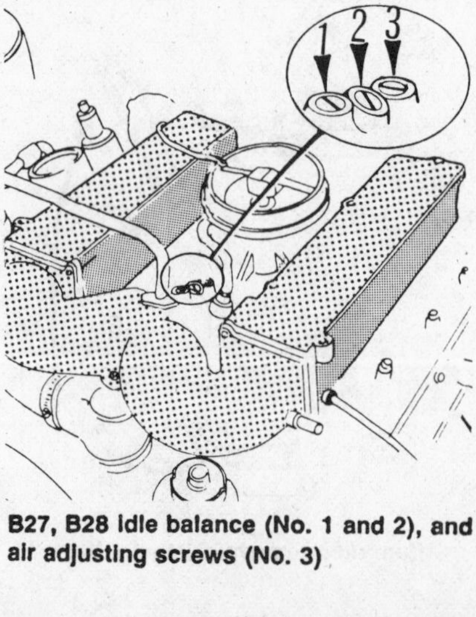


**B27, B28 idle balance (No. 1 and 2), and air adjusting screws (No. 3)**

**1983–85 B21F TURBO ENGINE**

1. Run the engine to normal operating temperature. Disconnect the throttle control rod at the lever. Make sure the cable and pulley run smoothly and do not bind in any position.

2. Remove the ECU cover panel. To deactivate the ECU, ground terminal 10 with the connector in place by inserting a copper wire along the terminal wire.

**NOTE: The same wire ends at the ignition coil but cannot be disconnected there.**

3. Connect a test light across the battery positive terminal and the orange wire terminal on the micro (throttle) switch. The test light must NOT light up while adjusting the idle speed (the electric circuit through the micro switch is open). If the test light illuminates, adjust the micro switch position by slackening the switch retaining screws and moving the switch down until the test light goes out. Tighten the screws. This is a temporary adjustment; the final adjustment will follow later on.

4. Run the engine to normal operating temperature if not already done. Connect a tachometer to the engine and check idle speed; idle speed should be 850 rpm. If idle speed is outside these limits, follow the procedure below.

5. Using the throttle position adjustment screw, adjust throttle position until the idle speed reaches 850 rpm. The test light must NOT light up. If necessary adjust the micro switch position **DOWN**.

6. Activate the ECU by disconnecting the ground wire that was inserted at terminal 10 of the blue connector.

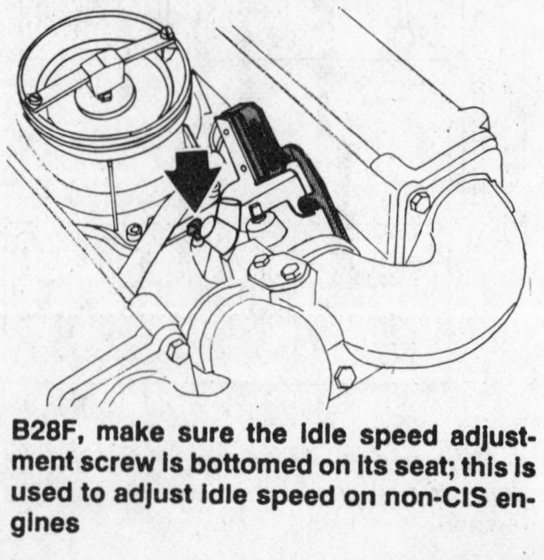

**B28F, make sure the idle speed adjustment screw is bottomed on its seat; this is used to adjust idle speed on non-CIS engines**

7. After activating the ECU, the idle speed should change to 900 rpm (880–920 rpm permitted). Stop the engine and install the ECU panel.

8. Reconnect and adjust the throttle control rod and cable, and the automatic transmission kickdown cable (if equipped) by following Step 6 of the 1983 B23E procedure.

9. Adjust the B21F Turbo throttle switch by inserting a 0.3mm feeler gauge between the throttle adjustment screw and the throttle control lever. Move the switch **UP** until the test light lights up. Set the switch by moving it **DOWN** until the test light just goes out. Disconnect all test instruments, install the ECU panel.

### 1983–86 B28F ENGINE

1. Disconnect the throttle rod at the cable pulley. Check the cable assembly, making sure the cable and pulley run smoothly and do not bind in any position. Check the throttle, make sure the throttle shaft and plate do not bind during operation.

2. Screw in the idle speed adjustment screw all the way until it just seats.

**NOTE: This screw is used to adjust the idle speed on engines without the CIS system.**

3. Remove the access panel to the ECU module. (The ECU is located on the passenger's side kick panel on all models except the 760 GLE, on which the ECU is mounted on the driver's side kick panel).

4. On 1983–86 models, ground terminal 10 with the connector in place. This can be done by inserting a copper wire along the No. 10 terminal wire.

5. Connect a test light across the positive battery terminal and the orange wire terminal on the throttle micro switch. The test light should NOT light up while adjusting the switch, indicating the electric circuit through the micro switch is interrupted.

6. Connect a tachometer to the engine, and run the engine up to normal operating temperature.

7. Adjust the idle speed by adjusting the throttle position adjustment screw. DO NOT adjust the idle speed screw (it should still be screwed in on its seat).

8. Activate the ECU. With the ECU activated, the idle speed should change to 750 rpm. Shut off the engine and install the ECU panel.

9. Reconnect the throttle control rod at the cable pulley. Disconnect the throttle cable and automatic transmission kickdown cable. The cable pulley should be completely retracted. Adjust the control rod length as necessary. Attach and adjust the throttle cable.

10. Check automatic transmission kickdown cable length at closed and open throttle with the engine **OFF**. Open throttle measurement should be checked with the throttle pedal in the car depressed, NOT by actuating the linkage by hand. Cable movement should be about 1.9 in. (50mm). Cable length with closed throttle should be 1mm with open throttle 51mm.

11. To adjust the throttle micro switch, insert 0.12 in. (3mm) feeler gauge between the throttle position adjustment screw and the throttle stop. Turn the adjustment screw until the test light lights up.

### Full Throttle Enrichment Switch

**NOTE: The B28F V6 is equipped with 2 micro switches actuated by throttle control. This second micro switch closes a Lambda-Sond (the oxygen sensor) circuit at full throttle to provide richer air/fuel mixture at maximum acceleration. Vehicles sold in high-altitude areas have this switch disconnected.**

1. To adjust the switch, loosen the micro switch retaining screws. Turn the switch sideways. The test light should come on, then go out 0.10 in. (2.5mm) before the pulley touches the full throttle stop. Tighten the retaining screws.

2. To check full throttle enrichment switch operations, disconnect the green wire at the micro switch. Connect a test light between the micro switch terminal and the positive battery terminal.

3. Turn the pulley slowly to the full throttle stop. The test light should light up 0.04–0.15 in. (1–4mm) before the pulley touches the stop. Adjust the switch as necessary, following the switch adjustment procedure above.

### *Electronic Injection (LH-Jetronic)*

### B23F, B230F and B234 ENGINES

1. Seat the throttle butterfly valve by loosening the stop nut on the adjuster screw. Unscrew the adjuster a couple of turns. Set the adjuster screw by screwing it in until it just touches the lever, then screw it in an additional ¼ turn. Tighten the lock nut.

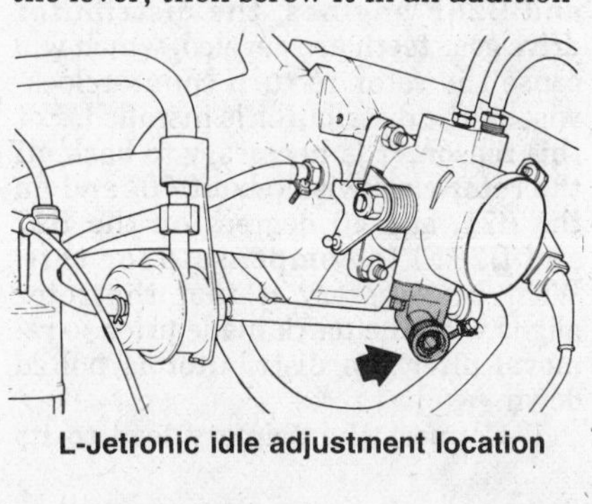

L-Jetronic idle adjustment location

2. Disconnect the CIS connector on the firewall. This is the connector that is directly behind the engine.

3. Connect a test light across the battery positive terminal and the orange wire terminal in the connector. Start the engine. The test light should light up at idle speed. If it does not, readjust the adjuster screw for the throttle butterfly valve position.

4. Open the throttle slightly by hand at the throttle control lever, with the engine running. The test light should go out. If it does not, run through the procedure again and try a new throttle switch.

### 1987–90 B280F ENGINE

1. Ground the CIS test point. The CIS test point is the red/white wire in the 2 wire connector which is located in the engine compartment across from the air conditioning compressor.

2. The green/white wire is the test point location for the oxygen sensor test.

3. Grounding the red/white wire will set the air valve in the wide open position.

4. Adjust the basic idle speed to 700 rpm. Disconnect the ground wire from the CIS test point. The idle speed should increase to 750 rpm.

## Diesel Fuel Injection

### SETTING THE IDLE SPEED

**NOTE: To correctly set the idle speed you will need either the Volvo Monotester and adapter 9950 or a suitable photoelectric tachometer, since a gasoline engine tachometer by itself cannot be used on a diesel engine owing to the fact that a diesel engine**

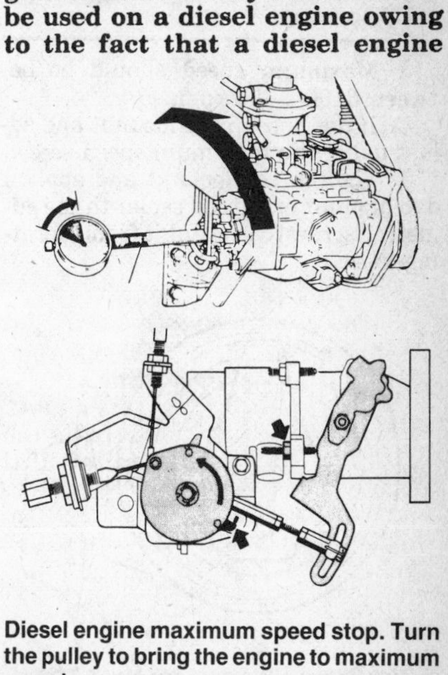

Diesel engine maximum speed stop. Turn the pulley to bring the engine to maximum speed.

**does not have an electric ignition system.**

1. Connect a suitable tachometer to the engine and run the engine to normal operating temperature.
2. Idle speed should be 720–880 rpm.
3. If not, adjust the idle speed by loosening the locknut and turning the idle speed screw on the fuel injection pump.
4. Tighten the locknut and apply a dab of paint or thread sealer to the adjusting screw to prevent it from vibration loose.
5. After adjusting idle speed and maximum engine speed, adjust the engine throttle linkage.

### SETTING THE MAXIMUM ENGINE SPEED

The diesel engine is governed by the fuel injection pump so that engine rpm will not exceed 5100–5300 rpm. Because of the extremely high compression ratio (23.5:1) and the great stored energy diesel oil contains, the diesel engine cannot be run at the high rpm levels of modern gasoline engines, as it would place a tremendous strain on the pistons, wrist pins, connecting rods and bearing of the engine.

To adjust the maximum idle speed you will need a special tachometer which will work on the diesel engine.

1. Connect the tachometer and run the engine to normal operating temperature.
2. Run the engine to maximum speed by turning the cable pulley counterclockwise.

**CAUTION**

***Do not race the engine longer than absolutely necessary.***

3. Maximum speed should be between 5100–5300 rpm.
4. If not, loosen the locknut and adjust using the maximum speed screw.
5. Tighten the locknut and apply a dab of paint or thread sealer to the adjusting screw to prevent it from vibrating loose.

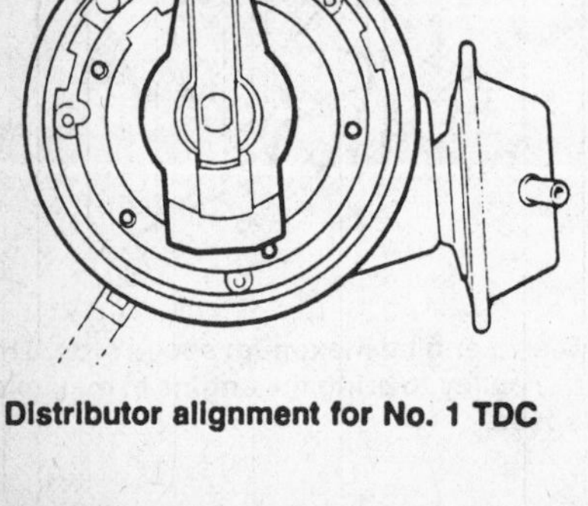

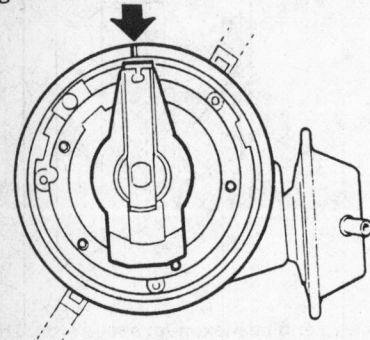

**Distributor alignment for No. 1 TDC**

**CAUTION**

***Do not attempt to squeeze more power out of your diesel by extending the maximum speed.***

6. After adjusting the maximum speed, adjust the engine throttle linkage.

# ENGINE ELECTRICAL

## Distributor

### REMOVAL & INSTALLATION

1. Unsnap the distributor cap clasps and remove the cap.
2. Crank the engine until No. 1 cylinder is at Top Dead Center (TDC). At this point, the rotor should point to the spark plug wire socket for No. 1 cylinder, and the 0 degree timing mark on the crankshaft damper should be aligned with the pointer. For ease of assembly, scribe a chalkmark on the distributor housing to note the position of the rotor.
3. Disconnect the negative battery terminal. Disconnect the primary lead from the coil at its terminal on the distributor housing. On electronic fuel-injected models, disconnect the plug for the triggering contacts. On all models except Canadian B21A, remove the retaining screw for the primary voltage wire connector and pull it from the distributor housing.
4. Remove the vacuum hose(s) from the regulator. Take care not to damage the bakelite connection during removal.
5. Remove the distributor attaching screw and lift out the distributor.
6. When ready to install the distributor, if the engine has been disturbed (cranked), find TDC for No. 1 cylinder. If the engine has not been disturbed, install the distributor with the rotor pointing to the No. 1 cylinder spark plug wire socket, or the chalkmark made prior to removal. On B21, B27 and B28F engines, the distributor drive gear teeth are beveled, which will cause the rotor to turn counterclockwise as the distributor is installed. For this reason, it is necessary to back off the rotor clockwise (about 60° and on the B21, and 40 degrees on the B27 and B28F) to compensate for this. What is necessary is that the rotor aligns with the mark made prior to removal after the distributor is bolted down.
7. Connect the primary lead to its terminal on the distributor housing. On electronic fuel injected models, connect the plug for the triggering contacts. Push the primary voltage wire connector into its slot in the distributor housing and tighten the retaining screw.
8. Connect the vacuum hose(s) to the bakelite connection(s) on the vacuum regulator, (if so equipped).
9. If the distributor was disassembled, or if the contact point setting was disturbed, proceed to set the point gap and/or dwell angle on B21A (Canadian) engines.
10. Install the distributor cap and secure the clasps. Proceed to set the ignition timing. Tighten the distributor attaching screw.

## Alternator

### PRECAUTIONS

Several precautions must be observed when performing work on alternator equipment.

- If the battery is removed for any reason, make sure that it is reconnected with the correct polarity. Reversing the battery connections may result in damage to the 1-way rectifiers.
- Never operate the alternator with the main circuit broken. Make sure that the battery, alternator, and regulator leads are not disconnected while the engine is running.
- Never attempt to polarize an alternator.
- When charging a battery that is installed in the vehicle, disconnect the negative battery cable. This is very important.
- When utilizing a booster battery as a starting aid, always connect it in parallel; negative to negative, and positive to positive.
- When arc welding is to be performed on any part of the vehicle, disconnect the negative battery cable, disconnect the alternator leads, and unplug the voltage regulator and all computers.

### DRIVE BELT ADJUSTMENT

Accessory drive belt tension is correct when the deflection made with light finger pressure on the at a midway point is about ½ in. Any belt that is glazed, frayed, or stretched so that it cannot be tightened sufficiently must be replaced.

Incorrect belt tension is corrected by moving the driven accessory (alternator, air pump, power steering pump or air conditioning compressor) away from or toward the driving pulley. Loosen the mounting and adjusting bolts on the respective accessory and tighten them, once the belt tension is correct. Never position a metal pry bar on the rear end of the alternator air pump or power steering pump housing, they can be deformed easily.

### REMOVAL & INSTALLATION

1. Disconnect the negative battery cable.
2. Disconnect the electrical leads to the alternator. Remove all necessary components in order to gain access to the alternator retaining bolts.
3. Remove the adjusting arm-to-alternator bolt and the adjusting arm-to-engine bolt.
4. Remove the alternator mounting bolt.
5. Remove the fan belt and lift the alternator forward and out.
6. Reverse the above procedure to install, taking care to properly tension the fan (drive) belt.

## Voltage Regulator

### REMOVAL & INSTALLATION

1. Disconnect the negative battery cable.
2. Disconnect the leads or plug socket from the old regulator taking note of their location.
3. Remove the hold-down screws from the old regulator and install the new one.
4. Connect the leads or plug socket and reconnect the negative battery cable.

### VOLTAGE ADJUSTMENT

#### *Motorola (S.E.V. Marchal) Regulator*

If the Motorola regulator is found to be defective, it must be replaced. No adjustments can be made on this unit.

The following test may be performed on the Motorola regulator to see if it is functioning properly. An ammeter, tachometer, and voltmeter are required.

1. Connect the testing equipment at the alternator.
2. Run the engine at 2500 rpm (5000 alternator rpm) for 15 seconds. With no load on the alternator, and the regulator ambient temperature at 77°F (25°C), the reading n the voltmeter should be 13.1–14.4 V.
3. Load the alternator with 10–15 amps (high-beam headlights) while the engine is running at 2500 rpm. The voltmeter reading should again be 13.1–14.4 V. Replace the regulator if it does not fall within these limits.
4. For a more accurate indication of the regulator's performance, drive the vehicle for about 45 minutes at a minimum speed of 30 mph. The regulator will be at the correct working temperature immediately after this drive.
5. With the engine running at 2500 rpm, and the regulator ambient temperature at 77°F (25°C), the voltmeter reading should be 13.85–14.25 V.

#### *Bosch A.C. Regulator (35, 55 and 70 Amp)*

The Bosch A.C. regulator is fully adjustable. To determine which adjustments are necessary (if any), perform the following test. (An ammeter, 12 V control lamp, tachometer, and voltmeter are required for this test.)

**NOTE: Where the numerical values differ for the 35 amp voltage regulator and the 55 amp unit, the figures for the 55 amp regulator will be given in parentheses.**

1. Connect the alternator and regulator as shown in the illustration.

**NOTE: The first reading must be taken within 30 seconds of beginning of test.**

2. While running the engine at 2000 rpm, load the alternator with 28–30 amps (44–46 for 55 amp alternator).
3. Rapidly lower the engine to idle speed or 500 rpm, and then return it to 2000 rpm. With a load of 28–30 amps (44–46 for 55 amp alternator), the voltmeter reading should be 14.0–15.0 V (13.9–14.8 V for 55 amp alternator). The regulator should be regulated on the left (lower) contact.
4. Reduce the alternator load to 3–8 amps. The voltmeter reading should not decrease more than 0.3 (0.4 for 44 amp, alternator) V. The regulator should be regulated on the right (upper) contact.
5. Adjustment is made by bending the stop bracket for the bi-metal spring. Bending the stop bracket down lowers the regulating voltage; bending it up raises the voltage. If the voltmeter reading for the low amp alternator load decreased more than 0.3 (0.4 for 55 amp alternator), V, compared to the reading for the high amp alternator load, adjust the regulator by bending the holder for the left (lower) contact and simultaneously adjust the gap between the right (upper) contact and the movable contact. The gap should be adjusted to 0.010–0.015 in. (0.25–0.40mm). If the holder is bent toward the right (upper) contact, the regulating voltage under high amp alternator load will be lowered.

To avoid faulty adjustments due to residual magnetism in the regulator core, it may be necessary to rapidly

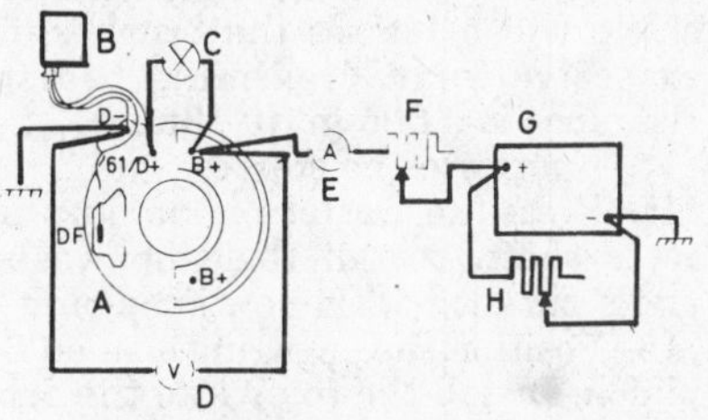


A. Alternator
B. Voltage lamp 12 volts
C. Control lamp 12 volts, 2 watts
D. Voltmeter 0-20 volts
F. Regulator resistance
G. Battery 60 amperehours
H. Load resistance
E. Ammeter 0-50 amps

**Wiring diagram for testing Bosch A.C. regulator**

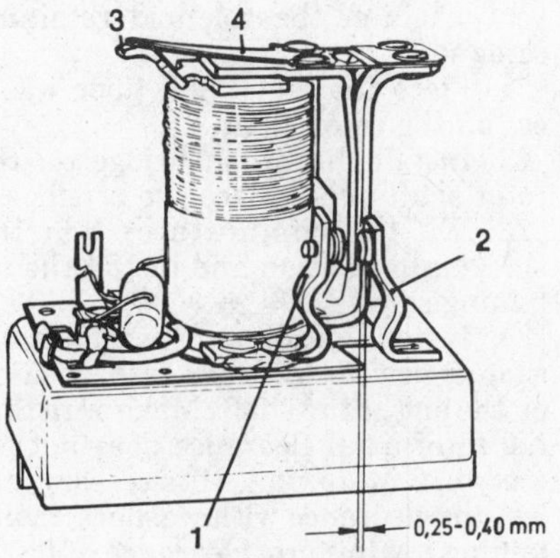


1. Regulator contact for lower control range (lower contact)
2. Regulator contact for upper control range (upper contact)
3. Spring tensioner
4. Spring upper section: Steel spring Lower section: Bimetal spring

**Bosch A.C. voltage adjustments**

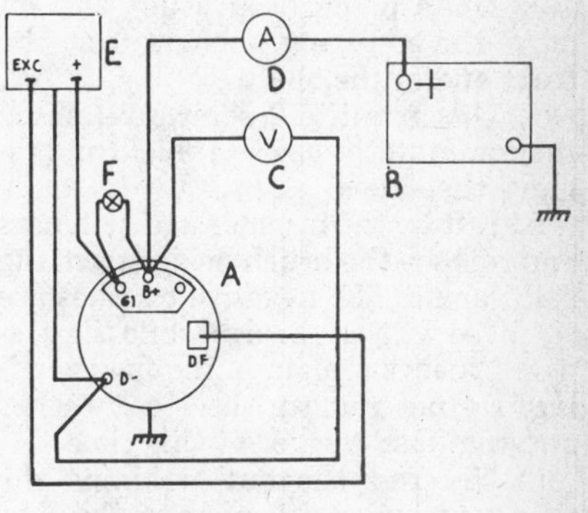


A. Alternator
B. Battery 60 Ah
C. Voltmeter 0—20 amps.
D. Ammeter 0—50 amps.
E. Voltage regulator
F. Warning lamp 12 volts. 2 watts

**Wiring diagram for testing Motorola regulator**

lower the engine rpm to idle after each adjustment, then raise it to 2000 rpm to take a new reading.

**NOTE: Warm regulators may be cooled to ambient temperature by directing a stream of compressed air on them. Final readings should be made with the regulator at ambient temperature.**

## Starter

### REMOVAL & INSTALLATION

1. Disconnect the negative battery cable at the battery.
2. Disconnect the leads from the starter motor. Remove the necessary components in order to gain access to the starter retaining bolts. Raise and support the vehicle, as required.
3. Remove the bolts retaining the starter motor brace to the cylinder block (B21 only) and the bolts retaining the starter motor to the flywheel housing and lift it off.
4. To install, position the starter motor to the flywheel housing and install the retaining bolts finger-tight. Torque the bolts to approximately 25 ft. lbs. (34 Nm), and apply locking compound to the threads.
5. Connect the starter motor leads and the negative battery cable.

### STARTER DRIVE REPLACEMENT

In order to remove the starter pinion drive, it is necessary to disassemble the starter. The procedure for disassembling the starter is as follows:

1. Remove the starter from the vehicle.
2. Unscrew the 2 screws and remove the small cover from the front end of the starter shaft.
3. Unsnap the lockwasher and remove the adjusting washers from the front end of the shaft.
4. Unscrew the 2 screws retaining the commutator bearing shield and remove the shield.
5. Lift up the brushes and retainers and remove the brush bridge from the rotor shaft. The negative brushes are removed with the bridge while the positive brushes remain in the field winding. Do not remove the steel washer and the fiber washer at this time.
6. Unscrew the nut retaining the field terminal connection to the control solenoid.
7. Unscrew the 2 solenoid-to-starter housing retaining screws and remove the solenoid.
8. Remove the drive end shield and rotor from the stator.
9. Remove the rubber and metal sealing washers from the housing.
10. Unscrew the nut and remove the screw on which the engaging arm pivots.
11. Remove the rotor, with the pinion and engaging arm attached, from the drive end shield.
12. Push back the stop washer and remove the snapring from the rotor shaft.
13. Remove the stop washer and pull off the starter pinion with a gear puller.

While the starter is disassembled, a few quick checks may be performed. Check the rotor shaft, commutator, and windings. If the rotor shaft is bent or worn, it must be replaced. Maximum rotor shaft radial throw is 0.003 in. (0.07mm). If the commutator is scored or worn unevenly, it should be turned. Minimum commutator diameter is 1.3 in. (33mm). Check the end shield which houses the brushes, for excessive wear. Maximum bearing clearance is 0.005 in. (0.13mm).

14. Lubricate the starter.
15. Press the starter pinion onto the rotor shaft. Install the stop washer and secure it with a new snap-ring.
16. Position the engaging arm on the pinion. Install the rotor into the drive end frame.
17. Install the screw and nut for the engaging arm pivot.
18. Install the rubber and metal sealing washers into the drive end housing.
19. Install the stator onto the rotor and drive end shield.
20. Position the solenoid so that the eyelet on the end of the solenoid plunger fits onto the engaging arm (shift lever). Tighten the solenoid retaining screws.
21. Place the metal and fiber washers on the rotor shaft.
22. Install the brush bridge on the rotor shaft and replace the brushes.
23. Fit the commutator bearing shield into position and install the retaining screws.
24. Install the adjusting washers and snap a new lockwasher into position on the end of the shaft. Make sure that the rotor axial clearance does not exceed 0.12 in. (3mm). If necessary, adjust the clearance with washers, maintaining a minimum clearance of 0.002 in. (0.05mm).
25. Replace the small cover over the front end of the shaft and install the 2 retaining screws.
26. Install the starter.

### STARTER SOLENOID REPLACEMENT

1. Remove the starter from the vehicle.
2. Unscrew the 2 solenoid-to-starter housing retaining screws and remove the solenoid.
3. As a final test, wipe the solenoid clean and press in the armature. Test its operation by connecting it to a battery. If the solenoid still does not function, replace it with a new unit.
4. Position the new solenoid so that the eyelet on the end of the plunger fits into the engaging arm. Tighten the retaining screws.
5. Replace the starter.

## Diesel Glow Plugs

### REMOVAL & INSTALLATION

1. Disconnect the negative battery cable.
2. Remove all necessary components in order to gain access to the glow plug.
3. Remove the electrical connector from the glow plug.
4. Carefully remove the glow plug from its mounting on the engine, using the proper tools.
5. Installation is the reverse of the removal procedure.

# ENGINE MECHANICAL

## Engine

### REMOVAL & INSTALLATION

#### *B23E and B230F Engines*

1. On cars equipped with manual transmission, remove the 4 retaining clips and lift up the shifter boot. Then, remove the snapring from the shifter.
2. Remove the battery.
3. Disconnect the windshield washer hose and engine compartment light wire. Scribe marks around the hood mount brackets on the under-side of the hood for later alignment. Remove the hood.
4. Remove the overflow tank cap. Drain the cooling system.
5. Remove the upper and lower radiator hoses. Disconnect the overflow hoses at the radiator. Disconnect the PCV hose at the cylinder head.
6. On cars equipped with automatic transmission disconnect the oil cooler lines at the radiator.
7. Remove the radiator and fan shroud.
8. Remove the air cleaner assembly and hoses.

9. Disconnect the hoses at the air pump. Remove the air pump and drive belt, if equipped.
10. Disconnect the vacuum pump hoses and remove the vacuum pump. disconnect the power brake booster vacuum hose.
11. Remove the power steering pump, drive belt and bracket. Position to one side.
12. On cars equipped with air conditioning, remove the crankshaft pulley and compressor drive belt. Then, install the pulley again for reference. Remove the A/C wire connector and the compressor from its bracket and position to one side. Remove the bracket.
13. Disconnect the vacuum hoses from the engine. Disconnect the carbon canister hoses.
14. Disconnect the distributor wire connector, high tension lead, starter cables, and the clutch cable clamp.
15. Disconnect the wiring harness at the voltage regulator. Disconnect the throttle cable at the pulley and the wire for the A/C at the intake manifold solenoid.
16. Remove the gas cap. Disconnect the fuel lines at the filter and return pipe.
17. At the firewall, disconnect the electrical connectors for the ballast resistor, and relays. Disconnect the heater hoses.
18. Disconnect the micro switch connectors at the intake manifold, and all remaining harness connectors to the engine.
19. Drain the crankcase.
20. Remove the exhaust manifold flange retaining nuts. Loosen the exhaust pipe clamp bolts and remove the bracket for the front exhaust pipe mount. On B21FT (Turbo) models, disconnect the turbo from the intake hose, disconnect the other hoses from the turbo unit, and disconnect the turbocharger from the exhaust system.
21. From underneath, remove the front motor mount bolts.
22. On cars equipped with automatic transmission, place the gear selector lever in **P** and disconnect the gear shift control rod from the transmission.
23. On manual transmission cars, disconnect the clutch cable. Then, loosen the set screw, drive out the pivot pin, and remove the shifter from the control rod.
24. Disconnect the speedometer and the driveshaft from the transmission.
25. On overdrive equipped models, disconnect the control wire from the shifter.
26. Raise and support the vehicle safely. Then, using a floor jack and a wooden block, support the weight of the engine beneath the transmission.
27. Remove the bolts for the rear transmission mount. Remove the transmission support crossmember.
28. Lift out the engine using the proper lifting equipment.
29. Reverse the above procedure to install. Adjust gear selector linkage, check and adjust throttle linkage.

### *B234 Engine*

1. Disconnect the battery, negative cable first.
2. Disconnect the ground connection at the top of the side frame rail.
3. Release the bolted joint at the exhaust manifold front bracket.
4. Attach the sling or lifting equipment to the rear of the motor and support the motor from above. Release any wiring harnesses from their clips and place the wiring out of the way of the lifting gear.
5. Remove the splashguard under the engine, drain the engine oil and remove the air intake duct.

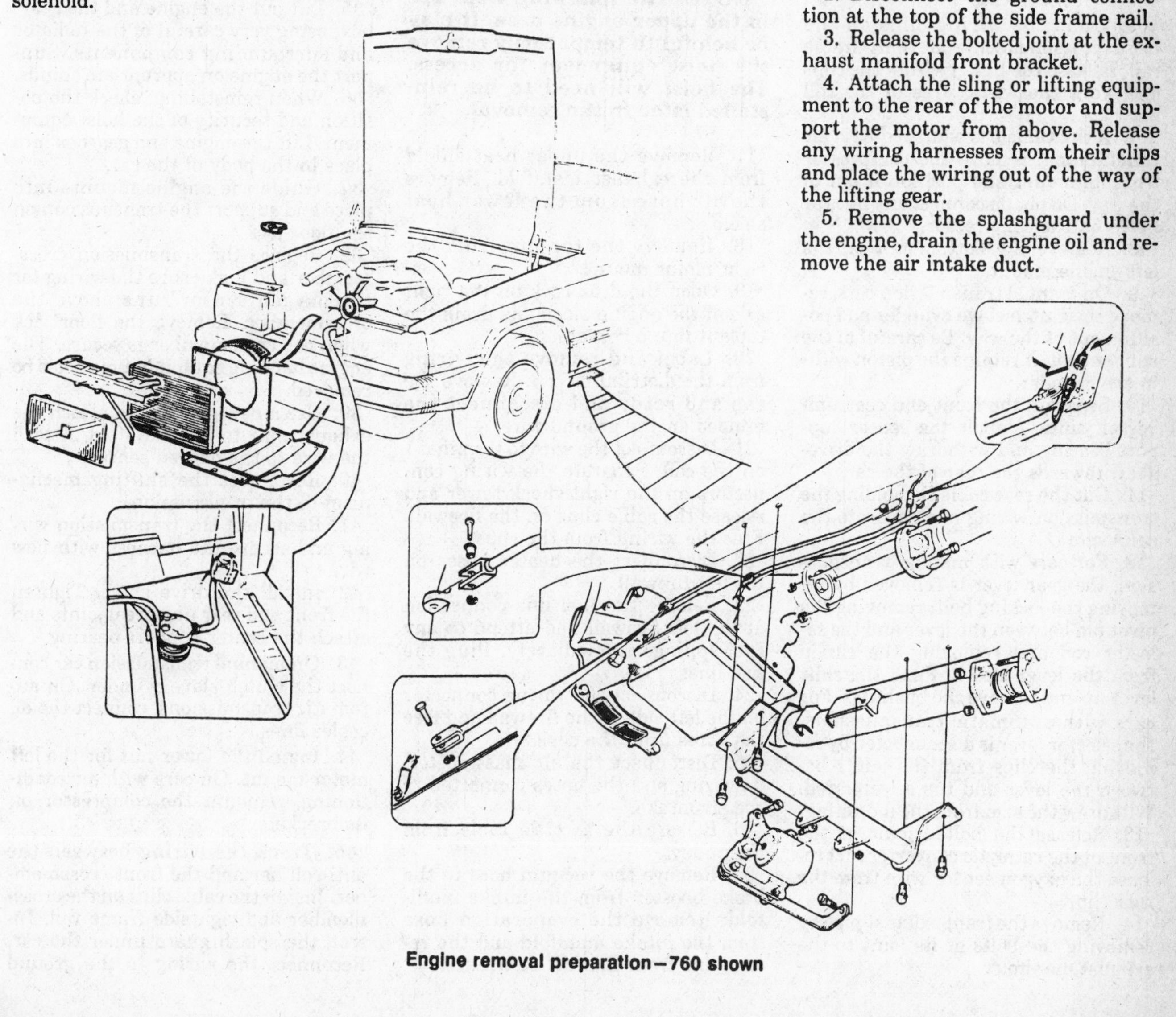

**Engine removal preparation—760 shown**

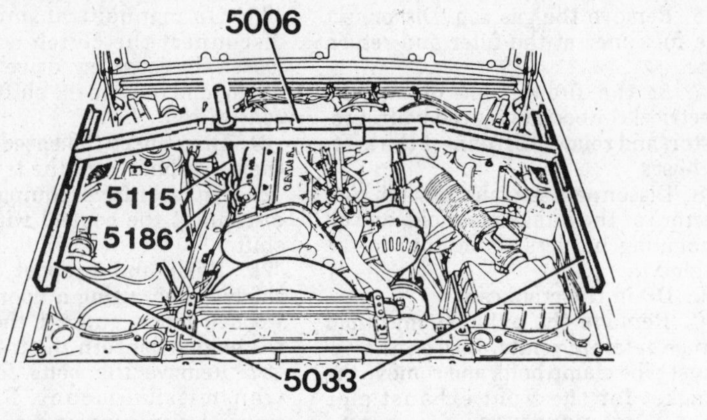


**Engine replacement tooling requirement—B234F engine shown, others similar**

**CAUTION**

*Used motor oil may cause skin cancer if repeatedly left in contact with the skin for prolonged periods. Although this is unlikely unless you handle oil on a daily basis, it is wise to thoroughly wash your hands with soap and water immediately after handling used motor oil.*

6. Undo the wiring clips on the front crossmember and right frame rail. Release the battery from the clips and work the wiring free of the roll bar.
7. If the vehicle is equipped with air conditioning, remove the compressor from its mount and position it out of the way. Do not disconnect any lines or hoses on the compressor.
8. Remove the bottom nut on the left engine mount.
9. On manual transmission cars, remove the clutch slave cylinder and position out of the way. Be careful of the rubber boot; it retains the piston within the cylinder.
10. Separate the front and rear universal joints. Unbolt the center support bearing and withdraw the driveshaft towards the rear of the car.
11. Cut the rear cable tie holding the transmission wiring and separate the connectors.
12. For cars with manual transmission, the gear lever is removed by removing the locking bolt, removing the pivot pin between the lever and the selector rod and removing the circlip from the lever sleeve. Push the shift lever up and remove the bushings. For cars with automatic transmissions, the selector lever is disconnected by removing the clips from the joints between the lever and the selector rod. Withdraw the arm from the mounting.
13. Release the bolted joint at the front of the catalytic converter and release the oxygen sensor wire from the rear clip.
14. Remove the front exhaust pipe by removing the bolts at its joint to the exhaust manifold.
15. If equipped with automatic transmission, disconnect the oil lines at the transmission and plug the lines.
16. Remove the transmission crossmember. As soon as it is removed, position a floor jack below the transmission to support it.

**NOTE: The following steps are in the upper engine area. It may be helpful to temporarily remove the hoist equipment for access. The hoist will need to be reinstalled later in the removal.**

17. Remove the upper heat shield from the exhaust manifold. Remove the air hose from the lower heat shield.
18. Remove the top nut from the right motor mount.
19. Open the draincock on the right side of the engine block and drain the coolant into a container.
20. Label and remove the wiring from the distributor cap. Remove the cap and rotor and disconnect the braided engine ground wire.
21. Disconnect the wire to terminal 1 on the coil. Separate the wiring connectors on the right shock tower and release the cable clips on the firewall. Free the wiring from the clips.
22. Disconnect the heater hoses on the left firewall.
23. Release the fuel line connection at the left firewall and attend to any fuel spillage immediately. Plug the fuel lines.
24. Disconnect the wiring connector on the left side of the firewall and free the wires from the clips.
25. Disconnect the air mass meter, its wiring and the hoses connected to the air intake.
26. Release the throttle cable from the pulley.
27. Remove the vacuum hose to the brake booster from the intake manifold. Remove the evaporation hose from the intake manifold and the return line from the fuel distributor.
28. At the left shock tower, release the engine wiring harness from its clips and disconnect the wiring connectors. Remove the power steering reservoir from its clips.
29. Disconnect the coolant hoses at the thermostat housing and at the water pump.
30. Remove the drive belts.
31. Remove the radiator fan, the fan shroud and the drive pulley.
32. Remove the power steering pump from its mount. Place the pump on paper or rags atop the left shock tower. Do not disconnect any hoses from the pump.
33. If the lifting equipment was removed earlier, reconnect it.
34. Check the surroundings of the engine and transmission unit. With the exception of the jack and the motor mounts, there should be nothing connecting the engine/trans assembly to the body of the car. Take slight tension on the hoist and check that the engine is balanced. Reposition the lift points if the engine is not balanced.
35. Lift out the engine and the gearbox, being very careful of the radiator and surrounding components. Support the engine on appropriate stands.
36. When reinstalling, check the position and security of the hoist equipment. Lift the engine and gearbox into place in the body of the car.
37. Guide the engine mounts into place and support the transmission on the floor jack.
38. Replace the transmission crossmember and make sure the wiring for the oxygen sensor runs above the crossmember. Remove the floor jack when the crossmember is secure. The engine hoisting equipment may also be removed.
39. Use a new gasket and attach the exhaust pipe to the manifold. Attach the wire to the oxygen sensor.
40. Reconnect the shifting mechanism to the transmission.
41. Reconnect the transmission wiring and secure the harness with new wire ties.
42. Install the drive shaft. Tighten the front and rear universal joints and attach the center support bearing.
43. On manual transmission car connect the clutch slave cylinder. On automatic transmissions, connect the oil cooler lines.
44. Install the lower nut for the left motor mount. On cars with air conditioning, remount the compressor on its brackets.
45. Track the wiring between the anti-roll bar and the front crossmember. Install the cable clips on the crossmember and rightside frame rail. Install the splash guard under the car. Reconnect the wiring to the ground

connection on the right frame rail.

46. Install the nut on the top of the right engine mount. Install the upper heat shield on the manifold and the air tube to the lower heat shield.

47. Reconnect the coolant hoses. The bottom hose connects to the water pump and the upper hose to the thermostat housing.

**NOTE: Note the marking on the upper hose. The hose must run at least 1 in. away from the alternator belt.**

48. Remount the power steering pump. Install its belt (and the air conditioning belt if so equipped) and adjust to the correct tension.

49. Install the fan, pulley and shroud. Secure the wiring below the fan with new wire ties. Install the drive belt and adjust to the correct tension.

50. Reconnect the rear wiring harnesses on the firewall. Plug all connectors carefully and secure harnesses within the clips. Don't forget the wire to terminal 1 on the coil.

51. Reinstall the distributor rotor, cap and wires. Connect the braided engine ground cable.

52. Reconnect the wiring at the left shock tower. Make sure the wiring is secure in its clips. Install the power steering reservoir.

53. At the intake manifold, connect the vacuum line to the brake booster, the evaporation line and the return line for the fuel distributor.

54. At the left side of the firewall, attach the heater hoses and connect the fuel line.

55. Reattach the throttle cable to the pulley.

56. Install the air mass meter with its hoses and connections.

57. Fill the engine with proper coolant, set the heater to its hottest setting and check the system for leaks.

58. Install the engine oil.

59. Reconnect the battery leads (positive first) and the protective cap on the terminals.

60. Double check all installation items, paying particular attention to loose hoses or hanging wires, untightened nuts, poor routing of hoses and wires (too tight or rubbing) and tools left in the engine area.

61. Start the engine and check for leaks. This engine may be somewhat noisy when started; the noise will disappear as the tappets fill with oil.

### B28F and B280F Engines

1. On cars equipped with manual transmission, remove the shifter assembly. From underneath, loosen the set screw and drive out the pivot pin. Then, pull up the boot, remove the reverse pawl bracket, and snap-ring for the shifter, and lift out the shifter.

2. Remove the battery.

3. Disconnect the windshield washer hose and engine compartment light wire. Scribe marks around the hood mount brackets on the underside of the hood for later hood alignment. Remove the hood.

4. Remove the air cleaner assembly.

5. Remove the splash guard under the engine.

6. Drain the cooling system.

7. Remove the overflow tank cap. Remove the upper and lower radiator hoses, and disconnect the overflow hoses at the radiator.

8. On cars equipped with automatic transmission, disconnect the transmission cooler lines at the radiator.

9. Remove the radiator and fan shroud.

10. Disconnect the heater hoses, power brake hose at the intake manifold and the vacuum pump hose at the pump. Remove the vacuum pump and O-ring in the valve cover. Remove the gas cap.

11. At the firewall disconnect the fuel lines at the filter and return pipe, disconnect the relay connectors and all other wire connectors. Disconnect the distributor wires.

**CAUTION**

***Use caution when disconnecting the fuel lines. The fuel lines may be under high pressure.***

12. Disconnect the evaporative control carbon canister hoses and the vacuum hose at the EGR valve.

13. Disconnect the voltage regulator wire connector.

14. Disconnect the throttle cable (and kickdown cable on automatic transmission cars), the vacuum amplifier hose at the T-pipe, and the hoses at the thermostat.

15. Disconnect the air pump hose at the backfire valve, the solenoid valve wire, and the micro switch wire.

16. Remove the exhaust manifold flange retaining nuts (both sides).

17. On cars equipped with air conditioning, remove the compressor and drive belt, and place it to one side. Do not disconnect the refrigerant hoses.

18. Drain the crankcase.

19. Remove the power steering pump, drive belt, and bracket. Position to one side.

20. From underneath, remove the retaining nuts for the front motor mounts.

21. Remove, as required, the front exhaust pipe.

22. On 49 states models, remove the front exhaust pipe hangers and clamps and allow the system to hang.

23. On cars equipped with automatic transmission, place the shift lever in **P**. Disconnect the shift control lever at the transmission.

24. On manual transmission cars, disconnect the clutch cylinder from the bell housing. Leave the cylinder connected (secure it to the car).

25. Disconnect the speedometer cable and driveshaft at the transmission.

26. Jack up the front of the car and place jack stands beneath the reinforced box member area to the rear of each front jacking attachment. Then, using a floor jack and a thick, wide wooden block, support the weight of the engine beneath the oil pan.

27. Remove the bolts for the rear transmission mount. Remove the transmission support crossmember.

28. Lift out the engine and transmission as a unit.

29. Reverse the above procedure to install. Adjust gear selector linkage, check and adjust throttle linkage.

### D24 and D24T Engines

1. Matchmark and remove the hood.

2. Disconnect the negative battery terminal.

3. Drain the radiator coolant.

4. Remove the 4 clips and pull up the rubber boot on the shift lever.

5. Disconnect the back-up light and overdrive connector if so equipped.

6. Remove the bracket for the reverse inhibitor.

7. Release the lock ring on the shift lever.

8. Move the lock ring, rubber ring, and plastic journal up on the lever.

**NOTE: On cars with automatic transmissions place the shift lever in P before disconnecting.**

9. Disconnect the top and bottom radiator hoses.

10. Disconnect the lower hose at the cold start device, and drain the coolant into a suitable container.

11. On vehicles with automatic transmissions remove the cooling lines from the radiator.

12. Disconnect the expansion tank hose.

13. Unbolt and remove the radiator.

14. Disconnect the electrical connection at the firewall.

15. Remove the heater hoses at the control valve.

16. Disconnect the hose from the vacuum pump.

17. Disconnect the accelerator cable from the pulley and bracket.

18. Disconnect the vacuum line to the brake booster.

19. Disconnect the fuel lines.

**NOTE: Thoroughly clean all**

**connections prior to disconnecting them.**

20. Plug all fuel lines to prevent dirt from entering them.
21. Disconnect the wires at the main terminal.
22. Disconnect the glow plug relay.
23. Remove the relay retaining screws and hang the relay and the wire bundle on the engine.
24. Remove the power steering pump and brackets, and tie it out of the way.
25. Remove the starter wires and the battery ground strap.
26. Remove the fan, spacer, pulley and drive belts.
27. Remove the air cleaner and all necessary hoses.
28. Disconnect the alternator wires.
29. Disconnect the exhaust pipe at the front exhaust manifold.
30. Drain the engine oil.
31. Disconnect the exhaust pipe at the rear exhaust manifold.
32. On D24T models, remove the inlet hose from the turbo pipe, and the snap-ring from the turbo intake pipe. Remove the compressor intake pipe and plug the hole immediately with a clean rag. Disconnect the oil return pipe bolts, and move the return pipe aside. Plug the holes. Remove the oil delivery pipe from the turbo unit, and plug the holes. Remove the compressor and exhaust pipes from the turbo unit, and remove the turbocharger.
33. Disconnect the clutch cable, return spring, vibration damper, and rubber buffer.
34. Pull out the clutch cable from the clutch lever and housing.
35. Disconnect the speedometer from the transmission.

**NOTE: On cars with automatic transmissions disconnect the shift lever.**

36. Disconnect the shift lever and push it up into the car.
37. Remove the driveshaft from the transmission.
38. Support the transmission with a jack and remove the rear crossmember.
39. Remove the engine mounts.
    a. Left side—Remove the nuts from the front axle member.
    b. Right side—Remove the lower nut from the rubber pad.
40. Gently put tension on your engine removal hoist.
41. Remove the left engine mount assembly.
42. Remove the engine using the proper lifting device.
43. Installation is the reverse of removal. Adjust gear selector linkage, and check and adjust throttle linkage. Use new gaskets on the turbocharger if equipped.

## Cylinder Head

### REMOVAL & INSTALLATION

**NOTE: To prevent warpage of the head, removal should be attempted only on a cold engine.**

#### *B23 and B230 Engines*

1. Disconnect the battery.
2. Remove the overflow tank cap and drain the coolant. Disconnect the upper radiator hose.
3. Remove the distributor cap and wires.
4. Remove the PCV hoses.
5. Remove the EGR valve and vacuum pump.
6. Remove the air pump, if equipped, and air injection manifold. Disconnect and remove all hoses to the turbocharger if equipped. Plug all open hoses and holes immediately.
7. Remove the exhaust manifold and header pipe bracket.
8. Remove the intake manifold. Disconnect the manifold brace and the hose clamp to the bellows for the fuel injection air/flow unit. Disconnect the throttle cable, and all vacuum hoses and electrical connectors to the fuel injection unit.
9. Remove the fuel injectors.
10. Remove the valve cover.
11. Loosen the fan shroud and remove the fan. Remove the shroud. Remove the upper belts and pulleys.
12. Remove the timing belt cover. Remove the timing belt.
13. Remove the camshaft (if so desired).
14. Remove the cylinder head 10mm Allen head bolts, and remove the cylinder head from the vehicle.
15. To install, reverse the removal procedure. Oil the head bolts. Tighten the head bolts in the prescribed torque sequence first to 44 ft. lbs. (60 Nm), then to 81 ft. lbs. (110 Nm). After the engine has been run 30 minutes, slacken the bolts to relieve any pretension, and then retorque to 81 ft. lbs. (110 Nm). To set the valve timing, follow the steps for timing belt installation later in this section.

#### *B234F Engine*

**NOTE: The use of the correct special tools or their equivalent is REQUIRED for this procedure.**

1. Disconnect the negative battery cable.
2. Remove the heat shield over the exhaust manifold.
3. Remove the cap from the expansion tank and open the draincock on the right side of the motor. Collect the drained coolant in a suitable container.
4. Unbolt the exhaust pipe from the bracket, remove the manifold nuts and remove the manifold from the head.
5. On the left side of the motor, remove the support under the intake manifold. and remove the bottom bolt in the cylinder block.
6. Remove the manifold intact and tie it or support it safely.
7. Disconnect the temperature sensor connectors, the heating hose under cylinders No. 3 and 4 and the upper radiator hose at the thermostat.
8. Remove the upper and lower timing belt covers.
9. Align the camshaft and crankshaft marks. Turn the engine to TDC on cylinder No. 1 and make sure the pulley marks and the crank marks align.
10. Remove the protective cap over the timing belt tensioner locknut. Loosen the lock nut, compress the tensioner (so as to release tension on the belts) and retighten the locknut, holding the tensioner in place.
11. Remove the timing belt from the camshafts. Do not crease or fold the belt.

**NOTE: The camshafts and the crankshaft MUST NOT be moved when the belt is removed.**

12. Remove the timing belt idler pulleys.
13. Remove the camshaft drive pulleys. Use a counterhold wrench to prevent the cam from turning.
14. Remove the plate or panel behind the pulleys. Remove the cover plate for the ignition wires. Label and disconnect the ignition wiring from the spark plugs and the distributor cap; remove the coil wire from the distributor cap.
15. Remove the valve cover and gasket. Clean the surfaces of any gasket remains.
16. Remove the distributor housing from the camshaft carrier. Remove the ignition wire clip next to the left bolt.
17. Plug the spark plug holes with crumpled paper. Remove the center bearing cap for each camshaft. Remove the third nut in the center. Mark the cam bearing caps for proper reinstallation.
18. Install a camshaft press tool, such as Volvo 5021 or similar on the exhaust side cam in place of the removed bearing cap. When it is securely in place, remove the remaining bearing caps and nuts. Remove the tool and remove the exhaust camshaft.
19. Remove the intake camshaft in identical fashion.

**NOTE: Label or identify each cam and its bearing caps. All removed components should be kept in neat order.**

20. Using a magnet or a small suction cup, remove the tappets. Store them upside down (to prevent oil drainage) and keep them in order; they are not interchangeable.

21. Remove the remaining 4 nuts in the center of the cam carrier and detach the carrier from the head. If it is stuck, tap it very gently with a plastic mallet. Remove the O-rings around the spark plug holes.

22. Wipe the remaining oil off the cylinder head and remove the bolts in the order shown. When all the bolts are removed, the cylinder head may be lifted free of the car.

**NOTE: The head is aluminum. Support it on clean wood blocks or similar to avoid scoring the face.**

23. Clean the camshaft carrier and the head assembly of all gasket material and sealer. Carefully scrape the joint surfaces with a plastic scraper. Do NOT use metal tools to scrape or clean. Wash the surfaces with a degreasing compound and blow the surfaces completely dry. Inspect the head bolts for any sign of stretching or elongation in the midsection. If this is observed or suspected, discard the bolt. Bolts may not be used more than 5 times.

24. Install the new head gasket and a new O-ring for the water pump. Carefully place the cylinder head into position; do not damage the gasket.

25. Clean the head bolts and apply a light coat of oil. Install them and tighten (in the order shown) in 3 steps: All to 15 ft. lbs. (20 Nm), then all to 30 ft. lbs. (41 Nm). Third Step is to tighten each bolt through 115 degree of arc in 1 continuous motion. The use of Volvo tool 5098 (protractor fitting) is strongly recommended for this task.

26. Install the exhaust manifold with a new gasket. Attach the front exhaust pipe to its bracket and install the heat shields.

27. On the left side of the motor, connect the temperature sensors, the heating hose under cylinders 3 and 4 and the upper coolant hose to the thermostat.

28. Fill the cooling system and check carefully for leaks, particularly around the head to block joint.

29. Install the intake manifold with a new gasket. Tighten the bottom bolts a few turns and place the manifold in position. Tighten all the bolts from the center outwards.

30. Reattach the support under the intake manifold and the cable clip. Double check all connections on and around the intake manifold.

31. Apply Volvo liquid sealing compound to the camshaft carrier. Use a small paint roller and coat the surfaces which match to the head and the bearing cap joint faces.

32. Install the cam carrier on the head and secure it with 4 of the 5 center nuts tightened to 15 ft. lbs. (20 Nm). Do not install the middle nut.

33. Oil all matching surfaces on the cam carrier, bearing caps and tappets.

34. Insert the tappets; they MUST be inserted in their original order and place.

35. Install the exhaust side camshaft by placing it in the carrier with the pulley guide pin facing up. Using the rear bearing cap as a guide, press the cam into place with the press tool. Install the bearing caps in the original order.

36. Install the bearing cap nuts and tighten them in stages to 15 ft. lbs. (20 Nm). Remove the press tool and install the center bearing cap; tighten it in stages to 15 ft. lbs. (20 Nm).

37. Install the intake camshaft in the carrier with the pulley guide pin facing upwards.

38. Turn the distributor shaft to align the driver with the markings on the distributor housing. Install new O-rings on the housing and rotor shaft.

39. Using the rear bearing cap as a guide, press the cam into place with the press tool. Install the bearing caps in the original order.

40. Install the bearing cap nuts and tighten them in stages to 15 ft. lbs. (20 Nm). Remove the press tool and install the center bearing cap; tighten it in stages to 15 ft. lbs. (20 Nm).

41. Install the center nut in the cam carrier and tighten it to 15 ft. lbs. (20 Nm).

42. Double check the tightness of all the camshaft carrier nuts and the bearing cap nuts. All should be 15 ft.lbs; do not overtighten.

43. Reinstall the distributor, connect the coil wire and install the ignition wire clip at the left bolt. Remove the paper plugs from the spark plug holes.

44. Use a silicone sealer and apply to the front and rear camshaft bearing caps. Install new gaskets for the valve cover and the spark plug wells. Install the spark plug gasket with the arrow pointing towards the front of the car and the word "UP" facing up. Make sure the valve cover gasket is correctly positioned and install the valve cover.

45. Reconnect the ground wire at the distributor.

46. Install the ignition wires and the cover plate.

47. Using a compression seal driver (Volvo tool 5025 or similar), install the oil seals for the front of each camshaft. Camshafts MUST NOT be allowed to turn during this operation.

48. Install the upper backing plate over the ends of the camshafts and adjust the plate so that the cams are centered in the holes.

49. Replace the idler pulleys and tighten their mounts to 18.5 ft. lbs. (25 Nm).

50. Install the camshaft drive pulleys, using a counterhold to prevent the cams from turning.

51. Making sure that the camshaft pulleys are properly aligned with the marks on the backing plate, position the timing belt so that the double mark on the belt coincides exactly with the top mark on the belt guide plate (at the top of the crankshaft). Place the belt onto the cam pulleys and make sure the single marks on the belt line up exactly with the marks on the pulleys. Fit the belt over the idler pulleys; right side idler first, then the left.

52. Double check that the engine is on TDC for cylinder No. 1 and that all the belt markings line up as they should.

53. Loosen the tensioner locknut. Rotate the crankshaft clockwise 1 full turn until the belt markings again coincide with the pulley markings.

**NOTE: The engine must not be rotated counterclockwise while the tensioner is loose.**

54. Turn the crankshaft smoothly clockwise until the pulley marks are 1½ teeth beyond the marks on the backing plate.

55. Tighten the tensioner locknut. Install the lower timing belt cover.

56. Install the radiator fan and pulley, the alternator drive belt and the negative battery cable.

57. Double check all installation items, paying particular attention to loose hoses or hanging wires, untightened nuts, poor routing of hoses and wires (too tight or rubbing) and tools left in the engine area.

58. Start the engine and allow it to run until the thermostat opens. Use extreme caution; the timing belt is exposed.

**NOTE: This engine may be somewhat noisy when started. The noise will subside as oil reaches the tappets. Do not exceed 2500 rpm while the tappets are noisy.**

59. Shut the engine off, rotate the crankshaft to bring the engine to TDC on cylinder No. 1 and use Volvo tool 998 8500 to check the belt tension. Correct deflection is 5.5 ± 0.2 units when measured between the exhaust camshaft pulley and the idler. If the tension is not correct repeat Steps 51-54, above.

60. Install the upper timing belt cov-

er. Start the engine and final check all functions.

### B28F and B280F Engines

1. Disconnect the battery. Drain the coolant.
2. Remove the air cleaner assembly and all attaching hoses.
3. Disconnect the throttle cable. On automatic transmission equipped cars, disconnect the kickdown cable.
4. Disconnect the EGR vacuum hose and remove the pie between the EGR valve and manifold.
5. Remove the oil filler cap, and cover the hole with a rag. Disconnect the PCV pipe(s) from the intake manifold.
6. Remove the front section of the intake manifold.
7. Disconnect the electrical connector and fuel line at the cold start injector. Disconnect the vacuum hose, both fuel lines. and the electrical connector from the control pressure regulator.
8. Disconnect the hose, pipe, and electrical connector from the auxiliary air valve. Remove the auxiliary air valve.
9. Disconnect the electrical connector from the fuel distributor. Remove the wire loom from the intake manifolds. Disconnect the spark plug wires.
10. Disconnect the fuel injectors from their holders.
11. Disconnect the distributor vacuum hose, carbon filter hose, and diverter valve hose from the intake manifold. Also, disconnect the power brake hose and heater hose at the intake manifold.
12. Disconnect the throttle control link from it pulley.
13. On cars equipped with an EGR vacuum amplifier, disconnect the wires from the throttle micro switch and solenoid valve.
14. At the firewall, disconnect the fuel lines from the fuel filter and return line.
15. Remove the 2 attaching screws and lift out the fuel distributor and throttle housing assembly.
16. On cars not equipped with an EGR vacuum amplifier, disconnect the EGR valve hose from underneath the throttle housing.
17. Remove the cold start injector, rubber ring, and pipe.
18. Remove the 4 retaining bolts and lift off the intake manifold. Remove the rubber rings.
19. Remove the splash guard beneath the engine.
20. If removing the left cylinder head, remove the air pump from its bracket.
21. Remove the vacuum pump and O-ring in the valve cover. Remove the vacuum hose from the wax thermostat.
22. If removing the right cylinder head, disconnect the upper radiator hose.
23. On air conditioned models, remove the A/C compressor and secure it to on side. Do not disconnect the refrigerant lines.
24. Disconnect the distributor leads and remove the distributor. Remove the EGR valve, bracket and pipe. At the firewall, disconnect the electrical connectors at the relays.
25. On air conditioned models, remove the rear compressor bracket.
26. Disconnect the coolant hose(s) from the water pump to the cylinder head(s). If removing the left cylinder head disconnect the lower radiator hose at the water pump.
27. Disconnect the air injection system supply hose from the applicable cylinder head. Separate the air manifold at the rear of the engine. If removing the left cylinder head, remove the backfire valve and air hose.
28. Remove the valve cover(s).
29. On the left cylinder head, remove the Allen head screw and 4 upper bolts to the timing gear cover. On the right cylinder head, remove the 4 upper bolts to the timing gear cover and the front cover plate.
30. From beneath the car, remove the exhaust pipe clamps for both header pipes.
31. If removing the right cylinder head, remove the retainer bracket bolts and pull the dipstick tube out of the crankcase.
32. Remove the applicable exhaust manifold(s).
33. Remove the cover plate at the rear of the cylinder head.
34. Rotate the camshaft sprocket (for the applicable cylinder head) into position so that the large sprocket hole aligns with the rocker arm shaft. With the camshaft in this position, loosen the cylinder head bolts in sequence (same sequence as tightening), and remove the rocker arm and shaft assembly.
35. Loosen the camshaft retaining fork bolt (directly in back of sprocket) and slide the fork away from the camshaft.
36. Next, it is necessary to hold the cam chain stretched during camshaft removal. Otherwise, the chain tensioner will automatically take up the slack, making it impossible to reinstall the sprocket on the cam without removing the timing chain cover to loosen the tensioner device. To accomplish this, a special sprocket retainer tool (Volvo No. 999 5104) is installed over the sprocket with 2 bolts in the top of the timing chain cover. A bolt is then screwed into the sprocket to hold it in place.
37. Remove the camshaft sprocket center bolt and push the camshaft to the rear, so it clears the sprocket.
38. Remove the cylinder head.

**NOTE: Do not remove the cylinder head by pulling straight up. Instead, lever the head off by inserting 2 spare head bolts into the front and rear inboard cylinder head bolt holes, and pulling toward the applicable wheel housing. Otherwise, the cylinder liners may be pulled up, breaking the lower liner seal and leaking coolant into the crankcase. If any do pull up, new liner seals must be used, and the crankcase completely drained. If the head(s) seem stuck, gently tap around the edges of the head(s) with a rubber mallet, to break the joint.**

39. Remove the head gasket. Clean the contact surfaces with a plastic scraper and lacquer thinner.
40. If the head is going to be off for any length of time, install liner holders (Volvo special tool No. 999 5093) or 2 strips of thick stock steel with holes for the head bolts, so that the liners stay pressed down against their seals. Install the holders width-wise between the middle 4 head bolt holes.
41. Reverse the above procedure to install, using the following installation notes:
    a. There are a pair of guide dowels at both outboard corners of the head. If they fell down during removal, pull them back out with a puller hammer. They can be propped up with a ⅛ in. drill shank.
    b. Remove the liner holders.
    c. The right and left head gaskets are different.
    d. Check the timing chain cover gasket. If damaged, replace only the upper section.
    e. Oil the head bolt threads. Position the head on the dowels and install (hand tight) 1 center head bolt. Then, slide the camshaft forward into position against the sprocket and install the sprocket center bolts, and remove the retainer tool.
    f. Before installing the head bolts, remove the guide dowel shanks, if used.
    g. On B28F engine, tighten the head bolts to 7 ft. lbs. (9.5 Nm) using the correct tightening sequence, then 22 ft. lbs. (30 Nm), and then 44 ft. lbs. (60 Nm). Next slacken the head bolts (in the tightening sequence) to relieve any pre-tension. Now, tighten the bolts to 11–14 ft. lbs. (15–19 Nm). Finally, tighten the head bolts exactly ⅓ of a full 360 degrees turn (116–120 degrees) in the tightening sequence. This is critical

for proper piston liner O-ring sealing. If necessary, use a protractor to ensure accuracy.

h. On 280F engine, tighten all head bolts in sequence to 44 ft. lbs. (60 Nm), then loosen bolt No. 1 and retorque it to 15 ft. lbs. (20 Nm), then tighten it to 106 degrees. Repeat for all bolts following number sequence and only loosening and tightening 1 bolt at a time. Adjust valves and run engine to operating temperature. Let cool for 2 hours. Tighten each bolt in sequence an additional 45 degrees.

i. Adjust the valves after completing assembly.

j. After running the engine to operating temperature, allow to cool for 30 minutes, and retorquing the head bolts. Following the tightening sequence slacken the bolts to relieve any pre-tension, then tighten to 11–14 ft. lbs. (15–19 Nm) and finally protractor torque them to 113–117 degrees (1/3 of a full turn).

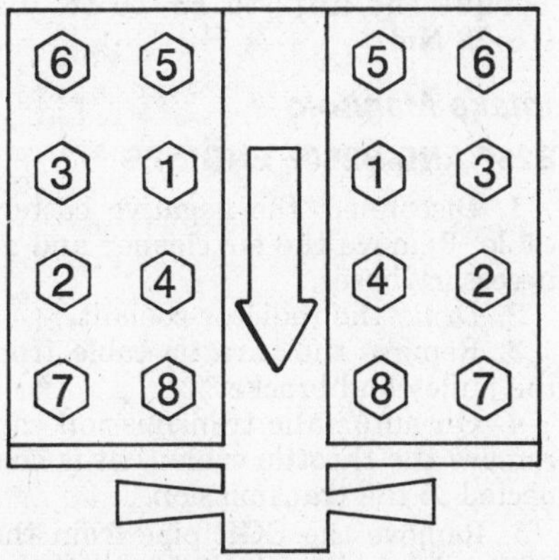


Cylinder head bolt tightening sequence – B21, B23 and B234

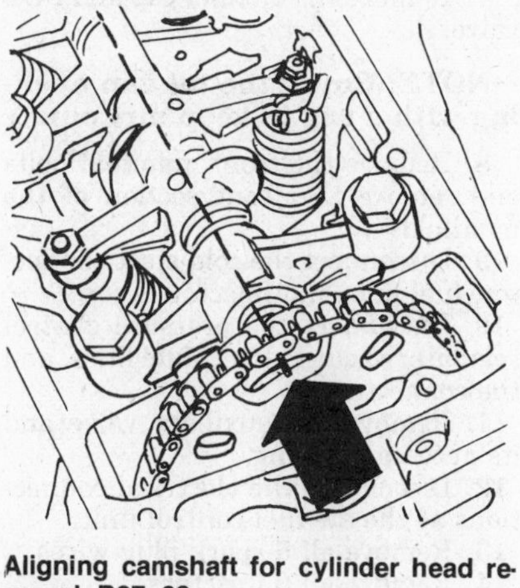

Aligning camshaft for cylinder head removal, B27, 28

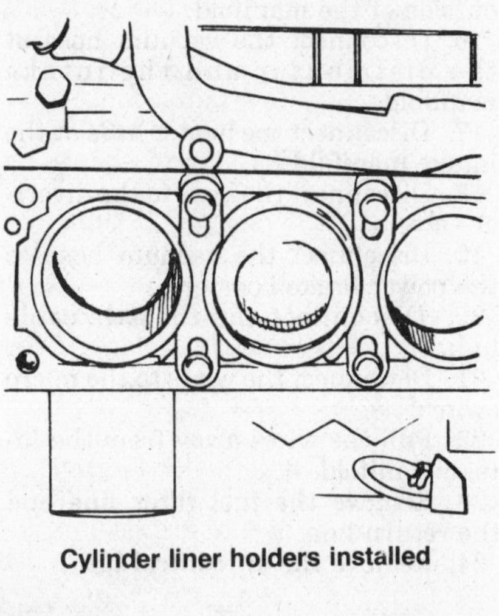

Cylinder liner holders installed

### D24 and D24T Engines

1. Disconnect the negative battery terminal.
2. Remove the engine splash guard.
3. Disconnect the exhaust pipe from the transmission bracket. On D24T models, disconnect all hoses to the turbocharger, and plug any open holes.

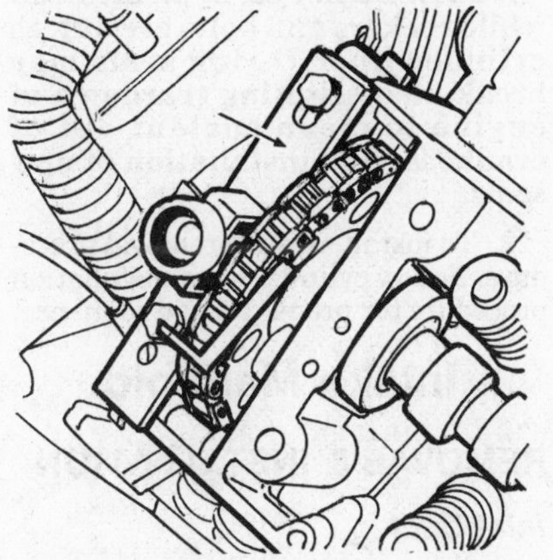

B27, 28 camshaft sprocket retainer tool

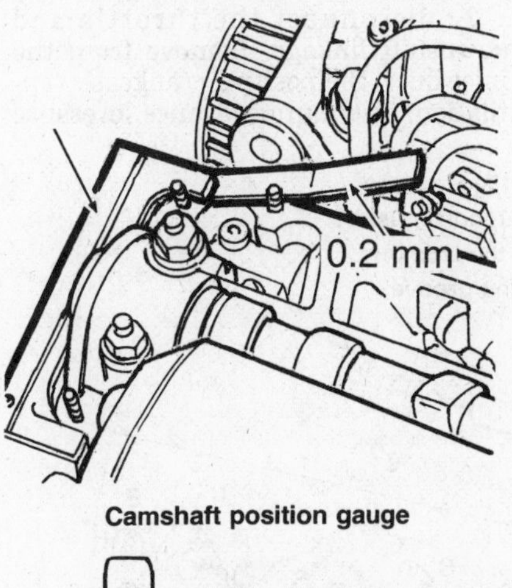


Camshaft position gauge

4. Disconnect the exhaust pipe from the rear exhaust manifold.
5. Disconnect the exhaust pipe from the front exhaust manifold.
6. Remove the air cleaner and all necessary hoses.
7. Drain the radiator.
8. Remove the bottom and top radiator hoses.
9. Remove the bottom hose from the cold start device and drain it into a suitable container.
10. Remove the top cold start hose.
11. Remove the vacuum pump and the plunger.
12. Remove all the fuel lines and plug the fuel line connections.

**NOTE: Carefully remove all dirt from the fuel line connections to prevent dirt from entering the system.**

13. Remove the glow plug wires and temperature sender wire.
14. Remove the rear injector return line hose.
15. Remove the valve cover.
16. Remove the front and rear timing belt covers.
17. Set the engine at top dead center and the fuel pump to the injection position for the No. 1 cylinder.
18. Remove the timing belt shield from the head.

**NOTE: Be careful not to drop the washers or bolts into the lower cover.**

19. Loosen the bolts on the water pump and the belt idler pulley.

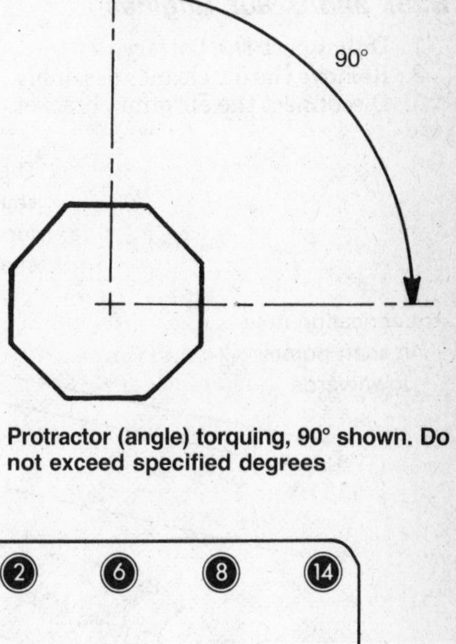


Protractor (angle) torquing, 90° shown. Do not exceed specified degrees

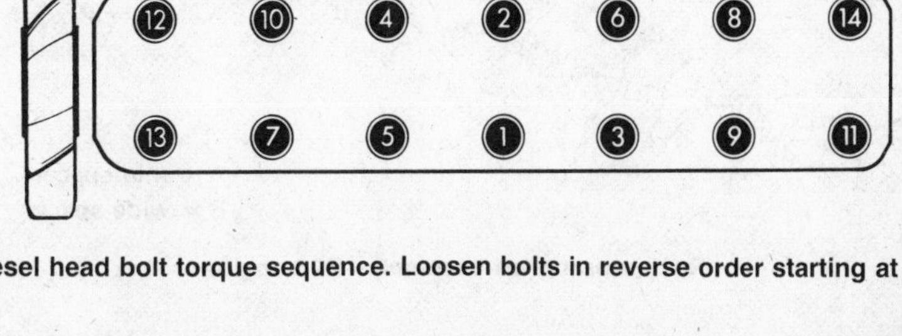


Diesel head bolt torque sequence. Loosen bolts in reverse order starting at 14

20. Remove the belt from the camshaft.
21. Use special tool No. 5199 or a suitable replacement to hold the cam gear steady while removing it.
22. Loosen the fuel pump bracket retaining screws to loosen the belt tension.
23. Remove the belt.
24. Remove the rear camshaft gear; see Step 21 for this procedure.
25. Remove the head bolts, and remove the head.
26. Installation is the reverse of removal. Always use a new gasket when replacing the head. Torque the cylinder head bolts in a 6 step procedure:
  a. Torque to 30 ft. lbs. (41 Nm)
  b. Torque to 44 ft. lbs. (60 Nm)
  c. Torque to 55 ft. lbs. (75 Nm)
  d. Tighten 180 degrees, in one movement, without stopping.
  e. Run engine until oil temperature is minimum 120°F (49°C).
  f. Tighten 90 degrees, in one movement, without stopping.
27. The following special tools are needed for reinstallation of the head: Belt tension gauge No. 5197, camshaft position gauge No. 5190.

## OVERHAUL

**For all overhaul procedures, please refer to "Engine Rebuilding" in the Unit Repair section.**

# Rocker Shafts

## REMOVAL & INSTALLATION

### *B28F and B280F Engines*

1. Disconnect the battery.
2. Remove the air cleaner assembly.
3. Disconnect the air pump bracket.
4. Remove the left valve cover (if so desired).
5. Tie the upper radiator hose out of the way and remove the oil filler cap and carbon canister hose.
6. On air conditioned models, remove the A/C compressor from it bracket. Do not disconnect the hoses.
7. Remove the EGR valve.
8. Remove the A/C compressor rear bracket.
9. Remove the control pressure regulator.
10. Disconnect any hoses or wires in the way. Remove the right valve cover (if so desired).
11. The rocker arm bolts double as cylinder head bolts. When loosening, follow the cylinder head bolt tightening sequence diagram. If removing both rocker shafts, mark them left and right.

**NOTE: Do not jar or strike head while rockers and bolts are out, as cylinder liner O-ring seals may break, necessitating teardown of engine to clean coolant out of crankcase and installation of new seals.**

12. To install, reverse removal procedure. Follow cylinder head installation procedure for proper torque sequence.

# Intake Manifold

## REMOVAL & INSTALLATION

### *Inlet Duct*

1. Disconnect the negative battery cable.
2. disconnect the throttle and downshift linkage. Remove from the inlet duct, the positive crankcase ventilation, distributor advance, pressure sensor (electronic fuel injection models only) and power brake hoses.
3. On electronic fuel injected models (B23F), disconnect the contact for the throttle valve switch, and remove the ground cable for the inlet duct.
4. Remove the bolts for the inlet duct stay. Remove the inlet duct-to-cylinder head retaining nuts and slide the inlet duct off the studs. Discard the old gasket.
5. To install, reverse the above procedure. Use a new inlet duct gasket. Torque the nuts to 13–16 ft. lbs. (18–22 Nm).

### *Intake Manifold*

#### B28F AND B280F ENGINES

1. Disconnect the negative battery cable. Remove the air cleaner and all necessary hoses.
2. Drain the radiator coolant.
3. Remove the throttle cable from the pulley and bracket.
4. On automatic transmission cars remove the throttle cable that is connected to the transmission.
5. Remove the EGR pipe from the EGR valve to the manifold.
6. Disconnect the EGR vacuum line.
7. Remove the oil filler cap and PCV valve.

**NOTE: Cover the oil cap opening with a rag to keep dirt out.**

8. Remove the front manifold bolts and remove the front section of the manifold.
9. Disconnect the cold start connector, fuel line, and injector.
10. Disconnect the pressure control regulator vacuum lines, fuel lines, and the connector.
11. Remove the auxiliary valve and its necessary piping.
12. Disconnect the electrical connections at the air fuel control unit.
13. Remove all 6 spark plug wires.
14. Remove all 6 injectors.
15. Move the wiring harness to the outside of the manifold.
16. Disconnect the vacuum hose at the distributor and the intake manifold.
17. Disconnect the heater hose at the intake manifold.
18. Disconnect the hose to the diverter valve.
19. Disconnect the vacuum hose to the power brake booster.
20. Disconnect the throttle cable link.
21. Disconnect the wires to the micro switch.
22. Pull the wires away from the intake manifold.
23. Remove the fuel filter line and the return line.
24. Remove the air control unit.

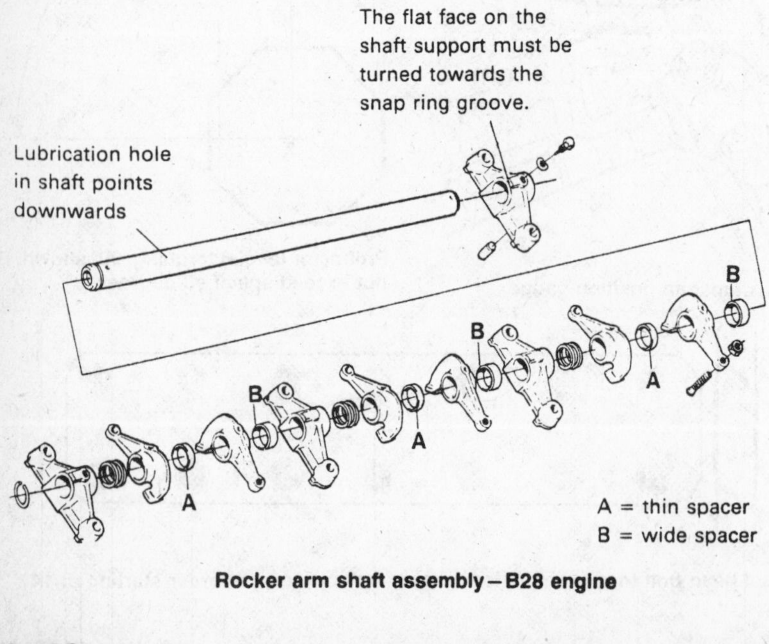
The flat face on the shaft support must be turned towards the snap ring groove.
Lubrication hole in shaft points downwards
A
B
A = thin spacer
B = wide spacer
**Rocker arm shaft assembly—B28 engine**

25. Disconnect the vacuum hose from the throttle valve housing.
26. Remove the pipe and cold start injector assembly.
27. Remove the intake manifold from the vehicle.
28. Installation is the reverse of removal.

**NOTE: Always use new gaskets when reinstalling the manifold.**

29. Torque the manifold bolts to 7–11 ft. lbs. (10–15 Nm).

### B21, B23 AND B230 ENGINES

1. Disconnect the negative battery cable. Remove the air cleaner and all necessary hoses.
2. Remove the PCV valve.
3. Remove the connector at the cold start injector.
4. Remove the fuel hose from the cold start injector.
5. Remove the cold start injector.
6. Remove the connector on the auxiliary valve.
7. Disconnect the hoses at the auxiliary valve.
8. Remove the auxiliary valve.
9. On turbocharged models, disconnect the turbocharger inlet hose (between turbo unit and intake manifold). Plug the hose immediately.
10. Remove the intake manifold brace.
11. Disconnect the distributor vacuum hose at the intake manifold.
12. Loosen the clamp for the rubber connecting pipe on the air-fuel control unit.
13. Remove the manifold bolts and remove the manifold.
14. Installation is the reverse of removal.

**NOTE: Remember to install new manifold gaskets before replacing the manifold.**

15. Torque the manifold bolts to 15 ft. lbs. (20 Nm).

### B234F ENGINE

1. Remove the air mass meter and the air intake hose.
2. Detach the throttle pulley from the intake manifold and remove the link rod from the throttle lever.
3. Separate the throttle housing from the intake manifold and cut the cable tie holding the wiring to the vacuum hose connections.
4. Disconnect the lines and hoses from the manifold, including the brake booster vacuum hose, the evaporation line, the oil trap, the fuel pressure regulator line and the air control valve line. If the car is equipped with a vacuum tank, disconnect its line at the manifold.
5. Disconnect the fuel return line at the distribution pipe. Disconnect the wiring to the injectors and remove the distribution pipe and injectors. Immediately protect these components from the entry of any dirt.
6. Unbolt and remove the intake manifold from the engine.
7. If installing a new manifold, it is necessary to transfer the various hose nipples and plugs to the new part. Install the manifold with a new gasket. Starting with the center bolts and working outward, tighten the bolts to 15 ft. lbs. (20 Nm).
8. Reconnect the hoses to their proper ports.
9. Position the injector wiring between cylinders 2 and 3 and reinstall the fuel distributor rail and the injectors. Tighten the pipe and the ground wires to the block. Connect the fuel pressure regulator line to the intake manifold.
10. Install the throttle pulley and connect the link rod.
11. Install the throttle housing with a new gasket. Check the operation of the throttle stops and switches.
12. Install the air mass meter and air inlet hose.

### D24 AND D24T ENGINES

1. Disconnect the negative battery terminal.
2. Remove the air cleaner and all necessary hoses.
3. Remove any other necessary vacuum or electrical lines.
4. On D24T models, disconnect the

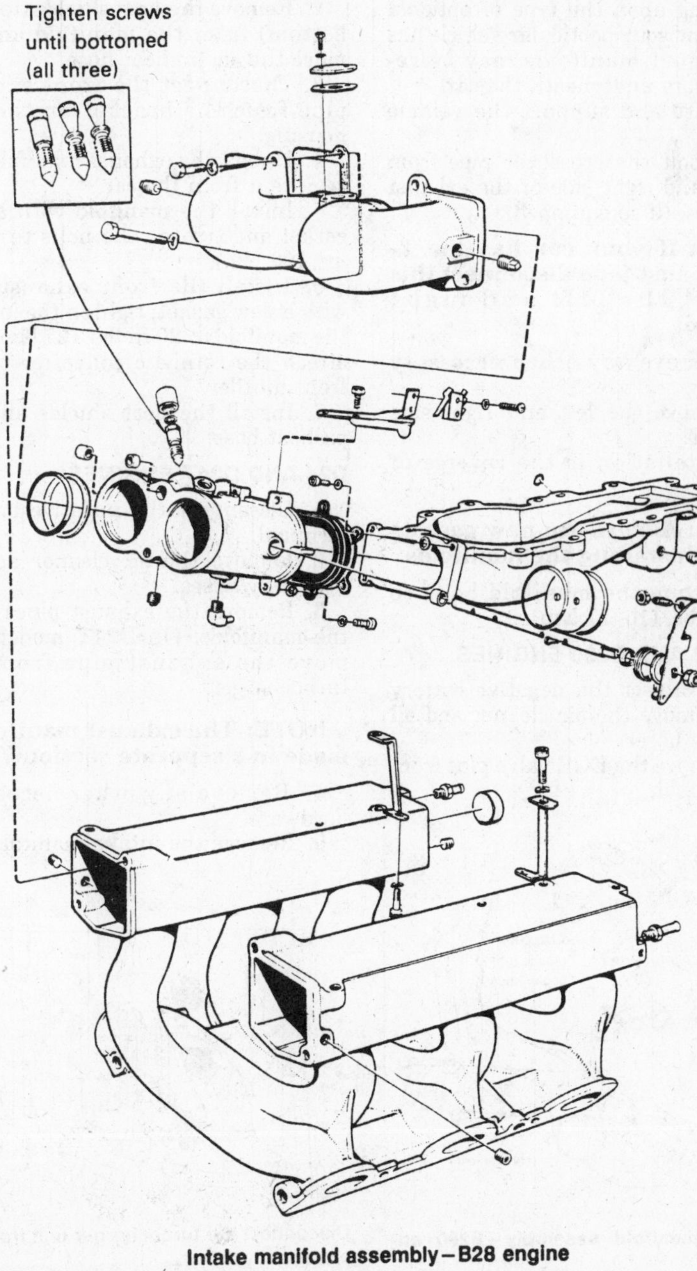
Tighten screws
until bottomed
(all three)

**Intake manifold assembly–B28 engine**

turbocharger inlet hose (between the intake manifold and turbo unit) and immediately plug the hose.

5. Remove the intake manifold bolts and remove the manifold.

6. Installation is the reverse of removal.

**NOTE: Always use a new gasket when reinstalling the intake manifold.**

7. Torque the intake bolts to 18 ft. lbs. (24 Nm).

## Exhaust Manifold

### REMOVAL & INSTALLATION

#### B28F AND B280F ENGINES

Depending upon the type of optional equipment your particular vehicle has the exhaust manifolds may be removed from underneath the car.

1. Raise and support the vehicle safely.
2. Unbolt the crossover pipe from the left and right side of the exhaust manifolds, (if so equipped).

**NOTE: If your car has the Y-type exhaust pipe disconnect this pipe at the left and right manifolds.**

3. Remove any other necessary hardware.
4. Remove the left and right side manifolds.
5. Installation is the reverse of removal.

**NOTE: Always use new gaskets when reinstalling the manifolds.**

6. Torque the manifold bolts to 7–11 ft. lbs. (10–15 Nm).

#### B21, B23 AND B230 ENGINES

1. Disconnect the negative battery cable. Remove the air cleaner and all necessary hoses.
2. Remove the EGR valve pipe from the manifold.

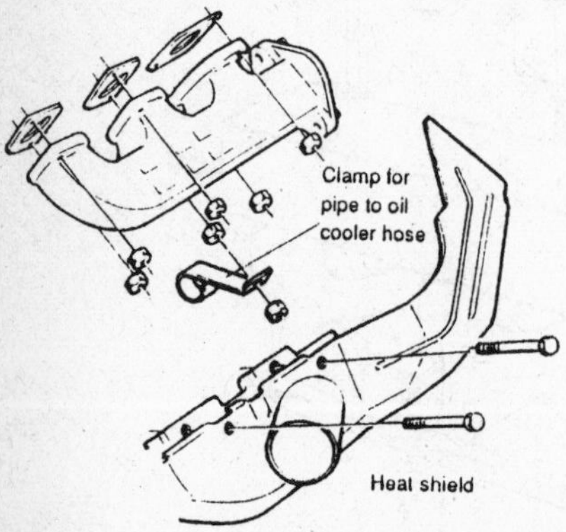

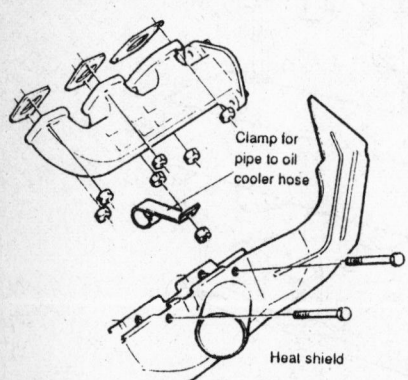


**Exhaust manifold assembly—B280 engine**

3. Remove the exhaust pipe from the exhaust manifold. On B21FT, remove the exhaust pipe from the turbocharger.
4. Remove the manifold bolts and remove the manifold.

**NOTE: Remember to install new manifold gaskets before installing the manifold.**

5. Installation is the reverse of removal.
6. Torque the manifold bolts to 10–20 ft. lbs. (14–27 Nm).

#### B234F ENGINE

1. Disconnect the front exhaust pipe from the manifold. Disconnect the catalytic converter from the front muffler.
2. Remove the heat shields (top and bottom) from the manifold and remove the air preheat hose.
3. Disconnect the front exhaust pipe from the bracket on the bell housing.
4. Unbolt the exhaust manifold and remove it from the car.
5. Install the manifold with a new gasket and tighten the bolts to 15 ft. lbs. (20 Nm).
6. Install the front exhaust pipe with a new gasket; tighten the joint to the manifold to 20 ft. lbs. (27 Nm). Reattach the catalytic converter to the front muffler.
7. Install the heat shields and the preheat hose.

#### D24 AND D24T ENGINES

1. Disconnect the negative battery terminal.
2. Remove the air cleaner and all necessary hoses.
3. Remove the exhaust pipes from the manifolds. On D24T models, remove the exhaust pipe from the turbocharger.

**NOTE: The exhaust manifold is made in 2 separate sections.**

4. Remove any other necessary hardware.
5. Remove the intake manifold.

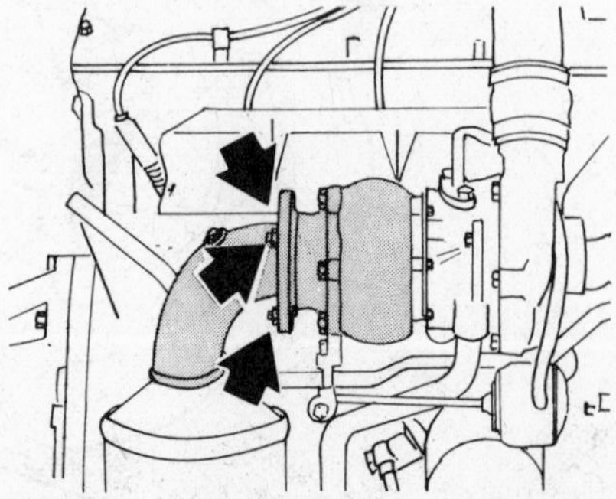

**Disconnect the turbocharger unit from the exhaust system**

6. Remove the exhaust manifold in 2 sections.
7. Installation is the reverse of removal.

**NOTE: Always use new gaskets when reinstalling the exhaust manifold.**

8. Torque the bolts to 18 ft. lbs. (24 Nm).

## Turbocharger

### REMOVAL & INSTALLATION

#### *B21FT, B23FT and B230FT Engines*

1. Disconnect the battery ground cable.
2. Disconnect expansion tank from retainer. Remove expansion tank retainer.
3. Remove preheater hose to the air cleaner. Remove the pipe and rubber bellows between the air/fuel control unit and the turbocharger unit. Pull out the crankcase ventilation hose from the pipe.
4. Remove the pipe and pipe connector between the turbocharger unit and the intake manifold.

**NOTE: Cover the turbocharger intake and outlet ports to keep dirt out of the system.**

5. Disconnect the exhaust pipe and secure it aside.
6. Disconnect the spark plug wires at the plugs.
7. Remove the upper heat shield. Remove the brace between the turbocharger unit and the manifold.
8. Remove the lower heat shield by removing the 1 retaining screw underneath the manifold.
9. Remove the oil pipe clamp, retaining screws on the turbo unit and the pipe connection screw in the cylinder block under the manifold. DO NOT allow any dirt to enter the oilways.
10. Remove the manifold retaining screws and washers. Let 1 nut remain in position to keep the manifold in position.
11. Remove the oil delivery pipe. Cover the opening on the turbo unit.
12. Disconnect the air/fuel control unit by loosening the clamps. Move the unit with the lower section of the air cleaner up to the right side wheel housing. Place a cover over the wheel housing as protection.
13. Remove the air cleaner filter.
14. Remove the remaining nut and washer on the manifold. Lift the assembly forward and up, Remove the manifold gaskets. Disconnect the re-

turn oil pipe O-ring from the cylinder block.
15. Disconnect the turbocharger unit from the manifold.
16. Installation is the reverse of removal. Be sure to use a new gasket for the exhaust manifold and a new O-ring to the return oil pipe. Keep everything clean during assembly, and use extreme care in keeping dirt out of the various turbo inlet and outlet pipes and hoses.

### D24T Engine

1. Remove the negative battery cable.
2. Remove the inlet hose from the turbo pipe.
3. Remove the complete air cleaner assembly, and the preheater hoses.
4. Remove the snap-ring form the turbocharger intake pipe, and remove the compressor intake pipe. Plug the hose immediately.
5. Disconnect the bolts securing the oil return pipe to the turbo unit. Move the pipe aside, and plug the holes immediately.
6. Remove the oil delivery pipe from the turbocharger and plug the holes.
7. Press the compressor pipe into the intake pipe. Remove the exhaust pipe from the turbocharger.
8. Raise and support the vehicle safely. Remove the exhaust pipe from the transmission support bracket and from the joint. Remove the exhaust pipe.
9. Remove the turbocharger securing nuts, and lower the front end of the turbo unit. Remove the turbocharger. Remove the compressor pipe.
10. If the turbocharger is replaced complete, transfer the necessary parts to the new unit. Always use new gaskets.
11. Installation is the reverse of removal. Make sure all hoses are connected without the addition of any dirt into the system. This is crucial to the life of the turbocharger and the engine.

## TROUBLESHOOTING

**For further information on turbocharging, please refer to "Turbocharging" in the Unit Repair section.**

# Front Cover

## REMOVAL & INSTALLATION

### B21, B23 and B230 Engines

1. Disconnect the negative battery cable. Loosen the fan shroud and remove the fan. Remove the shroud.
2. Loosen the alternator, air pump, power steering pump (if so equipped), and A/C compressor (if so equipped), and remove their drive belts.
3. Remove the water pump pulley.
4. Remove the 4 retaining bolts and lift off the timing belt cover.
5. Reverse the above procedure to install.

### D24 and D24T Engines

1. Disconnect the negative battery cable. Drain the engine coolant.
2. Remove the splash guard under the engine. Disconnect the lower hose at the radiator. Remove the expansion tank cap.
3. Remove the radiator.
4. Remove the cooling fan with spacer and pulley.
5. Remove the fan belt. Remove the drive belt for the power steering pump.
6. Remove the valve cover.

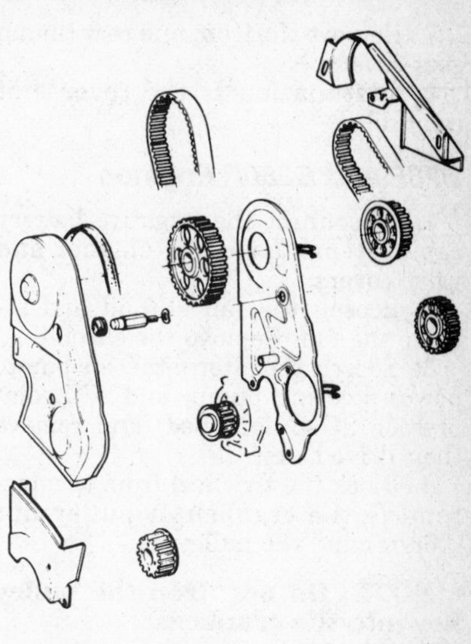

D24 Diesel timing belt cover and assembly

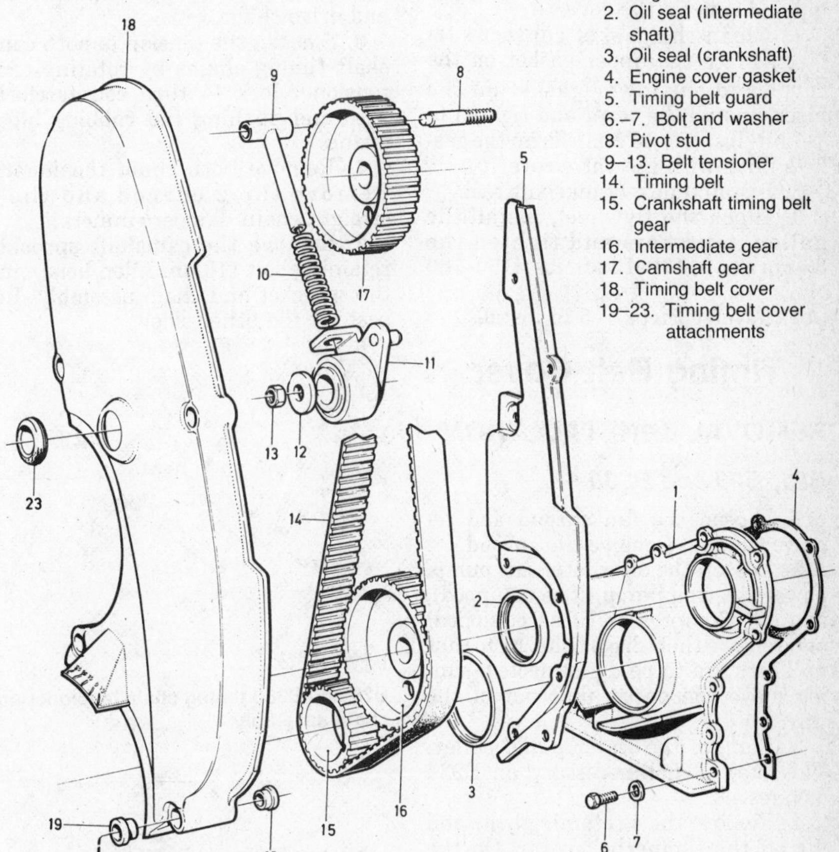

1. Engine front cover
2. Oil seal (intermediate shaft)
3. Oil seal (crankshaft)
4. Engine cover gasket
5. Timing belt guard
6.–7. Bolt and washer
8. Pivot stud
9–13. Belt tensioner
14. Timing belt
15. Crankshaft timing belt gear
16. Intermediate gear
17. Camshaft gear
18. Timing belt cover
19–23. Timing belt cover attachments

Timing belt assembly—all single cam 4 cylinder engines similar

7. Remove the front and rear timing gear covers.
8. Installation is the reverse of removal.

### *B28F and B280F Engines*

1. Disconnect the negative battery cable. Remove the air cleaner and valve covers.
2. Loosen the fan shroud and remove the fan. Remove the shroud.
3. Loosen the alternator, air pump, power steering pump, and A/C compressor (if so equipped) and remove their drive belts.
4. Block the flywheel from turning, remove the crankshaft pulley nut (36mm) and the pulley.

**NOTE: Do not drop the pulley key into the crankcase.**

5. Remove the power steering pump and place to one side. Remove the pump bracket.
6. Remove the timing chain cover retaining bolts (25 11mm hex bolts), tap and remove the cover.
7. Clean the gasket contact surfaces. Place the upper gasket on the cover and the lower gasket on the block. Install the cover and tighten to 7–11 ft. lbs. (10–15 Nm). Trim the gaskets flush with the valve cover.
8. Install a new crankshaft seal.
9. Block the flywheel, install the pulley, (and key) and tighten the 36mm nut to 118–132 ft. lbs. (160–180 Nm).
10. Reverse Steps 1–5 to install.

## Timing Belt Cover

### REMOVAL & INSTALLATION

### *B21, B23 and B230*

1. Loosen the fan shroud and remove the fan. Remove the shroud.
2. Loosen the alternator, air pump, power steering pump (if so equipped), and A/C compressor (if so equipped) and remove their drive belts. Note that no hcses are to be disconnected; simply move the entire unit out of the way.
3. Remove the water pump pulley. This step is not necessary on B234 engines.
4. Remove the 4 retaining bolts and lift off the timing belt cover. On the B234, the timing belt cover is in 3 sections; remove the upper section first and work to the lowest one.
5. Reverse the above procedure to install. Double check all installation items, paying particular attention to loose hoses or hanging wires, untightened nuts, poor routing of hoses and wires (too tight or rubbing) and tools left in the engine area.

### *Diesel D24, D24T*

### FRONT TIMING GEAR COVER

The front timing gear cover is removed by unsnapping the spring clips holding the cover and pulling the cover up and out. To install the cover, simply reverse the procedure.

### REAR TIMING GEAR COVER

To remove the rear timing gear cover, remove the 2 bolts in the cover and lift the cover out. When installing, adjust the cover in the bolt slots so that it is not touching the drive belt or other moving parts.

## Timing Chain and Sprockets

### REMOVAL & INSTALLATION

### *B28F and B280F Engines*

1. Remove the timing chain cover.
2. Remove the oil pump sprocket and drive chain.
3. Slacken the tension in both camshaft timing chains by rotating each tensioner lock ¼ turn counterclockwise and pushing the rubbing block piston.
4. Remove both chain tensioners. Remove the 2 curved and the 2 straight chain damper/runners.
5. Remove the camshaft sprocket retaining bolt (10mm Allen head) and the sprocket and chain assembly. Repeat for the other side.

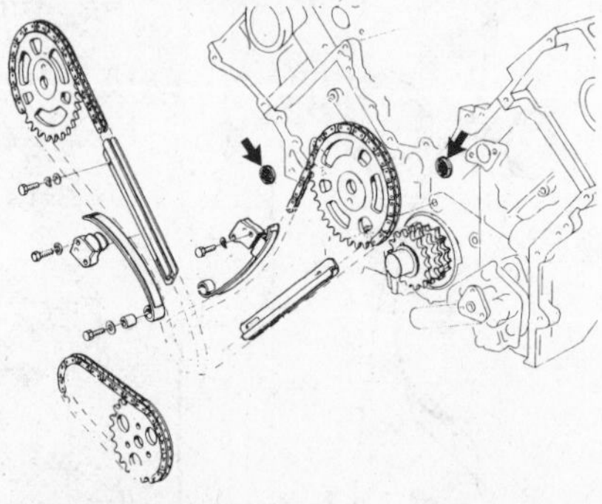

**B28 and B280 timing chain tensioner and chain assembly**

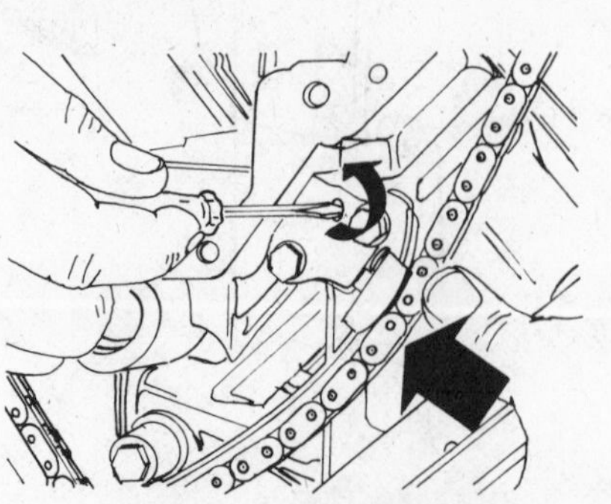

**Relieving chain tension**

6. Install the chain tensioners and tighten to 5 ft. lbs. (7 Nm). Install the curved chain damper/runners and tighten to 7–11 ft. lbs. (10–15 Nm). Install the straight chain damper/runners and torque to 5 ft. lbs. (7 Nm).
7. First install the left (driver) side camshaft sprocket and chain:
   a. Rotate the crankshaft (use crankshaft nut, if necessary) until the crankshaft key is pointing directly to the left side camshaft, and the left side camshaft key groove is pointing straight up (12 o'clock).
   b. Place the chain on the left side sprocket so that the sprocket notchmark is centered precisely between the 2 white lines on the chain.
   c. Position the chain on the crankshaft sprocket (inner), making sure that the other white line on the chain aligns with the crankshaft sprocket notch.
   d. While holding the left side chain and sprockets in this position, install the sprocket and chain on the left side camshaft (chain stretched on tension side) so that the sprocket pin fits into the camshaft recess.
   e. Tighten the sprocket center bolt to 51–59 ft. lbs. (69–80 Nm) (use a suitable tool to keep cam from turning).
8. To install the right side camshaft sprocket and chain:
   a. Rotate the crankshaft clockwise until the crankshaft key points straight down (6 o'clock).
   b. Align the camshaft key groove so that it is pointing halfway between the 8 and 9 o'clock positions (at this position, the No. 6 cylinder rocker arms will rock).
   c. Place the chain on the right side sprocket so that the sprocket notchmark is centered precisely between the 2 white lines on the chain.
   d. Then, position the chain on the middle crankshaft sprocket, making sure that the other white line aligns with the crankshaft sprocket notch.

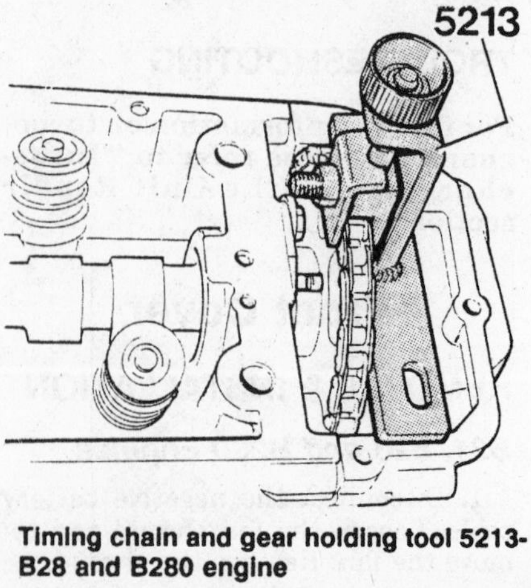


**Timing chain and gear holding tool 5213-B28 and B280 engine**

e. Install the sprocket and chain on the camshaft so that the sprocket notch fits into the camshaft recess.

f. Tighten the sprocket nut to 51–59 ft. lbs. (69–80 Nm).

9. Rotate the chain tensioners ¼ turn clockwise each. The chains are tensioned by rotating the crankshaft 2 full turns clockwise. Recheck to make sure the alignment marks coincide.

10. Install the oil pump sprocket and chain.

11. Install the timing chain cover.

## Timing Belt and Tensioner

### REMOVAL & INSTALLATION

#### *B21, B23 and B230 Engines*

1. Remove the timing belt cover.
2. To remove the tension from the belt, loosen the nut for the tensioner and press the idler roller back. The tension spring can be locked in this position by inserting the shank end of a 3mm drill through the pusher rod.
3. Remove the 6 retaining bolts and the crankshaft pulley.
4. Remove the belt, taking care not to bend it at any sharp angles. The belt should be replaced at 45,000 mile intervals, if it becomes oil soaked or frayed, or if it is on a car that has been sitting idle for any length of time.
5. If the crankshaft, idler shaft, or camshaft were disturbed while the belt was out, align each shaft with is corresponding index mark to assure proper valve timing and ignition timing, as follows:

   a. Rotate the crankshaft so that the notch in the convex crankshaft

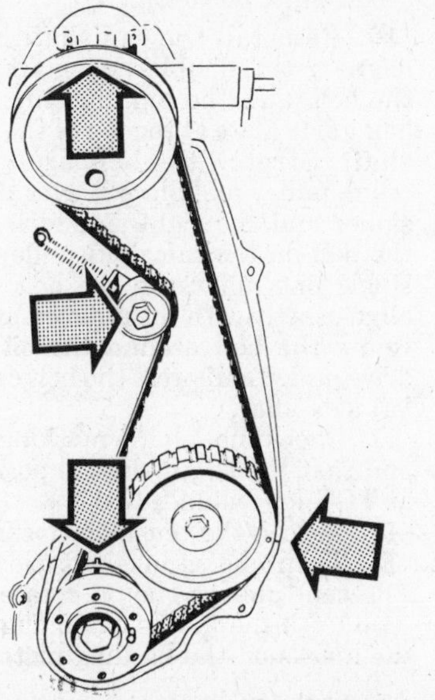

**Make sure all timing marks are lined up including marks on the new belt–B21 and B23 series**

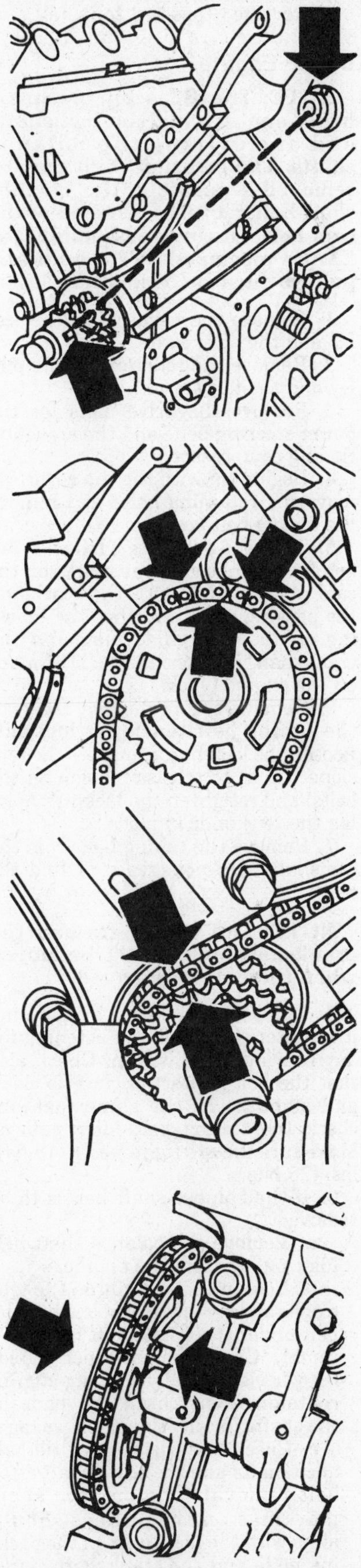

Left side camshaft timing chain installation sequence—V6 engines

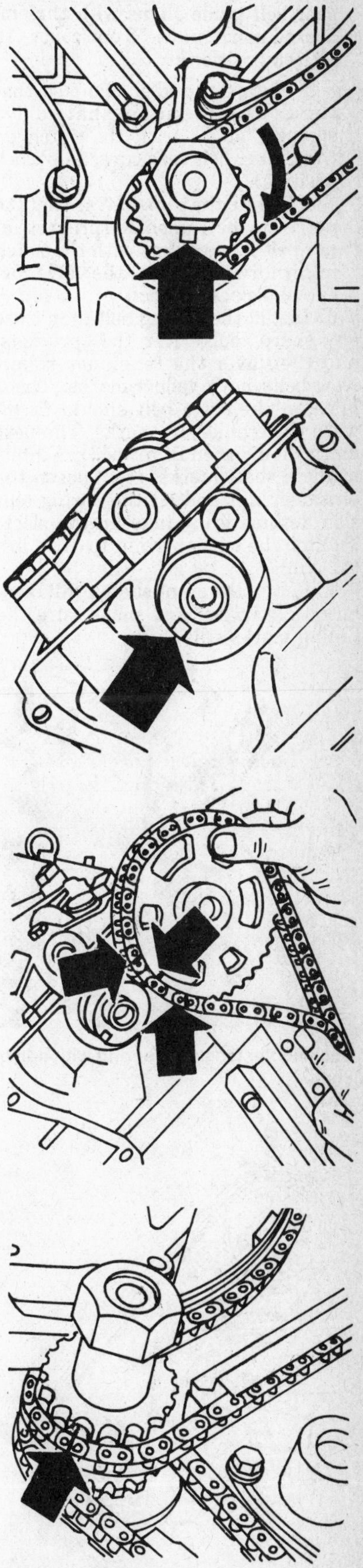

Right side camshaft timing chain installation sequence

gear belt guide aligns with the embossed mark on the front cover (12 o'clock position).

b. Rotate the idler shaft so that the dot on the idler shaft drive sprocket aligns with the notch on the timing belt rear cover (4 o'clock position).

c. Rotate the camshaft so that the notch in the camshaft sprocket inner belt guide aligns with the notch in the forward edge of the valve cover (12 o'clock position).

6. Install the timing belt (don't use any sharp tools) over the sprockets, and then over the tensioner roller. New belts have yellow marks. The 2 lines on the drive belt should fit toward the crankshaft marks. The next mark should then fit toward the intermediate shaft marks, etc. Loosen the tensioner nut and let the spring tension automatically take up the slack. Tighten the tensioner nut to 37 ft. lbs. (51 Nm).

7. Rotate the crankshaft 1 full revolution clockwise, and make sure the timing marks still align.

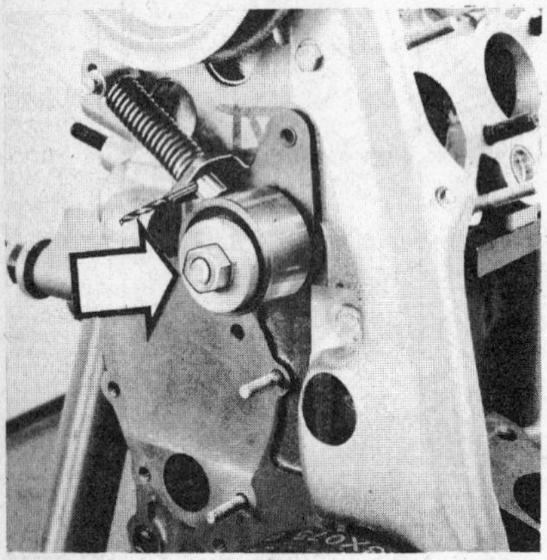

Locking the tensioner spring with drill bit shank

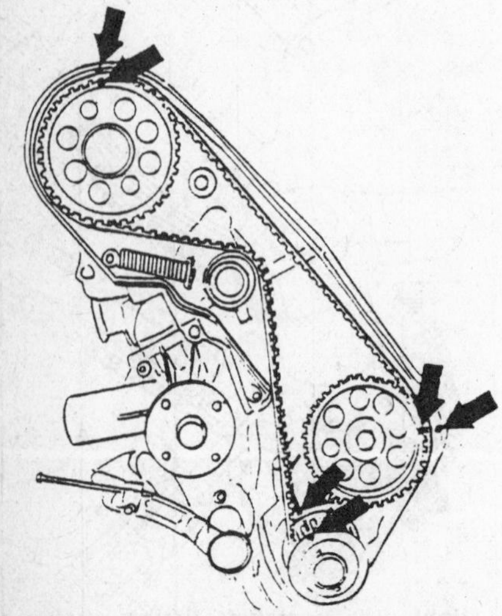

Timing belt alignment—B230 engine

8. Reverse Steps 1–3 to install.

### B234F Engine

**NOTE: The B234 engine has 2 belts, one driving the camshafts and one driving the balance shafts. The camshaft belt may be removed separately; the balance shaft belt requires removal of the cam belt. During reassembly, the EXACT placement of the belts and pulleys must be observed.**

1. Remove the negative battery cable and the alternator belt.
2. Remove the radiator fan, its pulley and the fan shroud.
3. Remove the drive belts for the power steering belts and the air conditioning compressor.
4. Beginning with the top cover, remove the retaining bolts and remove the timing belt covers.
5. Turn the engine to TDC on cylinder No. 1. Make sure the marks on the cam pulleys align with the marks on the backing plate and that the marking on the belt guide plate (on the crankshaft) is opposite the TDC mark on the engine block.
6. Remove the protective cap over the timing belt tensioner locknut. Loosen the lock nut, compress the tensioner (so as to release tension on the belts) and retighten the locknut, holding the tensioner in place.
7. Remove the timing belt from the camshafts. Do not crease or fold the belt.

**NOTE: The camshafts and the crankshaft MUST NOT be moved when the belt is removed.**

8. Check the tensioner by spinning it (counterclockwise) and listening for any bearing noise within. Check also that the belt contact surface is clean and smooth. In the same fashion, check the timing belt idler pulleys. Make sure the are tightened to 18.5 ft. lbs. (25 Nm).
9. If the balance shaft belt is to be removed:

a. Remove the balance shaft belt idler pulley from the engine.

b. Loosen the locknut on the tensioner and remove the belt. Slide the belt under the crankshaft pulley assembly. Check the tensioner and idler wheels carefully for any sign of contamination; check the ends of the shafts for any sign of oil leakage.

c. Check the position of the balance shafts and the crankshaft after belt removal. The balance shaft markings on the pulleys should align with the markings on the backing plate and the crankshaft marking should still be aligned with the TDC mark on the engine block.

d. When refitting the balance shaft belt, observe that the belt has colored dots on it. These marks assist in the critical placement of the belt. The yellow dot will align the right (lower) shaft, the blue dot will align on the crank and the other yellow dot will match to the upper (left) balance shaft.

e. Carefully work the belt in under the crankshaft pulley. Make sure the blue dot is opposite the bottom (TDC) marking on the belt guide plate at the bottom of the crankshaft. Fit the belt around the left (upper) balance shaft pulley, making sure the yellow mark is opposite the mark on the pulley. Install the belt around the right (lower) balance shaft pulley and again check that the mark on the belt aligns with the mark on the pulley.

f. Work the belt around the tensioner. Double check that all the markings are still aligned.

g. Set the belt tension by inserting an Allen key into the adjusting hole in the tensioner. Turn the crankshaft carefully through a few degrees on either side of TDC to check that the belt has properly engaged the pulleys. Return the crank to the TDC position and set the adjusting hole just below the "3 o'clock" position when tightening the adjusting bolt. Use the Allen wrench (in the adjusting hole) as a counter hold and tighten the locking bolt to 29.5 ft. lbs. (40 Nm).

h. Use Volvo tool 998 8500 to check the tension of the belt. Install the gauge over the position of the removed idler pulley. The tension must be 1-4 units on the scale or the belt must be readjusted.

10. Reinstall the camshaft belt by aligning the double line marking on the belt with the top marking on the belt guide plate at the top of the crankshaft. Stretch the belt around the crank pulley and place it over the tensioner and the right side idler. Place the belt on the camshaft pulleys. The single line marks on the belt should align exactly with the pulley markings. Route the belt around the oil pump drive pulley and press the belt onto the left side idler.
11. Check that all the markings align and that the engine is still positioned at TDC for cylinder No. 1.
12. Loosen the tensioner locknut.
13. Turn the crankshaft clockwise. The cam pulleys should rotate 1 full turn until the marks again align with the marks on the backing plate.

**NOTE: The engine must not be rotated counterclockwise during this procedure.**

14. Smoothly rotate the crankshaft further clockwise until the cam pulley markings are 1½ teeth beyond the marks on the backing plate. Tighten the tensioner locknut.

15. Check the tension on the balance shaft belt; it should now be 3.8 units. If the tension is too low, adjust the tensioner clockwise. If the tension is too high, repeat Step 8g above.

16. Check the belt guide for the balance shaft belt and make sure it is properly seated. Install the center timing belt cover (the one that covers the tensioner) the fan shroud, fan pulley and fan. Install all the drive belts and connect the battery cable.

17. Double check all installation items, paying particular attention to loose hoses or hanging wires, untightened nuts, poor routing of hoses and wires (too tight or rubbing) and tools left in the engine area.

18. Start the engine and allow it to run until the thermostat opens.

**CAUTION**

***The upper and lower timing belt covers are still removed. The belt and pulleys are exposed and moving at high speed.***

19. Shut the motor off and bring the motor to TDC on cylinder No. 1.

20. Check the tension of the camshaft belt. Position the gauge between the right (exhaust) cam pulley and the idler. Belt tension must be 5.5 ± 0.2 units. If the belt needs adjustment, remove the rubber cap over the tensioner locknut (cap is located on the timing belt cover) and loosen the locknut.

21. Insert a suitable tool between the tensioner wheel and the spring carrier pin to hold the tensioner. If the belt needs to be tightened, move the roller to adjust the tension to 6.0 units. If the belt is too tight, adjust to obtain a reading of 5.0 units on the gauge. Tighten the tensioner locknut.

22. Rotate the crankshaft so that the cam pulleys move through 1 full revolution and recheck the tension on the camshaft belt. It should now be 5.5 ± 0.2 units. Install the plastic plug over the tensioner bolt.

23. Final check the tension on the balance shaft belt by fitting the gauge and turning the tensioner clockwise. Only small movements are needed. After any needed readjustments, rotate the crankshaft clockwise through 1 full revolution and recheck the balance shaft belt. The tension should now be on the final specification of 4.9 ± 0.2 units.

24. Install the idler pulley for the balance shaft belt. Reinstall the upper and lower timing belt covers.

25. Start the engine and final check performance.

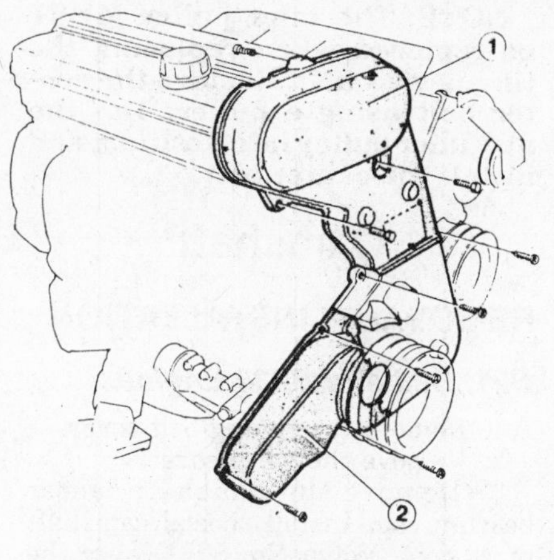


**Timing belt cover, upper cover (1), lower cover (2)—B234F engine**

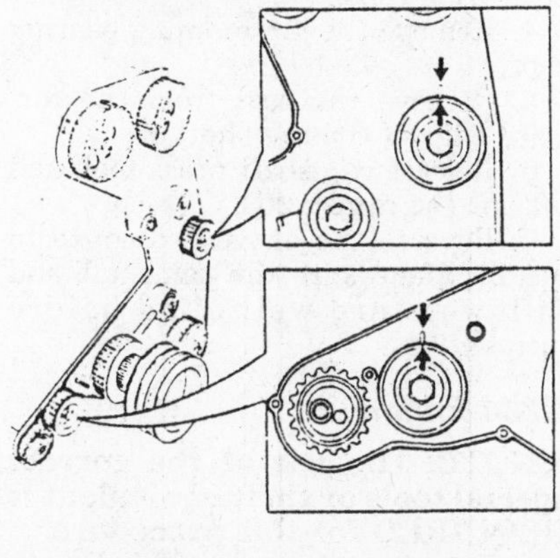

**Balance shafts alignment—B234F engine**

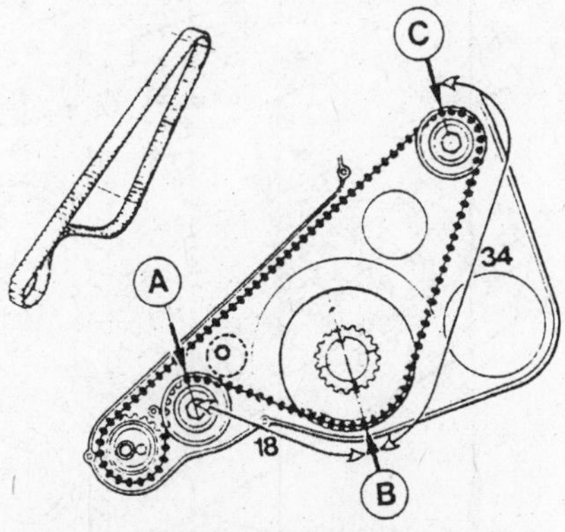


**Balance shaft belt markings, 18 teeth between A and B, 34 teeth between B and C—B234F engine**

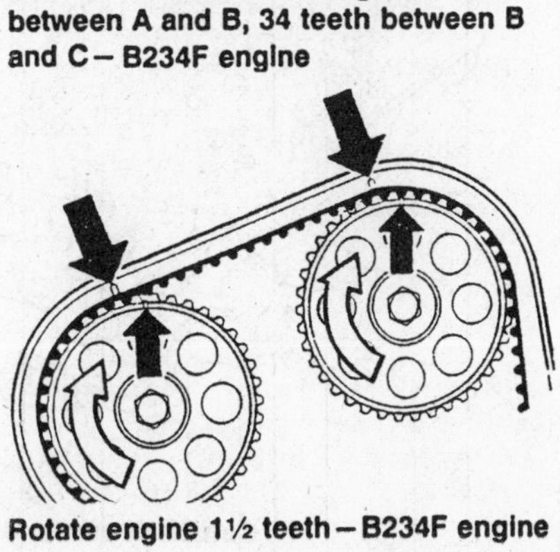

**Rotate engine 1½ teeth—B234F engine**

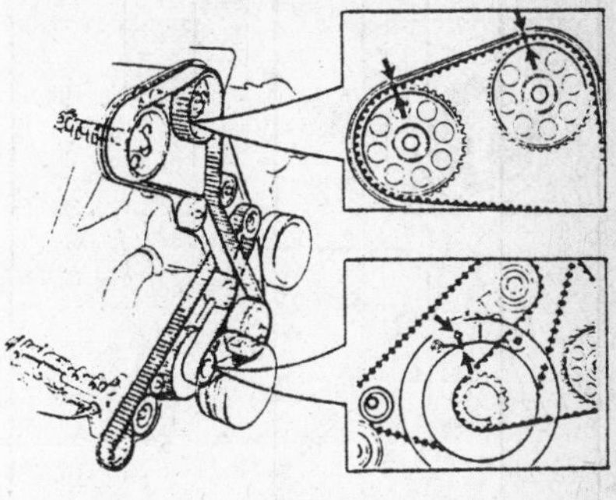

**Timing mark alignment—B234F engine**

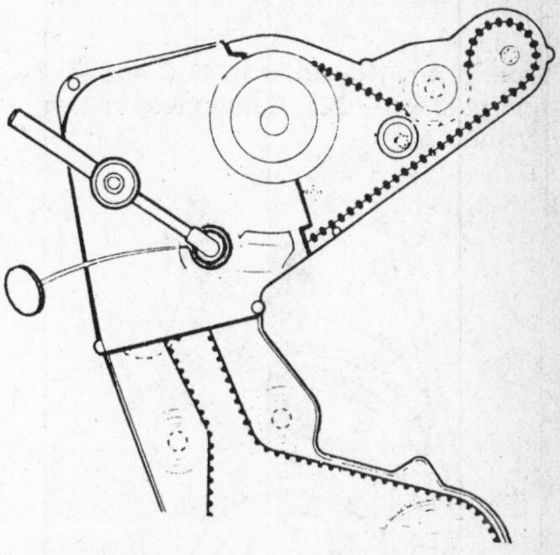

**Timing belt tensioner adjustment—B234F engine**

### *D24 and D24T Engines*

1. Remove the timing belt cover.

2. Set cylinder No. 1 to TDC and injection, using a 27mm socket on the vibration damper bolt to turn the engine to position for No. 1 cylinder injection. Both cam lobes should point up at equally large angles. The flywheel timing mark should be set a **0**.

3. Remove the vibration damper center bolt. It may be necessary to use Volvo special wrenches 5187 (to hold) and 5188 (to remove). The engine may have to be turned slightly to allow the holding wrench to rest temporarily on the cooling fan.

4. Check to make sure No. 1 cylinder is at TDC. If necessary, adjust the flywheel to the **0** mark.

5. Remove the vibration damper by removing the (4) 6mm Allen bolts.

**NOTE: The vibration damper and the crankshaft gear may be stuck together. You may have to tap them apart.**

6. Remove the camshaft gear belt by removing the lower belt shield, and releasing the retaining bolts for coolant pump.

7. Pull the gear belt straight out and off of the gears.

8. Installation is the reverse of removal.

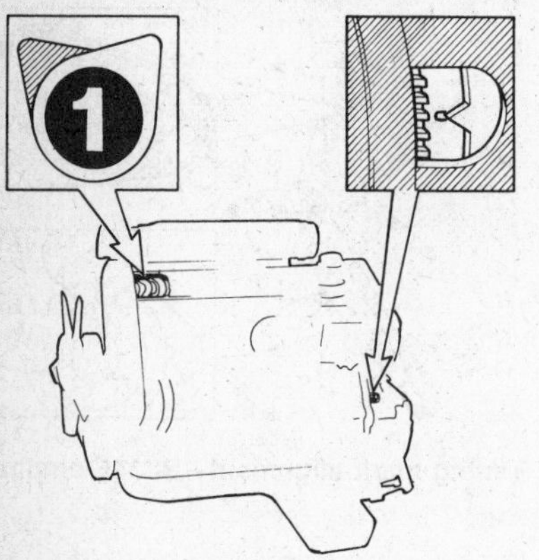

Setting No. 1 cylinder to TDC and injection position—D24. Cam lobes are "up", flywheel on 0

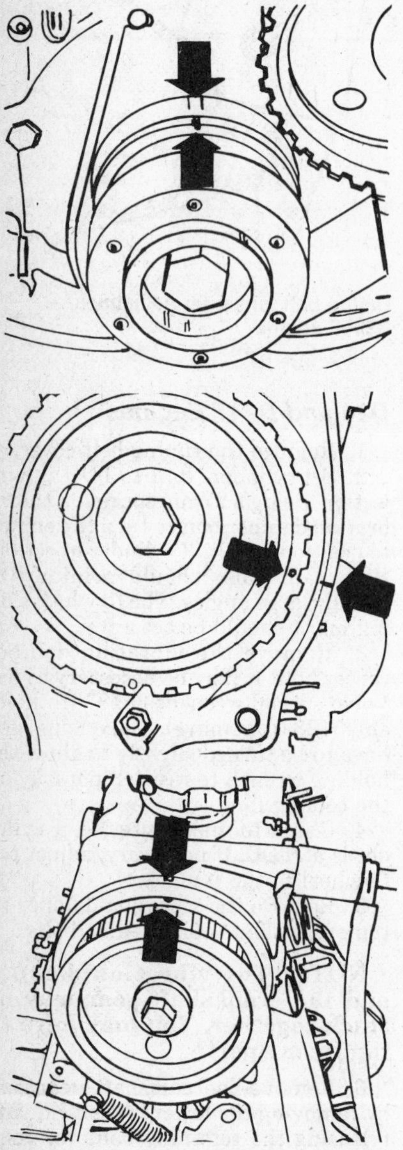

Aligning (top to bottom) crankshaft sprocket, idler shaft sprocket, and camshaft sprocket with their respective timing index marks prior to installing timing belt

**NOTE: The idler pulley MUST be replaced when replacing the timing gear belt. Remove the center bolt using a puller. Tap the new idler pulley into position, and install the center bolt.**

## Camshaft

### REMOVAL & INSTALLATION

#### *B21, B23 and B230 Engines*

1. Remove the timing belt cover.
2. Remove the valve cover.
3. Remove the camshaft center bearing cap. Install special camshaft press tool (Volvo No. 5021) over the center bearing journal to hold the camshaft in place while removing the other bearing caps.
4. Remove the 4 remaining bearing caps.
5. Remove the seal from the forward edge of the camshaft.
6. Release camshaft press tool, and lift out the camshaft.
7. Reverse the above procedure to install. Make sure the camshaft and followers are well oiled before installation.

#### *B234 Engine*

**NOTE: The use of the correct special tools or their equivalent is REQUIRED for this procedure.**

1. Disconnect the negative battery cable.
2. Remove the alternator drive belt, the radiator fan and its pulley.
3. Remove the upper and lower timing belt covers.
4. Align the camshaft and crankshaft marks. Turn the engine to TDC on cylinder No. 1 and make sure the pulley marks and the crank marks align with their matching marks on either the backing plate (cam pulleys) or the belt guide plate (crankshaft).
5. Remove the protective cap over the timing belt tensioner locknut. Loosen the lock nut, compress the tensioner (so as to release tension on the belts) and retighten the locknut, holding the tensioner in place.
6. Remove the timing belt from the camshafts. Do not crease or fold the belt.

**NOTE: The camshafts and the crankshaft MUST NOT be moved when the belt is removed.**

7. Remove the timing belt idler pulleys.
8. Remove the camshaft drive pulleys. Use a counterhold wrench to prevent the cam from turning.
9. Remove the plate or panel behind the pulleys. Remove the cover plate for the ignition wires. Label and disconnect the ignition wiring from the spark plugs and the distributor cap; remove the coil wire from the distributor cap.

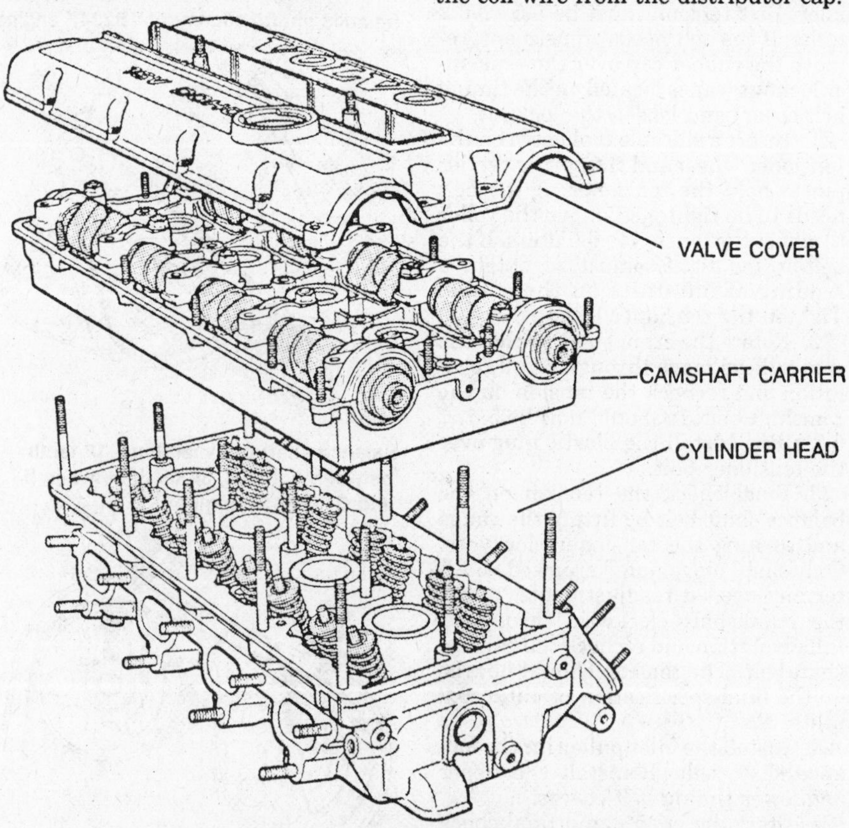


Camshaft carrier assembly–B234F engine

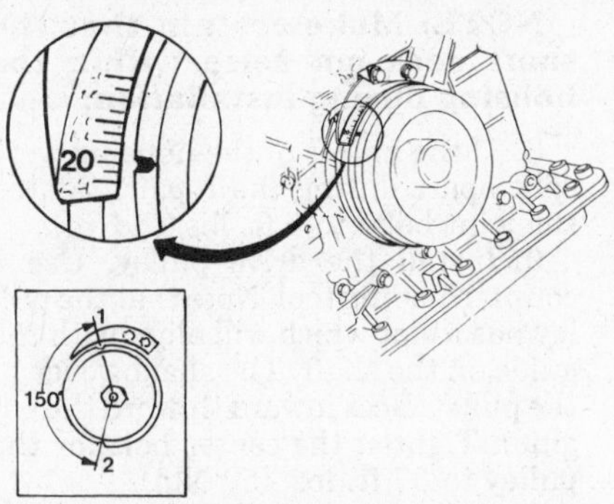


B28F static timing. Rotate the crankshaft until the engine is approximately 20° B.T.D.C. on cylinder 1. The pulley has two marks: "1" is T.D.C. for cylinder No. 1; "2" is T.D.C. for cylinder No. 6. The marks are 150° apart.

Four cylinder camshaft press tool installed

10. Remove the valve cover and gasket. Clean the surfaces of any gasket remains.
11. Remove the distributor housing from the camshaft carrier. Remove the ignition wire clip next to the left bolt.
12. Plug the spark plug holes with crumpled paper. Remove the center bearing cap for each camshaft. Mark the cam bearing caps for proper reinstallation.
13. Install a camshaft press tool, such as Volvo 5021 or similar on the exhaust side cam in place of the removed bearing cap. When it is securely in place, remove the remaining bearing caps and nuts. Remove the tool and remove the exhaust camshaft.
14. Remove the intake camshaft in identical fashion.

**NOTE: Label or identify each cam and its bearing caps. All removed components should be kept in neat order.**

15. Using a magnet or a small suction cup, remove the tappets. Store them upside down (to prevent oil drainage) and keep them in order; they are not interchangeable.
16. Clean and inspect the camshaft carrier and tappet bores for any sign of wear or scoring.
17. Oil all matching surfaces on the cam carrier, bearing caps and tappets.
18. Insert the tappets; they MUST be inserted in their original order and place.
19. Install the exhaust side camshaft by placing it in the carrier with the pulley guide pin facing up. Using the rear bearing cap as a guide, press the cam into place with the press tool. Install the bearing caps in the original order.
20. Install the bearing cap nuts and tighten them in stages to 15 ft. lbs. (20 Nm). Remove the press tool and install the center bearing cap; tighten it in stages to 15 ft. lbs. (20 Nm).
21. Install the intake camshaft in the carrier with the pulley guide pin facing upwards.
22. Turn the distributor shaft to align the driver with the markings on the distributor housing. Install new O-rings on the housing and rotor shaft.
23. Using the rear bearing cap as a guide, press the cam into place with the press tool. Install the bearing caps in the original order.
24. Install the bearing cap nuts and tighten them in stages to 15 ft. lbs. (20 Nm).
25. Double check the tightness of all the camshaft bearing cap nuts. All should be 15 ft.lbs; do not overtighten.
26. Reinstall the distributor, connect the coil wire and install the ignition wire clip at the left bolt. Remove the paper plugs from the spark plug holes.
27. Use a silicone sealer and apply to the front and rear camshaft bearing caps. Install new gaskets for the valve cover and the spark plug wells. Install the spark plug gasket with the arrow pointing towards the front of the car and the word "UP" facing up. Make sure the valve cover gasket is correctly positioned and install the valve cover.
28. Reconnect the ground wire at the distributor.
29. Install the ignition wires and the cover plate.
30. Using a compression seal driver (Volvo tool 5025 or similar), install the oil seals for the front of each camshaft. Camshafts MUST NOT be allowed to turn during this operation.
31. Install the upper backing plate over the ends of the camshafts and adjust the plate so that the cams are centered in the holes.
32. Replace the idler pulleys and tighten their mounts to 18.5 ft. lbs. (25 Nm).
33. Install the camshaft drive pulleys, using a counterhold to prevent the cams from turning.
34. Reinstall the camshaft belt by aligning the double line marking on the belt with the top marking on the belt guide plate at the top of the crankshaft. Stretch the belt around the crank pulley and place it over the tensioner and the right side idler. Place the belt on the camshaft pulleys. The single line marks on the belt should align exactly with the pulley markings. Route the belt around the oil pump drive pulley and press the belt onto the left side idler.
35. Check that all the markings align and that the engine is still positioned at TDC for cylinder No. 1.
36. Loosen the tensioner locknut.
37. Turn the crankshaft clockwise. The cam pulleys should rotate 1 full turn until the marks again align with the marks on the backing plate.

**NOTE: The engine must not be rotated counterclockwise during this procedure.**

38. Smoothly rotate the crankshaft further clockwise until the cam pulley markings are 1½ teeth beyond the marks on the backing plate. Tighten the tensioner locknut.
39. Reinstall the fan pulley and fan. Install all the drive belts and connect the battery cable.
40. Double check all installation items, paying particular attention to loose hoses or hanging wires, untightened nuts, poor routing of hoses and wires (too tight or rubbing) and tools left in the engine area.
41. Start the engine and allow it to run until the thermostat opens.

**CAUTION**

***The upper and lower timing belt covers are still removed. The belt and pulleys are exposed and moving at high speed.***

**NOTE: This engine may be somewhat noisy when started. The noise will subside as oil reaches the tappets. Do not exceed 2500 rpm while the tappets are noisy.**

42. Shut the motor off and bring the motor to TDC on cylinder No. 1.
43. Check the tension of the camshaft belt. Position the gauge between the right (exhaust) cam pulley and the idler. Belt tension must be 5.5 ± 0.2 units. If the belt needs adjustment, remove the rubber cap over the tensioner locknut and loosen the locknut.
44. Insert a suitable tool between the tensioner wheel and the spring carrier pin to hold the tensioner. If the belt needs to be tightened, move the roller to adjust the tension to 6.0 units. If the belt is too tight, adjust to obtain a reading of 5.0 units on the gauge. Tighten the tensioner locknut and remove the suitable tool.
45. Rotate the crankshaft so that the cam pulleys move through 1 full revolution and recheck the tension on the camshaft belt. It should now be 5.5 ±

0.2 units. Install the plastic plug over the tensioner bolt.

46. Reinstall the remaining belt covers. Start the engine and final check performance.

### B28F and B280F Engines

1. Remove the cylinder head.
2. Remove the camshaft rear cover plate.
3. Remove the camshaft retaining fork at the front of the cylinder head.
4. Pull the camshaft out the rear of the head.
5. Reverse the above to install. Oil the camshaft and followers before installation.

### D24 and D24T Engines

1. Disconnect the negative battery terminal.
2. Drain the radiator.
3. Remove the expansion tank hose.
4. Remove the top and bottom radiator hoses.
5. Remove the fan with the spacer and pulley.
6. Remove all the drive belts.
7. Remove the valve cover.
8. Remove the timing gear belt cover.
9. Set the No. 1 cylinder to TDC.

**NOTE: This is accomplished by turning the crankshaft pulley with 17mm socket. The flywheel timing mark should be set at "0".**

10. Remove the crankshaft pulley bolt.
11. Remove the 4 Allen head bolts in the center of the pulley and remove the pulley.

**NOTE: The pulley and the crankshaft gear may be stuck together. Gently tap them apart with a rubber hammer.**

12. Remove the lower belt shield.
13. Loosen and remove the timing belt.
14. Remove the front camshaft gear.

**NOTE: Use Volvo tool No. 5199 or another suitable tool to prevent the camshaft from turning.**

15. Remove the rear timing belt cover.
16. Loosen the injection pump bracket to release tension from the injection pump drive belt.
17. Remove the timing belt.
18. Remove the rear camshaft gear.
19. Remove the 1st and 4th bearing caps.
20. Remove the 2nd and 3rd bearing caps.

**NOTE: Loosen the bearing cap nuts on an alternating basis to prevent cam distortion.**

21. Remove the camshaft and discard the seals.
22. Installation is the reverse of removal, with the following suggestions.
    a. When reinstalling the cam you must use special tool No. 5190 available from your Volvo dealer.
    b. Place grease on the oil seal lips before installation. The seals must be driven into place with Volvo tool No. 5200 or a suitable substitute.
    c. Torque the cam bearing caps to 15 ft. lbs. (20 Nm).
    d. The 2nd and 3rd bearing caps should be installed first.
    e. The following torque specifications are needed: Front camshaft gear 33 ft. lbs. (45 Nm), rear camshaft gear 73 ft. lbs. (100 Nm), crankshaft pulley 330 ft. lbs. (450 Nm), crankshaft pulley Allen bolts 15 ft. lbs. (20 Nm).

## Balance Shafts

### REMOVAL & INSTALLATION

### B234 Engine

**NOTE: The use of the correct special tools or their equivalent is REQUIRED for this procedure.**

#### LEFT SHAFT AND HOUSING

1. Remove the timing and balance shaft belts.
2. Use a counterhold such as Volvo tool 5362 and remove the left side balance shaft pulley.
3. Remove the air mass meter and inlet hose.
4. Unfasten the bracket under the intake manifold and remove the bracket holding the alternator and power steering pump. These may be swung out of the way and tied with wire to the left shock tower.
5. Remove the bolts securing the balance shaft housing to the block. Using an extractor such as Volvo tool 5376 or similar, carefully separate the housing from the block. The housing must be removed evenly from both its front and rear mounts.
6. Clean the joint faces on the cylinder block. Place new O-rings in the grooves around the oil passages on the housing. The rings can be held in place with a light coating of grease.
7. Install the balance shaft housing. Make absolutely sure the housing is evenly mounted on the front and rear mountings. Tighten the bolts alternately in a diagonal pattern. Tighten each bolt ½ turn at a time; tighten them to 15 ft. lbs. (20 Nm). When all the bolts are at 15 ft. lbs. (20 Nm), loosen them individually and tighten each one to 7.5 ft. lbs. (10 Nm) plug 90 degrees of rotation.

**NOTE: Make certain that the shaft does not seize within the housing during installation.**

8. If the halves of the housing were split apart during the repair, tighten the joint bolts to 6 ft. lbs. (8 Nm).
9. Install the drive pulley. Use a counterholding tool. Note that the pulley has a slot which will align with the guide on the shaft. The shallow side of the pulley faces inward (toward the engine). Tighten the center bolt for the pulley to 37 ft. lbs. (50 Nm).
10. Reinstall the bracket for the alternator and power steering pump. Double check their connections and hoses. Attach the support under the intake manifold and don't forget the wire clamp on the bottom bolt.
11. Install the air mass meter and its intake hose.
12. Install the balance shaft belt and camshaft belt.

#### RIGHT SHAFT AND HOUSING

1. Remove the timing and balance shaft belts.
2. Use a counterhold such as Volvo tool 5362 and remove the left side balance shaft pulley.
3. Remove the balance shaft belt tensioner and remove the bolt running through the backing plate to the balance shaft housing.
4. Remove the air mass meter and its air inlet hose.
5. Remove the air preheat hose from the bottom heat shield at the exhaust manifold. Remove the nuts holding the right engine mount to the crossmember.
6. Connect a hoist or engine lift apparatus to the top of the engine. Lift the engine at the right side, being careful to maintain clearance between the brake master cylinder and the intake manifold.
7. Remove the complete motor mount from the block, including the pad and lower mounting plate.
8. Remove the bolts securing the balance shaft housing to the block. Using an extractor such as Volvo tool 5376 or similar, carefully separate the housing from the block. The housing must be removed evenly from both its front and rear mounts.
9. Clean the joint faces on the cylinder block. Place new O-rings in the grooves around the oil passages on the housing. The rings can be held in place with a light coating of grease.
10. Install the balance shaft housing. Make absolutely sure the housing is evenly mounted on the front and rear mountings. Tighten the bolts alternately in a diagonal pattern. Tighten each bolt ½ turn at a time; tighten them to 15 ft. lbs. (20 Nm). When all the bolts are at 15 ft. lbs. (20 Nm),

loosen them individually and tighten each one to 7.5 ft. lbs. (10 Nm) plus 90 degrees of rotation.

**NOTE: Make certain that the shaft does not seize within the housing during installation.**

11. If the halves of the housing were split apart during the repair, tighten the joint bolts to 6 ft. lbs. (8 Nm).
12. Install the drive pulley. Use a counterholding tool. Note that the pulley has a slot which will align with the guide on the shaft. The shallow side of the pulley faces inward (toward the engine). Tighten the center bolt for the pulley to 37 ft. lbs. (50 Nm).
13. Install the engine mount onto the block.
14. Using the studs on the crossmember as a guide, lower the engine into place on the front crossmember. When the engine is correctly seated, the lifting apparatus may be removed.
15. Reinstall the air mass meter and its air intake hose.
16. Reinstall the motor mount bolts and the air preheat tube at the lower part of the exhaust manifold.
17. Install the bolt through the backing plate and into the balance shaft housing. Reinstall the belt tensioner, tightening the bolt so that the pulley is movable when the belt is in position.
18. Reinstall the balance shaft and camshaft belts.

## Piston and Connecting Rod

**For all piston and connecting rod overhaul procedures, please refer to "Engine Rebuilding" in the Unit Repair section.**

### POSITIONING

On all engines, the notch or arrow stamped on top of the piston must face the front of the engine. On the B21 the connecting rod marking must face the front of the engine.

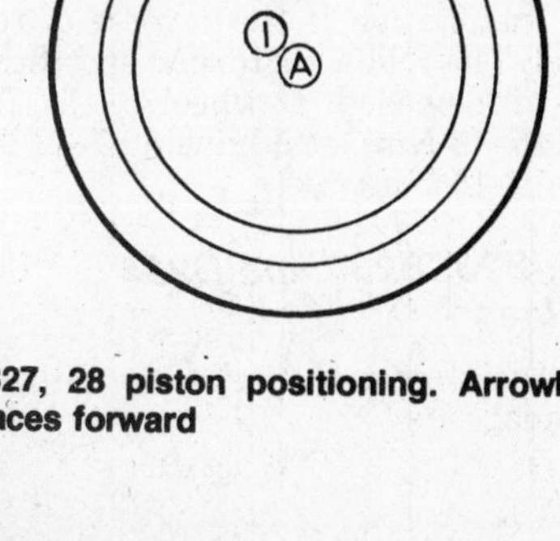

**B27, 28 piston positioning. Arrowhead faces forward**

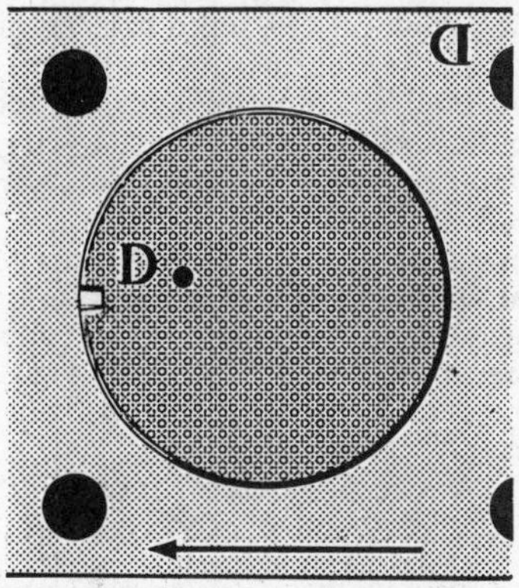


**B21FT series piston positioning. Notch faces forward**

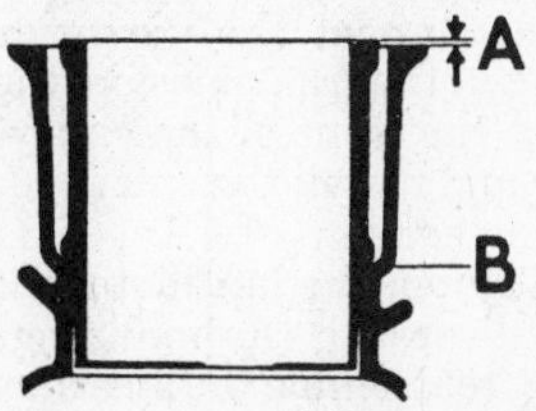


**Correct B27, 28 piston liner height "A" above block face is 0.0091 in. Shims are available for installation at point "B" and should be uniform for all cylinders**

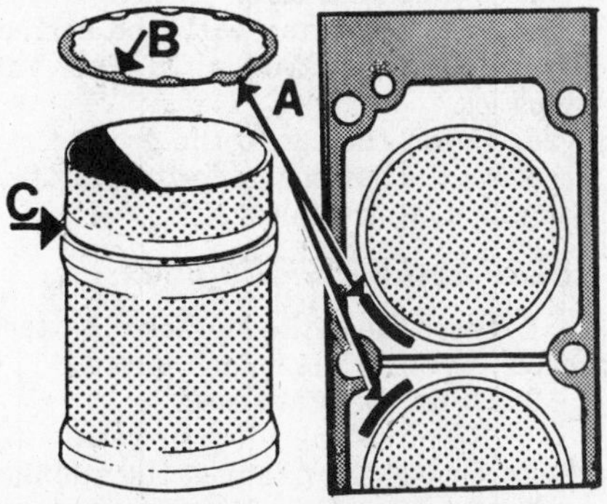


**When installing B27 and B28 liner shims, color marking "A" must face up and be positioned where shown. Inside tabs "B" fit into liner groove**

# ENGINE LUBRICATION

## Oil Pan

### REMOVAL & INSTALLATION

#### *B21, B23 and B230 Engines*

1. Disconnect the negative battery cable. Raise and support the vehicle safely.
2. Drain the engine oil.
3. Remove the splash guard.
4. Remove the engine mount retaining nuts.
5. Remove the lower bolt and loosen the top bolt on the steering column yoke.
6. Slide the yoke assembly up on the steering shaft.
7. Jack up the front of the engine.
8. Remove the retaining bolts for the front axle crossmember.
9. Remove the crossmember.
10. Remove the left engine mount.
11. Remove the pan support bracket.
12. Remove the pan bolts and remove the pan.
13. Installation is the reverse of removal.

**NOTE: Always use a new pan gasket when reinstalling the pan.**

The following torque specifications are needed:

Pan bolts – 8 ft. lbs. (11 Nm)

Steering yoke lower bolt – 18 ft. lbs. (24 Nm)

#### *B234 Engine*

1. Safely elevate the car and support it on jackstands. Disconnect the negative battery cable and remove the engine oil dipstick.

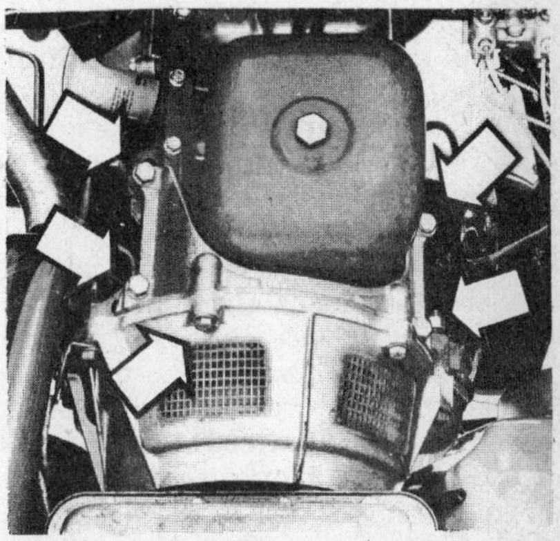

**Pan support bracket—B21 and B23 series engines (view from under car)**

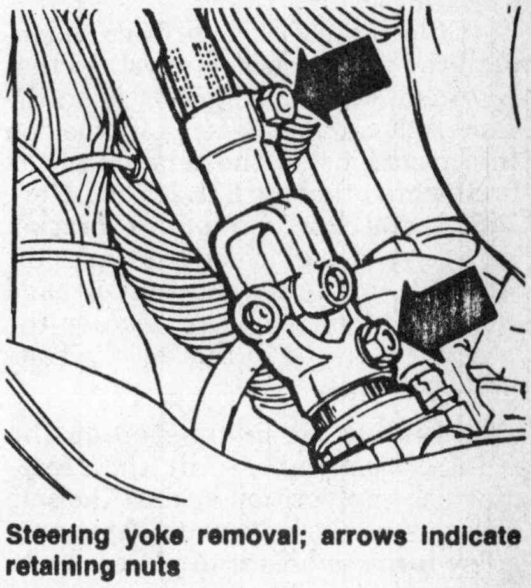

**Steering yoke removal; arrows indicate retaining nuts**

2. Remove the air mass meter and air inlet hose. Loosen the fan shroud.
3. Remove the bolts at both ends of the crossmember.
4. Fit a chain hoist or lifting apparatus to the top of the engine and relieve the weight of the engine by lifting the at the front.
5. At the right motor mount, unbolt the bottom mounting plate from the crossmember. At the left motor mount, unbolt the upper mounting plate from the cylinder block.
6. Drain the engine oil and replace the drain bolt when the pan is empty. Use a new washer and tighten the bolt to 44 ft. lbs. (60 Nm).

**CAUTION**

***Used motor oil may cause skin cancer if repeatedly left in contact with the skin for prolonged periods. Although this is unlikely unless you handle oil on a daily basis, it is wise to thoroughly wash your hands with soap and water immediately after handling used motor oil.***

7. Remove the splashguard from under the engine, the bottom nut for the left motor mount and the wiring harness bracket from the transmission cover.
8. At the steering shaft, remove the lower clamping bolt and loosen the upper bolt. Matchmark the position of the splined joint and slide the fitting up the steering shaft.
9. Remove the rubber bump-stop on the front crossmember and remove the reinforcing bracket between the engine and transmission.
10. Disassemble the bolted joint at the front of the catalytic converter.
11. Carefully elevate the engine with the hoist. Make very certain that no hoses or wires are strained and that clearance is maintained at the firewall. Raise the motor only enough to perform the next Steps of the procedure.
12. Remove the left motor mount.
13. Unbolt and remove the oil pan. It will need to be lifted and turned during removal.
14. Clean the gasket surfaces and install the new gasket (always!) so that the small tab on the gasket is on the same side as the starter. Lift the pan into place, install the retaining bolts and tighten them to 8 ft. lbs. (11 Nm).
15. Install the reinforcing bracket between the engine and transmission. Attach it first to the transmission and then to the engine block. Tighten the bracket in stages so that all the bolts pull up evenly.
16. Install the bump-stop on the front crossmember. Lift the crossmember into position against the side rails, install the bolts and tighten only a few turns to hold it in place.
17. When all the bolts are installed, tighten the crossmember bolts to 70 ft. lbs. (95 Nm). Install the left motor mount and secure the plate to the cylinder block. Don't forget to attach the cable clip on the upper bolt.
18. Paying close attention to the placement of the motor mounts, lower the engine into position. When the engine is correctly seated, the lifting equipment may be removed from the car.
19. At the right motor mount, tighten the plate onto the crossmember. Check the connection of the air preheat tube at the exhaust manifold.
20. Tighten the fan shroud. Adjust the position of the bottom bracket as needed.
21. Reconnect the wiring harness bracket at the transmission, the bolted joint at the front of the catalytic converter and install the splashguard under the engine.
22. Tighten the left motor mount.
23. Observing the markings made earlier, reassemble the steering shafts. Insert and tighten the bottom bolt to 15 ft. lbs. (20 Nm). Tighen the upper bolt the same. Don't forget to install the small spring clips on the bolts.
24. Install the air mass meter and its hoses and connectors.
25. Fill the engine with the correct amount of oil and reinstall the dipstick.
26. Lower the car to the ground, reconnect the battery cable and start the engine. Check for leaks.

### *B28F and B280F Engines*

1. Disconnect the negative battery cable. Remove the splash guard.
2. Drain the crankcase.
3. Remove the oil pan retaining bolts. Swivel the pan past the stabilizer bar and remove.
4. Reverse the above to install.

### *D24 and D24T Engines*

In order to remove the oil pan from the vehicle the engine must be remove first. After engine removal be sure that the engine is positioned in a suitable holding fixture.

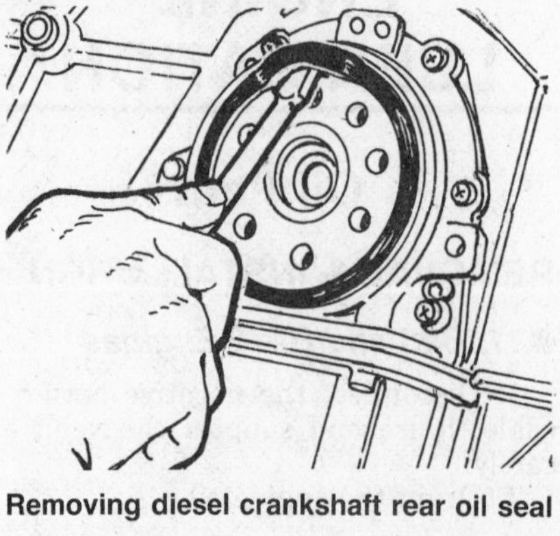

Removing diesel crankshaft rear oil seal

# Rear Main Bearing Oil Seal

## REMOVAL & INSTALLATION

### *D24 and D24T Engines*

1. Disconnect the negative battery terminal.
2. Remove the transmission.
3. Remove all but 1 starter bolt to keep it from falling out.
4. Remove the clutch and pressure plate assembly (if so equipped).
5. Remove the pilot bearing.
6. Remove the flywheel.

**NOTE: Use special tool No. 5112 or a suitable replacement to keep the flywheel from turning while removing the bolts.**

7. Remove the oil seal with a suitable tool.
8. Check the contact surfaces on the seal holder and crankshaft.
9. Installation is the reverse of removal. When reinstalling a new seal use special tool No. 5208 available from Volvo or a suitable replacement. Coat the seal with oil before installation. Torque the flywheel bolts to 55 ft. lbs. (75 Nm). Use a liquid sealer (Loctite® or similar product) on the bolts prior to installing them.

### *B28F and B280F Engines*

1. Disconnect the negative battery terminal.
2. Remove the transmission.
3. Remove the clutch and pressure plate (if so equipped).
4. Remove the flywheel (drive plate on automatic transmissions).

**NOTE: On automatic transmissions remove the crankshaft spacer.**

5. Remove the 2 rear pan bolts.
6. Remove the bolts in the seal housing and then the housing.

**NOTE: Gently remove the housing so as not to damage the oil pan gasket.**

7. Use special tool No. 5107 to remove the old seal and install the new one. This tool is available from Volvo or use a suitable replacement.
8. Installation is the reverse of removal. The following torque specifications are needed: flywheel 33–37 ft. lbs. (45–50 Nm), seal housing 7–11 ft. lbs. (10–15 Nm).

### *B21, B23, B230 and B234 Engines*

1. Disconnect the negative battery terminal.

2. Remove the transmission.
3. Remove the clutch and pressure plate (if so equipped).
4. Remove the pilot bearing snapring and remove the bearing.
5. Remove the flywheel or driveplate which ever is applicable.

**NOTE: Be careful not to press in the activator pins for the timing device.**

6. Remove the rear oil pan brace.
7. Remove the 2 center bolts from the pan that bolt into the seal housing.
8. Loosen 2 bolts on either side of the 2 in the seal housing.
9. Remove the 6 seal housing bolts, and remove the seal housing.

**NOTE: Be careful not to damage the oil pan gasket when removing the seal housing.**

10. Remove the seal using special tool No. 2817 or a suitable replacement.
11. Installation is the reverse of removal.

**NOTE: Use a new gasket on the seal housing and coat the seal with oil prior to installation.**

Torque the flywheel to 47–54 ft. lbs. (64–73 Nm). When installing the flywheel turn the crankshaft to bring the No. 1 piston to TDC. The lower flywheel pin should be installed approximately 15 degrees from the horizontal and opposite the starter. Install the bolts.

## Oil Pump

### REMOVAL & INSTALLATION

#### *B21, B23 and B230 Engines*

1. Remove the oil pan.
2. Remove the 2 oil pump retaining bolts, and pull the delivery tube from the block.
3. When installing, use new sealing rings at either end of the delivery tube. Also, make sure you **PRIME** the pump (remove all air) by filing it with clean engine oil and operating the pump by hand, before installation.

#### *B234 Engine*

1. Remove the timing belt.
2. Using a counterholding device such as Volvo tool 5039 or similar, remove the oil pump drive pulley.
3. Thoroughly clean the area around the oil pump. Place sheets of newspaper or a container on the splashguard to contain any spillage and remove the oil pump mounting bolts. Remove the pump from the engine.
4. Remove the seal from the groove in the block. Clean the area with solvent, making certain there are no particles of dirt trapped in the pump area.
5. Install the new seal in the groove and install the new oil pump. Lubricate the pump with clean engine oil before installation. Tighten the mounting bolts to 7.5 ft. lbs. (10 Nm).
6. Using the counterhold, install the drive pulley and tighten the center bolt to 15 ft. lbs. (20 Nm) plug 60 degrees of rotation.
7. Clean the area of any oil spillage; remove the paper or container from the splashguard.
8. Install the timing belt.

#### *B28F and B280F Engines*

The oil pump body is cast integrally with the cylinder block. It is chain driven by a separate sprocket on the crankshaft and is located behind the timing chain cover. The pick-up screen and tube are serviced by removing the oil pan. To check the pump gears or remove the oil pump cover:

1. Disconnect the negative battery cable. Remove the air cleaner and valve covers.
2. Loosen the fan shroud and remove the fan. Remove the shroud.
3. Loosen the alternator, air pump, power steering pump, and A/C compressor (if so equipped) and remove their drive belts.
4. Block the flywheel from turning, and remove the 36mm bolt and the crankshaft pulley.

**NOTE: Do not drop key into crankcase.**

5. Remove the timing gear cover (25 bolts).
6. Remove the oil pump drive sprocket and chain.
7. Remove the oil pump cover, and gears.
8. Reverse the removal procedure to install. Prime the pump (remove all air) by filling it with clean engine oil and operating the pump by hands, before installation.

#### *D24 and D24T Engines*

1. Remove the engine from the car.
2. Remove the oil pan and the oil suction pipe.
3. Remove the front timing belt cover, timing belt, vibration damper, and lower timing belt cover.

**NOTE: Do not allow the crankshaft to turn when disconnected from the camshaft. If this should happen the fuel injection timing must be reset.**

4. Remove the crankshaft gear and seal with a puller.
5. Remove the timing belt inner shield.

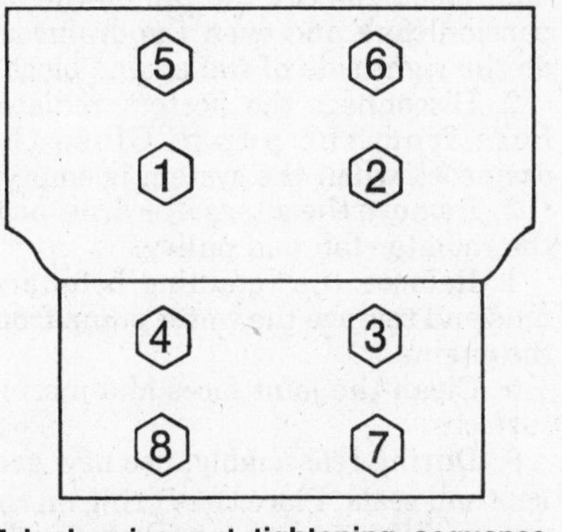


**Main bearing nut tightening sequence, B27, B28**

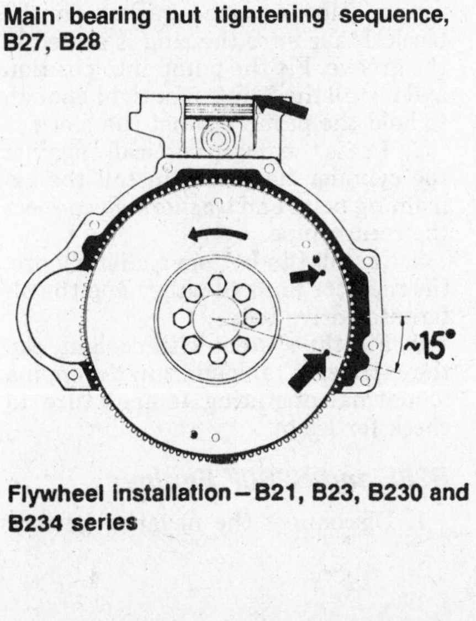


**Flywheel installation—B21, B23, B230 and B234 series**

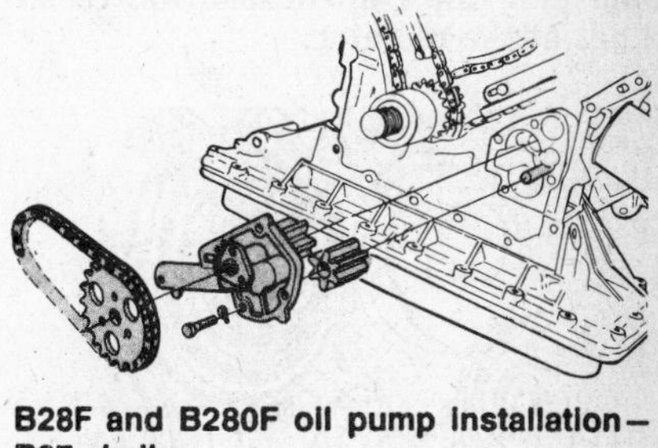

**B28F and B280F oil pump installation—B27 similar**

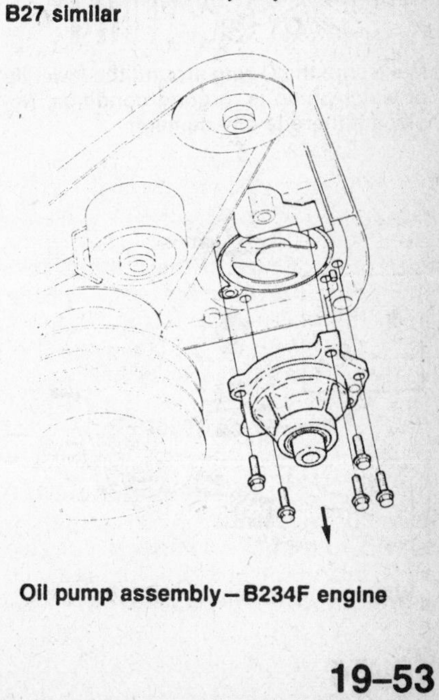

**Oil pump assembly—B234F engine**

6. Remove the oil pump bolts and remove the pump.

**NOTE: The oil pump can not be repaired. It must be replaced as a unit.**

7. When installing the oil pump the triangular mark on the pump outer gear must face the oil pump rear cover.
8. Installation is the reverse of removal. Fill the oil pump with clean engine oil and **PRIME** the pump by operating it by hand prior to installation.

# ENGINE COOLING

## Radiator

### REMOVAL & INSTALLATION

1. Disconnect the negative battery cable. Remove the radiator and expansion tank caps, disconnect the lower radiator hose, and drain the cooling system.
2. Remove the expansion tank and hose, and drain the coolant. Remove the upper radiator hose. On cars with automatic transmission, disconnect and plug the transmission oil cooler lines at the radiator.

Make sure the O-ring around the lower lip of water pump is in good condition. Replace if there is any damage

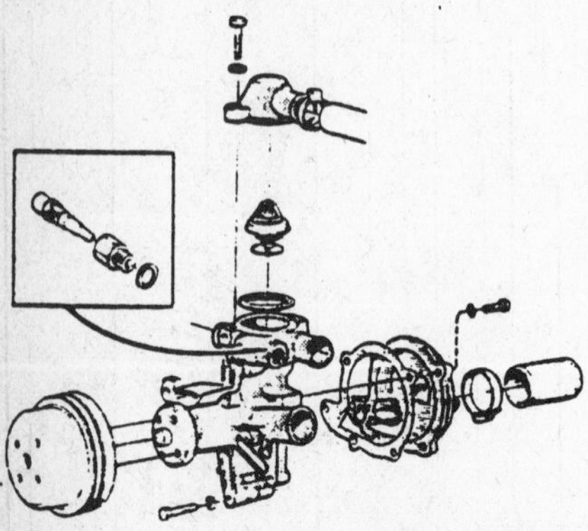

Water pump assemlby—B280 engine

3. Remove the retaining bolts for the radiator and fan shroud, if so equipped, and lift out the radiator.
4. Installation is the reverse of the removal procedure. Start the engine and check for leaks.

## Water Pump

### REMOVAL & INSTALLATION

#### *B21, B23 and B230 Engines*

1. Disconnect the negative battery cable. Remove the overflow tank cap. Drain the cooling system.
2. Remove the fan and fan shroud.
3. Remove the alternator and air pump drive belts. Remove the water pump pulley.
4. Remove the timing belt cover.
5. Remove the lower radiator hose.
6. Remove the retaining bolt for the coolant pipe (beneath exhaust manifold) and pull the pipe rearward.
7. Remove the 6 retaining bolts and lift off the water pump.
8. Clean the gasket contact surfaces thoroughly, and use a new gasket and O-rings (especially between the cylinder head and top of water pump).
9. Installation is the reverse of the removal procedure.

#### *B234 Engine*

1. Set the heater control for maximum heat, remove the cap on the expansion tank and open the draincock on the right side of the engine block.
2. Disconnect the bottom radiator hose from the pump. Close the draincock when the system is empty.
3. Remove the alternator drive belt, the radiator fan and pulley.
4. Remove the retaining bolts and nuts and remove the water pump from the engine.
5. Clean the joint faces and mating surfaces.
6. During reassembly, use new gaskets and seals. Place the O-ring on the return tube and the gasket on the block. Make sure the ring is seated in the groove. Fit the pump into position and install the 2 nuts just tight enough to hold the pump against the block.
7. Press the pump vertically against the cylinder head and install the remaining bolts and washers. Reconnect the return pipe.
8. Install the bottom radiator hose, the radiator fan and pulley and the alternator drive belt.
9. Fill the system with coolant, cap the expansion tank and run the engine to normal operating temperature to check for leaks.

#### *B28F and B280F Engines*

1. Disconnect the negative battery cable. Remove the front and main sections of the intake manifold.
2. Remove the overflow tank cap and drain the cooling system.
3. disconnect both radiator hoses. On automatic transmission cars, disconnect the transmission cooler lines at the radiator. Disconnect the fan shroud. Remove the radiator and fan shroud.
4. Remove the fan.
5. Remove the hoses from the water pump to each cylinder head.
6. Remove the fan belts. Remove the water pump pulley.
7. Loosen the hose clamps at the rear of the water pump.
8. Remove the water pump from the block (3 bolts).
9. Transfer the thermal time lender and temperature sensor to the new water pump.
10. Transfer the thermostat cover, thermostat, and rear pump cover to the new pump.
11. Reverse the removal procedure to install.

#### *D24 and D24T Engines*

1. Disconnect the negative battery cable. Drain the radiator.
2. Remove the splash guard shield from under the engine.
3. Remove the expansion tank.
4. Remove the top and bottom radiator hoses.

**NOTE: On cars with automatic transmissions remove the cooler lines from the radiator.**

5. Remove the radiator (and shroud if so equipped).
6. Remove all the drive belts.
7. Remove the fan with the spacer and pulley.
8. Remove the front timing gear cover.
9. Disconnect the cold start device.
10. Loosen screw No. 1 and push the lever forward, rotate the lever 90 degrees and push it backward against the stop.

**NOTE: Do not touch the 2nd screw. If it becomes loosened, the cold start device must be reset on a test bench.**

11. Remove the injection pump plug and install a dial indicator gauge with a measuring range of 0–0.118 in. (0–3mm).

**NOTE: This gauge must have adapter No. 5194 (available from Volvo) attached to it.**

12. Set the gauge to approximately 0.078 in. (2mm).
13. Set the No.1 cylinder to TDC.
14. The marking on the injection

pump gear should coincide with the marking on the injection pump bracket.

15. The flywheel timing mark should be at 0.

16. Turn the engine ¼ turn past zero and then back to zero again. This is done in order to place slack in the timing belt on the drive side. Otherwise the engine setting would be incorrect.

**NOTE: The gauge must not move during the remainder of the work. If it does the engine must be completely retimed.**

17. Loosen the water pump bolts to release the belt tension.
18. Remove the timing bolt from the camshaft gear.
19. Remove the camshaft gear.
20. Remove the vibration damper.
21. Remove the lower belt guard.
22. Loosen the bracket for the fan and alternator.
23. Remove the lower retaining bolt and move the bracket away from the engine.
24. Remove the inner belt shield and water pump.
25. Installation is the reverse of removal.

**NOTE: Grease the O-ring before installing it in the water pump.**

The following torque specifications are needed:

Vibration damper screws – 15 ft. lbs. (20 Nm)

Crankshaft center bolt – 255 ft. lbs. (345 Nm)

Camshaft gear – 33 ft. lbs. (45 Nm)

Pump setting – 0.0256–0.0287 in. (0.650–0.729mm)

## Thermostat

### REMOVAL & INSTALLATION

1. Disconnect the lower radiator hose and drain the cooling system.
2. Remove the 2 bolts securing the thermostat housing to the cylinder head and carefully lift the housing free.
3. Remove all old gasket material from the mating surfaces and remove the thermostat.
4. Test the operation of the thermostat by immersing it in a container of heated water. Replace any thermostat that does not open at the correct temperature.
5. Place the thermostat, with a new gasket, in the cylinder head. Fit the thermostat housing to the head and hand-tighten the 2 bolts until snug. Do not tighten the bolts more than ¼ turn past snug.

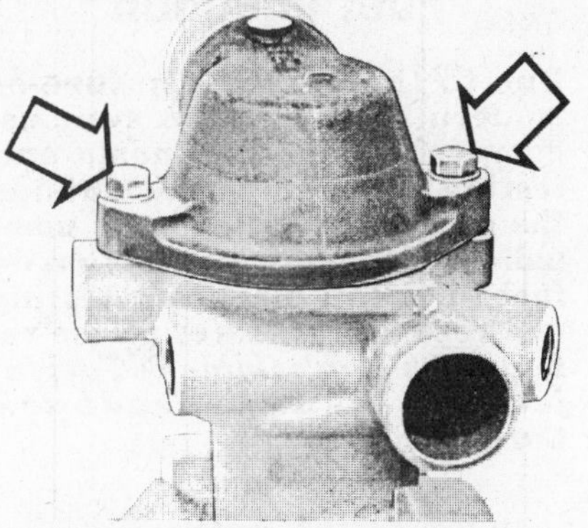

Remove the two top water pump bolts for access to the V6 thermostat

6. Connect the lower radiator hose and replace the coolant.

### COOLING SYSTEM BLEEDING

1. Fill the radiator with the proper type of coolant.
2. With the radiator cap off, start the engine and allow it to run and reach normal operating temperature.
3. Run the heater at full force and with the temperature lever in the hot position. Be sure that the heater control valve is functioning.
4. Shut the engine off and recheck the coolant level, refill as necessary.

# EMISSION CONTROLS

**Please refer to "Emission Control" in the Unit Repair section for system maintenance procedures. Due to the complex nature of modern electronic engine control system, comprehensive diagnosis and testing procedures fall outside the confines of this repair manual. For complete information on diagnosis, testing and repair procedures concerning all modern engine and emission control systems, please refer to *"Chilton's Guide to Electronic Engine Controls"*.**

# GASOLINE FUEL SYSTEM

**NOTE: All Volvos manufactured for sale in the U.S. are equipped with fuel injection. One Canadian engine, the B21A, is equipped with a 1 barrel carburetor.**

## Fuel System Service Precaution

When carrying out repairs to vehicle fuel system extreme care should be taken to prevent fuel spilling onto engine. If the engine is warm, the fuel can ignite. Also, petroleum spirit fumes contain benzene and lead, and are a serious danger to health.

### RELIEVING FUEL SYSTEM PRESSURE

**CAUTION**

***Before servicing any part of the fuel system, fuel pressure should be relieved.***

1. Place the proper size wrenches onto the fuel filter fittings.
2. Place a shop towel or rag around the fuel filter fittings and wrenches.
3. Slowly loosen the fuel line at the fuel filter until all pressure is relieved.
4. Tighten fuel filter fittings.

## Fuel Filter

### REMOVAL & INSTALLATION

1. Loosen the fuel cap.
2. Clean the filter connections carefully before removing.
3. Disconnect the nipples and remove the seals.
4. Remove the filter and clamp.
5. Transfer the nipples and clamp to the new filter.

**NOTE: Fuel flow direction arrow is marked on the new (and old) filter. Arrow follows direction from fuel tank to engine.**

## Electric Fuel Pump

### REMOVAL & INSTALLATION

1. Disconnect the negative battery cable. Remove the filler cap. Remove the electrical lead from the pump as well as the template to which the pump is mounted.
2. Clean around the hose connections. Pinch shut the fuel lines, loosen the hose clamps, and disconnect the lines.
3. Loosen the retaining nuts and remove the pump from its rubber mounts.
4. Install the new pump on its rubber mounts and tighten the retaining nuts.

5. Reconnect the fuel lines, tighten the hose clamps, and remove the pinchers.
6. Mount the template beneath the car and connect the electrical lead.
7. Start the engine and check for leaks.

## Carburetor

### REMOVAL & INSTALLATION

1. Disconnect the negative battery cable.
2. Remove the air cleaner. Remove all necessary components in order to gain access to the carburetor retaining bolts.
3. Remove all linkages, as required.
4. Disconnect the fuel line using the proper tools.
5. Remove the carburetor retaining bolts. Remove the carburetor from the vehicle.
6. Installation is the reverse of the removal procedure.

### ADJUSTMENT

1. Disconnect the air pump and plug the hose or crimp with pliers.
2. Start the engine and run until operating temperature is obtained.
3. Adjust the flow regulating screw to 900 rpm.
4. Check and, if necessary, adjust the CO content. CO content should be 1.5%.
5. When adjustments have been completed, connect the air pump.

### OVERHAUL

**For all carburetor overhaul procedures, please refer to "Carburetor Service" in the Unit Repair section.**

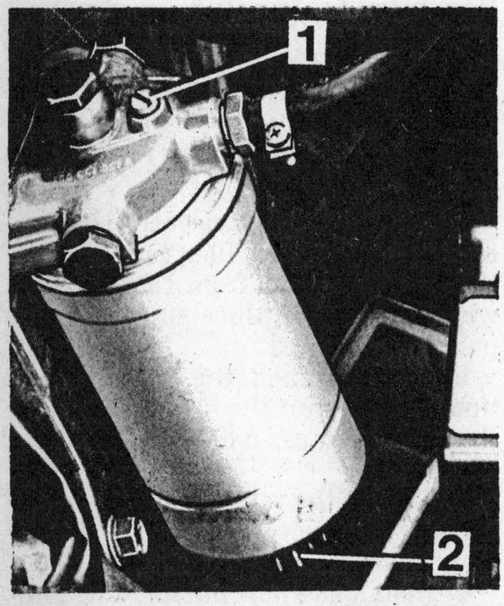


Diesel fuel filter service location. No. 1 is bleeder screw, No. 2 is drain

## Fuel Injection

**Due to the complex nature of modern fuel injection systems, comprehensive diagnosis and testing procedures fall outside the confines of this repair manual. For complete information on fuel injection diagnosis, testing and repair procedures please refer to *"Chilton's Guide To Fuel Injection And Feedback Carburetors"*.**

# DIESEL FUEL SYSTEM

## Fuel Filter

### REPLACEMENT

The fuel filter must be drained every 7500 miles. Place a drain pan under the drain screw to collect the condensate. Loosen the bleeder screw several turns. Loosen the drain screw and drain until clean fuel flows out. Tighten the drain screw and the bleeder screw.

## Diesel Injection Pump

### REMOVAL & INSTALLATION

**NOTE: Several special tools are needed to remove and install the pump and to set its timing. If these tools are not available, do not attempt to remove the pump. The tool numbers (Volvo part numbers) are given in the procedure.**

1. Pinch off and remove the 2 coolant hoses running to the cold-start device on the fuel pump.
2. Disconnect the accelerator linkage at the pump and disconnect the wire from the stop valve on the top of the pump.
3. Remove the rear timing belt cover and thoroughly clean the fuel lines, and their connections at the injection pump.
4. Disconnect the fuel lines at the pump and plug the open connections to prevent dirt from entering the fuel system.
5. Remove the vacuum pump and its plunger.
6. Clean and remove the delivery lines at the fuel injectors. Plug all connections.
7. Set cylinder No. 1 to TDC on the injection stroke. At this position, the O mark on the flywheel aligns with the pointer and the notch on the injection pump pulley aligns with the notch on the pump housing. Both valves on No. 1 cylinder are closed and their camshaft lobes are pointing up at equally large angles.
8. Loosen the retaining bolts for the injection pump and push the pump up, then remove the pump drive belt. Tighten 1 bolt to hold the pump in the upper position.
9. Loosen the center bolt in the rear camshaft gear while using wrench No. 5199 to the gear. The bolts will be easily accessible if wrench No. 5201 is used.

**NOTE: The camshaft must not rotate. Loosen the bolt only enough to rotate the gear on the camshaft.**

10. Insert pin No. 5193 into the injection pump gear to lock it in position and remove the injection pump gear nut.
11. With the pin still in position, use a puller to remove the pump gear.
12. Remove the bolts retaining the front injection pump bracket to the engine, then remove the hex screws retaining the pump and remove the pump from the engine.
13. Install the pump on the engine and tighten the bolts only finger-tight so that pump position can be adjusted.
14. Set the injection pump so that the mark on pump and the pump bracket align, then tighten the retaining bolts.
15. Make sure the shaft key is correctly installed and install the injection pump gear, washer and nut. Use pin No. 5193 to hold the gear while tightening the nut.
16. Unscrew and remove plug from injection pump distributor.
17. Install tool holder 5194 or equivalent and dial indicator in pump.
18. Turn engine 2 full turns until No. 1 cylinder is at TDC injection, again. If engine is turned too far it must be turned back approximately 1/4 turn and then to **0** mark; otherwise, setting will be incorrect.
19. Dial indicator should indicate:
1983 USA and Canada – 0.030–0.033 in. (0.77–0.85mm)
1984–90 USA Federal and Canada – 0.032–0.035 in. (0.82–0.90mm)
1984–90 USA California – 0.028–0.031 in. (0.72–0.80mm)
20. After completion, remove dial indicator and holder tool and install plug.
21. After the injection pump timing is set, fill the pump with clean diesel fuel through the fuel line connection only if a new fuel pump is being installed or if the old pump was drained and rebuilt.

22. Install the rear timing gear cover. Connect the fuel lines and fuel delivery pipes. Tighten the fuel delivery line cap nuts and the fuel line banjo bolts to 18 ft. lbs. (24 Nm). When installing the fuel line on the pump, do not mix the banjo bolts; the bolt for the fuel return line has a small hole in it and is marked OUT.

23. Install the vacuum pump and all remaining components in the reverse order of removal. Adjust the accelerator linkage.

## Diesel Injection Timing

### ADJUSTMENT

1. Unscrew and remove plug from injection pump distributor.
2. Install tool holder 5194 or equivalent and dial indicator in pump.
3. Turn engine 2 full turns until No. 1 cylinder is at TDC injection, again. If engine is turned too far it must be turned back approximately ¼ turn and then to **0** mark; otherwise, setting will be incorrect.
4. Dial indicator should indicate:
1983 USA and Canada – 0.030–0.033 in. (0.77–0.85mm)
1984–90 USA Federal and Canada – 0.032–0.035 in. (0.82–0.90mm)
1984–90 USA California – 0.028–0.031 (0.72–0.80mm)
5. After completion, remove dial indicator and holder tool and install plug.

## Injection Nozzle

### REMOVAL & INSTALLATION

1. Thoroughly clean the fuel delivery line connections around each fitting before removing.
2. Unscrew each fitting from its injector. Plug or tape the end of each fitting to prevent any dirt or grit from entering the fuel system.
3. Using a box-end wrench, unscrew the injector form the cylinder head. Remove the small heat shield and discard. Use care not to damage any part of the injector (especially the nozzle tip) while it is out of the engine. Plug each injector hole in the head with a piece of clean rag to prevent dirt from entering.
4. Installation is the reverse of removal. Be sure to use new heat shields with each injector. Note the proper way to install the heat shields as in the illustration.

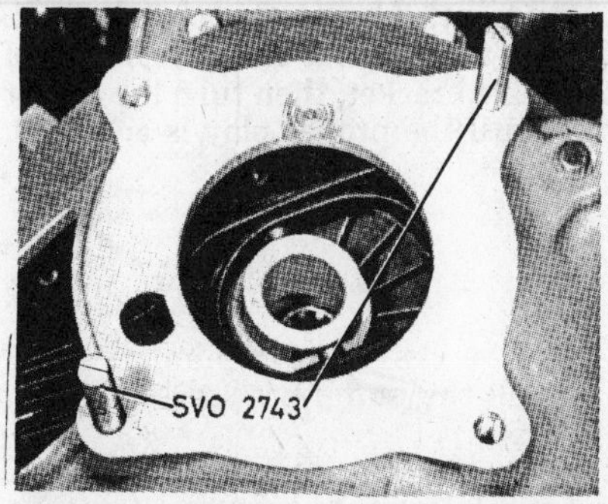

Transmission guide pins installed

# MANUAL TRANSMISSION

### REMOVAL & INSTALLATION

The transmission or the transmission overdrive assembly may be removed with the engine installed in the vehicle.

#### *240 Models*

1. Disconnect the battery. At the firewall, disconnect the back-up light connector.
2. Jack up the front of the car and install jack stands. Loosen the set screw and drive out the pin for the shifter rod. Disconnect the shift lever from the rod.
3. Inside the car, pull up the shift boot. Remove the fork for the reverse gear detent. Remove the snapring and lift up the shifter. If overdrive-equipped, disconnect the engaging switch wire.
4. On 240 series models, disconnect the clutch cable and return spring at the throw-out fork and flywheel housing.
5. Disconnect the exhaust pipe bracket(s) from the flywheel cover. Remove the oil pan splash guard.
6. Using a floor jack and a block of wood, support the engine beneath the oil pan. Remove the transmission support crossmember.
7. Disconnect the driveshaft. Disconnect the speedometer cable. If so equipped, disconnect the overdrive wire.
8. Remove the starter retaining bolts and pull free of the flywheel housing.
9. Support the transmission using another floor jack. Remove the flywheel (bell) housing-to-engine bolts and remove the transmission.
10. Reverse Steps 1–9 to install. Tighten the flywheel housing-to-engine bolts to 25–35 ft. lbs. (34–47 Nm).

#### *740, 760 and 780 Models*

#### 1983–85

1. Disconnect the battery ground cable.
2. Remove the ash tray and holder assembly. Remove the trim box around the gear shift lever.
3. Disconnect the shift lever cover from the floor. Remove the snap-ring at the base of the shift lever.
4. Jack up the car and safely support it with jackstands. From underneath the car, disconnect the gear shift rod at the gear shift lever. Remove the lock screw, and press out the pivot pin. Push up on the shift lever, and pull it up and out of the car.
5. Matchmark the driveshaft and transmission flanges for later assembly. Disconnect the driveshaft from the transmission.
6. Separate the exhaust pipe at the joint under the car. Detach the bracket from the front end of the exhaust pipe (near the bend).
7. Unbolt the transmission crossmember; at the same time, detach it from the rear support (rubber bushing).
8. Remove the rear support from the transmission.
9. Tag and disconnect the electrical connectors from the overdrive, back-up light connector and the solenoid.
10. Cut the plastic clamp at the gear shift assembly for the wiring harness.
11. Remove the starter motor retaining bolts. On models with the B28F V6, remove the cover plate under the bellhousing and the cover plate for the other starter motor opening.
12. On B28F models (hydraulic clutch), remove the slave cylinder from the bellhousing and upper bolts holding the bellhousing. On D24T models, (mechanical clutch), detach the clutch cable from the release fork and the bellhousing.
13. Place a transmission jack or a standard hydraulic floor jack underneath the gearbox (center section) of the transmission so that the transmission is resting on the jack pad. Remove the lower bolts holding the bellhousing, and carefully lower the transmission a few inches as you roll it back so the input shaft will clear. Stop the jack and make sure all wires and linkage are disconnected, then lower the transmission the rest of the way.

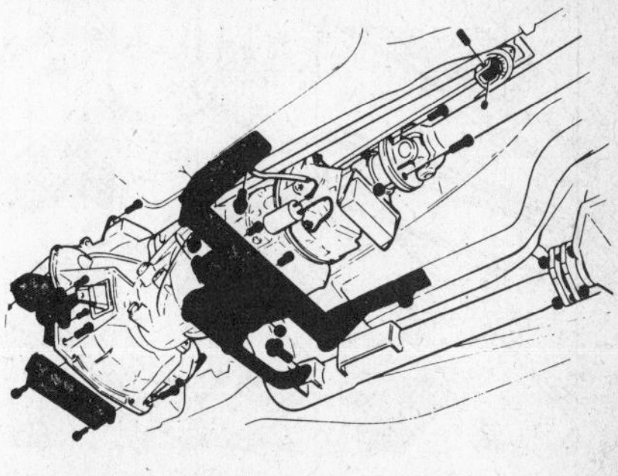
760 GLE manual transmission mounting—740 series similar

14. Reverse the above procedure for removal, making note of the following: use a plastic cable tie to secure the wiring harness to the gear shift assembly where the original plastic clamp was cut. Adjust clutch clearance on D24T models to 0.004–0.012 in. (1–3mm) between the release fork and bearing. When sliding the transmission into place make sure the release bearing is correctly positioned in the shift fork, and that the input shaft is aligned in the clutch disc. Adjust the shifter.

#### 1986–90

1. Disconnect the negative battery cable.
2. Attach a lifting beam, Volvo tool No. 5006, to the rear of the engine. This will support the engine once the transmission is removed.
3. Raise and support the vehicle safely.
4. disconnect the driveshaft at the transmission flange.
5. Disconnect the support bearing for the driveshaft at the crossmember.
6. Remove the driveshaft from the vehicle.
7. disconnect the exhaust system at the muffler.
8. Loosen the lock screw at the shifter assembly. Remove the pin through the gear shift lever. Remove the lock pin ring. Push the gear shift lever up.
9. Remove the transmission crossmember and bracket. Cut the wire straps and disconnect the wires at the transmission.
10. Disconnect the clutch cable at the clutch slave cylinder.
11. Disconnect the exhaust system attachment at the transmission cover.
12. Position a transmission jack under the transmission assembly. Remove the transmission to engine retaining bolts. Remove the transmission from the vehicle.
13. Installation is the reverse of the removal procedure.
14. Be sure to fill the unit with the proper type fluid. Adjust the clutch as required.

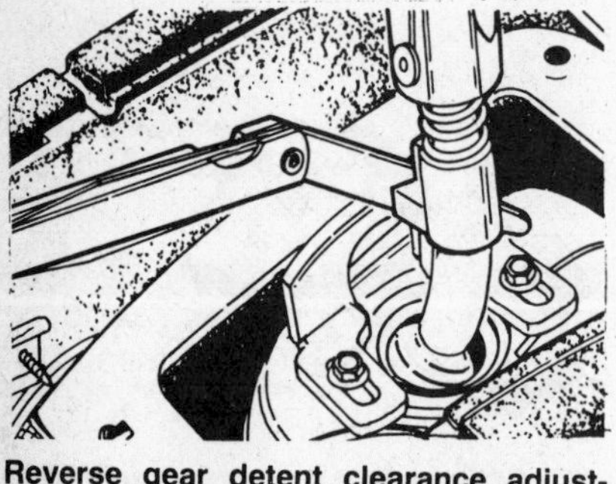

Reverse gear detent clearance adjustment—manual transmission models

### LINKAGE ADJUSTMENT

Reverse gear detent clearance is the only adjustment that can be made to the shift linkage. Remove the shift lever cover, trim frame and ash trav assembly. Engage 1st gear and adjust the clearance between the detent plate and the gear shift lever. Also check clearance should be 0.004–0.06 in. (0.1–1.5mm).

### TRANSMISSION LUBRICATION

The Volvo manual transmissions use Automatic Transmission Fluid type F or G. The oil level should be up to the filler plug hole.

### OVERHAUL

**For all overhaul procedures, please refer to "Manual Transmission Overhaul" in the Unit Repair Section.**

## OVERDRIVE

### REMOVAL & INSTALLATION

To facilitate removal, the vehicle should first be driven in 4th gear with the overdrive engaged, and then coasted for a few seconds with the overdrive disengaged and the clutch pedal depressed.

1. Remove the transmission from the vehicle.
2. Disconnect the solenoid cables.
3. If the overdrive unit has not already been drained, remove the 6 bolts and the overdrive oil pan.
4. Remove the bolts which retain the overdrive unit to the transmission intermediate flange. Pull the unit straight to the rear until it clears the transmission mainshaft.
5. Reverse the above procedure to install. Install the overdrive oil pan with a new gasket. After installation of the transmission (which automatically fills the overdrive) to the proper level with Automatic Transmission Fluid type F or G. Check the lubricant level in the transmission after driving 6–9 miles. The oil level should be up to the filler plug hole.

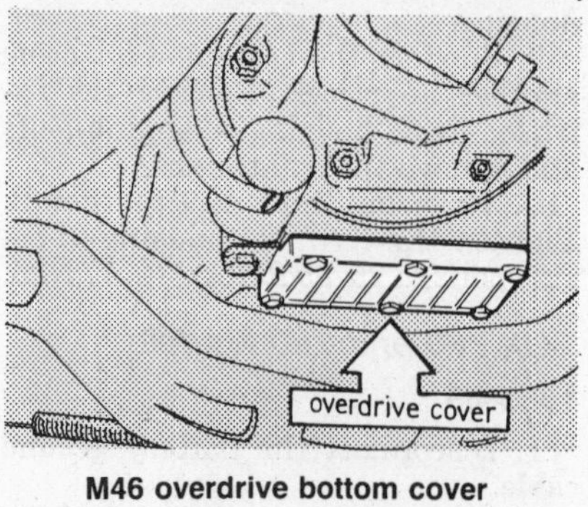


M46 overdrive bottom cover

## CLUTCH

### REMOVAL & INSTALLATION

1. Remove the transmission.
2. Scribe alignment marks on the clutch and flywheel. In order to prevent warpage, slowly loosen the bolts which retain the clutch to the flywheel diagonally in rotation. Remove the bolts and lift off the clutch and pressure plate.
3. Inspect the clutch assembly.
4. When ready to install, wash the pressure plate and flywheel with solvent to remove any traces of oil, and wipe them clean with a cloth.
5. Position the clutch assembly (the longest side of the hub facing backwards) to the flywheel and align the bolt holes. Insert a pilot shaft (centering mandrel or drift), or an input shaft from an old transmission of the same type, through the clutch assembly and flywheel so that the flywheel pilot bearing is centered.
6. Install the 6 bolts which retain the clutch assembly to the flywheel and tighten them diagonally in rotation, a few turns at a time. After all the bolts are tightened, remove the pilot shaft (centering mandrel).
7. Install the transmission.
8. On the 760 GLE, bleed the clutch hydraulic system, if necessary.

### CLUTCH ADJUSTMENT

#### *240, DL, GL, GLT Models and 760 GLE Model with D24T Turbodiesel Engine*

The play in the manually-operated clutches in these 4 cylinder Volvos can be adjusted. Clutch play is adjusted underneath the at the clutch fork. Loosen the lock nut on the fork side of the cable bracket, then turn the adjust nut until the proper play is achieved.

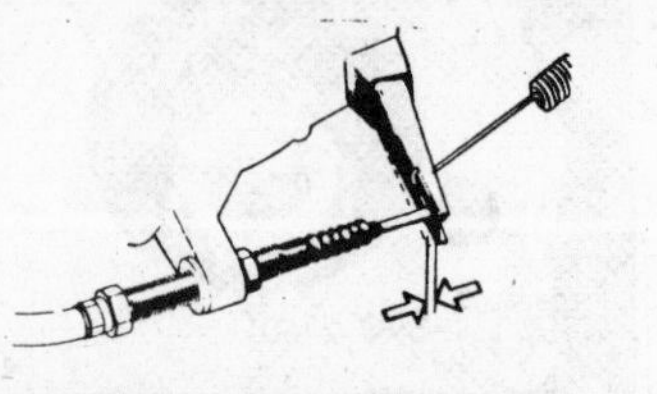

Clutch fork play adjustment, manual (non-hydraulic) clutches. Locknut at center, adjusting nut at left

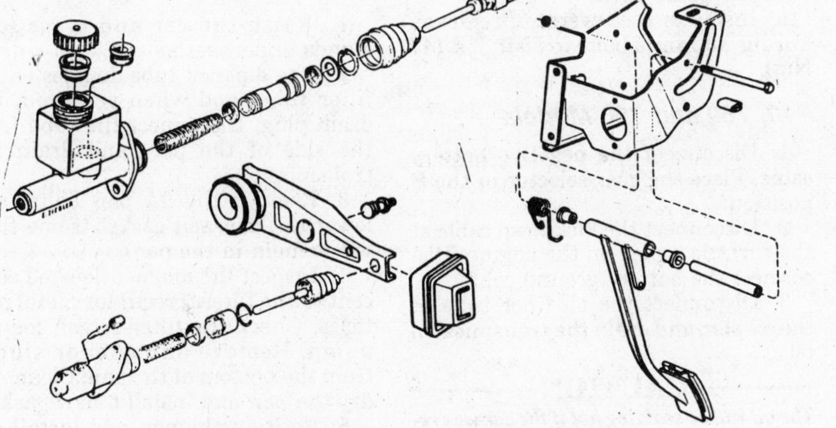

260 series clutch linkage—GLE (all V6) similar

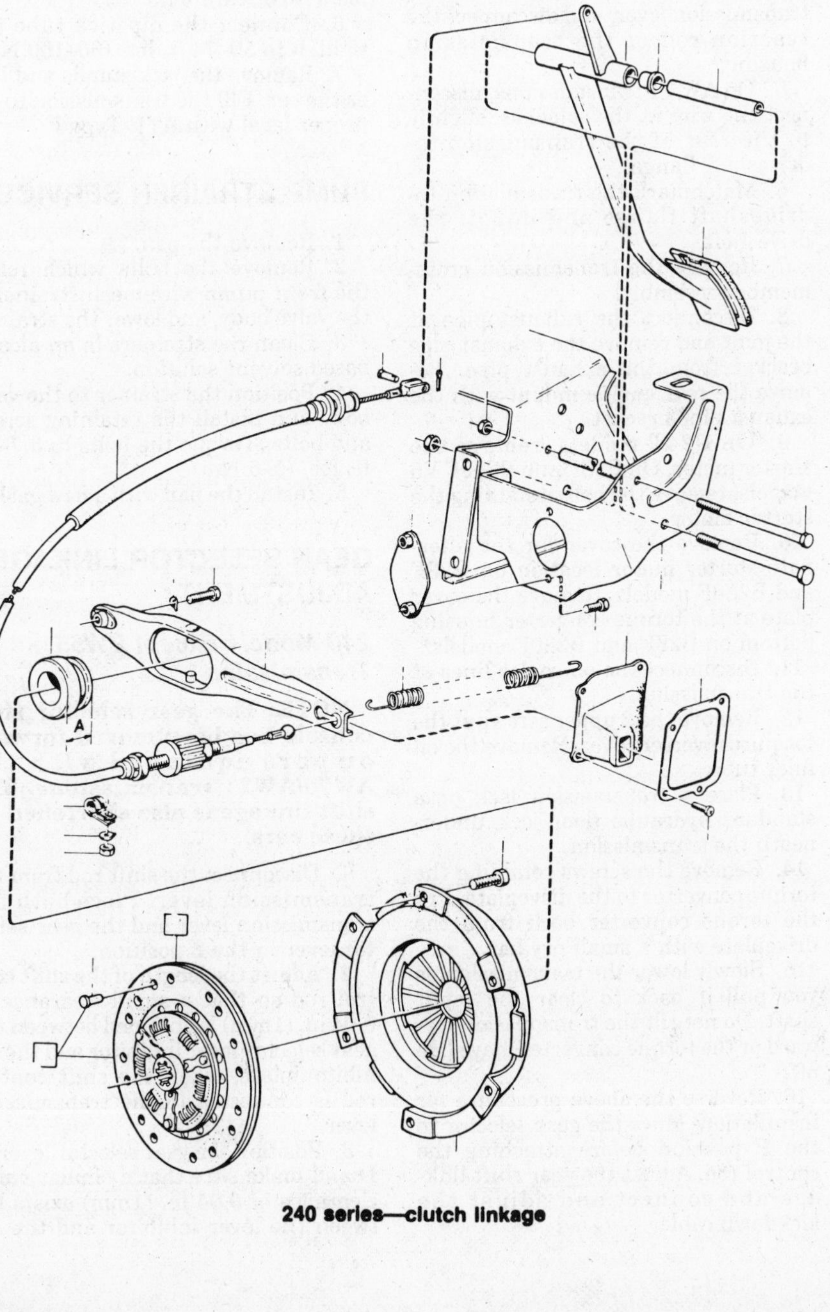


240 series—clutch linkage

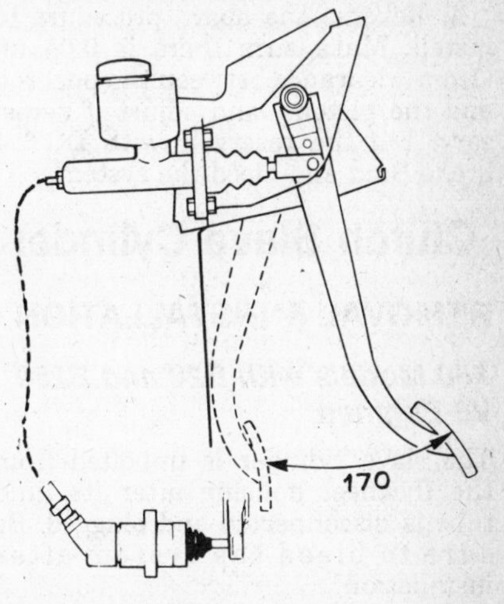


Clutch master cylinder and slave cylinder location—V6 models. Clutch travel is about 6.7 in. (170 mm)

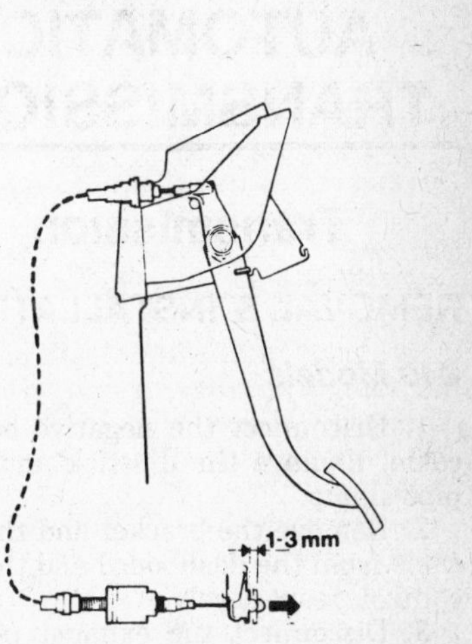


Clutch free-play clearance—B21F Turbo

Tighten the lock nut. Clutch play for all 4 cylinder engines except Turbo is 0.12–0.2 in. (3–5mm) Turbo clutch play (free movement rearward) is 0.04–0.12 in. (1–3mm). D24T clutch play is the same as the gasoline turbo above.

## Clutch Master Cylinder

### REMOVAL & INSTALLATION

#### *760 Model with B28F and B280F V6 Engine*

1. Remove the panel under the instrument panel. Remove the locking spring and pin from the clutch pedal assembly.

2. Disconnect the hose from the clutch fluid reservoir.

3. Unscrew the nipple from the cylinder housing. Place a container underneath the cylinder to catch the fluid that will spill out. Unbolt and remove the cylinder housing.

4. Reverse the above procedure to install. Make sure there is 0.04 in. (1mm) clearance between the pushrod and the pistons, and adjust if necessary. Fill the reservoir with DOT 4 brake fluid and bleed the system.

## Clutch Slave Cylinder

### REMOVAL & INSTALLATION

#### *760 Models with B28 and B280 V6 Engines*

The slave cylinder is unbolted from the flywheel housing after its fluid tube is disconnected and plugged. Be sure to bleed the system after installation.

# AUTOMATIC TRANSMISSION

## Transmission

### REMOVAL & INSTALLATION

#### *240 Models*

1. Disconnect the negative battery cable. Remove the dipstick and filler pipe clamp.
2. Remove the bracket and throttle cable from the dashboard and throttle control, respectively.
3. Disconnect the exhaust pipe at the manifold.
4. Raise the car and support it on jack stands at the front and rear axles.
5. Drain the fluid into a clean container.
6. Disconnect the driveshaft from the transmission flange.
7. Disconnect the selector lever controls and remove the reinforcing bracket from the pan.
8. Remove the torque converter attaching bolts.
9. Support the transmission with a jack equipped with a holding fixture.
10. Remove the crossmember.
11. Disconnect the exhaust pipe brackets and remove the speedometer cable form the case.
12. Remove the filler pipe.
13. Place a wooden block between the engine and firewall and lower the jack until the engine is against the block.

**NOTE: If the battery cable appears to stretch to much, remove it.**

14. Disconnect the starter wires, remove the converter housing bolts and pull the transmission backwards to clear the guide pins.
15. Install in the reverse of removal. Torque all 14mm bolts to 35 ft. lbs. (47 Nm).

#### *740, 760 and 780 Models*

1. Disconnect the negative battery cable. Place the gear selector in the **P** position.
2. Disconnect the kickdown cable at the throttle pulley on the engine. Disconnect the battery ground cable.
3. Disconnect the oil filler tube at the oil pan, and drain the transmission oil.

**CAUTION**

***The oil will be scalding hot if the car was recently driven.***

4. Disconnect the control rod at the transmission lever, and disconnect the reaction rod at the transmission housing.
5. On AW 71 transmissions, disconnect the wire at the solenoid (slightly to the rear of the transmission-to-driveshaft flange).
6. Matchmark the transmission-to-driveshaft flange and unbolt the driveshaft.
7. Remove the transmission crossmember assembly.
8. Disconnect the exhaust pipe at the joint and remove the exhaust pipe bracket from the exhaust pipe. Remove the rear engine mount with the exhaust pipe bracket.
9. On D24T models, remove the starter motor. On B28F and B280F V6 models, remove the bolts retaining the starter motor.
10. Remove the cover for the alternate starter motor location on B28F and B280F models. Remove the cover plate at the torque converter housing bottom on B28F and B280F models.
11. Disconnect the oil cooler lines at the transmission.
12. Remove the 2 upper screws at the torque converter cover. Remove the oil filler tube.
13. Place a transmission jack or a standard hydraulic floor jack underneath the transmission.
14. Remove the screws retaining the torque converter to the driveplate. Pry the torque converter back from the driveplate with a small pry bar.
15. Slowly lower the transmission as you pull it back to clear the input shaft. Do not tilt the transmission forward or the torque converter may slide off.
16. Reverse the above procedure for installation. Move the gear selector to the **P** position before attaching the control rod. Adjust the gear shift linkage and connect and adjust the kickdown cable.

### PAN REMOVAL

1. Raise the car and place jack stands underneath.
2. The dipstick tube doubles as the filler tube, and when removed, the drain plug. Disconnect the tube from the side of the pan, and drain the transmission.
3. Remove the 14 pan bolts, and lower the pan and gasket (some fluid will remain in the pan).
4. Inspect the magnet (located adjacent to the filter screen) for metal particles. Check the filter screen for the pump. Remove any gum or sludge from the bottom of the pan. Clean and dry the pan and install a new gasket.
5. Position the pan and install the bolts finger-tight. Then, stop torque, diagonally in rotation, to 4.4–7.4 ft. lbs. (7–10 Nm).
6. Connect the dipstick tube and tighten to 59–74 ft. lbs. (80–100 Nm).
7. Remove the jack stands and lower the car. Fill the transmission to the proper level with ATF Type F.

### PUMP STRAINER SERVICE

1. Remove the pan.
2. Remove the bolts which retain the front pump wire-mesh strainer to the valve body, and lower the strainer.
3. Clean the strainers in an alcohol based solvent solution.
4. Position the strainer to the valve body and install the retaining screws and bolts. Torque the bolts to 3.7–4.4 ft. lbs. (5–6 Nm).
5. Install the pan with a new gasket.

### GEAR SELECTOR LINKAGE ADJUSTMENT

#### *240 Models Except BW55 Transmission*

**NOTE: The gear selector shift console has been moved forward on cars equipped with the AW70/AW71 transmissions. The shift linkage is also shortened on these cars.**

1. Disconnect the shift rod from the transmission lever. Place both the transmission lever and the gear selector lever in the **2** position.
2. Adjust the length of the shift control rod so that a small clearance of 0.04 in. (1mm) is obtained between the gear selector lever inhibitor and the inhibitor plate, when the shift control rod is connected to the transmission lever.
3. Position the gear selector lever in **D** and make sure that a similar small clearance of 0.04 in. (1mm) exists between the lever inhibitor and the in-

hibitor plate. Disconnect the shift control rod from the transmission lever and adjust, if necessary.

4. Lock the control rod bolt with its safety clasp and tighten the locknut. Make sure that the control rod lug follows with the transmission lever.

5. After moving the transmission lever to the **P** and **1** positions, make sure that the clearances remain the same. In addition, make sure that the output shaft is locked with the selector lever in the **P** position.

### *Models with BW55 Transmission*

1. With the engine off, check that the distance between the **D** position and its forward stop is equal to the distance between the **2** position and its rearward stop, when the gear selector is moved. If you are not sure, remove the gear quadrant cover, and measure.

2. If adjustment is necessary, a rough setting is made by loosening the locknut and rotating the clevis on the control rod to the transmission. A fine adjustment can be made by rotating the knurled sleeve between the control rod locknut and the pivot for the gear selector lever. Increasing the rod length will decrease clearance between the **D** position and its forward stop, and vice versa. Maximum permissible length of exposed thread between the locknut and the control rod is 1.1 in. (28mm).

### *740, 760 and 780 Models*

**NOTE: Before adjusting the shift linkage, make sure the starter motor operates only in P or N positions; that the back-up lights light up only in R; that the shift lever is vertical in P with the car level; that the clearance between D and N is the same or less than the clearance between 2 and 1.**

#### BASIC ADJUSTMENT

1. Place the shift lever in **P**.

2. Loosen the locknuts on the adjustment and reaction rods (on the linkage under the car).

3. Make sure the shift lever is in **P**. Turn the driveshaft until it enters a locked position.

4. Position the adjusting rod arm (A) vertically and tighten the locknut. The gear shift lever may contact the dashboard if the adjusting rod arm is positioned too far backwards.

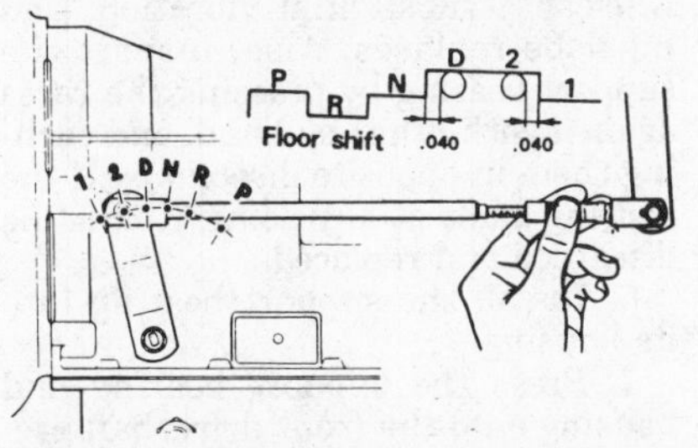


Adjusting automatic transmission gear selector. Clearance in position D toward position N is the same as the clearance in position 2 toward position 1. Adjust at the bottom end of the gear selector.

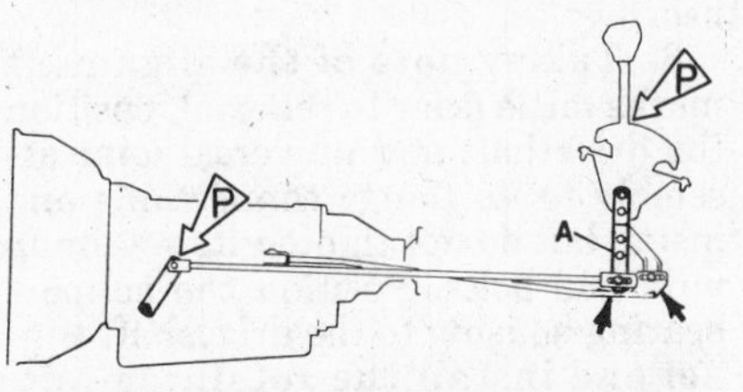


740 and 760 automatic transmission gear linkage. "A" is adjusting rod arm; arrows point to locknuts on adjustment (left) and reaction rod (right) arms

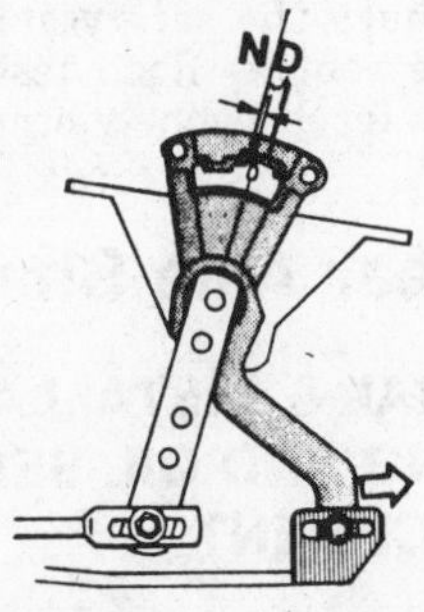


Checking clearance between D and N, and 1 and 2

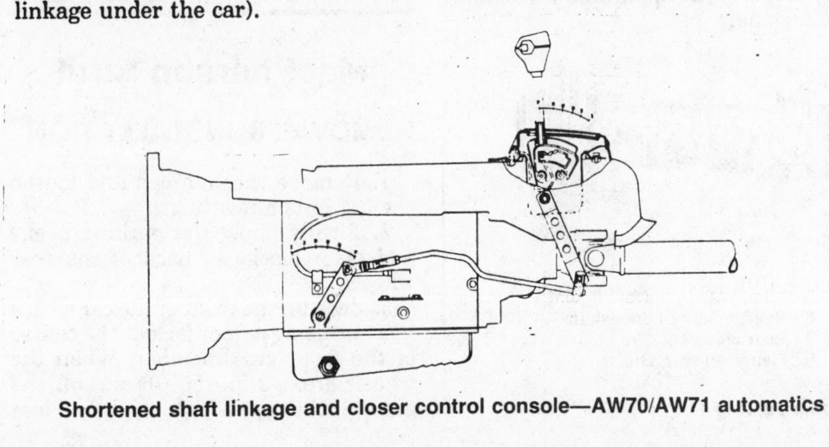

Shortened shaft linkage and closer control console—AW70/AW71 automatics

5. Press the reaction rod arm backwards until a slight resistance is felt. Tighten the locknut to 3.5 ft. lbs. (5 Nm).

#### ADJUSTING CLEARANCE

1. Check that the clearance between **D** and **N** is the same or less than the clearance between **2** and **1** on the shift lever. If clearance is correct, tighten the locknut to 12–17 ft. lbs. 16–23 Nm). If clearance is not correct, adjust as follows:

2. If no clearance is felt in **D**, move the reaction rod arm rearwards about 0.08 in. (2mm).

3. If no clearance is felt in position **2**, move the reaction rod arm forwards about 0.12 in. (3mm). Tighten the locknut.

4. After adjustment, check that the car starts only in **P** or **N**, and that the back-up light does NOT light up in **R**, reduce clearance in **D** by moving the rod arm forward slightly.

## THROTTLE AND DOWNSHIFT CABLE ADJUSTMENT

1. First, adjust the throttle plate angle and throttle cable. Disconnect the cable at the control pulley and the linkage rod at the throttle shaft. Set the throttle plate angle by loosening the adjusting screw locknut and backing off the screw. Then, turn in the screw until it just makes contact and then 1 additional turn. Tighten the locknut. Adjust the linkage rod so that it fits onto the throttle shaft pulley ball without moving the cable pulley. Attach the throttle cable to the pulley and adjust the cable sheath so that the cable is stretched but does not move the cable pulley. Finally, fully depress the gas pedal and check that the pulley contacts the full throttle abutment.

2. With the transmission cable hooked up, check that there is 0.010–0.040 in. (0.25–1mm) clearance between the cable clip and the adjusting sheath. The cable should be stretched at idle. Pull out the cable about ½ in. and release. A distinct click should be heard from the transmission as the throttle can returns to its initial position. Depress the gas pedal again to wide open throttle. Check that the transmission cable moves about 2 in. (50mm). Adjust as necessary at the adjusting sheath.

## NEUTRAL START SWITCH ADJUSTMENT

All models have an adjustable switch, located beneath the shifter quadrant on the tunnel. To adjust:

1. Remove the shifter quadrant cover.

2. Place the shifter lever in **P**. Check that the round switch contact centers over the indicating line for **P**. If not, loosen the 2 switch mounting screws and align the switch.

3. Place the shifter lever in **N**. Repeat the check and adjust as necessary.

4. Finally check that the engine starts only in **P** or **N**, and check that the back-up lights work only in **R**.

### BAND ADJUSTMENTS

#### *All Transmissions*

The BW55 and AW55, AW70 and AW71 transmissions are equipped with a multi-disc brake (band) system which does not require any adjustment. No provision is made for band adjustment, even at overhaul.

# DRIVE AXLE

## Driveshaft and U-Joints

### REMOVAL & INSTALLATION

1. Jack up the vehicle and install safety stands.

2. Mark the relative positions of the driveshaft yokes and transmission and differential housing flanges for purposes of assembly. Remove the nuts and bolts which retain the front and rear driveshaft sections to the transmission and differential housing flanges, respectively. Remove the support bearing housing from the driveshaft tunnel, and lower the driveshaft and universal joint assembly as a unit.

3. Pry up the lock washer and remove the support bearing retaining nut. Pull off the rear section of the driveshaft with the intermediate universal joint and splined shaft of the front section. The support bearing may now be pressed off the driveshaft.

4. Remove the support from it housing.

5. Inspect the driveshaft sections for straightness. Using a dial indicator, or rolling the shafts along a flat surface, make sure that the driveshaft out-of-round does not exceed 0.010 in. (0.25mm). Do not attempt to straighten a damaged shaft. Any shaft exceeding 0.010 in. (0.25mm) out-of-round will cause substantial vibration, and must be replaces. Also, inspect the support bearing by pressing the races against each other by hand, and turning them in opposite directions. If the bearing binds at any point, it must be discarded and replaced.

6. Install the support bearing into its housing.

7. Press the support bearing and housing onto the front driveshaft section. Push the splined shaft of the front section, with the intermediate universal joint and rear driveshaft section, into the splined sleeve of the front section. Install the retaining nut and lock washer for the support bearing.

8. Taking note of the alignment marks made prior to removal, position the driveshaft and universal joint assembly to its flange connections and install but do not tighten its retaining nuts and bolts. Position the support bearing housing to the driveshaft tunnel and install the retaining nut. Tighten the nuts which retain the driveshaft sections to the transmission and differential housing flanges to a torque of 25–30 ft. lbs. (34–40 Nm).

9. Remove the safety stands and lower the vehicle. Road test the car and check for driveline vibrations and noise.

## Rear Axle Shaft

### REMOVAL & INSTALLATION BEARING AND OIL SEAL REPLACEMENT

1. Raise the vehicle and install safety stands.

2. Remove the applicable wheel and tire assembly.

3. Place a wooden block beneath the brake pedal, plug the master cylinder reservoir vent hole, and remove and plug the brake line from the caliper. Be careful not to allow any brake fluid to spill onto the disc or pads. Remove the 2 bolts which retain brake caliper to the axle housing, and lift off the caliper. Lift off the brake disc.

4. Remove the thrust washer bolts through the holes in the axle shaft flange. Using a slide hammer, remove the axle shaft, bearing and oil seal assembly. You may be able to pull out the shaft by temporarily reinstalling the brake disc and using this to grab on to while pulling out the axle shaft.

5. Using an arbor press, remove the axle shaft bearing and its locking ring from the axle shaft. Remove and discard the old oil seal.

6. Fill the space between the lips of the new oil seal with wheel bearing grease. Position the new seal on the axle shaft. Using an arbor press, install the bearing with a new locking ring, onto the axle shaft.

7. Thoroughly pack the bearing with wheel bearing grease. Install the axle shaft into the housing, rotating it so that it indexes with the differential. Install the bolts for the thrust washer and tighten to 36 ft. lbs. (50 Nm).

8. Install the brake disc. Position the brake caliper to its retainer on the axle housing and install the 2 retaining bolts. Torque the caliper retaining bolts to 45–50 ft. lbs. (61–68 Nm).

9. Unplug the brake line and connect it to the caliper. Bleed the caliper of all air trapped in the system.

10. Position the wheel and tire assembly on its lugs and hand-tighten the lug nuts. Remove the jack stands and lower the vehicle. Torque the lug nuts to 70–100 ft. lbs. (95–135 Nm).

# FRONT SUSPENSION

## MacPherson Strut

### REMOVAL & INSTALLATION

1. Remove the hub cap and loosen the lug nuts a few turns.

2. Firmly apply the parking brake and place blocks in back of the rear wheels.

3. Jack up the front of the car with a hoist or using a floor jack at the center of the front crossmember. When the wheels are 2–3 in. (50–76mm) off the ground, the car is high enough. Place

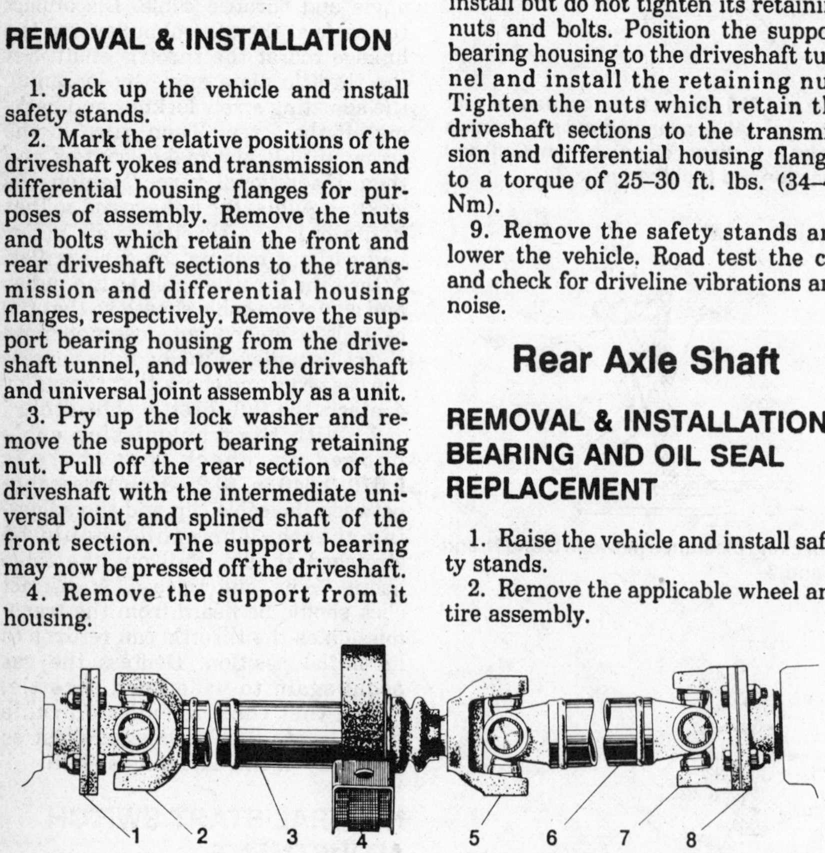


1. Flange on transmission
2. Front universal joint
3. Front section of driveshaft
4. Support bearing
5. Intermediate universal joint
6. Rear section of driveshaft
7. Rear universal joint
8. Flange on rear axle

**Driveshaft with support bearing**

jack stands beneath the front jacking points. Then, remove the floor jack from the crossmember (if used), and reposition it beneath the applicable lower control arm to provide support at the outer end. Remove the wheel and tire assembly.

4. Using a boll joint puller, disconnect the steering rod from the steering arm.

5. Disconnect the stabilizer bar at the link upper attachment.

6. Remove the bolt retaining the brake line bracket to the fender well.

7. Open the hood and remove the cover for the strut assembly upper attachment.

8. While keeping the strut from turning, loosen and remove the nut for the upper attachment.

9. Before lowering the strut assembly, wire or tie the strut to some stationary component, or use a holding fixture such as SVO 5045, to prevent the strut from traveling down too far and damaging the hydraulic brake lines. Then lower the jack supporting the lower arm and allow the strut to tilt out to about a 60 degree angle. At this angle, the top of the strut assembly should just protrude past the wheel well, allowing removal of the strut from the top.

10. Carefully lift and guide the strut assembly into its upper attachment in the spring tower. Connect the stabilizer bar to the stabilizer link. Guide the shock absorber spindle into the upper attachment and raise the jack beneath the lower control are. Install the washer and nut on top of the shock absorber spindle. While holding the spindle from turning, tighten the nut to 15–25 ft. lbs. (20–34 Nm). Install the cover.

11. Attach the brake line bracket to its mount. Tighten the nut retaining the stabilizer bar to the link. Connect the steering rod at the steering arm.

12. Install the wheel and tire assembly. Remove the jack stands and lower the car. Jounce the suspension a few times and then road test.

## OVERHAUL

**For all spring and shock absorber removal and installation procedures and any other strut overhaul procedures, please refer to "Strut Overhaul" in the Unit Repair Section.**

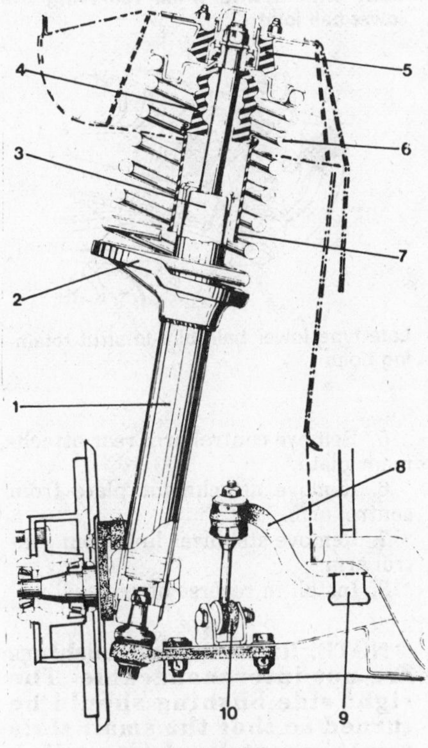


1. Strut assembly
2. Lower spring support
3. Shock absorber
4. Rubber bumper
5. Upper attachment
6. Coil spring
7. Ruber sleeve, protecting the shock absorber
8. Stabilizer bar
9. Stabilizer bar attachment
10. Stabilizer link

**Front suspension—240, 260 (DL, GL) series**

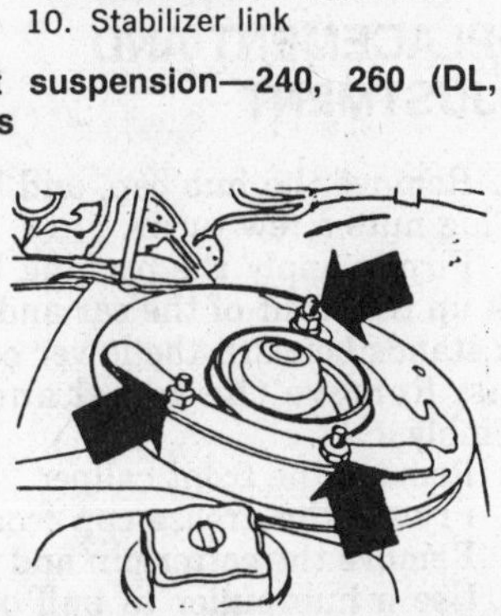

**Loosen the upper strut nuts to adjust the camber on 240, 260 (DL, GL) series**

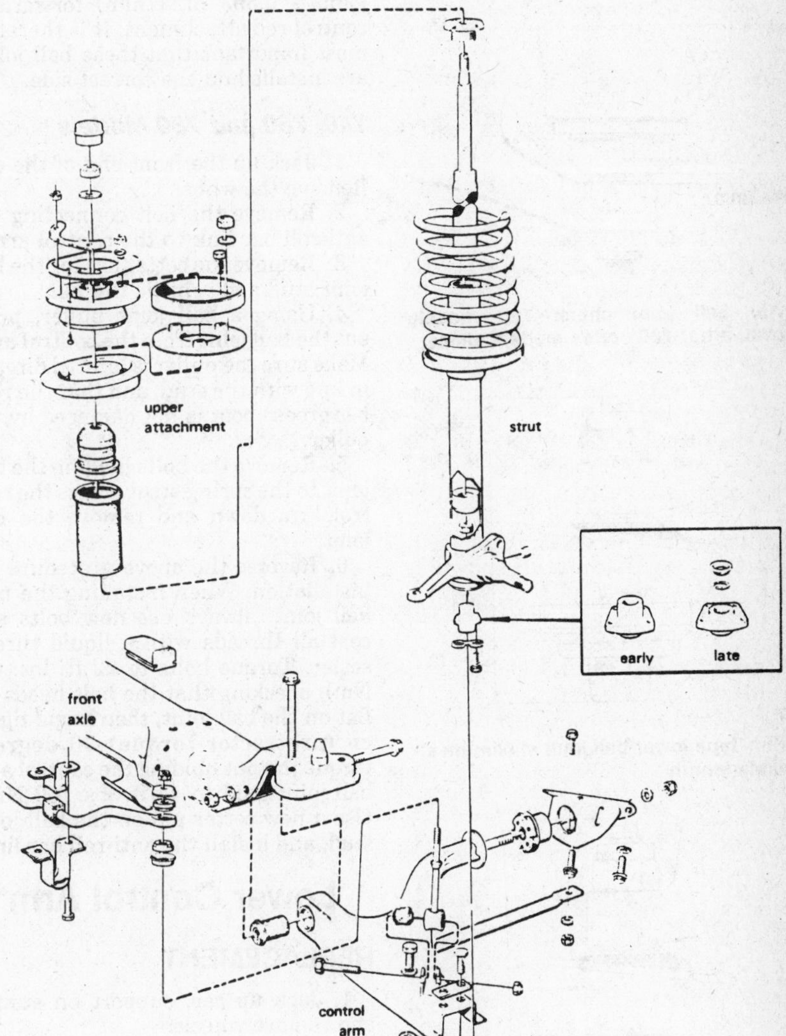


**Front suspension assembly—240 and 260 models**

## Lower Ball Joint

### INSPECTION

Maximum axial play with normally loaded front end is 0.12 in. (3mm). Maximum radial play is 0.02 in. (0.5mm).

### REMOVAL & INSTALLATION

#### *240 Models*

1. Jack up the front of the car and install jack stands beneath the front jacking attachments.
2. Remove the tire and wheel assembly.
3. Reach in between the spring coils and loosen the shock absorber cap nut a few turns.
4. Remove the 4 bolts (12mm) retaining the ball joint seat to the bottom of the strut.

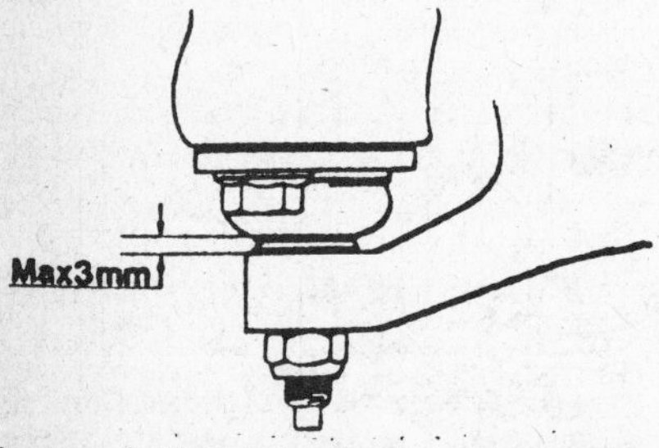


Lower ball joint check—760 models shown, other 700 series models similar

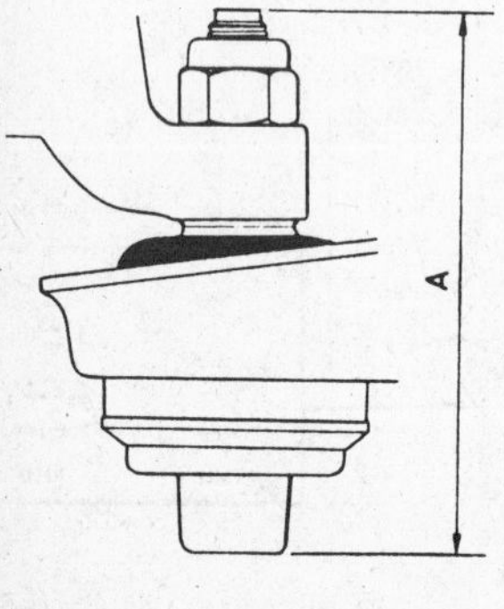


Spring-type lower ball joint maximum allowable length

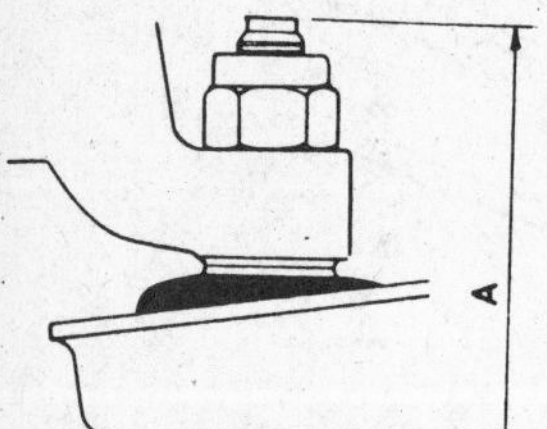

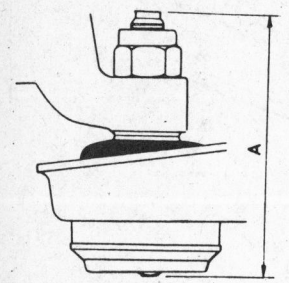


Non-spring type lower ball joint maximum allowable length

5. Remove the 3 nuts (19mm) retaining the ball joint to the lower control arm.
6. Place the ball joint and attachment assembly in a vise and remove the 19mm nut from the ball joint stud. Then, drive out the old ball joint.
7. Install the new ball joint in the attachment and tighten the stud nut to 35–50 ft. lbs. (47–68 Nm).
8. Attach the ball joint assembly to the strut. Tighten to 15–20 ft. lbs. (20–27 Nm).
9. Attach the ball joint assembly to the control arm. Tighten to 70–95 ft. lbs. (95–130 Nm).
10. Tighten the shock absorber cap nut. Install the wheel and tire. Lower the car and road-test.

**NOTE: On models with power steering, the ball joint are different for the left and right side.**

Compared to previous years, the ball joint is 0.393 in. (1mm) forward in control rod attachment. It is therefore most important that these ball joints are installed on the correct side.

#### *740, 760 and 780 Models*

1. Jack up the front end of the car. Remove the wheel.
2. Remove the bolt connecting the anti-roll bar link to the control arm.
3. Remove the cotter pin for the ball joint stud and remove the nut.
4. Using a ball joint puller, press out the ball joint from the control arm. Make sure the puller is located directly in line with the stud, and that the rubber grease boot is not damaged by the puller.
5. Remove the bolts holding the ball joint to the spring strut. Press the control arm down and remove the ball joint.
6. Reverse the above procedure for installation. When installing the new ball joint, always use new bolts and coat all threads with a liquid thread sealer. Torque bolts to 22 ft. lbs. (30 Nm), checking that the bolt heads sit flat on the ball joint, then angle-tighten (protractor-torque) 90 degrees torque the nut holding the control arm ball joint stud to 44 ft. lbs. (60 Nm). Use a new cotter pin on the ball joint stud, and install the anti-roll bar link.

## Lower Control Arm

### REPLACEMENT

1. Jack up car, support on stands and remove wheels.
2. Remove stabilizer bar.
3. Remove ball joint from control arm.
4. Remove control arm front retaining bolt.

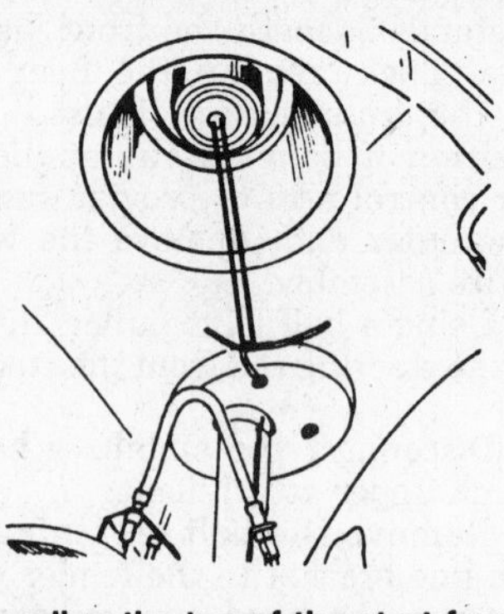

Suspending the top of the strut from the body with a wire while removing the lower ball joint

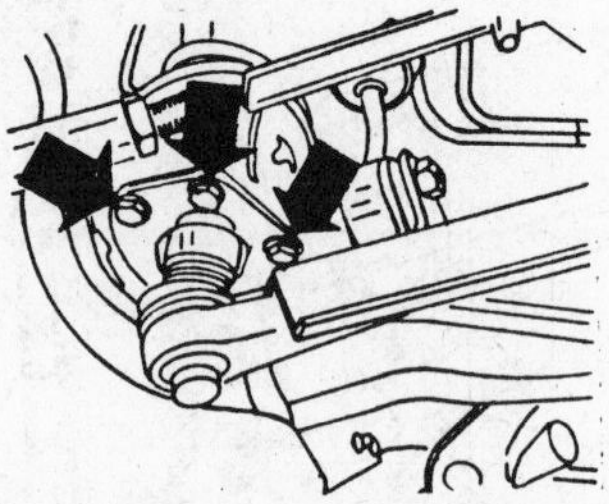

Late type lower ball joint-to-strut retaining bolts

5. Remove control arm rear attachment plate.
6. Remove attachment plate from control arm.
7. Remove stabilizer link from control arm.
8. Install in reverse of removal.

**NOTE: Right and left bushings are not interchangeable. The right side bushing should be turned so that the small slots point horizontally when installed. Torque the retaining bolt to 55 ft. lbs. (75 Nm), the rear bushing to 4 ft. lbs. and the rear attachment bolts to 30 ft. lbs. (40 Nm).**

## Front Wheel Bearings

### REPLACEMENT AND ADJUSTMENT

1. Remove the hub cap, and loosen the lug nuts a few turns.
2. Firmly apply the parking brake. Jack up the front of the car and place jack stands beneath the lower control arms. Remove the wheel and tire assembly.
3. Remove the front caliper.
4. Pry off the grease cap from the hub. Remove the cotter pin and castle nut. Use a hub puller to pull off the hub. On the 760, remove the brake disc. If the inner bearing remains

lodged on the stub axle, remove it with a puller.

5. Using a drift, remove the inner and outer bearing rings.

6. Thoroughly clean the hub, brake disc, and grease cap.

7. Press in the new inner and outer bearing rings with a drift.

8. Press grease into both bearing with a bearing packer. If one is not available, pack the bearings with as much wheel bearing grease as possible by hand. Also coat the outsides of the bearings and the outer rings pressed into the hub. Fill the recess in the hub with grease up to the smallest diameter on the outer ring for the outer bearing. Place the inner bearing in position in the hub and press its seal in with a drift. The felt ring should be thoroughly coated with light engine oil.

9. Place the hub onto the stub axle. Install the outer bearing washer, and castle nut.

10. Adjust the front wheel bearings by tightening the castle nut to 45 ft. lbs. (60 Nm) to seat the bearings. Then, back off the nut ⅓ of a turn counterclockwise. Torque the nut to 1 ft. lb. (1.5 Nm). If the nut slot does not align with the hole in the stub axle, tighten the nut until the cotter pin may be installed. Make sure that the wheel spins freely without any side play.

11. Fill the grease cap halfway with wheel bearing grease, and install it on the hub.

12. Install the front caliper.

13. Install the wheel and tire assembly. Remove the jack stand and lower the car. Tighten the lug nut to 70–100 ft. lbs. (95–135 Nm) and install the hub cap.

## Front Wheel Alignment

### ADJUSTMENT

#### *Caster and Camber*

Caster angle is fixed by suspension design and cannot be adjusted. If caster is not within specifications, check front end parts for damage and replace as necessary.

Camber angle, however, may be adjusted. At the strut upper attachment to the body, 2 of the 3 bolts holes are eccentric, allowing the upper end of the strut to tilt out or in as necessary. A special pivot lever tool SVO No. 5038, which attaches to the tops of the strut upper attachment retaining bolt threads is recommended for this job. To adjust, loosen the 3 retaining nuts, install the pivot lever tool, and adjust to specifications. After adjusting, torque the nuts to 15–25 ft. lbs. (20–34 Nm).

#### *Toe-In*

Toe in may be adjusted after performing the caster and camber adjustments. With a wheel spreader, measure the distance (X) between the rear of the right and left front tires, at spindle (hub) height, and then measure the distance (Y) between the front of the right and left front tires, also at spindle (hub) height. Subtract the front distance (Y) from the rear distance (X), and compare that to the specifications table. X – Y = toe-in. If the adjustment is not correct, loosen the locknuts on both sides of the tie rod, and rotate the tie rod itself. Toe-in is increased by turning the tie rod in the normal forward rotation of the wheels, and reduced by turning it in the opposite direction. After the final adjustment is make, torque the locknuts to 55–65 ft. lbs. (75–88 Nm), being careful not the disturb the adjustment.

# REAR SUSPENSION

## Shock Absorbers

### REMOVAL & INSTALLATION

1. Remove the hub cap and loosen the lug nuts a few turns. Place blocks in front of the front wheels. Jack up the rear of the car to unload the shock absorbers and place jack stands in front of the rear jacking points. Remove the wheel and tire assembly.

2. Remove the nuts and bolts which retain the shock absorber to its upper and lower attachments and remove the shock absorber. Make sure that the spacing sleeve, inside the axle support arm for the lower attachment, is not misplaced.

3. The damping effect of the shock absorber may be tested by securing the lower attachment in a vise and extending and compressing it. A properly operating shock absorber should off approximately 3 times as much resistance to extending the unit as compressing it. Replace the shock absorber if it does not function as above, or if it fixed rubber bushings are damaged. Replace any leaking shock absorber.

4. To install, position the shock absorber to its upper and lower attachments. Make sure that the spacing sleeve is installed inside the axle support (trailing) arm and is aligned with the lower attachment bolt hole. Install the retaining nuts and bolts, and torque to 63 ft. lbs. (85 Nm). On 240 and 760 series models, the shock fits inside the support arm.

5. Install the wheel and tire assembly. Remove the jack stands and lower the car. Tighten the lug nuts to 70–100 ft. lbs. (95–135 Nm), and install the hub cap.

## Springs

### REMOVAL & INSTALLATION

1. Remove the hub cap and loosen the lug nuts a few turns. Jack up the car and place jack stands in front of the rear jacking points. Remove the wheel and tire assembly.

2. Place a hydraulic jack beneath the rear axle housing and raise the housing sufficiently to compress the spring. Loosen the nuts for the upper and lower spring attachments.

**CAUTION**

***Due to the fact that the spring is compressed under several hundred pounds of pressure, when it is freed from its lower attachment, it will attempt to suddenly spring back to its extended position. It is therefore imperative that the axle housing be lowered with extreme care until the spring is fully extended. As an added safety measure, a chain may be attached to the lower spring coil and secured to the axle housing.***

3. Disconnect the shock absorber at its upper attachment. Carefully lower the jack and axle housing until the spring is fully extended. Remove the spring.

4. To install, position the retaining bolt and inner washer, for the upper attachment, inside the spring and then, while holding the outer washer and rubber spacer to the upper body attachment, install the spring and inner washer to the upper attachment (sandwiching the rubber spacer), and tighten the retaining bolt.

5. Raise the jack and secure the bottom of the spring to its lower attachment with the washer and retaining bolt.

6. Connect the shock absorber to its upper attachment. Install the wheel and tire assembly.

7. Remove the jack stands and lower the car. Tighten the lug nuts to 70–100 ft. lbs. (95–135 Nm) and install the hub cap.

# STEERING

## Steering Wheel

### REMOVAL & INSTALLATION

**NOTE: The use of a knock-off**

**type steering wheel puller, or the use of a hammer may damage the collapsible column and is not recommended.**

### *240 Models*

1. Disconnect the negative battery cable.
2. Remove the retaining screws for the upper half of the molded turn signal housing and lift off the housing.
3. Pry off the steering wheel impact pad.
4. Disconnect the horn plug contact.
5. Remove the steering wheel nut.
6. With the front wheels pointing straight ahead, and the steering wheel centered, install a steering wheel puller. Use a universal type puller, such as SVO 2263.
7. To install, make sure that the front wheels are pointing straight ahead, then place the centered steering wheel on the column with the plug contact to the left. Install the nut and tighten to 20–30 ft. lbs. (27–40 Nm).
8. Connect the horn plug contact and install the impact pad.
9. Install the upper turn signal housing half.
10. Connect the negative battery cable and test the operation of the horn.

### *740, 760 and 780 Models*

1. Disconnect the negative battery cable.
2. Gently pry up the lower edge of the steering wheel center pad and remove it.
3. Unscrew the steering wheel center nut, and pull off the wheel.
4. When installing, torque the center nut to 26 ft. lbs. (35 Nm).

# Turn Signal Switch

## REMOVAL & INSTALLATION

1. Disconnect the negative battery cable.
2. Remove the steering wheel.
3. Remove the upper and lower steering column casings.
4. Unscrew the turn signal switch/lever assembly.
5. Disconnect the wires from the switch.
6. Installation is the reverse of the removal procedure.

# Ignition Lock/Switch

## REPLACEMENT

### *240 Models*

1. Remove noise insulation panel and center side panel.
2. Disconnect the wires from the switch.
3. Pry out the switch with a suitable tool.
4. Install in reverse of removal.

### *740, 760 and 780 Models*

1. Remove the sound proofing under the instrument panel.
2. Disconnect the connector from the ignition switch.
3. Remove the upper steering column casing and the panel around the ignition switch.
4. Loosen the mounting screw for the switch.
5. Insert the key and turn it to the start position. Through the hole beneath the holder, press in the catch and remove the ignition switch.
6. To install, insert the key and turn and depress the locking tab. Remove the key. Position the switch and release the locking tab by inserting the key. Tighten the mounting screw and reverse the rest of the removal procedure. Test the switch.

# Manual Steering Gear

## REMOVAL & INSTALLATION

1. Disconnect the negative battery cable. Remove the lock bolt and nut from the column flange (at the steering gear). Bend apart the flange slightly with a suitable tool.
2. Jack up the front end. The stands should be positioned at the jack supports. Remove the front wheels.
3. Disconnect the steering rods from the steering arms, using a ball joint puller.
4. Remove the splash guard.
5. Disconnect the steering gear from the front axle member.
6. Disconnect the steering gear from the steering gear flange. Remove steering gear.
7. Install rubber spacers and plates for the steering gear attachment points.
8. Position the steering gear, and guide the pinion shaft into the steering shaft flange. The recess on the pinion shaft should be aligned towards the lock bolt opening in the flange.
9. Attach the steering gear to the front axle member. Check that the U-bolts are aligned in the plate slots. Install flat washers and nuts.
10. Install the splash guard.
11. Connect the steering rods to the steering arms.
12. Install the front wheels and lower the vehicle.
13. Install the lock bolt for the steering shaft flange.

## PITMAN ARM ADJUSTMENT

On a steering gear with a marked pitman arm and pitman arm shaft (on the steering gear), make sure that the marks align.

On a steering gear without the marks, lift up the front of the vehicle so that the front wheels are free. Turn the steering wheel to its center position (count the number of turns). Lower the vehicle. If the vehicle is correctly loaded, the wheels should now point straight forward. If the wheels do not, remove the pitman arm from the shaft with a puller. Then set the left wheel straight ahead should be in it center position. Tighten the pitman arm nut to 100–120 ft. lbs. (135–163 Nm).

# Power Steering Gear

## REMOVAL & INSTALLATION

1. Disconnect the negative battery cable. Loosen the steering column shaft flange from the pinion shaft. Remove the lock bolt and bend apart the flange slightly.
2. Jack up the front end. Position jack stands at the front jack supports. Remove the front wheels.
3. Disconnect the steering rods from the steering arms, with a ball joint puller.
4. Remove the splash guard.
5. Disconnect the hoses at the steering gear. Install protective plugs in the hose connections.
6. Remove the steering gear from the front axle member.
7. Remove the steering gear by pulling down until it is free from the steering shaft flange. On the 740 and 760 GLE, disconnect the lower steering shaft from the steering gear by removing the snaprings from the clamps. Loosen the upper clamp bolt, remove the lower clamp bolt and slide the joint up on the shaft. Then remove the unit on the left side of the vehicle.
8. Position the steering gear and attach the pinion shaft to the steering shaft flange.
9. Install right side U-bolt and bracket, but do NOT tighten the nuts.
10. Install left side retaining bolts, and tighten. Tighten the U-bolt nuts.
11. Connect the steering rods to the steering arms.
12. Install the lock bolt on the steering column flange.
13. Connect the return and pressure hoses to the steering gear.

# Power Steering Pump

## REMOVAL & INSTALLATION

1. Disconnect the negative battery

cable. Remove all dirt and grease from around the suction line connections and from around the delivery line of the pump housing.

2. Using a container to catch any power steering fluid that might run out, disconnect the lines, and plug them to prevent dirt from entering the system.

3. Remove the tensioning bolt and the attaching bolts.

4. Clear the pump free of the fan belt and lift it out.

5. If a new pump is to be used, the old brackets, fitting, and pulley must be transferred from the old unit. The pulley may be removed with a puller, and pressed on the pump shaft with a press tool. Under no circumstances should the pulley be hammered on, as this will damage the pump bearings.

6. To install, place the pump in position and loosely fit the attaching bolts. Connect the lines to the pump with new seals.

7. Place the fan belt onto the pulley and adjust the fan belt tension.

8. Tighten the tensioning bolt and the attaching bolts.

9. Fill the reservoir with Type A automatic transmission fluid and bleed the system.

### POWER STEERING SYSTEM BLEEDING

1. Fill the reservoir up to the edge with Automatic Transmission Fluid Type A. Raise the front wheels off the ground, and install safety stands. Place the transmission in neutral and apply the parking brake.

2. Keeping a can of ATF Type A within easy reach, start the engine and fill the reservoir as the level drops.

3. When the reservoir level has stopped dropping, slowly turn the steering wheel from lock to lock several reservoir if necessary.

4. Locate the bleeder screw on the power steering gear. Open the bleeder screw ½–1 turn, and close it when oil starts flowing out.

5. Continue to turn the steering wheel slowly until the fluid in the reservoir is free of air bubbles.

6. Stop the engine and observe the oil level in the reservoir. If the oil level rises more than ¼ in. past the level mark, air still remains the system. Continue bleeding until the level rise is correct.

7. Remove the safety stands and lower the car.

## Tie Rod Ends

### REPLACEMENT

The ball joints of the tie rod may be replaced individually. After the ball joint is disconnected, the locknut on the tie rod is loosened and the clamp bolt released. The ball joint is then screwed out of the tie rod, taking note of the number of turns. The new ball joint is screwed in the same number of turns, and the clamp bolt and locknut tightened. The ball joint is locked to the rod with 55–65 ft. lbs. (75–88 Nm) of torque. The new ball joint is pressed into its connection and the ball stud not tightened to 23–27 ft. lbs. (31–37 Nm).

After reconditioning of the rods and joints, the wheel alignment must be adjusted.

# BRAKES

**For all brake system repair and adjustment procedures not detailed below, please refer to "Brakes" in the Unit Repair Section.**

## Master Cylinder

### REMOVAL & INSTALLATION

1. Disconnect the negative battery cable. To prevent brake fluid form spilling onto and damaging the paint, place a protective cover over the fender apron, and rags beneath the master cylinder.

2. Disconnect and plug the brake lines from the master cylinder.

3. Remove the nuts which retain the master cylinder and reservoir assembly to the vacuum booster, and lift the assembly forward, being careful not to spill any fluid on the fender. Empty out and discard the brake fluid.

**CAUTION**

***Do not depress the brake pedal while the master cylinder is removed.***

4. In order for the master cylinder to function properly when installed to the vacuum booster, the adjusting nut for the thrust rod of the booster must not prevent the primary piston of the master cylinder from returning to its resting position. A clearance (C) of 0.004–0.04 in. (0.1–1mm) is required between the thrust rod and primary piston with the master cylinder installed. The clearance may be adjusted by rotating the adjusting nut for the booster thrust rod in the required direction. To determine what the clearance (C) will be when the master cylinder and booster are connected, first measure the distance (A) between the face of the attaching flange and the center of the primary piston on the master cylinder, then measure the distance (B) that the thrust rod protrudes from the fixed surface of the booster (making sure that the thrust rod is depressed fully with a partial vacuum existing in the booster). When measurement is subtracted from measurement (A), clearance (C) should be obtained. If not, adjust the length of the thrust rod by turning the adjusting screw to suit. After the final adjustment is obtained apply a few drops of locking compound, such as Loctite®, to the adjusting nut.

5. Position the master cylinder ana reservoir assembly onto the studs for the booster, and install the washers and nuts. Tighten the nuts to 17 ft. lbs. (23 Nm).

6. Remove the plugs and connect the brake lines.

7. Bleed the entire brake system.

## Proportioning Valve

### REPLACEMENT

Sophisticated pressure testing equipment is required to troubleshoot the dual hydraulic system in order to determine if the proportioning valve(s) are in need of replacement. However, if the car is demonstration signs of rear wheel lock-up under moderate to heavy braking pressure, and other variables such as tire pressure, tread depth, etc., have been ruled out, the valve(s) may be at fault. The valves are not rebuildable, and must be replaced as a unit.

1. Unscrew, disconnect and plug the brake pipe from the master cylinder, at the valve connection.

2. Slacken the connection for the flexible brake hose to the rear wheel a maximum of ¼ turn.

3. Remove the bolt(s) which retain the valve to the underbody, and unscrew the valve from the rear brake hose.

4. To install the valve, place a new seal on it, and screw the valve onto the rear brake hose and hand tighten. Secure the valve to the underbody with the retaining bolt(s).

5. Connect the brake pipe and tighten both connections, making sure that there is no tension on the flexible rear hose.

6. Bleed the brake system.

## Brake System Warning Valve

### VALVE RESETTING

1. Disconnect the plug contact and

screw out the warning switch so that the pistons inside the valve may return to their normal position.

2. Repair and bleed the faulty hydraulic circuit.

3. Screw in the warning switch and tighten it to a torque of 10–14 ft. lbs. (14–19 Nm). Connect the plug contact.

### REMOVAL & INSTALLATION

1. Placing a rag beneath the valve to catch the brake fluid, loosen the pipe connections, and disconnect the brake lines. Disconnect the electrical plug contact, and lift out the valve.

2. connect the new warning valve in the reverse order of removal, and connect the plug contact.

3. Bleed the entire brake system.

## Power Brake Booster

### REMOVAL & INSTALLATION

1. Disconnect the negative battery cable.

2. Remove the master cylinder to power booster retaining bolts and position the master cylinder to one side. Be careful not to damage the brake lines.

3. Disconnect the vacuum assist hose, from the booster.

4. From inside the vehicle, disconnect the brake pedal rod.

5. Remove the power booster retaining bolts. Remove the power booster from the vehicle.

6. Installation is the reverse of the removal procedure.

## Disc Brake Pads

### REMOVAL & INSTALLATION

#### *240 and 260 Models*

**NOTE: The brake pads should be replaced when there is approximately 0.12 in. (3mm) of the lining left. The linings should under no circumstances be less than 0.06 in. (1.5mm).**

#### FRONT BRAKES

#### ATE Type

1. Raise the vehicle and support safely.

2. Mark the position of the wheels on the hubs and remove the front wheels.

3. Remove the retaining pins using a punch.

4. Remove the retaining spring.

5. Remove the brake pads and identify the pads if they are to be reused.

6. To install, compress the pistons using a pair of pliers of special tool 2809 or equivalent.

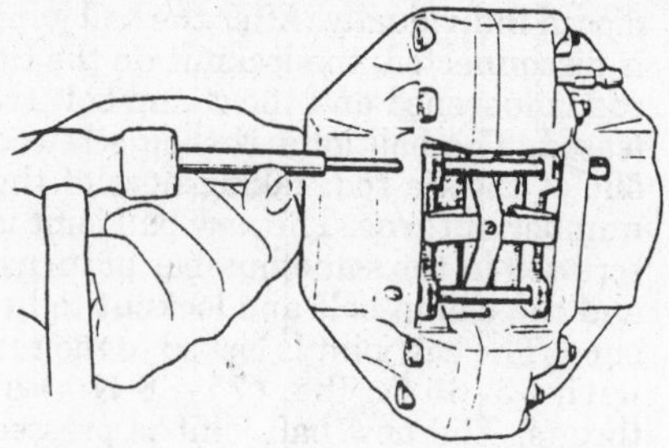

Retaining pin removal—200 series ATE type shown, Girling type similar

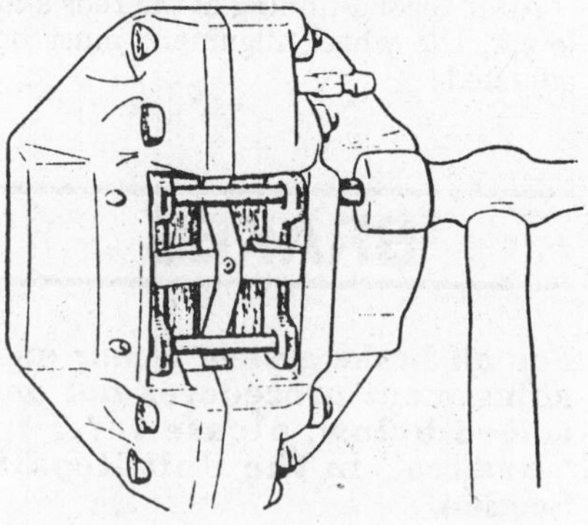

Retaining pin installation—200 series ATE type shown, Girling type similar

7. Install the brake pads.

8. Install 1 retaining pin and a new retaining spring.

9. Install the other retaining pin.

10. Check the brake fluid level and pump the brake pedal.

11. Install the front wheel assemblies and lower the vehicle.

**CAUTION**

***Check the brake pedal operation prior to driving the vehicle.***

#### Girling Type

1. Raise the vehicle and support safely.

2. Mark the position of the wheels on the hubs and remove the front wheels.

3. Remove the spring clips.

4. Remove the retaining pins.

5. Remove the retaining springs.

6. Remove the brake pads and identify the pads if they are to be reused.

7. To install, compress the pistons using a pair of pliers of special tool 2809 or equivalent.

8. Install the brake pads.

9. Install the retaining springs.

10. Install the retaining pins.

11. Install the spring clips.

12. Check the brake fluid level and pump the brake pedal.

13. Install the front wheel assemblies and lower the vehicle.

**CAUTION**

***Check the brake pedal operation prior to driving the vehicle.***

#### REAR BRAKES

#### ATE Type

1. Raise the vehicle and support safely.

2. Mark the position of the wheels on the hubs and remove the rear wheels.

3. Remove the retaining pins using a punch.

4. Remove the retaining spring.

5. Remove the brake pads and identify the pads if they are to be reused.

6. To install, compress the pistons using a pair of pliers of special tool 2809 or equivalent.

7. Install the brake pads.

8. Install 1 retaining pin and a new retaining spring.

9. Install the other retaining pin.

10. Check the brake fluid level and pump the brake pedal.

11. Install the rear wheel assemblies and lower the vehicle.

**CAUTION**

***Check the brake pedal operation prior to driving the vehicle.***

#### Girling Type

1. Raise the vehicle and support safely.

2. Mark the position of the wheels on the hubs and remove the rear wheels.

3. Remove the retaining spring.

4. Remove the spring clips.

5. Remove the retaining pins.

6. Remove the retaining springs.

7. Remove the brake pads and identify the pads if they are to be reused.

8. Remove any shims or damper washers fitted between the pads and the caliper pistons.

9. To install, compress the pistons using a pair of pliers of special tool 2809 or equivalent.

10. Install any shims or damper washers.

11. Install the brake pads.

12. Install the springs.

13. Install the retaining pins.

14. Install the spring clips.

15. Install the retaining spring.

**NOTE: If damper washers have been fitted, make sure that the large flat side faces the piston. A feeler gauge can be used to fit the washers.**

16. Check the brake fluid level and pump the brake pedal.

17. Install the rear wheel assemblies and lower the vehicle.

## CAUTION

***Check the brake pedal operation prior to driving the vehicle.***

### *740 and 760 Models*

**NOTE: The brake pads should be replaced when there is approximately 0.12 in. (3mm) of the lining left. The linings should under no circumstances be less than 0.06 in. (1.5mm).**

#### FRONT BRAKES

1. Raise the vehicle and support safely.
2. Mark the position of the wheels on the hubs and remove the front wheels.
3. Remove the bolt from the lower guide pin. On Girling type caliper, unscrew the upper bolt a few turns.
4. Swing up the piston housing and remove the pads.

**NOTE: Do not depress the brake pedal while the brake pads are not in position. Doing so could damage the pistons.**

5. To install, press the pistons in using a pair of adjustable pliers. Take care not to damage the rubber dust cap.

**NOTE: When the pistons are being pressed in, the level of the fluid in the reservoir will rise and the fluid may overflow.**

6. Fit the piston housing into the upper guide pin. Check that the rubber gaiter is fitted properly onto the mounting.
7. Install the brake pads.
8. Swing the caliper down and tighten the new lower guide pin bolt to 25 ft. lbs. (34 Nm). Check that the springs on the pads are correctly positioned.
9. Check the brake fluid level and pump the brake pedal.
10. Install the front wheel assemblies and lower the vehicle.

## CAUTION

***Check the brake pedal operation prior to driving the vehicle.***

#### REAR BRAKES

1. Raise the vehicle and support safely.
2. Mark the position of the wheels on the hubs and remove the rear wheels.
3. Remove the retaining pins using a punch.
4. Remove the retaining spring.
5. Remove the brake pads and identify the pads if they are to be reused.
6. To install, compress the pistons using a pair of pliers of special tool 2809 or equivalent.
7. Install the brake pads.
8. Install 1 retaining pin and a new retaining spring.
9. Install the other retaining pin.
10. Check the brake fluid level and pump the brake pedal.
11. Install the rear wheel assemblies and lower the vehicle.

## CAUTION

***Check the brake pedal operation prior to driving the vehicle.***

# Parking Brake Cable

## ADJUSTMENT

1. Remove the rear ashtray (between the front seat backs) or the rear of the center console on the 740 and 760.
2. Tighten the parking brake cable adjusting screw so that the brake is fully applied when pulled up 2–3 notches.
3. If one cable is stretched more than the other, they can be individually adjusted by removing the parking brake cover (2 screws) and turning the individual cable adjusting nut at the front of each yoke pivot.
4. Install the ashtray, and parking brake cover (if equipped).

## REMOVAL & INSTALLATION

### *240 Models*

1. Apply the parking brake. Remove the hub caps for the rear wheels and loosen the lug nuts a few turns.
2. Place blocks in front of the front wheels. Jack up the rearend and place jackstands beneath the rear axle. Remove the wheel and tire assembly. Release the parking brake.
3. Remove the bolt and the wheel from the pulley.
4. Remove the rubber cover for the front attachment of the cable sleeve and nut, as well as the attachment for the rubber suspension ring on the frame. Remove the cable from the other side of the attachment in the same manner.
5. Hold the return spring in position. Pry up the lock and remove the lock pin so that the cable releases form the lever.
6. Remove the return spring with washers. Loosen the nut for the rear attachment of the cable sleeve. Lift the cable forward after loosening both side of the attachments, and remove it.
7. To install, first adjust the rear brake shoes of the parking brake by removing the rear ashtray between the front seat backs.
8. Tighten the parking brake cable adjusting screw so that the brake is fully applied when pulled up 2–3 notches.
9. If one cable is stretched more than the other, they can be individually adjusted by removing the parking brake cover (2 screws) and turning the individual cable adjusting nut at the front of each yoke pivot.
10. Install the ashtray, and parking brake cover (if equipped).
11. Install new rubber cable guides for the cable suspension. Place the cable in position in the rear attachment and tighten the nut. Install the washers and return spring. Oil the lock pin and install it, together with the cable, on the lever. Install the attachment and rubber cable guide on the frame.
12. Install the cable in the same manner on the side of the vehicle.
13. Place the cable sleeve in position in the front attachments and install the rubber covers.
14. Lubricate and install the pulley on the pull rod. Adjust the pulley so that the parking brake is fully engaged with the lever at the 3rd or 4th notch.
15. Install the wheel and tire assemblies. Remove the jack stands and lower the vehicle. Tighten the lug nut to 70–100 ft. lbs. (95–135 Nm) and install the hub caps.

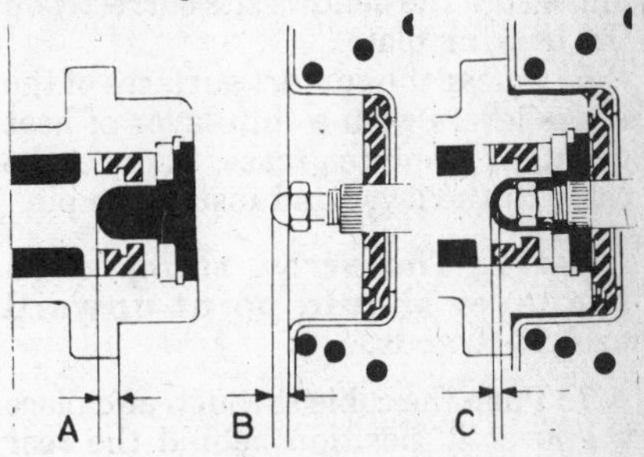


Adjusting thrust rod

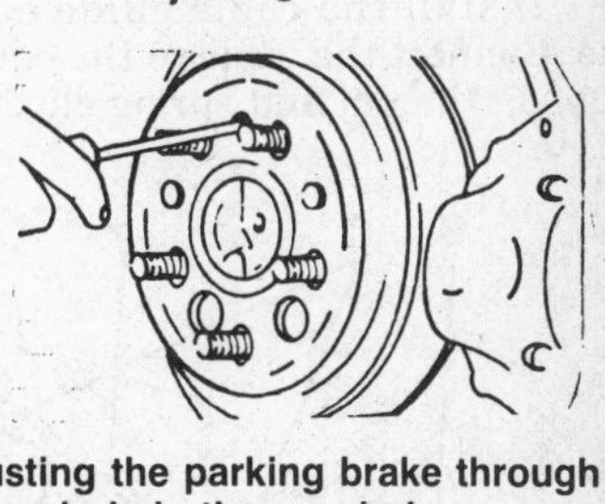

Adjusting the parking brake through the access hole in the rear hub

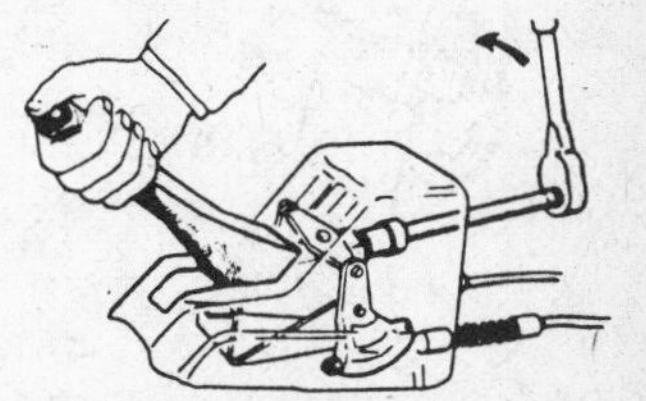

**Adjust the parking brake if it is not fully applied after pulling the lever 10–11 notches. After adjusting, good braking power should be obtained after pulling the lever 2–3 notches**

### *740, 760 and 780 Models*

The 700 series parking brake system employs 2 cable, a short one on the right hand side and long one on the left.

#### SHORT CABLE, RIGHT SIDE

1. Jack up the rear of the car and safely support it with jackstands.
2. Remove the right brake caliper rear wheel. Remove the right brake caliper and hang it from the coil spring with a wire. Remove the brake disc. Unhook the rear return spring and remove the brake shoes.
3. Push out the pin holding the cable to the brake lever. Remove the rubber bellows (boot) from the backing plate, and remove the bellows from the cable.
4. Remove the spring clip, pin and cable from the back of the differential housing. Remove the cable guide on the differential by removing the top bolt from the housing cover. Remove the cable.
5. Install the cable guide on the new cable. Check the rubber bellows for wear or damage and replace if necessary. Install the bellows and position it through the hole in the backing plate. Make sure the bellows sits correctly on the backing plate.
6. Smear the contact surfaces of the brake levers with a thin layer of heat resistant graphite grease. Connect the cable to the lever and install the pin.

**NOTE: The arrow stamped on the lever should point upward and outwards.**

7. Push the cable through and place the lever in position behind the rear axle flange.
8. Install the cable guide on the axle. Connect the cable to the equalizer using the pin and spring clip.
9. Install the brake shoes and rear return spring. Install the brake disc and caliper. Use new bolts. and torque to 43 ft. lbs. (58 Nm). Make sure the disc rotates freely. Adjust the parking brake. Install the wheel and lower the car.

#### LONG CABLE, LEFT SIDE

1. Remove the center console.
2. Slacken the parking brake adjusting screw. Remove the cable lock ring and remove the cable. Pull out the cable from the spring sleeve.
3. Jack up the rear end of the car and safely support it with jackstands. Remove the left rear wheel.
4. Remove the left rear brake caliper and hang it from the coil spring with a piece of wire. Remove the brake disc and rear return spring. Remove the brake shoes.
5. Push out the pin holding the cable to the lever. Remove the rubber bellows from the backing plate and remove the bellows from the cable.
6. Pull out the cable from the backing plate and the equalizer on top of the rear axle.
7. Remove the cable clamp on the sub-frame (above the driveshaft) and the cable.
8. Install the new cable through the grommet in the floor; check that the grommet sits correctly. Clamp the cable to the sub-frame.
9. Smear the contact surfaces of the brake levers with a thin layer of heat resistant graphite grease. Connect the cable to the lever and install the pin.

**NOTE: The arrow stamped on the lever should point upward and outwards.**

10. Push the cable through and place the lever in position behind the rear axle flange.
11. Install the cable guide on the axle. Connect the cable to the equalizer using the pin and spring clip.
12. Install the brake shoes and rear return spring. Install the brake disc and caliper. Use new bolts. and torque to 43 ft. lbs. (58 Nm). Make sure the disc rotates freely. Adjust the parking brake. Install the wheel and lower the car.

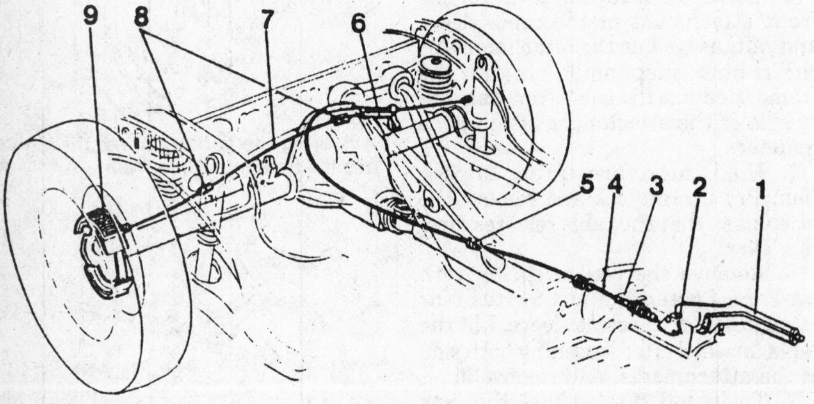


1 Lever
2 Bearing pin
3 Adjustment mechanism
4 Cable
5 Rubber covered clamp
6 Mounting
7 Cable
8 Guides
9 Brake shoe

**Parking brake cable assembly—760 models**

# CHASSIS ELECTRICAL

## Blower Motor

### REMOVAL & INSTALLATION

### *240 Models*

#### STANDARD HEATING SYSTEM

1. Disconnect the negative battery cable. Remove the heater unit.
2. Place the unit on its side with the control valve facing upward. Remove the spring clips and separate the housing halves.
3. Lift out the old fan motor and replace it with a new unit, making sure that the support leg without the "foot" points to the output for the defroster channel.
4. Assemble the heater housing halves with new spring clips, and seal the joint without clips with soft sealing compound.
5. Install the heater unit.

#### COMBINATION HEATER/ AIR CONDITIONER SYSTEM

In order to remove the blower motor, both the right and left blower wheels must first be removed. The heater unit does not have to be removed.

1. Disconnect the negative battery cable.
2. Lift the carpet and remove the central unit side panels.
3. Remove the retaining screws for the control panel and move the panel as for back on the transmission tunnel as the electrical cables will permit.
4. Remove the attaching screws for the rear seat heater ducts and disconnect the ducts from the central unit.
5. Remove the instrument cluster.
6. Remove the glovebox by unscrewing the 4 attaching screws, removing the glovebox door stop, and disconnecting the wires from the glovebox courtesy light. Remove the molded dashboard padding from beneath the glovebox.
7. Disconnect the vacuum hoses to the left and right defroster nozzle vac-

uum motors, then remove the nozzles and the left and right air ducts.

8. Remove the air hoses between the left and right inside air vents.

9. Remove the clamps on the central unit outer ends, and remove the ends.

10. Pry off the locking retainer for the turbines (blower wheels), and remove both left and right blower wheels.

11. Position the heater control valve capillary tube to one side.

12. Remove the left inner end (blower housing) from the central unit.

13. Unscrew the 3 retaining screws and remove the fan motor retainer.

14. Disconnect the plug contact from the fan motor control panel. Release the tabs of electric cables from the plug contact, and, removing the rubber grommet, pull the electrical cables down through the central unit right opening.

15. Remove the fan motor from the left opening.

16. Reverse the above procedure to install.

#### *740, 760 and 780 Models*

1. Disconnect the negative battery cable. Remove the panel beneath the glove compartment.

2. Unfasten the screws securing the fan motor, and lower the motor. Disconnect the hose for air cooling on the motor, and disconnect the wiring.

3. Remove the motor and fan.

4. To install, reconnect the wiring to the fan motor. Spread a sealer around the mounting face of the fan mounting flange, and install the fan motor. Reconnect the hose for cooling, and check fan operation. Reinstall the panel beneath the glove compartment.

## Heater Core

### REMOVAL & INSTALLATION

#### *240 Models*

##### STANDARD HEATING SYSTEM

1. Disconnect the negative battery cable. Remove the heater unit.

2. Place the unit on its side with the control valve facing upward. Remove the spring clips and separate the housing halves.

3. Disconnect the capillary tube from the heater core and then lift out the core.

4. Reverse the above procedure to install, being careful to transfer the foam plastic packing to the new heater core, and to install the fragile capillary tube carefully on the core.

##### COMBINATION HEATER/ AIR CONDITIONER SYSTEM

**CAUTION**

***Do not disconnect the refrigerant lines from the air conditioning system. These lines carry a dangerous refrigerant, the gas R-12.***

1. Disconnect the negative battery cable. Remove the combination heater-air conditioner unit.

2. Remove the left outer end of the central unit. Remove the locking retainer and the turbine (blower wheel).

3. Remove the 2 retaining screws for the left transmission tunnel bracket.

4. Remove the lockring for the left intake shutter shaft.

5. Remove the 3 retaining screws and lift off the inner end.

6. Remove the 3 retaining screws for the fan motor retainer.

7. Disconnect the heater hoses at the heater core.

8. Remove the clamps which retain the central unit halves together, lift off the left half, and remove the heater core.

9. Reverse the above procedure to install, taking care to transfer the foam plastic packing to the new heater core.

#### *740, 760 and 780 Models*

1. Disconnect the negative battery cable.

2. Pinch the hoses to the heater core near the firewall in the engine compartment. Use locking pliers. Make sure the hoses are pinched sufficiently so that the hose is completely blocked off. Remove the hose clamps on the engine compartment side of the hoses (close to the firewall).

3. Press down the clip under the ashtray and pull the tray out. Remove the cigarette lighter and the storage compartment.

4. Remove the engine console around the shift lever and parking brake. Unplug the connector.

5. Remove the panel beneath the driver's side dashboard, and remove the air duct to the steering column outlet.

6. Pull down the driver's side floor mat and remove the front and rear edge side panel screws. Remove the panels.

7. On the passenger's side, remove the 3 clips that fasten the panel beneath the glove compartment and remove the panel. Remove the glove compartment and its lighting.

8. Pull down the floor mat on the right side and remove the front and rear edge side panel screws.

9. Remove the radio compartment by pressing forward on the inner wall and removing the screw.

10. Remove the screws inside the center console and remove the side panel screws and the panels.

11. Remove the panel around the heater control. Remove the radio compartment console and remove the control panel. Free the central electrical unit and remove the mounting.

12. Remove the center panel vent, and the screw holding the distribution unit. Mark all air ducts to the panel vents and to the distribution unit with tape for later installation, and remove the ducts.

13. Remove the vacuum hoses from the vacuum motors.

14. Remove the distribution unit. Remove the heater core retaining clips and remove the heater core.

15. To reinstall, reverse the above procedure taking note of the following vacuum hose connections: On climate unit-equipped cars, connect the red hose to the upper shutter for the panel vents, and the light brown hose to the lower shutter. Connect the yellow and blue hoses to the floor/defrost shutter, the yellow to the lower one. On automatic climate control-equipped cars, connect the red hose to the upper shutter for the panel vent, and the blue hose to the defrost vent. Connect the light brown hose to the lower shutter for the panel unit.

## Radio

### REMOVAL & INSTALLATION

1. Disconnect the negative battery cable.

2. Remove the radio control knobs by pulling them straight out. Remove the control shaft retaining nuts.

3. Disconnect the speaker wires, the power lean (either at the fuse box or the inline fuse connection), and the antenna cable from its jack on the radio.

4. Remove the hardware which attaches the radio to its mounting (support) bracket(s), and slide it back and down from the dash.

5. Reverse the above procedure to install.

## Windshield Wiper Motor

### REMOVAL & INSTALLATION

#### *240 Models*

1. Disconnect the negative battery cable.

2. Disconnect the drive link from the wiper motor lever by unsnapping the locking tab underneath the dashboard.

3. Open the hood and disconnect the plug contact from the motor, located on the firewall.
4. Remove the 3 attaching screws and lift out the motor.
5. Reverse the above procedure to install, taking care to transfer the rubber seal, rubber damper, and spacer sleeves to the new motor.

#### 740, 760 and 780 Models

1. Disconnect the negative battery cable. Remove the wiper arms.
2. Lift up the hood to its uppermost position by pushing the catch on the hood hinges.
3. Remove the plastic clips and screw securing the wiper mechanism cover plate. Remove the cover plate by lifting it upwards and forwards. Close the hood.
4. Remove the cover below the windshield.
5. Unbolt the motor from its mount. Disconnect the motor wires at the connectors.
6. Installation is the reverse of removal.

## Tailgate Window Wiper Motor

### REMOVAL & INSTALLATION

1. Disconnect the negative battery cable.
2. Remove the upholstered finish panel on the inside of the tailgate.
3. Remove the screws which retain the reinforcing bracket beneath the wiper motor.
4. disconnect the wiper link arm. Bend the reinforcing bracket to one side and lower the wiper motor until it is clear of the bracket.
5. Disconnect the electrical wires from the motor and remove the motor.
6. Reverse the above procedure to install.

## Instrument Cluster

### REMOVAL & INSTALLATION

#### 1983–85 240 Models

A voltage stabilizer feeds a 10V current to both the temperature and the fuel gauges. Electrical malfunctions in these gauges must be checked with an ohmmeter, not a 12V test light. If malfunctions occur simultaneously in all 3 of the gauges that are fed by the stabilizer, the stabilizer itself is probably malfunctioning. When replacing the voltage stabilizer, the new unit must fit in the same position as the old one. If the stabilizer is not located correctly in the dash, the voltage output may be altered.

1. Disconnect the negative battery cable.
2. Remove the molded plastic casings from the steering column.
3. Remove the bracket retaining screw and lower the bracket toward the steering column.
4. Remove the cluster attaching screws.
5. Disconnect the speedometer cable.
6. Tilt the cluster out of its snap fitting and disconnect the plug contact. On vehicles equipped with a tachometer, disconnect the tachometer sending wire.
7. Lift the cluster out of the dashboard.
8. Reverse the above procedure to install.

#### 1986–90 240 Models and 740, 760 and 780 Models

1. Disconnect the negative battery cable. Remove the soundproofing above the foot pedals.
2. Remove the 2 catches and screws holding the panel.
3. Press the instrument panel forwards. Remove the panel from the dash.
4. Disconnect the connectors, and remove the instrument panel completely.

## Fuses

### LOCATION

On 240 series the fuse box is located beneath a protective cover, below the dashboard, in front of the driver's door. On the 740, 760 and 780 the fuses are located under a plastic panel in the center console, behind the ashtray.

On electronic fuel injected models, an additional fuse box is located in the engine compartment on the left wheel well. It houses a single fuse protecting the electrical fuel pump.

# Unit Repair Sections

# 20 Tools and Equipment

In addition to the normal assortment of screwdrivers and pliers, automotive service work requires an investment in wrenches, sockets and the handles needed to drive them, and various measuring tools such as torque wrenches and feeler gauges.

The best approach to gathering the required equipment is to proceed slowly, buying high-quality tools as they are needed. An initial investment should be made in a set of quality wrenches, ranging in size from ¼ inch to one inch, if your car has standard bolts, or from 5mm to 19mm if your car has metric fasteners. High quality forged wrenches are available in three styles; open end, box end, and combination open/box end. The combination tools are generally the most desirable as a starter set; the wrenches shown in the illustration are of the combination type.

**NOTE: Many later model American cars use both metric and standard nuts and bolts.**

The other set of tools inevitably required is a ratchet handle and socket set. This set should have the same size range as your wrench set. The ratchet, extension, and flex drives fro the sockets are available in many sizes; it is advisable to choose a ⅜ inch drive set initially. One break in the inch/metric sizing war is that metric-sized sockets sold in the U.S. have inch-sized drive (¼, ⅜, ½, etc.). Sockets are available in six and twelve point versions; six point types are generally cheaper and are a good choice for a first set.

The choice of a drive handle for the sockets should be made with some care. If this is your first set, take the plunge and invest in a flexhead ratchet; it will get into many places otherwise accessible only through a long chain of universal joints, extensions and adapters. An alternative is a flex handle; such a tool is shown in the illustration, below the ratchet handle. In addition to the range of sockets mentioned, a rubber-lined spark plug socket should be purchased. Spark plugs have either a 13⁄16 or a ⅝ inch hex; get the correct socket for the plugs in your car.

The most important thing to consider when purchasing hand tools is quality. Don't be misled by the low cost of "bargain" tools. Forged wrenches, tempered screwdriver blades, and fine tooth ratchets are a much better investment than their less expensive counterparts. The skinned knuckles and frustration inflicted by poor quality tools make any job an unhappy core. Another consideration is that quality tools sold by reputable firms come with an on-the-spot replacement guarantee; if the tool breaks, you get a new one, no questions asked.

The tools needed for basic maintenance jobs, in addition to those just mentioned, include:

1. Jackstands, for support;
2. Oil filter wrench;
3. Oil filler spout or funnel;
4. Grease gun;
5. Battery hydrometer;
6. Battery post and clamp cleaner;
7. Container for draining oil;
8. Many rags for the inevitable spills.

In addition to these items there are several others which are not absolutely necessary, but handy to have around. These include a transmission funnel and filler tube, a drop (trouble) light on a long cord, an adjustable wrench (crescent wrench), and slip joint pliers.

A more extensive list of tools, suitable for tune-up work, can be drawn up easily. While the tools involved are slightly more sophisticated, they need not be outrageously expensive. For example, there are several inexpensive tach/dwell meters on the market that are every bit as good for the average mechanic as a $100.00 professional model. The key to these purchases is to make them with an eye towards adaptability and wide range. Using the tach/dwell meter example again, if the model you buy runs up to at least 1,500 rpm on the tachometer scale, the dwell meter works on 4, 6, or 8 cylinder engines, and the tachometer unit is adaptable to both conventional and electronic ignitions, it will serve for a long time on a variety of automobiles. A basic list of tune-up tools could include:

1. A tach/dwell meter;
2. Spark plug gauge and gapping tool;
3. Feeler blades;
4. Timing light.

In this list, the choice of a timing light should be made carefully. A light which works on the DC current supplied by the car battery is the best choice; it should have a xenon tube for brightness. If your car has electronic ignition, the light should have an inductive pick-up (the timing light illustrated has one of these), and since nearly all cars will have electronic ignition in the future, this feature is a reasonable one to look for.

In addition to these basic tools, there are several other tools and gauges you may find useful. These include:

1. A compression gauge. The screw-in type is slower to use, but eliminates the possibility of a faulty reading due to escaping pressure.
2. A manifold vacuum gauge.
3. A test light.
4. An induction meter. This is used

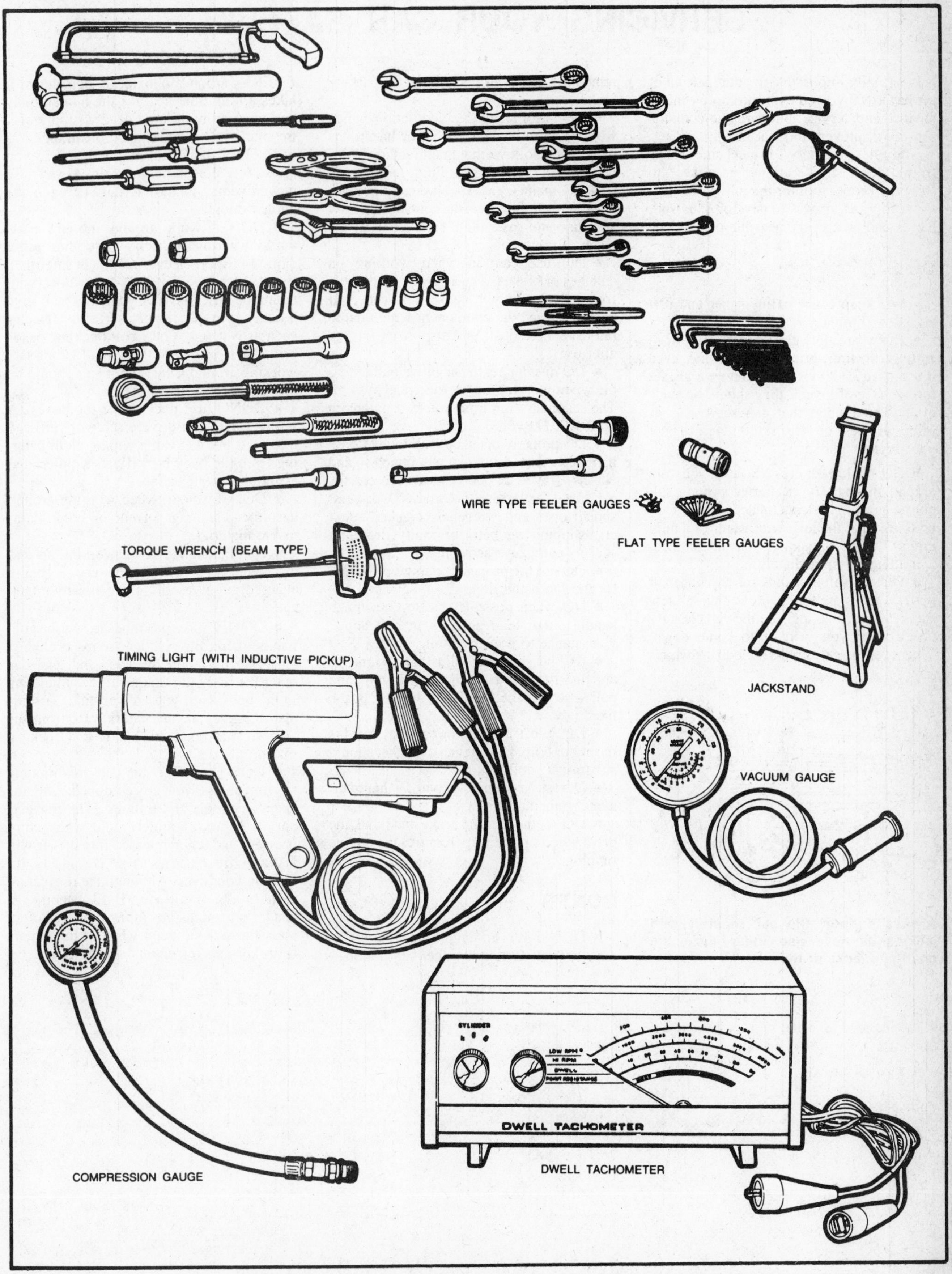


**A basic tool collection will handle almost any automotive repair work**

# SERVICING YOUR CAR SAFELY

It is virtually impossible to anticipate all of the hazards involved with automotive maintenance and service, but care and common sense will prevent most accidents.

The rules of safety for mechanics range from "don't smoke around gasoline," to "use the proper tool for the job." The trick to avoiding injuries is to develop safe work habits and take every possible precaution.

## DO'S

- DO keep a fire extinguisher and first aid kit within easy reach.
- DO wear safety glasses or goggles when cutting, drilling, grinding, or prying, even if you have 20-20 vision. If you wear glasses for the sake of vision, they should be made of hardened glass that can serve also as safety glasses, or wear safety goggles over your regular glasses.
- DO shield your eyes whenever you work around the battery. Batteries contain sulphuric acid. In case of contact with the eyes or skin, flush the area with water or a mixture of water and baking soda and get medical attention immediately.
- DO use safety stands for any undercar service. Jacks are for raising vehicles; safety stands are for making sure the vehicle stays raised until you want it to come down. Whenever the car is raised, block the wheels remaining on the ground and set the parking brake.

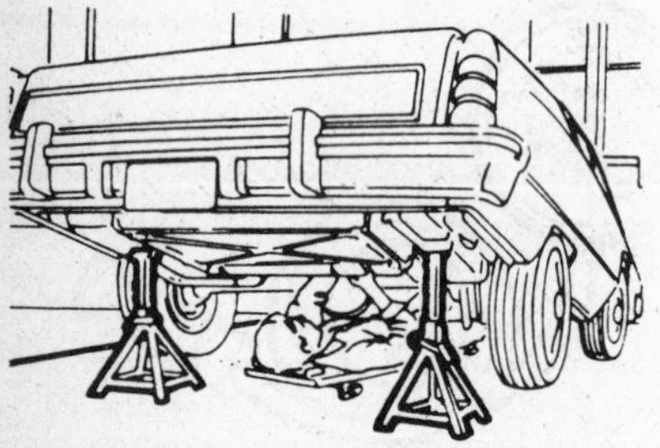

**Always support the car securely with jackstands; never use cinder blocks, tire changing jacks or the like**

- DO use adequate ventilation when working with any chemicals or hazardous materials. Follow the manufacturer's directions for usage. Brake fluid, anti-freeze, solvents, paints, etc. are all deadly poisons if taken internally. Seal the containers tightly after use and store them safely, out of the reach of children.
- DO use caution when working on clutches or brakes. The asbestos used in the friction material will cause lung cancer if inhaled. Wipe the component with a damp rag to remove dust, and dispose of the rag after use.
- DO disconnect the negative battery cable when working on the electrical system. The secondary ignition system can contain up to 40,000 volts.
- DO properly maintain your tools. Loose hammerheads, mushroomed punches and chisels, frayed or poorly grounded electrical cords, excessively worn screwdrivers, spread open-end wrenches, cracked sockets, slipping ratchets, or faulty droplight sockets can cause accidents.
- DO use the proper size and type of tool for the job being done.
- DO when possible, pull on a wrench handle rather than push on it, and adjust your stance to prevent a fall.
- DO be sure that adjustable wrenches are tightly closed on the nut or bolt and pulled so that the face is on the side of the fixed jaw.
- DO select a wrench or socket that fits the nut or bolt. The wrench or socket should sit straight, not cocked.
- DO strike squarely with a hammer; avoid glancing blows.
- DO set the parking brake and block the drive wheels if the work requires the engine running.

## DONT'S

- DON'T run an engine in a garage or anywhere else without proper ventilation—EVER! Carbon monoxide is poisonous; it takes a long time to leave the human body and you can build up a deadly supply of it in your system by simply breathing in a little every day. You may not realize you are slowly poisoning yourself. Always use power vents, windows, fans or open the garage doors.
- DON'T work around moving parts while wearing a necktie or other loose clothing. Short sleeves are much safer than long, loose sleeves; hard-toed shoes with neoprene soles protect your toes and give a better grip on slippery surfaces. Jewelry such as watches, fancy belt buckles, beads or body adornment of any kind is not safe working around a car. Long hair should be hidden under a hat or cap.
- DON'T use pockets for toolboxes. A fall or bump can drive a screwdriver deep into your body. Even a wiping cloth hanging from the back pocket can wrap around a spinning shaft or fan.
- DON'T smoke when working around gasoline, cleaning solvent or other flammable material.
- DON'T smoke when working around the battery. When the battery is being charged, it gives off explosive hydrogen gas.
- DON'T use gasoline to wash your hands; there are excellent soaps available. Gasoline may contain lead, and lead can enter the body through a cut, accumulating in the body until you are very ill. Gasoline also removes all the natural oils from the skin so that bone dry hands will suck up oil and grease.
- DON'T service the air conditioning system unless you are equipped with the necessary tools and training. The refrigerant, R-12, is extremely cold when compressed, and when released into the air will instantly freeze any surface it contacts, including your eyes. Although the refrigerant is normally non-toxic, R-12 becomes a deadly poisonous gas in the presence of an open flame. One good whiff of the vapors from burning refrigerant can be fatal.

# Basic Maintenance 21

## INTRODUCTION

Routine maintenance is probably the most important part of automobile care and the easiest to neglect. A regular program aimed at monitoring essential systems ensures that all components are in good and safe working order, and can prevent small problems from developing into major headaches. Routine maintenance also pays big dividends in keeping major repair costs at a minimum and extending the life of the car.

The owner's manual that came with your car includes a maintenance schedule, indicating service intervals in numbers of months or thousand of miles. This schedule should always be followed. We have provided, in each section, a guide to service intervals based on an averaging of manufacturer's recommendations. In most cases, the suggested interval offered here will be close to that given by the manufacturer of your car, but the manufacturer's schedule should always take precedence.

We have divided the maintenance work to be done into three categories: Under Hood, Under Car, and Exterior. The checks in each section require only a few minutes of attention every few weeks; the services to be performed can be easily accomplished in a morning. The most important part of any maintenance program is regularity. The few minutes or occasional morning spent on these seemingly trivial tasks will forestall or eliminate major problems later.

## UNDER HOOD

### Automatic Transmission, Automatic Transaxle

The fluid level in the automatic transmission or transaxle should be checked every three months or 6000 miles. All automatic transmissions have a dipstick for fluid level checks.

1. Drive the car until it is at normal operating temperature. The level should not be checked immediately after the car has been driven for a long time at high speed, or in city traffic in hot weather; in those cases, the transmission should be given a half hour to cool down.
2. Stop the car, apply the parking brake, then shift slowly through all gear positions, ending in Park. Leave the engine running.
3. Remove the dipstick, wipe it clean, then reinsert it, pushing it fully home.
4. Pull the dipstick again and, holding it horizontally, read the fluid level.
5. Cautiously feel the end of the dipstick to determine the temperature. Most dipsticks are marked with both cool and hot levels. If the fluid is not up to the correct level, more will have to be added.
6. Fluid is added through the dipstick tube. You will probably need the aid of a spout or a long-necked funnel. Be sure that whatever you pour through is perfectly clean and dry. Fluid recommendations can be found in the owner's manual.

Add fluid slowly, and in small amounts, checking the level frequently between additions. Do not overfill, which will cause foaming, fluid loss, slippage, and possible transmission damage.

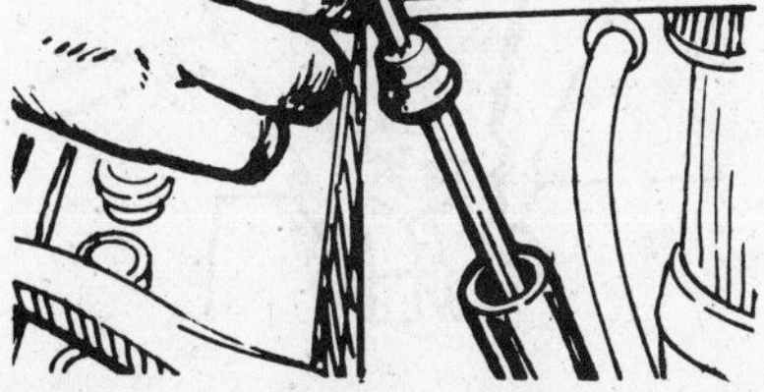

**Check the automatic transmission fluid level with the dipstick provided**

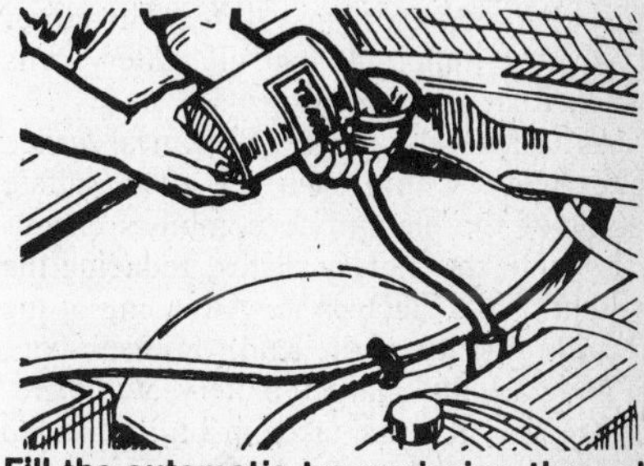

**Fill the automatic transmission through the dipstick tube**

### Battery

#### FLUID LEVEL (EXCEPT "MAINTENANCE FREE" BATTERIES)

Check the battery electrolyte level at least once a month, or more often in hot weather or during periods of extended car operation. The level can be checked through the case on translucent polypropylene batteries; the cell caps must be removed on other models. The electrolyte level in each cell should be kept filled to the split ring inside, or the line marked on the outside of the case.

If the level is low, add only distilled water, or colorless, odorless drinking water, through

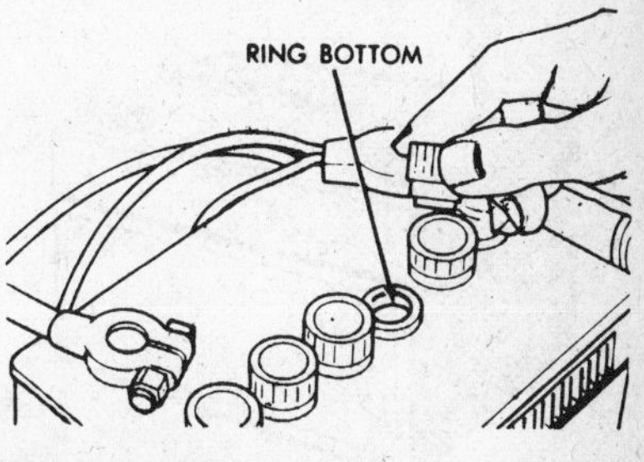


**Fill the battery cell to the bottom of the split ring**

the opening until the level is correct. Each cell is completely separate from the others, so each must be checked and filled individually.

If water is added in freezing weather, the car should be driven several miles to allow the water to mix with the electrolyte. Otherwise, the battery could freeze.

## SPECIFIC GRAVITY (EXCEPT "MAINTENANCE FREE" BATTERIES)

While not technically exact, a practical measurement of the chemical condition of the battery is indicated by measuring the specific gravity of the acid (electrolyte) contained in each cell. The electrolyte in a fully charged battery is usually between 1.260 and 1.280 times as heavy as pure water at the same temperature (80°F). Variations in the specific gravity readings for a fully charged battery may differ. Therefore, it is most important that all battery cells produce an equal reading.

As a battery discharges, a chemical change takes place within each cell. The sulfate factor of the electrolyte combines chemically with the battery plates, reducing the weight of the electrolyte. A reading of the specific gravity of the acid, or electrolyte, of any partially charged battery, will therefore be less than that taken in a fully charged one.

The hydrometer is the instrument used for determining the specific gravity of liquids. The battery hydrometer is readily available from many sources, including local auto replacement parts stores. The following chart gives an indication of specific gravity value, related to battery charge condition. If, after charging, the specific gravity between any two cells varies more than 50 points (.050), the battery is probably bad.

| Specific Gravity Reading | Charged Condition |
|---|---|
| 1.260–1.280 | Fully charged |
| 1.230–1.250 | Three-quarter charged |
| 1.200–1.220 | One-half charged |
| 1.170–1.190 | One-quarter charged |
| 1.140–1.160 | Just about flat |
| 1.110–1.130 | All the way down |

## CABLES AND CLAMPS

Once a year, the battery terminals and the cable clamps should be cleaned. Loosen the clamps and remove the cables, negative cable first. On batteries with posts on top, the use of a puller specially made for the purpose is recommended. These are inexpensive, and available in auto parts stores. Side terminal battery cables are secured with a bolt.

Clean the cable clamps and the battery terminal with a wire brush until all corrosion, grease, etc. is removed and the metal is shiny. It is especially important to clean the inside of the clamp thoroughly, since a small deposit of foreign material or oxidation there will prevent a sound electrical connection and inhibit either starting or charging. Special tools are available for cleaning these parts, one type for conventional batteries and another type for side terminal batteries.

Before installing the cables, loosen the battery hold-down clamp or strap, remove the battery and check the battery tray. Clear it of any debris, and check it for soundness. Rust should be wire brushed away, and the metal given a coat of anti-rust paint. Replace the battery and tighten the hold-down clamp or strap securely, but be careful not to overtighten, which will crack the battery case.

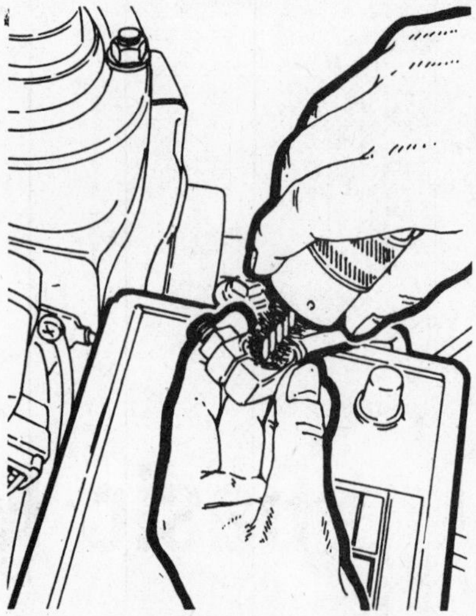

Clean the clamp with a wire brush

After the clamps and terminals are clean, reinstall the cables, negative cable last; do not hammer on the clamps to install. Tighten the clamps securely, but do not distort them. Give the clamps and terminals a thin external coat of grease after installation, to retard corrosion.

Check the cables at the same time that the terminals are cleaned. If the cable insulation is cracked or broken, or if the ends are frayed, the cable should be replaced with a new cable of the same length and gauge.

**NOTE: Keep flame or sparks away from the battery; it gives off explosive hydrogen gas. Battery electrolyte contains sulphuric acid. If you should splash any on your skin or in your eyes, flush the affected area with plenty of clear water; if it lands in your eyes, get medical help immediately.**

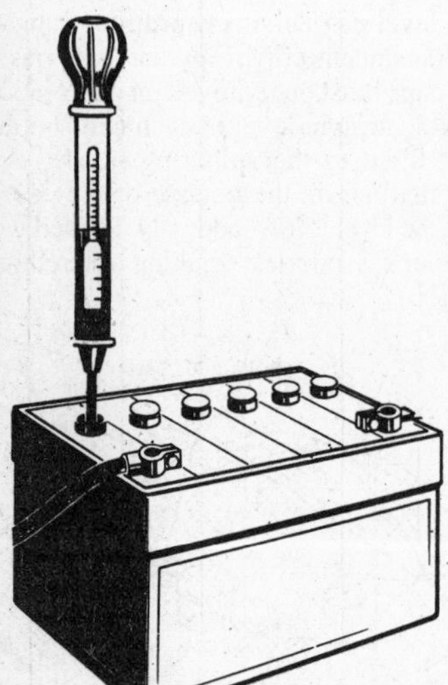

Testing battery specific gravity

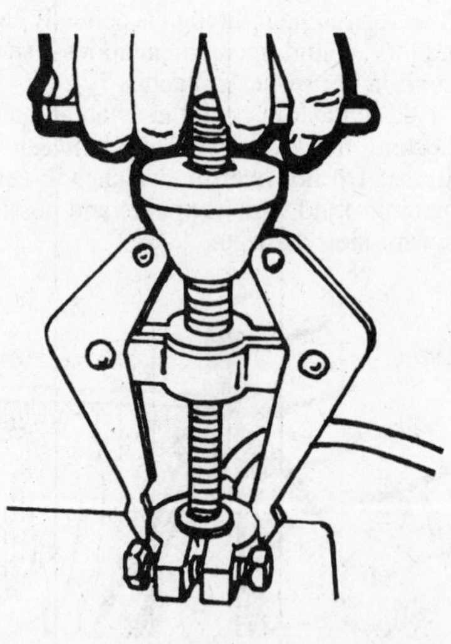

Use a puller to remove the clamp on post-type batteries

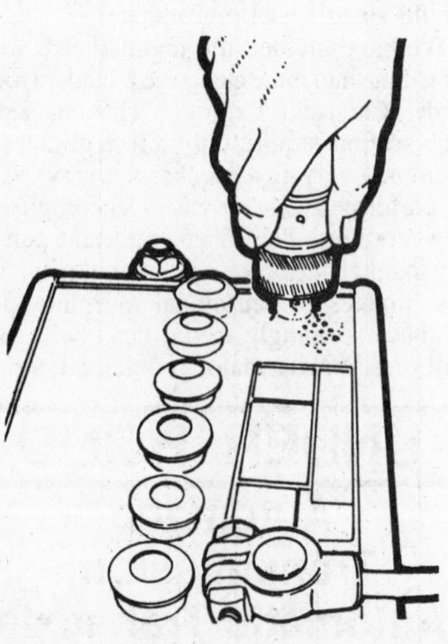

The posts are easily cleaned with a wire brush, or the battery post tool shown

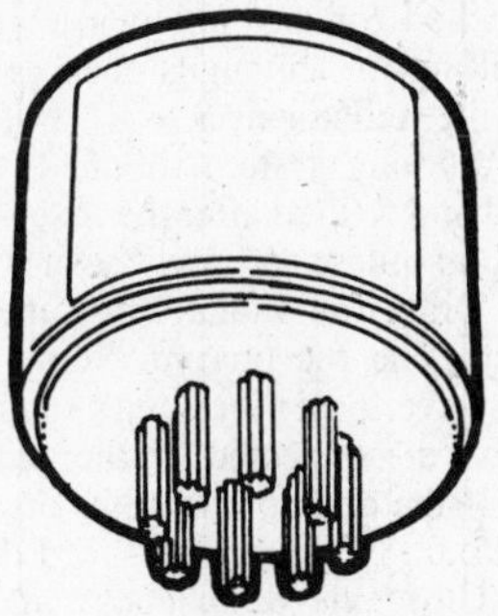

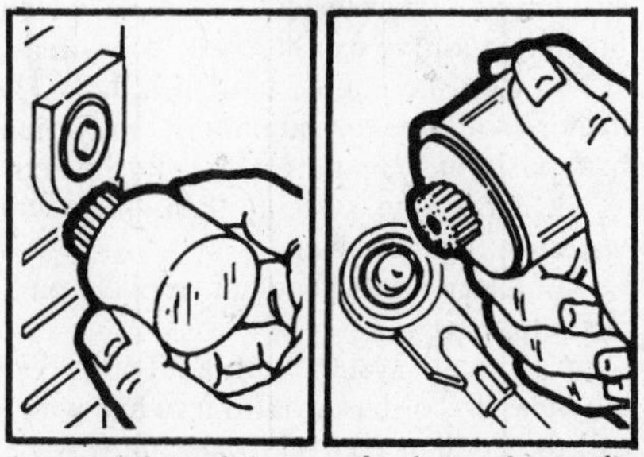

**A special tool is required to clean the terminals and clamps on side terminal batteries**

## Brake Fluid

Once a month, the fluid level in the brake master cylinder should be checked.

1. Park the car on a level surface.
2. Clean off the master cylinder cover before removal. Some covers are retained by a bolt. Some of the newer master cylinders with plastic reservoirs have screw caps. Remove the cover, being careful not to drop or tear the rubber diaphragm which will probably be underneath. Be careful also not to drip any brake fluid on painted surfaces, as it eats paint.

**NOTE: Brake fluid absorbs moisture from the air, which reduces effectiveness and will corrode brake parts once in the system. Never leave the master cylinder or the brake fluid container uncovered for any longer than necessary.**

3. The fluid level should be about ¼ inch below the lip of the master cylinder well.
4. If fluid addition is necessary, use only extra heavy duty disc brake fluid meeting DOT 3 or DOT 4 specifications. The fluid should be reasonably fresh, because brake fluid deteriorates with age.
5. Replace the cover, making sure that the diaphragm is correctly seated.

If the brake fluid is constantly low, the system should be checked for leaks. However, it is normal for the fluid level to fall gradually as the disc brake pads wear; expect the fluid level to drop about ⅛ inch for every 10,000 miles of wear.

## Belt Tension

Every six months or 12,000 miles, check

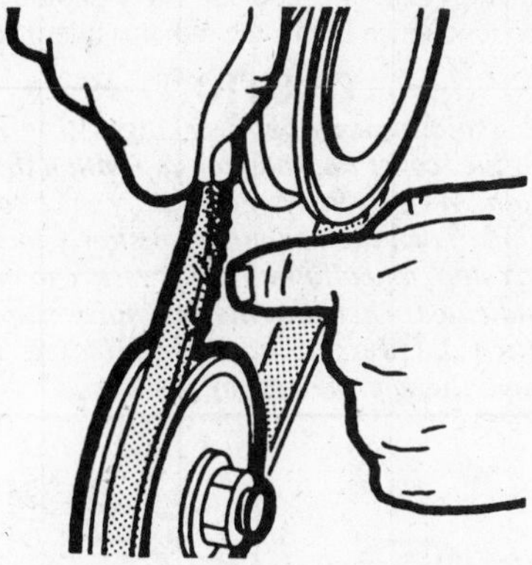

**Check the belts for wear**

the water pump, alternator, power steering pump, air pump, and air conditioning compressor drive belts for proper tension. Also look for signs of wear, fraying, separation, glazing and so on, and replace the belts as required.

Belt tension should be checked with a gauge made for the purpose. If a gauge is not available, tension can be checked with moderate thumb pressure applied to the belt at its longest span midway between pulleys. If the belt has a free span less than twelve inches, it should deflect approximately ⅛–¼ inch. If the span is longer than twelve inches, deflection can range between ⅛ and ⅜ inches.

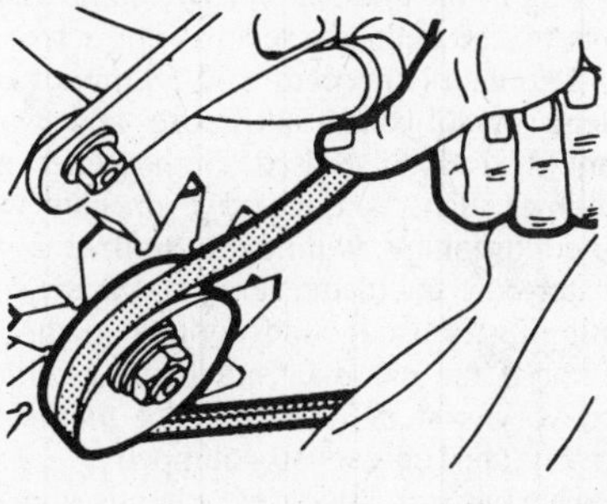

**Check the belt tension at the middle of the longest span between pulleys**

To adjust or replace belts:

1. Loosen the driven accessory's pivot and mounting bolts. Some air conditioning compressor belts are tensioned by an idler pulley; in this case, loosen the idler pulley and use a ½ in. drive ratchet in the square hole provided to lever the idler pulley up or down.
2. Move the accessory toward or away from the engine until the tension is correct. You can use a wooden hammer handle or broomstick as a lever, but do not use anything metallic.
3. Tighten the bolts and recheck the tension. If new bolts have been installed, run the engine for a few minutes, then recheck and readjust as necessary.

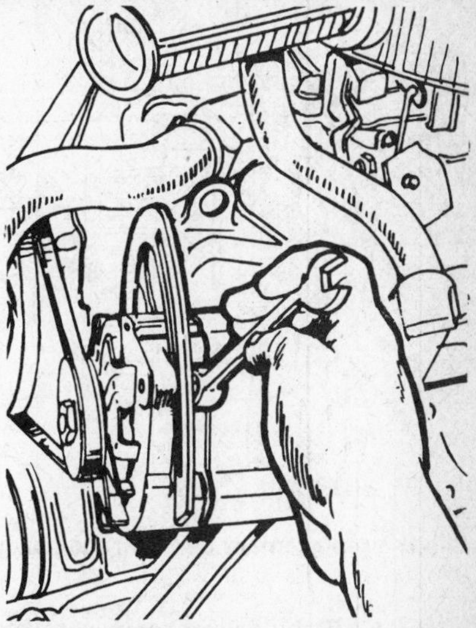

**To either adjust or remove a belt, loosen the driven component's adjusting bolt**

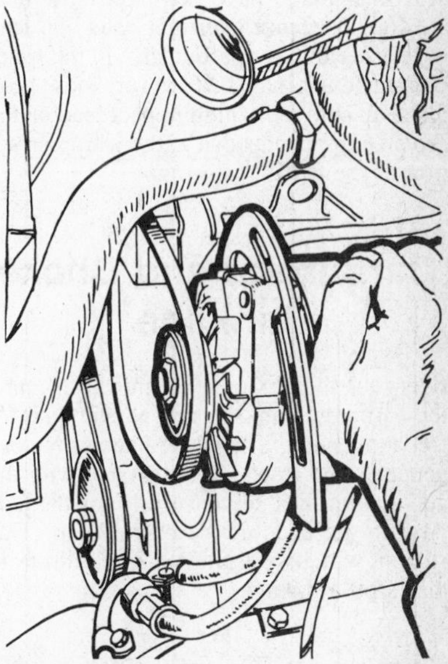

**Push the component toward the engine to remove the belt**

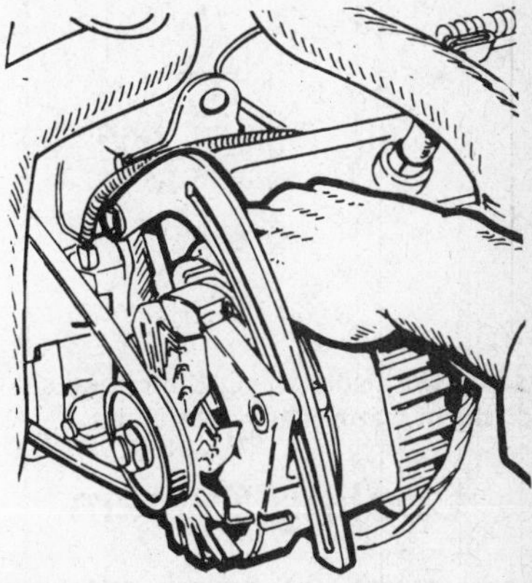

**Pull outwards on the component to tension the belt, then tighten the bolts; recheck the belt tension after tightening**

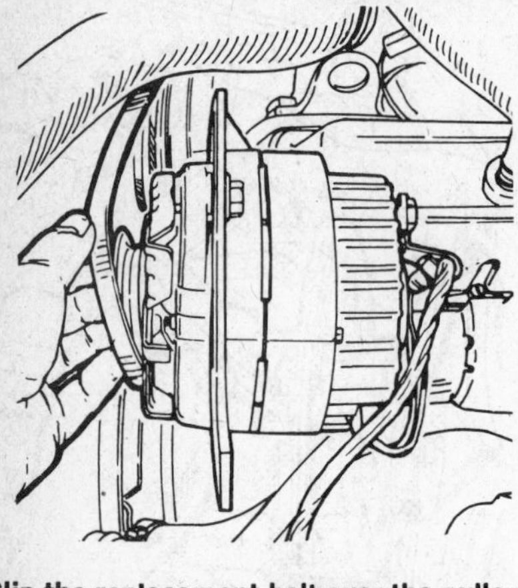

Slip the replacement belt over the pulley

**NOTE: If the driven component has two drive belts, the belts should be replaced in pairs to maintain proper tension.**

It is better to have belts too loose than too tight, because overtight belts will lead to bearing failure, particularly in the water pump and alternator. However, loose belts place an extremely high impact load on the driven components due to the whipping action of the belt.

## Carburetor and Choke Linkage

Every 12 months or 6000 miles, examine the carburetor linkage and choke plate for free movement. The choke plate action can generally be freed, if necessary, with the application of a solvent made for the purpose to the ends of the choke shaft. This solvent will also clean grease and dirt from the throttle linkage.

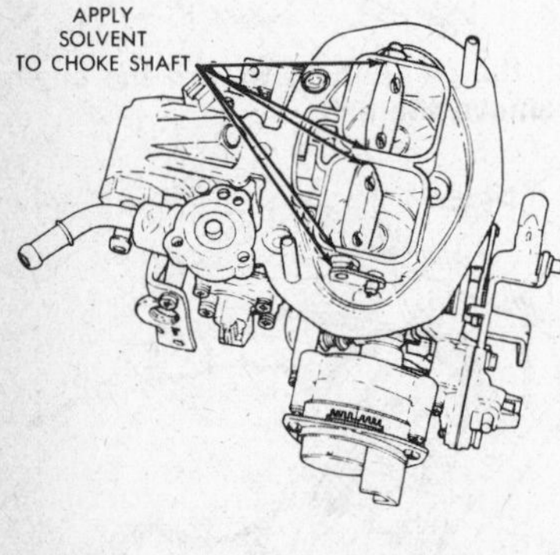


Use a spray solvent on the choke shaft, but do not apply any lubricants

## Cooling System

Once a month, the engine coolant level should be checked. On cars without a coolant recovery system, this should only be done when the engine is cold. Remove the radiator cap; the coolant level should be about one inch below the radiator filler neck.

**CAUTION**

***To avoid injury when working with a hot engine, cover the radiator cap with a thick cloth. Wear a heavy glove to protect your hand. Turn the radiator cap slowly to the first stop, and allow all the pressure to vent (indicated when the hissing noise stops). When the pressure has been released, remove the cap the rest of the way.***

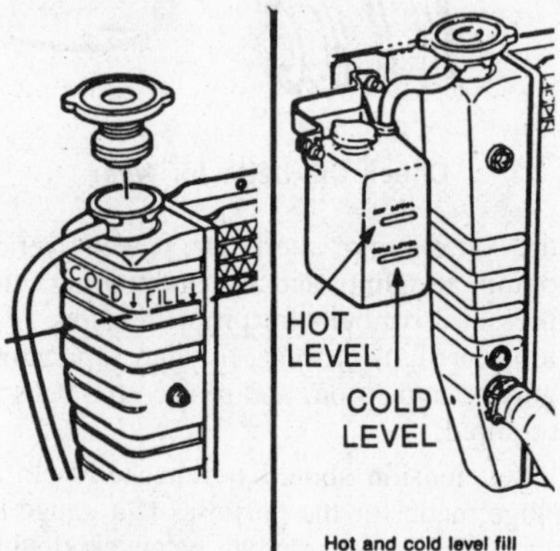


Fill level mark on crossflow radiator.

Hot and cold level fill marks, constant-full system.

Proper coolant level is about one inch below the radiator neck, or between the lines on the recovery tank

On cars with a coolant recovery tank, coolant should be visible within the tank; as long as the coolant is between the markings on the tank, the level is correct.

If coolant is needed, a 50/50 mix of ethylene glycol-based antifreeze and water should always be used, both winter and summer. This is imperative on cars with air conditioning; without the antifreeze, the heater core could freeze when the air conditioning is used. Add coolant to the radiator if the car does not have a coolant recovery system. Add coolant to the recovery tank on cars so equipped.

The radiator hoses and clamps and the radiator cap should be checked at the same time as the coolant level. Hoses which are brittle, cracked, or swollen should be replaced. Clamps should be checked for tightness (screwdriver tight only—do not allow the clamp to cut into the hose or crush the fitting). The radiator cap gasket should be checked for any obvious tears, cracks or swelling, or any signs of incorrect seating in the radiator neck.

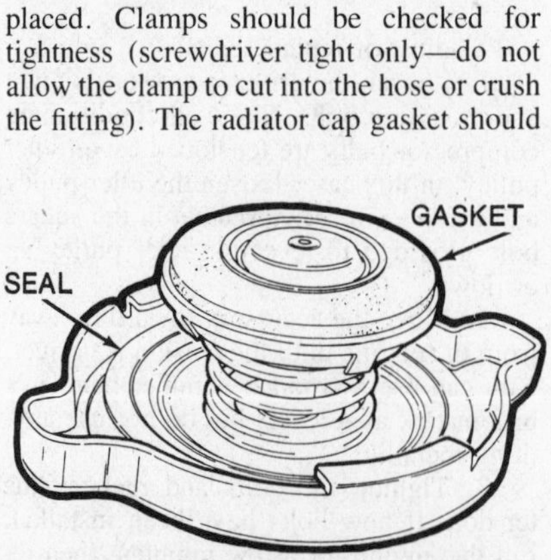


Check the radiator cap gasket and sealing surface

The cooling system should be drained, flushed and refilled after the first 24 months or 24,000 miles, and every year thereafter.

1. Drain the radiator by opening the drain cock at the bottom. Some radiators do not have these; the lower radiator hose must be disconnected at the radiator instead. If the engine block has drain plugs, they should be opened to speed draining.
2. Close the drain cocks and fill the system with clear water. A cooling system flushing additive can be used, if desired.
3. Run the engine until it is hot. The heater should be turned on to its maximum heat position so that the core is flushed out.
4. Drain the system, then flush with water until it runs clear.
5. Clean out the coolant recovery tank, if equipped.
6. Fill the system with a 50/50 mix of ethylene glycol-based antifreeze and water. Fill the coolant recovery tank midway between the marks with this mixture also.
7. Run the engine until it is hot, then let it cool and top up the radiator or coolant recovery tank as necessary with the antifreeze/water mixture.

## Heat Riser

The heat riser is a thermostatically or vacuum operated valve in the exhaust manifold (not all cars have one). It closes when the engine is warming up, in order to preheat the incoming fuel/air mixture. If it sticks open, the result will be frequent stalling during warmup, especially in cold and damp weather. If it sticks shut, the result will be a rough idle after the engine is warm.

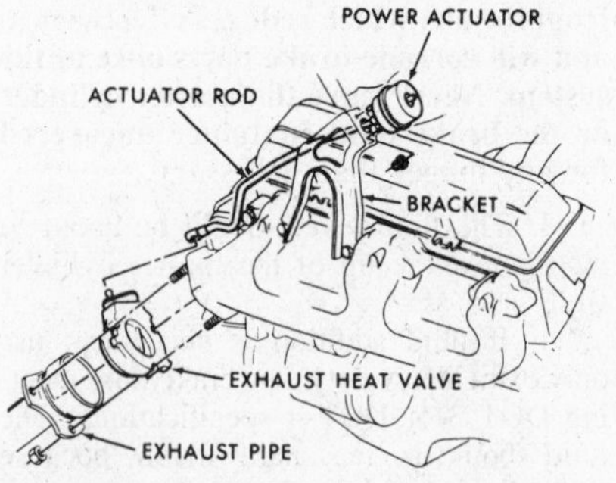


Exploded view of a vacuum-operated heat riser

The heat riser should move freely. It can be checked easily when the engine is cold by giving the counterweight on the valve shaft a twirl, or pulling the vacuum rod to open and shut the valve. If the valve is sticking or binding, a quick shot of solvent made for the purpose will free it up. This solvent should be applied every six months or 6000 miles to keep the valve free. If the valve is still stuck after application of the solvent, sometimes rapping the end of the

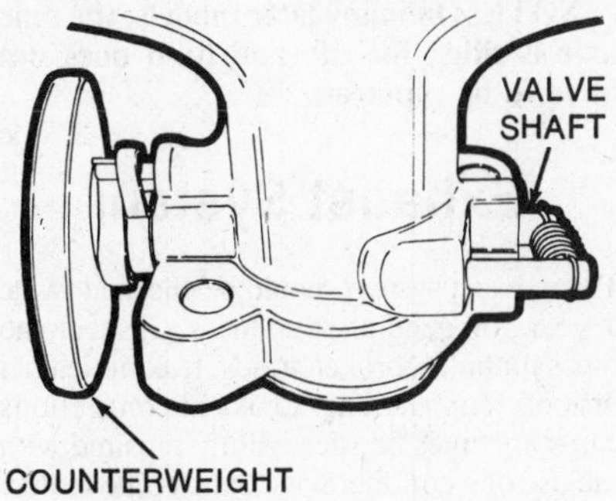


**Thermostatically-operated heat control valve**

shaft lightly with a hammer will break it loose. Otherwise, the components will have to be removed for further repairs.

## Ignition Cables

The ignition system (points, condenser, rotor, spark plugs, etc.) receives regular attention in the form of a tune-up, and thus is not covered here. But one of the most commonly overlooked components is the ignition cable, or spark plug wire.

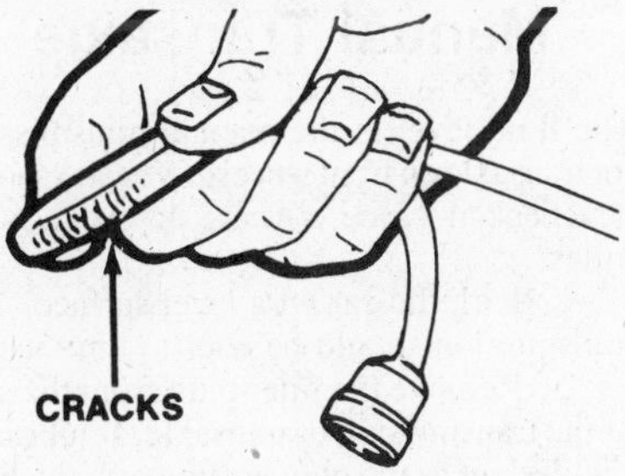


**Inspect the ignition cables for cracks or breaks in the insulation**

Although they rarely show any visible signs of deterioration, the ignition cables should be checked at every tune-up, and replaced at least every 50,000 miles. Cracking and embrittlement are of course obvious signs of wear, but most newer cables have silicone insulation and thus are not prone to display these conditions.

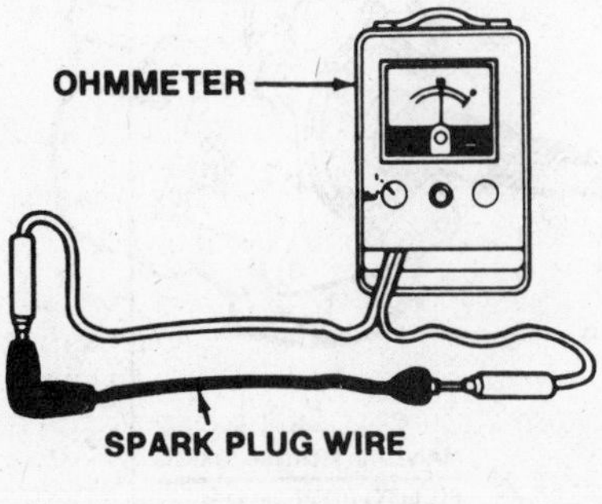


**Test the ignition cables with an ohmmeter. Conventional ignition cables should be removed from the distributor cap, but electronic ignition wires should first be tested through the cap**

The most reliable way to check the cables is with an ohmmeter. On conventional ignitions, the resistance should be less than 7,000 ohms per foot (wire removed). On cars with electronic ignitions, it is generally recommended to leave the wire attached to the distributor cap; test with one lead from the ohmmeter connected to the corresponding terminal in the distributor cap, the other lead touched to the disconnected end of the cable at the spark plug. Then, if resistance seems close to the limit, remove the wire from the cap and retest. In general, the spark plug wires on electronic ignitions should be replaced if the total resistance is over 36,000 ohms.

Always replace the cables with new ones of the same type. Replace the wires one at a time, working from the longest to the shortest.

## Oil Level

The engine oil should be checked on a regular basis, ideally at each fuel stop, or once a week. It is best to check when the engine is at operating temperature, but checking the level immediately after shutting off the engine will give a false reading, because all of the oil will not yet have drained back into the crankcase. The car should be parked on a level surface to obtain an accurate reading.

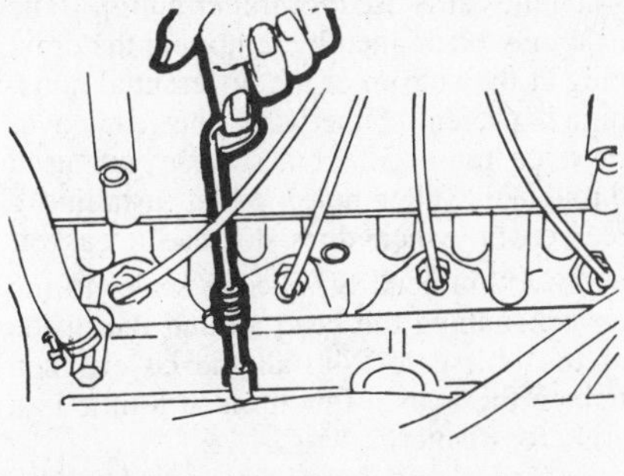

**Check the engine oil level with the dipstick**

1. Remove the oil dipstick. Wipe it clean, then replace it, seating it firmly.

2. Remove the dipstick again and hold it horizontally to prevent the oil from running. The level should be between the "Add" and "Full" marks on the dipstick. The dipstick may be marked "Add" and "Full," "Add" and "Safe," or may have lines scribed on it; in any case, the oil level should be above the lower marking.

3. If the oil is below the lower mark, enough oil should be added to the engine to raise the level to the upper mark. The markings are usually spaced so that one quart of oil will raise the level from the "Add" mark to the "Full" mark. Oil is added through the capped opening in the valve cover. Only oils labeled SF (gasoline engines) or CC (diesel engines) should be used; select a viscosity that will be compatible with the temperatures expected until the next drain interval.

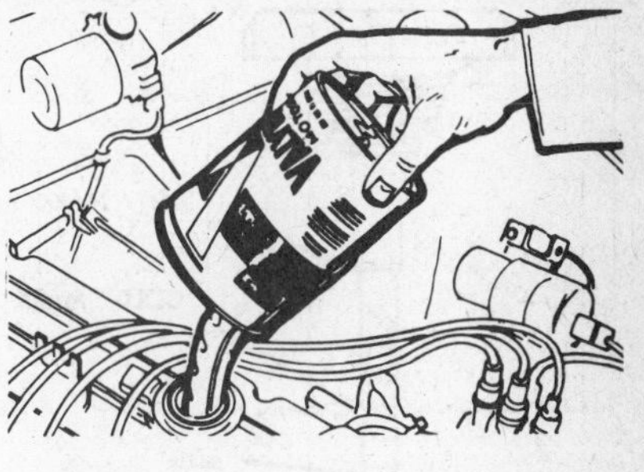

**Add oil through the valve cover**

4. Replace the dipstick, then check the level again after any additions of oil. Be careful not to overfill, which will lead to leakage and seal damage.

## Power Steering

The power steering fluid level is usually checked with a dipstick inserted into the pump reservoir. The dipstick may be attached to the reservoir cap, or inserted into a tube on the pump body. The level should be checked at every oil change. On some models, the power steering reservoir is translucent, allowing the level to be checked through the sides of the container without removing the cap. On others, the reservoir is a metal canister with a wingnut-attached cap. After the cap is removed, the level is checked with the scribed lines on the inside of the container.

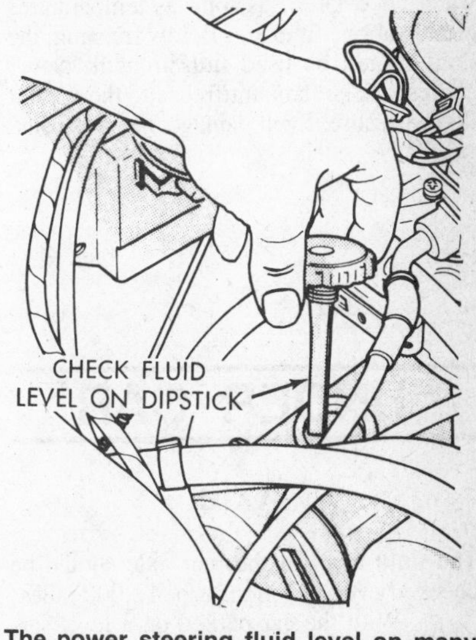


**The power steering fluid level on many models is checked by means of a dipstick installed in the reservoir**

On most models, the fluid level may be checked with the fluid either warm or cold. If checked with the fluid cold, the level will be slightly lower than with the fluid warm. If doubts arise about the specific procedures

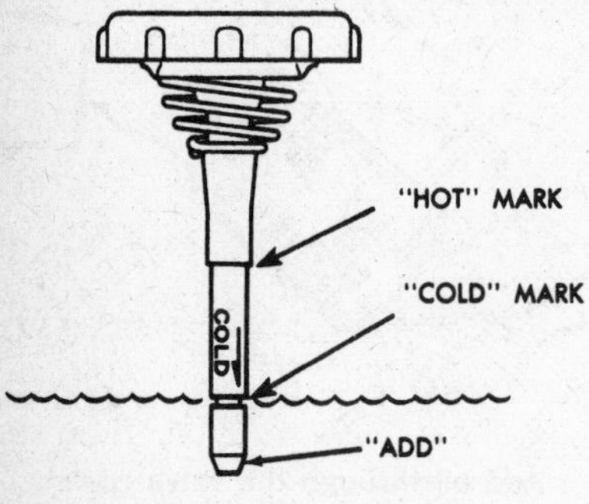


Typical power steering dipstick markings

for the car being checked, consult the owner's manual.

1. On all models, with the engine off, remove the dipstick, remove the cap or check the level through the side of the reservoir. If warm, the level should be between the "Hot" and "Cold" marks or even with the scribed line in the reservoir. If the fluid is cold, the level should be slightly lower.

2. If the level is low, add power steering fluid until the correct level is reached. Do not overfill the reservoir.

## Windshield Washer Fluid

Check the fluid level in the windshield washer tank at every oil level check. The fluid can be mixed in a 50% solution with water, if desired, as long as temperatures remain above freezing. Below freezing, the fluid should be used full strength. Never add engine coolant antifreeze to the washer fluid, because it will damage the car's paint.

# UNDER CAR

## Axle

The fluid level in the rear axle should be checked every 12 months or 12,000 miles.

1. With the car parked on a level surface, remove the filler plug. The plug can be found either in the rear cover of the differential, or on the front of the pinion housing.

2. If lubricant trickles out when the plug is removed, the level is correct. If not, stick your finger in the hole (watch out for sharp threads); the fluid level should be even with edge of the filler hole.

3. If lubricant is needed, use SAE 80W-90 GL-5 gear oil (SAE 80W GL-5 in very cold climates) to fill standard axles. Limited slip axles require a special lubricant, available in auto parts stores.

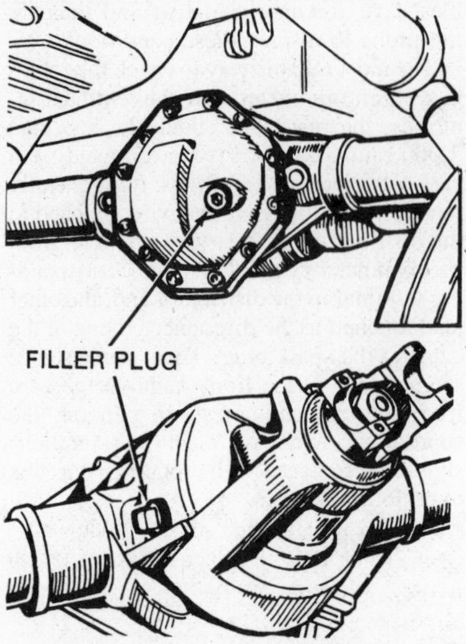


Rear axle filler plug locations

4. When the level is correct, install the plug and tighten until snug. Do not overtighten.

Standard axles should be drained and refilled with fresh lubricant every 15,000 miles when the car is used to pull a trailer. Limited slip axles should be drained and refilled at the first 7500 miles; the limited slip lubricant should be changed every 7500 miles when the car is used for trailer pulling. The axle may be drained by removing the drain plug at the bottom of the differential housing, if present. Otherwise, the rear cover must be removed, or a suction gun used through the filler hole. When installing a rear cover which does not use a gasket, apply a thin bead of silicone sealer to the cover, running the bead around the inside of the bolt holes. Install the cover, then tighten the bolts a few turns at a time in a crisscross pattern.

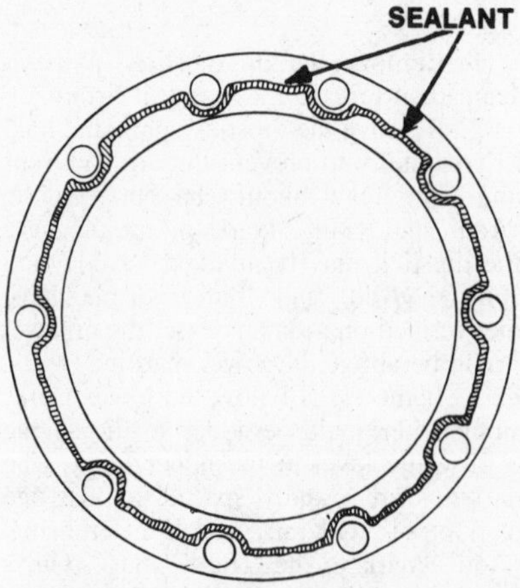


Apply a bead of silicone sealer to the rear cover if no gasket is used

**NOTE: On many later models, the rear axle is filled for life and fluid does not have to be replaced.**

## Exhaust System

The exhaust system should be checked twice a year for general soundness. Inspect the pipes for holes, broken welds, leaking seams, or loose connections. Leaks at connections can sometimes be successfully repaired with the use of a commercial exhaust pipe sealer, but holes or breaks warrant replacement of the part. The exhaust pipe hangers and straps should be examined for any breaks or cracks; replace these as necessary. Some slight cracking of rubber hangers is normal, but deep cracks or cuts are cause for replacement.

**CAUTION**

***Check the exhaust system only when it is cold. The temperature on an exhaust system using a catalytic converter can reach 1000°F after only a short period of engine operation.***

## Manual Transmission, Manual Transaxle

The fluid level in the manual transmission (or transaxle on front wheel drive cars) should be checked twice a year, or every 6000 miles.

1. Park the car on a level surface. The transmission should be cool to the touch.

2. Remove the filler plug from the side of the transmission or transaxle. If lubricant trickles out as the plug is removed, the fluid level is correct. If not, stick your finger into the hole (watch out for sharp threads); the lubricant should be right up to the edge of the filler hole.

3. If lubricant is needed, consult the owner's manual for the correct weight and type of fluid.

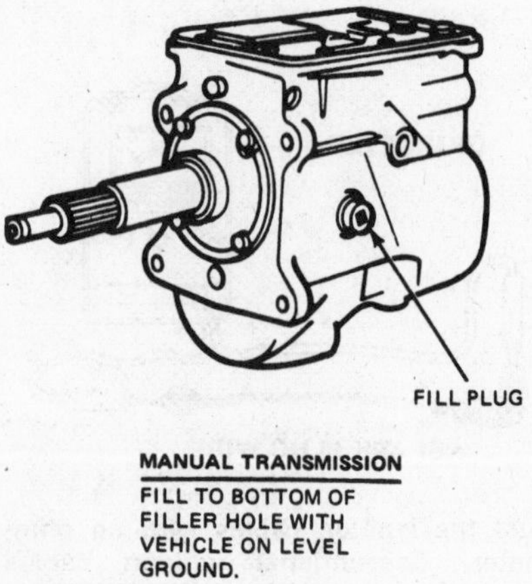

FILL PLUG
MANUAL TRANSMISSION
FILL TO BOTTOM OF FILLER HOLE WITH VEHICLE ON LEVEL GROUND.


Typical manual transmission filler plug location

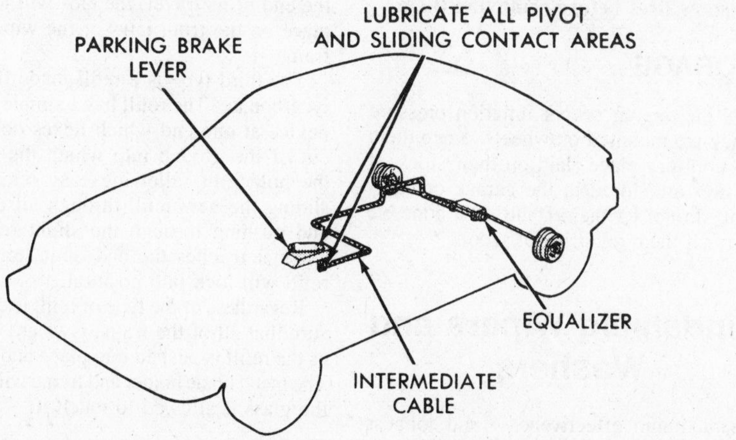


**Lubricate the parking brake cable with white waterproof grease**

**NOTE: Some manual transmission/transaxle assemblies are filled with automatic transmission fluid rather than gear oil. Consult the owner's manual for lubricant information.**

4. When the level is correct, install the filler plug and tighten until snug.

## Parking Brake Linkage

The parking brake cable assembly should be inspected twice a year for fraying, kinks, and binding. A smooth white waterproof lubricant should be applied at the same time to all pivot points and areas in sliding contact.

## Suspension Lubrication

Depending on the year of manufacture, there may be as many as twelve grease fittings on the suspension parts, or as few as two. Typical locations for grease nipples are on the ball joints, control arm pivot points, steering linkage, and the tie rod ends.

Lubricate these fittings with a small hand operated grease gun filled with EP chassis lubricant. Pump grease into the fitting slowly, until it begins to ooze out around the joint, or until the grease begins to expand the rubber boot around the fitting. Be extremely careful not to rupture any seals or boots, as this will lead to lubricant loss and contamination of the parts involved.

Occasionally, the grease nipples may become clogged with dirt or hardened grease. If so, unscrew them with a wrench of the proper size and clean them out with solvent. When reinstalled, they may be covered with plastic caps made for the purpose, or a piece of aluminum foil.

The chassis and suspension parts should be lubricated once a year, or every 7500 miles, whichever comes first.

## Transfer Case

The transfer case on the four wheel drive Subaru shares a common lubricant supply with the transmission, therefore the transfer case lubricant supply does not have to be checked separately.

# EXTERIOR

## Drain Holes and Underbody

Most cars have drain holes spaced along the lower edge of the rocker panels and doors. These holes should be cleared of any debris or rust twice a year. A small screwdriver can be used to open plugged drain holes.

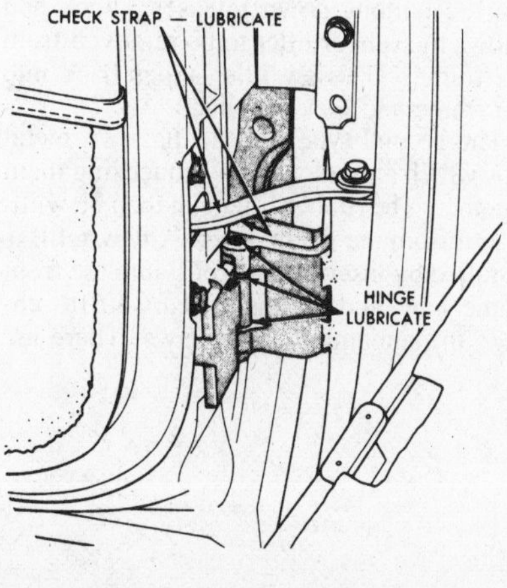


**Use engine oil to lubricate the door, hood, and trunk hinges**

Every spring, the underbody should be flushed with clear water to remove deposits of mud, road salt, and debris. It is advisable to loosen any packed-in sediment before flushing to assure a more thorough cleaning.

## Hinges and Locks

Once a year, the door, hood, and trunk hinges, and all locks should be lubricated to ensure smooth operation. The hinge points should be lightly oiled. Lock cylinders may be easily lubricated with a shot of silicone spray directed into the keyhole. Silicone lubricant also works well on the door latch mechanisms, and keeps the door, trunk, and window weatherseals pliable when applied in a light film.

## Tires

Tires should be checked weekly for proper air pressure. A chart, located either in the glove compartment or on the driver's or passenger's door, gives the recommended inflation pressures. Maximum fuel economy and tire life will result if the pressure is maintained at the highest figure given on the chart. Pressures should be checked before driving since pressure can increase as

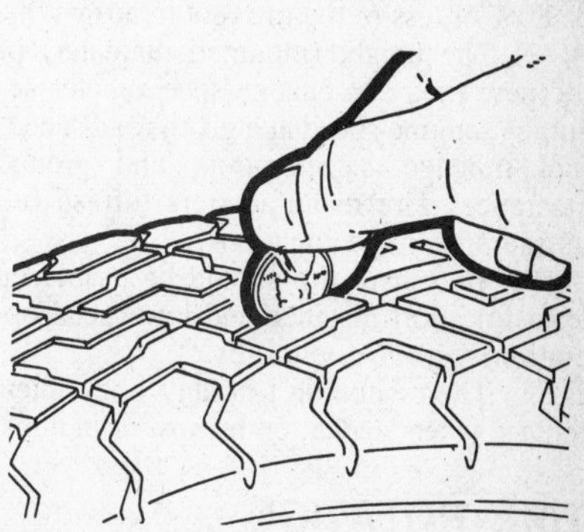

**Tire tread depth can be checked with a penny. If the top of Lincoln's head is visible, the tires are due for replacement**

much as six pounds per square inch (psi) due to heat buildup. It is a good idea to have your own accurate pressure gauge, because not all gauges on service station air pumps can be trusted. When checking pressures, do not neglect the spare tire. Note that some spare tires require pressures considerably higher than those used in the other tires.

While you are about the task of checking air pressure, inspect the tire treads for cuts, bruises and other damage. Check the air valves to be sure that they are tight. Replace any missing valve caps.

Check the tires for uneven wear that might indicate the need for front end alignment or tire rotation. Tires should be replaced when a tread wear indicator appears as a solid band across the tread.

**Tread wear indicators will appear as a band across the tire when the tread has worn out.**

When buying new tires, give some thought to the following points, especially if you are considering a switch to larger tires or a different profile series:

1. All four tires must be of the same construction type. This rule cannot be violated. Radial, bias, and bias-belted tires must not be mixed.
2. The wheels should be the correct width for the tire. Tire dealers have charts of tire and rim compatibility. A mismatch will cause sloppy handling and rapid tire wear. The tread width should match the rim width (inside bead to inside bead) within an inch. For radial tires, the rim width should be 80% or less of the tire (not tread) width.
3. The height (mounted diameter) of the new tires can change speedometer accuracy, engine speed at a given road speed, fuel mileage, acceleration, and ground clearance. Tire manufacturers furnish full measurement specifications.
4. The spare tire should be usable, at least for short distance and low speed operation, with the new tires.
5. There shouldn't be any body interference when loaded, on bumps, or in turns.

### TIRE ROTATION

Tire rotation is recommended every 6000 miles or so, to obtain maximum tire wear. The pattern you use depends on whether or not your car has a usable spare. Radial tires should not be cross-switched (from one side of the car to the other); they last longer if their direction of rotation is not changed. Snow tires sometimes have directional arrows molded onto the side of their carcass; the arrow shows the direction of rotation. They will wear very rapidly if the rotation is reversed. Studded tires will lose their studs if their rotational direction is reversed.

**NOTE: Mark the wheel position or direction of rotation on radial tires or studded snow tires before removing them.**

### STORAGE

Store the tires at proper inflation pressure if they are mounted on wheels. Keep them in a cool dry place, laid on their sides. If the tires are stored in the garage or basement, do not let them stand on a concrete floor; set them on strips of wood.

## Windshield Wipers and Washers

For maximum effectiveness, and longest element life, the windshield and wiper blades should be kept clean. Dirt, tree sap, road tar and so on will cause streaking, smearing and blade deterioration if left on the glass. It is advisable to wash the windshield carefully with a commercial glass cleaner at least once a month. Wipe off the rubber blades with the wet rag afterwards. For access to the blades on wiper systems which park below the hood line, turn the ignition key to "On" and run the wipers to the center of the windshield. Shut the wipers off with the ignition key, not the wiper switch. Do not attempt to move the wipers by hand; damage to the motor and drive mechanism will result.

If the blades are found to be cracked, broken or torn, they should be replaced immediately. Replacement intervals will vary with usage, although ozone deterioration usually limits blade life to about one year. If the wiper pattern is smeared or streaked, or if the blade chatters across the glass, the elements should be replaced. It is easiest and most sensible to replace the elements in pairs.

There are basically three different types of refills, which differ in their method of replacement. One type has two release buttons, approximately one-third of the way up from the ends of the blade frame. Pushing the buttons down releases a lock and allows the rubber filler to be removed from the frame. The new filler slides back into the frame and locks in place.

The second type of refill has two metal tabs which are unlocked by squeezing them together. The rubber filler can then be withdrawn from the frame jaws. A new refill is installed by inserting the refill into the front frame jaws and sliding it rearward to engage the remaining frame jaws. There are usually four jaws; be certain when installing that the refill is engaged in all of them. At the end of its travel, the tabs will lock into place on the front jaws of the wiper blade frame.

The third type is a refill made from polycarbonate. The refill has a simple locking device at one end which flexes downward out of the groove into which the jaws of the holder fit, allowing easy release. By sliding the new refill through all the jaws and pushing through the slight resistance when it reaches the end of its travel, the refill will lock into position.

Regardless of the type of refill used, make sure that all of the frame jaws are engaged as the refill is pushed into place and locked. The metal blade holder and frame will scratch the glass if allowed to touch it.

### WASHER NOZZLE ADJUSTMENT

#### *Centered Single Post–Non-Adjustable Nozzles*

This type is usually located on the rear center of the hood panel, directly in front of the windshield. By loosening the body retaining nut from under the hood, the nozzle body can be turned to provide the best spray discharge to cover the windshield. Tighten the retaining nut while holding the nozzle in position.

#### *Centered Single Post–Adjustable Nozzles*

This nozzle is adjusted with a wrench, screwdriver, or pliers. If the nozzle has no gripping area, the adjustment is made by inserting a stiff wire into the nozzle opening and moving the nozzle in the direction desired. When using the wire as an adjuster tool, do not force the nozzle; the wire can be broken within the nozzle opening.

#### *Individual Nozzles*

A tab is usually fastened to the nozzle stem to assist in turning the nozzle in the desired direction. If a tab is not present, use a pair of pliers to gently move the nozzle.

#### *Wiper Arm Nozzles*

No adjustment is necessary on this type of nozzle, because the opening is centered on the wiper arm and moves along with the arm.

# Air Conditioning Service 22

## AIR CONDITIONING SYSTEMS

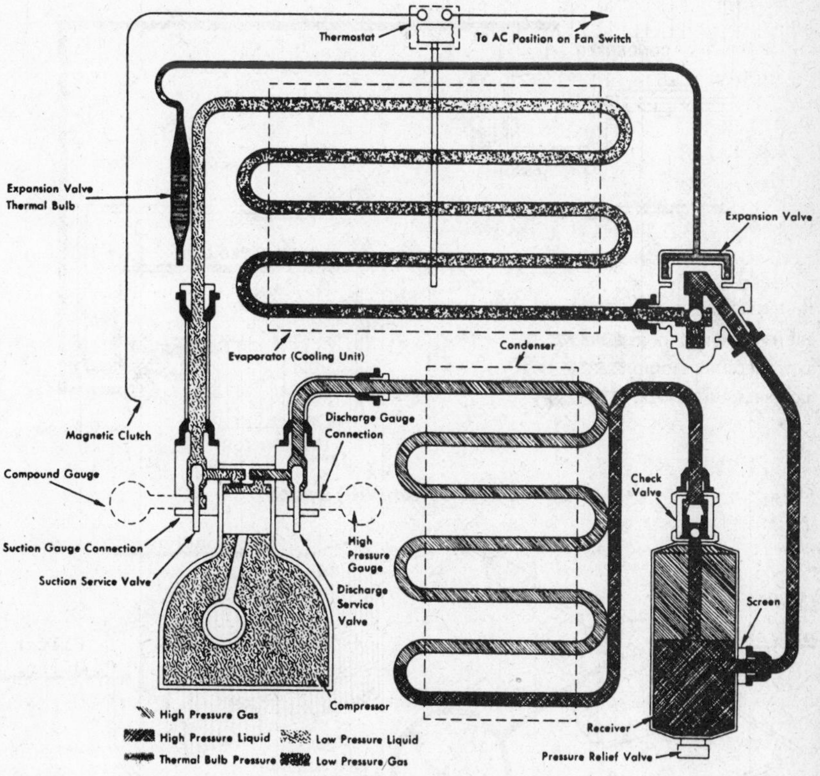

**Basic air conditioning system**

Automotive air conditioning systems are basic in design and operation, but many different components are used by the vehicle manufacturers to operate and control the systems to their specifications.

### Basic System

The basic air conditioning system utilizes the compressor, condenser, evaporator, receiver-drier, expansion valve and a thermostatic or ambient type switch to control evaporator freeze-up. The controls are manually operated and the unit is basic in design. This system is usually installed as an add-on or after-market unit. A sight glass may be used in the system.

### P.O.A. System

The P.O.A. (pilot operated absolute) suction throttling valve system contains the compressor condenser, evaporator, receiver-drier, expansion valve and a suction throttling valve. The suction throttling valve is used to keep the refrigerant gas in the evaporator at a pressure which will not allow the temperature of the evaporator core surface to go below 32 degrees F., thus preventing evaporator freeze-up. For the system to operate effectively, an equalizer line is connected between the suction side of the suction throttling valve and the expansion valve diaphragm. This modifies the operation of the expansion valve which now is controlled by the evaporator outlet temperature and compression suction pressure.

When a crank type compressor is used with the P.O.A. system, an accumulator is placed between the evaporator and the compressor. The accumulator operates as its name implies, accumulating any liquid refrigerant that may have passed from the evaporator and to prevent its moving to the compressor as a liquid, which may, in its form, cause internal compressor damage. A sight glass is normally used in this system.

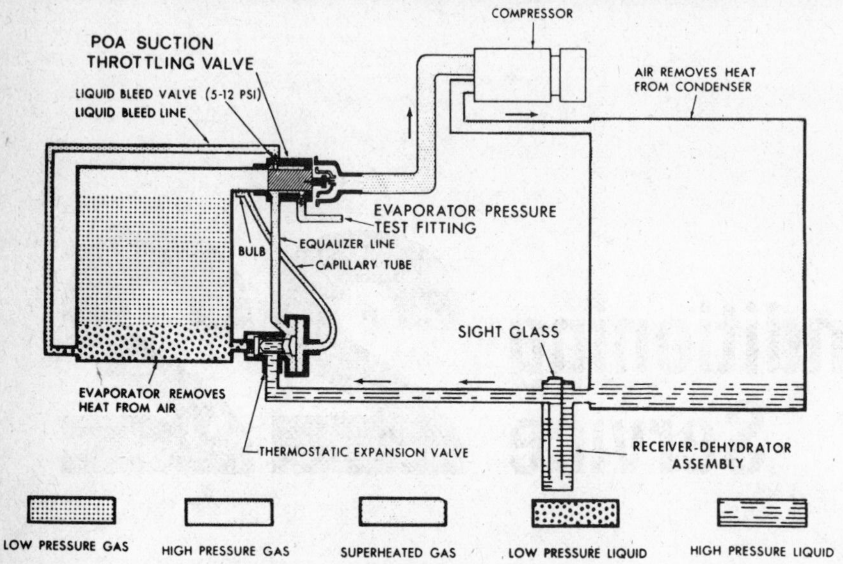


Pilot Operated Absolute (POA) system

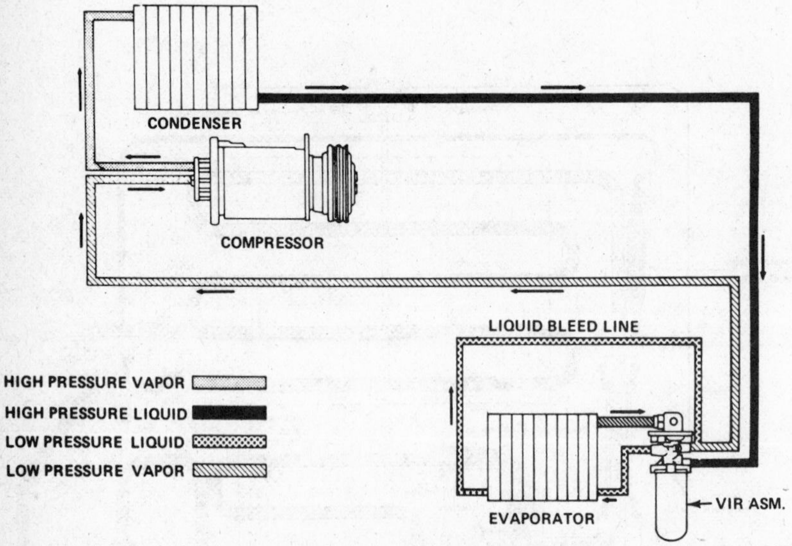


Valves In Receiver (VIR) system

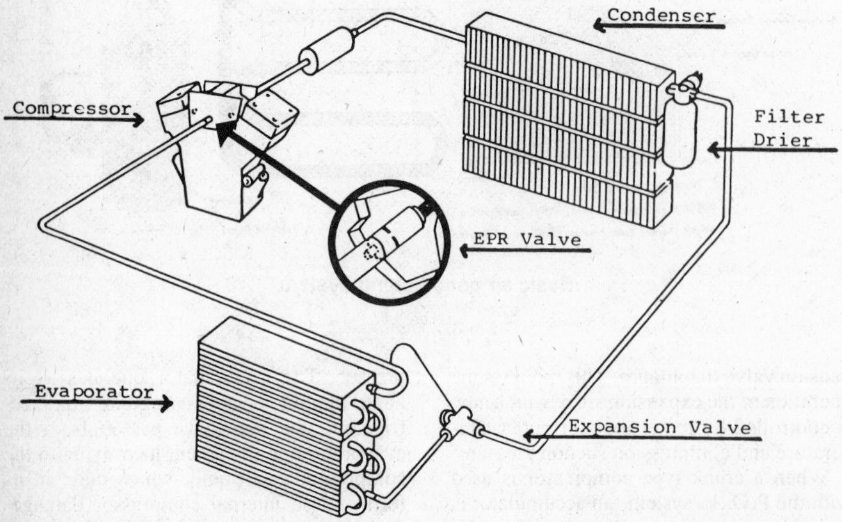


Evaporator Pressure Regulator (EPR) system

## V.I.R. System

The V.I.R. system contains the compressor evaporator, condenser, muffler and a unit containing the P.O.A. valve, expansion valve and the receiver-drier. This unit is called the V.I.R. (valves in receiver) assembly. A muffler is normally used with this system and is located between the compressor and the condenser to absorb the compressor pulsations.

The V.I.R. assembly eliminates the outside equalizer line between the outlet of the P.O.A. valve and the expansion valve. The equalizer is now a drilled orfice in the wall between the P.O.A. valve and the expansion valve cavities of the V.I.R. housing. Should the valve prove defective during tests, the unit should be replaced, as it is not repairable or adjustable. A sight glass is normally used with this system.

## E.P.R. System

The E.P.R. (evaporator pressure regulator) system includes the condenser, muffler, low pressure shut off valve receiver-drier, expansion valve, evaporator and a V-block, reciprocating crank type compressor. The E.P.R. valve is mounted on the suction side of the compressor and operates in conjunction with the expansion valve assembly, to regulate the flow of refrigerant from the evaporator to the compressor, under light air conditioning loads. By regulating the refrigerant flow, the evaporator temperature is controlled and freezing of the evaporator is prevented.

In contrast to other systems, the E.P.R. system uses the reheat procedure to control the temperature of the air, after it is cooled by passing through the evaporator fins. A manually controlled operating lever is connected to the heater water flow control valve and to a blend air door and the opening of the blend door proportions the amount of air around and through the heater core to control the mix of the cool and hot air for the desired inside temperature. A sight glass is used with this system.

Two types of expansion valves are used with this system. The first type has a capillary tube, mounted in a well on the suction line. The second type has no capillary tube, but senses the need to meter refrigerant into the evaporator by an internal sensing tube. This type of expansion valve is called the "H" type.

## "H" Valve System

As was described in the E.P.R. system, the "H" expansion valve can be used with the E.P.R. valve, located in the V-block, reciprocating crank type compressor, to control the amount of refrigerant metered into the evaporator and to control the temperature of the evaporator coils to prevent freeze-up of the condensed moisture. However, when the "H" valve is used with the three piston, axial compressor, a cycling switch is used to control the temperature of the evaporator to prevent freeze-up, rather than the E.P.R. valve, as used with the reciprocating crank type compressor. This can be called the "H" valve system for explanation purposes only and should be recognized as such. The "H" system uses the same components as the other systems, basically the compressor (axial type), condenser, evaporator, expansion valve without a capillary tube ("H" type), receiver-drier, muffler and a low pressure shut off valve. The cycling clutch switch uses a capillary tube, attached to the surface of the suction line, to sense the need for refrigerant movement and compressor operation, therefore causing the electrical clutch pulley and coil to operate the compressor on demand from the cycling switch and to open the circuit to the coil when the demand is not needed. A sight glass is used with this system.

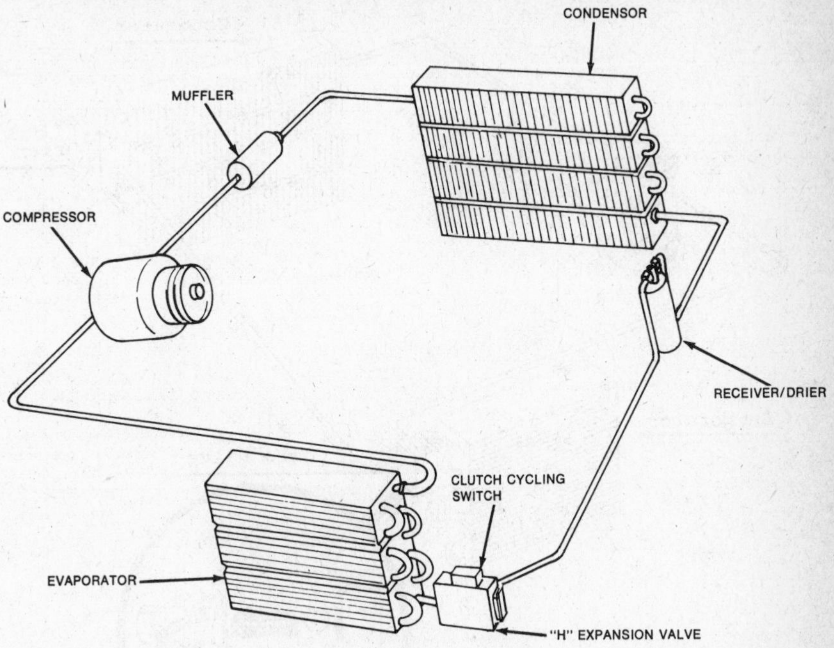

**H type expansion valve system**

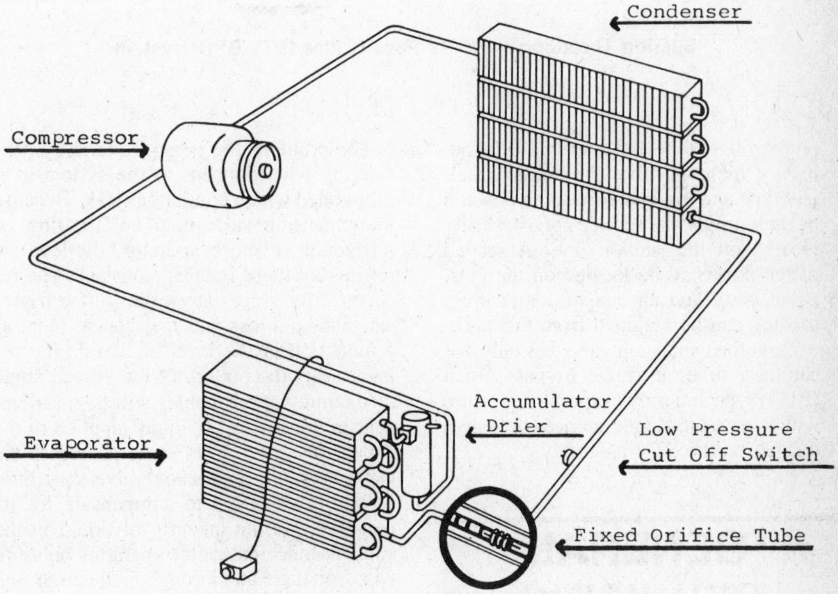

**Cycling Clutch Orifice Tube (CCOT) system**

## CCOT System

The CCOT (cycling clutch orifice tube) system includes the compressor, condensor, evaporator, an accumulator-drier, a clutch cycling switch with a capillary tube, and a fixed orifce tube, mounted to the evaporator, replacing the expansion valve.

The clutch cycling switch with a temperature probing capillary tube, cycles the compressor clutch off and on as required to maintain a selected comfortable temperature within the vehicle, while preventing evaporator freeze-up. Full control of the system is maintained through the use of a selector control, mounted in the dash assembly. The selector control makes use of a vacuum supply and electrical switches to operate mode doors and the blower motor. A sight glass is not used in this system and one should not be installed. When charging the system, the correct quantity of refrigerant must be installed by measurement.

## STV/BPO System

The STV/BPO (suction throttling valve/bypass orifice) system uses either two types of external expansion valves or a mini-combination valve assembly contains an expansion valve, suction throttling valve and a service port. The expansion valve is of the "H" block design and is used to regulate the flow of refrigerant into the evaporator core. It is also the dividing point for the high and low pressure within the system. The suction throttling valve is used to control the evaporator pressure and to prevent coil freeze-up. The suction throttling starts when the compressor suction pressure decreases below the valve setting. The compressor suction pressure can continue to drop, but the evaporator pressure is held steady by the controlling or throttling action of the STV. A pressure differential valve is used within the combination valve assembly, to allow oil–laden refrigerant to by-pass the restriction formed when the STV assembly is closed, to assure oil return to the compressor during times of reduced heat loads on the system. The by-pass valve remains closed under high heat loads since ample oil is moving through the system and compressor.

Evaporator pressure can only be measured on this system and a special type connector must be used to attach the high pressure gauge line to the service gauge port.

When either of the external type expansion valves are used, separate suction throttling valves are used. The operation of each is basically the same as the components of the combination valve assembly.

The type of external expansion valve used with the system will dictate either low suction or evaporator pressure measurements from the gauge service ports. To determine the pressure measurement that may be obtained from the system, examine the external expansion valve for one of the following conditions:

a. Should the expansion valve have

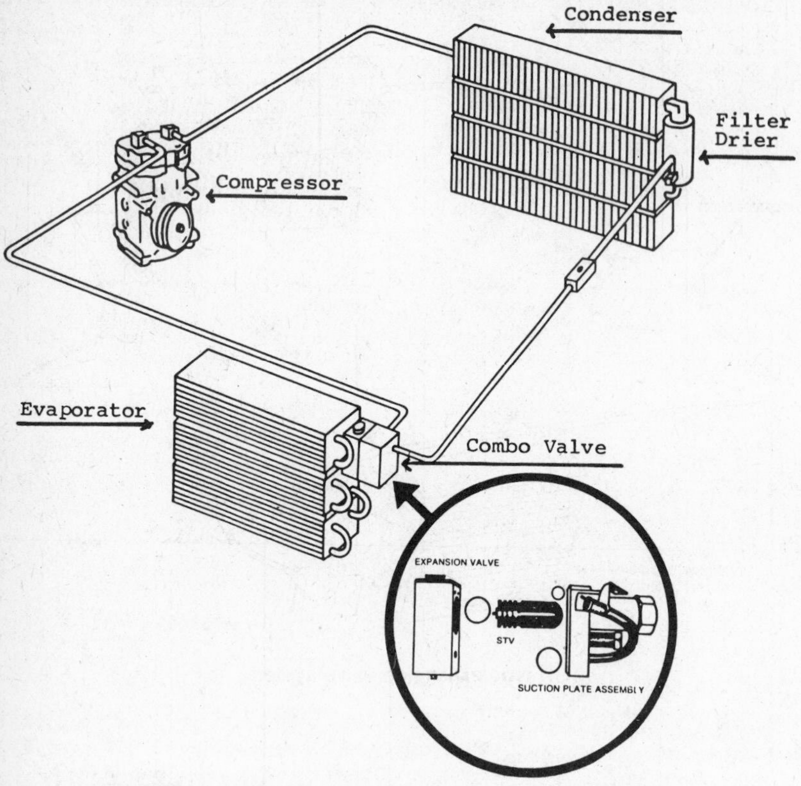


**Suction Throttling Valve/By-Pass Orifice (STV/BPO) system**

one capillary tube and one equalizer line, it is of the conventional external equalizer type and low pressure suction would be measured at the service port, normally located on the suction line. A second gauge port may be located on the POA valve body and an evaporator pressure reading can be obtained from this port.

b. If the expansion valve has only one capillary tube, it is the by-pass orfice (BPO) type and only evaporator pressure will be measured at the service port valve, located on the STV assembly.

# GENERAL SERVICING PROCEDURES

The most important aspect of air conditioning service is the maintenance of a pure and adequate charge of refrigerant in the system. A refrigeration system cannot function properly if a significant percentage of the charge is lost. Leaks are common because the severe vibration encountered in an automobile can easily cause a sufficient cracking or loosening of the air conditioning fittings; as a result, the extreme operating pressures of the system force refrigerant out.

The problem can be understood by considering what happens to the system as it is operated with a continuous leak. Because the expansion valve regulates the flow of refrigerant to the evaporator, the level of refrigerant there is fairly constant. The receiver-drier stores any excess of refrigerant, and so a loss will first appear there as a reduction in the level of liquid. As this level nears the bottom of the vessel, some refrigerant vapor bubbles will begin to appear in the stream of liquid supplied to the expansion valve. This vapor decreases the capacity of the expansion valve very little as the valve opens to compensate for its presence. As the quantity of liquid in the condenser decreases, the operating pressure will drop there and throughout the high side of the system. As the R-12 continues to be expelled, the pressure available to force the liquid through the expansion valve will continue to decrease, and, eventually, the valve's orifice will prove to be too much of a restriction for adquate flow even with the needle fully withdrawn.

At this point, low side pressure will start to drop, and severe reduction in cooling capacity, marked by freeze-up of the evaporator coil, will result. Eventually, the operating pressure of the evaporator will be lower than the pressure of the atmosphere surrounding it, and air will be drawn into the system wherever there are leaks in the low side.

Because all atmospheric air contains at least some moisture, water will enter the system and mix with the R-12 and the oil. Trace amounts of moisture will cause sludging of the oil, and corrosion of the system. Saturation and clogging of the filter-drier, and freezing of the expansion valve orifice will eventually result. As air fills the system to a greater and greater extent, it will interfere more and more with the normal flows of refrigerant and heat.

From this description, it should be obvious that much of the repairman's time will be spent detecting leaks, repairing them, and then restoring the purity and quantity of the refrigerant charge. A list of general precautions that should be observed while doing this follows:

1. Keep all tools as clean and dry as possible.
2. Thoroughly purge the service gauges and hoses of air and moisture before connecting them to the system. Keep them capped when not in use.
3. Thoroughly clean any refrigerant fitting before disconnecting it in order to minimize the entrance of dirt into the system.
4. Plan any operation that requires opening the system beforehand, in order to minimize the length of time it will be exposed to open air. Cap or seal the open ends to minimize the entrance of foreign material.
5. When adding oil, pour it through an extremely clean and dry tube or funnel. Keep the oil capped whenever possible. Do not use oil that has not been kept tightly sealed.
6. Use only refrigerant 12. Purchase refrigerant intended for use in only automatic air conditioning systems. Avoid the use of refrigerant-12 that may be packaged for another use, such as cleaning, or powering a horn, as it is impure.
7. Completely evacuate any system that has been opened to replace a component, or that has leaked sufficiently to draw in moisture and air. This requires evacuating air and moisture with a good vacuum pump for at least one hour.

If a system has been open for a considerable length of time it may be advisable to evacuate the system for up to 12 hours (overnight).

8. Use a wrench on both halves of a fitting that is to be disconnected, so as to avoid placing torque on any of the refrigerant lines.
9. When overhauling a compressor, pour some of the oil into a clean glass and inspect it. If there is evidence of dirt or metal particles, or both, flush all refrigerant components with clean refrigerant before evacuating and recharging the system. In addition, if metal particles are present, the compressor should be replaced.
10. Schrader valves may leak only when under full operating pressure. Therefore, if leakage is suspected but cannot be located, operate the system with a full charge of refrigerant and look for leaks from all Schrader valves. Replace any faulty valves.

## Additional Preventive Maintenance Checks

### ANTIFREEZE

In order to prevent heater core freeze-up during A/C operation, it is necessary to maintain permanent type antifreeze protection of +15 degrees F. or lower. A reading of −15 degrees F. is ideal since this protection also supplies sufficient corrosion inhibitors for the protection of the engine cooling system.

**NOTE: The same antifreeze should not be used longer than the manufacturer specifies.**

### RADIATOR CAP

For efficient operation of an air conditioned car's cooling system, the radiator cap should have a holding pressure which meets manufacturer's specifications. A cap which fails to hold these pressures should be replaced.

### CONDENSER

Any obstruction of, or damage to, the condenser configuration will restrict the air flow which is essential to its efficient operation. It is therefore a good rule to keep this unit clean and in proper physical shape.

**NOTE: Bug screens are regarded as obstructions.**

### CONDENSATION DRAIN TUBE

This single molded drain tube expels the condensation, which accumulates on the bottom of the evaporator housing, into the engine compartment.

If this tube is obstructed, the air conditioning performance can be restricted and condensation buildup can spill over onto the vehicle's floor.

## Safety Precautions

Because of the importance of the necessary safety precautions that must be exercised when working with air conditioning systems and R-12 refrigerant, a recap of the safety precautions are outlined.

1. Avoid contact with a charged refrigeration system, even when working on another part of the air conditioning system or vehicle. If a heavy tool comes into contact with a section of copper tubing or a heat exchanger, it can easily cause the relatively soft material to rupture.
2. When it is necessary to apply force to a fitting which contains refrigerant, as when checking that all system couplings are securely tightened, use a wrench on both parts of the fitting involved, if possible. This will avoid putting torque on refrigerant tubing.
(It is advisable, when possible, to use tube or line wrenches when tightening these flare nut fittings.)
3. Do not attempt to discharge the system by merely loosening a fitting, or removing the service valve caps and cracking these valves. Precise control is possible only when using the service gauges. Place a rag under the open end of the center charging hose while discharging the system to catch any drops of liquid that might escape. Wear protective gloves when connecting or disconnecting service gauge hoses.
4. Discharge the system only in a well ventilated area, as high concentrations of the gas can exclude oxygen and act as an anesthetic. When leak testing or soldering, this is particularly important, as toxic gas is formed when R-12 contacts any flame.
5. Never start a system without first verifying that both service valves are backseated, if equipped, and that all fittings throughout the system are snugly connected.
6. Avoid applying heat to any refrigerant line or storage vessel. Charging may be aided by using water heated to less than 125° to warm the refrigerant container. Never allow a refrigerant storage container to sit out in the sun, or near any other source of heat, such as a radiator.
7. Always wear goggles when working on a system to protect the eyes. If refrigerant contacts the eyes, it is advisable in all cases to see a physician as soon as possible.
8. Frostbite from liquid refrigerant should be treated by first gradually warming the area with cool water, and then gently applying petroleum jelly. *A physician should be consulted.*
9. Always keep refrigerant drum fittings capped when not in use. Avoid sudden shock to the drum, which might occur from dropping it, or from banging a heavy tool against it. *Never carry a drum in the passenger compartment of a car.*
10. Always completely discharge the system before painting the vehicle (if the paint is to be baked on), or before welding anywhere near refrigerant lines.

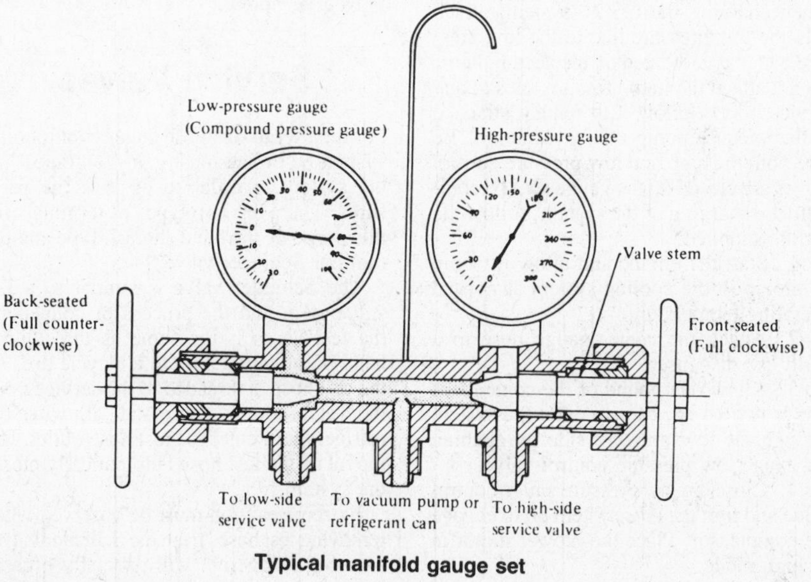


**Typical manifold gauge set**

# AIR CONDITIONING TOOLS AND GAUGES

## Test Gauges

Most of the service work performed on any air conditioning system requires the use of a set of two gauges, one for the high (head) pressure side of the system, the other for the low (suction) side.

The low side gauge records both pressure and vacuum. Vacuum readings are calibrated from 0–30 inches and the pressure graduations read from 0 to no less than 60 psi.

The high side guage measures pressure from 0 to at least 600 psi.

Both gauges are threaded into a manifold that contains two hand shut-off valves. Proper manipulation of these valves and the use of the attached-test hoses allow the user to perform the following services:

1. Test high and low side pressures.
2. Remove air, moisture, and contaminated refrigerant.
3. Purge the system of (refrigerant).
4. Charge the system (with refrigerant).

The manifold valves are designed so they have no direct effect on gauge readings, but serve only to provide for, or cut off, flow of refrigerant through the manifold. During all testing and hook-up operations, the valves are kept in a closed position to

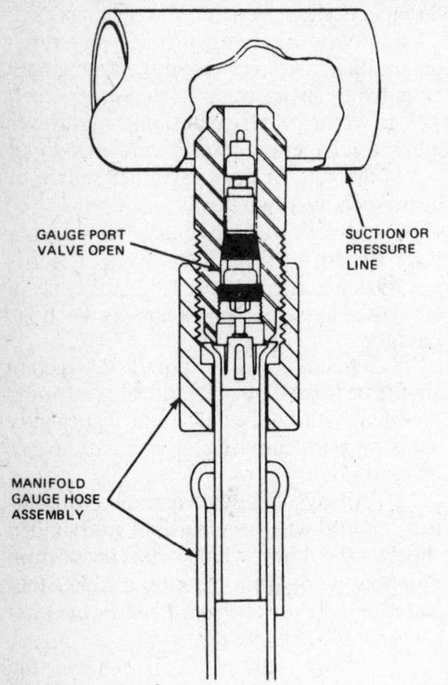


**Manifold gauge hose connected to a Schraeder type service port**

avoid disturbing the refrigeration system. The valves are opened only to purge the system of refrigerant or to charge it.

When purging the system, the center hose is uncapped at the lower end, and both valves are cracked open slightly. This allows refrigerant pressure to force the entire contents of the system out through the center hose. During charging, the valve on the high side of the manifold is closed, and the valve on the low side is cracked open. Under these conditions, the low pressure in the evaporator will draw refrigerant from the relatively warm refrigerant storage container into the system.

## SYSTEMS WITH A SIGHT GLASS

Air conditioning systems that use a sight glass as a means to check the refrigerant level should be carefully checked to avoid under or over charging. The gauge set should be attached to the system for verification of pressures.

To check the system with the sight glass, clean the glass and start the vehicle engine. Operate the air conditioning controls on maximum for approximately five minutes to stabilize the system. The room temperature should be above 70 degrees. Check the sight glass for one of the following conditions:

1. If the sight glass is clear, the compressor clutch is engaged, the compressor discharge line is warm and the compressor inlet line is cool, the system has a full charge of refrigerant.

2. If the sight glass is clear, the compressor clutch is engaged and there is no significant temperature difference between the compressor inlet and discharge lines, the system is empty or nearly empty. By having the gauge set attached to the system, a measurement can be taken. If the gauge reads less than 25 psi, the low pressure cut-off protection switch has failed.

3. If the sight glass is clear and the compressor clutch is disengaged, the clutch is defective, or the clutch circuit is open, or the system is out of refrigerant. Bypass the low pressure cut-off switch momentarily to determine the cause.

4. If the sight glass shows foam or bubbles, the system can be low on refrigerant. Occasional foam or bubbles is normal when the room temperature is above 110 degrees or below 70 degrees. To verify, increase the engine speed to approximately 1500 rpm and block the airflow through the condensor in order to increase the compressor discharge pressure to 225–250 psi. If the sight glass still shows bubbles or foam, the refrigerant level is low.

**CAUTION**

***Do not operate the vehicle engine any longer than necessary with the condensor airflow blocked. This blocking action also blocks the cooling system radiator and will cause the system to overheat rapidly.***

When the system is low on refrigerant, a leak is present or the system was not properly charged. Use a leak detector and locate the problem area and repair. If no leakage is found, charge the system to its capacity.

**CAUTION**

***It is not advisable to add refrigerant to a system utilizing the suction throttling valve and a sight glass, because the amount of refrigerant required to remove the foam or bubbles will result in an overcharge and potentially damage system components.***

## CCOT SYSTEM

When charging the CCOT system, attach only the low pressure line to the low pressure gauge port located on the accumulator. Do not attach the high pressure lines to any service port or allow it to remain attached to the vacuum pump after evacuation. Be sure both the high and low pressure control valves are closed on the gauge set. To complete the charging of the system, follow the outline supplied.

1. Start the engine and allow it to run at idle, with the cooling system at normal operating temperature.

2. Attach the center gauge hose to a multi-can dispenser.

3. Allow one pound or the contents of one or two 14 oz. cans to enter the system through the low pressure side by opening the gauge low pressure control valve.

4. Close the low pressure gauge control valve and turn the A/C system on to engage the compressor. Place the blower motor in its high mode.

5. Open the low pressure gauge control valve and draw the remaining charge into the system.

6. Close the low pressure gauge control valve and the refrigerant source valve on the multi-can dispenser. Remove the low pressure hose from the accumulator quickly to avoid loss of refrigerant through the Schrader valve.

7. Install the protective cap on the gauge port and check the system for leakage.

8. Test the system for proper operation.

# Leak Testing the System

There are several methods of detecting leaks in an air conditioning system; among them, the two most popular are (1) halide leak-detection or the "open flame method," and (2) electronic leak-detection.

The halide leak detection is a torch like device which produces a yellow-green color when refrigerant is introduced into the flame at the burner. A brilliant blue or violet color indicates the presence of large amounts of refrigerant at the burner. A small leak will cause the flame to turn a yellow-green color.

An electronic leak detector is a small portable electronic device with an extended probe. With the unit activated, the probe is passed along those components of the system which contain refrigerant. If a leak is detected, the unit will sound an alarm signal or activate a display signal depending on the manufacturer's design. It is advisable to follow the manufacturer's instructions as the design and function of the detection may vary significantly.

**NOTE: Caution should be taken to operate either type of detector in well ventilated areas, so as to reduce the chance of personal injury, which may result from coming in contact with poisonous gases produced when R-12 is exposed to flame or electric spark.**

# Service Valves

For the user to diagnose an air conditioning system he or she must gain "entrance" to the system in order to observe the pressures. There are two types of terminals for this purpose, the hand shut off type and the familiar Schrader valve.

The Schrader valve is similar to a tire valve stem and the process of connecting the test hoses is the same as threading a hand pump outlet hose to a bicycle tire. As the test hose is threaded to the service port, the valve core is depressed, allowing the refrigerant to enter the test hose outlet. Removal of the test hose automatically closes the system.

Extreme caution must be observed when removing test hoses from the Schrader valves as some refrigerant will normally escape,

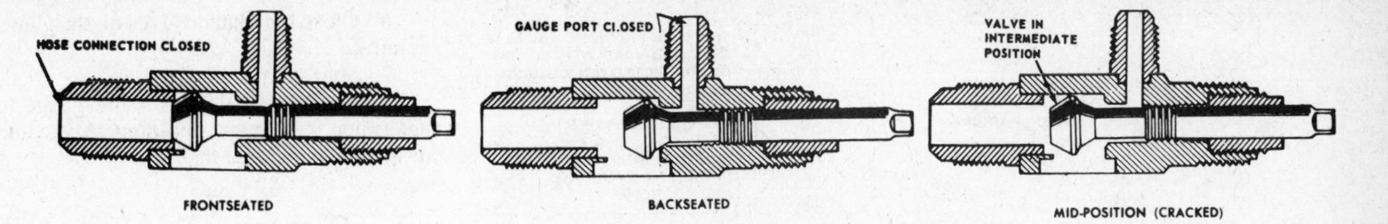


**Manual service valve positions**

## BAR GAUGE MANIFOLD AND COMPRESSOR SERVICE VALVE SETTINGS

| Condition | Manifold Valves | Compressor Valves |
|---|---|---|
| Testing System | Both fully closed | Both cracked off backseat |
| Depressurizing System | Both cracked open | Both at mid position |
| Evacuating the system | Both wide open | Both at mid position |
| Charging in gas form with compressor running | High pressure valve closed<br>Low pressure valve cracked | High pressure valve cracked off backseat<br>Low pressure valve at mid position |
| Charging in liquid form with compressor off | Low pressure valve closed<br>High pressure valve wide open | Both valves mid positioned |

**Note:** A very small leak, causing system discharge about every two weeks, can be caused by a leaky Schrader type service valve. Check these valves with extra care when testing for a small leak.

usually under high pressure (observe safety precautions).

Some systems have hand shut-off valves (the stem can be rotated with a special racheting box wrench) that can be positioned in the following three ways:

1. FRONT SEATED—Rotated to full clockwise position.

   a. Refrigerant will not flow to the compressor, but will reach the test gauge port. COMPRESSOR WILL BE DAMAGED IF SYSTEM IS TURNED ON IN THIS POSITION.

   b. The compressor is now isolated and ready for service. However, care must be exercised when removing service valves from the compressor as a residue of refrigerant may still be present within the compressor. Therefore, remove service valves slowly, observing all safety precautions.

2. BACK SEATED—Rotated to full counterclockwise position. Normal position for system while in operation. Refrigerant flows to compressor but not to test gauge.

3. MID-POSITION (CRACKED)—Refrigerant flows to entire system. Gauge port (with hose connected) open for testing.

## USING THE MANIFOLD GAUGES

The following are step-by-step procedures to guide the user to correct gauge usage.

1. WEAR GOGGLES OR FACE SHIELD DURING ALL TESTING OPERATIONS. BACKSEAT HAND SHUT-OFF TYPE SERVICE VALVES.
2. Remove caps from the high and low side of the service ports. Make sure both gauge valves are closed.
3. Connect the low side test hose to the service valve that leads to the evaporator (located between the evaporator outlet and the compressor).
4. Attach the high side test hose to the service valve that leads to the condenser.
5. Mid-position hand shutoff type service valves.
6. Start the engine and allow for warm-up. All testing and charging of the system should be done after the engine and system have reached normal operation temperatures (except when using certain charging stations).
7. Adjust the air conditioner controls to maximum cold.
8. Observe the gauge readings. When the gauges are not being used it is a good idea to:

   a. Keep both hand valves in the closed position.

   b. Attach both ends of the high and low service hoses to the manifold if extra outlets are present on the manifold, or plug them if not. Also, keep the center charging hose attached to an empty refrigerant can. This extra precaution will reduce the possibility of moisture entering the gauges. If air and moisture have gotten into the gauges, purge the hoses by supplying refrigerant under pressure to the center hose with both gauge valves open and all openings unplugged.

# DISCHARGING, EVACUATING AND CHARGING

## Discharging the System

**CAUTION**

***Perform this operation in a well-ventilated area.***

When it is necessary to remove (purge) the refrigerant pressurized in the system, follow this procedure:

1. Operate the air conditioner for at least 10 minutes.
2. Attach the gauges, shut off the engine and air conditioner.
3. Place a container or rag at the outlet of the center charging hose on the gauge. The refrigerant will be discharged there and this precaution will avoid its uncontrolled exposure.
4. Open the low side hand valve on the gauge slightly.
5. Open the high side hand valve slightly.

**NOTE: Too rapid a purging process will be identified by the appearance of an oil foam. If this occurs, close the hand valves a little more until this condition stops.**

6. Close both hand valves on the gauge set when the pressures read 0 and all the refrigerant has left the system.

## Evacuating the System

Before charging any system it is necessary to purge the refrigerant and draw out the trapped moisture with a suitable vacuum pump. Failure to do so will result in ineffective charging and possible damage to the system.

Use this hook-up for the proper evacuation procedure:

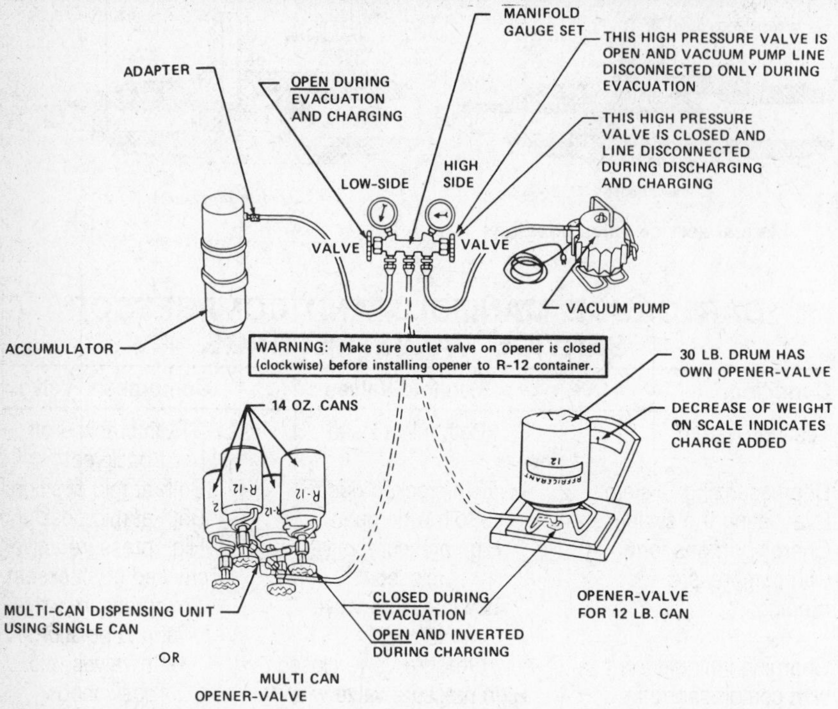


**Typical gauge connections for discharge, evacuation and charging the system**

1. Connect both service gauge hoses to the high and low service outlets.
2. Open both high and low side hand valves on the gauge manifold.
3. Open both service valves a slight amount (from back seated position), allow the refrigerant to discharge from the system.
4. Install the center charging hose of the gauge set to the vacuum pump.
5. Operate the vacuum pump for at least one hour (if the system has been subjected to open conditions for a prolonged period of time, it may be necessary to "pump the system down" overnight. Refer to the "System Sweep" procedure).

**NOTE: If the low pressure gauge does not show at least 28″ hg. within 5 minutes, check the system for a leak or loose gauge connectors.**

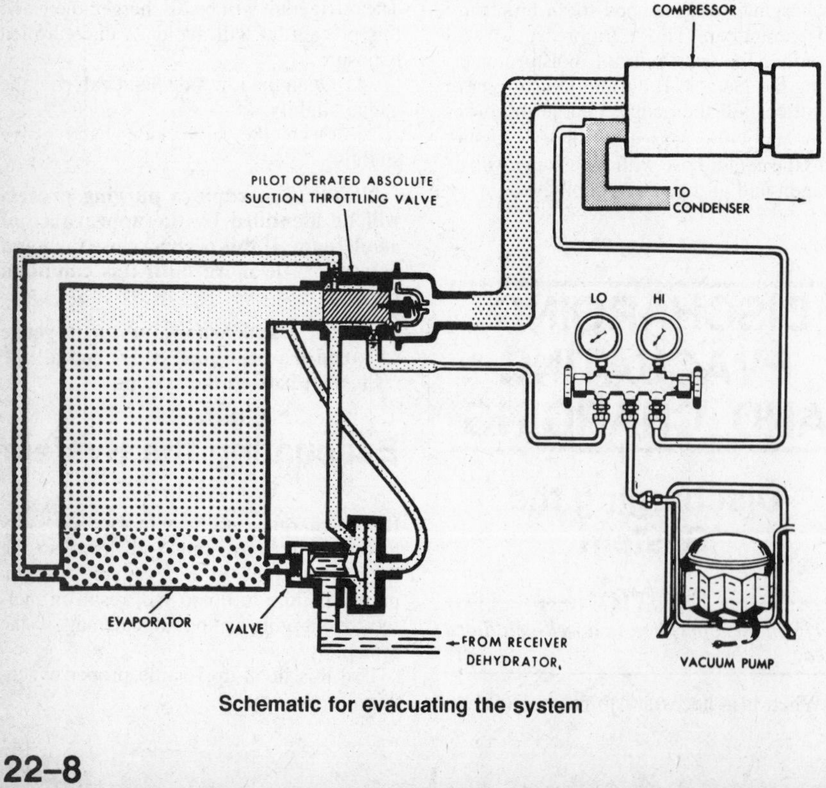


**Schematic for evacuating the system**

6. Close both hand valves on the gauge manifold.
7. Shut off the pump.
8. Observe the low pressure gauge to determine if vacuum is holding. A vacuum drop may indicate a leak.

## System Sweep

An efficient vacuum pump can remove all the air contained in a contaminated air conditioning system very quickly because of its vapor state. Moisture, however, is far more difficult to remove because the vacuum must force the liquid to evaporate before it will be able to remove it from the system. If a system has become severely contaminated, as, for example, it might become after all the charge was lost in conjunction with vehicle accident damage, moisture removal is extremely time consuming. A vacuum pump could remove all of the moisture only if it were operated for 12 hours or more.

Under these conditions, sweeping the system with refrigerant will speed the process of moisture removal considerably. To sweep, follow the following procedure:

1. Connect a vacuum pump to the gauges, operate it until vacuum ceases to increase, then continue operation for ten more minutes.
2. Charge the system with 50% of its rated refrigerant capacity.
3. Operate the system at fast idle for ten minutes.
4. Discharge the system.
5. Repeat twice the process of charging to 50% capacity, running the system for ten minutes, and discharging it, for a total of three sweeps.
6. Replace the drier.
7. Pump the system down as detailed in Step 1.
8. Charge the system.

## Charging the System

**CAUTION**

***Never attempt to charge the system by opening the high pressure gauge control while the compressor is operating. The compressor accumulating pressure can burst the refrigerant container, causing severe personal injuries.***

### BASIC SYSTEM

In this procedure the refrigerant enters the suction side of the system as a vapor while the compressor is running. Before proceeding, the system should be in a partial vacuum after adequate evacuation. Both hand valves on the gauge manifold should be closed.

1. Attach both test hoses to their respective service valve ports. Mid-position manually operated service valves, if present.

2. Install a dispensing valve (closed position) on the refrigerant container (single and multiple refrigerant manifolds are available to accommodate one to four 15 oz. cans).

3. Attach the center charging hose to the refrigerant container valve.

4. Open the dispensing valve on the refrigerant can.

5. Loosen the center charging hose coupler where it connects to the gauge manifold to allow the escaping refrigerant to purge the hose of contaminants.

6. Tighten the center charging hose connection.

7. Purge the low pressure test hose at the gauge manifold.

8. Start the engine, roll down the windows and adjust the air conditioner to maximum cooling. The engine should be at normal operating temperature before proceeding. The heated environment helps the liquid vaporize more efficiently.

9. Crack open the low side hand valve on the manifold. Manipulate the valve so that the refrigerant that enters the system does not cause the low side pressure to exceed 40 psi. Too sudden a surge may permit the entrance of unwanted liquid to the compressor. Since liquids cannot be compressed, the compressor will suffer damage if compelled to attempt it. If the suction side of the system remains in a vacuum, the system is blocked. Locate and correct the condition before proceeding any further.

**NOTE: Placing the refrigerant can in a container of warm water (no hotter than 125° F) will speed the charging process. Slight agitation of the can is helpful too, but be careful not to turn the can upside down.**

Some manufacturers allow for a partial charging of the A/C system in the form of a liquid (can inverted and compressor off) by opening the high side gauge valve only, and putting the high side compressor service valve in the middle position (if so equipped). The remainder of the refrigerant is then added in the form of a gas in the normal manner, through the suction side only.

## SYSTEMS WITHOUT SIGHT GLASS, EXCEPT CCOT SYSTEM

The following procedure can be used to quickly determine whether or not an air conditioning system has the proper charge of refrigerant (providing ambient temperature is above 70° F. or 21° C.). This check can be made in a manner of minutes, thus facilitating system diagnosis by pinpointing the problem to the amount of charge in the system or by eliminating this possibility from the overall checkout.

1. Engine must be warm (thermostat open).
2. Hood and body doors open.
3. Selector lever set at NORM.
4. Temperature lever at COLD.
5. Blower on HI.
6. Normal engine idle.
7. Hand-feel the temperature of the evaporator inlet and outlet pipes with the compressor engaged.

a. Both same temperature or some degree cooler than ambient—proper condition: check for other problems.

b. Inlet pipe cooler than outlet pipe—low refrigerant charge.

- Add a slight amount of refrigerant until both pipes feel the same.
- Then add 15 oz. (1 can) additional refrigerant.

c. Inlet pipe has front accumulation—outlet pipe warmer: proceed as in Step b above.

If during the charging process the head pressure exceeds 200 psi, place an electric fan in front of the car and direct the turbulent air to the condenser. If no fan is available, repeatedly pour cool water over the top of the condenser. These cooling actions may be necessary on an extremely warm day to help dissipate the heat emitted by the engine during idle.

If this fails and pressure on the discharge side continues to rise, the system may be overcharged or the engine might be overheating. *Never* allow head pressure to go beyond 240 psi. during charging. If this condition occurs, stop the engine, find and correct the problem.

8. Continue dispensing refrigerant until the container is no longer cool to the touch. On a humid day, the outside of the container will frost. When the frost disappears the can is usually empty. To detach the dispensing can:

a. close the low pressure test gauge hand valve.

b. crack open the low pressure test hose at the manifold until the remaining pressure escapes.

c. tighten the hose coupler.

d. loosen the hose coupler connected to the refrigerant can.

e. discard the empty can and repeat Steps 2–8.

9. Continue to add refrigerant to the required capacity of the system. (Usually marked on the compressor).

**CAUTION**

***DO NOT OVERCHARGE. This condition is usually indicated by an abnormally high side pressure reading and a noisy compressor resulting in ineffective cooling and damage to the system.***

## SYSTEMS WITH A SIGHT GLASS

Air conditioning systems that use a sight glass as a means to check the refrigerant level should be carefully checked to avoid under or over charging. The gauge set should be attached to the system for verification of pressures.

To check the system with the sight glass, clean the glass and start the vehicle engine. Operate the air conditioning controls on maximum for approximately five minutes

| Amount of refrigerant / Check item | Almost no refrigerant | Insufficient | Suitable | Too much refrigerant |
|---|---|---|---|---|
| Temperature of high pressure and low pressure lines. | Almost no difference between high pressure and low pressure side temperature. | High pressure side is warm and low pressure side is fairly cold. | High pressure side is hot and low pressure side is cold. | High pressure side is abnormally hot. |
| State in sight glass. | Bubbles flow continuously. **Bubbles will disappear and something like mist will flow when refrigerant is nearly gone.** | The bubbles are seen at intervals of 1 - 2 seconds. | Almost transparent. Bubbles may appear when engine speed is raised and lowered. **No clear difference exists betwen these two conditions.** | No bubbles can be seen. |
| | 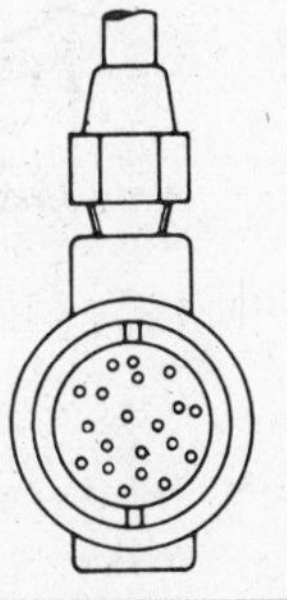 | 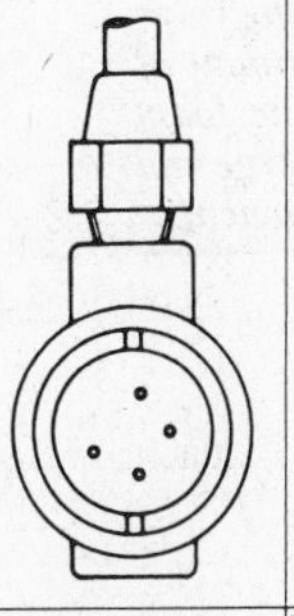 | 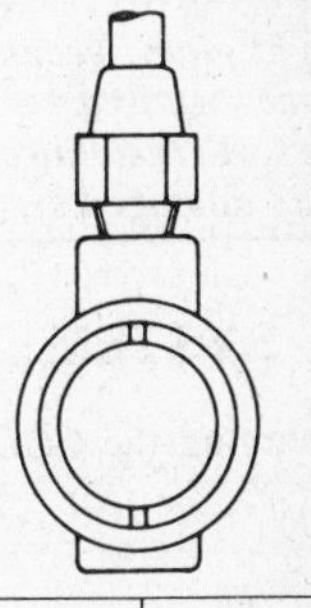 | |
| Pressure of system. | High pressure side is abnormally low. | Both pressure on high and low pressure sides are slightly low. | Both pressures on high and low pressure sides are normal. | Both pressures on high and low pressure sides are abnormally high. |
| Repair. | **Stop compressor immediately** and conduct an overall check. | Check for gas leakage, repair as required, replenish and charge system. | | Discharge refrigerant from service valve of low pressure side. |

**Using a sight glass to determine the relative refrigerant charge**

to stabilize the system. The room temperature should be above 70 degrees. Check the sight glass for one of the following conditions:

1. If the sight glass is clear, the compressor clutch is engaged, the compressor discharge line is warm and the compressor inlet line is cool, the system has a full charge of refrigerant.

2. If the sight glass is clear, the compressor clutch is engaged and there is no significant temperature difference between the compressor inlet and discharge lines, the system is empty or nearly empty. By having the gauge set attached to the system, a measurement can be taken. If the gauge reads less than 25 psi, the low pressure cut-off protection switch has failed.

3. If the sight glass is clear and the compressor clutch is disengaged, the clutch is defective, or the clutch circuit is open, or the system is out of refrigerant. By-pass the low pressure cut-off switch momentarily to determine the cause.

4. If the sight glass shows foam or bubbles, the system can be low on refrigerant. Occasional foam or bubbles is normal when the room temperature is above 110 degrees or below 70 degrees. To verify, increase the engine speed to approximately 1500 rpm and block the airflow through the condenser in order to increase the compressor discharge pressure to 225–250 psi. If the sight glass still shows bubbles or foam, the refrigerant level is low.

**CAUTION**

***Do not operate the vehicle engine any longer than necessary with the condenser airflow blocked. This blocking action also blocks the cooling system radiator and will cause the system to overheat rapidly.***

When the system is low on refrigerant, a leak is present or the system was not properly charged. Use a leak detector and locate the problem area and repair. If no leakage is found, charge the system to its capacity.

**CAUTION**

***It is not advisable to add refrigerant to a system utilizing the suction throttling valve and a sight glass, because the amount of refrigerant required to remove the foam or bubbles will result in an overcharge and potentially damaged system components.***

### CCOT SYSTEM

When charging the CCOT system, attach only the low pressure line to the low pressure gauge port located on the accumulator. Do not attach the high pressure line to any service port or allow it to remain attached to the vacuum pump after evacuation. Be sure both the high and the low pressure control valves are closed on the gauge set. To complete the charging of the system, follow the outline supplied.

1. Start the engine and allow it to run at idle, with the cooling system at normal operating temperature.

2. Attach the center gauge hose to a single or multi-can dispenser.

3. With the multi-can dispenser inverted, allow one pound or the contents of one or two 14 oz. cans to enter the system through the low pressure side by opening the gauge low pressure control valve.

4. Close the low pressure gauge control valve and turn the A/C system on to engage the compressor. Place the blower motor in its high mode.

5. Open the low pressure gauge control valve and draw the remaining charge into the system.

6. Close the low pressure gauge control valve and the refrigerant source valve, on the multi-can dispenser. Remove the low pressure hose from the accumulator quickly to avoid loss of refrigerant through the Schrader valve.

7. Install the protective cap on the gauge port and check the system for leakage.

8. Test the system for proper operation.

## Leak Testing the System

There are several methods of detecting leaks in an air conditioning system; among them, the two most popular are (1) halide leak-detection or the "open flame method," and (2) electronic leak-detection.

The halide leak detection is a torch like device which produces a yellow-green color when refrigerant is introduced into the flame at the burner. A purple or violet color indicates the presence of large amounts of refrigerant at the burner.

An electronic leak detector is a small portable electronic device with an extended probe. With the unit activated, the probe is passed along those components of the system which contain refrigerant. If a leak is detected, the unit will sound an alarm signal or activate a display signal depending on the manufacturer's design. It is advisable to follow the manufacturer's instructions as the design and function of the detection may vary significantly.

**CAUTION**

***Caution should be taken to operate either type of detector in well ventilated areas, so as to reduce the chance of personal injury, which may result from coming in contact with poisonous gases produced when R-12 is exposed to flame or electric spark.***

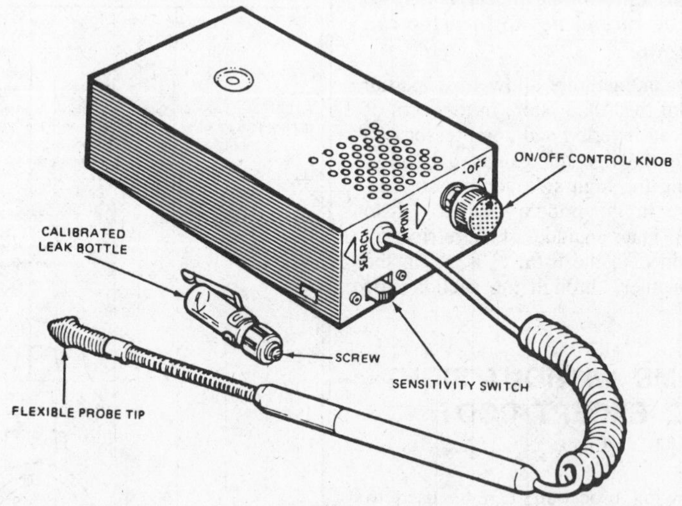

**Electronic leak detector**

# Diesel Service 23

**NOTE: Most procedures associated with diesel engined cars are similar to gas engined cars, although many parts of the diesel engine are unique compared to their gas engine counterparts. Standard maintenance and service procedures are given here while component removal, installation and adjustment procedures unique to diesel engines can be found in the appropriate section.**

## HOW THE DIESEL ENGINE WORKS

Four-stroke diesels require four piston strokes for the complete cycle of actions, exactly like a gasoline engine. The difference lies in how the fuel mixture is ignited. A diesel engine does not rely on a conventional spark ignition to ignite the fuel mixture for the power stroke. Instead, a diesel relies on the heat produced by compressing air in the combustion chamber to ignite the fuel and produce a power stroke. This is known as a compression-ignition engine. No fuel enters the cylinder on the intake stroke, only air. At the end of the compression stroke, fuel is sprayed into the precombustion chamber (prechamber). The mixture ignites and spreads out into the main combustion chamber, forcing the piston downward (power stroke). The fuel/air mixture ignites because of the very high combustion chamber temperatures generated by the extraordinarily high compression ratios used in diesel engines. Typically, the compression ratios used in automotive diesels run anywhere from 16:1 to 23:1. A typical spark-ignition engine has a ratio of about 8:1. This is why a spark-ignition engine which continues to run after you have shut off the engine is said to be ''dieseling''. It is running on combustion chamber heat alone.

Designing an engine to ignite on its own combustion chamber heat poses certain problems. For instance, although a diesel engine has no need for a coil, spark plugs, or a distributor, it does need what are known as ''glow plugs''. These superficially resemble spark plugs, but are only used to warm the combustion chambers when the engine is cold. Without these plugs, cold starting would be impossible, due to the enormously high compression ratios and the characteristics of the diesel fuel itself.

All diesel engines use fuel injection, be-

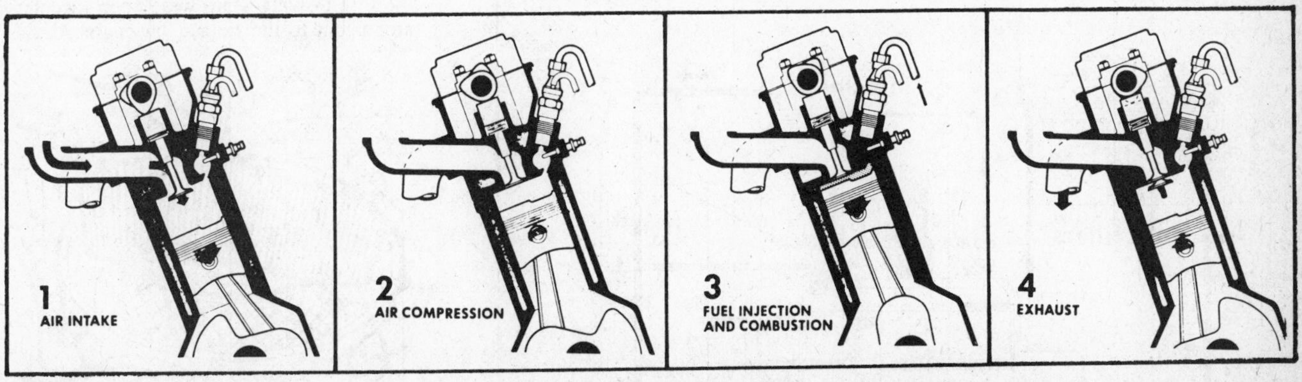


**4-stroke diesel engine cycle. At *air intake* (1), rotation of the crankshaft drives a toothed belt that turns the camshaft, opening the intake valve. As the piston moves down, a vacuum is created, sucking fresh air into the cylinder, past the open intake valve. *Air compression* (2): As the piston moves up, both valves are closed, and the air is compressed about 23 times smaller than its original volume. The compressed air reaches a temperature of about 1,650°F., far above the temperature needed to ignite diesel fuel. *Fuel injection and compression* (3): As the piston reaches the top of the stroke, the air temperature is at its maximum. A fine mist of fuel is sprayed into the prechamber, where it ignites, and the flame front spreads rapidly into the combustion chamber. The piston is forced downward by the pressure (about 500 psi) of expanding gases. *Exhaust* (4): As the energy of combustion is spent and the piston begins to move upward again, the exhaust valve opens, and burnt gases are forced out past the open valve. As the piston starts down, the exhaust valve closes, the intake valve opens, and the air intake stroke begins again.**

**Increasingly, modern diesel engines are being equipped with turbochargers, exhaust gas–driven devices that force more air into the engine to increase power output**

cause unlike spark-ignited engines, the fuel cannot be drawn through the intake tract

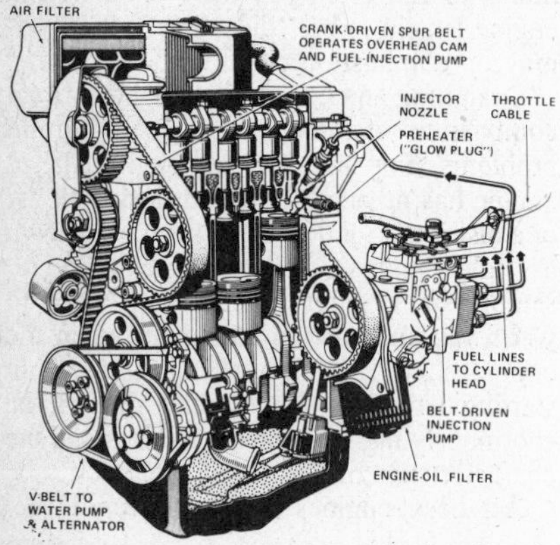


**Cutaway view of typical 4-cylinder diesel engine.**

and into the cylinders. The introduction of fuel into a diesel engine must be precisely timed so that each cylinder "fires" at the proper moment. Also, the fuel injection pressure (at the cylinder) must be great enough to overcome the high compression pressures, and properly atomize the fuel without the aid of a moving air mass (as in a carbureted gas engine). It is not uncommon for diesel engine fuel injection pressures to be set at 1500–1700 psi.

Diesel engines share many of their basic mechanical components with gasoline engines, though the cylinder block, head(s), crankshaft, connecting rods, pistons, etc., are manufactured to be much stronger for use in diesel engines. The additional strength of the components is necessary due to the very high cylinder pressure generated within the diesel engine.

## Maintenance and Service Procedures

Maintenance procedures for the diesel engine generally fall into three categories:

1. Fuel system
2. Starting system
3. Engine mechanical systems

Of these, the fuel system is usually the most likely source of engine troubles, and should be high on the list for regular maintenance attention.

### FUEL SYSTEM

The typical diesel engine fuel system consists of fuel tank, fuel feed and return lines, mechanical fuel injection pump, fuel injectors and lines, and a large capacity fuel filter. On some models, the engine may also be equipped with a small, low pressure fuel pump which feeds the injection pump.

In addition to these, the air intake system (air cleaner, inlet manifold) should be checked over regularly to insure unrestricted air flow into the cylinders.

In operation, fuel is sucked out of the fuel tank by the injection pump (or its feed pump) and fed by the injection pump to the injectors in the cylinder head at a very high pressure. Before the fuel is allowed to enter the main injection pump, it passes through a specially built fuel filter which traps solid particles (and water on some models) in the fuel. Fuel that is not used is pumped back to the fuel tank through the fuel return lines. This recirculated fuel helps cool the injection pump.

#### *Air Cleaner*

On a gasoline engine, the volume of air taken in by the engine is controlled by throttle valves. When the throttle valves are closed (engine idling), air intake is restricted. When the throttle valves are wide open (accelerator pedal to the floor), the engine draws

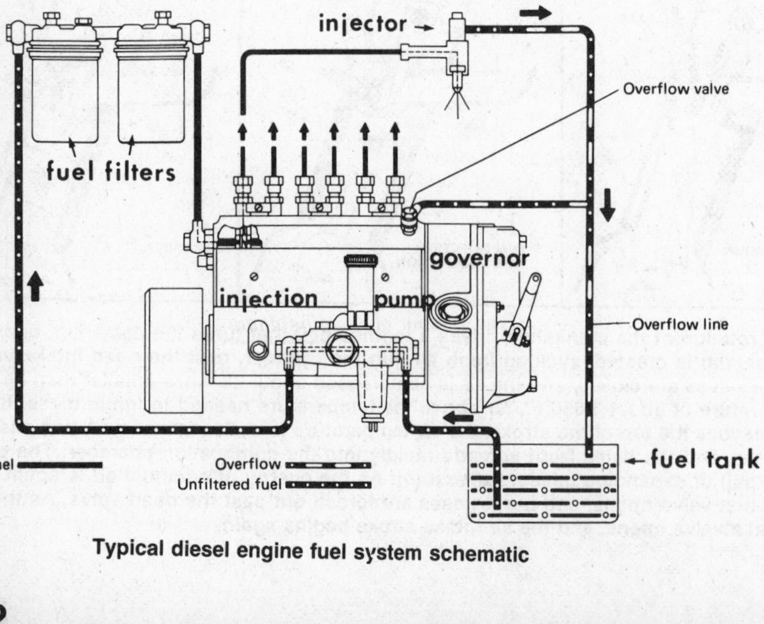


**Typical diesel engine fuel system schematic**

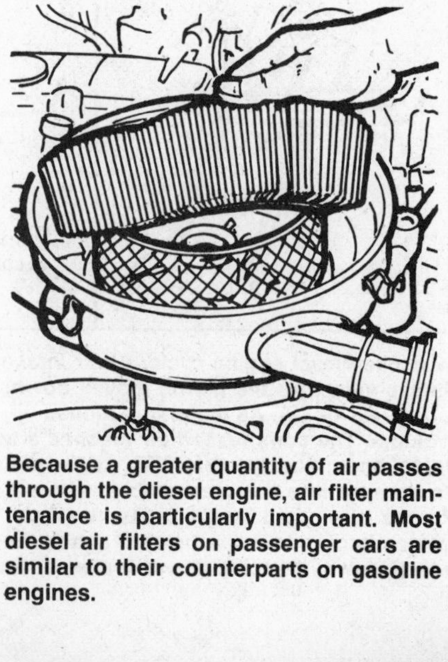

**Because a greater quantity of air passes through the diesel engine, air filter maintenance is particularly important. Most diesel air filters on passenger cars are similar to their counterparts on gasoline engines.**

in the maximum amount of air it possibly can. This applies to both carbureted and fuel injected gasoline engines.

The speed (rpm) of a diesel engine is controlled by the quantity of fuel which is injected into the engine; no air metering restrictions (throttle valves) are used. Because of this, diesel engines ingest as much air as they possibly can under all conditions. A much greater volume of air passes through the air cleaner of a diesel per mile, therefore, diesel air filters must either be larger or the filter replacement intervals more frequent than those of a similarly sized gasoline engine.

One word of caution: never remove the air cleaner on a diesel with the engine running, and never run the engine with the air cleaner removed. The volume of air drawn through the inlet manifold is very great, and, because the inlet manifold is unobstructed, anything drawn into the inlet manifold (air cleaner wing nut, etc.) goes straight to the combustion chambers, where it can cause major engine damage.

### Fuel Filter

The diesel engine fuel filter is usually larger than the filter used on gasoline engines. The extra capacity is needed to trap the suspended particles in diesel fuel, which is generally "dirtier" than gasoline.

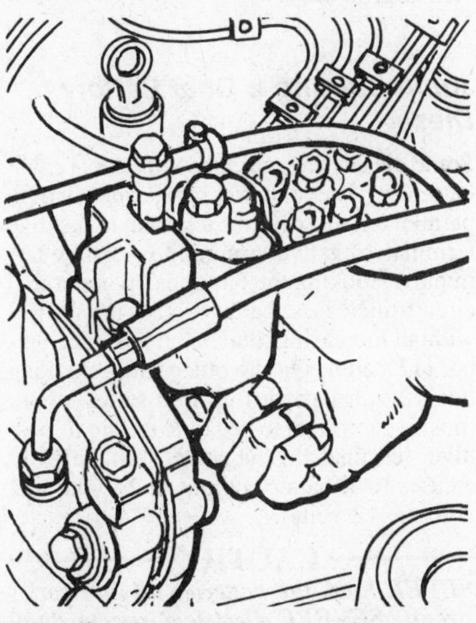

**Many diesel engines use a spin-on type primary fuel filter.**

On some engines, the fuel filter looks like a second engine oil filter, and is removed and installed in the same manner as the canister-type oil filter.

The fuel filter must be changed according to the manufacturer's suggested interval. See the owner's manual for information.

After installing the fuel filter start the engine and check for leaks. Run the engine for about two minutes, then stop the engine for the same amount of time to allow any air trapped in the injection system to bleed off.

Many diesels also have a small, in-tank filter which is usually maintenance-free.

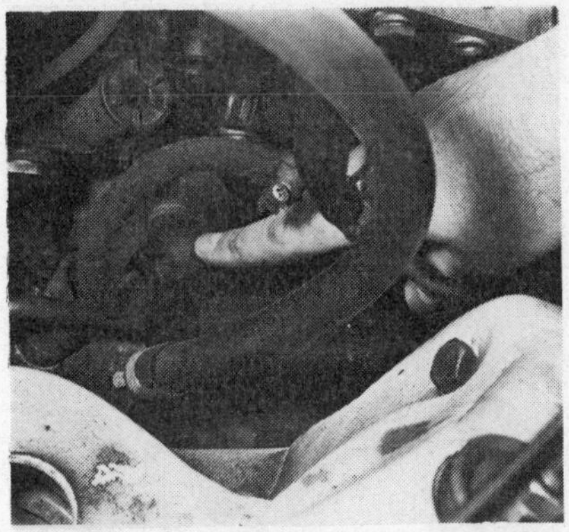

**A smaller, in-line secondary filter is used on many engines.**

**Check the tightness of the clamps securing the injector lines. Note that the injector lines are all the same length.**

**Mercedes-Benz diesel engines use this stop switch, which shuts off fuel delivery**

### Water In Fuel

Diesel fuel is a hydrophilic fluid, that is, it naturally attracts water. Since diesel fuel and water do not mix, the water remains floating beneath the fuel at the bottom of the tank. This water must be removed every now and then, or it will be sucked into the fuel circuit and pass through the injection system, causing corrosion and possible component failure (injection pumps can cost up to $1,000). Water in the fuel system will also cause the engine to run poorly, if at all.

Most diesel fuel tanks are equipped with a separator which can isolate from 1 to 3 gallons of water from the fuel.

Many diesels are also equipped with "Water in Fuel" lights in the dashboard which warn of the presence of water in the fuel tank. These warning systems can be installed on models not so equipped.

On some diesels, there is a water catcher in the bottom of the fuel filter which can easily be bled off. In addition, there are several bolt-on water filters on the market which attach to the fuel line under the hood and separate water from the fuel. Depending on which kind you buy, draining water from the system is simply a matter of opening the petcock at the bottom of the filter and letting the water drain out, or, if money is no object, a separator is available on which water is drained from the filter simply by activating a switch on the dashboard.

### Removing Water from the Fuel Tank

Treat diesel fuel with the same respect you would gasoline, and after the procedure, properly dispose of the fuel.

1. Remove the fuel tank cap.
2. Connect a pump or siphon hose to the ¼ in. fuel return hose (smaller of the two fuel hoses) above the rear axle, or under the hood near the fuel pump (on the passenger's side of the engine, near the front).
3. Siphon until all water is removed from the tank. Do not use your mouth to create siphon vacuum, EVER! The best method is to siphon the water into a large capacity see-through container. The water will collect at the bottom of the container.
4. When all water has been removed from the tank, be sure to reinstall the fuel return hose and fuel cap.

**NOTE: If the entire fuel system (not just the tank) is contaminated by water, the vehicle must be stopped immediately and the fuel system must be purged. This includes draining and removing the fuel tank, blowing low pressure compressed air backwards through the fuel feed and return lines, and bleeding the water out of all injection components. This job should be referred to a qualified technician.**

### Cold Weather Fuel System Maintenance

**CAUTION**

***NEVER use "starting aids" (e.g.—ether) to help start a diesel engine—serious engine damage will result.***

As will be explained later under "Fuel Recommendations", diesel fuel tends to become "cloudy", or thicker, as the temperature drops. The thicker the diesel fuel becomes, the slower it flows through the fuel system, until finally it stops flowing altogether somewhere near the bottom of the thermometer.

One way to fight sluggish fuel flow is to use winterized blends of diesel fuel, straight No. 1 diesel fuel or add cold weather additives to the fuel to improve flow in cold weather.

**NOTE: Consult your owners manual for recommendations and be sure to use a fuel conditioner compatible with water separators.**

Another way is to install an aftermarket fuel system pre-heater. These are generally canisters which connect into the fuel line and use coolant from the engine cooling system to heat the fuel before it reaches the injection pump. The one drawback with this system is the engine must be started before the pre-heater begins to work. Also available are electric fuel warmers. These preheat the fuel going into the filter and can be used in conjunction with the coolant-type fuel heater.

**Cold weather additives and fuel conditioners can help improve cold weather flow of diesel fuel.**

Some manufacturers offer an optional electric diesel fuel heater and engine block heaters. The fuel heater is thermostatically controlled to heat the fuel before it enters the fuel filter when fuel temperature is 20°F or lower. The fuel heater works only when the ignition key is in the RUN position. On these models, the fuel tank filter has a bypass valve which allows fuel to flow to the heater when the tank filter is covered with fuel wax. The engine block heater is equipped with an electrical cord wrapped up in the engine compartment. The cord

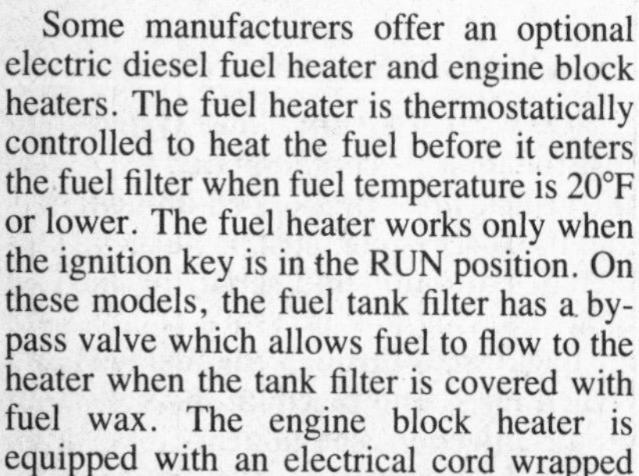

**Some diesel engines come equipped with a built-in heating system to keep the engine warm in cold temperatures.**
**Most OEM heaters work from 110-volt house current.**

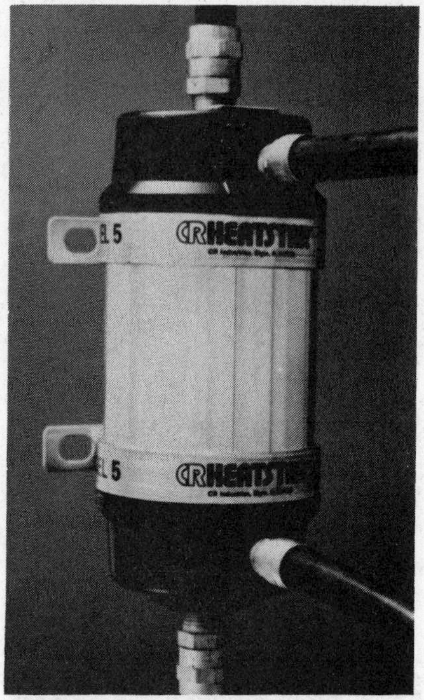

**Some aftermarket diesel fuel warmers are thermostatically controlled heat exchangers that use engine coolant to keep diesel fuel above its "cloud point," the temperature at which it gels and forms wax that can clog a fuel system.**

plugs into regular 110 volt household current. The block heater can be used, according to the type of oil in the crankcase, up to eight hours or overnight to warm up the block.

## STARTING SYSTEM

The diesel starting system includes one (sometimes two) heavy duty batteries, the starter, and the glow plug circuit. In addition to the heavy duty battery(ies), the majority of diesel engines also have starters and battery cables designed specifically as heavy duty items for diesel usage only. Because of the high compression of any diesel, the torque required to turn the engine is much greater than a gasoline engine. The starter must be powerful enough to handle the increased load; the battery cables must be thick enough to withstand the heat generated by the starter load.

For battery maintenance, see the regular "Maintenance" section. Jump starting procedures for a dual battery car are given below. Starter maintenance is included in the appropriate car section.

The glow plug circuit is used on the diesel to initially start the engine. When the ignition switch is turned to the ON position, a light will come on in the instrument panel signalling that the glow plugs are preheating the combustion chambers. After a certain interval (depending on how cold the engine is), the light will go off. This signals that the starter may be engaged and the engine started. If the glow plug circuit malfunctions, especially in cold weather, the engine will be almost impossible to start.

**CAUTION**

***NEVER use "starting aids" (e.g.—ether) to help start a diesel engine—serious engine damage will result.***

### Glow Plug Testing

To test each individual glow plug, disconnect the busbar and/or wire connector from the glow plug and connect a test light between the glow plug terminal and the positive battery terminal. If the test light lights, the glow plug is working. Replace individual glow plugs which do not work.

**NOTE: Some diesel engines are equipped with either "slow glow" or "fast glow" glow plugs. Do not attempt to interchange any parts of these two glow plug systems.**

To test the glow plug circuit, connect a test light to the terminal of one of the glow plugs (glow plug wiring still attached) and turn the ignition to the heating position. The test light should light for a short while. If not, the glow plug circuit is malfunctioning and must be diagnosed and repaired.

**NOTE: Perform this operation on a cold engine only.**

### Jump-Starting a Dual Battery Diesel

Some diesels are equipped with two 12 volt batteries. The batteries are connected in parallel circuit (positive terminal to positive terminal, negative terminal to negative terminal). Hooking the batteries up in parallel circuit increases battery cranking power without increasing total battery voltage output (12 volts). On the other hand, hooking two 12 volt batteries up in a series circuit (positive terminal to negative terminal, positive terminal to negative terminal) increases total battery output to 24 volts (12 volts + 12 volts).

**CAUTION**

***NEVER hook the batteries up in a series circuit; SEVERE electrical system damage will result.***

In the event that a dual battery diesel must be jumped started, use the following procedure.

1. Open the hood and locate the batteries.
2. Position the donor car so that the jumper cables will reach from its battery (must be 12 volt, negative ground) to the appropriate battery in the diesel. Do not allow the cars to touch.
3. Shut off all electrical equipment on both vehicles. Turn off the engine of the donor car, set the parking brakes on both vehicles and block the wheels. Also, make sure both vehicles are in Neutral (manual

transmission models) or Park (automatic transmission models).

4. Using the jumper cables, connect the positive (+) terminal of the donor car battery to the positive terminal of one (not both) of the diesel batteries.

5. Using the second jumper cable, connect the negative (−) terminal of the donor battery to a solid, stationary, metallic point on the diesel (alternator bracket, engine block, etc.). Be very careful to keep the jumper cables away from moving parts (cooling fan, alternator belt, etc.) on both vehicles.

6. Start the engine of the donor car and run it at moderate speed.

7. Start the engine of the diesel.

8. When the diesel starts, disconnect the battery cables in the reverse order of attachment.

## ENGINE MECHANICAL SYSTEMS

Included are engine lubrication and engine compression.

Although diesel engines are very low in carbon monoxide (CO) and hydrocarbon (HC) emissions, ''particulate'' emission output is very high from diesel engines. This is evident from the black smoke emitted by diesels, which is most noticeable during hard acceleration or high engine loads. The particulates are made up of mostly soot (carbon) and sulpher particles. The majority of these particulates are released into the atmosphere. However, some of the particulate matter, because it is produced within the engines cylinders, is left inside the engine and gradually contaminates the engine oil. This contamination makes the oil corrosive, due to the sulpher, and abrasive, due to the carbon. Serious engine damage will result if these contaminants continue to accumulate in the oil. Engine oil and filters of diesel engines must be changed more frequently than those of gasoline engines, due to the increased rate at which the contaminants form in the diesel. Consult the ''Maintenance'' section for oil and filter change procedures. The manufacturer's recommended oil change interval will be given in the owner's manual. An explanation of diesel engine oils is given at the end of this section.

As explained earlier, very high cylinder compression is the key to the operation of the diesel engine. The normal compression of most gasoline engines will rarely exceed 180 psi; whereas with diesel engines, compression pressures of 350–400 psi are commonplace.

**CAUTION**

***DO NOT attempt to check the compression of a diesel engine with a standard compression gauge—personal injury could result. A special, high pressure compression gauge is needed to safely check the compression of any diesel.***

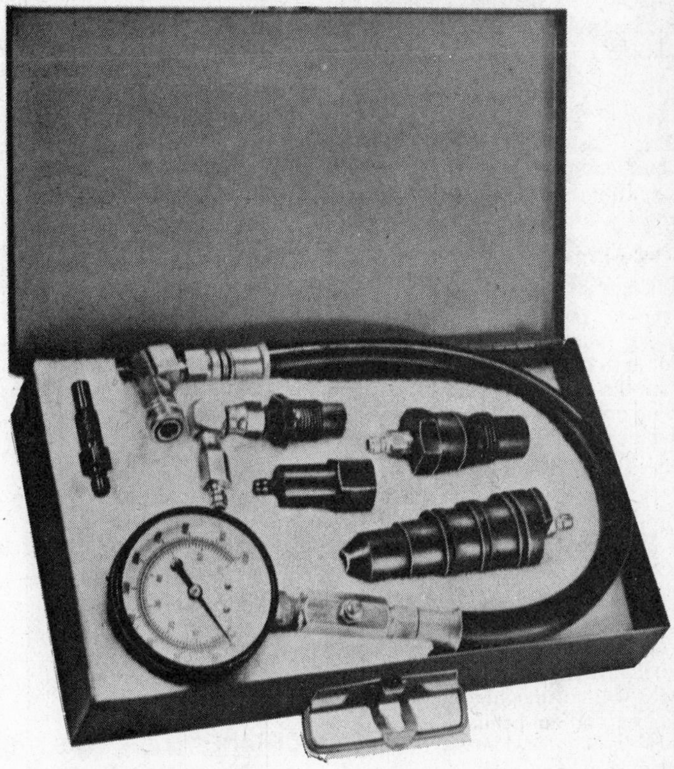

**A diesel compression tester kit with adaptors (Courtesy S & G Tools).**

### Compression Test

1. Remove the air cleaner.

2. Disconnect the wire from the fuel shutoff solenoid terminal of the injection pump.

3. Disconnect the wires from the glow plugs and remove all glow plugs.

4. Screw compression gauge into the glow plug hole in the cylinder being checked.

5. Crank the engine, allowing six ''puffs'' for each cylinder.

The lowest reading cylinder should not be less than 70% of the highest, and no cylinder should be less than 275 pounds.

### Idle Speed Adjustments

Idle speed adjustment procedures for individual diesel engines are given in the car section. Consult the following section for procedures to measure idle speed

### Connecting a Tachometer to a Diesel Engine

As mentioned earlier, the diesel engine does not require an electrical ignition system. Because of this, problems arise when attempts are made to connect a tachometer to the engine for the purpose of idle adjustments, etc. The average gasoline engine tachometer senses the ignition spark pulses and converts them into a readable engine rpm signal. This type of tachometer is useless on the diesel engine, because of the diesel's compression ignition system.

There are several magnetic and photoelectric tachometers available from various tool manufacturers which were designed specifically for use with the diesel engine. These units can run into a little more money than the average do-it-yourselfer may be willing to spend, in which case any adjustments requiring the monitoring of engine rpm should be performed by a competent service technician.

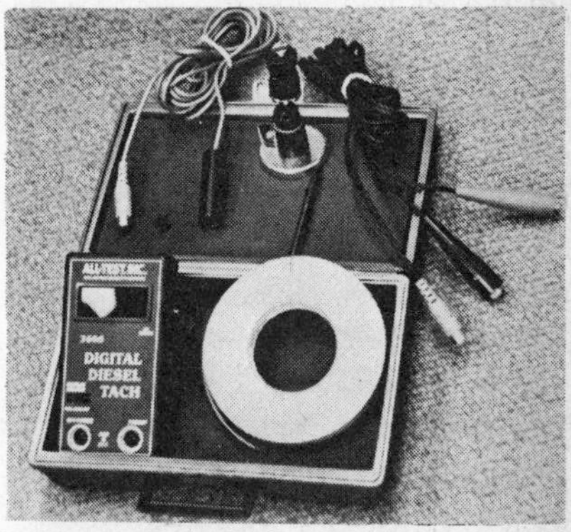


**The newest equipment for measuring idle speed on a diesel engine includes (clockwise from lower left) a digital diesel tach display, photomagnetic pick-up with display input, magnetic swivel base (holder), DC power source for the display unit and a roll of magnetic tape.**

The magnetic tape is attached to any moving part (such as the balancer). The pieces of tape must be at least 6 inches apart. Aim the photomagnetic pick-up at the moving object and adjust the position of the pick-up until the "on-target" light is lit. Flip the switch to TACH and read the rpm.

## Diesel Engine Precautions

- Never run the engine with the air cleaner removed: if anything is sucked into the inlet manifold it will go straight to the combustion chambers, or jam behind a valve.
- Never wash a diesel engine: the reaction of a warm fuel injection pump to cold (or even warm) water can ruin the pump.
- Never operate a diesel engine with one or more fuel injectors removed unless fully familiar with injector testing procedures: some diesel injection pumps spray fuel at up to 1400 psi—enough pressure to allow the fuel to penetrate your skin.
- Do not skip engine oil and filter changes.
- Strictly follow the manufacturer's oil and fuel recommendations as given in the owner's manual.
- Do not use home heating oil as fuel for your diesel.
- Do not use "starting aids" (e.g.—ether) in the automotive diesel engine, as these "aids" can cause severe internal engine damage.
- Do not run a diesel engine with the "Water in Fuel" warning light on in the dashboard.
- If removing water from the fuel tank yourself, use the same caution you would use when working around gasoline engine fuel components.
- Do not allow diesel fuel to come in contact with rubber hoses or components on the engine, as it can damage them.

## Fuel and Oil Recommendations

### FUEL

Fuel makers produce two grades of diesel fuel, No. 1 and No. 2, for use in automotive diesel engines. Generally speaking, No. 2 fuel is recommended over No. 1 for driving in temperatures above 20°F. In fact, in many areas, No. 2 diesel is the only fuel available. By comparison, No. 2 diesel fuel is less volatile than No. 1 fuel, and gives better fuel economy. No. 2 fuel is also a better injection pump lubricant.

Two important characteristics of diesel fuel are its cetane number and its viscosity.

The cetane number of a diesel fuel refers to the ease with which a diesel fuel ignites. High cetane numbers mean that the fuel will ignite with relative ease or that it ignites well at low temperatures. Naturally, the lower the cetane number, the higher the temperature must be to ignite the fuel. Most commercial fuels have cetane numbers that range from 35 to 65. No. 1 diesel fuel generally has a higher cetane rating than No. 2 fuel.

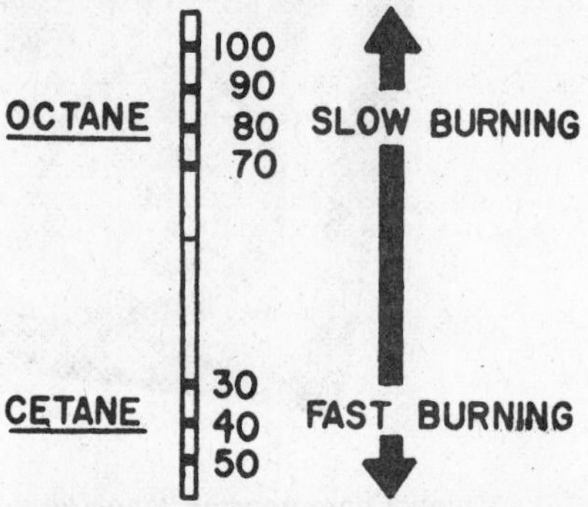


Cetane (diesel engine) versus octane (gasoline engine) ratings. The higher the cetane number, the faster the fuel burns

Viscosity is the ability of a liquid, in this case diesel fuel, to flow. Using straight No. 2 diesel fuel below 20°F can cause problems, because this fuel tends to become cloudy, meaning wax crystals begin forming in the fuel. In extreme cold weather, No. 2 fuel can stop flowing altogether. In either case, fuel flow is restricted, which can result in a "no start" condition or poor engine performance. Fuel manufacturers often "winterize" No. 2 diesel fuel by using various fuel additives and blends (No. 1 diesel fuel, kerosene, etc.) to lower its winter-time viscosity. Generally speaking, though, No. 1 diesel fuel is more satisfactory in extremely cold weather.

**NOTE: No. 1 and No. 2 diesel fuels will mix and burn with no ill effects, although the engine manufacturer will undoubtedly recommend one or the other. Consult the owner's manual for information.**

Depending on local climate, most fuel manufacturers make winterized No. 2 fuel available seasonally.

Many automobile manufacturers publish pamphlets giving the locations of diesel fuel stations nationwide. Contact the local dealer for information.

Do not substitute home heating oil for automotive diesel fuel. While in some cases, home heating oil refinement levels equal those of diesel fuel, many times they are far below diesel engine requirements. The result of using "dirty" home heating oil will be a clogged fuel system, in which case the entire system may have to be dismantled and cleaned.

One more word on diesel fuels. Don't thin diesel fuel with gasoline in cold weather. The lighter gasoline, which is more explosive, will cause rough running at the very least, and may cause extensive engine damage if enough is used.

### OIL

Diesel engines require different engine oil from those used in gasoline engines. Besides doing the things gasoline engine oil does, diesel oil must also deal with increased engine heat and the diesel blow-by gases, which create sulphuric acid, a high corrosive.

Under the American Petroleum Institute (API) classifications, gasoline engine oil codes begin with an "S", and diesel engine oil codes begin with a "C". This first letter designation is followed by a second letter code which explains what type of service (heavy, moderate, light) the oil is meant for. For example, the top of a typical oil can will include: "API SERVICES SC, SD, SE, CA, CB, CC". This means the oil in the can is a good, moderate duty engine oil when used in a diesel engine.

It should be noted here that the further

**COMPARISON OF #1 AND #2 DIESEL FUEL**

| Requirement | 1-D | 2-D |
|---|---|---|
| Flash Point, °F minimum | 100 | 125 |
| Cetane Number, minimum | 40 | 40 |
| Viscosity at 100°F, Centistokes | | |
| Minimum | 1.4 | 2.0 |
| Maximum | 2.5 | 4.3 |
| Water and Sediment, % by volume maximum | Trace | 0.05 |
| Sulfur, % by weight maximum | 0.5 | 0.5 |
| Ash, % by weight maximum | 0.01 | 0.01 |

Flash Point: The temperature at which diesel fuel ignites when exposed to a flame *in the open air.*
Cetane Number: See text

down the alphabet the second letter of the API classification is, the greater the oil's protective qualities are (CD is the severest duty diesel engine oil, CA is the lightest duty oil, etc.). The same is true for gasoline engine oil classifications (SF is the severest duty gasoline engine oil, SA is the lightest duty oil, etc.).

Many diesel manufacturers recommend an oil with both gasoline and diesel engine API classifications. Consult the owner's manual for specifications.

The top of the oil can will also contain an SAE (Society of Automotive Engineers) designation, which gives the oil's viscosity. A typical designation will be: SAE 10W-30, which means the oil is a "winter" viscosity oil, meaning it will flow and give protection at low temperatures.

On the diesel engine, oil viscosity is critical, because the diesel is much harder to start (due to its higher compression) than a gasoline engine. Obviously, if you fill the crankcase with a very heavy oil during winter (SAE 20W-50, for example), the starter is going to require a lot of current from the battery to turn the engine. And, since batteries don't function well in cold weather in the first place, you may find yourself stranded some morning. Consult the owner's manual for recommended oil specifications for the climate you live in.

## LUBE OIL ANALYSIS

From an oil sample a laboratory can diagnose many potential engine problems—from piston wear to impending bearing failure. What's more, the laboratory can spot them quicker, and with greater accuracy. Just as easily, the lab can give the diesel a clean bill of health, saving the car owner unnecessary servicing and other routine preventive maintenance, costly in time and money.

There's nothing new about engine lube oil analysis. Thousands of the nation's trucks and buses regularly have their engine's lube oil analyzed by laboratories specializing in this type of work. What is new is the availability of lube oil analysis to individual vehicle owners rather than, as before, almost exclusively to companies operating fleets of diesel equipment.

**Lube oil analysis can be a valuable indicator of internal engine condition.**

Here's how lube oil analysis works. You write one of the several laboratories that offer individual diesel vehicle owners lube analysis service. By return mail you'll receive an oil sampling kit. It will probably contain a two-ounce plastic oil sampling container with a screw-on plastic top. Instructions tell you how to take the sample. Usually, a lab-bound sample of diesel lube oil may be taken in any of three ways, but always right after the engine has been shut off, so that the sampled oil is as close as possible to normal engine operating temperature. That's important to assure that the lab's test will be accurate. Oil samples can be taken during normal oil changes, when lube oil is drained anyway. Between oil changes, a sample can be drawn from the engine through the dipstick tube (where you normally check the oil's level). In drawing an oil sample from the dipstick tube, a small suction bulb fitted with a length of disposable tubing is used. The tubing is merely inserted into the dipstick tube, the suction bulb depressed, and the oil sample drawn. The third method of sampling is by loosening the drain plug on the engine's bypass oil filter (if your diesel has one). A little oil is caught in the lube sampling container. In all cases, extreme cleanliness is a must, so as not to contaminate the sample with dirt, grease, or other substances not actually found inside the engine. For example, using a rag that contains solvents, metal filings, or other impurities can contaminate the oil sample, leading to false and even alarming lab reports. A bit of technique is required: In taking a sample of lube oil during a routine oil drain, about half of the crankcase's lube oil should be allowed to drain out before the sample is taken. The sample taken, the date, make and model of the engine, its mileage, mileage since last oil change, and sometimes oil type are noted on the container's label, and the container is mailed to the laboratory.

Shortly, you'll receive the lab's report, which, based on a number of tests, including spectrochemical analysis (using a spectrometer, which can detect the presence of virtually all basic elements and contaminants), tells what's in the oil in what quantities and analyzes both the probable source of what was found and whether it indicates trouble. For one example, the finding of more than trace amounts of copper in an oil sample may strongly point to excessive bearing wear in a particular diesel whose bearings contain copper. Some analyses report on as many as eighteen basic elements that may be found in a diesel's lube oil sample, and in the report's "recommendation" may pinpoint their probable source—as, "indicates piston ring wear." Also indicated is the presence of such contaminants as water, solids (the products of oxidation and engine blow-by), and fuel dilution. Noted, too, is the lubricity of the sample—whether, or not, in the lab's opinion, it is still doing its internal engine lubricating job.

**NOTE: Never use lube analysis and a lab's report of "good oil" to extend, beyond the manufacturer's recommendation, the mileage period between oil changes. Follow the manufacturers recommendations.**

The more frequently an engine is lube-sampled, the more accurate and meaningful the lab's reports. Infrequent samplings, although they can spot sudden, unusual changes in internal engine condition, may fail to show the gradual deterioration of engine parts. Ideally, you should have the laboratory analyze a lube sample every other oil change. For most automobile diesels, that's every 6,000 miles. Analysis costs from $7 to $11 per sample. Drive an average 18,000 miles a year and you'd change your diesel's oil three times. In that time, you'd submit three samples to the lab at an annual lube analysis cost of $21 to $33.

## Aftermarket Fuel System Accessories

Due to reasons described previously, most diesel engine problems can be attributed to either fuel contamination or cold weather fuel performance characteristics. Diesel-engined vehicle manufacturers have designed and installed various systems to combat these problems, but ultimately, their best efforts are limited by cost.

Inconvenience is a major concern to diesel owners. If water accumulates (in substantial quantities) in the diesel fuel system, the fuel and water must be siphoned from the fuel tank and purged from the remainder of the fuel system. It goes without saying that this operation is a messy, time-consuming process. Even if the vehicle is equipped with a water/fuel separator having a drain valve, the owner must manually open the valve from either under the hood or beneath the vehicle.

Although the fuel filter installed by the manufacturer offers adequate performance when maintained properly, the addition of another, separate diesel fuel filter is a wise improvement.

If you live in an extremely cold climate, you've probably experienced cold starting problems due to fuel "waxing", plugged filters, "gelled" fuel, etc. If your vehicle is not factory-equipped with the optional fuel line or cylinder block heaters, these

**Aftermarket fuel filter/water separator and fuel line heater**

heaters can be purchased from the after-market (retail auto parts manufacturers). The installation of either of these items can improve cold-starting dramatically.

## WATER/FUEL SEPARATORS

### Centrifugal Action

Sometimes referred to as a "cyclonic" water/fuel separator, this device uses baffles which spin the fuel as it comes through the separator inlet. Since water is heavier than diesel fuel, the water will spin away from the fuel, sink to the bottom of the separator, and collect in the sediment bowl.

This type of separator is most efficient in dealing with large water droplets. If the water is in emulsion with the fuel, that is, if the water is equally dispersed through the fuel in very small droplets, some of the water will remain with the fuel to travel through the fuel system.

### Coalescing Action

In this type of separator, the fuel must pass through a coalescent filtering media before proceeding through the fuel system. The idea behind the coalescent media is to trap even the smallest droplets of water on the media. As the small droplets combine into larger, heavier droplets, gravity acts on the droplets to pull them downward, off of the media and into the sediment bowl.

## FUEL FILTER/SEPARATOR COMBINATION UNITS

Most separators of either the centrifugal or coalescent types are available with disposeable fuel filtering elements which are built into the separator unit. If your car already has a large, disposeable filter, it would probably be more cost-effective to stay with a separator only, and to change the factory-equipped filter at the recommended intervals. Should your vehicle have a fairly small filter, and/or an inconveniently located water drain (or none at all), choose the filter/separator combination. The filter/separator offers both increased fuel filtering ability and efficient water separation.

### Convenience Add-Ons

Available with many separators and filter/separators are items such as dash-mounted water-in-fuel indicator lamps, audible water-in-fuel alarms, and dash-controlled water ejection systems. A properly chosen system would warn you of water in the fuel, and allow you to eject the water by simply "flipping" a dash-mounted switch.

### Installing a Separator

Clear installation instructions and the necessary installation parts will be provided with the separator kit. Follow those instructions exactly. A general list of suggestions follows:

1. Fuel additives should not be used unless approved by the separator manufacturer.
2. Do not install a separator within 4″ of any exhaust system component.
3. If plastic fittings are supplied with the kit, do not replace them with metal fittings. Also, use extreme caution when tightening the fittings, especially those made of plastic.
4. Use a fuel-proof sealer on all fitting threads, only if the threads are not factory-coated with sealer.
5. Use only fuel-proof hoses for the installation.
6. Do not eliminate the original equipment fuel filter, even if a filter/separator is installed.
7. For new car warranty purposes, a filter/separator should be located BEFORE the original equipment filter. The fuel must pass through the original filter last, before entering the fuel injection pump.
8. If any type of fuel line heater is installed, it is best to position the heater between the fuel tank and the separator inlet.
9. To ease the job of the separator, the separator should be installed between the fuel transfer pump and the tank (unless the separator manufacturer specifies otherwise). Fuel and water which have been churned through the fuel transfer pump will be more difficult to separate.
10. Be sure that any wiring (for warning lamps, water ejection, etc.) is routed and connected properly. If the wiring must pass through a drilled hole, be sure to use a rubber grommet between the drilled component(s) and the wire to prevent damage to the wire.

## FUEL LINE HEATERS

Two popular types of fuel line heaters are available for diesel passenger cars. Both types raise the temperature of the fuel to prevent "waxing" and "gelling" of the fuel in the lines during cold weather operation. One type uses engine coolant as a heating source. In order for this type to heat the fuel, the engine must first be started and allowed to run until the coolant temperature increases. Though this type of heater will usually increase fuel mileage, it offers no aid in starting ability.

The other type of heater uses a 12V DC electric heating element. This type is recommended, due to its ability to warm the fuel BEFORE the engine is started. This type of heater will also usually increase the overall fuel mileage.

### Installation

Follow the manufacturer's instructions exactly. Also, see suggestions 5, 8, and 9 under "Separator Installation".

## CYLINDER BLOCK HEATERS

A cylinder block heater electrically (usually 110V house current) heats the engine coolant, which in turn warms the cylinder block, heads, and engine oil. In this case, the warmth is not used to alter the characteristics of the fuel. Block heaters offer two main advantages when starting a diesel in cold weather:

1. The reduced viscosity (thinning) of the engine oil from the warmth allows the engine to be "turned over" easier (and faster) by the starter. Less strain is imposed on the starting system.
2. Because the diesel relies on the heat of compression to ignite the fuel, the increase in the base combustion chamber temperature results in a higher tempearture during compression. This allows the fuel to ignite easier than if just the glow plugs were used.

### Installation

Most cylinder block heaters replace one of the existing freeze (or expansion) plugs of the cylinder block. Follow the manufacturers installation instructions exactly. Also, refer to the manufacturers recommendations for usage.

# Carburetor Service 24

## Functions

Gasoline is the source of fuel for power in the automobile engine and the carburetor is the mechanism which automatically mixes liquid fuel with air in the correct proportions to provide the desired power output from the engine. The carburetor performs this function by metering, atomizing, and mixing fuel with air flowing through the engine.

A carburetor also regulates the volume of air-to-fuel mixture which enters the engine. It is the carburetor's regulation of the mixture flow which gives the operator control of the engine speed.

### METERING

The automotive internal conbustion engine operates efficiently within a relatively small range of air-to-fuel ratios. It is the function of the carburetor to meter the fuel in exact proportions to the air flowing into the engine, so that the optimum ratio of air-to-fuel is maintained under all operating conditions. Regulations governing exhaust gas emissions have made the proper metering of fuel by the carburetor an increasingly important factor. Too rich a mixture will result in poor fuel economy and increased emissions, while too lean a mixture will result in loss of power and generally poor performance.

Carburetors are matched to engines so that metering can be accomplished by using carefully calibrated metering jets which allow fuel to enter the engine at a rate proportional to the engine's ability to draw air.

### ATOMIZATION

The liquid fuel must be broken up into small particles so that it will more readily mix with air and vaporize. The more contact the fuel has with the air, the better the vaporization. Atomization can be accomplished in two ways: air may be drawn into a stream of fuel which will cause a turbulence and break the solid stream of fuel into smaller particles; or a nozzle can be positioned at the point of highest air velocity in the carburetor and the fuel will be torn into a fine spray as it enters the air stream.

### DISTRIBUTION

The carburetor is the primary device involved in the distribution of fuel to the engine. The more efficiently fuel and air are combined in the carburetor, the smoother the flow of vaporized mixture through the intake manifold to each combustion chamber. Hence, the importance of the carburetor in fuel distribution.

## Principles

### VACUUM

All carburetors operate on the basic principle of pressure difference. Any pressure less than atmospheric pressure is considered vacuum or a low pressure area. In the engine, as the piston moves down on the intake stroke with the intake valve open, a partial vacuum is created in the intake manifold. The farther the piston travels downward, the greater the vacuum created in the manifold. As vacuum increases in the manifold, a difference in pressure occurs between the carburetor and cylinder. The carburetor is positioned in such a way that the high pressure above it, and the vacuum or low pressure beneath it, causes air to be drawn through it. Fuel and air always move from high to low pressure areas.

### VENTURI PRINCIPLE

To obtain greater pressure drop at the tip of the fuel nozzle so that fuel will flow, the principle of increasing the air velocity to create a low pressure area is used. The device used to increase the velocity of the air flowing through the carburetor is called a venturi. A venturi is a specially designed restriction placed on the air flow. In order for the air to pass through the restriction, it must accelerate, causing a pressure drop or vacuum as it passes.

## Circuits

### FLOAT CIRCUIT

The float circuit includes the float, float bowl, and a needle valve and seat. This circuit controls the amount of gas allowed to flow into the carburetor.

As the fuel level rises, it causes the float to rise which pushes the needle valve into its seat. As soon as the valve and seat make contact, the flow of gas is cut off from the fuel inlet. When the level of fuel drops, the float sinks and releases the needle valve from its seat which allows the gas to flow in. In actual operation, the fuel is maintained at practically a constant level. The float tends to hold the needle valve partly closed so that the incoming fuel just balances the fuel being withdrawn.

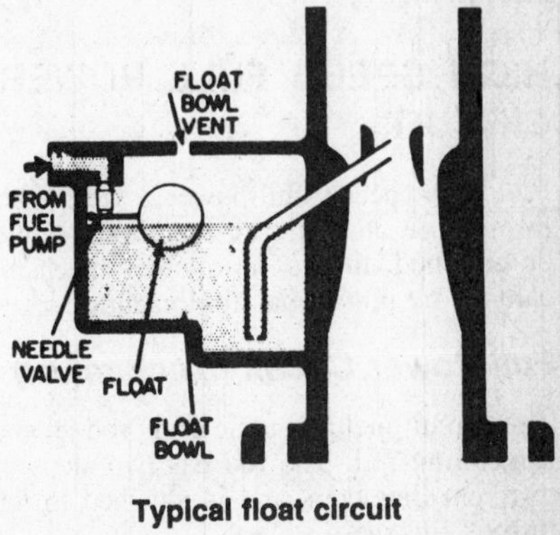


Typical float circuit

## IDLE AND LOW SPEED CIRCUIT

When the throttle is closed or only slightly opened, the air speed is low and practically no vacuum develops in the venturi. This means that the fuel nozzle will not feed. Thus, the carburetor must have another circuit to supply fuel during operation with a closed or slightly opened throttle.

This circuit is called the idle and low speed circuit. It consists of passages in which air and gas can flow beneath the throttle plate. With the throttle plate closed, there is high vacuum from the intake manifold. Atmospheric pressure pushes the air/fuel mixture through the passages of the idle and low speed circuit and past the tapered point of the idle adjustment screw, which regulates engine idle mixture volume.

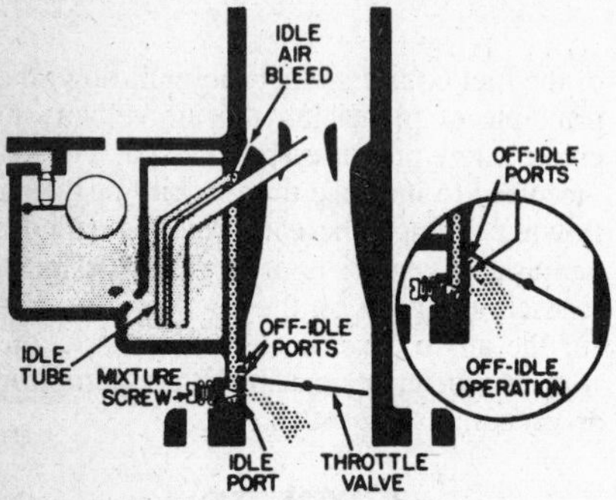


Typical idle and low speed circuit

## HIGH SPEED PARTIAL LOAD CIRCUIT

When the throttle plate is opened sufficiently, there is little difference in vacuum between the upper and lower part of the air horn. Thus, little air/fuel mixture will discharge from the low speed and idle circuit. However, under this condition enough air is moving through the air horn to produce vacuum in the venturi to cause the main nozzle or high speed nozzle to discharge fuel. The circuit from the float bowl to the main nozzle is called the high speed partial load circuit. A nearly constant air/fuel ratio is maintained by this circuit from part to full-throttle.

## HIGH SPEED FULL POWER CIRCUIT

For high-speed, full-power, wide open throttle operation, the air/fuel mixture must be enriched; this is done either mechanically or by intake manifold vacuum.

### *Full Power Circuit (Mechanical)*

This circuit includes a metering rod jet and a metering rod. The rod has two steps of different diameters and is attached to the throttle linkage.

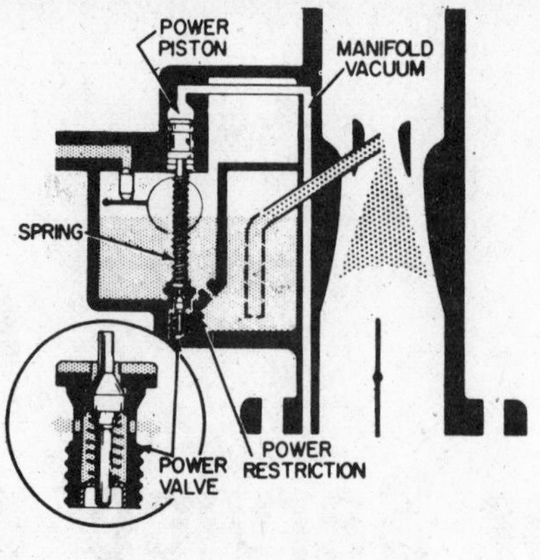


Typical power circuit

When the throttle is wide open, the metering rod is lifted, bringing the smaller diameter of the rod into the jet. When the throttle is partly closed, the larger diameter of the metering rod is in the jet. This restricts fuel flow to the main nozzle but adequate amounts of fuel do flow for part-throttle operation.

### *Full Power Circuit (Vacuum)*

This circuit is operated by intake manifold vacuum. It includes a vacuum diaphragm or piston linked to a valve.

When the throttle is opened so that intake manifold vacuum is reduced, the spring raises the diaphragm or piston. This allows more fuel to flow in, either by lifting a metering rod or by opening a power valve.

## ACCELERATOR PUMP CIRCUIT

For acceleration, the carburetor must deliver additional fuel. A sudden inrush of air is caused by rapid acceleration or applying full throttle.

When the throttle is opened, the pump lever pushes the plunger down and this forces fuel to flow through the accelerator pump circuit and out the pump jet. This fuel enters the air passage through the carburetor to supply additional fuel demands.

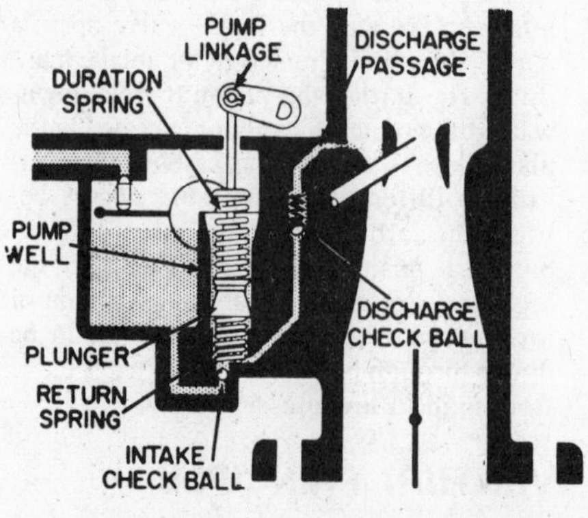


Typical accelerator pump circuit

## CHOKE

When starting an engine, it is necessary to increase the amount of fuel delivered to the intake manifold. This increase is controlled by the choke.

The choke consists of a valve in the top of the air horn controlled mechanically by an automatic device. When the choke valve is closed, only a small amount of air can get past it. When the engine is cranked, a fairly high vacuum develops in the air horn. This vacuum causes the main nozzle to discharge a heavy stream of fuel. The quantity delivered is sufficient to produce the correct air/fuel mixture needed for starting the engine. The choke is released either manually or by heat from the engine.

# OVERHAUL

Generally, when a carburetor requires major service, a rebuilt one is purchased on an exchange basis, or a kit may be bought for overhauling the carburetor.

The kit contains the necessary parts and some form of instructions for carburetor rebuilding. The instructions may vary between a simple exploded view and detailed step-by-step rebuilding instructions. Unless you are familiar with carburetor overhaul, the latter should be used.

There are some general overhaul procedures which should always be observed:

Efficient carburetion depends greatly on careful cleaning and inspection during overhaul since dirt, gum, water, or varnish in or on the carburetor parts are often responsible for poor performance.

Overhaul your carburetor in a clean, dust-free area. Carefully disassemble the carburetor, referring often to the exploded views. Keep all similar and lookalike parts segregated during disassembly and cleaning to avoid accidental interchange during assembly. Make a note of all jet sizes.

When the carburetor is disassembled, wash all parts except diaphragms, electric choke units, pump plunger, and any other plastic, leather, fiber, or rubber parts in clean carburetor solvent. Do not leave parts in the solvent any longer than is necessary to sufficiently loosen the deposits. Excessive cleaning may remove the special finish from the float bowl and choke valve bodies, leaving these parts unfit for service. Rinse all parts in clean solvent and blow them dry with compressed air or allow them to air dry. Wipe clean all cork, plastic, leather, and fiber parts with a clean, lint-free cloth.

Blow out all passages and jets with compressed air and be sure that there are no restrictions or blockages. Never use wire or similar tools to clean jets, fuel passages, or air bleeds. Clean all jets and valves separately to avoid accidental interchange.

Check all parts for wear or damage. If wear or damage is found, replace the defective parts. Especially check the following:

1. Check the float needle and seat for wear. If wear is found, replace the complete assembly.
2. Check the float hinge pin for wear and the float(s) for dents or distortion. Replace the float if fuel has leaked into it.
3. Check the throttle and choke shaft bores for wear or an out-of-round condition. Damage or wear to the throttle arm, shaft, or shaft bore will often require replacement of the throttle body. These parts require a close tolerance of fit; wear may allow air leakage, which could affect starting and idling.

**NOTE: Throttle shafts and bushings are not included in overhaul kits. They can be purchased separately.**

4. Inspect the idle mixture adjusting needles for burrs or grooves. Any such condition requires replacement of the needle, since you will not be able to obtain a satisfactory idle.
5. Test the accelerator pump check valves. They should pass air one way but not the other. Test for proper seating by blowing and sucking on the valve. Replace the valve if necessary. If the valve is satisfactory, wash the valve again to remove breath moisture.
6. Check the bowl cover for warped surfaces with a straightedge.
7. Closely inspect the valves and seats for wear and damage, replacing as necessary.
8. After the carburetor is assembled, check the choke valve for freedom of operation.

Carburetor overhaul kits are recommended for each overhaul. These kits contain all gaskets and new parts to replace those that deteriorate most rapidly. Failure to replace all parts supplied with the kit (especially gaskets) can result in poor performance later.

Some carburetor manufacturers supply overhaul kits of three basic types: minor repair; major repair; and gasket kits. Basically, they contain the following:

Minor Repair Kits:
- All gaskets
- Float needle valve
- Volume control screw
- All diaphragms
- Spring for the pump diaphragm

Major Repair Kits:
- All jets and gaskets
- All diaphragms
- Float needle valve
- Volume control screw
- Pump ball valve
- Main jet carrier
- Float
- Complete intermediate rod
- Intermediate pump lever
- Complete injector tube
- Some cover hold-down screws and washers

Gasket Kits:
- All gaskets

After cleaning and checking all components, reassemble the carburetor, using new parts and referring to the exploded view. When reassembling, make sure that all screws and jets are tight in their seats, but do not overtighten, as the tips will be distorted. Tighten all screws gradually, in rotation. Do not tighten needle valves into their seats; uneven jetting will result. Always use new gaskets. Be sure to adjust the float level when reassembling.

## Stromberg Carburetors Only

The preceding information applies to Stromberg carburetors also, but the following, additional suggestions should be followed.

1. Soak the small cork gaskets (jet gland washers) in penetrating oil or hot water for at least a half hour prior to assembly, or they will invariably split.
2. When the jet is fully assembled, the jet tube should be a close fit without any lateral play, but it should be free to move smoothly. A few drops of oil, or polishing of the tube may be necessary to achieve this.
3. If the jet sealing ring washer is made of cork, soak it in hot water for a minute or two prior to installation.
4. Adjust the float height.
5. Center the jet so that the piston will fall freely (when raised) and seat with a distinct click. If the jet is not centered properly, it will hang up in the tube.

# TROUBLESHOOTING

**NOTE: Carburetor problems cannot be isolated effectively unless all other engine systems are functioning correctly and the engine is properly tuned.**

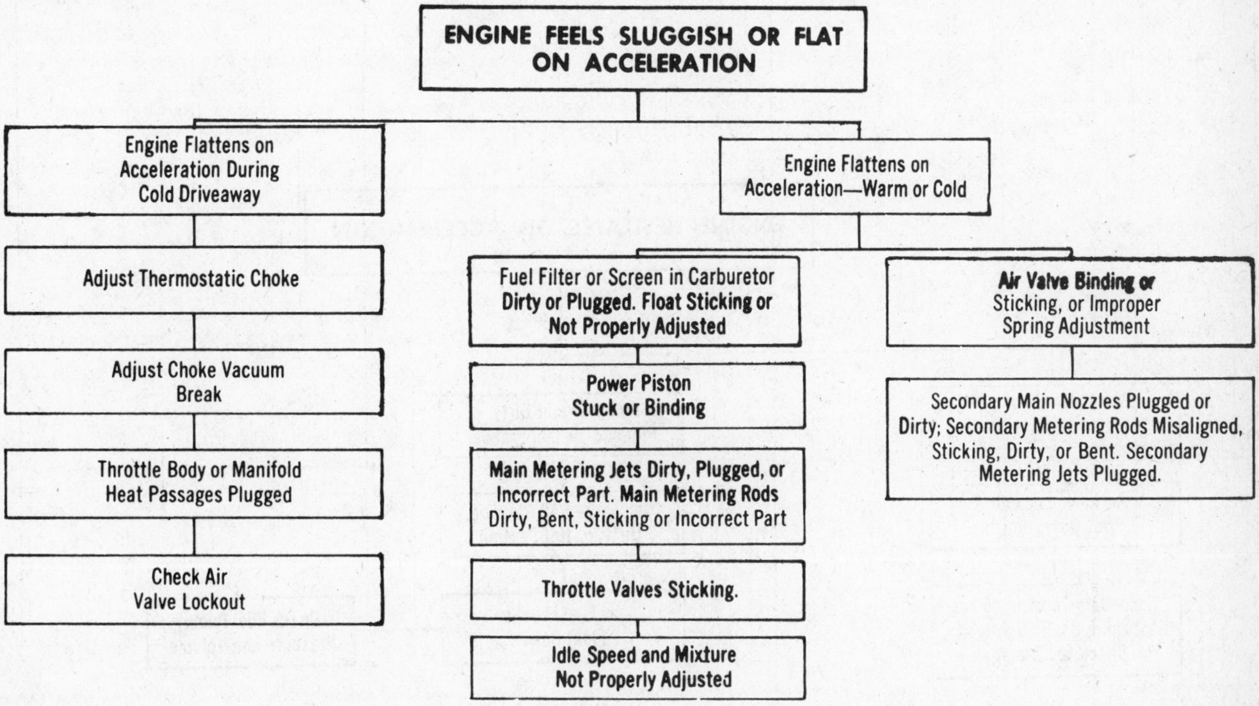

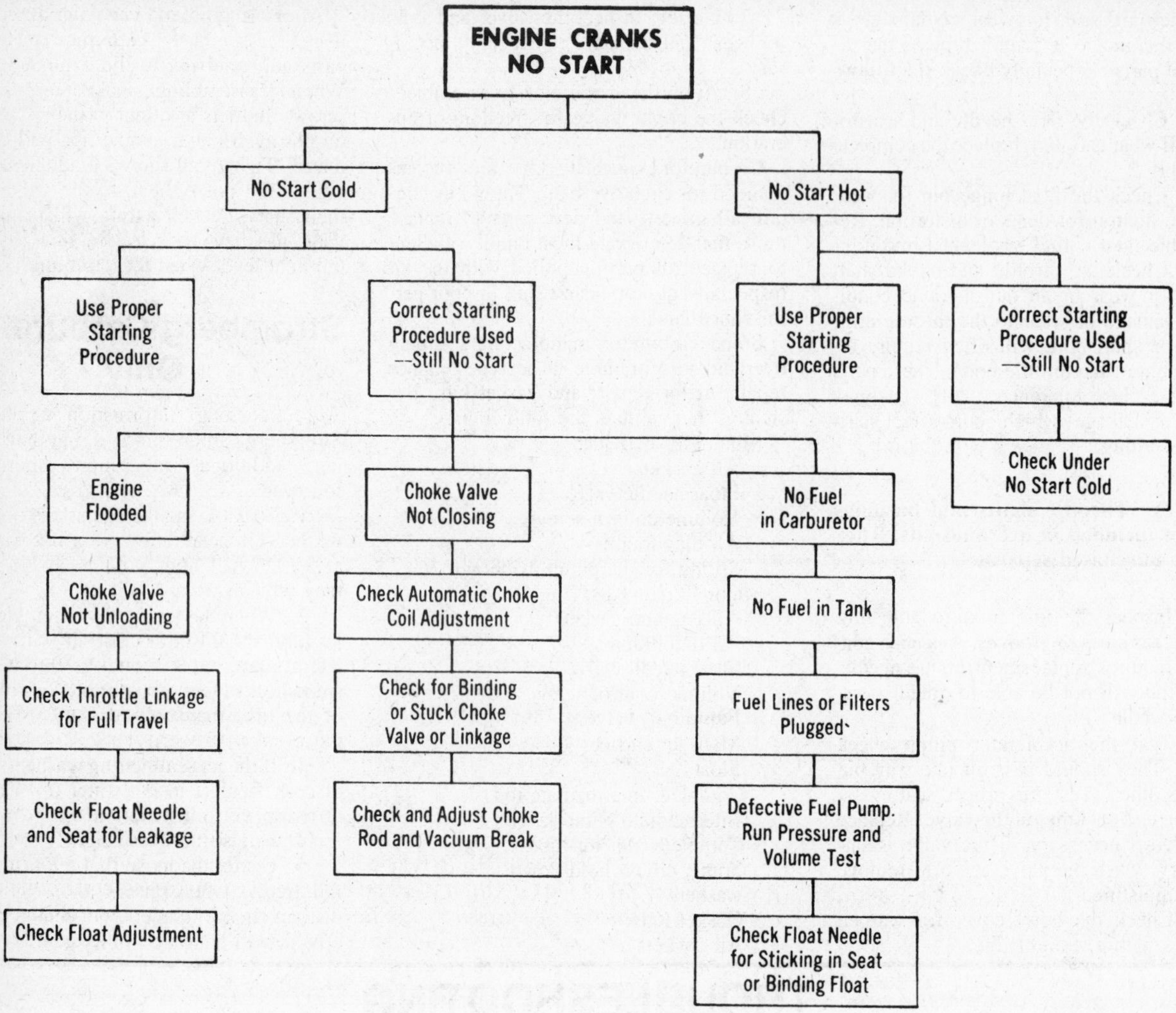
ENGINE CRANKS NO START
No Start Cold
No Start Hot
Use Proper Starting Procedure
Correct Starting Procedure Used --Still No Start
Use Proper Starting Procedure
Correct Starting Procedure Used —Still No Start
Engine Flooded
Choke Valve Not Closing
No Fuel in Carburetor
Check Under No Start Cold
Choke Valve Not Unloading
Check Automatic Choke Coil Adjustment
No Fuel in Tank
Check Throttle Linkage for Full Travel
Check for Binding or Stuck Choke Valve or Linkage
Fuel Lines or Filters Plugged
Check Float Needle and Seat for Leakage
Check and Adjust Choke Rod and Vacuum Break
Defective Fuel Pump. Run Pressure and Volume Test
Check Float Adjustment
Check Float Needle for Sticking in Seat or Binding Float

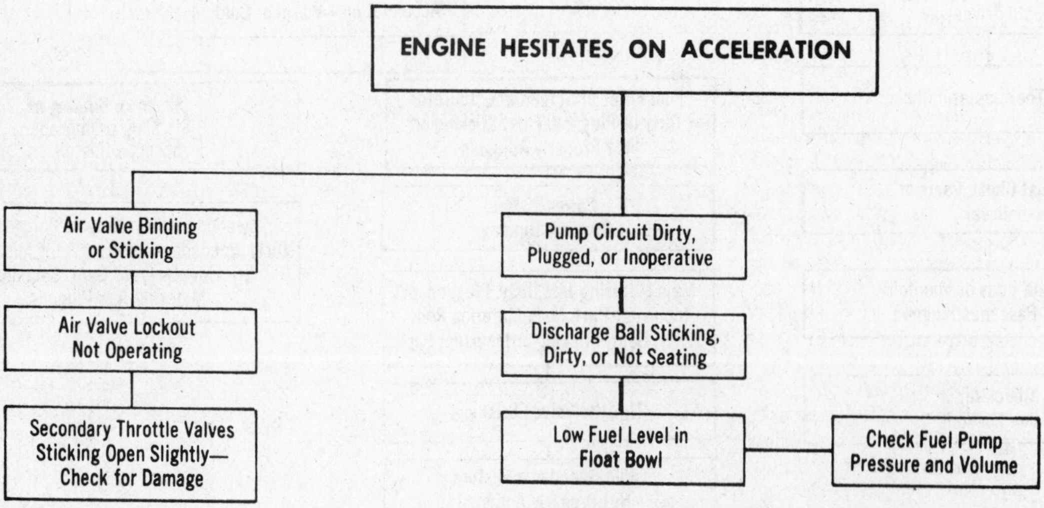
ENGINE HESITATES ON ACCELERATION
Air Valve Binding or Sticking
Pump Circuit Dirty, Plugged, or Inoperative
Air Valve Lockout Not Operating
Discharge Ball Sticking, Dirty, or Not Seating
Secondary Throttle Valves Sticking Open Slightly—Check for Damage
Low Fuel Level in Float Bowl
Check Fuel Pump Pressure and Volume

# Emission Controls 25

## EMISSION CONTROLS

### History

The first state to recognize the automobile pollution problem was California in 1959 and enacted the first standards for automobile emissions through the newly formed California Air Resources Board. The emission standards became effective in 1961.

In 1968, the United States Congress enacted the Clean Air Act, recognizing the work of the California Air Resources Board, by adopting California's test procedures and emissions standards as a beginning point. However, the federal regulations preempted those of any state enacting emission standards and legislation, meaning that federal regulations would override any state or state laws that may be in conflict with the federal act.

Waivers of federal preemption could be petitioned by a state or vehicle manufacturer for the purpose of advocating early establishment of emission standards, to delay the start of emission programs where the need is deemed necessary for the good of the people of the state or to further explore the development of emission control devices to be placed on the vehicles to control harmful emissions.

Federal approval of state applications for the waivers of federal preemption concerning stricter emission standards over the federal standards, forced the manufacturers to construct vehicles with emission components necessary to control emission in three areas, California, 49 State and High Altitude (over 4000 ft. in elevation).

Since the enactment of the first clean air legislation by California and the Federal Government, to date, thirty-one states have enacted automobile emission standards, either state wide or confined to heavily populated city areas within the state. The remaining states either rely on the federally mandated emission standards for clean air or have no regulations to date.

### Emission Types

Most pollution produced by an automobile comes from gasoline or gasoline by-products. The three main sources of pollutants are the fuel tank and carburetor, crankcase and exhaust. The exhaust is the major contributor of hydrocarbon pollutant, about 60%. The other sources account for the remaining 40% of the pollutants.

#### CRANKCASE EMISSIONS

The crankcase emissions are comprised of water, acids, unburned fuel, oil fumes and particulates. The emissions are classified as hydrocarbons (HC) and are formed by the small amount of unburned, compressed air/fuel mixture entering the crankcase from the combustion area during the compression and power strokes, between the cylinder walls and piston rings. The heat of the compression and combustion help to form the remaining crankcase emissions.

Since the conception of the internal combustion engine, these crankcase emissions are expelled into the atmosphere through a road draft tube, mounted on the lower side of the engine block. Fresh air was directed into the crankcase through an open oil filler cap or breather, with the air passing through the crankcase cavity and expelling part of the blow-by gases out the road draft tube by the movement of air as the vehicle was in motion and by the movement of engine fan air when the vehicle was stationary with the engine in the idle mode.

To control the crankcase emission, the road draft tube was deleted and in its place, a hose and/or tubing was routed from the crankcase to the intake manifold so that the blow-by emission could be burned with the air/fuel mixture. However, it was found that intake manifold vacuum would

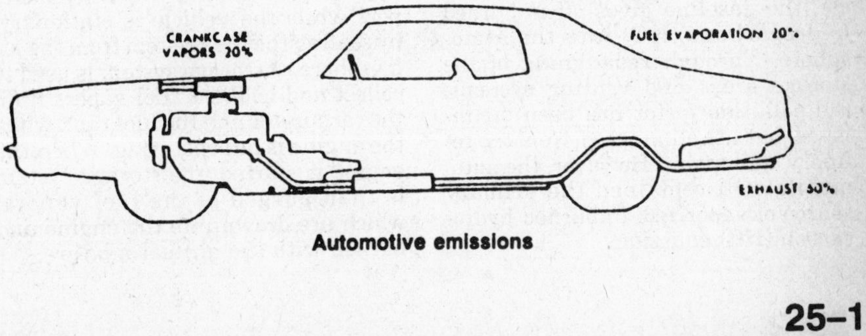


Automotive emissions

vary in strength at the wrong time and not allow the proper emission flow. A regulating type valve was needed to control the flow of air through the crankcase to relieve the volume of blow-by gases generated by the engine operation.

It was determined through testing, that the removal of the blow-by gases from the crankcase, as quickly as possible, was most important to the longevity of the engine. Should large accumulations of blow-by gases remain and condense, dilution of the engine oil would occur to form water, soots, resins, acids and lead salts, resulting in the formation of sludge and varnishes. This condensation of the blow-by gases occur more frequently on vehicles used in numerous starting and stopping conditions, excessive idling and when the engine is not allowed to attain normal operating temperature through short runs.

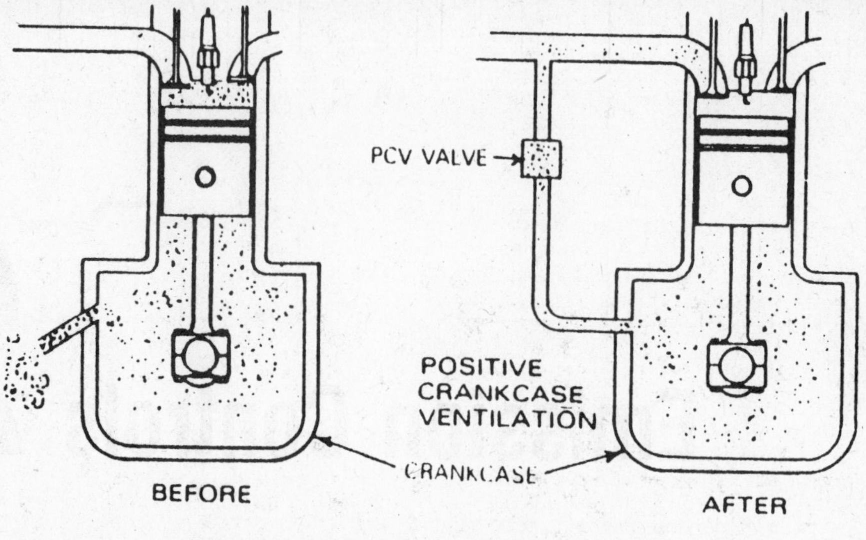


**Positive crankcase ventilation (PCV) systems**

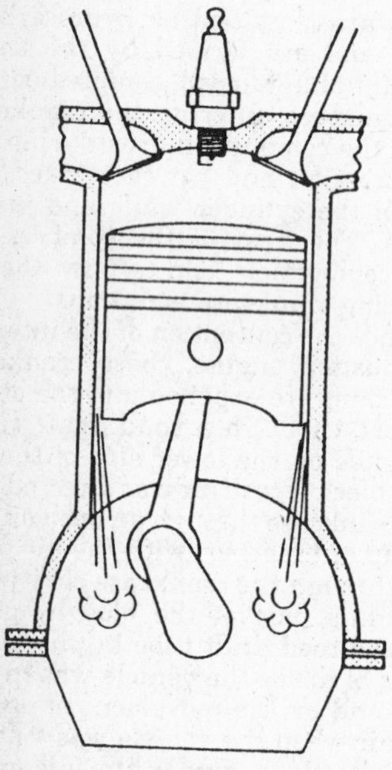

**Blow-by**

## EVAPORATIVE EMISSIONS

Gasoline fuel is a major source of pollution, before and after it is burned in the automobile engine. From the time the fuel is refined, stored, pumped and transported, again stored until it is pumped into the fuel tank of the vehicle, the gasoline gives off unburned hydrocarbons (HC) into the atmosphere. Through redesigning of the storage areas and venting systems, the pollution factor has been diminished, but not eliminated, from the refinery standpoint. However, the automobile still remained the primary source of vaporized, unburned hydrocarbon (HC) emissions.

Fuel pumped from an underground storage tank is cool, but when exposed to a warmer ambient temperature, will expand. Before controls were mandated, an owner would fill the fuel tank with fuel from an underground storage tank and park the vehicle for some time in warm area, such as a parking lot. As the fuel would warm, it would expand and should no provisions or area be provided for the expansion, the fuel would spill out the filler neck and onto the ground, causing hydrocarbon (HC) pollution and creating a severe fire hazard. To correct this condition, the vehicle manufacturers added overflow plumbing and/or gasoline tanks with built in expansion areas or domes.

However, this did not control the fuel vapor emission from the fuel tank and the carburetor bowl. It was determined that most of the fuel evaporation occurred when the vehicle was stationary and the engine not operating. Most vehicle will carry 5 to 25 gallons of gasoline and should a large concentration of vehicles be parked in one area, such as a large parking lot, excessive fuel vapor emissions would take place, increasing as the temperature would.

To prevent the vapor emission from escaping into the atmosphere, the fuel system is designed to trap the fuel vapors while the vehicle is stationary, by sealing the fuel system from the atmosphere. A storage system is used to collect and hold the fuel vapors from the carburetor and the fuel tank when the engine is not operating. When the engine is started, the storage system is then purged of the fuel vapors, which are drawn into the engine and burned with the air/fuel mixture.

## EXHAUST EMISSIONS

The exhaust gases emitted into the atmosphere are a combination of burned and unburned fuel. To understand the exhaust emission and its composition, we must recall basic chemistry.

When we introduce the air/fuel mixture into the engine, we are mixing air, composed of nitrogen (78%), oxygen (21%) and other gases (1%) with the fuel, which is 100% hydrocarbons (HC), in a semi-controlled ratio. As the combustion process is accomplished, power is produced to move the vehicle while the heat of combustion is transferred to the cooling system. The exhaust gases are then composed of nitrogen, a diatomic gas ($N_2$) the same as was introduced in the engine, carbon dioxide ($CO_2$), the same gas that is used in beverage carbonation and water vapor ($H_2O$). The nitrogen ($N_2$), for the most part passes through the engine unchanged, while the oxygen ($O_2$) reacts (burns) with the hydrocarbons (HC) and produces the carbon dioxide ($CO_2$) and the water vapors ($H_2O$). If this chemical process would be the only process to take place, the exhaust emissions would be harmless. However, during the combustion process, other pollutants are formed and are considered dangerous. These pollutants are carbon monoxide (CO), hydrocarbons (HC), oxides of nitrogen (NOx), oxides of sulfer (SOx) and engine particulates.

### *Hydrocarbons*

Hydrocarbons (HC) are essentially unburned fuel that has not been successfully burned during the combustion process or has escaped into the atmosphere through fuel evaporation. The prime sources of incomplete combustion are rich air/fuel mixtures, low engine temperatures and improper spark timing, while the prime sources of the hydrocarbon emission through fuel evaporation comes from the vehicle's fuel tank and carburetor bowl.

To accomplish the reduction of combustion hydrocarbon emission, engine modification were made to minimize dead space and surface area in the combustion chamber, leaning to the air/fuel mixture through improved carburetion, fuel injection and by the addition of external controls to aid in further combustion of the hydrocarbons outside the engine. Two such methods were the addition of an air injection system, to inject fresh air into the exhaust manifold(s) and the installation of a catalytic converter, a unit that is able to burn traces of hydrocarbons without affecting the internal combustion process or fuel economy.

To control hydrocarbon emissions through fuel evaporation, modifications were made to the fuel tank and carburetor bowl to allow storage of the fuel vapors during periods of engine shut-down, and at specific times during engine operation, to purge and burn these same vapors by blending them with the air/fuel mixture.

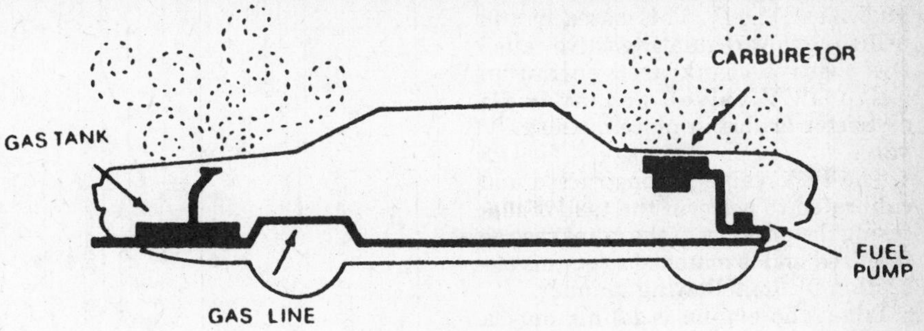

**Evaporative emissions**

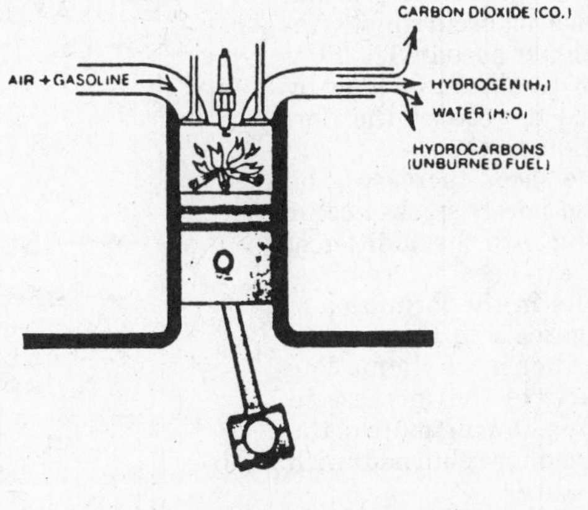

**Combustion products**

### *Carbon Monoxide*

Carbon monoxide (CO) is formed when not enough oxygen is present during the combustion process to convert carbon to carbon dioxide ($CO_2$). An increase in the carbon monoxide (CO) emission is normally accompanied by an increase in the hydrocarbon (HC) emission because of the lack of oxygen (O) to completely burn all of the fuel mixture.

Carbon monoxide (CO) also increases the rate at which the photochemical smog is formed by speeding up the conversion of nitric oxide (NO) to nitrogen ($NO_2$). To accomplish this, carbon monoxide (CO) combines with oxygen ($O_2$) and nitrogen dioxide ($NO_2$) to produce carbon dioxide ($CO_2$) and nitrogen dioxide ($NO_2$).

The dangers of carbon monoxide, which is an odorless, colorless toxic gas, are many. When carbon monoxide is inhaled into the lungs and passed into the blood stream, oxygen is replaced by the carbon monoxide (CO) in the red blood cells, causing a reduction in the amount of oxygen being supplied to the many parts of the body. This lack of oxygen causes headaches, lack of coordination, reduced mental alertness and should the carbon monoxide concentration be high enough, death could result.

### *Oxides of Nitrogen*

Normally, nitrogen is a diatomic, inert gas, but when heated to approximately 2500°F through the combustion process, this gas becomes active and causes an increase in the nitric oxide (NO) emission.

Oxides of nitrogen (NOx) are composed of approximately 97–98% nitric oxide (NO). Nitric oxide is colorless gas, but when it is passed into the atmosphere, it combines with oxygen (O) and forms nitrogen dioxide ($NO_2$). The nitrogen dioxide then combines with chemically active hydrocarbons (HC) and when in the presence of sunlight, causes the formation of photochemical smog.

## Emission Control Systems

### CRANKCASE EMISSION CONTROL SYSTEM

The crankcase emissions were responsible for approximately 20% of all harmful automotive pollutants before any emission controls were installed on the vehicles. The crankcase emissions are the result of compressed gases being forced past the piston rings on both the compression and power strokes, resulting in an accumulation of gases (known as blow-by gases), in the crankcase. These blow-by gases become mixed with vapors from the agitated lubricating oil and must be relieved from the crankcase area to prevent damaging pressures from building up.

Prior to the early 60's, a road draft tube was used to ventilate the crankcase, which allowed the pollutants to be emitted into the atmosphere. With the installation of a regulating valve and necessary plumbing, the road draft tube was eliminated and the gases routed to the air intake area, to be drawn into the engine vacuum was used as the controlling factor to draw the crankcase gases into the engine, but was found that the vacuum source varied at the wrong times.

Different systems were experimented with, some with flow control valves while others merely direct the gases to the air cleaner assembly. Other systems had open breather caps with the fresh air supply being tapped from the air cleaner snorkel.

By 1968, all vehicle manufactured in the United States were equipped with a closed crankcase ventilation system, which did not allow any of the blow-by gases and oil vapors to escape into the atmosphere. This system is known as Type IV. This closed system utilizes a flow regulating valve called the positive crankcase ventilation valve (PCV valve), or may use a restrictor orifice in place of the PCV valve.

The PCV valve is constructed and calibrated to perform the task of metering the gases from the crankcase as required and is matched to engine operation in the following manner.

When the engine is idling, only a small amount of air and fuel is needed for combustion, resulting in a small amount of blow-by gases being produced because the compression and power strokes are not occurring as frequently as at higher speeds. The PCV valve reacts to this lack of blow-by gases and tends to restrict the flow into the induction system.

As the engine speed increases, the compression and power strokes occur more often, along with the addition of more fuel and air need for combustion. This results in the formation of more blow-by gases and the need to purge the crankcase of them. The PCV valve reacts to the increase in blow-by gases by allowing more of the gases to be burned (or reburned) with the air/fuel mixture.

It should be noted that the PCV valve is constructed and calibrated in such a manner as to prevent engine backfires from entering the crankcase to avoid detonation of the accumulated blow-by gases.

In the closed crankcase ventilation system, the fresh air intake, located in the air cleaner or snorkel, has a dual role. Not only is it a source of fresh air for the crankcase ventilation system, but doubles as an overload release of blow-by gases into the carburetor air stream should the PCV valve fail to control the build up of blow-by gases, rather than allowing the excess gases to escape into the atmosphere. With the use of this closed system, the hydrocarbon (HC) emissions produced in the crankcase, are prevented from entering the atmosphere.

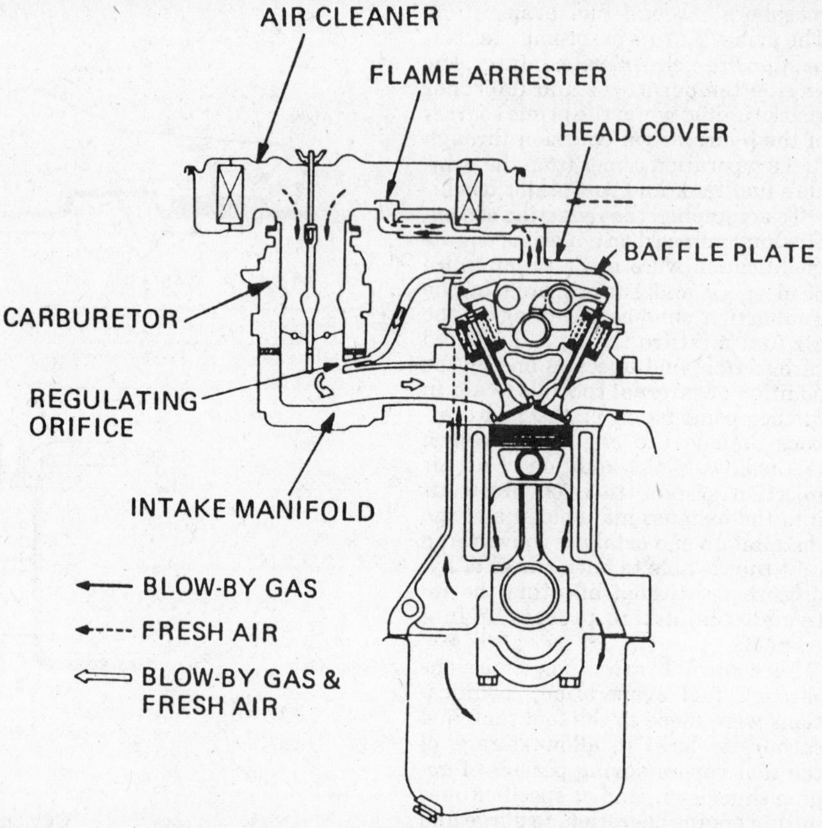

**Positive crankcase ventilation (PCV) system air flow**

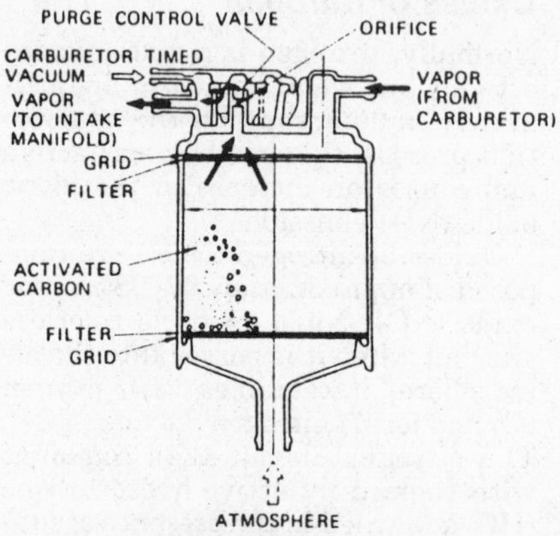

**Vapor canister**

## FUEL EVAPORATIVE EMISSION CONTROL SYSTEM

Fuel evaporation vapors were found to account for approximately 20% of the total automotive emission problem and was more severe with ambient temperature increases. The sources of the hydrocarbon vapor emissions were the fuel tank and carburetor bowl, both of which were vented to the atmosphere. Another problem was the overfilling of the fuel tank, which under changes of temperature or by having the vehicle parked on an incline, would spill gasoline from the tank. A means of trapping the vapor emission and preventing gasoline leakage was a major undertaking.

One of the early systems used, was the engine crankcase to store the fuel vapors when the engine was not running. When the engine was started, the vapors were purged from the crankcase by the positive crankcase ventilation system. Certain drawbacks were noted in this system, some of which were the dilution of engine lubricating oils with gasoline, an overrich air/fuel mixture during the purge cycle and danger of gasoline vapor detonation within the crankcase during engine start up.

To prevent fuel loss from the tank due to expansion, an expansion dome has been manufactured into the top to the fuel tanks and the fillpipes have been redesigned to prevent filling the fuel tank above a desired level. Certain vehicles use added plumbing to increase the area volume need, should the fuel expand. This added plumbing is normally part of the vapor control system with necessary valves to control both vapors and liquids included.

After much experimenting and testing, a general system was designed that could control both vapor and liquid emissions by sealing the fuel system from the atmosphere. Although each manufacture of vehicles has designed their own vapor control system, similar components are used, resulting in systems that are basically the same in the manner or vapor collection and storage. However, the manner in which the vapors are purged may vary greatly.

## EXHAUST EMISSION CONTROL SYSTEM

The exhaust emission control system encompasses the automotive engine

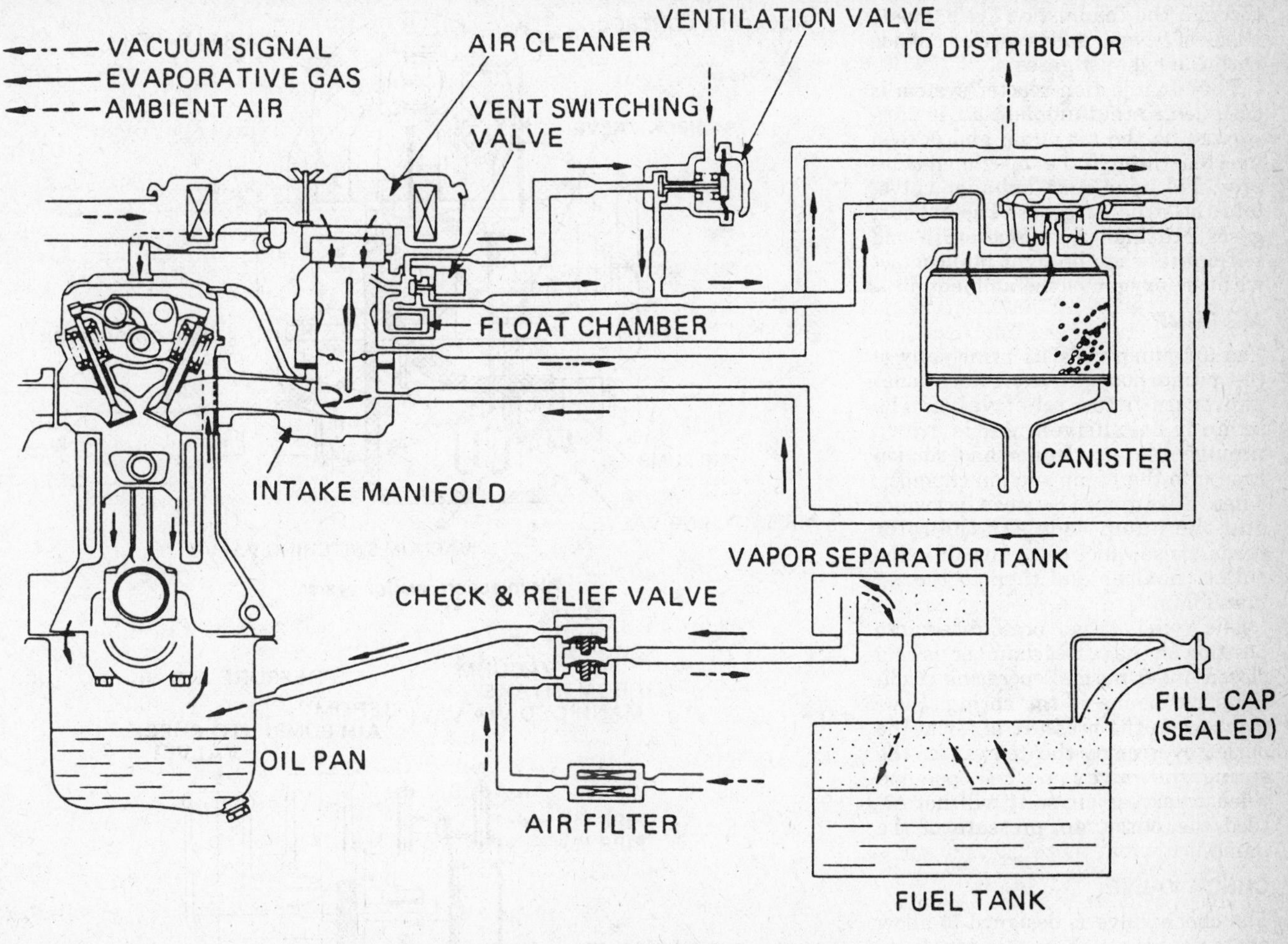


**Fuel evaporative emission control—early system**

from the entrance of air into the engine's induction system until the exhaust by-product of the combustion process emerges from the tail pipe.

The engine exhaust was found to be responsible for approximately 60% of all automobile emissions before any pollution controls were installed on the engines. Through the trail and error period of the late 60's and early 70's, many different systems were used, some separately and others in conjunction with other systems. While a number of the controls were dropped, others were refined and improved, resulting in greater emission control and driveability.

### *Air Injection Reactor System (AIR)*

In gasoline engines, it is difficult to burn the air/fuel mixture completely through combustion that takes place within the combustion chambers. Under certain operating conditions, more unburned gas is produced

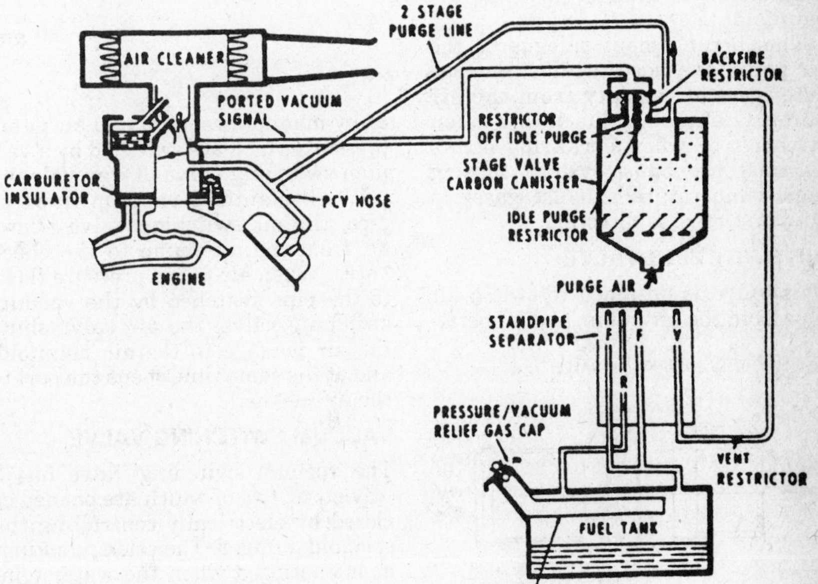


**Typical fuel evaporative emission control system**

through the combustion cycle, due to a lack of oxygen and is carried outside with the exhaust gases.

The air injection reactor system is designed so that ambient air is pressurized by the air pump and is then injected, through the injection nozzles provided near each exhaust valve, into the exhaust gases. The exhaust gases are high in temperature and self-ignite when brought into contact with the oxygen of the ambient air.

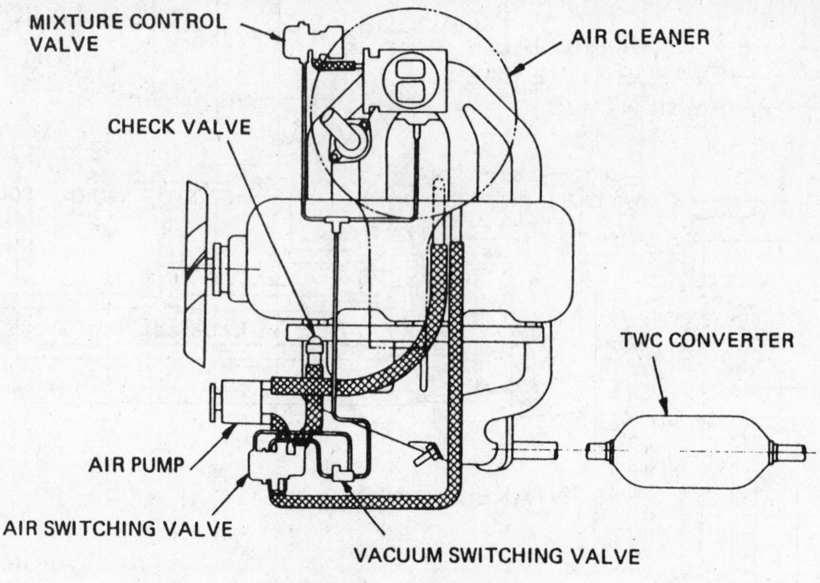


**Air injection reactor system**

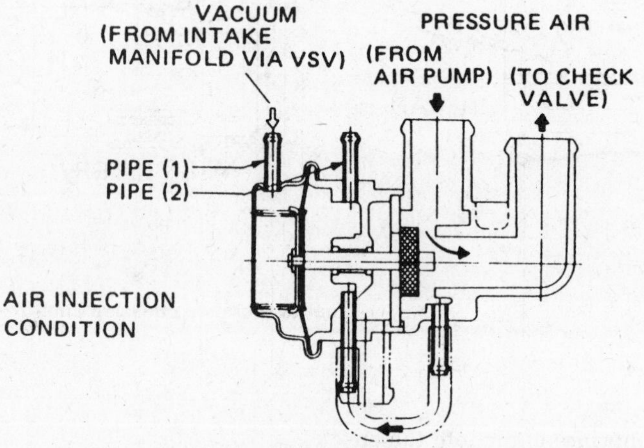


**Air switching valve**

### AIR PUMP

The air pump consists principally of the pump body, cover, rotor, vanes and press-fitted relief valve. The pump is belt-driven. Air is drawn through the air cleaner and suction hose into the pump suction chamber, where it is trapped between two vanes and the pump body. As the rotor turns, these vanes carry the air to the outlet chamber and then to the air manifold.

The relief valve, press-fitted into position on the outlet chamber, is held closed under normal operating conditions by means of the spring. However, when the pressure of air at the outlet overcomes the tension of the spring, the valve is pushed open and releases excess air so it will not exceed the outlet air pressure of the pump.

### CHECK VALVE

The check valve is designed to allow air to pass through in only one direction. The valve is pushed open when the pressure of air supplied from the air pump overcomes the valve spring tension, but closes with the counterflow of exhaust gas from the manifold.

This arrangement safeguards the air pump and hoses against damage when the air supply from the air pump is stopped, due to a broken drivebelt or when backfiring occurs within the exhaust system, causing high temperature exhaust gases to flow in a reverse direction.

### AIR SWITCHING VALVE

This valve is designed to switch air flow from the air pump, and is operated by manifold vacuum and air pump pressure which are switched by a vacuum switching valve (3 way valve).

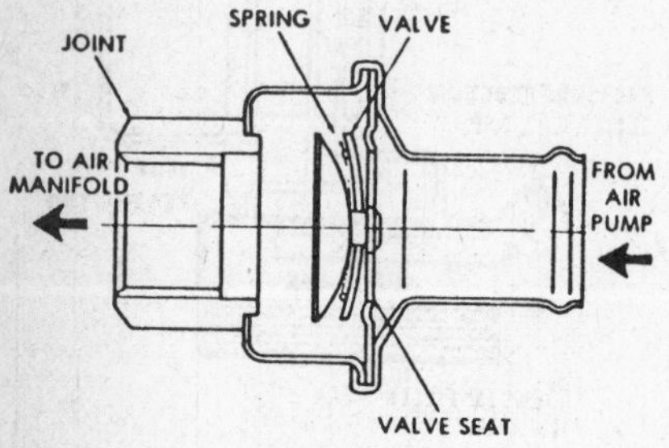


**Check valve**

When manifold vacuum flows to pipe, the air switching valve allows air from the air pump to the check valve. When air pump pressure flows to the pipe switched by the vacuum switching valve, the air valve shuts the air passage to the air manifold, and at the same time opens the port to the air cleaner.

### VACUUM SWITCHING VALVE

The vacuum switching valve has 3 way ports, two of which are opened or closed by electrically controlling the solenoid plunger. The solenoid plunger is energized when the water temperature is under 122° F (50° C) or for 10 seconds after the wide open throttle (WOT) switch is turned on with the condition that the water temperature is over 122° F (50° C). (However, the solenoid plunger is de-energized immediately when WOT switch is turned off within this 10 seconds). When energized, the vacuum switching valve connects the diaphragm chamber of the air switching valve to the intake manifold, permitting the manifold vacuum to be applied to the diaphragm chamber. When the solenoid plunger is de-energized, it plugs the ports, so the two inner diaphragm chambers of the air switching valve are connected.

### AIR MANIFOLD AND AIR INJECTION NOZZLES

Pressured air from the air pump is fed through the check valve, into the air manifold, where it is distributed to the nozzles. The nozzles are installed in position near the exhaust valves

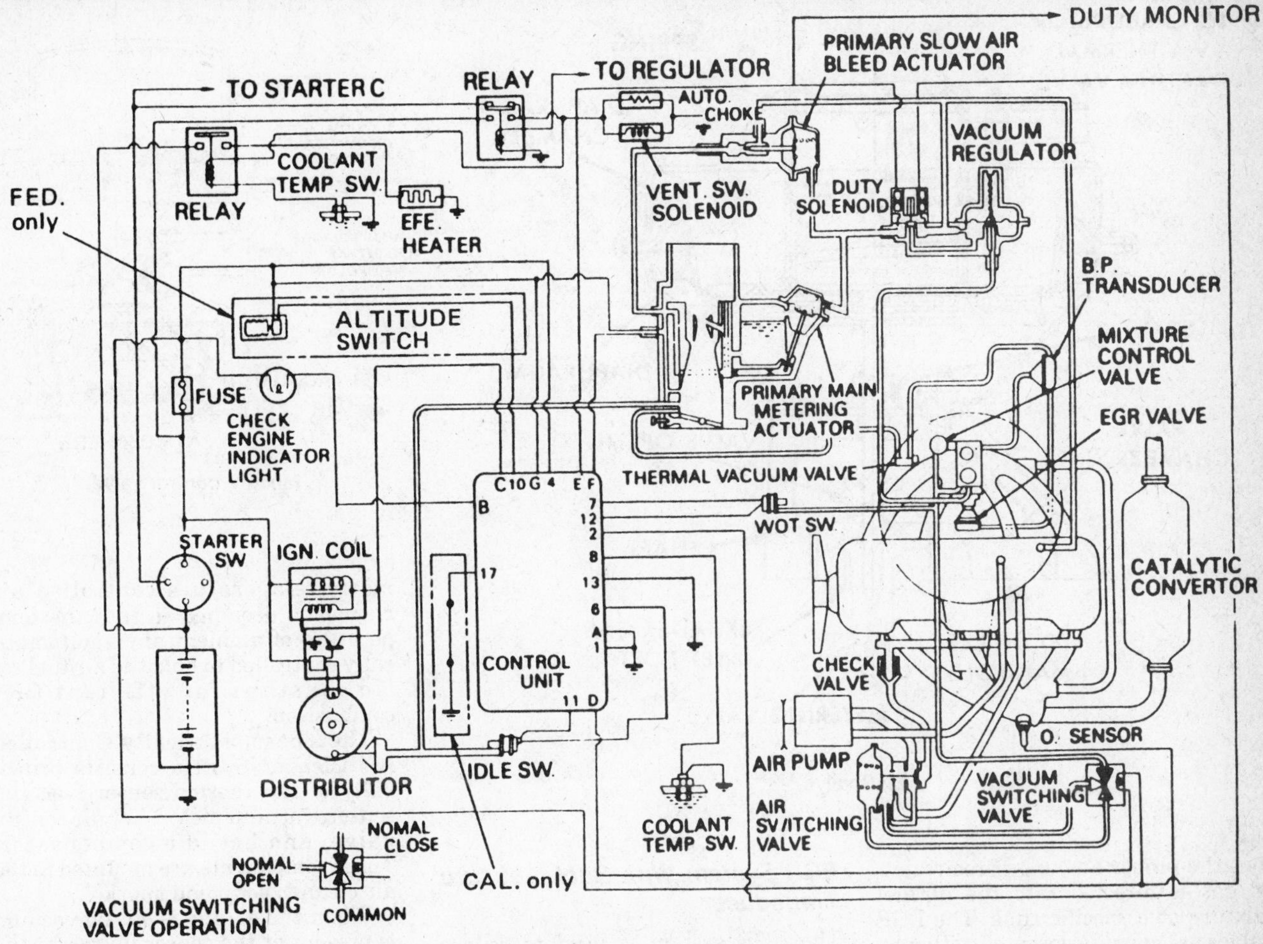


Emission control system

and pointed toward the valve. Thus, air is continuously injected into the exhaust manifold while the engine is running.

### Mixture Control Valve

The purpose of the mixture control valve is to prevent the backfiring in the exhaust system during deceleration. The mixture control valve is designed to supply air into the intake manifold to prevent over-enrichment of the air/fuel mixture, when the throttle valve in the carburetor is suddenly closed.

The mixture control valve is held closed under normal operating conditions. When the vacuum in the intake manifold increases rapidly, the valve opens, allowing the air into the intake manifold.

### Exhaust Gas Recirculation System (EGR)

Varied types of EGR valves are used with different control components, so

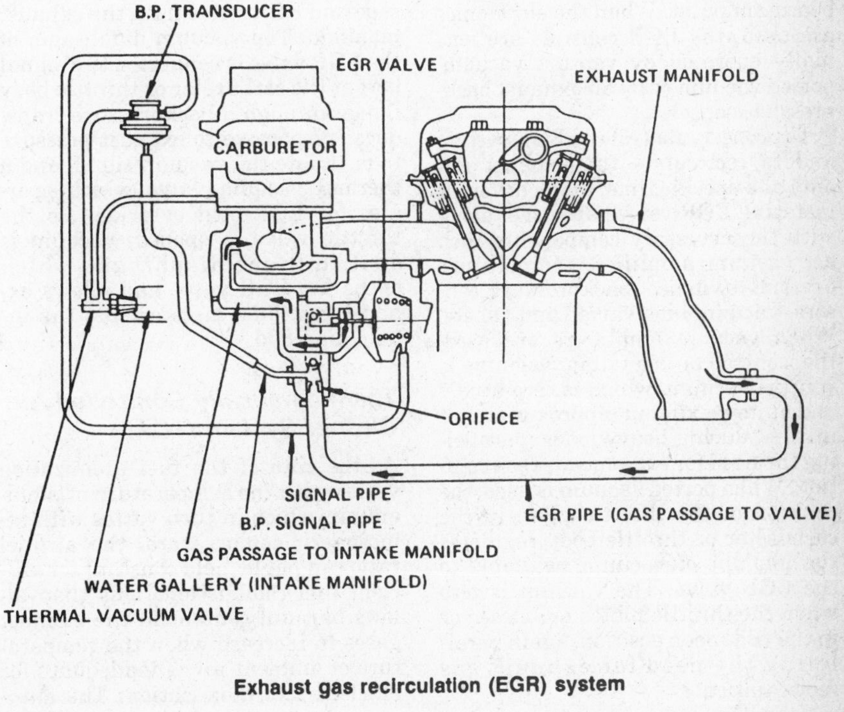


Exhaust gas recirculation (EGR) system

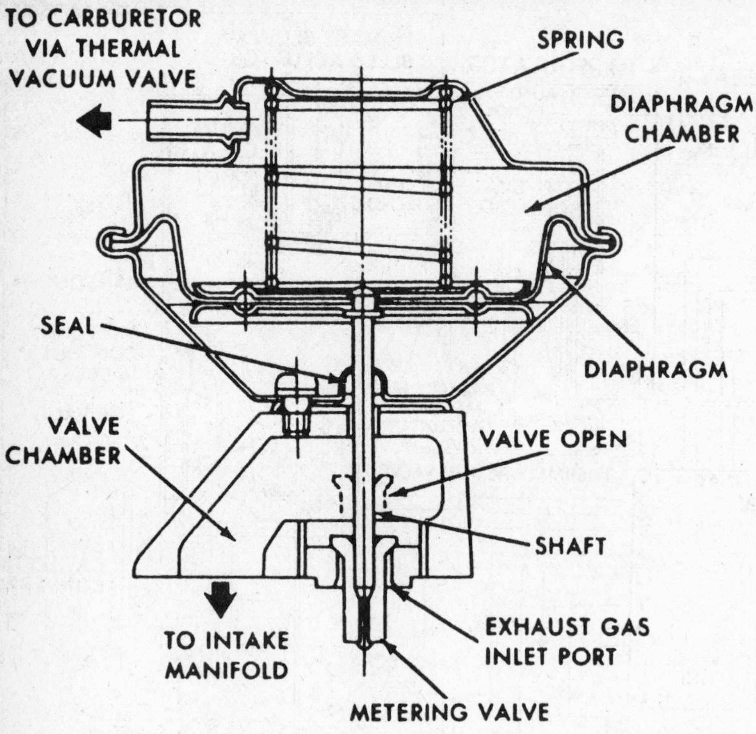

EGR valve

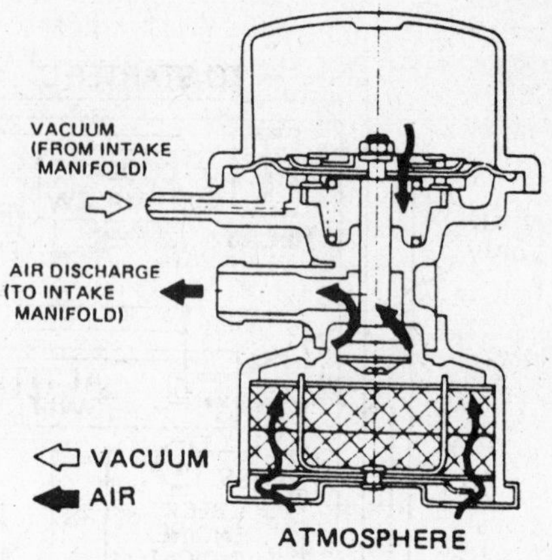

Mixture control valve

that the proper amount of recirculated gas is directed into the air/fuel mixture at a specific time. The EGR valves are vacuum operated, either by intake manifold vacuum or by ported vacuum. With the increased use of electronics, sensors and controlling solenoids are used to regulate the operation of the EGR valve by the onboard computer. When the electronics are used, the EGR controls are normally operated by venturi vacuum, ported vacuum or by an exhaust backpressure sensor.

To properly control the EGR system and to recirculate the exhaust gas only at a specific time, many different metering EGR valves are used, along with the necessary components such as; vacuum amplifier, temperature override switches, backpressure sensors, vacuum bias valves and timers. When vacuum amplifiers are used, the control or signaling vacuum is venturi vacuum, which is zero at idle and at its maximum (approximately 4 in. Hg.) during heavy loads, paralleling the need for exhaust gas recirculation. When ported vacuum is used, the position of the throttle plate in the carburetor or throttle body regulates the amount of vacuum available to the EGR valve. The vacuum is zero when the throttle plates are closed or in the wide open position, again paralleling the need for exhaust gas recirculation.

### EGR System With Backpressure Transducer

The EGR system is used to reduce combustion temperature in the combustion chamber, thereby reducing oxides of nitrogen emissions. The exhaust gas is drawn into the intake manifold through a steel pipe or passage and EGR valve from the exhaust manifold. The vacuum diaphragm of the EGR valve is connected to a signal port at the carburetor or throttle body flange through a backpressure transducer responsive to exhaust pressure to modulate the vacuum signal and a thermal vacuum valve which operates for EGR cold override. As the throttle valve is opened, vacuum is applied to the diaphragm, which opens the EGR valve and allows exhaust gas to be metered into the intake manifold.

### Thermostatically Controlled Air Cleaner System (TCA)

As the rate of the fuel atomization varies with the temperature of ambient air, which in turn varies with atmospheric temperature, the air/fuel ratio can not be held constant for efficient fuel combustion. This then allows harmful content in the exhaust gases to increase when the temperature of ambient air is inadequate for efficient fuel atomization. The automatic temperature controlled air cleaner is designed so that the temperature of ambient air is automatically controlled to hold the air/fuel ratio constant for efficient fuel combustion.

The Thermostatically Controlled Air Cleaner System consists principally of the thermo sensor, vacuum sensor, vacuum motor, hot air control valve, and hot idle compensator. These components are mounted to the air cleaner body and snorkel.

When the engine is off, no vacuum is present at the sensor unit or at the vacuum motor. The force of the vacuum motor spring closes off the heated air passage from the exhaust manifold heat stove (snorkel passage open).

When the engine is started cold, the thermo sensor is cool allowing maximum vacuum to the vacuum motor. Maximum vacuum at the vacuum motor completely opens the hot air control valve, closing off the ambient passage through the snorkel and opening the air passage from the manifold heat stove. Should the engine be heavily accelerated while in this mode, the vacuum level in the system will drop to a low enough level so that the diaphragm spring will overcome the vacuum an open the snorkel passage.

As the engine heats up and the air past the thermo sensor reaches between 100°–111° F (38°–44° C), the thermo sensor comes into operation and begins to bleed off the supply of vacuum from the intake manifold.

At approximately 111° F (44° C), the thermo sensor completely bleeds off all vacuum to the vacuum motor so that the diaphragm spring closes the hot air control valve to the heat stove passage and opens the ambient air passage through the snorkel.

Extended idling, climbing a slope or continuous high speed driving is immediately followed by a considerable increase in engine and engine compartment temperature.

With this heat build-up, excessive fuel vapors enter the intake manifold causing an over rich mixture that results in rough idle and increased carbon monoxide emission. To prevent this, the air cleaner is equipped with a hot idle compensator. As the engine heats up and air past the hot idle compensator reaches a specified temperature, the compensator opens to feed ambient air into the intake manifold to lean out the temporarily rich mixture.

### *High Altitude Emission Control System*

Altitude compensating system consists of altitude switch, solenoid valve and electronic control unit. The altitude switch senses from the atmospheric pressure and energizes the solenoid valve and ECU at high altitude. The solenoid valve opens and leans the air/fuel mixture by adding air to the carburetor altitude compensation passage. The ECU changes open duty cycle, also leaning the air/fuel ratio at high altitude and reducing hydrocarbon and carbon monoxide emissions. At low altitude, electric current from the altitude switch is shut off and altitude compensating system does not operate.

### *Closed Loop Emission Control System*

Closed loop emission control is a system that precisely controls the air/fuel mixture near the 14.7:1 ratio, allowing the use of a three-way catalyst to reduce oxides of nitrogen, oxidize hydrocarbons and carbon monoxide. The essential components are an exhaust gas oxygen sensor, an electronic controller, a vacuum controller with duty solenoid, a controlled air/fuel ratio carburetor and a three way catalytic converter.

The oxygen sensor used in the closed loop control system consists of a closed end zirconia sensor placed in the engine exhaust gas stream. This sensor is mounted in the exhaust manifold. The sensor generates a voltage which varies with the oxygen content in the exhaust gas stream. As oxygen content rises, (lean mixture) voltage falls, and as oxygen content falls, (rich mixture) voltage rises.

### *Early Fuel Evaporation System (EFE)*

The electric EFE system utilizes a ceramic heater grid located underneath

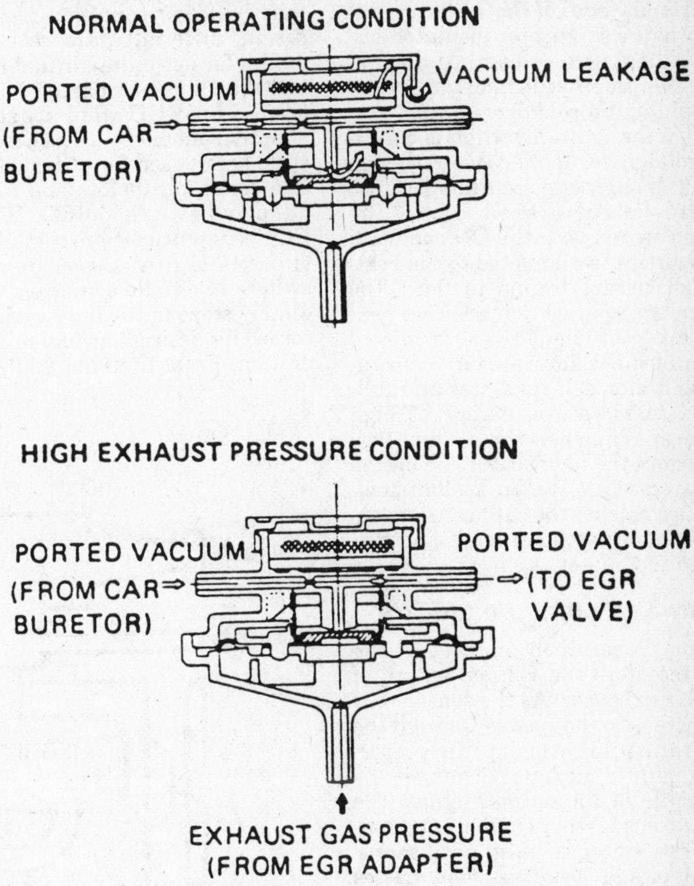


Backpressure transducer

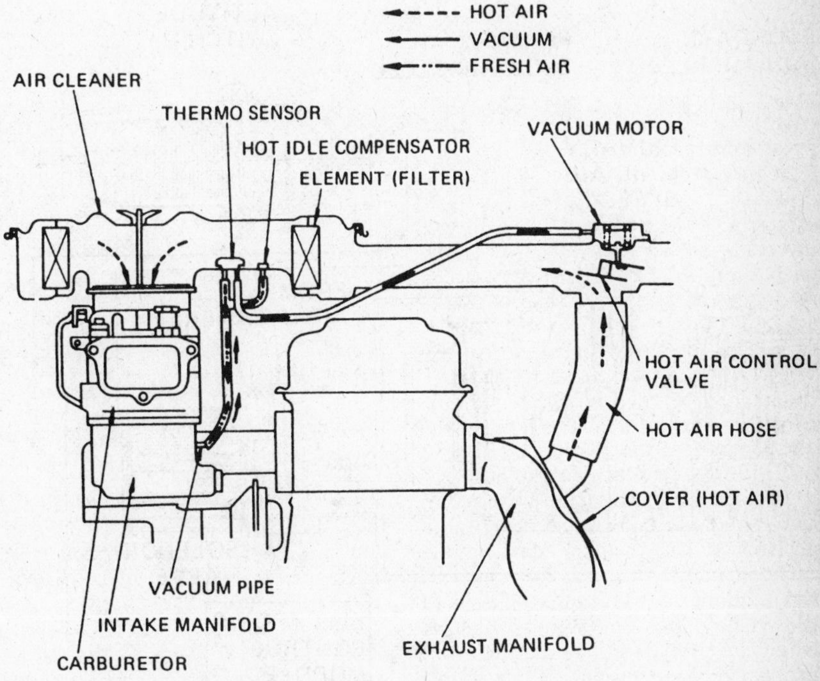


Thermostatically control air cleaner system

the primary bore of the carburetor as a part of the carburetor insulator gasket. It heats the incoming air/fuel charge for improved vaporization and driveability on cold drive-away.

When the ignition switch is turned on, voltage is applied to a thermo switch. If engine coolant temperature is below a calibrated value, the thermo switch is in the ON condition and a circuit is completed to the heater and current begins to flow. The heater, incorporating a positive temperature coefficient (PTC) semiconductor element, increases in temperature and then self-regulates at a calibrated temperature, except at high engine speeds when the air/fuel flow will reduce the temperature below the regulated value. When coolant temperature reaches the calibrated value, the thermo switch turns off and current to the heater is cut off.

### *Electronic Control Unit (ECU)*

During closed loop operation, the ECU monitors the voltage output of the oxygen sensor. As the sensor voltage increases and passes through the ECU threshold set point, the proportional gain immediately changes the duty cycle of the output signal. The duty cycle is further changed at a constant rate (integral gain) until sensor input voltage decreases and passes through the ECU threshold set point.

The selection of integral and proportional gain rates by the ECU is based on engine operating conditions (idle or off-idle condition). At idle condition, different gain rates are required for optimum air/fuel ratio control than those at partial load condition. The ECU also stores in an adaptive memory, the current duty cycle being used for either idle or off-idle condition (below and above the adaptive switch point). When the ECU sees a transition from idle condition (as signaled by the vacuum switch) to off-idle condition, it immediately steps to the duty cycle last recorded for desired air/fuel mixture operation. From then on, while at that engine operating condition, the system uses the basic proportional and integral gain controls as previously described.

### *Catalytic Converter*

The catalytic converters are mounted in the engine exhaust stream and works as a gas reactor in which its major function is to speed up the heat producing chemical reaction between the exhaust gas components, in order to reduce the carbon monoxide, hydrocarbon and oxides of nitrogen in the

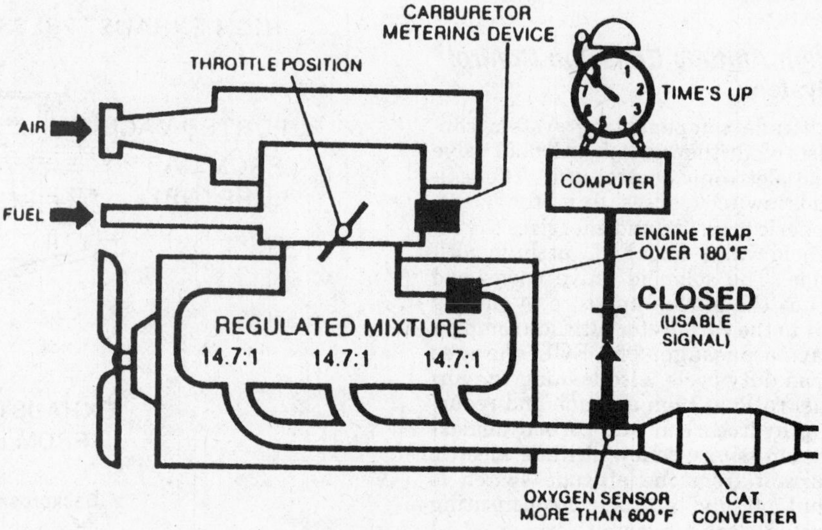


Closed loop system

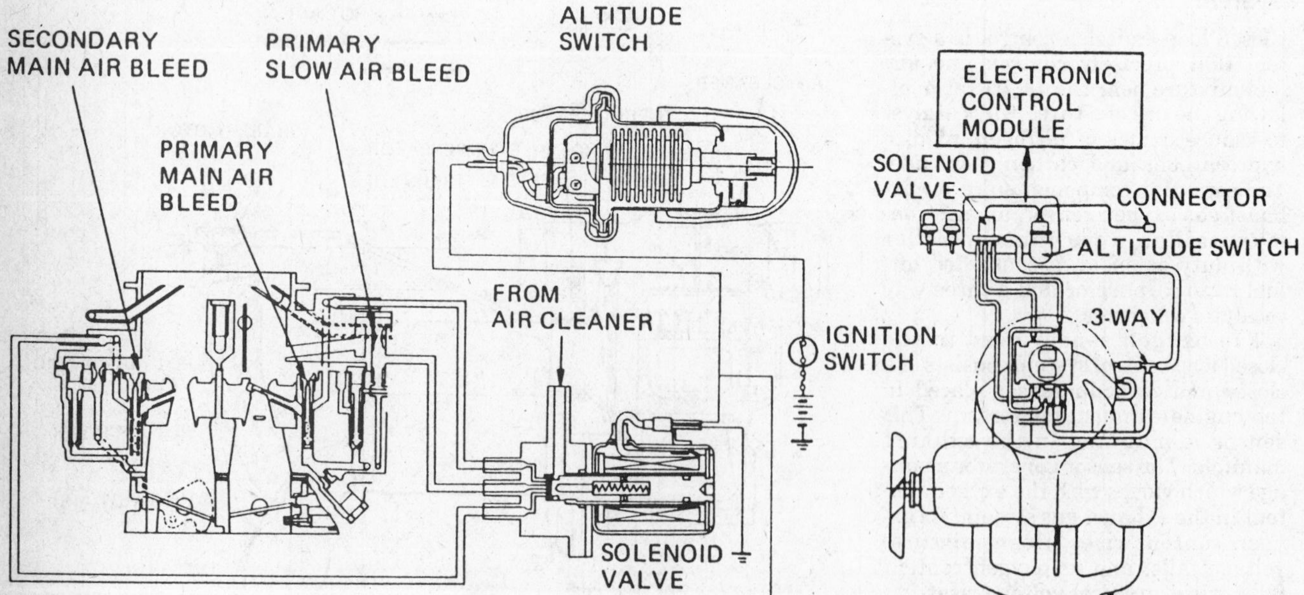


High altitude emission control system

engine exhaust. Unleaded fuel must be used in vehicles equipped with catalytic converters.

The catalyst material is either a ceramic substrate or pellets that are coated with a base of alumina and then impregnated with catalytically active, precious (noble) metals. It is the surface of the catalyst material that controls the heat producing chemical reaction.

Two main types of converters containing two precious (noble) metals, platinum and palladium to effectively catalyze the oxidation of the hydrocarbons and carbon monoxide. The second type converter used is considered a three-way catalyst, containing a small percentage of platinum and a greater percentage of rhodium in the front part of the converters to reduce the oxides of nitrogen, while platinum and palladium are used in the rear section to oxidize the hydrocarbons and carbon monoxide, as was done in the two way converters.

### *Three-Way Catalytic Converter*

The three-way catalytic converters use a combination of catalyst which produce two different chemical reactions, oxidation and reduction. By adding fresh air to the unburned hydrocarbons and carbon monoxide within the converter, the oxidizing of combustion process takes place.

Just the reverse process is required to lower the oxides of nitrogen emissions. The oxides of nitrogen already contains excessive oxygen and the process of separating the excess oxygen from the nitrogen is called a reducing reaction.

This reducing or reducing process is done in the front section of the converter while the oxidizing process is accomplished in the rear section. A fresh air connector is located on the center of the converter shell, to add fresh air from the air system as required.

To enable the three-way converter to operate properly, the engine's air/fuel ratio must be held within a tight range (the desired 14.7:1 air/fuel ratio). This is accomplished with the use of the latest computer controlled electronic engine components.

Different control components are used by the vehicle manufacturers to prevent converter damage and/or burnout. Unleaded fuels must be used in the vehicles equipped with the catalytic converters to prevent contamination failure.

### *Thermal Reactor System*

The thermal reactor is installed in place of the exhaust manifold. It is much heavier and heat resistant. Its purpose is to collect the exhaust gases in a common area, to keep their temperature higher for a longer period of time, thus allowing further oxidation or burning of the exhaust gas and secondary air mix burned emissions.

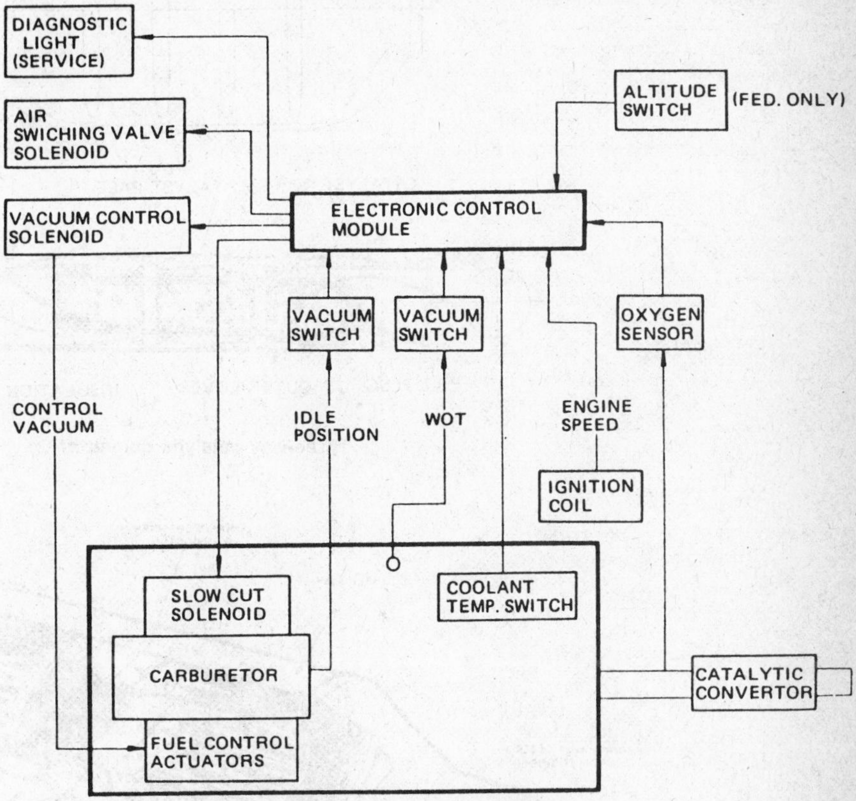


**Closed loop control system**

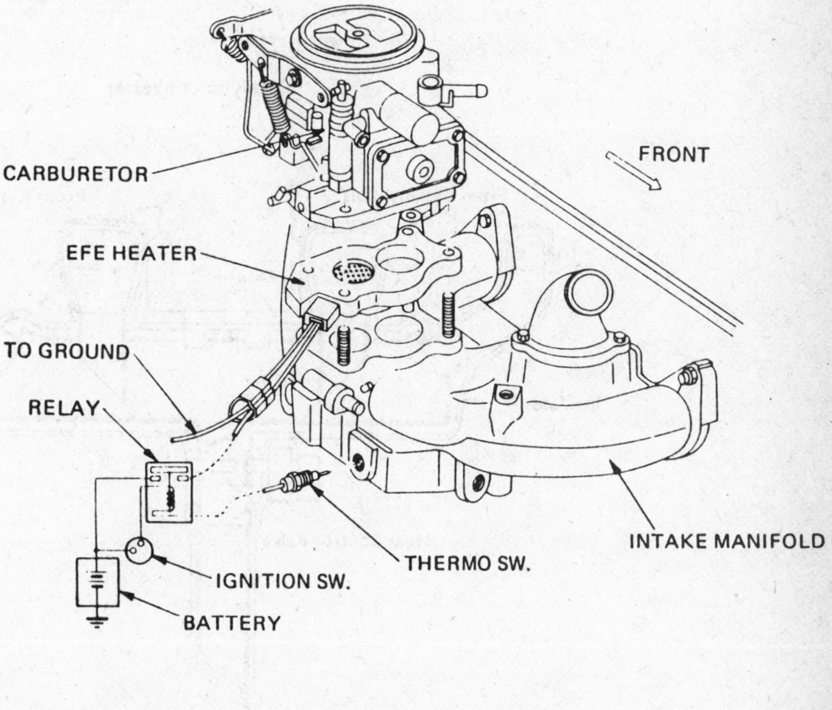


**Early fuel evaporation (EFE) system**

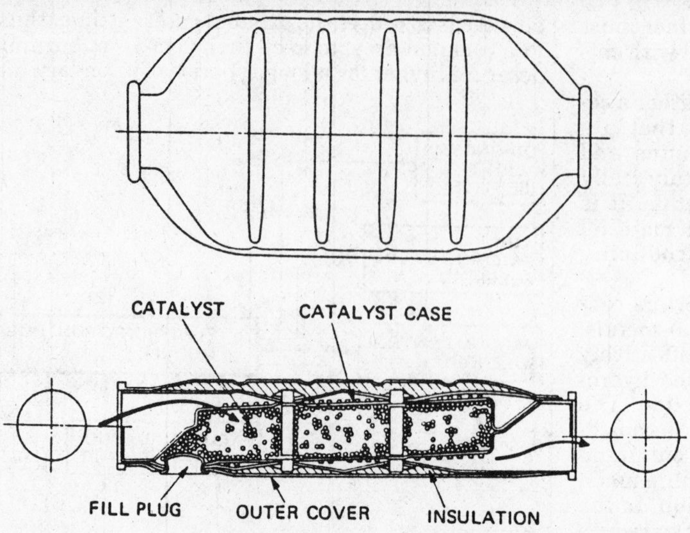


**Three-way catalytic converter**

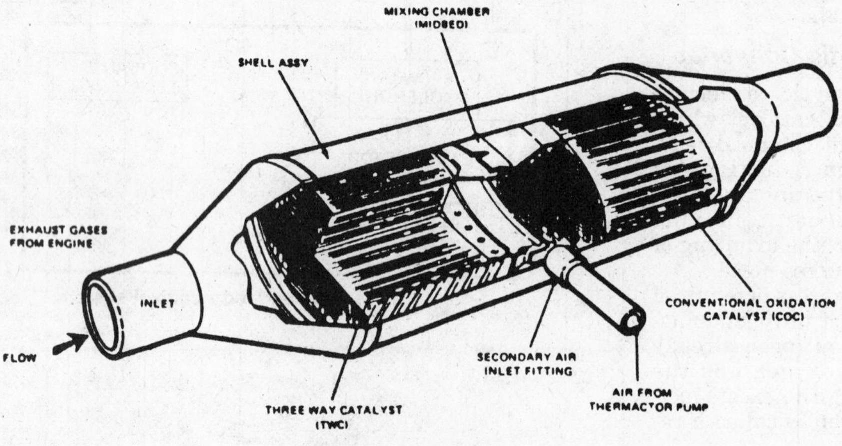


**Catalytic converter**

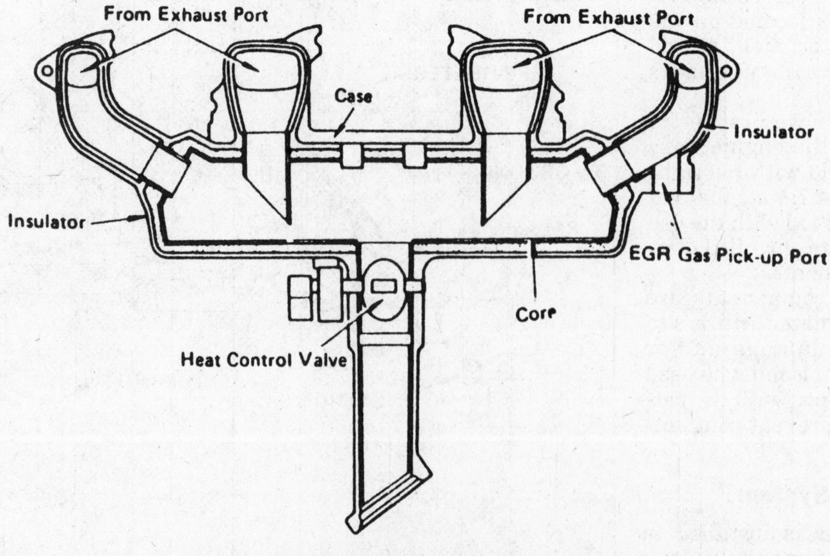


**Thermal reactor system**

# Engine Controls 26

## ENGINE ELECTRONICS

### History

In the latter part of the 1960's, Robert Bosch introduced the first true electronically controlled engine with an on-board computer. Today, almost every car produced has some kind electronic engine control. The once mechanically controlled engine functions of early model cars are all but extinct.

The first system, Bosch D-Jetronic, is comprised of electrically energized fuel injectors in which the injection time is controlled by an electronic control unit (ECU). The early system delivered a basic quantity of fuel and varied from this point depending upon engine load, engine speed and engine temperature.

Since the early days of the ECU, the controls have become more complex, with a much greater amount of computer memory and even the ability to learn.

In this section, the topics will include different types of electronically controlled fuel induction, spark control, the sensors and switches that provide the ECU with information, other non-engine related controls that the ECU might supply and some ECU self-diagnostics.

The most common fuel induction system with an ECU is electronic fuel injection. In this system, fuel can be delivered many different ways. One of which is the single point injection (SPI) were one or two injectors are mounted on a throttle body assembly. Fuel is delivered constantly through the injector(s), but in varying quantities. The SPI system very much resembles a carbureted system. SPI is more commonly known as throttle body injection (TBI). Another fuel injection system is multi-point injection (MPI). This system supplies one injector for each cylinder, usually positioned in the intake manifold, just above the intake valve. In MPI, fuel can be injected in two ways. One is to energize a group of injectors, thus atomizing fuel in the intake manifold and storing it for a short time until the intake valve opens. The second way is to sequentially energize each cylinder's injector as the intake valve is opened. This injection is the more efficient, effective and more complex system.

Another fuel induction system utilizing an ECU is the feedback carburetor (FBC). A conventional carburetor is still used, but it has a more precise air/fuel mixture control which is achieved through an integral mixture control solenoid. The solenoid is energized on and off by the ECU to maintain mixture demand. The ECU calculates air/fuel mixture demand changes by the data it receives through remote sensors. The most important sensor (and makes the system possible) is an oxygen ($O_2$) sensor (which will be discussed later in this section). The ECU monitors the exhaust gases for rich/lean conditions by way of the $O_2$ sensor and, in turn, controls the air/fuel mixture by increasing or decreasing the duty cycles (on and off) to the mixture control solenoid for an optimum 14.7:1 air/fuel ratio.

### ECU Self-Diagnostics

The ECU can detect a malfunction or abnormality in the sensors or in the ECU itself and display a warning light on the instrument panel when it does. When this occurs, the ECU stores a trouble code for future system diagnosis. If the problem is sever enough to where it inhibits closed loop operation, the ECU will assume a backup system. This fail-safe circuit is pre-programmed into the ECU for minimal driveability operation so the vehicle can be driven to a nearby service facility. The trouble codes are usually a two digit numbers identified by the number of diagnostic LED or check engine light flashes. The trouble codes assist the service technician in isolating a faulty circuit or component within the system.

### Electronic Data Sensors

The engine control system consists of various data sensors. Although data sensor names and applications vary from system to system, the most common input sensors/switches are:

- oxygen ($O_2$) sensor
- coolant temperature sensor
- manifold air pressure (MAP) sensor
- vehicle speed sensor (VSS)
- throttle position sensor (TPS)
- engine speed reference or distributor reference (rpm)
- air flow sensor
- air intake temperature sensor
- crankshaft sensor
- detonation (knock) sensor
- throttle body temperature sensor

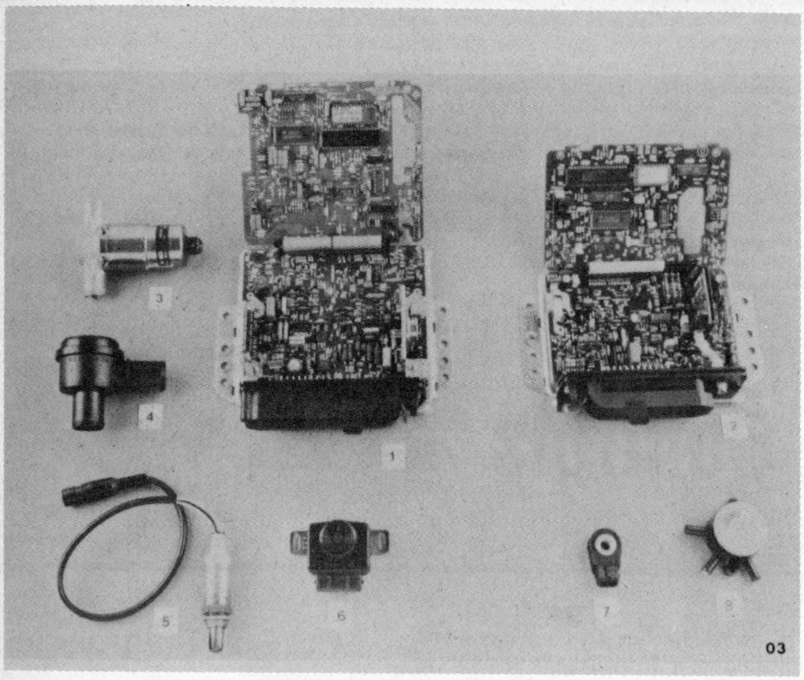

Engine electronic components

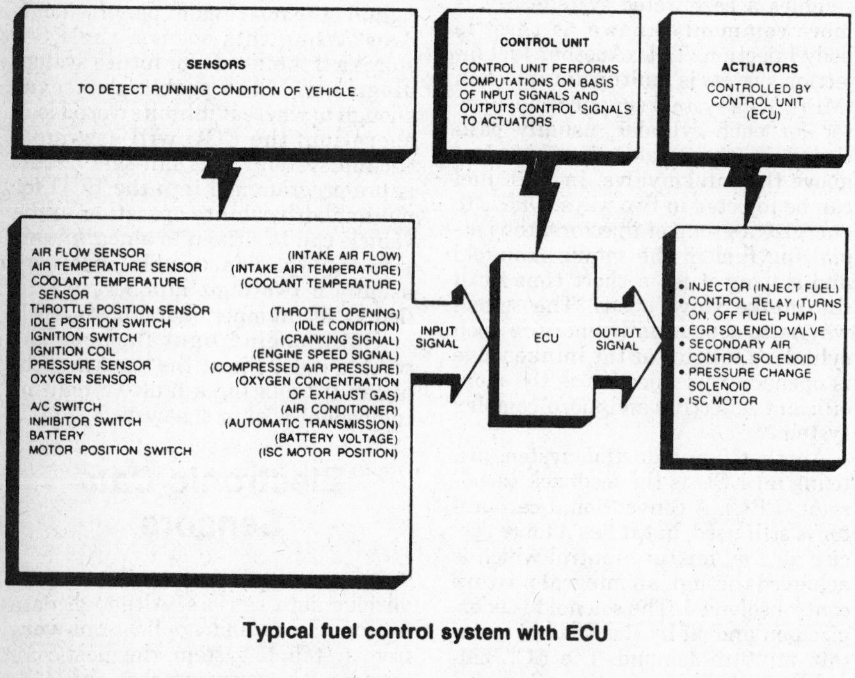


Typical fuel control system with ECU

- throttle idle switch
- transmission or drive switch
- a/c compressor clutch switch
- power steering pump switch
- altitude or barometric pressure sensor
- wide open throttle switch

## Electronically Controlled Devices

Some of the output devices that the ECU may control vary from system to system, but the most common output or ECU controlled devices are:

- fuel injector(s)
- air/fuel mixture solenoid
- fuel pump relay
- a/c compressor clutch relay
- idle air control (IAC) valve
- idle speed control (ISC) motor
- ignition spark/timing
- canister purge solenoid
- torque converter clutch solenoid (automatic transmission)
- air management system (air induction)
- idle-up or throttle kicker solenoid
- alternator field control (charging system)
- turbocharger boost wastegate
- cooling fan relay

## Component Description

### THROTTLE BODY

The throttle body, in most fuel injected systems, is usually an alumunum housing that consists of one or two throttle blades which are attached to a throttle shaft. The housing has a throttle position sensor (TPS) sensor, idle air control motor and, in some cases, throttle body temperature sensor. On SPI systems, the housing also has an injector(s) and (in some cases) a fuel pressure regulator. The throttle body throttle blade controls the amount of air that enters the engine as well as the amount of vacuum.

### ELECTRONIC CONTROL UNIT (ECU)

The ECU monitors and controls all engine control functions. The ECU consists of input and output devices, a central processing unit, a power supply and various memory banks. The input and output devices of the ECU convert electrical signals received by the data sensors and switches to the digital signal that are used by the central processing unit. The central processing unit receives digital signals that are used to perform all mathematical computations and logic functions necessary to deliver proper air/fuel mixture. The central processing unit is also responsible for calculating spark timing information. The main source of power that allows the ECU to function is generated from the battery of the vehicle and transported through the ignition system. The memory bank of the ECU is programmed with exact information that is used by the ECU during the open loop mode. This data is also used when a sensor of other component fails, allowing the vehicle to be driven to a repair facility.

### CALIBRATION ASSSEMBLY OR PROM (PROGRAMMABLE READ ONLY MEMORY)

Some vehicle manufactures use one

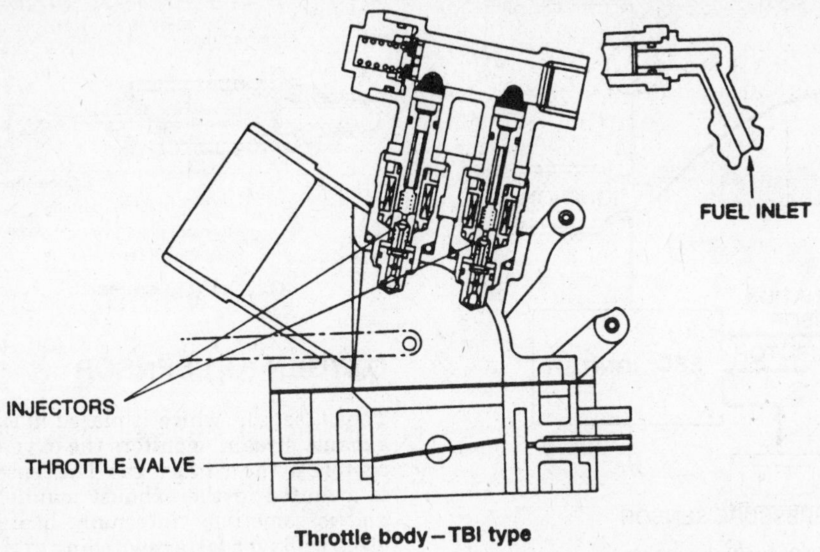


**Throttle body – TBI type**

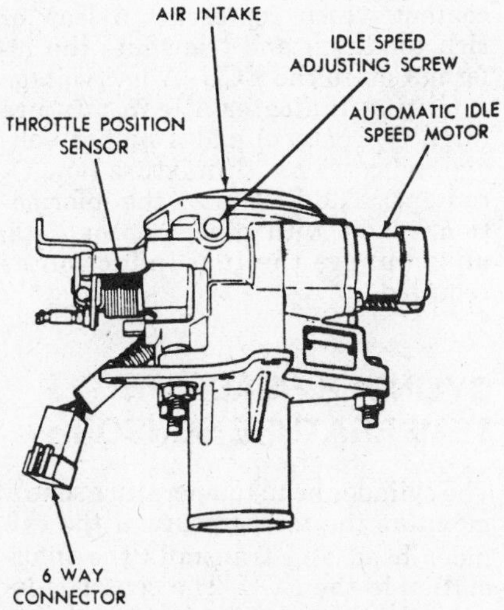


**Throttle body – MFI type**

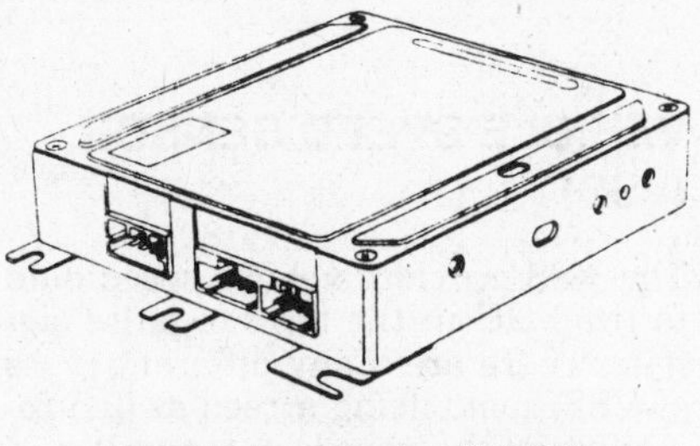

**Electronic control unit (ECU)**

ECU for several different model vehicles. This interchangeable ECU is possible through the use of a calibration assembly or prom. Information about the vehicle's engine, transmission, body and drive axle ratio are programmed and permanently stored into the assembly. If the battery supply should become disconnected from the ECU, the data stored into the assembly is not lost.

## ELECTRONIC SPARK CONTROL (ESC)

The vehicles equipped with an ESC have the ability to change the ignition timing under any and all operating conditions. Data from various remote sensors (coolant temperature, throttle position, rpm, etc.) is transmitted to the ESC. The ESC computes the information and triggers the ignition spark at precisely the right instant. Some ESC systems (ie.,turbocharged engines) use a detonation (knock) sensor which senses pre-ignition and transmits the information to the ESC. The ESC modifies spark advance and boost pressure in order to eliminate knock.

## MASS AIR FLOW SENSOR

The mass air flow (MAF) sensor is only incorporated in some Multi-point fuel injection systems. The MAF sensor is a very complex device which measures the air mass of the engine intake. Because the air mass is always changing with temperature, humidity and altitude, the fuel delivery rate must be adjusted to compensate for these changes so that a precise fuel mixture can be maintained.

## AIR TEMPERATURE SENSOR

The air temperature sensor is located in the air stream of the air flow meter. The sensor supplies incoming air temperature information to the ECU. The ECU uses this data, along with other data, to regulate fuel injection rate.

## THROTTLE POSITION SENSOR (TPS)

The TPS can be either a switch (or a combination of switches) or a variable resistor which is much more accurate in throttle position. The switch type TPS consists of switches that open and close at different throttle positions (usually at idle and wide open throttle) and sends the information to the ECU. The variable resistor type receives a reference voltage from the ECU and responds back to the ECU with a proportional voltage directly related to the position of the throttle plate.

## ENGINE COOLANT TEMPERATURE SENSOR

The coolant temperature sensor is located in the engine coolant passage, usually located in the intake manifold. The sensor is resistor based and changes resistance as coolant temper-

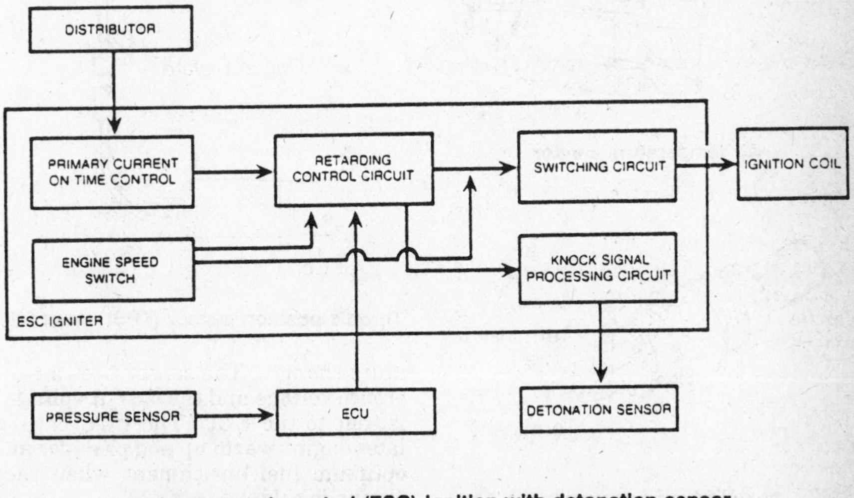


**Electronic spark control (ESC) ignition with detonation sensor**

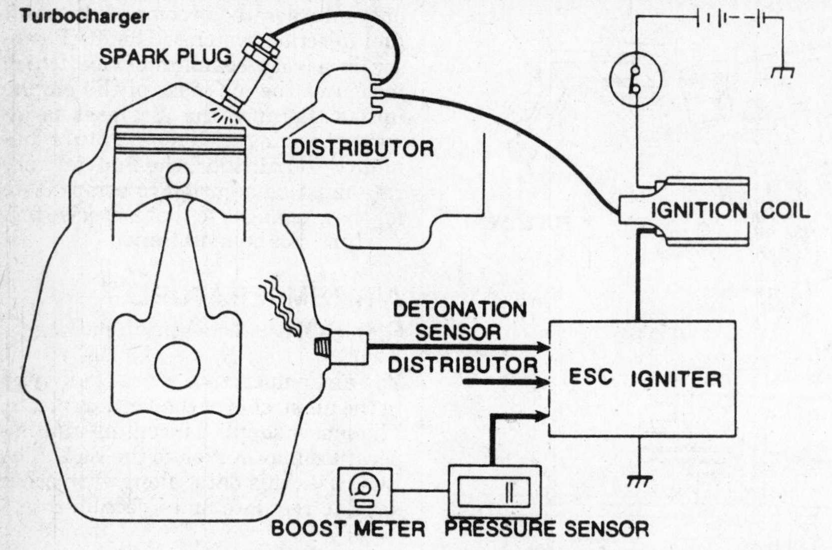


Electronic spark control (ESC) ignition system

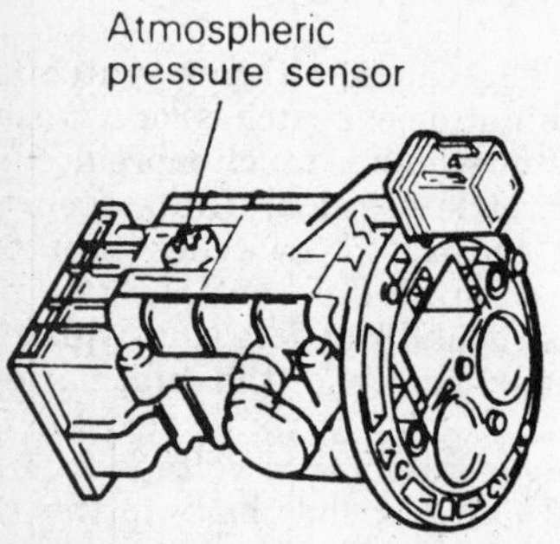


Mass air flow (MAF) sensor

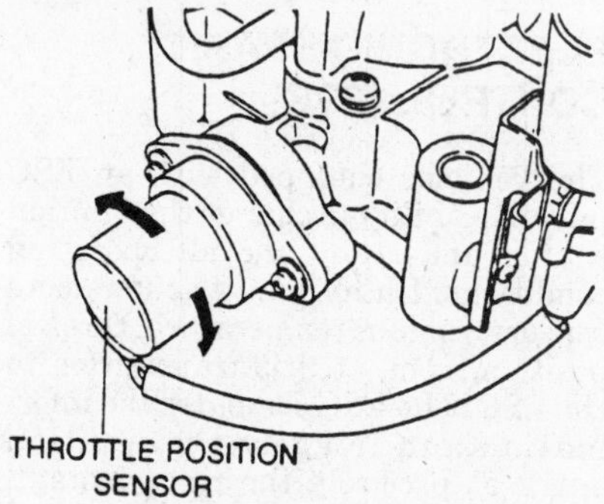


Throttle position sensor (TPS)

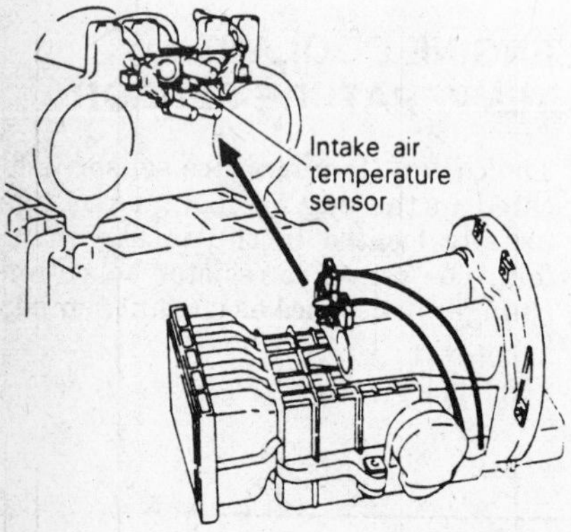


Air temperature sensor

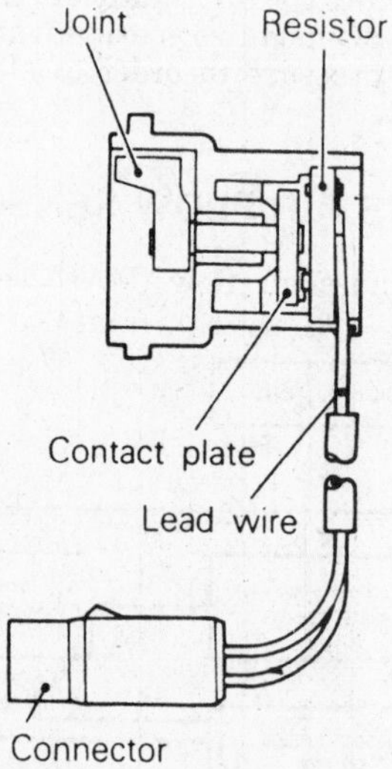


Throttle position sensor (TPS) – internal

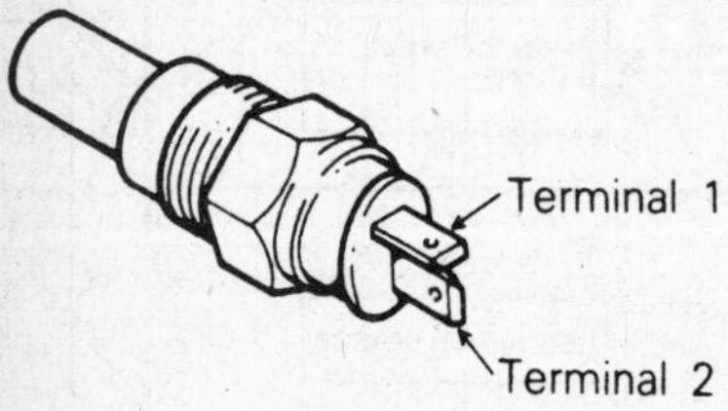


Coolant temperature sensor

ature changes. The sensor uses a reference voltage and the output voltage is sent to the ECU. The ECU calculates engine warm up and provides an optimum fuel enrichment when the engine is cold.

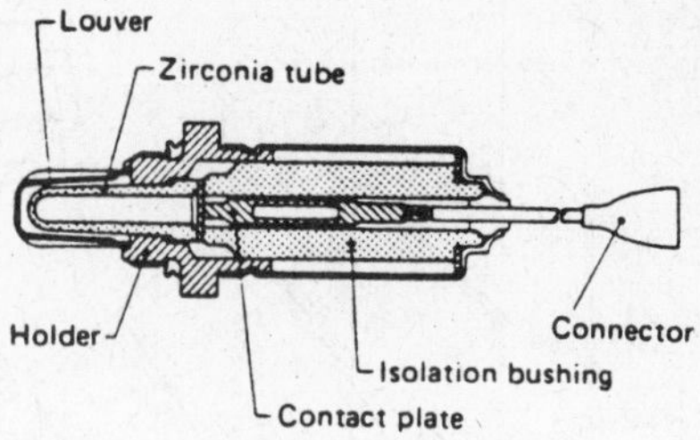


Oxygen ($O_2$) sensor

## OXYGEN ($O_2$) SENSOR

The $O_2$ sensor, which is placed in the exhaust stream, monitors the oxygen content in the exhaust gas. The sensor is mounted in the exhaust manifold and is sometimes internally heated electrically for faster switching to the closed loop mode. The sensor produces a voltage proportional to the oxygen content which represents a lean or rich condition and transmits the information to the ECU. A low voltage condition indicates a lean mixture (high $O_2$ content) and a higher voltage indicates a rich mixture (low $O_2$ content). The ECU uses the information, along with other sensor data, and changes the fuel induction as required.

## CYLINDER HEAD TEMPERATURE SENSOR

The cylinder head temperature sensor monitors the temperature of the cylinder head and transmits the information to the ECU. The sensor is located in the cylinder head and is a temperature sensitive resistive unit known as a thermistor.

## VEHICLE SPEED SENSOR (VSS)

The VSS provides vehicle speed data to the ECU in the form of pulse signals. There are many different types of VSS, some using a reed switch installed in the speedometer unit and others using a optical type. In the optical type a light emitting diode (LED) is used to transmit light and photo diode receives the light. A shutter device, which is usually in-line with the speedometer cable, allows the LED light to reach the photo diode in vehicle speed related pulses. The reed switch type relies on a reed switch that opens and closes by way of a rotating magnet. The magnet rotates proportionally with the vehicle speed.

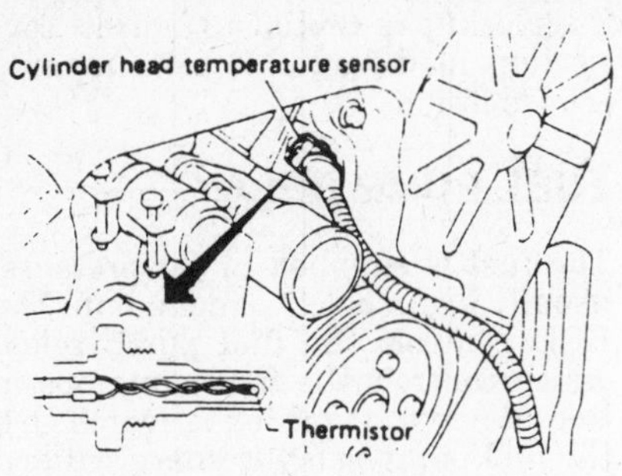


**Cylinder head temperature sensor**

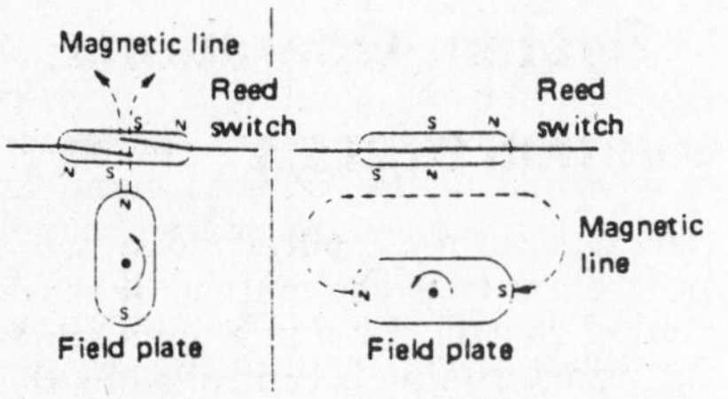


**Vehicle speed sensor (VSS)—reed switch type**

## MANIFOLD AIR PRESSURE (MAP) SENSOR

The MAP sensor is a device that monitors manifold absolute pressure. The sensor is mounted remotely and senses vacuum through a connecting hose. The MAP sensor has a reference voltage from the ECU and transmits remaining voltage to the ECU to calculate engine load. The ECU uses this data along with other data to determine fuel demands.

## DETONATION (KNOCK) SENSOR

The detonation sensor generates a signal when pre-ignition (knock) occurs in one or more combustion chambers. The sensor is made of a material that is sensitive to oscillation that the engine knock produces and sends signals to the ECU. The ECU, in turn, delays the ignition signal which retards the ignition timing and continues to do this until the engine knock ceases.

## CRANKSHAFT (REFERENCE MARK) SENSOR

The crankshaft sensor may be located at either the rear of the engine, at the flywheel, at the front of the engine, near the crankshaft pulley or mounted in the distributor. The sensor detects crankshaft position in relation to top dead center and transmits the signals to ECU.

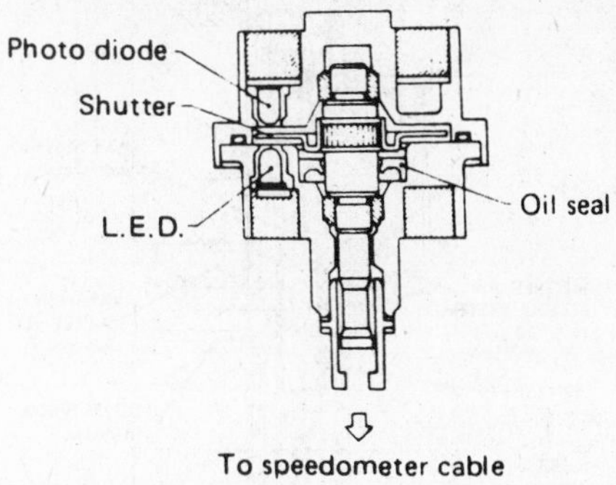


**Vehicle speed sensor (VSS)—photo type**

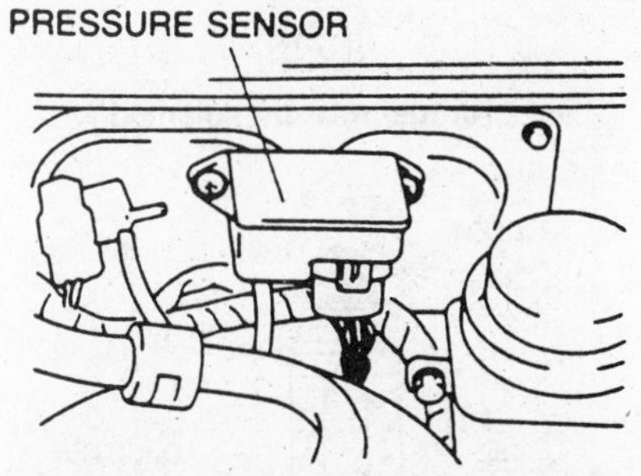


**Manifold air pressure (MAP) sensor**

**Detonation (knock) sensor**

## IDLE SPEED CONTROL (ISC) MOTOR

The ISC is sometimes included on a feedback carburetor system and mounted to the side of the carburetor. The motor driven ISC maintains a steady idle by way of the ECU. When an added load is put on the engine (air conditioning or when the vehicle is in drive) the ECU can increase the idle via the ISC by extending a plunger which opens the throttle valve.

## AIR/FUEL MIXTURE SOLENOID

The air/fuel mixture solenoid on a feedback carburetor operates in conjuntion with the fixed metering jets and/or the manually adjustable

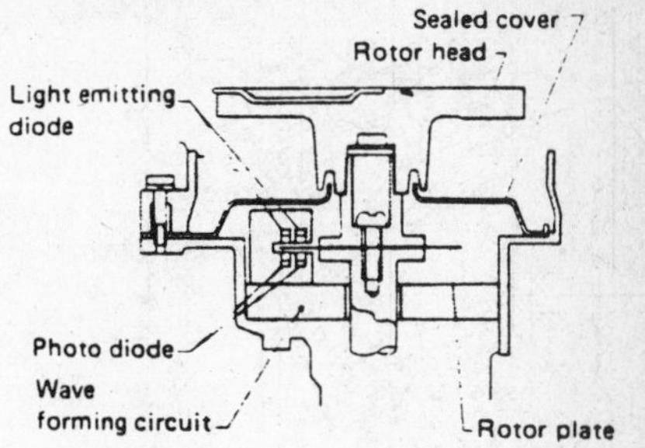


**Crankshaft position sensor—distributor mounted**

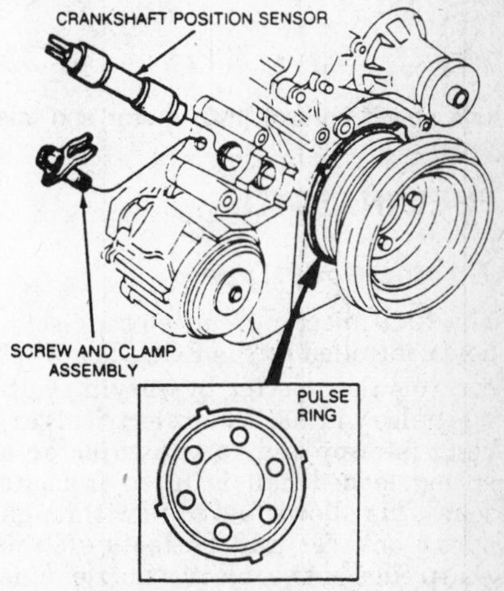


**Crankshaft position sensor—near crankshaft pulley**

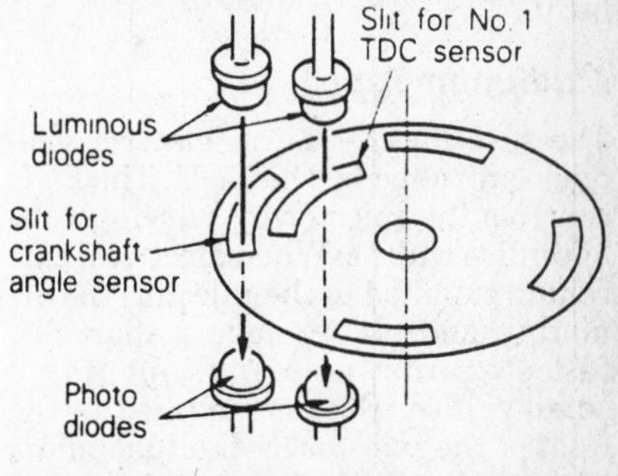


**Crankshaft position sensor—optical type**

idle speed mixture screw. The ECU energizes and de-energizes the solenoid in the closed loop mode. The solenoid usually controls a fixed air bleed and/or fuel discharge port.

## IDLE AIR CONTROL (IAC)

The IAC in a fuel injection system controls the air flow around the throttle plate by extending and retracting a bypass valve in the bypass port. The ECU controls the valve by sending voltage pulses called counts or steps to increase or decrease the bypass air flow, thus increasing and decreasing the idle speed.

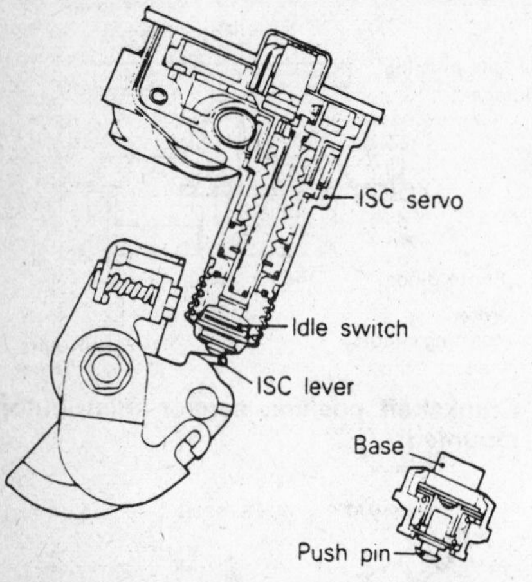


**Idle speed control (ISC) motor and idle switch**

## FUEL INJECTOR

### *Throttle Body Type*

The fuel injector is an electric solenoid controlled by the ECU. The ECU controls the injector by varying voltage pulse widths. When electrical current is supplied to the injector a spring loaded ball is lifted from its seat. This allows fuel to flow through spray orifices and deflects off the sharp edge of the injector nozzle. This action causes the fuel to form a 45° cone shaped spray pattern before entering the air stream in the throttle body.

### *Multipoint Type*

The fuel injector is an electric solenoid controlled by the ECU. The ECU controls the injector by varying voltage pulse widths. When electrical current is supplied to the injector, the armature and pintle move a short distance against a spring, opening a small orifice. Fuel is supplied to the inlet of the injector by the fuel pump, then passes through the injector, around the pintle and out the orifice. Since the fuel is under high pressure, a fine spray is developed in the shape of a hollow cone. The injector, through this spraying action, atomizes the fuel and distributes it into the air entering the combustion chamber.

## TORQUE CONVERTER CLUTCH (TCC) SOLENOID

The TCC solenoid is used on some automatic transmission, which allows for better fuel economy. When certain engine and vehicle speeds have been met, the ECU energizes the solenoid. This allows transmission fluid to flow into passages in the torque converter, which causes the converter to lock up.

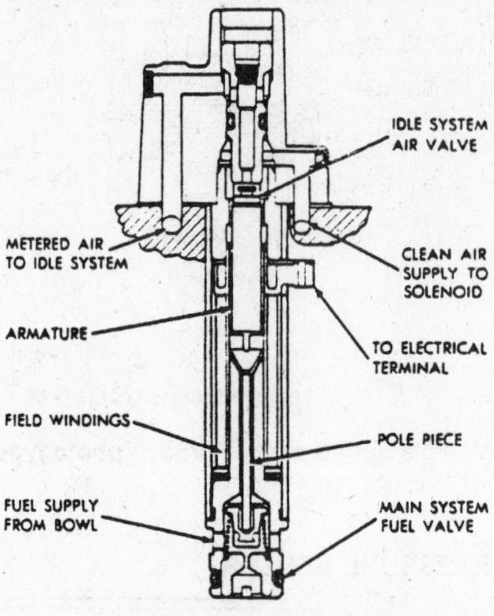


**Air/fuel mixture solenoid**

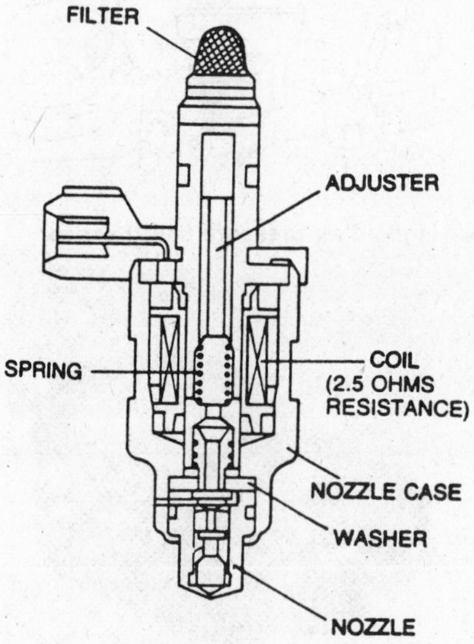


**Fuel injector – TBI type**

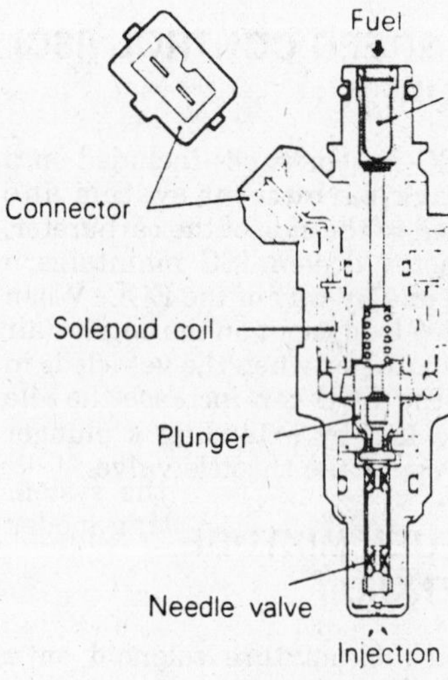


**Fuel injector – MFI type**

This lockup is similar to a direct connection made possible in a manual transmission.

## FUEL PUMP RELAY

The fuel is supplied under pressure, usually by an electric fuel pump. The ECU controls the fuel pump relay, which controls the fuel pump operation. When the ignition is switch ON, the fuel pump relay is energized and the fuel pump is activated. The pump primes the fuel system with fuel to a pre-determined pressure.

# System Operations

## IGNITION SYSTEM

The logic in a computerized system's program selects the method of spark timing control. During engine starting, spark timing is controlled by the mechanical setting of the distributor. Once the engine is running, spark timing is turned over to the ECU. This scheme ensures that the car will start regardless of whether the electronic control system is working or not.

The goal of electronic spark timing is to produce maximum engine power by adjustment the advance of the ignition firing in relationship to top dead center (TDC). The spark timing can be chosen to produce the best engine power with input variables of engine rpm, engine coolant temperature, initial and operating manifold or barometric pressure.

The total spark advance is determined by computing the information received from the various engine sensors which affect spark timing. The processor will then adjust the timing according to information that has been calibrated in it. The processor has programmed into it specific information on:

**Warm-Up Spark Advance** – this is used when the engine is cold, since a greater amount of advance is required while the engine warms up.

**Special Spark Advance** – to improve fuel economy during steady driving conditions.

**Spark Advance Due to Barometric Pressure** – this is used when barometric pressure exceeds a preset calibrated amount.

All of this information is then added together and the initial mechanical advance is subtracted to determine the final spark advance.

The processor receives a timing pulse from a sensor which indicates crankshaft position for top dead center and engines rpm. The processor makes a decision based upon this information and the information that was calibrated into it. At that time, the computer sends a pulse to the ignition actuator circuit, which opens the ignition coil primary circuit to generate a secondary voltage pulse to fire the spark plugs. In some cases, the circuitry to open the primary of the coil may be in the computerized controller. The spark selection is performed mechanically by the distributor and rotor contacts as it is done in a non-electronic controlled system.

The ignition timing works along with electronic fuel control to control emissions and provide for optimum fuel economy and driveability because engine power, fuel economy and emissions are dependent on spark advance of the engine timing.

The system just described is considered to operate in open-loop. There are some electronically controlled ignition systems which receive an input from a knock sensor. These systems operate in a closed-loop mode which allows the ignition system to monitor the engine for mechanical changes, such as engine knock.

Engine knock is a condition where the air/fuel mixture in the cylinder does not burn normally. The pressure rise during this burning is so rapid compared to normal combustion that it is accompanied by an audible "knock".

Through some low level knock is acceptable, it is important to avoid excessive knock. To control engine knock, a knock sensor is installed in the engine or intake manifold. This helps to detect excessive engine knock.

The knock sensor is a tuned accelerometer and produces an output voltage depending on the amount of engine vibration occurring in a certain frequency band. When the processor receives a signal from the knock sensor, it retards the spark advance until the knocking stops and then starts increasing it again. This cycle is repeated as long as engine knock occurs.

## FUEL CONTROL

In order for the processor to control fuel, it requires a sensor or sensors to monitor the state of the engine, and one or more actuators to do the actual controlling. The sensors measure: exhaust gas oxygen, manifold or barometric absolute pressure, engine rpm and speed, inlet air and coolant temperatures. Actuators are energized to control the air/fuel ratio.

The primary purpose of this control system is to maintain air/fuel ratio at or near 14.7:1 ratio. This is accomplished in two modes (during normal

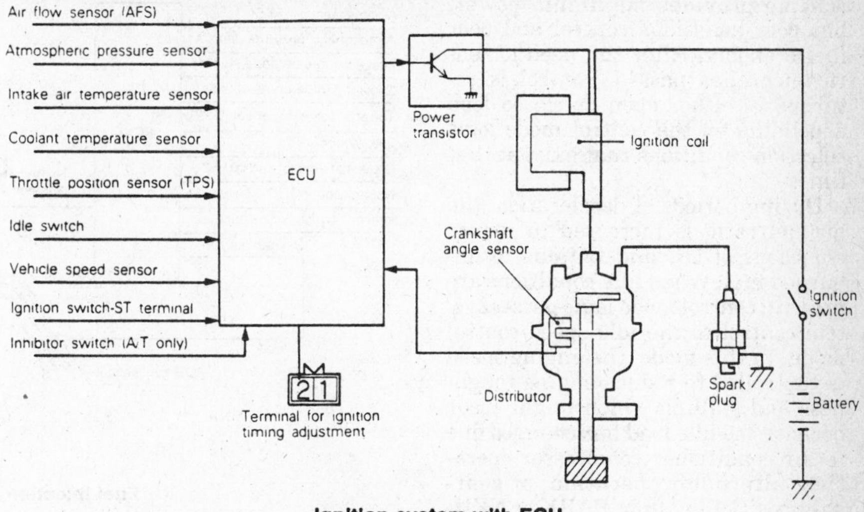


**Ignition system with ECU**

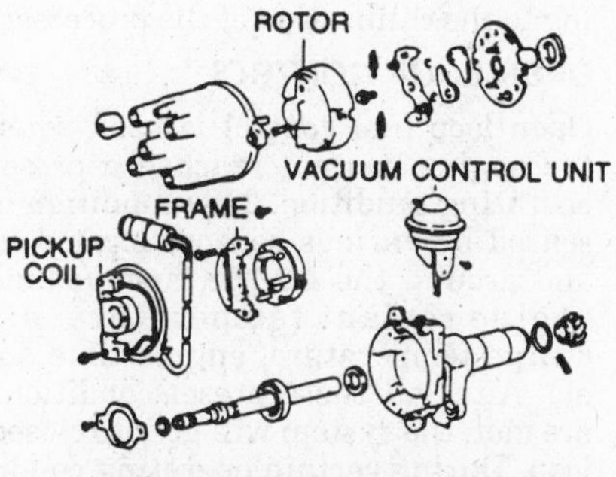


**Electronic distributor assembly**

engine operation) open and closed loop. The electronic fuel control system can operate in closed loop only when certain conditions are satisfied. Open loop mode is employed whenever these conditions are not satisfied. However, for either mode, the exhaust emissions will satisfy federal requirements if the average air/fuel ratio is held within the tolerance limits.

In addition to open and closed loop control modes, a practical fuel control system has other operating modes depending on engine conditions. These handle such conditions as starting, rapid acceleration or heavy load, sudden deceleration, idling, etc.

An automotive engine has various operating modes as the operating conditions change. Preprogrammed into the processor, control logic determines the operating mode from the engine conditions that exist. From these engine conditions, the system determines which operating modes are to be performed.

There are seven different engine operating modes which affect fuel control: engine crank, engine warmup, open loop, closed loop control, hard acceleration, deceleration and idle. The program for mode control logic determines the engine operating mode by reading various sensors.

When the ignition switch is initially switched on, the mode control logic automatically selects an engine-start control scheme which provides the low air/fuel ratio required for starting the engine. Once the engine rpm rises above the cranking value, the controller identifies the engine-started mode and passes control to the program for the engine warm-up mode. This operating mode keeps the air/fuel ratio low to prevent engine stall during cool weather until engine coolant temperature rises above a preset value.

When the coolant temperature rises, the mode control logic directs the system to operate in the open loop control mode until a certain time has elapsed and the exhaust gas sensor warms up enough to provide accurate readings. This condition is detected by monitoring the exhaust gas sensor's output for voltage readings above a certain minimum air/fuel mixture voltage set point. When the sensor has indicated a rich mixture a certain number of times (depending on calibration) and after the engine has been in open loop for a specific time, the control mode logic selects the closed loop mode for the system. The engine remains in the closed loop mode until either the exhaust gas sensor cools and fails to switch (from rich to lean) for a certain length of time, or a hard acceleration or deceleration occurs. If the sensor cools, the control mode logic selects the open loop mode again.

During hard acceleration of heavy engine loads, the control mode logic chooses a scheme which provides a rich air/fuel mixture for the duration of the acceleration or heavy load. This scheme provides maximum power, but poor emissions control and poor fuel economy. After the need for enrichment has passed, control is returned to either open or closed loop depending on the control mode logic selection conditions that exist at that time.

During periods of deceleration, the air/fuel ratio is increased to reduce emissions of HC and CO due to unburned fuel. When idle conditions are present, control mode logic passes system control to the idle speed control mode. In this mode, the engine speed is controlled to reduce engine roughness and stalling which might occur because the idle load has changed due to air conditioner compressor operation, alternator operation, or gearshift positioning from PARK or NEUTRAL to DRIVE.

### *Engine Crank*

While the engine is being cranked, the fuel control system must provide an intake air/fuel ratio anywhere from 2:1 to 12:1, depending on engine temperature. Low temperatures affect the carburetor's ability to atomize or mix the incoming air and fuel. At low temperature, the fuel tends to form into large droplets. The larger fuel droplets tend to increase the apparent air/fuel ratio because the amount of usable fuel in the air is reduced, therefore, the system must provide a decreased air/fuel ratio to provide the engine with a more combustible air/fuel mixture. The engine temperature is read by the processor through an analog to digital converter from a temperature sensor in the engine water coolant passage. The processor's calibration determines what the proper air/fuel ratio must be at that temperature. The air/fuel is determined and controlled as in the open loop mode.

### *Engine Warm-up*

While the engine is warming up, an enriched air/fuel ratio is still needed to keep it running smoothly, but the required air/fuel ratio changes as the temperature increases. Therefore, the fuel control system will stay in the open loop mode, but the air/fuel ratio commands continue to be altered due to the temperature changes. The emphasis in this control mode is on rapid and smooth engine warm-up. Fuel economy and emission control are still a secondary concern. The controller determines the warm-up time period based on the coolant temperature when the warm-up mode was selected. Naturally, an initially cold engine requires a longer warm-up time than a warm engine. The time allowed by the controller timer is chosen according to the calibration of the processor.

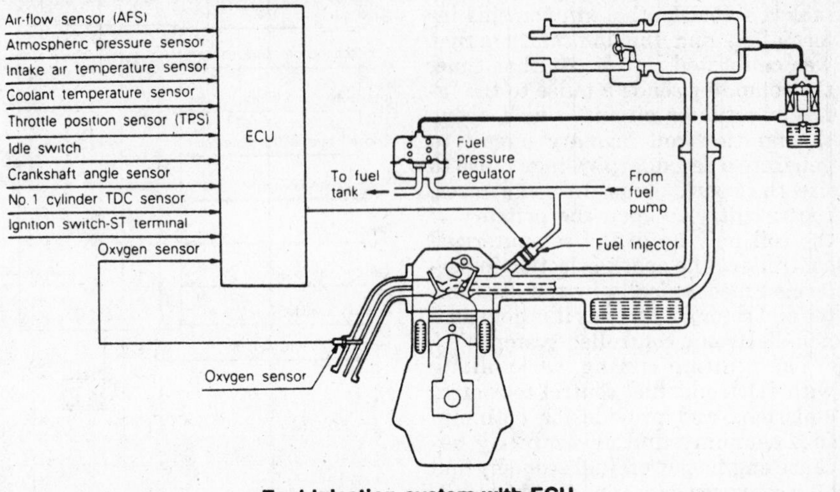


**Fuel injection system with ECU**

### OPEN LOOP CONTROL

Open loop fuel control is used when the engine has not reached a preset operating condition. This condition is sensed by various sensors located in and around the engine, and include engine coolant temperature, air charge temperature, engine time on, etc. After all these preset conditions are met, the system will go into closed loop. During certain operating conditions, such as a wide open throttle condition the system will go back into open loop.

### CLOSED LOOP CONTROL

Closed loop fuel control is selected when the engine is warm and the exhaust gas oxygen sensor exceeds its minimum operating temperature. The intake air/fuel ratio is controlled in a closed loop by measuring the exhaust gas at the exhaust manifold and altering the input fuel flow rate or the air entering the main metering systems (depending on the type of fuel system used).

### ACCELERATION ENRICHMENT (OPEN LOOP)

During periods of heavy engine load, such as wide open acceleration, fuel control is adjusted to provide an enriched ratio to maximize engine power while neglecting fuel economy and emission.

The computer detects this condition by reading the throttle position sensor voltage or the MAP sensor. Low intake manifold vacuum or throttle position corresponds to heavy engine loads. The fuel control system controller responds by increasing the amount of fuel to enter the intake manifold or to decrease the amount of air in the main metering system. This

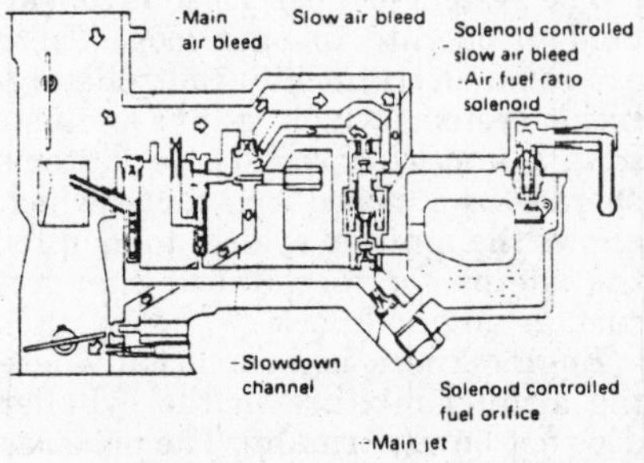


**Feedback carburetor air flow**

enrichment allows the engine to operate with a power greater than that allowed when emissions and fuel economy are controlled within specifications.

### DECELERATION AND IDLE SPEED CONTROL (OPEN LOOP)

During periods of light engine load and high rpm, such as during closed throttle deceleration, coasting or engine idle, the engine requires a very lean air/fuel ratio to reduce excess emissions of HC and CO. Deceleration is indicated by a sudden increase in manifold vacuum and throttle position, indicating a closed throttle. When these conditions are detected by the processor, it computes a change in the amount of fuel required or amount of air entering the main or idle speed passages (depending on type of fuel system used). On certain engine applications with electronic fuel injection, the fuel may even be turned completely off during closed throttle deceleration.

Idle speed control is used to prevent engine stall during idle. The goal is to allow the engine to idle at as low an rpm as possible, yet keeping the engine from running rough and stalling when power takeoff accessories such as air conditioning compressor is turned on.

# Turbocharging 27

## DESCRIPTION

A turbocharger is an exhaust-driven turbine which drives a centrifugal compressor wheel. The compressor is usually located between the air cleaner and the engine's intake manifold, while the turbine is located between the exhaust manifold and the muffler. Primarily, the turbocharger compresses the air entering the engine, forcing more air into the cylinders. This allows the engine to efficiently burn more fuel, thereby producing more horsepower.

All of the exhaust gases pass through the turbine housing. The expansion of these gases, acting on the turbine wheel, causes it to turn. After passing through the turbine the exhaust gases are routed to the atmosphere through the exhaust system. On some non-automotive applications, the turbocharger provides sufficient muffling of the exhaust noises to eliminate the need for a muffler.

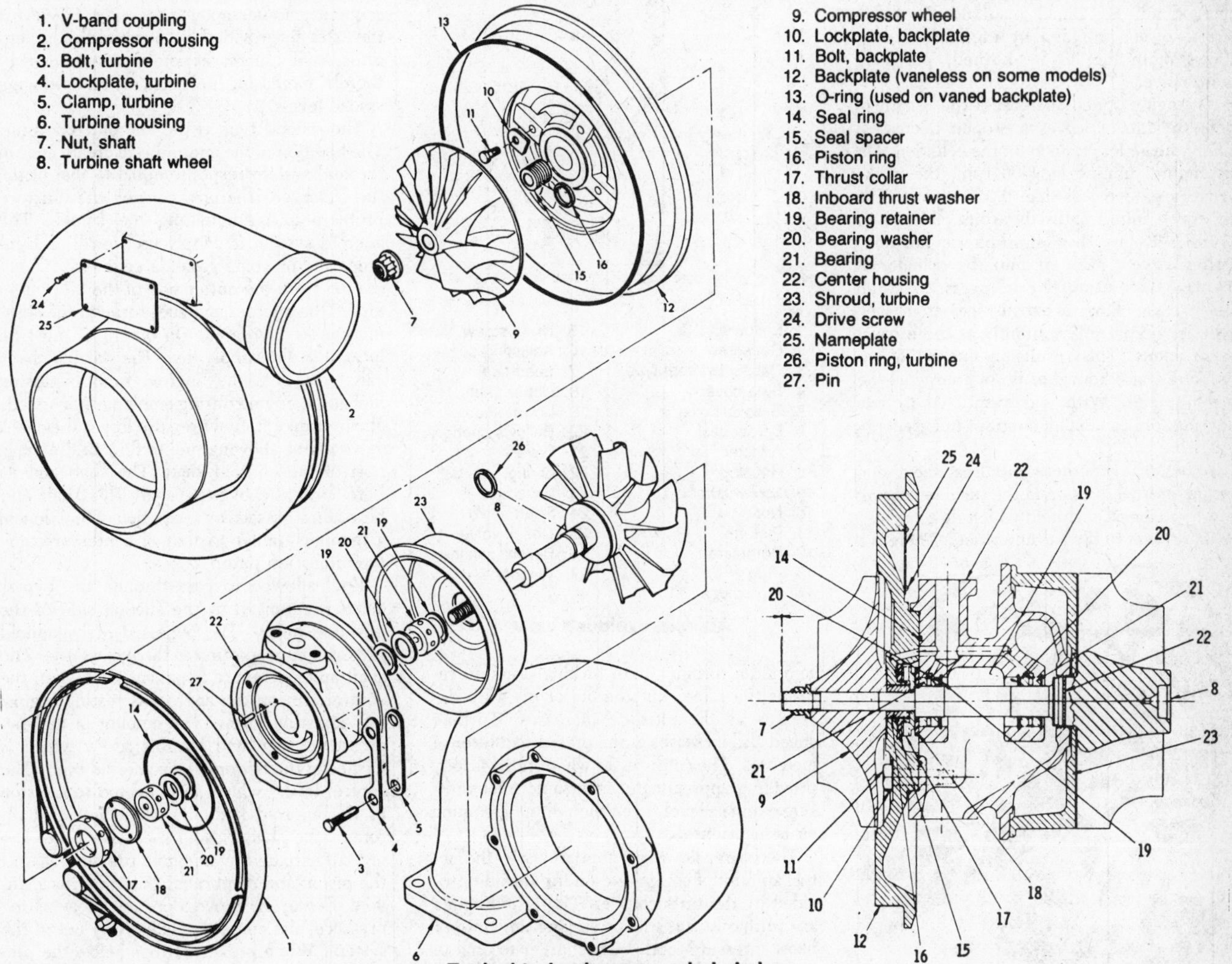

1. V-band coupling
2. Compressor housing
3. Bolt, turbine
4. Lockplate, turbine
5. Clamp, turbine
6. Turbine housing
7. Nut, shaft
8. Turbine shaft wheel
9. Compressor wheel
10. Lockplate, backplate
11. Bolt, backplate
12. Backplate (vaneless on some models)
13. O-ring (used on vaned backplate)
14. Seal ring
15. Seal spacer
16. Piston ring
17. Thrust collar
18. Inboard thrust washer
19. Bearing retainer
20. Bearing washer
21. Bearing
22. Center housing
23. Shroud, turbine
24. Drive screw
25. Nameplate
26. Piston ring, turbine
27. Pin

Typical turbocharger exploded view

# 27 TURBOCHARGING

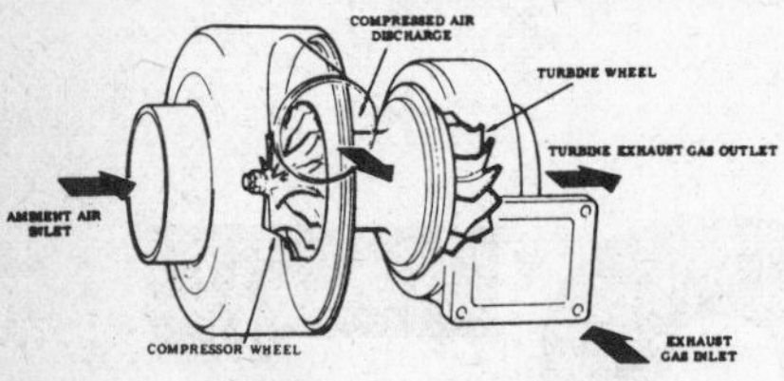


**Typical turbocharger air flow schematic**

The turbine also functions as a spark arrester. For example, the US Department of Agriculture recognizes the turbocharger as an adequate spark arrester for forestry operations.

## OPERATION

The compressor and turbine are each enclosed in their own housings and are directly connected by a shaft. The housings are constructed of light alloy and are designed for maximum heat dissipation. The only power loss from the turbine to the compressor is the slight friction of the shaft journal bearings. Air is drawn in through the filtered intake system, compressed by the compressor wheel and discharged into the intake manifold. The extra charge of air provided by the turbocharger allows more fuel to be burned, providing more power.

As engine speed increases, the length of time the intake valves are open decreases, giving the air less time to fill the cylinders. On an engine running at 2500 rpm, the intake valves are open less than 0.017 second. The air drawn into a naturally aspirated engine's cylinder is less than atmospheric pressure. Turbochargers pack air into the cylinder at greater than atmospheric pressure at all speeds. The flow of exhaust gas from each cylinder occurs intermittantly as the exhaust valve opens. This results in fluctuating gas pressures, also known as pulse energy, at the turbine inlet. With a conventional turbine housing, only a small amount of pulse energy is used.

To better utilize these impulses, one design has an internal division in the turbine housing and the exhaust manifold which directs these exhaust gases to the turbine wheel. There is a separate passage for each half of the engine cylinder exhaust.

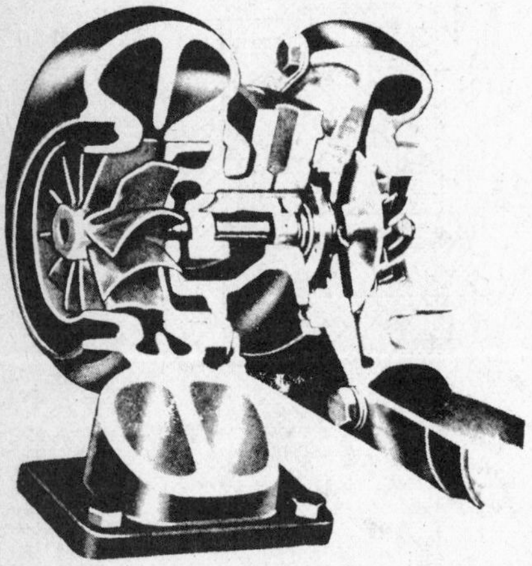

**Altitude compensator**

On some four and six cylinder engines built to accommodate turbochargers, there is a separate passage for the front two or three cylinders and another for the rear half.

By using a fully divided exhaust system combined with a dual scroll turbine housing, the result is a highly effective nozzle velocity. This produces higher turbine speeds and manifold pressures than can be obtained with an undivided system.

At high altitudes, a naturally aspirated engine drops 3% in horsepower per 1000 feet elevation due to a 3% decrease in air density per 1000 feet.

With a turbocharged engine, an increase in altitude also increases the pressure drop across the turbine. Inlet turbine pressure remains the same, but the outlet pressure decreases as the altitude increases. Turbine speed also increases as the pressure difference increases. The compressor wheel turns faster, providing approximately the same inlet pressure as at sea level, even though the incoming air is less dense.

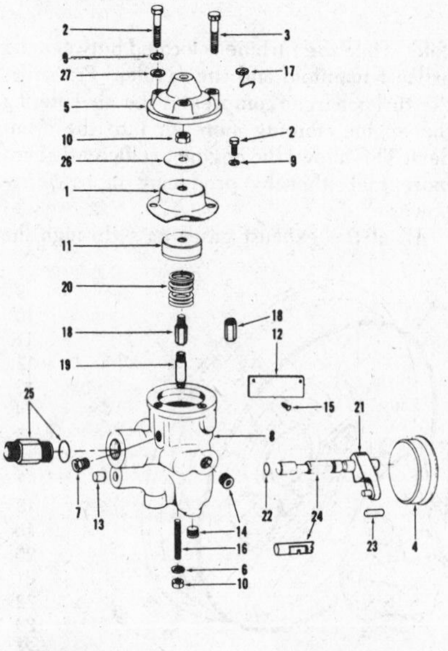

1. Bellows
2. Capscrew
3. Capscrew, seal type
4. Side cover
5. Bellows cover
6. Screw seal
7. Air filter
8. Housing
9. Lockwasher
10. Nut
11. Piston
12. Dataplate
13. Plug
14. Pipe plugs
15. Drive screw
16. Adjusting screw
17. Lead seal
18. Upper shaft
19. Lower shaft
20. Bellows spring
21. Lever
22. O-ring
23. Lever, pin
24. Shaft valve
25. Check valve
26. Bellows washer
27. Washer

**Aneroid exploded view**

There are, however, limitations to the actual amount of compensation for altitude provided by the turbocharger. These limitations are primarily a result of varying amounts of boost pressure and turbocharger-to-engine match. To make up for the difference in altitude compensation, an altitude compensator is added to the system. During rapid acceleration or rapid engine load changes, the turbocharger speed, reflected in manifold pressure, inherently lags behind the power or fuel demand exercised by the opening of the throttle. This lag does not exist in the fuel system, so an overly rich mixture accompanied by heavy smoke occurs until the turbocharger catches up.

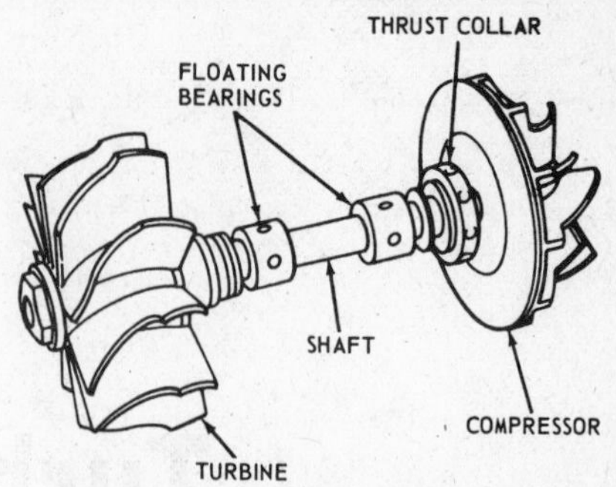


**Basic parts of the turbocharger**

On diesel engines, two types of altitude compensators are used. One is a compressed air type which is very similar in appearance to the turbocharger. This type supplies compressed air to the intake manifold at a pressure about equal to sea level pressure. There is no increase of fuel for combustion and consequently no horsepower increase. However, the extra air provided by the altitude compensator usually increases combustion efficiency, thereby increasing fuel economy and reducing smoke levels.

The second type is the aneroid type unit. The function of the aneroid is to create a lag in the fuel system response equal to that of the turbocharger, thereby control the mixture problem and eliminating the smoke. The aneroid system is widely used on diesel engines and on some gasoline engines.

Fuel from the outlet side of the fuel pump enters the aneroid and goes through the starting check valve area. On others, it must be located in the supply line. The starting check valve prevents the aneroid from bypassing fuel at the engine during cranking. For speeds above cranking, fuel pressure forces the check valve open, allowing fuel to flow to the valve port of the aneroid shaft. The shaft and its bore form the bypass valve. This shaft and bore allow passage or restriction of fuel flow in a manner similar to that of a pressure/time type injection pump.

Fuel allowed to pass through the bypass valve is returned to the suction side of the injection pump. The bypassed fuel manifold pressure in proportion to the bypass rate. The shaft and sleeve are bypassing fuel when the control arm on the aneroid is resting against the adjusting screw. The amount of fuel bypassed is regulated by this screw which is located at the bottom of the aneroid body. The control lever, which is connected to a piston in the aneroid body by an actuating shaft, rotates the shaft closing the valve port. The lever is actuated by manifold pressure against the piston and diaphragm. Anytime the manifold pressure is above a present air actuating pressure, the aneroid is effectively out of the system. When pressure drops below the preset figure, the aneroid comes into the system.

In modern automotive gasoline engine applications with their stricter emission control standards, turbocharger lag is compensated for by means of modified spark control and/or an enrichment vacuum regulator system. The spark control system changes the ignition timing on demand and the vacuum regulator system regulates vacuum flow at the carburetor through a remote power enrichment port.

Some engines, particularly passenger car applications, in which boost pressure must be held at low levels, utilize a wastegate unit. Since turbocharger operation is self-perpetuating, unchecked operation will increase boost pressure beyond the operating capabilities of these engines. Some method of limiting this boost increases must be used. The principle means is by the inclusion of a wastegate in the system. The wastegate, usually located in the outlet elbow assembly, is activated when boost pressure reaches a predetermined level (usually 3-7 psi depending on application). The wastegate opens and bypasses exhaust flow around the turbine.

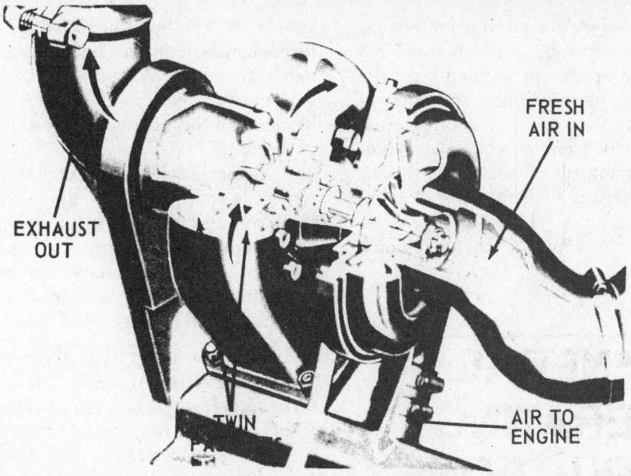

Twin passage turbine

## LUBRICATION

Since turbine speeds routinely reach 140,000 rpm, adequate lubrication is vitally important. Turbochargers are lubricated by engine oil. Depending on the application, the lubrication may be either pressure-fed or gravity-fed. In areas of very heavy load or when shut-down after peak operation is routine, pressure feeding, sometimes with a separate oil pump, is used. In cases where a separate oil pump is used, the pump continues operating during spin-down. Since all parts of the rotating assemblies are protected by a film of oil, no metal-to-metal contact occurs. Consequently, no appreciable wear should occur. If a constant supply of clean engine oil is maintained, bearing life should be indefinite. If the unit has floating sleeve type bearings, they provide oil clearance between the bearing and housing as well as between the bearing and shaft. When the turbocharger is operating, this allows the bearing to turn as the shaft turns. All clearances in the turbocharger are closely controlled and carefully machined. Any dirt in the oil will adversely affect service life of the working parts. Oil and filter changes should occur regularly. Some manufacturers recommend more frequent oil changes for turbocharged engines. In any case, on turbocharged engines, the oil filter(s) should ALWAYS be changed with the engine oil. ALWAYS use oil of the recommended viscosity for that particular engine application. Check the owner's manual for your engine or vehicle for recommended intervals and proper viscosity.

## TWO-CYCLE APPLICATIONS

Turbochargers may be used in addition to the regular scavenging process. In these cases, the air is drawn into the blower or scavenging pump and then transferred to the turbocharger where it is compressed and forced into the engine.

At light loads, there is little energy available to drive the turbocharger. The mechanically driven blower alone supplies scavenging air to cylinders. At increased loads, the turbocharger speeds up and takes in a sufficient amount of additional air to allow the inlet pressure to drop to atmospheric levels, causing the blower check valve to open. At this engine speed, the blower becomes unloaded, saving engine power, and the turbocharger enters the load range where it alone can provide scavenging and turbocharging. Under ideal conditions, the engine starting air contains enough energy to start the turbocharger and also supply enough air for combustion. In some applications, however, turbochargers can be equipped with additional methods for supplying necessary scavenging air while the engine is being started. This can be accomplished either mechanically by coupling the turbocharger to the crankshaft in such a manner that it is mechanically driven during starting and automatically disconnects when exhaust pressure is high enough or by jet air starting, where air is blown through jets into the turbocharger turbine or compressor. The air passing through the compressor also aids in scavenging during starting.

## INTERCOOLERS

When the air passing through the compressor is compressed it becomes heated and expands. Expanding air is less dense, therefore less air is forced into the engine. This helps defeat the turbocharging process. To overcome this condition, some engine applications use a heat exchanger, also known as an inter-

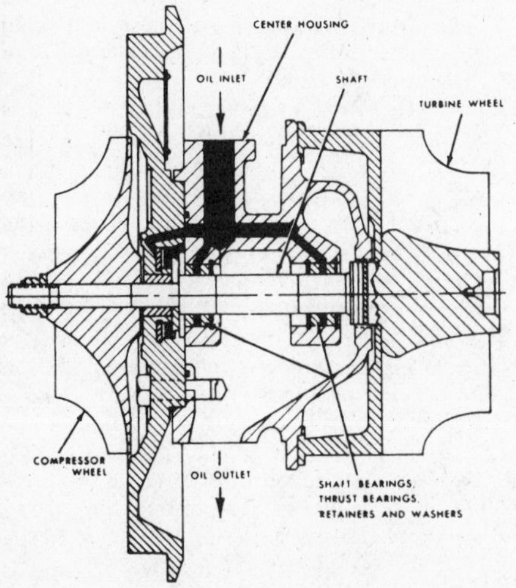

Turbocharger oil flow

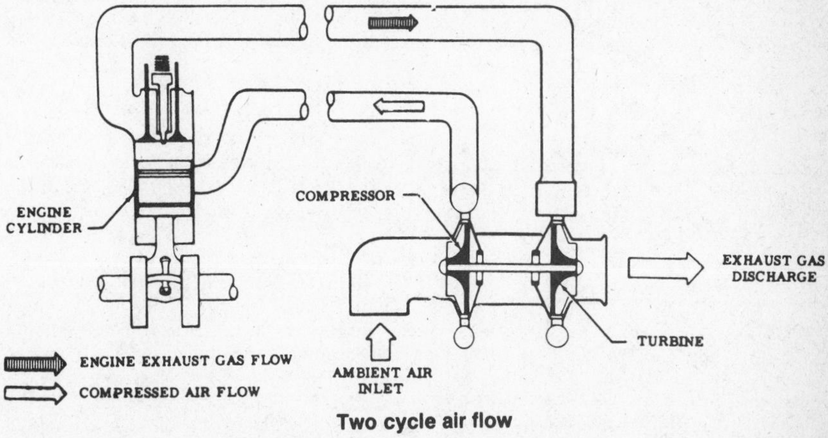

Two cycle air flow

cooler or after cooler. The intercooler reduces intake air temperature by as much as 90° F.

Located between the turbocharger and the intake manifold, the intercooler is a series of connected tubes, finned to provide dissipation, through which engine coolant is circulated. The carrying off of heat from the air makes the air denser, allowing more air to be forced into the engine. This provides more power, greater economy and quieter combustion.

## GENERAL OPERATING INSTRUCTIONS FOR TURBOCHARGED ENGINES

1. After starting the engine, make sure there is sufficient oil pressure before accelerating or applying load.
2. When starting in cold weather, allow the engine to run a sufficient length of time (up to five minutes for diesel engines in extreme cold) before applying load or accelerating. This will insure adequate lubrication.
3. Should the engine stall at normal operating temperature, restart it immediately. This will prevent a rapid rise in the turbocharger known as "temperature soaking". Also, the turbocharger, running hot during operation, may experience coking due to hot oil build-up in the center section. This coking will cause a blockage of the oil passages leading to failure of the unit.
4. Before stopping the engine, allow it to run for a short length of time (up to two or three minutes for some diesels) to allow internal engine temperatures to normalize or equalize. Failure to allow temperature normalization can lead to heat fatique and/or blockage of oil passages due to coking.

**CAUTION**

***When transporting an engine equipped with a turbocharger, always cover the exhaust outlet. This will prevent entrance of foreign material and/or the rotation of the turbine. Turbine rotation on a stopped engine could lead to bearing failure since no lubricating oil will be provided.***

## PREVENTIVE MAINTENANCE

1. Inspect all mountings and connections regularly to make sure they are secure and no leakage is present.
2. Make certain that there is no restriction in air flow at the crankcase ventilation system.
3. Run the engine at various, normal operating speeds and listen for unusual noises at the turbocharger.

Turbochargers normally emit a shrill whistle or whine. Bearings about to fail also emit a shrill whine, somewhat different from normal turbocharger noise. Try to distinguish between the two.

**NOTE: After engine shut-off, the turbocharger will whine during rundown. Don't confuse this with bearing failure noise. Grating or scraping noises could indicate improper turbine or compressor wheel-to-housing clearances. If any such noises are heard, the unit should be removed for inspection.**

4. Check the unit for unusual vibrations during operation.
5. Check for unusual smoking under load conditions. Excessive smoke means an incorrect air/fuel ratio.
6. Inspect and replace the air filter according to your owner's manual recommendations.

## TROUBLE-SHOOTING

The turbocharger is a relatively simple unit. Most problems occur in other parts of the engine such as the lubrication system or the fuel system. With proper routine maintenance, the unit should give troublefree operation.

# Engine Rebuilding 28

This section describes, in detail, the procedures involved in rebuilding a typical engine. The procedures are basically identical to those used in rebuilding engines of nearly all design and configurations.

The section is divided into two parts. The first, Cylinder Head Reconditioning, assumes that the cylinder head is removed from the engine, all manifolds are removed, and the cylinder head is on a workbench. The camshaft should be removed from overhead cam cylinder heads. The second section, Cylinder Block Reconditioning, covers the block, pistons, connecting rods and crankshaft. It is assumed that the engine is mounted on a work stand, and the cylinder head and all accessories are removed.

Procedures are identified as follows:

*Unmarked*—Basic procedures that must be performed in order to successfully complete the rebuilding process.

*Starred* (*)—Procedures that should be performed to ensure maximum performance and engine life.

*Double starred* (**)—Procedures that may be performed to increase engine performance and reliability.

In many cases, a choice of methods is also provided. Methods are identified in the same manner as procedures. The choice of method for a procedure is at the discretion of the user.

The tools required for the basic rebuilding procedure should, with minor exceptions, be those included in a mechanic's tool kit. An accurate torque wrench, and a dial indicator (reading in thousandths) mounted on a universal base should be available. Special tools, where required, all are readily available from the major tool suppliers. The services of a competent automotive machine shop must also be readily available.

When assembling the engine, any parts that will be in frictional contact must be prelubricated, to provide protection on initial start-up. Any product specifically formulated for this purpose may be used. NOTE: *Do not use engine oil.* Where semi-permanent (locked but removable) installation of bolts or nuts is desired, threads should be cleaned and coated with Loctite® or a similar product (non-hardening).

Aluminum has become increasingly popular for use in engines, due to its low weight and excellent heat transfer characteristics. The following precautions must be observed when handling aluminum engine parts:

—Never hot-tank aluminum parts.

—Remove all aluminum parts (identification tags, etc.) from engine parts before hot-tanking (otherwise they will be removed during the process).

—Always coat threads lightly with engine oil or anti-seize compounds before installation, to prevent seizure.

—Never over-torque bolts or spark plugs in aluminum threads. Should stripping occur, threads can be restored using any of a number of thread repair kits available (see next section).

Magnaflux and Zyglo are inspection techniques used to locate material flaws, such as stress cracks. Magnafluxing coats the part with fine magnetic particles, and subjects the part to a magnetic field. Cracks cause breaks in the magnetic field, which are outlined by the particles. Since Magnaflux is a magnetic process, it is applicable only to ferrous materials. The Zyglo process coats the material with a fluorescent dye penetrant, and then subjects it to blacklight inspection, under which cracks glow brightly. Parts made of any material may be tested using Zyglo. While Magnaflux and Zyglo are excellent for general inspection, and locating hidden defects, specific checks of suspected cracks may be made at lower cost and more readily using spot check dye. The dye is sprayed onto the suspected area, wiped off, and the area is then sprayed with a developer. Cracks then will show up brightly. Spot check dyes will only indicate surface cracks; therefore, structural cracks below the surface may escape detection. When questionable, the part should be tested using Magnaflux or Zyglo.

## REPAIRING DAMAGED THREADS

Several methods of repairing damaged threads are available. Heli-Coil® (shown here), Keenserts® and Microdot® are among the most widely used. All involve basically the same principle—drilling out stripped threads, tapping the hole and installing a prewound insert— making welding, plugging and oversize fasteners unnecessary.

Two types of thread repair inserts are usually supplied—a standard type for most Inch Coarse, Inch Fine, Metric Coarse and Metric Fine thread sizes and a spark plug type to fit most spark plug port sizes. Consult the individual manufacturer's catalog to determine exact applications. Typical thread repair kits will contain a selection of prewound threaded inserts, a tap (corresponding to the outside diameter threads of the insert) and an installation tool. Most manufacturers also supply blister-packed thread repair inserts separately and a master kit with a variety of taps and inserts plus installation tools.

Before effecting a repair to a threaded hole, remove any snapped, broken or damaged bolts or studs. Penetrating oil can be used to free frozen threads; the offending item can be removed with locking pliers or with a screw or stud extractor. After the hole is clear, the thread can be repaired as follows.

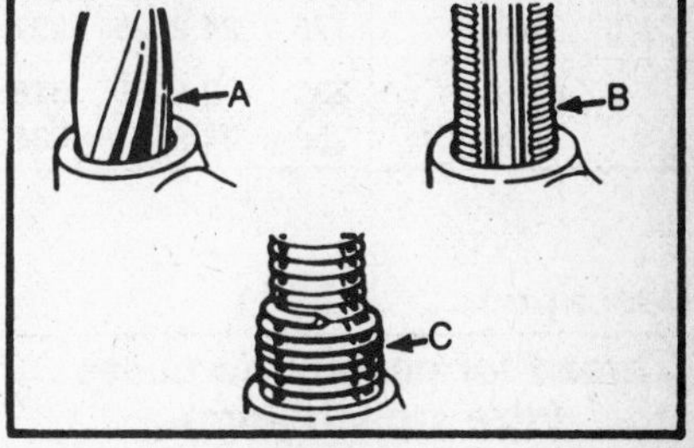


A. Drill out the damaged threads with the specified drill. Drill completely through the hole or to the bottom of a blind hole.

B. With the tap supplied tap the hole to receive the threaded insert. Keep the tap well oiled and back it out frequently to avoid clogging the threads.

C. Screw the threaded insert onto the installation tool until the tang engages the slot. Screw the insert into the tapped hole until it is ¼–½ turn below the top surface. After installation, break the tang off with a hammer and punch.

## STANDARD TORQUE SPECIFICATIONS AND CAPSCREW MARKINGS

Newton-Meter has been designated as the world standard for measuring torque and will gradually replace the foot-pound and kilogram-meter torque measuring standard. Torquing tools are still being manufactured with foot-pounds and kilogram-meter scales, along with the new Newton-Meter standard. To assist the repairman, foot-pounds, kilogram-meter and Newton-Meter are listed in the following charts, and should be followed as applicable.

### U.S. BOLTS

| SAE Grade Number | 1 or 2 | | | 5 | | | 6 or 7 | | | 8 | | |
|---|---|---|---|---|---|---|---|---|---|---|---|---|
| **Capscrew Head Markings** Manufacturer's marks may vary. Three-line markings on heads below indicate SAE Grade 5.  | 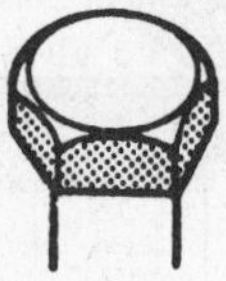 | | |  | | |  | | |  | | |
| **Usage** | Used Frequently | | | Used Frequently | | | Used at Times | | | Used at Times | | |
| **Quality of Material** | Indeterminate | | | Minimum Commercial | | | Medium Commercial | | | Best Commercial | | |
| **Capacity Body Size** | **Torque** | | | **Torque** | | | **Torque** | | | **Torque** | | |
| (inches)-(thread) | Ft-Lb | kgm | Nm | Ft-Lb | kgm | Nm | Ft-Lb | kgm | Nm | Ft-Lb | kgm | Nm |
| 1/4-20 | 5 | 0.6915 | 6.7791 | 8 | 1.1064 | 10.8465 | 10 | 1.3630 | 13.5582 | 12 | 1.6596 | 16.2698 |
| -28 | 6 | 0.8298 | 8.1349 | 10 | 1.3830 | 13.5582 | | | | 14 | 1.9362 | 18.9815 |
| 5/16-18 | 11 | 1.5213 | 14.9140 | 17 | 2.3511 | 23.0489 | 19 | 2.6277 | 25.7605 | 24 | 3.3192 | 32.5396 |
| -24 | 13 | 1.7979 | 17.6256 | 19 | 2.6277 | 25.7605 | | | | 27 | 3.7341 | 36.6071 |
| 3/8-16 | 18 | 2.4894 | 24.4047 | 31 | 4.2873 | 42.0304 | 34 | 4.7022 | 46.0978 | 44 | 6.0852 | 59.6560 |
| -24 | 20 | 2.7660 | 27.1164 | 35 | 4.8405 | 47.4536 | | | | 49 | 6.7767 | 66.4351 |
| 7/16-14 | 28 | 3.8132 | 37.9629 | 49 | 6.7767 | 66.4351 | 55 | 7.6065 | 74.5700 | 70 | 9.6810 | 94.9073 |
| -20 | 30 | 4.1490 | 40.6745 | 55 | 7.6065 | 74.5700 | | | | 78 | 10.7874 | 105.7538 |
| 1/2-13 | 39 | 5.3937 | 52.8769 | 75 | 10.3725 | 101.6863 | 85 | 11.7555 | 115.2445 | 105 | 14.5215 | 142.3609 |
| -20 | 41 | 5.6703 | 55.5885 | 85 | 11.7555 | 115.2445 | | | | 120 | 16.5860 | 162.6960 |
| 9/16-12 | 51 | 7.0533 | 69.1467 | 110 | 15.2130 | 149.1380 | 120 | 16.5960 | 162.6960 | 155 | 21.4365 | 210.1490 |
| -18 | 55 | 7.6065 | 74.5700 | 120 | 16.5960 | 162.6960 | | | | 170 | 23.5110 | 230.4860 |
| 5/8-11 | 83 | 11.4789 | 112.5329 | 150 | 20.7450 | 203.3700 | 167 | 23.0961 | 226.4186 | 210 | 29.0430 | 284.7180 |
| -18 | 95 | 13.1385 | 128.8027 | 170 | 23.5110 | 230.4860 | | | | 240 | 33.1920 | 325.3920 |
| 3/4-10 | 105 | 14.5215 | 142.3609 | 270 | 37.3410 | 366.0660 | 280 | 38.7240 | 379.6240 | 375 | 51.8625 | 508.4250 |
| -16 | 115 | 15.9045 | 155.9170 | 295 | 40.7985 | 399.9610 | | | | 420 | 58.0860 | 568.4360 |
| 7/8-9 | 160 | 22.1280 | 216.9280 | 395 | 54.6285 | 535.5410 | 440 | 60.8520 | 596.5520 | 605 | 83.6715 | 820.2590 |
| -14 | 175 | 24.2025 | 237.2650 | 435 | 60.1605 | 589.7730 | | | | 675 | 93.3525 | 915.1650 |
| 1-8 | 236 | 32.5005 | 318.6130 | 590 | 81.5970 | 799.9220 | 660 | 91.2780 | 894.8280 | 910 | 125.8530 | 1233.7780 |
| -14 | 250 | 34.5750 | 338.9500 | 660 | 91.2780 | 849.8280 | | | | 990 | 136.9170 | 1342.2420 |

### METRIC BOLTS

| Description | Torque ft-lbs. (Nm) | | | |
|---|---|---|---|---|
| **Thread for general purposes (size x pitch (mm))** | **Head Mark 4** | | **Head Mark 7** | |
| 6 x 1.0 | 2.2 to 2.9 | (3.0 to 3.9) | 3.6 to 5.8 | (4.9 to 7.8) |
| 8 x 1.25 | 5.8 to 8.7 | (7.9 to 12) | 9.4 to 14 | (13 to 19) |
| 10 x 1.25 | 12 to 17 | (16 to 23) | 20 to 29 | (27 to 39) |
| 12 x 1.25 | 21 to 32 | (29 to 43) | 35 to 53 | (47 to 72) |
| 14 x 1.5 | 35 to 52 | (48 to 70) | 57 to 85 | (77 to 110) |
| 16 x 1.5 | 51 to 77 | (67 to 100) | 90 to 120 | (130 to 160) |
| 18 x 1.5 | 74 to 110 | (100 to 150) | 130 to 170 | (180 to 230) |
| 20 x 1.5 | 110 to 140 | (150 to 190) | 190 to 240 | (160 to 320) |
| 22 x 1.5 | 150 to 190 | (200 to 260) | 250 to 320 | (340 to 430) |
| 24 x 1.5 | 190 to 240 | (260 to 320) | 310 to 410 | (420 to 550) |

CAUTION: Bolts threaded into aluminum require much less torque

**NOTE: This engine rebuilding section is a guide to accepted rebuilding procedures. Typical examples of standard rebuilding procedures are illustrated.**

## CYLINDER HEAD RECONDITIONING

| Procedure | Method |
|---|---|
| Identify the valves: | Invert the cylinder head, and number the valve faces front to rear, using a permanent felt-tip marker. |
| Remove the rocker arms (OHV engines only): | Remove the rocker arms with shaft(s) or balls and nuts. Wire the sets of rockers, balls and nuts together, and identify according to the corresponding valve. |
| Remove the camshaft (OHC engines only): | See the engine service procedures earlier in this book for details concerning specific engines. |
| Remove the valves and springs: | Using an appropriate valve spring compressor (depending on the configuration of the cylinder head), compress the valve springs. Lift out the keepers with needlenose pliers, release the compressor, and remove the valve, spring, and spring retainer. |
| Remove glow plugs and fuel injectors (Diesel engines only): | Label and remove all fuel injectors and glow plugs from the head. Glow plugs unscrew. See the appropriate car section for injector removal. Inspect glow plugs for bulges, cracks or signs of melting. Clean injector tips with a steel brush, then inspect for evidence of melting. |
| **Remove pre-combustion chamber inserts (Diesel engines only): 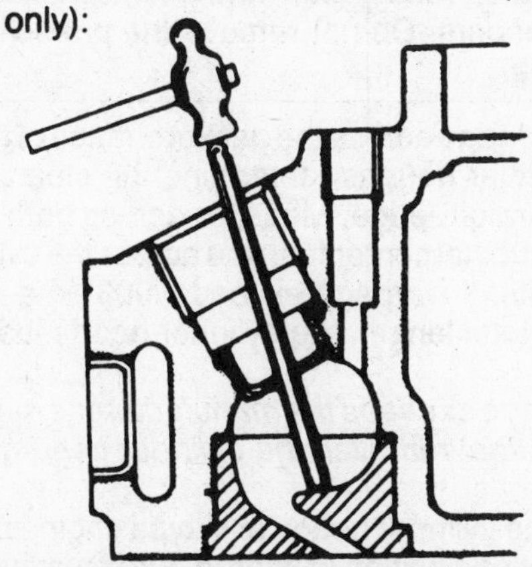 **Removing pre-combustion chamber with a drift (© G.M. Corp.)** | **Remove the pre-combustion chambers using a hammer and a thin, blunt brass drift, inserted through the injector hole (or glow plug hole, whichever is more convenient). If chamber is to be reused, carefully remove all carbon from it. NOTE: *Remove chamber only if being replaced, if a glow plug tip has broken off and must be removed, or if chamber is obviously damaged or loose.* |
| Check the valve stem-to-guide clearance: 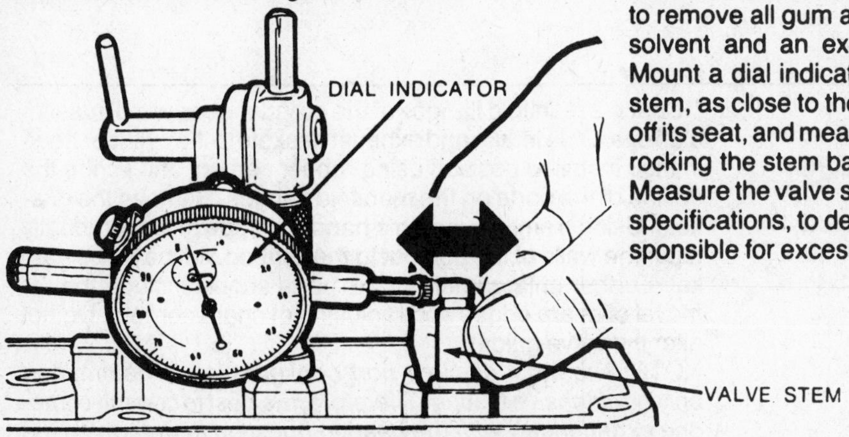  **Checking the valve stem-to-guide clearance** | Clean the valve stem with lacquer thinner or a similar solvent to remove all gum and varnish. Clean the valve guides using solvent and an expanding wire-type valve guide cleaner. Mount a dial indicator so that the stem is at 90° to the valve stem, as close to the valve guide as possible. Move the valve off its seat, and measure the valve guide-to-stem clearance by rocking the stem back and forth to actuate the dial indicator. Measure the valve stems using a micrometer, and compare to specifications, to determine whether stem or guide wear is responsible for excessive clearance. |

## CYLINDER HEAD RECONDITIONING

| Procedure | Method |
|---|---|
| De-carbon the cylinder head and valves:<br>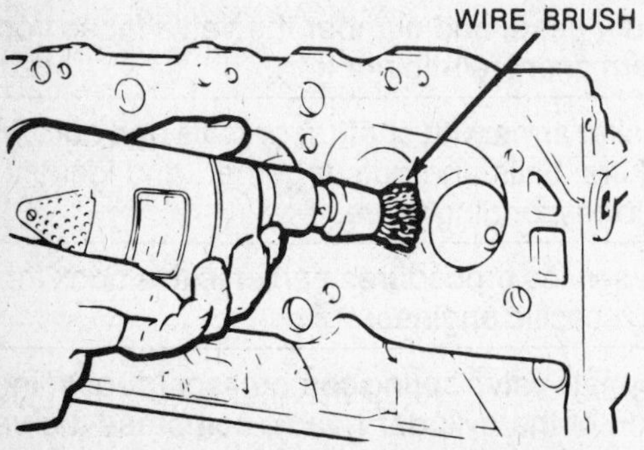<br><br>**Removing carbon from the cylinder head** | Chip carbon away from the valve heads, combustion chambers, and ports, using a chisel made of hardwood. Remove the remaining deposits with a stiff wire brush.<br>NOTE: *Ensure that the deposits are actually removed, rather than burnished.* |
| Hot-tank the cylinder head (cast iron heads only):<br>CAUTION: *Do not hot-tank aluminum parts.* | Have the cylinder head hot-tanked to remove grease, corrosion, and scale from the water passages.<br>NOTE: *In the case of overhead cam cylinder heads, consult the operator to determine whether the camshaft bearings will be damaged by the caustic solution.* |
| Degrease the remaining cylinder head parts: | Using solvent (i.e., Gunk), clean the rockers, rocker shaft(s) (where applicable), rocker balls and nuts, springs, spring retainers, and keepers. Do not remove the protective coating from the springs. |
| Check the cylinder head for warpage:<br>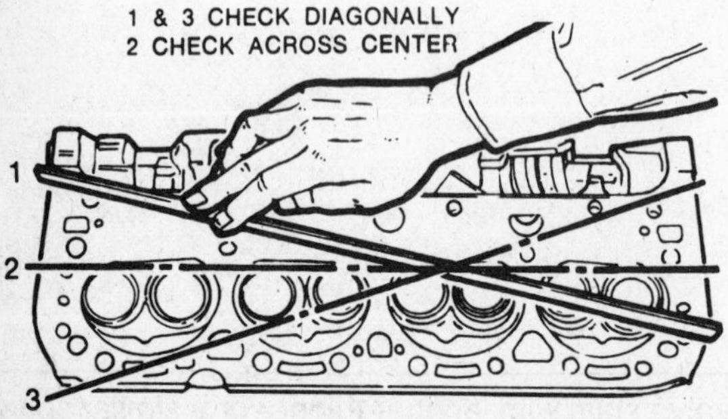<br><br>**Checking cylinder head for warpage** | Place a straight-edge across the gasket surface of the cylinder head. Using feeler gauges, determine the clearance at the center of the straight-edge. Measure across both diagonals, along the longitudinal centerline, and across the cylinder head at several points. If warpage exceeds .003′ in a 6′ span, or .006′ over the total length, the cylinder head must be resurfaced.<br>NOTE: *If warpage exceeds the manufacturer's maximum tolerance for material removal, the cylinder head must be replaced.*<br>When milling the cylinder heads of V-type engines, the intake manifold mounting position is altered, and must be corrected by milling the manifold flange a proportionate amount. |
| **Porting and gasket matching: | **Coat the manifold flanges of the cylinder head with Prussian blue dye. Glue intake and exhaust gaskets to the cylinder head in their installed position using rubber cement and scribe the outline of the ports on the manifold flanges. Remove the gaskets. Using a small cutter in a hand-held power tool gradually taper the walls of the port out to the scribed outline of the gasket. Further enlargement of the ports should include the removal of sharp edges and radiusing of sharp corners. Do not alter the valve guides.<br>NOTE: *The most efficient port configuration is determined only by extensive testing. Therefore, it is best to consult someone experienced with the head in question to determine the optimum alterations.* |

## CYLINDER HEAD RECONDITIONING

**Procedure** — **Method**

***Knurling the valve guides:**

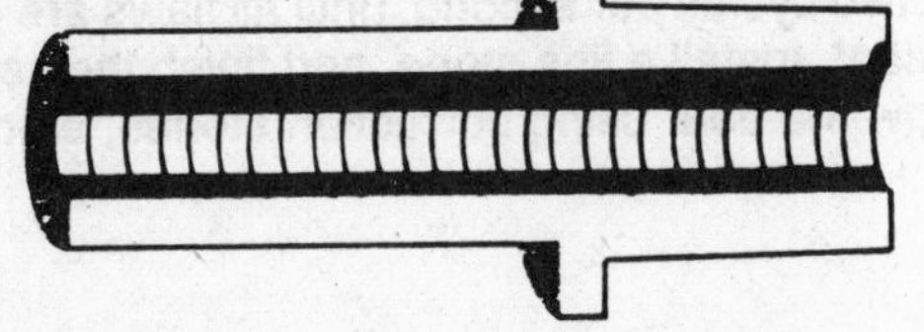

**Cut-away view of a knurled valve guide**

*Valve guides which are not excessively worn or distorted may, in some cases, be knurled rather than replaced. Knurling is a process in which metal is displaced and raised, thereby reducing clearance. Knurling also provides excellent oil control. The possibility of knurling rather than replacing valve guides should be discussed with a machinist.

---

**Replacing the valve guides:**
NOTE: *Valve guides should only be replaced if damaged or if an oversize valve stem is not available.*

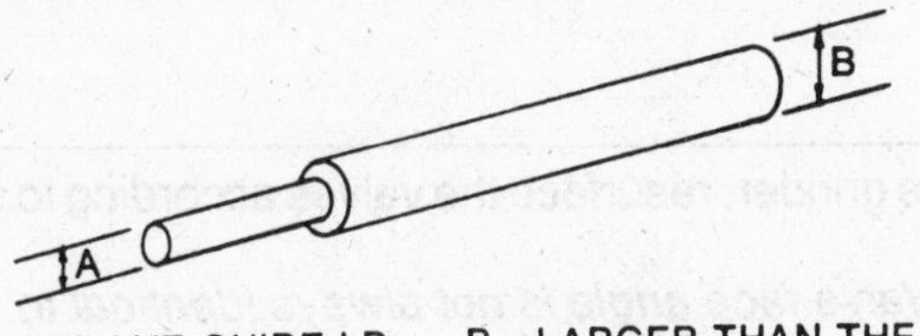


A—VALVE GUIDE I.D. B—LARGER THAN THE VALVE GUIDE O.D.
**Valve guide removal tool**

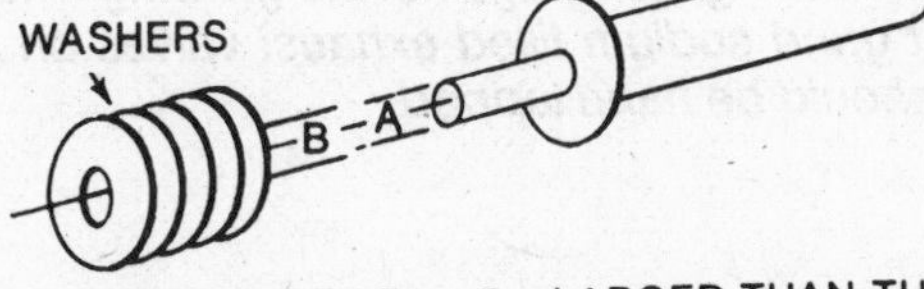


A—VALVE GUIDE I.D. B—LARGER THAN THE VALVE GUIDE O.D.
**Valve guide installation tool (with washers used for installation)**

Depending on the type of cylinder head, valve guides may be pressed, hammered, or shrunk in. In cases where the guides are shrunk into the head, replacement should be left to an equipped machine shop. In other cases, the guides are replaced as follows: Press or tap the valve guides out of the head using a stepped drift (see illustration). Determine the height above the boss that the guide must extend, and obtain a stack of washers, their I.D. similar to the guide's O.D., of that height. Place the stack of washers on the guide, and insert the guide into the boss.
NOTE: *Valve guides are often tapered or beveled for installation.*
Using the stepped installation tool (see illustration), press or tap the guides into position. Ream the guides according to the size of the valve stem.

---

**Replacing valve seat inserts:**

Replacement of valve seat inserts which are worn beyond resurfacing or broken, if feasible, must be done by a machine shop.

---

**Resurfacing the valve seats using reamers:**

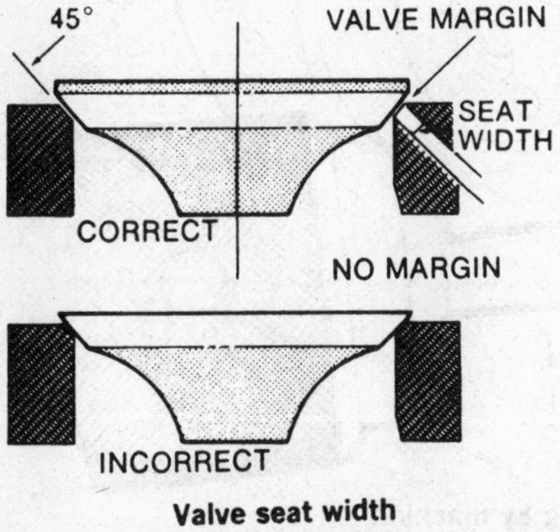


**Valve seat width and centering**

**Reaming the valve seat**

Select a reamer of the correct seat angle, slightly larger than the diameter of the valve seat, and assemble it with a pilot of the correct size. Install the pilot into the valve guide, and using steady pressure, turn the reamer clockwise.
CAUTION: *Do not turn the reamer counterclockwise.*
Remove only as much material as necessary to clean the seat. Check the concentricity of the seat (see below). If the dye method is not used, coat the valve face with Prussian blue dye, install and rotate it on the valve seat. Using the dye marked area as a centering guide, center and narrow the valve seat to specifications with correction cutters.
NOTE: *When no specifications are available, minimum seat width for exhaust valves should be 5/64", intake valves 1/16".*
After making correction cuts, check the position of the valve seat on the valve face using Prussian blue dye.
NOTE: *Do not cut induction hardened seats; they must be ground.*

## CYLINDER HEAD RECONDITIONING

| Procedure | Method |
|---|---|
| *Resurfacing the valve seats using a grinder: | *Select a pilot of the correct size, and a coarse stone of the correct seat angle. Lubricate the pilot if necessary, and install the tool in the valve guide. Move the stone on and off the seat at approximately two cycles per second, until all flaws are removed from the seat. Install a fine stone, and finish the seat. Center and narrow the seat using correction stones, as described above. |

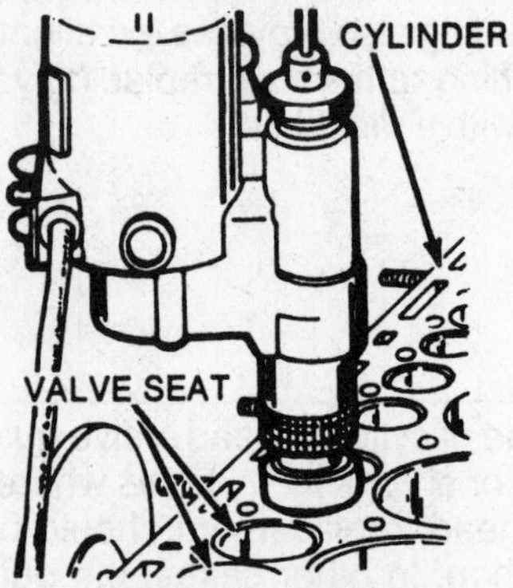

Grinding a valve seat

| Procedure | Method |
|---|---|
| Resurfacing (grinding) the valve face: | Using a valve grinder, resurface the valves according to specifications. CAUTION: *Valve face angle is not always identical to valve seat angle.* A minimum margin of 1/32" should remain after grinding the valve. The valve stem top should also be squared and resurfaced, by placing the stem in the V-block of the grinder, and turning it while pressing lightly against the grinding wheel. NOTE: *Do not grind sodium filled exhaust valves on a machine. These should be hand lapped.* |

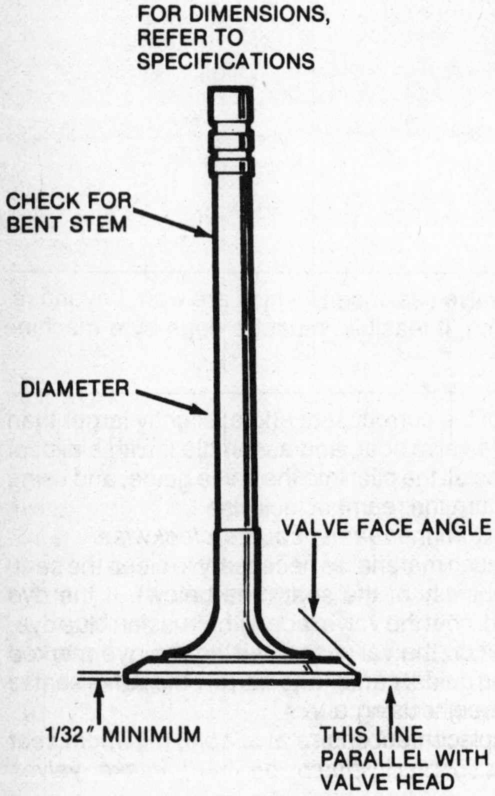

Critical valve dimensions

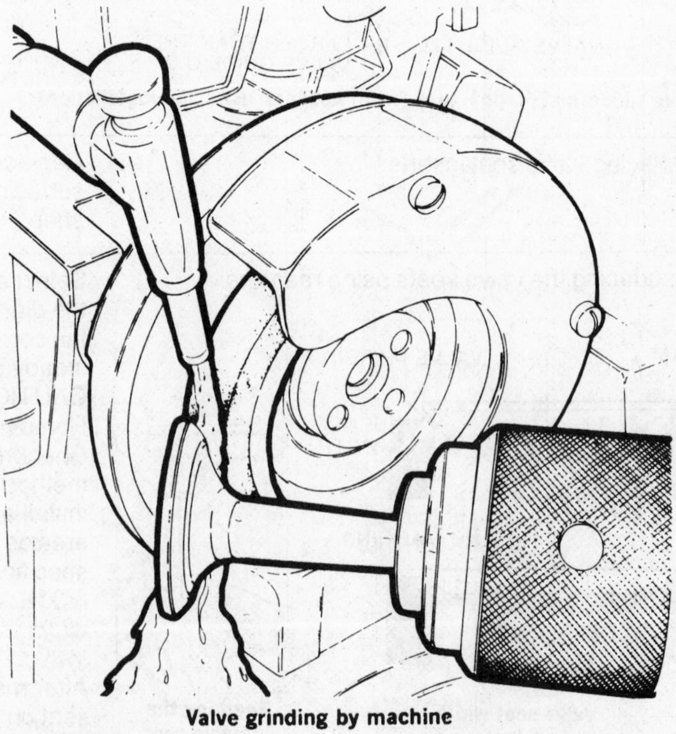
Valve grinding by machine

## CYLINDER HEAD RECONDITIONING

| Procedure | Method |
|---|---|
| Checking the valve seat concentricity: | Coat the valve face with Prussian blue dye, install the valve, and rotate it on the valve seat. If the entire seat becomes coated, and the valve is known to be concentric, the seat is concentric. *Install the dial gauge pilot into the guide, and rest the arm on the valve seat. Zero the gauge, and rotate the arm around the seat. Run-out should not exceed .002″. |

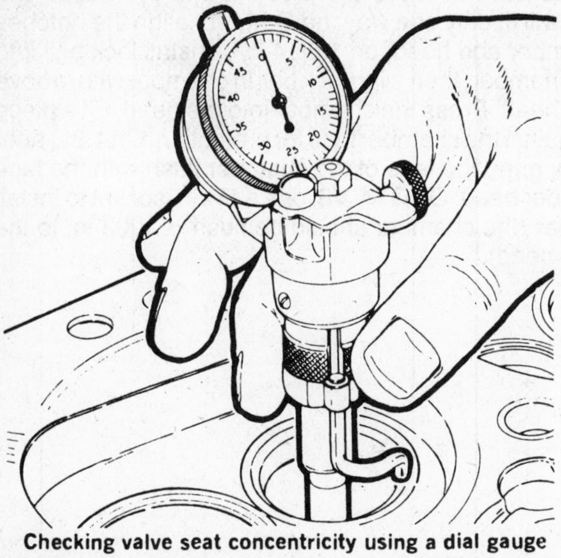

Checking valve seat concentricity using a dial gauge

| Procedure | Method |
|---|---|
| *Lapping the valves: NOTE: *Valve lapping is done to ensure efficient sealing of resurfaced valves and seats.* | *Invert the cylinder head, lightly lubricate the valve stems, and install the valves in the head as numbered. Coat valve seats with fine grinding compound, and attach the lapping tool suction cup to a valve head. NOTE: *Moisten the suction cup.* Rotate the tool between the palms, changing position and lifting the tool often to prevent grooving. Lap the valve until a smooth, polished seat is evident. Remove the valve and tool, and rinse away all traces of grinding compound. **Fasten a suction cup to a piece of drill rod, and mount the rod in a hand drill. Proceed as above, using the hand drill as a lapping tool. CAUTION: *Due to the higher speeds involved when using the hand drill, care must be exercised to avoid grooving the seat.* Lift the tool and change direction of rotation often. |

Hand lapping the valves

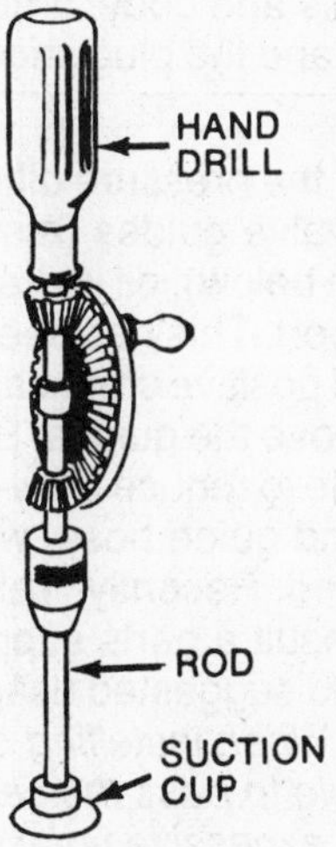


Home made mechanical valve lapping tool

| Procedure | Method |
|---|---|
| Check the valve springs: | Place the spring on a flat surface next to a square. Measure the height of the spring, and rotate it against the edge of the square to measure distortion. If spring height varies (by comparison) by more than 1/16″ or if distortion exceeds 1/16″, replace the spring. **In addition to evaluating the spring as above, test the spring pressure at the installed and compressed (installed height minus valve lift) height using a valve spring tester. Springs used on small displacement engines (up to 3 liters) should be ∓ 1 lb. of all other springs in either position. A tolerance of ∓ 5 lbs. is permissible on larger engines. |

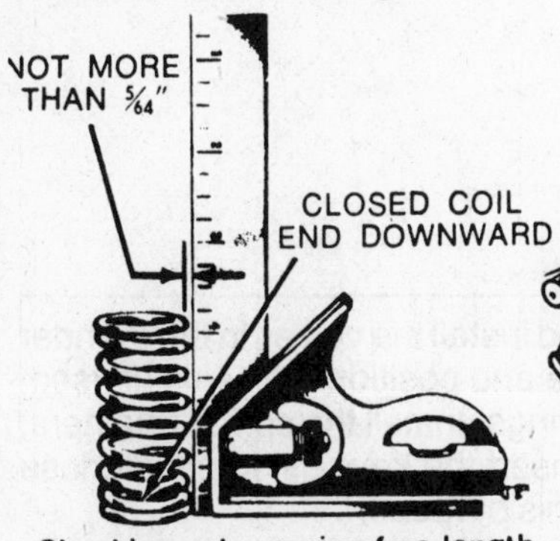


Checking valve spring free length and squareness

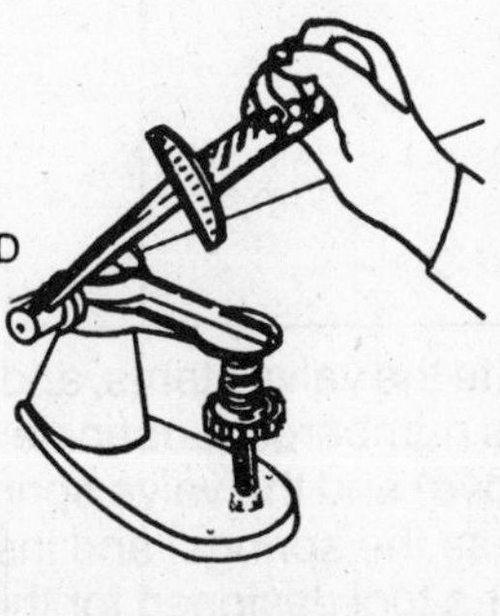

Measuring valve spring test pressure

## CYLINDER HEAD RECONDITIONING

| Procedure | Method |
|---|---|
| Install pre-combustion chambers (Diesel engines only) | Pre-combustion chambers are press-fit into the head. The chambers will fit only one way: on G.M. V8, align the notches in the chamber and head; on 1.8L 4 cyl., install lock ball into groove in chamber, then align lock ball in chamber with groove in cylinder head. Press the chamber into the head. Fit a piece of metal against the chamber face for protection. On 1.8L, after installation, grind the face of the chamber flush with the face of the cylinder head. On G.M. V8, use a 1¼ in. socket to install the chamber (the chamber should be flush ± .003 in. to the face of the head). |

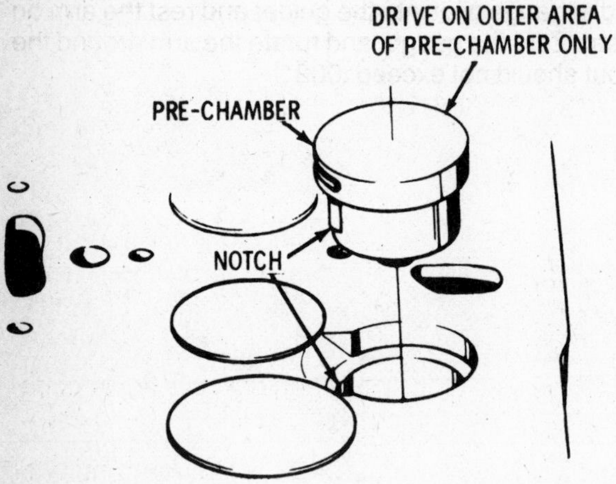


**Align the notches to install the pre-combustion chamber (© G.M. Corp.)**

| Procedure | Method |
|---|---|
| Install fuel injectors and glow plugs (Diesel engines) | Before installing glow plugs, check for continuity across plug terminals and body. If no continuity exists, the heater wire is broken and the plug should be replaced. |
| *Install valve stem seals: | *Due to the pressure differential that exists at the ends of the intake valve guides (atmospheric pressure above, manifold vacuum below), oil is drawn through the valve guides into the intake port. This has been alleviated somewhat since the addition of positive crankcase ventilation, which lowers the pressure above the guides. Several types of valve stem seals are available to reduce blow-by. Certain seals simply slip over the stem and guide boss, while others require that the boss be machined. Recently, Teflon guide seals have become popular. Consult a parts supplier or machinist concerning availability and suggested usages.<br>NOTE: *When installing seals, ensure that a small amount of oil is able to pass the seal to lubricate the valve guides; otherwise, excessive wear may result.* |

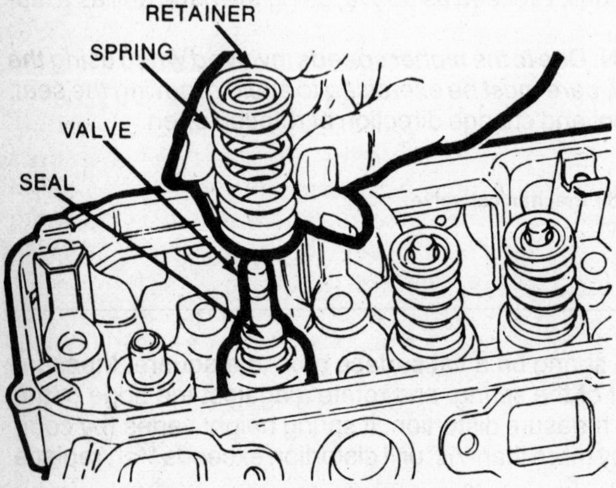


**Valve stem seal installation**

| Procedure | Method |
|---|---|
| Install the valves: | Lubricate the valve stems, and install the valves in the cylinder head as numbered. Lubricate and position the seals (if used, see above) and the valve springs. Install the spring retainers, compress the springs, and insert the keys using needlenose pliers or a tool designed for this purpose.<br>NOTE: *Retain the keys with wheel bearing grease during installation.* |

## CYLINDER HEAD RECONDITIONING

| Procedure | Method |
|---|---|
| Check valve spring installed height: | Measure the distance between the spring pad and the lower edge of the spring retainer, and compare to specifications. If the installed height is incorrect, add shim washers between the spring pad and the spring.<br>CAUTION: *Use only washers designed for this purpose.* |

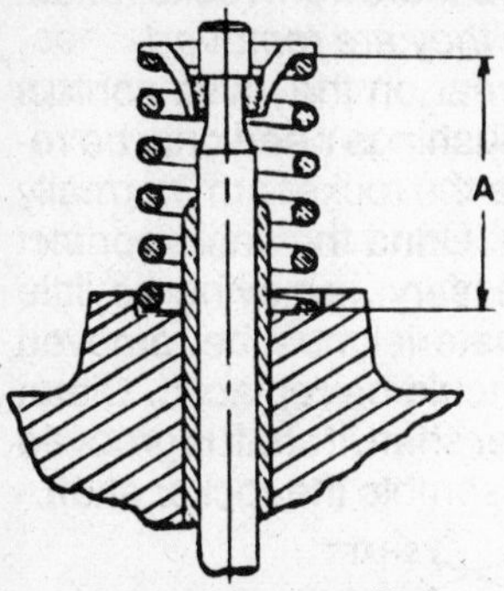


Valve spring installed height dimension

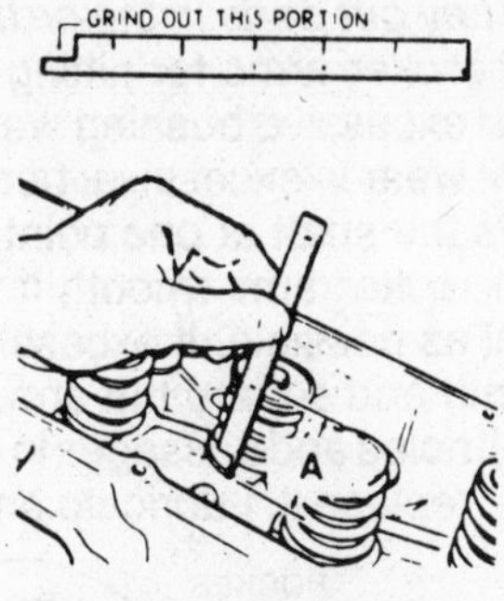


Measuring valve spring installed height

| Procedure | Method |
|---|---|
| Install the camshaft (OHC engines only) and check end play: | See the engine service procedures earlier in this book for details concerning specific engines. |
| Inspect the rocker arms, balls, studs, and nuts (OHV engines only): | Visually inspect the rocker arms, balls, studs, and nuts for cracks, galling, burning, scoring or wear. If all parts are intact, liberally lubricate the rocker arms and balls, and install them on the cylinder head. If wear is noted on a rocker arm at the point of valve contact, grind it smooth and square, removing as little material as possible. Replace the rocker arm if excessively worn. If a rocker stud shows signs of wear, it must be replaced (see below). If a rocker nut shows stress cracks, replace it. If an exhaust ball is galled or burned, substitute the intake ball from the same cylinder (if it is intact), and install a new intake ball.<br>NOTE: *Avoid using new rocker balls on exhaust valves.* |

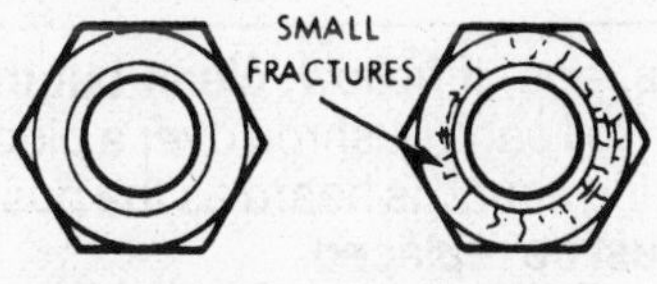


Stress cracks in the rocker nuts

| Procedure | Method |
|---|---|
| Replacing rocker studs (OHV engines only): | In order to remove a threaded stud, lock two nuts on the stud, and unscrew the stud using the lower nut. Coat the lower threads of the new stud with Loctite®, and install.<br>Two alternative methods are available for replacing pressed in studs. Remove the damaged stud using a stack of washers and a nut (see illustration). In the first, the boss is reamed .005–.006″ oversize, and an oversize stud pressed in. Control the stud extension over the boss using washers, in the same manner as valve guides. Before installing the stud, coat it with white lead and grease. To retain the stud more positively drill a hole through the stud and boss, and install a roll pin. In the second method, the boss is tapped, and a threaded stud installed. Retain the stud using Loctite® Stud and Bearing Mount. |

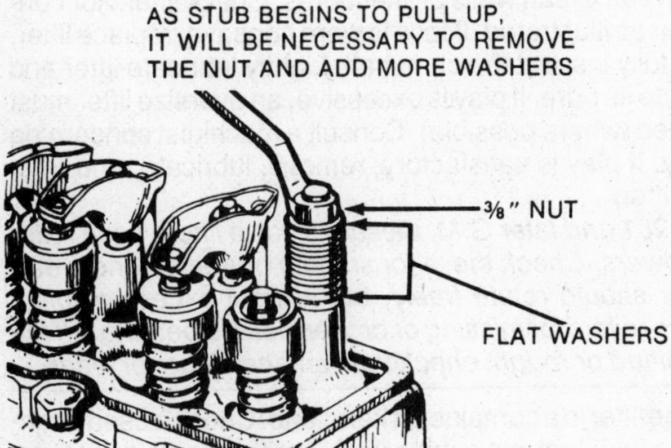


Extracting a pressed-in rocker stud

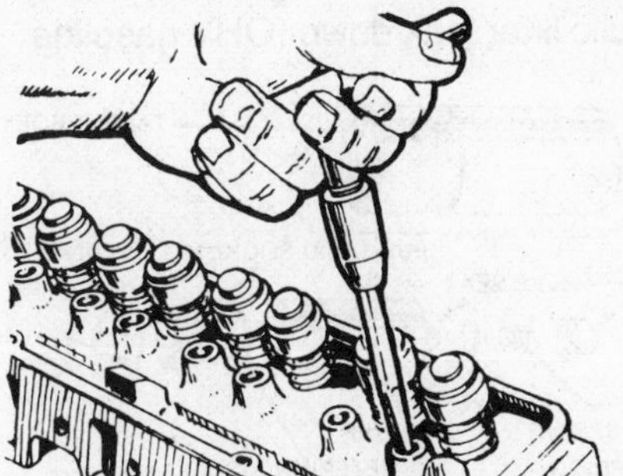

Reaming the stud bore for oversize rocker studs

## CYLINDER HEAD RECONDITIONING

**Procedure** | **Method**

**Inspect the rocker shaft(s) and rocker arms (OHV engines only):**

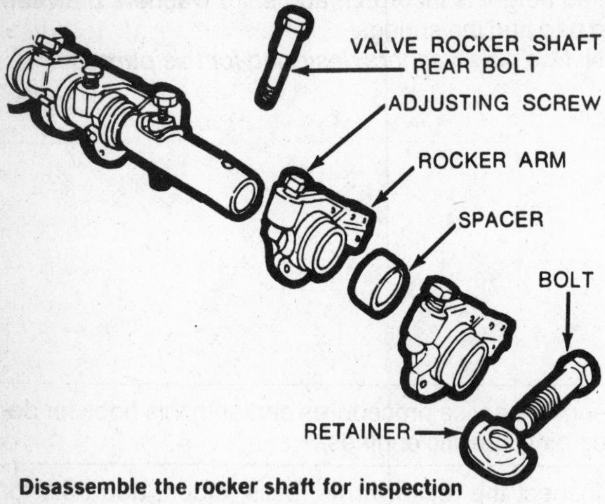


Disassemble the rocker shaft for inspection

Remove rocker arms, springs and washers from rocker shaft. NOTE: *Lay out parts in the order as they are removed.* Inspect rocker arms for pitting or wear on the valve contact point, or excessive bushing wear. Bushings need only be replaced if wear is excessive, because the rocker arm normally contacts the shaft at one point only. Grind the valve contact point of rocker arm smooth if necessary, removing as little material as possible. If excessive material must be removed to smooth and square the arm, it should be replaced. Clean out all oil holes and passages in rocker shaft. If shaft is grooved or worn, replace it. Lubricate and assemble the rocker shaft.

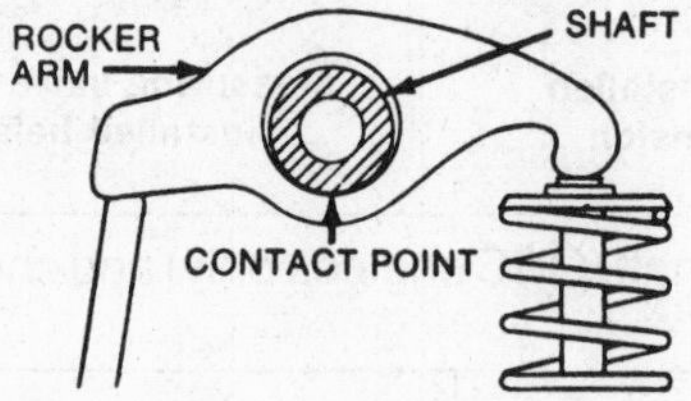


Rocker arm-to-rocker shaft contact area

---

**Inspect the camshaft bushings and the camshaft (OHC engines):**

See next section.

---

**Inspect the pushrods (OHV engines only):**

Remove the pushrods, and, if hollow, clean out the oil passages using fine wire. Roll each pushrod over a piece of clean glass. If a distinct clicking sound is heard as the pushrod rolls, the rod is bent, and must be replaced.

*The length of all pushrods must be equal. Measure the length of the pushrods, compare to specifications, and replace as necessary.

---

**Inspect the valve lifters (OHV engines only):**

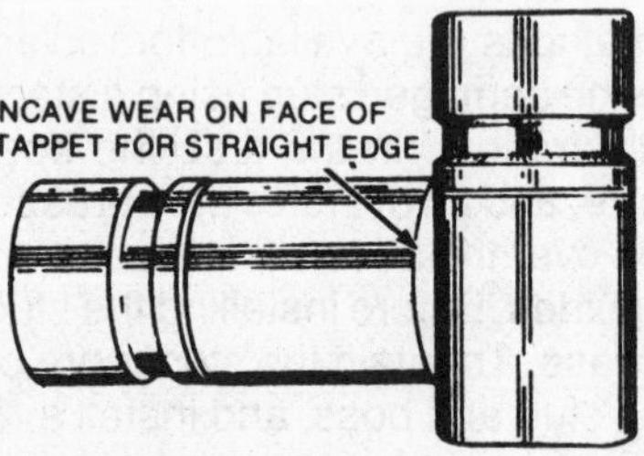


Checking the lifter face

Remove lifters from their bores, and remove gum and varnish, using solvent. Clean walls of lifter bores. Check lifters for concave wear as illustrated. If face is worn concave, replace lifter, and carefully inspect the camshaft. Lightly lubricate lifter and insert it into its bore. If play is excessive, an oversize lifter must be installed (where possible). Consult a machinist concerning feasibility. If play is satisfactory, remove, lubricate, and reinstall the lifter.
NOTE: *1981 and later G.M. diesel V8 valve lifters have roller cam followers. Check these for smooth operation and wear. The roller should rotate freely, but without excessive play. Check the rollers for missing or broken needle bearings. If the roller is pitted or rough, check the camshaft lobe for wear.*

---

***Testing hydraulic lifter leak down (OHV gasoline engines only):**

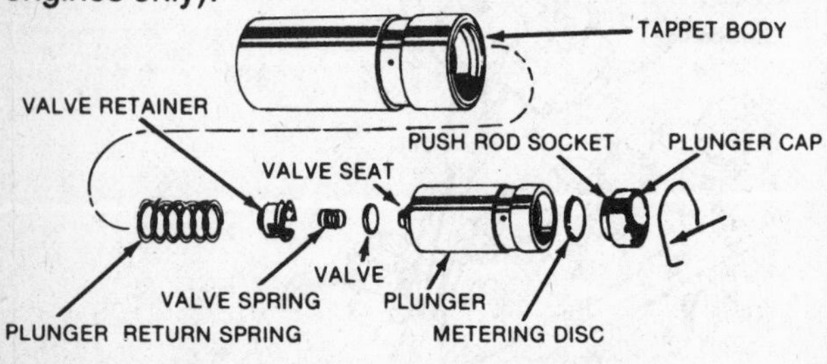


Typical exploded view of hydraulic valve lifter

Submerge lifter in a container of kerosene. Chuck a used pushrod or its equivalent into a drill press. Position container of kerosene so pushrod acts on the lifter plunger. Pump lifter with the drill press, until resistance increases. Pump several more times to bleed any air out of lifter. Apply very firm, constant pressure to the lifter, and observe rate at which fluid bleeds out of lifter. If the fluid bleeds very quickly (less than 15 seconds), lifter is defective. If the time exceeds 60 seconds, lifter is sticking. In either case, recondition or replace lifter. If lifter is operating properly (leak down time 15–60 seconds), lubricate and install it.

## CYLINDER HEAD RECONDITIONING

| Procedure | Method |
|---|---|
| Bleed the hydraulic lifters (diesel engines only): | After the cylinder heads are installed on G.M. V8 diesels, the valve lifters must be bled down before the crankshaft is turned. Failure to bleed down the lifters will cause damage to the valve train. See diesel engine rocker arm replacement procedure in Oldsmobile 88, 98, etc. car section for procedures. NOTE: *When installing new lifters, prime by working the lifter plunger while submerged in clean kerosene or diesel fuel.* |

## CYLINDER BLOCK RECONDITIONING

**Procedure** / **Method**

**Checking the main bearing clearance:**

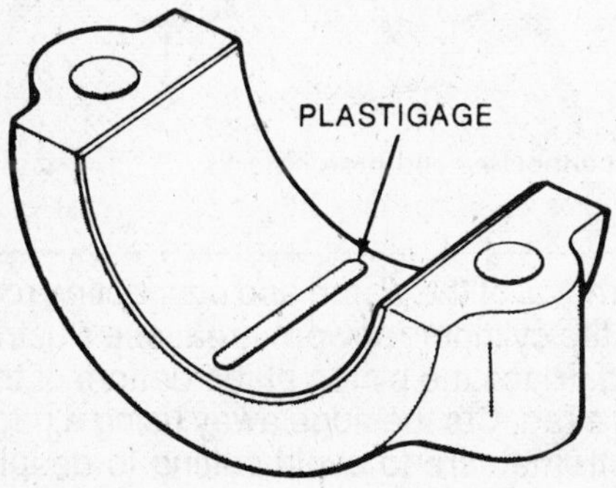


Plastigage® installed on the lower bearing shell

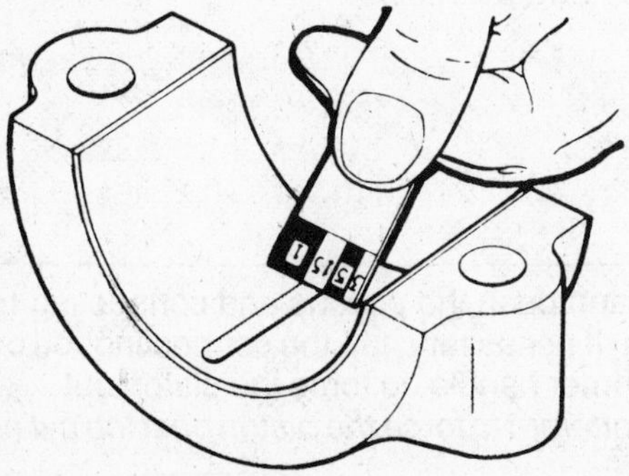

Measuring Plastigage® to determine bearing clearance

Invert engine, and remove cap from the bearing to be checked. Using a clean, dry rag, thoroughly clean all oil from crankshaft journal and bearing insert.
NOTE: *Plastigage is soluble in oil; therefore, oil on the journal or bearing could result in erroneous readings.*
Place a piece of Plastigage along the full length of journal, reinstall cap, and torque to specifications. Remove bearing cap, and determine bearing clearance by comparing width of Plastigage to the scale on Plastigage envelope. Journal taper is determined by comparing width of the Plastigage strip near its ends. Rotate crankshaft 90° and retest, to determine journal eccentricity.
NOTE: *Do not rotate crankshaft with Plastigage installed.*
If bearing insert and journal appear intact, and are within tolerances, no further main bearing service is required. If bearing or journal appear defective, cause of failure should be determined before replacement.

*Remove crankshaft from block (see below). Measure the main bearing journals at each end twice (90° apart) using a micrometer, to determine diameter, journal taper and eccentricity. If journals are within tolerances, reinstall bearing caps at their specified torque. Using a telescope gauge and micrometer, measure bearing I.D. parallel to piston axis and at 30° on each side of piston axis. Subtract journal O.D. from bearing I.D. to determine oil clearance. If crankshaft journals appear defective, or do no meet tolerances, there is no need to measure bearings; for the crankshaft will require grinding and/or undersize bearings will be required. If bearing appears defective, cause for failure should be determined prior to replacement.

**Checking the connecting rod bearing clearance:**

Connecting rod bearing clearance is checked in the same manner as main bearing clearance, using Plastigage. Before removing the crankshaft, connecting rod side clearance also should be measured and recorded.

*Checking connecting rod bearing clearance, using a micrometer, is identical to checking main bearing clearance. If no other service is required, the piston and rod assemblies need not be removed.

## CYLINDER BLOCK RECONDITIONING

**Procedure** | **Method**

**Removing the crankshaft:**

Using a punch, mark the corresponding main bearing caps and saddles according to position (i.e., one punch on the front main cap and saddle, two on the second, three on the third, etc.). Using number stamps, identify the corresponding connecting rods and caps, according to cylinder (if no numbers are present). Remove the main and connecting rod caps, and place sleeves of plastic tubing over the connecting rod bolts, to protect the journals as the crankshaft is removed. Lift the crankshaft out of the block.

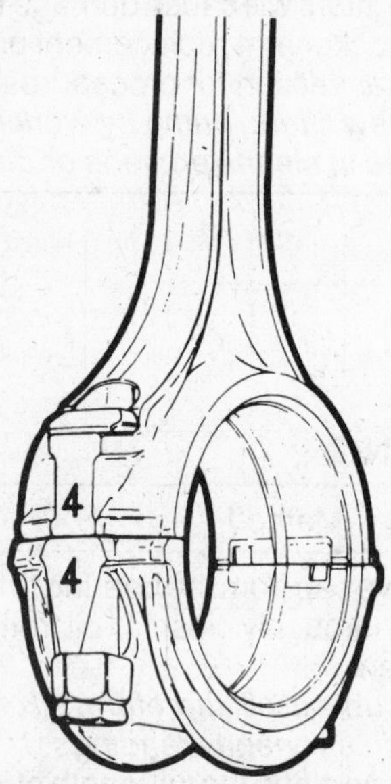

**Connecting rod matched to cylinder with a number stamp**

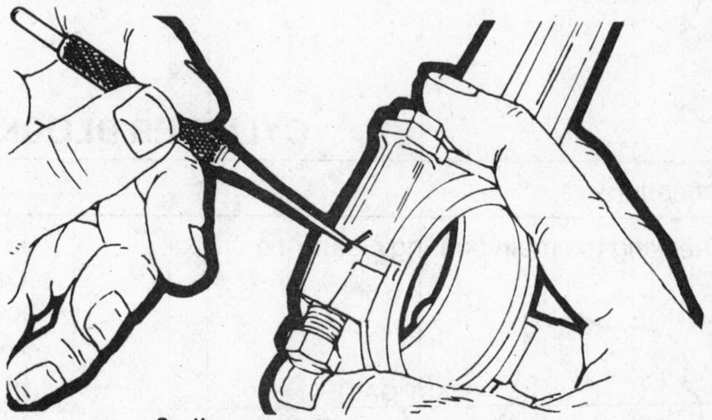
**Scribe connecting rod matchmarks**

**Remove the ridge from the top of the cylinder:**

In order to facilitate removal of the piston and connecting rod, the ridge at the top of the cylinder (unworn area; see illustration) must be removed. Place the piston at the bottom of the bore, and cover it with a rag. Cut the ridge away using a ridge reamer, exercising extreme care to avoid cutting to deeply. Remove the rag, and remove cuttings that remain on the piston.

CAUTION: *If the ridge is not removed, and new rings are installed, damage to rings will result.*

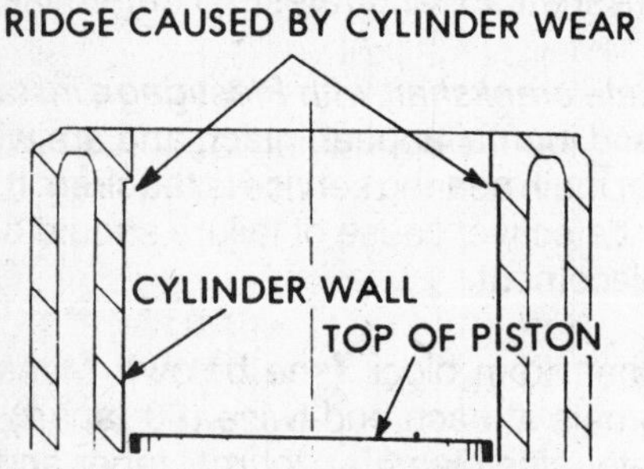

**Cylinder bore ridge**

**Removing the piston and connecting rod:**

Invert the engine, and push the pistons and connecting rods out of the cylinders. If necessary, tap the connecting rod boss with a wooden hammer handle, to force the piston out.

CAUTION: *Do not attempt to force the piston past the cylinder ridge* (see above).

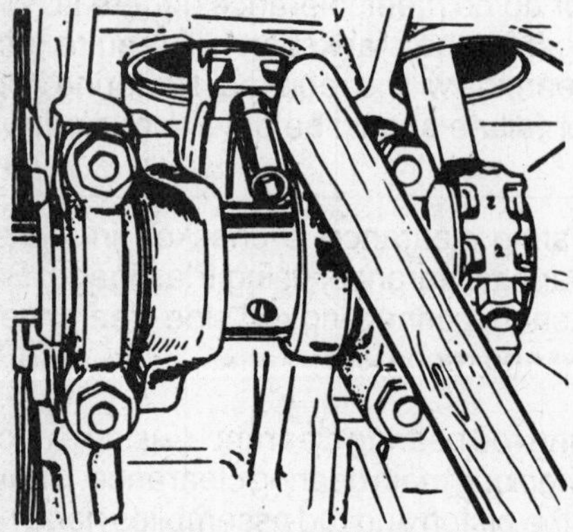
**Removing the piston**

## CYLINDER BLOCK RECONDITIONING

| Procedure | Method |
|---|---|
| Service the crankshaft: | Ensure that all oil holes and passages in the crankshaft are open and free of sludge. If necessary, have the crankshaft ground to the largest possible undersize.<br><br>**Have the crankshaft Magnafluxed, to locate stress cracks. Consult a machinist concerning additional service procedures, such as surface hardening (e.g., nitriding, Tuftriding) to improve wear characteristics, cross drilling and chamfering the oil holes to improve lubrication, and balancing. |
| Removing freeze plugs: | Drill a small hole in the middle of the freeze plugs. Thread a large sheet metal screw into the hole and remove the plug with a slide hammer. |
| Remove the oil gallery plugs: | Threaded plugs should be removed using an appropriate (usually square) wrench. To remove soft, pressed in plugs, drill a hole in the plug, and thread in a sheet metal screw. Pull the plug out by the screw using pliers. |
| Hot-tank the block:<br>NOTE: *Do not hot-tank aluminum parts.* | Have the block hot-tanked to remove grease, corrosion, and scale from the water jackets.<br>NOTE: *Consult the operator to determine whether the camshaft bearings will be damaged during the hot-tank process.* |
| Check the block for cracks: | Visually inspect the block for cracks or chips. The most common locations are as follows:<br>Adjacent to freeze plugs.<br>Between the cylinders and water jackets.<br>Adjacent to the main bearing saddles.<br>At the extreme bottom of the cylinders.<br>Check only suspected cracks using spot check dye (see introduction). If a crack is located, consult a machinist concerning possible repairs.<br><br>**Magnaflux the block to locate hidden cracks. If cracks are located, consult a machinist about feasibility of repair. |
| Install the oil gallery plugs and freeze plugs: | Coat freeze plugs with sealer and tap into position using a piece of pipe, slightly smaller than the plug, as a driver. To ensure retention, stake the edges of the plugs. Coat threaded oil gallery plugs with sealer and install. Drive replacement soft plugs into block using a large drift as a driver.<br><br>*Rather than reinstalling lead plugs, drill and tap the holes, and install threaded plugs. |
| *Check the deck height: | *The deck height is the distance from the crankshaft centerline to the block deck. To measure, invert the engine, and install the crankshaft, retaining it with the center main cap. Measure the distance from the crankshaft journal to the block deck, parallel to the cylinder centerline. Measure the diameter of the end (front and rear) main journals, parallel to the centerline of the cylinders, divide the diameter in half, and subtract it from the previous measurement. The results of the front and rear measurements should be identical. If the difference exceeds .005″, the deck height should be corrected.<br>NOTE: *Block deck height and warpage should be corrected at the same time.* |

## CYLINDER BLOCK RECONDITIONING

| Procedure | Method |
|---|---|
| Check the block deck for warpage: | Using a straightedge and feeler gauges, check the block deck for warpage in the same manner that the cylinder head is checked (see Cylinder Head Reconditioning). If warpage exceeds specifications, have the deck resurfaced. NOTE: *In certain cases a specification for total material removal (Cylinder head and block deck) is provided. This specification must not be exceeded.* |
| Check the bore diameter and surface: | Visually inspect the cylinder bores for roughness, scoring, or scuffing. If evident, the cylinder bore must be bored or honed oversize to eliminate imperfections, and the smallest possible oversize piston used. The new pistons should be given to the machinist with the block, so that the cylinders can be bored or honed exactly to the piston size (plus clearance). If no flaws are evident, measure the bore diameter using a telescope gauge and micrometer, or dial guage, parallel and perpendicular to the engine centerline, at the top (below the ridge) and bottom of the bore. Subtract the bottom measurements from the top to determine taper, and the parallel to the centerline measurements from the perpendicular measurements to determine eccentricity. If the measurements are not within specifications, the cylinder must be bored or honed, and an oversize piston installed. If the measurements are within specifications the cylinder may be used as is, with only finish honing (see below). NOTE: *Prior to boring, check the block deck warpage, height and bearing alignment.* CAUTION: *The 4 cyl. 140 G.M. engine cylinder walls are impregnated with silicone. Boring or honing can be done only by a shop with the proper equipment.* |

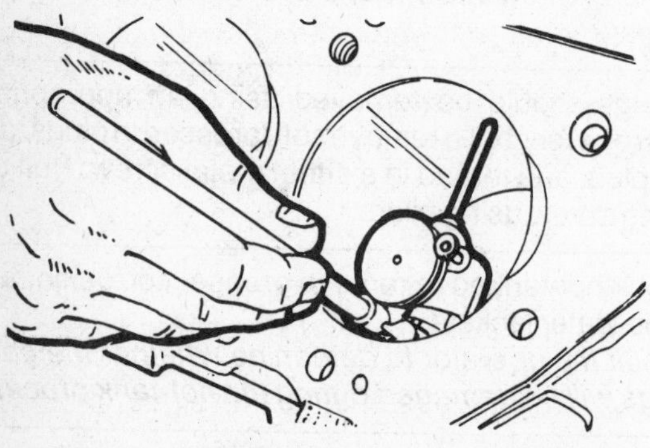

Measuring the cylinder bore with a dial gauge

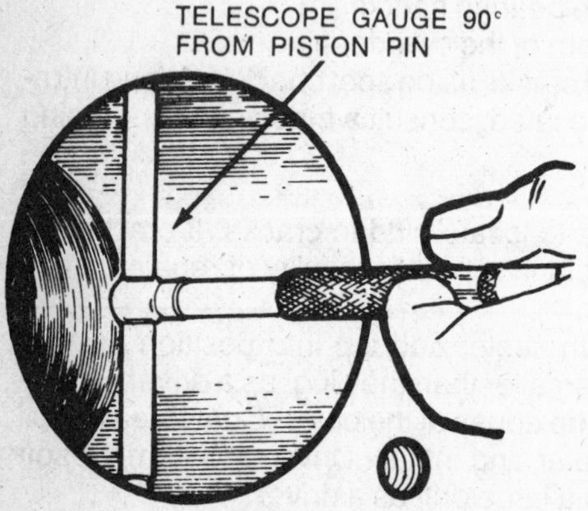


Measuring cylinder bore with a telescope gauge

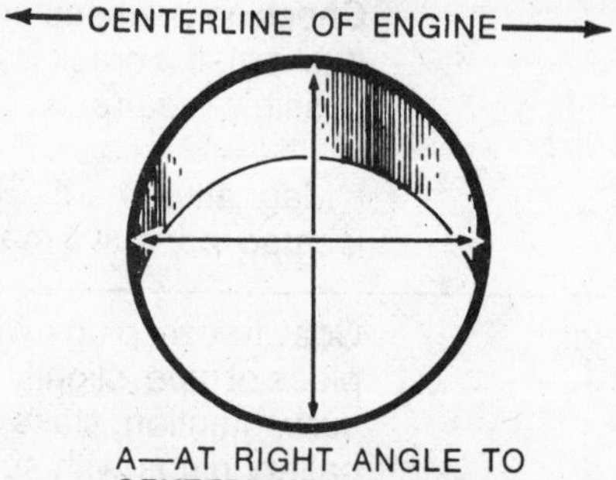


Cylinder bore measuring points

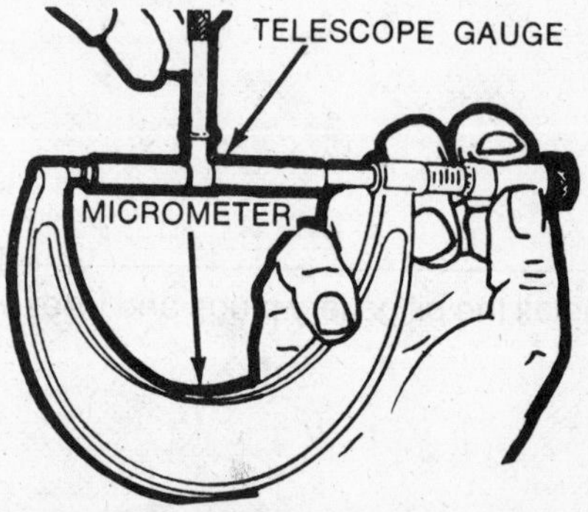


Determining cylinder bore by measuring telescope gauge with a micrometer

| Procedure | Method |
|---|---|
| Check the cylinder block bearing alignment: | Remove the upper bearing inserts. Place a straightedge in the bearing saddles along the centerline of the crankshaft. If clearance exists between the straightedge and the center saddle, the block must be alignbored. |

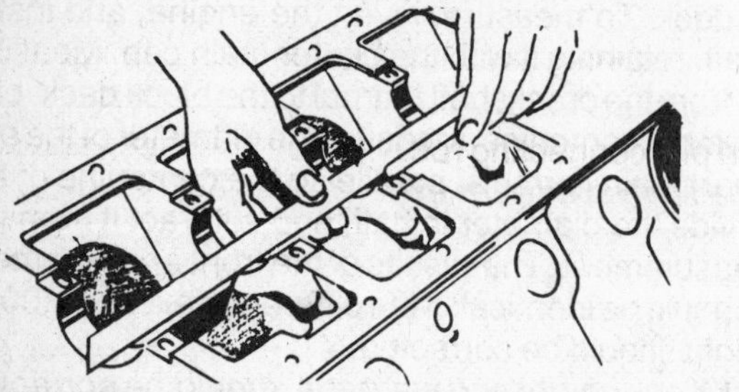

Checking main bearing saddle alignment

## CYLINDER BLOCK RECONDITIONING

| Procedure | Method |
|---|---|
| Clean and inspect the pistons and connecting rods: | Using a ring expander, remove the rings from the piston. Remove the retaining rings (if so equipped) and remove piston pin. NOTE: *If the piston pin must be pressed out, determine the proper method and use the proper tools; otherwise the piston will distort.* Clean the ring grooves using an appropriate tool, exercising care to avoid cutting too deeply. Thoroughly clean all carbon and varnish from the piston with solvent. CAUTION: *Do not use a wire brush or caustic solvent on pistons.* Inspect the pistons for scuffing, scoring, cracks, pitting, or excessive ring groove wear. If wear is evident, the piston must be replaced. Check the connecting rod length by measuring the rod from the inside of the large end to the inside of the small end using calipers (see illustration). All connecting rods should be equal length. Replace any rod that differs from the others in the engine. *Have the connecting rod alignment checked in an alignment fixture by a machinist. Replace any twisted or bent rods. *Magnaflux the connecting rods to locate stress cracks. If cracks are found, replace the connecting rod. |

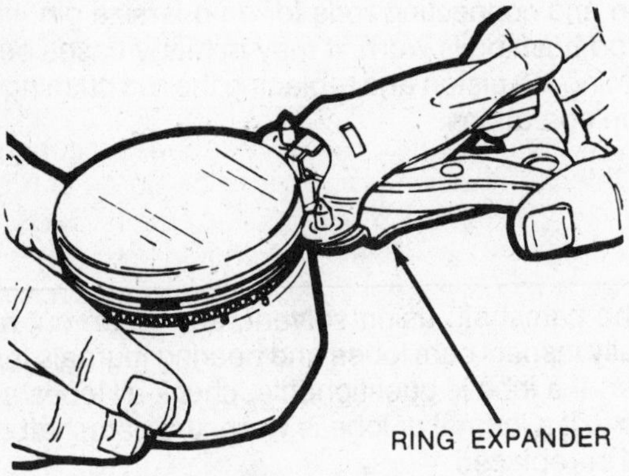

Removing the piston rings

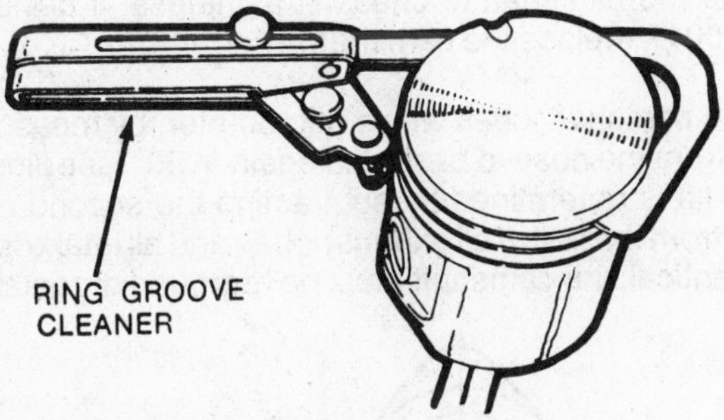

Cleaning the piston ring grooves

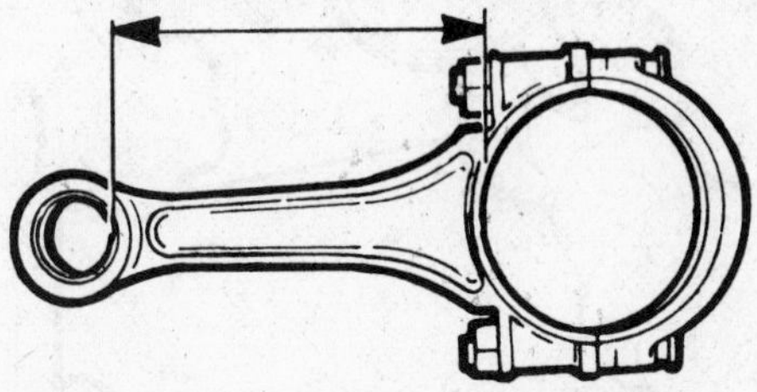
Check the connecting rod length (arrow)

| Procedure | Method |
|---|---|
| Fit the pistons to the cylinders: | Using a telescope gauge and micrometer, or a dial gauge, measure the cylinder bore diameter perpendicular to the piston pin, 2½" below the deck. Measure the piston perpendicular to its pin on the skirt. The difference between the two measurements is the piston clearance. If the clearance is within specifications or slightly below (after boring or honing), finish honing is all that is required. If the clearance is excessive, try to obtain a slightly larger piston to bring clearance within specifications. Where this is not possible, obtain the first oversize piston, and hone (or if necessary, bore) the cylinder to size. |

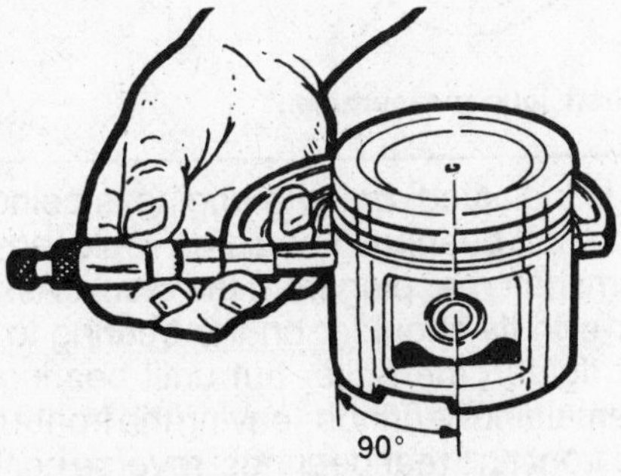

Measuring the piston prior to fitting

| Procedure | Method |
|---|---|
| Assemble the pistons and connecting rods: | Inspect piston pin, connecting rod small end bushing, and piston bore for galling, scoring, or excessive wear. If evident, replace defective part(s). Measure the I.D. of the piston boss and connecting rod small end, and the O.D. of the piston pin. If within specifications, assemble piston pin and rod. CAUTION: *If piston pin must be pressed in, determine the proper method and use the proper tools; otherwise the piston will distort.* |

## CYLINDER BLOCK RECONDITIONING

| Procedure | Method |
|---|---|
| 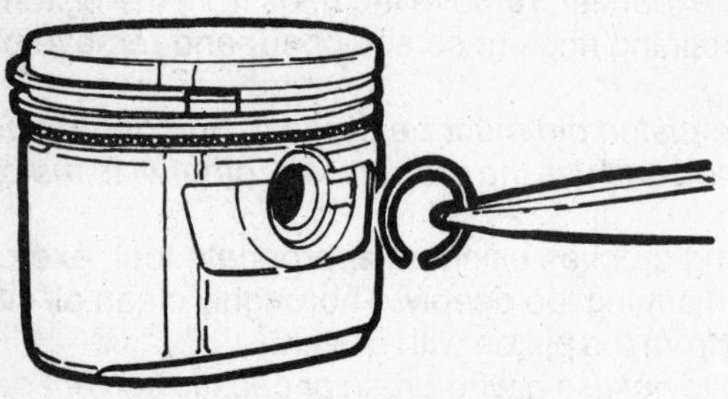 Installing piston pin lock rings | Install the lock rings; ensure that they seat properly. If the parts are not within specifications, determine the service method for the type of engine. In some cases, piston and pin are serviced as an assembly when either is defective. Others specify reaming the piston and connecting rods for an oversize pin. If the connecting rod bushing is worn, it may in many cases be replaced. Reaming the piston and replacing the rod bushing are machine shop operations. |
| Clean and inspect the camshaft: 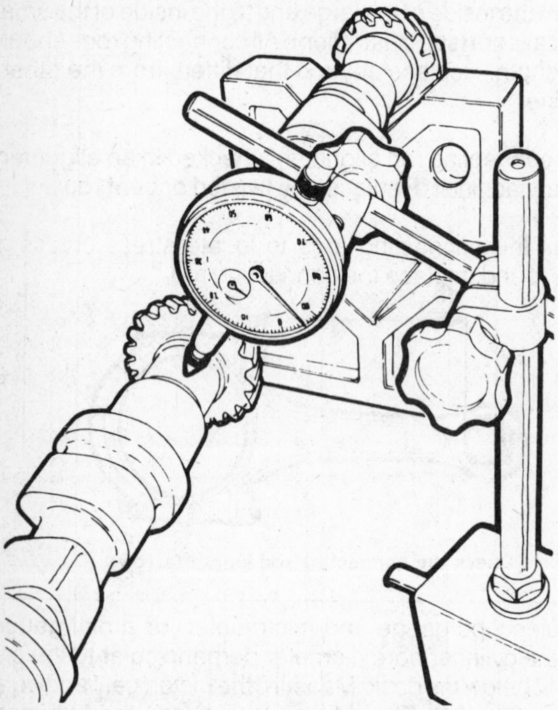 Checking the camshaft for straightness | Degrease the camshaft, using solvent, and clean out all oil holes. Visually inspect cam lobes and bearing journals for excessive wear. If a lobe is questionable, check all lobes as indicated below. If a journal or lobe is worn, the camshaft must be reground or replaced. NOTE: *If a journal is worn, there is a good chance that the bushings are worn.* If lobes and journals appear intact, place the front and rear journals in V-blocks, and rest a dial indicator on the center journal. Rotate the camshaft to check straightness. If deviation exceeds .001°, replace the camshaft. *Check the camshaft lobes with a micrometer, by measuring the lobes from the nose to base and again at 90° (see illustration). The lift is determined by subtracting the second measurement from the first. If all exhaust lobes and all intake lobes are not identical, the camshaft must be reground or replaced. 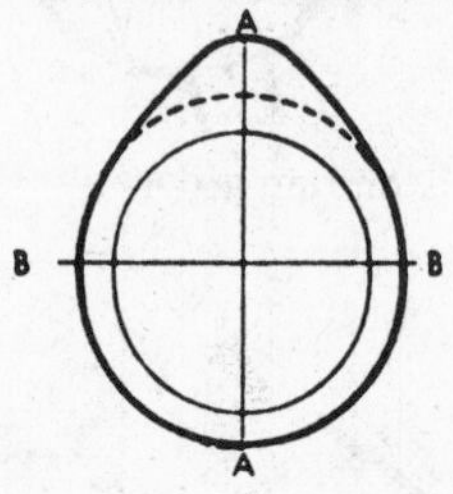  Camshaft lobe measurement |
| Replace the camshaft bearings (OHV engines only): 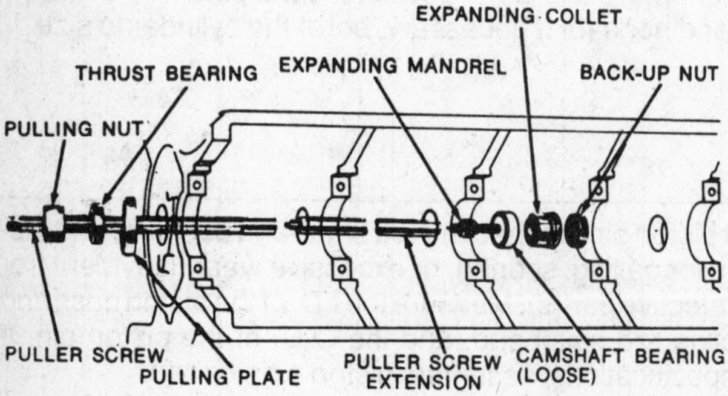  Camshaft removal and installation tool (typical) | If excessive wear is indicated, or if the engine is being completely rebuilt, camshaft bearings should be replaced as follows: Drive the camshaft rear plug from the block. Assemble the removal puller with its shoulder on the bearing to be removed. Gradually tighten the puller nut until bearing is removed. Remove remaining bearings, leaving the front and rear for last. To remove front and rear bearings, reverse position of the tool, so as to pull the bearings in toward the center of the block. Leave the tool in this position, pilot the new front and rear bearings on the installer, and pull them into position: Return the tool to its original position and pull remaining bearings into postion. NOTE: *Ensure that oil holes align when installing bearings.* Replace camshaft rear plug, and stake it into position to aid retention. |

## CYLINDER BLOCK RECONDITIONING

| Procedure | Method |
|---|---|

**Finish hone the cylinders:**

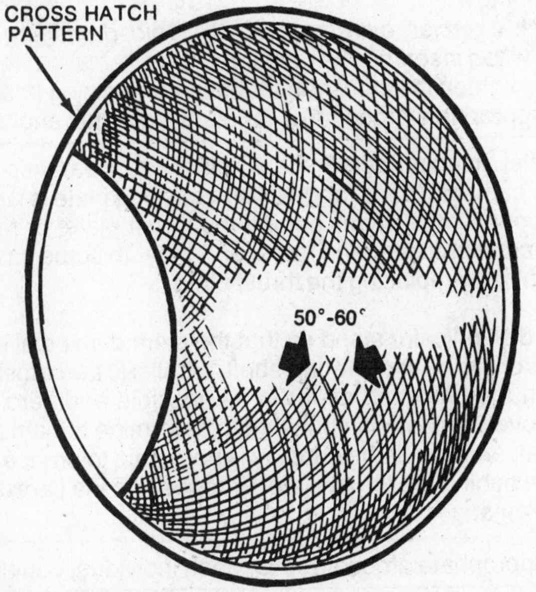


Chuck a flexible drive hone into a power drill, and insert it into the cylinder. Start the hone, and move it up and down the cylinder at a rate which will produce approximately a 60° cross-hatch pattern (see illustration).
NOTE: *Do not extend the hone below the cylinder bore.*
After developing the pattern, remove the hone and recheck piston fit. Wash the cylinders with a detergent and water solution to remove abrasive dust, dry, and wipe several times with a rag soaked in engine oil.

**Check piston ring end-gap:**

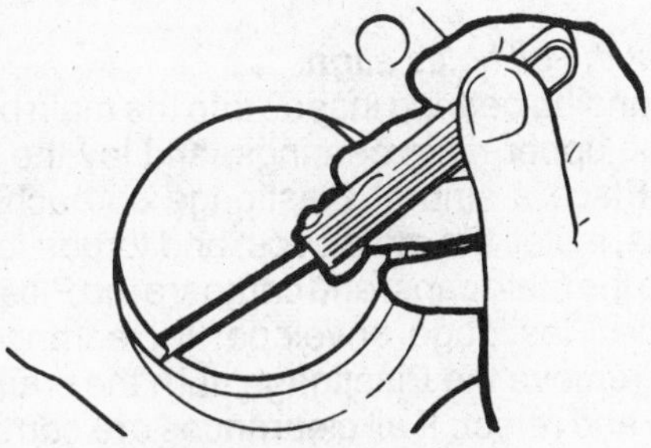

Checking ring end-gap

Compress the piston rings to be used in a cylinder, one at a time, into that cylinder, and press them approximately 1″ below the deck with an inverted piston. Using feeler gauges, measure the ring end-gap, and compare to specifications. Pull the ring out of the cylinder and file the ends with a fine file to obtain proper clearance.
CAUTION: *If inadequate ring end-gap is utilized, ring breakage will result.*

**Install the piston rings:**

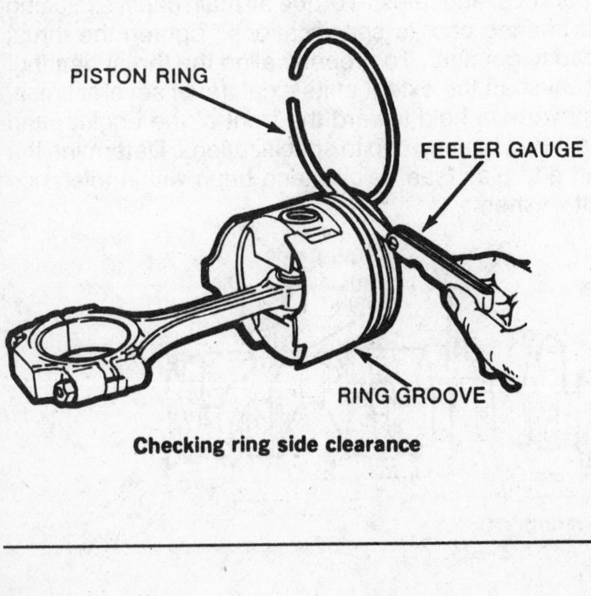


Checking ring side clearance

Inspect the ring grooves in the piston for excessive wear or taper. If necessary, recut the groove(s) for use with an overwidth ring or a standard ring and spacer. If the groove is worn uniformly, overwidth rings, or standard rings and spacers may be installed without recutting. Roll the outside of the ring around the groove to check for burrs or deposits. If any are found, remove with a fine file. Hold the ring in the groove, and measure side clearance. If necessary, correct as indicated above.
NOTE: *Always install any additional spacers above the piston ring.*
The ring groove must be deep enough to allow the ring to seat below the lands (see illustration). In many cases, a "go-no-go" depth gauge will be provided with the piston rings. Shallow grooves may be corrected by recutting, while deep grooves require some type of filler or expander behind the piston. Consult the piston ring supplier concerning the suggested method. Install the rings on the piston, lowest ring first, using a ring expander.
NOTE: *Position the ring markings as specified by the manufacturer (see car section).*

## CYLINDER BLOCK RECONDITIONING

**Procedure** — **Method**

**Install the camshaft (OHV engines only):**

Liberally lubricate the camshaft lobes and journals, and install the camshaft.

CAUTION: *Exercise extreme care to avoid damaging the bearings when inserting the camshaft.*

Install and tighten the camshaft thrust plate retaining bolts.

See the appropriate procedures for each individual engine.

**Check camshaft end-play (OHV engines only):**

Checking camshaft end-play with a feeler gauge

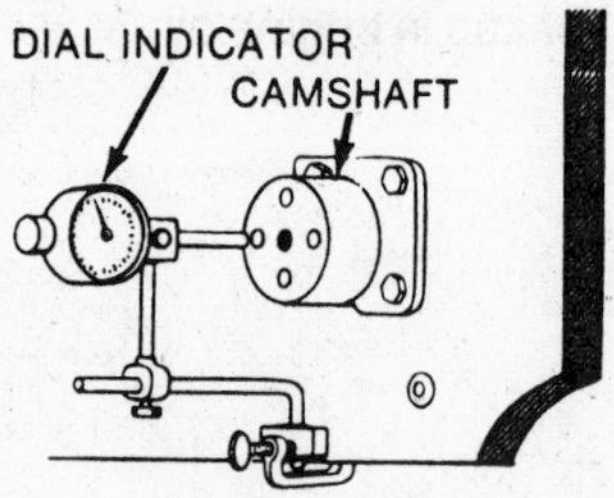


Checking camshaft end-play with a dial indicator

Using feeler gauges, determine whether the clearance between the camshaft boss (or gear) and backing plate is within specifications. Install shims behind the thrust plate, or reposition the camshaft gear and retest end-play. In some cases, adjustment is by replacing the thrust plate.

*Mount a dial indicator stand so that the stem of the dial indicator rests on the nose of the camshaft, parallel to the camshaft axis. Push the camshaft as far in as possible and zero the gauge. Move the camshaft outward to determine the amount of camshaft endplay. If the endplay is not within tolerance, install shims behind the thrust plate, or reposition the camshaft gear and retest.

**Install the rear main seal (where applicable):**

See the appropriate procedures for each individual engine.

**Install the crankshaft:**

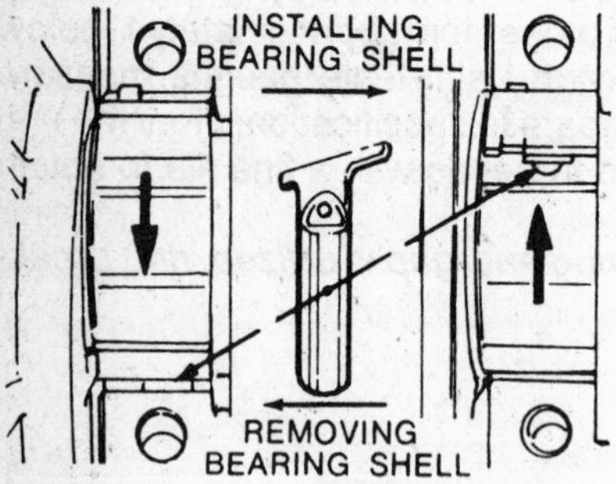


Removal and installation of upper bearing insert using a roll-out pin

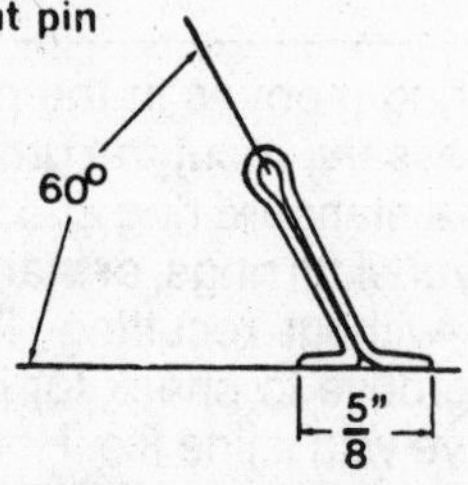


Home-made bearing roll-out pin

Thoroughly clean the main bearing saddles and caps. Place the upper halves of the bearing inserts on the saddles and press into position.

NOTE: *Ensure that the oil holes align.*

Press the corresponding bearing inserts into the main bearing caps. Lubricate the upper main bearings, and lay the crankshaft in position. Place a strip of Plastigage on each of the crankshaft journals, install the main caps, and torque to specifications. Remove the main caps, and compare the Plastigage to the scale on the Plastigage envelope. If clearances are within tolerances, remove the Plastigage, turn the crankshaft 90°, wipe off all oil and retest. If all clearances are correct, remove all Plastigage, thoroughly lubricate the main caps and bearing journals, and install the main caps. If clearances are not within tolerance, the upper bearing inserts may be removed, without removing the crankshaft, using a bearing roll out pin (see illustration). Roll in a bearing that will provide proper clearance, and retest. Torque all main caps, excluding the thrust bearing cap, to specifications. Tighten the thrust bearing cap finger tight. To properly align the thrust bearing, pry the crankshaft the extent of its axial travel several times, the last movement held toward the front of the engine, and torque the thrust bearing cap to specifications. Determine the crankshaft end-play (see below), and bring within tolerance with thrust washers.

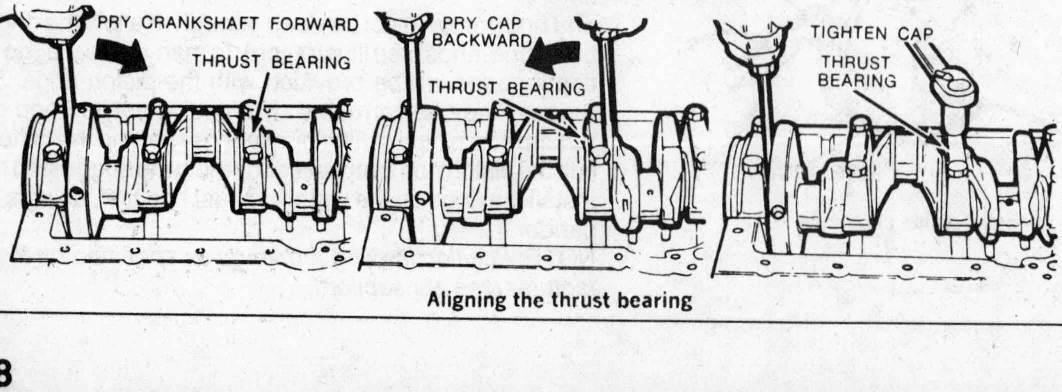


Aligning the thrust bearing

## CYLINDER BLOCK RECONDITIONING

| Procedure | Method |
|---|---|
| Measure crankshaft end-play: | Mount a dial indicator stand on the front of the block, with the dial indicator stem resting on the nose of the crankshaft, parallel to the crankshaft axis. Pry the crankshaft the extent of its travel rearward, and zero the indicator. Pry the crankshaft forward and record crankshaft end-play. NOTE: *Crankshaft end-play also may be measured at the thrust bearing, using feeler gauges* (see illustration). |

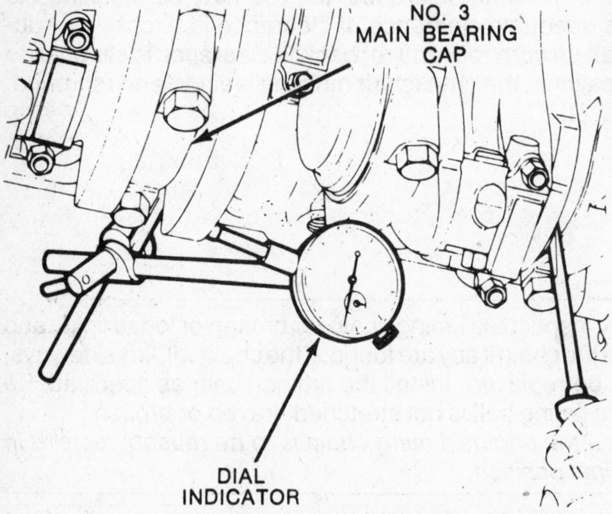


Checking crankshaft end-play with a dial indicator

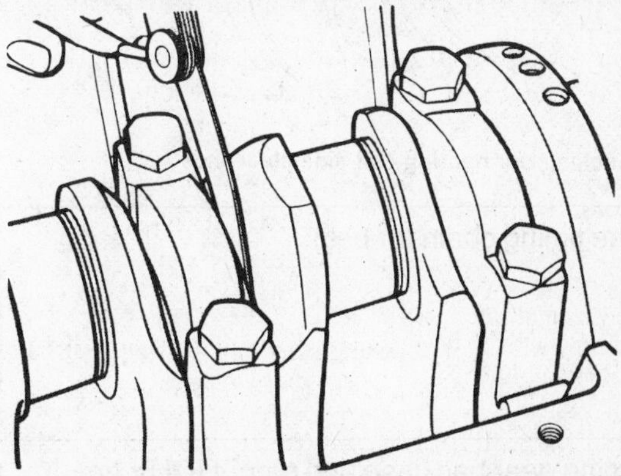

Checking crankshaft end-play with a feeler gauge

| Procedure | Method |
|---|---|
| Install the pistons: | Press the upper connecting rod bearing halves into the connecting rods, and the lower halves into the connecting rod caps. Position the piston ring gaps according to specifications (see car section), and lubricate the pistons. Install a ring compressor on a piston, and press two long (8″) pieces of plastic tubing over the rod bolts. Using the tubes as a guide, press the pistons into the bores and onto the crankshaft with a wooden hammer handle. After seating the rod on the crankshaft journal, remove the tubes and install the cap finger tight. Install the remaining pistons in the same manner. Invert the engine and check the bearing clearance at two points (90° apart) on each journal with Plastigage. NOTE: *Do not turn the crankshaft with Plastigage installed.* If clearance is within tolerances, remove *all* Plastigage, thoroughly lubricate the journals, and torque the rod caps to specifications. If clearance is not within specifications, install different thickness bearing inserts and recheck. CAUTION: *Never shim or file the connecting rods or caps.* Always install plastic tube sleeves over the rod bolts when the caps are not installed, to protect the crankshaft journals. |

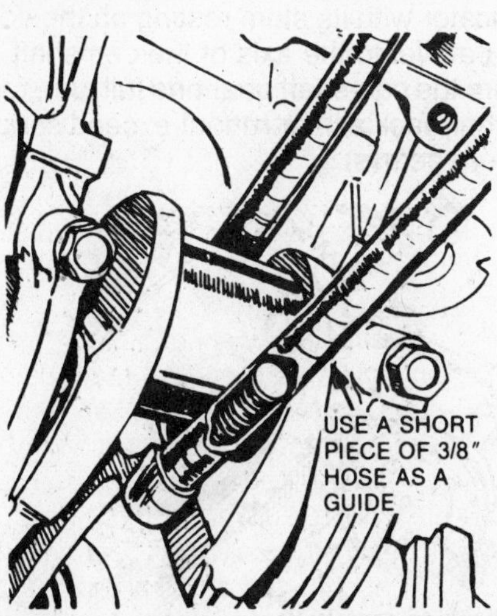


Tubing used to protect crankshaft journals and cylinder walls during piston installation

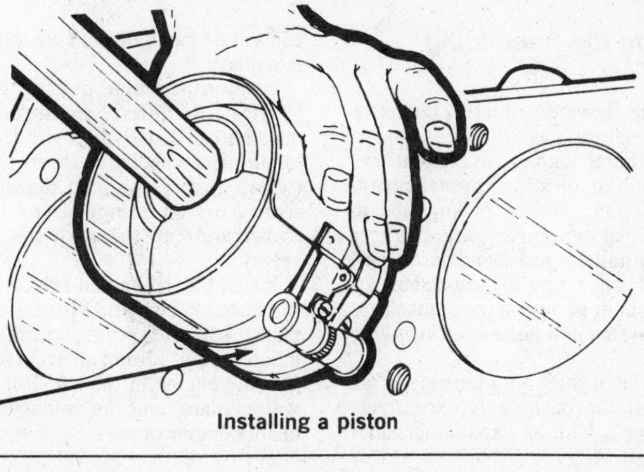


Installing a piston

## CYLINDER BLOCK RECONDITIONING

| Procedure | Method |
|---|---|
| Check connecting rod side clearance: 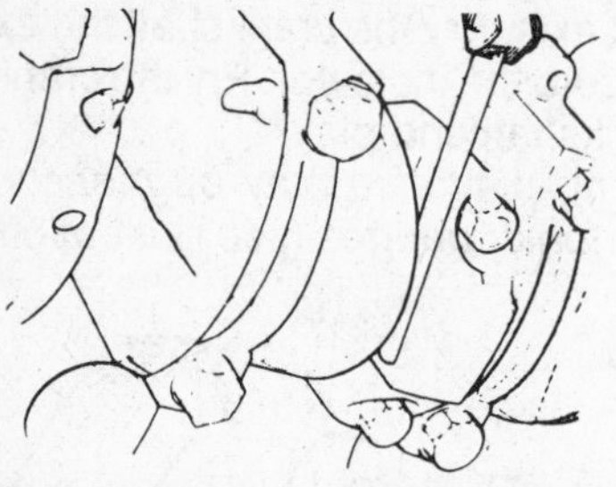 Checking connecting rod side clearance | Determine the clearance between the sides of the connecting rods and the crankshaft, using feeler gauges. If clearance is below the minimum tolerance, the rod may be machined to provide adequate clearance. If clearance is excessive, substitute an unworn rod, and recheck. If clearance is still outside specifications, the crankshaft must be welded and reground, or replaced. |
| Inspect the timing chain (or belt): | Visually inspect the timing chain for broken or loose links, and replace the chain if any are found. If the chain will flex sideways, it must be replaced. Install the timing chain as specified. Be sure the timing belt is not stretched, frayed or broken. NOTE: *If the original timing chain is to be reused, install it in its original position.* |
| Check timing gear backlash and runout (OHV engines): 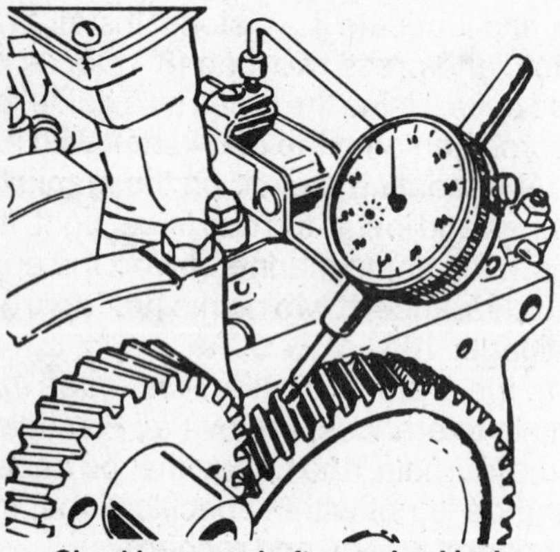 Checking camshaft gear backlash | Mount a dial indicator with its stem resting on a tooth of the camshaft gear (as illustrated). Rotate the gear until all slack is removed, and zero the indicator. Rotate the gear in the opposite direction until slack is removed, and record gear backlash. Mount the indicator with its stem resting on the edge of the camshaft gear, parallel to the axis of the camshaft. Zero the indicator, and turn the camshaft gear one full turn, recording the runout. If either backlash or runout exceed specifications, replace the worn gear(s).  Checking camshaft gear runout |

### *Completing the Rebuilding Process*

Following the above procedures, complete the rebuilding process as follows:

Fill the oil pump with oil, to prevent cavitating (sucking air) on initial engine start up. Install the oil pump and the pickup tube on the engine. Coat the oil pan gasket as necessary, and install the gasket and the oil pan. Mount the flywheel and the crankshaft vibration damper or pulley on the crankshaft. NOTE: *Always use new bolts when installing the flywheel.*
Inspect the clutch shaft pilot bushing in the crankshaft. If the bushing is excessively worn, remove it with an expanding puller and a slide hammer, and tap a new bushing into place.

Position the engine, cylinder head side up. Lubricate the lifters, and install them into their bores. Install the cylinder head, and torque it as specified. Insert the pushrods (where applicable), and install the rocker shaft(s) (if so equipped) or position the rocker arms on the pushrods. Adjust the valves.

Install the intake and exhaust manifolds, the carburetor(s), the distributor and spark plugs. Adjust the point gap and the static ignition timing. Mount all accessories and install the engine in the car. Fill the radiator with coolant, and the crankcase with high quality engine oil.

### *Break-in Procedure*

Start the engine, and allow it to run at low speed for a few minutes, while checking for leaks. Stop the engine, check the oil level, and fill as necessary. Restart the engine, and fill the cooling system to capacity. Check the point dwell angle and adjust the ignition timing and the valves. Run the engine at low to medium speed (800–2500 rpm) for approximately ½ hour, and retorque the cylinder head bolts. Road test the car, and check again for leaks.

Follow the manufacturer's recommended engine break-in procedure and maintenance schedule for new engines.

# CV-Joint/U-Joint Overhaul 29

## CONSTANT VELOCITY JOINTS

Front wheel drive vehicles present several unique problems to engineers because the driveshaft must do three things, simultaneously. It must allow the wheels to turn for steering, telescope to compensate for road surface vibrations, and it must transmit torque continuously without vibration.

To compensate for these three factors a two-joint driveshaft allows the front wheels to perform these functions. This driveshaft mates disc type straight groove ball joint design with the bell type Rzeppa CV universal joint.

The Rzeppa joint on the outboard end of each driveshaft provides steering ability by allowing drive wheels to steer up to 43° while transmitting all available torque to the wheels. The inboard joint allows telescoping (up to 1½″) through the rolling action of balls in straight grooves and operates at angles up to 20°. The combined action of these two ball type u-joints eliminates vibration.

The typical front wheel drive vehicle uses two driveshaft assemblies—one to each driving wheel. Each assembly has a CV-joint at the wheel end called the outboard joint. A second joint on each shaft located at the transaxle end is called the inboard joint. This joint may be either the ball or tripode type. It allows the slip motion required when the driveshaft must shorten or lengthen in response to suspension action when traveling over an irregular surface.

Constant velocity joints are precision machined parts that have difficult jobs to perform in a hostile environment. They are exposed to heat, shock, torque, and many thousands of miles of service. For this reason, the lubricants used are specially formulated to be compatible with the rubber boot and give proper lubrication. Most CV-joint repair kits have this special lubricant included.

**NOTE: Wear pattern in a used ball or tripode CV-joint are impossible to match during reassembly. If there are any signs of wear, abnormal operating noise, corrosion, heat discoloration, the joint must be replaced.**

### TROUBLESHOOTING

Noises from the engine, drive axles, suspension and steering in the front drive cars can be misleading to the untrained ear. Ideally a smooth road serves best for detecting operating condition(s) that cause noise.

- A humming noise could indicate that early stage of insufficient or incorrect lubricant.
- Worn driveshaft joints will cause a continuous knock at low speeds.

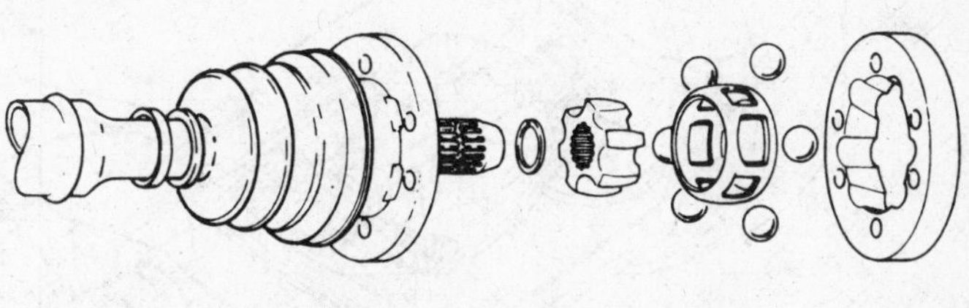

Ball style (Rzeppa) plunging CV joint

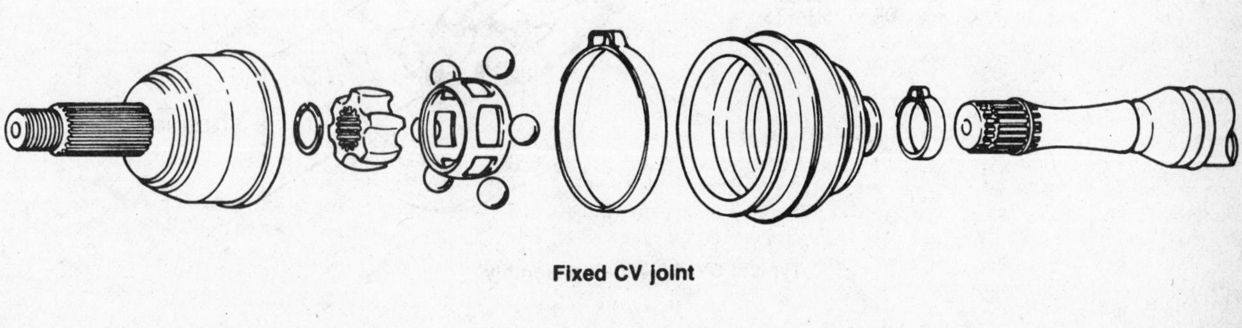

Fixed CV joint

• A popping or clicking sound on sharp turns indicates trouble in the outer or wheel end joint.

• The clunk noise at acceleration from coasting or deceleration from a load pull indicates two possibilities—damaged inner or transaxle joint or differential problem(s).

• An inner joint will create a vibration during acceleration due to plunging action hanging up and releasing repeatedly. Probable cause would be foreign particles or lack of lubrication, or improper assembly.

• Remember that tires, suspension, engine, and exhaust system are all up front to add their noises.

• Make a check with front wheels elevated off ground. Spin the wheels by hand to determine if wheel bearing could be noisy or if out of round tires are causing vibration. Many wheel bearings are prelubed and sealed at the factory.

**CAUTION**

***Personal injury can occur from spinning wheels by engine power. Spinning a wheel at excess speed may cause damage to CV-joints that could be operating at angles too steep when wheels are allowed to hang. Over speeding might also cause damage to tires and the differential.***

## SHAFT REMOVAL

1. Remove the hub nut and discard it.
2. Drain the lubricant from the transaxle.

**CAUTION**

***The lubricant may be hot.***

3. The speedometer pinion gear assembly must be removed before the right drive shaft can be removed. (Automatic transaxles only).
4. Rotate the driveshaft to view the circlip.
5. Compress the circlip tangs with needle nose pliers as you pry into the side gear. This compresses the circlip in position for shaft removal later. Keep an awl between the differential pinion shaft and the end face of the shaft to prevent circlip reentry to the groove.
6. Remove the ball joint clamp bolt. Drop the lower arm too allow clearance. This will permit the front wheel to swing free.
7. Pull the outer splined shaft from the wheel hub, when swinging wheel hub away. Do not pull on the shaft. Grasp the joint housing.
8. Remove the inner joint by pulling outward on the inner joint housing. Do not pull the shaft.

**NOTE: Do not allow the assembly to hang at either end. This can jam the CV-joint and cause vibration during operation. If necessary, support the shaft at either end by rope or wire.**

## INNER JOINT/BOOT

9. Place the assembly in a vise. Care must be taken not the crush the tubular shafts. Some shafts are solid steel.
10. If the inner joint needs replacement, cut the small rubber clamp, large metal clamp, and remove the rubber boot. These items must be discarded.
11. Inspect for internal wear and/or damage.
12. Clean the grease by hand from inside the joint housing and around the 3 ball trunnion assembly to inspect. Mark the tripod and housing for proper reassembly, if it is to be reinstalled.
13. To replace the boot, CV-joint, or both, remove the snap ring from the groove and tap the trunnion lightly with a brass drift pin. Leave the tripode bearings on the

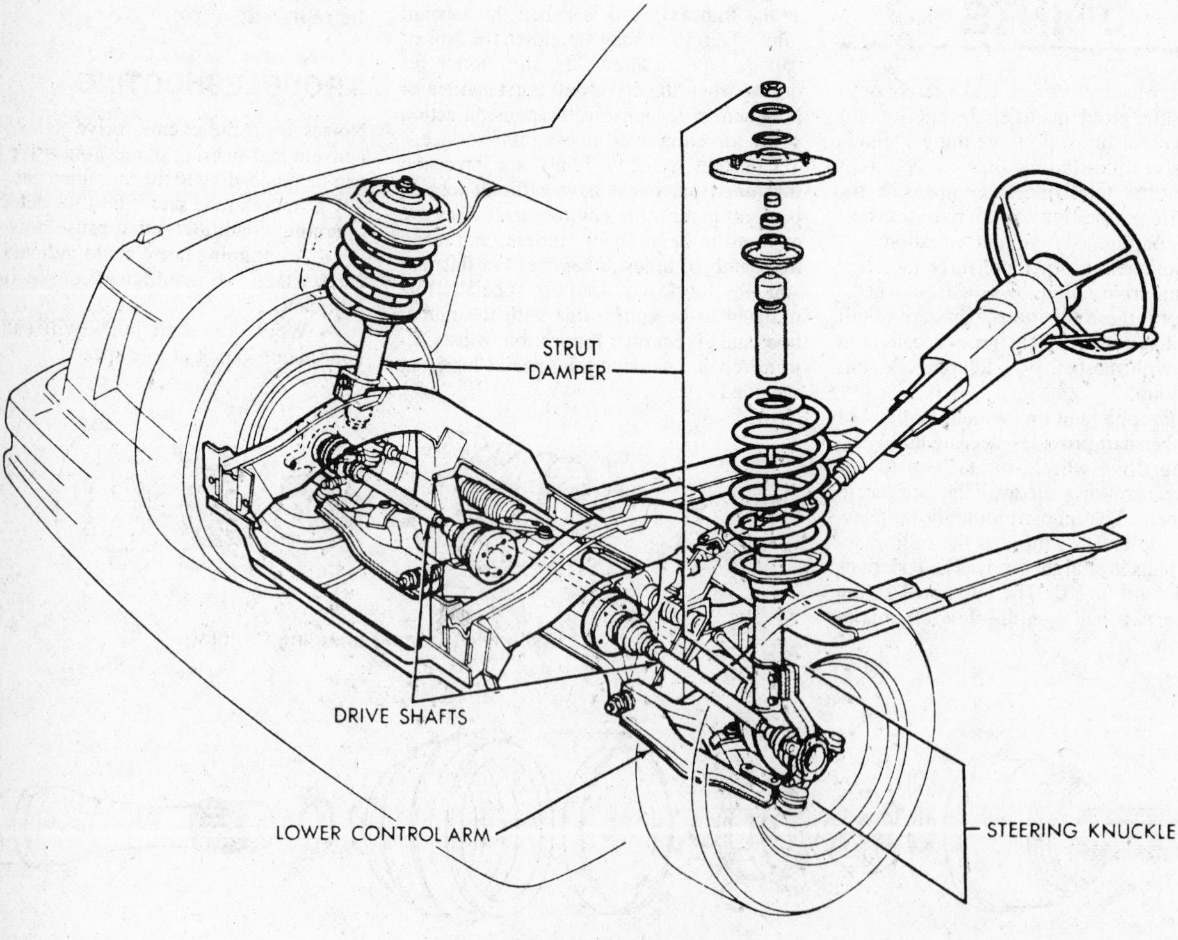


Typical CV driveshaft assembly

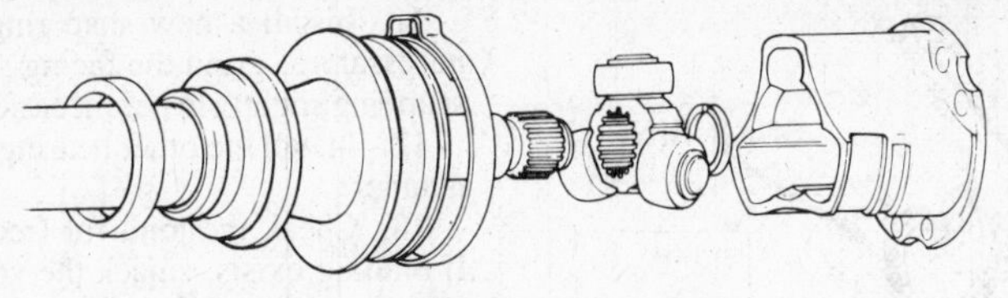

Closed tulip plunging CV joint

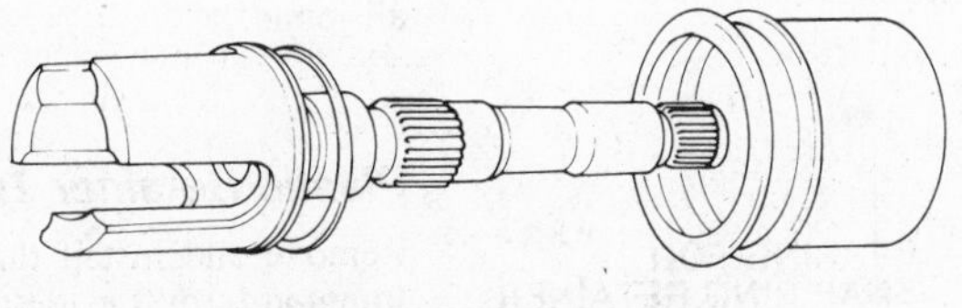

Open tulip plunging CV joint

trunnion. Care must be taken to support the bearings as they may fall off.

14. Installation is the reverse of removal with the following recommendations: When reinstalling the tripode on the shaft place the chamfer face toward the retainer groove. The grease provided with the repair kit must be used. It can not be substituted with any other type grease.

## OUTER JOINT/BOOT

1. Place the shaft in a vise. Be careful not to over tighten the vise thereby damaging the shaft.
2. Remove the boot and clamps. Discard these parts.
3. Using a soft hammer rap sharply on the housing. This forces the inner race over the internal circlip. Never remove the slinger from the housing.
4. Remove and discard the circlip. A new one is included with the boot kit. Leave the lock ring in place.

**NOTE: Never disassemble the cage and balls from the housing. Reuse the joint assembly with a new boot kit, unless the grease is contaminated and prior diagnosis indicated trouble. In that case replace the joint and boot.**

5. Installation is the reverse of removal.

# UNIVERSAL JOINTS

U-joint is mechanic's jargon for universal joint. U-joints should not be confused with U-bolts, which are U-shaped bolts used to connect U-joints to the differential pinion flange.

Universal joints provide flexibility between the driveshaft and axle housing to accommodate changes in the angle between them (changes of length are accommodated by the sliding splined yoke between the driveshaft and transmission). The engine and transmission are mounted rigidly on the car frame, while the driving wheels are free to move up and down in relation to the frame. The angles between the transmission, driveshaft and axle change constantly as the car responds to various road conditions.

To give flexibility and still transmit power as smoothly as possible, several types of universal joints are used.

The most common type of universal joint is the cross and yoke type. Yokes are used on the ends of the driveshaft with the yoke arms opposite each other. Another yoke is used opposite the driveshaft and when placed together, both yokes engage a center member, or cross, with four arms spaced 90° apart (the U-joint cross is alternately referred to as a spider, and the arms are called trunnions). A bearing cup (or cap) is used on each arm of the cross to accommodate movement as the driveshaft rotates. The bearings used are needle bearings.

A conventional universal joint will cause the driveshaft to speed up and slow down through each revolution and cause a corresponding change in the velocity of the driven shaft. This change in speed causes natural vibrations to occur through the driveline, necessitating a third type of universal joint: the constant velocity joint. A rolling ball moves in a curved groove, located between two yoke-and-cross universal joints, connected to each other by a coupling yoke. The result is a uniform motion as the driveshaft rotates, avoiding the fluctuations in driveshaft speed. This type of joint is found in cars with sharp driveline angles, or where the extra measure of isolation is desirable.

## CROSS AND YOKE U-JOINT OVERHAUL

There are two types of cross and yoke U-joints. One type retains the cross within the yoke with C-shaped snap rings. The second type of joint is held together by injection molded plastic retainer rings. The second type cannot be reassembled with the same parts, once disassembled. However, repair kits are available.

### *Snap-Ring Type*

1. Remove the driveshaft. For the correct procedure, see the car section for the model you are working on.
2. If the front yoke is to be disassembled, matchmark the driveshaft and sliding splined yoke (transmission yoke) so that driveline balance is preserved upon reassembly. Remove the snap rings which retain the bearing caps.
3. Select two sockets, one small enough

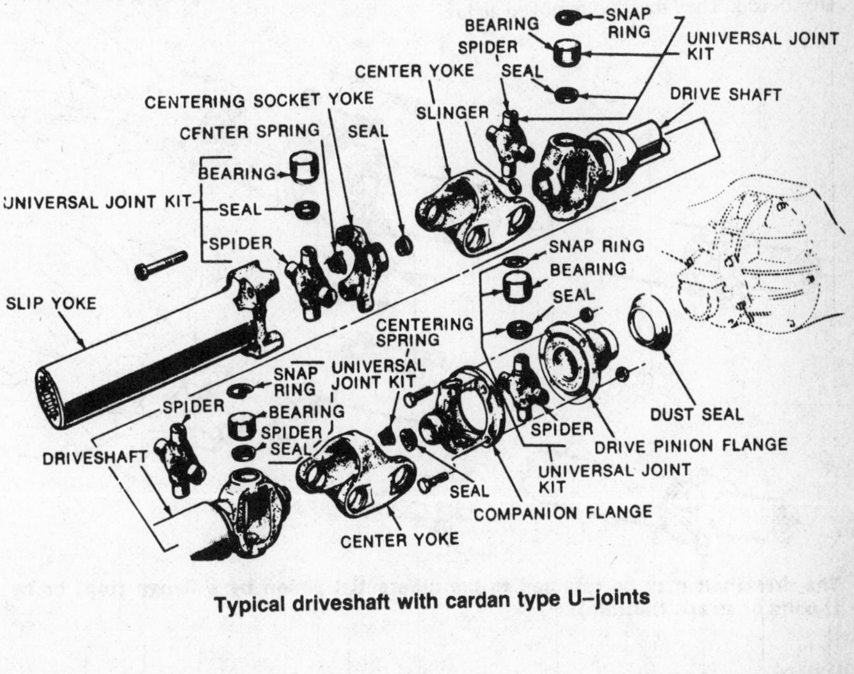


Typical driveshaft with cardan type U–joints

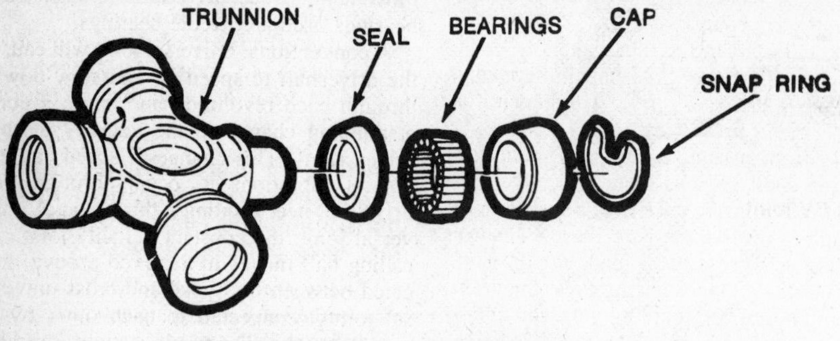


**Snap ring type universal joint**

11. Install a new snap ring. It may be necessary to grind the facing surface of the snap ring slightly to permit easier installation.

12. Install the other bearings in the same manner.

13. Check the joint for free movement. If binding exists, smack the yoke ears with a brass or plastic faced hammer to seat the bearing needles. Do not strike the bearings, and support the shaft firmly. Do not install the driveshaft until free movement exists at all joints.

to pass through the yoke holes for the bearing caps, the other large enough to receive the bearing cap.

4. Using a vise or a press, position the small and large sockets on either side of the U-joint. Press in on the smaller socket so that it presses the opposite bearing cap out of the yoke and into the larger socket. If the cap does not come all the way out, grasp it with a pair of pliers and work it out.

5. Reverse the position of the sockets so that the smaller socket presses on the cross. Press the other bearing cap out of the yoke.

6. Repeat the procedure on the other bearings.

7. To install, grease the bearing caps and needles thoroughly if they are not pregreased. Start a new bearing cap into one side of the yoke. Position the cross in the yoke.

8. Select two sockets small enough to pass through the yoke holes. Put the sockets against the cross and the cap, and press the bearing cap ¼ inch below the surface of the yoke. If there is a sudden increase in the force needed to press the cap into place, or if the cross starts to bind, the bearings are cocked. They must be removed and restarted in the yoke. Failure to do so will greatly reduce the life of the bearing.

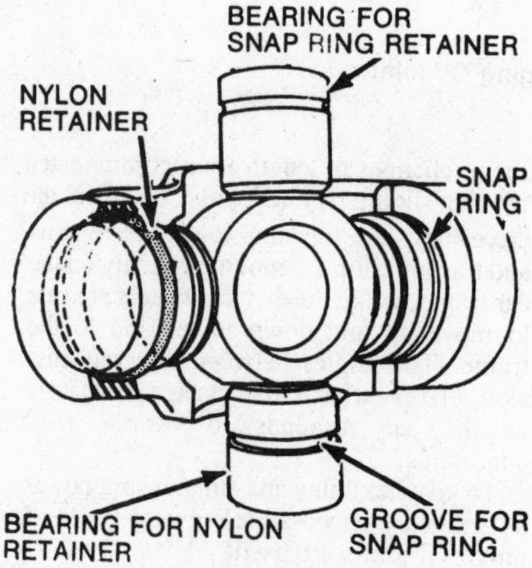


**U-joint locking methods**

9. Install a new snap ring.

10. Start a new bearing into the opposite side. Place a socket on it and press in until the opposite bearing contacts the snap ring.

### *Plastic Retainer Type*

Remove and install the bearing caps and trunnion (cross) as described for the snap-ring type universal joints. On an original universal joint, however, the bearing caps will be secured in the yokes with injected plastic. The plastic will shear when the bearing caps are pressed. Service snap-rings are installed in the groove on the inside (of yoke) of the installed caps.

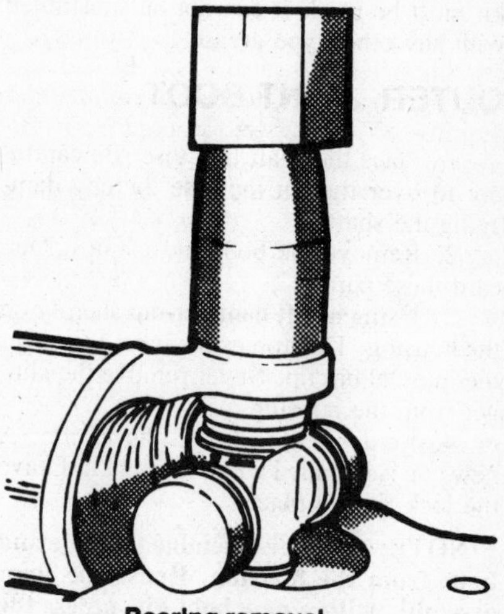

**Bearing removal**

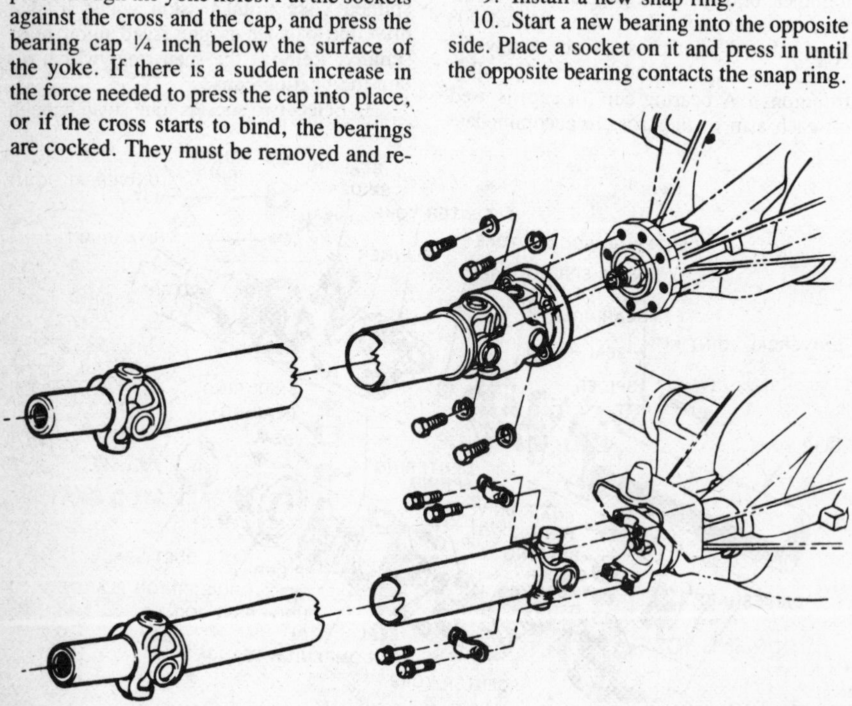

**The driveshaft may be retained to the differential pinion by a flange (top) or by U-bolts or straps (bottom)**

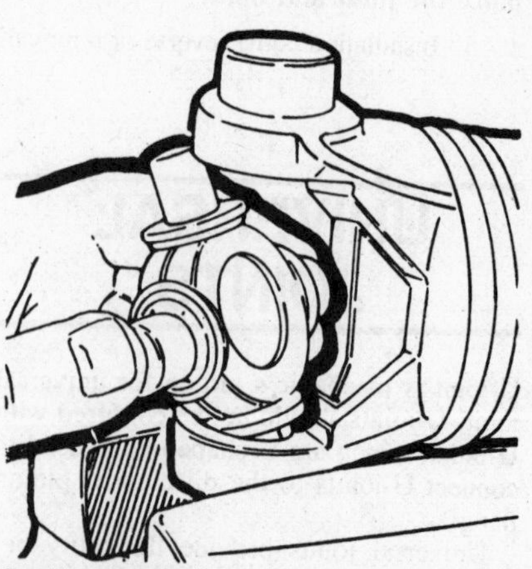

**Press a bearing cap into the yoke, then install the cross**

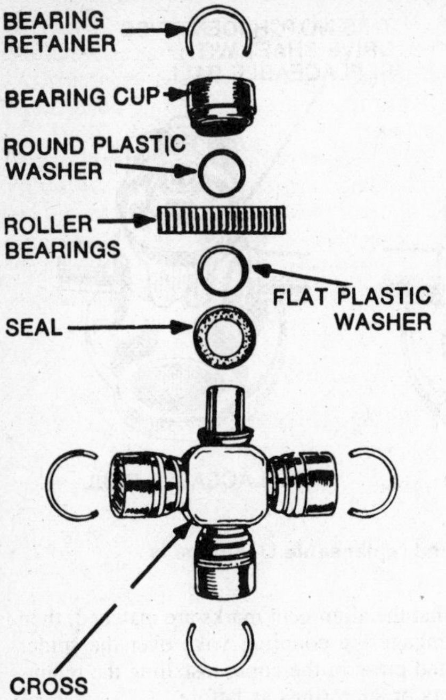


**Plastic retainer U-joint repair kit components**

**NOTE: The plastic which retains the bearing will be sheared when the bearing cup is pressed out. Be sure to remove the remains of the plastic retainer from the ears of the yoke. It is easier to remove the remains if a small pin or punch is first driven through the injection holes in the yoke. Failure to remove all of the plastic remains may prevent the bearing cups from being pressed into place and the bearing retainers from being properly seated.**

## CARDAN TYPE U-JOINT OVERHAUL

Some with Cardan type U-joints use snap rings to retain the bearing cups in the yokes. Other cars have plastic retainers. Be sure to obtain the correct rebuilding kit.

1. Use a punch to mark the coupling yoke and the adjoining yokes before disassembly, to ensure proper reassembly and driveline balance.

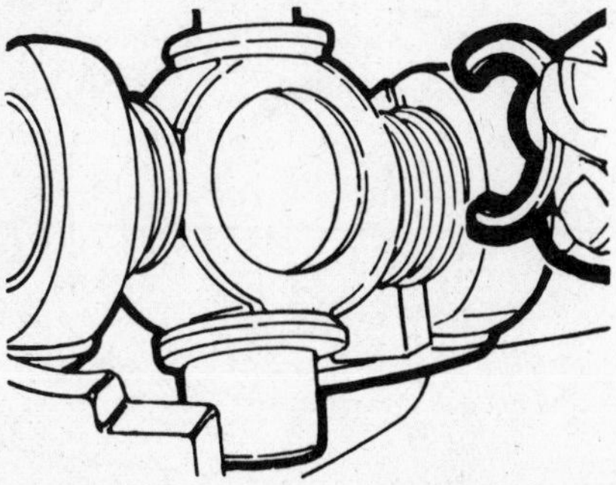

**Service snap rings are installed inside the yoke**

2. It is easiest to remove the bearings from the coupling yoke first. Follow the order indicated in the illustration.
3. Support the driveshaft horizontally on a press stand, or on the workbench if a vise is being used.
4. If snap rings are used to retain the bearing cups, remove them. Place the rear ear of the coupling yoke over a socket large enough to receive the cup. Place a smaller socket, or a cross press made for the purpose, over the opposite cup. Press the bearing cup out of the coupling yoke ear. If the cup is not completely removed, insert a spacer and complete the operation, or grasp the cup with a pair of slip joint pliers and work it out. If the cups are retained by plastic, this will shear the retainers. Remove any bits of plastic.
5. Rotate the driveshaft and repeat the operation on the opposite cup.
6. Disengage the trunnions of the spider, still attached to the flanged yoke, from the coupling yoke, and pull the flanged yoke and spider from the center ball on the ball support tube yoke.

**NOTE: The joint between the shaft and coupling yoke can be serviced without disassembly of the joint between the coupling yoke and flanged yoke.**

7. Pry the seal from the ball cavity, remove the washers, spring and three seats. Examine the ball stud seat and the ball stud for scores or wear. Worn parts can be replaced with a kit. Clean the ball seat cavity and fill it with grease. Install the spring, washer, ball seats, and spacer (washer) over the ball.
8. To assemble, insert one bearing cup

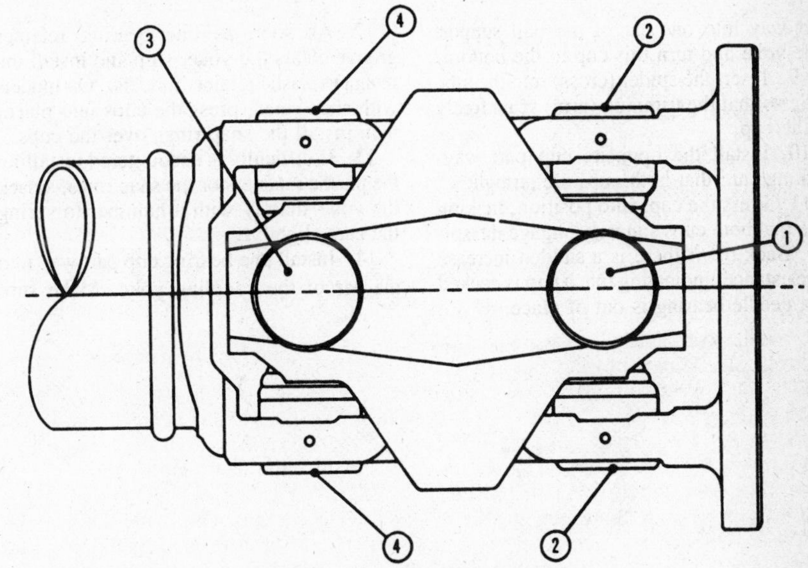


**Cardan joint disassembly sequence**

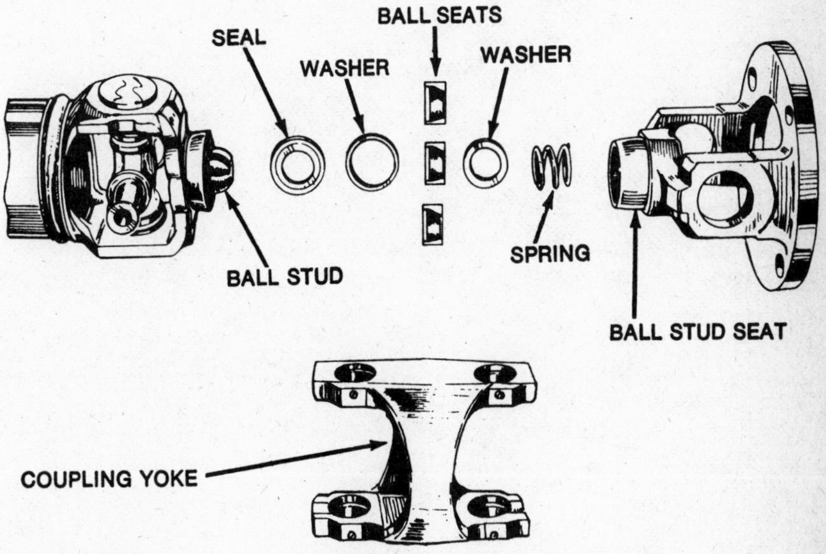


**Cardan type joint**

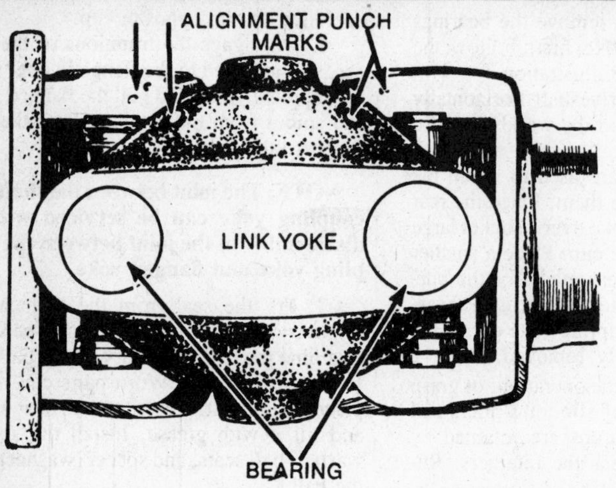


**Match marks for double cardan joint**

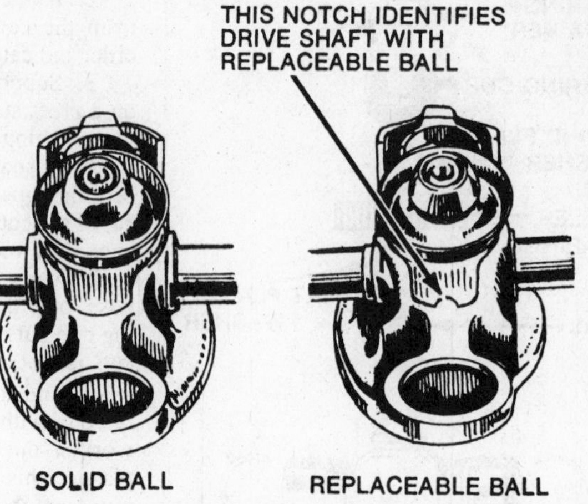


**Solid and replaceable U-joint balls**

part way into one ear of the ball support tube yoke and turn this cup to the bottom.

9. Insert the spider (cross) into the tube yoke so that the trunnion (arm) seats freely in the cup.

10. Install the opposite cup part way, making sure that both cups are straight.

11. Press the cups into position, making sure that both cups squarely engage the spider. Back off if there is a sudden increase in resistance, indicating that a cup is cocked or a needle bearing is out of place.

12. As soon as one bearing retainer groove clears the yoke, stop and install the retainer (plastic retainer models). On models with snap rings, press the cups into place, then install the snap rings over the cups.

13. If difficulty is encountered installing the plastic retainers or the snap rings, smack the yoke sharply with a hammer to spring the ears slightly.

14. Install one bearing cup part way into the ear of the coupling yoke. Make sure that the alignment marks are matched, then engage the coupling yoke over the spider and press in the cups, installing the retainers or snap rings as before.

15. Install the cups and spider into the flanged yoke as with the previous yoke.

**NOTE: The flange yoke should snap over center to the right or left and up or down by the pressure of the ball seat spring.**

# Strut Overhaul 30

## STRUT SERVICE AND REPAIR

MacPherson struts are appearing on the front (and rear) wheels of more and more cars. The strut design takes up less room in the engine compartment, compared to a conventional upper and lower arm with shock absorber arrangement. The trend toward smaller, lighter and more efficient vehicles mandates the use of a strut suspension to permit more room for engine accessories and front wheel drive components.

### Strut Suspension Design

In a conventional front suspension, the wheel is attached to a spindle, which is in turn connected to upper and lower control arms through upper and lower ball joints. A coil spring between the control arms (sometimes on top of the upper arm) supports the weight of the vehicle and a shock absorber controls rebound and dampens oscillations.

In a MacPherson strut type suspension, the strut performs a shock dampening function like a shock absorber, but unlike a conventional shock absorber the strut is a structural part of the vehicle's suspension.

The strut assembly usually contains a spring seat to retain the coil spring that supports the vehicle's weight. The shock absorber is built into the body of the strut housing. The strut is normally attached at the bottom to the lower control arm and at

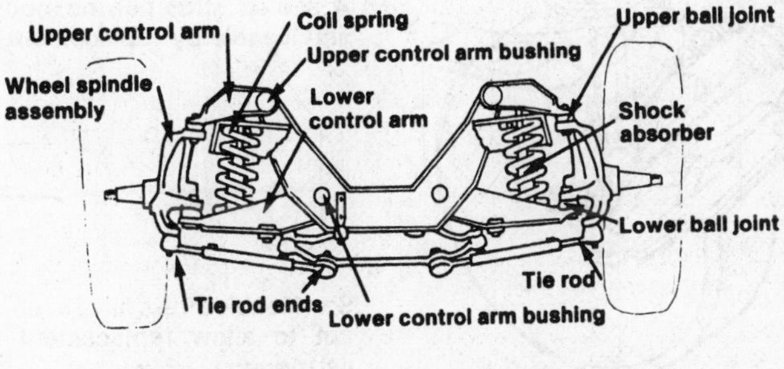

Conventional upper and lower arm suspension

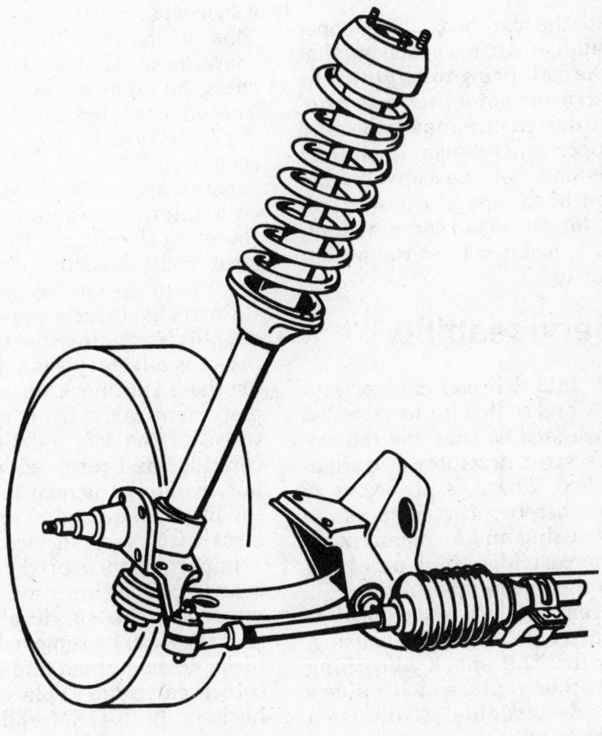
Strut with concentric coil spring (rear wheel drive)

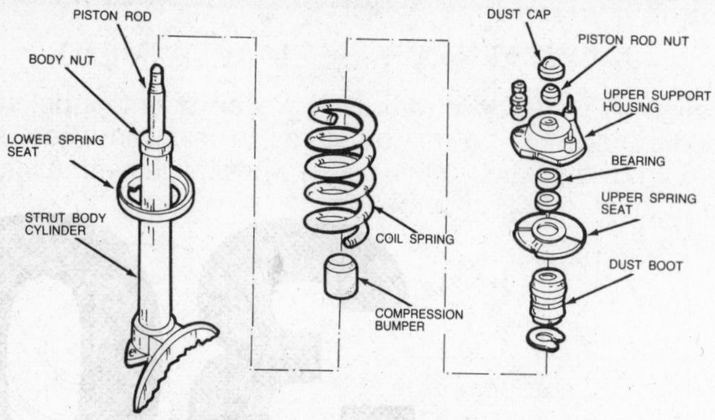


**Exploded view of a typical strut**

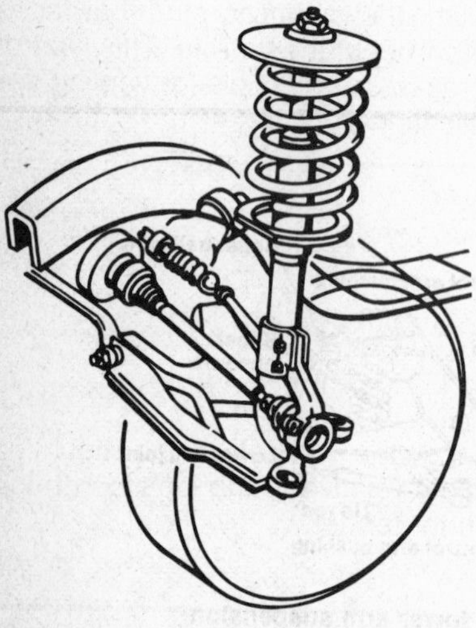

**Strut with concentric coil spring (front wheel drive)**

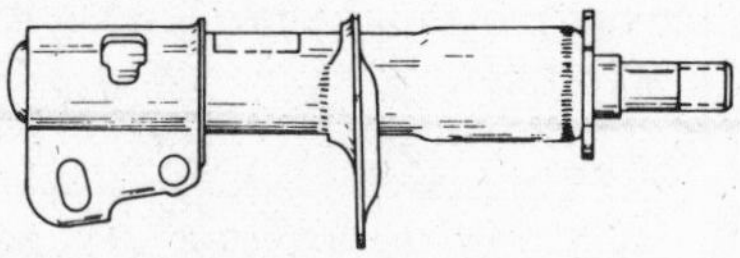

**A sealed strut has no body nut and is serviceable by replacement**

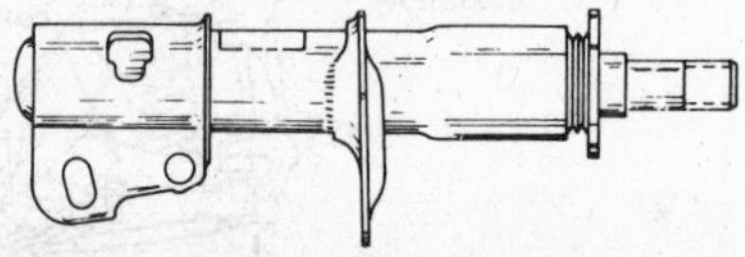

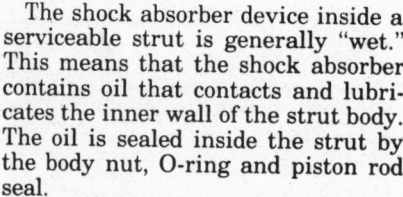

**Serviceable struts have a removeable body nut to allow replacement of the strut cartridge**

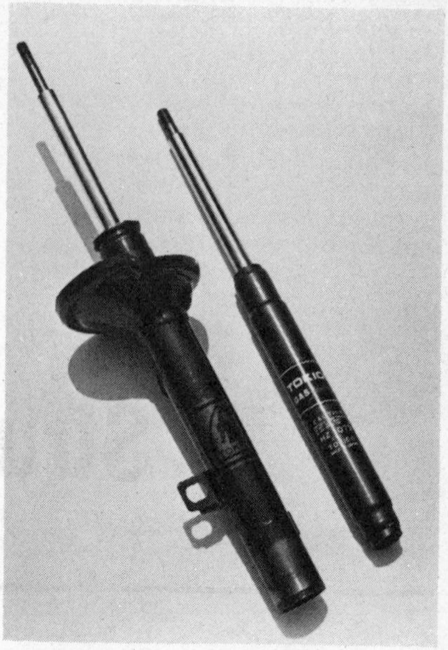

**A replacement sealed strut on the left, compared to a replacement strut cartridge used on serviceable type struts on the right**

the top to the car body. The upper mount usually features a bearing that permits the coil spring to rotate as the wheels turn for smoother steering. The entire design eliminates the need for the upper control arm, upper ball joint and many of the conventional suspension bushings. The lower ball joint is no longer a load carrying unit, because it is isolated from the weight of the vehicle.

## Serviceability

Struts fall into 2 broad categories – serviceable and sealed units. A sealed strut is designed so that the top closure of the strut assembly is permanently sealed. There is no access to the shock absorber cartridge inside the strut housing and no means of replacing the cartridge. It is necessary to replace the entire strut unit.

A serviceable strut is designed so that the cartridge inside the housing, that provides the shock absorbing function, can be replaced with a new cartridge. Serviceable struts use a threaded body nut in place of a sealed cap to retain the cartridge.

The shock absorber device inside a serviceable strut is generally "wet." This means that the shock absorber contains oil that contacts and lubricates the inner wall of the strut body. The oil is sealed inside the strut by the body nut, O-ring and piston rod seal.

Servicing a "wet" strut with the equivalent components involves a thorough cleaning of the inside of the strut body, absolute cleanliness and great care in reassembly.

Cartridge inserts were developed to simplify servicing "wet" struts. The insert is a factory sealed replacement for the strut shock absorber. The replacement cartridge is simply substituted for the original shock absorber cartridge and retained with the body nut, avoiding the near laboratory-like conditions required to service a "wet" strut with "wet" service components.

Import cars use predominantly concentric coil spring units and, for the most part are serviceable, meaning that they can be removed from the vehicle, disassembled and the shock absorber cartridge replaced in the old housing. Both OEM and aftermarket replacement cartriges can be used in these struts if they are serviceable.

Exceptions to the serviceable struts include some of the later model import cars, but even on these cars OEM struts can be replaced with aftermarket sealed strut assemblies.

### WHEEL ALIGNMENT

It is not always necessary to re-align the wheels after struts are serviced. If care is taken matchmarking affected components and in reassembling, alignment may be unaffected. However, if wheels were not in proper alignment prior to service, or if the entire strut assembly was replaced, a wheel alignment check should be made. Generally, only camber is adjustable, and then only within a narrow range.

Do not attempt to bend components to correct wheel alignment.

Since the majority of OEM struts are serviced by replacement, most manufacturers recommend wheel alignment following strut replacement.

On most serviceable import struts, the position of the upper bearing plate or lower mount can be matchmarked and wheel alignment will be maintained during reassembly.

## Tools

Without the right tools, a strut job will take longer than necessary and can be dangerous.

A normal selection of hand tools such as open end and box wrenches, sockets, pliers, screwdrivers and hammers are necessary to work on struts.

Extensions and universal joints will help reach tight spots. Be sure to have both metric and inch-sized wrenches on hand.

In addition to the normal handtools, some sort of spanner is necessary to remove the body nut on serviceable struts. Sometimes a pipe wrench can be used successfully. Also a strut vise should be used to avoid damage to the strut housing during the overhaul procedure.

Strut and cartridge replacement requires a spring compressor.

Makeshift tools for compressing coil springs – threaded rod, chains, wire or other methods – should never be used. The coil spring is under tremendous compression and can fly off causing personal injury and damage to equipment. Use only a good quality spring compressor such as described below.

Economy, or manual, spring compressors are the least expensive but more time consuming to use. Angle hooks grasp the spring coils and must be compressed with a wrench. For those who service struts infrequently, this is probably the wisest investment for purchase.

**CAUTION**

***When using an "economy type" spring compressor be certain to install J-Bolts or U-Bolts around the coil spring-to-the-tool. This is to prevent the tool from slipping off the spring and causing personal injury.***

Other manual spring compressors (jaws type) are faster to operate, have a more positive gripping action and can be used on or off the car. These types are probably not cost effective for the do-it-yourselfer, but can be rented from auto supply stores for single-time use. These are also safer to use than the "economy type" spring compressors.

## MAINTAINING WHEEL ALIGNMENT

The location and method of adjusting wheel alignment determines the components that must be match-marked to maintain wheel alignment. There are 4 basic methods of adjusting wheel alignment. Almost all cars use one of these or a slight variation.

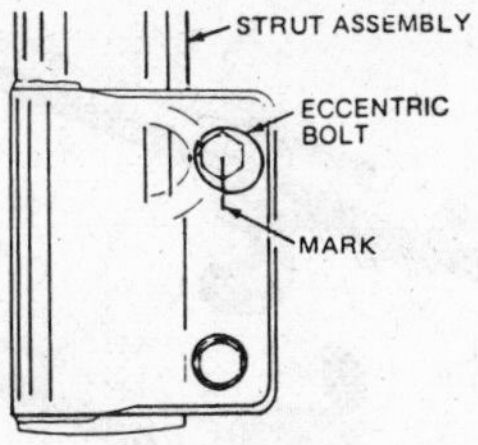


Mark the eccentric (camber adjusting bolt) relative to the clevis mounting bracket.

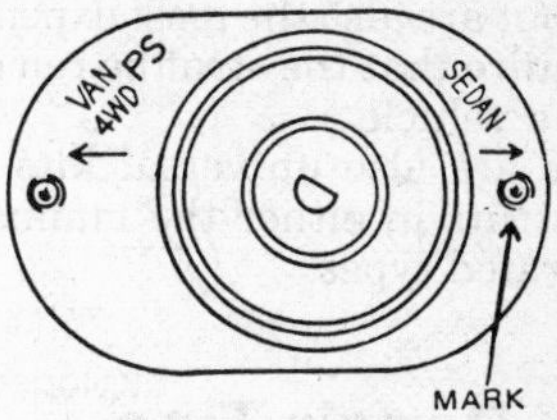


Mark the mounting stud that faces the front of the vehicle. This type of bracket is reversible for varying applications.

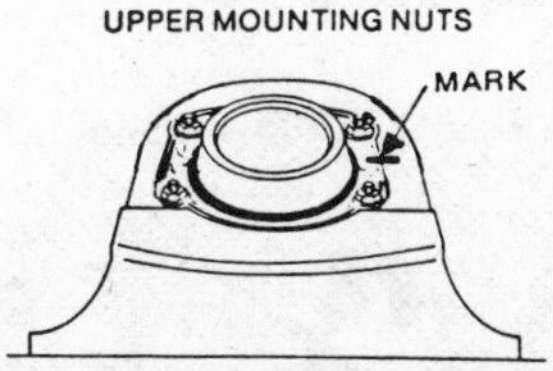


Mark the upper support housing relative to the inner fender before removing the strut from the upper mount.

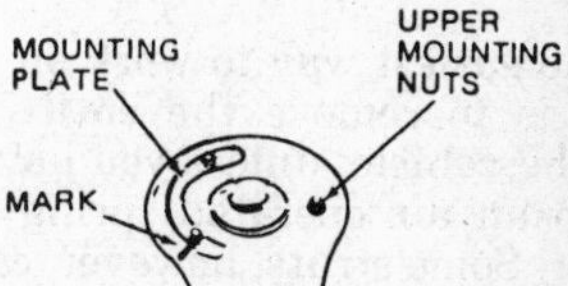


Mark the location of the mounting plate relative to the location on the inner fender.

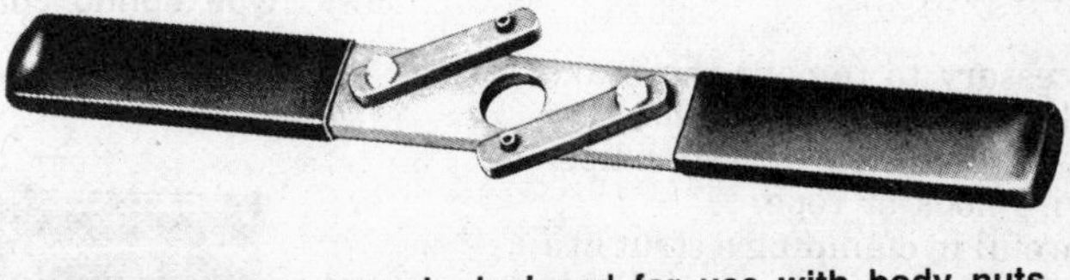

**A simple spanner wrench designed for use with body nuts equipped with recessed lugs. A pipe wrench is a frequent substitute**

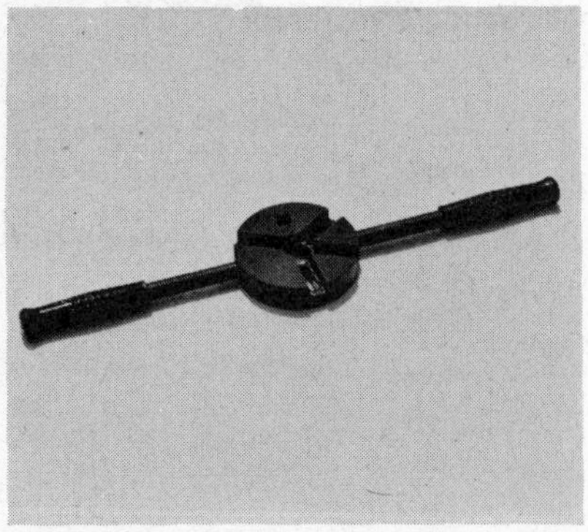

**This type of spanner wrench comes with adapter inserts for various applications of body nuts. A torque wrench can be used with this spanner for tightening the strut body nut**

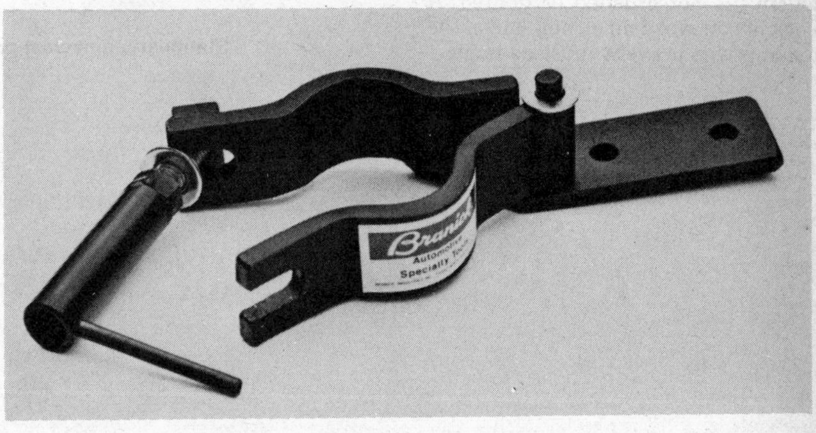


**A strut vise should be used to prevent damage to the strut housing during overhaul. It may be placed in a bench vise or mounted to a workbench**

For high volume work, compressors that are pneumatically or hydraulically operated are best. Air operated compressors are suitable for all types of struts (through use of adaptors), are lightweight and can be used on or off the vehicle. Bench mounted hydraulically operated units are probably the safest, but are also the most expensive and require that the strut be removed from the vehicle.

There are also universal kits that fit all struts in either the manual or air operated types.

## Repair Tips

• Make sure you have all the tools you'll need. NEVER IMPROVISE A SPRING COMPRESSOR.

• Normally both front struts should be repaired or replaced at the same time.

• The easiest way to work on most struts is to remove the entire unit from the vehicle, unless you have access to an air operated spring compressor. Some struts, however, can be repaired while installed on the vehicle.

• Always read the instructions packaged with any replacement parts. In particular, note whether the body nut is supplied new or re-used.

• Mark the position(s) of any bearing plate nuts or cam bolts to assure proper alignment after installation.

• Be sure to protect the rubber boot on the drive axle of front wheel drive cars.

• If necessary to remove the brake caliper, do not let the caliper hang by the brake hose. Suspend the caliper from a wire hook or rope.

• Be careful in clamping a strut in a vise. Special strut vises are available to hold struts, but are not absolutely necessary if care is used to be sure the housing is not crushed or dented. A block of soft wood on either side of the housing will prevent most damage.

• Use a spring compressor to relieve tension from the spring. Be sure to clean and lubricate the screw threads, particularly on hand operated (manual) spring compressors.

Some springs have a special coating that should not be scuffed.

• If you are replacing the strut cartridge, clean the inside of the strut housing and the body nut threads before replacing the oil and installing a new cartridge.

• Be sure to use OEM quality fasteners any time a fastener is replaced.

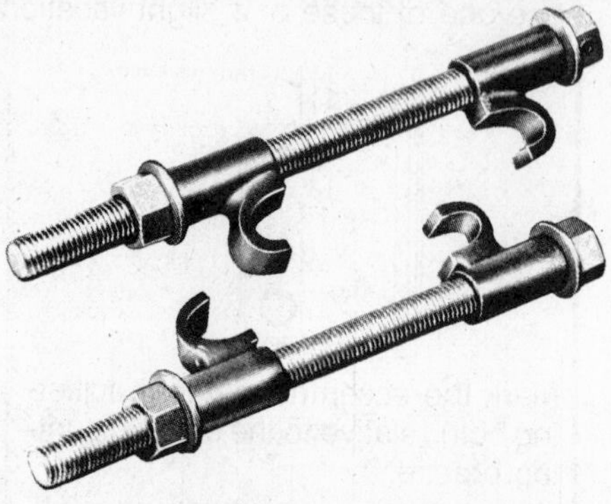

**An economical manual spring compressor**

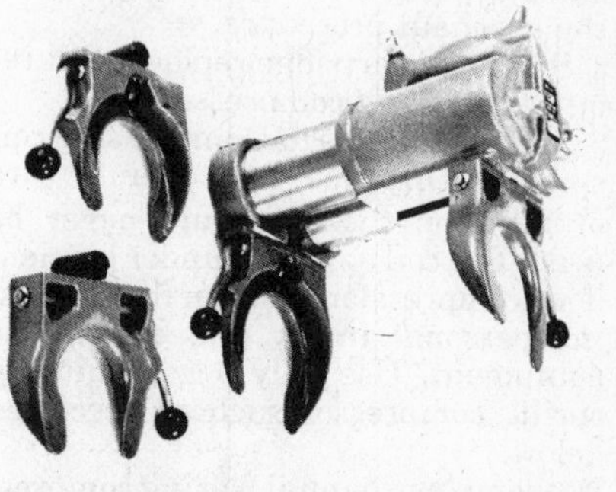

**Lightweight, air operated, portable spring compressor can be used on or off the vehicle. Extra shoes are available to handle all strut applications**

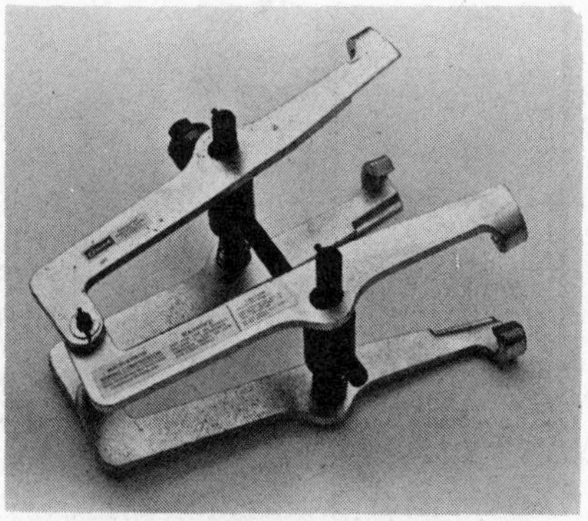

**"Jaws" type spring compressor**

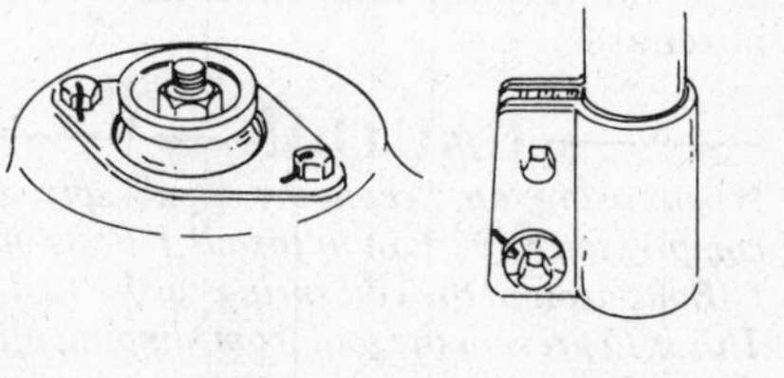

**Mark the position of the attachments that control wheel alignment. See Maintaining Wheel Alignment earlier in this section**

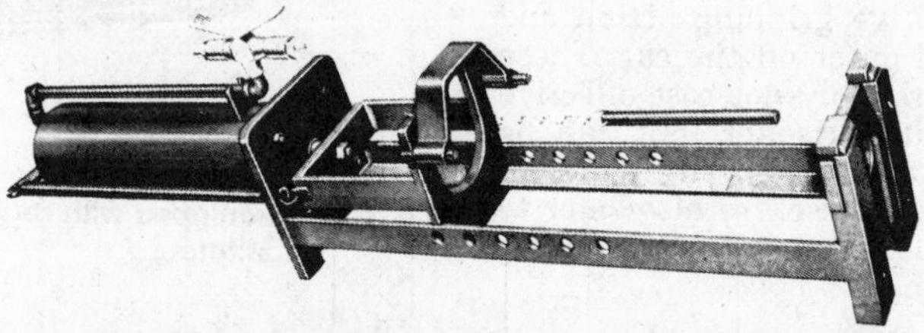

**Stationary, universal pneumatic spring compressor**

## STRUT OVERHAUL

Following is a typical overhaul procedure of a serviceable MacPherson strut, after having removed the strut from the vehicle. The vehicle should be firmly and safely supported on jackstands. If it is necessary, to separate the brake line from the strut for strut removal, the brakes will have to be bled after reinstallation. Examine the strut assembly for damage, dented strut body, spring seat, broken or missing strut mounting parts. Any of these will require replacement of the complete assembly. Also inspect other suspension components for wear or damage. See the manufacturer's car section for specific MacPherson strut removal and installation procedures.

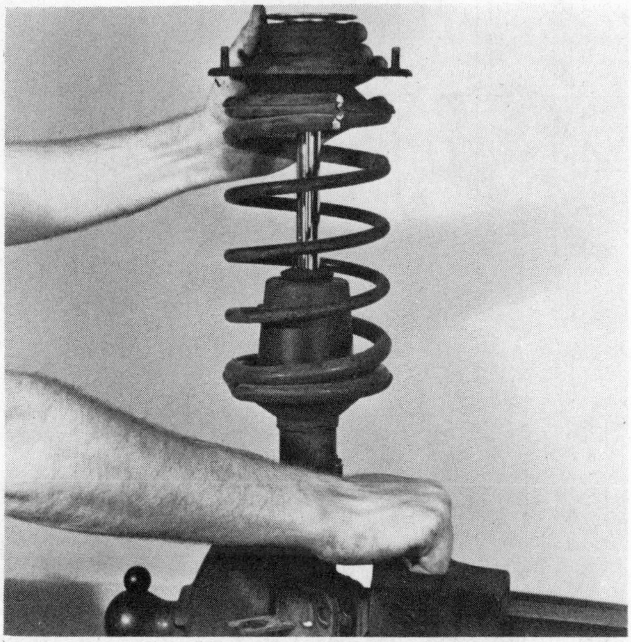

Step 1. **To make service easier, clamp the strut in a strut vise. The strut vise is designed to clamp the strut tight without damage to the strut cylinder. It is very handy for strut work and can be used in a bench vise or mounted to a workbench**

Step 2. **Matchmark the upper end of the coil spring and bearing plate to avoid confusion during reassembly**

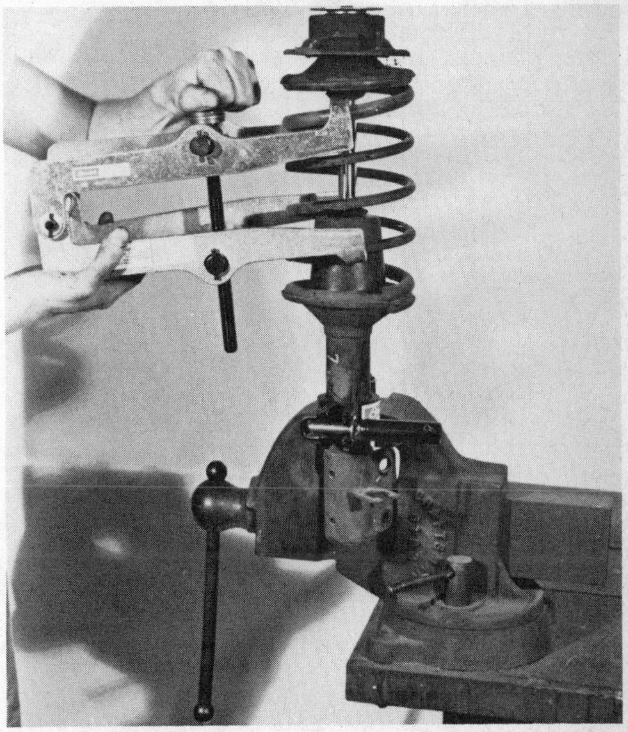

Step 3. **Position the spring compressor on the spring. Turn the load screw to open or close the compressor until the maximum number of spring coils can be engaged**

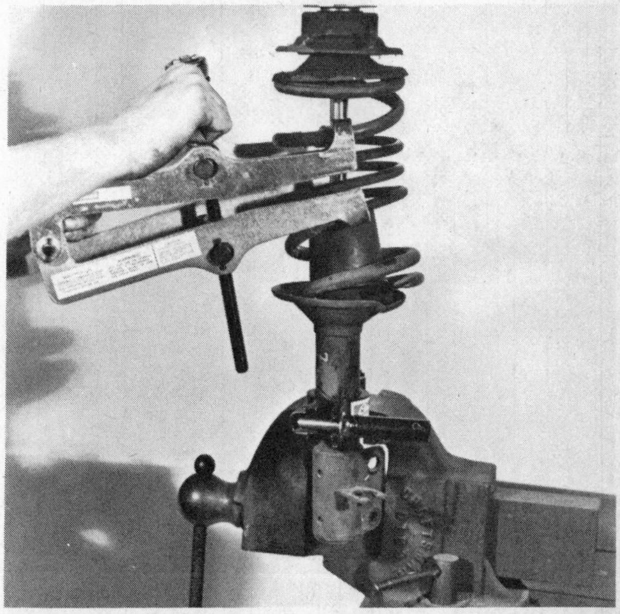

Step 4. **Tighten the load screw until the coil spring is loose from the spring seat. There is no need to compress the spring further than this point**

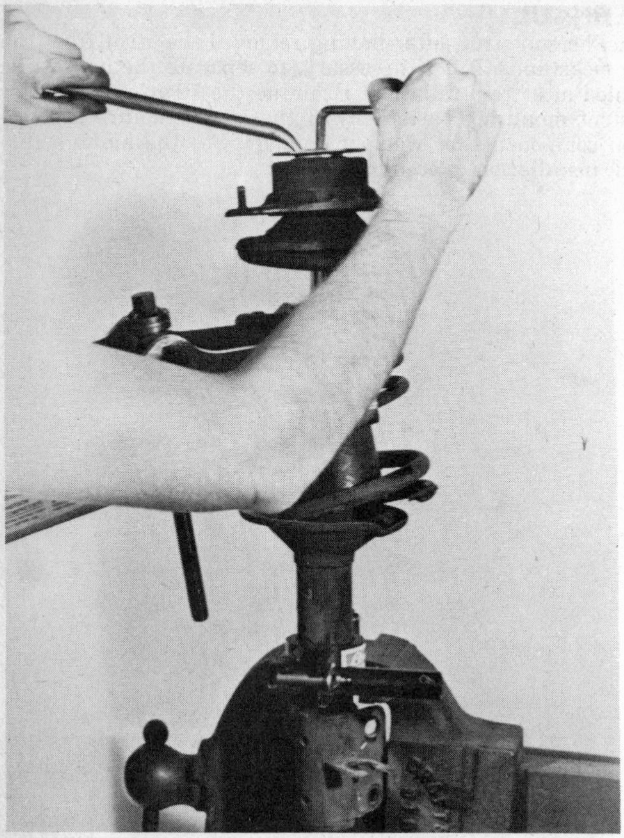

Step 5. **Using an offset wrench and an Allen wrench, loosen the piston rod nut**

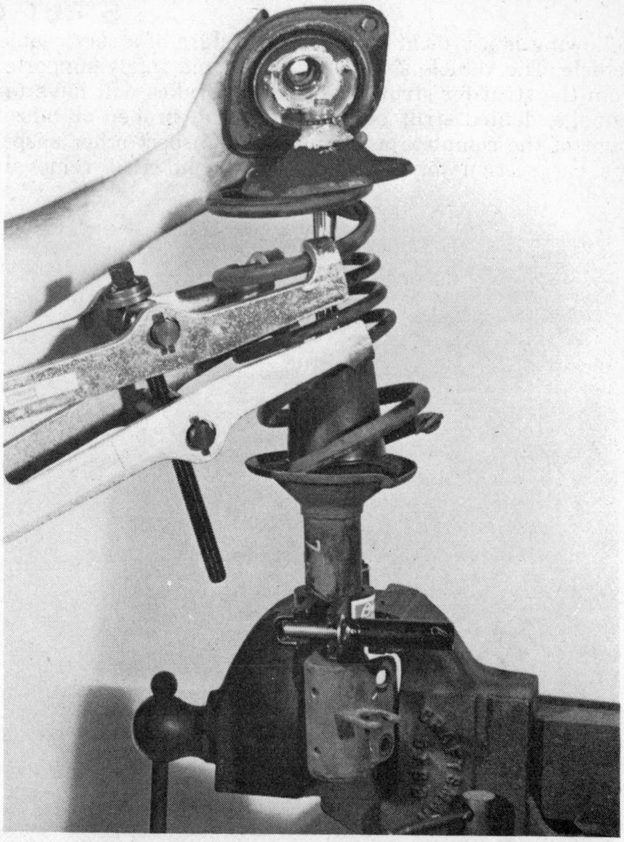

Step 7. **Disassemble the upper strut mounting parts. Keep the mounting parts in order of their removal. They'll be reassembled in reverse order**

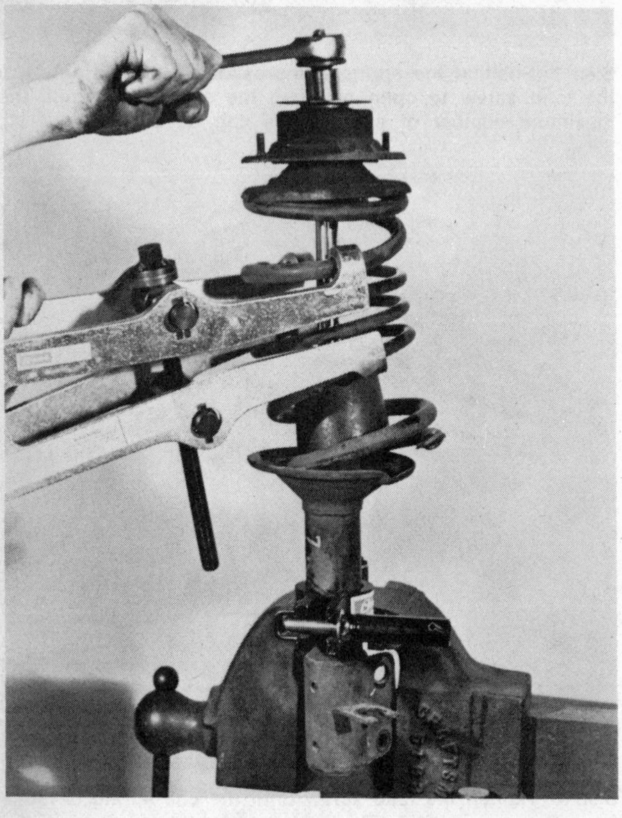

Step 6. **Remove the piston rod nut from the strut piston rod**

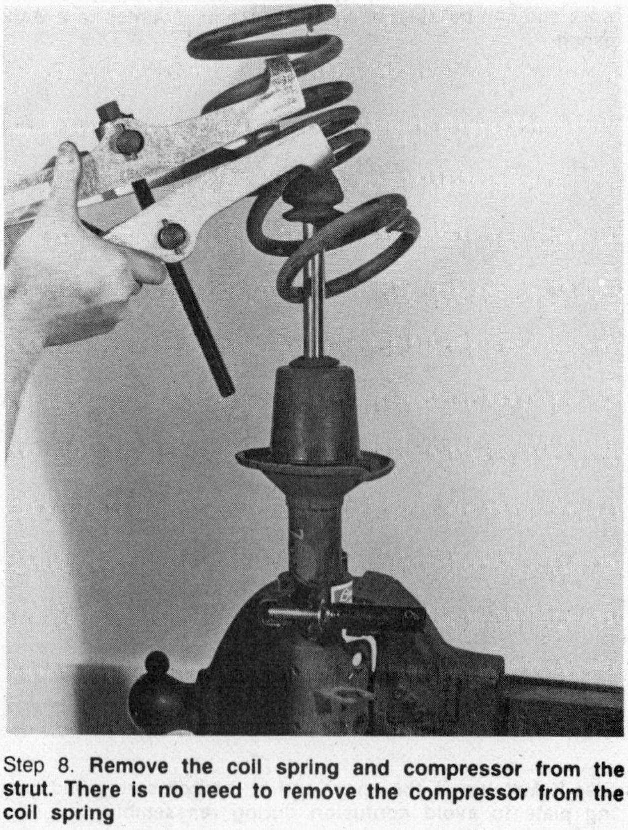

Step 8. **Remove the coil spring and compressor from the strut. There is no need to remove the compressor from the coil spring**

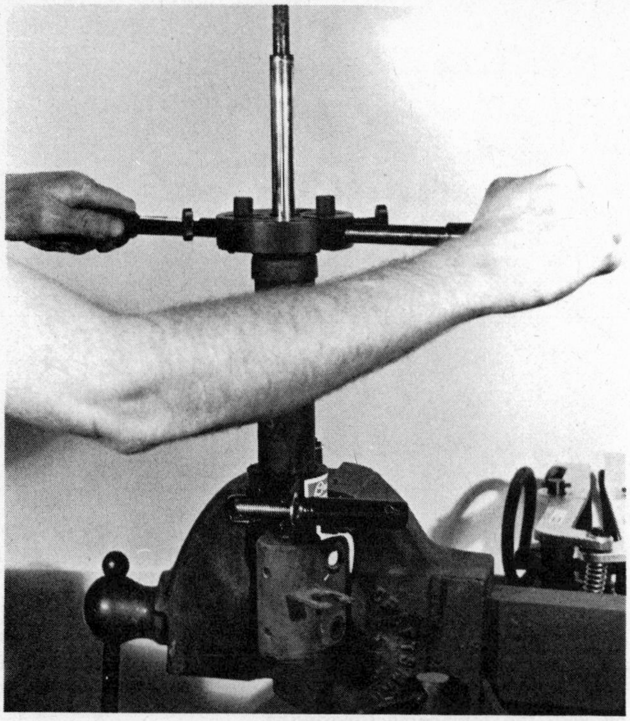

Step 9. **Use a spanner wrench or a pipe wrench to loosen the body nut**

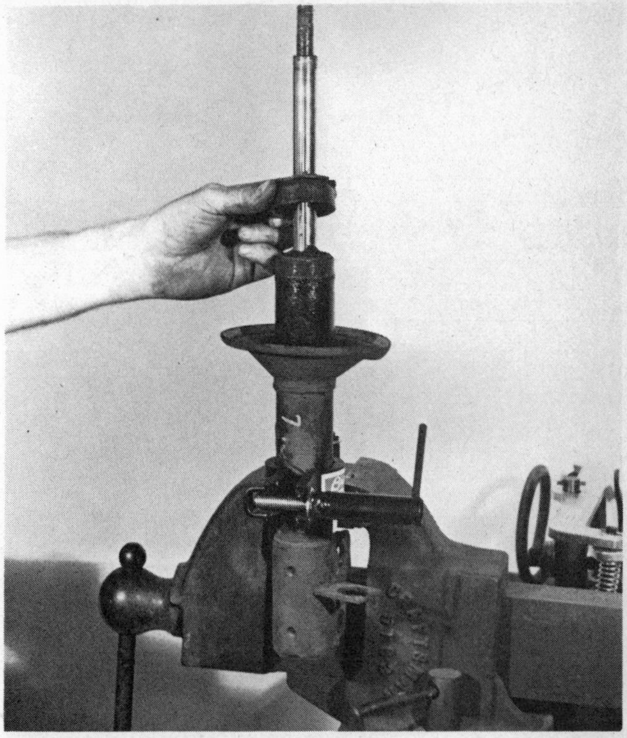

Step 10. **Remove the body nut and discard if a new body nut came with the replacement cartridge. If not, save the body nut**

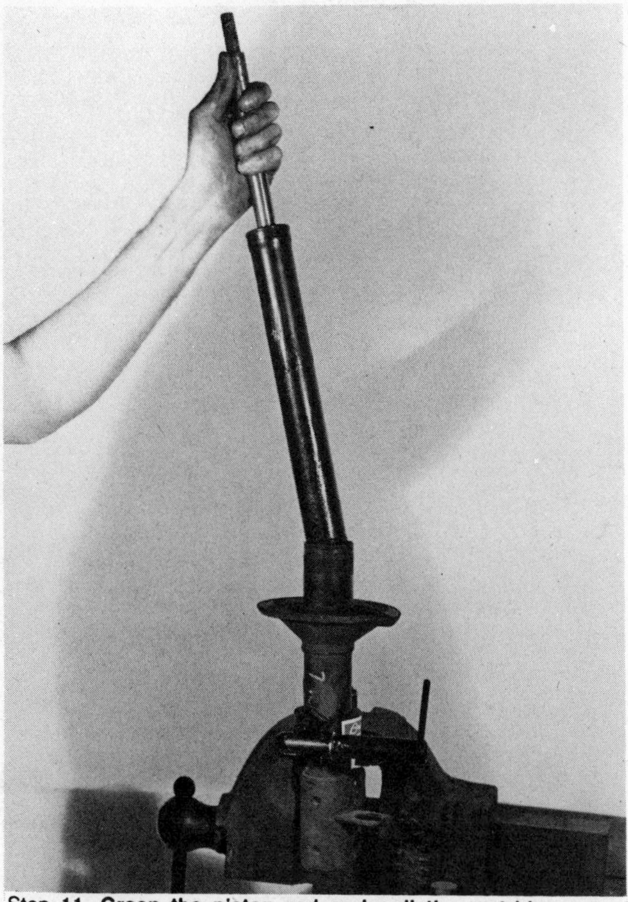

Step 11. **Grasp the piston rod and pull the cartridge out of the housing. Remove it slowly to avoid splashing oil. Be sure all pieces are removed from the housing**

Step 12. **Pour all of the strut fluid into a suitable container, clean the inside of the strut cylinder, and inspect the cylinder for dents and to insure that all loose parts have been remove from inside the strut body**

Step 13. **Refill the strut housing with approximately one once of the original oil or fresh oil. The oil helps dissipate internal cartridge heat during operation and results in a much cooler running, longer lasting unit. Do not overfill with oil—otherwise the oil may leak at the body nut after it expands when heated**

Step 15. **Insert any special bushings which should be included with the replacement cartridge**

Step 14. **Insert the new replacement strut cartridge into the strut body**

Step 16. **Place the body nut on the strut housing and start it by hand. Be sure not to cross-thread it**

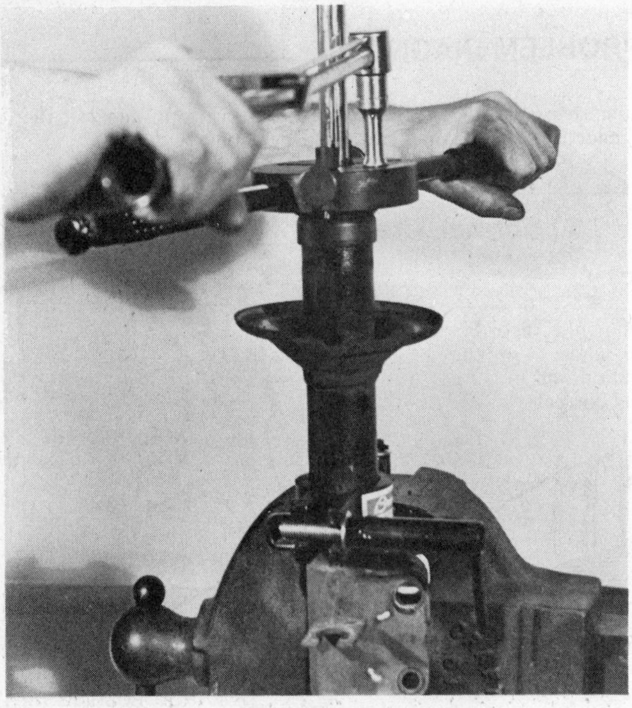

Step 17. **Tighten the body nut cap securely**

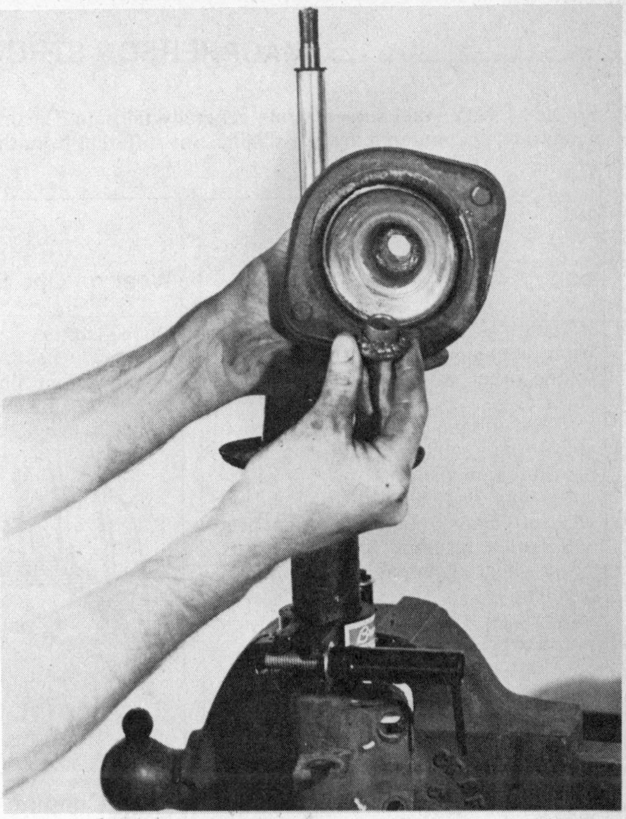

Step 19. **Repack the upper strut bearing with grease. Replace if excessive play is apparent**

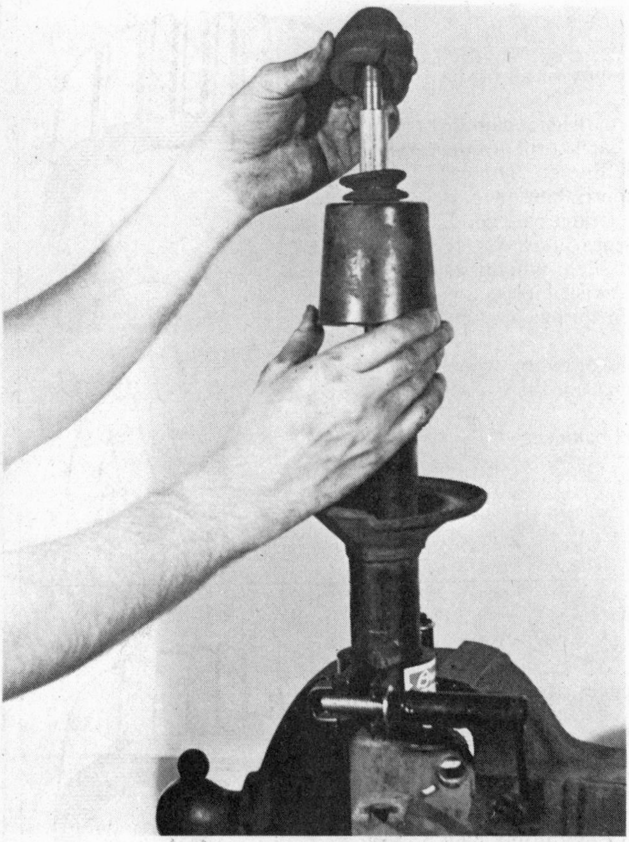

Step 18. **Inspect the upper strut mounting parts prior to reassembly. Replace any damaged components**

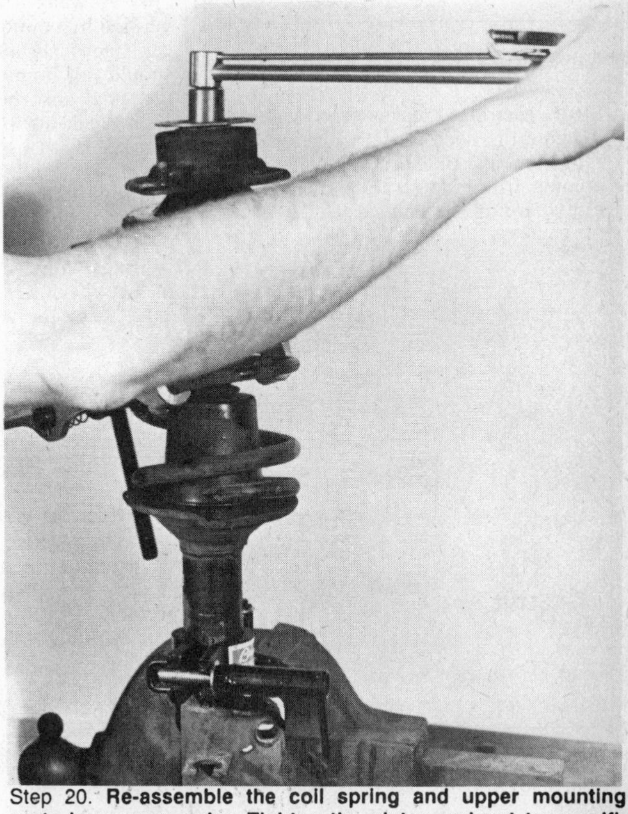

Step 20. **Re-assemble the coil spring and upper mounting parts in reverse order. Tighten the piston rod nut to specification and remove the spring compressor. Install the strut in the vehicle. See the car section for details**

## MACPHERSON STRUT PROBLEM DIAGNOSIS

Problems with MacPherson struts generally fall into 3 main categories: suspension, tire wear and steering. In general, the symptoms encountered are not significantly different from those encountered on conventional suspensions.

### Suspension

#### Sag

Vehicle "sag" is a visible tilt of the car from one side to the other or one end to the other while parked on a level surface.

Weak or damaged strut springs could cause this condition and should be repaired immediately.

Sag will also cause steering and tire wear problems to be more pronounced and vehicle instability on rough roads. Front wheel alignment will not solve the problem.

Weak strut springs increase vehicle sag. See "Tire Cupping".

#### Cartridge Leaks

Strut cartridge leaks (not seepage) indicate the need for cartridge or strut replacement. Be sure the leakage is coming from the strut, and not from elsewhere on the vehicle.

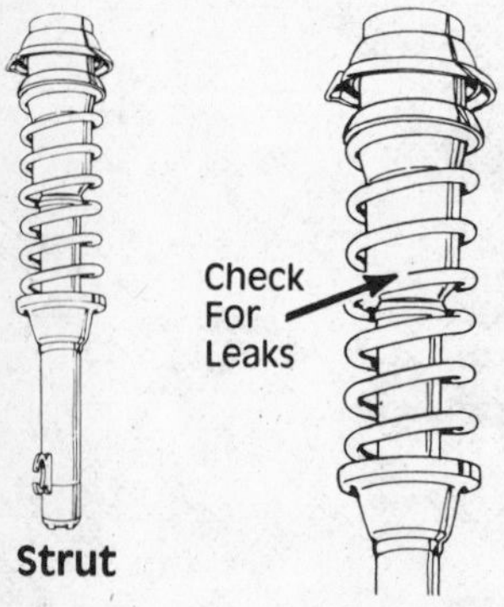


### Abnormal Tire Wear

#### Wear on One Side

One sided tire wear indicates incorrect camber. Check the causes in the accompanying illustration and be sure the wheel alignment is correct.

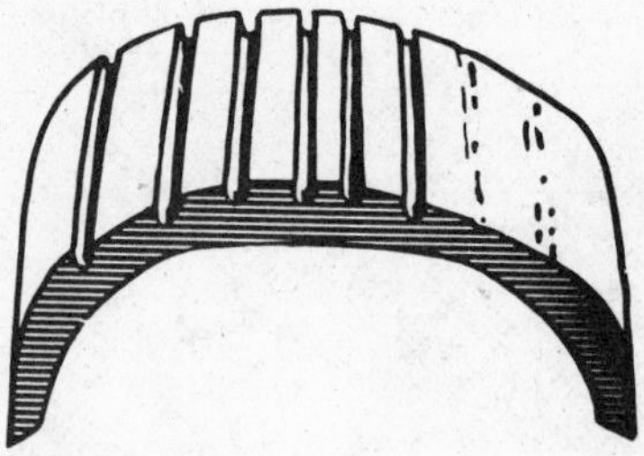

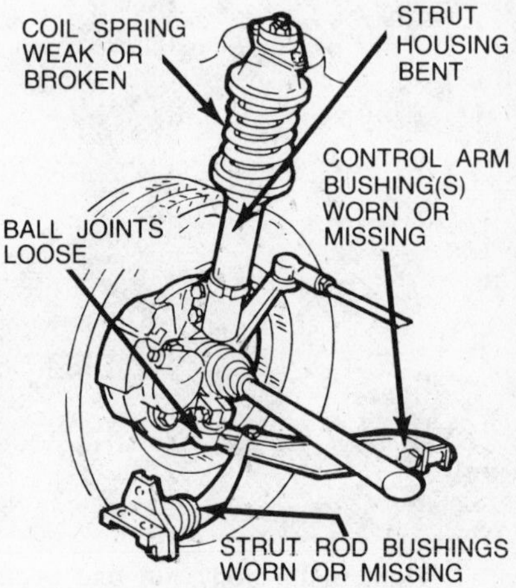


#### Tire "Cupping"

Cupped tires indicate any or all of the following problems.

1. A weak strut cartridge can be verified by bouncing each corner of the car vigorously and letting go. The car should not bounce more than once, if the shock absorber cartridges are good.
2. Weak strut springs allow sag to increase with only a slight amount of downward pressure. A visual inspection will reveal any broken springs or shiny spots.
3. Check for loose or worn wheel bearings with the weight of the car off of the wheel.
4. Check the wheel balance.

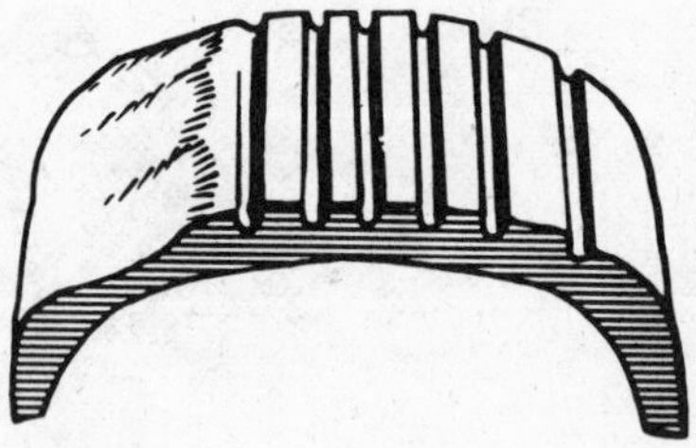

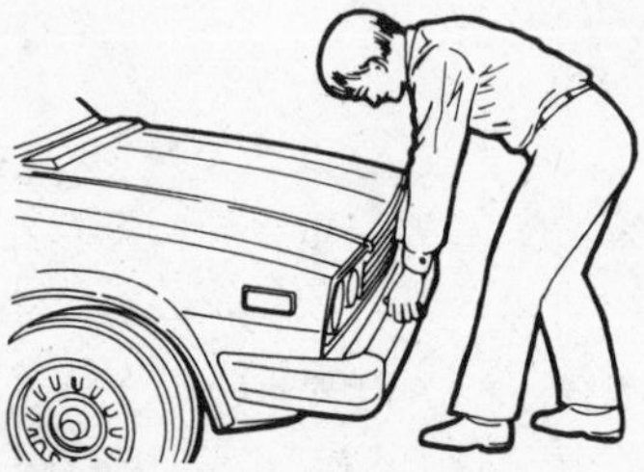

#### Tread Edge Wear

Wear along tread edges (feathering) indicates a suspension or steering system problem.

1. Strut rod bushings are worn or missing.
2. Tie rod end wear can be determined by grabbing the tie rod end firmly and forcing it up, down or sideways to check for lost motion.

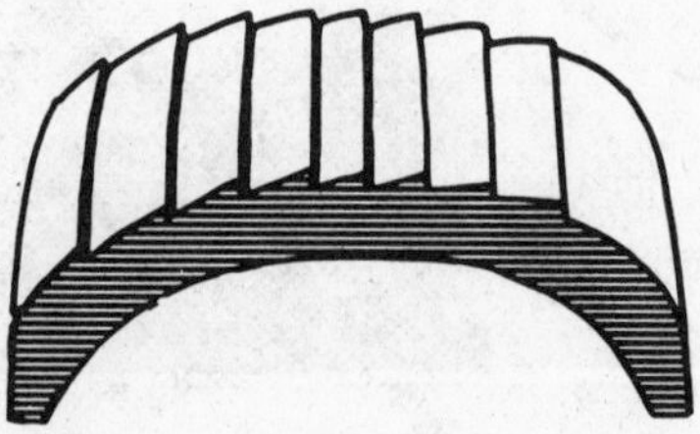

## MACPHERSON STRUT PROBLEM DIAGNOSIS

Problems with MacPherson struts generally fall into 3 main categories: suspension, tire wear and steering. In general, the symptoms encountered are not significantly different from those encountered on conventional suspensions.

### Steering

#### Tires

Both front tires should match and both rear tires should match. Be sure air pressure is correct.

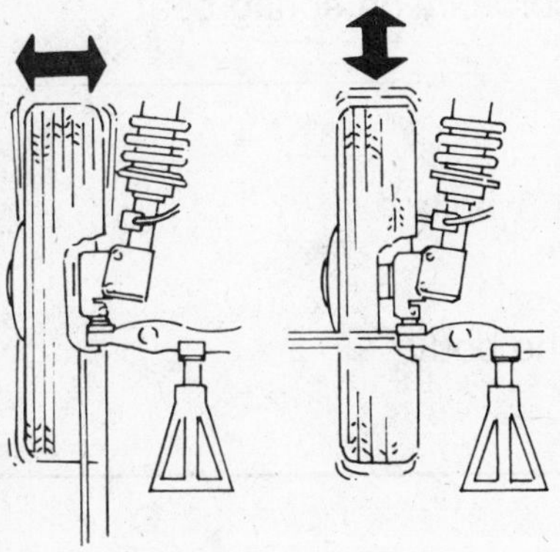

#### Strut Rod Bushings

Grasp the strut rod and shake it. Any noticeable play indicates excessive wear and need for parts replacement.

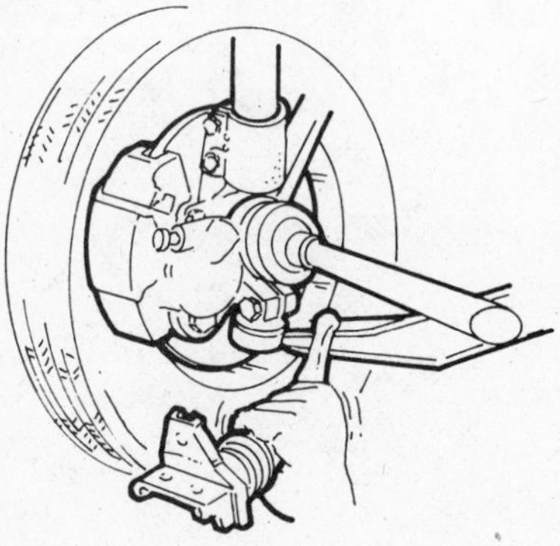

#### Ball Joints

Support the car under the frame or crossmember so that the jack does not interfere with the control arm. Rock the tire in and out and up and down. Excessive movement means that both ball joints should be replaced.

Struts with lower weight-carrying ball joints should be supported at the outer edge of the lower control arm. These vehicles usually have wear indicating ball joints that can be checked visually.

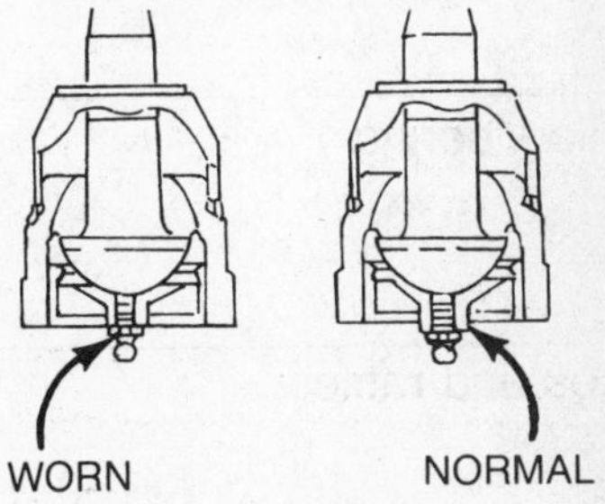


#### Stabilizer Bar Bushings

Check for worn bushings or lost motion with the vehicle level and the weight evenly distributed on all wheels.

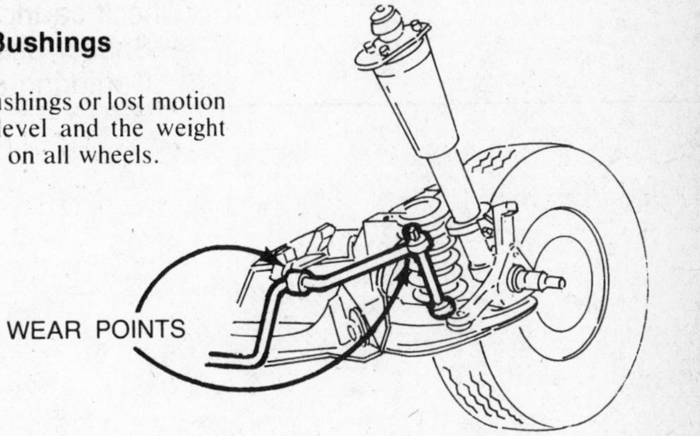


#### Control Arm Bushings

Support the car under the frame or body and remove the weight from the wheel and control arm. Check for free-play in the bushings at the pivot point, using a pry bar.

**NOTE: Some control arm bushings are serviceable only by replacing the entire arm.**

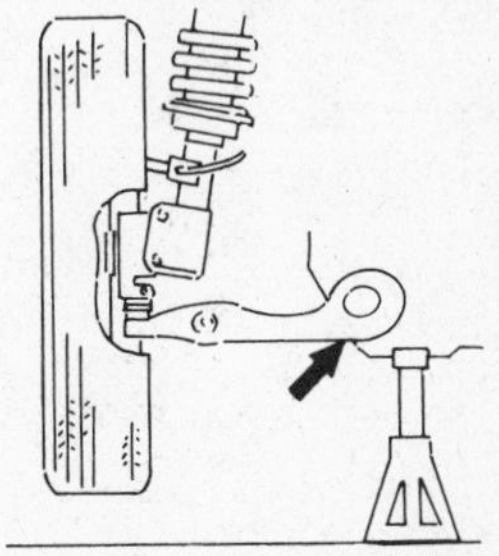

#### Strut Assembly

Check the strut assembly for cracks or dents in the housing. Look for worn, bent or loose piston rods or dents that will inhibit piston rod movement.

#### Steering Gear

Check for worn steering gear or loose or worn mounting bolts and bushings.

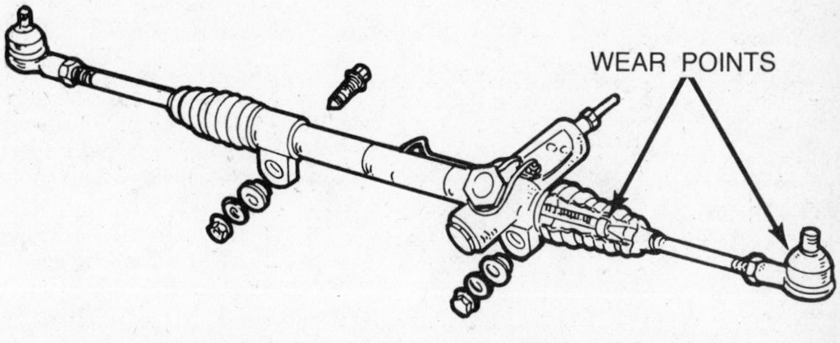

## ROAD TEST TROUBLESHOOTING

Following are possible solutions to common potential problems which might be noticed during the road test after strut service is completed. Many are not exclusively strut service related.

| Problem | Correction |
|---|---|
| Brake pedal low or soft | Bleed brakes<br>Check for leaks<br>Brake lines<br>Wheel cylinder<br>Caliper piston seal |
| Erratic steering | Check upper support housing components for proper assembly<br>Check spring assembly right side up<br>Check for spring helix riding correctly on spring seat<br>Check wheel alignment |
| Noises and rattles | Check torques<br>Piston rod nut<br>Upper support housing nuts & bolts<br>Lower mounting nuts & bolts<br>Body nut<br>Check cartridge assembly in the body<br>Spacer used<br>Centering collar used |

# Brakes 31

# BRAKE SYSTEM

## Understanding the Brakes

### HYDRAULIC SYSTEM

#### *Basic Operating Principles*

Hydraulic systems are used to actuate the brakes of all modern automobiles. The system transports the power required to force the frictional surfaces of the braking system together from the pedal to the individual brake units at each wheel. A hydraulic system is used for 2 reasons. First, fluid under pressure can be carried to all parts of an automobile by small hoses – some of which are flexible – without taking up significant amount of room or posing routing problems. Second, a great mechanical advantage can be given to the brake pedal end of the system, and the foot pressure required to actuate the brakes can be reduced by making the surface area of the master cylinder pistons smaller than that of any of the pistons in the wheel cylinders or calipers.

The master cylinder consists of a fluid reservoir and a double cylinder and piston assembly. Double type master cylinders are designed to separate 2 two-wheel braking systems hydraulically in case of a leak. The standard approach has been to utilize 2 separate two-wheel circuits; 1 for the front wheels and 1 for the rear wheels.

Most newer models now use a diagonally split system; i.e. 1 front wheel and the opposite rear wheel make up 1 braking circuit, while the remaining circuit consists of the other front wheel and its opposite side rear wheel.

Steel lines carry the brake fluid to a point on the vehicle's frame near each of the vehicle's wheels. The fluid is then carried to the wheel cylinders and/or calipers by flexible tubes in order to allow for suspension and steering movements.

The hydraulic system operates as follows: When at rest, the entire system, from the piston(s) in the master cylinder to those in the wheel cylinders or calipers, is full of brake fluid. Upon application of the brake pedal, fluid trapped in front of the master cylinder piston(s) is forced through the lines to the slave cylinders (wheel cylinders or calipers). Here, it forces the pistons outward, in the case of drum brakes, and inward toward the disc, in the case of disc brakes. The motion of the pistons is opposed by return springs mounted outside the cylinders in the drum brakes, and by internal springs or seals, in disc brakes.

Upon release of the brake pedal, a spring located inside the master cylinder immediately returns the master cylinder pistons to the normal position. The pistons contain check valves and the master cylinder has compensating ports drilled into it. These are uncovered as the pistons reach their normal position. The piston check valves allow fluid to flow toward the wheel cylinders or calipers as the pistons withdraw. Then, as the return springs force the shoes into the released position, the excess fluid flows back to the reservoir through the compensating ports. It is during the time the pedal is in the released position that any fluid that has leaked out of the system will be replaced through the compensating ports.

Dual circuit master cylinders employ 2 pistons, located 1 behind the other, in the same cylinder. The primary piston is actuated directly by mechanical linkage from the brake pedal. The secondary piston is actuated by fluid trapped between the 2 pistons. If a leak develops in the front of the secondary piston, it moves forward until it bottoms against the front of the master cylinder, and the fluid trapped between the pistons will operate 1 side of the split system. If the other side of the system develops a leak, the primary piston will move forward until direct contact with the secondary piston takes place, and it will force the secondary piston to actuate the other side of the split system. In either case, the brake pedal moves farther when the brakes are applied, and less braking power is available.

All dual circuit systems use a distributor switch to warn the driver when only half of the braking system is operational. This switch is located in

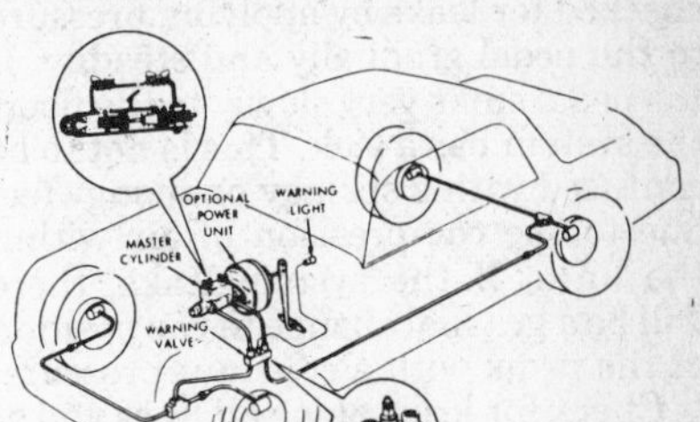


Dual braking system—front-to-rear split

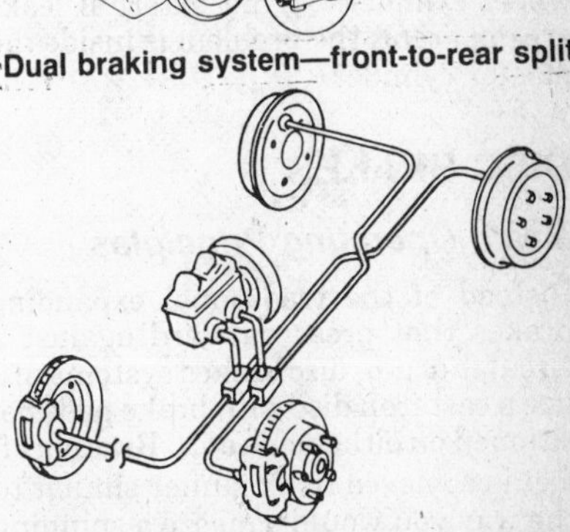

Dual braking system—diagonally split

a valve body which is mounted on the firewall, or the frame below the master cylinder. A hydraulic piston receives pressure from both circuits, each circuit's pressure being applied to 1 end of the piston. When the pressures are in balance, the piston remains stationary. When 1 circuit has a leak, however, the greater pressure in that circuit during application of the brakes will push the piston to 1 side, closing the distributor switch and activating the brake warning light.

In disc brake systems, this valve body also contains a metering valve and, in some cases, a proportioning valve (or valves). The metering valve keeps pressure from traveling to the disc brakes on the front wheels until the brake shoes or pads on the rear wheels have contacted the drums or rotors, ensuring that the front brakes will never be used alone. The proportioning valve throttles the pressure to the rear brakes so as to avoid rear wheel lockup during very hard braking.

These valves may be tested by removing the lines to the front and rear brake systems and installing special brake pressure testing gauges. Front and rear system pressures are then compared as the pedal is gradually depressed. Specifications vary with the manufacturer and design of the brake system.

Brake system warning lights may be tested by depressing the brake pedal and holding it while opening 1 of the wheel cylinder bleeder screws. If this does not cause the light to go on, substitute a new lamp, make continuity checks, and, finally, replace the switch as necessary.

The hydraulic system may be checked for leaks by applying pressure to the pedal gradually and steadily. If the pedal sinks very slowly to the floor, the system has a leak. This is not to be confused with a springy or spongy feel due to the compression of air within the lines. If the system leaks, there will be a gradual change in the position of the pedal with a constant pressure.

Check for leaks along all lines and at wheel cylinders. If no external leaks are apparent, the problem is inside the master cylinder.

## DISC BRAKES

### *Basic Operating Principles*

Instead of the traditional expanding brakes that press outward against a circular drum, disc brakes systems utilize a cast iron disc with brake pads positioned on either side of it. Braking effect is achieved in a manner similar to the way you would squeeze a spinning phonograph record between your fingers. The disc (rotor) is a one-piece casting which may be equipped with cooling fins between the 2 braking surfaces. The fins (if equipped) enable air to circulate between the braking surfaces making them less sensitive to heat buildup and more resistant to fade. Dirt and water do not affect braking action since contaminants are thrown off by the centrifugal action of the rotor or scraped off by the pads. Also, the equal clamping action of the 2 brake pads tends to ensure uniform, straight-line stops. All disc brakes are inherently self-adjusting.

There are 3 general types of disc brake:

1. A fixed caliper, 2 or 4-piston type
2. A floating caliper, single piston or double piston back-to-back type
3. A sliding caliper, single piston or double piston back-to-back type

The fixed caliper design uses 1 or 2 pistons mounted on either side of the rotor (in each side of the caliper). The caliper is mounted rigidly and does not move.

The sliding and floating designs are quite similar. In fact, these 2 types are often lumped together. In both designs, the pad on the inside of the rotor is moved into contact with the rotor by hydraulic force. The caliper, which is not held in a fixed position, moves slightly, bringing the outside pad into contact with the rotor. There are various methods of attaching floating calipers. Some pivot at the bottom or top, and some slide on mounting bolts. In any event, the end result is the same.

## DRUM BRAKES

### *Basic Operating Principles*

Drum brakes employ 2 brakes shoes mounted on a stationary backing plate. These shoes are positioned inside a circular cast iron (or aluminum) drum which rotates with the wheel assembly. The shoes are held in place by springs; this allows them to slide toward the drums (when they are applied) while keeping the lining and drums in alignment. The shoes are actuated by a wheel cylinder which is mounted at the top of the backing plate. When the brakes are applied, hydraulic pressure forces the wheel cylinder's 2 actuating links outward. Since these links bear directly against the top of the brake shoes, the tops of the shoes are then forced outward against the inner side of the drum. This action forces the bottom of the 2 shoes to contact the brake drum by rotating the entire assembly slightly (known as servo action). When pressure within the wheel cylinder is relaxed, return springs pull the shoes back away from the drum.

Most modern drum brakes are designed to self-adjust themselves during application when the vehicle is moving in reverse. This motion causes both shoes to rotate very slightly with the drum, rocking an adjusting lever, thereby causing rotation of the adjusting screw by means of a star wheel.

## POWER BRAKE BOOSTERS

Power brakes operate just as standard brake systems except in the actuation of the master cylinder pistons. A vacuum diaphragm is located on the front of the master cylinder and assists the drive in applying the brakes, reducing both the effort and travel he must put into moving the brake pedal.

The vacuum diaphragm housing is connected to the intake manifold by a vacuum hose. A check valve is placed at the point where the hose enters the diaphragm housing, so that during pe-

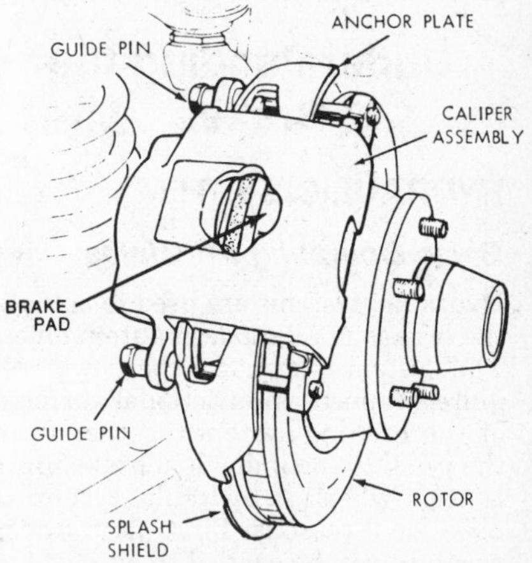


**Typical disc brake assembly**

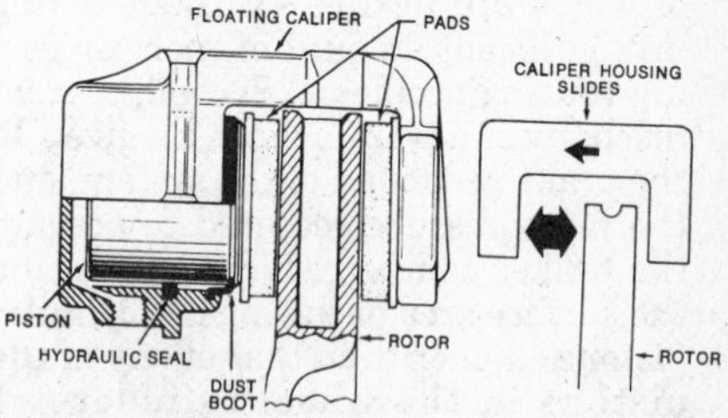


**Typical floating caliper disc brake (sliding caliper similar)**

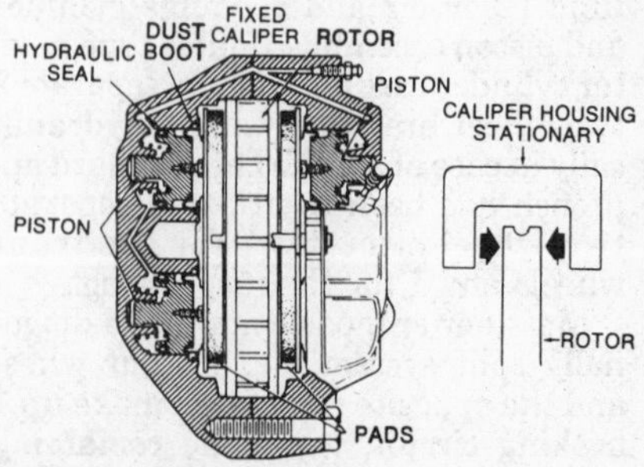


**Typical fixed caliper disc brake (four piston shown)**

riods of low manifold vacuum, brake assist vacuum will not be lost.

Depressing the brake pedal closes off the vacuum source and allows atmospheric pressure to enter on 1 side of the diaphragm. This causes the master cylinder pistons to move and apply the brakes. When the brake pedal is released, vacuum is applied to both sides of the diaphragm, and return springs return the diaphragm and master cylinder pistons to the released position. If the vacuum fails, the brake pedal rod will butt against the end of the master cylinder actuating rod, and direct mechanical application will occur as the pedal is depressed.

# HYDRAULIC CYLINDERS AND VALVES

## Master Cylinders

The master cylinder is a type of hydraulic pump that is operated by a push rod attached to the brake pedal or by a push rod that is part of the power brake booster. The cylinder provides a means of converting mechanical force into hydraulic pressure.

### DUAL MASTER CYLINDER

In this type there are 2 separate hydraulic pressure systems. 1 of the hydraulic systems may be connected to the front brakes, and the other to the rear brakes, or the system may connect diagonal wheels. If 1 system fails, the other system remains operational, thus providing an additional safety measure. There are 2 distinct fluid reservoirs and each has a vent and replenishing port that leads into the cylinder bore. These ports have been called compensating and inlet ports or bypass ports, and the terms have been used inconsistently causing confusion. The terms "vents" and "replenishing ports" are now standardized S.A.E. terms. An airtight seal for the reservoir is provided in the form of a rubber diaphragm, which is held in place by a metal cover. A bail type retainer or a bolt usually holds the cover on the reservoirs. The cover is vented to permit atmospheric pressure to enter above the diaphragm. The diaphragm prevents moisture and debris from contaminating the fluid. The cylinder bore contains the return springs, 2 pistons, and the seals. The piston stop bolt (if present) may be assembled in a thread hole in the bottom of the cylinder.

Some master cylinders have the piston stop bolt assembled in a threaded hole in the side of the bore or in the bottom of the front reservoir, and others do not have stop bolts at all. Do not install a stop bolt in the reservoir of a master cylinder if 1 was not originally there. Some cylinders have a tapped hole, but no bolt was ever installed in production. *This was done on purpose, and is not an error.*

A retaining ring fits into a groove near the end of the bore and holds the piston assemblies in the cylinder bore.

### *Dual System – Applied*

When the brake pedal is depressed, the push rod moves the primary piston forward in the cylinder bore. The primary vent port is sealed off by the lip of the primary cup. As a result, a solid column of fluid is created between the primary and secondary pistons.

With the help of the primary piston return spring, this column moves the secondary piston forward in the cylinder bore. This closes the secondary vent port. When both ports are closed, any further movement of the pushrod and pistons serves to increase the hydraulic pressure in the area ahead of each piston. This pressure is then transmitted through the 2 hydraulic brake systems to the brakes at each wheel.

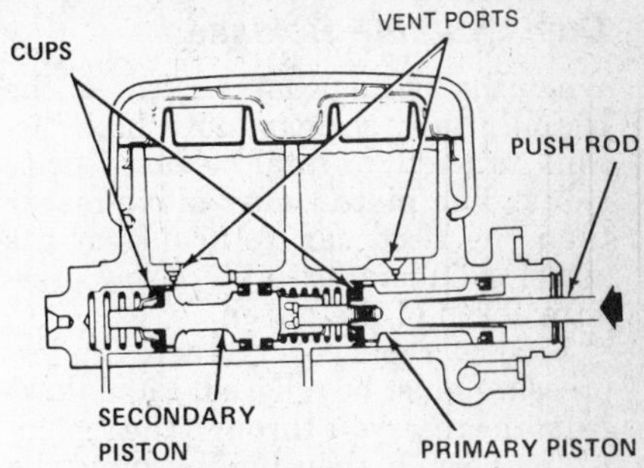

**Dual system—applied**

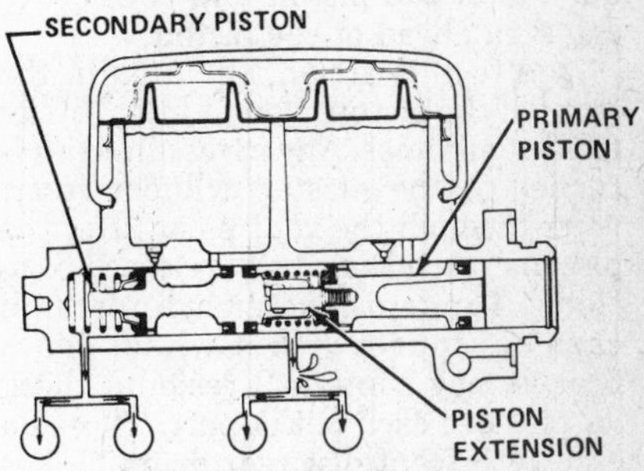

**Primary system failure**

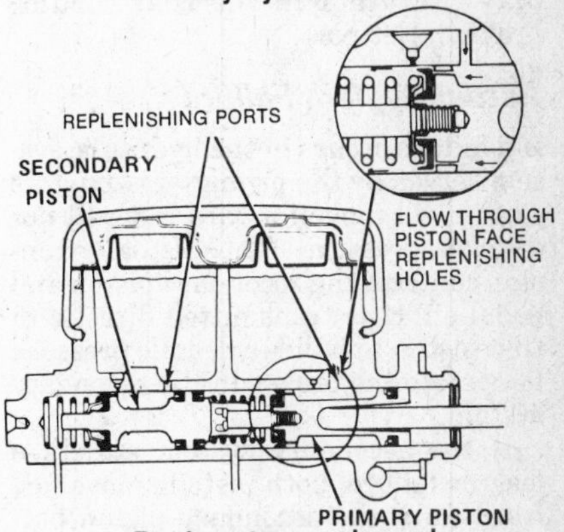

**Dual system—released**

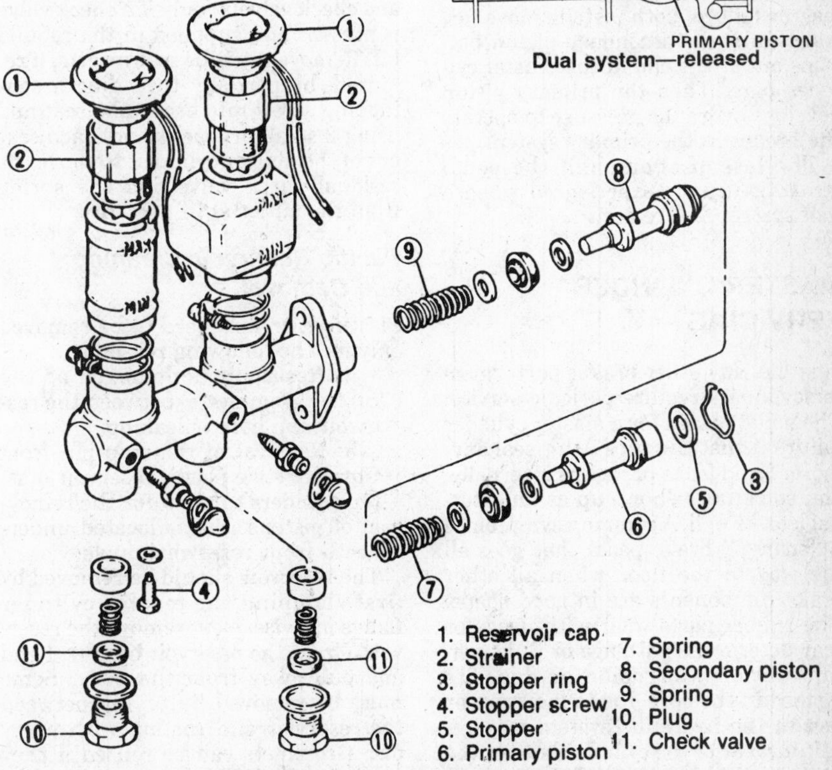

1. Reservoir cap
2. Strainer
3. Stopper ring
4. Stopper screw
5. Stopper
6. Primary piston
7. Spring
8. Secondary piston
9. Spring
10. Plug
11. Check valve

**Exploded view of a dual system master cylinder**

### Dual System—Released

When the brake pedal is released, the piston return springs move both pistons to their normal released positions. The piston may move faster than the fluid can return from the wheel cylinders, creating a low pressure ahead of the piston.

To allow rapid pedal return, this low pressure must be relieved. Fluid flows from the reservoir through the replenishing port. It then flows around the outside of the piston and cup lips to the area ahead of the piston.

Due to this action, the area in the front of the pistons if kept full of brake fluid at all times. Any excess fluid is returned to the master cylinder reservoirs through the vent ports after the pistons reach their fully released positions. Tandem master cylinders on cars equipped with 4 wheel drum brakes may contain 2 residual check valves, 1 in each outlet port. Those on cars with front disc/rear drum brakes may contain 1 in the rear (drum) brake outlet port.

### Partial System Failure

If a failure occurs in the hydraulic system served by the primary piston, this piston will move forward but will not develop pressure. The piston extension contacts the secondary piston and pedal effort is transmitted directly to that piston to build hydraulic pressure to operate the brakes in the secondary system.

If the secondary system suffers a leak or failure, both pistons move forward until the secondary piston bottoms out at the end of the master cylinder bore. Then the primary piston develops hydraulic pressure to operate the brakes in the primary system.

The loss of about half the pedal stroke is usually experienced when a half system failure occurs.

## MASTER CYLINDER SERVICING

Just like any other brakes parts, master cylinders require periodic service. The usual reason for a master cylinder failure is that the cups don't seal anymore. Fluid leaks past cups internally, and sometimes shows up as an external leak as well. A common symptom is a "spongy" brake pedal that goes all the way to the floor when all other brake components are in good shape. The rubber parts wear with usage or may deteriorate with age or fluid contamination. Corrosion or deposits formed in the bore due to moisture or dirt in the hydraulic system may result in wear of the cylinder bore or the parts therein. Also, the fluid levels in the reservoirs should be checked periodically. Whenever needed, clean brake fluid should be added to maintain the fluid level ¼–½ in. (6–13mm) from the top of the reservoir.

### Removal and Disassembly

1. Clean the area around the master cylinder to prevent dirt and grease from contaminating the cylinder or the hydraulic lines. Disconnect the tubes, remove nuts or bolts that secure the master cylinder to the firewall or power brake, and remove the master cylinder from the car (for further details, refer to appropriate car section).

On cars with manual brakes, the push rod must be disconnected from the brake pedal before removing the master cylinder from the car.

2. Remove the reservoir cover, and drain the brake fluid from the reservoir. Then remove the piston stop bolt, if present, from the master cylinder. Remove the boot and snap ring, then slide the primary piston assembly out of the master cylinder. Next, remove the secondary piston assembly by tapping the master cylinder, or by using needle nose pliers to pull it from its bore, or by carefully using compressed air. Disassemble the secondary piston assembly.

3. Clamp the master cylinder in a vise with the outlet ports facing up. Test for the presence of a check valve by probing with wire through the hole in the tube seats. Replace tube seat(s) and check valve(s) only if a check valve is present and supplied in the rebuild kit. Remove the tube seat inserts, if required, by partially threading a self-tapping screw into each tube seat and using 2 small prybars to pry each seat out of the master cylinder. Remove the residual check valve and the spring from the outlet(s) (if present).

### Plastic Reservoir Cleaning and Removal

Plastic reservoirs need to be removed only for the following reasons:

a. Reservoir is damaged or the rubber grommet(s) between the reservoir and bore is leaking.

b. Removal of the stop pin from Chrysler style plastic reservoir master cylinders to allow for the removal of pistons. Pin is located underneath front reservoir nipple.

The reservoir should be removed by first clamping the master cylinder flange in a vise. Next remove the reservoir. Grasp the reservoir base on 1 end and pull away from the body. Some must be removed by prying between the reservoir and casting with a pry bar. Grommets can be reused if they are in good condition. Whether or not the reservoir is removed, it and the covers or caps should be thoroughly cleaned.

### Cleaning and Inspection

Thoroughly clean the master cylinder and any other parts to be reused in clean alcohol. DO NOT USE PETROLEUM PRODUCTS FOR CLEANING. If the bore is not badly scored, rusted or corroded, it is possible to rebuild the master cylinder in some cases. A slight bit of honing is permissible to clean cups are facing.

**CAUTION**

***Aluminum cylinder bores cannot be honed. The cylinder MUST be replaced if the bore is scored.***

Lubricate all new rubber parts with brake fluid or brake system assembly lubricant.

#### CAST IRON BORE CLEAN-UP

Crocus cloth or an approved cylinder hone should be used to remove lightly pitted, scored, or corroded areas from the bore.

**CAUTION**

***If an aluminum master cylinder has pits or scratches in the bore, it must be replaced.***

Brake fluid can be used as a lubricant while honing lightly. The master cylinder should be replaced if it cannot be cleaned up readily. After using the crocus cloth or a hone, the master cylinder should be thoroughly washed in clean alcohol or brake fluid to remove all dust and grit. If alcohol is used, dry parts thoroughly before reinstalling.

**CAUTION**

***Other solvents should not be used.***

Then the clearance between the bore wall and the piston (primary piston of a dual system master cylinder) should be checked. If a narrow (⅛–¼ in. wide) 0.006 in. (0.15mm) feeler gauge can be inserted between the wall and a new piston, the clearance is excessive, and the master cylinder should be replaced. The maximum clearance allowed for units containing pistons without replenishing holes is 0.009 in. (0.23mm).

#### ALUMINUM BORE CLEAN-UP

Inspect the bore for scoring, corrosion and pitting. If the bore is scored or badly pitted and corroded the assembly should be replaced. *Under no conditions should the bore be cleaned with an abrasive material.* This will remove the wear and corrosion resistant anodized surface. Clean the bore with a clean piece of cloth around a wooden dowel and wash thoroughly with alcohol. Do not confuse bore discoloration or staining with corrosion.

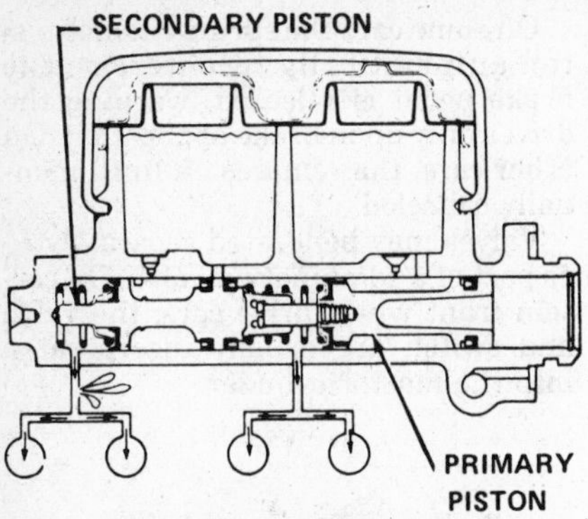


Secondary system failure

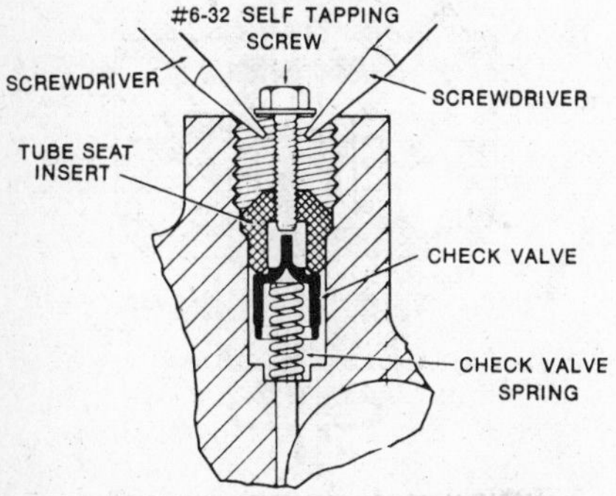


Removing the inserts from the master cylinder ports

### *Reassembly and Installation*

1. Carefully install the new cups or seals in the same positions and in reverse order of removal.
2. Use brake fluid or assembly fluid very generously to keep from damaging the seals.
3. Placing the small end of the pressure spring into the secondary piston retainer, slide the assembly into the cylinder bore, taking care not to nick or gouge any rubber part.
4. Place the spring retainer of the primary piston assembly over the secondary piston shoulder and push both assemblies into the bore.
5. Install and tighten the piston retaining screw and gasket, while holding the pistons in their seated positions. At the same time, reinstall any piston snap rings.
6. Install the residual check valve and spring in the proper master cylinder outlet (or both outlets, if originally present). If the tube seat inserts were removed, install new seats in both fluid outlets making sure that they are securely seated.

### *Bleeding and Checking*

1. Bleed the hydraulic system as described later in this section.

**NOTE: Be sure to bench bleed a rebuilt or new master cylinder before installation.**

2. Check master cylinder vent port clearance by watching for a spurt of brake fluid in both reservoir vent holes when the brake pedal is slightly depressed, indicating proper port clearance.

### *Master Cylinder Push Rod Adjustment*

After assembly of the master cylinder to the power section, the piston cup in the hydraulic cylinder should just clear the compensating port hole when the brake pedal is fully released. If the push rod is too long, it will hold the piston over the port.

A push rod that is too short, will give too much loose travel (excessive pedal play).

Apply the brakes and release the pedal all the way observing brake fluid flow back into the master cylinder.

A full flow indicates the piston is coming back far enough to release the fluid.

A slow return of fluid indicates the piston is not coming back far enough to clear the ports. The push rod adjustment is too tight, and should be shortened.

# Wheel Cylinders

## DRUM BRAKE WHEEL CYLINDER

The wheel cylinder performs in response to the master cylinder. It receives fluid from the hydraulic hose through its inlet port. As the pressure increases, the wheel cylinder cups and pistons are forced apart. As a result, the hydraulic pressure is converted into mechanical force acting on the brake shoes. The wheel cylinder size may vary from front to rear. The variation in wheel cylinder size (diameter) is 1 of the factors controlling the distribution of braking force in a vehicle.

## WHEEL CYLINDER OPERATION

The space between the caps in the cylinder bore must remain filled with fluid at all times. After depressing the brake pedal, additional brake fluid is forced into the cylinder bore. As a result of this, cups and pistons move outward in the cylinder bore pushing the shoe links an the brake shoes outward to contact the drum and apply the brakes.

On some designs, the end of the shoe web bears directly against the pistons and therefore, shoe links are not used.

## SERVICE PROCEDURES

Wheel cylinders may need reconditioning or replacement whenever the brake shoes are replaced or when required to correct a leak condition. On many designs, the wheel cylinders can be disassembled without removing them from the backing plate. On some designs, however, the cylinder is mounted in an indention in the backing plate or a cylinder piston stop is welded to the backing plate. When servicing brakes of this type, the cylinder must be removed from the backing plate before being disassembled.

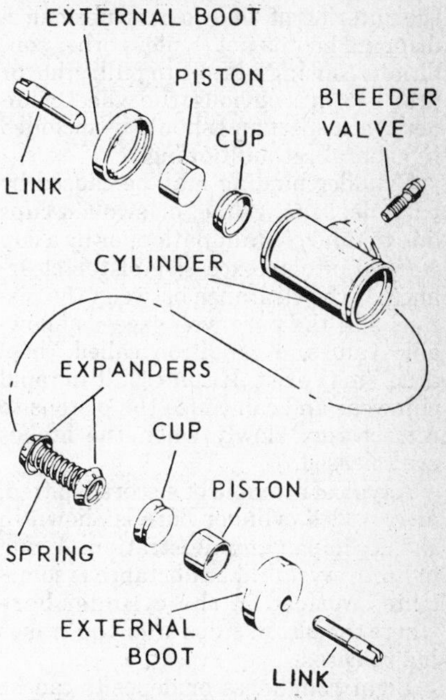


Typical wheel cylinder components

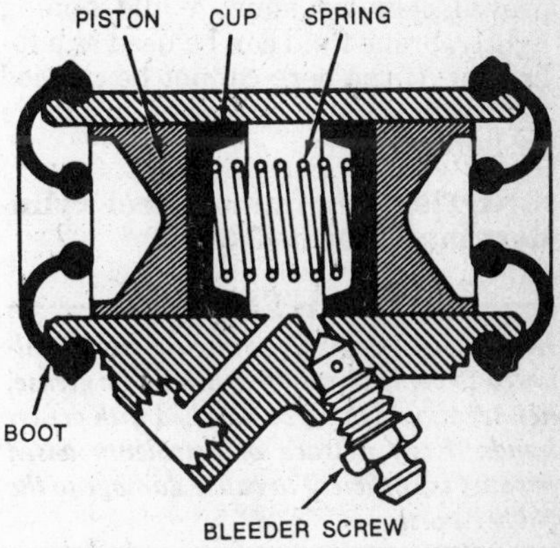


Double piston wheel cylinder

### *Diagnostic Inspection and Cleaning*

Leaks which coat the boot and the cylinder with fluid, or result in a dropped reservoir fluid level, or dampen or stain the brake linings are dangerous. Such leaks can cause the brakes to "grab" or fail and should be immediately corrected. A leakage, not immediately apparent, can be detected by pulling back the cylinder boot. A small amount of fluid seepage dampening the interior of the boot is normal; a dripping boot is not. Unless other conditions causing a brake to pull, grab, or drag becomes obvious, the wheel cylinder is a suspect and should be included in general reconditioning.

Cylinder binding may be caused by rust, deposits, grime, or swollen cups due to fluid contamination, or by a cup wedged into an excessive piston clearance. If the clearance between the pistons and the bore wall exceeds allowable values, a condition called "heel drag" may exist. It can result in rapid cup wear and can cause the pistons to retract very slowly when the brakes are released.

A typical example of a scored, pitted, or corroded cylinder bore is shown in the accompanying illustration. A ring of hard, crystal-like substance is sometimes noticed in the cylinder bore where the piston stops after the brakes are released.

Light roughness or deposits can be removed with crocus cloth or an approved cylinder hone. While honing lightly, brake fluid can be used as a lubricant. If the bore cannot be cleaned up readily, the cylinder must be replaced.

**NOTE: Aluminum wheel cylinders must not be honed.**

**CAUTION**

***Hydraulic system parts should not be allowed to come in contact with oil or grease, neither should those be handled with greasy hands. Even a trace of petroleum based product is sufficient to cause damage to the rubber parts.***

### *Reconditioning Wheel Cylinders*

It is common practice to recondition a wheel cylinder without dismounting it, however some brakes are equipped with external piston stops which prevent disassembly unless the cylinder is removed. In order to dismount, remove the shoe springs and spread the shoes apart, disconnect the brake line, remove the mounting bolts or retaining clips, and pull the cylinder free.

Pull the protective dust boots off the cylinder. Internal parts should slide out, or be picked out easily. Parts can be driven out with a wooden dowel, or blown out at low pressure by applying compressed air to the fluid inlet port. Parts which cannot be removed easily indicate they are damaged beyond repair and the cylinder should be replaced.

Clean the cylinder and the parts in alcohol and/or brake fluid (do NOT use gasoline or other petroleum based products). Use only lint-free wiping cloths. Crocus cloth can be used to clean minute scratches, signs of rust, corrosion or discoloration from the cylinder bore and pistons. Slide the cloth in a circular rather than a lengthwise motion. A clean-up hone may be used. After a cylinder has been honed, inspect it for excessive piston clearance and remove any burrs formed on the edge of fluid intake or bleeder screw ports.

**CAUTION**

***Do not rebuild aluminum cylinders.***

To check the maximum piston clearance, place a 1/4 in. (6mm) wide strip of feeler shim lengthwise in the cylinder bore.

If the piston an be inserted with the shim in place, the cylinder is oversize, and should be discarded. Depending upon the cylinder bore diameter, the shim (or the feeler gauge) thickness can vary as follows:

Assemble the cylinder with the internal parts, making sure that the cylinder wall is wet with brake fluid. Insert the cups and pistons from each end of a double-end cylinder; do not slide them through the cylinder. Cup lips should always face inward.

## Hydraulic Control Valves

### PRESSURE DIFFERENTIAL VALVE

The pressure differential valve activates a dash panel warning light if pressure loss in the brake system occurs. If pressure loss occurs in 1/2 of the split system, the other system's normal pressure causes the piston in the switch to compress a spring until it touches an electrical contact. This causes the warning lamp on the dash panel to light, thus warning the driver of possible brake failure.

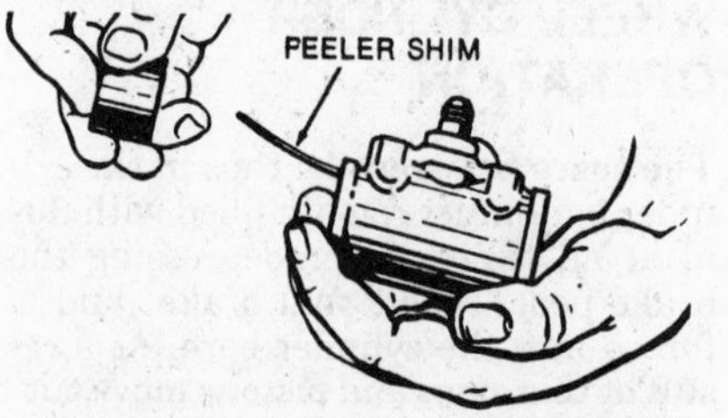


**Checking the maximum piston clearance**

| Cylinder Bore | Shim |
|---|---|
| ¾ in.–1 3/16 in. (19–30mm) | .006" (.15mm) |
| 1¼ in.–1 7/16 in. (32–37mm) | .007 in. (.18mm) |
| 1½ in. up (38mm) | .008 in. (.2mm) |

On some cars the spring balance piston automatically recenters as the brake pedal is released, warning the driver only upon brake application. On other cars, the remains on until manually canceled.

Valves may be located separately or as part of a combination valve. On certain front wheel drive cars, the valve and switch are usually incorporated into the master cylinder.

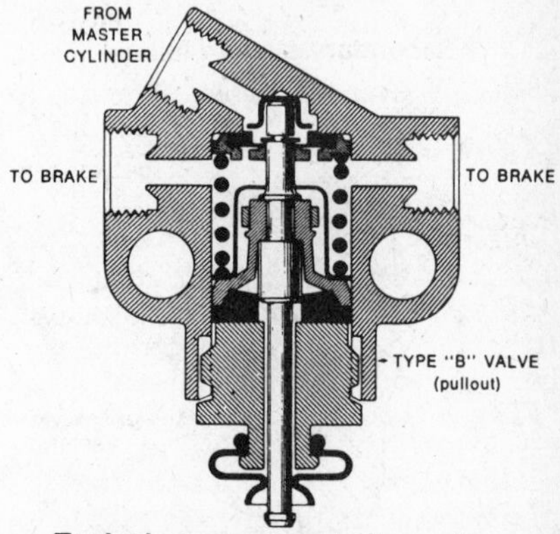


**Typical pressure metering valve**

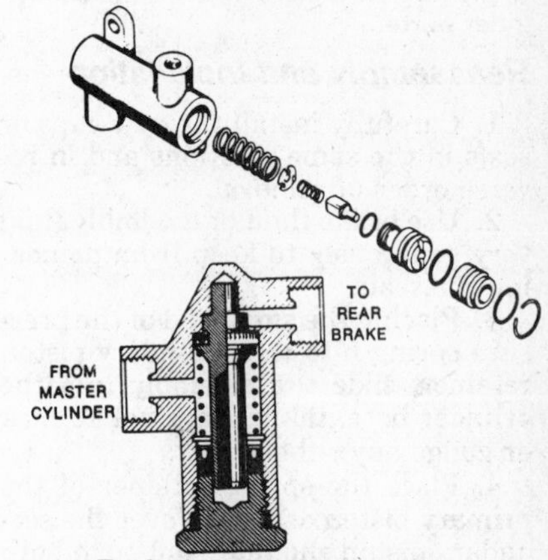


**Typical proportioning valve**

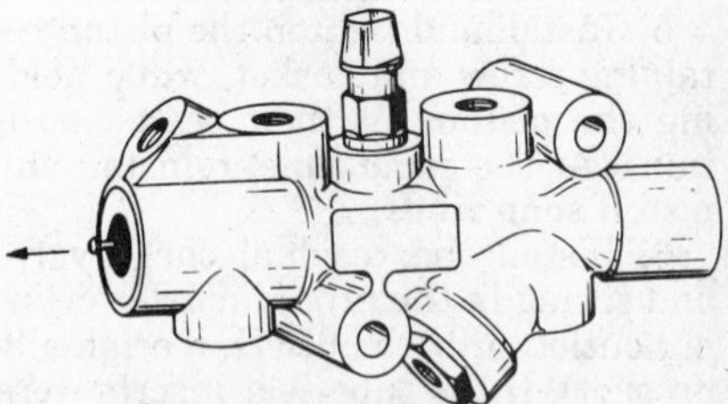

**3–way combination valve**

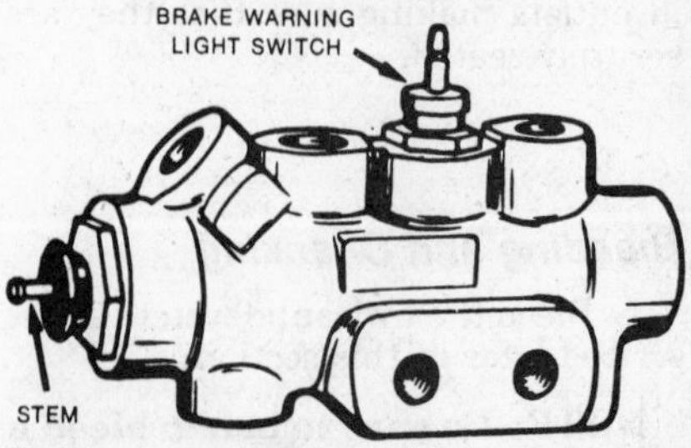


**Two–way combination valve (metering and brake warning light switch)**

### *ReSetting Valves*

On some cars, the valve piston(s) remain off center after failure, until necessary repairs are made. The valve will automatically reset itself (after repairs) when pressure is equal on both sides of the system.

If the light does not go out, bleed the brake system that is opposite the failed system. If the front brakes failed, bleed the rear brakes, this should force the light control piston toward center.

If this fails, remove the terminal switch. If brake fluid is present in the electrical area, the seals are gone, replace the complete valve assembly.

## METERING VALVE

The metering valve's function is to improve braking balance between the front and rear brakes, especially during light brake application.

The metering valve prevents application of the front disc brakes until the rear brakes overcome the return spring pressure. Thus, when the front disc pads contact the rotor, the rear shoes will contact the brake drum at the same time.

Inspect the metering valve each time the brakes are serviced. A slight amount of moisture inside the boot does not indicate a defective valve, however, fluid leakage indicates a damaged or worn valve. If fluid leakage is present, the valve must be replaced.

The metering valve can be checked very simply. With the car stopped, gently apply the brakes. At about an inch of travel, a very small change in pedal effort (like a small bump) will be felt if the valve is operating properly. Metering valves are not serviceable, and must be replaced if defective.

## PROPORTIONING VALVE

The proportioning (pressure control) valve is used, on some cars, to reduce the hydraulic pressure to the rear wheels to prevent skid during heavy brake application and to provide better brake balance. It is usually mounted in line to the rear wheels.

Whenever the brakes are serviced, the valve should be inspected for leakage. Premature rear brake application during light braking can mean a bad proportioning valve. Repair is by replacement of the valve. Make sure the valve port marked **R** is connected toward the rear wheels.

On some front wheel drive cars, the proportioning valve(s) is (are) screwed into the master cylinder. Since these cars usually have a diagonally split brake system, 2 valves are required. 1 rear brake line screws into each valve.

The early type valves were steel, an occasional "clunking" noise was encountered on some early models, but does not affect brake efficiency. Replacement valves are now made of aluminum. Never mix an aluminum valve with a steel valves, always use 2 aluminum valves.

## COMBINATION VALVE

The combination valve may perform 2 or 3 functions. They are; metering, proportioning and brake failure warning.

Variations of the 2-way combination valve are; proportioning and brake failure warning or metering and brake failure warning.

A 3-way combination valve directs brake fluid to the appropriate wheel, performs necessary valving and contains a brake failure warning.

The combination valve is usually mounted under the hood close to the master cylinder, where the brake lines can be easily connected and routed to the front or rear wheels.

The combination valve is non-serviceable and must be replaced if malfunctioning.

# Brake Bleeding

The hydraulic brake system must be free of air to operate properly. Air can enter the system when hydraulic parts are disconnected for servicing or replacement, or when the fluid level in the master cylinder reservoir(s) is very low. Air in the system will give the brake pedal a spongy feeling upon application.

The quickest and easiest of the 2 ways for system bleeding is the pressure method, but special equipment is needed to externally pressurize the hydraulic system. The other, more commonly used method of brake bleeding is done manually.

## BLEEDING SEQUENCE

Bleeding may be required at only 1 or 2 wheels or at the master cylinder, depending upon what point the system was opened to air. If after bleeding the cylinder/caliper that was rebuilt or replaced, the pedal still has a spongy feeling upon application, it will be necessary to bleed the entire system.

Bleed the system in the following order:

1. **Master Cylinder:** If the cylinder is not equipped with bleeder screws, open the brake line(s) to the wheels slightly while pressure is applied to the brake pedal. Be sure to tighten the line before the brake pedal is released. The procedure for bench bleeding the master cylinder is in the following section.
2. **Power Brake Booster:** If the unit is equipped with bleeder screws, it should be bled after the master cylinder. The car engine should be off and the brake pedal applied several times to exhaust any vacuum in the booster. If the unit is equipped with 2 bleeder screws, always bleed the higher 1 first.
3. **Combination Valve:** If equipped with a bleeder screw.
4. **Front/Back Split Systems:** Start with the wheel farthest away from the master cylinder, usually the right rear wheel. Bleed the other rear wheel, right front and then left front.

**NOTE: If you are unsuccessful in bleeding the front wheels, it may be necessary to deactivate the metering valve. This is accomplished by either pushing in, or pulling out a button or stem on the valve. The valve may be held by hand, with a special tool or taped, it should remain deactivated while the front brakes are bled.**

5. **Diagonally Split System:** Start with the right rear then the left front. The left rear then the right front.
6. **Rear Disc Brakes:** If the car is equipped with rear disc brakes and the calipers have 2 bleeder screws, bleed the inner first and then the outer.

**CAUTION**

***Do not allow brake fluid to spill on the car's finish, it will remove the paint. Flush the area with water.***

## MANUAL BLEEDING

1. Clean the bleeder screw at each wheel.
2. Start with the wheel farthest from the master cylinder (right rear).
3. Attach a small rubber hose to the bleeder screw and place the end in a clear container of brake fluid.
4. Fill the master cylinder with brake fluid (check often during bleed-

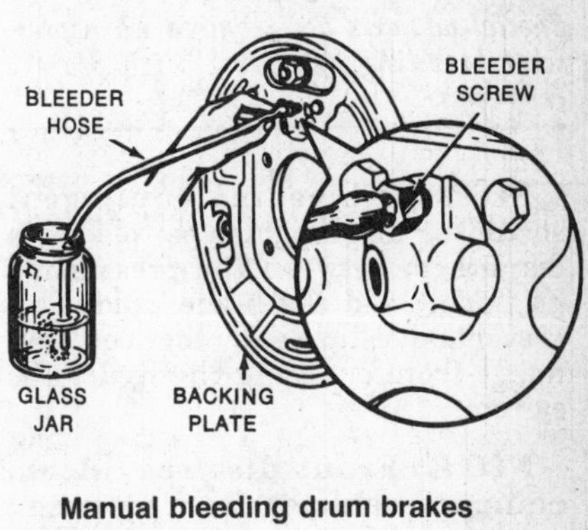


Manual bleeding drum brakes

ing). Have an assistant slowly pump up the brake pedal and hold pressure.

5. Open the bleed screw about one-quarter turn, press the brake pedal to the floor, close the bleed screw and slowly release the pedal. Continue until no more air bubbles are forced from the cylinder on application of the brake pedal.

6. Repeat the procedure on all remaining wheel cylinders and calipers.

Master cylinders equipped with bleed screws may be bled independently. When bleeding the Bendix-type dual master cylinder it is necessary to solidly cap 1 reservoir section while bleeding the other to prevent pressure loss through the cap vent hole.

**NOTE: The disc should be rotated to make sure that the piston has returned to the unapplied position when bleeding is completed and the bleed screw closed.**

**CAUTION**

*The bleeder valve at the wheel cylinder must be closed at the end of each stroke, and before the brake pedal is released, to ensure that no air can enter the system. It is also important that the pedal must be returned to the full up position so the piston in the master cylinder moves back enough to clear the bypass outlets.*

### PRESSURE BLEEDING DISC BRAKES

Pressure bleeding disc brakes will close the metering valve and the front brakes will not bleed. For this reason it is necessary to manually hold the metering valve open during pressure bleeding. Never use a block or clamp to hold the valve open, and never force the valve stem beyond its normal position. 2 different types of valves are used. The most common type requires the valve stem to be held in while bleeding the brakes, while the second type requires the valve stem to be held out (.060 in. minimum travel). Determine the type of valve by visual inspection.

**CAUTION**

*Special adapters are required when pressure bleeding cylinders with plastic reservoirs.*

Pressure bleeding equipment should be diaphragm type; placing a diaphragm between the pressurized air supply and the brake fluid. This prevents moisture and other contaminants from entering the hydraulic system.

**NOTE: Front disc/rear drum equipped vehicles use a metering valve which closes off pressure to the front brakes under certain conditions. These systems contain manual release actuators which must be engaged to pressure bleed the front brakes.**

1. Connect the tank hydraulic hose and adapter to the master cylinder.

2. Close the hydraulic valve on the bleeder equipment.

3. Apply air pressure to the bleeder equipment.

**CAUTION**

*Follow the equipment manufacturer's recommendations for correct air pressure.*

4. Open the valve to bleed air out of the pressure hose to the master cylinder.

**NOTE: Never bleed this system using the secondary piston stopscrew on the bottom of many master cylinders.**

5. Open the hydraulic valve and bleed each wheel cylinder and caliper. Bleed the rear brake system first when bleeding both front and rear systems.

### FLUSHING HYDRAULIC BRAKE SYSTEMS

Hydraulic brake systems must be totally flushed if the fluid becomes contaminated with water, dirt or other corrosive chemicals. To flush, simply bleed the entire system until *all* fluid has been replaced with the correct type of new fluid.

### BENCH BLEEDING MASTER CYLINDER

Bench bleeding the master cylinder before installing it on the car reduces the possibility of air getting into the lines.

1. Connect 2 short pieces of brake line to the outlet fittings, bend them until the free end is below the fluid level in the master cylinder reservoir(s).

2. Fill the reservoirs with fresh brake fluid. Pump the piston until no more air bubbles appear in the reservoir(s).

3. Disconnect the 2 short lines, refill the master cylinder and securely install the cylinder cap(s).

4. Install the master cylinder on the car. Attach the lines but do not completely tighten them. Force any air that may have been trapped in the connection by slowly depressing the brake pedal. Tighten the lines before releasing the brake pedal.

# POWER BRAKES

## Vacuum Operated Booster

Power brakes operate just as standard brake systems except in the actuation of the master cylinder pistons. A vacuum diaphragm is located on the front of the master cylinder and assists the driver in applying the brakes, reducing both the effort and travel he must put into moving the brake pedal.

The vacuum diaphragm housing is connected to the intake manifold by a vacuum hose. A check valve is placed at the point where the hose enters the diaphragm housing, so that during periods of low manifold vacuum brake assist vacuum will not be lost.

Depressing the brake pedal closes off the vacuum source and allows atmospheric pressure to enter on 1 side of the diaphragm. This causes the master cylinder pistons to move and apply the brakes. When the brake pedal is released, vacuum is applied to both sides of the diaphragm, and return springs return the diaphragm and master cylinder pistons to the released position. If the vacuum fails, the brake pedal rod will butt against the end of the master cylinder actuating rod, and direct mechanical application will occur as the pedal is depressed.

The hydraulic and mechanical problems that apply to conventional brake systems also apply to power brakes, and should be checked for if the tests and chart below do not reveal the problem.

Tests for a system vacuum leak as described below:

1. Operate the engine at idle with the transmission in Neutral without touching the brake pedal for at least 1 minute.

2. Turn off the engine and wait 1 minute.

3. Test for the presence of assist vacuum by depressing the brake pedal and releasing it several times. Light application will produce less and less pedal travel, if vacuum was present. If there is no vacuum, air is leaking into the system somewhere. Test for system operation as follows:

1. Pump the brake pedal (with engine off) until the supply vacuum is totally gone.

2. Put a light, steady pressure on the pedal.

3. Start the engine, and operate it at idle with the transmission in Neutral. If the system is operating, the brake

pedal should fall toward the floor if constant pressure is maintained on the pedal.

Power brake systems may be tested for hydraulic leaks just as ordinary systems are tested, except that the engine should be idling with the transmission in Neutral throughout the test.

## POWER BRAKE BOOSTER TROUBLESHOOTING CHART

The following items are in addition to those listed in the General Troubleshooting Section. Check those items first.

### *Hard Pedal*

1. Faulty vacuum check valve
2. Vacuum hose kinked, collapsed, plugged, leaky, or improperly connected
3. Internal leak in unit
4. Damaged vacuum cylinder
5. Damaged valve plunger
6. Broken or faulty springs
7. Broken plunger stem

### *Grabbing Brakes*

1. Damaged vacuum cylinder
2. Faulty vacuum check valve
3. Vacuum hose leaky or improperly connected
4. Broken plunger stem

### *Pedal Goes to Floor*

Generally, when this problem occurs, it is not caused by the power brake booster. In rare cases, a broken plunger stem may be at fault.

### *Overhaul*

Most power brake boosters are serviced by replacement only. In many cases, repair parts are not available. A good many special tools are required for rebuilding these units. For these reasons, it would be most practical to replace a failed booster with a new or remanufactured unit.

# ANTI-LOCK BRAKE SYSTEM (ABS)

## OPERATION

The Anti-Lock Braking System (ABS) is essentially a brake system enhancement. The purpose of ABS is to increase the driver's control over a vehicle during braking-especially steering control. When a vehicle equipped with a conventional brake system must brake suddenly, 1 or more wheels may lock up offering little or no steering control to avoid hazards. ABS is designed to prevent braked wheels from locking. The advantages of the system are considerable. For instance, during a high-speed stop while entering a curve, ABS is designed to allow the driver to steer through the curve while decelerating. Additionally, ABS is designed to enhance the braking action of each front wheel independently and the 2 rear wheels independent of the front wheels. This allows controlled braking even if 1 or more wheels encounters a slippery surface. In this situation, ABS will automatically sense the initial loss of adhesion in any 1 wheel and reduce or prevent further hydraulic pressure on that wheel's brake caliper, or if the rear wheels-both calipers until adhesion is regained.

## COMPONENTS

ABS is essentially the familiar split circuit hydraulic 4 wheel disc brake system in which a sophisticated electronic and mechanical override system has been carefully mated. 3 or 4 wheel speed sensors (depending on vehicle system design), an electronic control unit and a hydraulic unit that incorporates solenoid operated brakes line valves are the major components of the system. The sensors monitor the rotation speed of the wheels and provide data about wheel acceleration and deceleration over very small intervals of time. The signals from the sensors are transmitted to the control unit. The control unit monitors the signals and compares them to a contained program. If 1 of the sensors suddenly shows a deceleration rate that exceeds the threshold values of the programmed system-(indicating that a wheel is about to lock and skid)-the computer activates the hydraulic control unit to maintain the optimum brake pressure in that wheel, or both rear wheels to prevent lock-up. If, for any reason, the ABS should malfunction the brakes will operate as a normal system without ABS and a warning light will go on indicating service is required.

# SERVICING DISC BRAKES

## Disc Brake Caliper

An integral part of the caliper, the caliper bore(s) contains the piston(s) that direct thrust against the brake pads supported within the caliper. Since all braking forces (pad application force) are applied on each side of the rotor with no self energization, the cylinder and piston are large in comparison to a drum brake wheel cylinder.

### *Fixed Type*

A fixed type caliper is mounted solidly to the spindle bracket.

Pistons are located on both sides of the rotor, in inboard and outboard caliper halves. Fluid passes between caliper halves through an external crossover tube or through internal passages. A bleeder screw is located in the inboard caliper half. A dust boot protecting each cylinder fits in a circumferential groove on the piston.

### *Floating or Sliding Type*

Floating or sliding calipers are free to move in a fixed bracket or support.

The piston(s) is located only on the inboard side of the caliper housing, which straddles the rotor. The cylinder piston(s) applies the inboard brake shoe directly, and simultaneously hydraulic pressure slide the caliper in a clamping action which forces the caliper to apply the outboard brake shoe.

The actual applying movement is small. The unit merely grips during application, relaxes upon release, and the shoes do not retract an appreciable

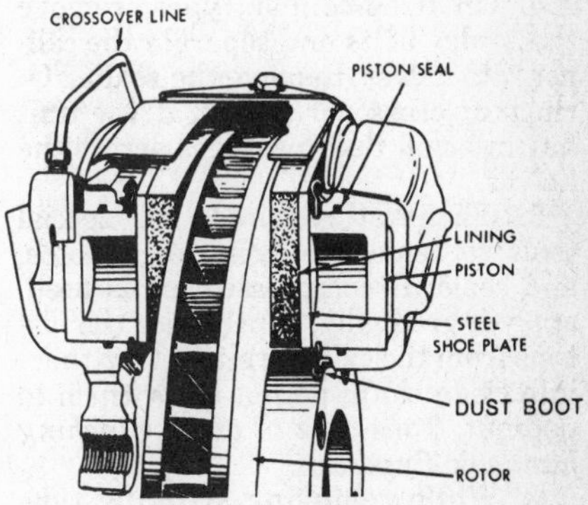

Fixed caliper disc brake

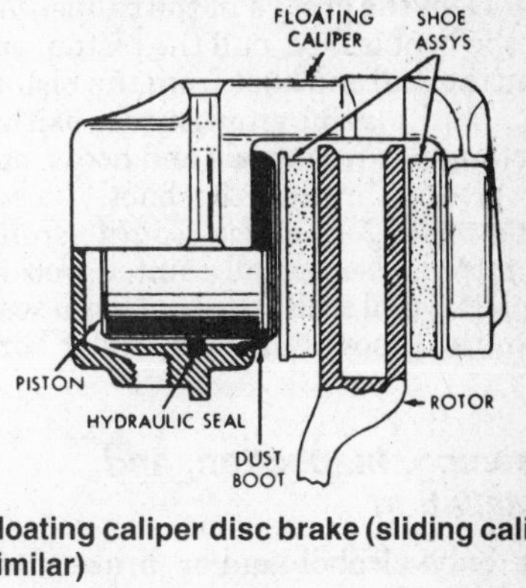

Floating caliper disc brake (sliding caliper similar)

distance from the rotor. The fluid inlet port and the bleeder screw are located on the inboard side of the caliper. A dust boot is fitted into a circumferential groove on the piston and into a recess at or near the outer end of the cylinder bore.

A scratched piston, nicked seal, or a sludge or varnish deposit which limits the sealing edge away from the piston will cause a fluid leak. A serious leak could develop if calipers are not reconditioned when new pads are installed. Then dust and road grime, gradually accumulating behind the dust boot, could be carried into the seal when the piston is shoved inward to accommodate new thick linings. Old seals may have taken a "set", thus preventing proper seating in the retainer groove and on the piston. Therefore, when reconditioning calipers, new seals should be installed.

## OVERHAUL PROCEDURES

Before servicing, siphon or syringe about $^{2}/_{3}$ of the fluid from the master cylinder reservoir; do not, however, lower the fluid level below the cylinder intake port.

1. To prevent a gravity loss of fluid, plug the brake line after disconnecting it from the caliper.
2. To overhaul, remove the caliper from the vehicle, allow the unit to drain, and remove the brake shoes.
3. For benchwork, clamp the caliper housing in a soft jawed vice.
4. On fixed-caliper types, remove the bridge bolts and separate the caliper into halves. Remove the sealing O-rings at crossover points, if the unit has internal fluid passages across the halves.
5. Whenever required, use special tools to remove pistons, dust boots, and seals. If compressed air is used, apply it gradually, gently ease the pistons from the cylinders, and trap them in a clean cloth; do not allow them to pop out. *Take care to avoid pinching hands or fingers.*
6. While removing stroking type seals and boots, work the lip of the boot from the groove in the caliper. After the boot is free, pull the piston, and strip the seal and boot from the piston.
7. While removing fixed position (rectangular ring) seals and boots, pull the piston through the boot. *Do not use a metal tool which would scratch the piston.* Use a small pointed wooden or plastic tool to lift the boots and seals from the grooves in the cylinder bore.

### *Cleaning, Inspection, and Installation*

Use only alcohol and/or brake fluid and a lint free wiping cloth to clean the caliper and parts.

**CAUTION**

***Other solvents should not be used. Blow out passages with compressed air. Always wear eye protection when using compressed air or cleaning calipers.***

1. To correct minor imperfections in the cylinder bore, polish with a fine grade crocus cloth working in a circular rather than a lengthwise motion.

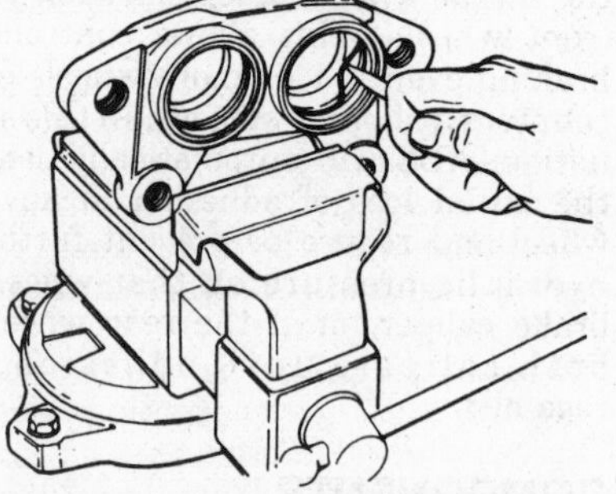

**Removing a fixed position rectangular ring seal**

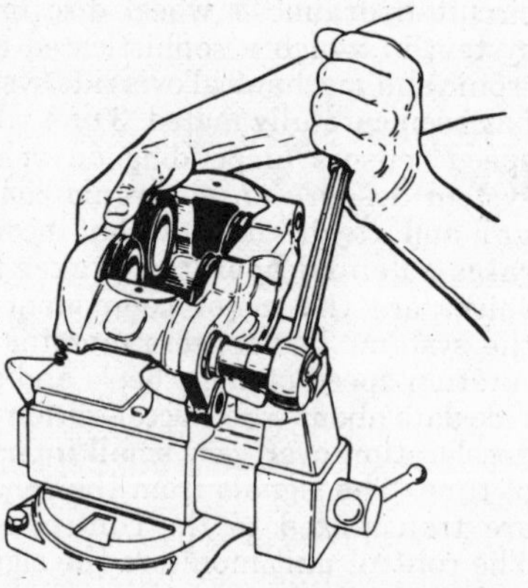

**Removing the fixed caliper bridge bolts**

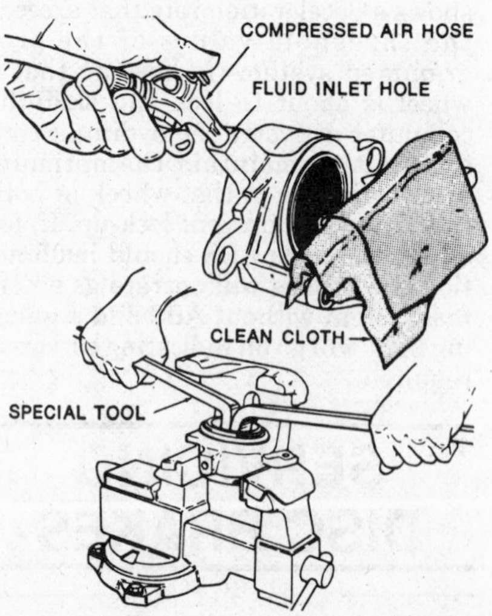


**Removing a hollow–end piston with compressed air (top) or the special tool (bottom)**

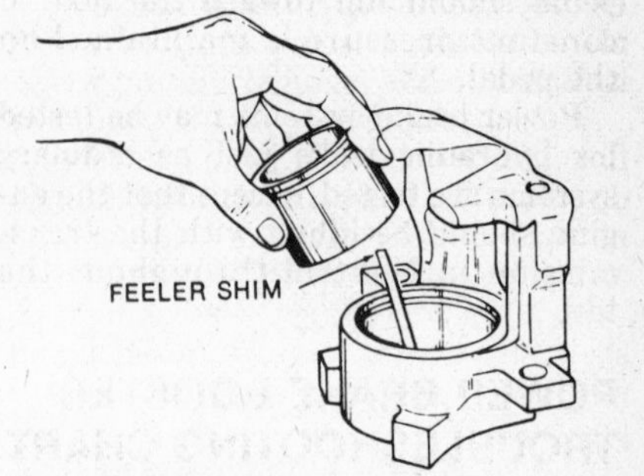


**Checking maximum piston clearance**

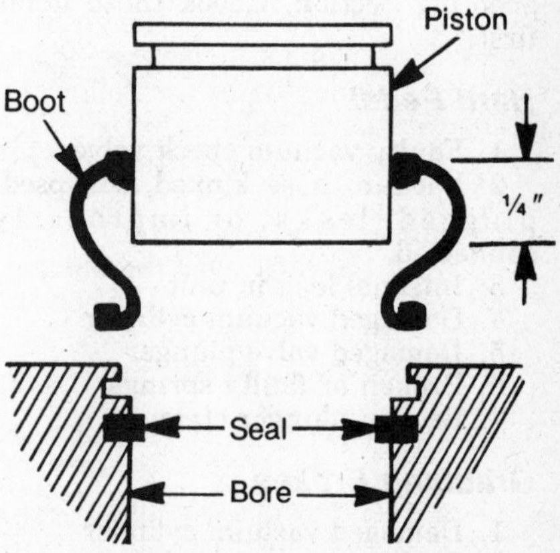


**Typical boot installation**

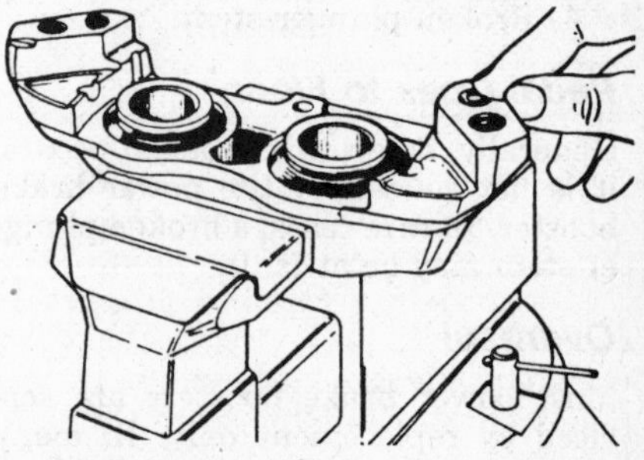

**Replacing the O–rings in the internal cross–over passages**

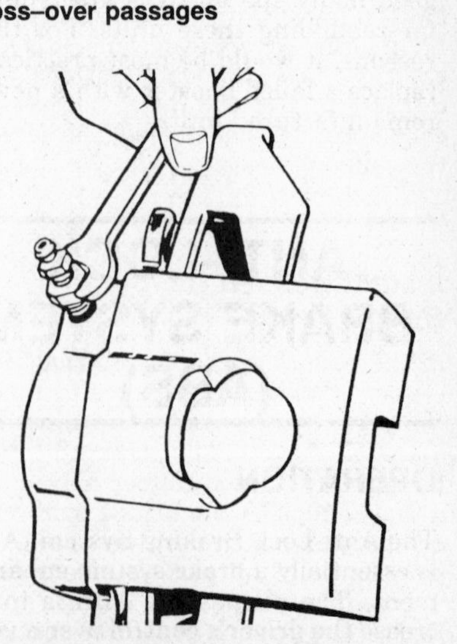

**Replacing a disc brake bleeder screw**

Do not use any form of abrasive on a plated piston. Discard a piston which is pitted or has signs of plating wear.

2. Inspect the new seal. It should lie flat and be round. If it had suffered a distorted "set" during its shelf life, do not use it. Lubricate the cylinder wall and parts with brake fluid.

3. While installing the stroking type seals and boots, stretch the boot and seal over the piston and seat then in position.

4. Use special alignment tools for inserting lip cup seals.

5. Install the fixed position (rectangular ring) seals and be sure the ring does not twist or roll into the groove.

6. Where the boot lip is retained inside the cylinder bore, the following method works as well:

a. Lubricate the bottom inside edge of the piston and brake seal in the caliper with brake fluid.

b. Pull the boot over the bottom end of the piston so that the boot is positioned on the bottom of the piston with the lip about ¼ inch up from bottom end.

c. Hold the piston suspended over bore.

d. Insert the back boot lip into the groove in the caliper.

e. Tuck the sides of the boot into the groove and work forward until only 1 bulge remains.

f. Tuck the final bulge into the front of the groove.

g. Push the piston carefully through the seal and boot to the bottom of the bore. The inside of the boot should slide on the piston and come to rest in the boot groove.

If the boot lip is retained outside the cylinder bore, first stretch the boot over the piston and seat it in its groove, then press the piston through the seal.

Fully depress the piston. You'll need 50–100 lbs. of force to fasten the boot lip in place. On some designs, it is necessary to use a wooden drift or a special tool to seat the metal boot in the caliper counterbore below the face of the caliper.

#### *Installing Fixed Caliper Bridge Bolts*

If the caliper contains internal fluid crossover passages, be sure to install the new O-ring seals at the joints.

Install high tensile strength bridge bolts on the mated caliper halves.

Never replace the bridge bolts with ordinary standard hardware bolts; order the bolts by part numbers only. Tighten the bridge bolts, using a specified torque wrench as follows specified by the manufacturer.

### OVERHAUL NOTES

Field reports indicate that 2 factors determine whether to replace or rebuild calipers:

- Can the piston or pistons be moved?
- Will the bleed screw break off when removal is attempted? (Rebuilders will not accept a caliper with a broken bleed screw.) Since there is no way to predict how a bleed screw will react, follow this procedure to attempt removal.

1. Insert a drill shank into the bleed screw hole (snug fit).

2. Tap the screw on all sides.

3. With a 6 point wrench apply pressure gently while working the drill up and down slightly.

4. If the drill starts to bind, the screw is beginning to collapse and cannot be removed intact.

Heating the caliper is another successful, but time consuming, bleed screw removal technique.

a. Remove the caliper from the car.

b. Heat the caliper.

c. Shrink the bleed screw by applying dry ice, and attempt removal.

### BLEEDER SCREW REPLACEMENT

1. Using the existing hole in the bleeder screw for a pilot, drill ¼ in. hole completely through the existing bleeder.

2. Increase the hole to $^{7}/_{16}$ in.

3. Tap hole using a ¼ in. × 18-National pipe thread, ½ in. deep-full thread.

4. Install bleeder repair kit.

5. Test for leaks and full brake pedal pressure.

### FROZEN PISTONS

#### *Sliding or Floating Caliper*

#### HYDRAULIC REMOVAL

1. Remove the caliper assembly from the rotor.

2. Remove the brake pads and dust seal. With flexible brake line connected and the bleed screw closed, apply enough pedal pressure to move the piston most of the way out of the bore. (Brake fluid will begin to ooze past the piston inner seal.)

#### PNEUMATIC REMOVAL

1. Remove the caliper from the car.

2. With the bleed screw closed, apply air pressure to force the piston out.

**CAUTION**

***Hydraulic and pneumatic methods of piston removal should be done carefully to prevent personal injury or piston damage.***

#### *Fixed Caliper*

**NOTE: The hydraulic or pneumatic methods which apply to the single piston type caliper will not work on the multiple type brake caliper.**

1. Remove the caliper from the car with the 2 halves separated.

2. Mount in a vise and use a piston puller (many types available) to remove the pistons.

## Brake Disc (Rotor)

### ROTOR RUNOUT

Manufacturers differ widely on permissible runout, but too much can sometimes be felt as a pulsation at the brake pedal. A wobble pump effect is created when a rotor is not perfectly smooth and the pad hits the high spots forcing fluid back into the master cylinder. This alternating pressure causes a pulsating feeling which can be felt at the pedal when the brakes are applied. This excessive runout also causes the brakes to be out of adjustment because disc brakes are self-adjusting; they are designed so that the pads drag on the rotor at all times and therefore automatically compensate for wear.

To check the actual runout of the rotor, first tighten the wheel spindle nut to a snug bearing adjustment, endplay removed. Fasten a dial indicator on the suspension at a convenient place so that the the indicator stylus contacts the rotor face approximately 1 inch from its outer edge. Set the dial at zero. Check the total indicator reading while turning the rotor 1 full revolution. If the rotor is warped beyond the runout specification, it is likely that it can be successfully remachined.

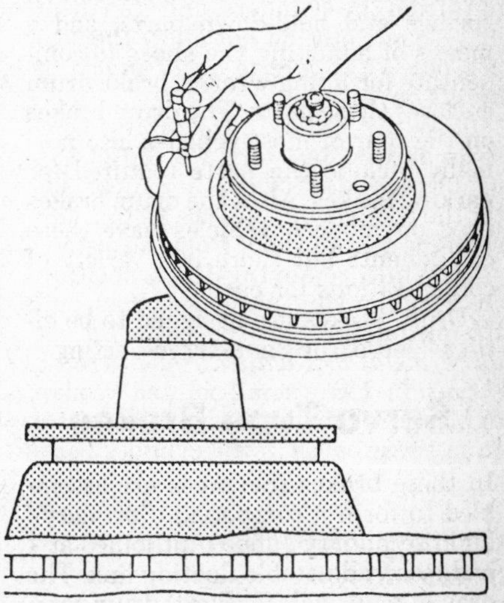

Parallelism

**Lateral Runout:** A wobbly movement of the rotor from side to side as it rotates. Excessive lateral runout causes the rotor faces to knock back the disc pads and can result in chatter, excessive pedal travel, pumping or fighting pedal and vibration during the braking action.

**Parallelism (lack of):** Refers to the amount of variation in the thickness of the rotor. Excessive variation can cause pedal vibration or fight, front end vibrations and possible "grab" during the braking action; a condition comparable to an "out-of-round brake drum". Check parallelism with a micrometer. "Mike" the thickness at 8 or more equally spaced points, equally distant from the outer edge of the rotor, preferably at mid-points of the braking surface. Parallelism is then the amount of variation between maximum and minimum measurements.

**Surface or Micro-inch finish, flatness, smoothness:** Different from parallelism, these terms refer to the degree of perfection of the flat surface on each side of the rotor; that is, the minute hills, valleys and swirls inherent in machining the surface. In a visual inspection, the remachined surface should have a fine ground polish with, at most, only a faint trace of non-directional swirls.

## SERVICING DRUM BRAKES

A typical drum brake assembly includes a backing or support plate, with 1 or 2 wheel cylinders attached to it. Mounted on the backing plate are 2 lined brake shoes with shoe return springs and hold-down parts, and a means of adjusting the shoes to compensate for lining wear. A brake drum encloses these parts. The drum brakes on the rear of most vehicles also normally include the parts required for parking brakes. All of the drum brakes used on modern vehicles have these components but there is a variety of configurations for each.

Drum brakes are designed to be either "servo" or "non-servo" acting.

### Servo Type Brakes

In these brakes the shoes are assembled to form a compound, "primary" and "secondary" shoe unit joined at 1 end by an adjustable floating link. The drag of a normal (forward) drum rotation causes the primary shoe to leave its anchor and holds the secondary shoe anchored.

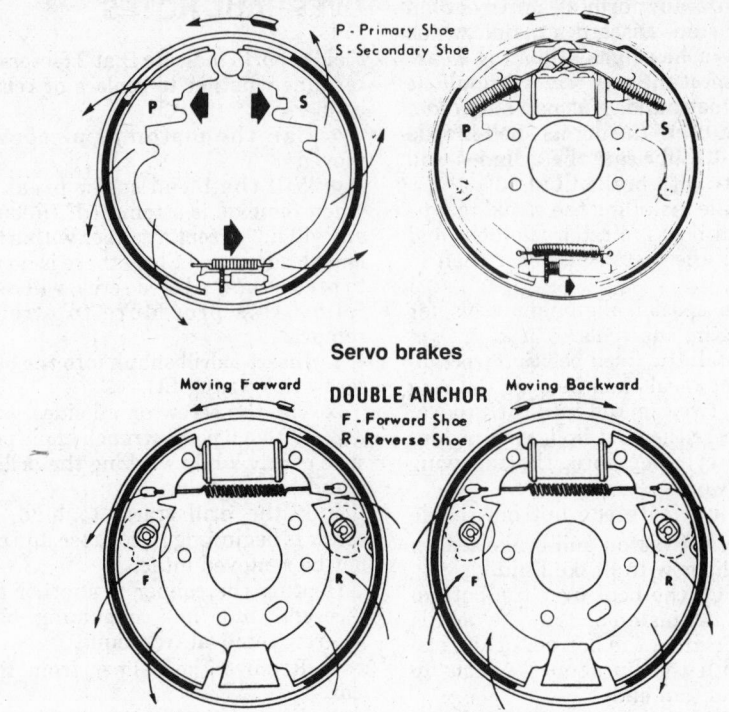

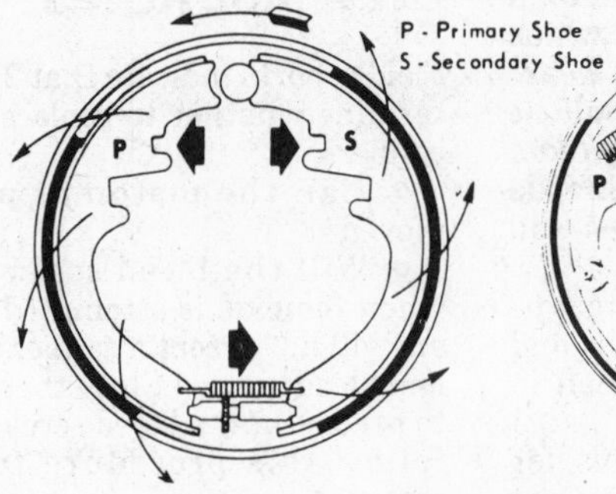


Servo brakes

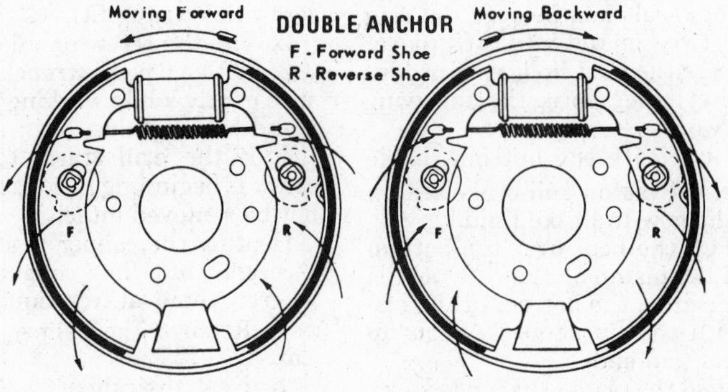


Non–servo brakes

All of the forces applying and anchoring the primary shoe are transmitted through the shoe link, in a servo action, and also apply the secondary shoe, thus compounding its braking effect. When the drum is rotated backward, this compounding action of the shoes is reversed. When equipped with a double-end wheel cylinder (two opposed pistons), brake effectiveness can be substantially the same with either forward or reverse movement of the vehicle. With a single-end wheel cylinder (one piston), the brake is energized in only 1 direction. Since the secondary shoe performs more of the work in forward movement, it shows more lining wear. A longer or thicker lining is often used to offset this wear.

### Non-Servo Type Brakes

In these brakes each shoe is separately anchored and their action is not compounded. On single cylinder brakes a "forward" or "leading" shoe is self-energized by the usual (forward) drum rotation while a "reverse" or "trailing" shoe is de-energized. When the drum is rotated backward, this action reverses, thus energizing the reverse shoe and de-energizing the forward shoe. The lining wear is unbalanced because the shoe perform different amounts of work; the wear is more rapid on the forward acting shoe during a forward stop.

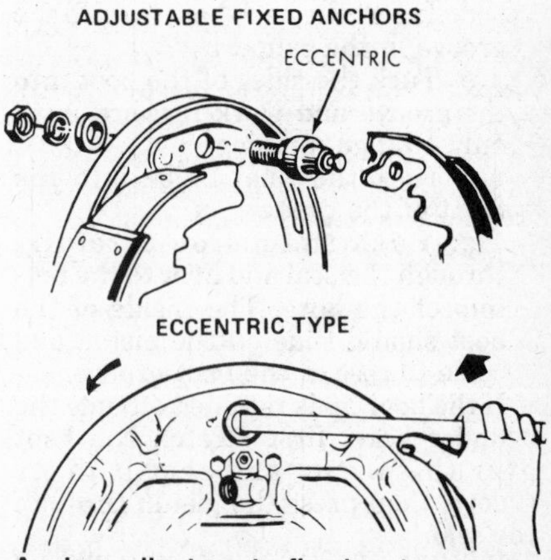


Anchor adjustment—fixed and eccentric

Large 2 cylinder non-servo brakes, found on certain models, make use of 2 double-end wheel cylinders which enable the shoes to be anchored or actuated at either end. This arrangement is non-directional in effectiveness. With two-cylinder brakes, lining wear is balanced on both sides.

### MECHANICAL COMPONENTS

To be sure of restoring the brake components correctly after servicing, closely observe the arrangement of shoe hook-up parts as the brake is disassembled. These arrangements may vary on different models. Usually the brake shoes are held in a sliding fit by spring tensions, at rest upon their anchor by the return springs, and against support pads by spring or clip type hold-downs. Opposite the anchor, a star wheel adjuster links the shoe webs and provides a threaded adjustment which permits the shoes to be expanded or contracted. Some rear brakes have adjustable links. The shoes are held against the adjuster by a spring.

### Shoe Hold-Downs

Various shoe hold-downs are shown in the illustration.

To unlock or lock straight pin hold-downs, depress the locking cup and coil spring, or the spring clip, and rotate the pin and lock 90 degrees. On certain lever type adjusters, the inner (bottom) cup has a sleeve which aligns the adjuster lever.

### Shoe Anchors

As shown in the illustration, there are various types of anchors such as the fixed non-adjustable type, or self-centering shoe sliding type, or, on some earlier models, adjustable fixed type providing either an eccentric or a slotted adjustment.

On adjustable anchors, when necessary to recenter the shoes in he drum or drum gauge, loosen the locknut enough to permit the anchor to slip out, but not so much that it can tilt.

On eccentric type anchors, tighten the star wheel to heavy brake drag. Rotate the eccentric anchor in the direction which frees the brake until drag cannot be relieved. Tighten the anchor nut. Back off the star wheel to a normal manual adjustment.

On the slotted type anchor, tighten the star wheel to heavy drag. Tap the support plate until the anchor slips and frees the brake. Repeat this sequence until drag cannot be relieved. Tighten the locknut to the proper torque. Back off the star wheel to a normal manual adjustment.

### Brake Shoes

In the same brake sizes, there can be differences in web thickness, shape of web cut-outs and positions of any reinforcements. Some vehicles require shoes made of higher tensile strength steels. Higher strength shoes usually are coded with a letter symbol stamped on the shoe web. Shoes with extra web holes or table nibs or tabs which do not cause interference generally are considered interchangeable with other shoes.

### Stops

An eccentric stop under the primary or secondary shoe web on tilted front brakes prevents the shoes from bumping against the drum. Before ad-

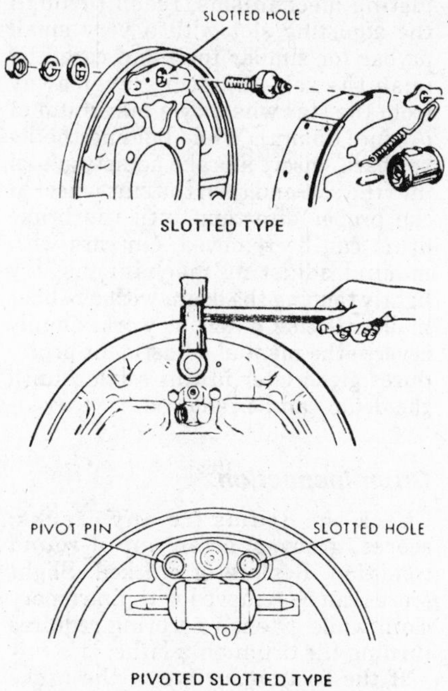


Anchor adjustment—slotted type

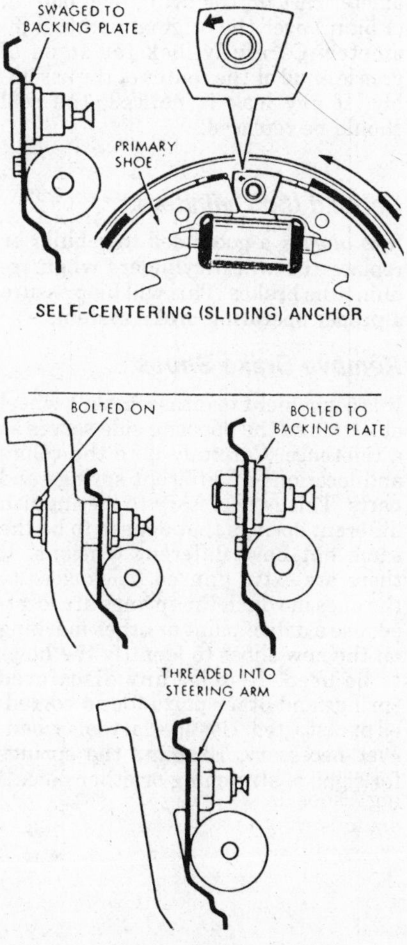


Different types of shoe anchors

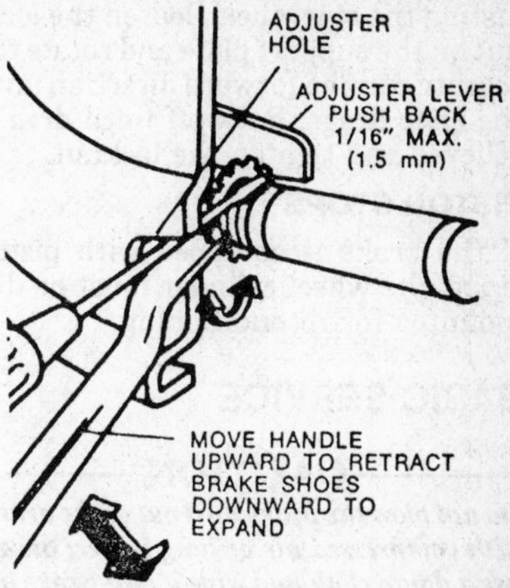


Some drums can be removed by backing off the self–adjuster

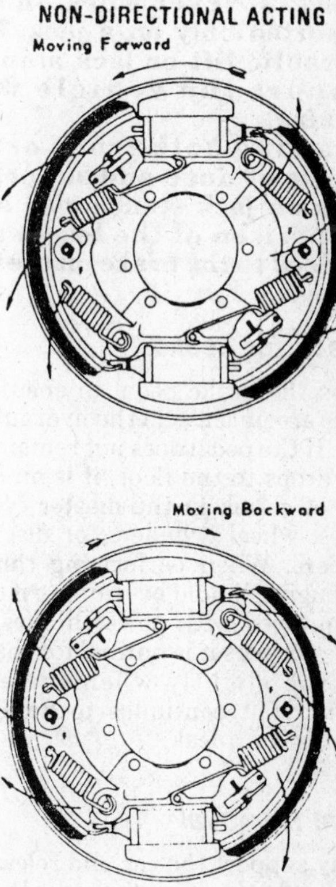


Two cylinder, non–servo brake

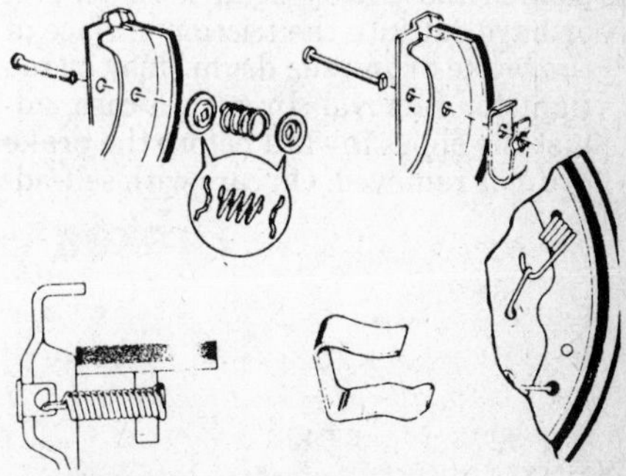

Different types of shoe hold–downs

justing the star wheel, loosen the locknut on the support plate and rotate the eccentric in the forward direction until the shoe drags. Back-off until drag is relieved and tighten the locknut.

### PISTON STOPS

If the brake is equipped with piston stops, the wheel cylinder must be dismounted for reconditioning.

## BASIC SERVICE

**CAUTION**

***Do not blow the brake dust out of the drums with compressed air or lung power; always use a damp cloth and wipe it out. Brake linings contain asbestos, a known cancer causing substance. Dispose of the cloth after use.***

**NOTE: Never work on a car supported only on a jack. Use a hydraulic lift or jack stands to support the vehicle while working.**

**Raising both front or rear wheels at once and supporting them on jack stands also allows comparison of the brake being serviced to the brake on the opposite side.**

### Check for Leaks

Press the brake pedal to ensure that there are no leaks in the hydraulic system. If the pedal does not remain hard, and drops to the floor, it is an indication of a leak in the master cylinder, hoses, wheel cylinders, or disc brake calipers. When performing this test, the engine should be running if the car is equipped with power brakes. With power brakes it is normal for the pedal to drop slightly when the engine starts. If it continues to drop, start looking for a leak.

### Drum Removal

Safely support the car and release the parking brake if working on the rear axle. Remove the lug nuts, the wheel/tire assembly and then pull off the drums. If the brake shoes have expanded too tightly against the drum, or have cut into the friction surface of the brake drum, the drums may be too tight for removal. In such a case, adjust the shoes inward before the brake drum is removed. On cars with self-adjusting mechanisms, reach through the adjusting slot with a very small prybar (or similar tool) and carefully push the self-adjusting lever away from the star wheel by a maximum of $1/16$ in. (1.5mm). While holding the lever back, insert a brake adjusting tool into the slot and turn the star wheel in the proper direction until the brake drum can be removed. On cars with manual adjusting mechanisms, try lightly tapping the drum with a rubber mallet. If this does not work, simply reverse the manual adjustment procedures given later in this section until the drum can be removed.

### Drum Inspection

Check the drums fro any cracks, scores, grooves, or an out-of-round condition. Replace of cracked. Slight scores can be removed with fine emery cloth while extensive scoring requires turning the drum on a lathe.

If the friction surface of the brake drum appears scored or otherwise damaged beyond repair, it will require reconditioning. After machining, the drum diameter must not exceed the diameter cast on the drum or 0.060 in. (1.5mm) over the original nominal diameter. Carefully look for signs of grease or oil at the center of the assembly. If any leak is noticed, the seal should be replaced.

### Rebuild the Cylinders

It is *always* a good idea to rebuild or replace the wheel cylinders when relining the brakes. This will help assure a proper operating brake system.

### Remove Brake Shoes

It is convenient to disassemble 1 wheel at a time so the opposite side serves as a reference. Carefully note the colors and locations of different springs and parts. This is necessary to distinguish different springs that appear to be the same but have different tensions. If there are extra unused holes close to the ones in which the springs are located, use a dab of paint or other marking on the new shoes to identify the holes to be used. Replace any discolored springs and other parts found corroded or distorted. Use special tools whenever necessary. Examine the springs for signs of stretching or other defects and replace if their condition is at all questionable. Examine the flexible brake hoses and replace any that show signs of cracking or other damage.

### Clean and Lubricate Shoes

With all the brake parts off, clean the backing plate with a damp cloth to avoid raising any asbestos dust, and dispose of the rag after use. Clean any rust with a wire brush. File smooth any ridges or rough edges on the contact points on the backing plate, and lubricate with approved brake lubricant. Clean and lightly lubricate the adjuster threads, and screw the adjuster all the way together to facilitate reassembly later on. Wash the wheel bearings with solvent and repack them with proper grease. Check backing plate bolts to make sure they are tight. Reassemble the brakes in the reverse order of disassembly. Make sure all parts are in their proper locations and that both brakes shoes are properly positioned in either end of the adjuster. Also, both brake shoes should correctly engage the wheel cylinder push rods and parking brake links, and should be centered on the backing plate. Parking brake links and levers should be in place on the rear brakes. With all parts in place, try the fit of the brake drum over the new shoes. If not slightly snug, pull it off and turn the star wheel until a slight drag is felt when sliding the drum on. The use of a brake pedal preset gauge will make this job easy. This makes final brake adjustment simpler. Then install the brake drum, wheel bearings, spindle nuts, cotter pins, dust caps, and wheel/tire assemblies, and make final brake adjustments as specified. Torque the spindle and lug nuts to specifications.

### Bleed and Road Test

Bleed the brakes to make sure of a high, hard brake pedal, and road-test the car. Most self-adjusting mechanisms are activated only during the rearward motion of the car. So, whenever servicing self-adjusting brakes, make sure that the road test included enough stops, traveling in reverse, to allow the self-adjusters to perform the proper match-up of all wheels. Or, operate the parking brake several times if that activates the automatic adjuster.